Who's Who In California

A Biographical Reference
Published Annually By
The Who's Who Historical Society

Who's Who in California

The Twenty-Fifth Edition
1996

Published by
The Who's Who Historical Society
1928 - 1996

TWENTY-FIFTH EDITION
Edna L. Barrett
Executive Director and Editor

International Standard Book Number ISBN 1-880142-04-X
Library of Congress Catalog Card Number 56-1715
International Standard Serial Number 0511-8948

PRINTED IN THE UNITED STATES OF AMERICA

Contents

Dedication

History can be formed from permanent monuments and records; but lives can only be written from personal knowledge, which is growing every day less, and in a short time is lost forever.

Dr. Samuel Johnson, 1709-1784
English Lexicographer and Critic

As it often happens the best men are but little known, and consequently cannot extend the usefulness of their examples a great way, the biographer is of great utility, as, by communicating such valuable patterns to the world, he may perhaps do a more extensive service to mankind than the person whose life originally afforded the pattern.

Sarah Fielding, 1710-1768
English Novelist

The highest reward for a man's toil is not what he gets for it, but what he becomes by it.

John Ruskin, 1819-1900
English Art Critic and Historian

First say to yourself what you would be; and then do what you have to do.

Epictetus, c.60
Greek Philosopher

How many things are looked upon as quite impossible until they have been actually effected.

Pliny the Elder, 23-79
Roman Writer

Biography is the best form of history.

Henry Wheeler Shaw, 1818-1885
American Humorist

Honorary Board of Directors

Abbreviations

AA Associate in Arts
AAAS American Association for the Advancement of Science
A.and M. Agricultural and Mechanical
AARP American Association of Retired Persons
AAU Amateur Athletic Union
AAUP American Association of University Professors
AAUW American Association of University Women
AB Arts, Bachelor of
ABA American Bar Association
ABC American Broadcasting Company
acad. academy, academic
accred. accredited, accreditation
achiev. achievement
ACLU American Civil Liberties Union
A.C.P. American College of Physicians
A.C.S. American College of Surgeons
ADA American Dental Association
adj. adjunct, adjutant
adj.gen. adjutant general
adm. admiral
admin. adminstration
adminstr. administrator
adminstrn. administration
adminstrv. administrative
adv. advisor, advanced
advt. advertising
advy. advisory
AEC Atomic Energy Commission
aero. aeronautical, aeronautic
AFB Air Force Base
AFL-CIO American Federation of Labor and Congress of Industrial Organizations
AFTRA American Federation TV and Radio Artists
agri., agric. agriculture, agricultural
agt. agent
agy. agency
AIA American Institute of Architects
AIAA American Institute of Aeronautics and Astronautics
AIEE American Institute of Electrical Engineers
AIM American Institute of Management

ALA American Library Association
Ala. Alabama
Am., Amer. American, America
AM Arts, Master of
AMA American Medical Association
A.M.E. African Methodist Episcopal
Amtrak National Railroad Passenger Corporation
anat. anatomical, anatomy
ANTA American National Theatre and Academy
anthropol. anthropological
AP Associated Press
APC A Professional Corporation
APICS American Production Inventory Control Society
APO Army Post Office
appt. appointment, appointed
arb. arbitrator, arbitration
ARC American Red Cross
archeol. archeological
arch. architecture
archtl. architectural
Ariz. Arizona
Ark. Arkansas
arty. artillery
ASCAP American Society of Composers, Authors and Publishers
ASCE American Society of Civil Engineers
ASME American Society of Mechanical Engineers
assn. association
assoc. associate, associated
asst. assistant
ASTM American Society for Testing and Materials
astron. astronomical
AT&T American Telephone & Telegraph Company
atty. attorney
AUS Army of the United States
aux. auxiliary
AVMA American Veterinary Medical Association

B. Bachelor
b. born
BA Bachelor of Arts
BAgr Bachelor of Agriculture
BBA Bachelor of Business Administration

BBC British Broadcasting Corporation
B.C. British Columbia
BCE Bachelor of Civil Engineering
Bch. Beach
BCL Bachelor of Civil Law
BCS Bachelor of Commercial Science
BD Bachelor of Divinity
bd. board
Bdo. Bernardino
BEdn Bachelor of Education
BEE Bachelor of Electrical Engineering
BFA Bachelor of Fine Arts
biblio. bibliographical
biog. biography
biol. biological
Biotech. Biotechnology
BJ Bachelor of Journalism
BL Bachelor of Letters
bldg. building
BLS Bachelor of Library Science
bn. battalion
bot. botanical
BPE Bachelor of Physical Education
br. branch
BRE Bachelor of Religious Education
brig.gen. brigadier general
Brit. British, Britannica
BS Bachelor of Science
BSA Boy Scouts of America
BSEE Bachelor of Science Electrical Engineering
BTh Bachelor of Theology
bur. bureau
bus. business

CAA Civil Aeronautics Administration
CAB Civil Aeronautics Board
Calif. California
Cal Poly California Polytechnic State University
Cal Tech California Institute of Technology
Can. Canada
cand. candidate
CAP Civil Air Patrol
capt. captain
Cath. Catholic
cav. cavalry
CBC Canadian Broadcasting Company
CBI China, Burma, India Theatre of Operations
CBS Columbia Broadcasting System
CC Country Club
CE, C.E. Civil Engineer, Corps of Engineers
CEO Chief Executive Officer
cert. certificate, certified, certification
CFO Chief Financial Officer

ch. church
ChD Doctor of Chemistry
chem. chemical, chemistry
ChFC Chartered Financial Consultant
Chgo. Chicago
chmn. chairman
chpt. chapter
CIA Central Intelligence Agency
CIC Counter Intelligence Corps
Cleve. Cleveland
clin. clinical
clk. clerk
CLU Chartered Life Underwriter
CMA California Medical Association
cmdr., cdr. commander
Co. Company, County
C.of C. Chamber of Commerce
col. colonel
coll. college
Colo. Colorado
com. committee
comd. commanded
comdg. commanding
comdr. commander
comdt. commandant
comm. community, communication
commd. commissioned
commdn. commendation
comml. commercial
commn. commission
commr. commissioner
comms. communications
conf. conference
Cong. Congress
congl. congressional
Conn. Connecticut
cons. consultant, consulting
consol. consolidated
constl. constitutional
constn. constitution
constrn. construction
contbd. contributed
contbg. contributing
contbr. contributor
contr. contractor
conv. convention
C.O.O. Chief Operating Officer
coop., co-op cooperative
coord. coordinator, coordinating
CORE Congress of Racial Equality
corp. corporation
corr. correspondent, corresponding
C.P.A., CPA Certified Public Accountant

C.P.C.U. Chartered Property and Casualty Underwriter
CPH Certificate of Public Health
cpl. corporal
CPR Cardio-Pulmonary Resuscitation
cred. credential/s, credentiales
ct. court
ctr. center
C.Z. Canal Zone

d., dau. daughter
DAgr Doctor of Agriculture
DAR Daughters of the American Revolution
DAV Disabled American Veterans
DC Doctor of Chiropractic
D.C., DC District of Columbia
DCL Doctor of Civil Law
DCS Doctor of Commercial Science
DD Doctor of Divinity
DDS Doctor of Dental Surgery
dec. deceased
def. defense
Del. Delaware
del. delegate, delegation
DEng Doctor of Engineering
dep. deputy
dept. department
desc. descendant
devel. development, developed
DFA Doctor of Fine Arts
DFC Distinguished Flying Cross
DHL Doctor of Hebrew Literature
dipl. diploma
dir. director
dist. district
distbg. distributing
distbn. distribution
distbr. distributor
disting. distinguished
div. division, divinity, divorced
DLitt Doctor of Literature
DMD Doctor of Medical Dentistry
DMS Doctor of Medical Science
DO Doctor of Osteopathy
DOD, DoD Department of Defense
D.P. Data Processing
DRE Doctor of Religious Education
DS, DSc Doctor of Science
D.S.C. Distinguished Service Cross
D.S.M. Distinguished Service Medal
DST Doctor of Sacred Theology
DTM Doctor of Tropical Medicine
DVM Doctor of Veterinary Medicine
DVS Doctor of Veterinary Surgery

E. East
ea. eastern
ecol. ecological
econ. economics, economical
ED Doctor of Engineering
ed. editor, edited
EdB Bachelor of Education
EdD Doctor of Education
edit. edition
editl. editorial
EdM Master of Education
edn. education
ednl. educational
EDP Electronic Data Processing
EE, E.E. Electrical Engineer
EEO Equal Employment Opportunity
E.Ger. German Democratic Republic
elec. electrical
elem. elementary
EM Engineer of Mines
empl. employee
ency. encyclopedia
Eng. England, English
engr. engineer
engring. engineering
entomol. entomological
environ. environmental
EOP Equal Opportunity Program
EPA Environmental Protection Agency
epidemiol. epidemiological
ERA Equal Rights Amendment
ESL English as a Second Language
ETO European Theatre of Operations
Euro. Europe, European
exam. examination, examining
exec. executive
exhib., exhbn. exhibit, exhibitor, exhibition
expo. exposition
exptl. experimental

FAA Federal Aviation Administration
FBI Federal Bureau of Investigation
FCC Federal Communication Commission
FDA Food and Drug Administration
FDIC Federal Deposit Insurance Corporation
Fdn. Foundation
fed. federal
fedn. federation
fgn. foreign
FHA Federal Housing Administration
fin. financial, finance
Fla. Florida
Flr Floor
fmr. former

Found. foundation
FPC Federal Power Commission
FPO Fleet Post Office
frat. fraternity, fraternal
FRS Federal Reserve System
Ft. Fort
f.t. full time
FTC Federal Trade Commission

Ga. Georgia
GAO General Accounting Office
gastroent. gastroenterological
GATT General Agreement of Tariff and Trades
GCM Good Conduct Medal
gen. general
geneal. genealogical
geog. geographical, geographic
geol. geological
geophys. geophysical
gerontol. gerontological
gov. governor
govt. government
govtl. governmental
grad. graduate
GSA General Services Administration
Gt. Great
gynecol. gynecological

hd. head, head of
hdqrs., hq. headquarters
HEW Department of Health, Education and Welfare
HHD Doctor of Humanities
hist. historical, historic, history
HM Master of Humanics
HOA Home Owners Association
hon. honorary, honorable
Ho. of Dels. House of Delegates
Ho. of Reps. House of Representatives
hort. horticultural
hosp. hospital
H.S. High School
HUD Department of Housing and Urban Development
Hwy. Highway

Ia. Iowa
IBM International Business Machines
ICC Interstate Commerce Commission
ICU Intensive Care Unit
Ida. Idaho
IEEE Institute of Electrical & Electronics Engineers
IGY International Geophysical Year

Ill. Illinois
illus. illustrated
ILO International Labor Organization
IMF International Monetary Fund
immun. immunology
Inc. Incorporated
incl. include, including
Ind. Indiana
indep. independent
Indpls. Indianapolis
indsl. industrial
inf. infantry
info. information
ins. insurance
insp. inspector
inst. institute
instl. institutional
instr. instructor
internat. international
intro. introduction
IRS Internal Revenue Service
ITT International Telephone & Telegraph Corp.

JAG Judge Advocate General
Jaycees Junior Chamber of Commerce
JD Juris Doctor
j.g. junior grade
jour. journal
jr. junior
jt. joint
jud. judicial

Kans. Kansas
K.C. Knights of Columbus
K.T. Knight Templar
Ky. Kentucky

L.A. Los Angeles
LA, La. Louisiana
lab. laboratory
L.A.C.C. Los Angeles City College
lang. language
laryngol. laryngological
ldr. leader
L.D.S. Latter Day Saints
lectr. lecturer
legis. legislation, legislative
LHD Doctor of Humane Letters
L.I. Long Island
lib. library
lic. license, licensed
lit. literature
LittB Bachelor of Letters
LittD Doctor of Letters

LLB Bachelor of Laws
LLD Doctor of Laws
LLM Master of Laws
Ln Lane
lt. lieutenant
Ltd. Limited
LWV League of Women Voters

m. married
M. Master
MA Master of Arts
mag. magazine
MAgr Master of Agriculture
maj. major
Mass. Massachusetts
math. mathematics, mathematical
MBA Master of Business Administration
M.C. Medical Corps
mcht. merchant
mcpl. municipal
MCS Master of Commercial Science
MD Doctor of Medicine
Md. Maryland
MDiv Master of Divinity
mdse. merchandise
mdsg. merchandising
ME, M.E. Mechanical Engineer
Me. Maine
mech. mechanical
med. medical
Med Master of Education
MEE Master of Electrical Engineering
mem. member
Meml., Mem. Memorial
met. metropolitan
metall. metallurgical
meterol. meteorological
Mex. Mexico
MF Master of Forestry
MFA Master of Fine Arts
mfg. manufacturing
mfr. manufacturer
mgmt. management
mgr. manager
M.I. Military Intelligence
Mich. Michigan
mil. military
Minn. Minnesota
MIS Management Information Systems
Miss. Mississippi
mktg. marketing
MLS Master of Library Science
M.L.S. Multiple Listing Service (real estate)
mng. managing

Mo. Missouri
Mont. Montana
M.P. Member of Parliament
MPA Master of Public Adminstration
MPH Master of Public Health
MPhil Master of Philosophy
Mpls. Minneapolis
MRE Master of Religious Education
MS, MSc Master of Science
MSD Master of Dental Surgery
MST Master of Sacred Theology
MSW Master of Social Work
Mt. Mount
mtg. mortgage
MTS member technical staff
mus. museum
MusB Bachelor of Music
MusD Doctor of Music
MusM Master of Music
mycol. mycological

N. North
NAACP National Association for Advancement of Colored People
N.Am. North America
NAM National Association of Manufacturers
NAREB National Association of Real Estate Boards
NASA National Aeronautics and Space Administration
NASD National Association of Securities Dealers
nat. national, naturalized
NATO North Atlantic Treaty Organization
NBC National Broadcasting Corporation
N.C., N.Caro. North Carolina
NCCJ National Conference of Christians and Jews
N.D., N.Dak. North Dakota
NE Northeast
NEA National Education Association
Nebr. Nebraska
neurol. neurological
Nev. Nevada
NG National Guard
N.H. New Hampshire
NHL National Hockey League
NIH National Institutes of Health
NIMH National Institute of Mental Health
N.J. New Jersey
NLRB National Labor Relations Board
N.M., N.Mex. New Mexico
No. Northern
NORAD North American Air Defense

NOW National Organization for Women
NRC National Research Council
nse. nurse
NSF National Science Foundation
nsg. nursing
num. numerous
numis. numismatic/s
NW Northwest
NY, N.Y. New York
NYC, N.Y.C. New York City
N.Z. New Zealand

OAS Organization of American States
ob-gyn obstetrics-gynecology
obstet. obstetrical
OD Doctor of Optometry
OEEC Organization of European Economic
Cooperation
OEO Office of Economic Opportunity
O.E.S. Order of Eastern Star
ofcl. official
ofcr. officer
Oh. Ohio
Okla. Oklahoma
OMD Doctor of Oriental Medicine
ophthal. ophthalmological
opr. operator
ops. operations
orch. orchestra
Ore., Oreg. Oregon
orgn. organization
orgzr. organizer
OSHA Occupational Safety and Health
Administration
OSS Office of Strategic Services
osteo. osteopathic
otol. otological
otolaryn. otolaryngology

Pa., Penn. Pennsylvania
PC, P.C. Professional Corporation
paleontol. paleontological
Pasa. Pasadena
path. pathology, pathological
PEN Poets, Playwrights, Editors, Essayists and
Novelists
P.E.O. women's organization
pfc private first class
pgm. program
pgmg. programming
pgmr. programmer
PHA Public Housing Administration
pharm. pharmacy, pharmaceutical
PharmD Doctor of Pharmacy

PharmM Master of Pharmacy
PhB Bachelor of Philosophy
PhD Doctor of Philosophy
Phila. Philadelphia
philos. philosophical
photog. photography, photographer, photographic
phys. physical, physician
physiol. physiological, physiology
Pitts. Pittsburgh
Pkwy, Pky Parkway
plnr. planner
POB, PO Box Post Office Box
Poli. Political
Poly. polytechnic, polytechnical
P.R. Puerto Rico, Public Relations
prep. preparatory
pres. president
Presbyn. Presbyterian
presdl. presidential
prin. principal
proc. proceedings, processing (data)
prod. produced, producer (theatrical)
prodn. production
prof. professor
profl. professional
prog. program
prop. proprietor
Prot. Protestant
pro tem pro tempore
PRSA Public Relations Society of America
PSRO Professional Services Review
Organization
psychiat. psychiatric
psychol. psychological, psychology
p.t. part-time
PTA Parent-Teachers Association
ptnr. partner
pub. publisher, publishing, published
publ. publication
publs. publications
pvt. private

radiol. radiological
RCA Radio Corporation of America
Rd Road
R&D Research & Development
R.E. Real Estate
re regarding, relevant to
rec. recreation
ref. reference
reg. region, regional, registered
regt. regiment
rehab. rehabilitation, rehabilitate
rels. relations

rep. representative
Res., res. Residence, Reserve, research
ret. retired
rev. review, revised
rhinol. rhinological
R.I. Rhode Island
RN, R.N. Registered Nurse
ROTC Reserve Officers Training Corps
R.R. Railroad
RV recreational vehicle

s. son
S. South
SAC Strategic Air Command
Sacto. Sacramento
SAG Screen Actors Guild
SALT Strategic Arms Limitation Talks
S.Am. South America
SAR Sons of the American Revolution
savs. savings
S&L Savings & Loan
SB Bachelor of Science
S.B. Santa Barbara
SBA Small Business Administration
S.C., S.Caro. South Carolina
ScB Bachelor of Science
ScD Doctor of Science
sch. school
sci. science scientific
SCLC Southern Christian Leadership
   Conference
S.Dak. South Dakota
S.D. San Diego
SE Southeast
sec. secondary
secty., sec. secretary
SEC Securities and Exchange Commission
sect. section
S.F. San Francisco
seismol. seismological
sem. seminary
s.g. senior grade
sgt. sergeant
S.J. Society of Jesus (Jesuit)
so. southern
soc. society
sociol. sociological
sor. sorority
spkr. speaker
spl. special
splst. specialist
splty. specialty
St. State, Saint, Street
sta. station

stats. statistics
STB Bachelor of Sacred Theology
STD Doctor of Sacred Theology
Ste Suite
subcom. subcommittee
subs. subsidiary
supr. supervisor
supt. superintendent
supvy. supervisory
surg. surgical, surgery
svc. service
svs. services
SW Southwest
sys. system

tchg. teaching
tchr. teacher
tech. technical, technology, technological,
   technologist
techn. technician
Tel, tel. telephone
Tel. & Tel. Telephone & Telegraph
temp. temporary
Tenn. Tennessee
Tex., Tx. Texas
ThD Doctor of Theology
theol. theology, theological
tng. training
transf. transferred
transl. translator, translation
transp. transportation
treas. treasurer
TV, t.v. television

UAW United Auto Workers
UC University of California
UCLA University of California at Los Angeles
UCSF University of California at San Francisco
U.K. United Kingdom
UN United Nations
UNESCO United Nations Educational,
   Scientific and Cultural Organization
UNICEF United Nations International
   Children's Emergency Fund
univ. university
UPI United Press International
urol. urological
US, U.S. United States
USA United States of America, U.S. Army
USAAF United States Army Air Force
USAF United States Air Fore
USAFR United States Air Force Reserve
USAR United States Army Reserve
USC University of Southern California

USCG United States Coast Guard
USCGR United States Coast Guard Reserve
USDA United States Department of Agriculture
USIA United States Information Agency
USMC United States Marine Corps
USMCR United States Marine Corps Reserve
USN United States Navy
USNR United States Naval Reserve
USO United Service Organizations
USPHS United States Public Health Service
USPS United States Postal Service
U.S.S. United States Ship
USSR Union of Soviet Socialist Republics

VA Veterans Administration
Va. Virginia
v.ch. vice chair
vet. veteran
VFW Veterans of Foreign Wars
v.p. vice president
vis. visiting
VISTA Volunteers in Service to America
vocat. vocational
vol. volunteer
vs. versus
Vt. Vermont

W. West
WAC Women's Army Corps
Wash. Washington
WAVES Women's Reserve, U.S. Naval Reserve
W.D.C. Washington D.C.
west., we. western
WHO World Health Organization
W.I. West Indies
Wis. Wisconsin
W.Va. West Virginia
Wyo. Wyoming

x-c cross-country

YMCA Young Men's Christian Association
YMHA Young Men's Hebrew Association
YWCA Young Women's Christian Association
yr. year
YR Young Republicans organization

zool. zoological
–, to date

Guide to Biographies

The biographical profiles in **Who's Who In California** are arranged alphabetically according to the surname of the biographee. Where identical surnames occur, the first name is used. If both surname and first given name are identical, the second given name is used to arrange the profiles alphabetically.

In the case of compound hyphenated surnames, the profiles are arranged according to the first member of the compound.

Some biographees delete part of their full name in ordinary usage. In those instances parentheses are used to indicate that portion of the name which is deleted. For example, SMITH, J(OHN) indicates that the usual form of the name is J. Smith.

Biographical profiles include the following data, offered in chronological order as a convenient guide:

1. Name
2. Occupation
3. Birthdate and Place
4. Parents
5. Marriage
6. Children
7. Education
8. Career
9. Career Related Activities
10. Awards and Honors
11. Memberships
12. Creative Works
13. Military Service
14. Political Affiliation
15. Religious Affiliation
16. Recreation/Hobbies
17. Residence Address
18. Office Address

* Noteworthy - Denotes a brief biographical sketch prepared by the Society on a noteworthy individual who did not submit biographical data, or whose complete profile was not received by press time.

Who's Who in California

AARONSON, SCOTT MICHAEL, plastic surgeon; b. April 14, 1952, Baltimore, Md.; s. Alfred Irving and Lorraine Mae (Galumbeck) A.; m. Sandra Lee Slisz, March 26, 1989; edn: BS magna cum laude, Univ. Miami 1974; MD, 1978; cert. Am. Bd. of Plastic Surgery 1986. Career: gen. surgery resident UC Irvine 1978-82; plastic surgery res. St. Joseph Hosp., Houston, Tx. 1982-84; pvt. practice plastic surgery, Palm Springs 1984–; honors: Phi Kappa Phi, Univ. Miami Pres.'s Honor Roll. (1972), Trustee Scholar (1974-78); mem: Am. Soc. Plastic & Reconstrv. Surgery, Palm Springs Acad. Medicine, Lipoplasty Soc. No. Am., Fellow of Am. College of Surgeons, Am. Soc. for Aesthetic Plastic Surgeons; articles pub. in sci. jours. (1981-85); rec: flute playing, photog., electronics. Ofc: 1080 N Indian Canyon Dr Ste 104 Palm Springs 92264

ABBATE, GERALDINE-VITTORIA, international business cross-cultural consultant and trainer; b. Mar. 27, 1952, Chgo.; d. Calogero Charles and Geraldine (Desborough) Abbate; m. Mahmoud Maghsoudi, Sept. 9, 1978; edn: BA, Univ. of Ill., Chgo. 1973; MA, N.E. Illinois Univ., 1975; tchg. credentials in English lang. and lit., Ill., and multiple-subject tchg. cred., State of Calif. Career: Western Regional Dir. ELS Educational Services Inc. 1974-79; founder/owner InterCultural Consultants, Internat.-USA, San Francisco 1979–; cons. and trainer in internat. business and inter-cultural skills development for internat. bus. execs.; honors: Phi Delta Kappa, 1973-74, official rep. ESL Language Centers, 1979–, listed Who's Who Am. Women, Who's Who Notable Italian-Americans, Community Leaders of Am.; mem: San Francisco C. of C., Calif. C.of C., Am. Soc. for Tng. & Devel., Nat. Assn. Women Business Owners, Soc. for Intercultural Edn., Tng. & Research, civic: Amnesty Internat., No. Calif. Consultative Grp. on Am. and World Affairs, World Affairs Council; rec: folk dancing, flute, writing, photog. Ofc: InterCultural Consultants International-USA, 278 Post St Ste 405 San Francisco 94108

ABBOTT, RICHARD BARRETT, shipping executive; b. Dec. 19, 1911, Lincoln, ebr.; s. Charles Howard and Lela Bell (Hunt) A.; m. Noradene Sproul, Nov. 8, 1939 (dec. 1969); 1 son, Richard B., Jr. b. 1947; m. Sandra Otto, July , 1972; edn: Oklahoma City Coll. of Law 1939-41; LLB, Pacific Coast Univ., Los Angeles 1950. Career: asst. mgr. Waterman Steamship, Los Angeles 1948-55; nat. mktg. mgr. Electro Products Div. Western Gear Corp., L.A. 1955-60; owner/pres. Pacific Steamship Agency Inc., Los Angeles, San Francisco, 1960-79; owner/pres R.B. Abbott & Co. Inc., 1970-79; cargo and ship broker, fgn. freight forwarder, chartered and operated vessels; rep. Splosna Plovba Yugoslav Line, Scandia Pacific Line, Retla Steamship Co., China Merchants Steam Nav. Co. (Rep. of China), Tiger Line, Ta Peng S.S. Co., and Sea King Lines; club: L.A. Transp. (dir. 1960-61, v.p. 64-65); author maritime autobiography, "Belo Horizonte", Around the World in 80 Years (1995, QED Press, Ft. Bragg, CA; distributors: Baker & Taylor); mil: lt. USNR 1944-46; Republican; Prot.; rec: sailing (has owned 8 yachts, cruised Atlantic, Pacific and the Caribbean). Res: 3201 Fiji Ln Alameda 94501

ABBOTT, RUSSELL JOSEPH, computer science educator; b. Mar. 1, 1942, Bklyn.; s. Samuel and Lillian (Ginsberg) A.; m. Gail Ann Whitley, May 6, 1981; children: Michael b. 1981, Julian b. 1985, Danielle b. 1987; edn: BA, Columbia Univ., 1962; MA, Harvard Univ., 1963; PhD, USC, 1973. Career: prof. computer sci. CSU Los Angeles, 1987–; author: Software Development (1986), various jour. articles. Ofc: Dept. Math. and C.S., CSULA, 5151 State University Dr L.A. 90032

ABDEL-AZIZ, SABRY MOHAMED, certified public accountant; b. May 8, 1934, Alexandria, Egypt, nat. 1974; s. Mohamed Abdel Aziz; m. Azima Hamad, Aug. 29, 1957; children: Samar and Sahar (twins) b. 1960; edn: BA, Alexandria Univ., 1955, dipl. in taxation, 1962; MBA, NY Univ. Grad. Sch. of Bus., 1973; C.P.A., Calif. Career: Russell & Co., Alexandria, Egypt 1952-55; Alex. Ins. Co., 1956-60; acctg. mgr. Rakta Pulp & Paper, 1960-70; credit analyst M.H.T. Co., NY, NY 1970-74; chief internal auditor/v.p. ABN Bank, Los Angeles 1974-88; cons. Crescent Accounting (CPA) 1988–; mem: Am. Inst. CPAs, Calif. Soc. CPAs, Egyptian Accts. and Auditors; civic: Islamic Ctr. of So. Calif., Islamic Soc. of Orange Co., Egyptian Am. Orgn.; Republican; Moslem; rec: travel. Res: 19132 E Gold Ln Walnut 91789 Ofc: 2127 E Ball Rd Anaheim 92806

ABDUL-JABBAR, KAREEM (ALCINDOR, LEWIS FERDINAND), former professional basketball player; b. NYC, Apr. 16, 1947; s. Ferdinand Lewis and Cora Alcindor; m. Habiba (Janice Brown), 1971 (div. 1973); children: Habiba, Kareem, Sultana, Amir; edn: BA, UCLA 1969. Career: basketball player Milw. Bucks 1969-75; Los Angeles Lakers 1975-89; honors: elected to Basketball Hall of Fame 1995, NBA all-time leading scorer 1984, Maurice Podoloff Cup, Most Valuable Player NBA (1971, 72, 74, 76, 77, 80), NBA All-Star Team (1970-87, 89), NBA 35th Anniv. All-Time Team 1980, NBA Playoff MVP (1971, 85), Rookie of the yr. 1970, NCAA Tournament Outstanding Player 1967, 68, 69; author (with P. Knobler) Giant Steps: An Autobiography of Kareem Abdul-Jabbar, 1983, (with M. McCarthy) Kareem, 1990; num. televi-

sion appearances incl. episodes: Mannix, Diff' rent Strokes, The Man from Atlantis, Tales from the Darkside, Pryor's Place, The After School Spl.; movies: Fletch 1985, Airplane 1980, The Fish that Saved Pittsburg 1979; Muslim. Ofc: c/o L.A. Lakers The Forum PO Box 10 Inglewood 90306

ABE, GREGORY, microbiologist, educator; b. Nov. 25, 1954, Los Angeles; s. Mabel (Tsumori) Abe; edn: AA, L.A. Valley Coll., 1978; PharmD, USC, 1988; BS, CSU Los Angeles, 1990, MBA, 1992. Career: virologist CSU Los Angeles, 1988-90, assoc. prof., 1990–; rec: tennis, golf, fishing. Res: 10404 Fairgrove Ave Tujunga 91042 Ofc: CSULA, 5151 State University Dr Los Angeles 90032

ABEL, ELIE, educator, journalist; b. Oct. 17, 1920, Montreal, Quebec, Can., nat. 1952; s. Jacob and Rose (Savetsky) A.; m. Corinne Prevost, Jan. 28, 1946; children: Mark b. 1948, Suzanne b. 1949; edn: BA, McGill Univ., 1941; MS, Columbia Univ., 1942. Career: rewrite man Los Angeles Times, L.A. 1947; UN corresp. Overseas News Agy., NY, NY 1947-49; corresp. New York Times, NY, NY 1949-59; Washington bur. chief Detroit News, Wash. DC 1959-61; corresp. NBC News, Wash. DC and London, 1961-69; dean and prof. Columbia Univ., NY, NY 1970-79; prof. Stanford Univ., 1979–; awards: G.F. Peabody award Univ. of Ga. 1968, excellence Overseas Press Club, NY 1970, hon. LLD McGill Univ. 1971, Univ. of Western Ontario 1975, 1st Amendment Defender, Catholic Univ., Wash. DC 1984; mem: Cosmos Club, W.D.C., Council on Fgn. Rels., World Affairs Council (S.F. bd. 1980-88); author: The Missile Crisis, 1966, Leaking: Who Does It..etc, 1987, The Shattered Bloc: Behind the Uprisings in Eastern Europe, 1990; coauthor: Roots of Involvement, 1971, Special Envoy, 1975, editor book: What's News, 1981; mil: sgt. Royal Canadian AF 1942-45; Democrat; Jewish. Ofc: Dept Communication Stanford University Stanford 94305

ABEL, TIMOTHY, lawyer; b. Dec. 30, 1929, Williams; s. Allen Raymond and Consuelo (Benham) A.; m. Louise, June 14, 1953; children: Elizabeth Ellen b. 1958, John Allen b. 1961, Robert William b. 1962; edn: AA, UC Berkeley 1953; JD, UC Hastings Coll. of Law 1957; lic. Real Estate Broker, Calif. Career: law practice, Hayward 33+ yrs., currently: senior ptr. law firm Abel & Abel, also pres. Hayward Properties, pres. West California Properties; mem: So. Alameda Co. Bar Assn. (pres.), Alameda Co. Bar Assn. (dir.); mil: sgt. UMSC 1950-52; (2) Pres. Unit Citation, (4) Battle Stars, Korean Campaign; Republican; Methodist; rec: skiing, tennis, golf. Res: 300 Sheridan Ave. Piedmont 94611 Ofc: Abel & Abel, 1331 B St Ste 3 Hayward 94541

ABELAR, INA MAE, equipment technician; b. July 18, 1926, Jay Em, Wyo.; d. Merritt Lyle and Leeta Mae (Worthen) Cameron; m. Michael Sandoval Abelar, Nov. 17, 1951 (div. 1966); children: Debora Jean, Michelle Elaine, Randolph Lee; edn: BA, Cal. Poly. Pomona 1978. Career: lumber estimator Keith Brown Bldg. Supply Salem, Ore. 1946-48, Whiting-Mead Bldg. Supply Vernon, Calif. 1949-51; lumber estimator, bookkeeper Trojan Lumber Co. Burbank 1952-55; bookkeeper Jerry Kalior Bkpg. Systems No. Hollywood 1959-66; chem. stock clerk to supv. instrl. support tech. II Physics Dept. Cal. Poly. Pomona 1967-88, staff council 1970-87, chmn. 1977-78, exec. bd. 1971-87, retired staff emeritus 1988; honors: Outstanding Staff Employee 1983-84, Service Award (SPS Physics Club); mem: Mu Phi Epsilon (profl. music frat., coll. advisor Gammi Chi chpt. 1980-82, treas. Claremont Alumni chpt. 1980-82, pres. 1983-86), Pace Setters (retired faculty & staff Cal. Poly. Pomona, v.p. 1991, treas. 1992, 94), Habitat for Humanity, Women's Blitz Build. (W.D.C. 1992, Denver 1993, Ark. 1994, S. Dakota 1994, v.p. Pomona affiliate 1994–); Democrat; Prot.; rec: wood carving, rebuilding pianos, hunting, swimming, hiking, travel. Res: 1833 Benedict Way Pomona 91767

ABELES, JUDITH, lawyer and loan broker; b. Nov. 28, 1937, New York; d. Jack and Minnie (Rubin) Abeles; edn: BA philosophy, Bklyn. Coll. 1958; JD, Western State Univ. Coll. Law, San Diego 1978; LL.M, Univ. Exeter, England 1980; diploma Private Internat. Law, Hague Acad. Internat. Law, Netherlands 1980; Europa Inst., Amsterdam 1981-82. Career: legal intern Council of Europe, Strasbourg, France 1982-83; sole practice, San Diego 1983-84; staff atty. ACLU, San Diego 1984; sole practice, San Diego 1984–; instr. Nat. Univ. Sch. Law 1985–; Univ. Redlands 1986-87; dir. Utility Consumers Action Network 1987–; Able-Disabled Advocates 1987–; honors: U.S. Congress Citizen of Month 1988, Vols. in Parole Outstanding Atty. of Year 1989; mem: Citizens Equal Opportunity Commn., City Watchdog Com. (chair 1985–), Vol. Lawyers Program, Legal Aid Soc.; Gallon Club; Nat. Women's Political Caucus; newsletter pub. 1980-81, articles in profl. jour. 1977, 78; rec: gardening. Res: 3318 Arthur Ave San Diego 92116

ABELES, KIM VICTORIA, artist; b. Aug. 28, 1952, Richmond Heights, Mo.; d. Burton Noel Wright and Frances Elizabeth (Sander) Hoffman; edn: B.F.A. in painting, Ohio Univ., 1974; M.F.A. in studio art, UC Irvine, 1980. Career: freelance artist, Los Angeles 1975–; lectr. various schs. and art ctrs. 1980–; vis. disting. artist Calif. State Univ., Fullerton, 1985-87; one woman shows include UC Irvine 1979, 80, Mcpl. Art Gallery, L.A. 1981, LA. City Hall 1982, Phyllis Kind Gallery, Chgo. 1993, Karl Bornstein Gallery, Santa Monica 1983, 85, 87, Pepperdine Univ., Malibu 1985, A.I.R. Gallery, N.Y.C. 1986, Chapman Coll., Orange 1986, Mount St. Mary's Coll., L.A. 1987, Atlanta Pavilion 1990, Calif. Mus. of Sci. and Industry, L.A. 1991, Laguna Art Mus. Satellite Gallery, Costa Mesa 1991, Turner-Krull Gallery, L.A. 1992, Lawrence Miller Gallery, NYC 1992, Santa Monica Mus. of Art (15 yr. survey), L.A. 1993; honors: outstanding student res. and creative achievement award UC Irvine 1972, U.S. Steel award Exhibition of Associated Artists of Pitts. 1977, Hand Hollow Found fellow 1984, grantee Pollock-Krasner Found. 1990, grantee Calif. Arts Council 1990, grantee L.A. Cultural Affairs 1991, recipient Clean Air award Air Quality Mgmt. Dist., Calif. 1992; fellow J. Paul Getty Trust Fund for the Visual Arts 1993, Design Team, Panorama City Lib., Calif. 1992-93; author, illustrator, Crafts, Cookery and Country Living, 1976; author, photographer: Impressions, 1979; work featured in Artery, 1979, Pacific Poetry and Fiction Review, 1980, Fiction Internat., 1985. Address: 2401 Santa Fe #100 Los Angeles 90058

ABERNETHY, ROBERT JOHN, real estate developer; b. Feb. 28, 1940, Indianapolis, Ind.; s. George Lawrence and Helen Sarah (McLandress) A.; edn: BA, Johns Hopkins Univ. 1962; MBA, Harvard Univ. 1968; cert. real estate, UCLA 1974; cert constrn. 1974. Career: asst. to deputy campaign mgr. Humphrey for Pres., Wash. D.C. 1968; asst. to chief scientist Phoenix missile program Hughes Aircraft Co., Los Angeles 1968-69, asst. program mgr., Iroquois Night Fighter and Night Tracker, Culver City 1969-71, asst. to controller, space and comm. group, El Segundo 1971-72, controller tech. div. 1972-74; pres. Am. Standard Devel. Co., Los Angeles 1974–; dir: Storage Equities, Glendale 1980–, Marathon Nat. Bank, L.A. 1982–, L.A. BanCorp. 1982-89, Self Serv. Stg. Assn., San Francisco 1978-83, L.A. Met. Water Dist. 1989-94; honors: Alpha Lambda; mem.: So. Calif. Planning Congress, Parker Found., L.A. City Planning Commn., 1984-89, L.A. Econ. Devel. Council (v.chmn. 1988-92), Ctr. for Study of Democratic Instns. (chmn. 1985–), L.A. Theatre Ctr., advy. council Peabody Conservatory, Davidson Coll. Bd. of Visitors, Los Angeles Comm. on Foreign Relations; bd. dirs.: Johns Hopkins Univ. (trustee), Pacific Council on Internat. Policy, Metropolitan Transportation Authority of Los Angeles County, World Children's Transplant Fund, Nitse School of Adv. Internat. Studies ; mil: lt. USNR 1962-66; rec: sailing, skiing. Res: 5800 W Century Blvd Los Angeles 90009-0855 Ofc: American Standard Development Co. 5221 W 102nd St Los Angeles 90045

ABRAHAM, ALBERT DAVID, retired railroad official, translator; b. Feb. 15, 1924, Baghdad, Iraq; naturalized U.S. citizen, Dec. 13, 1972; s. David and Mariam (Shawootha) A.; m. Lily, Jan. 12, 1958, (div. Dec. 1978); children: Peter b. 1962, Paul b. 1965; edn: BA, English (honors), San Francisco St. Univ., 1975; BA in Law, Blackstone, Chgo. 1976; master gardener Univ. Calif. Coop. Ext., 1985. Career: translator and interpreter (Eng., Arabic, Syriac) U.S. and Brit. Armed Forces, Basrah, Iraq 1942-45; translator Basrah Petroleum Co., Iraq 1947-54; chief translator Brit. Bank of the M.E., Baghdad 1958-67; claims investigator So. Pacific Transp. Co., San Francisco 1967-86, ret.; horticultural gardening cons. The Home Depot, San Leandro 1988-92; vol. horticultural cons. Alameda County; awards: military commendn. Hq. Persia & Iraq Command 1942-45, outstanding civic service San Leandro C.of C. 1989, Optimist Internat. Honour Roll 1989; author: Campanions in Misfortune, sched. publ. 9/94; clubs: Moose (Turlock), Optimist (San Leandro, pres. 1988-89); Democrat; Christian; rec: dancing, horticulture, writing. Res: 4045 Avatar Ct Turlock 95382

ABRAM, ALICE WILSON, manager, Info Technology, Service Request Management; b. Oct. 4, 1945, Glendale; d. Mack Lloyd and Jessie Lee (Andrues) Wilson; m. Wil C. Abram, June 8, 1974. Career: telephone svs. analyst Los Angeles County, 1980-85, supvg. analyst 1985-88, L.A. County voice mail mgr., respons. for pgm. devel, consulting, mktg. system with 10,000+ users; currently respons. for all voice and data comm. in L.A. Co.; telecom auditing, frequent speaker re Telecom; awards: employee of mo. L.A. Co., 1987, Family & Children Service Award 1995; mem. Telecommun. Assn. (nominating com. 1982–, So. Calif. chapt. mem. of yr. 1987); pres. Food Pantry-LAX (non-profit food source, feeds 35,000/yr., recipient, Cert. of Appreciation, L.A. City Council 1995) mem. L.A. Ladies Book Club; Democrat; rec: aerobics, travel, gourmet cooking. Ofc: County of Los Angeles 1100 N Eastern Ave Los Angeles 90063

ABSHIRE, LYNN THOMAS, computer scientist, executive; b. June 10, 1944, Twin Falls, Ida.; s. Joyce (Jack) and Viola M. (Bittner) Abshire; children: Mark b. 1968, Timothy b. 1971, Matthew b. 1979; m. 2d. Jean M., Aug. 12, 1993; 1 stepson: Stephen J. DeSanto b. 1981; edn: AS, Ore. Tech. Inst. 1967. Career: sr. tech., process control programmer Union Carbide Corp., S.D. 1969-70; d.p. mgr. Solitron Devices Inc. 1970-74; sr. res. and devel. programmer Gen. Automation Inc., Anaheim 1974-75; corp. d.p. mgr. VTN Corp., Irvine 1975-83; tech. support mgr. DMA Comm. 1983; customer service mgr. Studio Software, Costa Mesa 1983-85; computer systems mgr. Greiner Engring., Santa Ana 1985–; computer cons., v.p. PCG, Inc. 1986-93; mil: E-5 USN 1961-65; Republican; Prot.; rec: computers, electronics, music. Res: 27861 Perales Mission Viejo 92692 Ofc: Greiner Engineering, 1241 E Dyer Rd Ste 250 Santa Ana 92705

ABUL-HAJ, SULEIMAN K., physician; b. Apr. 20, 1925, Palestine, nat. USA 1955; s. Sheikh Khalil M. and S. Butheina (Oda) Abul-Haj; m. Elizabeth Abood, Feb. 11, 1948; children: Charles b. 1948, Alan b. 1957, Cary b. 1958; edn: BS, UC Berkeley 1949; MS, UC San Francisco 1951, MD, 1955. Career: research assoc. Univ. Calif. Sch. of Medicine, San Francisco 1950-54; fellow National Cancer Inst. 1955-56; surgical pathologist Brooke Army Gen. Hosp. 1957-59; chief Clinical & Surgical Pathology, Walter Reed Army Hosp. 1959-62; senior surgical pathologist USC-LA Co. Med. Center, 1962; pathologist-in-chief Community Memorial Hosp., Ventura 1964-80, and General Hosp. Ventura County 1964-74; assoc. clin. prof. USC 1963–; dir. Pathology Service Medical Group, 1970–; cons. Armed Forces Inst. of Pathology 1960–, Camarillo State Hosp. (1965-70), Tripler Army-Navy Hosp. (1964-68); awards: Borden's Award for Disting. Research 1955, Army Certificate of Achievement 1962; mem: AMA, Calif. Med. Assn., Coll. of Am. Pathologists, Am. Soc. of Clin. Pathologists, Internat. Coll. of Surgeons, NY Acad. of Scis., Internat. Platform Assn., AAAS, Am. Cancer Soc., Tricounties Blood Bank, Jonathan Club; num. publs. in fields of cancer, heart diseases, kidney diseases, skin diseases and pediatric diseases; mil: major M.C. US Army; Republican; rec: fine arts, antiques. Res: 105 Encinal Way Ventura 93001

ACHESON, LOUIS KRUZAN, JR., aerospace engineer and general systems analyst; b. Apr. 2, 1926 Brazil, Ind.; s. Louis Kruzan and Irene Ruth (Morrison) A.; edn: BS elec. eng. Case Inst. of Tech, l946; PhD, theoretical. physics, M.I.T., l950; m. Hyla Cook, July 12, 1958; children: Mari, b. 1961 William, b. 1964. Career: mem. tech. staff, chief scientist System Design Labs., Space and Communications Gp., Hughes Aircraft Co., Los Angeles 1950-89, ret.; Inst. for Defense Analyses (IDA), the Pentagon, 1958-59; awards: Cady Staley award, Case Inst. of Tech. 1946; Dr. of Celestial Cerebration (Blue Sky Thinker) 1959, Advanced Res. Projects Agy. (ARPA) award to orgzr. of US Missile and Space Pgm in First Yr. of the Space Age WDC; Destination 90 Award, 1968, Planning. Dirs. Co. and City, Los Angeles, Burbank, San Fernando; Maharishi Award 1979, World Govt. of the Age of Enlightenment; mem: Internat. Soc. for the Systems Scis., Am. Physical Soc., Am. Inst. of Aero and Astron., AAAS, World Federalists, Bertrand Russell Soc., ACLU, Mensa, Worldview Exploration Sem. (ed. 1970-94), Unity-and-Diversity Council, Sigma Xi, Tau Beta Pi, Eta Kappa Nu, Theta Tau, hon. frats., Sigma Chi (social); Publs: num. sci., mil. system studies; arts. in Physical Rev., Internat Jour of Gen. Systems: Destination Ninety Forum Reports 1967-68; LAPD Studies, 1969; reports on payload requirements for sci. satellites and spacecraft, 1970-80; ed. Satellite Handbook for Remote Environ. and Weather Determination, vol. 1, 1976, vol. 2, 1980; ed. Internat. Cooperation Council mag. 1970-75, annual dir. 1970-79; ed. Unity and Diversity Council mag., 1987-93; Democrat. Res: 17721 Marcello Place, Encino 91316

ADAMS, AUDREY LEE, physician; b. Mar. 27, 1952, Sioux Falls, S.Dak.; d. James R., Sr. and Louise (Lewis) Adams; edn: BS medicine, Univ. S.Dak. 1975; MD, Northwestern Univ. 1976. Career: asst. prof. anesthesiology Univ. of Chgo. 1981-82; asst. prof. anesthesia UC Irvine and chief surgical intensive care UCI 1982-85, assoc. prof. anesthesia, volunteer faculty, UCI, 1985-92; staff anesthesiologist Circle City Hosp. Corona 1985-92; chief of anesthesia Circle City Hosp., 1989-90; staff anesthesiologist Good Samaritan Healthcare Sys. 1994–; awards: Univ. of Chgo. Med. Housestaff tchg. award (1982), listed Who's Who in Am. Women (1984); mem: Soc. of Critical Care Medicine, Am. Soc. of Anesthesiology, Internat. Anesthesia Research Soc.; publs: numerous research articles; rec: backpacking, skiing, kayaking, photog./darkroom. Address: Los Gatos 95032

ADAMS, EARL RICHARD, architectural designer/artist; b. Aug. 6, 1930, McKee's Rocks, Pa.; s. Lloyd Theodore and Ruth (Rose) A.; m. Margaret D. Salazar Soto, May 2, 1955 (div.); children: E. Robert, Jonathan B., Gregory V., Wendy C.; edn: BSArch., Calif. St. Polytech. Univ., Pomona, 1982. Career: draftsman nuclear products div. ACF, Wash. D.C. 1956-57; design-drafter/facilities splst. Gen. Dynamics, Pomona 1958-81; c.e.o./founder ERA Design Consultants Ltd., Pomona 1981–; designer Exo Sensors, Anaheim 1984-86; tech. illustrator/graphic designer Sargent-Fletcher Co., El Monte 1986-89; sr. architect drafter C/L Builders-Developers, Inc. 1989; CEO/founder ERA Designs Ltd., 1990–; senior architl. designer Al Aguirre & Associates, Riverside 1991–; CEO/founder Revolution to Restore Citizens Rights, Pomona 1988; 3rd Party; Prot.; rec: photography, travel, fine art, industrial design, electronics. Ofc: ERA Designs Ltd. 12120 Raley Dr Riverside 92505

ADAMS, JACK, screenwriter, producer, director, educator; b. Sept. 15, 1952, Lakehurst, N.J.; s. John Carey and Dorothy Jeanne (Conover) A.; m. Shirley Janulewicz, June 28, 1975; children: Carey Miller, Chanine Angelina, Mikael Walter, Jozef Conover; edn: MusB in music edn., Univ. Dela., 1974. Career: pres. Koala Studio, Valencia 1977–; v.p. devel. Unifilms Inc., North Hollywood 1984–; founder Writers Anonymous, 1988; co-founder ScripTip, 1990; instr. film, TV writing and script analysis: Coll. of the Canyons, Valencia 1988–; L.A. City Coll. 1989–; EveryWoman's Village, Van Nuys, Info. Exchange, L.A., Learning Tree Univ. (Teacher of Year 1992), Chatsworth, Info. Network, S.Pasadena, 1990–; Univ. Wis., Madison and Milwaukee, USIA, W.D.C., Moorpark Coll., Oxnard Coll., Northwestern Univ., Classes Unlimited,

S.Pasadena, Glendale Comm. Coll., 1991–, Univ. of Calif., Fullerton 1995; founding mem. bd. dirs., ofcr. L.A. Filmmakers Workshop, 1989-91; founder, Santa Clarita Scriptwriters' Workshop; mem. Larry Wilson Devel. Workshop, Paramount Studios; mem. Storyboard Devel. Group, Paramount Studios, 1989–, Le Group; pres. Entertainment Writers' Workshop, 1990; pres. NBC Writers' Workshop; mem. KNX Speakers Bur. (CBS Radio) 1989–; mem. Independent Feature Project West; composer (film) EAT, 1980 (Filmex award 1981, best short film award Cinemagic mag. 1981); writer, co-creator sitcom pilot LOLA, Universal Studios, 1991; writer, developer sitcom pilot FAT FARM; writer, prod., dir. sitcom pilot BOX #22; line prod. sitcom pilot, ZEBRA, and IT'S NOT MY FAULT; mem: Am. Film Inst. (alumni assn. writers workshop), Scriptwriters' Network (bd. advrs.), Film Artists Network, Independent Writers So. Calif. Scriptwriters' Caucus, Assn. Information Systems Profls. (bd. 1983), Freelance Screenwriters' Forum (founding bd., TV editor, F.S.F. Newsletter 1990–, columnist Screenwrite Now mag. 1991–), Comedy Writers Co-op (founding ABC), Wis. Screenwriters Forum (cons., advr. 1989-91); active YMCA Indian Guides/Indian Princesses and Trailblazers pgms. (chief Apache Tribe 1990); columnist Creative Screenwriting mag. 1994–; rec: tennis, still photog., music. Res/Ofc: 22931 Sycamore Creek Dr Santa Clarita 91354-2050 Ph:805/297-2000

ADAMS, MICHAEL, physician; b. Aug. 1, 1933, Yosemite, Calif.; s. Ansel E. and Virginia Rose (Best) A.; m. Jeanne Victoria Falk, July 28, 1962; children: Sarah Jeanne b. 1965, Matthew b. 1967; edn: attended Stanford Univ. 1951-53; BA, Fresno State Coll., Fresno, Calif. 1962; MD, Washington Univ. Sch. Medicine, St. Louis, Mo. 1967. Career: mgr. Tuolunme Lode, Yosemite Park & Curry Co., Yosemite, Calif., summer 1958-61; asst. Mgr. Wawona Hotel, Yosemite, Calif., summer 1963; pilot USAF/Calif. Air Guard, 1953-63; pilot/physician (flight surgeon) USAF/Calif. Air Guard, 1967-88; Air Guard asst. SAC/SG and USAF/Surgeon General (Major Gen.), 1988-93; physician, pvt. practice, Fresno, Calif. 1974–; bd. chmn. Best's Studio, Inc. dba Ansel Adams Gallery, Yosemite, Calif. 1971–; asst. clinical prof. of medicine UCSF Med. Sch., Fresno 1976–; mem. Bd. of Fellows, Center for Great Photo., Univ. Ariz., Tucson, Ariz. 1989–; awards: Flight Surgeon of the Year, USAF Europe, Bitburg AB, Germany 1968, Disting. Alumnus, Calif. State Univ., Fresno 1990, Disting. Alumnus, Wasatch Acad., Mt. Pleasant, Utah 1994; mem: Aerospace Med. Assn. (fellow) 1991–, Am. Coll. of Physicians (fellow) 1994–, Alliance of ANG Flight Surgeons (fellow), Am. Soc. of Internal Medicine, Calif. Med. Assn., Civil Aviation Assn., Fresno-Madera Med. Soc. (v.p. 1984), Soc. of USAF Flight Surgeons, Soc. of Air Force Physicians, Internat. Assn. Military/Pilot Physicians; mil: major general, USAF/Calif. Air Nat. Guard 1953-93. Ofc: 4770 W. Herndon Ave, Fresno 93722

ADAMSON, GEOFFREY DAVID, reproductive endocrinologist, surgeon; b. , Sept. 16, 1946, Ottawa, Ont., Can.; came to U.S. 1978, naturalized 1986; s. Geoffrey Peter Adamson and Anne Marian Allan; m. Rosemary C. Oddie, Apr. 28, 1973; children: Stephanie, Rebecca, Eric; edn: BSc with honors, Trinity Coll., Toronto 1969; MD, Univ. Toronto, 1973; Diplomate Am. Bd. Ob-Gyn., Am. Bd. Laser Surgery; cert. Bd. Reproductive Endocrinology. Career: resident in ob-gyn. Toronto Gen. Hosp. 1973-77; fellow in ob-gyn., 1977-78; fellow reproductive endocrinology Stanford (Calif.) Univ. Med. Ctr., 1978-80; practice medicine specializing in infertility Los Gatos, Calif. 1990-84; instr. Sch. of Medicine Stanford Univ., Calif., 1980-84, clin. asst. prof., 1984-92; clin, assoc. prof. Stanford Univ., San Francisco 1992–, assoc. clin. prof. Sch. Medicine UC, San Francisco, 1992–; Ontario Ministry of Health fellow, 1977-78; fellow ACS, Royal Coll. Surgeons Can., Am. Coll. Ob-Gyns.; AAAS, AMA, Am. Soc. for Reproductive Medicine, Soc. Reproductive Surgeons (charter, dir.), Soc. Assisted Reproductive Tech. (dir.), Psychological Profl. Group (past pres.), Pacific Coast Fertility Soc. (dir.), Pacific Coast Ob-Gyn. Soc., Soc. Gynecologic Surgeons, San Francisco Ob-Gyn. Soc., Bay Area Reproductive Endocrinologists Soc., (founding pres.), Am. Assn. Gynecol., Laparoscopists, Gynecol. Laser Soc., NY Acad. Scis., Shufelt Gynecol. Soc., Peninsula Gynecol. Soc. (past pres.), Calif. Med. Assn., San Mateo Co. Med. Assn., Santa Clara Co. Med. Assn., Am. Fedn. Clin. Res., Nat. Resolve (bd. dir.), Can. Assn. Interns and Residents (hon. life, pres. 1977-79, bd. dir. 1974-79, rep. AMA resident physician sect. 1978-79, rep. Can. Med. Protective Assn. 1975-78, rep. Can. Med. Assn. 1975-78, disting. svc. award 1980), Profl. Assn. Interns and Residents, Ont. (bd. dir. 1973-76, v.p. 1974-75, pres. 1975-76), Royal Coll. Physicians and Surgeons Can. (Ont. exams. 1977-80), Ont. Med. Assn. (Sec. Interns and residents sect. 1973-74); mem. edit. advy. bd. Can. Doctor mag. 1977-83; contbr. num. articles to sci. jours. and books. Ofc: 540 University Ave # 200 Palo Alto CA 94301-1912

ADAMSON, MARY ANNE, utilities research analyst; b. June 25, 1954, Berkeley; d. A. Frank and Frances I. (Key) A.; m. Richard John Harrington, Sept. 20, 1974; edn: BA (highest honors) geography & gt. distinction in gen. scholarship, UC Berkeley, 1975, MA, 1976, postgrad. (cand. PhD) 1978. Career: scientist Lawrence Livermore Nat. Lab., Livermore 1978-83, cons. 1983-86; systems engr. ESL (Electromagnetic Systems Lab.), Sunnyvale 1986-90; res. analyst PG&E, San Francisco 1990–; awards: Phi Beta Kappa 1975, citation for outstanding undergrad. accomplishment dept. geography UC Berkeley 1975;

mem: Assn. of Am. Geographers (1975–, Life), UC Alumnae Assn. (1975–, Life), Commonwealth Club S.F., Toastmasters Internat. Blue Monday Club S.F. (edn. v.p. 1991), Nat. Speleol. Soc. Diablo Grotto Chpt. (exec. bd., editor 1982-86), Mountain Medicine Inst. Oakland (asst. chief engr. 1983–). Ofc: PG&E, 50 Fremont St Ste 2023 San Francisco 94105

ADEN, ARTHUR L., retired engineering executive; b. Feb. 1, 1924, Ford County, Ill.; s. Johann Franzen and Ida M. (Hafermann) A.; m. Leona Hoff, June 21, 1944; children: Donald b. 1945, Charles b. 1949, Sherry b. 1951, Gary b. 1953; edn: N. Ill. St. Coll. 1941-43, Univ. Mich. 1943-44; MA, Harvard Univ. 1948, M. Engring. Sci., 1949, PhD, 1950. Career: section hd. Cambridge Resrch. Center, Cambridge, Mass. 1950-53; engring. mgr./asst. lab. mgr. Sylvania Elec. Products, Mountain View, Calif. 1953-58; assoc. tech. dir. Mil. Electronics Div. and mgr. ops. Solid State Systems Div., Motorola Inc., Phoenix, Az. 1953-58; v.p. Electro Optical Systems and mgr. central engring. Information Products Div., Xerox Corp., Pasadena, Dallas, and Fremont, Calif., 1963-89; awards: scholarship N. Ill. State Coll. (1941-43), Gordon McKay Scholar (1947), Nat. Resrch. Council predoc. fellow (1948-50), Sigma Xi, Sigma Zeta; mem: Fellow IEEE (engr. of year Phoenix Sect. 1963, sect. chmn. Pasadena and Phoenix, chmn. Nat. Symp. of PGMTT, S.F., 1958), Am. Mgmt. Assn.; publs: 30+ tech. papers, contbg. writer one book; 1 Patent; mil: 1st lt. Army Air Corps 1943-46; Lutheran; rec: hiking, photog., music.

ADKINS, THOMAS JAY, financial executive; b. Sept. 12, 1953, Compton; s. Eugene L. and Faye Ilene (Kindy) A.; m. Marilee Kay Jennings, July 15, 1972; children: Benjamin b. 1973, Timothy b. 1976, Mark b. 1982, Stephen b. 1986; edn: AA, El Camino Coll. 1983; BS magna cum laude, USC 1986; Cert. Mgmt. Accountant (CMA). Career: sr. acct. Martin Marietta Aluminum, Torrance 1980-84; fin. adminstr. Internat. Light Metals 1984-87; dir. fin. Magna Mill Products, South Gate 1987-88; controller Internat. Light Metals, Torrance 1988-91; CFO, Direct Express, Inc.; owner Adkins Business Consulting, Padgett Business Services of Torrance; chmn. supervisory com. Martin Maretta Fed. Credit Union; honors: Alpha Gamma Sigma; mem: Nat. Assn. Accts., Controllers Council, Inst. of Mgmt. Accountants, So. Calif. Soc. of CMA's, Nat. Soc. of Public Accountants, USC Commerce Assocs.; Christian. Res: 2627 W 175th St Torrance 90504 Ofc: 20505 Annalee Ave Carson 90746

ADLER, ERWIN ELLERY, lawyer; b. July 22, 1944, Flint, Mich.; s. Ben and Helen M. (Schwartz) A.; m. Stephanie Ruskin, June 8, 1967; children: Lauren M. b. 1974, Michael B. b. 1977, Jonathan S. b. 1981; edn: BA, Univ. of Mich., 1963, JD, Harvard Law Sch., 1966, LL.M. Univ. of Mich. Law Sch., 1967. Career: assoc. Pillsbury Madison & Sutro law firm, 1967-73; assoc., partner law firm Lawler, Felix & Hall, 1973-82; ptnr. law firm Rogers & Wells, 1982-84; ptnr. law firm Richards, Watson & Gershon, Los Angeles 1985–; bd. dirs. Hollywood Opera Assocs. 1975-76; bd. dirs. Childrens Scholarships Inc. 1978-79; v.chmn. Appellate Advocacy Com. American Bar Assn.; honors: Phi Beta Kappa, Phi Kappa Phi; mem. Am. Bar Assn. 1967–, Calif. Bar Assn. 1967–, LA Athletic Club; Jewish; rec: photog., jogging. Res: 872 Norman Pl Los Angeles 90049 Ofc: Richards, Watson & Gershon, 333 So Hope St 38th Flr Los Angeles 90071

ADLER, JACK, writer, journalist; b. Jan. 8, 1940, New York; m. Barbro; Career: freelance columnist, travel section L.A. Times 1978-93; west coast bureau chief Travel Trade 1984–; leader, Travel Bulletin Bd., Prodigy; awards: grantee Yaddo Found. 1962; mem: Soc. Am. Travel Writers, Writers Guild of Am.; author: Exploring Historic Calif., 1974, Consumer's Guide to Travel, 1984, Travel Security (co-author 1988), Companion Guide to Southern India, 1991, plays: The Bed, Webs, The Retreat, Agis, Looking for Rosa. Res: 6122 Shadyglade Ave, North Hollywood 91606

AGRUSS, BERNARD, scientist, electrochemical engineer, ret.; b. Oct. 12, 1911, St. Louis, Mo.; s. Benjamin and Rose (Harris) A.; 1 dau., Jill b. 1943; edn: BSCE, Wash. Univ. St. Louis 1933; MS, 1934; PhD, Univ. Cincinnati 1937. Career: chief electrochemist ASARCO, Perth Amboy, N.J. 1941-44; research engr. Battelle Meml., Columbus, Ohio 1944-47; Engring. Research Inst., Univ. Mich. 1947-50; head battery dept. Nat. Lead Co., Bklyn. N.Y. 1950-59; tech. asst. to dept. head G.M. Allison Div., Indianapolis, Ind. 1959-67; sr. tech. staff G.M. Research, Warren, Mich. 1967-74; ret.; cons. First Ministry, China 1979; Tsing Hua Univ., Taiwan 1974; vol. exec. Hang Shin Battery, S.Korea 1943-44; pres. elect Sharp Cabrillo Hosp. Auxiliary 1989-90; instr. Grossmont Comm. Dist.; awards: Am. Electroplaters Soc. Prize Paper (1947); mem: Am. Chem. Soc., Electrochem. Soc. (life), Poly Photo Club (treas. 1987-90); ed. Electrochemistry (1980), 3 patents in field (1958, 66, 70), 26 articles pub. in tech. jours. (1935-71); Republican; Jewish; rec: photog. Res: 3950 Leland St San Diego 92106

AHDAN, PAUL S., marketing & sales company president; b. Apr. 20, 1942, Punjab, nat. U.S.A. 1964; s. G.S. and K.K. Ahdan; m. Jennie K., Mar. 26, 1965; 1 child, Ranbir; edn: AMIEX (MBA) Reg. St. Polytech Inst. of Export, London 1971; BSME, Heads Engring., S.F. 1975; MBA (Calif.) 1992. Career: asst. import-export mgr. Singer Bus. Machines, San Leandro, Calif. 1968-74; gen. traffic mgr. Commodore Bus. Machines, Palo Alto 1974-75; contracts mgr.

Granger Assocs., Menlo Park 1975-77; internat. mktg. mgr. Fairchild Camera & Instrument Corp., Mt. View 1977-83; internat. sales & mktg. mgr. Boschert Inc., Sunnyvale 1983-84; v.p. sales & mktg. PAD S.A., Paris, Fr., 1985-87; internat. sales & mktg. ops. mgr. Alcatel N.V., Info. Systems Div., 1987-88; dir. internat. sales PEGI, San Carlos 1988-89; pres. Rantronics Internat. Ltd., Los Altos 1989–, also pres. Rancor Internat. Ltd., W.Ger. 1990–; Sikh; rec: sports, stamps, coins, travel.

AHRENS, ERICK K.F., computer software executive; b. Feb. 22, 1949, Detroit, Mich.; s. Herman F. Ahrens and Evelyn V. (Metcalf) Finch; m. Dorothy A. Swiercz, June 22, 1972; edn: AA in math., Coll. of San Mateo, 1975; BS in engring., UC Berkeley, 1980; MBA, San Francisco St. Univ., 1987. Career: computer pgmr. Victor Comptometer, S.San Francisco 1975; res. and devel. engr. Earl and Wright, San Francisco 1976-83; v.p. Molecular Design Ltd., San Leandro 1984-93; v.p. UDI Software, Novato 1994–; honors: Alpha Gamma Sigma 1975; mem: Assn. for Computing Machinery 1979–, IEEE Computer Soc. 1988–, Am. Chem. Soc. 1985–; clubs: Marin Sail and Power Squadron, Novato (past comdr.), Corinthian Yacht, Tiburon (Harbor pres.); publs: tech. papers; mil: machinist mate USN 1969-73; rec: sailing. Res: PO Box 20984 Castro Valley 94546 Ofc: UDI Software 4 Commercial Blvd Novato 94949

AIJIAN, PAUL MISAK, minister, psychotherapist; b. Sept. 20, 1917, Detroit, Mich.; s. Misak Michael and Mabel Maude (Schuyler) A.; m. Arlys Ehlers, Dec. 19, 1950; children: Rachael b. 1952, Phillip b. 1954, David b. 1956, Rebecca b. 1958, Stephen b. 1962; edn: BA, UCLA, 1940; tchg. credential 1941; BD, San Francisco Theol. Sem., 1944, STM, 1946; PhD, USC, 1947. Career: pastor Hollenbeck Presbyterian Ch., Los Angeles 1947-49; pastoral asst. Wilshire Presbyterian Ch. 1950-54; head English dept. Biola Univ. 1949-54, faculty Talbot Theological Seminary 1951-53; pastor St. John's Presbyterian Ch., Long Beach 1955-63; faculty philosphy Univ. Mississippi, Oxford 1963-64; head. dept. philosophy North Central Coll., Naperville, Ill. 1965-66; pastor First Presbyterian Ch., North Hollywood 1966-80; dir. grad. study Am. Inst. Family Rels., Los Angeles 1980-83; dir. Am. Family Counseling Services, Woodland Hills 1983-85; sr. counselor The Healing Tree, Burbank 1985-88; adj. prof. U.S. Internat. Univ., San Diego 1985-88; honors: Phi Epsilon Theta, Phi Xi Phi, man of year No. Hollywood Community Adult Sch. 1981; mem: Kiwanis (pres. 1974-75), Long Beach Mental Health (pres. 1961-62); Democrat; Prot. Res/Ofc: 29854 Violet Hills Dr Canyon Country 91351-1932 also: 7041 Owensmouth Ave #202 Canoga Park 91503

AILSHIE, ROGER ALLEN, auditor; b. Sept. 27, 1962, Hutchinson, Kans.; s. Roger Howard and Jeanette Ray (McCall) A.; m. Jennifer Margaret Arkeder; edn: BS acctg., Baker Univ., 1987. Career: staff acct. Lindburg & Vogel, Hutchinson, Kans. 1987-88; senior auditor D.C.A.A., Mountain View, Calif. 1989-93; sr. auditor E.P.R.I., Palo Alto 1993-95; recipient profl. award for superior accomplishment DCAA (1989); mem: Assn. of Govt. Accts., Zeta Chi frat. (pres. 1987); Methodist; rec: basketball, raquetball, softball. Res: 1276 C St Hayward 94541 Ofc: EPRI 3412 Hillview Ave Palo Alto 94304

AIRES, RAMON HESS, consultant and technical advisor to management, ret. engineering executive; b. March 15, 1927, Lancaster, Pa.; s. Ray G. and Anna (Hess) A.; m. Jane Elizabeth Hawk, Sept. 6, 1952; children: Victoria b. 1953, David b. 1954, Mark b. 1957, Lisa b. 1959, Timothy b. 1962; edn: BEE, Cornell Univ. 1950; MSEE, Univ. Pa. Phila. 1959; reg. profl. engr. in control systems engr., 1978–. Career: engr. Philco, Phila., Pa. 1950-54; mgr., engr. RCA Defense Electronic Products, Camden, Princeton and Sommerville, N.J., 1954-65; chief engr. RCA Avionic Systems, Van Nuys, Calif. 1965-81; Sperry Avionics 1981-82; v.p. ops.and engring, Teloc Inc. 1982-86; v.p. and tech. adv. to the pres. Datatape Inc. (a Kodak Co.), Pasadena 1986-93; advy. bd. CSU Northridge 1974-92; awards: RCA Corp. David Sarnoff Tech. Achievement award (1978); mem: IEEE (sr.), Inst. Advancement Engring. (fellow), Masons; 10 patents (1952-86); mil: USN 1945-46; Presbyterian; rec: model trains, railroading, cars, music, pipe organs, computers, stock market. Res: 16653 Pineridge Dr Granada Hills 91344-1849

AIROLA, VIRGIL MARION, II, physician; b. Apr. 20, 1949, Oakland, Calif.; s. Virgil Raymond Airola and Caroline M. Lemon; m. Mary G.; children: David, Michael, John; edn: AB, UC Berkeley 1971; MD, Baylor Coll. of Medicine, Houston, Tx. 1974. Career: asst. prof. of anesthesiology, SUNY, Syracuse, NY 1980-81; clinical asst. prof. of pediatrics, U.C.S.F., Fresno, Calif. 1989–; honors: bd. certification: anesthesiology 1980, critical care 1989; mem: Am. Soc. of Anesthesiologists 1977–, AMA 1980–, CMA 1981–, Calif. Soc. of Anesthesiologists 1981- (Region 5 delegate), Fresno-Madera Med. Soc. 1981–, Pediatric Anesthesia Associates 1981–. Ofc: 3152 N. Millbrook Ave #D Fresno 93703

AKER, "DEE" DIANNE LEE, cross-cultural psychologist/anthropologist, educator, writer, consultant, university president; b. July 5, 1941, Kankakee, Ill.; d. Herald W. Stockton and Marjorie (Martin) Walley; m. William Bryson Smith, July 15, 1989; edn: BS biol./sociol., Southwest Mo. St. Univ., 1963; MA internat. affairs, Ohio Univ., 1973; PhD humanistic psych./cultural anthropology, The

Union Inst., Cinti. 1977. Career: vol. Peace Corps Colombia, S.A. 1963-64; resrch. asst. N.J. Neuro-Psychiat. Inst., Princeton 1965-67; soc. wkr. L.A. County Dept. Soc. Svs., 1968-72; vol. Kibbutz and archaeol. site, Israel 1968; coord. supr. Frontier Dist. Mental Health Ctr., Washington County, Oh. 1974-75; ldr. in residence Esalen Inst., Big Sur 1975-79; cons. prin., U.S., Canada, Europe, Israel, Africa, 1975-80; East-West Vis. Scientist Exchange, Poland, 1979; faculty U.S. Internat. Univ., San Diego 1978-79, faculty USIU-Africa, Nairobi, Kenya 1979-84, univ. dean 80-82, dir. 82-84, asst. v.p. USIU, San Diego 1984-87, dir. USIU Orange County Graduate Center, Irvine 1985-90; dean academic affairs Univ. for Humanistic Studies, 1991-93, pres. 1993–; prod./host weekly TV interview show "Women" KUSI-TV, San Diego 1985-91, Emmy Award nominee: "Women - The Uganda Women's Effort to Save the Orphan" 1990; cons./pres. Daker Cross-Cultural Prodns., 1986-91; prod./dir. video documentaries: Uganda: An African Phoenix 1987, Women of Gulfito 1988, Women Leaders of Uganda: A Quiet Revolution in Africa 1990; internat. correspondent Women's Times (monthly column "Human Terms" researched in Algeria, Turkey, Mex., Ireland, Uganda, Ea. Europe, Taiwan, China, 1992-94); numerous profl. papers and presentations; awards: Honors throughout academic career, Nat. Phys. Edn. Hon. Soc., Alpha Kappa Delta 1961-63, Who's Who Am. Colls. and Univs. 1963, Ohio Univ. grad. asst. 1972-3, Who's Who in Kenya 1982-84, lifetime achiev. Saddleback Comm. Coll. 1986, Philanthropy Award for profl. achiev. Nat. Soc. Fundraising Execs. L.A. 1987, career achiev. Rancho Santiago Coll. 1988, 'Wonderwoman 1990' Award for Edn. San Diego Women's Directory and Small Bus. Assn. 1990, Women of Merit Award in Education, San Diego 1994; mem: The Woman's Found./O.C. (advy. bd. 1986–), OEF/Women in Bus. for Women in Econ. Devel. 1986-90, San Diego Human Rels. Comm. Media Task Force 1987-92, Carl Rogers Inst. for Peace La Jolla (founding bd., staff 1986-90), Am. Women in Radio and TV (1990–, advy. bd. 1991–), Nat. Acad. TV Arts and Scis. 1989–, Assn. for Women in Devel. 1987–, World Trade Ctr. Inst./O.C., World Trade Ctr. Assn. O.C. 1985-86, Ctr. for Studies of the Person, La Jolla (fellow), The Union Inst. San Diego Ctr. (advy. bd. 1991-94), United Nations Women's Equity Council 1995– (official NGO rep. and official observer UN 4th World Conf. on Women, Bejing, 1995); rec: Asian art, photography, adventure travel. Res: 3340 del Sol Blvd #194 San Diego 92154 Ofc: University for Humanistic Studies 380 Stevens Ave., Solana Beach 92075

ALAIMO, TERRY ELLEN, artist; b. June 12, 1942, Rochester, N.Y.; d. Bernard and Mildred Michlin; m. S. Richard Alaimo, Jr., June 18, 1961 (div. 1979); children: Samuel b. 1966, Deborah b. 1969; edn: Rochester Inst. of Tech. Sch. of Art & Design 1961; cert. Am. Inst. Paralegal Studies 1983-84. Career: art dir. Monroe Litho Inc., Rochester, N.Y. 1961-66; fine arts Terry Alaimo Studio 1969-82; fine artist, Rockport, Mass. 1982-84; mediator Crime & Justice Found. Essex Co. Cts., Boston and Gloucester, Mass. 1982-84; paralegal Ross & Watson, Gloucester, Mass. 1984; Swartz & Swartz, Boston, Mass. 1983; fine artist, illustrator Terry Alaimo Studio, Laguna Beach 1984-93; art dir. Empringham, Bradley & Ho (EBH Publications) 1992; cons. TRW-Redi Property Data, Calif. 1993–; exhibits: poetry and visual arts, The Smithsonian, 1976; Miniature Painters, Sculptors & Engravers Soc., Wash. D.C. Art Club, 1975; Mus. of Duncans, Paris and N.Y.C., 1979; one woman shows Washington Art Expo. 1976, 78, 79, 80; awards: Miniature Art Soc. Fla. semi-abstract 1977, Chautaqua (N.Y.) Inst. Award Exh. of American Art 1977, Staudenmaier award Rochester Art Club 1978, 81, Laguna Art Mus. All Calif. Show small-scale 1986; mem: Am. Arbitration Assn., Printing Industries of Am., North Shore Art Assn.; publs: illustrator, Homeowners Guide to Re-roofing, Montage Pub., Jose Cuervo Internat. 1991; OC Ad News Illustration Issue 1991; Calif. Art Review 1989; Unitarian; rec: bicycling, golf, travel. Ofc: Terry Alaimo Studio 2233 Martin St Irvine 92715

ALANIZ, MIGUEL JOSE CASTANEDA, city librarian; b. Oct. 21, 1944, Los Angeles; s. Francisco Martinez and Amalia (Castaneda) A.; m. Mercedes, June 7, 1980; edn: AA edn., Chabot Coll. 1972; BS child/human devel., CSU Hayward 1974; MLS, CSU Fullerton 1975; MPA, CSU San Bernardino, 1988; Calif. Comm. Coll. Tchg. credential. Career: Spanish Services librarian, Alameda Co. 1975-77; branch lib. mgr. San Jose Public Library 1977-78, Santa Ana Public Library 1978-79; coord. Young Adult/ Outreach Svcs., San Bernardino Co. Library 1979-82, div. chief of tech. processing, 1982-84; city librarian City of Azusa 1984–; awards: grad. res. fellow in library sci., CSUF 1974-75; mem: Am. Library Assn., Calif. Library Assn., Reforma (Nat. Assn. Hispanic Librarians), cofounder Bibliotecas Para La Gente (orgn. providing lib. svcs. in Spanish lang.); mil: E5 AUS 1965-71; rec: collect exotic autos, rare books, unusual pets. Ofc: City of Azusa Library 729 N Dalton Ave Azusa 91702

ALARID, WILLIAM MORRIS, engineer, publisher; b. July 4, 1936, Santa Fe, N.M.; s. Jack Justice and Retha (Daniel) A.; m. Elsie Kathleen Sutherland, Nov. 20, 1965; children: Christine b. 1970, David b. 1973; edn: BSAE, Ind. Inst. Tech. 1957. Career: engr. Northwest Airlines, St. Paul, Minn. 1957-58; mgr. Aerojet Gen., Sacto. 1958-65; project engr. Aerospace Corp., Vandenberg AFB 1965–; pres. Puma Publishing, Santa Maria 1986–; awards: Pub. Library Assn. best of best 1989, Toastmasters Internat. 1st place humorous speech 1971, Aerojet Gen. engring. excellence 1956; mem: Am. Mensa Ltd., Publishers Mktg. Assn., Assn. Research & Enlightenment, COSMEP, Internat.

Assn. Indep. Publishers, Sertoma Internat. (membership chmn. 1966-71), Toastmasters Internat. (v.p. 1968-72), BSA (chmn. 1984-88), Explorer Post (chmn. 1988–), Alpha Gamma Epsilon (v.p. 1955-56); author: Free Help from Uncle Sam 1988, Money Sources for Small Business 1991; editor ESP newsletter 1980; Republican; R.Cath.; rec: skiing, hiking, writing. Res: 1670 Coral Dr Santa Maria 93454

ALBERS, CAROLYN JEAN, lawyer; b. July 22, 1947, Akron, Ohio; d. John Edwin and Martha Beryl (Taylor) Albers; m. Robert F. Perez, June 8, 1968, div. Oct. 1975; m. Ricardo R. Baca, Feb. 20, 1994; edn: BA, CSU Sacto., 1969; MS, CSU Fresno, 1974; JD (Valedictorian), San Joaquin Coll. of Law, 1984; reg. dietitian 1975; admitted Calif. bar 1984. Career: nutritionist Kaiser Hosp., Sacto. 1969-72; instr., vis., CSU Fresno, 1977, 78-83; clinical dietitian Valley Med. Ctr., Fresno 1975-84; law clk. Marderosian, et al, 1982; instr. para-legal courses San Joaquin Coll. of Law, 1985-87; atty., assoc. Blumberg, Kerkorian, 1984-87, partner Blumberg, Seng, Ikeda & Albers 1988–; treas. City Councilman Anaforian, Fresno 1984; honors: Delta Theta Phi law frat. scholarship key 1983, Fresno Co. Superior Ct. Judges Award 1983, disting. svc. Kidney Found. Fresno 1979, 85; mem: ABA, Fresno Co. Bar Assn. (judicial advy. and selection com. 1989-92), Cent. Valley, Calif. and Am. Dietetic Assn.; civic: Citizens Advy. Commn. to Fresno City Council (v.ch. 1985), Fresno-Madera Medical PAC (bd. 1987), Nat. Kidney Found. Fresno (cent. valley chpt. bd. 1978-89, pres. 1978-79), Am. Heart Assn. Fresno (cent. valley chpt. bd. 1985-89, chair 1988-89), Am. Diabetes Assn. Fresno (chpt. advy. bd. 1979-88, bd. dirs. 1986-89, pres. 1988), steering com. San Joaquin Coll. of Law, 1986; publs: nutrition bibliography and articles, 1978, 79; Republican; Presbyterian; rec: travel. Ofc: Blumberg, Seng, Ikeda & Albers 10 River Park Place East, Ste 220 Fresno 93720-1964

ALBERT, RONALD PETER, lawyer; b. Sept. 10, 1956, Utica, N.Y.; s. Raymond J. and Monica; edn: AB econs. (magna cum laude), UC Davis, 1979; JD, UC Berkeley, 1983; admitted bar: Calif.; lic. Calif. R.E. Broker. Career: acct. Davidson, Dreyer & Hopkins, San Francisco, 1979-80; atty. Law Offices of Ronald P. Albert, San Diego, 1983-87; prof. of law Syracuse Univ., Utica, N.Y., 1987-88; atty. law firm Griffinger Levinson Freed & Heinemann, San Francisco, 1988-93; Law Ofc. of Ronald P. Albert 1994–; lectr. in real estate law UC Berkeley 1993–; pro bono vol. Tax-Aid, S.F., 1989–, Volunteer Lawyers Service Progam, S.F., 1990–; honors: Moot Ct. Bd. and California Law Rev., UC Berkeley 1982-83; mem: Am. Bar Assn. (1983–, sect. taxation 1988–), State Bar Calif. 1983–, New York State Bar 1984–, Bar Assn. San Francisco 1988–; mem. Kts. of Col. Ofc: 60 Edwards Ave Sausalito 94965-2514

ALDEN, SCOTT DOUGLAS, company president; b. July 20, 1951, Covina; s. Charles and Adele Pearl (Coty) A.; m. Theresa Blanco; 2 sons, Desmond and Trevor; edn: BA fin., CSU Fullerton 1973; MBA, CSU Long Beach 1977; MSBA mktg., USC 1984; PhD (abd) urban planning, USC 1987; PhD marketing, PWU 1993. Career: owner, gen. mgr. Calif. Aquarium Leasing, Tustin 1970-74; mgr., buyer Menswear Retailers 1969-77; instr. Brooks Coll., Long Beach 1975-78; lectr. USC, L.A. 1978-84; instr. Purdue Univ., West Lafayette, Ind. 1985; Whittier Coll. 1986-91; owner, research dir. Alden & Assoc., Hermosa Beach 1977–; awards: USC 20 Best Tchrs. 1983; mem: Am. Mktg. Assn., Assn. Consumer Research, Acad. Mktg. Sci., Am. Planning Assn., Western Mktg. Educators; articles pub. in profl. jours., speaker at profl. confs.; Republican; Christian; rec: gardening, surfing. Res: 646 Sixth St Hermosa Beach 90254

ALDERMAN, ROBERT FRANK, civil engineer; b. Aug. 1, 1932, Los Angeles; s. Frank Edward and Frances Louise (Adams) A.; m. Eunice Alderman, Sept. 11, 1953; children: Jeffrey b. 1955, Karen b. 1957; edn: BSCE, Stanford Univ. 1954; Reg. Profl. Civil Engr., Calif. 1958. Career: engring. aide Calif. Div. of Highways, Los Angeles 1950-53; laborer Renz Constrn., Santa Clara 1954; design engr. Alderman & Swift, So. Pasadena 1955-58; asst. water supt. City of Alhambra, Alhambra 1958-64; project engr. Toups Engineering, Santa Ana 1964-66; v.p. Willdan Associates, Anaheim 1966-79; dir. of engring. San Luis Engring. Inc., Arroyo Grande 1979-90; sr. engr. Penfield & Smith, San Luis Obispo 1990-91; Alderman Engring. 1991-94 (ret.); instr. math and hydraulics Santa Ana Coll. 1970-79; instr. water and waste water treatment Allen Hancock Coll., Santa Maria 1980-83; honors: Award of Merit, Inst. of Transportation Engrs. 1978; mem: Am. Soc. of Civil Engrs. (br. pres. 1983-85), Am. Public Works Assn., Pub. Rels. Com., Inst. of Transportation Engrs, Am. Water Works Assn., Temple City Toastmasters (past pres. 1962); Republican; Nazarene; rec: golf, travel, photog. Res: 6080 Joan Pl. San Luis Obispo 93401

ALDRICH, DAVID LAWRENCE, public relations executive; b. Feb. 21, 1948, Lakehurst N.A.S., NJ; s. Clarence Edward and Sarah Stiles (Andrews) A., Jr., LCDR, USN (ret.); m. Benita Massler, Mar. 17, 1974; edn: Ocean Co. Coll., NJ 1967-8, Sophia Univ., Tokyo 1970-1; BA, CSU Dominguez Hills 1976. Career: reporter/columnist Ocean Co. Daily Observer, NJ 1967-68; asst. public information, City of Carson, Ca. 1974-77; pub. rels. mgr./adminstv. asst. Calif. Federal Svgs, Los Angeles 1977-78; v.p./group supr. Hill & Knowlton, L.A. 1978-81; v.p./mgr. W. Div., Ayer Public Relations, N. W. Ayer, L.A. (bd. Western Region) 1981-84; pres. Aldrich & Assoc., Inc. Public Relations Counsel, 1984–; mem. bd. dirs., chmn. mktg. advy. bd. Drum Corps Internat.;

mil: USAF 1968-72. Democrat; rec: travel, drum & bugle corps competitions. Res: 25 15th Pl #704 Long Beach 90802 Ofc: Aldrich & Assoc., Inc. 110 Pine Ave Ste 620 Long Beach 90802

ALDRICH, MICHAEL RAY, educator, librarian, historian; b. Feb. 7, 1942, Vermillion, S.D.; s. Ray J. and Lucile W. (Hamm) A.; m. Michelle Cauble, Dec. 26, 1977; edn: AB, Princeton, 1964; MA, Univ. So. Dak., 1965; PhD, St. Univ. N.Y., Buffalo 1970. Career: Fulbright tutor Govt. Arts and Commerce Coll., Indore, Madhya Pradesh, India 1965-66; founder Lemar Internat., 1966-71; faculty Sch. Critical Studies, Calif. Inst. Arts, Valencia 1970-72; workshop leader Esalen Inst., San Francisco 1972; co-director AMORPHIA, Inc. (non-profit nat. marijuana res. gp.), Mill Valley 1969-74; curator Fitz Hugh Ludlow Memorial Library, San Francisco 1974–; program coord. Youth Environment Study, AIDS Outreach Tng. Ctr., S.F. 1989-90; program coord. Calif. AIDS Intervention Tng. Ctr., 1990–; freelance writer, photographer, lectr., expert witness, cons. on drug research (splst. in drug laws, hist. & literature) colls., confs., publishers, service groups; author: The Dope Chronicles 1850-1950 (1979),Coricancha, The Golden Enclosure 1983; co-author: High Times Ency. of Recreational Drugs 1978, Fiscal Costs of Calif. Marijuana Law Enforcement 1986, Methods of Estimating Needle Users at Risk for AIDS 1989; editor drug edn. books, ed. Marijuana Rev. 1968-74, Ludlow Library Newsletter 1974–, mem. editorial rev. bd. Jour. Psychoactive Drugs (1981–, editor Marijuana theme issue 1987), contbr. Cocaine Handbook 1981, contbg. ed. High Times 1979-86, research photog. Life mag. 1984; mem. advy. bd. Nat. Orgn. for Reform of Marijuana Laws 1976–; mem. Princeton Univ. Working Group on Future Drug Policy 1990–; past mem. bd. dirs. Calif. Marijuana Initiative 1971-74, Ethnopharmacology Soc. 1976-84; NIDA grantee for AIDS research 1987-88. Ofc: Ludlow Library, POB 640346 San Francisco 94164

ALEKSICH, STEVEN, engineer; b. Apr. 7, 1920, Peoria, Ill.; s. Zivan and Matilda (Boda) A.; edn: BSME, Bradley Univ. 1955; Reg. Profl. Engr., Calif. Career: airframe design engr./standards engr., North Am. Aviation Inc., Downey 1955-60; mem. tech. staff Apollo/Saturn, Rockwell Corp. 1960-68; components engr. Lockheed Aircraft, Burbank 1968-70; components engr. Litton Systems, Inc. Van Nuys/ Woodland Hills 1970-73; mem. tech. staff, project engr. Space Shuttle, Rockwell Internat., Downey 1974-75; standards engr. Kirk Mayer Inc. (job shop) TRW, Redondo Beach 1975-76; senior prodn. design engr. Northrop Corp., Hawthorne 1976-87; sr. engr./scientist McDonnell Douglas Corp., Long Beach 1988-90; mem. US Marine Raider Assn. Inc. (v.p. bd. dirs.); mil: cpl. USMC 1942-45; Eastern Orthodox; rec: design, make and play tamburas (stringed musical instruments of Serbian origin similar to mandolins and guitars). Res: 8227 Arrington Ave Pico Rivera 90660

ALEN, RUPERT O., structural engineer; b. June 8, 1915, Kingsburg; s. Olaf and Julia Adelina (Nystrom) A.; m. Virginia Sandell (div. 1967); children: Helen b. 1942, James b. 1944; m. Eleanor Simon (div. 1981); son, Erich b. 1969; edn: BS, UC Berkeley 1937; MS, 1939. Career: sr. engring. aide Caltrans, Eureka 1937-38; jr. engr. Corps of Engrs., Los Angeles 1939-42; Concrete Ship Constrn., National City 1942-43; materials testing engr. Lockheed Aircraft, Burbank 1943-46; structural engr. Hillman & Nowell, Los Angeles; K. Bardizbanian, Beverly Hills 1947-50; St. Div. of Arch., Sacto. 1950-53; Earl Taylor Architects 1954-56; LeRoy F. Green Assoc. 1956-76; City of Oxnard 1976-83; R.O. Alen Cons. Engrs. 1983–; mem: Toastmasters (club pres. 1969, 72, 90), Calif. Farm Bureau (chapt. pres. 1964); author: History of My Family 1988; mil: seaman 1c. USN 1945-46; Republican; American Presbyterian; rec: photog., commodity trading, travel. Res: 1301 Glenwood Dr Oxnard 93030 Ofc: 995 W 7th St Oxnard 93030

ALEXANDER, GEORGE JONATHON, law professor, author; b. Mar. 8, 1931; married, 2 children; edn: AB (cum laude, Naval Scholar), Coll. of Univ. of Pa., 1953; JD (cum laude, Law Board Scholar), Univ. of Pa. Sch. of Law, 1959; LLM and JSD (Sterling Fellow), Yale Law Sch., 1965, 1969; admitted bar: Calif., Ill., N.Y., Supreme Ct. of U.S. and var. Fed. Cts. Career: instr. in law and Bigelow tchg. fellow Univ. Chgo. Law Sch. 1959-60; prof. of law, assoc. dean (2 yrs.) Syracuse Univ. Coll. of Law 1960-70; prof. of law Santa Clara Univ. Sch. of Law 1970–, dean of law 1970-85; dir. Inst. Internat. and Comparative Law 1986–; vis. scholar Stanford Law Sch. (1985-86, 92); pvt. law practice in antitrust, trade secrets and other trade regulations, civil liberties, problems of aging and invol. commitment; judge pro tem Santa Clara Co. Municipal Ct. 1979–; cons. on ednl. pgms., panelist Comptroller General's Resrch. and Edn. Advy. Panel (R.E.A.P.), 1977–; frequent lectr. univs. and bar assn. and med. assn. confs.; awards: Order of Coif 1968, Justinian Hon. Soc. 1970, Am. Inst. for Pub. Service finalist Nat. Jefferson Award for Gt. Pub. Service Benefiting Disadvantaged 1984, Edwin J. Owens Lawyer of Yr. Award 1985, Faculty Senate Distinguished Prof. of the Yr. 1994-95; mem: Soc. of Am. Law Tchrs. (bd. govs. 1974–, exec. com. 1975-80, pres. 1980-82), Nat. Senior Citizens Law Ctr. (bd. govs. 1983-90, exec. com. 1983-89, pres. 1986-89), Am. Bar Assn. (chair com. on legal problems of the aged 1969-83, chair subcom. on discrimination 1979-83), Assn. of Am. Law Schs. Sect. on Aging and the Law (founding mem., exec. com. 1985–, chair 1989-90), Calif. Bar Assn. (CEB advy. com. 1970-85, com. on law sch. edn. 1970-85, exec. com. sect. on legal svs. and chair com. on legal problems of aging 1976-79), N.Y. Civil Liberties Union (bd. 1962-70, v.ch. 1964-69), Specialized Suport Svs. (bd. 1984-87), Internat. Assn. for Adv. Tchg. and Resrch. in Intellectual Property 1982–, Internat. Assn. Constnl. Law 1983–, Internat. Fedn. of Aero. & Astro./ Internat. Inst. of Space Law (Life 1968–), Assn. of the U.S. (dir. and mem. 1970-83), Internat. Inst. of Human Rights 1984–, Internat. Commn. for Human Rights, London (hon. mem. advy. com. 1972–), Am. Assn. for Abolition of Involuntary Mental Hospitalization (co-founder, bd. ch. 1970-79); mil: ofcr. USN 1953-56, Reserve 1956-64; author book chapters in numerous law books, 11+ law books 1960–, incl. Honesty and Competition: False Advtg. Law and Policy Under FTC Adminstrn. (Syracuse Press, 1967, transl. into Mandarin 1987), Writing a Living Will: Using a Durable Power-of-Atty. (Praeger Press 1988); Internat. Perspectives on Aging (Nijhof Press 1992, editor), The Right to Be Responsible (unpub.). Res: 11600 Summit Wood Los Altos Hills 94022

ALEXANDER, HENRY ALAN, university vice president and dean, philosopher; b. Aug. 24, 1953, Berkeley; s. Ernest and Frances Evelyn (Conolley) A.; m. Shelley Tornheim, Aug. 24, 1975; children: Aliza b. 1979, Yonina b. 1982, Yehuda b. 1985; edn: AB philosophy (summa cum laude, highest dept. hons., Phi Beta Kappa) UCLA, 1976; BA, and B.Lit rabbinics, Univ. of Judaism, 1977; Rabbi, MA Judaic studies, Jewish Theol. Sem. of Am., 1982; EdS evaluation studies, Stanford Univ., 1982, PhD edn. and humanities 1985. Career: tchg. asst. Stanford Univ. 1979-80, also res. asst. San Jose Tchr. Corps Proj.; preceptor in edn., dir. of leadership devel. Jewish Theol. Sem. of Am., 1980-82; instr., asst. prof., asso. prof. of philosophy and edn. Univ. of Judaism, 1983–, dean, 1990–, and v.p. of academic affairs 1992–, also adminstr., bd. dirs. Lee Coll. (undergrad. sch.) 1984-89, dean 1989–; vis. lectr. UCLA Sch. of Edn., 1989–, Hebrew Univ. of Jerusalem 1982-83; author num. book chpts., essays and jour. articles; Jewish, Conservative. Ofc: University of Judaism 15600 Mulholland Dr Los Angeles 90077

ALEXANDER, JOHN DAVID, college president emeritus; b. Oct. 18, 1932, Springfield, Tenn.; m. Catharine Coleman, 1956; children: Kitty, John, Julia; edn: BS, Southwestern at Memphis, 1953; postgrad., Louisville Presbyterian Theol. Sem. 1953-54; PhD, Oxford Univ. 1957. Career: instr., asst. prof., assoc. prof. Old Testament, San Francisco Theol. Sem. 1957-65; pres. Southwestern at Memphis 1965-69; pres. Pomona Coll., Claremont 1969-91, president emeritus and Trustees Professor, 1991–; Am. Sec. Rhodes Scholarship Trust 1981–; bd. dirs., Am. Council on Edn. 1981–; Nat. Commn. on Acad. Tenure 1971-72, Panel of Gen. Profl. Edn. of the Physician, Assn. Am. Med. Colls. 1982-85; trustee, Tchrs. Ins. and Annuity Assn. 1970–; Woodrow Wilson Nat. Fellowship Found. 1978–, Webb Sch., Claremont 1970-72; dir. Great Western Fin. Corp. 1973–, British Inst. 1979–, Comm. Supported TV So. Calif., KCET, Inc. 1979–; bd. of overseers Huntington Library, Gardens and Art Gal., 1991–; trustee Seaver Inst., 1992–; bd. dirs., Louisville Presbyterian Theol. Sem. 1966-69; honors: Rhodes Scholar, Christ Ch. Coll., Oxford Univ. 1954; Hon. degrees: LLD, USC 1970, Occidental Coll. 1970, Centre Coll. of Kentucky 1971, LHD, Loyola Marymount Univ. 1984, LittD, Rhodes Coll. 1984; mem: Assn. Am. Colls. (commn. on liberal lng. 1967-69, chmn. commn. on instl. affairs 1970-73); So. Assn. Colls. and Schs. (exec. council of commn. on colls. 1969); Am. Council on Edn. (dir. 1981–); Am. Oriental Soc.; Soc. Bible Lit.; Soc. for Religion in Higher Edn.; Los Angeles C.of C. (dir. 1972-73); Phi Beta Kappa; Phi Beta Kappa Alumni So. Calif. (pres. Alpha Assn. 1974-76); Omicron Delta Kappa; Bohemian (San Francisco); Century Assn., NYC; Zamorano. Ofc: Pomona College, 333 College Way, Claremont 91711

ALEXANDER, KENNETH SIDNEY, mathematics educator; b. Mar. 3, 1958, Seattle; s. Stuart Murray and Elspeth (Dautoff) A.; m. Crystal Czarnecki, Aug. 21, 1982; children: Glenn b. 1992; edn: BS, Univ. Wash., 1979; PhD, M.I.T., 1982. Career: mem. Mathematical Scis. Resrch. Inst., Berkeley 1982-83; acting asst. prof. Univ. Wash., 1983-86; asst. prof. Univ. So. Calif., L.A. 1986-90, assoc. prof. 1990–; awards: Phi Beta Kappa 1979, Univ. Wash. Pres.'s Medal 1979; mem: Am. Math. Soc. 1988–, Inst. of Math. Stats. (fellow 1991); book editor: Spatial Stochastic Processes, 1991; jour. assoc. editor: Probability Theory and Related Fields, 1987-94, Annals of Probability, 1994–; contbr. numerous articles in profl. jours. 1982–; rec: flutist, photog. Ofc: Dept. Math. DRB 155 Univ. of So. Calif., Los Angeles 90089-1113

ALKIN, MARVIN CARL, university professor, department chair; b. Oct. 24, 1934, NY, NY; s. Enie and Faye (Berg) A.; m. Marilyn Renee Shenker, Sept. 9, 1959; children: Wendy b. 1960, Grant b. 1962; edn: AB, math., San Jose St. Coll. 1956, MA, edn., 1959; EdD, edn., Stanford Univ. 1964. Career: var. tchg., counseling and adminstrv. duties at high schs. and comm. colls. 1956-62; res. staff mem. Inst. of Govt. and Public Affairs, UCLA 1965-66; asst. prof. edn. Grad. Sch. of Edn., UCLA 1964-68; assoc. dir. Ctr. for Study of Evaluation of Instructional Progs., UCLA 1968-73, dir. 1968-75, mem. ops. mgmt. team 1981-86; pres. Ednl. Evaluation Assocs., Northridge 1969–; prof. of edn. Grad. Sch. of Edn., UCLA 1973–, chair, Div. of Social Res. Methodology 1987-89; chmn. Dept. of Edn., UCLA 1990–; assoc. dean Grad. Sch. of Edn. & Info. Studies, UCLA 1993–; chair Grad. Council, Academic Senate, UCLA 1987-89; chair res. methods and evaluation specialization, Grad. Sch. of Edn., UCLA 1981-83, chair

of faculty 1982-83; mem. res. panel So. Calif. Superintendent's Res. Council 1977-82; mem. com. on prog. evaluation in edn., Nat. Acad. of Sci. 1980-82; bd. mem. Calif. Ednl. Res. Assn. 1977-79; pres. Calif. Soc. of Ednl. Prog. Auditors and Evaluators 1975-76, bd. trustees 1974-75; cons. and contbr. num. evaluation reports for: L.A. Unified Sch. Dist. Vol. Integration Prog. and Year-Round Schs. 1981–, Chancellor's Ofc., Calif. Comm. Colls., EOPS 1981–, and Matriculation Prog. 1989–, others; awards: grantee UCLA: Ctr. for Study of Evaluation 1968-76, 76-85, Vocational Edn. Unit, St. of Calif. 1975, U.S. Ofc. of Edn. 1974, Agy. for Internat. Devel. 1974, Ofc. of Legis. Analyst, St. of Calif. 1973, Systems Devel. Corp. 1973, Career Edn. Prog. 1972, Dept. of Defense-Overseas Dependent Schs. 1972, Res. for Better Schs. 1972; recipient 5 awards Am. Ednl. Res. Assn. for Outstanding Policy Studies and Evaluation Reports 1980, 82, 87, 88, 89; mem: Am. Ednl. Res. Assn. (proposal reviewer 1972–, joint com. on standards for ednl. evaluation 1987–, com. chair to evaluate Ednl. Researcher 1988, bd. mem. special interest group on res. utilization 1987-91, chair selection com. Div. H, 1984-88, mem. selection com. 1978-80), Am. Evaluation Assn., Nat. Soc. for Study of Edn., Phi Delta Kappa; assoc. editor Studies in Ednl. Evaluation 1975–; editor Ednl. Evaluation and Policy Analysis 1994– (editl. bd. 1991-94); manuscript reviewer for var. jours.; proposal reviewer NSF and Exxon Found.; editor in chief Encyclopedia of Educational Research, 6th edit., 1988-92; co-editor The Costs of Evaluation (Sage Publications, 1983); co-author: Master Reading (reading course on cassettes, Reading Edn. & Devel., Inc., 1978), Using Evaluations: Does Evaluation Make a Difference? Vol. 76 (Sage Publs., 1979), How To Teach Reading Successfully (Little, Brown & Co., 1980); author: Framing the Decision Context (AERA cassette series, 1976), A Guide for Evaluation Decision-Makers (Sage Publs., 1985), Debates on Evaluation (Sage Publs., 1990), contbr. 46 articles to profl. jours., 1964-88, 48 chapters to encyclopedias and other books, 1966-93, 40+ papers to profl. assns., 1965–. Res: Northridge 91325 Ofc: UCLA Graduate School of Education & Information Studies 405 Hilgard Ave Los Angeles 90024-1521

ALKON, ELLEN SKILLEN, physician; b. April 10, 1936, Los Angeles; d. Emil and Jane (Skillen) Bogen; m. Paul Kent Alkon, Aug. 30, 1957; children: Katherine b. 1963, Cynthia b. 1965, Margaret b. 1968; edn: BA, Stanford Univ. 1955; MD, Univ. Chgo. 1961; MPH, UC Berkeley 1968. Career: staff physician Higland Alameda Co. Hosp., Oakland 1964-66; staff pediatrician No. Calif. Reg. Child Devel. Center 1968-70; chief sch. health Anne Arundel Co. Health Dept., Annapolis, Md. 1970-71; pediatrician Minneapolis Health Dept., Minn. 1971-73, dir. maternal and child health 1973-75, commr. of health 1975-80; chief preventive pub. health Coastal Region Los Angeles Co. Dept. of Health Services 1980-81, pub. health chief West area 1981-85, acting med. dir. pub. health 1986, med. dir. pub. health 1987-93; med. dir. Coastal County Health Centers 1993–; adminstr. Vis. Nurse Service, Mpls., Minn. 1975-80; adj. assoc. prof. Univ. Minn. 1971-80; adj. prof. Sch. Pub. Health UCLA 1981–; mem: Minn. Pub. Health Assn. (pres. 1978-79), So. Calif. Pub. Health Assn. (pres. 1986), Am. Coll. Preventive Medicine, Am. Acad. Pediatrics. Ofc: Los Angeles Dept. of Health Services 1333 Chestnut Ave Long Beach 90813

ALLAN, ROBERT MOFFAT, JR., executive, educator; b. Dec. 8, 1920, Detroit; s. Robert M. and Jane (Christman) A.; m. Harriet Spicer, Nov. 28, 1942; children: Robert M., III, Scott, David, Marilee; edn: BS, Stanford Univ., 1941; Stanford Grad. Sch. Bus., 1941-42; MS physics, UCLA, 1943; Loyola Law Sch., 1947-50. Career: economist res. dept. Security First Nat. Bank 1942; exec. Marine Insurance 1946-53; asst. to pres. Zinsco Elec. Prods. 1953-55, v.p., dir. 1956-59; asst. to pres. The Times-Mirror Corp., Los Angeles 1959-60, corporate v.p. 1961-64; pres., dir. Cyprus Mines Corp. 1964-67; pres. Litton Internat. 1967-69; pres. US Naval Postgraduate Sch. Found., prof. internat. mgmt., 1969-85; bd. dirs. US Naval Acad.; bd. trustees Monterey Inst. Fgn. Studies (senior fellow 1976), Pomona Grad. Sch., Claremont Grad. Sch., Boys Republic, Del Monte Forest Homeowners; awards: Helms Athletic Found. award 1947, 49, outstanding businessman of yr., L.A., Nat. Assn. Accts. 1966, Sailing Hall of Fame 1969, US Coast Guard Merit award, Medal for Heroism 1990, US Navy meritorious service award 1976; mem: Merchants and Mfrs. Assn. (bd.), Intercollegiate Yachting Assn., Phi Gamma Delta, Phi Delta Phi; mil: capt. US AAF, 1942-46, WWII; clubs: Newport Harbor Yacht (commodore 1962), Trans-Pacific Yacht, Carmel Valley Country. Res: 165 Del Mesa Carmel 93923

ALLARD, JOHN BRERETON, II, chief of staff California State Legislature; b. Mar. 12, 1957, Turlock; s. John Brereton and Betty LaRue (Brown) A.; m. Lisa Ann Duvall, Aug. 23, 1986; edn: BA political sci. and history, CSU Sacramento 1984, Pi Sigma Alpha. Career: state field coordinator Carol Hallett for Lt. Gov. 1982; adminstrv. asst. Huckaby Marsh & Rodriguez Inc., Sacto. 1984-85; campaign coordinator All Santa Cruz Coalition 1985; legislative aide Calif. State Legislature 1985-86; campaign coordinator Tim Leslie for Assembly 1986-90, Tim Leslie for Senate 1991–; chief of staff Calif. State Legislature 1986–; awards: Outstanding Young Men of Am. (1985), Who's Who Among Am. H.S. Students (1974, 75); mem: Roseville C.of C. (v.p. 1991-93, dir. 1989-93, City Council/C.of C. Task Force, edn., exec. dir. search, fin., gov. rels., special events coms.), Roseville Community Health Found. (chmn. 1994–, sec. 1991-93, dir. 1989–, Comm. Partnerships, Hosp. Replacement Proj., nominating, public relations, special events coms.), South Placer Transportation Management

Assn. (dir. 1991-93, Gov. Rels. Com.), Am. Political Sci. Assn., CSU Alumni Assn., Comstock Club; Calif. Republican Party State Central Com.; Presbyterian; rec: camping, skiing (snow, water), gardening, photography. Address: Roseville 95747

ALLEN, BETTIE CROSSFIELD, photographer, educator; b. July 14, 1931, Edmond, Okla.; d. Roy Lyman and Verdie Audrey (Tallent) Crossfield; m. Rex Whitaker Allen, Nov. 6, 1971; edn: BA art, S.F. St. Univ. 1979; MA edn., 1982. Career: owner, mgr. Crossfield Allen Gallery, S.F. 1972-84; exec. secty. AIA, East Bay chpt., Oakland 1964-70; freelance photographer, San Francisco 1978–; instr. Calif. Acad. Sci. 1984–, S.F. Zool. Soc. 1974–, Marin Mus. Am. Indian, Novato 1987–, Docent Council of Asian Art Mus., S.F. 1985; mem: Soc. Asian Art (dir. 1989–), AAUW (mem. v.p. 1989-90), Docent Council Asian Art Museum (sch. coord., bd.), S.F. Zoological Soc. (15 yr. service award 1988), Docent chair Sonoma State Historic Park Assn. Inc. 1994–; author First Displaced Homemakers Center, 1982; Democrat; Episcopalian; rec: skiing, swimming. Address: Sonoma 95476

ALLEN, CATHERINE ISABELLA, hotel executive; b. Nov. 29, 1953, Lennoxtown, Scotland; d. Albert Bertram and Nellie (Graham) Kelly; m. James Bernard Allen, March 29, 1984; edn: dipl., Glasgow Coll. Food Tech. 1973; BS, Nepean C.A.E. Australia 1982; cert. hospitality sales profl. (CHSP) Am. Hotel & Motel Assn. 1993. Career: personnel ofcr. F.W. Hughes, Sydney, Australia 1978-81; personnel mgr. Qantas Wentworth 1981-83; front office mgr. Days Inn, Santa Clara 1984-86; corp. sales mgr. Holiday Inn, San Jose 1986-87; front office mgr. Days Inn, Santa Clara 1987-88; dir. sales Ramada Silicon Valley 1988–; awards: Holiday Inns Inc. sales mgr. 1989; mem: Sacto. Soc. Assn. Execs., Am. Soc. Assn. Execs., San Francisco Bay Area Soc. Assn. Execs., Silicon Valley Business Travel Assn., Hotel Sales & Mktg. Assn. (pres. 1990-91), Music & Art Found. Santa Clara Co. (fund raising com. 1987-88), KTEH Channel 54 (vol. fundraiser 1989); author tng. manual Basic Front Office Procedures, 1985. Ofc: Ramada Silicon Valley 1217 Wildwood Ave Sunnyvale 94089

ALLEN, DAVID HARLOW, logistician, educator; b. May 26, 1930, Lynn, Mass.; s. Donald H. Allen and Miriam Ellsworth (Harlow) Wilson; m. Roberta Arlene Miller, July 15, 1952; children: Donald b. 1954, Richard b. 1956, William b. 1958; edn: BGS in business, Univ. Omaha, 1967; MBA, NM Highlands Univ., 1978; Certified Profl. Logistician, Cert. Cost Estimator/Analyst. Career: served to lt. col. US Air Force 1948-78: team dir. of mat. Air Force Insp. & Safety Ctr., Norton AFB, Ca. 1969-72; asst. dep. comdr. for maint., squadron comdr. SAC Bomb Wing, Dyess AFB, Tx. 1972-74; dep. dir. of logistics AF Test & Evaluation Ctr., Kirtland AFB, NM 1974-78, ret., decorated merit. svc., bronze star, commendn. medals; systems analyst, project engr., ARINC Research, Santa Ana 1978-84; dep. program mgr. logistics & logistics project mgr. Northrop Corp., Newbury Park, CA 1984-91; indep. consultant, Thousand Oaks, Ca. 1991–; sr. lectr. West Coast Univ. Coll. of Bus. and Mgmt., L.A. 1988–, mem. acquisition & contract mgmt. curricula com. 1991–, Faculty Senate 1992–, past asst. dean WCU/ Ventura Co. Ctr., 1988-91; mem: Soc. Logistics Engrs. (1975–, chpt. chmn. 1988-90, com. chmn. So. Calif. Logistics Workshop and Conf. 1988–, program com. chmn. Internat. Logistics Symposium 1994), Engrs. Week Com. Ventura-Santa Barbara Ctys. 1990–, Configuration & Data Mgmt. Assn. 1989–, Soc. Cost Estimating & Anal. 1983–, Am. Mgmt. Assn. 1983–, Am. Security Council (nat. advy. bd. 1983–), Phi Kappa Phi 1978–; pub. articles in field (1954, 67, 75, 76); Republican; Prot.; rec: swimming, racquetball, golf, bowling. Res: 428 Moondance St Thousand Oaks 91360

ALLEN, JEFFREY MICHAEL, lawyer; b. Dec. 13, 1948, Chgo.; s. Albert A. and Miriam F. (Feldman) A.; m. Anne Marie Guaraglia, Aug. 9, 1975; children: Jason b. 1978, Sara b. 1980; edn: BA with great distinction, UC Berkeley, 1970, JD, Boalt Hall Law Sch., 1973; admitted bar: Calif. (1973), U.S. Supreme Ct., U.S. Ct. Appeals (9th cir.), U.S. Dist. Cts. (No., Cent., So., E. dists. Calif.); lic. real estate broker 1975. Career: ptnr. Graves, Allen, Cornelius & Celestre (and predecessor firms), Oakland 1973–; lectr. St. Mary's Coll., Moraga 1975–; spkr. numerous cont. legal edn. pgms. for Am. Bar Assn.; dir: various computer consulting corps.. dir. var. real estate and related service corps.; judge pro tem Oakland Municipal Ct.; arbitrator Am. Arbitration Assn., Alameda County Superior Ct. Panel of Arbitrators; honors: Calif. Scholarship Fedn. (life), Varsity Forensics Team (state & nat. speech tournaments, 1st pl. USF invitational tournament 1965), Nat. Forensic League Student Senate (pres. 1966), recipient of Ford Grant Funds through the Ctr. for the Study of Law and Society 1965-66, Phi Beta Kappa 1970, Calif. State Scholar, Univ. Calif. Alumni Scholar 1966-69, staff/project editor Calif. Law Review 1971-73, staff Ecology Law Quarterly 1971-72; mem: Am. Bar Assn. (chair real prop. com., gen. practice sect. 1987-91, v.chair 1985-87 & 92, program bd. 1991-93, advocacy coord. 1993–, section counsel 1994–), State Bar of Calif., Alameda Co. Bar Assn.; former mem: Am. Trial Lawyers Assn., Calif. Trial Lawyers Assn.; civic: Rotary (former chmn. coms., bd. dirs 1992-94), Commonwealth Club of Calif., Oakland C.of C., Family Service of the East Bay (pres. 1989-92, 1st v.p. 1988-89, dir. 1987-92), PTA/Oakland (sch. pres. 1986-88, treas. 84-86), mem. various advy. coms. Oakland Public Schs., Oakland Metropolitan Forum 1987–, Oakland Strategic Planning Com. 1988-89; contbr. articles on computers and litigators in var. law

jours.; Democrat; rec: soccer coach (nat. "C" lic.) and USSF lic. state referee, state referee assessor and referee instr.: Bay Oaks Soccer Club (commr. 1988-93), CNRA Dist. 4 Referee Administr. 1993–, Jack London Youth Soccer League (dir. 1988-93), Calif. Youth Soccer Assn.- Dist. 4 (asst. dist. commr. 1990-93, mem. bd. dirs. 1990–, referee coord. 1993–), CYSA Dist. 4 Competitive League (pres. & mem. bd. dirs. 1990-93), secty., bd. dirs CYSA 1993–; soccer, skiing, computers, family activities. Ofc: Graves Allen Cornelius & Celestre, 2101 Webster St Ste 1590 Oakland 94612

ALLEN, LINDA JEAN, licensed acupuncturist; b. May 26, 1952, San Francisco; d. Sol Cecil and Sarah Doris (Herring) Allen; edn: BA in social sci., Univ. of Tex., Austin 1974, MA in foreign lang. edn., 1978; M.T.O.M., Emperor's Coll. of Trad. Chinese Medicine, Santa Monica 1989; H.M.D., PhD, College of Homeopathy, Marina del Rey 1993; lic. acupuncturist State of Calif. Dept. of Consumer Affairs 1989; bd. certified naturopathic physician. Career: assoc. acupuncturist Bodymind Systems Med. Ctr., Santa Monica 1989-92; acupuncturist, self-employed, L.A. 1993–; frequent guest speaker on Chinese medicine and women's health issues; honors: Dean's List Emperor's Coll. of Trad. Chinese Medicine 1989; mem. Calif. Acupuncture Assn. 1989–, Nat. Commn. for Cert. of Acupuncturists (Diplomate in Acupuncture cert. #6250) 1990–, Am. Assn. of Acupuncture & Oriental Medicine 1991–, Calif. State Homeopathic Med. Soc. 1993–, Am. Naturopathic Med. Assn.; rec: traveling, gardening, hiking.

ALLEN, MICHAEL B., lawyer; b. Oct. 17, 1949, Columbus, Oh.; edn: BSME, Univ. of Pittsburgh, 1972; JD, San Mateo Law Sch., 1978; admitted bar: Calif. 1978, and U.S. Dist. Ct. no. dist. Calif. Career: in-house counsel Fluor Corp., 1978-80; ptnr. law firm Himmelheber & Allen, 1980-85; pres. of law corp., Burlingame 1985-92, Redwood City 1992-94, San Mateo 1994–, special emphasis on real estate, construction matters, ins., bus. and bankruptcy; mem: Am. Bar Assn., San Mateo Co. Bar Assn., Lawyers Club of San Francisco, Exec. Council of Homeowners. Ofc: 411 Borel Ave Ste 445 San Mateo 94402

ALLER, SONIA KONIALIAN, director of training in communication disorders & speech/language pathologist; b. Sept. 10, 1944, Aleppo, Syria; nat. U.S. citizen 1976; d. Assadour Konialian and Yeghisapet Bezdikian; m. Wayne Kendall Aller, April 8, 1969; edn: BA, Beirut Coll. for Women (Lebanon) 1966; PhD, Indiana Univ. 1978; instr. Baakline High Sch., Lebanon 1966-67; asst. instr psychology Indiana Univ., Bloomington, Ind. 1969-74; research assoc. Center for Behavioral Research Am. Univ. of Beirut, Lebanon 1974-75; dept. chair, asst. prof. psychology St. Mary of the Woods Coll., Ind. 1978-83; speech pathologist II, USC Medical Ctr. 1983-87, acting chief speech pathology sect. 1987; supvr. speech/lang. pathology Children's Hosp. Los Angeles 1987-93; dir. of training in comm. disorders, coord., leadership training, Univ. of So. Calif. Affiliated Program-Childrens Hosp. Los Angeles 1993–, adj. asst. prof., Dept. of Comm. Disorders, California State Univ., Northridge 1992–; clinical asst. prof., USC Schools of Med. and Dentistry 1995–; v.p. Learning Unltd., Studio City 1983–; grants: Ford Foundation grant, 1974-75, Nat. Sci. Foundation grant, 1979-81, Nat. Endowment for the Humanities grant, 1982; mem: Am. Speech Language & Hearing Assn., Calif. Speech & Hearing Assn., Assn. for Women in Sci., Calif. Neuropsychological Soc., Computer Users in Speech & Hearing, Sigma Xi; co-author book chapt. (pub. 1979); rec: swimming, classical music. Res: 12045 Susan Dr. Granada Hills 91344 Ofc: Childrens Hospital of Los Angeles 4650 Sunset Blvd Los Angeles 90027

ALLISON, JAMES EDWARD, physician; b. Apr. 21, 1942, Rochester, NY; s. Ralph Allison and Sylvia Allison (Garelick) Kaplan; m. Margaret Gerty Lindenstein, Jan. 3, 1970; children: Ethan b. 1974, Annika b. 1978; edn: AB (major honors), Univ. Of Penn., Phila. 1964; MD, Univ. Of Rochester, NY 1969; diplomat, Nat. Bd. Of Examiners 1970; certified internist/gastroenterologist, ABIM 1972/74. Career: internship, internal med. UCLA 1971; resident, internal med. UC San Francisco 1972, NIH trainee, gastroenterology 1974; internist/gastroenterologist Permanente Med. Group, San Rafael 1974-77, Oakland 1977–; cons. Calif. Sch. Of Podiatry 1972-74, UC S.F. Med. Ctr. 1974–; asst. clinical prof. medicine, UC S.F. Med. Ctr. 1976-82, asst. clinical prof. 1982-92, clinical prof. 1992–; fellow Am. Coll. of Physicians 1989–; mem: Am. Gastroenterological Assn. 1974, No. Calif. Soc. For Clinical GI 1975- (mem. bd. of govs., program chmn. 1977-78, pres. 1980-81) Am. Soc. for GI Endoscopy 1976–, Alameda/Contra Costa Med. Assn. 1980–; author: num. articles and abstracts pub. in profl. jours. 1973-93, presentations in field 1988-93, peer reviews: Gastroenterology 1985-86, Annals of Internal Medicine 1990; 2 T.V. appearances 1990, mil: capt. US Army Reserve Med. Corps 1970-76. Ofc: Kaiser Oakland 280 W MacArthur Blvd Oakland 94611

ALLISON, LAIRD BURL, professor emeritus of management; b. Nov. 7, 1917, Saint Marys, W. Va.; s. Joseph Alexander and Opal Marie (Robinson) A.; m. Katherine Hunt, Nov. 25, 1943; 1 son, William, b. 1945; m. 2d. Genevieve Elmore, Feb. 1, 1957 (dec. 1994); edn: BS in personnel and indsl. rels., magna cum laude, USC 1956; MBA, UCLA 1958. Career: lectr., asst./assoc./ prof. of mgmt., CSU Los Angeles 1956-83, asst. dean undergrad. studies, Sch. of Business and Econ. 1971-73, and assoc. dean ops., 1973-83; prof. emeritus of mgmt., CSULA; vis. asst. prof. of mgmt. CSU Fullerton, summer 1970; collaborated in devel. of new degree program, BS Mgmt. Sci., CSULA 1963; honors: Phi Kappa Phi, Beta Gamma Sigma, Omicron Delta Epsilon, Phi Eta Sigma, Ford Found. Faculty Fellow (1960); mem: Acad. of Mgmt., Alpha Kappa Psi profl. Bus. Frat., Am. Assn. of Individual Investors, The Am. Acad. of Polit. and Social Sci., The Inst. of Mgmt. Scis. (TIMS), Western Econ. Assn. Internat., World Future Soc., Am. Assn. Retired Persons, Faculty Emeriti Assn. CSULA (v.p. programs 1986-87, v.p. adminstrn. 1987-88, pres. 1988-89, exec. com. 1990-91, treas. 1991-95), Calif. State Univ. Assn. of Emeriti Profs., Ret. Public Employees Assn. of Calif. (chpt. pres. 1990-92), U.S. Naval Inst., The Navy League of U.S., American Legion, USS Astoria Assn; mil: chief interior communications electrician, USN, 1936-51, decorated Am. Def., Am. Theatre, Asia-Pacific Theatre, WWII Victory, Good Conduct, battles: Coral Sea, Midway, Guadalcanal, Savo.; survivor of sinking of USS Astoria (CA 34) in Battle of Savo. Rec: history, travel, photog., hiking. Res: 2176 E Bellbrook St Covina 91724

ALLMETT, JOHN RAYMOND, business owner; b. Aug. 25, 1942, Los Angeles; s. Raymond Daniel and Gladys DeEtte (Walker) A.; m. Caroline Geiger, Apr. 25, 1981; edn: grad. So. Lake Tahoe H.S. 1960; vocational tchg. credentials, Nev. State. Career: patrolman to undersheriff Douglas County (Nev.) Sheriff's Dept., 1965-75, ret. (disabled by Multiple Sclerosis, confined to wheelchair 1975–); p.t. work Nevada State Crime Commn., instr. photography and fingerprinting to police agencies throughout Nevada; founder/owner w/wife Allmett's Fine Jewelry (Caroline also paralyzed by M.S., paints Christmas cards) 1982–; mem. Gardena Valley Chamber of Commerce (Amb. 1988–); Republican; R. Cath.; rec: people, photography, jewelry. Res: 15115 S Vermont Gardena 90247 Ofc: Allmett's Fine Jewelry POB 3126 Gardena 90247

AL-MATEEN, MAJEED, neurologist; b. Mar. 22, 1954, Los Angeles; s. Eddie Johnson, Jr. and Margaret (Strain) Johnson; m. Lillian Helen Koblenz, Nov. 22, 1989; children: Xavier Philip b. 1991, Sylvia Rose b. 1995; edn: biochemistry, Univ. of Calif., Davis 1975, MD, 1979; diplomate Nat. Bd. Med. Examiners 1980; physician and surgeon registration Calif. Bd. Med. Quality Assurance 1981; diplomate Am. Bd. Pediatrics 1985; diplomate Am. Bd. Psychiatry and Neurology 1989. Career: resident in pediatrics Children's Hosp. Med. Ctr., Oakland 1979-82, chief resident 1982-83; resident in neurology/fellow in pediatric neurology UCLA Ctr. for Health Scis. 1983-86; fellow in neuromuscular diseases Univ. of So. Calif. Sch. of Med. 1986-87; assoc. neurologist Children's Hosp. Oakland 1987-89; dir.dept. of neurology Children's Hosp. Oakland 1990–; mem. neonatal morbidity and mortality com. Children's Hosp. Oakland 1990–, vice chair multicultural com. 1992–, search coms. 1992-93; advy bd. mem. Epilepsy League of the East Bay 1991–; bd. dir. I Think I Can Found. 1994–; instr. UC Berkeley/ UCSF Jt. Med. Prog. 1994– awards: Mead Johnson award UCLA Sch. of Medicine-Dept. of Pediatrics 1986, Jean-Louis Riehl award UCLA Sch. of Medicine-Dept. of Neurology 1986, clinical fellowship award Muscular Dystrophy Assn. 1986, Teacher of Yr. award Children's Hosp. Oakland-Housestaff Assn. 1989, grantee NIH-AIDS Clinical Trials Group (No. Calif. Pediatric AIDS Treatment Ctr.) 1988-92, Stroke Prevention Trial in Sickle Cell (STOP) Study 1995–, AMA/CMA Physicians Recognition award 1992-95; mem: Am. Acad. of Pediatrics (fellow 1985–), Child Neurology Soc. 1989-(membership com. 1992–), Am. Assn. of Electrodiagnostic Medicine 1992–, Alameda-Contra Costa Med. Assn./CMA 1991–, East Bay Pediatric Soc. 1991–, Sinkler-Miller Med. Assn. 1991–; author: profl. papers/lectures 1986-92; author/co-author: numerous articles pub. in profl. jours, abstracts, commentaries and reviews 1986–; Democrat; Islam; rec: gardening, running. Ofc: Children's Hospital Oakland Dept of Neurology 747 52nd St Oakland 94609

ALOIA, ROLAND C., scientist, educator; b. Dec. 21, 1943, Newark, N.J.; s. Roland S. and Edna (Mahan) A.; edn: BS, St. Marys Coll. 1965; PhD, UC Riverside 1971; postdoctoral, City of Hope 1971-75. Career: research biologist UC Riverside 1975-76; asst. prof. Loma Linda Univ. Sch. of Medicine 1976-79, assoc. prof. 1979-89, prof. anesthesia 1989–; res. chemist J.L. Pettis Vets. Hosp. 1979–; pres. Cancer Hibernation Res. Found., San Bernardino 1988–; Loma Linda Vets. Assn. for Research & Edn. 1988–; awards: UC Riverside NIH predoctoral scholarship 1969-70, Calif. Heart Assn. postdoctoral fellowship 1971-74, Outstanding Service 1983-85, yearly Outstanding Performance award, VA Med. Ctr. 1985–; mem: Sigma Xi, AAAS, Am. Oil Chemists Soc., N.Y. Acad. Sci., Am. Soc. for Cell Biology, Calif. Heart Assn. (v.p. 1983-85, pres. 1980-81, 1984-86, v.p. 1979-80, 1982-84); sr. ed. Membrane Fluidity in Biology, vols. 1 & 2 (1983), vols. 3 & 4 (1985), sr. series ed. Advances in Membrane Fluidity, vols. 1-3 (1988), vol. 4 (1990), vol. 5 (1991), vol. 6 (1992); rec: flying, jogging, marksmanship. Ofc: Research Service, Pettis VA Hospital 11201 Benton St Loma Linda 92357

ALONZO, GREGORY, professional speaker and sales trainer; b. Apr. 9, 1954, San Bernardino; s. Rudy and Remi (Vicente) A.; m. Joanne Beth Reitz, June 18, 1992; edn: BA in internat. relations, Pitzer Coll., Claremont 1980. Career: sales mgr. CBS Advertising, Santa Barbara 1980-87; v.p. sales PacTel, Irvine 1987-90; profl. speaker Success Unlimited, Brea 1990–; mem: Profl. Speakers Network (Orange County chpt. pres. 1992-93), Nat. Speakers Assn., Toastmasters Internat. (speakers bur. chair 1991-92, TM of Yr. Orange Co.

1991-92, Speaker of the Year 1992), Internat. Platform Assn.; author tape series: Attitude Selling, 1992, Unlimited Success, 1993; Paths to Power, 1994, Wealth: Make It Yours Now!, 1994; author: (book) Say Yes to Success, pub. articles; mil: E5, sgt. USMC 1972-76; Democrat; R.Cath.; rec: collecting art, breeding Arabian horses. Ofc: R. Gregory Alonzo Unlimited 101 W Central Ave Ste B111 Brea 92621

ALPINIERI, LOUIS JOSEPH, executive; b. Aug. 12, 1936, Brooklyn, N.Y.; s. Salvatore and Virginia (Figurito) A.; m. Brenda Lee Porter, Sept. 15, 1962; children: Andrea b. 1969, Steven b. 1971; edn: BS aero. engring., Polytechnic Inst. N.Y. 1957; MS, CalTech. Pasadena 1960; PhD, Polytechnic Inst. N.Y. 1963. Career: staff engr. CalTech Coop. Windtunnel, Pasadena 1957-60; research assoc. Polytech. Univ. N.Y., N.Y.C. 1960-63; tech. staff Aerospace Corp., El Segundo 1963-65; prin. engr. Ford Aerospace, Newport Beach 1965-67; sr.v.p., gen. mgr. Acurex Corp., Mountain View 1967-79; pres. Vantage Assoc. Inc., San Diego 1980–; dir: Flow Internat. Inc., Seattle, Wash. 1980–, Life Support Systems Inc., Mountain View 1981–; mem: Sigma Xi, Soc. Aerospace Materials, Am. Inst. Aero. & Astro., Commonwealth Club S.F.; rec: sports, running, bicycling. Res: 2678 Prestwick Ct La Jolla 92037 Ofc: 6350 Nancy Ridge Dr San Diego 92121

AL-QAZZAR, AYAD, educator; b. Aug. 23, 1941, Baghdad, Iraq, U.S. citizen; s. Ali and Sharafa (Ahmad) Al-Q.; 1 child, Mayad b. 1964; edn: BA, Univ. Baghdad, 1963; BA, UC Berkeley, 1966, PhD, 1969. Career: asst. prof. CSU Sacramento, 1969-75, assoc. prof. 1975-81, prof. 1981–; vis. prof. Univ. Calif. Berkeley 1970–, Qatar Univ., Doha-Qatar, 1981; awards: Univ. of Calif. Award, UCB (1966-68), Meritorious award CSU Sacto. 1986; mem: AAUG, World Affairs Council, MESA, ASA, Comstock Club; author: Women in the Middle East (1979), The Arab World (1978), The Arab American Community (1978), The Arabs World Note Book (1989); Indep.; Islam; rec: tennis, walking, swimming. Res: 3501 Dutch Way Carmichael CA 95608 Ofc: California State Univ., 6000 J St Sacramento CA 95819

ALQUIST, ALFRED E., state senator; b. Memphis; m. Elaine A.; children: Alan; edn: Southwestern Univ.Career: former mem. Calif. State Assembly; mem. Calif. State Senate 1966–; chair fin. com., mem. govt. orgn. and public utilities coms.; candidate for Lt. Gov. State of Calif. 1970; mem. Little Hoover Commn.; mem. Calif. Seismic Safety Commn., Natl. Conf. Of State Legislators, Am. Legion, Com. Sci. And Tech.; trustee Good Samaritan Hosp.; Clubs: Elks, Commonwealth; mil: served with Air-Sea Emergency Rescue, USAAF, 1942-44; Democrat. Res: 100 Paseo De San Antonio San Jose 95113-1402 Ofc: Office of State Senate 100 Paseo De San Antonio #209 San Jose 95113

ALTER, GERALD L., business executive; b. Aug. 24, 1910, Rensselaer, Ind.; s. Leslie and Lettie (Willis) A.; m. Margaret A. Davis, Sept. 15, 1939; children: Judith Ann (dec.), John Edward; edn: Business Coll. 1927-28. Career: clk. and office mgr., 1929-35; bldg. contractor, 1936-45; real estate broker and insurance agt., 1946–; pres. Alter Realty & Ins., Leads, Inc., investments, Alter Ins. Agcy., Inc., REMCO Real Estate Mgmt. Co., Alter Devel. Co.; pres. Developers & Builders; mem: Torrance-Lomita-Carson Board Realtors (pres. 1978, v.p. 1980-81), Calif. Assn. Realtors (dir. 1978-81), Nat. Assn. Realtors, Torrance C.of C. (past dir.), Am. Legion, OX-5 (pioneer airmen org.), Rotary; civic: Torrance Police Reserves (1946-62), City of Torrance Planning Commn. (commr. 1966-82, chmn. 1982-83), Torrance Water Commn. (1984-92, chmn. 87-88), Harbor Area United Way (past bd.). Res: 1337 Engracia Ave Torrance 90501 Ofc: 2305 Torrance Blvd Torrance 90501

ALTERS, DENNIS BRIAN, psychiatrist; b. Dec. 11, 1948, Chgo.; s. Morris and Shirley Joyce (Zaglin) A.; m. Margaret Acree, Nov. 7, 1981; son, Brett Ryan b. July 5, 1987; edn: BS in chem., Univ. of Miami, Fla. 1970, MD, Univ. Miami Sch. of Med., 1976; diplomate Am. Bd. Psychiatry and Neurology 1985, Am. Bd. Child and Adolescent Psychiatry 1988. Career: surgical resident Mt. Sinai Med. Ctr., Miami 1976-77; ophthalmology res. Univ. Louisville, Ky. 1977-78, psychiat. res. Univ. Louisville, 1978, and UC San Diego, 1978-80, child psychiatric fellow UCSD, 1980-82; pvt. practice, San Diego 1982–; cons. psychiatrist Vista Conciliation Ctr. 1982–, Paradise Creek Ranch 1981-83, San Diego Sch. Dist. 1981-82, Big Brothers of San Diego Co. 1982-86 (v.p. agy. affairs 1984-86); chmn. Calif. chpt. Nat. Com. of Youth Suicide Prevention 1986–; exec. com. Mesa Vista Hosp. 1984-87; clinical dir. children's program Alvarado Parkway Inst., 1991-92; dir. child psychiatric svs. Charter Hosp., San Diego 1992-93; cons. Promise of Life 1994–; frequent lectr. and profl. seminars, speaker various profl. and comm. orgs., and guest local radio and t.v.; mem: San Diego Psychiat. Soc. (drug abuse and alc. com. 1984–), Am. Psychiat. Soc., Am. Acad. of Child Psychiatry, AMA, San Diego Co. Med. Soc., Child Psychiat. Council S.D., Am. Soc. for Adolescent Psychiatry, S.D. Soc. Adolescent Psychiatry, Phi Delta Epsilon; author: Wizard's Way™ a children's interactive therapeutic world; presentor at 1994 Calif. Psychiat. Assn. and 1995 Am. Psychiat. Assn. annual meetings; rec: tennis, SDSM Masters swimming, wt. tng., writing. Ofc: 2067 W Vista Way Ste 275 Vista 92083 also: 4550 Kearny Villa Rd Ste 214 San Diego 92123

ALTSHILLER, ARTHUR LEONARD, physics teacher; b. Aug. 12, 1942, N.Y.C.; s. Samuel Martin and Betty Rose (Lepson) A.; m. Gloria Silvern, Nov. 25, 1970 (div. 1975); m. Carol Heiser, Aug. 16, 1980; edn: BS physics, Univ. Okla., 1963; MS physics, CSU Northridge, 1971. Career: electronics engr. Garrett Corp., Torrance 1963-64, Volt Tech. Corp., Phoenix, Az. 1965, Aerojet Gen. Corp., Azusa, Calif. 1966-68, Magnavox Rsch. Labs., Torrance 1968-69; senior engr. Litton Guidance & Control, Canoga Park 1969; physics tchr. Van Nuys High Sch. (L.A. Unified Sch. Dist.), Van Nuys 1971–; math. instr., eve., Los Angeles Valley Coll., 1986–; foster teacher NASA Ames Research and SETI Inst. 1994; awards: Cert. of Honor Westinghouse Science Talent Search 1990, listed Who's Who in Am. Edn. 1992-93, Who's Who Am. Tchrs. 1992-93, Who's Who in West 1992-93, Who's Who in Sci. & Engring. 1994-95; mem: Am. Assn. of Physics Tchrs. (So. Calif. sect. 1971–), Am. Assn. of Sci. 1985–, Nat. Council of Math Tchrs. 1985–, Santa Monica Astronomical Soc. 1991–; So. Calif. region meeting presentations on teaching concepts & demonstrns. in physics edn.; AAPT 1971–; Democrat; rec: tennis, chess, table tennis, cycling, swimming, sr. masters track and field. Res: 6776 Vickiview Dr West Hills 91307 Ofc: Van Nuys High School 6535 Cedros Ave Van Nuys 91411

ALVAREZ, EDNA R. S., lawyer; b. March 16, 1939, Larchmont, N.Y.; d. Gustave and Edna (Rosenfeld) Simons; m. Rodolfo Alvarez, June 15, 1960 (div. 1984); children: Anica b. 1966, Amira b. 1970; edn: Inst. Am. Univs. Aix en Provence France 1959-60; BA, San Francisco St. Univ. 1961; Yale Univ. Sch. Law 1966-67; JD hons., Univ. Wash. Sch. Law 1967; admitted bar: Conn., 1967, Calif., 1973. Career: atty. Bergman Horowitz Reynolds & De Srto, New Haven, Conn. 1967-72; instr. USC Sch. of Law and Bus., 1972-75; atty. sole practice, Los Angeles 1975–; lectr. Calif. Cont. Edn. Bar, Practising Law Inst., UCLA, USC 1972–; honors: Order of Coif; mem: Am. Coll. Trust & Estate Counsel, Am. Bar Assn. (econ. of law practice sect. 1986-87), Westwood Bar Assn. (bd. dirs. 1985–), UCLA/CEB Annual Estate Planning Inst., USC Probate & Trust Conf. (planning com. 1984–), Calif. Bd. Accountancy, ACLU (bd. 1976-81), West Los Angeles C.of C. (bd. 1978-82); articles pub. in profl. jours. Ofc: 10850 Wilshire Blvd 4th Floor Los Angeles 90024-4316

ALY, NAEL ABBAS, professor of production management, department chair and director of training and consulting; b. July 2, 1952, Suez, Egypt; s. Abbas Elsayed Aly and Khairia (Morsi) Awad; m. Denys Baumgart, Jan. 4, 1986; children: Sammer b. 1987, Sarah b. 1989, Spencer b. 1992; edn: BS hon., production engring., Alexandria Univ. Egypt 1974; MS, 1978; MS indsl. engring., Univ. Okla. 1981; PhD, 1985. Career: production engr. AVD Engine Rebuilding, Alexandria, Egypt 1974-75; instr. Alexandria Univ. 1975-78; tchr., res. asst. Univ. Okla., Norman 1978-83, res. assoc. 1983-84; assoc. prof. CSU Stanislaus, Turlock 1984-89, prof. 1989–; dir. Quality and Prodn. Mgmt. Ctr. for Training and Cons. 1993–;chmn. Mgmt., Mktg. and Prodn. Dept., CSU Stanislaus 1994–; quality mgmt. cons., trainer Campbells Soups 1984-89; Proctor & Gamble 1986; Monte Cristo, Blue Diamonds, Calif. Almond, Gallo Glass, Louis Rich, 1989; Blommer Chocolate, Diamond Walnut 1990; TriValley 1991; Emanual Med. Ctr. 1993; St. Joseph's Med. Ctr., Con-Agra Butterball Turkey 1994, Supherb Farms, Ryan and Pierra Almond Co.; awards: RAB Certified Quality Systems Provisional Auditor, CSU Stanislaus Merit. Performance 1986, 89, Outstanding Scholarship Award 1992, Internat. Who's Who in Quality 1994, Who's Who Among Students Am. Univs. & Colls. 1983, Univ. Okla. Outstanding Internat. Student 1981, Alexandria Univ. 1st in Class 1970-74; mem: Inst. Indsl. Engrs., Prodn. & Ops. Mgmt. Soc., Am. Soc. Quality Control, Am. Production & Inventory Control Soc., Inst. Mgmt. Scis., Alpha Pi Mu, Tau Beta Pi, Turlock Sunrise Rotary (dir. internat. com. 1987-88, 94-95); 24 articles and 3 tng. manuals pub. 1983–; rec: travel, soccer, basketball. Res: 3909 Tanager Dr Denair 95316 Ofc: California State University Stanislaus 801 W Monte Vista Turlock 95382

AMANDES, RICHARD BRUCE, lawyer; b. March 29, 1927, Berkeley; s. Fernand Frederic and Nellie (McHoul) A.; m. Joanne Vivien Beran, June 9, 1950 (div. 1978); m. Janet Carol Sanford, Oct. 25, 1987; children: Christopher Bruce b. 1955, Robin Michelle b. 1956; edn: AB, UC Berkeley 1950; JD, UC Hastings Coll. Law 1953; LL.M, N.Y. Univ. 1956; admitted St. Bars Calif. 1954, Tx. 1967, Wash. 1959. Career: gen. counsel Planning Cons. Inc., Lubbock, Tx. 1983-85; atty. Isham & Lynch, Visalia 1985-89; solo practice, 1990–; founding dean, Tx. Tech. Univ. Sch. Law 1966-77; assoc. dean, Robert W. Harrison prof. law UC Hastings Coll. Law 1964-66; asst. dean, assoc. prof. law Univ. Wash. 1958-64; prof. law Vanderbilt Univ., Am. Univ., Santa Clara Univ., Univ. San Diego; ednl. dir. Seattle-King Co. Estate Planning Council 1960-64; pres. S. Plains Estate Planning Council, Lubbock, Tx. 1971-72; pres. Tulare-King Co. Estate Planning Council 1988-89; adminstr. Cont. Legal Edn. Bar, Wash. State 1958-64; honors: Order of Coif, Phi Kappa Phi (pres.), Tx. Tech. Univ. Man of Year 1971; mem: Am. Bar Assn. (ednl. dir. uniform real property acts), Nat. Conf. of Commission in Uniform State Laws (1978-88), Rotary Internat., Visalia C.of C. (indsl. chmn. 1988–); author: num. articles pub. in profl. jours., 1954–; mil: pfc US Army 1945-47; rec: tennis, racquetball, bicycling. Ofc: 3120 W Main St Visalia 93291

AMBROSE, RACHEL EBERLE, journalist; b. Dec. 10, 1942, New Albany, Ind.; d. Herman H. and Katherine M. (Andres) Eberle; m. George Ambrose, May 12, 1973; 1 son, Josiah b. 1977; edn: BA, St. Mary of the Woods Coll., 1964. Career: reporter, photographer New Albany tribune 1961-63; newswoman AP, Idpls. 1964-66, Indiana broadcast editor, AP 1966-67, newswoman AP, Los Angeles 1967-76, Calif.-Nev. broadcast editor AP 1976–; sec. treas. Associated Press TV-Radio Assn. of Calif.-Nev. 1976–; awards: AP Bdcstrs. best summary 1975, best enterprise 1976, and best spot news 1977, 90, 93, Internat. Press Inst. Japan Journalists Exchange 1978, alumnae in residence St. Mary of the Woods Coll. 1977, best of show prize Redondo Beach Photography Contest 1977, phot selected for Best of Photog. Annual 1994 and 1995 in Serbin Communications; mem: Am. Film Inst., AAUW (v.p. Torrance 1987-94), St. Mary's So. Calif. Alumnae (pres. 1969-75), St. Lawrence Cath. Ch. Renew Pgm.; Republican; R.Cath.; rec: philately, travel, photog. Res: 200 Via Colusa Palos Verdes Estates 90274 Ofc: Associated Press 221 S Figueroa St #300 Los Angeles 90012

AMBROSE, WILLIAM WRIGHT, JR., college administrator, educator, entrepreneur; b. Oct. 13, 1947, Norfolk, Va.; s. Wm. W., Sr. and Charlotte G. Ambrose; m. Marcelia Conerly, Aug. 7, 1971; children: William W., III b. 1978; Xandrea M. b. 1978; Mark S. b. 1982; m. 2d. Mildred Allen, Oct. 22, 1988; edn: BSBA Norfolk State Univ.; MBA Pepperdine Univ. 1982; PhD candidate Walden Univ.; Calif. Comm. Coll. Tchg. cred., lic. Ins. Broker, Notary Public, Enrolled Agent, Cert. Tax Profl. Career: mfg. and total quality mgr. Corning Glass, NY 1974-78; controller, plant supt. Philip Morris Auburn, NY 1978-79; plant mgr., corp. exec. mgmt. Kerr Glass Corp., Los Angeles 1979-84; instr. Nat. Edn. Corp., Anaheim 1985-87; owner The TAX INSTITUTE, Chino 1988–; assoc., dean of bus. acctg., prof. of accountancy DeVRY Tech., University Centre, Pomona 1988–; bd. dir. Profl. Translations, Santa Ana 1985–, The Spruell Comm. Learning Center, Compton 1990–, Kirtland Enterprises, Irvine 1990–, Francisco Realty Investors, San Bernardino 1993–; mem: Inst. of Mgmt. Accts., Nat. Assn. of Public Accts., Nat. Soc. of Tax Profls., Am. Soc. of Quality Control, Phi Beta Lambda (Profl. mem.), Sigma Beta Delta Assoc. of Acad. Affairs Adminstr., co-patentee: glass insp. Polarized Contaminate Viewer (1981); mil: sgt. E5 AUS Security Agy. 1968-71; Christian; rec: computing, reading, golf. Res: 13121 Robin Ct Chino 91710

AMDAHL, GENE MYRON, computer company executive; b. Nov. 16, 1922, Flandreau, S.D.; s. Anton E. and Inga (Brendsel) A.; m. Marian Quissell, June 23, 1946; children: Carlton Gene, Beth Delaine, Andrea Leigh; edn: BSEE, S.D. State Univ., 1948, DEng (hon.), 1974; PhD, Univ. Wis., 1952, DSc (hon.), 1979; D.Sc. (hon.), Luther Coll., 1980, Augustana Coll., 1984. Career: proj. mgr. IBM Corp., Poughkeepsie, N.Y., 1952-55; group ldr. Ramo-Wooldridge Corp., L.A., 1956; mgr. systems design Aeronutronics, L.A., 1956-60; mgr. systems design advanced data processing systems IBM Corp., N.Y.C., Los Gatos, Calif., Menlo Park, Calif., 1960-70; founder, chmn. Amdahl Corp. Sunnyvale, Calif., 1970-80; founder, chief exec. officer Trilogy Systems Corp. Cupertino, Calif., 1980-87; chmn. bd. Elxsi (name changed from Trilogy Systems Corp.), San Jose, Calif., 1987-89; founder, pres., chief exec. officer Andor Internat. Ltd., Cupertino, 1987-94, also bd. dirs.; founder, chmn. Commercial Data Servers, Inc., Mountain View, Calif. 1994–; awards: recipient Disting. Alumnus award S.D. State Univ., 1973 Data Processing Man of Yr. award Data Processing Mgmt. Assn., 1976 Disting. Svc. citation Univ. Wis., 1976, Miehelson-Morley award Case-Western Res. Univ., 1977, Harry Goode Meml. award for outstanding contbns. to design and manufacture of large, high-performance computers 1983, and Eckert- Mauchly award, 1987, Am. Fedn. Info. Processing Soc., Centennial Alumnus award S.D. State Univ., 1987, Good Samaritan award City Team Ministries, San lose, 1991, Man of Achievement award Computer Weekly mag., 1991; named to Info. Processing Hall of Fame, Infomart, Tex., 1985, named one of 1000 Makers of 20th Century, London Times, 1991, Junior Achievement Business Hall of Fame Laureate 1995, IBM fellow, 1965. Fellow IEEE, Brit. Computer Soc. (disting.); mem. Nat. Acad. Engring., IEEE (profl. group, W.W. McDowell award 1976), Quadrato della Radio, Pontecchio Marconi; clubs: Los Altos (Calif.) Country; patentee in field; mil: with USN, 1942-44; Presbyterian. Res: 165 Patricia Dr Atherton CA 94027-3922 Ofc: Commercial Data Servers Inc 1983 Landings Dr Mountain View 94043

AMELIO, GILBERT FRANK, electronics company executive; b. Mar. 1, 1943, N.Y., NY; s. Anthony and Elizabeth (DeAngelis) A.; m. Glenda Charlene; children: Anthony Todd, Tracy Elizabeth, Andrew Ryan; edn: BS, MS, and PhD in Physics, Georgia Inst. Tech., 1965, 1967, 1968. Career: mem. tech. staff Bell Tel. Labs, Murray Hill, N.J. 1968-71; v.p./gen. mgr. Fairchild, Mtn. View, Ca. 1971-83; pres. Semi. Products Div., Rockwell Internat., Newport Beach 1983-88, pres. Comms. Systems Div., 1988-91; pres. and c.e.o. Nat. Semiconductor, Santa Clara 1991–, elected chmn. 1995–; dir., Chiron Corp.; dir., Apple Computer; dir., nat. advy. bd. Georgia Inst. Tech. 1981-87; mem. c.e.o. roundtable UC Irvine 1985-89; recipient Masaru Ibuka Consumer Electronics Award, IEEE (1991); mem: Semiconductor Ind. Assn. (dir. 1983–, chmn. 1993-94), IEEE (Fellow, 1974-81), Bay Area Council (mem. exec. com.), Electronic Industries Assn. (bd. of govs.), Business Higher Edn. Forum, Wingspread Commn. on Higher Edn.; holder 16 patents; Republican; R.Cath. Ofc: National Semiconductor 2900 Semiconductor Dr MS 16-100 Santa Clara 95052-8090

AMIN, NAVINCHANDRA MANIBHAI, physician/professor family medicine; b. Sept. 13, 1937, Varnama, India; s. Manibhai C. and Shushilagauri M. Amin; m. Saroj Patel, Mar. 21, 1968; children: Manish b. 1972, Nimisha b. 1978; edn: Sen. Cambridge Cert., Racecourse Sec., Nairobi, Kenya 1955; undergrad. int. sci., MD, Wilson Coll., Bombay 1957, 1961; Diplomate Tropical Med. & Hygiene, Liverpool Sch. of Tropical Med., Liverpool, Eng. 1967; Fellow Royal Coll. Physicians (FRCP, MRCP), U.K. 1968; cert. Am. Bd. Internal Medicine, 1976, Infect. Disease, 1982, Tropical Medicine, 1983. Career: dist. physician and clin. instr. int. med. Lango Dist. Hosp., Uganda, E. Africa 1969-71; consulting phys. H.H., The Aga Khan Hosp., Dar es Salaam, Tanzania, E. Africa 1971-74, also hon. lectr. Univ. of Dar es Salaam 1971-74; chief resident phys. int. med. and cardiology Westminster Hosp., London, Ont., Canada 1974-75, and tchg. Hosp. for Trop. Dis.; asst. prof. int. med. Univ. Pittsburgh, Pa. 1976-79; physician assoc. dept. family practice Kern Med. Ctr., Bakersfield 1979–, chmn. depts. fam. practice 1982–, and pediatrics 1988–; adj. asst. prof., assoc. prof. medicine UC Los Angeles 1979–, assoc. prof., full prof. fam. medicine UC Irvine 1981–; honors: Alan Milane Gold Medal in tropical medicine, Kern Med. Ctr. med. faculty of year 1982-83, 1990-92; Fellow A.C.P. 1983, Am. Coll. Tropical Med. 1983, Royal Coll. Phys. & Surgeons Eng. 1968, mem. AMA, Am. Acad. Fam. Phys., Kern Acad. Fam. Phys.; editor "Emergency Pointers" and "Diagnostic Tips" J. Primary Cardiology, 1982, contbr. articles in var. med. jours. incl. Postgrad. Medicine, Consultant, Diagnosis, Am. Family Physician, Current Prescribing, Brit. Med. Jour., 1974-83; Hindu; rec: music, swimming, philately. Res: 4505 San Miguel Way Bakersfield 93306 Ofc: Kern Medical Ctr 1830 Flower St Bakersfield 93305-4197

ANARGYROS, NEDRA F. HARRISON, model, entertainer, retired cytologist; b. Dec. 3, 1915, NY, NY; d. Leverette Roland and Florence Martha (Pickard) Harrison; grandmother Florence Willingham Pickard, author, painter; m. Spero Drosos Anargyros, Oct. 21, 1940 (div. 1969); edn: att. pub. schs. Delray Beach, Fla., grad. Tifton (Ga.) H.S., att. Emerson Coll. Boston 1934-36, UC San Francisco 1957. Career: Power's model 1938; original model for The Dragon Lady of Milton Caniff's Terry & the Pirates 1939; posed for Salvador Dali for his painting "Madonna of the Sea;" rode the Quadrille on horseback for first year of the N.Y. World Fair in Wild West & Rodeo; small role in Albert Johnson's The American Jubilee 1939-40; lic. student pilot Tifton, Ga. 1941, grad. pilot tng. pgm. Avenger Field, Sweetwater, Tex. 1942; supr. cytology lab UCSF/San Francisco Gen. Hosp., ret. 1988; mem: Am. Soc. Clin. Pathologists (affil.), Am. Soc. Cytotechnology (affil.), Women Flyers of Am., DAR (nat. 1st v. regent 1970), DAR of S.F./La Puerta de Oro chpt. (regent 1990), Colonial Dames of Am., Huguenot Soc. of Calif., UDC, Phi Mu Gamma, Pres.'s Club of Mercer Univ. (Macon, Ga.), Who's Who of Amer. Women, Who's Who In The West; Republican; Christian Science; rec: travel, scuba (cert. 1972). Res: The Sequoias, 1400 Geary Blvd Studio Apt 5-N San Francisco 94109 and 2503 Clay St San Francisco 94115

ANASTASIOU, MARY M., pediatrician; b. June 11, 1954, England (nat. 1983); d. Thalis M. and Elli (Nicolopoulou) Michaelides; m. Stephen Anastasiou, Jan. 4, 1980; children: Alex b. 1981, Christine b. 1987; edn: MD, Univ. Athens Med. Sch. Greece 1979. Career: intern, resident, chief resident Kaiser Hosp., Oakland 1982-85; pvt. practice pediatrics, Pleasanton 1985–; mem: CMA, ACCMA; Christian; rec: swimming, tennis. Res: 3501 Kamp Dr Pleasanton 94588 Ofc: 5565 W Las Positas Blvd Ste 240 Pleasanton 94588

ANDERBERG, ROY ANTHONY, journalist; b. Mar. 30, 1921, Camden, N.J.; s. Arthur R. and Mary V. (McHugh) A.; m. Louise M. Brooks, Feb. 5, 1953; children: Roy, Mary; edn: AA, Diablo Valley Coll., 1975. Career: enlisted U.S. Navy, 1942, commd. officer, 1960, ret. 1970; waterfront columnist Pacific Daily News, Agana, Guam 1966-67; public relations officer Naval Forces, Mariana Islands, 1967; travel editor Contra Costa Times, Calif. 1968-69; entertainment and restaurant editor Concord Transcript, 1971-75; dining editor Rossmoor News, Walnut Creek, 1977-78; free-lance non-fiction journalist, 1976–; mem: U.S. Power Squadron, DAV, Ret. Officers Assn., American Legion, V.F.W., U.S. Submarine Vets. WWII Assn.; clubs: Martinez Yacht, Rossmoor Yacht (v. commodore 1994), Toastmasters. Democrat. Res: 1840 Tice Creek Dr #2228, Walnut Creek 94595 Ofc: PO Box 52 Concord 94522

ANDERSON, ANTHONY EDWARD, university librarian; b. Apr. 2, 1952, Pasadena; s. Herbert Raymond and Eugenia Caroline (Moore) A.; edn: AA, Pasadena City Coll., 1972; BA in Eng. lit./theater arts, Occidental Coll., 1974; MSLS, USC Sch. of Library and Information Mgmt., 1977, BA Slavic languages and literatures, USC, 1981. Career: librarian Jet Propulsion Lab., Pasadena 1983-85; librarian Univ. of So. Calif., 1981, 1985–; mem: Am. Lib. Assn., Calif. Acad. and Res. Librarians Assn., Edward Elgar Soc.; civic: Pasa. Sister Cities Com. (gen. chair 1986–), Friends of Pasa. Pub. Libs. (v.p. 1989–), People to People L.A. Co. chpt. (sec. 1986-87), mem. Pasa. Strategic Planning Com. 1984-86; Democrat; Episcopalian; rec: running, swimming, internat. relations, fgn. languages. Res: 1956 Woodlyn Rd Pasadena 91104-3244 Ofc: Von KleinSmid Library, USC, Los Angeles 90089-0182

ANDERSON, BRADFORD WILLIAM, food manufacturing company sales executive; b. Feb. 17, 1956, Redlands; s. B. W. and Helen Louise (Wisel) A.; m. Diane Hutt, Aug. 21, 1981; children: David B.; edn: BS mgmt., Univ. Redlands, 1978; MBA, CSU San Bernardino, 1982. Career: store mgr. Finger's Market, Redlands 1974-79; territory mgr., sr. terr. mgr./tnr. Carnation Co., Fullerton 1980-83, dist. sales coord. 1983-85, nat. mgr. sales planning Carnation Co., L.A. 1985-91, nat. mgr. & sales technology Nestle, Glendale, 1991–; instr. Chaffey Coll., 1985–; awards: Harris Memorial Scholar, Harris' Dept. Store, Redlands 1975, Pat Patterson Mem. Award, Santa Fe Fed. Savings, Redlands 1975, Outstanding Young Men in Am., Jaycees (1984, 87), listed Who's Who in West (1988, 90, 92), Who's Who in World 1992, Men of Achievement 1988, other biog. references; mem: Univ. Redlands Alumni Assn., Alpha Gamma Nu Alumni, CSUSB Alumni Assn., Inland Counties Food Industry Sales Club; civic: L.A. Zoo Support Group, Friends of Santa Ana Zoo, Muchenthaler Theater 1987–, Diamond Bar Ranch Festival, Diamond Bar Improvement Assn., Redlands Jaycees, trustee Diamond Bar Congregational Ch., Diamond Bar Children's Ctr. Parent's Aux.; publ: article in field, 1987; Republican; United Ch. of Christ; rec: skiing, racquetball, travel. Res: 24442 Rosegate Pl Diamond Bar 91765 Ofc: Nestle Food Co. 800 N Brand Blvd Ste 19 Glendale CA 91203

ANDERSON, CAROLE JOLENE, publishing executive; b. June 28, Tulare; d. James Pierce, Sr. and Helen Bernice (Walters) Slover; m. Douglas Robert Anderson, June 14, 1975; 1 dau: Sabrina Jo, b. 1955; edn: Riverside City Coll. 1973-76; Victor Valley Coll. 1970-73. Career: model Connor Sch. of Modeling, Fresno 1955; actress Kosloff Studios, Hollywood 1965; nat. sales mgr. Armed Services Publishers, Riverside 1966; pres. Armed Services Press, 1973; pres., dir., maj. shareholder Heritage House Publishing, Inc. until 1984; dir. Sullivan Pub. 1987-88; pres. Jolene S. Ander Publishing Consultants, Inc. 1988–; awards: Woman of Achievement (1989), Rotary Humanitarian of Yr. (1990); civic bds: Riverside Cultural Heritage (dir.), Tourist & Conv. Bur., YWCA, Soroptimists Internat., Riverside C.of C., Riv. Symphony (bd.), Riv. Year 2000 Com., Riv. County Philharmonic, Riv. Downtown Assn., March AFB (co-comdr.); rec: skiing, tennis, bicycling. Res: 10450 Dufferin Ave Riverside 92503

ANDERSON, COURTNEY ALFRED, writer; b. Dec. 22, 1906, Jamestown, N.Y.; s. Alfred Anders and Alice (Sundell) A.; m. Catherine Bullock, June 17, 1931; 1 son, James b. 1940; edn: BA, Dartmouth Coll. 1931; MA, Western Reserve Univ. 1934. Career: asst. prof. Fenn Coll., Cleveland, Ohio 1931-36; writer Indsl. Pictures Inc., Detroit, Mich. 1932-39; 1940-41; Carvavel Film, N.Y.C. 1941-42; First Motion Picture Unit, Culver City 1943-45; self-employed, L.A. 1945-60; v.p., writer Elba Systems Inc., Denver, Colo. 1960-72; awards: citations Los Angeles Co. Bd. Suprs. (1973), Judson Coll. (1976); mem: Nat. Assn. Sci. Writers, Am. Med. Writers Assn.; civic: L.A. Co. Commn. on Alcoholism (v.chmn. 1969-71, chmn. 1971-73); author (biographies): To The Golden Shore: The Life of Adoniram Judson (1952, 60, 88), Jonathan Edwards (1966); mil: 1st lt. USAAF 1942-45; Democrat. Res: 1447 17th St Apt 25 Santa Monica 90404

ANDERSON, DAVID CHARLES, librarian; b. Apr. 27, 1931, Oakland; s. Clarence Emil, Sr. and Alice P. (Smith) A.; m. Jean Lynn Hess, June 8, 1957; children: Alan b. 1958, David (Chris) b. 1959, Gregory b. 1960, Bradley b. 1962, Lisa b. 1967; edn: BA, UC Berkeley, 1952; BLS, UCB Sch. Librarianship, 1953. Career: librarian State Office of Local Planning, 1957-62, also State Dept. of Finance, 1960-62, Sacto.; serials cataloger Library, Univ. Calif. Davis, 1962-69, hd. Health Sci. Cataloging Pool 1969-71, hd. tech. svs. dept. Carlson Health Sci. Library 1971-91 (ret.); UC Ctr. for Animal Alternatives (p.t.) 1992–; mem: Medical Library Assn. (1973–, mem., chair pub. & info. industries rels. com. 1981-85, tech. svs. sect., veterinary med. libraries sect. 1975–, union list com. chair 1981-95, chair 1988-89, sect. newsletter ed. 1985-87), No. Calif.-Nev. Med. Library Group (1973–, chmn. union list com. 1988-90); num. profl. publs., bibliographies include Veterinary serials, a union list of serials in vet. collections in Canada, Europe, USA (2nd ed., 2 vols., MLA 1988); editor & pub. of qtrly. resource jour. on human-animal relationship, The InterActions Bibliography (v.1, 1990–); pub. poetry includes translations and poetic paraphrase: From Solomon's songbook: the Odes, 1984; mil: sp5 US Army 1953-56; Plymouth Brethren. Res: 8732 Rock Springs Rd Penryn 95663 Ofc: UC Center for Animal Alternatives, School of Veterinary Medicine, University of California Davis 95616-8684

ANDERSON, ERIC GEORGE, physician, author; b. April 22, 1932, Crieff, Scotland; nat. 1967; s. George Frederick and Jessie Sutherland (Thom) A.; m. Margaret Hunter, Sept. 14, 1955; children: Gillian b. 1958, Carolyn b. 1960, Michael b. 1962; edn: MB, Ch.B, Univ. Edinburgh Faculty of Medicine Scotland 1958. Career: pvt. practice, Groveton, Tx. 1960-64; founding mem. Derry Med. Center, Derry, N.H. 1964-85; physician Sharp Rees-Stealy Med. Group, San Diego 1985–; contbg. editor: Travel 50 & Beyond, Houston, Tx., 1995–, San Diego Magazine, S.D., Calif., 1995–, Relax, Cleveland, Ohio, 1994–, Medical Tribune, NYC, 1994–, Postgrad. Medicine, Minneapolis, Minn., 1992–, Geriatrics, Cleveland, Ohio, 1991–, Physician's Management, Cleveland, Ohio, 1983–; mem: N.H. Acad. Family Physicians (pres. 1974), Soc. of American Travel Writers, Motor Press Guild, Am. Soc. Journalists Authors; author: Lightplane Vacationing, 1976, Plane Safety & Survival, 1978, The Pilot's Health, 1984; mil: capt. Parachute Regiment British Army 1950-57; Republican; Presbyterian; rec: photog., automobiles, writing. Res: 10205 Rue Touraine San Diego 92131

ANDERSON, GARRY MICHAEL, physician, radiologist; b. May 17, 1955, Houston, Tx.; s. Dan Luther and Marcella Marie (Hanel) A.; edn: BS, Texas A&M 1979; MD., 1981; reg. Am. Bd. Radiology (1986). Career: fellow UC Los Angeles 1986-87; radiologist, Radiology Med. Group, Long Beach 1987–; attdg. clin. instr. UCLA Dept. Radiology 1987-88; chief resident, radiology Scott & White Hosp., Temple, Tx. 1985-86; awards: Tx. A&M Coll. Medicine Merit scholar 1978-79; mem: Am. Coll. Radiology, Radiological Soc. N.Am., AMA, L.A. Radiological Soc., L.A. Co. Med. Assn.; article pub. in med. jour., 1989; R.Cath. Res: 1811 Termino #7108 Long Beach 90815 Ofc: Community Radiology Medical Group, Inc. 1703 Termino Ave Ste 107A Long Beach 90804

ANDERSON, HOLLY GEIS, premenstrual syndrome clinic president and chief executive officer, educator; b. Oct. 23, 1946, Waukesha, Wis.; d. Henry H. and Hulda S. Geis; m. Richard Kent Anderson, June 6, 1969; edn: BA, Azusa Pacific Univ., 1970. Career: prop. Oak Tree Antiques, San Gabriel 1975-82; founder, pres. Premenstrual Syndrome Treatment Clinic, Inc. Arcadia 1982–; founder, pres. Hormonal Treatment Centers, Inc. (in-hosp. treatment prog.) 1992-94; lectr. seminars on womens' illnesses i.e. PMS, postpartum depression, hysterectomy, menopause, and the use of natural hormones; radio bdcst. personality "Women's Clinic with Holly Anderson" 1990–; TV guest authority on shows including: Mid Morning L.A., 1988, America, 1985, Tom Snyder Show, 1986, Montel Williams Show, 1992, Mo Show, 1993, Marilyn Kagan, 1994; mem. The Dalton Soc. (research PMS), Nat. Assn. Female Execs.; author: audio cassette, What Every Woman Needs to Know About PMS, 1987; audio cassette, PMS Talk, 1989; video cassette, The PMS Treatment Program, 1989; Republican; rec: writing poetry, travel. Ofc: 150 N Santa Anita Ste 755 Arcadia 91006 Tel: 818/447-0679

ANDERSON, IRIS ANITA, educator; b. Aug. 18, 1930, Forks, Wash.; d. James Adolphus and Alma Elizabeth (Haase) Gilbreath; m. Donald Rene Anderson; children: Karen C. b. 1952, Susan A. b. 1953, Gayle L. b. 1957, Brian D. b1959; edn: BA teaching, Univ. Wash. 1969; MA Eng., Seattle Univ. 1972; tchg. cred. English lang. K-12 (1977), Adminstrn. (1978), Comm. Colls. (1978). Career: tchr. Issaquah (Wash.) Sr. High Sch. 1969-77; tchr. Los Angeles Sr. H.S. 1977-79 (also dist. curriculum council chmn., middle sch. plan. dir. assn. curriculum chmn., planned programmed budget proj. chmn., edn. assn. instructional planning chmn. trimester system, accreditation evaluation, advisor Nat. Honor Soc., YMCA-YWCA v.p.); honors: W-Key Activities Scholarship Hon. (Univ. Wash.); mem: Wash. Speech Assn., Nat. Edn. Assn., CRTA, Sigma Kappa, AAUW, Palm Springs Press Women; civic: vol. UCLA Jules Stein Eye Inst., Santa Monica Hosp. Aux. Volunteers (hosp. nutrition vol.), active L.W.V., Nat. Thespians, Desert Beautiful, Palm Springs Panhellenic, Rancho Mirage Republican Women, Bob Hope Cultural Ctr., The Living Desert (Palm Desert), others; clubs: Palm Desert Women's, Rancho Mirage Women's, Indio Women's, CPA Wives, Desert Celebrities, Round Table West, D.A.R. (vice regent Cahuilla chpt.), Friends of Library-Coll. of Desert, World Affairs Council (Palm Springs chpt.); publ: Conservationist's Dilemma (Sea Pen, Marine Sci. Soc. of the Northwest 1975); Republican; Prot. Address: PO Box 6000 Palm Desert 92261

ANDERSON, JEFFREY LEE, physician; b. Feb. 3, 1959, Fontana, Calif.; s. Earle Richard and Joyce Elaine (Everington) A.; m. Crystal Gregory, Dec. 18, 1987; children: Kimberly b. 1991, Kristin b. 1993; edn: BS, USAF Acad. 1981; MD, Loma Linda Univ. Sch. of Medicine 1985; postdoctoral residency (anesthesiology), Loma Linda Univ. Med. Ctr. 1988; bd. cert., Am. Bd. of Anesthesiology 1989. Career: chief resident, dept. of anesthesiology Loma Linda Univ. Med. Ctr., Loma Linda, Calif. 1988-89; staff anesthesiologist USAF Hosp. Mather AFB, Sacramento, Calif. 1989-93, chief anesthesiologist, 1990-94; staff anesthesiologist Mercy Hosp. of Folsom, Folsom, Calif. 1990–, Mercy Gen. Hosp., Sacramento 1991–; assoc. clinical prof. of anesthesiology Univ. of Calif. at Davis Med. Ctr., Sacramento 1993–; cons. National Consultants, San Diego 1992–; awards: Outstanding Resident award, Loma Linda Univ. Dept. of Anesthesiology 1989, Meritorious Service Medal, USAF, Sacramento 1994; mem.: Am. Soc. of Anesthesiologists 1989–, Calif. Soc. of Anesthesiologists 1989–; co-author: Postanesthesia Care Unit Management, 1992; mil: major USAF 1989-94; rec: snow skiing. Res: 127 Goodell Road Folsom 95630 Ofc: 1650 Creekside Drive Folsom 95630

ANDERSON, MARJORIE BETH, marriage and family counselor; b. Oct. 9, 1914, Chgo.; d. Louis Saran and Margaret Zaida (Goodman) Strauss; m. Montague Allen Anderson, Mar. 27, 1938 (div.); children: Kent b. 1944 (dec.), Sherry b. 1945, Craig b. 1948; edn: BA psych., UCLA, 1932-36, 71-72; MA psych., Sierra Univ., 1982; lic. Marriage Family Child Counselor, Calif. 1985. Career: pvt. practice MFCC(current); volunteer profl. grief-support group ldr. Oasis Senior Citizens Ctr., Corona del Mar, and Irvine Senior Ctr., Irvine; steering com/ O.C. Hemlock; prior civic: Hoag Hosp. Aux. (original convenor), Orange Co. Panhellenic (founding mem.), Candy Stripers (1 of 3 founders), Nightengales (founding mem.), Children's Theater Guild (charter), Lido Isle Players (charter), Las Almas de Mardan (charter), active in Scouting, sch. room mother & PTA coms., Cotillion chaperone, sponsor Junior Board of Control Lido Isle; Agnostic; rec: photography, travel, crafts, gardening. Ofc: 3355 Via Lido, Newport Beach 92663

ANDERSON, MEL, college executive; b. Sept. 28, 1928, Oakland; s. Edwin Albert and Lillian Frances (Redmond) A.; edn: BA, Saint Mary's Coll. 1952, Hon. LittD, St. Albert's Coll., Oakland, Hon. DHL, Lewis Univ., Ill.; DHL (Honoris Causa) Univ. of San Francisco; Doctor of Pedagogy (Honoris Causa) Manhattan Coll., NY, NY. Career: instr. Sacred Heart High Sch., San Francisco 1952-56; v.prin. La Salle High Sch., Pasadena 1956-62; prin. San Joaquin Memorial High Sch., Fresno 1962-64; prin. Saint Mary's High Sch., Berkeley 1964-69; pres. Saint Mary's Coll. of Calif., Moraga 1969–, trustee 1968–; mem. advy. bd. Franciscan Sch. of Theology, Berkeley; bd. dirs. DeLaSalle Inst., Napa; awards: Alumnus of Yr. Saint Mary's Coll. 1987, inducted Contra Costa County Hall of Fame 1988, Dominican Sch. of Theol. and Philosophy Alemany award 1992, Anti-Defamation League Torch of Liberty award 1993, named 1994 Citizen of Yr. by Town of Moraga, recipient Papal "Pro Ecclesia" Medal 1994; mem: Assn. Independent Calif. Colls. & Univs. (exec. com. 1973, chmn. exec. com. 1988-89, 89-90), Indep. Colls. of No. Calif. (bd.), Regional Assn. East Bay Colls. & Univ. (chmn. 1979-81, 1990-91), Commonwealth Club of Calif.; Democrat. Roman Cath. Address: Bro. Mel Anderson, F.S.C., Saint Mary's College, PO Box 3005 Moraga 94575

ANDERSON, PAUL WAYNE, psychiatrist; b. Apr. 17, 1930, Janesville, Wis.; s. Elmer Evan and Helen Marie (Kidder) A.; edn: BA, Andrews Univ., Berrien Springs, Mich., 1950; MD, Loma Linda Univ., Calif. 1955; MPH, UC Berkeley, 1960. Career: preventive medicine ofcr. U.S. Army, France 1956-58; district health ofcr. King Co. Dept. of Public Health, Seattle, Wash. 1960-76; health ofcr. (p.t.) Kittitas Co. Dept. of Public Health, Ellensburg, Wash. 1966-76; health ofcr. Humboldt-Del Norte Co. Dept. of Public Health, Eureka, Calif. 1976-88; psychiatric resident Napa State Hosp., Napa, Calif. 1989-92, staff psychiatrist 1992–; mem.: AMA 1960–, Am. Psychiatric Assn. 1989–, No. Calif. Psychiatric Soc. 1989- (pres. No. Bay Chpt. 1994-95), Am. Rhododendron Soc. (v.p. Calif. chpt. 1993-94), No. Napa Rotary Club (sr. mem.); mil: col., U.S. Army, USAR, 1956-86; Seventh-day Adventist; rec: horticulture (specialty of growing rhododendrons). Ofc: Napa State Hospital 2100 Napa Vallejo Hwy Napa 94558

ANDERSON, RAYMOND HARTWELL, JR., engineer; b. Feb. 25, 1932, Staunton, Va.; s. Raymond Hartwell and Virginia Boatwright (Moseley) A.; m. Dana Wilson, Sept. 5, 1959; children: Kathryn, b. 1960, Margaret, b.1962, Susan, b. 1963; edn: BS, ceramic eng.,Va. Polytech. Inst. 1957, BS, metallurg. eng. 1958, MS, metallurg. eng. 1959. Career: metallurgical engr. Gen.Dynamics, Ft. Worth, Tex. 1959-61; senior metallurgical engr. Babcock & Wilcox Co., Lynchburg, Va. 1961-65, Douglas Aircraft Co., Santa Monica, Ca. 1965-67; materials R&D splst. McDonnell Douglas, Santa Monica 1967-71, senior technical splst. McDonnell Douglas, Huntington Bch. 1971-87, senior specialist Space Station Pgm., 1987–; mats., teaching staff Univ. Calif. Irvine, 1991–; asst. prof. metallurgy, Va. Poly. Inst. 1958-59; cons. engr., metallurgy, 1967-68; honors: Tau Beta Pi (earth sci.), Alpha Sigma Mu (metals), Omicron Delta Kappa (leadership), Sigma Gamma Epsilon, Scabbard & Blade (mil.); mem: Am. Soc. for Metals (1957–, tchg. staff 1966-69), Corrosion Soc. 1957-70, Am. Ceramic Soc. 1957-70, Am. Nuclear Soc. 1961-65, Am. Welding Soc. 1991–, De Molay 1952–; BSA Merit Badge Com. 1970. Patentee (2); publs: contbr. sci. jours. Mil: lst lt. AUS Ord.1954-56, Nat. Svc. ribbon.; Republican; Prot. rec: sports cars, philately, gardening, stereo music systems. Res: 1672 Kenneth Dr Santa Ana 92705 Ofc: McDonnell Douglas, 5301 Bolsa Ave Huntington Bch 92647

ANDERSON, RICHARD HAYDEN, physician, psychiatrist; b. Sept. 17, 1921, Hayden, Ariz.; s. Victor Emmanuel and LaVona (McClendon) A.; m. Bernice A. Meacham, Sept. 7, 1944; children: Michael b. 1946, Ronald b. 1950, Brian b. 1951; edn: BA, Univ. Utah 1943; MD, 1945; cert. Am. Bd. Psychiatry & Neurology 1952. Career: resident VA,. Palo Alto 1948-51, chief of psychiatry, Salt Lake City, Utah 1952-55, chief profl. services 1955-57; assoc. supt. Mendocino St. Hosp., Ukiah 1957-59; assoc. supt. Fairview St. Hosp., Costa Mesa 1959-60; pvt. practice, Santa Cruz 1960-92 (ret.); asst. clin. prof. Univ. Utah Med. Sch., Salt Lake City 1952-57; lectr. psychiatry UCSF Med. Sch. 1957-59; program chief Co. Mental Health, Santa Cruz 1960-63; dir. psychiatry Dominican Santa Cruz Hosp. 1969-75; honors: Phi Eta Sigma, Phi Kappa Phi, Phi Beta Kappa, Alpha Omega Alpha; mem: CMA, Am. Psychiatric Soc. (fellow), Santa Cruz Co. Med. Soc.; articles pub. in med. jours 1945-57; mil: capt. AUS Med. Corps 1946-48; rec: golf, photography, travel. Res: 22 Ortalon Ave Santa Cruz 95060

ANDERSON, RICHARD NORMAN, film actor; b. Aug. 8, 1926, Long Branch, N.J.; s. Henry and Olga (Lurie) A.; children: Ashley, Brooke Dominique, Deva Justine; edn: grad. University H.S., West L.A. 1944. Career: actor Metro Goldwyn Mayer, Culver City 1950-56; 20th Century Fox, Beverly Hills 1961-62; Columbia Bdcstg. Systems, Hollywood 1965-67; Quinn Martin Prodns., Hollywood 1970-71; Universal Studios, Universal City 1973-78 and 1986-89; film producer, pres. Richard Anderson Film Corp., Richard Anderson Films, Los Angeles 1973–; awards: Emmy nominee Bionic Woman TV Series (1976-77); mem. Acad. Motion Picture Arts & Scis., Ephebian Soc.; club: Friars (B.H. and N.Y.), The Players Club N.Y.; mil: t/sgt. US Army 1945-47; rec: tennis, bicycle touring, classic cars, travel. Ofc: c/o Lewis and Joffe 10880 Wilshire Blvd Los Angeles 90024

ANDERSON, TERRY MARLENE, civil engineer; b. Sept. 26, 1954, Honolulu; d. Stanley Dale and Anna Clara (Heigert) Anderson; edn: BS in aquacultural engring. and BS in biological scis., UC Davis; Reg. Civil Engr., Calif. 1983, Colo. 1986; Water Treatment Operator Grade 3, Calif. 1995. Career: project engr., proj. mgr. John Carollo Engring., Walnut Creek 1979-85; assoc. engr. Grice Engineering, Salinas 1985; consulting engr./prin., Durango, Colo. 1985-86; assoc. engr. Charpier, Martin Assocs., Sacto. 1986-87; proj. mgr. CWC-HDR, Inc. Cameron Park 1987; senior civil engr. El Dorado County Dept. Transp., Placerville 1987-90; dep. dir. pub. works Mendocino County Dept. Pub. Works, 1990; Engring. Div. mgr., sanitation, Sonoma Co. Dept. Pub. Works, 1991-94; dist. engr. Lake County Special Districts 1994–; honors: appreciation City of Gonzales 1984; mem: ASCE, Nat. Soc. of Profl. Engrs., Local Soc. of Surveyors, Architects, Geologists and Engrs. (profl. ethics com., chmn. gen. plan rev. com.); civic: volunteer Ofc. of Emergency Services County of Sonoma, 1991-94, Pollution Control, 1981–; Republican; Christian; rec: backpacking, sewing, designing, fish farming.

ANDERSON, THOMAS LEIF, physician, educator; b. Oct. 16, 1949, New Orleans, La.; s. Maurice John and Kitty Thordis (Thomstad) A.; m. Charlotte Ann Hull, Oct. 10, 1980; children: Laurel b. 1984, Timothy b. 1988; edn: BA, Denison Univ., 1971; MD, Yale Univ., 1975. Career: asst. prof. neurology UCLA /Harbor Med. Ctr., Torrance 1980-86, assoc. clin. prof. neurology 1987–; mem. med. advy. bd. Muscular Dystrophy Assn., L.A. 1983–; honors: Phi Beta Kappa, 1971; Prot. Ofc: Dept. Neurology Harbor-UCLA Medical Center 1000 W Carson St Torrance 90509

ANDERSON-IMBERT, ANA ISABEL, physician; b. Aug. 21, 1940, Buenos Aires, Argentina; nat. 1954; d. Enrique and Margarita (Di Clerico) Anderson-Imbert; m. Jack Himelblam, May 30, 1963 (div. 1993); children: Robert b. 1964, Vanessa b. 1968; edn: BA, Univ. of Mich., Ann Arbor 1961, MA, immunology, 1964, MD, 1968. Career: chief of medicine Kaiser Permanente, Fremont, Calif. 1980-87; chief of med. legal Kaiser Permanente, Hayward/Fremont 1983-87; physician-in-charge, Kaiser Permanente, Fremont 1987-88; asst. physician-in-chief, Kaiser Permanente, Hayward 1988–; apptd. mem. Med. Bd. of Calif. 1993; mem.: Am. Coll. of Rheumatology (fellow) 1973–, CMA 1987–, Am. Coll. of Physicians 1994–; rec: reading, music. Ofc: Kaiser Permanente 27400 Hesperian Blvd Hayward 94545

ANDIA, ANA MARIA, physician, psychiatric consultant; b. Aug. 3, 1949; d. Daniel C. and Dolores (del Gallego) Andia; edn: BA hons., Univ. Kans. Lawrence 1971; PhD, Utah St. Univ. 1977; MD, Univ. Tx. Houston 1984. Career: research asst. Univ. Kans., Lawrence 1971; Utah St. Univ., Logan 1971-76; jr. fellow Eleanor Roosevelt Cancer Research Inst., Denver, Colo. 1977; postdoctoral fellow Univ. Tx., Houston 1977-79, research scientist 1981-83; internal medicine resident UC San Diego, 1984-87, psychiatry resident 1987-90; outpatient clinical psychiatry fellow, 1989-90; psychiatric cons. Student Health Svs., San Diego St. Univ., 1989-90; adult psychiatrist, So. Calif. Permanente Med. Group 1990–; honors: BRINDIS award 1992, Alpha Omega Alpha 1984, Rotary Found. scholar 1970, Utah St. Univ. Delbert A. Greenwood award 1974, Univ. Texas merit scholar 1981; mem: Am. Psychiatric Assn., AMA, N.Y. Acad. Scis., Am. Group Psychotherapy Assn., San Diego Group Psychotherapy Soc. (pres.-elect 1995); 20+ articles pub. in med. jours., 1975-95; rec: poetry writing, acting. Ofc: Kaiser Permanente 990 Lane Ave Chula Vista 91903

ANDREWS, CANDACE LOU, radio executive; b. Apr. 20, 1957, Larson AFB, Wash.; d. Louis Warren Wilson and Lucie Elizabeth (Halley) A.; edn: BA psychology and BBA mgmt., Univ. Tx., Austin 1979. Career: with GranTree Furniture Rental: sales rep., then asst. sales/ mktg. mgr. in Austin, TX 1979-83, Denver, Colo. 1983-84, sales & mktg. mgr. Inland Empire, CA 1984-86; operations mgr. Shepherd Comms., Yucaipa, Calif. 1986-93, v.p. devel. & ops. 1993, general mgr. 1993–; mem: Nat. Religious Broadcasters., Nat. Assn. of Broadcasters., Christian Mgmt. Assn., Fellowship of Christian Athletes, Longhorn Assocs. (charter mem.), Tx. Exes Alumni Assn. (life), Yucaipa C.of C., Friends of Turkey (vol. 1987–), Awana Commander 1989-91, Faith Bible Ch. (asst. fin. secty 1988-90, fin. secty. 1990-91, deaconess 1993–); Republican; Christian; rec: outdoors, biking. Ofc: Shepherd Communications PO Box 1000 Yucaipa 92399-1000

ANDREWS, PATRICIA L., military human resources executive; b. Aug. 14, 1949, Clinton, Iowa; d. Henry and LaVonne Rose (Henning) Hinrichs; m. A. Kent Drechsler, March 16, 1969 (div. 1974); m. A.J. Andrews, Aug. 17, 1974; children: Nathan b. 1972, Stacey b. 1975, Melissa b. 1978; edn: Marycrest Coll. 1967-68; AA psychology, Blackhawk Coll. 1979; BA, Western Ill. Univ. 1982; MS, Fla. Inst. Tech. 1985. Career: dir. human resources. US Army Corps of Engrs. 1974-: personnel mgmt. intern, Rock Island, Ill. 1974-76, personnel staffing splst. 1976-78, dept. personnel ofcr. 1978-79, chief mgmt. employee relations and labor relations 1979-82, personnel ofcr. 1982-87; dir. human resources, Sacto. 1987–; appt. Program Evaluation Devel. Task Force, Corps of Engrs., Wash. D.C. 1986-88; awards: Corps of Engrs. Exceptional Performance 1982, 84, 85, 86, 88, 89, 90, Outstanding Achievement in EEO 1984, Dept. of Army Outstanding Personnel Program Leader 1986, appreciation 1984, 88, com-

mendn. 1987, 91, 92, 93, performance 1988; mem: Internat. Personnel Mgmt. Assn., Profl. Council of Engrs. & Scientists, S. Pacific Div. Career Planning Bd., No. Calif. Personnel Council; Greek Orthodox Christian; rec: walking, travel. Res: 1303 Meadowvista Way Roseville 95661 Ofc: 1325 J Street Sacramento 95814

ANDREYKO, JANICE LORRAINE, physician: reproductive endocrinologist; b. Nov. 27, 1953, Toronto, Can.; d. Norman Joseph and Stephanie Mary (Salivarski) Andreyko; m. Thomas George Arizmendi, Sept. 7, 1985; 1 son; edn: MD, Univ. of Toronto, Can. 1978; cert. ob/gyn, reproductive endocrinologist, Am. Bd. of Ob/Gyn 1987, 88. Career: asst. prof. Univ. of Toronto, Can. 1986-88; asst. clinical prof. UC San Francisco 1989-90; assoc. med. dir. Pacific Fertility Ctr., Sacramento 1990-92, med. dir. 1992–; awards: Med. Res. Council of Can. fellowship 1984-86; mem.: Royal Coll. of Physicians & Surgeons of Can. (fellow) 1983–, Am. Fertility Soc. 1984–, Am. Coll. of Ob/Gyn (fellow) 1989–, Soc. of Reproductive Endocrinologists 1989–, Bay Area Reproductive Endocrine Soc. 1990–. Ofc: Pacific Fertility Center 2288 Auburn Blvd #204 Sacramento 95821 Tel: 916/567-1302

ANDRIANO-MOORE, RICHARD GRAF, retired naval officer, teacher; b. Petaluma; s. Norvel Moore and Thelma Elizabeth (Cook) Koch-Andriano; desc. from the Grafen von Andriano and Brentano di Tremezzo of Italy and Germany; m. Janice Hironaka, Jan. 10, 1976 (div. Feb. 1990); children: Erika b. 1976, Stephen b. 1978; edn: BA, CSU San Jose 1956; grad. work UC Riverside; MBA, Pepperdine Univ. 1977; cert. Naval War Coll., Newport, R.I. 1980-81, 1981-82; Surface Warfare Ofcr., USN, 1972. Career: sch. tchr. (7th, 8th gr.) Oasis Sch., Thermal, Calif. 1960-63; commnd. ensign USN 1957, 1st lt., gunnery ofcr. USS Jefferson County (LST 1068) 1957-60; personnel and legal ofcr. USS Maury (AGS-16) 1963-65, CO Naval & Marine Corps Reserve Tng. Ctr., Pt. Arthur, TX 1965-68, dept. hd./ops. ofcr. USS Muliphen (LKA-61) 1968-69, asst. Surface & ASW Pgm. ofcr., 1970-72, Surface Pgm. ofcr. 11th Naval Dist. 1972-74, CO Hunters Pt. Naval Reserve Ctr., San Francisco 1974-75, CO Navy and Marine Corps Reserve Ctr., San Bruno 1975-79, dir. adminstrn. Nat. Com. for Employer Support of the Guard and Reserve, Office of Secty. Def., Wash DC 1979-82, comdr. recruiting coord. Region 1, Alameda 1982-84, chief of staff Naval Reserve Readiness Command Region 20, Treasure Is., S.F. 1984-85, ret. Comdr. USN, 9/1/85; decorated Def. Merit. Service 1982, Navy Commendn. 1973, 85, authorized by Sec. of Def. to wear the Office of the Secty. of Def. ID Badge 1980, Command Ashore Insignia 1974, Surface Warfare Insignia 1978, USN Recruiting Badge w/2 gold wreaths 1983, 84, Expt. Pistol Shot 1978; honors: War Service Medal 1974, Silver Good Citizenship Medal 1978, Patriot Medal 1985, Meritorious Service Medal 1987, Bronze Good Citizenship Medal 1993, SAR; Knight, Noble Company of the Rose 1986, recipient Coat of Arms of the Counts of Andriano Wappenrolle, Austria 1991, distinguished alumni San Jose State Univ. 1991; Guardian of Glasclune Castle 1993; 2d deg. Brown Belt, Kodakan Judo Assn., Tokyo; mem: Navy League of U.S. (hon. dir. San Mateo Co. Council 1975-79), Retired Ofcrs. Assn., Reserve Ofcrs. Assn., Sigma Nu Frat. (chpt. pres. 1955), Nat. Soc. SAR (pres. S.F. chpt. 1976-77, chmn. Nat. DAR Cmte 1979-81, v.p. N. Calif. Soc. SAR 1984-86, pres. Calif. Soc. SAR 1986-7), Mil. Order of Loyal Legion of U.S., Calif. Commandery (Recorder 1976-78, v.comdr. 1978-82, comdr. 1982-88), Calif. Soc. Children of the Am. Revolution 1986-87 (sr. state scholarships chmn. 1993-94), The Augustan Soc. (v.p. and mem. bd. dirs. 1988-94), Coast Range Soc. (sr. pres. 1987-88), Children of the Am. Revolution, Gen. Soc. of Mayflower Desc., Gen. Soc. of the War of 1812, Hospitaler Order of St. John of Jerusalem (Companion of Honor 1983, Knight 1991), Naval Order of U.S., Fedn. Des Combattants Allies En Europe; civic: Cultural Soc. of Marin, Webelos Scout Den Leader (1987-89, den leader award 1989), Scoutmaster Troop 18 (1989-92), Scouter's Tng. Award 1989, Scoutmaster Award of Merit 1992, camp dir. Boy Scout Camp Masonite-Navarro 1992-95, dist. Boy Scout exec. Redwood Empire Council BSA 1992-94; mem. Precinct Bd. (insp. 1987-90); chief ed. Calif. Compatriot 1986-87; Republican; Prot.; rec: travel, genealogy. Res: 197 Upland Dr Petaluma 94952

ANEMA, DURLYNN CAROL, education consultant, author; b. Dec. 23, 1935, San Diego; d. Durlin L. Flagg and Carolyn L. (Janeck) Owen; m. Charles J. Anema, Jan. 18, 1955 (dec. 1986); children: Charlynn Raimundi b. 1955, Charles Jay Jr. b. 1957, Richard F. b. 1963; edn: BA, CSU Hayward, 1968, MS, 1977; EdD, UOP, 1984; PhD Trinity Theological Seminary 1994. Career: secondary tchr. San Leandro Unified Sch. Dist., 1970-72, Hayward Unified Sch. Dist. 1972-75, vice prin. Hayward USD 1975-77, Lodi USD 1977-80; dir. Lifelong Learning, Univ. of the Pacific, Stockton 1981-84, faculty 1989–; prof. comm. Univ. of the Pacific 1984-89; instr. Nat. Univ., Sacto. 1989-91; edn. consultant statewide 1989–; columnist Stockton Record 1984-89; dir. San Joaquin Authors Symp., Stockton 1985-94; awards: Phi Kappa Phi 1984, Susan B. Anthony award San Joaquin Co. Commn. on Women 1989, listed Who's Who Am. Univs. 1982, Who's Who in West 1984–; mem. AAUW, Delta Kappa Gamma, Phi Delta Kappa; civic bds: San Joaquin Co. Childrens Commn. 1986-92, Tierro del Oro Girl Scouts (advy. bd. 1988-95); author 7+ books incl. Options, 1993, Don't Get Fired, 1978, 90, Get Hired, 1979, 90, Sharing an Apt., 1981; Christian; rec: biking, hiking, travel. Res/Ofc: 401 Oak Ridge Ct Valley Springs 95252

ANGELE, ALFRED ROBERT, law enforcement union executive director, retired police officer; b. Dec. 9, 1940, NYC; s. Alfred Otto and Alma Margaret (Branda) A.; m. Barbara Ann Chavez, Sept. 30, 1961; children: Cindy b. 1963, Lynda b. 1967; edn: AA, L.A. Valley Coll.; Calif. Comm. Colls. life tchg. cred. in police sci. Career: patrolman Burbank Police Dept., 1963-67, detective 1967-74, sgt. 1974-78; expert in narcotics and dangerous drugs; dept. self def. instr.; instr. self defense and pub. sector labor relations; car club youth advisor; exec. director Calif. Orgn. Police & Sheriffs, Sacto. 1978- (mem. 1975–, sec. 1976-78); sec.treas. Calif. Police & Sheriffs Found., Sacto. 1990–; mem., ofcr. Internat. Union of Police Assns. (IUPA), AFL-CIO, W.D.C., 1980-92 (dir. 1981-85, internat. sec.treas. 1985-90, sec.treas. emeritus 1990-92); A financial conservative, he is credited with bringing Burbank Police Ofcrs. Assn., Calif. Orgn. of Police & Sheriffs and the IUPA to sound fiscal positions. gov. appt. Commn. on Peace Officer Stds./Tng., Sacto. 1979-84; mem. AFL-CIO Observer Team sent to Nicaragua to monitor presdl. election (2-25-90); mem. Hon. Host Com. of the Nationwide Tour of the Bill of Rights, 1991, rep. Calif. Law Enforcement; awards: Mike Maggiora Memorial humanitarian award 1980, 1st recipient Burbank Jaycees officer of month award 1977, B.P.O.A. dir. of yr. 1972, Burbank Police Dept. profl. esteem award, law enf. editor of yr. I.U.P.A. 1987, commendns./ltrs. of appreciation from Burbank Bar Assn., BPO Elks, C.H.P., Burbank P.D., Houston Police Patrolmans Union, Women Peace Ofcr. Assn. Calif., Gov. of Calif., Gov. of Ala., Calif. Senate & Assembly, L.A. Mayor, Mayor's Drug & Alc. Abuse Com. Burbank, LA Co. D.A. Ofc., Calif. Dept. Corrections, Ret. Pub. Employees Assn. Calif., C.O.P.S.; mem: Calif. Narcotics Ofcrs. Assn. 1969-73, Calif. Narcotics Infor. Network 1972-74, Police Advy. Council for Car Clubs 1967-70, B.P.O.A. (1963–, only pres. to hold 5 consecutive terms 1976-81); contbr. articles in law enforcement jours., guest editorials for USA Today; mil: seaman USNR 1957-58, cpl. E4 USMC 1958-62, comms. instr. 3d Marine Div. Schs. 1960-61; Democrat; R.Cath.; rec: home remodeling, music, veh. restoration. Ofc: 175 E Olive Ave Ste 400 Burbank 91502

ANGELO, HOMER GLENN, educator; b. June 8, 1916, Alameda; s. Alfred Heath and Elizabeth (Glenn) A.; m. Ann Berryhill, Nov. 12, 1943; children: Christiane b. 1947, Alexander b. 1951, Nancy b. 1953; edn: AB, UC Berkeley 1938; JD, 1941; LL.M, Columbia Univ. N.Y. 1947. Career: prof. law UC Davis 1968; prof. Inst. D'Etudes Européennes Univ. Libre de Bruxelles, Brussels 1968; civic: The Family (S.F.), Bohemian (S.F.), The Carlton, Flyfishers, Savile (London), Cercle Royal Gaulois (Brussels), Club de la Fondation Univérsitaire (Brussels); Prot. Res: Sage House Jacks Valley Rd Genoe NV 89411 also: 100 Thorndale Dr Ste 150 San Rafael 94903

ANGLE, ROGER ROY, writer; b. Aug. 2, 1938, Wichita, Kans.; s. Roy Elmer Angle and Alice Virginia (Unger) Bostwick; m. Fontelle Slater, 1960 (div. 1968); son, Morgan Thomas b. 1967; edn: BA, Univ. Wichita, 1962; MFA creative writing, UC Irvine, 1972. Career: copy editor The Beacon, Wichita, Kans. 1964-67; investigative photojournalist The Gazette and Daily, York, Pa. 1967-69; So. Calif. coord. Poetry in the Schs., Nat. Endowment for the Arts, 1973-76; coll. instr. p.t. and freelance writer, 1973-81; reporter, then editor The Newport Ensign (weekly community newspaper), Newport Beach, Calif. 1979-82, 1983-85; editor Huntington Beach Independent, 1986; pub. relations cons., 1986–; author novels, plays, and screenplays; freelance writer: mag. articles in New West, Waterfront, Orange Coast, Bay Window, Orange County Home & Garden; short fiction, poetry- 20 appearances in eleven literary mags. (1962-94); awards: 1st Pl.- commentary Orange County Fair Best Reporter's Contest (1985), Best editorial page, large weeklies, and 2d best front page, Calif. Newspaper Publishers Assn. (1983), helped the Ensign win 34 state and nat. awards (1979-81), 2d best feature CNPA (1980), nominee Pulitzer Prize (1967), Heywood Broun Award nominee (1967), Fellow Squaw Valley Comm. of Writers (1974) and top fiction scholarship (1992), listed Who's Who in U.S. Writers Editors & Poets, Internat. Authors and Writers Who's Who, A Directory of Am. Poets and Fiction Writers; mem: Soc. of Profl. Journalists/Sigma Delta Chi (O.C. chapt. pres. 1983-84), O.C. Press Club; civic: Mus. Contemporary Art L.A., Mus. of Neon Art L.A., Am. Film Inst. L.A., Am. Ballet Theatre N.Y. Res: 2225-D Pacific Ave Costa Mesa 92627

ANJARD, RONALD P., administrator, technologist, international consultant and lecturer, educator, author; b. July 31, 1935, Chgo.; s. Auguste L. and Florence M. Byrne A.; m. Marie B. Sampler, Jan. 26, 1957; children: John R., Michele M., Michael M., Ronald P., Jr.; edn: BS in Metall. Engring., Carnegie Mellon Univ., 1957; MS/MBA in Indsl. Adminstrn., Purdue Univ., 1968; AS, Indiana Univ., 1973; BS in Bus. Adminstrn., U.S.N.Y., 1978; BA in Humanities, T.A. Edison Coll., 1979; PDE, Univ. of Wis., 1979; PhD in Edn.CPU, 1981; PhD in Metall. Engring., CPU, 1982; MS-CRM, Webster Univ., 1992. Career: div. qual. mgr. AVX/JMI, San Diego, 1981-83; corp. dir. Kaypro Corp., S.D., 1983-85;qual. mgr., CPT, S.D., 1985-89; pres., AIC/ASPT, S.D., 1987–; v.p. Triage Network, S.D., 1989–; SPC coord. & internal cons., General Dynamics/GDESI, 1989-94; adjunct faculty, USC, UCSD, Alabama A&M, Miracosta Coll. S.D. Comm. Coll., La Jolla Univ., Chapman Coll., Univ. of La Verne, Univ. of Phoenix, Mgmt. Inst., and others; awards: Who's Who in Am. 1975–, Gov. Voluntary Action Commendation 1975,1978, Who's Who in Technology Today 1984–, Jaycees Distinguished Service Award 1970, Am. Soc.

Registry 1980–, Who's Who in the World 1978–, Am. Men and Women of Sci. 1979–, Who's Who in Fin. and Ind. 1988–, Outstanding Ind. Young (Party) State Award 1970, Am. Bus. Reg. 1980–, U.S. Lib. of Cong. Listing of Engring. Authors 1974–, GM Comm. Service Award 1970, Notable Am. 1978–, Internat. Authors 1978–, Am. Edn. Reg. 1980–, Am. Scientific Reg. 1980–; Am. Pub. Who's Who 1988, Dict. of Internat. Biography 1976–, Who's Who in the Semiconductor Industry 1986–, Writer's Who's Who (UK) 1978–, Who's Who in History 1982–, Golden Poet Award, 1988, appointed Sagamore of the Wabash by Gov. of Ind. 1979, Personalities of the West and Midwest 1977–, Who's Who in Religion 1975–, Nat. Soc. Reg. 1977–, Sigma Xi Nat. Sci. Honorary 1973–, Layman of the Year Award 1971; Engr. of Distinction 1973–, Best Poets of 1988, Outstanding Young Men in Am. 1970, Who's Who in Am. Christian Leadership 1989, Am. Hall of Police 1987–, IBA Yearbook (UK) 1979, Biography of the Year 1986, Am. Cultural Arts Reg. 1980–, Howard Cty. Heart Citations 1973-75, Am. Civil Service Reg. 1988–, Am. Poetry Assn. Poet of Merit 1989, Two Thousand Notable Am. 1988, Internat. Dir. of Disting. Leadership 1989; mem: ISHM, ASQC, Deming Users Group, IEEE (exec. com.), ASTM (ed. rev. bd., coms.), IEPS, ACS, AIME., Sigma Xi, Am. Soc. for Metals, Internat. Soc. for the Investigation of Ancient Civilizations, Am. Bar Assn.; civic: councilman, Howard Co., Ind., 1980; township trustee, Clay Twnshp., Ind., 1970-75; Young Rep., state vice chmn, 5th dist. chmn, Ind.; S.D. Republican Central Comm.; chmn-small bus., United Fund; chmn cong. action com., C. of C.; active in many historical soc. and church councils; author: 1000 articles and publs. in 17 countries; mil: capt., Army; rec: history, archeology, anthropology, horticulture photography. Ofc: AIC Box 420950 San Diego 92124

ANSPACH, DENNY SYKES, radiologist; b. Feb. 5, 1934, Chgo.; s. William Earl and Rachel Mae (Sykes) A.; m. Carol Jacobs, June 22, 1958, and May 14, 1988; children: David b. 1962, Carolyn b. 1965; m. Polly Dakin, 1981, div. 1987; edn: AB, Stanford Univ., 1956, MD 1960, postgrad. splty. 1961-64; diagnostic radiologist Am. Bd. Rad., 1965. Career: capt. US Army and chief radiology Kirk Army Hosp., Aberdeen Proving Ground, Md. 1964-66; radiologist Radiolog. Assocs. of Sacramento Inc., Sacto., Ca. 1966-81; Green Mountain Radiology, Montepelier, Vt. 1981-87; indep. contr. radiologist 1987-90; radiologist (breast only) Univ. Calif. Davis Med. Ctr., Sacto. 1990–, Mammographia, Sacto. 1991–; asst. clin. prof. UC Davis 1970-77, 90–, founder Breast Imaging Study Gp. 1991–; awards: merit CalState Resources Agy., Sacto. 1978; mem: No. Calif. Radiological Soc. (pres. 1994-95), Am. Coll. Radiology (fellow 1982, councilor 197-81, 86-88), AMA 1966–, Calif. Radiol. Assn. (1966–); civic: Calif. State Railroad Mus., Sacto. (prin. founder 1964–), mem. Railway & Locomotive Hist. Soc. (Pac. Coast chpt. bd. 1961-81, 87-93), Antique & Classic Boat Soc. (bd. 1988-91), Motorcar Operators West, founding mem. and dir. 1992–; clubs: Sutter (bd. 1978-82); Republican; Prot.; rec: all RR subjects, antique boats. Res: 710 Coronado Blvd Sacramento 95864 Ofc: Mammographia, 920 29th St Sacramento 95816

ANTIN, MICHAEL, tax lawyer; b. Nov. 30, 1938, Milwaukee, Wis.; s. David Boris and Pauline (Mayer) A.; m. Evelyne Judith Hirsch, June 19, 1960; children: Stephanie b. 1967, Bryan b. 1970, Randall b. 1974; edn: BS, UCLA 1960; JD, UC Berkeley Boalt Hall 1963; admitted St. Bar Calif. 1964. Career: pres., chmn. of bd. Antin Litz & Gilbert, L.A. 1963-91; pres., chmn. of bd. Antin & Taylor, L.A. 1993–; dir: West Coast Bank, Encino 1979-83, Ventura Co. Nat. Bancorp 1985–, chmn. of bd. Conejo Valley Nat. Bank 1983-86; lectr. ABA Pgms. Dallas 1979, HI. 1980, WDC 1982, profl. tax seminars, and Cont. Edn. of the Bar, 1969–; instr. Solomon S. Huebner Sch. of CLU Studies 1977–; author: How to Operate Your Trust or Probate (Layman Pub. Co., 1983), num. articles on taxation, estate planning, probate law; coauthor med. & dental regulations-Profl. Corporations Act; Fellow Am. Coll. Trust & Estate Counsel, Fellow Am. Coll. Tax Counsel, mem: Am. Bar Assn. (tax sect., profl. svc. orgns., chmn.), Calif. Bar Assn. (tax, probate and trust law sect.), L.A. Co. Bar Assn. (tax sect.), Beverly Hills Bar Assn., W. Pension Conf., Beverly Hills Estate Planning Council (pres. 1981-82); civic: Harvard Sch. Parents Assn. (dir., treas. 1988-89), Bel Air Knolls Homeowners Assn. (pres. 1975-77), Sherman Oaks Little League (pres. 1983-4, 87-89); club: Regency; mil: airman USAF 1959-65, Reserve; Democrat; Jewish; rec: x-c skiing, tennis, jogging. Res: 16565 Park Lane Dr Los Angeles 90049 Ofc: Antin & Taylor 1875 Century Park E. Ste 700 Los Angeles 90067 Ph. 310/788-2733

ANTION, DAVID LEE, psychologist; b. May 6, 1937, Cannonsburg, Pa.; s. Leo and Freda Marie (David) A.; m. Molly Hammer, Aug. 16, 1959; 1 son, David Stephen b. 1961; edn: BA, Ambassador Coll. Pasadena 1959; MS, CSU Fullerton 1977; PhD, USC, 1982. Career: pastor Worldwide Ch. of God, Oklahoma City 1959-65, dist. supr., Akron, Ohio 1965-69; asst. prof. Ambassador Coll., Pasadena 1969-74, dir. coll. rels. 1974-78; dir. fund devel. St. Johns Hosp., Santa Monica 1978-80; pvt. practice, Pasadena 1980-83; Affiliated Counselors, Downey and Pasadena 1983–; honors: Who's Who West 1980, USC Educare scholar 1979; mem: Am. Psychological Assn., Calif. Assn. Marriage & Family Therapists; author: Pastor Care & Counseling, 1977, book chpt. pub. 1988; Democrat; rec: racquetball, music, photog. Res: 311 Waverly Dr Pasadena 91105 Ofc: Affiliated Counselors 9530 E Imperial Hwy Ste M Downey 90242

ANTONINI, MICHAEL JOSEPH, dentist; b. April 21, 1946, Livermore; s. Joseph and Doris Carolyn (Grana) A.; m. Linda Mae (Madigan), May 12, 1973; children: John b. 1978, Peter b. 1981, Gina b. 1984; edn: BA history, Univ. Santa Clara 1968; DDS, Univ. Pacific Sch. Dentistry 1972; lic. Calif. Bd. Dental Examiners (1972). Career: pres. Michael J. Antonini DDS Inc., San Francisco 1972–; examining com. Calif. St. Bd. of Dental Examiners 1982–; president's cabinet St. Ignatius Coll. Prep. 1993–; awards: Calif. Dental Assn. Best Editl. Newsletter 1983, 84, City of S.F. Cert. of Merit, 1994; mem: San Francisco Dental Soc. 1972- (ed. 1982-84, v.p. 1984-85, pres. elect 1985-86, pres. 1986-87), ADA 1972–, Calif. Dental Assn. 1972–, Olympic Club 1988–, The Godfather's Club 1993- St. Ignatius Fathers' Club 1992–, St. Brendans Mens Club 1978- (v.p. 1991-92, pres. 1992-93), St. Brendans Parish Advy. Bd. 1994–; trustee: San Fran-D-Pac 1994–; fabricated mouth guards for St. Ignatius Coll. Preparatory varsity basketball team 1994; Republican; R.Cath.; rec: running, golf, gardening. Res: 110 Broadmoor Dr San Francisco 94132 Ofc: 2827 Franklin St San Francisco 94123

ANTONOVICH, MICHAEL D., county supervisor; b. Aug. 12, 1939, Los Angeles; s. Michael and Francis (McColm) A.; single; edn: BA, CSU Los Angeles 1963, Secondary Teaching Cred., 1966, MA, 1967; grad. Pasadena Police Acad., Reserve Officer Sch. 1967; Rio Hondo Reserve Ofcr. Adv. Tng. Sch. 1978; Hoover Inst. and Intercollegiate Studies Inst. Stanford 1968-70; sr. exec. pgm. Harvard Univ. Sch. of Govt. 1984, 87; Air War Coll. 1984. Career: govt.-hist. tchr. L.A. Unified Sch. Dist. 1966-72; instr. Pepperdine Univ. 1980, CSU Los Angeles 1979, 85; mem. bd. trustees L.A. Comm. Coll. Dist. 1969-73;elected Calif. State Assembly 1972-78, Republican Whip 1976-78; L.A. Co. Bd. of Supervisors, 5th Dist., 1980- chmn. 1983, 1987, 1991; mem. Presdl. Fulbright Commn. 1991-93, Presdl. Commn. on Privatization 1987-88, Atty. Gen.'s Advy. Bd. for Missing Children 1987-88, County-wide Crim. Justice Coord. Com. (chmn. 1983, 87), Pres.'s U.S.-Japan Advy. Commn. 1984, Commn. of White House Fellowships Reg. Panel 1981-86, County Suprs. Assn. of Calif. (bd.), S. Coast Air Quality Mgmt. Dist., L.A. Coliseum Commn., chmn. Met. Transp. Authority 1995; honors: Outstanding Young Men Am., Menachim Begin achiev. medal Bar-Ilan Univ. 1983, alumni of yr., merit award CSULA (1977, 87), John Marshall H.S. disting. alumni 1984, Nisei VFW outstanding American 1985, Topanga C.of C. service 1983, L.A. Co. Deputy Sheriffs Assn. Victims of Violent Crimes Found. award (1981, 83), L.A. Co. Taxpayers Assn. award 1981, Nat. Taxpayers Union award 1984, dedication of Antonovich Canyon Wildlife Way Station 1984, Foster Parents Assn. Caring Award 1987, Didi Hirsch Comm. Mental Health award 1984, Brotherhood Crusade Award appreciation for leadership (1983, 87, 91), United Way Award for outstanding leadership to the comm. (1983, 87, 91), S.F.V. Interfaith Council award 1983, The Valley Shelter Award 1987, Good Scout Award 1987, Calif. Traditional Music Soc. commendn. of support 1991, L.A. Co. Probation Dept. commendn. of support 1991, Al-Impian of the Year 1991, Assn. of Comm. Health Agencies outstanding leadership 1991, The Ministers Fellowship and Focus 90's of S.F.V. outstanding leadership 1991, PTA hon. service 1991, Internat. Footprint Assn. outstanding citizen 1991, Thomas Jefferson Res. Ctr. Responsible Am. Award 1990, Chaplain's Eagles "Brother's Keeper" Award 1990, The Home Visitation Ctr. outstanding & invaluable svc. 1990, Nat. Fedn. of Indian-Americans public ofcl. of year 1989, Estonian League of W.Coast public ofcl. of yr. 1989; civic: Tournament of Roses Com., Glendale Sym. (bd. govs. 1973–), Glendale C.of C. 1975–, Elks, Good Shepherd Lutheran Home for Retarded Children, Native Sons of Golden West, L.A. Zoo Assn., So. Pasa. Police Dept. Reserves, The Philadelphia Soc., Sigma Nu Frat. Ofc: 869 Hall of Administration 500 W Temple St Los Angeles 90012

APPELBAUM, BRUCE DAVID, physician; b. Apr. 24, 1957, Lincroft, NJ; s. John S. and Shirley B. (Wolfson) A.; edn: BS pharm., Rutgers Univ., 1980; MS pharmacology, Emory Univ., 1983, PhD pharmacology 1985; MD, Med. Coll. of Ga., 1989; dipl. Nat. Bd. Med. Examiners, 1990. Career: research assoc. dept. pharmacology Emory Univ., Atlanta, Ga. 1985, dept. psychiatry Med. Coll. of Ga., Augusta 1989; resident physician dept. psychiatry UC Irvine, 1989-93; cons. psychiatrist Avalon Med. Group, Garden Grove 1990–; contracting psychiatrist Pacific Therapists, Huntington Beach 1993–; awards: NIH nat. resrch. service 1982, Eastern Student Res. Forum, Miami, Fla. 1984, Nat. Student Res. Forum, Galveston, Tx. 1987, listed Who's Who in West 1992-3, Who's Who in Sci. and Engring., 2nd edit., Dictionary of Internat. Biography 1993, Internat. Man of Year 1992-93; mem: AMA, Am. Psychiat. Assn., Calif. Psychiat. Assn., Orange Co. Psychiat. Soc., Internat. Platform Assn. 1994-95, N.Y. Acad. of Sciences 1994-95, Sigma Xi 1985–; publs: 7+ articles in peer jours., 1983, 84, 85, 86; rec: photography. Ofc: 18811 Huntington St #200 Huntington Beach 92648

APPELL, ALLEN L., marketing consultant/educator; b. Aug. 2, 1943, Worcester, N.Y.; s. Wm. and Martha (Morant) A.; m. 2d. Elizabeth Fuidge, Aug. 22, 1987; edn: BA sociol., UC Santa Barbara, 1965; MBA mktg., S.F. St. Univ., 1969; PhD bus. adm., Golden Gate Univ., 1981; att. Hastings Coll. of Law, 1965. Career: mktg. splst., coauthored bank's Mktg. Plan, ed. company newsletter Wells Fargo Bank, San Francisco 1967-69; dir. mktg., advtsg. & p.r. 26-hotel chain, Hyatt Corp., Inc. Burlingame 1969-72; mktg. dir., 9-rest. chain, Tia Maria Restaurants Inc., S.F. 1972-74; mktg. cons./pres. Marketing Unlimited, Sausalito 1974-89; principal Appell Properties 1989–; instr. Skyline Coll., San Bruno 1974-85; mktg. prof. San Francisco St. Univ., S.F. 1983–; author: A Practical Approach to Human Behavior in Business (C.E. Merrill Pub. Co., 1984), articles in bus. and banking jours. Res: 527 Woodland Road Kentfield 94904 Ofc: San Francisco State Univ. San Francisco

APPLEBERRY, WALTER THOMAS, aerospace engineer; b. Mar. 8, 1926, Wilmington, N.C.; s. William Pembrook and Carroll Ernesteen (Shingleton) A.; m. Mae Magdalene Bozeman, Feb. 21, 1953; children: Thomas Kent b. 1957, Robert William b. 1958, Rebecca Jean b. 1958; edn: BSME, CSU Long Beach, 1974. Career: supr. McDonnell Douglas, Long Beach 1965-69; dynamic test supr. Rockwell Intl., Downey 1982-84, crew systems project mgr., 1984-88, advanced engring. sr. staff engr., 1989–; awards: McDonnell Douglas design engr. award 1966, Rockwell Inventor of Yr. nom. 1977, Engr. of Yr. nom., Pi Tau Sigma 1970–; inventor mechanisms (24 patents); 5 pub. articles; Republican; Mormon; rec: music composition, violin, piano, choral. Res: 3440 Val Verde Ave Long Beach 90808 Ofc: Rockwell Intl. Corp. 12214 Lakewood Blvd Downey 90241

APPLETON, JAMES ROBERT, university president; b. Jan. 20, 1937, No. Tonawanda, N.Y.; s. Robert Martin and Emma (Mollnow) A.; m. Carol Koelsch, Aug. 8, 1959; children: Steven J. b. 1960, Jon M. b. 1963, Jennifer b. 1966; edn: AB, Wheaton Coll., 1958; MA, and PhD, Mich. State Univ., 1963, 1965. Career: assoc. dir. and vis. lectr. Mich. State Univ., 1963-65; assoc. dean Oakland Univ., Rochester, Mich. 1965-68, dean student life 1968-69, v.p./assoc. prof. 1969-72; v.p./assoc. prof. USC, L.A. 1972-87; pres. and univ. prof. Univ. of Redlands, 1987–; mem. NCAA Pres.'s Commn., 1992–; trustee S.F. Presbyterian Sem., San Anselmo 1985–; pres., ofcr. Nat. Assn. Student Personnel Adminstrs., 1969-76; awards: Phi Kappa Phi 1981, Fred Turner Award NASPA 1980, One of 100 Emerging Young Leaders of the Acad., Change & ACE, W.D.C. 1978; mem: Western College Assn. (pres. 1992-94), AAUP, Am. Assn. of Higher Edn., Am. Council on Edn., Western Assn. of Schs. and Colls. S.F. (accreditation com. 1990-94), Indep. Colls. of So. Calif. (dir.), Inland Action Inc. (dir.), Alpha Tau Omega frat.; clubs: University (LA), Redlands CC; author: Pieces of Eight (1978), guest editor NASPA J. (4/71), num. articles and monographs; mil: 1st lt. AUS 1958-60; Presbyterian; rec: vocal music, sports. Office of the President, Univ. of Redlands, Redlands 92373

ARABIAN, ARMAND, state supreme court justice; b. Dec. 12, 1934, NY, NY; s. John and Aghavnie (Yalian) A.; m. Nancy Megurian, Aug. 26, 1962; children: Allison Ann b. 1965, Robert Armand b. 1969; edn: BSBA (disting. military grad.), Boston Univ. Coll. of Bus. Admin., 1956; JD (class pres.), Boston Univ. Sch. of Law, 1961; LLM, USC, 1970; admitted Calif. St. Bar 1962. Career: dep. dist. atty. Los Angeles Co., 1962-63; pvt. practice law, Van Nuys 1963-72; apptd. by Gov. Reagan judge Municipal Ct., 1972-73, judge Superior Ct., L.A. Co., 1973-83; apptd. by Gov. Deukmejian assoc. justice Ct. of Appeal, 1983–; grad. Appellate Judges Sem., Inst. of Judicial Adminstrn., NYU, 1984, 91, 94, grad. Nat. Coll. State Court Judges, Univ. Nev., Reno 1974; honors: Silver Shingle of Boston Univ. Sch. of Law 1981, recogn. Calif. Sexual Assault Investigators Assn. 1978, San Fernando Valley Bar Assn. (1976, 77), Womens' Caucus of Western State Sch. of Law 1973, Senate and Assembly Resolutions, appreciation for 10-year dedicated judicial service- S.F.V. Crim. Cts. Bar Assn., L.A. Bd. of Police Commrs., L.A. Mayor, City Council and Co. Bd. Suprs. 1982, others; mem: Calif. Judges Assn. 1972–, S.F.V. Crim. Cts. Bar Assn. 1965-86, Internat. Footprint Assn. (chapt. founder 1970–), Sigma Phi Epsilon (1952–, dist. gov. 1968-69); mil: 1st lt. Army Inf. 1956-58, grad. Airborne Pathfinder and Jumpmaster Sch.; Republican; Armenian Apostolic. Ofc: Supreme Court 303 Second St San Francisco 94107

ARAI, RYOZO, trading company executive; b. Sept. 19, 1958, Hiratsuka, Japan; s. Gonpachi and Kazue (Fujisawa) A.; edn: Univ. of Pacific 1979-80; BA, Waseda Univ. Tokyo Japan 1982. Career: chief auditor Arai Shoji Co. Ltd., Hiratsuka, Japan 1981-84, resident dir. 1984-87, mng. dir. internat. 1988–; pres. Allied Holdings Inc., Torrance 1984–; exec. v.p. Allied Co. Ltd., Tokyo, Japan 1980–; mem: Loyola Marymount Univ. (bus. advy. council), Coll. of bus. Adminstrn.; Buddist; rec: travel, golf. Res: 67 Crest Rd E, Rolling Hills 90274 Ofc: Allied Holdings Inc. 19191 S Vermont Ave Ste 400 Torrance 90502

ARAKAWA, MITSUAKI, principal development engineer, management and professional consultant; b. Dec. 6, 1943, Japan; s. Kiyoshi and Suzuko (So) A.; m. Reiko, Oct. 16, 1970; children: Masahiro b. 1971, Kenji b. 1974; edn: BS, Seoul Univ., 1966. Career: engring. mgr. Japan Electron Optics Lab. (JEOL), Tokyo, Japan 1970-77; assoc. devel. engr. UC San Francisco Dept. of Radiology, 1977; product mgr. Bruker Instruments, Billerica, Mass. 1979; prin. devel. engr. and map engr. UCSF, 1979–; cons. mgmt. and profl. engr., prodn. cons. Toshiba America MRI Inc. 1980–; mem: IEEE, Soc. of Magnetic Resonance in Medicine; inventor: 18 patents in MRI field, 4 patents pending; author 40+ tech. publs. in MRI field; rec: literature, classical music, play piano. Res: 1005 Lakeview Dr. Hillsborough 94010 Ofc: UCSF-RIL 400 Grandview Dr. South San Francisco 94080

ARANDA, BENJAMIN, judge; b. Jan. 3, 1940, Brawley; s. Benjamin Aranda and Concepcion (Pesqueira) Calvin; m. Emma Salazar, May 29, 1965; children: Rebecca b. 1966, Maria Cristina b. 1968, Ruth b. 1970, Benjamin IV b. 1971, Andrea b. 1973, Danielle b. 1976, Carlos b. 1976, David b. 1977, Tania b. 1977, Frederick b. 1979, Eric b. 1980; edn: AB, and JD, Loyola Univ., L.A. 1962, 1969; admitted bar: Calif. 1970-79, U.S. Fed. Dist. Cts. (cent. dist. Calif. 1970, e. dist. Calif. 1978), US Ct. Appeals (9th cir. 1971). Career: atty., ptnr. Harris & Aranda, Marina del Rey 1970-79; judge municipal ct. South Bay Judicial Dist., Torrance 1979–; chair Mcpl. Ct. Judges Assn. 1987-88; justice pro tem St. Ct. Appeals, (1986, 92-93, 94-95); judge pro tem L.A. Superior Ct. 1987-88; vis. judge Avalon Justice Ct. 1986, 87, 88; appt. L.A. Co. jud. procedures commn. 1987-88, co. crim. justice coord. com. 1987-88, courthouse security task force 1988; honors: Loyola Univ. editor The Dial (pre-legal soc.) and The Cinder (stu. handbook), pres. YR, Pius X Medallion, Confrat. of Christian Doctrine 1975, disting. svc. Calif. Youth Auth. 1976, Alpha Delta Gamma nat. award of merit and man of yr. (1970, 79), Nat. Interfrat. Conf. Ho. of Dels. award of merit 1966, Hon. Ky. Col. 1965, hon. citizen City New Orleans 1963 and Kansas City 1964, commendn. Constl. Rights Found.1978, disting. citizen City of L.A. 1966, resolutions City and Co. of L.A., Santa Monica, Calif. St. Assem. and Senate 1979, White House Honors presented by First Lady Nancy Reagan 1987 and Great Am. Family award 1987, Adoption Family of yr. and Gov.'s proclamation (11/87), nat. judicial medallion Hispanic Nat. Bar Assn. 1988, role model of month Univision TV Network, Miami (1/89), others; mem: Hispanic Nat. Bar Assn. (1st nat. pres. 1978, 1979, 1980), Mex.-Am. Bar Assn. (pres. 1977, trustee 1973-80), ABA (commn. on opps. for minorities 1986-90, 94-95, host com. 1990, Judicial Admin. Div., Nat. Conf. of Spl. Ct. Judges, exec. comm. 1989–, secty. 1992-93, v.p. 1993-94, chair-elect 1994-95, chair 1995-96), St. Bar Calif. (editl. bd. Calif. Lawyer 1981-84, spkr. Conf. of Bar Presidents 1977, 80), Minority Bar Assn. (co-founder, chair 1977), L.A. Co. Bar Assn. (trustee 1977-79, pres.'s council 1981-82); civic: bd. dirs. Blue Cross of Calif., Woodland Hills 1982-89, bd. chmn. 1986-89; bd. dirs. Blue Cross of So. Calif. 1981-83; pres./chmn. Save Our Calif. Kids, Inc. L.A. 1985-89; bd. dirs. Little Company of Mary Hosp., Torrance 1991-93, Centurion Club, benefit hosp. (pres. 1976); mem. Alpha Delta Gamma Frat. (nat. pres. 1963-4, 64-66, 72-74, founding pres. Alpha Delta Gamma Edn'l. Found.), Phi Delta Phi, Public Advocates Inc., S.F. (dir. 1979-89), South Bay-Harbour Vol. Bur. (bd. 1984-89, chair nom. com. 1985, 87, 88), South Bay Assn. of Chambers of Commerce (founding dir., legal counsel 1976-79), El Segundo C.of C. (v.p. 1975, dir. 1972-75, 77-79), judges panel of Am. Family of the Yr. and Hispanic Am. Family of the Year (1987, 88), Kiwanis (El Segundo past pres. founder Torrance Club), LMU Alumni Assn. (dir. v.p. 89-90, pres. 90-92, Univ. Bd. of Regents 1993-), Westside Legal Svs. (dir. 81-83), AYSO Soccer Torrance (reg. bd. 1979-82); frequent speaker and lectr. profl. confs., author 5 books incl. History of the Hispanic Lawyer (Lawyear Pub. 1988), Directory of Minority Judges of the United States (ABA Press 1994); Republican; R.Cath.; rec: family. Ofc: 825 Maple Ave Torrance 90503

ARCADI, JOHN ALBERT, urologist, research professor; b. Oct. 23, 1924, Whittier; s. Antonio and Josephine Louisa (Ramirez) A.; m. Doris M. Bohanan, Apr. 11, 1951; children: Patrick, Michael, Judith, Timothy, Margaret, William, Catherine; edn: Whittier Coll. 1942-44, BS cum laude, Univ. Notre Dame, 1947, MD, Johns Hopkins Med. Sch., 1950. Career: intern, asst. resident, 1950-54, chief resident Brady Urol. Inst., The Johns Hopkins Hosp., 1954-55; urologist solo pvt. practice, Whittier 1955–; asst. prof. urol. Univ. So. Calif. Med. Sch., L.A. 1957-60; resrch. assoc. Whittier Coll., 1957-65, resrch. prof. 1965–; mem. bd. dirs. Presbyterian Hosp., Whittier 1989-95; coord. prostate cancer res. Huntington Med. Res. Inst., Pasadena 1993–; awards: Franklin Mall, Johns Hopkins 1948, pvt. practice urol. Am. Found. Urologic Disease 1986, 89; mem: Am. Assn. for the Adv. Scis. (fellow 1953), Am. Coll. Surgeons (fellow), Am. Urol. Assn., Am. Assn. Anatomists, Endocrine Soc.; civic: Whittier Hist. Soc. (bd. 1989-92); author 50+ sci. publs., 1948–; Republican; R.Cath. (pastoral coun. 1989-92); rec: photography, stamp & coin collection. Ofc: PO Box 9220, 6202 Washington Ave Whittier 90601

ARCADI, VICTORIA CARMELA, chiropractor, educator; b. July 9, 1954, New Brighton, Pa.; d. Victor Larry and Gloria Rose (LaGrotta) Arcadi; edn: BA, UCLA 1977; DC (magna cum laude), Cleveland Chiropractic Coll. 1984; lic. Chiropractor Calif. 1985; Diplomate Nat. Bd. Chiropractic Examiners; Cert. Practitioner Applied Kinesiology. Career: preceptorship, intern 1984-85; prof. Cleveland Chiro. Coll., Los Angeles; pvt. practice 1985–, cons. pre-natal and labor, staff chiropractor Gentle Birth Ctr. Med. Group, Glendale 1987–; mem: Cleveland Chiropractic and UCLA Alumni Assn., Calif. and Am. Chiropractic Assn., Assn. Childbirth At Home Internat.; civic: Women's Referral Svc., U.S. Tennis Assn; innovator new techniques in chiropractic treatment for women in labor and newborns (1985–); rec: tennis, swimming, running. Ofc: 14755 Ventura Blvd Ste 202 Sherman Oaks 91403 Ph: 818/905-5028

ARCINIEGA, TOMAS A., university president; b. Aug. 5, 1937, El Paso, Tx.; s. Tomas Hilario and Judith G. (Zozaya) A.; m. Concha Ochotorena, Aug. 10, 1957; children: Wendy M Heredia, Lisa, Judy A., Laura; edn: BA in edn. admin., N.M. St. Univ., 1960; MA and PhD in edn. admin., Univ. New Mexico,

1966, 1970; Grad., Inst. for Ednl. Mgmt., Harvard, 1989. Career: prof. of edn. Univ. New Mexico, Albuquerque 1970; admin. & supvn. Univ. of Texas, El Paso 1971-72, asst. dean Univ. Tex. Grad. Sch. 1972-73; dean Coll. of Edn. San Diego State Univ., 1973-89; v.p. academic affairs CSU Fresno, 1980-83; univ. pres. CSU Bakersfield, 1983–; short term cons.: Woodrow Wilson Found., NIE, U.S. Office of Edn., AACTE, N.M. Dept. Edn., Calif. Commn. for Tchr. Preparation and Licensing, Teacher Corps, Ministries of Edn.- Honduras, Panama, Bolivia, Ecuador and Guatemala; trustee emeritus Carnegie Corp. of N.Y.; secty., bd. dirs. Am. Council of Educ.; bd. dirs. The Aspen Inst.; awards: outstanding alumnus N.M. St. Univ. (1987), Tomas Rivera Award for achiev. in edn. RACHE (1984), list of 100 academic leaders Change Mag. (1978), among 100 Hispanic influentials Hispanic Bus. Mag. (1987); civic: Kern Citizens for Effective Local Govt. (dir.), Beautiful Bakersfield Advy. Bd., Junior League of Bakersfield (advisor), Rotary; clubs: Stockdale CC, Bakersfield Petroleum; cont-br. articles to scholarly jours.; mil: capt. Army; Democrat; R.Cath.; rec: racquet-ball. Res: 2213 Sully Ct Bakersfield 93311 Ofc: Calif. St. Univ. Bakersfield 9001 Stockdale Hwy Bakersfield 93311-1099

ARELLANO, EUGENE WALTER, physician-surgeon; b. Nov. 4, 1927, Los Angeles; s. Frederico and Petrita Beaubien (Abreu) A.; m. Judith Ellen Boam, Oct. 21, 1970; children: Debra b. 1952, Kimberlee b. 1956, Edward b. 1963, Eugene b. 1971, Melinda b. 1972; edn: undergrad. work Stanford Univ., AA, UCLA; DO, Coll. of Osteopathic Physicians & Surgeons, L.A. 1953; MD, UC Irvine 1962; bd. certified, Diplomate Am. Board of Family Practice. Career: solo practice physician-surgeon, Glendale 1953–; lt. col., by congl. appt., USAF Med. Corps, overseas duty 1977; group practice phys. Glendale Adventist Med. Diagnostic Center 1978-80, solo practice in Glendale, 1980–; attdg. staff Glendale Adventist Med. Ctr; Glendale Comm. Hosp. chief of staff 1975, pres. elect 1981-83; secty. bd. dirs. Assoc. Med. Group, Glendale 1979-80; asst. clin. instr. int. medicine, Coll. Osteo. Phys. & Surg. 1955-57; honors: physicians recogn. awards, AMA, CMA; Fellow Am. Acad. of Family Physicians 1978; mem: AMA, CMA, L.A. Co. Med. Assn., Glendale Dist. Med. Assn., UCLA Alumni Assn. (life), Calif. Acad. Family Phys., World Med. Assn., Assn. of Mil. Surgeons of the U.S., Royal Soc. of Medicine, Latin-Am. Advsy. Council, L.A. Dist. Atty. Advsy. Council, Calif. Thoroughbred Breeders Assn., Horsemens Benevolent Protective Assn.; breed and race throroughbred horses with stakes winners in USA, England, and France, 1962–; Republican; R.Cath.; rec: garden, swim, basketball, travel. Res: 605 Meadowgrove Pl La Canada-Flintridge 91011 Ofc: E.W. Arellano, MD, Inc. 609 S Glendale Ave Glendale 91205

AREND, ROBERT LEE, educator; b. Aug. 30, 1944, Bridgman, Mich.; s. Delbert Lee and Dorothy Evelyn (Martin) A.; m. Evelyn Kole, July 22, 1995; children: Julie Eve b. 1971, Joshua b. 1979; edn: BA, Moody Bible Inst., 1968; BA, W. Mich. Univ., 1968; MA, Trinity Evangelical Divinity Sch., 1970; MA, Northwestern Univ., 1971; postgrad. Purdue Univ., 1973-76; Calif. Comm. Colls. life instr. cred. Eng., suprvn., humanities, and speech. Career: asst. prof. English, Grace Coll., Winona Lake, Ind. 1971-76; instr. grad. asst. Purdue Univ. 1974-76; prof. and dept. chair Eng. dept. Christian Heritage Coll., El Cajon, Ca. 1977-90, also publs. advisor 1985-90, ann. judge literature contests 1990–; asst. prof. Eng., San Diego Miramar Coll., 1990–, p.t. faculty Cuyamaca Coll., El Cajon 1982-90, Palomar Comm. Coll., San Marcos 1981–; freelance tutor, writer, 1982–; editl. advy. bd. for new textbooks, Collegiate Press; awards: Outstanding Young Men of Am. 1974, tchg. award and yearbook dedication Christian Heritage Coll. 1990, listed Who's Who in West 1991, Who's Who Historical Soc. 1994, 2000 Notable Men 1994, Internat. Biography 1995; mem: Nat. Coun. of Tchrs. of Eng., Modern Language Assn., Shakespeare Assn., Sigma Tau Hon. Soc.; author 3 college textbooks, numerous articles in scholarly jours.; Republican; Baptist; rec: reading, tennis, hiking, writing, jogging. Res: 13881 Bassmore Dr, San Diego 92129 Ofc: 10440 Black Mountain Rd San Diego 92126

ARGUE, JOHN C., lawyer; b. Jan. 25, 1932, Glendale; s. J. Clifford and Catherine Emily (Clemments) A.; m. Leah Elizabeth Moore, June 29, 1963; children: Eliabeth Anne b. 1967, John Michael b. 1968; edn: AB in commerce, fin., Occidental Coll. 1953; LLB, USC Law Sch. 1956; (Hon.) LLD Occidental Coll. 1987; admitted bar: Calif. 1957. Career: atty., ptnr. Argue & Argue, Los Angeles 1958-59, Flint & MacKay, 1960-72, sr. counsel Argue Pearson Harbison & Myers, 1973–; advisory dir. LAACO, Ltd.; dir: Avery Dennison Inc., CAL MAT Inc., TCW/DW Family of Mutual Funds and Term Trusts, TCW Funds Inc., Rose Hills Memorial Park (chmn.); trustee: USC, Occidental Coll., Pomona Coll. (v.chmn.); pres. USC Assoc. 1988-93; chmn. L.A. Area C.of C. 1989; chmn. Amateur Athletic Found.; chmn. Criminal Justice Legal Found.; Nat. Advy. Council Autry Mus. of Western Heritage; honors: Sports Headliner of Year, L.A. Press Club 1978, Sparkplug Award as The Man Most Responsible for Bringing the 1984 Olympics to LA, LA Area C.of C. 1979, William May Garland award, So. Calif. Com. for the Olympic Games 1979, Spirit of Los Angeles award, L.A. Hdqtrs. City Assn. 1979, Centennial award 1980 and Hall of Fame 1984, LA Athletic Club, Track Hall of Fame, Occidental Coll. 1980, disting. service, Am. Heart Assn. LA 1982, Merit award, USC Gen. Alumni Assn. 1984, Disting. Eagle Scout Award, BSA 1984, Outstanding Citizen PRISMS award, Pub. Rels. Soc. Am. 1985, Calif. Ptnrship Award 1985,

The Emmett Award, 100 Club 1985, Brotherhood Award Los Angeles YMCA 1987, BSA's Vincent T. Lombardi Award 1985, Bill Of Rights Freedom Award 1986, Downtown Leadership Award 1987, Man of the Year 1988 by L.A.P.D., Salerni Collegian (hon.), Scapa Praetor (hon.), Olympic Order by Internat. Olympic Commn 1993; mem: Town Hall (pres. 1985), Chancery Club (pres. 1985), SCCOG (pres. 1972–), LAOOC (founding chmn.), So. Calif. Golf Assn. (pres. 1980), Republican Assocs., Am. Heart Assn. (pres. 1981-82, chmn. adv. bd. 1983–), Central City Assn., World Affairs Council, LA Hdqtrs. City Assn.; clubs: California (pres. 1992–), Oakmont Country (pres. 1972), Flint. Cyn. Tennis, Riviera CC, LA Athletic, LA Country, Rotary (LA), The Newcomen Soc., 100 Club of LA, Lincoln, Twilight (pres. 1993); mil: staff, Comdr.-in-Chief, US Army Europe, Heidelberg, Ger. 1957-58; Republican; Prot.; rec: golf, tennis, skiing. Res: 1314 Descanso Dr La Canada 91011 Ofc: Argue Pearson, 801 South Flower St Los Angeles 90017

ARIYASU, LAURENCE, physician; b. Sept. 11, 1957, San Fernando; s. George and Betty Tai (Hamamoto) A.; edn: BA in chem. and biol., CSU Northridge; MD, Univ. So. Calif, Los Angeles. Career: resident physician Kaiser Permanente, Oakland 1984-89; chief Head and Neck Surgery Dept., Kaiser Permante 1990–; sec. regl. chief Head and Neck Surgery 1994–; lab. instr. CSU Northridge 1979-80; honors: Phi Kappa Phi, Bay Area Residents Research Symposium 4th Prize 1988; mem: Am. Acad. Otolaryngology, Head & Neck Surgery, Am. Acad. Facial Plastic & Reconstructive Surgery; pub. article in med. jours., 1988, 89; rec: skiing, oil painting, photog. Res: 782 S Regatta Dr Vallejo 94591 Ofc: Kaiser Permanente 975 Sereno Dr Vallejo 94589

ARMER, MICHAEL SCOTT, marketing executive; b. May 4, 1953, Los Angeles; s. Alan Arthur and Elaine (Duschnes) A.; edn: BA, Stanford Univ. 1975; Univ. Tx. Austin 1972. Career: account exec. Carranza & Assoc., Los Angeles 1976-78; SSC&B Advtg. 1978-80; account supr. Keye Donna Pearlstein, Beverly Hills 1980-84; v.p., account supr. DDB/Needham, Los Angeles 1984-87; dir. mktg. Frozfruit Corp., Gardena 1987–; film comms. instr. St. Francis Sch., La Canada 1975-76; mktg. cons., Los Angeles 1981-82; electronic media cons. 1987-88; awards: Stanford Film Soc. Best Student Film 1974, Univ. Tx. Dean's List 1972; mem: Big Brothers of L.A. (bd. dir., comms. com. 1987–), speaker Ad. Club of Los Angeles, 1981; rec: tennis, basketball, bicycling. Ofc: Frozfruit Corp. 14805 S San Pedro St Gardena 90248

ARMINANA, RUBEN, university president; b. May 15, 1947, Santa Clara, Cuba; s. A.R. and Olga (Nart) A.; m. Marne Olson, Dec. 17, 1988; children: Tuly Arminana, Cesar Martino; edn: AA, Hill Jr. Coll., Hillsboro, Tx. 1966; BA, University of Texas, Austin 1968, MA, 1970; PhD, Univ. of New Orleans 1983. Career: v.p. Commerce Internat., New Orleans, La. 1978-83; v.p. of ops. Tulane Univ., New Orleans, La. 1983-85, asst. prof. internat. bus. & public adminstrn. 1983-88, assoc. exec. v.p. 1985-87, dir. inst. for study of change 1985-88, v.p. & asst. to pres. 1987-88; v.p. fin. and devel. Calif. St. Polytechnic Univ., Pomona, Calif. 1988-92, prof. political sci. 1988-92; pres. and prof. political sci. Sonoma St. Univ., Rohnert Park, Calif. 1992–; awards: Outstanding Leader award, United Citizens of La.; Phi Theta Kappa; mem.: Am. Assn. of Univ. Adminstrs., Western Coll. Assn. (pres.-elect 1993-94), Sonoma Co. Comm. Found. 1993-94; Catholic. Res: 1058 Gaddis Court Santa Rosa 95404 Ofc: Sonoma State University 1801 East Cotati Ave Rohnert Park 94928-3609

ARMSTRONG, JOANNA, educator, linguist; b. Feb. 3, 1915, Vienna, Austria; nat. 1948; m. David B. Armstrong, Biarritz, France, Mar. 12, 1946 (dec. 1992); edn: diploma Kindergarten Tchr. State Coll., Vienna, 1933, Sorbonne, 1935; MA, Univ. Utah, 1951; EdD, Univ. Houston, 1959. Career: caseworker, interpreter Czech Refugee Trust Fund, London, 1939-41; tchr. French Gt. Missenden, Bucks, 1941-43; secty. and interpreter U.S. Army, England and France, 1943-46; secty. US Forest Svc., Ely, Nev. 1948; instr. French, lang. dept. Coll. William and Mary, Williamsburg, Va., 1951-55, Univ. St. Thomas, Houston, 1957-59; chmn. fgn. languages sect. South Texas Coll., Houston, 1961-62; assoc. prof. fgn. languages Texas So. Univ., Houston 1962-68, also inst. dir. NDEA Inst., T.S.U., 1964, 1965; assoc. prof./dir. Head Start & Tchr. Tng. Pgm., Sch. Edn. Univ. Texas, El Paso, 1968-72; cons. HEW, Office of Child Devel., Kansas City, Mo., 1973; cons. Texas Edn. Agy., Austin 1965; honors: recipient Chevalier dans l'Ordre des Palmes Academiques 1967, Head Start award 1971, President's Plaque Alliance Francaise d'El Paso 1971, named Internat. Woman of Yr. 1972-73 by Internat. Biographical Inst., recipient Jubilé de la Liberté 1944-94 Medal given by Council Normandy, France; mem. Am. Biographical Inst. 1972–; mem. Long Beach Women's Music Club (pgm. chmn. 1986-88), U.S.-China People Friendship Assn. (sec. 1987–), vol. Long Beach Symphony (1978-80), Long Beach Grand Opera (1981-89), vol. Camodian Soc. (1981-84); author: Surprising Encounters (80 Yrs. of a 20th Century Woman's Life), 1994; pub. profl. articles in field; avocation: world travel (100+ countries) and study of peoples, their language & culture. Address: 120 Alamitos Ave #34 Long Beach 90802-5330

ARMSTRONG, JULIE ANN, accountant; b. Dec. 27, 1956, Bakersfield; d. Donald Redmond and Verna Mae (Allen) Langston; m. James Martin Armstrong, III, Sept. 30, 1989; edn: AA, Fresno City Coll. 1978; BS, CSU Fresno 1981; C.P.A. Calif. 1983. Career: staff acct. Martin Linger & Co., Fresno 1981-83; Ward Dedekian & Ezell 1983; CFO Manchester Mortgage 1983-88; v.p. fin. and adminstrn. Fresno Co. Employees Credit Union 1988–; honors: Fresno City Coll. dean's list 1975-78; mem: Calif. Scholastic Fedn. (life), Am. Inst. C.P.A., Calif. Soc. C.P.A. Ofc: Fresno County Employees Credit Union 4979 E University Fresno 93727

ARMSTRONG, MARGARET TEAGUE, lawyer; b. May 3, 1956, Pittsburgh, Pa.; d. Roy Wilson and Helen Seton (Klockman) Teague; edn: BA, Drake Univ. 1977; MPA, 1978; JD, Univ. San Diego, 1982; admitted St. Bar Calif. 1983. Career: fund raiser Calif. for Fair Taxation, Los Angeles 1980; law clk., atty. Ronis Ronis & Ronis, Chula Vista 1981-84; alumni dir. Bishops Sch., La Jolla 1984-85; atty. McCormick & Mitchell, San Diego 1985; atty. Ronis Ronis & Ronis 1985-89; Armstrong & Teague, San Diego 1989–; honors: Who's Who Collegians, Who's Who Among Women, Inns of Court; mem: Am. Bar Assn., Calif. Bar Assn., San Diego Co. Bar Assn., Trial Lawyers Assn.; rec: tennis. Ofc: Armstrong & Armstrong 444 Camino Del Rio S Ste 106 San Diego 92108

ARNDT, ROLF DIETER, radiologist, educator; b. Dec. 14, 1941, W. Germany; nat. 1957; s. Ernst and Lieselotte A.; m. Peggy Sue Sander, June 24, 1966 (div. 1988); children: Ava b. 1969, Lisa b. 1972; edn: BA, Occidental Coll. 1964; MD, UCLA Sch. Medicine 1968; cert. Am. Coll. Radiology 1974. Career: asst. prof. radiology UCLA Med. Center, Los Angeles 1974-75; staff radiologist St. John's Hosp. Health Center, Santa Monica 1975–; assoc. clin. prof. radiology UCLA Med. Center 1985–; honors: Phi Beta Kappa; mem: Am. Coll. Radiology, L.A. Co. Radiological Soc., L.A. Co. Med. Assn., Calif. Radiological Soc.; author: Clin. Arthrography, 1981, 85; translator: Mammography, 1977; num. articles pub. in med. jours., 1968-95; mil: lt. comdr. USN 1970-72; Protestant: rec: sailing. Ofc: St. John's Hospital Health Center Dept. Radiology 1328 22nd St Santa Monica 90404

ARNOLD, FRANK JOSEPH, consultant; b. July 24, 1929, Los Angeles; s. Francis Joseph and Bina Agnes (Cavanaugh) A.; m. Matea Rivera; son, Norman b. 1964; grad. Cathedral H.S., L.A. 1947. Career: peace and civil rights activist, San Francisco 1963-66; community organizer, San Jose 1967-75; exec. bd. Central Labor Council, Santa Clara County 1976-82, chair edn. com. 1979-81; founding mem. Southwest Labor Studies Conf., 1975–; workshop mgr. Rehab. Mental Health, San Jose 1980-81; business mgr. Catholic Charities, Vocational Learning & Treatment Ctr. (sheltered workshop for adults with emotional disabilities), Santa Clara County, 1981-92, ret.; appt. exec. bd. Mid-Peninsula Conversion Project, Mt. View 1978, labor studies advy. com. San Jose City Coll. 1978-79, exec. bd. Economic & Social Opportunities (ESO) City of San Jose 1979-80; recipient outstanding service award Cath. Charities S.C. Co. 1986; publs: numerous articles on labor issues (hist. & current), papers presented at univ. confs. in U.S. and Mexico, author payroll computer pgm. `Timecard' (1986). Res/Ofc: 3293 Aramis Dr San Jose 95127

ARO, GLENN SCOTT, environmental and safety executive; b. Jan. 18, 1948, Balt.; s. Raymond Charles, Sr. and Elizabeth Virginia (Coppage) A.; m. Marlene Rose Lefler, Jan. 8, 1972 (div. 1987); children: Vincent b. 1974, Marlena b. 1976; edn: BS in M.E., G.M. Inst., 1972; MBA fin. acctg., Wayne State Univ., 1980; reg. environmental assessor Calif., EPA, 1990. Career: staff engr. Gen. Motors, Balt., Detroit, and Van Nuys, Ca., 1966-84; sr. engr. New United Motor (GM-Toyota), Fremont, Ca. 1984-86; div. mgr. env. & maint. FMC Corp., San Jose 1986-89; cons. exec. sales Gaia Systems, Menlo Park 1990-92; mgr. Hughes Environmental Systems, El Segundo 1992–; corp. mgr. env. & safety Ampex Corp., Redwood City 1990-92; instr. env. compliance mgmt. Foothill Coll. 1992; lectr. Taiwan EPA and Taiwan Ind. Tech. Res. Inst., 1989; honors: judgeship Invest In Am., Mtn. View 1988; mem. Peninsula Indsl. & Bus. Assn. (dir., past v.p.), Calif. Bus. Roundtable (Toxics Awareness Proj. panel 1989–), Environ. Working Group. (tech. com. 1986-88); author: Developing a Nat. Environmental Policy in a Global Mkt., 1989; Republican; R.Cath.; rec: running, reading, movies. Res: 241 Palos Verdes Dr West #203 Palos Verdes Estates 90274

ARONI, SAMUEL, professor emeritus of architecture and urban design; b. May 26, 1927, Kishinev, Romania, naturalized US citizen 1972; s. David Aharoni and Haia (Apoteker) Zalmanovici-A.; m. Malca Corenfeld, Nov. 11, 1956; children: Ruth b. 1958, Miriam b. 1959; edn: BCE (hons.) Univ. of Melbourne, Australia 1955; MS, UC Berkeley, 1965, PhD, 1966; chartered engr., Austr. Career: in field of structures and concrete mats., Australia; lectr. Univ. Melbourne 1955-63; tchg. fellow UC Berkeley 1963-66; assoc. prof. San Francisco State Coll. 1966-67; res. engr. Am. Cement Corp., Riverside 1967-70; prof. Grad. Sch. Arch. and Urban Planning, UCLA 1970-91, actg. dean 1974-75, 83-85, emeritus prof. 1991–, dir. Spl. Acad. Cooperative Projects, Internat. Studies & Overseas Pgms., UCLA 1991–; mem. editl. advy. bd. Architl. Sci. Rev. (Australia) 1971–, Internat. Jour. for Devel. Technology 1984–; mem. bd. govs. Ben Gurion Univ. of Negev 1983–, bd. Architl. Res. Centrs. Consortium, Inc. (1982-93, exec. bd. 1983-86, 89-93, v.p. 1985-86), US Geol. Survey earthquake res. gp. 1989–, NSF Engring. Directorate MSME advy. com. 1985-90, NSF pgm. applied sci. and res. appl. (ASRA) panel of reviewers 1979–; awards: Austr. Town Pl. Inst. prize 1955, Hon. Founder Award Ben-

Gurion Univ. of Negev 1984, J. James R. Croes gold medal ASCE 1981; mem: ASCE 1965–, Am. Concrete Inst. 1958–, Sigma Xi 1967–, Earthquake Engring. Res. Inst. 1980–, ASTM, Instn. of Engrs. (Austr.); Jewish; rec: chess. Res: 24249 Martha St Woodland Hills 91367

ARONSON, JONATHAN DAVID, educator; b. Oct. 28, 1949, St. Louis, Mo.; s. Adam and Judith (Spector) A.; m. Joan Abrahamson, May 28, 1984; children: Adam b. 1987, Zachary b. 1989, James b. 1993 (dec. 1995); edn: AB, Harvard, 1971; MA, Stanford Univ., 1975, PhD, 1977. Career: res. fellow CFIA, Harvard, 1975-76; internat. economist US Trade Reps. Ofc., 1982-83; asst. prof. internat. rels., Univ. So. Calif., 1977-82, assoc. prof., 1982-88, prof. 1988–, prof. Annenberg Sch. USC, 1988, dir. 1995; author: Money and Power, 1977, coauthor: Trade Talks, 1985, When Countries Talk, 1988, Mng. the World Econ., 1993. Res: 10575 Fontenelle Way Los Angeles 90077-1901 Ofc: School International Relations Univ So Calif Los Angeles 90089-0043 Ph 310/740-2129

ARREDONDO, FREDERICK JOSEPH, computer technology recruiting company president; b. San Antonio, Tx.; s. Ephraim Alfonso and Margaret S. (Rios) A.; m. Mary Sue Bradford, Jan. 31, 1970; children: Anthony b. 1970, Russell b. 1973; edn: BS chemistry, Univ. Tx. Austin 1963; MBA, CSU Sacto. 1974; reg. rep. (1987). Career: instr. CSU, Sacto. 1973-74; sales rep. IBM Corp., San Francisco 1974-78; Digital Equipment Corp., Santa Clara 1978-80; cons. Coopers & Lybrand, San Francisco 1981-82, 82-85; cons. Alexander Grant 1982; MIS mgr. City and County of San Francisco 1985-89; pres. No. Calif. Search, Redwood City 1989–; honors: outstanding student CSUS 1974, Beta Gamma Sigma; mem: IEEE, BSA (cubmaster 1977-83); mil: lt. comdr. USN 1963-70, commendation medal 1969; Democrat; Presbyterian; rec: golf, skiing, jogging, violin. Ofc: Northern California Search 39899 Balentine Dr Ste 218 Newark 94560

ARROL, JOHN, corporate executive; b. Aug. 6, 1923, Cambuslang, Scotland; nat. 1934; s. William and Isabella (Gordon) A.; edn: BSBA, Xavier Univ. (Cincinnati) 1953, MA, Vanderbilt Univ. (Nashville) 1964; m. Jane Trice, June 18, 1949; children: Robert, b. 1950, Nancy Ann, b. 1952, David, b. 1961, William, b. 1964. Career: cost analyst Ford Motor Co., Mich. and Ohio, 1949-57; finl. analyst Curtiss Wright Corp., N.J. 1957-58; asst. controller Avco Corp., Oh., Tenn., Ind., 1958-64; v.p., controller Globe-Union Inc., Milw., Wis. 1964-70, v.p., chief fin. ofcr. 1971-73; sr. v.p. finance The Rucker Co., Oakland, Ca. 1973-77; sr. v.p. fin. NL Petroleum Svgs., Houston 1977-78; CFO/v.p. Gardner-Denver, Dallas 1978-79; exec. v.p. Systron-Donner Corp., Concord 1980-81, chmn. 1982-86; gen. ptnr. Thorn EMI Venture Fund, Ltd., Alamo 1983–; c.e.o. Personics Inc., Redwood City 1990–; advy. bd. dirs. Personics Inc., Menlo Park 1986-90, Gamma Link Inc. 1986-94, The Financial Center Bank, S.F. 1984-92; dir.: Hughes Electronic Devices (chmn. 1981-84), Paragon Technology Co., Pleasant Hill 1983-85, Lightgate Inc., Berkeley 1983-84, Pantle Mining Co., Grass Valley 1981-85, Roconex Corp., Milpitas 1979-84, Universal Semiconductor Inc., San Jose 1983-86, Thorn EMI America Fin. 1987-90, Optical Specialties Inc.. Fremont 1987-94, On-Site Technologies Inc. (v. chmn./dir. 1988-93), Nat. Water Mgmt. Corp. (v.chmn./dir. 1988-90), San Jose Capital Corp. (chmn. 1977-86), Advantage Realty Group (chmn. bd. 1991–); civic bds: Sch of Bus. Univ. S.F. Advy. Council, Mt. Diablo Council BSA (advy. bd.), Calif. Found. for the Retarded (trustee 1985–); author: (Arrol House Publishers), "A Brief Encounter", "A Rascal at Sea", "First Love", "I Love to Dance", Sir William Arrol, The Great Bridge Builder", "Memories of Mother", "My Final Love", and "A Brief Guide to the Greatest Composers", 1993–, pub. article in NAA Bull. 2/62; mil: US Maritime Svc. USNR 1942-45; rec: China Trade paintings, antique maps. Res: 2427 Alamo Glen Dr Danville 94526

ARROW, KENNETH J., economist, professor emeritus; b. Aug. 23, 1921, NY, NY; s. Harry I. and Lillian (Greenberg) A.; m. Selma Schweitzer, Aug. 31, 1947; children: David, b. 1962; Andrew, b. 1965; edn: B.Sc. soc. sci., The City Coll. 1940; MA, Columbia Univ. 1941; PhD, 1951. Career: res. assoc. Cowles Commn. for Research in Economics, Chgo., Ill. 1947-49; asst. prof. economics Univ. of Chgo. 1948-49; acting asst., assoc. and prof. of economics, statistics and ops. res., Stanford Univ., Stanford, CA 1959-68; prof. economics, James Bryan Conant Univ. prof., Harvard Univ., Cambridge, Ma 1968-79; Joan Kenney prof. of economics, prof. of ops. res., Stanford Univ., Stanford, Ca. 1979-91, prof. emeritus 1991–; pres. Soc. for Social Choice and Welfare, 1992-94; pres. Internat. Economic Assn. 1983-86; pres. Internat. Soc. for Inventory Res. 1983-88; dir: Varian Assocs., Inc., Fireman's Fund; honors: John Bates Clark Medal, Am. Economic Assn. 1957, Nobel Prize in Economic Sci. 1972, Order of the Rising Sun 2d class Govt. of Japan; mem: Econometric Soc. (fellow, pres. 1958), Am. Econ. Assn. (distng. fellow, pres. 1972), Inst. of Mgmt. Scis. (pres. 1962), Nat. Acad. of Scis., Am. Philosophical Soc., Am. Acad. of Arts and Scis., Finnish Acad. of Scis., British Acad., Pontifical Acad. of Social Scis.; author: Social Choice and Individual Values (1951, 2d edit. 1963), Essays in the Theory of Risk-Bearing, 1971, Limits of Organization, 1974; Collected Papers, 1983-85; Studies in the Mathematical Theory of Inventory and Prodn.; Studies in Linear and Nonlinear Programming; A Time Series Analysis of Interindustry Demands; Pub. Investment, the Rate of Return and Optimal Fiscal Policy; Studies in Resource Allocation Processes; Social Choice and

Multicriterion Decision-Making; mil: capt. U.S. Army Air Corps 1942-46; Democrat; Jewish; rec: bicycling, music. Res: 580 Constanzo St Stanford 94305 Ofc: Dept Economics Stanford Univ. Stanford 94305-6072

ARSHAM, GARY, medical educator; b. 1941, Cleveland, Oh.; s. Sanford Ronald and Florence A.; m. Diana Silver, 1971; edn: AB cum laud Harvard Univ., 1963; MD, Case-Western Reserve, 1967; PhD, Univ. Ill., 1971. Career: fellow in med. edn. Univ. Ill., Chgo. 1968-71; asst., assoc. dean curriculum devel., asst. prof. medicine and health scis. comm. State Univ. N.Y., 1971-72; assoc. prof., prof. health professions edn. Univ. of Pacific, San Francisco 1972-79; chmn. Coun. on Edn. Pacific Med. Ctr., S.F. 1976-81; v.p. Arsham Consultants Inc., S.F. 1981–; adminstr. Pacific Vision Found., 1977-84, dir. edn., 1983–; nat. advy. bd. John Muir Hosp. Med. Film Fest. 1981–; task force on interdisciplinary edn. Nat. Jt. Practice Commn. 1973-74; bd. dirs. US-China Ednl. Inst. 1980–, secty. 1986-88; chair, CEO Nat. Accreditation Commn. for Schs. and Colls. of Accupuncture and Oriental Med. 1993–; coauthor: Diabetes: A Guide to Living Well (1989, 2nd ed. 1992), chief editor Family Medicine Reports, S.F., 1983; mem: Am. Coll. Physicians (fellow), Am. Ednl. Res. Assocs., Assn. Am. Med. Colls., Assn. Study Med. Edn., Assn. Hosp. Med. Edn. (exec. com. 1980-84, sec-treas. 1982-84), Am. Diabetes Assn. (bd. S.F. chpt. 1984–, No. Calif. affil. 1986-87, Calif. affil. 1987–, pres. S.F. chpt. 1990-91, v.p. Calif. affil. 1992-93, pres. Calif. affil. 1994-95, nat. bd. dirs. 1995-98), Am. Assn. Diabetes Educators (assoc. editor 1985-92, bd. dirs. 1994-97), Calif. Med. Assn., S.F. Med. Soc., Am. Assn. Individual Investors (bd. S.F. chpt. 1984-88), Harvard Alumni Assn. (bd. dirs. 1993-96), Harvard Club S.F. (bd. 1981–, pres. 1984-86), Lane Med. Soc. (Sommelier 1985–), Tech. Security Analysts Assn. Ofc: PO Box 15608 San Francisco 94115

ARTHUR, BRENDA KAY, financial consultant, insurance broker; b. May 28, 1951, Charleston, W.Va.; d. Earl W. and Martena (Miller) Arthur; edn: BA sociology, W. Va. Univ., 1972; EdM in social agencies counseling, Univ. of Dayton, 1975; CLU 1993; ChFC and RHU studies in progress. Career: agent New York Life Ins. Co., Long Beach 1981-85, co-chair NY Life Ins. Co. Womens Network So. Pacific Region 1983-85; reg. rep. New York Life Securities Corp., Long Beach 1983-85; fin. cons. CIGNA Securities, CIGNA Ind. Fin. Services, Irvine 1985-87; fin. cons./planner Financial Services Unlimited, Inc. Newport Beach 1987-88; reg. rep./ Southmark Securities Corp., 1987-88; MKA Financial Services Inc., 1988-90; reg. rep. Corp. Benefit Svcs. 1988-90; BKA Consulting, 1990–; reg. rep. Sun Am. Securities 1990–; awards: recipient company and industry profl. awards 1981–, New Orgn. Leader CIGNA Individual Fin. Services Co. feature story in nat. mo. mag. Approach Mag. 1986, Outstanding Young Women Am. 1984, disting. West Virginian awarded by Gov. W.Va. 1986, life bd. govs. Am. Biographical Inst. 1988, listed World Who's Who of Women 1988, Who's Who of Am. Women (1989-90, 92), Who's Who in Profl. & Exec. Women (1987, 88, 89), 2000 Notable Am. Women, Internat. Register of Profiles 1988-89, Internat. Hall of Leaders 1988-89, Who's Who In Am. 1994; mem: Internat. Assn. for Fin. Planning, Nat. Assn. Life Underwriters/Long Beach Chpt., Am. Soc. CLU/ChFC, PACE participant, qualifyer; Charitable Giving Council Orange County (charter), Orange County Employee Benefit Council; Assn. Health Insurance Agents; civic: Zonta Internat. Irvine/Saddleback Valley chpt. (v.p., bd. 1986-88, 91-92), Adam Walsh Child Resource Ctr./affil. of Nat. Ctr. for Missing and Exploited Children (advy. bd., exec. bd.); rec: travel, biking, tennis. Res: 1737 N Oak Knoll Dr Anaheim 92807 Mail: PO Box 18353 Anaheim 92817-8353

ARTINGSTALL, THOMAS, electrical and mechanical engineer; b. Oct. 28, 1920, Chgo.; s. Wm. Thomas and Louise Mary (Hanson) A.; m. Laura Ann Swanson, June 23, 1946 (div. 1955); m. Arloah Darlene Norelius, June 25, 1965; edn: BME, Ill. Inst. Tech., 1944; grad. studies USC, 1956 and UCLA 1990-93; Reg. Profl. Engr., Calif., Ill. Career: designer Solar Capacitor Co., Los Angeles 1945-48; chief designer, developer Kollsman Instrument, 1948-55; mem. radar/antenna/transmitter devel. staff Autonetics, Anaheim 1956-70; tech. res. staff Los Angeles Aircraft, 1970-71, engring. splst. Rockwell Internat., Downey 1977-78; chief engr. Space Div. So. Calif., Yorba Linda, 1980-93; cons. engr. Pace-Arrow, Pomona 1970-78; engring., devel. and res., Swanson Electronics, Arcadia 1965-70; patents in field; mem. ASME, Nat. Mgmt. Assn., Profl. Engrs. Assn.; civic: ad hoc city incorporation com. 1966, archtl. com. 1968, parks & rec. dept. 1975 City of Yorba Linda; club: Langlauflers Ski; Democrat; R.Cath.; rec photography, skiing, camping, fishing. Res: 19622 Larkridge Dr Yorba Linda 92686-6423

ARULMOLI, KANDIAH, geotechnical engineer; b. June 5, 1955, Sri Lanka; s. Vinasithamby and Kangeswary (Nagalingam) Kandiah; m. Jayagowri Nakulendran, July 8, 1984; children: Janahan b. 1987, Vithuran b. 1988, Aarani b. 1991; edn: BS (eng. honors, 1st in Class 1977), Univ. Sri Lanka, 1977; MS, and PhD, UC Davis, 1980, 1982; reg. civil engr. Calif. 1985; reg. geotechnical engr. Calif. 1989. Career: instr. engring. Univ. Sri Lanka, 1977-78; postgrad. research engr. dept. civil engring. UC Davis, 1978-82; staff engr., project engr. The Earth Technology Corp., Long Beach 1982-85; senior engr. J.F.T. Agapito & Assocs., Inc. Grand Junction, Colo. also Rolling Hills Estates, Calif. 1985-87, sr. engr., mng. sr. engr., assoc. The Earth Technology Corp., Long Beach,

Huntington Beach & Irvine, Calif. 1987-94; sr. geotechnical engr. CH2M Hill, Santa Ana 1994–; adj. prof. CSULB 1984, guest lectr. 1986; lectr. UCI 1995 honors: Earle C. Anthony Fellow 1980-81, UC Regents' Fellow 1981-82; mem: ASCE (also, mem. soils properties com. Geotech. Div., 1988–); civic: The Hunger Project (sponsor 1981–), Save The Children Fedn. (sponsor 1981-83); publs: (research) A New Device for Characterizing Soils (1978-82), 20+ tech. papers and reports re earthquake engring., soil dynamics, lab. testing, computer modeling, expert systems; rec: travel, numismatics, jogging. Ofc: CH2M Hill 2510 Red Hill Ave Santa Ana 92705

ARYASINGHA, CHAND JASEN, physician, medical educator; b. Feb. 21, 1936, Sri Lanka; nat. 1984; s. Porolis and Mappie (de Silva) Jasentuliyana; m. Luxshimi de Silva, May 11, 1972; 1 child, Chanelle b. 1986; edn: MD, Univ. Ceylon 1961; MRCOG, Royal Coll. Ob-gyn. England 1974; dipl. Am. Bd. Obgyn. (1983). Career: dir. Chand Aryasingha MD Inc., Glendale 1981–; asst. clin. prof. ob/gyn Univ. So. Calif., Los Angeles 1984-93, chmn. dept. ob/gyn Calif. Medical Ctr. 1990-91; elected Fellow Royal Coll. Obstets. and Gynecols. Gt. Brit. (1989), Amer. Coll. Obstets. and Gynecols. (1980), Los Angeles County Ob/Gyn Soc. (1984); contbr. articles to med. jours.; rec: tennis, skiing, swimming. Res: 3120 Kingridge Way Glendale 91206 Ofc: 1510 S Central Ste 300 Glendale 91204

ASAMEN, JOY KEIKO, educator; b. Feb. 2, 1953, Calexico; d. Keigi and Kiyo (Koroda) Asamen; edn: BA, UCLA 1975; MA, CSU Northridge 1977; PhD, UCLA 1983; lic. psychologist Calif. 1986; lic. marriage and family therapist Calif. 1979. Career: counselor, clin. supr. Chabad Rehab. Program, Los Angeles 1977-80; research assoc. VA Hosp., Los Angeles 1981-84; clin. psychologist Riverside Co. Dept. Mental Health, Palm Springs, Indio 1984-86; research psychologist VA Hosp., Los Angeles 1986-87; research assoc. UCLA Neuropsychiatric Inst. 1986–; assoc. prof. Pepperdine Univ., Culver City 1987–; faculty mem. Kellogg Leadership Program for Minority Women in Mental Health 1986, 87; asst. project dir. suicide prevention evaluation program Los Angeles Unified Sch. Dist. 1987; project co-dir. Alternative Edn. and Work Ctr. Evaluation L.A. Unified Sch. Dist. 1989; program cons. Hayman Center Desert Alcoholism Coalition, Palm Springs 1984-86; honors: Pi Lambda Theta; mem: Am. Ednl. Research Assn., Am. Psychological Assn., Am. Psychological Soc., Nat. Assn. of Women in Edn.; jour. contbg. writer 1979-94, co-editor: Black Students, Psychosocial Issues and Academic Achievement, 1987, Children and Television: Images in a Changing Sociocultural World, 1993; Ofc: Pepperdine University Graduate School of Education and Psychology 400 Corporate Pointe Culver City 90230

ASAWA, GEORGE NOBUO, dentist; b. Apr. 29, 1925, Norwalk; s. Zen and Moto (Murata) A.; m. Masako Sadao, July 7, 1957; dau. Elizabeth b. 1967; edn: BA, UC Berkeley, 1950, BS, 1953; DDS, Wash. Univ., St. Louis, Mo. 1963; Fellow Acad. Gen. Dentistry, 1976. Career: analytical chemist Riker Lab., Los Angeles 1954-56; process engr. Douglas Aircraft, El Segundo 1956-58; research engr. Nat. Cash Register, El Segundo 1958-60; research assoc. Wash. Univ. 1960-63; clin. asst. prof. USC, 1963–, pvt. practice dentistry, Anaheim; mem: Internat. Assn. Dental Research, Am. Assn. Dental Research, Fedn. Dentaire Internat., Am. Dental Assn.; contbr. dental jour. articles, 1964, 72; mil: pfc US ARmy 1944-46; Democrat; Free Methodist. Res: 2801 Altivo Pl Fullerton 92635 Ofc: G.N. Asawa, Inc. 930 S Knott Ave Anaheim 92804

ASCHENBRENNER, FRANK ALOYSIOUS, manufacturing executive, ret.; b. June 26, Ellis, Kans.; s. Philip Albert and Rose Elizabeth (Schuster) A.; m. Gertrude Wilhelmina DeBie, Oct. 16, 1946; children: Richard David b. 1947, Robert Wayne b. 1951, Mary Lynne b. 1954; edn: BS in physics (high hons.), Kansas St. Univ., 1950; PhD physics, M.I.T., 1954. Career: mgr. physics and math General Electric, Evendale, Oh. 1954-61; asst. div. dir. Rockwell Internat. Space Div., Downey 1961-69, dir. technology Rockwell Internat. Commercial Prod. Div., Pittsburgh, Pa. 1969-72, v.p. and gen. mgr. yarn mach. 1972-75; chmn. bd., pres. and chief exec. COR Inc.h, Charlotte, N.C. 1975-77; v.p. Ball Corp., Muncie, Ind. 1977-86; chmn. bd. RAMZ Corp., Dunkirk, Ind. 1985–; mem. nat. advy. bd. Rose-Hulman Inst. of Tech., Terre Haute 1984–, nat. advy. bd. Univ. of Tenn. Space Inst., Tulahoma 1982–; mem: Am. Inst. Aero. & Astro. (assoc. fellow), Am. Physical Soc., Am. Assn. of Individual Investors, San Diego Venture Group; mil: capt. USNR 1942-73, ret.; Republican; R.Cath. Res: 14258 Palisades Dr Poway 92064

ASHE, JOHN H., neuroscientist, educator; b. Mar. 27, 1944, Phila.; s. John H. Ashe, Sr. and Gloria (Jones) Faison; div.; 1 child John Miles b. 1981; edn: AA, San Bdo. Valley Coll., 1970; BA in psych. (physiol.), highest honors, UC Riverside, 1972; PhD biol. scis (UC Regents grad. fellow), UC Irvine, 1977; postdoc. res. tng., 1977-80: UCSF Med. Sch. Dept. Physiology, NIH postdoc. fellow in neurophysiology 1977-78, NIMH interdisciplinary res. postdoc. fellow 1979. Career: tchg. asst. UC Irvine 1973-77; asst. res. physiologist UCSF Med. Sch. 1979-80; asst. prof. UC Riverside 1980-84, assoc. prof. 1984-90, prof. 1990–, mem. grad. pgm. biomed. scis. 1987–, grad. pgm. neurosci. 1989–; mem. UC Ctr. for Neurobiology of Learning and Memory, UC Irvine, 1984–; mem: AAAS, Am. Soc. for Cell Biology, Am. Physiol. Soc., Soc. for Neurosci., Internat. Brain

Resrch. Orgn./World Fedn. of Neuroscientsts, NY Acad. Scis.; rec: jazz. Ofc: Depts. Neuroscience and Psychology 075 Univ. Calif., Riverside 92521

ASHER, JERRY W., JR., retired military officer, trust administrator; b. Feb. 24, 1928, Pasadena; s. Jerry W. and Elsie R.H. (Lutz) A.;m.2d. Marlene Ann, 1992; children: William Jerald b. 1958, Katerine Jane b. 1960; edn: BA Stanford Univ. 1949; MBA, St. Matthews Univ. Ohio 1972; grad. USA Logistics Mgmt. Center 1966; Indsl. Coll. of Armed Forces 1971. Career: served to Col. (ret.) Field Arty. US Army, 1945-77, Reserve 1978-87: decorated Def. of Panama C.Z., Army Commendn. Medal awarded by Sec. of Army, Meritorious Service Medal (1988); Far East Cmd. in Korean Conflict 1951-52; Nat. Guard 40th Div. 1953-61, Artillery & Armor Cdr.; judicial asst. Superior Ct., Los Angeles 1960-70, in W.D.C. in Vietnam War 1966-72; gen. staff mem. HQ Dept. of Army, Pentagon; lt. col., congl. affairs ofcr., DofD staff re mobilization, 1973; Presdl. appt. mem. Council Small Bus. Adminstrn., 1973; US del. to NATO Conf., Bonn, W.Ger. 1978; publicist for group of nat. patriotic orgns., 1970-79, editor newspapers 1976-79; elected City Commr. (1976); recipient Am. Legion civic medal; mem: Reserve Ofcrs. Assn. (pres., nat. del.), Am. Security Council (founder 1971-82), VFW (Nat. del. 1971), C.of C., Am. Legion (comdr.), Kentucky Hist. Soc., Stanford Alumni Assn. (1950-87), SAR (Nat. Com.), NRA, MOWW Nat. Com., AUSA, Az. RPA, CRA (pres. 1977-78), 63rd Div. Assn. (1963–), Citizens for Republic (1978-85), Va. Hist. Soc., Pasadena Opera Co. (1965); num. pub. essays on defense, research on Am. army regts. in the Nat. Archives, W.D.C., Soc. of Cincinnati; Republican (state del. Calif. 1976-80, state del. Ariz. 1988-94); Lutheran; rec: waterskiing, boating, swimming. Res: Lake Havasu City, AZ 96403 Ofc: Security Ordnance Corp., Las Vegas NV

ASHLAND, CALVIN KOLLE, federal bankruptcy judge; b. Feb. 22, 1933, Mason City, Iowa; m. Ilse Doerr, 1957; edn: BS, Iowa St. Univ. 1957; JD, George Washington Univ. 1963. Career: credit mgr. Gen. Electric Co., Laurel, Md. 1957-67; atty. Office David S. Rubenstein, Bethesda, Md. 1967-72; Sulmeyer Kupetz Baumann & Rothman, Los Angeles 1972-76; judge U.S. Bankruptcy Ct., Los Angeles 1976–; chief bankruptcy judge Central Dist. Calif. 1991–; appellate judge 9th Circuit Bankruptcy Appellate Panel 1982–; mem: Am. Bar Assn., L.A. Co. Bar Assn., Am. Bankruptcy Inst., Comml. Law League, Fin. Lawyers Conf. (treas. 1987–), Masons, Am. College of Bankruptcy (fellow), Nat. Conf. of Bankruptcy Judges; mil: AUS 1954-56; Republican Ofc: U.S. Bankruptcy Court 255 E Temple St Ste 1634 Los Angeles 90012

ASHLEY, SHARON ANITA, pediatric anesthesiologist; b. Dec. 28, 1948, Goulds, Fla.; d. John Henry Ashley and Johnnie Mae (Everett) Mitchell; children: Cecili b. 1974, Nicole b. 1979, Erika b. 1986; edn: BA, Lincoln Univ., 1970; post baccalaureate certif. Pomona Coll., Claremont, 1971; MD, Hahnemann Univ., 1976; Diplomate, Am. Bd. of Anesthesiologists 1994. Career: physician-pediatric anesthesiologist specialist Martin L. King, Jr. Hosp., Los Angeles 1976–; honors: Nat. Merit finalist 1966, King Drew Med. Center Outstanding Tchr. of Yr., dept. anesth. 1988-89 and Outstanding Faculty of Year 1990-91, listed Who's Who in Am.; mem: AMA, CMA, Nat. Med. Assn., Am. Soc. Anesthesiology, Calif. Soc. Anesth. (alt. del. 1991), L.A. Co. Med. Assn., Alpha Kappa Alpha Sor.; pub. article in Jour. of Student Nat. Med. Assn., 1974, pub. article Anesthesia Analgesia, 1993; Democrat; Baptist; rec: sailing, reading. Res: 1555 5th St Manhattan Beach 90266

ASKREN, MISHA, physician; b. Jan. 27, 1952, Holton, Kans.; s. Melvin E. A.; m. Ruth Ellen Moskovitz, Sept. 11, 1979; children: Hana b. 1982, Ariella b. 1984, Shoshana b. 1987; edn: BA, Pomona Coll. 1974; MD, UC Davis 1978. Career: physician pvt. practice, Los Angeles 1981-93; adj. prof. Calif. Sch. Profl. Psychology 1984-89; comm. preceptor Santa Monica Family Practice Residency, Santa Monica 1984-93; physician cons. Staff Builders, Home Health, Los Angeles 1989; mem: Am. Acad. Family Physicians (fellow), La Leche League, Physicians for Social Responsibility. Ofc: FHP, Inc. 29050 S Western Ave #101 San Pedro 90732

ASMAR, ALICE, artist; b. Flint, Mich.; d. George and Helen (Touma) Asmar; m. Walter C. Smith (dec.); edn: BA magna cum laude, Lewis & Clark Coll., 1949; MFA, Univ. Wash., 1951; grad. work Ecole Nat. Superieure des Beaux-Arts, Paris 1958-59. Career: piano and French tutor, Portland, Oreg. 1949-51; instr. French, art & music St. Helen's Hall Private Sch., 1950-51; grad. reader Univ. Wash. Art Dept. 1950-51; archtl. draftsman Naramore, Bain, Brady & Johanson, Seattle 1951; engring. draftsman, aerodynamics, Boeing Aircraft Co., 1953; dir. Uitti Gallery, Seattle 1953; asst. prof. Lewis & Clark Coll., 1955-58; art instr. Portland (Oreg.) Tel. Co. 1956-58; art instr. Santa Monica City Coll. and Woodbury Coll., L.A. 1964-66; orig. line engraver and ptnr. Nambe Mills, Santa Fe, N.M. 1967-78; lectr. on SW Indians for t.v., museum and art groups, 1975-82; art instr. McGroarty Arts Ctr., a div. of L.A. City Cultural Affairs Dept., 1988-90; free lance illustrator. L.A. Times Home Mag., 1977-81; tchr. and artist commd. art pieces, currently; num. awards include: prize for mural design Oreg. Trail Centennial 1943, Lewis & Clark Coll. acad. scholar 1946-49, Poppleton Music Awards 1947-48, painting Seattle Art Mus. 1952, 1st prize (3) Oreg. State competitions in art (1955, 56, 57), west. reg. award for design Art Inst. Chgo. 1957, Harriet H. Wooley study grantee Paris 1958-59, Fulbright fellow Spoleto, Italy 1959, Mac Dowell Colony painting fellow 1959, Huntington Hartford painting fellow 1960, merit award Home Savings & Loan Assn./L.A. All-City Outdoor Art Festival. 1963, best in profl. class So. Calif. Expo. S.D. 1964, appreciation Mayor of Burbank, and Burbank Coord. Council 1977, 79, 1st prize Hancock Park Arts Council Beverly. Hills Annual Exhib. 1977, best of show for painting Coll. of the Desert 1978, selected list of Masters in the world Accademia Italia 1985, Lewis and Clark Coll. disting. alumni 1986, purchase award Westwood C.of C. 1987, Sale of the Century, NBC, purchase award 1988, 2000 Notable Am. Women 1989; mem: Audobon Society, L.A. Co. Art Mus., City of Burbank Art in Public Places Com. and Site Specific Com., Visual Artists and Galleries Assn. Inc., Calif. Lawyers for the Arts, Santa Monica, Nat. League of Am. Pen Women (honorary mem. 1991-), Internat Mus. and Artist Registration 1993-; major exhibits (solo & group): Southwest Mus., L.A.; Gallerie de Fondation des Etats-Unis, Paris; Roswell (N.M.) Mus. & Art Ctr.; Minneapolis Inst. of Art.; Salem (Ore.) Art Mus.; Downey (Calif.) Mus. Art; Framehouse Gallery, Louisville, Ky.; Edison Exhib. Ctr., Toledo, Ohio; Scottsdale (Ariz.) Civic Ctr.; Frye Art Mus., Seattle, Wash.; Circle Art Gallery, Houston, Tx.; Minneapolis Mus. Art nat. tour; Internat. Art Expo, LA Convention Ctr.; offices of Calif. Sec. of State March Fong Eu; Brand Lib. Art Galleries, Glendale; Calif. Mus. of Sci. & Industry, Retrospective; L.A. Co. Art Mus.; Seattle Art Mus.; St. Paul Art Ctr.; We. Assn. of Art Museums nat. tour; Minn. Mus. Art nat. traveling show; Am. Embassy, Brussels, Belgium; Museo de Arte Contemporaneo, Ibiza, Spain; Public Art Mus., Gabrova, Bulgaria; New England Fine Art Inst. Nat. Invitational Exhbn. of Contemporary Art; Internat. Print Biennale, Maastricht, Holland; Castaway R.E. & Art Show, Burbank; Internat. Consortium Exhib., Glendale; Art Auctions at Sheraton-Universal and Beverly Hills Hotel; Tusunga Art Assn., Sunland; Hancock Savings Bank, Toluca Lake; Sun Cities Art Mus., Sun City, Ariz.; Audobon Art Exhib., Portland, Ore.; Walt Disney Sch. Art Auction, Burbank; work in permanent collections: Smithsonian Mus. Kistler Collection; Franklin Mint Am. Art Collection; Roswell Mus. & Art Ctr.; Huntington Hartford Mus. Collection, NY; Southwest Mus., L.A.; Portland (Ore.) Art Mus.; Indian Wells City Hall; 7 profl. offices Toluca Lake, Beverly Hills, Hollywood, Portland, Ore. and Houston, Tx.; Electrocaine Med. Sys., Westwood; Phynque, Inc., Minneapolis, Minn.; Casa Pacifica Convalescent Home, Anaheim; Palmcrest Retirement Ctr., Long Beach; St. Jude's Hosp., Fullerton; Bonner Corp., Irvine; Mutual Savings & Loan, Pasadena; Glendale Fed. S&L (3 branches); McIntyre Oil Co., Roswell, N.M.; The Alan Casen Co., Beverly Hills; Burbank Studios; Calif. State Personnel Offices, L.A.; Security Pacific Internat Bank, NY; Public Art Museum, Gabrova, Bulgaria; Steve Garvey Art Collection; Vincent Price, Sears Collection of Art; Gene Autry Hotel. Palm Springs; City Hall, Burbank, and Indian Wells; Dreamscape Prod., Burnaby, B.C., Can.; Kaiser Permanente, Panorama City; Smith & Assoc., Boise, Idaho; Bangs Mfg., Burbank; Maple Collection, San Marino; Navarro Collection; Small Wilderness Area Preservation (SWAP); Dr. Nicholas H. Townell, Angus, Scotland. Mail: POB 1963 Burbank 91507

ASSISI, RITA F., investment company president; b. Sept. 27, 1943, Quilon, India; nat. 1978; d. Joseph M. and Roselyn M. Fernandez; m. Francis Clifford, Sept. 18, 1968 (div. 1990)Shashi b. 1969, Aruna b. 1971; edn: BS, Kerala Univ. India 1963; MS, Marquette Univ. 1967. Career: jr. lectr. Kerala Univ., Kerala, India 1963-64; research assoc. Stanford Univ. Med. Sch., Stanford 1974-87; pres. Tiara Investment Co., Los Altos 1987-; dir. FIABCI-USA 1988-89; awards: Marquette Univ. scholarship; Manca No. Calif. (pres. 1984-86), S. India Cultural Orgn. (v.p. 1983-84), India Cultural Assn. (pres. 1982-83); Democrat; rec: batik painting, pottery. Res: 755 Sunshine Dr Los Altos 94024 Ofc: Tiara Investment Co. 755 Sunshine Dr Los Altos 94024

ATCHLEY, BILL LEE, university president; b. Feb. 16, 1932, Cape Girardeau, Mo.; s. William and Cecil (Bicket) A.; m. Pat. Aug. 24, 1954; children: Julie b. 1957, Pam. b. 1961, David b. 1965; edn: BS civil engring., Univ. of Missouri, Rolla, Mo. 1957, MS civil engring., 1959; PhD civil engring., Texas A&M, 1965; attended Summer Inst. of O.C.D., Univ. of Hawaii, 1968; reg. Profl. Engr., S.C.. Career: profl. baseball pitcher, N.Y. Giants 1951-52; summer employment with: Mo. Hwy. Dept. 1959, Hughes Aircraft, Fullerton 1960, park engring. Grand Canyon Nat. Park, Ariz. 1962-63, U.S. Naval Civil Engring Lab. 1967; asst. prof. engring. mechanics, Univ. of Mo., Rolla 1957-61, assoc. prof., 1961-66; acting dept. chmn 1965-68, prof., 1966-75, asst. to dean Sch. of Engring. 1968-70, assoc. dean 1970-75; dean, Coll. of Engring., prof. mechanical engring. & mechanics, West Va. Univ., Morgantown 1975-79; pres. Clemson Univ. 1970-85; pres./CEO Nat. Sci. Center for Communications and Electronics Found. 1985-87; pres. Univ. of the Pacific, Stockton, Calif. 1987-; mem. Council of Govts. Habitat Policy Advy. Com., Calif. Campus Compact Exec. Com., Alpha Phi Omega (advy. bd. charter mem. 1992-), Nat. Edn. Advy. Com., U.S. Information Agency Sports Com., Am. Inst. for Public Svc. (bd. of nominators); honors: Ford Found. fellowship, Comm. Leader of Am. 1968, participant Continental Oil Co. conf. 1971, Knighted Honorary St. Patrick 1971, Chi Epsilon, Blue Key, Sigma Xi, Beta Gamma Sigma, Tau Beta Pi, Alumni Merit award for outstanding leadership and svc., Disting. Svc. award City of Rolla 1975, Service of Agriculture award S.C. Assn. of County Agricultural Agents 1981, Hall of Honor inductee Gamma Xi chpt. Sigma Nu Frat., Univ. of Mo. 1984, alumni mem. Clemson Univ. chpt. Gamma Sigma Delta 1984, Dept.

of the Army Outstanding Civilian Service Medal 1984, The Order of the Palmetto, St. of S.C. 1985, Prof. Emeritus Clemson Univ., Engineer of the Year S.C. Soc. of Profl. Engrs. 1985, Acad. of Civil Engrs., Rolla, Mo. 1986, hon. alumnus Clemson Univ. 1989, listed in: Who's Who in Midwest, Personalities of West and Midwest, Outstanding Young Men of Am. 1967, Who's Who in Engring. Edn., Outstanding Educators of Am., Who's Who in Am. 1980-83, Personalities of South 1982-83, Personalities of World, Internat. Who's Who in Engring. 1982-83, Registry of Am. Achievement 1982, Who's Who in Tech. Today 1982, Who's Who in West 1991, Bus. & Profl. Leaders Hall of Fame 1991, Who's Who Registry platinum edit. 1992, Who's Who in Calif. 1995; mem: Am. Soc. of Engring. Edn. (chmn. Midwest sect. 1971), Am. Soc. of Civil Engrs., Engrs. Club of St. Louis, The Newcomen Soc. of No. Am., Mid-Am. State Universities Assn., Nat. Soc. of Profl. Engrs., State Bd. of Registration for Profl. Engrs. (W.Va.); civic: mem: Stockton C.of C. (bd. dirs. 1994–), Stockton Beautiful (sub-com. mem. 1994–), Stockton Bus. Council, S.J. Partnership, Governor's Comm. on Energy, Economy and Environment (past chmn.), Willow Island Comm. (W.Va.), Rotary Club, Morgantown C.of C. (bd. dirs.), W. Va. C.of C., First Methodist Ch. (adminstrv. bd.), Wesley Methodist Ch. (chmn. council of ministers), Bicentennial, Rolla (dir.), Rolla Lions Club (bd. dirs.), Mo. C.of C., City of Rolla Third Ward Councilman (exec. bd.), Boy Scouts of Am. 1980-81; author: article pub. N.Y. Times 1982, numerous conf. addresses and articles pub. in profl. jours. 1971–; mil: U.S. Army 1952-54; Republican; rec: golf. Res: President's Home University of the Pacific Stockton 95211 Ofc: President, University of the Pacific Stockton 95211

ATIGH, STEPHANIE ANNE, lawyer; b. Feb. 19, 1951, Fresno; d. Hassan Atigh and Yolanda (Imperato) Trask; edn: BA, Engring., San Jose St. Univ. 1972; JD, Santa Clara Univ. Sch. Law 1975; admitted Supreme Ct. Calif. 1975. Career: staff atty. Comm. Legal Services, San Jose 1975-80; Legal Services Cape Cod, Hyannis, Mass. 1980-82, exec. dir. 1982-84; legal writer Matthew Bender, San Francisco 1984; asst. city atty. City of Salinas 1984-88, city atty. 1988–; instr. Mott Tng. Center, Pacific Grove 1988-90; awards: President's award Calif. Women Lawyers, Nat. Endowment for Humanities (fellowship 1979); mem: Monterey Co. Bar Assn., Monterey Co. Women Lawyers (pres. 1989-90), Nat. Lawyers Guild, Calif. Women Lawyers (bd. of gov. 1990-92). Res: 1080 Short St Pacific Grove 93950 Ofc: City Attorneys Office 200 Lincoln Ave Salinas 93901

ATKINSON, DOROTHY GILLIS, scholarly association executive; b. Aug. 5, 1929, Malden, Mass.; d. George Edward and Grace Margaret (Campagna) G.; m. Sterling K. Atkinson Jr., June 25, 1950, div. Dec. 1982; children: Kim b. 1955, Paul b. 1958; edn: BA, Barnard Coll., 1951; MA, UC Berkeley, 1953; PhD, Stanford Univ., 1971. Career: asst. prof. Stanford Univ., 1973-83; assoc. prof. UC Berkeley, 1984; exec. dir. Am. Assn. for the Advancement of Slavic Studies, Stanford 1981–; cons. fed. govt. agys., 1983–; awards: Pulitzer scholar, Mellon grantee, Stanford Univ. fellow, grantee Irex, Ford, and Fulbright; mem. advy. coun. US Dept. State 1984–; mem. Internat. Coun. for Soviet & East European Studies (exec. bd. 1985–), Nat. Coun. of Area Studies Assns. 1986–, Internat. Res. & Exchanges Bd. (exec. bd. 1991–); author: The End of the Russian Land Commune (1983), coeditor: Women in Russia (1976). Ofc: AAASS, Jordan Quad/Acacia Bldg, 125 Panama St Stanford 94305-4130

ATKINSON, RICHARD CHATHAM, university system president, cognitive psychologist, educator; b. Mar. 19, 1929, Oak Park, Ill.; s. Herbert and Margaret (Feuerbach) A.; m. Rita Loyd, Aug. 20, 1952; 1 dau. Lynn Loyd; edn: PhB, Univ. Chgo. 1948; PhD, Indiana Univ. 1955. Career: lectr. applied math. and stats. Stanford Univ. 1956-57, assoc. prof. psychology 1961-64, prof. psychol. 1964-80; asst. prof. psychol. UCLA 1957-61; dep. dir. NSF 1975-76, acting dir. 1976, dir. 1976-80; chancellor UC San Diego 1980-95; pres. Univ. of Calif. (nine-campus system) 1995–; Guggenheim fellow 1967; fellow Ctr. for Advanced Study in Behavioral Scis. 1963; awards: Disting. Research award Social Sci. Res. Council 1962; fellow APA (pres. exptl. div. 1974, Disting. Sci. Contribution award 1977, Thorndike award 1980); mem: AAAS (pres. 1989-90), Am. Psychol. Soc. (William James fellow 1985), Am. Acad. Arts & Scis., Soc. Exptl. Psychologists, Nat. Acad. Scis., Am. Philos. Soc., Nat. Acad. Edn., Inst. of Medicine, Psychonomic Soc., Cognitive Sci. Soc., Cosmos Club (Washington), Explorer's Club (N.Y.C.); author: (with Atkinson, Smith and Bem) Introduction to Psychology, 11th edit. 1993, Computer Assisted Instruction, 1969, An Introduction to Mathematical Learning Theory, 1965, Studies in Mathematical Psychology, 1964, Contemporary Developments in Mathematical Psychology, 1974, Mind and Behavior, 1980, Stevens' Handbook of Experimental Psychology, 1988; mil: AUS 1954-56. Res: 9630 La Jolla Farms Rd La Jolla 92037-1131 Ofc: Univ Calif at San Diego Office of Chancellor La Jolla 92093

ATKINSON, SHERIDAN EARLE, lawyer, financial analyst; b. Feb. 14, 1945, Oakland, Calif.; s. Arthur Sheridan and Esther Louise (Johnson) A.; m. Marjorie, Aug. 13, 1966; children: Ian b. 1972; edn: BS, Univ. Calif. 1966; JD, Univ. San Francisco 1969; MBA, Univ. Calif. 1971; postgrad. study, Univ. So. Calif., CSUH, Humboldt State Coll.; admitted Calif. State Bar 1970. Career: prin. Atkinson & Assoc. fin. and mgmt. cons. corp. and bus. valuations San

Francisco 1968–; assoc. Charles O. Morgan, Jr., S.F. 1972-76; solo law practice, San Francisco, Bay Area and Roseville, 1976–; mem: Am., Calif. bar assns.; mil: USAR 1970-76; Republican. Res: 1045 Key Route Blvd Albany 94706

AUERBACH, BRADFORD CARLTON, lawyer; b. April 17, 1957, Bethesda, Md.; s. Richard Carlton and Rita (Argen) A.; m. Jane Donnan Irwin, April 30, 1988; edn: BA, Hamilton Coll. 1979; JD, Boston Coll. 1982; admitted St. Bar Calif. Career: atty. Peter J. Sullivan, Marina del Rey 1984-89; atty. The Walt Disney Home Video, Burbank 1989-92; v.p. and gen. counsel Philips Interactive Media of America, 1992–; asst. prof. Loyola Univ., Los Angeles 1984; awards: Nat. Mock Trial Championships 1982; mem: Am. Trial Lawyers Assn., Am. Bar Assn., Santa Monica Bar Assn., Beverly Hills Bar Assn., Paladins of Temerity L.A.; article pub. in profl. jour. (1983), west coast correspondent Time Out mag. (London). Res: 1390 S Marengo Ave Pasadena 91106 Ofc: 10960 Wilshire L.A. 90024

AUERBACH, PHILIP BERNSTEIN, editorial director, international marketer; b. June 10, 1953, Philadelphia, Pa.; s. Isaac Levin Auerbach and Naomi Miriam (Bernstein) Diamond; m. Sands Tucker, Sept. 21, 1986; 1 dau., Aria Brianne b. 1988; edn: BA, Earlham Coll. 1975; MIM in internat. mgmt., Am. Grad. Sch. Internat. Mgmt. 1981. Career: assoc. ed. Auerbach Publishers, Pennsauken, N.J. 1975-77, dir. product mgmt. 1977-79; mktg. dir. Bophuthatswana Mgmt. Services, Southern Africa 1981-83; new product mgr. Springhouse Corp., Pa. 1983-85; cons. PBA Assoc., San Francisco 1985-88; editl. dir. Market Intelligence Research Co., Mountain View 1988-89; pres. Auerbach Internat. Inc. 1989–; pres. Translations Express!! 1993–; mem: Found. for Mideast Comms. (Bay Area co-founder), World Affairs Council, Concordia-Argonaut Club, Am. Jewish Congress (bd. mem. 1988, 89), Panel of Americans 1993-94; paper presented, 1988; speaker Profl. Bus. Women's Conf. 1993, 94; Democrat; Jewish; rec: travel, cultures, languages. Res: 2274 Bay St San Francisco 94123 Ofc: 2031 Union St Ste 2 San Francisco 94123

AULD, ROBERT HENRY, JR., biomedical engineer; b. Sept. 19, 1942, Akron, Ohio; s. Robert Henry and Elsie Mae (Rollans) A.; m. Karen Kay Atkinson, 1968 (div. 1981); children: Shiela Kay b. 1969, Jason Craig b. 1970; edn: BS, Univ. San Francisco 1978; internship: Stanford Univ. Med. Ctr., 1980, Univ. Calif. Med. Ctr., S.F. 1981; reg. profl. engr. Calif 1978, cert. clin. engr. 1976, internat. cert. 1984. Career: regional service mgr. Scientific Prods. Div. Am. Hosp. Supply Corp. Menlo Park, Calif. 1963-67; gen. mgr.,founder/owner Laboratory Instrument Service Campbell, Calif. 1967-77; nat. mgr. Lab. Mktg. Devel. Honeywell Inc. Biomedical Svcs. Denver, Colo. 1977-79; cons. biomed. engr./prin., dir. R&D, Robert Auld Enterprises 1970–; dir. clin. engring. St. Louis (Mo.) Regional Med. Ctr. 1987-90; nat. service mgr. RC Network, Cleveland Hts., Ohio 1990–; instr. workshops Stanford Sch. of Med. 1980; instr. Foothill Coll. Los Altos 1980-81; maintenance seminar & workshop dir. ASMT Phoenix 1978, Keene Coll., Union, NJ 1978, CAMLT-Calif. Monterey, Santa Clara, S.F., Marin chpts. 1977-79; mem: Nat. Soc. Profl. Engrs., Mo. Soc. Profl. Engrs. (chmn. Mathcounts, minority encouragement pilot project, St. Louis, Mo. NSPE/MSPE), Am. Soc. of Hosp. Engrs., Am. Coll. of Clin. Engrs., Assn. for Advancement of Med. Instrumentation, IEEE, ISA, Am. Soc. Med. Tech., Calif. Assn. Med. Lab. Tech., NY Acad. of Sciences, WESCON, L.A. (mem. convention attendance com. 1988-92), Masons; author: The Clone Factory, The Real Story About Police, 30+ articles pub. in med. trade jours.; concept developer Laser Fingerprint Analysis device for lifting latent prints, 1985, inventor device for Measurement of Oxygen Exchange in Blood, 1977; inventor "Dual-Beam" spotlight for public safety vehicles, 1992; devel. "Single Source Service," "Parts Banks" for healthcare facilities, 1964-67; mil: ET2 USN 1959-63; Republican (Presdl. Legion of Merit 1989–); Prot.; rec: restoration of antique instruments and telephone equipment. Res: 10445 Mast Blvd #140 Santee 92071

AULIK, DAVID JAMES, food industry executive, consultant, business and technology transfer specialist; b. Nov. 17, 1943, Antigo, Wis.; s. Raymond John and Emma (Schweitzer) A.; m. Susan Marie Foster, Aug. 2, 1981; children: Bond Aaron b. 1984, Taylor Jasmin b. 1987, Joshua Raymond b. 1988; edn: BS (athletic scholar), MS, and PhD in food chemistry, Univ. Wis., 1966, 1968, 1971, MBA in mktg./mgt., 1976. Career: mgmt. trainee Pet Inc., Hickory, N.C. 1966-67; res. asst. Univ. Wis., 1967-71, postdoctoral fellow 1971-72; exec. asst., interdeptl. coord., mgr. nutrition div., dir. client svs., WARF Institute Inc. (now Hazleton Labs. div. Corning), Madison, Wis., 1972-77; founder/c.e.o. Aulik Consulting Group Inc., 1977–, participant in devel. of 2500+ food products for 200+ client cos.; c.e.o. and v.chmn. bd. ITD Corp., Carpenteria, Ca. 1990-92; owner Pogen's Cookies, Compton 1991-93; v.p. Jack-In-The-Box and Foodmaker, San Diego 1994–; bd. dir. Henri's Food Products Co., Milw.; food counsel Nutri/System Franchisees (NSF), Janesville, Wis.; founder Freshen's Premium Frozen Yogurt, Atlanta, Ga.; consultant restaurant chains incl. Jack-In-The-Box, Winchell's, Internat. Dairy Queen, Hardee's, Marriott, Quaker Oats, Kraft General Foods, Pizza Hut, Arby's, Internat. House of Pancakes, Denny's, others; mem: Agricultural Research Inst., Am. Assn. of Cereal Chemists, Inst. of Food Technologists, Res. & Devel. Assocs., Sigma Xi; pub. research and tech. articles in field; Republican; rec: music, wine, gardening, football, basketball, running. Ofc: Aulik Consulting Group, Inc. 190 Alviso Dr Camarillo 93010

AUSENBAUM, HELEN EVELYN, psychologist/social worker; b. May 16, 1911, Chgo.; d. Herbert Noel and Mayme Eva (Bircher) Ausenbaum; edn: stu. Univ. of Ill., Urbana 1930-2; AB, UC Berkeley 1938, MSW 1956; postgrad. stu. CSU Hayward 1976-8, JFK Univ., Orinda 1976; lic. clin. social worker (LCSW), diplomate NASW, Calif. cred. school psychologist, 1956–. Career: social worker Alameda Co. Welfare Commn., 1939-42, American Red Cross, San Francisco 1942-43; exec. dir. ARC, Richmond 1943-51; Richmond Public Schs. 1951-53; sch. social worker/sch. psychologist Oakland Public Schs. 1953-76; program dir. Let's Rap prog. McChesney Jr. H.S., Oakland 1970-82; founder, pvt. practice Orinda Counseling Ctr. 1959-93; prog. dir. Diablo Valley Found. for Aging, Support Service for Elders, Walnut Creek 1980-84; apptd: Orinda Commn. on Aging (1976–, chair 1978-91), Contra Costa Co. Mental Health Com. on Aging, Lincoln Child Ctr. Oakland (bd. dirs. 1976-87), Contra Costa Co. Advy. Council On Aging 1977- (pres. 1985-86), Triple A Council of Calif. 1985-86, Calif. State Coordinating Com. for Mental Health and Older Adults, East Bay Elder Abuse Prevention (Consortium, Advy. Devel. Bd. 1987), mem. Martha Chickering Meml. Fund, UC Berkeley, Sch. of Social Welfare, Mary A. Sarvis Meml. Bd. 1965–; chair Rossmoor Comm. for Common Concern; co-chair: Rossmoor Mental Health Professionals, Democratic Club, Rossmoor Rotary Club 1995; awards: Am.Red Cross scholarship 1942-43, appreciation award Richmond Service Clubs, Oakland Principals Club Award 1976, certif. Orinda City Council; mem: Calif. Tchrs Assn., Nat. Assn. of Social Workers (charter), Calif. Assn. of Sch. Social Workers, Am. Soc. on Aging, AAUW; Democrat; Presbyterian; rec: photography, travel, coins & stamps. Res: 1637 Skycrest Dr #7 Walnut Creek 94595 Tel: 510/256-9847

AUTRY, ORVON GENE, singer, actor, broadcasting executive; b. Sept. 29, 1907, Tioga, Tex.; s. Delbert and Elnora (Ozmont) A.; m. Ina Mae Spivey, Apr. 1, 1932 (dec. 1980); m. 2d. Jacqueline Ellam, July 1981; edn: grad., Tioga High Sch. 1925. Career: railroad telegraph operator, Sepulpa, Okla. 1925; first phonograph record of cowboy songs 1929; radio artist Station WLS, Chicago 1930-34; motion picture actor in 93 films, 1934–; starred in 88 musical Western feature pictures, 91 half-hour TV pictures; pres., chmn. bd. Calif. Angels; chmn. bd. Golden West Broadcasters, owner radio station 101.9 FM, L.A.; chmn. Gene Autry Western Heritage Museum and several music publishing companies; mem: Internat. Footprinters; Masons (33 deg.); Shriners; Elks; composer 250+ songs incl. That Silver-Haired Daddy of Mine, 1931, You're the Only Star in My Blue Heaven, 1938, Dust, 1938, Tears On My Pillow, 1941, Be Honest With Me, 1941, Tweedle O'Twill, 1942; Here Comes Santa Claus, 1948; mil: USAAF, 1942-45. Address: 4383 Colfax Avenue Studio City 91604

AVERBOOK, BERYL DAVID, vascular surgeon; b. Aug. 17, 1920, Superior, Wis.; s. Abraham B. and Clara (Ziechig) A.; m. Gloria Sloane, Apr. 2, 1955; children: Bruce Jeffery b. 1956, Allen Wayne b. 1960; edn: Superior St. Tchrs. Coll. 1938-39; BS, Univ. Wis. 1942, MD, 1945; postgrad. tng. Univ. of Colo. 1948-50; diplomate, special qualifications in gen. vascular surgery, Am. Board of Surgery. Career: intern Akron (Ohio) City Hosp. 1945-46; surgical resident Fort Logan VA Hosp., Denver, Colo. 1948-50; Rochester (NY) Gen. Hosp. 1950-51; Wadsworth VA Hosp., Los Angeles 1951-54; chief surg. serv. Harbor Gen. Hosp., L.A. 1954-61; instr. in surg. Univ. Calif. Med. Ctr., L.A. 1954-58, asst. prof. surg. 1958-61, clin. asst. prof. surg. 1961-65; pvt. practise splst. in tumor and vascular surg., Torrance 1961–; Fellow A.C.S., mem. Soc. for Clin. Vascular Surgery, AMA, CMA, L.A. Co. Med. Assn., NY Acad. of Sci., Soc. of Head & Neck Surgeons, Long Beach Surg. Soc., L.A. Acad. of Medicine, Am. Geriatric Soc., UCLA Harbor Collegium (bd. dirs.), Am. Men of Medicine; mil: capt. M.C. AUS. Res: 6519 Springpark Ave Los Angeles 90056 Ofc: Beryl D. Averbook, MD 3640 Lomita Blvd #202 Torrance 90505

AVERILL, DONALD FREDERICK, college dean; b. Jan. 9, 1938, Los Angeles; s. Morton Anthony and Anita Marie (Moser) A.; m. Carol J., June 10, 1961; children: Margaret b. 1962, Kathleen b. 1963, Donald James b. 1965; edn: BA, CSU Los Angeles, 1960, MA, 1965; cred. gen. adminstr., USC; 1967; EdD, Univ. of La Verne, 1982; Calif. std. sec. tchg. cred., Calif. Comm. Colls. cred., adminstrn. Career: tchr. Norwalk La Mirada, 1960-63, Whittier UHSD, 1963-67; coord. work exper. Whittier UHSD, 1967-72; dir. career edn. Huntington Beach UHSD, 1972-77; vice chancellor Coast Comm. Coll. Dist., Costa Mesa 1977-85; dean of instrn./dir. cert. personnel Glendale Comm. Coll., 1985–, adminstrn. dean, human resources 1990–; faculty CSU Long Beach, 1980-89, UCLA, 1978-91; v.p. Alternatives, Marina del Rey, 1972–; assoc. Nat. Center for Development of Edn., Encina 1987–; awards: most promising tchr. Theta Rho Tau L.A. 1960, vocat. edn. adminstr. of yr. State Council Vocat. Edn., Sacto. 1972, Dr. Robert Moore Award Orange Count Edn. Council 1984, nominated Man of Yr. La Habra C.of C. 1988; mem: Calif. Assn. of Vocat. Edn. (pres. 1974-75), Calif. Assn. of Work Experience Edn. (pres. 1971-72), Calif. Adminstrs. of Vocat. Edn. (pres. 1977-78), Calif. Comm. Coll. Adminstrs. of Occupational Edn. (pres. 1984-85), ULV Doctoral Alumni Assn. (pres. 1987-88); civic: Glendale C.of C. (leg com.), Knights of Col., La Habra, Kiwanis, Glendale (pgm. chmn., pres. 1990-91, lt. gov. div. 3, 1994-95); author: AVA Year Book, 1984; mil: airman 2c USAF 1956-61; Republican; R.Cath.; rec: equestrian, woodworking, singing. Ofc: Glendale Community College 1500 N Verdugo Rd Glendale 91208

AXON, DONALD CARLTON, architect, consultant; b. Feb. 27, 1931, Haddonfield, NJ; s. William Russell, Sr. and Gertrude (Ellis) A.; m. Janice, Mar. 16, 1968; children: Donald b. 1953, James b. 1955, Marianne b. 1957, Darren b. 1958, William b. 1961, (step): Jonathan b. 1948, Elise b. 1956; edn: B.Arch., Pratt Inst. 1954; MS arch., Columbia Univ. 1966; arch. NY 1959, Calif. 1971, Pa. 1963. Career: ptnr. Bailey & Axon AIA Assocs. Long Beach 1960-66; programmer, project mgr. CRS, Houston 1966-69; pgmr./planner Kaiser Permanente Med. Care Group, Los Angeles 1969-75; pgmr./ med. dir. DMJM, L.A. 1975-79; proj. mgr. Lyon Assocs. L.A. 1979-80; pres. DCA/FAIA, Inc., L.A. 1980–; instr. Building Science Pgm., USC, 1978-82; instr., team leader AHA-UCLA sponsored planning & programming seminar 1975; guest lectr. UCLA Sch. of Arch. 1976, 77, Texas A&M Grad. Sch. Arch. 1977; liaison Kaiser Found. Hosps., UCLA Sch. of Arch. and Urban Planning Hosp. Pgm. 1973; profl. advisor Univ. Texas Dept. Arch. 1968-69; advisor to chmn. Rice Univ. Sch. of Arch. Masters Pgm. in Hosps. 1968-69; profl. dir. Future Archs. of Am. 1965-66; honors: Honor Award (Progressive Architecture Design Awards Pgm. 1955), First Prize (student team proj. 1953), Full Tuition Scholarship (Columbia Univ.), L.A. Beautiful Award (for KFH Norwalk Hosp.), Excellence in Design (Orange Co. chpt. AIA); Fellow AIA (nat. bd. dirs. 1987-89, chmn. com. on Arch. for Health 1980), mem. Los Angeles Chpt. AIA (bd. dirs. 1983-84, pres. 1986), Calif. Council AIA, Archtl. Found. of L.A. (founding mem., pres. 1987-89), Internat. Conf. Bldg. Officials, Forum for Healthcare Planning (dir. 1982–, chmn. regl. pgm. com., pres. 1993-94), Am. Hosp. Assn., Healthcare Forum, Internat. Hosp. Fedn., Fellow Royal Soc. Health, Archtl. Guild (USC), Crestwood Hills Assn. (bd. 1971-83, pres. 1973-75), Brentwood Comm. Fedn. (bd. 1973-75, 1st v.p. 1974-75); gubnat. appt. bd. mem. Hosp. Building Safety Bd., Ofc. of Statewide Health Planning & Devel. 1984, Calif. Seismic Safety Commn. Hosp. Act Task Force 1976-77, and Hosp. Act Legislation Task Force 1980. Ofc: Donald C. Axon FAIA 823 Hanley Ave Los Angeles 90049-1913

AXTELL, KEITH E., HUD-FHA housing regional official; b. March 10, 1942, San Bernadino; s. John Dewey and Nelta E. (George) A.; m. Pat Boster, Dec., 1964 (div. 1980); m. Holly Handler, Nov. 30, 1980; children: Andrea b. 1966, Jon b. 1969; edn: BA, UC Berkeley 1965; MA pub. adminstrn., 1966. Career: legislative cons. com. on ways and means Calif. St. Assembly, Sacto. 1966-67; U.S. Dept. HUD, San Francisco 1967-95, dir. San Francisco housing mgmt. branch 1971-74, Asst. Regional Adminstr. for adminstrn. 1974-78, dir. office of Indian housing 1978-80, spl. asst. field coordination 1980-82, Regional Dir. of Housing 1983-94, dir. of S.F. Housing/FHA ofc. 1994–; lectr. CSU Hayward, advy. com. mem. Sch. Pub. Adminstrn. 1989-95; honors: Phi Beta Kappa, Pres.'s Spl. Award for Mgmt. Improvement 1970, HUD Disting. Service 1972, ASPA Achievement award; mem: Am. Soc. Pub. Adminstrn. (pres. 1990-91, nat. council 1994-95); contbr. Democracy & Pub. Service, 1968; rec: gardening. Ofc: U.S. Dept. HUD 450 Golden Gate Ave POB 36003 San Francisco 94102

AYALA, RUBEN S, state senator; b. Mar. 6, 1922, Chino, Calif.; s. Mauricio R. and Erminia (Martinez) A.; student Pomona Jr. Coll., 1941-42; grad. Nat. Electronic Inst. Los Angeles, 1948; m. Irene Morales, July 22, 1945; children: Bud, Maurice Edward, Gary. Career: mem. sch. bd. Chino, Calif. 1955-62; councilman City of Chino, 1962-64, mayor, 1964-66; bd. suprs. 1966-73; chmn. San Bernardino Co. Bd. Suprs., 1968-72; mem. Calif. Senate from 34th Dist., 1974–, vice chair coms. on rules, agriculture and water resources, local govt., mem. bus. and professions, transportation, vets. affairs coms., mem. joint legis. audit com., com. fairs allocations; mem. Chino Sch. Bd. 1955-62; chmn. San Bernardino Co. Health Com. 1968-72, Chino Police Commn. 1964-66, Chino Parks and Recreation Commn. 1962-64; mem. Nat. Alliance of Businessmen Com., Washington, 1970; chmn. West Valley Planning Agy. 1968-72; mem. steering corn. County Hwy. Safety Orgn. 1968-72; bd. dirs. Pomona Freeway Assn. 1968; life mem. PTA, Chino; awards: recipient Outstanding Civil Leaders of Am. award 1967, Citizen of Year award Chino Valley C.of C. 1970, VFW of San Bdo. Co., Mex. Am. Polit. Assn., Disting. Citizens award Calif. Inland Empire council Boy Scouts Am. 1985, named Calif. Legislator of Yr. Democrats United 1982, named Citizen of Yr. Assn. Calif. Water Agys. and Am. Public Works Assn., San-Bdo.-Riverside branch, hon. City of Pomona 1971, 80, parks named in his honor, Chino and Bloomington, Calif., Chino Sch. Dist. high sch. named in his honor 1986; mem:. Assn. Calif. Water Agys, Assn. Calif. Engrs., Am. Legion, Native Sons of Golden West, Kiwanis; mil: served with USMC, World War II; PTO. Ofc: Office of State Senate 9620 Center Ave # 100 Rancho Cucamonga 91730 also: Office of State Senate State Capitol Sacramento 95814

AYER, JOHN D., professor of law; b. Feb. 18, 1936, Manchester, N.H.; s. Demeritt Colby and Esther Annette (Nordstrom) A.; m. Sue Ann Flesher, June 21, 1958 (div. 1978); children: Katherine Elizabeth b. 1962, David Colby b. 1964; m. 2d. Maryanne J. Bertran, 1990; edn: BA hons., Univ. Louisville 1963; JD cum laude, 1968; LL.M, Yale Univ. 1969; admitted St. Bar Calif. (1973). Career: reporter Louisville Times, Ky. 1960-68; Wash. correspondent Louisville Courier-Journal and Times, Wash. D.C. 1966; prof. law UC Davis 1969–; judge U.S. Bankruptcy Ct., Los Angeles 1983-84; adj. prof. USC 1983-84; counsel Stutman Treister & Glatt 1975, 1980-81; acad. vis. London Sch. of Econ., England 1976; vis. prof. Univ. Tx., Austin 1979-80; Stanford Univ., Palo Alto 1988-89, Univ. of Pa. 1993; awards: Am. Bar Assn. Ross Essay 1979, Silver Gavel 1965; mem: Am. Bar Assn., Am. Coll. of Bankruptcy (fellow), Univ. of Louisville Alumni Assn. (lifetime fellow); author Calif. Secured Transactions, 1984; mil: E-2 U.S. Army Nat. Guard 1958; Democrat. Res: 287 E 2d Ave Chico 95926 Ofc: Univ. Calif. Law School, Davis 95616

AYLOUSH, CYNTHIA MARIE, treasurer; b. July 2, 1950, Jackson, Mich.; d. Leonard Edward and Violet (Kroeger) Ullrich; m. Abbott Selim Ayloush, June 21, 1980; children: Sasha b. 1983, Nadia b. 1985, Ramsey b. 1989; edn: AA, Fullerton Coll. 1970; San Diego St. Univ. 1970-71; cert., Brooks Coll. 1973-74; BS, Pepperdine Univ. 1980. Career: secty. Hydraflow, Los Angeles 1968; dep. mgr. Robinsons, Cerritos 1973-79; secty., treas. Hydraflow 1979–; mem: Am. Soc. Personnel Adminstrs., Personnel Ind. Rels. Assn., Soroptimist Internat. (secty., pres. 1993-94), Cerritos C.of C. (bd. mem. 1983-89); Republican; R.Cath.; rec: boating. Address: Cerritos 90701

AYOUB, KAMEL JACK, miltary uniforms manufacturer, defense department contractor; b. Oct 24, 1933, Jordan; s. Jack and Nazilah A.; m. Majda Rihani, Aug. 30, 1974; children: Basil b. 1975, Mona b. 1978, Hana b. 1980; edn: BA, San Francisco State Univ. 1960. Career: owner Califashions, San Francisco 1970–; mem: World Affairs Council, U.N. Assn., Nat. Assn. Arab Am., Arab Cultural Center S.F. (past pres., co-founder), St. Nicholas Orthodox Church, Arab Am. Inst., Jordanian Am. Assn. (co-founder), U.S. Omen; Eastern Orthodox Christian. Ofc: Califashions 972 Mission St San Francisco 94103

AZCUE, PEDRO ARTURO, real estate marketing; b. Sept. 12, 1955, Mexico City, Mex.; s. Pedro Pabla Azcue and Lilly (Aderman) Mena; m. Ana Elena Attolini, Dec. 21, 1979; children: Pedro b. 1982, Derrick b. 1984, Axel b. 1987; edn: BS indsl. engring. (hons.), Univ. Iberoamericana, Mexico City, 1977; MBA, Stanford Grad. Sch. of Bus., 1981; reg. industrial engr. (with honorable mention), Mex. 1977. Career: investments ofcr. Banco de Mexico, Mexico City 1977-79; assoc. La Salle Partners, Chicago, Ill. 1981-84, v.p. La Salle Partners, Dallas, Tx. 1984-92, senior v.p. La Salle Partners, Los Angeles 1992–; dir. gen. La Salle Partners, Mexico 1993–; speaker Banco de Mexico, Mexico City, 1977, Indsl. Devel. Council, Nashville, Tenn., 1992; honors: best student of Mexico, Instituto Mexicano de Cultura, Mexico City 1977; mem. Calif.-Mexico Project 1989–, US-Mex. C.of C. 1989–; club: Jonathan (L.A.); publs: R.E. articles, 1991, 92, 93, 94; mil: Mexico 1976-77; R.Cath.; rec: travel. Res: 24939 Alicante Dr Calabasas 91302 Ofc: LaSalle Partners 355 S Grand Ave Ste 4280 Los Angeles CA 90071

BAAB, DAVID JOHN, architect, planning consultant; b. March 24, 1956, Dayton, Ohio; s. John Robert and Marilyn (Demmler) B.; m. Katherine Wright Mackey, July 12, 1980; edn: BArch, Univ. Cincinnati, 1980; MBA, UC Irvine, 1988; reg. architect Calif. 1983. Career: architect Blurock Partnership, Newport Beach 1980-84; mgr. The Irvine Company, Newport Beach 1984-88; planning cons. Baab & Assocs., Newport Beach 1988–; awards: Henry Adams Medal Ohio Soc. Architects, Cinti. (1980); mem: AIA-Orange Co. (CFO 1989-91, dir. profl. devel. 1986-87), Urban Land Inst., Willowgrove Assn. (pres.), Westpark Maintenance Dist. (bd.), Art Spaces, Irvine (bd.), Tustin Ranch Comm. Assn. (bd.); editor Insiders Guide to Orange Co., 1984; mem. building design team Orange County Performing Arts Center 1982-84, planning team community of Westpark 1984-88, building com. mem. Woodbridge Village Assn. 1983-87; Republican; Lutheran; rec: photog., hiking, gardening. Ofc: Baab & Associates 550 Newport Center Dr Ste 925, Newport Beach 92660

BABULA, WILLIAM, university dean, author; b. May 19, 1943, Stamford, Conn.; s. Benny F. and Lottie (Zajkowski) B.; m. Karen L. Gemi, June 19, 1965; children: Jared, Joelle; edn: BA, Rutgers Univ. 1965; MA, UC Berkeley 1967; PhD, 1969. Career: asst. prof. english Univ. Miami, Coral Gables, Fla. 1969-75, assoc. prof. 1975-77, prof. 1977-81, chmn. dept. English 1976-81; dean of arts and humanities Sonoma St. Univ., Rohnert Park 1981–; author: Shakespeare and Tragicomic Archetype, 1975, Shakespeare in Production 1935-79 (1981); short stories include: Motorcycle, 1982, Quarterback Sneak, 1983, The First Edsel, 1983, Ransom, 1983, The Last Jogger in Virginia, 1983, The Orthodontist and the Rock Star, 1984, Greenearth, 1984, Football and Other Seasons, The Great Am. Basketball Shoot, 1984, Ms. Skywriter Inc., 1987, Charlotte's Stones, 1989; plays: The Fragging of Lt. Jones (1st prize Gualala Arts Competition), Creatures (1st prize Jacksonville Univ. competition 1987), The Winter of Mrs. Levy (Odyssey Stage Co., artist in residence New Play Series, Nat. Playwrights Showcase Prodn., 1988), Production Theatre Americana (best play award 1989-90), Basketball Jones, Black Rep of Berkeley, 1988; productions: West Coast Ensemble, 1992, Mark Twain Masquers, 1994; novels: The Bombing of Berkeley and Other Pranks (1st prize 24th Annual Deep South Writers Conf. 1984), St. John's Baptism, 1988, According to St. John, 1989, St. John and the Saven Veils, 1990, St. John's Bestiary, 1994; contbr. articles to various journals, short stories in literary mags.; awards: Phi Beta Kappa, Fla. Endowment Humanities grantee 1980-81, Inst. for Study of Aging grantee; mem: Dramatists Guild, Authors League Am., Associated Writing Programs, Mystery Writers Am.. Ofc: School of Arts and Humanities Sonoma State University Rohnert Park 94928

BACHER, ROSALIE WRIDE, retired school administrator, counselor; b. May 25, 1925, Los Angeles; d. Homer Martin and Reine (Rogers) Wride; m. Archie Bacher, Jr., Mar. 30, 1963; edn: AB, Occidental Coll. 1947, MA, 1949; grad. work in counseling, sch. adminstrn., USC, 1949; Calif. life tchg. credentials: elem. and secondary tchg./ adminstrn., pupil personnel. Career: faculty Long Beach Unified Sch. Dist. 1959-89: English, Latin and history tchr. Jordan High Sch. 1949-55, counselor Jordan H.S. 1955-65, Lakewood H.S. 1966; research asst. Sch. Dist. Research Office 1967; v. principal Washington Jr. H.S. 1968, asst. principal Lakewood H.S. 1969, v. principal Jefferson Jr. H.S. 1970-81, v.principal John Marshall Jr. H.S., 1981-87, v. principal Lindbergh Jr. H.S. 1986-87; counselor Millikan H.S. 1988, Hill Jr. H.S. 1988-89, ret. 1989; mem. Vice and Asst. Principals Assn. (chair vocat. Guidance Steering Com., ofcr.); honors: Phi Beta Kappa 1947; mem: Pi Lambda Theta (pres. O.C. chpt.), Delta Kappa Gamma (pres. Delta Psi chpt., st. chair Profl. Affairs), Phi Delta Gamma (USC chpt. pres.), AAUW; MA thesis: A Hist. of the Long Beach oil fields and their influence on the city of L.B.; Republican; Christian Sci.; rec: home, garden, and dog. Res: 265 Rocky Point Rd Palos Verdes Estates 90274

BACON, LEONARD ANTHONY, university accounting professor; b. June 10, 1931, Santa Fe, N.M.; s. Manuel R. and Maria (Chavez) Baca; m. Patricia Balzaretti, June 6, 1964; children: Bernadine b. 1965, Jerry b. 1966, Tiffany b. 1978; edn: BE, Univ. Neb. 1965; MBA, Univ. Americas 1969; PhD, Univ. Miss. 1973. Career: vis. prof. Internat. Univ., Mexico City 1974; asst. prof. Delta St. Univ., Cleveland, Miss 1971-74; vis. prof. Univ. Americas, Mexico City 1975; assoc. prof. Delta St. Univ. 1975-79; W. Tx. St. Univ., Canyon 1976-79; prof. CSU, Bakersfield 1979–; cons. Kershen Triticale Co., Canyon, Tx. 1979-80; O'Neill Farms, Porterville 1987; Cath. lay minister Juvenile Hall, Bakersfield 1982–; listed Who's Who West, Who's Who Fin. & Industry, Who's Who Internat. Bus., Who's Who in World, Who's Who Am. Univs. & Colls.; mem: Jockey Club Rio de Janeiro, Lions, Kiwanis, United Campus Ministry, BSA, Am. Inst. CPA, Am. Acctg. Assn., Am. Assn. Spanish CPA, Inst. of Mgmt. Accts., Soc. of Cost Estimating & Analysis; author: articles and paper pub. 1980-94; mil: major AUS 1951-66; Republican; R.Cath.; rec: fishing, woodwork, flying. Ofc: California State University 9001 Stockdale Hwy Bakersfield 93309

BACON, RANDALL C., public administrator; b. Oct. 2, 1937, Youngstown, Ohio; s. Arthur E. and Audrey E. (Gross) B.; children: Randy b. 1956, Keith b. 1961, Kevin b. 1964; edn: AA, L.A. City Coll. 1958; BS, CSU Los Angeles, 1962; grad. work USC 1964-66. Career: chief dep. dir. parks and recreation Co. of Los Angeles 1968-74, asst. div. chief, CAO 1974-79; dep. chief adminstrv. ofcr. Co. of San Diego 1979-81, dir. social services 1981-87, dep. chief adminstrv. ofcr. 1987-88; gen. mgr. City of Los Angeles 1988–; guest lectr. USC 1975-79, UC San Diego also National Univ., 1980-88; awards: Am. Soc. Pub. Adminstrn. Nat. Pub. Service 1987, Combined Service Orgns. Comm. Service 1989, NFBPA Marks of Excellence 1990, Kappa Alpha Psi (nat. pres.); mem: Am. Soc. Pub. Adminstrn. (exec. council), NAACP, Nat. Forum Black Pub. Adminstrs. (nat. pres.), SCAPA Praeters USC, New Frontier Democratic Club, Common Cause; article pub. in profl. jour., 1985; Democrat; Methodist. Ofc: City of Los Angeles Department of General Services Room 800 City Hall E, 200 N Main St Los Angeles 90012

BAERG, RICHARD HENRY, podiatric physician, educator, medical-legal consultant; b. Jan. 19, 1937, Los Angeles; s. Henry Francis and Ruth Elizabeth (Loven) B.; m. Yvonne Marie Estrada, Nov. 23, 1987; children (by previous marriage): Carol b. 1963, William b. 1967, Michael b. 1969, Yvette b. 1970; gr.dau., Brie Ann b. 1991; edn: AA, Reedley Coll., 1956; BS, DPM, and MSc, Calif. Coll. Pod. Med., S.F. 1965, 1968, 1970; MPH, UC Berkeley, 1971; DSc, NYCPM, 1980; LittD, OCPM, 1984; postdoctoral intern Highland Hosp., Oakland 1969; surgical resident Pacific Coast Hosp., S.F. 1970; Inst. for Ednl. Mgmt. Harvard Univ., 1975; lic. podiatric physician Calif. BMQA 1968; bd. cert. Am. Bd. Pod. Orthopedics & Primary Pod. Med., Am. Bd. Pod. Surg., Am. Bd. Pod. Pub. Health. Career: academic dean NY Coll. of Pod. Med., NYC 1971-74; dean and exec. v.p. Calif. Pod. Med. Ctr., San Francisco 1974-78; pres. Ill. Coll. Pod. Med., Chgo. 1978-79; dir. pod. svs. Veterans Affairs, Wash. DC 1979-86; exec. dir. Am. Acad. of Podiatric Med., Wash. DC 1980-90; v.p./med. dir. Orthopedics Dr. Footcare, Montclair, Calif. 1986-90; asst. prof. Calif. Coll. Pod. Med., S.F. 1970-71, clin. assoc. prof. Stanford Med. Sch. 1974-76, clin. prof. NY Coll. Pod. Med. 1971-74, Calif. Coll. Pod. Med. 1974-78, Univ. of Osteo. Med., Des Moines, Ia. 1984–, Univ. N.C. Sch. of Medicine 1992–; Barry Univ. Sch. of Pod. Med., Fla. 1992–; private practice in Beverly Hills, 1976-78, Montclair, 1987-90, Redlands, 1990-92; appt. by Gov. Deukmejian to St. Dept. Consumer Affairs Bd. of Podiatric Medicine 1989-90; chmn. Pod. Health Sect. A.P.H.A., 1992-94; awards: USPHS fellow 1970-71, nominee Rockerfeller Pub. Svs. Wash. DC 1979, mem. Nat. Academies of Practice, Wash.D.C. (distinguished dr. honoree 1986), Kenison Award Assn. of Pod. Med. Wash. DC 1985; mem: Am. Pod. Med. Assn., Calif. Pod. Med. Assn., Am. Assn. of Colls. of Pod. Med. (pres. 1980), Am. Coll. of Foot & Ankle Surgeons (Fellow), Am. Coll. of Foot Orthopedists (Fellow), Acad. of Ambulatory Foot Surgery (Fellow), Assn. of Mil. Surgeons, Commonwealth Club Calif., Masons; author chapt. on Govt. Health Policy in Textbook of Pub. Health, 27 articles in J. of Am. Pod. Med. Assn.; mil: AUS Med. Corps 1958-66;

Republican; Prot.; rec: piano, opera, classical music. Res: 401 Baltimore #C Monterey Park 91754

BAEZ, JOAN CHANDOS, folk singer; b. Staten Island, N.Y., Jan. 9, 1941; d. Albert V. and Joan (Bridge) B.; m. David Victor Harris, Mar. 1968 (div. 1973); children: Gabriel Earl. Career: Appeared in coffeehouses, Gate of Horn, Chgo., 1958, Ballad Room, Club 47, 1958-68, Newport (R.I.) Folk Festival, 1959-69, 85, 87, 90, extended tour to colls. and concert halls, 1960's, appeared Town Hall and Carnegie Hall, 1962, 67, 68, U.S. tours, 197, concert tours, Japan, 1966, 82, Europe, 1970-73, 80, 83-84, 87-90, 93, Australia, 1985; rec. artist for Vanguard Records. 1960-72, A&M, 1973-76, Portrait Records, 1977-80, Cold Castle Records, 1986-89, (awarded 8 gold albums, 1 gold single), Virgin Records, 1990, European record albums, 1981, 83; other albums include: Play Me Backwards, 1992; author: Joan Baez Songbook 1964, (Biography) Daybreak, 1968, (with David Harris) Coming Out, 19;1, And A Voice To Sing With, 1987, (songbook) And then I wrote 1979, extensive tv appearances and speaking tours U.S. and Can. for anti militarism, 1967-68; visit to war torn Bosnia-Herzegovina, 1993; visit to Dem. Republic of Vietnam, 1972; founder, v.p. Inst. for Study Nonviolence (now Resource Ctr. for Nonviolence, Santa Cruz, Calif.), Palo Alto, Calif. 1965; mem. nat. adv. council Amnesty Internat., 1974-92; founder, pres. Humanities/Internat. Human Rights Com., 1979-92. Ofc: Diamonds and Rust Productions PO Box 1026 Menlo Park CA 94026-1026

BAHAN, JOSEPH ROBERT, doctor of chiropractic; b. July 29, 1963, Lynwood, Calif.; s. Joseph William and Judith Ann (Willenbring) B.; edn: BS and DC, Cleveland Chiropractic Coll., L.A. 1989; lic. DC, State of Calif. 1990. Career: dir. of radiology Ward Chiropractic, Long Beach 1988–, dr. of chiropractic 1990–; owner/DC Bahan Chiropractic Center, Dana Point 1993–; instr. for intact spine-meningeal systems at num. chiro. ctrs. 1989–, So. Calif. Coll. Chiro. 1993, So. Australia 1994, Canada 1994, 95; res. on S-M effects on muscular dystrophy Ward Chiro., Long Beach 1991–, Bahan Chiro., Dana Point 1993–; field dr.'s cons. Ward Chiro. and Capperauld Chiro. 1992–; featured guest/interviews on muscular dystrophy, num. radio and T.V. stas. 1992-93, KNBC-TV (Today Show), N.Y. 1993; interview/feature for 5 newspaper and 2 mag. articles 1992-93; mem. Calif. Chiro. Assn. 1993–; author: articles pub. in Chiropractic Economics 1991, The American Chiropractor 1992, 94, 94; Republican; Roman Catholic; rec: jet skiing (asst. tech. inspector for Internat. Jet Sports Boating Assn.), marlin fishing. Res: 8145 Woolburn Dr. Huntington Beach 92646 Ofc: Bahan Chiropractic Center 34207 Coast Hwy Suite 101 Dana Point 92629

BAHOSHY, BERNARD JOSEPH, food company technical administrator; b. Aug. 20, 1927, Baghdad, Iraq, nat. 1955; s. Dr. Razzouk and Rose (Andrea) B.; m. Mary Margaret Lee, Oct. 21, 1950; children: Robert b. 1951, Patricia b. 1956, Catherine b. 1956, Barbara b. 1958; edn: BS in chem., Fordham Univ. 1950. Career: research chemist E.F. Drew, Boonton, N.J. 1951-57; group leader/lab. mgr. Gen. Foods, Woburn, Mass. and Dover, Del. 1957-70, corp. research mgr. Gen. Foods, Tarreytown, N.Y. 1970-76, technical devel. mgr. 1976-80, representative dir. Ajinomoto GF Protein, Tokyo, Japan 1980-84, technical dir. Asia Pacific, Gen. Foods Honolulu, HI 1984-87, ret.; 11 U.S. Patents in food technology - fats & oils, desserts, chewing gum, 1958-80; recipient technical research innovation award Gen. Foods Corp. 1967; mem. Inst. of Food Technologists 1971–; pres. Chateau Bernardo Homeowners Assn. 1994; club: Bernardo Heights, San Diego; Republican; R.Cath.; rec: tennis, music, travel. Res: 11918 Avenida Consentido San Diego 92128

BAILEY, ALEX STUART, engineering manager; b. June 23, 1952, San Diego; s. Robert Earwood and Marcelle Adalyn (Groff) B.; m. Terri Anne Marsh, May 31, 1986; children: Kyle b. 1988, Corinne b. 1990; edn: AA, Canada Coll., 1972, BA, UC Berkeley, 1974; MBA, Santa Clara Univ., 1982. Career: satellite ops. engr. Lockheed Missiles & Space Co., Sunnyvale 1974-78, mgmt. devel. program 1978-80, senior res. engr. 1980-82; staff engr. Ultrasystems Def. & Space 1982-85, program mgr. 1985-88; engrg. mgr. GTE Government Systems, Mtn. View 1988–; honors: Calif. Scholarship Fedn. 1970, Outstanding Young Men of Am. 1989, listed Who's Who in West 1992; mem. Smithsonian Instn. (assoc. 1975–), US Fencing Assn., Bay Area Mil. Miniature Soc.; rec: European medieval history, medieval arms & armor, antiques, fencing, softball. Res: 1634 Juanita Ave San Jose 95125 Ofc: GTE Government Systems PO Box 7188 Mountain View 94039

BAILEY, HAROLD EARL, environmental engineer; b. June 16, 1944, Rochester, Ind.; s. Earl Joseph and Charlene Louise (Safford) B.; m. Mary Jane Norwood, March 10, 1984; edn: BS, Purdue Univ. 1966; MS, Univ. Ariz. Tucson 1972; reg. profl. engr. Calif., Tx. Career: owner Bailey Asocs., Jackson 1977-78; project mgr. Metcalf & Eddy, Houston, Tx. 1978-83; bus. devel. Kenneth Balk & Assoc., Houston, Tx. 1983-84; chief engr. Airdex Corp. 1985-86; dir. Bailey Cons., San Diego 1986-88; deputy dir. Engring. &Water Reclamation, City of San Diego 1989-93; dir. Water Reclamation, Padre Dam Municipal Water Dist. 1994–; reclamation advr. San Diego County Water Auth. 1989–; honors: Tau Beta Pi, Who's Who Young Am. Profls.; mem: ASCE, Water Environment Fedn., Am. Water Works Assn., Water Reuse Assn. of Calif. (v.chair potable reuse regulatory subcom. 1992-94), Optimists (program chmn. 1984-85), Exptl. Aircraft Assn., Volcano Pioneers Theatre (bd. dirs. 1977-78), Big Brothers/Big Sisters (bd. dirs. 1977-78); Republican; Methodist; rec: flying, photog., camping, auto restoration. Ofc: Padre Dam MWD 10887 Woodside Santee 92072

BAILEY, HARVEY A., advertising agency executive; b. Feb. 8, 1937, Chgo.; s. Joseph C. and Evelyn Ruth B.; m. Betsy Cohen, June 11, 1989; children: Dashiell b. 1979, Jodie b. 1960, Robin b. 1964, Nathaniel b. 1992; edn: BA, Univ. Mich., Ann Arbor 1958. Career: copywriter Edw. H. Weiss & Co., Chgo.; dir. creative strategy DMB&B, Bloomfield Hills, Mich.; group creative dir. Campbell-Ewald Co., Detroit; FCB, Chgo.; creative dir. TLK, Chgo.; dir. creative svs. Clinton E. Frank Inc., Chgo. 1977-83; chmn. bd. The Bailey Group Inc., Berkeley currently; vis. advtsg. profl. Mich. St. Univ., E. Lansing 1982; guest lectr. Univ. Mich., Ann Arbor 1987; recipient numerous CLIO awards, NYC, and sev. gold medals NY Film Fest.; clubs: Renaissance Club of Detroit (1983-), San Francisco Advt. (1988); frequent contbr. mag. articles to Advertising Age. Ofc: The Bailey Group, Inc. 41 Tunnel Rd Berkeley 94705

BAILEY, JOHN THOMAS, financial executive, pharmacist, educator; b. Jan. 19, 1931, Santa Paula; s. John Tom and Anna Gertrude (Terry) B.; m. Dona M. Cagnacci, Dec. 28, 1950; children: Steven b. 1952, Thomas b. 1960, Janine b. 1967; edn: AA, Ventura Coll. 1950; BS pharm., Univ. Ariz. 1954; MPH, CSU Northridge 1975. Career: pharmacist, owner Las Posas Pharmacy, Camarillo 1964-89; chief fin. ofcr. Specialty Food Service Equipment, Inc., 1989-91; nat. advy. bd. Univ. Ariz. Coll. Pharm., Tucson 1986-; bd. dirs. Calif. Pharmacists, Inc. 1991- (secty. 1992, v.p. 1993-94); bd. trustees St. John's Coll., Camarillo 1991- (secty. 1993-94); pharm. educator Project Hope, Barbados, W. Indies 1977-78; instr. Pan Am. Health Orgn. 1977-78; cont. edn. instr. Calif. Pharmacists Assn. 1980-85; instr. St. Johns Coll., Camarillo 1963-88; gubnat. appt. mem. state advy. bd. Calif. Drug Programs, 1986-89, 89-92, v.chair 1989-90; awards: Ventura Co. Pharmacist of Year 1978, Calif. Pharmacists Assn. Bowl of Hygeia 1979, Merck Sharp & Dohme award 1988; mem: Am. Pharmaceutical Assn. (Fellow 1991, Daniel B. Smith Medal 1992), Academy Pharm. Practice (exec. com. 1987-88), Calif. Pharmacists Assn. (pres. 1987), Am. Coll. Apothecaries (fellow), NARD (nat. com. 1987-89); civic: Habitat for Humanity (Ventura Co. chair 1994-), Camarillo Boys & Girls Club (dir. 1990-, v.p. 1991-92), City Planning Commn. Camarillo (commr. 1965-68), Ventura Co. YMCA (steering com.), Pleasant Valley Lions Club (pres. 1965); mil: capt. USAF 1955-57; Republican; R.Cath.; rec: track coaching, skiing. Res: 260 Mission Dr Camarillo 93010

BAILEY, K. DALE, psychologist; b. May 10, 1936, Belvedere, So.Carolina; s. Samuel K. and Emma M. (Thompson) B.; m. Gwendolyn McKeithen, 1964 (div. 1972); children: Brenda Susan b. 1967, Phillip Oliver b. 1969; m. Phyllis Kay Bekemeyer, June 23, 1984; edn: BA, Coll. of Wooster, Ohio 1958; STB, Harvard Div. Sch., 1961; ThD, Sch. of Theol. at Claremont 1967; cert. Manchester, Oxford, England 1960. Career: minister of counseling, First Methodist Ch., Pasadena 1963-64; priv. practice Albany 1994-95; cons. Pasadena Council of Churches 1966-69, S.F. General Hosp. 1974-75; Valencia St. Med. Clinic, S.F. 1974-84, Am. Internat. Assurance Co., Singapore 1978-79; mem: Am. Psychological Assn., Alameda Co. Psychological Assn.; Presbyterian; rec: remodeling, landscaping. Res: 1250 Washington Ave Albany 94706

BAILEY, MICHAEL JOHN, computer scientist; b. Oct. 16, 1953, Phila.; s. Theodore W. and Anne (Pomeroy) B.; edn: BSME, Purdue Univ., 1975, MSME, 1976, PhD, 1979; Calif. lic. EIT. Career: tech. staff Sandia Nat. Labs, Albuquerque 1979-81; asst., assoc. prof. Purdue Univ., 1981-85; dir. adv. devel. Megatek, San Diego 1985-89; mgr. of sci. visualization San Diego Supercomputer Ctr., San Diego 1989-; assoc. adj. prof. UC San Diego, 1989-; cons. in field; recipient Ralph Teeter Award SAE 1983; mem. Assn. Computing Machinery 1979-, ACM Siggraph (dir. 1986-90, conf. co-ch. 1991), Nat. Computer Graphics Assn. 1980-, Am. Soc. Mech. Engrs. 1976-. Ofc: SDSC, PO Box 85608 San Diego 92186

BAILEY, TRACEY LEIGH, acupuncturist, herbalist; b. Jan. 14, 1960, Torrance, Calif.; d. Barry C. and Susanne Mae (LeVan) B.; m. Gary Eugene Beck, Sept. 22, 1991; children: Carter b. 1992 dau. Bailey b. 1994; edn: El Camino Coll., Torrance, Calif., 1978-80, 1982-83; Coll. of the Virgin Islands, St. Thomas, 1980-81; Calif. Acupuncture Coll., L.A., 1984-86; MS, O.M.D., SAMRA Univ., L.A., 1986-88; adv. study in Oriental medicine, Zhejiang Univ., Hangzhou, China P.R.C., 1990; lic. acupuncturist, Doctor of Oriental Medicine, Calif. Career: staff acupuncturist, Turnaround Drug Treatment Ctr., L.A., 1987; acupuncturist/herbalist, Adv. Sports Care and Chiropractic Clinic, Redondo Beach, 1989-90; doctor of Oriental medicine, clinic dir., Ocean Side Acupuncture, Manhattan Beach, 1991-; tchr., South Bay Adult Sch., Manhattan Beach, 1990-; tchr./lectr., UC Long Beach, 1990-; lectr., Redondo Beach Sr. Citizens, 1990-; mem. Calif. Acupuncture Assn., 1987-, Am. Assn. of Acupuncture & Oriental Medicine, 1992-, Manhattan Beach C. of C.; editor: book, Dermatology-Chinese Medicine, 1990; rec: Koshiki karate. Ofc: Ocean Side Acupuncture 1104 Highland Ave Suite 1 Manhattan Beach 90266

BAINTON, DOROTHY FORD, pathologist; b. June 18, 1933, Magnolia, Miss.; d. Aubrey Ratcliff and Leta (Brumfield) Ford; m. Cedric R. Bainton, Nov. 28, 1959; children: Roland J. b. 1961, Bruce G. b. 1963, James H. b. 1968; edn: BS, Millsaps Coll., Jackson, Miss., 1955; MD, Tulane Sch. of Medicine, New Orleans, La., 1958; MS, UC San Francisco 1966. Career: postdoctoral res. fellow UC San Francisco 1963-69, postdoctoral res. pathologist 1966-69, asst. prof. path. 1969-75, assoc. prof. path. 1975-81, prof. path. 1981-, chair pathology dept. 1987-94, vice chancellor academic affairs 1994-; vis. prof. cell biology Univ. Tex., Dallas, 1983; mem. editorial bds.: Blood Cells 1974-, Jour. of Experimental Medicine 1981-84, Am. Jour. of Path. 1983-, Experimental Hematology 1984-88, Comparative Haematology Internat. 1991-; awards: Alpha Omega Alpha 1957-, NIH career devel. award 1970-75, Millsaps Coll. Alumna of Yr. 1978, NIH grantee cancer res. 1978-87, soc. adv. sci. 1979-89, heart, lung & blood 1983-86, NIH merit award HLB 1986-96, career recognition award Women in Cell Biology 1989, Inst. of Medicine, Nat. Acad. of Sci. 1990, Tulane Med. Sch. Outstanding Alumnus 1993; mem: Am. Soc. for Cell Biology 1966-, Am. Soc. for the Advancement of Sci. 1968-, Am. Assn. of Pathologists 1977-, Am. Heart Assn. 1987-, Assn. of Am. Physicians 1987-, others; author: numerous med. book chapters, jour. articles, abstracts; Democrat; Quaker; rec: gardening. Ofc: Office of Academic Affairs Box 0400 Univ. of Calif. San Francisco 94143-0400

BAIRD, RAND JAMES, chiropractor; b. Mar. 29, 1948, Chgo.; s. Arch Emery and Harriet Mary (Kowalski) B.; edn: BS in med. record adminstrn., Univ. Ill., Chgo. 1970; BA in psych., Univ. Ill., Urbana 1972; MPH, Univ. Ill. Med. Sch., 1975; DC, Cleveland Chiropractic Coll., 1982; lic. DC, Calif. 1982. Career: assoc. dir. med. records Michael Reese Hosp., Chgo. 1970-71; asst. dir. med. records Cook County Hosp., Chgo. 1971-74; asst. adminstr./dir. med. records Rush-Presbyn.-St. Luke's Med. Ctr., Chgo. 1974-77; dir. med. records Cedars-Sinai Med. Ctr., Beverly Hills 1978-79; pvt. solo practice of chiropractic, Torrance 1982-; bd. trustees Cleveland Chirop. Coll. Bd. of Trustees, 1989-; cons. various hosps., nursing homes, coll. clinics; instr., post-grad. faculty Thornton Comm. Coll., South Holland, Ill. 1975-77, Pierce Comm. Coll. 1978-82, Pasadena Coll. of Chirop. 1985, 86, Palmer Coll. of Chirop.-West 1986, Cleveland Chirop. Coll. of Kansas City 1985, 89, Logan Coll. of Chirop., St. Louis, Mo. 1987, Western States Chirop., Portland, Oreg. 1983, 1985-; med. staff Pacific Hosp., Long Beach 1988-; assoc. prof. L. A. Chiropractic Coll., 1985-; negotiator, rep. ACA, ICA, CCE, CCA and the Canadian Chirop. Assn. in negotiations with APHA, 1979-; mem: Internat. Chiropractors Assn. (seminar speaker 1987, 88, hosp. privileges com. 1985-, Disting. Fellow 1985, ICA merit award 1984), Internat. Coll. Chiropractors Inc. (Fellow 1987), Am. Chiropractic Assn. (pub. health com. 1987-, merit service award 1984), Calif. Chirop. Assn. (seminar speaker 1985, hosp. privileges com. 1985-, Disting. service award 1989-90), Los Angeles S.W. Chirop. Soc. (disting. service award 1983-84, 84-85, 89-90, L.A. Co. Chiro. Soc. (disting. service award 1989-90, Botterman Memorial award 1985-86), Am. Mensa, Am. Pub. Health Assn. (radiol. health sect., chirop. forum, Council Govs.), Am. Med. Record Assn., Council on Chirop. Edn. (chmn. pub. health panel 1984-), Delta Omega 1985-, NY Acad. Scis. 1985-; publs: 40+ articles in 10 different profl. jours., numerous seminars; Republican; R.Cath.; rec: ice hockey player, writing, bicycling, travel. Ofc: Chiropractic Health Center 3750 Sepulveda Blvd Torrance 90505-2513

BAISHIKI, SADAO, quality engineer; b. Apr. 26, 1922, Stockton; s. Toichi and Tsune (Wada) B.; m. Midori Yokoi, Sept. 30, 1944; children: Rodney S. b. 1945, Yukiye (Baishiki) b. 1946; edn: AA, Stockton Jr. Coll./Coll. of Pacific 1942, radio & TV tech. Am. Radio Inst. 1947, Univ. of Buffalo 1957, Capitol Radio Engring. Inst. 1961-63; cert. quality engr. ASQC, 1970; reg. prof. quality engr. Calif., 1976. Career: TV trouble shooter Colonial Radio, Buffalo, N.Y. 1948-49; insp. lab. tech. Sylvania Elec. Prod. Inc. 1950-53; supr. quality control lab., Batavia, N.Y. 1954-57; component engr., Batavia, N.Y. 1958-59; mgr. quality control, Santa Cruz, Calif. 1959-61; prod. mgr. 1962; mgr. vendor qual. control 1963-66; mgr. quick reaction prod. qual. control 1967-69; qual. mgr. Mt. View 1970-78; ret. Sylvania/Gen. Tel. 1978; qual. program mgr. ESL Sunnyvale 1978; qual. engr., cert. NASA soldering instr., set up program and taught at Aertech 1979; prod. engr. Varian Assocs. Santa Clara 1979-1984; prod. engr. mgr. Varian 1985; senior qual. engr. 1986-88, retired; instr. basic electronics Cabrillo Coll. 1959-66, Evening Sch. Santa Cruz H.S. 1961-62, total qual. control San Jose City Coll. 1966-68, advy. bd. Qual. Control San Jose City Coll. 1965-66; mem. IEEE (1959-/life mem.), ASQC (senior mem., Monterey Bay Area sect. organizer and ofcr. 1959-/life mem.), VFW Post 8985; civic: Sylvania GTE Quarter Century Club, Watsonville Adult Buddhist Assn. (pres. 1987), Brooklyn PTA (pres. 1959); mil: pfc. US Army 1944-45; Republican; Florin Buddhist Ch.; rec: water skiing, bowling, golfing, outdoors. Res: 1320 Valley Brook Ave Sacramento 95831

BAKER, CAMERON, lawyer; b. Dec. 24, 1937, Chgo.; s. D. Cameron and Marion (Fitzpatrick) B.; m. Katharine Solari, Sept. 2, 1961; children: Cameron b. 1963, Ann b. 1964, John b. 1967; edn: Univ. of Notre Dame 1954-57; AB, Stanford Univ. 1958; LLB, UC Berkeley 1961, admitted to practice: Calif. Supreme Ct. 1962, US Dist. Ct. (So. Dist. Calif. 1962, No. Dist. Calif. 1963), US Ct. of Appeals (9th Cir.) 1963. Career: atty., Adams, Duque and Hazeltine,

Los Angeles 1961-62; Pettit & Martin, San Francisco 1962-95 (exec. com. 1971-82, 1984-88, mng. ptnr. 1972-81, 1984-87); Farella, Braun & Martel, S.F. 1995–; dir. Lassen Volcanic Nat. Park Found.; elected City Council, Belvedere 1976-80, mayor 1978-79; mem: Am. Bar Assn. (sects. on bus. law, and internat. law and practice), San Francisco Bar Assn. (dir. 1966, 72-73), San Francisco Barristers' Club (pres. 1966), Belvedere Comm. Found. (trustee), Boalt Hall Alumni Assn. (dir. 1982-84); clubs: Bohemian, Tiburon Peninsula. Res: 38 Alcatraz Ave Belvedere 94920 Ofc: Farella, Braun & Martel 235 Montgomery St 30th Flr San Francisco 94104

BAKER, D. KENNETH, college president; b. Oct. 2, 1923, Glasgow, Scotland, nat. 1956; s. David Thomas and Edith Rose (Horner) B.; m. Vivian Christian Perry, Sept. 13, 1947; 1 son, Richard R., b. 1955; edn: BSc, McMaster Univ. (Hamilton, Can .) 1946; PhD, Univ. of Penna. 1953. Career: asst., assoc., prof. of physics, Union College, Schenectady, NY 1953-65; mgr. profl. personnel and univ. relations General Electric Resrch. and Devel. Ctr., Schenectady, NY 1965-67; acting pres. St. Lawrence Univ., Canton, NY 1969 (Feb.-Sept.), v.p. and dean, 1967-76; pres. Harvey Mudd Coll., Claremont, Calif. 1976–; cons.: Alco Products, Schenectady, NY 1954-55; Gen. Elec. Co., Schenectady 1956-57; Nat. Sci. Found., W.D.C. 1954-64; Agy. for Internat. Devel., W.D.C. 1962; Ronald Press Co., NYC 1964; advr. Advy. Council Los Angeles Council of Engrs. and Scientists, 1976-78; mem. (chmn. 1982, 83) Advisory Com. Inst. for the Advance. of Engring. 1978–; mem: American Inst. of Physics, Rotary (Claremont), California Club (LA), Newcomen Sunset, Sunset (Pasa.), University Club (Claremont); co-author w/A.T. Goble: Elements of Modern Physics. Res: 495 East Twelfth St Claremont 91711 Ofc: Harvey Mudd College, Kingston Hall, Claremont 91711

BAKER, DUANE RAYMOND, security systems company president; b. Los Angeles; s. Raymond H. and Nola Althea (Jones) B.; m. Margaret Jean Wadsworth, Sept. 7, 1951 (div. 1982); m. Janet H. Ekstrand, July 10, 1982; children: Lynn b. 1953, Robin b. 1954, Joy b. 1956; edn: BS police sci., CSU Los Angeles, 1958, spl. courses USC 1964-67. Career: dep. sheriff/lt. L.A. County Sheriff Dept., Los Angeles 1954-64; chief of police Glendora Police Dept., 1964-68; chief of police Glendale Police Dept., 1968-82; asst. director security L.A. Olympic Organizing Com., 1982-84; pres./gen. mgr. Baker Security Systems, Thousand Oaks 1985–; lectr. USC, CSU Long Beach, 1964-82; past pres. Calif. Police Chiefs Assn. (1977-78), Calif. Peace Officers Assn. (1978-79), L.A. Co. Peace Officers Assn. (1979-80); honors: outstanding citizen of year Glendale Bd. of Realtors (1978), outstanding public service Glendale C.of C. (1980); mem: Am. Soc. for Industrial Security (1984–), Rotary Internat., Glendale (dir., v.p. 1968-82); club: Sunset Hills CC; publs: numerous profl. articles, 1968-82; mil: cpl. USMC 1950-53; Republican; Methodist; rec: pvt. pilot, boating, golf. Res: 12446 Presilla Rd Camarillo 93012 Ofc: Baker Security Systems, Inc. 210 Conejo Ridge Ave Ste 200 Thousand Oaks 91360

BAKER, ELAINE MARGARET, healthfood restaurateur, cookbook author, nutritionist, artist; b. July 25, 1925, Vancouver, B.C. (Am. parentage); d. George McLeod and Olive Margaret (Marsh) Ross; m. James E. Baker, Aug. 25, 1952 (div. 1963); children: Beau b. 1953, Bart b. 1957, Ben b. 1963; edn: BA, and grad. studies, 1943-50: Univ. Wash., Seattle, Art Center Coll. of Design, Pasa., Chouinard Art Inst., L.A., Cal-Art (full scholarship 1949-50). Career: asst. fashion artist Best's Apparel, Seattle 1950-51; fashion layout artist J.W. Robinson, Los Angeles 1951-52; art dir. Coulter's Dept. Store, Los Angeles 1955-57; restaurateur, co-creator, ptnr. Aware Inn (pioneer gourmet health food restaurant), West Hollywood 1958-63, sole prop. 1963-78; creator, co-owner Old World Restaurant (pioneer family-style health food) West Hollywood, Beverly Hills, Westwood, Palm Springs, 1965-67, sold concept 1967; nutritionist/instr. Pritikin Longevity Center, Santa Monica 1980-83; prop. Aware Food Service (catering & food cons. service), Malibu 1984–; awards: million dollar club for selling most U.S. savings bonds USN Supply Depot, Seattle, 1944; best editorial art Pac. Northwest Art Directors Show, 1951; Aware Inn rated Three Star restaurant So. Calif. Rest. Writers Assn., L.A. (1971, 72, 73, 74, 75), rest. critic Paul Wallach's "E" award for Aware Inn (1974); mem. MOCA Art Mus. (charter 1985–), Malibu Community Ctr., 1985–, Gamma Phi Beta Sor.; Democrat; rec: drawing, crafts, int. decor, garden, parapsychology.

BAKER, GEORGE ALLEN, mathematics educator; b. Oct. 31, 1903, Robinson, Ill.; s. Edward Sheridan and Ida (Everingham) B.; m. Grace Elizabeth Cummins, June 12, 1930; children: George Allen Jr., John Cummins; edn: BS, Univ. Ill., 1926, PhD, 1929. Career: res. fellow Columbia Univ., N.Y.C., 1929-30; assoc. statistician USPHS, WDC 1929; prof. math. Shurtleff Coll., Alton, Ill. 1931-34, Miss. Women's Coll., Hattiesburg, 1934-36; statistician Dept. Agri. Bur. Home Econs., Birmingham and Wash. DC, 1936-37; prof. math., stats. UC Davis, 1937–, faculty research lectr. 1955-56; mem: Inst. Math. Stats. (fellow), Biometric Soc. (v.p. 1950), Am. Math. Soc., Math. Assn. Am., Am. Statis. Assn., Econometric Soc., AAAS (fellow), Sigma Xi, Pi Mu Epsilon, Gamma Sigma Delta; author: Statistical Techniques Based on Probabilistic Models (1962), contbr. articles to profl. jours. Res: 507 Eisenhower St Davis 95616 Ofc: Univ. Calif. Dept. Math., Davis 95616

BAKER, GUY EUGENE, insurance agent; b. April 16, 1945, San Bernardino; s. Luther Thomas and Kathlyn B.; m. Colleen Dee Hubbard, July 15, 1967; children: Stacie b. 1969, Todd b. 1971, Andrew b. 1980, Ellen b. 1982; edn: BS econ., Claremont McKenna Coll. 1967; MBA fin., USC 1968; MSFS, Am. Coll. 1984; MSM, 1985; chartered life underwriter, chartered fin. cons., cert. fin. planner, reg. health underwriter. Career: sales Pacific Mutual, Newport Beach 1966-81; pres. Assoc. Ins. Concepts 1977–; coboard Bayly Martin & Fay Compensation Strategies, Costa Mesa 1984-86; mng. ptnr. Baker Thomsen Assoc., Newport Beach 1986–; faculty UC Irvine 1985–; bd. dirs., faculty, speaker Am. Coll., Bryn Mawr 1985; speaker CLU Televideo Conf. (5/94, 11/95); awards: Preston Hotchkis Disting. Achievement Award 1995, elected to Pacific Mutual Council of Leaders 1995, Gen. Agents & Mgrs. Assn. Orange Co. agent of year 1978, Pacific Mutual agent of year 1977, Preston Hotchkiss Award 1971; mem: Top of the Table (bd. dirs.), Assn. Advanced Underwriting (bd. dirs.), Million Dollar Round Table (past dir.), Orange Co. Assn. Life Underwriters (past pres.), Am. soc. CLU and CHFC, Internat. Assn. Fin. Planners, Mexico Christian Missions (bd. dirs. 1989–), Mission Viejo CC; articles pub. in profl. jours., 1977–, 250 speeches on sales motivation, spoke in Australia, Singapore 1995; author: Bakers Dozen, 1989, The Box-The Key to Understanding Life Insurance, 1994, Why People Buy, 1995; Republican; Christian; rec: piano, writing, golf. Ofc: BTA Advisory Group 1001 Dove St Ste 240 Newport Beach 92660

BAKER, LAWRENCE COLBY, JR., insurance executive; b. Oct. 6, 1935, Carleton, Mich.; s. Lawrence Colby and Margaret Ellen (Close) B.; m. Ida Wasil, June 26, 1960; edn: BA, Univ. Mich., 1957. Career: underwriter Safeco, Panorama City 1960-61; dist. mgr. Travelers Ins. Co., Los Angeles 1961-71; chief dep. commr. Calif. Dept. Ins., Los Angeles 1971-75; pres. Argonaut Ins. Co., Menlo Park 1975-85; v.p., gen. mgr. Interins. Exchange of Automobile Club of So. Calif., L.A. 1985–; dir. Auto Club of So. Calif. Mgmt. Svs. Co.; trustee Am. Inst. of Chartered Property Casualty Underwriters, trustee Insurance Inst. of Am.; dir., past chmn. Calif. Workers Compensation Bd.; mem. Calif. Ins. Guarantee Assn. (past chmn.), Nat. Assn. Indep. Insurors (past gov.), Ins. Educational Assn. (past chmn.), Assn. Calif. Ins. Cos. (past treas.); mil: lt. jg USN 1957-60. Ofc: 2601 S Figueroa St Los Angeles 90007

BAKER, LILLIAN L., artist, writer, historian, lecturer, political activist; b. Dec. 12, 1921, Yonkers, N.Y.; m. Roscoe A. Baker; children: Wanda Georgia, George Riley; edn: El Camino Coll., 1952, UCLA, 1968, 77. Career: continuity writer Sta. WINS, N.Y.C. 1945-46; columnist, freelance writer, reviewer Gardena Valley News, Gardena, Ca. 1964-76; freelance writer, editor, 1971–; lectr. in field, founder/editor Internat. Club for Collectors of Hatpins and Hatpin Holders, monthly newsletter "Points" and annual Pictorial Jour., 1977–, conv. and seminar coordinator 1980-92; dir. Ams. for Hist. Accuracy, 1972, Com. for Equality for All Draftees, 1973; South Bay campaign chair S.I. Hayakawa for US Senate 1976; witness US Commn. Wartime Relocation 1981; witness US Senate Judiciary Com. 1983, US House Reps. appropriations subcom. 4/5/89, Judiciary com. 1986; honors: Freedoms Found. 1971, annual award Conf. Calif. Hist. Socs. 1983, Merit Award "for Contributions to Calif. History" scholarship category from Conf. of Calif. Hist. Socs., 1983, monetary award Hoover Instn. Stanford Univ. 1985, "The Lillian Baker Collection" estab. permanent archives Hoover Instn. Stanford Univ. 1990, Life Fellow Internat. Biographical Assn., Cambridge, Eng., listed Who's Who in World 1993-95, Who's Who in Am. 1991-95, Who's Who American Women 1988-95, Internat. Authors and Writers Who's Who 1995-96, semi-finalist No. Am. Open Poetry Contest (poem publ. in "The Coming Dawn" anthology), a 1990 Pulitzer Prize nominee, recipient 1991 "George Washington Honor Medal" in public comms. from Freedoms Found. at Valley Forge, recipient United States Flag (flown in the Capitol in remembrance of Pearl Harbor, Dec. 7, 1941, awarded by Congressman G.E. Sangmeister, 1994); mem: Nat. League Am. Pen Women, Nat. Writers Club, Art Students League N.Y. (life), Nat. Historic Soc. (founding), Nat. Trust Historic Preservation (founding), W.W.II Commemorative Assn. (adv. bd. 1993-95), The Ctr. for Civilian Internee Rights, Inc. (hon. life mem. 1995); author: Collector's Ency. of Hatpins and Hatpin Holders (1976, 2d edit. 1988, rev. 1993 3rd printing); 100 Years of Collectible Jewelry 1850-1950 (1978, rev. editions 1986, 88, 90); Art Nouveau and Art Deco Jewelry (1980, rev. editions 1985, 88, 91); The Concentration Camp Conspiracy: A Second Pearl Harbor 1981, Hatpins and Hatpin Holders: An Illustrated Value Guide (1983, updated 1988, 90); Creative and Collectible Miniatures 1984, Fifty Years of Collectible Fashion Jewelry: 1925-1975 (1986, 3d edit. 1991); Dishonoring America: The Collective Guilt of American Japanese (1988, Webb Research Group); American and Japanese Relocation in WWII: Fact, Fiction and Fallacy (1990, Webb Res. Group), The japanning of America: Redress & Reparations Demands by Japanese-Americans (1991, Webb Res. Group); 20th Century Fashionable Plastic Jewelry 1992; The Common Doom 1992 (pen-name Liliane L. Baker); Dishonoring America: The Falsification of WWII History (1994, Webb Res. Group); also articles and poetry; contbg. author Vol. VII Time-Life Ency. of Collectibles 1979; historian for Ex-POWs and Am. Survivors of Bataan and Corregidor (filed amicus curae brief Case 89-607 JG Penn Fed. Dist. Ct., WDC, testing constitutionality of PL100-383, 1988); columnist The World War II Times, 1994; num. radio and TV appearances. Address: 15237 Chanera Ave Gardena 90249-4042

BAKER, RICHARD W., structural engineer, engineering manager, architectural engineering consultant; b. Aug. 16, 1945, Glendale; s. Elwood V. and Eleanor J. (Vickers) B.; m. Judith K. Fields, July 5, 1969; children: Carrie A., Brian R.; edn: AA, Pasadena City Coll., 1965; BS in architectural engring., Calif. State Polytech. Coll., S.L.O. 1968. Career: naval architect Long Beach Naval Shipyard, 1968-69; stress engr. Lockheed Aero. Systems Co., Burbank 1969-73, 75-87, group engr. 1987-89, project structures engr., 1989-90, deputy chief engr. - F-117A, 1991-94, dir. of engring. 1994–; stress engr. Rockwell Internat., Downey, 1974; architectural engineering cons. prin., Cerritos 1972–; mem. AIAA; civic: youth coach City of Cerritos Parks & Rec. Dept. 1982-87, Frontier Little League, Cerritos (mgr. 1985-93); editor Aircraft Stress Analysis 1987; Republican; Methodist. Res: 23038 Parkview Dr Santa Clarita 91321 Ofc: Lockheed Adv. Development Co. Dept. 25-01, Bldg 608, 1011 Lockheed Way Palmdale 93599

BAKER, ROBERT M.L., JR., educator; b. Sept. 1, 1930, Los Angeles; s. Robert M.L. Baker, Sr. and Martha Ann (Harlan) Bricker; m. Bonnie Sue Vold, Nov. 14, 1964; children: Robert Randall b. 1960, Robert M.L. Baker III b. 1965, Robin Michele Leslie b. 1968; edn: BA in physics and math. (highest honors), UCLA 1954, MA in physics and applied math 1956; PhD in astronomy and engring., 1958. Career: sr. scientist Aeronutronic-Philco-Ford 1957-60; project ofcr. AFBMD (now Space Div.) 1960-61; dir. Lockheed Astrodynamics Res. Ctr. 1961-64; assoc. mgr. for math. analysis Computer Sciences Corp. (CSC) 1964-80; appt. CEO West Coast Univ. 1980, pres. 1981–; faculty, Dept. of Astronomy, UCLA 1959-63, Dept. of Engring. 1963-71; bd. dirs. Am. Data Systems, Canoga Park 1968-70; instr. USAF Acad. 1971-78; bd. dirs., treas. Internat. Information Systems Inc. 1975–; bd. mem. Transportation Sciences Corp. 1979–; dir. Dataware Devel. Corp., San Diego 1988; bd. trustees West Coast Univ. 1969, exec. com. chmn. 1973, bd. chmn. 1979–; awards: Phi Beta Kappa 1954, UCLA Physics Prize 1956, USAF rep. Internat. Astronautical Fedn., Sweden 1961, nat. chmn. astrodynamics tech. com. Am. Inst. of Aeronautics & Astronautics 1961-64, U.S. rep. Internat. Union of Theoretical and Applied Mechanics European Confs. 1962, 65, Outstanding Man of Year Jr. C. of C. 1965, invitee Astronomical Council of the Acad. of Scis. of USSR, Moscow 1967, recipient 1976 Dick Brouwer award for outstanding contributions in astrodynamics & flight mechanics; mem. Nat. Advy. Com. on Accreditation & Inst. Eligibility (appt. by Dept. of Edn. Sec. William J. Bennett) 1987; joint ed., Proceedings of the 1961 Internat. Astronautical Fedn. Cong.; ed., Journal of the Astronautical Sciences, 1963-75; author: 3 textbooks, 100+ tech. papers in astronautics and advanced marine vehicles; mil: major, USAF 1960-61; Republican; Lutheran; rec: electronics. Res: 8123 Tuscany Avenue Playa del Rey 90293

BAKER, WILLIAM P. (BILL BAKER), congressman; b. June 14, 1940, Oakland, Calif.; m. Joanne Atack; children: Todd, Mary, Billy, Robby; edn: grad. in bus. and indsl. mgmt., San Jose State Coll. Career: budget analyst State Dept. Fin., Calif.; assemblyman 15th dist. State of Calif., 1980-93; mem. 103rd and 104th Congresses from 10th Calif. dist., 1993–; vice chmn. budget writing Ways and Means Corn., 1994-91; exec. v.p. Contra Costa Taxpayers Assn.; active Contra Costa County Farm Bur.; mil: USCG, 1958-65; Republican. Ofc: House Of Representatives Washington DC 20515

BAKHOUM, YOUSSEF YASSA, pediatrician; b. Jan. 3, 1953, Cairo, Egypt; nat. 1987; s. Yassa Bakhoum and Linda Fakhry (Salama) Khalil; m. Nadia Hanna, Feb. 20, 1983; children: Jacob b. 1985, Christina b. 1988; edn: PNS, Sch. Sci. Ain Shams Univ. Cairo 1971; MBB Ch., MD w. hons. Ain Shams Univ. Sch. Medicine 1971; ECFMG 1977; bd. cert. Am. Board of Pediatrics, 1989. Career: intern Ain Shams Univ., Cairo, Egypt 1977-78; primary care physician mil. forces, Egypt 1978-79; flexible resident Zamalek Hosp. 1979-80; gen. practitioner Virgin Ch. Clin. 1980-81; clin. extern Brentwood VA Med. Center, L.A. 1981; pediatric resident Tod Babies & Children's Hosp., Youngstown, Ohio 1982-84; Tx. Tech. Univ., Lubbock 1984-85; pediatric group St. Mark Med. Group, Huntington Park 1985; pvt. practice pediatrics, Farmersville 1985–; mem: Am. Acad. Pediatrics, L.A. Pediatric Soc., CMA, Tulare Co. Med. Soc., N. Pacific Pediatric Soc., Visalia C.of C., YMCA, Farmersville C.of C., La Leche League; article pub. in med. jour. (1986-88); rec: chess, travel, music. Res: 3424 E Vasser Ct Visalia 93292 Ofc: 1014 San Juan Ste F Exeter 93221

BAKST, ABRAHAM ALFRED, engineer, real estate executive, investor, presidential advisor; b. Jan. 12, 1922, Palmer, Mass.; s. Isadore and Minnie (Kaplan) B.; a Manhattan synogogue (now a church) built in 1890 was named after his gr.gr.gr.grandfather Aaron David (orthodox rabbi in Russia); m. Pauline Day (Dep. Atty-Gen. of Hawaii 1948-9) July 10, 1948, div. 1959; 1 dau. Katherine (hd. tchr. Child Care Devel. Ctr., UCI and CSU Long Beach, 1973-6) b. 1949; edn: Bklyn. Coll. 1938-42, Univ. Hawaii 1946-7, Cal Poly 1949-50; AA in real estate, Long Beach City Coll. 1961; Orange Coast Coll. 1978-9; mil. certs., Bellevue/Naval Resrch Lab. 1943-44. Career: radar insp. War Dept., N.J. 1942; petty ofcr. USNR (radio, radar supr. P.T. Boat Squad.), So.Pac. 1942-5; teletype opr. War Dept., Hawaii 1946-7; electronic engr. all Naval and Marine Corps Air Stations, 14th Naval Dist. (H.I.), Pearl Harbor 1947-9, pioneered first VHF radio teletype and terminal network in Navy 1947, asst. proj. engr. VLF radio propa-

gation characteristic test, Pac. area 1948; electronic sci./staff Navy Dept., Inyokern 1950; electronic engr.: Douglas Aircraft, Rockwell Internat., Hughes Aircraft, Hoffman Radio, Varec Indus., 1951-8; supr. Nebeker Realty, Calif. 1958-61; owner/ broker/ investor Bakst Realty Enterprises, Anaheim 1961–; founder/ pub./ed. News Forecasting Newsletter 1958; advisor on news foresight to 8 Am. Presidents and the US Congress (1953-87, 1991-95). Honors: capt. (champion) Bklyn. Coll. chess team, H.S. champion chess team, listed in World Almanac-1942 for chess play in coll. tourn. 1941, later was Hawaiian Chess Champion; listed in P.T.Boats Knights of the Sea 1982. Jewish; rec: news analysis, chess. Address: 210 N Brookhurst St Anaheim 92801

BAKUS, GERALD JOSEPH, professor of biology; b. Dec. 5, 1934, Thorp, Wis.; s. Joseph John and Marie Loretta (Kalkstein) B.; m. Grace Elaine Munsey, Dec. 26, 1953; children: Melanie Ann b. 1962, Paul Gerald b. 1965; edn: BA in biol., CSU Los Angeles, 1955; MA zoology, Univ. Mont., 1957; PhD zool., Univ. Wash., 1962. Career: asst. prof. biol. CSU Northridge 1961-62; asst. prof. biol. USC 1962-67, assoc. prof. 1967-85, prof. biology, 1986–; staff officer Nat. Acad. Sci., Wash. DC 1969-70; chief biologist Tetra Tech Inc., Pasadena 1976-79; awards: Fulbright Fellow (1987); mem: Great Barrier Reef Com. of Australia (fellow 1976), AAAS (fellow 1981), Internat. Soc. Chemical Ecology, Pacific Sci. Assn., W. Soc. Naturalists; author: The Spanish Guitar (1977), Computers and Programs for Beginners (1984), Quantitative Ecology and Marine Biology (1990), Coral Reef Ecosystems (1994); rec: hiking, multimedia. Ofc: Dept. Biological Sciences Univ. of So. Calif., Los Angeles 90089-0371

BALASH, JEFFREY LINKE, investment banker; b. Nov. 2, 1948, N.Y., NY; s. George Everett and Jeanne Marie (Linke) B.; m. Brenda Sue Coleman, Nov. 22, 1991; stepsons: Blake S. Blivas, Ryan A. Blivas; edn: BA econs. (summa cum laude), Princeton Univ., 1970; MBA (Baker Scholar) Harvard Bus. Sch., 1974, JD (cum laude), Harvard Law Sch., 1974. Career: asst. to chmn. & CEO, Louis-Dreyfus Corp., N.Y., NY 1974-76; dir. Avon Products, 1976-79; mng. dir. Lehman Bros. Kuhn Loeb, 1979-85; mng. dir. Drexel Burnham Lambert, Beverly Hills 1985-90; founding ptnr. Anthem Partners, LP, Los Angeles 1991-92; chmn. Comstock Ptnrs., L.L.C. 1992–; awards: Churchill Scholar English Speaking Union S.F. 1970, Loeb Rhodes Fin. Prize Harvard Bus. Sch. 1973, civic: Joffrey Ballet, L.A. (bd. 1986-89), Harvard Bus. Sch. Alumni Council 1989-92, Princeton Univ. (class of 1970 major gifts com., alumni schools com.), Harvard Bus. Sch. (class of 1973 major gifts com.; prog. co-chair HBS Conf.: Information Technology, 3/96), West L.A. Little League (bd. dirs.); Republican; R.Cath.; rec: tennis, weight tng., jazz, wine, film. Res: 9430 Readcrest Dr Beverly Hills 90210-2552

BALCH, GLENN MCCLAIN, JR., clergyman, university administrator; b. Nov. 1, 1937, Shattuck, Okla.; s. Glenn McClain and Marjorie (Daily) B.; m. Diana Gale Seeley, Oct. 15, 1970; children: Bryan, Gayle, Wesley, Johnny; edn: student, Panhandle State Univ. 1958-60, So. Methodist Univ. 1962-64; BA, S.W. State Univ. Okla. 1962; BD, Phillips Univ. 1965; MA, Chapman Coll. 1973, MA in Edn. 1975, MA in Psych. 1975; PhD, U.S. Internat. Univ. 1978; postgrad., Claremont Grad. Sch. 1968-70, Univ. Okla. 1965-66; ordained minister Methodist Ch. 1962. Career: senior minister First Meth. Ch., Eakly, Okla. 1960-63, First Meth. Ch., Calumet, Okla. 1963-65, Goodrich Memorial Ch., Norman, Okla. 1965-66, First Meth. Ch., Barstow, Calif. 1966-70; asst. dean Chapman Coll., Orange 1970-76; v.p. Pacific Christian Coll., Fullerton 1976-79; pres. Newport Univ., Newport Beach 1979-82; sr. minister Brea United Meth. Ch. 1978-89; pres. and c.e.o. So. Calif. Inst., Brea 1988–; edn. cons. USAF 1974-75; mental health cons. U.S. Army 1969; cons. Hanford Police Dept. 1983–; civic bds: Comm. Advy Bd. Minority Depndents 1975, Mayor's rep. to County Dependency Prevention Commn. 1968-69, For Kid's Sake (chmn. bd. 1986-90), Brea Economic Devel. Com.; awards: man of yr. Barstow Jr. C.of C. 1969, Ea. Star religious tng. awards 1963, 1964, Broadhurst fellow 1963-65; mem. Calif. Marriage Therapists Assn., Am. Assn. for Marriage & Family Therapy, Rotary (532 dist. gov. 1987-88, 88-89), Masons, Shriners, Elks. Res: 1016 Steele Dr Brea 92621 Ofc: 1717 S State College Blvd Suite #100 Anaheim 92806

BALDWIN, JOHN DAVID, professor of sociology; b. June 24, 1941, Cincinnati, Ohio; s. Herman Jackson and Helen Thomas (Scrivner) B.; m. Janice Irene, Aug. 26, 1967; edn: BA, Johns Hopkins Univ. 1963; PhD, 1967; Albert Ludwig Univ. W. Germany 1966-67. Career prof. UCSB 1967–; awards: UCSB Prof. of Year, Pacific Soc. Assn. Disting. Scholarship; mem: AAAS, Am. Soc. Assn.; author: Behavior Principles in Everyday Life (1981, 86), Beyond Sociobiology, 1981, George Herbert Mead, 1986; rec: music, gardening, photog. Res: 4550 Via Esperanza Santa Barbara 93110 Ofc: Univ. of Calif. Santa Barbara 93106

BALDWIN, LEE EDWARD, import-export executive; b. Aug. 5, 1913, McGregor, Minn.; s. Archie H. and Ella N. (Pearthree) B.; m. Ines Muccioli; children: Edward Lee, Joyce Karen; edn: BS in engring., Univ. of Minn., 1937; reg. profl. mech. engr., Calif. (M00207). Career: chief engr. Weston Hydraulics, hydraulic & pneumatic specialists, Burbank 1945-51; chmn. bd. Ratron Internat., Ltd., 1951–, cons. in aircraft servo mechanisms and full engring. in gas purification work for the missile ind.; chmn. bd. Columbine Internat., Ltd.

1982–, builder and importer-exporter of plastic welding equipt.; cons. Flooring-Domco/Azrock 1994; mem. Nat. Roofing Contrs. Assn., Industrial Fabrics Assn., Inst. of Environmental Scis.; inventor: several servo-mechanisms patents; rec: gardening, classic autos. Ofc: Ratron International Ltd. 9471 Givens Pl. Northridge 91325

BALDWIN, PETER BARRY, tugboat company executive; b. July 16, 1941, Binghamton, N.Y.; s. Harold Scott and Mary Frances (Flemming) B.; m. Virginia Lee Federer, June 6, 1964; children: Scott b. 1965, Leslie b. 1967, Paul b. 1970, Jonathan b. 1972; edn: BA, Univ. Notre Dame 1963; MA, Georgetown Univ. 1964. Career: materials mgr. GATX, Sharon, Pa. and Chgo., Ill. 1966-73; mgr. fleet ops. Marine Transp. Lines, N.Y.C. 1973-78; gen. mgr. sales, asst. to pres. Williams Dimond & Co., Long Beach 1978-83; v.p., mgr. Foss Maritime PSW 1983–; dir., pres. Marine Exchange of Los Angeles Long Beach; mem: Propeller Club (pres. bd. govs.), Internat. Seafarers Center (founding dir., pres.); contbg. author: Handbook of Energy Tech. (McGraw Hill 1976); mil: capt. AUS 1964-66; R.Cath.; rec: sailing, tennis. Ofc: Foss Maritime Co-PSW POB 1940 Long Beach 90801

BALESTRERI, THEODORE JEROME, restaurateur/developer; b. June 30, 1940, Bklyn.; s. Vincent Jerome and Viola Georganne (Crispo) B.; m. Velma, May 16, 1971; children: Theodore, II b. 1972; Vincent Frank b. 1977; edn: Monterey Penin. Coll., 1959; grad. Lewis Hotel Mgmt. Sch., WDC; cert. (FMP) Food Mgmt. Profl., 1991. Career: ptnr/owner, founder Sardine Factory restaurant in Cannery Row area of Monterey, 1968- (respons. for redevel. of Cannery Row hist. area; corp. owns 70%), later acquired The Rogue restaurant (on Wharf #2), San Simeon Restaurant (nr Hearst Castle) San Simeon, The Gold Fork in Carmel (fmrly The Butcher Shop); current bd. chmn./pres. (parent co.) Restaurants Central/ Foursome Development; also active in commercial real estate and opr. franchise for Wendy's Internat. (3-county area, N.Calif.); guest lectr. var. state and nat. conventions, univs., bus. and financial instns., restaurant/ hotel seminars and convs.; apptd. commr. Tourism by Gov. Deukmejian, 1988–, Gov. Wilson, 1992–; honors: Gold Plate Award, Am. Acad. of Achievement 1982, Silver & Gold Plate Awards, Internat. Foodservice Mfrs. Assn. 1984, Hon. Dr. of Foodservice, NAFEM 1985, Hon. DBA in hospitality mgmt. Johnson & Wales Univ. 1987, Escoffier Soc. Award Medallion, Restaurant Bus. Mag. Leadership Award 1989, Edn. Found. of NRA Diplomate Award, numerous civic awards; feature cover article w/wife Velma, Money Mag. (11/81); restaurant awards for The Sardine Factory incl. The Ivy Award (Travel/ Holiday Mag., 1971–), Di Rona Award 1993, Nation's Rest. News Hall of Fame, Mobil Travel Guide Award, The Armstrong Gourmet Guide as one of Calif.'s Top 10 Restaurants, one of 50 restaurants in USA to serve at Pres. Reagan's Inauguration 1981, 1985; mem. Nat. Restaurant Assn. (dir., pres. 1985-86); NRA/ACF Culinary Team Found. (chmn. 1992), Edn. Found. of NRA (dir., chmn. 1991-92), Distinguished Restaurants of No. Am. (chmn. 1993-94), Calif. Restaurant Assn. (dir., pres. 1983-84), The Culinary Inst. of Am. (dir., corp. mem.), Monterey Peninsula Hotel and Restaurant Assn. (dir., past pres.), No. Calif. Restaurant Assn. (dir., past pres. & founder), Confrerie de la Chaine des Rotisseurs (dir., past chpt. pres.); mil: US Army; R.Cath.; rec: tennis, golf, racquetball. Res: POB 655 Pebble Beach 93953 Ofc: Restaurants Central/ Foursome Development 765 Wave St Monterey 93940

BALL, JOSEPH ANTHONY, lawyer; b. Dec. 16, 1902, Stuart, Iowa; s. Joseph Anthony and Ellen (Ryan) B.; m. Elinor Thon, April 21, 1931 (dec. 1972); m. Sybil Speer McEwen, Oct. 9, 1974; children: Mary Patricia b. 1936, JoEllen b. 1940; edn: BA, Creighton Univ. 1925; LLB, USC, 1927. Career: dep. dist. atty Los Angeles Co. Dist. Atty., 1928; sole practice, Long Beach 1929-48; sr. ptnr. Ball Hunt Hart Brown & Baerwitz, Long Beach and Los Angeles 1949-90; ptnr. Carlsmith Ball Wichman Murray Case & Ichiki 1990-95, Carlsmith Ball Wichman Case & Ichiki 1995–; counsel Commn. to Investigate Assassination of Pres. Kennedy 1964; instr. USC, 1958, 60, 62, 64, 68, 70; Loyola Law Sch., L.A. 1980; faculty Nat. Inst. Trial Advocacy, Boulder, Colo. 1975, 76; awards: L.A. Co. Bar Assn. Shattuck Price Meml. 1973, UCSF Hastings Coll. Law Great Advocate 1981, Am. Coll. Trial Lawyers Samuel E. Gates, Pepperdine Univ. Hon. LL.D; mem: Am. Coll. Trial Lawyers (past pres.), Am. Bar Assn., (litigation sect. spl. com. on discovery abuse); author textbook Criminal Law & Procedure, 1972; Democrat; R.Cath.; rec: golf. Res: 4281 Country Club Dr Long Beach 90807 Ofc: Carlsmith Ball Wichman Case & Ichiki POB 1287 Long Beach 90801

BALLINGER, CHARLES EDWIN, educator, association executive; b. June 3, 1935, West Mansfield, Oh.; s. William Edwin and Mildred Arlene (Jester) B.; m. Venita Dee Riggs, June 12, 1982; edn: BA, De Pauw Univ., 1957; MA, Ohio State Univ., 1958, PhD, 1971. Career: sch. tchr., Ohio, 1958-62; lab. sch. instr. Ohio State Univ., Columbus 1962-64; asst. supt. of schs. N. Canton City Schs., Ohio 1964-67; cons. Franklin County Schs., Ohio 1967-70; cons. Ohio Dept. of Edn., 1970-71; curriculum coordinator San Diego County Schs., San Diego, Ca. 1971–; exec. dir. Nat. Assn. for Year-Round Education, San Diego 1980–; mem: Assn. for Supvn. and Curriculum Devel. 1964–, Am. Education Research Assn. 1967–, Phi Delta Kappa 1967–; author: Year-Round School 1987; Republican; United Methodist. Ofc: Nat. Assn. for Year-Round Education, 6401 Linda Vista Rd San Diego 92111

BALLOT, MICHAEL HARVEY, professor of business administration; b. Jan. 8, 1940, NY, NY; s. Max and Claire (Bayer) B.; m. Nancy Dianne Christiansen, Feb. 23, 1963; children: Michele b. 1964, David b. 1968, Edward b. 1968; edn: BME, Cornell Univ., 1962; MBA, Univ. of Santa Clara, 1965; MA econ., PhD bus., econ., Stanford Univ., 1968, 1973. Career: mfg. engr. Lockheed Missles/Space, Sunnyvale 1962-64; stds. engr. Beckman Instruments, Palo Alto 1964-65; asst. prof. economics CSU Chico, 1968-71; asst., assoc., full prof. bus. adminstrn., Eberhardt Sch. of Bus., Univ. of the Pacific, Stockton 1971–; cons. U.S. Dept. Transp., Stockton 1973, Stockton Econ. Devel. Agy. 1971, 85-86, Stockton State Hosp. 1974; arbitrator Better Bus. Bur., Stockton 1979–; honors: Beta Gamma Sigma 1964, Stanford fellow 1965, 68; mem: Decision Scis. Inst., Am. Econ. Assn., Industrial Rels. Research Assn., Ops. Mgmt. Assn., Soc. for Computer Simulation; author: Dec.-Making Models in P/OM, 1986, Labor-Mgt. Rels. in Changing Environment, 1992, num. articles, papers for Labor Law Journal, DSI, AFIPS, SCS, 1968–; rec: racquetball, travel. Res: 5149 Gadwall Cir Stockton 95207 Ofc: Eberhardt School of Business, University of Pacific 3601 Pacific Ave Stockton 95211

BANCROFT, DAVID PHILLIPS, lawyer; b. Sept. 14, 1937, Hartford, Conn.; s. P.S. and Mildred Ann (Provost) B.; m. Cheryl H. Hagenberger, July 27, 1963; children: Jennifer b. 1966, James b. 1972, Jessica b. 1978; edn: BA, Swarthmore Coll., 1960; JD, Univ. Chgo. Law Sch., 1963; admitted bar: Dist. Col. 1964, Calif. 1976. Career: trial atty. U.S. Dept. Justice, Wash. DC 1963-66, asst. U.S. Atty., U.S. Dept. Justice, San Francisco 1966-69, 71-78, and chief Special Projects, S.F. 1971-78, assoc. dir. Nat. Com. on Reform Fed. Crim. Laws, Wash. DC 1969-71; ptnr. Sideman & Bancroft, S.F. 1978–; honors: Am. Jurisprudence Award in crim. law (1962), atty. generals award for superior performance U.S. Dept. Justice, Wash. DC (1977); mem. Calif. State Bar Assn., Bar Assn. S.F. (bd. 1980-82), Fed. Bar Assn. (v.p. 1989–); publs: articles on bus. crime P.L.I., A.B.A.; Republican; Prot.; rec: mountain hiking, travel, art hist., geographic explorations. Res: 2934 Broderick St San Francisco 94123 Ofc: Sideman and Bancroft, 8th Flr One Embarcadero Ctr San Francisco 94111

BANDMAN, EVERETT, molecular cell biologist; b. June 29, 1947, New York; s. Aaron and Dorothy (Feluren) B.; m. Elizabeth Mullenbach, May 1, 1982; children: Sherry b. 1969, Evan David b. 1984; edn: BS, City Coll. N.Y. 1969; PhD, UC Berkeley 1974. Career: postdoctoral fellow Harvard Med. Sch., Boston, Mass. 1974-76; UC Berkeley 1976-78, asst. research zoologist 1978-81; asst. prof. UC Davis 1982-86, assoc. prof. 1986-90, prof. 1990–; awards: Calif. Beef Council George M. Strathean Research 1987; mem: ASCB, AAAS, NYAS, IFT, Sigma Xi. Ofc: Univ. of Calif. Dept. of Food Science Davis 95616

BANDONG, PAUL ANTHONY, high-technology business consultant, investor; b. Ft.Carson, Colo., Apr 21, 1956; s. Isidro Sevidal and Rosalia (Martinez) B.; edn: grad. U. S. Military Academy, West Point 1977. Career: pres., owner Mgmt. Cons. Svc., Menlo Park 1978–; sr. Assoc., staffing and mgmt. Cons. Beckstead & Assoc. Santa Clara 1978-81; v.p. bus. devel. & mktg.Ward Cons. Group, San Jose, 1981-82; v.p. product devel. , mktg., fin., ops. Advanced Custom Computer Engring. Labs, Santa Clara 1982; exec. v.p. fin., ops. product devel. Daystar Learning Corp., Palo Alto 1983-84; v.p, fin., ops., bus. devel., product devel., mktg. Nat. Computer Tng. Inst., Fremont 1984; pres., c.o.o., c.f.o. PCC/Systems, Inc., Menlo Park 1985; group mgr,. quality assurance/product devel. Network Products Apple Computer, Cupertino 1986-88; pres. owner Prosperity Art/Investment, Prosperity Pubs. Prosperity Cons., Menlo Park 1989–; founder, prin., mng. ptnr. Future Vision Investment Group I & II, Menlo Park 1991–; lectr. seminars in leadership & mgmt., Natl. Right to Life Com.1985–, org., author, free lance writer; Nat. Rep. Congr. Com.1981–; deacon 1st Bapt. Ch., Menlo Park 1982-83; asst. coach girls varsity basketball Mountain View HS 1987-91; hd. coach batam div. Pop Warner Football 1980; asst. coach womens basketball De Anza Coll. 1987; asst. coach ASD/USA womens basketball teams, summer Internat. Champions, 1987-89; mem. Smithsonian Inst., Profl. and Tech. Cons. Assn., NRA, Churchill Club, Commonwealth Club (San Francisco), Nat. Assn. for the Self-Employed, Art Collectors Circle; mil: US Army 1975-77 Res: 106 Marigold Way Salinas 93905 Ofc: Management Cons Svc 1240 Hobart St Menlo Park 94025-5517

BANGASSER, RONALD P., physician; b. Jan. 25, 1950, Freeport, Ill.; s. Paul Francis and Florence (Ihm) B.; m. Susan, June 19, 1971; children: Debra b. 1978, Sandra b. 1981; edn: BA, Northwestern Univ. 1971; MD, Chgo. Medical, 1975. Career: hyperbaric oxygen research St. Lukes Presbyn. Hosp., Milw., 1975; navy diving med. officers tng., through Undersea Med. Soc., 1977; family practice residency, UCLA, 1978; pvt. practice physician Valley Family Medical Group, Yucaipa 1977-92; med. dir./bd. dir. Redlands Med. Group 1986-92; pvt. practice physician Beaver Meadow Medical Clinic 1993–; asst. med. dir. Beaver Meadow Clinic 1993–; pres. Sea To Sea Scuba Dive Shop, Inc. 1978-90; pres. Smart Center, sports medicine clinic 1987-90; med. staff Redlands Community Hosp. (hosp. bd. dirs. 1988–, chmn. continuous quality improvement com. 1992–, chief of staff 1990-92, exec. com. 1981, sec.treas. 1986-88, chmn. credentials com. 1987-89, chmn. hosp. util. rev. com. 1984-87, dir hyperbaric med. dept. 1989–, past chmn. F.P. Dept.); team phys. San Bernardino Valley Coll. 1977–, diving med. safety ofcr. CSU Long Beach 1982–, instr. nurse practitioner

UCSD 1980-82, Family Practice assoc. prof. Loma Linda Univ. 1992–; Family Practice staff instr. UCLA 1979; team phys. San Bernardino Spirit profl. baseball team 1987-92; dir. Just For You Volunteers (bd. pres. 1986-87); awards: Tiny Campora Award (1984), Sir Turtle Tourism Award Cayman (1984); mem: AMA (del. 1992–, alt. del. 1989-91, AMA HMSS chmn. REF Com. B, AMA HMSS com. on ops.), CMA (del. 1989–, alt. del. 1985-89, CMA HMSS v. chmn. 1991–, del. 1987–), San Bernardino Co. Med. Soc. (dir. 1977-78, 1980–, sec. 1988-89, v.p. 1989-90, pres. 1991-92), CALPAC (bd. dir. 1990–), Found. for Med. Care (med. dir. 1984-89, chmn. cent. practice & review com. 1986–, bd. 1984–, pres. 1986-88), Calif. Foundations for Med. Care (bd. 1987–, pres. 1991-94), Nat. Assn. Underwater Instrs. (diving instr. 1975–, reg. mgr. 1977-85, speaker annual Internat. Conf. on Underwater Edn. 8 yrs. 1976-86, conf. dir. So. Calif. Conf. on Underwater Edn. 1980-81, conf. dir. NAUI Dives Cayman 1984, instr. underwater photog.); R.Cath.; rec: scuba diving, snow skiing, swimming, hiking. Res: 12724 Valley View Redlands 92373 Ofc: Beaver Medical Group 11985 Fourth St Ste 100 Yucaipa 92399

BANGHAM, ROBERT ARTHUR, certified orthotist; b. Sept. 12, 1942, San Antonio, Tex.; s. Robert Dave and Marguerite Catherine (Wyckoff) B.; edn: orthotics and prosthetics and med. related courses Northwestern Univ., 1965, 71, 76, N.Y. Univ., 1969, Washtenaw Comm. Coll., 1971, Boston Childrens Hosp., 1979, Marshall Hale Mem. Hosp., 1980, Orthomedics Inc., Brea, Calif. 1981, Flex-Foot Inc., S.F., 1988, Nat. Orthotic Labs., Winter Haven, Fla. 1990; cont. edn. Am. Acad. of Orthotists and Prosthetists 1981-: Cert. Am. Bd. Orthotics (C.O. #821) 1971; VA B.K. Prosthetics Approved 1976–. Career: orthotist John R. Reets, C.O., Ann Arbor, Mich. 1960-65; orthotics supr. Dreher-Jouett Inc., Chgo. 1965-68; cert. orthotist, lectr. & clinician Univ. Mich. Med. Ctr., Ann Arbor 1968-75; pvt. practice, 1970-75; mgr., practitioner and clinician Wright & Filippis Inc., Alpena, Mich. 1975-78; Hittenbergers Inc., Oakland and Concord, Calif. 1978-90; western reg. mktg. mgr. Nat. Orthotic Labs., 1990;owner, founder, pres. and c.e.o. Mobile Orthotic & Prosthetic Assocs., Antioch, Calif. 1990–, patient care offices: Antioch, Oakland, and Sacramento; mem. VA Prosthetics and Orthotics Workshop Team (R&D) 1989–, author basic course "Intro. to Orthotics" taught in 100+ Acute and Extended Care Facilities 1982–, guest lectr. Tech. Sch. of Orthopedics, San Jose 1989–, lectr. profl. meetings and cont. edn. courses nat.; lic. Foster Parent and Home, Contra Costa Co., 1984–; advy. com. foster care edn. pgm. Diablo Valley Comm. Coll. 1989-92; advy. com. on ind. living svs. pgm. Los Medanos Comm. Coll., 1992; mem., past pres. 1989-90 Calif. Coalition of Allied Health Professions, appt. AB 1327 Advy. Com. (re staffing in Allied Health Professions) to Calif. Health & Welfare Agy. dept. hlth. planning & devel., 1990-92; mem: Am. Orthotic and Prosthetic Assn., Am. Acad. of Orthotists and Prosthetists (nat. bd. dirs. 1989-91, nat. sci. pgm. chmn. 1989-91, chmn. SIG/Spinal Orthotics Soc. 1991-93 and secty. SIG/Lower Extremity Orthotics Soc. 1992-93, N. Calif. Chpt. bd. dirs., rep. to Calif. Coalition of Allied Health Prof., AAOP liaison rep. to Am. Back Soc., past pres.), Internat. Soc. Orthotists and Prosthetists, Am. Acad. of Neurol. & Orthopedic Surgeons (Fellow, hd. dept. orthotics 1992), Am. Back Soc. (Fellow, inter-profl. rels. com., spinal orthotics workshop presentor 1991, v.ch. com. on orthotics); civic: Yosemite Assn.; publs: articles in profl. jours. (3), num. papers presented (1970s–); Jehovah's Witness minister; rec: reading, gardening, travel, computers. Ofc: Mobile Orthotic & Prosthetic Associates, PO Box 19600 Oakland 94619-0600 Tel: 510/482-6040 Fax 510/482-6043

BANGS, CATE (CATHRYN MARGARET BANGS), motion picture art director, interior designer; b. Tacoma, Mar. 16, 1951; d. Henry Horan and Belva Virginia (Grandstaff) B.; m. Steve Bangs, Nov 1, 1986. edn: Hammersmith Coll Art and Bldg., London, 1971; BA cum laude, Pfizer Coll., 1973; MFA– NYU, 1978. Career: owner Flying Pencil Design, Hollywood Hills 1981–; art dir. Cobra, Warner Bros. 1985; Who Framed Roger Rabbit 1986, A Year in the Life, Universal Studios 1986, Beverly Hills Cop 11, Paramount Studios 1986-87,The Seventh Sign 1987, Crime Story 1987-88, Spies, Partners and Lovers 1988, Far From Home, 1989, Hider in the House 1989, Lock Up, Tri-Star 1989, Die Harder, Fox 1989-90, Air America, Carolco 1990-91, RoboCop 3, (TV series), Man and Machine 1991-92, The Trapped, Universal 1992-93, The Birds II, Universal/Showtime 1993; production designer Lucky Day, 1990; bd. dir. Hollywood Hts. Assn.1985-87, Cahuenga Pass Porp. Owners Assn. 1990, 1st v.p. Friends of the Highland-Camrose Bungalow Village 1985–, Recipient and TV ArtDirs., Set Designers and Model Makers (cert., exec. bd. 1980–, v.p. 1989–90, pres. 1991–), United Scenic Artists; Democrat; Buddhist. Res: Angel Haven 3180 Oakshire Dr Hollywood 90068-1743

BANGS, JOHN WESLEY, III, international airport law enforcement administrator; b. Dec. 26, 1941, Phila.; s. John W., Jr. and Sarah Emily (Morcom) B.; m. Donna Louise McClanahan, June 1, 1963; children: Louis M., Terry M., John W., IV; edn: AA (summa cum laude), East L.A. Coll., 1976; Calif. Commn. on Peace Ofcr. Stds. and Tng. certs: basic, intermmediate, advanced, supvy., mgmt. Career: police ofcr. Los Angeles Police Dept., 1964–, sgt. 1970-74, lt. 1974-84, chief spl. ofcr. Los Angeles Dept. Airports Police, 1988–; lectr. USC, 1978-79; mem. Calif. Peace Ofcrs. Assn., Calif. Narcotics Ofcrs., L.A. Police Protective League, L.A. Police Relief Assn., Lions Internat.; civic: Cub Scouts Am., Ontario (cub master 1968), Boys Scouts Am., Ont. (scout master 1971),

Explorer Scouts Am., L.A. (ldr. 1976), mem. Greater L.A. Scouting Council (1976); mil: sgt. US Army 1959-62; Republican; Episcopalian. Ofc: Los Angeles Airport Police #1 World Way PO Box 92216 Los Angeles 90009-2216

BANGS, RICHARD JOHNSON, adventure travel company president; b. Aug. 24, 1950, New Haven, Conn.; s. Larry Cutler and Louise (Morton) B.; edn: BA in sociol., Northwestern Univ. 1972; MA in journalism, USC 1974. Career: pres., founder Sobek Expeditions and Sobek Productions 1973–; explorer; author: Rivergods: Exploring The World's Great Rivers. Ofc: Sobek Expeditions PO Box 1089 Hwy 49-1 Sobek Tower Angels Camp 95222

BANK, JONATHAN F., lawyer; b. May 4, 1943, Omaha, Neb.; s. Lloyd E. and Florence (Smeerin) B.; m. Carmen, Dec. 19, 1980; children: Melissa Flauren b. 1985, Andrew Lloyd b. 1990; edn: BBA, Univ. Okla. 1965; JD, Creighton Univ. 1968. Career: atty. Teledyne Inc., Los Angeles 1968-76; Buchalter Nemer 1976-94; Chadbourne & Park 1994–;mem:Excess and Surplus Lines Claims Assn., Internat. Assn. of INS Counsel (AIDA), Soc. of Fin. Examiners, counsel, Los Angeles Conf. Ins., Internat. Assn. Defense Counsel, Calif. Bar Assn., Ins. Soc., N.Y. Bar, Am. Bar Assn., Defense Research Inst.; num. articles on reinsurance pub. in profl. jours. Res: 167 Granville Ave Los Angeles 90049 Ofc: 601 S. Figueroa Los Angeles 90017

BANKS, ERNEST (ERNIE BANKS), business executive, former professional baseball player; b. Jan. 31, 1931, Dallas, Tex.; s. Eddie B.; m. Eloyee Ector, Apr. 6, 1953; edn: grad. high sch.; student Kellog Grad. Sch. of Bus., Northwestern Univ. Career: player with Kansas City Monarchs (Negro Am. League), 1950-51, 53; shortstop then 1st baseman Chgo. Cubs, 1953-71, mgr. group sales to 1982; formerly co-owner, v.p. Bob Nelson-Ernie Banks Ford, Inc., Chgo.; with Associated Films Promotions, Los Angeles, 1982-84; World Van Lines, Calif., 1984–; author (with Jim Enright) Mr. Cub; past mem. bd. Chgo. Transit Authority; active Boy Scouts Am., YMCA, named Most Valuable Player Nat. League, 1958, 59; recipient awards from Press Club 1969, awards from Jr. C. of C. 1971; inducted into Tex. Sports Hall Fame 1971, Baseball Hall of Fame 1977; mem. Nat. League All-Star Team, 1957-70; set major league record for most career grand slam home runs; mil: AUS, 1951-53, Europe. Ofc: New World Van Lines 14322 Commerce Dr Garden Grove CA 92643-4946

BANKS, GLADYS LUNELL, nurse; b. Oct. 1, 1941, Washington, Ga.; d. John W. and Magnolia (Martin) Huff; m. Howard Banks, Apr. 21, 1961; children: Sandra b. 1961, Howard Jr. b. 1963, Janet b. 1965; edn: AA, L.A. Southwest Coll., 1978; lic. Voc. Nse., 1978. Career: nse. Navy Reg. Med. Ctr. Hosp., Long Beach 1978-79; VA Hosp., Long Beach 1979-83; Las Flores Convalescent Hosp., Gardena 1984–; awards: medal of merit and Presdl. Task Force, White House, Wash. DC 1984; civic: Challengers Boys & Girls Club, L.A. 1971-75; Republican (Pres. Inner Cir., US Senatl. Club); Pentecostal, Acad. Cathedral Ch. Choir, Inglewood 1977–, Women of Faith 1983–; rec: sewing and designing, reading. Res: 1532 W 111th Pl Los Angeles 90047

BAO, JOSEPH YUE-SE, orthopaedist, microsurgery pioneer, educator; b. Feb. 20, 1937, Shanghai, China, naturalized U.S. citizen 1989; s. George Zheng-En and Margaret Zhi-De (Wang) B.; m. Delia Way, Mar. 30, 1963; children: Alice b. 1964, Angela b. 1968; edn: MD, Shanghai First Med. Coll., China 1958. Career: orthopaedist Shanghai 6th People's Hosp., Shanghai 1958-78, orthopaedist in charge 1978-79, v.chief orthopaedist 1979-84; research assoc. Orthopaedic Hosp./Univ. So. Calif., Los Angeles, 1985-90, 1994–, coord. microvascular svs. 1989-91; vis. clinical assoc. prof. Univ. So. Calif. 1986-89, clin. assoc. prof. dept. orthopaedics, 1989–, attdg. physician L.A. County-USC Med. Ctr., Los Angeles, 1986, 1990–; consulting specialist orthopaedics and reconstrv. surgery Rancho Los Amigos Med. Ctr., Downey 1986; mem: Internat. Microsurg. Soc. 1984–, Am. Soc. for Reconstrv. Microsurgery 1989–, Orthopaedic Research Soc. 1992–; author, coauthor publs. in med. jours., books on microsurgery, orthopaedic surgery 1963–, incl. Hand Replantation (1963, world's 1st reported replantation), rat toe replantation 1990 and transplantation 1993. Res: 17436 Terry Lyn Ln Cerritos 90703 Ofc: Dept. Orthopaedics LAC-USC Medical Ctr. 1200 N. State St GNH 3900 Los Angeles 90033

BARAD, JILL ELIKANN, toy company president and chief operating officer; b. May 23, 1951, NY, NY; d. Lawrence Stanley and Corinne (Schuman) Elikann; m. Thomas Barad, Jan. 28, 1979; children: Alexander b. 1979, Justin b. 1982; edn: BA English & psychology, Queens Coll. 1973. Career: product mgr. mktg. Coty Cosmetics, NY, NY 1976-78; acct. exec. Wells, Rich Green Advertising, L.A. 1978-79; product mgr. mktg. Mattel Toys, Inc. Los Angeles 1981-82, dir. mktg. 1982-83, v.p. mktg. 1983-85, sr. v.p. mktg. 1985-86, exec. v.p. product design 1986-88, exec. v.p. mktg. & product devel. 1988-90, pres., girls and activity toys div. 1989; pres. Mattel USA 1990–, pres. and C.O.O. 1992–; instrumental in more than doubling Mattel's Barbie sales since 1988, developing Mattel's successful portfolio of Disney toys, establishing Mattel as a serious contender in the activity toy category, and increasing internat. sales; dir: Bandai/Mattel, Tokyo 1987–, Arco Toys H.K., Reebok Internat. Ltd., BankAmerica Corp., Bank of Am. NT&SA, Mattel, Inc., Mattel Found. (nonprofit); bd. of trustees Queens Coll. Found.; bd. of governors Town Hall of

Calif.; honors: Business Week mag. list of Fifty Women to Watch (6/87), featured with John Amerman in Forbes Mag., 9/26/94; civic: chmn. exec. advy. bd. Children Affected by AIDS Found; Rainbow Guild/Amie Karen Cancer Fund L.A. (charter mem.), American Film Inst., L.A. Co. Mus.; rec: film, wt. lifting. Ofc: Mattel Toys, Inc.333 Continental Blvd El Segundo 90245

BARASH, ANTHONY H., lawyer; b. Mar. 18, 1943, Galesburg, Ill.; s. Burrel B. and Rosalyne J. (Silver) B.; m. Jean Anderson, May 17, 1965; children: Elizabeth b. 1965, Christopher b. 1969, Katherine b. 1970, Andrew b. 1970; edn: AB cum laude, Harvard Coll., 1965; JD, Univ. Chgo., 1968; admitted bar: Calif. 1969. Career: atty., assoc. Irell & Manella, Los Angeles 1968-71; assoc. Cox, Castle & Nicholson, 1971-74, ptnr. 1975-80; ptnr. Barash & Hill, 1980-84, Wildman, Harrold, Allen, Dixon, Barash & Hill, 1984-87, Barash & Hill, 1988-93; ptnr. Seyfarth, Shaw, Fairweather & Geraldson 1993–; bd. dir: Deauville Restaurants Inc. 1981–; trustee Pitzer Coll. 1981–, v.chmn. 1984–; bd. dir. St. Matthew's Parish Sch., Pacific Palisades 1975-78; trustee Windward Sch., 1985-86; mem: ABA (taxation, bus. law, real property sects.), Am. Bar Found. (Life Fellow), Calif. Bar Assn. (real property, bus. law and taxation sects., del. 1973-75, 76-93), L.A. County Bar Assn. (co-chmn. spl. com. prepaid legal ins. 1969-72, real property, bus. and corp. law sects., pro bono coun., trustee 1989-90), Beverly Hills Bar Assn. (bd. govs.1979-81, 88-94, pres. 1992-93), Beverly Hills Bar Assn. Found. (bd. dirs. 1981–, pres. 1983-86); Public Counsel (bd. dirs. 1980-87, pres. 1986-87, chmn. Capital Campaign 1989–);clubs: Regency (L.A.), Harvard of So. Calif. Res: 2102 Century Park Lane Los Angeles 90067 Ofc: Seyfarth, Shaw, Fairweather & Geraldson 2029 Century Park E Ste 3300 Los Angeles 90067 Ph: 310/277-7200

BARATTA, MARIO ANTHONY, civil engineer; b. Oct. 17, 1942, San Salvador, El Salvador; nat. US cit. 1961; s. Mario Augusto and Maria (Rivera) B.; m. Barbara Smith, June 13, 1964; children: Anthony Paul b. 1966, Lisa Marie b. 1969; edn: BCE, Santa Clara Univ. 1964, MBA 1983; MSCE (structures) Stanford Univ. 1971; bus. Creighton Univ. 1975-76; cert. Nat. Security Mgmt., Indsl. Coll. Armed Forces 1975; Reg. Civil Engr. Calif., Hawaii, Canal Zone. Career: mil. civil engr., cdr. US Navy 1961-84: ofcr. in chg. constrn., Yokosuka, Japan 1964-67, Canal Zone 1967-69; pub. works ops. ofcr. and co. cdr. CBMU 302, Vietnam 1969-70; asst. dir. pub. works dept. Marine Corps Air Station, El Toro, Calif. 1971-73; nuclear weapons effects ofcr. Offutt AFB, Nebr. 1973-76; ofcr. in chg. of constrn. and prodn. engring. ofcr. Naval Shipyard, Pearl Harbor, Hawaii 1976-78; asst. acquisition ofcr. Pacific Div. Naval Facilities Engring. Cmd. 1978-80; pub. works/ ofcr. in chg. constrn. Moffett Field Naval Air Sta. 1980-83; dir. Facilities Systems Ofc., Port Hueneme 1983-84, ret. 1984, decorated Bronze Star w/Combat V, Jt. Svc., Nat. Def. Svc., Navy Commdn. Medal, Nat. Defense Svc. Medal, Vietnam Svc. w/4 Stars, Rep. Vietnam Meritorious Unit Cit., Cross of Gallantry w/Palm; dir. constrn. svs. County of Santa Clara, 1984-86; v.p. Ruth & Going Inc. 1986-87; v.p. A-N West Inc./gen. mgr. San Jose br. 1987-93; proj. mgr. O'Brien-Kreitzberg & Assoc. 1993–; awards: energy conservation award Pearl Harbor Naval Shipyard 1978, commdn. Comdr. Naval Forces Southern Command 1969, Tau Beta Pi, J.H. Brunier Award ASCE/ S.F. 1989, Dean of Engineering SJSU comm. service award 1991, APWA meritorious svc. award 1991, APWA nat. merit. svc. award 1992, Santa Clara Univ. Dean of Engring. award 1994,various appreciation awards for coaching soccer teams; mem: San Jose St. Univ. Industry Advy. Bd. (chmn.), ASCE (chair nat. com. on equal opportunity pgms.), ASCE (San Jose pres. 1991-92, S.F. pres. elect 1994-95), SAME, NSPE, APWA (pres. South Bay Area chpt. 1992), CSPE, Silicon Valley Engring. Council (pres. 1990), ACELSCO (scholarship com. chair), Commonwealth Club (S.F.), CELSOC, Toastmasters Internat. (pres. Pearl Harbor Club 1978), Engineer's Club San Jose, U.S. Navy League (pres. Santa Clara Valley Council 1989, pres.'s plaque award); past pres. soccer clubs in Hawaii 1976-80 and Nebr. 1975-76; pub. article in Military Engineer 1974; rec: jogging, bowling, computers. Res: 3127 Rasmus Cir San Jose 95148 Ofc: O'Brien-Krietzberg & Assoc. 2001 Gateway Pl Ste 220W San Jose 95110

BARAZONE, MOUNQUE, holistic health practioner, massage & sports therapist, marketing executive, inventor, geosynthetic consultant, lecturer; b. Dec. 9, 1948, Cleveland, Ohio; s. Abraham and Helen (Leverstein) B.; m. Colleen S., July 12, 1992; edn: Cleveland State Univ. 1967-71; Mueller Coll. of Holistic Studies 1991-93. Career: floor supr. May Co. 1965-67; mgr., trainee F.W. Woolworth, 1967-69; mgr. Chagrin Valley "66", Moreland Hills, Ohio 1969-73; v.p. Data Information Services Corp., Chgo. 1973-78; adminstrv. asst. to the pres., W.J. Lazynski Inc. Contrs., Milwaukee 1978-80; founder/ pres./ bd. chmn. Earth Fabrics Inc., 1980-86; pres. Geotextile Apparatus and Consulting Co. (equip. mfr.) 1980–; v.p./dir. A.C.F. West Inc., Richmond, Va. 1986-89; comptroller, v.p./dir. Construction Computer Software Corp., 1989–; pres. BodyEngineering 1991–; therapist Team Dennis Conner - Stars & Stripes America's Cup Defense Boat, 1991-92, 94-95; asst. instr. Mueller Coll. 1992–; faculty ASCE Cont. Edn. course on geosynthetics; past dir. Data Info. Service Corp.; dir. Lake Calif. POA; lectr. Stanford Univ., ASCE stu. chapt. CSUF 1985, ASCE, So. Calif. 1987, US Forest Serv. 1984, 85, 86, 87; lectr. 1988–: Co. of Santa Barbara, Nev. Dept. Transp. (2), Caltrans, Calif. Geotech. Engrs. Assn., No. & So. sects., City of L.A. (5t 1989), L.A.Co. Pub. Works Dept. (5t 1988, 5t

1990), ASCE Kern br. 1991, Nat. Pavement Conv. 1993; internat. lectures 1989-Denmark (2), Sweden, Norway, Germany, Netherlands (2); awards: appreciation Geotech. Engr. Assn. 1989, tech. merit Los Angeles City Dept. Public Works 1989, tech. excellence So. Calif. Public Works Assn. 1989, lead sales distbr. Crown Zellerbach (1982, 83, 84, 85), mktg. excellence Exxon Chem. 1985, lead we. sales div. Amoco Fabrics & Fibers Co. (1986, 87, 88, 89) and top salesman distbr. 1987; mem. Assoc. Gen. Contrs. Am. (disaster assist. com.), Indsl. Fabrics Assn. Internat., Soc. Am. Mil. Engrs., Nat. Fedn. of the Blind. (Pres.'s Club), Greenpeace, PETA, Internat. Kempo Karate Assn., Am. Massage Therapy Assn., Calif. Massage Therapy Assn.; inventor: machinery to install paving fabrics on hwys. (6 US patents #4555073, 1985, continuation #4,669,330, 10/13/87), universal mounting brackets and mech. folding system (Pat. #4,705,229 11/10/87), Dual PVC Stretching mechanism for paving fabric (pat. #4,742,970 1987), material handling equip.: a fabric roll puller (pat. pend), braking mechanism for rotatable core support for a fabric roll (Pat. #4,657,199, 1987), multi-shafted adjustable roll mover (pat. pend.), device for supporting a roll of material to a vehicle (Pat. #4,664,332 1987); copyrighted Constrn. Bid Mgmt. computer system; pub. tech jours. articles and papers in geosynthetic fields, massage and sports; ednl. video in geosynthetic field; Messianic Jewish; rec: sailing, snorkel, karate, tennis, computers, flower gardening. Res: PO Box 6769 San Diego 92166-0769

BARBEE, MARGARET SOHL, organizational psychologist; b. Oct. 28, 1943, Bay City, Mich.; d. William Arthur and Carol Harmony (George) Sohl; m. Joel Ralph Barbee, July 15, 1967; edn: BA, Denison Univ. 1965; MS, No. Ill. Univ. 1967; PhD, Colo. St. Univ. 1976. Career: research asst. Ft. Logan Mental Health Center, Denver 1968-69; research psychologist Denver Gen. Hosp. Psychiatry Service 1969-72; program evaluator Law Enforcement Assistance Adminstrn., Denver 1973-75; orgn. devel. cons. Cummins Engine Co., Jamestown, N.Y. 1976-77; orgn. psychologist Univ. Calif. Lawrence Livermore Lab., 1977-94, womens' issues adv. to UN Internat. Atomic Energy Agency, 1994, Vienna, Austria; adj. faculty Univ. San Francisco 1982-88, chair, faculty of Center for Psychological Studies, Berkeley, 1985–; cons. various cos. and non-profit orgns., San Francisco 1978–; contbr. articles to profl. jours.; East Bay Volunteers for the Arts 1989–, Oakland; mem: Am. Psychological Assn., Orgn. Devel. Network (co-chair women in orgn. devel. 1985), Human Factors Soc., Inst. Noetic Scis., Alpha Kappa Delta, Psi Chi; rec: travel, jogging. Ofc: 11595 Betlen Drive Dublin 94568

BARBER, LAURAINE MARGARET, county executive; b. Sept. 14, 1930, Los Angeles; d. Fred Paul and Laura May (Sigafoose) Leonard; m. Robert Ellis Barber, Jan. 30, 1954; children: Paul Kevin, b. 1958, Cheryll Cecille, b. 1960, Michelle Louise, b. 1966; edn: AA, Glendale City Coll. 1951; BA edn., CSU Long Beach 1955. Career: tchr., Pre-School and Child Care, Glendale 1948-49, Baldwin park 1949-59; jr. high sch. tchr. Brethren Schs., 1955-72; dir. Pre-Sch., 1978-95; executive director Fedn. of Community Coordinating Councils, Los Angeles Co., 1978–, pres. 1978-85, re-elected pres. 1991-95, consultant to 80 councils and task forces re coordination of human services in L.A. County, community networking cons. to bus. corps., govt. agys. and civic orgns.; mem. L.A. Co. Commn. on Alcoholism, Narcotics And Dangerous Drugs; honors: Hannah Sullivan award, Kenyon Scudder award; mem. Calif. Assn. of Alc. & Drug Pgm. Execs.; civic: Film Advy. Bd., The Way Out Ministries (vice chmn.), Long Beach Health Advy. Com. (chmn.), So. Calif. Coalition Chemical People II (vol. coord.), L.A. Federal Exec. Bd. (v.chair U.S. Constn. Bicentennial Com.), Asian Svs. Coalition, Long Beach BACOLOD Sister City Com. (secty.), Fedn. of Filipino-Amer. Assns. Inc. (secty.), Calif. Youth Auth. Regional Citizens Com., Charles Drew Headstart Policy Council & Steering Com. (past), South Bay-Long Beach Svs. Area Advy. Com. (chair), Asian Advy. Com., Palos Verdes Substance Abuse Com., Long Beach Drug Suppression Com., L.A. Co. Dept. Mental Health Homeless & Housing Advy. Com. (chair), past ldr. Campfire Girls, Boy Scouts; author (book) You, Me, We; (record) It's Time for the We in America; devel. the community volunteer campaign theme: California Gold Rush; rec: travel, people; Republican; Prot. Res: 3109 Lees Ave Long Beach 90808 Ofc: F.C.C.C. 4060 Watson Plaza Drive Lakewood 90712

BARBER, THEODORE FRANCIS, aircraft mechanic; b. Jan. 29, 1931, Port Jervis, NY; s. Theodore and Frances Mary (Gross) B.; m. Beverly Ann Horton, Mar. 15, 1961 (div. Dec. 1965); l child, Theodore Francis Barber, Jr.; edn: student, Arlington Sch. Flight & Engring., Tillamook, Oreg., 1951-52; Jet Engine Specialist Sch., Chanute AFB, Rantou, Ill., 1952; lic. comml. eel fisherman State of Pa., 1964; career: laborer, Erie R.R., Port Jervis, NY, 1947-49; carpenter, Erie R.R., Port Jervis, NY, 1950; mail handler, Erie R.R., Jersey City, 1950-51; locomotive fireman Erie R.R., Port Jervis, 1951-59, locomotive engr., 1959-66; miniature golf course owner/operator, Matamoras, Pa., 1963-65; lipstick moulder, Kohmar Labs., Port Jervis, NY, 1966; interior installer Douglas Aircraft Co., Long Beach, Calif., 1966-67; field and svc. aircraft mechanic, Douglas and McDonnell Douglas Aircraft Co., Long Beach, 1967–; structure assembly mechanic Northrop Corp., Anaheim, Calif., 1969-70; exptl. flight test mechanic McDonnell Douglas Aircraft Co., Long Beach, 1971, 77; co-owner C&B Sabot Fiberglass Boat Mfrs., 1976; mech. test technician Space Shuttle Arrowhead Products, Los Alamitos, Calif., 1976077; B-1 bomber tool maker No. Am.

Rockwell, El Segundo, Calif., 1977; realtor, Real Estate Store, Fullerton, Calif., 1976-79; metal fitter, toolmaker, F-18, Northrop, Hawthorn, Calif., 1978-79; toolmaker, Satellite & Space Shuttle Div., No. Am. Rockwell, Seal Beach, Calif., 1984; walnut orchard grower, C&B Orchard, Fresno, Calif., 1982-83; mem: Jacksonville R.E. Investors Assn., Am. Legion, Moose, Gold Wing Road Riders, VFW; mil: USAF, 1951-55; rec: motorcycling, classic auto restoration, gourmet cooking. Res: 499 Creighton Rd Orange Park FL 32073

BARBERS, RICHARD GEORGE, academic physician, administrator; b. Jan. 12, 1949, Calasiao, Philippines, nat. US cit. 1975; s. Jesus Victor and Mary (Fernandez) B.; edn: BS, Loyola Coll. 1971, MD, Georgetown Univ. 1975; bd. cert. Internal Medicine, Pulmonary Disease, Allergy & Immunology. Career: intern Internal Medicine, USC-Los Angeles Co. Med. Ctr., 1975-76; resident, Int. Medicine, UCLA-Cedars Sinai Med. Ctr. 1976-78; postdoc. fellowship UCLA Med. Ctr. in Clin. Immunol. & Allergy, 1979-81, in Pulmonary Disease, 1981-82; adj. asst. prof. medicine UCLA Sch. of Medicine/assoc. dir., dir. UCLA Asthma and Immunologic Lung Disease Ctr., 1982-87; asst. prof. medicine Univ. Mass. Med. Sch., 1987-90; assoc. clin. prof. med. USC Sch. of Med. 1990–, dir. USC Bronchoscopy Service 1991–, medical dir. USC Lung Transplant Pgm. 1992–; participated in care of world's 1st adult living-related lung lobe transplantation performed at USC; honors: Tri Beta; Fellow Am. Coll. of Physicians, Fellow Am. Coll. of Chest Physicians, Fellow Am. Coll. of Allergy and Immunology, Fellow Am. Acad. of Allergy and Immunology, mem. Am. Thoracic Soc., Am. Fedn. of Clin. Research, Internat. Heart and Lung Transplant Soc.; publs: numerous research papers and articles in med. journals; Independent-Democrat; R.Cath.; rec: sailing, bridge, marathon runner. Ofc: Univ. of So. Calif. School of Medicine Div. Pulmonary and Critical Care Medicine, GNH 11-900, 2025 Zonal Ave Los Angeles 90033

BARGMAN, ALAN RICHARD, physician; b. June 18, 1945, Buffalo, NY; s. Max and Virginia (Breitung) B.; 1 dau. Alexandra b. 1986; edn: AB, Duke Univ., Durham, N.C. 1967; MS, Calif. St. Univ., Hayward 1971; MD UC Davis 1975; residency UC San Francisco 1978; bd. certified anesthesiologist, 1981. Career: attending staff St. Mary's Hosp., San Francisco 1978–; pres. No. Calif. Anesthesiology Soc., S.F. 1985-86; expert witness, anesthesiology 1992–; awards: Regents Scholarship, NY State 1963, Nat. Merit Scholarship (alt.) 1963, Sylvania Electric Co. scholarship, Duke Univ. 1964; mem: Am. Soc. Anesthesiology, Calif. Soc. Anesthesiology; co-author: jour. article, Protein Synthesis, 1972; rec: boating, astronomy. Ofc: St. Mary's Hospital 450 Stanyan San Francisco 94117

BARINGOLDZ, GREGG M., private practice psychologist; b. May 5, 1955, Allentown, Pa.; s. Leon and Jewel (Cooperman) B.; m. Cynthia L. Smith, Aug. 1, 1982; children: Sloan b. 1990; edn: BA, Temple Univ. 1977; MA, W.Chester St. Univ. 1982; PhD, Ball St. Univ. 1989; Licensed Psychologist, Calif. (1991). Career: naval psychologist U.S. Naval Hosp., Long Beach 1985-91, asst. hd. dept. psych. 1986-91; pvt. practice psychologist, Cerritos and Newport Beach 1991–; honors: Navy Achievement Medal, APA Letter of Commendation, Who's Who Young Profls. 1988; mem: Nat. Register for Health Svc. Providers in Psychology, Calif. Psychol. Assn., Orange Co. Psychol. Assn., Am. Bd. of Forensic Examiners, Am. Psychological Assn., Soc. Behavioral Medicine; mil: LCDR USNR 1984-91; Democrat; Jewish. Ofc: 17100 Norwalk Blvd Ste 116 Cerritos 90703

BARKER, GRACE KATHRYN, marriage and family counselor; b. June 16, Toms River, N.J.; d. Atwood Reynel and Eleanor Steinman (Magee) Applegate; son, Gregory; edn: AA, El Camino Coll., 1968; BA, CSU Long Beach, 1972; MA, Azusa-Pac. Univ., Calif. Family Study Ctr., 1977; certifs. in addictions counseling (CAARD) 1973, soc. services, 1974, adult tchg. cred., 1978, UCLA; lic. Marriage Family Child Counselor (M13716) Calif. Career: adminstrv. splst., Secty. special proj. of the Air Force, 1961-70; secty. to Dir. Engring., Internat. Pgm., USAF Space & Missile Sys. Org., 1971-74; staff counselor Drug Abuse Ctr., Ft. MacArthur, 1974-75; MFCC intern Clare Found. (alco.) 1976, and Harbor View House (comm. mental health), 1976-79; MFCC therapist pvt. practice, Torrance 1979–; originator and instr. course: Healthful Living; honors: Outstanding performance award USAF 1972-73; fmr. mem: Am. Red Cross (jr.), Am. Womens' Vol. Service, PTA (secty., hist., com. chair 1955-61), Calif. Student Soc. Welfare Assn. (state v.p. 1970-71); mem: Calif. Assn. Marriage, Family Therapists 1981–, Alumni Univ. Patrons CSULB 1986–, Azusa-Pac. Univ. 1977–, Calif. Family Study Ctr. 1981–, Soc. Work Aux. CSULB 1980–; civic: charter mem. Republican Presidential Task Force 1981–, Senatorial Club 1983–, Advy. Com. Cong. R. Dornan (1976, Dornan in '88), Gr. LA Zoo Assn. (charter 1967–), RRRC (charter 1987–), Women in the Arts (charter 1986–), L.A. Cty. Art Mus. Charter II 1987–, Natural Hist. Mus. 1983–, Nature Conservancy 1983–, Statue of Liberty Ellis Is. Found. 1984–, Friends of the Observatory 1986–, Nat. Trust for Historic Preservation 1987–, Nat. Parks Conserv. Assn. 1988–, Earthwatch 1988, Mono Lake Com. 1988–, The Wilderness Soc. 1987–; Am. Film Inst. 1988–; Clubs: Balboa Ski Club 1986–, Snowfliers Ski Club 1987–; Episcopalian; rec: tennis, dancing, travel, skiing. Res: 25819 Skylark Dr Torrance 90505

BARKER, GREG ALLEN, architect; b. Sept. 25, 1955, Minneapolis, Minn.; s. James Henry and Bonita Jean (Jacobson) B.; m. Jennifer Carol Allen, July 11, 1981; 1 dau., Jenna b. 1988; edn: BS, Calif. Polytech. St. Univ. 1978; M.Arch., Univ. Ill. 1983. Career: job captain Paul R. McAllister Architect, San Jose 1979-81; survey coordinator Hawley Stowers Architect 1981; instr., researcher Univ. Ill., Champaign 1983-84; intern architect Wallace Holm Architects, Monterey 1984-85; David Goldstein Architect, Solvang 1985-86; project mgr., v.p. Jay Farbstein & Assoc., San Luis Obispo 1986–; instr. aikido Cuesta Coll. 1987–; awards: Sch. Architecture Univ. Ill. Edward C. Earl prize 1983, Am. Collegiate Sch. Architecture Research 1983, Univ. Ill. Undergrad. Instruction 1984, Amoco Corp. award 1985; mem: Am. Inst. Architects, Environ. Design Research Assn., bd. dir. and secty., Environmental Design Res. Assn. 1995–; author: thesis pub. 1983; Democrat; Zen; rec: Aikido. Res: 120 Cerro Romauldo Ave San Luis Obispo 93401 Ofc: 1411 Marsh St Suite 204 San Luis Obispo 93401

BARKER, HAROLD N., police chief; b. Aug. 4, 1937, Ventura; s. Wm. Perry and Evelyn Inez (Beckwith) B.; children: Russell b. 1961, Terri b. 1963; edn: AA, Ventura Coll., 1966; BS, CSU Los Angeles, 1969; MPA, Univ. So. Calif., 1972; grad. Command Coll. 1987, FBI Acad., session 86. Career: police capt. Santa Paula Police Dept., 1957-74; asst. sheriff San Mateo County Sheriff, Redwood City 1974-83; chief of police San Francisco Internat. Airport, 1979-80; dir. security Shorenstein Co., San Francisco 1983-84; chief of police City of Folsom, 1984–; instr. Ventura Coll. 1968-72, La Verne Coll. 1969-72; awards: J. Edgar Hoover medal F.B.I., Wash. DC 1969, chair of year Calif. Peace Officers, Sacto. 1978, volunteer of year Folsom C.of C. 1986, chief of year Folsom P.D. 1987; civic: Rotary (pres. 1972), Shriners (provost marshal 1987-90), Elks, Folsom C.of C. (pres. 1993); mil: Col. State Mil. Reserve Army Nat. Guard; Prot.; rec: hunting, golf. Res: 2661 Larsen Dr Camino 95709 Ofc: Folsom Police, 46 Natoma St Folsom 95630

BARKOVICH, BARBARA ROSE, consultant; b. Dec. 18, 1950, Tokyo, Japan; d. Anthony and Mildred (Donner) B.; edn: BA, UCSD 1972; MS, St. Univ. N.Y. 1974; PhD, UC Berkeley 1987. Career: asst. energy policy analyst NSF, Wash. D.C. 1974-75; research splst. Calif. Pub. Utilities Commn., San Francisco 1975-78, dir. policy and planning 1978-83; asst. v.p. First Interstate Bancorp, Los Angeles 1983-84, v.p. 1984-85; cons. 1985-87; ptnr. Barkovich & Yap, Inc., Emeryville, Calif. 1987–; dir. Women Energy Associates, San Francisco 1985–; dir. Freewheelers Assn. Inc. 1989-93; dir. Pacific Energy and Resources Center, 1991-93; dir. Philharmonia Baroque Orchestra 1993–; apptd. energy engring. bd. Nat. Research Council, 1990-94; awards: Fed. Energy Adminstrn. energy conservation award, 1976; mem: Audubon Canyon Ranch (docent); author: Regulatory Interventionism in Utility Industry, 1989; rec: opera, chamber music, bird watching. Address: San Rafael 94901

BARNARD-WALTON, JO ELLEN, surgeon; b. Dec. 24, 1941, Los Angeles; d. Marion Cecil and Cleo Pauline (Fenderson) B.; m. Lewis Richard Walton, Dec. 19, 1971; children: Lewis Richard Walton, Jr. b. 1981; edn: BA, La Sierra Coll. 1962; MD, Loma Linda Univ. 1966; bd. cert. Am. Bd. of Surgery. Career: surgical res. Loma Linda Univ. White Meml. Hosp. 1972; intern Riverside Gen. Hosp. 1967. Career: surgeon Niles Surgical and Med. Group, Bakersfield 1973–; staff San Joaquin Comm. Hosp. (exec. com. 1985-), Greater Bakersfield Mem. Hosp.; honors: alumna of yr. Southwestern Adventist Coll. 1988, Personalities of the West & Mid West, Outstanding Young Women of Am.; mem: AMA, Calif. Med. Assn., Kern Co. Med. Assn., Loma Linda Univ. Womens Auxiliary (pres. 1974-75), Bakersfield Adventist Acad. School Board (chair 1985-86); author: How To Live Six Extra Years (Woodbridge, 1981); Seventh Day Adventist; rec: Arabian horses, travel, music, swimming, health lectures. Res: 2701 Rio Vista Bakersfield 93306 Ofc: Niles Surgical and Medical Group 2121 Nile St Bakersfield 93305

BARNES, ARTHUR DAVID, obstetrician-gynecologist; b. May 5, 1937, London, England; s. Arthur Reginald and Charlotte Elizabeth B.; m. Mary; children: Robert b. 1959, Stephanie b. 1962, Brooke b. 1976, Ben b. 1979, Bryn b. 1983, Brad b. 1983; edn: AKC, Univ. London, England 1958; MD, Royal Coll. Surgeons, 1966; MPH, UC Berkeley, 1978; PhD, Pacific Western Univ., L.A. 1992; bd. cert. Am. Bd. Ob-Gyn, FACOG. Career: assoc. dir. ob-gyn. Kern Med. Center, Bakersfield 1983-87; pvt. practice ob-gyn, Beverly Hills 1988-92, Palmdale Med. Ctr., Palmdale 1992–; mem: AMA, CMA, Am. Coll. Ob-gyn., Los Angeles Co. Med. Assn., Masons (master mason 1971–); 32 articles pub. in med. jours., 1 chpt. (1987); mil: col. M.C. USAR 1978–; rec: marathon running. Res: 2210 Garnet Ave Barstow 92311

BARNES, STANLEY NELSON, federal judge; b. May 1, 1900, Baraboo, Wis.; s. Charles L. and Janet B.; m. Ann Fisk, Oct. 18, 1929 (dec. Mar. 1983); children: Judith Melkesian, Joyce Robinson; m. Elizabeth MacDonald, Nov. 6, 1987; edn: AB, UC Berkeley, 1922; Harvard Law Sch. 1922-23, JD, Boalt Hall Sch. of Law, UCB, 1925; admitted bar, 1925. Career: atty. law firm Brobeck, Phleger & Harrison, S.F. 1925-28; Lucius K. Chase, L.A. 1928-28; Chase, Barnes, Chase, L.A. 1929-47; judge Superior Ct., Los Angeles 1947-53; asst. atty. general U.S. Anti-Trust Div., Wash. DC 1953-56; Pres. Eisenhower appt. judge Ninth Circuit Ct. of Appeals, Pasadena 1956–; appt. Pres.'s Conf. on

Adminstrv. Procedure 1953-54; co-chmn. Nat. Com. to Study Antitrust Laws 1954-56, coauthor w/ S.C. Oppenheim, Report of the Atty. Gen.'s Nat. Com. to Study the Antitrust Laws (1956); U.S. Judicial Conf. chmn. nat. advy. com. on Appellate Rules and Procedures 1954-56, chmn. Com. on Use of Land Commrs. and subcom. on Land Condemnation Cases 1960-62; Am. Bar Assn. sect. chmn. Judl. Admin. 1956-58; honors: Hon. LL.D. UCB (1961), Am. Bar Assn. disting. serv., anti-trust sect. (1955), UCB Alumnus of Yr. (1966), Boalt Hall Alumni award (1967), Shattuck-Price memorial L.A. Co. Bar Assn. (1971), St. Thomas Moore award Loyola Univ. Sch. of Law L.A. (1973), Nat. Collegiate Football Hall of Fame (1954), Helm's (now Citizens') Coll. Football Hall of Fame (1960), San Diego Hall of Champions (1969), All-Time/All-Pacific Coast Guard, First 50 yrs. (1970), Berkeley Fellow #38 (1968); mil: USN(R) active duty 1918-21. Res: 1800 S Sunrise Wy Palm Springs 92264 Ofc: POB 91510 Pasadena 91109-1510

BARNETT, GLEN, broadcasting executive; b. Feb. 19, 1924, Neodesha, Kans.; s. Harry Crawford and Irene Florence (Vining) B.; m. Opal Pogue; edn: grad. Hays H.S. 1942. Career: broadcast engr. KVGB radio, Gt. Bend, Kans. 1942-46; KTMC radio, McAlester, Okla. 1946-48; newscaster KAYS radio, Hays, Kans. 1948-57; owner KJFJ radio, Webster City, Iowa 1957-59; ops. mgr. KCMJ radio, Palm Springs 1959-64; owner KWXY radio 1964-; awards: Associated Press Best Disaster News Coverage (1951), Radio T.V. News Dir. Assn. Golden Mike (1988); mem: Pacific Poineer Broadcasters, Am. Radio Relay League; Republican; Prot.; rec: amateur radio. Ofc: KWXY AM/FM Broadcast Centre Palm Springs 92263

BARNETT, R(ALPH) MICHAEL, theoretical physicist; b. Jan. 25, 1944, Gulfport, Miss.; s. Herbert C. and Lisa M. (Brandt) B.; m. Suzanne Hamilton, Feb. 10, 1980; children: Julia b. 1981, Russell b. 1987; edn: BS, Antioch Coll. 1966; PhD, Univ. Chgo. 1971. Career: postdoctoral fellow UC Irvine 1972-74; research fellow Harvard Univ., Cambridge, Mass. 1974-76; research assoc. Stanford Linear Accelerator Center, Stanford 1976-83; vis. physicist Inst. Theoretical Physics, Santa Barbara 1983-84; staff scientist Lawrence Berkeley Lab., Berkeley 1984-89, senior scientist and hd. Particle Data Group 1990-; v.p. Contemporary Physics Edn. Project Inc. 1989-; Fellow Am. Physical Soc. (public info. coordinator, Div. Part. & Fields); author: Review of Particle Properties (1986, 88, 90, 92, 94), Teachers Resource Book, 1988, software and wall chart: Fundamental Particles & Interactions (1988, 95), 80+ papers pub. in sci. jours. on the Std. Model and extensions incl. studies of nature and validity of Quantum Chromodynamics, analyses of neutral current couplings, calculations of the prod. of hvy. quarks and predictions of properties and decays of supersymmetric parti-cles, 1971-. Ofc: Lawrence Berkeley Laboratory, MS 50-308 Berkeley 94720

BARNETTE, CHRISTOPHER KEVIN, lawyer; b. Dec. 16, 1957, Phoenix, Ariz.; s. Corwin James and Eleanor Almedia (Clow) B.; m. Catherine Ann, July 7, 1984; edn: BS, Ariz. St. Univ. Tempe 1981; MBA, 1987; JD, 1987. Career: atty. Luce Forward Hamilton & Scripps, San Diego 1987-; honors: Order of Coif, Beta Gamma Sigma; mem: San Diego Vol. Lawyer Program, Golden Hill Planning Com., Litigation Sect., State Bar of Calif.; editor-in-chief, Calif. Lit. News; article pub. in profl. jour., 1986; Democrat. Ofc: Luce Forward Hamilton & Scripps 600 West Broadway Ste 2600 San Diego 92101

BARON, NORMAN ARTHUR, physician; b. Nov. 16, 1946, NYC, NY; s. Sidney and Frieda (Worth) B.; m. Patrice Saenz; children: Pascale b. 1979, Jason b. 1981, Michelle b. 1985; 1 stepson Joe b. 1981; edn: BA, Boston Univ., Boston, Mass. 1968; MD, Univ. of Bologna, Italy 1974. Career: internship French and Polyclinic Hosp., NY 1974-75; resident, int. medicine Mt. Sinai Hosp., NY 1975-77; fellowship, rheumatology Rutgers Univ., N.J. 1977-79; pvt. practice, rheumatology/int. medicine, Santa Maria, Calif. 1979-91, St. Helena and Clearlake, Calif. 1991-; chmn. med. edn. com., St. Helena Hosp. 1992-; chmn. dept. of medicine Valley Comm. Hosp., Santa Maria 1980-81, 87-88; med. advr. bone densitometry unit The Women's Ctr. of St. Helena Hosp. & Health Ctr., Am. Lupus Soc., Santa Maria; mem: Napa Co. Arthritis Found. (advy. bd., med. edn. com.), Am. Soc. of Bone Mineral Res., Am. Coll. of Rheumatology, Osteoporosis Found., Am. Soc. of Internal Medicine, St. Helena Hosp Utilization Review Bd., listed Who's Who in Calif. 1985-; rec: carpentry, antique restoration. Ofcs: 1119 Hunt St Ste B St. Helena 94574 and 3400 Emerson St Clearlake 95422

BARR, WARREN PAUL, optometrist; b. Dec. 9, 1955, Hawthorne; s. Paul C. and Betty Patricia B.; m. Peggy Delite; edn: AA, El Camino Coll. 1976; BS, So. Calif. Coll. Optometry 1978; OD, 1980. Career: electrophysiology clin. Children's Hosp., San Diego 1980; optometry clin. VA Hosp., Los Angeles 1980; pvt. practice, Hermosa Beach 1980-; cons. South Bay Children's Hosp., Redondo Beach 1981-; awards: Gordon Optical Lens Design, Calif. Young Optometrist of the Yr. 1986; mem: South Bay Optometric Soc. (past pres.), Calif. Optometric Assn., Optometric Care Council So. Calif. (pres.), Hermosa Beach Jaycees (pres.), Hermosa Beach C.of C. (pres. 1993-94); 2 articles pub. in profl. jours. (1980, 81); rec: motorcycle racing, skiing, water skiing. Res: 1246 17th St Hermosa Beach 90254 Ofc: 1200 Artesia Blvd #1 Hermosa Beach 90254

BARRETT, REGINALD HAUGHTON, wildlife biologist, educator; b. June 11, 1942, San Francisco; s. Paul Hutchison, Sr. and Mary Lambert (Hodgkin) B.; m. Katharine Lawrence Ditmars, July 15, 1967; children: Wade Lawrence b. 1984, Heather Elizabeth b. 1987; edn: BS game mgmt., Humboldt State Univ., 1965; MS wildlife mgmt., Univ. Mich., 1966; PhD zoology, UC Berkeley, 1971; cert. wildlife biologist 1980; cert. senior ecologist 1993. Career: staff res. UC Berkeley, 1970-71; res. scientist C.S.I.R.O., Canberra, Australia 1972-75; prof. of wildlife mgmt. UC Berkeley, and dir. Sagehen Creek Field Sta., Dept. of Environmental Sci. Policy and Mgmt. 1976-; awards: Rho Sigma 1962, Chi Sigma Epsilon 1963, Xi Sigma Pi 1964, Who's Who Among Am. Univs. and Colls. 1964, undergrad. scholar Nat. Wildlife Fedn. 1964, Sigma Xi undergrad. res. award 1965, Bruce R. Dodd Award 1966, Phi Kappa Phi 1966, Union Found. Wildlife Res. Grant 1968-70, NSF grad. fellow 1965-70, Sigma Xi 1971, profl. achiev. Humboldt St. Univ. Alumni 1986, R.F. Dasmann profl. of yr. Wildlife Soc. we. sect. 1989; mem: The Wildlife Soc., Soc. for Range Mgmt., Soc. of Am. Foresters, Am. Soc. of Mammalogists, Ecol. Soc. of Am., Orinda Hist. Soc. (life), Nat. Wildlife Fedn. (life), Nat. Audubon Soc. (life), Sierra Club (life), Austr. Mammal Soc. 1972-, AAAS, Calif. Acad. Scis. (1975-), Pacific NW Natural Hist. Soc., Resource Modeling Assn., others; publs: 80+ profl. papers and jour. articles; Episcopalian; rec: hunting, fishing, hiking, boating, camping, photog. Ofc: Univ. of California 145 Mulford Hall Berkeley 94720

BARRETT, RICHARD HEWINS, oil company executive; b. Dec. 5, 1949, Pittsburgh, Pa.; s. Robert Hewins and Joan Lea (Mantler) B.; m. Virginia Kristine Arentzen, Apr. 14, 1973 (div. Jan. 1992); children: Robert b. 1975, Jeffrey b. 1977, Douglas b. 1980; m. 2d. Evelyn Paige Sexton, June 27, 1992; 1 son, David b. 1994; edn: BS, Penn State Univ., 1971, MBA, 1973; profl. desig. CCM, CDP, Treas. Mgmt. Assn. 1990. Career: senior cons. Gulf Oil Corp., Pittsburgh, Pa. 1982-85; supr. systems support Chevron Corp., San Francisco 19185-86, senior cash mgmt. analyst 1986-87, mgr. banking ops. 1987-90, mgr. receivables acctg. Chevron U.S.A., Concord 1990-91, mgr. bus. serv. Chevron Products Co., S.F. 1991-94, svcs. mgr., Chevron Products Co., La Habra 1994-; adj. prof. Salisbury State Coll., Md. 1975; instr. Golden Gate Univ., S.F. 1987-89; mem: Treasury Mgmt. Assn. 1987-; civic: Moon Area Soccer Assn., Coraopolis, Pa. (treas. 1983-85), Mustang Soccer League, Danville (treas. 1988-91); Republican; Presbyterian (trustee, elder 1981-84); rec: soccer, skiing, pers. computing, woodworking, music. Res: 1324 Carleton Way Fullerton 92633

BARRETT, ROBERT MATTHEW, lawyer; b. March 18, 1948, Bronx, N.Y.; s. Harry and Rosalind B.; edn: BA summa cum laude, Georgetown Univ. 1976; MSFS 1980; JD, 1980. Career: atty. Latham & Watkins, Los Angeles 1980-82; Morgan Lewis & Bockius 1982-84; Skadden Arps Slate Meagher & Flom 1984-87; Shea & Gould 1987-88; Donovan Leisure Newton & Irvine 1988-90; Barrett & Zipser 1990-93; asst. prof. Univ. of La Verne Law Sch. 1993-; honors: ed. Georgetown Law Journal, Who's Who in West, Who's Who Am. Law; mem: Vols. in Parole L.A. Co. Bar Assn. (bd. advisors 1981-), Calif. State Bar Standing Comm. on Profl. Responsibility and Conduct; Jewish. Res: 13816 Bora Bora Way #325-A Marina del Rey 90292-6870 Ofc: University of La Verne College of Law at San Fernando Valley 21300 Oxnard St Woodland Hills 91367

BARRICELLI, JEAN-PIERRE, professor emeritus of humanities and comparative literature, music critic; b. June 5, 1924, Cleve.; s. Giovanni Alfonso and Orfea (Malpezzi) B.; m. Norma Gaeta, Oct. 19, 1957; children: Marco, Laura, Franca; edn: BA, 1947, MA, 1948, PhD, 1953, Harvard Univ. Career: music dir. Radio Munich, 1945-46; teaching fellow Harvard Univ., Cambridge, Mass. 1948-50, 51-53; conductor Waltham Symphony 1955-62; asst. prof. humanities and comparative lit. Brandeis Univ., Waltham, Mass. 1953-62, 63, dir. Wien Internat. Sch. program, 1958-62, 63; prof. humanities and comparative lit. Univ. Calif. Riverside, 1963-; music critic Riverside Press, 1963-; vis. prof. Norwegian Sch. Bus. Adminstrn., Bergen, Norway 1962-63, New York Univ., N.Y.C. 1978, Distinguished Prof. Humanities chair Coll. of William and Mary 1988; awards: Phi Beta Kappa, Fulbright fellow 1950, 1962, grantee: Univ. of Calif. Humanities Inst. (2), 1968, 69, Rockefeller Found. (Bellagio), 1981; mem: Law and Humanities Inst. (bd. govs.), Internat. Comparative Lit. Assn., Am. Comparative Lit. Assn., MLA, Dante Soc. Am., Philol. Assn. Pacific Coast (pres. 1993-94), Am. Conf. on Romanticism (pres. 1994-); author: Alessandro Manzoni, 1976, Giacomo Leopardi, 1986, Melopoiesis, 1988, Dante's Vision and the Artist, 1992, Fireplaces of Civilization, 1993, and editor: Interrelations of Literature, 1982, Chekhov's Great Plays, 1981; mil: s/sgt. US Army 1943-46, European theatre, lt. USAR 1946-50; R. Cath. Res: 5984 Windemere Way Riverside 92506 Ofc: Chair of Dept. Literatures & Languages, Univ. Calif., Riverside 92521

BARRIOS, ALFRED ANGEL, psychologist; b. Oct. 1, 1933, N.Y., N.Y.; s. Arthur and Carmen (Vidal) B.; edn: BS, Caltech, 1955; MA, UCLA, 1964, PhD, 1969. Career: assoc. Dr. William S. Kroger, Inst. of Comprehensive Medicine, Beverly Hills, 1972-74; cons. City of Hope Pain Ctr., 1975; clin. psychologist, dir. Self Programmed Control Center, Culver City 1976-, specialist in stress management: inventor stress control biofeedback cards, pioneer in psychoneuroimmunol. approach to curing cancer, his self-programmed control pgm. introduced in schs. nat.; cons. Govt. Title III pgm. for minority students 1969-72; vis. prof. UCLA undergrad. recruitment & devel. dept. 1971-72; instr. psych. dept. East L.A. Coll. 1970-72; Santa Monica City Coll. 1975; Southwest Coll. 1975-76; honors: doc. diss. "Towards Understanding the Effectiveness of Hypnotherapy" nom. for Creative Talent Award 1969; speaker num. confs. and workshops; Christian; rec: beach volleyball. Res: 11959 Nebraska Ave Los Angeles 90025 Ofc: SPC Center, 11949 Jefferson Blvd Ste 104 Culver City 90230

BARRON, DAVID KRAIG, service company president; b. Feb. 3, 1954, Ottawa, Kans.; s. Pablo and Margarita Barron; edn: BS, Emporia St. Univ. 1976; MS, CSU Stanislaus 1980; cert., Nat. Career Inst. 1989; Rancho Santiago Coll. 1984-89. Career: job counselor Kans. Job Service, Ottawa 1976-78; welfare counselor Lawrence Social & Rehab. Services 1978-79; counselor Napa Resource Center 1981; craft supr. U.S. Postal Service, Santa Ana 1983–; owner Barron's Brokerage Consulting Co.; owner, pres. Baron's Building Maint. Co.; franchise owner Jani-King Inc.; mem. Image Inc., Kans. City, Mo. and Sacto. 1978-84; Lulac, Santa Ana 1989; awards: Lulac acad. scholarship 1972, Mex. Am. Com. acad. scholarship 1972, Tau Kappa Epsilon, St. of Kans. gov. appointee 1978; mem: Orange County C.of C., Hispanic C.of C., Am. Inst. Maintenance, MALDEF Leadership Prog.; Republican; R.Cath. Address: Lake Elsinore 92330

BARROZO, DONNA MARIE CALIMQUIM, psychiatrist; b. Oct. 28, 1956, Philippines; d. Irineo Salayog Barrozo, MD and Aurora (Calimquim) Barrozo, PhD.; edn: BS, biochem., Univ. of Calif., Davis 1978; MD, St. Louis Univ., Baguio City, Philippines 1983; lic. physician, Calif. Med. Bd. 1991. Career: intern (psychiatry) Chicago Med. Sch. 1989-90; resident (psychiatry) King/Drew Med. Ctr., L.A. 1990-94; staff psychiatrist San Bernardino County Med. Ctr., San Bernardino 1994–; res. asst. Univ. of Calif., Davis Med. Ctr., Davis and Sacramento 1986-87; mem. Am. Psychiatry Assn. 1994–, King/Drew Med. Ctr. Alumni Assn. 1994–; Democrat; Roman Catholic; rec: arts and travel. Address: La Mirada 90637

BARSAN, RICHARD EMIL, oral & maxillofacial surgeon; b. Dec. 18, 1945, Selma, Ala.; s. Emil O. and Letitia B.; m. Sandra Sherrick, June 22, 1974; children: Kelly Lynn b. 1982, Robert Scott b. 1984; edn: BSChE, Univ. Cincinnati 1968; DDS, Ohio State Univ. 1979; Oral & Maxillofacial Surg., La. State Univ. 1984; Diplomate Am. Bd. of Oral and Maxillofacial Surgery. Career: chem. engr. Tex., NY, Ill., Calif. 1968-76; gen. dental practice residency VA Hosp. Sepulveda, Calif. 1979-80; oral & maxillofacial sug. res. New Orleans 1980-84; pvt. practice oral & maxillofacial surg. La Jolla, Calif. 1985–; att. staff L.A. Co.-USC Med. Ctr. 1986; honors: Omicron Kappa Upsilon 1979, Chrysler Scholarship Grant 1964, dental class pres., student council (OSU 1978-79); mem: Am. Dental Assn., Calif. Dental Assn., San Diego Co. Dental Assn. (dir. 1988-92), Am. Assn. Oral & Maxillofacial Surg. (clinician annual meeting 1983), So. Calif. Soc. Oral & Maxillofacial Surg., San Diego County Oral & Maxillofacial Surgeons (pres. 1990); civic: Toastmasters La Jolla (pres. 1988), Paul Revere Study Club (pres. 1988); contbr. tech. article in dental jour.; clin. presentation First Internat. Congress on Preprosthetic Surg., 1985; mil: USAR 1969-76; Republican; rec: computers, diving, swimming. Ofc: 1745 S. Imperial Ave El Centro 92243

BARSKY, JONATHAN DANIEL, educator; b. Jan. 15, 1958, Aurora, Ill.; s. Morrey O. and Shirley Mae (Shapiro) B.; edn: BA Spanish/bus., Bucknell Univ., 1979; MS hotel, restaurant & travel adminstrn., Univ. Mass. 1980; PhD mktg. Golden Gate Univ. 1991. Career: cons. Pannell Kerr Forster, NY, NY 1981-82; asst. prof. Hotel Adminstrn., Univ. of New Hampshire 1982-84, Central Michigan Univ. 1984-86, Mktg. and Hospitality Mgmt., Univ. of San Francisco 1985–; cons. executive edn. U.S.F. McLaren Coll., cons. profl. devel. U.S.F. ARETE, 1988–; honors: Eta Sigma Delta (hon. mem. 1982), Acad. of Mktg. Sci. best paper 1984, Outstanding RSL Award McLaren Sch. of Bus. 1992; mem: S.F. Profl. Food Soc., Pan Pacific Bus. Assn. (charter), Calif. Restaurant Assn., Acad. of Internat. Bus., World Affairs Council S.F.; author: book, World Class Customer Satisfaction, num. scholarly articles in field; Jewish; rec: freestyle frisbee, aerobics tchr., dance. Res: 1890 Washington St #503 San Francisco 94109 Ofc: McLaren College USF, San Francisco 94117-1080

BARTALINI, MARILYN DARLENE, real estate broker; b. Sept. 1, 1938, Fort Bragg; d. Lyle James Robertson and Hilda Virginia (Lawrence) Roberts; m. Robert Bartalini, Aug. 16, 1958; children: Debora b. 1960, Cynthia b. 1962; edn: Coll. of the Redwoods, Lumbleau R.E. Schs., 1973; Anthony's R.E. Schs., 1973–; Calif. lic. R.E. Broker; desig: Realtor. Career: bookkeeper, teller, bank secty. Coast Nat. Bank, Ft. Bragg 1955-60, 1966-70; supr. teller line and bookkeeping dept. Savings Bank, 1970-73; R.E. sales agt. Spring Realty, 1973-74; Northern Calif. Prop., 1974-77; R.E. broker/owner Blue Pacific Realty, 1977-82; Head Realty, 1982-83; Seaside Real Estate, 1983-85; Century 21 Fort Bragg Realty, 1985-89; Mendo Realty, 1989-93, Mendo Realty Seaside, 1993–; Amway distbr. 1990-94, International Networking Assn. 1990-94; recipient profl. awards: million dollar producer 1977, 86, 87, $3mil. producer 1979, $2mil. producer 1978, 88, Century 21 R.E. Winners' Circle, highest units sales and listings Mendocino County, Lake County and a portion of Sonoma County 1988; mem: Coastal Mendocino Bd. of Realtors (by laws and long range plng.

coms. 1978-79, dir. 1979-82, treas. 85-86, MLS com. 86-88), Calif. Assn. Realtors, Nat. Assn. Realtors, Native Daus. of the Golden West 1967–, Mendocino Coast Hosp. Found., Norman Vincent Peale Positive Thinkers Club, Found. for Christian Living 1980–, AARP, Breakthrough, Intercessor; Democrat; R.Cath.; rec: fine arts, reading, travel, walking. Res: 1184 N Main St No.29 Fort Bragg 95437 Ofc: 690 S Main St Fort Bragg 95437

BARTOLOTTA, VINCENT J., JR., lawyer; b. May 23, 1945, Monongahela, Pa.; s. Helen Kurilko; m. Judith Ann, June 1, 1968; children: Nicolas Andrew b. 1981, Vincent, III b. 1971, Bret Anthony b. 1974, Garrett Michael b. 1979; edn: BA, Univ. Pitts., 1967, JD, 1970; admitted bar: Dist.Col., Pa., Calif. Career: trial lawyer pvt. practice, San Diego; mem. advy. bd. S.D. Sockers Profl. Soccer Team; mem. bd. American Ireland Fund; honors: List of 83 San Diegans to Watch 1983, Am. Lawyer Mag. list of top 20 small law firms in U.S., Best Lawyers in Am. (ann. 1986-94), master of Am. Inn of Court - Enright chpt.; mem: Am. Bar Assn., Am. Trial Lawyers Assn., Am. Bd. of Trial Advocates, Allegheny Co. Bar Assn., San Diego Co. Bar Assn. (code of conduct com.), San Diego Trial Lawyers Assn. (pres. 1990, Outstanding Trial Lawyer award 1981, 88, 89, 91), San Diego Co. Barristers Club; civic bds: St. Vincent de Paul/Joan Kroc Ctr. for Homeless (dir.), Am. Trauma Soc. (pres. S.D. chpt.), Rancho Santa Fe Youth (chmn. bd. govs., past pres. bd. dirs.), S.D. 1984 Olympic Com.; R.Cath.; rec: golf, soccer. Res: PO Box 2596 Rancho Santa Fe 92067 Ofc: 2550 Fifth Ave Ste 1100 San Diego 92103

BARTON, ANN ELIZABETH, financial executive; b. Sept. 8, 1923, Long Lake, Mich.; d. John and Inez Mabel (Morse) Seaton; m. H. Kenneth Barton, Apr. 3, 1948; children: Michael, John, Nancy; edn: att. Mount San Antonio Coll. 1969-71, Adrian Coll. 1943, Citrus Coll. 1967, Golden Gate Univ. 1976; CFP, Coll. Fin. Planning, 1982; Reg. Investment Advisor. Career: tax cons., real estate broker, Claremont, Ca. 1967-72, Newport Beach 1972-74; v.p., dir. Putney, Barton Assocs. Inc., Walnut Creek 1975-94; dir: FSC Securities; mem: Internat. Assn. Fin. Planners, Calif. Soc. Enrolled Agts., Nat. Assn. Enrolled Agts., Nat. Soc. Pub. Accts., Inst. Cert. Fin. Planners. Ofc: Putney Barton Associates, Inc. 1243 Alpine Rd #219 Walnut Creek 94596

BASCOM, EARL WESLEY, rodeo cowboy, sculptor-artist, writer; b. June 19, 1906, Vernal, Utah; s. deputy sheriff John W. and Rachel C. (Lybbert) B.; paternal cousin to western artists Frederic S. Remington and Charles M. Russell; m. Nadine Diffey, Dec. 20, 1939; children: Denise, Glen, Doris, John, Dona; edn: BS, Brigham Young Univ., 1940, postgrad. 1965, 66; postgrad. Univ. Calif. 1969; Career: profl. rodeo cowboy, 1918-40; dir. first rodeo, state of Miss. at Columbia, Miss. 1935, 36, 37; pres. Bascom and Wilkerson, 1947-51; owner Two Bar Quarter Circle Ranch 1951–; pres. High Desert Artists, Inc. 1964-65, pres. Bascom Fine Arts 1967–; owner Diamond B Ranch 1975–; art teacher Barstow H.S. and J.F. Kennedy H.S., Barstow, Calif. 1966, 67; pres., co-founder Buckaroo Artists of America 1978--; actor, western movie "The Lawless Rider" 1954; actor in Roy Rogers/Marriott Corp. commercials 1968, 69; art exhibits: Utah Artists, Provo (1971), Cowboy Artists, Temecula 1972, Desert Southwest Artists, Palm Desert and La Jolla (1974), Mormon Fest. of Arts 1975, Cochise Mus., Wilcox, Az. 1976, Wells Fargo Bank, San Brdo. 1976, Frank Tenney Johnson Invitational, Palm Springs 1979, Sun Valley, Idaho 1980, New Orleans 1981, Santa Anita Nat. Horse Show, Arcadia 1982, Cheyenne Frontier Days, Wyo. 1983, Weighorst/Bascom Exh., Alpine, Ca. 1984, Old Time Athletes, S.L.C., Utah 1985, National Salon, Springville, Utah 1986, Golden Boot Awards Exh., Woodland Hills, Ca. 1986, Internat. Art Exh., San Diego 1990, Equestrian Art Fest., Del Mar 1991, Oxford House, Salt Lake City 1992, World Cup Exh., Del Mar, Ca. 1992, Hollywood Park Exh., Cerritos, Ca. 1992, Brigham Young Univ., Provo, Utah 1992, Las Vegas, NV 1993; represented in permanent collections: Frederic S. Remington Art Mus., Gene Autrey Western Heritage Mus., Norwegian-Am. Mus., Danish Immigrant Mus., Denver Art Mus., Santa Barbara Mus. of Art, Whitney Mus. of Am. Art, Dallas Mus. of Fine Arts, Utah Mus. of Fine Arts, Tucson Mus. of Art, BYU Mus. Art, Old West Mus. (Cheyenne), Nat. Cowboy Hall of Fame (Oklahoma City), North Am. Cowboy and Pioneer Mus. (Ft. Worth), Canadian Rodeo Hall of Fame Mus. (Alberta), Univ. of Iowa, Art Mus.; producer first rodeo in Mississippi history at Columbia, Miss. 1935; awards: Reserve-Champion, steer decoration competition, North Am. Championship Calgary Stampede 1933, set arena record, Raymond, Alberta 1933, set world record time in steer decoration, Lethbridge, Alberta 1933, Third Pl. World Standings, Rodeo Assn. of Am. 1933, All-Around Rodeo Championships- Lethbridge Stampede, Lethbridge, Alberta 1934, Raymond Stampede, Raymond, Alberta (1935, 40), Ute Stampede, Nephi, Utah 1935, War Bonnet Roundup, Pocatello, Ida. 1937, Pacific Intl. Livestock Expo. Rodeo, Portland, Ore. 1939, named Stirling Stampede's First Rodeo Clown 1931, Sterling Sunset Soc. 1981, honoree Cardston Stampede Com. 1982, Raymond Stampede Com. 1984, Dinosaur Roundup Rodeo Assn. 1989, San Bdo. Co. Fair Rodeo Com. 1989, inducted Canadian Rodeo Hall of Fame 1984, Utah Sports Hall of Fame 1985, Raymond Sports Hall of Fame 1987, Hon. Parade Marshall-Cardston, Alberta 1982, Raymond, Alberta 1984, Columbia, Miss. 1985, Vernal, UT 1989, outstanding senior citizen award Dept. Gerontology BYU 1987, honoree Nat. Outlaw and Lawman Assn., Reno, Nev. 1990, special recogn. B.Y.U. Emeritus Club 1992; elected fellow, Royal Soc. of Arts, London 1993;

Resolutions from Calif. St. Senate, Miss. St. House & Senate, Co. San Bdo., and Cities of Victorville, Calif. and Vernal, Utah; mem: Am. Foundrymens Soc., Western Writers of Am., Profl. Rodeo Cowboys Assn. (hon. life), Canadian Rodeo Cowboys Assn., Cowboys Turtle Assn. (past), Nat. Old Timers Rodeo Assn., Canadian Rodeo Hist. Assn. (founder), Nat. Outlaw and Lawmen Assn. (life), Outlaw Trail Hist. Assn., Nat. Soc. Sons of Utah Pioneers (life), US Mormon Battalion Soc.(life), Western Heritage Soc. (life), Deseret Bus. & Profl. Assn., Interstake Bus. & Profl. Assn., Assn. Latter-Day Media Artists, BYU Emeritus Club; works: designed and made rodeo's 1st hornless bronc saddle (1922), also rodeo's 1st one-hand bareback rigging (1924), designed rodeo chaps (1926), invented rodeo exerciser (1928); bibliography: Who's Who in the West, Who's Who in Am., Who's Who in the World, Who's Who in Am. Art, Who's Who in Western Writers of Am.; Jon Scott (dir.) "Midnight's Last Ride - 1933" KBTV Denver (1983); Dick Dorwald (dir.) "Earl Bascom - An Artist and a Legend" K27-TV, Victorville (1984); "Cowboy Artist - Earl Bascom" KVVT-64 (1989); Michael Amundson (dir.) "Take Willy With You" (1989); author, illustr. "The Hist. of Bareback Bronc Riding" Western Horseman (6/90); illustr. book "Memories I Could Do Without and Other Short Stories" by Lyle Lybbert (1983); Cong. Jerry Lewis (author) "Earl Bascom - An American Hero" US Congl. Record (1985); Republican; Mormon; rec: saddle collection.; Res: Diamond B Ranch 15669 Stoddard Wells Rd Victorville 92392

BASSFORD, FORREST, journalist, livestock industry communications consultant; b. Feb. 2, 1906, Fountain, Okla.; s. Horace Albert and Vilura (McGinnis) B.; m. Marian Louise Horton, Oct. 12, 1929; children: Marilyn Ann b. 1937, Karen Lee (Kaytes) b. 1940, Dale H. b. 1944; edn: BS in animal husbandry, Colorado St. Univ., 1929. Career: county agric. ext. agt. Colo. Extension Service, Julesburg, Colo., 1929; editor Brush (Colo.) News, 1929; field rep. Denver Daily Record Stockman, 1930-34; American Hereford Journal, Kansas City, Mo. 1934-40; editor: The Record Stockman newspaper, Westerner Mag., Denver 1940-47; editor, gen. mgr., exec. editor, publisher Western Livestock Journal, Los Angeles then Denver, 1948-77; founding pub. Charolais Journal, Houston, Tx. 1977-78; sec.treas. then exec. dir. Livestock Publications Council, Denver then Houston, then Encinitas, Calif. 1974-92; awards: Colo. Cattlemen Assn. life mem. 1962, Am.-Intl. Charolais Assn. merit. svc. 1970, Iowa Beef Improvement Assn. friendship & svc. 1971, Mo. Charolais Breeders Assn. outstanding contbns. 1972, Marketeers livestock marketeer of yr. 1972, Mile Hi CowBelles father of yr. 1973, Nebr. Animal Agriculture Week commendn. 1973, Am. Polled Hereford Assn. spl. recogn. 1974, Am. Gelbvieh Assn. notable contbns. 1974, Beef Improvement Fedn. pioneer 1976, Calif. Beef Cattle Improvement Assn. commendn. 1976, Colo. St. Univ. Honor Alumnus 1977, Gamma Sigma Delta disting. svc. to agric. 1977, Colo. Cattle Feeders Assn. top choice 1977, Am. Soc. of Farm Mgrs. & Rural Appraisers merit. svc. in comms. 1977, Livestock Publs. Council headliner 1980, Alpha Gamma Rho Jerry Litton Memorial 1983, Intl. Stockmen's Sch. Honor Guest 1985, Beef Improvement Fedn. amb. 1989, Agricultural Communicators of Tomorrow Honored Profl. award 1993, American-Internat. Charolais Assn. Hall of Fame 1994; mem., dir. Western Stock Show Assn. 1940–, San Diego County, Calif. and Nat. Cattlemens Assns. 1978–; author: Century of Endurance, Hist. of Wyoming Hereford Ranch, 1983, thousands of livestock indus. features and reports, 1930–; mil: 1st sgt. Troop E, Wyo. Nat. Guard 1920-25, 2d lt. Field Arty. Reserve 1929-40; Republican; Episcopalian; rec: photog., fishing, writing. Res: 927 Elmview Dr Encinitas 92024

BASTIAN, JON ARNOLD, marketing and public relations consultant; b. May 29, 1949, Baltimore, Md.; s. Willard James and Jeanne Alice (Quigley) B.; edn: L.A. Valley Coll. 1967-72; UCSB 1972-75. Career: contbg. editor Four Wheeler Mag., Reseda 1969-70, freelance, Los Angeles 1971-72; contbr. Data Press, Santa Barbara 1979-80; pres. and c.e.o. Print Services, Santa Barbara 1980-89; Presentations Advertising, 1982–; mktg./pub. rels. KSBL Radio (101.7 FM), Santa Barbara 1989-90; assoc. publisher Country Music Today 1993–; nat. sales dir. Antenna Magazine 1993–; mem: Am. Advt. Fedn. (nat. bd. dirs. 1989-91, recipient AAF Dist. 15 Bell Ringer award 1992, Best AAF Ad Club award 1985-87, 90), Santa Barbara Advt. Club (past pres., sr. advisor 1989-91); civic: Am. Red Cross (S.B. Co. chpt. v.chair pgms. & svs., dir. p.r. com. 1988-91), S.B. C.of C., Santa Barbara Better Bus. Bureau, S.B. Rose Soc. (pres. 1986-87); rec: rosarian. Res: PO Box 849 Port Hueneme 93044 Ofc: Presentación Latino PO Box 849 Port Hueneme 93044

BATES, CRAIG DANA, museum curator; b. Aug. 2, 1952, Oakland; s. Dana Raymond and June (Robinson) B.; m. Jennifer Dawn Bernido, May 12, 1973, div. June 1987; child: Carson b. 1981. Career: park technician Nat. Park Service, Yosemite N.P., 1973-76, Indian cultural splst. 1976-80, asst. curator 1980-82, curator of ethnography 1982–; resrch. assoc. Santa Barbara Mus. Natural Hist. 1983–; cons. Brooklyn Mus. (N.Y.) 1988-89, Oakland Mus. 1991-92; instr. Yosemite Assn., 1977-88, Point Reyes Nat. Hist. Assn., 1978-88; publs: 100+ articles on Native Am. cultures, coauthor 2 books: Legends of the Yosemite Miwok 1981, Tradition and Innovation: A Basket Hist. of the Indian People of the Yosemite-Mono Lake Area 1990; avocation: Native Am material culture. Ofc: National Park Service PO Box 577 Yosemite National Park 95389

BATESOLE, DALE F., clergyman, television host; b. Oct. 1911, Ferguson, Iowa; s. John Floyd and Elsie Rebecca (Campbell) B.; m. Carolyn J. Dewey, Dec. 17, 1987; edn: Grad. Safety Engr., Kansas Univ. Ext. 1943; Ordained Minister, Unity Sch. of Christianity 1959. Career: br. mgr. Western Grocer Co., Marshalltown, Iowa 1930-48; sales rep. Schultz Burch Biscuit Co. 1948-56; minister Unity Christ Ch., St. Louis, Mo. 1958-64; co-founder Forsyth Sch., St. Louis, Mo. 1961; faculty Unity Sch. of Christianity 1960-61; founder, 1st exec. dir. Charles and Myrtle Fillmore Found., Lee's Summit, Mo. 1964-67; sch. bd. trustee Maricopa Co. Sch. Dist. 1970-71; cons. to psychiat. svc. VA Hosp., Phoenix, Ariz. 1971-76; founder Unity Ch. of Sedona, Ariz. 1973; orginator, presenter Psycho-Cybernetics Sems. nationwide 1973; instr. Psycho-Cybernetics, No. Ariz. Univ. Coll. of Bus. Admin. 1975-77; minister Unity of the Desert, Palm Springs 1977-79; prod./dir./host daily TV pgm. "There Is A Way" (fmr. "The Unity Way") 1979-86; pres. Unity Student Minister's Assn.; counselor, tchr., lectr. A.A. 1960–; mem. Assn. of Unity Churches; publs: newspaper articles, columns for Red Rock News, Sedona, Ariz. 1973, 1974, Carefree Enterprise, Carefree, Ariz. 1970-72; Republican; rec: tennis, music, jogging. Res: 909 Sandpiper Palm Desert 92260 Ofc: There Is A Way, 350 Prescott Ave El Cajon 92020

BATTIN, CYNTHIA ANN, electrical engineer; b. Aug. 29, 1957, Tucson, Ariz.; d. Gene and Peggy Ann (Purcell) Price; m. Richard Scott Battin, June 23, 1990; edn: BSEE, San Diego St. Univ., 1986; cert. qual. assur. ASQC 1989, electronics tech. USN 1976. Career: E-5, electronics tech. USN, 1975-81; electronics engr. Alexander Sys. Co., San Diego 1984-86; jr. engr. intern Naval Ocean Sys. Ctr., 1985-86; reliability engr. ARINC Res. Corp., San Diego 1987-94; communications engr. ARINC Res. Corp., Colorado Springs, Colo. 1993–; recipient athletic awards- mem. volleyball teams in USN, Inter-Service, and SDSU; mem. IEEE, SMTA, ASQC, Toastmasters S.D. (ofcr., TM of Yr. Club 1990, TM of Yr Area 1991, CTM, ATM); Republican; Christian; rec: sports, outdoors, dog. Res: 4315 Scotch Pine Dr Colorado Springs CO 80920 Ofc: ARINC Research 1925 Aerotech Dr Ste 212 Colorado Springs CO 80916

BATTLES, LARA, psychotherapist; b. Oct. 13, 1949, San Pedro; d. Willis Ralph Dawe and Roxy Edith (Baker) Battles; m. Thomas L. Morgan, Oct. 27, 1969; m. 2d. Dennis Lohof, Aug. 24, 1980; 1 son, Darien b. 1984; edn: undergrad. UCLA, 1967-8, El Camino Coll., 1968-9; BS, Montana St. Univ., 1971; MA, Loyola Marymount Univ., 1975; lic. marriage, family and child counselor Calif. 1978. Career: program coord., Straight Talk, Clinic, Cypress 1977; South County drug abuse prevention coord., San Luis Obispo County Drug Pgm., Arroyo Grande 1977-78; Tri-Counties coord. S.W. Montana Alcoholism Services, Helena, Mt. 1978-80; psychotherapist pvt. practice, Arroyo Grande 1981–; hospice vol. coord., San Luis Obispo Hospice, 1981; eating disorder tnr. and aftercare counselor, Pinecrest/ Cottage Care, Santa Maria 1985-86; founder, clin. supr., Inst. for the Study of Family Codependence 1988-90; honors: Nat. Merit Scholar; mem. Calif. Assn. Marriage & Family Therapists, Quota Club (pres. 1984), Women's Network Arroyo Grande (founding dir. 1985); rec: gardening, fostering global consciousness. Ofc: Lara Battles, MA, MFCC, 210 Traffic Way, Arroyo Grande 93420

BAUER, JEROME LEO, JR., chemical engineer; b. Oct. 12, 1938, Pitts.; s. Jerome L. and Anna Mae (Tucker) B.; div.; children: Lori, Trish, Jeff; edn: BSChemE, Univ. Dayton, 1960; MSChemE, Pa. State Univ., 1963; postgrad., Ohio State Univ., 1969; Reg. profl. engr., Ohio. Career: asst. prof. chem. engring. Univ. Dayton, Ohio 1963-67; mgr. advanced composites dept. Ferro Corp., Cleveland 1967-72; engring. material and process specifications mgr. Lockheed Missiles & Space Co. Inc., Sunnyvale, Calif. 1972-74; design specialist Convair div. Gen. Dynamics, San Diego 1974-76, project devel. engr. 1976-77; dir. research Furane div. M&T Chemicals Inc., Glendale 1980-82; mem. tech. staff Jet Propulsion Lab. Caltech, Pasadena 1977-80, 82-91; The Aerospace Corp., L.A. 1991–; awards: Phi Lambda Upsilon, Delta Sigma Epsilon, Meritorious Achiev. AIChE 1983; mem: Am. Inst. Chem. Engrs. (founder, chmn. Dayton sect. 1964-66, special projects chmn. Cleveland sect. 1968-69), Soc. for Advance. Material Process Engring. (No. Calif. sect. mem. chair 1973-74, San Diego secty. 1974-75, chmn. 1976, Los Angeles sect. chmn. 1977, nat. treas. 1978-82, gen. chmn. 31st internat. symposium exhibition, Las Vegas, Nev. 1986, internat. v.p. 1987-89, internat. pres. 1990, assoc. gen. chair 39th internat. symposium exhibit, Anaheim, Calif. 1994), Internat. Electronics Packaging Soc. (Los Angeles chpt. pres. 1982); editor: Materials Sciences for Future, 1986, Materials & Science Technology, 1994; contbr. articles to profl. jours.; St. Luke Episcopal Ch., La Crescenta (sr. warden 1981); Republican. Res: P.O. Box 3298 El Segundo 90245 Ofc: The Aerospace Corp. PO Box 92957 Los Angeles 90009

BAUER, PATRICIA MC COLLUM, college librarian; b. Nov. 29, 1920, Spreckles, Calif.; d. John Edgar and Maude Rae (Smiley) McCollum; m. Francis Harry, Apr. 12, 1945 (div. 1951); edn: BA, UC Berkeley, 1949, MA hist., 1951, MLS, 1959. Career: librarian Stanford Res. Inst., Menlo Park 1959-62; Livermore Rad. Lab., Livermore 1965-66; Head-Royce Sch., Oakland 1966-67; Oakland Pub. Schs., 1967-76; assoc. prof., head librarian Patten Coll., Oakland 1976-92; recipient numerous awards in photography; mem: Calif. Native Plant

Soc., Audubon Soc., Placer Art League, Fort Ross Interpretive Assn., Nat. Parks & Conserv. Assn., Camping Women, Calif. Acad. of Sci.; publs: article (1951), co. brochures (1960), 2 books in prog.; Democrat; R.Cath.; rec: photog., travel, camping, reading. Res: 40551 Airport Rd Little River 95456

BAUER, STEVEN MICHAEL, cost containment engineer; b. Nov. 8, 1949, Hemet; s. Donald Richard, Sr. and Jeanne Patricia (Lamont) B.; m. Myung-Hee Min, Sept. 10, 1983; children: Claudia Margaret b. 1984, Monica Anne b. 1985; edn: BA, CSU San Bernardino 1971, BS physics, 1984. Career: asst. then assoc. nuclear engr. SCE, Rosemead 1973-88, cost containment engr. 1988–; cons. res. JL Pettis VA Hosp., Loma Linda 1978-79; cons. mtn. planning San Bdo. County 1975-76; awards: volunteer of yr. Am. Red Cross 1990-91, listed Who's Who in Sci. & Engring. 1991, Who's Who in West 1995; civic bds: Am. for Energy Indep. (mem. chair 1991–), Neighborhood Watch Assn. San Bernadino (sec. 1991-92, v.p. 1993–, pres. 1994-95), Sierra Club (chpt. secty. 1991-92), Knights Columbus Fontana Pro-life 1984-92), Union of Concerned Scientists (chpt. orgnzr. San Bdo. 1991–), Newport Found. 1991–, Casa Colina Hosp. (fellow 1987-90), St. Labre Indian Sch. 1984–, LA Co. Mus. of Art 1984–, So. Poverty Law Ctr. 1986-91; Democrat (campaign worker, precinct leader. Re-elect Cong. G.E. Brown); R.Cath.; rec: gardening, writing. Res: 131 Monroe Ct San Bernardino 92408-4137

BAUERMEISTER, GILBERT E., insurance auditor; b. Nov. 23, 1923, Norfolk, Nebr.; s. Herman A. and Emma Sophia (Puls) B.; m. Marian V. Sebring, Oct. 5, 1968; children: Joan b. 1944, Larry b. 1948, Gary b. 1952; edn: BS, Univ. Neb. 1952. Career: tchr. Bennington H.S. 1952-53; merchandiser Cargill Grain Co., Omaha, Neb. 1953-56; auditor, field Travelers Ins., Los Angeles 1956-72; indep. field auditor, Cerritos 1972-73; chief field auditor Fremont Compensation, Foster City 1973-94 (ret. Mar. 30, 1994); tour guide at Crystal Cathedral, Garden Grove, Jan. 1995; mem: Nat. Soc. Ins. Premium Auditors, Fremont Elks #2121; mil: tech. sgt. Nat. Guard 1946-52; Republican; United Ch. of Christ; rec: golf, bowling, square dancing. Res: 707 West Santa Ana St #180 Anaheim 92805 Ofc: Fremont Compensation 100 California St San Francisco 94111

BAUMHOFF, WALTER HENRY, headmaster; b. May 27, 1937, N.Y.C.; s. Joseph and Elli (Schillig) B.; edn: BA, Wagner Coll., 1959; MS, Indiana Univ., 1961; postgrad. Harvard Univ., Stanford Univ. Career: asst. dir. scholarship/fin. aid Ind. Univ., Bloomington 1960-61; dean of freshmen St. Lawrence Univ., Canton, NY 1961-65, dean of students 1965-71; faculty dept. psychiat./behav. scis. Stanford Univ., 1973-74; dean of admissions Dominican Coll., San Rafael 1974-78; headmaster The Buckley Sch., Sherman Oaks 1978–; mem. Valley Coun., L.A. Co. Mus. of Natural Hist. 1987; Republican; rec: skiing, sailing. Res: 1964 North Kenmore Ave Los Angeles 90027 Ofc: 3900 Stansbury Ave Sherman Oaks 91423

BAXTER, LEONE (LEONE BAXTER WHITAKER), public relations executive; b. Kelso, Wash., Nov. 20, 1913; d. Leon W. and Grace P. (Hayes) Smith; m. Alexander D. Baxter. June 16, 1930 (dec. 1931) m. 2d, Clem S. Whitaker, Apr. 15, 1938 (dec. 1961); stepchildren: Clem Sherman, Milton G., Patricia (Mrs. Harry Sanders), Burdette (dec.). co-founder with Clem Whitaker of Campaigns, Inc., profl. mgmt. ballot issues and candidates, San Francisco 1934; v.p. Whitaker & Baxter, pub. relations counselor to industry, San Francisco 1934-58; co-founder, ptnr. Whitaker and Baxter Internat. l958-68, pres., 1962–; columnist 50 Calif. newspapers 1936-50, created Women in the News, Uncensored, Sparks from the News Circuit columns; editor-pub. Cal. Feature Service, San Francisco 1936-58; ptnr. Whitaker & Baxter, advt. San Francisco 1933-58; mng. ed. San Francisco Record 1940-45; pub. San Francisco Neighborhood Newspapers 1940-45; mgr. Earl Warren's campaign for gov. Calif. 1942, nat. campaign against compulsory health ins. for AMA 1949-52; mem. Nat. Profl. Com. for Eisenhower and Nixon 1952, Goodwin J. Knight's campaign for gov. Calif. 1954; poli. advisor Gov. Goodwin Knight 1946-58; gen. mgr. Calif. host com. to Rep. Nat. Conv. 1956; asst. mgr. Calif. campaign to create Central Valley Water Project 1933; trustee, Found. Pub. Relations Res. and Edn., Presbyn. Med. Ctr., Meals for Millions, Dooley Found., San Francisco Opera Auditions, Met. Opera Auditions, Am. Cancer Soc., Nob Hill Assn., Calif. Heritage Council, Artists Embassy; mem: Pub. Relations Soc. Am., San Francisco Opera Guild, DeYoung Mus. Soc., Internat. Pub. Relations Assn., U.S. People-to-People Com., Calif. Newspaper Pubs. Assn. Ballet Guild, Art Inst., San Francisco Symphony, Internat. Hospitality Center, Civic Light Opera; clubs: Metropolitan, Lake Shore, San Francisco Press; author, lectr. pub. relation aspects of govt., politics and industry. Res: 1250 Jones St San Francisco 94108 Ofc: Whitaker & Baxter International The Fairmont Nob Hill San Francisco CA 94108

BAYO, EDUARDO, educator; b. Sept. 3, 1954, Madrid, Spain; s. Candido and Ana Maria (Perez) B.; m. Elizabeth Anne Delgado, Sept. 25, 1982; children: Carolina b. 1983, Eduardo b. 1984, Joseph b. 1986, Annelise b. 1989, Christopher b. 1991; edn: BSCE, Polytech. Sch. Madrid Spain 1976; MSCE, UC Berkeley 1980; PhD civil engring., 1982. Career: civil engr. Gibbs & Hill, Madrid, Spain; research assoc. UC Berkeley 1980-83; research group supr. Initec, Madrid, Spain 1983-85; asst. prof. UC Santa Barbara 1986-89, assoc.

prof. 1989-93, full prof. 1994–; cons. E.D.O., Santa Barbara 1987–; Computer & Structure Inc., Berkeley 1985–; S.A.P. 1982–; assoc. ed. Jour. of Robotics & Automation, 1987–; awards: Fundacion Nacional Industria scholarship 1978, Ford Motor Co. scholarship 1981, UCSB regents jr. fellowship 1988, invited scientist by USSR Acad. of Sciences 1990; mem: ASME, Spanish Soc. Civil Engring.; author: 80 papers pub. in tech. jours., 1982-89, inventor of inverse dynamics of flexible manipulation, 1987; rec: philosophy, music, sailing. Res: 978 West Campus Ln Goleta 93117 Ofc: Univ. of Calif. Dept. of Mechanical Engineering Santa Barbara 93106

BEASLEY, BRUCE MILLER, sculptor; b. May 20, 1939, Los Angeles; s. Robert Seth and Bernice (Palmer) B.; m. Laurence Leaute, May 21, 1973; children: Julian Bernard, Celia Bernice; edn: Dartmouth Coll., 1957-59; BA, UC Berkeley, 1962. Career: sculptor in metal and plastic, major sculptures commd. by State of Calif. 1967, US Govt. 1976, Oakland Mus. 1976, Miami (Fla.) Internat. Airport 1978, San Francisco Internat. Airport 1981, Stanford Univ. 1982, Fed. Home Loan Bank, S.F. 1992, Cities of Eugene, Ore. 1974, San Francisco 1976, Salinas 1977, Anchorage, Alaska 1984, Gateway Ctr., Walnut Creek, Calif., Fresno Art Mus.; awards include Andre Malraux Purchase Award, Biennale de Paris 1961; One-man shows at Gal. Utermann, Dortmund, Ger., Gal. Rudolfinum, Prague, Czech Rep., Gal. Wirth, Zurich, Switzerland, Yorkshire Sculpture Park, W. Yorkshire, Eng.. Everett Ellin Gal., L.A., Kornblee Gal., N.Y.C., Hansen-Fuller Gal., S.F., David Stuart Gal., L.A., Andre Emmerich Gal., N.Y.C., De Young Mus., S.F., Santa Barbara Mus. Art, Fine Arts Gal., San Diego, Sonoma State Univ., Rohnert Park, The Oakland Mus., Fresno Art Mus., John Natsoulas Gal., Davis, Gal. Scheffel, Bad Homburg, Germany, Kunsthalle Mannheim, Mannheim, Germany; Group shows include Mus. Modern Art, NYC, Guggenheim Mus., NYC, Albright Knox Gal., Buffalo, La Jolla Art Mus., Musee d'Art Modern, Paris, S.F. Mus. Art, Krannert Art Mus. of Univ. Ill., Jewish Mus., NYC, Luxembourg Gardens, Paris, Calif. Palace of Legion of Honor, S.F., De Young Mus., Middleheim (Germany) Sculpture Park, Yorkshire (England) Sculpture Park, Santa Barbara Art Mus., others; represented in permanent collections of Fine Arts Mus. S.F., Mus. Modern Art, Guggenheim Mus., Musee d'Art Moderne, Paris, L.A. County Art Mus., Univ. Art Mus. of UC Berkeley, Oakland Mus., Wichita (Kans.) Art Mus., San Francisco Art Commn., Santa Barbara Art Mus., Dartmouth Coll., Kunsthalle Mannheim, Mannheim, Germany, Fresno Art Mus., Xantus Janos Mus., Gyor, Hungary, others; mem: Int. Sculpture Ctr. (bd. dir.), Washington, DC, Nat. Mus. Am. Art, Crocker Art Mus. Res: 322 Lewis St Oakland 94607-1236

BEATY, PAUL RICHARD, biologist; b. June 2, 1946, Ames, Iowa; s. Harold Huxford and Judith Helen (Skromme) B.; m. Sue Ann Weber, Sept. 7, 1968; children: Joel b. 1969, Christopher b. 1973, Michael b. 1978; edn: BS Eastern Illinois Univ., 1969; MS, Univ. Ill., Urbana 1976, PhD, 1979. Career: tchr. Unit 7 Schools, Tolono, Ill. 1969-72; refuge mgr. Illinois Dept. Conservation, Wilmington, Ill. 1972-73; assoc. scientist Illinois Natural History Survey, Urbana, 1974-78, asst. profl. scientist, 1978-79; dir. aquatic res. Coachella Valley Water Dist., Coachella, Calif. 1980-86; pres., prin. Southwest Aquatics, Beaty & Associates, Palm Desert, Calif. 1986–; mem: Calif. Lake Mgmt. Soc. (dir. 1986–, pres. 1993-94, 94-95), Western Aquatic Plant Mgmt. Soc. (mem. 1981–, v.p. 1992-93, pres. 1993-94), No. Am. Lake Mgmt. Soc. 1986–, Aquatic Plant Mgmt. Soc. 1981–, Am. Fisheries Soc. 1976–; civic: Riverside Co. Sch. Dist. Org. (1987–, chair 1989-95), Optimist (Palm Desert club pres. 1992-93), Palm Desert Planning Commn. 1993–, Desert Youth Sports Org. (dir.), Palm Desert Youth Sports (dir., League rep.), P.O.N.Y. Baseball (Region Palomino dir.); num. profl. articles and speeches in field; rec: golf, camping, fishing. Ofc: Beaty & Associates PO Box 13212 Palm Desert 92255

BEAUMAN, JOHN GERALD, aerospace group technical director; b. July 28, 1936, NYC; s. Lorenz and Constance; m. Sharon; children: Deborah Ann, Gerald, Brenda, and John Jr.; edn: engring. student SUNY, 1966-70; BSME, Calif. Coast Univ., 1976, MSME, 1983. Career: technical mgr. aircraft systems Fairchild Republic Co., Farmingdale, N.Y., 1965-82, participant in design of the F-105G, F-14, A-10, and Boeing's 767 and 757; technical mgr. flt. control hardware design & devel., tech. mgr. flt. controls integration, tech. mgr. systems integration, Northrop B-2 Div., Pico Rivera, Calif. 1982-88; group tech. dir. for systems and technology integration Parker Bertea Aerospace Group, Parker Hannifin Corp., Irvine 1988–; mem: AIAA, NCOSE; civic: Montefino Homeowners Assn. Diamond Bar (pres. 1982-86, newsletter editor & pub. Montefino Spotlight 82-86); author: Flight Control Iron Birds (1983); Republican; Presbyterian. Res: 824 Candlewood St Brea 92621

BECCHETTI, JOHN JOSEPH, surgeon; b. Nov. 13, 1935, Hibbing, Minn.; s. John L. and Mary Elizabeth (Pacioti) B.; m. Mary E. Ness, Sept. 22, 1962; children: Gina b. 1975, Teri b. 1978; edn: BS, Coll. of St. Thomas, St. Paul, Minn. 1958; MD, Univ. of Minn., Mpls. 1962. Career: pvt. practice gen. surgery, Oakland 1962–; mem. East Bay Surgical Soc. 1970–, Am. Bd. of Surgery (cert. mem. 1971–), Am. Coll. of Surgeons (fellow 1971–); mil: capt. USAF 1963-66; rec: reading, philately, bridge. Ofc: 3300 Webster St Oakland 94609 Tel: 510/834-7421

BECERRA, XAVIER, congressman, lawyer; b. Jan. 26, 1958, Sacramento, Calif.; s. Manuel and Maria Teresa B.; m. Carolina Reyes, 1987; edn: AB, Stanford Univ., 1980, JD, 1984. Career: atty., 1984–; dir. dist. office State Senator Art Torres, L.A.; dep. alty. gen. dept. justice, Calif., 1987-90; assemblyman, 59th dist. State of Calif., 1990-93; mem. 103rd and 104th Congresses from 30th Calif. dist., 1993–; mem. com. judiciary (courts and intellectual property subcom., immigration and claims subcom.) com. economic and educational opportunities (postsecondary edn., tng. and life-long learning subcom.); regional Dem. whip; awards: Outstanding New Mem. of Congress award, Com. for Edn. Funding 1993; mem. Congl. Hispanic Caucus, House Parliamentary Group, Mexican-Am. Bar Assn., Calif. Bar Assn., Assn. Calif. State Attys. and Admin. Law Judges; Democrat. Ofc: House of Representatives 1119 Longworth Bldg Washington DC 20515

BECHTEL, RILEY P., international engineering construction company president and chief executive; b. March 25, 1952, Oakland; s. Stephen Davison and Elizabeth (Hogan) B.; m. Susan Peters, Aug. 18, 1979; edn: BA, UC Davis 1974; combined JD/MBA, Stanford Univ. Sch. of Law and Grad. Sch. of Bus., 1979; admitted bar: Calif. 1979. Career: summer field constrn. work, var. jobs, Bechtel Group, Inc. 1966-79 (engring. & constrn. clients in 135+ countries on all 7 continents); atty. Thelen Marrin Johnson & Bridges, San Francisco 1979-81; rejoined Bechtel Group Inc. (BGI) 1981–, senior constrn. engr. later piping supt. at Belle River Power Plant, Mich., 1981-83, senior constrn. engr. and area supt. at Badak LNG Plant in Indonesia, 1983, gen. field supt. on N.Z. Gas-to-Gasoline project, 1984, asst. mgr. ops. for the London Div., and bus. devel. rep. in Middle East, No. Ireland and Africa, 1985, London Div. tech. mgr. 1986; mng. dir. Bechtel Ltd., London, U.K. 1986-87; dir., exec. v.p. and mem. exec. coms., Bechtel Group, Inc., 1987–, pres. and c.o.o. 1989–, c.e.o. 1990–, also chmn. exec. coms. BGI and subs. cos. incl. Bechtel Power, Bechtel Petroleum, Chemical & Industrial, Bechtel Civil, Bechtel Nat. Inc., Bechtel Constrn., Becon, and Bechtel Enterprises; trustee Thacher Sch., Ojai 1988–; mem. the Bus. Council, Bus. Roundtable, Calif. Bus. Roundtable, the J.P. Morgan Internat. Advy. Council, Pres.'s Commn. on Environmental Quality; rec: golf, tennis, fishing, hunting, skiing. Ofc Bechtel Group Inc PO Box 193965 San Francisco 94119-3965

BECHTEL, STEPHEN D., JR., industrialist; b. May 10, 1925, Oakland; s. Stephen D. and Laura (Peart) Bechtel; m. Elizabeth Mead Hogan, 1946; children: 2 sons, 3 daughters; edn: civil engr. stu. Univ. of Colo. 1943-44; BS, Purdue Univ. 1946; MBA, Stanford Univ. 1948; Hon. Dr. Engrg., Purdue Univ. 1972; Hon. Dr. of Sci., Univ. of Colo. 1981. Career: employed by Bechtel 1941–, held broad variety of jobs and responsibilities both in the field and San Francisco Home Office; dir. 1951–; v.p. 1952-55; sr. v.p. 195-57; exec. v. p. 1957-60; pres. 1960-73; chmn. 1973-90, chmn. emeritus 1990–; chmn. Fremont Group, Inc. and Sequoia Ventures, Inc., 1980–; bd. dir. Internat. Bus. Machines; mem. Nat. Acad. of Engineering (past chmn.), The Business Council (past chmn.), Conference Bd. (life councillor and past chmn.); fmr. mem: The Business Roundtable (policy com.), Labor-Mgmt. Group; mem: bd of trustees Calif. Inst. of Technology; Internat. Advy. Council, Inst. for Internat. Studies, Stanford Univ.; awards: Hon. Chairman NSPE 1990 Nat. Engineers' Week, French Legion of Honor Officer, Engineering News Record- Constrn. Man of Year 1974, Moles' Award for Outstanding Achiev. in Constrn. 1974, ASCE Civil Engring. Mgmt. award 1979, ASME Centennial award 1982, AAES Chmn.'s award 1982, Herbert Hoover Medal 1980, Washington Award 1985, Am. Jewish Com.'s Inst. of Human Relations award 1987, Nat. Medal of Technology 1991; clubs: The Beavers, Commonwealth of Calif., Augusta Nat. Golf, Bankers (SF), The Blind Brook (NYC), The Mount Royal (Montreal), Pacific Union (SF), Ramada (Houston), SF Golf, SF Tennis, Thunderbird CC (Palm Springs), Vancouver (B.C.), Villa Taverna (SF), The York (Toronto); publs: New Edisons and New Technologies (1979), Calif.'s Contbn. to the Multiplier Effect (1979), The Climate for Innovation (1979), Technology: Found. for America's Future Well Being (1980), others; mil: USMCR 1943-48; Prot.; rec: golf, tennis, hiking, photog., dog tng. Res: POB 3809 San Francisco 94119 Ofc: 50 Beale St San Francisco 94105

BECK, JOHN CHRISTIAN, physician/academic division director; b. Jan. 4, 1924, Audubon, Iowa; m. Dr. Arlene Fink; edn: BS, McGill Univ., 1944, MD, 1947, MS, 1951, diploma in experimental medicine, 1952; PhD (hon.) Ben Gurion Univ., Tel Aviv 1981; MD lic. Calif. BME, 1978. Career: prof. UC San Francisco, 1978-79; prof. UC Los Angeles, 1979–, dir. Multicampus Div. of Gerontological Medicine and Gerontology, UCLA, 1987-92; dir. Long Term Care National Res. Ctr., L.A. 1988–; dir. Older Americans Independence Ctr., L.A. 1991–; awards: Allan T. Bailey Memorial Award, Am. Coll. Physicians 1985, Bruce Hall Memorial Lecture, Garvan Inst. of Med. Res. Sydney, Australia 1989, Duncan Graham Award The Royal Coll. Physicians and Surgeons, U.K. 1989, Joseph T. Freeman Award Gerontol. Soc. of Am. 1990, Irving S. Wright Award Am. Fedn. on Aging Res. 1991; mem: AAAS, Am. Clin. and Climatol. Assn., Am. Coll. of Physicians, Am. Diabetes Assn., Am. Fedn. for Clin. Research, Am. Geriatric Soc. Ofc: UCLA, 10833 Le Conte Ave 32-144CHS Los Angeles 90024-1687

BECK, THOMAS EDWIN, studio furniture maker; b. Dec. 31, 1946, Stockton; s. Harold Marquis and Verna (Johnson); m. Ellen Marie Hill, June 11, 1973; 1 son, Alexander b. 1982; edn: San Francisco City Coll. 1964-66, UC Berkeley 1966-67, Coll. of the Desert 1984-85, Calif. Poly. State Univ. 1985. Career: journeyman carpenter United Brotherhood of Carpenters & Joiners, Portland, Oreg. 1972–; cabinetmaker apprentice to Drago Dimitri (Yugoslavian master), Calgary, Can. 1976-79; owner Thomas Beck Fine Furniture, Morongo Valley, Calif. 1981–; cons. San Bdo. Co. Regional Employment; awards: Best of Show Bellevue (Wash.) Art Mus. 1990, award for contemporary furniture So. Calif. Exposition 1993; conscientious objector Vietnam War; Democrat; rec: technical rockclimbing, bass fishing. Res/Ofc: 52355 Altadena Dr Morongo Valley 92256-9671 Ph: 619/363-6155

BECKEL, CARL LEE, lawyer; b. Aug. 27, 1948, Ventura; s. Carl Clifford and Esther Dorothy B.; m. Debra, Aug. 11, 1984; 1 dau: Monica, b. 1976; edn: AA, Ventura Coll. 1968; BA,summa cum laude, CSU Fresno 1974; JD, Ventura Coll. of Law 1979; admitted to Calif. Bar 1979. Career: sales Electrolux 1974; route sales Pepsi Cola Bottling 1979; former ptr. Beckel & Howard 1982; currently, atty. pvt. practice, Ventura; recipient Non-Commissioned Ofcr.'s Leadership Sch. Speech Award; mem: Phi Kappa Phi; Am., Calif. and Ventura Co. Bar Assn.; mil: staff sgt. USAF, Air Force Commdn., GCM, Marksmanship; Democrat; rec: black belt Kenpo Karate, bodybuilding, travel. Ofc: Law Ofcs. Carl L. Beckel 674 County Square Dr Ste 301 Ventura 93003

BEDRICK, JEFFREY KEITH, artist; b. Oct. 4, 1960, Providence, R.I.; s. Barry David and Ann Glenda (Rosenberg) B.; edn: pvt. apprenticeship Gage Taylor, artist, Woodacre, 1977-79; filmmaking, San Francisco St. Univ., 1983. Career: fine artist, exh. num. galleries internat. 1978–; muralist and decorative painting num. cos., San Francisco 1981–; prodn. artist/animator Colossal Pictures, S.F. 1982–; freelance illustrator var. corps. internat. 1986–; honors: internationally represented by Collector's Editions, Canoga Park, Calif.; illustrator, book: Weather (1989 Doubleday); mem. US Hang Gliding Assn. 1991–, World Affairs Council, S.F. Soc. of Illustrators; rec: hang gliding, raquetball, billiards, chess. Ofc: 2852 California Street No. 2 San Francisco 94115 Tel: 415/923-1122

BEEBE, JOHN ELIOTT, III, psychiatrist; b. June 24, 1939, Washington, D.C.; s. John Eliott, Jr. and Patricia (Boden) B.; edn: BA, Harvard Univ. 1961; MD, Univ. Chgo. 1965. Career: psychiatric resident Stanford Hosp., Stanford 1968-71; chief resident Adult Psychiatry Clinic, Stanford Hosp. 1970-71; pvt. practice psychiatry, San Francisco 1971–; asst. prof. psychiatry UCSF Med. Center 1977–; courtesy staff California Pacific Med. Center 1971–; mem: C.G. Jung Inst. S.F., Internat. Assn. Analytical Psychology, No. Calif. Psychiatric Soc., Am. Psychiatric Assn.; author/ed. Psychiatric Treatment, 1975; ed. Jung Inst. Library Jour., 1979–; ed. Money Food Drink Fashion, 1986; ed. Aspects of The Masculine, 1989; co-ed. Jour. of Analytical Psychology, 1990–; author Integrity in Depth, 1992; mil: sr. asst. surgeon USPHS; Democrat; rec: songwriting, screenwriting. Ofc: 337 Spruce St San Francisco 94118

BEFU, BEN, professor emeritus; b. Aug. 14, 1927, Los Angeles; s. Juma and Komaki B.; m. Grayce Yayoi Yano, Aug. 14, 1954; children: MaryLynn Midori b. 1960, AnneMarie Misayo b. 1968; edn: BA, UCLA, 1953; MA, UC Berkeley, 1962; PhD, Stanford Univ., 1966. Career: instr. Rafu Daini Gakuen, Los Angeles 1949-53; US Army 1954-57: linguist, intel. specialist US Army, Tokyo, Japan 1955-57; civilian mil. intel. analyst US DoD, Tokyo 1957-58, linguist, analyst US Govt., Tokyo 1958-60; actg. asst. prof. UCLA, Los Angeles 1964-66, asst. prof. 1966-72, assoc. prof. 1972-91, chmn. Oriental Lang. Dept. 1975-78, prof. emeritus 1991–; vis. asst. prof. Stanford Univ., summer 1965; awards: Commendn. Army Language Sch. Presidio of Monterey 1955, Commendn. 500th Mil Intel Gp Tokyo, Japan 1959, NDFL fellow 1961-64, Instrnl. Improvement award UCLA Academic Senate 1977; mem: Assn. of Asian Studies 1962–, Am. Oriental Soc. 1964-90, Assn. of Teachers of Japanese (1975–, bd. govs. 1983-86), Nat. Scholarly Advy. Council for the Japanese Am. Nat. Museum 1991–; Sierra Club, Nat. Audubon Soc., Nat. Parks and Conserv. Assn., Calif. Avocado Soc.; author: Worldly Mental Calculations (1976), articles "Monumenta Serica" (1968), Critical Survey of Short Fiction" (1987). Res: 1691 Yucatan Way Fallbrook 92028 Ofc: UCLA, Dept of EALC, 405 Hilgard Ave Los Angeles 90024

BEGOVICH, MICHAEL, government lawyer; b. Nov. 20, 1959, Burnaby, B.C., Can., nat. 1968; s. Steven and Helen (Tomich) B.; m. Diana Marie Lozano; edn: BA (summa cum laude), UC Davis, 1981; JD, UC Hastings Coll. of Law, 1985; admitted bar: Ind. 1987, Calif. 1988, U.S. Supreme Ct. 1993. Career: atty., assoc. Law Offices Ramon D. Asedo, Oceanside 1987-88; dep. pub. defender County of San Diego, Vista 1988–; adj. prof. criminal justice Palomar Coll. 1990–; adj. prof. paralegal studies Univ. of San Diego 1991; instr. Police Acad., Grossmont Coll. 1991-92; honors: Phi Beta Kappa, Phi Kappa Phi, Pi Sigma Alpha 1981, Who' Who in Am. Law 1990, Who's Who of Emerging Leaders in Am. 1992, Who's Who in the World 1995; mem: ABA, Calif. Public Defenders Assn., Indiana State Bar Assn., Serbian Bar Assn., San Diego Co. Bar Assn., No. S.D. Co. Bar Assn., Serb Nat. Fedn. (nat. bd. 1987–); civic: 44th

Congl. Dist. Advy. Com. S.D. Co. 1985–; pub. scholarly articles on Serbian hist., culture, poetry (4); Serbian Orthodox (ch. choir); avocation: Serbian hist. and culture. Ofc: Public Defender Co. of San Diego 400 S Melrose Dr Ste 200 Vista 92083

BEHRENDT, JOHN THOMAS, lawyer; b. Oct. 26, 1945, Syracuse, Kans.; s. Thomas Franklin and Anna Iola (Carrithers) B.; m., 1967 (div.); children: Todd Thomas, Gretchen Jean; m. 2d Theresa Ann Elmore, Oct. 27, 1985; edn: BA, Sterling Coll.; JD (cum laude), Univ. Minn.; admitted bar: Calif. 1971, Tex. 1973, N.Y. 1989. Career: atty. assoc., then ptnr. Gibson, Dunn & Crutcher, Los Angeles 1970-71, 1974–; mem: Am. Bar Assn., Los Angeles County Bar Assn.; clubs: Jonathan (L.A.), Union League (N.Y.), Tuxedo (Tuxedo Park, N.Y.); mil: capt. JAGC, AUS 1971-74. Ofc: Gibson Dunn & Crutcher, 333 S Grand Ave Los Angeles 90071 also: 200 Park Ave New York NY 10001

BEHRENS, B. LYN, university president; b. Apr. 14, 1940, Cooranbong, New South Wales, Australia; d. Amelia Sophia (Middleton) Behrens; m. Dave Basaraba, Dec. 24, 1968; children: Sherie b. 1971, Julie b. 1973; edn: M.B., BS (honors), Sydney Univ. Sch. of Medicine, Sydney, New So. Wales, Australia, 1964; cert. Am. Bd. of Pediatrics 1970; lic. physician Med. Bd. of Calif. 1972; cert. Am. Bd. of Allergy & Clinical Immunology 1983, A.B.P.-Sub-Bd. of Pediatric Pulmonary 1989. Career: instr. of pediatrics, Loma Linda Univ. Sch. of Medicine, Loma Linda, Calif., 1970-72; assoc. dir. med. edn. Florida Hosp., Orlando, Fla., 1972-75; asst. prof. pediatrics, Loma Linda Univ. Sch. of Medicine 1975-79; dir. pediatric residency prog. Loma Linda Univ. Med. Ctr., 1975-81; assoc. prof. pediatrics Loma Linda Univ. Sch. of Medicine, 1980-90, vice chair dept. of pediatrics, 1984-86, dean, 1986-91, prof. of pediatrics, 1990–, interim dean, 1993–; pres. Loma Linda Univ. 1990–; ptnr. gen. pediatric practice Loma Linda Univ. faculty 1971-72; employee of pediatric practice, Orlando Fla. 1972-75; pediatric cons. Inland Counties Developmental Disabilities Svs., San Bernardino 1975-81; dir. pediatric allergy/immunology svc. (inpatient & outpatient) Loma Linda Univ. Med. Ctr. 1975-81, dir. div. of allergy, immunology & pediatric pulmonary, 1984-86; awards: Outstanding Clin. Tchr., Loma Linda Univ. Sch. of Medicine 1971, 86, Outstanding Tchr., Fla. Hosp. Resident Staff 1974, Disting. Svc. award, Loma Linda Univ. Sch. of Medicine 1992, Adventist Woman of Year, Profl. Work Life award, Assn. of Adventist Women 1992, SAGUNA award, Sydney Univ. Grads. Union of No. Am. 1993, Alumni award for achievement in comm. svc. Univ. of Sydney 1993; mem.: Alpha Omega Alpha 1981–, Am. Thoracic Soc. 1982–, CMA 1984–, Sigma Xi 1987–, San Bernardino Co. Med. Soc. 1987–, Am. Acad. of Allergy & Clinical Immunology 1988–, Am. Acad. of Pediatrics (fellow) 1988–, Am. Coll. of Chest Physicians (fellow) 1988–, Am. Assn. of Presidents of Indep. Colls. and Univs. 1990–, AMA 1992–, Assn. of Academic Health Centers 1992–, Assn. of Health Services Research 1993–; author: Manual of Clinical Problems in Asthma, Allergy and Related Disorders, pub. Little, Brown & Co. 1984; co-author: num. pub. manuscripts and abstracts; internat. speaker and lecturer; Seventh-day Adventist; rec: travel, reading, entertaining, needlework. Ofc: Loma Linda University Magan Hall 111 Loma Linda 92350

BEIERLE, ROBERT THOMAS, scientist, electronics engineer, inventor; b. Nov. 3, 1945, Long Beach; s. William Frank and Dolores (Mounce) B.; m. Sally Jane Benson, Nov. 18, 1982; child: Troy Albert Emery b. 1988; edn: AS, Mt. San Antonio Coll. 1972; BSEE, Calif. St. Polytech. Univ. 1975, masters cand. Career: design engr. General Dynamics, Pomona 1975-79; principal designer Hughes Aircraft GEADGE pgm. (German Air-Ground Environ. Def. Sys.), Fullerton 1979-82; sr. mem. tech. staff/ hd. guidance control design gp. ADCAP pgm. Hughes Aircraft 1982-92, sr. staff engr., tech. supr.; tchg. asst., radar sys. & signal processing; staff engr. Space and Tactics Div., Santa Barbara Res. Ctr. 1993-94; mgr Engring. Dept. Hughes , AVICOM 1994–; honors: Cal Poly academic scholar 1975. IEEE Student Chpt. acad. outstanding scholar 1975, Hughes Aircraft Div. zero defects award 1984 also two patent awards 1989 and four div. invention awards; mem: IEEE; Nat. Mgmt. Assn.; patents: (3) issued U.S. and foreign; mil: sgt. USAF 1963-67, Vietnam, Nat. Defense Svc., GCM; R.Cath.; rec: landscape design, sailing, inventing. Res: 20980 E Gold Run Dr Diamond Bar 91765 Ofc: Hughes Aircraft, Ground Systems Group, Malvern and Gilbert Fullerton 92634

BEILBY, ALVIN LESTER, chemistry educator; b. Sept. 17, 1932, Watsonville; s. Claud Eldred and Elma Fern (Hockabout) B.; m. Ruby Irene Nelson, June 21, 1958; children: Mark Alfred b. 1959, Lorene Sigrid b. 1961; edn: BA (with great distinction), San Jose State Univ., 1954; Harvard Univ., 1954-55; PhD, Univ. Wash., Seattle 1958. Career: faculty Pomona Coll., Claremont, Calif. 1958-: chemistry instr. 1958-60, asst. prof. 1960-66, assoc. prof. 1966-72, prof. 1972–, dept. chair 1972-85, sci. div. chair 1987-90; vis. scholar Univ. Ill., Champaign-Urbana, 1964-65; guest worker and res. chemist Nat. Bur. of Stds., Gaithersburg, Md. 1971-72; guest wkr. Lockheed Palo Alto Res. Lab., Palo Alto 1979-80; guest prof. Uppsala Univ., Sweden 1986-87; honors: Phi Kappa Phi 1954, Phi Lambda Upsilon 1957, awards: Petroleum Res. Fund Faculty Award for adv. scientific study Am. Chem. Soc., Univ. Ill. 1964-65, NSF sci. faculty, profl. devel. award Lockheed Palo Alto Res. Lab. 1979-80; mem: A.C.S. 1956–, Soc. of Sigma Xi 1958–, AAAS 1983–, Assn. of Am. Med.

Colls. (1966-76, 81-93), Western Assn. of Advisors for the Health Professions (1970-76, 81-93, first chair 1970-71), Soc. of Western Analytical Professors (1968–, 10th annual mtg. co-chair 1977), Int. Univ. of Pure and Applied Chem. (affil. mem.); bd. dirs. Calif. Christian Home, Rosemead 1990-96 (treas. 1993-95, sec. 1995-96); corporation mem: Congregational Homes Inc., Pomona 1986–, Pilgrim Place, Claremont 1994–; publs: Lab. Manual for Chem.: A Quantitative Approach (co-author 1969), editor: Modern Classics in Analytical Chem. (vol. I 1970, vol. II 1976); Democrat; United Ch. of Christ (moderator Claremont United Ch. of Christ, Congl. 1975-77, bd. dirs. So. Calif. Conf. 1983-85, moderator So. Calif. Conf. 1984-85); rec: English handbell ringing, choral singing, travel, photography. Res: 663 Hood Dr Claremont 91711 Ofc: Pomona College 645 N College Ave Claremont 91711

BEILBY, RUBY IRENE, educator; b. Sept. 27, 1936, Seattle; d. Nels Vernon and Lillian Josephine (Johnson) Nelson; m. Alvin Lester Beilby, June 21, 1958; children: Mark b. 1959, Lorene b. 1961; edn: BS home econ., Univ. Wash., 1958; MA home econ., CSU Los Angeles, 1970. Career: home econ. tchr. Pomona (Calif.) Unified Sch. Dist., 1958-59, Pomona Adult Sch., 1967-69; instr. Mt. San Antonio Coll., Walnut 1970; prof. Calif. Poly. St. Univ., Pomona 1972–; honors: Phi Beta Kappa, Pi Lambda Theta, Omicron Nu (1958), Phi Upsilon Omicron (1970), Gamma Sigma Delta (1977), Phi Beta Delta (1988); mem: Am. Home Economics Assn., Internat. Microwave Power Inst., Inst. Food Technologists, Nat. Assn. for Edn. Young Childen; club: Swedish (Seattle); book cons.: Sunset Microwave Cookbook (1980); author Microwave Lab Manual (1979, 83); United Ch. of Christ. Res: 663 Hood Dr Claremont 91711 Ofc: CalPoly University 3801 W Temple Pomona 91768

BEILENSON, ANTHONY CHARLES, congressman; b. Oct. 26, 1932, New Rochelle, N.Y.; s. Peter and Edna (Rudolph) B.; m. Dolores Martin, June 20, 1959; children: Peter, Dayna, Adam; edn: BA, Harvard Coll., 1954; LL.B., Harvard U., 1957; admitted St. Bar: Calif. 1957. Career: mem. Calif. Assembly from 59th Dist., 1963-66, Calif. Senate from 22d Dist., 1967-76, 95th-104th Congresses from 23rd (now 24th) Calif. Dist., 1977–; Democrat. Ofc: House of Representatives 2465 Rayburn Bldg Washington DC 20515

BEKEY, GEORGE ALBERT, computer science and robotics institute executive; b. June 19, 1928, Bratislava, Slovakia; s. Andrew and Elizabeth (Magyar) B.; m. Shirley White, June 10, 1951; children: Ronald Steven; Michelle Elaine; edn: BSEE, UC Berkeley 1950; MS, UCLA 1952; PhD, 1962; Reg. Elec. Engr. & Control Sys. Engr., CA. Career: tchg. asst., research engr. UCLA Sch. of Eng. 1950-54; US Army Signal Corps. 1954-56; mgr. computer ctr. Beckman Instruments, L.A. 1956-58; group ldr., section hd., sr. staff engr. TRW Systems, L.A. 1958-62; asst. prof. Dept. Elec. Engring. USC 1962-64; assoc. prof. 1964-68, prof. Dept. Elec. Engring., Biomedical Engring. and Computer Sci., USC 1968–, co-dir. Sys. Simulation Lab. 1962-66, chmn. Elec. Engring.- Sys. Dept. 1970-72, 1978-82, dir. Biomed. Engring. Inst. 1972-75; dir. USC Robotics Inst. 1983–, chmn. USC Computer Science Dept. 1984-89, dir. Center for Mfg. and Automation Research, 1987-94; pres.-elect IEEE Soc. for Robotics and Automation; ed. IEEE Trans. on Robotics and Automation 1984-89; ed. Autonomous Robots; assoc. ed. Mathematics and Computers in Simulation, and Transactions of the Soc. for Computer Simulation; gen. chmn. 7th Internat. Symposium on System Identification and Process Parameter Estimation, Wash. DC 1982; honors: Sigma Xi nat. lectr. 1976-77, disting. faculty award USC Sch. of Engring. 1976, elected Nat. Acad. of Engring. 1989; mem: Soc. of Computer Simulation, AAAS (fellow 1992), Am. Inst. on Biol. and Med. Engring. (fellow 1991), IEEE (fellow 1972), World Affairs Council; publs: co-author Hybrid Computation, 1968, ed. Proceedings of Conf. on Mathematical Models of Public Systems, 1971, co-editor: Hospital Information Systems, 1972, Neural Networks and Robotics, 1993, num. book chpts. and tech. papers; mil: U.S. Army 1954-56. Ofc: Computer Science Dept. USC, Los Angeles 90089-0781

BELET, JACQUES HENRY, III, manufacturing executive, crisis management professional; b. Feb. 21, 1948, Akron, Ohio; s. Jacques Henry II and Harriet Jane (Hood) B.; m. Kathleen Ellen Williams, 1993; children: Richard b. 1968, Jeffrey b. 1971; edn: BA, Univ. of Akron, 1970. Career: indsl. engr. Am. Hard Rubber Co., Akron & L.A. 1966-67; indsl. engr. BF Goodrich Co. 1970-79; indsl. engr. Ameron Corp., Ventura, Calif. 1979; chief facility planning engr. Becton Dickinson & Co., Oxnard, Calif. 1979, mfg. mgr. 1979-80; plant mgr. Fesco Plastics div. Cities Service Oil Co., Tustin 1980-82, mgr. ops. Chgo. 1982; pres., chmn., c.e.o. The Belet Group, Inc., Newport Beach, Calif. 1983–; exec. v.p., c.o.o. Microwave Products of Am., Inc., Memphis, Tenn. 1989-91; pres., c.e.o., dir. Menumaster-U.K., Inc., 1990; pres., c.e.o., dir. Menumaster-Canada, Inc., 1990–, Menumaster, Inc. 1991–; ptnr. The Belet Partners, 1990–; pres., c.e.o. Rancho Dakota Niguel, 1991; pres., c.e.o. Belet Acquisitions, Inc. 1993–; mil: U.S. Army, 1967-70. Res: 23771 Mariner Dr #129 Laguna Niguel 92677 Ofc: The Belet Group, Inc 110 Newport Ctr Dr Ste 200 Newport Beach 92660

BELL, CAROL ANN, pathologist, educator, clinical laboratory director; b. July 29, 1935, Fresno; d. George Robert and Frances Eleanor (Young) Bell; edn: BS pharm., UCSF 1957; MD, 1961. Career: staff pathologist Cedars-Sinai Hosp., Los Angeles 1967-70, dir. blood bank 1970-72; asst. dir. clin. lab. UC

Irvine Med. Center, Orange 1972-73; director clinical lab. Brotman Med. Center, Culver City 1973–; clin. prof. pathology UC Irvine, 1978–, USC, 1980–; honors: Alpha Omega Alpha, ARC Candelite award (1984), Sigma Xi; mem: Am. Assn. Bloodbanks, Calif. Blood Bank Systems (pres. 1979), Coll. Am. Pathologists, ARC, Greater Los Angeles Zoological Assn.; author book chpts. and num. articles on blood banking (1962–), editor seminars for Am. Assn. of Blood Banks (1980-85); Methodist; rec: travel. Ofc: Memorial Pathology Medical Group Brotman Medical Center 3828 Hughes Ave Culver City 90230

BELL, WAYNE S., lawyer; b. June 24, 1954, Los Angeles; s. Joseph and Jane Barbara B.; 1st cousin, Richard Ellmann (dec.), fmr. prof. English lit. Oxford Univ., and biographer of James Joyce, Oscar Wilde; m. M. Susan Modzelewski, Apr. 1, 1989; edn: BA magna cum laude, UCLA, 1976; JD, Loyola Univ. Sch. Law, 1979; advanced mgmt. pgm. Rutgers Univ. 1992; admitted bar: Calif. (1980), U.S. Dist. Cts. Calif. (cent., so., no. dist.), U.S. Tax Ct., U.S. Ct. Appeals (9th circuit), U.S. Supreme Ct., Dist. Col. 1986; Calif. lic. R.E. Broker (1988). Career: intern Calif. Gov.'s Ofc., Sacto. summer 1976; law clk. LaFollette, Johnson, L.A. 1978-79; atty., assoc. Levinson, Rowen, Miller, Jacobs & Kabrins, L.A. 1980-82; sr. assoc. Montgomery, Gascou, Gemmill & Thornton, L.A. 1982-84; counsel, proj. devel. Thomas Safran & Assocs., L.A. 1984-85; of counsel Greenspan, Glasser & Medina, Santa Monica 1984-86; assoc. gen. counsel Am. Diversified, Costa Mesa 1985-88; legal cons., project atty., L.A. 1988-89; senior counsel Ralphs Grocery Co., L.A. 1989–; spec. master State Bar Spec. Master Pgm. 1991-92; judge pro tem South Bay Municipal Ct. 1987; judge pro tem L.A. Superior Ct., 1991, 94; mem. tech. adv. panel Legal Corps of L.A. 1994–; settlement ofcr. L.A. Municipal Ct. 1990-92; Gov. appt. mem. state advy. council to Legal Services Corp., Calif. 1982-88; vol. atty. Westside Legal Svs., legal aid, Santa Monica 1982-87; bd. dirs. Am. Theatre Arts, Hywd. 1983-84; legal ombudsman L.A. Co. Bar Assn. Olympics Ombudsman Pgm. 1984; bd. dirs., legis. strategy com., exec. com. Legal Assistance Assn. of Calif. 1984-86; mem., chmn. Bd. of Appeals for Handicapped Accommodations, Manhattan Beach 1986-88; honors: Phi Beta Kappa 1976, Pi Sigma Alpha 1975, Pi Gamma Mu 1975, chief Note and Comment ed. Loyola Law Rev., 1978-79, listed Who's Who in Amer. Law, Who's Who Emerging Leaders. in Am., Who's Who in the World, Who's Who in Am., Who's Who in West, Men of Achievement, Internat. Directory of Disting. Leadership; mem: ABA 1981-92, Calif. Bar Assn. (legal svs. sect. com. legal problems of aging 1983-86, chmn. legis. subcom. 1984-86; alt. Conf. of Dels. 1987), UCLA Alumni Assn. (life), Loyola Law Sch. (adv.), Phi Alpha Delta Law Frat.; civic: The Ralphs/Food 4 Less Found. (trustee, secty. 1995–), Foodbank of So. Calif. (dir., sec. 1991-94), Pgms. for the Developmentally Handicapped, Inc. (dir., pres. 1987-92), Autism Soc. of Am., So. Poverty Law Ctr.; contbr. poetry/articles to gen. pub. and articles in bar jours., Loyola Univ. Law Rev., 1978, Family Law News, 1981, Sr. Citizens Handbook (1984, 2d. ed. 1987), L.A. Daily Journal, 1989-90, Veterans Forum, 1991, Equipment Financing Jour., 1991, Mass Market Retailers, 1993, The Corporate Counselor, 1995; Democrat (contbg. mem. Dem. Nat. Com.); rec: travel, human behavior study, cycling, hiking, photog. Ofc: Ralphs Grocery Co. POB 54143 Los Angeles 90054

BELLANCA, LOUIS CHARLES, lawyer; b. June 26, 1943, Buffalo, NY; s. Russell Michael and Christine Mary (Fasciana) B.; m. Jayne Gardner, Sept. 5, 1970; children: Dayna, b. 1974, Erin, b. 1977; edn: AAS, Erie Comm. Coll. 1962; stu. Pasadena City Coll. 1962-3, Glendale Coll. 1963-4, Valley Coll. 1965-7; JD, LLB, Univ. San Fernando Valley, 1972; admitted bar: Calif. 1972, U.S. Dist. Cts. 1977. Career: optician, Superior Optical Co., Los Angeles 1962-72; pvt law practice, Beverly Hills 1973; staff atty. Mansell & Giddens, Los Angeles 1973-74; atty., assoc. Grancell, Kegel & Tobin, L.A. 1974-75; mng. atty. Levy, Koszdin, Goldschmid & Sroloff, Long Beach and Santa Ana, 1975-78; atty., sec., CFO law firm Towner, Kristjanson, Bellanca & Hill, Santa Ana and Tustin 1978-82, pres. 1980-82; pres. Kristjanson, Bellanca & Hill, 1982-85; pres. Kristjanson, Bellanca, Roselinsky, Gerrick & Hudes, 1985-87; v.p. Baziak & Bellanca, 1988–; Workers' Compensation judge pro tem 1982–, Workers' Compensation Arbitration Panel 1991–; awards: Master of Ophthalmic Optics 1972, Fellow Internat. Acad. of Opticianry 1965, James Bass and Loren Michael Mem. awards Jaycees (1967, 68); State Bar certified worker's compensation specialist 1994; mem: Workers Compensation Claims and Def. Counsel Assn. (secty.1978), Long Beach Bar Assn., Am. Bar Assn., Calif. Applicant's Attorneys Assn., Orange Co. Bar Assn. (chmn. Workers Compensation Sect. 1990), Lex Romana (sec. 1993, pres. 1994); civic: Northridge Jaycees (past pres. 1969-70), Sunland-Tujunga Jaycees (v.p. 1967, state dir. 1968); Republican; Christian; rec: boating, golf, bicycling, running. Res: Huntington Beach Ofc: Baziak & Bellanca, 1327 N Broadway St Santa Ana.

BELLEVILLE, PHILIP FREDERICK, lawyer; b. Apr. 24, 1934, Flint, Mich.; s. Frederick Charles and Sarah Adeline (Cottrell) B.; m. Geraldean Bickford, Sept. 2, 1953; children: Stacy, b. 1957; Philip II, b. 1958; Jeffrey, b. 1961; edn: BA, honors in econ. and high distinction, Univ. of Mich. 1956, JD, 1960; admitted to State Bar of Calif. 1961. Career: atty., assoc. Latham & Watkins, L.A., Calif. 1960-68, partner L.A. and Newport Bch. 1968-73, (chmn. Litigation Dept. L.A., Newport Bch., Calif. and Wash. D.C. 1973-80), partner L.A., Orange County, San Diego, Wash. D.C., 1980–, Chgo. 1983–, N.Y.C.

1985–, San Francisco 1990–, London 1990–, Moscow 1992–; awards: James B. Angell Scholar 1955-6, Phi Beta Kappa 1955, Phi Kappa Psi 1955, Order of the Coif 1960; mem. So. Calif. steering com. NAACP Legal Def. Fund Inc. 1979; advy. bd. San Pedro/Penninsula Hosp. 1980-88; mem: Am. Bar Assn. (Antitrust Law and Crim. Justice sects.), State Bar of Calif. (Antitrust, Trade Reg. Law & Bus. Law sects.), Los Angeles Co. Bar Assn. (Bus. Trial Lawyers sect.), Assn. of Bus. Trial Lawyers; clubs: City (Bunker Hill), Palos Verdes Golf, Jack Kramer Tennis, Rolling Hills Tennis, Caballeros, Portuguese Bend; Republican; Prot.; rec: antiques, classic autos, art and literature. Ofc: Latham & Watkins, 633 W Fifth St Los Angeles 90071-2007

BELLIS, CARROLL J., surgeon; b. May 11, 1908, Shreveport, La.; s. Joseph E. and Rose (Bloome) B.; m. Mildred E., Dec. 26, 1951; children: Joseph, b. 1940, David, b. 1944; edn: BS, 1930, MS, 1932, PhD in physiol., 1934, MD, 1936, PhD in surg., 1941, Univ. of Minn. Career: teaching fellow in Physiol., Univ. of Minn.; Alice Shevlin fellowship in physiology, Univ. of Minn.; instr. in surgery U. of Minn. Medical Sch.; surgical cons. to Surgeon-Gen. US Army; currently: pvt. practice of surgery; staff St. Mary Med. Ctr.; cons. in surgery, Long Beach Gen. Hosp.; prof./chmn. Dept. of Surgery, Calif. Coll. of Medicine. Honors: Sigma Xi, AOA, Phi Beta Kappa, recipient Charles Lyman Green Prize in Physiol., Mpls. Surgical Soc. Prize, Miss. Valley Med. Soc. Annual Awd. 1955. Dip. Am. Bd. of Surgery, Fellow Am. Coll. of Surgeons, Fellow Nat. Cancer Inst., Fellow Am. Coll. of Gastroenterol., Fellow Am. Geriatrics Soc., Fellow Internat. Coll. of Surgeons, Fellow of the Sci. Council, Internat. Coll. of Angiology, Fellow Phlebology Soc. of Am., mem. Am. Assn. for Study of Neoplastic Diseases, Am. Assn. of Hist. of Medicine, AAAS, NY Acad. of Scis., Am. Med. Writers Assn., Irish Med. Assn. (hon.), Hollywood Acad. of Medicine, Pan Am. Med. Assn. Author 51+ publs. in field incl. 3 books: Fundamentals of Human Physiology, Critique of Reason, Lectures in Medical Physiology; mil: col. US Army M.C., 1941-45. Res: 3 South Quail Ridge Rd Rolling Hills 90274 Ofc: 1045 Atlantic Ave Ste 1011 Long Beach 90813

BELLIS, DAVID JAMES, educator; b. May 1, 1944, Nashville, Tenn.; s. Carroll J. and Helen L. B.; m. Ann, Dec. 23, 1972; son, James; edn: BA, UCLA, 1965; MA, USC, 1969, PhD, 1977. Career: instr. Long Beach City Coll., 1970-78; lectr. USC, 1978-85; assoc. prof. CSU San Bernardino, 1985-91, prof. and acting chair dept. pub. adminstrn., 1991-92, prof. 1992–; asst. dir. Youth Gang Services, Los Angeles County, 1980-81; elected City Council, City of Signal Hill 1980-86, mayor 1984-85; cons. City of Highland 1991–, San Bernardino Co. Sheriffs Dept. 1994–, San Bernardino Police Dept. 1994–, St. Office of Criminal Justice 1987-88, Project Heavy, L.A. 1975-78; chmn. San Bernardino Downtown Mainstreet, 1987-91; honors: meritorious performance CSUSB, 1988, Outstanding Public Adminstrn. Educator of Yr. award ASPA, 1991, Excellence in Research awards, CSUSB, 1993, 94; mem., exec. bd. ASPA, 1987–; author: Heroin & Politicians, 1983. Res: PO Box 1064 Cedar Glen 92321 Ofc: California State Univ. 5500 University Pky San Bernardino 92407

BELTRAMI, ALBERT PETER, government executive; b. Feb. 26, 1934, Sacto.; s. Battista "Bob" and Anastasia "Annie" B.; m. Patricia J. Kearns, July 28, 1957; children: Katharine Clare b. 1964, Robert Richard b. 1965; edn: AA, Modesto Jr. Coll., AB pol. sci., UC Berkeley, and MA in pub. adminstrn., UC Berkeley. Career: dep. marshal Modesto Municipal Ct., 1954-55; adminstrv. asst. County of San Luis Obispo, S.L.O. 1960-61, asst. adminstrv. ofcr. 1961-65; county adminstrv. ofcr. County of Mendocino, Ukiah 1965-90; cons. local govt. fin. & ops., affil. Pub. Service Skills, Inc. Sacto. 1990-91; CEO County of Stanislaus, Modesto 1991-93; deputy dir. Intergovernmental Affairs, Office of Gov. Wilson, Calif. 1993- advy. com. Golden Gate Univ. Grad. Sch. Pub. Adminstrn. 1975-80; gov. appt. mem. Calif. No. Coast Reg. Water Quality Control Bd. 1972-93 (chmn. 1976, 81, 89); atty. gen. appt. mem. Calif. Law Enforce. Telecomms. Advy. Com. 1974-90; dir. Mendocino Devel. Corp., 1987-89; mem: Calif. Assn. Co. Adminstrv. Ofcrs. (sec. 1979-80, v.p. 80-81, pres. 81-82), AM Soc. for Pub. Adminstrn. 1965–, Inter City Mgmt. Assn. 1965–, U.S. Naval Inst., Navy League, Naval Reserve Assn. (life); clubs: Commonwealth of Calif. (SF), Elks (SLO), Lions (Ukiah), Elks (Ukiah); author: California- Golden Gate Report (6/88); mil: cdr. USNR Active 1957-60, 6/84 Ret.; Republican; R.Cath.; rec: chess, gardening. Res: 145 Mendocino Pl Ukiah 95482 Tel: 707/462-6230

BENEDICT, BURTON, professor emeritus of anthropology, museum director emeritus; b. May 20, 1923, Baltimore, Md.; s. Burton Eli Oppenheim and Helen (Dieches) Benedict; m. Marion MacColl Steuber, Sept. 23, 1950; children: Helen b. 1952, Barbara MacVean b. 1955; edn: BA cum laude, Harvard Univ. 1949; PhD, Univ. London England 1954. Career: sr. research fellow McGill Univ., Montreal, Canada 1954-55; sociological research ofcr. Colonial Social Sci. Research Council, Mauritius 1955-58; asst. lectr., sr. lectr. London Sch. of Econ., England 1958-68; prof. anthropology UC Berkeley 1968–, dean of social scis. 1971-74; dir. study center for U.K., London 1986-88; dir. Hearst Museum of Anthropology UC Berkeley 1988-94, chmn. dept. anthropology 1970-71, com on budget 1978-81; awards: NEH grant (1981-83), Colonial Social Scis. Conf. (1955-58, 60), Dept. of Tech. Coop. fellowship (1962), Humanites Research UC Berkeley fellowship (1974-76, 81-82); mem: Assn. Social Anthropologists,

Royal Anthropoligical Inst., Am. Anthropological Assn., Athenaeum; author: Indians in Plural Soc. (1961), People of Seychelles (1966), co-author: Men Women & Money in Seychelles (1982), author, ed. Anthropology of Worlds Fairs (1983); mil: sgt. USAF 1942-46; rec: museums, bird watching, collecting. Ofc: Dept. of Anthropology Univ. of Calif. Berkeley 94720

BENHAM, PRISCILLA CARLA, college president; b. Jan. 30, 1950, Berkeley, Calif.; d. Carl Thomas and Bebe (Harrison) Patten; m. Donald William Benham, Mar. 30, 1986; children: Charmaine Priscilla b. 1989; edn: BS, Patten Coll., Oakland 1969; BA, Holy Names Coll., Oakland 1970; MA (with honors), Wheaton Coll., Wheaton, Ill. 1972; PhD, Drew Univ., Madison, N.J. 1976. Career: teaching fellow Drew Univ. 1974-75; prof. Patten College, Oakland 1975–, pres. 1983–; co-pastor Christian Cathedral, Oakland 1964–, choral dir. 1975–; v.p. Christian Evangelical Churches of Am., Oakland 1989–; bd. dirs. Am. Assn. of Presidents of Indep. Colls. & Univs., Malibu 1990–; bd. dirs. Regional Assn. of East Bay Colls. & Univs., Oakland 1991–; editorial bd. Journal of Pentecostal Theology, Cleveland, Tenn. 1991–; listed in: Notable Americans 1979, Personalities of America 1979, Who's Who of Women 1982, Who's Who in Religion 1985, Who's Who in the West 1986, Men and Women of Distinction 1988; mem.: Am. Acad. of Religion/Soc. of Biblical Lit., Bar-Ilan Assn. of the Greater Bay Area 1984–, Assn. of Indep. Colls. & Univs. 1984–, Presidents of Small Indep. Colls. 1991–, Oakland C.of C. 1987–; co-author: Before the Times 1980, The World of the Early Church 1990; Christian Evangelical; rec: skiing. Ofc: Patten College 2433 Coolidge Ave Oakland 94601

BENJAMIN, ALFRED, medical photographer/educator; b. Aug. 14, 1916, Hamburg, Ger., nat. 1954; s. Martin Edmund and Roberta (Goldtree) B.; m. Selma Horovitz, Mar. 19, 1940; children: Roberta Feist Benjamin b. 1944, Wendy Benjamin Smith b. 1946; edn: dipl. in photography, sci. & med. photog., Reimann Sch., London, England 1938, 1939; adult edn. tchg. cred., UC Los Angeles, 1959. Career: photographer H. Hirsch Cancer Inst., Hamburg, Ger. 1934-36; chief med. photographer Queen Mary's Hosp., Roehampton, Eng. 1943-48; freelance medical & sci. photographer, Los Angeles 1948–; chief med photog. Rancho Los Amigos Hosp., Downey 1955-61; dir. A-V Dept. Orthopaedic Hosp. L.A. 1961-85, senior research photog. 1985-87; lectr. univs., med. centers, and profl. assns. USA and England, 1947–, tchr. photog. Hollywood Community Adult Sch., 1959-91; pvt. instr. in Santa Monica Studio, 1972–; exhibitor profl. assns. and galleries, 1949–; honors: display of photo of Electrical Field of Solanium Flower "Kodak's Journey into Imagination" Epcot Ctr. Disney World, Orlando (1989); mem: Royal Photographic Soc. London (asso. 1939–), Biol. Photographers Assn. (reg. mem. 1949–, pres. So. Calif. chpt. 1965, Fellow 1980), Soc. Photog. Scientists & Engrs. (1949), Am. Thermographic Soc. (1981–); inventor Cancer screening technique using electrical field of blood (pat. pend. 1987); publs: articles in Med. Tribune (1967), Visual/Sonic Medicine (1968), num. articles in BPA Jour. (1973-83), Perfusion Review (1993), Photonics (1994); Jewish; rec: painting, acting, adult counseling. Res: 1213 Pacific St Santa Monica 90405

BENJAMIN, ARLIN JAMES, physicist; b. Oct. 9, 1933, Guthrie, Okla.; s. Harold Dinsmore and Lulu Martha (Black) Yearout B.; m. Patricia Ann Crabb, Oct. 10, 1964; children: Arlin b. 1966, Cynthia b. 1968, Deborah b. 1972; edn: BS, Sam Houston St. Univ. 1955; MS, Okla. St. Univ. 1957; MIT 1959; Wichita St. Univ. 1959-60. Career: research engr. Boeing Co., Wichita, Kans. 1957-63; lead nuclear engr. LTV Corp., Dallas, Tx. 1963-64; ops. research analyst Research Triangle Inst., N.C. 1964-66; sr. ops. research analyst Gen. Dynamics Corp., Ft. Worth, Tx. 1966-68; mgr., sr. ops. research analyst Control Data Corp., Honolulu, Hawaii 1968-70; sr. scientist Southwest Research Inst., San Antonio, Tx. 1970-78; mgr., sr. scientist Hittman Assocs., Sacto. 1978-81; mgr. BDM Corp., Hawthorne 1981-86; prin. engr. Northrop Corp., Pico Rivera 1986–; honors: Alpha Chi, Pi Gamma Mu; mem: Am. Nuclear Soc. (treas. N. Texas section 1963-64), Am. Physical Soc., Am. Geophysical Union, Inst. Physics & Physical Soc. (London), European Physical Soc.; num. articles pub. in tech. and sci. jours.; Republican; rec: fishing, music, philately. Res: 3425 E Date St Brea 92621

BENJAMIN, KARL, painter, professor of art; b. Chgo., 1925; edn: Northwestern Univ. 1943; BA, Univ. of Redlands, 1949; MA, Claremont Grad. Sch., 1960. Career: mil: US Navy 1943-46; painter, 1951–, Loren-Barton Babcock Miller Prof. of Fine Arts/artist in residence Pomona Coll., also prof. of art Claremont Grad. Sch.; awards: NEA visual art grant, $15,000 (1983, 1986); permanent mus. collections internat.; major exhibits include: Univ. of Redlands, Falk-Raboff Gal., L.A., 1953, Pasadena Art Mus., L.A. Art Assn. 1954, Jack Carr Gal. Pasadena, "10th Ann. Newport Harbor Art Exh." Newport Beach, 1955, "Art in Architecture" Municipal Art Gal., L.A., 1956, "Calif. Drawings" Pomona Coll. and UC Riverside Art Depts. and Herschel Chipp, also shown Long Beach Mus. of Art 1957, Occidental Coll. 1958, "4 Abstract Classicists" L.A. Co. and S.F. Museums; "New Talent" Am. Fedn. of Arts: Wichita Art Mus., Time Inc. NY, Univ. Ala., Howard Univ., others, 1959, Esther-Robles Gal. L.A. (1959, 60, 62, 64), "West Coast Hard Edge" Inst. of Contemp. Arts London, Queen's Coll. Belfast; "Purist Painting" Am. Fedn. of Arts: Andrew Dickson White Art Mus. Ithaca, NY, Walker Art Ctr. Mpls., Speed Mus.

Louisville, Mus. of Art Syracuse, N.C. Mus. of Art, Columbus Gal. of Fine Arts Ohio; L.A. Co. Mus. of Art Ann. Exh, 1960, Auckland Art Gal. N.Z. (1961, 71), Bolles Gal. S.F., La Jolla Mus. of Art, 1961, "50 California Artists" Whitney Mus. N.Y., Walker Art Ctr. Mpls., Albright-Knox Art Gal., Buffalo, Des Moines Art Ctr., Ia.; "Geometric Abstraction in Am." Whitney Mus. NY, Boston Inst. Contemp. Art, others; "The Artist's Environment West Coast" Amon Carter Mus. of We. Art, Ft. Worth, Tx., UCLA Art Gals., Oakland Art Mus.; Santa Barbara Mus. Art, 1962, "Liturgical Art" Mount St. Mary's Coll. L.A., 1963, "New Accessions, USA" Colo. Springs Fine Arts Ctr., 1964, "The Responsive Eye" Mus. Modern Art N.Y., City Art Mus. St. Louis, Seattle Art Mus., Pasadena Art Mus., Balt. Mus. Art; "Art Across Am." Mead Corp., M. Knoedier & Co. N.Y., Toledo Mus. of Art, Cleve. Inst. Art, Wadsworth Atheneum Hartford, Contemp. Arts Ctr. Cinti., Isaac Delgado Mus. New Orleans, Commercial Mus. Phila., others; "The Colorists 1950-1965" S.F. Mus. Art; "Calif. Artists" Witte Memorial Mus. San Antonio; "Survey of Contemp. Art" Speed Mus. Art Louisville; "Denver Mus. Art Annual", 1965, "S.F. Art Inst. 85th Ann. Exh." S.F. Mus. Art; "Am. Painting" Va. Mus. Fine Arts, 1966, "30th Biennial Exh. of Am. Painting" Corcoran Gal. WDC; The White House, 1967, Henri Gal. WDC, Santa Barbara Mus. Art, 1968, "L.A. Ann. Art Exh." Municipal Art Gal., 1969, Wm. Sawyer Gal. S.F., 1971, Univ. Redlands, 1972, Tortue Gal. Santa Monica (1975, 77, 78, 80), "Painting and Sculpture in Calif.: The Modern Era" S.F. Mus. Art, Nat. Collection of Fine Arts WDC, 1976, "35th Biennial Am. Painting" Corcoran Gal.; "4 From Calif." Dorothy Rosenthal Gal. Chgo., 1977, Francine Seders Gal., Seattle (1978, 79, 80, 83, 86), "Art, Inc: Am. Paintings From Corp. Collections" Montgomery Mus. Fine Arts Ala., Corcoran Gal., Indpls. Mus. Art, San Diego Mus. Art; "Los Angeles Abstract Painting" Univ. N.M., UC Riverside, 1979, "survey, 1970-1980" Univ. Redlands, "partial retrospective" Cheney-Cowles Mus. Spokane, Wa., Whitman Coll. Sheehan Gal.; "West Coast: Art For the Pres.'s House" S.F. Mus. Art, The V.P.'s House WDC,1980, "Paintings of the 50s" Pepperdine Univ.; Nat. Mus. Am. Art, WDC, 1981, Univ. Wash., Stella Polaris Gal., L.A. 1982, "A Focus on Calif." L.A. Co. Mus. Art, "20th Century: S.F. Mus. Modern Art Collection", 1984, "The Calif. Colorists" Shasta Coll., Redding Art Mus., San Jose Inst. Contemp. Art, Palm Springs Mus., Pomona Coll.; "Color Forms" Sec. Pac. Nat. Bank Gal., L.A., 1985, "Insights" Laguna Art Mus., 1987, A Retrospective Exh., 1955-1987, CSU Northridge; "A Decade of Abstraction", Seattle Ctr., 1989, "Turning the Tide: Early L.A. Modernists 1920-1956" Laguna Art Mus., Oakland Mus., McNay Art Inst. San Antonio, 1990, "Survey of Geometric Abstractions" Marc Richards Gal., Santa Monica, "Ten Year Survey" D.P. Fong Gal., San Jose (one person show) 1991, "Paintings 1955-1990" Snyder Fine Art, N.Y. (one-person show) 1992. Res/Studio: 675 W Eighth St Claremont

BENJAMIN, STUART ALLAN, lawyer, film producer, entertainment company executive; b. Apr. 25, 1946, Los Angeles; s. Gerald T. and Victorine B. (Ritter); m. Alise Humple, 1991; children: Jennifer b. 1977, Matthew b. 1978; edn: BS in fin. (magna cum laude), USC, 1967; JD, Harvard Law Sch., 1970. Career: atty., assoc. Wyman, Bautzer, Christensen, Kuchel & Silbert, Los Angeles 1970-75, ptnr. 1975-88, of counsel 1988-91; pres. and c.o.o New Visions Inc. and New Visions Pictures (video and film prodn.), 1971-91; chmn. Stuart Benjamin Productions, 1991–; exec. prod. feature films: White Nights, LaBamba, Everybody's All American, Billy Galvin, Queens Logic, The Long Walk Home, Mortal Thoughts, Defenseless; exec. v.p./dir. New Visions Entertainment Corp., 1988-91; dir: Boston Celtics 1976-78, San Diego Clippers 1978-81, New Visions Pictures 1971-91; mem: Am. Bar Assn., Calif. State Bar, Beverly Hills Bar Assn., L.A. Co. Bar Assn.; civic: L.A. County Mus. of Art (sponsor); Democrat; Jewish; rec: tennis, politics, film, literature. Ofc: Stuart Benjamin Productions, 12725 Ventura Blvd Ste B Studio City 91604

BENNETT, ALAN JEROME, electronics executive, physicist; b. June 13, 1941, Philadelphia, Pa.; s. Leon Martin and Reba (Perry) B.; m. Frances Kitey, June 16, 1963; children: Sarah, Rachel, Daniel; edn: BA, Univ. Pa. 1962; MS, Univ. Chgo. 1963; PhD, 1965. Career: physicist research and devel. center GE, Schenectady, N.Y. 1966-74; branch mgr. research and devel. center 1975-79; dir. electronics lab. Gould Inc., Rolling Meadows, Ill. 1979-84; v.p. research Varian Assocs., Palo Alto 1984-91; dir prog. devel. Lawrence Livermore Nat. Laboratory 1992-94, dir. industrial partnerships and commercialization 1994–; awards: NSF fellow (1963-65, 1966); mem: AAAS, IEEE (sr.), Am. Physics Soc., Phi Beta Kappa, Sigma Xi; contbr. articles to profl. jours.; rec: linguistics, amateur radio. Res: 233 Tennyson Ave Palo Alto 94301 Ofc: Lawrence Livermore Nat. Laboratory PO Box 808 Livermore 94551

BENNETT, BRADFORD CARL, somatic educator; b. May 27, 1953, Dayton, Oh.; s. Carl Vernor and Norma June (Linkinhoker) B.; edn: BS, Univ. Wis., Madison,1975; MS, Stanford Univ., 1976, PhD, 1982. Career: staff engr. Acurex Corp., Mountain View 1983-88; sr. res. scientist MCAT Inst., 1988-93; assoc. Novato Inst. for Somatic Res. & Training, Novato 1990–; dir. Somatic Learning Center 1993–; instr. biomechanics Sonoma State Univ. 1994; res. assoc and lectr. San Francisco State Univ. 1994–; mem: Trager Inst., Somatics Soc., Assn. for Humanistic Psychol., Somatic Community; clubs: Cloud Hands West, S.F. (chair 1989-90, 91-92), Tai Chi; pub. articles in Somatics Jour., 1991, 92; rec: backpacking, basketball. Address: 120 Conrad St San Francisco 94131

BENNETT, BRIAN O'LEARY, electric utility executive; b. Dec. 5, 1955, Brooklyn, N.Y.; s. Robert Joseph and Barbara Ashton (Michael) B.; edn: BA econ., George Washington Univ. 1982; JD, Southwestern Univ. Sch. of Law 1982. Career: legislative caseworker U.S. Sen. James L. Buckley, W.D.C. 1973-77; legislative asst. Cong. Bob Dornan 1977-78, dist. field rep., L.A. 1978-83; dir. comms. Calif. Dept. Housing & Comm. Devel., Sacto. 1983-84; chief of staff, U.S. Cong. R.K. Dornan, WDC 1985-89, campaign mgr. Dornan in 84, 86, 88, Garden Grove; mem. Calif. Bush for Pres. Organizing Com., L.A. 1986-88, del. Calif. State Republican Party Platform Com., Burbank 1988, del. Republican Nat. Conv. 1988, 92 Calif. del. selection com. 1988, 92; regional affairs mgr., corp. municipal relations mgr. So. Calif. Edison Co., 1989-95, exec. dir., corp. public affairs, So. Calif. Edison Co., 1995–; honors: Outstanding Young Men of Am.; civic: Orange Co. Pro Life PAC, Calif. Republican Party (state central com., mem. resolutions com.), Orange Co. Forum (bd. dirs.) Orange Co. Public Affairs Assn. (bd. dirs.), Orange Co. Urban League (bd. dirs.), Orange Co. Boy Scout Council (bd. dirs.), World Affairs Council of Orange County (bd. trustees); contbr. Los Angeles Times; R.Cath.; rec: history, racquetball, travel, movies. Ofc: So. California Edison Co. 2244 Walnut Grove Ave Rm 417 Rosemead 91770

BENNETT, JOAN CAROL, government lawyer, prosecutor; b. Oct. 6, 1949, Los Angeles; d. Marvin Thomas and Gloria Natalie (Rinaldi) Bennett; div.; 1 dau. Anne Bernal b. 1976; edn: BA, Ripon Coll. 1971, grad. wk. Univ. de Toulouse, France 1972; JD, Univ. of La Verne 1977; admitted Calif. Bar. Career: sgt. US Army Reserve 1975-81, CDR. USNR 1981–, comdg. ofcr., NRSIMA 220 Alameda; cargo expert, decorated rifle expert, Army Letter of Appreciation, Navy Achievement Medals (2), USCG Unit Commendn. Medal, Navy Letter of Commendation, Navy Commendn. Medal; trial atty., mem. felony trial team Contra Costa County Dist. Atty. Office 1981-83; civil and criminal defense atty. law firm Gorelick and Gorelick, 1983; principal atty. Welfare Fraud Div. Head, Ofc. of San Francisco Dist. Atty., 1983–, Felony Rebooking Gen. Litigation Team I; active PTA San Lorenzo Unified Sch. Dist.; Democrat; Ch. of Rel. Sci. (past bd. dirs. Contra Costa); rec: piano, horticulture. Office of S.F. District Attorney 880 Bryant St San Francisco 94103

BENNETT, LAWRENCE ALLEN, psychologist, consultant in criminal justice; b. Jan. 4, 1923, Selma, Calif.; s. Allen Walter and Eva Eleanor (Hall) B.; m. Beth J. Thompson, Aug. 14, 1948; children: Glenn Livingston, Yvonne Irene Solis; edn: BA, Fresno St. Coll., 1949; MA, Claremont Grad. Sch., 1954, PhD, 1968. Career: supvg. psychologist Calif. med. facility Calif. Dept. Corrections, Vacaville 1955-60, departmental supr. clin. psychology, Sacto. 1960-67, chief of res., 1967-76; dir. Ctr. for Study of Crime, Delinquency and Corrections, So. Ill. Univ., Carbondale 1976-79; dir. Office of Program Evaluation, 1979-84; dir. Crime Prevention and Enforcement Div. Nat. Inst. of Justice, W.D.C. 1985-86; dir. Adjudication and Corrections Div. 1987-88; practicing clin. psychologist, also crim. justice consultant, Sacto. 1988–; faculty p.t. UC Davis, UC Berkeley, 1959-76, CSU Sacto. 1988–; appt. bd. Calif. Crime Technol. Res. Found. 1970-75, Calif. State Interdepartmental Coord. Council (1967-76, chmn. 1970); juvenile advy. bd. State of Ill. 1977-79; bd. dirs. Am. Justice Inst., Sacto. (1970-79, 88–, pres. 1991–); commr. Calif. Blue Ribbon Commn. on Inmate Population Mgmt. 1988-90; mem: Acad. of Crim. Justice Scis., Am. Psychol. Assn., Am. Soc. Criminology, Am. Correctional Assn., Evaluation Res. Soc., Assn. for Correctional Res. and Info. Mgmt. (pres. 1989-90); mil: US Army 1942-45, 50-51, decorated bronze star with o.l.c.; publs: coauthor (w/ T.S. Rosenbaum and W.R. McCollough) Counseling in Correctional Environments (1978), contbr. articles to profl. jours.; Unitarian. Res: 1129 Rivara Cir Sacramento 95864 Ofc: 2717 Cottage Way Ste 15 Cottage Center Sacramento 95825

BENNETT, WILLIAM PERRY, real estate lawyer/broker; b. Aug. 28, 1938, Inglewood; s. George William and Lenora (Perry) B.; m. Linda Lee Schneider, Aug. 19, 1961; children: Gregory b. 1962, Mark b. 1966, Carin b. 1968; edn: BA, CSU Long Beach 1961; MA (magna cum laude), Grace Theol. Sem.; JD (magna cum laude), USC Law Sch. 1964. Career: atty., ptnr. Powars Tretheway & Bennett, Long Beach 1964-79; atty., sr. ptnr. William P. Bennett, Seal Beach 1979-90; sr. atty. R.E. Dept., Wise, Wiezorek, Timmons & Wise, Long Beach 1991–; general counsel Campus Crusade for Christ 1991–; R.E. broker/pres. Century 21 Pacific Coast Realty 1979-87, Pacific Coast Properties 1987–; assoc. prof. CSU Long Beach 1965-87; awards: USC Law Sch. law review, 1965, Long Beach C.of C. businessman of year, 1987, Jaycees comm. service, 1973-74, Kiwanis kiwanian of year, 1971; mem: Long Beach Bd. Realtors, Long Beach Bar Assn. (bd. gov. 1970-71, 73-74, 75-76), Long Beach Area March of Dimes (bd. dir. & legal advr. 1973-90, Kiwanis (lt. gov. 1975-76), Long Beach Barristers (pres. 1971), Seal Beach C.of C. (pres. 1985-86, 89-90), CSU Advy. Bd., 1982-87, Am. Arbitration Assn. Panel 1965–, L.A. Co. Arbitration Panel 1989–; mil: 2d. lt. USMCR 1959-65; Republican; Christian; rec: edn. Res: 311 Ocean Ave Seal Beach 90740 Ofc: Pacific Coast Properties PO Box 2460 Seal Beach 90740

BENNIS, WARREN GAMELIEL, business administration educator, author, consultant; b. Mar. 8, 1925, NYC; s. Philip and Rachel (Landau) B.; m. Clurie Williams, Mar. 30, 1962 (div. 1983); children: Katharine, John Leslie, Will Martin; m. Mary Jane O'Donnell, Mar. 8, 1988 (div. 1991); m. Grace Gabe,

Nov. 29, 1992; edn: AB, Antioch Coll., 1951; hon. cert. econ., London Sch. Econ., 1952; PhD, MIT, 1955; LL.D. (hon.), Xavier Univ., Cin., 1972, George Washington Univ., 1977; L.H.D. (hon.), Hebrew Union Coll., 1974, Kans. State Univ., 1979; D.Sc. (hon.), Univ. Louisville, 1977, Pacific Grad. Sch. Psychology, 1987, Gov.'s State Univ., 1991; L.H.D. (hon.), Doan Coll., 1993; diplomate Am. Bd. Profl. Psychology. Career: asst. prof. psychology MIT, Cambridge, 1953-56, prof., 1959-67; asst. prof. psychology and bus. Boston Univ., 1956-59; prof. Sloan Sch. Mgmt., 1959-67; provost SUNY-Buffalo, 1967-68, v.p. acad. devel., 1968-71; pres. Univ. Cin., 1971-77; U.S. prof. corps. and soc. Centre d'Etudes Industrielles, Geneva, Switzerland, 1978-79; exec.-in-residence Pepperdine Univ., 1978-79: George Miller Disting. prof.-in-residence Univ. Ill., Champaign-Urbana, 1978; Disting. prof. Bus. Adminstrn. Sch. Bus., Univ. So. Calif., L.A., 1980-88; univ. prof. U. So. Calif., L.A., 1988–; vis. lectr. Harvard Univ., 1958-59, Indian Mgmt. Inst., Calcutta; vis. prof. Univ. Lausanne (Switzerland), 1961-62. INSEAD, France, 1983; bd. dirs. The Foothill Group; mem. Pres.' White House Task Force on Sci. Policy, 1969-70; mem. FAA study task force U.S. Dept. Transportation, 1975; mem. adv. com. N.Y. State Joint Legis. Corn. Higher Edn., 1970-71; mem. Ohio Gov.'s Bus. and Employment Council, 1972-74; mem. panel on alt. approaches to grad. edn. Council Grad. Schs. and Grad. Record-Exam Bd., 1971-73; chmn. Nat. Adv. Commn. on Higher Edn. for Police Officers, 1976-78; adv. bd. NIH, 1978-84; trustee Colo. Rocky Mountains Sch., 1978-82; bd. dirs. Am. Leadership Forum, 1984-89; mem. vis. com. for humanities MIT, 1975-81; trustee Antioch Coll., Salk Inst., Claremont Univ. Ctr.; awards: recipient Dow Jones award. 1987, McKinsey Fedn. award, 1967, 68; mem. Am. Acad. Arts and Scis. (co-chmn. policy coun. 1969-71), Am. Soc. Pub. Adminstrn. (nat. coun.), Am. Mgmt. Assn. (dir. 1974-77), U.S. C.of C. (adv. group scholars); author: Planning of Change, 4th edit., 1985, Interpersonal Dynamics, 1963, 3rd and 4th edits., 1975, Personal and Organizational Change, 1965, Changing Organizations, 1966, repub. in paperback as Beyond Bureaucracy, 1974, The Temporary Society, 1968, Organization Development, 1969, American Bureaucracy, 1970, Management of Change and Conflict, 1972, The Leaning Ivory Tower, 1973, The Unconscious Conspiracy: Why Leaders Can't Lead, 1976, Essays in Interpersonal Dynamics, 1979; (with B. Nanus): Leaders, 1985, On Becoming a Leader, 1989, (with I. Mitroff) The Unreality Industry, 1989, Why Leaders Can't Lead, 1989, Leaders on Leadership, 1992, An Invented Life: Reflections on Leadership and Change, 1993, Beyond Bureaucracy, 1993; assoc. editor Jour. Transpersonal Psychology, Community Psychology; cons. editor Jour. Creative Behavior, Jour. Higher Edn. Jour. Occupational Behavior, Ency. of Econ. and Bus., Jour. Humanistic Psychology, Calif. Mgmt. Rev., Mgmt. Series Jossey-Bass Pubs.; mil: capt. AUS, World War II; decorated Bronze Star, Purple Heart. Office: Univ of Southern Calif Sch Bus University Park Los Angeles CA 90089-1421

BENSON, JAMES BERNARD, instructor in police science; b. May 8, 1930, Phila.; s. James Bernard and Elizabeth Sloan (Smeaton) B.; m. Hiroko Nakamura, Apr. 14, 1955; edn: BA in police sci., Pacific Coll., Van Nuys 1978. Career: crim. investigator, ssgt. (E-6) US Marine Corps, El Toro 1947-66; delinquent loan ofcr. Bank America, Los Angeles 1966-85; clin. hypnotherapist practice, Anaheim 1985-91; instr. in police sci. St. John's Univ., Springfield, LA 1991–; awards: LLD (hon.) Nat. Law Enforcement Acad., Fla., Apr. 22, 1968, DD (hon.) Ch. of Gospel Ministry, San Diego, PhD in Hypnotherapy (hon.) St. John's Univ., Springfield, La. Jan. 10, 1988, Fellow in Clin. Hypnotherapy, Am. Assn. Profl. Hypnotherapists, Dec. 15, 1986; mem: Nat. Bd. for Hypnotherapy and Anesthesiology 1982, Nat. Soc. Clin. Hypnotherapists 1988–, Am. Assn. Criminologists 1960–, Internat. Assn. Counselors and Therapists 1991–; editor police poetry anthologies: Devotion in Blue, 1973, Lawman's Lament, 1974; Republican; Prot.; rec: photography, writing, cooking. Res: 1400 S Sunkist St, # 199 Anaheim 92806-5624

BENSON, JAMES ROBERT, technology company president; b. Oct. 5, 1942, Newark, N.J.; s. James W. and Nita E. (Webb) B.; m. Paula Mychack, Oct. 13, 1984 (div. 1991); children: Ashley b. 1987, Calvin b. 1989; edn: BS chemistry, Univ. Mich. 1964; MA, Dartmouth Coll. 1966; PhD, Stanford Univ. 1974. Career: pres. Dionex Chem. Corp., Sunnyvale 1968-79; pres., CEO Interaction Chemicals, Mountain View 1979-90, dir. 1979-90; pres. Sunstorm Research Corp. 1991–; chmn. Biopore Corp. 1993–; mem: Am. Soc. Biochemists & Molecular Biologists, Am. Soc. Microbiologists, ASTM, Protein Soc.; num. articles pub. in tech. jours.; Democrat; rec: skiing, running, windsurfing. Res: 15143 Kennedy Rd Los Gatos 95032 Ofc: Sunstorm Research Corp Box 33115 Los Gatos 95031

BENTLEY, JOSEPH IVINS, lawyer, church and community leader; b. Aug. 6, 1940, Safford, Ariz.; s. Israel Ivins and Anna Laura (Walser) B.; m. Marilyn Ann Brown, Dec. 18, 1964; children: Suzanne b. 1968, Michelle b. 1970, Marianne b. 1974, Mark b. 1980, Melissa b. 1985; edn: BA, Brigham Young Univ. 1965; JD, Univ. Chgo. Law Sch. 1968. Career: Latham & Watkins, assoc. atty. Los Angeles 1968-76, ptnr., Orange Co. 1976–; instr. Brigham Young Univ. Contg. Edn. Faculty, Provo, Utah 1980, 87; instr. Nat. Center for Constitutional Studies, Salt Lake City 1978-80; dir. Performing Arts Assn. Orange Co. 1987-89, Constl. Rts. Found. Orange Co. 1992– (dir.); honors: Order of Coif, Univ. Chgo. Law Sch. Nat. Hon. scholarship 1965-68, Jackson

Constitutional Law award 1967; mem: Ch. of Jesus Christ of Latter Day Saints (pres. Newport Beach Stake 1982-92, bishop Corona del Mar Ward 1980-81, bishop Harbor Hills Ward 1981-82, regl. rep. 1992-95), Opera Pacific (founder 1987), Pacific Chorale (dir. 1987-92), BSA (Eagle Scout dinner chmn. 1989, dir. 1995-, LDS Exec. Com. 1992-95); mng. ed. Univ. Chgo. Law Review, 1967-68, articles pub. in profl. jours. and Encyclopedia of Mormonism (1966, 76, 77, 90); mil: USAR 1963-69; Republican; Mormon; rec: sports, writing, geneaology. Ofc: Latham & Watkins 650 Town Center Dr Ste 2000 Costa Mesa 92626

BENZ, RONALD THOMAS, otolaryngologist; b. April 17, 1942, Milwaukee, Wisc.; s. Herman S. and Beatrice M. (Quinn) B.; m. Rita Kautza, Nov. 27, 1971; children: Michael, b. 1976, Jennifer, b. 1978, Nicholas, b. 1980; edn: BS, Carroll Coll. 1964; MD, Marquette 1968. Career: internship and residency in otolaryngology L.A. Co.-USC Med. Ctr. 1968-69, 1971-75; otolaryngologist pvt. practice 1976-, bd. dirs. Sharp Rees Stealy Med. Group, 1989-93, 94-95, corp. bd. 1991-93; asst. clin. prof. surgery UC San Diego Med. Sch.; pres. San Diego Academy of Otolaryngology 1987; staff Coronado Hosp. (chief of staff 1983), chief otol. dept. Childrens Hosp. 1986-92, Mercy Hosp. (v.chief 1984-90); mem: AMA, CMA, San Diego Med. Soc., Am. Coll. Surgeons (fellow 1987), Am. Acad. Otolaryngology (fellow), Head & Neck Soc.; club: Cottilian (pres. 1989-90); mem. San Diego Co. Umpires' Assn.; mil: lt. USNR (MC) 1969-71; R.Cath.; rec: sports, travel. Res: 8933 Activity Rd San Diego 92126 Ofc: 2001 4th Ave San Diego 92101

BERBERIAN, BERNARD, art director; b. Oct. 26, 1948, Hifa, Palestine, nat. Canadian; s. Nazar and Yevkine (Nalbandian) B.; m. 1978, div. 1986; children: Shaunt b. 1981, Ara b. 1983; edn: BA, advertising design, Ontario Coll. of Art, Can. 1972. Career: with Leonard Kurass Design Group, San Francisco 1972-74; Patterson and Hall Design 1974-78; Bernard Berberian Design, Los Angeles 1978-79; owner, pres., chief ed., art dir. UNIARTS Advertising, Glendale 1979-; honors: recognized in Armenian Who's Who Worldwide 1994; mem. Manougian/Demirdjian Sch. Festival Task Force Com. 1995; created Calif. UNIARTS Armenian Directory Yellow Pages, 1980-, Pocket Directory Yellow Pages, 1991; rec: music, travel tennis. Res: 1038 Alcalde Way Glendale CA 91207-1124 Ofc: UNIARTS Advertising, Glendale 91204

BERDELL, JAMES RUSSELL, venture capitalist; b. Mar. 23, 1944, Sellersville, Pa.; s. Russell Warren and Helen Dorothy (Schmidt) B.; m. Mary Clark, Nov. 27, 1971; 1 child: Lauren b. 1977; edn: BS engring., Drexel Univ. 1967; MS mgmt., MIT 1969; cert. fin. analyst (1975). Career: portfolio mgr. Hillsborough Capital Corp., San Francisco 1969-71; tech. analyst Mitchum, Jones, & Templeton 1971-73; research dir. Shuman, Agnew & Co. 1973-75; investment banker, Montgomery Securities 1975-82; pres. Berdell, Welling, & Co., Menlo Park 1982-; tchg./res. asst. MIT (1967-69); honors: Sigma Rho (1967), Phi Kappa Phi (1966); mem: Charter Fin. Analysts, S.F. Soc. of Security Analysts, Venture Capitalists Soc., Eletrosci. Soc., Computer and Elec. Soc., Commonwealth Club of Calif., Ladera Swim & Tennis Club; Republican; Lutheran; rec: ski, swim, travel. Ofc: Berdell Welling & Co 3000 Sand Hill Rd Ste 3-125 Menlo Park 94025

BERDON, SONDRA KAY, pharmacist, lecturer; b. Nov. 3, 1953, Paducah, Ky.; d. John and Laura Mae (Weaver) B.; edn: El Paso Comm. Coll., Colo. Spgs. 1971-72; BS pharm. scis., Univ. Ariz. Coll. of Pharmacy, 1976; lic. pharmacist Ariz., Calif. Career: intern Univ. Ariz. Health Scis. Ctr., Tucson 1972-76; pharmacist 3 clinic pharms. in Tucson and Marana, Az. 1976-77; pharmacy mgr. Tempe Store, Fed Mart Inc., Phoenix 1977-78; sr. staff pharmacist Dept. Pharm. Green Hosp. of Scripps Clinic and Res. Found., La Jolla 1978-; course instr. nursing certification pgms. in oncology, gerontology, sleep and drug treatment, pharmaceutical calculations, pain mgmt. and pharmacology, hypertension, and neurology; frequent speaker on drug topics in schs., univs., and various profl. and civic groups; video: "Recommended Handling for Cytotoxic Agents" for Winfield Corp., S.D. (c. 1984); honors: Pharmacist of Yr., San Diego Co. Pharmacists Assn. 1987; mem: Am. Soc. Hosp. Pharmacists, Calif. Soc. Hosp. Pharmacists, S.D. Soc. Hosp. Pharmacists, Am. Pharmaceutical Assn., Calif. Pharmacists Assn., S.D. Co. Pharmacists Assn. (pres. 1990-91, bd. 1987-, chair pub. affairs com. 1987-), Am. Inst. of History of Pharmacy, Am. Cancer Soc./S.D. (bd. 1985-87); rec: doll collector, history of pharmacy collection. Res: 4935 Via Lapiz San Diego 92122 Ofc: Green Hospital, Scripps Clinic 10666 N Torrey Pines Rd La Jolla 92037

BERESTYNSKI, ADAM S., architect, urban planner (retired); b. May 5, 1927, Krakow, Poland; s. Adam and Kazimiera B.; m. Magdalena Steinhagen, Oct. 4, 1957; 1 son, Peter b. 1958; edn: MSc in arch. and city planning, Polytechnic Univ., Krakow 1951. Career: mgr. arch. and planning dept. City of Krakow, Poland 1960-64; arch. and urban designer Royal Afghan Ministry of Pub. Works, Kabul, Afghanistan 1964-66; reg. planner Leslie Properties, Redwood City, Calif. 1967-69; assoc. planner City of Fremont, Calif. 1969-70; urban designer VTN Consol. Inc., Irvine 1970-76; asst. dir. planning Bein, Frost & Assocs., Newport Beach 1976-81; mgr. planning and devel. control Saudi Arabian Parsons Ltd., Yanbu, S.A. 1982-89; instr. Calif. Comm. Coll., 1977; awards: III gr. award Polish Soc. Architects 1963, 8 philatelic awards 1991-95;

mem: AIA (assoc. 1971-), Am. Inst. of Planners (assoc. 1972-), Am. Planning Assn. 1977-, Assn. of Environmental Profls. 1978-, Am. Philatelic Soc. 1989-; publs: articles in profl. jours., 1951-95, contbr. articles to mo. "Kultura" Paris, Fr., 1968-71; mil: Polish Underground Resistance Army (A.K.) 1943-45; Republican; R.Cath.; rec: philately, mtn. hiking, travel, distance swimming. Res: 2845 Chillon Way Laguna Beach 92651

BERETTA, GIORDANO BRUNO, computer scientist; b. Apr. 14, 1951, Brugg, Switz.; s. Modesto Carlo and Hildegard (Wenger) B.; edn: MS math., Swiss Fed. Inst. Tech., Zurich 1977, PhD in c.s., 1984; dipl. math. ETH Dr. Sc. Tech. ETH, Swiss Govt. (1984). Career: systems rep. Burroughs (Switzerland), Zurich 1977-80; asst. Swiss Fed. Inst. Tech., Zurich 1980-83; cons. Logitech S.A., Apples, Switz. 1984; scientist Xerox PARC, Palo Alto, Calif. 1984-90; senior scientist Canon Information Systems, Palo Alto 1990-93; mem. tech. staff Hewlett-Packard Labs., Palo Alto 1994-; recipient profl. achiev. award Xerox Corporate Resrch. Gp., Palo Alto 1989; mem: Swiss Math. Soc., IEEE Computer Soc., Internat. Soc. for Optical Engring., Intersociety Color Council; holder of patents in digital color reproduction; rec: photography. Res: 1760 Newell Rd Palo Alto 94303 Ofc: Hewlett-Packard Laboratories 1501 Page Mill Road Palo Alto 94304

BERETZ, PAUL B., manufacturing company executive; b. Oct. 15, 1938, Wash. D.C.; s. O. Paul and Marthe (Szabo) B.; m. Jane M., Nov. 9, 1963; children: Charles, Melissa, John, Michele, Claudine; edn: BBA, Univ. Notre Dame, 1960, MBA, Golden Gate Univ., 1974. Career: asst. treas. Crown Zellerbach, San Francisco 1983-86; prin. P.B. Beretz & Co., S.F. 1986-91; sr. fin. mgr., Applied Materials Inc., Santa Clara 1991-; adj. faculty: St. Mary's Coll., Moraga 1978-80, Golden Gate Univ., S.F. 1980, UC Berkeley 1990-; mem., past pres. Univ. Notre Dame Bay Area Alumni Org. (1975-, Award of Yr. 1987), nat. bd. dir. Univ. Notre Dame Alumni Assn. 1983-86; author: Managing Commercial Credit, 1981, articles on fin. & mgmt., 1980-95; Democrat; R.Cath.; rec: tennis, gardening, hiking. Res: Alamo 94507

BERG, DAVID, writer/artist; b. June 12, 1920, Brooklyn, NY; s. Morris Isaac and Bessie (Friedman) B.; m. Vivian Lipman, March 3, 1949; children: Mitchel b. 1952, Nancy b. 1955; edn: Art Students League 1937-38; Cooper Union 1939-41; Iona Coll. 1974; Coll. of New Rochelle 1975. Career: writer/artist Will Eisner The Spirit - Backgrounder; Death Patrol 1940-41; Fawcett 1941-43; Archie 1949-52; Timely 1941-42 and 1949-59; Mad Mag. The Lighter Side of.. 1956-; 15 paperbacks trans. into 12 lang., Mad's Dave Berg Looks at ..USA, ..People, ..Things, ..Our Sick World, ..Modern Thinking, ..Living, Mad's Dave Berg Takes a Loving Look, Mad's Dave Berg Looks Around, Listens, Laughs, Mad's Dave Berg Looks at You, ..The Neighborhood, .. Our Planet, ..Today, Dave Berg's Mad Trash, My Friend GOD, Roger Kaputnic and GOD, Japanese, German, French, English lang. tching. books, 1986; Mad Mag.; creative cons. NBC T.V. 1978; judge Miss Am. Contest; honors: David Berg Day mayoral proclamation Westchester Co. N.Y. (5/7/78), B'nai B'rith Youth Services Award 1978, Chair of Great Cartoonists, UCLA Student Body 1975, ThD (hon.) Reconstruction Rabbinical Coll., Lubavitchor Youth Service Award 1987; mem: Nat. Cartoonists Soc., Internat. Platform Soc., Author's Guild, Writer's Guild; civic: Boy Scouts, Girl Scouts, Little League, PTA, B'nai B'rith, Pioneer Skippers Assn., City of New Rochelle (chmn. of rec.), Thornton-Donovan Sch. (bd. dirs.); mil: staff sgt., chem. warfare tech., sta. chief 20th AF Pacific 1942-46; Army war corr. 1945; Democrat; Hebrew; rec: model building, photog. coin collecting. Res: 14021 Marquesas Way Ste 307C Marina del Rey 90292 Ofc: Mad Magazine 485 Madison Avenue New York 10022

BERGEN, RANDY E., pediatrician; b. Mar. 25, 1957, St. Paul, Minn.; edn: BA, St. Olaf Coll., Northfield, Minn. 1979; MD, Univ. of Minn., Mpls. 1982; MPH, UC Berkeley 1992; bd. cert. pediatrics 1988. Career: resident/intern Oakland Children's Hosp. 1983-86; fellow, pediatric infectious diseases Stanford Univ., Palo Alto 1987-90; gen. pediatrician The Permanente Med. Group 1992-; honors: Phi Beta Kappa, Alpha Omega Alpha. Address: San Lorenzo 94580

BERGER, BARBARA D., company president; b. May 4, 1931, Chicago, Ill.; d. Alfred (dec.) and Ruth (Shapiro) Lubin; m. Howard M. Berger, PhD, June 25, 1950; children: Teri Lawton, PhD, Patricia Wisley, Lisa Berger, MBA; edn: AA, Pasadena City Coll. 1950. Career: real estate sales E. Dunham, Arlington, Va. 1960-63; cons., mgr. Beverly Cross Agency, Torrance 1974-76; pres. and CEO, KMI dba Justin Bentley Agency and KMI Search 1977-, Justin Time Temps 1979-; dir: Keats Manhattan Inc., Justin Bentley Agy., Justin Time Temps awards: Calif. Assn. Profl. Cons. Maxine Taylor 1984-85, Kerr-Codera 1983-84; mem: Calif. Assn. Profl. Cons. (past pres., past 1st v.p.), Nat. Assn. Profl. Cons., Torrance C.of C., Santa Monica C.of C.; rec: boating. Ofc: Justin Bentley Agency 23326 Hawthorne Blvd Ste 300 Torrance 90505

BERGER, JAY VARI, executive recruiter; b. Aug. 31, 1944, San Francisco; s. Jack Vari and Ruth (Wasserman) B.; m. Meta Ahlberg, June 14, 1969; children: Karin b. 1971, John b. 1974; edn: BS, Univ. So. Calif., 1966, MS 1967, PhD 1971; Calif. life secondary tchg. cred. 1967. Career: assoc. dean admissions Univ. So. Calif., L.A. 1969-76, dir. admissions 1976-82, asst. v.p. devel. 1982-

86; ptnr. Morris & Berger, Pasadena 1986–; co-owner Berger & Berger Internat. (importer childrens apparel), Pasadena 1976–; awards: firm, Morris & Berger, on Executive Recruiter News list of 50 Leading Exec. Search Firms in No. Am., Jan. 1992; mem. Calif. Exec. Recruiters Assn. 1987–, USC Commerce Associates (nat. bd. 1991–); civic: Rotary Pasadena (dir. 1989–), The Sycamores, Altadena (pres. 1990–), The Chandler Sch., Pasa. (pres. 1988-90), Pasadena Pops (dir. 1989-92), Flintridge Prep. Sch. (bd. 1992–), Covenant House Calif. (dir. 1994–); author (childrens' book) Willie The Worm, 1988; rec: golf, travel, reading, writing, fishing. Res: 412 Oaklawn Ave So Pasadena 91030 Ofc: Morris & Berger, 201 S Lake Ave Ste 700 Pasadena 91101

BERGER, LISA SHARI, lawyer, appellate law; b. Oct. 24, 1959, Los Angeles; d. Richard Alvin and Jeanne (Skale) Berger; edn: BA, UCLA 1980; JD, Univ. San Diego 1983. Career: dep. city atty. L.A.City Atty. Office, L.A. 1985–; judge pro tem L.A.Co. Cts. 1989–; dep. atty. gen. Calif. Atty. Gen. Office 1988; mem: Calif. St. Bar Assn., L.A. Co. Bar Assn., Women Lawyers Assn. of L.A., Calif. Women Lawyers, Zeta Tau Alpha, UCLA Alumni Assn.; Democrat; Jewish. Ofc: 1700 City Hall E, 200 N Main St Los Angeles 90012

BERGESON, MARIAN C., state senator; b. Aug. 31, 1925, Salt Lake City, Utah; d. Ivan H. and Clara Greenwood (Hunter) Crittenden; m. Garth Bergeson, June 16, 1950; children: Nancy b. 1951, Garth b. 1953, Julie b. 1959, James b. 1961; 4 grandchildren; edn: UCLA; BA, Edn., Brigham Young Univ., Provo, Utah, 1949. Career: sch. bd. mem., Newport City Sch. Dist., Newport Beach, Calif., 1964-65; sch. bd. mem., Newport-Mesa Unified Sch. Dist., Newport Beach, 1965-77; state assemblywoman, Calif. State Legislature, Sacto., 1978-84; state senator, Calif. State Legislature, Sacto., 1984–; Minority Whip, Assembly and Senate; former pres., Calif. Sch. Boards Assn.; Republican Party nominee for Lt. Gov., 1990; chair, Women's Legislative Caucus, 1992; mem. State Allocation Bd; chair, Senate Local Gov. Com.; mem. of committees on Appropriations, Ethics, Health & Human Svs., Industrial Relations, Transp., Defense Base Closures; vice chair, Housing and Urban Affairs; chair, Select Com. on Planning for California's Growth; mem. Select Com. on Infant & Child Care and Devel., Select Com. on Source Reduction and Recycling Market Devel., Subcom. on Bonded Indebtedness and Methods of Financing; hon. advy. bd. mem., Concerned Citizens for Adolescent Pregnancy, Ad Hoc Legislative Tourism Caucus; serves on 3 Nat. Conf. of State Legislature Committees: State-Federal Assembly Com. on Fed. Budget & Taxation, Transp. & Communication Com., and Assembly on the Legislature Com. on State-Local Relations; awards & honors: over 50 awards as Legislator of Year, Senator of Year, Woman of Year, Outstanding Public Ofcl. and others; Disting. Svc. award, Brigham Young Univ., 1980-81; Hon. Doctor of Laws degree, Pepperdine Univ., 1993; listed in Who's Who of Am. Women, 2000 Notable Am. Women, Who's Who in US; mem: advy. bd. Oasis Sr. Citizens Ctr., Radio Station KBIG; bd. of adv., Calif. YMCA Model Legislature/Court; bd. of trustees Mem. Health Svs. of Long Beach, 1990-91; hon. dir., C.E.W.A.E.R., 1989; adv., UCI Grad. Sch. of Management Health Care Management Program Bd., 1992; mem. Bus./Industry Advy. Council, State ROP Assn., 1992; civic: charter mem., Advy. Bd. of Trustees, Bolsa Chica Wetlands; advy. bd., St. Jude Med. Ctr.; charter bd. mem., Maternal Outreach Management System; comm. advy. bd., Jr. League of Orange County; advy. council, Mardan Ctr. of Ednl. Therapy; advy. bd., Laguna Art Museum, Adam Walsh Child Resource Ctr., Program for Women Found., Advanced Resources for Foster Kids, Homeless Task Force Building Industry Assn.; hon. mem. bd. dir., Food Distribution Ctr.; mem: Comm. Devel. Council Bd., Rotary Internat. Newport Beach; author: article pub. in Land & Assembly Devel., 1987; legislation on pre-natal health care for low-income families, lower personal income tax, and improved efficiency of Caltrans; Republican; Mormon; rec: shopping. Ofc: 140 Newport Ctr. Dr, #120 Newport Beach 92660-6990

BERGIN, ROBERT WAYNE, manufacturing company executive; b. Feb. 13, 1954, Van Nuys; s. Fredrick Austin and Aileen E. (Hume) B.; m. Linda Ruth Webb, April 23, 1980; children: Austin b. 1981, Amanda b. 1985; edn: BS mgmt., Pepperdine Univ. 1985. Career: sr. planner Litton Guidance Control, Woodland Hills 1976-78; material control supr. Eaton Test Systems 1978-80; product and materials mgr. Magnetic Tech., Canoga Park 1980-85; v.p. Calif. Soap Co., Los Angeles 1985–; founder/pres. Calif. Minerals 1993–; mil: SK-5 USN 1972-76; Republican; R.Cath.; rec: numismatics. Ofc: California Soap Co. 1819 E 25th St Los Angeles 90058

BERGMAN, W. DIETER, physician, gynecological surgeon; b. July 3, 1920, Leipzig, Germany; nat. 1957; s. Ernst and Gertrud Helen (Landsberg) B.; m. Lore S. Meier, June 5, 1954 (div. 1963); children: Clifford b. 1955, Jeanne b. 1957; edn: MD, Univ. Bonn Germany 1948. Career: pvt. practice medicine, Hayward 1958-88; mem: Alameda Gyn. Soc. (pres. 1967), AARP, Calif. Soc. Chamber Music, Bohemian Club; author music column Flats & Sharps mag.; mil: lt.comdr. USNR; rec: violin, gourmet cooking, writing. Address: 22673 Wildwood St Hayward 94541

BERGO, EDWARD THOMAS, JR., construction executive; b. June 6, 1948, Los Angeles; s. Edward T., Sr. and Mary Agnes (Woods) B.; m. Dolores Anie, Apr. 3, 1971; son, Justin Bryan b. 1978; edn: BA, Stanford Univ., 1971; JD,

Univ. Santa Clara, 1975. Career: construction mgr. C. Aparicio Cement Co. Inc., San Jose 1975–; mem: No. Calif. Cement Masons (trustee Pension Fund 1983–), AGC Cement Masons (chmn. negotiation com. 1980–), AGC of Calif. (state dir. 1981-82, dist. chmn. 1982, trustee AGC Employers HealthTrust Fund 1988–); mil: s/sgt. USAF Reserve 1970-76; Republican; rec: water skiing, gardening. Res: PO Box 1311 Soquel 95073 Ofc: 506 Phelan Ave San Jose 95112

BERGSTROM, KARL A., specialty retail store chain president; b. Nov. 29, 1926, Gothenburg, Sweden, nat. 1956; s. Carl A. and Jenny A. (Bjorkman) B.; m. Conny Riis-Klausen, Nov. 28, 1957; children: Pierre, b. 1959; Vickie, b. 1961; edn: BS, summa cum laude, UC Berkeley 1950. Career: v.consul, Swedish Diplomatic Corps. 1946-50; mgr. Container Corp. of Am., San Francisco 1950-53; US Army Svc. 1953-56; mgr. Continental Can Co., Los Angeles 1956-63; founder/chief exec. Bergstroms Childrens Stores, Inc., Anaheim 1963–; chmn. bd. Stanford Distbg. Corp., Hayward; adv. bd: Nat. Bank of So. Calif., Santa Ana, Olympic Nat. Bank, L.A., Traweek Investment Co., Marina Del Rey; honors: Delta Sigma Pi, profl. bus. frat.; mem. Tustin Toastmasters Club (pres. 1978); mil: sgt. US Army 1953 interpreter in Germany, Norway, Denmark & France 1953-56, staff of Gen. Lucius Clay; Republican; Presbyterian; rec: skiing, art collection, classical music. Res: 1662 La Loma Dr Santa Ana 92705 Ofc: Bergstroms Childrens Stores, 1606 Clementine Anaheim 92802

BERKSON, BILL (WILLIAM CRAIG), poet, critic, teacher; b. Aug. 30, 1939, N.Y., NY; s. Seymour and Eleanor (Lambert) B.; m. Lynn Blacker, July 17, 1975; children: Siobhan b. 1969 (adopted), Moses b. 1976; edn: Lawrenceville (N.J.) Sch. 1955-57, Brown Univ. 1957-59, The New Sch. N.Y.C. 1959-60, Columbia Univ. 1959-60. Career: editorial assoc. Portfolio & Art News Annual, N.Y. 1960-63; assoc. prod. "Art/New York" WNDT-TV, N.Y. 1964-65; instr. The New Sch., 1964-69; guest editor Mus. of Modern Art, N.Y. 1965-69; vis. fellow Yale Univ., New Haven, Ct. 1969-70; ed. and pub. Big Sky press, Bolinas, 1971-78; prof. San Francisco Art Inst., 1984–, dir. Letters & Science 1994–; active in literary & art fields since 1959, author 11 books and pamphlets of poetry, incl.: Saturday Night: Poems 1960-61 (1961), Enigma Variations (1975), Blue Is the Hero (1976), Lush Life (1983); poetry transl. into Italian, Fr., Ger., Dutch, Romanian, and Hungarian; anthologies incl.: The Young Am. Poets, 10 Am. Poets, The Young Am. Writers, The World Anth., An Anth. of New York Poets, Best & Company, On the Mesa, Calafia, One World Poetry, Another World, Poets & Painters, Up Late: Am. Poetry Since 1970, Out of this World, A Norton Anth. of Postmodern Am. Poetry; poetry recordings on "Disconnected" (Giorno Poetry Systems), and "The World Record" (St. Marks Poetry Project) and in the Am. Poetry Archive (SFSU); writer revs. and articles, regular contbr. Artnews, 1961-63, Arts, 1964-66, Art in America, 1980–, Artforum, 1985–; num. pub. readings and lectures nat.; awards: Dylan Thomas Award, The New Sch. 1959, Poets Found. grantee 1968, NEA creative writing fellow 1979, Marin Arts Council Award 1987, award for criticism Artspace, S.F. 1990, vis. artist/scholar Am. Acad. in Rome 1991. Res: 787B Castro St, San Francisco 94114 Ofc: San Francisco Art Institute 800 Chestnut St San Francisco 94133

BERMAN, HOWARD LAWRENCE, congressman; b. Apr. 15, 1941, Los Angeles; s. Joseph M. and Eleanor (Schapiro) B.; m. Janis Schwartz, 1979; children: Brinley Ann, Lindsey Rose; edn: BA, UCLA, 1962, LLB, 1965; admitted St. Bar: Calif. 1966. Career: vol. VISTA, Balt., San Francisco, 1966-67; assoc. Levy, Van Bourg & Hackler, Los Angeles, 1967-72; mem. Calif. State Assembly from 43d dist., 1972-82 (majority leader), 98th-104th Congresses from 26th Calif. dist.; freshman rep. steering & policy com. 98th-103rd Congresses from 26th Calif. dist., 1983, mem. judiciary com. econ. and comml. law; intellectual property and jud. adminstrn. 98th-103rd Congresses from 26th Calif. dist., adminstrv. law and gov. rels. subcom., mem. budget com., fgn. affairs com., chmn. internat. ops., internal security, internat. orgns. and human rights; pres. Calif. Fedn. Young Democrats, 1967-69 (budget corn.); mem. adv. bd. Jewish Fund for Justice, Valley Internat. Trade Assn. Office: Rayburn House Office Bldg Rm 2201 Washington DC 20515

BERMAN, MYLES LEE, lawyer; b. July 11, 1954, Chgo.; s. Jordan and Eunice (Berg) B.; m. Mitra Moghimi, Dec. 19, 1981; children: Elizabeth b. 1983, Calvin b. 1990; edn: BA, Univ. Illinois, Champaign, 1976; JD, Kent Coll. of Law, Chgo., 1979; admitted bar: Ill., 1980, US Dist. Ct. No. Dist. Ill., 1980, Calif., 1987, US Dist Ct. Central Calif., 1988, US Supreme Ct., 1992. Career: asst. state's atty. Cook County, Ill., 1980-82; prin. law offices Myles L. Berman, Chgo., 1982-91, Los Angeles, 1988–; traffic court judge pro tem Beverly Hills Municipal Ct., 1990–, Traffic Ct. judge pro tem adminstr., 1991–; traffic court judge pro tem Culver City Municipal Ct., 1992–; probation monitor State Bar of Calif., 1992–; mem: Am. Bar Assn., Los Angeles Co. Bar Assn., Santa Monica Bar Assn., Beverly Hills Bar Assn., Century City Bar Assn. (crim. law sect. chair 1989–; Outstanding Svc. award 1990, 92, 93, 94, spl. recognition 1994; editor-Century City Lawyer; bd. of gov. 1991–, treas. 1994, secty. 1995), Calif. Attys. for Crim. Justice, Nat. Assn. of Crim. Defense Lawyers, Crim. Cts. Bar Assn.; Sinai Temple (L.A.); rec: golf. Ofcs: 9255 Sunset Blvd Ste 720 Los Angeles 90069; 4630 Campus Dr Ste 200 Newport Beach 92660; 100 E Thousand Oaks Blvd Ste 259 Thousand Oaks 91360

BERMAN, SAUL J., management consultant; b. Jan. 1, 1946, Phila.; s. Sherwood S. and Leona (Habelson) B.; m. Jann Gillen, June 6, 1980; 1 child, Ashley Scott b. 1984; edn: BS econ., Univ. of Penn. 1967; MBA, Columbia Univ. 1969, PhD 1973. Career: asst. prof. USC Sch. of Bus. 1972-7; divisional v.p. The Broadway 1977-82; case leader Boston Consulting Group,1982-86; managing ptnr. West Reg., Strategic Consulting, Price Waterhouse, Century City 1986–; advocate Calif. Coastal Commn. 1976-82, apptd. Los Angeles County Beach Commn. 1977-79; mem. LIFE/Love is Feeding Everyone, a charity (bd. dirs. 1987-88), Town Hall of Calif.; clubs: Wharton Sch., Columbia Bus. Sch. Club of So. Calif. (bd. dirs. 1992-94), Univ. Pa. Alumni (dir. 1987-89, So. Calif. Associate Alumni trustee); rec: tennis, running. Ofc: Price Waterhouse 1880 Century Park East Los Angeles 90067

BERNARD, ALEXANDER, city official; b. Apr. 23, 1952, Los Angeles; s. Louis and Hannah (Bergman) B.; m. Diana LoRee Winstead, Dec. 17, 1976; children: Michael, Andrew; edn: AA (magna cum laude), L.A. Valley Coll., 1976; BS (summa cum laude), CSU Los Angeles, 1989. Career: parking meter collector L.A. City Clerk's Office, 1973-79; police ofcr. Los Angeles Airport Police Div., 1979-95, Sergeant 1995–; honors: Golden Key (life), Phi Kappa Phi (life); mem: Internat. Police Assn. (life), Calif. Peace Ofcrs. Assn., L.A. County Peace Ofcrs. Assn., L.A. Airport Peace Ofcrs. Assn. (pres. 1981-89, 1994-95, dir. 1992-94), Peace Ofcrs. Research Assn. Calif. (state bd. dirs. 1984-85, 88–, chpt. pres. 1982-84, 85-87, ethnic relations com. 1993-94, exec com. 1994–), Indsl. Relations Research Assn., Airport Supvy. Police Ofcrs. Assn. of L.A., NRA (life), Calif. Rifle and Pistol Assn. (life), Boy Scouts of Am.; contbr. articles to profl. jours.; Democrat; Assemblies of God. Ofc: Police Services Division, Ontario Internat. Airport, 1070 S. Vineyard Ave Ontario 91761

BERNFIELD, LYNNE, psychotherapist; b. Mar. 16, 1943, NY City, NY; d. Meyer and Lillian Claire (Pastel) Bernfield; m. Arthur Dawson Richards 1982; edn: BA, Hofstra Univ., Hempstead, NY, 1964; MA, Azusa Pacific Univ., Azusa, Calif., 1981; Calif. Marriage, Family, Child Therapist License 1982. Career: founder/dir., Writers and Artists Inst., Calif., 1984–; honors: Who's Who of Am. Women 1995; mem: ASCAP 1970, C.A.M.F.T. 1990, A.A.M.F.T. 1994; author: When You Can You Will, 1993. Ofc: PO Box 35156 Sarasota, FL 34242 Tel 813/349-1010

BERNHARD, BRUCE C., municipal transit planning executive; b. April 15, 1950, Berkeley; s. Arthur Paul and Elsie Frances (Marsolek) B.; m. Judi Sui, June 19, 1971; children: Kyle b. 1977, Laura b. 1985; edn: BA geography, UC Berkeley 1972; MBA, 1976. Career: sr. economist Gruen Gruen & Assoc., San Francisco 1976-79; sr. planner Calif. Dept. of Transp. 1979-80; mgr. fin. analysis Pub. Utilities Commn., City and Co. San Francisco 1980-85; exec. asst. to gen. mgr. Municipal Railway, San Francisco 1985-87, dir. strategic planning 1987-89, dep. gen. mgr. 1989-91; dep. gen. mgr. Bechtel/Athens Metro 1992-93; project mgmt. cons. STV Group 1994-; awards: Metro-Transp. Comm. MTC 1983, Municipal Railway Gold 1987, 88; mem: Railway & Local Hist. Soc. (dir.), San Francisco Planning & Urban Research Assn., Berkeley Montessori Sch. (pres. bd. 1987-90); article pub. in profl. jour., 1988; rec: transp. history. Res: 1620 Arch St Berkeley 94709 Ofc: STV Group 425 Market St Ste 2835 San Francisco 94105

BERNHOFT, FRANKLIN OTTO, educational psychologist; b. Aug. 12, 1944, Fargo, N. Dak.; s. Otto Lawrence and Irene Viola (Ralston) B.; m. Dorothy Anne Larson, Aug. 11, 1973; children: Kimberley b. 1978, Brady b. 1980, Heather b. 1983; edn: BA, N. Dak. State Univ., 1966; MA, Univ. N. Dak., 1970; MA, CSU Sacto., 1978; PhD, Brigham Young Univ., 1985; Calif. lic. Marriage Family Child Counselor (1980), Sch. Psychologist (1984), Educational Psychologist (1988). Career: assoc. dir. Counseling Ctr., Grand Forks AFB, N.Dak. 1970-71; tchr./counselor Folsom/Cordova Unified Sch. Dist., Sacto. 1974-82; cons. Office of Edn., Sacto. 1978-82; instr. BYU, Provo, Ut. 1982-84; sch. psychologist Lodi (Calif.) Unified Sch. Dist., 1984–; assoc. prof. Chapman Coll. (Mather AFB), 1986–, U.S. Internat. Univ., 1988–; psychotherapist pvt. practice, 1980–, Sunrise Counseling Gp., Roseville 1986–, also Creative Therapy Ctr., Lodi 1990–; master tnr. Systematic Helping Skills, Utah and Calif., 1982–; psych. cons. Adolescent Group Homes, Sacto. 1979-82; honors: H.H. Kirk-R. Askanase scholar (1962-66), outstanding fraternity pledge (1963), "Joe College" NDSU (1964), Blue Key (corr. sec. 1964-66), Sigma Alpha Epsilon (ND Beta, pres. 1965-66), Circle K Service Org. NDSU (v.p.); mem: Am. Assn. for Couns. & Devel. (1970–, workshop presenter AACD Nat. Conv. New Orleans 1987), CAMFT, Calif. Assn. of Lic. Ednl. Psychologist, Calif. Cont. Edn. Assn. (treas. dist. II 1979-81, workshop presenter CCEA reg. and state convs. 1978-81), Mental Health Assn. of Sacto./Placer, Assn. of Mormon Counselors & Psychotherapists, Mensa; author: Eric- Brain Dominance/Personality (1987), Eric - Five Keys to Self-Concept Enhancement (1989), contbr. articles in profl. jours.; mil: 1st lt. USAR 1967-69, Bronze star, Combat badge; LDS Ch., Roseville 2nd Ward (Bishop's counselor 1986-89); rec: profl. bass/baritone soloist, radio announcer, jogging, golf, tennis. Ofc: Creative Therapy Associates, 310 W Lockeford Lodi 95240 and UOP Behavioral Medicine Clinic Stockton 95211

BERNSTEIN, BURTON M., company executive, lawyer; b. May 13, 1937, New York; s. Robert and Betty (Lieberman) B.; m. Judith Katz, June 23, 1962; children: Dina b. 1966, Mara b. 1968; edn: BA, City Univ. N.Y. 1959; JD, Santa Barbara Coll. of Law 1988. Career: sales man N.Y. Life, Bklyn., N.Y. 1959-62; life underwriter Mutual Life of N.Y., NYC 1962-65; v.p., corp. secty. Sovereign Life Ins. Co. Calif., Santa Barbara 1965–; instr. Santa Barbara Coll. of Law 1989; mem: Internat. Claims Assn., Western Home Office Underwriters Assn., Western Claims Assn., Am. Bar Assn., Santa Barbara Bar Assn.; med. article pub. in profl. jour. (1989); mil: sgt. AUS 1959-65. Ofc: Sovereign Life 30 W Sola St Santa Barbara 91101-93101

BERRY, EDWIN X., atmospheric physicist; b. June 20, 1935, San Francisco; s. Edwin and Frances Alice (Foley) B.; edn: BS, Caltech, 1957; MA, Dartmouth Coll., 1960; PhD, Univ. Nev., 1965. Career: research assoc. Desert Research Inst., Reno, Nev. 1961-72; program mgr. NSF, Wash. D.C. 1972-76; pres. Atmospheric Research & Tech., Sacto. 1976-87; Edwin X. Berry & Assocs. 1987–; ThinkNet Internat. 1994–; honors: Sigma Delta Psi, 1st pl. Canadian Olympic Regatta (1974), 1st pl. U.S. Sailing Championship (1975); mem: Am. Meteorological Soc., Am. Wind Energy Assn.; 42 papers pub. in sci. jours. (1962–); rec: running, sailing. Address: 6040 Verner Ave Sacramento 95841

BERRY, PHILLIP SAMUEL, lawyer; b. Jan. 30, 1937, Berkeley; s. Samuel Harper Berry and Jean Mobley (Kramer) Jenny; m. Michele Ann Perrault, Jan. 16, 1982; children: David b. 1962, Douglas b. 1964, Dylan b. 1966, Justin b. 1972, Matthew b. 1982; edn: BA, Stanford Univ. 1958; LLD, 1961. Career: atty., assoc. Berry Davis, Oakland 1962-69, ptnr. 1969-76; Berry & Berry 1976–; appt. State Bd. Forestry 1974-86; mem. advy. com. Coll. Natural Resources, UC Berkeley 1990–; honors: Sierra Club John Muir award 1978; mem: Sierra Club (nat. pres. 1969-71, 1991-92, dir. 1968–, v.p. 1971–), Sierra Club Legal Defense (trustee 1971-90), Pub. Advocates Calif. (trustee 1971-86), Nature Conservancy, Am. Farmland Trust, Common Cause, Nat. Cattlemans Assn., Am. Alpine Club; articles pub. in profl. jour. 1961-80; mil: 1st lt. USAR 1961-67; rec: mountaineering. Res: 2979 Rohrer Dr Lafayette 94549 Ofc: 1300 Clay St Oakland 94662

BERTACCHI, GLORIA MARIE, consultant pharmacist, entertainer; b. May 1, 1953, Sacramento; d. Jerome J. and Phyllis M. (Herr) B.; m. Laurence Freeman, 1987; edn: PharmD, Univ. Pacific, 1977. Career: lectr./tnr. and pres. National Medical Seminars Inc., Sacto. 1979–; cons. pharmacist and pres. Tempharmacists, National Medical Staffing Inc., 1979–; actress major feature films including: Raide on Entebbe, The Entertainer, Who Will Love My Children; guest host nat. t.v. and radio shows: Geraldo Rivera Show, Morton Downey, Jr. Show, News talk TV; civic: Carmichael Park Board (dir. 1987-88), Lodi Community Crusade vs. Drugs (drug abuse lectr. 1980–), UOP Stockton (street drug lab. anal. 1976-78); author 20+ med. books incl. Drugs of Abuse; Athletes and Drugs; Cocaine: Fact and Fantasy; Aids, Sex & Protection; Medical Emergency Drugs, Violence, Abuse, Depression and Suicide; Diet Secrets for Weight Control; Overview of Antibiotics; Osteoporosis: Prevention & Treatment; Drugs, Sex & Aging; Birth Control Choices; Treatment of Sexually Transmitted Diseases; (novel) Hawaiian Heat. Ofc: Dr. Gloria M. Bertacchi, National Medical Staffing Inc. PO Box 2699 Roseville 95746 Tel: 916/784-6200

BERTOLERO, OTTAVIO AMERIGO, civil engineer; b. March 3, 1954, Lima, Peru; nat. 1976; s. Ottavio and Juana Maria (Choza) B.; edn: BS, Calif. Polytech. Univ. 1979; reg. civil engr. Calif. 1987. Career: engr. Soil Conservation Service, Visalia 1979-85; engr. Contra Costa Co., Martinez 1986-89; sr. engr. City of Mill Valley 1989-90; asst. city engr. City of Vallejo Public Works 1990–; Democrat; Cath. Res: 115 Camino Alto Vallejo 94590 Ofc: City of Vallejo Public Works PO Box 3068 Vallejo 94590

BEST, GARY ALLEN, professor of education; b. July 27, 1939, Oceanside, Calif.; s. Charles Richard and Vivian Elaine (Misner) B.; m. Shirley J. Seelhammer, Dec. 18, 1962; 1 dau. Joanna b. 1964; edn: BA, elem. edn., Los Angeles St. Coll. of Applied Arts and Scis. 1961; MA, special edn., Calif. St. Coll., L.A. 1965; PhD, ednl. psychol., Univ. Minn. 1968; life tchg. cred. Calif., gen. elementary and orthopedically handicapped; cert. sex educator, Am. Assn. of Sex Educators, Counselors & Therapists 1991-93. Career: special edn. tchr. L.A. Unified Sch. Dist. 1961-65; tchg. asst., instr. special edn. Univ. Minn. 1966-68; instr. special edn. Wis. St. Univ. 1966; prof. special edn. CSU, Los Angeles 1968–, asst. prof. 1968-70, assoc. prof. 1970-75, prof. 1975–; chair Div. of Special Edn, CSU L.A. 1985-86, 87-91; acting dean Grad. Studies & Res., CSU, L.A. 1986-87; bd. dirs. CSU, LA. Found. 1987–, exec. com./sec. 1993–; mem. Commn. on Tchr. Credentialing, Special Edn. Advy. Panel 1994–; vis. prof. (summer): Univ. Victoria, BC, Canada 1970, 74, We. Mich. Univ. 1972, Univ. Oregon 1973, Univ. of LaVerne 1983; vis. prof. Nat. Taiwan Normal Univ., Taipei (12/89), sr. Fulbright scholar special edn. (fall 1991); cons. Calif. St. Dept. of Edn., 1985; honors: grantee Nat. Elks 1959-60, 60-61, Federal Fellow 1965-66, 66-67, 67-68, United Cerebral Palsy Assn. grant 1971, Registered Reader, Huntington Lib. Rare Books and Manuscript Lib. 1980-81, Outstanding Prof. award CSU, L.A. 1982-83, Friends of Edn., Faculty Devel. award Sch. of Edn.,

CSU, L.A. 1989, 91, 93, 95, Award of Merit, Intercomm. Med. Ctr., Covina 1987-89, 90, Dominic Longo Faculty Devel. award, Div. Special Edn., CSU, L.A. 1991, 94, Grant in Aid award CSU, L.A. 1991, Nat. Sci. Council of Republic of China Grant 1991, Disting. Alumnus award CSU, L.A. 1993, Alumnus of Yr., Riverside Comm. Coll. 1994, listed Who's Who in Am. Edn. 1992-95, Internat. Who's Who in Sexology 1986, Who's Who in West 1974-75, 80-81, 84-85, others; mem: Council for Exceptional Children (prog. advy. com. 1984, 86, 87, 91, nat. parliamentarian 1991-94), Div. for Physically Handicapped: Council for Exceptional Children (nat. level: v.p. 1982-83, pres. elect 1983-84, pres. 1984-85, exec. com 1975-78, 82-86, 87-90 as mem. of CEC Bd. Govs. 1987-90), Am. Assn. Sex Educators, Counselors & Therapists (cert. reg. sex educator), Calif. St. Fedn./Council for Exceptional Children (chair planning com. 1983), Calif. Educators of Physically Handicapped, Calif. Assn. of Professors in Special Edn., Calif. Professors in Physical and Health Disabilities (founder and first pres., 1985-); civic: vol. bd. dirs. Hospice of E. San Gabriel Valley Inc. 1980-86, bd. dirs. 1986-89, pres. 1987-89; bd. dirs. Intercomm. Med. Ctr. Found. 1989; mem. supt.'s. advy. com. on edn. and employment of persons with disabilities, L.A. Unified Sch. Dist. 1987-94; advy. council Calif. Coll. Health 2000, CSU, San Diego 1990-94; trustee and bd. dirs. Crippled Children's Soc. of So. Calif., Inc. 1993-; tng. cons., mem. Alliance 2000 Project, Dept. Special Edn., Coll. of Edn., Albuquerque, NM 1993-; assoc. edit. Exceptional Children 1971-78, DOPHHH Jour. 1976-78, 87-94; mem. review bd. Physical Disabilities: Edn. and Related Svs. 1994-; co-editor: Selected Readings in Special Education, 1970; pub. cons., author of the foreword to Private Zone, 1982; manuscript reviewer, Adaptive Mainstreaming: a primer for tchrs. and principals, 1988; author: Individuals with Physical Disabilities: An Introduction for Educators, 1978, Instructor's Manual, 1978, num. profl. papers and presentations; co-author: Getting and Spending; Fiscal Policies and Practices for Academic Leaders, 1991; contbg. author: res. reviews, num. book chpts and forewords, 1968-93, 40+ articles to profl. jours., 1967-. Ofc: Div of Special Education California State University 5151 State University Dr Los Angeles 90032

BEST, ROBERTA LOUISE, export executive; b. Apr. 8, 1941, Mpls.; d. Irving Wolfe and Beatrice Theresa (Marcus) Lichterman; m. Charles Patrick Best, Sept. 25, 1963 (div. 1966); son, Bennett Thomas; m. Masaharu Ichino, May 29, 1977; edn: AA, L.A. City Coll., 1962; paralegal cert., UCLA, 1974, postgrad. studies internat. bus., 1986-. Career: exec. legal secretary Litton Industries Inc., Beverly Hills 1967-73; life underwriter Connecticut Mutual Life Ins. Co., L.A., 1976-80, Mutual Benefit Life Ins. Co., L.A., 1977-86; c.e.o. Romac Export Mgmt. Corp., L.A., 1978-; owner, mgr. Canyon Gallery Two, L.A., 1978-82; appt. mem. Calif. Assembly Select Com. on Small Business Advy. Council; honors: named SBA Exporter of Yr. L.A. dist. & regional U.S. Small Bus. Adminstrn. 1990, Los Angeles Bus. Jour. list of 100 largest women-owned bus. firms in L.A. Co. (1990, 91, 92, 93, 94, 95), Alpha Pi Epsilon, apptd. by U.S. Sec. of Commerce to So. Calif. Dist. Export Council 1992; mem: Profl. Referral Orgn. (pres. 1980-81), Export Mgrs. Assn., Greater L.A. World Trade Ctr. Assn., Nat. Assn. Women Business Owners, Nat. Assn. Life Underwriters (Women's Leaders Roundtable 1978), Nat. Women's Political Caucus, B.H. Democratic Club (steering com. 1972), L.A. Bus./Profl. Democratic Club, West Adams Heritage Assn. (dir. 1985), Ctr. for Creative Change, Newbury Park (dir. 1987-), West Adams Heights Neighborhood Assn. 1986-, Tree People, World Wildlife Fund, City Club on Bunker Hill. Address: 2242 S Hobart Blvd Los Angeles 90018-2149

BESTE, IAN ROBERT, librarian; b. Jan. 28, 1960, Crescent City; s. Raymond F. and Pattie L. (Erwin) B.; m. Melissa C. Lathrop, April 5, 1986; edn: BA hist., UC Berkeley 1982, MLIS, 1985. Career: librarian UC Berkeley Center for Study and Law Soc. 1983-85; Brobeck Phleger & Harrison, Los Angeles 1985-88; Bryan Cave McPheetens & McRoberts 1988-; mem: So. Calif. Assn. Law Librarians, Am. Assn. Law Librarians; Democrat; Episcopalian; rec: equestrian sports. Ofc: Bryan Cave McPheetens 333 S Grand Ave Ste 3100 Los Angeles 90071

BETTS, BARBARA LANG, lawyer, rancher; b. Apr. 28, 1926, Anaheim; d. W. Harold and Helen (Thompson) Lang; m. Roby F. Hayes, July 22, 1948 (dec.); children: J. Chauncey, IV, b. 1953, Frederick Prescott, b. 1955, Roby F., b. 1957; m. 2d, Bert A. Betts (fmr. Calif. state treas.), July 11, 1962; children: Bruce Harold b. 1966, (step): Bert Alan b. 1950, Randy W. b. 1952, Sally (Joynt) b. 1949, Terry (Marsteller) b. 1946, Linda (Hansen) b. 1947, Leann (Wilson) b. 1954; edn: BA, magna cum laude, Stanford Univ. 1948; LLB, Calif. Western Univ. (fmr Balboa U.), 1951; admitted to calif. State Bar 1952, US Dist. Ct., S. and N. Dists. Calif. 1952, US Ct. of Appeals, 9th Circuit 1952, US Supreme Ct. 1978. Career: ptnr. law firm Barbara Lang Hayes & Roby F. Hayes, 1952-60; city atty. City of Carlsbad, 1959-63; pvt. law practice, Oceanside 1952-60, San Diego 1960-, Sacto. 1962-; rancher, 1948-62, 1967-; v.p. W.H. Lang Corp., 1964-70; secty. Internat. Prod. Assn., 1967-72; v.p. Isle & Oceans Marinas Inc., 1970-80; secty. Margaret M. McCabe, M.D., Inc. 1976-88; commr. Carlsbad Planning Commn. 1959, v.p. San Diego County Plng. Cong.; dir. North S.D. County chpt. for retarded children 1957-57; honors: Phi Beta Kappa 1948, Calif. Scholarship Fedn. (life), inducted Fullerton Union H.S. Wall of Fame 1986; mem: Am., San Diego Co., Calif. Trial Lawyers bar assns., Am. Judicature Soc., Nat. Inst. Municipal Ofcrs. 1959-63, Stanford Club (Sacto.),

Stanford Mothers' Club, US Supreme Ct. Hist. Soc., C.of C. (Oceanside, San Diego), North San Diego Co. Assn., Traveler's Aid (chmn. 1952-54), AAUW, Bus. & Profl. Womens Club 1953-63, Soroptimist Internat. (chapt. pres. Oceanside-Carlsbad; sec. pub. affairs San Diego - Imperial Counties 1954; pres. Presidents' Council - San Diego & Imperial Counties & Mexico 1958-59), San Diego Hist. Soc., Heritage League 2nd Air Div. USAAF, Fullerton Jr. Assistance League 1956-66, DAR 1956-64 (regent Oceanside chpt. 1960-61); Democrat (State Cent. Com. 1954-62, co-chair 28th C.D. 1960-62, del. Dem. Nat. Conv. 1960); Prot.; rec: fishing, hunting. Res: Betts Ranch, Elverta 95626 and 441 Sandburg Dr Sacramento 95819 Ofc: 8701 E Levee Rd Elverta;and 3119 Howard Ave San Diego 92104

BETTS, BERT A., former state treasurer; b. Aug. 16, 1923, San Diego; s. Bert A., Sr., and Alma (Jorgenson) C.; m. Barbara Lang; children: Terry Lou, Linda Sue, Sara Ellen, Bert Alan, Randy Wayne, John Chauncey, Frederick Prescott, LeAnn, Roby Francis, Bruce Harold; edn: BA, Calif. Western Univ. 1950; grad. Internat. Acctg. Soc.; lic. CPA, Calif. 1950. Career: ptnr. CPA firm, 1950, prin. 1951-59; college tchr., acct.-tax., 1950-58; elected State Treas. of Calif., 1958, re-elected 1962-67 (youngest statewide elected ofcl. and the first state-level exec. ofcr. from San Diego County in this century); cons. prin. Betts Fin., R.E. and Mgmt. Consultants, 1967-77; treas. and c.e.o. Internat. Prodn. Assocs. 1968-72; trustee Fidelity Mortgage Investors, 1970-78; dir. Lifetime Communities Inc., 1978-86; awards: hon. life mem. and award for outstanding leadership in mcpl. fin. Municipal Finance Ofcrs. Assn. of U.S. & Canada and the only state treasurer in U.S. awarded the gold medal and scroll of City of Louisville conferred on the most outstanding fiscal ofcr. in U.S. & Can. 1963, hon. life Beta Alpha Psi, hon. life Alpha Kappa Psi and award for bringing highest profl. stds. to Calif. Treasury ops. 1966; former mem. State Soc. Govt. Accts., Nat. Assn. of State Auditors, Comptrollers and Treasurers; mem: Calif. Municipal Treasurers Assn. (hon. life), Municipal Forum of NY (hon. life), Am. Inst. of CPAs, Nat. Assn. of Accts., Am. Accts. Assn., Calif. Soc. of CPAs (past v.p. S.D. chpt.), AF Assn. (past v-comdr.), Second Air Div. Assn., 8th Air Force Hist. Soc., Liberator Club, Sponsor Collings Found. "All American" B-24 Liberator, Friends USAF Mus., Colonel, Confederate Air Force, Smithsonian Air & Space (charter), Am. Mus. Natural Hist. (charter), VFW, Am. Legion, Intl. Order of Foresters, Lemon Grove Mens Club (past pres.), Lions Club, Masons, Sigma Phi Epsilon; civic bds: Lemon Grove Sch. Dist. (past pres. bd. trustees), Girl Scouts San Diego (past fin. com.), Boy Scouts Sacto., mem. citizen advy. coms. various govt. agys., S.D. Cerebral Palsy Found. (past treas.), Sacto. Co. Am. Cancer Soc. (pres. 1967-68); mil: B-24 Bomber Pilot 8th AF USAAF 1941-45, 30 combat missions over Europe WWII, decorated D.F.C., Air Medal w. 4 clusters. Res: Betts' Ranch, 8701 E Levee Rd, Elverta 95626; 441 Sandburg Dr Sacramento 95819

BEVERETT, ANDREW JACKSON, real estate and financial consultant; b. Feb. 21, 1917, Midland City, Ala.; s. Andrew J. and Ella L. (Adams) B.; m. Martha Sophia Landgrebe, May 26, 1951; children: Andrew J. III, James Edmund, Faye A.; edn: BS, Samford Univ. 1940; MBA, Harvard Univ. 1942. Career: exec. pos. in corp. plnng. and mgmt. United Air Lines, Chicago, Ill. 1946-66; senior mktg. & economic cons. Mgmt. & Economics Research Inc., Palo Alto 1966-71; senior economist Stanford Research Inst., Menlo Park 1971-72; pres. Edy's on the Peninsula Stores, Palo Alto 1972-78; real estate broker, fin. and tax counselor, Saratoga 1979-; mem: Phi Kappa Phi, Nat. Assn. of Enrolled Agents, Nat. Assn. of Realtors; mil: lt. USNR 1942-46. Res/Ofc: 6325 Whaley Dr San Jose 95135

BEYER, STEVE D., lawyer; b. Aug. 17, 1959, Anchorage, Alaska; s. David Dean and Reba (Pfaff) B.; m. Miriam Majofis; edn: BSME, Univ. Ariz. 1980; MS electro-mech. design, Stanford Univ. 1982; JD, George Washington Univ. 1985. Career: atty. Flehr Hohbach, San Francisco 1987-90; Onda Techno, Gifu City, Japan 1990-92; ptnr. Hickman & Beyer, Palo Alto 1993-; bd. dirs. Berg Store Fixtures of Calif., Carlsbad 1988-91. Res:748 9th Ave San Francisco 94118 Ofc: Hickman & Beyer 620 Hansen Way Palo Alto 94306

BHANDARI, SANJIV, architect; b. Mar. 10, 1959, Chandigarh, India; s. Om Parkash and Krishna (Sabherwal) B.; m. Arti, Mar. 10, 1985; children: Nipun B. b. 1991, Nakin B. b. 1993; edn: B.Arch., Chandigarh Coll. of Arch., 1979; postgrad. dipl. Inst. for Housing Studies, Rotterdam, Holland 1982; reg. arch. Council of Architecture, India 1982, reg. arch. Calif. 1992. Career: intern Virender Khanna & Assocs., New Delhi 1977; job captain Planners Group, Chandigarh 1979; architect/project dir. P.C.P. Ltd., Diwaniya, Iraq 1980-84; sr. v.p. and principal Brown/McDaniel Inc., San Francisco 1985-; awards: cash awards, outstanding performance P.C.P. Ltd. (1981, 82), merit scholar Punjab Univ. 1978; Editor's Choice Award for Outstanding Achievement in Poetry, Nat. Lib. of Poetry 1993; listed Who's Who in Interior Design 1992-93, The Internat. Who's Who of Intellectuals 1993, Dictionary of Internat. Biography 1993, Who's Who among Asian Americans 1994; full mem. Am. Inst. of Architects (AIA); Fellow Indian Inst. of Architects (FIIA) 1993-; founder/chairperson Asian Indian Architects Assn. (AIAA) 1994-95; author, pub. poems: Arcadia Poetry Anthology, 1993, "Where Dreams Begin" an Anthology, Nat. Lib. of Poetry, 1993, Outstanding Poets of 1994, Poetic Voices of America, 1994; thesis:

Evolutionary Housing for Urban Poor 1982; rec: internat. travel, sports, writing poetry. Res: 15 Vartan Ct Walnut Creek 94596 Ofc: Brown/McDaniel, Inc. 650 California St Ste 2205 San Francisco 94108

BIANCHINI, VICTOR E., judge; b. Feb. 21, 1938, San Pedro; s. Henry and Judith B.; children: Hannah b. 1971, Amber b. 1974, Amy b. 1989; edn: BA, San Diego St. Univ. 1960; JD, Univ. of San Diego 1963; admitted Calif. Bar 1964. Career: law clk. to Hon. James M. Carter, U.S. Dist. Ct., 1963-64; magistrate U.S. Dist. Ct. So. Dist. Calif., 1974; U.S. Commr. 1968-69; judge Municipal Ct., El Cajon 1982–; assoc. prof. CSU San Diego 1969-73; Western St. Univ. Sch. of Law 1975; founding dean 1980, prof. Nat. Univ. Sch. of Law, 1978-84; assoc. prof. Sch. of Mgmt. and Tech. Nat. Univ. Sch. of Law 1978–; prof. of evidence Western St. Univ. Coll. of Law 1990–; faculty Calif. Continuing Judicial Studies Pgm. 1986-88, Calif. Ctr. for Judicial Edn. and Res.; mem. faculty council Nat. Judicial Coll., Reno 1994–; chmn. bd. vis. Univ. San Diego Sch. of Law 1978; awards: Trial Judge of Yr. 1992, President's Award for contributions to legal edn. 1991, San Diego Trial Lawyers Assn.; mem: Nat. Council of U.S. Magistrates (chmn. by-laws com. 1978), Nat. Conf. of Spl. Ct. Judges, ABA 1974-82, Calif. State Bar Assn., San Diego Co. Bar Assn. (bd. dirs. 1978, treas., v.p. 1979-80, chmn. ethics com.), Calif. Agri. Labor Rels. Bd. (adminstrv. law ofcr.); vol. free legal clinic for youth (Ocean Beach 1970, S.D. region 1976–); cert. AAU boxing referee and judge; author: book reviews: How Can You Defend Those People? The Making of a Criminal Lawyer by James S. Kunen, 1984, Political Questions, Judicial Answers - Does the Rule of Law Apply to Foreign Affairs? by Thomas M. Franck, 1993; num. articles pub. in profl. jours., 1966–; mil: col. USMCR (ret.) 1960-91, gen. court-martial judge/dep. insp. gen. U.S. European. Command, Stuttgart, Ger., Bronze Star with V, 3 air medals, Meritorious Svc. Medal and Joint Svs. Commendation Medal; rec: tennis. Ofc: El Cajon Municipal Court 250 E Main St El Cajon 92020

BIANCO, MICHAEL F., corporate financial consulting firm executive; b. Dec. 27, 1940, West Pittston, Pa.; s. Joseph P. and Mary M. (Compitello) B.; m. Marcia E. Schroeder, Apr. 28, 1968; children: Suzanne b. 1972, Francesca b. 1973, Michael Joseph b. 1981; edn: AB, Wilkes Univ., 1962; MPA, Univ. Mich., 1968; Adv. Mgmt. Coll., Stanford Univ., 1981-84. Career: banking ofcr. Chase Manhattan Bank, N.Y.C., 1968-72; pres. and c.e.o. Loeb Rhoades Securities Corp., 1972-77; mng. dir. Security Pacific Leasing Corp., San Francisco 1977-80, Internat. Bank, W.D.C., 1980-81; with Bank of Calif., S.F., 1981-82; v.p. Barclay's Bank, S.F. 1982-84; v.p., mgr. The Hibernia Bank, S.F. 1984-88; pres. Asia Pacific Capital Corp., San Francisco 1987-91; mng. dir. corporate fin. consulting, Arthur Andersen & Co., S.F. 1991–; speaker Business Week Exec. Programs, N.Y., 1987, The Planning Forum, S.F., 1988; awards: fellow James A. Finnegan Found. 1960-61; mem: Calif. Council in Internat. Trade (bd. dirs., treas. 1987-88), Korean Am. C. of C. (dir. 1992–) Japan Soc. No. Calif., World Trade Assn., Univ. Mich. Alumni Assn., Stanford Univ. Alumni Assn.; civic: S.F. Library Assn. (bd. 1986-88); Pacific Basin Council grad. studies prog., Domincan Coll.; clubs: World Trade (S.F.), Foreign Correspondents (Japan); mil: lt. US Navy 1963-67; R.Cath. Res: 1420 Oak Rim Dr Hillsborough 94010 Ofc: Arthur Andersen & Co. 1 Market Plaza Ste 3500 San Francisco 94105

BICE, SCOTT HAAS, academic administrator, educator, lawyer; b. Mar. 19, 1943, Los Angeles; s. Fred Haas and Virginia M. (Scott) B.; m. Barbara Franks, Dec. 21, 1968; edn: BS, finance, Univ. of So. Calif. 1965, JD, 1968; admitted to bar, Calif. 1971. Career: summer assoc. Gibson, Dunn & Crutcher, L.A. 1967; law clerk to Chief Justice Earl Warren, Supreme Court of U.S., 1968-69; asst. prof., assoc. prof., prof. of law, Carl Mason Franklin prof. of law, Univ. of So. Calif., 1969–, assoc. dean for acad. affairs 1970-74, dean 1980–; vis. prof. of law, Calif. Inst. of Tech. 1977, Univ. of Va. 1978-79; exec. com. USC Council of Deans 1980-94, Provost's Council 1994–; mem. USC Radio Mgmt. Bd. 1994-95; chair, advy. com., Schoenberg Inst. 1992-95; bd. dirs. Residence Mutual Ins. Co. 1992–, Western Mutual Ins. Co. 1993–, Coalition for Justice 1993–, Extended School Day Programs Inc. 1986–, L.A. Family Housing Corp. 1987-94, Imagine Films Entertainment Inc. 1992-93, Jenny Craig Inc. 1995–; awards: Outstanding Province Grad., Phi Delta Phi, Order of the Coif, Phi Kappa Phi; affiliated scholar, Am. Bar Found. 1973-75; Fellow, Am. Bar Found. 1984–; mem: State Bar of Calif. 1970– (chair, Law Sch. Council 1987-88), Am. Law Inst. 1978–, L.A. Co. Bar Assn. 1980–, Chancery Club of L.A. 1985–; editl. advy. bd. Calif. Lawyer 1989-94; contbr. num. articles to law jours. Ofc: Univ of So Calif Law Center Univ Park Los Angeles 90089-0071

BICKMORE, EDWARD CLIFTON, JR., consulting executive; b. Oct. 12, 1929, Upland; s. Edward C. and Vira Jean (Sechrist) B.; m. Norma Kent, Mar. 17, 1950; children: Kennieth b. 1950, Charles b. 1954, Denise b. 1957; edn: AA, Reedley Coll., 1972; BS acctg., CSU Fresno, 1974, grad. studies, 1975. Career: served to lt. cmdr. US Navy, 1947-70; acct. Kings View Corp., Reedley 1974-75, controller 1975-77; gen. mgr. Orange Cove Irrigation Dist., Orange Cove, Calif. 1977-81; prin. Bickmore Bus. Services, Sacto. 1981–; pres. Bickmore & Assocs. Inc., 1987–; gen. mgr. Calif. Water Agencies Jt. Powers Auth. (JPA), Sacto. 1981-83; administr. Central San Joaquin Risk Mgmt. Auth., 1984–, also Vector Control JPA, 1986–, and Bay Cities Jt. Powers Ins. Auth., 1990–; bd.

dirs. Calif. Jt. Powers Ins. Auth. 1985–, bd. dirs./v.p. Local Agy. Workers' Compensation Excess Auth. 1992–, pres. 1993; honors: Beta Gamma Sigma, Phi Kappa Phi 1973; mem: Calif. Assn. of Jt. Powers Auth. (bd. 1984-88, state pres. 1986-87, legis. com. 1987–, chmn. 1987-88, accreditation com. 1991–), Public Agency Risk Mgrs. Assn., Public Risk & Ins. Mgrs. Assn., Californians for Compensation Reform (bd. 1990-93), Calif. Affiliated Risk Mgmt. Authorities (adminstr. 1993–); Republican; Prot.; rec: stamps, woodworking. Res: 6444 Pretty Girl Ct Citrus Heights 95621 Ofc: Bickmore & Associates, Inc. 6371 Auburn Blvd Citrus Hts 95621

BIERMA, RONALD SCOTT, anesthesiologist; b. Jan. 28, 1958, Denison, Iowa; s. Ronald Dean and Marcia Ann (Collins) B.; m. Lisa Hedwig Kirschner, Jan. 24, 1987; children: Michael b. 1990; edn: BS (with distinction), Iowa State Univ., Ames, Iowa 1980; MD, Univ. of Iowa, Iowa City 1984; lic. MD in Calif., Iowa, Arizona; diplomate, Am. Bd. of Anesthesiology 1989. Career: flexible internship Univ. of Ariz. Hospitals, Tucson 1984-85, anesthesia residency 1985-87, chief resident-anesthesiology 1986-87; anesthesiologist Anesthesia Consultants of Fresno 1987–, mgmt. bd. mem. 1993–; chmn. dept. of anesthesiology St. Agnes Med. Ctr., Fresno 1995–; awards: Bausch & Lomb Sci. award, Denison (Iowa) H.S. 1976; mem: Calif. Soc. of Anesthesiologists 1988–, Am. Soc. of Anesthesiologists 1988–, CMA 1988–, AMA 1988–, Fresno-Madera Med. Soc. 1988–; mem. Temple Beth Israel, Fresno; Republican; Jewish; rec: history. Res: 9254 N Hilltop Court Fresno 93720 Ofc: 6760 N West Ave Fresno 93711 Tel: 209/436-0871

BIGGERS, RALPH LEE, JR., structural engineer; b. Dec. 23, 1941, Charlotte, N.C.; s. Ralph Lee and Sara Wilma (Kidd) B.; m. Sally Miller, June 21, 1969; children: Lee Anne b. 1970; Sara b. 1971, Katie b. 1974; edn: BSCE, N.C. St. Univ. 1964; MSCE, San Diego St. Univ. 1973; reg. structural engr. Calif. 1973. Career: staff engr. Whitman Atkinson & Assoc., La Jolla 1969-70; expansion mgr. Scott Meml. Baptist Ch., San Diego 1970-71; assoc. engr. Inter-City Engrs. 1971-73; exec. v.p. Atkinson Johnson & Spurrier Inc. 1974–, corp. secty., dir. 1980–; prin. R.L. Biggers & Associates, La Mesa 1991–; lectr. civil engring, San Diego St. Univ. 1976, 77, 81; awards: ASCE Outstanding Achievement 1976; mem: ASCE, Structural Engrs. Assn. San Diego (v.p. 1992-93), Structural Engrs. Assn. Calif., Am. Concrete Inst., Christian Heritage Retirement Center (pres. 1979-82), Christian Unified Schs. El Cajon (v.p. 1983-85), Scott Meml. Baptist Ch. (trustee 1986-89), Shadow Mt. Comm. Ch. (deacon 1992-94, trustee 1994-96), Structural Engrs. Assn. of San Diego (pres. 1993-94); mil: Navy Civil Engr. Corps 1965-69; capt. USNR 1965-94; Republican; Baptist; rec: jogging. Res: 2409 Cerro Sereno El Cajon 92019 Ofc: 7777 Alvarado Rd Ste 261 La Mesa 91941

BIGGS, JULIE HAYWARD, lawyer; b. July 30, 1946, Providence, R.I.; d. Grant Arthur and Florida Emelia (Grenier) Hayward; m. Gerard Elden Biggs, June 3, 1967; children: Holly b. 1972, Justin b. 1974; edn: BA cum laude, USC 1966; MA, 1969; MS edn., 1970; JD, 1978; admitted St. Bar Calif. (1978), Colo. (1979). Career: tchr. Los Angeles City Schs. 1967-68; Monrovia Unified Schs. 1969-74; atty. Bank of Am., Los Angeles 1978-79; Holme Roberts & Owen, Denver, Colo. 1979-80; Fishman Geman 1980-83; Julie Hayward Biggs, Parker, Colo. 1983-89; Best Best & Krieger, Riverside 1988-93; city attorney City of Colton 1993–; candidate (R) for Colo. State Assembly, 1988; mem: Building Industry Assn.; Republican (Redlands Repub. Women Club, Colo. st. exec. com., Douglas Co. Rep. Party chmn. 1985-87); rec: politics. Ofc: City of Colton 650 N La Cadena Drive Colton 92324

BIKLE, DANIEL DAVID, physician; b. Apr. 25, 1944, Harrisburg, Pa.; s. Charles Augustus and Sarah Elizabeth B.; m. Elizabeth Wanner, June 20, 1965; children: Christine b. 1975, Hilary b. 1978; edn: AB, Harvard Univ. 1965; MD, Univ. of Pa., Phila. 1969, PhD, 1974. Career: med. residency Peter Bent Brigham Hosp., Boston, Mass. 1969-71; res. internist Letterman AMC, San Francisco 1974-79; asst. prof. Univ. of Calif., S.F. 1979-86, assoc. prof. 1986-91, prof. 1991–; co-dir. SDTU, VA Med. Ctr., S.F. 1979–; editorial bd. Endocrinology 1983-86; peer review bd. NIH, Bethesda, Md. 1986–; editorial bd. Endocrine Reviews 1989-93, Bone and Mineral 1992–; awards: Henderson Mem. Prize, Harvard Univ. 1965, Baldwin Lucke Mem. Prize, Univ. of Pa. 1966, Horatio C. Wood Prize, Univ. of Pa. 1969, Spencer Morris Prize, Univ. of Pa. 1969, fellow Am. Coll. Physicians 1982; mem.: Am. Soc. for Bone & Mineral Res. 1978–, Am. Soc. for Clin. Investigation 1986–, AAAS 1978–, Endocrine Soc. 1980–, Soc. for Investigative Dermatology 1990–, Assn. Amer. Physicians 1995–; clubs: Harvard (S.F.), Commonwealth (S.F.); civic: mem. Comm. Ch., Mill Valley (pres. of bd. 1981-82), chmn. bd. Wee Care, Mill Valley 1993–; editor (book): Calcium Regulating Hormones, 1983; author: 15 book chapters, 125 articles; mil: col. US Army 1974-79; rec: skiing, tennis, sailing, biking, hiking. Ofc: Veterans Admin. Med. Ctr. 4150 Clement St San Francisco 94121

BILECKI, RONALD ALLAN, financial planner; b. July 15, 1942, Cincinnati, Ohio; s. Allan Frederick and Ruth Hulda (Parker) B.; m. Judy B., Jan. 25, 1964; children: Sherry b. 1967, Sean b. 1970; edn: chem. major, CSU Los Angeles 1968; Cert. Financial Planner, Coll. for Fin. Planning 1982, Reg. Investment Adviser, SEC 1985, Calif. Dept. Corps. 1986. Career: insurance agt. New York Life Ins., Covina 1973-75, asst. mgr. Los Angeles office 1975-79; indep. fin. plnnr., Rosemead 1979-81; pres. Financial Designs Corp., San Gabriel 1981–; fin. planning cons. So. Calif. Edison Co. and So. Calif. Gas Co.; fin. planning seminars for So. Calif. Edison, City of L.A. and L.A. Dept. Water & Power employees, So. Calif. Gas Co., ABC Inc., Rockwell Intl., Pomona First Federal, Xerox, Loral EOS, the FAA, and the IRS; mem. Internat. Assn. for Fin. Plnng. Inc., Registry of Fin. Planning Practioners, Internat. Soc. for Retirement Planning; Republican; Christian; rec: western and square dancing, chess, jogging, hiking. Ofc: Financial Designs Corp. 7220 Rosemead Blvd Ste 206 San Gabriel 91775

BILHEIMER, STEPHEN C., business executive, civic leader; b. Arkadelphia, Ark.; s. Charles Wm. and Edna (Carpenter) B.; m. Jeanne Summerfield, May 5, 1928; children: Mary Flave, b. 1935, Peter, b. 1937; edn: BS, Ore. State Coll. 1927; USC; Dr. Bus. Adm., Woodbury Coll. Career: ptnr. dir. Phelps-Terkel, Inc., Los Angeles 1925-54; pres. Silverwoods Stores, 21 stores, 1964-67, chmn. bd. 1967–; dir. Calif. Federal S&L Assn. 1945–; bd. dirs. Good Samaritan Medical Ctr.; past pres. LA Airport Commn.; bd. dirs. Calif. Mus. Sci & Indus.; pres. Calif. Mus. Found.; past pres. LA Stock Exchange, So. Calif. Visitors Council, Central City Assn.; dir. Downtown Businessmen's Assn. 1954; dir. Better Bus. Bur. 1954–; dir. Bel-Air Bay Club 1954–; pres. LA C.of C. 1962-63, dir. 1963–; pres. All-Year Club So. Calif. 1966-67; past pres. LA Rotary Club No. 5; hon. dir. Who's Who Historical Soc.; honors: outstanding alumnus, USC Sch. of Bus. Adm., 1963, General Alumni Assn. Award for outstanding serv., 1968; Man of Year, L.A. Realty Bd., 1969; Humanitarian of Year, Aid-United Givers, 1972; Brotherhood Award, NCCJ, 1972; Bishop's Award of Merit, Episcopal Diocese of L.A., 1972; hon. trustee Repub. Assocs.; mem. Masons, Los Angeles Country Club; Episcopalian; rec: hunting, fishing, golf. Res: 142 S Rockingham Ave, West Los Angeles 90049 Ofc: 558 S Broadway Los Angeles 90012

BILLINGS, CHERYL SUSAN, software systems financial executive; b. Sept. 28, 1948, Hanford; d. Charles Elmer and Betty Jane (Hurt) Ruff; m. Michael Hunt Ottley, 1969 (div. 1971); m. John Sanborn Billings, Oct. 16, 1982; 1 son, Tony b. 1969; edn: BS, San Jose St. Univ. 1986; C.P.A. Calif. (1989); C.M.A. (1987). Career: controller A B Dick Products, Fresno 1977-81, A B Dick Co., Oakland 1981-83; sr. auditor Price Waterhouse, San Jose 1986-89; c.f.o. Alliance Data Systems, San Carlos 1989-90; financial projects mgr. Cisco Systems, Inc., Menlo Park 1990-92; corporate controller Silicon Valley Research 1992–; awards: Calif. Soc. C.P.A. outstanding sr. 1986, Beta Alpha Psi outstanding alumni 1988; mem. Inst. of Management Accountants (nat. com.), Am. Womens Soc. C.P.A. (bd. mem.), Calif. Soc. C.P.A.; club: Alpine Hills Tennis (treas. 1993–); Republican; rec: tennis. Res: 1160 Klamath Dr Menlo Park 94025 Ofc: Silicon Valley Research 300 Ferguson Drive #300 Mt. View 94043

BINDER, STEVE, filmmaker; b. Los Angeles; s. Irving and Ann (Fisher) B. Career: indep. producer, dir. 1963–; vis. prof. cinema depts. Univ. So. Calif. and UC Los Angeles; 1986-: filmmaker: T.A.M.I. Movie, 1963, 64, Give 'Em Hell Harry, 1978 (TV film), Innocent Love, 1982; prod., dir. TV series: The Steve Allen Show, 1963-65, 73, Mac Davis, 1978-79, Shields and Yarnell, 1979-80 (Emmy nominations), Hullabaloo, 1965, Motown Revue with Smokey Robinson, 1985, Zoobilee Zoo, 1986 (Emmy award, num. others), Pee-Wee's Playhouse, 1987, 88, 89 (winner awards: On the Television 1988-89, SK8 TV 1990), TV specials: The Elvis Presley Comeback Special 1968, Liza Minelli Special 1970, George Lucas' Star Wars Holiday Special 1977, Barry Manilow Specials 1977, 87 (Emmy award, 4 Emmy nominations), Diana Ross Special 1981 (Golden Globe Award), Emmy Awards Shows 1981-84, num. Ringling Bros. and Barnum and Bailey Circus specials, Diana Ross in Central Park 1983 (Ace award), Elvis: One Night With You 1985, Elvis Presley's Graceland, 1985, num. Annual Soul Train Music Awards 1987, 88, 89, Diana Ross at Wembley 1989, John Denver's Montana Christmas Skies 1991, Victory & Valor: The Special Olympics 1991, 4th Ann. Desi Entertainment Awards 1992, 1st Ann. ESPY Awards 1993, World Cup Soccer Rocks the Globe 1994, Disney's Music on Ice 1994; mem: Directors Guild Am., Writers Guild Am., Producers Guild Am., Nat. Acad. of Recording Arts & Scis. Nat. Acad. TV Arts & Scis.; mil: served US Army; Democrat. Ofc: Rodan Productions, Inc. 855 So. Bundy Dr. Los Angeles 90049

BINEGAR, GWENDOLYN ANN, clinical social work administrator; b. Sept. 23, 1924, Phoenix, Ariz.; d. Glenn Marvin and Mary Lenore (Cartwright) Redington; m. Lewis (Bert) Binegar, Nov. 2, 1951; children: Glen, b. 1952; Birne, b. 1954; William, b. 1957; Alan, b. 1959; edn: BS, Iowa St. Univ. 1948; MSS, Bryn Mawr 1967; LCSW Calif. 1974; Acad. of Cert. Soc. Wkrs. 1969. Career: psychiatric soc. wkr. Child Study Inst., Bryn Mawr Coll. 1967-71; med. soc. wkr. Casa Colina Hosp., Pomona 1973-74; supvg. counselor San Gabriel Valley Regional Ctr., Pomona 1975-79; pgm. mgr. high-risk infant projects at all six L.A. County Regional Ctrs., S.G.V. Regional Ctr. 1979; asst. chief, chief case mgmt. services San Diego Regional Ctr. 1981–, assoc. director 1988–, consultant 1992–; mem: AAMD, Assn. of Regional Center Agys. (chair, chief counselors), Nat. Assn. Soc. Wkrs., Assn. Chief Counselors, COACH (bd., treas.). Republican. Res: 28809 Lilac Rd Valley Center 92082

BINGHAM-NEWMAN, ANN MARIE, educator, child counselor; b. Feb. 14, 1943, Coronado; d. Carl Robert and Jane (Bingham) Newman; m. Arthur J. Gonchar; children: Rebecca b. 1977, Andrew b. 1979, Jonathan b. 1982; edn: BS, Univ. Wis. Madison 1966; MS, 1971; PhD, 1974; MA, Calif. Family Study Center 1980. Career: dir. Rhoades Terrace Sch., Dallas, Tx. 1967-70; coordinator Early Childhood Study Center, Univ. Wis., Madison 1971-74; coodinator Interdisciplinary Child Devel. Program CSU Los Angeles 1974-93; chair, Dept. of Child and Family Studies 1994–; bd. dirs. Resources for Infant Educators 1980-82; awards: CSU Merit. Performance & Profl. Achievement (1988); mem: Nat. Assn. Edn. of Young Children, So. Calif. Assn. for Edn. of Young Children, Calif. Profs. of Early Childhood Edn., Nat. Council Family Rels.; co-author Piagetian Perspective for Preschs. (1984), num. articles, presentations and workshops. Ofc: Calif. State Univ. 5151 State University Dr Los Angeles 90032

BIRD, KENNETH DEAN, public health physician; b. Mar. 20, 1952, Oklahoma City, Okla.; s. Earl Alford and Nancy Louise (Jessup) B.; m. Nettie, July 24, 1980; children: Celeste b. 1978, Kenny b. 1982; edn: BS in biol., highest honors, Univ. Texas (Arlington) 1975; MD, honors, Univ. Texas (Galveston) 1979; cert. Correctional Health Profl. by Nat. Commn. on Correctional Health Care. Career: pediatric residency, Univ. Texas Med. Branch 1980; stu. US Naval Aerospace Med. Inst. 1981, USNR flight surgeon NAS Lemoore, Calif. 1981-84; capt. USNR, comdg. ofcr. Naval Reserve Naval Hosp. Lemoore 1990-93, decorated Navy Achievement, Navy Expedit., Humanitarian medals; pvt. gen. practice medicine, Lemoore 1984-86; public health physician Fresno County Dept. of Health, 1986–, medical dir. Fresno County Detention Facilities, 1988–; honors: Alpha Chi, Alpha Omega Alpha, Mu Delta; mem. Naval Reserve Assn., Assn. of Military Surgeons of the U.S., Lemoore Union Elem. School Bd. 1984-94 (pres. 1992-94); rec: wt. lifting, jogging, backpacking. Res: PO Box 446 Lemoore 93245 Ofc: Adult Detention Facilities 1225 M St Fresno 93721

BIRD, ROBERT JAMES, electronic engineer; b. Oct. 20, 1939, Chgo.; s. Robert and Sally B.; m. Victoria, Jan. 9, 1971; children: Danny b. 1958, Pamela b. 1960, Tracy b. 1964, Robert b. 1980; edn: ASEE, Naval Electronics Acad., BSEE, Orange Coast Coll. Career: asst. engr. Collins Radio Co., Newport Beach 1962-64; project engr. Fender Musical Instruments, Fullerton 1964-67; chief engr. Altec Lansing, Anaheim 1967-74; dir. engring. E.S.S. Inc., Sacto. 1974-76; pres. AB Systems Design, Folsom 1976-86; pres. AB International Electronics, Roseville 1986–; mem: Audio Engring. Soc. 1968–, Nat. Assn. of Music Merchants 1977–, Nat. Sound & Comms. Assn. 1983–, Roseville C.of C., Altec Mgmt. Assn. (past mem., pres. 1971-72); invention: Multi Level Power Supplies (US Pat. 1974); author 3 books: Journal of A.E.S. (1969), Altec Technical Journal (1972, 1973); mil: ET6 USN 1957-62; Republican; Christian Sci.; rec: sailing, M/C riding, swimming, skiing. Res: 105 Strouse Ct Folsom 95630 Ofc: AB International Electronics, 1830-6 Vernon St Roseville 95678

BISSELL, JOHN ALBERT, physician and surgeon; b. Aug. 29, 1942, San Francisco; s. Dwight Montgomery and Geraldine (Etter) B.; m. Karen Alison Buchanan, July 13, 1991; children: Elizabeth Loraine b. 1975, John Albert II b. 1985; edn: AB, Stanford Univ. 1964; MD, Harvard Univ. 1969; lic. physician, Calif. Bd. Med. Examiners 1972. Career: chief of neurology Kaiser-Permanente, Sacramento 1975–; bd. dirs. Permanente Med. Group, Oakland 1985-91; mem: Calif. Acad. of Medicine 1976–; mil: USPHS 1970-72; Republican; Protestant. Ofc: Kaiser-Permanente Medical Ctr 6600 Bruceville Rd Sacramento 95823 Tel: 916/688-2269

BITAR, DAVID E., physician; b. Nov. 9, 1944, Portland, Ore.; s. Emmanuel and Margaret (Phillips) B.; m. Betty Jo Blanton, Aug. 10, 1946; children: Elizabeth b. 1977, David b. 1980; edn: BA, Westmont Coll., Santa Barbara 1967; MDCM, McGill Univ., Montreal, Quebec, Can. 1971. Career: physician, pvt. practice, Berkeley, Calif.; mem: Am. Soc. of Colon & Rectal Surgeons (fellow 1977–), Am. Coll. Surgeons (fellow 1978–); Republican; Presbyterian. Ofc: David E. Bitar, MD, Inc. 2900 Telegraph Berkeley 94705 Tel: 510/845-4638

BLACK, EILEEN MARY, teacher; b. Sept. 20, 1944, Bklyn.; d. Marvin Mize and Anne Joan (Salvia) Black; edn: liberal arts studies Grossmont Coll., El Cajon 1964; BA, San Diego State Univ., 1967; grad. work UCSD; NDEA grant Syracuse Univ., 1968; Calif. Std. Elem. Tchg. credential, 1967. Career: teacher Highlands Elem. Sch., Spring Valley 1967-83, Northmont Elem., La Mesa Spring Valley Sch. Dist., 1983–; award: 25 year svc. La Mesa Spring Valley Sch. Dist. 1992; mem: Calif. Tchrs. Assn. 1967–, Nat. Ednl. Assn. 1967–; Republican; R.Cath.; rec: reading, walking, baseball. Res: 9320 Earl St #15 La Mesa 91942 Ofc: Northmont Elementary, 9405 Gregory St La Mesa 91942

BLACK, KIRBY SAMUEL, healthcare management executive; b. Mar. 29, 1954, Salinas; s. Samuel McTarnahan and Rosilind (Strand) B.; m. Christine Mary Sharman, Mar. 5, 1977; children: Matthew, Colin, Meredith; edn: BSME, UCLA, 1976; PhD, UC Irvine, 1989; reg. profl. engr. Calif. Career: research asst. dept. surgery UCLA, 1973-77; research assoc. dept. pediatrics UC Irvine, 1977-78, dir reconstructive microsurgery labs., and assoc. dev. engr. div. plastic surgery, 1978–, co-dir. transplantation labs. and burn research labs. divs. plastic surgery and urology, 1981–; dir., proj. ldr. Advanced Tissue Sciences, La

Jolla 1993–; cons. Sandoz Pharmaceuticals, Beckman Instruments Inc., 1982-83, Am. Edwards, 1982-83; clin. instr. dept. surgery UC Irvine 1983–; awards: Ralph & Marjorie Crump award for Excellence in Med. Engring. 1975, report to the pres. of the Univ. 1985, 86, President's Educational award Am. Burn Assn. 1987, grantee NIH 1983-92, others; mem. AAAS, IEEE, Assn. for Advance. Med. Instrumentation, Am. Burn Assn., Assn. Clin. Faculty; numerous sci. publs.; Republican; rec: family activities, woodworking. Ofc: 13401 Sussex Place Santa Ana 92705

BLACK, NOEL ANTHONY, film and television director; b. Jun 30, 1937, Chgo.; s. Samuel A. and Susan (Quan) B.; m. Sandra Ann MacPhail, Dec. 2, 1968 (div.); children: Marco E. b. 1970, Nicole A. b. 1971; m. 2d Catherine Elizabeth Cownie, June 1, 1988; edn: att. Univ. Chgo. 1954-57; BA in theater arts - motion pictures, UCLA, 1958, MA, 1962. Career: film and tv dir., 1966–; director: Skaterdater UA, 1966 (short subject, his 1st film and Am. film winner of most internat. honors in 1966-67, won Grand Prix, Cannes Film Fest.; Statuette of Saint Finbarr Award, and the Waterford Glass Award for Best Film of Fest. from Cork, Ireland; Silver Medal from Moscow; First Prize from Colombo, and Silver Trophy from Cortina); writer-director: The River Boy, 1967 (his 2nd film and winner Lion of St. Mark Award, Venice Internat. Film Fest., 1st Prize Vancouver Internat. Film Fest.); I'm A Fool, PBS, 1977; The Golden Honeymoon, PBS, 1979; Electric Grandmother, NBC, Highgate Pictures, 1981 (George Foster Peabody Award 1982); Eyes of the Panther, Showtime "Nightmare Classics" 1989; The Hollow Boy, American Playhouse, 1991; Trilogy: The American Boy, ABC-TV (his first t.v. spl., U.S. entry at 8th Intl. Monte Carlo TV Fest., winner Cino del Duca, $2000 cash award); Pretty Poison, 20th Century Fox, 1968 (his first feature film, now a film-noire classic); A Man, A Woman & A Bank, Avco Embassy Pictures, 1980; Mischief, 20th Century Fox, 1985 (screenplay & exec. prod.); mini-series: Deadly Intentions (4 hrs.) ABC, 1985; MOW's: The Other Victim, CBS, 1981; Prime Suspect, CBS, 1981; Happy Endings, CBS, 1982; Quarterback Princess, CBS, 1983; Promises To Keep, CBS, 1985; A Time To Triumph, CBS, 1986; My Two Loves, ABC, 1986; Conspiracy of Love, CBS, 1987; The Town Bully, ABC, 1988; Pilots: The World Beyond (1 hr.) CBS, 1977; Mulligan's Stew (90 min.) NBC, 1977; Doctors Wilde (1 hr.) CBS, 1987; Meet The Munceys (1 hr.), ABC, 1988; Episodic: The Baby Sitters Club, Over My Dead Body, The Twilight Zone, Dolphin Cove, Kojak, Hawaii 5-0, Quincy; adj. asst. prof. N.Y. Univ. Graduate Pgm., Inst. of Film and Television, Tisch Sch. of the Arts, 1992-94; mem: Dirs. Guild Am. 1968–, Writers Guild Am. 1973–, Acad. Motion Picture Arts & Scis. 1969–, Acad. TV Arts & Scis. 1976–. Ofc: Starfish Productions 126 Wadsworth Ave Santa Monica CA 90405

BLACK, PATRICIA E., French educator, university international program director; b. Apr. 25, 1955, Amherst, Ohio; d. William Marion and Virginia Eileen (Davidson) B.; m. Douglas Scott Henderson, Oct. 11, 1980; children: Anna Elene, Camille May; edn: BA (high hons.), Oberlin Coll., 1977; MA French lit., Cornell Univ., 1980; DEA in French and Comparative Lit., Universite de Poitiers, 1982; PhD French lit., Cornell Univ., 1985. Career: prof. d'anglais Maison de la Formation de la Chambre de Commerce de Poitiers, 1982-83; lectr. in Fr. Potsdam Coll. of SUNY, 1984-86; asst. prof., assoc. prof. of French, CSU Chico, 1986–, named director of CSU Internat. Program in France for 1993-94; awards: Phi Beta Kappa 1976, Corson Fr. Prize 1980, Oberlin Coll. Alumni fellow 1980, Univ. de Poitiers fellow 1980, NEH Inst. for H.S. Tchrs. asst. dir. 1986, NEH Inst. fellow 1987, 95, Univ. Found. fellowship 1995; mem: Modern Language Assn., Soc. Rencesvals (Am.-Can. Br. sec. treas. 1992–), Soc. Guilhem IX, No. Am. Catalan Soc. Res: 2768 Ceres Ave Chico 95926 Ofc: Calif. State University Dept. Fgn. Languages, Chico 95929-0825 Tel: 916/898-5388

BLACKSTOCK, JAMES FIELDING, lawyer; b. Sept. 19, 1947, Los Angeles; s. James Carne and Justine Fielding (Gibson) B.; m. Kathleen Ann Weigand, Dec. 12, 1969; children: Kristin Marie, James Fielding; edn: BA English, USC, 1969; JD, USC Law Ctr., 1976; admitted bar: Calif. 1976, Tenn. 1994, U.S. Dist. Ct. 1977, U.S. Supreme Ct. 1980. Career: editor Bar Exam Information Book, BRC of Calif., 1974; atty. assoc. Hill, Farrer & Burrill, 1976-80; assoc., then ptnr. Zobrist & Vienna (and predecessor firm) 1980-83; v.p. and gen. counsel Tatum Petroleum Corp., 1983-84; ptnr. Sullivan, Workman & Dee, 1984-91; prin. James F. Blackstock, PLC, 1992-93; gen. counsel NATIONAL Auto/Truckstops, Inc. 1993–; mem: Am. Bar Assn., Calif. Bar Assn., L.A. Co. Bar Assn., Tenn. Bar Assn., USC Commerce Assocs. (pres. nat. bd. dirs.), USC Gen. Alumni Assn. (bd. govs.), USC Cardinal & Gold, USC Legion Lex (bd. 1988-91), Phi Alpha Delta, Sigma Nu; civic: Pasadena Tournament of Roses Assn., La Salle H.S. Bd. Regents (pres. 1990-93), Calif. Mus. Sci. and Ind. Advy. Bd. (1991), Breakfast Round Table, Somebody Cares for the Homeless Found. Pasa. (founding); club: Saddle & Sirloin (past pres.), Rancheros Visitadores, Pasadena BPOE; mil: lt. USN 1969-73, Navy Commendation Medal, Navy Achiev. Medal w/star; capt. USNR (Surface Warfare), c.o. Mobile Inshore Undersea Warfare Unit 105, 1991-93; rec: equestrian, racquetball, tennis, USC Rugby Club. Res: 5320 Stonewall Place Brentwood TN 37027 Ofc. Tel: 615/783-2690

BLADON, RICHARD ANTHONY, speech professional, b. March 7, 1943, Leicester, U.K.; s. Leonard Harry and Barbara Irene (Jones) B.; m. Deborah McGerry, July 31, 1992; edn: BA, Univ. of Cambridge, Eng., 1965; MA, Univ. of Cambridge, 1968; MPhil, Univ. of Reading, Eng., 1969; PhD, Univ. of Oxford, Eng., 1985; career: lectr. Univ. of Ghent, Belgium, 1965-67; lectr. linguistics, Univ. Coll., N. Wales, U.K., 1969-80; fellow, Wolfson Coll., Oxford, 1980-90; univ. lectr., phonetics Univ. of Oxford, 1980-88; assessor Univ. of Oxford, 1983-84; chair, computing/tchg. ctr. Univ. of Oxford, 1984-88; bd. of delegates Oxford Univ. Press, 1983-84; curator of Bodleian Lib., Oxford, 1983-84; assoc. prof. UC Santa Barbara 1988, UCLA 1989; res. scientist Infovox A.B., Stockholm, 1986-88; prin. mem. tech. Digital Sound Corp., Santa Barbara, Calif., 1988-92; engring. prog. dir. Digital Sound Corp., 1992-93; dir. product devel. Voice Processing Corp., Cambridge, Mass. 1993–; mem: The Philological Soc., 1969–; mem. of council, The Philological Society, 1982-86; Internat. Phonetic Assn., 1975–; mem. council, journal ed., Internat. Phonetic Assn., 1986-90; Acoustical Soc. Amer., 1975–; author: articles in profl. journals and several patents; rec: words, guitar, the outdoors. Res: 1024 San Diego Rd. Santa Barbara 93103

BLAETTLER, RICHARD BRUCE, school administrator/principal; b. Sept. 3, 1938, San Francisco; s. Henry Walter and Veronica (Smith) B.; m. Barbara Anne Crevier, June 1, 1968; children: Daniel, Derek and Janelle; edn: AA, City Coll. S.F., 1959; BA, San Francisco State Univ., 1962, MA, 1964; EdD, Univ. of La Verne, 1991; Bay Area Admin. Tng. Ctr. 1992; Supts. Acad. 1993; Personnel Acad. 1994; Calif. gen. secondary tchg. and adminstrn. credentials. Career: tchr. and coach Balboa High Sch., San Francisco 1964; Portola Jr. High Sch., S.F. 1964-65; Arroyo High Sch., San Lorenzo 1966-70; athletic dir. and dept. chair Richmond High Sch., Richmond 1970-83, dean of students 1983-90, 91–; principal/coordinator Kappa High Sch., Richmond 1994–; dean of students Richmond Adult Sch. 1990-91; also adult sch. instr. San Lorenzo U.S.D., 1968-80, Albany U.S.D., 1979-85; served to E9, sgt. major US Army Spl. Forces, 1960-89, corrective therapist Oakland Veterans Adminstrn. Hosp. 1962-64; awards: grantee Springfield Coll., Mass. 1965, Most popular artist Soc. Western Artists, DeYoung Mus., S.F. 1960, Meritorious Svc. Medal w/oak leaf cluster 1989; mem. Richmond Assn. Sch. Adminstrs. 1983–, Am. Rabbit Breeders Assn. 1984–, Tolenas Farms HOA (pres. 1981-82), City of Fairfield Vision 2020, Sounding Bd. & Sister City Com. 1992-95, Solano Irrigation Dist. (rural residential advy. com. 1995), Shriners (pres. Montezuma Club 1992-93, mem. Ben Ali Temple Pipes & Drums 1988–); publs: jour. articles re athletics 1966–, diss: Alternative to Suspension Programs in Calif., 1991; Republican; Prot.; rec: philately, raising show rabbits, playing bag pipes. Res: 4424 Tolenas Rd Fairfield 94533-6613 Ofc: Kappa High School 4300 Cutting Blvd Richmond 94804

BLAGDEN, JULIA WHITNEY, freight forwarder; b. Nov. 21, 1960, NYC, NY; d. George and Josephine Culter Stearns (Swan) Blagden; edn: H.S. diploma (with distinction), Dana Hall Sch., Wellesley, Mass., 1978; BA, psychology, Vassar Coll., Poughkeepsie, NY, 1982; M. of Internat. Management, The Am. Grad. Sch. of Internat. Management, Glendale, Ariz., 1986; NY State Elem. sch. tchr., NY Bd. of Edn., 1982. Career: trade dir./sr. dir., Tradecard of Boston, Inc., Boston, Mass., 1982-84; Eng. tchr. (through AFS Internat. & Chinese Ministry of Edn.), Hubei Univ., Wuhan, People's Republic of China, 1985; mgr., global sourcing, Pacific Marketing Consultants, So. S.F., Calif., 1987; mgr., internat. trade, ACA Pacific, Inc., S.F., 1988; cons., Barakat & Chamberlin, Inc., Oakland, Calif., 1989-91; assoc., Barakat & Chamberlin, Inc., Oakland, 1991-95; freight forwarder Able Freight Services Inc., So. San Francisco 1995–; pres. & speaker, Toastmasters Internat., Glendale, Ariz., 1985-86; mem./adv., Internat. Trade Assn., S.F., 1986-89; mem. Assn. of Demand-Side Management Professionals, Berkeley, 1992; mem. Am. Management Assn., NYC, NY, 1992; awards: Nan Coyle Citizenship award, Dana Hall Sch., 1978; student graduation speaker, Dana Hall Sch., 1978; Sr. Class Pres., Vassar Coll., 1982; student graduation speaker, Vassar Coll., 1982; mem: The Metropolitan Club of S.F., 1987-92; The Social Register, 1960–; The Ivy Club, 1987–; Thunderbird Alumnae Assn., S.F., 1986–; pres., Vassar Club of S.F. 1987-90; fund-raiser, Multiple Sclerosis Soc., Oakland, 1987-88, 91; vocalist: record (12 women a cappella) In The Mood, 1982; co-author, publ. article, 1992; Republican; Episcopalian; rec: rowing, singing, fund raisers, opera, symphony, and other cultural events. Res:1080 Church St San Francisco 94119 Ofc: Able Freight Services Inc 322 Littlefield Ave S San Francisco 94080

BLAINE, DEVON, public relations executive; edn: psych. and hist. studies, UCLA. Career: pres./CEO The Blaine Group Inc., Los Angeles; mem: The Consulting Consortium (co-founder), Nat. Small Bus. United (founding pres. Calif. chapt.), L.A. Venture Assn. (pres. 1989, 93), Assn. of Venture Founders, Nat. Assn. Women Bus. Owners (founding bd., past pres.), CEO Clubs (Boston, Chgo., Dallas, L.A., N.Y., S.F., W.D.C.), L.A. Area C.of C., Entrepreneur Club, United Fedn. of Small Bus., Ctr. for Entrepreneurial Mgmt., L.A. Women's Campaign Fund, Pub. Rels. Soc. Am. (Prism Award - on-going corp. comms. pgm. 1985, 88, hon. mention - fin. p.r., consumer media pgm., single-mkt. pgm., 1984), Publicity Club N.Y., Book Publicists So. Calif., Women in Bus., Women in Show Bus., Women's Nat. Book Assn., Variety Club (Tent 25). Ofc: The Blaine Group, Inc. 7465 Beverly Blvd Los Angeles 90036-2706

BLAKE, HERBERT, JR., university graduate programs director; b. June 1, 1942, Denver, Colo.; s. Herbert and Anna Lou (Morgan) B.; m. Nancy Lee Fiske, July 15, 1972; children: Chelsea b. 1980, Brook b. 1982; edn: BA, Univ. Colo. 1965; MBA, CSU Sacto. 1976; PhD, Univ. Santa Clara 1985. Career: branch mgr. Wash. Inventory Service, Sacto. 1969-74; lectr. CSU 1976-77; Univ. Santa Clara 1977-79; assoc. prof. CSU, Sacto. 1979-88, dept. chair 1988-94, grad. programs dir. 1994–; cons. Regional Transit 1980; Fed. Lab. Consortium, Minority Bus. Devel. Assn., Lawrence Livermore Nat. Lab. 1981-88, CalTrans 1992-94; honors: Beta Gamma Sigma; mem: APICS (pres. 1988-90), Tech. Transfer Soc., TIMS, Acad. Mgmt., Delta Upsilon; article pub. in profl. jour. (1988), ed. Teclab newsletter (1981-85); mil: lt.j.g. USNR 1966-69; Prot.; rec: computers. Res: 491 Windward Way Sacramento 95831 Ofc: California State University School of Business Sacramento 95819-6086

BLAKE, LOUIS MICHAEL, physician; b. June 4, 1957, Osaka, Japan; s. Edward K. Blake, Sr. and Setsuko (Inada) B.; edn: BA, biochem., Univ. of Calif., Santa Barbara 1979; MD, Case Western Reserve Univ. 1983. Career: intern, gen. surgery, Letterman Army Med. Ctr., San Francisco 1983-84; resident, internal medicine, Stanford Univ. Med. Ctr. 1988-90, chief resident, nuclear medicine, Stanford Univ. 1990-92; clin. fellow, cardiology, Calif.-Pacific Med. Ctr., San Francisco 1992-93; sr. fellow, echocardiography, UCSF Sch. of Medicine, S.F. 1993–; chief, ancillary svs., USAHC, Dugway, Utah 1985-86; chief, gen. outpatient clinic, US Army, Fort Ord, Calif. 1986-87; staff internist, East Valley Clinic, San Jose 1989-92; awards: US Army Commendation Medal 1986, US Army Commendation Medal with Oak Leaf Cluster 1988, AMA Physician Recognition award 1987, Evelyn Neiser Postdoctoral Res. award, Stanford Univ. 1992; mem: Am. Coll. of Nuclear Physicians, Am. Heart Assn. Council on Cardiovascular Radiology, Assn. of Mil. Physicians and Surgeons of U.S.; mem. in training, Am. Coll. of Cardiology; mil: capt. U.S. Army 1983-88; Republican; Roman Catholic; rec: alpine skiing, x-c skiing, running, tennis. Res: 351 Durant Way Mill Valley 94941

BLAKE, RICHARD RONALD, religious education consultant; b. Mar. 7, 1930, Parkers Prairie, Minn.; s. John Paul and Marian Dorothy (Magnuson) B.; m. Thelma Lucille Barnes, Nov. 3, 1956; children: Richard Jr. b. 1958, Kenneth b. 1960, James b. 1961, Robert b. 1965; edn: BBA, Armstrong Coll., 1957; M. Christian Edn., Golden State Sch. of Theology, 1985, D.Min., 1987. Career: reg. controller Boise Cascade Bldg. Co., Hayward 1968-74; Case Power & Equip. Sales, San Leandro 1975-80; controller Carpet Craft Inc., Hayward 1989-90; owner/opr. Family Book Center, 1980–; Christian edn. cons. Christian Education Resources, 1980–; customer advocate Nat. Tchr. Edn. Pgm., Durham, N.Caro. 1986-90; cons. Christian Edn. Leadership Service, Los Gatos 1987-90; instr. Golden State Sch. of Theol., Oakland 1984-94; advy. bd. Follow Up Ministries Inc., Castro Valley 1987-94; exec. com. Bay Area Sunday Sch. Conv., Castro Valley 1989-94; mem: Writer's Connection Cupertino, Assn. for Childhood Edn. Intl., Nat. Assn. Dirs. of Christian Edn., Christian Book Sellers Assn.; author (curriculum) A Children's Church Curriculum (1987), contbr. articles to Church Teacher Mag. (1988); mil: p.o.3c USN 1951-55; active Redwood Chapel Comm. Ch., Castro Valley (bus. administrator 1991-95). Res: 16630 Cowell St San Leandro 94578 Ofc: Christian Education Resources, 725 MacArthur Blvd San Leandro 94577

BLAKELY, EDWARD JAMES, educator; b. April 21, 1938, San Bernardino; s. Edward and Josephine Elizabeth (Carter) Proctor B.; m. Maaike C. Van Der Sleesen, Nov. 21, 1945; children Pieta b. 1974, Bretta b. 1981; edn: BA, UC Riverside 1960; MA, UC Berkeley 1963; PhD, UCLA 1970. Career: exec. Pacific Telephone & Telegram, Pasadena 1960-65; dir. W. Com. Action, San Francisco 1965-70; asst. secty. st. U.S. Dept. of State, W.D.C. 1970-72; asst. chancellor Univ. Pittsburgh, Pa. 1972-74; assoc. dean UC Davis 1974-77; asst. v.p. UC Berkeley 1977-85; chair dept. city and reg. planning UC Berkeley 1985–; dean Sch. of Urban & Regl. Planning, Univ. of So. Calif., Los Angeles ; awards: Fulbright fellow 1985, John Simon Guggenheim Found. Fellowship 1994-95; mem: Ecole Bilingue De Berkeley (pres. 1985), Bridge Housing Corp. (bd. 1987), Head Royce Sch. (bd. 1988); author: Planning Local Econ. Devel. (1988), Separate Socities (1993, Paul Davidoff Award for Best Book in Planning); mil: 1st lt. USAF 1961-63; rec: jogging, tennis. Res: 2709 Alida St Oakland 94602

BLANCHE, JOE ADVINCULA, aerospace engineer, scientist, real estate broker, registered tax preparer; b. Sept. 11, 1954, Santa, Ilocos Sur, Philippines, nat. 1978; s. Emilio Peralta and Concepcion Advincula (Burgonio) B.; m. Albine Selerio Lansangan, Oct. 9, 1982; children: Emmanuel Joseph b. 1985, Earl Jordan b. 1988; edn: certificate in mil. sci. & gen. edn., Univ. of the Philippines, 1973; BS, math., Adamson Univ., Manila, Philippines, 1976; post grad. work in accounting, Chapman Univ., Orange, Calif., 1978; assoc. in applied sci.-avionics systems, Comm. Coll. of the Air Force, Maxwell AFB, Ala., 1980; post grad. work in elec. engring., Calif. State Univ., Long Beach, 1982-85; certificate in mgmt., Central Texas Coll., Killeen, Tx., 1990; MA, organizational mgmt., Univ. of Phoenix, 1995; PhD in mgmt., Pacific We. Univ., L.A., 1993. Career: USAF, March AFB, Calif., avionics systems. splst., 1977-79, avionics systems. supr., 1979-80; tchr., Moreno Valley H.S. (Calif.), 1980-81; McDonnell Douglas

Corp., Long Beach, field svc electrical, 1981, assoc. engr./sci., 1981-83, engr./sci., 1983-86; lead engr., aerospace, Sikorsky ACFT-UTC, Stratford, Conn., 1986-87; McDonnell Douglas Corp., Long Beach, engr./sci. splst., 1987-88, sr. engr./sci., 1988-94; pres. J&A Blanche Ventures, Inc., Corona Hills 1994–; awards: scholarship, Univ. of Philippines, 1972-73; Humanitarian Svc. Medal, USAF, 1978; USAF Good Conduct Medal, 1979; USAF Nat. Defense Svc. Medal, 1976, 92; USAF Res. Meritorious Svc. Medal, 1984, 88, 92; USAF Armed Forces Res. Medal, 1992; mem: Internat. Soc. of Allied Weight Engrs., 1981–; So. Calif. Profl. Engring. Assn., 1981–; Corona-Norco Bd. of Realtors, CAR, NAR, 1988–; Nat. Notary Assn., 1989–; Am. Inst. of Aeronautics & Astronautics, 1991–;civic: mem., Santanians, USA, Inc., 1983– (bd. of dir., 1983-87, pres. 1994-96); mem., Marinduque Assn. of So. Calif., L.A., 1987–; U.P. Alumni Assn. of So. Calif., L.A., 1990–; FIL-AM Assn. of Corona, 1991–; author: status report on US Presidential Helicopter, 1987; management paper, 1992. Mil: tech. sgt., USAF, 1976-81; Republican; Roman Catholic. Ofc: J&A Blanche Ventures Inc 420 McKinley #111-333 Corona Hills 91719

BLANCHETTE, JAMES EDWARD, psychiatrist; b. Aug. 28, 1924, Syracuse, NY; s Joseph Marcel and Margaret Catherine (Vincent) Blanchette; m. Shirley Ruth Brisco, Sept. 1, 1948 (dec. May 4, 1981); edn: BA, Syracuse Univ., NY, 1950; MD, SUNY, Syracuse Coll of Med., 1953; Diplomate Am. Bd. Psychiatry and Neurology. Career: intern St. Vincent's Hosp., NYC 1953-54; res. Patton State Hosp., Calif. 1954-55; Met. State Hosp., Norwalk 1957-59; pvt. practice psychiatry, Redlands 1959–; chief profl. edn. Patton State Hosp., 1960-64; tchg. cons., 1964–; staff San Bernardino Comm. Hosp., St. Bernadine Hosp.; USAAF Band, WDC, 1945-47; USAAF Med. Corps, 1953-55; mem: Am. Psychiat. Assn. (life fellow), AMA, CMA, Pan-Am. Med. Assn., San Bernardino Med. Soc., So. Calif. Psychiat. Soc. (pres. Inland chpt. 1963-4, 1983-4), Royal Soc. Health, Am. Med. Soc., Am. Chemical Soc., AAAS, Internat. Platform Assn., Phi Mu Alpha, Arrowhead Allied Arts Council (San Bdo. past pres.), Elks, US Power Squadron, Dist. 13, P/D/C; USCG Aux., Hollywood Yacht club; musician ret. (string bass) fmrly with AF Band (WDC), Syracuse Sym., Univ. of Redlands Sym., Loma Linda Univ. Sym., Inland Empire Sym., Riverside Sym.; rec: boating. Res: 972 W Marshall Blvd San Bernardino 92405-2848 Ofc: 26 Cajon St Redlands 92373-5296

BLANKENSHIP, JUANITA CHAPMAN, court administrator; b. Feb. 25, 1935, Miles City, MT; d. Terry S. Chapman and June Brown Shelden; m. Thomas H. Blankenship, June 5, 1956 (div. July 1, 1974); edn: BA, Univ. of Montana 1956; MA, Univ. of Nevada 1970. Career: mgmt. asst. U.S. Atomic Energy Commn., Las Vegas 1962-65; administrative analyst Clark County, Las Vegas 1970-73; staff dir./criminal justice planner SRDAC, Las Vegas 1973-80; asst. dir. juror mgmt. Los Angeles Superior Ct. 1981-88, dir. 1988-92; administrnt. litigation support svs. 1992–; advy. com. USC Criminal Justice Training Ctr. 1977-81; awards: Phi Kappa Phi 1956, Public Admin. of Yr. Las Vegas Chapt. ASPA 1978, SCJA Annual Award, sect. on Crim. Justice Admin./ASPA 1983, named grant honoree EFP, AAUW Covina Br. 1986, comm. svc. award Covina Coordinating Council 1990, J.E.M. achievement award 1992; mem: Am. Soc. for Public Admin., Nat. Assn. for Court Mgmt., Jury Edn. & Mgmt. Forum, CASCA, L.A. Co. Mgmt. Council, Andalucia Townhomes Assn. (bd. dir.), Am. Assn. of Univ. Women, Covina Branch; contbg. author: Handbook for Court Specialists, 1976; Democrat; Protestant; rec: tennis, skiing. Ofc: 111 North Hill St Room 105E Los Angeles 90012

BLANTON, JOHN ARTHUR, architect; b. Jan. 1, 1928, Houston; s. Arthur Alva and Caroline Arnold (Jeter) Blanton; m. Marietta Newton, Apr. 10,1954 (dec. Apr. 3, 1976); children: Jill Lewis b. 1958, Lynette Rowe b. 1961, Elena Blanton b. 1965; edn: BS, arch., Rice Univ. 1949. Career: assoc. Richard J. Neutra, F.A.I.A., Los Angeles 1950-64; architect pvt. practice Manhattan Beach 1964–; instr. UCLA ext. 1967-75; instr. Harbor Coll. 1970-72; contbr. book revs. AIA Journal, 1972-75; appt. chmn. Manhattan Beach Bd. of Zoning Adjustment; Manhattan Beach Planning Commn. 1993; honors: Red Cedar Shingle nat. award AIA 1979, C.of C. awards: (1969, 70, 71, 74, 75, 82); mem: AIA; publs: 15-pg. monograph of completed works pub. L'Architettura, Italian archtl. mag. (5/88), work featured in Los Angeles: An Architectural Guide (9), Sunset Mag., L.A. Times Home mag., contbr. author Bicentennial edition AIA Journal, other prof. publs.; mil: US Signal Corps 1951-53. Ofc: John Blanton, AIA, Manhattan Beach 90266

BLASDALE, ALLAN WALTER, organist, choirmaster, pianist; b. July 5, 1953, Berkeley; s. Herbert Halsey and Jean Bevans (Coolbaugh) B.; edn: BA music, UC Berkeley 1976; postgrad. Ch. Divinity Sch. Pacific 1978-80. Career: organist Centennial Presbyterian Ch. Oakland 1971-72; organist, choirmaster North Congregational Ch., Berkeley 1972-83;organist Ch. Div. Sch. Of Pacific, Berkeley 1978-80; cir. music Ch. of Advent of Christ the King, San Francisco 1983-87; Holy Innocents Ch., S.F. 1987-88; minister music First Congregational Ch., S.F. 1988-91; St. Stephen's Episcopal Ch., Orinda 1991-92; dir music Pilgrim Congregational Ch., Walnut Creek 1976-92; concert organist 1972–; park ranger, Nat. Park Svc., Golden Gate Nat. Recreation Area, S.F. 1993–; mem.: Am. Guild Organists, Nat. Parks and Conservation Assn., Nat. Space Soc., Nat. Trust for Hist. Preservation, Yosemite Assn., Planetary Soc., Calif.

Hist. Soc., Nat. Assn. Of Park Rangers; Democrat; Episcopal; rec: hiking, mountaineering, history, astronomy, archaeology, geography. Res: 1400 McAllister St #17 San Francisco 94115

BLATT, BEVERLY FAYE, biologist, consultant; b. Mar. 17, 1944, Pittsburgh, Pa.; d. Simon and Sadie (Skigen) B.; m. Marc Harry Lavietes, Aug. 13, 1966 (div. July 31, 1987); children: Bryan Ross b. 1971, Jonathan David b. 1975; m. 2d David Herman Filipek, Dec. 28, 1987; edn: AB (magna cum laude), Vassar Coll., 1965; PhD, Case-Western Reserve Univ., 1969. Career: asst. prof. pathology N.Y.U. Med. Sch., 1971-80; asst. prof. medicine SUNY Downstate Med. Sch., Bklyn. 1980-84, SUNY Stony Brook Med. Sch. 1984-88; sect. hd. clin. immunol. res. Long Island Jewish Med. Ctr., New Hyde Park, NY 1986-88; cons. BFB Bioconsulting, Alameda, Calif. 1988–; awards: grad. fellow NSF 1967-69, postdoc. fellow Am. Cancer Soc. 1969-70, postdoc. fellow NIH 1970-71, grantee NIH 1971-77, 1981-85, grantee NY Arthritis Found. 1981-87; mem: AAAS, Assn. for Women in Sci., Harvey Soc., NY Acad. Scis., Am. Soc. Cell Biol., Vassar Coll. Class of 1965 (25th reunion gift chair, pres. 1990-95), co-chair organizing com. "Women in Bioscience: Opportunities in the 90's" (Stanford Univ. 1/93); publs: sci. res. reports, revs., 1969-88; Temple Israel, Alameda (bd. 1990-95, secty. 1990-91, v.p. 91-92, parliamentarian 1992-93, treas. 1993-95). Ofc: BFB Consulting 3265 Central Ave Alameda 94501-3108

BLAU, ERIC MARK, physician; b. Sept. 27, 1947, Sacramento; s. Sidney and Beatrice (Brainin) B.; m. Julie Gollin, Jan. 16, 1989; edn: BS, UC Davis 1969; MD, UCSD 1973; cert. Am. Bd. Internal Medicine 1977, F.A.C.P. 1992. Career: staff physician So. Calif. Permanente Med. Group, San Diego 1977–; asst. clin. prof. comm. medicine UCSD Sch. Medicine 1982-88, assoc. clin. prof. medicine 1988–; profl. photographer, San Diego 1982–; awards: Polaroid Corp. Artist Support grant 1988-95, City San Diego Pub. Arts Advy. Bd. grant 1988; author: Common Heroes, 1989; Stories of Adoption, 1993. Ofc: Kaiser Permanente 7060 Clairemont Mesa San Diego 92111

BLAWIE, JAMES L., lawyer, educator; b. Mar. 26, 1928, Newark, N.J.; s. Louis Paul and Ruth L. (Grish) B.; m. Marilyn-June Beyerle, May 30, 1952; children: Elias James b. 1958, Cecelia Ruth b. 1961, Christiana L. b. 1963; edn: BA w. distinction, Univ. Conn., 1950; AM, Boston Univ., 1951; JD, Univ. Chgo., 1955; PhD, Boston Univ., 1959. Career: asst. prof. polit. sci. Mich. St. Univ., E. Lansing 1955-56; assoc. prof. law Univ. Akron Law Sch., Oh. 1956-57; assoc. ed. State Constl. Law Proj., Columbia Univ., 1957-58; asst. prof. bus. law UC Berkeley, 1958-60; assoc. prof., prof. law Santa Clara Univ., 1960–; cons. Calif. Law Revision Commn., Palo Alto 1980-86; complaints examiner U.S. EEOC, Wash. DC 1980-86; honors: grantee Finnish Govt. Ministry of Edn., Helsinki 1980-81, tchg. fellow Boston Univ. 1951-53, law sch. scholar Univ. Chgo. 1953-55; mem: ABA, Calif. Bar Assn., Conn. Bar Assn., Am. Polit. Sci. Assn., Am. Soc. for Pub. Adminstrn., Western Polit. Sci. Assn., Nat. Municipal League, Lawyers in Mensa, Mensa, Intertel, Triple Nine, Internat. Soc. for Philosophical Enquiry; author (book) Mich. Township Board, 1956, assoc. ed. (ref. book) Index Digest of State Constns. (Oceana Press, 1958); mil: major JAGC USAR 1963-74; Republican; Prot.; rec: computers, fruit culture. Res: 41752 Marigold Dr Fremont 94539

BLECKSMITH, FRED RODRICK, JR., architect; b. Mar. 23, 1937, San Diego; s. Fred Rodrick and Margaret Luca (Scherring) B.; edn: BS in architectural engring., Calif. Polytech. Univ. 1960. Career: pres. Fred Blecksmith Architect, San Diego 1967–; chmn. Architects Consortium, San Diego 1977–; v. chmn. Park & Recreation Bd. Facilities Com. 1978–; mem. Pub. Review Com., S.D. 1978–; awards: Am. Inst. Architects Outstanding Achievement 1980, Exceptional Achievement 1970; mem: Am. Inst. Architects. Ofc: 1706 5th Ave San Diego 92101

BLEIBERG, LEON WILLIAM, surgical podiatrist, executive; b. June 9, 1932, Bklyn.; s. Paul Pincus and Helen (Epstein) B.; m. Beth Daigle, June 7, 1970; children: Kristina Noel, Kelley Lynn, Kimberly Ann, Paul Joseph; edn: student L.A. City Coll. 1950-51, USC 1951, Case Western Reserve Univ. 1951-53; DSc (honors) and DPM, Temple Univ. 1955; PhD, Univ. Beverly Hills, 1970. Career: rotating intern various hosps., Phila. 1954-55; resident various hosp., Montebello, L.A., Calif. 1956-58, surgical podiatrist So. Calif. Podiatry Group, Westchester, L.A., 1956-75; health care economist, researcher Drs. Home Health Care Services, 1976–; pres. Medica, Totalcare, Cine-Medics Corp., World-Wide Health Care Services; healthcare affiliate Internat. div. CARE/ASIA, 1987; pres. International Health Trust, 1991-92; track coach Westlake High Sch., Westlake Village 1990–; podiatric cons. USC Athletic Dept., Morningside and Inglewood High Schs., Internet Corp., Royal Naval Assn., Long Beach, Calif. Naval Sta.; writer, lectr. in field; producer 3 films: The Gun Hawk 1963, Terrified, and Day of the Nightmare; mem: Philippine Hosp. Assn. (appreciation cert. 1964, trophy award for outstanding svc. 1979), Calif. Podiatry Assn. (hon.), Am. Podiatric Med. Assn. (hon.), Royal Soc. Health (England), Western Foot Surgery Assn., Am. Coll. Foot Surgeons, Am. Coll. Podiatric Sports Medicine, Internat. Coll. Preventive Medicine, Acad. TV Arts and Scis., Masons, Shriners; clubs: Hollywood Comedy, Saints and Sinners, Hall Und Beinbruch Ski, Beach Cities Ski, Orange County Stamp, Las

Virgenes Track; mil: USN 1955-56, lt. cdr. med. svs. corps Brit.-Am. Cadet Corps, 1984–; civic: Hon. Sheriff Westchester 1962-64, chmn. Nat. Health Care Reform Com., United We Stand; Republican (Life mem. Rep. Nat. Com., Senatl. Inner Circle 1984-86, medal of merit U.S. Presdl. Task Force). Res: 1675 Berkshire Dr Thousand Oaks 91362

BLESSING-MOORE, JOANN CATHERINE, physician, medical educator; b. Sept. 21, 1946, Tacoma, Wash.; d. Harold R. and Mildred Benson B.; m. Robert Chester Moore, Feb. 1978; child: Ahna Blessing-Moore b. 1981; edn: BA, Syracuse Univ. 1968; MD, Syracuse Health Sci. Ctr., NY 1972; pediatric intern and res. Stanford Univ. Medical Ctr. 1972-75, Fellow in allergy, pediatric pulmonology 1975-77. Career: asst. clin. prof., full time, Stanford Univ. Hosp. 1977-84; private practice physician and assoc. clinical prof., Stanford Univ. 1984–; boarded in: pediatrics, allergy-immunology, pediatric pulmonology; FDA advy. com. on allergy pulm. drugs; cons. to various orgns. and companies; honors: NY State Acad. Scholarship, 1968-72, CF Found. Fellowship, 1975-77, listed Who's Who Am. Univ. Coll., 1968; fellow: Am. Acad. Allergy, Am. Coll. Allergy Immunology, Am. Acad. Pediatrics, Am. Coll. of Chest Physicians (com.), Am Thoracic Soc., Am. Coll. Asthma Allergy and Immunology, Am. Acad. Pediatrics; mem: No. Calif. Allergy Found. (bd.), Am. Acad. Allergy Imm. (com.), Am. Thoracic Soc., Am. Coll. Chest Physicians, Am Coll. of Asthma Allergy and Immunology, San Mateo and Santa Clara Co. Lung Assn. (bd. mem., com. Mem.), Nation Task Force for Establishment of Parameters of Care for Allergies and Asthma, Nat. Consortium on Asthma Camps for Children; civic: Medical Explorer Scouts, Presbyterian Church, Profl. Women's Orgn.; author: abstracts, articles, chapts. in 2 text books (allergy, pulmonary); co-editor 2 supplements for major jours., editorial bd. med. jour.; Republican; Presbyterian; rec: sailing, swimming, travel, gardening, cooking, music, horses.

BLINDER, BARTON JEROME, academic physician/psychoanalyst, b. July 30, 1938, Phila.; married; children: Madaline b. 1962, David b. 1966, Andrea b. 1968; edn: BA (distinction in psych.), Univ. Penn., 1960, MD (NIMH res. scholar), Univ. Penn. Sch. of Med., 1964; PhD psychoanalysis So. Calif. Psychoanalytic Inst., 1987; adv. studies Phila. Psychoanalytic Inst. 1967-69, Hamstead Child Therapy Clinic, London 1978, 79, Johns Hopkins Sch. Med., 1986, 87; diplomate Am. Bd. Psychiat. and Neurology, adult, child psychiatry (1970, 71). Career: intern Memorial Hosp., Long Beach 1964-65; inpatient child psychiatry and residential treatment E. Penn. State Sch. and Hosp. 1968-69; instr. child psychiat. Univ. Penn., 1969; maj. USAF M.C., asst. chief dept. mental hlth. svs. USAF Regional Hosp., Sheppard AFB Tx. 1969-71, commendn. medal 1971; dir. children's psychiatric svs. Long Beach Neuropsychiatric Inst., 1971-73; attdg. psychiatrist student hlth. ctr. UC Irvine, 1971-73, asst. clin. prof. dept. psychiat. and human beh. UCI, 1971-78, assoc. clin. prof. 1980-88, clin. prof. 1988–, dir. Eating Disorder Pgm. and Resrch. Studies anorexia/bulimia, UCI 1982–; co-dir. mental hlth. svs. for students Coast Comm. Coll. Dist., 1973-76; instr. So. Calif. Psychoanalytic Inst. ext. div., 1982-84; honors: Phi Beta Kappa (1959), Class of 1907 prize for psychiatric research Univ. Penn. Sch. Med. (1964); mem: Am. Acad. Child and Adolescent Psychiatry (fellow), Am. Psychiatric Assn. (fellow), So. Calif. Psychiatric Soc. (Exec. Council 1982-85), Am. Psychoanalytic Assn., Orange Co. Psychiat. Soc. (pres. 1980-82, APA rep. 1985–), Calif. Psychiatric Assn., Orange Co. Med. Assn., CMA, So. Calif. Soc. for Child and Adolescent Psychiatry (pres. 1988-89); author: Atypical Eating Disorders (in press 1989), The Devel. Line of Human Feeding: Normality and Pathology (in progress), numerous profl. jour. publs. and presentations. Address: 400 Newport Center Dr Ste 7 Newport Beach 92660

BLISS, EDWIN CROSBY, author, lecturer, consultant; b. Feb. 15, 1923, Salt Lake City, Utah; s. Edwin S. and Naomi (Crosby) B.; m. Mary Elizabeth Miller, Jan. 21, 1956; children: William, Rebecca, Roger, Kevin; edn: BS, Univ. Utah, 1948, MS, 1958. Career: editor Deseret News, S.L.C., Ut. 1948-52; lectr. Univ. of Utah 1952-54; magazine editor Columbus (Ohio) Dispatch, 1954-55; asst. to U.S. Senator, WDC 1955-63; public affairs dir. Nat. Assn. of Mfrs., WDC 1963-77; cons. prin. Edwin C. Bliss Assocs., Kingsburg, Ca. 1977–; lectr. Career Track, Boulder, Colo. 1983-91; mem. Am. Mgmt. Assn., Am. Inst. of Parliamentarians (advy. council 1984-92); author: Doing It Now (1983), Getting Things Done (1991), editor: Standard Guide to Parliamentary Procedure (1989); mil: lt. col. US Army, USAR 1944-74. Res/Ofc: 2220 Carolyn St Kingsburg 93631

BLOCK, ALVIN GILBERT, journalist; b. Sept. 15, 1946, Moline, Ill.; s. Sylvan Emory Block and Pauline (Kutten) Salzman; m. Ellen Marie Chapman Jan. 19, 1992; edn: BA, Bradley Univ., 1968. Career: editorial asst. Playboy Mag., Chgo. 1970; columnist, reporter Ketchum Tomorrow, Ketchum, Ida. 1973-74, editor 1975-76; reporter Idaho Statesman, Boise 1978-80; mng. editor California Journal, Sacto. 1983-93, editor, 1994–; freelance writer 1980–; radio sports commentator Sta. KXPR (NPR), Sacto. 1984-85; trek leader Himalayas Unlimited, Nepal 1978-82; elected councilman City of Ketchum, Ida. 1979; mem: Sacto. Press Club, Soc. for Am. Baseball Research, Sigma Delta Chi; mil: sp4 USAR/Idaho N.G. 1968-74; rec: baseball memorabilia, travel. Ofc: California Journal, 2101 K St Sacramento 95816

BLOCK, DEVON WESLEY, hotel chain general manager; b. Jan. 20, 1962, Grand Rapids, Mich.; s. Donald Wesley and Patricia Ann (Townsend) B.; m. Julie Kay Munson, Sept. 10, 1983; edn: BA chemistry, math., Cedarville Coll. 1982; MBA, Pepperdine Univ., 1991. Career: asst. controller Marriott, Houston, Tx. 1984-86; Sonesta Hotels, Orlando, Fla. 1986; controller Red Lion Hotels, Bellevue, Wash. 1986-89, Costa Mesa 1989-90, regional controller Red Lion Hotels, 1990-93; gen. mgr. Red Lion Los Angeles 1993–; honors: Cedarville Coll. nat. dean's list 1982; mem: Internat. Assn. Hospitality Accts.; Culver City Rotary, Culver City C.of C.; Republican; Baptist; rec: computers. Res: 111 Waterview St Playa del Rey 90293 Ofc: 6161 W Centinela Ave Culver City 90231

BLODGETT, ELSIE GRACE, business owner, retired teacher; b. Aug. 2, 1921, Eldorado Springs, Mo.; d. Charles Ishmal and Naoma Florence (Worthington) Robison; m. Charles Blodgett, Nov. 8, 1940; children: Carolyn Doyel, Charleen Bier, Lyndon, Daryl (dec.); edn: Warrensburg State Tchrs. Coll., 1939-40; BA, Fresno State Coll., 1953. Career: tchr. in Mo., 1940-42, and Calif., 1947-72; owner/mgr. rental units 1965–; exec. dir. San Joaquin County Rental Property Assn., Inc. 1970-81; ptnr. Key West Property Mgmt. 1980-84; owner Crystal Springs Health World, Stockton 1980-87; editor, News Bulletin; honoree w/husband as Mr. and Mrs. Apartment Owner of San Joaquin County 1977; mem: Stockton BBB (bd.), Nat. Apt. Assn. (state treas. 1977-79), Calif. Retired Tchrs. Assn.; civic: Zonta, PTA, Girl Scouts/Boys Scouts of Am., Stockton Goodwill Inds. (bd.), police svc. volunteer 1993, mem. Stockton Republican Women's Club and Calif. Republican Assembly 1993, capt. Delaware/Alpine Neighborhood Watch 1994; Republican; Methodist. Address: 2285 W Mendocino Stockton 95204-4005

BLOOM, ELLIOTT D., physicist; b. June 11, 1940, New York; s. Leo and Rose B.; m. Susan; children: Matthew (dec.), Wendy; edn: BA, Pomona Coll. 1962; PhD, Calif. Tech. Univ. 1967. Career: research assoc. SLAC, Stanford 1967-70; vis. asst. prof. Calif. Tech. Univ., Pasadena 1972-73; asst. prof. SLAC, Stanford 1970-74, assoc. 1974-80, prof. 1980–; awards: Humboldt Found. Sr. Scientist (1962); Fellow Am. Physical Soc., mem: Am. Astronomical Soc.; mem. of team that discovered quarks inside the nucleon, co-discoverer of ground state of the charmonium system. Ofc: Stanford Linear Accelerator Center MS 98 POB 4349 Stanford 94309

BLOSSOM, HERBERT JOHN, associate dean, physician; b. Sept. 22, 1944, San Diego; s. Herbert Henry Blossom and Grace Elizabeth (Tupper) LiCursi; m. Martha Elizabeth McConnell, Nov. 18, 1980; 1 dau. Susanne b. 1974; edn: BA, UC Davis 1966; MD, UC San Francisco 1970; internship, UCSF-Fresno 1970-71, residency 1971-73; lic. physician Med. Bd. of Calif. 1971; cert. Am. Bd. of Family Practice 1974, 80, 86, 92. Career: med. dir. Firebaugh-Mendota Health Ctr., Mendota, Calif. 1974-76; acting chief of family practice Valley Med. Ctr., Fresno 1976-78, chief of family practice 1978-92; interim assoc. dean med. edn. prog. UCSF-Fresno 1992, assoc. dean 1992–, prof. of clin. family & comm. medicine 1993–; mem. UCSF-Fresno Med. Edn. Com. 1991–; bd. dirs. UCSF-Fresno Found. 1991–; v.p. UCSF Alumni-Faculty Assn., Central Valley 1992–, mem. Tertiary Care Task Force 1993-94; mem. Valley Med. Ctr. nominating com. 1993-94; awards: Rudolph J. Taussig Scholarship 1967, Elliot J. Royer Scholarship 1968, Cary C. Gregory Scholarship 1969, fellow Am. Acad. of Family Physicians 1982, first annual Patient Care Mag. award for outstanding health edn. curriculum (with Diane Plorde), nat. award for innovation in edn. Soc. of Teachers in Family Medicine (with Diane Plorde), nominee-Kaiser Award for Excellence in Tchg. 1990, 91, 92; mem.: Calif. Acad. of Family Physicians (residency progs. com., risk reduction com. task force on legislative funding for family practice residencies 1987-89), Central Calif. Res. Symposium (planning com. 1992–), Fresno-Madera Med. Soc. 1974- (public health com. 1974-85, legislative com. 1983-88, bd. dirs. 1984-87, chair MedPAC 1984-88, editor MedPAC Advocate Newsletter 1985-88, finance com. 1986-87, v.p. 1987-88, chair CME com. 1987-89, prog. chair, moderator 1988), Hosp. Council of No. and Central Calif. 1993–, San Joaquin Valley Health Consortium 1983–, VMC Found. (bd. dirs. finance com. 1993–), Health Care Forum (panel mem. Concerned Citizens for Health Care Reform 1994); jour. reviewer We. Jour. of Medicine 1983–, Jour. of Family Practice 1983–; author: 25+ articles pub. in profl. jours. 1983–, book chpt., The Role of the Family Practice Program (Becoming a Family Physician, pub. 1989); grantee: Calif. Health Manpower Policy Commn. (14 special project grants 1976-91, 14 capitation grants 1978-92, minority recruitment grant 1988), Family Medicine Training grants 1977, 80, 83, 86, St. of Calif. 1988, Health Svs. Resources Adminstrn. Res: 708 East Carmen Fresno 93728 Ofc: UCSF-Fresno 2615 East Clinton Ave Fresno 93703

BLOUNT, HARRY NEIL, equipment marketing professional; b. Nov. 22, 1944, Blount, West Va.; s. Harry and Stella (Branard) B.; m. Dorothy Ann McDaniel, Oct. 1, 1965 (div. 1977); children: Harry Neil II, Patricia Suzette; m. Dolores Ruiz, Aug. 13, 1977; edn: West Va. Univ., 1963-65, bus. mgmt. major Hartnell Coll., 1974-77. Career: warranty adminstr. C.I. Walker Equipment Co., Charleston, W.Va. 1965-70; lt. Belle Fire Dept., Belle, W.Va. 1970-72; service advisor Quinn Co., Salinas, Calif. 1973-86; region sales mgr. Northwest Motor Welding, San Leandro 1986-87; founder, pres. Parts World, Salinas 1987–; ptnr. West World Mktg., 1988–; account exec. Empire Tractor Co., Newark 1988–;

group advr. Equipment Explorers, Belle 1970-73; cons. Industrial Safety Club, Salinas 1977-84; civic bds: Salinas C.of C., Lions/Salinas Club (bd. 1984-86, special svc. award 1986), Big Buddy Program, Monterey County 1981, Community Recycle Program, Salinas (asst. mgr. 1986), Citizen's Traffic Com., Salinas 1987, Friends Outside, Monterey 1988; author: Back Roads & Home, 1980, numerous pub. articles; Republican; Methodist. Res: 1605 Siskiyou Dr Salinas 93906 Ofc: Empire Tractor & Equipment Co. 415 9th Street Gilroy 95020

BLUE, JAMES GUTHRIE, city veterinarian, administrator; b. Oct. 22, 1920, Flora, Ind.; s. Van Calvin and Florence Amanda (Guthrie) B.; edn: ensign US Naval Acad., 1943; Northwestern Univ., 1943; AB, Wabash Coll., 1943; DVM, Ohio State Univ., 1950; AA in labor rels., L.A. Trade Tech., 1989. Career: active duty USN 1943-46, served to lt. comdr. USNR 1946-66; city veterinarian Los Angeles, North Hollywood, consultant in vet. medicine, surgery and dentistry; field veterinarian City of Los Angeles 1985-95; res. and projects consultant CSU Northridge, 1981-88; mem., secty. Arizona State Vet. Med. Bd., 1976-82; awards: sr. coll. award Am. Vet. Med. Assn.; mem: Calif. Vet. Med. Assn. (com. environ. health and ecology, state ethics com., profl. ethics com., wellness com. 1985-95), So. Calif. Vet. Med. Assn. (Council mem., PAC, contg. edn. com.), So. Ariz. VMA, Ariz. VMA, Am. VMA, San Diego VMA, Am. Fedn. of State Co. Muni. Employees (Profl. Med. Services) Local 2006 (secty., negotiator, 1983-95), Reserve Officers Assn. (pres. Tucson chpt. 1960, state pres. ROA Ariz. 1961-62), Am. Legion, Mil. Order of World Wars (comdr. Ariz., 1967-70), US Naval Reserve Assn., Scottish Rites, Shrine, Internat. 20-30 Club (hon. life); publs: Puppy Distemper Problem Series, Pulse (So. Calif. VMA jour.); Democrat; Episcopalian. Res: 6116 Fulton Ave #103 c/o Fulton Chateau Van Nuys 91401 Ofc: City of Los Angeles 13131 Sherman Way North Hollywood 91605

BLUM, NANCY ALLISON, clinical psychologist; b. Nov. 12, 1959, New York; d. Sander and Audrey Sheila (Goldsmith) Blum; m. Roger Bruce Lemberg, Aug. 24, 1986; edn: BA, Brandeis Univ. 1981; MA, Emory Univ. 1983; PhD, Emory Univ. 1993. Career: clin. psychology intern Camarillo St. Hosp., Camarillo 1985-86; psychotherapist, behavior cons. HELP Group, Sherman Oaks 1986-89; psych. asst., psych., neuropsych. and medicolegal evals., 1989-93; postdoctoral fellow clinical child psychol. UCLA-NPI 1993-94; asst. clinical dir. HELP Group, Sherman Oaks 1994–; awards: NIMH grantee 1985-86, Emory Univ. Grad. fellowship 1983-84, New Eng. Psychological Assn. Undergrad fellow 1980-81, Mass. Psychological Assn. Spl. Merit 1979; mem: Am. Psychol. Assn., Calif. Psychol. Assn., S.F.V. Psychol. Assn., Assn. Behavior Analysis, Assn. for the Advancement of Behavior Therapy, So. Calif. Assn. Behavior Analysis & Therapy, NOW, Sierra Club, Wellworth Minyan; articles pub. in profl. jours. 1984–, user manual pub. 1985, confs. presented 1984–; Democrat; Jewish; rec: computers, folk dancing, photog., exercise, music. Res: 17514 Arminta St Northridge 91325

BLUM, ROBERT M., obstetrician, gynecologist; b. Mar. 28, 1939, Jersey City, N.J.; s. Philip and Bertha (Hirsch) B.; m. Carole Lammer, June 13, 1964; children: Susan b. 1966, David b. 1968; edn: BA, Rutgers Univ. 1960; MD, Georgetown Univ. 1964. Career: intern Beth Israel Hosp., Newark, N.J. 1964-65; resident Sinai Hosp., Baltimore, Md. 1965-68; asst. chief Kaiser Permanente, Downey 1971–; assoc. prof. UCLA 1978–; mem: L.A. Co. Ob-Gyn. Soc., Am. Coll. Ob-Gyn.; mil: major AUS 1968-70; rec: skiing, fishing, tennis. Res: 4574 Shasta Circle Cypress 90630 Ofc: Kaiser Permanente 9449 Imperial Hwy Downey 90242

BLUSTEIN, ARNOLD JAY, physician, pediatrician; b. Feb. 2, 1949, Los Angeles; s. George and Ida (Shifrin) B.; m. Marjorie Elizabeth Yeager, Aug. 7, 1977; children: Rebecca b. 1978, Jonathan b. 1979, Gabriel & Benjamin b. 1986; edn: AB (cum laude), UCLA 1970; MD, UC Davis 1975. Career: physician Oak Hill Med. Group, San Leandro 1978-84; physician A. Blustein, MD, Inc., San Leandro 1984–; tchg. attending physician Children's Hosp., Oakland 1978–; chmn. pediatrics dept. Vesper Hosp., San Leandro 1982-84, Humana Hosp., San Leandro 1986-88; chmn. infection control Humana Hosp., San Leandro 1990-92; founder & pres. Gan Mah Tov Preschool, Oakland 1988-90; author, short story: Man Who Became Beethoven, 1971; rec: Irish music, gardening. Ofc: Arnold J. Blustein MD 1235 Harrison St San Leandro 94577 Tel: 510/352-2425

BOARINI, EDWARD JAMES, research and development executive; b. Sept. 26, 1949, Chgo.; s. Edward John and Celeste Mary (Butt) B.; m. Marla Bovar, Apr. 25, 1976; 1 son, David b. 1980; edn: BS biology, Univ. Ill., 1975; MS technology mgmt., Pepperdine Univ., 1991. Career: prin. engr. Travenol Labs., Round Lake, Ill. 1975-80, sect. mgr. 1980-82, program mgr. 1982-85; mgr. med. prods. Baxter Pharmaseal, Valencia, Ca. 1986-89, dir. med. prods. 1989-91, dir. tech. svs. 1991-93; v.p. tech. ops. P.S. Medical, Goleta 1993–; mil: PO2 USN 1970-74; rec: skiing, golf, neon art. Ofc: P.S. Medical 125-B Cremona Dr Goleta 93117

BOARMAN, PATRICK MADIGAN, economist; b. April 23, 1922, Buffalo, N.Y.; s. Marcus Daly and Virginia Benedict (Madigan) B.; children: Thomas b. 1954, Christopher b. 1957, Jesse b. 1958, Barbara b. 1961; m. Shi Chun (Shane) Hu, Dec. 18, 1988; edn: AB, Fordham Univ. 1943; MS, Columbia Univ. 1946;

PhD in econs., Grad. Inst. Internat. Studies, Univ. Geneva, Switz. 1965. Career: fgn. corr. CBS, Geneva 1946-48; dir. Office Cultural Affairs, US Catholic Welfare Conf., Bonn, W.Ger. 1951-55; asst. prof. econ. Univ. Wis. Milw. 1956-62; assoc. prof. Bucknell Univ., Lewisburg, Pa. 1962-67; prof. Long Island Univ., Greenvale, N.Y. 1967-72; dir. research Republican Conf., Ho. of Reps., Wash. D.C. 1967-68; dir. research Ctr. for Internat. Bus. Pepperdine Univ., L.A. 1972-75; apptd. San Diego Co. Bd. of Suprs. 3rd dist. 1983-85; prof. economics and bus. adminstrn., chmn. internat. bus., National Univ., San Diego 1979-93, prof. emeritus of economics 1993; mgr. econ. research div. employee rels. and mgmt. devel. Gen. Electric Co., N.Y.C. 1964-65; mgr. econ. reports div. econ. analysis AT&T, 1969; senior economist cons. World Trade Inst., N.Y.C. 1971; pres. Patrick M. Boarman Assocs., internat. bus. cons., 1975–; awards: Fulbright fellow Univ. Amsterdam 1949-50, Ford Found. fellow in econs. Univ. Mich. 195), GE Found. fellow Univ. Va. 1965, award of merit So. Calif. Assn. of County Suprs. 1984, spl. service Bd. Suprs. San Diego County 1984; mem. W. Econ. Assn. 1975–, Am. Econ. Assn. 1956-78, Philadelphia Soc. 1964–; author: Union Monopolies and Antitrust Restraints, 1963, Germany's Economic Dilemma, 1964; editor books: Trade With China, 1974, Multinational Corporations and Governments (w. Hans Schollhammer, 1975), World Monetary Disorder (w. D.G. Tuerck, 1976); contbr. numerous articles to profl. and gen. circ. periodicals; mil: pvt. US Army 1943, Disting. Service Cross, Order of Merit W. Ger.; Republican (S.D. Co. cent. com. 1981-84, Calif. st. cent. com. 1984-86); Cath.; rec: classical pianist. Res: 6421 Caminito Estrellado San Diego 92120

BOBROW, MICHAEL LAWRENCE, architect; b. April 18, 1939, New York City; s. Jack and Ruth (Gureasko) B.; m. Julia Dessery Thomas, March 24, 1980; children by previous marriage: Elizabeth Pressler b. 1964, Erica b. 1967, David b. 1969; 1 stepchild, Leslie Thomas; edn: B.Arch., Columbia Univ. 1963; grad. studies, UCLA Anderson Sch. Of Mgmt.; reg. architect 14 states and NCARB. Career: sr. architect Office of the Surgeon Gen. USAF, W.D.C., 1963-66; dir. arch. Med. Planning Assn., Malibu 1966-72; founder/chmn./design ptnr. BTA, Bobrow/Thomas & Assoc., Los Angeles 1972–; founder prog. in health facilities design Grad. Sch. Arch. and Urban Planning, UCLA 1972-80; adj. prof. and dean's advy. bd. Sch. Public Health, UCLA; regent, Mount Saint Mary's Coll., trustee, Otis Coll. of Art and Design; chmn. advy. bd. Arts & Arch. Mag.; pres. The Friends of the Schindler House, L.A.; dir. Am. Hosp. Assn. Annual Design Inst.; chair Arch. Record, UCLA, Columbia Univ. Internat. Hosp. Design Competition, "Outstanding Architects Under 40", Bldg. Design & Constrn. Mag. 1978; recipient AIA, NAVFAC, DOD, NARF, Bldg. Design & Constrn. Mag., L.A. Conservancy Design Awards; author: num. articles and projects pub. in profl. jours. and presented at insts. and univs. internationally; major projects: Otis Coll. of Art & Design, Arizona Cancer Ctr., Soc. of Singers Home, City of Hope Nat. Med. Ctr., Motion Picture & T.V. Hosp., Cedars Sinai Med. Ctr., Camp Pendleton Naval Hosp., Beckman Res. Lab., Shriners Hosps., Cook Co. Hosp., Cal Tech Parsons-Gates Hall, V.A. L.A. Clinic, San Bernardino Co. Med. Ctr., UCLA Arroyo Bridge, Daniel Freeman Mem. Hosp., Casa Pacifica Children's Crisis Ctr., St. Luke's Med. Ctr., St. Vincent's Med. Ctr., Shanghai Housing Towers, Hong Kong Hosp. Authority; clubs: Regency (L.A.), Beverly Hills Tennis Club. Ofc: BTA, Bobrow/Thomas and Associates 1001 Westwood Blvd Los Angeles 90024-2902

BODENSTEIN, KENNETH ALAN, financial consultant; b. Feb. 25, 1937, NY, NY; s. Wm. and Sylvia (Halperin) B.; m. Susan Sims, Sept. 4, 1960 (dec.); m. 2d. Diane Lerner, Sept. 6, 1992; children: Todd b. 1962, Leslie b. 1964; edn: AB, Columbia Coll., 1957, BS chem. eng., Columbia Univ. Sch. of Engring., 1958, MBA, Columbia Grad. Sch. of Bus., 1960; Chartered Fin. Analyst (CFA) ICFA 1977. Career: asst. to treas. Air Products and Chemicals Co., Allentown, Pa. 1960-64; senior investment analyst Armour & Co., Chgo. 1964-68; midwest reg. mgr. corp. finance Goodbody & Co., Chgo. 1968-70; dir. bus. research CNA Fin. Co., Chgo. 1970-74; senior v.p. Duff & Phelps Inc., Chgo. and Los Angeles, 1975–; dir. Intercargo Corp. 1987–, Driscoll Strawberry Associates 1990-94; mem: Assn. Corp. Growth (dir. 1982-84), Investment Analyst Soc. (Chgo. bd. 1984-87), Soc. CFA; clubs: Beverly Hills CC, Univ. (Chgo.); rec: tennis. Res: #503 2950 Neilson Way Santa Monica 90405

BOERSMA, LAWRENCE ALLAN, animal welfare administrator; b. Apr. 24, 1932, London, Ont., Can.; s. Harry Albert and Valerie Kathryn (DeCordova) B.; m. Nancy Noble Jones, Aug. 16, 1952 (div. 1962); children: Juliana b. 1954, Dirk b. 1956; m. June Elaine Schiefer, Nov. 22, 1962; children (by marriage) Kenneth McKim b. 1951, Mark McKim b. 1956; edn: BA, Univ. Nebr., 1953, MS, 1955; PhD, Sussex, Eng., 1972; Cert. Fund Raising Exec. (CFRE), Nat. Soc. FRE, 1988. Career: journalism tchr. Technical High Sch., Omaha, Nebr. 1953-55; dir. pub. relations and journ. chair Adams State Coll., Alamosa, Colo. 1955-59; advt. sales Better Homes and Gardens, N.Y.C. 1959-63; advt. account exec. This Week Mag., N.Y.C. 1963-66; Eastern sales dir., mktg. dir. Ladies' Home Journal, N.Y.C. 1966-75; v.p./assoc. publisher Saturday Evening Post also v.p./pub. Country Gentleman, N.Y.C., 1975; v.p., dir. mktg. and advt. sales Photo World Mag., N.Y.C., 1975-77; advt. mgr. La Jolla Light, Calif. 1977-80; photographer prin. Allan/TAnimal Photographers, 1980–, pres. and c.e.o. The Photographic Inst. Internat., 1982-86; dir. community relations San Diego Humane Soc. and S.P.C.A., 1985-94; bd. dirs. Spay/Neuter Action Project, 1991-93; founder, Feral

Cat Coalition San Diego (chmn. 1992-93); pres./c.e.o. United Animal Welfare Found. 1992-94; assoc. exec. dir., The Ctr. for Humane Edn. for So. Calif. 1994–; bd. dirs. Escondido Humane Soc. Found. 1994–; chmn./CEO, Internat. Dolphin Project 1995–; instr., prof. advt. Nat. Soc. of Fund Raising Execs., Alexandria, Va. 1992-93; author/photog. numerous articles in mags. in U.S., Mexico, Canada, Europe, Japan, Australia, S.Africa, S.Am.; named man of yr. Ladies' Home Jour. 1972; mem: Royal Photographic Soc., Bath, Eng. (Fellow 1985), Profl. Photographers of Calif. (Fellow 1986), Profl. Photographers of Am. (Master of Photography award, Chgo. 1985, Photographic Craftsman award, Chgo. 1986), Nat. Soc. Fund Raising Execs. 1986- (bd. dir. San Diego chpt. 1988-89, treas. 1990-91), Pub. Relations Soc. Am. 1987–, Soc. of Animal Welfare Adminstrs. 1986–, Shriners (pres. Businessmens Club Al Bahr Shrine, S.D. 1988), Scottish Rite, Masons 1967–, Am. Red Cross (vol. in public info. S.D./Imperial Cos. Chpt. 1993–), San Diego Co. Emergency Svs. Orgns. (mem. public info. ofcrs.); Republican; Presbyterian. Res: 3503 Argonne St San Diego 92117

BOGAARD, WILLIAM JOSEPH, lawyer; b. Jan. 18, 1938, Sioux City, Iowa; s. Joseph and Irene Mary (Hensing) B.; m. Claire Whalen, Jan. 28, 1961; children: Michele b. 1961, Jeannine b. 1963, Joseph b. 1966, Matthew b. 1972; edn: BS, Loyola Marymount Univ., L.A. 1959; JD w. honors, Univ. Mich. Law Sch., 1965; admitted Calif. St. Bar 1966. Career: atty., assoc. O'Melveny & Myers, Los Angeles 1965-66, 67-70; cons. Calif. Dept. of Corporations, L.A. 1966; ptnr. Hufstedler & Kaus, L.A. 1970-82; exec. v.p. and gen. counsel First Interstate Bancorp, Los Angeles 1982–; mem: Am. Bar Assn., Calif. Bar Assn., L.A. Co. Bar Assn. (exec. com. corp. law sect. 1984-86, Outstanding corporate counsel award 1987), Calif. Bankers Assn. (bd. dirs. 1987-91), Constl. Rights Found. L.A. (v.p. 1988–); mayor City of Pasadena 1984-86; mil: capt. USAF 1961-62. Ofc: First Interstate Bancorp 633 West Fifth St (T72-10) Los Angeles 90071

BOGART, WANDA LEE, interior designer; b. Feb. 26, 1939, Ashville, N.C.; d. Bob West and Virginia Elizabeth (Worley) McLemore-Snyder; m. Sterling X. Bogart, Feb. 12, 1962; children: Kevin Sterling, Kathleen Elisabeth; edn: BA, San Jose State Univ., 1961. Career: teacher Redondo Beach Sch. Dist., 1962-65; free-lance interior designer, Ladera 1970-75; designer MG Interior Design, Orange 1975-80; prin., pres. Wanda Bogart Interior Design Inc., Orange 1980–; honors: So. Calif. Ranch and Coast Mag. list of Top 20 Interior Designers 1987; profl. mem.: Internat. Soc. Interior Design, and Am. Soc. Interior Design; cert. interior designer #1609. Ofc: Wanda Bogart Interior Design, Inc. 1440 E Chapman Ave Orange 92666 Tel: 714/997-5991

BOGDAN, CAROLYN LOUETTA, accounting executive; b. Apr. 15, 1941, Wilkes-Barre, Pa.; d. Walter Cecil and Ethna Louetta (Kendig) Carpenter; m. James Bogdan, May 5, 1961; son, Thomas J. b. 1967; edn: spl. courses Am. Inst. of Banking. Career: head bookkeeper Forty Fort State Bank, Forty Fort, Pa. 1959-63; hd. bookkeeper U.S. Nat. Bank, Long Beach, Ca. 1963-65; office mgr. United Parts Exchange, 1976-81; contract adminstr. branch credit co-ordinator Johnson Controls Inc., Rancho Dominguez 1981–; acct./co-owner B.E.R.D. (Bogdan Electronic R&D), Lakewood 1981–; notary pub. Johnson Controls, L.A. 1987–; recipient sav. bond awards from Hire the Handicapped and Yearbook Club, Kingston, Pa. (1958, 59), listed Who's Who of Am. Women 17th edit., Who's Who in Finance & Industry, 2000 Notable Am. Women; mem. Nat. Notary Assn., Am. Inst. of Profl. Bookkeepers, Nat. Assn. for Female Execs.; civic: staff ofcr. L.A. Co. Sheriff/RACES (records keeper 1969-93, radio ofcr. 1994–), mem. Tournament of Roses Radio Assn. (pin chair 1975–); Republican; Prot.; rec: needlework, electronics, designing, amateur radio opr. Res: 3713 Capetown St Lakewood 90712 Ofc: Johnson Controls, Inc. 19118 S Reyes Ave Rancho Dominguez 90221

BOGERT, MARGOT INKSTER, trust company deputy division head; b. Feb. 18, 1953, Dunfermline, Scotland, U.K.; d. John Crisp and Elizabeth Fulton-Spence (Inkster) Yellowley; m. John Bogert, Feb. 1, 1975; children: Caitlin b. 1982, Rachel b. 1986, Ian Henry b. 1993; edn: BA, Edinburg Univ., Scotland; CTFA 1991. Career: chief of staff, sr. v.p. Trust Services of Am., Los Angeles 1975-92; mng. dir. and corp. secty. TSA Capital Mgmt. Inc. 1989-92; dep. div. hd. Sanwa Bank, 1992–; YWCA honoree, recipient Distinguished Profl. Woman award 1987; civic: Pasadena Child Edn. Ctr. (bd.), Townhall of Calif.; clubs: City Club on Bunker Hill, L.A. Athletic, La Canada CC; Presbyterian; rec: aerobics, swim, racquetball. Ofc: Sanwa Bank California 601 S Figueroa Los Angeles CA 90017

BOGGAN, DANIEL, JR., university administrator, b. Dec. 9, 1945, Albion, Mich.; s. Daniel, Sr. and Ruthie Jean (Crum) B.; m. Jacqueline Beal, Oct. 4, 1977; children: DeVone, Daniel, Dhanthan, Alike; edn: BA, Albion Coll., 1967; MSW, Univ. Mich., Ann Arbor 1968. Career: asst. chief adminstr. San Diego County, 1978-79; county adminstr. Essex County, NJ 1979-82; city mgr. City of Berkeley 1982-86; assoc. vice chancellor UC Berkeley, Mar.-Sept. 1986, actg. v. chancellor 1986-87, vice chancellor 1987–; dir: Clorox Corp., Oakland 1990–; civic bds: NFBPA (nat. pres. 1990-91, Oakland bd. 1985–), NAACP (nat. life), YMCA Berkeley (bd. 1988-90), Berkeley Booster (bd. 1986-90); awards: youth leadership NAACP 1965, outstanding pub. adminstr., chapter svc., and marks of excellence Nat. Forum. Black Pub. Adminstrs. (1975, 86, 87); Democrat; Baptist; rec: basketball, equestrian, reading, writing.

BOGGESS, JANE ELLEN, state government executive; b. April 29, 1946, Upland; d. Clayton Eli and Margaret Elmira (Miller) Boggess; m. Richard Arthur O'Neill, Oct. 24, 1977 (div.); children: Margaret Julia b. 1979; edn: BA hons., UC Berkeley 1969; PhD, 1976. Career: research fellow UC Berkeley 1976-81; dir. research Health Ofcrs. Assn., Sacto. 1981-84; dir. Family Planning, San Bernardino 1984-94; Chief Calif. State Ofc. of Family Planning 1994–; field researcher NIH, NIMH funded res., Himalaya 1972-74, 1976, 78, 91, 92; health researcher CDC funded res. 1981-84; awards: NIH traineeship (1969-74), UCB Dean's fellowship (1974-75); mem: Calif. Family Planning Council (bd. dirs.), Calif. Conf. Maternal Child & Adolescent Health, Inland AIDS Pediatric Task Force, N.Y. Acad. Scis., Nat. Family Planning & Reproduction Health Assn., Mt. Baldy Sch. Dist. Site Council; contbg. ed. Adult Male Reproductive Strategies (1983), 7 articles pub. in acad. and profl. jours. (1979-85); rec: travel, cross country skiing, gardening. Res: POB 309 Mount Baldy 91759 Ofc: California State Office of Family Planning 714 P St Rm 440 Sacramento 95814

BOGGS, DAVID ALLEN, transit executive; b. Apr. 24, 1943, Glendale; s. L. Wade and Lillian C. (Clarry) B.; m. Peggy, June 29, 1963; children: Debbie b. 1965, Christy b. 1969, Ryan b. 1973; edn: AA, Citrus Coll., 1973; BA, Evergreen State Coll., 1974. Career: asst. cashier/ops. ofcr. Bank of Am., Palm Springs 1963-66; ops. analyst Seattle First National Bank, Seattle 1966-68; supvg. acct. Wash. State Dept. Hwys., Olympia 1968-74; mgr. of admin. Wash. State Ferry System, Seattle 1974-77; finance dir./asst. to the exec. dir. Seattle Metro, 1977-80; finance dir./asst. exec. dir. Houston Met. Transit Auth., Houston 1980-83; gen. mgr. Reg. Transit Dist., Sacramento 1983-88; gen. mgr. Sacramento Municipal Utility Dist., 1988-90; utility and gen. mgmt. cons., 1990-91; dir. transit ops. Laidlaw Transit Fixed Route Ops., 1991–; mem: bd. dirs. Foundation Health Corp., Sacto. 1990–, Sacto. Safety Council 1986–, United Way 1986–, Chamber of Commerce 1986-1988, HIS Farm 1986-89; advy. bd. USC/Sacto. Pub. Affairs Ctr. 1986-89; active in Scouting (1950s–), Golden Empire Council BSA (pres. 1991), editorial bd. Calif. Executive 1987-89; awards: Masters fellowship Fed. Hwy. Adminstrn., Seattle 1977, Silver Beaver BSA, Sacto. 1986; mem. Rotary Club Modesto; Methodist (fin. chmn., bd. 1988-90); rec: collect military medals, square dance, spl. interest in personal orgn. & time mgmt. Res: 9350 Oak Dr Orangevale 95662 Ofc: Laidlaw Transit Services 1001 Ninth St Ste A Modesto 95354

BOGGS, GEORGE ROBERT, college president; b. Sept. 4, 1944, Conneaut, Ohio; s. George Robert Boggs, Sr. and Mary Ellen (Mullen) B.; m. Ann Holliday, Aug. 8, 1969; children: Kevin b. 1973, Ian b. 1977, Micah b. 1979; edn: BS, chem., Ohio State Univ., Columbus, 1966; MA, chem., Univ. of Calif., Santa Barbara, 1968; grad. study, ednl. adminstrn., Calif. State Univ., Chico 1969-72; PhD, ednl. adminstr., Univ. of Texas, Austin 1984; life credentials: std. tchg. cred. 1969, comm. coll. supr. cred. 1970, comm. coll. chief adminstrv. ofcr. cred. 1970. Career: tchg. asst. Ohio St. Univ. 1965-66, UC Santa Barbara 1966-68; instr. of chem. Butte Coll., Oroville, Calif. 1968-72, div. chair 1972-81, assoc. dean of instruction 1981-85; supt./pres. Palomar Coll., San Marcos, Calif. 1985–; guest lectr. CSU Chico, 1970, 77, 82, 83,84; adj. instr. Austin Comm. Coll. 1982; guest lectr. Univ. of Tex., Austin 1989, 90; cons.: Marin Comm. Coll. Dist. 1985, San Joaquin Delta Comm. Coll. Dist. 1986, Republic of So. Africa Dept. of Nat. Edn. 1993, Univ. of Hawaii Comm. Coll. 1994, El Camino Coll. 1994; mem. Am. Assn. of Comm. Colls., Wash., DC (federal relations com. 1990, 94, 95, bd. dirs. 1990–, chmn. bd. dirs. 1993-94); editorial advy. bd, Journal of Applied Res. in the Comm. Coll. 1993–; honors: Nat. Honor Soc. 1961 (scholarship recipient 1962), Scholastic "R" scholarship 1962, Stadium Dormitory scholarship 1962-65, Ohio St. Univ. scholarship 1963, Upsilon Pi Upsilon 1964 (pres. 1965-66), Phi Kappa Phi 1983, Richardson fellowship 1982-83, listed Who's Who in the West 1987, Am. Pub. Who's Who 1988, San Diego Hall of Success 1988, Who's Who in Calif. 1988, 95, Who's Who of Emerging Leaders in Am. 1988, 5,000 Personalities of the World 1989, Who's Who Worldwide 1993, Who's Who in Am. Edn. 1993, Men of Achievement 1993, 94; Disting. Grad. award, Univ. of Tex. 1990, Pacific Region CEO award, Assn. of Comm. Coll. Trustees, British Columbia 1993, Stanley A. Mahr Comm. Svc. award, San Marcos C.of C. 1994, Proclamation of Jan. 15th as Dr. George R. Boggs Day in Vista, Calif. 1994, Harry Buttimer Disting. Adminstrs. award, Assn. of Calif. Comm. Coll. Adminstrs. 1994, Professional of Yr. award, The Leadership Alliance 1994; mem: Assn. of Calif. Comm. Coll. Adminstrs. 1980- (comm. on mgmt. devel. 1985–, conf. presenter 1988, 89, 90, 91, 94), Calif. Comm. Coll. CEO's Assn. 1985–, Faculty Assn. of Calif. Comm. Colls. 1971- (presenter 1989, 94), Phi Rho Pi Speech Frat. 1987–, San Diego and Imperial Counties Comm. Coll. Assn. 1985- (pres. 1991-92), So. Calif. Comm. Coll. CEO's Assn. 1985- (sec./treas. 1990–), Nat. Res. Council (undergrad. sci. edn. com. 1993-95), The College Bd. (we. regional meeting prog. planning com. 1992, 93, 94, 95 presenter 1994), Calif. Comm. Coll. CEO Acad. (steering com. 1986–), Calif. Comm. Coll. Trustees Assn. (presenter 1988, 89, 94), Assn. Comm. Coll. Trustees (presenter 1993, 94) BECA Found. (bd. dirs. 1987–, v.p. 1989-90), Calif. Center for the Arts (Escondido bd. trustees 1993–, v.p. for edn. and chair edn. com. 1993-94), Lake San Marcos Chamber Music Soc. (bd. dirs. 1990–), Rotary Club of Escondido 1985- (scholarship chair 1988-91, bd. dirs. 1991-93), Vista New Beginnings (exec. council 1991–);

author: numerous articles publ in profl. journals, 1969–; rec: photography, wood working. Ofc: Palomar College 1140 W Mission Rd San Marcos 92069-1487

BOGREN, HUGO GUNNAR, academic physician; b. Jan. 9, 1933, Sweden, nat. 1983; s. Gunnar Hugo and Signe Victoria (Holmstrom) B.; m. Elisabeth Faxen, Nov. 1, 1956 (div.); children: Cecilia b. 1961, Niclas b. 1964, Joakim b. 1966; m. 3d. Gunilla Lady Whitmore, July 2, 1988; edn: pre-med. Univ. of Lund, Sweden 1954; MD, Univ. Gothenburg 1958, PhD in med., 1964; bd. certified in diagnostic radiology (1966). Career: med. resident Univ. Gothenburg, Sweden 1958-64, asst., assoc. prof. 1964-69; vis. assoc. prof. UC San Francisco 1970-71, assoc. prof., prof. of radiology and med. UC Davis 1972–; vis. prof. Univ. London, Eng. 1986-87, 1993-94; awards: Sr. Internat. Fogarty Fellow 1986-87; mem: Am. Heart Assn. - Golden Empire, Radiological Soc. of No. Am., No. Am. Soc. for Cardiac Imaging,, No. Calif. Radiol. Soc., Soc. Thoracic Radiology, Swedish Soc. of Med. Radiology; Rotary Internat.; author numerous articles in the field of cardiovascular radiology, exophtalmos research and gall stone research; mil: lt. Swedish Army Med. Corps; Lutheran; rec: ocean sailing, skiing. Res: 347 Rio Del Oro Ln Sacramento 95825 Ofc: Univ. Calif. Davis Medical Center Div. of Diagnostic Radiology 2516 Stockton Blvd Sacramento 95817

BOHN, RALPH C., dean of continuing education (emeritus), San Jose State University; b. Feb. 19, 1930, Detroit, Mich.; s. Carl and Bertha (Abrams) B.; m. Adelle Stanul, Sept. 2, 1950 (dec. 1975); m. JoAnne Olvera, Feb. 19, 1977 (div. 1990); children: Cheryl b. 1954, Jeffrey b. 1957; stepchildren: Kathryn b. 1962, Kimberly b. 1964, Gregory b. 1965; m. 3d. Mariko Tajima, Jan., 1990; stepchild, Diachi b. 1982; son, Thomas b. 1992; edn: BS, Wayne St. Univ. 1951; Ed.M, 1954; Ed.D, 1957. Career: tchr. Detroit Pub. Schs., Mich. 1947-51, 54-55; comdg. ofcr. USCG, San Diego 1951-54; dean of continuity edn., div. tech. San Jose St. Univ. 1955-92, emeritus 1992; cons. on coll. & univ. programs on mil. bases for USAF 1990–; cons. Calif. State Univ. System 1992–; chmn. bd. dirs. Sci. & Human Values Inc., San Francisco 1975–; chair, committees WASC 1975-92; mem. & chair of 40+ accreditation teams for WASC, NCASC & NWASC; chair of 12 mil. base assessments of collegiate progs. on base for USAF, USN & Marine Corps; mem: Tahoe Tavern Homeowner Assn. (pres.), Nat. Univ. Contg. Edn. Assn. (chmn. accreditation com.); author: Fundamentals of Safety Education, 3rd Edition, 1981, Energy, Power and Transportation Technology, 1987, Power & Energy Techology, 1990; mil: capt. USCGR 1951-78; Republican; Lutheran. Res/Ofc: 105 Manresa Ct Aptos 95003

BOHN, ROBERT HERBERT, lawyer; b. Sept. 2, 1935, Austin, Tx.; s. Herbert and Alice (Heinen) B.; m. Gay, June 4, 1957; children: Rebecca b. 1958, Katherine b. 1965, Robert, Jr. b. 1968; edn: BBA, Univ. Texas, 1957, LLB, 1963. Career: tax law editor Commerce Clearing House Inc., San Francisco 1964-65; atty., ptnr. The Boccardo Law Firm, San Jose 1965-87, ptnr. Law Firm of Alexander & Bohn, 1987-91; ptnr. Bohn, Bennion & Niland, 1992–; judge pro tem Superior Ct. Santa Clara Co.; lectr. Calif. Contg. Edn. of the Bar; arbitrator Am. Arbitration Assn.; Am. Bd. of Trial Advocates; Nat. Board of Trial Advocates; listed Best Lawyers in Am., Who's Who in Am. Law; mem: Calif. Trial Lawyers Assn., Assn. of Trial Lawyers of Am., Calif. State Bar Assn., Santa Clara Co. Bar Assn., Commonwealth Club, Phi Gamma Delta, Churchill Club, World Forum, Silicon Valley Capital Club; mil: capt. USAF 1958-61; First Baptist Ch. of Los Altos. Res: 14124 Pike Rd Saratoga 95070 Ofc: 50 W San Fernando St Ste 1020 San Jose 95113

BOLAND, LLOYD E., III, chiropractor; b. Nov. 29, 1953, Culver City; s. Lloyd E., Jr. and Louise E. (Appleby) B.; edn: BS biol., CSU Northridge 1977; D.C., Los Angeles Coll. of Chiropractic 1980; diplomate Nat. Bd. Chirop. Examiners 1980; cert. disability examiner, indep. med. examiner, 1984. Career: chiropractor pvt. practice, Simi Valley 1980–; honors: Delta Sigma, Dean's List CSUN and LACC (1976, 77, 80), Norka Image award (1988); mem: Calif. Chiropractic Assn., Ventura Co. Chiropractic Assn., Simi Valley Chiropractic Assn.; civic: Simi Valley C.of C. (pres. 1990-91), Govtl. Review Council (1990-91), Rotary Club Rancho Simi (bd. dirs.), Simi Valley Jaycees (pres. 1983), Simi Valley Days (co-founder, chmn. 1985-90, exec. com. 1990-91), Seniors' Easter Breakfast (sponsor 1985-89). Ofc: Boland Chiropractic 2139 Tapo St Ste 106 Simi Valley 93063

BOLAND, PAULA L., assemblywoman, State of Calif.; b. Jan. 17, 1940, Oyster Bay, N.Y.; d. Pellegrino and Joannina (Stellabotte) Mazzarelli; m.2d. Lloyd E. Boland, Jr., Aug. 13, 1976; children: Craig Wroe b. 1958, Maryssa D'Angelo b. 1959, Lloyd E. Boland III. Career: broker/owner, G.H. Realty Corp., Granada Hills, 1980-90; assemblywoman, 38th A.D., Calif. State Assembly, Granada Hills, 1990–; awards: Comm. & Political Vol. of Year, Calif. Republican Assn., 1979; Citizen of Year, Granada Hills C.of C., 1986; Woman Pioneer of Year, City of L.A., 1989; listed Who's Who in Calif., 1988; fellow mem., S.F. Valley Bd. of Realtors, 1973–; fellow mem., Calif. Assn. of Realtors, 1973–; pres., Granada Hills C.of C., 1979-81; founding dir., Bank of Granada Hills, 1983-94; pres., Granada Hills Comm. Hosp. Found., 1984-88; L.A. County delegate, Calif. Republican Party, 1974–; commr., Consumer Affairs, L.A. County, 1980-84; commr., LAFCO, L.A. County, 1985-90; Republican; Catholic. Ofc: 10727 White Oak Ave. Ste. 124 Granada Hills 91344

BOLDREY, EDWIN EASTLAND, physician, retinal surgeon; b. Dec. 8, 1941, San Francisco; s. Edwin Barkley M.D. and Helen Burns (Eastland) B.; m. Catherine Oliphant, Oct. 20, 1973; children: Jennifer Elizabeth b. 1981, Melissa Jeanne b. 1984; edn: BA w.hons., DePauw Univ. 1963; MD, Northwestern Univ. 1967; lic. physician Bd. Med. Examiners Calif. 1968. Career: intern King Co. (Harborview) Hosp., Seattle, Wash. 1967-68; gen. surgery resident Univ. Minn., Mpls. 1968-69; resident ophthalmology UCSF 1971-74; fellow diseases and surgery of retina and vitreous Wash. Univ., St. Louis, Mo. 1974-75; retinal surgeon Palo Alto Med. Clinic 1975-91, chmn. dept. ophthalmology 1990-91; clinical instr. Stanford Univ. 1975-79, clin. asst. prof. 1979-87, clin. assoc. prof. 1987–; attdg. physician VA Hosp. Palo Alto 1975-76, cons. physician 1976–; awards: UCSF Asbury 1973, Heed Ophthalmic Found. fellowship 1974-75, Honor award Am. Acad. of Ophthalmology 1989; mem: Western Retina Study Club (charter mem.; exec. secty., treas. 1983-95), Am. Acad. Ophthalmology, Vitreous Soc. (charter mem.), Retina Soc., Peninsula Eye Soc. (secty., treas. 1985-86, v.p. 1986-87, pres. 1987-88), A.C.S., AMA, CMA, Santa Clara Co. Med. Soc., Cordes Eye Soc. (pres. 1995–), Good Samaritan Hosp., San Jose (vice chmn. 1993-95, chmn. 1995–); 25+ articles pub. in sci. jours. (1966–); mil: lt. cmdr. USNR 1969-71; rec: skiing, hiking. Ofc: 2485 Hospital Drive Mountain View 94040, and 2512 Samaritan Ct. Ste A San Jose 95124

BOLEN, JOHN E., art dealer; b. Aug. 27, 1953, Fort Gordon, Ga.; s. James L., Sr. and Peggy J. (Sandstrom) B.; m. Lynne N. Uyeda, July 25, 1976; children: James b. 1979, Kate b. 1982, Claire b. 1988, Paul b. 1992; edn: BA, UCLA, 1975. Career: pres. Bolen Gallery, Inc. Santa Monica 1978-84; owner, pub. Bolen Publishing, Los Angeles 1981-84; art dealer Bolen Fine Arts, Huntington Beach 1984–. Ofc: Bolen Fine Arts PO Box 5654 Huntington Beach 92615-5654

BOLEN, LYNNE N., art dealer, consultant; b. Feb. 19, 1954, San Diego; d. Leon R. and Maria N. (Ishida) Uyeda; m. John E. Bolen, July 25, 1976; children: James b. 1979, Kate b. 1982, Claire b. 1988, Paul b. 1992; edn: BA, UCLA, 1976. Career: v.p. Bolen Gallery, Inc. Santa Monica 1978-84; owner/pub. Bolen Pub., L.A. 1981-84; mgr. Carrington Garrett, Irvine 1984-88; art dealer Bolen Fine Arts, Huntington Beach 1984–, consultant, 1988–. Ofc: Bolen Fine Arts PO Box 5654 Huntington Beach 92615-5654

BOLLINGER, WILLIAM ANTHONY, information resources manager; b. Sept. 7, 1949, Long Beach; s. Robert Louis and Marcella Ceceile (Daigle) B.; m. Coleen Joyce Petersen, Dec. 22, 1984; stepson, Christopher b. 1973; edn: BA, CSU Long Beach 1971; MS, USC, 1973. Career: info. splst. Bechtel Corp., Norwalk 1973-74, info. researcher, San Francisco 1974-78; tech. librarian Sabco, Jubail, Saudi Arabia 1978; info. mgr. Fluor Engrs. Inc., Redwood City 1978-83; document control ofcr. Lawrence Livermore Nat. Lab., Livermore 1983–; prof./lectr. Golden Gate Univ., San Francisco 1986-95; awards: USC Inez Dean scholarship 1973; Pacific Telecomm. Council Conf. invited presentation 1989-91; mem. Who's Who Info. Sci., Am. Soc. Info. Sci.; numerous papers pub. on information policy and transborder data flow; rec: mountaineering, skiing, shooting. Res: 3647 Kirkcaldy Ct Pleasanton 94588 Ofc: LLNL NAI Directorate PO Box 808 L-389 Livermore 94551

BOLMAN, ROBERT HILL, management consultant; b. Jan. 13, 1906, Lawton, Okla.; s. Robert Oliver and Sylvia (Hill) B.; m. Nevada Hayward, Apr. 7, 1930; m. 2d Edith Bain, Jan. 23, 1937; children: Gay (Stern) b. 1931, Sylvia (Fones) b. 1942; edn: grad. Shattuck Sch. 1919-23; BA, Stanford Univ. 1927. Career: asst. secty. Bishop Trust Co. Ltd., Honolulu 1927-36; asst. v.p. Union Bank, Los Angeles 1936-44; exec. v.p., dir. Pasadena 1st National, also pres., dir. Bank of Beaumont, 1944-47; v.p., dir. Oakland Bank of Commerce, 1947-54; exec. v.p., dir. Bank of California Internat., also senior v.p. The Bank of Calif., 1954-69; management cons., 1970–; resident advisor Dow Banking Corp., Zurich 1971-73; dir: Products Research and Chemical 1972-74, Computer Sci. Corp. 1973-86; past dir: Mercantile Printing Co., Bergstrom Music Co. (Honolulu), Western Die Casting, Home Found. Sav. & Loan; past mem. Bankers Assn. Fgn. Trade 1967-69, Calif. Bankers Assn., Indep. Bankers Assn. (pres. So. Calif. 1943, No. Calif. 1953); civic: Monterey Co. Bd. Suprs. 1974, chmn. bd. trustees Calif. Coll. of Arts & Crafts (emeritus), Stanford Assocs. (bd. govs., treas. 1961-62), Arthritis Found./ East Bay (pres.), Merritt-Peralta Hosp. Found. Oakland (dir.); past active mem. Honolulu Jr. Chamber (dir), Los Angeles C.of C. (govt. affairs com. 1939), San Francisco C.of C., U.S. C.of C., US Treasury War Fin. Com. 1941-45, Russian War Relief (So. Calif. dir./treas. 1942), United War Relief (dir. So. Calif. 1943), Pasa. Art Inst. (trustee 1945), Crippled Children's Fund. (dir. 1950), Alameda Co. United Fund (pres. 1958), San Francisco Ordnance Bd. of Review 1950, United Bay Area Crusade (dir. 1957), Monterey Inst. of Fgn. Studies (trustee 1972-73), Japan Soc. of S.F., World Affairs Council Palm Springs (dir. 1973), Am. Security Council (nat. advy. bd.); clubs: Claremont CC, Bohemian, Pacific Union.; Republican; Episcopalian. Address: 1860 Tice Creek Dr Waterford #1402 Walnut Creek 94595

BOMMER, WILLIAM J., professor of medicine; b. June 4, 1946, Batavia, NY; s. Roger Herbold and Gladys E. (Goade) B.; m. Marla Clary, July 26, 1976; children: Ashley b. 1977, Zachary b. 1979, Nicholas b. 1982; edn: AB, Cornell Univ., Ithaca, NY 1968; MD, SUNY, Buffalo, NY 1972. Career: med. residency SUNY, Buffalo 1972-75; cardiology fellowship UC Davis 1975-77; prof. of medicine UC Davis 1977–. Ofc: UCDMC 2315 Stockton Blvd Sacramento 95817 Tel: 916/734-2640

BONNER, JOHN ARTHUR, motion picture sound engineer; b. Jan. 21, 1929, Pueblo, Colo.; s. Arthur Dewey and Luella Marie (McCown) B.; m. Lila Cumings, Oct. 24, 1948, div. 1972; children: Diane Marie Kane, Carol Anne Collins, Nadine Brock; m. Shirley, Mar. 23, 1973; edn: undergrad. Occidental Coll.; BS, UCLA, 1962. Career: sound engr. 20th Century Fox Film Corp., Beverly Hills 1954-60, dir. sound 1968-75; engr. TODDAO, Hollywood 1960-63; dir. special proj. Warner Hollywood Studios, 1975–; awards: Acad. of Motion Picture Arts & Scis. Medal of Commendation 1995; mem: Soc. Motion Picture and TV Engrs. (Fellow, Samuel L. Warner award 1989), Audio Engring. Soc., Academy Motion Picture Arts and Scis. (bd. govs., chmn. sci. technology 1988–); mil: capt. USAF 1949-53, ETO; Republican; Presbyterian; rec: bicycling, woodworking. Ofc: Warner Hollywood Studios, 1041 N Formosa Ave Hollywood 90046

BONO, SONNY SALVATORE, congressman, singer, composer, former mayor; b. Feb. 16, 1935, Detroit, Mich.; m. Donna Rankin; children: Christy, Santo, Jean; m. Cher LaPiere, Oct. 27, 1964 (div.); 1 child, Chastity; m. Susie Coehlo (div.); m. Mary Whitaker, Mar. 1986; 1 child, Chesare Elan. Career: songwriter, later artist and repertoire man for Speciality Records; singer with Cher as team Sonny and Cher, 1964.-74, co-star The Sonny and Cher Show, 1976-77; solo night club act; numerous recs., TV, concert and benefit appearances; has appeared on TV series The Love Boat; composer, lyricist, appearance in Good Times, 1966; films include: Escape to Athena, 1979, Airplane 11-The Sequel, 1982, Hairspray, 1988; producer film: Chastity, 1969; composer: A Cowboy's Work is Never Done, I Got You, Babe. others; TV video Nitty Gritty Hour with Cher, 1992. Restaurateur; mayor Palm Springs, Calif., 1988-92; cand. U.S. Senate, 1992; mem. 104th Congress from Calif. dist. 1995–. Ofc: c/o LaRocca Talent Group 3800 Barham Blvd Ste 105 Los Angeles CA 90068-1042 also: PO Box 1786 32 E Tahgutz-McCullum Way Palm Springs CA 92262 also: U.S. House of Representatives Washington DC 20515

BOOK, RONALD VERNON, professor of theoretical computer science; b. March 5, 1937, Los Angeles; s. Vernon LeRoy and Agnes Pearl (Andersen) B.; m. Celia Wrathall, July 12, 1975; edn: BA, Grinnell Coll. 1958; MAT, Wesleyan Univ. 1960; MA, 1964; PhD, Harvard Univ. 1969. Career: instr. Boston State Coll., Mass. 1965-66; lectr. Boston Coll. Chestnut Hill, Mass. 1967-69; asst. prof. Harvard Univ., Cambridge, Mass. 1969-73, assoc. prof. 1973-75; Yale Univ., New Haven, Conn. 1975-77; prof. UCSB 1976–; ed. Theoretical Computer Sci. 1974–; Math. Systems Theory 1975–; editl. bd. Jour. Symbolic Computation 1985–; ed. in chief Research Notes in Theoretical Computer Sic. 1984–; ed. in chief Progress in Theoretical Computer Sci. 1991–; honors: hon. prof. Univ. Nacional San Antonio Abad, Cuzco, Peru 1975, hon. faculty mem. Beijing Computer Inst., People's Republic of China 1988, sr. U.S. scientist award Alexander von Humboldt Found. 1990-91, res. fellowship Japan Soc. for Promotion of Sci. 1992; mem: Assn. Computing Machinery, Soc. Indsl. & Applied Math., European Assn. Theoretical Computer Sci. (bd. govs. 1977-85); ed. Formal Language Theory: Perspectives & Open Problems, 1980, Studies in Complexity Theory, 1986; author: String-Rewriting Systems (with Friedrich Otto, 1993), 95+ articles pub. in research and profl. jours. Address: Goleta 93117

BOOLOOTIAN, RICHARD A., software systems company president; b. Oct. 17, 1927, Fresno; s. Vanig and Vivian (Ohannesian) B.; m. Mary Jo Blue, Oct. 18, 1972 (div. 1981); m. Yvonne Morse, Aug. 12, 1988 (div. 1995); children: Mark b. 1958, Alan b. 1959, Craig b. 1960; edn: BA, CSU Fresno 1951; MA, 1953; PhD, Stanford Univ. 1957. Career: research asst. Stanford Univ., Pacific Grove 1957; assoc. prof. UCLA 1957-67; sci. cons. Univ. Colo., Boulder 1967-68; pres. and c.e.o. Science Software Systems Co., Inc., Sherman Oaks 1968–; cons. Morler Internat., Burbank 1985-93; Mira Assoc., Costa Mesa 1974–; sci. cons. Mirman Sch. for Gifted, Los Angeles 1974–; dir. Mirman Sch. Summer Sci. Explorations 1989–; awards: Lalor fellow 1964, 65, NIH fellow 1965, outstanding tchr. award Johns Hopkins Univ. 1990, nominee excellence in tchg. Presdl. Award (1990, 91, 92, 93); mem: AAAS, Challenger Soc., Aircraft Owners & Pilots Assn; author: 22 text books on ecology, zoology, physiology, human anatomy and biology, 3000+ audio visual programs pub. and copyrighted, 200+ articles pub. in scholarly jours. (1955-70); mil: USAF 1944-46; Democrat; Prot.; rec: scuba diving, flying, tennis. Res: 3576 Woodcliff Rd Sherman Oaks 91403

BOOS, WAYNE WILLIAM, tax consultant, certified public accountant; b. June 20, 1963, Reedley; s. August George and Helen Marie (Froehmer) B.; edn: AA, Kings River Coll. 1983; BS business admin.-acct., CSU Fresno 1985; MS fin. acctg., 1986; C.P.A. Career: inventory acct. Ito Packing Co. Inc., Reedley 1979-86; staff acct. Ernst & Young, Fresno 1986-87, sr. tax cons. 1987-89; tax mgr. Ernst & Young 1989-94, tax senior mgr. 1994; tax sr. mgr. Deloitte & Touche LLP, 1994–; awards: Kings River Coll. Bus. Student of Year 1983; mem: Inst. of Mgmt. Accountants, Calif. Soc. CPA, Am. Inst. CPA, Kings River

Country Club, Sherwood Forest Mens Club; Lutheran; rec: golf, skiing, travel. Res: 4919 N Millbrook #112 Fresno 93726 Ofc: Deloitte & Touche LLP 5260 N Palm Ave Ste 300 Fresno 93704

BOOTH, GENE, publishing executive; b. June 24, 1932, Springfield, Ill.; s. Forrest Everett Booth and Mary Eloise (Hill) Sapp; m. Dolores Annabel Porter, April 18, 1954 (div. 1959); m. Dagny Palmer Tennyson, July 2, 1976; children: Mark Eugene b. 1954, David Eric b. 1956, Britt Erinn b. 1982; edn: BS, Bradley Univ. 1954; tchg. credential Calif. Comm. Colls. Career: reporter, ed. Peoria Jour. Star, Peoria, Ill. 1951-61; ed., co-pub. The Observer 1961-62; assoc. ed. Road & Track Mag., Newport Beach 1962-66; freelance photojournalist 1966-75; pub. mgr. Golden West Coll., Huntington Beach 1975-79; KOCE-T.V. 1979-82; pub. cons. Moonlight Press, Westminster 1982-90; ed. Touring America Mag., Irvine 1990-94; pub. Bowtie Press, Irvine 1994-; cons Express Pictures, Westminster 1993-; mem: Pub. Mktg. Assn. (bd. mem. 1989-91), Calif. Press Photographers Assn. (exec. dir. 1989-92), Western Pub. Assn.; articles pub. in automotive and aviation mags., 1962-75, pub. book Countdown to Retirement for Educators (Riles Heinzman 1989); mil: 1st lt. USAFR 1956-61. Address: EXPRESS Pictures Box 994 Westminster 92684-0994

BOOTH, GEOFFREY KEMP, physician, associate professor of psychiatry; b. Feb. 4, 1947, Dayton, Ohio; s. Alfred B. and Jacqueline (Kinney) B.; edn: BA, Yale Univ. 1969; MD, Georgetown Univ. Med. Sch., W.D.C. 1973; residency in psychiatry Naval Regional Med. Ctr., Oakland, Calif. 1973-76; med. lic., St. of Calif. 1976; diplomat Nat. Bd. of Med. Examiners 1976; cert. Am. Bd. of Neurology & Psychiatry 1981. Career: chief of psychiatry Naval Hosp., Roosevelt Roads, Puerto Rico 1976-78; dir. of residency tng. Naval Regional Med. Ctr., Oakland, Calif. 1978-80; asst. med. dir. Veterans Affairs Med. Ctr., S.F. 1980-82, asst. chief of mental hygiene clinic 1982-86, chief of psychiatric outpatient svs. 1986-; asst. clin. prof. psychiatry UC San Francisco Sch. of Medicine 1981-92, assoc. tng. dir. psychiatry 1982-86, assoc. clin. prof. 1992-; clin. investigator Eli Lilly Co. 1993-; indep. academic reviewer, US Army Letterman Army Med. Ctr.; participant NIH task force on psychiatry edn. on minority issues; awards: Naval Med. Corps Commendation, Puerto Rico 1978, Tchr. of Yr. award NRMC, Oakland 1979, Faculty Tchg. award UC S.F. 1984; mem: AMA 1976-, Am. Psychiatric Assn. 1976-, No. Calif. Psychiatric Soc., Assn. of Mil. Surgeons of U.S., Nat. Assn. Veterans Affairs Physicians, Faculty UC S.F. Alumni Assn. 1982-; author: num. articles pub. in profl. jours., textbook chapters, 1984-; mil: comdr. USN 1972-80; rec: horticulture/botany, med. writing and clinical research. Ofc: San Francisco 94121

BORGES, CARLOS R., professor of mathematics; b. Feb. 17, 1939, Sao Miguel, Azores, nat. U.S. citizen 1965; s. Jose Jacinto Rego and Maria (Rego) Borges; m. Margaret Freitas, Jan. 30, 1958; children: Mary Lou b. 1960, Carlos b. 1961, Michael b. 1962; edn: BS in math., Humboldt State Coll., Arcata 1960; MS in math., Univ. Wash., Seattle 1962, PhD in math., 1964. Career: asst. prof. Univ. of Nevada, Reno 1964-65; asst. prof. Univ. Calif., Davis 1965-68, assoc. prof. 1968-72, full prof. math. 1972-; awards: Fulbright-Hayes, Univ. Coimbra, Portugal 1972; Republican; R.Cath.; rec: tennis. Res: 921 Fordham Dr Davis 95616 Ofc: Dept. Math. Univ. of California, Davis 95616

BORGES, DAVID JOSEPH, lawyer; b. May 10, 1955, Tulare; s. Joseph R., Jr. and Rosemary (Rogers) B.; children: David J., Jr. b. 1981, Derek J. b. 1983, Dylan J. b. 1985, Daniel J. b. 1987; edn: BA (magna cum laude), CSU Northridge, 1977; JD (magna cum laude), USC, 1980; admitted bar: Calif. 1980, US Dist. Ct. ea. dist. Calif. 1980, US Supreme Ct. 1986, Fla. Supreme Ct. 1994, Wash. D.C. Ct. of Appeals 1995; cert. splst. in family law 1985-. Career: atty., assoc. Stringham, Rogers & Graves, Tulare 1980-83, ptnr. 1983-86; pres. David J. Borges, A Law Corp., Visalia 1985-; bd. dirs. Assn. of Cert. Family Law Specialists 1995; honors: Phi Alpha Theta, Pi Gamma Mu, USC Scholar 1977-80; mem: ABA, Calif. Bar Assn., Assn. of Trial Lawyers of Am., Calif. Trial Lawyers Assn., Tulare Co. Bar Assn. (dir. 1982-89), Tulare Co. Trial Lawyers (dir. 1982-90), Kings Co. Bar Assn., Calif. Orgn. of Small Bar Assn., Stockton (dir. 1987-); Republican (life mem. Rep. Nat. Com. 1980-, life mem. Rep. Nat. Lawyers Assn. 1985-); life mem. Shotokan Karate of Am. 1973-. Ofc: David J. Borges, ALC, 3330 W Mineral King Ste H Visalia 93291-5762

BORNEMAN, JOHN PAUL (JAY), pharmaceutical executive, writer; b. Oct. 18, 1958, Darby, Pa.; s. John A., III and Ann E. (Conway) B.; m. Anne Marie Albert, July 18, 1980; children: Elizabeth b. 1983; edn: BS in chem., St. Joseph's Univ., 1980, MS chem. 1983, MBA fin. 1987. Career: v.p. Boiron Borneman, Norwood, Pa. 1980-86; dir. mktg. Standard Homeopathic Co., Los Angeles 1986-88, vice pres. 1988-; bd. dirs. Nat. Ctr. for Homeopathy, W.D.C. 1986-; editor Homeopathic Pharmacopoeia of U.S., W.D.C. 1988-; chmn. Council on Homeopathic Edn., W.D.C. 1988-; columnist Resonance Mag., 1986-; mem. Am. Pharmaceutical Assn. (chmn. legal & regulatory affairs 1986-), Am. Chem. Soc., Am. Pharmaceutical Assn., Nat. Assn. of Chain Drug Stores, Sigma Xi.

BOROW, RICHARD HENRY, lawyer; June 19, 1935, New York; s. Joseph and Dorothy (Graze) B.; m. Trudy F., June 8, 1958; children: Harlan b. 1959, Carolyn b. 1961, Jennifer b. 1964; edn: BA econ. Hunter Coll. 1956; LLB,

Columbia Univ. Sch. Law 1959; admitted Bar N.Y. 1959, Calif. 1966, Me. 1985. Career: atty., assoc. Paul Weiss Rifkind Wharton and Garrison, N.Y.C. 1959-60; Poletti Freidin Prashker Feldman and Gartner 1961-65; Irell & Manella (listed in every edit. of The Best Lawyers in Am.), Los Angeles 1965-, ptnr. and chair litigation group, 1968-; adj. prof. UCLA Sch. Law 1971-83; appt. advy. com. of Cent. Dist. of Calif., Civil Justice Reform Act; awards: Hunter Coll. Athletic Hall of Fame, Harlan Fiske Stone scholar, Rev. Charles Parkhurst honor scholar, bd. eds. Columbia Law Review; mem: State Bar Assns. of Calif., N.Y. & Maine, Am. Law Inst., Am. Judicature Soc., Am. Bar Assn., L.A. Co. Bar Assn. (Judiciary Com. chmn 1983-84, Assn. Bar of N.Y.C., Assn. Bus. Trial Lawyers (bd. govs. 1983-84); civic bds: trustee Public Advocates Inc. (S.F. 1983-93), Ctr. for Pub. Resources Inc. (alternative dispute resolution panel); clubs: Brentwood Country Club, Falmouth Country Club; bd. eds. Fed. Litigation Guide; num. lectures and articles for contg. edn. of bar programs sponsored by Practising Law Inst., ABA Am. Law Inst., Calif. CEB, Legal Times Wash., USC Law Center; rec: golf. Ofc: Irell & Manella, 1800 Ave of the Stars Ste 900 Los Angeles 90067 Ph: 310/277-1010

BOROWSKY, PHILIP, lawyer; b. Oct. 9, 1946, Phila.; s. Joshua and Gertrude (Nicholson) Borowsky; m. Judith Goldwasser, Sept. 5, 1970; children: Miriam, b. 1971, Manuel b. 1975, Nora, b. 1981; edn: BA, UCLA 1967, JD, Univ. of S.F. Law Sch. 1973. Career: atty. law firm Cartwright, Slobodin, Bokelman, Borowsky, Wartnick, Moore & Harris, Inc., San Francisco 1973-, ptnr. 1978-, pres. 1988-; currently pres. Cartwright, Bokelman, Borowsky, Moore, Harris, Alexander & Gruen, Inc.; arbitrator Am. Arbitration Assn., mem. Arbitration Panel S.F. Superior Ct.; adj. faculty Hastings Las Sch. 1981-82; spkr. for Practising Law Inst.; mem. Calif. Trial Lawyers Assn. (legis. com.); McAuliffe Hon. Soc. U.S.F. Law Sch.; contbr. law revs.; publ: co-author, Unjust Dismissal; bd. of Editorial Consultants of Bad Faith Law Update; mil: spec.4th cl. US Army, Army Commendn. Medal; Democrat; Jewish; rec: sports. Ofc: 101 California St 26th Flr San Francisco 94111

BORRELL, JERRY, company president; b. May 23, 1952, El Paso, Tx.; s. Gerald and Harriet B.; edn: BA, Univ. Miami 1976; MS, Catholic Univ. Wash. D.C. 1981. Career: researcher Library of Congress, Wash. D.C. 1976-79; co-editor Electronic Publishing Review, Oxford, England 1979-80; sr. editor Computer Graphics World, San Francisco 1980-81; ed. in chief Digital Design, Boston, Mass. 1981-83; sr. ed. Mini Micro Systems 1983-85; ed. in chief Macworld, San Francisco 1985-92; pres. and ed. in chief, Sumeria 1992-; mem: Soc. Profl. Journalists. Res: 2000 Broadway #712 San Francisco 94115 Ofc: 329 Bryant St Ste 3D San Francisco 94107

BORT, RICHARD, consultant, author; b. Aug. 2, 1941, Glen Ridge, N.J.; s. Louis and Eleanor (Goldberg) B.; m. Judi Leisten, June 20, 1963; 1 son, Randall b. 1964; edn: BA econ. (with honors), Colgate Univ. 1963; MBA banking, fin., N.Y. Univ. 1969. Career: asst. treas. Bankers Trust Co., N.Y.C. 1964-70; mgr. bank rels. Daylin Inc., Beverly Hills 1970-75; asst. treas. 20th Century Fox Film Co. 1975-82; Computer Scis. Corp., El Segundo 1982-84; v.p., sales mgr. Wells Fargo Bank, Los Angeles 1984-85; treasury mgr. Circus Circus Enterprises, Las Vegas, Nev. 1985-86; pres. Richard Bort & Assoc., Sherman Oaks 1986-; mem: Treasury Mgmt. Assn., ANSI ASCX12, Treasury Assn. So. Calif.; author: Corp. Cash Mgmt. Handbook, 1989, Handbook of EDI, 1994, articles pub. in profl. jours., 1984-89; exec. editor Jour. of Working Capital Mgmt.; rec: gardening, golf. Ofc: Bort & Company Inc POB 55394 Sherman Oaks 91413

BORUN, GEORGE ANTHONY, scientific instruments company president; b. July 27, 1932, Milwaukee, Wis.; s. Thaddeus Theopholus and Sophia Barbara (Synowitz) B.; m. Bernys Jo Veverka, May 10, 1958; children: Mark Anthony b. 1959, Michael George b. 1960; edn: Wright Jr. Coll. 1950-52; Ill. Inst. Tech. 1952; BS, Northwestern Univ. 1963; MA, CSU Los Angeles 1975; PhD, Calif. Pac. Univ. 1978. Career: chief chemist Martin Marietta Div., Wheeling, Ill.; dir. pollution control Bataille Engrs., Barrington, Ill. 1967-69; product mgr. Culligan Internat., Northbrook, Ill. 1969-72; founder, v.p. engring. Ecotech Inc., Los Angeles and Cardiff 1971-72; v.p. sales and mktg. Sci. Application Internat. Inc., La Jolla 1972-78; founder, pres. La Jolla Scientific Co., San Diego, currently; honors: BSA scouters key; mem: Am. Nuclear Sco., Health Physics Soc., Am. Soc. Testing of Materials, Am. Chem. Soc., So. Calif. Assn. Violin Makers; papers pub. in Analytical Chemistry, ed. 2 symposia proceedings; mil: pvt. 1c. AUS 1952-54; Methodist; rec: violin making, art. Address: San Diego 92121

BOSSEAU, DON L., library services director; b. Nov. 28, 1936, Pittsburg, Kans.; s. Demar and Jessie (Bartoletti) B.; m. Dawn, Nov. 19, 1983; edn: BS in engring., Kans. State Univ. 1958; MS in nuclear engring., Univ. Kans. 1961; MLS, Univ. Hawaii 1966. Career: nuclear engr. Gen. Atomic, La Jolla 1960-65; asst. univ. librarian UC San Diego 1966-72; univ. librarian Univ. Tx., El Paso 1972-73; dir. libraries, Emory Univ., Atlanta, Ga. 1973-77; Univ. Hawaii, Honolulu 1977-82; dir. library svcs. San Diego State Univ., Calif. 1982-; co-chair Mayor of San Diego's City of the Future Task Force on a Wired City 1993-94; v.p./pres. elect Calif. Academic/Res. Librarians Assn. 1994-96; chair Calif. State Univ. Library Directors' Council 1990-91; No. Am. editor Information Mgmt. Report (Oxford, England 1993-); co-editor Jour. of Academic

Librarianship, VISIONS column 1994–; mem. Calif. State Lib. Networking Task Force 1995–; cons. Ednl. Data Systems Corp., Newport Beach 1969-72; v.p., bd. dirs. INFILL PHOT, Oceanside 1971-75; ed. Jour. of Library Automation-Tech. Comm. 1972-77; honors: Kappa Mu Epsilon (1956), Phi Beta Delta; mem: Library Automation Research and Cons. Assn. (pres. 1975), Am. Library Assn., Library Automation Discussion Gp. (chmn. 1970-75); civic: Univ. City Racquet Club (bd. dirs. 1986–), Marine Towers Honolulu (bd. dirs. 1981); author: Impact of Inflation on American Libraries, Library Assn. of Australia, 1982, and The Computer in Serials Processing and Control, Advances in Librainanship, vol. 2 (Academic Press 1971), presentation "Ramifications of New Technologies on Libraries: The Good and the Bad" Gov.'s Conf. on the Future of Libraries, Las Vegas (2/7/90); Democrat; Christian Ch.; rec: surfing, tennis, film making. Res: 3257 Erie St San Diego 92117 Ofc: San Diego State Univ San Diego 92182

BOSSEN, DAVID AUGUST, manufacturing company president; b. Jan. 9, 1927, Clinton, Ia.; m. Darlene Phelps, Aug. 10, 1991; children: Alison, Amy, Julie, Laura; edn: US Naval Acad., Annapolis 1946-49; BS, M.I.T., 1951. Career: indsl. engr. Alcoa, Davenport, Ia., 1951; v.p./gen. mgr. Industrial Nucleonics, Columbus, Oh., 1951-67; founder, chmn. and c.e.o. Measurex Corp., Cupertino 1968–; mem.: M.I.T. Corporation Devel. Com., Santa Clara Co. Mfg. Group (dir.), Bay Area Council (dir.); patentee: several in process control; mil: USMC 1945-46. Ofc: Measurex Corp. One Results Way Cupertino 95014

BOST, THOMAS GLEN, lawyer; b. July 13, 1942, Oklahoma City, Okla.; s. Burl J. and Lorene (Croka) B.; m. Sheila Kay Pettigrew, Aug. 27, 1966; children: Amy b. 1970, Stephen Luke b. 1974, Emily b. 1976, Paul b. 1980; edn: BS (summa cum laude) Abilene Christian Univ., 1964; JD, Vanderbilt Univ. Sch. of Law, 1967. Career: instr. David Lipscomb Coll., Nashville, Tenn. 1967; asst. prof. of law Vanderbilt Univ. Sch. of Law, 1967-68; atty. Latham & Watkins, Los Angeles 1968–; honors: Vanderbilt Univ. Sch. of Law Founder's Medal, Order of the Coif 1967; chmn. bd. of regents Pepperdine Univ., also mem. exec., religious stds. coms., and bd. visitors Sch. of Law; mem: Am. Bar Assn. (tax. sect., chair com. on stds. of tax practice 1988-90); clubs: California (L.A.), The Beach (L.A.); State Bar of Calif., L.A. County Bar Assn. (1968–, taxation sect. 1981-82); publs: articles on taxation in Vanderbilt Law Rev., NYU Inst. on Fed. Taxation, Major Tax Planning (USC), Calif. Lawyer; Republican; Culver-Palms Ch. of Christ; rec: reading, hiking. Ofc: Latham & Watkins, 633 W Fifth St Ste 4000 Los Angeles 90071-2007

BOSTIC, BYRON MICHAEL, electronic manufacturers' representative; b. Oct. 17, 1952, Royal Oak, Mich.; s. Clyde Wm. and Barbara Joanne (Kinshella) B.; m. 4th. Melanie D. Lavell, Mar. 15, 1984; children: Byron, II b. 1975, Vanessa b. 1977; edn: electronic engr. E.I.T., Detroit, Mich. 1974; lic. R.E. agt. Calif. Career: quality control tech. Allen Bradley, Ann Arbor, Mich. 1972-73; computer engr. Litton A.B.S., Long Beach 1974-76; q.c. engr. Rockwell Internat., Newport Beach 1977-79; video engr. J.V.C. Corp., Compton 1979-81; sales engr. Sencore Corp., 1981-82; Stanford Applied Engring., 1982-83; sales mgr. So. Calif., Basic Systems Corp., 1983-85; sales engr. Lambda Power Supplies, 1985-86; owner Dynamic Planning Consultants, So. Calif., 1983–, ptnr. West Coast Reps, Western USA, 1986–; mem. Lancaster C.of C.; realtor assoc. Century 21 LWL Realtors, Granada Hills 1988-89, Century 21 Tabor Realtors, 1989-90; High-Speed Data Transmission - HYBRICON, Real-Time Transfers - C.E.S., Geneva, Switz. 1990; recipient corporate awards for tech. and sales excellence Litton 1974, Rockwell 1977, Sencore 1981, image processing Datacube, Peabody, Mass. 1986, live multiprocessing Ironics, Ithaca, N.Y. 1987; VMEBUS+ Force Computers, Campbell 1990; complete image processing, Imaging Technology 1991; vectorizing code on: 860 Sky Computers, Chelmsford, Mass. 1992; Fiber-optic data distbn. interface Interphase, Dallas, Tx. 1992; multiprocessing VME /SUN /PC /Futurebus- Elma, Fremont 1992; real-time data acquisition interfaces- Acromag, Wixom, Mi. (1992); transducers/ strain gages/ load cells/ and accelerometers, Kyowa/Soltec, San Fernando 1992; Songwriter award, So. Calif. Songwriters Guild 1979, winner Battle of the Bands, Gazarri's, Hollywood 1980; organic fruit tree & vegetable farmer; guitar player/ singer/ songwriter, author song and lyrics: Sweet Southern Gal, 1979, Joy of Life, 1979, Flying Down the Highway Again, 1981, I Just Want to Rock N' Roll, 1982; Democrat; rec: pets. Ofc: 441 E Whittier Blvd Ste 3A La Habra 90631 Ph: 310/690-9960 FAX 310/697-6167

BOTKIN, DANIEL BENJAMIN, biologist, educator; b. Aug. 19, 1937, Oklahoma City, Okla.; s. Benjamin Albert and Gertrude (Fritz) B.; m. Ellen Chase, Dec. 22, 1962 (div. 1976); children: Nancy, Jonathan; m. Erene Victoria Youngberg, Apr. 7, 1978; edn: BA, Univ. Rochester, 1959; MA, Univ. Wis., 1962; PhD, Rutgers Univ., 1968. Career: from asst. to assoc. prof. Yale Univ., New Haven, 1968-76; assoc. scientist Marine Biol. Lab., Woods Hole, Mass., 1976-78; prof. biology Univ. Calif., Santa Barbara, 1978-93; pres. Ctr. for the Study of the Environment, Santa Barbara 1992–; dir. Prog. on Global Change, Geo. Mason Univ., Fairfax, VA 1993–; chmn. environ. studies prog. 1978-85; awards: Bernard Edward Ferow Award for International Forestry 1995, First Prize, Mitchell Internat. Prize for Sustainable Devel. 1991; fellow Rockefeller Bellagio Inst., Italy, 1985, East-West Ctr., Honolulu, 1985-88, Woodrow Wilson Internat. Ctr. for Scholars, Wash., 1977-78; grantee NSF, NASA, NOAA, Mellon Found., Pew Charitable Trusts, W. Alton Jones Found., World Wildlife Fund, SOHIO Alaska Corp.; mem: AAAS, Ecol. Soc. Am., Am. Soc. Naturalists, Brit. Ecol. Soc.; author: Environmental Science: Earth as a Living Planet, 1995, Our National History: The Lessons of Lewis and Clark, 1995, Forest Dynamics: An Ecological Model, 1993, Discordant Harmonies: A New Ecology for the 21st Century, 1990; co-editor: Changing The Global Environment, 1989; coauthor: Environmental Studies, 1982, 87, software, JABOWA model of forest growth, 1970; contbr. articles to profl. jours.; rec: aircraft piloting, music, photog., hiking. Ofc: Center For The Study Of The Environment Santa Barbara 93101

BOTWIN, HARVEY JEROME, economist; b. Dec. 5, 1940, NY, NY; s. Abraham and Lillian Pearl (Kiel) B.; m. Harriet Lefkovits, Jan. 26, 1963; children: Alan b. 1967, Michele b. 1971; edn: BA, Univ. Miami, 1961, MA, 1963; MA, Princeton Univ., 1965. Career: asst. instr. econs. Univ. of Miami, Coral Gables 1962-63; Princeton Univ. 1965-66, instr. econs. 1966-67; asst. prof., assoc. prof. prof. economics Pitzer Coll., Claremont 1967–, prof. econs. The Claremont Grad. Sch. 1982–; cons. in economics, Los Angeles 1984–; fellow Found. for Econ. Edn., Bank of Am., San Francisco 1968; vis. research assoc. The Internat. Labor Orgn., Geneva, Switz. (1979), The European Univ. Inst., Florence, Italy (1983), The European Econ. Community, Brussels, Belgium (1986). Res: 696 W Tenth St Claremont 91711 Ofc: Pitzer College Claremont 91711; (consulting) Beverly Towers Ste 215 1115 S Elm Dr Los Angeles 90035

BOUCHARD, PAUL EUGENE, artist; b. Sept. 26, 1946, Providence, R.I.; s. Paul Marcel and Anna Thersa (Dullea) B.; m. Ann Marie Jones, Nov. 18, 1971, div. 1976; 1 son, Michael Paul; edn: att. Chouinard Art Inst. 1964, El Camino Coll., Torrance 1976; BFA, CSU Long Beach, 1978. Career: E-3, US Navy, 1967-68; recipient award for contbn. to the arts City of Torrance 1985; art in permanent collections: Grants Pass (OR) Mus. of Art, El Camino Coll., Angeles Gate Cultural Ctr. (San Pedro), Art Mus. (CSULB), Municipal Art Collection (Bev. Hills), Sanctuario de Chimayo (NM), Maturango Mus. (Ridgecrest, CA), Coos Art Mus. (Coos Bay, OR), Constnl. Rights Found. (L.A.), Univ. South Dakota, US Dept. of State Art in Embassies Pgm., Combined Forces Mus. of Art, Milperra, NSW Australia; solo exhibitions include: Tylan Intl. Corp. Ofcs. (Carson), Joslyn Ctr. for Arts (Torrance) 1982; Cassman Group (Torrance), El Camino Coll., 1984; Rogue Coll. (Grants Pass, OR) 1987; Maturango Mus., Richmond (CA) Art Ctr., 1988; Franklin Furnace Mus. (NYC) 1988/9; Chabot Coll., Steve Bush Exh. Room (NYC), 1989; Univ. S.D. 1991, Brand Library Art Gals. (Glendale, CA) 1992; numerous group exh. incl. The Australian Nat. Gallery. Res: 33140 Baldwin Blvd Lake Elsinore 92530 Ph: 909/678-7384

BOURGAIZE, LINDA HARPER, special education administrator; b. May 1, 1947, Tacoma, Wash.; d. Donald William and Helen (Harper) Bourgaize; son, Matthew b. 1977; edn: BA, San Jose St. Univ. 1971; MS, 1973. Career: psychologist Whitman Sch. Dist., Mountain View 1973; psychologist, coordinator, dir. Mount Pleasant Sch. Dist., San Jose 1973-81; dir. San Benito/Santa Cruz Counties Spl. Edn. Local Plan Area (SELPA), Aptos 1981-91; pvt. educational cons. 1991-93; dir. Washington Township SELPA and dir., Special Svs., Fremont Unified Sch. Dist.; past chair La Selva Beach Recreation Dist.; appt. Calif. St. Dept. Edn. Spl. Edn. Funding Model Task Force 1986-88; mem. Interag. Task Force, Assemblyman Sam Farr 1984-90; steering com. Coalition for Adequate Funding for Disabled Children, 1987-93; cons. Calif. State Dept. Edn. 1975–; awards: La Selva Beach Recreation Dist. SCOPE 1986; mem: Phi Delta Kappa, Calif. SELPA Adminstrs. (chair 1989-90, legislative/finance chair 1991–), Assn. Calif. Sch. Adminstrs. (chair spl. edn. conf. 1986, 87), Council for Exceptional Children-Calif. Assn. of Sch. Bus. Officials, Am. Assn. Sch. Adminstrs., Assn. Supervision & Curriculum Devel., PEO, League Women Voters; Am. Assn. of Univ. Women; Democrat; rec: needlework, travel, politics. Res: 27 Altivo Ave La Selva Beach 95076

BOWER, KATHLEEN ANN, communications and marketing professional; b. Feb. 10, 1962, Stanford, Calif.; d. E. George and Joan Martine (Sorensen) Bower; edn: BS in bus. adminstrn./mktg., San Jose St. Univ. 1984. Career: editl. splst. Regis McKenna Inc., Palo Alto 1980-82; dir. mktg. InterSight Comms. Inc., Los Gatos 1982-84; account exec. Rudolph Design Inc., Santa Cruz 1985; promotional programs mgr. 3Com Corp., Santa Clara 1986-88; group mktg. comms. mgr. Software Pub. Corp., Santa Clara 1988-92; dir. mktg. commn. Global Village Communication, Inc., Mountain View 1993–; columnist San Jose FILM CLIPS Newsletter, San Jose 1982-84; editor PARTNERS Newsletter, Santa Clara 1986-87; co-founder, CONNECT, The Jour. of Computer Networking 1987; honors: ballet Royal Acad. Dance 1968; mem: Am. Mktg. Assn., Peninsula Women in Advt., Pub. Rels. Soc. Am., San Jose Film Commn., S.F. Film & Video Commn., Profl. Media Network (bd. dirs. 1985-86), Beta Gamma Sigma. Res: 509 26th Ave Santa Cruz 95062 Ofc: Global Village Communication, Inc. 685 E. Middlefield Rd Mountain View 94043

BOWER, PAUL GEORGE, lawyer; b. April 21, 1933, Chicago, Ill.; s. Chester Lee and Retha Mae (Dausman) B.; m. Elreen Lore Thurlow, June 23, 1962; children: Stephanie b. 1964, Julienne b. 1966, Aimee b. 1970; edn: BA, Rice Univ.

1955; postgrad., Calif. Inst. Tech. 1959-60; LL.B, Stanford Law Sch. 1963. Career: atty., assoc. Gibson Dunn & Crutcher, L.A. 1963-67; asst. dir. Nat. Advy. Com. Civil Disorder, Wash. D.C. 1967-68; spl. asst. to Dep. Atty. Gen. U.S. Dept. Justice 1968-69, consumer counsel 1969; ptnr. Gibson Dunn & Crutcher, L.A. 1971–; mem: L.A. Co. Bar Assn., Calif. Bar Assn., Am. Bar Assn., Sierra Club Legal Defense Fund Inc. (trustee 1982–), Legal Aid Found. (dir. 1975-80, pres. 1979-80), Legal Svs. Trust Fund Commn. (mem. 1990-93, chair 1993), deputy gen. counsel Webster Commn.1992; mil: sgt. AUS 1956-59; Democrat. Ofc: Gibson Dunn & Crutcher 2029 Century Park E Ste 4000 Los Angeles 90067

BOWERS, JOHN EDWARD, director, optical switching technology center, professor, physicist; b. June 7, 1954, St. Paul, Minn.; s. Charles Edward and Audrey Sigurd (Hanson) B.; m. Cynthia Merle Durbahn, Aug. 14, 1978; children: Eric David b. 1982, Steven Michael b. 1985; edn: BS, Univ. Minn. 1976; MS, Stanford Univ. 1978; PhD, 1981. Career: scientist Honeywell Corp., Materials Sci. Center, Mpls. 1978-79; research asst. Ginzton Lab., Stanford Univ. 1976-78, 1979-81; research assoc. 1981-82; mem. tech. staff AT&T Bell Labs., Holmdel, N.J. 1982-87; prof. UC Santa Barbara 1987–; meeting chmn. IEEE, LEOS, chair IPRM Conf. 1994; program chair CLEO Conf. 1994; advy. bd. Internat. Jour. Optoelectronics, England 1986–; local arrangements chmn. Device Research Conf., Santa Barbara 1990; guest ed. Jour. Quantum Electron., N.Y. 1989, chmn. LEOS Subcom. on Semiconductor Lasers; cons. Rockwell, Optical Concepts; honors: Phi Beta Kappa, Sigma Xi, Pres.'s Young Investigator award 1988; mem: IEEE (fellow), OSA, APS, SPIE; 16 patents in field, 4 book chpts. pub., 170+ papers pub. in tech. jours.; rec: tennis, sailing, chess. Ofc: Dept. ECE, Univ. of Calif., Santa Barbara 93106

BOWERS, WILLIAM JAMES, data corporation executive, ret.; b. Oct. 31, 1928, San Diego; s. James Parsons and Elizabeth (Richert) B.; m. Joanne Grassl, Aug. 2, 1958; children: Laura b. 1960, Kerry b. 1962, Bill b. 1967; edn: BS advt., USC 1951; BSEE, UCLA 1958. Career: founder MSI Data Corp., Costa Mesa 1967-1989 (ret.); dir: Storage Concepts Inc., Quality Systems Inc., D H Technology mil: s.sgt. USMC 1951-54; Republican; Episcopalian; rec: skiing, wind surfing, sailing. Res: 45 S La Senda, South Laguna 92677

BOWKER, LEE HARRINGTON, dean; b. Dec. 19, 1940, Bethlehem, Pa.; s. Maurice Harrington and Blanche Emma (Heffner) B.; m. Nancy S. Bachant, 1966 (div. 1973); m. Dee Constantine Thomas, May 24, 1975; children: Kirsten b. 1971, Jessica b. 1978, Gwendolyn b. 1980; edn: BA, Muhlenberg Coll. 1962; MA, Univ. Pa. 1965; PhD, Wash. St. Univ. 1972. Career: assoc. prof. sociology Whitman Coll., Walla Walla, Wash. 1967-77; assoc. dean social welfare Univ. Wis., Milwaukee 1977-82; dean grad. sch. and research Ind. Univ., Pa. 1982-85; provost Augustana Coll., Sioux Falls, So. Dak. 1985-87; dean coll. behavioral and social sciences Humboldt St. Univ., Arcata 1987–; cons. to univs. and publishers, expert witness Calif. courts on battered woman syndrome; awards: grants received from num. orgns. incl. Wash. Arts Commn., Wash. Office Comm. Devel., Nat. Inst. Mental Health; mem: Am. Sociological Assn., Am. Correctional Assn., Am. Assn. Univ. Professors, Pacific Sociological Assn., Humboldt Women for Shelter; author 16 books incl. Ending the Violence, 1986, 96 articles pub. in profl. jours., (1974–), 71 sci. book reviews (1975–), 84 papers presented at sci. confs. (1973–); rec: music, flyfishing, geology. Res: POB 208 Bayside 95524 Ofc: Humboldt State Univ. College of Behavioral and Social Sciences Arcata 95521

BOWLING, LANCE CHRISTOPHER, recording and publishing executive; b. May 17, 1948, San Pedro; s. Dan Parker and Sylvia Lois (Van Devander) B.; edn: BA polit. sci. and history, Pepperdine Univ., 1966-70, MPA, 1973. Career: owner, founder Cambria Records and Pub., Palos Verdes 1972–; editor: Joseph Wagner: A Retrospective of Composer-Conductor 1900-1974 (1976), Hazards Pavilion, Jour. of Soc. for Preservation of So. California Musical Heritage 1985–; author: Eugene Hemmer: Composer-Pianist (1983); producer 50+ Am. Classical records including works by Charles W. Cadman, Madeleine Dring, Mary Carr Moore, John Crown, Ed Bland, Elinor Remick Warren, Florence Price and Erich Wolfgang Korngold; also produced classical music for radio stations KPFK, KFAC, NPR and APR; mem: ASCAP, Assn. Recorded Sound Collections, Music Library Assn., Sonneck Soc., Soc. for the Preservation of Film Music (bd. dirs. 1991–), Los Angeles Ballet (bd dirs.); clubs: Variety Arts (L.A.), Musical Arts (Long Beach); civic: United Way L.A. (allocation com. region V 1978-85); rec: collect early Calif. books and ephemera, restore 78-RPM recordings, antique autos. Res: 2625 Colt Rd Rancho Palos Verdes 90275 Ofc: Cambria Records and Pub. PO Box 374 Lomita 90717

BOWMAN, LESLIE GREENE, curator; b. Nov. 9, 1956, Springfield, Ohio; d. Robert H. and Phyllis Jane (Weikart) Greene; m. Bradley Guy Bowman, Oct. 10, 1981 (div. Feb. 1991); m. 2d. Cortland Neuhoff, May 1, 1994; edn: B. Philosophy (summa cum laude) interdisciplinary studies, Miami Univ., Oh. 1978; MA, Winterthur Pgm. in Early Am. Culture, Henry Francis du Pont Winterthur Mus./Univ. Dela., 1981. Career: editl. asst., The Papers of Frederick Law Olmsted, W.D.C. 1979-80; curatorial intern Dela. Art Mus. 1980; curatl. asst. decorative arts L.A. Co. Mus. of Art 1980-81, asst. curator 1981-84, assoc. curator 1984-88, curator and dept. hd. decorative arts, 1989–, coord. of exhibi-

tion programs 1994–; adj. prof. Sch. Fine Arts, USC, 1988–, instr. design pgms., UCLA Ext., 1988–; frequent lectr. univs., art symposiums; presidential appointee Com. For the Preservation of The White House; mem. bd. dirs. UCLA Internat. Student Ctr., Decorative Arts Study Ctr., San Juan Capistrano; awards: Charles F. Montgomery Award of Decorative Arts Soc./ Soc. of Architectural Historians, Florence J. Gould Found. seminar scholar at Fontainebleau (10-89); listed Who's Who in West 1991, Who's Who in Am. Women 1991-92, World Who's Who of Women (11th edit.); exhibitions: "Am. Arts & Crafts: Virtue in Design," 1990 (author exh. catalogue); (co-curator W. Morrison Heckscher, Met. Mus. of Art) "American Rococo, 1750-1775: Elegance in Ornament," 1992 (coauthor w/ M. Heckscher of exh. catalogue); cons. curator "Silver in the Golden State" Oakland Mus. 1986-87; installation curator "The Art that is Life: The Arts & Crafts Movement in Am., 1875-1920" (org. by Mus. Fine Arts, Boston, expanded for L.A. Co. Mus. of Art), 1987; rec: equestrienne. Ofc: L.A. Co. Museum of Art 5905 Wilshire Blvd Los Angeles 90036

BOWYER, C. STUART, educator, astrophysicist; b. Aug. 2, 1934, Toledo, Ohio; s. H.D. and Elizabeth (McEuen) B.; m. Jane Anne Baker, Feb. 27, 1957; children: William, Robert, Elizabeth; edn: BA, Miami Univ., OH 1956; PhD, Catholic Univ. of Am., W.D.C. 1965. Career: research physicist Naval Research Lab, W.D.C. 1959-67; prof. Catholic Univ. of Am., 1965-67; prof. Univ. Calif., Berkeley 1967–, dir. Ctr. for Extreme Ultraviolet Astrophysics, UCB 1989–; pres. Berkeley Photonics Inc., Orinda 1986–; cons. NASA 1970–, NSF 1970–, Israel Space Agy. 1989–; awards: Vis. Prof. Sci. Research Council, England 1973, Miller Found. Fellow Univ. Calif. Berkeley 1978, Humbolt Prize Prof., Ger. 1982, Fulbright Prof. 1983, Centre Nat. d'Etudes Spatiales Prof., Fr. 1989, Guggenheim Fellow 1992; mem: Am. Inst. of Aeronautics & Astronautics, Internat. Astronomical Union 1970–, Am. Astronomical Soc. 1965–, Am. Geophysical Union 1965–, Astronomical Soc. of Pacific 1980–, Internat. Acad. Astronautics 1982–; author sev. patents in space instrumentation, 400+ astrophysics/geophysics articles (1965–), editor 2 conf. proceedings. Ofc: Center for Extreme Ultraviolet Astrophysics, Univ. of California, Berkeley 94720

BOXER, BARBARA, United States senator; b. Nov. 11, 1940, Brooklyn, N.Y.; d. Ira and Sophie (Silvershein) Levy; m. Stewart Boxer; children: Doug, Nicole; edn: BA, Brooklyn Coll. 1962. Career: stockbroker, N.Y.C. 1962-65; journalist, assoc. editor Pacific Sun 1972-74; congl. aide to rep. 5th Congl. Dist. San Francisco 1974-76; mem. Marin County Bd. Suprs., San Rafael 1976-82, pres., 1980-81; mem. 98th-102d Congresses from 6th Calif. dist., 1983-92, mem. armed services com., select com. children, youth and families; majority whip at large, co-chair Mil. Reform Caucus, chair subcom. on govt. activities and transp. of house govt. ops. com. 1990-92, author Violence Against Women Act, cosponsor Freedom of Choice Act; mem. U.S. Senate, Wash. DC 1993–, mem. Senate com. on banking, housing and urban affairs (subcoms. on internat. fin. (ranking mem.), on securities, on financial institutions), com. on environment and public works (subcoms. on superfund, waste control and risk assessment, on clean air, wetlands, private property and nuclear safety, on drinking water fisheries and wildlife), com. on the budget, founder Calif. Unit Working Group; mem. Bay Area Air Quality Mgmt. Bd., S.F. 1977-82, pres., 1979-81; bd. dirs. Golden Gate Bridge Hwy. and Transport. Dist., S.F. 1978-82; founding mem. Marin Nat. Women's Polit. Caucus, Marin Community Video; pres. Dem. New Mems. Caucus 1983; awards: Govt. award Common Cause 1980, Rep. of Yr. award Nat. Multiple Sclerosis Soc. 1990, Margaret Sanger award Planned Parenthood 1990, honored for leadership in Congress by. Consumer Fedn. of Am., Coalition to Stop Govt. Waste, League of Conservation Voters, Public Citizen, Sierra Club, Ctr. for Environmental Edn. Ctr. for Defense Info., and Am. Assn. of Univ. Women, recipient awards from Anti-Defamation League, Human Rights Campaign Fund and Leadership Conf. on Civil Rights; Jewish. Ofc: 112 Hart Senate Office Bldg Washington DC 20510

BOXER, MICHAEL E., investment banker; b. Denver, Colo.; m. Caryn; edn: BSBA, Colorado State Univ. 1983; MBA, Univ. Chicago Grad. Sch. of Bus., 1991. Career: fin. analyst Am. Home Video Corp., Englewood, Colo. 1982; ofcr. United Bank of Denver, N.A., Denver, Colo. 1983-86; v.p. Birr, Wilson & Co., Inc., San Francisco 1986-88; Furman Selz, San Francisco, 1991–; mem. Anti-Defamation League (bd.); publs: Special Research Report on Bank Mergers, Colo. St. Univ. Press, 1982; Republican; Jewish. Address: San Francisco

BOYD, CULLEN DICKSON, businessman; b. Aug. 30, 1910, Cleburne, Tx.; s. Samuel Edgar and Lula Maye (Dickson) B.; m. Margurite Lee Dickson, Mar. 17, 1945; edn: Godley (Tx.) H.S. grade 11; grad. Army Air Corps regs. in Airplane & Engine Mechs., 1945. Career: p.t. clk. Armstrong's Mercantile Store & Co., Godley, Tx. 1927-30, also harvest and cotton gin work summers; day laborer, 1931; ranch work in Post City, Tx. 193233; baseball catcher sand-lot baseball, 1928-34, Johnson County, Tx. baseball champions (1934); sales and installation awnings & canopies, Stuckert-Owens Lumber Co. and O.J. Johnston Co., Fort Worth, Tx. 1935-39; roofing contr. and supplier assoc. Moncrief-Lenor Mfg. Co., Dallas 1939-42; with Van Buren Lino & Shade, Anaheim 1945-48; owner/contr. Boyd's (floor and window coverings), Oceanside 1948–; Hough Mfg. Co. HUFCOR/Airwall distributor 1955–; civic: Lions Internat. (life. mem. 1986, Perfect Att. Award 1951-86, Old Monarch 1951-61, 100 Percent pres.'s award 1971-72; Carlsbad Club pres. 1954-55; Oceanside Host Club pres. 1971-72; Zone chmn. Dist. 4L6 1974-75; Internat. Conv. del. Las Vegas 1971-72, Dallas 1986-86, St. Louis 1989-90); mil: sgt., radar opr. QM Supply Tech. Army Air Corps 1942-45, Euro., African, Middle E. Svc. medals, GCM; Democrat; Prot. (gov. bd. S. Oceanside Comm. Ch.); rec: photog., miniature trains, story telling. Address: Boyd's 1101 S Hill St Oceanside 92054-5101

BOYD, ROBERT GIDDINGS, JR., mental health agency executive; b. March 16, 1940, San Juan, P.R.; s. Robert Giddings and Laura Jean (Stephenson) B.; m. Denise Ann Ryll, Dec. 10, 1978; edn: BA, William and Mary Coll., 1962; George Washington Univ., 1966. Career: budget mgr. Goodbody & Co., N.Y.C. 1968-70; bus. mgr. Westminster Sch., Simsbury, Conn. 1970-76; gen. mgr., ptnr. F&R Enterprises Inc., Scottsdale, Ariz. 1976-78; bus. mgr. Orme Sch., Mayer, Ariz. 1978-81; mng. dir. San Diego Symphony Orch. Assn. 1981-84; v.p. San Diego Center for Children 1985-94, exec. v.p. adminstrn. & finance 1994–; mem: Am. Symphony Assn., Am. Mgmt. Assn., Rotary Internat.; mil: 1st lt. AUS 1962-64; Prot.; rec: tennis, swimming, hiking. Ofc: San Diego Center for Children 3002 Armstrong St San Diego 92111

BOYER, CARL, III, educator, city official; b. Sept. 22, 1937, Phila., Pa.; s. Carl Jr. and Elizabeth Campbell (Timm) B.; m. Ada Christine Kruse, July 28, 1962; children: Michele, b. 1963; Denise, b. 1965; Danielle, b. 1967; edn: Univ. of Edinburgh, Scotland 1956-57; BA, Trinity Univ., Tex. 1959; MEd, Univ. Cincinnati, 1962; postgrad. studies BYU, CSUN; Calif. Gen. Secondary (life) Tchr. Credential 1968. Career: sch. tchr. in Tex., Ky., Ohio 1959-63; social studies tchr. San Fernando H.S. 1963–; faculty chmn. 1969-70, dept. chair 1980-83; instr. Kennedy-San Fernando Comm. Adult Sch. and Mission Coll.; genealogical publisher & compiler/author of references, manuals & family histories 1971–; cons. City of Sofia, Bulgaria 1991; elected supvr. Canyon County 1976; chmn. City of Santa Clarita Formation Com., 1987, council mem. City of Santa Clarita 1987–, mayor 1990-91; mem. Calif. Contract Cities Assn., exec. bd. 1991-93, treas. 1992, secty. 1992-93; pres. Santa Clarita Valley Internat. Prog. 1991–; treas. Healing the Children Calif. 1994–; trustee Santa Clarita Comm. Coll. Dist. 1973-81, pres. 1979-81; bd. dirs. Castaic Lake Water Agy. 1982-84; pres. Del Prado Condominium Assn., Inc.; awards: United Way Sweepstakes 1972, Respected Tchr. San Fernando H.S. Students 1982; mem: United Tchrs. of Los Angeles, Nat. Geneal. Soc., Newhall-Saugus-Valencia Fedn. of Homeowners Assns. (pres.), Civic Inc. (pres.), Canyon Co. Formation Com., Internat. Municipal Consortium of Nat. League of Cities 1991–, League of Calif. Cities (Revenue and Taxation Com. 1991–); works: Slade-Babcock Genealogy, 1971; Ancestral Lines (2 eds., 1975, 81); Ship Passenger Lists (4 vols. 1976-79); How To Market and Publish Your Family History (1982, 85, 87, 93); mil: USNR 1955-63; Republican; Methodist; rec: travel, photog. Res: POB 220333 Santa Clarita 91322 Ofc: San Fernando High School 11133 O'Melveny San Fernando 91340

BOYKIN, RAYMOND FRANCIS, educator; b. Nov. 18, 1953, Santa Monica; s. Francis Raymond and Doris Elaine (Davis) B.; m. Shelley Lynne Ladd, July 30, 1977; children: Jennifer b. 1979, Whitney b. 1981; edn: BA, CSU Fullerton, 1975; MS, San Diego St. Univ., 1976; PhD, St. Louis Univ., Mo. 1986. Career: research scientist Rockwell Internat., Richland, Wa. 1976-80; mgmt. scientist Monsanto, St. Louis, Mo. 1980-86; prof. CSU Chico 1986–; senior cons. PLG, Inc. Newport Beach 1986–; v.chmn. bd. Makaira Ministries, La Mirada 1991–; awards: "innovator" Monsanto 1982, achiev. TIMS, Balt., Md. 1984, CSU Chico: merit performance 1987, 89, Pres.'s achiev. award 1988, outstanding faculty 1988, 93, 94, outstanding researcher 1991; mem. Soc. for Risk Analysis (treas. 1989-94, recipient outstanding contribution award, 1994); author: Test Bank - Production Mgmt. (1989, 92, 95), 20+ pub. articles, 1979–; Democrat; Christian; rec: basketball, volleyball, golf. Res: 862 Westmont Dr Chico 95926 Ofc: California State University, Chico 95929-0011

BOYLAN, RICHARD JOHN, psychologist; b. Oct. 15, 1939, Hollywood; s. John Alfred and Rowena Margaret (Devine) B.; m. Charnette Marie Blackburn, Oct. 26, 1968 (div. 1984); m. 2d. Judith Lee Sanders, Nov. 21, 1987; children: Christopher b. 1972, Jennifer b. 1973, Stephanie b. 1975; edn: BA, St. John's Coll. 1961; MS edn., Fordham Univ. 1966; MSW, UC Berkeley 1971; PhD, UC Davis 1984; lic. clin. psychologist 1987. Career: supervising counselor S. Campus Comm. Ministry, Berkeley 1970-71; chief, forensic unit Marin Co. Mental Health Dept., San Rafael 1971-77; dir. Calaveras Co. Mental Health Alcohol/Drug Dept., San Andreas 1977-85; sr. mental health counselor Sacto. Co. Mental Health Center, Sacto. 1986-87; lectr. CSU, Sacto. 1985-90; regional dir. U.S. Behavioral Health 1988-89; pvt. practice, psychol. counseling 1973–; instr., coordinator Nat. Univ., Sacto. 1985-86; lectr. Sierra Comm. Coll., Rocklin 1986-87; UC Davis 1986; preceptor in psychology UC Davis Sch. Medicine 1987-88; psychologist cons. to fed. TOPH study UC Davis Sch. Medicine 1994–; awards: Calif. St. Undergrad. scholarship 1958, Calif. St. Grad. scholarship 1969, Who's Who in West, Who's Who in Sci. & Engring., Who's Who in Am. Edn., UC Davis Exptl. Station grant 1983, AARP Davis chpt. scholarship 1984; mem: Am. Psychological Assn., Calif. St. Psychological Assn., Sacto. Valley Psychol. Assn. (past pres.), Acad. of Clin. Close Encounter Therapists (bd. dirs. 1993–) Calaveras Co. (pres. bd. edn. 1981-84), Sacramentans for Safe Energy, Natural Resources Defense Council, Marin Municipal Water Dist. (bd. dirs.); author:

Extraterrestrial Contact & Human Response, 1992, Close Extraterrestrial Encounters (Wild Flower Press, 1994), num. articles, documents and conf. papers pub. 1984-95; Democrat; Native Am. Taoist; rec: snorkeling, photography, backpacking. Res: 6724 Trudy Way Sacramento 95831 Ofc: Richard Boylan, PhD 2826 O Street Ste. 2 Sacramento 95816

BRADFORD, DAVID PAUL, state court judicial assistant; b. Mar. 23, 1955, Lynwood; s. William H. Johnson and Barbara O'Leary; edn: AA, Citrus Coll., Azusa, Calif. 1975; BA in poli. sci., UCLA, 1978; postgrad., Calif. State Univ., L.A. 1984-85, Univ. W. L.A. 1990-91. Career: prin. clerk UCLA Brain Research Inst. 1977-81; adminstrv. asst., supr. UCLA Hosp. and Clinics 1977-81; dep. to atty. in residence matters ofc. of registrar UCLA, 1981-85; ofc. of clerk L.A. County Bd. Suprs., L.A. 1987-88; judicial asst., ct. clerk L.A. Co. Superior Ct., Los Angeles 1988–; founder and dir. Bradford & Assocs., L.A. 1987–; research dir. Citizens Protection Alliance, Santa Monica 1992–; active L.A. County Domestic Violence Council; awards: Chancellor's marshal UCLA 1978, Award of Recognition, UCLA Employees Advy. Council 1981, Cert. of Recognition, Domestic Violence Council L.A. Co. 1990, Commendation, L.A. Co. Bd. Suprs. 1993, Award of Recognition, L.A. Police Dept. and Assn. of Threat Assessment Profls. 1994 Threat Mgmt. Conf., listed in Who's Who in Am. Law, Who's Who in Sci. and Engring., Who's Who in Finance and Industry, Who's Who in Calif., Who's Who in West, Who's Who in World, Internat. Who's Who of Intellectuals, Two Thousand Notable Am. Men, Dictionary of Internat. Biography, Men of Achievement; mem: Am. Psychol. Soc., NY Acad. Scis., Acad. of Political Scis., L.A. Co. Supr. Ct. Clerk's Assn. (local 575 AFSCME pres. 1993-94), UCLA Alumni Assn., Citizenship Protection Fund, Santa Monica (res. dir./advy. bd. 1991–); address before Calif. State Assembly Com. on Edn. regarding undocumented aliens, 1993; rec: music, movies, numismatics. Ofc: Bradford & Associates 3921 Wilshire Blvd Ste 303-V Los Angeles 90010

BRADLEY, DONALD EDWARD, lawyer; b. Sept. 26, 1943, Santa Rosa; s. Edward Aloysius and Mildred Louise (Kelley) B.; m. Marianne Stark, Apr. 22, 1990; children: Evan b. 1970, Matthew b. 1972, Andrea b. 1974; edn: BA, Dartmouth Coll. 1965; JD, UCSF Hastings Coll. Law 1968; LL.M Tax., N.Y. Univ. 1972; admitted St. Bar Calif. (1968). Career: assoc. atty. Pillsbury Madison & Sutro, San Francisco 1972-77, ptnr. 1978-84; Wilson Sonsini Goodrich & Rosati, Palo Alto 1984–; adj. prof. Golden Gate Univ. 1973-82; pres., dir. Attys. Ins. Mutual Risk Retention Group, Honolulu, Hawaii 1992–; awards: Bureau of Nat. Affairs Merit Award 1968, N.Y. Univ. Charles M. Ruddick Award 1972; mem: Am. Bar Assn., Internat. Bar Assn., Santa Clara Bar Assn., San Francisco Bar Assn., Internat. Fiscal Assn., Peninsula Tax Club, Internat. Tax Club; mil: capt. AUS 1968-70; Democrat; R.Cath. Ofc: Wilson Sonsini Goodrich & Rosati 650 Page Mill Rd Palo Alto 94304

BRADLEY, KENNETH DANIEL, reinsurance executive; b. Feb. 13, 1949, Ft. Clayton, Panama C.Z.; s. William Perry and Dorothy (Gill) B.; m. Millajean Miller, Nov. 21, 1987; 1 son, Ian Perry b. 1992; edn: BS in B.A., Seton Hall Univ., South Orange, N.J. 1971; desig: CPCU. Career: rating analyst N.C.C.I., Lyndhurst, N.J. 1971-73; casualty underwriter Central Mutual Ins. Co., N.Y.C. 1973-75; v.p. American Home Assurance, N.Y.C. and Los Angeles, 1975-87; exec. v.p. Alliance Insurance Group, Burbank 1987-92; insurance cons. 1992-95; asst. secty. Sorema N.A. Reinsurance Co., Universal City, Calif. 1995–; mem. N.A.P.S.L.O. 1980–; rec: tennis, golf. Res: 4758 D La Villa Marina Marina Del Rey 90292

BRADLEY, TOM, former mayor; b. Dec. 29, 1917, Calvert, Tex.; s. Lee Thomas and Crenner (Hawkins) B.; m. Ethel Mae Arnold, May 4, 1941; children: Lorraine, Phyllis; edn: undergrad. UCLA 1937-40, LLB, Southwestern Univ., 1956, LLD, 1980; LLD, Brandeis Univ., Oral Roberts Univ., Pepperdine Univ., Loyola Marymount Univ., Calif. Lutheran Univ., Wilberforce Univ., 1974, Whittier Coll., 1976, Yale Univ., USC, Princeton Univ., 1979, Bus. Nat. Univ. Korea, 1979, Antioch Univ., N.C. Central Univ., 1983; PhD (hon.) Humanity Res. Ctr. Beverly Hills, 1976; admitted bar: Calif. 1956. Career: police ofcr. Los Angeles P.D., 1942-62; law practice, 1956-73; mem. Los Angeles City Council, 1963-73; mayor of Los Angeles, 1973-93; sr. counsel Brobeck Phleger & Harrison, L.A. 1993–; founder, dir. Bank of Fin.; bd. dirs. Nat. Urban Coalition, Nat. League Cities (pres. 1974, nat. bd.), League of Calif. Cities (pres. 1979), So. Calif. Assn. Govts. (pres. 1968-69), Nat. Assn. Regional Councils (pres. 1969-71), U.S. Conf. Mayors (advy. bd., v.ch. transp. com.); mem. Nat. Energy Advy. Council, Nat. Commn. on Productivity and Work Quality; awards: African Methodist Episcopal man of yr. 1974, Dr. Martin L. King, Jr. award 1974, Pub. Ofcl. of yr. Los Angeles Trial Lawyers Assn. 1974, CORO Found. award 1978, award of merit Nat. Council Negro Women 1978, J.F.Kennedy Fellowship award Govt. of N.Z. 1978, internat. humanitarian M.E.D.I.C. 1978, city employee of yr. All City Employees Benefits Serice Assn. 1983, Magnin award 1984; mem: L.A. Urban League, NAACP (Spingarn medal 1985), So. Calif. Conf. on Community Rels., L.A. Conf. Negro Elected Ofcls., UN Assn. Los Angeles (bd.), Kappa Alpha Psi; Democrat (Calif. Dem. Central Com., del. Dem. Nat. Mid-Term Conf. 1974, co-ch. Dem. Nat. Conv. 1976); AME (trustee). Brobeck Phleger & Harrison 550 S Hope St Los Angeles 90071-2604

BRADLEY, WILLIAM MARVIN (BILL SILBERT), radio station executive; b. Jan. 1, 1921, Detroit; s. Louis and Helen (Krause) Silbert; edn: BS, Univ. Detroit 1936; postgrad. So. Methodist Univ. 1945; MS, N.Y. Univ. 1953. Career: disc jockey num. radio - TV shows, Detroit 1947-52; panelist Songs for Sale, CBS-TV, 1952; emcee Bill Silbert Show, Let's Go Bowling WABD-DuMont TV 1952-53, Bill Silbert Show, WMGM radio; announcer Red Buttons Show, NBC-TV, Philco Show, emcee Nat. Radio Fan Club NBC Mag. of Air, Mut., KLAC, Los Angeles; Bill Bradley Show, KTLA, Hollywood, Crime Story, Greet the People, Ad Lib, Hollywood Diary; gen. sales mgr., retail sales mgr. Radio Station KLOS-FM (ABC), Los Angeles 1969-; appeared in motion pictures: Bundle of Joy, Thunderjets, Alligator People, Young Jesse James, Lost Missile, Breakfast at Tiffanys, Return Payton Place, Goonies; TV shows: Bronco, 77 Sunset Strip, Hawaiian Eye, Sugarfoot, Combar, Adventures in paradise, Police Station, Michael Shayne, Roaring 20's, Outlaws; songwriter ASCAP "Heavenly Feeling" later used in "Chock Full of Nuts" commercial; awards: Damon Runyon Memorial Fund fellow Nat. Assn. Mental Health (1970-74), Billboard mag. "Most Popular D.J. in Am." (1955); mem: Screen Actors Guild, AFTRA, Variety Clubs Internat., Nat. Acad. TV Arts & Scis., So. Calif. Bdcstrs. Assn., mil: 1st lt. USAAF 1944-46. Res: 13802 Northwest Passage Marina Del Rey 90292 Ofc: 3321 S La Cienega Blvd Los Angeles 90016

BRADPIECE, THEODORE GRANT, mutual fund administrator; b. Aug. 31, 1965, Los Angeles; s. Sidney and Naomi Grena (Silton) B.; edn: AB Freeman Sch. of Bus., Tulane Univ., 1987. Career: owner Bradpiece Advising Los Angeles 1987-; brokers' asst. Prudential-Bache, Beverly Hills 1986-88; acct. exec. Baraban Securities, Los Angeles 1987-88; mutual fund supr. Associated Financial Group Inc., L.A. 1988-93; investment counselor Montano Securities Corp. 1993-94; mutual fund adminstr. Pacific Financial Research, Inc. 1993-; acct exec. Quest Capital Strategies, Inc. 1995-; lic. NASD series 7; mem: Sierra Club, Tau Epsilon Phi Frat. (dir. 1987-, co-chair fin. com. 1992-); Epsilon Kappa Alumni Holding Corp. (v.p. 1987-); Tulane Alumni Admissions Com. 1987-; TEP Found. (trustee 1990-); Young Adult Network (co-chmn. 1991-94); Nat. Assn. Securities Dlrs. (Bd. of Arbitrators 1992-); Young Adults for Alumni & Friends of United Synagogue Youth (co-chmn.); Democrat; Jewish; rec: philately, computers, securities, sports, travel, music. Res: 651 Andalusia Ave Los Angeles 90065 Ofc: Pacific Financial Research, Inc. 9601 Wilshire Blvd Ste 800 Beverly Hills 90210 Tel: 310/247-3939

BRADSHAW, CARL JOHN, investor, business consultant, lawyer; b. Nov. 1, 1930, Oelwein, Iowa; s. Carl John and Lorraine Lillian (Thiele) B.; m. Katsuko Anno, Nov. 5, 1954; children: Carla K. b. 1956, Arthur H. b. 1961, Vincent M. b. 1963; edn: BS, Univ. Minn. 1952; JD, 1957; LLM, Univ. Mich. Ann Arbor 1958; MJ, Keio Univ. Japan 1962. Career: atty. Graham James & Rolph, Tokyo, Japan 1961-63; assoc. prof. Univ. Wash., Seattle 1963-64; sr. v.p., dir. Oak Industries Inc., Crystal Lake, Ill. and San Diego, 1964-85; of counsel Seki and Jarvis, Bell, Boyd and Lloyd, Los Angeles 1985-87; prin. Pacific Law Group, L.A. and Tokyo, Japan 1987-; The Asian Mktg. Group, Torrance 1992-; honors: Order of Coif; mem: Radio Club Am. (fellow), Calif. Bar Assn., Westwood Bar Assn., Minn. Bar Assn., San Diego Co. Bar Assn., Am. Bar Assn., Regency Club (L.A.); articles pub. in profl. jours. (1961-75); mil: lt.j.g. USN 1952-55; rec: tennis. Res: 12958 Robleda Cove San Diego 92128 Ofc: Pacific Law Group Wilshire-Bundy Plaza 2d Fl 12121 Wilshire Blvd Los Angeles 90025

BRAHM, STEPHEN MARSMAN, podiatrist; b. Aug. 29, 1951, Upland; s. Robert Dempster and Gertrude (Marsman) B.; m. Donna Hamilton, July 19, 1980; children: Amanda Danielle b. 1985, Chelsea Anna b. 1989; edn: AA, Chaffey Jr. Coll. 1972; BA, Fullerton St. Univ. 1975; DPM, San Francisco Sch. Podiatric Medicine 1982; diplomate Am. Bd. Podiatric Medicine (1982), Am. Bd. Podiatric Surgery (1989), Fellow Am. Coll. of Foot Surgeons (1989). Career: lifeguard Parks & Recreation, Santa Monica 1970, pool mgr., Ontario 1971-73; librarian Childrens Hosp., San Francisco 1977-80; med. asst. pvt. practice, Covina 1974-75; San Bruno 1976-77; surgical resident VA Hosp. Loma Linda 1982-83; pvt. practice, Hemet 1984-89; vol. L.I.G.A. Flying Doctor 1987-89; lectr. Hemet Valley Hosp. 1987-89; honors: Pi Delta, Who's Who Am. Colls. & Univs., Si Sikosky Memorial award (1970), Trainable Handicapped Equestrians Appreciation (1987); mem: Rotary, AOPA, Hemet Model Masters (bd. 1985-); 3 articles pub in med. jours. (1982-88); Republican; Baptist; rec: aeronautics, flying. Res: 24926 Cologne Dr Hemet 92344 Ofc: 1225 E Latham Ste 3 Hemet 92343

BRAHTZ, JOHN FREDERICK PEEL, engineering, research & development planning consultant; b. Jan. 29, 1918, St. Paul, Minn.; s. John Henry August and Charlotte Beatrice (Peel) B.; m. Lise Vetter, May 11, 1991; edn: AB in civil engring., Stanford Univ. 1939, MSME, 1947, PhD applied mechs., 1951; reg. profl. engr. Calif. Career: structural res. engr. Consolidated Vultee Aircraft Corp, San Diego 1939-41; project engr. Northrop Aircraft Co., Hawthorne 1951-53; assoc. prof. UC Los Angeles 1953-57; v.p engring J.H. Pomeroy & Co., Inc., San Francisco 1957-59; dir. ops. John F. Brahtz Assoc., L.A. 1959-60; res. dept. mgr. Stanford Res. Inst. 1960-63; sr. lctr. UCLA 1963-70; cons. to White House Commn., Nat. Council on Marine Resources and Engring. 1964-68; staff cons. Navy Engring. Lab., San Diego and Port Hueneme 1963-70; cons. res. prof. Stanford Univ. 1986-, on loan by Stanford to US Navy 1986-89, completed 3-yr.

investigation into feasibility of floating bases as alternative to fixed land bases overseas, and author NCEL Tech. Report re Modularized Ocean Basing System circa 2000 (R-928, Naval Civil Engring. Lab., Port Hueneme); honors: military commendation U.S. Navy 1944, elected mem. Honorary Res. Sigma Xi 1950, grad. fellowship Stanford Univ. 1946; fellow, Am. Soc. of Civil Engrs.; mem.: Am. Soc. for Engring. Edn., Nat. Ocean Res. and Exploration Ctr. (fellow 1992-), Float, Inc., San Diego (bd. dirs.1993-); clubs: Old Capital Club (Monterey), Beach and Tennis Club (Pebble Beach), La Jolla Beach & Tennis; U.S. patent (navy sponsored) 1971; author books (pub. John Wiley & Sons): Ocean Engineering, 1968, Coastal Zone Management: Multiple Use with Conservation, 1972; ed. book series: Construction Management & Engineering, 1970-88; mil: Comdr. U.S. Navy (Ret.); rec: writing non-fiction. Res./Ofc: John F. Peel Brahtz Associates, Planning and Engineering Consultants, 2740 16th Ave Carmel 93923

BRAITHWAITE, CHARLES HENRY, JR., chemical engineering executive, forensic consultant; b. Dec. 16, 1920, Chgo.; s. Charles H., Sr. and Wilhelmina (Hoth) B.; m. Bernice Hyde, Apr. 29, 1949; children: Charles III, Betty Susan; edn: AB chem., UCLA, 1941; BSE in chem. eng., Univ. Mich., 1943; MS chem., Carnegie Inst. of Tech., 1948, DSc organic chem., 1949; reg. cons. engr. Calif. Career: engr., elec. insulation devel., Westinghouse Electric, 1943-46; senior res. chemist in petroleum chemistry Shell Oil Co., 1949-51; div. dir. of res. Chlor-Alkali Div., F.M.C. Corp., 1951-57; dir. R&D Productol Co., 1957-59; founder, pres. Cal Colonial Chemsolve, 1959-87, Subsidiaries & Divs. Jack Sons Products Corp., Lee Potter Co., Nat. Testing Standards (analytical lab.); forensic consulting prin. Braithwaite Consulting, 1988-, cons. W.R. Grace Corp., U.S. Borax Corp., Piezo Products Div., Gulton Inds., Fairchild - Stratos Div., Henkel Corp., Monsanto; patentee 8 U.S. patents issued, sev. pending; contbr. articles in trade jours. Res: 11232 Tigrina Whittier 90603

BRAKENSIEK, JAY CLEMENCE, risk manager, safety officer, industrial hygienist; b. Apr. 23, 1954, Troy, Mo.; s. Clemence Ernst and Juanita Geraldine (Gaylord) B.; m. Kathleen Lorraine Edmonds, July 25, 1981 (div. Aug. 1991); children: Gregory b. 1983, Matthew b. 1987; edn: BS biology, Northeast Mo. State Univ., 1977, MA biosci. edn./biology, 1981; MS indsl. hygiene, USC, 1991; USC cert. in Hazardous Waste Mgmt. 1991, Associate Safety Profl. (A.S.P.) certification, 1992, Calif. Registered Environmental Assessor, 1992. Career: pulmonary splst. Huntington Memorial Hosp., Pasadena 1979-89; safety ofcr. L.A. County Dept. Pub. Works, Alhambra 1990-93, risk mgr. 1993-; instr. biology Citrus Coll., Glendora 1984-85, life scis. Pasadena City Coll., 1985-88; awards: fellow Nat. Inst. of Occ. Health & Safety 1989-91, citations Who's Who Environment Registry 1992, 93, listed Who's Who in the West 1991, 92, 93, L.A. Co. Outstanding Job Performance award 1993, L.A. Co. Productivity Commn. awards: Computerized Safety Prog. 1992, High Hazard Review Prog. 1993, MEDVAN Mobile Med. Monitoring Prog. 1993, Nat. Assn. of Counties award, Mobile Med. Monitoring Prog. 1994; mem: Am. Indsl. Hygiene Assn., Am. Conf. of Govt. Indsl. Hygienists, Am. Soc. of Safety Engrs., Calif. Safety Ofcrs. Org., USC Inst. of Safety & Systems Mgmt. (Triumvirate), USC Gen. Alumni Assn. NE Mo. State Univ. Alumni Assn.; pub. article in field, 1992; Democrat; Lutheran; rec: backpacking, photography, skiing, sailing, AYSO soccer. Res: 1618 E South Mayflower Ave Monrovia 91016 Ofc: L.A. County Dept. Public Works, Risk Management, 7th Fl Alhambra 91803

BRANCA, JOHN GREGORY, lawyer; b. Dec. 11, 1950, Bronxville, NY; s. John Ralph and Barbara (Werle) B.; edn: AB, cum laude, Occidental Coll., 1972, JD, UCLA Law Sch., 1975. Career: songwriter, recording artist, Original Sound Records, 1968-70; atty. law firm of Kindel & Anderson, 1975-77; Barovick Konecky Braun Schwartz Kay & Schiff, 1977-81; ptnr. Ziffren, Brittenham & Branca, 1981-; exec. com. UCLA Athletic Dept.; exec. com. UCLA Law. Sch.; bd. of trustees Occidental Coll., Musicians' Asst. Program; honors: chief editor UCLA-Alaska Law Rev. 1974-75, Am. Jurisprudence Award; mem: Am. Bar Assn., Calif. Bar Assn., Bev. Hills Bar Assn., Phi Alpha Delta law frat, Wm. Stewart Young Soc./Occidental Coll., UCLA Chancellor's Assocs.; numerous publs. incl. Attorney Fee Schedules and Legal Advertising: The Implications of Goldfarb, 24 UCLA Law Rev. 475-522 (1977); rec: travel - Carribbean, basketball, music. Ofc: Ziffren, Brittenham, Branca & Fischer 2121 Avenue of the Stars 32nd Flr Los Angeles 90067

BRANDENBURGH, DONALD CARTER, literary agent; b. July 4, 1931, Stuart, Ia.; s. Wilbur H. and Esther Hadley (Carter) B.; m. Mary Isabelle Moore, June 5, 1953; children: Gregory b. 1955, Curtis b. 1957, Brenda b. 1965; edn: BA, William Penn Coll., Oskaloosa, Ia. 1953; MA, Whittier Coll., 1960; MDiv, Talbot Sch. of Theology, La Mirada 1970; tchg. cert. ESL, UC Riverside Ext., 1991; recorded minister, Iowa Yearly Meeting of Friends, 1956. Career: minister Friends Ch., Paton, Ia. 1955-57; minister of Christian edn. Friends Ch., Garden Grove, Ca. 1959-68; bus. adminstr. Calif. Yearly Meeting of Friends, Whittier 1968-73; exec. dir. Nat. Sunday Sch. Assn., Wheaton, Ill. 1973-74; exec. dir. Evangelical Christian Publishers Assn., La Habra 1974-80; assoc. publisher Homes & Land Mag., La Habra 1981-85; prin. Brandenburgh & Associates Literary Agy., Murrieta 1986-; ESL tchr. UC Ext., Riverside 1991-; Republican; Episcopalian. Ofc: 24555 Corte Jaramillo Murrieta 92562

BRANNAN, WILLIAM WAYLAND, real estate broker; b. July 13, 1923, San Francisco; s. Wm. Smith and Ramona Cora (Hoag) B.; m. Marian Gimby, Mar. 26, 1951; children: Carol b. 1954, John b. 1955, Ann b. 1957, Thomas b. 1959, James b. 1962, Paul b. 1965, Kathleen b. 1969; edn: AB, Stanford Univ. 1952. Career: life ins. salesman Guardian Life, 1951-55; real estate salesman Timmer Realty, 1955-71, Fox & Carskadon, 1971-76, Frank Howard Allen, 1977-82; self-empl. realtor and appraiser, San Rafael 1982–; condr. workshops on telephone techniques throughout No. Calif., 1978-82; honors: Realtor Assoc. of the Year 1980, Marin Co.; dir. St. Vincent's Sch. for Boys; dir. Marin Co. Bd. of Realtors; mem. Kiwanis Club, Serra Club, Knights of Columbus; chmn. 1st Annual Town Picnic Parade, San Rafael 1980; author book and cassette tapes on tel. techniques (1981), art. in Calif. Real Estate Assn. Mag. (1980); mil: company scout, pfc, 517th Parachute Inf. Regt. 1943-45, Purple Heart, Presdl. Citation; Republican; R.Cath.; rec: handwriting analyst, golf. Res: 304 Mission Ave San Rafael 94901 Ofc: Brannan Associates, 4340 Redwood Hwy Ste 17 San Rafael 94903

BRAUN, JEROME IRWIN, lawyer; b. Dec. 16, 1929, St. Joseph, Mo.; s. Martin H. and Bess (Donsker) B.; m. Dolores F.; children: Aaron b. 1959, Susan b. 1963, Daniel b. 1967; edn: AB (w/distinc.), Stanford Univ., 1951, LL.B, Stanford Law Sch. 1953; admitted bar: Mo. 1953, Calif. 1953, U.S. Supreme Ct., U.S. Dist. Ct. (no. dist. Calif.), U.S. Ct. Appeals (9th cir.), U.S. Tax Ct., U.S. Ct. of Mil. Appeals. Career: atty., assoc. Long & Levit, San Francisco 1957-58; Law Offices of Jefferson Peyser, 1958-62; founding ptnr. Elke, Farella & Braun (now Farella, Braun & Martel), San Francisco 1962–; law instr. San Francisco Law Sch. 1958-69; speaker State Bar convs. in Calif., Ill., Nev., Mont.; frequent moderator, participant Calif. Contg. Edn. of Bar pgms.; past chair, Ninth Circuit Sr. Advy. Bd., past chmn. lawyer reps. to Ninth Cir. Judicial Conf.; mem. U.S. Dist. Ct. Civil Justice Reform Act Advy. Com.; mem. Calif. Ct. of Appeal First Dist. Appellate Lawyers' Liaison Com.; honors: Order of the Coif, revising ed. Stanford Law Rev., Lloyd W. Dinkelspiel Outstanding Young Leader, Jewish Welfare Fedn. 1967, honoree Mex.-Am. Legal Defense Fund 1979; mem: Am. Bar Assn., Calif. State Bar Assn. (mem., past chmn. Adminstrn of Justice Com.), Bar Assn. San Francisco, Calif. Academy of Appellate Lawyers (past pres.), Am. Judicature Soc. (past dir.), Am. Coll. of Trial Lawyers, mem. Teaching of Trial and Appellate Advocacy Com., Ninth Cir. Hist. Soc. (immediate past pres.), No. Dist. Calif. Hist. Soc. (dir.); civic: Jewish Community Fedn. of S.F., the Peninsula, Marin and Sonoma Counties (past pres.); S.F. United Jewish Comm. Ctrs. (past pres.); contbr. numerous articles to profl. jours.; author Calif. St. Bar bill on comparative negligence and contbn.; mil: 1st lt. JAG Corps US Army 1954-57, capt. Active Reserve 1957-64; Democrat; Jewish. Ofc: Farella, Braun & Martel, 235 Montgomery St San Francisco 94104

BRAUN, RICHARD RODMAN, real estate agent; b. Feb. 8, 1951, Boston, Mass.; s. Stanley S. and Claire (Rodman) B.; edn: BA, Hartwick Coll. 1973; Univ. London 1972; Univ. Pa. 1971. Career: account exec. Promotional Planning Service, Boston, Mass. 1973-79; Bernard Hodes Advt. (div. Doyle Dane Bernbach), Los Angeles 1979-85; account supr. Thompson Recruitment Advt. (div. J. Walter Thompson 1985-90; R.E. agt. James R. Gary & Co. Ltd., Real Estate, Woodland Hills 1990–; mem: San Fernando Valley Bd. Realtors; Democrat; Unitarian; rec: photography. Res: 22493 Venido Rd Woodland Hills 91364

BRAY, ABSALOM FRANCIS, JR., lawyer; b. Nov. 24, 1918, San Francisco; s. A.F., Sr. (presiding Justice, Ct. of Appeal) and Leila (Veale) B.; grandson of Sheriff R.R. Veale, Contra Costa Co., 1895-1935; m. Lorraine Paule, June 25, 1949; children: Oliver Whitney, b. 1954, Brian Keith, b. 1955, Margot Elizabeth, b. 1957; edn: AB, Stanford Univ. 1940; JD, USC Sch of Law 1949. Career: legal dept. Iowa Ord. Plant, Burlington 1940-42; pvt. practice law, 1949–, pres. Bray, Breitwieser, Costanza & Bray, APC, attys. at law; advy. bd. Bank of Am. 1953-65; founder and dir. John Muir Nat. Bank, Martinez, 1983-92; awards: Silver Beaver Award BSA 1988, A.F. Bray Award estab. in his father's honor by Kiwanis Club of Martinez; mem: Vets. of Fgn. Wars (cmdr.), Am. Legion (cmdr.), Contra Costa Co. Devel. Assn. (pres. 1959-60), Contra Costa Council (pres.), Navy League of U.S. (pres. Contra Costa council 1981-83), State Bar of Calif., Contra Costa Co. Bar Assn. (past pres.), Contra Costa Co. Tuberculosis and Pub. Health Assn. (past pres.); civic: Martinez High Twelve Club (pres. 1987), Contra Costa Co. Hist. Soc., E. Clampus Vitus, Martinez Historical Soc. (pres. 1984), Soc. of Calif. Pioneers, Camp Fire Girls (chmn. nat. bd. dirs. 1959-61, 1969-71 and past chmn. Region V, CA, NV, UT, AZ, HI), Boy Scouts Am. John Muir Dist. (chmn. 1968), John Muir Memorial Assn. (pres. 1989-92), Salvation Army (com.), Martinez PTA (life), Rotary Intl. (past pres.), Masons, Elks; mil: lt. USNR 1942-46, WWII, Navy Commendn., Navy Unit Citation; Republican; Episcopalian (Vestry); rec: photog., ship models, hiking. Res: 600 Flora St Martinez Ofc: Bray, Breitwieser, Costanza & Bray, APC, Ward and Ferry Sts., Martinez 94553

BRAZIER, JOHN RICHARD, lawyer, physician; b. Mar. 11, 1940, Olean, N.Y.; s. John R. and Edith (Martin) B.; m. 1968, div. 1978; children: Mark b. 1970, Jennifer b. 1975; edn: AAS, SUNY, 1960; BS engring. physics, Univ. Colo., Boulder 1963; MD, Univ. Colo. Med. Ctr., Denver 1969; JD, Santa Clara Sch. of Law, 1989. Career: instr. surg. and adj. prof. phys. therapy & rehab.,

N.Y. Univ. 1975-77; asst. prof. surg., div. thoracic & cardiovascular surg., UCLA Med. Ctr., Los Angeles 1977-78, also asst. chief CV surg. Wadsworth VA Hosp.; pvt. practice thoracic & cardiovascular surg., Los Angeles 1978-84; Newport News, Va. 1984-86; mem: Am. Coll. Surgeons, Am. Coll. Chest Physicians; publs: articles (1972–); Indep.; rec: pvt. pilot. Res: 1401 36th St Sacramento 95816

BRENNEMAN, MARY LOUISE, physician, psychiatrist; b. Oct. 14, 1923, Sewickley, Pa.; d. George Edward and Laura Marjory (Dryden) Black; m. Richard Henry Brenneman (div. 1971); children: Gayne Slay, James, Donna, Heidi; edn: MD, Univ. Toronto, Ont., Can. 1947; MA in pub. health, Univ. Pittsburgh, 1958; postgrad. C.G. Jung Inst., 1975-78. Career: rotating intern Western Pa. Hosp., Pittsburgh, 1947-48, resident in pediatrics 1948-49, Children's Hosp., Pitts. 1949-50; pediatrician Pittsburgh Pub. Health Dept. and B.C.G. Vaccine Pgm., 1950-57; pediatrician, med. staff Kaiser Hosp., Hollywood, Calif. 1957-58, Santa Monica Hosp., 1961-62; sch. physician L.A. Bd. Edn., 1962-68; 3 yr. psychiat. residency, 1968-71, psychiatrist Camarillo State Hosp., 1968-73; pvt. psychiatric practice West L.A. 1973-87; staff cons. Rancho Los Amigos Hosp., Downey 1973-75; day-care psychiatrist St. John's Hosp., Santa Monica 1975-88, estab. Prolixin Clinic St. John's 1974-75; psychiat. cons. St. John's Hosp. and Health Ctr., 1975–, Beverlywood Mental Health Ctr., L.A., 1975-88; psychiatric dir. Penny Ln. Inst. for Teenage Emotionally Handicapped, Sepulveda 1975-80; psychiatric cons. St. John of God Nursing Hosp., Los Angeles 1975-87; staff psychiatrist Metropolitan State Hosp., Norwalk 1987–, Robert F. Kennedy Hosp., Hawthorne 1985-88; psychiat. dir. El Portal Guest Home, L.A. 1985-88; clin. instr. peds. Univ. Pitts. 1950-57, UCLA, 1957-68; awards: H.E.W. research grantee (1965, 66); mem: Am. Psychiatric Assn., So. Calif. Psychiatric Soc., L.A. Co. Med. Womens Assn., L.A. Soc. Adolescent Psychiatry, West Soc. for Sci. Study of Sex, Am. Med. Womens Assn.; civic: YMCA, Sierra Club; rec: clog dancing, organ playing. Address: 1330 19th St Manhattan Beach 90266-4004

BRENNER, RICHARD JAMES, physician, medical educator; b. Sept. 27, 1949, Los Angeles; s. John Hans and Dorothy (Cohen) B.; edn: BA, UC Santa Cruz 1971; Univ. Edinburgh Scotland; MD, UCLA 1975; JD, Univ. San Francisco 1981. Career: assoc. clin. prof., lectr. UCLA Med. Sch. 1981–; dir. Tower Breast Imaging Center 1983–; attdg. physician, chief section on mammography John Wayne Cancer Inst., Los Angeles 1993–; bd. dirs. Central L.A. ACS; pres., founder Calif. House Ofcr. Med. Assn. 1979; honors: Order Gran Chevalier, Alpha Omega Alpha, UCLA Regent scholar 1971-75, NIH fellow 1976-80; mem: AMA, CMA, L.A. Co. Med. Assn., LARS, Soc. Breast Imaging; num. articles pub. in med. jours., 1978–, novelist; Democrat. Ofc: Tower Imaging 8635 W 3rd St Los Angeles 90048

BRENT, IRA M., psychiatrist; b. Nov. 1, 1944, N.Y., NY; married, 1 dau.; edn: BS, Long Island Univ., 1966; MD, Chicago Med. Sch., 1970; Qualified Med. Examiner, US Dept. of Labor. Career: rotating intern UC Irvine Orance Co. Med. Ctr., 1970-71; resident gen. psychiatry Cedars-Sinai Med. Ctr., L.A. 1973-76; psychoanalytic tng. 1974-80; cons. So. Calif. Counseling Ctr., 1976; staff psychiatrist L.A. Co. Dept. Mental Health 1976-77; staff psychiatrist Calif. Med. Gp. 1977-78; med. dir. L.A. Co. Health Dept. Methadone Maint. Clinic, West Hollywood 1979-89, also clin. dir. Day Treatment Pgm. Gateways Hosp. 1980-81; pvt. practice, L.A., 1976-81, pvt. group practice gen. psychiatry, Long Beach, 1981-84, pvt. practice Decatur, Ill. 1984-89, Roseville, Ca. 1989–; med. dir. Spl. Care Unit, Hillhaven-Fair Oaks (Ca.) Healthcare Ctr. 1989–, The Ctr. for Med. Wt. Mgmt., Sacto. 1991–; cons. Calif. St. Dept. Soc. Svs., Sacto. 1991–; faculty So. Ill. Univ. Sch. of Med. 1986-89, UC Davis Sch. of Med. 1991–; mem: Am. Assn. of Psychoanalytic Physicians (Fellow), Am. Psychiat. Assn., Placer-Nev. Co. Med. Soc., Cent. Calif. Psychiat. Assn., Sacto-El Dorado Co. Med. Soc., Calif. Med. Assn., Am. Soc. Bariatric Physicians, No. Am. Assn. for Study of Obesity, Am. Coll. of Nutrition; mil: capt., flt. surgeon US Air Force, 1971-73. Ofc: 87 Scripps Dr Ste 214 Sacramento 95825 Tel: 916/567-0111

BRENT, RICHARD S., marketing manager; b. July 30, 1949, Pittsburgh, Pa.; s. Irving J. and Sarah Evelyn (Weiss) B.; m. Sharon I., Aug. 17, 1969; children: Andrew, Sarah, Kirah; edn: BA, Sonoma State Coll., Rohnert Park 1972; tchg. cred., 1973. Career: gen. mgr. Solar Warehouse, El Cajon 1980-82; plant mgr. Jet Air Inc., El Cajon 1982-85; program mgr. Solar Turbines Inc., San Diego 1985–; awards: outstanding vol. of year Combined Health Agys. San Diego 1989, Point of Light, Solar Turbines Inc. 1990-91; mem. Solar Profl. Mgmt. Assn. S.D. (bd. pres. 1989); civic: Combined Health Agencies Drive (exec. bd. 1991, 92), Zool. Soc. San Diego Keeper's Club, United Cerebral Palsy S.D. (v.p. 1984), Nat. Kidney Found. S.D. (chmn. 1990-91), United Way S.D. Loaned Exec. 1986, Combined Health Agy. S.D. (exec. com. 1992); club: Sports Chalet Dive; publs: booklet, Who Says You Can't Do Anything? An ecology primer, 1970; rec: scuba, reading, touring, gardening.

BRESSAN, PAUL LOUIS, lawyer; b. June 15, 1947, Rockville Centre, N.Y.; s. Louis Charles and Nance Elizabeth (Batteley) B.; edn: BA, Fordham Coll. 1969; JD, Columbia Law Sch. 1975. Career: atty., assoc. Kelley Drye & Warren,

N.Y.C. 1975-84, ptnr., N.Y., Los Angeles 1984–; mem: Am. Bar Assn., Calif. Bar Assn.; mil: lt. USN 1970-72; Republican; R.Cath. Ofc: Kelley Drye & Warren 515 S Flower St Ste 1100 Los Angeles 90071

BRETT-ELSPAS, JANIS E., public relations and marketing consultant; b. Sept. 6, 1956, Hackensack, N.J.; d. Charles and Jean Estelle (Hawrey) Brett; m. Shlomo Elspas, Sept. 14, 1986; edn: BA political sci., Univ. Ariz. 1978; profl. designation in Public Relations, UCLA 1983. Career: asst. pub. rels. dir. SSC&B, Los Angeles 1979-81; pub. rels. mgr. Informatics Gen. Corp., Woodland Hills 1981-84; account exec. Hill & Knowlton, San Jose 1984-85; corp. account exec. Rogers & Cowan, Los Angeles 1985-86; pres., founder Rachel P.R. Services, Santa Monica 1984–; honors: Who's Who in the West, Who's Who in Advtg., Who's Who of Am. Women, O'Dwyer's Dir. of P.R. Execs., Informatics Gen. Corp. CEO Employee of Quarter (1983); mem: Pub. Rels. Soc. Am., Internat. Assn. Bus. Comms., Publicity Club L.A., Indep. Writers So. Calif., Delta Zeta; articles and feature stories pub. in profl. jours. (1983–), syndicated column Copley News Service (1986-87); Ofc: 1650 S Pacific Coast Hwy #200-C Redondo Beach 90277

BREUER, MELVIN A., professor; b. Feb. 1, 1938, Los Angeles, Calif.; s. Arthur and Bertha Helen (Friedman) B.; m. Sandra Joyce Scalir, Apr. 7, 1963; children: Teri b. 1966, Jeffrey b. 1968; edn: BS, UCLA, 1959, MS, 1961; PhD, elec. engring., UC Berkeley 1965. Career: prof. elec. engring. and computer sci., Univ. of So. Calif. 1965–; chmn. Dept. of Elec. Engring.-Systems, USC 1991-94; honors: Fulbright-Hays scholar 1972, recipient Assocs. Award for Creativity in Res. and Scholarship, USC 1991, USC Sch. of Engring. Award for Exceptional Svc. 1991, IEEE Computer Soc.'s Taylor L. Booth Edn. Award 1993, Charles Lee Powell chair of computer engring., USC 1995; fellow, IEEE 1985–; editor and co-author: Design Automation of Digital Systems: Theory and Techniques; editor: Digital Systems Design Automation: Languages, Simulation and Data Base; co-author: Diagnosis and Reliable Design of Digital Systems, Digital System Testing and Testable Design, 1990 (reprinted 1995), 160+ tech. papers, co-editor Computer Hardware Description Languages and Their Applications; co-editor and contbr. Knowledge Based Systems for Test and Diagnosis; Democrat; Jewish. Res: 16857 Bosque Dr Encino 91436 Ofc: Univ. of Southern California Los Angeles 90089-2562

BREWER, KARA PRATT, university planned giving executive; b. Oct. 29, 1930, Reno, Nev.; d. Kenneth and Kara (Lucas) Pratt; m. David P. Brewer, Sept. 10, 1949; children: Margaret b. 1950, Martin b. 1951, Kenneth b. 1953, Paul b. 1954, Elena b. 1957, Clare b. 1959, Sam b. 1961, Matthew b. 1965; edn: Smith Coll. 1948-49; BA, Univ. of Pacific 1969; MA, 1972; DA, 1976. Career: asst. ed. Pacific Historian, Univ. of Pacific, Stockton 1971, instr. 1971-75, writer in residence 1976, dir. of alumni and parent programs 1977-90, dir. of planned giving, 1990–; conf. chair CASE Dist. VII 1983, conf. co-chair Dist. VII 1982; awards: Danforth Found. fellowships 1969-71; mem: Pope John XXIII Found. (bd. mem.), St. Marys Interfaith Dining Room (bd. mem.), Am. Com. for Irish Studies (conf. chair We. region 1991); author: Pioneer or Perish: A History of Univ. of Pacific (1977), contbr. book preface to Pacific: Yesterday & The Day Before That (H.S. Jacoby 1989); Democrat; R.Cath.; rec: reading. Res: 94 W Knoles Way Stockton 95204 Ofc University of Pacific Planned Giving Office Stockton 95211

BREWER, LEO, scientist, educator; b. June 13, 1919, St. Louis, Mo.; s. Abraham and Hanna (Resnik) B.; m. Rose Strugo, Aug. 22, 1945; children: Beth b. 1952, Roger b. 1954, Gail b. 1956; edn: BS, Caltech, 1940; PhD, UC Berkeley, 1943. Career: res. assoc. US Army Manhattan Project, Berkeley 1943-46; principal investigator Lawrence Berkeley Lab. (previously known as Radiation Lab.), Berkeley 1943-94, assoc. dir. LBL 1967-75, hd. inorganic mats. res. div. 1961-75; asst. prof. dept. chemistry UC Berkeley 1946-50, assoc. prof. 1950-55, prof. 1955–; awards: Great Western Dow Fellow 1942, Guggenheim Fellow 1950, E.O. Lawrence award AEC 1961, R.S. Williams lectr. M.I.T. 1963, H. Werner lectr. Univ. Kans. 1963, O.M. Smith lectr. Okla. St. Univ. 1964, G.N. Lewis lectr. UCB 1964, Faculty lectr. UCB 1966, Corn Products lectr. Penn. St. Univ. 1970, disting. alumni Caltech 1974, W.D. Harkins lectr. Univ. Chgo. 1974, Oak Ridge Nat. Lab. lectr. 1979, Frontiers in Chemistry lectr. Texas A&M 1981, Eyring Lectr. Chemistry, Ariz. St. Univ. 1989, Louis C. Jordy res. scholar lectr. Drew Univ. 1983, Leo Brewer Special Festchrift Modern High Temperature Science 1984, Louis Jacob Bircher lectr. Vanderbilt Univ. 1986, Berkeley Citation UCB 1989, Leo Brewer retirement symposium on high temperature and materials chemistry Lawrence Berkeley Lab. 1989, Berkeley Fellow UCB 1992; mem: Alpha Chi Sigma, AAAS (fellow 1960), Am. Acad. of Art and Scis. 1979, AAUP, Am. Ceramic Soc. (Hon. mem. award 1991), Am. Chem. Soc. (Leo Hendrick Baekeland award N.Jersey Sect. ACS 1953, W.Coover lectr., Ames, Iowa sect. ACS 1967), Am. Physical Soc. (fellow 1973), Am. Soc. for Metals (fellow 1989), Calif. Acad. of Scis., Calif. Assn. of Chemistry Tchrs., Calif. Botanic Soc., Calif. Native Plant Soc., Calorimetry Conf. (H. Huffman lectr. 1966), Coblentz Soc., Combustion Inst., Electrochemical Soc. (lectr. 1970, Palladium Medalist 1971, Henry B. Linford award for disting. tchg. 1988), Fedn. of Am. Scientists, Internat. Plansee Soc. for Powder Metallurgy, Materials Res. Soc., Metallurgical Soc. of AIME (Wm.

Hume-Rothery Award 1983, Extractive Metallurgy Sci. Award 1991), Nat. Acad. of Scis. 1959, Optical Soc. Am., Royal Soc. Chemistry, Soc. of Sigma Xi, Tau Beta Pi; coauthor: Thermodynamics (1961), 170+ sci. publs. Ofc: Dept. Chemistry, University of California, Berkeley 94720

BREWSTER, RUDI MILTON, federal judge; b. May 18, 1932, Sioux Falls, S.D.; s. Charles Edwin and Wilma Therese (Rud) B.; m. Gloria Nanson, June 27, 1954; children: Scot b. 1956, Lauri b. 1958, Julie b. 1960; edn: AB Princeton Univ., 1954; JD, Stanford Law sch., 1960. Career: civil trial lawyer and ptnr. law firm Gray, Cary, Ames & Frye, San Diego 1960-84; judge U.S. Dist. Ct., San Diego 1984–; faculty Calif. State Bar cont. edn. seminars; mem: Am. Bar Assn., San Diego Co. Bar Assn. (v.p. 1981-82, dir. 1969-72, del. state conv. 1965-74, mem: State Bar Com. on Unauthorized Practice of Law 1965-68), Am. Coll. of Trial Lawyers, Am. Board of Trial Advocates, Am. Inns of Ct. (pres. Louis M. Welsh Chapt. #9), San Diego Rotary Club (pres. 1980-81, bd. 1977-82); mil: USN 1954-81, capt. USNR-Ret. JAG Corps; Republican; Lutheran; rec: skiing, hunting, fishing, gardening. Ofc: U.S. District Court, 940 Front St San Diego 92189

BRICHTA, EDGAR S., physician, psychiatrist; b. Feb. 5, 1930, Bratislava, Czechoslovakia; nat. 1972; s. Maximillian and Regina (Lustig) B.; m. Judy, Apr. 16, 1954; children: Danny b. 1955, Eric b. 1958, Karen b. 1960, Paul b. 1962, Jenny b. 1964; edn: BS, Concordia Univ., Montreal, Quebec, Can. 1957; MD, McGill Univ., Montreal 1961; MPH, UC Berkeley, Calif. 1965; lic. physician and surgeon, Calif. 1965. Career: chief MHS, USAF, Pentagon, W.D.C. 1974-81; psychiatrist, pvt. practice, Yreka, Calif. 1981-86; psychiatrist SCMHC, Sacramento 1986-93, Psychiatry West, Sacto. 1987-93; sr. psychiatrist CMF-CDC, Vacaville 1988-92; locum tenens Vista Staffing Solution, Salt Lake City, Utah 1993–; asst. prof. Univ. of N.D., Minot 1978-80; awards: Mappin Medal, SGWU, Montreal, Quebec 1955, 1st prize Can. Chem. Inst., Montreal 1956, Wyeth Pediatric Fellowship, Radnor, Pa. 1962-64; M&CH Fellowship, UC Berkeley 1964-66; mem: Sierra Club., Audubon Soc.; author: pub. articles on alcohol dependency, 1969, mental health treatment in AF, 1976; mil: col. (0-6), USAF 1974-81; Democrat; Atheist; rec: hiking, gardening. Res: 9471 Fort Worth Way Sacramento 95827 Ofc: Vista Staffing Solution Salt Lake City Utah

BRIGGS, DONALD CLIFFORD, engineering manager; b. Sept. 19, 1932, Los Angeles; s. Clifford Russell and Mildred Louise Wainscott (Shriner) B.; m. Sonja Louise Schwab, May 11, 1963; children: Robin b. 1956, Tammie b. 1960, Linda b. 1964; edn: BSME, Stanford Univ. 1957; MSME, 1958; engring., 1960; MBA, Univ. Santa Clara 1965; MSEE, 1973. Career: engr. AiResearch, Los Angeles 1959-61; engr. ITEK, Palo Alto 1961-65; mgr. Ford Motor Co. 1965-90; mgr. Loral 1990–; awards: Stanford Univ. William Eckert Prize 1959, Sigma Xi, Tau Beta Pi, Beta Gamma Sigma; mem: AIAA (com., assoc. fellow), Nat. Mgmt. Assn., Masons, Elks, Dodge Car Club (v.p.); author: 50+ tech. papers pub.; 5 patents; mil: USN 1953-55; Republican; Protestant; rec: fishing, antique cars. Res: 10141 Prado Vista Dr Cupertino 95014 Ofc: Space Systems/Loral 3825 Fabian Way Palo Alto 94303

BRIGGS, ROBERT NATHAN, electronics engineer (communications); b. Dec. 22, 1946 Miami Beach, Fla.; s. Donald Hicks and Harriett Martha (Mercer) B.; m. Polly Elizabeth Partridge, Dec. 22, 1970; children: Nathan Michael, Carey Robert, Christopher Alan; edn: BSEE, Northrop Inst. of Tech., Inglewood, Calif., 1974; Univ. of Nev., Las Vegas, Nev., 1978-81. Career: electronic engr., Telcom, Inc., Las Vegas, Nev., 1974-75; sr. optics engr., Holmes and Narver, Las Vegas 1975-81; dir. of QA, Am. Fiber Optics, Signal Hill, Calif., 1981-83; sr. section head, TRW, Inc., Redondo Beach, Calif., 1983-85; optics R&D engr., TRW, Inc. 1985-91; TDRSS project engr., TRW, Inc. 1986-90; AXAF-I project engr., TRW, Inc. 1991–; chmn., IEEE Student Chpt., Inglewood, Calif., 1973-74; class pres., Northrop Inst. of Tech., Inglewood, Calif., 1973-74; com. mem., Electronics Industries Assn., Wash., DC, 1978-86; awards: President's award, Northrop Inst. of Tech., 1974; Certificate of Appreciation, Electronics Industries Assn., Wash., DC, 1986; Certificate of Appreciation, NASA, Goddard Space Flight Ctr., 1989; mem: Optical Soc. of Am., 1976-90; Am. Inst. of Aeronautics & Astronautics, Inc., 1985-90; Boy Scouts of Am., L.A. County: Cub Master 1986-91; Scout Master 1991-94; inventor, Security System for Dept. of Energy, 1975; author: FO Standards & Procedures, Electronics Industries Assn., 1978-86; prin. investigator, spacecraft res. projects: Spacecraft Comm. Tech. 1984, Spacecraft Fiber Optic Local Area Network 1984-88; mil: sgt., USAF, 1967-71; Republican; Episcopal. Res: 6532 Verde Ridge Rd. Rancho Palos Verdes 90275. Ofc: TRW Inc. S&TG One Space Park Redondo Beach 90274

BRIGGS, WINSLOW RUSSELL, biologist-plant physiologist; b. Apr. 29, 1928, St. Paul, Minn.; s. John DeQuedville and Marjorie (Winslow) B.; m. Ann Morrill, June 30, 1955; children: Caroline, Lucia, Marion; edn: BA, MA, and PhD, Harvard Univ., 1951, 52, 56. Career: instr. biol. scis. Stanford Univ. 1955-57, asst. prof. 1957-62, asso. prof. 1962-66, prof. 1966-67; prof. biology Harvard Univ. 1967-73; dir. dept. plant biology Carnegie Instn. of Washington, Stanford, 1973-93; awards: John Simon Guggenheim fellow 1973-74, Alexander von Humboldt U.S. senior scientist award 1984-85, Deutsche Akademie der

Naturforscher Leopoldina 1986, Nat. Acad. Scis., Am. Acad. Arts and Scis., Stephen Hales Award Am. Soc. Plant Physiologists; mem: AAAS (fellow), Sigma Xi, Am. Soc. Plant Physiologists (pres. 1975-76), Calif. Botanical Soc. (pres. 1976-77), Am. Inst. Biol. Scis. (pres. 1980-81), Am. Soc. Photobiology, Botanical Soc. Am., Nature Conservancy; contbg. author: Life on Earth (1973), Annual Rev. of Plant Physiology (assoc. ed. 1961-72, editor 1972-83), profl. jour. articles on plant growth & devel., photobiology. Res: 480 Hale St Palo Alto 94301 Ofc: Dept. Plant Biology Carnegie Institution of Washington, 290 Panama St Stanford 94305

BRILL, JOEL VICTOR, physician, educator; b. Jan. 28, 1956, Phila.; s. Earl Burton and Lois Elaine (Werner) B.; m. Laurie Ann Lissner, May 17, 1980; children: Jacob b. 1989, Zachary b. 1991; edn: AB in biology, UCLA, 1976; MD, Chicago Med. Sch., 1980. Career: resident internal medicine UCLA, Sepulveda 1980-83; fellow gastroenterology USC, L.A. 1983-85; pvt. practice gastroenterology, Ventura 1985–; instr. in medicine USC Med. Sch. 1983–; med. staff Ventura Co. Med. Ctr. (dir. gastroent. svs.), Community Memorial Hosp. Ventura (dir. gastrointestinal lab., v.chmn. dept. medicine 1992, chmn. 1993, CQI/TQM Task Force, med. staff exec. com. 1993-95, chmn. quality assurance & quality improvement 1993-94); medical dir. VIP-IPA, Oxnard 1994; mem: Am. Coll. Gastroent. (fellow), Am. Gastroenterol. Assn., Am. Soc. for Gastrointestinal Endoscopy, Am. Soc. Parenteral & Enteral Nutrition, Am. Coll. Physicians, Am. Coll. of Physician Execs.; rec: reading, travel, cooking. Res: 32 Cerro Crest Dr Camarillo 93010 Ofc: 168 N Brent St Ste 404 Ventura 93003

BRISBIN, ROBERT EDWARD, management consultant, insurance executive; b. Feb. 13, 1946, Bklyn.; m. Sally Ann Norton; edn: BS in B.A., San Francisco State, 1968; cert. safety exec., World Safety Org. Career: field rep. Index Research, San Mateo 1969-82; mgr. loss control Homeland Ins. Co., San Jose 1982-87; ins. exec. Morris & Garritano, San Luis Obispo 1987–; pres. Robert E. Brisbin & Assocs., San Francisco 1975–; mem. Am. Soc. Safety Engrs. 1982–, World Safety Org. 1984–; author: Loss Control for the Small to Medium Size Business (1990), w/ Carol Grant, Workplace Wellness (1992); composer song: America the Land of Liberty (1986); Republican; rec: scuba, writing, flying, musical performance, photography. Address: PO Box 341 Pismo Beach 93448

BRITTON, RANDIE SUE, stockbroker; b. Jan. 25, 1955, Cleveland, Ohio; d. Sol and Esther (Kolinsky) Olshansky; m. Jonathan Britton, Dec. 23, 1980, div. 1983; edn: cert. pgm. in law enforcement Lakeland Comm. Coll., Mentor, Oh. 1973-75, commd. police ofcr. S. Euclid, Oh. 1975. Career: probation ofcr. S. Euclid Police Dept. 1975-76; sales asst. Dean Witter, Cleveland, Oh. 1976-79, Encino, Calif. 1979-83; sales asst./stockbroker A. G. Becker, Los Angeles 1983-86; Shearson Lehman, Woodland Hills 1986-87; stockbroker PaineWebber Inc., Woodland Hills 1987-89; fin. cons. Shearson Lehman Hutton Inc., Sherman Oaks 1989; Dean Witter, Encino 1990-92; Guide Dogs of Am., Sylmar 1992–; asst. instr. fin. plng. prog. UCLA 1987-90; volunteer Internat. Guiding Eyes, Sylmar (recipient recogn. award 1987); mem. Norwegian Elkhound Assn. So. Calif., Police Benevolent Assn., Fraternal Order Police (Cleve.), Valley Sword Club, Tri-Valley Polo; publs: editorial Wall St. Jour. (1986); Republican; Jewish; rec: polo, fencing, dog shows. Address: Canoga Park 91306

BROADHURST, NORMAN NEIL, manufacturing company executive; b. Dec. 17, 1946, Chico; s. Frank Spencer and Dorothy Mae (Conrad) B.; m. Victoria Thomson, Aug. 7, 1976; 1 son, Scott; edn: BS, CSU Chico 1969; MBA, Golden Gate Univ. 1975. Career: marketing staff Del Monte Corp., San Francisco 1969-76; brand mgmt. Colgate-Palmolive, Riviana Foods Div., Houston 1976-78; mktg. mgr. Coca-Cola Foods, Houston 1978-83; v.p. mktg. Beatrice Cos., Chgo. 1983-86; pres/COO Famous Amos Chocolate Chip Cookie Corp., Van Nuys 1986-88; sr. v.p./pres. of consumer prods. div., Kerr Group Inc., 1988-95; chmn./CEO, Double Eagle Holdings Inc. 1995–; mem: Am. Mktg. Assn., Am. Mgmt. Assn.; civic: Cystic Fibrosis Found. (chmn. Youth Soccer Pgm., Houston 1982-83), South Coast Symph. (chmn./pres. 1985-88, exec. com. 1988–), Literacy Volunteers of Am. (nat. bd. 1988–, vice chmn. 1993–), Toastmasters Internat. S.F. (chpt. pres. 1974-76); mil: s/sgt USAFR 1966-73; Republican; Presbyterian. Ofc: Double Eagle Holdings Inc 19528 Ventura Blvd #420 Tarzana 91356

BRODERICK, EDWARD MICHAEL, III, corporate lawyer; b. Nov. 4, 1947, Stamford, Conn.; s. Edward Michael Broderick Jr. (dec.) and Lois Caroline (Brown) Contaras; m. Jeanine Lynn Anglea, Mar. 4, 1989; children: Courtney Elizabeth b. 1990, Ashley Noelle b. 1991; edn: BA, St. Anselm Coll., Manchester, N.H. 1969; JD, St. John's Univ. Sch. of Law, 1973; admitted bar: N.Y., 1974, Conn., 1974. Career: adminstrv. asst. legislative affairs Royal Globe Ins. Cos., NY, NY 1969-73, staff atty. 1974-75; asst. counsel and secty. G.E. Credit Corp./Puritan Ins. Co., Stamford, Conn. 1975-79; asst. gen. counsel ITT Financial Corp., also gen. counsel and secty. ITT Lyndon Ins. Group, St. Louis, Mo. 1979-86; v.p. and gen. counsel CalFarm Ins. Cos., Sacramento, Ca. 1986–; mem. Am. Bar Assn. (mem. coms. 1971–), NY State Bar Assn. 1973–, Conn. Bar Assn. 1973–; civic: St. Louis (Mo.) Squires 1985-86; Republican; R.Cath.; rec: skiing, sailing. Ofc: CalFarm Insurance Cos. 1601 Exposition Blvd Sacramento 95815

BRODSKY, STANLEY JEROME, physics professor; b. Jan. 9, 1940, St. Paul, Minn.; s. Sidney Charles and Esther Rene (Levitt) B.; m. Judith Ellen Preis, June 29, 1986; children: Stephen Andrew, David Jonathan; edn: B.Physics, Univ. Minn., 1961, PhD Physics, 1964. Career: research assoc. Columbia Univ. 1964-66; Stanford Linear Accelerator Ctr. (SLAC), Stanford Univ., 1966-: res. assoc. 1966-68, permanent staff 1968-75, assoc. prof. 1975-76, full prof. 1976–, head Theoretical Physics Dept. 1994–; vis. AVCO assoc. prof. Physics Dept. Cornell Univ. 1970, vis. prof. natural scis. Inst. for Adv. Study Princeton 1982, vis. prof. Max Planck Inst. for Nuclear Physics Heidelberg Sept. '87 and Mar.-Sept.'88; mem. sci. and ednl. advy. com. Lawrence Berkeley Lab. Univ. Calif. 1986–; mem. bd. referees and editl. bd. Physical Review (Am. Physical Soc.) 1978-79, 85-86; awards: Sr. Disting. U.S. Scientist Award (Humboldt Award) Alexander von Humboldt Found. 1987–, External Sci. Mem. Max Planck Inst. for Nuclear Physics in Heidelberg (3/89–), assoc. editor Nuclear Physics B (1987–), lectr. Disting. Speaker Colloquium Series, Univ. Minn. (2/89), res. grantee U.S./Israel Binat. Found., Weizmann Inst. 1986-90; apptd. bds: NSF Review Panel for Theoretical Physics (chmn. 1980-81), Weizmann Inst. of Science Forum (exec. bd. 1977–), mem. com. on fundamental constants Nat. Res. Council- Nat. Acad. of Scis. 1972-75; fellow, Am. Physics Soc.; coauthor 4 books: Lectures on Lepton Nucleon Scattering and Quantum Chromodynamics (1982), Quarks and Nuclear Forces (1982), Nuclear Chromodynamics: Quarks and Gluons in Particles and Nuclei (1986), Perturbative Quantum Chromodynamics (1989). Res: 2339 Branner Dr Menlo Park 94025 Ofc: Bin 81, Stanford Linear Accelerator Center, 2575 Sand Hill Rd Menlo Park 94025

BROGDON, RALPH EWING, JR., judge; b. Aug. 12, 1927, Fresno; s. Ralph E. and Doris Elaine (Nilmeier) B.; children: John Arthur b. 1946 (dec.), Joan Marie b. 1951, Dirk Ewing b. 1956, Lisa Mary b. 1959, Gregory Ralph b. 1961, Aleta Marcelle b. 1979; edn: att. Menlo Coll., 1947-48; AA, CSU San Jose 1949; BA econ., Stanford Univ. 1951; Stanford Univ. Sch. of Law 1951-53; JD, Southwestern Univ. Sch. of Law 1956; admitted Calif. State Bar 1959. Career: atty. assoc. w/ Boris S. Woolley, Torrance 1959-60; ptnr./assoc. w/ William N. Willens, Lawndale 1959-64; assoc. w/ Truman R. Adkins, Redondo Bch. 1964-67; assoc. w/ Gerald F. Moriarty, Edward Gorman, Norman Miller, John Holtrichter, John Chevalier, R.B. 1967-73; assoc. w/ Tunney & Carlyle, San Jose 1973-74; atty. pvt. practice, Cupertino 1974-89; judge Municipal Ct., Santa Clara Co., 1989–; honors: CSF, Triad Hon. Soc., Menlo Coll. #1 scholar Freshman Class 1947-48, coll. athletics (baseball, basketball); mem: ABA, Calif. Trial Lawyer's Assn., L.A. Co. Bar Assn., Criminal Cts. Bar Assn., Calif. Judges Assn. (exec. bd. 1994-97); past mem: Santa Clara Co. Bar Assn. (bd. 1976-78), Sunnyvale-Cupertino Bar Assn. (pres. 1978), Santa Clara Co. Trial Lawyers Assn., South Bay Bar Assn. (pres. 1972, chmn. Annual Golf Tourn. 1962-71, chmn. South Bay Legal Aid Found. 1963-65), civic: Am. Cancer Soc. (featured in ACS video of 3 survivors of cancer of larynx, 1985), frequent speaker var. comm. groups and schs. and support counselor for laryngectomy patients pre/post surgery; mem. Stanford Alumni Assn. (life, dir. Stanford Buck Club 1978-87), Stanford Law Soc. of Santa Clara Co., Phi Alpha Delta legal frat. 1952–, Canyon Lake Property Owners Assn. (bd., past pres.), C.of C., Kiwanis (pres. Redondo Bch. 1964), Canyon Lake Men's Golf Club (charter pres. 1970-71) past leader Cub Scouts, Babe Ruth Baseball League; mil: Yeoman 3/c USN 1945-46; Republican: active precinct wkr., campaigner 1950-89, charter chmn. Stanford Univ. Young Repubs. Club 1949; Prot.; rec: golf. Res: 4950 Cherry Ave #84 San Jose 95118-2714 Ofc: 200 W Hedding St San Jose 95110-1774

BROKL, STANLEY SCOTT, senior staff engineer, inventor; b. Apr. 20, 1941, Hutchinson, Minn.; s. Arnold Stanley and Annette (Chidlaw) B.; m. Christina Gutierrez; children: Timothy, b. 1961, James, b. 1963, Diana, b. 1964, Deborah, b. 1966; edn: West Coast Univ. 1969-73; AA, Pasadena City Coll. 1971; BS bus., Univ. of La Verne, 1988; USN Grad. Electronic Tech Sch. Career: jr. engr./tech. var. cos. 1960-69; sr. tech. Jet Propulsion Lab., Pasadena 1969, sr. engring. asst. 1973-77; sr. mem. tech. staff RCA Somerville, NJ 1977-80; sr. engr. JPL, 1980-83, tech. group leader and cognizant engr. for Goldstone Solar System Radar, 1984-88; systems engr. LORAL EOS, 1988-90, project engr. for MAIS, Nov. 1991–; proj. engr., show/ride electronics engring. Walt Disney Imagineering, Glendale, 1990-91, in Euro Disney, France, 8/90-7/91; awards: NASA Group Achievement Award "Series X" (10/85), NASA Monetary Award, tech. brief "A General Monitor and Control Interface To The VAX Unibus" (11/86), recognition for var. inventions, NASA (1972, 74, 77, 80); three monetary awards for Patent Appls., RCA (1977, 78, 79); Patentee: Peripheral Interactive Device with Manual Controls (1973), Jam Resistant TV System (1982), Jam Resistant Receiver (1983), Multiple Synchronous Counters with Ripple Read (1984); mem: IEEE, American Radio Relay League (life, section mgr. L.A. Sect. 1980-84); club: Sierra La Verne CC; mil: ETRSN, USN 1958-60; Democrat; Prot.; rec: amateur radio opr. N2YQ (1955–). Res: 2126 E Iron Club Dr La Verne 91750 Ofc: LORAL EOS, 600 E Bonita Pomona CA 91767

BROOKE, CHARLES THOMAS, consulting electrical engineer (retired); b. April 29, 1911, Cincinnati, Ohio; s. Clarence Martin and Stella Louella B.; m. Annabel Hoem, Aug. 9, 1952, dec. 1979; children: Michael Thomas b. 1943, Charles Dean b. 1954, Cherilyn Dianne b. 1956; edn: EE, Univ. of Cincinnati 1929-35; Reg. Profl. Elec. Engr., Calif. 1949. Career: design engr. Auto Lite

1934-37; Underwriters Laboratory Inc.: inspector, Cincinnati and Cleveland 1937-41, project engr., Chicago 1946-47, supvsg. inspector, Los Angeles 1947-54, assoc. field engr., Santa Clara 1954-76; currently, p.t. cons. engr. to computer cos. in the Bay area; cons. engr. computer design and safety, Ramtek 1978-85, Ford Aerospace 1977-78, National Semiconductor 1984-94, RAMCO 1983-84, Elsenhower Tunnel (Denver) 1982-83; honors: Highest Award, IBM 1985 Magicians Order of Merlin, Excalibur, award of hon. Who's Who Calif. 1992; mem: Internat. Brotherhood of Magicians 1936–, Hollister Masons; publs: Switchboard Handbook, 1974; Fixture Handbook, 1973; How to Speak In Public, 1972; Elec Fuse Table, 1970; mil: capt. US Army CAC (Radar) Active 1941-46, Pacific Area 1942-43, Army War Coll. 1944-46, Army Reserve 5 yrs., ROTC 1929-35; Republican; Prot.; rec: profl. magician, lapidarist, golf, wood carving. Res: 460 Donald Dr Hollister 95023

BROOKS, GLENN ALLEN, audio engineer, video service company buyer; b. Mar. 23, 1960, Pasadena; s. Robert Allen Brooks and Sarah Eloise (Merritt) Bogenreif; m. Tracy Jo Williams, June 11, 1983 (div. 1994); children: Joshua Allen-Ray b. 1984, Ashleigh Nicole b. 1987, Jonathan Lincoln b. 1988; edn: AA, Goldenwest Coll., 1983; BS, San Diego State Univ., 1985; Orange Coast Coll. 1978-79; Coastline Comm. Coll. 1983; MBA cand., Univ. of Phoenix, Fountain Valley, Calif. 1995; lic. foster parent, Orange Co. 1990–, Notary Public, Orange Co. 1988-92. Career: audio engr. KPBS-TV, San Diego 1984-85; Group W Productions, Los Angeles 1985-86; KSCI-TV, L.A. 1986-88; conformist Chace Productions Inc., Hollywood 1988; materials coord. Rank Video Svs. Am., Garden Grove 1989–, also TQM facilitator, 1992–, sys. controller II, 1993–; pres. Brooks Concepts Inc., Huntington Beach 1990-92; owner Moriah Recording, San Diego, 1985, Small World Prodns., H.B. 1986-90; proprieter Celluloid Research, Westminster 1994- Republican; Christian; rec: water/snow sports, radio controlled gliding. Res: Huntington Beach 92648 Ofc: Rank Video Services America, 12691 Pala Dr Garden Grove 92641

BROSCHE, PAUL H., marketing executive, educator, percussionist; b. Seattle, Wash.; m. Susan Rose Kaelin (Santa Ana Jr. Miss 1971), Sept. 20, 1972; children: Paul, Jr. b. 1973, Elisabeth Lorena b. 1976, Susan Catherine b. 1979; edn: BS mktg., USC, 1974, grad. work in mktg., 1974. Career: advertising acct. exec. N.W. Ayer, Los Angeles 1974-75; regional supr. Foster & Kleiser, Los Angeles 1975-78; mktg. proj. mgr. The Bekins Co., L.A. 1978-79, dir. advt. The Bekins Co., Glendale 1979-80, national mktg. mgr. 1980-82, v.p. mktg. 1982-84; co-founder and exec. v.p. The Practice Builder Agency, Irvine, Calif. 1984–; musician- Percussion Section leader, USC Band, 1970-74, percussion instr./arranger, USC, 1974-80, freelance percussion performer/arranger, 1980–, co-prod. two commercial record albums for Rage Music Internat., North Hollywood 1984-85; guest lectr. Art Ctr. of Design, Pasadena 1978-79, paid speaker on mgmt., mktg. and advt. strategies throughout U.S., 1983–; p.t. mktg. faculty CSU Fullerton, 1984–. Ofc: PHB Marketing Inc., 1881 Hawkbrook Dr San Dimas 91773

BROWN, CLYDE WILSON, certified public accountant; b. Dec. 31, 1935, San Francisco; s. Stitt Wilson and Rose Eilene (Dolan) B.; m. Norlene Sharon Tendler, May 5, 1978; prior m. Carol Suzanne Clayholt, Dec. 31, 1955 (div.); edn: BA, San Francisco St. Univ. 1958. Career: posting clk. Anglo Nat. Bank, S.F. 1954-55; cost acct. J.L. Stuart Mfg. 1955-58; C.P.A. Stevens & Maness, Salinas 1960-61; Touche Ross Bailey & Smart 1961-62; Wilbur H. Stevens & Co. 1962-70; Elmer Fox Westheimer & Co. 1970-79; Clyde W. Brown Associates, Salinas 1979–; mem: Calif. Soc. C.P.A. (dir. 1983-88, 89-93, exec. com. 89-92, pres. San Jose chpt. 83-84), Am. Inst. C.P.A., Am. Acctg. Assn., Rotary (Paul Harris Fellow, treas. 1990-94), Salinas C.of C. (v.p. fin. 1976-77), Commonwealth Club of Calif.; mil: sp4 AUS 1958-60; rec: sailing, golf. Address: Salinas 93901

BROWN, DAVID R., corporate rehabilitation director; b. May 9, 1956, Orange, N.J.; s. George R. and Beatrice C. (Hansen) B.; m. Marilyn Escalle, Nov. 15, 1986; edn: BS, E. Carolina Univ. 1979; MPH, San Diego St. Univ. 1989; reg. physical therapist Calif. Career: staff physical therapist St. Barnabas Med. Center, Livingston, N.J. 1979-80; sr. physical therapist UC San Diego, 1980-83; supr. physical therapy Alvarado Med. Center, San Diego 1983-86; dir. rehab. Pomerado Hosp., Poway 1986-94; corporate dir. rehab. Kennon S. Shea and Associates, El Cajon 1994–; cons. UCSD Phase I Surgical Cardiac Rehab. Program 1983; honors: Phi Kappa Phi, Pomerado Hosp. Dept. Head of Year 1988, Bethany Coll. All-Am. Swimmer 1976; mem: Am. Heart Assn., Am. Lung Assn.; article pub. in profl. jour., 1983; rec: swimming, softball. Address: El Cajon 92021

BROWN, DIANNA LEE, promotional sales management; b. Jan. 4, 1947, Knoxville, Tenn.; d. Henry O. and Irene J. (Letner) Hanson; m. Kenneth F. Brown, May 3, 1986; children: Matthew Brooks b. 1976, Michael Brooks b. 1978; edn: attended Centralia (Wash.) Jr. Coll. 1965-66; completed legal secretarial course, Wash. Tech. Inst., Seattle 1967. Career: sec., The Boeing Co., Renton, Wash. 1966-70; dir. sales promotions, Communication Resources, Costa Mesa, Calif. 1970-80; pres. and CEO, Center Promotions, Running Springs, Calif. 1981–; awards: 3rd place, state typing contest, Future Bus. Leaders of Am. 1965; mem: Future Bus. Leaders of Am. (sec. 1963-65), Women's Club of Running Springs (v.p. 1992-94); created "Shopping Sitter," in

1981, a promotional svc. for shopping ctrs. and convention ctr. shows (supervised play ctr. for children ages 2-12). Ofc: Brooks Management Corp dba Center Promotions PO Box 776 Running Springs 92382

BROWN, DONNA MARIE, deputy city manager; b. Jan. 5, 1943, Hopkinsville, Ky.; d. John Wm., Jr. and Cola Marie (Hocker) B.; edn: BA, Western Ky. State Coll., 1965; Univ. N.M., 1967; MLS, Univ. of Ky., Lexington 1970. Career: tchr. Logan County Pub. Sch., Russellville, Ky. 1965-66; sch. librarian Albuquerque (N.M.) Pub. Sch., 1966-69; county librarian Amherst Co., Va. 1970-73; pub. library cons. Virginia State Library, Richmond 1973-78; br. librarian City of Stockton, Calif. 1978-79, coord. branch services, 1979-81, asst. dir. library services, 1981-92; deputy city mgr City of Stockton 1992–; mem: ALA, Calif. Lib. Assn. (councilor 1983-88), Calif. Inst. of Libraries (pres. 1987-88), Am. Soc. for Pub. Adminstrn., AAUW, LWV (chapt. pres. 1987-88), Pilot Club, Marion, Va. (pres. 1977-78), Stockton Delta Rotary Club (pres. 1994-95); Democrat; Methodist. Res: 737 N Central Stockton 95204 Ofc: City of Stockton 425 N El Dorado Stockton 95202

BROWN, EDMUND G. "PAT", lawyer, former governor of California; b. April 21, 1905, San Francisco; s. Edmund and Ida (Schuckman) B.; m. Bernice Layne, Oct. 30, 1930; children: Cynthia, Barbara, Jerry, Kathleen; edn: Univ. Calif. Ext.; LLB, JD, S.F. Coll. Law, 1927. Career: dist. atty. San Francisco, 1943-50; elected State Atty. Gen., Calif., 1950-58; Gov. of Calif., 1959-67; name ptnr. law firm Ball Hunt Hart Brown & Baerwitz, Los Angeles 1968-91; honorary chair Edmund G. "Pat" Brown Inst. of Public Affairs, CSULA, guest lectr. CSU Los Angeles, 1988–; emeritus trustee Univ. Calif., Berkeley Found.; Democrat; R.Cath.; rec: golf, travel.

BROWN, EDMUND GERALD, JR. (JERRY BROWN), former governor of California; b. Apr. 7, 1938, San Francisco; s. Edmund Gerald and Bernice (Layne) B.; edn: BA, UC Berkeley 1961; JD, Yale Univ. 1964; admitted Calif. Bar 1965. Career: research atty. Calif. Supreme Ct. 1964-65; atty. Tuttle & Taylor, Los Angeles 1966-69; secty. State Calif. 1970-74; Governor of State of Calif. 1975-83; chmn. Calif. Democratic Party 1989-90; Democratic cand. for Pres. of United States 1992; trustee Los Angeles Comm. Colleges 1969. Address: 3022 Washington St San Francisco 94115

BROWN, ELEANOR PHYLLIS, economics educator; b. April 18, 1954, Los Angeles; d. Robert James Sidford and Phyllis Jeanne (White) Brown; m. Jules Benge Prag, May 26, 1984; children: Robert Benjamin b. 1986, Thomas Maxwell b. 1990; edn: BA, Pomona Coll. 1975; MA, Princeton Univ. 1977; PhD, 1981. Career: asst. prof. Univ. Fla., Gainesville 1980-84; vis. asst. prof., lectr. Princeton Univ., N.J. 1985-86; asst. prof. Pomona Coll. 1986-89, assoc. prof. 1989–, assoc. dean of the college 1994–; tchr. Found. for Am. Comms., Los Angeles 1989; awards: Pomona Wig Tchg. (1989, 94); mem: Am. Econ. Assn., Western Econ. Assn., Nat. Tax Assn. (com. on status of women in econ. profession); ed. Readings Issues & Questions in Pub. Fin. (1988), 10 articles pub. in profl. jours. Res: 220 W Eigth St Claremont 91711 Ofc: Pomona College Dept of Economics 425 N College Ave Claremont 91711

BROWN, ELIZABETH LILLIAN, retired physician; b. Aug. 12, 1916, NY, NY; d. Joseph and Dora (Engel) B.; m. William Brown, M.D.; edn: MD, Albany Med. Coll. 1940-41, New York Med. Coll., 1941-43; bd. cert. Am. Bd. Allergy, Am. Bd. Pediatrics, subsplty., pediat. allergy. Career: research physicist NASA, 1937-40; intern pediat. Fordham Hosp. 1944; resident pediatrics Flower & Fifth Avenue Hosp., 1944; fellow Mayo Clinic, Rochester, Minn. 1944-45; resident peds. Greenpoint Hosp., Bklyn. 1949-50; pvt. practice pediatrician 1950-92, and allergy only 1970–, med. staff West Hills Med. Ctr. Canoga Park, Calif., West Park Hosp., Canoga Park Hosp., retired May 8, 1992; Fellow Am. Acad. Pediatrics (FAAP), Fellow Am. Acad. Allergy (FAAA), mem. Nat. Soc. Asthma Care Phys. (treas.), L.A. Allergy Soc., L.A. Pediat. Soc., Am. Allergy Assn; author: Yearbook of Pediatrics, Eczema Vaccinatum, Report of a Recovery; Jewish; rec: fishing, ranching. Address: 23300 Erwin St Woodland Hills 91367

BROWN, GEORGE EDWARD, JR., congressman; b. Mar. 6, 1920, Holtville, Calif.; s. George Edward and Bird Alma (Kilgore) B.; 4 children; edn: BA, UCLA, 1946; grad. fellow, Fund Adult Edn., 1954. Career: mgmt. cons. Calif., 1957-61; v.p. Monarch Savings & Loan Assn., Los Angeles, 1960-68; mem. Calif. Assembly from 45th Dist., 1959-62, 88th-91st Congresses from 29th Dist. Calif., 93rd Congress from 38th Dist. Calif., 94th-104th Congresses from 36th (now 42nd) Dist. Calif.; mem. standing com. on agri., chmn. sci. space and tech. com. 94th-101st Congresses from 36th Dist. Calif., 1987; mem. agriculture com. , mem. sci., space and tech. com., chmn. Office of Tech. Assessment; coll. lectr., radio commentator 1971; mem. Calif. Gov.'s Adv. Com. on Housing Problems, 1961-62; mem. Mayor Los Angeles Labor-Mgmt. Com., 1961-62, councilman, Monterey Park, Calif., 1954-58, mayor, 1955-56; candidate for U.S. Senate, 1970; mem. Am. Legion, Colton C. of C., Urban League, Internat. Brotherhood Elec. Workers, AFL-CIO, Friends Com. Legislation, Ams. for Dem. Action, Kiwanis; mil: served to 2d lt., inf. AUS, World War II; Democrat; Methodist. Ofc: US House of Representatives 2300 Rayburn House Office Bldg Washington DC 20515-05420

BROWN, GEORGE STEPHEN, physics professor; b. June 28, 1945, Santa Monica; s. Paul Gordon and Frances Ruth (Moore) B.; m. Annaclare von Dalen, Sept. 17, 1966, div. 1979; children: Sonya Elena b. 1972; m. Nohema del Carmen Fernandez, Aug. 8, 1981, div. 1992; edn: BS, Caltech, 1967; MS, Cornell, 1968, PhD, 1973. Career: mem. tech. staff Bell Labs, Murray Hill, N.J. 1973-77; senior res. assoc., Stanford Univ., 1977-82, research. prof. 1982-91; prof. of physics UC Santa Cruz, 1991–; Fellow Am. Physical Soc. (1985–); author, ed., Handbook on Synchrotron Radiation Research (1992), 100+ sci. articles (1972–); mem. editorial bd. Rev. Scientific Instr. 1983-86; rec: music performance. Res: 10699 Empire Grade Santa Cruz 95060 Ofc: Physics Dept. University of California, Santa Cruz 95064

BROWN, GLENN A., JR., lawyer; b. Oct. 1, 1955, Los Angeles; s. Glenn A. and Martha Lee (Day) B.; edn: BA, UCLA 1978; JD cum laude, Loyola Law Sch. 1978-82; admitted St. Bar Calif. (1982), U.S. Dist. Ct. (1983). Career: atty., assoc. Grace Neumeyer & Otto, Los Angeles 1982-83; Parkinson Wolf Lazar & Leo 1983–; O'Flaherty Prestholt & Bennington 1985–; Wasserman Comden & Casselman, Tarzana 1987–; judge pro tem Los Angeles Municipal Ct. 1988–; arbitrator Los Angeles Superior Ct. 1993–; mem: L.A. Co. Bar Assn. (ethics com. 1987-93), Am. Bar Assn. (ins. litigation com., torts & ins. practice sect.); Republican. Ofc: Wasserman Comden & Casselman 5567 Reseda Blvd Ste 330 Tarzana 91356

BROWN, HARRY F., physician, ophthalmologist; b. June 2, 1919, Pittsburgh, Pa.; s. Harry and Olive (Page) B.; m. Anne C. Murray, March 20, 1943; children: Christine b. 1947, Larry b. 1949, Sharon b. 1950, Lynne b. 1952, Russell b. 1954, Stephanie b. 1961; edn: BS, UCLA 1943; MD, USC 1950; Calif. Tech. Univ. Grad. Sch. 1942-43; lic. Am. Bd. Ophthalmology (1955). Career: pvt. practice ophthalmology, Arcadia, Pasadena 1954–; clin. tchr. USC Med. Sch., Los Angeles 1954-74; head ophthalmology dept. Methodist Hosp., Arcadia 1976, 78, 80; mem: Am. Ophthalmology Soc., CLAO, Internat. Coll. Surgeons, Los Angeles Soc. Ophthalmology, Calif. Soc. Ophthalmology; articles pub. in med. jours.; mil: USAF 1942-45, 1950-51. Res: 408 Via Lido Nord Newport Beach 92663

BROWN, J. MOREAU, corporate philanthropies consultant; b. June 1, 1916, Evanston, Ill.; s. Dr. James Moreau and Edna Veronica (Cullen) Brown; children: Christine b. 1942, Moreau Stoddard b. 1944, Pamela Ashton b. 1948, Mallory b. 1952; edn: AB, Dartmouth Coll., 1939; M.Ed., St. Lawrence Univ., 1953. Career: dir. admissions St. Lawrence Univ., 1944-52; asst. dean admissions New York Univ., 1952-54; adminstr. edn. support/supr. ednl. awards and grants, General Electric, also assoc. secty. GE Found., 1954-72; v.p. Council Financial Aid to Edn., N.Y.C. 1972-77; cons./prin., San Francisco 1977–; mem. advy. council Beta Theta Pi 1960–, gen. sec./trustee 1960-63; development dir. Found. Teach. Econ., San Francisco 1980-81; awards: outstanding community service GE Elfun Soc., NY 1966-67, patriot medal, gold good citizenship medal SAR, NY (1968, 69), N.Y. St. American Revolution Bicentennial Commn. 1969-77, Bicentennial Council 13 Original States 1973-77; mem: Montefiore Sr. Ctr. (3 term pres. 1985-92), United Jewish Comm. Centers (bd. 1985-92, exec. com. ex officio), Mason Blue Lodge, Shriner, Scottish Rite, SAR (Empire State pres. 1968-69), Marines Memorial Club, Dartmouth Coll. Club; authored first corporate gift matching program "Corporate Alumnus Program" 1954; avocation: public service. Res: 545 Teresita Blvd San Francisco 94127 Ofc: Montefiore Senior Center 3200 California St San Francisco 94118

BROWN, JAMES EDWARD, biochemist; b. Jan. 9, 1945, Columbus, Ind.; s. Edward Alvin and Shirley L. (Hazelleaf) B.; m. Diane Howe, Aug. 14, 1971 (dec. May 29, 1988); children: Peter b. 1972, Roger b. 1978; edn: BS chem., Iowa St. Univ., 1967; PhD chem., Penn State Univ., 1971. Career: postdoctoral fellow Worcester Found. for Exptl. Biology, Shrewsbury, Mass. 1971-73; res. biochemist UCSD Pathology Dept., La Jolla 1973-82; res. mgr. Hemostasis Systems, Helena Laboratories, Beaumont, Tx. 1982-84; sr. staff scientist Bayer, Pharmaceutical Div., Berkeley 1984–, seminar com. chmn. 1987-88; recipient of 8 science & technology awards, Cutter Labs. div. sci. award 1989, Otto Bayer Science Award 1992; mem. ACS, AAAS, Alpha Chi Sigma, Internat. Soc. on Thrombosis and Haemostasis; inventor: Phospholipid Affinity Purification of Factor VIII:C (pat. 1989), Immunoassay for Cellular Proteins (pat. 1992); pub. 29jour. articles; Methodist (trustees bd.); rec: tennis, golf. Res: 914 Anita Ct Lafayette 94549 Ofc: Bayer Pharmaceuticals 4th and Parker Sts Berkeley 94701

BROWN, KATHLEEN, lawyer, state treasurer; d. Edmund G. and Bernice Brown; m. George Rice (div. 1979); children: Hilary, Alexandra, Zebediah, m.2d. Van Gordon Sauter, 1980; 2 stepsons; edn: BA History, Stanford Univ. 1969; grad., Fordham Univ. Sch. of Law. Career: atty. O'Melveny & Myers, N.Y.C. and Los Angeles; commr. Los Angeles Bd. Pub Works 1987-89; elected Treas. of Calif., 1990–; mem: L.A. Bd. Edn. 1975-80; Democrat. Ofc: Office of State Treasurer PO Box 942809 Sacramento 94209-0001

BROWN, LILLIAN ERIKSEN, nurse administrator; b. Feb. 7, 1921, Seattle; d. Peter Louis and Lena (Lien) Eriksen; m. Wm. W. Brown, Jan. 21, 1942, div. Nov. 1962; children: Patricia Lee b. 1952, Michael b. 1954, Kevin b. 1957; edn: att. UC Berkeley 1939-40, dipl. St. Luke's Hosp. Sch. Nursing, San Francisco 1943; AB, CSU San Francisco, 1952; MPA, USC, 1975. Career: RN, Calif. Pub. health nse. San Francisco Dept. Health, 1946-50; asst. dir. nsg. S.F. General Hosp., 1950-56; dir. nsg. Weimar Med. Ctr., Weimar 1956-62, Orange County Med. Ctr., Orange 1962-76; assoc. dir. hosp. and clinics, dir. nsg., lectr. Univ. Calif. Med. Ctr., Irvine 1976-82; assoc. hosp. adminstr. King Khalid Eye Specialist Hosop., Riyadh, S.A., 1982-86; cons. AMI-Saudi Arabia Ltd., Jeddah, 1986-90; mem. advy. bds. various coll. nursing pgms., Consortium to Enhance Grad. Edn. in Nsg., advy. coun. 1970; Gov. Reagan appt. to Calif. Dept. Rehab. planning proj. com. 1967-69, advy. com. 1970-73; Univ. Calif. Ad Hoc Pres.'s com. on hosp. governance 1981-82; Calif. Hosp. Assn. personnel com. 1978-80, nsg task force 1982; Orange County Health Planning Council com. on emergency med. svs. 1977-78, health promotion task force 1977-78; awards: Lauds and Laurels UCI 1981, Lillian E. Brown award estab. in her honor Calif. Nurses Assn. 1989; mem: Am. Acad. Nurses (fellow), ANA (cert. Nse. Adminstr. Advanced), Orange County Dirs. of Nsg. (chair 1968-69), Nat. League for Nsg., APHA, Am. Orgn. Nse. Execs., Nat. Critical Care Inst., Calif. Hosp. Assn. (personell com. 1978-80, nsg. task force 1982), Calif. Nurses Assn. (dir. at lg. 1961-65, treas. 1965-69, chair Com. on Stds. of Care 1969-73), Calif. Orgn. for Nse. Execs. (hon.), Calif. Soc. for Nsg. Svc. Adminstr., NOW; mil: capt. (Res.) ANC 1946-52; contbr. articles in profl. jours.; Republican; rec: travel, philately. Res: 1806 Nordic Pl Orange 92665

BROWN, LINDA LOUISE, company owner and industry consultant; b. Oct. 7, 1946, Trenton, Mo.; d. Herbert Shanklin and Dorothy Mae (French) Brown; edn: BA, Tx. Christian Univ., 1968; MBA, Univ. Tx., Austin 1975. Career: mktg. rep. Chevron U.S.A., Seattle 1974-75, Portland, Oreg. 1975-77, mktg. services splst. Chevron U.S.A., San Francisco 1977-79, chartering specialist Chevron Shipping Co., S.F. 1979-80, facilities & transportation splst. Chevron U.S.A. Inc., S.F. 1980-85, coordinator transp., legis. and regulation, 1985-92; tng. cons. HazMat, San Francisco 1992-94; principal HazMasters, Oakland 1994–; honors: outstanding bus. grad. Univ. of Texas 1974; mem: Calif. Mfrs. Assn. (chair T&D com. 1987-88), Nat. Indsl. Transp. League (SEEI com. 1985-8), Women Entrepreneurs S.F. (treas. 1985-6), Big Brothers/Big Sisters (1983-90), Bay Area Texas Exes (co-founder, pres. 1979-83); mag. articles on Negotiations pub. 1984; Democrat; Prot.; rec: skiing, trekking in Nepal. Res: 2609 Chelsea Dr Oakland 94611-2421

BROWN, LOUIS DANIEL, lawyer; b. Aug. 31, 1908, San Francisco; s. Louis Thomas and Ella Rose (Kelly) B.; m. Felice, Sept. 9, 1932; children: Lawrence Louis, Ronald Stamper, Carol Felice; edn: AA, Univ. S.F. 1929; AB, Stanford Univ. 1931; LL.B, Southwestern Univ. 1944; JD, 1944. Career: pres. Romer O'Connor & Co., S.F. and L.A., ptnr. Romer Brown atty. 1944-68; Romer Brown Miller Murphy 1968-72; sole practice 1972–; honors: Who's Who in West, Who's Who in Calif., Men of Achievment, Martindale Hubbell Law Dir., Who's Who Western States, and others; mem: Calif. St. Bar Assn., L.A. Co. Bar Assn., Am. Bar Assn., Am. Judicature Soc., L.A. Lawyers Club; civic: Stanford Univ. Alumni Assn., Southwestern Univ. Alumni Assn., UC Hastings Law Sch. Alumni Assn., Borrego Springs C.of C., Internat. Lions Club, Elks Club, La Quinta Dessert Club, BSA, Univ. S.F. Law Soc., Stanford Univ. Law Soc., Southwestern Law Soc.; author: num articles on legal aspects of credit (Nat. Assn. Credit Petroleum Assn.), var. articles Lions Club Bulletin and Consumer Credit Assn.; Republican; R. Cath.; rec: church and charity work. Res: 6630 Newcastle Ave Reseda 91335

BROWN, LOUIS M., lawyer, emeritus professor law; b. Sept. 5, 1909, Los Angeles; s. Emil and Anna B.; m. Hermione Kopp, 1937; children: Lawrence David, Marshall Joseph, Harold Arthur; edn: AB cum laude, USC, 1930; JD, Harvard Univ., 1933; LLD, Manhattan Coll., Riverdale, NY 1977; admitted bar: Calif. 1933, US Supreme Ct. 1944. Career: law practice, Los Angeles 1933-35; with Emil Brown & Co., Dura Steel Products Co., both Los Angeles 1936-41; counsel RFC, Wash. DC 1942-44; ptnr. law firm Pacht, Warne, Ross and Bernhard, L.A. 1944-47; ptnr. Irell & Manella, L.A. 1947-69, of counsel 1969-72; of counsel Sanders Barnet Goldman Simons & Mosk 1980–; lectr. in law Southwestern Univ. Law Sch., 1939-41, UCLA, 1944-46, USC, 1950-51; lectr., adj. prof. law USC, 1960-74, prof. law 1974-80, emeritus prof. 1980–, acad. dir. program for legal para-professionals 1970-77, mem. plng. com. Tax Inst. 1948-69; vis. prof. law Loyola-Marymount Law Sch., L.A. 1977-82; distinguished vis. prof. Whittier Coll. Sch. Law 1980–; mem. nat. panel arbitrators Am. Arb. Assn., 1956-63; chmn. bd. trustees Nat. Ctr. for Preventive Law. Univ. Denver Coll. Law, 1987–; author: Preventive Law, 1950, How to Negotiate a Successful Contract, 1955, Lawyering Through Life: The Origin of Preventive Law, 1986; also case books, articles in law jours.; coauthor: Planning by Lawyers: Materials on a Non-Adversarial Legal Process, 1978; editor: Major Tax Problems, 3 vols. (1948-51); mem. community relations com. Jewish Personnel Relations Bur., 1950-60; founder, adminstr. Emil Brown Fund Preventive Law Prize Awards, 1963-85, Hermione and Louis Brown Found., 1985–; founder, adminstr. Client Counseling Competition, 1968-73 (cons. 1973-74, 1993 became Louis M. Brown Internat. Client Counseling Competition); pres. Friends of Beverly Hills Publ. Library, 1960; awards: Order of Coif, an issue of So. Calif. Law Rev. pub. in his honor 1975, merit award USC Gen. Alumni Assn. 1979, disting. svc.

Beverly HIlls Bar Found. 1984, Disting. Emeritus Award, USC 1995, Fellow Am. Bar Found., Fellow Soc. for Values in Higher Edn.; mem: ABA (chmn. standing com. legal assistance for servicemen 1969-72, mem. accreditation com. sect. legal edn. and admissions to bar 1978-81), Beverly Hills Bar Assn. (pres. 1961, disting. svc. award 1981), L.A. Co. Bar Assn. (chmn. prepaid legal svs. com. 1970-71), State Bar Calif., Town Hall of Calif., Masons, B'nai B'rith, Harvard Club So. Calif.; honors: Am. Bar Assn. est. perpetual Louis M. Brown Legal Access Award 1994, L.A. Co. Bar Assn. est. annual Louis M. Brown Conflict Prevention Award 1994; Democrat; Jewish; rec: music performance (viola, Am. Community Symphony Orch., European Tour, 1968), world peace edn., photography; motto: The obvious is too often overlooked. Find it. Identify it. Explore it. There is much that lies hidden in the fundamentals and complexities of the obvious. Res: 606 N Palm Dr Beverly Hills 90210 Ofc: 1901 Ave of Stars Ste 850 Los Angeles 90067

BROWN, RONALD STAMPER, builder, engineer; b. Feb. 20, 1943, Los Angeles; s. Louis Daniel and Felice (Stamper) B.; children: Deborah Lee b. 1963, Darren C. b. 1966; edn: Mount Carmel H.S., 1961; AA, Los Angeles City Coll., 1965; BS, CSU Long Beach, 1969; Sencore Electronics Sch. 1987, 88, 89; postgrad. studies: math., Northrop Inst. of Tech.; architectonics in constrn., USC; geology, oil & water well drilling, astrophysics, astronomy & relativity, UCLA; Univ. Mich. Ext. courses in laser engring., superconductors, fiberoptics, electronics; entomology, Calif. Acad. of Sci.; cosmology, Caltech; organic arch. and struct. engring., Architect Geo. Frank Ligar; infrared detectors & systems applications engring., UC Santa Barbara, 1991-92 and 94, Assoc. res. UNI elec. ground systems, lighting protection and elec. fault locating; continuing edn. PhD, electrical sci. & cosmology, Columbia Pacific Univ. 1995; Lic: Electrical Engr.; Bldg., Electrical, Plbg. Htg. A/C, Solar, Roofing, Well Drilling, Struct. Pest Control, Air Frames & Power Plants; FCC commercial gen. radio tel. lic. w. GMDSS/M and GMDSS/O radar endorsement; cert. electronic tech. Career: Romer O'Conner Co. Inc., 1965; builder 1970; Brown Termite 1980; Digital Products 1980; Stamper Louis Co. 1981-; mem: IEEE, Nat. Notary Assn., Astronomical Soc. of Pacific, Planetary Soc., Wrightian Soc. of Organic Architecture, Am. Inst. of Wine & Food, Internat. Soc. for Optical Engring., Am. Radio Relay League, NRA, L.A. Co. Mus. of Art, Opera Club, Anza-Borrego Desert Natural Hist. Assn., Nat. Chevy Truck Assn., Mercedes Benz Club Am.; publs: articles on non linear optics; Republican; rec: flying, sailing, skiing, scuba, amateur radio (EXTRA class lic. #KN6DJ), enology. Res: 6630 Newcastle Ave Reseda 91335

BROWN, THAD, tax official; b. May 5, 1927, Vicksburg, Miss.; s. Jack and Ada (Parker) B.; m. Geri Litzius, Jan. 5, 1979; children: Gwendolyn, Janice, Kenneth; edn: BA, S.F. St. Univ., 1950; MPA, Golden Gate Univ., 1965. Career: staff City and County of San Francisco, 1957-: auditor Assessor 1957-65; adminstrv. asst. Mental Health Dept., 1965-68; adminstrv. analyst Office of Chief Adminstr., 1968-69; tax collector, 1969–; honors: disting. service Black C.of C. San Francisco 1982, vol. of yr. United Way Bay Area 1983, outstanding vol. Cal/Neva Community Action, Sacto. 1986, recogn. Econ. Opportunity Council S.F. 1989, resolutions Calif. St. Assembly, Senate, and San Francisco Board of Suprs. 1989; mem: Alpha Phi Alpha (life), Calif. Acad. of Scis. (life, fellow, bd. 1974-89); civic: Econ. Opp. Council of S.F. (bd. chmn. 1978–), United Way of Bay Area (bd. chmn. 1981-83), NAACP (life), World Affairs Council No. Calif. (bd. 1989), S.F. Fine Arts Mus. (bd. 1989), Nat. Fedn. of Neighborhood Ctrs. (v.p. 1975-76), Lions Intl. S.F.; mil: cpl. USAF 1945-46; Prot.; rec: photog., bicycling. Ofc: City Hall Rm 107 San Francisco 94102

BROWN, WILBUR KNIGHT, physicist/astrophysicist, consultant; b. July 6, 1932, Oakland; s. Herbert Walter and Donna Louise (Anderson) B.; m. Kathryn Lomilla Lind, June 27, 1954; children: Walter b. 1962, Craig b. 1966; edn: AB physics, UC Berkeley, 1954, MS nucl. engr., 1957, PhD enrg. sci., 1962; reg. Profl. Engr. (nuclear) Calif. Career: staff mem. Research Estab. Riso, Roskilde, Denmark 1962-64; staff mem. Los Alamos Nat. Lab., N.Mex. 1964-70, 72-87, cons. 1987-92; assoc. prof. Univ. Wyoming, 1970-72; instr. p.t. Lassen Coll., Susanville, Calif. 1987-95; honors: Phi Beta Kappa 1954, Sigma Xi 1958; mem: Am. Physical Soc., Am. Nuclear Soc., Am. Astronomical Soc., Astron. Soc. of Pacific; publs: numerous articles in sci. jours., 1957–; mil: lt. jg USN 1954-56; Democrat. Res: 5179 Eastshore Dr Lake Almanor 96137

BROWN, WILLIAM EDWIN, construction executive, educator; b. Jan. 11, 1934, Belknap, Ill.; s. Samual Edwin and Sarah Elizabeth (Kean) B.; edn: BS, So. Ill. Univ., 1956, MS, 1957; Univ. of Tenn., 1956-57; PhD, The Ohio State Univ., 1964. Career: grad. instr. So. Ill. Univ., 1955, instr. Univ. Tenn. 1956; asst. prof. engring. graphics The Ohio State Univ., 1957-65, asst. to the dean of engring. 1965-67; prof. and dept. engring. technology chair Trenton State Coll., N.J. 1967-76 (devel. curr. and gained State approval for 4 yr. baccalaureate pgm., BS in mech., electrical, and indsl. engring. technology; appt. N.J. Advy. Bd. on Tech. Edn., also State Engring. Tech. Master Planning Com., 1969-76); regional dir. Pub. Employment Rels. Bd., Sacto., 1976-80; gen. contr., prin. Bear Tavern Assoc., Sacto. 1980–; faculty mech. engring. dept. CSU Sacto. 1986–; franchise seminar dir./bus. mgmt. for Dial One of No. Calif., Sacto. 1985–; mem: NEA, Am. Indsl. Arts Assn., Am. Coun. on Indsl. Arts Tchr. Edn., Am.

Soc. Engring. Edn., AAU honors: Phi Delta Kappa, Epsilon Pi Tau, Iota Lambda, Phi Alpha Delta profl.-social frat. (advr. 8 yrs.), Outstanding Tchr. Award 1976; United Methodist. Res: 1110 La Sierra Dr Sacramento 95864 Tel: 916/486-9054

BROWNE, DIANA GAYLE, artist, clinical social worker; b. Aug. 31, 1924, San Francisco; d. Clarence Luther and Elsa Henrietta (Ericson) Sidelinger; m. Alfred Britton, Jr. Sept. 2, 1942; children: Alfred, III, b. 1944, Kathryn (Lumbert) b. 1950, Patrick b. 1950; m. James S. Browne, MD, May 19, 1963; children: Bruce P. b. 1966, Julia R. b. 1970; edn: att. Stanford Univ., 1947; BA (magna cum laude), San Jose St. Univ., 1949; MSW, UC Berkeley, 1958; BFA, S.F. Art Inst., 1973; att. Inst. for Clinical Social Work, Berkeley 1981-83; lic. clin. soc. worker, Calif. Career: clin. soc. wkr. Dept. of Mental Hygiene, Sacto. 1958-59, UCSF, 1960-61, Langley Porter Clinic, S.F. 1961-66, Napa State Hosp., Napa 1980-85; pvt. practice 1982-85; freelance artist, Marin County, 1966-80, 85–; profl. awards: Calif. State Fair Fine Arts Div. merit award 1989, Marin County Fair- Fine Arts Div. merit 1990, also Photo Div. best of show & 4 merit awards 1977-78, Mill Valley Arts Guild best of show, hon. mention & cash awards 1977, 78, 79, Eastbay Watercolor Soc. merit 1987, Marin Soc. of Artists, Ross 3 merit & 2 cash awards 1974-79, 2 merit awards 1990; mem: Indian Valley Artists 1992-93, Artisans' Gallery 1988-90, Marin Watercolor Soc., Calif. Soc. of Printmakers, Marin Soc. of Artists (signature mem., advy. council 1979, 87-89, 92-93), Marin Arts Guild (rental chair 1987-88), Eastbay Watercolor Soc. (signature mem., bd. 1986-87), S.F. Women Artists (1977-78, 87, 89; bd. 1978-79), Outdoor Art Club Mill Valley, Alliance of Women Artists 1988-89, AAUW, Alpha Chi Omega (San Jose St. Univ.); civic: Family Service League, Mill Valley 1985-89. Res: 178 Ignacio Valley Circle Novato 94949

BROWNE, LEE F(RANKE), academic administrator, lecturer emeritus; b. Dec. 18, 1922, N.C.; m. Dorothy G.; children: Gail, Daryl, Alice, Adriene, Scott (dec.); edn: BS chem./biol., West Va. State Coll., 1944; postgrad. UCLA, 1946-48; MS, N.Y. Univ., 1950, postgrad. 1950-53. Career: chemist, asst. to pathologist N.Y. Dept. Hosps., 1953-55; asst. prof. Langston (Okla.) Univ., 1955; chemistry instr. Valley Jr. Coll., Van Nuys, Calif. 1956-57, John Muir High Sch., Pasadena 1958-64; chemistry instr., dept. chmn. Blair High Sch., Pasa. 1964-70; sci. coord. Pasadena Schs., 1970; dir. secondary sch. relations Calif. Inst. Tech., Pasa. 1971–, dir. spl. student projects, lecturer 1977–; mem. grading team for chemistry, Advanced Placement Pgm. Coll. Entrance Exam. Bd. and Ednl. Testing Service, 1971-72, 74, 75, 76, 78; lectr. local radio stas.; mem. monitoring com. Los Angeles Bd. Edn., mem. Multicultural Edn. Resource Bd.; bd. dirs. NACME, Inc.; founding ed. Pasadena Eagle newspaper, 1968-73; honors: Tchr. of Year, Industry and Ednl. Council (1968), Raymond Pitts Human Rels. award Pasadena Star News (1970, 76); civic: CORE (chmn. 1963-64), Pasa. Commn. on Human Need and Opportunity (chmn. 1973-74), Pasa. Community Svs. Ctr. (chmn. 1974), Ad-Hoc Integration Com. (chmn. 1970), Northwest Community Conv. (chmn. 1969, v.chmn. 1970), Monrovia Job Resources Bd. (bd., chmn. 1973, 75, 76), Pasadena Hall of Sci. (dir.), Westside Study Ctr. Bd., Co-op Village Pasa., Help Invest in People, Pasa. Urban Coalition (Turner Sch. ESSA Project advy. council), Project Head-Start Parent Policy Council; mem: Am. Chem. Soc., AAAS, AAUP, Nat. Sci. Tchrs. Assn., Nat. Assn. Curriculum Splsts., Calif. Chemistry Tchrs. Assn., Am. Inst. Chemists, Calif. Assn. Afro-Am. Tchrs. (v.chmn. 1970-72). Res: 871 W. Ventura St Altadena 91001-4965 Ofc: Calif. Institute of Technology 104-6, Pasadena 91125

BROWNING, ROBERTA FULLERTON, university administrator; b. Aug. 23, 1937, Swedesboro, N.J.; d. John and Josephine (Broome) Fullerton; m. Lee A. Broadbent, May 6, 1977; 1 son, John Jarvis b. 1965; edn: BS psychology, Bucknell Univ. 1959; MS counseling, CSU 1974. Career: tchr. Salem Elem. Sch., N.J. 1960; statistican Research Inst. of Am., N.Y.C. 1960-64; coordinator of testing CSU Fullerton 1970-82, lectr. 1975-82, acting asst. dean 1982-84, dir. career devel. 1984–; chair California State Univ. Directors of Career Centers, 1991–; honors: Phi Kappa Phi, Phi Sigma Tau, CSU Fullerton Ernest Becker award (1989); mem: CSU Womens Ctr. (founder 1972), Am. Assn. Counseling & Devel., Am. Coll. Personnel Assn., Womens Council of St. Univ. Coll. Placement Council, Western Coll. Placement Assn., YWCA (bd. dirs. 1985-93); article pub. in profl. jour. (1988, 94); rec: walking, gardening. Ofc: CSU Fullerton Career Development & Counseling, Fullerton 92634

BRUBAKER, CRAWFORD FRANCIS, JR., international management consultant; b. April 23, 1924, Fruitland, Ida.; s. Crawford Francis and Sue (Flora) B.; m. Lucile May Christensen, May 5, 1945; children: Eric b. 1949, Alan b. 1951, Craig b. 1954, Paul b. 1957; edn: BA econ., Pomona Coll. 1947; MBA mgmt., Univ. Pa. Wharton 1948. Career: office mngr., field rep., contracts adminstrn. Lockheed Calif., Burbank 1948-60, asst. mgr. export contracts 1960-69, mgr. bid and proposal dept., 1969-74, sr. sales mgr. fighters 1974-76, dir. internat. market devel. Lockheed Corp., Calabasses 1976-83; dep. asst. secty. of commerce for aerospace Dept. of Commerce, Wash. D.C. 1983-87; internat. mgmt. cons. Brubaker & Assoc., Glendale 1987–; lectr. mgmt. schs. So. Calif. 1988–; dir. D-3 Technologies Inc., San Diego 1989-92, So. Calif. Presbyterian Homes, Glendale 1988-94, Interloc Inc., Glendale 1989-90; honors: Who's Who in Am., Dept. of Commerce Merit. Achievement 1984, St. of Fla. Export Support 1985; mem: So. Calif. Dist. Export Council (v.chmn. 1979-83, 1987-91, chair 1992-93), Aero. Policy Review Com. OSTP, Am. Inst. Aeronautics & Astronautics, Air Force Assn., Am. Defense Preparedness Assn., Gateway Kiwanis (pres. 1993-94); mil: lt.j.g. USN 1943-46; Republican; Presbyterian; rec: fishing, golf, philately. Address: Brubaker Associates 1538 Irving Ave Glendale 91201

BRUCE, JOHN ANTHONY, western artist, art consultant; b. Apr. 8, 1931, Los Angeles; s. Merle VanDyke and Katherine Mary (Butler) B.; m. Barbara Jean Kennedy, May 29, 1967 (div. 1988); children: Marsha Lee, Margaret Lorren, James Cole, Glenn Allen, Mark Corwin, Leslie Ann; edn: BA psychology/art, CSU Los Angeles, 1965. Career: design engr. North Am. Aviation Corp., Downey 1952-57; commercial artist Aerojet Gen. Corp., Sacramento 1957-59; advt. mgr. Flow Equipment Co., Santa Fe Springs 1959-63; art dir. Barnes-Camp Advt., Santa Ana 1963-66; Long Beach Independent Press-Telegram News, 1970-73; freelance art cons. Epcot project Walt Disney Enterprises, 1976-77; recipient num. art awards including John B. Grayback Award Am. Profl. Artists League 1988, Philip Isinberg Award Knickerbocker Artists 1988, Eagle Feather Award Am. Indian and Cowboy Artists (1988, 1989); represented by Bartfield Gal., N.Y.C., Texas Art Gallery, Dallas, Tex.; one man shows Ghormley Gal., L.A., 1966, Les Li Art Gal., L.A., 1970, Upstairs Gal., Long Beach, 1973, El Prado Gal., Sedona 1987; group shows Newport Beach Invitational, 1964, Laguna Beach Art Festival, 1962, 63, 64, 64, Butler Inst. American Art, Youngstown, Oh. 1970, Allied Artists, 1988; rep. in permanent collections Smithsonian Inst., W.D.C.; mem. Knickerbocker Artists, Am. Indian and Cowboy Artists; mil: AUS 1949-52, Korea; Republican: Studio: 5394 Tip Top Rd Mariposa 95338

BRUDER, EUGENE MILAN, dentist; b. June 29, 1947, Oakland; s. Alexander and Gloria (Schlackman) B.; m. Diann Rose Weiss, Sept. 25, 1973; children: Michelle b. 1968, Patrick b. 1982, Joshua b. 1985; edn: UC Davis 1965-6, UC Berkeley 1966-8; DDS, BS in dentistry, UCSF Sch. Dentistry, 1972. Career: intern Queens Med. Center, Honolulu, Hawaii 1972-73; pvt. practice, Anchorage, Alaska 1975-76; Honolulu, Hawaii 1976-86; Chico 1986–; tchg. staff Queens Med. Center 1976-86; advy. com. Enloe Hosp. Found., Chico 1988-93; honors: Calif. Scholarship Fedn. (life); mem: Acad. of General Dentistry (Fellow 1990), ADA, Calif. Dental Assn., No. Calif. Dental Assn., Rotary Internat. (sec. Hawaii Kai 1981-2), Chico Coin Club (pres. 1988–), Am. Numismatic Assn., Liberty Seated Collectors Club, Early Am. Coppers Club, Am. Philatelic Soc., Brit.-No. Am. Philatelic Soc., Royal Philatelic Soc. of Canada, C.Z. Study Group, Bureau Issues Assn.; mil: capt. AUS 1973-75; Republican; rec: boating, camping, philately, numismatics. Ofc: 650 Rio Lindo Ave Ste 11 Chico 95926

BRUHN, JOHN CARL, extension food technologist; b. Aug. 23, 1940, Cleveland, Ohio; s. Henry Ralph and Laura (Hauschild) B.; m. Christine M. Mattson, July 18, 1970; children: Laura b. 1974, Aron b. 1978; edn: BS, Mich. St. Univ. 1962; PhD, UC Davis 1969. Career: ext. food tech. UC Davis 1969–; awards: Internat. Milk Food & Environ. Sanitarians Educators award (1983), Am. Dairy Sci. Assn. DeLaval Ext., Mich. St. Univ. Outstanding Alumni; mem: Calif. Dairy Industries Assn., Am. Dairy Sci. Assn., Internat. Milk Food & Environ. Sanitarians, Calif. Assn. Dairy & Milk Sanitarians, Inst. Food Techs.; 72 articles pub. in sci. jours., 1 book pub.; Prot. Res: 627 Georgetown Pl Davis 95616 Ofc: Univ. of Calif. Dept. of Food Science & Technology Davis 95616-8598

BRUNSON, MARIA NIKI, real estate broker; b. Mar. 3, 1948, Youngstown, Ohio; d. Nicholas George and Sophia N. (Pamfilis) Loijos; m. Marvin D. Brunson; children: Michael Nicholas Loijos b. 1969; edn: grad. Ukiah H.S. 1966; bus. mgmt. CSU Sacto. 1966-67, CSU Sonoma 1983-84; Calif. R.E. lic. 1974, R.E. Broker/Notary Public 1986; C.R.S. designation, 1990. Career: former real estate sales staff MacElhenny, Levy & Co. Inc., Merrill Lynch Realty, sales and tng. supr. 1979-83, subdiv. sales mgr. 1980-83; owner/broker Foust & Co., Santa Rosa, 1985-90; broker assoc. Polley Polley & Madsen, 1990–; dir. Golden Pacific Financial 1984; honors: Virginia Kline Memorial award Board Member of Year, Am. Red Cross 1987, life mem. Million Dollar Club, Sonoma Co. M.L.S. 1976; mem: Sonoma Co. Bd. Realtors (bd. dirs. 1983-84, Ethics instr. 1982-83), Ducks Unlimited (charter mem. Womens Chpt.), Womens Council of Realtors, Am. Red Cross Redwood Empire Chpt. (chair bd. dirs. 1988-90, fin. devel. chair 1987-88), Soroptimists Internat. (recording secty. 1989–); Republican; Eastern Orthodox; rec: tennis, racquetball, skiing, golf. Res: 930 Buckingham Dr Windsor 95492 Ofc: Polley Polley & Madsen 2725 Mendocino Ave Santa Rosa 95403

BRUTON, LAURENCE "BRYAN", advertising, public and international government relations executive; b. Feb. 25, 1947, Altadena; s. L. B. and Mary Jayne (Moore) B.; m. Karen, Feb. 2, 1969; children: Wendi Nicole b. 1977; edn: BS telecomms. mgmt.; Air Univ. 1965-69, East N.M. Univ. 1966-68, Am. River Coll. 1969-70, Mt. San Antonio Coll. 1971-73. Career: public relations, advt. and mktg. strategy cons., internat. relations; ptnr. COM3 Multi-Media

Productions 1983-84, sole owner 1984–; gen. ptnr., now sole owner Green-Bruton & Associates, gen. bus. consulting (local, nat., internat.), offices in Sacto. and San Francisco, Calif., Austin and San Antonio, Tx.; owner COM3 Communications Network, Commercial Powerwash Systems, and GO-SOAP; mem: Retired Officer Assn., Internat. Platform Speakers Assn., Soc. Am. Engrs., Nat. Guard Assn. Calif. Nat. Guard Assn. of U.S.; comm. bds. (PTA, Softball League); invention: anti-syphon device utilized for home and crop applications of insecticides etc.; mil: E3 USAF 1965-69, LTC (Ret.); Republican; Baptist; rec: art, reading, fishing, garden. Res: Rt 2 Box 218C Burnet TX 78611 Ofc: Green-Bruton & Associates Rt 2 Box 24-0 Burnet TX 78611 Tel: 800/883-8569

BRUYERE, DENNIS PAUL, real estate broker, general building contractor, entrepreneur; b. Apr. 7, 1947, Ogdensburg, N.Y.; s. Joseph Paul and Audrey L. (Paulsen) B.; div.; children: Garey b. 1967, Paula b. 1970; edn: AA, Compton Jr. Coll. 1968; CSU Los Angeles, UCLA Ext., 1969-72, Pepperdine Univ., 1973; desig: Grad. Realtors Inst. (GRI) Calif. Assn. Realtors 1976, Cert. Residential Splst. (CRS) Nat. Assn. Realtors 1978, Gold Card Exchangor, Nat. Exch. Counselors 1978; var. Century 21 certs. (CIS inv. splst., CRS res. splst., VIP 301 referral broker). Career: sales person Hallmark Realty 1970, LCOA Investment & Realty Inc. 1971, Verpet Devel. 1972, Viren Realty 1973-75; broker/owner and gen. sales mgr. Century 21 Granada Realty (50+ lic. sales agts. in 2 branch offices), Bellflower 1975-89, current owner Granada Realty with Mgmt. & Maint. depts.; real estate investor, Calif., Tex.; tchr. seminars 1977-80; mem: Calif. Assn. Realtors (CAR), Rancho Los Cerritos Bd. Realtors, Long Beach Bd. Realtors; contbg. author "Residential Real Estate Financing" (CAR, 1978); Republican; rec: surf, swim, travel. Res: Paramount 90723

BRYAN, JOHN RODNEY, consultant; b. Dec. 29, 1953, Berkeley; s. Robert Richard and Eloise (Anderson) Putz; m. Karen Nelson Bryan, Jan. 20, 1990; edn: BA, UC San Diego, 1975; MBA, Rutgers Univ., 1984. Career: associated with Brooks Internat. Corp., West Palm Beach, Fla. 1985–; owner Applied Control, Management & Effectiveness Systems, San Diego, Calif. 1989–; associated with Western Productivity Group, Palo Alto 1989–; honors: Beta Gamma Sigma 1985; mem: Inst. of Indsl. Engrs. 1986–, ASPA 1993–; Republican; La Jolla Presbyterian Ch. (elder 1991–); rec: singing (classical), gardening. Res: 6265 Hurd Court San Diego 92122-2917

BRYANT, ALAN WILLARD, human resources executive; b. Aug. 17, 1940, Glen Ridge, N.J.; s. Alan Willard and Clara Sherman (Clark) B.; m. Karen Koenig; children: Hilary Ann, Christopher Bowman; edn: AB, Dartmouth Coll., 1962, MBA, 1963; postgrad. St. Mary's Univ. Law, San Antonio 1964-65. Career: with General Electric Co., 1965-93: specialist profl. placement Spacecraft Dept. GE Co., King of Prussia, Pa. 1965-66; foreman, methods analyst Television Dept., Syracuse, N.Y. 1966-67; specialist salaried employment Armament Dept., Springfield, Mass. 1967-68; specialist profl. and salaried compensation Information Systems Equip. Div., Phoenix, Ariz. 1968-70; mgr. personnel relations Nuclear Energy Dept., Wilmington, N.C. 1970-72; mgr. relations practices TV Receiver Products Dept., Portsmouth, Va. 1972-76; mgr. employee and community relations Meter Bus. Dept., Somersworth, N.H. 1976-85; mgr. human resources op. Nuclear Energy, San Jose, Calif. 1985-93, mem. senior staff GE leadership course in positive mgmt., Fairfield, Conn. 1981-93, adj. staff, exec. assessment and devel., 1987-93; v.p. Computer Curriculum Corp. 1993–; speaker Am. Mgmt. Assn. Nat. Conf. 1986, speaker US-Japan Institute 1991; recipient awards for public service Gov. Ariz. (1970), Gov. N.H. (1982-84); mem: Soc. for Human Resource Mgmt., Bay Area Human Resource Execs. Council (pres. 1992-93), No. Calif. Human Resources Council, Dover C.of C. (pres. 1984-85), Rotary (disting. svc. award 1985); civic bds: United Way (pres., campaign chair of Strafford Co., Dover, N.H. 1980-81), Strafford Hospice Care, Somersworth (founding pres. 1982-85), Wentworth Douglass Hosp., Dover (trustee 1982-85); mil: capt. US Army 1963-65; author/subject several pub. articles; Republican. Res: 1285 Poker Flat Place San Jose 95120-1766 Ofc: Computer Curriculum Corp. 1287 Lawrence Station Road Sunnyvale 94089

BRYANT, STEVEN HARRY, design engineer; b. Nov. 28, 1946, Des Moines, Iowa; s. Harry Kenneth and Hannah (Levey) B.; edn: AA engring., Fullerton Coll., 1968; BA hist., CSU Long Beach, 1970. Career: sr. structural design engr., aerospace indus., So. Calif., 1966-88; aerospace engring. contr., 1976–, pres. Hawkeye Enterprises (contract engring.), Cathedral City 1986–; listed Who's Who in West, Who's Who in World, Who's Who in Fin. and Ind., Who's Who of Emerging Leaders Am.; mem. Am. Soc. of Engrs. and Architects S. Pasa., Nat. Writers Club, Am. Corvette Owners Assn., Calif. Astrology Assn., U.S. Hist. Soc.; civic: Cathedral City Citizens for Progress 1989, World Vision for Africa 1985–, Cystic Fibrosis Found. 1987–, Chino Hills Area #19 (commr. 1979-82), Riverside Raceway Booster's Club 1976-82, Statue of Liberty Ellis Island Found. (charter 1984–); contbr. poetry to American Poetry Anthology (1987); Democrat (sec. San Bdo. Co. Dem. Party 1985); Christian/Jew; rec: dancing, skiing, swimming, poetry. Res: 3540 Autumn Ave Chino 91709 Ofc: 31-200 Landau Blvd Ste 1604 Cathedral City 92234

BUAAS, SHARON, marketing director; b. Jan. 15, 1950, Chicago, Ill.; d. Harry H. and Miriam (Gitlin) Shapiro; m. Robert Andrew Buaas, June 22, 1985; edn: BS, So. Ill. Univ. 1972; cert. of hyperalimentation/nutrition, Univ. Tx. Houston 1977; MBA mktg. and mktg. research, Roosevelt Univ. 1982. Career: nutrition territory mgr/splst. American McGaw, Irvine 1978-82; acct. exec. Vicom Assocs., San Francisco 1982-83; sr. account exec. V. Montegrande & Co., Irvine 1983-85; pres. The Buaas Corp., Huntington Beach 1985-89; account supr. Forsythe Marcelli Johnson, Newport Beach 1987-88; dir. mktg. Los Alamitos Med. Ctr., Los Alamitos 1988-92; corp. dir. mktg. & comm. relations Community Hospice Care, Anaheim Hills 1992-93; pres. The Buaas Corp., Huntington Beach 1993–; dir. marketing Bergen Brunswig Corp., Orange 1994–; awards: HPRMA Golden Advocate award 1992, listed World Who's Who of Women, Directory of Disting. Americans, Community Leaders of Am., Who's Who of Am. Women, Internat. Who's Who of Intellectuals, Book of Honor; mem: Women in Bus. (bd. dirs.), Med. Mktg. Assn. Ofc: The Buaas Corporation 10044 Adams Ave Ste 108 Huntington Beach 92646

BUBB, BRIAN DAVID, lawyer; b. June 22, 1962, Baltimore, Md.; s. Donald L., Sr. and Louise Mary (Masimore) B.; edn: BS in bus. admin./fin., Albright Coll., Pa. 1985; JD, Pepperdine Univ. Sch. of Law 1988. Career: partner Howarth & Smith, Los Angeles 1993–; tchg. asst. Pepperdine Univ., Malibu 1987-88; mem: Am. Trial Lawyers Assn., L.A. Co. Bar Assn., Calif. Bar Assn.; Republican. Ofc: Howarth & Smith 700 So Flower St Ste 2908 Los Angeles 90017

BUCHANAN, PEGGY KATHRYN, real estate broker; b. Nov. 1, 1943, Los Angeles; d. Howard Eugene and Geraldine Stowe (Young) Kutepoff; m. Donald Gene Buchanan, June 21, 1963; children: Jeffrey Dwayne b. 1965, Kathryn Anna b. 1969, Ryan Eugene b. 1973; edn: AA, Imperial Valley Coll. 1963; real estate courses Coll. of Redwoods 1979-80. Career: real estate broker/owner, Community Realty; mem. Calif. Assn. Realtors (regional v.p. 1988, state dir. 1988-94), Humboldt Co. Bd. Realtors (pres., bd. dirs., chair 1988), Humboldt Light Opera Co. (bd. dirs. 1986-95); articles pub. 1988; Republican; Mormon; rec: camping. Ofc: 2823 E St., Eureka 95501

BUCKEL, HARRY J., publisher; b. March 7, 1944, Indpls., Ind.; s. Harry J. and Delia (Spellman) B.; m. Helen McGrady, Dec. 16, 1966; children: Susan, Hailey, Sean, Brendan, Megan; edn: BS, BA, Xavier Univ., 1966. Career: pub. San Francisco Progress 1978-80; pub. Gloucester Times, Woodbury, NJ 1980-81; pub. Journal News, Hamilton 1981-82; pres. Pennysaver, Brea 1982–; v.chmn.Third Class Mail Marketing Assn. 1985-92, chmn. Advertising Mail Marketing Assn.; mem. Balboa Bay Club (Newport Beach); mil: 1st lt., U.S. Army, 1967-69; Irish Cath.; rec: hunting, fishing. Ofc: 2830 Orbiter, Brea 92622

BUCKLEY, JAMES WHITNEY, city librarian; b. Aug. 16, 1933, Los Angeles; s. George W. and Alta L. (Hale) B.; m. Margaret Wall, Aug. 7, 1965; children: Kathleen Ann, b. 1966, James W., b. 1972, John W., b. 1979; edn: AA, LA Harbor Coll. 1953; BA, CSU Long Beach 1960; MLS, USC 1961, MPA, 1974. Career: br. librarian Los Angeles County Pub. Library, 1961-68; regional librarian Orange County Public Lib. 1968, dir. pub. services 1969-74; county librarian San Mateo County 1974-77, Marin County 1978; city librarian City of Torrance 1979–; mem. advy. bd. Friends of Calif. Libraries, 1974-89; mem. Calif. Library Assn., Am. Soc. for Pub. Adminstrn.; Rotarian; mil: sp3 US Army Med. Corps 1955-57; rec: sports, walking, music. Ofc: Torrance Public Library, 3301 Torrance Blvd Torrance 90503

BUCKLIN, LOUIS PIERRE, professor of business administration; b. Sept. 20, 1928, New York; s. Louis Lapham and Elja (Barricklow) B.; m. Weylene Edwards, June 11, 1956; children: Randolph b. 1960, Rhonda b. 1965; edn: BA, Dartmouth Coll. 1950; MBA, Harvard Univ. 1954; PhD, Northwestern Univ. 1960. Career: asst. prof. Univ. Colo., Boulder 1954-56; instr. Northwestern Univ., Evanston, Ill. 1958-59; UC Berkeley asst. prof. 1960-67, assoc. prof. 1967-72, prof. bus. adminstrn. 1972–; dir. PhD program grad. sch. of bus. adminstrn. 1975-81, assoc. dean, 1981-83; vis. prof. Stockholm Sch. Econ., Sweden 1983; INSEAD, Fountainbleau, France 1984; Unilever Erasmus vis. prof. of mktg. Erasmus Univ., Rotterdam, The Netherlands 1993-94; awards: Am. Mktg. Assn. Paul D. Converse 1986, Alpha Kappa Psi award for best mgmt. article in Jour. of Mktg. 1993; mem: Am. Mktg. Assn., Inst. Mgmt. Sci., Lafayette Langeac Soc. (bd. 1987-92); civic bds: City of Lafayette Planning Commn. 1991-93; ed. Research in Marketing: Channels, 1986, author: Productivity in Mktg., 1979, Competition & Evolution in Distributive Trades, 1973, A Theory of Distbn. Channel Structure, 1966; mil: capt. USMC 1951-53; Republican; rec: micro computers. Res: 1061 Via Alta Lafayette 94549 Ofc: Haas School of Business University of California, Berkeley 94720

BUDLONG, DUDLEY WEBSTER, engineering executive; b. May 9, 1922, Mount Prospect, Ill.; s. Dudley W. and Louise B. (Schiller) B.; children: Gerald, Steven, Bruce, Roger; edn: BS, Ill. Inst. Tech., 1948, postgrad., 1951-53; postgrad., USC, 1953-54; reg. profl. engr. Calif., N.J., N.Y., Nev., Va., Fla., Mich.,

Minn., Ak., Utah. Career: asst. staff engr. Standard Oil Co. of Indiana (now AMOCO), Whiting, 1948-51; plant engr. Argonne Nat. Lab., Ill. 1951-53; senior job engr. Bechtel Corp., Los Angeles 1953-54; chief engr. May Engring. Co., Van Nuys 1954-58; pres., chief engr. Budlong and Assocs., Sherman Oaks 1958-69; exec. v.p. Quinton-Budlong Architects, Engrs. and Planners, L.A. 1969-73; pvt. practice cons. Northridge, 1973; pres. Killian Assocs. West Inc., Northridge 1973-78; v.p. facilities systems group Boyle Engring. Corp., Northridge 1974-81; pres. Dudley W. Budlong Cons., Woodland Hills 1981-86, past pres. and chmn. Budlong & Moore Assocs., 1986-90; pres. and ceo Budlong & Associates, Inc. 1990–; mem. planning cabinet Am. Cons. Engrs. Council U.S., 1970-76, chmn. 1975; mem. engring. profl. advy. council, dean's advy. bd. Sch. of Engring. and Computer Science CSU Northridge, 1976–; honors: Tau Beta Pi, Eta Kappa Nu, Alpha Phi Omega, recipient distinguished achiev. L.A. Council Engrs. and Scientists 1986, distinguished internat. engring. achiev. Calif. Council Industrial and Bus. Assocs. 1986, Fellow Inst. Advancement of Engring.; mem. Am. Inst. Plant Engrs. (cert.), Assn. Energy Engrs. (charter), Consulting Engrs. Assn. Calif. (past bd. dirs. and sec.), Consulting Engrs. and Land Surveyors of Calif. (L.A. chapt. pres. 1993), Calif. Soc. Profl. Engrs. (past pres., state dir.), Consulting Elec. Engrs. So. Calif. (past pres., bd. dirs.), Illuminating Engring. Soc., Mech.-Elec. Engrs. Council Calif. (past state chmn.), Industrial Assn. S.F.V.; mil: 2d lt. USAF 1943-45; Emmanuel Presbyterian Ch., Thousand Oaks (deacon). Ofc: Budlong & Associates, Inc. 28720 Roadside Dr Agoura Hills 91301

BUFFALOW, OSCAR THOMAS, oil company executive; b. May 15, 1924, Chattanooga, Tenn.; s. Oscar Thomas and Mamie (Van Dusen) B.; m. Jean Carolyn Hart, Feb. 2, 1946 (div. 1979); m. Marie Antoinette Briggs, Jan. 9, 1988; children: Victor Thomas, Edward Hart; edn: B. Chemical engring., Cornell Univ. 1948. Career: engr. Standard Oil Co. Calif., San Francisco 1948-57, supervising engr. 1960-63; research engr. Chevron Research Co., Richmond 1958-59; asst. Chief engr. Standard Oil Co. of Calif. western ops. 1964-68, supt. 1968-69, El Segundo 1969-70, chief engr. 1970-71, mgr. ops., Pascagoula, Miss. 1971-72, chmn. bd. engrs., asst. v.p., Standard Oil Co. of Calif., San Francisco 1973-76; gen. mgr. mfg. dept. Chevron USA, San Francisco 1977-89 (ret.); dir. Kentucky Agr. Energy Corp. 1985-87; dir. Oahu Gas Service, Inc., 1989–; mem Olympic Club; mil: 1st lt. USAAC 1943-46; Republican; Methodist; rec: golf, dominoes. Res: 1345 San Raymundo Rd Hillsborough 94010

BUIE, ROBERT FRANK, real estate developer; b. May 29, 1942, Washington DC; s. Paul Douglas and Mary Margaret (Bullock) B.; m. Pamela Nosler, Jan. 2, 1984; children: Tatia b. 1969, Garrett b. 1975, Catherine Nicole b. 1987, Erica Anne b. 1988; edn: BS civil engring., Virginia Tech. 1964; MBA, Harvard Univ. 1971. Career: naval flight ofcr. USN, S.E. Asia 1964-69; var. positions Avco Community Developers 1971-75, v.p. gen. mgr. San Diego Div. Avco 1975-78, exec. v.p. Avco Community Developers 1978-83; pres. The Buie Corp., real estate developer San Diego, Orange, and Riverside counties 1983-93; pres. Buie Communities 1993–; mem. Building Industry Assn. (bd. dirs.), Presidents Council, Marbella Assn. (pres.); clubs: San Diego Yacht, Fairbanks Ranch CC, The Centre; mil: lcdr. USN-R, active duty 1964-69; Republican; Methodist; rec: skiing, boating. Res: PO Box 8365 Rancho Santa Fe 92067 Ofc: Buie Communities 380 Stevens Ave Solano Beach 92075

BUKRY, JOHN DAVID, geologist; b. May 17, 1941, Baltimore; s. Howard Leroy and Irene Evelyn (Davis) Snyder; edn: undergrad., Colo. Sch. of Mines 1959-60; BA, The Johns Hopkins Univ. 1963; Univ. Ill. 1965-66; MA, PhD, Princeton Univ. 1965, 1967. Career: geologist US Army Corps of Engrs., Baltimore 1963; research asst. Mobil Oil Co., Dallas 1965; geologist US Geological Survey, La Jolla 1967-75, geologist in charge 1975-84; geologist US Minerals Mgmt. Service, La Jolla 1984-86; geologist US Geological Survey, Menlo Park 1986–; research assoc. Geol. Research Div. UC San Diego 1970–; cons. Deep Sea Drilling Project, La Jolla 1967-1987; guest lectr. Vetlesen Symposium, Columbia Univ., N.Y. 1968, 3d Internat. Planktonic Conf., Germany 1974, British Petroleum Exploration Sem. on nannofossil biostratigraphy, Houston 1989; shipboard micropaleontologist on D/V Glomar Challenger (5 DSDP Cruises 1968-78); mem. NSF-JOIDES Stratigraphic Correlations Panel 1976-79; ed. Marine Micropaleontology 1976-83, editl. bd. Micropaleontology 1985-90; awards: fellowships at Princeton Univ., Mobil Oil Co. 1965-67, Am. Chem. Soc. 1966-67; elected fellow AAAS 1981, Explorers Club 1979, Geol. Soc. of Am. 1975; mem. Am. Assn. of Petroleum Geologists, European Union of Geosciences, Internat. Nannoplankton Assn., The Oceanography Soc., Paleontol. Research Instn., Sigma Xi; civic: S.D. Shell Club, UCSD Ida and Cecil Green Faculty Club, S.D. Soc. Natural Hist., Hawaiian Malacological Soc., Nat. Sci. Tchrs. Assn., The Nature Conservancy, Zool. Soc. of S.D., Calif. Acad. of Sciences; author two sci. books in field; contbr. identification and definitions for 300 new species of fossil marine phytoplankton used to give geological ages for ocean bottom sediments pub. in sci. jours.; rec: basketball, photog., shell collector. Ofc: USGS (MS-915), 345 Middlefield Rd Menlo Park 94025

BUKWICH, ANTHONY MICHAEL, county juvenile detention administrator; b. Feb. 13, 1937, Los Angeles; s. Michael and Wilhelmina Maria (Noordman) B.; m. Geraldine Fay Bourland, Sept. 3, 1955; children: Michael A. b. 1956,

Tersea A. b. 1959, Stephen J. b. 1963, Kathleen M. b. 1964; edn: BA pub. mgmt., St. Marys Coll. 1978. Career: counselor Orange Co. Juvenile Hall, Orange 1962-69; supt. Solano Co. Juvenile Hall, Fairfield 1969-94 (ret.); mem: Calif. Juvenile Detention Adminstrs. Assn. (st. pres. 1972-73, st. secty., treas. 1976-78), Calif. Assn. Probation Inst. Adminstrs. (st. secty., treas. 1986-88); mil: cpl. USMC 1954-57; Democrat; R.Cath. Res: 159 Carlsbad Circle Vacaville 95687 Ofc: Solano County Juvenile Hall 2010 W Texas St Fairfield 94533

BULLOCK, JOHN ROLAND, minority program coordinator; b. March 29, 1936, Chicago, Ill.; s. John Roland and Nellie Beatrice (Croyle) B.; m. Mary Helen Nunez, Oct. 27, 1979; children: John b. 1959, Laura b. 1961, Pamela b. 1962, Kevin b. 1963, Dante b. 1974; edn: civil engring., L.A. City Coll., Columbia Pacific Univ.; AA, labor relations, L.A. Trade-Tech. Coll. Career: asst. civil engring. draftsman Los Angeles Dept. Water & Power 1956-57, civil engring. draftsman 1957-64; sr. civil engring. draftsman City of L.A. Bureau of Engring., 1964-70, engring. designer I 1970-86, engring. designer II 1986-95; mem: Engrs. & Architects Assn. (exec. com. 1975-95, sec. 1995, treas. 1992-94, v.p. 1982-89, sec.-treas. 1975-82, unit council gov. 1974-95), Am. Public Works Assn. (com. on equal opportunity), Am. Water Works Assn., Assn. Quality & Participation, Inst. of Indsl. Relations Assn., So. Calif. Mediation Assn., Calif. St. Sheriffs' Assn., NRA, MADD; Republican; Lutheran; rec: boating, skeet and target shooting. Ofc: MJB Productions 8596 Phlox Dr Buena Park 90620-2276

BUNGER, DEBRA LYNNE, psychiatrist; b. Apr. 12, 1959, Louisville, Ky.; d. Kenneth E. and Marijane (Simpson) Bunger; children: Melissa Nicole Bunger Cherpas b. 1992, Madison Lynne Bunger Cherpas b. 1994; edn: MD, Univ. of Louisville Sch. Medicine 1989; med. internship Cabrini Med. Ctr., NYC, NY 1990; psychiatry residency Boston Univ., Boston, Mass. 1991. Career: dept. chair Palo Alto Med. Clinic Fremont Ctr., Fremont, Calif. 1991–; med. dir. St. Luke's Partial Hospitalization Program, Union City, Calif. 1994–. Ofc: Palo Alto Medical Clinic 39500 Liberty Fremont 94538 Tel: 510/490-1222

BUNKER, MARY LOUISE, elected city official; b. Aug. 11, 1923, Logan, Utah; d. James I. and Mary (Lloyd) Condie; m. Earle R. Bunker, May 22, 1944; children: Robert b. 1945, Thomas b. 1955, Carol b. 1960; edn: BA (cum laude) CSU Los Angeles, 1971, MA, 1977; reg. dietitian Am. Dietetic Assn. (1978). Career: pres. J.I. Condie & Assocs., Alhambra 1965-68; dir. Progressive Savs. & Loan, Alhambra 1977-87; chief clinical dietitian St. Luke Medical Ctr., Pasadena 1976-88; elected mayor and mem. Alhambra City Council, 1982–; instr. Pasdena Community Coll., 1978-80; awards: Alumni honor award, graduate award CSULA (1973, 75), Phi Kappa Phi (1971–), Pi Lambda Theta (1976–); mem. Am. Dietetic Assn., Soroptomists Internat., Alhambra C. of C. (bd.); publs: 6 articles in profl. jours. (1972-79); Republican; L.D.S. Res: 132 S El Molino Alhambra 91801

BUNKIS, JURIS, plastic surgeon; b. Aug. 27, 1949, Lubeck, Ger.; s. Janis and Jadviga (Buzinskis) B.; m. Dr. Ruta Sternbergs, Oct. 12, 1974; children: Justin S. b. 1986, Jessica S. b. 1989; edn: pre-med, MD, Univ. of Toronto Med. Sch. 1968-74; lic. MD, Canada (1975), Calif.; diplomate Am. Bd. of Surgery 1980, Am. Bd. of Plastic Surgery 1982. Career: gen. surgery residency, Mary Imogene Bassett Hosp. (Columbia P&S), 1974-79; plastic surg. res. Peter Bent Brigham Hosp., and Childrens Hosp. Med. Ctr. (Harvard) 1979-81, chief res. 1980-81; asst. chief/ chief of plastic surgery, San Francisco Gen. Hosp. 1981-83; asst. prof. of surgery, UC San Francisco 1981–; pvt. practice, Danville, Hayward and Tracy; med. dir. Blackhawk Surgery Ctr. 1990–; pres. United Bridges, Inc. (global mktg. firm); grants: Woodroof Mfg. Inc. (study biosynthetic temporary wounddressings) 1983, Cox-Uphoff Internat. (study digital fluorometric quantification of expanded skin ischaemia) 1983; mem: Fellow Am. Coll. Surgeons, Calif. Med. Assn., Alameda Contra Costa Co. Med. Soc., Internat. Soc. of Aesthetic Plastic Surgery, Lipoplasty Soc. of N. Am., Plastic Surgery Res. Council, Pan Pacific Surgical Assn., Am. Assn. for Hand Surg., Am. Soc. Plastic & Reconstrv. Surgeons, Calif. Soc. Plastic Surgeons, Am. Soc. for Aesthetic Plastic Surgery; author book chapts., numerous med. journal articles, invited lectures; R.Cath.; rec: golf, tennis, skiing. Res: 99 Oak Ridge Ct Danville 94506 Ofc: Juris Bunkis, MD, Inc. 4165 Blackhawk Plaza Circle Ste 150 Danville 94506; 1320 Apple Ave Ste 201 Hayward 94541, 530 W Eaton Ave Ste E Tracy 95376

BUNZEL, JOHN H., senior research fellow; b. Apr. 15, 1924, NYC; s. Ernest Everett and Hariett (Harvey) Bunzel; m. 2d Barbara Bovyer, May 11, 1963; children: Cameron, Reed; edn: AB, pol.sci., magna cum laude, Princeton Univ. 1948; MA, sociol., Columbia Univ. 1949; PhD, pol. sci., UC Berkeley 1954; LL.D.(hon.), Univ. Santa Clara 1976. Career: tchr. CSC San Francisco, 1953-56, Mich. State Univ. 1956-57; pres. San Jose State Univ., 1970-78; sr. res. fellow, Hoover Instn., Stanford Univ., 1978–; awards: Presidential Award, No. Calif. Polit. Sci. Assn. 1969, cert. of honor, S.F. Bd. of Suprs. 1974, Hubert Humphrey award as an outstanding public policy practioner 1990; research grantee: Ford Found. Fund for the Republic 1958-60, Com. on resrch in pub. affairs Stanford Univ. 1960-61, vis. scholar Ctr. for Adv. Study in Behavioural Scis. 1969-70, Rabinowitz Found. 1961-62, Rockefeller Found. 1965-66, No. Calif. Citizenship Clearing House (dir. 1959-61); mem. Am. Polit. Sci. Assn. (No. Calif. pres. 1962-63); author: The American Small Businessman (Knopf 1962), Issues of

American Public Policy (Prentice-Hall 1964, 2d ed. 1968), Anti-Politics in America (Knopf 1967), New Force On the Left: Tom Hayden And The Campaign Against Corporate America (Hoover 1983); Challenge To American Schools (Oxford, 1985), Political Passages: Journeys of Change Through Two Decades, 1968-88 (The Free Press, 1988), Race Relations on Campus: Stanford Students Speak (The Portable Stanford, 1992); coauthor monograph: The Calif. Democratic Delegation of 1960; columnist (biwkly) San Jose Mercury-News; contbr. NY Times, Wall St. Jour., scholarly and polit. jours.; conducted wkly TV pgm. (KPIX-S.F.) 1964; Democrat (del. 1968 Nat. Conv.). Res: 1519 Escondido Way Belmont 94002 Ofc: Hoover Instn. Stanford Univ. Stanford 94305

BURCHAM, THOMAS HERBERT, lawyer; b. Oct. 13, 1936, Los Angeles; s. James Edward and Elizabeth Shera (Redpath) B.; m. Julie Briggs, Dec. 19, 1964; children: Stephen b. 1965, John b. 1967, Peter b. 1970, Simon b. 1976; edn: AA, UC Berkeley 1956; BA, 1958; JD, 1961; admitted St. Bar Calif. 1962. Career: asst. counsel Calif. Farm Bureau Fedn., Berkeley 1965-72, assoc. counsel 1977-82; atty. practice, 1973-74; assoc. counsel West Coast Life Ins., San Francisco 1974-77; solo law practice, Berkeley and Albany 1982–; dir. Berkeley Cares 1991–, pres. 1991-94; dir., pres. Serological Research, Richmond 1978–; dir. Worldwide Farmers Exchange, Berkeley 1984–; mem: Berkeley-Albany Bar Assn. (past pres.), Berkeley C.of C. (dir. 1988–, pres. 1989-90), Berkeley Convention & Visitors Bureau (chmn. 1994-95); mil: col. USAR 1958-89; Republican; Episcopalian. Ofc: 2320 Shattuck Ave Ste B Berkeley 94707

BURDSALL, DEAN LEROY, certified public accountant; b. June 4, 1935, Indianapolis, Ind.; s. Ralph K. and Florence G. (Duncan) B.; m. Georgia Vent, June 1, 1957; children: Kevin b. 1960, Craig b. 1962, Scott b. 1968, Jeffrey b. 1970; edn: BA, Pasadena Coll. 1957; CPA, Calif. 1968. Career: staff acct. Peat, Marwick, Mitchell & Co., San Jose 1960-68; corp. controller GRT Corp., Sunnyvale 1968-71; staff acct. Brooks, Stednitz & Rhodes Accty. Corp., San Jose 1971-74, prin. 1974–; mem: Am. Inst. CPAs (PCPS Peer Review com. 1991-93, PCP Exec. com. 1993–), Calif. Soc. CPAs (Quality Review com. 1989-93, state Acctg. Prin. & Auditing Stds. com. 1987–, and S.J. Chpt. chmn. AP & AS com. 1987-89), CAL GAF Assn. (Peer Review com. chmn. 1987-88), Calif. State Bd. of Accountancy Reporting Standards Com. 1994; civic: Cupertino Rotary Club, Rotary Internat. (Paul Harris Fellow, dist. club service chmn. 1988-89, dist. 517 area rep. 1986-87, pres. West Valley San Jose 1984-85), Youth for Christ Santa Clara Co. (past dir., treas.), past mem. San Jose C.of C.; mil: sp4 AUS 1958-60; Republican; Prot.; rec: tennis, boating, fishing. Res: 6531 Gillis Dr San Jose 95120 Ofc: Brooks, Stednitz & Rhodes Acctncy. Corp. 1600 Willow St San Jose 95125

BURGESON, NICHOLAS R., health care executive/management consultant; b. July 4, 1943, Portland, Oreg.; s. Randolph Benjamin and Grace Ruth (Nimlos) B.; m. Donna Irene MacGlashen, Oct. 17, 1964; children: Tina Lynn b. 1965, Robert Gene b. 1967; edn: AS nsg. sci., Pacific Union Coll., 1964; BS bus. adm., Golden Gate Univ., 1977, MBA, Univ. Beverly Hills, 1981; RN, Calif., W.D.C.; lic. nursing home adminstr. Calif. Career: staff nse. Napa State Hosp. 1964-66; nsg. coord. Adolescent Pgm., Napa State Hosp., 1968-70, asst. to the med. dir. 1970-71; pgm. adminstr. I, II, Hosp. Svs. Sect. Calif. Dept. of Mental Hygiene, Sacto. 1971-72, Calif. Dept. of Health, 1973-77; adminstr. Metropolitan State Hosp., Norwalk 1977-81; assoc. adminstr., chief ops. Loma Linda Comm. Hosp., Loma Linda 1981-82; pres. NRB & Associates, Sacto. 1982–; mgr. psychiatric hosp. devel. Am. Med. Internat. Inc., Beverly Hills 1983-84; stds. compliance coord. Atascadero State Hosp., 1984-86, then dir. info. resources dept., 1986-90; spl. advisor Hosp. Accreditation, Calif. Dept. of Mental Health, Sacto. 1990-91, cons. on hosp. adminstrn. 1992–; narrated and appeared in 90-min. NBC-TV White Paper "Cry Help" (1970); recipient commendn. Secty. Calif. Health and Welfare Agy., Sacto. 1979, sustained superior accomplishment award Calif. Dept. Mental Hlth. 1987, leadership and scholarship award National Univ. Bd. Trustees, Sacto. 1987, recipient commendn. Dir. Calif. Dept. Mental Health 1993; biographical listings in Who's Who in West (22d), Who's Who in Fin. and Industry (26th), Dir. of Top Computer Execs., Men of Achiev. (14th); mem: Calif. Assn. of Mgmt. Sacto. (secty. 1974-76, pres. 1976-77, dir. 1988-92), Forensic Mental Health Assn. of Calif. (dir. 1988–, pres. 1990-92); contbr. articles in Forensic Forum J. (1988–); mil: chief warrant ofcr., staff nse. US Army Nurse Corps, Walter Reed Army Med. Ctr., W.D.C. (hon. disch.) 1966-68; Republican; Prot. Res: 5612 Gitta Ria Ct Citrus Heights 95610 Ofc: 1600 Ninth St Rm 120 Sacramento 95814 Ph: 916/654-3600

BURGESS, MICHAEL, librarian, author, publisher; b. Feb. 11, 1948, Fukuoka, Kyushu, Japan, came to U.S. 1949; s. Roy Walter and Betty Jane (Kapel) B.; m. Mary Alice Wickizer, Oct. 15, 1976; stepchildren: Richard Albert Rogers, Mary Louise Reynnells; edn: AB (honors), Gonzaga Univ., 1969; MLS, USC, 1970. Career: periodicals librarian CSU San Bernardino, 1970-81, prof. and chief cataloger CSU San Bernardino, 1981-94, head of collection development and tech. svs. 1994–; editor Newcastle Pub. Co., North Hollywood 1971-92, pub. Borgo Press, San Bernardino 1975–; advy. editor Arno Press, N.Y.C., 1975-78; author of 80 books, editor, publisher approx. 1250 books; including: Cumulative Paperback Index 1973, Things to Come 1977, Science Fiction and Fantasy Literature 1979, Tempest in a Teapot 1984, Lords Temporal & Lords

Spiritual 1985 (2nd. ed. 1994), Futurevisions 1985, Arms Control, Disarmament, & Military Security Dict. 1989, The Work of Colin Wilson 1989, Reference Guide to Science Fiction, Fantasy, and Horror 1992, House of the Burgesses 1994; editor 15 scholarly series incl. Milford Series: Popular Writers of Today (60 vols.), Science Fiction (63 vols.), Stokvis Studies in Historical Chronology and Thought (10 vols.), ed. 6 reprint series, 2 jours.; 145+ pub. articles and revs., 80+ publishers' catalogs, 1 pub. short story, 15 major state documents, designer and prodn. mgr. 100+ pub. vol.; awards: Title II fellow USC 1969-70, $2500 MPPP Award 1987, Lifetime Collectors Award 1993, Pilgrim Award 1993; mem: ACLU, NEA, AAUP, Calif. Tchrs. Assn., Am. Library Assn., Calif. Library Assn., Kent Hist. Soc., Sci. Fiction Writers Am., Horror Writers of Am., Calif. Faculty Assn. (Librarians' Task Force 1987-89, sec., librarian, Libr. Affairs Com. 1993–), Sci. Fiction Res. Assn., Blue Earth County (Minn.) Hist. Soc., City of San Bdo. Hist. and Pioneer Soc., Grant County (Ky.) Hist. Soc., Internat. Assn. for the Fantastic in Arts, Nat. Geneal. Soc., Internat. P.E.N., Ky. Hist. Soc., Upper Cumberland Geneal. Assn., World SF. Res: PO Box 2845 San Bernardino 92406 Ofc: Calif. State Univ. Library, 5500 University Pkwy San Bernardino 92407

BURKE, RAE LYN, virologist; b. April 25, 1948, Cape Girardeau, Mo.; d. Charles and Marian (Rideout) Conrad; m. Arthur Roger Cooke, May 8, 1983 (div. 1989); m. 2d. Regis Kelly; 1 dau., Virginia b. 1983; edn: BS high hons., chemistry, Univ. Nev. 1971; PhD, St. Univ. N.Y. 1977. Career: postdoctoral fellow UCSF Dept. Biochemistry 1977-81; scientist Chiron Corp., Emeryville 1981-84, prin. scientist 1984-86, senior scientist 1986-90, assoc. dir. virology 1990-92, project leader 1982–, dir. virology 1992–; bd. dirs. Pacific Dental Research Found., San Francisco 1986–; honors: Sigma Sigma Kappa, Phi Kappa Phi, Lyndon B. Johnson Presdl. scholar 1966, Biophysical Soc. Lamport award 1977, Bank of Am. Giannini fellowship 1980, NIH fellowship 1981; mem: ASAS, Am. Soc. Microbiology, Am. Soc. Virology; 54 papers pub. in sci. jours. (1977–), 9 issued patents in vaccine devel.; Democrat; rec: tennis, sailing, travel. Ofc: Chiron Corp. 4560 Horton St. Emeryville 94608-2916

BURKE, YVONNE BRATHWAITE, lawyer; b. Oct. 5, 1932, Los Angeles; d. James A. and Lola (Moore) Watson; m. Louis Brathwaite; m. 2d, William A. Burke, June 14, 1972; dau. Autumn Roxanne b. 1973; edn: BA in polit. sci., UCLA, 1953, JD, USC, 1956; admitted Calif. Bar 1956. Career: practicing atty., dep. corporation commr. Calif., 1956-66, hearing ofcr. Police Commn. 1964-66, and staff atty. McCone Commn. (investig. Watts Riots) 1965; rep. 63d dist. Calif. State Assembly, 1966-72, chair com. on urban devel. and housing 1971-72; elected 93d-95th Congress, rep. 37th dist. Calif. 1972-78 (1st woman in 20 yrs and 1st black woman ever elected to Congress from Calif.) mem. House appropriations com., select com. on assassinations; ptnr. Calif. law firm Burke, Robinson & Pearman, 1984-87; Jones, Day, Reavis & Pogue, Los Angeles 1987-92; supr. L.A. County Bd. of Supervisors 1992–; awards: fellow Kennedy Sch. of Politics at Harvard, Chubb fellow at Yale, profl. achiev. UCLA 1974, 84, 200 future leaders Time Mag. 1974, woman of year LA Times, Nat. Assn. of Blk Mfrs., num. citations various orgns., listed Who's Who Am., Who's Who among Blk Am.; appt: bd. regents Univ. Calif. 1991–, bd. Brookings Inst. 1990–, bd. Ednl. Testing Svc. 1990–, bd. Ford Found. 1993–, bd. chair Federal Reserve Bank of S.F. 1990–, bd. Founders Sav. & Loan 1989–, bd. Amateur Athletic Found. 1989–, L.A. 2000 Com. 1989–, bd. Coalition of 100 Blk Women L.A. 1989–; rec: tennis, equestrienne. Ofc: Room 866, Hall of Adminstrn. 500 West Temple Los Angeles 90012

BURKETT, NANCY SCHALLERT (Mrs. William Andrew Burkett), educator, artist, philanthropist; b. May 11, 1917, Winston-Salem, N.C.; d. Dr. Paul Otto and Grace (Jackson) Schallert; m. Richard Morrison Lofton, Aug. 20, 1938 (dec. 1966); children: Nancy Lofton Faridany, and Melissa Lofton; m. Dr. Dwight W. Morrow, Jr., Nov. 25, 1970 (dec. 1976); m. William Andrew Burkett, June 20, 1992; edn: att. Salem Coll., Winston-Salem, 1934-36; AB in English, Univ. N. Carolina, Chapel Hill 1938; grad. study UC Berkeley; Calif. life tchg. credential 1955. Career: feature writer Winston-Salem Journal and Sentinel, 1938-40; Monterey Herald, and Carmel Pine Cone, 1945-50; tchr. Monterey-Carmel Schs., 1952-73; cons. and lectr. on Textbook Edn., 1961-63; designer of Carmel Bach Festival Heraldic Banners, 1951-91, fest. cons. and artist, 1979-89; dir. Burkett Land Co., 1990–; appt. by Gov. Edmund G. Brown to Calif. Curriculum Commn., 1964-68; appt. Calif. Com. to Create Humanities Framework for Schs., 1969-74; appt. Nat. Commn. U.S.M.E.S., supported by AAAS tp improve tchg. of sci. and math., 1969; civic bds: endowment com. Univ. N.Carolina, Chapel Hill (bd. 1977-89), Carmel Bach Festival (dir. 1977–), Friends of Music, Smithsonian Mus., Met. Mus. of N.Y., The Nat. Trust, Monterey Mus. of Art, Carmel Music Soc., Carmel Art Assn., Garden Club Am., Carmel-by-the-Sea Garden Club (bd.), Casa Abrego Club of Monterey (pres. 1985-86), Mt. Rushmore Hall of Records Commn. (trustee 1988–), Sierra Club, Nat. Audubon Assn., Monterey Co. Symphony Assn., Carmel PTA (bd.); mem: Monterey Tchrs. Assn. (bd.), Monterey Hist. and Art Assn., Stanford Univ. Alumni Assn., Univ. N.C. Alumni Assn., Monterey Inst. Internat. Studies, Chi Omega Sor.; clubs: Carmel Valley Golf & Country, Rocky Creek, Monterey Peninsula Golf & Country, Beach and Tennis, Pebble Beach; All Saints Episcopal Ch., Carmel (vestry). Res: 1548 Viscaino Road Pebble Beach 93953 and PO Box 726 Pebble Beach 93953

BURKETT, WILLIAM ANDREW, banker, business executive, former state superintendent of banks; b. July 1, 1913, Herman, Nebr.; s. William H. and Mary (Dill) B.; 7th generation desc. of Stuffel Burkett, farm emigre to Pa. from Ger., 1700; desc. Maj. Gen. Edward Dodge and Judge John F. Williams, Calif. pioneers, 1849; m. Juliet Ruth Johnson, Oct. 5, 1940 (dec. Mar. 13, 1976); children: Juliet Ann (Mrs. Rodman L. Hooker, Jr.), Katherine C. (Mrs. Jeffrey H. Congdon), William Cleveland; m. Nancy Schallert Morrow, June 20, 1992; edn: stu. Univ. Nebr. 1931-32, Creighton Univ. Law Sch., 1932-33; LLB, Univ. Omaha, 1936. Career: elected nominee Secty. of State Nebr. (R) 1936; candidate for U.S. Congress, Nebr., 1938; regional chief of enforcements War Prodn. Board, 1941-43, ofcr. in chg. Secret and Confidential Sect., chief prosecutor of subversives, USCG, 12th Naval Dist., WWII; sr. spl. agt. intelligence unit US Treasury Dept. 1945-50; cons. and witness Calif. Crime Commn. and US Senate Kefauver Crime Com., 1950-52; exec. v.p. Calif. Employers Assn. Group, Sacramento 1950-53; dir. Calif. Dept. Employment, 1953-55; Supt. Banks, chmn. Dept. Investments Calif., 1955-59, credited by state legis. com. for discovery and correction of State Unemployment Ins. abuses, and for reorgn. of State Dept. Employment and State Banking Dept.; nominee of Nat. Assn. Supts. of Banks & Am. Bankers Assn. for Presdl. appt. to chair FDIC, Wash. DC; dir. Liquidation Yokohama Specie Bank, also Sumitomo Bank, San Francisco, 1955-59; cons. Western Bancorp, S.F., 1959-61; chmn. bd., pres. Security Nat. Bank Monterey Co., Monterey-Carmel 1961-66; chmn. bd. Burkett Land Co., Monterey, 1966–; cons. United Calif. Bank, L.A. 1966–; chmn. bd. Securities Properties Corp., Monterey 1966–; appt. dir. Calif. Emergency Manpower Commn. 1953-55, chmn. Gov.'s Com. Refugee Relief 1953-55, commr. Calif. Securities Commn. 1955-59; candidate for Gov. of Calif. (D) 1978; witness US Senate Banking Com. 1984, US Congress Banking Com. 1991; nat. chmn. Bank and Savings & Loans League, 1991–, guest spkr. on "Needed Reforms" Wash. Press Club 1986; guest spkr. Am. Bankers Assn. 84th Annual Nat. Conv., Chgo.; mem: Internat. Platform Assn., Am., Calif., Independent Bankers Assns., Nat. Assn. Supts. State Banks (pres. 1958-59), Amvets (dept. comdr. Calif. 1947, nat. v.comdr. 1948), Disabled Am. Veterans (life), American Legion (life), Stanford Univ. Alumni Assn., Soc. Calif. Pioneers; civic: Pine Manor Jr. Coll., Chestnut Hill, Mass. (fin. bd. 1967–), Mt. Rushmore Hall of Records Commn. (nat. co-chr. 1991–, co-chr. bd. trustees/founder 1987–), Mt. Rushmore Nat. Memorial Soc. (life, trustee), Nat. Hist. Found. (bd. chmn.), Monterey Co. Hist. Commn., Monterey Hist. and Art Assn. (life mem.), Monterey Sym. Assn. (bd. dirs.), Monterey Mus. Art (trustee), Bishop Kip Sch., Carmel Valley (trustee), Robert Louis Stevenson Sch., Pebble Beach (advy. bd. 1971–), Smithsonian Assocs., Met. Mus. of Art, Bach Festival Assocs., Nat. Trust Found. 1986, The Royal Oak Found. 1986; clubs: Monterey Peninsula Golf & Country, Beach and Tennis, Stillwater Yacht (Pebble Beach), Carmel Valley Golf and Tennis, Commonwealth of Calif., Rotary (S.F.), Sutter Lawn (Sacto.); author: Mount Rushmore National Memorial's History of America, 1776-1904 (1971); Episcopalian; rec: swim, golf. Res: Pebble Beach Ofc: 1548 Viscaino Rd (POB 726) Pebble Beach 93953

BURKETT, WILLIAM CLEVELAND, investment banker and management consultant; b. June 3, 1956, San Mateo; s. William Andrew and Juliet Ruth (Johnson) B.; m. Wynn McClenahan, July 4, 1992; children: Elizabeth Locke Burkett; edn: BA (hons.), Stanford Univ. 1978; MBA (honors), Yale Univ. 1983. Career: fin. analyst corp. fin. dept. merger and acquisitions, First Boston Corp., 1978-80, New York; internat. coord. Credit Suisse First Boston Ltd., London, England 1980-81; pres. Security Properties Inc. 1981–; mgmt cons. staff McKinsey & Co., San Francisco 1983-88; v.p. Mehta Burkett Co. Inc. Investment Bankers 1989-90; spl advisor to the Pres., Takata Corp.,Tokyo, Japan 1990–; v.chmn. bd./c.e.o European Components Corp., Belfast, Ireland, 1991–; exec. v.p. and dir. Takata Inc. 1993–; pres. Takata Fabrication Corp. 1993–; dir. Burkett Land Co. 1974–; pres. Burkett & Co., Inc. 1990–; awards: recogn. for unusual ability and personal initiative Conservation Div. U.S. Geol., Dept. of Interior; mem: Delta Upsilon, Stanford Alumni Assn. (life), Yale Univ. Alumni Assn.; civic: Commonwealth Club, Nat. Hist. Found. (pres. 1984–), Mt. Rushmore Nat. Memorial Soc. (life. 1983), Soc Calif. Pioneers (life 1987), MtRushmore Hall of Records Commn.; clubs: Yale, N.Y. Athletic, Pebble Beach; Episcopalian; rec: ski, sailing, tennis. Res: 1901 Pacific Ave San Francisco 94109 also: PO Box 726 Pebble Beach 93953

BURKETT, WYNN MCCLENAHAN (Mrs. William Cleveland Burkett), financial analyst, consultant; b. July 16, 1959, San Francisco; d. James Brice and Sharon (Rosengreen) McClenahan; m. William Cleveland Burkett, July 4, 1992; children: Elizabeth Locke Burkett; edn: BA, Stanford Univ., 1981; MA in mgmt., Yale Univ. 1987. Career: legal asst. Wilmer, Cutler & Pickering, W.D.C., 1981-83; financial analyst Morgan Stanley & Co. Inc., NY, NY, 1983-85; consultant, Exec. Office of the President - Office of Mgmt. & Budget, W.D.C., 1986; assoc. The First Boston Corp., NY, NY, 1987-88, San Francisco, 1988-91; cons., Sotheby's, London 1991-92; exec. asst. Ofc. of Federal Housing Enterprise Oversight, Wash., D.C. 1993–; dir: Burkett Land Company, Pebble Beach; mem. Kappa Kappa Gamma Soc., Stanford Alumni Assn.; Prot.; rec: tennis, running. Res: 1901 Pacific Ave San Francisco 94109

BURNS, FRANKLYN, real estate broker; b. Sept. 30, 1933, Los Angeles; s. Milton and Belle Miriam (Cytron) B.; m. Frieda Joyce Tannenbaum, June 30,

1962 (div.); children: Michelle Dorene b. 1964, Kimberly Rachel b.1966; edn: student Los Angeles City Coll. 1951-53, 1954-55, Univ. Ariz. 1953-54, Chounaird Art Inst. 1959; Calif. lic. R.E. sales 1972, R.E. broker 1974; Master Senior Appraiser (MSA), NAMA. Career: mgr. Jerome Ehrlich Realty 1972-75; ptnr., broker Jones Burns Realty, Golden Rule Realty 1975-78; broker, owner Franklyn Burns, Realtor 1978-83; Viking Realty 1983-85; salesman, realtor, cons. R.R. Gable Inc. Northridge 1985-88; Mike Glickman Realty Inc. 1988-90; Paramount Properties, Northridge 1990-95; S & R Financial 1992-94; Leyden Financial 1994–; owner/broker Franklyn Burns Realtor 1994–; instr. L.A. City Schs.: 4-part seminar "How to Select A Broker" 1987, 10-part course "Real Estate Practices; How To Buy & Sell Property" 1989; mem: Nat. Assn. Master Appraisers /No. L.A. Co. (chapt. sec. 1989), Nat. Assn. Realtors, Calif. Assn. Realtors, S.F.V. Bd. of Realtors (grievance com. 1990, political affairs com. 1992), Kiwanis Internat. (chapt. pres. 1992-93); Republican; Jewish. Res/Ofc: 11552 Gothic Ave Granada Hills 91344-2933

BURROUGHS, KATE, entomologist; b. Oct. 31, 1953, Hayward; d. Erwin S. and Mary Adele (Henderson) Burroughs; m. David L. Henry, July 12, 1975; 1 son, Michael b. 1985; edn: BS entomology, UC Berkeley, 1975; bd. cert. entomologist E.S.A., 1980. Career: entomologist Calif. Dept. Food & Agr., Sacto. 1975-78; entomologist, cons., Sebastopol, 1978-80; entomologist Harmony Farm Supply, Sebastopol 1980–; mem: Assn. of Applied Insect Ecologists (1976–, past pres.), Am. Soc Enology & Viticulture 1989–, Calif. Certified Organic Farmers 1976–, Com. for Sustainable Agriculture 1980–, USDA Nat. Sustainable Agriculture Advy. Council 1993–; civic: Organic Gardening & Nutrition Club Santa Rosa, Graton Community Club, Sonoma Co. Orchid Soc.; contbg. author: Future Is Abundant (1980), book editor: Controlling Vegetable Pests (1991), num. articles in field; rec: orchidist. Ofc: Harmony Farm Supply, 3244 Hwy 116 No, Sebastopol 95472

BURSTEEN, DAVID BRUCE, marketing executive; b. Sept. 16, 1957, Highland Park, Ill.; s. Jack D. and Annette Vivian (Turen) B.; m. Donna Marie Grider, Jan. 15, 1978; children: Amanda, b. 1983, Marisa Jaye b. 1985; edn: AA, L.A. Valley Coll. 1977. Career: past dir. advtg. Malibu Grand Prix Corp.; v.p. mktg. Phone-In-Drive Thru Markets, Inc., W. Los Angeles; v.p. sales Essex Video, Inc., Northridge 1985-86; regional v.p. Ja-Ru Inc. (peg toy mfg.-import co.), 1987–; founder Elite Home Video, new home video prodn. co., 1986–, G-Whiz, mail-order cat. of childrens videos & movies 1988–, New City Releasing Cable (pay & free t.v. movie distbr.), 1989–; pres. & founder Split Screen Media, Inc. (producers representation) 1994–; cons: Laff Stop 1979-80, Video Vision 1981-82, Infobase 1983-84, USC Food Ind. Pgm. 1983; sem. spkr: Pierce Coll., Students in Advtg. 1981, Promise and Pitfalls of Electronic Shopping 1983; honors: Player of the Year, M.G.P. 1980; hon. citizen Louisville, Ky. 1980; mem: L.A. C.of C.; Chatsworth C.of C.; Bnai Brith; Gateway Hospital; L.A. Ad Club; rec: skiing, cars, high tech. Ofc: Split Screen Media 22120 Clarendon Ave #250 Woodland Hills 91367

BURTON, BERTHA L., case management specialist; b. Apr. 19, 1949, Columbia, S.C.; d. Burt T.N., Sr. and Georgie L. (Lott) Burton; m. Herbert L. Stocker; edn: BA (cum laude), Johnson C. Smith Univ., Charlotte, N.C. 1971; MSW, Univ. S.C., 1974. Career: tchr. Columbia (S.C.) Public Schs., 1971-72; acting dir. Gaston Memorial Hosp., Gastonia, N.C. 1972; instr. Benedict Coll., Columbia, S.C. 1974-76; addiction coord. Mid-Carolina Council, 1976-78, Columbia; tnr. counselor Urban Mgmt., San Francisco, Calif. 1980-82; sch. cons. Community Human Services Proj., Monterey, Calif. 1981-85; prison rep. Friends Outside, Correctional Tng. Facility (CTF), San Jose, Calif. 1987–; mem. Friends Outside Monterey Co. (bd. 1987–), Family & Corrections Network 1988–, Pan-Hellenic Council Monterey (sec. treas. 1984-85), Seaside Kiwanis (chair 1984-85), Executive Internat. (Col., S.C. pres. 1977-80), Delta Sigma Theta Sor., W.D.C. (v.p. 1970-71); pub. jour. article "Nurturing Today" (1988); Democrat; Rel. Sci.; rec: swimming, jogging, reading, arts & crafts. Ofc: Friends Outside PO Box 686 - CTF Soledad 93960-0686

BURTON, DONALD EUGENE, physicist; b. Apr. 24, 1941, Kans, City, Mo.; s. Charles Marcelan and Alice Agnes (Gillis) B.; m. Chong Su Im, Oct. 11, 1970; children: Michael b. 1976, Jennifer b. 1979; edn: BS in engring. physics, Univ. Mo.-Rolla 1962; PhD in theoretical nuclear physics, Kans. State Univ. 1968. Career: capt., res./devel. coord. AUS Corps of Engrs. 1968-69, 1970-73; physicist Earth Scis. Dept. Lawrence Livermore Nat. Lab. 1973-77, gp. leader code devel. 1977-82, project leader ground motion effects 1982-86, gp. leader GROK design code Def. Scis. Dept. 1986-93, project ldr. FLAG develop. 1993–; awards: commendation medal for res. AUS 1973, NDEA Fellowship, KSU 1963-65, Phi Beta Kappa award 1959, Mo. Curators Scholarship 1960, Gen. Motors Scholarship 1960-62, Sigma Xi, Sigma Pi Sigma, Kappa Mu Epsilon, Phi Kappa Pi, Tau Beta Pi; mem: Internat. Assn. for Mathematics and Computers in Simulation, Am. Geophysical Union, Internat. Soc. Rock Mechanics, Am. Inst. Physics Tchrs., Am. Physical Soc., AAAS; 70+ sci. papers in field (-1986); rec: genealogy. Res: 2802 Waverly Way Livermore 94550 Ofc: Lawrence Livermore Nat Lab PO Box 808 Livermore 94550

BUSCH, PETER JONATHAN, lawyer; b. June 24, 1952, Evanston, Ill.; s. Albert Eliot and Vera (Ellman) B.; m. Catharine S. Barnes, June 6, 1982; children: Frank b. 1983, Emily b. 1987; edn: BA, magna cum laude, Yale Coll. 1974; JD, Univ. Va. Sch. Law 1977; admitted St. Bar Calif. Career: law clk. U.S. Ct. Appeals 1st Circuit 1977-79; Justice W. J. Brennan, U.S. Supreme Ct., Wash. 1979-80; atty. Howard Rice, San Francisco 1980–; article ed. Univ. Va. Law Review; mem: San Francisco Legal Aid Soc. (past mem. bd. dirs.), Bar Assn. San Francisco, Am. Bar Assn., Cal. State Bar (co-chair com. on women in the law 1989-90). Ofc: Howard Rice 3 Embarcadero Center 7th Floor San Francisco 94111

BUSH, ELMER W., corporate president; b. Nov. 26, 1923, Sacramento; s. Charles J. and Alice Ellen (Pitiman) B.; m. Felomena T. Cimaroli, Nov. 26, 1973; children: Michael M. b. 1959; edn: Master Engr. Aircraft, Dallas Aircraft Engring. Coll. 1943; Mastr Engr. Internal Combustion Engines, Chevrolet Motor Div. 1943; Technical Splst. Turbo Superchargers, Honeywell 1944; Splst. Aircraft Hydraulics, Army Air Force Sch. of Hydraulics 1944; Splst. Hydramatic Props. & Controls, Hamilton Standards Propeller Div. 1944; Master Mech. Engr., US Army Air Force 1944. Career: welding insp. Kaiser Shipbldrs., Richmond 1940-42; master aircraft engr. US Army Air Force; founder, pres., chief chemist Pal-Pen Chemical Corp. 1950–; pres., exec. engr. Condensator Inc. 1975–; inventor: dry cleaning chemicals; patent, Pal-Gun, for spotting garments; patent, condensator supplementary carburetor; farm machinery; mil: m/sgt. US Army Air Force 1943-46, (2) Pres. Unit Citations, 9 Battle Stars, European Theatre, WWII; R.Cath.; rec: boating, water skiing, skin diving. Address: 433 Bull River Rd Noxon MT 59853-9707

BUSH, WILLIAM MERRITT, lawyer; b. June 23, 1941, Long Beach; s. Lloyd Merritt and Barbara Ann (Bufkin) B.; m. Dorothy Irene Vasvary, June 25, 1966; children: Steven b. 1967, Amy b. 1972; edn: BA, Stanford Univ. 1963; JD, UC Hastings Coll. Law 1966; admitted Calif. Supreme Ct. 1967. Career: law clk. Dannemeyer & Tuohey, Fullerton 1966-67, atty., assoc. 1967; ptnr., shareholder Miller Bush & Minnott 1967-88; sole practice, Fullerton 1989–; awards: Calif. St. PTA Hon. Service award 1988; mem: Calif. St. Bar (bd. legal specialization chmn. 1982-88, family law advy. commn. chmn. 1979-85), Orange Co. Bar Assn. (dir. 1982-85), Am. Acad. Matrimonial Lawyers, Kiwanis (pres. 1971-72), City of Fullerton Human Rels. Commn. (commr. 1971-77), Fullerton Union H.S. Site Council 1986-88; Republican; Methodist; rec: jogging, computers, weight training. Res: 1400 Avolencia Dr Fullerton 92635-3705 Ofc: 110 E Wilshire Ave Ste 210 Fullerton 92632-1998

BUSKA, SHEILA MARY, corporate financial executive; b. May 9, 1941, Brewer, Me.; d. George Wm. and Owenita Margaret (Harrah) Sanderlin; m. Roland Buska, Nov. 28, 1959; children: Bryan b. 1960, Craig b. 1961, Christy b. 1962, Paul b. 1964; 6 grandchildren: Tobyn b. 1988, Blake b. 1991, Breanna b. 1991, Garrett b. 1993, Shelby b. 1994, Ryan b. 1994; edn: AA liberal arts, Univ. San Diego, 1959; BS acctg. (magna cum laude), San Diego St. Univ., 1984; CMA, Inst. Cert. Mgmt. Accts., 1988; Calif. lic. CPA, 1989. Career: sr. acct. Peak Health Plan, San Diego 1984-86; sr. acct. M/A-COM Govt. Systems Inc, 1986-87; sr. acct. Lois A. Brozey, CPA, 1987-89; controller Crown Chemical Corp., 1989–, chief fin. ofcr. 1990–; honors: Beta Gamma Sigma 1984, Beta Alpha Psi 1983; mem. Inst. Cert. Mgmt. Accts., Calif. Soc. of CPAs, Inst. of Mgmt. Accts. (Chapter v.p. mem. 1985-86, assoc. dir. meetings 88-89, dir. 1989-90, dir. corporate devel. 1992-93, treas. 1993-94, dir. membership 1995-96); publs: poems selected in nat. competition Am. Poetry Soc., Nat. H.S. Poetry Assn.,1957, acctg. article in Mgmt. Accountant, 1992; Democrat; R. Cath.; rec: poetry, music, theater, travel in U.S. Res: 509 Burgasia Path El Cajon 92019 Ofc: 1888 Nirvana Ave Chula Vista 91911

BUSKE, KENNETH EUGENE, consulting engineering company owner; b. June 18, 1942, Rochester, N.Y.; s. Gilbert Eugene and Genevieve June (Strutt) B.; m. Mary Lawler, April 1, 1961 (div. 1982); children: Richard b. 1961, Scott b. 1975, Joan b. 1975; edn: BSEE, Purdue Univ. 1963; MSEE, 1964; MS indsl. adminstrn., 1965; reg. profl. engr. Va. 1973. Career: engr. IBM, Endicott, N.Y. 1965-68; USN, Wash.. DC 1968-73; ARINC Research, Annapolis, Md. 1973-74; Trident Engring. 1974-76; engr., owner Buske Engring. 1974-83, Benicia 1983–; mem: Nat. Soc. Profl. Engrs., Nat. Fire Protection Assn., Assn. Testing Materials, IEEE, Sierra Club; rec: sailing, photography, flying. Res: 302 Marina Village Way Benicia 94510 Ofc: Buske Engineering 302 Marina Village Way Benicia 94510

BUSS, DIETRICH GOTTHILF, historian; b. Sept. 20, 1939, Tokyo, Japan; s. Bernhard August and Katharina Martha (Wenzel) B.; m. Miriam Eleanore Epp, July 10, 1943; children: Eric b. 1970, Julie b. 1972, Natalie b. 1974; edn: BA in edn., Biola Univ., 1963; MA social sci., CSU Los Angeles, 1965; PhD history, Claremont Grad. Sch., 1976. Career: social studies faculty Culter Acad., L.A. 1965-66; history faculty Biola Univ., La Mirada 1966–; mem. City of La Mirada Hist. Heritage Commn., 1977–, chair 1992-94; recipient Charles J. Kennedy Award Econ. and Bus. Hist. Soc. 1978; mem: Org. of Am. Historians 1965–, Econ. and Bus. Hist. Soc. 1976–, Conf. of Faith and History 1976–; author: Henry Villard (econ. biography), Giving Wings to the Gospel (internat. history of Mission Aviation Fellowship), 1995; contbr. (rel. biog.) Dict. of Christianity in Am., 1991, Blackwell Dict. of Evangelical Biog., 1995, contbr. Encyclopedia USA, 1994; Republican; Evangelical Free Ch. of Am.; rec: outdoorsman, naturalist. Ofc: Biola Univ. 13800 Biola Ave La Mirada 90639

BUTLER, BRIAN ANDREW, auto dealership executive; b. Sept. 27, 1951, Enid, Okla.; s. Robert Andrew Butler and Bette Mae (Clark) Raiser; m. Peggy Ann Baldwin, July 6, 1980; children: Jenifer b. 1976, Judy b. 1982, Jimmy b. 1985. Career: construction work as carpenter 1972-82; salesman to sales mgr. Villa Honda, Hemet, Calif. 1982-88; sales mgr. to gen. mgr. to pres./CEO Villa Ford, Orange, Calif. 1988–; awards: Ford Motor Co. 100 Club 1992, 93 (awarded to top 100 Ford dealerships in U.S.), Villa Ford #1 in Orange Co. (24 straight yrs.), as high as 11th in nation with Ford Motor Co., #49 with Ford Motor Credit; mem: National Auto Dealers Assn. 1989–; rec: golf, fishing, bicycling. Ofc: Villa Ford 2550 N. Tustin Orange 92665 Tel: 714/637-8222

BUTLER, DONALD EARNEST, association executive; b. Mar. 2, 1927, Coatesville, Pa.; s. John Minor and Jane B. (Hanthorn) B.; m. Laura Eaton, Aug. 28, 1948; children: Donald E. b. 1952, Jeffrey E. b. 1956; edn: BS, Franklin & Marshall, 1949. Career: mgmt. staff, 19 yrs., then pres./c.e.o. SSP Industries, 12 yrs., ret. 1979; elected pres. and c.e.o. The Employers Group (human resources mgmt.) 1979–, mem. bd. dirs. 1973–; dir: Calif. Casualty Ins. Cos., Keenan Properties Inc., C.Itoh, Calif. Offset Printers Inc., Master Halco Inc., Unique Mfg.; awards: man of yr. Calif. Bus. Edns. 1970, SME pres.'s award, L.A. 1969, best dressed L.A. Bus. Jour. 1985; mem. Nat. Assn. of Mfs. (dir.), L.A. C.of C. (internat. commerce exec. com.), Japan Amer. Soc. (dir.); civic bds: Verdugo Hills Hosp. (advy. bd.), Glendale Sym. Orch. Assn. (dir., past pres.), BSA L.A. (advy. bd.); clubs: Oakmont CC, Jonathan, Univ. Club of S.F., Rotary (L.A.); mil: aviator USN 1944-47; Republican; rec: golf, sailing. Res: 1710 Ivy Bridge Rd Glendale 91207 Ofc: 1150 S Olive St Ste 2300 Los Angeles 90015

BUTLER, RUSSELL, artist; b. Mr. 7, 1949, N.Y.C.; s. Milton W. and Dorothy Ann (Adams) B.; edn: BFA, Univ. Buffalo, 1971; San Francisco Art Inst., 1977. Career: art director Annelieses Sch., Laguna Beach 1977–, Willowbrook, Calif., 1987-88; owner Russ Butler School of Art, Laguna Beach, 1981-84; artist Stein/Brief Corp., Newport Beach, 1983, Xerox, S.F., 1985, City of Laguna Beach, 1986, Transamerica Corp., L.A., 1987, UC Irvine Med. Ctr., Orange 1987-88; principle works incl. commemorative murals: Dreamer, 1983, Delusions of Grandeur, 1987, Legend of the Waters, 1988, 5 major paintings UCI Med. Ctr., large paintings Greater L.A. World Trade Ctr. 1992, paintings and installations: Pres. & Mrs. Bill Clinton, The White House 1993, Landmark Tower, Osaka, Japan 1994, Shinjuku Royal Host Hotel, Tokyo, Japan 1995, Pukuoka Mall, Japan 1995, Walt Disney Inst. 1995; exhibns: Los Angeles Art Expo 1988, Sheraton Rosemead, Newport Harbor Yacht Club, Magic Internat, 1989; calendar and exhibn. Am. Cancer Soc. 1993; one-man exhibns. Nat. Acad. of Sci. & Engring., Irvine, Calif. 1992, Robert Mondavi Wine Ctr., Santa Ana 1993; mem. Aliso ArtistsAlliance (pres. 1981-84). Res: 165 Dumond Dr Laguna Beach 92651

BUTTCHEN, TERRY GERARD, company president; b. July 15, 1958, Madison, Wis.; s. Elmer John and Margaret (Falkenstein) B.; edn: BS, Univ. Wis., Platteville, 1980, MS, 1981. Career: sales mgr. Searle Pharmaceuticals, Chgo. 1982-84; sales mgr. Am. Hosp. Supply, Chgo. 1984-86; pres. Titan Consultants, San Francisco 1986–; instr. Dale Carnegie Seminars, St. Louis, Mo. 1984–; awards: Humanitarian, CSU Northridge 1988, Outstanding Young Man of Am., Montgomery, Ala. 1988, listed Who's Who in West 1992, Who's Who Worldwide 1992; mem: Delta Sigma Phi (v.p. 1987–), Univ. Wis., Platteville (v.p. bd. dirs. 1990–), Order of Omega Hon. Frat. 1989–, Alpha Zeta 1978–, Nat. Interfrat. Conf. 1987–; civic: March of Dimes, S.F. (v.chmn., budget & fin. chair 1990-92); author: How To Buy A Business (1990); Republican; R.Cath. Res: 1800 Pacific Ave #705 San Francisco 94109

BUTTS, KAREN LYNN, clinical social worker, psychotherapist; b. Nov. 30, 1956, Reedley; d. George and Viola Frances (Marshall) Long; m. Kevin Butts, Aug. 5, 1979; children: Devon b. 1987, Nolan b. 1989; edn: BA soc. welfare (cum laude), CSU Fresno, 1978, MSW, 1980; Calif. lic. therapist, lic. clin. soc. wkr. (LCS 10968) 1984; Calif. tchg. cred. adult edn., 1988. Career: medical soc. wkr. Kaweah Delta Dist. Hosp., Visalia 1981-87; Fresno Comm. Hosp., Fresno 1987; soc. wkr. Kings View Psychiat. Ctr., Reedley 1987; childbirth educator and perinatal social wkr. pvt. med. practice of A. Peters M.D. (Ob-Gyn), Fresno 1988-93; owner Growing Families, Child Birth Educ. Svcs. 1993–; pvt. practice therapist, 1991–; initiator and facilitator Visalia community support groups: I Can Cope (oncology edn.) 1983-85, SHARE (perinatal loss gp.) 1983-87, Premature (parent gp.) 1985, Source of Support (parent bereavement gp.) 1986-87; cons. Parents of Murdered Children, Fresno-Tulare 1986; mem: Nat. Assn. Soc. Wkrs., Internat. Childbirth Edn. Assn., Nat. Perinatal Assn., Calif. Perinatal Assn., Central Valley Perinatal Soc. Wk. Cluster (past chair), Tulare Co. Victim-Witness Coord. Council 1985-86, Central Valley Continuity of Care Assn. 1984-86. Res: 272 N Ezie Fresno 93727 Ofc: 5150 N Sixth Ste 149 Fresno 93710

BUZUNIS, CONSTANTINE (DINO), lawyer; b. Feb. 3, 1958, Winnipeg, Manitoba, Canada; s. Peter and Anastasia (Ginakes) B.; edn: BA, Univ. Manitoba Canada 1980; JD, Thomas M. Cooley Law Sch. 1985; admitted bar: Mich. 1986, Calif. 1987, U.S. Dist. Ct., E. and W. Dist. Mich. 1985, U.S. Dist. Ct., So. Dist. Calif. 1987. Career: juvenile counselor Manitoba Provincial Govt., Dept. of Comm. Services & Corrections, Winnipeg 1981-83; legal intern Sixty Plus Legal Clinic, Lansing, Mich. 1985; atty. Church Kritselis Wyble & Robinson 1986; Neil Dymott Perkins Brown & Frank, San Diego 1987–; vol. moot ct. judge Univ. San Diego Law Sch. 1987–; honors: Thomas M. Cooley Law Sch. Dean's List, Who's Who Am. Law, Who's Who in World, Who's Who in West, Who's Who in Emerging Leaders of Am., Who's Who among Young Am. Profls, Internat. Directory Disting. Leadership; mem: Am. Bar Assn., Assn. Trial Lawyers of Am., Fed. Bar Assn., San Diego Co. Barristers Soc. (bd. 1991-92), Phi Alpha Delta, San Diego Co. Bar Assn., Calif. Trial Lawyers Assn., AHEPA (Chpt. 223 v.p. 1995-96), State Bar of Calif. Young Lawyers Div. (gov. 9th Dist. 1991-94, 1st v.p. 1993-94, pres. 1994-95), State Bar of Calif. Bd. of Governors 1995-96, Volunteers in Parole, Sixty Plus Law Center (sec. treas. 1985); Democrat; Greek Orthodox. Res: 3419 Overpark Rd San Diego 92130

BYRD, RONALD FRANK, librarian; b. Aug. 17, 1940, Fresno; s. Frank Malroy and Lola Marie (Exley) B.; m. Cecelia Marie Sturgis, June 18, 1966; children: Bryan Hamilton b. 1967, David Clark Harrington b. 1968; edn: BA, CSU Fresno, 1962; MA, CSU San Jose, 1967. Career: tchr. Rio Linda Jr. High, Rio Linda 1963-65; school librarian Ft. Miller Jr. High, Fresno 1966-68; college librarian Fresno City Coll., 1968–; mem: Am. Fedn. Tchrs., Calif. Tchrs. Assn., Fresno Area Lib. Council (1980–, past pres.); civic: SPEBSQSA Fresno (1973–, past pres.), Fresno City Coll. Friends of the Arts (1987–, past sec.); mil: sgt. Calif. Air Nat. Guard 1964-71; Republican; Ch. of Christ; rec: barbershop quartet and chorus singing, gardening, owner That Special Touch (florist). Res: 721 E Alluvial Ave Fresno 93720 Ofc: Fresno City College Library 1101 E University Ave Fresno 93741

BYRNE, MARIE MARTIN, educator; b. May 6, 1925, New York; d. Arthur Lawrence and Josephine Lillian (Repp) Byrne; edn: BA, Marymount Coll. 1947; MBA, UCLA 1953; PhD, 1959. Career: asst. prof. bus. econ. Marymount Coll., L.A. 1947-59; prof. 1960-68; prof. finance Loyola Univ., L.A. 1968–; Loyola Marymount Univ. 1971–; treas. Religious of Sacred Heart of Mary, L.A. 1947-72; honors: Beta Gamma Sigma; mem: Danforth Found. (assoc. 1981), Fin. Mgmt. Assn., Bus. Assn. for Latin Am. Studies, Atlantic Econ. Soc.; articles pub. in profl. jours. (1959, 69); R.Cath. Res: 7100 W 85th St Los Angeles 90045 Ofc: Loyola Marymount Univ. W 80th St Los Angeles 90045

BYRNE, NOEL THOMAS, sociologist, educator; b. May 11, 1943, San Francisco; s. Joseph Joshua and Naomi Pearl (Denison) B.; m. Dale Elrod, Aug. 6, 1989; 1 dau. by previous marriage, Ginger Melyn b. 1966; edn: BA in sociol., CSU Sonoma 1971; MA in sociol., Rutgers Univ. 1975, PhD in sociol., 1987. Career: instr. sociology Douglass Coll., Rutgers Univ., 1974-76, Hartnell Coll. 1977-78; lectr., asso. prof. mgmt. and sociology CSU Sonoma Sch. Business and Econs., 1978–; also consulting prof. Emile Durkheim Inst. for Advanced Study, Grand Cayman, British West Indies, 1990–; review ed. Symbolic Interaction (1980-83); awards: Dell Publishing Award, grad. sociol., Rutgers Univ. (1976-77), Louis Bevier Fellow (1977-78); mem: Am. Sociol. Assn., Soc. for the Study of Social Problems, Soc. for the Study of Symbolic Interaction, N.Y. Acad. of Scis., AAAS, Pacific Sociol. Assn., Commonwealth Club; contbr. num. articles and reviews in profl. jours., presentations profl. confs.; Democrat; rec: photog., collect sequential art (splst. Carl Barks). Res: 4773 Ross Rd Sebastopol 95472 Ofc: Sociology Dept, School of Social Sciences, Sonoma State University, Rohnert Park 94928

CADDELL, ROGER LOUIS, health care administrator; b. March 9, 1939, Odessa, Tx.; s. Louis Fletcher and Juanita (White) C.; m. Peggy Rhodes Livezey, Aug. 22, 1958; children: Roger b. 1958, Jay b. 1963, Lyle b. 1967; edn: BBA, and MBA, National Univ., S.D. 1983, 1985. Career: chief hosp. corpsman USN, San Diego 1957-69; chief mil. personnel, supr., instr. Naval Sch. Health Sci. 1969-75; chief mil. personnel Naval Hosp., Camp Pendleton 1975-76; dir. ops., CE of nursing home adminstr. Carroll Enterprises, El Cajon 1976-81; instr. National Univ., San Diego 1981-87; c.e.o., adminstr. Paradise Hills Convalescent Center 1982–; preceptor for adminstr. tng. State Calif. 1980-90; cert. activity dir. San Diego Co. Activity Coordinators 1987–; awards: San Diego County Council comm. service award 1988, San Diego Health Care Assn. service awards (1977-81, 1986-91), appreciation Sweetwater H.S. 1986-89; mem: Am. Coll. Health Care Adminstrs. (fellow), S.D. Health Care Assn. (pres.), CAHF Health Care Assn. (bd. mem.), Fleet Reserve Assn.; lodge: Masonic, Albahr Shrine, Albahr Drum & Bugle Corps, York Rite; mil: USN 1957-76; Republican; SDA; rec: collect eagles. Ofc: Paradise Hills Convalescent Center 6061 Banbury St San Diego 92139

CAESAR, CAROL ANN, psychologist; b. June 10, 1945, Jacksonville, Fl.; d. David Union and Helen (Casper) Richards; m. Vance Roy Caesar, Apr. 22, 1967; 1 son, Eric b. 1971; edn: BA Univ. Fla.; MA Fla. Atlantic Univ.; PhD Calif. Sch. of Profl. Psychology; lic. clin. psychologist, Calif. Career: counselor

Family Guidance Ctr., Long Beach 1980-84; behavioral scientist Long Beach Memorial Med. Ctr., 1987-90; owner/pres. Life Improvement Ctr., Seal Beach 1989–; mem. bds. Long Beach Family Services 1981-87, Am. Cancer Soc. Long Beach 1985–; mem: Calif. Psychol. Assn., Am. Psychol. Assn., Long Beach Psychol. Assn.; clubs: Old Ranch CC, Long Beach Jr. League (sustaining); Indep.; L.D.S. Ch.; rec: walking. Res: 110 Ocean Seal Beach 90740 Ofc: Life Improvement Ctr. 550 Pacific Coast Hwy Ste 203 Seal Beach 90740

CAESAR, VANCE ROY, publishing executive; b. Dec. 22, 1944, New Kensington, Pa.; s. Jack and Norma N. (Wiles) C.; m. Carol Ann, Apr. 22, 1967; 1 son, Eric Caesar b. 1971; edn: BS, The Citadel; MBA, Fla. Atlantic Univ.; grad. Stanford Exec. Pgm.; PhD, Walden Univ. Career: (past) assoc. ed. Detroit Free Press; dir. consumer mktg., dir. prodn., and adminstrn., asst. to exec. v.p. Detroit Free Press; senior v.p./gen. mgr. Press-Telegram, Long Beach 1978-88; current owner P.C.H. Pub. Co. and The Vance Caesar Group (bus. and career builders), Seal Beach; mem. Calif. Newspaper Publishers Assn.; bd. mem.: Am. Women Enterprise Movement, Rancho Los Alamitos Found., L.A. World Trade Ctr. Assn. ; civic: United Way (bd. chair Region III), Long Beach C.of C., Memorial Medical Ctr. (trustee), Am. Cancer Soc., Boy Scouts of Am. (bd.); club: Old Ranch CC; mil: AF Reserves; Republican; rec: mountaineering, skiing, gardening. Res: 110 Ocean Ave Seal Beach 90740 Ofc: 3020 Old Ranch Parkway #300 Seal Beach 90740

CAGLE, THOMAS M., electronics engineer; b. Apr.26,1927, Chillicothe, TX; s. William Robert and B. Clyde (White) C.; m. Jane E. De Bute, May 16,1964; children: Kent b. 1965, Thomas b. 1967; edn: BS, Univ. of So. Calif., L.A. 1968. Career: engr. N. Am. Rockwell Corp., L.A. 1950-71; engring. cons., Scottsdale, AZ 1971-77; electronics engr. Dept. of Defense, L.A. 1977–; mem: Inglewood Jaycees (pres., dir.), YMCA Inglewood (pres.), Inglewood Youth Counseling Orgn. (pres.), Ch. of Foothills; copyright held for calculator - nuclear weapon, 1962, num. papers pub. in tech. jours., 1954-76; mil: U.S. Navy 1945-46. Res: 10461 Greenbrier Rd Santa Ana 92705

CAHILL, JOHN DAVID, lawyer; b. May 12, 1929, Niagara Falls, N.Y.; s. David John and Julia (Kot) C.; m. Fae Muriel Smith, Oct. 20, 1956; children: Kevin b. 1958, Tara b. 1959, Kennon b. 1965; edn: Canisius Coll. 1950; LL.B, St. Univ. N.Y. 1953; UCLA Law Sch. 1956; USC Law Sch. 1958. Career: chief tax sect., deputy co. counsel Los Angeles Co. Counsel, 1957-70; atty., assoc. Simon Sheridan Murphy Thornton & Medvene 1970-72; ptnr. Simon Sheridan Murphy Thornton & Hinerfeld 1973-74; Murphy Thornton Hinerfeld & Cahill 1975-83; Rodi Pollock Pettker Galbraith & Phillips 1983–; honors: Alpha Kappa Psi (gold disting. svc. 1971, silver 1965), disting. svc. awards L.A. Co. (1970), City of Arcadia (1971); mem: Catholic Big Brothers (bd. dirs. 1963-65), Alpha Kappa Psi (exec. com. 1968-89), L.A. Co. Bar Assn., Calif. Bar Assn. (tax sect. 1965–), Arcadia Planning Com. (chmn. 1968-71), H.A. Sch. Bd. (chmn. 1970-73), La Salle H.S. Ambassadors (chmn. 1975-76); mil: capt. USNR 1950-86; R.Cath.; rec: skiing, jogging, surfing. Res: 65 La Sierra Dr Arcadia 91007 Ofc: 801 S Grand Ave Ste 400 Los Angeles 90017

CAHILL, PATRICK JEREMIAH, physician-radiologist; b. Jan. 15, 1943, Dublin, Ireland; nat. 1978; s. Timothy Joseph and Mary Frances (McCann) C.; m. Jacqueline Walter, Nov. 24, 1979; 1 dau. Allison b. 1982; edn: MB, B.Ch., B.A.O., Nat. Univ. of Ireland, Dublin 1967; DMRD, Edinburgh Univ., Scotland 1971. Career: surgical intern St. Vincents Hosp., Dublin 1967, med. resident St. Kevins Hosp. 1967-68, radiology registrar Royal Infirmary, Edinburg 1968-72, sr. registrar 1972-73, lectr. Edinburgh Univ. 1972-73; vis. prof. and chief urological radiology UC Los Angeles 1973-76; staff radiologist St. Mary Med. Ctr., Long Beach 1976–, co-dir. radiology 1982–, chief med. staff 1984; honors: Faculty of Radiologists fellow Royal Coll., London (1973); mem: Royal Coll Radiologists London (1971–), Am. Coll. Radiology (1978–), Calif. Rad. Soc., Am. Med. Assn.; num. articles in radiology and surgical jours. (1973-78); rec: golf. Res: 28011 Lobrook Dr Rancho Palos Verdes 90274 Ofc: St. Mary's Radiology Medical Group Ste 1050 Linden Ave Long Beach 90813

CAI, DUNG VAN, obstetrician-gynecologist; b. Oct. 10, 1942, Vietnam; nat. 1981; s. Trang Van and Chi Thi (Tran) C.; m. Ngoc Hong Truong, Dec. 1, 1965; children: Tung b. 1966, Tuyet Mai b. 1967, Hoang Mai b. 1969, Thuy Tien b. 1970, Bach b. 1976; edn: MD, Saigon Med. Sch. 1968; certs: ECFMG 1977, Calif. lic. 1981; diplomate Am. Bd. Obstetrics & Gynecology (1987); Career: intern Bucks County Hosp., Bristol, Pa. 1978-79; resident Presbyterian Hosp., Phila. 1979-80, Hahnemann Hosp., Phila. 1980-81, Albany Hosp., Albany, N.Y. 1981-84; ob-gyn. physician pvt. practice, San Jose 1984–, med. staff O'Connor Hosp., San Jose Hosp.; Fellow Am. Coll. Obstets. and Gynecols. (1988), mem. Calif. Med. Assn., Santa Clara Co. Med. Soc., Vietnamese Physicians San Jose; club: Indian Father & Son (NY); civic: City of San Jose Human Rights Commn. (1989-91); pub. med. jour. articles (83, 84, 87); mil: capt. Vietnamese Med. Corps 1968-74; Buddist; rec: singing, dancing. Res: 17540 Elaine Ct Monte Sereno 95030 Ofc: 259 Meridian Ave Ste 5 San Jose 95126

CAIN, HARVEY D., physician; b. June 26, 1930, Lake Forest, Ill.; s. Harvey S. and Ruth A. (Dunning) C.; children: Harvey b. 1957, Norman b. 1958, Lori b.

1959, Phillip b. 1961, Thomas b. 1963; edn: BA summa cum laude, Lake Forest Coll. 1952; MD, Northwestern Med. Sch. 1956; JD, Lincoln Law Sch. 1976; admitted St. Bar Calif. (1978). Career: L.A. Co. Gen. Hosp., 1956-57, internal medicine resident, chief resident communicable disease unit 1957-60; clin. instr. Loma Linda Med. Sch. Communicable Disease, L.A. 1958-61; National Heart Inst. post doctoral res. fellow 1960-61; staff physician Kaiser Found. Rehab. Center, Vallejo 1961-67, assoc. dir. 1965-69; sr. cons., occupational medicine and rehab. Permanente Med. Group and Kaiser Found. Hosp., Sacto. 1969–; asst. clin. prof. physical medicine and rehab. UC Davis Sch. Medicine 1970–; intensive residence occupational medicine U.S. Med. Sch., S.F. 1979-80; author Flint's Emergency Treatment & Mgmt. 6th ed. 1980, 7th ed. 1985; author w. Thomas Flint 4th ed., 1970, 5th ed. 1975; honors: Phi Beta Kappa; mem: Calif. Heart Assn. (rehab.com., legislative subcom.), Am. Coll. Cardiology, Am. Soc. Clin. Research, Am. Congress Physical Medicine & Rehab., Calif. Arthritis Found. (med. com., exec. com.). Solano Co. Heart Assn. (pres.); num. articles pub. in med. jours.; Christian; rec: running, swimming, bicycling. Res: Carmichael 95608 Ofc: Kaiser Permanente Medical Center 2025 Morse Avenue Sacramento 95825

CAIN, PATRICIA JEAN, financial executive; b. Sept. 28, 1931, Decatur, Ill.; d. Paul George and Jean Margaret (Horne) Jacka; m. Dan L. Cain, July 12, 1952; children: Mary Ann, b. 1963; Timothy, b. 1965; Paul, b. 1967; edn: Univ. of Mich. 1949-52; Pasadena City Coll. 1975-76; BS, CSU Los Angeles, 1977; MBA, 1978; M.Taxation, Golden Gate Univ., 1988; CPA, Calif. 1981; cert. in advanced personal finl. plnng. 1985; Career: CPA/tax supr. Stonefield & Josephson Accty. Corp., Los Angeles 1979-87; controller/CFO Loubella Extendables Inc., Los Angeles 1987–; lectr. CSULA 1983, participant in USC business ethics program 1986; instr. Becker CPA Review Course 1989-93; honors: Thanks Badge, Highland Rim Girl Scout Council, Oakridge, Tenn. 1959, Thanks Badge, Sierra Madres Girl Scout Council, Pasa. nat. del. Girl Scouts 1975; mem: Am. Inst. CPAs taxation com.), Calif. Soc. CPAs (state profl. conduct com., state and L.A. chpt. taxation com.), Microcomputers Users Discussion Gp., speaker/mem. state plng. com. Microcomputer Conf. & Show for CPAs 1987, 88, 89), AWSCPA (L.A. chpt. dir. 1986-7, v.p. 1987-9), Internat. Arabian Horse Assn., Beta Alpha Psi, Girl Scouts USA, Wrightwood C.of C.; recipient Diploma in Pastry, Ecole de Gastronomie Francaise Ritz-Escoffier, Hotel Ritz, Paris, France 1991; Democrat; Episcopalian; rec: fishing, skiing, rug making. Res: 3715 Fairmeade Rd Pasadena 91107 Ofc: Loubella Extendables, Inc. 2222 S Figueroa St Los Angeles 90007

CALANTAS, THOMAS DE LA CRUZ, JR., real estate and mortgage broker; b. Feb. 9, 1948, Philippines, nat. 1987; s. Tomas Calderon, Sr. and Fermina Eslabon (De La Cruz) C.; m. Ruth, Dec. 29, 1974; 1 son, Thomas Jeff b. 1976; edn: BS, biol., Phil. Union Coll. 1970; respiratory therapy, Am. Vocat. Sch. 1974; grad. De Loux Sch. of Cosmetology 1984; tchr. tng. Riverside City Coll. 1987; Calif. lic.: lic. adminstr. handicapped adult care facility 1980, cosmetologist 1984, R.E. lic. 1989 R.E. broker 1991, Notary Pub. 1991. Career: respiratory therapist San Gabriel Comm. Hosp. 1974-75; respiratory therapist La Vina Hosp. 1975-76; respiratory therapist White Memorial Med. Center 1977; owner/mgr. Orange Blossom Motel, San Bernardino 1979; owner/adminstr. Sunset Plaza Guest Home, Beaumont 1980-86; owner/adminstr. Lolinda Rancho Guest Home (facility for independent living rehabilitated handicapped) 1983–; ABBA Acad. For Hair (hairstyling sch.) 1986; cosmetologist, owner beauty salons: Delta Con Hair Design, San Bernardino 1986--, and Hair Gallery, Riverside 1987-88; real estate agt. Century 21 Home & Investment, 1989-91; broker, owner Ambassadors Realty, San Bdo. 1991–; broker, pres. Renet Financial-Greater California Mortgage Inc., 1992–; v.p. Adventist Mission Soc. of Am. 1994–; pres., founder, Calantas Found., Philippines, 1994–; pres., founder Good Samaritan Ministries 1995–; sr. dir. Melaleuca Inc. 1995; awards: student of mo., 1st place Inter-school competition hair show 1984; mem. City of Loma Linda Citizen Patrol (1992); mem: Bd. of Realtors: San Bernardino, Redlands, and Riverside, Nat. Cosmetologist Assn., Loma Linda, Riverside, and Gr. Riverside Hispanic C.of C. (dir., treas. 1988-89); Loma Linda Filipino 7th-Day Adventist Ch. (fund chmn. 1979-81); rec: classical music, singing. Res: 10630 Coloma St Loma Linda 92354 Ofc: Ambassadors Realty 24674 Redlands Blvd San Bernardino 92408

CALDEN, ANN CATHERINE, attorney; b. Feb. 20, 1952, Oakland; d. Gilbert Dana Calden and Mary Jane (Dinkens-Calden) Babcock; div.; edn: BA, UC Berkeley 1982; JD, Univ. S.F. 1985. Career: Surety Counsel, Fireman's Fund Ins. Co., San Francisco 1986–; mem: Am. Bar Assn., Hawaiian St. Bar Assn., United States Dist. Court, No. Dist. of Calif., No. Calif. Surety & Fidelity Assn. (pres. 1994); Republican; Episcopalian; rec: gardening, hunter-jumper equestrienne, cooking, travel. Res: 30 Newport Way San Rafael 94901 Ofc: Fireman's Fund Insurance Co. PO Box 3136 San Francisco 94105

CALDERA, LOUIS EDWARD, legislator; b. Apr. 1, 1956, El Paso, Tx.; s. Benjamin Luis and Soledad (Siqueiros) C.; m. Evagren Orlebeke, Nov. 9, 1991; edn: BS, US Mil. Acad., West Point, NY, 1978; JD, Harvard Law Sch., Cambridge, Mass., 1987; MBA, Harvard Bus. Sch., Boston, Mass., 1987. Career: Army ofcr. (capt.), US Army, 1978-83; assoc., O'Melveny & Myers,

L.A., Calif., 1987-89; assoc., Buchalter Nemer Fields & Younger, L.A., 1990; deputy county counsel, County of L.A., 1991-92; Assembly mem., Calif. State Assembly, Sacramento, 1992-94, chair Assembly Banking and Fin. Com.; Democrat; Roman Catholic. Ofc: 304 S. Broadway Ste. 580, Los Angeles 90013

CALDWELL, COURTNEY LYNN, lawyer, higher education consulting company executive; b. Mar. 5, 1948, W.D.C.; d. Joseph Morton Caldwell and Moselle (Smith) Caldwell; edn: undergrad. Duke Univ. 1966-68; BA, UC Santa Barbara, 1970, MA, 1975; JD (highest hons.) George Washington Univ., W.D.C. 1982; admitted bar: D.C. 1984, Wash. 1986, Calif. 1989. Career: summer assoc. law firm Arnold & Porter, W.D.C., 1982, law firm Hufstedler, Miller, Carlson & Beardsley, Los Angeles 1982; judicial clerk US Ct. Appeals, Seattle 1982-83; lawyer, assoc. Arnold & Porter, W.D.C. 1983-85, Perkins Coie, Seattle 1985-88; dir. western ops. MPC Associates, Inc. Irvine, Calif. 1988-91, senior v.p. 1991–; bd. dirs. Habitat for Humanity of Orange Co. 1993-94 (chair adminstrv. com. 1994–); bd. dirs. Univ. Town Center Assn. 1994; awards: John Ordranaux Award Geo. Washington Univ. 1980, sr. articles editor G.W. Law Rev. 1981-82, listed Who's Who in Am. Law 1989–, of Practicing Attorneys, of Emerging Leaders in Am., of Am. Women 1992, in the West 1992, in U.S. Execs. 1992, in the World 1992-93, in Fin. & Industry 1994-95; publs: law summaries (Martindale-Hubbell, 1986), articles in law revs., texts; rec: fgn. languages. Ofc: MPC Associates, Inc. 1451 Quail St Ste 212 Newport Beach 92660

CALDWELL, JONI, chief executive officer and general manager, retail furniture, and educator; b. Aug. 8, 1948, Chgo., Ill.; d. Bruce and Eloise (Ijams) Caldwell; m. David H. Weisbach, Apr. 23, 1988; div. Oct. 7, 1990; edn: diploma, Marquette (Mich.) H.S., 1965-66; BS, home econ., Mich. State Univ., 1966-70; grad. studies, Mich. State Univ., 1970-75; MA, clinical psychol., Lone Mt. Coll., San Francisco, 1978; career: educator, Grand Blanc H.S., Grand Blanc, Mich., 1970-73; educator, Northwestern Mich. Coll., Traverse City, Mich. 1972-78; educator, Mott Comm. Coll., Flint, Mich., 1974-78; educator, Clio H.S., Clio, Mich., 1974-79; work/study, Esalen Inst., Big Sur, 1979-81; parent educator/vol. coord., Family Resource Ctr., Seaside, 1981-82; c.e.o. and gen. mgr., Futons & Such, Monterey, 1982–; prof. psychology Hartnell Coll., Salinas 1993–; awards; Small Business Excellence Award, Monterey C. of C., 1990; Congressional Award, US Congress, 1990; mem: v.p. (past pres.), New Monterey Bus. Assn., charter mem. 1983–; past pres. and v.p., Monterey Church of Religious Sci., 1984-87; past v.p., Pacific Coast Church, 1987-92; bd. of dirs., Monterey YWCA; 1986-88; com. mem., Monterey C. of C., 1985-87; membership com., Profl. Womens Network, 1989–; listed in Who's Who in the West 1992, Who's Who in the World 1993; civic: fundraising for the Buddy Program, YWCA and MCRS, Monterey; author: home econ. article, 1970; Greens; Metaphysian; rec: travel, reading, personal growth, skiing, sailing, white water rafting, kayaking, remodeling houses. Res: 29 Portola Ave. Monterey 93940. Ofc: Futons & Such 484 Lighthouse Ave. Monterey 93940

CALDWELL, WALTER EDWARD, newspaper editor and publisher; b. Dec. 29, 1941, Los Angeles; s. Harold Elmer and Esther Ann (Fuller) C.; m. Donna Edith Davis, June 27, 1964; children: Arnie-Jo; edn: AA, Riverside City Coll., 1968. Career: sales staff Sears Roebuck & Co., Riverside 1963-65; dispatcher Rohr Corp., 1965-67; trainee Aetna Fin., 1967-68; mgr. Aetna Fin., San Bruno 1968-70, Amfac Thrift & Loan, Oakland 1970-74; free lance writer, 1974-76; news dir. Sta. KAVA Radio, Burney 1977-79; editor/pub. Mountain Echo, Fall River Mills 1979–; contbr. Yearbook of Modern Poetry, 1976; announcer Intermountain Fair Parade, McArthur 1983–, Burney Basin Days Parade 1985-92, Big Valley Days Parade, Adin 1988; candidate Shasta County Bd. Supervisors, Dist. 3, 1992; mem. Calif. Newspaper Publishers' Assn.; civic bds: Intermountain United Way, Burney (pres. 1979, chmn. 1978), Am. Red Cross, Redding (disaster relief wkr. 1988–, disaster action team ldr. 1992–), Shasta County Women's Refuge (bd. dirs. 1988-91), Shasta County Econ. Devel. Corp., Redding (1986-87, 89-91, exec. bd. dirs. 1987), Ea. Shasta County Econ. Devel. Corp. (pres. 1987-89), Shasta County Econ. Devel. Task Force (bd. 1985-86), Girl Scouts, San Jose (troop ldr. 1973-76), Burney Fire Protection Dist. (commr. 1987-91, pres. 1991), Mosquito Abatement Dist., Burney (trustee 1978-87, 1989–, pres. 1990), Burney Basin Days Com. (pres. 1985-86, 88-89, chmn. Hay Days celebration 1995), Ea. Shasta County Sheriff's Flying Posse (observer 1988–); mem. Am. Legion, Burney Basin C.of C. (advt. chmn. 1982), Fall River Valley C.of C. (dir. 1990–, v.p. 1994-95, pres. 1995-96), Rotary (chmn. bike race 1981-85, pres. 1987), Masons, (master 1995) Surprise Valley Lodge 1995, Intermountain Shrine Club (sec. 1992-94), Lions/ Fall River (youth spkr. 1983-88, dist. bulletin chmn. 1989-91, pres. 1992), Moose; cpl. USMC 1959-63; Republican. Res: 20304 Elm St Burney 96013 Ofc: Mountain Echo Hwy 299 Fall River Mills 96028

CALE, CHARLES GRIFFIN, lawyer, international sports executive; b. Aug. 19, 1940, St. Louis, Mo.; s. Julian Dutro and Judith Hadley (Griffin) C.; m. Jessie Leete Rawn, Dec. 30, 1978; children: Whitney Rawn, Walter Griffin, Elizabeth Judith; edn: BA, Principia Coll., 1961; LLB, Stanford Univ., 1964; LLM, USC, 1966; admitted Calif. Bar 1965. Career: law practice, Los Angeles 1965–; ptnr. Adams, Duque & Hazeltine, 1970-81, Morgan, Lewis & Bockius, 1981-90; c.e.o. and co-chmn. bd. World Cup USA 1994, Inc. 1991;dir. World

Cup USA 1994, Inc. 1991–; group v.p. sports L.A. Olympic Organizing Com., 1982-84; assoc. counselor U.S. Olympic Com. (USOC), 1985, special asst. to pres. USOC 1985-88, asst. Chef de Mission of the 1988 U.S. Olympic Team, asst. to pres. USOC and dir. Olympic Delegation (Barcelona) 1988; civic bds: Hallum Prevention Child Abuse Fund, L.A. (dir.), St. John's Hosp. and Med. Ctr., Santa Monica (trustee); awards: Gold Medal of Youth and Sports, France (1984); mem. ABA, State Bar of Calif.; clubs: California, Los Angeles CC, The Beach. Ofc: PO Box 688 Pacific Palisades 90272

CALESCIBETTA, C.C., physician; b. Oct. 1, 1932, Auburn, N.Y.; s. Frank and Maria (Bauso) C.; m. Genevieve Atkins, April 1955 (div. 1974); m. Diane M. Bunkers, Aug. 6, 1976; children: Marcus b. 1957, Carlo b. 1959, Gina b. 1968, Chris b. 1977, Cara Mia b. 1980; edn: BA, San Diego St. Univ. 1956; MD, St. Univ. N.Y. 1960; JD, Pacific Coast Univ. 1988; admitted Calif. St. Bar 1989. Career: dir. med. edn. St. Mary Med.Center, Long Beach 1967-74; med. dir. Renal Center 1970–; pres. Long Beach Med. Assn. 1994-95; pres. Renal Disease Network of So. Calif.; clin. prof. medicine UCLA Sch. of Medicine 1984–; bd. dirs. ESRD Network 1985–, med. review bd. 1982–; Western Med. Review, Torrance 1984–; mem: Am. Bar Assn., Am. Soc. Nephrology, Nat. Health Lawyers Assn., F.A.C.P., CMA, AMA, Calif. Bar Assn., So. Calif. Kidney Found.; Republican. Res: 5500 El Parque Long Beach 90815 Ofc: St. Mary Medical Center 1050 Linden Ave Long Beach 90801

CALLAN, TERRENCE ALOYSIUS, lawyer; b. Sept. 20, 1939, San Francisco; s. Harold A. and Viola A. (Briese) Martin C.; m. Gail Rita Raine, April 20, 1968; 1 son, Ryan b. 1978; edn: BA, Univ. San Francisco 1961; JD, Univ. of Calif. Hastings Coll. Law 1964; admitted St. Bar Calif. (1965), Supreme Ct. Calif. (1965). Career: research asst. Pillsbury Madison & Sutro, San Francisco 1964-65, atty., assoc. 1965-72, ptnr. 1973–; mem. Calif. State Bar coms: exec. com. Antitrust & Trade Regulation Sect. 1985- (chair 1987); San Francisco Bar Coms.: judiciary com. 1982-84, merit screening com. for bankruptcy judgeships No. Dist. Calif. 1985–; honors: Order of Coif, Thurston Hon. Soc., Am. Jurisprudence award 1963, Authur Newhouse scholar 1962, Phi Alpha Delta; mem: Presidio Soc. (dir., secty., gen. counsel 1981-94), Fort Point & Presidio Historical Assn. (dir., secty., legal counsel 1984–), Am. Bar Assn., Univ. San Francisco Green & Gold Club (bd. dirs.), Hastings Coll. Law Found. Bd. of Trustees; 1 comment pub. in profl. jour., 1962; Cath.; rec: basketball, bicycling, theatre. Ofc: Pillsbury Madison & Sutro 225 Bush St San Francisco 94104

CALLO, JEFFREY FRANCIS, computer software company marketing manager; b. Jan. 29, 1947, Jersey City, N.J.; s. Sylvester Francis and Jeanne Barbara (Murray) C.; m. Janet Hacker, Jan. 21, 1984; edn: BS in mgmt. sci., Kean Coll., 1976. Career: service engr. G.E. Medical System, Whippany, N.J. 1972-77; internat. engr., technical specialist G.E. Med. System, Milwaukee 1977-82; logistic mgr., then product mgr. Picker Internat., Cleveland, Oh. 1982-86; senior product mgr. Sun Microsystems, Mountain View 1986-90; group mktg. mgr. Motorola, Phoenix, Ariz. 1990-92; product line mgr. Novell, Monterey, Ca. 1992-93; bus. devel. mgr. Novell, San Jose 1993–; honors: Alpha Lambda Sigma (1976); Republican; R.Cath.; rec: skiing, biking. Res: 43713 Cameron Hills Dr Fremont 94539 Ofc: Novell 2180 Fortune Dr San Jose 95131

CALVERT, ANN MARCINE, publisher, marketing director; b. Jan. 17, 1943, Cheyenne, Wy.; d. Harold McClure Forde and Elizabeth Ann (Farthing); m. John Jolley, Jr., 1965, div. 1989; m. 2d. David W. Calvert, 1991; children: Helen b. 1968, Kendall b. 1971; edn: BA, Univ. Wyoming, 1964. Career: admin. asst. San Diego Mag. 1964-65; admin. asst. Colo. Women's Coll. 1965-66; reporter Desert Dispatch, Barstow 1976-77; bus. devel. First Interstate Bank, San Diego 1980-82; owner RB Network, S.D. 1982-84; owner, editor and pub. Rancho Magazine, San Diego 1984-93; assoc. puiblisher/mktg. dir. Pomorado Newspaper Group 1993–; mem. civic bds: BECA Hispanic Scholarship Found. 1988-90, Palomar Coll. Found. 1982-90; awards: meritorious service Navy Relief Soc. 1975, 78, San Bernardino Co. Grand Jury 1976; mem. Chamber of Commerce (Rancho Bernardo pres. 1989-90, Poway bd. mem. 1993–, Diamond Gateway), Rotary Internat., San Diego Press Club; Presbyterian Ch. USA (San Diego Presbytery moderator 1986); rec: folk singing, skiing, sailing. Ofc: Pomerado Newspaper Group 13247 Poway Rd Poway 92064

CALVERT, KEN, congressman; b. June 8, 1953, Corona, Calif.; edn: AA, Chaffey Coll., 1973; BA econ., San Diego State Univ. 1975. Career: Corona/Norco youth chmn. for Nixon, 1968, 82; county youth chmn. rep. Vesey's Dist., 1970, 43d dist., 1972; congl. aide to rep. Vesey, Calif., 1975-79; gen. mgr. Jolly Fox Restaurant, Corona, Calif., 1975-79, Marcus W. Meairs Co., Corona, Calif., 1979-81; pres., gen. mgr. Ken Calvert Real Properties, Corona, Calif., 1981–; Reagan-Bush campaign worker, 1980; co-chmn. Wilson for Senate Campaign, 1982, George Deukmejian election, 1978, 82, 86, George Bush election, 1988, Pete Wilson senate elections, 1982, 88, Pete Wilson for Gov. election, 1990; mem. 103rd and 104th Congresses from Calif. dist., 1993–; mem. natural resources corn., sci., space and tech. corn., 1993–; former v.p. Corona/ Norco Rep. Assembly; chmn. Riverside Rep. Party, 1988-90; County Riverside Asset Leasing; bd. realtors Corona/ Norco; exec. bd. Corona Community Hosp. Corp. 200 Club; mem. Corona Airport adv. commn.; adv. com. Temescal/ El Cerrito

Community Plan; mem. Riverside Count Rep. Winners Circle (charter), Lincoln Club (co-chmn., charter, 1986-90), Corona Rotary Club (pres. 1991), Elks, Navy League Corona Norco, Corona C. of C. (pres. 1990), Noroco C. of C., Monday Morning Group, Corona Group (past chmn.), Econ. Devel. Ptnrship., Silver Eagles (March AFB support group, charter). Ofc: US House Representatives 1523 Longworth Washington DC 20515-0543

CALVIN, MARGARET H., business manager, corporate executive; b. June 10, 1940; m. Travis H. Calvin, M.D., 1969; children: Elizabeth b. 1974, Travis b. 1978, Kathleen b. 1984; edn: att. Gonzaga Univ.; BA w. distinction, San Diego St. Univ. Career: asst. to supt. E. Oregon Hosp., The Dalles, 2 yrs.; dir. volunteers, asst. adminstr. So. Pacific Hosp., San Francisco, 1965-69; bus. mgr. T.H. Calvin, M.D., 16 yrs., Neurological Assocs., 5 yrs.; c.f.o. Commercial Cotton Co., 10 yrs., Artesia Inc., 5 yrs.; c.f.o. Imperial Imaging 1984–; adminstr. Desert Rehabilitation Inst. 1991–; honors: Imperial Co. woman of yr. nom. 1983, Silver Beaver Award S.D. Area Council of Boy Scouts; mem. Mensa Internat.; civic: AMA Aux. (pres. Imperial Co. 1978, 84), Imperial Co. Child Abuse Prev. Council (founding mem., pres. Children's Fair), parent vol. El Centro Area Schs. (vol. coord. 1979-83, pres. El Centro Swim Team 1981-88, McCabe Sch. Dist. advy. council 1987-88, GATE tchr. 1987–); publs: newsletter editor for hosp. "The Pulse", for health care assn. "Across the Tracks"; author: A Med. Hist. of Imperial Valley (Holtville Press, 1989), newsletter "Wellness News", sev. articles. Address: 1505 W Ross El Centro 92243

CAMENZIND, MARK J., research chemist; b. Nov. 17, 1956, Palo Alto; s. Paul Vincent and Mildred Martha (Glover) C.; m. Dorothy L. Hassler, Apr. 11, 1992; edn: SB, M.I.T. 1978; PhD, UC Berkeley, 1983. Career: postdoctoral fellow Univ. of British Columbia, Vancouver, B.C. 1983-86; research chemist Salutar, Inc. Sunnyvale, Ca. 1986; Balazs Analytical Lab., Sunnyvale 1986–; mem. Am. Chem. Soc. (1978–), ASTM (com. 1988–), SEMI (stds. com. 1990–); publs: tech. papers in chemistry & semiconductor ind. (1981–); rec: x-c skiing, electronics. Ofc: Balazs Lab. 252 Humboldt Ct Sunnyvale 94089-1315

CAMERON, ELSA SUE, curator, art consultant, educator; b. Nov. 19, 1939, San Francisco; d. L. Don and Betty (Jelinsky) C.; m. Michael Lerner, Dec 24, 1979; edn: BA, San Francisco State Univ., 1961, MA, 1965, tchg. credential, 1962. Career: curator Randall Jr. Mus., San Francisco 1963-65, Fine Arts Mus. Downtown Center 1976-80, San Francisco Airport Galleries 1980–; exec. dir. Community Arts, Inc., S.F. 1973–; reporter Council on Museums, N.Y.C., 1973-80; asst. prof. art edn. Univ. So. Calif., L.A. 1982-83; cons. University Art Mus., Berkeley 1980-82, instr. 1981; instr. 101 California Venture, S.F. 1986–; exhibitions curator OM & M/Olympia & York, L.A. 1988–; cons. Art in Public Places, Miami, Fla. 1988; awards: NEA fellow (1973, 77); mem. Western Regional Conf. (v.p. 1974-75), Am. Assn. Museums; publs: (book) The Art Museum as Educator 1977, (exhibit cat.) Airport Cafe 1986; Ofc: San Francisco International Airport Exhibition Box 8097 San Francisco 94128

CAMERON, JOANNA, actress/producer/director; b. Greeley, Colo.; d. Harold and Erna (Borgens) Cameron; edn: Univ. Calif. 1967-68, Pasadena Playhouse 1968. Career: discovered by Walt Disney while special tour guide at Disneyland, motion picture debut in How to Commit Marriage, 1969; actress in The Amazing Spiderman, other feature films; appear in numerous TV commercials; named in Guiness Book of Records as having the most nat. network programmed TV commercials; actress TV network prime time serial shows including Name of the Game, Medical Center, The Bold Ones, Marcus Welby, Columbo, High Risk, Switch; guest star numerous network TV shows incl. Merv Griffin Show, The Survivors, Love American Style, Mission Impossible, The Tonight Show; star weekly TV series The Shazam-I IS Hour, CBS, 1976-78; host/dir. US Navy closed circuit network pgm. for TV equipped ships 1977, 78, 79, 80; dir. commercials, dir. CBS Preview Special; prod./dir. documentary Razor Sharp, 1981; media cons. to Catholic Bishops on Papal Visit of Pope John Paul II, Calif. 1987; mem: Directors Guild Am., Acad. TV Arts and Scis., AFTRA, Screen Actors Guild, Delta Delta Delta; club: L.A. Athletic. Ofc: Cameron Productions PO Box 1011 Pebble Beach CA 93953

CAMERON, JUDITH LYNNE, mentor teacher in space science, hypnotherapist; b. Apr. 29, 1945, Oakland; d. Alfred Joseph and June Estelle (Faul) Moe; m. Richard Irwin Cameron, Dec. 17, 1967; son, Kevin Dale; edn: AA psych., Sacto. City Coll., 1965; BA psych./German, Calif. St. Univ., 1967; MA reading specialization, San Francisco St. Univ., 1972; postgrad., Chapman Coll.; PhD, Am. Inst. Hypnotherapy, 1987; Calif. tchg. cred. Career: tchr. St. Vincent's Catholic Sch., San Jose 1969-70; Fremont Elem. Sch., 1970-72; LeRoy Boys Home, LaVerne 1972-73; Grace Miller Elem. Sch., LaVerne 1973-80, resource specialist 1980-84; resource specialist, dept. chair Bonita High Sch., LaVerne 1984–, H.S. advisor Peer Counseling Pgm. 1987–, mentor tchr. in space sci. Bonita Unified Sch. Dist. 1988–, Teacher-in-Space dist. cons. 1987–; selected as mem. of internat. faculty Challenger Ctr. for Space Edn., 1991–; adj. faculty Challenger Learning Ctr, Calif. St. Univ., 1989–; owner/therapist So. Calif. Clinical Hypnotherapy 1988–; mem. Civil Air Patrol, Sq. 68, 1988–; vol. advi-

sor Children's Home Soc., Santa Ana 1980-81; awards: Toyota Tchr. of Yr., Bonita H.S. 1994; mem: Council Exceptional Children, Calif. Assn. Resource Specialists, Calif. Elem. Edn. Assn., NEA, Calif. Tchrs. Assn., Calif. Assn. Marriage and Family Therapists, Planetary Soc., Orange County Astronomers, Com. Sci. Investigation L5 Soc., Challenger Ctr. for Space Edn., Calif. Challenger Ctr. Crew for Space Edn.; clubs: Chinese Shar-Pei Am., Concord, Rare Breed Dog. Res: 3257 La Travesia Dr Fullerton 92635 Ofc: Bonita High School 115 W Allen Ave San Dimas 91773

CAMERON, MARK ALAN, lawyer; b. Aug. 20, 1954, Boston, Mass.; s. Alan Bruce and Marilyn Ruth (Waldron) C.; m. Sandra Karen Bakko, June 18, 1983; children: Mathew Bruce b. 1987, Gregory Cronquist b. 1990; edn: BA econ., UC Davis 1976; MA econ., 1978; JD, Hastings Coll. of Law 1981; admitted St. Bar Calif., Calif. Supreme Ct. 1981, U.S. Dist. Ct. No. and Central Dist. 1982, U.S. Ct. Appeals 9th Circuit 1983, U.S. Supreme Ct. 1985. Career: atty. Kindel & Anderson, Los Angeles 1981-83; Miller Starr & Regalia, Oakland 1983-; mem: San Francisco Bar Assn.; Republican; rec: tennis, skiing, volleyball. Ofc: Miller Starr & Regalia 1 Kaiser Plaza Ste 1650 Oakland 94612

CAMERON, WILLIAM JAMES, teacher; b. June 24, 1933, Santa Rosa; s. Douglas Meacham and Avola May (Newberry) C.; m. Lois Sowers, June 14, 1953 (dec. 1980); children: Laura b. 1957, Shirley b. 1959, Bruce b. 1964; m.2d. Jean C., Feb. 14, 1992; edn: AA, Santa Rosa Jr. Coll., 1954; BA, San Francisco St. Univ., 1964; Calif. general tchg. creds., 1959. Career: pub. sch. tchr. Anderson Valley Sch. Dist., Booneville 1959-60, Fremont Unified Sch. Dist., Fremont 1960-93 (ret.); nurseryman, Home Depot, Modesto; mem: Calif. Tchrs. Assn. (past nat. del.), Nat. Educators Assn. (past nat. del.), Fremont Unified Tchrs. Assn. (past treas.), A.S.C.A.P., Am. Fedn. of Musicians, The Commonwealth Club, Alpha Gamma Sigma; composer ballads: Lois (1977), Avola (1980); mil: sp4 AUS 1954-56; Indep. Democrat; rec: trombonist, racquetball, hiking. Ofc: Cameron Enterprises 916 Crater Ave Modesto 95351

CAMMACK, ROBERT JAMES, engineering executive; b. May 8, 1950, Monterey Park; s. James Clarence and Elizabeth Lucille (Morrison) C.; m. Carla, Feb. 15, 1975; children: Carrie b. 1978, Marie b. 1980; edn: BSME, Univ. Fla. 1973; MBA, UC Irvine, 1991; Reg. Profl. Engr. Calif. (1983). Career: plant mgr. Delta Truck Body, Bell Gardens 1973-74, gen. mgr. 1974-75, div. pres., Parsons, Kans. 1975-78; design engr. Taylor-Dunn, Anaheim, Calif. 1978-79, mgr. engring. 1979-80, v.p. engring. 1980-90; mgr. Pioneer Electronics Service, Long Beach 1991-92; dir. engring. Accuride Internat., Santa Fe Springs 1992–; pres. Orange County Engring. Council 1983-85; mem: Inst. Advancement of Engring. (fellow 1984, dir. 1984-87), ASME (Orange Co. chmn. 1986-87, EIT review course instr. 1985-86, Region IX pub. affairs chmn. 1987-88), Order of the Engineer (life 1982), IEEE, SME, SAE, CSPE, NSPE, North Orange Co. Computer Club; civic: PTA, Girl Scout Olympics ofcl., AYSO soccer coach, ofcl.; contbg. author, Modern Materials Handling Handbook (1984); Republican; Lutheran; rec: computer programming, model R.R. Ofc: Accuride International 12311 Shoemaker Ave Santa Fe Springs 90670

CAMPBELL, ARTHUR WALDRON, law professor, writer; b. Mar. 29, 1944, Bklyn.; s. Wilburn Camrock and Janet Louise (Jobson) C.; m. Drusilla Newlon, June 7, 1969; children: Wilburn b. 1976, Matthew b. 1979; edn: AB, Harvard Coll., 1966; JD, West Va. Univ. Coll. of Law, 1971; LLM, Georgetown Univ., 1975; admitted bar: W.Va., 1971, Dist. Col., 1971, Calif. 1974. Career: def. atty. Prettyman Fellows, Georgetown Univ., W.D.C. 1971-72; asst. U.S. Atty., U.S. Justice Dept., W.D.C. 1972-73, senior staff atty. Dist. Col. Law Students in Ct. Pgm. 1973-74, chief civil div. 1974-75, dep. dir. 1975-76; adj. law prof. Georgetown, George Washington, Howard, Catholic, Am. Univ., 1973-76; law prof. Calif. Western Sch. of Law, San Diego 1976–; c.e.o. Trudar Prodns., Inc. 1981–; advr. W.Va. Legis. Com. to recodify juv. code 1971-72; honors: First law student to argue case W.Va. Supreme Ct. Appeals 1971, merit award Freese Elem. Sch., San Diego 1987, appreciation San Diego Sch. Dist. 1989; mem: Am. Bar Assn., Nat. Assn. Crim. Def. Lawyers (task force ldr.), Assn. of Am. Law Schs., Pub. Defenders Inc. San Diego (bd. 1979-86), Appellate Defenders Inc. S.D. (bd. 1979-), Fed. Defenders Inc. S.D. (bd. 1979–); San Diego Repertory Theater (bd. 1992-93); author: Entertainment Law (3rd ed. 1994), treatise, Law of Sentencing (1978, 2d. edit. 1991); mil: 1st lt. USAF 1968-69; rec: tennis, backpacking, running. Ofc: Calif. Western School of Law, 350 Cedar St San Diego 92101

CAMPBELL, CHERYL DIANE, meeting planner; b. Oct. 24, 1960, Orange; d. Donald George and Edith Maxine (Dunkleberg) Campbell; edn: BS mgmt., Pepperdine Univ. 1991. Career: account rep. North Island F.C.U., Coronado 1983-86; data splst. Allergan Inc., Irvine 1986-88, meeting planner 1988-92; meeting planner Price Waterhouse 1993–; mem: Meeting Planners Internat., Le Premier, Cystic Fibrosis, The Guilds of the Orange Co. Performing Arts Ctr.; Democrat; Lutheran; rec: tennis, rollerblading, dancing, sports. Res: 702 1/2 Poinsettia Corona del Mar 92695

CAMPBELL, DONALD OTIS, physician; b. March 3, 1936, Loma Linda; s. Otis W. and Delia E. (Nasser) C.; m. Elizabeth Short, June 22, 1963; children: Catherine D. b. 1964, Julie S. b. 1967; edn: Stanford Univ. 1954-57; MD, USC

1961; Diplomate Am. Bd. Quality Assurance and Utilization Rev. Physicians, 1991. Career: intern, surgical res. Santa Fe Coast Lines Hosp., Los Angeles 1961-63; house physician Santa Fe Hosp., Los Angeles 1965-66; individual pvt. practice of medicine, family and gen. practice, 1966–; med. dir. Torrance Hosp. Independent Practice Assn. (THIPA) 1987–; staff Torrance Memorial Med. Center, Torrance 1966–, chief dept. fam. practice 1983 and 1986, med. staff secty. 1987-88, asst. chief staff 1989-90; mem: Am. Acad. of Family Physicians (Fellow 1981), Am. Coll. Med. Quality (Fellow 1991), AMA, Calif. Med. Assn., L.A. Cty. Med. Assn., Am. Acad. of Medical Dirs., Am. Coll. of Physician Execs., Torrance Health Assn. (life), Salerni Collegium, Phi Chi Med. Frat., Palos Verdes Penin. C.of C. 1968-78 (dir. 74-76) Kiwanis 1966-80; mil: capt. Med. Corps USAF 1963-65; rec: cooking, gardening, woodwork, photog., plate collector. Ofc: 927 Deep Valley Dr Rolling Hills Estates 90274

CAMPBELL, DOUGLAS A., securities broker-dealer; b. Jan. 13, 1929, Toronto, Ont.; s. Douglas and Dorothea Owen (Turner) C.; m. Allegra, Dec. 1970 (div. 1974); edn: BA, McGill Univ., 1951; MBA, Harvard Bus. Sch., 1953; PhD, Columbia Univ., 1972. Career: pres. D.A. Campbell Co. Inc., Los Angeles 1960–; mem: AAAS, Am. Electronics Assn., Nat. Assn. of Petroleum Investment Analysts, NASD Dist. 2 (v.chmn. bus. conduct com. 1986, internat. com. 1988); clubs: Knickerbock (NY), Racquet & Tennis (NY); publs: Environmental & Economic Implications of Enhanced Oil Recovery Processes - An Overview; The Third Market: A Catalyst for Change in Securities Market; Mexico - A Korea On Our Doorstep; The Internat. Telephone Cos.- An Opportunity for Growth; A North American Common Market: Mexico's Manifest Destiny; Republican; Episcopalian; rec: skiing, travel. Address: 1150 Brooklawn Dr Los Angeles CA 90077

CAMPBELL, GARY J., management consultant; b. Feb. 21, 1944, Hartford City, Ind.; s. Lloyd W. and Charlotte G. (Stover) C.; children: Clark b. 1968, Stephanie b. 1972, Chad b. 1975; m. Kristin A. Menge, Oct. 13, 1989; edn: BSIE, Purdue Univ., 1966; MBA, Washington Univ., 1968. Career: Emerson Electric, St. Louis, Mo. 1966-68; McDonnell Douglas, Santa Monica 1968-70; prin. A.T. Kearney Inc., internat. mgmt. consultants, Chgo., Ill. 1970-76; v.p. First Nat. Bank of Chgo. 1976-78; prin. Booz Allen & Hamilton, Chgo., Ill. 1978-80; v.p. A.T. Kearney Inc., Internat. Mgmt. Cons., Chgo. 1980-84, v.p., ptnr. in charge west coast ops. Los Angeles 1984–; mem: Cert. Mgmt. Cons., Assn. of Mgmt. Cons., Univ. Club of Chgo., Jonathan Club (Los Angeles), Rotary Five, Sports Club of L.A., Riveria Tennis Club, Kappa Sigma Frat.; Republican; Presbyterian; rec: skiing, running, tennis. Res: 7 Sea Colony Dr Santa Monica 90405 Ofc: A.T. Kearney Inc, Biltmore Tower 500 S Grand Ave Los Angeles 90071

CAMPBELL, GREGORY SCOTT, real estate executive; b. May 5, 1948, Blue Earth, Minn.; s. Dallas L. and Ida G. (Leland) C.; m. Ruth Elizabeth Barnett, Jan. 1, 1972; children: Lisa b. 1975, Jonathan b. 1978; edn: BA, Wheaton Coll. 1970. Career: regional mgr. Service Master, Downers Grove, Ill. 1970-72; v.p. J. Emil Anderson & Son, Des Plaines, Ill. 1972-79; sr. v.p. Richard Ellis Inc., Chgo., Ill. 1979-84; sr. v.p. Homart Devel. Co. 1984-89; exec. v.p. Coldwell Banker Corp., Mission Viejo, Calif. 1989–; mem: Internat. Council Shopping Centers, Chgo. Real Estate Bd., Nat. Assn. Realtors, Timothy Project (bd. dirs.), Honey Rock Camp (bd. mem.). Res: 27226 Westridge Ln Laguna Hills 92653

CAMPBELL, HARRY MEIKLE, consulting civil engineer; b. Feb. 4, 1922, Los Angeles; S. Harry, Sr. and Grace (Alward) M.; m. Karen E. Hose, Apr. 3, 1964; children: Tyrra Jo b. 1948, Nancy June b. 1950, Martin James b. 1960; edn: BSCE, UC Berkeley 1943; BS in bus., UC Los Angeles 1964; tchg. credential, El Camino Coll. 1966; Reg. Profl. Civil Engr., Calif. Career: engring. ofcr., capt. US Marine Corps 1942-46; resident engr. and project engr. Am. Bridge Co., 1946-50; structural designer Fluor Corp. 1950-54; transp. engr. Div. of Hwys. State of Calif. 1955-73; pres. Harry M. Campbell Engring. Corp., Los Angeles 1973–; Fallout Shelter Analysts, 1988–; Blast Design Specialist, 1990–; condr. seminars, hwy. engring. fundamentals and civil engring. registration, Calif. State Div. of Hwys. 1958-73; chmn. Nat. Com. for Integration of Engring. Edn. and Practice, 1974-78; mem. ASCE (chmn. Engr. Edn. Com.), Am. Soc. of Engring. Edn.; civic: 25 yr club for CalTrans, First Aid instr. Am. Red Cross, Doves Pgm. for L.A. Unified Sch. Dist., Marines Meml. Club (S.F.), VFW Post 3261, Disabled Am. Vets #101; publs: T6 (Thoughtful training tends toward tremendous transactions) 1976, composer of music, 1940-42; Republican; Baptist; rec: music, fishing, gardening. Res: 15912 Chanera Ave Gardena 90249 Ofc: Campbell Engineering Co. 1052 West 6th St Los Angeles 90017

CAMPBELL, IAN DAVID, opera company director; b. Dec. 21, 1945, Brisbane, Australia; s. Colin David and May (Irwin) C.; m. Ann Roslin Spira, Sept. 1, 1985; children: Benjamin b. 1987, David b. 1989; edn: BA, Univ. Sydney, 1967; Assoc. Fellow Australian Inst. of Mgmt., 1991. Career: prin. tenor singer Australian Opera, Sydney 1967-74; senior music ofcr. The Australia Council, 1974-76; gen. mgr. State Opera South Australia, Adelaide 1976-82; asst. artistic adminstr. Met. Opera, NY 1982-83; gen. dir. San Diego Opera, 1983–; prod. and host San Diego Opera Radio Prog. and At The Opera With Ian

Campbell 1985–; masterclasses, Music Acad. of the West 1990–; awards: Peri Award, Opera Guild So. Calif., L.A. 1985, Headliner of Yr. San Diego Press Club 1991; mem. bd. Opera America, W.D.C. 1986-94; mem. Australian Inst. of Arts Adminstrn. 1990–, Rotary Intl. S.D.; rec: golf, squash. Ofc: San Diego Opera PO Box 988 San Diego 92112

CAMPBELL, JOHN TIMOTHY, executive, international attorney; b. July 8, 1945, Lake Charles, La.; s. Aubrey Dorriss and Helen Teresa (Wilson) C.; m. Pamela Johnston, Apr. 18, 1987; edn: BA, Principia Coll., 1967; JD, So. Methodist Univ., 1970; admitted bar: Texas 1970. Career: atty./land Amoco Prodn., Houston 1970-71; atty./negotiator Amoco Internat., Chgo. 1971-72; v.p. Amoco Tunisia, Tunis 1972; pres. Campbell Energy Corp., Santa Barbara, Calif. 1972–; bd. chmn., pres. Alaska Pacific Refining Inc., Anchorage, Ak. 1986-92; chmn., CEO Paramount Petroleum Corp. 1988-89, bd. dirs. 1988-93; dir.: Montecito Water District 1991–, Central Coast Water Authority 1991–, Santa Barbara Co. Water Purveyors Agency 1991–; chmn. special dist. advy. com. Santa Barbara Co. 1994–; commissioner Santa Barbara Co. Local Agency Formation (LAFCO) 1994–; honors: silver key Am. Bar Assn. 1970; mem: Am. Bar Assn., Interam. Bar Assn., L.A. Petroleum Club, Phi Alpha Delta law frat.; club: Birnam Wood Golf; Republican; Christian Sci. Res: 1275 Spring Road Santa Barbara 93108

CAMPBELL, L. ANDREW, mathematician; b. May 9, 1942, Detroit, Mich.; s. Laughlin Austin and Mary Kennerly (Holmes) C.; m. Janet Rhonda Gore, May 28, 1971, div. July 1978; life ptnr. Roberta Grubb; edn: ScB, M.I.T., 1963; Lic. es Sc., Univ. of Paris, Fr. 1964; MA, Princeton Univ., 1967, PhD 1970. Career: asst. prof. UC San Diego, La Jolla 1969-76; mem. tech. staff, engring. splst., resrch. scientist The Aerospace Corp., El Segundo 1978–; mem. AMS (1966-69, 79-), IEEE Computer Soc. 1985–, IEEE Control Soc. 1988–, ACM (1983–, chair L.A. chpt. 1991-92); civic: volunteer reader Recording for the Blind 1967–; rec: contract bridge ACBL Life Master. Ofc: The Aerospace Corp. M1-102, PO Box 92957 Los Angeles 90009

CAMPBELL, MICHAEL LEE, computer scientist; b. Nov. 25, 1958, Los Angeles; s. Earl Junior and Lee (Fitch) C.; m. Asya Glozman, July 11, 1981; children: Sasha b. 1988, Alice b. 1991; edn: BS in math., UC Riverside, 1980; MS in c.s., UCLA, 1982, PhD in c.s., 1986. Career: tchg. asst., res. asst. UCLA Sch. Engring. and Applied Sci., 1980-82, lectr.1987-88; mem. tech. staff math, Hughes Aircraft Co., Electro-Optical and Data Systems Gp., 1982-88, staff engr., sr. staff computer scientist Hughes Aircraft Research Labs., 1988-92; engring. spec. The Aerospace Corp., Computer Systems Div. 1992–; awards: Howard Hughes doctoral fellow 1983-86; mem. Sigma Xi (chpt. pres.), IEEE Computer Soc., Assn. for Computing Machinery; author 10+ publs. re parallel computer software, applications, fault tolerance and architecture, patentee (1 granted, 1 pending); Indep.; Jewish; rec: karate, photography, travel. Ofc: The Aerospace Corp. - M1/102 P.O. Box 92957 Los Angeles 90009-2957

CAMPBELL, REA BURNE, insurance brokerage executive; b. Aug. 13, 1954, Niceville, Fla.; d. Charles Burnette Campbell and Phyllis (Burgan) Patty; edn: BSBA, Univ. So. Miss. 1976; C.P.A. Miss. (1984). Career: mgt. trainee Deposit Guaranty National Bank, Jackson, Miss. 1976-77, credit dept. ofcr. 1977-80, asst. v.p. and asst. mgr. commercial loan ops. 1980-81, v.p./mgr. customer profitability analysis, 1981-83; acctg. mgr. Fred S. James of Miss. 1983-85, controller, Phoenix and Tucson, Ariz. 1985-87; v.p., c.f.o. Sedgwick James Consulting Group, San Francisco 1987-90; employee benefits cons. Sedgwick James of CA, Inc. 1990–; mem: Kappa Delta Alumni Assn. (treas. 1991), Calif. Soc. CPAs (bd. dir. S.F. Chpt.,chair State Com. on Members in Industry); civic: Sierra Club, ARC (CPR instr. vol.), Tax-Aid Volunteers (v.p. publicity 1990-92, bd. dir. & chair of vol. development 1992–); rec: balllroom dance, backpacking, tennis, kayaking. Res: 850 Powell #103 San Francisco 94108 Ofc: Sedgwick, 600 Montgomery 9th Flr San Francisco 94111

CAMPBELL TOM, state senator; b. Aug. 14 1952, Chgo.; s. William J. and Marie Campbell; m. Susanne Martin; edn: BA, MA in econ. with highest honors, Univ. Chgo. 1973, PhD in econ. with highest dept. fellowship, 1980; JD magna cum laude, Harvard Univ., 1976. Career: law clerk to Judge MacKinnon, U.S. Ct. Appeals (DC Cir.), 1976-77; law clerk to Justice Byron R. White U.S. Supreme Ct. Washington, 1977-78; Winston & Strawn, Chgo., 1978-80; White House Fellow, Office Chief of Staff and White House Counsel, Washington, 1980-81; exec. asst. to dep. atty. gen. Dept. Justice, Washington, 1981; dir. Bur. Competition, FTC, Washington, 1981-83; mem. 101st-102nd Congresses from 12th Calif. dist., 1989-92; mem. com. on judiciary, com. on banking, fin. and urban affairs; mem. Calif. State Senate, 1993–; mem. com. budget & fiscal review, com. on edn., com. on judiciary, com. on revenue and taxation (vice chair), com. on housing and land use (chair); prof. Stanford Law Sch., 1983–. Ofc: 373 First St Ste 100 Los Altos 94022; also State Capitol Sacramento 95814

CAMPBELL, WESLEY GLENN, economist, educator; b. Apr. 29, 1924, Komoka, Ont., Can.; nat. 1953; s. Alfred Edwin and Delia (O'Brien) C.; m. Rita Ricardo, Sept. 15, 1946; children: Barbara Lee (Gray), b. 1954, Diane Rita (Porter), b. 1956, Nancy Elizabeth, b. 1960; edn: BA, Univ. W. Ont. 1944, MA,

Harvard Univ. 1946, PhD, 1948. Career: instr. in econ. Harvard Univ. 1948-51; res. econ. US Chamber of Commerce, Wash. DC 1951-54; res. dir. Am. Enterprise Inst. for Public Policy Res., Wash. DC 1954-60, program adviser 1960–; director Hoover Instn. on War, Revolution and Peace, Stanford 1960-89, counselor 1989–; bd. trustees Ronald Reagan Presdl. Found. 1985-89, chmn. 1985-87; chmn. Pres's Intelligence Oversight Bd. 1981-90, mem. Pres's Fgn. Intelligence Advy. Bd. 1981-90; chmn. Japan-US Friendship Commn. 1983-89; mem. Univ. Calif. Bd. of Regents 1968–, chmn. 1982; NSF Nat. Sci. Bd. 1972-78, 1990–; Presdl. Com. on Sci. and Tech. 1976; Pres's Commn. on White House Fellow 1969-74; chmn. Reagan-Bush Task Force on Edn. 1980, mem. R.-B. Task Force on Fgn. Policy, and on Inflation Policy, 1980; Personnel Advy. Com. to Pres. Reagan 1980-81; bd. dirs. Com. on the Present Danger, 1976–; advy. bd. Ctr. for Strategic and Internat. Studies 1980–; trustee Herbert Hoover Presdl. Lib. Assn. 1964–; mem. Mont Pelerin Soc. (dir. 1980-86), Philadelphia Soc. (pres. 1965-67), George Washington Boyhood Found. (bd. dirs. 1993–); clubs: Bohemian, Cosmos, Commonwealth; mil: Canadian Navy 1943-44. Res: 26915 Alejandro Dr Los Altos Hills 94022. Ofc: Hoover Institution, Stanford 94305-6010

CAMPBELL, WILLIS PRESTON, JR., photographer; b. May 16, 1945; s. Willis Preston Campbell and Dorothy Lee (Eshman) Collier; m. Sherelyn Douglas, Dec. 13, 1975; children: Jonathan, Paul; edn: BA, Westmont Coll. 1967; MA, UCSB 1972. Career: photographer Westmont, Santa Barbara 1974-77; self-employed photographer, Santa Cruz 1977–; mem: Profl. Photographers Calif. (fellow), Profl. Photographers Am. (certified, master photographer), PPMBA; Republican; Baptist; rec: gardening. Ofc: 1015 Cedar St Santa Cruz 95060

CAMPOS, LEONARD P., psychologist; b. Dec. 24, 1932, Arecibo, P.R.; s. Joseph Campos and Emma (Crespi) Roman; m. Lee Barrett, June 12, 1986; children: David b. 1954, Elizabeth b. 1956, Barbara b. 1962; edn: PhD in clin. psych., Mich. St. Univ., 1963; Diplomate Am. Bd. Profl. Psych. (1984), Am. Bd. Forensic Psych. (1985), Am. Bd. Med. Psychotherapy (1987). Career: asst. prof. Univ. of Pacific, Stockton 1963-66; staff psychologist Calif. Youth Auth., Stockton 1966-69; consultant psychologist pvt. practice, Sacto. 1969–; mem: Am. Psychol. Assn., Am. Group Psychotherapy Assn., Calif. St. Psychol. Assn., Internat. Transactional Analysis Assn., Nat. Hispanic Psychol. Assn.; author: You Can Redecide Your Life (1987), coauthor 2 books: Intro Yourself to TA (1985), Intro Your Marriage to TA (1972); mil: sp4 US Army 1957-58; Democrat; Unitarian; rec: tennis, skiing, travel, golf. Res: 1606 Oakview Roseville 95661 Ofc: Leonard P. Campos & Associates 1820 Professional Dr Ste 5 Sacramento 95825

CANNING, BRUCE R., doctor of Oriental medicine, acupuncturist, herbalist; b. Sept. 21, 1955, Whittier, Calif.; s. Glenn R. and Vada (Schurtz) C.; edn: diplomate, Emperors Coll., Santa Monica, 1987; diplomate, DaLian Med. Sch., DaLian, China, 1988; diplomate, Acad. of T.C.M., Beijing, China, 1988; doctor of Oriental Medicine, S.A.M.R.A. Univ., L.A., 1988; diplomate acupuncture, N.C.C.A.; lic. acupuncturist, State of Calif. Career: doctor of Oriental medicine, Westwood Ctr. for Acupuncture, Westwood, Calif., 1988; doctor of Oriental medicine, M. M. Van Benschotten & Assoc., Reseda, Calif., 1989–; tchr. of Qi Gong, Emperors Coll., Santa Monica, 1988; awards: 5th Degree Black Belt, (Chinese) Kung Fu S.S., L.A. County, 1986; author: doctoral dissertation, Current Traditional Oriental Medicine in China, 1988; rec: Shing Yi Chuan (internal Kung Fu), Qi Gong, Nei Gong, Yoga, meditation. Ofc: M. M. Van Benschotten OMD, M.A., C.A., & Assoc. 19231 Victory Blvd #151 Reseda 91335

CANOVA-DAVIS, ELEANOR, research biochemist; b. Jan. 18, 1938, San Francisco, Calif.; d. Gaudenzio Enzio and Catherine (Bordisso) Canova; m. Kenneth Davis, Feb. 10, 1957; children: Kenneth b. 1958, Jeffrey b. 1960; grandson: Scott b. 1985; edn: BA, S.F. State Univ. 1968; MS, S.F. State Univ. 1971; PhD, UC Med. Ctr., S.F. 1977; career: lab. asst., Frederick Burk Found. for Edn., S.F.. Calif. 1969-71; res. and tchg. asst., UC Med. Ctr., S.F. 1972-77; NIH postdoctoral fellow, UC, Berkeley 1977-80; asst. res. biochemist, UC Med. Ctr., S.F. 1980-84; sr. scientist, Liposome Tech., Menlo Park, Calif. 1984-85; sr. scientist, Genentech, Inc., So. S.F. 1985–; awards: Honors Convocation award, Dept. of Chem., S.F. State Univ. 1966; grad. div. fellowship, UC Med. Ctr., S.F. 1972-73; Earl C. Anthony Trust for Grad. Student Res., UC, S.F. 1975; Chancellor's Patent Fund award, Grad. Div., UC, S.F. 1976; Nat. Res. Service award, NIH, Berkeley 1977-80; mem: Calif. Scholarship Fedn. 1951–, Am. Chemical Soc. 1971–, The Protein Soc. 1988–; civic: Foxridge PTA and Westborough PTA, So. S.F.; Tiny Tots, S.F., St. Patrick's Circle, So. S.F.; author: numerous pub. articles in prof. journals, articles in various symposia; Catholic; rec: reading, sewing, knitting, bridge. Ofc: Genentech, Inc. 460 Point San Bruno Blvd South San Francisco 94080

CANTY, TIMOTHY GILES, pediatric surgeon; b. July 23, 1940, Oakland; s. Wm. Charles and Marjorie (Clark) C.; m. Maxine Schuhmann, June 21, 1962; children: Sean Todd b. 1964, Timothy Jr. b. 1966, Tabitha Lynn b. 1969; edn: BA cum laude, Stanford Univ., 1961; MD summa cum laude, UCLA Med. Sch. 1966; cert. Am. Bd. of Surgery (1975), splty. pediatric surg. (1976, 85). Career: pathology fellow UCLA Med. Sch. 1963-64; intern in surg. Mass. Gen. Hosp.,

Boston 1966-67, chief resident pediatric surg. 1970; clin. assoc. NIH/Nat. Cancer Inst., Bethesda, Md. 1967-69; sr. res. in cardiovascular surg. Children's Hosp. Med. Ctr., Mass. 1971, chief resident pediatric surg. 1971-72; sr. resident gen. surg. Mass. Gen. Hosp. 1973-74; assoc. prof. of surg. Univ. of Louisville, Ky. 1974-77, also surgeon-in-chief Children's Hosp., Louisville; assoc. prof., clin. prof. of surgery UC San Diego, 1977–; sr. surgeon Children's Hosp., S.D. 1983–; honors: Alpha Omega Alpha 1964, Regents scholar UCLA 1961-66, Dean Stafford Warren Award and Wm. Longmire Surgical Award for highest achiev. in surgery UCLA 1966, Hon. Kentucky Col.; mem: Am. Trauma Soc., F.A.C.S. (com. of fellows trauma care and prevention), Assn. for Acad. Surg., Am. Acad. Pediatrics (fellow), AAUP, S.D. Co. Med. Soc., Am. Ped. Surg. Assn., Pacific Assn. Ped. Surg., Calif. Children's Services (cons.), L.A. Ped. Soc., N.Y. Acad. Scis., British Assn. Ped. Surgeons, AMA, Soc. Internat. De Chirugie, Royal Soc. of Med. (London), Ped. Oncology Gp., Galen Club, Calif. Perinatal Assn., AAAS, Soc. of Gen. Surgeons of S.D., Am. Inst. of Ultrasound in Medicine, Calif. Inst. Assn. Ped. Surgeons, Pacific Coast Surg. Assn., Soc. Alpine de Chirugie Ped.; mem: Le Chavalier du Tastevin; coauthor Ultrasonography of Pediatric Surgical Disorders (Grune and Stratton, 1982), contbr. med. book chapter in Hernia (JB Lippencott, 1987), 46+ articles in med. jours.; mil: lt. cmdr. USP215 1967-69; Republican; rec: music, skiing, surfing, tennis. Res: 1846 Castellana La Jolla 92037 Ofc: Timothy G. Canty, Sr., MD, 3030 Children's Way Ste 401 San Diego 92123-4228

CAPLES, MICHAEL EDWARD, lawyer; b. October 1, 1951, Glendale; s. Edward Warren and Frances Maude (Bulla); m. Therese Ann Mueller; children: Connor b. 1986, Robert b. 1988, Andrew b. 1990, Emily b. 1993; edn: BA, CSU Fullerton 1973; JD cum laude, Whittier Coll. Sch. of Law 1980; LL.M, N.Y. Univ. Law Sch. 1981; admitted St. Bar Calif. 1980, N.J. 1981. Career: tchr. Conejo Valley Unified Sch. Dist., 1975-77; assoc. atty. Pitney Hardin Kipp & Szuch, Morristown, N.J. 1981-82; Barlow & Attaway, Los Angeles 1982-86; ptnr. Barlow Kobata & Caples 1986-87; assoc. atty. Jackson Lewis Schnitzler & Krupman, San Francisco 1987-90; ptnr. Jackson Lewis Schnitzler & Krupman 1991–; mem: Calif. St. Bar Assn., Reserve Ofcrs. Assn., Civil Affairs Assn.; 5 articles pub. in profl. jours. (1980-88); mil: maj. USAR 1984–; rec: skiing, travel. Ofc: Jackson Lewis Schnitzler & Krupman 525 Market St Ste 3400 San Francisco 94105

CAPORASO, FREDRIC, food science and nutrition educator; b. May 28, 1947, Jersey City, N.J.; s. Pat and Florence C.; m. Karen Denise Kuhle, Dec. 5, 1981; children: Robert b. 1968, Michael b. 1972, Daniel b. 1976, Allison b. 1989; edn: BS, Rutgers Univ. 1969, MS, 1972; PhD, Penn. State 1975. Career: asst. prof. food sci. Univ. of Nebraska 1975-78; mgr. food sci. Am. McGaw, Irvine 1978-82; chmn. food sci. & nutrition Chapman Univ. 1982–, dir. food sci. research ctr. Chapman Univ. 1988–; mem: So. Cal. Inst. of Food Technologists (chmn., ch.-elect, pgm. ch.), Inst. of Food Technologists, coord. Food Sci. Administrators, scientific lectr. 1993-96; author 30+ pub. research articles; rec: running. Ofc: Chapman University Food Science & Nutrition Dept. Orange 92666

CAPPS, ANTHONY T. (CAPOZZOLO), international public relations executive; b. April 19, Pueblo, Colo.; s. Nicolo and Ann (Salomone) Capozzolo; Career: dance dir., choreographer, prod. mot. pic. TV and radio; feat. Profl. Dance Team, Biltmore Bowl, Cocoanut Grove, L.A.; St. Catherine Hotel, Catalina 1939-42; dance dir., prod. NBC, ABC, KCOP-TV, Columbia Pictures, 20th Century Fox and Calif. studios 1940-60; govt. tours, P.R., Cuba, Jamaica, Dominican Rep., Haiti, 1954; prod. "Latin Holiday" t.v. series; exec. dir. activities Lockheed and Vega Aircraft Co., Burbank, L.A., Glendale, Pomona, Pasadena, Bakersfield, and Taft plants; internat. pub. rels. dir: Howard Manor, Palm Springs Key Club, Country Club Hotel, Palm Springs Ranch Club; Desert Sun Newspapers, KDES Radio P.S., Cameron Ctr. and Cameron Enterprises and Oil Co., Burbank radio sta., Murietta Hot Springs Hotel, Health and Beauty Spa P.S.- Coachella Valley; founder, pres., dir. Tony Capps Ents.; frequent t.v. guest re religion & politics, hist. of ballet & opera; founder/chmn. Nat. Artists Art Patrons Soc., St. Martin's Abbey (Lacey, Wash.), founder Capps-Capozzolo Gallery, St. Martin's Abbey & Coll. (Lacey, Wash.) 1988; fundraiser for num. charities: chair/exec. dir. golf and tennis tournaments, benefit dinners for civic ldrs. and elected ofcls., United Fund, City of Hope (3t), Nat. Cystic Fibrosis Fund, P.S. Bob Hope Golf Classic; created advtsg. gimmick for Colgate and Cugat, Coca Cola; Eisenhower Med. Ctr.; mem. Nat. Football Found. and Hall of Fame (founder/pres. Tri-Co. chpt., founder/ co-ch. Annual Golf Classic), Nat. Artists and Art Patrons Soc./ City of Hope (founder/pres.), Eisenhower Mem. Hosp. Aux (charter), Opera Guild of the Desert, P.S. Pathfinders, Desert Art Ctr. Coachella Valley, P.S. Desert Mus., AFTRA, Smithsonian Instn., Am. Security Council, LA Co. Mus. Art (Patron), Nat. Trust for Hist. Preserv.; publs: Am. Film Inst., The Reporter, Desert Sun P.S., L.A. Daily News; Republican: Life mem. Presdl. Repub. Task Force, US Senatl. Club (Wash. DC), Repub. Senatl. Inner Circle, The Ronald Reagan Presdl. Found. (charter sponsor), Who's Who in the Republican Party (Wash. D.C.); R.Cath. Res: 2715 Junipero Ave Palm Springs 92262

CARBONE, JUNE ROSE, law professor; b. June 14, 1953, Rochester, N.Y.; d. Joseph L. and Jane (Saraceno) Carbone; m. William Kurt Black, July 28, 1979; children: Kenny b. 1982, Genina b. 1984, Galen b. 1988; edn: AB, Princeton

Univ. 1975; JD, Yale Law Sch. 1978; admitted St. Bar Wash. D.C. 1978. Career: trial atty. U.S. Dept. of Justice Civil Div., Wash. D.C. 1978-83; asst. prof. George Mason Univ. Sch. Law, Arlington, Va. 1983-87; assoc. prof. Santa Clara Univ. Sch. Law 1987–; mem: Am. Bar Assn.; 11 articles pub. in profl. jours., 1982-94. Ofc: Santa Clara Univ. School of Law Santa Clara 95053

CARDENAS, ROBERT LEON, military officer, experimental test pilot (ret.), corporate executive, economic development consultant; b. Mar. 10, 1920, Merida, Yucatan, Mexico, nat. 1936; s. Robert L., Sr. and Maria de Jesus Lopez (Alonzo) C.; m. Gladys Gisewite; children: Diana b. 1949, Richard b. 1951, Robin b. 1955, Debra b. 1956, Michael b. 1958, Mark b. 1960, Maria b. 1962; edn: BSME, Univ. N.M., 1955; grad. USAF Air War Coll., 1958, Command and Staff Sch.; MBA/JD, National Univ., 1984; comml. pilot rating, multi-engine, jet with instrument rating. Career: served to brigadier general US Air Force 1939-73: exptl. test pilot- XF-86, XB-45, XB-47, YB-49 Flying Wing (chief test pilot), XF-87, and X-4; flew the 1st jet fighter, 1st jet bomber, overall project dir. 1st rocket aircraft to break the sound barrier (was pilot of the B-29 that dropped the XS-1 and Capt. Yeager) 1945-51; chief Aircraft and Missiles Pgmmg. Div., Hq. USAF, Wash. DC (devel. annual pgm. and 5-yr forecasts) 1957-61; chief Spl. Ops. Plans Div., U.S. Strike Command, MacDill AFB, Fla. 1961-64; comdr. 18th Tactical Fighter Wing Okinawa (TFW)(first to fly F-105 over N. Vietnam 1964-66; comdr. 835th Air Div., McDonnell AFB Kansas 1966-68; USAF Spl. Ops. Force, Eglin AFB, Fla. (policy and plng. SOF worldwide) 1968-69; vice comdr. 16th AF, Torrejon Air Base, Spain (negotiater base agreements in Spain and w. Muommar Quadaffi in Libya) 1969-70; classified mission Live Oak 1970-71; chief Nat. Strategic Target List Div., Jt. Strat. Target Plng. Staff (JCS) SAC Hq. 1971-73, ret.; decorated Disting. Service Medal, D.F.C., Legion of Merit, Air Medal, Purple Heart; Grand Cross of Order of Aeronautical Merit and spl. cit. Gen. Franco, Spain; dir. intelligence and spl. projects/exec. asst. to the pres., Sci. Applications Inc., 1973-78, bd. dirs./asst. v.p. SAI 1975-78, corp. v.p./internat. bus. SAI 1978-80; dir. internat. ops. System Devel. Corp., Santa Monica 1980-82; chmn. bd./ceo ROCAR Internat., San Diego; cons. to White House on econ. devel. of Cal.-Mex. border, presdl. apptd. state co-ordinator SW Border Action Gp. 1983-85; commr. San Diego Crime Commn. 1983; Gov. Deukmejian apptd. chmn. State Advy. Gp. on Juvenile Justice and Delinquency Prevention, 1985–, and mem. Calif. Council on Criminal Justice, mem. Calif. Veterans Bd.; mem: Fellow AIAA, Soc. Exptl. Test Pilots, Phi Kappa Phi, Sigma Chi, Pi Tau Sigma, Am. Def. Preparedness Assn., AF Assn., Am. Security Council (nat. advy. bd.), Swiss Internee Assn., Order of Daedalians, AOPA, TROA; Republican; Cath.; rec: golf, youth work; "Going to travel and smell the roses for a few years to recharge the batteries." Res: 6143 Madra Ave San Diego 92120

CARDINALE, LORETTA ANN, real estate broker; b. Oct. 24, 1913, Beloit, Kans.; d. Charles Edward and Frances (Spannan) Rasher; m. Glen Clinton Lowry, Feb. 20, 1946 (dec. 1973); children: Nancy Ann (Mrs. Larry Powers), Elizabeth Jane (Mrs. Thomas K. Krupka); m. 2d Frank Cardinale (dec. 1984); stepchildren: Frank, Dominic, Raymond; edn: grad. Am. Inst. Banking 1941; att. San Bernardino Valley Coll. 1965. Career: asst. cashier First Nat. Bank, Beloit, Kans. 1943-46; co-owner Lowry Real Estate & Ins., Beloit 1946-62; Lowry Real Estate, Calimesa, Calif. 1962–; registrar of voters Riverside County 1965-70, mem. Citizens Com. for New Gen. Plan for Riverside County, Residential and Commercial, 1970-73; troop ldr. Girl Scouts, Beloit 1951-60; mem: Nat. Assn. Realtors, Calif. Assn. Realtors, Yucaipa Valley Bd. Realtors (treas.) 1966), Calimesa C.of C. (dir.1965-71), Assn. Indep. Businessmen Redlands, AARP, Am. Field Svc. Assn.; VFW Aux.; Cath. Daus. Am., Bus & Profl. Women, Sons and Daus. Soddies; Redlands Yucaipa Horticulture Soc., Soroptimist (charter), Yucaipa Womens Club; Republican; Cath. Res: POB 117 Calimesa 92320 Ofc: 543 W County Line Rd Calimesa 92320

CAREY, STEVENS ANTHONY, lawyer; b. Mar. 30, 1951, Los Angeles; s. Edward Macdonald and Elizabeth (Heckscher) C.; m. Indy Shriner, Mar. 20, 1987; children: Lauren b. 1987, Meagan b. 1989; edn: BA, MA, and JD, UC Berkeley, 1973, 1975, 1978; admitted bar: Calif. 1978, N.Y. 1988. Career: assoc. Lawler, Felix & Hall, Los Angeles 1978-83; invitation to participate on Hastings Law Jour., 1976, Phi Beta Kappa, offered 4-yr. fellowship from UCLA, 1974, 1st place winner at UCLA Shakespeare Festival, 1969; mem: Calif. State Bar Assn., Los Angeles Co. Bar Ass., Am. Bar Assn.; publs: articles, "Profit Participations: Coping with the Limitations Faced by Pension Funds and REITs", 1986, "Shared Appreciation Loans by Tax-Exempt Pension Funds", 1990, "UBTI: A Primer for Real Estate Investments", 1991, "Workouts: A Borrower's Guide to Shared Appreciation Formulas", 1992; contbg. editor Real Estate Finance Jour., 1991–, Board of Advisors for Real Estate, Workouts & Asset Management 1993–; Republican; Catholic; rec: piano, tennis. Ofc: Pircher, Nichols & Meeks 1999 Avenue of the Stars, 26th Flr Los Angeles 90067

CARICATO, CHARLES ROBERT, a.k.a. CHUCK CARR, dance studio executive; b. June 28, 1931, Monessen, Pa.; s. Charles Patrick and Anne (Hurrianko) C.; m. Nancy Willis, Nov. 4, 1967 (div. July 1989); children: Charlene b. 1968, Tiffany b. 1969, Charles b. 1971, Christian b. 1972; m. Yoni Eisnor, Oct. 28, 1989; edn: BA, Penn State, 1953. Career: account exec.

Prudential Ins., Monessen, Pa. 1953-54; instr.- counselor Arthur Murray, Los Angeles 1955-60; mgr. Arthur Murray Studio, Glendale 1960-63; franchisee, pres. Arthur Murray, San Diego 1963–, area dir. Arthur Murray Internat., Coral Gables, Fla. 1985-94; pres. Gloria Marshall Figure Salons, San Diego 1973-81; awards: industrious franchisee Arthur Murray (Miami 1980), Studio of Year (1989, 90, 91), VIP Honors and Arthur Gold Award 1991; mem. Penn St. Alumni, Alpha Chi Rho Alumni; Republican; R.Cath. (parish council 1984-85); rec: golf, tennis, sports. Ofc: Arthur Murray 3919 4th Ave San Diego 92103

CARINI, MICHAEL JOSEPH, certified public accountant; b. June 7, 1951, San Francisco; s. Fred Joseph and Anna Elizabeth (Lamb) C.; m. Patricia Anne Vince, Oct. 3, 1981; 1 dau., Gina b. 1983; edn: BS, Univ. San Francisco 1973; C.P.A. Calif. 1979. Career: external auditor Hood & Strong, San Francisco 1973-76; acctg. mgr. Cutter Labs., Emeryville, mgr. MIS 1976-84; controller Kinney Wall Coverings, Oakland 1984-86; Crittendon Publishers, Novato 1986-87; New Zealand Milk Products, Petaluma 1987-89, Regan Holding Co., Petaluma 1989-92, Fritzi California, San Francisco 199294; asst. controller MTC Telemanagement, Inc., Petaluma 1994–; mem: Am. Inst. CPA, Calif. Soc. CPA; rec: historical autographs and accordionist. Res: 662 Hudis St Rohnert Park 94928

CARLETON, FINIS EWING, consulting chemical engineer; b. June 27, 1940, Houston, Tx.; s. Finis Ewing and Lillian Frances (Bridges) C.; m. Mary Elizabeth McLaughlin, Oct. 1, 1966; 1 dau., Jennifer b. 1976; edn: BSCE, Univ. Tx. Austin 1962; MSCE, Univ. Mich. 1963; PhD, 1970; reg. profl. engr. Tx. 1971, reg. chem. engr. Calif. 1985; reg. environmental assessor Calif. 1989, qualified environmental prof. 1994. Career: sr. engr. Atlantic Richfield Co., Dallas and Los Angeles 1968-79; v.p. Semarck Calif., Houston, Tx. 1979-80; pres. Carleton Engrs. and Cons. Inc., Pasadena 1980–; indsl. prof. So. Methodist Univ., Dallas, Tx. 1970; mem: Am. Inst. Chem. Engrs., Air and Waste Mgmt. Assn., Pacific Energy Assn., San Marino City Club, San Marino Comm. Ch. (trustee 1983-85, pres. 1985), San Marino Comm. Ch. Found. (trustee 1988-90), Flintridge Riding Club; patent held for apparatus and method for producing hydrogen, 1971, articles and papers pub. in sci. jours., 1972-83; thesis pub., 1970; Republican; Presbyterian. Res: 2495 Coniston Pl San Marino 91108 Ofc: Carleton Engineers & Cons. Inc. 690 E Green St #203 Pasadena 91101

CARLETON, JOHN LOWNDES, psychiatrist; b. Dec. 26, 1925, Seattle; s. John Phillip and Lillian (Lowndes) C.; m. Marie Pak, June 12, 1948 (div. 1968); m. Ellen Andree Masthoff, Apr. 14, 1985; children: John b. 1949, Pakie b. 1950, Daniel b. 1952, Kip b. 1986, Talitha b. 1988; edn: BA, Univ. of Louisville, Ky. 1946; MD, Northwestern Univ. Med., Chgo. 1950; cert. in psychiatry Am. Bd. Psych. & Neurology, 1959. Career: intern Swedish Hosp., Seattle, 1949, resident in surgery, 1952, 1954-55; industrial physician Howe Sound Mining Corp., Holden, WA 1950-52; capt. Med. Corps US Army Reserve, 1952-54; resident psychiatry Johns Hopkins Univ. Med. Sch., Balt. 1955-57; asst. psychiatrist Sheppard & Enoch Pratt Hosp., Towson, Md. 1957-58; private practice, Santa Barbara, Calif. 1958–; trustee Masserman Found., Chgo. 1985–; awards: Founders Award Am. Assn. for Soc. Psych., W.D.C. 1984, Silver Camellia award City of Opatija, Yugoslavia 1976, congress hon. medals World Assn. for Soc. Psych.: Israel, Opatija, Yugo., Lisbon, Portugal, Santa Barbara, CA (1972, 76, 78, 79); mem: Am. Psychiatric Assn. (1957–, life fellow), Am. Coll. Psychiatry (fellow 1973–), Am. Coll. Physicians (fellow 1973–), World Assn. for Social Psychiatry (3d. hon. pres. 1970–), Am. Assn. for Social Psychiatry (past pres. 1970–, jour. ed. in chief 1980-87), Nuclear Age Peace Found. Santa Barbara; author 25+ sci. publs., 1957–, co-editor 3 books: Man for Man, 1973, What is Alcoholism, 1976, The Dimensions of Soc. Psych., 1979; Republican; Unitarian; rec: carpentry, gardening, sailing, hiking. Res/Ofc: 656 Romero Canyon Road Santa Barbara 93108-1527

CARLIN, JEAN EFFAL, psychiatrist; b. July 24, 1930, Hibbing, Minn.; d. Earl William and Effal Octavia (Anderson) Carlin; edn: BA, Univ. of Minn. 1950, BS, 1952, MA, 1953, MD, 1954, PhD, 1959. Career: intern Mpls. Gen. Hosp. 1954-55, resident in psychiatry Univ. of Minn. 1955-56; faculty, chief student health svc. North Park Coll., Chgo. 1956-58; UCLA Brain Res. Inst. staff at theVA Hosp., Long Beach, Calif. and mem. faculty CSU Long Beach 1958-60; pvt. practice general medicine, Long Beach 1961-67; resident in psychiatry UC Irvine 1967-69; volunteer physician to Viet Nam in 1969, 1971; faculty UC Irvine Med. Sch. at Med. Ctr. 1969-71, faculty UCI 1971-80, chief profl. edn. Fairview State Hosp. 1971-75; assoc. dean UCI Coll. of Med. 1974-78; also staff psychiatrist Fairview St. Hosp. 1978-80; assoc. prof. and dir. Residency Edn. in Psychiatry, Drew Med. Sch., Martin Luther King Hosp. 1980-82; assoc. prof., 1982-86, dir. Residency Edn. in Psychiatry, Univ. Oklahoma Med. Sch., Oklahoma City 1982-86; cons. Indian Health Svc. 1984-86; fellow in psychiatry and law USC/L.A. Co. Med. Ctr. 1986-87; cons. Fed. Dept. of Prisons 1986-87; forensic psychiatrist Calif. State Dept. of Mental Health, So. Regional Office, L.A. 1987-88; pvt. practice gen. psychiatry adults and children plus forensic and cross-cultural psychiatry, Santa Ana 1989-91, Seal Beach 1991–; mem: AMA, CMA, Am. Coll. Psychiat., Pacific Rim Coll. Psychiat. (charter), Soc. for the Study of Psychiatry & Culture, Am. Psychiat. Assn., S. Calif. Psychiatric Assn., NGAS; mil: col. Army Nat. Guard, 143rd Evac. Hosp.; Covenant Ch. of Am. Ofc: 500 Pacific Coast Hwy Ste 208 Seal Beach 90740

CARLISLE, JOHN B., probation officer; b. July 29, 1947, Beloit, Wis.; s. William George and Jo Ann (Green) C.; m. Veronica A. Nord, March 17, 1979; 1 son, Jeremy John; edn: Stanford Univ. 1966-68; BA, CSU Chico 1971. Career: dep. probation ofcr. Colusa Co. Probation Dept., Colusa 1970-71; dep. probation ofcr. I Merced Co. Probation Dept., Merced 1971-72, dep. probation ofcr. II 1972-87, dep. probation ofcr., office mgr. III 1987-89; traffic hearing ofcr. Merced Co. Juvenile Ct. 1987–; specialized Drug Supervision Program dir. 1989–; traffic sch. instr., Modesto and Turlock 1986–; tch. law awareness classes, Fresno 1988–; cons. Merced Co. Supt. of Schs. 1986–; mem. Merced Co. Grievance & Appeals Bd. 1980–; Merced Co. Affirmative Action Advy. Com. 1980-85; awards: U.S. Jaycees Outstanding Young Men Am. (1978, 79), Merced Youth Soccer Assn. Coaching (1980, 81); mem: Merced Co. Student Attendance Review Bd. (chmn. 1987-89), Central Valley Investigators Assn., Calif. Narcotic Ofcrs. Assn. (life), Calif. Juvenile Ofcrs. Assn., Am. Fedn. St. Co. and Mun. Employees Local 2703 (exec. bd.), Calif. Probation Parole & Corrections Assn., Merced Youth Soccer; articles and papers pub. in profl. jours., 1979-93; Cath.; rec: gardening, travel. Ofc: Merced County Probation Department 2150 M Street Merced 95340

CARLSON, CHARLES LONG, financial executive, business consultant; b. Jan. 10, 1917, Olean, N.Y.; s. Charles Julius Carlson and Edna Long; m. June Kreamer, Apr. 10, 1948; children: Yvonne, Shaun, Linda, Maria; edn: BS in B.A., Univ. Buffalo, 1938; CPA, Calif. Career: ptnr. Merle Moore & Co., CPAs, Tucson 1954-55; sec.-treas., comptroller Infilco, Tucson 1955-64; comptroller Traveler Boat Div., Stanray Corp., Chgo. and Danville, Ill. 1964-65; comptroller Dorsett Plastics Co., Santa Clara, Calif. 1966; v.p., sec.-treas. Daniel, Mann, Johnson & Mendenhall, Los Angeles 1966-82, bus. cons., sec. 1982-84, asst. sec. 1984–; dir.: subs. of Infilco & DMJM; sec., dir. Infilco (Australia) Ltd., Infilco (Can.) Ltd., Infilco Mexicana; sec. Gale Separator Co. (Tucson), Catalina Constrn. Co. (Tucson); sec.-treas. Beach Ocean Inc., 1985–, Honolulu Condo Inc. 1985-86; bus. mgr. Westwil Ltd. 1986-92, Hampwil Ptnrs. 1986–; asst. treas. Fuller Co., Catasauqua, Pa.; dir. Gen. Steel Co., Ft. Worth 1960-64; instr. St. Bonaventure Univ., Olean 1948; mem. Am. Inst. CPAs; civic: (Olean): Republican county committeeman 1939, Community Chest (cpgn. gen. chmn. 1950), Olean Gen. Hosp. drive (team chmn. 1952); Tucson C.of C. (tax study com. 1960); mil: 2d lt. USAAF 1944-45; Nazarene Ch. Res./Ofc: 4515 Prairie Rd Paso Robles 93446

CARLSON, GARY WALLACE, political scientist, college instructor; b. July 31, 1937, Albany; s. Wallace Frederick and Elsa (Hendrickson) C.; m. Boonruen Sakulma, Jan. 11, 1985; children: Erik b. 1967, Superath b. 1977, Petchara b. 1985; edn: BA, San Jose St. Univ. 1964; MA, 1966; linguist: Thai, German, Swedish, Norwegian, Russian. Career: instr. Ft. Hay Kans. St. Univ. 1966-67; San Jose St. Univ. 1969-70; UC Santa Cruz 1970; Cabrillo Coll., Aptos 1967-86, chair social scis. 1986-89; cons. Calif. Spl. Tr. Inst., San Luis Obispo 1980-82; Calif. St. Dept. of Justice, Sacto. 1979-82; mem: Fgn. Correspondents Club Thailand, Reserve Ofcrs. Assn., Commonwealth Club Calif.; mil: major USAR mil. intelligence 1954-94, lt. col. State Mil. Reserve 1994–, Army Commend. Medal 1988, China Svc. Medal (USMC 1956); rec: investments. Ofc: Cabrillo College 6500 Soquel Dr Aptos 95003

CARLSON, M. JOEL, real estate broker-developer; b. May 24, 1952, Hollywood; s. Franklin Joel and Evelyn (Knutson) C.; m. Mary, June 26, 1982; edn: BA, Chapman Univ., 1974; Calif. Comm. Colls. life instr. cred., 1982; profl. credits, desig: RECI, Santa Ana Coll., 1979, CREC (cert. R.E. cons.), American Coll., Idpls. 1980, G.R.I., Grad. Realtors Inst. Career: asst. mgr. Walker & Lee Realty, Villa Park 1976-78; branch mgr. Strout Realty, Buena Park 1978-80; owner/broker Carlson Realty, Orange 1980-85; pres. MJC Realty, Newport Beach 1985–; awards: sales agt. of month Walker & Lee (1st mo. in bus.), $1 Million Club, Strout (1979), Multi-Million $ Club, MJC Realty (1986–); mem: Calif. Assn. Realtors (Master Instr. 1984, author CAR course Intro to R.E. Counseling, 1989), Nat. Assn. Realtors, Newport Mesa Bd. Realtors (edn. chair 1983, 88, dir. 1984, 90, 91), Calif. R.E. Educators Assn. (past pres., Desig. R.E. Instr.-DREI 1989), Kiwanis (past pres. Villa Park 1979, Corona del Mar 1984, 90); publs: (workbook w. 8 tapes) The Secrets of Equity Sharing, 1984; (booklet) So... You Wanna ,Make A Deal, 1985; seminar lectr. (w. workbook) On Your Mark, Get $et, Go!, 1986; Republican; Christian; rec: skiing, golf, lecturing. Ofc: MJC Realty, Inc. 471 N Newport Blvd Ste 100 Newport Beach 92663

CARLSON, PAUL EDWIN, television writer, real estate developer; b. June 29, 1944, San Francisco; s. Carl John and Margueritte E. (Kovatch) C.; m. Sharon Hammond, 1963; children: Kim, b. 1964, Davin, b. 1971, Christina, b. 1979; edn: AA, Yosemite Coll. 1964; BA, CSU Long Beach 1971; Cert. Shopping Center Mgr. (CSM) Internat. Council of Shopping Ctrs. Mgmt. Sch. 1981. Career: police ofcr. (vice & narcotics) Modesto Police Dept. 1964-69; owner Universal Prodns., NYC and Modesto, Ca. 1969-73; gen. mgr. City Investing Co., Beverly Hills and NYC 1973-75; v.p. The Koll Co., Newport Beach 1975-79; v.p. Irvine Co., Newport Beach 1979-80; owner Willows Shopping Center, Concord 1980-83; sr. vice pres. Lee Sammis Co. 1983-85; pres. Am. Devel. Co., 1985-87; bd. chmn. The Carlson Co., 1987–; writer 3

screen plays for NBC's Police Story, comedy writer for NBC-TV Tonight Show, Saturday Night Live, and Late Night with David Letterman; special projects comedy writer for British Bdcstg. Co. (BBC), London; pub. Property Managers Handbook; guest lectr. USC, UCLA, Orange Coast Coll.; real estate cons. Bank of Am., Union Bank, Chevron USA, Aetna Life Ins. Co., James Lang Wooten (G.Brit.), Peoples Rep. of China; commr. Calif. State Juvenile Justice Commn.; ops. chmn. Internat. Council of Shopping Ctrs.; advy. bd. mem. UC Irvine Bus. Sch., CSU Fullerton Bus. Sch.; sr. advr. Chapman Coll.; mem. Concord Visitors & Conv. Bur. (bd.), Am. Cancer Soc. (bd. Contra Costa Co.), Mt. Diablo Hosp. (pres. bd. trustees), City of Concord Pavillion (v.p., bd.), past chmn. City of Newport Bch. Traffic Commn.; Republican; Prot.; avocation: youth counseling. Res: 37 Rue Fontainebleau Newport Beach 92660 Ofc: The Carlson Co. #3 Corporate Plaza Ste 100 Newport Beach 92660

CARLSON, RICHARD WARNER, journalist, government official, broadcasting executive; b. Feb. 10, 1941, Boston, Mass.; s. W.E. and Ruth Carlson; m. Patricia Caroline Swanson, Feb. 18, 1979; children: Tucker McNear b. 1969, Buckley Peck b. 1971. Career: journalist Los Angeles Times 1962-63; United Press Internat. 1963-65; ABC-TV, San Francisco and Los Angeles 1966-75; freelance writer, stringer Time Magazine, Look, others 1966-70; dir., prod. documentaries NBC-TV, Burbank 1975; anchorman CBS-TV, San Diego 1975-76; sr. v.p., v.p. fin. Great American Fed. Savings Bank 1976-84; dir. pub. liaison U.S. Info. Agency 1985-86, dir. The Voice of Am., Washington DC 1986-91; U.S. Ambassador to the Republic of Seychelles 1991-92; pres., c.e.o. Corp. for Public Broadcasting 1992–; dir: Delmar News Press 1976, Calif. Gen. Mortgage Inc. 1978, San Diego C.of C.; awards: recipient AP tv & radio awards for investigative reporting, news analysis and commentary (6 awards), Golden Mike awards (4), Emmy awards (3), San Diego Press Club awards (2), Geo. Foster Peabody Award for investigative reporting, L.A. Press Club Grand Award, Nat. Headliners Award; apptd. by Pres. Reagan to President's Council on Peace Corps 1982; mem: Jr. League of San Diego (fin. advy. bd.), La Jolla Soccer League (sponsor), Muscular Dystrophy Assn. (dir. San Diego), Actors & Others (pres. L.A. 1972-76), Rosalind Russel Arthritis Found. (dir.), Fund for Animals (dir. N.Y.), San Diego Coalition (chmn.), Sigma Delta Chi; clubs: La Jolla Beach, Thunderbird CC, Mid Ocean, Capitol Hill, Metropolitan, City Tavern, Georgetown; Episcopalian. Res: 7718 Georgetown Pike McLean, VA 22102 Ofc: Corporation For Public Broadcasting 901 E St NW Washington DC 20004

CARMAN, ERNEST DAY, lawyer; b. Mpls.; s. Ernest Clarke and Juanita (Howland Day) C.; m. Deborah Daynes; children (by previous m.): Eric C., Christiane M., and Dayna H.; edn: BA, USC; MA, Stanford Univ.; Dr. es Sci. Pol., Univ. Geneva, Switz.; JD, Univ. San Francisco; admitted bar: Calif., U.S. Supreme Ct. Career: law ptnr. E. Day Carman & Associates, Newport Beach, currently; mil: maj. USMC Reserve (ret.). Res: 720 Cliff Dr Laguna Beach 92651 Ofc: E. Day Carman & Associates 567 San Nicholas Dr Ste 207 Newport Beach 92660

CARNIGLIA, STEPHEN CHARLES, author, educator, consultant on materials science; b. Jan. 15, 1922, San Francisco; s. Harold Chester and Muriel Carlotta (Skinner) C.; m. Phebe Davis, June 20, 1947; children: Stephen Davis b. 1950, William Douglas b. 1955; edn: BS, MS, and PhD in chemistry, UC Berkeley, 1943, 45, 54; Calif. std. gen. secondary tchg. cred., 1946. Career: instr., hd. dept. chemistry, Coll. of Marin, Kentfield 1946-51; dept. hd. inorganic chemicals res. & devel. FMC Corp., Newark, Calif. and Princeton, N.J., 1953-56; sect. chief mats. R&D, Atomics Internat. Div., Rocketdyne Div., Rockwell Internat. Corp., Canoga Park 1956-70; dept. mgr. chem. and mats. R&D, Kaiser Aluminum and Chemical Corp., Pleasanton 1970-86; indep. cons., frequent guest lectr. on materials sci., 1986–; W.W. Clyde Prof. of Engring. Univ. of Utah, 1988, lectr. UCLA and UC Davis, 1987-90; adj. prof. of M.S.&E., UC Davis, 1991–; honors: Phi Beta Kappa 1943, Sigma Xi 1945, Ross Coffin Purdy Award Am. Ceramic Soc. 1974, listed Who's Who in the West, Am. Men and Women of Sci.; mem: Fellow Am. Ceramic Soc. (v.p. 1980), Catalysis Soc. 1982–; civic: Marin Co. Jr. C.of C. 1950; 40+ pub. res. papers, 4 patents, 2 books; mil: pvt. US Army Inactive Res. 1942-43; Republican; United Ch. of Christ; rec: sailing, tennis, bicycling. Address: 115 Wilshire Ct Danville 94526

CARON, DAVID DENNIS, lawyer, educator; b. June 28, 1952, Hartford, Conn.; s. Laurier Dennis and Rita Gertrude (Lafond) C.; m. R'Sue Popowich, May 24, 1975; children: Peter, Marina; edn: BS, USCG Acad., 1974; MSc, Univ. Wales, 1980; JD, UC Berkeley, 1983; diploma, Hague Acad. Internat. Law, 1984; Drs, Leiden Univ. 1985; Dr.Jur., Leiden Univ. 1990; admitted bar Calif. 1983. Career: lt. US Coast Guard, 1974-79; legal asst. Iran-U.S. Claims Tribunal, The Hague, The Netherlands, 1983-86; atty., assoc. Pillsbury, Madison & Sutro, San Francisco, 1986-87; prof. law UC Berkeley, 1987; dir. studies Hague Acad. Internat. Law, The Hague, The Netherlands, 1987; vis. prof. Cornell Law Sch., 1990; awards: Fulbright scholar U.S./U.K. Fulbright Comm., U.K. 1979-80, Environmental Conservation fellowship, Nat. Wildlife Fedn. 1980-81, Deak Prize for Writing Am. Soc. of Internat. Law 1990, Thelen Marrin Prize for writing UC Berkeley 1983, Order of the Coif; mem: UN Assn., Internat. Studies Assn., S.F. Commn. on Fgn. Rels., Am. Soc. Internat. Law (exec. com., exec. council 1990-94), Ocean Goverance Study Group (steering com. 1990-94), U.S. Dept. of State Advy. Com. on Public Internat. Law 1993–; publs: numerous articles in law jours., editor-in-chief Ecology Law Quarterly 1982-83, ed. Law of the Sea: U.S. Policy Dilemma, 1983, Perspectives on U.S. Policy Toward the Law of the Sea, 1985, bd. editors Am. Jour. of Internat. Law, 1991-95; rec: classical choral works. Res: 2750 Elmwood Ave Berkeley 94705 Ofc: University of California School of Law Boalt Hall Berkeley 94720

CAROTHERS, ROBERT ALEXANDER, certified public accountant; b. Aug. 31, 1940, Redwood City; s. Troy Luther Carothers and Christena Augusta (Berg) Shinn; stepfather Orville Herbert Shinn; m. Mary Deane Ray, June 25, 1961 (div. June 30, 1985); children: Rhonda b. 1962, Shelley b. 1964, Gwyn b. 1966; m.2d. Ida Lou Louise Mezzetti, Sept. 28, 1985 (div. Mar. 1, 1995); edn: AA acctg., Chabot Coll., 1964; BS acctg., CSU Hayward, 1967; MS taxation, Golden Gate Univ., 1978; C.P.A., Calif. 1973, Nev. 1989; lic. investment adv. SEC (1988); desig: Cert. Fin. Planner (CFP) 1987; Arbitrator, Am. Arbitration Assn. 1992; Bus. Appraiser 1992. Career: rate clk. Consol. Freightways, San Leandro 1959-67; revenue agt. U.S. Treasury Dept., Oakland 1967-70; tax mgr. Wood, Nye & Co., CPAs, Palo Alto 1970-73; ptnr. Carothers & Ito., CPAs, Fremont 1973–; guest lectr. Ohlone Coll. 1976-81, Mission S.J. High 1982, Fremont C.of C. 1984, cable t.v. Union City 1986; mem: Am. Inst. CPAs, Calif. Soc. CPAs, So. Alameda Co. CPA Discussion Group (past pres.), Soc. CPA Financial Plnrs.; civic: Fremont Rotary (Paul Harris Fellow 1983), Fremont Boys Club (pres. 1980-81), S. Fremont Lions (dir. 1973-75), Wash. Township Mens Club, The 100 Club, Rodent Soc. of Fremont, Inc. (founder), Tri-City Executives Assn. (founder); Republican; Presbyterian; rec: travel, fishing, hunting. Res: 1210 Ocaso Camino Fremont 94539 Ofc: Carothers & Ito, CPAs, 39221 Paseo Padre Pkwy Ste F Fremont 94538

CARPENTER, DONALD BLODGETT, real estate appraiser, educator; b. Aug. 20, 1916, New Haven, Conn.; s. Prof. Fred Donald and Gwendolen (Blodgett) C.; m. Barbara Marvin Adams, June 28, 1941 (dec. Aug. 1978); m. 2d Lee Burker McGough, Dec. 28, 1980 (div. Apr. 1987); children (nee McGough): Edward G. b.1952, John D. b.1957, William V. b.1959, Andrew J. b.1960, Dorothy J. b.1962, James J. b.1964; edn: Ph.B., Univ. VT 1938; Sonoma St. Univ. 1968-69, Mendocino Comm. Coll. 1977, Coll. of the Redwoods 1984-85; Career: reporter Burlington Daily News, VT, 1938-39; guide chair opr. Am. Express Co., NY World's Fair, 1939; underwriter Gen. Exchange Ins. Corp., Newark, NJ 1939-40; sales correspondent J.Dixon Crucible Co., Jersey City, NJ 1940-41, asst. ofc. mgr., priorities splst., 1941-42; sales rep., San Francisco 1946-52; field supr. The Travelers Ins. Co., 1952-58; gen. agent Gen. Am. Life Ins. Co., 1958-59; western reg. supr. Provident Life & Accident Ins. Co., 1959-60; brokerage supr. Aetna Life Ins. Co., 1960-61; maintenance cons. J.I. Holcomb Mfg. Co., Mill Valley 1961-68; sales rep. Onox Inc., Mendocino 1965-68; ednl. svs. rep. Marquis Who's Who, Inc., Mill Valley 1963-68; tchr. and coach Mendocino Jr.-Sr. H.S., 1968; real prop. appraiser County of Mendocino, 1968-81; indep. R.E. appraiser 1982-88, ret. 1988; dir: Mendocino Coast Land Devel. Corp. 1991–, exec. v.p. 1995; instr. Coll. of the Redwoods 1985-87; mem. Nat. Retired Tchrs Assn.; awards: scholarship and leadership Kappa Sigma Internat. Frat. 1937-38, Community Sportsman of the Year 1971; mem: Mendocino Co. Employees Assn. (1968-81, dir. 1981), Kappa Sigma Intl. Frat. (life), Univ. Vt. Catamount Club (charter), Univ. Vt. Alumni Assn./S.F. (founding pres. 1964), Rotary Internat. (club pres. 1975-76, dist. gov. area rep. 1977-8, club historian 1989–, Paul Harris Fellow 1979–, Rotarian of the Yrs. 1969-88), Am. Legion (1945–, Post Cdr. 1972-3, Past Comdrs. of Calif. (life), Mendocino Cardinal Boosters (charter, life, pres. 1971), Ret. Ofcrs. Assn. (life), Reserve Ofcrs. Assn. of U.S. (life, chpt. pres. 1954, 56, state v.p. 1958-61), Marines Memorial Assn., Naval Order of U.S. (life), Naval Reserve Assn. (life), Mil. Order World Wars (life), U.S. Naval Inst. (life), Nat. Assn. Uniformed Svs. (life), Navy League of U.S. (Life), Am. Diabetes Assn., Mendocino Art Ctr. (sponsor 1965–), Save the Redwoods League, Mendocino Co. Hist. Soc., Mendocino Hist. Res. Inc. (docent 1982-88), Mendocino Coast Geneal. Soc. (pres. 1991-93), Mendocino Coast Stamp Club (charter, dir. 1983-92, v.p. 1993, 95, pres. 1994); chief editor univ. newspaper, ed. internat. frat. chpt. alumni publ., and ed. Univ. Frosh Handbook (Univ. Vt. 1937-38), ed. Rotary Club Membership Directory 1971–, ed. Univ. Vt. 50th Yr. Class Reunion Handbook 1983-88, Nat. Assn. Fleet Tug Sailors (1990–, v.p. 1991); mil: lt. cdr. USNR, active duty WWII 1942-46, Reserve unit comdg. ofcr. 1967-68, ret. 1968, commendations U.S. Sec. of Navy, 1946, and Comdt. 12th Naval Dist., 1968; Republican; Congregational; rec: genealogy, philately, history, writing, tennis, football, youth work. Res: PO Box 87, 10801 Gurley Ln Mendocino 95460-0087

CARPER, JOHN KIRKENDALL, family physician; b. Nov. 30, 1961, Covina, Calif.; s. Clarence Spahr and Elizabeth Anne (Kirkendall) C.; m. Therese-Marie Hewett, June 13, 1992; edn: BA, Stanford Univ. 1983; MD, Univ. of Calif. San Francisco 1987. Career: resident physician San Pedro Peninsula Hosp., San Pedro 1987-89, UC Davis/Mercy Med. Ctr., Redding 1989-90; physician Salinas Family Practice, Salinas 1991-92; physician, ptnr. Alameda Family Physicians, Alameda 1992–; medical staff mem: Natividad Med. Ctr., Salinas 1990-92, Salinas Valley em. Hosp. 1990-92, Summit Med. Ctr., Oakland 1992–, Alameda Hosp. 1992–; mem: Alameda H.S. Health Ctr. Advy. Bd. 1993–, CMA 1992–, Am. Academy of Family Physicians 1990–,

Alameda Contra Costa Med. Assn., Salinas Jaycees 1990-92; Episcopal; rec: bicycling, hiking, bird watching, sea kayaking, sailing. Ofc: Alameda Family Physicians 2100 Otis Dr Alameda 94501 Tel: 510/521-2300

CARR, THOMAS LEE, public affairs executive, mechanical engineer; b. July 2, 1946, N. Tonawanda, N.Y.; s. Robert Myron and Phyllis (Kinne) C.; m. Virginia Holty, May 30, 1981; edn: BS engring., Hrvey Mudd Coll., 1969; MS, ops. research, USC, 1973; Fuller Theol. Sem., 1977; Reg. Profl. Mech. Engr., Calif. Career: engr. Bechtel Power Corp., Los Angeles 1969-86, Bechtel Div. Public Affairs coordinator, L.A. 1976-86; pres. TLC Ministries, Inc. 1988–; awards: North Am. Ministerial Fellow, Fund for Theol. Edn. 1977, Mainstream Milestones award L.A. Jaycees 1980, Outstanding Young Men of Am. 1981; bd. trustees Harvey Mudd Coll. 1978-82; bd. trustees So. Calif. Multiple Sclerosis Soc. 1979-83, Patient Services Com. 1980-83; mem: Bechtel Employees Club (pres. 1978), Am. Nuclear Soc., Americans for Energy Independence, Harvey Mudd Coll. Alumni Assn. (pres. bd. govs. 1978-79); coauthor with wife Ginny: Waiting Hearts: a story of extraordinary love (Harold Shaw Pubs., 1989); cont-br. numerous articles in newspapers and periodicals, T.V. appearances; Conservative Democrat; Evangelical Christian; rec: swimming. Res: 2749 Quail Ridge Circle Fullerton 92635

CARR-CASANOVA, ROSARIO, psychotherapist/college counselor; b. Nov. 12, 1940, Lima, Peru; d. Domingo Casanova Baca and Blanca Torres de Casanova; edn: AA, Coll. of Marin, 1970; BS, San Francisco State Univ., 1973, MS 1975; PhD, The Wright Inst., Berkeley 1985; MPA, JFK Sch. of Govt. Harvard Univ., 1988; Coro Found. pub. affairs leadership tng. fellow 1977, MALDEF leadership tng. 1981; lic. MFCC 1975; Calif. Comm. Colls. counselor cred. 1977. Career: coordinator Marin County Honor Farm Career Ctr., Coll. of Marin, 1976; marriage, family and child counselor in pvt. practice, San Rafael 1975–, college counselor Skyline Coll. 1977–; founder New Horizons S&L Assn.; apptd. del. rep. State of Calif. to the White House Conf. on Families 1980; awards: AAUW 1978, Marin Co. Womens Agencies leadership award 1981, Marin Co. vol. activist 1981, United Way vol. 1987, women leadership fellow Harvard Univ. 1987-88, Outstanding Comm. Svc. Award YWCA Mission Girls Prog. (1990, 92), Bay Area Urban League Comm. Svc. Award 1994-95; mem: Marin Co. Mental Health Advy. Bd. 1978–, United Way Bay Area (treas. 1986-87), Chicana, Latina Found. (bd. 1988–), Interam. Soc. of Psychologists, Am. Psychol. Assn., Ross Hosp. (Calif. Adv. Bd. 1992–), Am. Heart Assn. (bd. dir Marin Co. 1993–), Marin Co. Policy Acad. 1993–; Democrat. Res: 116 Jefferson Dr Tiburon 94920 Ofc: Skyline College, 3300 College Dr San Bruno 94066

CARRIGAN, JOHN LIONEL, information specialist/library consultant; b. Sept. 9, 1948, Leadville, Colo.; s. Lionel R. and Helen R. (Plake) C.; m. Brenda L. (div. 1987); children: Jeff b. 1969, Patrick b. 1974; edn: BS, Tx. A&M Univ. 1970; MS, Cal Tech Pasadena 1973; MS, CSU Fullerton 1979. Career: res. tech. City of Hope Nat. Med. Center, Duarte 1973-74, asst. librarian 1974-76, chief librarian 1976, dir. of library services 1977-85, info. splst. 1985–; indep. library consultant 1976–; mem: Med. Library Assn., Special Library Assn., Am. Library Assn., Assn. Coll. & Research Libraries, Am. Soc. Info. Sci., N.Y. Acad. Scis., Montclair Little League (past bd. mem.), Am. Red Cross (bd. mem. Inland West chpt.), San Bernardino Co. Mus. Commn. Res: 4811 Orchard Montclair 91763 Ofc: City of Hope National Medical Center 1500 E Duarte Duarte 91010

CARRILLO, GILBERTO, engineer; b. Sept. 22, 1926, San Diego; s. Manuel C. and Francisca (Ruiz) C.; m. Maria de Lourdes Paez, Jan. 21, 1957; children: Gilbert A., Elizabeth, Evelyn, Fernando, Maria De Lourdes; edn: BS (honors), San Diego State Univ., 1951. Career: materials and process engr. Convair Div. Gen. Dynamics, San Diego 1950-56; Douglas Aircraft Co., El Segundo 1956-60; tech. dir. Turco Products Inc., Mexico City 1960-68; mgr. environmental engring. Rohr Industries, Riverside, Calif. 1969-92 (ret.); founder and CEO, Enviro-Safe Systems, Riverside, Calif. 1992–; mem.: Soc. for Advancement of Materials and Process Engring. (gen. chmn. 1st internat. SAMPE symp. & tech. exhib. dedicated to environmental issues 6/91; nat. gen. chmn. internat. symposium & tech. conf. 1988), SAMPE Inland Empire (chpt. chmn. arrangements com. 1972-76, scholarships chmn. 1976-82, gen. chmn. 1982-83, Best Paper award 1983), VFW; patentee, tech. publs. in field; mil: sgt. USAAF 1945-46; Republican; R.Cath. Res: 5535 Montero Dr Riverside 92509 Ofc: Enviro-Safe Systems Riverside

CARRILLO, RICHARD, steel company executive; b. Oct. 29, 1938, Tucson, Ariz.; s. Joseph Gil and Esther (Mendoza) C.; m. Georgia Elinore Armenta, May 7, 1960; children: Veronica Ann b. 1961, Richard Gerard b. 1964; edn: Univ. Ariz. 1961-63, Met. Coll. L.A. 1974. Career: traffic mgr., sales desk mgr. M.S.L. Industries, Los Angeles 1964-65; ops. mgr., adminstrv. mgr. Comstock Steel Co., Tucson, Phoenix, 1960-64, 65-69; adminstrv. mgr. Rio Grande Steel, Phoenix 1969-71; tubular products mgr. Ducommun Metals, Los Angeles 1972-74; sales rep., tubular products mgr. Bernard Epps Co., 1974-83; regional sales mgr. Maruichi American Corp., Santa Fe Springs 1983–; mil: ADR3 USN 1956-59; Democrat; R.Cath.; rec: golf, vintage autos, rare plants. Res: Huntington Beach Ofc: Maruichi American Corp. 11529 S Greenstone Ave Santa Fe Springs 90670

CARROLL, DAVID MCKENZIE, photographic illustrator; b. Aug. 15, 1954, Los Angeles; s. David Warrren and Beverly (Spicer) C.; m. Pamel Elaine Peterson, June 18, 1978; edn: BS marine biology, Calif. Polytech. St. Univ. 1978; BA photog., Brooks Inst. Photography. Career: lab. tech. Calif. Polytech. St. Univ., San Luis Obispo 1975-77; production supr. The Association, Newport Beach 1977-79; photographic cons. Jaffes Camera, Ventura 1979-81; owner The Black & White Lab. of Ventura 1980-83; Carroll Studios 1981-83; The Photique, Pismo Beach 1983-; awards: Gold Coast Profl. Photographers Photographer of Year (1984, 86, 87, 89), Portrait of Year (1985-89, 92-93), Profl. Photographers of Am. Print Exhibition Merit (1987-92), Profl. Photographers of Calif. fellowship (1989); mem: Gold Coast Profl. Photographers (pres. 1986-87, 1987-88, bd. dirs.), Profl. Photographers Calif. (2d. v.p. 1987-88, 1st v.p. 1988-89), Profl. Photographers of Am. (councilman 1983-89, Craftsmen Degree 1991, Master Photog. Degree 1992), Wedding Photographers Internat.; Republican; Christian; rec: scuba diving, marine aquariums. Ofc: The Photique 600 Dolliver St Pismo Beach 93449

CARROLL, JOEL, retired mathematician; b. Apr. 8, 1924, Hallettsville, Tx.; s. Norman and Otealia (Hargrove) C.; m. Anne M. Merriweather, Aug. 20, 1960; children: Joel Anson b. 1961, Bernard Eugene b. 1963, Harlan Patrick b. 1969; edn: BA, Roosevelt Univ., Chgo. 1950; MS, DePaul Univ., Chgo. 1952. Career: analytical statistician, U.S. Railroad Retirement Bd., Chgo. 1952-54; asst. mathematician, Argonne Nat. Lab., Lemont, Ill. 1954-55; computing engr., No. Am. Aviation, Inc., L.A. 1955-58; mathematician, Land-Air, Inc., Point Mugu 1958-61; mathematician, General Precision, Inc., Glendale 1961-63; sr. engr., Northrup Corp., Hawthorne 1963-65; computer scientist, Douglas Aircraft, Santa Monica 1965-66; mathematician, Naval Ocean System Ctr., San Diego 1966-88; awards: Superior Accomplishment, Dept. of Navy 1968; Special Achievement, Naval Ocean System Ctr. 1974; mem: A.C.L.U., Town Hall of Calif., Harry S. Truman Lib. Inst. (hon. fellow), Am. Mathematic Soc., Am. Assn. for Advancement of Sci., N. Y. Academy of Sci., Pi Mu Epsilon; civic: past secr., Kiwanis; S.D. Assoc. United Church of Christ (moderator 1980-81); Congregational Church (past moderator and treasurer); mil: aviation metalsmith 3/c, Navy, 1943-45; Congregationalist. Res: 13307 Olive Grove Poway 92064

CARR-RUFFINO, NORMA J., management consultant, business educator; b. Dec. 15, 1932, Ft. Worth; d. Robert Leroy and Lorene (Dickeson) Carr; m. Alfred Ruffino, Jan. 6, 1979; children: Randy, Brian, Carrie; edn: BA, Tx. Wesleyan Univ. 1968; MBE, Univ. of North Texas 1969; PhD, 1973. Career: v.p. Randys Inc., Ft. Worth 1965-72; vocat. office educator coordinator Ft. Worth Pub. Schs. 1969-72; prof. bus. San Francisco St. Univ. 1973–; referee Calif. St. Bar Ct.; mem: Acad. Mgmt., Internat. Assn. of Business & Society, World Future Soc.; author Theory Reinforcement & Skill Building (2d edit. 1981), Writing Short Bus. Reports, 1980, The Promotable Woman, (1982, rev. 1985, 2d. edit. 1992), The Bus. Students Guide, (1987, 2d. edit. 1991), Building Personal Power, 1990, Managing Cultural Diversity, 1995, ed. Calif. Bus. Edn. Assn. Jour., 1975-76. Ofc: School of Business San Francisco State Univ. 1600 Holloway St San Francisco 94132

CARSON, RICHARD TAYLOR, JR., economics professor; b. Feb. 24, 1955, Jackson, Miss.; s. Richard Taylor and Alice (Goldthwaite) C.; m. Julia W. Carson; edn: BA, Miss. St. Univ. 1977; MAIA, George Washington Univ., 1979; MA, UC Berkeley; PhD, UC Berkeley 1985. Career: prof. econ. UCSD, La Jolla 1985–; co-author: Using Surveys to Value Pub. Goods, 1989. Ofc: Univ. of Calif. San Diego Dept. of Economics La Jolla 92093

CARTER, KENNETH, medical science administrator; b. Feb. 6, 1914, Morecambe, England; s. Herbert and Ethel (Halstead) C.; m. Dorothy Crossley, March 16, 1940; m. 2d. Hylkia van Nouhuys, Oct. 2, 1970; edn: MPS, Manchester Univ. Eng. 1937; MD, London Univ. Eng. 1947; lic. Royal Coll. Physicians 1947. Career: intern Royal Post-Grad. Med. Sch., London 1947-48; corp. secty. Therapeutic Research Corp. Gt. Britain 1946-48; sci. dir. Glaxo Labs., Buenos Aires, 1948-51; dir. devel. med. dir. Smith Kline & French Internat., Phila. 1951-54, London 1954-57; v.p. research and med. affairs Ames Co., Elkhart, Ind. 1957-61; Miles Labs. Inc. 1961-65; v.p. Syntex Internat., Mexico City 1965-71, Syntex Corp., Palo Alto 1971-79; cons., Los Altos Hills 1979–; mem: Pharmaceutical Soc. Gt. Britain (fellow), British Med. Assn., AMA; rec: photog., hiking, wood carving. Address: 246 Olive Tree Ln Los Altos Hills 94024

CARTER, LUCIAN C., college administrator; b. Aug. 27, 1940, Beaumont, Tx.; s. Lucian C. and Ruth (McKenzie) C.; edn: BA in math., BS in Chem., Univ. Tx., Austin 1960, BS in physics 1961; MS physics, Cal Tech, 1968. Career: instr. physics CSU Los Angeles, 1967-75; physics instr. L.A. Trade Tech Coll. 1975-81, dept. chair, sci. and math. 1981-86, asst. dean electronics 1986-88; dean acad. affairs L.A. Southwest Coll. 1988-89; sr. dir. personnel L.A. Comm. Coll. Dist. 1989–; awards: L.A. Trade Tech Coll. innovator of year 1986; mem: Am. Assn. Physics Tchrs. (secty. So. Calif. 1973-91), LACCD Adminstrs. Assn. (pres. 1990-91), Madison Heights Neighborhood Assn. (treas.); Clipper software developer; Democrat; Baptist. Res: 1033 S Euclid Pasadena 91106 Ofc: Los Angeles Community College District 770 Wilshire Blvd Los Angeles 90017

CARTER, MICHAEL RAY, artist, singer and composer, poet and author; b. Dec. 2, 1953, Los Angeles; s. Richard Eugene and Sarah Ann (Carter) C.; edn: Cypress Jr. Coll. Career: freelance artist of Wildlife and Western Art,, 1976–; indep. collector and appraiser memorabilia, oak antiques, Americana, San Diego 1965–; pres. M.R. Carter's American Character Co., San Diego 1988; awards: 2d pl. Fort Verde Days Assn. Inc. 1985, art in permanent collection Roy Rogers-Dale Evans Mus. 1986 and 1994, best of show UNISYS Corp. (1987 and 1990); listed Who's Who in West, 22d and 23d, Who's Who in Am., 46th, Intl. Dir. of Distinguished Leadership, 3d and 4th, Who's Who in World, 10th, Personalities of Am., 5th and 6th, & award for contbn. to preserv. we. music 1990, Who's Who Emerging Leaders in Am., 3d (1990); mem. Gene Autry Western Heritage Mus., L.A. (charter, founding mem. 1988), Buffalo Bill Hist. Ctr., Cody, Wyo. (patron 1985), Buck Jones Western Corral 1, Lompoc (asst. nat. treasure 1989-90), Western Music Assn. Inc. (founding mem. 1988), N.Am. Hunting Club Inc. (charter, founding mem. 1980–), Statue Liberty Ellis Island Found. (patron 1985), Internat. Platform Assn.; served as co-chair pgm., mktg., New Year's Live at Sea World, San Diego, 1991, Christian Celebration Prodns.; rec: collector art of Am. West, actors' autographs & movie memorabilia of Western film (esp. Roy Rogers and Sons of the Pioneers), Am. oak antiques, photog. Address: PO Box 27464 San Diego 92198

CARTER, WARREN G., agriculture and real estate executive; b. Jan. 19, 1937, Delano, Calif.; s. Henry Frank and Catherine M. (Offutt) C.; m. Lenore Jane Wilkinson, Aug. 10, 1957; children: Doug b. 1961, Ken b. 1963, Karen b. 1966; edn: AA, Mt. San Antonio Coll., Pomona, 1958; BA, Univ. of La Verne, 1958, Ph.D., 1985. Career: instr. Bakersfield City Sch. 1958-60; ins. broker Carter & Ritchey, McFarland 1959-74; farming pres., Kern Farming Co. 1965–; real estate chmn. Watson Corp., Bakersfield 1982–; cons. agri-bus., almond industry, real estate 1965–; pres./dir. Kern Farming Co.; mng. ptnr. Oak Co. (R.E. devel.); chmn. bd./dir. Watson Corp., and Watson Devel. Co.; appt. USDA tech. advy. com. on fruit & vegetables for multilateral internat. trade negotiations (appt. by former US Sectys. of Agri. Earl Butz, Robert Bergland, John Block, Dick Lyng and Clayton Yuetter); grower orgn. bds: Sun Giant Growers Services (past pres.), Calif. Almond Growers Council (chmn. bd., dir.), Kern County Farm Bureau (dir.), Kern Co. Water Assn., Almond Bd. of Calif., So. Central Farmers Com., Am./Calif. Soc. Farm Mgrs. and Rural Appraisers, Agricultural Leadership Assocs.; chmn. 1985 Kern County Bus. Outlook Conf.; trustee and v.chmn. exec. com. Univ. La Verne; chmn. bd. trustees McFarland Unified Sch. Dist.; Pres.'s Advy. Coun. Bethany Seminary; agri. advy. bd. Bakersfield Coll.; guest lectr. Bakersfield Coll. and CSU Bakersfield; honors: merit and service awards Kern Co. BSA, merit Kern Co. Cancer Soc., Kern Co. Farm Bureau, Kern Co. FFA, man of year Manufacturer's Life Ins. Co., grand marshall McFarland Christmas Parade (2x), father of year McFarland Elem. Sch. (2x), hon. life mem. and father of year McFarland Future Farmers Am., Outstanding Kern Co. Young Farmer, Outstanding Calif. Young Farmer runner-up, Outstanding Civic Leader of Am., Outstanding Young Men of Am., alumni of year Univ. La Verne (1972); civic bds: Calif. Living Mus. Found. (trustee), CSU Bakersfield Found. (dir.), Commonwealth Club of Calif., Kern Co. Youth For Christ (dir.), McFarland FFA Booster Club (past chmn.), Lions Club; Republican (fin. chmn. Don Rogers Calif. Senate Campaign); Christian; rec: golf, tennis, travel. Ofc: Kern Farming Co. POB 577 McFarland 93250, 2100 H St Bakersfield 93301

CARUSO, JOSEPH MICHAEL, orthodontist/educator; b. Sept. 20, 1946, Los Angeles; s. Thomas Angelo and Letha Mae (Carter) C.; m. Julie Jensen, June 23, 1968; children: Michael b. 1973, Christopher b. 1977; edn: BA biology La Sierra Coll. 1968; DDS, Loma Linda Univ. 1973, MPH 1975, MS orthodontics 1975; Dipl. Am. Bd. of Orthodontics. Career: estab. dental practice in Newhall, 1975–; assoc. with Dr. Ruel W. Bench, Reseda 1976-80; consulting staff Henry Mayo Newhall Memorial Hosp. for TMJ and Orthognathic surg. 1982–; adj. faculty USC, 1976-77; clin. instr. dept. orthodontics Loma Linda Univ. 1977–, dept. orthodontics co-chmn., pgm. dir. 1989–; clin. lectr. profl. seminars in orthodontics, TMJ and practice mgmt. 1979–, lectr. on ceramics, TMJ & orthodontics in U.S., Brazil, Austr., Japan 1988, 89; awards: 3-M Golden Step Award 1988; mem. San Fernando Dental Soc., LLU Orthodontic Alumni Assn. (pres. 1985-6, 86-7); civic: mem. Cleft Palate team Kaiser Hosp. 1978-79, Boys & Girls Club of Santa Clarita Valley 1977, Newhall Rotary (pres. 1982-83, dir. 1978-84), Coll. of the Canyons Found. Bd. 1983, Friends of Hart Park (dir. 1984), YMCA (advy. bd., dir. 1985); research: devel. cold slab at Unitek 1972, cons. design & devel. of Transcend (TM) ceramic bracket for Unitek/3M 1986–, 2+ res. projects annually LLU 1977–; Republican; Seventh-day Adventist; rec: woodcarving, fish, hunt, inventions. Ofc: Joseph M. Caruso, DDS, MS, Corp. 25044-200 Peachland Ave Newhall 91321

CASAÑAS, DOMINGO IVAN, motivational speaker and writer, insurance consultant; b. May 22, 1957, Pinar Del Rio, Cuba, naturalized U.S. cit. 1976; s. Homobono and Josefa (Rodriguez) C.; m. Laura Sanabria, May 2, 1981; children: David b. 1985, Olivia b. 1987, Kristina b. 1989; edn: BSBA, Univ. San Francisco, 1980. Career: walkathon coord. March of Dimes, S.F. 1972-75; sales cons. Moore Business Forms, Pleasant Hill 1980-81; insurance cons. Allstate Ins. Co., Concord 1981–; speaker Western Ins. Information Svs., 1984–; reporter/writer La Nueva Prensa, Concord; honors/awards: U.S.F. Varsity NCAA Div.1 Soccer Team 1976-

80, Gus Donahue award U.S.F. 1980, Am. Legion achiev. award Calaroga Jr. H.S. Hayward 1971, Allstate sales achiev. awards (1981, 84, 85, 86, 93); founder, pres., newsletter editor Success Achievement Club, Pittsburg 1985–; clubs: Toastmasters Intl. (pres. Delta TM Club, Antioch 1990), Am. Intl. Soccer Club (player 1987–), Delta Investment Club 1993–; civic: Salesian Missions (sponsor 1982–), East Contra Costa Little League (vol. 1988–), Delta Youth Soccer (coach, referee 1988–), S.F. Olympic Club Soccer (youth coord. 1976-80), coach summer soccer camps in No. Calif., Neighborhood Watch Pgm. 1985–; mem: Contra Costa Co. Adv. Bd. on Aging 1992-94; Republican; R.Cath.; rec: soccer, motivation tnr., reading, dancing, investing in penny stocks. Res: 1110 Jewett Ave Pittsburg 94565 Ofc: 3135 Clayton Rd Ste 203 Concord 94519

CASCIOLA, STEVEN GEORGE, manufacturing and distribution company executive; b. Mar. 25, 1948, Detroit, Mich.; s. Guy and Josephine (Tarantino) C.; m. Anne Ryan, June 17, 1989; edn: courses in arch., engring., mktg., Ariz. State Univ., 1966–. Career: nat. sales dir. Alexia Alexander, Los Angeles 1991-93; v.p. sales & mktg. Ed Wyse & Co., Seattle, Wash. 1994-95; speaker, lectr. SC. Comms., L.A. 1973–, writer, nat. cons., 1986–; mem: F&A Masons of Calif., Burbank Lodge #406 (worshipful master 1992, Grand Lodge Committeeman, Speakers Panel), Nile Shrine, Seattle 1994–, Pasadena Scottish Rite (orator 1992), Seattle Scottish Rite 1994–, St. John's Lodge #9 (Seattle), Philosophical Research Soc. (vol. 1982–), Internat. Platform Assn. 1992–; publs. in field; Republican; R.Cath.; rec: history, comparative religion, Am.'s Destiny. Res: 909 N Palm Ave #102 West Hollywood 90069

CASE, DOUGLAS NELSON, university student services specialist, fraternities and sororities advisor; b. Dec. 20, 1954, Chgo.; s. Ronald Nelson and Anna Jean (Brown) C.; edn: undergrad. Georgia Tech. 1972-73, Ga. State Univ. 1973-75, BBA (summa cum laude) San Jose State Univ., 1976; grad. bus. adminstrn. San Diego State Univ. 1976-78. Career: univ. student svs. specialist, fraternities and sororities adv., San Diego State Univ., 1978–; mem. bd. dirs. Gay and Lesbian Alliance Against Defamation/S.D. 1993–; mem. San Diego Mayor's Advy. Bd. on Gay and Lesbian Issues, 1992; bd. dirs. Lobby for Individual Freedom and Equality (LIFE) 1987–; bd. dirs. Project Concern Internat., 1972-82, advy. council 1982-94; awards: San Diego City Council spl. commendn. 1990, San Diego Mid-City C.of C. college citizen of yr. 1990, S.D. Democratic Club Doug Scott polit. action award 1990, Decade Club Award ACLU 1992, Assn. of Frat. Advrs. disting. service award 1993, Outstanding Greek Advisor Award, We. Reg. Greek Conf. 1994, Presl. Award for Poli. Action, S.D. Gay/Lesbian Comm. Nicky Awards, listed in Outstanding Young Men of Am. 1981, 86, Who's Who in West 1992-94, Who's Who in Am. Edn. 1994; mem: Assn. of Fraternity Advisors (bd. 1980-90, nat. pres. 1991), Nat. Assn. Student Personnel Adminstrs. 1986–, Am. Coll. Personnel Assn., Kappa Sigma Frat. (scholarship com. 1987–), Coll. Area Comm. Coun. San Diego (exec. bd. 1980-90, 1994–, pres. 1989-90), San Diego Dem. Club (pres. 1991-92), ACLU (bd. San Diego affil. 1978-92), Calif. State Dem. Central Com. 1991–, Uptown Dem. Club (pres. 1993); Democrat (del. Dem. Nat. Conv. 1992, San Diego County Cent. Com. parliamentarian 1987–, chair, 76th Assembly Dist. Dem. Com. 1993–); avocation: political activism. Res: 5444 Reservoir Dr #D-20 San Diego 92120 Ofc: Housing & Residential Life San Diego State Univ 5500 Campanile Dr San Diego 92182

CASEY, JOHN MICHAEL, orthopedic surgeon; b. June 23, 1940, St. Louis, Mo.; s. John Charles and Hildagarde Mary (Temmeyer) C.; m. Carolynne Cay Chapman, June 12, 1965; children: Timothy M. b. 1966, Bridget K. b. 1968, Kevin M. b. 1969, Anne C. b. 1971; edn: BS, St. Louis Univ. 1961; MD, Univ. Mo. Columbia 1965; cert. Am. Bd. Orthopedic Surgery 1974. Career: served to CDR, USN, 1964-75: intern Oakland 1965-66, student flight surgeon Pensacola 1966-67, flight surgeon Virginia Beach 1967-69, resident orthopedic surgeon San Diego 1969-73, staff orthopedic surgeon Portsmouth, Va. 1973-75; pvt. med. practice orthopedic surgery, San Diego 1975–; cons. Naval Hosp., San Diego 1976–; asst. clin. prof. surgery UC San Diego 1978–; staff Children's Hosp. San Diego, chief staff 1990-91; fellow Am. Acad. Orthopedic Surgeons; mem: ACOS, Western Orthopedic Assn., Irish Am. Orthopaedic Assocs; club: Stardust CC; mil: Capt. M/C. USNR 1976-92 (ret.); Catholic; rec: golf, jogging. Ofc: 8901 Activity Road San Diego 92126

CASILLAS, MARK, lawyer; b. July 8, 1953, Santa Monica; s. Rudolph and Elvia C.; m. Natalia Settembrini, June 2, 1984; edn: BA in hist., Loyola Univ., L.A. 1976; JD, Harvard Law Sch., 1979. Career: clk. to Chief Judge Seth, U.S. Ct. of Appeals, Santa Fe, N.M. 1979-80; atty., assoc. Breed, Abbott & Morgan, NY, NY 1980-82; counsel Bank of America NT & SA, San Francisco 1982-84; assoc. Lillick & Charles, S.F. 1984-87, ptnr. 1988–; counsel Internat. Bankers Assn. in Calif., 1984-89; honors: mng. editor Harvard C.R.-C.L. Law Rev. (1978-79); mem: Am. Bar Assn. (appt. Airfinance Subcom. 1991–), N.Y. Bar, Calif. Bar (v. chmn. Fin. Instns. Com. 1987-88), Internat. Bar Assn., Bankers Club of S.F., Japan Soc.; Democrat; rec: ski, opera, travel. Ofc: Lillick & Charles, Two Embarcadero Center Ste 2600 San Francisco 94111

CASSEL, RUSSELL N(APOLEON), research psychologist; b. Dec. 18, 1911, Harrisburg, Pa.; s. Herman Irwin and Sallie Agnes (Hummer) C.; m. Lan Mieu Dam-Cassel, Oct. 5, 1965; children: Louis b. 1939, Angelica b. 1942, Gary b.

1953, Lynn and Gail b. 1955, Sallie b. 1965, Susie b. 1967; edn: pre-law, Penn. State. Univ. 1932; BS, edn., Millersville St. Univ. 1937; MEd., Penn. St. Univ. 1939; EdD, Univ. of So. Calif., L.A. 1949; grad. Army Personnel Cons. Sch., Air War Coll.; dipl. Am. Bd. Profl. Psychology 1968, dipl. Biofeedback Soc. 1970–. Career: rural sch. tchr., No. Annville, Pa. 1935-38; sch. psychologist, Dauphin, Pa. 1939-40; personnel cons. U.S. Army, Calif./Pacific 1940-46;psychologist pvt. practice, Cassel Clinic, Fontana, Calif. 1946-48; asst. prof. San Diego St. Univ. 1949-51; res. psychologist U.S. Air Force, Calif./Tx. 1951-57; psychologist Phoenix H.S., Phoenix, Ariz. 1957-59; dir. pupil pers. schools Lompoc Unified Sch. Dist., Calif. 1959-61; res. psychologist Dept. of State in Vietnam and Liberia 1961-66; prof. ednl. psychol. Univ. of Wis., Milwaukee, Wis. 1967-74; ed. and pub. Project Innovation, Chula Vista, Calif. 1974–; cons. in chem. dependency rehab.; past ed/pub. 3 nat. jours.; awards: num. military awards 1940-70, civilian awards and merit plaques 1944-93, Co-Patriot award Sons of Am. Rev., San Diego 1994; mem. Correctional Psychol. Assn. (v.p. 1954-55, pres. 1955-56), fellow Am. Psychol. Assn. 1949–, fellow Rorschach Inst. 1952–, fellow Humanistic Soc. 1992–;mem.: Chula Vista Masonic Lodge (chair, drug abuse), Scottish Rite, Shrine, Constitution Renewal, S.D. 1987–; author: 8 books including The School Dropout Odyssey, 1950-93, 400+ articles pub. in profl. jours., over 24 psychol. tests by 6 test publs., num. computer programs for use in health care by several pubs.; mil: served to col. USAF 1940-70; Republican; Lutheran; rec: airplane pilot, tennis, bridge. Res: 1362 Santa Cruz Ct Chula Vista 91910 Ofc: Project Innovation Chula Vista 91910

CASSIDY, JOHN JOSEPH, retired engineering executive; b. June 21, 1930, Gebo, Wyo.; s. Valentine Patrick and Elizabeth Johannah (Johnson) C.; m. Alice Willman, March 15, 1953; children: Val Patrick b. 1956, Jon Allan b. 1957, Debra Kay b. 1962; edn: BSCE, Mont. St. Univ. 1952; MSCE, 1960; PhD, Univ. Iowa 1964; reg. profl. engr. Calif. 1975, Montana 1959, Idaho 1988, Washington 1979, Wyoming 1995, Nebraska 1995. Career: design engr. Mont. Water Conservation Bd., Helena 1955-58; instr. Mont. St. Univ., Bozeman 1958-60; res. asst. Univ. Iowa 1960-63; asst. prof. civil engring. faculty Univ. Mo., Columbia 1963-66, assoc. prof. 1966-68, prof. 1968-74, dept. chmn. 1972-74; asst. chief hydraulic engr. Bechtel Inc., S.F. 1974-76, chief hydrologic engr. 1976-79, 1981-85; dir. Wash. St. Water Resources Res. Ctr., Pullman 1979-81; mgr. engring. hydraulics/hydrol. Bechtel Corp., S.F. 1985-94, mgr. geotech. and hydraulic engring svs. 1994-95, (ret.); hydraulic cons. Morrison Knutsen Co. 1980; spl. cons. New Eng. Power Co. 1985-86, World Bank 1990-91; mem. Nat. Research Council Com. on Global Climate Change 1991-94; mem. advy. com. civil engring. Calif. Polytech. St. Univ., San Luis Obispo 1986–; awards: elected to U.S. Nat. Acad. of Engring. 1994, elected hon. mem. Am. Soc. Civil Engrs. 1994, Bechtel fellow 1985, Ford Found. fellow 1968-69, Hydraulics Div. (chmn.), Am. Soc. Civil Engrs. (exec. com. 1980-81); Am. Soc. Civil Engrs. (fellow), Am. Geophysical Union, Am. Water Resources Assn., US Com. on Large Dams (bd. dirs. 1989-95), Internat. Assn. for Hydraulic Res. (chmn. Com. on Hydraulics for Dams, Internat. Commn. on Large Dams 1987–); civic: Walnut Creek United Meth. Ch.; publ. 50+ tech. papers on hydraulic engring. and hydrol., coauthor textbook on hydrol., textbook on hydraulic engring., book on hydropower engring.; mil: cpl. AUS 1953-55; Republican; Methodist; rec: woodworking. Res: 4400 Capitol Ct Concord 94518

CASTAGNA, JOSEPH VINCENT, JR., business executive, consultant, investor; b. Dec. 4, 1931, Baltimore, Md.; s. Joseph Vincent and Margaret (Bosson) C.; m. Chalya Regas, June 2, 1956; edn: undergrad. John Hopkins Univ. 1950-51; BA, USC, 1953; Exec. Pgm. Grad. Sch. of Mgmt., UC Los Angeles 1972-73; desig: GRI, Grad. Realtors Inst. 1970, CRB, Cert. R.E. Brokerage Exec. 1972, CRS, Cert. R.E. Mktg. Splst. 1979. Career: insurance broker Alexander & Alexander Inc., Los Angeles 1956-61; sales mgr. Vincent Realty, 1961-63; sales mgr. Mt. Olympus 1963-65; gen. mgr. Vincent Realty 1965-66; bd. chmn. Castagna, a Calif. Corp.; pres. Castagna Realty, 1966–, pres. Castagna Insurance 1971-76, pres. Castagna Yachts 1984–, bd. chmn. Escrow Center, Inc.; dir: Lincoln Title Co., Pacifica Encinitas, Ponto Corp.; mem: Nat. Assn. Realtors, Calif. Assn. Realtors (dir. 1975-80), Los Angeles Board Realtors (dir. 1975-80), Rec. Boaters of Calif. (dir. 1993–); clubs: Calif. Yacht, Fourth of July Yacht, Pacific Coast Yachting Assn. (dir. 1980–, Commodore 1989), North Am. Cruiser Assn. (dir. 1980-83) U.S. Coast Guard Aux. 1974–, Santa Monica Bay Power Fleet (Commodore 1978), So. Calif. Cruiser Assn. (Commodore 1981), SAR Internat. Order of Blue Gavel, Beta Beta Pi; awards: So. Calif. Cruiser Racing Champion 1975, Santa Monica Bay Power Fleet Champion 1979, Nat. Cruiser Racing Co-champion 1981; Republican; R.Cath.; rec: boat racing & cruising, travel, bus. consulting. Ofc: Castagna 5701 Hollywood Blvd Los Angeles 90028

CASTOR, WILBUR WRIGHT, consultant, lecturer; b. Feb. 3, 1932, Harrison Township, Pa.; s. Wilbur W. and Margaret (Grubbs) C.; m. Donna Ruth Schwartz, Feb. 9, 1963; children: Amy, Julia, Marnie; edn: BA, St. Vincent Coll., 1959; PhD, Calif Univ. Advanced Studies, 1986–. Career: sales rep. IBM, Pittsburgh and Cleveland, 1959-62; v.p. data processing ops. Honeywell, Waltham, Mass. 1962-80; pres./c.e.o. Aviation Simulation Tech., Lexington, Mass. 1980-82; senior v.p. Xerox Corp., El Segundo, Calif. 1982-89; pres. bd. dirs. Internat. Acad., mem. bd. trustees Information Inst., Santa Barbara; mem.

World Future Soc.; clubs: Caballeros (Rolling Hills), Tennis, U.S. Senators; author: (play) Un Certaine Soirire 1958, (musical comedy) Breaking Up 1960; contbr. articles to profl. jours.; mil: capt. USN 1953-58; Republican; rec: flying, scuba, music, writing. Res: 19 Georgeff Rd Rolling Hills 90274

CASTRICONE, BENJAMIN LOUIS, sales executive; b. Apr. 26, 1946, Roseburg, Oreg.; s. Benjamin Louis and Marie (Petersen) C.; m. Kimmerly Sue Haddy, May 19, 1983; children: Benjamin L., III, Matthew James and Gabrille Lynn; edn: BSEE, Oreg. Inst. Tech., 1972; MBA, Univ. of Santa Clara 1974; PhD, UC Berkeley 1993. Career: reg. sales mgr. Microtest, Sunnyvale, 1975-80; owner Focus Data, Mountain View 1980-85; v.p. sales Graphic Strategies, 1985-86; sales mgr. West Coast Data, Milpitas 1986-; pres./CEO, Uniforce Sales & Engring. 1986-; mem: IEEE, AFCEA, AOC, ERA, Am. Legion, DAV, San Leandro Y.C.; author: Maya Magic, 1988; mil: USN 1964-72; Republican; Cath.; rec: archaeology, sailing, writing. Ofc: 536A Valley Way Milpitas 95035

CASTRO, DONALD STEVEN, university professor and administrator; b. June 27, 1940, Bakersfield; s. Emilio and Lilia (Meyers) Castro-Galvez; m. Connie Lee Picella, June 12, 1970; children: Antonia Carolina b. 1978, Daniela Emilia b. 1982; edn: BA, UCLA 1962; MA, 1964; PhD, 1970. Career: asst. prof., assoc. prof., prof. of history Calif. St. Polytech. Univ., Pomona 1967-93, chmn. Chicano St. Dept. 1970-72; dean, Sch. of Humanities and Social Scis., CSU Fullerton 1993-, prof. of history 1993-; assoc. dir. internat. studies CSU Chancellors Office, Long Beach 1972-78; dean of undergrad. studies Calif. St. Polytech. Univ., Pomona 1980-81, univ. dean 1981-87; assoc. v.p. CSU Northridge 1987-88; cons. CSU campuses 1980-; honors: Phi Gamma Mu, Phi Alpha Theta, Phi Beta Delta, Gold Key, Fulbrights scholar 1965-67, UCLA Regents scholar 1962-64; mem: Pacific Coast Council on Latin Am. Studies (exec. bd. 1978-, bd. govs., secty.; recipient Herbert Herring Award for Excellence in Res., 1995), Latin Am. Studies Assn., Modern Language Assn., Social Sci. Assn., Claremont City (commr. 1980-86), Claremont Dist. Advy. Com. to Sch. Dist.; author: several books, contbr. 25+ articles to profl. jours., 1978-, book chpts. pub. internationally; rec: gardening. Res: 293 E Carver Dr Claremont 91711 Ofc: School of Humanities and Social Sciences CSU Fullerton 92634

CASTRO, JOSEPH R., physician, professor of radiation oncology emeritus; b. Apr. 9, 1934; s. Cosimo Castro, MD and Agnes (Lenhart) C.; m. Barbara A. Kauth, Oct. 10, 1957; children: Joseph b. 1958, Margaret b. 1959, Anne b. 1960, Eileen b. 1962, Michael b. 1963, Kathleen b. 1964; edn: BS, Loyola Univ., Chgo., Ill. 1956; MD, Stritch Sch. of Medicine, Chgo. 1958; intern Memorial Hosp., Rockford, Ill. 1958-59; resident, radiology U.S. Naval Hosp., San Diego 1960-63. Career: head radiotherapy sect. US Naval Hosp., Oakland, Calif. 1964-66; PHS sr. clin. trainee, Univ. of Tx. M.D. Anderson Hosp. & Tumor Inst. 1966-67, asst. & assoc. prof. radiotherapy; assoc. mem. res. staff 1967-71; assoc. clin prof. and clin. prof. radiology Sch. of Medicine UC San Francisco 1972-75; prof. of radiology UCSF 1975-78, prof. of radiation oncology in residence 1978-94, dir. UC Lawrence Berkeley Lab. heavy charged particle clin. res. trial 1975-94, vice-chmn. dept. radiation oncology 1980-94, res. assoc. Cancer Res. Inst. 1972-94; chief, dept. radiation oncology Mt. Zion Hosp. & Med. Ctr. 1972-81; bd. of trustees N. Calif. Cancer Ctr. 1976-92, pres. & chmn. bd. trustees 1980-83; mem. Nat. Cancer Inst. (cancer fellowship review com. 1977-80, clin. prog. project review com. 1981-85; pres. Gilbert H. Fletcher Soc. 1987-88; faculty sr. physician UC Lawrence Berkeley Lab. 1990-94; prof. dept. of surgery UC Davis Med. Ctr. 1991-94; exec. dir. radiation oncology UC Davis Cancer Ctr. 1992-94; prof. of radiation oncology emeritus UCSF 1994–; honors: Honors Program Loyola Univ. 1951-54, hon. mem. Rocky Mt. Radiological Soc. 1970, Excellence in Tchg. award Mt. Zion Hosp. & Med. Ctr. 1972, Special award Univ. of Tokyo Faculty of Medicine 1982, fellow Am. Coll. of Radiology 1983, Silver Pin Club Award Am. Soc. for Therapeutic Radiology & Oncology 1991, Vis. Scientist award Nat. Inst. of Radiological Sci., Japan 1992, hon. mem. European Soc. Therapeutic Radiology & Oncology 1993; author: 89 original articles in field, 63 abstracts, 63 proceedings and chapters, 1977–. Ofc: University of California San Francisco 94143

CATE, BENJAMIN WILSON, journalist; b. Sept. 28, 1931, Paris, France; s. Karl Springer and Josephine (Wilson) C.; div.; children: Christopher b. 1965, Stephanie b. 1968; edn: BA, Yale Univ., 1955. Career: staff TIME Mag., 1965-87: Houston Bureau chief 1965-68, corresp. Paris, Fr. 1968-69, Bureau chief Bonn, W. Ger. 1969-72, dep. chief of corresp. NY, NY 1972-75, Midwest Bureau chief Chgo. 1975-81, West Coast Bureau chief Los Angeles 1981-85, special asst. to pub. 1985-87; political editor KCRW-Radio, Los Angeles 1987-88; mem. Sigma Delta Phi; mil: sgt. AUS 1955-57; rec: sailing, photog., skiing, tennis. Res: 10583 Dunleer Dr Los Angeles 90064

CATRAMBONE, EUGENE DOMINIC, public relations consultant; b. June 5, 1926, Chgo.; s. Nicola and Maria Theresa (Catrambone) C.; m. Mary Gloria Gaimari, Mar. 26, 1951; children: Mary, Eugene Jr., Jane, David, Jill; edn: BA, St. Benedict Coll., 1950; postgrad., Kansas State Univ., 1952-54; MA, DePaul Univ., 1960; postgrad. UCLA 1962-63; cert. secondary tchr., coll. instr.,Calif. Career: tchr. high schs. Chgo. 1950-62, Los Angeles 1963-88; public relations cons., Westlake Village, Calif. 1986-; tech. writer Univ. Chgo. 1956-59,

Douglas Missile div. USN, L.A. and Ventura, 1962-75; reporter, editor Las Virgenes Enterprise, Calabasas 1968-75; evening instr. L.A. City Coll. 1965-68; awards: Fostering Excellence award L.A. Unified Sch. Dist. 1986-87, nominee Apple award 1986; mem. NEA (life), Calif. Tchrs. Assn., United Tchrs. L.A., Book Publicists So. Calif., Am. Legion, Westlake Village Men's Golf Club (public rels. editor 1986–, dir., pres. 1989–); author: Requiem for a Nobody, 1993, The Golden Touch: Frankie Carle, 1981; poem "Exit dust", 1982; contbr. articles on edn. to profl. pubs., 1959-60, feature stories to local newspapers, 1968-75; mil: sgt. US Army 1944-46; Democrat; R.Cath.; rec: coins, World War II history, golf, poetry. Res: 31802 Tynebourne Ct Westlake Village 91361 Ofc: Golden Touch Associates 31802 Tynebourne Ct Westlake Village 91361-4132

CATTOLICA, STEPHEN JOHN, health care sales executive, former national swimming coach; b. Dec. 2, 1951, Berkeley; s. Joseph Louis and Anne Ellicott (Davis) C.; m. Joan Elmer, June 15, 1975; children: Sara b. 1982, Erin b. 1985, Katie b. 1986, Emily b. 1988, Molly b. 1990, Daniel b. 1993; edn: BS, UC Berkeley, 1974; secondary tchg. cred. St. Mary's Coll., Moraga 1975. Career: hd. asst. swim coach Pleasant Hill Swim Club, Pleasant Hill, Ca. 1974-79; hd. swim coach Mesa Aquatics Club, Mesa, Ariz. 1979-81; Dad's Club YMCA, Houston 1981-82; coach U.S. Nat. Swimming, Colorado Springs 1983, mem. bd. dirs. 1982-83; account exec. Dean Witter & Co., Santa Ana 1983-85; Redhill Medical, Santa Ana 1986-88; v.p. sales Beech Street Inc., Irvine 1989-90; v.p. bus. development P.H.S. Management Group, 1990-94; dir. of svs. and product devel. Foothil Industrial Med. Ctr. 1995–; academic recruiter UC Berkeley 1986, 87; lectr. World Swim Coaches Clinic, Seattle 1979; lectr. Univ. Miami, Fla. 1989; lectr. Calif. Soc. of Indsl. Medicine & Surgery, and Calif. Workers' Compensation Inst.; awards: alumni scholar UCB Alumni Assn. 1969-70, excellence Am. Swim Coaches Assn., Ft. Lauderdale (1980, 81, 82, 83); mem. UC Berkeley Alumni Assn. (life 1974–), Med. Mgmt. Assn.; Republican (YR); Lutheran; rec: woodworking, running, biking. Res: 25192 Northrup Dr Laguna Hills 92653

CAUDRON, JOHN ARMAND, forensic engineer, expert witness, b. Sept. 26, 1944, Compton; s. Armand Robert and Evelyn Emma (Hoyt) C.; m. Marilyn Fairfield, Mar. 16, 1968; children: Melita b. 1973, Rochelle b. 1976; edn: AA, Ventura Coll. 1965; BA, CSU Fullerton 1967; civil engring. Univ. Nevada, Reno 1975-78; MSS, USC 1980; cert. instr. in rifle, pistol, and shotgun. Career: mgr. Snyder Research Labs-Reno, Reno, Nev. 1976-78; v.p. Snyder Research Labs, Inc. Pico Rivera, Calif. 1978-83, pres. El Monte 1983-85; tech. evaluation cons./ pres. Fire & Accident Reconstruction, Rowland Hgts 1985–; mem: Firearms Research & Identification Assn. (pres.), Nat. Soc. of Profl. Engrs., Nat. Assn. of Profl. Accident Reconstrn. Specialists, ASCE, Am. Soc. Safety Engrs., Am. Soc. Metals, Nat. Fire Protection Assn.; civic: Boy Scouts Am. (counselor), Fort Tejon Hist. Assn.; publish newsletter re: tech. aspects of accidents - product failure, property damage, personal injury; mil: US Army, Inf. fire team ldr. Vietnam, then M.I. (S-2) aerial observer Tactical Op. Ctr., decorated Army Air Medal, Army Commendn., Cross of Gal., Combat Inf. Badge (1969); Republican; Christian; rec: mil. hist., firearms, photog., exploring. Ofc: 17524 Colima Rd Ste 360 Rowland Heights 91748

CAUGHLIN, STEPHENIE JANE, organic farmer; b. July 23, 1948, McAllen, Tex.; d. James Daniel and Betty Jane (Warnock) Caughlin; edn: BA in family econs., San Diego St. Univ., 1972, MEd, 1973; MS psychology, U.S. Internat. Univ., 1979; Calif. tchg. cred., secondary life. Career: prop. Minute Maid Service, San Diego 1970-75; prin. Rainbow Fin. Services, 1975-78; tchr. S.D. Unified Sch. Dist., 1973-80; mortgage broker Santa Fe Mortgage Co., S.D. 1980-81; commodity broker Premex Commodities, 1981-84; owner/gen. mgr. Seabreeze Organic Farm 1984–; owner/pres. Nationwide Futures Corp. 1984-88, owner/secty. Nationwide Metals Corp., owner/dir. Nationwide Broker's Resources 1987-88; civic: Arroyo Sorrento Assn., Del Mar (secty. 1978–), Greenpeace, Nature Conservancy, Sierra Club, DAR, Jobs Daus.; Republican; rec: equestrienne, dancing. Res: 3909 Arroyo Sorrento Rd San Diego 92130

CAVANNA, CESAR EDMUND, cryogenic engineer; b. Dec. 1, 1932, Modesto; s. Cesar and Emilia (Luchessa) C.; m. Arleen Louise (Lucchesi) C., Oct. 6, 1962; children: Cynthia b. 1963, Catherine b. 1966, Christina b. 1967, Cheryl b. 1969, Colette b. 1972; edn: AA Modesto Jr. Coll. 1953; BSME Univ. Calif. Berkeley 1956; lic. profl. mechanical engr. Calif. 1977, reg. assoc. engr. Canada 1978. Career: Lox Equipment Co., Livermore, project engr. 1960-69, chief engr. 1969-77, v.p. engring. 1977-86, exec. v.p. 1986-87; cons. engr. Boster Kobayashi Assoc. 1987-93; owner Cesar Cavanna Cons. Engr., Livermore 1993–; subcom. chmn. Compressed Gas Assn., N.Y.C. 1977-86; mem. Internat. Oxygen Mfg., Chgo. 1975-86; chmn. Cryogenic Soc. of Am. 1973; mem: Soc. Automotive Engrs., ASME, Soc. of Forensic Engrs. and Scientists, St. Michaels Parish Council (fin. chmn. 1981-85); mil: comdr. USNR 1956-78; Republican; R. Cath.; rec: photog., classic automobiles. Res: 529 Tyler Livermore 94550 Ofc: Cesar Cavanna Consulting Engineer 1336 Concannon Blvd Bldg J Livermore 94550

CAVE, G. TRENT, environmentalist; b. May 13, 1950, San Francisco; s. William G. and Donna Grace (Gunthrope) C.; m. Loralin L. Bracco, March 31, 1973; children: Zachary b. 1977, Sam b. 1985; edn: BS, San Jose St. Univ.

1973; reg. environ. health splst. St. Dept. Pub. Health 1973. Career: sanitarian Napa Co. Dept. of Pub. Health, Napa 1973-80, dir. of environ. health 1980-84; dir. Napa Co. Dept. of Environ. Mgmt. 1984–; mgr. South Napa Waste Mgmt. Authority 1993–; bd. dirs. Calif. Conf. of Dir. of Environ. Health, Auburn 1987-89, chmn. food com. 1986-89; bd. dirs. Calif. Environ. Health Assn., Sacto. 1976-78; pres. Justin Siena Sports Assn. Inc. 1994-95; mem: Napa Sunrise Rotary, Napa Valley Co. Club, No. Calif. Golf Assn., Calif. Environ. Health Assn., Native Sons of Golden West; rec: golf, hiking, softball. Ofc: Napa County Environmental Management 1195 3rd St Ste 101 Napa 94559

CEDOLINE, ANTHONY JOHN, psychologist, real estate developer, winery executive; b. Sept. 19, 1942, Rochester, N.Y.; s. Peter Ross and Mary Jane (Anthony) C.; m. Clare DeRose, Aug. 16, 1964; children: Maria b. 1967, Antonia b. 1971, Peter b. 1976; edn: BA, San Jose State Univ., 1965, MS, 1968, PhD, Columbia Pacific Univ., 1983; Calif. lic. ednl. psychologist; sch. psychologist, sch. administr. credentials; lic. marriage, fam. child counselor (MFCC); lic. real estate broker 1984. Career: counselor Oak Grove Sch. Dist., San Jose 1968; intern 1968, staff sch. psychologist 1969-72, coord. psychol. services 1972-76, asst. dir. pupil svs. 1977-81, dir. pupil services 1981-85; assessment cons. Newark and Campbell Union Sch. Dists., special edn. cons. Modoc County Schs., special programs auditor Calif. State Dept. of Edn., stress/distress cons. Morgan Hill Unified Sch. Dist.; educational psychologist pvt. practice, ptnr. Cypress Center, 1978-84; co-director Biofeedback Inst. of Santa Clara Co., 1976-85; current pvt. practice with wife, Educational Associates, 1985–; ptnr. DeRose-Cedoline-DeRose (shopping centers); owner/pres. Sound Investments; mng. ptnr. Cardillo Properties, 1984–; owner/ptnr. Cienega Valley Winery (formerly Almaden Vineyards, now renamed) Hollister 1988–, a Nat. Landmark, begun in 1851 as Vache Winery, now with 358 acres of vineyard and covered wine cellar of over 4 acres, largest in we. world according to Guiness Book of Records; jt. venture developer under contract Santa Clara County Housing Auth. to build Sr. Citizen Complex, 1988–; instr. La Verne Coll. ext. courses, guest speaker on ednl. psych., SJSU; frequent lectr. various profl. groups statewide; co-founder, bd. dirs. Lyceum of Santa Clara County (serving gifted students) 1971–; honors: Tau Delta Phi (1963-68), special recogn. Almaden Pre-School, Lyceum of Santa Clara County 1976, Optimist Club, outstanding tchr. in field of Exceptional Edn. 1975, listed Who's Who in the World, Who's Who in the West; mem: Santa Clara County Assn. Sch. Psychologists (bd.), NEA, Calif. Tchrs. Assn., Nat., Calif. Assn. Sch. Psychologists, Council for Exceptional Children, Calif. Assn. for the Gifted, Assn. Calif. Sch. Adminstrs., Calif. Personnel & Guidance Assn., Biofeedback Soc. Am., The Wine Inst.; sustaining mem. San Jose Hist. Soc. and the Children's Museum; author: Parent's Guide to School Readiness 1971, The Effect of Affect 1975, Occupational Distress and Job Burnout 1982; contbr. articles local newspapers; Republican; R.Cath.; rec: antique cars, antiques, coins, fishing. Res: 1183 Nikulina Ct San Jose 95120

CEPPOS, JEROME MERLE, journalist; b. Oct. 14, 1946, Wash. DC; s. Harry and Florence (Epstein) C.; m. Karen E. Feingold, Mar. 7, 1982; children: Matthew b. 1989, Robin b. 1991; edn: BS in journ., Univ. Md., 1969. Career: asst. city ed., exec. news ed., asst. mng. editor The Miami Herald, Miami, Fla. 1972-81;exec. editor., mng. edit., assoc. edit. San Jose Mercury News, San Jose, Calif. 1981–; advy. bd. Knight Center for Specialized Reporting, Univ. of Md., College Park 1988–; mem: AP Managing Editors (bd. 1989–, com. chair 1987–), AP News Execs. Council (bd. 1985–), Am. Soc. Newspaper Editors, Calif. Soc. Newspaper Editors (pres. 1993-95). Ofc: San Jose Mercury News, 750 Ridder Park Dr San Jose 95190

CERETTO, WILLIAM J., physician-cardiologist; b. Sept. 19, 1947, Rock Springs, Wyo.; s. Alvin M. and Bobbie Dees (Clayton) C.; m. Marietta Bonello, June 10, 1978 (div. 1992); children: Mario Dante, b. 1982, Gian Marco, b. 1979; edn: BS, Univ. of Wyo. 1969; MD, Univ. of Colo. 1973. Career: med. intern, resident internal med., US Naval Hosp., San Diego 1973-76, fellowship in cardiology 1976-78, staff cardiologist and dir. Coronary Care Unit 1978-80; staff cardiologist Alvarado Hosp. Med. Ctr., San Diego, dir. Non-invasive Cardiology 1980–; asst. clin. prof. UC San Diego Dept. of Med. 1980–; Fellow Am. Coll. Cardiology, Fellow Am. Coll. Chest Physicians, Fellow Council of Clin. Cardiol./Am. Heart Assn., Fellow American Coll. Physicians, mem. San Diego County Med. Soc., S.D. Co. Heart Assn. (bd. dirs. spkrs com.); mem. Am., San Diego Soc. of Echocardiography; bd. dirs. The Cardiovascular Technology Found. of Grossmont Coll.; publs: arts. in med. journals; mil: lcdr. USNR 1973-80; Republican; R. Cath.; rec: skiing, jogging, windsurfing, pro football & baseball. Ofc: Alvarado Hospital Medical Center 6655 Alvarado Rd San Diego 92120

CHABRA, DEEPAK DEV RAJ, urologic surgeon; b. Sept. 23, 1951, Nairobi, Kenya (nat. 1985); s. Dev Raj and Savitri Devi (Arya) C.; m. Debra Jean Kahn, Dec. 26, 1980; children: Aman b. 1983, Nikhil b. 1987; edn: Int. SC., Elphinstone, Bombay, India 1969; M.B., BS, G.S. Medical, Bombay, India 1975; lic. MD, Calif.. Career: attending urologist Kaiser-Permanente, Sacramento 1983–; assoc. clinical prof. UC Davis Medical Ctr., Sacramento 1986–; mem: AMA 1988–, AUA 1986–, Sacto. El Dorado Med. Soc. 1988–; Republican; L.D.S.; rec: tennis, running, reading. Res: 4921 Puma Way Carmichael 95608 Ofc: 2345 Fair Oaks Blvd Sacramento 95864 Tel: 916/978-1377

CHAFKIN, RITA MELNICK, physician, dermatologist; b. April 11, 1929, Brooklyn, N.Y.; d. Joseph and Dora (Winslow) Melnick; m. Samuel Chafkin, June 29, 1952; children: Elise Ceil b. 1955, Marc David b. 1957; edn: BA cum laude, N.Y. Univ. 1949; MD, 1953; cert. Am. Bd. Dermatology (1959). Career: intern internal medicine St. Univ. N.Y. Kings City Hosp., Bklyn. 1953-54; dermatology resident Bellevue Hosp., N.Y.C. 1954-55; fellow in dermatology N.Y. Univ. Med.Sch. 1955-56, preceptee 1956-57; pvt. practice dermatology, Modesto 1958-94 (retired); asst. clin. prof. UC Davis, Modesto 1958–; cons. Scenic Gen. Hosp. 1958–, pres. of staff 1965-66, 1975-76; honors: Phi Beta Kappa, UC Davis Tchr. of Year; mem: Stanislaus Co. Med. Soc. (pres. 1983-84), CMA (del. 1984-93), AMA, Pacific Dermatology Assn., San Francisco Dermatology Soc., Am. Acad. Dermatology, Scenic Gen. Hosp. Found. (pres. 1988-89), Zonta Internat.; recreation mem. 1963-65); num. pencil sketches and oil paintings. Address: Modesto 92350

CHAIT, ARTHUR L., management consultant; b. March 20, 1947, Philadelphia, Pa.; m. Susan Smith; children: Stephen, Audrey; edn: BS, Rutgers Univ. 1969; MBA, Univ. Pittsburgh 1974. Career: research dir. Dresser Industries, Pittsburgh, Pa. 1969-80; program dir. Booz Allen & Hamilton, N.Y.C. 1980-82; pres. bus. cons. div. PA Cons., Princton, N.J. 1982-88; senior v.p. Business & Policy Group, formerly dir. tech. mgmt. and strategic practice, SRI Internat., Menlo Park 1988–; mem: Planning Forum, Am. Ceramic Soc., Tech. Transfer Soc. Ofc: SRI Intl. 333 Ravenswood Ave Menlo Park 94025

CHAMBERLIN, EUGENE KEITH, historian, educator; b. Feb. 15, 1916, Gustine; s. Charles Eugene and Anina Marguerite (Williams) C.; m. Margaret Rae Jackson, Sept. 1, 1940; children: Linda (Davies) b. 1941, Thomas Wayne b. 1944, Rebecca (Washburn) b. 1948, Adrienne Colleen (1950-1981), Eric Carl b. 1963; edn: BA in hist., UC Berkeley 1939, MA in Mexican hist. 1940, PhD in Latin Am. hist. 1949; seminar and field work CSU San Diego and Peru (Fulbright Hays grantee) 1982. Career: reader UC Berkeley in Mex. hist., 1938-40, in Calif. hist., 1945-46; misc. work 1940-41; tchr. Spanish and Latin, Lassen Union High Sch. and Jr. Coll., Susanville 1941-43; tchr. hist., Elk Grove Jt.Union H.S. 1943-45; tchg. asst. UC Berkeley 1946-48; instr., asst. prof. hist. Mont. State Univ., Missoula 1948-54; summer instr. Mont. State Coll., Bozeman, 1953; prof. hist. & govt., San Diego City Coll. 1954-78; vis. lectr. Latin Am. hist., S.D. State Coll. 1965-67, UCLA Ext.1964-66, UCSD Ext. 1966-67; TV lectr. on Mexican and SW hist., recent world hist., S.D. Comm. Colls., 1969-77; prof. hist., Miramar Coll., 1978-83; prof. Calif. and Latin Am. hist., S.D. Mesa Coll. 1983-86; cab driver p.t. S.D. Yellow Cab Co., 1955-76, 86; awards: Rockefeller / Huntington Library grantee 1952, outstanding educator San Diego City Coll. 1970, merit award San Diego Cong. of Hist. 1978, Fulbright-Hays grantee in Peru 1982, award for years of dedicated service to local history, San Diego Hist. Soc. 1991, Resolution of Commendn. from Calif. State Hist. Resources Comm. for over 20 years of installing 30 Calif. Registered Historical Landmark Plaques (11/1/91), honoree San Diego Pub. Library Local Authors Exh. for contbns. to literature in 1990, 91, 92, 93, 94, 95, Plaque award from Squibob Chpt. E Clampus Vitus for 30 years of dedication to preserve Calif. history; mem. Phi Alpha Theta (1946–, Mont. St. Univ. chapt. founder, faculty adv. 1949-54), AAUP (1949–, MSU chapt. secty. 1953-54, pres. S.D. City Coll. chpt. 1956-57, Nat. Council 1967-70, pres. Calif. Conf. 1968-70, acting exec. secty. Calif. 1970-72), Am. Hist. Assn. (mem. 1940–, Hon. 50-yr. mem. 1990–, chmn. Beveridge-Dunning Com. 1984, mem. 82-84), The Westerners/ Calafia Corral & San Diego Corral 1973–, San Diego Co. Congress of Hist. (pres. 1976-77, newsletter ed. 1977-78), Pac. Coast Council on Latin Am. Studies 1955-93, Cultural Assn. of the Californias 1964–, E Clampus Vitus (mem., chpt. offcs. 1962–, historian 1970–, bd. proctors 1983-89), Transierra Roisterous Alliance of Sr. Humbugs (1975–, bd. 1980-93, pres. 1982-83), Mont. Acad. Scis. 1949-54, San Diego Histo. Soc. (1954-65, 88–); civic: tech. advr. Quechan Indian Tribal Council on Yuma Crossing Master Plan Proj. 1989-90, active vol. Food Bank and Ch. Food Distbg. Ctr. 1989-90; publs: 80+ articles and num. book revs. in profl. jours. and separate pamphlets mostly on NW Mex., American SW, Calif. hist., church hist., hist. comparison of Mex. and Peru 1951–; Democrat; Ch. of the Brethren (nat. conf. del. 1986); rec: hist., gardening. Res: 3033 Dale St San Diego 92104

CHAMPLIN, CHARLES DAVENPORT, writer; b. Mar. 23, 1926, Hammondsport, N.Y.; s. Francis Malburn and Katherine Marietta (Masson) C.; m. Margaret, Sept. 11, 1948; children: Charles, Jr. b. 1950, Katherine Ann b. 1951, John b. 1953, Judith b. 1954, Susan b. 1962, Nancy b. 1964; edn: AB, Harvard Coll. 1948. Career: Life mag. reporter N.Y.C. 1948-49, corr. Chgo. 1949-52, corr. Denver 1952-54, asst. ed. N.Y. 1954-59; Time mag. corr. Los Angeles 1959-62, corr. London 1962-65; entertainment ed. Los Angeles Times, 1965-80, and prin. film critic 1967-80, arts ed. and Critic at Large columnist, 1980-91; t.v. host: Film Odyssey (PBS, 1970), Homewood (PBS, 1970-71), Citywatchers (KCET, 1976-82), On the Film Scene (Z Channel, L.A., 1978-90); Champlin on Film, Bravo Cable 1990-94; adj. prof., cinema-t.v., USC 1986–, adj. prof. Loyola-Marymount Univ., L.A. 1969-86, instr. Occidental Coll. 1983-86; awards: Order of Arts and Letters, French Govt.; mem: Nat. Book Critics Circle, Los Angeles Film Critics Assn. (founding sec.); trustee: Am. Cinematheque 1993–; Cinema Circulus (USC support gp.) 1987–; author: How

To Swim Well (w/Charles Sava) (Simon & Schuster 1960); The Flicks (Ward Ritchie 1977), rev. and retitled as The Movies Grow Up (Swallow Press/Ohio U. Press 1980); George Lucas: The Creative Impulse (Abrams 1992); Back There Where The Past Was (Syracuse Univ. Press 1989); John Frankenheimer: A Conversation with Charles Champlin (Riverwood 1995); mil: cpl. AUS Inf. 1944-46, Purple Heart, 3 battlestars. Res: 2169 Linda Flora Dr Los Angeles 90077-1408

CHAN, ALFRED, JR., dentist; b. Mar. 7, 1940, Colon, Rep. of Panama, nat. US cit. 1977; s. Alfred and Edith Victoria (Low) C.; m. Lisa, Feb. 2, 1987; children: (step nee Yen) Willie, Chas; edn: BA, Whittier Coll. 1962; PhD, Univ. of Ill. 1968; DDS, UC Los Angeles 1978. Career: research scientist Bio Science, Van Nuys 1969-70; dir. research & devel., Reference Labs., N.H. 1970-71; dentist assoc. George Mizushima, DDS, Los Angeles 1984-85, Gregory Robins, DDS, Montebello 1985-87; owner dental practice Sepulveda Dental Group, Torrance 1987–; asst. clin. prof. USC Sch. of Dentistry 1983-85; mem. Am. Dental Assn., Calif. Dental Assn., L.A. Dental Soc., South Bay Chinese Am. Assn. (pres. 1985), South Bay P.C. Users Group (pres. 1992); Republican; Methodist; rec: computer, classical guitar. Res: 3523 W 226th St Torrance 90505 Ofc: Sepulveda Dental Group 3706 Sepulveda Blvd Torrance 90505

CHAN, DAVID RONALD, certified public accountant, lawyer; b. Aug. 3, 1948, Los Angeles; s. David Yew and Anna May (Wong) C.; m. Mary Anne Chan, June 21, 1980; children: Eric David, b. 1981, Christina Mary, b. 1982; edn: AB econ., UCLA, 1969; MS bus. adm., UCLA, 1970; JD, UCLA Sch. of Law, 1973; admitted bar: Calif., US Ct. of Appeals 9th Cir., US Claims Ct., US Tax Ct. Career: staff acct. Touche Ross & Co., Los Angeles 1970; acct. Oxnard Celery Distbrs. Inc., L.A. 1971-73; tax. dept. Kenneth Leventhal & Co., L.A. 1973–, presently dir. in Nat. Tax Office; real estate broker; co-dir. KL Tax Hall of Fame, 1980–; awards: John Forbes Gold Medal, Calif. Soc. CPA 1970, Elijah Watt Sells Cert. AICPA 1970, Newton Becker Award 1970, Phi Beta Kappa, Beta Gamma Sigma, Beta Alpha Psi, others; mem: Chinese Hist. Soc. of So. Calif. (founder, past bd. dir.), N.Y. Chinatown Hist. Project, Chinese for Affirmative Action, Hawaii Chinese Hist. Center, Chinese Hist. Soc. of Am. (appreciation award 1975), L.A. Co. Bar Assn., So. Calif. Chinese Lawyers Assn., Am. Inst. of CPA, Calif. Soc. CPA, Chinese Am. CPA Soc. So. Calif., Legends of Tax (tax profl. social org.), UCLA Alumni Assn. (life), UCLA Bruin Bench, UCLA Coll. of Letters and Scis. Dean's Council, L.A. Bicentennial 200 Speakers Bur., Am. First Day Cover Soc., L.A. Bd. of Realtors (MLS), Asian Business League; publs: num. articles on taxation, philately, and Chinese-Am. studies incl: The Five Chinatowns of Los Angeles, A Postcard View of Chinatown, The Tragedy and Trauma of the Chinese Exclusion Laws, Chinese-American Heritage: Hist. and Contemporary Perspectives, Structuring the R.E. Syndicate, Pre-Combination First Day Covers, Sale of Property Developed on Leased Land; contbg. author: The Chinese American Experience; restaurant revs. in East West Chinese Am. Jour., and A. Asian Magazine; mng. editor Tax Perspectives newsletter; frequent spkr. on Chinese hist. in US: 1st, 2d Nat. Confs. Chinese-Am. Studies, KCBS TV, Calif. Conf. Hist. Socs., Hist. Soc. So. Calif., L.A. City Schs. Project Follow-Through, 2d Asian Pacific Am. Heritage Week Commemoration (keynote), CHSSC; tax presentations: UCLA Grad. Sch. Mgmt. Advy. Com., Drexel Burnham Lambert; Republican (Nat. Com.); rec: philately, post cards, sports memorabilia, Chinese cuisine. Res: 2540 Wild Oak Dr Los Angeles 90068 Ofc: 2049 Century Park East Ste 1700 Los Angeles 90067

CHAN, YVONNE Y., marketing specialist; b. Dec. 21, 1955, San Francisco; d. S.P. and B.K. (Ho) Chan; edn: BA econ., USC, 1978; MBA fin., Northrop Univ., 1980. Career: fin. planning analyst Rockwell Internat., L.A. 1981-82; corporate lending ofcr. Bank of Am., San Francisco 1982-83; asst. corp. treas. First Pacific Group, San Francisco 1983-87; asst. v.p. corporate banking American Express Bank, 1988; leveraged-lease splst. merchant banking CEF Capital; mktg. dir. corporate promotions, Great Western Internat. Inc., 1989–; Republican; Presbyterian; rec: skiing, sailing, water polo. Ofc: 9080 Santa Monica Blvd PO Box 606 Santa Monica 90406

CHANDLER, BRUCE FREDERICK, physician; b. Mar. 26, 1926, Bohemia, Pike Co.,Pa.; s. Frederick Arthur and Minnie Flora (Burkhardt) C.; m. Janice Piper, Aug. 14, 1954; children: Barbara b. 1955, Betty b. 1956, Karen b. 1959, Paul b. 1961, June b. 1965; edn: pre-med. Penn State, 1942-44; MD, Temple Univ. 1948; renal dialysis Harvard, 1953. Career: rotating intern Temple Univ. Hosp., Phila. 1948-49; med. resident Valley Forge Gen. Hosp., Phoenixville, Pa. 1949-50 and Walter Reed Gen. Hosp., WDC 1950-53; batt. surgeon 2d div. arty. Korea 1953-54; chief renal dialysis unit 45th Evac. Hosp., Korea 1954, and Tokyo Army Hosp., Japan 1954-55; chief gen. med. svc. #3 Walter Reed Gen. Hosp., 1955-58; comdg. ofcr. 45th Field Hosp., Vicenza, Italy 1958-62; pulmonary disease fellow Fitzsimons Gen. Hosp., Aurora, Colo. 1962-63, chief pulmonary service, 1963-64; chief pul. svc. Letterman Gen. Hosp., San Francisco 1964-70; internist in pvt. practice, Ridgecrest, Calif. 1970-76; chief med. svc. VA Hosp., Walla Walla, Wash. 1976-77; outpatient physician VA Med. Ctr. Spokane, Wash. 1977-82; med. cons. Social Security Adminstrn., Spokane 1983-87, ret.; asst. clin. prof. of med. UC San Francisco 1964-70; contbr. 33+ articles in med. jours.; lectr. extensively esp. in field of pulmonary diseases,

including in 1963-66 on the true incidence, in sarcoidosis, of pleural effusion and pulmonary cavitation, neither of which had previously been known to occur in that disease; 3 TV appearances on medical panels re Malaria, Shock, Tuberculosis; honors: gold medal, outstanding student Temple Univ. Sch. of Med. 1948, achievement award Walter Reed Gen. Hosp. 1955-58, 45th Field Hosp., Vicenza, Italy 1958-62; mem: AMA, Am. Coll. Physicians (fellow, life mem.), Am. Coll. Chest Physicians (fellow, life mem., gov. 1968-70), Am. Thoracic Soc., N.Y. Acad. of Scis., SETAF Med.-Dent. Soc. Vicenza, Italy (pres. 1958-62); Masons 1960–; vol. Boy Scouts Am. (com. chair 1970-76); mil: col. Med. Corps U.S. Army 1948-70, Legion of Merit; Republican; Methodist; rec: photography, fishing, travel, collect Agatha Christie and Jules Verne books. Res: 6496 N Callisch Ave Fresno 93710

CHANDLER, JOHN HERRICK, college president; b. Aug. 7, 1928, San Francisco; s. Ralph William and Gwen Thornton (Herrick) C.; m. Nancy Gordon Phillips, Dec. 10, 1955; children: John, Seth, Will; edn: AB, UCLA 1952; BD (Danforth fellow), Univ. Chgo. 1958, PhD (fellow), 1963. Ordained to ministry Episcopal Ch. 1960. Career: instr. English Dartmouth Coll., 1961-63; asst. prof. UCLA, 1963-64; assoc. prof., dean spl. programs Ohio Univ., 1964-67; v.p. Danforth Found., St. Louis, 1967-71; pres. Salem Coll. and Acad., Winston-Salem, N.C. 1971-76; pres. Scripps Coll., 1976–; trustee Newton Coll. Sacred Heart, 1970-75, Thacher Sch., 1977-86; dir. Clayton (Mo.) Bd. Edn. 1970-71; clubs: University (LA), Bohemian, Twilight. Ofc: Scripps College, Balch Hall, Claremont 91711

CHANDLER, MARK JOSEPH, municipal executive/international business coordinator; b. June 30, 1956, Albuquerque, New Mex.; s. Everett Marston and Arlene Byrdell (Bahr) C.; edn: AB, UC Davis 1978; MBA, UC Berkeley 1983; stu. Tokyo Acad., Japan 1983-84. Career: mgr. mkt. develop. PIE Nationwide, Walnut Creek 1980-83; mgr. sales & mktg. US Sprint, Burlingame 1984-87; internat. business coordinator City of San Francisco 1987–; Advy. Council, ctr. for Internat. Trade CCSF 1991–; bd. dirs. S.F. Trade Office; honors: outstanding sr. UC Davis 1978, grad. w/honors UC Davis 1978; mem: World Affairs Council, Pacific Rim Communications Forum, Commonwealth Club, SPUR, Nature Conservancy, Golden Gate Nat. Parks Assn., Maritime Mus. Assn., Shanghai Sister City Com. (S.F.), Taipei Sister City Com. (S.F.); Democrat; rec: baseball, travel, reading, beachcombing, chanty singing. Res: 1557 Noe St San Francisco 94131

CHANDLER, OTIS, communications company executive; b. Nov. 23, 1927, Los Angeles; s. Norman and Dorothy (Buffum) C.; m. Bettina Whitaker, Aug. 15, 1981; children (by previous marriage): Norman Brant, b. 1952, Harry Brant, b. 1953, Cathleen, b. 1955, Michael Otis, b. 1958, Carolyn, b. 1963; edn: The Cate Sch., Phillips Acad.; BA, Stanford Univ. 1950. Career: var. mgmt. pos., Times Mirror, 1953-: trainee in mech., editorial, circulation, advt. depts. 1953-57; asst. to pres., 1957-58; mktg. mgr. Los Angeles Times, 1959-60; publisher 1960-80; v.p. Newspaper Div. Times Mirror, 1961-65, dir. 1962–; pres. Newspaper and Forest Products, 1965-66; mem. exec. com., bd. dirs. 1966–, bd. chmn./ editor-in-chief, 1981-86, chmn. exec. com. 1986–; dir: Found., Chandis Securities Co., Chandler-Sherman Corp.; dir. Pres.'s Council on Physical Fitness and Sports; dir. World Wildlife Fund-US; honors: Delta Kappa Epsilon (pres. 1950), 4-Yr. Letterman, capt. Track Team 1950 (Stanford Univ.); co-capt. USAF Track Team 1952; hon. LL.D., Colby Coll. 1966; hon. LL.D., Claremont Grad. Sch. 1978; num. journalism awards: USC 1962, Lovejoy 1966, Columbia Univ. 1967, Univ. Mo. Honor Medal 1969, Ohio Univ. Sch of Journ. Carr Van Anda 1973, Univ. of Ks. Allen White 1975, CORO 1978, Nat. Collegiate Athletic Assn. Theo. Roosevelt 1979, Gallagher Report 1980, Univ. Tex. Coll. Comm. DeWitt Carter Reddick 1982; mem: Am. Newspaper Pubs. Assn. (dir. 1968-77; Found. trustee 1969-78), Am. Soc. Newspaper Editors, Inter-Am. Press Assn., Soc. Profl. Journalists, Sigma Delta Chi; clubs: California, Regency, So. Calif. Safari; mil: Navy midshipman 1946-48; lst lt. USAF 1951-53; rec: classic & sports cars, surfing, hunting, weightlifting, track & field. Ofc: Times Mirror, Times Mirror Square Los Angeles 90053

CHANDLER, TERTIUS, historian; b. Feb. 6, 1915, Dedham, Mass.; s. Theophilus & Sarah (Chase) C.; m. Margot Tegelstrom, Sept. 18, 1961; edn: BA, Harvard Univ. 1937; PhD, Clayton of Mo. 1988; author (with Gerald Fox): 3000 Years of Urban Growth, 1974; author: 4000 Years of Urban Growth, 1987; editor: Digsig (1977-82), Solutions (1978-82); contbr. of articles to profl. journals; specialties: early biblical chronology, size of cities down the ages, Egyptian and Norse contacts to early America, origin of Zimbabwe city, origin of democracy in Moses's Egypt. Res: 2500 Buena Vista Berkeley 94708 Tel: 510/849-1850

CHANEY, FREDERICK BENNETT, management education company executive; b. Sept. 8, 1936, Boulder, Colo.; s. Marjorie (Elliott) Hendrickson; m. Linda S. Spearman; children: Melanie, Andrew, Kira, Ari; edn: BS in psych., Purdue Univ., 1959, MS in exptl. psych., 1960, PhD in mgmt. psych., 1962. Career: research asst. The Boeing Co., Seattle 1962-63, N.Am. Ops. div. Rockwell Internat. Corp., 1964-68; pres. Continuing Education Corp., 1968-81; pres./CEO successor firm Vedax Sciences Corp. Santa Ana 1981–; instr. managerial psychology USC, 1969-70; adj. prof. mgmt. Pepperdine Univ., 1970-74; cons. Xerox Corp., Collins Radio, Lockheed Corp., State of Calif., 1969–; awards: NSF fellow 1964; author: (with D.H. Harris) Human Factors in Quality Assurance 1969, articles in profl jours. Ofc: Vedax Sciences Corp. 5000 Birch Blvd Ste 6200 Newport Beach 92660

CHANG, CHI-CHI, acupuncturist; b. Nov. 14, 1945, Bejing, China; d. Joseph Tze-Hsuan and Maria Hsu-Ling (Shen) C.; m. Philip Zee-Pee Hsing, Dec. 12, 1971; div. July 1, 1978; children: Marie T. Hsing b. 1973, Caroline Hsing b. 1982; edn: PhD, SAMRA Univ., Los Angeles, 1984; Doctor of Oriental Medicine, SAMRA Univ., L.A., 1984. Career: acupuncturist, Acupuncture Clinic, Millbrae, Calif. 1980, Piedmont, Calif. 1982-90, Walnut Creek, Calif. 1991; acupuncturist, Oriental Acupuncture Clinic, Hacienda Hts., Calif. 1992–; bd. dir./secty. Acupuncture Inst. for Addiction-Free Life, 1992–; res. com. mem. Amer. Inst. of Chinese Medicine, Inc., S.F., 1992; awards: Outstanding Performance and Service award, Acupuncture Medicine Assn. of So. Calif., 1993; honors: Acupuncture Inst. for Addiction-Free Life, Calif., 1993; mem: United Acupuncturists of Calif. 1980, Calif. Certified Acupuncturists Assn. 1991; Acupuncture Medicine Assn. of So. Calif. 1992; mem. La Puente, Calif. C.of C., 1992; author (2 books): Low Back Pain 1984, Acupuncture Treatment of Arthritis 1984. Ofc: Oriental Acupuncture Clinic 243 Sunnyside Ave Piedmont 94611

CHANG, EDWARD I., real estate broker, management consultant; b. Aug. 31, 1948, Taipei, Taiwan; s. Ming Cheng and Ching Ling (Li) C.;m. Lan, Dec. 14, 1977; 1 dau. Caroline, b. 1981; edn: BS, Tankang Univ. 1972; cert., Univ. of Santa Clara 1977; cert., Western Real Estate Sch. 1982, PhD. Century Univ. 1991; gen. contractor, Calif. 1981; R.E. broker, Calif. 1982. Career: mgr. Chang Brothers Co., Palo Alto, 1975-77; pres. Chinese Fast Food Devel. Ctr., L.A., 1978-81; pres. Eastern Group, L.A., 1981–; v.p. Excom, Inc. 1982–; exec. dir. Wok King Chain Commn., Rep. of China 1978; mem: Calif. Chinese Assn. of Construction Profls.; Chinese-Am. R.E. Profls. of So. Calif.; Chinatown Lions Club; publs: Overseas Chinese Restaurant Operation, 7/78; columnist, World Jour., 1978; Catholic; rec: golf, skiing. Res: P.O. Box 80760 San Marino 91118. Ofc: Eastern Group Inc. 2451 W Main St #107 Alhambra 91801

CHANG, JANICE MAY, doctor, lawyer and psychologist; b. May 24, 1970, Loma Linda, Calif.; d. Belden Shiu-Wah and Sylvia So Lan (Tan) Chang; edn: BA, Calif. State Univ., San Bernardino 1990, cert. in paralegal studies 1990, cert. in creative writing, 1991; JD, La Salle Univ. 1993; Doctor of Naturopathy, Clayton Sch. of Natural Healing 1993; Doctor of Homeopathic Medicine, Internat. Univ. 1993, PsyD, 1993, PhD in psychology, 1994; Doctor of Preventive Medicine, Bernadean Univ. 1994; DO, Anglo-Am. Inst. for Drugless Therapy 1994. Career: general counsel, JMC Enterprises Inc. 1993–; adj. prof. La Salle Univ. 1994–; listed in Who's Who in U.S. Writers, Editors, and Poets 1992-93, 95-96; mem: Am. Soc. of Law, Medicine and Ethics, Am. Naturopathic Med. Assn., Am. Psychol. Assn., Am. Psychology-Law Soc., Assn. of Trial Lawyers of Am.; author: Writingscapes: An Approach to Creative Writing, 1991; Herbal Qualities of German Chamomile, 1993; Psychological Ramifications of Child Sexual Abuse, 1993; Republican; Seventh-Day Adventist; rec: poetry, literature, drama, music. Res: 11466 Richmont Rd Loma Linda 92354

CHANG, SYLVIA TAN, administrator, educator; b. Dec. 18, 1940, Bandung, Indonesia, naturalized 1972; d. Philip Harry and Lydia Shui-Yu (Ou) Tan; m. Belden Chang, Aug. 30, 1964; children: Donald Steven b. 1968, Janice May b. 1970; edn: dipl. nursing, Rumah Sakit Advent, Indonesia 1960; BS, Philippine Union Coll., 1962; MS, Loma Linda Univ., 1967; PhD, Columbia Pacific Univ., 1987. Career: head nurse Rumah Sakit Advent, Indonesia, 1960-61; critical care nse., team ldr., medicine nse., treatment nse., spl. duty nse. White Mem. Med. Ctr., Los Angeles 1963-64; team coord./team ldr. (med. & surgical units) Loma Linda Univ. Med. Ctr., Loma Linda 1964-66; relief hd. nse., team ldr., critical care nse. Pomona Valley Hosp. Med. Ctr., Pomona 1966-67; relief supr. obstets. Loma Linda Univ. Med. Ctr. 1967, evening supr. 1967-69, noc. supr. 1969-79, adminstrv. supr. 1979–, dir. health service La Sierra Univ. 1988–; faculty mentor Columbia Pacific Univ., 1986–, CPR instr. La Sierra Univ. 1988–, First Aid instr. Phil. Union Coll. 1961-63; annual blood drive coord. La Sierra Univ.; site coord. Health Fair Expo, La Sierra Univ.; honors: Sigma Theta Tau, profl. awards for Teaching Excellence, Disting. Adminstrv. Service to Profession, Women of Achievement Award, Disting. Leadership, Outstanding Contbn. to Health Edn.; listed in Who's Who in Sci. & Engring., Who's Who Among Asian Americans, Who's Who in Am. Nursing, Internat. Who's Who of Profl. & Bus. Women, Who's Who of Am. Women, Internat. Dir. of Disting. Leadership, Personalities of Am., Internat. Book of Honor, Internat. Register of Profiles, Internat. Leaders in Achiev., Dir. of Disting. Americans, 5,000 Personalities of World; mem: Am. Assn. Critical-Care Nurses, Am. Coll. Health Assn., Assn. of Seventh-day Adventist Nurses, Pacific Coast Coll. Health Assn., Sigma Theta Tau Intl. Inc., Adventist Student Personnel Assn. Intl., alumni assns. Philippine Union Coll., LLU Grad. Sch., LLU Sch. of Nsg., Col. Pac. Univ.; Republican; Seventh-day Adventist; rec: music (organ, piano), coin, jade carving, shell & stamp collecting. Res: 11466 Richmont Rd Loma Linda 92354 Ofc: La Sierra Univ., Riverside 92515

CHANG, WILLIAM JERRY, physician, medical educator; b. March 23, 1955, Youngstown, Ohio; s. William J. H. and Mollie (Yee) C.; m. Leslie M. Itano, Feb. 22, 1986; edn: BA, Harvard Coll. 1977; MD, Stanford Med. Sch. 1982. Career: physician Santa Clara Valley Med. Center, San Jose 1982-83; physician, ophthalmologist Stanford Med. Center, Stanford 1983-86; staff ophthalmologist Kaiser Permanente Med. Group, Redwood City 1986–, dir. patient edn. ophthalmology dept. 1988–; clin. asst. prof. Stanford Univ. Hosp., Stanford 1988–, and Palo Alto VA Hosp., 1989–; awards: Stanford Dept. Ophthalmology McCaskill scholar (1985); mem: Calif. Med. Assn., Am. Acad. Ophthalmology, San Mateo Co. Med. Soc.; mem. Calif. Cello Club, classical music performer, 1975–; rec: cello, piano. Ofc: Kaiser Permanente Medical Group 1150 Veterans Blvd Redwood City 94063

CHANG, WILLIAM S.C., professor of electrical and computer engineering; b. April 4, 1931, Nantung, China; s. Tung Wu and Phoebe Yung-Sun (Chow) C.; m. Margaret Hua-Chen Kwei, Nov. 26, 1955; children: Helen Nai-Yee, Hugh Nai-Hun, Heidy Nai-Lin; edn: BSEE, Univ. Mich. 1952; MSEE, 1953; PhD, Brown Univ. 1957. Career: lectr. Stanford Univ., Stanford 1957-59; asst. and assoc. prof. Ohio St. Univ., Columbus 1959-65; prof., head, dir. lab. for applied electronics Wash. Univ., St. Louis, Mo. 1965-79; prof. UCSD, La Jolla 1979–; chair ECE Dept., UCSD, 1993–; honors: Eta Kappa Nu, Tau Beta Pi, Univ. Mich. Dist. Profl. Achievement 1978, Wash. Univ. Samuel Sachs Chair; mem: IEEE (fellow), OSA (fellow), AIP; 100+ research papers pub., 1959–, author Principle of Quantum Electronics. Res: 9654 Clairborne Square La Jolla 92037 Ofc: Univ. of Calif. San Diego Dept. of Electrical and Computer Engineering La Jolla 92093-0407

CHAO, FRANK W., network engineer; b. May 21, 1951, Oakland; s. Dr. Fu-Chuan and Lydia Lai-Yuk (Chui) C.; edn: AA, El Camino Coll., 1981; BA, UC Los Angeles, 1973; MBA, USC, 1975; lic. Gen. Radio Tel. Opr., FCC (1979). Career: sales research analyst Mattel Inc., Hawthorne 1976-77; alarm techn. Morse Signal Devices of Calif.,. L.A. 1977-79; radio services techn. Northrop Grumman Corp., Hawthorne 1979-82, radio services engr., 1982-92, computer equipment design analyst 1992-94, systems integrator 1994-95, network engr. 1995–; mem: Internet Soc., L.A. Netware Users, Orange Co. Netware Users, Nat. Computer Security Assn., Nat. Assn. of Radio and Telecomm. Engrs., Nat. Wildlife Fedn., Uniforum; rec: computer networks. Ofc: Northrop Corp. PO Box 2548 El Segundo 90245-2548

CHAO, JAMES MIN-TZU, architect; b. Feb. 27, 1940, Dairen, China; nat. 1962; s. T. C. and Lin Fan (Wong) C.; m. Kirsti Helena Lehtonen, May 15, 1968; edn: B.Arch., UC Berkeley 1965; cert. architect Calif.; cert. architect Ariz. 1994. Career: intermediate draftsman Spencer Lee & Busse Architects, S.F. 1966-67; asst. to pres. Import Plus Inc., Santa Clara 1967-69; job. capt. Hammaberg & Herman Architects, Oakland 1969-71; project mgr. B.A. Premises Corp., S.F. 1971-79; constrn. mgr. The Straw Hut Restaurant Corp., 1979-81; sr. mgmt., dir. real estate and constrn. 1981-87; sole practice architect 1987–; pres., c.e.o. Stratsac, Inc. 1987-91; pres. Food Service Consultants, Inc. 1987-89; princ. architect Alpha Cons. Group, Inc. 1991–; v.p. Intersyn Industries of Calif. 1993–; bd. dirs. Ambrosia Best Corp. 1992–; lectr. comml. real estate site analysis and selection for profl. real estate seminars; coordinator minority vending program, solar application program Bank of Am.; guest faculty mem. Northwest Center for Profl. End.; patentee tidal electric generating system; author first comprehensive consumer orientated performance specification for remote banking transaction; awards: hon. mention Future Scientists Am. (1955); mem. AIA; club: Encinal Yacht; Republican.

CHAPIN, JOHN KEITH, lawyer, author, editor; b. Nov. 15, 1946, Goodland, Kans.; s. Orville Edward and Florence Ada (Updike) C.; div.; edn: BA, Univ. Colo., Boulder 1968; JD, Univ. Texas Sch. of Law 1971; admitted to state bars: Texas 1971, Colo. 1972, Calif. 1973. Career: atty. advisor US Gen. Services Adminstrn. reg. office, San Francisco 1972-78; dep. county counsel Sonoma County 1979-80, Solano County 1980-85; editor Construction Litigation Reporter 1981-83; govt. editor California Tort Reporter 1983-85; appeals editor Federal Litigator 1985-88, legal editor Univ. of Calif. Continuing Edn. of the Bar 1985–; dir., secty. New Gate Theatre Co., SF 1976; dir., secty. San Francisco Poverty Theatre Co., SF 1974-75; dir. Shaman's Drum mag., 1985–; recipient Presidential Citation (Pres. Jimmy Carter) for outstanding achievement 1978; author: Tort Claims Against Public Entities and Employees, Div. VII Calif. Torts (Matthew Bender & Co., 1985); mil: USAR, JAGC, 1968-74; rec: fiction and poetry writing; drama (acting, writing). Res: PO Box 208 Inverness 94937-0208 Ofc: Continuing Education of the Bar, 2300 Shattuck Ave Berkeley 94704

CHAPMAN, MICHAEL WILLIAM, physician, surgeon, medical educator; b. Nov.29, 1937, Newberry, Mich.; m. Elizabeth Casady; children: Mark John, Craig David; edn: AA, Am. River Coll., 1957; BS, UC San Francisco, 1959, MD, 1962; diplomate Am. Bd. Orthopedic Surg. 1969, 83. Career: intern, mixed med.-surg., S.F. Gen. Hosp. 1962-63, resident orthop. surgery UCSF, 1963-67; fellow Royal Nat. Orthopedic Hosp., London 1967-68; served US Army Med. Corps 1968-70; asst. prof. orthopedic surgery UC San Francisco 1971-76, assoc. prof. 1976-79; asst. chief orthop. surgery S.F. Gen. Hosp. 1971-79, actg. chief orthop. surgery 1972-73; chmn. orthop. surgery UC Davis Med. Ctr., Sacto. 1979–, prof. orthop. surg. 1981–; physician U.S. Nat. Olympic Ski Team, 1976–; assoc. editor: Clin. Orthopaedics and Related Res., J. of Orthopedic Trauma, J. of Bone and Joint Surgery; book revs. New England J. of Medicine 1988–; num. publs. in med. and profl. jours.; awards: Alpha Omega Alpha, AOA guest resident 1967, Fogarty Sr. Internat. Fellow, Switz. 1978-79, outstanding tchg. UCSF 1972, tchr. of yr. UC Davis 1984, annual Gill Memorial Lectr. Phila. Orthopedic Soc. 1988, Most outstanding book in clin. medicine category "Operative Orthopaedics" Assn. Am. Publishers 1989, AMA physician recogn. award 1989-92; Hon. mem. British Orthopaedic Assn., corr. mem. South African Orthopaedic Assn.; mem: Internat. Soc. for Skiing Safety, Assn. for Study of Internal Fixation (A-O Internat.), Am. Acad. Orthopedic Surgeons, Am. Assn. for Surgery of Trauma, Am. Bd. of Orthopedic Surgeons (bd. dirs. 1985–, oral examiner 1981–, exams. com. 1985–), Am. Orthopedic Assn. (pres. 1990-91, bd. dirs. 1985-88, 88–), Am. Coll. Surgeons, Pan-Pac. Surg. Assn., Internat. Soc. for Fracture Repair, Am. Assn. for Surgery of Trauma AMA, Am. Bd. of Med. Splties, Am. Orthopedic Assn., Am. Orthopedic Soc. for Sports Medicine, Am. Trauma Soc., Assn. of Am. Med. Colls., Assn. of Bone and Joint Surgeons, LeRoy C. Abbott Orthopedic Soc., Paul R. Lipscomb Soc., NW Med. Assn., Orthopedic Research Soc., Orthopedic Trauma Assn. (pres. 1985-6), We. Orthopedic Assn., CMA, Calif. Orthopedic Assn., Sacto.-El Dorado Med. Soc., Wilson Interurban Orthopedic Soc., Sierra Club; Republican; Prot.; rec: skiing, mountaineering, scuba, tennis. Ofc: Dept. Orthopedics, Univ. Calif. Davis Medical Ctr. 2230 Stockton Blvd Sacramento 95817

CHAPPLE, CHRISTOPHER KEY, professor; b. Sept. 4, 1954, Medina, NY; s. Hugh Edward and Julia Dolores (Peton) C.; m. Maureen Shannon, Aug. 10, 1974; children: Dylan b. 1985, Emma b. 1989; edn: BA, SUNY, Stony Brook, NY 1976; MA, Fordham Univ., Bronx, NY 1978, PhD, 1980. Career: asst. dir. Inst. for Advanced Studies of World Religions, Stony Brook, NY 1980-85; lectr. SUNY, Stony Brook 1980-85; prof. Loyola Marymount Univ., L.A. 1985–; honors: Casassa Chair of Social Values, Loyola Marymount Univ. 1989-91, Nat. Endowment for the Humanities summer stipend 1990; mem: Am. Acad. of Religion 1979–, Soc. for Asian and Comparative Philosophy 1980–, Soc. for Buddhist-Christian Studies 1984–, Coll. Theology Soc. 1985–, Am. Inst. of Indian Studies (trustee 1990–); author: Karma and Creativity, 1986, Non-Violence to animals, Earth, and Self in Asian Traditions, 1993, Ecological Prospects, 1994; co-translator: Yoga Sutras, 1990. Ofc: Dept of Theological Studies Loyola Marymount University Los Angeles 90045

CHARLES, ANNE H., state bar communications director; b. May 5, 1941, Bethlehem, Pa.; d. Clement R. and Ethel (Grein) Hanlon; m. Peter Charles, May 2, 1964; children: Eric b. 1966, Susan b. 1967, Jeffrey b. 1970, Leslie b. 1971; edn: BA magna cum laude, Marymount Coll. 1963. Career: exec. dir. Marin Arts Council, San Rafael 1979-83; prin. Anne Charles & Assoc., Kentfield 1975-85; dep. dir. State Bar of Calif., San Francisco 1985-; bd. dirs. No. Calif. Mediation Ctr. 1984–; mem. cost control com. Calif. St. Senate; honors: achiev. Womens Campaign Fund 1988, listed Worlds Who's Who of Women, Who's Who in Am. Politics, Biography Internat.; mem. Pub. Relations Soc. Am.; civic: Nat. Women's Political Caucus (state pres. 1979), Marin Arts Council (pres. 1979-81); Calif. Dem. state central com.; R.Cath.; rec: cooking. Res: 33 Terrace Ave Kentfield 94904

CHARLSON, MICHAEL LLOYD, lawyer; b. Sept. 1, 1958, Pittsburgh, Pa.; s. Benjamin Charlson and Sheila (Ostrow) Flodberg; m. Elizabeth Stone, Aug. 31, 1986; edn: BS biol., Stanford Univ. 1981; MS, 1981; JD, UC Berkeley 1985; admitted St. Bar Calif. (1985). Career: law clk. Hon. William C. Canby Jr., U.S. Ct. Appeals 9th Circuit, Phoenix, Ariz. 1985-86; atty. Heller Ehrman White & McAuliffe, San Francisco 1986-92, ptnr. 1992–; honors: Order of Coif; mem: Am. Bar Assn. (editl. bd. Litigation mag. 1989-94), Bar Assn. San Francisco; article pub. in Calif. Law Review, 1984; Democrat; Jewish. Res: 3405 Westwood Court San Mateo 94403 Ofc: Heller Ehrman White & McAuliffe 525 University Ave Palo Alto 94301

CHARNY, ROBERT DAVID, executive; b. Dec. 16, 1953, Los Angeles; s. Frank and Laura (Burstein) C.; m. Paula, May 1, 1976; children: Heather Kathlene b. 1979, Jonathan Robert David b. 1981; edn: Santa Monica Coll. 1971-2, UCLA 1972-75; lic. dental tech. Tx. (1976); Calif. State and NRA cert. firearm tng. instr., Calif. cert. hunter safety instr. Career: Raydent Lab., Los Angeles 1972; dept. hd. Superdent Lab., Westwood 1975; c.e.o. The Pet Shop, Inc. 1978; trustee Pabst Farms Inc., Oconomowoc, Wis. 1980; c.e.o. Paragon Farm West, 1982; c.e.o. Charny, Coyan & Co. Inc., Diamond Springs, Calif. 1984; c.e.o. Charny Co., 1987–; pres. and c.e.o. Frontier Sports Inc., Placerville 1990-93; owner D & R BBS, 1991–; owner DRCSS Systems, 1993–, Glock, Inc. Police Service Div. cert. armorer; El Dorado Co. Sheriff Dept. citizen firearm course instr.; firearms cons. and instr. Frontier Armory, El Dorado Gun Club; listed Am. Biog. Inst. Directory of Distinguished Leadership (1991 Man of Yr.); mem. Encino Town & Country Merchant Assn. (pres. 1980), El Dorado Rod & Gun Club (pistol chmn. 1987-90, dir. 1988-90, pres. 1991-92), NRA (life), CRPA (life), IHMSA (life); rec: internat. handgun metallic silhouette shooting, combat shotgun & handgun shooting, internat. trap shooting. Ofc: 791 N Circle Dr Diamond Springs 95619

CHATTERJEE, SATYA NARAYAN, surgeon, educator; b. Dec. 31, 1934, Calcutta, India; s., Radha Nath and Jyotirmoyee (Mukherjee) Chatterjee; m. Patricia Sheppard, Sept. 26, 1964; children: Sharmila b. 1966, Shalini b. 1968, Arun b. 1972; edn: M.B.B.S., R.G. KAR Med. Coll., 1957; F.R.C.S., Royal Coll. of Surgeons of Glascow, 1963; F.R.C.S., Royal Coll. of Surgeons of Edinburgh, 1964; F.R.C.S., Royal Coll., of Surgeons of England, 1964. Career: assoc. prof., surg., dir. Renal Transplantation Service UC Davis, Sch of Med., 1977-84; prof. surgery UC Davis 1984-88; asst. prof. surg. UCLA, Sch. of Med., 1975-77; assoc. prof. surg. Charles Drew Postgrad. Med. Sch., 1977, asst. prof. 1975-76; res. fellow transplant Univ. of So. Calif., Sch. of Med., 1973-75; registrar in surg. Univ. of Edinburgh, Sch. of Med. 1970-73; also visiting prof. Univ. of Ottawa (Canada), Univ. of Oxford (England), Univ. of Cardiff (England), Univ. of Guadalajara (Mex.), Univ. of Bologna (Italy), Univ. of Milan (Italy), Univ. of Basle (Switzerland), Univ. of Ankara, Turkey, and Univ. of Kuwait; awards: A.K. Banerjee Scholarship for Academic (First Certificate of Honors); mem.: Intl. Transplant Soc. European Dialysis and Transplant Assn.; Amer. Soc. of Transplant Surgs.; Assn. for Acad. Surg.; Western Assn. of Transplant Surgs. (past pres.), fellow Amer. Coll. of Surgs., Calif. Med. Assn., Kidney Found. of No. Calif., Sacto Co. Med. Soc. Calif. Soc. of Transplant Surgs; author: books "Manual of Renal Transplantation" (Springer, Verlag, NY), "Transplantation: A Multidisciplinary Approach" (Raven Press, NY); editor: Surgical Clinics of No. Amer.; published 106 papers in scientific jours.; Hindu; rec: tennis, traveling. Res: 3267 Clubhouse Dr. El Macero 95618 Ofc: 2705 K Street Ste 2 Sacramento 95816

CHAVEZ, LEO E., college chancellor, educational administrator; b. June 4, 1947, Chicago, Ill.; s. Salvador and Angelina C.; m. Judy Chavez, Aug. 14, 1985; children: Timothy b. 1983, Christopher b. 1987; edn: BA, Univ. of Texas, El Paso 1969; MA, Univ. of Michigan, Ann Arbor 1973, PhD, 1976. Career: instr. San Jose City Coll., San Jose, Calif. 1976-81, asst. dean 1981-86, dean of instruction 1986-89; pres. West Valley Coll., Saratoga, Calif. 1989–, history instr. 1992–; mem: Edn. Subcom. Joint Venture Silicon Valley 1992–; Am. Leadership Forum, Class V 1993–; rec: golf, gardening, biking. Ofc: Foothill/DeAnza Community College District 12345 El Monte Rd Los Altos Hills 94022

CHEN, CHUN-I PHILIP, management information systems executive; b. Dec. 23, 1946, Fu-Chien, China; nat. 1986; s. Shui-Cheng and Jim-Kwong (Lin) C.; m. Chen-Yann Judy, Feb. 12, 1972; 1 son, Stephen Hao b. 1974; edn: LL.B, Central Police Univ. 1969; BCS, Univ. Windsor Canada 1974; MSTM, Am. Univ. Wash. D.C. 1982; Phd cand., Nova Univ., Ft. Lauderdale, Fla. 1990–. Career: systems analyst Computer Resource 1974-75; programmer, analyst Reed Paper, Toronto, Canada 1975-76; programmer, analyst Shell Canada, Don Mills 1976-79; group leader U.S. C.of C., Wash. D.C. 1979-82; data base adminstr. Freddie Mac 1982-84; project mgr. Computer Data Systems, Rockville, Md. 1984; mgr. IRM Western Airlines, Los Angeles 1984-87; mgr. DBA The Capital Group Inc., Brea 1987–; awards: outstanding service South Bay Chinese Sch. 1986, 88, Joint Chinese Univ. 1987; mem: Data Processing Mgmt. Assn., Data Adminstrn. Mgmt. Assn., Chinese Am. Engrs. & Scientists Assn. So. Calif., Chinese Am. Assn. So. Calif.; Republican; rec: travel. Ofc: The Capital Group, Inc. 135 S State College Blvd Brea 92621

CHEN, DAVID Y. C., acupuncturist; b. May 8, 1950, Taipei, Taiwan; nat. U.S. citizen 1985; s. Frank H.Y. and Josephine S.Y. (Chang) C.; m. Christina, Aug. 2, 1977; children: Phillip b. 1978, David, Jr. b. 1984; edn: Dr. of Oriental Medicine, Scientific Acupuncture Med. Ctr., 1970; OMD, Internat. Acupuncture. Univ. and Res. Inst., 1973; field surgeon, Nat. Def. Med. Coll., 1974; cert. acupuncturist, Calif. 1978; Calif. Comm. Coll. instr. cred., 1982–; provider of Cont. Edn. for RNs, LVNs, Physician's Assistants, Dentists and Podiatrists, Calif. 1983, 86. Career: clinic dir. Scientific Acupuncture Med. Ctr., Whittier, 1978–; staff mem. Calif. Inst. for Spinal Injuries and Disorders, Whittier, 1987–; appt. State Bd. of Med. Quality Assurance. 11th Dist. 1989-93; appt. chief examiner Acupuncture Examining Com 1989, chmn. Acupuncture Com. 1990; mem. Acupuncture Com. 1991, chairperson 1992-93; lectr. Rio Hondo Comm. Coll. 1982–, Fullerton Jr. Coll. 1979, Whittier Presbyn. Hosp. 1982, 83. 85, La Mirada Comm. Hosp. 1985, UC Irvine Med. Ctr. 1984; speaker var. civic groups; awards: appreciation award for comm. svc. Rio Hondo Coll. 1982, Kiwanis Club, Whittier 1984; award for dedication, contributions. & achievements in acupuncture, Acupuncture Res. Inst. 1990; mem: A.R.I. Hollywood Presbyn. Hosp., Chinese Medicine and Herb Assn. (res. fellow 1974), Asian Am. Republican Assn.; research herbal and acupuncture pain control; mil: capt. MC Army, hon. discharge. 1976; Republican; Christian; rec: classical music, homing pigeon racing, fishing. Ofc: Scientific Acupuncture Medical Center, Calif. Pain Control Clinic 14632 E. Whittier Blvd Whittier 90605

CHEN, HENRY TAAN, export-import executive; b. Nov. 19, 1927, Prome, Burma, naturalized U.S. cit. 1975; s. Ko Sein and Manip (Kok) C.; m. Won Fen Thuei, May 10, 1953; children: Alice H. b. 1954, Ohn b. 1955, Dorothy K. b. 1956, Mark b. 1958, Alan b. 1960, Angie K. b. 1967; edn: H.S. dipl. Fuzhou Coll., Fuzhou, China 1946; BS, National Tun Chi Univ., Shanghai, 1949; BS, Rangoon Univ., Burma 1954; reg. chem. engr., Rangoon 1954; PhD, Coll. of Buddhist Studies, U.S.A. 1991. Career: asst. engr. Kachin Chemical Work,

Rangoon 1952; engr. State Planning Board, Rangoon, Burma 1954; pres., owner Maung Sein Industries, 1954-64; pres., ptnr. Hong Kong Hosiery Works, 1954-63; pres., owner Pandeda Export & Import Corp., 1956-63; pres., ptnr. Kachin Mining Corp., Mykyina, Burma 1956-63; owner Oriental Trading Center, San Gabriel, Calif. 1968–; pres. Lucky and Happy Inc., 1972–; chmn. bd. Arahat Investment and Devel. Group Inc., 1983–; honors: fellow The Inst. of Commerce, London (1961); mem: U.S. C.of C., Alhambra C.of C., UCLA Alumni, Fuzhou Coll. Alumni/ China (pres. Overseas); Kiwanis Club (San Gabriel), San Marino Masonic Temple; inventor, 2 U.S. Patents (1973, 76); Buddhist; rec: Chinese violin, photog., travel (50+ countries), languages. Ofc: Lucky and Happy, Inc. 324 S San Gabriel Blvd San Gabriel 91776

CHEN, KUO-CHING, acupuncturist; b. Oct. 17, 1924, Hsiaoshan, Chekiang, China; s. Wen-Jui and Shih (Kung) C.; m. Yuan-Yuan, Mar. 4, 1967; children: Ju-Ching b. 1969, Chi-Yu b. 1972; edn: Chinese Literature & Art Coll., China 1942-45; Chih-Chiang Univ., China 1946-47; advanced acupuncture 1-yr. course, Taiwan 1960; A.M.D., PhD in oriental medicine, Asian Am. Acupuncture Med. Univ., USA 1984; cert. acupuncturist, Calif. St. Bd. (1978); cert. acupuncture instr. Calif. Supt. of Public Instr. (1984). Career: acupuncturist prin., Kuo-Ching Chen Acupuncture and Tui-Na Manipulation Clinic, Taipei, Taiwan 1949-83, acupuncture master of 15 apprentices 1964-85; Chen's, K.C. Acupuncture, South Pasadena 1983–; splst. in clin. treatment of neck pain, back pain and infertility; clinic supr. Acupuncture Coll. of Los Angeles Univ. 1985-87; honors: first doctor in Rep. of China to treat Pres. M. Hubert Maga, Rep. of Dahomey with Acupuncture and Tui-Na Manipulation 1963, plaque inscribed "The Doctor that Performs Wonders" from Fernando Sanchez R., Amb. of Costa Rica 1982, Silver medal from Chinese Acupuncture Soc. 1980, listed Men of Achievement, Internat. Biog. Ctr., Cambridge, Eng. 1989; mem: Taipei Acupuncture Assn. (gen. adminstr. 1961-67), Chinese Acupuncture Assn. (1960–, chmn. edition & paper-selection com. 1966-68, chmn. promotion com. 1969), Nat. Commn. for Certification of Acupuncturists (1984-85), Acupuncture Medicine Assn. of So. Calif. (1984–, dir. 1985-86, supr. 1987-88, chmn. 1993-94), Acupuncture Inst. for Addiction Free Life (founding mem. 1993–); PhD diss: Intro. of Chinese Acupuncture (1983-84); research: clin. diagnosis using reflex points on hands, face, feet, ears, extra points, Tui-Na Manipulation and acupuncture techniques 1962–; Buddhist; rec. gardening, Chinese brush painting. Ofc: Chen's, K.C. Acupuncture, APC, 2130 Huntington Dr Ste 216 South Pasadena 91030

CHEN, MILTON, educational broadcaster; b. Feb. 6, 1953, Negaunee, Mich.; s. Wen-Lan and Jeanne Chen; m. Ruth Cox, Aug. 18, 1985; children: Margaret b. Nov. 27, 1986; edn: AB (social studies), Harvard Coll. 1974; MA (communication), Stanford Univ. 1983, Ph.D. (communication) 1986. Career: dir. research Children's TV Workshop, New York, N.Y. 1978-80; asst. prof. Harvard Grad. Sch. of Edn., Cambridge, Mass. 1985-87; center dir., KQED Ctr. for Edn., San Francisco 1987–; consultant and advy. committes, Children's TV Workshop, Scholastic, PBS, Agency for Internat. Devel.; frequent speaker to parents' and ednl. groups; awards: Agency for Instructional Technology, Pacific Mountain Network, Children's TV Workshop, Internat. Communication Assn.; author: The Smart Parent's Guide to Kids' TV (KQED Books, 1994), 25+ pub. papers and chapts. on ednl. tech.; edit. book "Children & Microcomputers" pub. 1985; Democrat; rec: tennis, golf, running, parenting. Ofc: KQED 2601 Mariposa St San Francisco 94110

CHEN, YEAMOW, professor of finance; b. April 12, 1953, Taiwan; s. Shade and Yung-Young (Hsieh) C.; m. Shu-ru Chiang, Aug. 8, 1981; children: Elaine b. 1983, Allen b. 1984, Edward b. 1989; edn: BA econ., Nat. Taiwan Univ. 1976; MA, Ohio St. Univ. 1980; PhD, 1984. Career: assoc. prof. and prof. San Francisco St. Univ. 1984–; indep. cons., San Francisco 1988–; dir. U.S.-Chinese Business Inst. 1991–; awards: S.F. St. Univ. grantee 1988-89, Merit. Performance & Profl. Promise 1985-89, Chicago Bd. Options Exchange Competitive Res. Award 1992; mem: Chinese Am. Faculty Assn. (pres. 1988-89), Am. Fin. Assn., Am. Econ. Assn., Asian Bus. League, Chinese for Affirmative Action, Career Resources Devel. Center (planning and advy. com. 1986–), The City Club S.F.; articles pub. in profl. jours. (1984–); Republican; rec: travel, music, golf. Res: 655 Ulloa St San Francisco 94127 Ofc: San Francisco State Univ. School of Business 1600 Holloway Ave San Francisco 94132

CHESS, ROBERT BRUCE, company president; B. Jan. 31, 1957, Inglewood; s. Samuel and Shirley (Ablewitz) C.; edn: BS, Cal Tech, 1978; MBA, Harvard Univ., 1980. Career: strategic bus. segment chmn. Intel, Santa Clara 1980-83; segment mgr. Metaphor, Mountain View 1983-85; ptnr. Chess Frederick & Co., Palo Alto 1985-86; pres., dir. Penederm, Foster City 1986-89; dir: T.V. Mag. Network, Merion Station, Pa. 1985–, Mayfield Clinic, Palo Alto 1989-90; White House Fellow 1990-91; pres. and CEO, Inhale Therapeutic Systems 1991–; cons. Theater Bay Area, San Francisco 1987-88; rec: golf. Res: 60 San Mateo, Menlo Park 94301

CHESSER, STEVEN BRUCE, public relations specialist; b. Sept. 28, 1951, Lakeland, Fla.; s. Gordon Stuart (dec.) and Shirley Ann (Hoff) C.; m. Mary Sennholtz, 1972 (div. 1989); children: Bethany b. 1974, Michelle b. 1978; m.Karole Gwen Sense, Feb. 28, 1993; edn: BA, Univ. So. Caro. 1973; MA,

Univ. Okla. 1985. Career: U.S. Navy: public affairs splst., duties in Phila., Puerto Rico, Wash. D.C., Battleship New Jersey, and Long Beach 1973-93; media relations splst. L.A. Metropolitan Transit Authority 1993–; awards: Key to the City, Long Beach 1993; mem: Long Beach D.A.R.E. (bd. dirs., pres. 1993-94); technical advisor movie Marine Mammals-Naval Undersea Ptnrs. 1986; tech. adv. and mil. coord. for mini-series "Family of Spies" (CBS) and movies "Hunt for Red October" and "Flight of the Intruder" (Paramount), 1989; mil: lt. comdr. USN 1973-93, Navy Achievement Medal 1988, Navy Commendation Medal 1989, 1993; Republican; Prot.; rec: flying, bicycling, hiking. Res:2747 Altura Ave La Crescenta 91214 Ofc: Los Angeles MTA PO Box 194 Los Angeles 90053

CHEUNG, KAM YUEN, medical doctor; b. May 18, 1956; s. Kai Kei Cheung and Fuk Wa Chan; m. Anne Lai Siu, Feb. 8, 1983; children: Constance b. 1988, Crystal b. 1992; edn: BS, Long Island Univ., Brooklyn, NY 1981; MD, Albert Einstein Coll. of Medicine, Bronx, NY 1988. Career: internist, Beth Israel Med. Ctr., NY, NY 1988-91; MD, internist Buenaventura Med. Clinic Inc., Verona, Calif. 1991-93; pres. Kan Y. Cheung, MD, Inc., Oakland 1993–; awards: Long Island Univ. Dean's award and Med. Sch. honors-Endocrine and Neurology 1978-80; Richard 'St, M.D. Memorial award 1980, Alpha Epsilon Delta 1979, Soc. of Optimata 1980; mem: AMA 1988–, Calif. Med. Assn. 1993–, Ventura Co. Med. Assn. 1993–, Chinese C.of C., Oakland, Chinese Am. Physician Assn., Oakland; researcher: "The Contribution of Uridine and Oritic Acid to the Intracellular UPM Pool in Rat Liver Slices", 1978-81, "Heat of Hydroponation", 1979-81, "Properties of P19 Protein", 1988; rec: tennis, running, swimming. Ofc: 388 9th St #203 Oakland 94607

CHIA, HSIN-PAO, banking executive; b. May 6, 1920, Shanghai, China; s. Yang-Shan and Jui-Hsueh (Chang) C.; m. Beatrice, Oct. 9, 1943; children: Edward and Amy; edn: BA econs., St. John's Univ., Shanghai 1943. Career: gen. mgr. The Central Bank of China 1962-81; pres. Bank of Communications (now Chiao Tung Bank), Taipei, Taiwan 1981-85; chmn. bd. and c.e.o. Bank of Canton of California, San Francisco 1985–; chmn. Pacific Heritage Museum, S.F. 1985; honors: Most Outstanding in govt. services, R.O.C. 1969, Man of Year Chinatown Neighborhood Ctr., S.F. 1987, Resolution, Board of Suprs. S.F. City and County 1987, bd. dir. YMCA 1991–; clubs: World Trade, Bankers, Lake Merced G&C, Olympic G&C; rec: golf (USGA Honor Club). Ofc: Bank of Canton of California, 555 Montgomery St San Francisco 94111

CHICKS, CHARLES HAMPTON, mathematician; b. Nov. 10, 1930, Sandpoint, Ida.; s. Ralph Raymon and Emma Marie (Robbins) C.; m. Barbara Jean Thomson, June 19, 1956; children: Kathryn Montano b. 1957, Steven b. 1960, R. David b. 1968, Vicki Boatsman b. 1970; edn: BA, Linfield Coll., 1953; MA, Univ. Oregon, Eugene 1956, PhD, 1960; Stanford Univ., 1956-57. Career: mathematician GTE-Sylvania, Mt. View, Calif. 1957-69; ESL Inc., Sunnyvale, 1969-91, ret.; p.t. instr. Univ. of Santa Clara, 1964-86; trustee Linfield Coll., McMinnville, Oreg. 1972–; trustee Am. Bapt. Seminary of West, Berkeley 1982-91, chmn. 1995–; v.p. Am Baptist Churches of the West, 1992-93, pres. 1993-94; mem.: Am. Math. Soc. 1959–; Republican; Am. Baptist. Res: 925 Kamsack Ct Sunnyvale 94087

CHILDS, ALFRED WHEELER, physician; b. Oct. 11, 1922, San Francisco; s. Alfred Augustus and Genieve Estelle (Meloche) C.; m. Eunice Concordia Mahler; edn: BA, UC Berkeley 1943; MD, UCSF 1946; MPH, UC Berkeley 1964. Career: vis. fellow Columbia Coll. Physicians and Surgeons, N.Y. 1954-56; physician, San Francisco 1956-62; faculty UC Berkeley Sch. of Pub. Health, Berkeley 1964-75; physician, Berkeley 1976-95; med. resident UCSF 1949-53; mil: major USAF 1947-49. Ofc: 2500 Milvia St Ste 218 Berkeley 94704

CHIN, LLEWELLYN PHILIP, real estate lawyer; b. June 4, 1957, Saigon, Vietnam; s. Thomas and Quoc Kim (Sam) C.; edn: AA, Glendale Comm. Coll., 1980; BA (summa cum laude), USC, 1982; JD, Columbia Univ. Law Sch., 1986; admitted Calif. St. Bar 1988. Career: budget adminstr. USC, Los Angeles 1980-83; sr. counsel Calif. Assn. of Realtors, L.A. 1989–; Robert Kwan for School Bd., Monterey Park 1988; dist. coord. S.W. Voter Registration Proj., Monterey Park 1988; Alhambra City Council cand. 1992; legal counsel for: Elderly Indochinese Assn. 1992–, Chinese Am. Garment Contractor Assn. 1993–, Chinese Consolidated Benevolent Assn. 1993–, Multicultural Comm. Assn. 1993–, Chee How Oak Tin Family Assn. 1993–, Chinese Am. Entrepeneur Assn. 1993–, Hai Ninh Assn. 1994; prof. of law Southwestern Univ. Sch. of Law; honors: Totten Anderson Award, USC 1981, Phi Beta Kappa 1982, Beren Found. Scholar 1983-86, Harlan Fisk Stone Scholar 1986, Who's Who Among Am. Law Students 1986, Who's Who Among Practising Attys. 1989, Who's Who in Am. Law 1991; mem: Am. Bar Assn. (chair Real Prop. Sect. Improvement, Construction, Sales & Purchases of Residential R.E. Com.), Am. Immigration Lawyers Assn., Calif. State Bar (real property sect., co-chair Sales & Brokerage Subsect., and cons., Adv. Com. Continuing Educ. of the Bar), L.A. Co. Bar Assn., Fed. Bar Assn., Calif. Trial Lawyer Assn., Chinese Am. PAC (bd. dir. 1987-93), Chinese Am. Educ. Assn. (pres. 1994), planning commr. City of Alhambra; rec: organizing political/social events. Ofc: Calif. Assn. of Realtors, Legal Services Div. 525 S Virgil Ave Los Angeles 90020

CHIN, MARJORIE SCARLETT, corporate controller; b. Mar. 24, 1941, Reno, Nev.; d. Wing Yee and Jessie (Wong) Echavia; m. Manford Jeffrey Chin, Dec. 26, 1969; edn: AA, Contra Costa Coll., 1969; BS, John F. Kennedy Univ., 1988. Career: treas./controller Maya Corp., South San Francisco 1977-78; fin. and personnel coord. Garretson Elmendorf Zinov, San Francisco 1978-82; bus. mgr. Cyclotomics Inc., Berkeley 1982-85; controller JTS Leasing Corp., South S.F. 1985-88; controller and office mgr. Barbary Coast Steel Corp., Emeryville 1988–; bd. dirs. Experience Unlimited, Pleasant Hill 1992–; mem: Nat. Assn. Accts. (Oakland chpt. bd. 1984-85), Calif. Fedn. Bus. & Profl. Womens Club (S.F. chpt. sec. 1980-82), AAUW 1988–, Nat. Assn. Female Execs. 1990–, Am. Mgmt. Assn. (recogn. award 1990); civic: Am. Red Cross (vol. 1978), UNICEF (vol. 1980); rec: photog., gym, hiking, nature studies.

CHIN, PENNY, interior designer; b. Feb. 29, 1948, N.Y.C.; d. Peter and Celia (Goon) Chu; m. Chester Chin, May 1967 (div.); children: Wendy, Michelle, Kenneth, Cynthia, Karina; edn: AS in Interior Design (honors), Canada Coll. 1984; cert. kitchen & bath design, cert. ASID. Career: new accounts teller Lincoln Savs., Bklyn., 1965-66; exec. sec. Stauffer Chem. Co., N.Y.C., 1966-69; kitchen sales designer KBA Design, Palo Alto, 1982–; designer, planner Intraplan Design (formerly PC Design Assocs.), San Mateo, 1984–; v.p. Hildebrandt Assoc., 1990–; coord. health lectrs. Am. Cancer Soc., San Mateo, 1981; dir. health edn. San Francisco Med. Soc., 1980-81; mem. int. design advy. com. for Coll. San Mateo 1988-94; advy. bd. Kasmar Publications; honors: named Miss N.Y. Chinatown 1965, Miss Congeniality Miss USA Chinatown 1966, nat. award Health & Edn. Med. Soc. 1980-81; mem: Am. Soc. Interior Designers (Student Affairs liaison com., edn. pgm. & project chair, YWCA Comm. Svc. project, Am. Cancer Design House Com. 1994), Internat. Interior Designer Assn., Internat. Soc. Interior Designers, Inst. of Business Designers, Calif. Council Interior Designer Certification, Nat. Kitchen & Bath Assn., Gals for Am. Lung Assn., Asian Am. Mfg. Assn.; publs: Kitchen By Professionals, (Vol. I, II, III, IV, V, VII), Designer Kitchens & Baths (Fall '89), Kitchen By Designers, 1990. Calif. Kitchen & Bath (12/89), Bathroom & More By Professional Designers (Vol. I, II, III, IV, V), Designer's Calif. Kitchen & Bath Ed. '89, Kitchen & Bath Specialist (July 1990), Who's Who in Kitchen Design; rec: tennis. Address: 161 West 25th Ave San Mateo 94403

CHING, ERIC S.H., health care and insurance administrator; b. Aug. 13, 1951, Honolulu; s. Anthony D.K. and Amy K.C. (Chong) C.; edn: BS in biol. scis., Stanford Univ., 1973, Stanford-in-Germany, 1973; grad. stu. in marine pop. ecology, UCSB, 1973-74; MBA mktg. & org. beh., Stanford Univ. Sch. of Bus., 1977; MS in hlth. svs. adminstrn., Stanford Univ. Sch. of Medicine, 1977. Career: actg. dep. exec. dir. Santa Clara Co. Health Systems Agy., San Jose (short term contract), 1978; program officer Henry J. Kaiser Fam. Found., Menlo Park 1978-84; dir. strategic planning Lifeguard Inc., Milpitas 1984-90, also dir. ops./v.p. strategic planning Foundation Life Ins. Co. (startup co., subs. Lifeguard), Milpitas 1986-90; coord., product and competitive analysis Kaiser Found. Health Plan, Oakland 1990–; mem.: Stanford Alumni Assn. (life), Stanford Bus. Sch. Alumni Assn. (life), Stanford Swordmasters (pres. 1980-89, mem. varsity fencing team Stanford 1972-73); civic vol. United Way S.C.Co. 1985-90, L.A. Olympic Org. Com. 1984. Ofc: Kaiser Foundation Health Plan, Inc. One Kaiser Plaza 25th Fl Oakland 94612

CHINN, ROGER, architect, city official; b. May 22, 1933, Isleton; s. Gee and Bessie (Toy) C.; m. Rachel Han, Feb. 10, 1961; children: Annette b. 1961, Robert b. 1965; edn: AB arch., UC Berkeley 1957. Career: prin. Roger Chinn Architect AIA, San Francisco 1968-72, 1977–; gen. ptnr. Hertzka & Knowles 1972-77; apptd. planning commr. City of Foster City 1972-80, elected City Council Foster City 1980–; mayor 1981, 84, 85, 89, 91; chmn. S.F. Airport Roundtable 1982-92; mem: Am. Inst. of Arch.; civic: Foster City Lions (past pres., dist. gov. 1983-84, Lion of Yr. 1970, Melvin Jones Fellow 1987, Helen Keller Fellow 1988), Foster City Chinese Club (past pres.); author: Rehabilitation Plan of Isleton, Ca., 1982; contbr. Foster City Gen. Plan 1974, County Housing Plan 1976; mil: sp4 AUS 1958-60; Republican; Methodist; rec: hunting, fishing. Res: 833 Constitution Dr Foster City 94404 Ofc: 1485 Bayshore Blvd San Francisco 94124

CHIU, DOROTHY, physician, pediatrician; b. Aug. 8, 1917, Hong Kong; nat. 1955; d. Yan T. and Kwei-Ching (Wan) Chiu; m. Kitman Au, Dec. 29, 1949; children: Katherine b. 1950, Margo b. 1952, Doris b. 1955, James b. 1959, Richard b. 1962; edn: BS, Lingnan Univ. China 1939; MD, Nat. Shanghai Med. Coll. 1945. Career: sch. physician Burbank Unified Schs., Burbank 1957-58; Los Angeles Unified Schs. 1954-56; pediatrician pvt. practice, San Fernando 1956–; clin. instr. outpatients Childrens Hosp. Los Angeles 1955-70; awards: Childrens Hosp. L.A. 25 Year Service (1981); mem: Am. Acad. Pediatrics (fellow), L.A. Co. Med. Assn., CMA, Calvary Bible Ch.; Republican; Christian; rec: hand crafts. Res: 510 N Sunset Canyon Dr Burbank 91501 Ofc: 11273 Laurel Canyon Blvd San Fernando 91340

CHLAD, ARNOLD JOSEPH, physician, surgeon; b. Aug. 18, 1914, St. Paul, Minn.; s. Joseph B. and Otilia (Ekhaml) C.; m. Helen Marie Murphy, Nov. 17, 1948 (dec. 1985); children: Cheryl b. 1949, Michele b. 1950, Arnold P. b. 1953,

Gary b. 1956, Gregory b. 1962; edn: BS summa cum laude, St. Thomas Coll. 1934; MB, Univ. Minn. 1938; MD, 1939; residency and fellowship in surgery Univ. of Minn. and Charles T. Miller Hosp. 1942-46; diplomate Am. Bd. of Surgery 1947. Career: pvt. practice 1946–; honors: Alpha Omega Alpha; retired mem: CMA, AMA, San Diego Co. Med. Assn.; mil: 1st lt. AUS 1939; Catholic; rec: thoroughbred racehorses. Res: 7514 Girard Ave. C La Jolla 92037

CHONG, MARY DRUZILLEA, nurse; b. March 8, 1930, Fairview, OK; d. Charles Dewey and Viola Haddie (Ford) Crawford; m. Nyuk Choy Chong, Aug. 24, 1952 (div. 1968); children: Anthony b. 1954, Dorlinda b. 1955; edn: AA El Camino Jr. Coll. 1950; grad. nurse L.A. County Gen. Hosp. Sch. of Nursing 1953; BSN, PhN, CSU Los Angeles 1968. Career: staff nurse USC-L.A. Cty Gen. Hosp. 1957; UCLA-Harbor Gen. Hosp., Torrance 1958-69; hd. nurse Chest Med. Unit 1969-72; instr. Voc. Nurse Program, YWCA Job Corps, L.A. 1972-74; mobile intensive care nurse Victor Valley Hosp., Victorville 1974-79; dir. nursing San Vincente Hosp., L.A. 1980-82; Upjohn Healthcare Svcs., L.A. 1982-85, Bear Valley Comm. Hosp. Home Health Agcy., Big Bear Lake 1986-87; asst. dir. of nursing Care West Palm Springs 1987-88; instr. Valley Coll. of Med. & Dental Care Careers, N. Hollywood 1988-90; staff nurse Hi-Desert Continuing Care Ctr., Joshua Tree 1991-92; mem: AAUW, CSULA Alumni Assn., Internat. Platform Assn.; Democrat; Prot.; rec: gardening, crafts. Res: POB 697 Lucerne Valley 92356

CHOU, ALLEN CHINPIN, physician; b. Jan. 1, 1951, Taiwan, nat. 1985; s. Kwanhwei and Lanfong (Chen) C.; m. Annie Wentzu Huang, Feb. 25, 1978; children: Kenneth b. 1979, Emily b. 1982, Andrew b. 1990; edn: MD, Kaohsiung Med. Coll., Taiwan 1975; Fellow Am. Coll. of Physicians, 1991; Diplomate Am. Bd. Internal Medicine, 1985, and Geriatric Medicine, 1990. Career: family practice resident Barberton (Oh.) Citizen Hosp., 1978-79; med. resident Mt. Sinai Hosp. Chgo. 1979-80, St. Joseph's Hosp. of Phoenix, Az. 1980-82; attdg. physician Coastal Communities Hosp., Santa Ana 1982–, Western Med. Ctr., Santa Ana 1982–, Medical Ctr. Garden Grove 1983–; mem: AMA, Am. Coll. Physicians, Am. Soc. Geriatrics; rec: tennis, travel. Res: 45 St Tropez Newport Beach 92660 Ofc: 2621 S Bristol St Ste 203 Santa Ana 92704

CHOU, CHUNG-KWANG, biomedical engineer; b. May 11, 1947, Chung-King, China, naturalized U.S. citizen 1979; s. Chin-Chi and Yu-lien (Shiao) C.; m. Grace Wong, June 9, 1973; children: Jeffrey b. 1974, Angela b. 1979; edn: BSEE, Nat. Taiwan Univ., 1968; MSEE, Washington Univ., 1971; PhD, Univ. Wash., 1975. Career: res. assoc. Univ. Wash., Seattle 1976-77, asst. prof. 1977-81, res. assoc. prof./assoc. dir. 1981-85; res. scientist City of Hope Med. Center, Duarte 1985–, dir. radiation res. 1991–; cons. Los Alamos Lab. 1986-90, Nat. Council Radiation Protection 1978–; mem. NIH spl. study session 1987–; awards: postdoc. fellow NIH 1976-77, 1st Spl. Award of Decade, Internat. Microwave Power Inst. 1981, outstanding paper award Jour. of Microwave Power 1985, Electromagnetic Acad. 1990–; mem: Bioelectromagnetics Soc. (charter, 1979–; recipient Curtis Carl Johnson Mem. Award 1995), Inst. Elect. and Electronics Engring. (Fellow 1989–), IEEE SCC28 1979–, IEEE USA COMAR (subcom. chmn. 1990–, vice chmn. 1994-95, chmn. 1996-97), No. Am. Hyperthermia Soc. (charter 1984–), Internat. Microwave Power Inst. 1979–, Radiation Res. Soc. 1984–; author: 130+ book chapters and articles in Bioelectromagnetics and Hyperthermia (1973–), Patent on Intracavitary Microwave applicator (1989); assoc. ed. J. of Bioelectromagnetics 1987–, mem.: editl. bd. IEEE Trans. on Microwave Theory and Techniques 1987–; mil: 2d lt. Army Taiwan 1968-69; Republican; Christian; rec: gardening, fishing. Res: 11 E Longden Ave Arcadia 91006 Ofc: City of Hope National Medical Ctr. Duarte 91010

CHOU, YUE-HONG, professor, cartographer; b. Oct. 14, 1952, Taipei, Taiwan, naturalized U.S. citizen 1991; s. Chang-Shong and Chin-Lien (Cheng) C.; m. Grace Liau, Aug. 11, 1978; children: Jason H. b. 1982, Jonathan W. b. 1990; BS, Nat. Taiwan Univ., 1975; MA, Ohio State Univ., 1979; PhD, 1983; Career: asst. prof. Northwestern Univ., Evanston, Ill. 1984-87; asst. prof. to assoc. prof. Univ. Calif., Riverside 1987–; prin. investigator: US Forest Service, Riv. 1989–, US Dept. of Navy, San Bruno 1990-92, So. Calif. Assn. of Govts., LA 1990, US Marine Corps, Yuma, Az. 1990-92; cons. Air Pollution Ctr., Riv. 1991-92; awards: CBJ and CKF awards: Nat. Taiwan Univ. 1974, 75; Huntington award Ohio State Univ. 1983, Faculty Honor award Northwestern Univ. 1987, res. grantee US Forest Svc. Berkeley 1990; mem: Assn. of Am. Geographers 1979–, Am. Congress on Surveying & Mapping 1987–, Am. Soc. Photogrammetry & Remote Sensing 1988–, Am. Cartographic Assn. 1988–, Urban Reg. Info. Systems Assn. 1989–; publs: articles in Transp. Research, 1993, Forest Sci., 1993, Geographical Analysis, 1991, Transp. Planning & Tech., 1991, Photo. Engring. & Remote Sensing, 1990, Taiwan Tribune, 1990; Evangelical Formosan Ch., Cerritos (chmn. 1992-93); rec: travel. Ofc: Dept. Earth Scis. Univ. California, Riverside 92521

CHOUDHARY, SUSHIL KUMAR, manufacturing company president; b. Apr. 2, 1937, Darbhanga, Bihar, India; s. Uttam Lal and Karpoor C.; m. Lalita, Jan. 7, 1973; children: son Rajesh b. Oct. 22, 1973, dau. Neeta b. Dec. 19, 1979; edn: MBA, Golden Gate Univ., 1968. Career: consular officer Govt. of India, San Francisco 1964-79; pres. Indo-U.S. Industries 1977–, pres. American Gage

& Medical Products, Inc., San Francisco 1985–; mem. Rotary Club Intl., N.Am. Hunting Club, Nat. Rifle Assn. of Am. Res: 1550 O'Farrell St #5 San Francisco CA 94115 Ofc: FAWSCO, PO Box 420552 San Francisco CA 94142-0552

CHOUNG, JOON HO, physician; b. Feb. 17, 1938, Kyunggi-do, Korea; s. Won Bock and Han Soon (Kim) C.; m. Jong, Oct. 9, 1967; children: Clara b. 1968, Rosa b. 1970, Paul b. 1978; edn: MD, Cath. Medical Coll., Seoul 1963. Career: instr. Cath. Medical Coll., Seoul 1971-73; clin. asst. prof. Hahnemann Med. Coll., Phila. 1978; pvt. practice internal med., Los Angeles 1979–, attdg. physician Good Samaritan Hospital; mem. Am. Soc. of Internal Medicine, Los Angeles County Med. Assn., LA Cancer Soc. (bd. 1981-83); rec: tennis, golf. Ofc: LA Medical Center 3671 West Sixth St Los Angeles 90020

CHOY, ALLAN KINN, architect; b. Dec. 5, 1920, Canton, China; s. K.C. and Wong (Shee) C.; m. Mary Yee, July 16, 1950; children: Terence b. 1952, Timothy b. 1954, Bryan b. 1960; edn: BArch, USC 1948. Career: chief architect E.L. McCoy, Bakersfield 1948-59; ptnr. Goss/Choy 1959-67; ptnr. Harding/Choy/Gaines 1967-71; county architect Co. of Kern 1971-88; ret.; architect: Co. Services Bldg., Independence; Am. Nat. Bank, Bakersfield; FBI Bldg., Las Vegas, Nev.; Co. Library, Shafter; mem: Am. Arbitration Assn., AIA, Bakersfield E Rotary Club (dir.); mil: s.sgt. USAAF 1943-46; Republican; Congregationalist. Res: 500 Jamaica Way Bakersfield 93309

CHRISTENSEN, DONN WAYNE, insurance executive; b. Apr. 9, 1941, Atlantic City, NJ; s. Donald F. and Dorothy L. C.; m. Sue H. Kim, Feb. 14, 1987; children: Donn Jr. b. 1964, Lisa b. 1965; edn: BS, Univ. Santa Clara 1964. Career: West Coast div. mgr. Ford Motor Co. 1964-65; agt. Conn. Mutual Life Ins. 1965-68; founder, pres. Christensen & Jones Mgt. & Ins. Svcs. Inc. 1969–; bd. dirs. Research Devel. Systems Inc., Duarte Drug Abuse Council, Mid-Valley Mental Health Ctr.; mem. White Mem. Hosp. Instl. Review Bd. 1975–, and Com. for Animal Care 1987–; mem. Friends Med. Research Instl. Review Bd. 1993-; honors: LA Gen. Agents and Mgrs. Assn. Man of Year (4 yrs.); mem: Nat. Assn. Life Underwriters, Nat. Assn. Music Mfrs. & Merchants, Am. Soc. Pension Actuaries; civic: Duarte Drug Abuse Council (pres. 1974-75), Foothill Comm. Concert Assn. (pres. 1970-73), Woodlyn Property Owners Assn. (pres. 1972-73), L'Ermitage Found. 1985; rec: tennis, bicycling, travel. Res: 4000 Pulido Ct Calabasas 91302 Ofc: Christensen & Jones Inc. 77 N Oak Knoll Ste 101 Pasadena 91101

CHRISTENSEN, TED, artist; b. Mar. 20, 1911, Vancouver, Wash.; s. Ted and Francine Catherine (Christensen) C.; edn: Art Center Sch., L.A. 1945, Portland (Ore.) Museum Sch., grad. Otis Art Inst., L.A. 1949. Career: free lance artist-painter, printmaker, potter, San Francisco Bay area since 1949; exhibited in museums and galleries, 60+ one man shows nat., represented in permanent collections in USA, Canada, Denmark, Germany, Switzerland, Turkey, Spain, Chile, China, and Japan; instr. Coll. of Marin, 1952-60; awards: 50+ awards, 1941–, listed Who's Who in Am. Art, Who's Who in West, Internat. Biographical Inst. (England), World Art Diary (Italy); mem. Marin Watercolor Soc., Mendocino Art Ctr.; publs: feature article, America Artists Mag., 1976, Artist Mag., London, 1978, cover and feature article, Art of Calif. Mag., 1993; included in book: 20 Landscape Artists & How They Work (pub. Watson Guptil, 1977). Studio: 573 Third St East, Sonoma 95476

CHRISTOPHER, GAYLAIRD WILEY, architect; b. Dec. 14, 1951, Los Angeles; s. Wiley S. and Eleanor A. (Smith) C.; m. Gayle Ann Gibbons, Sept. 25, 1976; children: Katie Marie b. 1981, Whitney Gayle b. 1983, Hayley Suzanne b. 1986; edn: AA, Pasadena City Coll. 1972; B.Arch., Calif. Polytech. St. Univ. 1976. Career: project mgr. Powell Morgridge Richards & Coghlan, Los Angeles 1976-77; project designer VETCO, Ventura; assoc. architect Barmakian Wolff & Assoc., Upland 1977-81; pres. Wolff Lang Christopher Architects Inc., Rancho Cucamonga 1981–; educator Chaffey Coll.; lectr. Council of Ednl. Facility Planners; juror Am. Soc. Sch. Bus. Officials; awards: Am. Assn. Sch. Adminstrs. Design award (1988), Council Ednl. Facility Planners Ruben S. Ayala award (1987); mem: St. Calif. Allocation Bd. Legislative Implementation Com., CASBO (So. section facilty com.), Architecture for Edn. Com., Soc. Am. Reg. Architects, Coalition for Adequate Sch. Housing; author: Developing the Master Plan (1987), jour. articles (1988); Democrat; Episcopalian. Res: 1055 W 25th St Upland 91786 Ofc: Wolff/Lang/Christopher Architects Inc. 10470 Foothill Blvd Tower Ste Rancho Cucamonga 91730

CHU, MORGAN, lawyer; b. Dec. 27, 1950, New York; m. Helen M. Wong, Dec. 29, 1970; edn: BA, UCLA 1971; MA, 1972; PhD, 1973; MSL, Yale Univ. 1974; JD magna cum laude, Harvard Univ. 1976; admitted St. Bar Calif. (1976), U.S. Dist. Ct. Central Dist. Calif. (1977), U.S. Ct. Appeals 9th Circuit (1980), U.S. Dist. Ct. No. Dist. Calif. (1980), U.S. Dist. Ct. So. Dist. Calif. (1984), U.S. Dist. Ct. Eastern Dist. Calif. (1986), U.S. Ct. Appeals Fed. Cir. (1989). Career: law clk. to judge of U.S. Ct. Appeals 9th Circuit, S.F. 1976-77; atty., assoc. Irell & Manella, L.A. 1977-82, ptnr. 1982–; adj. prof. UCLA Sch. Law 1979-82; judge pro tem L.A. Municipal Ct. 1980-88; assoc. ed. Litigation 1981-84; postdoctoral fellow Yale Univ. 1974; mem: Am. Bar Assn. (chmn. high tech. intellectual property and patent trials subcom. 1986-89, trial practice com. litiga-

tion sect.), Calif. Bar Assn., L.A. Co. Bar Assn. (judiciary com.). Ofc: Irell & Manella 1800 Ave of Stars Ste 900 Los Angeles 90067-4276 Tel: 310/277-1010

CHUNG, EILEEN LOUIE, corporate designer; b. March 26, 1954, New York; d. Louie W. and Doris Mo Han (Chan) Chung; m. Russell A. LeDet, June 28, 1986; edn: grad. John Adams Sch., 1973; career: jewelry sales buyer Gary Sales Inc. San Francisco, 1970-1973; printing clk. Ready Copy Service, 1973-1974; acctg. clk. Tia Maria Inc., 1974-75; mgr., graphic designer, typesetter, Monarch Graphics, 1975-1981; owner, corporate graphic designer, typographer, graphic/printing cons. Spectrum Graphics, San Francisco 1981–; minister, tchr. Church of Divine Man 1994–; also fashion model Barbara Davis Sch. of Modeling and Agency, San Francisco 1982-92; Democrat; Christian; rec: travel, photo., music. Res: 169 Homestead Blvd Mill Valley 94941 Ofc: Spectrum Graphics, 55 New Montgomery Street, Ste 514, San Francisco 94105

CHURCHMAN, DAVID ALAN, educator; b. July 20, 1938, New York; s. Stanley and Elizabeth (Lawson) C.; edn: BA, Mich. Univ. 1960; MA, 1964; PhD, UCLA 1972. Career: tchr. Internat. Sch., Tangier, Morocco 1965-66; Marple Newton H.S., Newtown Square, Pa. 1966-68; research assoc. UCLA 1972-76; prof. CSU, Dominguez Hills 1976–; Calif. chmn. Nat. Council on US-Arab Relations 1993-95; dir. Orangutan Found., Los Angeles 1985-92; treas., dir. Wildlife on Wheels 1982–; cons. Nat. Drug Abuse Center, Wash. D.C. 1974-78; Tribal Am. Corp., Los Angeles 1972-78; Melbourne & Singapore Zoos, Australia 1986-87; mem: Am. Assn. Zoological Parks & Aquariums, Internat. Assn. Zoo Educators, L.A. Mediation Roundtable, NRA; author: Negotiation Tactics, 1993, 95, Basic Negotiating Tactics, 1988, co-author Evaluation Workshop (I in 1971, II in 1973); columnist Armchair General, 1982-89, articles and papers pub. in profl. jours., 1969–; mil: lt. AUS 1960-62; Republican; rec: shooting, jogging, chess, cooking, photog., travel. Ofc: California State University Dominguez Hills 90747

CIESLAK, WILLIAM MARION, president, Franciscan School of Theology; b. Sept. 12, 1946, East Chicago, Ind.; s. Walter Bernard and Irene Joan (Koziol) C.; edn: BA, St. Joseph Coll., Rensselaer, Ind. 1969; MDiv, Franciscan Sch. of Theology, Berkeley, Calif. 1973; PhD, Graduate Theol. Union, Berkeley 1979. Career: asst. prof. St. Francis Seminary, Milwaukee, Wis. 1976-80; vis. prof. Franciscan Sch. of Theology, Berkeley 1980-82, prof. 1982-92, pres. 1992–; vis. faculty Inst. of Spirituality and Theology, Santa Barbara 1981–; mem. editorial bd. Modern Liturgy, San Jose 1982-88; adv. U.S. Bishops' Com. on Liturgy, Wash., DC 1985-89; vis. lectr. Vatican II Inst., Menlo Park 1985–; mem.: Catholic Theol. Soc. of Am. 1980–, No. Am. Acad. of Liturgy 1982–, Societas Liturgica 1982–; author: Console One Another, 1990, pub. articles 1981–; Democrat; Roman Catholic; rec: travel, racquetball. Ofc: Franciscan School of Theology 1712 Euclid Ave Berkeley 94709

CIONE, JOHN P., mutual funds broker, dealer, company executive; b. Sept. 1, 1933, Brooklyn, N.Y.; s. Michael and Grace (Chille) C.; m. Roberta Catherine Irwin, Oct. 1, 1960; children: John b. 1961, Robert b. 1962, Christine b. 1964, Cynthia b. 1967; edn: BA, St. Francis Coll. 1955; JD, St. Johns Univ. 1961; admitted St. Bar N.Y. 1962. Career: dir. legal and compliance Blyth Eastman Dillon & Co. Inc., N.Y.C. 1965-80; indep. floor broker and mem. Am. Stock Exchange 1980-86; mem. New York Stock Exchange 1981-86; v.p. Seligman Securities Inc. 1982-85; sr. v.p., gen. counsel/compliance dir. Sutro & Co. Inc., S.F. 1985-86; cons., Sausalito and Santa Monica 1987-88; pres. Foresters Equity Services Inc., San Diego 1988-94; securities cons. 1994–; pres. Legal & Compliance Div. Securities Industry Assn., N.Y.C. 1970-72; instr. Inst. of Fin. 1970-90; arbitrator Am. Stock Exchange 1976–, N.Y. Stock Exchange 1993–; Nat. Assn. Securities Dealers 1972, 1985–; mem: Am. Bar Assn. (corp. law div.), Am. Arbitration Assn. 1992; mil: 1st lt. USMCR 1953-57; Republican; Cath.; rec: racquetball, sailing, fishing. Res: 474 Palmitas St Solana Beach 92075 Tel: 619/259-7346

CISLO, DONALD M., patent lawyer; b. Jan. 21, 1935, Chicago, Ill.; s. Marion J. and Marie (Kurzek) C.; m. Sharon A., May 2, 1970; edn: BS, Ill.Inst. Tech. 1957; LL.B, DePaul Univ. 1964. Career: patent agent, atty. Pure Oil Co., Palatine, Ill. 1963-65; patent atty. Mahoney Schick Cislo, Santa Monica 1970-79; Cislo & Thomas 1979–; mem: Am. Bar Assn., Santa Monica Bar Assn. (trustee), L.A. Co. Bar Assn. (trustee), Marina Bar Assn. (trustee, pres.); rec: painting. Ofc: Cislo & Thomas 233 Wilshire Blvd Ste 900 Santa Monica 90401

CITRIN, WILLIE, physician; b. Mar. 18, 1947, Amberg, Germany; naturalized U.S. citizen 1962; s. Abe and Dora (Bril) C.; edn: BA, Rutgers Univ., 1968; MD, N.J. Coll. Med., 1972. Career: served to major US Army, Korea, 1975-77; med. staff Parkview Hosp., Riverside, Calif., 1977–; dir. Parkview Clinic 1977-81; chief dept. medicine 1983-86; chief of staff 1986-88; pvt. med. practice, 1981–; mem. Am. Coll. Physicians 1975–, Am. Soc. Internal Med., Calif. Soc. Int. Med., Am. Med. Assn., Calif. Med. Assn., Riv. 1978–. Ofc: W. Citrin MD, Inc. 3975 Jackson St Ste 203 Riverside 92503

CLABAUGH, ELMER EUGENE, JR., lawyer; b. Sept.18, 1927, Anaheim; s. Elmer Eugene and Eleanor Margaret (Heitshusen) Clabaugh; children: Christopher Chapman, Matthew Martinson; edn: BBA cum laude, Woodbury

Coll. 1951, BA summa cum laude, Claremont McKenna Coll. 1958, JD, Stanford Law Sch. 1961; Career with US State Dept., Jerusalem, and Tel Aviv, 1951-53; Pub. Adminstrn. Service, El Salvador, Ethiopia, and USA, 1952-57; admitted Calif. Bar 1961; deputy dist. atty. Ventura Co., Calif. 1961-62; atty. law firm Hathaway, Clabaugh, Perrett & Webster in Ventura 1962-79; individual practice, 1979–; State Inheritance Tax referee, 1968-78; city atty. City of Thousand Oaks, 1964-69, City of Simi Valley, 1969-71; mem: bd. dirs. San Antonio Water Conservation Dist., Ventura Co. Found. Port-Harbor 1985–, Ventura Co. Maritime Museum 1988–; bd. dirs. Ventura Community Mem. Hosp.; trustee Ojai Unified Sch. Dist. 1974–; mem: Calif. Bar Assn., Am. Arbitration Assn., Phi Alpha Delta; Rep. rec: hunting, tennis, sailing. Res: 241 Highland Dr Channel Islands Harbor 93035 Ofc: 1190 S Victoria Ave Ste 305 Ventura 93003

CLAES, DANIEL JOHN, medical research director; b. Dec. 3, 1931, Glendale; s. John Vernon and Claribel (Fleming) Claes; m. Gayla Blasdel, Jan. 19, 1974; edn: AB magna cum laude, Harvard Univ. 1953; MD cum laude, Harvard Med. Sch. 1957. Career: intern UCLA, 1957-58; Boywer Found. Fellow, resident in medicine, L.A., 1958-61; pvt. practice spec. in diabetes mellitus, Los Angeles 1962–;Am. Eye Bank Found. vice pres. 1978–, dir./med. res. 1980–; awards: Boywer Found. award for excellence in medicine, 1958; mem. Los Angeles Co. Med. Assn.; clubs: Royal Commonwealth (London) Harvard (So. Calif.), Harvard Med. Sch. (So. Calif.); contbr. to profl. literature on computers in med. and on diabetes mellitus. Ofc: Daniel J. Claes, MD, Inc. 15327 Sunset Blvd Ste A236 Pacific Palisades 90272

CLARK, ALBERT G., physician; b. Dec. 14, 1906, New York; s. Clarence G. and Margaret A. (Rastenberg) C.; m. Helen Hoegh, Nov. 11, 1935; children: Barbara b. 1937, Albert b. 1938, Patricia b. 1941, William b. 1946; edn: BA, UC Berkeley 1928; MD, UCSF 1932. Career: surgeon, Boulder City, Nev. 1934-35; asst. clin. prof., assoc. clin. prof. UCSF Med. Sch. 1938-78; pvt. practice surgery 1935-41, 1945-78; mem: San Francisco Co. Med. Soc. (pres. 1967), CMA (councillor 1968-75, secty. 1974-75), Univ. Calif. Emeritus Faculty Orgn. (pres. 1989), San Francisco Rose Soc., Monterey Heights Assn. (pres. 1985-87), San Francisco Comp. Health Planning (pres. 1967-70), Calif. Blue Shield (trustee 1972-75), Calif. St. Health Advy. Council, Peer Review Orgn. San Francisco (pres. 1975-79); 7 articles pub. in surgical jours. (1937-69); mil: lt. col. AUS 1941-45; Republican; rec: woodworking, gardening. Res: 68 Fernwood Dr San Francisco 94127

CLARK, DIDDO, mediator,arbitrator,attorney; b. Jan. 20, 1950, Oakland; d. Johnson and Louise Clark; m. Paul Reiche; edn: AA, Diablo Valley Coll., 1968; BA, UC San Diego, 1973; JD, Georgetown Univ., 1976. Career: gen. civil litigation Solomon, Ward, Aguirre and Seidenwurm, San Diego 1978; federal appellate litigation U.S. Dept. of Labor, Wash. DC 1979-83; bus. law pvt. practice, Law Offices of Diddo Clark, Wash. DC and Lafayette, Calif. 1984-92; prin., Dispute Resolvers, mediation and arbitration law firm, Lafayette 1992–; court-apptd. mediator 1976–, mediation trainer for businesses, bar assns., ednl. institutions; court-apptd. arbitrator for U.S. Dist. Ct., Superior Cts. (S.F. Bay area), Diverse ADR Inc., ADR Inc. and since 1980, The Am. Arbitration Assn.; judge pro tem Contra Costa Co. Superior Ct.; litigator (retired); profl. marathon swimmer, and profl. writer in law, pub. affairs, and recreation; dir. Dublin Land Co. 1989–, pres. 1993–; dir. Nat. Amateur Sports Found. 1989–; awards: nat. champion Jessup Internat. Moot Ct. Competition, Am. Soc. Internat. Law 1975, Women's Record: for swimming around Manhattan in 6 hrs. 52 min. 15 sec., Manhattan Is. Swimming Assn. N.Y. 1983, for swimming Bay Bridge to Golden Gate Bridge, South End Rowing Club, S.F. 1983; mem: State Bar of Calif. (acting co-chair ad hoc ADR com. 1994; mem. ADR bar ldrs. roundtable and litigation sect. ADR com.), Contra Costa Co. Bar Assn., Alameda Co. Bar Assn., Golden Gate Swimmers (race organizer and pres. 1988-93), Am. Bar Assn. 1987–, League Women Voters (bd. 1986-90), Artists Equity Assn. (local bd. 1977-78, nat. fund bd. 79-84); publs: (book of poetry) The Train, 1967, law jour. article re criminal justice, 1973, numerous mag. articles; avocation: marathon swimming. Ofc: 6 Blackthorn Rd Lafayette 94549-3307

CLARK, R. BRADBURY, lawyer; b. May 11, 1924, Des Moines, Ia.; s. Rufus Bradbury and Gertrude Martha (Burns) C.; m. Polly King, Sept. 6, 1949; children: Cynthia b. 1954, Rufus B. b. 1956, John A. b. 1961; edn: BA, Harvard Coll., 1946; JD, Harvard Law Sch., 1951; Dipl.L. Oxford Univ., 1952; D.H.L. (hon.) Ch. Divinity Sch. of the Pacific, 1983. Career: atty., assoc. O'Melveny & Myers, L.A. 1952-61, ptnr. 1962-93, of counsel 1993–, mem. mgmt. com. 1983-90; chancellor Episcopal Diocese of L.A. 1967–; dir.: So. Calif. Water Co., San Dimas; Brown Internat. Corp., Covina; Automatic Machinery & Electronics Inc., Covina; Automatic Machinery Corp., Covina; The John Tracy Clinic, L.A.; Economic Resources Corp., L.A.; Prot. Episcopal Ch. Diocese of L.A.; awards: Hon. Canon, Diocese of Los Angeles 1981, Phi Beta Kappa, Fulbright grantee 1951-52; mem. Am. Bar Assn. (subcom. on audit letter responses, com. on law and acctg., com. on legal opinions), Calif. Bar Assn. (corporations com. 1976-77, chmn. drafting com. on gen. corp. law 1977-78, chmn. drafting com. on nonprofit corp. law 1980-84, bus. law sect. exec. com. 1977-78, 1984-87, mem. com. on nonprofit corp. law 1991–), L.A. Co. Bar Assn.; clubs: Harvard (So. Calif.), Alamitos Bay Yacht, Chancery (L.A.); editor: Calif. Corp. Laws (Ballantine &

Sterling), contbr. various articles on corp. matters in law jours.; mil: capt. US Army 1943-46, Bronze star w. OLC, Purple Heart w. OLC, other service awards; Republican; Episcopalian; rec: sailing. Res: 615 Alta Vista Cir South Pasadena 91030 Ofc: O'Melveny & Myers, 400 S Hope St Los Angeles 90071

CLARK, RICHARD WARD, food industry executive, consultant; b. Oct. 23, 1938, N.Y., N.Y.; s. Richard Leal and Dorothy Jane (Whittaker) C.; edn: BA (distinction) Univ. Rochester, 1960; MBA fin., Wharton Sch. Univ. Pa., 1962. Career: corp. planning analyst Campbell Soup Co., Camden, N.J. 1965-67; asst. product mgr. General Mills Inc., Mpls. 1967-70; sr. fin. analyst McKesson Corp., San Francisco 1970-71, asst. div. controller 1971-72, division controller 1972-78, gen. mgr. Grocery Prods. Devel. 1978-79, v.p./ controller McKesson Foods Group 1979-84, dir. strategic planning McKesson Corp. 1985-87; v.p. fin. and c.f.o. Provigo Corp. (market wholesale grocery), San Rafael 1987-89; hotel devel. prin. and cons. Napa Valley Assocs., S.A., San Francisco 1990–; bd. dir. Taylor Cuisine Inc., S.F. 1990-92; awards: Sherman fellow Univ. Rochester 1960, Beta Gamma Sigma 1962; mem. Fin. Execs. Inst. 1981-90; civic: Salvation Army Rehab. Ctrs., S.F. (advy. bd. dir. 1984–, chmn. 1993–), Services for Seniors Bd., S.F. (dir. 1990-93); club: Bohemian (S.F.); author: Some Factors Affecting Dividend Payout Ratios, 1962; recording artist (tape cassette) "I Love a Piano" Quicksilver Records, 1990 and (compact disc)"I Play the Songs", 1993; mil: lt. jg. USNR 1962-65; Republican; Presbyterian; rec: piano, singing, skiing, tennis, jogging. Res: 2201 Sacramento St #401 San Francisco 94115

CLARK, ROGER WILLIAM, lawyer, educator; b. Aug. 29, 1954, Savanah, Ga.; s. Joseph Logan and Norell (Roper) C.; m. Kathy Kacerek; son, Joseph Roger b. 1986; edn: BS, Florida St. Univ., Tallahasee 1975; JD, Rutgers Sch. of Law, 1978; admitted bar: Calif. 1983, Fla. 1978. Career: atty., assoc. Blackwell et al, Miami, Fla. 1978-80; ptnr. Engstrom, Lipscomb & Lack, Los Angeles 1983-92; ptnr. Bienstock & Clark, Santa Monica 1992–; instr. bus. law Fla. Internat. Univ., 1979, Univ. of Phoenix, L.A., 1989–; pres. and chmn. The Iraida Found. Inc.; honors: Beta Gamma Sigma; mem: Am. Bar Assn., L.A. Co. Bar Assn.; author radio program & newpaper articles: You and the Law (1982-83); mil: USAF Acad., hon. disch. 1973; Democrat; Prot.; rec: scuba diving. Res: 23334 Berdon St Woodland Hills 91367 Ofc: Bienstock & Clark 3340 Ocean Park Blvd Suite 3075 Santa Monica 90405

CLARK, THOMAS SULLIVAN, lawyer; b. Dec. 12, 1947, Bakersfield; s. Walter J. and Ruth Virginia (Sullivan) C.; edn: BA in hist., USC, 1969, JD, 1973. Career: gen. counsel Income Equities Corp., Los Angeles, 1972-74; polit. campaign cons. 1974-75; dep. dist. atty., prosecutor Office of Kern County Dist. Atty., Bakersfield 1975-78; pvt. practice, ptnr. law firm Arrache, Clark & Potter (formerly Rudnick, Arrache & Clark), Bakersfield 1978–; cons. Volunteer Atty. Pgm., 1985–; Kern Co. Dem. Cent. Com. 1976-80; mem: Calif. Bar Assn., Kern County Bar Assn. (client cons. 1984–), USC Alumni Assn. (Kern Co. bd. 1985–, pres. 1988-89); civic: Kern Bridges Youth Found. (pres. 1987-89, bd. 1987–), Kern County Hist. Soc., Rotary (bd. 1982), Bakersfield City Sch. Dist. Edn. Found. (bd. 1989–); club: Petroleum; mil: Calif. Nat. Guard 1970-76; Republican; R. Cath. Ofc: Arrache, Clark & Potter, 5401 California St Ste 301 Bakersfield 93309

CLARKE, DAVID WILLIAM, information systems director; b. Feb. 23, 1948, Gary, Ind.; s. Ralph Harding and Eleanor Margurite (Koopmann) C.; m. Donna Lynn Avery, Oct. 6, 1979; 1 son, John Edward b. 1969; edn: BS, Purdue Univ. 1970. Career: systems analyst Amoco, Chgo., Ill. 1970; life underwriter New York Life, Fremont 1974-75; gen. mgmt. Shaklee U.S. Inc., San Francisco 1975–; awards: Shaklee U.S. Inc. Pres.'s award 1981; mem: Am. Production & Inventory Control Soc., BSA, United Way; mil: lt. USN 1970-74; Republican; Presbyterian. Ofc: Shaklee Corp 444 Market St T-323 San Francisco 94111

CLARKE, RICHARD ALAN, electric and gas utility executive; b. May 18, 1930, San Francisco; s. Chauncey Frederick and Carolyn (Shannon) C.; m. Mary Dell Fisher, Feb. 5, 1955; children: Suzanne b. 1958, Nancy C. Stephen b. 1960, Douglas b. 1964; edn AB in polit. sci. (cum laude), UC Berkeley, 1952, JD, Boalt Hall, 1955; admitted Calif. St. Bar 1955. Career: atty. Pacific Gas and Electric Co., 1955-60; ptnr. law firm Rockwell, Fulkerson and Clarke, San Rafael 1960-69; staff atty. Pacific Gas and Electric Co., 1969, sr. counsel 1970, asst. gen. counsel 1974, v.p. and asst. to chmn. of bd. 1979, exec. v.p. and gen. mgr. utility ops. 1982, pres./dir. 1985, chmn. bd. and chief exec., 1986-94; chmn. of bd. 1994-95; dir.: Pacific Gas and Electric Co., Bank of America, Potlatch Corp.; mem.: President's Council on Sustainable Development 1992–; Com. on Jobs, S.F. (past chmn.), Bay Area Council (dir., past chmn.), Bay Area Econ. Forum, The Business Council, Indep. Colls. of No. Calif., Calif. C. of C. (past dir.), S.F. C. of C. (past dir., v.p. econ. devel.); advy. bd. Haas School of Bus., UC Berkeley; trustee Boalt Hall Trust, UC Berkeley; dir. S.F. Symphony; clubs: Marin Tennis; mil: capt. USAR 1952-60; Presbyterian; rec: tennis, gardening, reading. Ofc: Pacific Gas and Electric Co. 77 Beale St. 32nd Flr. San Francisco 94106

CLARKE, ROGER GLEN, investment advisor; b. Aug. 9, 1948, Ogden, Utah; s. Glen Wallace and Lulu Fern (Meyers) C.; m. Janet Rounds, Aug. 11, 1971; children: Angela b. 1973, Stephanie b. 1975, Mary Ann b. 1980; edn: BA,

Brigham Young Univ. 1972; MBA, 1974; MA econ., Stanford Univ. 1977; PhD, 1978. Career: asst. prof. Brigham Young Univ., Provo, Utah 1978-81, assoc. prof. 1981-85; sr. v.p. Trust Services of Am., Los Angeles 1985-87, pres., CIO, 1987, v.chmn., CIO, 1988-91; pres. TSA Capital Management 1991–; bd. dirs. Nat. Applied Computer Technologies, Orem, Utah 1982-90; cons. num. organizations incl. Marriott Corp., Utah St. Housing Authority, Intermountain Health Care; awards: Western Fin. Assn. Trefftz 1978, Inst. Quantitative Research in Fin. Roger F. Murray 1982, Fin. Analysts Fedn. Graham & Dodd Scroll 1985; mem: Western Fin. Assn., Am. Fin. Assn., Fin. Mgmt. Assn. (institutional dir.); author: Strategic Fin. Mgmt., 1988, Option Strategies for Institutional Investment Mgmt., 1983; articles pub. in profl. jours.; Republican; Mormon. Ofc: TSA 888 West 6th Street Los Angeles 90017

CLAUSON, STEVEN LLOYD, chiropractor; b. Aug. 2, 1955, Alamagordo, N.M.; s. Lloyd Allen Clauson and Shirley Ann (Hughes) Pollen; m. Lauren Rose Mooney, April 3, 1982; 1 son, Kyle Bjorn b. 1988, 1 dau. Zoe Chloe-Rae; edn: AS, Valley Coll. San Bernardino 1983; DC, Life Coll. 1986. Career: race car mechanic Jim Flores Racing, Crestline 1976-79; foreman Home Centers, San Bernardino 1980-82; lectr. Calif. Chiropractic Assn., Sacto. 1988-89; Sacramento Valley Chiropractic Assn. 1988-89; awards: CGM Chiropractic Humanitarian 1988; mem: Calif. Chiropractic Assn. (key dr. 1989), Sacramento Valley Chiropractic Assn.; Republican; Episcopalian; rec: skiing. Ofc: 7000 Franklin Blvd Ste 190 Sacramento 95823

CLAUSSEN, RONALD VERNON, federal agency transportation administrator (retired); b. Feb. 6, 1938, Davenport, Iowa; s. Elmer Arthur and Mary Elizabeth (Negus) C.; m. Martha Elizabeth Walls, Jan. 26, 1961 (div. 1988); children: Terry, Traci; m. 2d. Angelita H. Bautista, July 20, 1993; edn: AA in bus. admin., Palmer Jr. Coll., 1970; BA in pub. admin., Upper Iowa Univ., 1974; MBA, Central Mich. Univ., 1977; cert. contract mgr. Career: police ofcr. City of Davenport, Ia. 1961-67; with US Dept. of Defense 1967–: transp. splst. Rock Island (Ill.) Arsenal Activity 1969-69; traffic mgr. Savanna (Ill.) Army Depot 1969-70; storage splst. personal property Dept. of Def., Chgo. and Atlanta, 1970-73, traffic mgmt. splst. Rock Island Arsenal DOD, 1973-74, sr. storage splst. personal property DOD, Falls Church, Va. 1974-82, chief transp. Army Aviation Ctr. DOD, Ft. Rucker, Ala. 1982-85, dep. dir. personal property DOD Mil. Traffic Mgmt. Command We. Area, Oakland, Calif. 1985-88, dep. dir. inland traffic 1988-93, dep. asst. chief of staff ops. 1993 (ret.); pres. and CEO, Claussen Associates Inc., Carson City, NV 1993–; bd. dirs. Oakland Traffic Club 1994–; pres. Greater Bay Area Transportation Assn. 1994–; bd. dirs. and supervisory com. ILWU Fed. Credit Union 1988–; bus. instr. Fairfax County (Va.) Adult Edn. 1977-83; seminar instr. George Mason Univ., Fairfax 1977-83; adj. faculty Univ. Va. 1977-83, Embry-Riddle Aero. Univ., Daytona Beach, Fla. 1983–; owner Claussen Assocs., p.t. cons., car swap meet, T-shirt sales, San Pablo, Calif.; awards: recipient Mil. Traffic Mgmt. Command Western Area Cmdr.'s Award and Meritorious Civilian Service award 1990, Disting. Mem. of Transportation Corps Regiment 1993, biog. listings in Who's Who in Am., Who's Who in Calif., Who's Who in the West; mem: Meeting Planners Internat., Nat. Defense Transp. Assn. (bd. 1987–, chapter pres. San Francisco Bay Area 1991-92, recipient Regional, and Internat. Chapter of Year Award, 1992, in recogn. of providing outstanding ednl. & profl. devel. opportunities for members, scholarship pgms., and service to comm., recipient Disting. Service award 1993), Soc. of Govt. Meeting Planners (nat. pres. 1987-89, founding mem. and past pres. No. Calif. chpt., recipient Sam Gilmer Award, Planner of Yr. 1990, Member's Choice award 1992), No. Calif. Meeting Planners Internat., Am. Legion, Shriners, Masons (32 degree), Scottish Rite, Delta Nu Alpha (internat. bd. dirs., Pac. Southcoast reg. v-p. 1990-91, 91-92 past pres. S.F. chpt., recipient Presidential Citation for Leadership award 1991); coauthor: Warehouse Emergency Operations, 1982, contbr. to profl. orgns.; mil: sgt. USAF 1956-60; Republican; Lutheran. Res/Ofc: 1009 Cedar Terrace Ste 101 San Pablo 94806

CLAYTON, LAURA ANCELINA, lawyer; b. Aug. 22, 1960, St. George's, Bermuda; nat. 1978; d. Sylvester Valentine and Barbara Joan (Milton) Clayton; edn: AA, De Anza Coll. 1980; AS, 1980; BS internat. bus., San Jose St. Univ. 1981; MBA, UC Berkeley 1985; JD, UC Berkeley Boalt Hall 1985; admitted St. Bar Calif. 1986, Wash. D.C. 1988. Career: atty. Lillick McHose & Charles, San Francisco 1985-86; Pettit & Martin, San Francisco 1986-89; corp. counsel Apple Computer, Inc., Cupertino 1989–; v.chair bd. Youth Entrepreneurial Services Internat., Oakland 1988-90; bd. dir. Nat. Econ. Devel. Law Center, Berkeley 1988-90; advy. bd. dir. Street Law Project 1989-90; bd. dir. Acad. Fin., S.F. 1989-90; advy. bd. dir. Bus. & Fin. Acad. McClymonds H.S., Oakland 1988-90; awards: Women of Achievment S.F. Bus. and Profl. Women's Club 1990, Outstanding Women of Am. 1987, 88, 91, Boalt Hall Sch. Law Best Oral Argument 1982, Nat. Black MBA Com. of Year 1988, Nat. Black MBA Community Svc. award 1990, Who's Who Am. Law; mem: Nat. Black MBA Assn. (pres. S.F. Bay Area chpt. 1989-90, chair student affairs com. 1988), Charles Houston Bar Assn., Am. Bar Assn., Bar Assn. San Francisco, Santa Clara Co. Bar Assn. (pres. Barristers Section 1994, sec. Barristers Sect. 1993, bd. of trustees 1994, exec. com. 1994), Black Women Lawyers No. Calif.; Democrat; rec: bicycling, fencing, tennis. Address: Oakland 94610

CLEGG, JAMES STANDISH, biochemist; b. July 27, 1933, Aspinwall, Pa.; s. Arthur Standish and Helen (Gaskill) C.; children: Elizabeth b. 1959, Susan b. 1962, Cynthia b. 1963; edn: BS, Pa. St. Univ. 1958; PhD, Johns Hopkins Univ. 1961. Career: asst. prof., assoc. prof., prof. Univ. Miami, Coral Gables 1962-85; adj. prof. Univ. Miami Sch. Medicine, Miami 1983-85; prof. UC Davis 1986–; dir. Univ. Calif. Bodega Marine Lab., Bodega Bay 1986–; vis. scientist Oak Ridge Nat. Lab., Tenn. 1966; Queen Elizabeth Coll., London, England 1978; Centre Nat. de la Recherche Sci., Thiais, France 1981, 82; honors: Phi Beta Kappa, Johns Hopkins Univ. Woodrow Wilson fellow 1958-60, Univ. London Fulbright senior research fellow 1978; mem: AAAS (fellow), Am. Soc. Cell Biology, Am. Soc. Zoologists, Biophysical Soc., Soc. Cryobiology; 100+ aricles pub. in sci. jours., 1961–, 4 books pub., 1973-87. Ofc: Univ. of Calif. Bodega Marine Laboratory Bodega Bay 94923

CLEMENT, CLAYTON EMERSON, lawyer; b. Dec. 3, 1943, Oakland; s. Robert Emerson and Dorothy (Deacon) C.; m. Barbara Jonas, Sept. 4, 1965 (div. 1983); m. Kimberly Anderson, Nov. 30, 1991; children: Robert b. 1968, Jason b. 1970; edn: BA w. hons., Univ. Pacific Stockton 1965; JD, UC Berkeley 1968. Career: atty., assoc. Cox & Cummins, Martinez 1968-71; ptnr. Misuraca & Clement, Santa Rosa 1972-75; Clement Fitzpatrick & Kenworthy 1975–; assoc. prof. law John F. Kennedy Univ., Martinez 1970-72; instr. Santa Rosa Jr. Coll. 1978-86; Sonoma St. Univ., Rohnert Park 1981-83; mem: Assn. Bus. Trial Lawyers, Sonoma Co. YMCA (dir. 1986-91), Sonoma Co. Citizens for Transp. Solutions (treas. 1989-90); Democrat; Congregationalist; rec: flying, fly fishing. Res: 1313 St. Helena Ave Santa Rosa 95404 Ofc: Clement Fitzpatrick & Kenworthy POB 1494 Santa Rosa 95902

CLEVELAND, CARL SERVICE, (JR.), college president; b. Mar. 29, 1918, Webster City, Ia.; s. Dr. Carl S., Sr. and Dr. Ruth R. (Ashworth) C. (both parents Drs. of Chiropractic); grandmother, Dr. Sylvia L. Ashworth, D.C.; m. Mildred S. Allison, D.C., Mar. 28, 1939 (dec. 1979); son, Dr. Carl S. Cleveland III, D.C., pres. Cleveland Chiro. Coll., Kansas City, Mo., b. 1946; edn: BS physiology, Nebr. Univ., 1947; DC, Cleveland Chiro. Coll., K.C., Mo., 1945, postgrad. studies Cleveland Chiro. Coll., K.C., Mo.; lic. DC Missouri 1945, Kans. 1947, Calif. 1950. Career: instr., prof., dean and pres. Cleveland Chiropractic Coll., K.C. and L.A., pres. Cleveland Chiropractic Coll., Los Angeles, 1982–; v.p. Parker Res. Found., Dallas; staff lectr., personal relations counselor; speaker nat., internat. lecture tours, appeared on "So You May Know" tv show (5 yrs.); past mem. Mo. State Anatomical Bd.; awards: Hon. mem. Delta Sigma Chi, distinguished res. award Parker Chiro. Res. Found., Man of Year PCRF, The Sci. Award Medallion Palmer Coll. of Chiro. Davenport, Ia., Res. Award World Chiro. Congress, Montreux, Switz. 1970; mem. Internat. Chiro. Assn. (Distinguished Fellow, ICA Chiropractor of Year 1969, mem. bd. of control, pres. cabinet, ednl. comm., res. found.), No. Am. Assn. of Schs. & Colls., Mo. State Assn. (past pres. res. com.), Nu-Med. Soc., Acad. of Mo. Chiropractors, Beta Chi Rho Frat., Sigma Chi Frat., Sigma Chi Psi Frat.; publs: `Pilot Research Program' Science Rev. (Aug. 1965), studies pathology resulting from subluxating the vertebra in the domestic rabbit with a mechanical splint; Unity Soc. of Practical Chritianity (past pres. Unity Temple, Country Club Plaza). Ofc: 590 N Vermont Ave Los Angeles 90004

CLEWETT, RAYMOND WINFRED, design engineer, business executive; b. Nov. 7, 1917, Upland, Calif.; s. Howard Jasper and Pansy Gertrude (Macy) C.; m. Hazel Royer, June 11, 1938; children: Alan b. 1943, Patricia b. 1945, Charles b. 1948, Richard b. 1956, Beverly b. 1958; edn: Chaffey Jr. Coll. 1936-37. Career: exptl. mechanic, research mech., research dept. foreman, test lab. foreman, wind tunnel model builder, master machinist Douglas Aircraft Co. Santa Monica, Calif. 1937-45; shop mgr., design engr. new prod. devel. Lear Inc., L.A. 1945-51; shop mgr., design engr. The Rand Corp., Santa Monica 1951-83; owner, chief engr. Hy-Tech Engrg. & Devel. Lab., Malibu 1983–; designer specialized optical-mechanical equipt. for US Army, Navy and Air Force; instr. Curtis Wright Tech. (on leave from Douglas Aircraft); cons. Pacific-Sierra Research Corp. L.A., Rand Corp.; mem: Soc. Mfg. Engrs., Am. Soc. Metals, AAAS; publs: num. articles on reading aids for visually handicapped, patent held; Republican; Prot.; rec: photog., nat. history, travel, family. Ofc: Hy-Tech Engineering & Development Laboratory 7069 Fernhill Dr Malibu 90265

CLODIUS, ALBERT HOWARD, educator; b. Mar. 26, 1911, Spokane, Wash.; s. William, Sr. and Mary Hebner (Brown) C.; m. Wilma Charlene Parker, June 3, 1961; children: Helen-Lou (Parker) Namikas b. 1951, John Charles Parker b. 1953; edn: BA, East Wash. State Univ., Cheney 1937; grad. studies Univ. Wash., Seattle 1937-40, Stanford Univ. 1940-42; MA in history, The Claremont Grad. Sch., 1948, PhD in history, 1953. Career: actg. instr. Stanford Univ. 1942-43; instr. Claremont-McKenna Coll., Claremont 1946-50; asst. prof. Pepperdine Coll., L.A. 1952-53; instr. Ventura Comm. Coll., 1953-76, ret.; adj. prof. humanities Northrop Univ., L.A. 1977-87, National Univ., L.A. 1987-89 (ret.); awards: Clarence D. Martin scholar Ea. Wash. State Univ. 1936-37, editl. asst. Pacific Northwest Qtrly. U.Wash. 1938-40, John R. & Dora F. Haynes Found. Fellow 1950-57; mem. Plato Soc. (Perpetual Learning and Tchg. Org.) UCLA Ext., 1980–, vol. tchr. English conversation, UCLA Internat. Student Ctr., 1979–; mil: cpl. US Army Air Corps 1943-46; Democrat; Unitarian; rec: classical music, walking, swimming. Res: 4832 Salem Village Pl Culver City 90230

CLOUD, JAMES MERLE, hospital and education administrator, mnemonics educator; b. Feb. 16, 1947, Winston-Salem, N.C.; s. Merle Vail and Jane (Moore) C.; edn: French lang. studies, Univ. of Paris, 1967; BA in comparative lit., Univ. N.C., 1970; MA in edn. adminstrn., Columbia Pacific Univ., 1979, PhD health care adminstrn., 1980; Calif. lic. nursing home adminstrn., 1989, FAA lic. pvt. pilot, 1980. Career: co-founder, mem. bd. dirs., dir. of edn. Wholistic Health & Nutrition Inst. (pioneer in wellness edn.), Mill Valley 1974-79; co-founder, secty. bd. dirs., dir. admissions Columbia Pacific Univ. (devel. it into the largest non-traditional univ. in USA), San Rafael 1978-84; asst. to the pres. Posada Del Sol (unique solar powered senior residence complex), Sausalito 1985-87; co-founder, v.p. Am. Assn. of Active Seniors, 1988-89, editor & pub. Nat. Directory of 250 Active Senior Orgs. and Communications Resources"; acquisition resrch. and administr. convalescent hosps. in Oakland, 1989-90, Ukiah, 1990-91, Berkeley, 1991; founder Steel Trap Memory Systems (mnemonics edn. for adults, seniors, H.S. and coll. students), 1992–; author: The Foreign Language Memory Book, 1995, The Bible Memory Book, 1995; publs: weekly columns in New Penny Pincher, Ukiah 1990-91, editor: Internat. Mounted Police Assn. Newsletter 1989, The Healthscription, 1978, Guide to Personal Wellness (C.P.U. Press), poetry anthologies (1969, 71); photography exh. "Renaissance Faire Faces" featured in Bay Area cafes 1989; rec: aviation, chess, trap shooting, foreign languages, archeology, travel. Res/Ofc: 4286 Redwood Hwy San Rafael 94903 Tel: 415/677-4779

COATES, ROBERT CRAWFORD, judge, adjunct law professor; b. Jan. 31, 1937, Torrance; s. H Crawford and Genevieve Dorothy (Teachout) C.; m. Catherine Dehorst Rozendaal, May 12, 1974 (div. 1980); m. Margaret Lynn LaPlace, Jan. 17, 1981; children: M. Whitney b. 1981, R. Cameron b. 1983; edn: BA engring. geology, San Diego St. Univ. 1959; JD, Calif. We. Coll. Law 1970; Hon. JD, We. St. Law Sch. 1987. Career: jr. civil engr. Engring. Dept. City of San Diego 1959-61; budget analyst City of San Diego City Mgrs. Office 1961-63; owner Coates & Assoc. 1963-70; atty., ptnr. Coates & Miller 1971-82; judge San Diego Municipal Ct. 1982–; instr. CJER Inst., Sacto. 1988; mem. CJA Comp. & Retirement Com. 1982-92; adj. law prof. Univ. San Diego and Western State Law Schools 1982–; trustee Co. Law Library 1986–; awards: Warren William Award (U.S. and Calif. Psychiatric Assn.), San Diego Mag. list of San Diegans to Watch in 1989, pres.'s award S.D. Trial Lawyers Assn. 1986, Silver Beaver BSA 1987, geology disting. grad. SDSU 1984, La Jolla H.S. MVP Baseball 1954; mem: San Diego Co. Judges Assn. (bd. dirs. 1985, 87), Rocky Mountain Mineral Law Found. (law profs. com. 1981–), San Diego Natural hist. Museum (trustee, v.p. 1988-89), SDSU Geology Alumni (chair 1984-89), S.D. Ecology Centre (pres. 1985-86), Rotary Club, Baja Group, Sierra Club, Anza Borrego Assn., Calif. Mining Assn., Theodore Roosevelt Assn., Eagle Scout Alumni Assn. (pres. 1984-85); author: A Street is Not a Home: Solving Americas Homeless Dilemma, 1990, Ships Crossing At Dead of Night, 1983, The Guys Who Can't Cook's Cookbook, 1992, 15+ articles in law jours., 1980–; mil: USNR 1955-63; Democrat; Ch. of God in Christ; rec: camping, swimming history, mining. Ofc: San Diego Municipal Court 220 West Broadway San Diego 92101

COBB, GEORGE EDWARD, physician-surgeon; b. Aug. 10, 1930, Oklahoma City, Okla.; s. George Thomas and Nell (Norvell) C.; m. Marilyn Idema, Dec. 11, 1954; children: Deborah b. 1956, Sheryl b. 1962, Christopher b. 1965; edn: BS, Univ. Okla., 1951; MD, Harvard, Boston 1955; bd. certified Am. Coll. of Surgeons 1962;. Career: intern and resident, surgery, Johns Hopkins, Md. 1955-58; resident in general surgery, resident surgery USPHS Hosp., San Francisco 1958-62; surgeon pvt. practice, 1962–, staff John Muir Hosp., Walnut Creek 1962–, Merritt Hosp., Oakland 1962–, Providence Mt. Diablo Hosp., Concord 1986–; bd. certified honors: Phi Beta Kappa 1951, Alpha Omega Alpha 1955; mil: lt.cdr. USPHS 1955-62; Presbyterian (deacon); rec: swimming, biking, snow & water skiing. Ofc: 3501 School St Lafayette 94569

COBB, ROY LAMPKIN, professional services company executive; b. Sept. 23, 1934, Oklahoma City, Okla.; s. Roy Lampkin Sr. and Alice (Ellis) C.; m. Shirley Ann Dodson, June 21, 1958; children: Kendra b. 1959, Cary William b. 1962, Paul Alan b. 1967; edn: BS, Univ. Okla., Norman 1972; grad. work in environmental planning, CSU Northridge, 1978. Career: naval aviator, cdr. US Navy, 1955-78, decorated Air Medal (13), Navy Commendn. svc. in Vietnam 1967; engr. General Dynamics, NAS Pt. Mugu, 1978-81; senior engr. Advanced Technology, Camarillo 1981-91; dept. head Computer Services Corp., Pt. Mugu 1991–; indep. computer cons., 1991–; adj. instr. tchg. computer graphics UC Santa Barbara, 1991; cons. RhC Graphics, Camarillo 1990–; awards: service Boy Scouts Am. Ventura County Coun. 1979; mem: Missile Technology Hist. Assn. editor "Launchings" (1989–), Assn. of Naval Aviators 1988–, Navy League 1991–, Town Hall of Calif. (L.A.); clubs: Las Posas CC (Camarillo), Spanish Hills CC (Camarillo); Republican; Disciples of Christ; rec: computers, design. Res: 2481 Brookhill Dr Camarillo 93010

COBB, SHIRLEY ANN, public relations professional, public information official; b. Jan. 1, 1936, Oklahoma City, Okla.; d. William Ray and Irene (Fewell) Dodson; m. Roy Lampkin Cobb, June 21, 1958; children: Kendra b. 1959, Cary Wm. b. 1962, Paul Alan b. 1967; edn: BA journ., Univ. Okla., 1958; coursework Univ. Jacksonville, 1962, Univ. Okla., 1972, UCLA, 1976. Career: information specialist Pt. Mugu Naval Air Station, 1975-76; splty. editor fashion, religion, News Chronicle, Thousand Oaks 1977-81; media services mgr. City of Thousand Oaks, 1983–; appt. Task Force on Telecomms., League of Calif. Cities, 1991–; honors: Phi Beta Kappa 1958, Who's Who Univs. and Colls. 1958, listed Who's Who Am. Women, Who's Who in the West, in the World 1985–; mem: Calif. Assn. Public Information Officials (pres. 1989-90, recipient Paul Clark award as Outstanding Public Info. Official in State 1993), Pub. Rels. Soc. Am. (com. chair 1989–), Nat. Assn. Telecomms. Officials (speaker nat. confs. 1989–), Pt. Mugu Officers Wives (pres. 1975-76); civic: Town Hall of Calif., Hospice Camarillo (bd. 1986, aux. 1990-91), Ocean View Sch. Dist. Pt. Mugu (trustee 1976-79); contbr. articles to various publs. (1979–); Republican; Methodist. Res: 2481 Brookhill Dr Camarillo 93010 Ofc: City of Thousand Oaks 2510 Hillcrest Dr Thousand Oaks 91320

COBBLE, JAMES WIKLE, professor of chemistry, university dean; b. Mar. 15, 1926, Kansas City, Mo.; s. Ray and Crystal Edith (Wikle) C.; m. Margaret Ann Zumwalt, June 9, 1949; children: Catherine Ann C. Dozier b. 1952, Richard James b. 1955; edn: BA, No. Ariz. Univ., 1946; MS, USC, 1949; PhD, Univ. of Tenn. and the Oak Ridge Inst. of Nuclear Studies, 1952. Career: chemist Oak Ridge Nat. Lab., Oak Ridge. Tenn. 1949-52; postdoctoral research assoc. UC Berkeley 1952-55; instr. 1954; asst., assoc., and prof. of chemistry Purdue Univ., 1955-73; prof. chemistry and dean Grad. Div. and Resrch., San Diego St. Univ., 1973–; v.p. and chmn. bd. SDSU Found., 1975–; mem. Joint Graduate Bd. of Univ. of Calif. and the Calif. St. Univ., Long Beach 1978–, mem. Calif. Postsecondary Commn. Joint Graduate Bd., Sacto. 1978–; cons. Oak Ridge Nat. Lab., E.R. Squibb and Sons Inc., GE Co., Gt. Lakes Chem. Corp., C.T.S. Corp., Uniroyal, Lawrence Berkeley and Livermore Labs., Allison Div. (G.M.), Argonne Univs. Assn., Battelle Pacific Northwest Labs., Babcock and Wilcox Co.; appt: chmn. ad hoc com. on geothermal energy Nat. Mats. Advy. Bd. of NAS/NRC, W.D.C. 1977-78, corrosion advy. com. Elec. Power Resrch. Inst., Palo Alto 1974-79; Bd. of Visitors U.S. Air Force Air Univ. (1984-93, chmn. 1988-89), trustee, Calif. Western Law Sch. 1989-93; awards: Guggenheim Fellow 1966, E.O. Lawrence Award U.S. Atomic Energy Commn. 1970, Welch Found. Lectr. 1971; mem: Am. Physical Soc. (Fellow), Am. Chemical Soc., Sigma Xi, Phi Kappa Phi, Alpha Chi Sigma, Phi Lambda Upsilon; mil: lt. j.g. USN 1945-46; rec: swimming, jogging, music (piano). Ofc: Graduate Div. and Research San Diego State Univ. San Diego 92182-1641

COBIANCHI, THOMAS THEODORE, marketing executive; b. July 7, 1941, Paterson, N.J.; s. Thomas and Violet Emily (Bazzar) C.; m. Phyllis Linda Asch, Jan. 6, 1964; children: Michael Douglas b. 1964; edn: elec. engr. program Clemson Univ. 1960-62; BS, Monmouth Coll., 1968, MBA 1973; Doctorate in Bus. Adminstrn., U.S. Internat. Univ., San Diego 1994; grad. exec. program The Wharton Sch., 1987. Career: various mgmt. pos. Westinghouse Electric, in Norman, Ok., Phila., N.Y.C., Balt., 1968-80, internat. mgr. Bus. Devel. Westinghouse Electric, Pittsburgh, Pa. 1980-82, dir. Mktg. Westinghouse Electric, Arlington, Va. 1982-86; actg. dir., engring. mgr. General Dynamics, San Diego 1986-89; dir. bus. devel. Teledyne-Ryan Aeronautical, San Diego 1989-90; pres. Cobianchi & Assocs., 1990-91; v.p. strategic planning & pgm. devel. S-Cubed Div. Maxwell Labs., San Diego 1991–; past instr. Towson St. Univ., staff Penn State Univ., guest lectr. intl. bus. Monmouth Coll. and Geo. Washington Univ.; mem. bd. Bus. Advy. Council, U.S. Internat. Univ., 1992–; mem: Armed Forces Comms. & Electronics Assn. 1983–, Navy League S.D. 1989-90, Air Force Assn. 1983-84, Assn. of US Army 1989-90, Assn. of Old Crows 1991–, The Princeton Club (W.D.C., San Diego); civic bds: United Way S.D. (sect. chair 1987–), Cath. Charities S.D. (1989); rec: golf, tennis, skiing, hunting, target shooting. Ofc: S-Cubed Div. Maxwell Labs 3020 Callan Rd San Diego 92121

CODDINGTON, IQBAL JWAIDEH, anthropologist; b. Nov. 25, 1935, Baghdad, Iraq, naturalized U.S. citizen 1985; d. Abdul Massih Elias and Jamila (Jwaideh) J.waideh; m. Joseph Mark Coddington, June 20, 1970 (div. 1992); edn: BA English lit., Baghdad Univ., 1955; Dipl. in English ednl. theory and practice, Univ. London, 1961, Assoc. in Comparative Edn., 1962; MSc in edn., Indiana Univ., 1964, MA anthropology, 1970, PhD anthropology, 1980. Career: tchr. high sch., Baghdad 1955-60; adj. asst. prof. Oklahoma Univ., Norman 1981-85; dept. hd. res. & data collection, asst. dir. Arab Gulf States Folklore Ctr., Doha, Qatar 1985-87; asst. prof. De Anza Coll., Cupertino, Calif. 1989; lectr. p.t. Cogswell Coll. 1991, 92; res. assoc. UC Berkeley, 1988-91, vis. scholar 1992; awards: Baghdad Ministry of Edn. govt. scholar 1960-65; mem. Middle East Studies Assn., Assn. M.E. Womens Studies, AAUW (Palo Alto bd.); civic: Neighbors Abroad, Palo Alto (co-chair internat. vis. com.), Palo Alto Cultural Ctr. (vol.); pub. res. articles in jours., 1985, 86, 87; Democrat; R.Cath.; rec: reading. Res: 1945-3 Mount Vernon Court Mountain View 94040

COFER, BERT (BERDETTE) HENRY, consultant; b. Apr. 4, 1928, Las Flores, Tehama Co.; s. William Walter and Violet Ellen (Elam) C.; m. Ann McGarva, June 27, 1954 (dec. Feb. 20, 1990); m. Sally Shepherd, June 12, 1993; children: Sandra Cofer-Oberle b. 1960, Ronald b. 1962; edn: AB, Csu Chico, 1950; MA, UC Berkeley, 1960. Career: tchr. Westwood Jr. - Sr. High Sch., Westwood (Lassen Co.), Ca. 1953-54; Alhambra High Sch., Martinez, Ca. 1954-59; prin. Adult and Summer Sch., Hanford High Sch., Hanford, Ca. 1959-60, asst. supt. 1960-67; dean of bus. services West Hills Coll., Coalinga, Ca. 1967-76; vice chancellor Yosemite Community Coll. Dist., Modesto, Ca. 1976-88, v.chancellor emeritus, 1988–; pres. BHC Associates Inc., Modesto 1988–; chmn. Valley Insurance Jt. Powers Agy., Modesto 1986-88; interim chancellor No. Orange County Comm. Coll. Dist., Fullerton, Ca. 1989-90; pres. Coalinga Indsl. Devel. Corp. 1972-74; mayor City of Coalinga 1974-76; pres. Assn. of Chief Bus. Officers, Calif. Comm. Colls., 1981-82; awards: Coalinga C.of C. Outstanding Citizen 1976, Walter Starr Robie Outstanding Bus. Officer Calif. Comm. Colls. Bus. Officials 1988, Foreman Stanislaus Co. Grand Jury 1987-88; mem: Calif. Assn. of Comm. Coll. Adminstrs. (charter, hon. life 1988), Commonwealth Club, Phi Delta Kappa (1956–, pres. King-Tulare chpt. 1962-63), Lions Clubs Intl. (Hanford/Coalinga/Modesto dist. gov. 1965-66), Am. Legion 1987–, Elks 1987–; publs: com. mem. Nat. Assn. of Coll./Univ. Bus. Ofcls. com. to write 4th Ed. of Coll. & Univ. Bus. Admin. 1977-81, author 2 articles and coauthor 3 articles in profl. jours. (1987, 88); mil: 1st lt. USAF 1951-53; Democrat; Prot.; rec: reading, travel, bowling, golf. Res: 291 Leveland Ln #D Modesto 95350-2255

COFFMAN, WILLIAM BRENT, dentist; b. Nov. 6, 1945, Wytheville, Va.; s. William Henry and Esther Virginia (Brent) C.; m. 1967, div. 1991; children: William Brent b. 1971, Amy Louise b. 1973; edn: BA, ColumbiaUnion Coll. 1969; MA, Andrews Univ. 1971; DDS, Loma Linda Univ. 1983; ordained minister Seventh-day Adventist, SE Calif. Conf. 1974. Career: pastor Ohio Conf. of SDA, Kettering, Ohio 1968-72, University Ch., Loma Linda Univ., S.E. Calif. Conf. 1973-80; pvt. practice gen. family dentistry, Yucaipa Valley 1983–; vol. Am. Dental Assn. Internat. Mexico Mission, Chgo., Ill. 1983-88; Dental Clinical Services of Salvation Army; honors: ADA internat. service award 1983, listed Who's Who Am. Colls. & Univs. 1969, Outstanding Young Men Am. 1971, Who's Who in Religion 1977, Personalities of West and Midwest 1978, Internat. Who's Who Comm. Service 1979, Who's Who in West 1988, 90, Dict. Internat. Biography 1990, Personalities of Am. 1990, 92, Internat. Directory of Disting. Leadership 1990, Who's Who of Emerging Leaders in Am. 1990, Dict. of Internat. Biography 1990, Men and Women of Distinction, 14th; elected mem. Historical Commn., Loma Linda, Ca.; mem: Am. Dental Assn., Calif. Dental Soc., TriCounty Dental Soc., Andrew Soc. for Religious Studies, Assn. Adventist Forums, Yucaipa Valley C.of C., Columbia Union Coll. Alumni Assn. (pres. 1983–); Seventh-day Adventist (bd. mem. UC of SDA 1973–); rec: collect antique med.-dental instruments, bicycling, off-road motorcycling, skiing, travel. Res: 613 E Sunset Dr N, Redlands 92373-6404 Ofc: 11834 Bryant St Ste 101 Yucaipa Valley 92399

COHEN, ALAN JAY, psychiatrist; b. Aug. 30, 1956, Phila.; s. Harry Wallace and Shirley Vita (Berman) C.; m. Shannon Bowman, June 25, 1989; children: Brendan Harris b. 1990, Hallie Patricia b. 1992; edn: BA in biology (cum laude), Oberlin Coll., 1978; MD, Jefferson Med. Coll., 1982; intern med./psych. Langley Porter Inst., UC San Francisco, 1982-86, resident psychiatry, 1986-87; fellow psychiatry Inst. of Pa. Hosp., 1986-87. Career: res. fellow, clin. instr. psychiatry Univ. Pa. Hosp., 1986-87; asst. clin. prof. psychiatry UC San Francisco, 1987–; attdg. psychiatrist San Francisco Gen. Hosp., UCSF, 1987-90; pvt. practice, 1990–; attdg. physician East Bay Hosp. (chief of staff 1993, dir. clinical research 1993–, co-dir. of lab. svs. 1994–), Brookside Hosp.; lectr. No. Calif. Psychiatric Soc. annual mtg. 1995; lectr. Center for Psychol. Studies, Albany, Calif.; cons. U.S. Postal Service; mem. S.F. Dept. Pub. Hlth. Div. of Mental Hlth., Substance Abuse, and Forensic Svs. Pharmacy and Therapeutics Com. and Stds. Subcom.; mem. Thomas Bond Soc. of Pa. Hosp.; awards: Nat. Merit Commendn., Haverford Sch. 1974, Sigma Xi 1978, Baldwin Keyes Prize in psychiat. 1982, Harrity Res. Fund fellow 1986-87, NIH fellow 1979; mem.: No. Calif. Psychiat. Soc., AMA, Am. Psychiat. Assn., Calif. Med. Assn., Alameda Contra Costa Med. Assn., Calif. Psychiatric Assn. Ofc: Comprehensive Psychiatric Svs., 37 Quail Ct Ste 200 Walnut Creek CA 94596 Tel: 510/944-1733

COHEN, BRUCE IRA, physicist; b. Oct. 26, 1948, Los Angeles; s. Elliott E. and Joyce May (Ruby) C.; m. Sharon Ann Krause, April 6, 1975; 1 dau., Jenny b. 1984; edn: BS, Harvey Mudd Coll. 1970; MA, UC Berkeley 1971; PhD, 1975. Career: postdoctoral research physicist Princeton Univ., N.J. 1975-76; research physicist Lawrence Livermore Nat. Lab., Livermore 1976–; adj. lectr. elec. engring. UC Berkeley 1981-85; dep. program leader magnetic fusion theory and computation Lawrence Livermore Nat. Lab. 1984–; awards: NSF fellow (1970-73), Woodrow Wilson fellow (1970); mem: Am. Physical Soc. (fellow); author, ed. Multiple Time Scales (Acad. Press 1985), 75+ articles pub. in sci. jours. (1972); Democrat; Jewish; rec: golf, hiking, biking. Ofc: Lawrence Livermore National Laboratory POB 808 L-630 Livermore 94550

COHEN, CYNTHIA MARYLYN, lawyer; b. Sept. 5, 1945, Brooklyn, NY.; d. Bernard and Evelyn (Berman) C.; edn: AB Cornell Univ. 1967; JD cum laude N.Y.U. Sch. of Law 1970; admitted bar: NY 1971, Calif. 1980, Federal Cts. NY and Calif., 1972, 80, 81, 86, U.S. Supreme Ct. 1975. Career: atty., assoc. Simpson Thacher & Bartlett, NYC 1970-76; Kaye, Scholer, Fierman, Hays & Handler, NYC 1976-80; atty., shareholder Stutman, Treister & Glatt Profl. Corp., LA 1980-87; atty., ptnr. Hughes Hubbard & Reed, LA 1987-93; atty., ptnr. Morgan, Lewis & Bockius, LA 1993–; student res. advisor N.Y.U. and

mem. student-faculty curriculum and clin. prog. coms. 1968-70; honors: Order of the Coif 1970, Founder's Day Cert. 1969, John Norton Pomeroy Scholar 1968-70, Law Rev. 1968, N.Y.U.; Am. Jurisprudence Awards; Cornell Dean's Scholarship 1963-67; NY State Regents Scholarship 1963-70; mem: Am. Bar Assn. (Antitrust, Litigation sects.), Bar Assn. of City of NY (Trade Reg. Com. 1976-79), NY State Bar Assn. (ch. Class Action Com. 1979), Assn. of Bus. Trial Lawyers, L.A. County Bar Assn. (Antitrust, Comml. Law and Bankruptcy Sects.), Calif. Bar Assn. (Antitrust, Bus. Sects.), Financial Lawyers Conf.; Girl Scouts 1954-59; Delta Gamma Sor.; NY chpt. Am. Cancer Soc. (dir. 1977-80); rec: tennis, collector rare books and wine. Res: 4818 Bonvue Ave. Los Angeles 90027 Ofc: Morgan, Lewis & Bockius, 801 S. Grand Ave. 22nd Floor Los Angeles 90017-3189 Tel: 213/612-2500

COHEN, DAVID E., newspaper publisher; b. Nov. 17, 1950, Springfield, Mass.; s. Philip J. and Marjorie (Rednor) C.; m. Barbara Elia; children: Daniel b. 1981, Dustin b. 1984; edn: BA, Windham Coll., 1971. Career: advt. mgr. Advocate Newspapers, Springfield, Mass. 1976-79; assoc. publisher L.A. Weekly, Los Angeles 1979-84; pub./co-founder Metro, Santa Clara Valley's weekly newspaper and Metro Community Newspapers, San Jose 1985–; mem. Assn. of Alternative Newsweeklies (bd. 1989-90, pres. Western Region 1994, 95), Rotary Club of San Jose; civic bds: San Jose Symphony Orch. 1986- (vice chmn. 1993-94), San Jose Jazz Soc. 1987–. Ofc: Metro, 550 S First St San Jose 95113

COHEN, ELAINE LINENBERG, graduate school dean; b. Nov. 7, 1939, Philadelphia, Pa.; d. Herman and Goldie (Greenberg) Linenberg; m. George Harris Cohen, June 19, 1960; children: Sheryl b. 1963, Jeffrey and Jonathan b. 1968; edn: BS, Univ. Pa. 1960; MEd, Trinity Univ. 1969; EdD, Univ. San Francisco 1978. Career: tchr. Lower Merion Sch. Dist., Ardmore, Pa. 1960-63; tchr., prin. San Antonio Sch. Dist., Tx. 1968-69; tchr. Millbrae Sch. Dist., Millbrae 1970-74; instr. Univ. San Francisco 1974-76; prof. Coll. of Notre Dame, Belmont 1975-84, dean grad. sch. 1984–; mem. Council Grad. Schs., Wash. D.C. 1984–; honors: Kappa Delta Pi, Univ. San Francisco Commencement Speaker (1989), Phi Delta Kappa; mem: Assn. Calif. Sch. Adminstrs., Am. Assn. Univ. Women, Am. Bus. Womens Assn., San Mateo Co. Med. Aux., Mills Peninsula Hosp. Found. (trustee), Hillsborough Schs. Found. (founding dir. 1980-82), Univ. Pa. (assoc. trustee 1989), S.F. Symphony, S.F. Opera; articles pub. in profl. jours. (1980, 91); Republican; Jewish; rec: travel, cooking. Res: 1350 Brandt Rd Hillsborough 94010 Ofc: College of Notre Dame 1500 Ralston Ave Belmont 94002

COHEN, LAWRENCE MARK, mechanical engineer; b. Oct. 17, 1956, New York; s. Robert Irwin and Beverly Eleanor (Greenstein) C.; edn: BS (summa cum laude), SUNY at Buffalo, 1978; MS, MIT, 1980; PhD, Stanford Univ., 1990. Career: tchg. asst. SUNY 1976-78; analytical engr. Pratt & Whitney Aircraft, E. Hartford, Conn. 1978; research asst. MIT 1978-80; mem. tech. staff TRW Space & Technology, Redondo Beach, Calif. 1980-90; res. asst. Dept. Mech. Engring. Stanford Univ. 1984-90; sr. engr. specialist Aerojet Propulsion, Sacramento 1991–; honors: Pi Tau Sigma, Tau Beta Pi, Cummins Engine Co. Fellow, TRW, Inc. Industrial Fellow; mem: ASME, AIAA, OSA; publs: 8+ articles in sci. jours. (1984–); Democrat; Jewish; rec: hiking, opera, bicycling. Ofc:Aerojet Propulsion PO Box 13222 Sacramento 95813

COHEN, MARLENE ZICHI, clinical nursing researcher; b. June 1, 1951, Brooklyn, NY; m. David M. Cohen, Mar. 5, 1978; edn: BSN, Univ. of Mich., Ann Arbor, 1974 (magna cum laude); MS, Psychiatric-Mental Health Nsg., Univ. of Mich., 1981; PhD, Nsg., Univ. of Mich., 1984. Career: clinical nsg. (various positions), Ann Arbor, Mich., 1974-84; asst. prof., Ea. Mich. Univ., Ypsilanti, Mich., 1984-85; asst. prof., Univ. of Iowa, Iowa City, 1985-90; res. scientist, City of Hope, Duarte, Calif., 1990-92; dir. Office of Nsg. Res., Univ. of So. Calif. Dept. of Nsg. and Norris Comprehensive Cancer Ctr., L.A., 1992–; Sigma Theta Tau, Gamma Chpt. Pres. 1986-90; com. mem, Sigma Theta Tau Internat., Reg. 2 1988-90; collateral reviewer, Sigma Theta Tau Res. Grants Prog.,1989-92; manuscript reviewer: We. Jour. of Nsg. Res. 1985–, Image 1989–, Qualitative Health Res. 1989–, Res. in Nsg. and Health 1990–, Clinical Nsg. Res. 1991–; reviewer, Oncology Nsg. Soc. grant study sect. 1991; faculty mem., Oncology Nsg. Soc. and Nat. Cancer Inst. Cancer Nsg. Res. Short Course 1992; mem., Hadassah Nurses Council Internat. Advy. Bd.; awards: Sigma Theta Tau, induction 1973, Shirley C. Titus Grad. Scholarship 1981, 1984, Rackham Grad. Sch. Fellowship 1981-82, Outstanding Young Woman of Am. award 1982, Am. Assn. of Critical Care Nurses Res. award, Nat. Tchg. Inst. 1988; invited consultation, Hebrew Sch. of Nsg. and Hadassah Med. Orgn., Jerusalem, Israel 1992; mem: Am. Nurses Assn. 1974–, Council of Nurse Researchers 1985–, Iowa Acad. of Sciences 1985-90, Iowa Nurses Assn. 1985-90, Mich. Nurses Assn. 1974-85, Calif. Nurses Assn. 1990–, Midwest Alliance in Nsg. 1982-90, N.Am. Nsg. Diagnosis Assn. 1986–, Sigma Theta Tau 1973–, Oncology Nsg. Soc. 1990–, We. Soc. for Res. in Nsg., We. Inst. of Nsg. 1990–, Soc. for Edn and Res. in Psychiatric-Mental Health Nsg. 1991–, Council on Psychiatric and Mental Health Nsg. 1991–; author: numerous articles and abstracts publ. in profl. nsg. and health journals 1982–,over 50 res. papers presented, keynote speaker and lectr. Nsg. Res. Soc. Conferences 1982–. Ofc: University of Southern California, Dept. of Nursing, 1540 Alcazar St. Los Angeles 90033

COHEN, MISHA RUTH, doctor of Oriental medicine; b. Nov. 8, 1951, Tallahassee, Fla.; d. Bart Leonard and Jacqueline (Freeman) Cohen; edn: student, Oberlin Coll., Oberlin, Ohio 1969-72; doctorate, San Francisco Coll. of Acupuncture and Oriental Medicine 1986; attended Lincoln Detox. Acupuncture Sch., Bronx, NY; lic. acupuncturist, Calif. Career: clin. & didactic prof. S.F. Coll. of Acupuncture, 1981-86; investigator (herbal) S.F. General Hospital Ward 86, 1992-93; dir. S.F. AIDS Alternative Healing Project 1985-90; dir. Quan Yin Acupuncture & Herb Ctr., S.F. 1984-90; clinical dir. Quan Yin Healing Arts Ctr. 1986–; internat. tchr. Quan Yin HIV Certificate Prog., S.F. 1990–; pvt. practice, dir. Chicken Soup Chinese Medicine, S.F. 1990–; mem.: AIDS Care Project, Boston, Mass. (advy. bd. 1990–), Nat. Council of Schools of Acupuncture & Oriental Medicine (doctoral subcom., 1992), Calif. Acupuncture Assn. (v.p., 1992), Am. Assn. of Acupuncture & Oriental Medicine (bd. dirs., 1992), Quan Yin Healing Arts Ctr. (bd. dirs. 1992–). Ofc: San Francisco 94103

COHEN, PATRICIA FELTZ, educator, nursing consultant, author; b. June 7, 1932, Idpls.; d. Walter Frederick and Marie Ziegler Feltz; m. Stanley J. Cohen, Sept. 1, 1966; children: David Walter b. 1968, Susan Marie b. 1969; edn: RN, St. Joseph Infirmary Sch. of Nursing, 1953; BSN, Indiana Univ., 1960; MA nsg. edn., Teachers Coll. Columbia Univ., 1963, MA edn., 1964. Career: Capt. Nurse Corps US Air Force, 1955-58; nursing consultant and educator; res. assoc. in breast cancer Univ. of Calif., Irvine; coauthor 6 books on nsg., Nursing Care Planning Guides; mem. bd. trustees (elem.) Huntington Beach City Sch. Dist. 1981-90; recipient award for outstanding contbn. to edn. Orange County Dept. Edn., honorary & cont. service awards PTA, Orange Co. Commn. on Status of Women award; mem. AAUW; Democrat; R.Cath.; rec: computers, genealogy. Res: 21731 Saluda Circle Huntington Beach 92646

COHEN, ROBERTA SHERRI, marketing - promotions executive; b. April 23, 1955, Winnipeg, Canada; d. H. Jerome and Frances Helen (Lyon) Cohen; edn: BS bus., Univ. Colo. Boulder 1976; BA, Univ. Redlands 1979. Career: adminstrv. asst. Direct Mktg. Corp. Am., Los Angeles 1976-77; corp. mgmt. trainee 1977-79, mdsg. adminstr. 1979-82, Toyota Motor Sales USA Inc., Torrance; sales promotion mgr. Jafra Cosmetics Inc., Westlake Village 1983-85; Redken Labs., Canoga Park 1985-87; dir. of mktg. services Physicians Formula Cosmetics, City of Industry 1987-91; pres. Fait Accompli 1991–; dir. corporate commns. Treasure Chest Adv. Co., Inc. 1992–; alumni rep. Univ. Colo. 1985–; mem: Am. Soc. Advtg. & Promotion, Nat. Assn. Female Execs., Advertising Club of L.A., Les Amis du Vin, Spl. Olympics; paper pub. in profl. jour., 1976; rec: travel, theatre, dance, literature, blues, jazz, cycling. Res: 3180 Cadet Court Los Angeles 90068

COHEN, RONALD MORTON, physician, surgeon, ophthalmologist; b. July 9, 1947, Los Angeles; s. Eli Bertran and Aimee (Salomon) C.; m. Ricki Ruth Pasternak, June 23, 1968; edn: BS, UCSF 1968; MD, 1971. Career: intern pathology Harbor Gen. Hosp., Torrance 1971-72; resident ophthalmology UCLA/Jules Stein Eye Inst., Los Angeles 1972-75; pvt. practice ophthalmology, La Mirada 1975-89; ret.; attdg. physician VA Hosp., Long Beach 1975–; mem: L.A. Co. Med. Assn., Orange Co. Soc. Ophthalmology, CMA; article pub. in med. jour. 1970; mil: major USAR 1970-82; Democrat; Jewish; rec: aviation, playing piano, computers. Res: PO Box 3541 Anaheim 92803

COHEN, SEYMOUR I., lawyer; b. Apr. 15, 1931, N.Y.C.; s. Fred and Nettie (Sederer) C.; m. Rhoda Goldner, July 22, 1956; children: Cheryl Lynn, Marcy Ann, Lori Beth; edn: BBA (cum laude) City Coll. N.Y., 1951; LLB, Bklyn. Law Sch., 1954, JD, 1967; MBA, N.Y. Univ., 1960; admitted bar: N.Y. 1954, U.S. Tax. Ct. 1954, Calif. 1973, U.S. Dist. Ct. (cen. dist.) Calif. 1973, U.S. Ct. Appeals (9th cir.) 1973, U.S. Supreme Ct. 1976; CPA, Ohio, Calif. Career: staff acct. S.D. Leidesdorf, N.Y.C., 1958-61; mgr., acct. Rockwell, Columbus, Ohio and Los Angeles, 1961-69; mgr. contracts Logicon, L.A. 1970-71; mgr. internal audit Daylin, 1971-72; contr. NYSE Co., 1972-73; atty., pvt. practice personal injury, probate and gen. practice law, Torrance, Calif. 1973–; mem: Am. Inst. CPA, L.A. County Bar Assn. (appellate ct. com. 1979–, svs. com. 1981-82), South Bay Bar Assn. (pres. 1986-87, chair referral svc. 1977-81), Calif. Bar Assn. (client trust fund commr. 1983, 84), Ohio Inst. CPAs, N.Y. Inst. CPAs, Calif. Inst. CPAs, L.A. Trial Lawyers Assn., N.Y. State Bar Assn.; Jewish; Republican. Res: 30691 Via La Cresta Rancho Palos Verdes 90274 Ofc: 18411 Crenshaw Blvd Ste 411 Torrance 90504 Ph: 310/329-6384

COHEN, SHELDON ERVIN, physician/surgeon; b. Sept. 10, 1941, Detroit, Mich.; s. Abraham and Lillian (Schulman) C.; m. Joanne Kass, Dec. 12, 1965; children: Amy Cohen Lesher b. 1968, Robert Brian b. 1970, Heather b. 1977; edn: 2-4-2 program, Wayne State Univ. Coll. of Medicine 1961-62; MD, Univ. of Mich. Med. Sch., Ann Arbor 1966; surgical internship Univ. of Rochester, Strong Mem. Hosp., Rochester, NY 1966-67; resident, gen. surgery Univ. of Rochester 1967-69, UC Davis, Sacto. Med. Ctr. 1969-70, chief resident 1970-71; resident, thoracic surgery Case Western Reserve Univ. Sch. of Medicine, Univ. Hosps. of Cleveland 1980-82; med. lic. Mich. 1967, N.Y. 1969, Calif. 1969, Idaho 1972, Ohio 1980; diplomate Am. Bd. of Surgery 1972, cert. Am. Bd. of Thoracic Surgery 1983, recertified 1993. Career: chief surgical svs. USAF Hosp., Mountain Home AFB, Idaho 1971-73; asst. prof. of surgery UC Davis, Sacto. Med. Ctr. 1971-74, asst. clin. prof. of surgery 1974-80; adminstrv.

chief, white surgical svc. Sacto. Med. Ctr., UC Davis Med. Sch. 1972-74; gen. surgeon Fresno Comm. Hosp. & Med. Ctr, Fresno 1974–, St. Agnes Med. Ctr., Fresno 1974–, Sierra Hosp., Fresno 1974–, Valley Children's Hosp., Fresno 1974–; cons. physician Valley Med. Ctr., Fresno 1974–, VA Hosp., Fresno 1976–; cardiothoracic surgeon Valley Cardiac Surgery, Fresno 1982–; currently chmn., hosp. council Fresno Comm. Hosp. & Med. Ctr. (pres. elect med. staff, mem. exec. com., cont. med. edn. com., strategic planning. com., regional med. ctr. com., chmn. cardiovascular surgery com., v. chmn. critical care com.); mem. cardiovascular subsection com., St. Agnes Med. Ctr.; instr., cont. med. edn. Central San Joaquin Valley Area Health Edn. Ctr. 1974-80; clin. res. Medtronic Pacemakers 1974-82; instr., patient care audits, CMA 1978-80; awards: Am. Coll. of Surgery Meeting Tour, Genesee Hosp., NY 1968, Frederick A. Coller Clin. Tour, Univ. of Mich. 1970; mem: Sigma Alpha Mu, Phi Delta Epsilon, Am. Coll. of Surgeons (fellow), Fresno-Madera Med. Soc., Assn. of Academic Surgeons, Fresno Surgical Soc., Earl F. Wolfman, Jr. Surgical Soc. (past pres.), CMA, AMA, Soc. of Clin. Vascular Surgery, Internat. Coll. of Angiology (fellow), Am. Physicians Fellowship, Soc. of Thoracic Surgery (fellow), Am. Coll. of Cardiology (fellow), Central Valley Am. Heart Assn. (past pres., mem. bd. dirs.), CPS Nat. Registry for Emergent Application (mem. nat. advy. bd.); author or co-author: 16 articles pub. in profl. jours., 1974-93; mil: maj. USAF 1971-73; Jewish; rec: tennis, snow skiing, flying, boating. Res: 2216 W Roberts Ave Fresno 93711 Ofc: Valley Cardiac Surgery 110 N Valeria #204 Fresno 93701

COHEN, (STEPHEN) MARSHALL, professor of philosophy and law; b. Sept. 27, 1929, N.Y.C.; s. Harry and Fanny (Marshall) C.; m. Margaret Dennes, Feb. 15, 1964; children: Matthew, Megan; edn: BA, Dartmouth Coll., 1951; MA, Harvard Univ., 1953, Jr. fellow Soc. of Fellows 1955-58; spl. student Magdalen Coll., Oxford 1953-54, MA (Oxon.) 1977. Career: asst. prof. of philosophy and of gen. edn. Harvard Univ. 1958-62; asst., assoc. prof. philosophy Univ. of Chgo. 1962-64, 1964-67, actg. chair Coll. Philosophy 1965-66; assoc. prof. philosophy Rockefeller Univ. 1967-70; prof. philosophy Richmond Coll. (now Coll. of Staten Island) also The Grad. Sch. CUNY, 1970-83; exec. ofcr. Program in Philosophy, The Grad. Sch., CUNY 1975-83; prof. philosophy and law 1983–, dean of humanities Univ. of So. Calif. 1983-84; interim dean Coll. of Letters, Arts & Scis. USC 1993-94; vis. prof. UC Berkeley 1971, Harvard Univ. 1972, New Sch. for Social Resrch. 1973-74, Cornell Univ. 1974, Yale Coll. 1975, Barnard Coll. Columbia Univ. 1979-81, US Mil. Acad., West Point, 1982; awards: Fellow A.C.L.S. 1951-52, Harvard Univ. Sheldon Traveling 1953-54, Soc. Fellows 1955-58, Santayana 1962-63, Yale Law Sch. 1964-65, hon. fellow Trumbull Coll. Yale 1968-73, grantee NEH 1975, vis. fellow All Souls Coll., Oxford 1976-77, Guggenheim fellow 1976-77, Rockefeller Found. Humanities fellow 1977, Inst. for Adv. Study, Princeton 1981-82, prin. investigator: Andrew W. Mellon Found. 1981-83, 91-95, NEH Instnl. Challenge Grant 1988-92; lectureships: "The Meaning of Metaphor" Lowell Inst. Lectures, Boston 1957-58, "Aesthetics and Poetics" Christian Gauss Seminars in Criticism, Princeton 1964-65, Phi Beta Kappa vis. scholar 1975-76, N.Y. Coun. for Humanities Lectr. 1982-83; mem: Am. Philosophical Assn., Soc. for Philosophy and Pub. Affairs, Amintaphil; author: 10+ books incl. Film Theory & Criticism (ed. with Gerald Mast Oxford, 1974; 2d. edit. 1979, 3d. edit. 1985, 4th edit. with Leo Braudy, 1992), num. essays, articles and reviews in scholarly and literary jours.; editor: Philosophy and Public Affairs (Princeton Univ. Press, 1971–). Ofc: Law Center, Univ. So. Calif., Los Angeles 90089-0071

COHN, DANIEL HOWARD, research scientist, educator; b. Aug. 24, 1955, Santa Monica; s. Sidney Lorber and Mynda Ellen (Zimmerman) C.; m. Ludmila Bojman, May 16, 1982; children: Zachary b. 1986, Marissa b. 1988, Rachel b. 1988; edn: BA, UC Santa Barbara, 1977, PhD, UC San Diego, 1983; grad. student Scripps Inst. Oceanography, UCSD, 1977-83, postdoc. fellow Univ. Wash., Seattle 1983-88. Career: resrch. scientist, asst. prof. Cedars-Sinai Med. Ctr., UC Los Angeles, 1988-93, assoc. prof. 1993–; awards: Deans list UCSB 1977, Phi Beta Kappa 1977, Outstanding senior in biology UCSB 1977, Martin Kamen Award UCSD 1983, Eckhardt Prize, Scripps Inst. 1983, NIH postdoc. fellow 1985, Cedars-Sinai Young Investigator Award 1993; mem. AAAS 1977–, OI Found. 1988–, Concern Found. L.A. 1988–; author 40+ book chapters and sci. articles (1978–); Democrat; Jewish; rec: fatherhood, golf, volleyball, cooking, wine. Ofc: Medical Genetics, SSB-3, Cedars-Sinai Med. Ctr. 8700 Beverly Blvd Los Angeles 90048

COHN, ROBERT GREER, professor of French literature; b. Sept. 5, 1921, Richmond, Va.; s. Charles Alfred and Susan (Spilberg) C.; m. Dorrit Zucker, 1948 (div. 1963); children: Stephen b. 1949, Richard b. 1955; m. Valentina Catenacci, Oct. 26, 1965; edn: BA Romance languages, Univ. Va., 1943; MA, Yale Univ., 1947, PhD French, 1949. Career: instr. Yale Univ. 1949-50; asst. prof. Swarthmore Coll. 1952-54, Vassar Coll. 1954-59; assoc. prof. Stanford Univ., 1959-62, prof. French literature 1962-92; founding editor, Yale French Studies, 1948-49; awards: Croix de Guerre Fr. Army, France 1946, Guggenheim fellow (1956-57, 1986-87), Nat. Endowment for Humanities fellow (1969-70, 79-80), ACLS (1969-70); mem. advy. bd. Calif. Assn. of Scholars 1992–; author: L'Oeuvre De Mallarme (1951), Toward The Poems of Mallarme (1965), The Poetry of Rimbaud (1973); mil: t/5 US Army 1943-46; rec: gardening, music. Res: 6 Maywood Ln Menlo Park 94025

COLBERT, LINDA WHEELOCK, elementary school principal; b. Dec. 23, 1948, San Diego; d. Richard Hastings and Betty J. (Watters) Wheelock; m. James Raymond Colbert, July 25, 1981; 1 son, Brett b. 1983; edn: BS, San Diego St. Univ. 1971; MA, 1977; admin. credential 1984. Career: tchr. Lakeside Union Sch. Dist. 1972-84, tchg. vice prin. 1984-87, vice prin. 1987-89, principal 1989-; chair Dist. History Social Sci., Lakeside 1988-; chair Dist. Jr. Olympics, Schoolhouse Planning Com.; honors: Phi Delta Kappa Service (1989, pres. 1988-89), Pi Lambda Theta Outstanding Young Educator 1978; mem: Assn. Calif. Sch. Adminstrs., San Diego Council Women Adminstrs. in Edn., Assn. Supervision & Curriculum, Lakeside Hist. Soc., Friends of Library Lakeside; rec: photog, reading. Res: 14263 Jennings Vista Dr Lakeside 92040

COLE, RALPH NOBLE, commercial real estate broker; b. Apr. 17, 1924, Long Beach; s. Ralph Gideon Cole and Louise Noble (Carter) C.; m. Susan, Sept. 6, 1946; children: Alan b. 1953, Alice b. 1955, Randall b. 1956, Charles b. 1959; edn: AB, Stanford Univ., 1947, MBA, Stanford Grad. Sch. of Bus., 1949; certificates: Coro Found., S.F. 1947, Command & Gen. Staff Coll. 1969, USA War Coll. 1976; Calif. lic. real estate broker, realtor 1947. Career: economist US Dept. of Labor, San Francisco 1950-52; dist. mgr. Pacific Tel., S.F. and Seattle, 1952-83; commercial real estate broker Grubb & Ellis, San Rafael 1984-; honors: Phi Beta Kappa, Knight, NATO Grand Priory of St. Sebastian SMOTJ (Knights Templar); mem: Nat. Assn. Realtors, Marin County Assn. of Realtors, Commonwealth Club of Calif., Assn. of US Army, Reserve Officers Assn., Stanford Grad. Sch. of Bus. Alumni Assn., Phi Gamma Delta Frat. Alumni Assn., SAR; clubs: Elks; mil: Col. AUS 1943-46, 1949-79; Republican; Presbyterian; rec: boating. Res: 3348 Paradise Dr Tiburon 94920 Ofc: Grubb & Ellis, 899 Northgate Dr Ste 210 San Rafael 94903

COLE, RICHARD CHARLES, lawyer; b. April 23, 1950, Albany, N.Y.; s. Charles Stanley and Doris Jean (Hatch) C.; edn: BA, Cornell Univ. 1972; JD, Harvard Univ. 1975; St. Bar of New York and Calif., 2d Circuit, 5th Cir., 9th Cir., U.S. Supreme Court, Federal Dist. Cts., S.D.N.Y., E.D.N.Y., all Calif. Dist. Cts. Career: assoc. atty. LeBoeuf, Lamb, Greene & MacRae, N.Y.C. 1975-83, ptnr., N.Y. and San Francisco 1984-; mem: Am. Bar Assn.; rec: woodwind music. Res: 41 Buena Vista Mill Valley 94941

COLEMAN, PAUL JEROME, JR., physicist, educator; b. Mar. 7, 1932, Evanston, Ill.; s. Paul Jerome and Eunice Cecile (Weissenbergh) C.; m. Doris Ann Fields, Oct. 3, 1964; children: Derrick b. 1968, Craig b. 1971; edn: BSE physics, BSE math, Univ. Mich., 1954, MS physics, Univ. Mich., 1958; PhD physics, UCLA, 1965. Career: res. scientist Ramo-Wooldridge Corp. (now TRW Systems), 1958-60; hd. interplanetary scis. pgm. NASA, Wash. DC 1961-62; res. scientist Inst. of Geophysics and Planetary Physics, UCLA, Los Angeles 1963-66, prof. of geophysics and space physics UCLA 1966-; asst. lab. dir./mgr. Earth and Space Scis. Div./chmn. Inst. of Geophysics and Planetary Physics, Los Alamos Nat. Lab., Los Alamos, N.M. 1981-84; dir. Inst. of Geophysics & Planetary Physics, UCLA 1989-92; dir. Nat. Inst. for Global Environmental Change 1994-; bd. dirs: Universal Monitor Corp. 1971-76, Univ. Technology Transfer, Inc. 1984-88, Lasertechnics, Inc. 1985-, Fairchild Space & Def. Corp. 1989-, CACI Internat., Inc. 1990-; apptd. bds. public and non-profit orgns.: LLNL and Los Alamos Nat. Lab., UC (sci. advy. com. 1975-81), Calif. Space Inst., UC (steering com. 1979-82), Univ. Space Resrch. Assn. (trustee 1981-, pres. 1981-), Nat. Inst. for Space Commercialization (dir. 1983-86), San Diego Supercomputer Ctr. (steering com. 1984-, chmn. 1986-88), West Coast Univ. (bd. advisors 1986-), External Tanks (Space Shuttle) Corp. (tech. advy. bd. 1986-), American Technology Initiative (bd. trustees 1990-), Small Satellite Orgn. (bd. trustees 1992-); cons. num. govt., internat. and public agencies (U.S., Ger., Italy, Australia, Euro. Space Agy.), cons. num. indsl. corps. 1963-; honors: Phi Eta Sigma 1950, Tau Beta Pi 1953, exceptional sci. achievement medal for contbns. to exploration of the solar system NASA 1970 and for contbns. to the exploration of the moon 1972, spl. recogn. by NASA for contbns. to the Apollo Pgm. 1979, John S. Guggenheim Memorial Fellow 1975-76, Sr. Fulbright Scholar 1975-76, Internat. Acad. of Astronautics (elected 1975), Presdl. appointee Nat. Commn. on Space 1985-86, appt. Vice Pres.'s Space Policy Advy. Bd. 1991-; mem: AAAS 1959-, Am. Geophysical Union 1959-, Am. Inst. of Aero. and Astro. 1966-, Am. Physical Soc. 1956-, Soc. of Exploration Geophysicists 1975-90, Fulbright Alumni Assn. 1978-; clubs: Cosmos (WDC), Explorers (NY), Bel Air Bay (LA), Birnam Wood Golf (Montecito), Eldorado CC (Palm Desert); mil: 1st lt. USAF 1954-56; R. Cath. Res: 1323 Monaco Dr Pacific Palisades 90272 Ofc: UCLA, 405 Hilgard Ave Los Angeles 90024

COLEMAN, ROBERT TRENT, vocational rehabilitation and career counselor, consultant human relations; b. Feb. 4, 1936, Gary, Ind.; s. Robert Clinton and Lucille Verna C.; m. Dorothy Agnes, Aug. 1957; children: Sean, Bryce, Daniel; m. 2d, Patricia Lou, June 13, 1976; m. 3d Polly Anderson, Sept. 15, 1984; edn: BA in Speech Therapy, Univ. Wash., Seattle, 1962; postgrad. in speech Univ. Redlands, 1963-64; MS in Rehab. Counseling, Univ. Oreg., 1971; cert. rehab. counselor, career counselor. Career: social worker, San Bernardino City Welfare Dept., 1963-64; correctional counselor Calif. Rehab. Ctr., Norco, 1964-67; sr. counselor Job Corps, Clearfield, Utah, 1967; assoc. dir. Ednl. Systems Corp., Washington, 1968-69; ptnr. Black Fir Jade Mines, Big Sur,

1971-76; vocat. specialist Internat. Rehab. Assn., San Diego, 1976-77; vocat. rehab. counselor Sharp Hosp., San Diego, 1977-80; clin. coordinator San Diego Pain Inst., 1981; cons. in rehab. counseling, career guidance, human relations, Carlsbad, 1981-83; propr. R.T.C. Cons. Services, Escondido, 1983-; commr., Handicapped Appeals Commn., San Marcos, 1981-83; mem. Am. Assn. for Counseling and Devel. (pres.), San Diego Career Gudance Assn. (pres. 1984), Assn. Indsl. Rehab. Reps. (pres. 1983), Am. Rehab. Counseling Assn., Nat. Assn. Rehab. Profls. in Pvt. Sector (standards and ethics com. 1986-); mil: U.S. Army, 1955-58; Republican. Res: 538 Glenheather Dr San Marcos 92069 Ofc: 218 E Grand #6 Escondido 92025

COLENZO, SALVATORE JOHN, clinical social worker; b. Dec. 14, 1942, Utica, N.Y.; s. Lugo Peter and Concetta Margaret (Armao) C.; m. Patricia, Nov. 26, 1970; children: Karin b. 1972, Kenneth b. 1975, Kristi b. 1980; edn: BA, Univ. Toronto Canada 1964; MSW, Univ. Ottawa 1966; bd. certified diplomate in clin. social work (1988). Career: caseworker Family Service Agency, Utica, N.Y. 1966-67; clin. social worker UC Davis Med. Center, Sacto. 1970-78; Kaiser Med. Center 1979-, chief of clin. social work 1987-94; social sci. instr. Solano Comm. Coll., Suisun City 1970-77; field work instr. CSU Sch. Social Work 1971-78, methods instr. 1975-76; sociology instr. Univ. Md., Viet Nam 1968-69; honors: USAF Bronze Star medal (1969), Univ. Ottawa Father Molloy bursary (1964); mem: Nat. Assn. Social Work, Acad. Cert. Social Workers; mil: capt. USAF 1967-70; Democrat; R.Cath.; rec: writing. Res: 812 Burr St Davis 95616 Ofc: Kaiser Permanente Medical Center 10725 International Dr Rancho Cordova 95670

COLES, CLARENCE WARREN, author, publisher; b. Oct. 13, 1925, Beloit, Wis.; s. Venice Virgil and Corienne Lois (Marsh) C.; m. Joan Darlene Lorton, Jan. 18, 1981; children: Mark, Greg, Julie, Brian, Liz; edn: B.Journ., Univ. Wash., 1959. Career: writer, staff various newspapers, 1945-50, 1959-61; mem. Cmdr. Hect Expedition charting Arctic Ocean, 1953; personnel recruiter Boeing Airplane Co., Seattle 1954-56; editor/writer McDonnell-Douglas, El Segundo, Calif. 1961-70; technical writer Hughes Helicopters, Long Beach 1970-74; author or coauthor 24 books; owner/pub. Seloc Publs., Cucamonga 1974-, and Ebb Tide Writers, Inc. 1990-; mem. Nat. Marine Mfrs. Assn.; mil: pfc USMC 1942-45, 50-51; Democrat; rec: sailing, woodworking, poetry writing. Ofc: 10693 Civic Center Dr Rancho Cucamonga 91730-3804

COLEY, ROBERT BERNARD, software company executive; b. Aug. 10, 1951, Bethesda, Md.; s. Robert and Anna C.; m. Denise Bolden, July 4, 1976; children: Robert, Jr. b. 1977, Elena b. 1978; edn: AB, Harvard Univ. 1973; JD and MBA, Stanford Univ. 1977. Career: mgmt. cons. McKinsey & Co., N.Y.C. 1976; mgmt. cons. Am. Mgmt. Systems, Inc., Foster City, Ca. 1977-79; adminstrv. mgr. of ISD, ADPAC Corp., San Francisco 1979-80; pres., CEO and CFO, Avalanche Prodns. Inc., Palo Alto 1980-83, PRIMS, Inc., Redwood City 1984-86, PSMG, Inc., Palo Alto 1986-; dir: Avalanche 1980-83, PRIMS 1984-86, RBC Acquisition Corp. 1982-, PSMG, Inc. 1986-; honors: Nat. Merit Achievement 1969, Nat. Honor Soc. 1968-69, academic fellowships 1970-77, Harvard Book Club award, Civitan award 1969, Nat. Tech. Assoc. achievement award 1987, YMCA Disting. Service Award 1993, listed Who's Who in Fin. and Ind.; mem: Nat. Assn. of Corp. Dirs., Stanford Bus. Sch. Alumni Assn., Kiwanis Internat.; civic: Little League Basketball (commr., coach 1987-89), Palo Alto Little League (asst. coach 1986-90), Palo Alto Bobby Sox League (pres., bd. v.p., chair fundraising com., coach 1988-92), St. Elizabeth Seton School Board (chair fin. com. 1984-87), Palo Alto YMCA Bd. Mgrs. (chair 1992, fin. com. chair 1989-95), SAY Basketball League (commr., coach 1984-), YMCA of the Mid-Peninsula (bd. 1992-), SFHS Tech. Advy Bd. 1992-, Stanford Univ. Alumni Cons. Team (chair bd, chair fin. com. 1992-); recipient hon. mention Phillip Gerry Poetry Contest 1969; TV guest on topic entrepreneurship; keynote speaker FAMU's 25th Annual Cluster Conf.: The Information Super Highway; Democrat; Baptist; rec: basketball, tennis, travel. Ofc: PSMG, Inc. 2124 Clarke Ave Palo Alto 94303

COLGREN, RICHARD DEAN, flight controls engineer; b. June 13, 1961, Seattle; edn: BSAA, Univ. Wash., 1982; MSEE, Univ. So. Calif., 1987, PhD in EE, 1993. Career: engr. Northrop Corp., Pico Rivera 1982-84; res. specialist Lockheed Martin Corp., Palmdale 1984-; mem. Am. Inst. Aero. & Astro. (secty. nat. tech. com. 1989-95, sect. chair 1989-90, Sr. Mem. 1989, Assoc. Fellow 1991, sect. treas. 1991-, ACC Review chmn. 1992, GNC Review chmn. 1993, 94, GNC Tech. Prog. chmn. 1996), Inst. Electrical & Electronics Engrs. (sr. mem. 1993, session organizer 1993); assoc. editor: Jour. of Theoretical & Computational Graphics, 1988-91, Workstation News, 1992-93; co-author: Progress in Simulation, 1995, num. papers, tech. confs., 1987-, article in CSS Mag., 1989; inventor Miniature Jet Engine (pat. 1991). Ofc: Lockheed Martin Skunk Works 1011 Lockheed Way Palmdale 93599-2525

COLLEY, PETER MICHAEL, playwright, screenwriter; b. Jan. 3, 1949, Scarborough, England, nat. U.S. citizen 1985; s. Thomas and Irene (Firth) C.; m. Ellen Ross Jenkins, Nov. 22, 1983; edn: Royal Grammar Sch. High Wycombe, Eng. 1968 (Victor Laudorum award as top athlete of yr.); BA (hons.) Univ. of Sheffield, 1971; grad. studies Univ. of W. Ont., Nat. Arts Centre, Can. Career:

resident playwright Grand Theatre, London, Ont. 1973-76; instr. of playwright-ing Theatre Ont. summer courses; resident playwright Actors' Alley Repertory Theatre, Los Angeles 1989-93; pres. Buckingham Internat. Productions; winner of six nat. and 4 regional awards Can.; stageplays: The Saga of Regin, 1971; The Donnellys, 1974 (pub. MacMillans anthology, and Simon & Pierre); musical, You'll Get Used To It, 1975 (Canadian tour 1988, pub. Simon & Pierre); The Huron Tiger, 1978; I'll Be Back Before Midnight, 1979 (sole credit film version titled "Illusions" 1992; most prod. stage thriller in Can., prodns. in 13 countries and 42 states in U.S., Nat. Brit. tour 1988; pub. Samuel French Inc., NY, Baker's Plays, Boston, Samuel French Ltd., (London); Heads, You Lose! 1981; psycho-logical thriller, The Mark of Cain, 1984 (coauthor of film 1985); philosophical thriller, When The Reaper Calls 1990; Beyond Suspicion, 1991 (Petro-Canada Stage One Awards); feature films: The Mark of Cain, 1990; Illusions, 1992; mem.: Writers Guild of Am./West, ACTRA Writers Guild (Can.), Dramatists Guild (NY), Playwrights Union of Canada, Acad. of Canadian Cinema and TV. Ofc: 20929-47 Ventura Blvd Ste 123 Woodland Hills CA 91364

COLLIER, CHARLES ARTHUR, JR., lawyer; b. Apr. 18, 1930, Columbus, Ohio; s. Charles Arthur and Gertrude Clara (Roe) C.; m. Linda, Aug. 5, 1961; children: Sheila b. 1963, Laura b. 1965; edn: AB magna cum laude, Harvard Coll. 1952; LLB, Harvard Law Sch. 1955. Career: law clerk US Dist. Ct. cent. dist. Calif. 1959-60; atty., assoc. Freston & Files, Los Angeles 1960-66; assoc., ptnr. Mitchell, Silberberg & Knupp 1967-82; ptnr. Irell & Manella 1982-95, of counsel 1995–; lectr. Contg. Edn. of Bar, var. assns. and seminars; Fellow Am. Coll. Trust and Estate Counsel, State Laws Com. mem. 1983-89, chmn. 1986-89, Office Mgmt. Com. 1986-88, exec. com. and regent 1989–, Expanded Practice Com. (chmn. 1989-92, treas. 1992-93, secr. 1993-94, v.p. 1994-95, pres.-elect 1995-96); mem. jt. editorial bd. Uniform Probate Code 1988–, rep. Am. Coll. Trust and Estate Counsel; mem. Calif. State Bar (Taxation sect., trust and probate com. 1975-77, Estate Plnng., Trust and Probate Law sect. chmn. 1980-81, exec. com. 1977-82, advisor 1982-85), ABA (mem. Real Property, Probate and Trust Law Sect. Council 1989-93, mem. Nat. Conf. of Lawyers and Corporate Fiduciaries Rep. Sect. 1989-92, trust law com. chmn. 1982-86, Task Force on Fiduciary Litigation chmn. 1986-89, Task Force on Changing Role of Probate Lawyer 1985-88), Am. Bar Found. Fellow 1990–; advr. restatement of property, donative transfers 1990–; Internat. Acad. Estate & Trust Law, L.A. Co. Bar Assn. (Probate & Trust Law sect.), Harvard Club of So. Calif. (pres. 1971-73, dir. 1966-74), Harvard Alumni Assn. (reg. dir. 1975-79, v.p. at large 1979-82); recipient Arthur K. Marshall Award L.A. Co. Bar Assn. Probate & Trust Law Sect. (1989), listed Best Lawyers in Am., Who's Who in Am.; contbr. num. articles in legal jours.; mil: USN 1955-57; Republican; Prot.; rec: travel, garden-ing. Res: 1075 S El Molino Ave Pasadena 91106 Ofc: 1800 Ave of the Stars Ste 900 Los Angeles 90067

COLLINGS, MICHAEL ROBERT, professor of English, poet; b. Oct. 29, 1947, Rupert, Idaho; s. Ralph Willard and Thella Marie (Hurd) C.; m. Judith Lynn Reeve, Dec. 21, 1973; children: Michael-Brent b. 1974, Erika b. 1975, Ethan b. 1977, Kendra b. 1979; edn: AA, Bakersfield Coll. 1967; BA, Whittier Coll. 1969; MA, UC Riverside 1973, PhD, 1977. Career: instr. of English UCLA 1978-79; prof. English, Pepperdine Univ. 1979–;cons. editor, Poet, 1992–; poet guest BYU SF/F Symposium 1993, 94, 95; Scholar Guest of Honor, Mytheon XXVI, 1995; poetry editor "Dialogue", Salt Lake City 1983-89; awards: 1st pl. award Calif. Poetry Assn.,1982, finalist Odyssey Poetry Contest, Brigham Young Univ., 1988, nom. Rhysling award Sci. Fiction Poetry Assn., 1981, 82, 86, 93, Recommendation/Nebula award, Sci. Fiction Writers of Am., 1986, 1st pl. award Calif. Fed. of Chaparral Poets, 1982; mem: Calif. State Poetry Soc., Sci. Fiction Poetry Assn.; author num. books, monographs, short stories, poetry, book reviews and articles pub. profl. jours. Res: 1089 Sheffield Pl Thousand Oaks 91360-5353 Ofc: Humanities Div., Pepperdine Univ. Malibu 90263

COLLINS, CURTIS ALLAN, oceanographer, educator; b. Sept. 16, 1940, Des Moines, Ia.; s. Ralph Charlie and Noma Lovella (Buckley) C.; m. Judith Ann Petersen, Dec. 21, 1962; children: Nathaniel, Hillary; edn: BS. US Merchant Marine Acad., Kings Pt, NY, 1962; MS, Oregon State Univ., 1964, PhD, 1967. Career: Third mate S.S. Inger, 1967-68; research scientist Pacific Ocean Gp., Nanaimo, Brit. Col., 1968-70; ocean engr. Cities Service Oil, Tulsa, Ok. 1970-71; program mgr. Nat. Sci. Found., W.D.C., 1972-87; prof. Naval Postgrad. Sch., Monterey, Ca. 1987–; dir. MBARI, Monterey 1988–; commissioner, Moss Landing Harbor District, 1993-94;awards: Am. Geophy. Union Ocean Scis., W.D.C. 1985, NSF meritorious svc. 1987, Fulbright Garcia-Robles Scholar, Instituto Investigaciones Oceanologias, Universidad Autonoma de Baja Calif., Ensenada, BC, Mexico 1995; mem. AGU Ocean Scis. (pres. 1993-94), Oceanographic Soc. (Council 1989-91), Am. Meterol. Soc. 1980–, Oceanographic Soc. of Japan 1967–; mil: capt. USNR 1963–, decorated Armed Forces Reserve Medal 1973, 83, 93, Nat. Def. Svc. 1991; Democrat; Prot. Rds: 24010 Ranchito del Rio Ct Salinas 93908 Ofc: Code OC/CO, Naval Postgraduate School, Monterey 93943

COLLINS, GERALD CHESTER, bank vice president, mortgage banking division manager; b. July 28, 1946, Los Angeles; s. Chester and Harriet (Hart) C.; m. Midge Bigham, May 31, 1968; children: Julie b. 1975, Bart b. 1977; edn:

BA, CSU Northridge 1971. Career: asst. loan dept. head California Federal, head ofc. 1974-76, asst. v.p., loan dept. head, regl. loan mgr., Visalia 1979-85; regional loan mgr. N. Calif., Gibraltor Savings 1985-87, senior v.p. residential loans, 1987-88; branch mgr. Wells Fargo Bank, 1989-93; branch mgr. United Valley Bank 1993; mortgage banking div. mgr. United Valley Bank 1993–; bd. dirs. The King's Strategist, Inc.; past pres. VIAH Inc.; past pres. Energy Com., City of Visalia; past pres. Cal Fed PAC; tchr. Inst. of Fin. Edn. chpt. 208; instr.: Am. Inst. of Banking, Fresno State Univ.-Fresno Extension, Coll. of Sequoias; mem. Rotary, past mem. West Visalia Kiwanis, Visalia United Methodist Ch. Commn. on Edn., Calif. Nevada Conf. of United Methodist Ch. (Ch. Expansion of Bd. of Conf. Life div.), Christian Bus. Mens Com.; devel. Personal Money Mgmt. System used in seminars & counseling statewide; mil: sp5 AUS 1966-69, GCM; Republican; Methodist; rec: tennis. Res: 1313 Chatham Dr Visalia 93277 Ofc: United Valley Bank 140 E Tulare Ave Tulare 93274

COLLINS, WILLIAM LEROY, telecommunications engineer; b. June 17, 1942, Laurel, Miss.; s. Henry L. and Christene E. (Finnegan) C.; edn: La Salle Univ., 1969; BS computer sci., Univ. Beverly Hills, 1984. Career: sr. computer opr. Arizona Dept. Public Safety, Phoenix, 1975-78, data communications spe-cialist, 1978-79, supr. computer ops., 1981-82; sr. network control specialist Valley Nat. Bank, Phoenix, 1979-81; mgr. data communications Ariz. Lottery, Phoenix 1982-85; mgr. telecommunications Calif. Lottery, Sacramento 1985–; listed Who's Who Worldwide, Who's Who in Am., Who's Who in West, Who's Who in Sci. & Engring., Intl. Leaders in Achiev., Intl. Directory of Disting. Leadership, Am. Biog. Inst. Man of the Year 1991; mem: AT&T T1 User Group, Sacto. Valley Centrex User Group, Telecommunications Assn. (v.p. edn. Sacto. Valley Chpt. 1990-94, Corp. Educ. Com., chmn. 1994-95, pres. Sacto. Chpt. 1995), Assn. of Data Comms. Users, Data Processing Mgmt. Assn., Am. Mgmt. Assn., Assn. Computing Machinery, Soc. Mfg. Engrs., K.C., Communications Mgrs. Assn. (CMA), Inst. of Electrical Engrs. (IEEE); mil: sgt. USAF 1964-68; R. Cath. Res: 116 Valley Oak Dr Roseville 95678 Ofc: Calif. State Lottery, 600 N 10th St Sacramento 95814

COLOGNE, GORDON BENNETT, jurist, educator; b. Aug. 24, 1924, Long Beach; s. Knox Mason and Ione C.; m. Patricia R., Sept. 28, 1957; children: Steven J. b. 1959, Ann Maureen b. 1960; edn: BS, USC, 1948; LLB, Southwestern Univ., 1951. Career: elected mayor City of Indio 1954-56; Riverside Co. Bd. Freeholders, 1957-58; st. legislator Calif. St. Assembly 1961-65, Calif. St. Senate 1965-72; appt. justice State Ct. of Appeal, San Diego 1972-84; pvt. practice atty. Gordon Cologne & Assocs., San Diego 1984–; prof. Univ. San Diego, 1974-84; awards: Freedoms Found. (1967), Sears Roebuck Found.-water conservation (1967); contbr. article: Chaos to Confusion, St. Bar Jour. (1981); mil: USN 1944-46. Res: POB 1877 Rancho Santa Fe 92067

COLVIN, IRIS VENITA IOLA, construction/property management executive; b. Apr. 15, 1914, Ashland, Ore.; d. Clarence Victor and Cozensa Delvina (Clark) Atterbury; m. Lloyd Colvin, Aug. 11, 1938; dau., Joy b. 1940; edn: BA, UC Berkeley 1937; cert. Univ. Heidelberg, Germany 1955; FCC Extra Class radio opr. lic.; Calif. lic. gen. contr./real estate broker. Career: staff W. A. Bechtel Corp., bldg. the Alaska Hwy. and CANOL oil line project during WWII; with US Govt. GSA in Japan after WWII; v.p./treas. Drake Builders, Calif. Corp. (constrn. internat.), 1947–; honors: Delta Epsilon; life mem. No. Calif. DX Club (past pres.), life mem. Am. Radio Relay League (fmr. Calif. QSL mgr.), mem. Radio Club of Am.; author: How to make a Million Dollars in the Construction Business (Prentice Hall), Book of the Month Club selection and also Best Seller list; rec: amateur radio opr. (W6QL), art, writing. Address: 5200 Panama Ave Richmond 94804

COMPOMIZZO, URIL EDWIN, outdoorsman and conservationist, anti-drug youth volunteer, fishing news reporter, retired energy company mechanic; b. Sept. 15, 1923, Hartford, Ark.; s. Angelo (dec. 1933) and Emed (Strickland) C.; m. Anna E., Jan. 12, 1947; children: Edwin L. b. 1949, Mrs. Susan E. Bluel b. 1953, Walter A. b. 1957; ed. pub. schs. Antioch, Calif.; learned fishing & nature lore from mentor Guy Chappell (b. 1903, dec. 1990) of Rio Dell, Calif. Career: line mechanic Standard Pacific Gas Lines Inc., Antioch 1946-79, instr. safety class 1 yr., ret. 1979; outdoorsman, fisherman (caught 36-lb. bass at age 15 dis-played in Roosevelt Jubilee parade); writer camping and fishing column for newspapers: Antioch Ledger, Pittsburg Post Dispatch, Martinez Morning Gazette, Concord Transcript and The San Jose Mercury, 1970-85, writer guest articles for Mendocino Beacon and Fort Bragg Advocate, contbg. writer Rivertown Express, Antioch 1988–; frequent guest local radio & t.v.; reporter local fishing news for KKIS 990 Pittsburg (sev. yrs.), weekly fishing report on Shasta Lake for KQMS Redding (annually in May), radio interviewer in Fort Bragg area for KBIC Clear Lake, KVRE and KQTE Santa Rosa; speaker on issues affecting the Delta, wildlife and saving the outdoors before state legisla-ture, and U.S. Congress; presents youth seminars "Get Hooked on Fishing Not On Drugs" in schools with demonstrations and gifts of freshly caught fish, fish-ing rods & tackle (aided by local service clubs) 1988–, videos of his drug pgm. distbd. to schools districts nat. (85+), and the pgm. was feature story in North American Fisherman Mag. (Feb., Mar. 1992); rec'd letter of appreciation from The White House signed by Barbara Bush (3/91); conservation activist since successful campaign to save Russian Gulch State Park for overnite camping, 1965; spearheaded campaign to create release of reserved state park campsites after 24-hr. hold, 1966; organized 268-mile trip in small boats for fathers and sons from Red Bluff to Antioch for Antioch Centennial 1972, and led annual event 7 yrs.; co-hosts annual C.of C. fish derby for boys and girls at Antioch Fishing Pier; active in re-instatement of Golden Eagle Permit to nat. parks (for seniors); honors: John A. Britton Gold Medal for saving drowning youth at Donner Lake St. Park, Standard Pacific Gas Lines 1965, Compy Compomizzo Week estab. by mayoral proclamation City of Antioch (4-23-78), citizen of yr. Antioch C.of C. 1978, hon. citizen City of Ft. Bragg 1980, hon. mem. Ft. Bragg C.of C. 1982, hon. mem. Ft. Bragg Footlighters 1984, City of Antioch birthday party celebration in honor of his 66th (9/15/1989), Humanitarian of Year Kiwanis Club of the Delta Antioch 1992, preservation work cited U.S. Congl. Record, Wash. (1970s), featured numerous media articles, local & nat., including life story in nat. mag. `Trailer Life', 1988, originator ranger recognition pgm. for state and nat. park rangers w/ aid of US Sen. Alan Cranston and sev. state senators, 1978-83, appt. public school consultant by Masonic Grand Lodge of Calif. for his anti-drug work with youth 1991; mem: Calif. Striped Bass Assn. (charter), Masons Antioch Lodge, Antioch C.of C., Antioch Historical Soc., Delta Drifters Square Dance Club (charter pres. 1962-67, hon. life); rec: gardening, fishing, outdoor writing, fishing seminars, camping, civic special events. Res: 2712 Bautista St Antioch 94509

COMRIE, BERNARD STERLING, linguist; b. May 23, 1947, Sunderland, England; s. Clifford Reginald Herbert and Ellen (Coulton) C.; m. Akiko Kumahira, 1985; children: Amanda b. 1987, Michael b. 1989; edn: BA, modern and medieval languages, Univ. of Cambridge 1968; PhD, Linguistics, Univ. of Cambridge 1972. Career: jr. res. fellow King's Coll., Cambridge 1970-74; sr. asst. in res. Dept. of Slavonic Studies, Univ. of Cambridge 1972-74; univ. lectr. in linguistics, Univ. of Cambridge 1974-78; assoc. prof. linguistics, Univ. of So. Calif., Los Angeles 1978-81; prof. of linguistics 1981–; vis. prof. Linguistic Soc. of Am. Linguistic Inst. (summer 1978); vis. fellow Australian Nat. Univ., Canberra (July-Dec., 1979); vis. res. fellow Max Planck Inst. for Psycholinguistics, Nijmegen, The Netherlands (summer 1983, 84, 88, 90, 91, 92); vis. prof. Univ. of Santiago de Compostela, Spain (June 1993); vis. prof. Tokyo Univ. of Fgn. Studies, Tokyo, Japan 1993-94; internat. guest lectr. in 26 countries; co-editor (with Georg Bossong) Empirical Approaches to Language Typology, Mouton Grammar Library; co-ed. Studies in Language; author (books): Aspect: An Introduction to the Study of Verbal Aspect and Related Problems (Cambridge Univ. Press, 1976; transl. into Japanese), Language Universals and Linguistic Typology: Syntax and Morphology (Basil Blackwell and Chicago; Univ. of Chgo. Press, 1981, 89; transl. into Italian, Spanish, Chinese, Japanese), The Languages of the Soviet Union (Cambridge Univ. Press, 1981), Tense (Cambridge Univ. Press, 1985); editor (books): The World's Major Languages (Oxford Univ. Press, 1987), (with Maria Polinsky) Causatives and Transitivity (Amsterdam: John Benjamins, 1993), (with Greville G. Corbett) The Slavonic Languages (London: Routledge, 1993); editor or co-editor: 15 pub. articles, 1975-93. Ofc: Dept of Linguistics GFS-301 University of Southern California Los Angeles 90089-1693

COMRIE, KEITH BRIAN, city administrator; b. Oct. 3, 1939, Schnectady, N.Y.; s. Arthur James and Therese (Johnson) C.; m. Sandra Lee McNutt, Jan. 8, 1989; children: Shannon, Colleen; edn: BBA, USC, 1963, Mof Pub. Adminstrn. in local govt., 1966. Career: administrv. analyst city adminstrv. office City of Los Angeles, 1963-69, city adminstrv. officer, 1979–; prin. adminstrv. analyst chief adminstrv. office County of Los Angeles 1969-71, bur. dir. dept. pub. social services, 1971-73, asst. dir. dept. pub. social services 1973-75; dir. social svs. 1975-79; Fellow Nat. Acad. Pub. Adminstrn. (1986); bd. councillors USC Sch. Pub. Adminstrn., 1984–; recipient Bowron award USC 1986, All Pro Mgmt. Team award City and State mag. 1987, USC Award of Merit 1989; mem. Internat. City Mgmt. Assn., Am. Mgmt. Assn., Am. Soc. Pub. Adminstrn. (Dykstra award 1986), Govt. Fin. Officers Assn.; civic: Los Angeles C.of C. (centennial mem. 1986-87), Los Angeles 2000 Com. (1986-89), United Way (L.A. bd. dirs. 1985–); rec: autos, architecture. Ofc: City of Los Angeles Rm 300 City Hall E Los Angeles 90012

CONDIT, GARY A., congressman; b. Apr. 21, 1948; edn: AA, Modesto Jr. Coll.; BA, Calif. State Coll. Career: councilman, City of Ceres, Calif. 1972-74, mayor 1974-76; supr. Stanislaus County, Calif. 1976-82; assemblyman State of Calif. 1982-89; mem. 101-104th Congresses from 15th (now 18th) Calif. Dist. 1989–; mem. agriculture com., mem. govt. ops. com.; Democrat. Ofc: US House of Representatives 1123 Longworth Washington DC 20515-0518

CONE, JAMES ELMER, physician; b. July 3, 1949, Eugene, Ore.; s. Elmer R. and Eleanor (Scott) C.; m. Blanche Grosswald, June 30, 1991; edn: AB, Stanford Univ. 1971; MD, UC San Francisco 1978; MPH, UC Berkeley 1978; bd. certified, internal medicine and occupational medicine, 1982, 83. Career: intern and resident Cook Co. Hosp., Chgo., Ill. 1978-80; epidemic intelligence svc. CDC, Niosh, Cincinnati, Oh. 1980-82; resident in medicine Worcester Mem. Hosp., Worcester, Mass. 1982-83; chief, occupational med. clinic San Francisco Gen. Hosp. 1983-91; asst. clin. prof. medicine UCSF 1983–; chief, HESIS Calif. Dept. of Health Svs., Berkeley 1994–;cons. Assn. of Flight

Attendants, W.D.C. 1987–; asst. clin. prof. UCSF Sch. of Nsg., S.F. 1985-92; cons. Univ. of Fla., Gainesville 1987-90; health effects dir. Carpenter's Health & Safety Fund, W.D.C. 1992-93; honors: Nat. Honor Soc. scholarship and Nat. Merit finalist, Eugene, Ore. 1967, grad. of distinction Stanford Univ. 1971; mem: Am. Public Health Assn. 1977–, Assn. of Occupational & Environ. Clinics (bd. dirs. 1991–), Berkeley City Club 1991–; editor (book): Problem Buildings, 1989; author: articles in field, 1994; mil: O3, Public Health Svc. 1980-92; rec: sailing. Res: 1517 Henry St Berkeley 94709 Ofc: HESIS 2151 Berkeley Way Berkeley 94704 Tel: 510/540-2115

CONGER, JOHN PEYTON, psychologist, writer; b. Mar. 3, 1935, NY, NY; s. Frederic DePeyster and Elizabeth (Mallett) C.; m. Judith Donovan, Dec. 27, 1961, dec. 1969; m. Jane Marie Reynolds, Oct. 14, 1979; children: Timothy b. 1965, Gregory b. 1987, Rhys b. 1991; edn: BA, Harvard Univ., 1957; STB, Gen. Theol. Sem. NYC 1960; Cooper Union Art Sch., 1962-64; MA in english, New York Univ., 1967; PhD, Calif. Sch. of Profl. Psych., 1974; lic. psychologist Calif. (PP4778) 1976. Career: faculty, Eng. tchr. Pingry Sch., Elizabeth, N.J. 1964-69, Horace Mann Sch., N.Y.C. 1969-70, College Prep. Sch., Berkeley 1971-72, student, instr. Calif. Sch. Profl. Psych., 1972-74; intern Probation Guidance Clinic, San Leandro 1973-74; clin. dir. Phoenix House, Concord, Ca. 1974-78; psychologist pvt. practice, Berkeley 1978–; assoc. prof. grad. psych. dept. John F. Kennedy Univ., 1978–, tnr. Bioenergetic Soc. of No. Calif., 1981–; mem: Am. Psychol. Assn./Calif., Bioenergetic Soc. of No. Calif. (pres., treas. 1982-86, founder/ed. The Bioenergetic Rev.), Inst. for Jungian and Reichian Studies (founder, dir. 1984–); author: Jung and Reich: The Body as Shadow (No.Atlantic Books, Berkeley 1988), The Body in Recovery: Somatic Psychotherapy and the Self (N. Atlantic Books, Berkeley 1994), profl. jour. articles; mng. ed. Internat. Inst. for Bioenergetic Analysis Jour.; Episcopalian Priest; avocation: painting. Address: 851 Regal Rd Berkeley 94708

CONLEY, SUSAN B., pediatric nephrologist, physician; b. Feb. 3, 1948, Coldwater, Mich.; d. Kenneth D. and Mary F. (Spence) Conley; edn: MD, Univ. of Mich., Ann Arbor 1973. Career: instr. Wash. Univ. Sch. of Medicine, St. Louis, Mo. 1977-78; asst. prof. to assoc. prof., Univ. of Tex. Med. Sch., Houston 1978-91; dir. Pediatric Renal Ctr., Calif. Pacific Med. Ctr., San Francisco 1991-94; prof. of pediatrics Stanford Univ. Med. Sch. 1994-; recipient Disting. Svc. award Nat. Kidney Found., NY, NY 1992; mem: Am. Academy of Pediatrics (exec. com. sect. on nephrology), Nat. Kidney Found. (pres. Region V 1994–); author: 60+ articles pub. in med. journals. Res: 2397 Sharon Rd Menlo Park 94025 Ofc: Dept. of Pediatrics Stanford University Medical School Stanford 94305 Tel: 415/498-5480

CONLIN, WILLIAM RICHARD, journalist; b. Apr. 14, 1913, Sacto.; s. Wm. Richard and Clara Mabel (Schaadt) C.; m. Olivia Moore, Aug. 15, 1940; 1 son, William R., III b. 1955. Career: AB in econ., Stanford Univ. Career: staff writer Sacramento Union, 1937-76, sports editor 1945-59, 65-76, editor 1959-62, asst. to the pub. 1962-65; columnist Sacramento Bee 1976–, sports editor 1980-82; awards: Ring of Truth, 7 times, Copley Newspapers (1966-72), Sigma Delta Chi, No. Calif. Athletic Hall of Fame, World Boxing Hall of Fame; mem. Alpha Sigma Phi, Military Order of World Wars, Am. Philatelic Soc.; contbr. articles in mags., trade papers, philatelic topics; mil: lt. USN 1942-45; Republican; Cath.; rec: philately. Res: 1362 Eighth Ave Sacramento 95818 Ofc: Sacramento Bee 2100 Q St Sacramento

CONLON, JACK MARTIN, real estate executive; b. Oct. 8, 1931, Parsons, Kans.; s. John Thomas and Alice M. Conlon; m. Kathi Bergman, Feb. 29, 1984; children: Lisa b. 1955, Catherine b. 1957, Julia b. 1958 (dec.), Casey b. 1985; edn: BS, Kansas Univ., 1957; USC, 1957-58; Calif. lic. C.P.A. 1960. Career: CPA, Peat Marwick Mitchell, Los Angeles 1957-59, Kansas City 1960-63; pres. Coachella Valley Sav. & Loan, Palm Springs 1963-72; exec. v.p. Sunrise Co., Los Angeles 1972-76, pres. Sunrise Co., Palm Desert 1976–; instr. Am. Sav. & Loan Inst. 1965-66; mem. Tri-County Soc. of Sav. & Loan Controllers (pres. 1966), Palm Springs Conv. & Vis. Bur. (dir., treas. 1967-72), Palm Springs C.of C. (pres. 1971), Phi Kappa Psi Frat., PGA West, Rancho Santa Fe Farms Golf Club; civic: United Way (dir., treas. 1966-67), Coachella Valley Mountains Conservancy 1991–; mil: US Navy; Republican; rec: golf. Ofc: 42-600 Cook St Palm Desert 92260

CONNOLLY, J. JOSEPH, lawyer; b. July 4, 1948, Pasadena; s. John J. Connolly and Paula (Lowry) Galbraith; m. Dana Brooks, Dec. 18, 1971 (dec. 1982); m. Cynthia Sprague, June 9, 1984; edn: BA, Stanford Univ., 1969; JD, USC, 1972. Career: dep. dist. atty. Los Angeles Co. 1972-73; trial atty. U.S. Dept. Justice, Wash. D.C. 1974-76; assoc. atty. Adams Duque & Hazeltine, Los Angeles 1976-79, ptnr.` 1979-87; O'Neill & Sun, Santa Monica 1988–; hearing examiner Los Angeles Police Commn. 1977-83; judge pro tem Municipal Ct. Los Angeles 1986. Ofc: O'Neill & Sun 100 Wilshire Ste 700 Santa Monica 90401

CONOVER, DUANE, lawyer; b. July 31, 1937, Long Beach; s. Wesley Winfrey and Margaret Virginia (Mathews) C.; edn: BA, Dartmouth Coll. 1959; MA hist., UC Berkeley 1960; JD, Loyola Univ. 1974; LL.M tax., Univ. San Diego 1986; admitted U.S. Supreme Ct. (1979), U.S. Tax Ct. (1981). Career: controller Ralph

Edwards Productions, Hollywood 1968-74; ptnr. Button & Conover, Marina del Rey 1975; owner Conover & Assoc., Torrance 1976–; mediator Los Angeles Superior Ct., Santa Monica 1977–; mem: Peninsula Symphony (pres. 1992-94), L.A. Opera Assocs. (pres. 1977-79), El Segundo Alumni Assn. (treas.), El Segundo Edn. Found. (dir.); mil: lt.j.g. USN 1960-65; Democrat; Cath.; rec: flying, music. Ofc: 2780 Skypark Dr Ste 330 Torrance 90505

CONRAD, JOHN WILFRED, ceramic artist, educator; b. Aug. 3, 1935, Cresson, Pa.; s. Wilfred Lee and Elizabeth (Bouch) C.; m. Barbara Jean Daugherty, June 5, 1963; children: William T. b. 1969, Kristin E. b. 1973; edn: BS art edn., Ind. State Univ., 1958; MFA ceramics, Carnegie-Mellon Univ., 1963; PhD ceramic res., Univ. Pittsburgh, 1970. Career: art instr. Penn Hills (Pa.) High Sch., 1959-64; instr. Carnegie-Mellon Univ., 1961-64; prof. of fine arts Mesa Coll., San Diego 1966–, chmn. art dept. 1980-82, 85-88, academic senator 4 terms; consultant: Kennywood Amusement Park, Pitts., float bldr., artist and cons. 1960-63, Am. Cement Corp., Riverside, Ca. 1968-73, Baby Keepsakes, Thousand Oaks 1990–, KD Corp., Dallas, Tx. 1983–, various local potteries; devel. unique glazes and clay bodies for individual studio ceramists; exh. ceramics and ceramic sculpture 1963-: Three Rivers Fest., Pitts.; Allied Artists, Pitts.; Tiffany Invitational; Small Sculpture, Nat., Cypress Gal.; Sculpture Gal., San Diego; Soup Tureens, Campbell Mus.; one man show Oceans West Gal., Sa Diego; Group Ceramics Exhibits, Seattle; Ceramic Artists of San Diego; Allied Craftsmen, San Diego; mem.: Ceramic Artists S.D. (bd.), Nat. Coun. Edn. Ceramic Arts (bd.), Allied Craftsmen SD.; author: Ceramic Formulas: The Complete Compendium (MacMillan 1973), Contemporary Ceramic Techniques (Prentice Hall 1976), Contemp. Ceramic Formulas (MacMillan 1980), Ceramic Windchimes (Falcon Pub. 1984), Adv. Ceramic Manual (Falcon Pub. 1988), Studio Potters Dict. (Falcon 1989), Cone Six Ceramics (Falcon 1994), contbr. mag. articles; rec: skiing, ocean fishing, scuba. Res: 770 Cole Ranch Rd Encinitas 92024 Ofc: Art Dept. Mesa Coll. Mesa College Dr San Diego 92111

CONRAD, ROBERT WILLIAM, photographer; b. Oct. 19, 1953, Plainfield, N.J.; s. Robert Carl and Norma Anne (Montgomerie) C.; m. Gail Joanne Ransom, Jan. 10, 1976; children: Jenny Lynne b. 1984, Robert Michael b. 1987; edn: BA photojournalism, San Jose St. Univ. 1976; cert. W. Coast Sch. 1980-84; Golden Gate Sch. 1984–; tchg. credential, Humboldt St. Univ. 1982; Certified Professional Photographer (CPP). Career: owner Gillard Photog., Fortuna 1977–; p.t. instr. Coll. of Redwoods 1980-86; awards: Profl. Photographers of Calif. fellowship, 1986; mem: Profl. Photographers of Am., Profl. Photographers of Calif.; Republican; Evangelical; rec: sailing, windsurfing, backpacking, guitar. Ofc: Gillard Photography 1136 Main St Fortuna 95540

CONROE, MARK GUSTAV, real estate developer b. Jan. 21, 1958, Hartford, Conn.; s. Wallace Weller Conroe and Marie-Anne (Langenskiold) Conroe-Harris; edn: undergrad. US Mil. Acad., West Point 1976-78; BSCE, Stanford Univ., 1980, MSCE, 1981, MBA, 1985; E.I.T. cert., Calif. 1980. Career: staff scientist Energy Resources Co., Walnut Creek 1981-82; prodn. engr. Sohio Petroleum Co., San Francisco 1982-83; cons. McKinsey and Co., Dallas, Tx. 1984; ptnr. Mozart Devel. Co., Palo Alto 1985–; awards: Pepsico Found. fellow 1984, Ctr. for Engrepreneurship Best Service Co. award- $1500 1984-85, grantee The Shidler Group, Stanford 1985; civic: founder Ctr. for Entrepreneurship, E.Palo Alto 1989–, steering com. Bayshore Workers 1991–, Cancer Support & Edn. Ctr. Menlo Park (bd. 1989–), S.F. Child Abuse Council (bd. 1983-85); pub. article in Real Estate Rev. (1985); Christian; rec: tennis, triathlons, travel. Ofc: Mozart Development Co. 435 Tasso St Ste 300 Palo Alto 94301

CONSIDINE, SHARON CULVER, restauranteur; b. June 6, 1942, San Diego; d. Harold Bell Wright and Elaine Lois (Smith) Culver; m. Timothy Malcolm Considine, Aug. 18, 1962; children: Kevin b. 1963, Kenneth b. 1965, Kelly b. 1970; edn: San Diego St. Univ. 1960-63 (treas. Assoc. Women Students). Career: owner/opr. Mexican Village Restaurant, 1973–; owner/agent TNT Travel Agency, 1975-82; real estate agt., 1976–; bd. dirs. Bank of So. Calif., 1983-93; bd. dirs. Danielson Trust Co. 1993–; awards: Co. of San Diego Merit Certif. for devel. of Las Ayudantes Aux. 1974, Peninsula YMCA Woman of Yr. 1986, service Coronado Rotary 1988, San Diego Restauranteur of Yr. 1990, Mex-Am. Found. "Amiga de Mexico" 1990, Alumnus of 1994 SDSU College of Arts & Letters, listed Who's Who in We. States 1983, Who's Who in World of Internat. Women 1994; mem: San Diego Restaurant Assn. (founding mem., pres. 1981), Calif. Restaurant Assn. (state bd. 1983–), Coronado C.of C. (dir. 1988–, pres. 1990), Coronado Rotary 1990–, Min. Wage Bd. State of Calif. 1993-95, SDSU Alumni Assn. (dir. 1980-84), Pi Beta Phi Sor. Alumnae (past pres.); civic bds: USO (ofcr., dir. 1987–, pres. 1993-95), Aztec Athletic Found. (dir., pres. 1981-85), San Diego Super Bowl Com. (rep. 1984-88), Coronado Hosp. Found. (dir. 1984-89, 1993-96, v.p. 1994-95), SDSU Pres.'s Council 1984-89, Industry Council for Hotel and Rest. Mgmt. 1985-86, U.S. Internat. Univ. (dir. 1985-86), Mercy Hosp. Aux. (Pink Lady 1964-69), Ladies Aux. for Retarded Children (mem. and pres. 1970-76), Las Ayudantes for teenagers on probation (founder 1973-75), Pt. Loma Cub Scout Ldr. 1974-75, Sunset View Sch. (tchr.'s asst. 1978-79), Pt. Loma Girl Scout Ldr. 1980-82; Republican; R.Cath.; rec: running, skiing, travel. Ofc: Mexican Village Restaurant 120 Orange Ave Coronado 92118

CONSIDINE, TIMOTHY MALCOLM, certified public accountant; b. Nov. 20, 1940, Palo Alto; s. Charles Ray and Thalia Houston (Kelly) C.; m. Sharon Elaine Culver, Aug. 18, 1962; children: Kevin b. 1963, Kenneth b. 1965, Kelly b. 1970; edn: BS, San Diego St. Univ. 1962; C.P.A. Career: staff Considine & Considine, San Diego 1960-62, sr. 1962-64, mgr. 1964-65, ptnr. 1965–; chmn. San Diego Co. Civil Service; awards: San Diego St. Univ. outstanding alumnus; mem: Am. Inst. C.P.A., San Diego Space & Sci. Found. (bd. trustees); articles pub. in profl. jours. (1970–); Republican; R.Cath.; rec: philately, travel. Res: 545 Ocean Blvd Coronado 92118 Ofc: Considine & Considine 1501 5th Ave Ste 400 San Diego 92101

CONSTANTINE, DENNY GEORGE, public health veterinarian; b. May 5, 1925, San Jose; s. Gordon and Lucy Belle Brimblecom (Olson) C.; m. Peggy Jean Panabaker, July 25, 1952 (div. 1971); children: Gordon b. 1953, Kenneth b. 1962; edn: L.A. City Coll. and L.A. St. Coll., 1945-49; BS, UC Davis, 1953, DVM, 1955; MPH, UC Berkeley, 1965. Career: asst. mammalogist Los Angeles Co. Museum, 1942-46; cons. mammalogist Project X-Ray, Calif., N.M. and Tx. 1943-44; biologist USPHS, Anchorage, Alaska 1950-51; curator UC Davis Zoology Museum 1951-56, mammalolgist, lab. tech. 1954-55; chief CDC wildlife rabies investigations USPHS, Newton, Ga. 1955-56; Carlsbad Caverns, N.M. 1956-58; Las Cruces, N.M. 1958-64; chief CDC investigations U.S. Naval Biomed. Res. Lab., Oakland 1966-76; pub. health veterinarian St. Calif. Dept. Health, Berkeley 1976-91; consultant in rabies virology, epidemiology and control, mammology, ecology, wildlife management, environmental impact assessments 1991–; mem: AVMA, Wildlife Disease Assn., Am. Soc. Mammalogists, Calif. Vet. Med. Assn., U.S.-Mex. Border Pub. Health Assn.; 79 articles, monographs and chpts. pub., 1946–; mil: capt. USPHS 1955-76; Christian; rec: mammalogy, ecology, history. Ofc: 1899 Olmo Way Walnut Creek 94598

CONTI, ISABELLA, psychologist, consultant; b. Jan. 1, 1942, Turin, Italy; came to U.S., 1964; d. Giuseppe and Zaira (Melis) Ferro; m. Ugo Conti, Sept. 5, 1964; 1 son, Maurice b. 1970; edn: JD, Univ. Rome, Italy 1966; PhD in psychology, UC Berkeley 1975; lic. psychologist. Career: sr. analyst Res. Inst. for Study of Man, Berkeley, Calif. 1967-68; postgrad. res. psychologist Personality Assessment and Res. Inst., UC Berkeley 1968-71; intern UC Berkeley and VA Hosp., San Francisco 1969-75; asst. prof. St. Mary's Coll., Moraga 1978-84; cons. psychologist Conti Resources, Berkeley 1977-85; v.p., pres. Barnes & Conti Assocs., Inc., Berkeley 1985-90; pres. Lisardco, El Cerrito 1989-; v.p. ElectroMagnetic Instruments Inc., El Cerrito 1985-; awards: NIMH predoctoral res. fellow 1972-73; Regents fellow UC Berkeley 1972; mem: Am. Psychological Assn.; author (with Alfonso Montuori): From Power to Partnership, 1993; contbr. articles on creativity and mgmt. cons. to profl. jours. Ofc: Lisardco 1318 Brewster Dr El Cerrito 94530

COOK, KATHLEEN MARIE, librarian; b. Aug. 13, 1947, Los Angeles; d. William Patrick Roach and Elizabeth Jane (Reilly) Howes; m. Steven Kenneth Cook, Aug. 24, 1968; children: Jerret b. 1975, Colin b. 1976; edn: BA psychology, Univ. R.I. 1981; MLS, 1983. Career: mgr. tech. library, AiResearch Mfg. Co., Torrance 1983-85; staff Cubic Defense Systems, San Diego 1985–, mgr. tech. library 1989–; honors: Beta Phi Mu; mem. Spl. Libraries Assn. (com. chair 1986–); pub. articles in profl. jours. (2, 1983); Democrat; Christian; rec: camping. Ofc: Cubic Defense Systems POB 85587 San Diego 92186-5587

COOK, LYNETTE RENE, illustrator, educator; b. Jan. 1, 1961, Herrin, Ill.; d. Kenneth Severin Cook and Charlotte Cecelia Cook-Fuller; edn: BS, Miss. Univ. for Women, 1981, BFA, 1982; MFA, Calif. Coll. of Arts & Crafts, Oakland 1984. Career: freelance artist, San Francisco 1983–; artist, photographer Morrison Planetarium, Calif. Acad. of Scis., S.F. 1984–; art instr. Calif. Acad. of Scis. 1988–, UC (Ext.) Berkeley 1989–, Academy of Art Coll. 1994; guest lectr. UC Santa Cruz 1989–; fine artist; exhibits include. "Spaceweek Internat. Space Art Exhibit", Space Ctr. Houston, Tx. 1994, "Ancient Myths, Legends, and Future Dreams," NASA Ames Res. Ctr., Moffett Field, Calif. 1994, and "Artists and the Universe," 1993, "Free Hand: The Fine Art of Commercial Illustration," Bedford Gallery, Walnut Creek, Calif. 1993, "Reflections of O'Keefe," Miss. St. Univ., Starkville, Miss. 1993, "Space Art: Probing the Outer Limits," Cleveland Mus. of Nat. Hist., Cleveland, OH 1993, Art of the Cosmos, Hayden Planetarium, Am. Mus. of Natural Hist., NY, NY 1992, Guild of Natural Sci. Illustrs. Nat. Exh. Durham, N.C. 1991, Santa Barbara, Ca. 1989, Denver 1988, Mus. of Natural Hist., Smithsonian, W.D.C. 1986, Naturalists: Paintings and Drawings of Life, Reese Bullen Gal., Humboldt State Univ. 1991, Strybing Arboretum 50th Ann. Exh., S.F. 1990, illustr. Notecubes, gift wrapping paper, cards, mugs, posters for various cos., 1990–; awards: Guild of Natural Sci. Illustrs. (GNSI) Traveling Exh., art selected for permanent collection 1985, 89, 1st pl., 2-dimensional category "Bridge Works" art contest commemmorating 50th ann. of Golden Gate Bridge 1987, DESI Award, Graphic Design: USA 1988, juror "Calif. Species: Biol. Art and Illustrn." The Oakland Mus. 1989, winner Spaceweek Internat. Assn. Poster Competition 1995, listed Outstanding Young Women Am. 1985, American Artists 1989, Who's Who in the West 1992, 94, Who's Who in Calif. 1993, 94, Who's Who in Am. Edn. 1994, The World Who's Who of Women 1993, Internat. Woman of Yr. 1993; mem: GNSI (mem. 1980–, exec. bd. 1986-92), Internat. Assn. for the

Astronomical Arts 1988–, San Francisco Soc. of Illustrators 1994–; rec: gardening, cooking, hiking. Ofc: Morrison Planetarium, Calif. Academy of Sciences, Golden Gate Park, San Francisco CA 94118

COOK, RUDOLPH EMANUEL, psychologist; b. May 30, 1928, Chgo.; m. Shirley Thrower, Aug. 3, 1973; edn: Ph.D., Northwestern Univ., 1949; M.A., Loyola Univ., Chgo., 1956; Ph.B., Univ. Oreg., 1965; lic. psychologist, Calif. Career: counselor Cook County Juvenile Home, Chgo., 1952-56; psychologist Elgin State Hosp., Illinois, 1956-62; teaching asst. Univ. Oreg., Eugene, 1962-65; poverty worker Portland Urban League, 1965-66; psychol. counselor San Jose State Univ., 1966-90 (ret.); pvt. practice psychologist 1968–; forensic evaluator Santa Clara Co. Superior Court; psychologist Calif. Disability Evaluation Div.; recipient Service award Continental Socs., 1982-83; Fellow Am. Orthopsychiat. Assn., Royal Soc. Health; mem. Nat. Register Health Service Providers in Psychology, Pathway Socs. (Service award 1977), Afro-Am. Community Ctr., Campus Christian Ctr., Kappa Alpha Psi (Service award 1975, 76); Democrat. Res: 1094 Pomeroy Ave Santa Clara 95051 Ofc: 95 S Market St Ste300 San Jose 95113 Tel: 408/995-3215

COOLEY, CHESTER WINSLOW, psychologist, educator; b. April 14, 1919, Cottage Grove, Ore.; s. Clarence Waldo and Lida Louise (Dimick) C.; m. Alice Iverne Eymard, Sept. 6, 1940; 1 son, Robert W. b. 1942; edn: BA, San Francisco St. Univ. 1951; MA, 1952; cert. psychologist Calif. St. Bd. Med. Examiners 1959. Career: social sci. tchr. Napa Valley Unified Sch. Dist., Napa 1952-54, spl. edn. tchr. 1954-55, dean of boys 1955-58, sch. psychologist 1958-64, dir. pupil personnel services 1964-79; ret.; vis. lectr. San Francisco St.; mem. advy. bd. Napa Co. Mental Health 1960-88; honors: Calif. PTA Life Membership 1956; mem: Nat. Assn. Pupil Personnel Adminstrs. (charter), Assn. Calif. Sch. Adminstrs. (charter), Napa Valley Retired Tchrs. Assn., Calif. Retired Tchrs. Assn.; mil: s.sgt. AUS 1944-46; Democrat; Prot.; rec: photog., philately. Res: 2132 Janette Dr Napa 94558

COOLEY, FRED EVERETT, retired physician-surgeon; b. Apr. 3, 1912, Phoenix, Ariz.; s. Fred E., Sr. and Jessie Gertrude (Rosen) C.; m. Mildred Elfrieda Peterson, Apr. 30, 1939; edn: AB, USC, 1932; MD, Washington Univ., St. Louis, Mo. 1936. Career: surgical resident Gen. Hosp. of Fresno Co., Fresno, Calif. 1936-40; pvt. practice physician and surgeon, Fresno 1946-74, emergency med. Community Hosp. Fresno, 1974-76, dist. surgeon Southern Pacific R.R., Fresno 1946-71; med./surg. staff Community Hosp., St. Agnes Hosp., 1946-77, Valley Childrens Hosp., 1954-64, ret. 1977; pres. Central Calif. Blood Bank, Fresno 1956-59; honors: 'Others' Award for estab. substance abuse pgm. Salvation Army Fresno (1973), O.D.A.S. internat. award for estab. health care pgm. for Adult Rehab. Ctr. Fresno and 35 yrs. of volunteer svc. The Salvation Army London, Eng. (1983), Paul Harris Fellow Fresno Rotary (1988), Frontiersman of Yr. 1990 award for outstanding service to Adult Rehabilitation Ctr. Fresno the We. terr. of Salvation Army (6/9/90); mem: Fresno Madera Med. Soc. (pres. 1954), Calif. Med. Assn., Fellow A.C.S.; civic: The Salvation Army Fresno (coord. health care pgms. 1982–, past chmn. and life mem. Advy. Bd. 1954–, mem./past chmn. Advy. Council 1976–); lodges: Shrine, Royal Order of Jesters (past dir.); mil: major USAR 1st Aux. Surgical Gp. 1941-46; Republican; Prot.; rec: music/ player mem. Fresno Philharmonic Orch. (1953-68), travel, woodworking, Salvation Army volunteer service.

COOMBS, ROBERT HOLMAN, educator/medical sociologist; b. Sept. 16, 1934, Salt Lake City; s. Dr. Morgan Scott, M.D., and Vivian (Holman) C.; m. Carol Jean Cook, May 29, 1958; children: Robert Scott, Kathryn, Lorraine, Karen Youn Jung, Holly Ann, Krista Ho Jung, David Jeremy; edn: BS, Univ. Utah, 1958, MS, 1959; PhD, Wash. State Univ., 1964. Career: asst., assoc. prof. sociology Iowa State Univ. 1963-66; postdoc. fellow Behavioral Sci. Ctr. Bowman Gray Sch. Med. Wake Forest Univ., 1966, asst. prof. 1966-68, assoc. prof. 1968-70; career research specialist Calif. Dept. Mental Hygiene, Camarillo 1970-73; assoc. research sociologist UCLA 1970-77, assoc. prof. biobehavioral scis. UCLA Sch. Med. 1977-78, prof. behavioral sci. 1978–, chief Camarillo/ Neuropsychiatric Inst. 1970-78, dir. UCLA Family Learning Ctr., Oxnard 1977-84; asst. dir. res. UCLA Neuropsychiatric Inst. Ctr. for Health Scis. 1978-81; dir. Office Edn. of Neuropsychiatric Inst. 1980-90, mem. Calif. Atty. General's Commn. on the Prevention of Drug and Alcohol Abuse, 1986-87; dir. Grief and Bereavement Prog., UCLA Neuropsychiatric Hosp.; honors: Sigma Xi, Phi Kappa Phi, grantee NIMH 1968-73, Nat. Fund Med. Edn. 1969-71, Law Enforcement Adminstrn. 1971-76, Nat. Inst. Drug Abuse 1977-80, Calif. Dept. Alcohol and Drug Pgms. 1977-78, Father Flanagan's Boys Home 1977-79, CETA, Ventura Co., Calif. 1978; mem: Internat., Am. Sociol. Assns., Assn. Am. Med. Colls., Am. Psych. Soc. (fellow), Internat. Family Therapy Assn., World Fedn. for Mental Health, Internat. Sociology Assn., World Fedn. for Med. Edn., AAAS (fellow), Am. Assn. Applied and Preventive Psychol. (fellow); author 10 books: Psychosocial Aspects of Med. Training, 1971, Junkies and Straights: The Camarillo Experience, 1975, Socialization in Drug Abuse, 1976, Mastering Medicine: Profl. Socialization in Med. School, 1978, Making it in Med. School, 1979, Inside Doctoring: Stages and Outcomes in the Profl. Development of Physicians, 1986, The Family Context of Adolescent Drug Use, 1986, Drug Testing: Issues and Options, 1991, Drug Impaired Professionals, 1995,

Handbook on Drug Prevention: A Comprehensive Strategy to Prevent the Abuse of Alcohol and Other Drugs, and num. book chapters, jour. articles; assoc. ed. Family Relations: J. Applied Family and Child Studies, 1970-80, Clin. Sociology Rev., J. Clin. Sociology, J. Marriage and the Family; contbg. ed. J. Drug Issues, 1977–, corresp. ed. Medical Education, 1991-95, editorial bd. Qualitative Health Res.; mil: spE6 US Army 1958-64; Democrat; Ch. Jesus Christ of Latter-day Saints (bishop Winston-Salem, NC Ward 1969-70, Camarillo, CA Ward 1972-77). Res: 29439 Green Grass Ct Agoura Hills 91301 Ofc: UCLA School of Medicine 760 Westwood Plaza Los Angeles 90024-1759

COOMES, GERALDINE SAWYER, youth counselor, teacher; b. Mar. 20, 1935, San Francisco; d. Albert Pierce and Margaret (Bird) Sawyer; m. Joseph E. Coomes, Jr., June 17, 1955, div. 1985; children: Bryan b. 1960, Harlan b. 1961; edn: AA, Santa Rosa Jr. Coll. 1954; AB with honors, Sacramento State Coll., 1960, grad. work 1965; Univ. of La Verne 1981; Inst. of Children's Literature, Conn. 1987-88, 95; Calif. std. tchg. cred., gen. K-8 (1960). Career: recreation dir. Co. of Sonoma, Santa Rosa 1954, playground dir. City of Berkeley 1955, clk. Registrar's ofc. UCB 1955-58; substitute tchr. Sacto. Unified Sch. Dist. 1967-69, San Juan U.S.D., Carmichael 1968-71, Elk Grove U.S.D. 1980-84, Sacto. Co. Office Edn. (2 dists.) 1985-89, Yolo Co. (1 dist.) 1986-89; lab. svs. helper Calgene Inc. (plant bio-genetics firm), Davis 1989-91; tchr. aide The Poppy Patch Child Care Ctr., Sacto. 1991–, also youth counselor Royal Gardens Youth Care Home, Sacto. 1992-93; p.t. lobby usher United Artists Theatre Circuit, Inc., Sacto. 1993-95; p.t. dining room host Burger King #1841, Sacto. 1994-95; apptd. Sacto. Co. Office of Voter Reg. & Elections (judge 1964-79, supr. election bd. 1980-85); awards: 3d pl./named Miss Personality, Miss Sonoma County comp. 1953, World of Poetry Golden Poet Award 1985, 86, 87, 92, Silver Poet Award 1990, Editor's Choice Award 1994, 95; civic: mgr. singing group The Mockingbirds (vol. entertain nsg. homes), vol., co-chair and Easter bunny for Easter Egg Hunt, Calgene Inc., Davis 1991, PTA (pres. Thos. Jefferson Elem. 1967-68); club: College Greens Swim & Racquet; publs: World of Poetry Anthols. (1983, 84, 85, 86), The National Library of Poetry Anthols. (1994, 95, 96); Democrat; Presbyterian; rec: write stories for children, write song lyrics, feed blue jays. Res: 3057 Great Falls Way #89 Sacramento 95826

COOPER, JAMES L., television executive producer/talk-show host; b. May 21, 1921, Chgo.; s. Charles L. and Gladys (Flynn) C.; m. Elinore Mary Worrell, Aug. 7, 1943; children: Leslie b. 1948, James L. Jr. b. 1950; edn: BA in polit. sci., journ., Univ. Nebr., Lincoln 1947. Career: police reporter Omaha World Herald, Nebr. 1938-40; editor VFW Mag., Vet. Foreign Wars, Lincoln, Nebr. 1957-59; city editor Orange County Evening News, Garden Grove, Calif. 1953-66; TV on-air reporter KCBS-TV, Ch. 2 (CBS), Hollywood 1966-72; v.p. community affairs KOCE-TV, Ch. 50 (Orange Coast Comm. Coll. sta.), Huntington Beach 1966–, exec. prod./talk show host, univ. student intern supr.; producer-host 30-min. TV Specials: Homeless Women, 1987, AIDS: Fighting Ignorance, 1988, Schizophrenia: New Hope for Families, 1989; awards: 2 Emmy awards also 10 Emmy nominations Acad. TV Arts & Scis. (1983, 86), George Washington Medal Freedoms Found. at Valley Forge 1988, 1st Amendment award B'nai Brith, Santa Ana 1984; mem. Orange County Press Club (pres. 1954), Marine Corps Aviation Assn.; civic: March of Dimes Orange Co. (1966–, v.p.), NCCJ (bd. 1974–), O.C. Old Courthouse Mus. (bd. 1981–), Advy. Com. Brea Neuropsychiatric Hosp. (bd. 1987–), O.C. Performing Arts Ctr. Board Emeritus 1980–, Orange Co. Grand Jury 1993-94; mil: pilot/lt. col. USMC 1942-45, South Pacific, 1949-53, Korea; Cath.; rec: woodworking, classic autos, gardening, stamps, reading. Res: 1541 E Wellington St Santa Ana 92701

COOPERSMITH, HENRY JOSEPH, lawyer; b. March 17, 1943; s. Paul C.; edn: AA, Oakland City Coll. 1963; BS, Calif. St. Coll. Hayward 1965; JD, UC Berkeley 1969; LL.M tax., N.Y. Univ. 1969. Career: pres. Henry J. Coopersmith Inc., Santa Ana 1976–. Ofc: 611 Anton Blvd Ste 1110 Costa Mesa 92626

COPENHAVER, BRIAN PAUL, academic administrator, historian; b. Dec. 21, 1942, Baltimore, Md.; s. Olin Franklin and Rose Mary (Fitzpatrick) C.; m. Kathleen Ann Gulick, Sept. 4, 1965; children: Gregory b. 1966, Rebecca b. 1971; edn: AB, Loyola Coll., Baltimore, Md. 1964; MA, Creighton Univ., Omaha, Nebr. 1966; PhD, Univ. of Kansas 1970. Career: asst. instr. Univ. of Kans. 1966-70; instr. Kans. City Art Inst. 1970, Drake Univ. 1971; asst. prof. gen. studies Western Washington Univ. 1971-74, assoc. prof. 1975-77, dir. honors prog. 1974-80, prof. liberal studies 1978-81, assoc. dean Coll. of Arts & Scis. 1977-81; dean coll. of arts & scis./prof. of hist. Oakland University, Rochester Hills, Mich. 1981-88; dean coll. of humanities & social sci./prof. of hist. & philosophy Univ. of Calif. Riverside 1988-93; provost coll. of letters & sci./prof. of hist. UCLA 1993–; v.p. Mich. Council of Arts & Scis. Deans 1987, pres. 1987; bd. of editors Annals of Sci. 1986–; ctr. assoc. Ctr. for Medieval and Renaissance Studies, UCLA 1988–; bd. of editors Jour. of the Hist. of Philosophy 1988–; cons. editor Jour. of the Hist. of Ideas 1991–; editorial bd. Renaissance Quarterly 1992–; honors: Fulbright Scholar, Universite de Lyon 1968-69, fellow Medieval Acad. Inst. on the Basic Disciplines 1974, fellow Am. Council of Learned Societies 1975-76; mem.: Am. Historical Assn. 1966–, Hist. of Sci. Soc. 1975–, Renaissance Soc. of Am.(editorial bd., council 1993–), Soc. for the Hist. of Alchemy and Chem., Am. Soc. for Ch. Hist., Internat. Assn. for Neo-Latin Studies, Sixteenth Century

Studies Soc., Sigma Xi; author: Symphorien Champier and the Reception of the Occultist Tradition in Renaissance France (Mouton, 1978), Hermetica (Cambridge, 1993), Renaissance Philosophy (Oxford 1993), num. pub. articles, book chapters and reviews, essay reviews, 1969–; mil: 1st lt. arty., USAR 1970; Democrat; Roman Catholic. Ofc: College of Letters & Science UCLA 405 Hilgard Ave Los Angeles 90024-1438

COPPERMAN, WILLIAM HAROLD, value engineering consultant; b. Dec. 4, 1932 Cleve., Oh.; s. Jack Jason and Ruth (Rollnick) C.; m. Rena June Dorn, Dec. 26, 1954, div., 1978; children: Randy Lee b. 1956, David Marc b. 1962; edn: BS, Duquesne Univ., Pitts., Pa., 1954; MBA, Univ. So. Calif., L.A., 1962; JD, Univ. San Fernando, L.A., 1977; career: corp. mgr. of value engring. Hughes Aircraft, L.A., 1957-89; pres. Cave, Inc., L.A., 1983–; certified value spec. (CVS) Soc. of Am. Value Engrs., 1983; mem. Miles Value Found., 1977-84; exec. v.p. Soc. of Am. Value Engr., 1984-88; dir. certification bd., SAVE, 1986-88; instr. engring. extension, No. Caro. State, 1986–; dir., Miles Value Found. 1988–; awards: Outstanding Achievement, US Army AMC, 1986; Value Engring. Award, Purchasing Mag., 1987; Achievement in VE, US Army (Huntsville, Ala.), 1977-82; mem: Soc. of Am. Value Engrs (SAVE), 1975–; civic: mem, Nat. Rifle Assn., Am. Legion, Disabled Am. Vet.; author: book, Guide to Value Engring., 1986; ed., dod handbook on Value Engring, 1986; author video tape series, Value Engring., 1987; over 30 pub. articles on Value Engring., 1976–; mil: capt. USA, 1954-62; rec: computer programming, tennis, golf. Ofc: P.O. Box 5488 Playa del Rey 90296

COPPOLA, FRANCIS FORD, director, producer, film writer; b. Apr. 7, 1939, Detroit; s. Carmine C.; m. Eleanor Neil; children: Gian-Carlo (dec.), Roman, Sofia; edn: B.A., Hofstra Univ., 1958; Master of Cinema, UCLA, 1968. Career: pub. mag. San Francisco, 1975-76; artistic dir., Zoetrope Studios; dir. motion pictures including Dementia 13, 1964, You're a Big Boy Now, 1967, Finian's Rainbow, 1968, The Rain People, 1969, One from the Heart, 1981; writer: motion pictures This Property Is Condemned, 1966, Reflections In a Golden Eye, 1967, The Rain People, 1969, Is Paris Burning, 1966, Patton 1970, The Great Gatsby, 1974; writer, producer and dir. motion pictures The Godfather (Acad. awards for Best Screenplay and Best Picture, nominee for Best Dir., Film Dir.'s award Dirs. Guild 1972), The Godfather, Part II, 1974 (Acad. awards for Best Screenplay, Best Dir. and Best Picture), The Conversation, 1974 (Golden Palm award Cannes Film Festival 1974), Apocalypse Now, 1979, Rumble Fish, 1983; producer TV movie The People; producer, dir. motion picture The Outsiders, 1983; producer: motion pictures THX 1138, 1971, The Escape Artist, 1982, The Black Stallion Returns, 1983; exec. producer motion picture Black Stallion, 1979; exec. producer motion picture Hammett; dir., co-screenwriter The Cotton Club, 1984, co-exec. producer Mishima, 1985; dir. Peggy Sue Got Married, 1986, Gardens of Stone, 1987, Tucker: The Man and His Dream, 1988, The Godfather, Part III (also writer), 1990, Bram Stoker's Dracula, 1992; dir. play Private Lives, opera The Visit; exec. producer motion picture Lionheart; dir., co-screenwriter Life Without Zoe segment in film New York Stories, 1990; mem. Dirs. Guild Am. Inc. Ofc: Am Zoetrope 916 Kearny St San Francisco 94133-5138

CORBANI, CANDACE BEDFORD, antique dealer, civic activist; b. Sept. 1, 1944, Sellersville, Pa.; d. Harry Clay and Gwendolyn (Murdoch) Bedford; m. John Corbani, July 3, 1963; children: Kim Marie b. 1968, Donna Alene b. 1972; edn: BA, UC Santa Barbara, 1968; AA in hotel restaurant mgmt., S.B. City Coll., 1977. Career: certified owner/tchr. Swim School, Santa Barbara 1970-75; organizational cons. Partymakers, 1977-84; owner/author Liberated Logo's, 1982–; antique dealer/prop. C&G Collection, 1984–; co-owner Hidden Oaks Country Club, Santa Barbara 1989–; pub. relations cons. Brinkerhoff Merchants Assn., 1988-90; awards: woman of yr. Commn. for Women S.B. (1987), woman of achiev. Calif. Senate 1987, recogn. cert. Calif. State Assembly 1987; civic: S.B. American Cancer Soc. (exec. bd. 1986–), S.B. Co. Affirmative Action Commn. (commr. 1986-88), Calif. Republicans for Choice (state advisor 1985–), Calif. Fedn. Repub. Women (former state dir.), S.B. Sch. Dist. Affirm. Action Com. (past chair, mem. 1982), Alumni Assn. Hotel Rest. Culinary SBCC (pres. 1987–), S.B. Bus. & Profl. Women (1st. v.p. 1988), Mesa Improvement Assn. S.B. (1987–, pres. 1990-91), L.W.V. 1984-86, Planned Parenthood 1984–, Mental Emotional Social Health Task Force S.B. Sch. Dist. 1986-88; author 2 books: Bright Ideas I, II (1982, 84); edit.: Inside Antiques, 1993-94; radio talk show host: KTMS 1250AM Collector's News Hour, The Whole Woman, co-host Literary Lunch, 1990-95, NARTSH, 1993-94 (C. Corbani and Collector's Resource Network nat. computerized antique info. & referral svc., consignment locations in Ventura and Santa Monica, 1990–); Republican (alt. S.B.Co. Repub. Central Com. 1990-91); rec: calligraphy. Ofc: 4760 Calle Camarada Santa Barbara 93110-2053

CORDELL, LADORIS HAZZARD, judge; b. Nov. 19, 1949, Bryn Mawr, Pa.; d. Lewis Randall and Clara Beatrice (Jenkins) H.; children: Cheran b. 1975, Starr b. 1980; edn: BA, Antioch Coll., 1971; JD, Stanford Univ. Law Sch., 1974; admitted Calif. St. Bar 1975. Career: atty. pvt. practice, East Palo Alto 1975-82; asst. dean Stanford Law Sch. 1978-82; judge Muni. Ct., Santa Clara Co., San Jose 1982-88, judge Superior Ct. 1988–; awards: woman of achiev. Santa Clara

Co. 1985, achiev. W. Ctr. on Domestic Violence, San Francisco 1986, Juliette Gordon Low Award, Girl Scouts of Santa Clara Co. 1987, Volunteer of Yr., United Way of Santa Clara Co. 1990, San Jose Baha'i Community Svc. Award 1992; mem: Nat. Assn. of Women Judges, Calif. Judges Assn., Nat. Bar Assn., Am. Bar Assn.; civic: United Way Santa Clara Co. (bd. 1986–), NCCJ, Santa Clara Co. (bd. govs. 1988–), Sierra Club Legal Defense Fund, Inc. (chair, bd. of trustees 1994-95), Am. Red Cross (bd. dirs. Santa Clara Co., 1995), Packard Children's Hosp. (bd. dirs. 1994–); contbr. articles to bar jours. and law revs.; Democrat. Ofc: Superior Court 191 N First St San Jose 95113

CORDIER, MARC ANDRE, computer systems analyst; b. June 3, 1958, Bakersfield; s. Robert Joseph, Sr. and Peggy Loranne (Lewis) C.; m. Cathy Lynn Rambo, Mar. 22, 1980; 2 sons, Alexander Jordan b. 1989, Cody Jack b. 1994; edn: AA in comp. sci., Bakersfield Coll., 1986. Career: computer svc. mgr. Achievements in Microsystems, Bakersfield 1984; computer svc. mgr. Valcom of Bakersfield, 1985; computer telecomms. tech. County of Kern, 1985-88; dept. systems coord. Kern Co. Assessor, 1988; dept. systems coord. Kern Co. Dist. Atty., 1988–; instr. computer software & systems Kern Co. Information Systems, Bakersfield 1986-87; awards: cert. of achiev. in d.p. Bakersfield Coll. 1974, Eagle Scout BSA 1974; mem. Calif. District Attorney's Check Enforcement Assn.; civic: Nat. Eagle Scout Assn., Am. Cancer Soc. (vol. 1972-73), Council of Churches 1971-75; mil: E5 USNR 1975-89, hon. discharge; Republican; Presbyterian; rec: systems design, auto restoration. Res: 4700 Chaney Ln Bakersfield 93311 Ofc: Kern Co. District Atty. 5357 Truxtun Ave Bakersfield 93309

CORDOVA, RON, lawyer; b. Aug. 18, 1946, Los Angeles; s. Reuben and Lya (Gruber) C.; m. Mariann Pehrson, June 2 1970; children: Danielle b. 1976, Andrea b. 1981; edn: Trinity Coll. Dublin 1966; AB, Dartmouth Coll. 1967; JD, USC 1972. Career: dep. dist. atty. Orange Co. Dist. Attys. Office, Santa Ana 1973-76; mem. Calif. Legislature, Sacto. 1976-78; atty., Newport Beach 1979–; adj. prof. UC Irvine, Sch. Social Ecology 1975-77, 1981-82; awards: Jaycees Outstanding Young Men Am. (1977, 78); mem: Lincoln Club Orange Co.; 4 articles pub. in profl. jours. (1975, 77, 84); Republican; Jewish; rec: travel, photog. Ofc: Cordova & Ruzicka 130 Newport Center Dr Newport Beach 92660

COREY, JOSEPH ROBERT, regional manager; b. Aug. 28, 1944, Corning, N.Y.; s. Joseph Marshall Corey and Betty (Waters) Snyder; m. Sally J. Davis, Aug. 24, 1967 (div. 1988); m. Cynthia Joan Clinton, April 22, 1989; children: Joseph b. 1969, Matthew b. 1972, Lara b. 1976; edn: BA, Taylor Univ. 1966. Career: mfrs. rep. Lincoln Mercury (div. Ford Motor Co.), Cincinnati, Ohio 1972-77; promotion coordinator Ford, Detroit, Mich. 1977-82; media dealer advt., assoc. mem. Toyota Motor Sales, Torrance 1982-85; nat. advt. mgr. Hyundai Motor Am., Garden Grove 1985-89, western regional mgr. 1989-91, nat. advt./merch. mgr. 1991-93; regional mgr. Automotive Acceptance Co. 1993–; mil: capt. AUS 1967-72; Republican; Prot.; rec: swimming, gardening. Res: 23001 Ceccila Mission Viejo 92691 Ofc: Automotive Acceptance Company 5800 Jameel Road Houston TX 77040

CORMIER, MARK S., poet; b. Nov. 25, 1960, Dover, Del.; s. Rene Victor and Margaret Mary (Moreau) C.; m. Catherine Elizabeth Breitman, May 30, 1992; edn: H.S. diploma, St. John's Prep., Danvers, Mass. 1978; AB, Dartmouth Coll. 1982. Career: reporter, North Shore Weeklies, Danvers, Mass. 1982-83; caller, Pacific Stock Exchange, S.F. 1983-93, market maker Kessler-Asher 1994–; mem. Sutter Station Historical Soc., S.F. 1986–; lectr., Toronado Tempest Oratorical Club, S.F. 1988-92; awards: runner-up Time Capsule, Mills Bldg., S.F. 1992; mem. Dartmouth Alumni Assoc. 1982–; Am. Legion, S.F.; poetry moderator, Cafe Babar, S.F. 1986, 88, Cafe Malvina 1993-94; ed., 2 books: Dr. Irony 1987, 26 Numbers in the Alphabet 1989; author, 2 books: I Hear a Tear,1988, Lilly 1992; Democrat; Catholic; rec: trapshooting, history. Res: 2230 Taylor St San Francisco 94133 Ofc: Pacific Stock Exchange, 2nd Flr Options Flr 220 Bush St. San Francisco 94114

CORNWALL, KENT NEELEY, architect; b. Feb. 26, 1954. Salt Lake City; s. J. Shirl and Lenore (Neeley) C.; m. Susan Hodgkinson, June 19, 1979; children: Jason, 1980; Robert, 1982; Kathryn, 1984; Jeffrey, 1986; Rachel, 1989; Sarah, 1992; edn: BA, Calif. Polytechnic Institute, Pomona, 1979; licensed architect, Calif. State Reg. Bd. Career: vice pres. Cornwall Assoc., Pasadena, 1980-92, pres., 1992–; mem: Nat. Trust for Historic Preservation, 1988–; Monrovia Preservation Group, 1987–; leader, Boy Scouts of Am., 1989–; Calif. and Nat. A.I.A. (dir. Pasadena/Foothill Chpt. A.I.A.), 1979–; Republican; Ch. Jesus Christ Latter-Day Saints; rec: house restorations; skiing. Res: Monrovia.

CORRIGAN, FRANCIS JOSEPH, professor of finance; b. Feb. 27, 1919, St. Louis, Mo.; s. John F. and Catherine A. (Costello) C.; edn: BS, St. Louis Univ. 1941; MBA, Stanford Univ. 1943; PhD, St. Louis Univ. 1952. Career: financial analyst, Monsanto Co. 1943-46; investment broker, Dempsey-Tegeler & Co. 1946-49; prof. fin. St. Louis Univ., Mo. 1949-67; Santa Clara Univ. 1967–; mem: Knights of Malta, Fin. Execs. Inst., Mo. Athletic Club; co-author: Investments (1978, 84); Republican; Cath.; rec: travel, sports, theatre. Res: 18400 Overlook Rd #8 Los Gatos 95030 Ofc: Santa Clara Univ. Santa Clara 95053

CORRIGAN, ROBERT ANTHONY, university president; b. Apr. 21, 1935, New London, Conn.; s. Anthony John and Rose Mary (Jengo) C.; m. Joyce Mobley, Jan. 12, 1975; children: Kathleen Marie b. 1960, Anthony John b. 1963, Robert Anthony b. 1965, Erika Mobley b. 1968; edn: dipl. Classical High Sch., Springfield, Mass. 1953; AB, Brown Univ., 1957; MA, Univ. Pa., 1959, PhD 1967. Career: researcher Phila. Historical Commn. 1957-59; lectr. Univ. Gothenburg, Sweden 1959-62, Bryn Mawr Coll. 1962-63; instr. Univ. Pa. and vis. lectr. Phila. Mus. Coll. of Art, 1963-64; instr. Univ. Iowa, 1964-66, asst. prof., assoc. prof. of Eng. and Am. Civilization 1966-1973; vis. prof. Am. Studies, Grinnell Coll. 1970; dean Coll. of Arts and Scis./prof. of Eng., Univ. Mo., Kansas City 1973-74; provost for Arts and Humanities and prof. of English, Univ. Md., College Park 1974-79; chancellor and prof. English, Univ. Mass., Boston 1979-88; pres. and prof. English & Humanities, San Francisco State Univ., 1988–; mem. Calif. St. Univ. Educational Equity Advy. Council 1988-92, Asian Pacific Am. Edn. Advy. Gp. 1989–; dir. First Trade Union Savings Bank, FSB, 1986-88; mem. Econ. Devel. Corp., 1989-91, Modern Greek Studies Found., 1989–, Advy. Council Calif. Acad. Scis., 1988–; mem. ednl. advy. com. JFK Library 1979-88, bd. dirs. JFK Library Found. 1983-91, Friends of the JFK Library, 1983–; trustee Boston Coll. High Sch. 1984-90; editl. advy. bd. Yale Univ. Black Periodical Fiction Proj.; awards: Phi Beta Kappa, full tuition scholar Brown Univ. 1953-57, Clarkson Able Collins, Jr. maritime hist. prize 1956, Univ. Pa. Carnegie fellow 1957-59, Pa. Colonial Soc. essay award (1st pl. 1958, 1959), Smith-Mundt vis. prof. 1959-60, Fulbright lectr. 1960-62, Standard Oil Found. of Ind. tchg. excellence 1968, Nat. Endowment for Humanities/Ford Found. grantee 1969, NEH grantee 1970) NEH proj. grantee to develop Afro-Am. Studies Pgm. 1970-71, 71-74, Rockefeller Found. grantee 1972-75, Mo. State grantee for Summer Inst. on the Black Woman in Am. Culture 1974, US State Dept. lectr. in Africa and Asia 1977, comm. svc. award Freedom House 1985, comm. svc. award Action for Boston Comm. Devel. 1986, Wm. Lloyd Garrison Award of Mass. Ednl. Opp. Assn. 1987, named Distinguished Urban Fellow of The Assn. of Urban Univs. 1992–; mem: No. Am. Council Internat. Assn. of Univ. Presidents (steering com. 1981–), Mass. Council of Pub. Presidents and Chancellors (chmn. 1983-84), Assn. of Urban Univs. (chmn. 1988-92), World Affairs Council (dir. Boston 1983-88, dir. Bay Area 1991-94), San Francisco C.of C. (dir. 1989-92); clubs: University, City; numerous pub. lectures, frequent speaker nat. confs. and assn. annual meetings; contbr. numerous articles in literary jours. Ofc: San Francisco State Univ. 1600 Holloway Ave San Francisco 94132

CORTELYOU, ROBERT JOHN, water agency engineering executive; b. July 2, 1937, Taft, Calif.; s. John Taylor and Mildred Louise (Kessel) C.; m. Barbara Watson, May 26, 1962; children: Robert Jr. b. 1965, John b. 1968; edn: att. UCLA, 1955-57; BSME, Cal Poly SLO, 1960; reg. Profl. Civil and Mech. Engr. (C-23790, M14113) Calif. Career: engr. Gen. Electric. Co., Calif., Ky., Mass., 1960-61; mech. engr. Calif. Dept. Water Resources, Sacto. 1965-70; mech. engr. Sonoma Co. Water Agy., Santa Rosa 1970-78; supvg. engr. Western Municipal Water Dist. Riverside Co. 1978-80; supvg. engr. Sonoma Co. Water Agy., Santa Rosa 1980–; mem: ASME (1968–), ASCE (1991–), SF Bay Engrs. Council (scholarship chmn. 1984-94), Naval Reserve Assn., Navy League; mil: capt. USNR 1961-92 (ret.), active 1961-64; rec: Model A Ford cars, backpacking, camping, volleyball. Res: 6640 St. Helena Road Santa Rosa 95404 Ofc: Sonoma County Water Agency 2150 W College Ave Santa Rosa 95401

CORTESE, DOMINIC L., assemblyman, farmer, businessman; b. Sept. 27, 1932, San Jose, Calif.; m. Suzanne; children: David, Rosanne, Mary, Thomas and James; edn: grad., Bellarmine Coll. Prep. 1950; BS, poli. sci., Univ. of Santa Clara 1954. Career: served in U.S. Army 1954-56; mem. Santa Clara Co. Bd. of Suprs., 1968-80, chmn., 1971-79; chmn. Santa Clara Co. Transit Dist. 1976, 1980; elected Calif. State Assembly, 23rd Dist., 1980–; served as chmn. of Assembly Com. on Local Govt. (7 yrs.), chmn. Assembly Com. on Water, Parks and Wildlife 1990–; current chmn.: Assembly Select Com. on Calif. Wine Prodn. and Economy, Wine Industry Task Force of Nat. Conf. of St. Legislatures; com. mem: Governmental Orgn., Transportation, Public Employees, Retirement and Social Security, Governmental Orgn. Subcom. on Veteran's Affairs, Joint Legis. Audit Com., Rural Caucus; commr. Seismic Safety Com.; awards: League of Calif. Cities Legislator of Yr. 1983, Co. Suprs. Assn. of Calif. President's Award 1983, Calif. Contract Cities El Matador Award 1984, We. Fairs Assn. Blue Ribbon Award 1986, Am. Planning Assn., Calif. Chpt., Legislator of Yr. 1984, 1989, Co. Suprs. Assn. Disting. Svc. Award 1988, Am. Cancer Soc. Legislator of Yr. 1988, Calif. Assn. for the Edn. of Young Children Commitment to Children Award 1988, Assn. of Calif. Water Agencies Legislators Merit Award 1988, Calif. Council Am. Inst. of Architects Legislator of Yr. 1990, Mt. Lion Found. Outstanding Service Award 1991, Sierra Club Commendation for Environ. Leadership 1992, Safari Club Recognition Award 1992, Calif. Trucking Assn. Legislator of Yr. 1994; mem: Civic Club of San Jose, Am. Legion Post 250, B.P.O.E. Lodge 522, Italian Am. Heritage Found., BSA; mil: 1st lt. U.S. Army 1954-56. Ofc: 100 Paseo de San Antonio Ste 300 San Jose 95113

CORTSEN-DIAZ, LENE, accountant, historical preservation activist; b. Jan. 23, 1941, Copenhagen, Denmark; d. Thorvald Cortsen and Gerda (Christophersen) Jansberg; m. Joseph Jimenez Diaz, Aug. 2, 1969 (div. Apr. 1976); son, Rodrigo Ximenez Diaz b. 1971; edn: Mar Vista H.S., San Diego, 1959; eve. sch., Sacto., 1959-60. Career: asst. lab. tech. Pillsbury, Sacto. 1961-63; asst. accts. payable Soule Steel, San Francisco 1963-64, Beckman & Jurgensen, Copenhagen, Dk. 1964-67, Mechanics Tool, 1968-71; acctg. Transbay Security, San Leandro, Calif. 1980–; civic bds: San Leandro Historical Marker Commn. (chair 1989–), Casa Peralta Found. (pres. 1990-92), mem. Nat. Trust for Historic Preservation, Oakland Heritage Alliance, San Leandro Hist. Soc., Alameda Co. Hist. Soc.; Democrat; Lutheran; rec: Early California history & preservation. Res: 139 Williams St #B San Leandro 94577

CORWIN, JACK B., industrialist; b. July 10, 1951, New York; s. Howard Stanley and Sydelle (Friedman) C.; edn: BS bus. adminstrn., Univ. Md. 1978; MS mgmt., Yale Univ. 1980. Career: assoc. corp. fin. Advest Inc., Hartford, Conn. 1980-82; Drexel Burnham Lambert, N.Y.C. 1982-83; assoc. exec., corp. service E.F. Hutton 1983-84; v.p. PruCapital, Los Angeles 1984-86; pres. Huntington Holdings 1987–; chmn. Bianchi Holdings Inc., Temecula 1987; dir. Fairchild Industrial Products Co., Winston-Salem, N.C. 1989; mem. bd. dirs. Ketchum-Downtown YMCA; clubs: City Club on Bunker Hill, Yale; Neighborhood Ch. Pasadena, Young Presidents Orgn. (L.A. chpt.); rec: classic autos. Res: 1051 Prospect Blvd Pasadena 91103 and 99 Emerald Bay Laguna Beach 92651

CORY, WILLIAM NICHOLAS, investor; b. June 20, 1911, Walsenberg, Colo.; s. Abraham Namen and Melia (Mittry) C.; m. Faye, May 18, 1946; children: William b. 1948, Robert b. 1949, Carol b. 1952; edn: stu. L.A. City Coll. 1930, Glendale City Coll. 1931-33. Career: mgr./opr. Idaho Motor Co. (400 car storage & service facility), Idaho Falls, Ida. 1934-38; owner/opr. Idaho Motor Co. - Oldsmobile Dealership Automotive Sales, Service and Storage, 1938-41; owner/opr. Cory Motor Co. - Oldsmobile, Packard, Cadillac, Automotive Sales and Service, Marshfield, Wis. 1941-51; capital investor, real estate acquisition, devel. & mgmt., 1951–; honors: life mem. The President's Club, Presdtl. Task Force, Presdtl. Found.; civic: sponsor Heritage Found., Inter-Am. Security Council, Peace Through Strength, Nat. Freedom Found.; contbr. Freedom Fighters Nicaraguan and Afghanistan, African Famine Relief, Inter-American Def.; mil: lt. USNR 1943-46; Republican; Episcopalian; club: San Diego CC; rec: golf. Res: Bonita 92002

COSTA, JOHN ANTHONY, family service agency coordinator; b. Oct. 20, 1946, San Francisco; s. Henry Milton and Martha Florence (Seineke) C.; edn: BA, San Francisco St. Univ., 1969; grad. studies George Washington Univ. 1969-73, Univ. of San Francisco 1987-88; legal asst. diploma, ICS Paralegal Sch., Scranton, Pa. 1994. Career: analyst internat. rels. Library of Congress Congressional Research Service, Wash. D.C. 1969-82; coordinator Family Service Agency of San Mateo Co., Burlingame 1984–; civic: Internat. Studies Assn. (chpt. sec. W.D.C. 1970-71), Commonwealth Club S.F., World Affairs Council No. Calif., Bentana Park Condominium Reston, Va. (pres., v.p., secty., 1977-81), bd. mem. St. Dunstan Sch. 1991-92. Res: 2250 Shelter Creek Ln San Bruno 94066 Ofc: Family Service Agency 1870 El Camino Real Ste 107 Burlingame 94010

COTTAM, CALVIN, chiropractor, international lecturer and teacher; b. Mar. 28, 1925, Salt Lake City; s. Nephi Livesay Cottam DC (originator of cranial adjusting, craniopathy) and Edwardena (Parry) C.; edn: grad. Chouinard Art Inst. (now Cal Arts) 1949; MA psych., David Seabury Sch. Psychology, 1953; DC, Cleveland Chiro. Coll., 1965; DC lic. Calif., New Zealand. Career: dr. of chiropractic; co-founder, instr. Found. for Living, Problems Anon., Creative Self Research, 1953-64; radio pgm. co-host: Living Today, L.A. 1954-55; dir. Inst. for the Study of Human Resources 1985–; extensive travel w/parents on cranial adjusting tchg. tours U.S. and Canada; internat. conf. World Chiropractic Cong. Switz. 1970; lecture tours incl. Spain 1971, Greece, USSR, Turkey, Yugoslavia, 1972, Japan, Taipei, Hong Kong, Singapore, Thailand, 1972, France, England, Ireland, Scotland, 1973, Scandinavia, England 1974, Australia, N.Z., Fiji, Tahiti, 1975, U.S., Mex., Can., 1976–, Egypt, Israel, 1983, China, 1983, 84 (invited by Chinese govt., mem. first official chiropractic information exchange group to China 1983), Europe, 1984, Brazil, Argentina, Alaska, 1986, Costa Rica, Panama, Colombia, Mex., 1987, U.K., Ireland, 1988, U.S. cities, Vancouver B.C. 1989, Carribbean 1990; mem: Nat. Writers League (nat. pres. 1958), David Seabury Sch of Psychol. Alumni Assn. (pres. 1955-6), Internat. New Thought Alliance (ch. Govt. Affairs 1957), C.of C., Civil Def., Nat. Vocat. Guidance Assn., Wilshire Center, Country Club Park Assn. (dir., Info. Council); author: Head First for Health (1952, House-Warven); Fun, How To Take a Vacation Every Day; Living Without Strain; Don't Be Afraid of your Mind; Magic of Meditation; w/Bert M. Anderson: How To Write True To Yourself 1960; w/Reid Rasmussen DC (brother by adoption): Craniopathy for You and Others 1975; Cranial/Facial Adjusting/Craniopathy Step-by-step 1985, Technique in Pictures 1987; Illustrated Seminars 1986; co-prod. w/R. Rasmussen DC: 6 one-hr video tapes re cranial technics 1981; publs: Digest of Chirop. Economics 1981, The Smithsonian 1981; mil: s/sgt M.C. US Army WWII, Korea; rec: comparative studies of ancient/current philosophies. Address: 1017 S Arlington Ave Los Angeles 90019

COUGHLIN, JAMES PATRICK, chemical consultant; b. July 6, 1924, Los Angeles; s. Frank Patrick and Catherine Cecilia (Crimmins) C.; m. Mary Rosaleen Healey, Apr. 26, 1952; childen: Catherine b. 1954, Kevin b. 1955; edn: BS chemistry, Univ. San Francisco, 1944; MS chem., Univ. Nev., Reno 1946; postgrad. work Stanford Univ., 1947. Career: physical chemist U.S. Bureau of Mines, Berkeley 1948-58; assoc. scientist Aerojet Solid Propulsion Co., Sacramento 1958-87; indep. cons. scientist, 1987–; conf. participant Nat. acad. of Scis. conf. on thermodynamics and nat. energy problems (6/74); NSF tech. evaluator of coal resrch. proposals; evaluation panel "Jannaf Thermochemical Tables"; honors: R.B. Young tech. innovation award Aerojet Gen. Corp. (1983), listed Am. Men of Sci. (1955–), Who's Who in West (1964–); mem: Am. Chem. Soc. (referee tech. jour.), Sigma Xi, AAAS; author book chapt. in Experimental Thermochemistry, Vol. II (Intersci. Pub.), 1962), 33+ tech. papers on thermodynamics of rocket propulsion (1958-87), 21 tech. papers re calorimetry and thermodynamics of extractive metallurgy (1948-58); Democrat; R.Cath.; rec: running, x-c skiing, gardening, personal computer. Address: Coughlin Chemical Consultant 3712 Atwater Rd Sacramento 95864-1543

COULTER, GEORGE PROTHRO, lawyer, vintner; b. June 8, 1930, El Dorado, Ark.; s. Edward Herbert and Estella Martha (Prothro) C.; brother of Murray W. Coulter, hd. biol. dept. Texas Tech Univ.; m. Gloria `Corky' Cohn, Dec. 28, 1952; children: Craig R. b. 1953, Christopher N. b. 1955, Cameron M. b. 1960; edn: AB in polit. sci., UC Los Angeles, 1951; JD, Geo. Washington Univ., 1957; adv. law, USC, 1958. Career: Lt. US Navy 1951-56, decorated Korean Service, K-1 to K-3 clusters, China Service (extended), UN Service; Nat. Security Agy. 1956-57; atty., assoc. Gordon & Weinberg, Los Angeles 1958-63; ptnr. Coulter & Coulter, 1964-78; atty. prin., now of counsel, Coulter, Vernoff & Pearson, P.C., 1979–; dir. Parade Properties Inc., 1963-87; gen. ptnr. Welsh Hill Orgn. (vineyard and winery), Temecula Valley 1980–; honors: student body pres. Geo. Washington Univ. Law Sch. 1956-57; three-time individual winner Van Vleck Case Club appellate competition; mem: Theta Xi soc. frat., Phi Delta Phi legal frat., Alpha Phi Omega service frat., Scabbard & Blade mil. hon., Conning Tower naval hon., Hon. Soc. of Cymmrodorion, Les Amis Du Vin; author: "Parallel Lines: The Proth(e)ro(e) Genealogies" (1980), contbr. articles in legal jours. and philatelic jours., chapter author and cons. Calif. State Bar CEB books; Democrat; Presbyterian (elder); rec: genealogy, enology, philately, travel. Res: 589 Cocopan Dr Altadena 91001 Ofc: Coulter, Vernoff & Pearson, P.C., 490 S Fair Oaks Ave Pasadena 91105

COVINO, JOSEPH, JR., writer; b. Jan. 24, 1954, Phenix City, Ala.; s. Joseph, Sr. and Eleanor Josephine (Bowen) C.; m. Elizabeth Perkins, June 1978 (div. Apr. 1981), 1 son, Michael John Perkins b. 1980; edn: AA, Pensacola (Fla.) Jr. Coll., 1974, AS law enf., 1980; BA crim. justice, Univ. W.Fla., 1976, BA econs., 1979, BA internat. studies, 1981; law enforcement cert. Fla., 1981. Career: social studies tchr. Cardinal Newman High Sch., West Palm Beach, Fla. 1978-79; author: ...And War For All (1983); Lab Animal Abuse (1990); awarded Alexander Wilbourne Weddell Prize, Geo. Washington Univ., D.C. 1975; Democrat; R.Cath.; rec: trumpet, Japanese Shotokan karate. Ofc: New Humanity Press PO Box 215 Berkeley 94701

COWDEN, ROBERT HAPGOOD, educator; b. Nov. 18, 1934, Warren, Pa.; s. Wallace Hapgood and (Sundelof) C.; m. Jacqueline Viviane Mailloux; children: Christopher b. 1961, Jonathan b. 1964, Jennifer b. 1965, Marc b. 1967, Adrienne b. 1969; edn: BA, Princeton Univ. 1956; BM, Eastman Univ. 1959; MM, 1960; DMA, 1966. Career: hd. fine arts Wayne St. Univ., Detroit, Mich. 1972-74; chair music dept. Univ. Omaha 1974-76; San Jose St. Univ. 1976-82, prof. music 1976–; chair music CSSSA, Sacto. 1987–; awards: Fulbright scholar, 1959-61, Univ. Neb. grad. fellow, 1976, Univ. Mich. NEH fellow, 1985, NEH grant, 1987, 89, San Jose St. Univ. merit. prof., 1987, 88, 90; author: Concert & Opera Singers, Conductors, Instrumental Viruosi: A Bibliography of Biographical Materials, 1985, 87, 89; Opera Companies of the World: Selected Profiles, 1992; contbd. International Dictionary of Opera, 1993; Am. Nat. Biography, 1993; Classical Singers of the Opera and Recital Stages, 1994; Episcopalian; rec: bibliography, gardening, book collecting. Ofc: San Jose State University School of Music. San Jose 95192

COWLES, R. VERN, information systems executive; b. Feb. 20, 1943, Imperial, Nebr.; s. Arnold Riedler and Minnie Mable (Hatterman) C.; edn: BA, Doane Coll. 1965; MA, Wash. Univ. St. Louis 1968; MA, Sch. Theology Claremont 1989. Career: data systems analyst Registrar Recorder, City of Norwalk, 1975-77, head tally and mgmt. systems 1977-80, head elec. systems 1981-83, chief elec. systems 1984-91, mgr. election systems 1991–, AIDS tng. ofcr. 1988; alt. rep. GIS Advy. Body, L.A. 1988–, chair GISAB stds. com. 1988-94, chair GISAB tech. group 1988-91, GIS steering com. 1986-88; L.A. County Mgmt. Council 1984–; awards: L.A. County Prod. Com. plaque 1988, 90, certificate 1989, 92, 93, NACO awards 1979, 85, 89, 94; literary reviewer G.C. Stone Library; articles in profl. jours., 1987-91; mil: lt. USN 1967-72; Republican; Episcopalian (L.A. Diocese coms. human sexuality, viable parishes, group on small parishes, mem. vestry Christ Ch., Ontario 1985-88); rec: reading, gardening. Res: 23702 Dunemear Lake Forest 92630 Ofc: Registrar Recorder County Clerk 12400 Imperial Hwy Norwalk 90650

COX, CHRISTOPHER, congressman; b. Oct. 16, 1952, St. Paul, Minn.; s. Charles C. and Marilyn A. (Miller) C.; edn: BA, Univ. So. Calif., 1973; MBA, JD, Harvard Univ., 1977; admitted to Bar: Calif. 1978, DC 1980. Career: law clk. to judge U.S. Ct. Appeals (9th cir.), 1977-78; assoc. Latham & Watkins, Newport Beach, Calif., 1978-82, ptnr., 1985-86; sr. assoc. counsel to the Pres. The White House, Washington, 1986-88; mem. 101st-104th Congresses from 40th (now 47th) dist. Calif. 1989–; mem. budget corn., mem. govt. ops. corn.; prin., founder Context Corp., St. Paul, 1984-86; lectr. bus. adminstrn. Harvard Univ., 1982-83; editor Harvard Law Rev., 1975-77; Republican; Roman Catholic. Res: E Tower Ste 430 4000 MacArthur Blvd Newport Beach CA 92660 Ofc: US House of Representatives 206 Cannon Bldg Washington DC 20515-0547

COX, FRANCES NORALLEN, educator; b. Oct. 15, 1919, Goodyear, Ariz.; d. Arthur Clinton and Florence E. (Miller) Plake; m. N. James Cox, Nov. 24, 1948; children: James b. 1950, Douglas b. 1958; edn: BA, Ariz. State Univ. 1941; stu. CSU San Francisco, Santa Clara Univ., Notre Dame Coll., UC Santa Cruz, UC Berkeley, CSU San Jose; tchg. credentials: elementary-life, Ariz. 1941, Ore. 1950, Calif. 1954, resource splst.-Learning Handicapped, Calif. 1972. Career: classroom tchr. Phoenix, Ariz. 1941-49, Fresno (Ca.) City Schs. 1949-50, Fresno Cty. Schs. 1953-56, Portland (Ore.) City Schs. 1960-64, tchr./resource splst. Palo Alto Unified Schs., 1964-87, ret.; devel. curriculum in Kdg. literature and elem. sci., Phoenix 1941-43; lead panel Assn. for Childhood Edn. Conv., Ariz. St. Univ. 1946, lead demonstr. for 2d gr. games Fresno County Schs., Fresno St. Coll. 1954, lead demonstr. for social studies for Portland City Schs., Portland Tchrs. Inst. 1962, master tchr. Fresno St. Coll. 1953, Ore. St. Univ.; biog. listins in Dir. of Disting. Americans (5th), Internat. Directory of Distinguished Leadership 3rd ed. 1991, World Who's Who of Women 1990-93, World Biog. Hall of Fame 1989; mem: Palo Alto Tchrs. Assn. (recipient WHO Award for outstanding svc. 1986), Remedial Reading Tchrs. 1961-73, Resource Splst. Orgn., Nat. Tchrs. Assn., Calif. Tchrs. Assn. (Polit. Action rep.), NEA, Calif. Retired Tchrs Assn. Mid-Penin. Div., Ariz. St. Univ. Valley of the Sun Mortar Board Alumni, tchr. orgns. in Phoenix, Fresno, and Portland, PTA 1941-, Sigma Phi Gamma Internat. Sor. 1941-47, Commonwealth Club Calif., Internat. Platform Assn., Sierra Club; mil: pilot Civil Air Patrol 1941-42, Pilot Wings 1941; Prot.; rec: travel, politics, environment, art. Res: 911 La Mesa Dr Menlo Park 94028 Ofc: Palo Alto Unified Schools 25 Churchill Ave Palo Alto 94306

COX, JAMES A., photographer; b. Aug. 15, 1947, Wichita Falls, Tx.; s. Jack L. and Betty Jean (Castle) C.; m. Rebecca Jo Wisdom, Nov. 5, 1969 (div. 1975); m. Diane P. Murphy, Oct. 13, 1989; children: Chris (dec.), Dustin Ashley b. 1974; edn: Tx. Tech. Univ. 1965-66; Midwestern Univ. 1966-69. Career: photographer The Salk Inst., La Jolla 1975-77, dir. Multimedia Resources 1977-95; owner, photographer Earthlight Photog., San Diego 1976-94; awards: pres.'s award Profl. Photographers of S.D. 1986-87, Photographer of Year 1987-88; mem: Biological Photographers of S.D. (pres. 1980-81), Profl. Photographers of S.D. (bd. 1984-85, secty. 1985-86, treas. 1986-88); mil: USN 1969-74; Republican; Methodist. Res: 11930 Thomas Hayes Ln San Diego 92126 Ofc: The Salk Institute 10010 N Torrey Pines Rd La Jolla 92037

COX, J(OHN) WILLIAM, physician/health administrator/retired naval officer; b. Aug. 31, 1928, St. Louis, Mo.; s. Wm. E. and Evelyn Ann (Schenck) C.; m. Anne Maczewsk, June 11, 1949; son, William E. b. 1952; edn: MD, PhD, St. Louis Univ., 1952, 1953. Career: served to vice admiral US Navy 1954-83: dir. research VA Hosp., St. Louis, Mo. 1953-54; intern, resident Naval Hosp., San Diego 1954-59, staff supr. 1959-61; chief profl. services Naval Hosp., Subic Bay, Rep. Philippines 1961-63; head cardio pulmonary svc. Naval Hosp., Phila., Pa. 1963-65, chief of medicine and dir. research, 1965-69; assoc. prof. medicine Jefferson Univ. Med. Sch. 1965-72; head. clin. services USN, Wash. D.C. 1969-72; dir. med. edn. Navy Dept. 1971-77; asst. chief Bureau for Personnel & Profl. Ops., Navy Dept. 1976-78; commdg. ofcr. Naval Regional Med. Center, San Diego 1978-80; surgeon general of the Navy, Navy Dept., Wash. D.C. 1980-83; assoc. dir. and prof. Graduate Sch. of Pub. Health, San Diego St. Univ. 1983-87; dir. dept. health svs. San Diego Co. 1987-94 (ret.); awards: St. Louis Univ. Borden Med. 1951, Disting. Alumnus Merit 1981, AMA Bd. Trustees Merit. Service 1983, Uniformed Services Univ. Disting. Service 1983; mem: Am. Coll. Cardiology (fellow), Am. Coll. Chest Physicians, A.C.P. (fellow), Phila. Coll. Physicians (fellow), AMA (alt. Ho. Dels. 1970-92, Delegate 1992-94), AMA Forum for Med. Affairs (pres. 1989-90), CMA (Ho. Dels. 1983-94), Rotary Internat., Hospice San Diego Inc. (bd. 1988-92), BSA (bd.), Am. Cancer Soc. (bd., exec. com. 1986-93); publs: 40+ sci. med. & physiology articles (1949-70); Republican; Prot.; rec: swimming, music.

COZAD, LYMAN HOWARD, city manager; b. May 22, 1914, Painesville, Ohio; s. Wm. Howard and Ethyl (Phelps) C.; m. Arliss Smith, Sept. 6, 1978; children: Bradford b. 1949, Roberta b. 1958, Kimberly b. 1965; edn: BS bus. adminstrn., Ohio St. Univ., 1935, MSPA, 1936; postgrad. studies Yale, 1936-37, USC, 1948-57. Career: dir. examinations Los Angeles City Civil Service Commn., 1939-42; personnel officer Nat. Housing Agy., Wash. DC 1942-43; personnel dir. UNRRA, Wash. DC 1944-47; So. Calif. mgr. Louis J. Kroeger & Assocs., Los Angeles 1947-56; city mgr. City of Colton, 1957-64; adminstrv. ofcr. City of Beverly Hills, 1964-66; city mgr. City of Arcadia, 1966-77; So.

Calif. mgr. League of Calif. Cities, 1977-84, ranger rider, p.t. 1985–; v.p. and So. Calif. rep. Public Service Skills Inc., Sacto., 1986–; instr. USC, 1941-42, 48-58, UC Riverside, 1961-63, CSU Long Beach, 1974-77; awards: Fletcher Bowron Award, Scapa Praetor USC 1985; mem: Am. Soc. for Pub. Adminstrn. 1939–, Internat. City Mgmt. Assn. 1957–, life mem. City Mgrs. Dept. LCC Sacto. (pres. 1972), So. Calif. Pub. Pers. Assn. L.A. (pres. 1942); Rotarian (dir. Colton 1961-62, Arcadia 1970-71); pub. articles (1941, 46); mil: pvt. US Army 1943-44; rec: hiking, gardening. Res: 952 Canyon View Dr La Verne 91750 Ofc: Public Service Skills, Inc. 1400 K St Ste 400 Sacramento 95814

CRAIN, CLAIRE VIRGINIA (YEGGE), civic historian, teacher, reading specialist; b. Oct. 14, 1914, Sedro Wooley, Washington; d. Robt. Martin and Corinne Queen (Stiles) Yegge; m. John G. L. Crain, Dec. 30, 1939 (dec. Jan. 3, 1991; Industrial R.E. Broker and lic. Practitioner ICC, charter commr. Torrance Airport Commn.); children: Lawrence D. b. 1941, Cliff G. b. 1944; edn: BA in English, UC Los Angeles; MA, CSC Long Beach 1969; Calif. lifetime tchg. creds., cert. to counsel, child welfare and social work. Career: tchr./reading splst. Torrance Unified Sch. Dist., Active Reading orgns. 1955-79; mem: Torrance Library Commn. 1956-74, organizer and Hon. Life mem. Torrance Friends of the Library, initiated the library transfer from County library services to City of Torrance Library System (1966), honored by name on plaque in front of all Torrance City Libraries; named citizen of year Torrance Lions Club, Torrance City Council (1980), AAUW award, Hon. life mem. and recogn. as organizer of both Torrance Hist. Soc. and Museum (1987); Founder Associated Hist. Societies of Ventura Co. (1988); Life mem. Conf. of Calif. Historical Socs. (regional v.p. for Ventura County); mem. Centinela Valley Hist. Soc., Ventura County Hist. Soc. (docent), Olivas Adobe (docent); Republican; Prot. Res: 85 Poinsettia Gardens Dr Ventura CA 93004

CRAMER, EUGENE NORMAN, engineer - nuclear power; b. Apr. 26, 1932, Arkansas City, Kans.; s. Norman Charles and Hulda Margaret (Maier) C.; m. Donna (Gagliardi) C., May 18, 1957 (dec. 1984); m. 2d. Marlene (Marjenhoff) C., Dec. 29, 1985; children: Lorene b. 1958, Kristine b. 1959, Eileen b. 1964, Carla b. 1965; edn: BS physics, BS math., Kansas St. Coll. 1955; grad. Oak Ridge Sch. Reactor Tech. 1959; Claremont Grad. Sch. (MA mgmt. 1976; MBA 1984); reg. profl. engr. Calif. Career: engr. Westinghouse Bettis, Pittsburg 1955-57; devel. engr. Oak Ridge Nat. Lab., Oak Ridge, TN 1959-69; engr. advanced energy systems S. Calif. Edison, Los Angeles 1969-88; mgr. nuclear comms. 1988-95; pres. Assistance to Education 1995–; cons. U.S. Atomic Energy Commn. 1961-73; sect. ed. Nuclear Soc. Jour. 1964-69; secty. Task Force Nuclear Safety Res., Electric Res. Council 1969-74; dir. programs Western Forum for Edn. 1982–; bd. dirs. Am. Nuclear Soc. 1978-81; awards: Am. Nuclear Soc. Merit Award 1981; Inst. Advancement of Engrs. (fellow); mem: Health Physics Soc. (secty. 1982), Am. Nuclear Soc. (v.chmn. Public Info. Com 1994); 39 articles pub. in tech. jours. 1957–; civic: Capistrano Unified Sch. Dist. Educ. Found. (v.p. 1994); mil: 1st. lt. AUS 1957-59; Republican; R. Cath. Res/Ofc: 2176 Via Teca San Clemente 92673

CRAMER, HAROLD DAVIDSON, physician; b. Sept. 30, 1908, Lake Geneva, Wis.; s. David Harold and Florence (Davidson) C.; m. Claire Burke, Dec. 15, 1935; children: Anita b. 1939, Catherine b. 1941, Jean b. 1947; edn: San Jose St. Univ. 1928; BA, Stanford Univ. 1930; MD, 1934; lic. physician Calif. (1934). Career: examining physician Stanford Univ., Palo Alto 1935-38; univ. physician Univ. Idaho, Moscow 1938-49; resident internal medicine VA Hosp., San Francisco 1949-51; pvt. practice internal medicine, Los Altos 1951-85; Long Term Care Com., Santa Clara Co. Med. Assn., San Jose 1970–; mem: Santa Clara Co. Med. Assn., CMA, AMA; mil: capt. AUS MC 1944-46; Democrat; Methodist; rec: gardening, photog. Res: 13445 Robleda Rd Los Altos 94022

CRANDALL, IRA CARLTON, II, engineering consultant, b. Oct. 30, 1931, South Amboy, N.J.; s. Carlton Francis and Claire Elizabeth (Harned) C.; m. Jane Leigh Ford, Jan. 29, 1954; children: Elizabeth Anne b. 1954, Amy Leigh b. 1959, Mtthew Garrett b. 1964; edn: BS in radio engring., Indiana Inst. of Tech., 1954, BS in E.E., 1958; BS engring. electronics, US Naval Postgrad. Sch., 1962; BCS computer sci., LaSalle Univ., 1986; LLB (magna cum laude) Blackstone Sch. of Law, 1970; MA humanities (cum laude) Piedmont Univ., 1967; PhD engring. adminstrn. (cum laude) Univ. of Sussex, 1964; reg. Profl. Engr., Calif. (electrical, control systems), Fla., Hawaii, Mich., N.C., Oreg., Wash.; Cert. Profl. Engr., Nat. Council Engring. Examiners; Cert. Energy Mgr., Assn. Energy Engrs. Career: elem. sch. tchr., 1954-55; ofcr. USN, tech. and engring. duties, 1955-72, decorations incl. Vietnam Cross of Valor, Nat. Def. Svc., Unit Cit., Expt. Rifle, Expt. Pistol; engring. cons., pres./bd. chmn. I. C. Crandall and Assocs., Inc., 1972-82; exec. v.p. and chief engring. Williamson Engineering, Inc., 1972-82; v.p. Dickinson Ents., 1973-76; v.p./chief elec. engr./dir. Gayner Engineers, Inc., 1982-92; sr. engr. Ajmani and Pamidi, Inc. 1992–; research cons./pres. Internat. Research Assocs., 1982–; gen. ptnr. White Crane Properties, 1985–; ptnr. C & H Ents., 1988–; awards: Pi Upsilon Beta 1967, Gamma Chi Epsilon 1970, hon. ScD (soc. scis.) Piedmont Univ. 1968, hon. LittD St. Matthew Univ. 1970, hon. EdD Mt. Sinai Univ. 1972; mem: Am. Coll. Engrs. (Fellow), Assn. Energy Engrs. (charter sr.), Am. Inst. of Tech. Mgmt. (sr.), IEEE, Industrial Applications Soc., Soc. Am. Mil. Engrs., Assn. of Old Crows,

US Naval Inst., Assn. of Naval Aviation (life), Am. Bus. Women's Assn.; works: asstd. in devel. of Radar systems for ground control of aircraft traffic, pioneered use of solid-state electronics in indsl. control systems, resrch. design & devel. of 1st 2-way cable tv system installed in US, devel. various energy conservation systems; publs: tech. articles in J. Am. Inst. of Tech. Mgmt., J. Am. Coll. of Engrs., author misc. E.E. computer pgms. and manuals; Republican (Nat. Com.); Methodist. Res: 5754 Pepperidge Pl Concord 94521

CRANE, STEVEN, company executive; b. Jan. 21, 1959, Los Angeles; s. Roger Deppen and Violet (Heard) C.; m. Peggy Anne Gilhooly, Apr. 25, 1987; dau. Allison Nicole b. 1989; edn: grad. Kurt T. Shery H.S., Torrance, Ca. 1976. Career: sales mgr. Mobar Inc., Torrance 1976-78; v.p. internat. mktg. Fluid Control Internat., Marina del Rey 1978-79; pres. and CEO, Energy Devel. Internat., Torrance 1979-85; pres. and CEO, Kaempen USA Inc., Anaheim 1985-91; senior ptnr., chmn. bd. Western Finance Group Inc., Huntington Beach 1991–; chmn. Tarison G.P., Redondo Beach; dir., CEO, Artist Network 1992–; awarded Legion d'Honneur, Am. Savate Fedn., Chgo. 1989; mem. Vanguard Bus. Leaders 1990-91; pub. papers: Accessing Public Capital, 1992, A Guide to Exempt Equity Offerings, 1992; Republican; Prot.; rec: photog., savate, basketball, bird hunting. Ofc: Artist Network 20422 Beach Blvd #245 Huntington Beach 92648

CRAWFORD, JANE WEBB, university professor of classics; b. Oct. 11, 1945, Huntington, W. Va.; d. Joseph P. and Katherine (Miller) Webb; m. Bernard Frischer, Dec. 1, 1979; 1 dau. Katherine b. 1966; edn: BA in classics, Boston Univ. 1968; MA, Latin, UCLA 1974, MA, Greek, 1976, C.Phil. in classics 1979, PhD in classics 1981. Career: vis. prof. of classics, dept. of classics Loyola Marymount Univ. 1982-84, asst. prof. 1984-88, assoc. prof. 1988-93, prof. 1993–, chair, dept. of classics 1985–, acting chair, dept. of modern langs. 1987-88; Loyola Marymount Univ. freshman adv. 1984–, dir. Humanities major 1991–, mem. selection com. for Trustee Scholarship Awards 1993–, mem. Univ. Planning Council 1994–, chair, task force on advising, Coll. of Liberal Arts 1994–; evaluator, secondary schs. cred. waiver prog., Latin, Calif. Public Sch. Sys. 1984–; mem. com. for test devel., advanced placement Latin, Ednl. Testing Svc., Princeton, NJ 1994–; honors: Disting. Tchg. Assistant's award UCLA 1975, 78, Rome Prize Fellowship in Classical Studies, Am. Acad. in Rome 1982, Faculty Research award Loyola Marymount Univ. 1982, 85, 87, 91, 93, 94, NEH Summer Inst., USC 1987, res. fellowship Sch. of Historical Studies, Inst. of Advanced Study 1988-89, Disting. Tchg. award Am. Philological Assn. 1989; mem: Am. Philological Assn. (com. on excellence of tchg. 1990-92, chair 1992; referee, Monograph Series 1993–), Am. Acad. in Rome (mem. advy. council 1987–, bd. 1993–), Calif. Classical Assn. (bd. mem. 1993–); author: M. Tullius Cicero: The Fragmentary Speeches. An Edition with Commentary, 1994, M. Tullius Cicero: The Lost and Unpublished Speeches, 1984, Reading the Other, Reading God. A Translation and Analysis of Baudonivia's Life of Radegunde (with Dr. M.A. Mayeski, 1995), contbr. articles and reviews to profl. pubs. Ofc: Loyola Marymount University 7101 W 80th St Los Angeles 90045

CRAWFORD, LEONARD E., JR. medical doctor; b. Mar. 4, 1941, Monterey, Tenn.; s. Leonard Elroy and Gladys Estelle (Castleman) C.; edn: BS, Tenn. Tech. Univ., Cookeville 1962; MD, Univ. of Tenn. Med. Sch., Memphis 1965; internship City of Memphis Hosps. 1966-67, internal medicine residency 1967-68; urology residency UC Davis, Sacto. Med. Ctr. 1971-74; urology cancer fellowship Memorial Sloan-Kettering Cancer Ctr., NY, NY 1974-75; med. lic. Tenn. 1966, Calif. 1969. Career: physician Capitol Urology Med. Group Inc., Sacto. 1975–; clin. instr. of urology UC Davis Sch. of Medicine and Sacto. Med. Ctr. 1975–; sr. staff Sutter Comm. Hosp., Mercy Gen. Hosp., Mercy Folsom Hosp.; mem: AMA, CMA, Sacto. Med. Soc., Sacto. Surgical Soc., Am. Urological Assn., We. Section Am. Urological Assn., No. Calif. Urologic Assn.; contbr. articles to profl. jours., 1966, 73; presentations on prostate cancer at med. conferences, 1983-89; mil: capt. USAF, Castle AFB 1968-70; Republican; Protestant. Res: 414 Powers Dr El Dorado Hills 95762 Ofc: Capitol Urology Medical Group Inc. 2801 K St #325 Sacramento 95816

CRAWFORD, WAYNE HALBURTON, JR., retired naval officer, financial executive; b. Apr. 20, 1927, Covina; s. Wayne H. and Emogene Victoria (Crews) C.; m. Camille Lamar Tribelhorn, May 15, 1948 (dec. Nov. 24, 1990); children: Gary M.; m. Lillian M. Frank, Sept. 1, 1991; edn: BA, USC, 1947, MS, 1978; MS, US Navy PG Sch., 1961. Career: commd. ensign, advanced through ranks to capt. US Navy, 1947-77: chief naval ops. info. systems div. USN, W.D.C., 1969-72, asst. for automation orgn. joint chiefs of staff, 1972-75, staff, 1975-77, ret.; decorated Meritorious Service Medal 1975; branch mgr. Downey Savings, La Costa 1978-80; v.p., br. mgr. Central Savings, Coronado 1980-87; Coast Savings, Coronado 1987-88; honors: Phi Kappa Tau; mem. Navy League (v.p. 1985-86, pres. 1994-95), TROA/Coronado (v.p. 1986-87), Optimist (bd. 1985-87), Hammer Club/S.D., Aerospace Internat. Hall of Fame, Poets/S.D. Res: 82 Port of Spain Rd Coronado 92118

CREIGHTON, JOHN WALLIS, (JR.), professor emeritus, consultant; b. Apr. 7, 1916, Yeung Kong, China (parents Am. citizens); s. John Wallis and Lois (Jameson) C.; m. Harriet Harrington, June 30, 1940; children: Carol (Mrs. Brian LeNeve) b. 1944, Joan (Mrs. Robert Nielsen) b. 1945; edn: BS in forestry, Univ.

Mich. 1938; AB, Hastings Coll., 1939; PhD in indsl. engrg., Univ. Mich. 1954. Career: sawmill owner Cuyahoga Falls, Ohio 1939-40; cost estimator Goodyear Aircraft, Akron, Ohio 1940-41; lumber insp. head Bd. of Economic Warfare, Guyaquil, Ecuador 1941-44; asst. gen. mgr. R.S. Bacon Veneer Co., Chgo. 1944-45; v.p./gen. mgr. Bacon Lumber Co., Sunman, Ind. 1944-46; prof., wood technology, Mich. State Univ., E. Lansing 1946-54; asst. gen. mgr./v.p. Baker Furniture Inc., Holland, Mich. 1954-58; pres. Creighton Builders (home constrn.), Santa Barbara, Calif. 1958-65; prof. mgmt. Colo. State Univ., Ft. Collins 1965-67; prof. mgmt. US Naval Postgraduate Sch., Monterey, Calif. 1967-86, dean Sch. of Mgt., 1967-71, prof. emeritus 1986–; recipient numerous research grants and awards for work on wood technology, indsl. engring. and tech. transfer; assoc. ed. Jour. of Tech Transfer, 1973-88; listed Who's Who in Am., in the West, in the World; mem: Am. Mgmt. Assn. 1965-85, Technology Transfer Soc. 1973–, Forestry Commn., Carmel 1987–, Sons in Retirement, Carmel Valley Property Owners Assn.; club: Carmel Golf & Country; Republican; Presbyterian; rec: woodworking. Res: 8065 Lake Place Carmel 93923

CRETIN, SHAN, consultant, educator; b. Dec. 5, 1946, New Orleans, La.; s. Theodore David and Rosemary Mamie (Lombardinno) C.; m. Burns Woodward, June 15, 1968 (div. 1976); m. Emmett Brown Keeler, Sept. 26, 1976; children: Mikala b. 1969, Lauren b. 1977, Alexis b. 1979; edn: BS, MIT 1968; MPH, Yale Univ. 1970; PhD, MIT 1975. Career: research assoc. Yale Univ., New Haven, Conn. 1970-71; asst. prof. Harvard Univ., Cambridge, Mass. 1975-76; asst. prof. UCLA 1976-81, assoc. prof. UCLA 1981-88, prof. UCLA 1988-90, dept. chair 1986-90; cons. Rand Corp., Santa Monica 1977–, co-dir. Rand-UCLA Center for Health Policy Study 1988-90; pres. Shan Cretin & Assoc. 1990–; honors: Sigma Xi, Pi Tau Sigma, Delta Omega; mem: ASQC, APHA, ORSA (health applications sect. chair 1985-87); author Cholesterol Children & Heart Disease, 1980, num. articles pub. in profl. jours.,1976–; Quaker. Res: 402 15th St Santa Monica 90402 Ofc: Shan Cretin & Assoc. 1431 7th St Ste 204 Santa Monica 90401

CREVELT, DAVID CHRISTOPHER, insurance broker; b. June 10, 1958, Redwood City; s. John Theodore and Audrey Joan (Stanford) C.; edn: BS, CSU Fresno, 1981. Career: sales, br. mgr. Lundberg & Assoc. Ins. Brokers, Fresno 1980-85; Leland West Ins. Brokers 1985-87; Alburger DeGrosz Ins. Brokers, Palo Alto 1988-90; Richard N. Goldman & Co. 1990-91; Nationwide Ins. Co. 1991-93; Wausau Ins. Group 1993-94; pres. Innovative Insurance Services 1994–; seminar spkr. Small Bus. Adminstrn., Fresno 1988-90; mem: Theta Chi Alumni Assn. (pres. 1985-86, dep. reg. counselor Theta Chi Nat. Frat. 1985, nat. seminar spkr. 1984, pres. S.F./Bay Area Alumni Assn. 1992-94), Fowler C.of C. (pres. 1984-86), Fresno C.of C. (Amb. Club 1983), Redwood City Sunrise Lions (secty. 1988-90), Redwood City Elks Lodge (Exalted Ruler 1994, Leading Knight 1993, Loyal Knight 1992, Inner Guard 1991); bd. mem. Woodside H.S. Found.; varsity soccer coach Woodside H.S.; Republican: 1986 cand. U.S. Cong., Calif. Congl. Dist. 18, founder/pres. Fresno Co. YR 1985-86, pres. San Mateo Co. YR 1988-89, mem. chair 1989-90, mem: San Mateo Co. Republican Central Com. 1988-92, Selective Svc. Bd. 1988–, R.Cath.; rec: softball, water skiing, travel. Res/Ofc: 1434 Mitchell Way Redwood City 94061

CREWS, WILLIAM O., JR., theological seminary president; b. Feb. 8, 1936, Houston, Tx.; s. William O. and Ola Juanita (Pearson) C.; m. Jo Ann Cunningham, Sept. 1, 1955; children: Ronald Wayne b. 1956, Rhonda Ann b. 1960; edn: BA, Hardin Simmons Univ. 1957; BD, Southwestern Baptist Theological Seminary 1964; LHD, Hardin Simmons Univ. 1987; DD, Calif. Baptist Coll. 1987. Career: pastor Grape Creek Baptist Ch., San Angelo, Tx. 1953-54; Plainview Baptist Ch., Stamford, Tx. 1955-57; First Baptist Ch., Sterling City, Tx. 1957-60; Seventh St. Baptist Ch., Ballinger, Tx. 1960-65; Woodland Heights Baptist Ch., Brownwood, Tx. 1965-67; Victory Baptist Ch., Seattle, Wash. 1967-72; Metro. Baptist Ch., Portland, Ore. 1972-77; dir. comms. Northwest Baptist Convention 1977-78; pastor Magnolia Ave. Baptist Ch., Riverside 1978-86; pres. Golden Gate Baptist Theological Seminary, Mill Valley 1986–; awards: SW Portland Rotary Club Service Above Self (1976), Lake View H.S. Citizen of Year (1954); mem: Evergreen Baptist Assn. (moderator 1969-72), NW Baptist Convention (pres. 1975-77), Calif. So. Baptist Convention (pres. 1983-85), So. Baptist Convention (peace com. 1983-86), Golden Gate Baptist Seminar (bd. trustees 1982-86), SW Portland Rotary (pres. 1974-75), Rotary Club Riverside (pres. elect 1985-86), Rotary Club San Rafael, Marin C.of C.; Republican; Baptist; rec: walking. Res: 157 Chapel Dr Mill Valley 94941 Ofc: Golden Gate Baptist Theological Seminary Strawberry Point Mill Valley 94941

CRICK, FRANCIS H.C., scientist, research professor; b. June 8, 1916, Northampton, England; s. Harry and Anne Elizabeth (Wilkins) C.; m. Ruth Doreen Dodd, Feb. 18, 1940 (div. 1947); m. Odile Speed, Aug. 13, 1949; children: Michael b. 1940, Gabrielle b. 1951, Jacquelyn Nichols b. 1954; edn: BSc physics/math., University Coll., London 1937; PhD (X-ray diffraction: polypeptides and proteins), Cambridge Univ., 1954. Career: scientist with British Admiralty, 1940-47; Medical Research Council student at the Strangeways Lab., Cambridge 1947-49; scientist Med. Research Council Lab. of Molecular Biology, Cambridge 1949-77; protein structure proj. Bklyn. Polytechnic, N.Y. 1953-54; vis. lectr. Rockefeller Inst., N.Y. and vis. prof. chem. dept. Harvard

Univ., 1959; fellow Churchill Coll., Cambridge 1960-61; vis. prof. of biophysics Harvard Univ., 1962; non-resident fellow Salk Inst. for Biological Studies, San Diego 1962-73, Ferkauf Found. Vis. Prof. 1976-77, J.W. Kieckhefer Distinguished Res. Prof. Salk Inst. for Biol. Studies also adj. prof. chemistry dept UC San Diego, 1977–; pres. Salk Inst. for Biological Studies 1994–; distinguished sci. lectr. numerous univs. internat., 1959–; awards: Warren Triennial Prize Lecture 1959, Lasker Award 1960, Prix Charles Leopold Mayer, French Academies des Scis. 1961, Research Corp. Award 1961, Nobel Prize for Physiology or Medicine (w. J.D. Watson and M.H.F. Wilkins) 1962, Gairdner Found. Award, Toronto 1962, Royal Medal, Copley Medal, Royal Soc. of London (1972, 75), Michelson-Morley Award, Cleveland 1981, Benjamin P. Cheney Medal, Spokane 1986, Golden Plate, Acad. of Achiev., Malibu 1987, Albert Medal for 1987 Royal Soc. of Arts, London 1987, Joseph Priestly Award, Dickinson Coll. 1988, Wright Prize VIII, Harvey Mudd Coll. 1988, Disting. Achievement Award, Oregon State Univ. Friends of the Library 1995; honors: Fellow: Royal Soc. 1959, Univ. Coll., London 1962, AAAS 1966, Indian Nat. Sci. Acad., India 1982, Rochester Mus., N.Y. 1984, Order of Merit 1991, Hon. Fellow: Churchill Coll., Cambridge 1965, Royal Soc. of Edinburgh 1966, Caius Coll., Cambridge 1976, Indian Acad. of Scis., India 1985, John Muir Coll. UCSD 1986, Hon. mem: Am. Acad. of Arts and Scis. 1962, Am. Soc. Biol. Chemists 1963, Royal Irish Acad. 1964, Hellenic Biochem. and Biophysical Soc. 1974; fgn. assoc. Nat. Acad. of Scis. USA 1969, fgn. mem. Am. Philosophical Soc., Phila. 1972, assoc. fgn. mem. French Acad. of Scis. 1978, mem. German Acad. of Sci., Leopoldina 1969; publs: 125+ sci. jour. articles; 4 books; mil: lt. comdr. British Navy 1945. Ofc: Salk Institute PO Box 85800 San Diego 92186-5800

CRILLY, EUGENE RICHARD, engineering consultant; b. Oct. 30, 1923, Phila., Pa.; s. Eugene John and Mary Virginia (Harvey) C.; m. Alice Royal Roth, Feb. 16, 1952; edn: BA, Central H.S. Phila. 1941; Mech. Engr., Stevens Inst. Tech. 1944; MS, 1949, MS, Univ. Pa. 1951; UCLA 1955-58. Career: res. engr. Keasbey & Mattison Co., 1951-54; sr. engr. L.A. div. No. Am. Aviation, 1954-57; process engr. Northrop div., Northrop Corp., 1957-59; project engr., Q.C. mgr. HITCO, Gardena 1959-62; sr. engr. Rocketdyne & Space divs. No. Am. Aviation 1962-66; sr. res. splst. Lockheed Calif. Co. 1966-74; engring. specialist Rockwell Internat., North American Aircraft, 1974-89; engring. cons., 1989–; instr. econ. of engring. Stevens Inst. Tech. 1946-49; honors: Sigma Xi 1984, Award of Merit Soc. Advancement of Material and Process Engring. 1986, Who's Who Engring.; mem: Soc. Advancement of Material and Process Engring. (L.A. chpt. chmn. 1978-79, nat. dir. 1979-86, nat. treas. 1982-85, chmn. symposium and exhib. 1981), Soc. of Mfg. Engrs. (sr. mem.), Assn. Former Intelligence Ofcrs. (treas. San Diego Chpt. 1990–), Naval Intelligence Profls., Am. Soc. Composites, ASM Internat., V.F.W., Naval Reserve Assn., Mil. Order of World Wars, (adj. S.F.V. chpt. 1985-87, 2nd v. comdr. 1986-87, comdr. 1987-89, v.comdr. West, Dept. Central Calif. 1988-89, comdr. Cajon Valley-San Diego Chpt. 1990-92, Region XIV Adjutant 1990-91 and ROTC chmn. 1989-91, comdr. Dept. of So. Calif. (1991-93), v. comdr. Region XIV (1992-93), dep. comdr./gen. staff ofcr. (1993-94), Region XIV comdr. (1994-95) Retired Ofcrs. Assn. (treas. Silver Strand Chpt. 1990–), Navy League of US, US Naval Inst., British United Services Club of L.A., Naval Order of the U.S., Sigma Nu, Marine Meml. Club, S.F. 1993–; author: numerous tech. papers re adhesive bonding and advanced composites; mil: apprentice seaman & ensign USNR 1943-46, comdr. (ret.) 1975; Republican; R.Cath.; rec: Am. & W.W.II history. Address: 276 J Ave Coronado 92118-1138

CRONEN, MICHAEL JAMES, lawyer; b. Feb. 8, 1958, Monterey Park; s. James L. and Katherine Mary (Vincent) C.; m. Nelle P. Shutman, Sept. 19, 1987; edn: BA (honors), CSU Los Angeles 1983; JD, UC Hastings Coll. Law 1987. Career: supr. Calif. Conservation Corp. 1978-80; asst. dir. Bi-Lingual Edn. Center, Los Angeles 1981-84; atty. Law Offices of Harris Zimmerman, Oakland 1986–; assoc. prof. CSU Hayward; honors: Phi Kappa Phi, Moot Ct. Hastings Coll. Law; mem: Am. Trial Lawyers Assn., Calif. Bar Assn., Alameda Co. Bar Assn., Calif. Trial Lawyers Assn., S.F. Intellectual Property Law Assn., Am. Bar Assn. (intellectual property sect.); Democrat; rec: trumpet, golf. Res: 1974 Altura Dr Concord 94519

CRONK, MILDRED (Mili) SCHIEFELBEIN, special education consultant; b. May 29, 1909, Waverly, Iowa; d. Emil August and Nettie Marie (Berger) Schiefelbein; m. Dale Cronk, July 20, 1930; children: Barbara (Burress), Bruce, Margaret, Michael; edn: att. Wartburg Coll., Waverly 1927, Tampa Univ., Fla. 1944-45, Los Angeles City Coll., 1957; BA in psych., Calif. State Univ., 1960, MA in spl. edn. supervision, 1971. Career: aircraft communicator, weather observer CAA, Fla. and Calif., 1942-49; dir. Parkview Nursery Sch., Los Angeles 1956-57; tchr. trainable mentally retarded Hacienda-La Puente Unified Sch. Dist., 1961-74; cons. special edn. La Mirada, 1975–, ins-service tnr. for tchrs.; mem. coms: Special Olympics SE Los Angeles Co. 1977, Very Special Arts Orange Co. (bd. 1977–), Internat. Very Special Arts Festival 1981, Very Special Arts Calif. (bd. 1986–, treas. 1987); mem: Am. Assn. on Mental Deficiency (bd. reg. II, ed. Newsette 1975-77, chair publicity com. 1977-79, presenter annual confs.), Council for Exceptional Children (state bd., ed. Calif. State Fedn./Council for Exceptional Children J. 1977-80, past pres. San Gabriel Valley chpt.538, mem. at lg. So. Calif. div. Mental Retardation 1976-79, pres.

Calif. div. Mental Retardation 1980-81, chair com. on ofcrs.' handbook, nat. council, div. Mental Retardation 1977-78, presenter Nat. Confs., recipient spl. recognition awards 1976, 77, 78, 79, 89), Assn. for Retarded Citizens SELACO (secty. 1980-81), Nat. Soc. Autistic Children, Nat. Retired Tchrs. Assn., Am. Ceramic Soc. (design div.), Psi Chi; civic: Common Cause, Smithsonian Instn., Wilderness Soc.; author: Create With Clay, 1976, Vocational Skills Taught Through Creative Arts, 1978, Attitude Change Toward TMR Students/ Mainstreaming in Reverse, 1978, Career Education for Trainable Mentally Retarded Students -- It's For Life!, 1982, others; Democrat. Res: 13116 Clearwood Ave La Mirada 90638

CROSBY, GEORGE HYDE, stockbroker; b. Jan. 19, 1927, Ely, Nevada; s. Kent Miller and Janice (Hyde) C.; m. Nadine Potter, June 16, 1949; children: Janet, b. 1951; Kent, b. 1952; Mary, b. 1956; Marc, b. 1958; edn: BA, Brigham Young Univ. 1948; Univ. of Utah Law Sch. 1948-51; MBA, Golden Gate Coll. 1965; reg. principal, NASD. Career: Bank of Am., Sunnyvale 1952-54; op. ofcr./ asst. mgr. First Western Bank, Sunnyvale, San Francisco, Riverdale 1954-64; asst. mgr. United Calif. Bank, Gustine, Santa Maria 1964-68; mgr./ v.p. Mid-State Bank, Arroyo Grande, Santa Maria 1968-76; senior v.p.-economist and director Maguire Investments, Inc., Santa Maria 1976–; instr. bus. admin, Allan Hancock Coll., Santa Maria 1967-85; dir. T.T.O.C. 1977-79; chair. Fin. Commn., Santa Barbara Co. Ret. Bd. 1975-84; mem: Santa Maria C.of C. (pres. 1974); Santa Maria Kiwanis Club (pres. 1973-74, lt. gov. div. 29, 1980-81); Boys Club, Santa Maria (pres. 1979-80); Santa Maria Valley Developers; mil: USN 1944-45 Republican; Latter-day Saints; rec: fencing. Res: 4182 Glenview Santa Maria 93455 Ofc: Maguire Investments, Inc. 1862 S Broadway Santa Maria 93454

CROSBY, WILLIAM MARSHALL, lawyer; b. Jan. 26, 1945, Pasadena; s. Joseph Marshall and Margaret Jane (Aldridge) C.; m. Dori Templeton; children: Mary Beth b. 1977, Joseph b. 1978, Christopher b. 1995; edn: BA, UC Berkeley 1967; JD, Loyola Law Sch. 1970; admitted bar Calif. 1971; Career: dept. dist. atty. County of Riverside 1971; dep. city atty., Anaheim 1972; atty. pvt. practice in Irvine 1973, 1976–, San Francisco 1974-75; in-house counsel Monex Internat. Ltd., Newport Beach 1975-76; law practice, William M. Crosby Law Corp. 1980-91; ptnr. Barnes, Crosby & Fitzgerald, 1991–; lectr., author re wrongful termination of employment, Calif. Contg. Edn. Bar, trial practice articles OCTLA and CTLA Jours., OCBA Jour.; awards: Repub. Youth Assocs. award 1980; mem: Am. Bd. of Trial Advocates, Orange County Bar Assn., Am., Calif., Orange County (bd. 1983–) Trial Lawyers assns., ABA, Plaintiff and Employment Lawyers Assn., Calif. Employment Lawyers Assn. (founding mem.), Sigma Nu, Phi Delta Pi, Calif. Alumni Assn.; civic: Exchange Club Irvine (pres. 1980), Irvine C.of C. (chair govtl. affairs 1992), Newport Harbor Area C.of C., Industrial League of Orange Co., Republican Assocs., Lincoln Club Orange Co., Irvine Workforce Com., South Coast Symphony (dir. 1990-92), Pacific Symphony (dir. 1992), Silver Circle Com. Services Commn. Irvine, Eisenhower Scholarship Found. (trustee 1987), High Hopes Neurol. Recovery Group Inc.; Republican (cand. Calif. State Assembly 1976); Prot.; rec: boating, fishing; Ofc: Barnes, Crosby & Fitzgerald, 18200 Von Karman Ave Ste 820 Irvine 92715

CROSS, GLENN LABAN, engineering/construction executive; b. Dec. 28, 1941, Mt. Vernon, Ill.; s. Kenneth Edward and Mildred Irene (Glenn) C.; m. Kim Lien Duong, Aug. 30, 1968; m. 2d. Tran Tu Thach, Dec. 26, 1975; children: Cindy b. 1977, Cristy b. 1983, Crystal b. 1987, Cassandra b. 1992; edn: BS, Calif. Western Univ. 1981; MBA, 1982. Career: med. splst. USA Spl. Forces, Machinato, Okinawa 1962-65; hosp. adminstrn. splst. USAID Dept. State, Wash. D.C. 1966-68; staff asst. to v.p. and gen. mgr. Pacific Architects & Engrs. Inc., Los Angeles 1968-75; contracts adminstr. AVCO Internat. Services div., Cincinnati, Ohio 1975-77; contract adminstrn. supr. Bechtel Hydro & Comml. Facility, San Francisco 1977-85, cons. Bechtel Power Corp. 1985-90; mgr. field contract adminstr. Ralph M. Parsons Co. Los Angeles Metro, Los Angeles 1990-93; contract adminstr. Parsons-Brinckerhoff, Costa Mesa, CA 1993; proj. adminstr. Pacific Architects and Engrs. Inc., Singapore 1993–; awards: Wash. Univ. Nat. Merit scholarship 1960; mem: Nat. Contract Mgmt. Assn., Constrn. Mgmt. Assn. of Am., Am. Mgmt. Assn., Am. Arbitration Assn., Assn. MBA Execs., Assn. Human Research System Profls., Internat. Personnel Mgmt. Assn., Human Resource Planning Soc., Nat. Contract Mgmt. Assn., Constrn. Mgmt. Assn. of Am., Order of DeMolay, Republican Party; author Living With a Matrix 1983; mil: AUS Spl. Forces 1962-64; Republican; Christian; rec: swimming. Res: 25935 Faircourt Ln Laguna Hills 92653 Ofc: Ralph M. Parsons Co. 100 W Walnut Pasadena 91124

CROSS, JAMES FRANCIS, workfare program coordinator; b. Oct. 11, 1950, Montebello; s. Marshall Lane and Rose C.; edn: East L.A. Coll. 1968-70; Whittier Coll. 1970-72; grad., So. Calif. Broadcast Workshop 1975. Career: Los Angeles Co. Dept. of Pub. Social Services eligibility worker 1972-76, eligibility supr. 1976-80, data systems analyst 1980, operations analyst 1981-85, workfare project coordinator 1985-87, division chiefs asst. 1987, dep. district dir. 1987-91, Workfare Program coordinator 1991–; program host KBW AM/FM 1976-77; awards: Brotherhood Crusade leadership (1988, 89, 90, 91), United Way silver (1987, 88, 90, 91), Dept. Pub. Social Services productivity and efficiency

1989; mem: Neighborhood Watch, Los Angeles Co. Mgmt. Council, Citizens Allied for Understanding & Social Awareness (co-founder 1970-73), Kerner Commn. Action Group 1970-71, Wilderness Conf. musical group (co-founder w/Joseph Maldonado 1967-73); song writer "Window to Cry From" 1971; R.Cath.; rec: musician, artist, mil. history. Ofc: DPSS Bureau of Assistance Payments, Workfare Program Section 12860 Crossroads Parkway South, Industry 91746 Tel: 310/908-8437

CROSS, K. PATRICIA, educator; b. Mar. 17, 1926, Normal, Ill.; d. Clarence L. and Katherine (Dague) Cross; edn: BS in math., Ill. State Univ., 1948; MA psychology, Univ. Ill., 1951, PhD social psych., 1958. Career: math. tchr. Harvard Community H.S., Harvard, Ill. 1948-49; resrch. asst. dept. psych. Univ. Ill., Urbana 1949-53, asst. dean of women 1953-59; dean of women Cornell Univ. 1959-60, dean of students 1960-63; dir. coll. and univ. pgms. Educational Testing Service, Princeton, N.J. 1963-66, Berkeley, Calif. 1966-69, sr. resrch. psychologist ETS, Berkeley 1969-76, distinguished resrch. scientist 1976-80; also resrch. educator Ctr. for R&D in Higher Edn., UC Berkeley 1966-77; prof. and chair dept. adminstrn., planning and social policy Harvard Grad. Sch. of Edn., 1980-88; Elizabeth and Edward Conner Prof. of Edn., UC Berkeley 1988–; vis. prof. Univ. Nebr. 1975-76; keynote speaker and del. internat. and confs.; author 6 books, num. monographs and book chapters, jour. articles; book awards: Am. Council on Edn. Borden Medal for Accent on Learning 1976, Sch. and Soc. outstanding bk. in edn. for Beyond the Open Door 1971, Pi Lambda Theta best books award for The Junior Coll. Student 1968, other awards include 1990 Leadership award Am. Assn. Community and Jr. Colls. 1990, disting. lectr. Am. Soc. for Engring. Edn. 1991, Nat. Coun. of Instrnl. Adminstrs. Award 1990, master tchr. Nat. Inst. for Staff and Orgnl. Devel. 1990, Howard R. Bowen Lectr. Claremont Grad. Sch. 1989, nat. person of yr. Nat. Coun. on Comm. Svs. and Cont. Edn. 1988, Adult Educator of Yr. Coalition of Adult Edn. Orgs., W.D.C. 1987, DeGarmo Lectr. Soc. Profs. of Edn. 1987, E.F. Lindquist award Am. Ednl. Resrch. Assn. 1986, Regents Medal of excellence SUNY 1984, fellow Nat. Policy Ctr. on Edn., Leisure and Cont. Opportunities for Older Ams. 1982–, Delta Sigma Epsilon nat. lectr. 1981, disting. alumni Ill. State Univ. 1980, Delbert Clark award for contbns. to adv. adult edn. 1979, Nat. Acad. of Edn. (elected 1975, v.chair 1981-83), Hon. Degrees- Ill. St. Univ., 1970, Grand Valley State Colls., Mich., 1975, Northeastern Univ., 1975, Our Lady of the Lake Univ., Tx. 1977, Hood Coll., Md. 1979, Loyola Univ. Chgo., Ill. 1980, Marymount Manhattan Coll., NY 1982, Coll. of St. Mary, Neb. 1985, DePaul Univ., Chgo. 1985, Thomas Jefferson Univ., Pa. 1987, SUNY, 1988, Open Univ. of Netherlands 1989. Res: 904 Oxford St Berkeley 94707 Ofc: Univ. of Calif. School of Education Berkeley 94720 Tel: 510/642-7441

CROSSER, JAMES M., certified public accountant, ret.; b. Apr. 1, 1927, Dupo, Ill.; s. James J. and Agnes (McVicker) C.; m. Blue Bell Foster, June 20, 1992; children: Kim b. 1951, Kathryn b. 1954, Susan b. 1957, Janice b. 1964; edn: BBA, and MBA, Univ. of Wis., Madison 1951; C.P.A., Calif. Career: bus. trainee General Electric, Schenectady, NY 1951-53; staff acct. Touche Ross & Co., Detroit, Mich. 1953-59, Los Angeles 1959–, ptnr. 1964, senior ptnr. Deloitte & Touche, L.A. 1987-90, ret.; mem: Am. Inst. CPA (past chmn. sav. & loan com., mem. real estate com.), Calif. Soc. CPA (past chmn. sav. & loan com.), FASB (Task Force on R.E. acctg.); mil: midshipman USN 1945-47; Republican; Prot.; rec: sailing, golf. Res: 93 Pollock Ln Ventura 93003 Ofc: Deloitte & Touche 1000 Wilshire Blvd Ste 1500 Los Angeles 90017

CROSSETT, JERRY WAYNE, export management company owner; b. May 19, 1938, Wellman, Iowa; s. Merle Omer and Marjorie Evelyn (Loeffler) C.; m. Mary Lou Palmer, June 10, 1961; children: Joy Ann b. 1966, Donald Wayne b. 1971; edn: BSME, Iowa State Univ. 1961; MSME, CalTech, 1964; business certificate, UCLA, 1970. Career: engr., scientist Naval Missile Ctr., Pt. Mugu 1961-63; engr. Douglas Aircraft Co., Santa Monica 1964-71; engr., splst. MDAC Tech. Services, Nagoya, Japan 1971-74; engr. McDonnell Douglas, Huntington Bch. 1974-75; owner, mgr. Action International, Fountain Valley 1975–; honor socs.: Phi Eta Sigma, 1958, Pi Tau Sigma, 1960, Tau Beta Pi, 1961; mem: Orange Co. Internat. Mktg. Assn., Am. Defense Preparedness Assn., NRA, So. Calif. Internat. Skeet Assn. (treas. 1987-89); patent for sounding rocket staging device, 1962; Republican; Christian; rec: skeet shooting. Res: 18609 Santa Ramona Fountain Valley 92708

CROWELL, ANN HULT, strategic planning, marketing and advertising executive; b. Aug. 16, 1938, Chicago, Ill.; d. Stanley Earl and Elizabeth (Yakel) Hult; m. Alton Ingram Crowell, Jr., May 29, 1971; 1 dau., Catherine Elizabeth b. 1981; edn: BS, Univ. Ariz. 1960; grad. studies, USC 1965. Career: co-owner Betty Hult Shops, Tucson, Ariz. 1952-60, 63-65; mgmt. tng. program Joseph Magnin, S.F. 1961-63; advt. exec. Carson Roberts, L.A. 1965-67; Erwin Wasey 1967-69; pres. Crowell McKay Inc. Advt., Irvine 1970-84; pres./c.e.o. Crowell & Assoc., Laguna Beach 1984–; awards: City of L.A., Advt. clubs of L.A., N.Y., Orange Co. 1971-84, The One Show, Calif. Mag., BPAA, MAME, SAMY, BIA; mem: Womens Round Table of Orange Co. (bd. dirs.), Orange Co. Womens Forum; author The Ad Agent (1986), articles pub. in newspapers and jours. (1986–); Republican; Episcopalian; rec: bicycling, skiing, art history. Ofc: Crowell & Associates, 801 Glenneyre Laguna Beach 92651

CROWLEY, DAVID JOSEPH, public relations professional; b. June 25, 1934, Malden, Mass.; s. David Joseph and Mary Veronica (O'Donnell) C.; m. Carolyn Ann Parker, June 8, 1957; children: Pamela Ann, Jill Elizabeth, Paul David; edn: AA, Boston Univ., 1953, BS Pub. Rels., 1956. Career: reporter, editor Haverhill Jour., Mass. 1958-62; publicist, sr. publicist GE News Bur., Schenectady, N.Y. 1962-67; supr. GE Western News Bur., Los Angeles 1967-69; mgr. GE Info. Systems, Phoenix, Az. 1969-70; assoc. Carl Byoir and Associates Pub. Rels., Phoenix 1970-72; mgr. GE Nuclear Energy, San Jose, Calif. 1972-88; pres. Pacific News Bur., Campbell, Calif. 1988-; ghost writer speeches, position papers; mem. Nat. Assn. Sci. Writers, Peninsula P.R. Roundtable, Los Altos (chmn. 1988-92), Marines Memorial Club, Rotary Club; civic: Rotocare Inc. (med. help for homeless) San Jose (founding mem. 1988-90), San Jose Hist. Mus. (bd. mem.-at-lg. 1992-, chmn. p.r. com. 1989-92); mil: US Army 1956-58; Republican; R.Cath.; rec: skiing, photog., reading. Res: 1111 Casual Way San Jose 95120 Ofc: Pacific News Bureau 880 E Campbell Ave Ste 202 Campbell 95008 Ph: 408/559-7774

CROWLEY, JOHN W., lawyer; b. May 6, 1938, Portland, Me.; s. Patrick J. and Mary (Finnerty) C.; m. Patricia H. Hebert, April 7, 1968; 1 son, John Mark b. 1970; edn: BS, Tufts Univ. 1960; LL.B, UCLA 1966. Career: atty. Bronson Bronson & McKinnon, San Francisco 1966-88; Cyril & Crowley 1988-; mem: Am. Bd. Trial Advocates, Am. Coll. Trial Lawyers (fellow); mil: lt. USAF 1960-63. Ofc: Cyril & Crowley 456 Montogery St 17th Floor San Francisco 94104

CRUMP, GERALD FRANKLIN, lawyer; b. Feb. 16, 1935, Sacramento; s. John Laurin and Ida May (Banta) C.; m. Glenda Roberts Glass, Nov. 21, 1959; children: Sara Elizabeth, b. 1972, Juliane Kathryn, b. 1974, Joseph Stephen, b. 1977; edn: AB, UC Berkeley 1956, JD, 1959; MA, Baylor Univ. 1966. Career: judge advocate USAF 1960-63; deputy county counsel Los Angeles County 1963-73; legislative rep. 1970-73; chief Public Works Div. 1973-84; sr. asst. co. counsel 1984-85; chief asst. co. counsel 1985-; lectr. Pepperdine Univ. 1978, Univ. Calif. 1982; vice pres. San Fernando Valley Girl Scout Council; mem: State Bar of Calif. (delegate, 1984-), Am. Bar Assn., Los Angeles County Bar Assn. (chmn. Govt. Law Sect. 1983-84), Am. Judicature Soc., Am. Acad. of Polit. and Social Sci., Calif. Historical Soc., Reserve Officers Assn., Air Force Assn., Phi Alpha Delta, Delta Sigma Phi; mil: capt. USAF 1960-63, Reserve 1963-, major general, USAFR, 1993; mobilization asst. to the Judge Advocate Gen., decorated Legion of Merit, Meritorious Service w. 2 o.l.c., AF Commendn. Res: 4020 Camino de la Cumbre, Sherman Oaks 91423 Ofc: Los Angeles County Counsel 648 Hall of Administration Los Angeles 90012

CRYER, RODGER EARL, school administrator, author, counselor, educator; b. Apr. 2, 1940, Detroit, Mich.; s. Earl Wilton and Mary Venetia (Miller) C.; m. Bellaflor, June 22, 1986; children: Joseph b. 1970, Noel b. 1978; edn: undergrad., Ohio Wesleyan Univ. 1958-60; AB, San Diego St. Univ. 1965; AM, Stanford Univ. 1974; PhD, Columbia-Pacific Univ. 1985. Career: counselor/tchr. J.W. Fair Intermediate Sch., San Jose; summer sch. tchr. The Foundry Sch. (Juvenile Ct. Sch. pgm.); principal McKinley Neighborhood Sch., 1988-91, principal G.W. Hellyer Sch., 1991-; counseling pvt. practice; adj. prof. CSU San Francisco and CSU San Jose; chmn. San Jose Parks & Recreation Commn. 1993-; dir. Our City Forest 1993-; dir. San Jose Beautiful 1994- (steering com., chmn. nominating com. 1993); dir. Monopoly In The Park, Inc. 1994-; dir. Commonwealth Central Credit Union 1990-94, v.chmn. 1989-90; chmn. Recycle Grove Task Force 1989-90; co-owner Guided Learning Assocs. 1987-; awards: summer fellow in sociol., Western Interstate Commn. for Higher Edn.; doctoral dissertation grantee Colgate-Palmolive Fund, Stanford Univ.; mem: Calif. Tchrs. Assn. (State Council rep., budget com. 1983-), Parental Stress Hotline and Services of San Jose, Inc. (vol. counselor 1984-85), Pine Ridge Assn. of Henry Coe St. Park 1989-, Nat. Bicycle Safety Bd. 1991-, Guadalupe River Park Task Force 1993, San Jose Bicycle Adv. Com. 1994-, block capt. City Council Dist. 8, 1994-; author & editor: Shared Decision Making Study (US Dept. Edn., Title XI Edn. Profl. Devel. Act., 1976), Decision-Making Heuristic; Democrat; Unitarian; rec: bicycling, x-c skiing. Res: 3529 Milburn St San Jose 95148 Ofc: POB 21917 San Jose 95151-1917

CSENDES, ERNEST, finance and technical executive; b. Mar. 2, 1926, Satu-Mare, Rumania, nat. US cit. 1955; s. Edward O. and Sidonia (von Littman) C.; m. Catharine Tolnai, Feb. 11, 1953; children: Audrey Carol b. 1959, Robert A. Edward b. 1963; edn: BA, Protestant Coll., Hungary 1944; BS, Univ. of Heidelberg 1948, MS 1950, PhD, 1951. Career: res. asst. organic chem., Univ. of Heidelberg 1950-51; res. assoc. biochem. Tulane Med. Sch., New Orleans 1951-52, fellow Harvard Univ. Chem. Dept., Cambridge, Mass. 1952-53; research chemist, Organic Chemicals Dept., E.I. Du Pont de Nemours & Co., Wilmington, Del. 1953-56, Elastomer Chems. Dept. 1956-61; dir. R&D, Armour & Co., Agric. Chem. Div., Atlanta, Ga. 1961-63; v.p. corp. devel. Occidental Petroleum Corp., L.A. 1963-64, exec. v.p. Res., Engring. & Devel. 1964-68, exec. v.p./c.o.o. Occidental Res. & Engring. Corp., L.A., London, Moscow, 1963-68; managing dir. Occidental Res. & Engring., Ltd., London (UK) 1964-68; pres./bd. chmn./CEO TRI Group (offshore finance, investment mgmt. & trusteeing), London, Amsterdam, Rome and Bermuda, 1968-84; bd. chmn./CEO Micronic Technologies Inc., L.A. 1981-85; mng. ptnr. Inter-

Consult, Ltd. (technical, finance & corporate mgmt.), L.A. 1984-; pres./chief tech. ofcr. General Grinding Corp., LA 1991-; chmn./c.e.o. Edew Management Corp., LA, London 1993-; res. in the areas of organic & biochemistry, dyestuffs, elastomers and plastics, fertilizers and pesticides, energy raw materials, petrochemicals, coal utilization & acid rain, advanced bldg. materials, size reduction of solids, corporate finance, Eurodollar securities and off-shore trusts; honors: Pro Mundi Beneficio gold medal, Brazilian Acad. of Humanities 1976, acclaimed for reg. devel. programs related to agric. and natural resources in Europe, N. Africa, former USSR, Far East and India; Fellow AAAS, Fellow Am. Inst. of Chemists, Fellow Royal Soc. of Chem. (London), mem. N.Y. Acad. of Sci., Am. Chem. Soc., Am. Inst. of Chem. Engrs., Am. Concrete Inst., Soc. of Mining, Metallurgy & Exploration, IEEE, Am. Inst. Aero. & Astro., Sigma Xi, German Chem. Soc., Global Action Economic Inst. (NY), Explorers Club (NY); works: 250+ books, reports, articles in sci. and trade papers and patents; rec: collect 18th Century decorative arts/France, music (violin & chamber music; graduate Music Conservatory). Res: 514 Marquette St Pacific Palisades 90272

CUADRA, CARLOS ALBERT, computer company president; b. Dec. 21, 1925, San Francisco; s. Gregorio and Amanda (Mendoza) C.; m. Mary Eleanor Dwyer, 1942 (div.); m. Gloria Nathalie Adams, May 3, 1947; children: Mary Susan b. 1942, Neil Gregory b. 1953, Dean Arthur b. 1956; edn: BA, UC Berkeley 1949, PhD, 1953. Career: staff psychologist Vets. Hosp., Downey, Ill. 1950-53; tech. staff System Devel. Corp., Santa Monica 1953-68, mgr. library and documentation systems dept. 1968-71, mgr. edn. and library systems dept. 1971-74, gen. mgr. SDC Search Service 1974-78; pres. Cuadra Assoc. Inc., Los Angeles 1978-; commr. Nat. Commn. on Libraries & Info. Sci., Wash. D.C. 1971-84; mem. governing bd. Chemical Abstracts Soc. 1991-; awards: Am. Soc. Info. Sci. Award of Merit 1968, Best Info. Sci. Book 1970, Nat. Fedn. Abstracting & Indexing Services Miles Conrad 1980, Info. Industry Assn. Hall of Fame 1980; founder, ed. Annual Review of Info. Sci. & Tech., 1964-75; mil: USN 1944-46; rec: jazz piano playing. Ofc: Cuadra Associates Inc. 11835 W Olympic Blvd Ste 855 Los Angeles 90064

CUBRE, ALAN P., physician; b. May 22, 1949, Fresno; s. Anthony Francis and Diana Elinor (Lubisich) C.; m. Jacquelyn Rita Lindt, Nov. 10, 1979; children: Alan Joseph b. 1981, Alison Jacquelyn b. 1983, Paul James b. 1986; edn: BA, UCLA 1971; MD, UC Irvine 1975; cert. internal medicine (1978), pulmonary medicine (1980), critical care (1987). Career: intern Univ. Mich., Ann Arbor 1975-76, resident 1976-78; fellow UCLA Health Center, Los Angeles 1978-80; staff Roseville Comm. Hosp., Roseville 1980-; honors: Alpha Omega Alpha; mem: Am. Thoracic Soc., Am. Coll. Chest Physicians, Soc. Critical Care, CMA, Sacto. Med. Soc.; Cath. Ofc: 3637 Mission Ave Carmichael 95608

CUCCHISSI, MICHAEL SALVATORE, lawyer; b. Aug. 29, 1953, Brooklyn, N.Y.; s. Michael Anthony and Grace Anne (Del Casino) C.; m. Barbara V. Barbella, April 12, 1980; children: Gregory b. 1982, Jennifer b. 1985; edn: BS mgmt., MIT 1975; JD, Univ. Pa. 1978; admitted St. Bar Calif. 1978. Career: law clk. Judge Samuel P. King U.S. Dist. Ct., Honolulu, Hawaii 1978-79; atty., assoc. Gibson Dunn & Crutcher, Newport Beach 1979-86, ptnr. 1987; ptnr. Pettis Tester Kruse & Krinsky, Irvine 1987-94; ptnr. Newmeyer & Dillion 1994-; mem: Am. Bar Assn., Orange Co. Bar Assn., Homebuilders Council, Calif. Building Industry Assn.; author book chpt., 1987, ed. book chpt., 1989; Republican; Protestant. Res: 28481 Avenida La Mancha San Juan Capistrano 92675-3341 Ofc: 3501 Jamboree Road North Tower 6th Flr Newport Beach 92660

CUCITI, LESLIE MARTIN, accountant; b. May 16, 1953; d. Gene A. and Donna M. Martin; m. Richard B. Cuciti, Aug. 8, 1981; edn: BS microbiol., San Diego St. Univ. 1974; MBA, USC 1985; cert. mgmt. accountant 1985. Career: fin. analyst Gen. Dynamics 1980-81; bus. mgr. Hughes Aircraft Co., Fullerton 1981-90; cost acctg. mgr. Emerson Computer Power, Irvine 1990-92; controller Sigmapower, Inc., Carson 1992; controller Beckman Instruments, Inc., Carlsbad; honors: Sigma Iota Epsilon, Beta Gamma Sigma, USC Dean's List; mem: Inst. of Mgmt. Accountants, CMA Soc. So. Calif. (pres. 1992), Alpha Gamma Delta; Republican; Protestant; rec: white water rafting, sailing.

CULLER, FLOYD LEROY, JR., electric utility R&D executive and consultant; b. Jan. 5, 1923, Washington, D.C.; s. Floyd Leroy (dec.) and Ora L. (Labee) Culler (dec.); m. Della Hopper, July 3, 1946; 1 son, Floyd Leroy, III; edn: BS, chem. engr., Johns Hopkins Univ., Baltimore, MD 1943; engr. Tenn. Eastman, Oak Ridge, Tenn. 1943-47; design engr. Clinton Labs. 1947-48; section chief Oak Ridge Nat. Lab. 1948-53, dir. chem. tech. div. 1953-65, asst. lab. dir. 1965-70, deputy dir. 1970-73, acting dir. 1973-74, deputy dir. 1974-77; pres. Elec. Power Research Inst., Palo Alto 1978-88, pres. emeritus 1988-; dir: Houston Industries, Inc. and Houston Lighting & Power, 1988-89; mem. U.S. Dept. of Energy Research Advy. Bd. 1984-88; mem. IFS fusion oversight com. Lawrence Livermore Lab., DOE; magnetic fusion oversight com., DOE; advy. com. on nuclear facility safety, DOE; advy. council Oak Ridge Nat. Lab.; awards: E.O. Lawrence Award of AEC, 1967, UN Atoms for Peace Award, 1969, Exceptional Svc. award Am. Nuclear Soc., 1980 and Walter Zinn Award, 1988, Fellow Am. Inst. of Chemists, Fellow Am. Inst. of Chem. Engrs., 1981,

TN Outstanding Scientist Award, 1988, inducted Nat. Acad. of Engineering, W.D.C., 1974. Res: 1385 Corinne Ln Menlo Park 94025 Ofc: Electric Power Research Institute 3412 Hillview Ave Palo Alto 94304

CULTON, PAUL MELVIN, educator; b. Feb. 12, 1932, Council Bluffs, Iowa; s. Paul Roland and Hallie Ethel Emma (Paschal) C.; edn: AB, Minn. Bible Coll., Minneapolis, Minn., 1955; BS, Univ. of Nebr., Omaha, 1965; MA, CSU-Northridge, Calif., 1970; EdD, Brigham Young Univ., Provo, Utah, 1981. Career: tchr., Iowa Sch. for the Deaf, Council Bluffs, 1956-70; ednl. splst., instr., dir. Disabled Students Program, Golden West Coll., Huntington Beach, Calif., 1970-88; visiting prof. Univ. of Guam, Agana, Guam, 1977; freelance cons., sign language interpreter, So. Calif., 1988-90; counselor, acting assoc. dean for spl. resource ctr., El Camino Coll., Torrance, Calif., 1990–; cons. on deafness and other disabilities, Calif. Comm. Colleges, other univs. and colls., businesses, K-12 schools, Calif, other states and Guam 1970-90; svc. on task force related to edn. of disabled, Calif. Comm. Colls., 1971-87; part-time instr., Golden West Coll., El Camino Coll., Saddleback Coll., Rancho Santiago Coll., Calif,. other states and Guam, 1971-74, 1980, 88-90; part-time asst. prof., CSU Dominguez Hills, Northridge, Fresno, Calif., 1973, 76, 80, 87-90; co-chair Hearing Impaired Subcom. Task Force on Mental Health for the Disabled, Calif. Conf. of Mental Health Directors; mem. Com. to Establish Qualifications for Tchrs. of Sign Language, Calif.; awards: mem. Nat. Honor Soc. 1950, Nat. Leadership Training Prog. in the Area of Deafness, CSU Northridge 1970; mem. Olympic Honor Chorus US Internat. Olympic Com. L.A. 1984, Disting. Svc. award, Registry of Interpreters for the Deaf, 1989; Fellow, League for Innovation in the Comm. Coll.; mem. journal bd., founding v.p., treas., Calif. Assn. of Postsecondary Educators of the Disabled; chair, postsecondary edn. com., Conf. of Ednl. Administrators Serving the Deaf; founding sec. Dayle McIntosh Ctr. for the Disabled; mem journal bd., standards com., pres. So. Calif. chpt., Registry of Interpreters for the Deaf; mem: Am. Deafness and Rehabilitation Assn., Nat. Assn. of the Deaf, Calif. Court Interpreters Assn., Calif. Assn. of Persons with Handicaps; founding second v.p. Greater L.A. Council on Deafness; treas., bd. mem. Gay Men's Chorus of Long Beach; bd. dirs., hotline, Gay & Lesbian Comm. Ctr., Garden Grove; mem: Common Cause, Am. Civil Liberties Union, Americans for Separation of Ch. and State, Nat. Com. for an Effective Congress, Ctr. for Nat. Independence in Politics, NAACP; author: A Vocabulary Guide For Parents of Preschool Deaf Children, 1970; ed., conf. proceedings, 1970, 71; composer, song: Carry The Light, 1985; Democrat; Am. Humanist Assn.; rec: languages, vocal music, politics, community activism. Res: 2567 Plaza Del Amo 203 Torrance 90503 Ofc: El Camino College 16007 Crenshaw Blvd Torrance 90506

CUMMING, JOHN WILLIAM, lawyer; b. Aug. 14,1950, Los Angeles; s. George W. and Barbara Norine (Jones) C.; m. Lilli Sommer, Oct. 13, 1977; m. 2d. Nancy Pennekamp, July 26, 1987; Children: Noble b. 1978; edn: AB, UC Berkeley 1971; JD, George Washington Univ. 1974. Career: law clk. Fulbright & Jaworski. WDC 1974-75; staff atty. Calif. Indian Legal Svs., Eureka 1975-76; Redwood Legal Assistance 1976-79; adminstr. Lawyer Referral Svs. 1976-79; founder, directing atty. Northcoast Legal Svs., Crescent City 1979-81; atty. John Wm. Cumming, Eureka 1979–; columnist The Recorder, San Francisco 1985-86, L.A. Daily Journal 1987-90; weekly commentator KFLI Radio, Eureka 1991–; mem: Calif. Young Lawyers Assn. (bd. 1982-86, pres. 1984-85), Calif. Bar Assn. (bd. gov. 1985-88, v.p. 1987-88, mem. Judicial Nominees Evaluation Com. 1989), Calif. Orgn. Small Bar Assn. (bd. 1987-89), Humboldt Co. Bar Assn., Del Norte Co. Bar Assn.; honors: Commendations Northcoast Workers Ctr. 1982, Calif. State Bar Assn. 1983, Northcoast Legal Svs. 1983, Humboldt Open Door Clinic (bd. 1976-86, v.p. 1981-84), Humboldt Co. Housing Commn. (commr. 1983-86), Humboldt Youth Soccer League (coach 1984-85, 87-91); Democrat (exec. bd. Calif. St. Central Com., chair Humboldt Co. Central Com. 1990–); Episcopal; rec: soccer, politics, music. Res: POB 704 Eureka 95502 Ofc: John Wm. Cumming 517 3rd St Ste 30 Eureka 95501

CUMMING, RICK (FREDERICK LITTLEFIELD), III, risk management professional; b. Nov. 20, 1943, Bklyn.; s. Frederick Littlefield and Corinne Marie (Kast) C.; children: Sean b. 1970, Kirk b. 1972; edn: BA, Holy Cross Coll., 1965; AA, San Diego Comm. Coll., 1972; MA, CSU Los Angeles 1975. registered profl. safety engr. Calif. Career: safety dir. City of San Diego, 1969-87; loss control mgr. San Diego Schs. JPA 1987-91; risk mgmt. dir. Imperial Co. Schools JPA 1991–; adj. prof. San Diego Comm. Coll. 1976–, San Diego St. Univ. 1979–; indep. consultant, 1974–; mem: Am. Soc. of Safety Engrs. (pres. 1978, named Safety Profl. of Yr. 1982, Outstanding Mem. award 1986), Nat. Safety Mgmt. Soc. (pres. 1980-81, nat. v.p. 1982-84), Am. Soc. Testing Materials; civic: Youth Baseball San Diego (ofcr. 1977-86), Madeleine Sch. Bd. (1984), San Diego Safety Council (bd. 1970-80); publs: ed. Readings In Stress Management, 1986, 14+ articles pub. in profl. jours., 1978–; mil: 1st lt. US Army 1965-68, Vietnam; rec: running, winetasting, cooking. Res: 4544 Mt. Bigelow Dr San Diego 92111 Ofc: Imperial County Schools 1398 Sperber Rd El Centro 92243

CUMMINGS, ALAN COFFMAN, physicist; b. March 20, 1944, Joy, Tx.; s. Kermit Clyde and Beulah Elsie (Crawford) C.; m. Suzette Yeats, Oct. 27, 1973; child: Travis b. 1975; edn: BA (summa cum laude), Rice Univ., 1966; PhD, Caltech 1973. Career: scientist Caltech, Pasadena 1973-79, sr. scientist 1979-81,

mem. profl. staff 1981–; awards: Phi Beta Kappa 1965, Sigma Xi 1966, NSF Fellowship 1966, Woodrow Wilson Fellowship 1966, U.S. Churchill Found. Fellow, plus other awards incl. Voyager Project Cert. of Appreciation; mem: Am. Physical Soc., Am. Geophysical Union; author and co-author 50+ scientific articles; rec: tennis, birdwatching. Res: 531 Mariposa Ave Sierra Madre 91024 Ofc: Caltech MC 220-47 Pasadena 91125

CUMMINGS, CYNTHIA LOUISE, physician; b. March 11, 1948, Houston, Tx.; d. William Frances and Arlene Josephine (Peter) Cummings; m. Michael A. Boutte, Jan. 30, 1988; edn: BS biol., Univ. Santa Clara, 1971; MD, Emory Univ. Sch. Med., 1982; bd. cert. Am. Bd. Family Practice 1985, 1991. Career: tech. to coordinator adminstr. No. Calif. Transplant Bank 1971-77; cons. Banco de Oidos Ruben Lenero Hosp., Mexico City 1976; intern internal med. Columbia Univ., Mary Imogene Bassett Hosp., Cooperstown, N.Y. 1982-83; resident family practice Goppert Family Care Center Baptist Med. Center 1983-85; family practice San Jose Med. Group, Los Gatos 1985–, chmn. Dept. Family Practice; psychiatry exec. bd. Good Samaritan Hosp. 1986-91; bd. dirs. Planetree Project, San Jose Hosp. 1987–; asst. med. coordinator U.S. Figure Skating Championships 1985; Hepatitis Vaccine Trials, Alaska 1982; awards: So. Calif. Industry Edn. Medal for Sci. 1965, Bausch & Lomb Medal for Sci. and Math. 1966, Rotary Internat. Exchange Student (1968, 69); mem: Am. Acad. Family Practice 1983–, Calif. Acad. Family Practice 1985–, AMA 1979–, Primary Care Sports Med. Network Santa Clara 1985–, Am. Coll. of Sports Med. 1989–; civic: Nat. Geographic Soc., Smithsonian Inst., Wilderness Medical Soc., Hispanic Arts Cultural Council (San Jose), Calif. Council of Youth (edn. chmn. 1967, 69), Alviso Tutorial Project (coordinator 1967, 68); res. in transplant tissues (1971-76), parasitic infections (Mexico 1976); R.Cath.; rec: x-c skiing, travel, handicrafts, languages (Spanish, Norwegian, French, German). Ofc: San Jose Medical Group 14651 S Bascom Ave Ste 110 Los Gatos 95032

CUMMINGS, GREGG ALEX, senior civil engineer; b. May 18, 1963, Oakland; s. Garth Ellis and Shirley Elaine (Wolfe) C.; m. Donna Marie Cavalieri; edn: BSCE, UC Berkeley, 1985; MSCE, San Jose St. Univ., 1989; reg. profl. engr. (civil) Calif. Career: staff engr. Metcalf & Eddy, Palo Alto 1986-89; sr. engr. Dames & Moore, San Francisco 1989–, project mgr. lectr. 1991-92; awards: IFC scholar Acacia Frat., Berkeley 1985; mem.: Am. Soc. Civil Engrs. 1983– (H.S. Outreach chmn. 1994–), Water Pollution Control Fedn. 1989–, Chi Epsilon, Acacia Frat. Berkeley (house mgr. 1984-85, dir., secty. 1991–); Republican; Methodist; rec: reading, gardening, music. Res: 53 Gladys St San Francisco 94110 Ofc: Dames & Moore 221 Main St Ste 600 San Francisco 94105

CUMMINGS, MARILYN LOUISE, tutoring service owner; b. Sept. 20, 1932, Chgo.; d. Blaine and Ruth Louise (Niekamp) C.; div.; edn: grad. Southern Sem. 1952; CSU Long Beach, 1957-61; spl. courses w/Mae Carden 1969. Career: engring. dept. Pac. Tel. Co., Compton 1953-55; music tchr. Music Center Studios, San Pedro 1955-7, founder/co-dir. Musicland Studios (main ofc., S.P.) 1957-64; music tchr./coord., Betty Thomas Music Sch., Torrance 1965-67, others; dist. mgr. Field Ent. Ednl. Corp. 1967-69; tutor/field rep. Wingrock Sch. Inc., Torrance 1969-71; area mgr. Am. Incentive to Read, L.A. 1969; founder/director Marilyn Cummings Tutoring Ctr., San Pedro 1969-94, Marilyn Cummings Tutoring Service 1994–; also: sr. area mgr. 1989–, dist. mgr. World Book - Childcraft, 1990-92; advt. rep. Christian Sci Monitor, (1971-73, 76); honors: Southern Seminary Coll. Dean's list 1951, Alumnae secty. 1988–, sales award Field Ent. Educational Corp. 1967; mem: Accordion Fedn. of No. Am. (judge Music Contest 1956-64, 78–), Sweet Adelines (bd. 1982-4), San Pedro C.of C. 1982- (chair Bus. & Edn. Com. 1986-87), Bus. & Profl. Womens Club; Accordion Tchrs Guild, Toastmistress, Hermosa Harmony Singers (v.p. 1977-80); Chorale of Sun Lakes 1991–; asst. coordinator for chartering of Leads Club/San Pedro 1986; devel. successful method for teaching reading to illiterate and slow learners 1969; listed Who's Who Profl. and Exec. Women, Two Thousand Notable Am. Women (1st ed., Hall of Fame), Five Thousand Personalities of World; Christian Science (ch. bd. 1973-76, 90, v.p. C.S. Assn. 1987-90). Res: 730 La Quinta Dr Banning 92220

CUMMINGS, THOMAS GERALD, professor of management & organization; b. Mar. 23, 1944, Batavia, N.Y.; s. Gerald E. and Arlene T. (Steg) C.; m. Nancy A. Hanks, May 8, 1971; children: Seth b. 1973, Sarah b. 1975; edn: BS, and MBA, Cornell Univ., 1966, 67; PhD, UC Los Angeles, 1970. Career: prof. Case Western Reserve Univ., 1970-76, Univ. So. Calif., 1976–; organizational cons., 1970–; mem. Acad. of Mgmt. (chair orgn. devel. div. 1982), Western Acad. of Mgmt. (pres. 1986); editor-in-chief Jour. of Management Inquiry, 1990–, assoc. editor Jour. of Organizational Behavior, 1982–; author 12 books, 35+ jour. articles. Res: 345 Palos Verdes Dr W Palos Verdes Estates 90274 Ofc: Univ. of So. Calif. University Park Los Angeles 90089

CUMMINS, PATRICIA ANN, real estate specialist, educator; b. Sept. 29, 1945, Portland, Me.; d. Arther M. and Eunice G. (Swan) Peterson Griggs; m. Gerald D. Cummins, July 4, 1964 (div. 1971); children: Mark David, Christine Diane, Scott David; m. Michael A. Hoxsey, Dec. 30, 1988, (div. 1992); edn: AA, San Diego City Coll., 1967; BA, National Univ., 1977, MBA, 1977; Dr. Bus. Adminstrn., U.S. Internat. Univ., 1980. Career: real estate broker Carlton

Oaks Realty and Investment, Santee 1967-85, Century 21 Ryan & Ryan, Santee 1987; tax acct. Larson CPA, San Diego 1966-86, asset mgr. Mesa Mortgage, San Diego 1970-80; bus. prof. U.S. Internat. Univ., San Diego 1980-82; instr. Grossmont Coll., El Cajon 1982; mem: Nat. Assn. Realtors, Calif. Assn. Realtors; civic: Nat. Rifle Assn., Planned Parenthood, Santee C.of C., Calif. Performing Arts, S.D. (dir. 1980–, prod. broadway mus. 1980), active Boy Scouts Am., Pop Warner youth softball league Santee 1972-80; clubs: Flying, Ancianos; Republican; 1st Ch. Christ Scientist, Lakeside (reader); rec: performing arts, numismatics, target shooting. Res: PO Box 710187 Santee 92072

CUNNINGHAM, LINDA BURKE, psychologist; b. April 2, 1943, Dallas, Tx.; d. Harold M. and Irla Jean (Severance) Waite; m. Macyl Burke, Aug. 31, 1963 (div. 1978); 1 dau. Lauren Burke b. 1971; edn: BA psychology, Univ. Tx. Austin 1964; MA, 1966; PhD, 1968; lic. Calif. Bd. Med. Examiners (1971). Career: psychologist Peace Corps, Austin, Tx. 1966-68; clin. psychologist UC Berkeley 1968-71, lectr. psychology 1971-73; pvt. practice clin. psychology, San Francisco 1972-73, San Diego 1989–; research assoc Synanon Research Inst. 1972-76; psychology Synanon Coll., Badger 1977-89, lectr. 1977-89; dir. clin. services Professional Community Services, San Diego 1989-92; awards: NIMH Fellow Comm. Mental Health 1966-67; pub. PhD dissertation, 1968, contbr. articles to profl. jours., 1973, 74; liason minister, Divine Govt. Ofc: 4350 Executive Dr Ste 200 San Diego 92121

CUNNINGHAM, RANDY, congressman; b. Dec. 8, 1941, Los Angeles; m. Nancy Jones; 3 children; edn: BA, Univ. of Mo., MA; MBA, Nat. Univ.. Career: mem. 102-104th Congresses from Calif. Dist. 44 (now 51), 1991–; mem. Armed Svcs. com., mem. edn. and labor com., mem. merchant marine and fisheries com.; Republican; Baptist. Ofc: US House of Representatives 117 Canon Washington DC 20515-0551

CURNUTTE, JOHN TOLLIVER III, physician, biochemist; b. Sept. 9, 1951, Dixon, Ill.; s. John Tolliver Curnutte, Jr. and Elizabeth Ann (Mueller) C.; m. Karen Diane Northrop, June 21, 1975; children: Jacqueline b. 1978, John IV b. 1980, Margaret b. 1982; edn: AB, Biochem., Harvard Univ. 1973; MD, Harvard Med. Sch. 1979; PhD, biological chem., Harvard Grad. Sch. of Arts & Sciences 1980. Career: asst. prof., Univ. Mich. Med. Sch., Ann Arbor, Mich. 1983-86; asst. mem. (prof.) The Scripps Res. Inst., La Jolla, Calif. 1986-87, assoc. mem. (prof.) 1987-93; assoc. dir., Gen. Clinical Res. Ctr., The Scripps Res. Inst. 1989-93; dir. immunology, Genentech, Inc., San Francisco 1993–; clinical prof. pediatrics, Stanford Univ., Palo Alto 1993–; awards: Established Investigator, Am. Heart Assn., Dallas, Tex. 1986-91; Outstanding Young Investigator, 1st Internat. Congress on Inflammation, Barcelona, Spain 1990; mem: Am. Soc. for Clinical Investigation 1988, Am. Soc. of Hematology 1983–; editorial bd.: Blood 1989–, Jour. of Immunology 1992–, Jour. of Biological Chem. 1994–; author: 80 res. articles in prof. journals 1973–; Hematology chapters. in 3 textbooks 1985–; Independent; Roman Catholic; rec: mountain climbing, football, piano. Ofc: Dept of Immunology, Genentech Inc. 460 Pt San Bruno Blvd So. San Francisco 94080

CUROTTO, RICKY JOSEPH, lawyer; b. Dec. 22, 1931, Lomita Park; s. Enrico and Nora Marie (Giusso) C.; m. Anne Kathryn Drobac, June 12, 1954 (div. 1970); m. Lynne Therese Ingram, Dec. 31, 1983; children: Dina b. 1960, John b. 1962, Alexis b. 1969; edn: BS cum laude, Univ. San Francisco 1953; JD, Univ. S.F. Sch. Law 1958; admitted St. Bar Calif. 1959. Career: assoc. atty. Peart Baraty & Hassard, San Francisco1958-60; sr. counsel, asst. secty. BHP Minerals International, Inc. (formerly BHP Utah Internat. Inc.), San Francisco 1961–; dir: Garden Hotels Investment Co., Santa Rosa, Fathom Mgmt. Corp., S.F., Newco Trading Corp., S.F.; Broken Hill Proprietary (USA) Inc., S.F., BHP Transport USA Inc., Oakland, BHP Internat. Marine Transport Inc., Oakland, Family Housing & Adult Resources Inc., Belmont; v.p./dir. Shorebird HOA; trustee emeritus Univ. San Francisco; honors: Pi Sigma Alpha, Phi Alpha Delta, Bureau Nat. Affairs award 1958, U.S.F. disting alumni service 1981, Athletic Hall of Fame 1985, Alumnus of Year USF 1989; mem: Am. Arbitration Assn. (nat. panel of arbitrators 1962–), Bar Assn. San Francisco, Am. Bar Assn., Am. Corp. Counsel Assn., Commonwealth Club Calif., Univ. S.F. Alumni Assn.; article pub. in profl. jour. 1975; mil: 1st lt. AUS 1954-56; Republican; R.Cath. Res: 8201 Shorebird Circle Redwood City 94065 Ofc: BHP Utah International Inc. 550 California St Rm 800 San Francisco 94104

CURRAN, DWIGHT, wholesale lumber company president; b. Sept. 28, 1938, Santa Ana; s. Frank, Jr. and Nan (Mead) C.; m. Linda Kemble, July 15, 1967; children: Dennis b. 1969, Mike b. 1972, Katie b. 1975; edn: courses, Loyola Univ. 1956-61; BS, CSU Hayward 1972. Career: w/lumber indus. 1955–; ops. mgr. Ga. Pacific, San Jose 1972-75; gen. mgr. Redwood Empire, Morgan Hill 1975-76; lumber sales Ore.-Pacific, Concord 1976-78; pres. DMK-Pacific Corp., Fremont 1978–; bd. dirs. N.Am. Wholesale Lumber Assn., Chgo. 1987–; Oakland Lumbermans Club 1967-90, pres. 1970, treas. 1980-86; contbr. ed. Merchant Mag. 1969–; awards: Lumbermen of Yr., Oakland Lumbermens Club (1982); mem: Nat. Assn. Credit Mgmt., Hoo-Hoo Internat. (1963–); civic: Moreau High Sch., Hayward (fin. com.), Centerville Am. Little League, Fremont City Soccer Club; Republican; R.Cath. (Holy Spirit Ch. catechist). Res: 37925 Palmer Dr Fremont 94536 Ofc: DMK Pacific Corp. 4529 Mattos Dr Fremont 94536

CURRY, WILLIAM SIMS, procurement executive; b. Feb. 6, 1938, Mt. Vernon, Wash.; s. Eli and Winona (Davis) C.; m. Kirsten Arms, May 20, 1971; children: William, II b. 1960, Kevin b. 1961, Randal b. 1965, Kim b. 1967, Derek b. 1972; edn: BS, Fla. St. Univ., 1967; MBA, Ohio St. Univ., 1968; cert. profl. contracts mgr. Nat. Contract Mgmt. Assn. (1976). Career: served to capt. US Air Force, 1955-77, meritorious service w. cluster; procurement/d.p. analyst USAF Electronic Systems Div., Hanscom AFB, Bedford, Mass. 1968-73; procurement/d.p. analyst USAF Space & Missile Systems Orgn., Los Angeles 1973-74; bus. mgmt. branch chief USAF Plant Office, Rockwell Internat., Anaheim 1974-77, ret. USAF; asst. purch. ofcr. Stanford Linear Accelerator Ctr., Stanford 1977-80; subcontract adminstr. Space Telescope Pgm., Lockheed, Sunnyvale 1980-81; materials mgr. Altus Corp., San Jose 1981-86; purch. mgr. Litton Systems Inc., Electron Devices Div., San Carlos 1986–; speaker Subcontracts, Procurement & Small Business Seminar; honors: Psi Chi 1966, Beta Gamma Sigma 1967; mem: Nat. Contract Mgmt. Assn. (fellow 1983), Am. Mensa Limited, Industry Council for Small Bus. Devel. (bd. dirs. 1992–, exec. v.p. 1994–), AF Acad. Ski Club 1960; contbr. articles in profl. jours. and yearbooks; Republican; (treas. Newark Rep. Assem. 1981); Lutheran; rec: chess, cycling. Res: 8289 Del Monte Newark 94560-2129 Ofc: Litton Electron Devices, 960 Industrial Rd San Carlos 94070-4194

CURTIS, JEROME JAMES, JR., law professor; b. Sept. 21, 1942, Hinsdale, Ill.; s. Jerome James and Lorraine June (Brettner) C.; m. Diane Elna Eaton, Dec. 26, 1965; children: Jeffrey b. 1968, Jason b. 1971; edn: BA, UCSB 1964; JD, UC Hastings Coll. Law 1967; LL.M, Univ. Va. Charlottesville 1972; admitted St. Bar Calif. (1967), Va. (1970). Career: instr. Univ. Va., Charlottesville 1969-71; asst. prof. Coll. of William and Mary, Williamsburg, Va. 1972-73; private practice, Williamsburg 1973-74; prof. McGeorge Sch. of Law, Univ. of Pacific, Sacto. 1974–; honors: Order of Coif, Hastings Coll. Law Thurston Soc., AUS Outstanding Young Man (1971); mem: Am. Law Inst., Am. Bar Assn., Sons of Norway (pres. Roald Amundsen Lodge 1986-91), St. Johns Lutheran Ch. (council 1988-91); author: Anatomy of Real Estate Transaction, 1985, num. articles pub. in profl. jours.; mil: capt. AUS 1968-72; Republican; Lutheran; rec: amateur radio, piano. Ofc: McGeorge School of Law 3200 5th Ave Sacramento 95817

CURTIS, PAUL N., computer consultant; b. Feb. 1, 1944, San Francisco; s. Claude Hamilton and Kathleen Geralda (Starr) C.; m. Mary Louise Parchen, July 6, 1986; children: Sharon Kathleen b. 1965, Teresa Marie b. 1966; edn: Calif. State Coll. 1964-68. Career: pres. West Coast PC Exchange, Newport Beach 1989-92; dir. Information Security and Technology Ltd., Swinden, England 1989-93; ptnr. Coast Computer Technology, Anaheim Hills 1986–; instr. Coastline Comm. Coll., Huntington Beach 1989; mem: Orange Coast IBM PC User Group (pres. 1988-89, dir. 1986-88); author: Development Finance, 1972; computer programs (FIX.COM, PROMPTER.EXE), Certified Mustang Software Integrator, Network System Administrator, GLOBALNET (APCUG, Wash., D.C.) 1989-94; mil: USN 1962-66; rec: flying, sailing, computers. Address: Newport Beach

CURTIS, THERESE DODGE, corporate secretary; b. May 1, 1935, Niagara Falls, N.Y.; d. Edward Francis and Agnes (Dell) Dodge; m. Charles R. Curtis, July 30, 1967, div. 1979; edn: cert. Katherine Gibbs Sch., NY, NY, 1956. Career: corporate secty. of dur. Topa Equities, Ltd., L.A. 1964–, also corp. secty. and dir.: Ace Beverage Co., L.A. 1964–, Paradise Beverages, Honolulu 1980–, West Indies Corp., St. Thomas, V.I. 1982–. Ofc: 1800 Ave of the Stars Ste 1400 Los Angeles 90067

CURTIS, WILLIAM CLAUDE, university safety officer; b. May 24, 1947, Oakland; s. Ralph Lester and Mary Louise (Sparkman) C.; m. Donna, Mar. 31, 1975; children: Roger b. 1970; edn: BS, Loma Linda Univ. 1970; FFL (Fed. Firearm Lic.), NASD Series 7 lic., NASD Series 63 lic., Life & Disability Ins. lic., Calif. R.E. sales agent. Career: plant foreman Loma Linda Univ. Farms, Riverside 1970-71; carpenter Ralph Curtis Co., Susanville 1972; security ofcr. Sierra Security, San Bernardino 1972-73, Calif. Plant Protection, Colton 1973; patrolman LLU, 1973-75, safety ofcr. LLU Med. Center 1975-76, sgt. 1976–; reg. rep. Quest Capital Strategies, Inc. 1994–; owner Curtis Firearms (firearms & knives); life mem: Nat. Rifle Assn., Calif. Rifle and Pistol Assn., Nat. Knife Assn., Classic Chevy Club Internat., Sierra Club, Nat. Geographic Soc., Nat. Wildlife Fedn., Am. Assn. of Individual Investors; Republican; Seventh Day Adventist; rec: gun collector, outdoorsman, investor. Res: 26329 Cardigan Place (Box 81) Loma Linda 92354

CUSHMAN, ELLIOTT LOUIS, media publisher-owner; b. Jan. 22, 1915, Los Angeles; s. Philip Ralph and Sara (Levin) C.; m. Helen Newbauer, Jan. 27, 1940; children: Stephen b. 1941, Lawrence b. 1943; edn: AA, San Diego State Coll., 1937. Career: news carrier, dist. mgr. Glendale News Press 1925-32; circ. mgr., asst. to publ. San Diego Shopping News, 1932-39; pres./owner/general mgr. Southwest Color Press, San Diego 1943-66; founder, owner, publisher San Diego Independent -1966; owned 11 percent NBC-KOGO Radio and TV Chan.10 San Diego, family owned 50% Hawaii KHNL-TV Chan.13; apptd. commr. State Scholarship Commn. 1958-68, San Diego Citizen's Charter Review Com., Pres. Reagan's Economic Com. 1985-86; mem. bd. dirs.: San

Diego Convention & Visitors Bureau, Donald N. Sharp Memorial Hosp (sec. 1962–, exec. com.), Salvation Army Advy. Bd. (exec. com. 1952–, chmn. 1959-61), Tri-Hosp. Bldg. Fund (trustee), Alumni Assn. San Diego State Coll., Greater San Diego Sports Assn., Navy League of U.S. (dir. San Diego Council), Army League (chmn. San Diego), Anti-Defamation League (regional dir., chapt. bd.), Am. Jewish Com. (nat. dir., San Diego chapt. bd.), Better Bus. Bureau (pres. 1948-50), San Diego Downtown Assn., C.of C., San Diego County Heart Assn., Sharp Hosp. Heart Ctr. (campaign co-chmn.), Community Chest, San Diego Jewish Appeal, Am. Cancer Soc. (San Diego Council), Am. Red Cross, Campfire Girls, Temple Beth Israel (past pres.), Controlled Newspapers of Am., San Diego Symphony, San Diego/Army Advy. Bd. (chmn.), YMCA (city and co. bds.); recipient ACLU award, San Diego; mem: Friends of the Library UCSD (past pres.), Calif. Newspapers Pub. Assn., Ariz. Newspaper Assn., Sigma Delta Chi (charter), Rotary Club of San Diego; Temple Solel, B'nai B'rith, Soc. of Prof. Journalists S.D.; Republican, vol. cons. Cong. Bob Wilson, 1952-70's, San Diego co-chmn. Eisenhower, 1952, fmr. mem. San Diego Repub. Fin. & Exec. Com., alt. del. Nat. Repub. Conv. 1956; rec: collector, Mark Twain, tennis. Ofc: Cushman Associates 2901 Fifth Ave San Diego 92103

CUSUMANO, JAMES ANTHONY, chemical company executive, former recording artist; b. April 14, 1942, Elizabeth, N.J.; s. Charles Anthony and Carmela Madeline (Catalano) C.; m. Jane La Verne Melvin, June 15, 1985; children: Doreen Ann b. 1967, Polly Jean b. 1976; edn: BA chemistry, Rutgers Univ. 1964; PhD, 1967; grad. Exec. Mktg. Program, Stanford Univ. 1981, Harvard Univ. 1988. Career: mgr. catalyst research Exxon Research & Engring., Linden, N.J. 1967-74; pres., CEO, founder Catalytica Inc., Mountain View 1974-85, chmn., bd. dirs. 1985–; pres., CEO Catalytica Fine Chems., Inc., Mountain View, Calif.; lectr. chem. engring. dept. Stanford Univ. 1976; advisor to Inst. Internat. Edn. Fulbright Scholar Program; lectr. Rutgers Univ. 1966-67; Charles D. Hurd lectr. Northwestern Univ. 1989-90; speaker to chem. and physics. grads. Univ. Wis. 1992; mem. NSF Com. on Catalysts and Environment; exec. briefings with Pres. George Bush and Cabinet mems. 1990, 92; fellow Churchill Coll., Cambridge Univ. 1992–; awards: Henry Rutgers scholar 1963, Continental Oil Co. Surface Chemistry award 1964, Lever Bros. fellow 1965, Phi Lambda Upsilon; mem: Am. Chemical Soc., Am. Inst. Chemical Engrs., Am. Physical Soc., N.Y. Acad. Scis., Am. Mus. Natural History, Pres.'s Assn., Smithsonian Assocs., Sigma Psi; author: Catalysis in Coal Conversion, 1978, (with others) Critical Materials Problems in Energy Production, 1976, Advanced Materials in Catalysis, 1977, Liquid Fuels from Coal, 1977, Kirk-Othmer Encyclopedia of Chemical Technology, 1979, Chemistry for the 21st Century, Perspectives in Catalysis, 1992; contbr. articles to profl. jours., chpts. to books; founding editor Jour. of Applied Catalysis, 1980; 20 patents held in catalysis, 1964–; rec. artist with Royal Teens and Dino Take Five for ABC Paramount, Capitol and Jubilee Records, 1957-67; single records include Short Shorts, Short Shorts Twist, My Way, Hey Jude, Rosemarie, Please Say You Want Me, Lovers Never Say Goodbye; albums include The Best of the Royal Teens, Newies But Oldies; appeared in PBS TV prodn. on molecular engring., Little by Little, 1989. Republican; Roman Cath.; rec: skiing, hiking, sailing, swimming, travel. Res: 1644 Candace Way Los Altos 94024 Ofc: Catalytica Inc. 430 Ferguson Dr Bldg 3 Mountain View 94043-5215

CUTHBERTSON, JOHN BROWN, mechanical contractor executive; b. June 7, 1929, Glasgow, Scotland; s. William and Beatrice (Brown) C.; m. Anita Straley, July 16, 1983; children: Stephen John b. 1958; edn: Creighton Selective Central, England 1945; Carlisle Tech. Coll. 1947. Career: apprentice steamfitter David Thompson Ltd. 1947-53; mech. supt. R.D. Purdie 1953-55; Canadian Comstock Co., Canada 1956-60; Harry Lee Inc., Burlingame 1961-68; exec. v.p. Thermal Mechanical, Santa Clara 1968-85; pres. 1985-90 (ret.); mem: Calif. St. Assn. Plumbing Heating Cooling Contrs. (state dir. 1990-92), Greater Bay Area Assn. Plumbing Heating Cooling Contrs. (dir. 1978-84, secty. 1985, v.p. 1986, pres. 1987-88, treas. 1989); mil: RAF 1947-49; rec: skiing, golf. Address: 575 Fulton Way Danville 94526

CUTINO, BERT PAUL, restauranteur, developer; b. Aug. 7, 1939, Monterey; s. Paul and Rose (Aiello) C.; m. Bella, Nov. 12, 1972; children: Marc b. 1964, Michele b. 1968, Bart b. 1974; edn: grad. Monterey Union H.S., 1957, AA in bus., Monterey Peninsula Coll., 1964; Certified Executive Chef, Am. Culinary Fedn. (ACF) 1983; Dr. of Culinary Arts (hon.), Johnson & Wales Coll., 1988. Career: founder, ptnr./owner Sardine Factory, Monterey 1968- (award winning restaurant: Mobil Travel Guide - 1977-1992; one of 50 restaurants chosen by Pres. Reagan to serve at Presdl. Inauguration in 1981 & 1984; "Taste of America" and Restaurants and Instns. Mag. "Ivy Award"), responsible for redevelopment of Cannery Row area; corp. owns 70%, ptnr. of Foursome Devel. Co. and active in real estate; v.chmn. and c.e.o. Restaurants Central, 1973–, franchisee Wendy's (5); bd. dirs. Calif. Culinary Acad.; mem. advy. bd. Monterey Peninsula Coll. Culinary Pgm.; initiated bill intro. by Calif. Assembly Sam Farr to fund culinary arts pgms. in Calif. Community Colls.; instrumental in forming the 1st W. Region Culinary Team that participated in 1988 Culinary Olympics, Frankfurt, W.Ger.; honors: distinguished alumni Calif. Assn. of Colls. 1982, honor soc. American Acad. of Chefs 1984, Antonin Careme Medal for highest achiev. in gastronomy and food service 1987, Fellow for Life in Hon.

Order of the Golden Toque (past comdr.-dir.), medal of honor Internat. Les Amis d'Escoffier Soc. (past Amb.-at-large for N.Y. chpt.), several gold medals in culinary competition, chef of yr. ACF Monterey Bay Chapter 1983, chef of yr. Calif. Restaurant Assn. 1984, nat. chef of yr. American Culinary Fedn. 1988, honored as "Diplomat" Calif. Culinary Acad. 1992, recipient 1st Soviet-Am. Culinary Exchange Medallion 1988, spl. award resolutions for community service from Calif. St. Senate (presented by Hon. Henry J. Mello) and Calif. St. Assembly, proclamation Mayor of Monterey, spl. honor from U.S. Congress entered into Congl. Record by Hon. Leon Panetta 1988, listed Who's Who Food Service Execs. 1990-92, Am. Biog. Inst. life fellow, internat. medal of honor; mem: Am. Culinary Fedn. (senior v.p. 1985-89, ACF presdl. medl #3 award, nat. chmn. mil. affairs com., protocol chmn. 1992 USA Nat. Culinary Team, bd. dir. ACF Chef and the Child Found., recipient ACF Presdl. Recognition Award 1994, ACF Presdl. Medal #22 Award 1995), Calif. Travel Industry Assn. "F. Norman Claek Entrepreneur Award" 1993; mem: Monterey Peninsula Chefs Assn. (1977–, bd. chmn., past pres.); Internat. Bd. of Les Toques Blanches, Paris, France (Mont. chpt. founder), 1st pres. Les Toques Blanches, USA 1994; Soc. for American Cuisine (founding mem.), Am. Inst. of Food and Wine, Confrerie de la Chaine des Rotisseurs (Bailli 1995–), Wine Investigation for Novices and Oenophiles, Kts. of the Vine (Master), Guild of Sommeliers (England), Wine Inst., Internat. Assn. of Cooking Profls., Advance. of Food Service Research, Calif. Rest. Assn., Nat. Rest. Assn., Rest. Bus. Research Advy. Panel 1985–; civic: Sheriff's Advy. Council (charter), Mont. Penin. C.of C. (past v.p.), Monterey Schs. Found. (life hon. mem., founding bd.), Am. Red Cross (recipient Award of Honor 1989), active fundraising events for March of Dimes (Gala co-chair and hd. culinary judge since 1988), other charities; club: Beach and Tennis, Spanish Bay; mil: p.o., hosp. corpsman USNR 1961-67. Res: Jack's Peak, Monterey Ofc: Restaurants Central 765 Wave St Monterey 93940

CUTINO, LOUIS VICTOR, lecturer, nutritionist, poetic, oratorical and philosophical essayist; b. Sept. 7, 1920, Passaic, N.J.; s. Salvatore and Mary (Gullo) C.; father, noted poet, philosopher, scholar and biologist (discoverer of the plant kingdom biochemical equivalent of mother's milk in the animal kingdom; social scientist corresp. with Albert Einstein, Helen Keller, Jan Sibelius, Geo. Santayana re world problems and solutions; literary contbr. many mags. in Italy, and quarterly rev. "Personalist" USC Sch. Philosophy; Italian translator of Prometheus Bound by Aeschylus, hon. by world's great academies); nephew of Leopold Cutino (industrialist, blt. world's largest watch material bus.) and Rudolph Cutino M.D. (prof. ophthalmology Johns Hopkins, and chief of svs. Bklyn. Coll. Hosp.); Louis, a verified child prodigy, at 2 years of age answered questions and gave 20-minute recitations on hist., literature & music in 3 languages (Fr., Eng., Ital.); m. Avery, July 6, 1946; children: Mary Louise b. 1948, Louis K. b. 1949; m. 2d Geneva, May 15, 1971 (dec.); m. 3d. Donna Marie Thrush, June 4, 1994 (granddaughter of John Thrush, an Oregon pioneer who came over the Oregon Trail in the mid-1800's); edn: BA, major Sp. and Latin Am. Affairs, USC, 1954. Career: publications secty. to Gen. Buckner US Army, Alaskan Defense Command 1943-44; duty ofcr. USAF/Material Command, San Bernardino 1955-60; personal rep. and talent scout of Grace Mullen (the founder Redlands Bowl) 1955-60; founder `Project Tijuana' cultural crusade to break psychological barrier between the Anglo-Saxon and Latin cultures to benefit border areas of both Mexico and U.S.A., San Diego-Tijuana 1960-: recent push by Pres. Bush to create common markets between Canada, Mexico and the U.S. was first suggested by L.V. Cutino in his widely circulated letter to Pres. Diaz Ordaz, 12/1/65 (copies to Pres. L.B. Johnson, Am. and Mex. diplomats); began leading Am. pioneer discovery visits to `the other Tijuana' 1960–, frequent lectr. bus. and profl. groups on the true Mexican culture and erroneous Am. conceptions, 1962–; awards: listed Am. Biog. Inst., Man of Year Award 1990, Hall of Fame and Gold medal award 1991–, Fellowship 1992; Man of the Year 1993, Hall of Fame 5,000 personalities of the World 1993 (ded. to L.V. Cutino 1993), listed in ABI's 500 Leaders of Influence 1993; author/pub. book: Project Tijuana (1966, 1970), in library archives Hist. of San Diego, San Diego St. Univ. and San Diego Pub. Lib.; book: A Symphony of Thoughts 1989, essays on universal problems & solutions, containing unpub. letters of Helen Keller to Salvatore C., and also Louis' hist. letters to Mrs. Lyndon B. Johnson, Vice Pres. Humphrey, Pres. Diaz Ordaz, Helen Keller and Billy Graham; booklet "The Soul of God," collection of free-verse spiritual poems 1991; recipient appreciation Pres. L.B. Johnson, Mexican Minister Tourism, ed.-in-chief L.A. Times 1966; rec: gardening. Address: P.O. Box 162 Aberdeen, WA 98520

CUTLER, LEONARD SAMUEL, physicist; b. Jan. 10, 1928, Los Angeles; s. Morris and Ethel (Kalech) C.; m. Dorothy Alice Pett, Feb. 13, 1954; children: Jeffrey b. 1956, Gregory b. 1960, Steven b. 1961, Scott b. 1962; edn: BS physics, Stanford Univ. 1958; MS, 1960; PhD, 1966. Career: v.p. engring. Gertsch Products Inc., L.A. 1949-57; engr. Hewlett Packard Co., Palo Alto 1956-64, dir. quantum electronics 1964-67, mgr. frequency and time div., Beverly, Mass. 1967-69, dir. physical sci. lab., Palo Alto 1969-84, dir. instruments and photonics lab. 1984-87, dir. superconductivity lab. 1987-91, disting. contributor, technical staff 1991–; cons. Kern Co., Danvers, Mass. 1981–; awards: IEEE Morris Leeds 1984, Centennial 1984, Rabi 1989, AIP Industrial Applications of Physics 1993; mem: IEEE (fellow), Sigma Xi, APS, Nat. Acad. Engring.; 20 tech. articles pub. (1957-89), 20 patents in field (1950-89); mil: USN 1945-46; rec: computers, music, photog. Address: Los Altos Hills 94022

CUTRI, ALBERT ANTHONY, oral and maxillofacial surgeon; b. Sept. 21, 1947, San Diego; s. Joseph Anthony and Vanda (Alibrandi) C.; m. Sharon Marie Heinz, May 17, 1969; children: Albert Michael b. 1974, Nicholas James b. 1981; edn: BS, Villanova Univ. 1969; DDS, USC 1973; MD, Univ. Neb. Omaha 1976; lic. Am. Bd. Oral & Maxillofacial Surgery 1980. Career: resident, 1976-78; pvt. practice 1978–; cons. Cleft Palate Team, Children's Hosp., San Diego 1978–; dept. dentistry San Diego VA Hosp. 1980, 81; dept. plastic surgery binational surgery team, UCSD Med. Ctr. 1985–; chmn. dept. oral surgery and dentistry Sharp Meml. Hosp. 1986-88, 91-93; mem: Am. Assn. Oral & Maxillofacial Surgery, So. Calif. Acad. Oral Pathology, ADA, So. Calif. Soc. Oral Maxillofacial Surgery, Internat. Microsurgical Soc., Internat. Congress Oral Implantologists, Acad. of Osseointegration, St. Augustine H.S. (bd. trustees 1987–), Laguna Art Museum Historical Collections Council (pres. 1992–); Republican; Catholic; rec: gardening, bicycling, skin diving, collecting artwork, studying history. Ofc: 9855 Erma Dr #100 San Diego 92131

CYMET, PAULINE, employment agency owner; b. Nov. 13, 1942, San Francisco; d. Max M. and Rose S. (Rabinowitch) Cymet; edn: BA in Spanish, UC Los Angeles 1968; Calif. Lic. Personnel Counselor 1982. Career: employment agcy. mgr. Creative Counseling, San Francisco 1968-71, Cosmopolitan Personnel, S.F. 1971-76; exec. medical recruiter Druthers Agency, Marina Del Rey 1978; dir. pub. relations Great Western Cities, No. Hollywood 1979; office mgr./adminstr. Heritage Ents. (film distbn. co.), Los Angeles 1980; owner The Right Connections Personnel Service (entertainment ind. splsts.), L.A. 1982–; seminar spkr./tchr. Careers for Women, Santa Monica Comm. Coll. 1979; mem: Nat. Assn. for Female Execs. Inc., Women in Show Business, Hollywood C.of C.; jewelry designer: products displayed in nat. catalog, sold in boutiques in S.F. and Sausalito; Democrat; Jewish; rec: gemology, plastercraft, backgammon. Ofc: The Right Connections Personnel Service, 511 N La Cienega Ste 218 Los Angeles 90048

DAGGETT, ROBERT S., lawyer; b. Sept. 16, 1930, La Crosse, Wis.; s. Willard Manning and Vida Naomi (Sherman) Daggett; bro. Willard M. Daggett, Jr., M.D. (heart and vascular surgeon; Harvard Med. Sch. faculty, staff Mass. Gen. Hosp., Boston; Fellow Am. Coll. of Physiol.; lectr, writer on med. subjects); m. Helen Hosler Ackerman, July 20, 1976; children: Ann Daggett McCluskey b. 1962, John Sullivan Daggett b. 1964; edn: AA, Univ. Wis., 1950; AB with honors in polit. sci. and highest honors in journalism, UC Berkeley, 1952, and JD, 1955; admitted bar: Calif. 1955, US Supreme Ct. 1967, various Fed. Cts. Career: ptnr. San Francisco law firm of Brobeck, Phleger & Harrison, 1966–; major commercial litigation esp. antitrust, intellectual prop., securities, product liability and other corp. litigation; adj. prof. Hastings Coll. of Law and mem. acdle. bd. Hastings Center for Trial and Appellate Advocacy; instr. Federal Ct. Practice Pgm. and mem. teaching com. No. Dist. Calif.; demonstrator-instr. Nat. Inst. for Trial Advocacy; arbitrator S.F. Superior Ct., and pvt. commercial arb.; evaluator Fed. Early Neutral Evaluation Pgm.; frequent lectr., writer on legal subjects; judge in Nat. Moot Court competition, occasional host Face to Face KQED-TV, Winner Joffre Debate between UC and Stanford, 1952; asst. coach of debate, Univ. Calif., 1954-55. Mem: Am. Law Institute, Bohemian Club (SF), Commercial Club (SF, dir. 1989–, pres. 1993), Commonwealth Club (SF), State Bar of Calif., Am. Bar Assn.(Sects. on Litigation, Antitrust, Judicial Adminstrn.), Bar Assn. of S.F., Am. Judicature Soc., Fed. Bar Assn. (pres. S.F. ch. 1992–), Phi Delta Phi legal frat., Theta Xi frat., Order of the Golden Bear, Republican Nat. Lawyers Assn.; past mem. Bd. Visitors, UC Santa Cruz: Coll. V.; Fellow, Am. Bar Found.; Coauthor Rev. of Selected Code Legislation, Cal.Cont.Edn.of Bar 1955; participant in legal pgms., seminars; mil: served to 1st lt. US Army JAGC, QMC 1956-60; Republican; Prot.; rec: photog., music. Ofc: Brobeck, Phleger & Harrison, One Market Plaza, San Francisco 94105

DAHLMAN, ANTON RAY, surgeon; b. Nov. 10, 1947, Denver, Colo.; s. Rynol A. and Alice (Ray) D.; m. Marie, May 29, 1971; children: Nicholas b. 1975, Katrina b. 1981; edn: BA, UCSB 1974; MD, UCLA 1979; diplomate Am. Bd. Surg. 1987. Career: intern surg. LAC-USC Med. Center 1979-80; resident in surg. UC Irvine and affliated hosps. 1980-84, chief resident 1983-84; attending surgeon L.A. and Orange Co. hosps. 1984–; co-chmn. Dept. Surg., Greater El Monte Comm. Hosp.; mem: AMA (1981–); 6 publs. on cancer therapy resrch. (1981-82); mil: staff sgt. USAF 1968-72; Republican; Episcopalian; rec: tennis, piano, sailing. Res: 1724 Crestview Seal Beach 90740 Ofc: 3325 Palo Verde Ste 101 Long Beach 90808

DAILY, JOSEPH ABELARDO, lawyer; b. Nov. 4, 1945, Tucson, Ariz.; s. Leonard and Suzanne (Castro) D.; m. Barbara Jean Maiolo, Oct. 21, 1972; 1 son, Patrick E. b. 1968; edn: AA, Rio Hondo Coll. 1971; LL.B, Glendale Univ. of Law 1976; admitted St. Bar Calif. (1976). Career: atty. Law Office John Murphy, Los Angeles 1976-78; ptnr. Murphy & Daily, 1978-79; Murphy Gold Daily & Ruiz 1979; sole practice, Crescent City 1979-82; dist. atty. Co. of Del Norte 1983-84; deputy dist. atty. Co. of Riverside, Indio 1984–; mem. advy. bd. Project CEASE; mem. CV Juvenile Delinquency Prevention Com., named Juvenile Prosecuter of the Yr. (1989-90); mem: Am. Bar Assn., Rotary (pres. 1987-88, secty. 1988-91, dist. secty. Dist. 5330, 1992-94), Desert Users Group (pres. 1988-91), Elks, Am. Legion; mil: E-5 USMC 1963-67, Vietnam;

Republican; R.Cath.; rec: computers, fishing. Ofc: Office of District Attorney 46-209 Oasis Room 4020 Indio

DALABA, O. GENE, consulting psychologist; b. Jan. 27, 1928, Kansas City, Kans.; s. Orin B. and Gladys Jeanette (Miller) D.; m. Margaret Jean; children: Lesli T. b. 1954, (step): Nathan Lane b. 1970, Susannah Lane b. 1973; edn: BA, UC Berkeley, 1952, PhD, 1960; lic. psychologist Calif. 1962. Career: v.p. we. region The McMurry Co., San Francisco 1960-69; prin. TPF & C, 1969-76; founder, pres. Dalaba Associates Inc., 1977–; founder, pres. The Executive Forum, 1978-85 (sold); graduate instr. Golden Gate Univ. 1964-77; lectr. Am. Mgmt. Assn., WDC 1970-80, British Inst. of Mgmt., London 1974; advisor Safe Rides of Alameda 1985-88; mem. ASPA (regl. v.p., S.F. 1975-76); mem. Park Webster HOA (v.p. 1987–); inventor: Adjustable tire chain installer (pat. #4703675 1987), Locking & Alarm device (pat. #4776188 1988); publs: 6+ profl. articles, 1970–; mil: sgt. USMC 1947-50; rec: sailing. Res: 980 Harness Ct #22 San Ramon 94583

DALAL, KANU B., biochemist; b. Jan. 1, 1941, Bombay, India; s. Bhaidas P. and Lalita B. D.; m. Mayuri K., Jan. 20, 1968; children: Manish, Jai; edn: BS, Bombay Univ., 1956, BS (Tech), 1959; MS, Seton Hall Univ., 1961; MS, Utah St. Univ., 1963, PhD, 1967. Career: CSIR fellow Univ. Dept. of Tech., Bombay, India 1960-61; NIH res. fellow Utah State Univ., Logan 1963-69; postdoctoral fellow UC San Francisco 1968-73; res. scientist UC Berkeley 1974-76; sr.res. scientist MRI Preb. Med. Center, San Francisco 1977-82; cons. W.R.L., Albany 1983-84; staff scientist L.B.L., Berkeley 1985–; awards: NIH res. fellow 1963-69, fgn. travel grantee Soc. MS Found. 1970, Sigma Xi; mem: Soc. Nuclear Medicine, Internat. Soc. Neurochemists, Am. Chemical Soc., Soc. Food Technologists, Plant Sci. Club (secty., treas.), Internat. Student Assn. (pres.), S.F. Day Care Assn. (secty., pres.); articles pub. in sci. jours., 1963–; Hindu; rec: swimming, tennis, arts. Ofc: L.B.L. 74/157 One Cyclotron Rd Berkeley 94720

DALIS, IRENE, opera singer, opera company founder-executive; b. Oct. 8, 1925, San Jose; d. Peter Nicholas and Mamie R. (Boitano) Dalis; m. George Loinaz, July 16, 1957 (dec. Mar. 10, 1990); 1 dau., Alida Mercedes b. 1959; edn: AB, San Jose State Coll., 1946, MA, Teachers Coll. Columbia Univ., 1947; Hon. MusM, San Jose St. Univ., 1957, Hon. MusD, Univ. Santa Clara, 1987. Career: principal artist Berlin Opera, Ger. 1955-65, Hamburg Statsoper, Ger. 1966-71, San Francisco Opera, 1958-73, Metropolitan Opera, 1957-77; prof. of music San Jose State Univ., 1977–; exec. dir., founder Opera San Jose, San Jose, Calif. 1984-86, gen. and artistic director 1988-92, general director 1992–; awards: distinguished svc. Tchr.'s Coll., Columbia Univ. 1961, 20th Ann. Honor, Met. Opera, NY, Wagner medallion Bayreuth Fest., Bayreuth, Ger. 1963, Presdl. appt. SJSU 1977, medal of achiev. Acad. of Vocal Arts, Phila., Pa. 1988, Phi Kappa Phi 1980–; mem: Beethoven Soc. (advy. bd. 1985–), San Jose Arts Roundtable 1983–, AAUW (1980–), San Jose Opera Guild, Italian-Am. Heritage Found. S.J., Mu Phi Epsilon; Recording: Parsifal (Wagner) 1964; cont-bg. editor, Book Revs., Opera Quarterly (1983). Ofc: Opera San Jose, 2149 Paragon Drive San Jose 95131

DALLARA, KEN BRADLEY, production/plant manager; b. Jan 10, 1963, Mtn. View, Calif.; s. George Peter and Nadine (Vill) D.; m. Julia Brooke Fairchild, Dec. 6, 1987; 1 son, Dominic Anthony b. 1991; edn: BS in indsl. and systems engring., Univ. of So. Calif., 1985; currently att. Univ. of La Verne Law Coll. (JD candidate). Career: mfg. engr. Apple Computer, Garden Grove 1984-85; indsl. engr. Hughes Aircraft Co., El Segundo 1985-88; pres. Genoa and Assocs. (industrial and systems engring. consulting firm), Hollywood 1988-89; prodn./plant mgr. Raindrip, Simi Valley 1989–; mem: Am. Inst. Industrial Engrs. (v.p., past dir.), Am. Soc. Mech. Engrs., Archemedes Circle (v.p.), USC Engineering Alumni Assn. (bd.); creator software: Client Maintenance System for Non-Profit Orgns. 1988; pub. papers: Effects of Psychogenic Diseases on Sedentary Workers; Inventory Control Through Use of Vertical Integration; club: Cabrillo Beach Yacht; Republican (task force); Christian (mem. diaconate, First Christian Ch. of N. Hollywood); rec: golf, sailboat racing ("Earl of Tasmania"). Res: 12352 Laurel Terrace Dr Studio City 91604 Ofc: Raindrip, Inc. 2250 Agate Ct Simi Valley 93065

DALY, THOMAS JAMES, patent attorney; b. Aug. 10, 1957, Chicago, Ill.; s. Thomas Joseph and Catherine Ann (Radloff) D.; m. Laurie Rene Pulskamp, Dec. 17, 1983; edn: BS chem. engring., Univ. Ill. 1979; JD magna cum laude, Loyola Law Sch. 1985; reg. profl. chemical engr. Calif. 1983; admitted U.S. Patent & Trademark Office 1986. Career: project engr. PPG Industries, Pittsburgh, Pa. 1979-80; process engr. C.F. Braun Co., Alhambra 1980-83; law clk. Christie Parker & Hale, Pasadena 1983-85, atty., assoc. 1985-88; ptnr. 1988–; moot ct. judge Loyola Law Sch. 1988; scorer mock trial Constitutional Rights Found., L.A. 1988; judge Center for Civic Edn., Pasadena 1988; honors: Alpha Sigma Nu, W. Publishing Co. Hornbrook award 1986; mem: Am. Bar Assn., Pasadena Bar Assn., Am. Judicature Soc., L.A. Patent Law Assn. (dir. 1990-, ofcr. 1995-), Resolve of L.A. (secty. 1987-88, legal advisor 1988-90); 1 article pub. in profl. jour., 1984; Republican; Cath.; rec: painting. Ofc: Christie Parker & Hale 350 W Colorado Blvd Ste 500 Pasadena 91105

D'AMICO, JOSEPH THOMAS, manufacturing company executive; b. Jan. 16, 1930, New York; s. Stanislao and Mary (Maniscalco) D'A.; m. Lucille Smith, Dec. 30, 1966; edn: BS mgmt., Fordham Univ. 1951. Career: dir. materiel Loral Electronics, Bronx, N.Y. 1954-65; Philco Ford Corp., Phila., Pa. 1965-70; v.p. materiel Varadyne Industries, Santa Monica 1970-76, v.p. internat. sales 1976-80; dir. materiel Superior Industries, Van Nuys 1981-84, v.p. materiel 1984–; mem: Purchasing Mgmt. Assn. L.A., Export Mgmt. Assn. of L.A.; Republican; R.Cath.; rec: sports, music. Res: 521 Muskingum Ave Pacific Palisades 90272 Ofc: Superior Industries Internat. 7800 Woodley Ave Van Nuys 91406

DANA, DEANE, county supervisor; b. July 9, 1926, N.Y.C.; s. Deane andDorothy Bartlett (Lawson) D.; m. Doris Agath Weiler, July 14, 1951; children: Deane III b. 1952, Marguerite b. 1953, (twins) Diane and Dorothy b. 1956; 4 grandchildren; edn: ME, Stevens Inst. of Tech., 1951; Reg. Profl. Engr. Calif. Career: dist. mgr. Pacific Tel. Co. 1953-80; elected supr. 4th Dist. Los Angeles Co. Bd. of Suprs., 1980–, re-elected 3d term 1988–, chmn. bd. 2t, mem. Coliseum Commn. (past pres.), LA. Co. Transp. Commn. (chmn. 1986), So. Calif. Reg. Airport Auth. (chmn. 1987-88); honors: Hon. LLD, Pepperdine Univ. 1985, named Most Caring Pub. Ofcl. by Calif. Ctr. for Fam. Survivors of Homicide 1985, Torch of Liberty Govt. of Israel (1986); mem: Calif. Assn. of Compensatory Edn., Navy League U.S., Am. Legion, Elks, Calif. Motion Picture Council, Californians for A Strong Am., Calif. Shore and Beach Preservation, Pepperdine Univ. Assocs., Santa Monica Coll. Assocs., Internat. Footprint Assn., Venice-Marina Rotary Club, Exec. Bd. L.A. Area Council BSA, Town Hall of Calif.; mil: lt. USAF 1945-47, 1951-53; Republican (Rep. Central Com. of Calif.); Episcopalian; rec: golf, tennis, water skiing. Res: Palos Verdes Estates Ofc: County of Los Angeles 500 W Temple St Ste 822 Los Angeles 90012

DANANDEH, SAEED, civil engineer, building plans examiner; b. Aug. 21, 1952, Tehran, Iran; s. Nosrat and Ghodsieh D.; m. Oranous, June 11, 1983; 1 son, Andalib b. 1985; edn: BSC (CNAA) w/honors, Univ. of East London 1976; M.Engr., Sheffield Univ. 1977; Reg. Profl. Civil Engr., Calif; Reg. Profl. Engr., St. of Oregon. Career: structural eng. asst. Computer Engring., NCR Nat. Cash Register, London, UK 1972; struct. eng. S.B. Tietz and Partners, U.K. 1973-76; civil engr. VTN Consol. Inc., Irvine 1978-80; civil engr. City of Long Beach, 1980-90; spl. essential plan checking engr. P.E., City of Ontario, 1990-91; res. into advanced composite materials, Dept. of Mechanical & Process Engring., Univ. of Sheffield, UK, England, 1992-94; plans examiner City of Lancaster, Calif. 1994–; mem: ASTM, ASCE, Prestressed Concrete Inst., Am. Concrete Inst., Internat. Conf. of Building Ofcls., Struc. Engrs. Assn. of Calif.; research in field of composites and concrete; Bahai World Faith; rec: sports, movies, cars, travel. Res: 12550 Okahda Ct Apple Valley 92308 Ofc: City of Lancaster Dept of Public Works Bldg & Safety Div 44933 Fern Ave Lancaster 93534-2461

DANIEL, ERNO S., physician; b. Dec. 15, 1946, Budapest, Hungary; Derivative Citizen 1964; s. Erno and Katinka (Scipiades) D.; m. Martha Peaslee, Aug. 14, 1976; children: Kristina b. 1977, Michael b. 1979, Mary b. 1980, Monica b. 1987; edn: BS chem., Calif. Inst. of Tech. 1968; MS chem., UC San Diego 1970, PhD phys. chem., 1971; MD, UC Los Angeles 1975; cert. Am. Bd. Internal Medicine, 1981, bd. cert. Geriatrics, 1988, cert. in vascular physics and technology by Am. Registry of Diagnostic Medical Sonographers (ARDMS). Career: teaching and res. asst., UC San Diego 1968-71; resident phys. dept. internal medicine UCLA 1975-78; geriatric and vascular med. specialist, dept. internal med. Santa Barbara Medical Foundation Clinic, 1978–, dept. chmn. int. med. 1984–, mem. Res. and Edn. Com.; med. advy. bd. Alzheimer's Assn. Santa Barbara; awards: Conger Prize CalTech 1967, NSF undergrad. res fellow 1968, Calif. St. Univ. grad. fellow 1968, Outstanding Young Men Am. 1983, travel grantee Internat. Res. and Exchanges Bd. N.Y. 1985, recipient Chairman's award S.B.M.F. Clinic 1986; Fellow A.C.P. 1983, mem. Soc. of Vascular Med. & Biol., Soc. of Vascular Tech., CalTech Alumni (life), UCLA Alumni (life); violinist Santa Barbara Sym. Orch. 1961-64; prod./ co-host TV weekly series "Senior Forum" KCOX TV 3, Santa Barbara 1985-86; contbr. articles in other med. and sci. jours.; rec: computers in health care, American Indian hist. and arts. Ofc: Santa Barbara Medical Foundation, 215 Pesetas Ln Santa Barbara 93102

DANIEL, GARY WAYNE, music industry executive; b. June 22, 1948, Wendall, Ida.; s. Milan Chauncy Daniel and Ila Fay (Cox) Harkins; m. Jeanne L. Blandford (div. 1972); m. Sandi Kay Modey, July 24, 1974; children: Kelly Jean b. 1970, Marcus Chauncy b. 1981; edn: AA, Boise Bus. Coll. 1969; MA, Westbrook Univ. 1993; PhD, Westbrook Univ. 1994. Career: program dir. KYME Radio, Boise, Ida. 1968-69; gen. mgr., dir. KSPD Radio, Boise 1964-72; on air personality KBBK Radio, Boise 1972-74; account exec. ABC TV KIVI, Nampa, Ida. 1974-77; owner Video Magic Co., Caldwell, Ida. 1978-85; pres., CEO Victory Media Group, Santa Rosa, Calif. 1985–; mktg. cons. Capital Bus. Systems, Napa, Calif. 1986–; dir. Firenze Records, San Francisco, Calif. 1987–; Victory Artists, Petaluma, Calif. 1985–; Agri Devel., Caldwell, Ida. 1979-82; founder, owner Bay City Records, Petaluma, Calif. 1988–, recording exec. producer: (Shelly T.) Out of Control, 1987, Shelly T., 1989; record cons. (Raiders) Indian Reservation, 1971; record mktg. cons. (Markus James) Green Eyes, 1988, Season of Dread, 1989; owner Neuro Achievement Ctr., Petaluma; awards: Idaho St. Broadcast Assn. Top Radio Personality 1971, Most Humorous TV

Commercial 1975, Boise Advt. Club Most Creative TV Commercial 1976, top sales Agri Steel Corp. 1977; mem: Video Software Dealers Assn., Indep. Record Mfg. & Distributing Assn., ASCAP, Nat. Assn. Broadcasters, Gospel Music Assn., U.S. Jaycees; Christian. Address: Petaluma 94954

DANIEL, THOMAS LUTHER, corporate executive; b. July 19, 1947, Santa Monica; s. Loyd Richard and Leila May (Phipps) D.; m. Mary Ann Brackin, Sept. 7, 1968 (div. 1993); children: Lita b. 1974, Justin b. 1980, Syrii b. 1994; m. 2d. Cindy Kae Hall, Mar. 19, 1994; edn: BSME, Cal Poly 1969. Career: production engr. Beaumont Concrete, Beaumont 1969-71, pres. 1971–; mem: Young Presidents Orgn., The Valley Group; rec: skiing, softball. Ofc: Beaumont Concrete Co. POB 216 Beaumont 92223

DANIELS, LYDIA M., assistant director, humaan resources; b. Dec. 21, 1932, Louisville; d. Effort and Gladys (Turner) Williams; children by previous marriage: Danny Winston, Jeffrey Bruce, Anthony Wayne; edn: undergrad. Central State Coll., Ohio 1950-52; cert. Samuel Merrit Hosp. Sch. Med. Record Adminstrs., 1959; BA, Golden Gate Univ. 1992, MS, 1993. Career: secty. chem. dept. Central State Coll., Wilberforce, Ohio, 1950-52; co-dir. Indian Workcamp, Pala Indian Reservation, Pala, Calif. 1956-58; clk.-typist Camarillo State Hosp., 1956-58; student asst., 1958-59, asst. chief, then chief med. record adminstr. Samuel Merritt Hosp., Oakland 1962-72; med. record adminstr. Albany Hosp., 1964-65; asst. med. record adminstr. Children's Hosp., S.F. 1960; co-dir. interns in community service Am. Friends Service Com., S.F. 1960-61; med. record adminstr. Tahoe Forest Hosp., Truckee 1969-73; chief med. record adminstr. Highland Gen. Hosp., Oakland 1972-74; dir. med. record services UCSF Hosps. and Clinics, 1975-82; mgr. patient appts., reception and registration Kaiser Permanente Med. Ctr., Oakland 1982-88, dir. ambulatory adminstrv. svcs. KPMC, 1988-94; pres. Daniels Consultation Svs., 1988–; adj. prof. mgmt., office automation Golden Gate Univ., 1978–; awards: Outstanding Graduate in Human Resources, Golden Gate Univ. 1994, Mgmt. fellow UCSF 1979-80; mem: Am. Med. Record Assn., Calif. Med. Record Assn. (pres. 1974-75), East Bay Med. Record Assn. (pres. 1969-70), Assn. Systems Mgmt., Am. Mgmt. Assn., S.F. Med. Records Assn. (pres. 1983-84); civic: Girl Scout leader Oakland area council 1960-62, Sunday Sch. tchr. Soc. of Friends, Berkeley (1961-63, edn. com. 1965-68), advy. bd. Far West Lab. Demonstration Sch., Oakland 1973-75; publs: editorial bd. CMRA, 1976-77, issues ed. Topics in Health Record Management, I, II, 1983, articles and tng. manuals in field. Res: 545 Pierce St #1105 Albany 94706 Ofc: Kaiser-Permanente Medical Ctr. 280 W MacArthur Blvd Oakland 94611

DANIELS-MEADE, CAREN VIRGINIA, elections specialist, Office of the Secretary of State of California; b. Oct. 19, 1950, Sacramento; d. Allen Lyle and Virginia Maxine (Thompson) Daniels; m. John W. Meade, July 1, 1984 (dec. June, 1994); 1 son, Bryce Matthew b. 1987; edn: BA, UC Davis 1972. Career: media dir., Calif Secty. of State, Sacto. 1972-89, elections chief, 1989-93, chief, legis. and constituent svs. 1993-94; elections splst., prog. mgr. for voting, voter registration and outreach, 1995–; awards: Good Housekeeping Mag. Young Women of Promise 1985, Sacto. Mag. Best & Brightest 1985, Downtown Capitol B.P.W. Woman of Achievement 1987; mem: Calif. Fedn. Bus. & Profl. Women, Sacto. Press Club, State Info. Ofcrs. Council, Calif. Democratic Party, Firefighters SOS Fund San Joaquin Co. (bd. 1989-94), Nat. Council Future of Women in Workplace; handbook Pub. Rels. Guide pub. (1982, 86); Democrat; Methodist; rec: writing, softball, sewing, jigsaw puzzles, reading. Res: 4601 Clay Ct Rocklin 95677 Ofc: Calif. Secretary of State 1500 11th St Sacramento 95814

DANIELSON, WALTER G., lawyer, diplomat; b. July 3, 1903, Anaconda, Mont.; s. John and Tekla Christina (Jonsson) D.; m. Beryl Marie Pearce, Aug. 17, 1935; children: Karin Lynn Godfrey, John Howard; edn: LLB, Univ. Mont., 1929, JD (Hon.), 1970; Pepperdine Univ. Diploma of Honor, 1980, Doctor of Laws, 1991; admitted bar Calif. 1929. Career: sole practice, Los Angeles 1986–; former ptnr. Danielson & St. Clair; vice consul for Sweden, Los Angeles, 1937-55, consul 1955-69, consul gen., 1969-76, consul general emeritus, 1976; sec. Los Angeles Consular Corps, 1976–; honors: cmdr. and Knight Royal Order Vasa, cmdr. Royal Order North Star (Sweden), Officers Cross of Hungary, Knight Royal Order St. Olav, Norway, Knight's Cross 1st class Royal Order Dannebrog, Denmark, disting. service Calif. Lutheran Univ. (2/24/86) first recipient Sven A. Eliason Merit Award (9/16/88), first recipient annual Chmn's. Award Calif. Med. Ctr. Found. (3/28/89), disting. service Republic of Honduras (3/12/91), Ellis Island Medal of Honor, NY (5/22/94), Proclamation City of Redlands (6/14/94); mem. Calif. State Bar, Los Angeles Co. Bar Assn.; clubs: California, Vasa Order Am., Swedish (L.A.), Sigma Chi, Chaine des Rotisseurs. Res: 68 Fremont Pl Los Angeles 90005

DANKANYIN, ROBERT J., business executive; b. Sept. 4, 1934, Sharon, Pa.; s. John and Anna (Kohlesar) D.; m. Dorothy Jean Kuchel, Aug. 9, 1958 (div. June 1975); children: Douglas, David, Dana; m. Georgia C. Oleson, Apr. 2, 1988 (dec. Sept. 5, 1990); edn: BS, Pa. State Univ., 1956; MBA, USC, 1961; M.Engring., UCLA, 1963. Career: with Hughes Aircraft Co., Culver City: mgr. Mobile ICBM Systems engring. dept., pgm. mgr. Surveyor Sci. Payloads, mgr. Space System Labs, 1956-68; Litton Industries, Beverly Hills: assoc. pgm. mgr.

for DD-963 Class Ships, pgm. mgr. for LHA Class Ships, v.p. of pgm. mgmt., 1968-73; group exec. Whittaker Corp., Westwood Village, also pres./chmn. bd. Whittaker Community Devel. Corp., Englewood, Colo., Knoxville, Tenn., and Westwood Village, Calif., 1973-75; Hughes Aircraft Co., Canoga Park: asst. mgr. for U.S. Roland Pgm. 1975-77, asst. div. mgr. Missile Devel. Div. 1977-84, div. mgr. Land Combat Systems Div. 1984-86, group v.p., then v.p., asst. group exec. Missile Systems Gp. 1986-88, v.p. and asst. group exec. Space & Comms. Gp. Hughes Aircraft Co., El Segundo 1988-89, corporate senior v.p. diversification Hughes Aircraft Co., L.A. 1989-92; senior v.p. bus. devel. 1992-93; sr. v.p. and pres. Hughes Industrial Electronics Co., Torrance 1993-95; internat. mktg. and bus. cons. 1994–; chmn. of bd./CEO, ITI 1994–; chmn. bd. Light Valve Products Inc., San Diego; chmn. bd. Hughes/Japan Victor Tech., Inc., Calsbad, Calif. 1990-92; chmn. bd.: Hughes Identification Devices, Hughes Europa, Hughes Lexington, Hughes Mexico; dir.: ADPA, W.D.C. 1986-95, Hughes Micro Elec. Ltd., Scotland 1984-95, Hughes Environmental Systems Inc., Hughes Espana; profl. ski instr., Bear Mtn. 1991–; awards: editor Inter Frat./Sor. Newsletter Penn State Univ. 1955-56, La Vie 1956, outstanding engring. alumni Penn State Univ. 1992, laid the Kell of LHA-1, Litton Ship Building, Pascagoula, Miss. 1971, Penn State Outstanding Engineering Alumnus 1991, Kappa Delta Rho Ordo Honorium 1992; mem.: Hughes Mgmt. Club, Am. Def. Preparedness Assn. (dir.), Indsl. & Profl. Advy. Coun. Coll. of Engring. Penn State Univ. (chmn.); clubs: Marina City (Marina Del Rey), Riviera CC, Aero Club of So. Calif.; rec: skiing, skin diving, sailing, hiking, fishing, golf. Res: One Catamaran St Marina Del Rey 90292 Ofc: ITI Co. PO Box 7118 Big Bear Lake 90213

DARBY, GEORGE HARRISON, lawyer; b. Jan. 24, 1942, New York; s. Stephen John and Madge Buzzard (Leh) D.; edn: BA, Muhlenberg Coll. 1963; JD, Brooklyn Law Sch. 1967; admitted N.Y. Bar (1967). Career: atty., resident ptnr. L.A. office Jackson, Lewis, Schnitzler & Krupman, mgmt. labor & employment law firm, N.Y.C., S.F., L.A., Chgo., Pittsburgh, Pa., Atlanta, W.D.C., Boston, Orlando, Fla., Morristown, N.J. and Dallas, Tx.; adv. mgmt. research, 1970-76; mem. Am. Bar Assn., N.Y. Bar Assn.; contbg. writer Winning NLRB Elections (Practising Law Inst.). Res: 3553 Summerfield Dr Sherman Oaks 91423

DARBY, JOHN LESLIE, consultant, non-profit administration/management, deafness and disabiliy issues; b. Dec. 5, 1926, Vancouver, Canada; nat. 1945; s. Leslie and Ida May (Mallory) D.; edn: AB, Stanford Univ. 1950; 1951-53; cert. adminstrn. Coll. Speech & Hearing Adminstrn. 1978. Career: Rotary fellow in audiology San Francisco Hearing Center 1953-54; clin. audiologist San Francisco Hearing & Speech Center 1954-56; exec. dir. Hearing Soc. for Bay Area 1956-92; grad. research audiologist UCSF 1956-64; v.chair advy. bd. UCSF Center on Deafness 1979-90; advy. group for people with disabilities, Pacific Bell 1993-95; bd. dirs. Nat. Assn. Hearing & Speech Action, Wash. D.C. 1966-72; profl. advy. com. Vis. Nurse Assn. 1970-87; chair Calif. Coalition Indep. Health Profls. 1978-80; profl. advy. com. St. Dept. Rehab., Sacto. 1984-90; founding mem. and 1st v.p. S.F. Assn. of Executives of United Way Member Agencies, United Way of Bay Area Inc.; honors: Calif. Speech Language Hearing Assn., United Way 30 Year Service, N.Y. League Hard of Hearing Herbert H. Lehman award, Who's Who Among Human Service Profls.; mem: Am. Speech Language Hearing Assn. (fellow; legis. council 1972-91, fin. planning bd. 1988-92, num. coms., chair com. on honors 1995), Calif. Speech Language Hearing Assn. (pres. 1972-73, commr. for legislation 1976-79, num. coms., bds.), Commonwealth Club Calif., Marines Meml. Club, Californians for T.V. Access, Health Council of Marin Co., Mgmt. Ctr. of S.F./Chevron Found. Awards for Excellence (judging panel), Mayor's Disability Council (S.F.), On Lok Sr. Health Svs. Inc. (bd. dirs., Dr. William L. Gee Ctr. Capital Campaign Com.), Self Help for Hard of Hearing People (nat. profl. advy. bd.); ed. Innovative Ednl. Tech. & Design of Instruction for Deaf Children, 1968, Students of Sixties, 1973, article pub. in profl. jour., 1979; mil: s.sgt. AUS 1945-46, 1950-51; Republican; rec: community service. Res: 54 Hazel Ave Mill Valley 94941 Ofc: PO Box 640533 San Francisco 94164-0533

DARLING, SCOTT EDWARD, lawyer; b. Dec. 31, 1949, Los Angeles; s. Dick and Marjorie Helen D.; m. Cynthia D. 1970 (div.); m. Deborah L., Aug. 22, 1981; children: Ryan b. 1976, Jacob b. 1978, Smokie b. 1980; edn: BA, Univ. of Redlands 1972; JD, USC 1975; admitted bar: Calif. Career: travel counselor World Travel Inc., Riverside 1968-72, asst. mgr. 1972-76; campaign mgr. Grant Carner for Congress, Riverside 1976; asso., ptnr. law firm Falsetti, Crafts, Pritchard & Darling, Riverside 1978-84; senior ptnr. Darling, Miller & King, Riverside 1984-92; pres. Newport Harbor Devel. Co., Inc. 1983-87; grant reviewer U.S. Dept. HUD 1984-88; bd. dirs. Tel-Law, Inc. (nat. public svc. legal info. system) 1978-80; judge protem Riverside Superior Ct. 1980, 87; mem. Atty's panel Calif. Assn. Realtors; honors: Who's Who In Am. Law 1986–, Who's Who in World 1989–, Outstanding Young Men Am. 1979-86, Calif. Scholarship Fedn. (life), charter mem. H.S. Hall of Fame, Eddie D. Smith award Sickle Cell Orgn. 1981; mem: ABA, Calif. Bar Assn., Riverside Co. Bar Assn. (speakers' bur.), Native Sons of Golden West; civic: Survival Ministries (bd. 1986-89), Am. Red Cross (dir. 1982-84), Am. Heart Assn. (dir. Riv. Co.), UCR Citizens Com. 1978-81, Inland Area Sickle Cell Orgn. (dir. 1980-84), World

Affairs Council (1978-84, Friends of Mission Inn 1980-82, Lions Club, Hispanic C.of C. (bd. 1978-82), Riv. Jaycees 1976-86; Republican: cand. for Congress 36th Dist. 1982; asst. treas. Calif. State Republican Party 1980-82; Bible Fellowship of Riverside. Ofc: 3697 Arlington Ave Riverside 92506

DARMSTAETTER, JAY EUGENE, educator; b. Nov. 30, 1937, Altadena; s. Eugene Jamison and Virginia (Fagans) D.; edn: AA, LA City Coll., 1958, BA, L.A. State Coll., 1960, MA, 1962, postgrad., USC, 1962-1965. Career: tchr. Los Angeles City Schs. 1960-: athletic dir. 1965-83, announcer CIF so. sect. Artesia 1964-85, L.A. Unified Schs. district announcer 1970–, master tchr. 1983-84; training instr. CSULA, UCLA and Whittier Coll. 1966-95; apptd. L.A. County commr. Citizens Community Planning Commn., 1988–; recipient Nat. Def. Edn. Assn. award 1968; mem.: NEA 1977–, United Tchrs. L.A., Calif. Tchrs. Assn., Phi Mu Alpha Sinfonia 1958–; rec: music, announcing, reading. Ofc: Wilson High School 4500 Multnomah St Los Angeles 90032

DASH, HARVEY DWIGHT, artist; b. June 28, 1924, Bklyn.; s. Irving and Ann (Walters) D.; m. Ruth Strom, May 30, 1946 (dec. June 1975); children: Stefanie Marvel b. 1948, Eric b. 1950, Stuart b. 1952; m. Beverly Leonora Fields, June 26, 1976; edn: BFA, BS in edn., Temple Univ., 1948, MFA, 1949. Career: supr. art Pub. Schs. of Boundbrook, N.J. 1949-51; dir. Dash Art Sch., Plainfield, N.J. 1951-54; head dept. art Tenafly High Sch., N.J. 1954-57; dir. creative arts Paramus High Sch., N.J. 1957-67; founder, dir. Lighthouse Sch. of Art, Upper Grandview, N.Y. 1967-81; pres. Lighthouse Galleries Inc., Nyack, N.Y. 1967-70; curator Gallery Five, Grandview, N.Y. 1970-80; one man shows Melbourne Gal., N.Y.C., 1960, Aker Gal., N.Y.C., 1963; group shows Penn. Acad., Phila., Fairleigh Dickenson Univ., others; awards: Berley grantee Italy 1964, Paramus Sch. Sys. 1965; mem. Common Cause, People for the Am. Way; mil: sgt. US Army 1942-44; Democrat; rec: landscape designing, philateley, model R.R. Res: 16345 Bassett Ct Ramona 92065

DAUER, DONALD D., loan agent, consultant, investor; b. June 1, 1936, Fresno; s. Andrew and Erma Mae (Zigenman) D.; m. Laverne, Jan. 23, 1971; children: Gina b. 1971, Sarah b. 1977; edn: BS in B.A., CSU Fresno, 1958; postgrad. work Univ. Wash., Seattle 1964; desig: SRA, Soc. of Real Estate Appraisers, 1965. Career: loan officer First Savings & Loan, Fresno, 1961-71, senior v.p. 1971-78, exec. v.p. 1978-81; pres. Uniservice Corp., Fresno 1976-81; prin. Don Dauer Investment, 1981–; pres. and c.o.o., dir. Riverbend Internat. Corp., Sanger 1985-89; loan agent Equity Lending Group, Fresno 1989-91; loan ofcr. Norwest Mortgage, Fresno 1993–; dir: University Sav. & Loan 1981-92, Riverbend Internat. 1987-91; mem. Soc. of R.E. Appraisers (past pres. Fresno), past mem. Calif. Mortgage Lenders Assn. (past pres. Cent. Calif.), Fresno Bldg. Material Dealers Assn. (past pres.); civic bds: Valley Childrens Hosp. Foundation, Fresno (1984-93, chmn. 1986-90), Valley Childrens Hosp. (bd. trustees 1987-93, chmn. 1990-92), Youth for Christ/USA (nat. trustee 1989–), Cent. Calif. United Cerebral Palsy Assn. (past), City of Fresno Gen. Svs. Retirement Bd. (past chmn.), CSU Fresno Alumni Trust Council (past pres., bd.); mil: s/sgt. Calif. Air Nat. Guard 1958-65; Republican; Prot.; rec: sports. Ofc: Norwest Mortgage 1616 W. Shaw Ste D-7 Fresno 93711

DAUGHADAY, DOUGLAS ROBERT, electronics engineer; b. Mar. 13, 1954, Highland Park, NJ; s. Robert Owings and Mary (Kirkpatrick) D.; m. Ilene D. Eichel, Feb. 14, 1987; son, Brian Douglas b. 1989; edn: BSEE, cum laude, W. Va. Inst. of Tech. 1976; MSEE, USC 1979; engr. in tng., State of W.Va. 1976. Career: tech. staff Hughes Aircraft Co., Culver City 1977-79; senior engr. Litton Guidance and Control Systems, Woodland Hills 1979-80; lab. engr. Airesearch Mfg. Co. of Calif., Torrance 1980-84; proj. engr. The Aerospace Corp., El Segundo 1984–; awards: Masters fellowship, Hughes Aircraft Co. (1977-79), Eta Kappa Nu (life), Aerospace Corp. President's Quality Team Award (1993); mem: Assn. Computing Machinery, IEEE Computer Soc., pres., Soc. of Am. Magicians Assembly #22, Nat. Assn. of Underwater Instrs. (1982–), USC Gen. Alumni Assn. (life); Democrat; Christian; rec: magic, scuba diving, photog. Res: Los Angeles; Ofc: The Aerospace Corp. 2350 East El Segundo Blvd El Segundo 90245

DAUGHERTY, RICHARD BERNARD, lawyer; b. Aug. 30, 1915, Los Angeles; s. Edwin Matthew and Mabel Boye (Dunbar) D.; m. Margaret Eaton Amey, Nov. 15, 1941; children: Richard, Jr. b. 1943, Patricia Anne b. 1945; edn: BA, Stanford Univ. 1937; LL.B, Harvard Univ. Law Sch. 1940; admitted Calif. Supreme Ct. 1940, U.S. Dist. Ct. No. Dist 1940, U.S. Ct. Claims 1964, U.S. Supreme Ct. 1974. Career: atty., assoc. Pillsbury Madison & Sutro, San Francisco 1940-41, 1945-55, ptnr. 1955–; gen. atty. Pacific Telephone & Telegraph Co. 1969-79; Presidio Soc., S.F. 1978-83; secty., counsel Ft. Point Army Museum Assn. 1969-79, pres. 1979-80; mem: Calif. St. Bar Assn., Am. Bar Assn., Stanford Alumni Assn., Harvard Law Sch. Assn., Presidio Ofcrs. Club, Irish Beach Water Dist. (pres. dir. 1975-79), Irish Beach Improvement Club (v.p., dir. 1970-73), Bohemian Club; mil: lt. col. AUS 1937-53; Army Commend. 1945; Republican; R. Cath.; rec: travel, swimming, woodworking. Res: 100 Thorndale Dr #102 San Rafael 94903 Ofc: Pillsbury Madison & Sutro 225 Bush St San Francisco 94104

DAVENPORT, DAVID, university president; b. Oct. 24, 1950, Sheboygan, Wis.; s. E. Guy and Beverly Jean (Snoddy) D.; m. Sally (Nelson), Aug. 13, 1977; children: Katherine b. 1982, Charles b. 1984, Scott b. 1988; edn: BA, Stanford Univ. 1972; JD, Univ. Kans. 1977; admitted Calif. St. Bar; ordained minister Ch. of Christ. Career: atty. Gray, Cary, Ames & Frye, San Diego, 1977-78; minister Ch. of Christ, San Diego 1979; law prof. Pepperdine Univ., 1980–, gen. counsel 1981-83, exec. v.p. 1983-85, pres. Pepperdine Univ. 1985–; mem. bds: Hoover Instn. of Stanford Univ., Merchants and Mfrs. Assn., L.A. Area C.of C., Indep. Colls. of So. Calif., Am. Assn. of Indep. Colls. and Univs.; honors: Order of the Coif 1977, nat. and internat. champion, Phillip C. Jessup Moot Ct. Competition 1977; mem: Young Presidents Orgn, State Bar of Calif., Am. Bar Assn., Am. Council on Edn., Nat. Assn. of Coll. and Univ. Attys.; Republican; Ch. of Christ. Ofc: Pepperdine University, 24255 Pacific Coast Hwy Malibu 90265

DAVIDIAN, S(HARON) J(OSEPH), risk management consultant; b. Oct. 14, 1927, Fresno; s. David and Grace Darling (Toutjian) Davidian; m. Marise Charlotte Fairbanks, Apr. 2, 1948; children: Isaac, b. 1949; Rebekah, b. 1951; Keren, b. 1959; Barak, b. 1962; edn: BA, Columbia Pacific 1982; CPCU (Chartered Prop. Casualty Underwriter), Am. Inst. of CPCU 1983; ARM (Asso. in Risk Mgmt.), Ins. Inst. of Am. 1978, AIC (Assoc. In Claims) Ins. Inst. of Am. 1986. Career: bookkeeper Shell Oil Co., 1948-49, United Fairway/Borelli Produce Co., 1949-55, Producers Cotton Oil Co., 1955-58, all in Fresno; office mgr. Borelli Produce Distbrs., Fresno 1958-9, secty-treas., 1959-70; pres./ gen. mgr. Hallmark Ins. Assocs., Inc., Fresno 1970-92; mem. Soc. of CPCU (founding dir. Central Calif. Chpt.); publs: ed./writer, Keeping Covered, quarterly ins. consumer publ., 1981-92; Jehovah's Witness (elder, wt study cond.); rec: astronomy, music. Res: 1784 E Lester Fresno 93720 Ofc: Hallmark Insurance Assocs., Inc. (POB 5539, Fresno 93755) 5150 N 6th St Ste 124 Fresno 93710

DAVIDOW, GLENN ROBERT, financial planner; b. Aug. 8, 1958, Winnipeg, Manitoba, Can.; s. Harold and Corrine (Trester) D.; m. Laura Cheryl Droker, Nov. 6, 1988; 1 dau. Rachel Sarah b. 1991; edn: spl. courses, USC, 1987; CFP, Coll. for Fin. Planning, 1987. Career: dist. asst. mgr. Equitable Life Ins., Burbank 1979-82; owner Davidow Financial, Tarzana 1982–; appt. commr. State Senate Com., 1988–, fund raising chmn. CAHU, 1989–; mem. Internat. Assn. Fin. Plnrs., Nat. Assn. Health Underwriters (legis. com. 1982–), Nat. Assn. Life Underwriters; Republican; rec: skiing, travel, cooking. Res: 5815 Wheelhouse Ln Agoura Hills 91301 Ofc: Davidow Financial Services, 19510 Ventura Blvd Ste 101 Tarzana 91356

DAVIDSON, WILLIAM HARLEY, educator; b. Sept. 25, 1951, Albuquerque, N.M.; s. Harley Frederick and Joan (Anderson) D.; m. Anneke Marina Rozendaal, June 16, 1973; children: Ben b. 1977, Jay b. 1981, Brad b. 1986; edn: BA, Harvard Univ. 1973; MBA, 1975; PhD, 1979. Career: asst. prof. Dartmouth Coll., Hanover, N.H. 1978-82; assoc. prof. Univ. Va., Charlottesville 1982-86; Univ. So. Calif., 1986–; chmn. Mesa Research Inc., Redondo Beach 1984–;mem: Acad. of Internat. Bus. (v.p. 1988–); author: 2020 Vision, 1991, Managing The Global Corp., 1989, U.S. Competitiveness, 1987, The Amazing Race, 1984, Global Strategic Mgmt., 1982; rec: sailing, skiing, golf. Res: 1605 Chelsea Palos Verdes 90274 Ofc: Mesa Research Inc. 1720 Catalina Ave Ste 204 Redondo Beach 90274

DAVIES, EDWARD DAVID, architect; b. Sept. 4, 1911, Madison, Wis.; s. Rev. Howell David and Julia Hosford (Merrell) D.; m. Marjorie Scheflow, Jan. 30, 1936; 1 son, Robert Huntington b. 1936; edn: ME, Ill. Inst. of Tech. 1931; arch., Univ. Ill., Urbana 1931-34; arch. scholarship Cranbrook Acad. of Art, Mich. 1934-35; reg. architect, Calif. (1948), Ariz., Nev.; Calif. Comm. Colls. life tchr. cred. 1966. Career: arch. design/draftsman J. Robt. F. Swanson AIA, Detroit 1936-37; body designer (Buick) Gen. Motors Corp., 1937; power plant engr. Bigelow-Liptak, 1938; arch. Chicago YMCA 1939; arch. layouts new stores, Montgomery-Ward Co. 1940; proj. coord./chief Convair Aircraft (PB4Y, B-32 USN and Army Contracts) San Diego and Fort Worth Plants, WWII 1941-46, created Master Scheduling System and Prodn. Illustration Div. for Aircraft; archl./office designer/dftsman for Richard J. Neutra FAIA, Los Angeles Studio; chief arch. for S. Charles Lee (theatres), mgr. Los Angeles ofc. (indsl./hosp.), 1948-53; pvt. practice, 1954-64: worked with Walt Disney on New Orleans project at Disneyland, 1954; assoc. arch. George V. Russell, Planner UC Riverside Campus and CSC Dominguez Project; spl. projects for Lockheed Corp. and McDonnell-Douglas Corp.; project arch. Calif. Inst. of Tech. (Planetary and Seismology Lab.), Pasadena; arch. 27 Lutheran Chs., Calif.; faculty (Arch., Hist. & Practice) East Los Angeles Coll., 1956-66; mem: AIA, Calif. Council of Archs. (trustee Ins. Trust Fund 1960-63), AIA/Pasa. (pres. 1959), USC (20 Club), Navy League, Nat. Aeronautic Assn., Chi-Beta frat.; civic: Calif. Planning and Conserv. League (founding 1st v.p.), Pasa. Urban Redevel. Commn. (1st v. chmn. 1951-52), Pasa. Study Downtown Area Renewal (1959-60), Pasa. Beautiful Found. (founding pres.), Pasa. C.of C. (sec. 1961-64), Pasa. Citizens Council for Planning (pres. 1962), Pasa. Art Mus., Mus. of Modern Art N.Y., Los Angeles Co. Art Mus.; designed "Chief Illiniwek" logo for Univ. Ill. (1932); Republican; Prot.; rec: gardening, travel (worldwide). Res: 45100 Brest Rd c/o PO Box 1081 Mendocino 95460

DAVIES, JACK L., vintner; b. June 19, 1923, Cinti.; s. John Lloyd and Celia (Davis) D.; m. Jamie Peterman, March 19, 1960; children: William b. 1961, John b. 1964, Hugh b. 1965; edn: Northwestern Univ. 1942-43, Stanford Univ. 1946-48, MBA, Harvard Univ., 1950. Career: v.p. Avalon Mfg. Co., Los Angeles 1950-52; sr. analyst Kaiser Aluminum, Oakland 1952-55; assoc. McKinsey & Co., San Francisco 1955-60; v.p. mktg. Fiberboard Corp., San Francisco 1960-63; v.p. acquisitions Ducommun Inc., Los Angeles 1963-65; pres. Schramsberg Vineyards, Calistoga 1965–; pres. Caves Transmontanas Lda., Vila Flor, Portugal 1989–; dir. and past chmn. Wine Inst., San Francisco 1975–; honors: Cook's Mag. list of Who's Who of Cooking in Am., N.Y. 1985, wine man of year Friends of Jr. Art Mus. Los Angeles 1984, Junipero Serra award Calif. Wine Patrons L.A. 1984; club: Bohemian (SF); contbr. numerous articles to wine publs. internat.; mil: sgt. USAAF 1943-46; Republican; Prot.; rec: archeology, hiking, historic textiles. Address: Schramsberg Rd Calistoga 94515

DAVIS, COLEEN COCKERILL, teacher, bed & breakfast owner, consultant; b. Sept. 20, 1930, Pampa, Texas; d. Charles Clifford and Myrtle Edith (Harris) Cockerill; m. Richard Harding Davis, June 22, 1952, (div. 1984); children: David Christopher, Denis Benjamin (dec. 1979); edn: BS, Univ. Oklahoma, 1951; MS, UCLA, 1952; postgrad. studies UCLA, Whittier Coll., USC; Calif. std., sec. tchg. cred. Career: tchr. and dept. chair home econs. Whittier Union High Sch. Dist., 1952-85, substitute tchr., home tchr. 1985–; cons. 1986–; founder, pres., exec. dir. CoHost, America's Bed & Breakfast, Whittier 1983–; mem. Calif. Tchrs. Assn., NEA, Internat. Tour Mgmt. Inst.; civic bds: Whittier C.of C. (amb.), Children of Murdered Parents, Whittier (founder 1984), Parents of Murdered Children, Whittier (S.E./Long Beach chapt. leader 1984), Coalition of Organizations and People, Whittier (founder 1984), Whistle Ltd., Whittier (founder 1984), Fred C. Nelles Sch. (citizen advy. bd.); contbr. articles to newspapers; Republican; Episcopalian; rec: volunteer work. Address: PO Box 9302 Whittier 90608

DAVIS, DONALD GLENN, finance and business executive, lawyer; b. Sept. 15, 1949, Los Angeles; s. Maurice G. and Elinore C. (Leigh) D.; 4th generation Californian, family active in finance, real estate and law since 1920s; m.. Sandy D. (PhD physicist); edn: BS acctg., CAL Univ., Pomona; JD (rank 2d in class), USC; lic. R.E. Broker, lic. Securities Broker. Career: atty., assoc. O'Melveny & Myers, Los Angeles -1973; prin. Davis & Assoc. 1973–; pres. The Bluechip Financial Group, 1977–; prof. law Southwestern Univ. 1972-80; chmn. SEC Cooperative Inst. 1987; mem. ABA, Calif. Bar Assn., L.A. Co. Bar Assn. (sect. chmn. Bus. & Corporate Law 1985-86; Legion Lex (bd. dirs.) Wine & Food Soc. of So. Calif.; honors: Student Body v.p. CAL Univ. Pomona, Order of Coif, exec. editor USC Law Rev.; clubs: California, L.A. Yacht, Balboa Peninsula Point Beach, Palos Verdes Beach, Arrowhead Lake Assn.; Republican (elected L.A. Rep. Cent. Com. 1992-94, Calif. Rep. Party, Senatorial Inner Circle, Congl. candidate 42nd C.D., primary 1988). Res: Villa Del Monte, Palos Verdes Estates; The Island House, Avalon; Whispering Point, Lake Arrowhead; Motor Yacht Papillon, Newport Beach. Ofc: Davis & Associates 300 S Grand 14th Fl Los Angeles 90021 also Beverly Hills and Newport Beach offices.

DAVIS, EDMOND RAY, lawyer; b. Sept. 4, 1928, Calif.; s. Archie Allen and Eva (Hoover) D.; m. Ruby Evelyn, Oct. 17, 1954; children: Phillip b. 1958, Sandra b. 1960; edn: att. Pepperdine Coll. 1946-49, JD, Hastings Coll. Law 1952; admitted Calif. Bar and Fed. Cts. 1952. Career: atty., assoc. Bailie, Turner & Sprague, Los Angeles 1955-60; trust counsel Security Pacific Nat. Bank, 1960-67; estate planning, probate and trust atty./ ptnr. Overton, Lyman & Prince 1967-87; Brobeck, Phleger & Harrison, 1987–; chmn. legal advy. com. San Marino Unified Sch. Dist. 1981–; mem. legal com. Music Ctr. Found., Performing Arts Council, L.A. Co. 1980–; chmn., pub. adminstr. Pub. Guardian Advy. Commns., L.A. Co. Bd. Suprs. 1974-76; bd. dirs. Braille Inst. Am. Inc. 1974–, Childrens Bur. L.A., Childrens Bur. Found.; honors: Order of Coif (1952), Pepperdine Coll. Alumni award (1962), the Arthur K. Marshall Award 1991 L.A. Co. Bar Assn. Probate & Trust Law Sect.; mem: Am. Coll. Trust & Estate Counsel (fellow, chmn. Calif. chpt. 1981-86), Internat. Acad. Estate and Trust Law (academician), Calif. Bar Assn. (chmn. estate planning, trust and probate law sect. 1977-78), Los Angeles County Bar Assn. (exec. com., probate and trust law sect. 1988); past pres. L.A. Jaycees (1962); clubs: Rotary, Calif., Chancery, Breakfast; mil: n.c.o. AUS 1952-54; Republican; rec: fishing, biking, tennis. Ofc: Brobeck, Phleger & Harrison 550 S Hope St Los Angeles 90071-2604

DAVIS, GRAY, lieutenant governor; b. Dec. 26, 1942, NY, NY; m. Sharon Ryer, Feb. 20, 1983; edn: BA (cum laude) Stanford Univ., 1964; JD, Columbia Univ. Law Sch., 1967. Career: chief of staff to Gov. Jerry Brown, 1974-81, served as chmn. Calif. Counsel on Crim. Justice, initiated statewide Neighborhood Watch Pgm.; elected rep. 43rd dist. Calif. St. Assembly, 1982-84, 1984-86, chmn. Housing and Community Devel. Com. (authored legis. requiring 10 percent of all apts. blt. with tax-exempt bonds be for very low income tenants; estab. stds. for removal of asbestos from pub. schs.); elected state controller, 1986-90, re-elected 11/90, respons. acctg. and disbursement of all state funds, mem. 56+ state boards and commns. including Bd. of Equalization, State Lands Commn., Commn. on State Finance, St. Bd. of Control, various bond fin. coms., chmn. Franchise Tax Bd.; founder/chmn. Calif. Found. for the Protection of Children (non-profit), co-op. with bus. and labor union to publicize photos of missing children, 1985 award for best pub./pvt. partnership in Calif.; mil: served to capt. US Army, Vietnam, Bronze Star 1969; Democrat. Ofc: Lieutenant Governor, State Capitol Rm 1114 Sacramento 95814

DAVIS, JOHN JACOBS, JR., lawyer; b. March 20, 1949, Beaumont, Tx.; s. John Jacobs and Julia (Herzfeld) D.; edn: BA, Univ. Tx. Austin 1970; JD, UC Hastings Coll. Law 1975; admitted St. Bar Calif. 1975. Career: atty., assoc. McCarthy Johnson & Miller, San Francisco 1975-80, ptnr. 1980-89, ofcr., dir., shareholder 1989–; mem: Am. Bar Assn., ACLU, AFL-CIO Lawyers Co-ordinating Com., Calif. Lawyers for Arts (dir. 1979–), St. Bar (exec. com. Labor and Employment Law sect. 1982-83); Democrat. Address: 595 Market St, Ste 2200, San Francisco 94105

DAVIS, JOHN WARREN, contracting specialist; b. Feb. 14, 1946, York, Pa.; gr.grandson, W.F. Davis, founder Anchor Serum Co. and St. Joseph (Mo.) Stockyards and mem. Mo. State Legislature; gr.son, Frank A. Davis Sr., lawyer, St. Joseph, Mo.; son, Lillian M. (Billings) and Frank A. Davis Jr., real estate broker; edn: AA in real estate, San Diego City Coll. 1976; BA in pol. sci., Drake Univ. 1968; MS in acquisition & contract mgmt., West Coast Univ. 1987; Calif. lic. real estate broker ; Cert. Profl. Contract Mgr. (CPCM), Nat. Contract Mgmt. Assn. (1985, recert. NCMA -1995), cert. in contract mgmt., AF Inst. Tech. and NCMA 1989; profl. designation in contracting, US Army Logistics Mgmt. Coll. (ALMAC) and NCMA, 1991, panel mem. Nat. Panel of Arbitrators, Am. Arbitration Assn.; num. profl. tng. studies, DOD. Career: enlisted US Army, service in Vietnam, 1968-72; real estate sales and mgmt./student 1972-79; Naval Ocean Systems Center, San Diego 1979-80; contract intern/adminstr. Ofc. of Naval Research, resident rep. Stanford Univ., 1980-84; contract splst. Naval Weapons Sta., Seal Beach Corona site 1984-86, contract splst. jt. service (Navy/AF) assigned to def. meteorological satellite pgm. Navy Space Systems Activity, Los Angeles AFB, 1986-88; procurement analyst Comdr. Naval Air Force Pacific Fleet, 1988–; instr. West Coast Univ. (chmn. curriculum rev. com. for acquisition Coll. of Bus., WCU), instr. San Diego State Univ. Ext. (chmn. curriculum rev. com. for acquisition Coll. of Extended Studies, SDSU; SDSU del. Nat. Acamenic Conf. for Academic Educators 1991, 1992); listed Roster of Neutrals, Admin. Conf. of U.S.; author of several prof. jour. articles and presenter at prof. acquisition meetings; awarded Royal Order of Trident for Equatorial Crossing; listed state, nat., internat. biographical directories; mem: Am. Mgmt. Assn., Nat. Contract Mgmt. Assn. (Fellow, ednl. chmn., mentor, Pony Express Award 1992, San Diego chpt.), Am. Bar Assn. (assoc.), Am. Arbitration Assn., Soc. of Govt. Meeting Planners (chpt. v.p.); clubs: San Diego Writer's and Editor's Guild (pres.), San Diego Athletic, Sons of the Am. Revolution (SAR); author: (book) Paperless Contracting: The EDI Revolution, Holbrook & Kellogg 1994; mil: E5 US Army 1968-72, Vietnam Campaign (2/60 device) and Vietnam Svc. (2 stars) medals, Army Commendation, medals,; Episcopalian; rec: sailing, swim, travel. Res: PO Box 620657 San Diego 92162 Ofc: COM-NAVAIRPAC (41A) NAS North Island San Diego 92135-5100

DAVIS, JOSEPH HAROLD, pediatrician, clinical professor emeritus; b. Mar. 16, 1914, San Francisco; s. Casper and Phoebe (Shipper) D.; m. Carol May Michels, Aug. 4, 1938; children: Leland b. 1941, Nancy b. 1946, Betsy b. 1950; edn: AB, Stanford Univ., 1933, MD, Stanford Univ., 1938; Calif. Lic. A07906, 1938. Career: pediatrician pvt. practice, San Francisco 1940-42; capt. Medical Corps US Army 1942-45; pediatrician Palo Alto Med. Clinic, Palo Alto 1946–; clin. prof. Stanford Univ. Sch. of Med., 1942–, emeritus prof. 1979–; honors: AOA, Stanford Med. Sch. 1937, Distinguished Eagle Scout 1989 and Scouter of Yr. Stanford Area Council BSA, Palo Alto 1989, lifetime service award Senior Coord. Council Palo Alto 1991; mem: AMA, Calif. Med. Assn., Santa Clara Co. Med. Soc. 1946–, Am. Acad. Pediatrics (1942–, Fellow, newsletter editor No. Calif. chpt. 1981–); civic: adv. Med. Explorer Post 63, Stanford Area BSA 1963–; club: University (Palo Alto); contbr. num. sci. articles in med. jours.; Democrat; Jewish; rec: philately. Res: 40 Anderson Way Menlo Park 94025 Ofc: Palo Alto Medical Clinic 300 Homer Palo Alto 94301

DAVIS, LOWELL LIVINGSTON, cardiothoracic surgeon, educator; b. Urbanna, Va.; edn: BS, Morehouse Coll., 1949; MS biology, Atlanta Univ., 1950; MD, Howard Univ., 1955; postgrad. Univ. Penn. Grad. Sch. of Med., 1959-60; diplomate Am. Bd. of Surgery (1966), Am. Bd. Thoracic Surgery (1969), cert. x-ray supr. Calif. Career: rotating intern Jersey City Med. Ctr., N.J. 1955-56; resident obstetrics Margaret Hague Maternity Hosp., Jersey City, N.J. 1956-57; res., chief resident ob-gyn Elmhurst (N.Y.) Gen. Hosp. 1957-58, 58-59; res., chief resident gen. surgery VA Hosp., Tuskegee, Ala. 1960-61, Nassau County Med. Ctr., Hemstead, N.Y. 1961-64; res., senior resident cardiothoracic surgery Cook County Hosp., Chgo. 1967-68, 68-69; gen. surgeon solo practice, N.Y.C., 1964-65; sr. surgeon US Naval Hosp., St. Albans, N.Y. 1965-67, staff, then senior thoracic and cardiovascular surgeon 1969-70, then chief thoracic and cardiovascular surgeon 1970-71; pvt. practice thoracic and cardiovascular surgery, 1975–; clin. assoc. prof. of surgery, sect. cardiothoracic surg., USC Medical Sch., Los Angeles, 1991–; vis. surgeon cardiothoracic surg. Royal Brompton and Nat. Heart Hosp., London, Eng. (July 1990), vis. surgeon (1991): Hanover Med. Sch. and Univ. Hosp., Ger.; German Heart Ctr., Munich, Ger.;

Cardiac Surgery Ctr. of West Berlin, Ger.; Univ. of Dusseldorf Med. Sch. and Univ. Hosp.; fellowships: Univ. Oreg. Med. Sch. Hosp. and Clinics, Portland 1972, St. Vincent Hosp., Portland 1972, Med. Coll. of Wisconsin, Milw. 1973, Pacific Med. Ctr. Inst. of Med. Scis., Presbyterian Heart Research Inst., San Francisco 1974, Allen-Bradley Med. Sci. Research Lab., Milw. 1975, Hosp. for Sick Children London, 1978, Texas Heart Inst., Houston 1983; vis. prof. and research fellow in cardiac surgery sect. Hadassah Med. Sch. and Univ. Hosp., Jerusalem 1987; Fellow Internat. Coll. Angiology, Am. Coll. Angiology, Internat. Coll. Surgeons, N.Y. Acad. Med., Am. Coll. Chest Physicians, A.C.S., Am. Coll. Cardiology, mem. Assn. of Mil. Surgeons of U.S., Am. Assn. for Thoracic Surgery, Soc. of Thoracic Surgeons, Albert Starr Cardiac Surg. Soc. (founding mem. 1974), Am. Coll. Emerg. Physicians, Lyman Brewer III Internat. Surg. Soc., Royal Soc. Med. England (affil.), Am. Fedn. of Police (police surgeon, honor roll, nat. med. advy. bd.), AAAS, Denton A. Cooley Cardiovasc. Surgery Soc., Western Thoracic Surg. Assn., L.A. Surg. Soc.; contbr. articles in med. jours.; mil: USNR 1943-46, capt. (surgeon) USNR M.C. 1965-67, 69-71, Am. Campaign, Asiatic Pacific Campaign, WWII Victory, Presdl. Unit Cit., letters of thanks from Sec. of Navy James Forrestal (1946), Pres. Harry Truman (sent postwar), Occup. Asia, Nat. Def., certif. signed by Pres. Richard M. Nixon (1971). Ofc: 123 South Figueroa Ste #1644 Los Angeles 90012

DAVIS, OAKLEY, JR., engineer; b. Sept. 20, 1930, Heilwood, Pa.; s. Oakley M. and Emabel (Decker) D.; m. Gloria T. Foresi, Aug. 7, 1957 (dec. 1981); m. Miriam Joy Berwick, Sept. 28, 1985; children: Jan M. b. 1960, Jeffrey E. b. 1962; edn: BSME, Pa. St. Univ. 1960. Career: waiter Hot Shoppes/Marriott, Arlington, Va. 1949-50; shoe sales Brown Boot Shop 1950-51; design draftsman Penna Dept. Hwys., Ind., Pa. 1951-55; design engr. Green Engring. Co., Sewickley, Pa. 1955-57; devel. engr. Aerojet Gen. Corp., Azusa 1961-64; v.p., gen. mgr. W.A. Whitney of L.A. 1965-68; v.p. sales Pow-R-Tron Inc., Home, Pa. 1968-69; gen. mgr. Fabri-Quipt Systems Co., Arcadia 1969–; awards: Outstanding Representative over 20 yrs. Unittool Punch & Die Co. Inc. 1993, First Baptist Ch. mem. of year 1985, Hydra Tool top dealer 1973; mem: Am. Baptist Credit Union (dir. 1977-92), Fabrications Mfrs. Assn., Am. Mgmt. Assn., The Music Theatre, So. Calif. (dir. 1984-87); articles pub. in tech. jours. 1970-75, seminars on metal fabricating methods 1985–; mil: pfc AUS 1952-54; Republican; Baptist; rec: classic and spl. interest vehicles. Ofc: Fabri-Quipt Systems Co. 125 E Santa Clara #19 Arcadia 91006

DAVIS, RANDALL BARTON, psychotherapist; b. Oct. 16, 1955, Hollywood; s. Kenneth Cord and Joyce Jeanette (Watson) D.; m. Dena Mintz, June 15, 1985; edn: BA psych. with honors, CSU Fullerton, 1978, MS counseling, CSU Fullerton, 1981; lic. Marriage Family and Child Counselor, Calif. (1984). Career: dir. adolescent pgm. Care Unit Hosp., L.A. 1981-82; dir. adol. psychiatric pgm. Charter Grove Hosp., Corona 1982-84, dir. eating disorders pgm. 1984-85, dir. chem. dependency pgm. 1986-88, in-service tng. dir. 1982-89, med. staff 1987-89; dir. child/adol. psychiatric program Canyon Ridge Hosp., 1989-94; psychotherapist pvt. practice, Corona 1983–; cons. tchg. So. Calif. Coll. Optometry, Fullerton 1988-90; mem: Calif. Assn. MFTs, Internat. Assn. Eating Disorder Counselors (charter), Corona/Norco Drug Advy. Council (chmn. 1987–), Riverside Drug Abuse Advy. Council 1986–; rec: music. Ofc: 802 Magnolia Ave Ste 207 Corona 91719

DAVIS, RICHARD, aviation insurance executive; b. March 11, 1947, Pittsburg, Calif.; s. Morgan William and Margaret (Jacobs) D.; m. Valerie Jean Hart, March 18, 1967; children: Kellie Susanne b. 1970, Scott Richard b. 1975; edn: BS, CSU 1971. Career: sr. v.p., western regional mgr. Assoc. Aviation Underwriters, Universal City 1971–; mem: Am. Inst. Chartered Property & Casualty Underwriters, West Hills Property Owners Assn. (v.p. 1988, bd. dirs. 1988, 89); Republican; rec: flying, skiing, travel. Ofc: Associates Aviation Underwriters 10 Universal City Plaza Ste 2350 Universal City 91608

DAVIS, RODNEY, state appellate court justice; b. Feb. 14, 1949, Sacramento; s. Lester Thomas and Pauline Lillian (Vakoch) D.; m. Susan Baxter, Aug. 10, 1974; children: Kevin b. 1981, Brian b. 1985; edn: BA, UC Davis, 1971, JD, UC Hastings Coll. Law, 1974, MA, USC, 1979. Career: dep. atty. gen. Calif. Dept. Justice, Sacto. 1974-78; actg. dist. atty. Co. of Sierra, 1978; supvg. dep. atty. gen. Calif. Dept. Justice, Sacto. and S.F. 1978-83; chief Medi-Cal Fraud Unit 1983; appt. judge Sacto. Municipal Ct. 1983-85; Sacramento Superior Ct. 1985-89; assoc. justice Calif. Ct. of Appeal 3d dist., Sacto. 1989–; instr. Calif. Cont. Edn. of Bar, 1985–; mem. Calif. Judges Assn., Cal Aggie/ UC Davis Alumni Assn. (pres. 1990-92), UC Davis Found. (trustee 1989–), Sacto. Welsh Cir., Del Dayo Soccer Club (pres. 1992–), Crocker Art Mus. Assocs., Sacto. Tree Found.; Republican; Episcopalian; rec: running, tennis. Ofc: Court of Appeal 914 Capitol Mall Ste 119 Sacramento 95814

DAVIS, WILLIAM, lawyer; b. Oct. 13, 1942, Lexington, Ky.; s. Evan Jefferies and Martha Louise (Crain) D.; m. Constance Shrawder, Aug. 24, 1968; children: Marya Elizabeth b. 1969, Hillary Louise b. 1974; edn: AB, Transylvania Lexington 1964; JD, Univ. Ky. 1973. Career: vol. Peace Corps, Lautaro, Chile 1964-66, trainer, Univ. N.M., Albuquerque 1966-67, Univ. Wash., Seattle 1967-68, reg. rep., Valdivia, Chile 1968-69, actg. dep. dir., Santiago, Chile 1969-71;

staff atty. Judicial Council, S.F. 1973-75; dir. Admin. Office of Cts., Frankfort, Ky. 1975-79; personnel ofcr. Bahai World Center, Haifa, Israel 1979-81; circuit exec. U.S. Ct. (9th circuit), S.F. 1981-87; exec. dir. Bronson Bronson & McKinnon 1987; dir. Admin. Office of Cts. 1987-91; sr. advisor Nat. Ctr. for State Courts, Williamsburg, VA; principal DPR Consulting, San Francisco; honors: Vol. Fireman of Yr. 1968, Transylvania Univ. Athlete of Year 1964, Ky. St. Bar Assn. outstanding contbr. 1979, Transylvania Univ. Disting. Svc. Award 1994; mem: World Affairs Council, Internat. Women's Judges (adv. mem.), Libra Found. (adv. mem.) Buenos Aires, Argentina; civic: Commonwealth Club, 9th Circuit Hist. Soc. (bd. dirs.); publs: 2 law jour. articles (1979, 86); Bahai (treas. Nat. Spiritual Assembly of Bahai's of U.S.); rec: golf, travel. Res: 414 Bay Rd Menlo Park 94025

DAWES, DAVID FORD, land and development company president; b. July 29, 1909, Muskogee, Okla.; s. Maurice and Ethel (Ford) D.; m. Dorothy L. Snyder, Jan. 5, 1933; children: David Alan b. 1934, Stuart Edward b. 1936, Mary Lou b. 1943; edn: Okla. Univ. 1927-28; realtor 1945. Career: store mgr., salesman Safeway Stores 1931-37; milk route sales Golden Gate Creamery Long Beach 1938-39; salesman Automobile Club of So. Calif. 1939-42; personnel Northrup Aircraft Hawthorne 1942-45; realtor David Dawes Realty Torrance 1945-68; pres. Western Land & Devel. Co., pres. Am. Self Storage, Hawthorne; mem: Rancho Carlsbad Country Club 1969–, Calif. Assn. of Realtors (Hon. Life), Gardena Bd. Realtors (1956-69, pres. 1957, Realtor of Year 1962, Hon. Life), Carlsbad Bd. Realtors (pres. 1974), Hawthorne Bd. Realtors, Torrance Bd. Realtors, Masons (32 degree, Worshipful Master 1984), Scottish Rite, San Luis Rey Shrine Club (pres. 1994, past v.p.), Knights Templar, Rotary, Carlsbad Boys Club; secty., v.p. commr. San Diego County Flood Control 1975-80, Carlsbad Municipal Water Dist. Special Citizens Com. 1973-74. Republican; Prot.; rec: swimming, golf. Res: 3428 Don Juan Dr Carlsbad 92008 Ofc: Western Land & Devel. Co. 5200 El Camino Real 92008

DAWSON, CHANDLER ROBERT, physician; b. Aug. 24, 1930, Denver, Colo.; s. Irvin Milo and Helen (Quick) D.; m. Paula Whitlock Schilt, Oct. 2, 1954; children: Seth b. 1955, Ethan b. 1960, Matthew b. 1962; edn: BA, chemistry, Princeton Univ., 1952; MD, Yale Univ., 1956; cert. Am. Bd. of Ophthalmology, 1967. Career: intern N.C. Memorial Hosp., Univ. N.C., 1956-57; sr. asst. surgeon Ctrs. for Disease Control, USPHS Epidemiology Br., 1957-60; resident dept. ophthal. UC San Francisco 1960-63; spl. fellow Bland-Sutton Inst. of Pathology, Middlesex Hosp. Med. Sch., London 1963-64; res. fellow Francis I. Proctor Found. UCSF, 1959-63, asst. res. ophthalmologist 1964-66; asst. clin. prof., asst., assoc. prof. ophthalmology UC San Francisco 1963–, prof. ophthal. in residence 1975-85; co-dir. World Health Orgn. res. ctr. trachoma and prev. of blindness, Francis I. Proctor Found., UCSF, 1970-79, dir. 1979–; assoc. dir., 1970-84, dir. Francis I. Proctor Found. for Res. in Ophthal. UCSF, 1984–; cons. Div. of Indian Health, USPHS, 1965-80; cons. in ophthalmology Marine Hosp. (USPHS) S.F. 1979-84; cons. Pan Am. Health Orgn. 1966; cons. WHO 1966–; counsellor Internat. Orgn. against Trachoma 1974–; mem: NIH visual sci. study sect. 1974- 78 (chmn. 1976-78); mem. Am. Acad. Ophthal. (edn. com. 1974-75), AMA (pgm. com. 1974-77), Internat. Agy. for Prevention of Blindness (exec. bd. 1978–), Internat. Eye Found. (med. advy. bd. 1981–), Assn. for Res. in Vision and Ophthalmology, Ophthalmic Soc. of U.K., Electron Microscope Soc. No. Calif., Am. Soc. for Microbiology, AAAS; awards: Knapp Award 1969, AMA ophthal. sect. hon. mention for exhibit "Trachoma - still world's leading cause of preventable blindness" 1976, Medaille d'Or du Trachoma, La Ligue Contre le Trachome 1978, Am. Acad. of Ophthalmology Honor Award 1979and exhibit prize 1983; author, coauthor 200+ med. jour. articles, books and book chapters. Ofc: Francis I. Proctor Foundation for Research in Ophthalmology UCSF San Francisco 94143-0412

DAWSON, FRANCES EMILY, writer-poet, civic volunteer; b. Augsburg, Germany, Dec. 7, 1952; d. Emmett C. Jr. and B. Louise (Boddie) Dawson; edn: BSN, nursing, Penn State Univ., 1974; R.N., Dist. Col. Career: staff nurse Howard Univ. Med. Ctr., Wash. D.C., 1974-75, charge nurse 1975-77; model, Operation Confidence, Beauty Ind. Skilled Ctr. for Physically Challenged 1985-86; head cheerleader Disabled Drill Team 1985-86; recipient Golden Poetry award 1985-92, Excellence in Lit. award Pinewood Poetry, 1987, 88, 89, Merit Poet award APA, 1989, listed Who's Who in West, 1989, 91, 93, Who's Who in World 1990, 5000 Personalities of World 1991, 93, 95, 2000 Notable Am. Women 1990, 91; mem. Walt Whitman Guild, Detroit Black Poets Guild 1989, Internat. Soc. of Poets (hon. charter mem. 1993), Penn State Univ. Alumni Assn.; civic: mem. Long Beach Task Force for Ams. with Disabilities Act 1994–, Disabled Resource Ctr., Lupus Found. Am., Calif. Assn. Physically Handicapped; pub. poems include: Live for Today, 1986, With You In Mind, 1987, Reflections, 1988; Democrat; Baptist. Res: 315 West 3rd St #511 Long Beach 90802

DAY, LUCILLE ELIZABETH, educator, author; b. Dec. 5, 1947, Oakland; d. Richard Allen and Evelyn Marietta (Hazard) Lang; edn: A.B., UC Berkeley, 1971, M.A., 1973, Ph.D., 1979; m. Frank Lawrence Day, Nov. 6, 1965; children: Liana Sherrine; m. 2d. Theodore Herman Fleischman, June 23, 1974, (div. 1985); children: Tamarind Channah. Career: teaching asst., U.C., Berkeley, 1971-72, 75-76, research asst., 1975, 77-78; tchr. sci. Magic Mountain Sch.,

Berkeley, 1977; specialist math. and sci. Novato Unified Sch. Dist., 1979-81; instr. sci. Project Bridge, Laney Coll., Oakland, Calif., 1984-86; sci. writer and mgr. of precollege edn. programs Lawrence Berkeley Lab., 1986-90, life sciences staff coord. 1990-92; mgr. Hall of Health, Berkeley 1992–; honors: Phi Beta Kappa, Iota Sigma Pi, NSF Grad. fellow (1972-75), Joseph Henry Jackson award in lit. San Francisco Fdn. (1982); mem. Women in Communications, Nat. Assn. Sci. Writers, AAAS, No. Calif. Sci. Writers Assn.; publs: (w. Joan Skolnick and Carol Langbort) How to Encourage Girls in Math and Science: Strategies for Parents and Educators (1982), (collected poems) Self-Portrait with Hand Microscope (1982), numerous pub. poems, articles and book reviews; Res: 1057 Walker Ave Oakland CA 94610

DEADRICH, PAUL EDDY, lawyer, realtor (retired); b. Jan. 30, 1925, Lakeport, Ca.; s. John A. and Grace E. (Jackson) D.; m. Connie Washburn; children: Marjanne Robinson b. 1947, Nancy Wolfer b. 1950, Dianne Deadrich-Rogers b. 1952, Bettianne Buck b. 1955, John F. b. 1963, David b. 1968; edn: AA, UC Berkeley 1946; JD, Hastings Coll. of the Law 1949. Career: real estate sales agt., 1947-50; self-empl. attorney, San Leandro 1950-61; atty., realtor, ins. agt. in Twain Harte, 1961-73; law practice in Loomis 1973-75, in Cameron Park 1975-78; missionary at Apostolic Alliance Mission, Gibi, Liberia 1978-82; atty., realtor in San Leandro 1982-92; atty., Santa Clarita, Ca. 1992–; judge Justice Court, Tuolumne 1964-67; dir. Alameda Contra Costa Transit Dist. 1956-61; phys. edn. instr., coach Mother Lode Christian Sch., Tuolumne 1969-73; adminstr., coach, tchr. Loomis Christian Sch. 1974-75; dir. Calif. Conservatory Theatre 1988-91; past pres. Family Counseling Agy. of So. Alameda Co.; named Outstanding young man of year San Leandro Jr. Chamber 1955; mem: So. Alameda Co. Bd. of Realtors, Tuolumne Co. Bd. of Realtors (pres. 1973), So. Alameda Co. Bar Assn., DAV (past comdr. Chap. 67), Veterans Battle of the Bulge, 11th Armored Div. Assn., Am. Legion Post 117 (San Leandro), Sons in Retirement- Seven Hills; clubs: San Leandro Breakfast (pres. 1985-86) So. San Leandro Kiwanis (pres. 1985-86), Full Gospel Business Mens Fellowship Intl. (San Leandro chpt. pres. 1988-91, exec. v.p. 1983-86, dir. 1986-91), Twain Harte Rotary (pres. 1966-67), Broadmoor Mens (pres. 1958), Chabot Lions (pres. 1956-7), Twain Harte Hi-12 (past pres.), Loyal Order of Moose- Oakland, Clowns of Am. Internat.- Golden Gate (#80), East Belt Lodge F&AM No. 391, Cryptic Masons of CA Lodge No.5, Royal Arch Masons Chpt. 2, Kts. Templar of CA Commandery No.3, Old West Ch. 642 Order of Eastern Star; mil: pfc 11th Armored Div. WWII, France and Belgium, 1943-45, Bronze Star, Purple Heart, Combat Inf. Badge; Creation Missions Ch. (missionary in Liberia 1978-82); rec: gardening, fishing, backpacking. Res: 41440 30th St W, Palmdale 93551

DEAN, NAT, artist, educator; b. Jan. 13, 1956, Redwood City; d. Richard Wm. and Marianne Ridley (Smith) D.; m. Paul Singdahlsen, May 24, 1987; edn: att. Cooper Union 1975, Calif. Inst. of Arts 1973-76, BFA, San Francisco Art Inst. 1977. Career: profl. artist: paintings, sculptures, drawings and artists' books, 1970-, cons., lectr. various schs. and tchr. workshops nat., 1978-, dir. career devel. and planning Calif. Inst. of Arts, Valencia 1986-89, Ringling Sch. of Art & Design, Sarasota, Fla. 1989-92; travelling lectr. on "Artist Survival Skills & Business of Art" and owner, cons./counselor for "A.R.T.S.: Artist Resources & Tools for Survival" (a resource orgn.), 1978-; awards: Bemis Project artist in residence Omaha, NE (1986), best of show S.F. Art Inst. (1977); mem: NSIEE, CCEA, CPC, Center for Book Arts, Coll. Art Assn. Res: 32679 Seagate Dr #202 Rancho Palos Verdes 90274 Res/Studio: Sierra Azul Route 10 Box 94-N.D. Santa Fe NM 87501

DEAN, RICHARD MASON, educator, company president; b. Apr. 4, 1951, Pomona; s. Louis Mason and Mary Louise (Fandre) D.; edn: BS bus. mgt., Calif. State Polytech. Univ. 1974, BS econs. 1978, MSBA 1980, MS econs. 1984; Calif. Life Community Coll. tchg. credentials: bus. edn. 1978, bus. and indsl. mgmt. 1979, administrator 1986, economics, office and related technols., computer & related technols., profl. edn. (Life, 1985), clear single subject Bus. Edn. 1979 (life), Supp. Auth. Math. 1990; Lic. Pvt. Pilot 1988. Career: acct. Rowland Unified Sch. Dist., Rowland Hts. 1975-79; work experience coord. Chaffey Joint Union H.S. Dist., Ontario 1979-82; lectr. Mgmt. Human Resources Dept. Cal Poly Univ., Pomona 1982-85; tchr. Arroyo H.S., El Monte Unif. Sch. Dist. 1985–; pres. University Word Processing, Fullerton 1982–; cons. Gentek Corp., La Verne 1984; guest lectr. General Dynamics, Pomona 1984; cons. Houghton Mifflin Pub. Co., Boston 1984–; mem: Nat. Business Educators Assn., Calif. Bus. Educators Assn., Apartment Owners Assn.; sponsor Arroyo H.S. Info. Systems Club; publs: Easy Computations Software (for appls. in mktg., fin., acctg. and stats.), How to Program in B.A.S.I.C., Easy Librarian Software, (all copyrighted 1982); Republican; Congregational; rec: golf, skiing (snow, water), scuba, travel. Ofc: University Word Processing 2733 Pine Creek Circle Fullerton 92635-2936

DE BRE, ALVIN JACK, dentist; b. Mar. 29, 1922, Marshall, Tx.; s. Leon and Zelma (Sorkin) De B.; father born in Alsace-Lorraine, desc. House of Bre, Count 1600; m. Anita Derchan, Dec. 1, 1946 (div.); children: Greg b. 1950, Kevin b. 1960; m. 2d. Susan Solomon, June 15, 1980; edn: BS, Univ. Texas, Austin 1945; DDS, Univ. Texas Dental Sch., Houston 1945; lic. Calif. Bd. Dental Exam. 1952. Career: dental practice, 1952–; mem. Am. Dental Assn.,

Calif. Dental Assn. (bd. trustees 1962-71), Am. Coll. of Dentists (Fellow), L.A. County Dental Soc. (pres. 1965-66), Western Dental Soc./ L.A. (pres. 1964-65); active num. civic coms., past pres. Sherman Oak Homeowners (1955-58), mem. Calif. Country Club Homeowners (pres. 1986-88); clubs: Elks, Masons, Shriners, Beverly Hills CC; publs: several profl. articles and dental clinics; mil: ltcdr. USNR 1945-60, WWII; Republican; Jewish; rec: photography, tropical fish, tennis. Ofc: Alvin J. De Bre, DDS, 7060 Hollywood Blvd Ste 412 Hollywood 90028

DEBRIE, CAROL JEAN (PERALTA), nurse; b. Apr. 14, 1955, Encino, Calif.; d. Harold Richard Wallinger and Beverly Jean (Tuckett) DiDonato; m. Jimmy Lee Peralta, Jan. 19, 1974 (div. Feb. 14, 1985); m. Glen Ray DeBrie, June 15, 1991 (div. Apr. 28. 1993); children: Seth James Peralta b. 1976, Shelbi Jean Peralta b. 1978, Aubrie Anna Peralta b. 1981; edn: diploma, AA Stagg H.S., Stockton, Calif.; assoc. degree, San Joaquin Delta Coll., Stockton; BSN prog., CSU, Dominguez Hills. Career: staff nurse ICU, SJGH, French Camp, Calif. 1986-90. LaSalette Conv., Stockton, Calif. 1990: venipuncture RN, Delta Blood Bank, Stockton 1990-91; utilization review coord., Interplan, Stockton 1991; nsg. supr., CarePoint/HSSI, Stockton 1991-93; dir. of clinical svs. Agostini & Assoc., Stockton 1993–; PRN Registry, home visit nurse 1989-91; Certified Birth Educator, Babes; CPR instr., Amer. Heart Assn.; HHA certification instr. 1993; staff nurse, ICU Doctors Hosp., Manteca, Calif. 1990-94; nurse cons., PCA, Stockton 1994; awards: Volunteer of the Year, Amer. Cancer Soc., Stockton 1989; mem: bd. of dirs. ACS 1987-88; vol., ACS 1987–; vol., ADA 1989–; Republican. Res: 2352 Polk Way Stockton 95207

DEBS, JOHN FREDERICK, investor/dentist; b. June 26, 1937, Los Angeles; s. John Nickola and Bathie (Joseph) D.; m. Anne Louise Russell, July 1961; children: Anthony David b. 1962, Julianna Marie Purner b. 1964; edn: BS, Loyola Univ., 1959; DDS, Creighton Univ., 1962; cert. DDS Calif. St. Bd. of Dental Examiners. Career: lt.-lcdr. United States Navy Dental Corp., Camp Pendleton, Calif. 1962-64, Taipei (Taiwan) 1964-67; assoc. dentist Douglas B. Ryan, DDS, Santa Ana 1967-71; gen. practice dentist San Clemente Medical Plaza 1971–; founder, cons. Mission Valley Bank, San Clemente 1981–; adj. prof. Nat. Taiwan Univ., Taipei (Taiwan) 1965-67; mem: Am. Dental Assn., Calif. Dental Assn., Orange Co. Dental Assn., Newport Harbor Acad. of Dentistry, San Clemente C.of C. (bd. dirs.), Lions Club (secty. 1973, v.p. 1974, pres. 1975); mil: colonel U.S. Army Reserves, 1954–, Army Achievement Award 1982, Meritorious Service Medal 1986; Republican; R.Cath.; rec: reading, history.

DE CAMPLI, WILLIAM MICHAEL, physician, cardiovascular surgeon; b. Dec. 7, 1951, Allentown, Pa.; s. William J. and Bernadine Laura (Diehl) DeCampli; m. Kristi Lynn Peterson, M.D., May 27, 1989; edn: BS, MIT 1973, PhD Harvard 1978; MD, Univ. Miami 1982. Career: Chaim Weizman Fellow in theoretical astrophysics, Caltech 1978-80; Carl and Leah McConnell Fellow in cardiovascular physiology, Stanford Medical Center, Stanford 1984-85, chief resident in general surgery 1987-88, Fellow in peripheral vascular surgery 1988-89, Fellow in cardiovascular surgery 1989-92; Diplomate Am. Bd. of Surgery 1989 and Am. Bd. of Thoracic Surgery 1993; pediatric cardiac surgeon Children's Hospital, Oakland, Calif.; cons. Nat. Acad. of Scis., Wash., D.C. 1985-86; mem. NASA Life Scis. Strategic Planning subcom. 1985-88, NASA Space Station Sci. & Applications subcom. 1988-89; mem: Am. Coll. of Surgeons, Am. Coll. of Chest Physicians, N.Y. Acad. of Scis., Sigma Xi Research Soc.; author or coauthor papers in fields of astronomy, astrophysics, cardiovascular physiology, pediatric cardiac surgery; rec: PADI rescue scuba diver, AA cert. parachutist. Ofc:Center for Cardiac Surgery 2500 Milvia Ave Berkeley 94704

DE CIUTIIS, ALFRED C.M., physician, television producer; b. Oct. 16, 1946, N.Y.C.; s. Alfred Ralph and Theresa Elizabeth (Manko) de C. (the deCiutiis family was first ranked among the nobles of Italy in 893 AD, designated princely family and titled Princes of the Holy Roman Empire in 1629); m. Catherine L. Gohn, Aug. 31, 1987; edn: BS (summa cum laude), Fordham Univ., 1967; MD, Columbia Univ., 1971; Dipl. Am. Bd. Int. Medicine (ABIM), Am. Bd. Med. Oncology. Career: intern N.Y. Hosp. Cornell Med. Ctr., NYC 1971-72, resident 1972-74; fellow clin. immunology Memorial Hosp. Sloan Kettering Cancer Ctr. 1974-75, fellow clin. oncology 1975-76, spl. fellow in immunology 1974-76; guest investigator, asst. physician exptl. hematology Rockefeller Univ., 1975-76; med. practice, splst. in med. oncology, Los Angeles 1977–; producer num. med. TV shows; host cable TV shows, 1981–, med. editor Cable Health Network, 1983–, Lifetime Network 1984–; mem. med. advy. com. 1984 Olympics; co-founder Meditrina Med. Ctr., free out-patient surg. ctr., Torrance; syndicated columnist Coast Media News "The Subject is Cancer" 1980s; awards: Phi Beta Kappa, Alpha Omega Alp[ha, Sigma Xi, Mensa, Leukemia Soc. Am. fellow 1974-76, NY State Regents scholar (1963-67, 67-71), AMA Physicians Recogn. (1978-80, 82-85, 86-89, 89-91, 91-94), Proclamation Calif. State Senate Rules Com. 1982; mem. Fgn. Policy Leadership Proj. The Ctr. for Internat. Affairs, Harvard Univ.; mem: Am. Coll. Physicians (Fellow), Internat. Coll. Physicians and Surgeons (Fellow), AMA, Am. Union Physicians and Dentists, Am. Soc. Clin. Oncology, NY Acad. Sci. (life), CMA, LA Co. Med. Assn., Internat. Health Soc., Am. Pub. Health Assn., AAAS, Am. Geriatrics Soc., Chinese Med. Assn., Drug Info. Assn., Am. Soc. Hematology (emeritus mem.), Nat. Geog.

Soc., Internat. Platform Assn.; civic: Italian-Am. Med. Assn. (founder 1982), Italian-Am. Med. Legal Alliance LA (co-founder 1982–), Italian-Am. Civic Com. L.A. 1983, Italian-Am. Found. (gov. bd. med. coun.), UCLA Chancellor's Assocs., Cath. League for Civil and Rel. Liberty, Nature Conservancy, Nat. Wildlife Fedn., World Affairs Council LA, Am. Coll. Heraldry Confedn. Chivalry, Fondazione Giovanni Agnelli, Smithsonian Instn. (assoc.), Boston Mus. Fine Arts, Met. Mus.; publs: author first clinical comprehensive description of Chronic Fatigue Syndrome as a neuro-immunologic disorder probably caused by a retrovirus with multi-system complications (Audio Digest Internal Med. Vol. 37 #21, 11/90), extensive bibliography, contbr. num. articles to profl. jours.; mil: capt. Med. Corps US Army 1972-74; Republican; R.Cath.; rec: collecting, reading, hunting, fishing, astronomy. Res: 32062 1/2 Lobo Canyon Agoura Hills 91301 Tel: 818/706-3308

DECKER, PATRICIA ANNE, television news videotape editor; b. Mar. 23, 1956, Blackwell, Okla.; d. Otto and Elfriede Maria (Schaul) Decker; m. Fabian Victor Rodriguez, July 9, 1983; edn: BA in communications, Univ. N.Mex., 1979. Career: news intern Sta. KOB-TV, Albuquerque, 1979, news videotape editor, 1979-81; TV and news videotape editor Sta. KABC-TV, Hollywood, Calif. 1982–; honors: Alpha Chi Omega (chapt. v.p. 1978-79); mem. NABET; Republican. Res: 422-B E Harvard Rd Burbank 91501 Ofc: Sta KABC-TV 4151 Prospect Ave Hollywood 90027

DECKER, PHILIP E., lawyer; b. June 17, 1943, Montclair, N.J.; s. Everett N. and Mary E. (Davey) D.; m. Judith S., June 18, 1968; dau., Christina M. b. 1980; edn: AB (honors pgm., Great Distinction), UC Berkeley, 1969; JD, Boalt Hall Sch. of Law UC Berkeley, 1972; admitted Calif. State Bar, U.S. Dist. Ct. (No. Dist. Calif.), U.S. Ct. Appeals (9th Cir.), 1974. Career: atty., San Jose 1974–; judge pro tem Santa Clara County Superior Ct. 1986–; apptd. (first Public Member appointee) Contractor's State License Bd., St. Calif., 1976-80; chmn. Mayor's Task Force on Condominiums, 1976; co-founder Pub. Interest Law Ctr., San Francisco, 1972, and Pub. Interest Res. Ctr., Berkeley, 1971; honors: Phi Beta Kappa; mem: Calif. Trial Lawyers Assn., Santa Clara Co. Bar Assn., Santa Clara Co. Trial Lawyers Assn., Marin Co. Bar Assn., Exec. Council of Homeowners, S.J. (pres. 1977, bd. dirs. and chmn. Legal Resource Panel), Inverness Yacht Club, Sports Car Club Am., I.M.S.A.; author: Moving in California: A Hard Way to Go (P.I.R.C., 1972); lectr. and author - construction law, condominium law, consumer protection law, 1972–; rec: gardening, auto racing. Law Offices of Philip E. Decker, P.C., 50 W San Fernando St 13th Flr San Jose 95113

DEDEAUX, PAUL J., orthodontist; b. Feb. 22, 1937, Pass Christian, Miss.; s. Mack and Harriet D.; m. Janet Louise Harter, June 29, 1971; children: Michele b. 1965, Kristen b. 1980, Kelly b. 1983; edn: BA, Dillard Univ., 1959; DDS, Howard Univ., 1963; MS, Farleigh Dickinson Univ., 1975. Career: instr. Howard Univ., Wash. D.C. 1967-69; program planner Dr. Martin Luther Kind Center, Bronx, N.Y. 1969-70, actg. dental dir. 1969-70; assoc. prof. Columbia Univ., N.Y.C. 1970-72; pub. health dentist Martin Luther King Center, Bronx, N.Y. 1969-73; cons. Hostos Comm. Coll. 1970-78; orthodontist pvt. practice, Santa Ana 1978-93; chief dentist Calipatria State Prison, Calipatria, Calif. 1993-; honors: Who's Who in E., Who's Who Among Black Americans, Notable Americans; mem: Am. Assn. Orthodontist, Pacific Coast Soc. Orthodontist, ADA, Calif. Dental Assn., Assn. Mil. Surgeons of U.S.; articles pub. in profl. jours., 1970-77; mil: col. USAR 1963-; Democrat; Methodist; rec: photog., fishing. Res: 12181 Anzio St Garden Grove 92640 Ofc: Calipatria State Prison PO Box 5001 Calipatria 92233

DEEDWANIA, PRAKASH C., physician, medical administrator, educator; b. Aug. 28, 1948, Ajmer, India; s. Gokul C. and Paras (Garg) D.; m. Catherine E.; children: Anne, Ravi, David; edn: pre-med. Univ. of Rajasthan 1963, MD (honors in pharmacol.), 1969; Diplomate in internal med. 1975, pulmonary 1976, and cardiol. 1977, ABIM. Career: rotating intern, postgrad. res. in medicine J.L.N. Med. Coll. Hosp. Center, Ajmer, India 1970-71; med. intern Coney Is. Hosp./Maimonides Med. Ctr., Bklyn. 1971-72; med. res. VA Med. Ctr., Bronx/Mt. Sinai Sch. of Med., N.Y. 1972-73, chief res. 1973-75; cardiol. fellow Univ. of Ill. Abraham Lincoln Sch. of Med., Chgo. 1975-76, sr. res. fellow in cardiology 1976-77; supv. att. phys. St. Joseph's Hosp., N.Y. 1973-75, Weiss Meml. Hosp., Chgo. 1975-77; cons. in cardiology and pulmonary Bd. of Health, Chgo. 1976-77; chief Cardiology, VA Med. Center/Univ. of Va., Salem 1977-78; dir. Non-Invasive Lab VAMC/Univ. of Ill., Chgo. 1978-80, also dir. Electrophysiology and co-dir. Critical Care Unit; chief Dept. Cardiology and dir. Coronary Care Unit, VAMC/UCSF Sch. of Med., Fresno 1980–, clin. prof. medicine UC San Francisco, 1988–; lectr. in var. areas of cardiovascular disorders at hosps. in the UCSF Med. Edn. Pgm. and comm. hosps.; vis. prof., faculty num. internat. med. confs. and seminars; honors: Dean's List, Govt. Coll., Kota, India 1963-64 and J.L.N. Med. Coll. 1968-69, recipient num. res. awards 1973-94; mem: Am. Coll. of Chest Physicians (fellow 1977), Am. Coll. of Physicians (fellow 1978), Am. Coll. of Cardiol. (fellow 1978), Am. Heart Assn. Clin. Coun. Cardio. (fellow 1978), Am. Fedn. of Clin. Res., The N.Y. Acad. of Sci.; num. publs. in med. jours. 1975–; rec: study of cultures, photog., travel, pen pals. Ofc: VA Medical Center 2615 East Clinton Fresno 93703

DEETS, DWAIN AARON, aeronautical research engineering manager; b. Apr. 16, 1939, Bell, Calif.; s. Kenneth Robert and Mildred E. (Bergman) D.; m. Catherine Elizabeth Meister, June 18, 1961; children: Dennis, Danelle; edn: AB in physics, Occidental Coll., 1961; MS physics, San Diego St. Univ., 1964; ME, UCLA, 1978. Career: research engr. NASA, Edwards 1961-78; laison mgr. NASA Hq., Wash. DC 1978-79; flight controls mgr. NASA Dryden, Edwards 1979-86, dep., 1986-88, 89-90, chief research engring. div. 1990–, mgr. flight research NASA Hq., Wash. DC 1988-89; awards: Wright Brothers lectr. in aeronautics Am. Inst. of Aeronautics & Astronautics, Wash. DC 1987, exceptional service medal NASA, Wash. DC 1988; mem: AIAA (assoc. fellow; mem. soc. and aerospace technology tech. com. 1990–), Soc. of Automative Engrs. (chmn. aerospace control and guidance sys. com. 1988-90); lodge: Masonic; publs: 20+ tech. papers re aero. flt. controls (1966-87); Republican; Christian. Res: 769 E Oldfield St Lancaster 93535 Ofc: NASA Ames-Dryden POB 273 Edwards 93523-5000

DE FONVILLE, PAUL BLISS, western history museum and library administrator; b. Mar. 3, 1923, Oakland, Calif.; s. Marion Yancy and Charlotte (Bliss) de F.; m. Virginia Harpell, June 17, 1967; edn: Calif. St. Poly. Univ., S.L.O., 1942-44; Michael Chekhov Group, Hollywood, 1947-52. Career: cowboy various ranches Calif., 1926-52; film actor, Hollywood, 1947–; artist, prin., L.A., 1957-73; pres., Alexandria Coeur de Lion, L.A., 1969-80; founder, pres., adminstr., Cowboy Meml. and Lib. (a museum), Caliente, 1980–; instr. outdoor edn. CSU Bakersfield, 1980; mem. Rep. Presdl. Task Force 1984–, Rep. Senatorial. Inner Circle. 1989–, Nat. Com. 1987, Nat. Rep. Congl. Com. 1990, US Senatorial Club 1988–, Calif. Rep. Assembly 1990–, Rep. Senatorial Commn. 1991; awards: Slim Pickens award Calif. State Horsemen, 1980; Marshall Working Western award Rose Parade Pasadena, 1980; County of Kern Recognition, 1984; Proclamation of Mayors of Bakersfield, 1984, 85; Proclamation Gov. of Calif., 1984; St. of Calif. recognition for Walker Basin Resolution 008, 1987; Senate Resolution No. 914, 1988; Calif. Legislative Assembly Resolution No. 2681; Presdl. Order of Merit, 1991; Congl. Cert. of Merit, 1992; Rep. Presdl. Legion of Merit, 1992; Hon. Marshall Lake Isabella Christmas Parade 1993; Presdl. Commn. on Am. Agenda -The Presdl. Trust 1992, Delegate 1992; Rep. Nat. Com. Cert. of Recognition 1992; Nat. Rep. Senatorial Com. Presdl. Commn. 1992; Rep. Nat. Hall of Honor 1992; Rep. Presdl. Advy. Commn. Cert. of Award 1993; Congl. Cert. of Appreciation 1993; Wash. Legal Found. Cert. of Commendation 1993; Internat. Man of Yr. 1993-94; ABI (fellow, dep. gov. 1993); Internat. Directory of Disting. Leadership Hall of Fame 1993; Internat. Biog. Ctr. Life Mem. (fellow, patron 1993), Internat. Order of Merit 1993; Biog. Honor Award 1993; 20th Century Award of Achievement 1993; Most Admired Man of Yr. 1993; Rep. Congl. Order of Liberty 1993; Most Admired Man of Decade 1994; Rep. Presdl. Award 1994; Medal of Freedom 1994; listed Who's Who in Rep. Party 1990, Who's Who in West 1992, Who's Who in America-Index 1992-93, Who's Who in America 1993-94, Men of Achievement 1993, Internat. Who's Who of Intellectuals 1993, First Five Hundred 1993, Five Hundred Leaders of Influence 1994; mem: Calif. State Horsemen (life), Equestrian Trails Inc. (life), Forty Niners (life), PRO Rodeo Cowboys Assn. Colo. (Gold Card holder #480), Turtles and Rodeo Cowboys Assn. (life); Baptist; rec: Heritage, horses, cowboys, mountain men, Indians. Res/Ofc: 40371 Cowboy Ln Caliente 93518

DE GARMO, E. PAUL, emeritus professor of mechanical and industrial engineering; b. Jan. 29, 1907, Lucerne, Mo.; s. Arthur and Editha (Snider) DeG.; m. Mary Elizabeth Turner, Dec. 26, 1934; children: Richard b. 1938, David b. 1942; edn: BS, Univ. Wash., 1930; MS, Calif. Inst. of Tech., 1937; reg. profl. engr., mech., indsl., Calif. (1949, 1967). Career: engr. Converse Co. Inc., Seattle 1930-31; engr. Firestone Tire & Rubber, Los Angeles 1934-37; prof. indsl. engring. and mech. engring., UC Berkeley, 1937-72, emeritus prof. 1972–; indep. cons. engr., Berkeley 1940-85; U.S. AID mission Japan, 1962; guest prof. Korea Advanced Inst. of Sci., 1975; honors: Lincoln Gold Medal Am. Welding Soc. 1948, Phi Beta Kappa, Sigma Xi, Alpha Pi Mu, Fellow Inst. Industrial Engrs. 1966–, mem. ASME, Am. Welding Soc. (life), Am. Soc. for Metals; coauthor 3 texts: Technical Lettering (2 eds 1941, 1943), Engineering Economy (7 eds 1942–), Materials & Processes in Manufacturing (7 eds), contbr. numerous engring. papers; Republican; Prot.; rec: woodworking. Res: 1860 Tice Creek Dr #1302 Walnut Creek 94595

DEGOLIA, RICHARD C., JR., lawyer; b. May 12, 1950, Cincinnati, Ohio; s. Richard Case and Sallie (Van Dyke) DeG.; m. Jennifer Howard, June 12, 1983; children: Alexander b. 1985, Benjamin b. 1987; edn: BA, UC Berkeley 1981; JD, Harvard Law Sch. 1985. Career: member Wilson Sonsini Goodrich & Rosati, Palo Alto 1984–; honors: Phi Beta Kappa; mem: Am. Bar Assn., Calif. Bar Assn., Santa Clara Co. Bar Assn., Wilderness Soc., Sierra Club Legal Defense Fund; Independent; Episcopalian; rec: wilderness exploration, wine. Ofc: Wilson Sonsini Goodrich & Rosati, PC, 650 Page Mill Road Palo Alto 94304

DEGRAVE, DOUGLAS MICHAEL, lawyer; b. May 23, 1954, Rochester, N.Y.; s. Gorman Joseph and Elaine (Best) DeG.; m. Deborah Jean Horn, Jan. 11, 1975; children: Jacob b. 1978, Jennifer b. 1982, Joshua b. 1987; edn: AS in crim. justice, Univ. Hawaii, 1976; BA pol. sci., CSU Long Beach, 1978; JD,

Loyola Univ. L.A., 1981; admitted bar Calif. 1981, US Dist. Ct. cent. dist. Calif. 1982, so. dist. Calif. 1985, US Ct. Appeal 9th cir. 1986, US Supreme Ct. 1987. Career: atty., assoc. Stockdale, Peckham & Werner, Tustin 1981-86; ptnr. Behrens, Recht, Finley & Hanley, Santa Ana 1986-87; ptnr. Parker, Stanbury, Babcock, Combs & Bergsten, 1987–; cons., guest spkr. Orange Co. Adj. Assoc. Orange, 1981–; honors: Pres.'s List CSULB 1976-78, Dean's List Loyola Univ. 1978-81, staff, ed. Entertainment Law Jour. 1979-81, Scott Moot Ct. honors pgm. 1980-81, co-winner trial advocacy comp. 1981; mem: Am. Bd. of Trial Advocates, Assn. of S. Calif. Defense Counsel, Internat. Assn. of Defense Counsel, Defense Res. Inst., Phi Alpha Delta law frat.; civic: YMCA Orange (dir., v.p. 1986-89), Indian Guides/Princess (chief 1984-85, 89-90, 93-95), Orange Junior Soccer Club (coach 1982-90, v.p. 86-87, pres. 87-88, chmn. bd. 89-91), Little League (mgr. 1993–); contbr. 3 articles pub. in law jours.; mil: sp4 AUS 1973-76; Republican; R.Cath.; rec: golf, scuba diving. Res: 369 Jennifer Ln Orange 92669 Ofc: 888 N Main St 7th Flr Santa Ana 92701

DEIBEL, FARRELL LEE, aerospace engineer; b. Sept. 22, 1959, Paris, France; s. Karl Edward and Sandra Sue (Jackson) D.; m. Karlyn, June 23, 1984; children: Taylor b. 1988, Brent b. 1990, Riley b. 1992; edn: BS, Calif. Polytech. St. Univ. 1981; MS, USC, 1987; MSME, USC, 1990; lic. profl. mech. engr. Calif. 1985. Career: engr. Garrett Corp., 1979-80; tech. staff Hughes Aircraft Co. 1981-85, staff engr. 1985-90, sr. staff engr. 1990–; cons. Sigma Power, Carson 1987-88; honors: Tau Beta Pi, Phi Kappa Phi, Who's Who Am. H.S. Students, Nat. Merit Hon. Mention; 2 articles pub. in tech. jours. (1986, 87); Republican; Presbyterian; rec: basketball, bowling. Ofc: Hughes Aircraft 3100 W Lomita Blvd Torrance 90509

DELANEY, MARION PATRICIA, advertising executive; b. May 20, 1952, Hartford, Conn.; d. William Pride Delaney and Marian Patricia (Utley) Murphy; edn: BA, Union Coll., 1973. Career: acct. exec. Foote, Cone & Belding, N.Y.C., 1974-78; senior acct. exec. Dailey & Assocs., Los Angeles 1978-81; prin., Marnie Delaney Public Relations, L.A. 1981-83; acct. supr. BBDO/West, L.A. 1983-85; v.p., mgmt. supr. Grey Advt., L.A., S.F., 1985-89; sr. v.p., group acct. dir. McCann-Erickson, San Francisco 1989–; bd. dirs. JED Found. 1991–, Easter Seals Soc./Bay Area 1995–; Democrat; Congregationalist.

DELAURENTIS, ROCCO EUGENE, company founder; b. May 10, 1919, Shelton, Conn.; s. Rocco Joseph and Flora (Bianco) DeL.; m. Marion Ruth Youngblood, Oct. 5, 1959; children: Robin b. 1960; edn: Stone Bus. Coll. 1940; Balboa Coll. 1950; San Diego City Coll. 1952-56. Career: balancer and vibrations USN Repair, San Diego 1950-58; Calif. Elec. Works 1958-80; chmn. Rocky's Balancing Inc. 1980- ; instr. San Diego City Coll. 1960-65; IBEW 1965-67; awards: Shrine plaque (1986, 87), Defense Mfrs. cert. 1988; one of the first to play with a `Frisbe' recorded in the 1939 yearbook of Shelton (Conn.) H.S., the football team that yr. were called "Pie-Eaters" because they ate Frisbe Pie Co. pies (then only 10 cents) during lunch break & then played catch with the `Frisbe' pie plates; mem. IBEW (pres. motor shop div. 1972-78); Shriners (pres. 1986, 87), Masons (master 1987), San Diego Marine Square Club (pres. 1990), Order Ea. Star (patron 1990), Book Publicists of San Diego, VFW (trustee 1947-49), Am. Legion; author: Laughing & Griping with 97th Seabees, columnist Corp. News 1970-76, Past Masters 1989–, inventor of safety device (1955); mil: USN 1942-47; Lutheran; rec: golf, writing. Res: 3476 Mt Aachen Ave San Diego 92111 Ofc: Rocky's Balancing, Inc. 2525 Southport Way F National City 92050

DELL, OWEN EUGENE, landscape architect and contractor; b. Nov. 20, 1950, Chicago, Ill.; s. Arthur Joseph and Irene Anna (Williams) D.; edn: Santa Barbara City Coll. 1971-73. Career: owner County Landscape & Design, Santa Barbara 1972–; instr. Santa Barbara Botanic Gardens 1988–, UC Santa Barbara 1989-90; founder, chmn. Firescape Garden 1983–; awards: Calif. Landscape Contractors Assn. 1st residential landscape 1983, 2d. specialties 1984, 1st hardscape 1986, 1st xeriscape (statewide) 1991; mem: Calif. Landscape Contractors Assn. (pres. 1983-84, bd. dirs. 1981-90, profl. review com. 1983–, co-chair state edn. com. 1984-86), South Coast Landscape Water Mgmt. Task Force, Santa Barbara City Coll. Landscape Horticulture Advy. Com.; author: How To Open & Operate a Home-Based Landscaping Business, profl. jour. articles (1988–), non-tech. writings pub. in The Sun, Brussels Sprout (a haiku jour.), others; Democrat; rec: nature, sports, photography, writing/poetry. Ofc: County Landscape & Design PO Box 30433 Santa Barbara 93130

DELLUMS, RONALD V., congressman; b. Nov. 24, 1935, Oakland; m. Leola Roscoe Higgs; 3 children; edn: AA, Oakland City Coll. 1958; BA, San Francisco State Coll. 1960; M.S.W., Univ. of Calif. 1962. Career: psychiatric social worker Calif. Dept. Mental Hygiene 1962-64; program dir. Bayview Comm. Ctr., San Francisco 1964-65; from assoc. dir. to dir. Hunters Point Youth Opportunity Ctr. 1965-66; planning cons. Bay Area Social Planning Council 1966-67; dir. concentrated employment prog. San Francisco Econ. Opportunity Council 1967-68; sr. cons. Social Dynamics Inc. 1968-70; mem. 92nd-103rd Congresses form 9th Calif. Dist.; chmn. house com. on D.C. 1979-92, chmn house armed svs. com. 1992-94, ranking minority mem. house com. on nat. security 1995–; lectr. S.F. State Coll., UC Berkeley; mem. U.S. Del. North

Atlantic Group; mem. Berkeley City Council 1967-71; author: Defense Sense: The Search For A Rational Military Policy, 1983; mil: USMCR 1954-56; Democrat. Ofc: U.S. House of Representatives 2108 Rayburn House Office Bldg Washington DC 20515

DELONG, MARY KATHERINE, artist, designer, writer; b. July 25, 1917, Kansas City, Mo.; d. Harvey Alvaro and Katherine Pearl (Ruble) DeLong; m. Frank Basil Haylock, July 6, 1935 (div. 1967); children: David Gordon b. 1938, Douglas Gregory b. 1939, Susan Elizabeth Parma b. 1943, Jonathan Michael b. 1946; 4 grandchildren; edn: student, Baker Univ., Baldwin, Kans. 1933-34; AA (cum laude), interior design, Fashion Inst. of Design & Merchandising, San Francisco 1985. Career: founding dir., Young Horizons Nursery Sch. with Dr. Benjamin Spock as cons. pediatrician; adminstrv. asst., media buyer, and printing prod. supr. for Frank Haylock (mktg. cons. in electronics and sci. instrumentation); assoc. editor, Grid (monthly pub. of S.F. section of IRE, then IEEE); editor, monthly pub. for Women's Assn. of Electronic Industry; founder, prin., DeLong Properties, San Mateo and Marin County 1977-91; charter mem. WAEI; mem: San Francisco Quilters Guild (served on design team for S.F. Peace Quilt for Leningrad, now St. Petersburg, Russia), San Mateo-Burlingame Bd. of Realtors, Marin Assn. of Realtors, Am. Bus. Women's Assn., Navy League, ASID (student mem.), Mensa, San Mateo Co. Human Relations Commn. (commr.), Com. on Race, Religion and Social Concern (co-chmn. for peace and world order), Samaritan House, San Mateo (co-founder and bd. mem.), Sister City Assn., Phoenix on the Hill (founder and chmn. of bd.), Citizens' Com. for Student Affairs, Red Cross; designer, num. church banners and altar frontals; Republican; Episcopalian (lic. lay reader, choir singer). Res: 515 San Rafael Ave #3C Belvedere 94920

DE LORCA, LUIS, educator/program developer, professional speaker; b. Oct. 18, 1959, Los Angeles; s. Naomi (Rodriguez) Garcia; m. Lori Ann Vanzant, Mar. 23, 1991; edn: AA, Rio Hondo Comm. Coll., Whittier, 1983; BA, Calif. St. Poly Univ., Pomona, 1989. Career: lifeguard Los Angeles City Rec. Dept., 1980-87; high sch. football coach various schs. So. Calif., 1980–; pres. Exclusive Concepts, Los Angeles, 1987-89; pub. rels. dir. Cal Poly Pomona Music Dept. 1987-89; English tchr. Cathedral High Sch., L.A. 1989-90; resource specialist Special Edn., Whittier High Sch., 1990–; elementary sch. tchr. St. Paul of the Cross 1993-95; founder, director The Learning Advantage Ctr., Whittier 1991–; CEO, New Educational Wave Corp., Whittier 1993; founder Homework Club, Whittier H.S., 1990–; founder So. Calif. Latino Students Assn., Pomona, 1987-88; civic: Greenpeace, Fair Housing 1983–, Cousteau Soc., Big Brothers of Am. 1979-81, Operation Share 1977-81; Democrat; Unity; rec: scuba, martial arts, coaching, swimming, handball, skiing. Res: 9427 Tarryton St Whittier 90605

DEL PIERO, MARC JEFFREY, lawyer, state board official; b. Jan. 6, 1953, Watsonville; s. Richard Domenic and Patricia Ann (Borcovich) Del P.; m. Tina Tomlinson, Jan. 6, 1979; children: Paul Richard b. 1984, John George b. 1988; edn: BA, Univ. Santa Clara, 1975, JD, Univ. Santa Clara Sch. Law, 1978; admitted Calif. St. Bar, 1980. Career: atty. pvt. practice, Salinas 1980–; bd. mem. Calif. State Water Resources Control Bd., Sacramento 1992–; elected Monterey Co. Bd. Suprs., 1981-92, v.chmn. Monterey Co. Plng. Commn. 1978-80, v.chmn. Monterey Co. Transp. Commn. 1982-83, chmn. Monterey Bay Unified Air Pollution Control Dist. 1985, chmn. Monterey Co. Agric. and Hist. Lands Conservancy 1984-86, State Dredging Coord. Calif. Environmental Protection Agy.,hearing ofcr. Nat. Audubon Soc and The Com. to Save Mono Lake v. the L.A. Dept. of Water and Power; mem. Assn. Monterey Bay Area Govts. 1981, 85, Monterey Co. Flood Control & Water Conserv. Dist. 1981–, San Felipe Div. Com. (Cent. Water Proj.) 1981–, chmn. Local Agy. Formation Commn. 1981–; awards: honors scholar Univ. Santa Clara 1971-73, Calif. State scholar 1971-75, Who's Who in Am. Univs. 1975; mem: Calif. Bar Assn., Mont. Co. Bar Assn., County Suprs. Assn. Calif., Rotary Castroville (pres. 1986-87), Eagles; mil: capt. Calif. Army Nat. Guard 1978-89; Republican; Cath.; rec: swimming, fishing. Res: 11765 Tam O'Shanter Dr Salinas 93906 Ofc: State Water Resources Control Board PO Box 100 Sacramento 95814

DE LUCHI, STEPHEN F., oral and maxillofacial surgeon; b. May 11, 1952, Alameda; s. Frank S. De L.; edn: BS, UC Berkeley 1974; BS, DDS, UCSF 1978; cert. 1978-79, 1979-82. Career: clin. instr. UCSF 1978-85; pvt. practice oral surgery, San Francisco 1982-92; cons. 1992-94; mem: Am. Assn. Oral & Maxillofacial Surgeons (fellow), Guardsmen S.F.; Republican; Catholic; rec: golf. Ofc: PO Box 193055 San Francisco 94119-3055

DEMANES, DAVID JEFFREY, physician; b. Apr. 14, 1948, Champaign, Ill.; s. Floyd A. and Eve (Douquet) D.; edn: BA, zoology, UC Berkeley 1970; MD, UCLA 1974. Career: dir. Calif. Endocurietherapy Med. Corp. 1981–. Ofc: California Endocurietherapy Medical Corporation 365 34th St Oakland 94609 Tel: 510/658-9824

DE MASSA, JESSIE G., media specialist; edn: BS in journ., Temple Univ., Phila.; MLS, CSU San Jose, 1967; postgrad. Univ. Okla., USC, others. Career: tchr. Palo Alto Unified Sch. Dist., 1966; librarian Antelope Valley Joint Union High Sch. Dist., Lancaster 1966-68, ABC Unified Sch. Dist., Artesia 1968-72; dist. librarian Tehachapi Unified Sch. Dist., 1972-81, also media splst.; free lance writer, 1981–; Fellow Internat. Biog. Assn.; mem. Calif. Media and Library Educators Assn., Calif. Assn. Sch. Librarians (exec. council), AAUW (bull. editor, assoc. ed. state bulletin), Nat. Writer's Club, Women's Roundtable of Orange County; civic: charter supporter U.S. Holocaust Mem. Mus., W.D.C., Statue of Liberty, Ellis Island Found. Inc. (1988), Nat. Mus. of Women in the Arts (charter 1988), Hon. Fellows of John F. Kennedy Lib. (founding mem.); publs: articles in profl. jours. Res: 9951 Garrett Circle, Huntington Beach 92646

DE MET, EDWARD MICHAEL, neurochemist, educator, consultant; b. July 27, 1949, Elmhurst, Ill.; s. Michael Constantine and Elvira Linnea (Franson) DeM.; m. Aleksandra Chicz, Oct. 22, 1983; edn: student Ill. Inst. of Tech., Chgo. 1963-66, AS, Harper Coll., Palatine, Ill. 1969; BS, Univ. Ill., 1971; PhD, Ill. Inst. of Tech. 1976. Career: res. asst. prof. Univ. Chicago, 1976-80; asst. prof. dept. psychiatry UCLA, 1980-83; UC Irvine 1983-87, assoc. prof. 1988–; res. chemist VA Med. Ctr., West L.A., 1980-83, cons. 1983–; dir. clinical res. (psychiatry) VA Med. Ctr., Long Beach 1991–; cons. VA Med. Ctr. Long Beach 1986-91, Spectra Physics Corp. 1982-84, Stuart Pharmaceuticals 1983, Vydak Inc. 1983, IBM Instruments 1984–, Pfizer Pharmaceuticals 1985–, Fairview State Hosp. 1985–, Abbott Lab. 1986–, Kronos Inc. 1986, In Vitro Int. 1994; awards: USPHS Fellow 1976-78; mem: Soc. Neuroscis., AAAS, N.Y. Acad. Sci.; rec: backpacking, rock climbing, sailing. Res: 26322 Los Alamitos Ave Laguna Hills 92653 Ofc: UCI Dept. Psychiatry and Human Behavior Irvine 92717

DE NECOCHEA, FERNANDO, public accountant; b. May 30, 1916, Calexico; s. Gabriel and Adelaida (Castro) de N.; m. Margarita Padilla, Feb. 4, 1940; children: Fernando b. 1940, Ruben b. 1942, Margarita b. 1944, Gloria b. 1947, Yvonne b. 1951, Robert b. 1955, Michelle b. 1959; edn: bus. & acctg. San Diego Coll. Commerce 1940-43; Amer. Ext. Sch. of Law, Chgo. 1943-44; lic. Pub. Acct. Calif. 1946. Career: credit mgr. Sears Roebuck, El Centro 1943-44; chief acct. Desert Valley Seed Co. 1944-47; pvt. acctg. Calexico 1947–; appt. by Gov. Goodwin Knight, Calif. Commr. of Deeds for Mexico, 1955-59; honors: 7th gen. Californian, mem. Native Sons of Golden West, mem. Mexico-U.S. Interparliamentary (1962), liaison Interparliamentary U.S.-Mexico Congress, recipient City of Calexico pioneer award; mem: Nat. Soc. Pub. Accts., Calif. Soc. Accts., Calexico C.of C. (pres. 1958-60, rep. Border Cities Conf. 1958-60, del. Imperial Valley Assoc. Chambers of Commerce 1958-60), AARP, Lions; Calexico Planning Commn. 1965-67; Democrat; R.Cath.; rec: golf, horseback riding, hunting, camping. Res: 506 Mary Ave Calexico 92231 Ofc: F. de Necochea, 4th St Calexico CA 92231

DENNY, JAMES CLIFTON, tree farm owner; b. Aug. 3, 1922, Palo Alto; s. James Milton and Alma May (Siler) D.; m. Shirley Ann Elliott, Oct. 31, 1948; children: Christine b. 1951, Stuart b. 1953, James b. 1957, Matthew b. 1960, Katharine b. 1963; edn: BS forestry, UC Berkeley 1948; reg. profl. forester 1973. Career: forestry dispatcher Calif. Div. Forestry, Redding 1948-50, forester I, II and III 1950-62, asst. dep. state forester, Sacto. 1962-71, ops. ofcr., Santa Rosa 1971-75; chief resources mgmt. Calif. Dept. Forestry, Sacto. 1975-80; ret.; cons., Shingletown 1984–; dir. Forest Landowners of Calif., Sacto. 1988-95; mem: Soc. Am. Foresters; mil: 1st lt. USAF 1942-45; Republican; Presbyterian; rec: woodworking, gardening, travel. Address: Shingletown 96088

DENVIR, QUIN ANTHONY, lawyer; b. May 27, 1940, Chicago, Ill.; s. Paul Francis and Dorothy (Ryan) D.; m. Ann Gallagher, June 11, 1966; children: Karen b. 1968, Paul b. 1971; edn: BA cum laude, Univ. Notre Dame 1962; MA, Am. Univ. 1966; JD hons., Univ. Chgo. Law Sch. 1969; admitted St. Bar Calif. 1971, Wash. D.C. 1969. Career: assoc. atty. Covington & Burling, Wash. D.C. 1969-70; dir. atty. Calif. Rural Legal Assistance, El Centro and Salinas 1971-74; dep. pub. defender Monterey Co., Monterey 1974-75; chief counsel St. Dept. of Health, Sacto. 1975-77; Calif. St. pub. defender, Sacto. 1977-84; ptnr. Marron Reid & Sheehy 1984-87; atty. sole practice 1987–; instr. Monterey Sch. of Law 1975; Hastings Coll. of Advocacy 1987-88; mem: Calif. Council on Criminal Justice, St. Bar Appellate Com., Central Calif. Appellate Program (pres. 1987–), Am. Bar Assn., Calif. Attys. for Criminal Justice, Calif. Academy Appellate Lawyers; articles pub. in profl. jours., 1986-88; mil: lt. USN 1962-66; Democrat; Cath.; rec: bicycling. Res: 1614 Orange Ln Davis 95616 Ofc: 660 J St Ste 200 Sacramento 95814

DEOL, SHIVINDER SINGH, physician; b. June 4, 1953, Ahmedgarh, India, nat. USA 1979; s. Col. Tej Bhan Singh and Joginder Kaur (Benepal) Deol; m. Harjit Kaur, Apr. 9, 1977; children: Randeep b. 1980, Vikramjit b. 1982, Amartej b. 1992; edn: premed., DAV Coll., Chandigarh, India 1971; MBBS, Armed Forces Med. Coll., Poona, India 1975; MD, Univ. of Tenn. Center for Health Scis., Memphis 1981; Diplomate Am. Board of Family Practiee 1981, 87, 93; Fellow Am. Acad. of Family Physicians. Career: group practice Manor Medical Group Inc., Bakersfield 1982-83; solo med. practice, 1983–; bd. dirs. Good Samaritan Hosp. 1992–; pres. Kern Acad. of Family Physicians 1988–; bd. dirs. Physicians Radiology Group, Bakersfield 1985-88; chief of staff Alliance Comm. Hosp. 1991-92; bd. dirs. Bakersfield Meml. Hosp. IPA 1987-92, dept. chmn. fam. practice 1985-86, 89-90; v. chief of staff Bakersfield Comm. Hosp. 1985; mem: Kern Co. Med. Soc., CMA, AMA, Indian Med. Assn., Am. Acad.

of Cosmetic Surgery (Assoc. Fellow), Am. Coll. of Internat. Physicians (Fellow), Am. Geriatric Soc., Am. Soc. of Contemporary Med. & Surg. (Fellow), Intl. Soc. of Plastic Anesth. & Reconstrv. Surgery (assoc. fellow), Am. Assn. Physicians from India, Am. Acad. of Home Care Physicians, Nat. Stroke Assn., Am. Liver Found., Am. Acad. Sclerotherapy, Nat. Headache Found., AFMC Alumni Assn. Am. (exec. com.), Rotary Intl. (Paul Harris Fellow 1983-88); civic: vol. physician to inpatients Salvation Army Rehabilitation Ctr. 1985-87, donor Xray machine to Mexico, Computer to KMC FP residency, free sch. physicals Highland H.S. 1989–; Republican; Sikh; rec: comm. affairs, sports. Res: 10909 Princeville Ct Bakersfield 93311 Ofc: Shivinder S. Deol, MD, 4000 Stockdale Hwy Ste D Bakersfield 93309

DEPNER, THOMAS ARNOLD, physician, professor of medicine; b. Apr. 8, 1943, Medford, OR; s. Arnold Martin and Helen Lois (Swan) D.; m. Celeste Marie White, June 22, 1968; children: Charles b. 1969, Kristine b. 1970, Ivy b. 1979; edn: BS, biology, Univ. of Portland 1965; MD, Johns Hopkins Med. Sch. 1969; intern, internal medicine Univ. Hosps., Case-Western Reserve Univ. Sch. of Medicine, Cleveland, Ohio 1969-70, resident, internal medicine 1970-72, fellow in nephrology, internal medicine 1972-73; fellow in nephrology UC Davis Med. Ctr., Sacto., Calif. 1973-74; med. lic. Ohio 1970; cert. Am. Bd. of Internal Med. 1972; lic. Calif. Bd. Med. Examiners 1973; cert. in nephrology, Am. Bd. of Internal Medicine 1974. Career: asst. prof. Sch. of Medicine, UC Davis 1974-81; med. dir. Dialysis Ctr., UC Davis Med. Ctr., Sacto. 1980–; assoc. prof. Sch. of Medicine UC Davis 1981-91, prof. 1991–; dir. Univ. Dialysis Clinic, Sacto. 1988–; co-dir. Southgate Dialysis Clinic, Sacto. 1991–; dir. Hemodialysis Svs., UC Davis Med. Ctr. 1979–; chmn. med. dirs. advy. com., Dialysis Clinic, Inc. 1992–; honors: NIH res. grant (co-investigator) 1977-85, invited speaker/lectr. U.S., Scotland, Israel, 1991-93, NIH res. grant (prin. investigator) 1994-2001, listed in Best Doctors in Am. 1994; mem: Am. Soc. of Nephrology 1973- (annual meeting prog. com. 1991, 94, 95, joint clin. vol. res. & devel. com. 1993–, annual meeting prog. com. chmn., dialysis modeling and hemodynamics 1994), Internat. Soc. of Nephrology 1973–, Am. Fedn. for Clin. Res. 1974–, Am. Soc. for Artificial Internal Organs 1979- (prog. com., annual meetings 1994, 95), Internat. Soc. for Artificial Organs 1980–, Kidney Found. of No. Calif. 1974–, Nat. Soc. for Patients on Hemodialysis and Transplantation 1976–, Calif. Dialysis Council 1980–, Am. Heart Assn. kidney & cardiovascular disease council 1987–, Friends of Nat. Lib. of Medicine 1986–, Transpacific Renal Network (bd. dirs. 1992–), Comstock Club of Sacto. 1990–; mem. editl. bd. and reviewer: Seminars in Dialysis (guest ed. "Optimal Hemodialysis 1994"), Advances in Renal Replacement Therapy (guest ed. "Kinetic Modeling in Dialysis"), Jour. of Am. Soc. for Artificial Internal Organs; reviewer: Kidney Internat., Am. Jour. of Kidney Diseases, Nephron, Jour. of AMA, Jour. of Am. Soc. of Nephrology, Jour. of Artificial Organs; co-author: 5 book chpts., 1979; author or co-author: 50+ pub. jour. articles, 1975–, 38 pub. abstracts, 1967–; Democrat; Roman Catholic; rec: golf, computer development. Ofc: University of California-Davis 4301 X St Sacramento 95817

DERBIN, ROBERT C., JR., departmental administrative officer, lawyer; b. Oct. 30, 1948, Highland Park, Mich.; s. Robert D. and Mary Margaret (O'Brien) D.; edn: BS acctg., Univ. Detroit 1970; JD, Lincoln Univ. 1979; admitted St. Bar Calif. 1983. Career: atty. sole practice, S.F. 1983–; acct. City of Detroit, Mich. 1970-74; assoc. acct. City of Berkeley 1976-80, sr. acct. 1980-87, sr. mgmt. analyst 1987-90; dept. admin. ofcr. 1990–; awards: City of Berkeley Employee of Month 1985; mem: Am. Bar Assn., Am. Library Assn., Friends of Berkeley Pub. Library; Democrat; Cath.; rec: sailing, skiing, photog., music, poetry. Address: Berkeley 94709

DE REGT, JOHN STEWART, real estate and small venture executive; b. San Francisco; s. Christian Anthony and Mary Margaret (Stewart) deR.; children: Kenneth, Thomas, James, Lauren, Mary, Keith, Stewart; edn: BCE, Univ. Santa Clara. Career: pres. Carl Holvick Co., Palo Alto 1957-75; v.p. Holvick deRegt Koering, Sunnyvale 1960-75, pres., owner 1975-86; industrial and office park counsel, Urban Land Inst. 1978-90; pres., owner Golden Eagle Devel. Co. Inc. 1987–; contbr. feature articles to Corporate Times, Santa Clara; mem. Nat. Assn. Indsl. Office Parks; civic: Bellarmine High Sch., San Jose (regent 1977-93), Food Bank, San Jose (dir. 1980-88), San Mateo County Devel. Assn. 1975-93, YMCA 1984-88, Santa Clara Univ. Sch. of Bus. (advy. bd. 1984-90), The Exec. Com. 1980-88; mil: AUS 1951-53. Res: 1700 Sand Hill Rd #408 Palo Alto 94304 Ofc: PO Box 716 Menlo Park 94026; Tel: 415/321-7277

DERSHEM, STEPHEN MICHAEL, research chemist; b. Dec. 1, 1954, San Diego; s. William Aaron and Helen Maureen (Ullery) D.; m. Amanda Margaret Smith, Apr. 19, 1980; edn: BS, San Diego State Univ., 1978, MA, 1981; PhD, Mississippi State Univ., 1986. Career: organic chemist Johnson Matthey, Inc. San Diego 1980-83, cons. 1983-84; res. chemist, dir. of research Quantum Materials Inc., San Diego 1986–, cons. 1985-86; awards: life Calif. Scholarship Fedn., Clairemont H.S. 1972, grad. student of yr. chem. dept. Miss. State Univ. 1984; mem. Am. Chem. Soc. (mem. 1981–, mem. at lg. 1990-93, San Diego sect. exec. bd. 1990-93, S.D. newsletter advt. mgr. 1990-92); inventor, 7 U.S. Patents (issued 1990-95); Republican; Christian; rec: backpacking. Res: 9097 Truman St San Diego 92129 Ofc: Quantum Materials Inc. 9938 Via Pasar San Diego 92126

DESAI, JITENDRA NANUBHAI, physician, pediatrician; b. June 29, 1942, India; nat. 1978; s. Nanubhai R. and Padmaben N. D.; m. Bharti J., Aug. 24, 1969; children: Shital b. 1972, Premal b. 1975; edn: MD, Baroda Med. Coll. India 1967. Career: fellow pediatric hematology Univ. Wis. Med. Center, Madison 1970-73; pediatrician Cigna Health Plan, Canoga Park 1973–; staff Cedars Sinai Med. Center, Beverly Hills 1981–; Tarzana Med. Ctr. 1994–, St. Joseph Hosp., Burbank 1994–; courtesy staff Childrens Hosp. Los Angeles 1975–; mem: Am. Acad. Pediatrics (fellow), L.A. Pediatric Soc.; rec: tennis, skiing, swimming. Res: 11728 Monte Leon Way Northridge 91326 Ofc: Cigna Health Plan of California 10605 Balboa Blvd Granada Hills 91344

DESDIER, STEVEN ROSS, accountant; b. Oct. 11, 1952, San Diego; s. Don Desdier and Audree LaVerne Leischner; edn: BA, summa cum laude, U.S. Internat. Univ. 1970; Cert. in Taxation, UC San Diego 1981; Enrolled Agent, IRS; cert. fin. planner (CFP) Coll. for Fin. Planning; accredited tax advisor and accredited business acct. Accreditation Council for Accountancy & Taxation. Career: asst. menswear buyer Miller's West Dept. Store 1970-77; life & disability ins. agent Home Life Ins. Co. 1976-78; acct. San Francisco AIDS Found. 1985-87; reg. rep. Am. Pacific Securities 1982-89; pres. Desdier Inc. dba DESCO 1977–; honors: recogn. for contbns. GSDBA Found. 1985; appt. Advy. Bd. Calif. Senate Select Com. on Small Bus. Enterprises 1986-91; appt. Senate Small Bus. Advy. Bd. 1991-92, selected as 1995 Fin. Services Advocate of Yr., U.S. Small Bus. Adminstrn., No. Calif.; mem: Am. Uniform Assn. (treas. 1990-94, steering com. 1989-93, 94-96), Gr. San Diego Bus. Assn. (pres. 1984-85, treas. 1980-84, bd. 1980-85), Castro Community & Bus. Alliance (treas., bd. 1991-92), Golden Gate Bus. Assn. (v.p. admin. 1985-86, bd. mem.), Nat. Assn. of Bus. Councils (treas. and bd. mem. 1982-84), San Diego Co. Citizen's Scholarship Found. (treas. 1982-84, bd. mem. 1981-84), Calif. Assn. of Indep. Accts. (v.p. 1985-87, pres.-elect 1987-88, pres. 1988-89), Nat. Soc. of Public Accts. (Calif. state dir. 1991-95, chmn. Soc. Rel. Com. 1993-94, mem. Edn. Com. 1994-95, mem. Nat. Affairs com. 1995-96), Nat. Assn. of Enrolled Agents, Calif. Soc. Of E.A. (Golden Gate Chpt. bd. 1990-92, 2d v.p. 1992-93), Inland Soc. of Tax Cons.; Republican; Lutheran; rec: coins, oriental art.

DESROCHES, DIANE, educator, writer, director, co-producer, conference speaker, actress; b. Nov. 17, 1947, Webster, Mass.; d. Victor Joseph and Rose Blouin; m. Roger John DesRoches, Aug. 27, 1966 (div. 1974); son, Bill b. 1970; edn: AA in French (magna cum laude), Mesa Coll., 1976; BA in English (magna cum laude), San Diego St. Univ., 1979, MA in English, 1981; Calif. Comm. Colls. instr. creds. in lang. arts, literature, and ESL, 1981. Career: freelance writer and editor Word Factory, San Diego 1979–; English as a Second Language instr. San Diego Comm. Coll. Dist., 1982–, Coll. of English Language, San Diego 1982–; awards: Gregg Inst. bus. award, 1965, D.B. Williams scholar SDSU, 1979, Calif. State fellow, 1979, Phi Kappa Phi, Psi Chi, Pi Delta Phi; mem: AFT, CATESOL, TESOL; civic: Neighborhood Watch Pgm. #711 S.D. (founder & block capt. 1985–); Democrat; R.Cath.; rec: ice skating, boogie boarding, swimming, horseback riding. Ofc: Word Factory 2029 Cerrissa Ct Ste F San Diego 92154

DESSELLE, KELLY ANN, real estate broker; b. Oct. 14, 1960, Redondo Beach; d. Robert Lee and Lynda Rae (Hurlbut) Desselle; m. John Sandy Pontrelli; lic. R.E. broker Calif., 1985; Cert. Property Mgr. (CPM) cand. Nat. Inst. R.E. Mgmt. (IREM). Career: real estate agent MDR Devel., Marinna del Rey 1980-81; real estate rental agent Palm Springs Rental, Palm Springs 1981; real estate agent Century 21-Van Lizzen 1981-82; Walker & Lee Realty, Palm Desert 1982-83; real estate cons. Oster-McNeel, Palm Springs 1983-85; broker, owner Desselle Properties Inc., Cathedral City 1985–; owner Kelly's Katering, Palm Springs 1978-79; driver Frontier Catering, Beaumont 1976-78, cook 1973-76; awards: Century 21 Salesperson of Month (1981); mem: Nat. Assn. Realtors, Calif. Assn. Realtors, Palm Springs Bd. Realtors, IREM Orange County Chpt., Calif. Apartment Assn., Nat. Apartment Assn.; sculptor and potter; rec: art, tennis, skiing. Res: 68640 Hermosillo Rd Cathedral City 92234 Ofc: Desselle Properties and Investments 68545 Ramon Rd Ste C-101 Cathedral City 92234 Ph: 619/328-4227

DETELS, ROGER, professor of epidemiology; b. Oct. 14, 1936, Bklyn.; s. Martin Paul and Mary J. (Crooker) D.; m. Mary M. Doud, Sept. 14, 1963; children: Martin, Edward; edn: BA, Harvard Univ., 1958; MD, New York Univ., 1962; MS preventive med., Univ. of Wash., Seattle 1966. Career: fellow N.Y.C. dept. of health summer 1956; USN fellow Naval Med. Research Unit, Taipei, Taiwan 1961-62; postdoc. fellow Nat. Inst. Infectious Diseases, Univ. Wash. 1963-66; med. ofcr. USN Med. Research Unit, Taipei 1966-69; med. ofcr./epidemiologist NIH/Nat. Inst. Neurol. Disease and Stroke, Bethesda, Md. 1969-70; assoc. prof., prof. epidemiology UCLA Sch. Pub. Health, 1970-73, 1973–, hd. div. epid. 1972-80, dean UCLA Sch. Pub. Health, 1980-85, dir. UCLA/Fogarty internat. tng. grant in epidemiology related to AIDS; prin. investigator state and nat. research grantee 25+ awards, 1972–, current research: Natural Hist. of AIDS in Homosexual Men (1983-87, 87-99); dir. UCLA/Fogarty Internat. Tng. Prog. in Epidemiology 1988-98; dir. UCLA Tng. Prog. on Epidemiology of HIV in Drug Abusers; dir. UCLA Tng. Prog. in Epidemiology of AIDS; invited spkr. numerous nat., internat. profl. confs.; editor Oxford Textbook of Public Health (4 vols., 1985, 2d edition 1991); contbr. 150+ articles, book chapts. on various topics, 1966–; honors: Delta Ometa 1971, Sigma Xi 1971; mem: Internat. Epidemiol. Assn. (treas. 1984-90, pres. 1990-93, exec. com. 1984-96), Am. Coll. Epidemiology (fellow 1984, pgm. chmn. 1987, bd. 1987–), Internat. AIDS Soc., Am. Pub. Health Assn., AAAS (fellow 1995), Soc. Epidemiologic Research (fellow 1969, pres. 1976-78), Am. Coll. Preventive Med. (fellow 1969), Am. Epidemiol. Soc., Concerned Faculty UCLA, Assoc. Schs. of Pub. Health (1980-85, sec. treas. 1984-85), Physicians for Soc. Responsibility; mil: lt. cdr. USN 1966-69; rec: chamber music, surfing. Ofc: UCLA School of Public Health Los Angeles 90024-1772

DETHLEFSEN, ROLF, consulting engineer, scientist; b. Aug. 30, 1934, Niebuell, Germany, naturalized U.S., 1970; s. Andreas Christian and Clara D.; m. Ingrid Baars, July 28, 1961; children: Olaf b. 1961, Stefan b. 1964, Karin b. 1965, Tanja b. 1974; edn: Dipl. Ing., Technical Univ., Braunschweig, Ger. 1961; MS, M.I.T., 1962, ScD, 1965. Career: lab. asst. M.I.T., 1962-65; staff scientist General Dynamics Convair, San Diego 1965-68; assoc. dir. Allis Chalmers, Milw. 1968-72; sr. project mgr. Brown Boveri Electric, Colmar, Pa. 1972-83; prin. engr. Maxwell Labs., San Diego 1983-94; cons. engr. Marx Technologies 1994–; pres. Gould Mgmt. Assn., Greensburg, Pa. 1976-77; nat. secty. Electric Launch Assn., 1988-89; awards: NATO fellow M.I.T. (1961-62); mem: IEEE (senior mem. 1966–), AIAA (senior 1990–), VDI (Assn. German Engrs., 1966), Am. Def. Preparedness Assn. 1986–, Am. Radio Relay League 1990–, New York Acad. of Scis. 1992–; civic: Calif. Rare Fruit Growers, German-Am. Socs. (San Diego), Corps Frisia (Braunschweig, Ger.); patentee, 9 US Patents 1971-92; author 30+ tech. papers (1966–); Republican; Lutheran. Ofc: Marx Technologies 13476 Samantha Ave San Diego 92129-2119

DEUKMEJIAN, GEORGE, lawyer, former governor of California; b. June 6, 1928, Menands, NY; s. George and Alice (Gairdan) D.; m. Gloria M. Saatjian, Long Beach, Feb. 16, 1957; children: Leslie Ann, b. 1964, George Krikor, b. 1966, Andrea Diane, b. 1969; edn: BA, Siena Coll., 1949, JD, St. John's Univ. Sch. of Law, 1952. Career: deputy county counsel, Los Angeles; former ptnr. law firm Lucas, Lucas & Deukmejian; former ptnr.Riedman, Dalessi, Deukmejian & Woods, Long Beach; elected rep. Calif. State Assembly 1963-67, elected Calif. State Senate 1967-78, senate majority leader 1969-71, senate minority leader 1974-78; elected state atty. gen. 1979-83, elected state gov. 1983-87, re-elected 1987-91; currently ptnr. law firm Sidley & Austin, L.A. mil: US Army 1953-55; mem.Calif. Club., Calif. C.of C., Chancery Club, 100 Club of L.A., Am. Legion, Elks Club; Episcopalian. Ofc: Sidley & Austin 555 W Fifth St 40th Flr Los Angeles 90013

DEU PREE, PAUL JAY, mechanical engineer; b. March 15, 1952, Denver, Colo.; s. Frank Earl and Virginia Chapman (Ward) Deu Pree; edn: BSME, Colo. St. Univ. Ft. Collins 1974; reg. profl. engr. Calif. 1976. Career: tech. staff II Rockwell Internat., Downey 1974-78; project engr. J.M. Ney Co., Yucaipa 1978-82; sr. mech. engr. Baldwin Tech., San Bernardino 1982-; mem: ASME. Res: 1924 Duke St Redlands 92374 Ofc: Baldwin Technology Corp. 1351 E Riverview Dr San Bernardino 92408

DE VEY, RICHARD E., instructor; b. July 30, 1932, Washington, D.C.; s. Ernest E. and Emily (Holweg) De Vey; m. Kathleen, Apr. 5, 1953; children: Chris b. 1954, Karlyn b. 1957, Michael b. 1958, David b. 1960, Claudia b. 1960, Richard b. 1969, Sheri b. 1970; edn: BA in edn. (honors), Mich. State Univ., 1954, MA in English/edn., 1959; crim. justice law, UCLA, 1979; MPA with cert. in judicial admin., USC Sch. Public Adminstrn., 1980, PhD criminology/juvenile law USC 1992. Career: high sch. tchr., English, Whittier Union HSD, 1963-69; juvenile probation ofcr. Los Angeles County Probation Dept., 1969–; pres./CEO De Vey Data Inc., Whittier 1985–; instr. Delinquency Control Inst. USC 1992-94; volunteer profl: "In Jesus Si Se Puede", E.L.A. store front therapy for juvenile gang members, 1970-79; bd. mem. Project Jade, Juvenile Div. City of South Gate 1989–; Commr. South Gate Commn. For Youth, 1989–; awards: full tuition scholar MSU Bands 1950-59, All University writing awards, poetry and short stories, MSU (1953, 54); mem: USC Alumni Club Pasa. chpt. 1990–, Phi Mu Alpha music frat. 1954–, Univ. Alumni Symphonic Band (1954–, solo clarinet 1988), Pi Sigma Alpha, Lambda Chpt. Poli. Sci. USC 1980–, Circle Squares Social Square Dance Club (pres. 1985-86); Democrat; Charismatic Christian; rec: gun collector, hunting, fishing. Ofc: L.A. Co. Probation, South Gate Police Dept. 8620 California Ave South Gate 90280

DE VITA, JOSEPH STEPHEN, JR., insurance company executive; b. Dec. 1, 1941, Philadelphia, Pa.; s. Joseph Stephen and Yolanda Grace (Di Padova) De V.; m. Joan Theresa Allen; children: Joseph b. 1966, John b. 1969, Deborah b. 1971; edn: BSBA, St. Josephs Univ.; MBA, Drexel Univ.; CPA, Pa. Career: v.p. Fremont Gen. Corp., Santa Monica 1977-86; senior v.p. and CFO Western Employers Ins. Co., Santa Ana 1986-87; exec. v.p. and CFO Great States Ins. Co., Anaheim 1987–; mem: Am. Inst. CPA, Pa. Inst. CPA; mil: USAF 1960-64; Republican. Res: 3267 S Downs Dr Chino Hills 91709

DE VORE, DAUN ALINE, lawyer; b. Ft. Worth, Tx.; d. Jacques Le Roy and Madelyn Norma (Schwartz) De Vore; edn: fgn. studies Univ. Paris IV, Sorbonne, 1976-77; BA magna cum laude, philosophy, UC Irvine 1977; JD,

Univ. San Francisco Sch. Law, 1981; MPA, internat. affairs and security, Harvard Univ. 1983; grad. Hastings Sch. of Advanced Advocacy 1991; admitted bar: Calif. 1981, U.S. Court of Internat. Trade and U.S. Court of Appeals, Ninth Circuit 1988, U.S. Court of Veterans Appeals 1990. Career: with U.S. EPA, Region IX, 1979; law clk. U.S. Senate Subcom. on U.S. Constn., U.S. Dept. Justice Civil Rights Div., Fed. Enforcement Honors Prog. 1980; law offices of Melvin M. Belli, San Francisco 1981; dep. pub. defender City and County of San Francisco, 1982; mem. Harvard Jour. for Policy Analysis and Mgmt. 1982, 83; atty. Central Internat. Law Firm, Seoul, Korea 1984-85; U.S. atty. Othniel H.K. Ltd., Hong Kong 1986-89; atty. Internat. Bus. Law Firm, WDC 1989-92; first woman lecturer Seoul Nat. Univ. Sch. of Law 1985; speaker, panelist: Am. Nuclear Soc., Seoul, Korea 1986, U.S. Info. Service, Korea 1988, Calif. Bar Internat. Law Sect. 1990, UC Santa Barbara 1990, Conf. on Soviet Am. Trade and Econ. Cooperation, Moscow 1991; honors: Phi Delta Phi, Aldrich Senior Merit Scholar UC Irvine 1977, Golden Gate Bus. & Civic Women's Assn. Outstanding Senior Legal Scholar in Calif. 1981, regional finalist White House fellowship 1983, Judge Fulbright fellowship 1985, Disting. Leadership award Am. Biographical Inst. 1988, Palm Springs City Council Commendation for Svc. to the City 1990, listed Who's Who in Am. Law, Who's Who of Emerging Leaders of Am. 1990, Who's Who in Calif.; mem: Am. Bar Assn. (chair internat. law com., standing com. liaison to fgn. and internat. bars, gen. practice sect. 1992-93; chair Asia/Pacific subcom. of internat. svs. com., internat. law sect. 1990), State Bar of Calif.(mem. internat. law sect. 1990-), Union Internat. des Avocats, Asia Pacific Lawyers Assn., Armed Forces Comms. and Electronics Assn., Harvard Club (bd. dirs., Korea 1986), Stephens Inn (Magistrar); publications: National Security Issues to be Considered by Foreign Investors (12 Whit. L.R., 1990); fgn. languages: French and Korean; Christian; rec: music (singer, write songs, flutist). Mail: PO Box 8987 Palm Springs 92263

DEVOSS, DAVID ARLEN, journalist, news service editor; b. Aug. 4, 1947, Dallas, Tx.; s. Hugh Arlen and Barbara Helen (Cooper) DeV.; m. Elizabeth Ann Rushton, Dec. 28, 1975; children: Thomas Arlen b. 1981, Matthew Richard b. 1988; edn: BA Univ. of Texas, Austin 1968. Career: corresp. Time Magazine, Houston, Montreal, Detroit, Saigon, 1968-80, Time Mag.bureau chief Bangkok, Mexico City, 1981-85; special reporter Los Angeles Times, L.A. 1985-89; editor East-West News Service, L.A. 1990–; corresp. Asia, Inc. Hong Kong, 1991–; awards include: best sport story of 1987 Sporting News, St. Louis 1987, best sports story AP, L.A. 1987, best education reporting Unity Awards in Media, Lincoln Univ., Jefferson City, Mo. 1989; mem. bd. dirs. Inst. for Democracy in Viet Nam 1988–, L.A. Council World Affairs; clubs: Foreign Correspondent Hong Kong (bd. 1978-81), Fgn. Corresp. Thailand (bd. 1981-83); author: Insight Guide to Thailand, 1982, Bordering on Trouble - Resources & Politics of Latin America, 1986, Day in the Life of California, 1988, Day in the Life of China, 1989, Insider's Guide to Indonesia, 1993, Thailand, 1994. Ofc: East-West News Service, 4159 Stansbury Ave Sherman Oaks 91423-4621

DE VOTO, TERENCE ALAN, broadcasting executive; b. Aug. 2, 1946, San Francisco; s. Albert Anthony and Virginia Louise (Kohnke) De V.; m. Christine McKannay, Jan. 24, 1976; children: Tommy b. 1977, Mark b. 1980, Julie b. 1983, Carolyn b. 1985; edn: BBA, Gonzaga Univ. 1968. Career: v.p. trading dept. Birr, Wilson & Co., 1968-74; account exec. KFOG Radio 1974-78, KSFO Radio 1978-81; local sales mgr., nat. sales mgr., gen. sales mgr., gen. mgr. KYUU Radio 1981-88; v.p. Fuller-Jeffrey Bdcstg., gen. mgr. KHTT and KSRO Radio, 1989-91; pres. radio div. Americom, 1991–; civic bds: Marin Assn. Retarded Citizens (bd., pres. 1989-91), Hanna Boys Ctr. (bd. 1991–); clubs: Olympic, Guardsmen; Republican; R.Cath.; rec: sports, music. Res: 115 Hillcrest Lane Kentfield 94904

DEWAR, NICHOLAS ALAN RICHARD, CPA, mediator, forensic accountant; b. April 5, 1950, London, England; s. Richard Alistair Robert and Monica Joan D.; edn: BA, MA, Trinity Coll. Cambridge England 1972; MS, Antioch Univ. 1982; C.P.A. Calif. 1988. Career: asst mgr. J. Henry Schroder Wagg, London, England 1972-76; gen. mgr. World Wildlife Fund, Caracas, Venezuela 1976-78; tax acct. Seifer Murken Levy & Despina, San Francisco 1983-85; Deloitte Haskins & Sells 1985-88; owner Nicholas Dewar CPA 1988-94; Kinsel Accountancy Corp. 1995–; awards: Fundacion Gran Mariscal de Ayacucho grant 1980; mem: Comm. Bd. Program Inc. (chairperson, bd. mem. 1988), Soc. of Professionals in Dispute Resolution, Bar Assn. of San Francisco, Am. Inst. CPA, Calif. Soc. CPA, Leander Club Henley-on-Thames England; rec: gardening, rowing. Ofc: 433 California St Ste 810 San Francisco 94104

DEWEY, DONALD WILLIAM, editor and publisher; b. Sept. 30, 1933, Honolulu; s. Donald Wm. and Theckla Jean (Engeborg) Dewey; m. Sally Ryan, Aug. 7, 1961; children: Michael b. 1962, Wendy b. 1968; edn: Pomona Coll. 1953-55; Career: sales engr. Pascoe Steel Corp., Pomona 1955-56, div. Reynolds Aluminum Co., Los Angeles 1956-58, Switzer Panel Corp., Pasadena 1958-60; sales and gen. mgr. Western Pre-Cast Concrete Corp., Ontario 1960-62; founder, editor & pub. R/C Modeler Magazine, 1963–, Freshwater and Marine Aquarium Mag., 1978–; pres., bd. chmn. RC Modeler Corp., RCM Publications; v.p., co-dir. Project Alert, Inc. 1981-84; author: Radio Control From the Ground Up (1970), Flight Training course (1973), For What It's Worth (vol. 1 1973, vol. 2 1975), num. sci. articles; mem: Am. Radio Relay League, Nat. Assn. Radio Amateurs, Acad. Model Aeronautics, Sport Flyers Assn., Nat. Aeronautic Assn., Oceanic Assn., Internat. Oceanographic Found., Smithsonian Assocs., Fedn. of Am. Aquarium Socs., Am. Philatelic Soc., Soc. of Philatelic Americans, Am. Topical Assn., APS Writers Unit 30, Am. First Day Cover Soc., United Postal Stationery Soc., Confederate Stamp Alliance, Am. Air Mail Soc., Bureau Issues Assn., Am. Revenue Assn., Canal Zone Study Group, Pitcairn Islands Study Group, Smithsonian Instn., Sierra Madre Hist. Soc., Friends Sierra Madre Library (life), Ludwig von Mises Inst., Rutherford Inst., The Endowment Found., The Claremont Inst., Heritage Found.; mil: HM-3, Hosp. Corps, USNR 1951-53; Republican (nat. com., US Presdl. Trust, US Congl. & Senatl. Clubs, Conservative Caucus, Presdl. Task Force); Lutheran; rec: writing, R/C modeling, am. radio, stamps. Res: 410 W Montecito Ave Sierra Madre 91024 Ofc: R/C Modeler Corp. 144 W Sierra Madre Blvd Sierra Madre 91024

DEWITT, JOHN BELTON, conservation executive; b. Jan. 13, 1937, Oakland; s. Belton and Florence D.; m. Karma Lee Sowers, Sept. 17, 1960; edn: BA in wildlife conservation, Univ. Calif. Berkeley, 1959. Career: Forest Service, El Dorado Nat. Forest, 1955-56; ranger naturalist Nat. Park Service, Yosemite Nat. Park 1957-58, Mt. Rainer Nat. Park 1959, Death Valley Nat. Monument 1960; Land Law examiner, information ofcr. and land appraiser Bur. of Land Mgmt., 1960-64; asst. secty. Save-the-Redwoods League, 1964-71, exec. dir. and secty., 1971–; dir. Nature Conservancy No. Calif. Chapter 1976-77, advy. council Trust for Public Land 1975-78, dir. Tuolumne River Preserv. Trust 1981-85, advisor to U.S. Secty. of Interior on nat. conserv. policy 1964-1994), advy. council Anza Borrego Desert Com. 1983–; awards: Nat. Conserv. Award, DAR 1982, Golden Bear Award, Calif. State Park & Rec. Commn. 1982, Gulf Oil Conserv. Award 1985, Calif. State Park Rangers Assn. Honorary Ranger 1985, Calif. State Park Partnership Award 1995, hon. National Park Ranger 1995, hon. recognition Calif. State Assembly 1995; mem: Sierra Club (conserv. com. 1953-63), Am. Forestry Assn., Nat. Parks Assn., Wilderness Soc., Nat. Audubon Soc.; publs: California Redwood Parks & Preserves (1982, reprinted 3rd edition 1993); Prot.; rec: fishing, hiking, historical resrch., gardening. Ofc: Save-the-Redwoods League 114 Sansome St Ste 605 San Francisco 94104

DEY, SAMUEL EUSTACE, JR., psychiatrist; b. Sept. 5, 1958, Guyana, S.A.; s. Samuel Ezekiel and Pauline Elizabeth (Pollydore) D.; m. Andrea Leona Jenkins, Apr. 1, 1986; children: Samuel Everett b. 1988, Brandon b. 1990; edn: BS in chem. (hons.), Loma Linda Univ., 1981; MD, LLU Sch. of Med., 1983; bd. certified ABPN - Psychiatry 1991, Geriatric Psychiatry 1992. Career: resident phys. LLU Med. Ctr. Dept. Psychiatry, Loma Linda 1983-88; staff psychiatrist Patton State Hosp., Patton 1987-89, 1990–; pvt. practice, San Bernardino 1988-92; pvt. practice, Riverside 1988–; staff psychiatrist San Bdo. County Dept. Mental Health 1989-90; mem: AMA, Am. Psychiat. Assn., CMA, San Bdo. Co. Med. Soc., Riv. Co. Med. Soc., Am. Orthopsychiatric Assn., So. Calif. Psychiat. Soc. (Inland Chpt. pres. 1991-92, sec. treas. 1989-90, pres. elect 1990-91), Am. Profl. Practice Assn., Nat. Med. Assn., Black Psychiatrists of Am., Am. Assn. for Geriatric Psychiatry; rec: stamps, sports, travel. Res: PO Box 51059 Riverside 92517 Ofc: PO Box 51030 Riverside 92517

DIAZ, RAUL ZARAGOZA, university administrator; b. Feb. 18, 1953, Visalia; s. Angel and Benita (Zaragoza) D.; m. Ana Maria Leos, Feb. 18, 1977; children: Raul Alejandro b. 1979, Mauricio Inocencio b. 1983; edn: AA, Coll. of Sequoias 1973; BA, UC Santa Cruz 1975; MS, CSU Sacto. 1977. Career: adminstrv. asst. Campesinos Progresistas, Dixon 1976-77; counselor Dinuba H.S. 1977-79; coordinator, RSVP program CSU Fresno 1979-81, dir. CAMP program 1981-88, dir. UMS 1988–, ag. leadship mentor ALD program 1984–, res. assoc. Nat. HEP CAMP Eval. 1985, cons. sch. of ag. 1986; amnesty instr. SER West 1989; awards: MAPA El Concilio Noche de Hechos; mem: Year Round Task Force Fresno Unified Sch. (affirmative action com. 1989), HEP CAMP Nat. Assn. (pres. 1985-86), Citizens Advy. Com. City of Fresno, Raza Advocates for Calif. Higher Edn., El Concilio de Fresno Inc., Chicano Staff Orgn. (pres. 1981), Mex-Am. Political Assn. (v.p. Fresno chpt. 1988), Tri-Co. Migrant Head Start (bd. pres. 1983, 84); Democrat; Cath. Res: 15874 Mark Rd Madera 93638 Ofc: Calif. State University Fresno 93740-0067

DI BARTOLOMEO, JOSEPH R., physician; b. Aug. 31, 1937, NY, NY; s. Thomas Albert and Antoinette (Dionisio) DiB.; m. Ericka Theckla, Sept. 8, 1962 (div. 1984); children: Phillip b. 1964, David b. 1967, Raymond b. 1977; m. Maxine Gwen Schalk, Aug. 20, 1989; edn: BS, St. John's Univ., Jamaica, NY, 1959; MD, Georgetown Med. Sch., 1963; bd. cert. Nat. Bd. Med. Examiners, 1964, Am. Bd. of Otolaryngology, 1968. Career: rotating intern Waterbury (Conn.) Hosp., 1963-64; resident gen. surg., 1964-65; resident otol. NY Univ. Bellevue Med. Ctr., 1965-68; att. otolaryngologist Cottage Hosp., Santa Barbara, and chmn. dept. otol. St. Francis Hosp., 1968, 1983-85, chief of staff 1986-87; medical dir. The Ear Foundation, Santa Barbara, 1980–; pres. of Am. Neurotology Soc.; currently cons. Hard of Hearing Pgm. Santa Barbara Sch. Dist., cons. Speech Comms. Research Lab. Inc., ednl. assoc. Ear Internat.; med. dir. hearing sect. Lions Sight and Hearing Conservation Ctr., 1975; resrch. assoc. dept. speech and hearing UCSB, 1969; mem. med. staff UCLA and clin. prof. UCLA Div. Head and Neck Surg., 1976; cons. Wadsworth VA Hosp.,

1982; instr. Am. Acad. of Otolaryngology, 1976-84; awards: outstanding tchg. UCLA 1978-79, honor award Am. Acad. Otol.-Head and Neck Surg. 1986, Fellowship awards: Am. Acad. of Ophthal. and Otol. 1969, Am. Acad. of of Facial Plastic and Reconstrv. Surg. 1969, Am. Coll. of Surgeons sect. otol. 1971, The Triological Soc. 1979; mem: AMA, CMA, Santa Barbara Co. Med. Assn., Royal Soc. of Medicine (London), World Med. Assn., Triol. Soc. (sec. we. sect. 1982-86), Dizziness and Balance Disorders Assn. of Am., Pacific Coast OtoOphthalmol. Soc., Internat. Correspondence Soc. of Ophthalmologists and Otolaryngologists, Centurion Club, Am. Hearing and Speech Assn., Pan Am. Soc. of Otolaryngologists and Bronchoesophagologists, SENTAC, Am. Council of Otol., Am. Auditory Soc., Am. Soc. for Laser Medicine and Surgery, Undersea Med. Soc., The Prosper Meniere Soc.; inventions: Nasal therapy for treatment of patulous Eustachian tube, Prosthesis - middle ear ventilation tube obturator (Oto-Med Inc. Products), Argon Laser for otologic surg. (Coherent Lasers, Med. Div.), A Cable Carrying Guide for Accessory Cords on the Operating Microscope; author chapters in med. books, med. jour. articles; mil: s/sgt. US Army 1955-59; Republican; R.Cath.; rec: scuba, skiing. Ofc: 2420 Castillo St Santa Barbara 93105-4346

DICKERSON, WILLIAM ROY, lawyer, lecturer, judge pro tem; b. Feb. 15, 1928, Uniontown, Ky.; s. Benjamin Franklin and Honor Mae (Staples) D.; edn: BA in acctg., Calif. St. Univ., 1952; JD, UCLA, 1958; admitted bar: Calif. 1959. Career: dep. atty., city prosecutor ex-officio, City of Glendale, 1959-62; atty., assoc. James Brewer, Los Angeles 1962-68, LaFollette, Johnson, Schroeter & DeHaas, 1968-73; solo law practice, 1973–; arbitrator L.A. Superior Ct., L.A. Municipal Ct.; judge pro tem L.A. Superior Ct. Appellate Dept., L.A. Municipal Ct., Small Claims Ct., Traffic Ct.; lectr. in field; mem: Am. Bar Assn., Calif. Bar Assn., L.A. County Bar Assn., Fed. Bar Assn., Soc. Calif. Accts., Am. Film Inst., Internat. Platform Assn.; civic: Los Feliz Improvement Assn. (bd. 1986-88), Zoning Commn., Streets and Hwys. Commn. (co-chair). Address: 813 N Doheny Dr Beverly Hills 90210

DICKEY, GARY ALAN, clergyman; b. Jan. 25, 1946, Santa Monica; s. Charles Harry and Audrey Winifred (White) D.; m. Tamara Jean Kimble, Jan. 11, 1976; edn: BA, UC Los Angeles, 1968; MDiv, Fuller Theol. Sem., Pasadena 1972; DMin, Sch. of Theology, Claremont 1974; Phd. cand., Trinity Theol. Sem. 1994; ordained minister United Methodist Ch. Career: assoc. pastor Magnolia Park United Meth. Ch., Burbank 1974-78; senior pastor St. James United Meth. Ch., Pasadena 1978-90; First United Meth. Ch., Canoga Park 1990–; supvg. pastor Bd. of Higher Edn., Nashville, Tn. 1978–; exec. com. Calif. Pacific Conf. Bd. of Ordained Ministry, 1980-88, mem., chair Pasadena Dist. com. ordained ministry 1978-90; awards: Meritorious Service award Calif. St. Soc. Sons of the Am. Revolution 1995, Citizenship award Sons Am. Rev., Pasa. 1990, Polonia Restituta Polish People's Republic 1990, Paul Harris Fellow Altadena Rotary 1986; mem: Sons Am. Rev. (Calif. Soc. chaplain 1988, pres. 1994, 95), Soc. Descendants of Washington's Army Valley Forge, Rotary Intl. (Altadena pres. 1989-90), Order of the Colonial Acorn 1992–, Sons of Colonial Wars (Calif. Soc. chaplain 1990–), Soc. War of 1812 (Calif. Soc. chaplain 1990–, editor 1991–), Soc. Sons of Am. Colonists, Royal Soc. of St. George, London, United Empire Loyalists Assn., Toronto, Can.; Vet. Corps of Artillery, New York; Soc. Sons of Union Vet. of Civil War; Republican; rec: genealog. res., photography, travel. Res: 22167 Bryant St West Hills 91304 Ofc: First United Methodist Church 22700 Sherman Way West Hills 91307

DICKEY, ROBERT RICHIE, business consultant and artistic director, "Les Chanteurs du Lycée"; b. March 25, 1932, Chicago, Ill.; s. Forrest Clark and Dorothy Lucille (Schuman) D.; m. Joyce Orr, Sept. 16, 1951 (div. 1973); children: Susan Carol b. 1953, Kathy Diane b. 1955, Karen Ann b. 1957, Robert Forrest b. 1963; m. Harriet Dayton, Oct. 4, 1974 (div. 1983); m. Cristina Allen Stevens, April 11, 1984; children: Cristina Michelle b. 1986, Anthony Alexander b. 1988; edn: BA (high hons.), Univ. Ill. 1954. Career: exec. Honeywell, Minneapolis, Minn. 1960-77, Mexico City 1977-80, Santa Clara 1980-83; owner Dickey & Assoc., Palo Alto, Paris, Mexico City 1983–; dir. U.S. C.of C. in Mexico 1977-80; honors: Who's Who in Fin. & Industry, Internat. Bus. Who's Who; articles pub. on Mexico and music (1960–); mil: capt. RA 1954-60; Republican; Episcopalian; rec: organ, choral singing. Ofc: Dickey & Associates 1259 El Camino Real Ste 325 Menlo Park 94025

DICKINSON, RUSSELL IRA, school district superintendent; b. Mar. 5, 1932, Newfane, N.Y.; s. Clarence Lee and Iona Helen (Schaffer) D.; m. Elaine Theis, July 2, 1955; children: Douglas b. 1957, Craig b. 1959, Scott b. 1966; edn: EdB, Univ. of Buffalo 1954, EdM, 1962. Career: school tchr. Kenmore (N.Y.) Public Schs., 1954-62; Fontana (Calif.) Unified Sch. Dist. 1962-68; cons., bus. advy. service San Bernardino County Supt. of Sch. 1968-76; asst. supt. bus. Chaffey High Sch. Dist., Ontario 1976-85; asst. supt. bus. Colton Joint Unified Sch. Dist., Colton 1985-86, supt. of schs. 1986–; honors: accreditation mem. Western Assn. of Schs. & Colls., Guam (1983-84, 84-85); mem: Assn. of Calif. Sch. Adminstrs. 1986–, Calif. Assn. of Sch. Bus. Officials (1968–, San Bernardino Co. pres. 1978-79, state pres. S.S. 1982-83); Kiwanis Club Colton (dist. pres. 1989); rec: camping, fishing. Res: 11991 Reche Canyon Rd Colton 92324 Ofc: Colton Joint Unified School Dist. 1212 Valencia Dr Colton 92324

DICKINSON, WADE, company president; b. Oct. 29, 1926, Hickory Township, Pa.; s. Ben Wade Oakes and Gladys Grace (Oakes) D.; m. Eleanor C., June 12, 1952; children: Mark b. 1955, Katherine b. 1957, Peter b. 1960; edn: Carnegie Inst. Tech. 1944-45; BS, U.S. Mil. Acad. Westpoint 1949; Univ. Tenn. 1950; Oak Ridge Sch. Reactor Tech. 1951. Career: physicist, cons. RAND Corp., Santa Monica 1952-54; tech. advisor U.S. Congress-Joint Com. on Atomic Energy, Wash. D.C. 1956-57; prin. engr., cons. Bechtel Corp., San Francisco 1954–; pres. Agrophysics Inc. and Radialphysics Inc., San Francisco 1972–; pres. W.W. Dickinson Corp. and Petrolphysics Inc., San Francisco 1978–; sr. lectr. UC Berkeley 1984–; cardiology staff UCSF, Mt. Zion, San Francisco 1972–; mem: Soc. Petroleum Engrs., Am. Physical Soc., Petroleum Soc. CIM, Bohemian Club, Guardsmen; 100+ patents held, 50+ articles pub. in tech. jours.; mil: capt. USAF 1949-54; Republican; Episcopalian. Ofc: Petrolphysics Inc. 2101 3rd St San Francisco 94107

DICKSON, RICHARD BARRY, realtor; b. Jan. 25, 1940, South Gate; s. Frederick Winston and Doris Willina (Miller) Green; m. Sally Ann Moore, July 15, 1961 (div.); m. Eleanor LaRae Firpo, July 1, 1972; children: Lance b. 1962, Kimberly b. 1964; edn: BA econ., Chapman Coll. 1973. Career: indsl. rels. Ford Aerospace, Newport Beach 1961-72; comm. rels. Irvine Co. 1972-73; acct. exec. Crosson Advtg. 1973-75; owner Dickson Advtg. 1975-92; Realtor, Grubb & Ellis, Newport Beach 1992–; mem: Newport-Balboa Rotary (pres. 1989-90), Commodores Club (skipper, pres. 1979-80), Big Brothers-Big Sisters (bd. dirs. 1970-86), Ducks Unlimited (bd. dirs. 1970-89); Republican; Cath.; rec: running, racquetball. Res: 980 Bayside Cove W, Newport Beach 92660 Ofc: Grubb & Ellis 23 Corporate Plaza #190 Newport Beach 92660

DIEKMANN, GILMORE FREDERICK, JR., lawyer; b. Jan. 14, 1946, Evansville, Ind.; s. Gilmore Frederick and Mabel Pauline (Daniel) D.; m. Katherine Etta Westlake, July 12, 1969; children: Anne b. 1973, Andrew b. 1975, Matthew b. 1982; edn: BS bus. adminstrn., Northwestern Univ. Evanston 1968; JD, Northwestern Univ. Chgo. 1971; admitted St. Bar Calif. 1972. Career: atty., assoc. Bronson Bronson & McKinnon, San Francisco 1971-78, ptnr. 1978–; seminar panelist Calif. CEB Berkeley 1989–, DRI, IAIC, Exec. Enterprises, PLI 1978–; honors: Order of Coif, Best Lawyers in Am.; mem: Am. Bar Assn., Defense Research Inst.; author: chpts. pub. 1987; Republican; Lutheran; rec: travel, outdoor activities. Res: POB 1433 51 Winship Ave Ross 94957 Ofc: Bronson Bronson & McKinnon 505 Montgomery St San Francisco 94111

DI LIBERTI, CHER, lawyer, real estate broker; b. June 2, 1951, Jersey City, N.J.; d. Joseph and Margaret (Mackin); m. Gene J. Goldsman, Dec. 18, 1980 (div. Dec., 1989); children: Aron Matthew, b. 1981, Marisa Becca b. 1981, Alyssa Hali b. 1985, Jacob Alexander b. 1987; edn: BA, Univ. of Md., 1972, JD, Pepperdine Univ. Sch of Law, 1976. Career: claims evaluation analyst Social Security Adminstrn. 1974-76; law clerk Beam & Ure, Santa Ana 1976-77; law offices of Di Liberti & Goldsman, Santa Ana 1977–; apptd. by Gov. Brown to bd. dirs. Area Board XI, Disability Rights Dept., 1983-86; legal advisor, Orange Co. Epilespsy Soc., 1980-; mem: Am., Calif. Bar Assns., Am., Calif. Trial Lawyers Assns., Orange County Bar Assn., ACLU, participant-profl. Orange Co. Regional Occupational Advis. Bd.; Law Rev., Pepperdine Univ. Sch of Law 1975-76. Res: 24 N. Vista de Catalina Laguna Beach 92677 Ofc: Sea View Properties/Law Offices of Di Liberti-Goldsman 15 Monarch Bay Plaza Ste 240 Monarch Beach 92629

DILLIER, WERNER CHRISTIAN, insurance and security sales agent; b. Aug. 8, 1923, Sursee, Luzerne, Switzerland, naturalized U.S. citizen 1963; s. Julian and Kathryn (Yurt) D.; m. Alice Maria Hodel, Oct. 1, 1949; children: Judy b. 1951, Irene b. 1955, Donald b. 1958; edn: acctg. degree Fed. Sch. of Bus., Sarnen, Obw., Switz., 1943; fgn. banking Obw. State Bank, 1945; chartered life underwriter (CLU) and enrolled agent (EA) Am. Coll. of Life Ins., 1959, ins. mgmt. cert., 1963. Career: banking ofcr. Obw. State Bank, Sarnen, Switz. 1943-45; office mgr. Renggli & Co., Willisau, Switz. 1945-47; credit mgr. Made Rite Saus. Co., Sacramento, Calif. 1947-53; ins. agent Transamerica Life, Sacto. 1953-69, general agent, 1969–; pres. Valley Thrift Co., Sacto. 1973-74; bd. dirs. Capital Plywood Inc., Sacto. 1957-84; awards: Leading Prod. Club Transam. Life L.A. (1954-65), man of year Barr Agy. Sacto. (1968), Conservation award Sacto. Hist. Soc. (1989); mem: Sacto. Life Ins. Assn. (1953–, instr. 1967-69), Sacto. CLU Soc. (1959–, pres. 1964), Sacto. Soc. Enrolled Agts. (1975–); clubs: Elks #6 (Sacto.), Sacto. Helvetia Verein (pres. 1964), United Swiss Lodge (Sacto. pres. 1979-85), Sacto. Swiss Sport Club, Council for the Swiss Abroad of Bern, Switz. (elected del. to represent the 11 western states); founder, chmn. and creator Gen. John A. Sutter Monument and Found. (1987–); mil: cpl. Swiss Army 1943-47; Republican; R.Cath.; rec: swimming, hiking, skiing. Ofc: Dillier Agency 6229 Fordham Way PO Box 22526 Sacramento 95822

DILLON, FRANCIS PATRICK, human resources executive, management consultant; b. March 15, 1937, Long Beach; s. Wallace Myron and Mary Elizabeth (Land) D; m. Vicki Lee Dillon, Oct. 1980; children: Cary Randolph, Francis Patrick Jr., Randee, Rick; edn: BA, Univ. Va. 1959; MS, Def. Fgn. Affairs Sch. 1962; MBA, Pepperdine Univ. 1976. Career: traffic mgr., mgr. personnel services Pacific Telephone Co., Sacto. and Lakeport 1966-69; asst. mgr. manpower planning and devel. Pan-Am World Airways, NYC 1969-71; mgr. personnel and orgn. devel. Continental Airlines, Los Angeles 1971-74; dir. human resources Bourns Inc., Riverside 1974-80; v.p. employee and comm. rels. MSI Data Corp. 1980-83; pres./CEO Pavi Enterprises 1983–; mgmt. cons. 1983–; pres., CEO Personnel Products & Services Inc. 1983-88; v.p. Executive Horizons, Inc. 1988-94; sr. profl. svs. cons. Right Assoc. 1994–; bd. dirs. Health Services Maintenance Orgn. Inc., Youth Services Center Inc.; secty., bd. dirs. Lake Mission Viejo Assn. 1990-94; vol. precinct worker; awards: Disting. Service Jaycees 1969, Jack Cates Meml. Vol. of Year Youth Service Center 1977; mem: Assn. Internal Mgmt. Cons., Am. Soc. Personnel Adminstrn., Personnel Indsl. Rels. Assn., Am. Soc. Tng. & Devel., Am. Electronics Assn. (human resources com., chmn. human resources symposium), Mission Viejo Sailing Club, Toastmasters (pres. 1966-67), Have Dirt Will Travel, Capo Valley 4 Wheelers; mil: lt. cdr. USN 1959-66; asst. naval attache Brazil 1963-65; Republican; Episcopalian. Ofc: Pavi Enterprises 27331 Via Amistoso Mission Viejo 92692

DIMMICK, KEVIN C., organizational change consultant; b. Aug. 21, 1953, Redwood City; m. Debra Herring; 1 dau., April Louise; edn: BA in speech comm., San Diego State Univ.; grad. studies in human resources and organizational devel., Univ. of San Francisco. Career: general mgr. All American Janitorial Services and Supply Co., San Diego 1975-78; personnel rep. Varian Assoc., Palo Alto 1978-81; personnel mgr. Arrowhead, Inc., San Rafael 1981-84; dir. of human resources Coherent Auburn Group, Coherent, Inc., Auburn 1984-93; pres. Dimmick & Assocs., Auburn 1993–; frequent speaker & expert on self-managed work teams and drug-free workplace programs; past instr. Sierra Coll., Rocklin; civic: bd. mem. (past chmn.) Sierra Coll. Mgmt. Advy. Bd.; v.p. The Workplace Found.; mem: (past pres.)The Employers Group Sacto. Advy. Bd., former crisis intervention counselor Marin Suicide Prevention Ctr.; author: The Legal Aspects of Management 1992. Res: 11175 Rosemary Dr Auburn 95603

DINER, DANIEL BRUCE, biomedical engineer; b. Sept. 14, 1947, Kew Gardens, NY; s. Harry Diner and Miriam Greenberg; edn: BA in physics, Johns Hopkins Univ., Baltimore, Md. 1969; MA in creative writing, Johns Hopkins Univ. 1971; MS, computer sci., Calif. Inst. of Tech., Pasadena 1973; PhD in engring. sci., Calif. Inst. of Tech. 1978. Career: asst. prof., neurology, Univ. of Zurich, Switzerland 1979-81; asst. prof., computer sci., NY Inst. of Tech., Old Westbury, NY 1982-85; human vision cognizant engr. for robotics and teleoperation, Jet Propulsion Lab./Calif. Inst. Tech./NASA, Pasadena 1985-93; v.p. of Am. affairs, Hans Wälischmiller GmbH (Ltd.) 1994; co-owner, Fundamental Magic of Hollywood 1991–; awards: NIH Fellow, Calif. Inst. Tech., Pasadena 1974-78; guest researcher, Hoffman-La Roche, Zurich 1979-81; Jet Propulsion Lab./Calif. Inst. Tech./NASA, Pasadena: NASA Summer Faculty Fellow 1985, recipient NASA New Tech. Innovator awards (11) 1986-93, NASA patent filing awards (4) 1988-93, NASA Group Achievement award 1991; listed Who's Who in the West 1991; mem: Robotics Internat./SME (bd. dir. 1988-90, sr. mem. 1983–); magician mem. Magic Castle of Hollywood; co-author of book, Human Engring. in Stereoscopic Viewing Devices, 1993; contbr. numerous scientific papers to profl. jours.; rec: backpacking, chess, magic, travel. Ofc. PO Box 1658 Sag Harbor NY 11963-0060

DING, MAE LON, personnel management consultant; b. May 7, 1954, Norwalk, Calif.; d. Lock Gee and Ruth (Tang) Ding; m. David J. Mashaw, July 2, 1995; edn: BA, UCLA, 1976; MBA, USC, 1978; cert. compensation profl. Am. Compensation Assn. 1986. Career: mgmt. intern 20th Century Fox, L.A. 1976-77; cons. Forum Corp., Boston, Mass. 1978; senior cons. Wyatt Co., Boston 1978-81; senior cons. R.A. Smith & Assocs., Laguna Hills 1981-83; compensation mgr. Allergan Pharmaceutical, Irvine 1983-85; pres. Personnel Systems Assocs., Tustin 1985–; instr. CSU Pomona 1988-89, CSU Long Beach 1988-90, Chapman Univ., Orange 1991; instr. Am. Compensation Assn., Scottsdale, Az. 1985-95; mem. Assn. of Professional Consultants (Orange Co. chpt. bd. 1989-95), Am. Compensation Assn. 1983–, Forensic Consultants Assn. of Orange Co. (bd.1994-95), Forensic Consultants Assn. of San Diego 1995–; civic: SHARE, Corona Del Mar (pres. 1991-92); author: Survey Sources (1991, 92, 93, 94), articles in Personnel News, 1992, Personnel, 1991, Jour. of Compensation & Benefits, 1991, Chapman Univ. Econ. Review, 1992; rec: skiing, mtn. biking. Ofc: Personnel Systems Associates 2282 Aspen St Tustin 92680

DI ROCCO, GREGORY CHRISTOPHER, obstetrician-gynecologist; b. Oct. 11, 1951, Los Angeles; s. George Anthony and Marie Virginia (Anastasia) Di R.; m. Saranne Roberta Gangi, Sept. 16, 1978; children: Phillip b. 1980, Mark b. 1981, David and Jason (frat. twins) b. 1984, Micheal b. 1989, Marcella b. 1993; edn: BS, and MD, USC, 1973, 1980. Career: intern and resident in OB/Gyn, USC and affil. hosp., 1980-84; pvt. med. practice obstets. and gynecol., Newport Beach 1984–; med. staff Hoag Hosp., coms: ER 1985-86, edn. 1986-87, utilization rev. 1987-88, Surgicenter 1987-88, 90-92; mem: AMA, CMA, Am. Fertility Soc., Fellow Am. Coll. OB/Gyn; club: Pacific (N.B.), Santa Anna Country Club; research: Hemopoietic Stem Cell Growth & Differentiation, 1981, Fetal Lung Maturity, 1982; Republican; R.Cath.; rec: golf. Ofc: 351 Hospital Rd Ste 514 Newport Beach 92663

DISHNO, DUANE ALLAN, school district superintendent; b. Oct. 26, 1941, Missoula, Mong.; s. Thomas Charles and Nellie Montana (Managhan) D.; m. Pauline Schwandt, Aug. 17, 1968; children: Joel b. 1969, Chris b. 1972; edn: BA, Eastern Wash. St. Univ., 1963; MA, CSU Long Beach, 1972; EdD, Univ. of La Verne, 1984. Career: tchr., reading specialilst, learning analyst, coord. compensatory edn. Westminster Sch. Dist., 1963-74; lectr. CSU Los Angeles, 1973-74; principal, dir. spl. services, asst. supt. ednl. services Huntington Beach City Sch. Dist., 1975-84; supt. of schools El Monte City Sch. Dist., 1984-88; supt. of schools Bonita Unified Sch. Dist., 1988-91; supt. of schools, Huntington Beach City Sch. Dist. 1991–; cons. Calif. St. Dept. Edn.; mem. advy. coms. Bilingual Tchr. Preparation and Ethnic Heritage Studies, CSU Long Beach; v.p./mem. policy bd. West Orange County Tchrs. Center; honors: Supt. of Yr. Alhambra/San Gabriel chpt. DAR 1987; mem: Assn. of Calif. Sch. Adminstrs. 1973–, West San Gabriel Valley Adminstrs. Assn., Orange Co. Reading Assn. 1968-72, Calif. Assn. for Compensatory Edn. 1968-84, Calif. Assn. for Bilingual Edn., Orange Co. Adminstrs. of Spl. Edn. 1977-84, Educare 1982-84, Assn. for Supvn. and Curriculum Devel. 1982–; civic: West S.G.V. Boys Club (bd.), El Monte/South El Monte Comm. Coordinating Council (pres. 1986-88), El Monte Kiwanis Club, El Monte/South El Monte C.of C., San Dimas C.of C. (bd. dirs. 1989-91), ARC-SGV 1989-94, Am. Heart Assn. 1992–; publ: Impact of Collective Bargaining on Policy Formation as Perceived by Calif. Personnel Adminstrs. (1984); Republican (sustaining); Cath.; rec: spectator sports, literature, family activities. Res:1 Ribera Irvine 92720 Ofc: Huntington Beach City School District PO Box 71 Huntington Beach 92648

DIVOLA, JOHN, artist, educator; b. June 6, 1949, Santa Monica; s. John M. and Marion (Foster) D.; edn: BA, CSU Northridge, 1971; MA, UCLA, 1973, MFA, 1974. Career: grad. tchg. asst. art, photography, UCLA, 1972-74; instr. UCLA summer qtr. 1977, Immaculate Heart Coll., L.A. 1975-79, Loyola Marymount Univ., L.A. 1976-80; vis. instr. USC, 1981; vis. artist Claremont Grad. Sch., 1981; vis. lectr. UCLA, 1982-83; instr. art/photography, Calif. Inst. of the Arts, Valencia 1978-88; prof. art dept. UC Riverside, 1988–, art dept. chair 1991-93; awards: NEA photography fellow (1973-74, 76-77, 79-80, 90-91), John Simon Guggenheim Meml. fellow 1986-87, Mellon fellow Calif. Inst. of Arts 1987-88, fellow Ctr. for Ideas in Soc., UCR 1991-92; num. one person exhs. since 1975 incl. Visual Studies Workshop, Rochester, N.Y., Camerawork Gal., Cinti., Ctr. for Creative Photog. Univ. Az., Tucson, Image Gal., Aarhus, Denmark, L.A. Inst. of Contemp. Art, Vision Gal., Boston, Print Galleri, Copenhagen, Blue Sky Gal., Portland, Ore., Camera Obscura, Stockholm, Sweden, Henry Gal. Univ. Wash., Seattle, Madison (Wis.) Art Ctr., Catskill Ctr. Photog., Woodstock, N.Y. Paul Cava Gal., Phila., Lightwork, Syracuse, N.Y., Grapestake Gal., S.F., Robert Freidus Gal., N.Y.C., Photographers Gal., Melbourne, Aust., No. Kentucky Univ., Gal. Del Cavallino, Venice, Italy, Univ. N.M. Art Mus., Albuquerque, Susan Spiritus Gal., Newport Beach, Jones Troyer Gal., W.D.C., Film in the Cities, St. Paul, Minn., L.A. Municipal Gal. Barnsdall Park (retrospective 1974-85), Jayne Baum Gal., N.Y.C., Gallery Min, Tokyo, Japan (catalog, 1987), Photo Interform, Osaka, Japan, Seibu Gal., Tokyo, Richard Green Gal., L.A., Jayne Baum Gal., N.Y.C., Jan Kesner Gal., L.A., Galerie Niki Diana Marquardt, Paris, Fr. (1990), Univ. Art Gal., UCR (1991), Rewdex Contemporary Art Gal., Koyoto, Japan (1992); num. group exhs., nat., internat., traveling, since 1973; rep. in permanent collections of corporate and public instns. Res: 245 Ruth Ave Venice 90201 Tel: 310/396-0334

DIXON, DEAN OWEN, executive; b. July 25, 1945, Baraboo, Wis.; s. Myer Eldon and Ruby Luvera (Hupenbecker) D.; m. Gail, May 8, 1965; 1 son, Todd b. 1968; edn: Ariz. St. Univ. 1963-65, CSU Long Beach 1965-67; Career: mgr. Factory Sales/ Traffic, Varec Inc., 1967-70; asst. nat. sales mgr. Merit Abrasive Prods. Inc., 1970-78; territory mgr. Sancap Abrasives Inc., 1978-79; v.p. sales & mktg. Jet and Western Abrasives Inc. 1979-91; gen. mgr. Marathon Abrasives/ Sunmight Abrasives 1991–; awards: Rotary Found. Group Study Exchange to New South Wales, Australia 1980; civic: City of Buena Park Centennial (exec. bd. 1986-87), B.P. Hist. Soc (1974–, trustee 1978-79, v.p. 1979-84, treas. 1992–), Orange County Hist. Commn. 1980-82, O.C. Hist. Soc. 1978–, B.P. C.of C. 1974-80, Silverado Days Com. 1974-88, B.P. Boys Club (com. 1980-87), Am. Found. for Sci. of Creative Intelligence 1973–, Cultural Arts Found. Buena Park (bd., v.p., v.chmn. 1989-93), Buena Park Civic Theater artistic review com. 1986-88, SAR, Calif. Soc. SAR, United Scottish Soc., Clan Keith Soc. (USA); coauthor: GSE Report 1980, A Hundred Years of Yesterdays: A Centennial Hist. of the People of Orange County & Their Communitites 1988, Orange Countiana Vol. V 1992; columnist Buena Park Independent Newspaper 1990–; writer/prod. cable-t.v. prodn.: Natural Hist. in No. Orange County 1985; Republican; Methodist; rec: bibliophile. Ofc: Marathon Abrasives/Sunmight Abrasives 12101 Western Ave Garden Grove 92641

DIXON, GAIL S., community leader; b. Jan. 3, 1943, Northampton, Mass.; d. Walter and Mary Jane (Elder) Hargesheimer; m. Dean O. Dixon, May 8, 1965; son, Todd b. 1968; edn: W. Wash. St. Univ., Bellingham 1960-64. Career: reprographics ind., self-empl., 1964-70; v.p. Great Western Sav. & Loan Assn., Beverly Hills 1970-87; reg. rep. Lincoln National Life, Santa Ana 1987-93; Fullerton Chamber of Commerce 1993–, exec. dir. 1994–; bd. dirs. Humana Hosp., Anaheim 1976-84, Beach Comm. Hosp., Buena Park 1978-85; honors:

Cypress Coll. Americana award 1983, Woman of Achiev. Buena Park Mall Assn. 1984, citation U.S. Congl. Record 1978; mem: Calif. Municipal Treasurers Assn. 1986-93, Am. Found. for the Sci. of Creative Intell. 1974–, Assn. of Calif. Water Agys. 1985-93, Public Affairs Com. 1988-93, Calif. Assn. of Sanitation Agys. 1988-93, Buena Park C.of C. (1st woman pres. in 51 yr. hist. 1978-79, dir. 1974-80), Buena Park Noon Lions Club (1st woman mem. 1989-94), Silverado Days Com., B.P. 1974-94, North Orange Co. Girls Club, Fullerton (1974-82, v.p. 1977), Buena Park Coord. Council (sec.treas. 1976-84), Boys Club of Buena Park (assoc. bd. 1974-84), Hugh O'Brian Youth Found. So. Calif. (dir. 1989-92), City of Buena Park Vision 2010 Core Com. (1990-92); Republican; Methodist; rec: entertaining. Ofc: Fullerton Chamber of Commerce 219 E. Commonwealth Ave. Fullerton 92632

DIXON, JULIAN CAREY, congressman; b. Aug. 8, 1934, Washington; m. Bettye Lee; 1 son, Cary Gordon; edn: BS, Calif. State Univ., Los Angeles, 1962; LL.B., Southwestern Univ., L.A., 1967. Career: mem. Calif. State Assembly, 1972-78; mem. 96th-104th Congresses from Calif. 32nd Dist., 1979–; mem. House Appropriations Com. 96th-104th Congresses, mem. subcom. on commerce, justice, state and judiciary, subcom. on legislative; ranking Democratic mem. subcom. on DC, mem. permanent select com. on intelligence, regional rep. Democratic steering and policy com., served on Bipartisan Task Force on Disasters 1994; past chair House com. on standards of official conduct; pres. Congl. Black Caucus Found. 1986-90; chmn. standing com. on rules for Democratic Nat. Convention 1984; chair; Congl. Black Caucus 1981-82; awards: named one of twelve Unsung Heroes in Congress by Politics in Am. 1985, cited as one of State's Most Effective Legislators by Calif. Congl. Recognition Prog. 1992, hon. chairperson of Nat. Sickle Cell Month 1993, acknowledged for invaluable support by Nat. Marrow Donor Prog. 1994, num. others; mem. NAACP, Urban League, Calif. Arts Commn.; mil: U.S. Army, 1957. 60; Democrat. Ofc: US House of Representatives 2252 Rayburn Washington DC 20515-0532

DJANG, SAM SUKHYUNG, dentist, b. Nov. 12, 1947, Seoul, Korea; s. Doohoon and Oksoo D.; m. Shihee, July 2, 1978; children: Mabel b. 1979, Robin b. 1983, Benzamin b. 1984; edn: pre-dental, Seoul Univ. Sch. Liberal Arts & Sci., 1970, DDS, Seoul Univ. Dental Sch. 1975; DDS, USC Dental Sch. 1984. Career: dental intern and resident Nat. VA Hosp. Seoul, Korea 1975-77; Army dentist in Korea, 1977-80; practicing dentist, 1984–; mem. Am. Soc. for Geriatric Dentistry, Am. Acad. of Implant Dentistry; publs: Ordinary Dentist, 1987, contbg. columnist "Oral Hygiene" in Korean Street Jour., comm. weekly newspaper, 1984-85; mil: capt. Army Med. Corps 1977-80. Res: 11456 Edenberg Ave Northridge 91326 Ofc: 15424 Nordhoff St Sepulveda 91343

DLUGIE, PAUL DAVID, physician; b. June 17, 1940, Chgo.; s. Samuel R. and Ruth (Mesirow) D.; m. Lida Pira, July 23, 1965; edn: AB, Johns Hopkins Univ. 1961; MD, Chgo. Med. Sch. 1965. Career: physician, capt. Med. Corps USAF, 1966-68; physican pvt. practice, 1968–; medical dir. Testing 1-2-3, subs. of E.N. Phillips Co., Woodland Hills 1991-92; dir. Columbia S&L, Beverly Hills (1984-92); mem. bd. dirs.: Indio Community Hosp. 1975-80, bd. chmn. 1978-80, bd. pres. 1980-85; The Lentz Inst., Indio 1984-91; United Stroke Found., L.A. 1985–; advy. bd. the Foundation for Sight, Palm Desert 1989–; recipient service award The Desert Medical Community, Palm Springs & Indio 1986; mem: AMA, Am. Assn. Family Physicians, Calif. Med. Assn., Riverside Co. Med. Soc.; host weekly medical t.v. show: The Medicine Show, KMIR-TV, NBC affil. 1983–. Ofc: Palm Desert Medical Center, 72-840 Hwy 111 Ste 165-D Palm Desert 92260

DOBRIS, JOEL CHARLES, law professor; b. Jan. 19, 1940, Albany, N.Y.; s. M. Michel and Frances (Lazoroff) D.; m. Linda Sue Wasserberg, June 8, 1970; son, Eliot Michel b. 1975; edn: BA, Yale, 1963; LLB, Univ. Minn., 1966; admitted bar: N.Y. 1967. Career: lawyer, assoc. Milbank, Tweed, Hadley & McCloy, NY, NY 1966-76; actg prof. of law UC Davis, 1976-81, prof. of law 1981–; Nat. Conf. of Commrs. on Uniform State Laws co-reporter apptd. to amend the Revised Uniform Principal & Income Act and the Uniform Prin. & Income Act; mem., adviser American Law Inst., 1987-92; Hess Lecture 1992; publs: num. law jour. articles re transfer taxes, probate and trust law; Democrat; Jewish; rec: reading, travel. Ofc: Law School Univ. Calif. Davis 95616

DOCKSON, ROBERT RAY, savings and loan executive; b. Oct. 6, 1917, Quincy, Ill.; s. Marshal Ray and Letah L. (Edmondson) D.; m. Katheryn Virginia Allison, Mar. 4, 1944; child, Kathy Kimberlee, b. 1948; edn: AB, Springfield Jr. Coll. 1937; BS, Univ. Ill. 1939; MS fgn. service, USC, 1940, PhD 1946. Career: lectr. USC 1940-41, 45-46, prof., head dept. mktg. 1953-59; dean USC Sch. Bus. Adminstrn. and prof. bus. econs. 1959-69; vice chmn bd. Calif. Fed. Savings & Loan Assn., Los Angeles 1969-70; pres. Calif. Fed. Savs. & Loan Assn. 1970-77, chmn. 1977-88, chief exec. ofcr. 1973-83; chmn. CalFed Inc. 1984-88, chief exec. ofcr. 1984-85, also dir.; instr. Rutgers Univ. 1946-47, asst. prof. 1947-48; economist western home ofc. Prudential Ins. Co. 1948-52, Bank of Am., San Francisco 1952-53; econ. cons., 1953-57; bd. dirs. IT Corp., Computer Scis. Corp.; Am. specialist for U.S. Dept. State; mem. Town Hall 1954–, bd. govs. 1963-65, hon. bd. govs. 1965–, pres. 1961-62; trustee John Randolph Haynes and Dora Haynes Found., Com. for Econ. Devel., Calif. Council for Econ. Edn.; chmn bd. Rose

Hills Meml. Park Assn. 1990-92; trustee, pres. Orthopedic Hosp.; bd. councilors USC Grad. Sch. Bus. Adminstrn.; bd. regents, chmn. univ. bd. Pepperdine Univ.; chmn. housing task force Calif. Roundtable; chmn. Commn. on the Future of the Calif. Cts. 1991-93; awards: decorated Star of Solidarity Govt. of Italy, Asa V. Call Achievement award, Disting. Comm. Service award Brandeis Univ., Whitney M. Young Jr. award Urban League 1981, Albert Schweitzer Leadership award, Man of Yr. award Nat. Housing Conf. 1981, Industrialist of Yr. award Calif. Mus. Sci. and Industry 1984; mem: Am. Arbitration Assn., Newcomen Soc. N. Am., Hugh O'Brian Youth Found., Calif. C.of C. (pres. 1980, bd. dirs. 1981-86), L.A. C.of C. (bd. dirs.), Phi Kappa Phi (Diploma of Honor award 1984), Beta Gamma Sigma, Bohemian Club, Calif. Club., L.A. CC, One Hundred Club, Birnam Wood Golf Club, Thunderbird CC; mil: lt. USNR 1942-44. Ofc: 6310 San Vicente Blvd Ste 402 Los Angeles 90048-5426

DODDS, MICHAEL JOHN, theologian, academic dean; b. Nov. 14, 1950, Des Moines, Iowa; s. John Joseph and Margaret Evelyn (Farrell) D.; edn: MA philosophy, St. Alberts Coll. 1975; MA theology, Grad. Theological Union, 1978; M.Div., Dominican Sch. of Philosophy and Theology 1978; STD, Univ. Fribourg Switzerland 1985. Career: Dominican priest; acad. dean Dominican Sch. of Philosophy & Theology, Berkeley 1988–; mem: Am. Cath. Philosophical Soc., Cath. Theological Soc. Am.; author: The Unchanging God of Love, 1986; Cath. Res: 2006 Berryman St Berkeley 94709Ofc: Dominican School of Philosophy and Theology 2401 Ridge Rd Berkeley 94609

DODGE, PETER H., architect; b. July 1, 1929, Pasadena; s. Irving Crow and Edna (Allison) D.; m. Janice Coor-Pender, Aug. 30, 1952; children: Susan b. 1958, Sarah b. 1963; edn: Art Center Sch., L.A. 1947-49; AB arch., UC Berkeley, 1956; reg. arch. 1961, NCARB 1973. Career: architect Joseph Esherick, Architect, San Francisco 1956-63; assoc. Joseph Esherick and Associates 1965-72; prin. Esherick, Homsey Dodge and Davis, 1972–, corp. pres. 1979-85; proj. architect The Cannery, S.F., Graduate Residence Facility UC Davis, 1960-68; project mgr. TWA Passenger Facilities Expansion, S.F. Intl. Airport, Promontory Point Master Plnng., Newport Bch., 1971; prin.-in-chg. Ctr. for Ednl. Devel., 1973; Chimpanzee Res. Facility, UCSB 1974; We. Airlines Passenger Facilities Expansion, S.F. Intl. Airport 1975; Theater Arts Bldg. CSU Sonoma 1976; Ekahi Village (297 condo. units) Maui, HI 1976; Great American Hamburger Place Bldg., Davis 1977; Citizens Utils. Svc. Ctr., Susanville 1983; R.A.B. Motors Mercedes-Benz Showroom, San Rafael, Mills Coll. Life Sci. Bldg., Boarding Area "B" Expansion S.F. Intl. Airport, 1984; Mills Coll. Art Ctr., 1986, Mills Coll. F.W. Olin Library, 1989; Rand Corp. Facilities, Santa Monica 1985-90; Golden Gate Univ., S.F. 1985–; U.S. Embassy, La Paz, Bolivia 1989; Walter Stearn Library CSU Bakersfield, 1991; Geary Theater Restoration Master Plan, S.F. 1992; Olney Hall Rehab. Project and Mills Hall Restoration Project (recognized by Calif. Preservation Found. 1995 design award), Mills Coll., Oakland 1994; lectr. dept. arch. UC Berkeley 1964-69, 71, vis. lectr. S.F. Art Inst. 1965; mem: Am. Inst. of Arch. (corp. mem. 1966–, fellow 1980, dir. Calif. Council AIA 1978-80, dir. No. Calif. 1977-78) AIA San Francisco (pres. 1981, nom. com. 1989); publs: chmn. editl. bd. Architecture California (1986-88), mem. editl. bd. Landscape 1987–; mil: 1st lt. US Army Corps Engrs. 1956-58. Res: 67 El Camino Real Berkeley 94705 Ofc: Esherick Homsey Dodge and Davis 2789 25th St San Francisco 94110

DOKE, MIMI IRENE, wedding consultant/photographer; b. Nov. 15, 1949, Covina; d. Charles Marshall and Suvia (Dominguez) Anderson; m. Martin L. Huggett, Feb. 13, 1966; children: Lisa b. 1966, Amber b. 1970, Melissa b. 1977; m. James Thomas Doke, Dec. 31, 1984; edn: grad. Sierra Vista H.S., Baldwin Park 1967; accredited bridal cons. (first to be granted cert.). Career: co-owner Alaska Roofing Co., Ukiah 1974-82; photographer, co-owner G.M.I. Studios, 1976-78; photographer cons., owner the Darkroom, Sun Valley, Ida. 1979-81, also owner the Coffee Break, 1979-81; wedding cons./photographer, owner The Wedding Specialist, Redwood Valley, Calif., Lake Havasu City, Ariz., 1982–; owner Party Express (party rental store), Lake Havasu City, Ariz. 1994–; cons. ABC News-Bride's Mag. 1994; nat. t.v. wedding cons. CBS News 1991-92, 95, ABC News 1994, 95, NBC News 1995, AZ State coord. 1991-94; judge, internat. print and album competitions, Wedding & Potrait Photographers Internat. 1995; honors: 1st in nation to achieve designation of Master Bridal Cons.; mem: Internat. Assn. of Bridal Consultants (speaker and state coord. 1982–), Wedding Photographers Internat. (1982–, nat. speaker 1988–, mem. bd. advisors), Profl. Photographers of Am. (speaker statewide 1988–); publs: poems in Today's Best Poetry, 1976, articles in photog. jours., (1988, 89, 93), Bridal Fair mag., 1991, Brides mag.,1994, Rental Mgmt. mag., 1994, editl. and photo layout for ALBUM '94 (book); Prot. Ofc: The Wedding Specialist, 1425 McCulloch Blvd #F Lake Havasu City AZ 86403

DOLAN, MARYANNE MCLORN, antique dealer, educator, author, lecturer; b. July 14, 1924, N.Y.C.; d. Frederick Joseph and Kathryn Cecilia (Carroll) McLorn; m. John Francis Dolan, Oct. 6, 1951; children: John Carroll, James Francis McLorn, William Brennan; edn: BA, San Francisco St. Univ., 1978, M.A., 1981. Career: owner antique shop, Benicia 1970–; tchr. classes and seminars in antiques and collectibles 1969–; UC Berkeley, UC Davis, UC Santa Cruz, Coll. of Marin, Mills Coll., St. Mary's Coll. Moraga, Solano Coll.; tchr.

writing Dolan Sch., 1978-92; lecture tours nat. and internat.; author books: Vintage Clothing 1880-1980 (1983), Collecting Rhinestone Jewelry 1984, Old Lace & Linens 1989, Commonsense Collecting 1991, 300 Years of American Silver Flatware 1992; weekly column: The Collector 1979-89, numerous articles in various periodicals; mem: Antique Appraisal Assn. of Am. Inc., New England Appraisers Assn., Nat. Soc. of Jewelry Appraisers, Internat. Soc. Appraisers, Calif. Writers Club, The Costume Soc. of Am., Internat. Platform Assn., Questers, Women's Nat. Book Assn., AAUW; Republican; R.Cath. Res: 138 Belle Ave Pleasant Hill 94523 Ofc: 191 West J St Benicia 94510

DOLICH, ANDREW BRUCE, sports executive; b. Feb. 18, 1947, Brooklyn, N.Y.; s. Mac and Yetta D.; m. Ellen Fass, June 11, 1972; children: Cory b. 1978, Caryn Lindsay b. 1983; edn: BA govt., Am. Univ. 1969; Ohio Univ. 1971. Career: adminstrv. asst., gen. mgr. Phila. 79ers., Pa. 1971-74; v.p. adminstrn., Md. Arrows, Wash. D.C. 1974-76; dir. mktg. Wash. Capitals 1976-78; exec. v.p., gen. mgr. Wash. Diplomats 1978-80; v.p. ops. Oakland A's, Oakland 1989–; exec. v.p Oakland A's 1993–; pres., COO, Golden State Warriors 1995–; bd dirs: Ohio Univ. Sports Adminstrn. 1975–, Oakland Conv. Bureau 1985–, Bay Area Sports Hall of Fame, S.F. 1986–, Sports & Special Events Commission, Oakland 1989, Internat. Sports Mktg. Assn., Oakland 200; listed Who's Who in Am. 1993–.

DOMBROSKE, LEONA JEAN, manager, home health pharmacy; b. Dec. 31, 1957, Garden Grove; d. Ray James and Marlene Jean (Madison) Dombroske; m. John Stanley Ross, Aug. 6, 1983 (div. Sept. 1990); edn: AA, Golden West Coll. 1983; Pharm.D, USC 1987; reg. pharmacist Calif. 1987. Career: foods and attraction hostess Disneyland, Anaheim 1976-78; 1979 Disneyland Ambassador to World 1979; pharm. tech. UC Irvine Med. Center, Orange 1977-78; St. Josephs Hosp. 1980-87, pharm. resident 1987-88; assoc. clin. prof. UC San Francisco Sch. of Pharmacy, S.F. 1987-95; drug usage evaluation coord. Kaiser Permanente, Anaheim 1988-90, home health coordinator, 1990-92; Fellow Calif. Soc. of Hosp. Pharmacists, mem: Am. Soc. Hosp. Pharmacists (recipient Hosp. Practitioner award 1992); author Drug Usage Evaluation, 1989, speaker: Drug Usage Evaluation seminar, 1989, Home Care Standards, 1994. Res: 14122 Hereford St Westminster 92683

DOMBROW, RICHARD LYLE, lawyer; b. Mar. 5, 1944, Flagstaff, Ariz.; s. Roman J. and Clementine C. (Casmire) D.; m. Eileen C., Apr. 3, 1976; children: Derian C. b. 1967, Kathleen b. 1983; edn: BS, San Jose St. Univ. 1966; JD, USC 1969; cert. family law specialist (CFLS) Calif. State Bar 1980. Career: dep. dist. atty. Los Angeles Dist. Atty's Office, 1969; pvt. practice law, Orange 1971-75; senior ptnr. Dombrow and McKenna, Orange 1975-79, pvt. practice, Tustin 1979-84, Santa Ana 1984–; planning commnr. City of Tustin 1972-74; honors: Active 20-30 Intl. Member of the Decade (1970s), Falstaff Mgmt. achievement award 1966; mem: Am. Bar Assn., Calif. Bar Assn. (Family Law Splst. Advy. Com. 1989-93), Orange County Bar Assn. (Family Law Sect. pgm. chmn. 1984-85, pres. 1985-86, exec. com. 1987-91), Family Law Bd. of Specialization 1989-93, State Bar Bd. of Specialization 1993-96; civic: Amicus Publico (bd. 1985-89), Active 20-30 Club Intl. (past pres. Santa Ana 1978, dist. gov. 1979-80), World Council of Young Mens Service Clubs (v.chmn. 1981), Helios at Mammoth HOA (pres. 1985-90), Monarch Bay Terrace HOA (pres. 1989-90); Republican; St. Margaret's of Scotland Episcopal Ch., San Juan Capistrano (Bishop's Com. 1989-92, School Bd. Trustees 1990-93); rec: skiing, hunting, fishing, model bldg. Ofc: 444 W 10th St 2nd Fl Santa Ana 92701

DOMBROWER, MARIO, civil engineer; b. June 26, 1941, La Paz, Bolivia, nat. U.S. citizen 1959; s. William G. Dombrower and Jenny C. (Gotthelf) Feigenblatt; m. Beatriz Horowitz, Oct. 30, 1965; children: Michael b. 1967, Shirley b. 1969; edn: BSE, CSU Los Angeles, 1966; MPA, CSU Dominguez Hills, 1985. Career: student profl. wkr. County of Los Angeles, 1961-65; civil engr. Dept. Pub. Works, City of Los Angeles 1965–; awards: outstanding scholar Mayor of New York 1959, Tau Beta Pi 1966, Pi Alpha Alpha 1985, Pub. Works Supr. of Mo. City of L.A. DPW (1990); mem. Am. Soc. Civil Engrs. 1977–, Engrs. and Architects Assn. (bd. govs. L.A. chapt. 1982-88, 92–); Democrat; rec: numismatics, plate collecting, music, crosswords, walking. Res: 6215 Rustling Oaks Dr Agoura Hills 91301-1638 Ofc: DPW, City of Los Angeles,650 S Spring St Ste 900 Los Angeles 90014

DOMINGUEZ, JOHN CHRISTOPHER, systems engineer; b. Oct. 25, 1954, Los Angeles; s. Camilo and Janet Aileen (Lister) D.; m. Maria Eugenia Claveran, June 11, 1977; edn: BS biology, BS computer sci., UC Irvine, 1977; MS Computer Sci., Calif. State Univ., Fullerton, 1993. Career: systems programmer Burroughs Corp., Mission Viejo, 1977-81; systems engr. Hughes Aircraft Co., Fullerton 1981–; rec: photography, baking, gardening. Res: 21202 Cranbridge Dr Lake Forest 92630 Ofc: Hughes Aircraft Co. MS 675/D229 PO Box 3310 Fullerton 92634

DOMONDON, OSCAR, dentist; b. July 4, 1924, Cebu City, Philippines; s. Antero B. and Ursula L. (Maglasang) D.; m. Vicky DeGuzman, Oct. 29, 1983; children: Reinelda b. 1944, Carolyn b. 1954, Catherine b. 1957, Oscar Jr. b. 1961; edn: DMD, Philippine Dental Coll. 1951; AA, St. Marys Univ., San

Antonio Coll. 1960; DDS, Loma Linda Univ. 1964. Career: dentist Sanitarium Hosp., then the U.S. Embassy, Manila; came to U.S. 1954, dental lab technician US Army 1954-60; dentist pvt. practice, Long Beach 1964–; bd. mem. and examiner Calif. State Dental Bd.; awards: Pierre Fauchard Acad. comm. service award; mem: Fellow Am. Coll. Dentists, Fellow Internat. Coll. of Dentists, Fellow Acad. of Dentistry Internat., Nat. Assn. of Filipino Dentists in Am. (pres.), Fellow Acad. of Continuing Edn., Fellow Acad. of Internat. Dental Studies, Lions (past pres.), Elks, Masons; mil: m/sgt. AUS 1946-49, 1954-60; Repub; Prot.; rec: fishing, flying, camping. Res: 3570 Aster St Seal Beach 90740 Ofc: Oscar Domondon, DDS 3714 Atlantic Ave Long Beach 90807

DONALD, PAUL J., professor of medicine; b. Oct. 3, 1938, British Columbia, Canada (nat. 1979); married; four children; edn: BS, Univ. of British Columbia, Vancouver 1960; student, Univ. of Manitoba, Winnipeg 1960-61; MD, Univ. of British Columbia 1964; internship Royal Jubilee Hosp., Victoria, B.C. 1964-65; residency, gen. surgery Canadian Forces Hosp. Esquimalt, Victoria, B.C. 1966-68, St. Paul's Hosp., Vancouver, B.C. 1968-69, Univ. of Iowa Hosps., Iowa City 1969-73, M.S. June 1973; lic. MD British Columbia 1964, Calif. 1973; diplomate Am. Bd. of Otolaryngology 1973, Am. Bd. of Facial Plastic and Reconstructive Surgery 1991. Career: asst. prof. Dept. of Otorhinolaryngology, UC Davis Sch. of Medicine 1973-79, vice chmn. 1978, 1987–, assoc. prof. 1979-84; chief of staff UC Davis Med. Ctr. 1983-85; prof. Dept. of Otolaryngology/Head & Neck Surgery, UC Davis Sch. of Medicine 1984–, coord. of residency tng. 1987-95, fellowship prog. preceptor: adv. tng. in head & neck oncologic surgery, facial plastic & reconstructive surgery 1987–, skull base surgery 1991–; unit dir. Specialty Care Unit, UC Davis Med. Ctr. 1988–; dir. Ctr. for Skull Base Surgery, UC Davis Med. Ctr. 1990–; mem. UC Davis cancer com. 1974–, grad. med. edn advy. com. 1988-95, intensive care unit policies & practice com. 1989–, operating rm. policies com. 1975–, privilege & tenure investigative subcom. 1991–, skull base surgery prog. subcom. 1990–, subcom. on innovative surgery, surgical scis. group coord. com. (chmn.) 1978–; vis. prof. Nat. Taiwan Univ. Hosp., Taipei, Chung Shan Med. & Dental Coll. Hosp., Taichung 1989; oral examiner Am. Bd. of Otolaryngology 1985-86, assoc. 1994–; internat. lecturer; awards: Isbister Scholarship 1961, Mosby Book Award, Psychiatry Prize 1963, H. MacIntosh Award, Psychiatry Prize, Univ. of B.C. 1964, Travel Award, Am. Assn. of Academic Otolaryngology Chairmen, Toronto, Can. 1974, Honor Award, Am. Acad. of Otolaryngology-Head & Neck Surgery 1982, Honorable Mention Thesis - The Triological Soc. 1986, Medal of the City of Paris 1990; mem: Am. Acad. of Facial Plastic and Reconstructive Surgery (bd. dirs., oral examiner, delegate to ACS Bd. Govs. 1992-95, legislative affairs com. 1993–, craniomaxillofacial com 1990–, We. Region v.p. 1992-93), Am. Acad. of Otolaryngology-Head & Neck Surgery (fellow 1974–, instr. 1978–, skull base surgery com. 1988–), Am. Coll. of Surgeons (fellow 1975–), Am. Council of Otolaryngology, Am. Rhinologic Soc. (cons. to bd. dirs. 1991-92), Am. Soc. for Head & Neck Surgery 1982- (councilor 1991-94, ad hoc com. on skull base surgery 1989–), B.C. Med. Assn., CMA (advy. panel for otolaryngology 1976–, advy. com. on legislation 1977–), Calif. Otolaryngology/Head & Neck Surgery Soc. (exec. com. 1989–), Canadian Soc. of Otolaryngology-Head & Neck Surgery 1975–, Head and Neck Intergroup Res. Team 1984–, N. Am. Skull Base Soc. (bd. dirs., founding pres. 1989), Royal Soc. of Medicine 1992–, Sacto. Soc. of Otolaryngology and Maxillofacial Surgery 1978- (sec. 1978, pres. 1979), The Royal Coll. of Physicians and Surgeons of Canada 1975–, The Triological Soc. 1986–, Yolo Co. Med. Soc. 1986–; editor The Otolaryngology Jour. Club Jour.; co-editor Current Controversies in Otolaryngology-Head & Neck Surgery 1989–; reviewer: Jour. of Am. Med. Assn. 1982–, Jour. of Otolaryngology-Head & Neck Surgery 1983, 1985–; author: Head and Neck Cancer: Management of the Difficult Case (W.B. Saunders, Phila., 1984), 19 research papers (others in progress), 1962–, 100+ articles and abstracts pub. in profl. jours., 1962–, numerous papers and lectures; co- author: The Sinuses (Raven Press, NY, 1995), 50+ pub. jour articles, 1962–. Ofc: UC Davis Medical Center Dept. of Otolaryngology/Head & Neck Surgery 2521 Stockton Blvd #7200Sacramento 95817 Tel: 916/734-2832

DONALDSON, JOHN RILEY, physicist, emeritus professor; b. Nov. 24, 1925, Dallas, Tx.; s. John Riley and Marguerette Hoover (Atkinson) D.; m. Shirley Jean Brown, June 30, 1951; children: Nancy b. 1955, Dorothy b. 1957, Jack b. 1960, Jane b. 1960; edn: BS, Rice Univ., 1945, MA, 1947; MS, Yale Univ., 1949, PhD, 1951. Career: physicist Calif. Res. & Devel., Livermore, 1950-53; assoc. prof. Univ. Arizona, Tucson 1953-54; physicist U.S. Army, Frederick, Md. 1954-56; prof. of physics CSU Fresno, Ca. 1956-91, chair dept. physics 1983-91, emeritus prof. 1991–, vol. CSUF, 1991–; honors: All-American Discus, Volleyball AAU (1945, 1951); elected mem., chair Fresno County Bd. of Supervisors 1973-80, Fresno; elected mem. of exec. bd. Calif. Supervisors Assn. of Calif., Sacto. 1979, 80; mem: Am. Physical Soc. 1956–, AAAS 1965–, Am. Assn. of.Physics Tchrs. 1956–; mil: SP3 US Army 1954-56; Democrat; United Ch. of Christ (Coll. Comm. Congl. Ch. 1956–, moderator 1960, 61, chair, trustees 1993, 94, choir dir., soloist); rec: music, singing. Res: 4559 N DeWitt Fresno 93727 Ofc: Physics Dept. Calif. State Univ., Fresno 93740-0037

DONKER, RICHARD BRUCE, hospitals organization executive, clinical services administrator; b. Sept. 29, 1950, Modesto; s. Luverne Peter and Ruth Bernice (Hoekenga) D.; m. Susan Gail Content, May 3, 1986; children:

Elizabeth Anne, Danica Ruth; edn: BS biol./chem., Calvin Coll., 1972; grad. work physiology, UC Davis, 1973; MA in ednl. adminstrn. (high honors) CSU Stanislaus, 1978; EdD in ednl. adminstrn. (med. edn.), Univ. of the Pacific, 1980; paramedic cert. Modesto Junior Coll., 1974. Career: EMT instr. Modesto Jr. Coll., 1973-77; paramedic & ops. mgr. Modesto-Ceres Ambulance Co., 1972-75; grant coord. Yosemite Jr. Coll. Dist., 1975-77; hosp. educator Memorial Hosps. Assn. of Stanislaus County, 1977-78, emergency svs. supr. 1977-80, adminstr. flt. ops., trauma svs. cons., dir. ground ambulances, 1978-87, dir. "HealthPlus" community edn. pgms. and employee asst. pgms., also coord. urgent care ctrs. (Meml. Hosp. Med. Ctr., Modesto; Meml. Hosp. Ceres; St. Rose Hosp., Hayward; Emanuel Hosp. Med. Ctr., Turlock; Sonora Comm. Hosp.; Dominican Hosp., SantaCruz; 4-hosp. Mercy Health Care System, Sacto.; Stanford Univ. Med. Ctr., Pal Alto; Moses Taylor Hosp., Scranton, Pa.), 1983-87; also dir. "Golden HealthPLUS" pgm. for seniors with Medicare, 1986-87; negotiator for HMO and PPO contracting 1986-87; v.p. bus. strategies Memorial Hosps. Assn., 1987-89, v.p. clinical svs., 1989-92; mng. director Global Business Network, Emeryville, Calif. 1992-93; div. pres. Coastal Healthcare Group, Durham, N.C. 1993–; indep. cons. 1979–; pres. Calif. Aeromedical Rescue & Evacuation Inc., opr. Medi-Flight in Modesto and Stockton and Flight Care in Chico, 1985–; exec. dir. MediPLUS Inc., Preferred Provider Org. (4 hosp., 285+ physicians, other health care providers) 1986-92; appt. Stanislaus Co. Dept. Edn. R.O.P. advy. coun. 1980-90, Stanislaus Co. ER Med. Care Com. (1975-77, 88-90), Calif. St. Task force on Air Ambulance Policies 1984-86, Calif. Assn. of Hosps. and Hlth. Systems Trauma/EMS Com. 1987–, NAS Inst. of Medicine Com. on Pediatric ER Med. Svs., WDC 1991-92; del. People-to-People Intl. Citizens Amb. Pgm., PROC 1988; mem: Am. Acad. Med. Adminstrs. (fellow), Phi Delta Kappa 1978–, Commonwealth Club of Calif. 1980–, Calif. Assn. of Air Medical Svs. (founding pres.); composed, recorded sound tracks for 2 children's films: Snail and Friend, The Spell of Bigfoot (distbd. intl.); numerous publs. and profl. presentations in field; rec: pvt. pilot, scuba, sailing, jazz percussionist, classical pianist, travel. Res: 1322 Edgebrook Dr Modesto 95354

DONNELLY, BERNARD PHILIP, JR., state executive, retired; b. April 28, 1927, Washington, D.C.; s. Bernard Philip and Evelyn (Smoot) D.; m. Loraine Louise Barry, June 18, 1951; 1 dau., Cathlin Loraine b. 1961; edn: BA, State Univ. New York, 1950; USC, 1950-51. Career: organization and methods examiner McClellan AFB, Sacto. 1951-53; personnel cons. State Personnel Bd. 1953-58, personnel mgmt. analyst 1959-60; sr. mgmt. analyst State Dept. of Corrections 1960-61; asst. chief surveys S.P. Bd. 1962-66; sr. program and policy cons. Fin. 1966-68; asst. to secty. State Health & Welfare Agency 1968-71; dep. dir. Office of Criminal Justice Planning 1971-74; prin. program budget analyst Fin. 1974-75, chief program evaluation, Fin. 1975-81, prin. program review analyst, Fin. 1981-86; honors: Phi Beta Kappa, Carnation Com. Adminstr. Vol. of Year 1988; mem: Am. Soc. Pub. Adminstr. (pres. 1968-69, chair w. region conf. 1983), Govs. Scholar Com., dep. dir. Conf. 1971-72, Interngovtl. Bd. EDP, Sacto. Co. Adult & Aging Commn., Calif. Capital Enterprises; articles and monograph pub. in profl. jours., 1962-77, ed. Calif. Historic Capitol, 1983; mil: sgt. AUS 1947; Republican; Prot.; rec: community work, Am. Indian crafts, writing. Res: 729 Columbia Dr Sacramento 95864

DONNER, NEAL ARVID, teacher; b. Aug. 17, 1942, Wernigerode, Germany; s. Otto Richard Donner and Jane Hilton (Esch) Sweeney; m. Carol Anne Linnell, May 4, 1968 (div. Dec. 1981); children: Erich b. 1971, Rebecca b. 1971; edn: BA, Oberlin Coll., 1964; MA, Univ. Mich., 1968; PhD, Univ. Brit. Col., 1976. Career: tchr. Peace Corps, Ethiopia, 1964-66; asst. prof. Univ. Va., Charlottesville 1976-78; scholar in residence Cimarron Zen Ctr., Los Angeles 1978-79; violin tchr., L.A., 1981–; awards: Canadian Ministry of Edn. grad. fellow in Japan 1974, Japanese Ministry of Edn. grad. fellow 1975, Karl Bray Award of Libertarian Party Calif. 1991; mem. Suzuki Music Assn. 1981–, Amnesty Internat., ACLU, Citizens Against Govt. Waste, Zen Ctr. of L.A.; translator books: (Japanese) Entrepreneur & Gentleman, 1976, History of Hindu-Buddhist Thought, 1977, (Chinese) The Great Calming & Contemplation, 1993, (French/German) The Legacy of Pythagoras, 1994; Libertarian Party candidate: Calif. State Assembly 1984, 86, Calif. State Senate 1994; outreach dir. L.A. 1991–, Calif. state v.chair 1989, L.A. Westside chair 1984-88; Buddhist; rec: running. Res: 2739 Westgate Ave Los Angeles 90064

DOOLEY, DENNIS JOSEPH, lumber broker, executive; b. May 20, 1950, Los Angeles; s. Joseph George and Edna May (Taylor) D.; m. Jennifer Lynn Starkey, Feb. 20, 1983; children: Tara b. 1983, Daran b. 1988; edn: grad. San Marino H.S. 1969. Career: v.p. Dooley Forest, Industry 1973-85; pres. Studio America, Pasadena 1978-86; pres. American Republic Mills, City of Industry, 1979-84; CEO Dooley Lumber Co., 1987–; CEO Dooley Industries Inc., 1989–; mem: Western Wood Assn., Lumber Assn. So. Calif., City of Industry Mfg. Council (1972-87), Hoo-Hoo Frat. Order of the Forest Product Industry, Pasadena C.of C.; R.Cath.; rec: surfing, sailing, woodworking.

DOOLITTLE, DONALD CHASE, management consultant; b. July 12, 1949, Lincoln, Nebr.; s. Glayne D. and Eleanor (Chase) D.; m. Patricia Joan Stines, Sept. 5, 1970; children: Abigail b. 1976, Andrew b. 1979, Greg b. 1981, James

b. 1986; edn: BS (Magna Cum Laude), Univ. of Nebr., 1971; MBA (high distinction), Harvard Bus. Sch.; CPA, Nebr. Career: mktg. and fin. 3M Co., St. Paul, Minn., 1971-79; v.p. Bain & Co., San Francisco 1979-88; dir. APM Inc., 1988–; dir. Heals Health Plan, Oakland, 1990; awards: Dean's list Univ. Nebr. 1971, Phi Mu Alpha, Phi Eta Sigma, Baker Scholar Harvard Bus. Sch. 1979; mem. Harvard Bus. Sch. of No. Calif.; civic: March of Dimes Gr. Bay Area (past chmn.; dir. 1990–); Republican; rec: instrumental music, sports. Ofc: APM, Inc., 1 Bush St Ste 400 San Francisco 94104

DOOLITTLE, WILLIAM LAWRENCE, information systems management consultant; b. Aug. 15, 1959, Burlington, Vt.; s. William Hotchkiss and Arvilla Jean (Boswell) D.; edn: BBA mgmt., Univ. Alaska 1984; MBA fin., Claremont Grad. Sch. 1987; cert. data processor 1988; cert. info. sys. auditor 1993. Career: firefighter, dispatcher, security ofcr. Univ. Alaska, Fairbanks 1979-84; ops. mgr. Personal Page Inc., Anchorage, Alaska 1985; office systems coordinator OCLC Pacific Network, Claremont 1986-87; mgr. The Warner Group, Woodland Hills 1987–; mem: Info. Systems Security Assn.; Republican; rec: sports. Ofc: The Warner Group 5950 Canoga Ave Ste 600 Woodland Hills 91367

DOR, YORAM, accountant, health care executive; b. April 17, 1945, Tel Aviv; s. Simon and Shulamit (Remple) D.; m. Ofra Lipshitz, April 9, 1967; children: Gil, Ron; edn: Hebrew Univ. Jerusalem 1969; BA econ., Tel Aviv Univ. 1971; MBA, UCLA 1977; C.P.A. Calif. Career: sr. auditor Somekh Chaikin CPA, Tel Aviv 1969-72; c.f.o. E. African Hotels, Dar-es-Salaam, Tanzania 1972-74; staff acct. Hyatt Med. Enterprises Inc., Encino 1974-75, controller 1977-79, v.p. fin. 1979-82, sr. v.p. fin., c.f.o. 1987–, bd. dirs.; mem: Am. Inst. C.P.A., Calif. Soc. C.P.A. Ofc: NU Med Inc. 16633 Ventura Blvd Encino 91436

DORN, ROBERT MURRAY, psychiatrist, educator; b. May 1, 1921, Cleveland, Ohio; s. Karl and Frieda (Cohan) D.; m. Natalia Ivanavna Borokhovich, Nov. 28, 1964; children: Mrs. Nancy Dorn-Stuart, Robert, Mary Beth, Anthony J.; edn: BS, Western Reserve Univ. 1941; MS, 1944; MD, 1945. Career: intern Strong Meml. Hosp., Univ. Rochester, N.Y. 1945-46; tng. Univ. London 1948-49; clin. clk. Nat. Hosp. Queens Sq. Inst. Neurology 1948-49; psychoanalytic trainee British Inst. Psychoanalysis 1948-51; pvt. practice psychoanalysis, Beverly Hills 1953-75; pvt. practice psychiatry, Davis 1986–, Sacto. 1986–; prof. psychiatry UC Davis 1981-86, clin. prof. 1986–; attdg. psychiatrist L.A. Psychiatric Services, 1955-59; instr. Davis Clinic Child Guidance, L.A. 1955-59; lectr. Los Angeles Inst. Psychoanalysis 1958-65, sr. faculty 1965-68, tng. analyst 1968-75, analyst supr. 1969-75; cons. Whittier Family Service Agy. 1960-68, Reiss Davis Child Study Center, 1960-75; asst. clin. prof. Sch. Med. UCLA 1962-69, assoc. clin. prof. 1969-75; prof. Med. Sch. E. Va. Univ., Norfolk 1975-81; contbr. articles to profl. jours.; civic: chmn. psychiatric div. Comm. Chest, L.A. 1959-60, instr. Beverly Hills YMCA 1964-75, mem. Town Hall Calif. 1964-75, founding patron Huntington Hartford Theatre Wing, Greek Theatre, sustaining mem. Comm. TV, L.A. Co. Mus. Art, mem. Tidewater Assembly on Family Life 1977-81, Task Force on School-Age Parents 1977-81, profl. advy. bd. Parents with Heart 1982-86, advy. bd. Yolo Co. Mental Health 1986-88; awards: Sigma Xi, disting. service YMCA 1966; Fellow: Am. Orthopsychiatric Assn., Royal Soc. Health, Am. Coll. Psychiatrists, Am. Coll. Psychoanalysts, Am. Acad. Child & Adolescent Psychology; mem: AMA, CMA, So. Calif. Med. Assn. (council 1964-68), Yolo Co. Med. Soc. (exec. com. 1986-91), British Psychoanalytical Soc., Internat. Psychoanalytical Soc., Am. Psychiatric Assn., Am. Psychoanalytical Assn. (del. 1960-63, 1968-75), Crocker Art Museum, Crocker Soc., Sacto. Symphony (concertmaster 1986–), Sacto. Opera (patron), Internat. House Davis; club: El Macero CC; mil: capt. USAF 1946-47, AUS 1953-55; rec: golf, tennis. Ofc: 79 Scripps Dr Ste 212 Sacramento 95825; 433 F St Davis 95616

DORNAN, ROBERT KENNETH, congressman; b. Apr. 3, 1933, N.Y.C.; s. Harry Joseph and Gertrude Consuelo (McFadden) D.; m. Sallie Hansen, Apr. 16, 1955; children: Robin Marie, Robert Kenneth II, Theresa Ann, Mark Douglas, Kathleen Regina; edn: student, Loyola Univ., Westchester, Calif., 1950-53. Career: host TV polit. talk shows in Los Angeles, 1965-73; host, producer: Robert K. Dornan Show, Los Angeles, 1970-73; combat photographer/broadcast journalist assigned 8 times to Laos-Cambodia-Vietnam, 1965-74; nat. spokesman Citizens for Decency Through Law, 1973-76; mem. 95th-97th Congresses from 27th Calif. dist., 1977-83, 99th-104th Congresses from 38th (now 46th) Calif. dist., 1985–; chmn. House Reps. Study Commn. 99th-102d Congresses from 38th Calif. dist., 1989-91,103d Congress from 46th Calif. dist.; mem: Am. Legion, Navy League, Air Force Assn., Res. Officers Assn., AMVETS, Assn. Former Intelligence Officers, Special Forces Assn., AFTRA; lodge: K.C.; originator POW/MIA bracelet; mil: served to capt.; as fighter pilot USAF, 1953-58, as fighter pilot and amphibian rescue pilot USAFR, 1958-75; Republican; Roman Catholic. Ofc: Rm 1201 Longworth Office Bldg Washington DC 20515

DORNBUSCH, SANFORD MAURICE, sociologist; b. June 5, 1926, New York; s. Meyer and Gertrude (Weisel) D.; m. Barbara Anne Farnham, Feb. 28, 1950; children: Jeffrey Neil b. 1953, Steven Samuel b. 1957; edn: BA, Syracuse Univ. 1948; MAUniv. Chgo. 1950; PhD 1952. Career: assoc. prof. sociology

Univ. Wash. 1958-59; asst. prof. sociology Harvard Univ., Cambridge, Mass. 1955-58; prof. sociology Stanford Univ., Stanford 1959–, prof. edn. 1977–, Reed Hodgson Prof. of Human Biology 1978–, dir. center for study of families children and youth 1987-91; awards: Walter J. Gores award Excellence in Tchg. 1984, Who's Who in World; mem: Am. Sociological Assn. (chmn. social psychology sect., sociology of edn. sect., methodology sect.), Pacific Sociological Assn. (pres. 1963-64), Soc. for Res. on Adolescence (pres. 1992-94), Feminism Children & New Families, 1988, Tchr. Evaluation Standards Student Effort, 1984. Res: 841 Pine Hill Rd Stanford 94305 Ofc: Stanford University Dept. of Sociology Stanford 94305-2047

DORNETTE, RALPH MEREDITH, church administrator; b. Aug. 31, 1927, Cincinnati.; s. Paul August and Lillian (Bauer) D.; m. Betty Jean Pierce, May 11, 1948; 1 dau., Cynthia Anne Orndorff; edn: AB (Valedictorian), Cincinnati Bible Coll., 1948; Cincinnati Bible Sem., 1948-51; Talbot Theol. Sem., La Mirada, Calif. 1967. Career: assoc. prof. Cincinnati Bible Coll., Oh. 1948-51; senior minister Indian Creek Christian Ch., Cynthiana, Ky. 1946-51; First Christian Ch., Muskogee, Ok. 1951-57; founding minister Bellaire Christian Ch., Tulsa, Ok. 1957-59; exec. dir. So. Calif Evangelistic Assn., Torrance, Calif. 1959-62, 68-77; founding minister Eastside Christian Ch., Fullerton 1962-68; c.e.o. Church Devel. Fund., Fullerton (1968-77, 79-94, ret.); prof. of ministries Cincinnati (Ohio) Bible Sem. 1977-79, bd. dirs. 1973-77; bd. secty. Midwest Christian Coll., Oklahoma City, 1955-62; honoree, Churchman of Yr., Pacific Christian Coll., Fullerton 1973; mem. No. Am. Christian Conv., Cincinati. (v.p. 1972, exec. com. 1963, 70-72, 80-82); So. Calif. Christian Ministers Assn., Fullerton (pres. 1975), Financial Planning Ministry (pres. 1986-94), Homeowners Assn. Anaheim (bylaws com. 1979-80, pres. 1980-82, exec. bd. 1983); author: Bible Answers to Popular Questions (1954, Book II, 1961), Walking With Our Wonderful Lord 1955; rec: travel, photography. Res: 2133 Begonia Ct Hemet 92545

DORR, LAWRENCE D., physician, orthopaedic surgeon; b. April 13, 1941, Storm Lake, Iowa; s. M. Everett and Evelyn (Knoll) D.; m. Marilyn Minard, April 2, 1962; children: Michael b. 1963, Kristina b. 1967, Randy b. 1969; edn: BA, Cornell Coll. 1963; BA, Iowa Med.Sch. 1963; MS, 1965; L.A. Co.- USC Med. Sch. 1967-68. Career: staff physician Rancho Arthritis, Downey 1977-; assoc. clin. prof. UC Irvine 1983-; assoc. Kerlan-Jobe, Inglewood 1983-92; prof. orthopedic surgery, USC 1992–; dir. Ctr. for Arthritis and Joint Implant Ctr. 1992–; awards: USC Outstanding Resident 1975-76; mem: Am. Acad. Orthopaedic Surgeons, Knee (founding mem., pres. 1990), Hip Soc., Assn. of Arthritic Hip and Knee Surgery (founding mem., v.p. 1991); club: Annandale Golf; editor Techniques in Orthopaedics, 1985-, founding editor Journal of Arthroplasty, 1983-; designer of APR Hip System, 1983, and designer of Apollo Knee System, 1992; mil: lt. cmdr. USN 1968-71; Republican; Methodist; rec: sports. Ofc: 501 E Hardy Ste 300 Inglewood 90301

DOUGHERTY, BETSEY OLENICK, architect; b. Oct. 25, 1950, Guantanamo Bay, Cuba; d. Everett Jacob and Charlotte (Kristal) Olenick; m. Brian Paul Dougherty, Aug. 25, 1974; children: Gray Brenner b. 1979, Megan Victoria b. 1986; edn: BA Arch., UC Berkeley, 1972, MArch., 1975; reg. architect Calif., 1978. Career: designer, drafter HO&K, San Francisco 1975-76; job capt. Wm. Blurock & Ptnrs., Newport Beach 1976-78; assoc. architect UC Irvine 1978-79; ptnr. Dougherty & Dougherty, Newport Beach 1979–; awards: design awards Design Internat. 1981, AIA Orange Co. (1981-86, 1990), Illuminating Engr. Soc. 1987, Pacific Coast Builders Conf. grand award, Con. Mas. Design 1992, NSBA 1993-94, CASH Dessign award 1992-94; Fellow AIA; mem. AIA/Wash. D.C. (secty. 1993-94, nat. bd. 1989-91), AIA/Calif. (state pres. 1988-89), AIA/Orange Co. (pres. 1984), Calif. Women in Environ. Design; rec: sailing, travel. Ofc: Dougherty & Dougherty, 3 Civic Plaza Ste 230 Newport Beach 92663

DOUGHERTY, HOWARD WILLIAM, oil and gas producer; b. Jan. 5, 1915, Kansas City, Mo.; s. Frank C. and Elsie (Braecklein) D.; m. Violeta van Ronzelen; edn: BS, Stanford Univ. 1938. Career: oil and gas producer, Pasadena 1947–; dir. Los Angeles Turf Club; pres. Pioneer Kettleman Co., Book Cliffs Oil & Gas Co.; pres. Trend Oil Co.; pres. Bret Harte Realty Co.; dir. and v.p. Hollywood Turf Club 1954-80, dir. emeritus 1980–; mem: Conservation Com. Calif., Ind. Petroleum Assn. of Am., API, IPAA, Am. Inst. Mech. Engrs. (past), Beta Theta Pi; civic: San Gabriel Valley Boy Scouts, Los Angeles Boy Scouts, Pres.'s Circle L.A. Co. Mus., Founders L.A. Music Center, So. Calif. Tennis Assn. (dir.), Youth Tennis Found. of So. Calif. (pres.), Loyola Marymount Univ. (former regent), St. Mary's Coll. (past bd. trustees), Villanova and Woodside Priory (past bd. trustees), Soc. of Calif. Pioneers; clubs:, California, Bohemian, Valley Hunt, Riviera (Coral Gables, Fla.), New Orleans. Ofc: 304 N Canyon Blvd Monrovia 91016

DOUGHERTY, WILLIAM ANDERSEN, lawyer; b. April 18, 1924, Arlington, Mass.; s. William Leonard and Alice A. (Andersen) D.; m. Sharlee Powers, April 14, 1961 (div. 1978); children: Robyn b. 1963, William P. b. 1965, Shannon b. 1970; edn: BA, Bowdoin Coll. 1948; JD, Cornell Law Sch. 1955. Career: asst. U.S. atty. Dept. of Justice, Wash. D.C. 1955-58; asst. counsel U.S. Sentate Judiciary Com. 1959-60; asst. U.S. atty. Strike Force, L.A. 1960-

61; atty. pvt. practice, Orange Co. 1970–; mil: col. USMC 1942-76, 2 Disting. Flying Crosses, 4 Air Medals; Republican (Cent. Com.); Episcopalian; rec: flying, railroads. Res: 18352 Serrano Ave Villa Park 92667

DOUGLASS, ENID HART, educator, oral history program director; b. Oct. 23, 1926, Los Angeles; d. Frank Roland and Enid Yandell (Lewis) Hart; m. Malcolm P. Douglass, Aug. 28, 1948; children: Malcolm Paul Jr., John Aubrey, Susan Enid; edn: BA, Pomona Coll., 1948; MA, Claremont Grad. Sch., 1959. Career: research asst. World Book Ency., Palo Alto 1953-54; exec. secty., asst. dir. oral history pgm. Claremont Grad. Sch., 1963-71, dir. oral history pgm., 1971–, history lectr., 1977–; appt. Calif. Heritage Preservation Comn. 1977-85, chair 1983-85; Planning & Research Advy. Council Calif.; mem. Claremont City Council 1978-86, mayor pro tem 1980-82, mayor 1982-86; recipient disting. alumna award Claremont Graduate Sch. 1981, J.V. Mink award Southwest Oral Hist. Assn. 1984, award for outstanding svc. to community L.W.V. 1986; founder Claremont Heritage Inc., 1977-80, bd. dirs. 1986-89; bd. dirs. Pilgrim Place, Claremont; founder, bd. dirs. (v.p. 1990, pres. 1990-94) Claremont Community Found.; mem. Oral Hist. Assn. (pres. 1979-80), Southwest Oral Hist. Assn. (founding steering com. 1981), Nat. Council Pub. Hist., L.W.V. (bd. 1957-59); Democrat. Res: 1195 Berkeley Ave Claremont 91711 Ofc: Oral History Pgm. Claremont Graduate School 710 N College Ave Claremont 91711-5908

DOVE, DONALD AUGUSTINE, city and regional planner; b. Aug. 7, 1930, Waco, Tx.; s. Sebert Constantine and Amy Delmena (Stern) D.; m. Cecelia Mae White, Feb. 9, 1957; children: Angela b. 1958, Donald b. 1961, Monica b. 1963, Celine b. 1964, Austin b. 1965, Cathlyn b. 1968, Dianna b. 1970, Jennifer b. 1972; edn: BA, CSU Los Angeles, 1951; MPA, USC, 1966; Cert. Planner, Am. Inst. Cert. Planners, 1975. Career: regional planner L.A. County Regional Planning Commn., 1954-59; cons./rep. King Associates, L.A. 1959-60; research analyst Calif. Div. of Highways, L.A. 1960-66, planner, Sacto. 1966-72; br. mgr. planner Calif. Dept. Transp., L.A. 1972-93; guest lectr. urban affairs, pop. forecasting, transp., envir. mgmt., Univ. Calif., Calif. St. Univs., 1966-91; planning commr. (chair) City of Lynwood, and previous cities, 1979–; dir. Dove Found., L.A. 1985-91; mem. Am. Planning Assn. 1955–, So. Calif. Assn. for Pub. Adminstrn. (dir. L.A. 1983-87), Que-Up Found. 1993–, Kts. Col. 1982–, Kts. of Peter Claver (1959–, fin. sec 1976-88), L.A. Civic Ct. Optimist Club (dir., sec. 1973–); author: Preserving the Urban Environment, 1975, articles on travel, environ., urban concensus, etc., 1964-81; mil: cpl. US Army 1952-54; R.Cath.; rec: model making, sailing. Ofc: Better Neighborhoods 11356 Ernestine Ave Lynwood 90262-3711

DOW, FREDERICK WARREN, university professor of international management; b. Aug. 2, 1917, Boston; s. Frederick Vincent and Marcia (McMahon) D.; m. Patricia Rathbone, Oct. 2, 1943; edn: BS in chemistry (magna cum laude) Boston Coll. 1940; MS physical chem. (high distinction) Univ. Mass. 1942; AM ednl. psych. Yale Univ. 1949, PhD adminstrn., 1954. Career: sales personnel mgr. Dow Chemical Co., 1951-59; asst. to gen. mgr. of chem. sales, 1959-61; gen. sales mgr., New York, Dow Chemical Internat., 1961-64; mng. dir. Dow Chemical France, 1964-66; gen. mgr. assoc. cos. Latin Am. and Pacific, Dow Chem. Co., 1966-67; pres. Econ. Devel. Corp., Southbend, Ind., A Model Cities Agy., 1970-74; chmn. exec. com. Minority Venture Co. (Univ. Notre Dame) 1973-77; mng. ptnr. KCD & Assocs., Mgmt. Cons., South Bend, Ind. 1967-79; chmn. bd. Kestrel Inc., Mgmt. Consultants, Carlsbad, Calif. 1979–; Dir.: Berkel Inc., Laporte, Ind. 1975–, Rambend Inc., South Bend (also v.p., treas.) 1970–, Arrar Group N.V. internat. holding co. (v.chmn. bd.) 1985–; apptd. cons. Pres. Johnson's McKinney Commn. (to decrease travel gap), 1968; sci. advy. com. Italy Ministry of Tourism, 1973-89; Sr. Fulbright Scholar, lectr. Catholic Univ. of Ecuador, Quito, 1973-74; prof. mktg., Hayes-Healy Prof. Grad. Sch. of Bus. Univ. Notre Dame, 1967-77; prof. bus. adminstrn. U.S. Internat. Univ., San Diego, 1977-81, prof. internat. mgmt. 1981–, dean USIU Sch. of Bus. and Mgmt., 1986-88; mil: major USAAF, 1943-46, command meteorologist 9th Bombardment Cmd., ETO, awarded Bronze star and Air medal 3 o.l.c.; mem. Sigma Xi, Am. Chem. Soc., Soc. de Chemie Industrielle, Union League Club (NY), Travellers Club (Paris); author book: Estrategia de Planeamiento (1974), articles in bus. jours.; Republican; Episcopalian. Res: 5080 Carlsbad Blvd Carlsbad 92008 Ofc: U.S. International Univ., 10455 Pomerado Rd San Diego 92121

DOW, JAMES RICHARD, industrial designer, set designer, art director; b. Mar. 8, 1943, Long Beach, Calif.; s. Frederic Arthur and Marion Laurine (Lemon) D.; m. Susan Claire Petroni, Apr. 10, 1980; children: Jameson Chase, Ian Thomas Scot; edn: BS design, CSU Long Beach, 1967. Career: designer Universal Pictures, Studio City 1969-72; coordinator, designer Columbia Pictures, Hollywood 1973-76; art dir., creative dir. Paramount Pictures, Hollywood 1976-81; show designer Disney Studios, Burbank 1983-84, Walt Disney Imagineering, Burbank 1984; art dir., designer Dow Design, Newport Beach 1980–; film credits include: Silent Running, Close Encounters of the Third Kind, Star Trek: The Motion Picture, Heavenly Kid, Russkies; TV shows: Cosmos (Emmy award 1980), Mork and Mindy, Little House on the Prairie, Greatest American Hero; various TV commercials; mem: Industrial Designers Soc. Am., Acad. TV Arts and Scis., Am. Film Inst., Exhibit Designers and Producers Assn.; mil: sgt. Nat. Guard 1963-69; rec: sailing, painting, sculpting. Ofc: Dow Design 872 W 18th St Costa Mesa 92627

DOW, MAY M., pediatrician; b. Aug. 25, 1947, Jerusalem, nat. 1987; d. Ibrahim and Antoinette Mudarry; m. Tony Dow, Dec. 25, 1976; edn: MD, Damascus Univ., Syria 1972; postgrad. splty. tng. in pediatrics Emory Univ., Atlanta, Ga.; diplomate Am. Bd. Ped., 1975. Career: pvt. practice pediatrician, Whittier, Calif. 1978–; v.p. internat. & med. affairs Lifecare Internat. Inc.; chief pediatrics Presbyterian Intercomm. Hosp., Whittier 1986; examiner Med. Quality Assur. Bd. Calif.; honors: ranked No. 1 student among among 10,000+ High Sch. graduates (1963); mem: Am. Pediatrics Soc., L.A. Co. Med. Assn., Calif. Med. Assn., Whittier Med. Assn., Assn. Women Physicians, Am. Assn. Physicians and Surgeons; research: diabetes and digestive diseases. Ofc: Lifecare Intl., Inc. 14831 Whittier Blvd Ste 103 Whittier 90605

DOWELL, ROBERT VERNON, entomologist; b. Sept. 13, 1947, San Francisco; s. Robert Leroy and Clare Adel (Smith) D.; m. Linda Kay Wange, March 15, 1974; children: Elizabeth b. 1987, Alexander b. 1994; edn: BS, UC Irvine 1969; MS, CSU Hayward 1972; PhD, Ohio St. Univ. 1976. Career: asst. res. scientist Univ. Fla., Ft. Lauderdale 1977-80; pest mgmt. splst. Calif. Dept. Food & Agri., Sacto. 1980-83, assoc. econ. entomologist 1983-86, sr. econ. entomologist 1986–; cons. Marine World, Vallejo 1988; instr. UC Davis 1985–; bd. dirs. San Francisco Insect Zoo 1985–; awards: Calif. Dept. Food & Agri. superior accomplishment 1985, 94; mem: Calif. Acad. Sci. (fellow), N. Calif. Entomology Club (pres. 1988), Pacific Coast Entomological Soc. (pres. 1990), AAAS, Entomological Soc. Am.; author: 60 articles pub. in sci. jours., 1974–, ed. Apple Maggot in West, 1989; assoc. ed. Pan-Pacific Entomologist 1993-95, editor 1996–; rec: fishing, butterfly collecting. Ofc: California Dept. of Food and Agriculture 1220 N St Sacramento 95814

DOWNEY, PAUL SCOTT, chief executive officer; b. May 1, 1959, San Diego; s. Albert Russell and Joan Hastie (Scott) D.; m. Mary Katherine Curran, Jan. 8, 1983; 1 child, Colin b. 1988; edn: BA, San Diego St. Univ. 1981. Career: ed., reporter KSDO Radio, San Diego 1979-82; political reporter KWMS Radio, Salt Lake City, Utah 1982; mng. ed. Copley Videotex, San Diego 1982-84; editl. mgr. Times Mirror Videotex, Santa Ana 1984-86; press secty. Mayors Office, San Diego 1986-92; asst. CEO, San Diego Consortium & Private Industry Council, 1992-94; CEO, Senior Community Centers of San Diego, 1995–; num. articles and speeches pub.; Democrat; rec: running, gardening. Ofc: Office of the Mayor 202 C St San Diego 92101

DOWNING, JACQY LESLEY HARRISON, registered nurse, administrator; b. July 17, 1941, Stone, England; nat. 1958; d. J. Norman Standage and Murielle Mercer (Wood) Harrison; m. Dennis Robert Rowe, April 26, 1959 (div. 1969); m. Robert Downing, Nov. 28, 1970; children: Russell b. 1959, Robert b. 1961; edn: AA summa cum laude, Barstow Coll., 1974; ASN (honors), Grossmont Coll., 1978; BSN, Regents Coll., 1984; MBA health care adminstrn., National Univ., 1986. Career: office mgr. So. Calif. Water Co., Barstow 1965-74; sr. nurse aide Barstow Hosp. 1974-75; vocational nurse Kelly & Profl. Nurses Bureau, San Diego 1976-77; emergency room nurse, nursing supr. Valley Med. Ctr., El Cajon 1977-86; nursing supr., quality assurance coord. Inland Valley Reg. Med. Ctr., Wildomar 1986-88; health facilities evaluator nurse supr. Calif. Dept. Health Svs., San Diego 1988-94 (ret.); asst. adminstr. Golden State Manor, S.D. 1994-95 (ret.); critical care transp. nurse Schaeffer Amublance, S.D. 1982-86; nursing inservice instr. Valley Med. Ctr., El Cajon 1984-86; Inland Valley Reg. Med. Center Wildomar 1986-88; emergency med. tech. instr. Mt. San Jacinto Jr. Coll. 1987-88; student mem. Am. Coll. Healthcare Execs.; Eastern Star; Republican; Episcopalian; rec: golf, swimming. Res: 10334 Rancho Carmel Dr San Diego 92128

DOYLE, DONALD WILLIAM, real estate developer; b. June 6, 1945, Los Angeles; s. William and Helen (Barrett) D.; m. Mary Nocerine, Dec. 3, 1969 (div. 1977); m. Dollee Stillwell, June 20, 1986; children: Sean b. 1971, Bridget b. 1973, Meghan b. 1976; edn: BBA, Loyola Univ. 1967. Career: freight service supr. trainer Am. Airlines, Los Angeles 1966-70; real estate sales, mgmt. Sail Realty, Marina del Rey 1969-77; pres., Calif. Devel. Co. 1977–; founding dir. Exec. S&L, Marina del Rey 1983-85; citizen advy. commn. City Council 6th Dist. Venice 1983; awards: Venice Marina del Rey Bd. Realtor of Year 1982, Calif. Assn. Realtors GRI 1978, Pres.'s Circle 1985; mem: Venice Bd. Realtors (dir. 1972–), Calif. Assn. Realtors (speakers bureau 1981-86), Venice Marina del Rey Area Bd. Realtors (pres. 1981), Long Range Planning Com. (1987, 88, 89), Calif. Assn. Realtors (chmn. land use com. 1983, 20th dist. reg. v.p. 1984, chmn. state condominium/ shared ownership com. 1986, budget & fin. com. 1990), Marina Peninsula Property Owners Assn. (pres. 1973-75), Playa del Rey Penn. Neighborhood Assn. (bd. mem. 1989–, pres. 1989), L.A. Co. Beach Advy. Com. (bd. mem. 1989–); mil: USCG 1967-69; Republican; Cath. Res: 6206 Pacific Ave #2 Playa del Rey 90293 Ofc: Calif. Development Corp. 6206 Pacific Ave #2 Playa del Rey 90293

DOYLE, MICHAEL JAMES, school principal; b. Aug. 24, 1939, Bell, Calif.; s. Joseph Edward and Irma Louise (Smith) D.; m. Mina Katherine Martensen, Feb. 8, 1964; children: Michael II b. 1967, Mary b. 1970, Matthew b. 1974; edn: BA, Whittier Coll., 1961, ME, 1971. Career: tchr. El Rancho Unified Sch. Dist., Pico Rivera 1961-79, jr. high dept. chair 1967-74, actg. principal 1979; tchg. asst. prin.

Alta Loma Sch. Dist., 1979-86, summer sch. prin. 1985, elementary sch. principal, Alta Loma, 1986–; organist and choir director various Luth. chs. So. Calif. 1955-86, St. Paul's Lutheran Ch., Pomona 1986–; mem.: Calif. State Rev. Team, Rancho Cucamonga, 1982-83, Calif. Sch. Leadership Acad., San Bdo. 1986-89; tchg. awards: Outstanding tchr. of yr. Burke Jr. H.S. PTA, Pico Rivera 1973, Honor svc. Jasper Sch. PTA, Alta Loma 1983, cont. svc. Jasper Sch. PTA 1988, employee recogn. Alta Loma Sch. Dist. 1985; mem: So. Calif. Music Clinic (v.p. 1978-81), Assn. Calif. Sch. Adminstrs. 1979–, Assn. of West End Sch. Adminstrs. 1979–, Am. Guild Organists 1961–, Phi Delta Kappa 1980- (ch. pres. 1993–); civic bds.: Zion Luth. Sch. Bd., Maywood (1962-67, chmn. 1966-67), Downey City Water Board 1977-78, Luth. H.S. Edn. Com. 1988–, Cucamonga Hist. Soc. 1981–; Democrat; Lutheran, Mo. Synod; rec: music. Res: 2085 N Palm Ave Upland 91784 Ofc: Jasper School 6881 Jasper St Alta Loma 91701

DOYLE, OWEN PAUL, physician-cardiac anesthesiologist; b. Nov. 30, 1934, Mpls.; s. Dr. Larry Oscar and Veronica Anastasia (Walsh) D.; m. Barbara Taylor, Jan. 7, 1961; children: Owen b. 1965, Megan b. 1974; edn: BA (cum laude) Univ. of Minn., 1956, BS (cum laude), 1957, MD, 1960. Career: resident in anesthesiology, UC San Francisco, 1963-65; cardiac anesthesiologist Peninsula Hosp. and Med. Center, Burlingame 1966–; asst. clin. prof., anesth., Stanford Univ. Hosp. and Med. Ctr., 1981-87; mem. and pres. SPEBSQSA/ San Mateo Co. chpt., barbershop singing orgn., Bass singer in "Fog City Four" & "Regular Rhythm Boys" quartets; pub. article in med. jour. (1965); mil: 1st lt. Med. Corps USN 1962-64; Republican; R.Cath.; rec: water sports, flying, tennis, golf. Ofc: 1838 El Camino Real Ste 107 Burlingame 94010

DOYLE, ROBERT ALAN, psychiatrist; b. June 12, 1935, Chgo.; s. Robert Morrison and Carmen Clara (Dorweiler) D.; m. Cary Tilton, May 10, 1969; children: Anne de Peyster Cary b. 1970, Brude Dickinson Stoever b. 1968, Henry von Hoff Stoever b. 1966; edn: BS, Mich. State Univ. 1957; MD, Yale Univ. 1961; MD, Duke Univ. Med. Sch. 1963; psychiatrist Am. Assn. Psychiatry 1969. Career: psychiatric residency Duke Hosp., Durham, N.C. 1963-69; staff psych. Broward Gen. Hosp. Ft. Lauderdale 1969-84; chief of staff Coral Ridge Psych. Hosp. 1969-84; assoc. med. dir. Brightside ACT Carmel 1984-86; staff psychiatrist Community Hosp. Monterey Peninsula 1984–, chief psychiat. div. 1989-90; mem: Am. Psych. Assn., AMA, Carmel Valley Garden Club, Royal Horticultural Soc., Am. Horticultural Soc., Asian Art Soc.; mil: capt. USAF 1966-68; Republican; Episcopalian; rec: gardening, Chinese Armorial Porcelain collector. Ofc: 3855 Via Nona Marie Ste 109 Carmel 93923

DRACHNIK, CATHERINE MELDYN, art therapist; b. June 7, 1924, Kansas City, Mo.; d. Gerald Willis and Edith (Gray) Weston; m. Joseph Brennan Drachnik, Oct. 6, 1946; children: Denise Elaine, Kenneth John; edn: BS, Univ. Md., 1945; MA, CSU Sacramento, 1975; Calif. lic. Marriage, Family & Child Counselor (MFCC), reg. Art Therapist. Career: art therapist Vincent Hall Retirement Home, also Fairfax (McLean, Va.) and Arlington (Va.) Mental Health Day Treatment Ctrs., 1972-73; art therapist Hope for Retarded, San Jose, Calif., also Sequoia Hosp., Redwood City, 1972-73; supvg. tchr. adult edn. Sacto. Soc. Blind, 1975-77; ptnr. Sacramento Div. Mediation Svs., 1981-82; instr. CSU Sacto. 1975-82, Coll. Notre Dame, Belmont 1975–; art therapist, mental health counselor Psych West Counseling Ctr., Carmichael 1975-93; private practice, Sacramento 1994–; instr. Univ. Utah, S.L.C., 1988–; lectr. in field; art exhs., solo and group juried shows, U.S. and internat.; mem: Am. Art Therapy Assn. (pres. 1987-89, hon. life 1991), No. Calif. Art Therapy Assn., Calif. Coalition of Rehab. Therapists, Nat. Art Edn. Assn., Am. Assn. Marriage and Family Therapists, Kappa Kappa Gamma Alumnae Assn. (chpt. pres. 1991-92), Alpha Psi Omega, Omicron Nu; Republican; rec: swimming, golf, theater. Res/Ofc: 4124 American River Dr Sacramento 95864 Tel: 916/489-0316

DRACHNIK, JOSEPH BRENNAN, retired naval officer, lawyer; b. June 11, 1919, Ross, Calif.; s. George and Mary Ann (Brennan) D.; m. Cay Weston, Oct. 6, 1946; children: Denise b. 1952, Kenneth b. 1957; edn: junior cert. UCB, 1939; BSEE, US Naval Acad. 1942; MS Internat. Affairs, George Washington Univ. 1967; JD, McGeorge Sch. of Law UOP 1981; admitted Calif. St. Bar. Career: served to Capt. US Navy 1942-72, participated in invasion of Guadalcanal 8/7/42, served in major campaigns of WWII on destroyers in Pacific, Comd. Fleet Tug, Destroyer Escort, Destroyer; promoted Capt. USN 1962, Chief of Naval Advy. Mission in Vietnam 1961-64, staff, Secty. of Def. McNamara, 1964-66, staff del. to Australia New Zealand-U.S. (ANZUS) Treaty Conf. 1966, and to SEATO Treaty Conf. 1965; Nat. War College 1967; Comdr. Amphibious Task Force, US Sixth Fleet 1968; c/s to Comdr. Amphib. Force, Atlantic Fleet 1969-70, ret. 6/1/72; Exec. Asst. to Calif. Lt. Gov. Ed Reinecke 1973-74; Cabinet Secty. to Gov. Reagan 1974; atty. in pvt. practice 1982-91; mem. Calif. State Bar, U.S. Naval Acad. Alumni Assn.; mil. decorations: Navy Unit Cit. (1942), Legion of Merit w/combat star (1964), Merit. Svc. (1966), var. cpgn. medals; rec: woodworking, gardening, golf. Res: 4124 American River Dr Sacramento 95864

DRAKE, FRANK D., professor of astronomy and astrophysics; b. May 28, 1930, Chgo.; s. Richard Carvel and Winifred (Thompson) D.; m. Elizabeth Bell, Mar. 7, 1953 (div. 1977); children: Stephen, Richard, Paul; m. Amahl Zekin Shakhashiri, Mar. 4, 1978; children: Nadia, Leila; edn: BA engring. physics (honors), Cornell Univ., 1952; MS and PhD astronomy, Harvard Univ., 1956, 58. Career: electronics ofcr. USN, 1952-56; Agassiz Station Radio Astronomy Project, Harvard Univ. 1956-58; hd. telescope ops. & sci. svcs. div. Nat. Radio Astronomy Observatory, Green Bank, W.Va. 1958-63 (discovered the radiation belts of Jupiter, organized 1st search for ETI signals, Project OZMA 1960; devised Drake Equation- an estimate of communicative extraterrestrial civilizations in our galaxy 1961); chief of lunar & planetary scis. Jet Propulsion Lab, 1963-64; prof. astronomy Cornell Univ. 1964-84: dept. chmn. 1969-71, Goldwin Smith Prof. Astronomy 1976-84, dir. Arecibo (P.R.) Observatory 1966-68, first dir. Nat. Astronomy & Ionosphere Ctr. 1970-81 (constructed first interstellar message transmitted via radio waves from our planet to any ETI "Arecibo Message of 1974"); prof. astronomy & astrophysics UC Santa Cruz, 1984–, dean natural scis. div. 1984-88, acctg. assoc. v. chancellor 1989-90; apptd: SETI Inst. (pres. 1984-), Astronomical Soc. of Pacific (pres. 1988-90), NRC bd. physics and astronomy (chmn.), NSF (astronomy advy. com., Alan T. Waterman Awards com.), Nat. Acad. of Scis. of U.S.A. (1972-, NAS/NRC astronomy survey coms: Whitford, Greenstein and Field coms.); mem: Internat. Astronomical Union (1960-, chmn. U.S. Nat. Com.), Am. Astronomical Soc. (1958-, chmn. AAS Div. Planetary Scis. 1973), AAAS (fellow 1986, nat. v.p. and chmn. sect. astronomy 1973), Am. Acad. Arts and Scis. (fellow), British Interplanetary Soc. (fellow), Explorers Club, Soc. Sigma Xi; author: "Is Anyone Out There?" (with Dava Sobel) Delacorte Press, 1992; 150+ articles and books, lectr. numerous symposia, documentaries and interviews nat. and internat. media. Ofc: Univ. Calif. Observatory, Santa Cruz 95064

DRAKE, HAROLD ALLEN, historian; b. July 24, 1942, Cinti.; s. Morris and Mollie (Cooperstein) D.; m. Kathleen Ann Senica, May 31, 1969; children: Susan Jennifer b. 1972, Katherine Jessica b. 1978; edn: AB journ., USC, 1963; MA in English hist., Univ. Wis., 1966, MA classics, 1969, PhD ancient hist., 1970. Career: staff reporter UPI, Los Angeles 1962-65; tchg. asst. Univ. Wis., Madison 1965-68; lectr., asst. prof., assoc. prof., prof. history Univ. Calif. Santa Barbara, 1970–, chair dept. history 1987-90; NEH fellow Inst. Advanced Study Princeton, NJ 1976-77; senior fellow Annenberg Resrch. Inst., Phila., Pa. 1991-92; mem. editl. bd. Classical Antiquity, Berkeley 1986-93; awards, UCSB: outstanding tchg. Assoc. Students 1973, Plous award Acad. Senate 1976, prof. of year Mortar Board 1986-87; mem: Phi Beta Kappa (pres. Calif. Lambda 1986-88), Phi Alpha Theta (Internat. Coun. 1982-84), Am. Philol. Assn., Am. Hist. Assn., Soc. for Promotion of Roman Studies; author: In Praise of Constantine, 1976, coauthor: Eudoxia and the Holy Sepulchre, 1980; articles incl. "Eusebius on the True Cross", 1985, "The Genesis of the Vita Constantini", 1988; Democrat; R.Cath. Res: 423 Los Verdes Dr Santa Barbara 93111 Ofc: Dept. History Univ. of Calif. Santa Barbara 93106

DREIER, DAVID TIMOTHY, congressman; b. July 5, 1952, Kansas City, Mo.; s. H. Edward and Joyce (Yeomans) D.; edn: BA cum laude, Claremont McKenna Coll., 1975; MA in Am. Govt., Claremont Grad. Sch., 1976. Career: dir. corp. relations Claremont McKenna Coll., 1975-78; dir. mktg. and govt. relations Indsl. Hydrocarbons, San Dimas, Calif., 1978-80; mem 97th-104th Congresses from 33rd (now 28th) Calif. dist., 1980–; v.p. Dreier Devel. Co., Kansas City, Mo., 1985–; mem. rules com., ranking Rep. rules of the house subcom., chmn. task force on fgn. policy, mem. task force on POW/MIAs; mem. spl. task force on the devel. of parliamentary instns.; mem. U.S.-Mex. Interparliamentary Caucus; bd. dirs. Nat. Rep. Inst. for Intenat. Affairs, Internat. Rep. Inst.; vice co-chmn. joint com. on orgn. of Congress; vice chmn. GOP Calif. Congl. Del.; asst. regional whip; mem. task force on fed. mandates; awards: Golden Bulldog award Watchdogs of the Treasury, 1981-92, Taxpayers Friends award Nat. Taxpayers Union, 1981-92, Clean Air Champion award Sierra Club, 1988. Ofc: US Congress House of Representatives Washington DC 20515*

DREVER, RICHARD ALSTON, JR., consulting architect; b. Feb. 9, 1936, Kearny, N.J.; s. Richard A. and Dorothy L. (Farrer) D.; m. Ellen M. Cornell, Dec. 21, 1957 (div. Oct. 1978); children: Richard A. III, Diana J., Beverly K.; m. Jane L. Cash, June 1, 1981; edn: AB, Columbia Univ., 1957, B.Arch, 1963, M.Arch, 1963; reg. architect, Calif., Alaska, Ariz., Nev., NCARB. Career: intern Frederick Frost & Associates, N.Y.C., 1961, 63; mem. firm Allen-Drever-Lechowski, Architects, San Francisco, 1963-85, pres. 1983-85; cons. architect, prin., Drever Consulting & Architecture 1985–; ofcr., dir. Medos Corp., S.F. 1979-81; mem: AIA, The Forum for Health Care Planning; chair architect's sect., The Healthcare Forum 1983-84; civic bds: Tamalpais Community Svs. Dist. Marin Co. 1970-75, Tamalpais Parks & Rec. Commn. 1968-70; mil: lt. USNR 1957-59; contbr. articles in field. Res/Ofc: 314 Vista De Valle Mill Valley 94941 Tel: 415/381-1380

DREW, STEPHEN E., museum curator; b. Feb. 6, 1949, Oakland; s. Leland Stanford, Jr., and Barbara Lois (Sprague) D.; m. Beverly K. King, Apr. 7, 1973; children: Jeremy b. 1982, Amanda b. 1986; edn: BA, UC Berkeley, 1973; grad. Museum Mgmt. Inst., Berkeley 1982. Career: asst. librarian Bancroft Library Berkeley 1971-76; curator Calif. State Railroad Mus., Sacto. 1976–; dir: Carson & Colorado R.R., Carson City, Nev. (1969–), Virginia & Truckee R.R., Virginia City, Nev. 1971–; cons. Nevada St. Parks, 1973-75, Calif. St. Parks, 1974-76,

Kansas State Mus. Topeka 1983-88; mem: Railway & Locomotive Hist. Soc. Pac. Coast Chpt. 1971–, Lexington Group in Transp. Hist. 1981–, Am. Guild of Organists 1967–, Calif. State R.R. Mus. Assn. Sacto. (secty. 1984-87), Friends of Calif. State R.R. Mus. Sacto. (v.ch. 1980-83, dir. 1980-85); publs: 12 tech. reports on R.R. topics; Republican; Presbyterian (ch. organist). Ofc: Calif. State Railroad Museum 111 I St Sacramento 95814

DREW, WALLACE THOMAS, investment counselor; b. Sept. 16, 1917, Wausau, Wis.; s. Walter Stanley and Christine Elizabeth (Noren) D.; m. Katherine House (dec. Jan. 16 1991); children: Wallace T., Jr. b. 1943, Elizabeth (Carlsson) b. 1946, Katherine (Margolin) b. 1951; m. Ursula Henderson M.D., Oct. 3, 1992; edn: BA, Univ. of Wis. 1937. Career: advt. mgr. Bristol Myers Co., N.Y. 1948-54; sr. v.p./acct. supvr. Cunningham & Walsh, N.Y. 1954-59; v.p., dir. Coty Inc., N.Y. 1959-64; v.p. Beech Nut-Lifesavers, N.Y./pres. Lander Co., N.Y. (wholly owned subs.), 1964-68; mng. dir. Revlon Internat., London, Eng. 1968-71; financial cons./ v.p. Smith Barney, Santa Barbara 1971–; honors: City of Santa Barbara distinguished citizen 1984, recognition award ADL, B'nai B'rith, Santa Barbara Man of Year 1986, Santa Barbara News - Press lifetime achievement award fin. 1989; past mem. Drug Chemical & Allied Trades Assn., NYC (pres. 1968, dir. 1961-68); civic bds: Santa Barbara City Coll. Found. (dir. 1990–), Lobero Theatre Found., S.B. (pres. 1978), Work Inc. handicapped workshop, S.B. (pres. 1979), United Boys Clubs of S.B. (pres. 1987–), S.B. Symphony Assn. (exec. v.p. 1980–), S.B. Arts Council (pres. 1983), Tres Condados Girl Scout Council (treas. 1982-86), Nuclear Age Peace Found., S.B. (chmn. 1983–), S.B. United Way (treas. 1987–), Piney Woods Country Life Sch., Piney Woods, MS (dir. 1992–); club: Santa Barbara, Church Club (NYC), Bascom Hill Soc. (Univ. Wis.); mil: major US Army Corps of Engr. 1941-46, First US Army Hq., Europe and Philippines, decorated Bronze Star, 7 Battle Stars; Republican; Episcopalian (sr. warden All Saints By The Sea 1984); rec: sailing, collect books. Res: 131 La Vereda Rd Santa Barbara 93108 Ofc: Smith Barney Inc 1014 Santa Barbara St Santa Barbara 93101

DREYER, LEONARD H., restaurant chain executive; b. Aug. 27, 1943, St. Louis, Mo.; s. Leonard Michael and Marion Veronica (Petchow) D.; m. Grace Victoria Ulberg, May 22, 1965; children: Christine b. 1965, Rachel b. 1966, Jennifer b. 1969, Anne b. 1971; edn: BA, fin./accounting., Calif. State Univ., Fullerton 1972; CPA, 1976. Career: audit mgr. Arthur Young & Co., Santa Ana 1972-78; corp. controller Denny's Inc., La Mirada 1978-87; staff v.p. & controller TW Services, Inc.-Denny's, La Mirada 1987-89; v.p. and CFO, Acapulco Restaurants Inc., Long Beach 1989-90; exec. v.p. and CFO, Marie Callender Pie Shops, Inc., Orange 1990-94, pres. and CEO, 1994–; bd. dirs. Orange Co. Financial Soc. 1989–; dir., CFO, pres., sec. Wilshire Restaurant Group, NY 1991–; dir., sec. Marie Callender Pie Shops, Inc. 1994–; mem: Internat. Forum for Corporate Directors, Orange Co. 1994–; civic: bd. dirs. Canning Hunger, Brea 1992–; mil: cpl. U.S. Marine Corps 1961-66; Republican; Friends Church; rec: carpentry, boating. Ofc: Marie Callender Pie Shops, Inc. 1100 Town & Country Rd #1300 Orange 92668

DRINNAN, MICHAEL J., ophthalmologist; b. April 29, 1957, Bristol, England; nat. 1970; s. Alan James and Rita D.; m. Caroline Rachel, May 30, 1982; children: Andrew b. 1985, Jonathan b. 1988, Alex b. 1993, Jacob b. 1993; edn: BA, Cornell Univ. 1978; MD, McGill Univ. 1982; cert. ophthalmologist 1988. Career: physician emergency, Fresno 1983; asst. clin. prof. Stanford Univ. 1989–; mem: AMA, Am. Acad. Opthalmology, ASCRS, PEPMA-IPA (v.p.); rec: tennis, scuba diving, music. Ofc: 215 N San Mateo Dr #1 San Mateo 94401

DRISCOLL, JOSEPH EDWARD, lawyer; b. June 18, 1941, Floral Park, N.Y.; s. John Edward and Mary Rose (Laurer) D.; m. Patricia Ann Tezuka, July 31, 1982 (div. 1984); 1 dau., Crystal b. 1983; edn: BS mil. sci., USAF Acad. 1964; MS engring. adminstrn., S.M. Univ. 1973; JD, McGeorge Sch. Law Univ. Pacific 1982; admitted St. Bar Calif. (1986). Career: pilot USAF, Vietnam and Thailand 1965-72; Air Force Inst. of Tech., Dallas, Tx. 1972-73; Elec. Systems Div., Hanscom AFB 1973-77; pilot 454 Flying Squ., Mather AFB 1978-82; lt. col. Aeronautical Systems Div., Wright-Patterson AFB 1982-85; ofcr. Air Force Space Div., Los Angeles 1985-88; vol. atty. San Diego Co. Bar Assn. 1989–; advisor to Royal Thai Air Force 1969-72; honors: Internat. Moot Ct.; mem: S.D. Co. Bar Assn., Am. Bar Assn., Air Force Assn., U.S. Navy League; author: articles pub. in law and aviation jours. (1982, 89); mil: lt. col. USAF 1964-88; Cath.; rec: bicycling, flying, skiing. Ofc: POB 910406 San Diego 92191-0406

DRISCOLL, PATRICK JOSEPH, psychologist; b. May 8, 1918, Antigo, Wis.; s. Daniel and Melvina (Duquette) D.; edn: BA in journ., MA and PhD psych., Univ. Wis., Madison 1941, 1949, 1956. Career: state cons. Wis. Health & Soc. Svs. Div., Madison 1947-51; employee counsellor S.C. Johnson & Son Inc., Racine 1951-56, tng. mgr. 1956-61, employee rels. mgr. 1962-69; pres. Peer Consultant Group, San Jose, Calif. 1969-88, ret.; lectr. Univ. Wis. bur. industrial psychology, Ext. Div., 1956-59; mem: Wis. Mental Health Assn. (pres. 1958-59), Am. Psychol. Assn.; research papers pub. in profl. jours. include: Concommitants of adjustment of prison inmates, 1947, Salesman helped by bringing out job's critical incidents, 1959, A probe into future of police ops., 1971; mil: s/sgt US Army Ord. 1942-45. Res: 43 Wistaria Way Santa Clara 95050

DROHOJOWSKA-PHILP, HUNTER, writer/art critic; b. Sept. 5, 1952, Schenectady, NY; d. Richard A. and Carol Gleason; m. David Anthony Philp, Feb. 6, 1993; edn: BFA, Instituto Allende, Mexico 1975. Career: art ed., L.A. Weekly 1979-85; art writer, Herald Examiner, L.A. 1985-87; chair, dept. liberal arts & sciences, Otis Coll. of Art and Design, L.A. 1987–; film critic, The Japan Times, Tokyo; west coast ed., Artnews Magazine 1983–; contbg. ed., Art Issues 1991–; co-host, story cons., Arts Illustrated TV series, KCET, L.A. 1985-86; architecture ed., L.A. Style 1986; bd. dir., Found. for Adv. Critical Studies, L.A. 1992; mem: Internat. Assn. of Art Critics 1986–, Coll. Art Assn.,1988–; author: numerous pub. articles in Artnews and Architectural Digest and others; pilot for the L.A. Mus. of Contemporary Art radio series, 1983; radio program on photography, 1983; catalog essays for many contemporary artists; regular contbr. of profl. articles to the L.A. Times; book, Tempest In A Teapot: The Ceramic Art of Peter Shire, 1991; book (in progress), Georgia O'Keeffe (pub., Alfred Knopf); Ofc: Otis College of Art & Design 2401 Wilshire Blvd. Los Angeles 90057

DROR, ALAN, physician, anesthesiologist; b. Dec. 9, 1956, Los Angeles; s. Jess and Norma (Rosen) D.; edn: BS in biochemistry (cum laude), UCLA, 1978; MD, UC Davis, 1982; diplomate Am. Bd. Anesthesiology 1988, Nat. Bd. Med. Examiners 1983, Am. Acad. of Pain Mgmt. 1990. Career: intern internal medicine UCLA, anesthesia resident Yale Univ., New Haven, Conn. 1984-86; fellow in obstetric anesthesia USC, 1986-87; med. staff Placentia Linda Hosp., Placentia 1987–; Fountain Valley Hosp. 1988–; presentor Am. Soc. Anesthesiologist, Atlanta, Ga. 1987; Soc. Obstetric Anesthesia & Perinatology, Halifax, Nova Scotia 1987; 25th Annual Western Anesthesia Residents Conf., San Francisco 1987; honors: Phi Eta Sigma, NSF grant 1980, UCLA Hons. Program 1979-82; mem: Am. Soc. Anesthesiologists, Soc. Obstetric Anesthesiologists & Perinatologists, Internat. Anesthesia Research Soc., Calif. Soc. Anesthesiologists; author: 4 profl. jour. articles, 1982–; Jewish; rec: tennis. Res: 320 20th St Huntington Beach 92648 Ofc: Spring Anesthesia Group POB 22222 Los Angeles 90022

DROTT, CHARLES RAY, certified public accountant, certified fraud examiner, business and litigation consultant; b. Dec. 3, 1939, Plaquemine, La.; s. Wm. Martin and Mamie (Anstead) D.; m. June Ring, Oct. 18, 1986; stepson, Ryan; edn: BS acctg., La. State Univ., Baton Rouge 1964; C.P.A., Calif. and La. Career: audit supr. Touche Ross & Co., 1964-70; chief fin. ofcr. A.C.W., Inc., New Orleans 1970-74; senior ptnr. Allen & Drott, New Orleans 1974-78; audit ptnr. Touche Ross & Co., Los Angeles and other cities, 1978-82; owner Charles R. Drott, CPA, CFE, San Francisco 1982–; key expert witness in large Calif. court cases for various law firms, S.F., San Jose, 1984–; instr. CPA courses, 1978–; evaluate other CPAs' work, 1978–, evaluated acctg. programs Univ. of Nebr. 1981; cons., investigator US Dept. Justice, Calif. State Bd. Acctncy., Calif. Atty. Gen.'s Office, 1989–; appt. Calif. State Bd. Acctncy. tech. review panel 1986–, reporting stds. com. 1989–; honors: Dean's List L.S.U. 1963, Beta Alpha Psi 1963, functional dir. Touche Ross & Co. 1979-82; mem: Am. Inst. CPAs, Calif. Soc. CPAs, Nat. Assn. Cert. Fraud Examiners; civic: Omaha C.of C. 1980-82, New Orleans Symphony (fundraiser 1974-76), Combined Health Agencies Omaha, Nebr. (bd. dirs. 1980-82); coauthor SEC Practice Manual (1981); 2 pub. manuals: Auditing Quality Control (1982), Personnel Counseling (1981); Prot.; rec: water sports, travel, golf. Res: 15 Pensacola Ct Novato 94949 Ofc: Charles R. Drott, CPA, CFE, One Sansome St Ste 2100 San Francisco 94104

DROWN, EUGENE ARDENT, forest management and development professional; b. Apr. 25, 1915, Ellenburg, N.Y.; s. Frank Arthur and Jessie Kate D.; m. Florence Marian Munroe, Mar. 5, 1938; children: Linda Harriett Oneto, Margaret Ruth Lunn; edn: BS, Utah State Univ., 1938; postgrad. Mont. St. Univ. 1939-40; PhD in pub. adminstrn., Univ. Beverly Hills, 1979; reg. profl. engr., profl. land surveyor, profl. forester, Calif. Career: park ranger National Park Service, Yosemite Nat. Park, 1940-47; forest ranger U.S. Forest Service, Calif. Region, 1948-56; forest mgr. and devel. specialist U.S. Bur. of Land Mgmt., Calif. 1956-70; forest engring. cons., 1970–; R&D coord. US Army at UC Davis, 1961-65; advy. bd. Sierra Coll., Rocklin 1962–; awards: nat. service medal Am. Red Cross 1964; mem: Nat. Soc. Profl. Engrs., Soc. Am. Foresters, Am. Inst. Biol. Scientists, Ecol. Soc. Am., Reserve Ofcrs. Assn. U.S., NRA, Internat. Rescue and First Aid Assn., Internat. Platform Assn., Bulldog Sentinels of Superior Calif., Masons, Shriners; civic: Am. Red Cross (instr. 1954), Boy Scouts Am.; mil: US Army 1941-45, decorated Bronze star, Silver star; Methodist. Res: 5624 Bonniemae Way Sacramento 95824

DROZ, HENRY, music distribution company executive; b. Sept. 26, 1926, Detroit, Mich.; s. Joseph and Katie (Zallman) D.; m. June Jacyno, May 31, 1959; 1 dau., Kathy Ann b. 1961; edn: BA, Wayne St. Univ. 1950. Career: branch mgr. Decca Distbg. Co., Detroit, Mich. 1952-54; pres. ARC Distbg. Co., Detroit 1954-63; v.p. Handleman Co., Detroit 1963-72; v.p. Warner Elektra, Atlantic Corp., Burbank, Calif. 1973-77, pres. and c.e.o. 1977–; awards: T.J. Martell Found. humanitarian of year 1989, City of Hope spirit of life 1989; mem: Sigma Alpha Mu, City of Hope (bd. chmn. music chpt. 1980-82, pres. 1978-80, trustee 1979–); mil: T-4 US Army 1945-46; rec: tennis. Res: 12053 Crest Ct Beverly Hills 90210 Ofc: W.E.A. Corp. 111 N Hollywood Way Burbank 91505

DRUCE, MARY EULALIA, telecommunications manager; b. Aug. 20, 1955, Fort Stockton, Tx.; d. Camilo and Eulalia (Nunez) Garcia; m. Robert Lee Druce, Dec. 3, 1977; edn: BBA, Texas Tech Univ., 1977; MBA, Univ. N.Mex., Albuquerque 1982; lic. CPA, Tx. 1984. Career: acct. Texas Tech Univ., Lubbock 1977-80; software devel. engr. Hewlett Packard, Palo Alto, Calif. 1982-84, cost acctg. analyst 1984-85, gen. acctg. mgr. 1985-86, sr. fin. analyst 1987, networks services mgr., 1988–; awards: math & sci. Soc. of Women Engrs. Ft. Stockton, Tx. 1973, dean's list Texas Tech Univ. 1974-77, fellow Washington Campus Pgm., WDC 1981, Beta Sigma Phi (pres. 1979); mem. Texas Soc. CPA 1984–, Data Proc. Mgmt. Assn. (chpt. pgm. dir. 1985-87), World Affairs Council 1991-92; civic: advisor Junior Achievement Palo Alto 1983; publs: articles in field, 1987–, newsletter ed. Net Gazette, 1989. Res: 32801 Oakdale Ct Union City 94587 Ofc: Hewlett Packard 3000 Hanover Palo Alto 94304

DRYDEN, ROBERT EUGENE, lawyer; b. Aug. 20, 1927, Chanute, Kans.; s. Calvin Wm. and Mary Alfreda (Foley) D.; m. Jetta Burger, Dec. 19, 1953; children: Lynn b. 1954, Thomas b. 1957; edn: AA, City Coll. San Francisco 1948; BS, Univ. San Francisco 1951; JD, 1954; Dipl. Am. Bd. Trial Advocates. Career: atty., assoc. Barfield & Barfield, San Francisco 1955-65, ptnr. Barfield Dryden & Ruane, 1965-88; senior mem. Dryden, Margoles, Schimaneck, Hartman & Kelly, 1988–; faculty Hastings Nat. Coll. Advocacy; mem. Lawyer to Lawyer Consulting Panel; lectr. Calif. Contg. Edn. of Bar; arbitrator Am. Arbitration Assn., S.F.; Master of the Bench, S.F., Am. Inn of Ct.; evaluator U.S. Dist. Ct., Early Neutral Evaluation Pgm.; mem. Pro-tem Judges Panel, Product Liability Advy. Council; mem: Am. Coll. Trial Lawyers (Fellow), Internat. Acad. of Trial Lawyers (Fellow), Am. Bar Endowment (Fellow), Internat. Assn. of Defense Counsel, Fedn. of Insurance & Corporate Counsel, Phi Alpha Delta, USF Law Soc. (nat. exec. com. 1973-74), USF Alumni Assn. (bd. govs. 1977–); mil: USMC 1945-46; R.Cath.; rec: tennis, ski, golf. Res: 1320 Lasuen Dr. Millbrae 94030 Ofc: Dryden, Margoles, Schimaneck, Hartman & Kelly, 1 California Ste 3125 San Francisco 94111

DRYSDALE, GEORGE MARSMAN, venture capitalist; b. Sept. 16, 1954, Manila, Philippines; s. George and Anne (Marsman) D.; m. Diane Elizabeth Rogers, Aug. 17, 1991; edn: BS engring., Harvey Mudd Coll., 1976; MBA, Stanford Univ., 1980, JD, 1980; admitted bar: N.Y., Calif. Career: cons. Braxton Associates, Boston 1980; lawyer Davis Polk & Wardwell, N.Y.C., 1981-83; gen. ptnr. Hambrecht & Quist Venture Partners, San Francisco 1983-87; asst. to Secty. US Dept. Ag., W.D.C., 1987-88; mng. gen. ptnr. Westar Capital, Costa Mesa, Calif. 1988-91; v.chmn. Marsman-Drysdale Group; pres. Drysdale Enterprises, San Mateo 1991–; dir: H&Q Ventures, Marsman Estate Plantations, Skyvision, Upside Publ.; Wireless Holdings; Internat. Wireless Communications, Pocketbell, RCPI, UTS; exec. dir. Nat. Advy. Council Small Bus., W.D.C. 1991; bd. trustees Harvey Mudd Coll.; mem. Western Assn. Venture Capitalists (bd.); clubs: Guardsmen S.F. 1985, Pacific, N.Y. Athletic, Bahia Corinthian Yacht; Republican; Prot. Ofc: Drysdale Enterprises 177 Bovet Rd Ste 600 San Mateo 94402

DUCKOR, JEROME NOAH, financial consultant; b. Dec. 7, 1942, Fort Wayne, Ind.; s. David and Natalie (Liff) D.; edn: AB, Univ. Miami, 1965; MBA, Golden Gate Univ., 1977. Career: account exec. Parke-Davis & Co., Morris Plains, N.J. 1969-83; gen. mgr. Maternal Care Prod., San Francisco 1984-86; pres. & CEO Best Selection, Inc. San Francisco 1986-88; fin. cons. Shearson Lehman Brothers Inc., 1989-91; account exec. Dean Witter Reynolds, Inc., 1991–; cons. Dental Pik, Mill Valley 1981-83, Infotech, Palo Alto 1987-88; recipient sales excellence award Parke Davis Co. 1977; mem. Med. Mktg. Assn. Irvine, S.F. Ad Club, Commonwealth Club Calif., Am. Heart Assn., Am. Sport Inst., The Museum Soc., The Official Registry of Who's Who of Am. Business Leaders; club: Harbor Point, Mill Valley; catalog editor: Mother & Baby Selection 1986-87; rec: tennis, skiing. Res: 450 E Strawberry Dr Mill Valley 94941 Ofc: Dean Witter Reynolds, Inc. PO Box 66 Corte Madera 94976

DUFFEY, PAUL S., microbiologist, immunologist; b. Nov. 24, 1939, Oakland; s. Norman David and Saphrona Carol (Korkus) D.; m. Marlen Gregory, Jan. 1961 (dec. June 1975); m. Dixie Anita Herrick, June 26, 1988; edn: BA, San Jose St. Univ., 1963; PhD, Univ. Mich., Ann Arbor, 1974. Career: asst. prof. Univ. of Mich. Med. Sch., Ann Arbor, 1974-75; Univ. of Texas Health Sci. Ctr., San Antonio, Tx. 1976-81; res. microbiologist Calif. St. Dept. of Health Svs., Berkeley 1981-93, chief, biologics/immun. 1993–; appt. Gov.'s Task Force on Biotechnology, Sacto. 1985–; mem: Assn. of Immunologists 1978–, N.Y. Acad. of Scis. 1980–, Sigma Xi 1970–; publs: sci. articles, 1976–; R.Cath.; rec: computer design, assembly, programming. Res: 166 Miramonte Dr Moraga 94556 Ofc: Dept. of Health Services 2151 Berkeley Way Berkeley 94704

DUFFUS, JAMES E., research plant pathologist; b. Feb. 11, 1929, Detroit, Mich.; s. John and Dorothy J. (Pellow) D.; m. Rachael B. Anderson, May 17, 1952; children: Mark C. b. 1954, John S. b. 1956, Lisa K. b. 1958; edn: BS hons., Mich. St. Univ. 1951; PhD, Univ. Wis. 1955. Career: plant pathologist U.S. Dept. Agri. ARS, Salinas 1955-81; vis. scientist Tasmanian Dept. Agri., Hobart 1980-81; supvy. research plant pathologist, res. leader U.S. Dept. Agri. ARS, Salinas 1982–. location coord. 1989–; assoc. exptl. station UC Davis and UC Berkeley, 1962–; adj. prof. Univ. Ark., Fayetteville, Ark. 1984–; awards: ARS superior svc. USDA 1968, 83, Scientist of Yr. 1982, Am. Soc. Sugar Beet Technologists Merit. Svc. 1985; mem: Am. Phytopathological Soc. (fellow), Am. Soc. Sugar Beet Technologists (bd. dirs.), Internat. Soc. Plant Pathology (virus epidemiology com.), Internat. Soc. Horticultural Sci. (chmn. vegetable), Internat. Working Group Legume Viruses, Lutheran Ch. Good Shepherd (congregational pres. 1965); 220+ res. articles pub. in profl. jours., 1955–, ed. Compendium of Beet Diseases & Insects, 1986; Lutheran. Ofc: U.S. Dept. of Agriculture 1636 E Alisal St Salinas 93905

DUGONI, ARTHUR A., academic administrator; b. June 29, 1925, San Francisco; m. Katherine Groo, Feb. 5, 1949; children: Steven b. 1952, Michael b. 1953, Russell b. 1955, Mary b. 1956, Diane b. 1957, Arthur b. 1962, James b. 1964; edn: BS, Gonzaga Univ., Spokane, Wash.; DDS, Coll. of Physicians and Surgeons, San Francisco, 1948; MSD, Univ. of Wash., Seattle, 1963. Career: dentist/orthodontist, pvt. practice, San Francisco 1948-87; chmn. dept. of orthodontics Univ. of the Pacific Sch. of Dentistry, S.F. 1964-66, prof. of orthodontics 1977-95, dean 1978–; pres. Calif. Dental Assn. 1982-83; pres. Am. Dental Assn. 1988-89 (trustee 13th Dis. 1984-87, House of Delegates mem., cons. to Council on Dental Edn. 1973-82, 1991-95); treas. Fedn. Dentaire Internationale, London 1992-96; pres. Am. Assn. of Dental Schools 1994-95; awards: Disting. Svc. award Pierre Fauchard Acad. 1982; Alumnus of Yr. awards: Univ. of the Pacific 1983, Univ. of Wash. 1984, Univ. of S.F.; Hinman Medallion for Leadership in Dental Progress 1989; Medallion of Distinction, Univ. of the Pacific Sch. of Dentistry; Alumni Merit award Gonzaga Univ. 1992; Gold Medallion and Merit award, Orthodontic Edn. and Res. Found. 1993, Albert H. Ketcham Award 1994, Am. Dental Assn. President's Citation 1994, Am. Dental Trade Assn. Chairman's Award 1994; listed: Who's Who in Calif., Who's Who in the West, Who's Who in Am., Am. Acad. of Sci.; founding mem. Nat. Academies of Practice; hon. mem/fellow Acad. of General Dentistry; mem.: Am. Coll. of Dentists (fellow) 1960–, Internat. Coll. of Dentists (fellow) 1970–, Acad. of Dentistry Internat. (fellow), Am. Bd. of Orthodontists (diplomate 1970–, dir. 1979-86, pres. 1986), Pierre Fauchard Acad. 1970–, Pew Health Professions Commn. (commissioner 1993–); mem: Concordia Argonaut Club, S.F. 1978–, Olympic Club 1978–; author: over 100 pub. articles in field, 1978–; mil: lt. comdr. U.S. Navy, 1943-51; Republican; Catholic; rec: golf, tennis.

DUHL, LEONARD J., educator, psychiatrist, health planning consultant; b. May 24, 1926, N.Y.C.; s. Louis and Rose (Josefsberg) D.; m. Lisa June 8, 1980; children: Pamela, Nina, David, Susan, Aurora; edn: AB, Columbia Univ., 1945; MD, Albany Med. Coll., 1948; dipl. Menninger Sch. of Psychiatry, 1954, Wash. Psychoanalytic Inst., 1964. Career: intern Jewish Hosp., Bklyn. 1948-49; resident in psychiatry Winter VA Hosp., 1949-51, 1953-54, also fellow Menninger Found. Sch. Psychiatry 1949-51; sr. asst. surgeon Health Dept. Martinez, Calif. 1951-53; med. director (Ret.) Pub. Health Svc. 1954-72: psychiatrist NIMH, Bethesda, Md. 1954-64, chief cons. psychiatry Peace Corps 1961-64, chief Office of Planning NIMH 1964-66, special asst. to Secty. Dept. Housing & Urban Devel., W.D.C. 1966-68; prof. of public health and city planning, UC Berkeley 1968–, prof. psychiatry Univ. Calif. Med. Sch., San Francisco, 1968–; cons. to WHO, UNICEF, State of Calif. Health Dept., Nat. Civic League, Healthy Cities pgms., other agys.; appt. World Hlth. Orgn. Expert Com. on Env. Hlth. in Urban Devel. 1991; mem. bd. dirs: Partners for Democratic Change 1991, Consultation to Religious Personnel 1991-92, Calif. Inst. for Integral Studies 1990, Louis August Jonas Found. 1989–, Menninger Found. (bd. trustees 1994–); mem. Am. Psychiatric Assn., Am. College of Psychiatrists, The Charles F. Menninger Soc.; author: City and Health: Governance of Diversity, 1992, Social Entrepreneurship of Change, 1990, Health Planning & Social Change, 1986, contbr. articles in N.E. J. Med., J. Prevention, Future Choices, Calif. Architecture, B of NY Acad. of Medicine, World Health; rec: photography, sailing. Ofc: Univ. Calif. Sch. of Public Health 410 Warren Hall Berkeley 94720

DULLY, FRANK EDWARD, JR., physician, aviation safety educator; b. Jan. 19, 1932, Hartford, Conn.; s. Frank Edward and Monica Theresa (Cooney) D.; m. Rebecca Sue Akers, Apr. 23, 1982; children: Kathleen, Ann, Margaret, David, Nancy, Tammy; edn: BS, Coll. of Holy Cross, 1954; MD, Georgetown Univ., 1958; MPH, UC Berkeley, 1970; diplomate Am. Bd. Preventive Medicine. Career: intern D.C. Gen. Hosp., Washington, 1958-59; resident Bridgeport (Conn.) Hosp. 1959-60; pvt. med. practice Shelton, Conn. 1960-64; served to capt. US Navy 1964-87: with Destroyer Squadron 14, 1964-65; USN student flt. surgeon 1965-66; senior med. officer USS Hornet 1966-68, Naval Air Sta., Glynco, Ga. 1968-69; aerospace medicine resident USN, Pensacola, Fla. 1970-72; senior med. officer USS Enterprise, 1972-74; dir. tng. Naval Aerospace Med. Inst., Pensacola 1974-77, comdg. officer 1982-85; senior med. officer First Marine Aircraft Wing, 1977-78, Pacific Fleet Naval Air Force, 1978-82; aviation safety instr. US Naval Postgrad. Sch., Monterey, Calif. 1985-87; ret. 1987; decorated Legion of Merit, Air medal o.l.c., Meritorious Svc. medal; co-editor USN Flight Surgeon manual, 1976; assoc. prof. USC Inst. Safety and Systems Mgmt., Los Angeles 1987-90; cons. in aviation medicine USC Inst. Safety & Systems Mgmt. 1990–; writer and lectr. on aviation safety worldwide 1978–; instr. safety Northwest Airlines, Mpls. 1988-91; mem: Am. Coll. Physicians (Fellow), Am. Coll. Preventive Medicine (Fellow), Aerospace Med. Assn. (Fellow), Internat.

Acad. Aviation and Space Medicine, US Naval Flt. Surgeons (pres. 1980-83), Internat. Soc. Air Safety Investig., Am.Helicopter Soc., Acad. Model Aeros., Flight Safety Found., Scale Ship Modelers Assn. of N. Am.; Republican; R.Cath. Res: 8991 Kingfisher Lake Rd Maceo KY 42355-9737

DUNBAR, MICHAEL PATRICK, water district executive; b. July 31, 1949, Chgo.; s. Thomas Patrick and Patricia (Kocourek) D.; m. Cynthia Long, June 6, 1981; children: Erica b. 1982, Ashley b. 1984, Taryn b. 1986; edn: BS in C.E., Univ. Notre Dame, 1972, MS in E.H.E., 1974; reg. profl. engr. Ind., Calif. Career: engr. John Carollo Eng., Fountain Valley, Calif. 1979-84; senior engr. Dan Boyle Eng., Santa Ana 1984-87; gen. mgr. South Coast Water Dist., Laguna Beach 1987–; dir. Aliso Water Mgmt. Agy., 1992–; dir. South Orange County Reclamation Auth., 1992–; civic: YMCA Laguna Niguel (bd. 1990–); Indep.; R.Cath.; rec: golf, reading, cards. Res: 29521 Los Osos Laguna Niguel 92677 Ofc: South Coast Water District PO Box 30205 Laguna Niguel 92607-0205

DUNCAN, ANDREW MALCOLM, mathematician, audio engineer; b. May 27, 1960, London, England (Am. parentage); s. Glen Malcolm and Eleanor Jane (Watson) D.; m. Gabriella Clementine Borsay, Aug. 23, 1986 (div. Oct. 1987); edn: BS engring., Calif. Inst. of Tech., 1983; MA pure math., UC Santa Cruz, 1989. Career: physics tchr. Pasadena Sch. Dist., 1983-84; pgmr. Cerwin-Vega, Arleta, Ca. 1984-86; cons. E-mu Systems, Scotts Valley 1987-89; cons. Cerwin-Vega, Simi Valley 1989-90; recording engr. MAMA Found., Studio City 1990-92; engr. Philips Media, Los Angeles 1992–; mem.: Audio Engring. Soc. (1983–, exec. com. L.A. chpt. 1990-92, nat. publication award AES, N.Y.C. 1989), Am. Math. Soc. 1987–, Math. Assn of Am. 1992–; inventor: Z-board MIDI controller; publs: math. papers 1988, 91; rec: competitive swimming, music, Shakespeare. Res: 641 Las Lomas Ave Pacific Palisades 90272-3355 Ofc: Philips Media 10960 Wilshire Blvd Los Angeles 90024

DUNCAN, THOMAS OSLER, botanist, educator; b. Jan. 15, 1948, Cambridge, Ohio; s. George Wendall and Elizabeth (Fuller) D.; edn: BS, Ohio St. Univ., 1970; MS, and PhD, Univ. Mich., 1975, 1976. Career: asst. prof. UC Berkeley, 1976-82, assoc. prof. 1982–, director Univ. Herbarium 1982-91, assoc. curator of seed plants 1982–, faculty asst. for Museum Informatics 1991-mem. Internat. Assn. for Plant Taxonomy, Am. Soc. of Plant Taxonomists, Calif. Botanical Soc.; publs: (software) MorphoSys, 1988, Meka, 1989, 30+ sci. articles, 1970–, ed. (book) Cladistics: Perspectives on the Reconstruction of Evolutionary History; research: Systematics of Ranunculus; application of numeical methods to systematic problems; floristics of alpine regions; rec: travel, music. Ofc: Integrative Biology, Valley Life Sciences Bldg Berkeley 94720

DUNLAP, JACK STUART, fraud investigator; b. Jan. 6, 1930, Mullens, W.Va.; s. James Edward and Mary Katherine (Carpenter) D.; m. H. June Foglesong, Sept. 26, 1952 (div. 1975); children: Katherine b. 1953, James b. 1957, Jack b. 1962; m. Linda Sue Hayes, May 1, 1978; edn: BS in bus. adminstrn., Concord Coll., 1958; computer courses, Saddleback Coll., 1985-90; cert. fraud examiner 1990, E.A., IRS 1980, lic. pvt. investigator 1981, cert. internat. investigator 1992. Career: fireman, engr. Virginian Railway Co., 1947-59; IRS spl. agt. Toledo, Ohio 1959-64, Charleston, W.Va. 1965-67, San Diego (1967-72, 1977-80, ret. 1980), Los Angeles 1972-75, Santa Ana 1975-77; pvt. investigator Dunlap Investigations, El Cajon 1980-83; pres. Intelligence Investigations Inc., San Diego 1983-86; assoc. Breese & Dunlap Assocs., Lakeside 1986-92; fraud investigator, expert witness, enrolled agt., Dunlap Investigations, San Clemente 1984–; recipient superior performance awards IRS (1976, 78); honors: Eagle Scout BSA 1946; mem: Calif. Assn. Lic. Investigators, San Diego Co. Investigators Assn., Nat. Assn. Cert. Fraud Examiners, Coun. Internat. Investigators Inc.; civic: Singing Hills Little League, El Cajon (coach 1968-72), BSA, Mullens, W.Va. (asst. scoutmaster 1949-52); lodge: AF&A Masons 1951–, Royal Arch Masons 1954–; mil: sgt. US Army 1951-53; Democrat; Prot.; rec: numismatics, gardening. Ofc: Dunlap Investigations PO Box 4328 San Clemente 92674-4328

DUNN, CAROL M., educator, university athletic director; b. Dec. 11, 1949, Washington, D.C.; d. John E. and Evelyn (Kelly) Dunn; edn: BS, Frostburg St Univ. 1973; M.Ed, 1976. Career: tchr., coach Glenridge Jr. H.S., Woodlawn, Md. 1973-75; Bishop Walsh H.S., Cumberland, Md. 1975-78; prof., coach, dept. chair Kans. Newman Coll., Wichita, Kans. 1978-81; prof., coach CSU, L.A. 1981-82, assoc. athletic dir. 1982-88, dir. athletics 1988–; mem: NCAA (mem. council, steering com. and eligibility com. 1995), Nat. Assn. Collegiate Directors of Athletics; rec: golf, tennis. Res: 5359 Delta St San Gabriel 91776 Ofc: California State University 5151 State University Dr Los Angeles 90032

DUNN, EDWARD THOMAS, dermatologist, educator; b. Mar. 12, 1925, Miami, Ariz.; s. Clyde Frederic and Imogene (Brewer) D.; m. Beverly Jean Dixon, July 19, 1946, div. 1969; m. Rebecca Jane Kline, Dec. 19, 1969; children: Edward T. Jr. b. 1954, Beverly Ann b. 1956, Robert b. 1962, Kelly b. 1970, Jenny b. 1972, Justin b. 1975, Matthew b. 1975; edn: AB, USC, 1951, MA 1954; MD, Loma Linda Univ., 1961; lic. M.D. Calif. 1962; Diplomate Am. Acad. Family Practice. Career: prodn. staff NBC Television, Hollywood 1948-50; youth minister Evangelical Free Ch., L.A. 1950-52, Trinity Methodist, L.A. 1952-54; pastor Covina Village Ch., 1954-57; prof. and pub. relations dir. Azusa

Pacific Univ., 1952-54; physician solo practice, Whittier 1962-70, ptnr. FR Hills Med. Group, La Habra 1970–, practice limited to dermatology 1985–; clin. instr. USC, 1981-92; chief of staff Whittier Hosp. 1966; chief of staff La Habra Hosp. 1982, bd. trustees 1982-87; bd. trustees Azusa Pacific Univ. 1966-69; Fellow Am. Acad. Family Practice, mem. ASCAP; author, composer numerous songs and song books incl. "The Tree of Life" (1960–) mil: lt. USNR 1943-46; Republican; Baptist; rec: photographer, musician, songwriter, writer. Res: 14257 Bronte Dr Whittier 90602 Ofc: 951 S Beach Blvd La Habra 90631

DUNN, ROBERT ALAN, management consultant; b. Aug. 22, 1941, Wilmar; s. Evans DeWitt and Olive Marie (Canning) D.; m. Diane Jensen, Sept. 21, 1963; children: Paul b. 1965, Timothy b. 1967, Thomas b. 1967; edn: BS forestry, Oreg. St. Univ. 1963; MBA, Univ. Oreg. 1970; PhD mktg., 1975. Career: asst. prof. Pacific Lutheran Univ., Tacoma, Wash. 1975-77; mktg., sales mgr. Internat. Paper Co., N.Y.C. 1977-80; v.p. mktg. Shakertown Corp., Winlock, Wash. 1980-83; pres. Furniture Byte, Longview, Wash. 1983-84; v.p. mktg. Standard Structures, Santa Rosa 1984-87; owner Action Mgmt. Co. 1987–; lectr. UC Berkeley, San Francisco St. Univ. 1987–, John F. Kennedy Univ., Orinda 1987–; visiting prof., Advanced Mgmt. Inst., Shanghai Univ. 1989; honors: Beta Gamma Sigma; mem: Am. Mktg. Assn., Santa Rosa Sunrise Rotary (dir. 1986–, pres. 1988-89); author book and seminar Mktg. Planning Using Lotus, 1988, Field Sales Mgmt. Using Lotus, 1989, co-author: Mgmt. Sci., 1980; mil: capt. AUS 1963-68; Republican; Lutheran; rec: computers, travel. Res: 1385 Quail Ct Santa Rosa 95404 Ofc: Action Management Co. POB 9580 Santa Rosa 95405

DUNNEBACKE-DIXON, THELMA HUDSON, research biologist; b. Dec. 23, 1925, Nashville, Tenn.; d. Frederick Charles and Allie Thelma (Hudson) Dunnebacke; m. Jonathan Stanton Dixon, June 9, 1954; children: James Dunnebacke b. 1958, Lindsay Ann b. 1959, Frederick Charles b. 1965; edn: BA, Wash. Univ. St. Louis 1947; MA, 1949; PhD, 1954. Career: instr. zoology Smith Coll., Northampton, Mass. 1949-50; research biologist Virus Lab. UC Berkeley 1955-76, lectr. Electron Microscopy Virus Lab. 1974-76; res. scientist Viral and Rickettsial Disease Lab. Calif. Dept. Health Services, Berkeley 1976–; mem: Sigma Xi, Tissue Culture Assn., Am. Soc. Cell Biology, Electron Microscope Soc., Soc. Protozoologists; 50+ papers pub. in sci. research jours., 1953–; rec: photog., painting, gardening. Res: 2326 Russell St Berkeley 94705 Ofc: California State Dept. of Health Services Viral and Rickettsial Disease Laboratory 2151 Berkeley Way Berkeley 94704

DUNSON, BETTY WALKER, clinical social worker; b. Mar. 7, 1947, Fairfield, Ala.; d. Elijah James and Verna Rea (Calloway) Walker; m. Leroy H. Dunson, June 17, 1989; edn: BA, Univ. of Ala. 1968; MSW, Atlanta Univ. 1970; Calif. lic. clin. soc. worker (LCSW); Calif. Comm. Colls. counselor, instr. cred. in pub. svcs. and adminstrn. Career: med. soc. wkr. Atlanta Southside Comp. Health Ctr. 1970; dir. soc. svcs. Trenton Neighboorhood Family Health Ctr, Trento, NJ 1970-3; dir. soc. svcs. Trenton Head Start Pgm. 1973-74; cons./ pgm. analysis & job tng. New Era Learning Corp., Greenvale, NY 1972-3; instr./ mgmt. & supvr. Los Angeles Southwest Coll. Evening div. 1976-79; supervising children's social worker Los Angeles Co. Dept. of Children's Services/Adoptions Div., 1974–; social worker, cons. and trainer, pvt. practice; honors: Delta Sigma Kappa; mem: Nat. Assn. Social Wkrs., Alpha Kappa Alpha Sor., Univ. of Ala. Alumni Assn., Top Ladies of Distinction, Inc. (adv. Top Teens of Am., L.A. chpt.); works: initiated techniques for mainstreaming special-needs children into the regular child care sys.; Democrat; Abundant Life Christian Ch. (chmn. bd. dirs.); rec: acting, floral design, arts & crafts. Res: 2425 Hines Dr Los Angeles 90065 Ofc: L.A. Co. Dept. Childrens Services Adoption Div. 695 S Vermont Ave Los Angeles 90005

DURANCEAU, CHRISTINE MARIE, physician; b. Sept. 25, 1949, Chartres, France; nat. 1960; d. Jacques Louis and Marcelle Marie (Violeau) Duranceau; m. Patrick Abergel, June 1982 (div. 1985); edn: BA, UC Irvine 1971; PhD, 1977; MD, Yale Sch. Medicine 1981. Career: intern Harbor UCLA Med. Center, Torrance 1981-82, resident emergency medicine 1981-84; emergency physician Glendale Adventist Med. Center, Glendale 1984-86; Eisenhower Med. Center, Rancho Mirage 1986-91, base station dir. 1986-91; co-director Eisenhower Immediate Care Centers, Coachella Valley 1991-92; physician Eisenhower Idyllwild Clinic, Idyllwild 1991-93; mem: Am. Coll. Emergency Physicians, Am. Heart Assn., Riverside Emergency Services (directors com. 1987-91), Club Francais Du Desert, Yale Alumni Assn., UC Irvine Alumni Assn. Address: Palm Desert 92255

DURFLINGER, JEFFREY DUANE, pharmaceutical validation engineer; b. Mar. 15, 1961, Oakland; s. Laurence Duane and Patricia Etta (Cord) D.; m. Kelly Denise Evans, June 24, 1989; 1 dau., Jenna b. 1991; edn: BS, CSU Chico, 1986; MS Golden Gate Univ. 1993; cert. senior indsl. technologist Nat. Assn. Indsl. Tech., 1992. Career: product devel. mgr. Omni Scientific, Martinez 1986-87; process engr. Alza Corp., Palo Alto 1987-89, Vacaville 1989-92, validation engr. 1992–; tchg. asst. Chico St. Univ., 1986; cons. Polytex Consulting, Sacto. 1988–; recipient profl. awards for spl. achievement Alza Corp. (1991, 92); mem. Soc. of Plastics Engrs. 1984–, Soc. Mfg. Engrs. 1990–; Republican; Methodist. Res: 245 Foster Ln Dixon 95620 Ofc: Alza Corp. 700 Eubanks Dr Vacaville 95688

DURHAM, DON D., restauranteur; b. Sept. 3, 1947, Belmont, Iowa; s. Sherman Kenneth and Elenor Levon (Kendal) D.; m. Carmel Columbell, July 25, 1955; children: Rene L., Tamie L., Danielle; ed. pub. schs., Pierce H.S., Colo. Career: farm work on family dairy farm, Pierce, Colo. 1956-62; cook, mgr., reg. supr. Doggie Diner chain rests., San Francisco 1963-71; cook, mgr., gen. mgr., owner Bill's Place rest., S.F. 1972–; honors: rated Best restaurant in category San Francisco Focus guide (1984, 85, 86, 87, 88), Three Stars, Paul Wallach's Guide (1987, 88), achiev. certif. Nat. Restaurant Assn. 1980, commendn. Calif. State Senate 1985; mem: Clement Street Merchants Assn. (pres. 1988, 91, 92), Council of District Merchants, Nat. Restaurant Assn., Golden Gate Restaurant Assn., S.F. Visitors Bur.; civic: Boutiqe de Noel, Paralysis Project, Friends of Quentin Kopp, Friends of Milton Marks; med. disch. AUS; R.Cath.; rec: video tape archiving & cataloging. Ofc: Bill's Place, 2315 Clement St San Francisco 94121

DURKIN, WILLIAM THOMAS, JR., physician; b. Feb. 5, 1953, Danbury, Conn.; s. William Thomas and Anne Marita (Deakin) D.; m. Patricia K. Sung, June 11, 1994; edn: grad. La Salle Acad., Providence, R.I.; BS, and MD, Georgetown Univ., 1975, 1980; diplomate Am. Bd. Emergency Medicine. Career: intern Georgetown Univ. Med. Center, Wash. D.C. 1980-81; resident Harvard Surgical Service New England Deaconess, Boston, Mass. 1981-83; staff physician Charlton Memorial Hosp., Fall River, Mass. 1983-84; Associated Emergency Physicians Med. Group, San Diego 1987–, emergency physician Community Hosp. of Chula Vista; emergency physician St. Jude Hosp., Fullerton; chief emergency svs. Paradise Valley Hosp. 1994–; instr. adv. cardiac life support Am. Heart Assn. 1985–, instr. adv. trauma life support; instr. EMS Tng. Inst., San Diego; instr. USN Sch. of Health Scis., San Diego, 1985-87; asst. res. coord. Paradise Valley Hosp. 1989–; appt. San Diego Co. Emergency Care Com. 1991-93; recipient AMA Physicians Recognition awards (1987, 90, 94); Am. Coll. Emergency Physicians (fellow), Am. Acad. of Emergency Medicine (fellow); mem: AMA, Mass. Med. Soc., San Diego Emergency Physicians Soc., N.Y. Acad. Scis., S.D. Zool. Soc., Harvard Med. Alumni Assn.; mil: lt. cdr. USN 1984-87, Letter Commendation 1985; Republican (Medal of Freedom 1994); R.Cath.; rec: sailing, skiing, investing, autos. Address: P.O. Box 3880 Rancho Santa Fe 92067

DUSANIC, LINDA ANN NELSON, bank examiner; b. May 22, 1959, Sioux City, Iowa; d. Charles Howard and Mary Joyce (Forney) N.; m. Matthew Dusanic; edn: BA bus., Univ. Wash., Seattle 1981; MBA fin., Boston Coll., 1987. Career: ins. cons. Washington Mutual Ins., Seattle 1982-85; cons. Manassa Systems Inc., Boston 1986; budget analyst Kendall Corp., 1986; bank examiner Fed. Reserve Bank of Boston, 1987-89; cons. Welling & Woodard, San Francisco 1990; bank examiner Fed. Reserve Bank of San Francisco 1990–; mem. Nat. Assn. Bus. Economists (v.p. S.F. chpt. 1993-94); rec: skiing, scuba. Ofc: FRB of S.F. 101 Market St San Francisco 94105

DUSTIN, FRANK ARTHUR, physician (neurologist); b. Sept. 4, 1962, Pasadena., Calif.; s. Douglas Frank and Adelheid Gisela (Thiel) D.; m. Katherine Ann Leydorf, June 24, 1989; edn: BA, philosophy and religious studies, Stanford Univ. 1984; MD, Baylor Coll. of Medicine, Houston, TX 1988; cert. Am. Bd. of Psychiatry and Neurology 1994. Career: intern Kaiser Med. Ctr., Oakland 1988-89; neurology resident UC Davis, Martinez, CA 1989-92, neurology fellow 1992-93; pvt. practice neurology, Alameda, Oakland and Berkeley 1993–; clin. instr. UCSF Dept. of Neurology 1993-94; mem: Am. Academy of Neurology 1990–, Am. Assn. of Electrodiagnostic Medicine 1992–. Ofc: Frank A. Dustin, MD 947 Marina Village Parkway Alameda 94501

DUTTON, DONALD STEVEN, information systems executive; b. Mar. 10, 1947, Kalispell, Mont.; s. Donald Zedoc and Roberta Estella (Lewis) D.; edn: Grays Harbor JC 1965-6; BBA, summa cum laude, National Univ. 1977, MBA 1980; cert. computer sci., Coleman Coll. 1973; cert. data processing, Inst. for the Cert. of Computer Profls. 1982. Career: asst. data processing supr. Allied Administrators, San Diego 1972-73; computer ops. Rohr Ind., Inc., Chula Vista 1973-77, comp. pgmmr. analyst 1977-79; sr. pgmmr./analyst Foodmaker Inc., S.D. 1979-80, system project leader 1980-81, software apps. mgr. 1981-84; mgr. Systems, Denny's Inc., La Mirada 1984-86; systems splst. County of Los Angeles, Downey 1986–; adj. faculty National Univ. 1980–, UCSD 1983-84; information systems cons. City of Carlsbad 1983-84; profl. seminars, S.D. Regl. Tng. Ctr. 1983-4; mem: D.P. Mgmt. Assn. (bd. dirs. S.D. chpt. 1981-83, com. chmn.), Toastmasters (past pres.); mil: E4 US Navy 1966-70; Christian. Res: 23426 Coso, Mission Viejo 92692 Ofc: CLA-ISD 9150 E. Imperial Hwy Downey 90242

DUVAL, VIRGINIA HENSLEY, psychologist, research professor; b. Nov. 27, 1948, Marion, N.Caro.; d. Fess Vernon and Shirley Lee (Simpson) Hensley; m. Thomas Shelley Duval, Oct. 4, 1975; edn: BA, USC 1971; MA, 1975, PhD, 1979. Career: behavioral scis. cons. Los Angeles Co. Dept. of Mental Health 1980-84, chief info. systems support bureau 1984-90; res. prof. dept. psych. USC, 1990–; awards: Case Western Reserve Univ. Gen. Motors scholarship 1968-70, USC scholar 1970-75, 8 Nat. Assn. Cos. awards 1985-90; mem: Productivity Mgrs. Network, Am. Psychological Assn., Psychologists in Pub. Service, Soc.

Psychological Study of Social Issues, Internat. Assn. Social Sci. Info. Service & Tech.; author: Consistency & Cognition (1983), ed. book chpt. in New Directions in Attribution Research (1976), 20+ articles and papers pub. in profl. jours. (1974–). Ofc: Dept. Psychology, Univ. of So. Calif., Los Angeles 90089-1061

DUXBURY, ANDREW SAUNDERS, assistant clinical professor of medicine; b. May 11, 1962, New Haven, Ct.; s. Alyn Crandall and Alison Beatrix (Saunders) D.; m. Jon Steven Spivey, Feb. 14, 1989; edn: BS, chem. and biology (with distinction), Stanford Univ. 1984; MD, Univ. of Wash., Seattle 1988; resident in internal medicine, UC Davis 1988-91; vis. post doctoral scholar in geriatrics UC Davis 1991-93; med. lic. Calif. 1989; DEA 1989; diplomate Nat. Bd. of Med. Examiners 1989; diplomate Am. Bd. of Internal Medicine 1991; Cert. of Added Qualifications in Geriatrics 1994. Career: staff physician Stanford Med. Group, Sacramento 1991-93, Kaiser Permanente Med. Group, Sacto. 1991-92; assoc. med. dir. geriatric nursing unit UC Davis Med. Ctr. 1991-; assoc. med. dir. Sacto. Co. Multipurpose Sr. Svs. Program 1991-93, med. dir./prin. investigator 1993-; physician cons. Dept. of Comm. and Internat. Health, UC Davis 1991-; asst. prof. of clin. medicine Sect. of Geriatrics, Div. of Gen. Med. UC Davis 1993-; dir. geriatrics clinics UC Davis Med. Ctr. 1994-; attending physician gen. internal medicine clinic Gen. Medicine Consultation Svc. 1991-; adminstr. and tchr. Dept. of Internal Medicine Home Care Program 1992-; attending physician Geriatric Clinic, Memory Disorders Clinic, Geriatric Pre-operative Clinic 1993-; tchr. Internal Medicine Core Clerkship Lecture Series 1993-, Freshman Seminar - Social Problems and Modern Medicine 1994-; mem. UC Davis Dept. of Internal Medicine student clerkship com. 1993-, housestaff selection com. 1989-, UC Davis Dept. of Comm. and Internat. Health acad. geriatric resources program 1993-, UC Davis Med. Ctr. geriatrics programs devel. com. 1992-; res. asst./investigator num. research projects 1980-; lectr. in field, 1991-; awards: National Merit Scholar 1980, Presdl. Scholar Finalist 1980, John Pearce Mitchell Scholarship in Chem. 1983, Glaxo Geriatric Fellow Scholarship 1992, Univ. of Calif./Healthnet Wellness Found. Disting. Lectr. for UC Davis 1993; mem: Am. Geriatrics Soc., Gerontological Soc. of Am., Am. Coll. of Physicians, AMA, CMA, Sigma Xi, Physicians for a Nat. Health Program, Physicians for Social Responsibility; civic: Asian Free Health Clinic (physician), Alzheimer's Assn. (bd. dirs.), Boulevard Park/Marshall Sch. Neighborhood Assns. (bd. mem., fund-raising chair), cons. on elder abuse: Sacto. Co. Sheriff's Dept., Sacto. Co. Dist. Atty., St. Dept. of Health Svs., cons. on aging issues to num. local agys. and organizations; contbr. articles and abstracts to profl. jours., 1987-; dir., stage mgr. and performer in num. theater productions (awards for direction and writing); Democrat. Res: 2721 H Street Sacramento 95816 Ofc: UCDMC 2221 Stockton Blvd #3107 Sacramento 95817

DYCK, ANDREW ROY, philologist, educator; b. May 24, 1947, Chicago, Ill.; s. Roy H. and Elizabeth (Beck) D.; m. Janis Mieko Fukuhara, Aug. 20, 1978; edn: BA, Univ. Wis., Madison 1969; PhD, Univ. Chicago, 1975. Career: sessional lectr. Univ. of Alberta, Edmonton, Can. 1975-76; asst. prof. Univ. Minnesota, Mpls. 1977-78; asst. prof., prof. Univ. Calif., Los Angeles 1976-77, 1978–; awards: Alexander von Humboldt-Stiftung fellow, Bonn, Ger. 1980-89, NEH fellow 1991-92, mem. Inst. for Adv. Study, Princeton 1991-92; mem: Am. Philol. Assn., Calif. Classical Assn., Byzantine Studies Conf. (govng. bd. 1989-93), U.S. Nat. Com. for Byzantine Studies; editor (books): Epimerismi Homerici, II (1995), Michael Psellus, Essays on Euripides & George of Pisidia and on Heliodorus & Achilles Tatius (1986). Ofc: Dept. Classics UCLA 405 Hilgard Ave Los Angeles 90024-1475

DYER, ALICE MILDRED, psychotherapist; b. July 4, 1929, San Diego; d. Wm. Silas Cann and Louise Lair (Addenbrooke) Vaile; m. James Wm. Vawter, PhD, Dec. 26, 1972; children: Alexis b. 1949, Bryan b. 1954, Christine b. 1956; edn: BA, CSU Fullerton, 1965, MA 1967; PhD, U.S. Internat. Univ., 1980; Calif. lic. educational psychologist 1978, marriage family therapist 1979 Career: psychotherapist Academic Success, Fountain Valley 1975-82; school psychologist Cypress Sch. Dist. 1972-86; pvt. practice psychotherapist, Brea 1985–; cons. Orange County M.S. Soc., Irvine 1986–; family therapist La Habra Comm. Hosp. 1988; juvenile connection therapist Orange Co. Juvenile Connection 1988–; instr. Fullerton Coll., and Adult Edn., Fullerton 1875-78; alumni cons. CSU Fullerton 1982–; awards: Psy. Chi 1967, svc. awards Orange Co. M.S. Soc. 1987, Gary Ctr. La Habra 1975; mem: Orange County Assn. Educational Psychologists, Orton Dyslexic Soc., Learning Disabilities Adults & Children, Calif. Assn. Marriage & Family Therapists, Orange Co. MFTs; civic: Fullerton Arboretum Friends (bd. 1980–), Fullerton Beautiful (bd. 1987–), Soroptimists Internat. Brea (health chmn. 1988), YWCA (bd. 1988, chair Women of Distinction luncheon 1988); Republican; Unitarian (bd. 1981-85); rec: gardening, travel. Ofc: Brea Mental Health Associates 1203 W Imperial Hwy Brea 92621

DYER, CHARLES ARNOLD, lawyer; b. Aug. 29, 1940, Blairstown, Mo.; s. Charles Arnold and Mary Charlotte (West) D.; m. Marilyn Abadie, Dec. 5, 1983; children: Kristine b. 1965, Erin b. 1973, Kathleen b. 1975, Kerry b. 1986; edn: BJ, Univ. Mo. 1962; JD, UC Hastings Coll. of Law 1970; admitted St. Bar Calif. 1971. Career: atty. Cotchett Hutchinson & Dyer, San Mateo 1971-84; Dyer & White, Menlo Park 1984-; awards: Boys Club Am. Man & Boy 1978; mem: Am. Bd. of Trial Advocates, Am. Arbitration Assn. (Arb.), San Mateo

County Bar Assn., Santa Clara County Bar Assn., Palo Alto Bar Assn., San Mateo Co. Trial Lawyers Assn. (pres. 1982), Calif. Trial Lawyers Assn. (v.p. 1983), Assn. Am. Trial Lawyers (st. committeeman 1983); mil: capt. USNR 1963-, Navy Commendn. Medal 1967, Merit. Svc. Medal 1990; Democrat; R.Cath. Ofc: Dyer & White 800 Oak Grove Ave Ste 200 Menlo Park 94025

EAGLE, G. DONOVAN, advertising executive; b. Nov. 7, 1937, Minot, N.D.; s. Gerald Stewart and Ellen Rose (Donovan) E.; m. Barbara Ann Butcher, Aug. 22, 1964; children: Paul b. 1965, Patrick b. 1967, Jennifer b. 1970; edn: AA, Cabrillo Coll. 1960; BA, San Jose Univ. 1962; cert., Advanced Advt. Inst. San Francisco 1965. Career: account exec. Foote Cone & Belding, San Francisco 1962-67; merchandising mgr. Castle & Cooke, San Jose 1967-72; advt. mgr. FMC Corp. 1972-74; account exec. Bergthold Fillhardt & Wright 1974-77; pres. Eagle Advt., Auburn 1978-88; advt. mgr. WEMCO, Sacto. 1988-; tchr. Sierra Coll., Rocklin 1985-; awards: Point of Purchase Advt. Inst. Gold 1970, Silver 1970, Printing Industry Am. 1st Place 1970; mil: USN 1957-59; Republican; R.Cath.; rec: writing, art, music. Res: 21380 Cameron Way Grass Valley 95949 Ofc: WEMCO 1796 Tribute Rd Sacramento 95852

EARLE, MARLOWE D., music education teacher/director; b. Dec. 3, 1926, Wilmington; s. Haskell K. and Ellen Amelia (Davis) E.; m. Idabelle Bauerle, Aug. 2, 1947; children: Maryanne b. 1948, Gaylen b. 1949; m. Leslie Anne Lane, Dec. 17, 1983; edn: AA, Long Beach Comm. Coll., 1950; BM, USC, 1953; MA, CSU Long Beach, 1957. Career: music tchr. Paramount Unifed Sch. Dist., 1953-63; dir. music edn. Fountain Valley Sch. Dist. 1963-87, music tchr. 1987-94 (ret.); pres. Calif. Music Educators Assn. (CMEA) All-State Honor Orch., 1985-86; awards: PTA hon. life mem. Paramount (1961), recogn. JFK Cent. for Performing Arts Long Beach (1981), named outstanding state music educator CMEA Sacto. (1987), youth service award Huntington Union Council PTA (1987); mem: Music Ed. Nat. Conf. (life 1953-, govtl. rels. com. Calif. 1978-79), Calif. Music Ed. Assn. (life 1953-, pres. So. Sect. 1970-72, state pres. 1974-76), Orange. Co. Music Ed. Assn. (life 1963-, pres. 1968-70, Irene Scheffle Award 1967), Orange Co. Music Adminstrs. (mem., chmn. 1963-87), So. Calif. Sch. Band & Orch. Dirs. 1963-, Calif. Arts Alliance 1974-78, Calif. Coord. Council for Fine Arts 1974-78, O.C. Phil. Assn. 1963-; contbr. numerous articles CMEA Jour., 1972-78; mil: cpl. USAF 1946-47; Democrat; rec: performance on saxophone, photography, travel. Res: 4532 Adenmoor Lakewood 90713

EARLY, ALEXANDER RIEMAN, III, judge; b. Sept. 22, 1917, Phila.; s. Alexander Rieman, Jr. (R.Adm. USN) and Elizabeth (Dence) E.; m. Mary C. Worland, Aug. 15, 1959; children: Alexander R., IV b. 1960, Lucia b. 1961, Elizabeth b. 1964, John b. 1967; edn: BA, Cornell, 1938; LLB, Harvard, 1941. Career: pvt. practice law, Los Angeles 1947-50; senior atty. Div. of Hwys. State of Calif., Los Angeles 1950-55; asst. U.S. atty. Lands Div., 1955-57; asst. county counsel Los Angeles County, 1957-72; judge Los Angeles Superior Court, 1972-87; adj. prof. law Southwestern Univ. Sch. of Law, 1970-79; Nat. Conf. of State Tax Judges, 1982-; mem: Sigma Alpha Epsilon, Soc. of the Cincinnati, Aztec Club of 1847, Soc. of the War of 1812, Order of Polonia Restituta, Am. Legion, Mil. Order of the World Wars, Reserve Ofcrs. Assn., Maryland Hist. Soc., Order of the Holy Sepulchre, U.S. Naval Inst.; mil: comdr. USNR-Ret. 1941-46 (active); Republican; Cath.; rec: raising camellia seedlings, US Civil War hist. Res: 3017 Kirkham Dr Glendale 91206

EARLY, AMES S., health system executive; b. April 18, 1937, Allison, Iowa; s. W.C. and F. Eva Early; m. Beryl J.; children: Barbara C. Berlat; edn: BA, Drake Univ., Des Moines, Iowa, 1958; Masters, Health Admin., Univ. of Iowa, 1961. Career: admin. resident, admin. asst. Univ. Minnesota Hosp., Minneapolis 1961-67; exec. dir. Mary Francis Skiff Meml. Hosp., Newton, Iowa 1967-68; asst. admin. Mercy Hosp., Miami, Fla. 1968-70, exec. dir. 1970-76; pres. Scripps Meml. Hosp., La Jolla, Calif. 1976-91; exec. v.p. & C.O.O. Scripps Institutions of Medicine & Sci. and pres./CEO, Scripps Health, San Diego 1992-; award: Headliner of Yr. in Healthcare, San Diego Press Club 1987; mem: So. Fla. Hosp. Assn. (pres. 1974-75, bd. 1971-76), Fla. Hosp. Assn. (bd. 1974-76, var. com.'s 1973-76), Fla. Blue Cross Assn. Hosp. Peer Review Panel 1975-76, Comprehensive Health Planning of So. Fla. (bd. 1974-76, var. com's 1970-76), Calif. Assn. of Hosp. and Health Systems (trustee 1984-92, exec. com. 1984-90, legis. com. 1985, hosp. med. staff bylaws com. 1985-86, treas. 1987, chmn. 1989), Nat. Council of Comm. Hosp. (bd. 1974, bd. chmn. 1985-94), Hosp. Council of San Diego and Imperial Counties (bd. 1978-80, 1983-86, secty. 1979-80, bd. chmn. 1985), The Healthcare Forum (conv. pgm. & mktg. com. 1987-88), Calif. Polit. Action Com. (bd. 1979-85), United Way San Diego (chmn. hosp. div. 1977, chmn. prof. div. 1980), Blue Cross/Hosp. Advy. Com 1982, Voluntary Hosp. of Am. (bd. 1984, nom. com. 1989-92), Voluntary Hosp. of Am. West (bd. 1986-91, exec. com. 1986-91); mem: Am. Coll. of Healthcare Execs., Am. Hosp. Assn., Am. Assn. of Hosp. Planning. Ofc: Scripps Health 4275 Campus Point Court San Diego 92121

EAST, JOHN CLIFFORD, electronics executive; b. Jan. 20, 1945, Amarillo, Tx.; s. John Prather and Francis Louise (Holly) E.; m. Pamela Ann Mattson, June 16, 1968; children: Erin b. 1977, Amber b. 1980; edn: BSEE, UC Berkeley

1966; MBA, 1968. Career: engr. Fairchild, Mountain View 1968-76; ops. mgr. Raytheon 1977-78; v.p. AMD, Sunnyvale 1979-88; pres., CEO ACTEL 1988-. Ofc: Actel 955 E Arques Sunnyvale 94086

EASTON-HAFKENSCHIEL, CYNTHIA RUTH, architect; b. March 27, 1949, San Francisco; d. Ellis Herbert and Mary Alice Easton; m. Joseph Henry Hafkenschiel, Sept. 28, 1972; children: Erin Thomas b. 1983, Alexander Scott b. 1985; edn: BA environ. design, UC Berkeley 1972; B.Arch. w/honors, Univ. Md. 1975; lic. architect Calif. (1979). Career: intern architect Living Systems Inc., Winters 1972-75; architect Alan Oshima, Sacto. 1976-80; Cynthia Easton 1980-; CBAE Exam Com. mem. 1990-; exam. writer Calif. Arch. Lic. Examiners, Monterey 1987-90; awards: Legal Services Achievement 1986, AIA Mentor Citation, AIA; bd. dirs. CVAIA, 1981-82, 90-94; bd. dirs. Soc. Mktg. Profls., 1980-81, mem: Constrn. Specifications Inst. (co-ed. 1980-81), Soroptimist Internat. Res: 1600 Alvina Ave Sacramento 95822

EATON, BARRY DAVID, city planner; b. Dec. 1, 1937, Oakland; s. Joseph Lloyd and Dorothy (Stockton) E.; children: Colleen Ann, Cathleen Anissa; edn: AB, UC Berkeley 1960; postgrad., USC 1960-62. Career: planning asst. City of Los Angeles 1960-62; city planner and planning dir. City of Azusa 1962-64; planning dir., Stanton 1964-66; Thousand Oaks 1966-70; chief planner, Boise-Cascade Bldg. Co., Los Angeles 1970-71; dir. planning VTN Corp., Irvine 1972-74; dir. gen. planning Raub Bein Frost & Assocs., Newport Beach 1974; chief planner Fullerton 1975-; honors: spl. ecology awards from local environ. groups Thousand Oaks 1960, and Escondido 1961; mem: Am. Inst. Certified Planners, Am. Planning Assn., Calif. Planning and Conservation League, Reg. Plan Assn.; civic: So. Calif. Sierra Club, Mensa, Calif. Tomorrow. Res: POB 802 Corona del Mar 92625 Ofc: City Hall Fullerton 92632

EBINER, ROBERT MAURICE, lawyer, b. Sept. 2, 1927, Los Angeles; s. Maurice and Virginia (Grand) E.; m. Paula H. Van Sluyters, June 16, 1951; children: John, Lawrence, Marie, Michael, Christopher, Joseph, Francis, Matthew, Therese, Kathleen, Eileen, Brian, Patricia, Elizabeth, Ann; edn: JD, Loyola Univ., Los Angeles 1953; admitted bar: Calif. 1954, U.S. Dist. Ct. Calif. 1954. Career: solo practice, West Covina 1954-; judge pro tem Los Angeles Superior Ct. 1964-66, 1991-, arbitrator 1978-; judge pro tem Citrus Muni. Ct. 1966-70; mem. disciplinary hearing panel Calif. State Bar, 1968-75; organizer/incorporator Queen of Valley Hosp., 1959, bd. dirs. Hospital Men's Club 1973-76, bd. dirs. Queen of Valley Hosp. Found. 1983-89; founder/incorporator West Covina Hist. Soc. 1982, bd. dirs. 1982-89; bd. dirs. West Covina United Fund 1958-61, organizer Jt. United Funds East San Gabriel Valley, 1962, bd. dirs. 1961-68; bd. dirs. S.G.V. Cath. Social Svcs., 1969-, pres. 1969-72; bd. dirs. Region II Cath. Social Service, 1970-, pres. 1970-74; trustee L.A. Cath. Charities (fmr. Cath. Welfare Bur.) 1978-; charter bd. dirs. N.E. Los Angeles Co. unit Am. Cancer Soc., 1973-78, chmn. by-laws com. 1973-78; mng. meet dir. Greater La Puente Valley Special Olympics 1985-89, mng. meet dir. BishopAmat Relays 1981-, mem. MSAC Relays Com. 1978-; awards: L.A. Co. Human Relations Commn. disting. service award 1978, West Covina "Citizen of Year" 1986, S.G.V. Daily Tribune "Father of Year" 1986, Thomas Kiefer Humanitarian Award 1993; mem: ABA, Calif. Bar Assn., L.A. Co. Bar Assn., L.A. Trial Lawyers Assn., Eastern Bar Assn. L.A. Co. (pres. Pomona Valley 1965-66), West Covina C.of C. (pres. 1960), Am. Arbitration Assn.; clubs: K.C., Bishop Amat H.S. Booster (bd. 1973-, pres. 1978-80), Kiwanis (charter West Covina, pres. 1976-77, lt. gov. Div. 35 1980-81, Kiwanian of Yr. 1978, 82, Disting. Lt. Gov. 1980-81, bd. dirs. Cal-Nev-Ha Found. 1986-92, 1993-); mil: US Army 1945-47, Korea; active Calif. State Democratic Central Com. 1963-68, campaign mgr. for Congressman Ronald B. Cameron 1964; rec: collector memorabilia: historical, Olympic, and political. Res: 2734 Sunset Hill Dr West Covina 91791 Ofc: 1000 E. Garvey Ave. So., Suite 365, The Lakes Bldg., West Covina 91790

EBSEN, ROGER ROY, marriage and family therapist; b. Jan. 11, 1947, Santa Monica; s. Christopher Frederick and Irene S. (Simson) E.; m. Kathleen Wage, June 26, 1971; edn: BA sociology, CSU Northridge 1979; MA, EdPsych: counseling, 1981. Career: researcher, counselor VA Hosp., Brentwood 1979; staff Woodview Calabasas Hosp., Calabasas 1979-82; clin. dir. CareUnit, Glendale Adventist Hosp. 1982-84; staff Valley Counseling Clin., Sherman Oaks 1980-87; pvt. psychotherapy practice, Woodland Hills 1988; Sherman Oaks 1988, Westlake Village 1994; mem: Am. Assn. Marriage & Family Therapists, Calif. Assn. Marriage & Family Therapists, Assn. Humanistic Psychology, Am. Counseling Assn., Assn. Transpersonal Psychology, Group Psychotherapy Assn. So. Calif.; mil: sgt. AUS XXIV Corps, Vietnam 1966-68; rec: photography, camping, philosophy. Ofc: 32107 West Lindero Canyon Blvd Ste 214 Westlake Village 91361

ECHEVARRIA, SANTIAGO, company president; b. Aug. 23, Vitoria, Spain; s. Felix and Blanca (Manzanares) E.; m. Susan Mortrude; 1 son, Victor b. 1979; edn: BSME, Nat. Polytechnic Inst., Mexico City; Exec. MBA, The Claremont Grad. Sch. Career: reg. mgr. American Optical, So. Calif., 1969-72; div. mgr. The Southland Corp., So. Calif., 1972-80; v.p. overseas devel. Denny's Inc., Orange, 1980-84; pres. and CEO Internat. Food Concepts., Anaheim, 1984-86; pres. and CEO Intermart Inc., Anaheim Hills, 1986-; gubnat. appt. mem. Calif. State Task Force on Calif.- Mexico Relations; frequent lectr. on internat. mgmt., mktg. & franchising; mem: The Claremont Grad. Sch. Alumni Council, The Peter F. Drucker Grad. Mgmt. Ctr. Alumni Assn., World Trade Ctr. Assn., Internat. Mktg. Assn., Rotary Internat. (Anaheim). Ofc: Intermart, Inc. 5360 E Honeywood Ln Anaheim 92807 Tel: 714/974-9071

ECONOMOS, KIRK WILLIAM, real estate executive; b. Sept. 3, 1947, N.Y.C.; s. Wm. Charles and Florence Lillian (Szylage) E.; m. Peggy Bergstrand, Oct. 11, 1986; edn: BBA, St. Bonaventure Univ. 1969; lic. R.E. Broker Calif. 1977; Certified Commercial Investment Mem. (CCIM) Nat. Assn. Realtors. Career: fin. analyst Dun and Bradstreet, Long Island, N.Y. 1969-71; independent promoter musical prodns., Amsterdam, Holland 1971-76; dir. musical prodns. Curriculum Concepts Inc., N.Y.C. 1976-77; real estate agent Ashwill Burke Inc., Oakland, Calif. 1977-82; investment broker Fuller Comml. Brokerage, San Francisco 1982-85; co-founder, pres. Meridian Real Estate Services, Fremont 1985-88; founder/pres. Hospitality and Investment Real Estate (hotel brokerage and consulting co.), San Francisco 1988–; owner/founder Meridian IPAD (computer sales & cons., multimedia prods.) 1985–; mem. Nat. and Calif. Assn. Realtors; civic: Multiple Sclerosis (fundraising com. 1988), Police Athletic League, S.F. Art Inst., Kts. of Col.; club: San Francisco Tennis Club (capt. men's 3.5 USTA tennis team 1994); publs: article: Fremont, Calif., the Jewel of the Silicon Valley Crown, Barron's, 1987 and Real Estate Indus. Out of Synch with Silicon Valley, San Jose Bus. Jour., 1987; rec: tennis, music, art, scuba, sailing. Res: 2606 Buchanan St San Francisco 94115 Ofc: Hospitality and Investment Real Estate, 2606 Buchanan St San Francisco 94115

EDBERG, STEPHEN J., astronomer; b. Nov. 3, 1952, Pasadena; s. Joseph and Sophie (Pasternak) E.; m. Janet Lynn Greenstein, Dec. 23, 1979; children: Aaron b. 1985, Shanna b. 1989, Jordan b. 1990; edn: AB, UC Santa Cruz, 1974; grad. work UC San Diego, 1974-75, UCLA 1975-77, AM, 1976. Career: solar observer CSU Northridge, 1978-79; calibration scientist Jet Propulsion Lab., Pasadena 1979-81, discipline specialist IHW, JPL, 1981-88, investigation scientist CRAF, JPL, 1986-92, sci. coordinator GLL, JPL, 1989–, investigation scientist Cassini, JPL, 1992–; freelance speaker, cons. 1978–; exec. dir. Riverside Telescope Makers Conf. Inc., Riverside 1992–; chmn. Corp. for Research Amateur Astronomy, S.F. 1990–; awards: profl. award Astronomical Assn. of No. Calif. 1988, G. Bruce Blair Medal Western Amateur Astronomers 1988, Minor Planet 3672 Stevedberg Internat. Astronomical Union, Paris, Fr. 1988, Sigma Xi research grantee 1974, Chancellor's intern fellow UCLA 1975-77; mem. Am. Astronomical Soc. 1971, Internat. Amateur Profl. Photoelectric Photometry 1982-95; author: Int'l Halley Watch Amateur Observers' Manual, 1983, co-author: Observe Comets, 1985, Observe Meteors, 1986, lead author: Observing Comets, Asteroids, Meteors, and the Zodiacal Light, 1994; rec: bicycling. Ofc: Jet Propulsion Laboratory 4800 Oak Grove Dr Pasadena 91109

EDGETT, STEVEN DENNIS, transportation consultant; b. June 3, 1948, Idpls.; s. Robert Neil and Elizabeth Catherine (Hatch) E.; m. Catherine Ann, June 19, 1971; children: Jeffrey b. 1974, Christopher b. 1977; edn: N.M. State Univ. 1965-67, Univ. of Cincinnati, Oh. 1967-68, Grossmont Coll., La Mesa, Calif. 1970-72. Career: lead designer U.S. Elevator Corp., Spring Valley 1970-76; safety engr. State of Calif., San Diego 1976-78; assoc., dept. head Skidmore, Owings & Merrill, San Francisco 1978-86; pres. Edgett Williams Consulting Group Inc., Mill Valley 1986–; advisor ASCE Coun. on Tall Buildings, 1990–; mem. Constrn. Specs. Inst. 1978–; pub. articles in mags. 1985, 92; rec: mtn. biking, computers, reading. Res: 541 Shasta Way Mill Valley 94941 Ofc: Edgett Williams Consulting Group 100 Shoreline Hwy Ste 250 Mill Valley 94941

EDMISON, LYLE DUANE, university administrator; b. Dec. 2, 1925, Columbus, Neb.; s. Thomas Howard and Lucy Jeannette (Ellis) E.; m. Phyllis Jane Arnold, May 30, 1952; children: Barbara Lynn b. 1954, Patricia Jean b. 1957, Joanne Faye b. 1959; edn: BA, Univ. Neb. 1950; MA, 1951; PhD, 1955. Career: prof. San Jose St. Univ. 1955-59; assoc. dean of students CSU, Hayward 1959-62, dean of students 1962-84, v.p. student svs. 1984-91; v.p./prof. emeritus CSU Hayward 1991; consultant 1991–; civic bds: Fremont-Newark Comm. Coll. dist. (pres., v.p. 1965-69), Am. Coll. Testing Program, Iowa City (dir. 1960-65, sec. 1973-79), Bay Area Mental Health Assn., S.F. (1974-77), Alameda Co. Mental Health Assn., Oakland (v.p. 1970-77), Alameda Co. Greater Avenues for Independence, Oakland 1986-88; awards: Scott Goodnight award NASPA, Wash. DC 1982, Sigma Xi 1954; mem: Am. Psychological Assn., Nat. Assn. Student Personnel Adminstr. Ofc: 620 Curtner Rd Fremont 94539

EDMUNDS, ALAN VAUGHAN, attorney at law; b. July 17, 1948, Akron, Oh.; s. Burt Vaughan and Rita Ansel Edmunds; m. Kelly Edmunds, June 2, 1975 (div.); m. Julie A. Edmunds, Oct. 21, 1995 children: Danielle b. 1976, Trevor b. 1979, Christopher b. 1983; edn: BA, Univ. of Miami, 1970; JD, Western State, San Diego 1975; MBA, Univ. of Phoenix, San Diego, 1994. Career: atty., Law Office of Alan V. Edmunds, San Diego, 1976–; instr., Southwestern Coll., Chula Vista, Calif., 1973-75; dir. Childrens Council, San Diego, 1990–; dir. San Diego Missionary Pilots 1990–; mem. San Diego Bar Assn. 1977–, San Diego Trial Lawyers Assn. 1977–; civic: Lions Club, San Diego (program dir. 1976-77); rec: flying, tennis, traveling. Ofc: Alan V. Edmunds, Attorney at Law 2121 5th Ave San Diego 92101

EDWARDS, ARDIS LAVONNE QUAM, teacher, writer, church and civic volunteer; b. July 30, 1930, Sioux Falls, S.Dak.; d. Norman Alvin and Dorothy Margaret (Cade) Quam; m. Paul Edwards (airline capt.), Apr. 18, 1953 (dec. Sept. 12, 1988); children: Kevin b. 1954 (dec. 1980), Kendall b. 1956, Erin b. 1958, Sally b. 1959, Kristin b. 1961, Keely b. 1962; 4 grandchildren: David Paul, Tiffany, Nicole and Brittany; edn: tchg. cred. Augustana Lutheran Coll. 1949; provisional tchg. cred., San Jose St. Coll., San Francisco St. Coll. ext. and summer sessions 1953-1957; FAA lic. pvt. pilot (1984). Career: all pos. to mgr. The Cottage (restaurant), Sioux Falls, S.Dak. 1943-50 (became largest restaurant within 5 state area); one-room school tchr., 8 grades, Colman, S.D. 1949-50, Sioux Falls, S.D. 1950-51; tchr. 1st grade Decoto (Calif.) Sch. Dist. 1952-58; recreation dir. City of Albany, 1951-52; mem. Calif. Tchrs. Assn., Nat. Edn. Assn., PTA, Southwest Airways Pilots Wives, Republic Airlines Retired Pilots Sitting Ducks Assn., Northwest Airlines Retired Pilots Assn., Aircraft Owners and Pilots Assn., AARP, Concerned Women for Am., Nat. Assn. Female Execs.; honors: commendn. from March Fong Eu 1954, special service award Girl Scouts Am. 1971, service awards Arthritis Found. (1974, 75), Who's Who in America, Who's Who in the West, World Who's Who of Women, others; civic: Mission Swim Club, Philomathian Literary Soc., Mission San Jose Restoration Com., Mental Health Assn., Cancer Soc., Heart Assn., March of Dimes, School Room Mother (15 yrs) and Team mother (9 yrs), Brownie co-leader; author: Health Instruction Unit, Study Packet for Tchrs., 1954, quotation: "My greatest sense of fulfillment is in being a Christian wife, mother, teacher and writer...in that order."; Republican; Our Savior Lutheran Ch.: charter mem., ch. historian, mem. adminstrv. bd., Christian Concern and Pastoral Call coms., hon. life mem. Altar Guild, co-chair Silver Anniv. Celebration, tchr. Sunday Sch., Bible Sch. and Christian Week Day Sch., mem. choir, prayer chain, founder/chair O.S.L.C. Blood Bank 1968–, past pres. L.W.M.L., past hospitality chair, Fraternal communicator and education ofcr., RespecTeen ofcr. for Lutheran Brotherhood; rec: Bible study, grandchildren, flying, history, antiques.

EDWARDS, BRUCE GEORGE, physician, ophthalmologist; b. Apr. 6, 1942, Idaho Springs, Colo.; s. Bruce Norwood and Evelyn Alice (Kohut) E.; edn: BA, Univ. Colo., Boulder 1964; MD, Univ. Colo. Sch. Medicine 1968. Career: intern U.S. Naval Hosp., San Diego 1968-69, med. officer USS Long Beach 1969-70; U.S. Naval Hosp., Taipei, Taiwan 1970-72; resident, ophthalmology U.S. Naval Hosp., Oakland 1973-76; staff ophthalmologist U.S. Naval Hosp., Camp Pendleton 1976-83; chair med. staff U.S. Naval Hosp., Naples, Italy 1983-85; head, ophthalmology U.S. Naval Hosp., Camp Pendleton 1985–; mem: Am. Acad. Ophthalmology (fellow), AMA, Am. Assn. Ophthalmology, Assn. Mil. Surgeons of U.S., Pan-Am. Assn. Ophthalmologists, Marines Meml. Club (assoc. marine); mil: capt. USN Med. Corps 1980–, Naval Achievement Medal 1970; Republican; Protestant; rec: piano playing, hiking, swimming. Ofc: U.S. Naval Hospital Camp Pendleton 92055

EDWARDS, CHARLES CORNELL physician, research administrator, b. Sept. 16, 1923, Overton, Nebr.; s. Charles Busby and Lillian Margaret (Arendt) E.; m. Sue Cowles Kruidenier, June 24, 1945; children: Timothy, Charles Cornell, Nancy, David; edn: student, Princeton Univ., 1941-43; BA, Univ. Colo., 1945, M.D., 1948; MS, Univ. Minn., 1956; LL.D. (hon.), Phila. Coll. Pharmacy and Sci.; LHD (hon.), Pa. Coll. Podiatry, Univ. Colo.; Diplomate: Am. Bd. Surgery. Career: intern St. Mary's Hosp., Mpls., 1948-49; resident surgery Mayo Found., 1950-56; pvt. practice medicine specializing in surgery Des Moines, 1956-61; mem. surgical staff Georgetown Univ., WDC, 1961-62; also cons. USPHS; dir. div. socio-econ. activities AMA, Chgo., 1963-67; v.p., mng. officer health and sci. affairs Booz, Allen & Hamilton, 1967-69; commr. FDA, WDC, 1969-73; asst. sec. for health HEW, WDC, 1973-75; sr. v.p., dir. Becton, Dickinson & Co., 1975-77; pres., Scripps Clinic and Research Found., La Jolla, Calif., 1977-91; pres., CEO Scripps Insts. Medicine and Sci., La Jolla, 1991–; bd. dir. Bergen Brunswig Corp. Biomagnetic Techs., Inc., Molecular Biosystems, Inc., Nova Pharm Corp., IDEC Pharmaceuticals Corp.; bd. regents Nat. Lib. Medicine, 1981-85; mem. Nat. Leadership Commn. on Health Care, 1986–; bd. govs. Hosp. Corp. Am. 1986-89; mem: Inst. Medicine, Nat. Acad. Scis.; clubs: Chevy Chase, Princeton; La Jolla Country, La Jolla Beach and Tennis; Fairbanks Ranch Country; mil: served to lt. M.C. USNR, 1942-46. Ofc: Scripps Inst Medicine & Sci 4275 Campus Point Ct San Diego CA 92121

EDWARDS, DAVID ELBERT, charitable fundraising and organization consultant; b. July 8, 1933, Los Angeles; s. C. Olin and Ruth Adelia (Crego) E.; m. Elisabeth Battin, June 16, 1957; children: Mark b. 1958, Michael b. 1963, Susan b. 1967; edn: BA, Cascade Coll. 1958; M.Div. Asbury Theol. Sem. 1962; ordained United Methodist Ch. 1968. Career: asst. to the pres., Asbury Theol. Sem., Ky. 1961-68; parish pastor United Meth. Churches in Taft, El Cajon, Pomona, 1968-80; cons. D.M. Lawson Assocs., N.Y. 1980-82; exec. dir. Methodist Hosp. Found., Arcadia 1982-83; v.p. Univ. Advancement, Azusa Pacific Univ., 1983-84; pres. Life Span Concepts, Claremont 1984–; assoc. ptnr. The ProSource Group, L.A. 1986-90; prin. Planned Gift Associates, 1990–; trustee Asbury Theol. Sem.; founding bd. Calif. Parks Ministry; cons. in fundraising, human resource assessment, organization structure various nonprofit orgns.; honors: Outstanding Young Men of Am. 1965, Kentucky Col. 1968, hon. D.Div., ATS 1972; mem. Rotary Internat. (dir. Claremont); publs:

num. sermons, promotional copy; mil: sgt. AUS 1953-55; Republican; rec: cabinetry, ceramic potting, golf, sailing. Res: 310 Miramar Claremont 91711 Ofc: Planned Gift Associates 675 W Foothill Blvd Ste 320 Claremont 91711

EDWARDS, GEORGE HENRY, technical writer; b. Feb. 19, 1932, Hammond, Ind.; s. Samuel Finley and Eula Gertrude (Gruber) E.; m. Marian Joan Weiss, May 24, 1958; children: Susan b. 1959, Judith b. 1960, Sandra b. 1961; edn: BA, American Univ., Washington DC 1959; grad. study MSEE, Johns Hopkins Univ., 1974. Career: assoc. engr. Motorola, Chgo. 1955-56; jr. engr. to engr. Cook Research Labs., Wash. DC 1956-59; engr. to sect. mgr. Litton Amecom, College Park, Md. 1959-73; sr. engr. Vitro Laboratories, Silver Springs, Md. 1973-76; mem. tech. staff Rockwell Internat., Anaheim, Calif. 1976-81; dep. program mgr. Lockheed, Ontario 1981-83; pgm. mgr. Flight Systems Inc., Newport Beach 1983-87; div. IR&D pgm. mgr. Litton Applied Technology, San Jose 1987-88; engring. mgr. 1988-89; broker Edwards Real Estate, San Jose 1989-91; contract technical writer, San Jose 1991–; honors: Kappa Mu Epsilon nat. math. hon. soc. (1950); mem: Electronic Defense Soc. (bd. 1983-84), Assn. of Old Crows (pres. Mission Club 1982-83), Mensa 1973–; active civic assns. Calif. and Md., mem. Pres.'s Assn. Prince George Co., Md. (pres. 1971-72), Toastmasters (v.p. 1974-75), Anaheim Hills Comm. Assn. (sec. 1979-80), San Jose Dist. 8 Comm. Leaders Council (facilitator 1994); co-inventor Radar Counter-Counter (classified 1961); pub. article in J. of Electronic Def., 1985; mil: electr. tech 2c p.o. USN 1951-54; Republican; Prot.; rec: personal computing. Res/Ofc: 2921 Glen Darby Ct San Jose 95148

EDWARDS, JAMES RICHARD, lawyer; b. April 14, 1951, Long Beach; s. Nelson James and Dorothy June (Harris) E.; m. Joan Marie Carriveau, Sept. 24, 1988; edn: BS psychology, Colo. St. Univ. 1973; JD, Univ. San Diego Law Sch. 1977. Career: atty. Downtown Legal Center, San Diego 1977-78; Getty Oil Co., Los Angeles 1978-80; gen. counsel, secty. Logicon Inc., Torrance 1980-85; ptnr. Mirasson Nyznyk & Edwards, Redondo Beach 1985-87; v.p., gen. counsel, secty. Gen. Atomics, San Diego 1987–; dir. Sequoyah Fuels Corp., Gore, Okla. 1988–; Chembond Corp., Eugene, Oreg. 1979-80; awards: U.S. Parachute Assn. nat. championship team 1977, 79, 80, F.I.A. world skydiving records 1977, 78, 86, 88, 92; mem: State Bar of Calif., Am. Corp. Counsel Assn., San Diego Bar Assn., U.S. Parachute Assn.; articles pub. 1986; Republican; rec: skydiving, flying, golf. Ofc: General Atomics POB 85608 San Diego 92186

EFRON, THEODORE, wholesale meat packer; b. May 26, 1944, New York; s. Morris and Pearl E.; m. Barbara Goldstein, June 26, 1965; Career: Efron & Son Meat Packers Inc., Brea, currently; awards: Kiwanis man of year 1980; mem: Fullerton Elks Lodge, Orange Co. Chefs Assn., Am. Culinary Federation, Kiwanis (life, pres. 1980-81), Orange Empire Chefs Assn., Fullerton Elks, Yorba Linda Kiwanis (pres. 1981-82), Placentia Elks (treas. 1965-66). Ofc: Efron & Son Meat Packers Inc. 154 Viking Brea 92621

EGAN, EDWARD JOSEPH, JR., adhesives manufacturing company president; b. Oct. 4, 1943, NY, NY; s. Edward Joseph, Sr. and Ann (Coakley) E.; m. Elizabeth Schwartz, Jan. 17, 1964 (div.); children: Elisabeth b. 1964, Edward, III b. 1966, Kevin b. 1970, Daniel b. 1977; m. Anne Marie Glennon, Oct. 7, 1989; children: Lillian Anne b. 1990; edn: BA, Notre Dame Univ. 1965; MBA, USC 1969. Career: nat. mktg. mgr. American Can Co., Greenwich, Conn. 1970-73, region mgr. 1973-76, dir. mktg. & sales 1976-77; pres. General Can Co., Los Angeles 1977-82; pres. W.W. Henry Co., Los Angeles 1982–; pres. West Coast Container, Los Angeles 1986–; mem: Can Mfrs. Inst. (bd. dirs., exec. com.), Carpet Mfrs. of the West, Carpet & Rug Inst., Adhesives & Sealants Council, Nat. Assn. of Floor Covering Dist., Am. Tile Mfrs. Inst., Nat. Paint & Coatins Assn., Co. Calif. Paint & Coatings Assn., Los Angeles C.of C., Town Hall of Calif., Who's Who in Am. Bus.; civic bds: Intra-Sci. Research Found. (chmn. & pres. 1982-92), La Canada Little League (coach 1977–), Am. Heart Assn., Nat. Kidney Found., Am. Cancer Res. Found., Sacred Heart High Sch. Advy. Bd. 1978-83, St. Francis H.S. 1979-87, St. Bede Grammar Sch. (treas. 1976–); clubs: Jonathan, Annandale Golf, La Canada-Flintridge Golf, Winged Foot Golf; Republican (pres. La Canada Young Rep. 1968); R. Cath.; Knight of Malta; rec: golf, swim, tennis, theatre arts. Res: 1437 Edgehill Pl Pasadena 91103 Ofc: W.W. Henry Co. 5608 Soto St Huntington Park 90255

EHRLER, DANIEL LYNN, association executive; b. June 27, 1945, Long Beach; s. Claude William and Jessie Mildred (Ernst) E.; m. Carole Jean Schmidt, March 13, 1982; edn: BA, CSU Long Beach 1967; MA, 1970. Career: asst. to exec. dir. Eugene Hearing & Speech Center, Ore. 1977-79; exec. dir. Jr. Achievement, Corvallis, Ore. and Orange Co. 1979-81; tchr. Long Beach Unified Sch. Dist. 1981-84; exec. dir. Sonoma Valley Chamber of Commerce 1984-85; exec. v.p. Pacifica Chamber of Commerce 1986-87; exec. v.p. Palm Desert Chamber of Commerce 1987-92; CEO, Santa Cruz Area Chamber of Commerce 1992-95; exec. dir. Santa Monica Chamber of Commerce 1995–; adj. instr. Coll. of Desert 1988, 89; awards: Active 20-30 Club outstanding new mem. 1978, Long Beach City Coll. silver key 1965; mem: Santa Monica Rotary, Palm Desert Rotary, Sonoma Kiwanis, Eugene Kiwanis, Corvallis Rotary, Eugene Active 20-30 Club; rec: auto racing, sailing, golf. Ofc: 501 Colorado Ave Ste 150 Santa Monica 90401

EHRSAM, ELDON EDWARD, operations research analyst; b. July 8, 1936, Bern, Kans.; s. Loyd and Elma Elizabeth (Bauman) E.; m. Clara Louise Schwartz, Nov. 20, 1958; children: Elizabeth Sue b. 1959, Jeffrey b. 1961, John b. 1968, Brian b. 1969; edn: BS, Washburn Univ. 1962; MS, USC 1969; cert. (MS equiv.) UC Santa Barbara 1973; Calif. lic. real estate broker. Career: physicist Naval Ordnance Lab, Corona, Ca. 1962-65; electronic engr. AF Western Test Range, Vandenberg AFB, 1965-68, project engr. Space & Missile Test Center, VAFB 1968-73, telemetry systems mgr. 1973-76, ops. research analyst 1976–; real estate broker, Danish Village Realty, Solvang 1976-90, ERA Hunter Realty, Santa Ynez/ Lompoc, 1991–; securities rep. Vestcap Sec. Corp., Solvang 1982-89; honors: BSA District Award 1979, listed Who's Who in West, Jane's Who's Who in Aviation & Aerospace; mem: AIAA (Vandenberg chpt. Council 1980-81), Internat. Platform Assn., Nat. Assn. of Realtors, Nat. Assn. Securities Dealers, Sigma Pi Sigma, Masons, Elks; coauthor 7 tech. papers, presented AIAA and Internat. Telemetry Confs. 1969-94; Republican; United Methodist; rec: racquetball, jogging, camping. Res: 3087 Fairlea Rd Santa Ynez 93460 Ofc: Det. 9 Space & Missile Systems Center, Code TA Vandenberg AFB 93437

EIGNER, WILLIAM WHITLING, lawyer; b. Feb. 4, 1959, Dover, Ohio; s. Stanley Spencer and Jeraldine (Lippy) E.; m. Jeanne Beach, May 24, 1987; edn: BA, Stanford Univ. 1981; JD, Univ. Va. Sch. Law 1986; admitted St. Bar Calif. 1986, U.S. Dist. Ct. So. Dist. 1986. Career: Judicial Intern U.S. Supreme Ct., Wash. D.C. 1981; atty. Higgs Fletcher & Mack, San Diego 1986-89; ptnr. Procopio Cory Hargreaves & Savitch 1989–; land use chmn. La Jolla Town Council 1989-90, trustee 1988-92; mem: Greater San Diego C.of C. (chmn. bus. recognition and awards com. 1989–), Stanford Alumni S.D. (bd. mem. 1987-89), Bishop's Sch. Headmaster's Advy. Council 1993-94; Republican; Jewish; rec: Civil War history, tennis. Ofc: Procopio Cory Hargreaves & Savitch 530 B St San Diego 92101-4469 Tel: 619/238-1900 x312

EISEMANN, KURT, mathematics professor; b. June 22, 1923, Nuremberg, Germany, naturalized U.S. citizen 1953; s. Dr. Lazarus and Lina (Bacharach) E.; m. Marlene K. Cross, June 22, 1969 (div. 1988); children: Jamin Albert b. 1970, Caroline Ruth b. 1974; edn: BA, Yeshiva Univ., NY 1950; MS, M.I.T., 1952; PhD, Harvard Univ., 1962. Career: sr. and res. mathematician Internat. Business Machines Corp., N.Y.C. and Cambridge, Mass., 1952-61; mgr. mathematical res. Sperry Rand Corp., W.D.C., 1961-63; dir. Computer Ctr. and assoc. prof. Catholic Univ. of Am., W.D.C., 1963-66; tech. dir. Computer Usage Devel. Corp., Boston 1966-68; dir. acad. computing svs. and prof. computer scis. Northeastern Univ., 1968-74; dir. computer svs. and prof. math. and computer sci. Univ. of Missouri, Kansas City, Mo. 1974-82; dir. univ. computing ctr. and prof. math. & compter scis. San Diego State Univ., (1982-92, prof. emeritus (ret.) 1992); lectr. Yeshiva Univ. 1953-55, Cath. Univ. of Am. 1962-63; dir. chem. lab. pgms. Children's Science Camps, Pa. 1970-73; awards: Yeshiva Univ. prize for excellence in math., prize for scholarship, ethics & character 1950, M.I.T. scholar 1950-52, commendn. Gov. Indiana; civic bds: Singles Cultural Club, Boston (founder, chmn. 1967-69), Private School Bd. of Edn. Greater Kansas City (mem., chmn. 1977-80), Private Schs. Regional Edn. Coun., Met. K.C. (bd. 1979-81); publs: numerous papers in math. Ofc: Dept. Math. San Diego State Univ., San Diego 92182

EISENBERG, RONALD LEE, physician; b. July 11, 1945, Philadelphia, Pa.; s. Milton and Betty (Klein) E.; m. Zina Leah Schiff; 2 children; edn: AB, chem., Univ. of Pennsylvania 1965, MD, 1969; cert. Am. Bd. of Radiology 1975. Career: staff radiologist VA Med. Ctr., San Francisco 1975-80; chmn. of radiology LSU Med. Ctr., Shreveport, La. 1980-91; chmn. of radiology Highland Hosp., Oakland 1991–; clin. prof. of radiology UC San Francisco and UC Davis 1991–; honors: Phi Beta Kappa 1965, Alpha Omega Alpha 1969, Am. Physicians Fellowship Man of the Year 1985; mem: Radiological Soc. of N. Am. 1975–, Am. Roentgen Ray Soc. 1975–, Am. Coll. of Radiology fellow 1980–), Soc. for Gastrointestinal Radiology 1980–; Am. Physicians Fellowship (bd. dirs. 1980–), Kol Shofar, Tiburon (v.p. 1993–); author: 15 books, 75 articles, newspaper column Doctor/Doctor, 1992–; editor: journal; mil: maj. US Army 1971-73; rec: law, piano. Ofc: Highland Hospital 1411 E 31st St Oakland 94602

EISNER, MICHAEL DAMMANN, entertainment executive; b. Mar. 7, 1942, Mt. Kisco, N.Y.; s. Lester and Margaret (Dammann) E.; m. Jane Breckenridge, July 21, 1967; children: Breck, Eric, Anders; edn: BA in Eng. lit. & theater, Denison Univ., Granville, Oh. 1964. Career: pgmmg. dept. CBS-TV, N.Y.C. 1964-66; asst. to nat. pgmg. director ABC-TV, N.Y.C. 1966-68, mgr. Specials & Talent/dir. pgm. development- East Coast 1968-71, v.p. Daytime Pgmg. 1971-75, v.p. Pgm. Plng. & Devel. 1975-76, sr. v.p. Prime Time Prodn. & Devel. 1976; pres./c.o.o. Paramount Pictures, Los Angeles 1976-84; bd. chmn./c.e.o. The Walt Disney Co., Burbank 1984–; trustee Georgetown Univ.; bd. dirs: Denison Univ., Calif. Inst. of the Arts, Am. Hospital of Paris Found., Environmental Media Assn., L.A. Music Center. Ofc: The Walt Disney Co. 500 S Buena Vista St Burbank 91421

EKELUND, JOHN JOSEPH, college president, admiral; b. Jan. 19, 1928, Washington; s. Kenneth Oscar and Marjorie (Buscher) E.; m. Lynn Marie Schumacher, May 3, 1952; children: John, Jr. b. 1953, Christopher b. 1954, Terri

b. 1956, Peter b. 1958, Tracy b. 1960, Patricia b. 1962, Kent b. 1967; edn: BS, US Naval Acad. 1949; MS systems analysis, Univ. Rochester 1969. Career: officer U.S. Navy 1945-83, commnd. ensign 1949, advanced through grades to rear adm. 1976, service in Korea and Vietnam; chief staff Naval Forces, Vietnam, 1972-73; cmdr. guided missile cruiser USS Albany, 1973-75; dean Naval War Coll., 1975-76; dep. dir. naval edn. and tng. Office Chief Naval Ops., WDC 1976-77; nat. intelligence officer CIA, 1977-78; cmdr. US South Atlantic Force, 1978-80; supt. Naval Postgrad. Sch., Monterey, Calif. 1980-83; decorated Legion of Merit (1973, 79, 83), Meritorious Service 1972, Presdl. Unit Cit. 1950, Nat. Intelligence Achiev. U.S. Intelligence Community 1978; pres. Calif. Maritime Acad., Vallejo, 1983–; civic: Napa Solano United Way (pres. 1988–), Vallejo Rotary (dir. 1986–), Vallejo C.of C. (dir. 1986–); mem. US Naval Acad. Alumni Assn., US Naval Inst.; works: devel. modern submarine torpedo fire control solution methodology used internat. (1957); Republican; Cath.; rec: golf, reading. Res: 2 Faculty Dr Vallejo 94590 Ofc: California Maritime Academy, P.O. Box 1392, Vallejo 94590

ELAINE, KAREN, musician; b. Nov. 6, 1965, San Jose; d. Gaston Ortega and Alice Lee (Ray) Sanders: edn: H.S. grad. Sch. of Creative & Performing Arts, San Diego, 1983; dipl. music, viola performance profl., Curtis Inst., Phila. 1984-87. Career: principal, solo viola New American Chamber Orch., Detroit 1986-87; prin. viola San Diego Sym. Orch., 1987-90, also asst. prin. viola San Diego Chamber Orch., 1987-90; prin. viola Orquesta Sinfonia de Tijuana, B.C., Mexico 1988–; prof. viola San Diego State Univ. 1989–; prof. viola Chanterelle Music Festival, Pouidoux, Switz. (summers 1989, 90); prin. viola, soloist Sun Valley Summmer Sym., Sun Valley, Idaho 1991–; asst. prin. viola Pro Musica Chamber Orch., Santa Fe 1994–; guest lectr., soloist Internat. Viola Cong., Ithaca, NY 1991; guest soloist Am. Youth Sym., L.A. 1992; awards: 1st pl. grand prize Bruno Giuranna Internat. Viola Competition, Brazil 1988, 1st pl. Rio Hondo Young Artists Comp., Whittier, Ca. 1989, Commn. grant (Gordon Kerry's Viola Concerto) Australia Arts Council, Sydney 1991, Commn Concert Piece by David Baker 1989, Cinnabar Concerto by David Ward-Steinman 1993, 1992 Grammy Music Com. award nominee, N.Y. 1992; mem. Am. Viola Soc. 1988–, Musicians' Union (Locals #47, #325); recording soloist: Bartok, Orq. Sinfonia de Paraiba/ Delos 1988, Dello Joio, City of London Sinfonia/ Harmonia Mundi 1990, Bloch, London Sym.Orch. /Laurel 1990, Kerry with Melbourne Sym. Orch., Hill, Glanville-Hicks with Queensland Sym. Orch./ABC 1994, ABC Radio Live broadcast archive; contbr. article in J. Am. Viola Soc., 1991, 92; Democrat; rec: karate, body surfing, sci. fi., chamber music. Res: 208 Welling Way San Diego 92114-5947

ELGIN, GITA, clinical psychologist; b. Santiago, Chile, nat. 1987; d. Serafin and Regina (Urizar) Elgin; m. Bart Bödy, Oct. 21, 1971; children: Dio Christopher Karoly Elgin-Bödy b. 1986, Alma Ilona Raia Julia Elgin-Bödy b. 1990; edn: PsyD (summa cum laude), Univ. of Chile, 1964; PhD, UC Berkeley, 1976; lic. psychologist (PSY 6901). Career: hosp. psychologist, Santiago, Chile 1964-65, clin. and exptl. psychologist Univ. of Chile 1965-68; clin. psych. intern Alameda County Mental Health Svs., 1968-69; res. asst. UCB, also pre-doctl. intern Kaiser Found. Med. Ctr., Oakland 1970-71; post-doctl. intern Contra Costa Co. Mental Hlth. Svs., 1977; co-founder, clin. dir. Holistic Health Assocs., Montclair, Oakland 1979–; co-founder Montclair Mediation Group 1994; writer, lectr. and workshops on holistic health; publs. in profl. jours. and local newspapers; mem: Am. Psychol. Assn., Calif. Psychol. Assn./Alameda Co. Chpt., Montclair Health Profls. Assn. (founding pres. 1983-84), Assn. for Holistic Health, UCB Alumni Assn., No. Calif. Soc. for Clin. Hypnosis, Assn. for Cognitive Behavior Therapy, Assn. for Transpersonal Psych., Psychosynthesis Network, Am. Holistic Psychological Assn. (founder 1995), Commonwealth Club of Calif.; awards: research fellow Found. for Research on the Nature of Man, Durham, N.C. 1968, res. grantee on psychol. correlates of EEG-alpha, UCB 1973, NIMH res. fellow in biofeedback, UCB 1973-74; Self-Realization Fellowship; rec: writing, windsurfing, swimming, R.E., Chinese med.& homeopathy. Ofc: Holistic Health Associates, Montclair Professional Bldg 2080 Mountain Blvd Ste 203 Oakland 94611

ELIAS, JAMES MORROW (natus ALLAIS), mining geologist; b. May 12, 1929, Los Angeles; s. Arthur M. and Melba (Wightman) E.; edn: BA, USC 1951; grad. work, Univ. of Utah 1952; Reg. Geologist (No. 1972), Calif. 1970; cert. profl. geologist, Am. Inst. Profl. Geol. 1967. Career: staff/sr./mining geologist for various cos. incl. Getty Oil, Interpace, Gladding McBean, Anaconda, US Geol. Survey, Cyprus Mines, 1952-67; chief geologist, Exploration, US Smelting Refining & Mining Co., NY, NY and Salt Lake City, Utah 1968-72; dir. Oil & Gas Devel., 1973, chief geologist, UV Industries, Salt Lake City and NY, NY 1973-76; pres. J. Morrow Elias & Assocs. (cons. geologists), Rutherford, Ca. 1976–; awards: Golden Award, Pyrite Hall of Fame 1983; mem: Am. Inst. of Mining Engrs. (chmn. So. Calif. Sect. 1966-8), Northwest Mining Assn., Soc. of Economic Geologists, Nev. Mining Assn., Canadian Inst. of Mining; num. articles in profl. jours.; Republican; rec: vineyardist and winemaker (Cabernet & Sauvignon Blanc) Allais Vineyards in Napa Valley. Res: 8278 St Helena Hwy Napa 94558 Ofc: J. Morrow Elias & Associates, PO Box 23 Rutherford 94573

ELIOT, MARK STEVEN, public relations executive, graphic designer; b. Oct. 19, 1954, Burbank; s. Gerald and Eileen (Dougherty) E.; m. Ellen Mary Steinberg, Sept. 20, 1981; 1 dau., Ashley Elizabeth b. 1986; edn: BA, CSU Long Beach 1976. Career: arts and feature writer Orange Coast Mag., Irvine 1977; pub. rels. promotion dir. KWIZ AM & FM Radio, Santa Ana 1977-82; self employed P.R.Graphic Design, Laguna Hills 1982-83; regional media coord. Rogers Cablesystems, Garden Grove 1983-85; comms. splst. Tustin Unified Sch. Dist. 1985–; com. Tustin Tiller Days 1986–; awards: Cable Advt. Mag. advt. and promotion award 1984, Orange Co. Fair art awards 1982-88, Film Festival award 1979, Orange Co. Advt. Fedn. Awards of Excellence 1978; mem: Tustin C.of C. (bd. dirs. 1986-88), Assn. Tustin Sch. Adminstrs., Nat. Sch. Pub. Rels. Assn., So. Calif. Schs. Pub. Rels. Assn., Masons, Rotary Club, Kiwanis, Tustin Hist. Soc., United Way, BSA; mural artist PepperTree Fair 1973, pub., ed. Cobblestone Art Newspaper, 1974-76, Blvd. Comm. Newspaper, 1976-77; rec: collect buttons, old toys and books, swimming, basketball. Res: 124 Rockview Drive Irvine 92715 Ofc: Tustin Unified School District 300 South C St Tustin 92680

ELIZONDO, SERGIO D., educator; b. Apr. 29, 1930, El Fuerte, Sin. Mex., nat. U.S. 1955; s. Cristino Santiago Elizondo and Feliciana (Dominguez) Maldonado; m. Sharon Mowrey, June 8, 1958 (div. Mar. 1971); children: Even D. b. 1959, Sean S. b. 1962; edn: BA, Findlay Coll., Ohio 1958; MA, Univ. N.C., Chapel Hill 1961, PhD in Spanish, 1964. Career: asst. prof. Univ. Texas, Austin 1963-68; assoc. prof. CSU San Bernardino, 1968-71; dean of coll. West Washington St. Univ., Bellingham 1971-72; prof. and hd. Spanish dept. New Mexico State Univ., Las Cruces 1972-90, dir. Inst. Chicano Studies, 1975-90; vis. prof. Mex.Am. literature San Diego State Univ., 1990–; prof. Spanish, San Diego State Univ. 1994–; vis. prof. Texas A&I Univ., Kingsville, Tx. 1979; awards: Ford Found. fellow Colegio de Mexico 1971, postdoc. grantee N.Mex. st. univ., Seville, Spain 1973, NEA fellow, W.D.C. 1981, mencion -short story Revista Cultural Plural, Mexico, D.F. 1985, Gold medal literature Univ. Ciudad Juarez, Mexico 1990; mem: Am. Assn. Tchrs. Spanish and Portuguese 1958–, Calif. Faculty Assn., ACLU, Amnesty Internat., Hemlock; author 5 books: Perros (1972), (fiction) Suruma (1990), Muerte En Una Estrella (1984), (short fiction) Rosa, La Flauta (1980), (poems) Libro Para Batos (1977); mil: pfc US Army 1954-56; Indep.; rec: travel, writing. Res: 5040 Comanche Dr #114 La Mesa 91941

ELLENBERG, ALEXANDER H., plastic surgeon; b. Oct. 13, 1933, Stockton; s. Morris and Gertrude (Barron) E.; m. Maureen Aronow, Aug. 8, 1955; children: Steven b. 1963, Gary b. 1966; edn: BA, UC Berkeley 1954, MD, UCSF 1958; bd. cert. plastic surgery (1967). Career: intern Los Angeles County Gen. Hosp., 1958-59; resident gen. surgery UC Med. Sch., San Francisco 1959-61; surgeon American Hosp., capt. Med. Corps AUS, Paris, Fr. 1961-63; resident plastic surgery UC Med. Sch., S.F. 1963-65; pvt. practice in plastic surgery, San Jose 1965–; chief plastic surg. Good Samaritan Hosp.; instr plastic surgery Stanford Univ., 1965–; lectr. in plastic surgery in US, Eng., Fr., Israel, Mex., Japan; honors: Phi Beta Kappa (1954); mem: AMA, CMA, Santa Clara Co. Med. Soc., San Jose Surgical Soc., Calif. Soc. Plastic Surgery (exec. com.), Am. Soc. Plastic Surg., Am. Soc. Aesthetic Plastic Surg.; civic: San Jose Rotary (chmn. coms.), Jewish Fedn. S.J. (dir. 1967–), S.J. Mus. Art (dir. 1975-85, pres. 83-85); coauthor Textbook of Plastic Surgery, numerous plastic surg. articles in med. jours. nat., internat.; Democrat; Jewish; rec: music, art. Ofc: 2550 Samaritan Dr San Jose 95124

ELLICKSON, DEANE LOUIS, insurance brokerage executive; b. Sept. 16, 1934, Chgo.; s. Ray and Madeline G. (Morris) E.; m. Lorraine, May 31, 1955 (div. July 1991); children: Suzanne b. 1958, Sherri b. 1961, Debra b. 1964, Lorne b. 1968, Deanna b. 1971; edn: stu. law LaSalle Univ. 1958-61, spl. courses, U.S. Internat. Univ., Golden Gate Univ., comm. colls.; Calif. lic. Ins. Broker, life & disab. agent 1960. Career: ins. investigator supr. Retail Credit Co., Santa Monica 1958-60; spl. agt. Bankers Life Co. of Iowa, L.A. 1960-62; group ins. rep. Occidental Life Ins. of Calif., L.A. 1962-65; profl. staff cons. Calif. Tchrs. Assn., Burlingame 1965-79, dept. supr. 1967-75; staff cons. and agcy. coord. Ednl. Comm. Ins. Services Inc., San Mateo 1979–, currently dir. and corp. ofcr.; prop. Rancho Pistachio Co. (pistachio orchard devel. co.), Temecula 1981–; dir. First Finl. Credit Union, Glendale 1985-88; recipient suggestion award Retail Credit Co. 1958, achievement award, Occidental Life (1962, 64), service awards: City of Huntington Beach, H.B. Rotary, H.B. Neighborhood Watch 1978, Liberty Bell Award, Orange Co. Bar Assn. 1978, La Cresta Prop. Owners Assn. golden telephone award 1984; civic: Arevalos Elem. Sch. Site Council 1968-79, Fountain Valley Dist. Supt.'s Spl. Advis. Com. 1974-77, H.B. Neighborhood Watch (founding com., bd., pres., 1975-78; secured O.C. grant funds for org. 1977), cons. var. Neighborhood Watch groups in So. Calif. 1975-84, H.B. Police Dept. and Civil Def. Aux. (spl. communs. team 1976-78), LaCresta Prop. Owners Assn. (pres. 1982-83); life mem. Calif. Rifle and Pistol Assn., Nat. Rifle Assn.; publs: Fgn. Dinner Menu & Cookbook (1986); mil: sgt.-major US Army Corps of Engrs., Pres. Unit Cit., Korean War, Good Conduct, 1957; Democrat; rec: shooting, avocado ranching, woodworking. Res: 24850 Hancock Ave, I106, Murrieta 92562 Ofc: Rancho Valley Services, Inc. PO Box 909 Murrieta 92564-0909

ELLINGTON, JAMES WILLARD, mechanical engineer; b. May 26, 1927, Richmond, Ind.; s. Oscar Willard and Leola Lenora (Sanderson) E.; m. Sondra Elaine Darnell, Dec. 6, 1952; children: Ronald b. 1953, Roxanna b. 1956; edn: BSME (summa cum laude), West Coast Univ., L.A. 1978. Career: designer NATCO, Richmond, Ind. 1954-67; design engr. Burgmaster, Gardena, Calif.

1967-69; senior mfg. engr. Xerox Corp., El Segundo 1969-84, consulting mem. engring. staff Xerox, Monrovia 1984-87; staff engr. Photonic Automation, Santa Ana 1987-88; sr. mech. engr. Optical Radiation, Azusa 1988; senior staff engr. Omnichrome, Chino 1988–; awards: 2d prize nat. design contest Gray & Ductile Iron Founders Soc., Richmond, Ind. 1966, Team Excellence Xerox Corp., Monrovia (1985); mem. Soc. Mfg. Engrs. 1962–, W.C.U. Alumni Assn., L.A. (bd. 1988–, v.p. budget & fin. 1993-94); mil: BT2/c US Navy 1945-52; Republican; Baptist; rec: gardening. Res: 6221 Mitchell Ave Riverside 92505

ELLIOT, DAVID CLEPHAN, historian; b. Sept. 17, 1917, Larkhall, Scotland; nat. 1954; s. John James and Edith Emily (Bell) E.; m. Nancy Franelle Haskins, Dec. 3, 1945; children: Enid b. 1947, John b. 1949, Nan b. 1951; edn: MA, St. Andrews Univ. Scotland 1939; MA, Harvard Univ. 1948; PhD, 1951; MA, Oxford Univ. England 1956. Career: Indian Civil Service 1941-48; tchg. fellow Harvard Univ., Cambridge, Mass. 1948-50; asst. prof. history Calif. Inst. of Tech., Pasadena 1950-53, assoc. prof. 1953-60, prof. 1960-86, prof. emeritus 1986–, chmn. 75 Ann. 1965-67, v.chair faculty 1965-67, exec. ofc. hum./social sc. 1967-71, secty. faculty 1973-85; co-chair exec. com. Calif. Seminar on Internat. Sec. and F.P. 1970-88; cons. Rand Corp., Santa Monica 1960-66, Fgn. Area Fellowship Pgm., N.Y.C. 1967-69; awards: Ford fellowship 1956-57, NATO fellowship 1980; mem: Inst. Current World Affairs, L.A. Com. of Fgn. Rels.; mil: gunner Royal Artillery 1940; rec: golf, bridge. Res: 1251 Inverness Dr Pasadena 91103 Ofc: Calif. Institute of Technology Pasadena 91125

ELLIOTT, GORDON JEFFERSON, educator; b. Nov. 13, 1928, Aberdeen, Wash.; s. Harry Cecil and Helga May (Kennedy) E.; m. Suzanne Tsugiko Urakawa, Apr. 2, 1957; children: Meiko Ann, Kenneth Gordon, Nancy Lee, Matthew Kennedy; edn: AA, Grays Harbor Coll., 1948; BA, Univ. Wash., 1950; cert. in Russian Army Language Sch., Monterey 1952; MA, Univ., Hawaii, 1968; Calif. Community Colls. lifetime tchg. credential. Career: English prof. Buddhist Univ., Ministry of Cultures, The Asia Found., Phnom Penh, Cambodia 1956-62, also cons. on Buddhist edn. The Asia Found., San Francisco, 1956-62; English instr. Univ. Hawaii, Honolulu 1962-68, also cons. on English edn., Hawaii State Adult Edn. Dept., 1966-68; dir. orientation English Coll. of Petroleum and Minerals, Dhahran, Saudi Arabia 1968-70; asst. prof. English and linguistics, Univ. Guam, Mangilao, 1970-76; tchr., French and English, Medford Mid High Sch., Oreg. 1976-77; instr. English Merced Coll. 1977–; spkr. conf. on English Edn. in Middle East, American Univ., Cairo 1969; vis. prof. English Shandong Tchrs. Univ., Jinan, China 1984-85; coauthor Cambodian/English (textbooks): English Composition 1962, Writing English 1966, (test) Standard English Recognition Test 1976; pub. articles in profl. jours.; mem. editl. advy. bd. Collegiate Press;awards: tchg. fellow Univ. Mich., Ann Arbor 1956, summer seminar stipend Nat. Endowment for the Humanities, UW, Seattle 1976, travel grantee People's Rep. of China, Beijing 1984-85; mem. Merced Coll. Found., Am. Assn. Woodturners, BPOE, NRA, Am. Near East Refugee Aid, Statue of Liberty Centennial Commn. 1983, Heritage Found., Lincoln Inst.; mil: sgt. US Army Security Agy. 1951-55, Japan; Republican (Rep. Presdl. Task Force 1980-86). Res: 680 Dennis Ct Merced 95340 Ofc: Merced College 3600 M St Merced 95340

ELLIOTT, JOHN GREGORY, aerospace engineer; b. Nov. 9, 1948, Dutch East Indies, came to U.S. 1956; s. Frans Jan and Charlotte Clara (Rosel) E.; m. Jennifer Lee Austin, May 7, 1988; edn: AA, Cerritos Coll., 1974; BS, CSU Long Beach, 1978. Career: design engr. Douglas Aircraft Co., Long Beach 1978-82, lead engr. 1983-89, sect. mgr. elec. installations group 1989–; mem. So. Calif. Profl. Engring. Assn., Douglas Aircraft Co. Management Club, Tennis Club, Surf Club; mil: US Navy 1969-73; Republican; Presbyterian. Ofc: Douglas Aircraft Co., MC 800-53, 3855 Lakewood Blvd Long Beach 90846

ELLIOTT, REED OAKLEY, JR., speech/language pathologist; b. Feb. 7, 1947, Altadena; s. Reed O., Sr. and Doris Josephine (Holland) E.; m. Christine Hinds, Sept. 3, 1976; children: Laine Elizabeth b. 1979, Kyle Walker b. 1982; edn: BA psych., Antioch Coll., 1970; MA commun. disorders (summa cum laude), CSU Northridge, 1986. Career: staff State Dept. of Devel. Services, 1970–; psych. tech. Pomona 1971-73, sr. psych. tech. Camarillo (1973-75, 78-85), unit mgr. 1975-78, Tchr. of Communicatively Handicapped, Dept. of Devel. Services, Camarillo 1985-93; Vocational Opportunities Coord. Regional Project at Camarillo 1993–; speech pathologist pvt. practice, Camarillo 1986-89; expert witness, cons. Dist. Atty., Maui, Hawaii 1986; cons. ednl. staff Lanterman Devel. Ctr., Pomona 1988; p.t. faculty Dept. Communicative Disorders CSU Northridge, 1989–; cons. Horrigan Enterprises group homes, Oxnard, 1991-93; exec. com. Mental Health Advy. Bd. Ventura County, 1989-92; profl. presentations Soc. of Neurosci. Conv., New Orleans, 1987, The Assn. for Persons with Severe Handicaps, S.F., 1989, Research & Program Devel. Conf., Dept. of Mental Health, S.F. 1990; Supported Living Connection Conf., VCSELPA, Oxnard, 1991, Employment of Persons with Disabilities Conf., Palm Springs 1993; awards: NSF research grantee 1969, Calif. Dept. of Devel. Serv. research grantee, 1989, 90, 91, profl. promise award CSUN Sch. of Comm. & Profl. Studies 1990, listed in Men of Achievement (pub. Cambridge, Eng. 1990); cert. mem. Am. Speech, Language & Hearing Assn. 1985–; civic: Am. Youth Soccer Orgn. (coach 1987–), YMCA Youth Basketball (coach 1988); publs: book chapt.

Using STRETCH to tch. comm. skills to people with developmental disabilities" in STRETCH, a life skills curriculum, 1990 pub. by Calif. Dept. of Devel. Svs.; A Critical Life Skills Vocabulary, 1988; contbr. articles to profl. jours.; Republican; rec: backpacking, musical composition, gourmet cooking, youth coaching. Ofc: Box 6022 Regional Project Camarillo 93011

ELLIOTT, ROLAND MEREDITH, II, real estate broker, rancher; b. June 16, 1933, Hollywood; s. Roland Meredith and Merle Vera (Chapman) E.; m. Sandra G., July 10, 1954 (div. 1979); m. Dale F. Hammes, Dec. 24, 1981; children: Kimberly b. 1956, Roland M., III b. 1957, Darin b. 1959, Tracy b. 1962; edn: AA, San Jose City Coll. 1955; BS, San Jose St. Univ. 1957; AA, W. Valley Coll. 1970; AA, Columbia Jr.Coll. 1979. Career: owner Elliott Enterprises, San Jose 1963-78; Lake Forest Properties, Groveland 1967–; awards: J.C. Penney's Golden Rule Award, past officer Hwy. 120 Assn.; mem: I.O.O.F. Yosemite #97 (past dep. dist. grand master), San Jose Bd. Realtors (dir. 1973-75), Calif. Assn. Realtors (dir. 1977-78), Groveland Real Estate Assn. (life, dir. 1980-), Hetch Hetchy Bd. of Realtors (co-founder), South Side Emergency Med. Svs. (co-founder), Tuolumne Co. Hosp. (trustee), Tuolumne Co. C.of C. (dir.), Sons Grand Army of the Republic, So. Tuolumne Co. Hist. Soc. (charter and life), Garrote Lions (charter and life), Am. Legion Post 300 (charter and life), Helping Hands (co-founder), SAR, Nat. Sons of Golden West, NRA (life), CRPA (life), DAV Post 119 Sonora (life), Korean War Veterans Assn. Sonora (life), patron Sierra Rep. Theater; mil: pvt. 1c. AUS 1953-54; Prot.; rec: swimming, exercise. Ofc: Lake Forest Properties Main St Groveland 95321

ELLIOTT, THOMAS JOSEPH, educator; b. Jan. 25, 1941, Boston; s. Thomas Joseph and Anne Teresa (Regan) E.; m. Eugenia Marie Coleman, June 18, 1966; 1 dau., Christine b. 1979; edn: AB (cum laude), Boston Coll., 1963, MA, 1967; PhD, Univ. Mich., 1970. Career: tchr. English and Latin, St. Dominic Savio H.S., East Boston, Mass. 1963-67; tchg. fellow Univ. Mich., Ann Arbor 1968-69; asst. prof. to full prof. English, Calif. Polytech. State Univ., Pomona 1970–; vis. fellow Univ. Kent, Canterbury, Eng. 1984; awards: fellow Southeastern Inst. of Medieval & Renaissance Lit., Duke Univ. 1976; mem. Modern Language Assn., Irish Am. Cultural Assn., Medieval Acad. of Am., New Chaucer Soc., others; author: A Medieval Bestiary (1971); textbook essay, College English (1980); talks: "Pilgrimage" Chaucer Congress, Eng., 1990, "Education" UC Berkeley, 1992; Democrat; R.Cath. Res: 982 Richmond Dr Claremont 91711-3348 Ofc: Dept. English Calif. State Polytechnic Univ., 3801 W Temple Ave Pomona 91768

ELLIS, EUGENE JOSEPH, cardiologist, professor emeritus medicine; b. Feb. 23, 1919, Rochester, N.Y.; s. Eugene Joseph and Violet (Anderson) E.; m. Ruth Nugent, July 31, 1943; children: Eugene J., Susan Ellis Renwick, Amy Ellis Miller; edn: AB, USC, 1941, MD, 1944; MS medicine, Univ. Minn., 1950; Diplomate Am. Bd. Internal Medicine and Cardiovascular Diseases. Career: intern USC/L.A. Cty. Hosp. 1944, resident 1946; fellowship Mayo Clinic, 1947-51; dir. dept. cardiology St. Vincent's Hosp., Los Angeles 1953-55, Good Samaritan Hosp., 1955-84, ret.; prof. medicine Univ. So. Calif., L.A. 1965-84, prof. emeritus medicine, 1984–; appt. Med. Bd. of Calif., 1984–, bd. pres. 1988; pres. Calif. State Div. of Med. Quality, 1985-89; exec. com. trustees Univ. Redlands, 1976-86; clubs: Los Angeles CC, Valley Club of Montecito, Birnam Wood G.C., Montecito; mil: lt. USN 1944-46; contbr. articles to med. jours.; Republican. Res: 450 Eastgate Lane Santa Babara 93108

ELLISON, TERI HALL, public health nutritionist; b. June 24, 1956, Fresno; d. Harold Robert and Patricia Ann (Dettinger) Hall; m. David Lee Ellison, Sept. 9, 1989; edn: BS, San Jose Univ. 1981; MPH, UC Berkeley 1985. Career: nutrition asst. Santa Clara Co. Health Dept., San Jose 1980-81; dietetic tech. O'Connor Hosp. 1981-83; pub. health nutrition con. Calif. Dept. Health Services, Sacto. 1984-86; ed., res. analyst Calif. Health Fedn. 1986-87; perinatal nutritionist Vacaville Comm. Clinic 1987-88; supervising dietitian Sacto. Co. Health Dept. 1988–; mem: Calif. Conf. of Local Health Dept. Nutritionists (pres. 1991-92, sec. 1989-90); honors: Phi Kappa Phi, San Jose St. Univ. Pres. scholar 1981, Yale Book award 1973, Outstanding Young Woman of Am. 1982, UC Berkeley Regents Fellow 1984, Helen R. Stacey award Am. Pub. Health Assn. 1984; civic: Hispanic Democratic Club Sacto. (v.p. 1986-87), Community Resource Project (bd., treas. 1987-90), Los Medicos Voladores; frequent profl. speaker on diabetes & nutrition in the Mexican Am. population; contbr. articles and pamphlets on nutrition (1984-86); Democrat; Prot.; rec: Spanish. Res: 8178 Heather Grove Ct Sacramento 95828 Ofc: Sacramento County Dept. of Health and Human Services 2251 Florin Rd Ste W Sacramento 95822

ELSWICK, WILLIAM ERNEST, software/audio engineer; b. July 6, 1955, Omaha, Nebr.; s. Wm. Robert and Lillian E.; edn: UCLA, 1972-74. Career: engr. Record Plant, Los Angeles 1974-79; engr. Concorde Recording, L.A. 1979-80; chief engr. Record Plant Sausalito, 1980-81; chief engr. Sound City Inc., Van Nuys 1982-85; software engr. Compact Video, Burbank 1986-89; dir. audio engring. Ediflex Systems, Glendale 1989-92; principal Entertainment Technology Assoc. 1992–; cons. Paramount Pictures 1978, Broadway Prodns., NY 1979, Marcus Electronic Devel., Van Nuys 1982; mem: Soc. Motion Picture and TV Engrs., Assn. for Computing Mach., IEEE (Computer Soc.), Audio

Engring. Soc.; author (software): Audio Prelay Sys., 1986, Dialog Replacement Sys., 1987, Digital Dialog Editor, 1988; rec: biking, sci-fi books. Ofc: Entertainment Technology Associates 1007 Montana Ave. Ste 102 Santa Monica 90403 EMAIL: belswick@entertech.com and elswick@primenet.com

EL-WARDANI, SAYED ALY, oceanographer; b. Feb. 26, 1927, Alexandria, Egypt; s. Aly M. and Bahgat (Elba) El-W.; m. Joan Margaret Newman, June 15, 1956 (div. 1973); m. Mary Elizabeth Houston, July 17, 1989; children: Ramsey Walter and Nile Regina b. 1957; Aladdin Sayed b. 1960; edn: BS hons., chem., Univ. Alexandria Egypt and Kings Coll. London 1948; UC Berkeley 1950-51; MS, Scripps Inst. Oceanography 1952; PhD, 1956. Career: instr. faculty of chemistry, Univ. Alexandria, Egypt 1948-49; asst. research prof., sr. oceanographer dept. oceanography, Univ. Wash., Seattle 1956-59; asst. prof. chemistry and environ. scis. San Jose St. Univ. 1959-63; staff scientist Lockheed Ocean Systems, Sunnyvale and San Diego 1963-68; assoc. prof. Calif. Western Univ., S.D. 1966-68; chief scientist, ptrn. Gen. Ocean Sci. & Resources Ins. 1968-74; mgr. internat. programs Lowry & Assoc., San Diego 1974-77; ptnr., environmental cons. Elwardani & Assocs., 1977-87, cons. environmental impacts, waste water mgmt. for So. Calif. and Orange Co. and Middle East countries; ret. 1987; mem: AAAS, Am. Chem. Soc., Am. Geophysical Union, Geochem. Soc., Marine Tech. Soc., Optimists Club; num. tech. and research articles and papers pub. in sci. jours.; Republican; Moselem; rec: tennis, swimming, travel. Address: 1730 Avenida Del Mundo Coronado CA 92118 also: 5525 E Lincoln Dr #122 Paradise Valley AZ 85253

EMAMJOMEH, JAVAD S., computer company president; b. Aug. 20, 1951, Teheran, Iran; s. Abolghasem S. and Hormat (Raesi) E.; m. Azam Mirshojaee, Jan. 20, 1974; children: Tannaz, Ranna, Neda; edn: BS, Univ. So. Louisiana; HND, ITT (Iran). Career: mgr. Epic Computer, Lafayette, La. 1978-82; mgr. Triad Systems, Sunnyvale 1982-84; mgr. Mainstreet Systems, Carlsbad 1984-86; pres. Computer Power, Ann Arbor, Mich. 1986-87; v.p. Salepoint, Del Mar 1987-88; pres., CEO Computer Profls., Carlsbad 1988–; rec: fishing.

ENEA, SANTO, dental technician; b. June 2, 1954, Pittsburg, Calif.; s. Joseph Paul and Rosa (Geraci) E.; edn: AA, Diablo Valley Coll. 1974; stu. Los Medanos Jr. Coll. 1978-80; desig: Dental Techn. Career: dental techn., lab. mgr. Yosemite Dent. Lab., Pittsburg, 1975-77, owner 1977-81; dental techn./owner Enea Dent. Lab., Pittsburg 1982–; mem. Nat. Assn. Dental Labs. 1978-84; civic: Pittsburg CofC (named Citizen of Year 1985), Sons of Italy, Pittsburg Bus. & Profl. Assn., Nat. Fedn. of Indep. Businessmen, Pittsburg Hist. Soc.; works: Italian-Am. Fishing Boat Monument (1984), Pittsburg Columbus Day Fest./Parade (84, 85, 86), Delta Fest. Fun Run (82, 83, 84, 85, 86); Democrat; R. Cath.; rec: genealogy. Address: Enea Dental Lab 112 Pueblo Dr Pittsburg 94565

ENGLE, RAPHAEL, graphic designer; b. June 6, 1934, Calgary, Canada; nat. 1978; s. Ely and Lilian (Belkin) E.; m. Anne Mary Jiry, March 24, 1963 (div. 1972); children: Elysa b. 1963, Shaena b. 1965; edn: BA, Art Center Coll. Design, L.A. 1959; MA, UCLA, 1972. Career: designer Porter & Goodman, Los Angeles 1959-60; cons. McCann Erickson 1960-63; pres. Ray Engle & Assoc. 1963–; faculty Art Center Coll. of Design, Pasadena 1960-87, UC Northridge 1975-77, Am. Coll 1994–; advy. bd. L.A. Trade Tech. Coll., Los Angeles 1978–; awards: N.Y. Art Dirs. Club Cert. Merit (1963, 65), Art Dir. Mag. (1987), Fin. World (1987), Pub. Rels. Soc. Am. (1987), Art Museum Assn. Am., Internat. Assn. Bus. Communicators (1986); mem: Art Center Alumni, UCLA Alumni, Am. Inst. Graphic Arts, Del Rey Yacht Club, Toastmasters (pres. 1983); articles pub. in profl. jours. (1960–), lectr. seminars and panels (1960–); rec: sailing, tennis, cooking. Res: 4726 La Villa Marina Marina del Rey 90292

ENGLEHORN, THEODORE DAVID, orthopedic surgeon (retired); b. June 18, 1903, Wagner, S.Dak.; s. Louis F. and Katie (Loepp) E.; m. Arleta Lane, Feb. 19, 1930; children: Frances Arleta b. 1932, Theodore D. b. 1934; edn: BS, Northwestern Univ. 1929; MD, 1930; orthopedic resident Hosp. for Ruptured & Crippled,N.Y.C. 1930-31. Career: chief orthopedics Monterey County Hosp., Salinas 1947-66; chief of surgery Salinas Valley Memorial Hosp. 1959-60, chief of staff 1960-61; med. dir. Casa Serena de Salinas extended care hosp., 1980-92; awards: AMA Fifty Year Club 1980, Northwestern Univ. Med. Sch. Half Century Club 1980, Salinas C.of C. Mem. of Month 1976, 79, Salinas Lodge F&AM Golden Veteran 1986, Scottish Rite Fifty Year Cap 1988; mem: Monterey Co. Med. Soc. (state del. 1954-66), Calif. Med. Soc., AMA, Internat. Coll. Surgeons, We. Orthopedic Assn.; civic: Pop Warner Football (med. dir. 1975-80), Nor-Cal Swim Meets (area med. dir. 1972-84), Salinas Area C.of C. (chmn. legislative com. 1975-77, 1986), Commonwealth Club of Calif. (S.F.), Am. Forestry Assn. (life); lodges: Masonic, Scottish Rite, Shrine, Salinas Elks (40-yr. mem.), Islam Temple Shrine (50-yr. mem.); mil: Major AUS M.C. 1934-52, WWII Am. Theater and South Pacific 1942-44 as orthopedic surgeon at McCaw Gen. Hosp., Walla Walla, Wash. 1944-46; Republican; Methodist; rec: camping, fishing, photog., woodwork and stitching, gourmet cooking & barbecueing. Res: 95 San Clemente Ave Salinas 93901

ENGLISH, CHRISTOPHER B.M., biotechnology company executive; b. June 12, 1947, Beckenham, Kent, U.K.; s. Clifford William Frederick and Pamela Marguerite (Schrod) E.; m. Sandra E., Feb. 17, 1977; son, Damien B.M. b. 1979; edn: BA (honors), Durham Univ., U.K., 1968. Career: advt. exec. G.D. Searle & Co., High Wycombe, Bucks, U.K., 1968-69, market res. asst. 1969-70, sales rep. 1970-71, coordinator overseas 1971-72; managing dir. Baird & Tatlock Ltd., Ndola, Rep. of Zambia, 1972-76; Euro. ops. mgr. G.D. Searle & Co., 1976-78; mktg. mgr. Bio-Rad Labs, Richmond, Calif. 1978-81, gen. mgr. 1981-83; dir. clin. cytometry Becton Dickinson, San Jose 1983-85, v.p. ops. 1985-90, v.p./gen. mgr. 1990-93; pres./CEO Biolumin Corp., San Jose 1993–; Fellow Chartered Inst. of Mktg. (FCIM) London, U.K. 1987; mem: No. Calif. Cricket Assn. (v.p. 1980, capt. 1982), Marin Cricket Club (capt. 1980-81, 88, chmn. 1982-84), Lions Club 1973-76; rec: cricket, golf, drama, music. Ofc: Biolumin Corporation 2154 Paragon Drive San Jose 95131

ENGORON, EDWARD DAVID, food service consultant, cookbook author and radio show host; b. Feb. 19, 1946, Los Angeles; s. Leo and Claire (Gray) E.; m. Charlene Scott, Oct. 7, 1970 (div. 1982); edn: BArch, USC, 1969, MBA, 1973, PhD, 1974; MA, Cordon Bleu, Paris 1975. Career: art director ABC, Los Angeles 1964-67, Paramount Pictures, 1967-68, Warner Bros. Pictures, 1968-69; mktg. dir. Lawry's Foods Inc., Los Angeles 1969-74; v.p. Warehouse Restaurants, Marina del Rey, 1968-72; pres. Perspectives, The Consulting Group Inc., San Francisco 1974-82, Los Angeles 1986–; pres. China Rose Inc., Dallas 1982-86; exec. v.p. T.G.I. Fridays Inc., Dallas 1986-87; pres., dir. and c.e.o. Guilt Free Goodies Ltd., Vancouver, B.C. 1986-90, Sugarless Co., Los Angeles 1987-90; pres. Sweet Deceit, Inc.; cons. The Southland Corp., Dallas 1982-86, Pizza Hut Inc., Wichita, Kans. 1975-87, Frank L. Carney Ents., Wichita 1982-87; co-host radio show The Food Show, KABC-AM 790; author cookbook: Stolen Secrets 1980; patentee Pasta Cooking Station 1981, micro-wave controller 1982; mem: Internat. Assn. of Culinary Professionals, Chaine des Rotisseurs, Foodservice Cons. Soc. Internat., Soc. Motion Picture Art Dirs., Food, Wine & Travel Writers Assn., Masons; civic: Los Angeles Parks (bd. govs. 1971-74), Fine Arts Commn., Tiburon (commr. 1974-76); Republican. Ofc: 11030 Santa Monica Blvd Ste 301 Los Angeles 90025

ENIS, BEN M., marketing educator; b. Jan. 5, 1942, Baton Rouge, La.; s. Ben, Sr. and Marjorie (Wood) E.; children: Ben M., III; edn: BS, MBA, and PhD, Louisiana St. Univ., 1963, 65, 67. Career: sales supr. So. Bell Tel. Co. 1964; tchg. fellow La. St. Univ. 1966; asst., assoc. prof., prof. Univ. of Houston, 1967-78; Howard Prof. Univ. of Mo. at Columbia 1978-82; vis. prof. Univ. Queensland, Brisbane 1982; prof. USC, 1982–; dir: Countrywide Credit Inc., Pasadena 1984–; dir. Protection One , Inc. 1994–; tng. cons. L.A. Times 1986-90; cons. US Bur. of Census, 1975-81; cons. (expert testimony) O'Melveny & Myers, L.A. 1983-85, 1987-89, 1991-92, Lane Powell, 1989, Gibson Dunn & Crutcher 1992-93, Munger Tolles & Olson 1993-94; awards: Humble Oil doctl. fellow 1965-66, Ford Found. doctl. fellow 1966-67, tchg. excellence award Univ. Houston Faculty Senate 1973, list of top 20 Leaders in Marketing Thought, Marketing News (22/21/85), USC Dean's fellowship for tchg. excellence 1987-89, tchr. of yr. MBA Assn. Univ. Mo. 1978-79; mem: Am. Mktg. Assn., Mensa; co-author: Marketing, 1985, ed. 8th edit. Marketing Classics, 1994, author: The Marketing Audit, 1994, 85+ articles in res. and tech. jours.; Libertarian; Deist; rec: scuba, skiing, swimming. Res: 4097 Robin Hill Rd La Canada 91011 Ofc: Univ. of So. Calif. University Park Los Angeles 90089-1421

ENNIS, C. BRADY, editor; b. Mar. 19, 1954, Alton, Ill.; s. Calvin Franklin and Virginia Jo (Moody) E.; edn: BA journ., Texas Christian Univ., 1978. Career: advt. copywriter Concordia Publishing House, St. Louis, Mo. 1978; display ad rep. Ft. Worth Star-Telegram, 1979; proofreader Deloitte Haskins & Sells, San Francisco 1980-83; assoc. editor ASU Travel Guide, 1983-86, mng. editor, 1986-89; copy editor Unix World Mag., Mountain View 1990; San Francisco General Hosp. 1991-92; S.F. Dept of Bldg. Inspection 1992–; co-founder and publicist Different Spokes Bicycle Club, S.F. 1982-83; awards: Sigma Delta Chi citation best news story of yr. Texas Christian Univ. 1975, gay sports award Gay Sports mag., S.F. 1983; mem. S.F. Advt. Club 1983-89, Am. Advt. Fedn. 1983-89, Soc. Profl. Journalists 1986-89, S.F. Creative Alliance 1994–; rec: drawing, cycling. Res: 1201 Green St #7 San Francisco 94109

ENOCH, JAY M., vision scientist, educator; b. April 20, 1929, New York; s. Jerome Dee and Stella Sarah (Nathan) E.; m. Rebekah Ann Feiss, June 24, 1951; children: Harold b. 1955, Barbara b. 1957, Ann b. 1962; edn: BS, Columbia Univ., N.Y.C. 1950; PhD, Ohio St. Univ., Columbus 1956; hon. DSc, S.U.N.Y. Career: prof. of the Grad. Sch., prof. and dean emeritus, UC Berkeley Sch. Optometry 1980-, chmn. grad. group in physiological optics 1980-94; prof. dept. ophthalmology UCSF Sch. Medicine 1980-; fmr. 2-term mem. Nat. Advy. Eye Council NIH, Bethesda, Md.; honors: Am. Acad. Optometry Glenn A. Fry award, Charles Prentice Medal, Assn. Research in Vision & Ophthalmology Francis Proctor medal, Am. Acad. Ophthalmology Honor award. Res: 54 Shuey Dr Moraga 94556-2621 Ofc: School of Optometry University of California Berkeley 94720-2020

ENRIGHT, KEVIN A., lawyer; b. April 23, 1953, San Diego; s. William Benner and Bette Lou (Card) E.; m. Judith Karen Wright, Aug. 12, 1978; children: Kelly b. 1984, Erin b. 1987, Megan b. 1991; edn: BA, Stanford Univ. 1975; JD, McGeorge Sch. Law 1979; admitted State Bar Calif. 1979, U.S. Supreme Ct. 1988; AV-rated by Martindale-Hubbell. Career: dep. dist. atty. Mendocino Co., Ukiah 1979-84; atty. Butz Lucas Dunn & Enright, San Diego 1985-95; judge, San Diego Municipal Ct., 1995–; instr. Nat. Inst. of Trial Advocacy 1994–; workshop leader S.D. Inn of Ct. 1989-94, dir. 1995–; barrister Am. Inns of Ct. Louis M. Welsh Chpt., S.D. 1985-87; mem: State Bar Calif. (del. Conf. of Delegates 1991), San Diego Co. Bar Assn. (Superior Ct. com. 1989-92, Justice System Funding com. 1994), San Diego Defense Lawyers Assn. (dir. 1991-93, pres. 1993), Am. Bar Assn., Defense Research Inst., Assn. So. Calif. Defense Counsel (dir. 1994-95), Calif. Defense Counsel (dir. 1994-95), Assn. Business Trial Lawyers, Stanford Club of S.D., Gr. San Diego Barristers Club (dir. 1987-88); Republican; Presbyterian; rec: basketball, tennis, sports. Ofc: San Diego Municipal Court 220 W Broadway San Diego 92101

ENSMINGER, MARK DOUGLAS, chemist; b. Oct. 11, 1955, Escondido; s. Douglas Lloyd and Mary Theresa E.; m. Marsha Lynn Westerhold, Dec. 20, 1980; edn: BA in economics and BS in chemistry, UC Santa Barbara, 1977; AM in chem., Univ. Ill., 1979, PhD chem., 1982. Career: research chemist Chevron Oil Field Research Co., La Habra, Calif. 1982-86; engring. specialist Northrop Aircraft Div., Hawthorne 1987-91, Northrop Grumman B-2 Div., Pico Rivera 1991–; instr. 1990 ISFTA, L.A. 1990; cons. Getty Conservation Inst., Marina del Rey 1986-87; mem: Sigma Xi 1983–, Am. Chem. Soc. 1983–, Am. Physical Soc. 1983–, Optical Soc. of Am. 1983–, Soc. for Applied Spectroscopy 1989–; contbr. articles to profl. jours.; Evangelical Free Ch.; rec: audio engring. Ofc: Northrop B-2 Div. Dept. T631/GS 8900 E Washington Blvd Pico Rivera 90660

ENSOR, KAREN JOYCE, college professor; b. Oct. 8, 1946, Oakland; d. William Dean and Charlotte Joan (Jacobs) Isom; m. William Evan Ensor, April 8, 1965 (dec. 1987); children: Karena b. 1974, Jeremy b. 1977; edn: BS, Western Baptist Bible Coll. 1969; BA, Am. Coll. Jerusalem 1970; MA, Am. Inst. Holy Land Studies 1975; MA, Holy Names Coll. 1976; EdD, Univ. San Francisco 1983. Career: social worker Ministry of Social Welfare, Jerusalem, Israel 1970-71; tchr. Acad. of Christian Edn., Oakland 1971-73; prof. Patten Coll. 1974–, chair dept. of profl. studies 1976-87, library club dir. 1975-76, com. chair Patten Coll. Library 1976-87; sch. cons. DeVoss Sch., San Jose 1981; dir. of credential Patten Coll. 1987–; awards: Patten Coll. hon. student 1965, Gold P 1968, Talent Piano 1969, service 1981, Outstanding Young Woman of Am. 1976; mem: Nat. Assn. Christian Edn., Am. Edn. Res. Assn., Assn. Christian Schs. Internat., Religious Edn. Assn., Phi Delta Kappa, Credential Counselors & Analysts of Calif., Christian Cathedral (ministry bd. co-dir.), Youth Coalition (conf. coordinator), Bay Area Sunday Sch. Convention (mem. program com.); publs: diss., thesis, profl. paper presentation, 1979; Republican; Prot.; rec: skiing, swimming, crafts. Ofc: Patten College 2433 Coolidge Ave Oakland 94601

EPCAR, RICHARD, actor, writer, director; b. Apr. 29, 1955, Denver; s. George B. and Shirley (Learner) E.; m. Ellyn Jane Stern, Aug. 15, 1982; children: Jonathan b. 1983, Jacqueline b. 1987; edn: BFA in performing arts, Univ. Arizona, Tucson 1978; postgrad., USC, 1980, UCLA, 1981, Am. Film Inst., 1982. Career: pres. Trouble Shooter Productions, L.A. 1986–; actor (films) including Memoirs of an Invisible Man, D.C. Collins, Columbo, Incident of War, Street Hawk, Escape to Love, Not of This World, (TV series) Diagnosis Murder, Cheers, General Hospital, Guns of Paradise, Matlock, Beverly Hills 90210, Who's the Boss?, Sonny Spoons, Moonlighting, Highway to Heaven, Amazing Stories, Fast Times, Crazy Like a Fox, Hell Town, Stir Crazy, Santa Barbara, (on stage) Why a Hero, Dracula, An Evening With Lincoln, Real Inspector Hound, Richard II; actor, writer (stageplay) Take My Wife...Please!, 1980; writer, director English adaptation of Academy Award winning film: Cinema Paradiso Belle Epoque; awards: Academy Award nominee for Women on the Verge of A Nervous Breakdown, Fencing Master, Eat Drink Man Woman, and Kika, Haldeman Found. scholar Univ. Ariz. 1973-78, named Nat. Best Actor of Year, Nat. Players 1977, CPC Repertory Group 1980, Irene Ryan Soloist award 1978; civic: L.A. Zoo Assn. 1983-91, Natural History Mus., L.A. 1989-91, Earth Save, L.A. 1990, L.A. Mus. Art 1991, host fall festival Sta. KCET-Pub. TV, L.A. 1980, active Am. Cancer Soc. Ofc: Trouble Shooter Prodns. PO Box 5429 North Hollywood 91616-5429

EPSTEIN, ERVIN HAROLD (SR.), dermatologist, editor; b. May 17, 1909, Vallejo, Calif.; s. Nathan and Lilly (Levin) E.; m. Selma Zinman, June, 1936; children: Ervin, Jr. b. 1942, Kenneth b. 1948; edn: AB, UC Berkeley 1931; MD, UC San Francisco 1935. Career: resident, dermatology, Los Angeles City Hosp. 1935-37; private practice, Oakland 1937–; awards: Practitioner of Yr., Dermatology Found., Evanston, Ill. 1936; honorary mem. Am. Dermatologic Assn. 1970-90; pres., sec. Pacific Dermatologic Assn. 1948-52; author: 8 books on dermatology, 1954-93; mil: capt. US Army 1942-44. Res: 5 Sotelo Ave Piedmont 94611

EPSTEIN, JOHN HOWARD, physician, dermatologist; b. Dec. 29, 1926, San Francisco; s. Norman Neman and Gertrude (Hirsch) E.; m. Alice Thompson, 1953; children: Norman H. b. 1954, Janice A. b. 1957, Beverly A. b. 1958; edn:

BA, UC Berkeley 1949; MD, UCSF 1952; MS, Univ. Minn. Minneapolis 1956. Career: pvt. practice, San Francisco 1956–; clin. prof. dermatology UCSF Med. Center 1972–; cons. USN Calif. 1962–; AUS 1962-86; faculty UCSF 1956–; honors: Am. Acad. Dermatology Silver award (1962), Gold award (1969), Phi Beta Kappa (1949), hon. mem. Polish, French, Spanish, Danish, No. American, Iowa and British Socs. Dermatology, Acad. Mex. de Dermatologia; mem: Am. Acad. Dermatology (pres.), Am. Bd. Derm. (fellow, pres. 1958–), Pacific Dermatological Assn. (press.), A.C.P. (fellow), A.C.S. (fellow), Soc. Investigative Dermatolkogy (v.p.); 255 articles pub. in med. jours (1956–), chief ed. Archives Dermatology (1973-78), asst. ed. Jour. Am. Acad. Dermatology (1978-88); editl. bd. Video Jour. Dermatology (1986–), mil: seaman 1c. USN 1944-46; rec: tennis, jogging, skiing. Ofc: 450 Sutter St Ste 1306 San Francisco 94108

EPSTEIN, LOIS BARTH, physician, professor; b. Dec. 29, 1933, Cambridge Mass.; d. Benjamin and Mary Frances (Perlmutter) Barth; m. Dr. Charles Epstein, June 10, 1956, Brookline, Mass.; children: David Alexander b. 1961, Jonathan Akiba b. 1963, Paul Michael b. 1967, Joanna Marguerite b. 1975; grandchildren: Jeffrey Mark Epstein b. 1990, Kendra Ann Epstein b. 1994; edn: AB, Radcliffe (cum laude), 1955; MD, Harvard Med. Sch., 1959. Career: resident in pathology Peter Bent Brigham Hosp., Boston 1959-60; internship New England Center Hosp. 1960-61; research med. ofcr. Nat. Inst. of Health 1962-63, 1966-67; NIH Post doctoral and NIH Spec. Fellow 1963-64, 1964-65; asst., then assoc. research physician Cancer Research Inst., Univ. Calif., S.F. 1969-74, assoc. dir. 1974-77, research assoc. 1977–; assoc. prof. of pediatrics Univ. Calif. Sch. of Med. 1974-80, prof. of pediatrics 1980–; UCSF Faculty Council 1989-94 (vice chair 1991-93); mem.: NIH Study Sect. on Immunological Sci. 1977-81, Allergy & Immunology Com. 1974-76; mem. bd. of sci. counselors Div. of Cancer Biology, Diagnosis and Cancer Ctrs., Nat. Cancer Inst., NIH 1991-95; mem. Nat. Cancer Inst. Cancer Ctr. Support Review Com. 1984-87; honors: Phi Beta Kappa, honoris causa, Radcliffe Coll. 1980, NIH Merit Award 1987-97, nominee Harvard Univ. Bd. of Overseers 1988; mem.: Assn. Am. Physicians 1980–, Am. Soc. Clin. Investigation 1977–, Am. Assn. Immunologists 1972–, Internat. Soc. for Interferon and Cytokine Res. 1983– (chair, membership com. 1988–), Soc. for Pediatric Research 1977–, Am. Pediatric Soc. 1994- Am. Soc. Hematology 1972–, Am. Assn. Cancer Edn. 1975–, Am. Soc. Cancer Research 1977–, AMA, CMA; bd. dirs.: Marin Symphony Assn. 1979-85 (chair, Endowment Subcom. 1983-85), Marin Dance Assn. 1980-85 (pres. of bd. 1984-85); assoc. editor: Cancer Research 1989-94, Jour. of Immunology 1983-85; editorial bds: Biotechnology Therapeutics 1988–, AIDS Patient Care 1987-94, Jour. of Experimental Pathology 1986–, Cellular Immunology 1984-92, Jour. of Clin. Immunology 1980-85; contbr. 120+ sci. papers to med. jours. and books; Jewish; rec: working with glass, sewing. Res: 19 Noche Vista Lane Tiburon, 94920 Ofc: Cancer Research Inst. Box 0128 Univ. of California 505 Parnassus Ave San Francisco 94143.

EPSTEIN, ROBERT ALAN, psychiatrist; b. Apr. 3, 1946, Brooklyn, N.Y.; s. Samuel Epstein, MD and Blanche (Mendlowitz) E.; m. Rebecca Bluestone, Aug. 2, 1981; children: Daniel b. 1978, Laura b. 1982, Sara b. 1986; edn: AB (magna cum laude), Brown Univ., Providence, RI 1966; MD, Yale Univ., New Haven, Ct. 1970; internship, internal medicine and gen. psychiatry Mt. Zion Hosp. & Med. Ctr., S.F. 1970-71, residency in adult psychiatry 1971-73, residency in child psychiatry 1973-75; adult psychoanalysis, S.F. Psychoanalytic Inst. 1978-90, child & adolescent psychoanalysis 1982-91; diplomate, gen. psychiatry, Am. Bd. of Psychiatry & Neurology 1977, diplomate, child & adolescent psychiatry 1980; cert. in adult psychoanalysis, Am. Psychoanalytic Assn. 1992, cert. in child & adolescent psychoanalysis 1992. Career: pvt. practice, child, adolescent & adult psychiatry & psychoanalysis 1975–; asst. chief, dept. of psychiatry Mt. Zion Hosp. and Med. Ctr., S.F. 1975–, staff child psychiatrist 1975-78; staff child psychiatrist Ann Martin Children's Ctr., Piedmont 1976-78; clin. asst. prof. UCSF 1977–; med. dir. East Bay Agency for Children, Oakland 1980–; cons. psychiatrist Oakland Comm. Counseling Ctr. 1982–, St. Mary's Coll., Moraga 1988–; med. staff Alta-Bates Herrick Hosp., Berkeley 1989–; faculty S.F. Psychoanalytic Inst. 1990–, faculty council 1993–; exec. com., capitated psychiatry group Alta Bates Med. Group 1992–; honors: Phi Beta Kappa 1965, Sigma Xi 1966; mem: Am. Academy of Child and Adolescent Psychiatry, Am. Coll. of Forensic Psychiatry, Am. Psychiatric Assn., Am. Psychoanalytic Assn., Assn. for Child Psychoanalysis, No. Calif. Psychiatric Soc., Regional Orgn. of Child and Adolescent Psychiatrists; contbr. article to profl. jour. 1990, num. papers and presentations, 1985-93; mil: USPHS Reserves 1968-74; rec: running, classical music. Ofc: 2702 Dana Street Berkeley 94705

ERICKSON, ARTHUR CHARLES, architect; b. June 14, 1924, Vancouver, B.C., Canada; s. Oscar and Myrtle (Chatterson) E.; edn: Univ. Brit. Col., Vancouver 1942-44; BArch, McGill Univ., 1950; LLD (hon.) Simon Fraser Univ. 1973, Univ. Manitoba 1978, Lethbridge Univ. 1981, D.Eng. (hon.) Nova Scotia Tech. Coll., McGill Univ. 1971, Litt.D. (hon.) Univ. Brit. Col. 1985, Lake Head Univ. 1988. Career: asst. prof. Univ. Oregon, Eugene 1955-56; asst. prof. Univ. Brit. Columbia 1957, asst. prof. 1961-63; ptnr. Erickson-Massey Architects, Vancouver, B.C. 1963-72; prin. Arthur Erickson Architects, offices in Vancouver and Toronto, 1972-90, Los Angeles 1981-91; dir.: Campus Planning Associates, Toronto; appt. com. on urban devel. Council of Canada, 1971; bd. dirs. Can.

Conf. of Arts, 1972; design advy. council Portland Devel. Commn., Can. Council Urban Research; trustee Inst. Research on Pub. Policy 1973; principle works: Canadian Pavilion at Expo '70, Osaka, Japan (1st prize nat. competition Can., best pavilion award Architectural Inst. of Japan), The Law Courts/Robson Square (honor award and Gov. General's Medals, Arch. Inst. of B.C. award for Law Courts 1983), Mus. of Anthropology (honor award), Eppich Residence (honor award), Habitat Pavilion (honor award), Sikh Temple (award of merit), Champlain Heights Community Sch. (award of merit); exhibitions: Vancouver Art Gallery 1965, 85-86, Centre for Internat. Relations, NY 1985, Decorative Arts Museum, Montreal 1985, Canada House, London 1986; awards: Can. Council fellow 1961, recipient Molson prize Can. Council for Arts 1967, Triangle award Nat. Soc. Interior Design, Royal Bank of Canada award 1971, Gold medal Tau Sigma Delta 1973, titled Officer and Companion Order of Canada 1973, 1981, residential design award Can. Housing Council 1975, August Perret award Internat. Union of Architects' Congress 1975, Pres.'s award Excellence Am. Soc. Landscape Architects 1979, Chgo. Architecture award 1984, Gold medal French Acad. Arch. 1984, McLennan Travelling scholar; subject of 4 books (1970, 75, 81, 88) monograph, Time mag. cover article, 1979, and New Yorker Mag. profile, 1979; mem: AIA (hon. Fellow, Pan Pacific citation Hawaiian chpt. 1963, Gold medal 1986), Royal Archtl. Inst. Can. (Fellow 1980, Gold medal 1984), Archtl. Inst. B.C., Ontario Assn. Architects, Royal Can. Acad. Arts (academician), Internat. Assn. of Architects (academician), Am. Soc. Interior Designers, Order des Architectes du Quebec, Am. Soc. Planning Officials, Community Planning Assn. Can., Heritage Can., Planning Inst. B.C., Urban Land Inst., Mus. of Modern Art (internat. council mem. 1986-92), Americas Soc. 1985-88, Friends of Nat. Symphony 1992-94, Llambda Alpha Internat. 1991-, Vancouver Art Gallery (life); clubs: Vancouver, U.B.C. Faculty, University; author: num. pub. articles and lectures, incl. Time Mag. cover article, 2/14/72; mil: served to capt. Can. Intelligence Corps 1945-46. Ofc: Arthur Erickson Architectural Corp. AE Architect Inc., PO Box 48007 Los Angeles 90048

ERICKSON, ERIC DOUGLAS, chemist; b. July 31, 1955, Astoria, Ore.; s. Douglas Leon and Patricia (Thiebes) E.; m. Barbara Marie Davenport, Sept. 3, 1977; children: Ivy b. 1980, Benjamin b. 1982; edn: BS in chem., Oregon State Univ., 1977; cert. indsl. hygiene, San Diego City Coll., 1980; PhD analytical chem., Mich. State Univ., 1989. Career: chemical technician Amtech Labs, San Diego 1977-78, asst. lab. mgr. 1978-80; res. chemist Naval Weapons Ctr., China Lake 1980-94, pollution abatement pgm. mgr. 1983-84; res. chemist, environmental R&D coord. Naval Air Warfare Ctr., China Lake 1992-93, dir. Environmental Lab 1992-94; recipient long term tng. fellowship Naval Weapons Ctr. 1984-85; mem: Am. Chemical Soc. (1977–, Mojave Desert sect. treas. 1990-91), Sigma Xi (1981–, chpt. pres. 1992); civic: Cub Scouts Ridgecrest (Webelos ldr. 1990-93), Sci. Explorer (post adv., Ridgecrest 1992–); inventor: Indicator Tubes for the Detection of TNT in Water (pat. 1984); author: 24+ book chapters and sci. jour. articles, 1982-91; rec: computer pgmg., reading. Res: 406 S Gordon Ridgecrest 93555 Ofc: Naval Air Warfare Ctr Weapons Div. Code 474230D China Lake 93555

ERICKSON, JAMES H., vice chancellor for university relations and development; b. May 18, 1939, Oak Park, Ill.; s. Chester E. and Ethyl M. (Jackson) E.; m. Janet J. Selburg, June 18, 1966; children: Michael James b. 1971, Richard James b. 1974; edn: BS, Bradley Univ., Peoria, Ill. 1961, MA, 1966; EdD, Indiana Univ., 1970. Career: dir. pub. info. Bradley Univ., Peoria, 1963-69, adj. prof. 1969-84, asst. to the pres. and chancellor, 1970-78, dean of student svs., 1978-82, assoc. v.p., 1982-85; dir. news bureau Indiana Univ., Bloomington, 1969-70, mag. editor: Chalkboard; v. chancellor univ. rel. and devel. UC Riverside, Calif. 1985–; dir. Riverside Co. Economic Devel.; cons. Council on Soc. for Advancement of Edn. (IL); dir. Illinois-Iowa Higher Edn. Consortium (IL); fundraising cons. colls. and charitable orgns., IL and CA, 1980–; commencement speaker for high schs., IL, 1970-85; awards: One of Ten Outstanding Young Men, IL 1971, Citizen of Yr. Peoria 1970, Distinguished service Urban League, IL, Pres.'s Cup United Way IL 1978, Merger Award for Pub. Svc. IL 1981, Citizen of the Year, Riverside 1993, Fulbright Fellowship to U.K. 1995, Urban League Vernon Jordan Humanitarian Award 1995; mem: Greater Riverside Urban League (pres. 1992), Gr. Riverside C.of C. (bd.), Raincross Club, Riv. Philharmonic Assn. (bd.), Coun. for Advancement and Support of Educ., Assn. of Urban Univs. (newsletter editor); author (Master Plan) "Illinois Private College," contbr. articles to edn. jours.; mil: s/sgt. US Army 1961-63; rec: jogging, basketball. Ofc: Univ. Calif. Riverside 900 University Ave Riverside 92521

ERICKSON, RANDALL ROBERT, advertising creative director; b. Aug. 14, 1949, Great Falls, Mont.; s. Robert Francis and Anna Lee (Dauwalter) E.; edn: Rocky Mountain Coll. 1967-68; Univ. Hawaii 1968-69; BS profl. arts, Woodbury Coll. 1972. Career: account exec. Jon Sandvick Studios, Los Angeles 1979-81; production mgr. Jones Agency, Palm Springs 1981-84; v.p. creative services, Walt Disney Home Video, Burbank 1984–; Democrat; Methodist; rec: painting, drawing. Ofc: The Walt Disney Co 500 S Buena Vista St Burbank 91521

ERIKSON, GREGORY ROBERT, corporate banking executive; b. Aug. 7, 1964, Chgo., Ill.; s. Robert Victor Erikson and Patricia (McPike) Hewlett; m. Cassie Diane McCollum, Sept. 22, 1991; edn: BBA, Calif. State Poly. Univ.,

Pomona (emphasis on mktg./fin.), 1986; Claremont Coll., Claremont, Calif. (minor in mil. sci.), 1987. Career: stockbroker Dean Witter Reynolds, Long Beach, Calif. 1987-88; internat. stockbroker Internat. Assets Advy. Corp., Irvine, Calif. 1989-90; asst. v.p./mgr. PFF Funding, Irvine, Calif. 1990; private banker Union Bank, City of Industry, 1990-19; asst. v.p., entertainment industries World Trade Bank, N.A., Beverly Hills, 1991-92; v.p./branch mgr. of corp./private banking Rancho Vista Nat. Bank, Orange, Calif. 1992–; cons. So. Calif., 1986–; awards: ranked #2 in So. Calif. by Dean Witter, Long Beach, Calif. 1988; mem: Calif. Rep. Party 1986–, Nat. Rifle Assn. 1986–, Indsl. League of Orange County 1990–, Orange County C. of C. 1990–, Amer. Marketing Assn. 1986–; civic: Sigma Chi Fraternity, Evanson, Ill., chapter adv. to Loyola Marymount univ. pres. and current alumni, 1986-92; active in Masonic Lodge #419, Upland, Calif.; author: frequent contributor to Bus. Sect. of Long Beach Press Telegram, 1987-91; mil: first lt. (promotable) AUS, armored cavalry br., 1987–; Republican; Lutheran; rec: scuba, skiing, sailing, golf, tennis. Res: 3625-J Bear St., South Coast Metro 92704

ERNST, ELDON GILBERT, seminary dean and professor; b. Jan. 27, 1939, Seattle; s. Kenneth Gilbert and Bydell (Painter) E.; m. Joy Skoglund, June 12, 1959; children: Michael b. 1962, David b. 1963, Peter b. 1968, Samuel b. 1973, Rachel b. 1982; edn: BA, Linfield Coll., 1961; MDiv, Colgate Rochester, 1964; MA and PhD, Yale Univ., 1965, 1968. Career: prof. American Baptist Sem., Berkeley 1967-82, Franciscan Sch. of Theology and Graduate Theological Union, 1982-90; dean and prof. American Baptist Sem. of the West, Berkeley 1990–; ed., Foundations, Rochester, NY 1975-78; cons. Lutheran History Ctr. of the West, Berkeley 1984–; organizer and convenor GTU Archives Council, 1986-89; awarded Howd Sociology Prize, Linfield Coll. 1961; mem: Am. Hist. Assn. 1988–, Am. Acad. of Religion 1974–, Am. Soc. of Church History 1967–, Calif. Hist. Soc. 1986–; author: Moment of Truth for Protestant America, 1974, Without Help Or Hindrance, 1977, 1987, Pilgrim Progression, 1993, 30+ jour. and encyclopedia articles, 1969–; Democrat; Prot.; rec: piano and singing. Res: 1855 San Antonio Ave Berkeley 94707 Ofc: American Baptist Seminary of the West 2606 Dwight Way Berkeley 94704

ERSKINE, JOHN MORSE, physician; b. Sept. 10, 1920, San Francisco; s. Morse and Dorothy (Ward) E.; edn: BS, Harvard Univ., 1942; MD, Harvard, Boston 1945; Diplomate Am. Bd. of Surgery, 1953. Career: surgical intern Univ. of Calif. Hosp., San Francisco 1945-46; research fellow Mass. Gen. Hosp., Boston 1948; resident in surgery Peter Bent Brigham Hosp., 1948-53; Georg Görham Peters Fellow, St. Mary's Hosp., London, England 1952; med. practice specializing in surg., San Francisco 1954–; asst. clin. prof. Stanford Med. Sch., S.F. 1956-59; asst., assoc. clin. prof. UC Med. Sch., San Francisco 1959–; surg. cons. S.F. Veterans Hosp. 1959-73; founder No. Calif. Artery Bank, 1954-58; mem. Irwin Memorial Blood Bank Commn., 1969-74; bd. dirs. Am. Cancer Soc., S.F. 1963-75; mem: S.F. Surgical Soc. (1956–, v.p. 1984), Pacific Coast Surgical Assn. 1968–, Am. Coll. Surgeons 1956–, S.F. Med. Soc. (1954–, bd. 1965-75), Calif. Med. Assn. 1954–; civic: Greenbelt Alliance S.F. (bd. 1984–), Dorothy Erskine Open Space Fund (chmn. advy. coun. 1988–); author chpts. in books, articles in profl. jours. (1950–); mil: capt. US Army 1946-47; Unitarian; rec: mountaineering, tree farming. Res: 233 Chestnut St San Francisco 94133 Ofc: 2340 Clay St San Francisco.

ERVIN, PATRICIA CONNELLY, association executive; b. Dec. 23, 1924, Owatonna, Minn.; d. James B. and Mavilda D. (Scoville) Connelly; edn: BA, USC 1950, MA, 1954, UCLA Law Sch. 1958. Career: tchr. public schools 1954-58; founder and leader Holistic Healing Group 1972–; lectr. on holistic healing and philosphy Philosophical Research Soc. (PRS), L.A. 1979-88, vice pres. PRS, 1982-88; founding mem. Assn. for Holistic Health 1976–; recipient Peace award UN Assn. of U.S., So. Calif. div. (1978); civic bds: United Nations Assn. of L.A. (pres.), Valley Mayors Fund for The Homeless (bd. dirs.), Excellence in Media (bd. dirs.); Independent; Christian. Ofc: Mission Viejo 92692

ESHOO, ANNA GEORGES, congresswoman; b. Dec. 13, 1942, New Britain, Conn.; d. Fred and Alice Alexandre Georges; children: Karen Elizabeth, Paul Frederick; edn: AA with honors, Canada Coll. 1975. Career: chmn. San Mateo County Dem. Central Com. 1978-82; chair Human Relations. Com. 1979-82; former me. Calif. State Dem. Central Exec. Com.; mem. Dem. Nat. Com., 103-104th Congresses from 14th Calif. Dist. 1993–; active mem. League of Women Voters; Roman Catholic. Ofc: US House of Representatives Office of House Members Washington DC 20515

ESTABROOK, WILLIAM CHARLES, engineer; b. Dec. 27, 1920, Odessa, NY; s. Harold Charles and Edith Alleine (Smith) E.; edn: BSEE, Purdue Univ. 1949; reg. Profl. Engr., control sys., Calif. 1977. Career: field svc. engr. Am. Locomotive Co. Schenectady, NY 1949-55; test engr. Lockheed-Calif. Co. 1955-74; senior design engr. Lockheed Missiles & Space Co. Sunnyvale 1974; power sys. study leader, design splst. Lockheed Aircraft Svc. Co., Jet Propulsion Lab. 1974-77; prin. engr. Boeing Aerospace Co., Jet Propulsion Lab. 1977-83 (ret.); mem: Disabled Am. Vets. (life), Am. Ex-Prisoners of War (life), Masons 1942–, Caterpillar Club 1944; Am. Legion 1945 68 (v.cdr.), VFW 1945-54, Kappa Sigma Frat. 1945–, La Canada CofC and Community Assn. 1955-82,

Western Collaborate Heart Study Group 1960–; Montrose Community Ch. (deacon, trustee 1964–, treas. 1984–); mil: 1st lt. US Air Corps 1942-45, ETO, Purple Heart (POW Germany 5/44-5/45), Air Medal; publs: 20+ tech. reports. Res: 1730 Bonita Vista Dr La Canada 91011-1614

ESTEBAN, MANUEL A., university president; b. June 20, 1940, Barcelona, Spain (nat. 1987); s. Manuel and Julia (Beltran) E.; m. Gloria Ribas, July 7, 1962; 1 dau. Jacqueline b. 1964; edn: BA, French & Spanish (first class honors), Univ. of Calgary, Calgary, Canada 1969, MA, Romance studies, Univ. of Calgary 1970; PhD, French, Univ. of Calif., Santa Barbara 1976. Career: asst. prof. Univ. of Michigan, Dearborn, 1973-80, assoc. prof. 1980-86, prof. and assoc. dean Arts & Sci. 1984-86, interim dean 1986-87; dean Arts & Sci., CSU, Bakersfield, Calif. 1987-90; provost/v.p. Humboldt State Univ., Arcata, Calif. 1990-93; pres. CSU, Chico, Calif. 1993–; bd. mem. Nat. Council Colleges of Arts & Sciences 1988-90; editorial bd. Catalan Review, Wash., DC; bd. mem. Inst. For Teaching & Learning, CSU Long Beach 1991–; honors: Woodrow Wilson Fellow 1969, Canada Council Doctoral Fellow 1970-73, Phi Kappa Phi 1992, listed Who's Who in Hispanic Americans 1991, Who's Who in the West (23rd & 24th edits.); mem: No. Am. Catalan Soc. 1984–, Nat. Assn. of Academic Administrators 1984–, Am. Assn. of Higher Edn. 1990–,Calif. State Univ. Inst. for Tchg. and Learning 1990–, Am. Council on Edn. 1993–, U.S. Distance Learning Assn. 1995–; civic: bd. dirs. Mercy Hosp., Bakersfield 1989-90, bd. dirs. Kern Am. Cancer Soc., Chico C. of C.; author: (book) Georges Feydeau, 1983, 14 pub. articles, num. presentations and speeches; rec: racquetball, jogging. Res: 630 Marshall Court Chico 95926 Ofc: California State University Chico 95929

ETCHESON, CRAIG CARLYLE, social scientist; b. June 28, 1955, Huntington, N.Y.; s. Kenneth Carlyle and Rosemarie (Dickson) E.; edn: Spoon River Coll. 1973; BA, Univ. Ill. 1977; MA, 1979; PhD, USC 1985. Career: mgr. data processing RPS Electronics, Los Angeles 1979; instr. USC 1980-89; tech. staff Jet Propulsion Lab., Pasadena 1984; database adminstr. Pacific Telesis, Los Angeles 1985-88; mgr. bus. systems Paramount Pictures, Hollywood 1988–; res. assoc. Inst. Transnational Studies, Los Angeles 1980–; cons. Center for Public Internat. Edn. 1982; Vietnam Vets. of Am. 1983; Computer Tng. Splst. 1984; N. Am. Rockwell 1984; ABACUS Programming Corp. 1985; awards: Univ. Ill. Merriam fellowship 1977, USC Hermann fellowship 1978, Harris fellowship 1980, Haynes Found. 1981, Pi Sigma Alpha; mem: Am. Assn. Artificial Intelligence, Internat. Studies Assn., Am. Political Sci. Assn., Acad. Political Sci., Internat. Political Sci. Assn.; author: Arms Race Theory, 1989, Rise & Demise of Democratic Kampuchea, 1984, num. articles in profl. jours., PhD diss. on Strategy and Structure of Behavior, 1985. Ofc: Paramount Pictures 5555 Melrose Ave Balaban 113 Los Angeles 90038

ETTLICH, WILLIAM F., consulting engineer; b. Jan. 7, 1936, Spokane, Wash.; s. Fred E. Ettlich and Dorothy S. (Olney) Nicholls; m. Dianne L. Lawton, Aug. 24, 1958; children: Pamela b. 1970, Daniel b. 1971; edn: BSEE, Ore. St. Univ. 1957; Harvard Bus. Sch. 1973; reg. profl. engr. Ore., Calif., Nev., Ohio and Colo. Career: project engr. CH2M Hill, Corvallis, Ore. 1959-65; pres. Neptune Micro Floc 1965-74; v.p. CWC, Cameron Park 1974-86; CWC HDR Inc. 1986-87; sr.v.p. HDR Engring. 1987–; dir. CWC 1980-85; trustee CWC ESOT 1980-86; sr. mem. IEEE, ISA; v.p. Marshall Hosp. Found.; bd. trustees Marshall Hosp.; club: Rotary (pres. 1987-88); U.S. patents held; articles pub. in tech. jours.; mil: capt. AUS 1957-59; Republican; Presbyterian; rec: sports, skiing. Res: 3417 Strolling Hills Rd Cameron Park 95682 Ofc: HDR Engineering, Inc. 5175 Hillsdale Circle El Dorado Hills 95630

EU, MARCH FONG, U.S. ambassador, former state official; b. Mar. 29, 1927, Oakdale; d. Yuen and Shiu (Shee) Kong; children by previous marriage: Matthew Kipling, Marchesa Suyin; m. Henry Eu, July 30, 1973; stepchildren: Henry, Adelina, Yvonne, Conroy, Alaric; edn: BS, UC Berkeley, M.Ed, Mills Coll., EdD, Stanford Univ., postgrad. work Columbia Univ., CSC Hayward; LL.D., Lincoln Univ. 1984; Calif. State Teaching Creds., Jr. Coll. Adm.-Supr. Career: div. chmn. Univ. California Medical Ctr., San Francisco; dental hygienist Oakland Public Schs.; div. supr. Alameda County Schs.; lectr. Mills College; mem. (pres. 1961-62) Alameda Co. Bd. of Edn. 1956-66, pres. Alameda County Sch. Bds. Assn. 1965; spl. cons. Calif. State Dept. Edn.; edn., legislative cons. Santa Clara Co. Office of Edn., Sausalito Public Schs., others 1962-66; elected rep. to Calif. State Legislature 15th Assem. Dist., 1966-68, 70-72; elected Calif. Secty. of State, 5 terms, 1974-94; apptd. Calif. Chief of Protocol, 1975-83; chair Calif. State World Trade Commn., 1983–; bd. councillors USC Sch. of Dentistry; apptd. US ambassador to Micronesia by Pres. Clinton 1994–; awards: Eastbay Intercultural Christian Fellows outstanding achiev. intercultural & interracial relations, Hearst Newspapers' Phoebe Apperson Hearst Bay Area Disting. Bay Area Women of Yr., Sacto. Dist. Dental Soc. honor award, Calif. Chiropractic Assn. legislative merit, appreciation Calif. R.E. Assn., Lamplighter Award for achiev. in crime prevention Oakland R.E. Bd., V.F.W. Nat. Loyalty Day Award, svc. to edn. Alameda Co. Edn. Assn., achiev. L.A. Chinese Drum and Bugle Corps, Outstanding Legislator of 1973 Calif. Assn. of Marriage and Family Counselors, service March of Dimes, Hon. Law Degree We. State Univ. Coll. of Law of San Diego, service to comm. Irish Israeli Italian Soc. of S.F., Disting. Alumni Calif. Community Coll. and Jr. Coll. Assn., Hon. Law Degree

Univ. San Diego Sch. of Law, annual award Nat. Notary Assn., Daisy award Calif. Lndscp. Contrs. Assn., Milton Shoong Hall of Fame humanitarian of yr. 1981, citizen of yr. Council for Civic Unity S.F. Bay Area 1982, woman of achiev. in govt. Calif. Asian/Pac. Womens Network 1983, Democrat of Yr. San Mateo Dem. Cent. Com. 1983, C.A.R.E. Award 1985, leadership S.F. Filipino-Am. C.of C. 1985, woman of yr. Democrats United San Bdo. 1986, disting. service Rep. of Honduras 1987, outstanding Asian Am. Byanihan Jaycees of L.A. 1987, achiev. Calif. Dem. Party Black Caucus 1988, Ladies' Home J. list of America's 100 Most Important Women 1988, BSA L.A. Co. Good Scout Award 1989, spl. appreciation Union of Viet. Student Assns. of So. Calif. 1990, comm. leadership Torat-Haijun Hebrew Acad. 1990, spl. appreciation Nat. Assn. Chinese Am. Bankers 1990, Orange Co. Buddhist Assn. 1990, Internat. Bus. award West Coast Univ. 1992; mem: Am. Dental Hygienists Assn. (pres., life), No. Calif. State Dental Hygienists Assn. (life), L.W.V./ Oakland, Delta Kappa Gamma, AAUW (Oakland br. area rep. in edn.), Calif. Tchrs. Assn., Alameda Co. School Bds. Assn. and Calif. Sch. Bds. Assn., Calif. Interagency Council on Family Planning, Calif. B.P.W. (Woman of Achiev. Golden Gate chpt.), Nat. Womens Political Caucus (outstanding woman 1980), Mental Health Assn. of Alameda Co., Navy League (life), Ebell Club (L.A.), Hadassah (life, woman of achiev. L.A. chpt. 1983); hon. mem: L.A. Advt. Women and Am. Advt. Fedn., Chinese Retail Food Mkts. Assn., So. Calif. State Dental Assn., Calif. Agricultural Aircraft Assn., Calif. Landscape Contrs. Assn., Calif. Women for Agriculture, Folsom Hist. Soc., Phi Alpha Delta Law Frat. Intl., Soroptimist; Democrat (del. Nat. Conv. 1968, exec. com. Calif. Dem. Central Com.). Ofc: Secretary of State State of California 1230 J Street Sacramento 95814-2924

EVANS, FERN MILDRED, teacher; b. Jan. 22, 1911, Okeene, Okla.; d. Wm. Fletcher and Elizabeth (Lively) Wallace; m. I.J. Evans, June 20, 1949; edn: BS, and MS, Okla. State Univ., Stillwater 1946, 1948; postgrad. work Univ. Calif., 1958-60. Career: tchr. Elem. Schs. Oklahoma, 1933-45; hd. English dept. Perry H.S., Perry, Okla. 1946-49; tchr. Potter Valley Sch. Dist., Potter Valley, Calif. 1949-54; Owens Valley Unif. Sch. Dist., Independence 1954-57; Los Angeles Unif. Sch. Dist. 1957-76, ret. 1976; appt. mem. Com. to Rewrite English course of Study for St. Oklahoma, 1948; awards: commendns. for devel. of Tchrs. Guide to Moral and Spiritual Values, Calif. St. Dept. Edn. 1953, hon. life mem. 32nd Dist. PTA L.A. 1971, hon. svc. award PTA Calif. 1971, Outstanding Elementary Tchr. of Am. 1975, disting. leadership award 1988; mem: United Tchrs. of L.A. 1957-76, L.A. City Elem. Sch. Music Assn. 1957-76, Calif. Tchrs. Assn. 1949-76, Nat. Edn. Assn. 1947-76, current: Calif. Ret. Tchrs. Assn., Nat. Ret. Tchrs. Assn., Calif. PTA 1949–, AARP; contbr. poetry anthologies: Great Poems of Today, 1987, World Poetry Anthology, 1987, Our W. World's Most Beautiful Poems, 1985, recipient Golden Poet Awards, 1985-88; Republican; Prot.; rec: writing, music, travel, photog. Res: 16741 Armstead St Granada Hills 91344

EVANS, HILTON BERNARD, consulting petrophysicist; b. Jan. 7, 1929, Moab, Utah; s. Hilton Byrd and Flora Fontella (Peterson) E.; children: Teri b. 1948, Jama b. 1955, Kelle b. 1959; edn: cert., UC Daivs 1988; BA, Univ. Utah 1954; Univ. Colo. 1961-69; PhD, Univ. Utah 1959; computer prog., Santa Barbara City Coll. 1992-94; reg. geologist in So. Carolina; reg. geophysicist in Calif. Career: nuclear physicist U.S. Geological Survey 1955-59; advanced research scientist Marathon Oil Co. Research Center 1959-73; dir. formation evaluation Gearheart Industries. 1973-76; dir. advanced tech. div. Bendix Field Engring. Corp. 1976-78; mgr. Integrated Seismic Well Logging Services 1979-80; cons. formation evaluation 1980-86; cons. in measurements while drilling EXLOG, Sacto. 1986-89; prof. Univ. Fed. do Para, Brazil 1989-91; cons. and tchr. Univs. in Colo. and Utah; awards: SPWLA Disting.Service (1980), ed. Log Analyst (1980-81), Who's Who in the West, Who's Who in the Southwest, Personalities of Am., Internat. Directory Disting. Leadership; mem: num. profl. mems. incl. Soc. Profl. Well Log Analysts, Soc. Exploration Geophysicists, Soc. of Petroleum Engrs., Assn. Groundwater Scientists & Engrs., Am. Geophysical Union, European Assn. Exploration Geophysicists, Sigma Xi; 300+ tech. papers and books pub., patentee in field; mil: sgt. USAAF 1946-49; Republican; Prot.; rec: writing, theatre, ballet. Address: Applied Petrophysics 924 San Andres Santa Barbara 93101

EVANS, JAMES HANDEL, architect, academic administrator; b. June 14, 1938, Bolton England; s. Arthur Handel and Ellen Bowen (Ramsden) E.; m. Carol Mulligan, Sept. 10, 1966; children: Jonathan b. 1971, Sarah b. 1976; edn: diploma of arch., Univ. of Manchester, England 1965; M. Arch., Univ. of Oregon, Eugene 1967. Career: assoc. dean/prof. Arch. Cal Poly, San Luis Obispo 1967-68; prof. of art San Jose State Univ. 1979–, assoc. exec. v.p. 1978-81, interim exec. v.p. 1981-82, exec. v.p. 1982-91, interim pres. 1991-92, pres. 1992–; sci. res. coun. fellow Cambridge Univ., England 1969-70; cons. Ibiza Nueva, Ibiza, Spain 1977-80; vis. prof. Ciudad Universitaria, Madrid, Spain 1977; vis. lectr. Herriott Watt Univ., Edinburgh 1970; mem. advy. com Army Command Staff Coll., Ft. Leavenworth, Kan. 1988; trustee Good Samaritan Hosp., San Jose 1987-90; bd. dirs. San Jose Shelter 1988-90; awards: AIACC Service award for excellence in edn. 1993, Juror, AIACC Awards Program 1994; mem: AIA (fellow), SCVAIA (fellow), NCARB, Internat. Assn. of Univ. Presidents, Calif. Business/Higher Edn. Forum, Royal Inst. of British Architects,

San Jose Rotary, Joint Venture-Silicon Valley, San Jose C.of C., Tech. Museum of Innovation; rec: golf. Res: 6060 Guadalupe Mines Court San Jose 95120 Ofc: San Jose State University One Washington Square San Jose 95192-0002

EVANS, JAMES WILLIAM, metallurgical educator; b. Aug. 22, 1943, Dobcross, Yorkshire, England, naturalized U.S. citizen 1976; s. James Hall and Alice Maud (Dransfield) E.; m. Beverley Lynn Connor, July 22, 1967 (div. 1978); m. Sylvia Marian Johnson, Jan. 5, 1985; children: James b. 1971, Hugh Edmund b. 1987, Claire Meredith b. 1989; edn: BSc chemistry, Univ. of London, Eng. 1964; PhD chem. engring., SUNY at Buffalo, 1970. Career: tech. advisor Internat. Computers, Ltd., London, Eng. 1964-65; chemist Cyanamid of Canada, Ltd., Niagara Falls, Ont., Can. 1965-67; engr. Ethyl Corp., Baton Rouge, La. 1970-72; asst. prof. 1972-76, assoc. prof. 1976-80, prof. metallurgy, dept. mats. sci. and mineral engring. UC Berkeley, 1980-, dept. chmn. 1986-90; prin. investigator Energy and Environment Div., Lawrence Berkeley Lab, 1977-; awards: C.C. Furnas Memorial fellow SUNY, Buffalo 1969-70, extractive metallurgy science award of AIME for best paper 1973, 83, Champion H. Mathewson Gold Medal of Metallurgical Soc. of AIME 1984, Extractive Metallurgy Lecturer of Minerals, Metals and Materials Soc. 1994, C.C. Furnas Distinguished Alumnus Award SUNY Buffalo 1994; mem: Am. Inst. Chem. Engrs., The Minerals, Metals and Materials Soc., The Electrochem. Soc., Iron and Steel Inst. of Japan; inventor, patentee (with G. Savaskan) Battery Using a Metal Particle Bed Electrode (1991); author 150+ tech. publs. Ofc: Dept. Materials Science and Mineral Engineering, Univ. of California, Berkeley 94720 Tel: 510/642-3807

EVANS, LOUISE, clinical psychologist, investor, philanthropist; b. San Antonio, Tex.; d. Henry Daniel and Adela (Pariser) Evans; m. Tom R. Gambrell, MD, Feb. 23, 1960; edn: BS, Northwestern Univ. 1949; MSc in psychol., Purdue Univ. 1952, PhD in cliln. psychol., 1955; Diplomate in Clin. Psychol., Am. Bd. of Examiners in Profl. Psychol., 1966. Career: tchg. asst. Purdue Univ. 1950-51; intern Menninger Found., Topeka State Hosp., 1952-53; staff psychologist Kanakee State Hosp., 1954; post-doc. fellow in child clinical psych. USPH Menninger Found., 1955-56; hd. staff psychologist Child Guidance Clinic Kings County Hosp., Bklyn. 1957-58; dir. of psychol. clin. Barnes-Renard Hosp., and instr. Washington Univ. Sch. of Med., St. Louis, Mo. 1959; clin. research consultant Episc. Diocese, St. Louis 1959; pvt. practice, Fullerton, Calif. 1960-92; psychol. cons. Fullerton Comm. Hosp., 1961-81, staff cons. Martin Luther Hosp., Anaheim 1963-70; frequent keynote speaker civic and academic pgms. 1950-; del. state and nat. traffic safety confs. 1964; hon. mem. Am. Biog. Inst. nat. resrch. bd. (A.B.I. "Most Admired Woman of Decade" 1994), Internat. Biog. Ctr. advy. council (I.B.C. "World's leading biographee" 1987, "One in a million" award 1991, "World Intellectual" award 1993), hon. life fellow Internat. Biog. Assn., Hist. Preservations Am. (biographee of yr. 1986); awards: Disting. Alumni award Purdue Univ. Sch. of Liberal Arts 1993, Old Master award Purdue Univ. 1993, Am. Biog. Assn. "Most Admired Men & Women of Yr. 1992-93", Statue of Victory prize Centro Studi E. Ricerche Delle Nazioni, Acad. Italia 1985, Purdue Alumni Assn. 1st citizenship award for local, state and nat. service 1975, Internat. Who's Who in Comm. Svc. Publishers (England) gold medals 1972-75,Yuma, Az. Headstart Pgm. service award 1972, Hall of Fame Central H.S. 1966, Northwestern Univ. scholar 1945, Evansville, Ind. First PTA scholar 1945; Fellow: Internat. Council of Psychologists Inc., Royal Soc. of Health (U.K., emeritus), AAAS (emeritus), Am. Orthopsych. Assn. (life), Am. Psychol. Soc. (charter), Am. Psychol. Assn. (fellow, Divs. of Psychotherapy, Clin. Psychology, Psychology of Women, and Consulting 1995), Internat. Council of Sex Edn. & Parenthood, Worldwide Acad. of Scholars (New Zealand), Acad. of Clin. Psychology, ABPP; mem: Am., Calif., L.A. Soc. Clin. Psychology, Orange Co. Soc. Clin. Psychology, Am. Pub. Health Assn., NY Acad. Scis., Internat. Platform Assn., AAUP, Soc. Jewelry Historians USA, alumni assns., President's Council and Dean's Club Pacesetters-Purdue Univ., Pi Sigma Pi frat., Ctr. for Study of the Presidency; rec: antiques, collectibles. Ofc: PO Box 6067 Beverly Hills 90212-1067

EVANS, PETER HOLLINGSHEAD, composer, classical guitarist, nurse; b. Jan. 26, 1942, Durham, N.C.; s. Frank Moore and Marion (Haase) E.; m. Barbara Jean Segal, March 3, 1968; children: Dylan b. 1972, Sarah b. 1981; edn: Julliard Music Sch. 1978-81; AS nursing, Monterey Peninsula Coll. 1983-85; Flamenco Masters Madrid, Sp. 1961-62. Career: concert soloist Weston Agy., tours U.S., Spain, Canada and France, 1966-72; featured soloist w. Sergio Mendez, Brazil, U.S., Japan and So. Am., 1970-74; concert soloist U.S. 1975-; reg. nurse, IV nurse splst. VNA, Monterey 1985-; v.p. Carmel Classic Guitar Fest. 1981-83; bd. dirs. Carmel Classic Arts Fest. 1986-; mem: ASCAP, AACN, Am. Philatelic Soc., Musicians Union; recording soloist: An American in Spain (RCA Victor 1966), Peter Evans "Guitar Solos Vol. I" (BDS Records, 1989); composer: Concert Solos for Classical Guitar (G.Schirmer Inc. 1982), Hums of Edward Bear, 1984, Sevillanans-Guitar & Orchestra, 1989, Monterianans-Guitar & Orchestra, 1993; rec: philately. Address: PO Box 222181 Carmel 93922

EVANS, SUSAN K., publisher, art consultant, landscape architect; b. March 14, 1956, Sidney, N.Y.; d. John Cary and Rachel Ann (Burbank) Youmans; m. William Edward Fee, Oct. 12, 1980 (div. 1989); m. 2d., David Becker, Oct. 14,

1994; edn: BS cum laude, environ. sci., St. Univ. N.Y. 1978; B.Arch. cum laude, 1979. Career: landscape architect Marmon Mok & Green, Houston, Tx. 1980-83; John Blevens Assoc., Fremont 1984-85; gallery dir. Victor Fischer Gallery, Oakland 1985-87; western mgr. Calif. Fine Art Directory, San Francisco 1987; art cons. Editions Ltd. 1988, 1989-; we. mgr. Kraus Sikes Publishers The Guild 1989-, v.p. 1994; seminar leader Am. Soc. Landscape Architects, Yosemite Valley 1989, Landscape Architect and Specifier News mag. conf., Las Vegas, Nev. 1987; awards: Am. Soc. Landscape Architects Hon. Service 1988, Juryleader 1990, 91, 92, Calif. Fine Arts Directory Hi Sales 1987; mem: Women's Bldg. Craft Show (bd. dirs. 1993-94), Contemporary Extension of S.F. Mus. of Modern Art 1993, Pub. Art Works (bd. dirs. 1989-92), Am. Soc. Landscape Architects, Toastmasters, N. Montrose Civic Assn., Chi Omega; ed. The Guild 1989, landscape architect San Antonio airport 1983; Democrat; rec: clothes designing, kayaking, travel. Res: 279 Mangels Ave San Francisco 94131

EVERDING, ROBERT GEORGE, university dean; b. Apr. 25, 1945, St. Louis, Mo.; s. R. G. and Elizabeth Jane (Lehman) E.; m. Sarah Page Monroe, June 1, 1969; children: Brian b. 1974, Julia b. 1977; edn: BA, Univ. Mo., Columbia 1967; MA, Univ. Minn., 1969; AM, Stanford Univ., 1972, PhD 1976; lifetime secondary edn. credentials, Mo. and Calif., 1967. Career: program dir. humanities Univ. of Houston, Clear Lake, Tx. 1976-84; external reviewer Univ. of Tx., Dallas 1983; artistic director Houston Shaw Festival, Houston 1978-84; dir. Sch. of Art and Architecture, Univ. of Southwestern Louisiana, Lafayette, La. 1984-88; dean Coll. of Visual & Performing Arts, Humboldt State Univ., Arcata, Calif. 1988-91, dean CSU Summer Arts Program 1989-91, course dir. CSU Faculty Arts Exchange 1992-93 prin. investigator Redwood Arts Project, Arcata (1991-, dir. Redwood Arts Proj. 1992-93); mgmt. bd. Center Arts, Arcata 1988-92; honors: Omicron Delta Kappa 1975, Phi Beta Kappa 1976, Phi Kappa Phi 1991, Am. Bus. Women Assn. bus. assoc. of year, Redwood Chpt. 1991, listed Who's Who in West 1992; mem: Bernard Shaw Soc. 1983-, Phi Beta Kappa Soc., Phi Kappa Phi Soc., Stanford Alumni Assn.; civic bds: Humboldt Arts Council (bd. dirs. 1988-91), City of Arcata Design Review Com. (chair 1988-92), Acadiana Arts Council, Lafayette, La. (bd. 1986-88), Boy Scouts Am. (asst. scoutmaster 1985-8 publs: (play) Kindergarden (1985), articles in nat., internat. jours. (1979-), editor "Arts Review" UH/CLC Arts (1980-84); mil: sp5 US Army 1971-74. Res: 2711 Hilltop Ct Arcata 95521 Ofc: Humboldt State University, Arcata 95521

EVERHART, THOMAS EUGENE, college president, professor of electrical engineering and applied physics; b. Feb. 15, 1932, Kansas City, Mo.; s. William Elliot and Elizabeth Ann (West) E.; m. Doris Arleen Wentz, June 21, 1953; children: Janet S. b. 1956, Nancy J. b. 1959, David W. b. 1961, John T. b. 1963; edn: AB, Harvard Coll., 1953; MSc UCLA 1955; PhD, Clare Coll., Cambridge Univ., England 1958. Career: mem. tech staff Hughes Aircraft Co., Culver City, Calif. 1953-55; research work, Cambridge Univ., England 1955-58; asst. prof. to prof. UC Berkeley 1958-78; dean Coll. of Engring., Cornell Univ., Ithaca, NY 1979-84; chancellor Univ. of Ill., Urbana-Champaign, Ill. 1984-87; pres. Calif. Inst. of Technology, Pasadena 1987-; pres. Electron Microscopy Soc. of Am. 1977; bd. dirs. General Motors, N.Y., NY 1989-; bd. dirs. Corp. for Nat. Res. Initiatives, Reston, Va. 1990-; bd. dirs. Hewlett-Packard Co., Palo Alto 1991-; honors: Phi Beta Kappa, Harvard Coll. 1953, sr. post doctoral fellowship Nat. Sci. Found., Wash. 1966-67, John Simon Guggenheim Mem. Fellowship 1974-75, B.G. Lamme award Am. Soc. of Engring. Edn., Wash., D.C. 1989, Clark Kerr award, UC Berkeley 1992; mem: Nat. Acad. of Engring. (council mem. 1988-), The Royal Acad. of Engring. (foreign mem. 1990-), Council on Competitiveness (v. chmn. 1990-), Am. Acad. of Arts and Scis. (fellow 1990-), Assn. of Am. Universities (exec. com. 1992-); author: one book, over 90 technical publications; patentee (6); Methodist; rec: hiking, fishing. Ofc: California Institute of Technology 204-31 Pasadena 91125

EWALD, WILLIAM RUDOLPH, development consultant; b. Jan. 10, 1923, Detroit, Mich.; s. William Rudolph and Rhea Elizabeth (Allen) E.; m. Janeth Hackett, 1948 (div. 1969); dau., Annalisa b. 1953; m. Katharina Clark, 1975 (div. 1976); edn: ScB civil eng., Brown Univ., 1944; grad. work Univ. Mich., Ann Arbor; degree cert. Harvard Univ. Career: planner Saarinen, Swanson, Saarinen 1946-47; planner-writer Skidmore, Owings, Merrill 1948; planner Detroit City Planning Comm. 1949-51; asst. mgr. Baltimore Assn. of Communities 1951-55; chief of devel. Arkansas Indsl. Devel. Commn. 1955-59; asst. commr. Urban Renewal Adminstrn. 1959-61; sr. v.p. Doxiadis Assoc. 1961-63; decision support systems, graphic communications and analysis: sole prop. William R. Ewald, Development Consultant, WDC, Santa Barbara, (currently) Los Angeles, 1963-, clients include Edison Electric Inst., NASA, EPA, Commerce, Interior, HEW, US Pub. Health Svc., NSF, Conservation Found., Gen. Electric, Exxon, Am. Inst. of Architects, Am. Inst. of Planners, Weyerhaeuser, Ark. Indsl. Devel. Commn., Commonwealth of Puerto Rico, Gov. Nelson R. Rockefeller, Gov. Winthrop Rockefeller, Appalachian Regional Commn., N.Y. State Office Reg. Planning, Baltimore County, Md., Tom's River, N.J., Albuquerque, N.M., Columbus, Ind., Flagstaff, Ariz.; vis. fellow Ctr. for Study of Democratic Instns., Santa Barbara, 1970; lectr. Univ. Texas Sch. of Arch., 1971; mem. policy bd. Change in Liberal Edn. Project (Carnegie Corp.) 1973-76; awards: James Manning Scholar, Brown Univ. 1943, Lambda Alpha hon. internat. land econs. frat. 1960, citation Ark. Indsl. Devel. Commn., Little Rock, Ark. 1957; spl. design award Southwest Printing & Graphic Arts Assn. 1959; commendn. Housing & Home Finance Agy. 1960; resolution Am. Inst. of Planners 1966, 67; Earth Day principal speaker Sch. of Arch. Univ. of Mich. 1968; spl. design award (film) Mexico Olympics 1968; nat. lectr. Danforth Found. 1970-72; prin. investigator NSF 1973-76; citation Am. Revolution Bicentennial Award 1976; club: Cosmos (W.D.C. 1969–); works: (author/illustrator childrens' book) Neighbor Flap Foot the City Planning Frog (1952), The Arkansas Ency. (4 vol. reference, 1958), Change Challenge Response, 60 Years Development Policy in New York State (1964), Environment For Man, Environment and Change, Environment and Policy (3 vols., commissioned, edited 1967-68), Signals in The Environment (exhibit USPHS, 1967), Pandora's Easy Open Pop Top Box (film, 1967), Street Graphics (book & film, 1971, HUD Spl. Design Award 1972), A Whole New Way To Think (video, 1978), Street Graphics & The Law (coauthor book, 1988), 100 Short Films About the Human Environment (editor book, 1981), contbr. articles in Brown Alumni Monthly (11/69), Information, Perception & Regional Policy (GPO,1976), Ekistics (1976), Computer Graphics World (4/82); mil: s/sgt. US Inf. 1943-46; Episcopal; rec: sailing, skiing. Ofc: 1888 Century Park E #1990 Los Angeles 90067

EWELL, A. BEN, JR., lawyer, businessman; b. Sept. 10, 1941, Elyria, Ohio; s. Austin Bert and Mary Rebecca (Thompson) E., Sr.; desc. John Ewell, b. 1734, Scotland, settled in Plymouth Co., Mass. 1751; m. Suzanne Ewell; children: Austin B., III b. 1978, Brice B. b. 1982; edn: BA, Miami Univ. 1963; LLB, JD, UC Hastings Coll. of Law 1966; admitted Calif. State Bar 1966, US Dist. Ct., E. Dist. Calif. 1967, US 9th Circuit Ct. Appeals 1967, US Supreme Ct. 1982. Career: atty., ptnr. law firm McCormick, Barstow, Sheppard, Wayte & Carruth, Fresno 1970-84; pres. A.B. Ewell, Jr., APC, 1984–; chmn. Millerton New Town Devel. Co. 1987–; pres. Brighton Crest Country Club 1990–; past general counsel various water dists. and assns.; appt. Task Force on Prosecution, Courts and Law Reform, Calif. Council on Criminal Justice 1971-74, Fresno County Econ. Dev. Corp. 1987–, Fresno County Water Advy. Com., San Joaquin River Flood Control Assn. (chmn. 1984-88), San Joaquin Valley Agri. Water Com. 1979-88, U.S. SBA Nat. Advy. Council (1981–, co-chmn. 1981-82), mem: Calif. Bar Assn., Fresno County Bar Assn.; civic: Commonwealth Club of Calif., Citizens for Community Enrichment (bd.) Fresno, City of Fresno Historic Preservation Commn., City-County Hist. Soc., Fresno City-County C.of C., Fresno State Univ. Pres.'s Club and Bulldog Found., Univ. Calif. Valley Medical Education Found. (fmr. trustee), Firelands Hist. Soc., Spirit of '76 Museum and Hist. Soc., Fresno Met. Museum of Art, History & Sci. (trustee 1983-89, sustaining); pub. research: "The Sufferers Lands" (hist. and settlement of Huron and Erie Cos., OH); Republican (State Central Com. 1974-76, State Exec. Fin. Com. 1978–, Fresno Co. Central Com. treas./exec. com. 1971-72, past v.p. Calif. Repub. Assn. of Fresno, chmn. The Lt. Gov.'s Club Fresno Co. 1980, campaign chmn. var. campaigns; Congregational; rec: hist. research, antique books, jogging. Ofc: 516 W. Shaw Ave., Ste 200 Fresno 93704

FAGIN, DAVID KYLE, mining executive; b. April 4, 1938, Dallas, Tx.; s. Kyle Marshall and Francis (Gaston) F.; m. Margaret Ann Hazlett, Jan. 24, 1959; children: Kyle b. 1959, Scott Edward b. 1966; edn: BS petroleum engring., Univ. Okla. 1960; So. Methodist Univ. 1968; Am. Inst. Banking 1966-67. Career: engr. Bednar Petroleum Cons., Dallas, Tx. 1959-63, ptnr. 1963-65; bank ofcr. First Nat. Bank 1965-68; v.p. oil and gas Rosario Resources, Greenwich, Conn. 1968-75, exec.v.p., COO 1975-78, pres., COO 1978-80, 80-82; chmn., CEO Fagin Exploration Co., Denver, Colo. 1982-86; dir., pres. and COO Homestake Mining Co., San Francisco 1986–; dir: T. Rowe Price mutual funds, Balt., Md. 1987–, Homestake Gold of Australia, Adelaide 1986–; mem: Internat. Lightning Class Assn. (commodore 1980), Am. Inst. Mining Engrs. (chmn. endowments com.), Soc. Mining Engrs., Am. Petroleum Inst., Dallas Geological Soc., Soc. Petroleum Engrs. (pres. 1970); civic: BSA (dir. 1989), San Francisco C.of C. (dir. 1989–), United Way (v.chmn. S.F.); clubs: Pacific Union (S.F.), World Trade (S.F.), Commonwealth (S.F.), Petroleum (Dallas and Denver); Republican; United Methodist (bd. chmn. 1979); rec: fishing. Res: 2382 Ironwood Pl Alamo 94507 Ofc: Homestake Mining Co. 650 California St San Francisco 94108

FAHDEN, NANCY MARIE, county supervisor; b. July 14, 1923, Martinez; d. Antonio and Jennie (Fontana) Cardinalli; m. Wilbur J. Fahden, Oct. 15, 1945; children: Antone b. 1946, Lyall b. 1949; grad. Alhambra H.S., Martinez. Career: registrar Alhambra High Sch., Martinez 1941-45; elected Contra Costa Co. Board of Supervisors, 1977–, first woman elected in 125 yr. hist. of co.; currently mem. bds.: Assn. Bay Area Govts., CC Med. Services Jt. Conf. Com., CCC Mental Health Advy. Bd., LAFCO, CCC Solid Waste Commn.; recipient appreciation awards: VFW 1988, Kiwanis Club Martinez 1988, Peace Officers Assn. 1984, Nutrition Proj. for Elderly 1984, Contra Costa Co. Child Care Council (1987 Kiddie Award), Contra Costa Co. Bd. Suprs. 10-yr. service 1987, John Muir Memorial Assn. conservation award 1986, Contra Costa Dental Soc. 1986, Martinez Boys Club citizen award 1974, woman of yr. Martinez C.of C. 1975, woman of yr. Rodeo C.of C. 1984, J.C. Penney Co. Golden Rule Award 1985, Nat. Women's Polit. Caucus 1985, Rubicon Programs Inc. pub. service award 1985, others; Democrat; Christian; rec: walking, jogging, gardening. Res: 1153 Hillside Dr Martinez 94553

FAISON, JAMES IVER, medical services company executive; b. Mar. 10, 1941, Oakland; s. James Hughes and Elinore Ruth (Iverson) F.; m. Linda C. Stewart, Dec. 14, 1968; children: Jamie b. 1979, Heidi b. 1980, Ian b. 1986; edn: AA, Staten Island Comm. Coll. 1972; AB, UC Berkeley 1977. Career: self-empl. insurance safety engineer 1962-77; criminal investigator New York State Tax Commn. 1969-72; owner Faison Medical Services, (retail med. supplies for the severely retarded), Concord, Ca. 1978–; Gov. Deukmejian apptd. mem. Area Board V for Developmental Disabilities; mem: Calif. Assn. Med. Prods., Nat. Assn. of Med. Equipment Suppliers, NRA (life); mil: info. splst. US Army, disch. 1962; Republican (past chmn. 51st Assy. Dist. Repub. Club); Cath.; rec: hunter. Res: 836 Rosemount Rd, Oakland 94610 Ofc: Faison Medical Services 836 Rosemount Rd Oakland 94610

FALCONE, ALFONSO BENJAMIN, physician; b. July 24, Bryn Mawr, Pa.; s. B. and Elvira (Galluzzo) F.; m. Patricia J. Lalim, Oct. 22; children: Christopher L., Steven B.; edn: AB chem. (with distinction), Temple Univ., 1944, MD (with honors), 1947; PhD biochem., Univ. Minn., 1954; Diplomate Am. Bd. Internal Medicine. Career: intern Phila. Gen. Hosp. 1947-48, asst. resident internal medicine, 1948-49; tchg. fellow internal medicine Univ. Hosps., Univ. Minn., 1949-51; asst. clin. prof. med. Univ. Wis., Madison 1956-59, assoc. clin. prof., 1959-63, asst. prof. Inst. Enzyme Research, 1963-66, vis. prof. Univ. Wis. 1966-67; med. practice specializing. in endocrine and metabolic diseases, Fresno, Calif. 1968–; staff Fresno Community Hosp. (chmn. dept. med. 1973), St. Agnes Hosp.; hon. staff Valley Med. Ctr., Fresno; senior corr. Ettore Majorana Ctr. for Sci. Culture, Erice, Italy; awards: NIH postdoctoral fellow 1951-53, NIH res. grantee 1958-68, listed Who'w Who in West, in Am., in World; mem: A.C.P. (fellow), AMA, Am. Soc. Biochemistry and Molecular Biology, Endocrine Soc., Central Soc. for Clin. Res., Am. Fedn. Clin. Res., Am. Chem. Soc., Am. Assn. for Study of Liver Disease, Am. Diabetes Assn., AAAS, Calif. Acad. Medicine, Sigma Xi, Phi Lambda Upsilon; civic: assoc. Fresno Co. Assn. for UC Campus 1988–, co-chair Univ. of Calif. Fresno Com. 1987–, alternate mem. Univ. of Calif. 10th Campus Citizens Advy Council 1991–, Archeol. Inst. of Am.; pub. works: contbr. num. articles to profl. jours.; research and publications in the following areas: Mechanisms of energy/transduction in biological systesms, Mechanism of oxidative phosporlyation, Mechanism of enzyme action, Mechanism of drug action; mil: US Army 1944-46, lt.cdr. Med. Corps USNR 1954-56, US Naval Radiological Defense Lab. Ofc: 2240 E Illinois Ave Fresno 93701-2191 Tel: 209/486-0666

FALERO, FRANK, economist, educator; b. Dec. 22, 1937, New York; s. Frank Falero and Lydia M. (Camis) Del Castillo; children: Lisa Ann b. 1963, Sara Francine b. 1968; m. Verna Downing Whittier, Nov. 22, 1990; edn: AA, St. Petersburg Jr. Coll. 1962; BA hons., history, Univ. S. Fla. 1964; MS, Fla. St. Univ. 1965; PhD, 1967; Career: asst. prof. VPI & SU, Blacksburg, Va. 1967-72; Fulbright scholar Univ. del Pacifico, Lima, Peru 1968-69, res.economist Fed. Reserve, Richmond, Va. 1968; prof. economics and finance CSU Bakersfield, 1972–; economist, Springville 1972–; vis. prof. Univ. Colo., Boulder 1976; commentator KERO TV, Bakersfield 1979-90; CTA & CPO Calfutures commodity trader, 1987–; awards: Golden Mike 1985, CAPTRA excellence 1984, APTRA excellence 1986; Dipolmate, Am. Bd. of Forensic Examiners; RFE, AREA; author: 30+ articles and 7 monograms pub. (1964–); mil: AUS 1955-58; rec: scuba diving, skiing. Res: POB 950 Springville 93265-0950

FALICOV, LEOPOLDO MAXIMO, physicist, educator; b. June 24, 1933, Buenos Aires, Argentina, naturalized U.S. citizen 1967; s. Isaias Felix and Dora (Samoilovich) F.; m. Marta Alicia Puebla, Aug. 13, 1959; children: Alexis and Ian; edn: Licenciado chemistry, Buenos Aires Univ. 1957; PhD physics, Cuyo Univ. Inst. J.A. Balseiro, Argentina 1958; Cambridge Univ.1960; ScD, Cambridge Univ., Eng. 1977. Career: res. assoc. dept. physics Inst. Study Metals, Univ. Chicago 1960-61, instr. physics 1961-62, asst. prof., assoc. prof., prof. physics 1962-69; prof. physics UC Berkeley, 1969–, Miller res. prof. 1979-80, chmn. dept. physics 1981-83; cons. internat.; awards: Alfred P. Sloan Found. fellow 1964-68, vis. fellow Fitzwilliam Coll., Cambridge, Eng. 1966, Fulbright fellow 1969, OAS vis. prof. Argentina 1970, Nordita vis. prof. Univ. Copenhagen 1971-72, 87, Fulbright lectr. Spain 1972, Guggenheim fellow 1976-77, vis. fellow Clare Hall, Cambridge, Eng. 1976-77, exchange prof. Univ. Paris 1977, 84; mem: Third World Acad. Scis. (fellow), Nat. Acad. Sci. (U.S. 1983), Royal Danish Acad. Scis. and Letter Academico Correspondiente, Academia Nacional de Ciencias Exactas, Fisicas y Naturales, Argentina 1990; author: Group Theory and Its Physical Applications, 1966, La Estructura Electronica de los Solidos, 1967; contbr. articles in profl. jours. Res: 90 Avenida Dr Berkeley 94708 Ofc: Dept. of Physics Univ. of Calif. Berkeley 94720 Tel: 510/642-5993

FALKENROTH, CHARLES FREDERICK, wholesaling company executive; b. Nov. 11, 1949, Indianapolis, Ind.; s. Frederick Samuel and Dorothy Wilhelmena (Frische) F.; m. Jacqueline Rae Ennis, Jan. 18, 1970; 1 son, John b. 1972; edn: BS acctg., Univ. Nev. 1971. Career: acct. McKesson Drug, San Francisco 1972-75, regional controller 1975-85; v.p. fin. Rawson Drug & Sundry, San Leandro 1985-87; v.p., controller McKesson Office Products, San Francisco 1987-88; v.p. planning and control Rawson Drug & Sundry, San Leandro 1988-

90, v.p. controller McKesson Drug, San Francisco 1990–; mil: E-5 USAF 1971-72; Republican; Lutheran; rec: travel, camping, skiing. Res: 89 Tumbleweed Ct San Ramon 94583 Ofc: McKesson 1 Post St San Francisco 94104-5296

FALVEY, MARY C., management consultant; b. Oct. 28, 1941, Detroit; d. Lawrence C. and Mathilde G. Falvey; edn: BA in econs. (honors), Cornell Univ., 1963; MBA, Harvard Univ., 1967. Career: systems engr. IBM Corp., N.Y.C. 1963-65; mgmt. cons. McKinsey & Co. Inc., 1967-75; v.p. Citibank, N.A. 1975-78, head asset servicing div., 1977-78; senior v.p., dir., head adminstrn. div., mem. exec. com., mem. operating com. Blyth Eastman Dillon & Co. Inc., 1978-80; pres. M.C. Falvey Assocs. Inc., 1980-81; v.p. fin. Shaklee Corp., San Francisco 1981-82; pres., dir. Falvey Autos Inc., Troy, Mich. 1978-93; pres. Falvey & Assoc. 1992–; dir. Access Healthnet 1994–; mem. Composite Com., U.S. Med. Licensing Examination 1995–; mem. of the Corporation of The Jackson Lab., 1995–; trustee Fed. Hosp. Ins. Trust Fund, Fed. Old Age and Survivors Ins. Trust Fund, Fed. Disability Ins. Trust Fund, 1984-90; dir. Tech. Funding Inc., 1983-91; mem. regional dealer advy. council Toyota Motor Sales Corp., 1986-88; apptd. Advy. Council on Social Security 1979-80, Nat. Commn. on Social Security Reform 1982-83; awards: Harvard Bus. Sch. grantee 1965-77; civic: Com. for N.Y. Philharmonic 1975-77, Williamsburg Charter Found. (trustee 1987-90), Cornell Univ. (trustee fellow 1988–, Council adminstrv. bd. 1984-86, Alumni Assn. dir. 1988–), St. Francis Hosp. Found. (dir. 1992–), Harvard Bus. Sch. Assn. of No. Calif. (dir. 1991–), Mills Coll. Advy. Council (adminstrn. and legal processes, 1982-85), S.F. Performances (trustee 1981-93, chmn. bd. trustees 1984-91), Internat. Women's Forum 1993–, Commonwealth Club Calif. (chmn. Asia Pac. study sect. 1985-86), Univ. Club (dir. 1993–); Republican; Episcopalian. Address: 2100 Pacific Ave. #4A San Francisco 94115

FALZONE, NICHOLAS, lawyer; b. Nov. 12, 1945, Chicago, Ill.; s. Nicholas and Eleanor (Geske) F.; m. Sally Peterson, May 17, 1975; edn: AB, Coll. Holy Cross 1967; JD, Univ. Ill. 1970. Career: atty. Samuel H.Young P.C., Chgo., Ill. 1970-73; asst. gen. counsel Trailer Train Co. 1973-80; ptnr. Arvey Hodes et al 1981-84; v.p. law CIS Corp., San Francisco 1984-90; v.p. Bank of America Leasing & Capital 1990-95; dir. Chgo. String Ensemble, Ill. 1981-84; mem: Calif. St. Bar Assn. Res: 265 Currey Ln Sausalito 94965

FAN, HUNG Y., biologist, cancer research director; b. Oct. 30, 1947, Beijing, China; s. Hsu Yun and Li Nien (Bien) F.; edn: BS, Purdue Univ., 1967; PhD, M.I.T., 1971. Career: postdoc. fellow M.I.T., Cambridge, MA 1971-73; asst. resrch. prof. Salk Inst., San Diego 1973-81; asst. prof. to full prof. biology Univ. Calif. Irvine 1981–, dir. UCI Cancer Research Inst., 1985–; cons. venture capital firms 1989–; mem. grant rev. panels NIH 1979-94, Am. Cancer Soc. 1986-90; awards: Woodrow Wilson fellow 1967-68, Helen Hay Whitney fellow 1971-73, AAAS fellow 1992, Am. Acad. Microbiology fellow 1993; mem. AAAS 1985–, Am. Soc. Microbiology 1978–, Am. Soc. Virology 1985–, Am. Cancer Soc. (Orange Co. chpt. bd. 1986-90); author: Biology of AIDS (1989, 2d edit. 1991, 3rd edit. 1994), 90+ jour. articles & reviews, 1969–, symp. editor: Viruses That Affect the Immune System, 1991; Democrat; rec: chamber music. Ofc: Dept. Molecular Biology & Biochemistry Univ. Calif., Irvine 92717

FAN, JERRY YU, project engineer; b. May 16, 1939, Szechwan, China, nat. 1973; s. Chin and Wen-Su (Tsu) F.; m. Lucia Yue Chen, June 10, 1967; children: Vincent b. 1970, Larry b. 1972; edn: BS, Nat. Taiwan Univ., 1961; MS, Univ. Minn., 1965, PhD 1968; MMgt., West Coast Univ., 1985; reg. profl. engr. R.O.C., 1961. Career: asst. designer K.W. Engring. Consultants, Taipei 1962-63; research asst., adj. prof. Univ. Minn., Mpls. 1963-68; research, then senior engr. Uniroyal Inc., Middlebury, Ct. 1968-74; senior engr. Westinghouse Elect. Corp., West Mifflin, Pa. 1974-80; structural engr. (GS-14) US Nuclear Regulatory Commn., Bethesda, Md. 1981; senior cons. Santa Fe Internat., Alhambra, Calif. 1981-82; engring. specialist, then project engr. Rockwell Space Sys. Div., Downey 1982–; awards: scholar Nat. Taiwan Univ. (1957-61), fellow Univ. Minn. (1965-68); mem: ASME, Nat. Mgmt. Assn. (v.p. profl. devel. 1994–), Chinese Engrs. & Scientists Assn. of So. Calif (chair membership 1992-93), Nat. Taiwan Univ. Alumni Assn. of So. Calif., Chinese Student Assn. Univ. Minn., Mpls. (v.p. 1964-65); author: patent disclosure New Process of Curing Twin Rubber Hoses, 1972, tech. papers pub. in Surface Mechanics Symp., 1969, CAAPA Convention Yearbook, 1985, case study: Quality Management Systems in Aerospace Applications (pub. CAAPCON Yearbook 1993), numerous co. res. reports, 1968-86; mil: 2d lt. Marine Corps 1961-62; Republican; Lutheran; rec: photog., stamps & coins, dancing, tennis, golf, travel, skiing. Res: 4907 Rockvalley Rd Rancho Palos Verdes 90274 Ofc: Rockwell Space Systems Div., MS FC96, 12214 Lakewood Blvd Downey 90241

FARGHER, LAWRENCE LE ROY, real estate broker; b. Sept. 16, 1932, Helena, Montana; s. Lawrence Arthur and Maude Cecilia (Lauson) F.; m. Camille Marie Augusta, May 16, 1953; children: Larry Lee (dec.), b. 1954; Leighton Lynn, b. 1956; Lauson Layne, b. 1957; Lindel Lee, b. 1959; Laure Lynne, b. 1962; edn: BS, Univ. Nebr., Omaha 1954; MBA, Univ. Santa Clara, 1965; designations: CRB & CRS, Nat. Assn. of Realtors 1979, GRI & RECI, Calif. Assn. of Realtors; cert. Master Instr., Calif. Assn. of Realtors. Career: navigator, aircraft performance engr., USAF 1955-8; engr. Boeing Airplane Co.,

Wichita 1958; engring. writer, Polaris Launcher, Westinghouse, Sunnyvale 1958-62; hd. systems engring. United Technology Ctr., Sunnyvale 1962-71; owner Realcom Assoc. (gen. real estate brokerage), Santa Clara 1969–; real estate instr. (Lifetime Com. Coll. Cred.), West Valley and Mission Colls.; city councilman 1962-71, mayor 1964-5, City of Santa Clara; awards: Realtor of Year, San Jose R.E. Bd. 1982, various civic awards; mem: San Jose Bd. Realtors (pres. 1983, dir. 1984-7), Calif. Assn. of Realtors (dir. 1969–, regl. v.p. 1986, dir. for life 1990), Nat. Assn. of Realtors (dir. 1987-93, 95-98); contbr. articles in Real Estate Today (NAR), and California Real Estate (CAR); mil: 1st Lt. USAF, S.A.C. 1955-8; Republican (State Central Com. 1968–, Reagan del. to nat. conv. 1976, 80, 84); R.Cath.; rec: hunting, fishing. Res: 2831 Fargher Dr Santa Clara 95051 Ofc: Realcom Associates, 830 Kiely Blvd, Kiely Center, Santa Clara 95051

FARHA, JIMMIE LEROY, commercial real estate brokerage president; b. Feb. 12, 1932, Alva, Okla.; s. Henry S. and Saada Elizabeth (Zakoura) F.; m. Patricia A. Connor, Sept. 14, 1957; children: Jimmie, Jr., b. 1958; Catherine, b. 1961; edn: BA, Wichita Univ., 1954; MA, Webster Univ., 1974. Career: comptroller Travis AFB 1975-77; mgr. Ashwill- Burke, Vacaville 1978-82; broker/mgr. Bishop-Hawk, Vacaville 1982-87; owner/pres. Farha Commercial Real Estate, 1987–; appt. Solano County Grand Jury 1988; recipient award for spl. service Calif. Human Devel. Group 1983; mem: No. Solano Co. Bd. of Realtors, Bay Area Brokers Assn., Solano Commercial Brokers Assn. (pres. 1994-95), Council of Military Orgns. (chmn. 1982-83), Air Force Assn. (pres. 1989-90, Community Leader of Yr. award 1982); civic: United Way Vacaville (chmn. 1989), Solano Economic Devel. Corp. (dir. 1987-91), Private Industry Council Solano Co. (dir. 1983–, chmn. 1985-87), Vacaville C.of C. (pres. 1987-88, dir. 1983-92), Ctr. for Employment Training (indsl. rels. advy. bd. 1982-84), Travis Air Mus. (dir. 1989-92); clubs: Rotary Internat. (dir. 1982-83, Paul Harris Fellow), Masons (Hiram Award 1988), Shriners; mil: col. USAF 1954-77, decorated Disting. Service, D.F.C., 8 Air medals, 2 USAF Commendns., Vietnam; rec: walking, swimming. Res: 560 Ridgewood Dr Vacaville 95688 Ofc: Farha Commercial Real Estate, 406 Main St Vacaville 95688

FARLEY, BARBARA SUZANNE, lawyer; b. Dec. 13, 1949, Salt Lake City, Ut.; d. Ross Edward and Barbara Ann (Edwards) F.; m. Arthur Hoffman Ferris, Apr. 9, 1982 (div.); children: Barbara Whitney b. 1986, Taylor Edwards b. 1988; edn: BA, Mills Coll., 1972; JD, UC Hastings Coll. of Law, 1976; admitted bar: Calif. 1976. Career: extern Calif. Supreme Ct., San Francisco 1975; atty., assoc. Pillsbury, Madison & Sutro, S.F. 1976-78; Bronson, Bronson & McKinnon, S.F. 1978-80; Goldstein & Phillips, S.F. 1980-84; ptnr. Rosen. Wachtell & Gilbert, S.F. 1984-89; of counsel Lempres & Wulfsberg, Oakland 1989–; arbitrator U.S. Dist. Ct., no. dist. Calif.; S.F. 1980–, S.F. Superior Ct. 1985–, judge pro tem S.F. Municipal Ct. 1982–; settlement panelist S.F. Bar Assn. 1987–; hearing ofcr., probation monitor Calif.; awards: editorial scholar Hastings, mng. editor Hastings Constnl. Law Qrtly. 1975-76; mem: S.F. Bar Assn., Alameda Bar Assn., Am. Trial Lawyers Assn., Calif. Trial Lawyers Assn., S.F. Trial Lawyers Assn.; pub. article in Cont. Edn. of the Bar 1985; speaker Nat. Business Inst. 1993; avocation: artist. Ofc: Lempres & Wulfsberg 300 Lakeside Dr Ste 2400 Oakland 94612

FARMER, JANENE ELIZABETH, artist, educator; b. Oct. 16, 1946, Albuquerque, NM; d. Charles Watt and Regina M. (Brown) Kruger; edn: BA art, San Diego State Univ., 1969; tchg. credentials, SDSU, 1984, UC San Diego, 1985. Career: freelance artist, San Diego 1970–, environment art: paintings of rare and endangered animals from around the world; instr. UC San Diego, La Jolla (1979-83, 1992–); tchr. Diocese of San Diego, 1984-87, Ramona Unified Sch. Dist., Ramona 1987–; awards: Calif. Arts Council grantee, UC San Diego Resident Artist 1980-81, Coronado Art & Humanities Council 1983, Univ. San Diego grad. fellow 1984; design affil. Am. Soc. Interior Designers 1980–, mem. Calif. Tchrs. Assn. 1987–; Democrat; R.Cath.; rec: the arts, nature, sports. Res: 4435 Nobel Dr Ste 35 San Diego 92122

FARNUM, NICHOLAS ROBERT, statistician, educator, consultant; b. Dec. 19, 1946, Bremerhaven, Ger.; s. Charles Wm. and Doreen Jean (Spencer) F.; edn: BA math. (cum laude), UC Irvine 1969; PhD, 1975. Career: postdoctoral res. fellow Sch. Pub. Health & Hygiene Johns Hopkins Univ., Balt. 1975-76; prof. dept. mgmt. sci., CSU Fullerton, 1976–; sr. statistician Ford Aerospace, Newport Beach 1983-85; cons. Ford Aerospace, McDonnell Douglas, Carter Hawley Hale, McGaw Labs, Paramount Citrus, Nature's Best, Ford Motor Co., 1976–; mem: Am. Statistical Assn., Am. Soc. Quality Control, Ops. Res. Soc., Mathematical Assn. of Am.; author: Quantitative Forecasting Methods (Duxbury Press 1989), Modern Statistical Quality Control and Improvement (Duxbury Press, 1994), Business Statistics (HBJ/Dryden 1997), num. articles pub. in profl. jours., 1976–; rec: jogging, volleyball, music. Ofc: Dept. Mgmt. Sci. California State University Fullerton 92634

FARR, SAM, congressman; b. July 4, 1941, Calif.; m. Shary Baldwin; 1 dau. Jessica; edn: BSc biology, Willamette Univ. 1963; student Monterey Inst. Internat. Studies, Univ. Santa Clara. Career: vol. Peace Corps, 1963-65; budget analyst, cons. Assembly com. Constitutional Amendments; bd. suprs. Monterey

County, Calif.; rep. Calif. State Assembly 1980-93; mem. 103-104th Congresses from 17th Calif. Dist., 1993–; awards: named Legislator of Yr. Calif. 9 times; Democrat. Ofc: House of Representatives 1117 Longworth House Bldg Washington DC 20515-0517

FARSADI, NAY, educational institute president; b. Oct. 15, 1946, Tehran, Iran, nat. 1979; d. Mohammad A. and Kobra (Pirouzian) Shirkhani; children: Lisa b. 1968, Laura b. 1974; edn: AA, Citrus Coll., 1968; BSBA, CSU Los Angeles, 1970; C.P.A. Calif. 1972, real estate lic. 1980. Career: U.S. tax mgr. and audit mgr. Price Waterhouse and Price Waterhouse Internat. in Los Angeles, Houston and Iran, 1970-78, lectr. Price Waterhouse seminars on U.S. taxes for Am. citizens employed by lg. U.S. corps. abroad 1973-78; pres. LCP Internat. Inst., Irvine 1978–, dir. 3 divs: English Language Studies, Ednl. Contract Adminstrv. Svcs., and Internat. Educative and Profl. Tng. Inst.; cons. to internat. sponsors in area of language tng., acquisition, orientation, intercultural communication and pgm. mgmt., 1979–; mem: Am. Inst. CPAs, Tchrs. of English to Speakers of Other Languages (TESOL), Nat. Assn. Fgn. Student Advisors (ATESL chair W.Coast Reg. 1987-88, local arrangements com. chair exhibs. NAFSA Nat. Conf. Long Beach 1987), Am. Mideast Ednl. & Tng. Svc. Inc.; publ: U.S. Tax Booklet for U.S. Citizens Abroad, Price Waterhouse (1975-76); Moslem; rec: flying (lic. pvt. pilot), tennis, swimming, jogging, skiing (snow, water). Res: 27521 Lost Trail Laguna Hills 92653 Ofc: LCP International Institute, 930 AT&T Tower, 8001 Irvine Center Dr Irvine 92718

FASSEL, VELMER ARTHUR, physical chemist, professor and science administrator emeritus; b. Apr. 26, 1919; s. Arthur Edward and Alma (Poppitz) F.; m. Mary Alice Katschke, July 25, 1943; edn: BA, S.E. Missouri State Univ., 1941; PhD, Iowa State Univ., 1947. Career: chemist Manhattan Project, Iowa State Univ., Ames 1942-47, mem. faculty Manhattan Project, Iowa State Univ., 1947–, Disting. prof. sci. and humanities, 1986, prof. chemistry, emeritus sr. scientist, 1986–; sect. chief Ames Lab. US Dept. Energy, 1966-69, dep. dir. Ames Lab. Energy and Mineral Resources Research Inst. 1969-84, prin. scientist Ames Lab. 1984-87, ret.; titular mem., secty., chmn. Commn. Spectrochemistry; Methods of Analysis, Internat. Union Pure and Applied Chemistry; awards: Disting. Alumni S.E. Mo. State Univ. 1965, award Spectroscopy Soc. Pitts. 1969, Maurice F. Hasler award 1971, Anachem award 1971, IR-100 award Res. and Devel. Mag. 1986, Iowa Gov.'s Sci. Medal, Iowa State Univ.'s Disting. Achievement Citation 1987, Eastern Analytical Symp. award 1987; mem: AAAS (Fellow), Optical Soc. Am. (Fellow), Soc. for Applied Spectroscopy (Ann. medal 1964, Strock medal 1986), Am. Chem. Soc. (Fisher award 1979, Chem. Instrumentation award 1983, Iowa award 1983, Analytical Chem. Div. award in Spectrochem. Analysis 1988), Japan Soc. Analytical Chemistry (Hon. mem., medal 1981), Assn. Official Analytical Chemists (Harvey Wiley award 1986), Am. Inst. Physics, Sigma Xi; author 10 patents, 212+ sci. rsch. publs. (on analytical atomic emission and absorption spectroscopy, spectroscopic instrumentation, analytical chemistry), coauthor 1 book. Res: 17755 Rosedown Pl San Diego 92128

FATEMAN, RICHARD J., professor of computer science; b. Nov. 4, 1946, N.Y.C.; m. Martha, June 15, 1968; children: Abigail b. 1971, Johanna b. 1974; edn: BS, Union Coll., 1966; PhD applied math., Harvard Univ., 1971. Career: lectr. math. dept. M.I.T., 1971-74; prof. computer sci., electrical engring. and comp. scis. dept. UC Berkeley, 1974–; mem. Sigma Xi, SIAM, Assn. Computing Machinery; publs: 50+ jour. articles. Ofc: EECS Dept. Univ. California, Berkeley 94720-1776

FATERI, FARDAD, university executive, cross-cultural and organizational behavior expert; b. July 12, 1964, Tehran, Iran; s. Mohammad and Farideh (Miri) F.; m. Farnaz Abdollahi, Nov. 17, 1989; edn: BA, UC Irvine, 1985; MA, CSU Fullerton, 1987; PhD, U.S. Internat. Univ., San Diego, 1989. Career: constrn. supt. New World Developers, Hawthorne, Calif. 1984-86; exec. asst. to the CEO, TiGeh Corp., Tehran, 1986-88; adj. prof. U.S.Internat. Univ., 1988–, grad. advisor 1988-89, asst., then dir. USIU Orange County Ctr., Irvine 1989–, actg. dir. USIU L.A. Co. Ctr., Eagle Rock, 1991–; civic bds: City of Irvine Multi-Cultural Task Force 1990–, Hist. and Cultural Found. of Orange Co. (bd. dirs. 1990–), Iranian New Year Task Force (Irvine coordinator 1989–); pub. articles in profl. jours. incl.: Alternatives to Deadly Force (1990), Methods Dealing with Cross-Cultural Concerns (1990), The Politics of Diversity: From the Melting Pot to the Salad Bowl (1992), The Future of Cultural Diversity: A Paradigm Shift (1992); rec: tennis and volleyball, collect bronze sculptures, community svc. Res: 5 Haggerstone Irvine 92715 Ofc: U.S.I.U., 2500 Michelson Dr Bldg 400 Irvine 92715

FATTORINI, HECTOR OSVALDO, researcher, mathematics professor; b. Oct. 28, 1938, Buenos Aires, Argentina, naturalized U.S. citizen 1980; s Osvaldo Franco and Concepcion (Marti Ros) F.; m. Natalia Lubow Karanowycz, Nov. 4, 1961; children: Maria Elena b. 1961, Sonia b. 1962, Susana b. 1965; edn: lic. in math. scis. Univ. de Buenos Aires, 1960; PhD math., New York Univ., 1965. Career: adj. prof. Univ. Buenos Aires, 1965-66; res. asso. Brown Univ., 1966-67; asst. prof. to full prof. Univ. Calif. Los Angeles, 1967–; prof. titular Univ. of Buenos Aires, Argentina 1973-75; editor and referee sev. scientific jours., revs. for Math. Reviews and Zentralblatt fur Mathematik; rev. Nat. Sci. Found. propos-

als; awards: ann. research grantee NSF 1967–; mem: Union Matematica Argentina 1958–, Circulo Unidad (Buenos Aires, 1962–), Am. Math. Soc. 1962–, Soc. for Indsl. and Applied Math. 1965–; author: The Cauchy Problem (1983), Second Order Linear Differential Equations in Banach Space (1985), 60+ sci. papers in various jours. incl. Comm. Pure Appl. Math., SIAM Jour. Control Optim., Math Zeitschrift, others; rec: music. Res: 14701 Whitfield Ave Pacific Palisades 90272 Ofc: Dept. Mathematics Univ. California, Los Angeles 90024

FAUL, DAVID CHARLES, logistics systems analyst, educator; b. July 24, 1936, Hastings, Mich.; s. Charles Ludwig and Geneva (McQuarrie) F.; m. Helen Schultz, June 11, 1960; children: James b. 1962, Jeffrey b. 1964, Scott b. 1965; edn: BBA, Univ. Mich., 1958, MBA, 1959; USN War Coll. Naval Commd. & Staff, 1972; Cert. Profl. Logistician (CPL) Soc. of Logistic Engrs. Career: served to comdr. U.S. Navy 1959-81: shipbd. supply ofcr. USS Mahan (DLG-11) San Diego 1960-62, adminstrv. asst. Naval Supply Depot Seattle 1962-64, shipbd. supply ofcr. USS Preble (DLG-15) San Diego 1964-66, fin. mgr. Fleet Mat. Support Office Mechanicsburg, Pa. 1966-69, inventory control ofcr. Naval Supply Depot Guam 1969-71, instr. and student Naval War Coll. Newport, R.I. 1971-74, aviation repairables pgm. mgr. Phila. 1974-77, supply ofcr. Naval Air Sta. Point Mugu, Calif. 1977-80, inventory & fin. mgr. Naval Support Forces Antartica 1980-81, decorated Meritorious Service 1980; sr. project engr. Hughes Aircraft Co., El Segundo 1981-87; program mgr. Automated Scis. Group, Camarillo 1987-88; logistics analyst Science Applications Internat. Corp., Camarillo 1989-92; Technology Applications Inc. 1992-93 ; bus. adminstrn. lectr. and asst. dean COBM, West Coast Univ., 1988–, instr. LaVerne Univ., 1992–; active Boy Scouts Am. (commr. Camarillo Dist. 1984-90, commr. Ventura County Council 1990-92), Silver Beaver Award 1991, Dist. Award of Merit 1987; mem: Nat. Contract Mgmt. Assn., Soc. of Logistic Engrs. (chpt. chmn. 1990-92), Assn. of Naval Aviation, Missile Tech. Hist. Assn. (bd. 1990–), Point Mugu Fed. Credit Union (bd. chmn. 1987-90), Am. Red Cross Ventura Co. (bd. 1990-93), Sigma Alpha Epsilon Frat., Toastmasters, Optimist Club (v.p. Oxnard 1981-82); publs: ed. corresp. course Defense Economics & Decision Making 1974; Republican; Methodist. Res: 1310 Lantana Camarillo 93010 Ofc: Veda, Inc. Camarillo 93010

FAUST, G. THOMAS, executive; b. Sept. 22, 1931, Mt. Carmel, Ill.; s. Gilbert Sefton and Helen Esther (Morray) F.; m. Barbara Lee Roberts, May 9, 1956 (dec. Mar. 5, 1993); m. Mary Kathleen Bousquet, Feb. 24, 1995; children: Jonathan Scott b. 1956, Gilbert Sefton b. 1960, David Thomas b. 1963, Nina Marie b. 1964; edn: BA, UCLA 1953; MBA, 1961. Career: account exec. Hixson & Jorgensen, Los Angeles 1956-62; pres., CEO Faust Day Advt., 1962-68; v.p. Foremost McKesson Inc., S.F. 1968-70; founder, COO Intra Leisure Inc., Redondo Beach 1970-72; Pennsylvania Co., NYC 1972-75; co-founder, ptnr. Enterprise Mgmt. Group, LA 1975-85; Holley & Faust, Redondo Beach 1985-88; owner, CEO G. Thomas Faust & Assoc. Inc., Costa Mesa 1988–; guest prof. Claremont Coll. 1980-81; faculty USC Bus. Sch., 1972-74; CEO and owner Masterite Connector Corp., mfr. electronic connectors, Costa Mesa 1994–; UCLA Sch. Bus. 1964-66; mil: 1st lt. AUS 1953-56; Republican; rec: golf, skiing, oenology. Res: 24903 Moulton Pkwy #133 Laguna Hills 92653 Ofc: 3000 A Airway Costa Mesa 92626

FAWCETT, J. SCOTT, real estate developer; b. Nov. 5, 1937, Pittsburgh, Pa.; s. William Hagen and Mary Jane (Wise) F., Jr.; m. Anne Mitchell, Dec. 30, 1960; children: Holly b. 1961, John (1965-1983); edn: BS, Ohio State Univ. 1959. Career: dist. dealer rep. Shell Oil Co., San Diego 1962-66; dist. real estate rep. Shell Oil, Phoenix 1967-69; region real estate rep. Shell Oil, San Francisco 1970-71; head office land investments rep. Shell Oil, Houston 1972-75; pres./CEO Marinita Devel. Co., Newport Beach 1976–; lectr. in land devel. related fields; mem: Internat. Council of Shopping Centers (ICSC), Inst. of Business Appraisers, Nat. Assn. of Review Appraisers and Mortgage Underwriters, Calif. Lic. Contractors Assn., Building Indus. Assn., Internat. Right of Way Assn., Internat. Inst. of Valuers, Am. Assn. of Certified Appraisers, Urban Land Inst., Nat. Assn. Real Estate Execs. (pres. L.A. chpt. 1975), US C.of C., Town Hall of Calif., Internat. Platform Assn., Toastmasters (pres. Scottsdale, Ariz. Club, pres. Hospitality T. Club, San Diego 1964), Univ. Athletic Club, Ohio State Univ. Alumni Assn., Phi Kappa Tau Alumni Assn.; mil: M.P., US Army, Mil. Dist. of Wash. 1960-61; Republican; R.Cath.; rec: antiques, tennis, skiing. Res: 8739 Hudson River Circle Fountain Valley 92708 Ofc: Marinita Development Co. 3835 Birch St Newport Beach 92660

FAZIO, VIC, congressman; b. Oct. 11, 1942, Winchester, Mass.; m. Judy Kern; children: Dana Fazio, Anne Fazio, Kevin Kern, Kristie Kern; edn: BA, Union Coll., Schenectady, 1965; postgrad., Calif. State Univ., Sacramento. Career: journalist, founder Calif. Jour.; congl. and legis. cons., 1966-75; mem. Calif. State Assembly, 1975-78; mem. 96th-104th Congresses from Calif. 3rd Dist., 1979–, chmn. Dem. Congl. Campaign Com., vice chair Dem. caucus, house steering policy com., chmn. legis. br. appropriations subcom., vice chmn. appropriations subcom. energy and water, appropriations subcom. mil. constrn.; majority whip-at-large 96th-103rd Congresses; also co-chmn. Fed. Govt. Svcs. Task Force 96th-101st Congresses, former chmn. bipartisan com. on ethics; former mem. Sacramento County Charter and Planning Commns.; bd. dirs. Asthma

Allergy Found.; honors: Jr. Statesman, Nat. Italian-Am. Found., Coro Found. fellow; named Solar Congressman of Yr.; mem: Air Force Assn., Navy League, UNICO. Ofc: US House of Representatives Washington, DC 20515*

FEARN, DEAN HENRY, mathematics educator; b. June 8, 1943, Portland, Oreg.; s. Clyde Henry Fearn and Sylvia Adele (Dahl) Christensen; m. Gloria June Wilber, Oct. 1, 1966; children: Neal b. 1971, Justin b. 1976; edn: BS, Univ. Wash., Seattle 1965; MA, Western Wash. Univ., Bellingham 1967; PhD, UC Davis, 1971. Career: tchg. asst. Western Wash. Univ., 1965-66, Univ. Calif. Davis, 1967-71; senior mathematician Aerojet-General, Rancho Cordova, Ca. 1970; prof. CSU Hayward, 1971–; honors: Pi Mu Epsilon 1965; mem: Am. Stat. Assn. (pres. S.F. chapt. 1991-92), Math. Assn. Am. 1980–, Inst. of Math. Stats. 1980–, SPC Apple computer club Fremont (pres. 1992-93); contbr. articles in profl. jours. (1971–); Democrat; Lutheran; rec: computers. Res: 3255 Sunnybrook Ct Hayward 94541 Ofc: Dept. Statistics, Calif. State University, Hayward 94542

FEATHER, LAWRENCE STEVEN, company executive director; b. Jan. 4, 1955, Hackensack, N.J.; s. Leo and Della Bertha (Shupetsky) F.; m. Barbara Lynn Krone, June 26, 1982; edn: BA (cum laude), Boston Coll., 1977, MEd (hons.), 1978; postgrad. U.S. Internat. Univ., San Diego. Career: child welfare specialist Dept. Soc. Svs., Brockton, Mass. 1978-79; sales/purch. Manor Steel Corp., Park Ridge, Ill. 1979-83; personnel administr. Kevan Industries, L.A. 1983-84; cons. Mark Miller & Assocs., Van Nuys 1985-87; personnel tng. supr. Walden Environment, Mission Hills 1987-88, district dir. 1988-92; executive dir. Inner Circle Foster Family Agy., Van Nuys 1990–; mem: Am. Psychol. Assn., Soc. for Industrial & Organizational Psychologists, Personnel & Industrial Relations Assn., Calif. State Psychol. Assn.; Jewish; rec: golf, tennis, books, travel. Res: 20737 Roscoe Blvd Ste 201 Canoga Park 91306

FEDER, STEVEN S., tax attorney; b. May 22, 1959, Detroit, Mich.; s. Jakob and Marilyn F.; m. Catherine Weir, July 4, 1985; edn: BS computer engring., Univ. Mich. 1980; JD, Univ. San Diego 1982; LL.M tax., 1987; admitted St. Bar Calif. (1983). Career: computer engr. U.S. Postal Service, San Diego 1983-85; dist. counsel I.R.S., S.F. 1985; atty. Levitz Zacks & Ciceric 1985-86; Muegenburg Normand Dowler, Ventura 1986-88; Hathaway Perrett Webster Powers & Chrisman 1988–; assoc. prof. Ventura Coll. Law 1989–; honors: Eta Kappa Nu, Tau Beta Pi, Univ. S.D. Moot Ct. semi-finalist (1982); mem: Am. Bar Assn., Calif. Bar Assn., Ventura Co. Bar Assn.; rec: skiing. Ofc: Hathaway Law Firm 5450 Telegraph Rd Ste 200 Ventura 93003

FEICHTMEIR, EDMUND FRANCIS, retired agricultural chemist; b. July 6, 1915, Ainsworth, Iowa; s. Edmund and Emma (Theis) F.; m. Barbara Elizabeth Wright, Jan. 20, 1943; children: Wendi b. 1946, Kurt b. 1949, Janis b. 1952, Kris b. 1956; edn: BA, UC Berkeley 1937; PhD, 1947. Career: agri. chemist Shell Oil, Modesto 1947-50, field devel., NYC 1950-52, mgr. product devel., Denver, Colo. 1953-57, Modesto 1957-72, mgr. consumer product and agri. research Shell Devel. Co. 1972-79; mem: Ripon Council (councilman 1965-72, mayor 1972-92, councilman 1992-94), Lions; mil: lt. USN 1942-46. Res: 408 Linda Ripon 95366

FEILDER, CLIVE LEE, (screen name: LEE MASON), screen producer, writer; b. Jan. 10, 1939, Brentford, England, perm. resident U.S., 1968–; s. Rt. Hon. Arthur Leonard Feilder (14th Earl of Denbigh) and Lady Dorathy Florence (Packer) Hagger; m. Kathlean M. Quillan, Oct. 4, 1972 (dec. 1980); children: Rachel Eden b. 1974; m. Florence Thorsteinson, Sept. 7, 1991; edn: British GCE, Sir Godfrey Kneller Private, London 1953; BA, Kingston Art Coll., London 1957; MA, Univ. St. Thomas, U.S. Virgin Islands, 1966. Career: head instr. Ron Bailey Sch. Broadcasting, San Jose 1975-76; instr. De Anza Coll., San Jose 1985-87; art director Molesworth Films, USA and Hong Kong, 1986, Artistic Films, Sacramento, Calif. 1987, Transbay Pictures, L.A. 1987–, Penny Ante Films, L.A. 1987–; video producer Ancha Audio Video, Chgo. 1989-91; screen writer, self-empl., Santa Cruz 1991–; awards: Best Designer Set (for 1st film) No. Calif. Film Board, S.F. 1987, Best poem Great Poems Am., Sacto. 1991; mem. Free Lance Writers Union 1979–, Writers Guild Am. 1986–; author: (book) How Far to Neptunas, 1976, (t.v. plays) Chicken Little Comedy Hour, 1976, (radio play) High Wire Radio Choir, 1977, (TV series) It's A Wrap, 1991, (book) Box Car of Dreams, 1992; mil: flt. lt. Royal Air Force 1957-62; Unitarian; rec: writing, theater, sailing, travel. Ofc: Edenwood Productions PO Box 67145 Scotts Valley 95067-7145

FEIMAN, THOMAS EDWARD, certified public accountant, investment manager; b. Dec. 21, 1940, Canton, Ohio; s. Daniel Thaviu and Adrienne (Silver) F.; m. Marilyn Judith Miller, June 26, 1966; children: Sheri b. 1969, Michael b. 1971; edn: BS econ., Univ. Pa. 1962; MBA, Northwestern Univ. 1963; C.P.A. Calif. 1965. Career: staff auditor Arthur Young & Co., Los Angeles 1963-66; field auditor I.R.S. 1966-68; owner Thomas Feiman CPA 1968-69; ptnr. Wideman Feiman & Co. 1969-74; pres., stockholder Wideman Feiman Levy Sapin & Ko 1974-93; investment mgr., v.p. Schroder, Wertheim & Co., Inc. 1993–; sr. instr. UCLA 1968-85; pres. Urological Science Research Found. 1992–; honors: Beta Gamma Sigma, Delta Sigma Rho, Pi Gamma Mu, Omicron Chi Epsilon, IRS Cert. of Award 1968; mem: Northwestern Alnuni Club So.

Calif. (former treas., bd. mem.), Northwestern Bus. Club So. Calif. (former pres., founder), Temple Israel Hollywood; Republican; Jewish; rec: golf. Ofc: 10877 Wilshire Blvd Ste #300 Los Angeles 90024

FEIN, WILLIAM, ophthamologist/educator; b. Nov. 27, 1933, NY, NY; s. Samuel and Beatrice (Lipschitz) F.; m. Bonnie Fern Aaronson, Dec. 15, 1963; children: Stephanie Paula b. 1968, Adam Irving b. 1969, Gregory Andrew b. 1972; edn: BS, Coll. of the City of N.Y., 1954; MD, UC Irvine Med. Sch., 1962; diplomate Am. Bd. Ophthamology, 1969, Fellow Am. Coll. Surgeons, 1988. Career: resident ophthalmol., L.A. County Gen. Hosp. 1963-66; post res. tng. in ophthalmic plastic surgery, Manhattan Eye and Ear Hosp. 1966-67; instr. ophthalmol. UCI Med. Sch. 1966-69, instr./assoc. clin. prof. ophthalmol. USC Med. Sch. 1969–; chmn. Dept. Ophthalm. Midway Hosp. 1975-79; v.p. California Eye Med. Clinic, Inc. 1969-83; chief of Ophthalm. Clinic Svcs., Cedars Sinai Med. Ctr. 1979-81, chmn. Div. of Ophthalm., 1981-86; dir. Ellis Eye Ctr. 1984–; frequent lectr. on new techniques in ophthalm. plastic surgery, var. hosps. and convs.; Fellow Am. Coll. of Surgeons 1988, Internat. Coll. of Surgeons 1988; mem. Royal Soc. of Medicine, Am. Soc. of Ophthalmol. Plastic and Reconstrv. Surgery, Am. Acad. Ophthalmology, L.A. Soc. of Ophthalmology, AMA, Calif. Med. Assn., L.A. Co. Med. Assn.; author numerous articles in med. books and jours. describing new ophthalmic surgeries; editorial bd. Internat. Jour. of Cataract and Ocular Surgery; Jewish. Res: 718 N Camden Dr Beverly Hills 90210 Ofc: 415 N Crescent Dr Beverly Hills 90210

FEINSTEIN, DIANNE, U.S. senator; b. San Francisco, June 22, 1933. d. Leon and Betty (Rosenburg) Goldman; m. Bertram Feinstein, Nov. 11, 1962 (dec.); 1 child, Katherine Anne; m. Richard C. Blum, Jan. 20, 1980; edn: BS, Stanford Univ. 1955; LLB (hon.), Golden Gate Univ. 1977; D. Pub. Adminstrn. (hon.), Univ. Manila 1981; D. Pub. Service (hon.), Univ. Santa Clara 1981; JD (hon.), Antioch Univ. 1983, Mills Coll. 1985; LHD (hon.), Univ. San Francisco 1988. Career: fellow Coro Found., San Francisco 1955-56; with Calif. Women's Bd. Terms and Parole 1960-66; mem. Mayor's com. on crime, chmn. advy. com. Adult Detention 1967-69; mem. Bd. of Suprs., San Francisco 1970-78, pres., 1970-72, 74-76, 78; mayor of San Francisco 1979-88; mem. exec. com. U.S. Conf. of Mayors 1983-88; Dem. nominee for Gov. of Calif. 1990; mem. U.S. Senate, Washington, DC 1992–; mem. Nat. Com. on U.S.-China Rels; mem. Bay Area Conservation and Devel. Commn. 1973-78; awards: Woman of Achievement award Bus. and Profl. Women's Clubs San Francisco 1970, Disting. Woman award S.F. Examiner 1970, Coro Found. award 1979, Coro Leadership award 1988, Pres. medal UC S.F. 1988, Scopus award Am. Friends Hebrew Univ. 1981, Brotherhood/Sisterhood award NCCJ 1986, Comdr.'s award U.S. Army 1986, French Legion of Honor 1984, Disting. Civilian award USN 1987, named Number One Mayor All-Pro City Mgmt. Team City and State Mag. 1987; mem: Trilateral Commn., Japan Soc. of No. Calif. (pres. 1988), Inter-Am. Dialogue, Nat. Com. on U.S.-China Rels. Ofc: 1700 Montgomery St Ste 305 San Francisco 94111

FEIT, MICHAEL D., physicist; b. Nov. 15, 1942, Easton, Pa.; s. Joel E. and Kathryn T. (Bracken) F.; m. Lorraine R. Mauriel, Dec. 31, 1967; children: Sean M. b. 1971, Kathryn R. b. 1973; edn: BA, Lehigh Univ., 1964; PhD, Rensselaer Polytechnic Inst., 1970. Career: res. assoc. dept. physics Univ. of Illinois, Urbana 1969-72; physicist dept. physics Lawrence Livermore Nat. Lab., Livermore, Calif. 1972–, optical physics group leader 1992; adj. faculty dept. applied sci. Univ. Calif., Davis 1984–; awards: Phi Beta Kappa, Sigma Xi 1964, physics distinguished achiev. LLNL 1990; mem. AAAS 1964–, Am. Physical Soc. (1964–, Fellow 1988), Optical Soc. of Am. (1990–, Fellow 1992); publs: 90+ tech. jour. articles (1964–). Ofc: LLNL, PO Box 808 MS L-438 Livermore 94550

FEKETE, GEORGE OTTO, trial lawyer; b. Budapest, Hungary, nat. U.S. citizen 1952; s. Bela and Ilona (Mehr) F.; m. Amy; children: Jacquelyn, and Jeanette; edn: BS, Wayne State; PhD, USC; JD, Pepperdine Univ.; reg. pharmacist Calif.; admitted Calif. St. Bar, 1973. Career: aircraft cdr./capt. USAF S.A.C.; chief pharmacist various pharmacies, Los Angeles; pres. and chief trial lawyer G.O. Fekete Law Corp., Anaheim 1973-85, San Francisco Bay Area 1988–; lead trial lawyer M. M. Belli, Sr. law offices, S.F. 1988; honors: outstanding citizenship Wayne Univ. 1954, Dean's Honor Roll Pepperdine 1972, 73; mem: Assn. Trial Lawyers of Am., ABA, Calif. Bar Assn., Calif. Trial Lawyers Assn., Contra Costa County Bar Assn., ex-dir. Orange Co. Trial Lawyers Assn. 1973-84; publs: article "Drug Product Liability" CTLA Jour., 1978, "Pharmaceutlical Litigations" Iowa Trial Lawyers Jour., 1979; Republican; Prot.; rec: reading, writing, music, photography. Ofc: 495 Goheen Cir Ridge Crest Vallejo 94591-4114

FELACTU, ODESSA J., executive recruiter; b. Oct. 21, 1945, Bristow, Okla.; s. John Odessa and Elizabeth (Simiodies) F.; m. Mary Agatha, Aug. 16, 1969; children: John 1970, George b. 1973, Tom b. 1977; edn: BS fin., USC 1969. Career: stockbroker Kidder Peabody, N.Y.C. 1969-71; cons. Paul R. Ray, Los Angeles 1971-74; v.p. Eastman & Beaudine 1974-80; pres. THE ODESSA GROUP 1980–; mem: USC Assoc., Sigma Chi, L.A. Athletic Club, Calif. Exec. Recruiters Assn.; Republican; Greek Orthodox; rec: handball, soccer. Ofc: 523 W 6th Ste 807 Los Angeles 90014

FELDMAN, DANIEL, federal agency administrator; b. Jan. 16, 1917, Pittsburgh, Pa.; s. Jerome Feldman and Jennie (Schott) Solomon; m. Rose Solomon, Aug. 15, 1937 (dec. 1985); m. Sylvia Swartz Dobkin, Aug. 31, 1986; edn: Univ. Pittsburgh 1969. Career: pres. Automatic Catering, Swissvale, Pa. 1946-56; Interstate United, Pittsburgh, Pa. 1956-61; Dynamic Products 1961-76; mgr., adminstr. U.S. Dept. Energy 1976-80; cons. Score, San Diego 1987-89; mem: SCORE (Service Corps of Retired Execs.) Jewish Comm. Center; invention: automatic dispenser (1960); mil: p.o. USN 1944-45; rec: sports, tennis, table tennis. Res: 13391 Heston Pl San Diego 92130

FELDMAN, LOUIS ARNOLD, mathematics professor; b. Nov. 26, 1941, Bay City, Mich.; s. Henry and Rebecca F.; m. Rosetta Sue Croom, Aug. 3, 1975 (div. April 1981); m. Marry Ellen Rhodes, Oct. 7, 1988; edn: dipl. Arthur Hill H.S., Saginaw, Mich. 1959; BS, Univ. Mich., Ann Arbor 1963; MA, UC Berkeley, 1965, PhD mathematics, 1969. Career: asst. prof. math. CSU Stanislaus, Turlock 1968-71, assoc. prof., 1971-76, prof. math., 1976–, chair, dept. of math, 1993–, coordinator of Applied Studies, 1992–, AMP coordinator, 1994–; awards: Woodrow Wilson fellow 1963, NSF grad. fellow 1963, Phi Beta Kappa 1963, Phi Kappa Phi 1963; pub. profl. jour. articles; rec: exercise. Ofc: Calif. State Univ. Stanislaus Dept. Math., 801 W Monte Vista Ave Turlock 95380 Tel: 209/667-3461

FELDMAN, RON LYLE, hotel negotiation specialist, information technology inventor; b. Apr. 15, 1950, Los Angeles; s. Julian and Sarah (De Norber) F.; m. Linda, June 16, 1973; children: d. Anna b. 1984; edn: BS, CSU Hayward, 1972, MS, 1974; Calif. sch. counselor credential 1974. Career: counselor Livermore Unified Sch. Dist., 1974-75; profl. bridge player American Contract Bridge League, N.Am., 1975-81, member U.S. Bridge Team, World Championships (1982, 1986, 1994); hotel negotiation splst. Hotel Connections, Inc. 1981–, appt. v.chmn. exec. com. Assn. of Travel Marketing, 1990; developed worldwide system w. Citicorp providing discounted hotel rooms & payment in the local currency; invented & designed new automated technology to interpret order requests electronically (via sequential routing of computer file transfer & send data for transaction processing to multiple parties) for inventory based corporations, 1991 (patent pending 1993); pres. World Business Services, Inc. 1981–; honors: Congressional recogn. for work with children; mem: Am. Hotel and Motel Assn. 1987–, Meeting Planners Intl. 1991–, Am. Soc. of Assn. Execs. 1986–, Am. Contract Bridge League (nat. conduct and ethics com. and nat. goodwill com. 1977), Assn. of Profl. Bridge Players (pres. 1982–, oldest ACBL accredited group), Found. for Glaucoma Research 1983–; Indep.; Jewish; avocation: bridge. Res: 606 Western Ave Petaluma 94952 Ofc: Hotel Connections, Inc. 6 Petaluma Blvd North Petaluma 94952

FELICITA, JAMES THOMAS, aerospace company executive; b. May 21, 1947, Syracuse, NY; s. Anthony Nicholas and Ada (Beech) F.; edn: Syracuse Univ. 1965-66; AB, Cornell Univ. 1969; Harvard Univ. 1969; Univ. So. Calif. 1970; Govt. Contract Mgmt., UC Los Angeles 1974-77. Career: motion picture editor/ producer Jacques Descent Prodns. Hollywood 1970-71; social welfare examiner Onondaga County Dept. of Social Svcs. Syracuse, NY 1972-73; underwriter Transamerica Corp. L.A. 1974; contract negotiator US Naval Regional Contracting Ofc., Long Beach 1974-80; contract negotiator Hughes Aircraft Co. El Segundo 1980-81, head NASA contracts 1981-83, mgr. major pgm. contracts 1983–; organized aerospace wing of Calif. Mus. of Sci. & Industry L.A. 1983; honors: NY State Regents Scholar 1965-69, Syracuse Univ. Trustee Scholar 1965-66, Cost Savings Commdn. (Pres. Gerald Ford 1976), Cape Canaveral Missile Space Range Pioneer, Sustained Superior Performance Award (USN 3 yrs.); mem: Nat. Space Club, Planetary Soc., Hughes Mgmt. Club, Cornell Alumni Assn. of So. Calif., Nat. Contract Mgmt. Assn.; Republican; Prot.; rec: military & space models, rare books, modern art. Res: 8541 Kelso Dr Huntington Beach 92646 Ofc: 1700 E Imperial Hwy El Segundo 90245

FELT, JAMES WRIGHT, professor of philosophy, Jesuit priest; b. Jan. 4, 1926, Dallas, Tx.; s. Wright Lafayette and Freda Marie (Brown) F.; edn: AB (hons. Classical), and MA in philosophy, Gonzaga Univ., Spokane 1949, 1950; STL theology, Alma Coll., Calif. 1957; MS physics, St. Louis Univ. 1962, PhD philosophy, 1965. Career: asst. prof. phil. Santa Clara Univ., Santa Clara, Calif. 1965-69, asso. prof. 1970-83, prof. phil. 1984–, Jesuit Comm. prof. phil. 1993–, dept. philosophy chair (1967-69, 74-80, 82-83), estab. ann. phil. conf. S.C. Univ., founding editor Logos: Philosophic Issues in Christian Perspective (pub. ann. S.C. Univ. 1980-91); co-dir. of 6 wk. Summer Inst. on Process Metaphysics, S.C. Univ. 1986–; vis. prof. Inst. European Studies, Vienna 1971, Gonzaga Univ. 1976; lectr.univs., confs., symposiums, presentations nat., internat.; recipient Santa Clara Univ. Pres.'s Recognition Award 1984; mem: Am. Philosophical Assn. 1965–, Am. Cath. Philosophical Assn. (1962–, exec. coun. 1977-80, 89-92), Metaphysical Soc. Am. (1964–, exec. coun. 1994–), Jesuit Philosophical Assn. (1962–, nat. pres. 1981-82); author (book): Making Sense of Your Freedom (Ithaca: Cornell Univ. Press 1994); contbr. numerous essays in phil. jours., 1965–; rec: model R.R. Res: Jesuit Residence, Santa Clara Univ., Santa Clara 95053 Ofc: Dept. Philosophy, Santa Clara Univ., Santa Clara 95053

FENTON, DONALD MASON, chemist, new technology development executive; b. May 23, 1929, Los Angeles; s. Charles Youdan and Dorothy Chaplan (Mason) F.; m. Margaret Keehler, April 24, 1953; children: James Michael b. 1957, Douglas Charles b. 1959; edn: BS, UCLA 1952; PhD, 1958. Career: chemist Rohm & Haas Co., Phila., Pa. 1958-61; sr. res. chemist Union Oil Co., Brea 1962-67, res.assoc. 1967-72, sr. res. assn. 1972-82, mgr. planning devel. 1982-85, mgr. new tech. devel. 1985-94 (retired), cons. (AMSCO div.) 1967-73; chmn. Petroleum Environ. Res. Forum 1986-88; Gordons Research Cong. Hydrocarbon Chem. 1975; dir. Calif. Engring. Found., Sacto. 1989–, chmn. of bd. 1991-92; honors: Sigma Xi; mem: Am. Chem. Soc., Am. Inst. Chemists, Alpha Chi Sigma; author: 1 book chpt. pub., 10 papers pub. in tech.jours.; over 100 patents held; mil: cpl. AUS 1953-55; rec: photography. Res: 2861 E Alden Pl Anaheim 92806

FERENCE, HELEN MARIE, director; b. Sept. 1, 1946, Youngstown, Ohio; d. Emery and Josephine (Terlecki) Ference; m. William Verill Nick; edn: diploma, nsg., Youngstown Hosp. Assn., Youngstown, Ohio, 1967; BS, Youngstown Univ., 1970; MS, Ohio State Univ., Columbus, 1972; PhD, NY Univ., NYC, 1979. Career: charge nurse ICU, Youngstown Hosp. Assn., 1967-70; instr. Youngstown Univ., 1970; clinician ICU's, Ohio State Univ., Grant Hosp., Columbus, 1970-80; instr. Ohio State Univ., 1972-79; asst. prof. Ohio State Univ., 1980; cons. VA, Chillicothe, Ohio, 1973-81; cons. Battelle Mem. Inst., Columbus, 1973-81; cons. Arlington Surgery Ctr.; bd. of dir. Arlington Surgery Ctr.; dir. Nsg. Prog., Arlington Surgery Ctr.; dir. res. qualification, Mt. Sinai Hosp., NYC; clinician Cedars-Sinai Hosp., L.A.; awards: Mary Wright Toelle award, Youngstown Hosp. Assn. 1967; Sigma Theta Tau Achievement award, Indpls. 1985; Nightingale award, Nightingale Soc., Carmel, Calif. 1990; Nightingale Prize, Nightingale Soc., Eng. 1992; mem: Sigma Theta Tau (v.p.1979-94), Nightingale Soc. (dir. 1986–), Spanish Bay, Pebble Beach; author: Notes on Nsg. Sci., 1991-94. Res: P.O. Box 862 Pebble Beach 93953

FERER, HARVEY S., aviation consultant; b. Dec. 24, 1924, St. Louis, Mo.; s. Sidney Sapot and Hannah (Cooper); stepfather Allen Ferer; children: Aaron b. 1960, Andrew b. 1965, Ana Michelle b. 1968; edn: Univ. Omaha 1942-43, Doane Coll. 1943-44, UCLA 1947-49; IFR Procedures Splst., FAA (1963). Career: air transport plane cmdr. US Navy, lcdr. USNR-ret. 1943-46, 1949-61, decorated Air Medal, Reserve Medal, Good Conduct, 12 campaign ribbons; IFR procedures splst. FAA, N.Y.C., Atlantic City, Los Angeles 1963-85, tng. ofcr. various units FAA 1970-85; aviation cons./prin. H. Ferer & Assocs. 1985–; cons. Mexican govt. on new Mexico City Airport 1975, cons. to South Jersey AirWays, Rocky Mtn Airways, SkyWest 1967-81; recipient commendns. control towers of Atlantic City and Phila. (1968, 70), superior performance award FAA 1980; docent/instr. Santa Monica Mus. of Flying; mem. Inst. of Navigation, Wild Goose Assn.; Republican; Jewish; rec: flying, tennis (trophies 1947-70), photog. Address: 14028 Tahiti Wy Ste 413 Marina Del Rey 90292

FERGUS, GARY SCOTT, lawyer; b. Apr. 20, 1954, Racine, Wis.; s. Russell Malcolm and Phyl Rose (Muratore) F.; m. Isabelle Sabina Beekman, Sept. 28, 1985; children: d. Mary Marckwald Beekman F. b. 1988, s. Kirkpatrick Russell Beekman F. b. 1989; edn: JD, Univ. Wis. Sch. of Law, 1971; SB, Stanford Univ., 1976; LLM, N.Y. Univ., 1981; admitted bar: Wis., 1979, Calif., 1990. Career: atty., assoc. Brobeck, Phleger & Harrison, San Francisco 1980-86, ptnr. 1986–, trial atty. first major consolidated asbestos trial in U.S. 1990; lectr. trial advocacy pgm. Stanford Law Sch., 1990, speaker, instr. trial advocacy pgm. Harvard Law Sch., 1991; supvg. instr. Fed. Trial Practice Pgm. & Negotiations Sem., U.S. Dist. Ct. no. dist. Calif., 1992; mem. Am. Bar Assn.; author (software) Nat. Case Mgmt. for Asbestos Litigation; Recognized leader in use of technology for lawyers in law jour. articles Nat. Law Jour. (7/27/87), and California Lawyer (10/87), "High Tech Attorneys Get the Business" Profit Magazine; rec: sailing, racing. Ofc: Brobeck, Phleger & Harrison, One Market Plaza Spear St Tower San Francisco 94105

FERGUSON, ROLLINGTON, physician; s. David and Cetia F.; edn: advance level cert., chem. biology, physics, Coll. of Bahamas, Univ. of London 1975-77; BS, chem., biology, Mankato State Univ., Minn. 1980, MS, comm. health 1982; MPH, UCLA 1986; MD, UCLA/Drew 1990; residency, internal medicine, Highland Gen. Hosp. 1990-93; approved supr. of physician assistants, Med. Bd. of Calif. Career: bank trainee Central Bank of Bahamas 1975-76; lab asst. Bahamas Oil Refinery Co. 1977; security dispatcher M.S.U. 1979-80, bindery supr. 1980-82; res. asst., academic project 1980; res., academic project 1981; store mgr. Bond Street 1981; vol. lab asst. Minn. State Health Dept. 1982; mgr. Insty-Prints Inc. 1982-84; vol. Cedars-Sinai Med. Ctr. 1985; tutor HCOP Prog., UCLA 1985; staff res. assoc. Jonsson Comprehensive Cancer Ctr., UCLA 1985-86; sr. res. assoc. King/Drew Med. Ctr. 1985-90; cons. physician Bonner Med. Clinic 1992–, Ctr. for Elder Independence, Highland Gen. Hosp. 1993, St. Lukes Hosp. Out-Patient Psychiatric Unit 1993-94; primary and sole physician provider La Clinica La Esperanza, Los Banos, Calif. 1993-94; fellow cardiology, VA Fresno and Valley Med. Ctr., Fresno 1994–; awards: John A. Morris, MD award, Drew Univ. 1987; Pfizer Scholarship 1988, nominated nat. James H. Robinson, MD Mem. Prizes in Surgery award 1989, recipient Dr. Richard Allen Williams Nat. Scholarship 1990, Best Scientific Paper award Drew Univ. 6th

Annual Sci. Conf. 1990, selected Steven's Who's Who in Health and Med. Svs. 1991, NHLBI award Cleveland Clinic Found. and Am. Heart Assn. 1992; mem: AMA, Assn. of Black Cardiologists, Nat. Med. Assn. NY Acad. of Scis., UCLA Sch. of Public Health Dean's Council; co-editor: Health Transition: UCLA Sch. of Public Health Jour. 1985; co-author, abstracts and papers presented at profl. soc. conferences, 1986-93; contbr. num. articles to sci. jours., 1987-93. Address: Clovis 93612

FERNANDEZ, FERNANDO LAWRENCE, company president; b. Dec. 31, 1938, New York; s. Fernando and Luz Esther (Fortuno) F.; m. Carmen Dorothy Mays, Aug. 26, 1962; children: Lisa Marie b. 1963, Christopher John b. 1965; edn: ME, Stevens Inst. Tech. 1960; MS, 1961; PhD, Cal Tech Pasadena 1969. Career: thermodynamicist Lockheed Missiles, Sunnyvale 1963-65; div. and dept. mgr. Aerospace Corp., El Segundo 1965-72; program mgr. R&D Assoc., Santa Monica 1972-74; v.p. Physical Dynamics, La Jolla 1974-76; pres. Arete Assoc., Sherman Oaks 1976-93; pres. Arete Engring. Tech. Corp. 1993-; cons. to chief of naval ops. USN, Wash. D.C. 1983-; naval studies bd. 1986; DARPA Dept. of Defense 1980-89; rec: bicycling, skiing. Res: 2159 El Amigo Rd Del Mar 92014 Ofc: Arete Engring. Tech. Corp. POB 8050 La Jolla 92038

FERRILL, V. MIKKI, photographer, photojournalist; b. May 12, 1937, Chgo.; d. Edward R. and Gladys Marie (Black) F.; edn: Wilson Jr. Coll., Chgo. 1957-60, Chicago Art Inst., 1960-63. Career: staff photog. assignments: Mexico This Month; photog. asst. to Ted Williams; Astra Photo Service; black and white printer, Chgo.; Let's Save The Children Pub. Co.; Sigma Photo Agency; SCLC; Photo Cell Inc.; Phototechtronics Inc.; current free-lance in b&w color illstrn., ednl. media, filmstrips, textbooks, and documentary journ.; lectr., workshops Malcolm X Coll., guest lectr. Northeastern Univ. Inner City Studies, Chgo.; instr. Cook County Jail, Urban Gateways Artist-In-Residence Pgm., Chgo.; vis. prof. Calif. Coll. of Arts & Crafts; graphic cons.; works appeared in nat. and internat. magazines and newspapers incl. Life, Time, Chicago Tribune, Chicago Defender, Muhammad Speaks, Ebony, Jet, Institutions, Downbeat, What It Is, Chicago Urban League Newsletter, Muzkiki Pub. Co., Matanan Pub. Co., Knees Pub. Co., Mousenik Pub. Co., Design and Environment, The Woodlawn Org., Photo Cell Inc., U.S. Commn. on Civil Rights, U.S. Embassy, Black Photog.'s Annual, Vols. I and II, Standard Oil, Scott Foresman Pub. Co., Noble Advt., Doyle Dane & Bernbach, Mexico This Month, Burda Publs., Chicago Mag., Pamoja Mag., Black Bus. & Profl. Women, BART, UC Berkeley Alumni House, East Bay Municipal Dist., San Francisco Examiner, Image Mag., Oakland Tribune, Ten 8 Mag.; exhibits: New World (Dis)Order at Ctr. for the Arts, Yerba Buena Gardens, S.F.; one woman show and group exh. Sheppard Gal., Chgo., South Side Comm. Art Ctr., Chgo., Lincoln Center, NY, Ea. Wash. State Coll., Mus. of Sci. & Ind., Chgo., Evanston (Ill.) Art Ctr., B&W Photog. Exh. U.S.S.R., Black Photog.'s Annual, NY, Mus. of Modern Art, S.F., Onyx Gal. Jazz Photo Exh., NY, William Grant Still Comm. Art Ctr., LA, Kenkiliba House, NY, Cinque Gal., Studio Mus. of Harlem, NY, Camera Works, London; rep. in permanent collections: C.N. Gormann Mus. of UC Davis; The Blues Aesthetic, Traveling Show, Wash. Projects of the Arts, WDC. Mail: PO Box 4060 Berkeley 94704 Ph:510/533-0911

FIDLER, RONALD W., lawyer; b. April 3, 1932, Moberly, Mo.; s. Eldon Herbert and Mae (Roberson) Coyner F.; m. Maureen P. Richardson, Nov. 25, 1959 (div. 1977); Linda P. Pieri, Aug. 19, 1977; children: Denise b. 1960, Paul b. 1962; edn: BA, Central Methodist Coll. 1954; Univ. Okla. 1957-59; JD, UCLA 1962; admitted St. Bar Calif. 1963, U.S. Dist. Ct. for So. Dist. of Calif. 1963. Career: research asst. US Dist. Ct. Appeals, 2d Dist., Los Angeles 1962-63; atty. Brody Grayson & Green 1963; sr. trial atty. Early Maslach Form & Williams 1963-73; ptnr. Fidler, Bell, Orrock & Watase, Riverside 1973-; honors: Tau Beta Pi, Sigma Tau, SEA scholarship (1958); Diplomate, Am. Bd. Trial Advocates; mem: Am. Bar Assn., L.A. Co. Bar Assn., K.C. (grand knight), Valley Dolphins Youth Football (coach, pres., treas., athletic dir.); article pub. in profl. jour. (1986); mil: 1st lt. USMC 1954-57; Republican; Cath.; rec: coaching football. Res: 3003 Greentree Ct Bel Air 90077 Ofc: Fidler, Bell, Orrock & Watase 2000 Market St Riverside 92501

FIELDS, MARK STEPHEN, acupuncturist; b. April 8, 1949, Chicago, Ill.; s. Harry Carter and Mary Louise (Kinney) F.; m. Adelyn R. Sept. 26, 1993; edn: BA, CSU Dominguez Hillls 1971; MS, Univ. Oreg. 1974; PhD, UC Davis 1974-78; BS, SAMRA Univ.; cert. acupuncturist (1983). Career: dir. Health Enhancement Center, Santa Cruz 1979-81; instr. SAMRA Univ., Los Angeles 1983-84; acupuncturist Pain Mgmt. Group, Long Beach 19885-86; East-West Clinic, Los Angeles 1985-86; Mark Fields Acupuncture Clin., Sacto. 1986-; mem: Calif. Acupuncture Assn. (chpt. rep. 1985-); rec: tennis, racquetball, wind surfing. Ofc: Mark Fields Acupuncture Clinic 87 Scripps Dr Ste 306 Sacramento 95825

FIELDS, NINA S., clinical social worker; b. New York; d. John and Gladys Marshall (Salit) Shepard; m. Maurice Fields, Mar. 23, 1952; children: Abbie b. 1957, Laura b. 1959, Kenneth b. 1961; edn: BA, Roosevelt Univ. 1953; MSSA, Case Western Reserve 1956; PhD, Calif. Inst. Clin. Social Work 1979. Career: pvt. practice, Encino 1960-; cons. editor, NASW Jour. "Social Work"; lectr. UCLA Ext. 1979-, Northridge Hosp. 1980-, Reiss-Davis Seminars, Los Angeles 1980-; honors: Psi Chi; chairperson, San Fernando Valley Child Guidance Clinic Profl. Adv. Bd. (v.p. bd. trustees); mem: Inst. Clin. Social Workers (trustee, treas., pres. 1989-91), Nat. Assn. Social Workers (Diplomate); author: The Well-seasoned Marriage, 1986; article pub. in profl. jour. 1983. Ofc: 5353 Balboa Blvd Ste 311 Encino 91316

FIELER, JAMES H., advertising executive; b. Nov. 9, 1942, Cincinnati, Ohio; s. Howard William and Evelyn (Lehmkuhl) F.; m. Margaret Mary Pope, June 28, 1969; children: Sean b. 1972, Erin b. 1976; edn: Cincinnati Art Acad. 1961-62; BS advt., Univ. Cincinnati 1968; Univ. Md. 1971. Career: exec. Ford Motor Co., Dearborn, Mich. 1966-68; account exec. Young & Rubicam, Detroit, Mich. 1968-70, WDC 1970-72, office head, S.F. 1972-79; pres., owner AIM Inc., Foster City 1979-91; chmn. coll. fund review Menlo Sch. & Coll., Atherton 1987-88; pres. A & M, Foster City 1992-94; awards: City of Foster City Design 1977, Chrysler Plymouth Advt. 1976, Dandy Nat. Advt. award 1978; mem: Foster City Townhomes (pres. 1976), No. Chrysler Plymouth Dealers (com. 1972-89, adminstrn. 1979-89), Rotary, BSA (chmn. Belmont 1976-77), St. Lukes Fundraiser (co-chmn. 1987), Concours Lyons; author: Autobile Mktg. 1980; Republican; R.Cath.; rec: art, golf, tennis. Res: 308 Pompano Circle Foster City 94404

FIFE, LORIN MERRILL, III, lawyer; b. Aug. 25, 1953, Los Angeles; s. Lorin M., Jr. and Marian Ruth (Stromwall) F.; m. Linda Suzanne Schein, June 22, 1975; children: Yoni b. 1979, Ari b. 1983; edn: BS, US Naval Acad., 1975; JD, USC, 1983. Career: midshipman, ofcr. US Navy, 1971-78; English tchr. Ulpan Amerikai, Tel Aviv, Israel 1979, data analyst Israel Ministry of Commerce, 1979-80; law clk. Donovan Leisure Newton & Irvine, L.A. 1980-82; atty., assoc. O'Melveny & Myers, L.A. 1983-89; dir., sr. v.p. and general counsel SunAmerica Life Companies (SunAmerica Life Ins. Co., Anchor Nat. Life Ins. Co., First SunAmerica Life Ins. Co.), v.p. and general counsel-regulatory affairs SunAmerica Inc. (formerly Broad Inc.), L.A. 1989-; dir. Aurora Nat. Life Assurance Co. (formerly Exec. Life Ins. Co.) 1994-95; mem.: Nat. Alliance of Life Cos. (inv. com., 1990-), Conf. of Ins. Counsel, Calif. 1989-, Assn. Calif. Life Ins. Cos. (exec. com. 1992-), mem. advy. com. Ins. Commr. John Garamendi Calif., 1990-94, Assn. of Life Ins. Counsel 1992-; awards: USC Law Ctr. moot ct. honors, best brief 1982, merit scholar, Legion Lex fellow 1981-83, Fellow of Life Mgmt. Inst. 1994-; mem.: Calif. State Bar (insurance law com., chmn. investments subcom. 1991-94), L.A. County Bar Assn. (intl. law sect. exec. com. 1987-89), Adat Ari El, North Hollywood (v.p., dir. 1987-); author: pub. articles in Municipal Fin. Jour., 1985-87, Urban Lawyer, 1986; Jewish; rec: reading, politics, sports. Ofc: SunAmerica Inc., 1 SunAmerica Ctr, Century City, Los Angeles 90067-6022

FILIPOW, LILLY, commercial photography company executive; b. Oct. 20, 1951, Chicago, Ill.; d. Wladimir and Galina Filipow; m. Richard Ran, Jan. 14, 1950; 1 dau., Sofia b. 1984; edn: Univ. Kans. Career: mgr. Herb Lubaun Inc., N.Y.C. 1970-75; Pushpin Studio 1975-78; exec. recruiter Jerry Fields Assn. 1978-84; owner Ace Repping Co. 1984-85; gen. mgr. Image Bank West, Los Angeles 1985-92, artist relations mgr. 1992-; cons. ASMP and APA 1985-; speaker APA and schs. 1985-; mem: Art Dirs. Club Calif., Art Dirs. Club N.Y., Hollywood C.of C., ASMP, APA; Russian Orthodox. Ofc: The Image Bank One Sansome Street #2100 San Francisco 94104

FILNER, BOB, congressman; b. Sept. 4, 1942, Pittsburgh, Pa.; s. Joseph H. and Sarah F. F.; m. Jane P. Merrill, Dec. 29, 1985; children: Erin b. 1969, Adam b. 1973; edn: BA, Cornell Univ. 1963; MA, Univ. Delaware 1966; PhD, Cornell Univ. 1973. Career: prof. history San Diego St. Univ. 1970-92; legislative asst. U.S. Senate, Wash. D.C. 1974-75; mem. San Diego Bd. Edn. 1979-83, pres. 1982; spl. asst. U.S. House of Representatives, Wash. D.C. 1984; city councilman City of San Diego 1987-93, dep. mayor 1991; mem. 103rd Congress from 50th Calif. dist. 1993-; chmn. Schs. of Future Commn. 1986-87; mem. Regional Employment Tng. Consortium 1987-91; San Diego Housing Commn. 1987-91; awards: SDSU Outstanding History Prof. 1981; mem: San Diego Urban League, San Diego City Club, San Diego Navy League, Lead Alumni, Sierra Club; articles pub. in profl. jours., 1976-. Ofc: US House of Representatives 504 Cannon Washington DC 20515-0550

FIMMEL, RICHARD OSCAR, research scientist/spacecraft missions executive; b. Nov. 29, 1924, Somerville, N.J.; s. Gustav Adolf and Olga (Harmel) F.; m. `Judy' Edeltraud Anna Franke, May 15, 1946; children: Richard Roy b. 1950, Sandra Ileen b. 1953; edn: BS in E.E., MS in E.E., Rutgers Univ., 1949, 1954. Career: research assoc. Rutgers Univ., 1949-51; supr. electronic engr. Evans Signal Lab, Neptune, N.J. 1951-56; sect. chief U.S. Army Signal Research & Devel. Lab, Ft. Monmouth, N.J. 1956-60; mgr. computer products dept. Ampex Internat., Redwood City, Ca. 1960-63; Pioneer project sci. chief NASA- Ames Research Ctr., Moffett Field, Ca. 1963-80, Pioneer missions mgr., 1980-; awards: spl. achiev. NASA-Ames Res. Ctr. (1973, 86), exceptional svc. medals NASA (1974, 80), group achiev. NASA, Wash. DC & Moffett Field (6), superior perf. Ames Res. Ctr. 1986; civic: Los Altos Sister Cities Inc. (bd. 1988-); author 4 books: Pioneer Odyssey, Encounter with a Giant, 1974, Pioneer Odyssey, 1977, Pioneer, First to Jupiter, Saturn & Beyond, 1980, Pioneer

Venus, 1983, booklet: The Space Pioneers & Where They Are Now, 1987; mil: T5 US Army Air Corps 1943-47; Republican; Presbyterian; rec: piano & organ, photog. Res: 12350 Hilltop Dr Los Altos Hills 94024 Ofc: NASA-Ames Research Center MS244-14 Moffett Field 94035

FINDLEY, GERALD LEE ELMER, banking consultant; b. Oct. 27, 1920, Truman, Ark.; s. Burl Clinton and Gertrude A. (Tolar) F.; m. Myrtle L. Royer, June 11, 1948; children: Melinda Ann, b. 1952; Gary Steven, b. 1954; Pamela Ann, b. 1956; edn: BS, UCLA 1949, MBA, 1950; Public Acct., State of Calif. 1951. Career: mgr. Research Engring. Dept. Union Bank, Los Angeles 1950-4; mgr. Spl. Projs. Dept. Calif. Bank, L.A. 1954-5; West Coast regl. mgr. Cunneen Co., L.A. 1955-6; pres./owner Gerry Findley & Assoc., Temple City 1956-81; pres./owner Gerry Findley Inc., Brea 1981–; editor The Findley Reports, 1965-92; ed. newsletters: California Banking, 1975-92, Directors' Compass, 1979-92; instr. Univ. Calif. Ext. comml. fin. & factoring, 1952-4; mem: USS Maryland Assn.; Pearl Harbor Survivors Assn.; Masons; Shriners; author: Mergers & Acquisitions of California Banks, (4 vols.) 1955-75; Get Richer - Own the Local Bank, 1978; The Buying and Selling of Banks & Bank Holding Cos. 1981; Promises Kept (autobiog., 1986); author: California Banking - In Pursuit of Premier Performances, 1988; mil: Chief Quartermaster (permanent), USN 1939-45, GCM, Bronze star, Am. Defense, Bronze Letter-A, Am. Cmpgn., Asia-Pac. Cpgn., WWII Victory medals; Republican; Methodist; rec: collector miniatures, buttermolds, Early Am. paintings. Address: Gerry Findley, 169 N Morning Glory St Brea 92621

FINE, RICHARD ISAAC, lawyer; b. Jan. 22, 1940, Milwaukee; s. Jack and Frieda F.; m. Maryellen Olman, Nov. 25, 1982; dau. Victoria Elizabeth; edn: BS, Univ. Wis. 1961; JD, Univ. Chgo. 1964; PhD internat. law Univ. London 1967; cert. Hague Acad. Internat. Law, Netherlands 1965, 66; cert. comparative law Internat. Univ. Comparative Sci., Luxembourg 1966; dipl. superiere Faculte Internat. pour l'Enseignment du Droit Compare, Strasbourg, Fr. 1967; admitted bar: IL 1964, DC 1972, Calif. 1973. Career: trial atty. fgn. commerce sect. antitrust div. U.S. Dept. Justice, 1968-72; chief antitrust div. Los Angeles City Atty.'s Office, also spl. counsel gov. efficiency com., 1973-74; prof. internat., comparative and EEC antitrust law Univ. Syracuse (N.Y.) Law Sch. (overseas program), summers 1970-72; pvt. practice Richard I. Fine and Assocs., Los Angeles 1974; mem. antitrust advy. bd. Bur. Nat. Affairs 1981–; chmn. L.A. advy. com. London School of Economics, 1992–; mem. vis. com. Univ. Chicago, 1992–; mem: ABA (chmn. subcom. internat. antitrust and trade regulations, internat. law sect. 1972-77, co-chmn. com. internat. econ. orgn. 1977-79), Am. Soc. Internat. Law (co-chmn. com. corp. membership 1978-83, corr. ed. Internat. Legal Materials 1983-, mem. exec. council 1984-87, budget com. 1992–, reg. coord. for Los Angeles 1994, 1995 annual prog. com. 1994-), Am. Fgn. Law Assn., Internat. Law Assn., Brit. Inst. Internat. and Comparative Law, Calif. Bar Assn. (chmn. antitrust and trade reg. law sect. 1981-84, exec. com. 1981-88), Retinitis Pigmentosa Internat. (bd. dirs. 1985-90), Los Angeles Cty. Bar Assn. (chmn. antitrust sect. 1977-78, mem. exec. com. internat. law sect. 1993-), IL Bar Assn., Am. Friends London Sch. Econ. (bd. dirs. 1984-, cochmn. S. Calif. chpt. 1984–), Am. Trial Lawyers Assn., Phi Delta Phi; publs. in legal jours. Address: 10100 Santa Monica Blvd Ste 1000 Los Angeles 90067

FINEFROCK, JAMES ALAN, journalist, editor; b. May 4, 1947, Bellefontaine, Ohio; s. Richard Harvey and Mary Jane (Smith) F.; m. Diane Curtis, Oct. 31, 1981; children: Jessica b. 1982, John b. 1987; edn: AB, Princeton Univ.; fellow Journalists in Europe, Paris, Fr. Career: reporter South San Francisco Enterprise-Journal, 1971; reporter San Francisco Examiner, 1972-82, investigative editor 1982-87, metro editor 1987-89, op-ed editor 1989-91, editor of editorial pages 1991–; honors: Silver Gavel award Am. Bar Assn., W.D.C. (1986, 87), Mark Twain award AP 1979, Best story Investigative Reporters and Editors, Columbia, Mo. 1986. Ofc: San Francisco Examiner 110 Fifth St San Francisco 94103

FINERMAN, MATTHEW LAWRENCE, physician; b. July 4, 1951, Los Angeles; s. Wilmore Bernart and Muriel Ruth (Weinstein) F.; m. Jill Radin; edn: BA, UCLA 1973; MD, Loyola Stritch Univ. 1976. Career: resident UCLA 1976-81; pvt. practice, Los Angeles 1981–; chief otolaryngology Calif. Med. Center, Los Angeles; asst. clin. prof. UCLA; honors: Phi Eta Sigma (pres. 1972-73), UCLA Clin. Prof. of Year Head & Neck Surgery (1983-84); mem: AMA, CMA, L.A. Co. Med. Assn., Am. Acad. Otolaryngology Head & Neck Surgery (fellow); article pub. in med. jour. (1984); rec: travel. Res: 605 N Trenton Dr Beverly Hills 90210 Ofc: 1245 Wilshire Blvd Ste 603 Los Angeles 90017

FINGARETTE, HERBERT, philosopher, educator; b. Jan. 20, 1921, New York; m. Leslie Swabacker, Jan. 23, 1945; 1 dau., Ann b. 1947; edn: BA, UCLA 1947; PhD, 1949. Career: instr., prof. UC Santa Barbara 1948–; spl. asst. to pres. UC Berkeley 1971; cons. World Health Orgn. Alcohol & Drug Addiction, Wash. D.C. 1980; vis. fellow Center for Addiction Research 1978; awards: Harvard Univ. William James lectr. in Religion 1971, Stanford Univ. Evans Wetz lectr. 1977, Dartmouth Univ. Gramlich lectr. 1978, Phi Beta Kappa; mem: Am. Philosophical Assn. Pacific Div. (pres. 1976-77); author 7 books, including: Self in Transformation, 1963, Self-Deception, 1971, Heavy Drinking, 1988; mil: lt. AUS 1943-46. Ofc: Philosophy Dept. Univ. Calif. Santa Barbara 93106

FINK, BARRY EVAN, lawyer; b. Nov. 22, 1938, Bay City, Mich.; s. Louis Russell and Ida Carol (Meyers) F.; m. Arlene, June 24, 1962; children: David b. 1966, Steven b. 1969; edn: BS in commerce, De Paul Univ., 1960; JD (honors), Univ. Chgo. Law Sch., 1963; C.P.A., Ill. 1963) admitted bar: Ill. 1963, Dist. Col. 1968, Calif. 1969, U.S. Supreme Ct., and var. Fed. Cts. Career: clk. to Hon. Richard B. Austin, U.S. Dist. Ct., No. Dist. Ill., also faculty John Marshall Law Sch., Univ. Chgo., 1964-66; trial atty. Tax Div., U.S. Dept. of Justice, Wash. DC, 1966-69; atty., sr. ptnr. Christensen, White, Miller, Fink & Jacobs, Los Angeles, (specialize in taxation, transactional and internat. law); mem: Am. Bar Assn., Bar Assns. of Dist. of Col., Ill., Calif., Los Angeles County, and Beverly Hills, Am. Inst. of CPAs; civic: Arrowhead Lake Assn. (pres. 1985-87), advisor L.A. Co. Sheriff's Dept., past mem. Pres. Carter's Tax Advy. Com., active numerous charitable orgs.; lectr. Calif. Continuing Edn. of the Bar (CEB), contbg. author "Advising California Partnerships" CEB (1988), contbg. author "USC Tax Inst. (1987, 89); Res: Pacific Palisades Ofc: Christensen, White, Miller, Fink & Jacobs, 18th Flr 2121 Avenue of the Stars Los Angeles 90067

FINK, HOWARD JOEL, financial services executive; b. Aug. 4, 1944, Los Angeles; s. Irving Isadore and Ruth (Alexander) F.; m. Hanne Brurberg, May 21, 1966; children: Pauline, b. 1966; Lisa, b. 1969; Vikki, b. 1971; edn: bus. acctg. courses, L.A. Valley Coll. 1962-66; CLU Am. Coll. 1981; Registered Financial Cons. 1985. Career: dist. sales mgr. (13) stores Firestone Tire and Rubber Co., 1966-72; insurance industry, 1973–; pres. PFP Fin. & Ins. Services Inc., 1977–; pres. Fin. Mgmt. Services, Inc. 1989–; Registered Principal NASD 1987; moderator Life Underwriters Tng. Council, 1982; chmn. advy. bd. Security Life of Denver, 1991-94; awards: sales mgr. of the yr., Pacific Mutual (1979); mem.: Million Dollar Round Table (Kt.), Internat. Assoc. of Profl. Financial Cons., Estate Counselors Forum in Bev. Hills (pres. 1990-91), S.F.V. Life Underwriters, UCLA Chancellor's Associates, Valley Industry & Commerce Assoc. (VICA); rec: golf, tennis. Res: 24537 Peachland Ave Newhall 91321 Ofc: Financial Management Services, Inc. 17750 Sherman Way Reseda 91335

FINK, STUART HOWARD, certified public accountant; b. Dec. 13, 1948, New York; s. Arthur Milton and Mollie (Wrubel) F.; m. Robin Heather Heacock, Aug. 25, 1984; children: Laura b. 1987, Allison b. 1992; edn: BA cum laude, acctg., Queens Coll., N.Y. 1970; MBA fin., Univ. Rochester Grad. Sch. Mgmt 1972; MBA taxation, Golden Gate Univ. 1986; C.P.A., N.Y. 1975, Calif. 1979. Career: sr. accountant Brout & Co., N.Y.C. 1972-78; audit review mgr. Grant Thornton, San Francisco 1978-82; acctg. tax mgr. Jones Schiller & Co. 1982-92; self-employed C.P.A. 1992–; Credit Grantors Com., Calif. Soc. CPA 1980-83; awards: Outstanding Young Men Am. 1985, Arista Hon. Soc. 1965, N.Y. Regents scholarship 1965, Dean's List 1968; mem: Am. Inst. CPA, Calif. Soc. CPA, Commonwealth Club, Stonegate Terrace Homeowners Assn. (pres. 1983-84), Jewish Comm. Red. Social Com., San Francisco Fair (vol. 1983, 85), March of Dimes (vol. 1985); Democrat; Jewish; rec: bicycling, walking, writing. Res: 19715 Michaels Ct Castro Valley 94546

FINKEN, MARJORIE MORISSE, restaurant columnist; b. June 29, 1918, St. Louis, Mo.; d. William J. and Alice (Seidler) Morisse (O'Hern); gr.granddau. of Ferdinand Diehm, 1842-1916, Imperial and Royal Consul of Austria-Hungary in St. Louis, Mo. 1882-1915; grandniece of Albert Diehm, apptd. food admr. two Ill. counties by Pres. Hoover, 1914-18; bro. Richard Diehm Morisse (dec. 1968), aud. of USC, 20 years; m. John W. Finken, Apr. 26, 1940, div. 1957; 1 son Richard Dale, b. 1943; edn: grad. Los Angeles H.S. 1936; stu. dress design Chouinard Inst. of Art 1937-38; art maj., L.A. City Coll. 1938-40. Career: profl. photographer; freelance photog. and rep. Daily Breeze/News Pilot, 1956–, Copley L.A. Newspapers; restaurant ed. 1956-86, columnist: Munchin' with Marge 1956–; Marge to Midnight 1956-84; apptd. Calif. Rec. Commnr., Manhattan City Sch. Adminstr. 1954-60; awards: first Rose & Scroll, Manhattan Bch C.of C., 1954; mem: Phi Epsilon Phi (secty.-treas. L.A. chpt. 1942-43, 44-45), So. Bay Sym. Assn. (pub. chmn. 1954-55), So. Bay Comm. Arts Assn. (pub. chmn. 1954-56), Women of Moose Lodge No. 323 (secty. 1957-59), South Bay Hosp. Aux. (charter secty., dir. 1959-61), Greater L.A. Press Club, Calif. Press Women (bd., L.A. chpt.), Restaurant Writers Assn. (secty. L.A. Co. 1967-70), Calif. Restaurant Writers Assn. (pres. 1977-79), Los Angeles Mus of Art, Altrusa Internat. Inc. (pres. Redondo Beach chpt. 1983-85), Internat. Brotherhood of Kts. of the Vine (1986–), Greater Los Angeles Press Club (bd. dirs. 1995); rec: theater, concerts, art. Res: 223 Ave F Redondo Beach 90277 Ofc: Daily Breeze, 5215 Torrance Blvd Torrance 90509

FINN, SARA, public relations firm president; b. Cincinnati, Ohio; edn: BA in English, Maryville Coll., St. Louis. Career: advtg. and pub. relations rep. San Diego Magazine, 1964-71; dir. pub. relations Univ. San Diego, 1971-1987; founder/pres. Sara Finn Public Relations, 1987, pres. Finn/Hannaford, a division of The Hannaford Co., W.D.C. 1987–; honors: Internat. Papal Soc., Equestrian Order of the Holy Sepulchre (Pope John Paul II 1982, elevated to Lady Comdr. with Star, 1988); mem: Public Relations Soc. of Am. (APR, accredited mem.) PRSA Counsellors Acad., San Diego Press Club, Alumnae of the Sacred Heart (nat. pres. 1979-81), AASH; civic: Women Together, Sister City San Diego/Tijuana, Inst. Latin Professionals; Partners for Livable Places (pres.), San

Diego C.of C., San Diego Mus. of Art; R.Cath./All Hallows Ch. La Jolla; rec: travel, painting. Res: La Jolla Ofc: Sara Finn, APR, 7817 Ivanhoe Ave Ste 300 La Jolla 92037 Tel: 619/454-1128

FINNEY, J. SPURGEON, community leader, retired corporate financial executive; b. June 7, 1907, Omaha, Neb.; s. Charles Spurgeon and Ora Jean (Stephenson) F.; m. Mildred Elise Bostwick, March 3, 1932; children: Carleen b. 1934, Lynda b. 1937, MaryLou b. 1945, James b. 1946; edn: BA, UCLA, 1930, grad. Exec. Program, UCLA, 1958-59. Career: acct. The Texas Co., Los Angeles 1930-37; office mgr. The Ediphone Co., L.A. 1937-38; asst. chief acct. M.G.M. Studios, Culver City 1938-45; fin. v.p. Bell Brand Foods Inc., Santa Fe Springs 1945-70; corp. secty., treas. Tom Sawyer Foods Inc., Vernon 1957-59; honors: Fellow of the College, Rio Hondo Comm. Coll. (1976); civic bds: Santa Fe Springs Industrial League (pres. 1959), Santa Fe C.of C. (dir. 1958-59), City of Whittier Personnel Bd. (bd. chmn. 1964-66), Friendly Hills Property Owners Assn. (pres. 1965-66), Rio Hondo Coll. Bd. Trustees (1968-77, pres. 1974-75), Emeriti Assn. Rio Hondo Coll. (pres. 1987-89), Whittier Area School Trustees Assn. (pres. 1972), Presbyterian Hosp. Whittier (dir., v.chmn. 1977-87, dir. emeritus 1987–), Interhealth Corp., Whittier (1983-86, dir. emeritus 1988–), United Way Rio Hondo (dir.), Whittier Rose Float Com. (dir.); mem: Nat. Assn. of Accts. (1949–, pres. L.A. chapt. 1960-61, nat. dir. 1961-62, N.A.A. gen. chmn. So. Calif. Bus. Show, Ambassador Hotel, L.A.), McLeod Soc., Toreador Club, Kappa Sigma, UCLA Club Whittier (pres. 1957, 1972), Lions; club: Friendly Hills CC; Republican; United Presbyterian; rec: golf, swimming. Res: 8612 Enramada Ave Whittier 90605

FISCHER, COLETTE BARBARA, municipal business manager; b. Sept. 22, 1947, Chgo.; d. Aloysius Michael and Ruth Mary (Thomas) Fanning; m. Donald Andrew Walker, Jan. 22, 1968 (div. 1974); m. Robert Eugene Fischer, June 5, 1976; 1 dau., Nicole Marie Fischer b. 1973; edn: Vassar Coll. 1964-66; BS in bus., Calif. Coast Univ., L.A. 1987, MBA, 1990, PhD bus. (cand.). Career: owner, opr. The Bounty Restaurant, Santa Barbara 1976-79, Foremost Dairy 1976-82, The Spur Restaurant 1984-87; bus. office supr. Police Dept. Santa Barbara 1984-85, accts. payable payroll supr. City of Santa Barbara, 1984-87, waterfront bus. mgr., 1987–; Republican; R.Cath.; rec: travel, gourmet cooking, skiing, reading, creative writing. Ofc: 321 E Cabrillo Blvd Santa Barbara 93101

FISCHER, CRAIG LELAND, physician; b. Feb. 17, 1937; s. Emil Carl and Ruth Barbara (Minarcik) F.; m. Sandra L., Feb. 17, 1962; children: Emil Lewis b. 1965, Lisa Anne b. 1968; edn: BS in zool./chem., Kansas State Univ. 1958, MD, Kansas Univ. 1962; Diplomate Am. Board of Family Practice, Cert. in anatomical & clinical pathology, Cert. in nuclear medicine; designated FAA Aviation Medical Examiner 1991–. Career: resident in anatomical pathology (USPHS res. fellow path.) Kans. Univ. Med. Ctr. 1962-64; res. fellow in nuclear medicine Baylor Univ. 1965-66, resident in clin. pathology 1967-68; res. med. ofcr. biomed. res. br. NASA Manned Spacecraft Center, Houston 1965-68; pathologist/chief Preventive Medicine Div., Clinical Laboratories, NASA Manned Spacecraft Ctr., Houston 1968-71, dir. clin. labs. Abbot & Assocs., 1971; chief clin. pathol. Eisenhower Med. Ctr., Rancho Mirage 1971-73, dir. labs./hd. pathol. dept. 1973-78, dir. oncol. & immunol. labs. 1976-78; family practice phys. and pathologist/co-dir. Valley Clin. Labs., Palm Desert 1978-80; chief Med. Ops. Br. NASA, Johnson Space Ctr., Houston 1980-82; assoc.dir. Immunopathol. & Toxicol., Univ. of Tx., Galveston 1980-82; pathologist/dir. clin. labs. John F. Kennedy Memorial Hosp., Indio 1982–, dir. postgrad. med. edn.; med. dir. V-Tech Corp., Pomona 1983-94; pres. Diametrix, Inc., Indio 1985-89; pres. Fischer Associates 1989–; ptnr. Fischer & Starke Assocs., 1995–; honors: distinguished military cadet Kans. St. Univ. 1967, NASA Manned Spacecraft Ctr. achievement awards (8), Presdl. Medal of Freedom, Apollo 13 Mission Ops. Team (4/70), Skylab Med. Team, NASA Johnson Space Ctr. 1974, Space Shuttle Launch & Landing Ops. Team STS-3, NASA 1982, Dept. of the Air Force award for meritorious civilian service 1990; Fellow Coll. of Am. Pathologists (coms.), Am. Soc. Clin. Pathologists (Council on Spl. Topics 1979), Am. Coll. Nuclear Physicians, Am. Pub. Health Assn.; mem. AMA, Riverside County Med. Assn. (councilor 1983–, pres. 1989-90), Aerospace Med. Assn., Soc. of NASA Flight Surgeons (pres. 1991), AAAS, Calif. Soc. Pathologists, Palm Springs Acad. of Medicine (pres. 1988-89), Explorers Club; publs: articles in sci. and aerospace med. jours., NASA tech. reports; mil: lt. col. USAFR, Dept. of Air Force Sci. Advy. Bd. HQ, USAF, Wash. D.C. (1986), Nat. Acad. of Engring., Nat. Research Council, mem. NASA Advy. Council Task Force on Shuttle-MIR Rendezvous and Docking Missions 1995, Nat. Def. Service Medal. Res: 45-800 Cholame Indian Wells 92260 Ofc: 81715 Ste A2 Dr. Carreon Blvd Indio 92201

FISCHER, DALE SUSAN, lawyer; b. Oct. 17, 1951, E. Orange, N.J.; d. Edward LeRoy and Audrey Selma (Tenner) Fischer; edn: BA magna cum laude, Univ. S. Fla. 1977, JD, Harvard Law Sch. 1980. Career: assoc. atty. Kindel & Anderson, Los Angeles 1980-86, ptnr. 1986–; awards: Constitutional Rights Found. Lawyer in Classroom 1981; mem: Am. Bar Assn., L.A. Co. Bar Assn., Orgn. of Women Execs., Faculty Nat. Inst. for Trial Advocacy, judge pro tem Los Angeles Municipal Court, arbitrator, Am. Arbitration Assn. Res: 3695 Hampton Rd Pasadena 91107 Ofc: Kindel & Anderson 555 S Flower St Los Angeles 90071

FISCHER, JEANETTE LUCILLE, occupational therapist; b. Nov. 13, 1937, Albert Lea, Minn.; d. Stewart Joseph and Bessie Lucille (Junk) Stockett; m. Richard Fischer, Oct. 22, 1960; children: Richard Arnold b. 1962, Robert Andrew b. 1966; edn: BS occupational therapy, Washington Univ., 1960; MA in health facility mgmt., Webster Coll., 1981; Reg. Occ. Therapist (OTR) 1960. Career: occupational therapy dept. aide St. Louis (Mo.) State Hosp., 1958-59; dir. psych. occup. therapy Alexian Brothers Hosp., St. Louis, Mo. 1960-61; dir. occup. therapy Americana Healthcare Center, Florissant, Mo. 1975-79; mgmt. cons. Occupational Therapy Consultants, St. Louis 1978-81; chief occup. therapist Physical Medicine and Rehab. Dept., St. Mary's Health Center, 1979-81; dir. occup. therapy Fullerton Care Convalescent Hosp., Fullerton 1981-84; Orange Region coord. Intermountain Health Care, Rehab. Services, Div. Occup. Therapy, Orange 1984-88, regional clinical edn. cons. Therapy Management, (subs. Intermtn. Health Care), 1988-89; OTR prin., co-owner Gerontic Therapy Services, Seal Beach 1989–; instr. Loma Linda Univ. 1994–; mem: Am. Occupational Therapy Assn. (com. of state assn. presidents 1979-81), Occup. Therapy Assn. of Calif. (Gr. Orange Co. chpt. v.p. 1983-84), L.A. Occup. Therapy Director's Forum, Mo. Occup. Therapy Assn. (1960-81, pres. 1980-81, newsletter ed. 1960-62), World Fedn. of Occup. Therapy; civic: Midland Valley Estates Improvement Assn. (dir. 1974-81, pres. 1972-74); publs: 4 profl. papers 1967, 80, 82, 84, speaker and panelist profl. meetings; Lutheran; rec: travel. Ofc: Gerontic Therapy Services, 4217 Elder Ave Seal Beach 90740

FISH, JONATHAN S., corporate financial officer; b. June 6, 1944, Brooklyn, N.Y.; s. James B. F.; m. Wendy W. Weinstein, May 24, 1969; children: Erica A. b. 1973, Warren G. b. 1975; edn: BA, Middlebury Coll. 1966; MBA, Harvard Grad. Sch. of Bus. Adminstrn. 1968. Career: controller, dir. adminstrn. Wickes Homes, 1974-76; asst. to controller Wickes Corp. 1976-77; v.p. adminstrn. Wickes Furniture 1977-78; v.p., treas. Wickes Cos. 1978-82; v.p. fin. United Publishers 1982-88; v.p., treas. Magma Power Co. 1988-90; exec. v.p. fin. Advanced Marketing Services, Inc. 1990–; mil: USN 1968-71; rec: skiing, backpacking, jogging. Ofc: Advanced Marketing Services, Inc. 5880 Oberlin Dr Ste 400 San Diego 92121

FISHEL, HOWARD EDGAR, physician; b. Mar. 3, 1922, Raleigh, N.C.; s. Allen Thurman and Mattie Ann (Eller) F.; edn: BA, Gettysburg Coll. 1945; MD, Temple Univ. Sch. Medicine 1950; dipl. Nat. Bd. Med. Examiners 1951, Am. Bd. Orthopaedic Surgery 1960. Career: intern Los Angeles Co. Gen. Hosp., L.A. 1950-51; gen. surgery resident S.D. Co. Gen. Hosp., S.D. 1952-53, orthopaedic surgery resident 1953-55; children's orthopaedic resident Shriners Hosp., L.A. 1955-56; pvt. practice orthopaedic surgery, Redondo Beach 1956-84; med./legal cons., Carson 1984-91; ret.; cons., tchr. Orthopaedic Hosp., L.A. 1957-70; UCLA/Harbor Med. Center, Carson 1956-70; awards: S. Bay Hosp. Dist. Disting. Pub. Service 1965; mem: AMA, CMA, Western Orthopaedic Assn., Calif. Orthopaedic Assn., L.A. Co. Med. Assn., Am. Acad. Orthopaedic Surgeons (fellow); 6 articles pub. in med. jours. 1954-75; rec: golf, flying, cabinet making. Address: Torrance 90505

FISHER, ALISON LOUISE, program and membership director, government consultant; b. Oct. 25, Fullerton; d. William Herbert and Rosalie (Plotnick) Fisher; edn: BA pub. adminstrn., San Diego St. Univ. 1987. Career: project mgr. Calif. Republican Party, Burbank 1988; chmn. asst. Supr. Susan Golding, San Diego 1989; asst. to Dep. Mayor Wolfsheimer, San Diego 1990; govt. cons. 1990-93; prog. and membership dir. San Diego TMA 1993–; mem: San Diego Jr. C.of C. (past pres.), SDSU Young Alumni; Republican (state & co.); Jewish; rec: softball, golf. Res: 550-210 Camino De La Reina San Diego 92108

FISHER, BRUCE DAVID, teacher, resource specialist, consultant; b. Dec. 24, 1949, Long Beach; s. Oran Wilfred and Irene May (Genero) F.; m. Mindi Beth Evans, Aug. 15, 1976; children: Jenny b. 1982; edn: BA, Humboldt State Univ., 1976, Calif. Std. Elem. tchr. cred., 1976, Learning Handicapped cred., 1977. Career: instructional svs. specialist Blue Lake Elementary Sch., Blue Lake, Calif. 1977-78; resource specialist Fortuna Elem. Sch., Fortuna 1978-82, 3rd Grade tchr. 1982-87, 5th Grade tchr. 1987-92; cons. Learning Mag., Springhouse, Pa. 1991-94; cons. Ctr. for Teaching Resources 1991-92; dir. Whale Celebration, Eureka, 1989-91, co-dir. Redwood Environmental Edn. Fair, 1989-94; cons. PITSCO Sci., 1995; cons. NASA Top Gun Aviation Challenge, 1995 awards: 1994 U.S. Space Found./NASA fellowship, 1993 Newest award NSTA, NASA, NCTM, Calif. Tchr. of the Year, Calif. State Dept. Edn. 1991, Nat. Educators Award, Milken Found., L.A. 1991, Profl. Best Leadership Learning Mag., Pa. 1991, Favorite teacher award ABC-TV, Burbank 1991, Humboldt Co. Teacher of the Year 1991, Disting. Grad. Long Beach Unified 1991, Leadership excellence Calif. Assn. of Sci. Specialists, Long Beach 1990, Excellence in Teaching 1987; mem: CTA, Calif. Sci. Tchrs. Assn., Calif. Assn. Hlth., Phys. Edn., Rec. & Dance; civic: Sequoia Park Zool. Soc. 1987-94, Am. Heart Assn., Spl. Olympics; publs: article in Learning Mag. 1991, coauthor (curriculum): Cardiovascular Fitness 1995, Educational Psychology 1993, Zoo Edn. 1990, Green Box Environmental Edn. 1989, Family Wellness 1988; Democrat; rec: whalewatching, photog., sports, travel. Res: 4810 14th St Fieldbrook 95521

FISHER, DELBERT ARTHUR, academic physician; b. Aug. 12, 1928, Placerville; s. Arthur Lloyd and Thelma (Johnson) F.; m. Beverly Carne, Jan. 1951; children: David b. 1956, Mary b. 1958, Thomas b. 1958; edn: BA, UC Berkeley 1950, MD, UC San Francisco 1953; Diplomate Am. Bd. of Pediatrics 1959. Career: pediatric resident UC San Francisco 1953-55; pediatric endocrinology fellow Univ. Oregon Med. Sch. 1957-60; asst. prof., assoc. prof., prof. of pediatrics Univ. Arkansas Med. Sch. 1960-68; prof. pediatrics UCLA Sch. of Medicine 1968-73, prof. peds. and internal medicine 1973-93, emeritus 1993–, chief Pediatric Endocrinology, Harbor-UCLA Med. Ctr., Torrance 1968-75, research prof. developmental & perinatal biology 1975-85, assoc. chmn. Pediatrics, Harbor-UCLA Med. Ctr. 1974-85, prof./chmn. Dept. Pediatrics, 1985-89, dir. Walter P. Martin Research Ctr., 1987-91; pres. Nichols Institute Reference Laboratories, 1991-93; pres. Nichols Academic Associates, chief sci. ofcr. 1993-94; pres. Corning Nichols Institute Academic Associates, chief sci. ofcr. 1994–; chief editor J. Clin. Endocrinol. Metab. 1978-83, Pediatric Research 1984-89; subspecialty com. Pediatric Endocrinology, Am. Acad. Ped. 1976-79, Written Exam com. 1977-80; author 6 books: Research in Congenital Hypothyroidism (Plenum Press, London, 1989); w/ F. DeLange, D. Glinoer, Pediatric Thyroidology (Karger AG, Basel, 1985); 100+ book chpts.; 400+ sci. articles; research in developmental biology and endocrinology and clin. endocrinology; awards: Phi Beta Kappa 1964, Alpha Omega Alpha 1985, NIH Research career devel. award 1964-68, Am. Acad. of Ped. Research Award 1982, Inst. Med. Nat. Acad. Sci. 1988; mem: W. Soc. for Ped. Research (pres. 1982-83), The Endocrine Soc. (pres. 1983-84), Am. Acad. Pediatrics 1960, Soc. Pediatric Research (v.p. 1973-74), Am. Pediatric Soc. (pres. 1992-93), Am. Thyroid Assn. (pres. 1988-89), Am. Soc. Clin. Invest., Assn. Am. Physicians, Lawson Wilkins Ped. Endocrine Soc. (pres. 1982-83); mil: capt. USAF Med. Corps 1955-57; Democrat; Prot.; rec: indian art collecting, swimming, jogging. Res: 24581 Santa Clara Ave Dana Point 92629 Ofc: Corning Nichols Institute, 33608 Ortega Hwy San Juan Capistrano 92690 also: Walter Martin Research Center, Harbor UCLA Medical Center, 1124 W Carson St Torrance 90502

FISHER, PHILIP A., investment manager; b. Sept. 8, 1907, San Francisco; s. Arthur Lawrence and Eugenia (Samuels) F.; m. Dorothy Whyte, Aug. 14, 1943; children: Arthur b. 1944, Donald b. 1947, Kenneth b. 1950; edn: AB, Stanford Univ., 1927, Stanford Grad. Sch. of Bus., 1928. Career: founder mgr. Fisher & Co., 1931–; author: Common Stock and Uncommon Profits (1958), Paths to Wealth Through Common Stocks (1960), Conservative Investors Sleep Well (1975); served to capt. US Army Air Corps, 1942-45. Ofc: Fisher & Co., 520 El Camino Real Ste 422 San Mateo 94402

FISHER, SEYMOUR, physician, retired; b. Apr. 23, 1907, Chicago, Ill.; s. Mandel and Ida Sarah (Burman) F.; m. Gussie W. Wish, May 1, 1938 (dec. Jan. 7, 1994); children: Ruth Ann b. 1941, Judith Sue b. 1944; edn: BA, Univ. Ill. 1928; MD, Northwestern Univ. 1933. Career: pvt. practice, Chgo., Ill. 1935-38; Ill. Sol and Sail Children's Sch., Normal 1938-40; dir. handicap program St. of Ill., Springfield 1940-41; dir., chief of staff VA Hosps., Indianapolis, Phoenix, S.F. and L.A. 1946-70; cons. Co. of Los Angeles 1970-84; cons. allergy VA Hosp., L.A. 1970-82; mem: Am. Coll. Allergy & Immunology (fellow), A.C.P. (fellow), Am. Coll. Hosp. Adminstrs. (fellow), Assn. Mil. Surgeons (fellow), Am. Acad. Pediatrics (fellow), Masons, Shriners, B'nai B'rith; articles pub. in med. jours 1938-70; mil: Ill. NG 1928-32, AUS 1932-41, col. AUS 1941-46; USAR 1926-64; Democrat; Jewish; rec: lapidary, bridge. Res: 32120 Village 32 Camarillo 93012

FISK, IRWIN WESLEY, writer; b. Nov. 20, 1938, Byers, Kans.; s. Walter Roleigh and Mae Pearle (Irwin) F.; m. Susie Walters, Sept. 9, 1973; children: Mark b. 1968, Paul b. 1970; edn: CSU Los Angeles. Career: asst. exec. dir. Stores Protective Assn., Los Angeles 1964-66; investigator Calif. Dept. Corps., 1966-71, sr. investigator 1971-83, chief investigator, So. Calif. Dist., Calif. Dept. Corps., 1983-92; chief investigator, Calif. Dept. Corps. 1992-94; freelance writer, 1994–; mem. Multistate Law Enforcement Task Force on Fraudulent Telemktg. 1987–; frequent guest speaker comm. colls. and univs., and law enforcement classes; featured guest KWHY-TV, 1986, 87, 88; mem: So. Calif. Fraud Investigators Assn. 1968–, Authors Guild, Nat. Rifle Assn., U.S. Chess Fedn., Masons; publs: articles on white collar crime and business; Republican; rec: ham radio (KC6QJB), genealogy, photog., chess. Res: 374 Malcolm Dr Pasadena 91105

FITCH, JOHN RICHARD, newspaper executive; b. June 1, 1938, Newark, Ohio; s. John Clyde and Mildred Josephine (Nethers) F.; children: Joanne b. 1959, Troy b. 1962, Victoria b. 1968, Valerie b. 1973, Megan b. 1984; edn: Baylor Univ. 1958-59; Imperial Valley Coll. 1962-86. Career: advt. sales Associated Desert Newspapers, El Centro 1960-64, advt. mgr. 1964-65, bus. mgr. 1965-66, gen. mgr. 1966-69, ed., publisher 1976-78, pres., editl. publisher 1988–, pres., exec. bd. mem.; awards: CNPA best editl. cartoon 1981, 83, 84, 85, best editl. page 1978, 1st comml. service 1967, Kiwanis lt. gov. disting. 1982; mem: Regional Econ. Devel. Inc. (founder), Calif. Newspaper Publishers Assn. (bd. mem., govtl. affairs chair), El Centro C.of C. (past pres.), El Centro Kiwanis (past pres.), Kiwanis Div. 31 (lt. gov. 1981-82); mil: airman 2c. USAF 1956-60; Prot.; rec: horse ranching. Res: 903 W McCabe El Centro 92243 Ofc: Imperial Valley Press 205 N 8th St El Centro 92243

FITCH, NOEL RILEY, educator, author; m. Dr. Albert Sonnenfeld, Aug. 23, 1987; 1 dau. Gailyn; edn: PhD, Washington State Univ.; post-doctoral work, Princeton and Yale Universities. Career: lecturer, Univ. of Southern Calif. & prof. American Univ., Paris; awards: fellow N.E.H. 1980-81, listed in Directory of American Scholars, Contemporary Authors, Who's Who in West, Internat. Author and Writers' Who Who; mem: Authors Guild of America, PEN Center-West; author: Anais: The Erotic Life of Anaïs Nin (Boston: Little Brown, 1993; named Outstanding Literary Biography, DLB), Erotique Anaïs Nin (Paris: Filipacchi, 1994; nominated Le Prix des Lectrices de Elle), Anais: Dàs erotische Leben der Anais Nin (Munich: Europaverlag, 1995), Sylvia Beach and the Lost Generation: A History of Literary Paris in the Twenties and Thirties (W.W. Norton, 1983; now in its 11th printing; pub. in Japanese, Spanish, German; named by L.A. Times as one of the five best histories pub. in U.S. 1983), Faith and Imagination: Essays on Evangelicals and Literature (ed. with Richard W. Etulain, Far West Books, 1985), Literary Cafés of Paris (WDC: Starrhill Press, 1989), Hemingway in Paris (London: Thorson, 1989; Dutch trans. 1990), Walks in Hemingway's Paris (St.Martin's Press, N.Y., 1990; Plantin in Europe, 1995), "Djuna Barnes" (American Writers Supplement III; N.Y.: Scribners, 1991), "The Elusive 'Seamless Whole': A Biographer Treats or Fails to Treat Lesbianism" (in Lesbian Texts and Contexts: Radical Revisions; N.Y. Univ. Press, 1990, pp.59-69), "Introduction" (in transition: A Paris Anthology, N.Y.: Doubleday, 1990, pp. 11-16), "The Literate Passion of Anais Nin & Henry Miller" (in Significant Others: Creativity and Intimate Partnership; London: Thames & Hudson, 1993). Res: 11829 Mayfield Ave, Los Angeles 90049 and 74 rue de Sèvres, Paris, France 75007

FITZGERALD, JERRY (JOHN MATHIAS), management consultant; b. April 21, 1936, Detroit, Mich.; s. John Middleton and Jessie Lucy (Call) F.; m. Ardra Elizabeth Finney, Dec. 1, 1962; edn: BS, Engring., Mich. State Univ., 1959; MBA, Univ. Santa Clara, 1964; M.Bus. Econs., Claremont Grad. Sch., 1971, PhD, 1972; CDP (Certificate in Data Processing) 1967, CISA (Certified Information Systems Auditor) 1978. Career: industrial engr. Parke Davis, Detroit 1959-61; stock broker McDonnell & Co., Detroit 1961-62; engr. Lockheed Mis. & Space, Sunnyvale 1962-64; systems analyst Friden, Inc., San Leandro 1964-66; systems analyst UCSF Med. Ctr., San Francisco 1966-69; prof. CSU Pomona, Hayward 1969-74; sr. mgmt. cons. SRI Internat., Menlo Park 1974-77; mgmt. cons./prin. J. FitzGerald & Assoc., Redwood City 1977–; mem: EDP Auditors Assn. (1978–, recipient Joseph J. Wasserman Memorial Award N.Y.`1980), Inst. of Internal Auditors 1977–, Info. Systems Security Assn. 1987–; author six books, 40+ articles; mil: priv. U.S. Marine Corps, 1959. Ofc: Jerry FitzGerald & Associates 506 Barkentine Ln Redwood City 94065-1128 Ph: 415/591-5676

FITZGERALD, JOHN EDWARD, III, lawyer; b. Jan. 12, 1945, Cambridge, Mass.; s. John E. and Kathleen (Sullivan) F.; m. Nancy Sharon Balik, Sept. 23, 1984; edn: BSCE, U.S. Mil. Acad., 1969; JD, Univ. Pa. Law Sch., and MPA, Wharton Sch., 1975. Career: atty., Saul Ewing Remick & Saul, Phila., Pa. 1974-77; atty. Shearman & Sterling, N.Y.C. 1977-78; legal counsel, dir. govt. rels. PepsiCo. Inc., Purchase, N.Y. 1978-82; sr. v.p. Security Pacific Corp., Los Angeles 1982-83; atty. John E. FitzGerald & Assocs., Palm Springs 1983–; adj. prof. law Wharton Sch., Temple Univ., Phila., Pa., Redlands Univ. 1977–; v.p., bd. govs. Desert Hosp. Found., Palm Springs 1988–; v.p. Palm Springs Boys and Girls Clubs; trustee Nat. Council Trustees of Freedoms Found. at Valley Forge; mem: Calif. Bar Assn., N.Y. Bar Assn., Pa. Bar Assn., ATLA, CTLA, Army Athletic Assn.; articles pub. in profl. jours.; mil: capt. AUS 1969-72; rec: sports. Ofc: John E. FitzGerald & Associates 901 E Tahquitz Way Ste A-202 Palm Springs 92262

FITZGERALD, WILLIAM BRENDAN, lawyer; b. May 4, 1936, Waterbury, Conn.; s. Wm. Brendan, Sr. and Margaret (Cunning) F.; m. Teresa Vannini, Oct. 12, 1963 (div. 1980); edn: BA, Yale Univ., 1958; JD, Harvard Univ., 1961; admitted bar: Conn. 1961, Calif. 1985. Career: ptnr. Fitzgerald & Fitzgerald, Waterbury, Conn. 1961-72; ptnr. Carmody & Torrance, Waterbury and New Haven, Conn. 1972-85; ptnr. Haight, Dickson, Brown & Bonesteel, Santa Monica 1985-88; ptnr. Dickson, Carlson & Campillo, 1988–; state trial referee Conn. Superior Ct. 1983-85; mem: Am. Coll. of Trial Lawyers (fellow), Nat. Board of Trial Advocacy (diplomate), Am. Board of Trial Advocates, Am. Bar Assn. (v. chmn. trial techniques com. 1988–), Roscoe Pound Found. (fellow), Conn. Trial Lawyers Assn. (pres. 1985, ed. monthly law report `Forum' 1983-85), Rotary Intl. (fellow); contbr. article in law book "The Trial Masters" (1983); Republican; R.Cath. Res: 979 Bel Air Rd Los Angeles 90077 Ofc: PO Box 2122, 120 Broadway 3rd Fl Santa Monica 90407-2122

FLAMM, DANIEL LAWRENCE, chemical engineer, consultant, educator; b. Sept. 14, 1943 San Francisco, Calif.; s. Gerald R. and Esther Lucile (Zwerling) F.; m. Lois Ellen Canter, Oct. 30, 1965; children: Jonathan, Stephen; edn: BS, math., Mass. Inst. of Tech. 1964; MS, chem. engring., Mass. Inst. of Tech. 1966; ScD, chem. engring., Mass. Inst. of Tech. 1970; reg. profl. engr., Tex. Career: asst. prof., Northeastern Univ., Boston 1969-70; sr. design programmer, Foxboro (Mass.) Co. 1970-72; asst. prof., Tex. A&M Univ., College Sta., Tex. 1972-77; disting. mem. tech. staff, AT&T Bell Labs., Murray Hill, N.J.,1977-89;

McKay lectr. dept. elec. engring, UC Berkeley 1988–; co-founder, Crystalline Materials, Inc. 1989; v.p. for tech., Mattson Technology, Sunnyvale,1991-92; mem., advanced x-ray optics group, Lawrence Livermore Nat. Labs. 1992-93; lectr., cons. in field; chmn, Am. Water Works Assn. Task Force for Standard Methods, Ozone, 1975-85; chmn., Gordon Conf. Plasma Chemistry, 1980; mem. Internat. Union of Pure and Applied Chemistry subcommittee on Plasma Chemistry 1980-87, advy. bd., rev. bd., NSF 1981-83, 88; awards: recipient, Certificate of Recognition, NASA, Moffett Field, Calif. 1978, 79, Thinker award, Tegal Corp., Petaluma, Calif. 1985, Japanese Soc. Promotion of Science Fellowship 3/94-6/94; mem: Am. Inst. of Chem. Engrs., Am. Vacuum Soc., Am. Radio Relay League, Materials Res. Soc., Internat. Soc. for Optical Engring., Sigma Xi, Pi Lambda Upsilon; author, co-editor: Plasma Materials Interaction Series; co-editor: Plasma Diagnostics Vol. I, Discharge Parameters and Chemistry, 1989, Plasma Diagnostics Vol. II, Surface Analysis and Interactions, 1989, Plasma-Surface Interactions and Processing of Materials, 1990; mem. editorial bd. profl. journals; contbg. West Coast features ed., Solid State Tech., 1990–; contbg. ed., Microlithography World, 1992–. Res: 476 Green View Dr. Walnut Creek 94596-5459. Ofc: Univ. of Calif. Dept. Elec. Engring. Berkeley 94720-1330

FLAMM, MELVIN DANIEL, JR., cardiologist, clinical professor of medicine; edn: BA, UCLA 1956; MD, Stanford Univ. Sch. of Medicine 1960; rotating intern Walter Reed Gen. Hosp., W.D.C. 1960-61; honor grad., primary course in aerospace medicine Sch. of Aerospace Medicine, Brooks AFB, Texas 1961; med. resident Stanford Univ. Sch. of Medicine 1964-66, fellow in cardiology 1966-68; cert. Am. Bd. of Internal Medicine 1968, Subspecialty Bd. in Cardiovascular Disease 1970. Career: 2nd lt. to col. USAF Med. Corps 1959-74; cmdr. 408th USAF Dispensary, and flight surgeon 322nd Fighter Interceptor Squadron, Kingsley Field, Ore. 1961-64; cardiologist David Grant USAF Hosp., Travis AFB, Calif. 1968-69, chief of cardiology and dir. cardiology fellowship prog. 1969-74; USAF mil. cons. to the Surgeon Gen. in cardiology and internal medicine 1968-74; special cons. in cardiology for the New Generation of Mil. Hosps. Project 1973-74; cons. in cardiology USAF Hosp. Mather, Mather AFB, Calif. 1975-83; cardiologist, pvt. practice, No. Calif. Cardiology Assocs., Sacramento; clin. instr. in medicine (cardiology) Stanford Univ. Sch. of Medicine 1968-71, clin. asst. prof. (cardiology) 1971-78; clin. asst. prof. of medicine (cardiology) UC Davis Sch. of Medicine 1969-73, clin. assoc. prof. (cardiology) 1986-90, clin. prof. of medicine (cardiology) 1990-; guest lectr. in field, 1969-89; examiner, subspecialty bd. of cardiovascular disease Am. Bd. of Internal Medicine 1971-78; med. dir. cardiac catheterization labs., Sutter Mem. Hosp., Sacto. 1976-92; vis. prof. in cardiology: Nat. Defense Med. Sch., Veterans Gen. Hosp., Taiwan Univ. Sch. of Medicine, Queen Mary Hosp. of Hong Kong Univ. Sch. of Medicine, and Hong Kong Cardiologic Soc. 1978; chmn. and mem. instl. review com. Sutter Comm. Hospitals 1985-93; honors: Phi Beta Kappa 1956, Alpha Omega Alpha 1959, Casimir Funk Award for accomplishment in field of cardiovascular disease, Assn. of Mil. Surgeons of U.S. 1973; mem: Am. Coll. of Cardiology (fellow), Am. Coll. of Physicians (fellow), Am. Heart Assn. (fellow, Council on Clin. Cardiology; chmn. and mem. res. com. and res. allocation com. Golden Empire Chpt.; bd. dirs. Golden Empire Chpt. 1982-83), Am. Fedn. for Clin. Research, CMA (grievance com. 1985-90), AMA, Sacto.-El Dorado Med. Assn.; trustee Sutter Hospitals Found. 1987-89; contbr. 26 articles and 30 abstracts pub. in profl. jours., 1967-89; mil: col. USAF Med. Corps. 1959-74, active reserve 1974-83, ret. reserve 1984. Ofc: Northern California Cardiology Associates 5301 F St Ste 117 Sacramento 95819

FLANAGAN, JAMES HENRY, JR., lawyer; b. Sept. 11, 1934, San Francisco; s. James Henry and Mary Patricia (Gleason) F.; m. Charlotte Anne Nevins, June 11, 1960; children: Nancy, Christopher, Christina, Alexis, Victoria, Grace; edn: BA political sci., Stanford Univ. 1956; JD, 1961; admitted St. Bar Calif. 1962, U.S. Dist. Ct. Calif. 1962, U.S. Ct. Appeals 1962, U.S. Dist. Ct. so. dist. 1964, U.S. Dist. Ct. ea. dist. 1967, Oreg. 1984. Career: assoc. atty. Creede Dawson & McElrath, Fresno 1962-64; ptnr. Pettitt Blumberg & Sherr 1964-75; sole practice, Clovis, 1975-92, North Fork, 1992–; pres. Am. Benefit Development Corp. 1994–; instr. Humpreys Coll. Law 1964-69, adj. Nat. Univ. 1990–, bus. CSU Fresno 1986–; judge pro tem Fresno Co. Superior Ct. 1974-77; gen. counsel Kings River Water Assn. 1976-79; author Calif. Water Dist. Laws 1962; awards: Fresno Jaycees Pres. award 1964; mem: Fresno Co. Rep. Center Com., St. Helens Parish Council (exec. com. 1982-85, chmn. 1985), Fresno Opera Assn. (pres. 1965-69), St. Johns Cathedral Parish Council, Fresno Facts Found. (bd. dirs. 1969-70), Fresno Dance Repertory Assn., St. Anthonys Retreat Center, Three Rivers, Calif. Bar Assn., Oreg. Bar Assn., Fresno Co. Bar Assn., Assn. Trial Lawyers Am., Calif. Trial Lawyers Assn. (pres. Fresno chpt. 1975, 83, bd. of govs. 1990-94), Oreg. Trial Lawyers Assn., Fresno Trial Lawyers Assn., Stanford Alumni Assn. (life, service award), Fresno Region Stanford Club (pres. 1979-80), Celtic Cultural Soc. Central Calif. (pres. 1977-78), Fresno Co. and City C.of C. (chmn. natural resources com. 1977-78, award of merit 1982), Clovis C. of C. (bd. 1980-90), pres. North Fork C. of C. 1993–, Clovis-Big Dry Creek Hist. Soc. (past v.chmn.), Internat. Platform Assn., Phi Alpha Delta, Serra Club (Fresno chpt. pres. 1980-81, v.p. 1986-87), Elks Lodge, Rotary; mil: 1st lt. USMC 1956-59; Republican; Cath.; rec: writing, music, fishing. Res/Ofc: PO Box 1555 North Fork 93643-1555 Tel: 209/877-2677

FLANDERS, ALLEN F., architect; b. Mar. 26, 1945, Paynesville, Minn.; s. Harold E. and Beatrice E. (Schultz) F.; m. Cathleen A. Pomatto, Sept. 13, 1986; children: Derek b. 1974, Lyndsey b. 1988; edn: Bachelor of Architecture, Univ. of Minn., 1969; lic. architect, State of Calif., 1974. Career: draftsman George Mastney Assoc., Minneapolis, Minn., 1967-69; draftsman Carl Schulz Assoc., S.F., Calif., 1972-74; proj. architect H. E. Bermudez Assoc., S.F., 1974-75; proj. architect Hellmuth, Obata, Kassabaum, S.F. 1975-77; pres. Hope Design Group, San Diego, 1977-93; v.p. Coleman Caskey Architects Inc. 1993–; bd. dir. San Diego Taxpayers Assn. 1990-92, San Diego Kiwanis 1991-93, San Diego C.of C. 1991-94; awards: design award, Robert Presley Detention Ctr., AIA, Riverside, Calif., 1986; design award, Bob Wiley Detention Facility, AIA, Visalia, Calif., 1988; mem: AIA 1974–, Am. Correctional Assn. 1980–; civic: Kiwanis Club, San Diego, 1990-93; author publ. article, 1991; mil: lt., USN, 1969-72; rec: travel, woodworking. Ofc: Coleman Caskey Architects Inc. 100 Pacifica Ste 300 Irvine 92718

FLANTER, JILL SELEVAN, entertainer, television show host; b. July 8, 1960, Miami Beach, Fla.; d. Bernard E. and Phyllis Anita (Gordon) Selevan; edn: BA, Univ. Tex., 1982. Career: TV host Palm Springs and Los Angeles, Calif. 1985–, host: The Golf Club, Home View Magazine, Flying Fisherman, Visitors Video, United Artists Entertainment Guide, Hilton Video Magazine, Fashion World, The Silver Strategy; neurolinguistic programming expert Advanced Community Technologies, Glendale 1986–; mem. Internat. Brotherhood Magicians, SAG, AFTRA, Recording for the Blind, Am. Cancer Soc., City of Hope, Concern II; Republican. Ofc: PO Box 46381 Los Angeles 90046

FLEER, JOHN LAWRENCE, lawyer, psychologist; b. Dec. 24, 1951, Council Bluffs, Iowa; s. John Wilhelm and Pearl Marie (Garber) F.; m. Kathleen Daugherty; children: Jason b. 1978, Juna b. 1986, Alex b. 1986, Jake b. 1987; edn: BA, Gustavus Adolphus Coll. 1974; MA, PhD, Univ. of Wyo. 1975, 1979; intern USC, 1977-78; JD, UC Boalt Hall 1981; admitted Calif. Bar 1981. Career: counselor Central Wyoming Counseling Center, Casper, Wyo. 1977; clin. psych. intern L.A. County Med. Center, Los Angeles 1977-78; co-dir. Center for Psycholog. and Legal Research, Berkeley 1979-81; trial atty. Crosby, Heafey, Roach and May, Oakland 1981-86; trial atty. Bjork, Fleer and Lawrence, 1986-91; Fleer & Daugherty, 1991–; law/mental health cons.; legal counsel Rape Crisis Svc. of Central Contra Costa Co. 1984–; awards: NIMH Fellow 1974-75, Nat. Endowment for Humanities Fellow 1976-77; mem: Am. Bar Assn., Calif. Bar Assn.,Am. Psychology-Law Soc., W. Psychol. Assn.; profl. jour. publs. in fields of mental health law, offender rehab., profl. liability and suicide; rec: musician, writer, pub. Istanbul Diary (1981). Ofc: Fleer & Daugherty, 2831 Telegraph Ave Oakland 94609

FLEISCHER, WAYNE NEAL, financial planner; b. Jan. 9, 1945, Pittsburgh, Penn.; s. Benjamin and Edna Leatrice (Krauss) F.; m. Rosemarie, Sept. 2, 1979; children: Jennifer b. 1980, Jonathan b. 1982; edn: MS in Mgt. and MS Fin. Svs., American Coll., Bryn Mawr, Pa.; Cert. Fin. Planner (CFP), Chartered Fin. Cons. (ChFC), Chartered Life Underwriter (CLU); Calif. lic. Life & Disability Analyst, Accredited Tax Advisor, Reg. Tax Interviewer; Enrolled Agt., IRS. Career: senior v.p. Planned Asset Management, Inc.; instr. fin. plnng. practitioner, IAFP, LUTC; honors: Top Ventura Fin. Plnng.; mem: IAFP, VALU, ICFP, Nat. Soc. of Pub. Accts., Nat. EA Soc., Registry of Fin. Plng. Practitioners; author: articles for industry; Republican; rec: flying. Ofc: Planned Asset Management, Inc. 300 Esplanade Dr Ste 907 Oxnard 93030 Tel: 818/708-6888

FLEISCHMANN, ROGER JUSTICE, lawyer; b. Sept. 23, 1934, Buffalo, N.Y.; s. Edwin and Clover (Seelig) F.; m. Martha Ann Stennis, June 29, 1959; children: Roger J. b. 1964, Susan b. 1972; edn: BA magna cum laude, Harvard Univ. 1956; LL.B, Harvard Law Sch. 1959; admitted St. Bar Calif. (1960). Career: assoc. atty. Bledsoe Smith Cathcart, San Francisco 1961-62; Graham & James 1962-67; ptnr. Graham & James 1967-69; ptnr. Fleischmann & Fleischmann 1969–; lectr. internat. comml. transactions Golden Gate Univ. Law Sch., S.F. 1973; mem: Japan Soc. No. Calif. (pres. 1979-81, dir. 1977); author article on Letters of Credit in CEB Publ. on Calif. Comml. Code, article on "U.S. Trade Law Issues Relating to Countertrade" in "Countertrade: Internat. Trade Without Cash" (Harcourt Brace Jovanovich); mil: AUS 1959-60; rec: golf, tennis, swimming. Res: 12 Lower Dr Mill Valley 94941 Ofc: Fleischmann & Fleischmann 650 California St Ste 2550 San Francisco 94108

FLEMING, JOHN GUNTHER, professor of law; b. July 6, 1919, Berlin, Germany; nat. 1974; m. Valerie Joyce Beall, April 16, 1946; children: Anthony P. b. 1947, Barbara b. 1949, Colin b. 1954, Stephen b. 1958; edn: BA, MA, PhD, DCL, Oxford Univ.; LLD, York Univ. 1985. Career: prof., dean Australian Nat. Univ., Canberra 1949-60; prof. law, UC Berkeley Boalt Hall Sch. of Law 1960–; Shannon Cecil Turner prof. of law 1974-90; ed. in chief Am. Jour. Comp. Law 1971-87; mem: Am. Law Inst., Am. Acad. Fgn. Law, Internat. Acad. Comp. Law; author: Law of Torts (8th edit. 1992), Am. Tort Process (1988); mil: British Army 1941-45. Res: 401 Western Dr Point Richmond 94801 Ofc: Univ. of Calif. School of Law Berkeley 94720

FLEMING, RICHARD SCOTT, organization executive; b. Aug. 9, 1947, Oakland, s. William Fleming and Cornelia Burton (Leas) Crowley; m. Eleanor MarieIto, Nov. 21, 1971 (dec. Jan. 3, 1989); children: Cynthia b. 1974, William b. 1978, Kimberly b. 1980, Creed b. 1981;m. Debra Kay Thomson, Feb. 27, 1993; edn: grad. Tennyson H.S., Hayward 1965, att. CSU Hayward 1965-66, Chabot Jr. Coll. 1969-71. Career: deliveryman Allied Meat Service, San Leandro 1970; claims adjuster Calif. State Auto Assn., Hayward 1970-72; life ins. agt. Conn. Mutual, Oakland 1972-83; independent ins. broker, Ceres 1983-84; exec. v.p. Ceres Chamber of Commerce, 1984-85; gen. mgr. Antioch Chamber of Commerce, 1985-90; exec. dir. Livermore Chamber of Commerce, 1990–; recipient numerous Jaycee Awards at dist., state and nat. levels: Calif. Jaycee of Yr. (1981-82, 1983-84), Calif. Jaycee Recruiter of Yr. 1981-82, US Jaycees Hall of Fame (Tulsa, Okla. 1984), outstanding state chaplain US Jaycees 1982-83, Hamilton Award for best v.p. US Jaycees (1983-84); mem: Oakland Magic Circle (pres. 1979-80), Calif. Assn. C.of C. Execs. 1984–, Am. Assn. C.of C. Execs. 1985–, Livermore Rotary 1991–, Masons 1988–, Jaycees 1981–, DAV 1969–, VFW 1969–; mil: cpl. USMC 1966-69, Vietnam Veteran decorated Purple Heart, s/sgt. USMCR 1972-80; Republican (pres. Hayward area YR 1972); Mormon. Res: 479 Stanford Ct Livermore 94550 Ofc: Livermore Chamber of Commerce 2157 First St Livermore 94550

FLETCHER, LOIS LORETTA, real estate broker; b. Sept. 13, 1926, Leflore Co., Okla.; d. Alec L. and Ruth (Cox) Burnett; m. Eugene Fletcher, Nov. 18, 1959; edn: San Diego State 1942-44, Mesa Coll. 1970-72, UC San Diego 1972, City Coll. 1973; desig: GRI, CRS, CRB, CE, Senior Appraiser, Cert. Counselor. Career: asst. librarian National City Public Library 1942, 43; bookkeeper, asst. prop. mgr. Burnett & Horning, National City 1944-55; real estate sales agent, broker, 1955–, broker/owner Fletcher Realty, Smyrna, Ga. 1955-70, San Diego 1970–; real estate exchange splst., author Beginning Exchange Course for R.E. (1977), instr. R.E. exchange courses; awards: 15 plaques for Exchanging, 52 certs. of Merit and Outstanding Service, R.E. Exchangor of the Year, Past Pres.'s Award S.D. Bd. Realtors 1988, B.P.W. Woman of Achievement, Pres.'s Council of Womens Service, Bus. & Profl. Clubs of San Diego 1980, listed Who's Who Creative R.E., Who's Who Repub. Party; mem: NAR, RAP-Realtors Active in Politics (life), NAR Nat. Mktg. Inst., CRS/Certified R.E. Residential Sales Council (So. Calif. Chpt. pres. 1992), Calif. Assn. Realtors (dir. 1978-89, 1992–, v.chair conv. com. 1988, mem. credentials com. and conv. com. 1990–, Living Scholarship estab. in her name 1990, appt. 5-yr. trustee CAR Scholarship Found., state chair Scholarship Trustees 1991), San Diego Bd. Realtors (v.p., exec. com. 1990, and 1978–, v.p. 1984, 1986, pres. 1987, Past Pres.'s Award recipient), San Diego Assn. Realtors (dir. 1992–, election com.), Calif. Womens Council of Realtors (gov. 1983), 99 Club (pres. So. Calif. chpt. 1986), FLI, NCE, WCR, NIREC, NIREA, University Ave Bus. Assn., Paradise Hills- San Diego Planning Com. 1990-91; Republican (life mem. Presdl. Task Force); R.Cath.; rec: oil painting, gourmet cooking, fishing, piano. Ofc: Fletcher Realty 3583 University Ave San Diego 92104

FLIEGE, STEWART EDWARD, educator; b. Oct. 8, 1927, Alhambra; s. J. Stewart and Mary G. (Nysewander) F.; m. Mary Jo Perry, Sept. 1952 (div. 1989); m. Charlayne Rowsell, May, 1995; children: Malcolm b. 1959, Kevin b. 1961, Heather b. 1963; edn: BA, UCLA 1950; MA, PhD, Univ. Mich. 1955; lic. psychologist Calif. (1967). Career: dept. mgr. Rand/SDC, Santa Monica 1955-64; v.p. Computer Sci. Corp., El Segundo 1964-71; UMF Systems, Los Angeles 1971-72; prof. Pepperdine Unv., Malibu 1972–; exec. dir. Calif. Inst. Bus. Mgmt., Los Angeles 1980-90; dir. Computer Scis. Canada, Montreal 1969-71, Computer Scis. Australia, Sydney 1969-71, Computer Scis. S. Africa, Johannesberg 1969-71; chmn. Cory Computer Corp., Newport Beach 1981-82; pres. Westward Travel & Tours Inc., Los Angeles 1973-86; honors: Phi Beta Kappa, Sigma Xi; mem: Am. Psychological Assn., Psychometric Soc., Assn. Computing Machinery; mil: pfc AUS 1945-47; rec: travel, theatre, bridge. Res: 12115 San Vicente Blvd #409 Los Angeles 90049 Ofc: Pepperdine University 400 Corporate Point Ste 369 Culver City 90230

FLINT, ROBERT THOMAS, clinical psychologist; b. Sept. 16, 1935, Los Angeles; s. Thomas and Louise (Jones) F.; m. Winifred Watters, Aug. 29, 1955 (div. 1971); Gayla Kaibel, May 28, 1974 (div. 1990); children: Jerretta Villines b. 1952, Sean b. 1957, Kathleen Deakins b. 1967, Deirdre b. 1969; edn: BA, San Francisco State Coll. 1961, MA, 1963; PhD, Univ. Minn. 1970; lic. psychologist Calif. 1981. Career: res. psychologist Am. Rehab. Found., Mnpls. 1966-68; instr., asst., assoc. prof. Univ. Minn. 1968-77; psychotherapist pvt. practice/v.p. Judson Family Center 1977-80; chief psychol. svcs Ashby Med. Gp., Berkeley, Calif. 1980-83; staff psychol. Paul S.D. Berg and Assocs., Oakland 1983-85; pres. Robert T. Flint, PhD, Psychologist, Concord 1986–; pvt. practice psychotherapy; forensic psychologist, cons. law enforcement agencies; instr. psychol. profl. tng.; awards: spotlight award Minn. Rehab. Assn. 1968, recogn. for contributions to contg. legal edn. Minn. Bar Assn. 1975, recogn. for contributions to law enforcement Internat. Assn. Women Police 1977, Hon. Mem. Juvenile Ofcrs. Assn. 1979; mem: Am. Psychol. Assn., Calif. State Psychol. Assn., Calif. Soc. of Ind. Med. and Surgery (bd. dirs. 1994-95), Internat. Assn. Chiefs of Police (asso. mem.), Minn. Health Careers Council (founder, pres. 1965), Central Contra Costa Co. Rape Crisis Svc. (secty. bd. dirs. 1982-83); 24+ sci. publs., 1966-86; 12 video and film tng. pgms. for law enforcement; mil: yeoman 2/c USN 1954-58; Democrat; rec: gardening. Ofc: Robert T Flint, PhD, Psychologist, 1868 Clayton Rd. Ste 126 Concord 94520

FLOR, LOY LORENZ, chemist, corrosion engineer, consultant; b. Apr. 25, 1919, Luther, Okla.; s. Alfred Charles and Nellie Marguerette (Wilkinson) F.; m. Virginia L. Pace, Oct. 1, 1946; children: Charles b. 1950, Scott b. 1952, Gerald b. 1954, Donna Jeanne b. 1959, Cynthia Gail b. 1960; edn: BA in chem., San Diego State Coll. 194 1; Reg. Profl. Engr., Calif. Career: Helix Water Dist., La Mesa 1947-84, supr. corrosion control 1956-84, chief chemist and supr. of water quality 1963-84; indep. cons., 1984–; mem: Am. Chem. Soc. (chmn. San Diego Sect. 1965), Am. Water Works Assn. (chmn. Water Quality Div., Calif. Sect. 1965), Nat. Assn. of Corrosion Engrs. (chmn. W. Region 1970), Masons; mil: 1st lt. U. S. Army Air Force 194145; Republican; Presbyterian; rec: travel/camping, hiking, swimming.

FLORES, DANIEL ALEXANDER, orthodontist, educator; b. Sept. 25, 1955, Iquitos, Peru; parents: Daniel and Adelina (Grey) F.; m. Lin Diana Day; children: Hayden Alexander b. 199 1, Mackinsie Day b. 1994; edn: BS in bus., DDS, MS in orthodontics, Loma Linda Univ., 1978, 82, 88. Career: dentist pvt. practice, Loma Linda, Calif. 1982-83; orthodontist pvt. practice Riverside, Calif. 1988–, and Fallbrook, Calif. 1990–; dental ofcr. USPHS, Martinsville, Va. 1983-86; asst. prof. orthodontics Loma Linda Univ., 1988–, ETM Advy. Bd. 1992–; reviewer & referee The Angle Orthodontist (jour.) 1981–; cons. REI Associates Inc., Claremont 1988–; awards: Nat. Dean's List LLU 1986-87, Unitek Clinic Award 1988, Nat. Health Service Corp. Scholar 1979-82, BEOG Scholarship grantee, Riverside 1974-78; mem: Fallbrook Village Rotary, Fallbrook C.of C., CDA, ADA, PCSO, AAO, NASDAD, LLU Century Club; thesis: The Fracture Strength of Ceramic Brackets, 1988; pub. article in The Angle Orthodontist (winter 1990), pub. article Deformation of Metal Brackets in The Angle Orthodontist (1994, vol. 64, no. 4); mil: lt. USPHS 1983-88; Republican; Seventh-day Adventist; rec: surfing, sailing, water skiing, snow skiing, biking, travel. Res: 964 Cookie Lane Fallbrook 92028 Ofc: Orthodontic Dept. LLU School of Dentistry, Loma Linda 92350 also: 645 E Elder Ste B Fallbrook 92028-3084

FLORES-ORTIZ, YVETTE GISELE, clinical psychologist; b. Feb. 24, 1952, Colon, Panama; nat. 1980; d. Claudio Angel and Aura María (Perigault) Flores; m. Arthur Ignacio Ortiz, May 5, 1978; children: Xochitl b. 1981, Alejandro b. 1983; edn: BA, UCSB 1973; MS magna cum laude, CSU Long Beach 1975; PhD, UC Berkeley 1982; lic. clin. psychologist Calif. (1987). Career: asst. prof. CSU Long Beach 1975-76; clin. fellow Westside Comm. Mental Health Center, San Francisco 1979-80; psychologist ARC 1980-81; lectr. UC Berkeley 1981-88; asst. prof. John F. Kennedy Univ., Orinda 1983-89; Calif. Sch. Profl. Psychology, Alameda 1987-80; asst. prof. UC Davis, 1989–; cons. Escuela de la Raza, Long Beach 1984-76; Humboldt Co. Schs. 1976-80; Latino Family Alcohol Center, San Francisco 1987–; Inst. Familiar de la Raza 1989–; Inst. for Arts of Living 1988–; honors: Fulbright Scholar to Panama 1994, CSU Long Beach Dean's scholar 1975, UC Berkeley Minority Research fellow 1985-86, Bassta Outstanding Contbn. to Mental Health 1989; mem: Calif. St. Psychological Assn., Nat. Hispanic Psychological Assn., Calif. Assn. Marriage & Family Therapists, Am. Ortho-psychiatric Assn., Contra Costa Co. Mental Health Advy. Bd., Bicultural Assn. Spanish Speaking Therapists & Advocates; 16+ articles pub. in profl. jours. 1982-94; Democrat; R.Cath.; rec: travel, dancing, modern jazz. Ofc: Univ. Calif. Davis Chicano Studies TB 101 1079 Davis 95616

FLOREY, JERRY JAY, aerospace company executive, consultant; b. Apr. 3, 1932, Geddes, S.Dak.; s. Henry Clifford and Lizzie M. Florey; m. Mary E. Richey, Sept. 17, 1955; children: Glenn David, Janet Renee; edn: BS chem. engring., Oregon State Univ., 1955; Cert. in electronics. Career: from res. engr. to engring. supr. Rockwell Internat., Canoga Park 1955-66, sr. project engr. Rockwell Internat., Downey 1966-67, engring. mgr., engring. dir., chief engr. Rockwell Internat., Seal Beach 1967-85, dir. advanced systems, res. and tech. 1985-89; sr. staff mgr. strategic planning/mkt. analysis McDonnell Douglas Space Co., Huntington Beach 1989-95; participant on several industry workshop panels which advised USAF regarding its mil. space systems tech. planning activities; awards: Astronaut Person Achievement award NASA 1969, NASA Cert. Appreciation Marshall Space Flight Ctr., Huntsville, Ala. 1972, Skylab achievement award NASA 1973, AIAA and USAF Recognition of Svc. certs. AFSTC 1985; Fellow AIAA (assoc., bd. dirs. 1993–, nat. space and missile systems tech. activities com. 1989–); mem: Nat. Mgmt. Assn., Nat. Mktg. Soc. Am., U.S. Space Found., BSA (scoutmaster, Costa Mesa 1970), Republican Presidential Task Force. Res: 2085 Goldeneye Pl Costa Mesa 92626

FLYNN, JOHN ALLEN, lawyer; b. Jan. 12, 1945, Riverside, Ill.; s. Wm. and Marian Rae (Gustafson) F.; children: Judson b. 1972, Erin b. 1972; m. Georgette A. Kaleiki, Dec. 31, 1988; edn: AB, Stanford Univ. 1966; JD, UC Hastings Coll. of Law 1969; admitted to State Bar of Calif. 1970, US Dist. Cts., US Ct. of Appeals Ninth Cir. 1970, US Sup. Ct. 1975. Career: partner Graham & James, Attys., San Francisco 1969–; guest spkr., Practicing Law Inst., 'Maritime Personal Injury,' Los Angeles 1980, San Francisco 1982; guest spkr. Lloyd's of

London Press, `Maritime Claims,' S.F. 1984; recipient Am. Jurisprudence Award. in Community Property 1969; mem: Am Bar Assn.; Maritime Law Assn. (Practice and Procedure com. 1983-90, Uniformity of Maritime Law com. 1990–); San Francisco Bar Assn. (chmn. Admiralty Com. 1978–); R.Cath.; rec: golf, swimming. Res: 315 Castle Crest Rd Walnut Creek 94595 Ofc: Graham & James, One Maritime Plaza, Ste 300, San Francisco 94111

FOCH, NINA, actress, educator; b. Apr. 20, 1924, Leyden, Netherlands, nat. 1932; d. Dirk (composer-condr., founder NYC Sym.) and Consuelo (Flowerton) Foch; m. James Lipton, June 6, 1954; m. 2d Dennis R. Brite, Nov. 27, 1959; 1 son, Dirk de Brito; m. 3d Michael Dewell (founder, pres. Nat. Repertory Theatre Found.), Oct. 31, 1967 (div. 1991); edn: Miss Hewitt's Classes, NYC; grad. Lincoln Sch., Columbia Univ. 1939; stu. painting, Parsons Sch. of Design, stu. acting w/ Stella Adler. Career: film actress, 1942-: starred in 18 feature films with Warner Bros., then Columbia Pictures, 24 feature films var. other studios, incl.: Ten Commandments, American In Paris, Executive Suite (Oscar nom.), Spartacus, etc...recently Skin Deep (1989), Sliver (1993), Morning Glory (1993); Broadway stage debut in John Loves Mary, 1947-48, followed by num. stage roles, fund raising tour for Am. Shakespeare Festival, 1967; founder w/ John Housman, The L.A. Theatre Group, now at LA Music Center; sang Anna in The Seven Deadly Sins, S.F. Ballet and Opera, 1966; spl. guest Seattle Repertory Theatre in west coast premiere of Albee's All Over, 1973, and Chekhov's The Seagull, 1974; lead roles in num. TV dramas, 1947–, appearances on all major talk shows; co-host 3 seasons, CBS News series with Walter Cronkite; guest star num. TV series incl. Lou Grant Show (1980 Emmy nom.), series star ABC's Shadowchasers, 1985, and War and Remembrance, 1988; assoc. film dir. The Diary of Anne Frank, 1959; adj. prof. of drama Univ. of So. Calif. 1966-8, 78-80; artist-in-res. Univ. of N.C., 1966, Univ. Ohio, Columbus, 1967, CalTech, 1969-70; sr. faculty Am. Film Inst. Ctr. for Advanced Film Studies, 1974-77; adj. prof. cinema USC, 1987–; founder/tchr. Nina Foch Studio, Hywd 1973–; directors cons. 1982–; mem: Acad. Motion Picture Arts & Scis. (cochair Fgn. Film Award), Am. Cancer Soc. (hon. Crusade co-chair L.A. 1970), Hollywood Acad. of TV Arts & Scis. (gov. 1976-7); rec: cooking, work. Address: Nina Foch Studio, POB 1884 Beverly Hills 90213

FOERTMEYER, WILLIAM LOUIS, artist; b. Feb. 6, 1921, San Francisco; s. William Adolphus and Nelle Mae (Stangle) F.; edn: BA (honors), Yale College, 1943, graduate study Columbia Univ. 1948-50, National Academy of Design 1954-55; mem. Alpha Sigma Phi frat., Yale Club of Monterey; mil: pfc Army Enlisted Reserve 1942-44; Republican. Studio: Carmel-By-Sea 93923

FOGEL, NORMAN I., synagogue administrator; b. Dec. 23, 1939, Los Angeles; s. Edward G. and Frieda (Moder) F.; m. Helaine; children: Melissa b. 1972, Stephanie b. 1974, Jeremy b. 1976; edn: BS, UC Los Angeles 1962; desig: Fellow in Temple Adminstrn. (FTA), Board of Certifications, Union of Am. Hebrew Congregations. Career: asst. dir. Temple Emanuel, Beverly Hills 1962-65; exec. dir. Temple Solael, Woodland Hills 1965-66, Temple Beth Israel, San Diego 1966-71; adminstrv. v.p. Brandeis Inst., Simi Valley 1971-78; exec. dir. Temple Israel, Boston, Mass. 1978-83; exec. dir. Stephen S. Wise Temple (largest synagogue in the world), Bel Air 1983–; mem. nat. MUM Com., UAHC; honors: Commendations, County of Ventura, City of Simi Valley; mem. Nat. Assn. of Temple Adminstrs. (past pres.); civic: past mem. (chmn.) Simi Valley Plnng. Commn., Ventura County Human Rels. Commn.; mil: US Army Reserve 1957-65; Republican; Jewish; rec: tennis, racquetball. Ofc: Stephen S. Wise Temple, 15500 Stephen Wise Dr Los Angeles 90077

FOILES, STEPHEN MARTIN, physicist; b. July 20, 1956, Tonasket, Wash.; s. Otis Wilson and Bertha Elouise (Cowen) F.; m. Linda Gayle Duncan, Aug. 2, 1986; children: Matthew b. 1989, Jenna b. 1993; edn: BS physics, Stanford Univ. 1978; MS, Cornell Univ. 1981; PhD, 1983. Career: tech. staff Sandia Nat. Labs. 1983–; awards: U.S. Dept. Energy Outstanding Research Metallurgy (1987); mem: Am. Physical Soc., Materials Research Soc.; 88+ articles in jours. and books. Address: Pleasanton 94566

FOLLICK, EDWIN DUANE, college dean, chiropractic physician; b. Feb. 4, 1935, Glendale; s. Edwin Fulfford and Esther Agnes (Catherwood) Follick; m. Marilyn Kay Sherk, March 24, 1986; edn: BA, CSU Los Angeles, 1956, MA, 1961; MA, Pepperdine Univ., 1957; MPA, 1977; PhD and DTheol, St. Andrews Theol. Coll., Seminary of the Free Prot. Episcopal Ch. London, 1958; MS in LS, USC, 1963; MEd, 1964; LLB, Blackstone Law Sch., 1966, JD, 1967; DC, Cleveland Chiropractic Coll., L.A. 1972; PhD, Acad. Theatina, Pescara 1978; MAOM orgn. mgmt., Antioch Univ., L.A. 1990. Career: teacher/lib. administr. Los Angeles City Schs. 1957-68; law librarian Glendale Univ. Coll of Law 1968-69; coll. librarian Cleveland Chiropractic Coll., L.A. 1969-74, prof. jurisprudence, 1975–, dir. edn. and admissions 1974-85, dean student affairs 1976-92, chaplain of the coll. and dean of edn. 1986–; extern prof. St. Andrews (London) 1961; assoc. prof. Newport Univ. 1982; dir. West Valley Chiropractic Health Center, 1972–; honors: Cavaliere Intl. Order Legion of Honor of Immaculata (Italy); Knight of Malta, Order St. John of Jerusalem; Ritter, Der Intl. Legion Friedrich II von Schwaben Teutonische Miliz; Comdr. Chevalier, Byzantine Imperial Order of Constantine the Great; Comdr. Ritter, Order of St. Gereon;

Knight, Order of Signum Fidei; mem: Am. Chiro. Assn., Internat. Chiro. Assn., ALA, NEA, Am. Assn. Sch. Librarians, Assn. Coll. and Resrch. Librarians, Am. Assn. Law Librarians, Calif. Sch. Lib. Assn., Intl. Platform Assn., Nat. Geographic Soc., Phi Delta Kappa, Sigma Chi Psi, Delta Tau Alpha. mil: chaplain's asst. US Army Air Def. Command 1958-60; Democrat; Episcopalian. Res: 6435 Jumilla Ave Woodland Hills 91367 Ofc: 7022 Owensmouth Ave Canoga Pk 91303 Ofc: 590 N Vermont Av Los Angeles 90004

FOLTZ, ELDON LEROY, professor of neurological surgery; b. Mar. 28, 1919, Ft. Collins, Colo.; s. Leroy Stuart and Emily Louise (Proctor) F.; m. Catherine C. Crosby, Oct. 18, 1943; children: Sally Jean b. 1946, James Stuart b. 1948, Janice Ann b. 1951, Suzanne Ellen b. 1955; edn: BS (magna cum laude), Mich. St. Univ., E. Lansing, 1941; MD, Univ. Mich., Ann Arbor, 1943. Career: intern dept. surg. University Hosp., Ann Arbor, Mich. 1943-44, asst. resident, surgery, 1946-47; Horace H. Rackham Sch. of Grad. Studies, Univ. Mich., neuropathology and neuroanatomy, 1947; neurosurg. resident Dartmouth Med. Sch. and Hitchcock Clinic, Hanover, N.H., 1947-49; Univ. of Louisville, Ky., 1949-50; resrch. assoc. div. neurosurg. Univ. of Washington, 1950-51, instr. 1951-53, asst. prof. 1953-58, assoc. prof. 1958-64, prof. neurological surgery, 1964-69; cons. neurol. surg. VA Hosp., Long Beach, Calif. 1969–; prof. UC Irvine, 1969–, and chmn. div. neurol. surg. 1969-80; prof. emeritus UC Irvine, 1989–; program dir. Neurol. Surgical Resident Tng., UCI, 1970-80, 85-86; dir. of neurosurgical resrch. UCI, 1982-86; awards: NIMH postdoctoral fellow, 1950-51, Markle Scholar in Med. Sci., 1954-59, Alpha Omega Alpha, Prototype instructional materials in the clin. neuroscis. Dept. HEW, CDC, Atlanta, 1972-74, Outstanding Alumnus Award Coll. of Natural Sci. Mich. St. Univ. ,1980, Schulte Research Fellow Schulte Research Inst., 1983-84, Emeritus Prof. Univ. of Calif., 1989; mem: AMA, Am. Assn. Neurol. Surgeons (ped. neurosurg. subsect.), Am. Coll. of Surgeons, Am. Acad. of Neurology, Am. Electroencephalographic Soc., AAAS, We. Neurosurg. Soc. (pres. 1976-77), We. Electroencephalographic Soc., Calif. Assn. of Neurol. Surgeons, CMA, Neurosurgical Soc. Am. (pres. 1979-80), Phi Chi Med. Frat., Am. Acad. of Neurol. Surgeons, Research Soc. Neurol. Surgeons, Assn. of Am. Med. Colls., Soc. of Sigma Xi, Soc. of Neurol. Surgeons, Orange Co. Med. Assn., Soc. of Neurol. Surgeons of O.C. (pres. 1976-77), Internat. Soc. Pediatric Neurosurgeons, Internat. Soc. Psychiatric Surg., Internat. Soc. for Stereoencephalotomy and Functional Neurophysiology; civic: Irvine Cove Comm. Assn. (coms. chmn. 1982-83), Annual Parents Hydrocephalus Conf., Golden West Coll. (dir. annual all day cont. edn. conf. 1982-90); publs: 120+ articles in peer-reviewed jours. (primary author 58), numerous abstracts, research studies and acad. lectures; mil: lt. MC-USNR 1944-46; Laguna Beach Congregational Ch. (choir 1971–, music com. 1982–, Com. of Elders 1975-77); rec: sailing. Res: 2480 Monaco Dr Laguna Beach 92651 Ofc: UCI Medical Center 101 City Dr - Rt.81 (Neurosurgery) Orange 92668-5397

FONES, MONTY GARTH, consultant, computer graphics specialist, writer, retired teacher; b. Dec. 5, 1932, Dalhart, Tx.; s. Wilbur Leslie and Bernice Hazel (Wiley) F.; m. Nancy Jeanne Mills, Dec. 23, 1972; edn: BS math., Panhandle A&M 1955; grad. work, UC Berkeley 1960; MA, San Diego St. Univ. 1964. Career: tchr. Redwood H.S., Visalia 1960-61; Newport Mesa Unified Sch. Dist., Newport Beach and Costa Mesa 1961-89; consultant, 1989–; awards: grantee CAEMAT Media Assn., 1974, NMEA Edn. Assn. Beacon Education Award, 1975, Back Bay High Sch. Teacher of Year, 1983, Newport Schs. Found. grantee, 1987-88, 88-89; civic: Rainbow Warriors of Green Peace, Lions (pres. 1973-4); ed. Colonizing a Planet, 1968, author: Model Rocket Guidebook, 1972, editor Metric Guidebook, 4 Editions, 1972-75, author/editor Tech. in Curriculum, 1989; mil: lt.jg USNR 1956-59; Methodist; rec: music, photog., computing.

FONG, ALBERT J., physician; b. Jan. 13, 1925, San Francisco; s. Bing Shun and Emily (Lee) F.; m. Marigold Fong, July 30, 1950 (widowed 1972); m. 2d. Jo-Anne K. Curr, Dec. 27, 1975; children: Jonathon Fong b. 1957, Joel Fong. b. 1960, Michael Curr b. 1964, Susan Curr b. 1966; edn: BA, Stanford Univ. 1950, MD, 1956. Career: internship, Stanford, San Francisco Gen. Hosp. 1956-57; residency, Sonoma County Hosp., Santa Rosa 1957-59; medical doctor, pvt. practice, Novato, Calif. 1959–; mil: cpl., USAF 1943-46; Republican; Protestant; rec: photography. Res: 11 Jennifer Lane Novato 94947 Ofc: Bel Marin Medical Center 372 Bel Marin Keys Blvd Novato 94949

FONG, CARL S., systems and operations analyst; b. June 11, 1959, Sacramento; s. John Y. and Amy F.; edn: AS, Consumnes River Coll. 1979; BS, Cal Poly Pomona 1985; MBA pgm. Univ. La Verne 1990-93. Career: tutor Cal Poly, Pomona 1983, lab. cons. 1984-85; peripheral opr. Security Pacific Automation Corp., Brea 1984-85; programmer analyst I, and II, Orange Co. Dept. of Edn., Costa Mesa 1985-86, 86-88, systems programmer 1988-89, systems & ops. analyst 1989–, indep. d.p. cons., Corona 1988–; honors: Who's Who H.S. Students 1975-76, 76-77, Dean's list Consumnes River Coll. 1977-79, Pres.'s list and Dean's list CalPoly 1982-84, 84-85, Who's Who in the West 1992-93; mem: Mgmt. Info. Systems Student Assn., Data Proc. Mgmt. Assn., AMBA Assn.; rec: skiing, tennis, bowling. Ofc: Orange County Dept. of Education 200 Kalmus Dr Ste C1016 Costa Mesa 92626

FONG, DARRYL LES, pastor, professor, chiropractor; b. Dec. 7, 1959, Los Angeles; s. Benjamin and Carol F.; m. Cora; edn: AA, Long Beach City Coll. 1980; Long Beach St. Univ. 1980-82; BS human biol., Los Angeles Chiropractic Coll. 1986; DC, 1986; M.Div. Talbot Sch. of Theology, Biola Univ. 1993. Career: chiropractor, Santa Ana 1987-88; owner Darryl L. Fong D.C., Anaheim 1988-91; pastor, Cerritos 1994–; prof. La Mirada 1994–; honors: Who's Who Chiropractic, Dean's List 1986, Who's Who in Coll., Who's Who in Calif., Louis Talbot Award 1992; mem: Calif. Chiropractic Assn., Christian Chiropractors Assn., Found. Chiropractic Edn. & Research, Parker Research Found., Am. Chiropractic Assn., Evangelical; Theol. Soc.; Chinese Congregational Ch. (deacon 1985-88), Chinese Baptist Church of Orange County 1990–, Evangelical Formosan Church of Cerritos. Address: 5820 Via Santana Yorba Linda 92687-3416

FONG, DAVID, psychiatrist; b. Mar. 20, 1921, Stockton, Calif.; s. Ying King and Sutie (Wong) F.; m. Nancy Nai-Sien Wong, May 8, 1955; children: Heather M., Celia L.; edn: AB, UC Berkeley 1942; MD, UCSF Med. Sch., San Francisco 1944; grad. S.F. Psychoanalytic Inst. & Soc. 1964; Diplomate, Am. Bd. of Psychiatry & Neurology. Career: psychiatrist, pvt. practice, Berkeley, Calif. 1950–; psychiatrist UC Berkeley Student Health Svc. 1950-71; med. dir. Chinatown/North Beach Clin. Svs., S.F. Dept. Public Health, S.F. 1972–; lectr. Calif. State Univ., Hayward 1970-71; cons. Herrick Hosp. Residency Tng. Prog., Berkeley 1966-71, Internat. Inst. of Alameda, Oakland 1973-75, Asian Comm. Mental Health Svs., Oakland 1974-75, Highland Hosp. Asian Mental Health Component, Oakland 1976-79; mem: Am. Psychiatric Assn. (life fellow), CMA, No. Calif. Psychiatric Soc., Alameda Contra-Costa Med. Assn., Mental Health Advy. Bd. of Berkeley 1972-76; mil: capt. U.S. Army Med. Corps, Germany 1945-47; rec: photography, drawing, painting, copper enameling, carpentry. Ofc: David Fong, M.D. 2232 Carleton St Berkeley 94704

FONG, KEVIN MURRAY, lawyer; b. Jan. 25, 1955, San Francisco; s. William W. and Lillian (Chew) F.; m. Rosalia Han-Ming Ting, March 22, 1980; 1 son, Elliot b. 1987; edn: BA, Harvard Coll. 1976; JD, Harvard Law Sch. 1979. Career: law clk. Hon. Constance Baker Motley, U.S. Dist. Ct., N.Y.C. 1979-80; assoc. Pillsbury Madison & Sutro, San Francisco 1980-86, ptnr. 1987–; mem: Asian Am. Bar Assn. Greater Bay Area (pres. 1989), Asian Pacific Bar of Calif. (pres. 1990); ed. in chief Harvard Civil Rights - Civil Liberties Law Review (1978-79); Democrat. Ofc: Pillsbury Madison & Sutro POB 7880 San Francisco 94120

FONS, RUSSELL JOHN, public relations executive; b. Mar. 14, 1944, Milwaukee, Wis.; s. Jerome Joseph and Lucille Helen (Fischer) F.; m. Mary Lorrayne Kurtz, Apr. 24, 1965 (div. 1973); children: Tracy b. 1965, Denise b. 1967; Roni Louise Naiman, Jan. 31, 1983 (div. 1988); edn: BS, Univ. Wis. 1966. Career: publications supr. Miller Brewing Co., Milw. 1966-69; pub. rels. dir. The Patton Agy., Phoenix, Az. 1969-73; ptnr. Sooy, Brejtfus, Fons, 1973-74; pub. rels. mgr. Best Western Internat., 1975; pub. rels. dir. McAward & Assocs., 1976-78; group supr. Harshe, Rotman & Druck, Los Angeles 1978-80; owner Russ Fons Public Relations, Van Nuys, CA and Las Vegas, NV 1980–; dir. Media Research Inst., Santa Monica 1985–, dir. Satellite Information Resources Network, Van Nuys 1986–; awards: best mktg. PRSA/L.A. 1979, best annual PR program PRSA/Orange Co. 1980, best PR program for a specific problem L.A. Advtsg. Women 1985; mem: Soc. of Profl. Journalists 1965–, Phoenix Press Club 1969–, L.A. Press Club 1978–; civic: Leukemia Soc. of Am. (trustee 1986-88), L.A. Co. Sheriffs Dept. (civilian vol. 1986–); author: The Executive Crisis Manager (1987); Republican; Lutheran. Ofc: Russ Fons Public Relations 7509 Turtle Dove Ct Las Vegas NV 89129

FONSECA, EMIDIO LOPES, general building contractor; b. Feb. 9, 1933, Portugal, naturalized May 15, 1964; s. Alfredo Lopes and Maria Augusta (de Jesus) da Fonseca; m. Mary, July 27, 1958; children: Anna Maria b. 1962, David b. 1965, Sandra b. 1968; edn: grad. Internat. Trade Sch., Lisbon; spl. courses Naval Tng. Sch., Radio TV Sch., Gen. Contractors Sch., Mechanics Sch.; lic. B-1 gen. building contr., Calif. Career: carpenter trainee Pacheco Constrn. Ltd., Guimaraes, Portugal 1947-52; machinist mate 1/c Portuguese Navy, 1953-58; gen. contr./prin., Orinda 1966–; projects include hotel restoration of the York, The Lombard, Chancellor, Hyde Park, Richelieu hotels (all in S.F.); prop. Elekai Motel, South Lake Tahoe 1978-87; awards: scholastic honor roll Portuguese Navy, 1957; Portuguese Govt. medal of honor for service to community 1992; Sears, Roebuck, Concord excellence in contracting award, 1978, 79, 80; biog. listings 5,000 Personalities of World, Internat. Who's Who of Intellectuals, ABIRA life fellow, nat. advr., medals of honor (gold, silver, brass); mem: Licensed Contrs. Assn., 1966–; Carpenters Local #180, Vallejo, 1958–; Nat. S. Bus. United, Better Bus. Bur. (Contra Costa, Alameda, Solano Cos.), Elks Club, Our Lady of Fatima Soc. Thornton, Nat. Trust for Hist. Preservation, ASPA/Portuguese Navy Veterans in USA (Calif. pres. 1992-96);Master Bldrs. Assoc.,Internat. Conf. of Blg. Officials, Republican (Nat. Congl. Club, Presdl. Task Force charter mem. & Honor Roll 1981–, Rep. Nat. Com. 1979–); R.Cath.; rec: travel. Res: 52 Orchard Rd Orinda 94563 Ofc: Emidio Fonseca Remodeling and Construction, 52 Orchard Rd Orinda 94563

FORBES, JOHN CARTER, manufacturing and securities brokerage company executive; June 7, 1947, Pontiac, Mich.; s. Walter Rucker and Caroline (Giles) F.;

m. Patricia Ann Collins, May 15, 1971 (div. 1993); children: Sarah b. 1974, Chelsea b. 1976; m.2d. Cecilia Ann Baxter, Jan. 29, 1994; edn: BA, Western Mich. Univ. 1969; 1971-75. Career: supt. constrn. Simax Devel. Corp., Portage, Mich. 1972-73; union carpenter Don Smith Gen. Contractor 1973-75; coordinator venereal disease control Kalamazoo Co. Health Dept., Mich. 1975-77; ops. and personnel mgr. Gen. Copy Corp., Ann Arbor, Mich. 1977-78; realtor Cambridge House Realtors, Kalamazoo 1978-79; account v.p. Paine Webber, San Diego 1979–, asst. branch mgr. 1987-89; pres. EnviroBest Corp. 1994–; dir. Elizabeth Hospice, Escondido 1986-89; Western Mich. Univ., Pres. of Mens Union 1968-69; awards: Calif. Ballet Presidential Award 1993, San Diego Found. for Performing Arts Star Award - Vol. of Yr. Calif. Ballet 1994; mem: Calif. Ballet (bd. trustees 1987-95, pres. 1990-94), Westwood Elem. PTA (pres. 1980-81), Meadowbrook Middle Sch. PTA (pres. 1987-88), Bernardo Soccer Club (coach 1983-89, girls commr. 1984-85), San Diego Soccer Club (coach 1990-92); Bahai; rec: soccer, tennis, golf, skiing. Ofc: Paine Webber 16890 Bernardo Ctr Dr San Diego 92128 and EnviroBest 11610 Iberia Pl Ste 204 San Diego 92128

FORBES, JUDITH L., engineering executive; b. Sept. 27, 1942, Fullerton; d. James Franklin and Lois Virginia (Couse) Forbes; m. Thomas Wilkins, June 8, 1961 (div.); m. Edward Resha, Aug. 2, 1967 (div.); m. Ralph M. Hawk, Nov. 10, 1990; children: Laurel b. 1962, James b. 1963, John b. 1967; edn: BA physics, CSU Fullerton 1974; MS engring., 1979; MBA, USC 1983; PhD, exec. mgmt., Claremont Grad. Sch. 1993. Career: engr. Northrop Electromech., Anaheim 1975-79; tech. staff TRW, San Bernardino 1979-80; project engr., mgr. Northrop Electronics, Hawthorne 1980-87; project mgr. Gen. Research, El Segundo 1987-89; prog. mgr. TRW Technar, Irwindale 1989-94; v.p. D.C. Caldwell & Co., Monrovia 1987-92; pres. Jandr Assoc., Inc. 1993–; asst. prof. CSU Fullerton 1974-75; adj. prof. DeVry Inst. of Tech., Pomona 1993–; adj. prof. Univ. of La Verne 1994–; awards: Orange Co. Engring. Council Engr. of Merit 1985, CSU Fullerton Disting. Alumni 1987; mem: Soc. of Women Engrs. (pres. L.A. 1981-82, nat. v.p. 1983-85), Am. Inst. Aero. & Astro. (pres. Orange Co. 1986-87), Town Hall of Calif.; articles pub. in tech. jours., 1974-76, 77; author column on tech. mgmt., 1982-87, speaker on engring. and mgmt., 1980–; mil: AC3 USN 1960-61; Democrat; rec: piano, flying, theater. Res: 23557 Casa Loma Dr Diamond Bar 91765-2125 Ofc: Jandr Associates Inc 564 N Diamond Bar Ste 248 Diamond Bar 91765

FORD, ELIZABETH BLOOMER (MRS. GERALD R. FORD), First Lady during 38th U.S. Presidency; b. Apr. 8, 1918, Chgo.; d. Wm. Stephenson and Hortence (Neahr) Bloomer; m. William Warren, 1942, div. 1947; m. 2d Gerald R. Ford (elected to Congress 2 weeks after wedding), Oct. 15, 1948; children: Michael Gerald, John Gardner, Susan Elizabeth; edn: Bennington Sch. Dance, 1936-38; LLD (hon.), Univ. Mich. 1976. Career: dancer Martha Graham Concert Group, NYC 1939-41; model John Powers Agcy., NYC 1939-41; fashion dir. Herpolsheimer's Dept. Store, Grand Rapids, Mich. 1943-48; dance instr. Grand Rapids, 1932-48; raised 4 children, also active in GOP, Episcopal Ch. and family, 1950s-60s; as First Lady focused on the arts, handicapped and women's issues 1974-78, mem. Nat. Commn. on Observance of Internat. Women's Year 1977; ongoing svc. in field of chemical dependency recovery: trustee Eisenhower Med. Ctr., Rancho Mirage, and chmn. bd. dirs. Betty Ford Ctr. (chem. dependency recovery unit), 1982–; Betty Ford cancer resrch., screening & prevention ctrs. opened at Cedars Sinai Hosp., L.A. 1978, Columbia Hosp. for Women, W.D.C. 1980, Blodgett Memorial Hosp., Grand Rapids, Mich. 1987; other affils: co-ch. ERA Countdown Campaign 1981-82, advy. com. State of Calif. Chem. Dependency Recovery Hosp., The Lambs, Inc. nat. tng. ctr. for mentally retarded adults, Libertyville, Ill. (hon. bd. dirs.), Center Theatre of the Performing Arts, P.S. (hon. Golden Cir. Patrons), P.S. Desert Mus. (hon. chair bd. trustees), Nsg. Home Advy. Com. (bd. trustees), White House Preserv. Fund (hon. co-chair), Martha Graham Dance Ctr. (trustee), Nat. Arthritis Found. (hon. trustee); honors: hon. Dr. of Laws Univ. Mich. 1976, recipient num. humanitarian and service awards including Women's Div. Anti-Def. League, B'nai Brith 1975, Ladies Home Jour. 1976, ICCJ 1978), Albert Einstein Coll. of Med. 1979, Friends of Hebrew Univ. 1981, Am. Cancer Soc. 1982, Am. Lung Assn. 1983, Nat. Fedn. of Press Women 1983, Susan G. Komen Found. 1983, Abraxas Found. 1983, Calif. Women's Commn. of Alcoholism 1984, YWCA of Nat. Capitol Area 1985, L.A. Girl Scouts Council 1985, L.A. AIDS Project 1985, Nat. Ctr. for Health Edn. 1986, Nat. Council on Alcoholism 1986, Internat. Ctr. for the Disabled 1987, Gateway Rehab. Ctr. 1987, others; publs: autobiography: The Times of My Life (1979), Betty: A Glad Awakening (1987); Address: PO Box 927 Rancho Mirage 92770

FORD, GERALD RUDOLPH, JR., 38th President of the United States, b. July 14, 1913, Omaha; s. Gerald R. and Dorothy (Gardner) F.; m. Elizabeth Bloomer, Oct. 15, 1945; children: Michael Gerald, John G., Steven M., Susan Elizabeth; edn: AB, Univ. Mich. 1935; LLB, Yale Univ. 1941; LLD (hon) Mich. State Univ., Aquinas Coll., Spring Arbor Coll., Albion Coll., Grand Valley State Coll., Belmont Abby Coll., Western Mich. Univ.; admitted to Mich. State Bar, 1941. Career: law practice in Grand Rapids, Mich. 1941-49; assoc. firm Butterfield, Amberg, Law & Buchen, 1946-51, ptnr. Amberg, Law, Buchen & Fallon, 1951-59, Buchen & Ford, after 1960; elected mem. 81st to 93d congresses from 5th Mich. Dist., mem. Appropriations Com., minority leader, 1954-73;

apptd. vice president United States of Am., 1973-74, elected US President, 1974-77; dir: Shearson Lehman Bros., Tiger Internat.; honors: distinguished service award, Grand Rapids Jr. C.of C. 1948, one of ten outstanding young men in US, US Jr. C.of C. 1950, Sports Illus. Silver Anniversary All-American 1959, Congl. distinguished service, Am. Polit. Sci. Assn. 1961, George Washington award, Am. Good Govt. Soc. 1966, Gold Medal award Nat. Football Found. 1972; mem. Am., Mich., Grand Rapids bar assns., Delta Kappa Epsilon, Phi Delta Phi, Masons, University Club, Peninsular (Kent Co.) Club; author: A Time To Heal: The Autobiography of Gerald R. Ford (1979), Global Stability (1982); coauthor: Portrait of the Assassin; mil: served to lcdr. USN 1942-46; Republican; Episcopalian. Address: PO Box 927, Rancho Mirage 92270

FORD, JOHN T., JR., teacher; b. Feb. 17, 1953, Rotan, Tx.; s. John T. and Lala Fern (Shipley) F.; m. Betty Jean Crawford, Aug. 21, 1976; children: Casey b. 1980, Craig b. 1983, Kirk b. 1986; edn: BA, Univ. of Redlands, 1974. Career: tchr. Yucaipa Jt. Unified Sch. Dist., 1976-88; creative coordinator (conceptual art) "Whole Sch. Environments" Green Valley H.S. 1980-84; Vacaville Sch. Dist., 1990–; mem.: dist. task force on technology, and on vocat. edn., 1992–; producer TV4U 1992; awards: Golden Bell award Calif. Sch. Board Research Found. 1987, tchr. of year Calif. Continuation Ednl. Assn. Dist. VIII 1987; mem. Calif. Tchrs. Assn. 1979–; Prot.; rec: reading. Ofc: Will C. Wood High School 998 Marshall Rd Vacaville 95687

FOREMAN, JOHN PATRICK, electrical engineer; b. Aug. 16, 1954, Lake Charles, La.; s. John Calvin Foreman and Daisy Mae (Finley) F. Milsted; edn: BSEE, McNeese St. Univ., 1976; reg. profl. engr. Calif., Tx. La., Ore. Career: electrical engr. Flour Corp., Houston, Tx. 1977-83; Jacob Engring. Group 1983-84; Burgess & Niple Inc. 1984-86; project mgmt. Turpin & Rattan Engring. Inc., S.D. 1986-92; T.H. Rogers & Assoc., Oakland 1993; Alfa-Tech Bouillon, San Jose 1994–; mem: Nat. Soc. Profl. Engrs., Calif. Soc. Profl. Engrs. (S.D.chpt.), Tx. Soc. Profl.Engrs. (San Jacinto chpt.), La. Engring. Soc., IEEE; rec: skiing. Res: 596 N 2nd St San Jose 95112

FOREST, IRA, developer; b. Feb. 18, 1920, Milwaukee, Wis.; s. Harry and Frances (Pelsinger) F.; m. Joyce Levine, Nov. 23, 1944 (div. 1970); m. Myrna Miller Snyder, Jan. 9, 1982; children: David b. 1948, Michael b. 1955, Adam b. 1960; edn: BS, Stanford Univ. 1942. Career: engr. Standard Oil Calif., Los Angeles 1942-43, 46-47; sales engr. Kelley Petroleum, Long Beach 1947-49; retail owner Discount Stores 1950-60; builder, developer Forest & Co., Los Angeles 1960–; bd. dirs. Am. West Bank 1987–; mem: BSA (commr. 1967-70), Building Industry Assn. L.A. (past pres., bd. dirs.), Internat. Conf. of Shopping Centers, Stanford Univ. Alumni Assn., Mountain Gate Tennis Club, Palm Springs Racquet Club, Marina City Club; report pub. Congressional Record, WDC "Opportunity for U.S. Builders in Middle East", US Dept. Commerce Trade Missions (1967, 78); mil: capt. USAF 1943-46, 4 air medals, Disting. Flying Cross, presdl. citation 1944; Republican; Jewish; rec: tennis, bicycling, walking. Ofc: Forest & Co. 16861 Ventura Blvd Ste 200 Encino 91436

FORESTIER, DANIELLE, master baker; b. Feb. 28, 1943, Ray, Ariz.; d. Earl Francis Ruth and Dorothy Margaret (Steil) Toms; m. Charles H. Schley II, Nov. 10, 1962 (div. 1982); m. Warren David Vail, Oct. 2, 1994; children: Sara b. 1963, Charles III b. 1964; edn: BA in art, Bennington Coll., 1966; desig: Maitre Boulanger (Master Baker) Chambre de Commerce, Paris, France 1977; cert. tchr. Internat. Assn. of Cooking Professionals, W.D.C. 1986. Career: baker Boulangerie Candalot, Paris, France 1974-77; owner, opr. Les Belles Miches, Santa Barbara, Calif. 1977-81; cons. Forestier, Boulanger, Oakland 1982–; cons. Chopin, Paris, Fr. 1986-89, Anheuser-Busch, St. Louis, Mo. 1985, Am. Inst. of Baking, Manhattan, Ks. (1984, 86), General Mills (1991,92), Calif. Apricot Adv. Bd. 1992, Calif. Walnut Com. 1993-95; awards: "Best bread in Calif." California Mag., L.A. 1980, listed Who's Who in West 1991; mem: Am. Inst. of Wine & Food (founder 1981–), San Francisco Soc. of Food Profls. 1992–, Amicale de Bon Pain 1987–; contbr. articles in Cook's Mag., 1986-87, Am. Inst. Baking, 1990; Democrat; rec: ballet, opera, dining, golf. Res: 470 Weldon Ave Oakland 94610 Ofc: D. Forestier, Maitre Boulanger, 470 Weldon Ave Oakland 94610

FORGHANI, BAGHER, virologist; b. Mar. 10, 1936, Bandar-Anzali, Iran; s. Baba and Jahan (Rahimi) F.; m. Nikoo Alavi, June 12, 1969; children: Niki b. 1971, Nikta b. 1975; edn: PhD, Justus Liebig Univ., Giessen, Ger. 1965. Career: postdoctoral fellow Utah State Univ., Logan 1965-67; asst. prof. Nat. Univ. of Iran, Tehran 1967-69; postdoctoral fellow Calif. State Dept. Health Svs., Berkeley, Calif. 1970-72, research specialist, 1972-82, research scientist, 1982–; scientific advy. bd. Varicella-Zoster Virus Research Found., Inc. N.Y. 1991–; mem: Am. Soc. for Microbiology 1969–, Nat. Registry of Microbiologists 1974–; author: 7 chapters in virological books, 45+ original papers in virology in nat. and internat. sci. jours. (1966–); Moslem. Res: 134 Lombardy Ln Orinda 94563

FORMAN, SANFORD, transportation services executive; b. Sept. 22 1932, New York; s. Louis and Rose (Fenster) F.; m. Marilyn Resnick, Aug. 29, 1954; children: Suzanne b. 1956, Jody b. 1959; edn: BS, Fairliegh Dickinson Univ. 1960. Career: nat. ops. mgr. W.T. Grant, N.Y.C. 1958-69; gen. traffic mgr. Mattel Inc., Hawthorne 1970-78; v.p. A. Cesana & Assoc., Los Angeles 1979-

88; AFSAC 1979-88; pres. Alliance Air Freight 1985–, Alliance Courier Service 1986–, Alliance Travel Svs. 1986–, Air Freight Forwarding Co. of Los Angeles, 1988-90; chmn. and CEO Alliance Logistics Resources 1990–; pres. Mercury Internat. 1992–; CEO, Air Freight Forwarding Corp., 1995–; pres. GFZ Imports; tchr. L.A. Trade Tech. 1971-78; U.S. Congl. Com. on Trans. Regulatory Reform 1972-78; instr. Golden West Coll., Hungtington Beach 1980-94; mem: Western Traffic Conf., Toy Mfg. Am., Traffic Mgrs. Conf. of Calif., Morclay Internat., Transp. Exec. Council, Jewish War Vets., DAV; mil: sgt. USAF 1951-55; Democrat; Jewish; rec: skiing, fishing, tennis, running. Address: PO Box 88549 Los Angeles 90009

FORMAN, TERRI, marketing/communications consultant; b. Oct. 1, 1954, Wash. D.C.; d. Joseph and Ethel Frances (London) Pincus; m. Max Robert Forman, Aug. 20, 1978; 1 child, Hallie b. 1988; edn: BA, Univ. of Miami, 1975. Career: media splst. Staff Devel. Tng. Ins., Dept. of Health and Rehab. Svs., St. of Fla; assoc. devel. dir. Easter Seal Rehabilitation Ctr., Dade County, Fla. 1979-81; assoc. United Way of Dade County, 1981-82; staff exec. United Way, San Francisco, 1983-91; sr. assoc. 1983-87, mgr. advtg. creative services 1987-88, v.p. communications 1988-90, group v.p. advtg. and communications 1990-91; principal, Mindshare, mktg. communications consortium 1991–; dir. of devel. Congregation Emanu-El 1993–; awards: MOBIUS Award 1991, CLIO Awards (1987, 89), `Best in the West' Am. Advt. Fedn. 1983-89, Compass Award 1986; mem: Nat. Soc. of Fund Raising Executives. Ofc: Mindshare 1513 Golden Gate Ave San Francisco 94115; Congregation Emanu-El 2 Lake St San Francisco 94118

FORNIA, DOROTHY LOUISE, educator; b. Feb. 14, 1918, Youngstown, Ohio; d. Joseph Victor and Margaret Alice (Berner) Fornia; edn: BS in edn., Ohio State Univ., 1941, MA, 1944, EdD, USC, 1957, postdoctoral, 1976. Career: instr. Ohio Soldiers & Sailors Home, Xenia, Ohio 1941-43; grad. asst. Ohio St. Univ., Columbus 1943; asst. prof. Wilmington (Ohio) Coll. 1944-45; Ohio Wesleyan Univ., Delaware, Ohio 1945-47; Bowling Green St. Univ., 1947-53; tchg. asst. USC, Los Angeles 1953-56; asst., assoc. prof., prof. CSU Long Beach 1956-92, dir. graduate studies and research 1962-72, dir. gerontology pgm. 1972-92, coordinator of grad. studies 1982-92; honors: Soroptomist Internat. 1989, Delta Epsilon, Delta Kappa Gamma, Delta Psi Kappa, Phi Kappa Phi (v.p. 1978), Fellow Am. School Health Assn. 1956, founder's award Senior Care Action Network, Long Beach 1987 Outstanding faculty Calif. Women in Higher Edn. 1987, listed Who's Who of Am. Women, Who's Who in West, World Who's Who of Women, Directory of Internat. Biography, London 1966; apptd. advy. bds: Interfaith Action for Aging, Long Beach Comm. Hosp. - gerontology, L.A. Co. Commn. on Aging, University Graduate Council (1966-92, chair 1973-92); mem: Senior Care Action Network (founder, dir. 1978–), Calif. Council on Gerontology and Geriatrics (co-chair 1978-81), Chancellor's Task Force on Gerontology and Geriatrics (1981-92), Phi Kappa Phi (v.p. 1978); publs: articles in higher edn jours. (1959–), current research: Life Satisfaction of Retirees; Presbyterian; rec: photog., travel. Res: 6941 Driscoll St Long Beach 90815 Ofc: Calif. State University, Long Beach 1250 Bellflower Blvd Long Beach 90840

FORTIN, JEFFREY ALLEN, safety and risk management consultant, entrepreneur; b. June 26, 1957, Worcester, Mass.; s. Albert Alfonse and Bette Louise (Arcand) F.; edn: AA, San Bdo. Valley Coll. 1981; AA in journ., Amers. Am. River Coll. Sacto. 1982; grad. Calif. Mil. Acad. 1988; desig: REA, cert. indep. paralegal. Career: pres. and c.e.o. J.Fortin & Assocs., Inc., San Jose 1986-92; pres. and c.e.o. Nat. Environmental & Safety Technologies Inc., San Jose 1992–; safety cons./risk mgr. Central Concrete Supply Co. Inc., 1977–; Central Transport, Inc., 1982–; Quikrete of No. Cal, Inc., 1988-94; recipient disting. service award Am. River Coll. (1982); mem. Calif. Trucking Assn. (chmn. Santa Clara County (SCC) Unit 1991-92); civic bds: San Bdo. City Police Commn. (1981), Santa Clara Co. Personnel Bd. (chmn. 1988-94), SCC Social Services Advy. Commn. (v. chair 1983-90), SCC Justice Advy. Bd. (1986-88), SCC Youth Found. Inc. (founder, chmn. 1987-93), Timpany Ctr. Found. (dir 1989-90), Community Kids to Camp Inc. (dir. 1986-88), student advy. com. Calif. Postsec. Edn. Commn. (1980-81); past mem. Calif. Comm. Coll. Student Govt. Assn. (exec. bd. 1981-82); mil: sgt. USAF 1974-79, AF Reserve (TSG) 1979-82, Calif. Nat. Guard/USAR (2LT) M.P. 1985-93, decorated USAF Commendn. w/oak leaf, Humanitarian, Presdl. unit cit., USAF Outstanding unit cit., Good Conduct, Longevity; Democrat; rec: philately, racquetball, swimming, jogging. Ofc: NEST Inc. PO Box 610966 San Jose 95161-0966

FOSSUM, LYNN BARRICKS, psychotherapist, business consultant; b. Oct. 9, 1944, Des Moines, Iowa; d. Joseph Bernard and Helene Barricks; children: R. Cory b. 1973, Cheney E. b. 1975; edn: BA cum laude, Univ. Iowa, 1965; MA, Drake Univ., 1968; SDS, PPS, San Jose St. Univ., 1972; PhD cand. Calif. Coast Univ.; Calif. adminstrv. cred. (life), std. designated svs. pupil personnel (life), Comm. Coll. instr. (life), Marriage Family Child Counselor (MFCC), Ednl. Psychologist. Career: lic. vocat. counselor Iowa St. Employment Svc. 1965-67; resrch. analyst Drake Univ., 1967-68; parole ofcr./fam. counselor Iowa St. Bd. of Control, 1968-70; instr. West Valley Coll., 1970-73; school psychologist Cupertino Union Sch. Dist., 1971-75, coord. pupil personnel svcs. 1975-76; proj. dir./cons., devel. statewide child abuse intervention pgm. Calif. Bd. of Edn.,

1976-82; cons., pgm. plng. & eval. to schools and agys., 1980–; pvt. practice marriage and fam. counselor/ednl. psychologist, 1982–, spkr., bus. cons. in areas of stress mgmt., interpersonal comm., mgmt. of change, 1982–; pres. VisionTec; honors: Phi Beta Kappa, Mortar Board, Murray Scholar, recipient commendations Santa Clara Co. Bd. Suprs., Calif. St. Legislature, and US House of Reps.; appt. Calif. Consortium of Child Abuse Councils (past exec. com.), Iowa Gov.'s Commn. on Children & Youth (past), Child Advocacy Council of Sta. Clara-San Mateo Counties (past exec. com.); mem: Nat. Speakers Assn., Calif. Assn. Sch. Psychologists (past exec. com.), past com. Santa Clara Annual Symp. on Child Abuse, Calif. Assn. Marriage Fam. Therapists (past sec. Santa Clara Valley MFT), Peninsula Profl. Women's Network, Am. Soc. Tng. & Devel., Crippled Childrens Soc. (S.C.Co. exec. com.), AAUW (past woman's chair), San Jose Repertory Theatre (bd.), Silicon Valley Capital Club (bd.); author: Understanding Organizational Change (Crisp Publs., 1989), Overcoming Anxiety (Crisp Publs. 1990), ednl. handbooks and articles. Ofc: 812 Nash Rd Los Altos 94024

FOSTER, BEVERLY BUTLER, educator; b. Dec. 21, 1934, San Diego; d. Ralph C. and Vera Aileen (Anderson) Butler; m. Jerry L. Foster, March 24, 1956; 1 dau., Amy Aileen b. 1965; edn: BA, San Diego St.Univ. 1956; MA, 1961; Ed.D, No. Ariz. Univ. Flagstaff 1981. Career: tchr. San Diego City Schs., San Diego 1956-63, prin. 1963-83, ops. mgr. 1983-85, asst. supt. 1985–; adj. faculty Pt. Loma Nazarene Coll., San Diego 1984–; honors: Outstanding Young Women Am. (1966), Phi Kappa Phi (1981), EDUCAP Lighthouse award (1987), YMCA Tribut to Women (1987); mem: Assn. Calif. Sch. Administrs. (1983–), profl. studies exec.com.), Phi Delta Kappa (1971–), San Diego Council Adminstrv. Women in Edn. (1980–); civic: KPBS Pub. Bdcstg. System (S.D.). Res: 6106 Caminito Sacate San Diego 92120 Ofc: San Diego Unified School District 4100 Normal Room 2131 92103

FOSTER, CLYDE THURSTON, gold mine owner-operator; b. Apr. 30, 1911, Ukiah (his birth cert. is No. 59 in Mendocino Co.); s. Raymond Osborne and Grace Lorain (Thurston) F.; married and widowed twice; edn: Santa Rosa Jr. Coll. 1928-29, Macky Sch. of Mines, Univ. of Nev. 1930-31, Stanford Univ. 1943. Career: first underground mining for father at Twin Sisters Mine in Nevada County, 1927, and Sweetwater Mine (acquired 1933); miner (and owner) Sleeping Beauty Mine 1931-52, and Sweetwater Mine, 1931-93; advisor Sweetwater Mine 1993–; owner/opr. (smith) Blacksmith Shop, Sweetwater Mine of Calif., Yountville 1993–; also worked as micropaleontologist (w/micro fossils from Artic Slope) USGS, Fairbanks, Alaska 1946; computer US Corps of Engrs., Anchorage 1948; survey party chief AEC, Atomic Test Site Nev. and hydro elec. projects (Merced River, Tuolumne River, American River, Yuba River, Rancho Seco Nuclear Generating Plant), 1951-73; owner/opr. Sweetwater Mine, Mariposa (mining with the machinery, methods & language of the 1930s), 1952–; instr. Stamp Mill Sch. (the only sch. of its kind) Mariposa Hist. Soc., donated considerable gold collection to the Calif. State Mus., Mariposa; mil: tech. sgt. US Army WWII & Korea, 6 yrs Active Duty, 9 decorations. Address: Veterans Home of Calif. PO Box 1200 Yountville 94599-1297

FOSTER, JAMES MARK, television producer; b. April 6, 1947, Los Angeles; s. John (Glen) Leonard and Artiemese M. (Couturier) F.; m. Linda Kay Rhodes, Jan. 10, 1970 (div. 1981); children: Chelsie Lynn b. 1973, Evan James b. 1977; edn: AA, Pasadena City Coll., 1971; BS, USC, 1973. Career: v.p. Pathfinder Equipment, San Gabriel 1973-76; owner Alignment Enterprises, Costa Mesa 1976-80; pres. Gemini Productions, Irvine 1980–, pres. Ski Dazzle, Inc. 1979–, pres. Orange Co. Post Production, 1991–; honors: Beta Gamma Sigma, Houston Internat. T.V. Soc. Gold 1987; mem: Commerce Captains USC, So. Calif. Ski Writers Assn., E. Clampus Vitas; author (tv series) Ski Scene, 1986-89; mil: E-5 sgt. USMC 1967-69; Republican; R.Cath.; rec: skiing. Ofc: 2082 Business Center Dr # 160 Irvine 92715

FOSTER, WILLIAM JAMES, III, gemologist, city official; b. Dec. 9, 1953, Princeton, N.J.; s. William James, Jr. and Frances Alberta (Savidge) F.; m. Lynn Marie McDonald, June 9, 1975; children: Trevor b. 1979, Tracy b. 1982; edn: BA in geology, Carleton Coll., Northfield, Minn. 1976; CDP, Inst. Certification of Computing Profls., 1983. Career: pgmr., information splst. Univ. of Mo., Kansas City 1979-81; staff cons. DST Systems Inc., K.C., Mo. 1982-86; ptnr. Carats and Crystals, Pismo Beach, 1986–; property mgr. Cypress Landing, 1986–; elected city council, Westwood, Kans. 1980-86, mayor 1986, councilman City of Pismo Beach, 1988-92; founder, dir. Facts About Tomorrow's Energy (non-profit, citizens' edn. group) 1981-84; mem: Nat. Assn. of Jewelry Appraisers (NJA), Am. Gem Soc. (reg. jeweler), Pismo Beach C.of C. (pres. 1988); Republican; Methodist; rec: trees (dwarf conifers), flying. Res: 2054 Ocean Blvd Pismo Beach 93449 Ofc: Cypress Landing PO Box 1132 Pismo Beach 93448

FOUST, ROSANNE SKIBO, foreign industrial development executive; b. Feb. 28, 1964, Derby, Ct.; d. John Andrew and Claire Frances (Fallon) Skibo; m. Joseph Victor Foust, Dec. 30, 1989; edn: BA, Stonehill Coll., North Easton, Mass. 1986; UCLA exec. mgmt. prog. 1993. Career: program coord., dir. spl. events, dir. mktg. Internat. Bus. Ctr. of New England Inc., Boston 1986-88;

assoc. dir., regional dir., dir. U.S. ops., V.P. global devel. Alsace (France) Devel. Agy., Los Angeles 1988–; mem: French Am. Chamber, L.A. (v.p. sec 1993, v.p. mem. 1992, bd. 1990-91), Junior Achiev. Alumni Assn. 1988–, Am. Mgmt. Assn. 1990–, Nat. Assn. Female Execs. 1989–; LA Co. Mus. of Art 1990–; Republican; R.Cath. Ofc: 2029 Century Park East Ste 1115 Los Angeles 90067

FOWLER, MURRAY ELWOOD, professor emeritus of veterinary medicine; b. July 17, 1928, Glendale, Wash.; s. Harry Cyrenus and Elizabeth Hannah (Ruegg) F.; m. Audrey Cooley, June 5, 1950; children: Alan b. 1952, Gene b. 1954, Janet b. 1956, Linda b. 1959, Patricia b. 1962; edn: BS, Utah St. Univ. 1952; DVM, Iowa St. Univ. 1955. Career: practitioner pvt. practice, Van Nuys 1955-58; instr., prof. UC Davis 1958–; honors: BSA Silver Beaver 1979, UC Davis Outstanding Tchr. 1968, 74, Iowa St. Univ. Stange Alumni 1989; mem: Am. Bd. Vet. Toxicology, Am. Coll. Vet. Internal Medicine, Am. Coll. Zoological Medicine, AVMA, Am. Assn. Zoological Vets. (pres. 1978), Morris Animal Found. (trustee 1976-88), Sacto. Zoo. Soc. (dir. 1968–); editor: Zoo & Wild Animal Medicine, 1978-86; author: Restraint & Handling of Wild & Domestic Animals, 1978, 2nd edit., 1995, Med. & Surgery of S. Am. Camelids, 1989, 190+ articles in sci. jours.; mil: USN 1946-48; Mormon; rec: photog., bird watching. Ofc: Univ. of Calif. School of Veterinary Medicine Dept. Medicine and Epidemiology Davis 95616

FOWLER, PETER NILES, lawyer; b. April 3, 1951, Hamilton, Ohio; s. Richard Allen and Blanche Marie (Niles) F.; edn: BA, John Carroll Univ. 1973; MA edn., Univ. Ala. Tuscaloosa 1977; MA political sci., Ball St. Univ. 1979; JD, Golden Gate Univ. 1984; admitted St. Bar Calif. (1984), Nev. (1986). Career: asst. to mayor City of Marion, Ind. 1973-74; chief investigator, asst. Prosecuting Atty. 1975; social studies instr. Colegio Cristobal Colon, Medillin, Colombia 1976-78; social services coordinator Grant-Blackford Devel. Center, Marion, Ind. 1978-80; law library staff Golden Gate Univ., San Francisco 1980-84; law clk. Nev. Supreme Ct., Carson City 1984-85; atty., assoc. Lilienthal & Jacobson, San Francisco 1985-87; ptnr. Lilienthal & Fowler 1988–; adj. law prof. Golden Gate Univ. Sch. Law 1988–; lectr., cons. Television Edn. Inc., Berkeley 1989; awards: Certs. of Appreciation St. Bar Calif. 1989, Bay Area Lawyers for Individual Freedom 1988, Am. Cancer Soc. Cert. Hon. 1980, Am. Bar Assn. Hon. Mention 1983; mem: Nat. Gay & Lesbian Task Force (bd. dirs. 1983-89), Nat. Ednl. Found. Individual Rights (bd. dirs. 1984–), Frameline S.F. Internat. Lesbian Gay Film Fest. (bd. dirs. 1987–), Bay Area Lawyers for Individual Freedom, Bar Assn. San Francisco; articles pub. in profl. jours.; contbr. Sexual Orientation and the Law (1985); Democrat; Cath.; rec: weightlifting, racquetball, films. Ofc: Lilienthal & Fowler 220 Montgomery St Ste 1500 San Francisco 94104

FOX, EDWARD C., III, data processing executive; b. Sept. 28, 1954, Cleveland, Ohio; s. Edward C. and Edith R. (Yerga) F.; m. Robbie M. Whitehead Fox, June 26, 1976 (div. 1982); m. Lena M. Ranaldi, April 21, 1984; 1 son, Edward b. Aug. 29, 1985; edn: BS chemistry, John Carroll Univ. 1976. Career: computer operator, programmer Cook United Inc., Maple Heights, Ohio 1974-77; mgr. data control Revco D.S. Inc., Twinsburg, Ohio 1977-78; mgr. computer ops. Mandate Corp., Cleveland, Ohio 1978-79; mgr. ops. Shared Health, Independence, Ohio 1979-82; dir. info. systems Compucare Baxter, Orlando, Fla. and Hollywood, Fla. 1982-88; Cleveland Clinic, Ft. Lauderdale, Fla. 1988-89; v.p. info. sys. services, TDS Healthcare Systems Corp., San Jose 1989–; cons. Central Bank, Cleveland, Ohio 1982; honors: Who's Who in Computers; mem: Am. Fedn. Aviculture, DPMA; Republican; R.Cath.; rec: aviculture. Ofc: TDS Healthcare Systems Corp. 160 E Tasman Dr San Jose 95134

FOX, JACK, author, consultant; b. Mar. 8, 1940, Brooklyn, NY; s. Benjamin and Rebecca (Shure) F.; m. Carolyn Gleimer, Apr. 16, 1967 (div. Dec. 1975); m. 2d. Carole Olafson, July 8, 1987; children: Neal, Stuart; edn: BBA, CCNY 1961; MBA, CUNY 1969. Career: sales specialist Am. Can Corp., NYC 1962-63; talent agent Gen. Artists Corp., NYC, 1963-66; bus. specialist NY Times, 1966-70; pres. Ednl. Learning Systems, Inc., Washington, 1971-78; budget dir. Nat. Alliance of Bus., Wash., 1979-80; pres. computerized Fin. Services, Rockville, Md., 1980-87; regional v.p. Govt. Funding Corp., L.A., 1987-90; owner, mgr. Jack Fox Assocs., San Diego, 1990–; adj. prof. Am. Univ., Wash., 1983-85; tchr. fin. Montgomery Coll., Rockville, 1978-86; mem: Internat Platform Assn., Nat. Assn. Accountants; author: How to Obtain Your Own SBA Loan, 1983, Starting and Building Your Own Accounting Business, 1984, 2d. rev. edit., 1991; Democrat; Jewish. Res/Ofc: 6115 Gullstrand St San Diego 92122

FOX, JOSEPH MICKLE, III, consulting chemical engineer; b. Nov. 20, 1922, Philadelphia, Pa.; s. Joseph Mickle and Ruth Louise (Martin) F.; m. Elizabeth Jane Larkin, Oct. 16, 1948 (dec. Aug. 5, 1992); children: Joseph, Elizabeth, Martha, Thomas, Harry, Justin; edn: BSChE, Princeton Univ. 1943; MSChE, 1947; reg. chem. engr. Calif. 1988. Career: tech. service engr. Am. Oil Co., Tx. City, Tx. 1943-45; research engr. M.W.Kellogg Co., Jersey City, N.J. 1947-58, section head, Piscataway, N.J. 1958-66; process design mgr. Bechtel Group Inc., San Francisco 1966-92 (ret.); consulting chemical engr. 1992–; del. Calif. Leg. Council for Profl. Engrs., Sacto. 1968-72; Bay Area Engring. Council, S.F. 1972-83; awards: Am. Inst. Chem. Engrs. Profl. Devel. award 1985; mem: Am. Inst. Chem. Engrs. (fellow, dir. 1975-78), Am. Petroleum Inst. (tech. data com.

1984–), Oakland Mus. (art docent), Orindawoods Tennis Club (TAC com. 1980-82); 15 articles pub. in tech. jours.; patentee in field; Democrat; Cath.; rec: tennis, hiking, computer programming. Res/Ofc: 3396 Angelo St Lafayette 94549 Ofc (p.t.): Bechtel Group Inc POB 3965 San Francisco 94119

FOX, SHEILA, advertising agency president; b. Feb. 11, 1947, Los Angeles; d. James Winton and Sheila (Doyle) Schooler; m. Charles S. Fox, Feb. 14, 1970; edn: BA, CSU Northridge 1969. Career: Leo Burnett Co., Los Angeles 1969-74; Boylhart, Lovett & Dean, L.A. 1974-78; Chapman/Warwick Advtg., San Diego 1978–, pres. 1984–; awards: Irish Woman of Yr. Irish Cong. of So. Calif. 1985; mem: San Diego State Univ. Ad Club (lectr.), Ad Club of S.D. (bd. dirs. 1982-86, lectr.), Am. Advertising Fedn. (we. region leadership panel), S.D. Museum of Art, La Jolla Museum of Contemporary Art, S.D. Zoological Soc., Travel & Tourism Research Assn., Am. Film Inst., co-founder Irish Olympic Host Com., S.D. 1982-84, S.D. Super Bowl Task Force (vol. 1989-90), S.D. C.of C., S.D. Conventions & Visitors Bur. (mktg. com. 1980–), Irish Cong. of So. Calif. (St. Patrick's Day Parade Com. 1982-85); mem. mktg. com. Old Globe Theatre 1986-89, Muscular Dystrophy Assn. (Jerry Lewis Labor Day telethon vol., Rainbow Auction com.); frequent guest speaker on tourism. Ofc: Chapman/Warwick Advertising 2445 Fifth Ave Ste 401 San Diego 92101

FRAHMANN, DENNIS GEORGE, computer manufacturing company executive; b. June 25, 1953, Medford, Wis.; s. George Henry and Aini (Siikarla) F.; edn: BA, Ripon Coll., 1974; MS, Columbia Univ., 1975; postgrad. Univ. Minn., 1979. Career: free lance writer, Mpls., 1975-77, contbg. editor Mpls.-St. Paul Mag., 1976-79; instructional designer Control Data Corp., Mpls. 1977-80; mgr. customer edn. Xerox Corp., Los Angeles 1980-84, mgr. Xerox Systems Inst., Palo Alto 1984-89, mgr. consultant relations Xerox Corp., L.A. 1989–; speaker trade & profl. assns., 1984–; honors: Phi Beta Kappa 1976; mem. Ripon Coll. Alumni Assn. (bd. 1978-80), MECLA 1983-87; civic: Silver Lake Improvement Assn. (dir. 1988-90); numerous pub. articles in field (1975–); Democrat; rec: running, gourmet cooking.

FRAITAG, LEONARD ALAN, project/mechanical engineer; b. Dec. 23, 1961, N.Y.C.; s. David and Lucille Renee (Jay) F.; children: Shoshana b. 1989, Aaron b. 1992; edn: AA, Grossmont Coll., 1983; BSME, San Diego State Univ., 1987. Career: design engr. Restaurant Concepts, San Diego 1987; mech. engr. Vantage Assocs. Inc. 1988-89; design engr. Mainstream Engineering Co. Inc. 1989; manufacturing engr. Sola/Barnes-Hind 1989–; honors: Pi Tau Sigma 1987–, cash award Vlier Enerpac, Burbank 1990; lodges: Al Bahr Shrine (noble 1989–), Scottish Rite (32nd deg., class pres.), F&AM Blackmer Lodge #442 (1994 master); Democrat; rec: camping, computers, sports. Ofc: Sola/Barnes-Hind, 8006 Engineer Rd San Diego 92111

FRANCIS, TIMOTHY DUANE, chiropractor; b. Mar. 1, 1956, Chgo.; s. Joseph Duane and Barbara Jane (Sigwalt) F.; edn: BS biol., Los Angeles Coll. of Chiropractic 1982, DC (magna cum laude), 1984; MS nutrition/biol., Univ. of Bridgeport 1986; bd. qual. as team physician, LACC Postgrad. Sch. 1984-85. Career: pvt. practice chiropractic, 1984–; faculty Univ. of Nev., Reno 1976-80, L.A. Coll. of Chiropractic 1983-85; honors: Phi Kappa Phi (1978; Scholar of Year award 1980), Charles F. Cutts Scholar 1980, Delta Sigma 1982, Nat. Dean's List 1981-84; Republican; R.Cath.; rec: karate, bodybuilding, shooting. Res: PO Box 81961 Las Vegas NV 81380 Ofc: 3750 S Jones Las Vegas NV 89103

FRANCO, CRAIG ANTHONY, numismatic investment company executive; b. Nov. 30, 1959, Los Angeles; s. Abelardo Fernandez and Joan Marie (Loveland) F.; m. Erin S.; edn: Calif. Polytech. St. Univ. Pomona, 4 yrs., Univ. La Verne, 2 yrs. Career: numismatist Miller-Contursi, Inc. Newport Beach 1982-86; v.p. fin. DNI, Claremont 1986-87; founder, bd. chmn. and c.e.o. Pacific Rarities Inc., Redlands 1988–; cons. T.G. M. Inc., St. Paul, Minn. 1984-86, Am. Telesis, Newport Beach 1985-88; recipient scholarship Univ. La Verne 1982-84; mem: ANA, IAPF, CSNA, NGC, PCGS, NSDR, CABDAP, PNG, ICTA; civic: speaker for Holy Family Adoption Agency, and Saint Anne's Hosp. 1978–, tchr. Elizabeth Anne Seton Ch. and St. Joseph's Ch., Upland 1986-91, youth minister St. Adelaide's Ch. 1991-92, founder/chmn. The Give Back Foundation (nonprofit orgn. for underprivileged youth), bd. dirs. Children's Fund 1993–; publs: numerous pub. articles in field, ed. fin. newsletter "Market Report" (1988–), asst. ed. "MarketWise" 1986-87; Republican; R.Cath.; rec: music, art, literature. Address: PO Box 1064 Redlands 92373 Tel: 909/798-6103

FRANEY, PHILIP D., county treasurer and tax collector; b. Feb. 5, 1948, Bakersfield; s. James Thomas and Dorothy Mary (Ross) F.; m. Dina, Jan. 24, 1976; children: Shelly b. 1968, Dina b. 1969; edn: AA, Bakersfield Jr. Coll., 1968; BS, BPA, CSU Bakersfield, 1973, graduate work 1976-77. Career: supvy. acct. Bakersfield City Sch. Dist., 1973-77; systems acct. Kern County Auditor-Controller 1977-81, asst. treas. County of Kern, 1981-86, elected county official, treasurer and tax collector County of Kern, 1987-91; mem. and county rep. State Assn. of County Retirement Systems 1987–, mem. audit com. Calif. Assn. of County Treasurers & Tax Collectors 1987–; mem: Am. Soc. for Pub. Adminstrn., Cal-State Alumni Assn., Bakersfield Coll. Found., Kern County Mgmt. Council, Nat. Assn. of Co. Treasurers & Finance Ofcrs. 1990–, Kern Co.

Bd. of Retirement; civic: Bakersfield East Rotary Club (dir. 1988-89, past sgt. at arms), United Way (county employees campaign chmn. 1987-88), Am. Legion 1988–, Lloyd Plank Found. (treas., 1992–), Walter Stiern Libr. Found. 1992–; num. pub. reports; mil: sp4 AUS 1968-71; rec: golf, fishing, running. Ofc: County of Kern 1115 Truxtun Ave Bakersfield 93301

FRANKE, RICHARD H., mathematician, educator; b. Apr. 11, 1937, Herndon, Ks.; s. Claude E. and Beulah E. (Tannehill) F.; m. J. Amelia Franklin, July 6, 1963; children: Evan b. 1967, Tanna b. 1970, Hailey b. 1970; edn: BS math. & physics, Ft. Hays State Coll., Ks. 1959; MS math., Univ. of Utah, S.L.C., 1961, PhD math., 1970. Career: research engr. Boeing Co., Wichita, Ks., Huntsville, Ala., New Orleans, La., 1961-64; research scientist Kaman Nuclear, Colorado Springs, Co. 1964-66; prof. Naval Postgraduate Sch., Monterey, Calif. 1970–, chmn. dept. math 1992–; liaison scientist Office of Naval Research, European Ofc., London 1988-89; vis. prof. Univ. of Utah, S.L.C. 1977, Drexel Univ., Phila. 1980-81; awarded 20-Yr. Service pin USN 1990; mem: Soc. for Indsl. & Applied Math. 1973–, Sigma Xi 1972–, Am. Math. Soc. 1970-75, Math. Assn. of Am. 1978-82, Slant 6 Club of Am. 1990–; civic: AFS, Monterey chpt. 1983-88, Old Town Neighborhood Assn. (treas. 1994–); editor (book) Mathematical Linkages (1981), 30+ profl. jour. articles (1970–); rec: auto mechanics, sailing. Res: 877 Jefferson St Monterey 93940 Ofc: Naval Postgraduate School Dept. Math., Monterey 93943

FRANKEL, JAMES BURTON, lawyer; b. Feb. 25, 1924, Chicago, Ill.; s. Louis and Thelma (Cohn) F.; m. Louise Untermyer, Jan. 22, 1956; children: Nina, Sara, Simon; edn: Univ. Chgo. 1940-42; BS, U.S. Naval Acad. 1945; LL.B. Yale Univ. 1952; M.P.A. Harvard Univ. 1990; admitted St. Bar Calif. (1953). Career: Steinhart Goldberg Feigenbaum & Ladar, San Francisco 1954-72; of counsel Cooper White & Cooper 1972–; sr. fellow, lectr. in law Yale Univ. 1971-72; lectr. Stanford Univ. Law Sch. 1973-75; vis. prof. Univ. Calif. Law Sch. 1975-76, lectr. 1992–; lectr. Univ. of S.F. Law Sch. 1994–; mem: Council Civic Unity of S.F. Bay Area (pres. 1964-66), S.F. Citizens Charter Revision Com. (chmn. 1968-70), S.F. Pub. Schs. Commn., Natural Resources Defense Council (trustee 1972-77, 1979-92, hon. trustee 1992–, staff atty. 1977-79), S.F. Citizens Energy Policy Advy. Com. (chmn. 1981-82), Am. Bar Assn., Calif. Bar Assn., S.F. Bar Assn.; Democrat. Ofc: 201 California St 17th Floor San Francisco 94111

FRANKLIN, SCOTT H., manufacturing company executive; b. Oct. 27, 1954, Inglewood, Calif.; s. Harrison H. and Marjorie June (Johnson) F.; grad. Pacific Palisades H.S., 1972, stu. Santa Monica Coll., 1975-76. Career: auto sales Sun West Volkswagon, Hollywood 1972-76, Bob Smith Volkswagon, 1976; agt. Royal Ins. Agy., Encino 1976; mechanic Union Plastics Corp., North Hollywood 1977-78; rubber div. mgr. Calif. Gasket & Rubber, Gardena 1978-81, quality control mgr. 1981-82, v.p. ops. 1982-84, pres., CEO and chief ops., 1984–; mem: The Los Angeles Rubber Group Inc. 1981–, Am. Chem. Soc. 1984–, Soc. Mfg. Engrs. (sr. mem. 1987–), Am. Soc. for Quality Control 1990–, ASM Internat. 1990–, Instrument Soc. Am. 1992–, Calif. Mfrs. Assn., Precision Metalforming Assn., Calif. C.of C.; developer: mfg. process CALBOND (US reg. TM, 1988), material "Self-Lubricating Flouroelastomer" 1990; publs: tech. paper, Mixing Silicone Rubber (1986), essay, People Make The Difference (1989); Republican (GOP nat. com.); rec: gourmet cooking, computers. Ofc: California Gasket and Rubber Corp. 1601 W 134th St Gardena 90249

FRANKO, ROBERT MATTHEW, banking, finance and real estate executive; b. 1947, Pittsburgh, Pa.; s. Robert M., Sr. and Ursula F.; m. Melanie Anne, 1980; edn: BS, Univ. Notre Dame, 1969; MBA, Central Mich. Univ., 1978; MIM, Am. Grad. Sch. of Internat. Mgmt. (Thunderbird Sch.), Phoenix, Az. 1979; NASD Reg. Securities & Options Principal & Rep.; lic. gen. contractor, Calif. Career: sales rep. Coulter Electronics, Hialeah, Fla. 1974-75; mktg. mgr. Smith Kline Corp., Valley Forge, Pa. 1975-79; pres. Quality First Internat. Co., Phoenix, Az. 1980-84; sr. v.p. Citibank Arizona (now Norwest Bank), Phoenix 1984-86; mng. dir. Docklands Financial Services, Inc. Costa Mesa, Calif. 1986-95; CFO, Canary Wharf Devel. Co., London, England 1986-87; CEO, Pacific Point Partners, Newport Beach 1988-95; cons. Morningside Group 1988–; pres., CEO, Springfield Bank & Trust of Gibraltar 1993-95; mng. dir. & CEO, Springfield Fund Mgmt. Ltd., Springfield Investment Advisors Ltd. and Springfield Securities Ltd., Gibraltar 1993-95; chmn. and dir. Imperial Trust Co., L.A. 1993–; exec. v.p. and CFO, Imperial Bank 1995–; author: Export Import Operations - A Managers Guide, 1979; rec: running, skiing. Ofc: Imperial Bank Box 92991 Los Angeles 90009

FRASER, EARL DONALD, city planning consultant; b. Sept. 9, 1912, Missoula, Mont.; s. William I. and Grace M. (Beeman) F.; m. Elizabeth Argento, May 16, 1942; edn: B.Arch. in city planning, M.I.T., 1937; M. in regional planning, Harvard Grad. Sch. of Design, 1939; desig: A.I.C.P., Am. Planning Assn. Career: city planner State Planning Boards, Ala. and Miss., 1939-41; senior planner Maryland Nat. Capital Park & Plan. Commn., Silver Spring, Md. 1942-43; planning dir. Kalamazoo, Mich., 1946-53; exec. dir. Redevelopment Agy., San Bernardino 1954-55; planning dir. County of Sacramento, 1955-77; city planning cons. prin., Sacto. 1978–; honors: Alpha Phi

Omega disting. service award M.I.T. 1936; mem. Am. Inst. Planners 1948–; civic: Internat. Assn. of Torch Clubs (mem., ofcr., bd. various chpts. 1946–), SIRS (Sacto.); works: dir. local, city, county and reg. plans incl.: American River Pkwy. 1962, Sacramento Met. Airport - Natomas Area Plan 1967, Sacramento County Plan 1973; mil: lt. USN 1943-45; Unitarian-Universalist; rec: numismatics. Res: 2237 Ehrborn Way Sacramento 95825

FRASER, GLORIA JILL, composer; b. Oct 11, 1952, Cincinnati; d. David and Gloria Anna (Sgritta) Fraser; m. Gregg Gower Arreguin, Aug. 18, 1989; edn: MusB, E.Caro. Univ., Greenville 1974; MFA, Calif. Inst. of Arts, 1977. Career: composer, prin. dba Broadscore Music, Beverly Hills; original music feature films: Cutting Class, Personal Best, Hardcore, Reckless, Spirit of the Wind, When You Comin' Back Red Ryder; TV: Carlin on Campus, Breaking the Ice, Sesame Street; TV and radio commercials: Apple Computers, Baskin Robbins, California Cooler, Carl's Junior, Esso, Gen. Foods, Mattel, Lexus, Nissan, Mazda, Mexicana Airlines, Nat. Geographic Mag., Nike, Porsche, Safeway, Shell Oil, Yamaha Motorcycles, others; awards: Clio best local campaign "Buffy's Bedtime", "Confessions" 1986, Clio finalist :60 Radio "Grizzly" Great America, 1987; mem: Am. Fedn. of Musicians, ASCAP, Screen Actors Guild; mag. columnist: Music, Computers & Software Mag. 1986-88. Ofc: Broadscore Music POB 2252 Beverly Hills 91405

FRASER-SMITH, ELIZABETH BIRDSEY, biologist; b. April 19, 1938, Pasadena; d. William Canvin and Elizabeth Armstrong (Creswell) Birdsey; m. Antony Charles Fraser-Smith, April 6, 1968; children: Julie b. 1968, Bill b. 1970; edn: BA biology, Stanford Univ. 1960; MA, 1962. Career: assoc. scientist, sr. scientist Lockheed Missiles & Space Co., Palo Alto 1960-69; biologist cons. Enviros, Los Altos 1973-77; biologist II, staff researcher II Syntex Research Corp., Palo Alto 1977–; mem: Am. Soc. Microbiology, Internat. Soc. Virology, AAAS, Nat. Wildlife Fedn., Zero Population Growth, Sempervirens Fund; 24 research articles pub. in profl. jours. (1962–), 4 book reviews pub. (1968–), 2 patents for antimicrobiol. drugs (1984–). Res: 71 Alma Ct Los Altos 94022 Ofc: Syntex Research 3401 Hillview Ave Palo Alto 94304

FRASSINELLI, GUIDO JOSEPH, aerospace long-range planning advisor, ret.; b. December 4, 1927, Summit Hill, Penn.; s. Joseph and Maria (Grosso) F.; m. Antoinette Clemente, 1953; children: Lisa b. 1954, Erica b. 1956, Laura b. 1957, Joanne b. 1960, Mark b. 1961; edn: BS, MS aeronautical engring., M.I.T., 1949; MBA, Harvard Bus. Sch., 1956. Career: res. engr. MIT Aeroelastic Lab, 1949-52; project engr. USAF Flight Dynamics Lab, 1952-54; dynamics engr. Raytheon Co., 1956-58; co-founder/v.p. bus. mgmt. AviDyne Research, 1958-64; asst gen. mgr Kaman AviDyne Div., Kaman Corp., Burlington, Mass. 1964-66; plans integration mgr. L.A. Div., Rockwell Internat., 1966-68; asst dir. Strategic Planning, N. Amer. Aircraft Opns., Space Shuttle Cost/Schedule/Technical Reporting Gp., 1972-76; staff asst. to v.p. Shuttle Integ. and Ops., 1976-78; R & D proj. ldr. 1978-79; chief analyst, strategic planning, space transp. system div., 1980-85; sr. tech. advisor Advanced Engring., Rockwell Internat., 1985-89, project mgr. 1990-94; honors: Sigma Xi, Tau Beta Pi, Phi Kappa Theta, NASA Technology Utilization Award 1971, Astronaut Personal Achievement Award 1985; Assoc. Fellow Am Inst. of Aero. & Astro (tech. comm. on econ. 1983, v. chair. fin. L.A. Sect. 1986-87); civic: The Planning Forum, Town Hall of Calif., EDICT (treas. 1971-76); works: Atomic weapons effects on aircraft, Wind shear design criteria on launch vehicles, Space transp. strategic planning software; mil: lt. USAF, 1952-54, ret. lt. col. Reserve 1976; Republican; R.Cath. (founding com. chmn. St. John Fisher Parish Council 1978-85); rec: accordion, photography, reading Res: 29521 Quailwood Dr Rancho Palos Verdes 90275

FRAYSSINET, DANIEL FERNAND, software company executive; b. June 25, 1956, Rodez, France; s. Leon Privat and Fernande Marie (Foulquier) F.; m. Chantal Luce Hebrard, June 30, 1979 (div. 1988); m. Corinne Yollande Guillaud, March 4, 1989; children: Jennifer b. 1989, Malorie b. 1991; edn: DEUG math., INSA Villeurbanne France 1976; MSME, 1979. Career: research asst. O.N.S.E.R., Bron, France 1977-78; devel. engr. Centech, Glenview, Ill. 1979-82; pres. I.M.S. Inc., Camarillo 1985–; pres. and dir. D.P. Technology Corp. 1982–; dir. ACASO Business Ctr., Oxnard, Calif. 1992–; mem: S.M.E., Acad. of Magical Arts. Inc.; author: Adverse Effect of Intertia & Rigidity of Truck Colliding with Lighter Vehicle, 1978; coauthor (software) Arcade, 1979, Esprit, 1984; R.Cath.; rec: flying, windsurfing, jetskiing, magic, hypnosis. Ofc: D.P. Technology 1150 Avenida Acaso Camarillo 93010

FREEDMAN, STANLEY DAVID, physician; b. Oct. 12, 1935, Pittsburgh, Pa.; s. Joseph and Mary (Shelkrot) F.; m. Saralyn Cohen, Aug. 11, 1957; children: Joseph b. 1962, Eric and Douglas b. 1964; edn: AB, Harvard Coll. 1957; MD, N.Y. Univ. 1961. Career: chief div. of infectious diseases York Hosp., York, Pa. 1969-76; Mercy Hosp., San Diego 1976-77; pres. med. staff Green Hosp. of Scripps Clin., La Jolla 1985-87; head div. on-call physicians Scripps Clin. & Research Found. 1980-84, dir. grad. med. edn. 1984-92, chmn. dept. grad. med. edn. 1992–, Ann Dobbins chair in grad. med. edn., 1995– head div. infectious diseases 1977–; asst. prof. medicine Univ. Md. Sch. Medicine, Baltimore 1972-76; asst. clin. prof. medicine UCSD, La Jolla 1976, assoc. clin. prof. 1976-87, clin. prof. 1987–; awards: York Hosp. Outstanding Tchr.

Medicine 1974-75, Scripps Clin. Med. Group Disting. Service 1984, Scripps Clinic & Research Found. Outstanding Tchr. Medicine 1990-91; mem: Am. Soc. Microbiol., Infectious Diseases Soc. Am. (fellow), A.C.P. (fellow), San Diego Co. Med. Soc., CMA, UCSD Faculty Club; num. articles and textbook chapters pub. in med. jours.; mil: capt. USAF 1963-65; rec: photography, hiking. Res: 5901 Avenida Chamnez La Jolla 92037 Ofc: Scripps Clinic and Research Foundation 10666 N Torrey Pines Rd La Jolla 92037

FREEDOM, NANCY, neurolinguistic programmer, librarian; b. Sept. 16, 1932, Wash. D.C.; d. William Heman and Lillian Blanche (Martin) Clements; m. Gerald P. Brierley, Apr. 9, 1954 (div. 1969); children: Glenn Anthony, Lynn Hope; edn: BS, Univ. Maryland, 1954; MS, Univ. Wis., 1961; cert. behavioral sci., Univ. Mich., 1971; accelerated tchg. cert., cert. neurolinguistic pgmmg.; Calif. tchg. credential. Career: librarian (I) Madison (Wis.) Public Library, 1961-62; reference and circulation librarian Grandview-Arlington Pub. Lib., Worthington Pub. Lib., Columbus, Ohio, 1964-66; medical librarian Ohio State Univ. Med. Sch., Columbus 1966-68; reference librarian Gen. Motors Inst., Flint, Mich. 1969; librarian (III) Detroit Pub. Lib., 1969-76, Stockton (Calif.) San Joaquin County Pub. Lib., 1977-79; yoga tchr. adult schs. and libraries, Detroit, 1970-76, Calif., 1976–; neurolinguistic cons. and tnr. Freedom Workshop, Oakland 1981–; freelance book editor and indexer; librarian Alameda County Pub. Lib., Berkeley Pub. Lib., 1988–; librarian City of Alameda Free Lib., 1992, Oakland Pub. Lib. 1993–; contbr. book revs. to lib. jours.; mem: Progressive Library Workers, Internat. Assn. Neurolinguistic Pgmmg. (Western states rep., bd.), Calif. Lib. Assn., Assn. Profls. Treating Eating Disorders (speaker), Last Monday Club Womens Network, Omicron Nu, Beta Phi Mu; civic: Open Housing Com. Upper Arlington, Ohio 1967, Pledge of Resistance S.F.Bay Area 1984-88, LWV (chapt. bd. 1957), NOW; Democrat; Soc. of Friends; rec: early jazz collection, Asian philosophy, social justice. Res/Ofc: Freedom Workshop 540 Alcatraz Ave Ste 205 Oakland 94609-1140 Tel: 510/428-1184

FREEMAN, CHARLES LAWRENCE, researcher; b. Aug. 18, 1905, Newton, Mass.; s. Charles Alfred and Grace Edith (Rumery) F.; m. Phyllis Yates, June 29, 1929; children: Nancy b. 1931, Phyllis b. 1934; edn: BS, US Naval Acad., Annapolis, Md. Career: naval officer U.S. Navy, world wide service 1923-57: cruiser duty 1927-29, submarine duty, New London Co. 1929-34, post grad. sch., Annapolis, Md. 1934-36, submarine command, Honolulu 1936-39, instr. submarine sch., New London Co. 1939-41, submarine command, Southwest Pacific 1941-42, staff command 1942-44, staff command, Atlantic Ocean 1944-46, comdg. ofcr. USS Drew, Pacific Fleet 1945-46, comdg. ofcr. USS Williamsburg (Truman's presidential yacht), Atlantic Fleet 1946-48, comdr. naval sta. U.S. Naval Acad. and USS Reina Mercedes, 1948-51; NATO staff, Paris 1951, then Sixth Fleet, Mediterranean and Pentagon service to 1957 (ret.); researcher Rand Corp., Santa Monica 1957-91; author var. research papers; rec: golf. Res: 601 Country Club Ln Coronado 92118-2035

FREEMAN, JEFF, film editor; b. Sept. 12, 1951, Santa Monica; s. Joel Freeman and Jo (Stack) Napoleon; m. Kathryn Lynnchild, June 5, 1983; 1 dau. Caroline Louise b. 1990; edn: UC Northridge 1973; BA magna cum laude, UCLA 1975. Career: film editor New Century, Paramount, 20th Century Fox, 1986-87, NBC, 1988-89, Joe Wizan Prodns., 1989; faculty UCLA 1984-89; mem. IATSE; editor feature films: Mad Love, 1994, Deep Red, 1993, A Family Torn Apart, 1992, The Waterdance, 1991, Favorite Son, 1988, Bad Dreams, 1988, Split Decisions, 1987, Bullet Proof, 1987, Quiet Cool, 1986, Oceans of Fire, 1986, Dirt Bike Kid, 1985, Joni & The Whales, 1984, others; Democrat; rec: music. Res: 1132 19th St #1 Santa Monica 90403

FREEMAN, MARTIN, computer research company, principal scientist; b. Sept. 26, 1944, Paterson, N.J.; s. Reubin and Minnie (Kahn) F.; m. Barbara Frutiger Cechmanek, Aug. 17, 1975; children: Robert b. 1979, Michael b. 1985; edn: BEE, Rensselaer Polytechnic Inst., 1965; MSEE, Columbia Univ., 1966; PhD, computer sci., Univ. Pa., 1971. Career: assoc. prof. computer sci. American Univ., Washington, 1971-77; vis. prof. Stanford Univ., Palo Alto 1977-78; mem. tech. staff Bell Laboratories, Whippany, N.J. 1978-82; sr. microprocessor architect Signetics, Sunnyvale, Calif. 1982-86; vis. fellow Stanford Univ., 1986-87; principal scientist Philips Res., Palo Alto 1988–; gen. chmn. Internat. Symp. on Archtl. Support, Palo Alto 1987, Workshop on Transaction Machine Arch., Lake Arrowhead 1988, Hot Chips Symp., Stanford 1991; vice chmn. Hot Chips Symposium 1995; chmn. SPIE Conf. of Multimedia Computing and Networking 1996; awards: Tau Beta Pi, Eta Kappa Nu, appreciation IEEE Computer Soc., W.D.C. (1987, 1988), Assn. for Computing Mach., N.Y.C. 1987, IEEE Meritorious Service Award 1994, listed Am. Men & Women in Sci. 1976, Who's Who in Technology Today 1982, Who's Who in the West 1992; Who's Who in Sci. & Tech. 1993; mem: IEEE (1964–, chmn. tech. com. on microprocessors, W.D.C. 1986-88, chmn. nat. stds. com PI285 Scalable Storage Interface 1990–), Assn. for Computing Machinery 1966–, AAAS 1986–, Internat. Platform Assn.; inventor: Memory Mgmt. & Pattern Matching Units (2 patents, 1985, 87); guest editor IEEE Transactions on Computers: Archtl. Support for Pgmg. Languages and Operating Systems, 1988, num. journal articles, 1971–; rec: film, theater. Res: 4189 Donald Dr Palo Alto 94306 Ofc: Philips Research 4005 Miranda Ave Palo Alto 94304

FREEMAN, MYRNA FAYE, government employee benefits manager; b. Oct. 30, 1939, Danville, Ill.; d. Thomas Gene, Sr. and Dorothy Olive (Chodera) Freeman; m. Lonnie Choate, Aug. 16, 1959 (div. 1987); children: Leslie b. 1965, Gregory b. 1967; edn: BA, San Diego St. Univ., 1977, MA, 1987. Career: employee benefits mgr. City of San Diego, 1974-84; asst. risk mgr. San Diego Co. Office of Edn., 1984–; instr. Ins. Edn. Assn. for the CEBS prog., Internat. Found. of Employee Benefit Plans and Wharton Sch. of Univ. of Pa.; honors: appreciation, COMBO, S.D. 1977, Phi Kappa Phi 1986, listed Who's Who Among San Diego Women 1983, Who's Who of Am. Women 1992; mem. Calif. Assn. of Sch. Bus. Officials (chair risk mgmt. R&D com. 1987-88), Calif. Women in Govt. (S.D. exec. bd. 1983-84), Risk & Ins. Mgmt. Soc. (San Diego chapt. pres. 1988), S.D. Employers Health Cost Coalition (bd. v.chair 1988), S.D. Group Ins. Claims Council (pres. 1987, treas.), Kaiser Consumer Council (1977-84, pres. 1980), Internat. Found. of Employee Benefits, S.D. Workers' Compensation Forum, Pub. Agency Risk Mgmt. Assn., Calif. Assn. Jt. Powers Authorities, Council of Self-Insured Pub. Agencies, Pub. Risk and Ins. Mgmt. Assn., S.D. Co. Affirmative Action Advy. Bd. 1984-85, Vista Health Plan (pub. policy advy. com. 1994), Kaiser on-the-job (advy. council 1994–, Internat. Platform Assn., Sigma Kappa Sor.; publs: Administrative Impact of Implementing Legislation AB: 528 Retiree Health and Dental Coverage, 1987, articles in field, 1985-92; Republican; Prot.; rec: sports, numismatics, swimming, cards. Res: 4345 Cartulina Rd San Diego 92124-2102 Ofc: San Diego Co. Office of Education, 6401 Linda Vista Rd #405 San Diego 92111-7399

FRENCH, GEORGINE LOUISE, guidance counselor; b. May 15, 1934, Lancaster, Pa.; d. Richard Franklin and Elizabeth Georgine (Driesbach) Beacham; m. Barrie J. French, Feb. 4, 1956; children: Joel B., John D., James D., Jeffrey D.; edn: BA, CSU San Bernardino, 1967; MS, No. Ill. Univ., 1973; DD, Am. Ministerial Assn., 1978; cert. guidance counselor Nat. Board Cert. Counselor, 1985; secondary tchr.; cert. coll. counselor. Career: personnel counselor Sages Dept. Store, San Bernardino, 1965-66; asst. bookkeeper Bank Calif., San Bernardino, 1964-65; tchr. Livermore Sch. Dist., 1968-69; guidance counselor Bur. Indian Affairs, Tuba City, Ariz., 1974-80, guidance counselor Sherman Indian H.S., Riverside, Calif., 1980-82; guidance counselor Ft. Douglas Edn. Ctr., U.S. Army, Salt Lake City, 1982-86; USAF guidance counselor Los Angeles Air Force Base, 1986-87, education services ofcr. Comiso Air Force Base, Italy 1987-88; counselor Los Angeles Air Force Base 1988-95 (ret.); extension tchr. Navajo Comm. Coll., Yavapai Coll.; personnel counselor USNR, 1976-86; ordained to ministry Am. Ministerial Assn., 1979; mem: Am. Counseling Assn., AARP; mil: USAF 1954-56. Res: PO Box 33298 Laughlin, NV 89028

FRENCH, PRESLEY BURDETTE, life insurance sales executive; b. May 10, 1921, Central City, Nebr.; s. Crawford Hunter and Ida Maurine (Dughman) F.; m. Violetta Hill, Mar. 27, 1943; children: Linda, b. 1944; Brian, b. 1946; Patricia, b. 1950; Bette Jean, b. 1955; edn: UC Berkeley 1946-7; BSc, cum laude, Armstrong Univ. 1950; Life Ins. Mktg. Inst., Purdue Univ. 1957; Life Ins. Agcy. mgmt. courses, 1961; Adv. Sch. Ins. Mktg., So. Methodist Univ. 1961. Career: agent Mutual Life of New York 1946; agt. Western Life Ins. Co. 1947-68; exec. agcy. asst. Home Ofc. 1950-4, general agent (co's leading agcy.) 1954-9, supt. of agencies for No. Calif. & Hawaii 1959-68, mng. gen. agent Western Life & AMEV (now Fortis) Investors 1968-81; sr. agcy. consultant Western/ St. Paul Life Cos. 1981-83, ret.; charter mem. Western Agcy. Officers Conf.; charter mem. Western/ St. Paul Cos. Communique Panel; awards: Ins. Exec. of 1955, Armstrong Univ. Alumnus Assn.; Pres. Trophy 1964; Western Life Million Dollar Round Table; mem: NALU, Nat. C.of C., DAV, Commonwealth Club of Calif., Amer. Legion, VFW, Calif. Wildlife Fedn., NRA (life), 4th Marine Div. Assn. (life), Navy League, Masons 32 degrees Islam Temple Shrine, De Molay Alumni Assn. (life), Beta Phi Gamma, Kappa Sigma Kappa, mil: CPhM USN Fleet Marine Force: sev. personal cits., commends., Purple Heart, Pres. Unit Cit., Navy- Marine Corps. Medal, Navy Unit Commendn.; Republican; Presbyterian; rec: hunt, fish, golf. Res: 28 Eastwood Dr San Mateo 94403

FRESQUEZ, ERNESTO CLIFFORD, executive recruiting consultant; b. May 24, 1955, Roswell, N.M.; s. Bonifacio Archuleta and Lucilla (Lucero) F.; m. Jeanette Acosta, July 20, 1985; children: Eric, Marissa; edn: BABA, N.M. Highlands Univ. 1977; John F. Kennedy Univ. 1980-83; Golden Gate Univ. 1983-85. Career: acctg. asst. Chevron USA, Concord 1977-80, assoc. acct. Chevron Internat., San Francisco 1980-81, budget analyst Chevron Overseas 1981-85; mgmt. auditor ADC Ltd. DOE IG, Albuquerque, N.M. 1985-89; exec. recruiter Fresquez & Assoc., Oakland; mentor Puente Project, Berkeley 1989–; Metas Project, El Cerrito 1989; dir. of public relations Nat. Soc. Hispanic MBA 1994, dir. at large 1995, S.F. Chpt. treas. 1991-92; awards: Bus. Hons. Club student of month, 1977; nat. vice-chair-bd. Personnel Mgrs. Assn. Aztlan, 1992-93; mem: Contra Costa Hispanic C.of C. (bd.), Alameda Co. Hispanic C.of C.; Democrat; Congregational; rec: backpacking, tennis. Ofc: Fresquez & Associates 405 14th Street Suite 1040 Oakland 94612

FREW, BARRY ALBERT, information services administrator, educator; b. Feb. 10, 1948, Portland, Oreg.; s. Howard Albert and Dorothy Estelle (Marcum) F.; m. Jeanne Lynn, June 29, 1985; children: Arlen b. 1968, Brian b. 1973; edn: AS, Umpqua Comm. Coll. 1968; BS, Miami of Ohio 1976; MS Info. Systems,

Naval Postgrad. Sch. Monterey, 1984. Career: dir. environ. dept. Naval Maintenance & Supply Support Office, Norfolk, Va. 1979-82; dir. inventory control dept. Naval Supply Center, Pearl Harbor, Hawaii 1981-82; prof. Naval Postgrad. Sch., Monterey 1984–, dir. and dean 1990, Computer and Information Services, 1989-93; gen. ptnr. J&B Cons., Monterey 1982–; award: Meritorious Civilian Service Award 1993; bd. dirs. Monterey Fed. Credit Union 1989–, v.chmn. bd. 1991-94, chmn. bd. 1995; instr. Learning Tree Internat. seminars, L.A. 1989-91; mem: Spl. Interest Group on CD-ROM Applications & Tech.; thesis advisor 1984-92, researcher optical storage tech. 1986-92, workshop leader Federal Computer Conf. 1991-92, Navy Microcomputer Conf. 1990, 92, leader Profl. Dept. Seminar 1989, keynote speaker Am. Soc. Mil. Comptrollers 1988; mil: LCDR USN 1968-88, Navy Commend. 1982, 84; rec: flying, softball, running. Ofc: J&B Consulting 25565 Boots Rd Monterey 93940

FRICK, OSCAR LIONEL, physician, educator; b. Mar. 12, 1923, New York; s. Oscar and Elizabeth (Ringger) F.; m. Mary Elizabeth Hubbard, Sept. 2, 1954; edn: AB, Cornell Univ. 1944; MD, Cornell Univ. Sch. Medicine 1946; MMS, Univ. Pa. Grad. Sch. Medicine 1960; PhD, Stanford Univ. Grad. Sch. Medicine 1964; lic. Am. Bd. Pediatrics 1960, Am. Bd. Allergy & Immunology 1978. Career: intern, Babies Hosp., Columbia, N.Y.C. 1946-47; resident Children's Hosp., Buffalo, N.Y. 1950-51; postdoctoral fellow Univ. McGill-Allergy, Montreal, Canada 1958-59; UCSF 1959-60; Inst. Immunologie, Paris, France 1960-62; Stanford Univ. 1962-64; asst. prof. pediatrics UCSF 1963-67, assoc. prof. 1967-72, prof. 1972–; awards: Georgetown Univ. Von Pirquet, 1974, Am. Acad. Pediatrics Bret Ratner, 1982; mem: Am. Acad. Allergy & Immunology (pres. 1977-78), Internat. Assn. Allergy & Immunology (secty. 1975-94), Coll. Internat. Allergy & Immunology (exec. com. 1988-92), Am. Pediatric Soc., Am. Acad. Pediatrics, Am. Coll. Allergy & Immunology (fellow), Am. Assn. Immunologists, Am. Thoracic Soc., Am. Lung Assn., FDA (advy. com. allergic drugs 1984-88, chmn. 1987-88); author: 100 articles pub. in sci. jours., 1950–; mil: lt., USNR, USN 1947-49; Republican; Protestant; rec: photography, hiking. Res: 370 Parnassus Ave San Francisco 94117 Ofc: University of California 505 Parnassus Dr San Francisco 94143

FRIDLEY, SAUNDRA LYNN, internal audit executive; b. June 14, 1948, Columbus, Ohio; d. Jerry Dean and Esther Eliza (Bluhm) Fridley; edn: BS, Franklin Univ., 1976; MBA, Golden Gate Univ., 1980; Cert. Fraud Examiner (CFE). Career: accounts receivable supr. Internat. Harvester Inc., Columbus, Ohio, San Leandro, Calif., 1972-80; senior internal auditor Western Union, San Francisco 1980; internal auditor II, County of Santa Clara, San Jose 1980-82; senior internal auditor Tymshare Inc., Cupertino 1982-84, div. contr. 1984; internal audit mgr. VWR Scientific, Brisbane 1984-88, audit dir. 1988–; internal audit mgr. Pacific IBM Employees Fed. Credit Union, 1989-90; dir. quality assurance Western Temporary Svs. 1990–; owner/founder Dress Fore The 9's, 1994–; mem: Inst. Internal Auditors (pres., founder Tri-Valley chpt., Speakers Bur., Internat. Seminar Com.), Nat. Assn. Female Execs., Assn. of Cert. Fraud Examiners (pres. S.F. Bay Area chpt.); civic: Friends of the Vineyards; rec: woodworking, gardening, golf. Res: 19 Windmill Ct Brentwood 94513 Ofc: Western Temporary Services 301 Lennon Lane Walnut Creek 94598

FRIED, ELAINE JUNE, insurance agent, civic activist; b. Oct. 19, 1943, Los Angeles; m. Howard I. Fried, Aug. 7, 1966; children: Donna Marie, Randall Jay; edn: grad. Pasadena H.S. 1963, various coll. courses. Career: v.p. Sea Hill Inc., Pasadena 1973–; ins. agt., office mgr. Howard I. Fried Agy., Alhambra 1975–; frequent speaker on Insurance Medicine, Psycho-social aspects of diabetes, Insurance and the Diabetic; recipient Vol. award Am. Diabetes Assn. of So. Calif. 1974-77; former mem. Visiting Nurses Assn., Pasadena and San Gabriel Valley (bd., pub. rels. com., personnel com.); mem: Women's Am. ORT (past publicity chair S.G.V. region), B'nai B'rith Women, Hadassah, Temple Beth Torah Sisterhood (co-recipient Ner Tamid award), Congregation Shaarei Torah (publicity chair 1993–, outside publicity chair, Sisterhood 1993–); contbr. articles to profl. jours. Res: 404 N Hidalgo Ave Alhambra 91801-2640

FRIEDMAN, GARY DAVID, physician, epidemiologist; b. Mar. 8, 1934, Cleveland, Ohio; s. Howard N. and Cema (Cort) F.; m. Ruth Helen Schleien, June 22, 1958; children: Emily b. 1960, Justin b. 1963, Richard b. 1965; edn: student, Antioch Coll., Yellow Springs, Ohio 1951-53; BS, Univ. of Chicago 1956, MD (with honors), 1959; MS, Harvard Univ. Sch. of Public Health 1965; lic. physician Calif. 1965; cert. Am. Bd. Internal Medicine 1966. Career: intern/resident Harvard Med. Svs., Boston City Hosp. 1959-61; resident Univ. Hospitals, Cleveland Ohio 1961-62; med. ofcr. Heart Disease Epidemiology Study, Nat. Heart Inst., Framingham, Mass. 1962-66; chief Epidemiology Unit, Heart Disease Control Prog., USPHS, San Francisco 1966-68; sr. epidemiologist Kaiser Permanente, Div. of Res., Oakland 1968-76, asst. dir. for Epidemiology & Biostatistics 1976-91, dir., 1991–; res. fellow, then res. assoc. Harvard Med. Sch. 1962-66; lectr. Univ. Calif. Sch. of Medicine, S.F. 1980- (asst. 1967-75, assoc. 1975-92, clin. prof. Depts. of Medicine and Family & Comm. Medicine); lectr. UC Berkeley Sch. of Public Health 1968–; editorial. bd. HMO Practice 1991–; editor Am. Jour. of Epidemiology 1988–; mem: Scientific Review Panel on Toxic Air Contaminants, St. of Calif. 1988–; advy. com. Merck Found./Soc. for Epidemiologic Res., Clin Epidemiology Fellowships 1990-94; sr. advy.

Expert Panel on Preventive Svs., USPHS 1991–; com. on Epidemiology & Veterans Follow-up Studies, Nat. Res. Council 1980-85, Subcom. on Twins 1980–; NIH Epidemiology and Disease Control Study Sect. 1982-86; U.S. Preventive Svs. Task Force 1984-88; US/USSR Working Group, Sudden Cardiac Death, Nat. Heart Lung & Blood Inst. 1975-82; honors: Phi Beta Kappa, Alpha Omega Alpha, Roche Award for outstanding performance as a med. student, Delta Omega, Nat. Cancer Inst. Merit Award 1987 and Outstanding Investigator Grant 1989-2001, Cleveland Heights. H.S. Disting. Alumni Hall of Fame 1991; mem: Am. Epidemiological Soc. (membership com. 1982-86), Soc. for Epidemiological Res., Internat. Epidemiological Assn. Am. Coll. of Physicians (fellow) Council on Epidemiology, Am. Heart Assn. (fellow, chmn. Com. on Criteria & Methods 1969-71, chmn. Prog. Com. 1973-76), Am. Public Health Assn., Am. Soc. for Preventive Oncology, Internat. Soc. for Twin Studies, Chamber Musicians of No. Calif. (bd. dirs. 1992–), S.F. Recreation Symphony (oboist); author (book): Primer of Epidemiology 4 editions, 1974, 80, 87, 94); author/co-author: 225+ scientific papers; mil: sr. surgeon USPHS 1962-68; rec: music: playing oboe and English horn. Ofc: Division of Research, Kaiser Permanente Medical Care Program 3505 Broadway Oakland 94611

FRIEDMAN, LOUIS, winery executive, lawyer; b. Sept. 24, 1939, St. Louis, Mo.; s. Abraham and Elinor (Rubin) F.; m. Kennicia Gillett; children: Cary b. 1965, Stacey b. 1968; edn: BS, Ariz. St. Univ. 1960; LL.B, Loyola Univ. 1964; LL.M, N.Y. Univ. 1967. Career: Price Waterhouse & Co., Los Angeles 1961-64, N.Y.C. 1964-73; exec. v.p., treas. E. & J. Gallo Winery, Modesto 1973–; mem: Calif. Bar Assn., N.Y. Bar, Am. Inst. C.P.A., Calif. Soc. C.P.A., Am. Bar Assn., Stanislaus Co. Bar Assn., Modesto Rotary Club (pres. 1992-93); trustee Sylvan Union Sch. Dist. 1976-81; Jewish. Res: 508 Andover Ln Modesto 95350 Ofc: E. & J. Gallo Winery 600 Yosemite Blvd Modesto 95354

FRIEDMAN, MICHAEL ELLIOTT, lawyer; b. Nov. 3, 1951, Los Angeles; s. Selma B. (Himovitz) F.; m. Janet M. Kiniry, Dec. 1971; 1 son, Paul b. 1981; edn: BA, UC Berkeley 1973; JD, UC Davis 1976. Career: atty. Beardsley Hufstedler & Kemble, Los Angeles 1977-81; Nagata Masuda & Katayama 1981-83; sole practice, Pasadena 1983–; arbitrator PSE, NASD, NFA, 1988–; honors: UC Davis Moot Ct. (1974), Law Review ed. (1975-76); mem: Am. Arbitration Assn., Pasadena Bar Assn. (secty. 1988-89); 1 article pub. in profl. jour. (1975). Ofc: 215 N Marengo Ave #204 Pasadena 91101

FRIEDMAN, MILTON, economist, author; s. Jeno Saul and Sarah Ethel (Landau) F.; m. Rose Director, June 25, 1938; children: Janet, David; edn: AB, Rutgers Univ. 1932, LLD, 1968; AM, Univ. Chgo. 1933; PhD, Columbia Univ. 1946; hon. degrees: LLD, St. Paul's (Rikkyo) Univ. 1963, Kalamazoo Coll. 1968, Lehigh Univ. 1969, Loyola Univ. 1971, Univ. N.H. 1975, Harvard Univ. 1979, B.Y.U. 1980, Dartmouth 1980, Gonzaga Univ. 1981; ScD, Rochester Univ. 1971, LHD, Rockford Coll. 1969, Roosevelt Univ. 1975, Hebrew Union Coll. L.A. 1981, Jacksonville Univ. 1993; LittD, Bethany Coll. 1971; PhD (hon.), Hebrew Univ. Jerusalem 1977; DCS, Francisco Marroquin Univ. Guatemala 1978. Career: assoc. economist Nat. Resources Com., W.D.C. 1935-37; res. staff Nat. Bur. Econ. Res., NY, 1937-45, 48-81; vis. prof. econs. Univ. Wis. 1940-41; prin. economist, tax res. div. US Treasury 1941-43; assoc. dir. res., stats. res. group, war res. div. Columbia Univ. 1943-45; assoc. prof. econs. and bus. adminstrn. Univ. Minn. 1945-46; assoc. prof. econs. Univ. Chgo. 1946-48, 1948-62, Paul Snowden Russell Disting. Service Prof. 1962-82, Emeritus, 1983–; Fulbright lectr. Cambridge Univ., 1953-54; vis. Wesley Clair Mitchell Res. prof. econs. Columbia Univ., 1964-65; fellow Ctr. for Advanced Study in Behavioral Sci., 1957-58; mem. Pres.'s Commn. All-Vol. Army, 1969-70, Pres.'s Commn. on White House Fellows, 1971-74, Pres.'s Econ. Policy Advy. Bd. 1981-88; vis. scholar Fed. Reserve Bank, San Francisco, 1977; sr. res. fellow Hoover Instn., Stanford Univ., 1977–; awards: John Bates Clark medal Am. Econ. Assn. 1951, Nobel prize in econs. 1976, Pvt. Ent. Exemplar medal Freedoms Found. 1978, Chicagoan of year Chgo. Press Club 1972, educator of yr. Chgo. Jewish United Fund 1973, Grand Cordon of the First Class Order of the Sacred Treasure Govt. Japan 1986, Nat. Medal of Sci. U.S. Govt. 1988, Presdl. Medal of Freedom U.S. Govt. 1988; Fellow Inst. Math. Stats., Am. Stats. Assn., Econometric Soc., Jewish Acad. of Arts and Scis., mem. Nat. Acad. Scis., Am. Econ. Assn. (exec. com. 1955-57, pres. 1967), Royal Econ. Soc., Western Econ. Assn. (pres. 1984-5), Am. Philos. Soc., Mont Pelerin Soc. (dir. 1958-61, pres. 1970-2); club: Quadrangle; author: Taxing to Prevent Inflation (w/ C. Shoup, R.P. Mack) 1943; Income from Independent Professional Practice (w/ S.S. Kuznets) 1946; Sampling Inspection (w/ H.A. Freeman, F. Mosteller, W.A. Wallis) 1948; Essays in Positive Economics, 1953; A Theory of the Consumption Function, 1957; A Program for Monetary Stability, 1960; Price Theory, 1962; (w/ R.D. Friedman) Capitalism and Freedom, 1962, Free To Choose, 1980, Tyranny of the Status Quo, 1984; (w/ A.J. Schwartz) A Monetary History of the U.S., 1967-1960, 1963, The Great Contraction, 1965, Monetary Statistics of the U.S., 1970, Monetary Trends in the U.S. and the U.K., 1982; Inflation: Causes and Consequences, 1963; The Balance of Payments: Free vs. Fixed Exchange Rates (w/ R. Roosa) 1967; Dollars and Deficits, 1968; The Optimum Quantity of Money and Other Essays, 1969; Monetary vs. Fiscal Policy (w/ W.W. Heller) 1968; A Theoretical Framework for Monetary Analysis, 1972; Social Security (w/ W.J. Cohen) 1972; An Economist's Protest,

1972; There Is No Such Thing As A Free Lunch, 1975; Price Theory, 1976; Milton Friedman's Monetary Framework (w/ R.J. Gordon et al) 1974; Bright Promises, Dismal Performance: An Economist's Protest (w/ W.R. Allen) 1983; Money Mischief, 1992; ed. Studies in the Quantity Theory of Money, 1956; bd. eds. Am. Econ. Rev., 1951-53, Econometrica, 1957-69; advy. bd. Jour. of Money, Credit, and Banking, 1968-94; columnist Newsweek mag. 1966-84, contbg. ed. 1972-84; contbr. articles. to profl. jours. Ofc: Hoover Institution Stanford Univ. Stanford 94305-6010

FRIEMAN, EDWARD ALLAN, university administrator, educator; b. Jan. 19, 1926, NY, NY; s. Joseph and Belle (Davidson) F.; m. Ruth Paula Todman, June 19, 1949 (dec. May 6, 1966); m. Joy Fields, Sept. 17, 1967; children: Jonathan, Michael, Joshua, Wendy, Linda Holiner; edn: BS, Columbia Univ., 1946; MS, Polytechnic Inst. of Brooklyn, 1948, PhD, 1952. Career: instr. physics, res. assoc. Polytechnic Inst. Bklyn., 1945-52; head theoretical div. Plasma Physics Lab., Princeton Univ., 1953-64, prof. dept. astrophysical scis. 1961-64, dep. dir. Plasma Physics Lab, 1964-79; dir. of energy research U.S. Dept. of Energy, W.D.C., 1979-81; exec. v.p. Science Applications Internat. Corp., La Jolla 1981-86; adj. prof. physics UC San Diego, 1981-91, dir. Scripps Institution of Oceanography, and vice chancellor marine scis. UC San Diego, 1986–; apt: V.Pres.'s Space Advy. Bd. 1992-93, White House Sci. Council (v. chmn. 1981-88), President's Com. on the Nat. Medal of Science (chmn. 1992-93), Secty. of Energy Advy. Bd./SEAB 1990-94, SEAB Task Force on DOE Nat. Labs. (chmn. 1991-92), Defense Sci. Bd. ASW Task Force (chmn. 1991-92), Dept. Energy Task Force on Energy Res. Priorities (mem. 1992–), Jt. Oceanographic Institutions Inc. (1986–, chmn. 1991–), NASA/Earth Observing Sys. engring. rev. advy. com. (chmn. 3/91–), NRC/Ocean Studies Bd. 1987-94, editl. bd. Jour. of Defense Research 1987-91; cons.: Jason Div. The Mitre Corp. 1960–, AMAX Inc. 1993-94; dir: Science Applications Internat. Corp. 1987–; Sci. Advy. Com. General Motors 1987-93, The Charles Stark Draper Lab., Inc. 1989–, planning and steering advy. com. of Adv. Tech. Panel for Vice Chief Naval Ops. 1990–, exec. com. Calif.-Israel Task Force 1992-95, Nat. Coalition of Indep. Scholars Advy. Council 1994–, Ctr. for Oceans Law and Policy Advy. Bd. 1994-98, DOD Panel on Defense Sci. and Engring. Prog., Defense Sci. Bd. task force on tactical directed energy weapons, Naval Res. Advy. Com. (chmn. tech. base study, mem. special study group 1995–), com. on Internat. Security and Arms Control, NSF Physics Advy. Panel, NASA Nuclear Processes Res. Advy. Com., DOD Nat. Security Agency Special Task Force 1995–; awards: NSF senior postdoc. fellow 1964, John Simon Guggenheim fellow 1970, DOE Disting. Service Medal 1980, Richtmyer Award, Am. Physical Soc. 1984, Disting. Alumni, Polytechnic Inst. Bklyn. 1984; mem: Nat. Acad. Scis. (mem. BISE review panel on U.S./USSR Sci. & Tech. agreements, chmn. NAS/NRC Bd. on Global Change 1993–95 and Bd. on Sustainable Devel. 1995–98), Am. Philosophical Soc., Am. Physical Soc., Astronomical Soc., AAAS, Sigma Xi, N.Y. Acad. Scis.; publs: 80+ in statistical mechanics, theoretical plasma physics, magnetohydrodynamics and kinetic theory; mil: ensign USN 1943-46; rec: piano, tennis, literature. Ofc: Scripps Institution. of Oceanography, UCSD 9500 Gilman Dr La Jolla 92093-0210

FRISCH, JOHN HENRY, financial executive; b. March 3, 1932, Joliet, Ill.; s. Henry P. and Helen W. (Riley) F.; m. Karen M. Blitz, Nov. 22, 1956; children: Penni J. b. 1957, Gary J. b. 1959, Wendi J. b. 1960, Kristi K. b. 1963; edn: BS, Lewis Univ. 1954. Career: controller Fairchild Industries, Manhattan Beach 1956-64; dir. fin. planning Planning Research Corp., Los Angeles 1965-74; corp. controller, treas. Holmes & Narver Inc., Orange 1974-80; controller Bethlehem Steel Corp., Los Angeles 1980-81; v.p., corp. controller Becket Group, Santa Monica 1981-84; corp. controller Modern Alloys Inc., Stanton 1985-86; v.p. fin. and adminstrn. E&L Engring. Inc., Long Beach 1986-90; corporate controller/CFO, Geoservices, Long Beach 1990–; chmn. Planning Commn., Manhattan Beach 1972-74; pres. Think Bridge 1984–; prin., founder FGM Assoc. 1984–; mem: Manhattan Beach Badminton Club (past pres.), Nat. Assn. Accts. (past bd. dirs.), Calif. Assn. Realtors, Nat. Assn. Realtors, Elks; mil: lt.j.g. USN 1954-56; Republican; R.Cath.; rec: badminton, bicycling. Res: 920 John St Manhattan Beach 90266

FRISCH, JOSEPH, college professor; b. April 21, 1921, Vienna, Austria; nat. 1946; s. Abraham and Rachel (Liebermann) F.; m. Joan S. Assert, May 26, 1962; children: Nora Theresa, Erich Martin, Jonathan David; edn: BSME, Duke Univ. 1946; MS, UC Berkeley 1950; reg. profl. engr. Calif. (1948). Career: faculty UC Berkeley 1947–, asst. prof. 1951-57, assoc. prof. 1957-63, prof. 1963–, chmn. div. mechanical design 1966-70, assoc. dean. 1972-75; cons. 1950–; honors: Phi Beta Kappa, Sigma Xi, Pi Tau Sigma, Tau Beta Pi; mem: ASME (fellow), Faculty Club; research papers and articles pub. in tech. jours. (1950–). Res: 986 Wildcat Canyon Rd Berkeley 94708 Ofc: Univ. of Calif. Dept. of Mechanical Engineering 5130 Etcheverry Berkeley 94720-1740

FROEHLICH, CHARLES W., JR., state appellate court justice; b. Dec. 5, 1928, San Jose; s. Charles W., Sr. and Ruth (Eddy) F.; m. Millicent Gene Davis, May 24, 1951; children: Marion b. 1952, Susan (Marvin) b. 1955, Helen (Trevelyan) b. 1957; edn: AB, Stanford Univ., LLD, UC Berkeley. Career: atty. pvt. practice, San Diego 1956-62, 65-72, 82-88; prof. of law UC Berkeley,

1962-65; judge Superior Ct., San Diego 1972-82; justice Ct. of Appeal, State of Calif., San Diego 1988–; honors: Phi Beta Kappa 1951, Order of the Coif 1956; mem. ABA; mil: 1st lt. AUS 1951-53, Bronze star; Republican; Methodist; rec: farming, winemaking. Res: 1444 Windsong Ln San Diego 92026

FROEHLY, BERTRAM MARTIN, JR., physician, neurologist; b. Aug. 26, 1947, St. Louis, Mo.; s. Bertram Martin and Elaine Ernestine (Bost) F.; m. Heather Ann Fike, March 28, 1981; children: Brittany b. 1984, Courtney b. 1988; edn: BS, Tulane Univ. 1969; MD, Cornell Univ. Med. Coll. 1973. Career: med. resident Cornell Univ.-N.Y. Hosp., N.Y.C. 1973-75; Case Western Reserve Univ., Univ. Hosp. Cleveland, Ohio 1975-76; neurology resident UCSF Moffitt Hosp., San Francisco 1976-79; attdg. neurologist Riverside Med. Clinic., Riverside Comm. Hosp. and Parkview Hosp., Riverside 1979–; honors: Phi Beta Kappa; mem: L.A. Acad. Medicine, Am. Acad. Neurology, AMA, CMA, Riverside Co. Med. Assn.; rec: golf, astronomy, chess. Ofc: Riverside Medical Clinic 6780 Indiana Ave Riverside 92506

FROST, PATRICIA JOYCE ROSE, entrepreneur, model; b. Feb. 11, 1939, Wewoka, Okla.; d. Mayhon Tiner and Frances Nell (Carl) Rose; m. Sterling Newell Frost, Aug. 18, 1957; children: Patricia (Wiscarson) b. 1958, Richard b. 1960, Lindy (Harrington) b. 1962; edn: Orthodontic Nurse, Johns Hopkins, Balt., 1972. Career: orthodontic nse. Baltimore and Chgo., 1972-76; exec. asst. to the v.p. Chemical Dynamics, Chgo. 1977-78; freelance model, San Francisco 1985–; owner/opr. bed and breakfast Paradise Retreat, Tiburon, Calif. 1988–; frequent marital counseling var. churches No. Calif. 1980-82, conduct Marital Enrichment Seminar: Four Steps to Ectasy, Tiburon 1987; appt. Marin County Grand Jury, San Rafael (chair hlth. and human svs., 1988), Marin Co. Adult Law & Justice Commn. 1989-92, Marin Co. Jail Liason Commn. 1989-92; owner/mgr. Prima Pacific Inc. (custom design clothing) 1992-93; mem. Marin Newcomers (pres. 1987-88, dir. 1988-89); Republican; Baptist; rec: painting, travel, gourmet cooking, hot air ballooning, Mercedes sports car. Address: Paradise Retreat, 4144 Paradise Dr Tiburon 94920

FRYE, DOUGLAS MCDONALD, physician; b. Dec. 8, 1956, Fresno, Calif.; s. John William and Jeanette Laverne (Frazier) F.; edn: BS biology (magna cum laude), Santa Clara Univ. 1979; MD Med. Coll. of Wisconsin, Milwaukee 1983; lic. physician Nat. Bd. of Med. Examiners 1984. Career: surgical resident Univ. of Hawaii, Honolulu 1983-85; flight surgeon USAF Med. Corps, Castle AFB, Calif. 1985-88; missionary doctor Migori Christian Centre, Migori/Suna, Kenya 1989; urgent care physician Westminster Med. Group, Westminster, Calif. 1989-90; HIV/urgent care physician Tom Waddell Clinic, San Francisco D.P.H. 1991–; instr. UC S.F. 1992–; honors: valedictorian San Joaquin Mem. H.S., Fresno 1974; Phi Beta Kappa 1979; Commendation Medal USAF 1987, Humanitarian Svs. Award USAF 1988; vol. physician Haight-Ashbury Free Med. Clinic, S.F. 1992, Holy Cross Clinic, Fresno 1991; vol. aide Kaiser Hospice, S.F. 1991-92; vol. counselor Youth Advocates, San Anselmo 1993-94; vol. speaker Marin AIDS Project, San Rafael 1993–; youth group advisor 1st Presbyn. Ch., San Rafael 1993–; vol. speaker's bureau Spectrum Ctr. for Gay, Lesbian, Bisexual Concerns, San Anselmo 1994–; author: articles pub. in Santa Clara Mag. 1990, 93; mil: capt. USAF and USAFR 1980-88; Democrat; Christian; rec: basketball, tennis, photography, writing. Ofc: Tom Waddell Clinic 50 Ivy St San Francisco 94102

FRYXELL, KARL JOSEPH, educator; b. June 12, 1953, Las Cruces, N.M.; s. Paul Arnold and Greta (Albrecht) F.; m. Patty P.Y. Pang, July 19, 1987; edn: BA and BS, Univ. Texas, 1975; PhD, Caltech, 1983. Career: Helen Hay Whitney postdoctoral fellow, Caltech, 1983-86, mem. profl. staff Caltech 1986-88; asst. prof. biology UC Riverside, 1988–; awards: NSF individual grad. fellow Caltech (1977-80), Helen Hay Whitney postdoc. fellow (1983-86), Phi Beta Kappa, Phi Kappa Phi (1974); mem. Genetics Soc. of Am. Ofc: Dept. Biology Univ. Calif., Riverside 92521

FUJIKAWA, EVA, aerospace/automotive company business management; b. May 27, 1958, Santa Monica; d. Osamu Sam and Teruko (Nakamizo) Fujikawa; edn: BA psychology, social sci., Univ. of Pacific 1979; MBA, Loyola Marymount Univ. 1985. Career: program controls splst. Hughes (subs. of GM), El Segundo 1979-88, program controls splst. comml. and automotive products, Culver City 1988-89, Program Controls Supr. Bus. Ops., El Segundo 1989-92, Bus. Staff 2 1992-94, team ldr. 1994–, Corporate ATEP 1991; instr. EDSG, El Segundo 1987-88; mem: Los Angeles World Affairs Council, Am. Mgmt. Assn., Nat. Contract Mgmt. Assn., Soc. Tech. Comm., Internat. Tng. in Comm. (secty.), Japanese Am. Nat. Museum (econ. devel. com. 1988-92), So. Calif. Am. Nikkei (bd. mem. 1988–), El Segundo C.of C. (indsl. activities com., govt. activities com.); Methodist; rec: French, Japanese, violin. Res: 1633 E Palm Ave #4 El Segundo 90245 Ofc: Hughes Bldg S52 M/S K308, PO Box 92919 Los Angeles 90009

FUKUHARA, HENRY, artist, instructor, consultant; b. Apr. 25, 1913, Los Angeles; s. Ichisuke and Ume (Sakamoto) F.; m. Fujiko Yasutake, Aug. 18, 1938; children: Joyce b. 1941, Grace b. 1943, Rackham b. 1946, Helen b. 1948; edn: grad. Santa Monica High Sch., 1931. Career: nurseryman, landscape contr.

Las Palmas Nurseries, Los Angeles 1935-41; wholesale florist Fukuhara Greenhouses, Deer Park, Long Is., N.Y. 1946-87; artist, instr./cons., L.I., N.Y. 1980-87, Santa Monica, Ca. 1987–; instr. watercolor Huntington (N.Y.) Township Art League 1983-87, East Islip (N.Y.) Mus., 1985-86, Oakdale (N.Y.) Arboretum 1984-86, Parrish Art Mus., Westhampton, N.Y. 1981-86, Jacqueline Penney Studio, Cutchogue, N.Y. 1980-84, Palos Verdes (Calif.) Art Center 1988-91, Joslyn Center of the Arts, Torrance, Ca. 1990, Venice H.S. Adult Sch. 1992-93; Santa Monica Emeritus CollegeMaster Watercolor Workshop 1992, 93, 94; art in permanent collections: Heckscher Mus. of Art, N.Y., Abilene Mus., Texas, Nassau Comm. Coll., N.Y., S.U.N.Y. Stonybrook, N.Y., Los Angeles County Mus. of Art, Blaine (Mont.) County Mus., Ralston Mus., Sidney, Mont., San Bernardino (Calif.) County Mus., Santa Monica (Calif.) Comm. Coll., Riverside (Calif.) Mus. of Art, Nagano Mus. of Art, Japan, Hiroshima Mus. of Art, Japan; exhibitions: Stary-Sheets Galleries, Irvine, Calif. 1994, "Living Legend", Mira Costa Coll., Oceanside, Calif. 1994; awards: Rosohkai Watermedia Exhib., Setagaya Mus. of Art, Tokyo, Japan 1988, 89, 90, 91, 92, 93, 94, 95, Strathmore Paper Co., Creative Connection, Golden, Mont., purchase award Nassau Comm. Coll., N.Y., num. other awards; mem. Watercolor Soc. of Ala., Nat. Watercolor Soc., Pittsburgh Watercolor Soc.; publs: Watercolor Energies by Frank Webb, 1983, Am. Artist mag. "Working with Abandoned Control", 5/93, Learning Watercolor the Edgar Whitney Way by Ron Ranson, 1994, Splash 3 by Rachel Wolf, 1994; represented by Stary Sheets Galleries, Irvine, Calif. Res: 1214 Marine St Santa Monica 90405

FUKUMOTO, BRIAN MICHAEL, manufacturing engineer/program manager; b. June 13, 1967, Offutt AFB, Nebr.; s. Malcolm Tatsumi and Lorraine Sachiko (Noguchi) F.; edn: BSME, UC Berkeley, 1989. Career: mfg. engr. Solectron Corp., Milpitas 1991-92, program mgr. 1992–; mem: Amer. Soc. Mech. Engrs. (assoc. 1985–), Calif. Alumni Assn. 1989–, Berkeley Engring. Alumni Soc. 1989–; Republican (sustaining GOP Nat. Com. 1990–); Prot.; rec: tennis, audio/video-phile, sports cards, piano. Res: 1703 Parkview Green Circle San Jose 95131-3222 Ofc: Solectron Corp. 777 Gibraltar Dr Milpitas 95035

FULD, FRED, III, financial/computer consultant; b. July 31, 1952, San Pedro; s. Fred Jr. and Gloria Mary (Cameron) F.; m. Sharon Elizabeth; one son, Fred Fuld IV; edn: BA in bus., BA in econ., Rockford Coll. 1974; Reg. Investment Advisor, SEC; Gen. Securities Sales Supr., NASD. Career: investment broker San Diego Securities, S.D. 1974-78; market maker, Pacific Stock Exchange, San Francisco 1978-79; vice pres. fin. planning. CGR Consultants, S.F. 1979-83; pvt. practice financial/computer cons., Concord, Calif. 1983–; mem: Am. Mensa Soc.; author: 101 Most Asked Questions about the Macintosh Computer; rec: swimming, running, collecting antique stock certificates. Ofc: 3043 Clayton Road Concord 94519

FULGHUM, BRICE ELWIN, employee benefits consultant; b. Aug. 27, 1919, Fredonia, Kans.; s. Byron Harmon and Myrtle (Broderick) F.; married; children: Linda Lee Fulghum McDonald; edn: Univ. Kansas City, The American Coll., San Francisco State Coll.; Chartered Life Underwriter (CLU). Career: asst. to sales mgr. Gas Service Co., Kansas City, Mo. 1939-41; sales mgr. Ace Auto Rental & Sales Co., K.C., Mo. 1945-48; asst. mgr. Owl Drug Co., San Francisco, 1948-50; mgr. Pacific Mutual Life Ins. Co., 1950-61; v.p. Gordon H. Edwards Co., 1959-64; v.p. Federated Life Ins. Co. Calif., 1964-66; gen. mgr. Los Angeles Fulghum Agy. Pacific Mut. Life Ins. Co., 1966-71; v.p. Hendrie Bonding & Ins. Corp., Huntington Beach 1976-77; chmn. bd. PGA Ins. Services Inc., Torrance 1976–; cons. Am. Health Profiles Inc., Nashville; sr. fin. cons. Shearson Hayden Stone Inc., Newport Beach 1977-79; cons. Penn Gen. Agys., L.A. and Employee Benefits Consultants, Santa Ana, 1979-80; cons. Assn. Calif. State Univ. Profs., 1959–, Profl. Sponsoring Fund, 1979–; mem: Am. Soc. C.L.U.s (Golden Key Soc.), Leading Life Ins. Producers No. Calif. (life mem., pres. 1955), S.F. Peninsula Estate Planning Council (charter), L.A.-S.F.V. Estate Planning Councils (life), Orange Co. Life Underwriters Assn. (editorial advy. bd. Western Underwriter); civic: March of Dimes /La Quinta (chmn. 1991), Am. Cancer Soc. (chmn. fundraising), Comm. Chest, Am. Heart Assn., Opera Pacific (founder), Town Hall of Calif. (charter mem. Charitable Giving Council Orange Co.); clubs: La Quinta CC, El Niguel CC, Commonwealth Club, Desert Diabetes Club (v.p., bd.dirs. 1992–); mil: Q.M.C., U.S. Army 1941-43; contbr. articles to ins. publs. Res: 77-030 Avenida Fernando La Quinta 92253 Ofc: PO Box 1750 La Quinta 92253

FULLER, JAMES WILLIAM, financial director; b. Apr. 3, 1940, Rochester, Ind.; s. Raymond S. and Mildred (Osteimeier) F.; m. Mary Falvey, Aug. 22, 1981; children: Kristen Anne, Glen William; edn: AA, San Bernardino Valley Coll., 1960; BS, San Jose State Univ., 1962; MBA, Calif. State Univ., 1967. Career: v.p. Dean Witter, San Francisco, 1967-71; v.p. Shields & Co., S.F., 1971-74; fin. mgr. SRI International, Menlo Park, 1974-77; sr. v.p. N.Y. Stock Exchange, NYC, 1977-81, Charles Schwab & Co., S.F., 1981-85; pres. Bull & Bear Corp., NYC, 1985-87; dir. Bridge Info. Systems, S.F., 1987–; bd. dir. Action Trac Inc., L.A., Current Techs. Inc., Vancouver, B.C., Bridge Info. Systems, St. Louis; bd. dirs. Security Industry Protection Corp., Wash., 1981-87, Global Econ. Action Inst., NYC 1989- (chmn. 1993–), Pacific Res. Inst., S.F., 1991–; bd. trustees UC Santa Cruz; mem: The Family Club (S.F.), Olympic

Club (S.F.), Jonathon Club (L.A.), Univ. Club (NYC); Republican; Presbyterian Res: 2584 Filbert St San Francisco 94123 Ofc: Bridge Info. Systems 555 California St San Francisco 94104

FULLER-VON BOZZAY, GEORGE DENNIS, biofeedback institute director, clinical psychologist; b. Oct. 9, 1942, Gyor, Hungary; s. George and Judy (Fuller) von B.; m. Pennie L. Sempell, Oct. 14, 1979; edn: Whitman Coll. 1962; BS psychology, Wash. St. Univ. 1964; MS, PhD clin. psychology, Univ. Mass. Amherst 1967; lic. clin. psychologist Calif. Career: fellow med. psychology UCSF Med. Center 1967-68, assoc. clin. prof. dept. biology, assoc. clin. prof.; clin instr. psychiatry Stanford Univ. Sch. Medicine; pvt. practice psychology; psychology faculty behavioral scis. dept. City Coll. San Francisco ; dir. Biofeedback Inst., San Francisco ; cons. to num. orgns. incl. num. VA Hosps., Herrick Hosp., Berkeley, Vallejo Gen. Hosp. Pain Clinic; awards: num. profl. and pub. service awards; mem: Biofeedback Soc. Am. (pres. 1976, ins. com.), Am. Psychological Assn., Am. Assn. Biofeedback Clinicians, Assn. for Humanistic Psychology,, Am. Assn. Univ. & Coll. Profs.; author textbooks and workbooks incl. Projects in Biofeedback (1980), Biofeedback: Methods and Procedures in Clin. Procedure (1977). Ofc: 3428 Sacramento St San Francisco 94118

FULLERTON, GAIL JACKSON, university president; b. Apr. 29, 1927, Lincoln, Nebr.; d. Earl Warren and Gladys Bernice (Marshall) Jackson; m. Stanley Fullerton, Mar. 27, 1967; 2 children by previous marriage, Gregory and Cynde Putney; edn: AB, Univ. Nebr. 1949, AM, 1950; PhD, Univ. Oreg. 1954. Career: lectr. sociology Drake Univ., Des Moines 1955-57; asst. prof. Fla. State Univ., Tallahassee 1957-60; prof. sociol. San Jose State Univ., 1963-72, dean, 1972-76, exec. vice pres., 1977-78, pres., 1978–; bd. dirs. San Jose Symphony 1979–, Associated Western Univs., Inc. 1981–; bd. govs. NCCJ of Santa Clara Co., 1981–; trustee Nat. Commn. Cooperative Edn., 1982–; awards: Carnegie fellow, Doherty fellow, 1951-52; mem: AAAS, Internat. Sociol. Assn., Am. Sociol. Assn., Western Coll. Assn. (pres. 1982), San Jose C.of C. (dir. 1978–); author: Survival in Marriage (1972, ed. 1977); coauthor: The Adjusted American (1964). Ofc: San Jose State University, Washington Sq San Jose 95192

FULMER, SCOTT GORDON, archaeologist, environmental planner; b. March 30, 1950, Lawton, Okla.; s. Richard Proctor and Evelyn Marie (Westlind) F.; edn: BA, UC Santa Barbara 1975; grad. study San Diego State; cert. hazardous mat. mgmt., UC San Diego, 1990. Career: cons. archaeologist to various companies 1977-82; archaeologist Caltrans, San Diego 1982-83; archaeologist Calif. Dept. of Parks & Recreation, San Diego 1983-84; environ. mgmt. splst., Co. of San Diego 1984-85; environ. analyst, Port of San Diego 1985-89; sr. project manager Recon, San Diego 1990–; juror of comm. design awards (Orchids & Onions) Am. Inst. Architects, 1989; judge of sci. fair Greater San Diego Sci. Fair, 1984-90; mem: Soc. for Calif. Achaeology (pgm. ch. annual meeting 1983), Nat. Assn. of Environ. Profls., Assn. of Environ. Profls. (past ofcr.), Soc. of Profl. Archaeologists, Soc. for Am. Archaeology; author article pub. 1985, co-auth. article pub., 1987; co-auth. monograph BLM Pubs. in History, Anthropology pub. 1981; rec: golf. Ofc: Recon 7460 Mission Valley Rd San Diego 92108

FULTZ, PHILIP NATHANIEL, management analyst; b. Jan. 29, 1943, NY, NY; s. Otis and Sara L. (Gibbs) F.; m. Bessie L. McCoy, Mar. 11, 1972; edn: AA in bus., Coll. of the Desert, 1980; BA and MA in mgmt., Univ. Redlands, 1980, 1982; Calif. Comm. Colls. instr. credential, bus. mgmt. Career: served to capt. US Marine Corps 1964-78; CETA coord. Morongo Unified Sch. Dist., 29 Palms 1978-80; manpower specialist San Bdo. County, Yucca Valley 1980-85; analyst/tech. writer Advanced Technology Inc., 29 Palms 1985-89; MIK, Inc., 1989-91; mgmt. analyst Morale, Welfare & Recreation, USMC, 29 Palms, 1991–; adj. asst. prof. Chapman Univ., 29 Palms 1989–; civic bds: 29 Palms Water Dist. (elected dir. 1991–), Morongo Basin Coalition for Adult Literacy, 29 Palms (founding dir., tutor 1985–), Unity Home Battered Womens Shelter, Joshua Tree (founding dir. 1983-86); Republican; rec: hunting. Ofc: Morale, Welfare & Recreation, Marine Corps Air Ground Combat Ctr. 29 Palms 92278

FUOTI, JAMES CHARLES, insurance agency president; b. Jan. 13, 1951, Reading, Pa.; s. James and June Elizabeth (Witman) F.; m. Susan, June 24, 1972; edn: BS indsl. mgmt., Purdue Univ. 1972; Chartered Property Casualty Underwriter, Am. Inst. PLU 1976; Accred. Advisor Ins., 1983, Assoc. in Risk Mgmt., 1992, Ins. Inst. of Am. Career: with Hartford Ins. 1972-74; surplus lines broker M.J. Hall & Co. Inc. 1974-77; v.p., ins. agent/broker J.P. Burris Ins. 1977-82; Pickett, Rotholz & Murphy 1982-84, Nationwide Ins. 1984-86; pres. Fuoti Insurance Agency Inc., 1986–; instr. San Joaquin Delta Coll. 1975-76, instr. Insurance Edn. Assn. 1981–; Risk Mgmt. Day Panelist, 1983; awards: USN ROTC Scholar 1968, Continuing Profl. Devel. CPCU 1983–, Independent Agents of No. Calif. Insurance Profl. of Year 1984, PGA Senior Gold Rush Pro-Am Winner 1987; mem: Chartered Property Casualty Underwriters (Sacto. Valley pres. 1983, edn. chmn. 1990); Purdue Alumni Assn., RIMS Chapter; clubs: Comstock, North Ridge CC, Nat. Assn. of Lefthanded Golfers; rec: golf, music. Ofc: POB 621718 Orangevale 95662

FURNAS, DAVID WILLIAM, physician, plastic surgeon; b. April 1, 1931, Caldwell, Ida.; s. John Doan and Esther Bradbury (Hare) F.; m. Mary Lou Heatherly, Feb. 11, 1956; children: Heather Jean b. 1957, Brent David b. 1959, Craig Jonathan b. 1963; edn: BA, UC Berkeley 1952; MD, 1955; MS, 1957. Career: assoc. in surgery Univ. Iowa, Iowa City 1964-66, asst. prof. surgery 1966-68; assoc. prof. surgery UC Irvine 1969-74, prof., chief div. plastic surgery 1974-80; awards: UC Irvine Excellence in Tchg. (1971, 79, 80, 81), Orange Co. Press Headliner of Year (1982), Council Exceptional Children Exceptional Person (1984); mem: Am. Bd. Plastic Surgery (dir. 1979-85), African Med. & Research Found. (bd. dirs. 1987–), Am. Assn. Plastic Surgeons (treas. 1988–, pres. 1995), Am. Soc. Surgery of Hand, Am. Soc. Plastic & Reconstructive Surgery; 200+ articles pub. in med. jours. and textbooks; mil: capt. USAF 1957-59; col. Med. Corps. U.S. Army Nat. Guard 1989-92, col. (ret.) USAR 1992; Prot.; rec: photog., music, exercise. Ofc: UC Irvine Div Plastic Surgery 1310 Stewart Dr #610 Orange 92668

FUTCH, ARCHER HAMNER, JR., physicist; b. Mar. 21, 1925, Monroe, N.C.; s. Archer, Sr. and Emma (Covington) F.; m. Patricia Anne West, June 13, 1964; children: Lisa b. 1957, Jacqueline b. 1960, Tina b. 1961; edn: BS, and MS, Univ. of N.C., Chapel Hill, 1949, 1951; PhD, Univ. Maryland, College Park, Md. 1956. Career: physicist Du Pont, Aiken, S.C., 1955-58; Univ. Calif., Lawrence Livermore Nat. Lab., Livermore 1959-91; honors: Phi Beta Kappa 1949, Sigma Xi 1951; civic bds: Livermore Planning Commn. 1968-72, Livermore City Council (1972-76, Mayor 1976), Alameda County Water Dist. 1976-80; author: Excited Energetic Nuclear Particle Prodn. (Pat. 1969), numerous plasma physics papers (1971–); mil: pfc US Army 1944-46; Republican; Methodist.

FUTTERMAN, JOHN ARTHUR HARDT, physicist; b. Apr. 25, 1955, USNB Yokosuka, Japan; s. Perry and Zelda F.; m. Dorothea Hardt, 1978; edn: BA in physics (honors) Swarthmore Coll., 1977; PhD physics, Univ. of Texas, Austin 1981. Career: mem. tech. staff AT&T Bell Labs., Holmdel, N.J. 1981-84, MTS supr. 1984-86; physicist Lawrence Livermore Nat. Lab., Livermore, Ca. 1987–; honors: Sigma Xi 1977; mem. IEEE (sr. mem. 1988), Am. Physical Soc.; coauthor: Scattering from Black Holes (1988), 5+ sci. papers; rec: photography. Ofc: LLNL Code L-85 PO Box 808 Livermore 94550

GAAB, THOMAS ANTHONY, physician (psychiatry); b. Jan. 17, 1953, Fresno, Calif.; s. Edward Martin and Florian Virginia (Suglian) G.; m. Maria Ann Rubino, Mar. 19, 1994; edn: BA, Calif. State Univ. Fresno 1975; MusM, Univ. of So. Calif. 1977, MusD, 1980; MD, Texas Tech. Univ., Lubbock 1992; lic. physician & surgeon, Calif. Med. Bd. 1994. Career: music instr. El Camino Coll., Torrance, Calif. 1977-83, USC, L.A. 1978-82, Univ. of Tex. at San Antonio 1983-85; asst. prof. of music, Univ. of Tex. at San Antonio 1985-88; resident in psychiatry, UCSF 1992-94, UC Irvine 1994–; awards: The Baroque Consortium Music Competition, L.A. 1977, Sigma Alpha Iota Music Scholarship Competition 1977, Rotary Young Artists award, Fresno 1982, listed Who's Who in Am. Music 1983, 85, Outstanding Young Men of Am. 1986, Internat. Who's Who in Music 1986, 92; arranger, musical composition: Bach, J.S. - Sonata in D Major, BWV 1028, for Guitar and Keyboard (Southern Music Publishers, 1987); Roman Catholic; rec: classical guitar performance, cycling. Address: Long Beach

GABELMAN, JOHN WARREN, consultant geologist; b. May 18, 1921, Manila, P.I.; s. Charles Grover and Cyprienna Louisa (Turcotte) G.; m. Olive Alexander Thompson, Sept. 22, 1945; children: Barbara Grace b. 1952, Joan Lynn b. 1955; edn: Geological Engr., Colo. Sch. of Mines, 1943, Master Geol. Engring., 1948, DSc, 1949; cert. profl. geologist (#1613) Am. Inst. Profl. Geol., 1967, reg. profl. engr. Colo. (#1226), reg. geol. Calif. (#003790). Career: jr. engr./geol. New Jersey Zinc Co., Gilman, Colo. (1943-44, 46); p.t. instr. Colo. Sch. of Mines, Golden 1946-49; geologist Colo. Fuel & Iron Corp., Pueblo, Colo. 1949-52; Am. Smelting & Refining Co., Salt Lake City, 1952-54; dist. geologist US Atomic Energy Commn., Gr. Junction, Colo. 1954-58, geol. adviser, Latin Am. US AEC, Lima, Peru 1958-61, chief resource appraisal US AEC, Wash. D.C., 1961-74, program mgr. Geothermal, US AEC, 1974-75; mgr. exploration res. Utah Internat. Inc., San Francisco 1975-83; consultant, pres. J.W. Gabelman & Assocs., Danville, 1983–; mem: Geol. Soc. Am. (1949–, Fellow), Soc. Economic Geologists (1948–, Fellow), Am. Assn. Petroleum Geol. (1943–, Emeritus mem.), Soc. Mining Engrs. AIME (1941–), Legion of Honor 1993, Assn. of Exploration Geochemists 1985–, Computer-Oriented Geol. Soc. 1990–; author: Migration of Uranium & Thorium (1977), 114+ profl. papers and jour. articles (1947–); mil: aviation electronic tech. mate 3/c USN 1944-46; Republican; R.Cath.; rec: skiing, fishing, hunting, photography. Res/Ofc: 23 Portland Ct Danville 94526

GABRIEL, MICHAEL, hypnotherapist, educator, author; b. Sept. 27, 1927, Brooklyn, NY; s. Benjamin and Martha (Buslow) Waldman; m. Marie Woltjer, May 27, 1989; children: Celina Waldman b. 1961; edn: BA, Brooklyn Coll., Brooklyn, NY 1950; MA, Sierra Univ., Costa Mesa, Calif. 1987; MA, Columbia Univ., NY, NY 1993. Career: eligibility worker, County of Santa Clara, San Jose, Calif. 1970-72; workshop dir., Wellhouse Seminars, San Jose 1973–; hypnotherapist, private practice, San Jose 1973–; instr., West Valley Coll., Saratoga,

Calif. 1979-93; instr. DeAnza Coll., Cupertino, Calif. 1993–; presenter at nat. conferences: Assn. for Past Life Res. & Therapies, Assn. for Pre and Peri-Natal Psychol. and Health, Am. Bd. of Hypnotherapy. Nat. Guild of Hypnotherapy; mem. Assn. for Pre and Peri-Natal Psychol. and Health 1991–; author: jour. article, 1989; book, Remembering Your Life Before Birth, 1992; rec: gardening. Res: 1102 Camino Pablo San Jose 95125. Ofc: P.O. Box 8030 San Jose 95155

GABRIEL, ROBERT MICHAEL, insurance executive; b. Oct. 8, 1923, Detroit, Mich.; s. Andrew and Nazara (Karam) G.; m. Louise B. Rassey, Dec. 29, 1946; children: Susan (Potter) b. 1948, Robert b. 1950, Sharyl b. 1959; edn: BS and gen. secondary tchg. cred. UCLA, 1948; grad. Midshipman Sch. Columbia Univ.; Career: ptnr. Gabriel's Food Market, Santa Monica 1946-52; tchr. Los Angeles Sch. Dist., 1949-50, Santa Monica Sch. Dist., 1953-54; owner Bob Gabriel Co., Ins. and Real Estate, Santa Monica 1954–; instr. Navy Ofcr. Tng. Pgm. 1953, instr. real estate Santa Monica Coll. 1962-64; honors: Eagle Scout 1938, service award Santa Monica Bd. of Edn. 1974, recipient 1st Boss of Year awarded by S.M. Jaycees, NCCJ Humanitarian Award, citizen of yr. Santa Monica Bd. of Realtors 1985, medallion award Boys Club Am. (1987, community service Santa Monica Kiwanis Club 1987, citizen of yr. Santa Monica Lions Club 1990; mem. Santa Monica Indep. Ins. Agents (pres. 1964), Reg. Producer Advy. Council- Commercial Union Ins. Cos. (chmn.); civic: Santa Monica Conv. & Visitors Bur. (chmn. bd. 1989-90, 91-92), Santa Monica C.of C. (pres. 1981-82), S.M. Boys Club (pres. 1985-87), S.M. Medical Ctr. (chmn. bd. 1990-92, dir. 1977–), S.M. Med. Found. (bd. 1978–), Santa Monica City Council (councilman 1971-73), S.M. Rec. and Parks Commn. (chmn. 1968), S.M. Hist. Soc. (advy. bd. 1991–), Optimist Club, NCCJ (past chmn.); mil: lcdr USNR-R 1942-64, WWII, Korea; Republican; Eastern Orthodox; rec: sports, volunteerism. Ofc: Bob Gabriel Co. 2325 Wilshire Blvd POB 620 Santa Monica 90406

GADBOIS, RICHARD A., JR., federal district judge; b. June 18, 1932, Omaha, Nebr.; s. Richard A., Sr. and Margaret Ann (Donahue) Bartlett; m. Vicki Cresap children (prev. m.): Richard, Gregory, Guy, Geoffrey, Thomas; edn: AB, St. John's Coll., Camarillo 1955; JD, Loyola Univ., L.A. 1958; postgrad. law, USC, 1958-60. Career: dep. atty. gen. Calif., Los Angeles, 1958-60; assoc. Atty. Forste & Gemmill 1960-62; ptnr. Musick, Peeler & Garrett, 1962-68; v.p. Denny's Inc., La Mirada 1968-71; judge Municipal Ct., Los Angeles 1971-72, Superior Ct., 1972-82, U.S. District Ct., 1982–; decorated Kt., Order of Holy Sepulchre by Pope John Paul II; mem. ABA, Calif. State Bar (profl. ethics com. 1965-70), L.A. County Bar Assn. (trustee 1966-67); Republican; R.Cath. Ofc: 176 U.S. Courthouse, 312 N Spring St Los Angeles 90012

GAGNON, CATHY ANN, paramedic program instructor; b. Aug. 2, 1949, Los Angeles; d. Charles William Fry and Priscilla C. (Hanssler) Eger; m. Neil Edward Gagnon, April 25, 1989; 1 child, Amity b. 1970; edn: AA, AS, Mt. San Antonio Coll. 1978; BSN, CSU Dominguez Hills 1995. Career: staff nurse Inter-Comm. Hosp., Covina 1978-79; Presbyterian Inter-Comm. Hosp., Whittier 1979-80; San Dimas Comm. Hosp., San Dimas 1980-85, coordinator 1985-86; staff nurse Inter-Comm. Med. Center, Covina 1986-1991, Queen of Valley Hosp., West Covina, 1994; instr. Mt. San Antonio Coll., Walnut 1987–; life support instr. Am. Heart Assn. 1982–; trauma life support instr. Calif. Am. Coll. Emergency Physicians 1988–; awards: Am. Heart Assn. Cert. of Merit 1986, Emergency Nurses Assn. C.E.N. 1989, Am. Assn. Critical Care Nurses C.C.R.N. 1980, San Dimas Hosp. Employee of Year 1985; mem: Am. Assn. Critical Care Nurses, Emergency Nurses Assn., Am. Assn. Women in Comm. Jr. Colls., Calif. Tchrs. Assn., Am. Heart Assn.; rec: baking. Ofc: Mount San Antonio College 1100 N Grand Ave Walnut 91789

GAHAN, KATHLEEN MASON, educational counselor; b. May 23, 1940, Long Beach; d. Robert Elwyn Fisher and Jean Mason Campbell; m. Keith Victor Gahan, Apr. 21, 1961; children: Carrie, 1962; Christie, 1966; edn: MA, Calif. State Univ., Long Beach, 1966; BA, Calif. Sate Univ., Long Beach, 1962; Calif. General Secondary Cred., 1965; Calif. Admin. Cred., 1978; Calif. Pupil Services Cred., 1979. Career: tchr. Long Beach Unified Sch. District, Long Beach 1963-70; tchr. Porterville Union High Sch. District, Porterville 1970-76, counselor 1976–; coordinator, Gifted and Talented Edn., Porterville 1976-83; adminstr., Adv. Placement Program, Porterville 1979–; proprietor, El Mirador Ranch, Strathmore 1978–; tchr.-organizer, SAT Workshop 1981-83; exec. com., Math-Science Conference, Tulare Cty. 1982-85; coach, Academic Decathlon Team, Porterville 1977-82, 85; advisor, Drop Out Retention Program, Porterville 1986–; adminstr., Counseling for College-able Hispanics, Porterville 1988-90; Counselor, Partnership Academy in Business, Porterville 1990–;tchr., faculty, staff computer workshops 1992-93; awards: 1st place, Museum of Art, Long Beach 1961; champion Tulare Cty. Academic Decathalon Team 1982, 85; 1st and 2nd place, Orange Blossom Festival Art Show, Lindsay 1988; 2nd place, Coll. of Sequoias Art Show, Visalia 1988;commendation Porterville Sch. Gov. Bd. 1975, 82; 20 Year Service Award, Porterville Public Sch. 1990; Who's Who in the West 1992; hon. mention, Orange Blossom Festival Art Show, Lindsay 1992; Who's Who Am. Women 1994; mem: Calif. Teachers Assn. 1963–, Am. Assn. of Univ. Women 1970–, Porterville Educators Assn. 1970–, Am. Assn. of Individual Investors 1984–, Bible Study, 1986–; civic: 4-H Club, Lindsay, proj. leader 1971-79; Tulare Cty. Herb Soc., Visalia, charter mem. 1983-85; author:

pub. articles and poems; ed., Mexican Cooking in Am., 1974; ed., Glory Bee, craft patterns 1979-84; Republican; Ch. of Nazarene; rec: painting, gardening, bridge, travel. Res: Lindsay Ofc: Porterville High Sch. 465 W. Olive Ave. Porterville 93257

GAHRING, DEAN RAY, veterinarian, educator; b. Mar. 29, 1946, Maywood; s. Harry Ray Gahring and LaRue (Luck) Keenan; m. Lillian Frances Delatorres, Dec. 5, 1970; children: Taralyn b. 1973, Lisa b. 1975; edn: BS, UC Davis, 1968, DVM, 1970; diplomate Am. Coll. Vet. Surgeons 1975. Career: intern, res. and chief resident in surgery The Animal Med. Ctr., N.Y.C. 1970-73; instr., asst. prof. small animal surgery dept. vet. clin. scis. Coll. of Vet. Med., The Ohio St. Univ. 1973-76, surgical residency tchg. in small animal tng. pgms. 1973-76; hd. surg. Main Street Small Animal Hosp., San Diego 1976-78; hd. surg./co-owner San Carlos Vet. Hosp. & Critical Care Ctr., San Diego 1978–; mem: Am. Animal Hosp. Assn., Am. Vet. Med. Assn., Calif. Vet. Med. Assn. (cont. edn. com. 1980-85), San Diego Co. Vet. Med. Assn. (pres. 1989, del. state Ho. Dels. 1981-82), Assn. for Vet. Orthopedic Resrch. & Edn. (pres. 1985-86), Assn. of Certified Veterinary Med. Specialists (reg. dir. 1984-85), Am. Coll. of Vet. Surgeons (mem., chmn. nomination com. 1986-88), Alpha Psi frat. (hon.), Alpha Gamma Rho, Phi Zeta (hon.), Vet. Orthopedic Soc., Vet. Cancer Soc.; Republican; rec: water & snow skiing. Res: 4626 Katy Ct La Mesa 92041 Ofc: San Carlos Veterinary Hospital 8618 Lake Murray Blvd San Diego 92119

GAIBER, MAXINE D., museum education/publications executive; b. May 6, 1949, N.Y.C.; d. Sidney and Junia Estelle (Gruberg) Oliansky; m. Stuart Gaiber, May 11, 1971; children: Scott Cory b. 1979, Samantha Lauren b. 1981; edn: BA art hist. (magna cum laude, Phi Beta Kappa), Brooklyn Coll., 1970; mgmt. devel. pgm. Harvard Inst. in Arts Adminstr., 1976; MA art hist./museology, Univ. Minn., 1972, PhD studies 1978; cont. edn. Mpls. Coll. of Art and Design, 1973-78, Art Ctr. Coll. of Design, 1985, profl. tng. Smithsonian Instn., Univ. Minn., UC Irvine. Career: tchg. asst. Univ. of Minn., 1970-71; instr. Mpls. Inst. of Arts (MIA), 1972-79, dev. arts-in-edn. pgms. 1972- 73, supr. tours & curriculum svs. 1973-79, assoc. chair edn. div. 1977-79; museum edn. cons. Art Inst. of Chgo., 1979-82, instr. Fall 1980; Kellogg Found. pgm. coord. (tng. pgms. for mus. profls.) Field Mus. of Natural History, Chgo. 1982-83; instr. humanities div. Coll. of DuPage, 1981-83; publications dir., then dir. campaigns and funding res. Art Center Coll. of Design, 1983-88, faculty 1986-89; pub. rels. dir. Newport Harbor Art Mus., Newport Beach 1988-94, edn. & publications dir. 1994–; instr. L.A. Co. Mus. of Art, 1985–; exhibitions: Assimilation: Japan, MIA/Univ. Minn. Sch. Arch. 1974, Japanese Art from the Burke Collection, MIA 1977, Art and Technology, MIA 1979; author teacher's guides and discovery units (American Indian Art, 1972, Native Arts, 1980, Imperial China, 1980, Indians of the Northwest Coast, 1981, Alaska's Coastal Eskimos, 1981), articles in museum and art jours., annual reports, catalogs, newsletters. Ofc: 850 San Clemente Dr Newport Beach 92660

GAITHER, JAMES CASTLE, lawyer; b. Sept. 3, 1937, Oakland; s. Horace Rowan, Jr. and Charlotte Cameron (Castle) G.; m. Susan, Apr. 30, 1960; children: James b. 1962, Stanley b. 1964, Reed b. 1968, Kendra b. 1970; edn: BA econ., Princeton Univ. 1959; JD, Stanford Law Sch. 1964; admitted to practice: Calif. Supreme Ct. 1966, US Dist. Ct., (Dist. Col. 1966, No. Dist. Calif. 1972), US Ct. of Appeals (7th Cir. 1966, 9th Cir. 1975), US Supreme Ct. (1969). Career: intern, UN (ECOSOC), Geneva, Switzerland. 1957; clerk. Draper, Gaither & Anderson, Palo Alto 1962; law clerk. Orrick, Dahlquist, Herrington & Sutcliffe, San Francisco 1963; law clerk. to Earl Warren, US Chief Justice, 1964-65; spl. asst. to John W. Douglas, Asst. Atty. Gen. Civil Div. US Dept. Justice, 1965-66; staff asst. to the President of the US, 1966-69; lawyer Cooley, Godward, Castro, Huddleson & Tatum, San Francisco 1969–, ptnr. 1971–, mng. ptnr. 1984-1990; dir: Basic American Inc., Levi Strauss & Co., Stanford Mgmt. Co.; chmn. Dean's Advisory Council, Stanford University Law Sch.; exec. com., Bd. of Visitors, Stanford Law School; mem. bd. trustees and exec. com. for the Carnegie Endowment for Internat. Peace; RAND (exec. com.), The James Irvine Found., The Scripps Res. Inst., The William and Flora Hewlett Found., former mem. bd. trustees Marin Comm. Found. (chmn.), The Branson Sch. (pres.), Marin County Day Sch. (pres.), Stanford Bd. of Trustees (pres. bd. of trustees, chmn. investment com.), Rosenberg Found., Evelyn and Walter Hass, Jr. Fund; honors: disting. pub. svc. US Dept. HEW 1977, Order of the Coif, Hilman Oehlmann, Jr. Award, Phi Delta Phi (graduate of year 1964, Province 12), note ed. Stanford Law Review 6 qtrs.; mem. Am., Calif., S.F. Bar Assns.; mil: capt. USMCR 1959-61; Democrat; Presbyterian; rec: tennis, camping, fishing, photog. Ofc: Cooley Godward Castro Huddleson & Tatum One Maritime Plaza Ste 2000 San Francisco 94111

GALANOS, JAMES, designer; b. Sept. 20, 1924, Phila.; s. Gregory D. and Helen (Gorgoliatos) G. Career: with Hattie Carnegie, 1944; asst. to designer Columbia Pictures Corp., Hollywood 1946-47; trainee Robert Piguet, Paris, France 1947-48; founder, designer Galanos Originals, Beverly Hills 1951–; awards: distinguished service in field of fashion Neiman-Marcus 1954, Am. Fashion Critics award Met. Mus. Art, Costume Inst. 1954, Return award 1956, Hall of Fame 1959, creativity award Internat. Achievments Fair 1956, Filene's Young Talent design award, Boston 1958, Cotton Fashion award 1958, Coty

Hall of Fame 1959, London Times Internat. Fashion Award 1965, Lifetime achiev. Council Fashion Designers of Am. 1985, Stanley award Fashion Collectors of Dallas Hist. Soc. 1986, Otis-Parsons design achiev. award 1987; retrospective exhibns. Costume Council L.A. County Mus. Art (1974), Fashion Inst. Tech. 1976. Ofc: 2254 S Sepulveda Blvd Los Angeles 90064

GALES, ROBERT SYDNEY, acoustical physicist; b. Dec. 12, 1914, Boston, Mass.; s. Robt. Joseph and Grace Risley (Moore) G.; m. Dorothea Yocum, Aug. 29, 1942; children: Robert T. b. 1944, Patricia F. b. 1952, Michael J. b. 1956; edn: BA, UCLA 1938, MA, 1942. Career: res. asst. UCLA 1938-42; physicist Div. of War Research UC San Diego 1942-46; physicist Naval Electronics Lab. 1946-67; supr. physicist Naval Ocean Systems Center 1967-80; staff sci. Computer Scis. Corps. 1981-83; prin. cons. Young and Gales, Cons. in Acoustics 1983–; naval res. assoc. Inst. of Naval Studies 1964-65; adj. prof. San Diego State Univ. 1977-86; awards: San Diego Co. Bd. Suprs. commendation of svc. on Noise Control Hearing Bd. 1978, World Champion Coronado 25 Class, sailing (1972); mem: Acoustical Soc. Am. (fellow 1950, pres. 1975-76), Sigma Xi (v.ch. San Diego chpt. 1968), Fedn. Profl. Assn. (pres. San Diego chpt. 1966); Alamitos Bay Yacht Club (commodore 1942), Mission Bay Yacht Club (commodore 1948), San Diego Noise Abatement Bd.; contbg. author 6 books, 1946-79; author 60+ tech. articles; co-inventor 4 U.S. patents on noise abatement devices; Presbyterian, elder. Ofc: RS Gales Cons in Acoustics 1645 Los Altos Rd San Diego 92109

GALES, SAMUEL JOEL, army logistics specialist (retired), equal employment opportunity counselor (retired); b. June 14, 1930, Dublin, Miss.; s. James McNary McNeil and Alice Francis (Smith) Broadus-Gales; m. Martha Ann Jackson (div. Jan. 1978); children: Samuel, II (dec. 1985), Martha Diane Bryant, Katherine Roselein, Karlmann Von, Carolyn B., Elizabeth Angelica McCain; edn: BA, Chapman Univ., 1981, MS, 1987; tchr credential 1987. Career: enlisted, served to master/1st sgt. US Army, 1948-76, ret., decorated Air medal; tchr. Monterey Unified Sch. Dist. 1981-82; Dept. of Army civilian empl. Directorate of Logistics, Fort Ord, 1982-93, equal employment opportunity counselor (collateral) DoD 1987-93 (ret.); Ombudsman, Monterey County, long term care program 1993–; mem: American Legion (post comdr. 1973-74), Monterey Aquarium Found. 1994–, vol. Aquarium Guide; clubs: Forty and Eight (chef-degare 1979, 80), Monterey Chess (pres.), Past Commanders' Club Calif. (pres. Outpost #28 1981-82); civic bds: Family Service Agency, Monterey 1979-85, Episcopal Soc. for Ministry on Aging, Carmel 1980-86, Task Force on Aging, Carmel 1983-87; Peer Counselor 1982-84; Republican; Episcopalian (Eucharist minister, vestry man 1982-85, 1991-94). Res: 1617 Lowell St POB 919 Seaside 93955-0919

GALIPEAU, STEVEN ARTHUR, psychotherapist/psychoanalyst; b. Nov. 10, 1948, Summit, N.J.; s. Arthur Harmars and Theresa Louise (Levesque) G.; m. Teresa Louise Shelton (div. 1983); m. Linda Carlotta Holmwood, Apr. 22, 1984; children: Brendan b. 1985, Owen b. 1988; edn: AB, Boston Coll., 1970; MA psychol. counseling, Univ. of Notre Dame, 1972; MDiv, The Church Divinity Sch. of Pacific, Berkeley 1977; lic. Marriage Family, Child Counselor, BBSE, 1975; cert. Jungian Psychoanalyst, C.G. Jung Inst., Los Angeles 1993. Career: psychotherapist Family & Children's Center, Mishawaka, Ind. 1972-74; vicar St. Luke's Ch., Fontana 1977-78; assoc. rector St. Edmund's Ch., San Marino 1978-82; psychotherapist pvt. practice, Studio City, 1975–, dir. Coldwater Counseling Ctr., 1983–; lectr. churches, psych. profl. orgs. in So. Calif. 1977–, lectr. C.G. Jung Inst., L.A. 1986–; mem: Am. Assn. for Marriage and Family Therapy 1990-91, Calif. Assn. of Marriage and Family Therapists 1987–, C.G. Jung Inst. of L.A. 1982–, Nat. Assn. for the Advancement of Psychoanalysis 1992–, Internat. Assn. Of Analytical Psychol. 1993–; author: Transforming Body and Soul: Therapeutic Wisdom in the Gospel Healing Stories (1990); Democrat; Episcopalian. Ofc: Steven A. Galipeau, 4419 Coldwater Canyon Ave Ste E Studio City 91604

GALLARDO, ALBERT JOHN, county transportation authority executive (retired); b. Apr. 8, 1927, Oakland; s. Frank Navarro and Emily (Luque) G.; m. Margaret Theresa McAuliffe, Sept. 25, 1954; children: Albert b. 1955, Susan b. 1957, Julie b. 1963; edn: BSCE, UC Berkeley 1950; lic. civil engr. Calif. 1956. Career: transp. engr. Fed. Hwy. Adminstrn., Sacto. 1950-83; project mgr. Bissell & Karn Inc. 1984-86; exec. dir. Alameda Co. Transp. Authority, Oakland 1987-94; nat. dir. ASCE, Sacto 1986-88; awards: U.S. Dept. Transp. Silver Medal 1978, Engrs. Council Service to Profession 1987; mem: ASCE (fellow), Am. Pub. Works Assn.; mil: USN 1945-46; Catholic; rec: history and service at Calif. Railroad Museum. Res: 3814 Moddison Ave Sacramento 95819

GALLEGLY, ELTON WILLIAM, congressman; b. Mar. 7. 1944, Huntington Park, Calif.; married; four children; edn: attended Calif. State Univ., L.A. Career: businessman, real estate broker Simi Valley, Calif. from 1968; mem. Simi Valley City Council 1979; mayor City of Simi Valley 1980-86; mem. 99-104th Congresses from the 21st (now 23rd) Dist. of Calif. 1986–; mem. fgn. affairs com., mem. judiciary com., mem. natural resources com.; mem. exec. com Task Forces on Crime and Strategic Defense Initiative, U.S. House of Reps. Rep. Study Com.; mem. Congressional Human Rights Caucus, Congressional Fire Svcs. Caucus; former vice-chmn., chmn. Ventura County Assn. govts., Calif. Bd. dirs Moorpark Coll. Found.*

GALLISON, H(AROLD) BAILEY, youth agency executive; b. Apr. 6, 1924, Orange, N.J.; s. Harold Hobron and Stella Camilla (Holm) G.; m. Janet C. Frazier, June 23, 1951 (div. 1983); m. Sharilyn Leone Lemkuil, Jan. 27, 1984; children: Claudia Jean (M.D.), and Harold Bailey, II; edn: BA, Univ. Mo., 1948. Career: sales mgr. Carll Mercury Dealership, La Jolla 1951-53; exec. dir. La Jolla Town Council, 1953-63; advt. mgr. Security Pacific Bank, San Diego 1963-70; dir. p.r. Mercy Hosp. and Med. Ctr., San Diego 1970-83; commun. rep. Citadel Communications, San Diego 1983-84; exec. dir. Community Campership Council, 1985–; past pres. So. Calif. Bank Advertisers Assn.; past chmn. La Jolla Civic Ctr. Corp.; awards: outstanding alumni Univ. of Mo., 1987, profl. of yr. San Diego Public Rels. Club S.D., 1973, good neighbor award Miramar Naval Air Station S.D., 1957;mem. Nat. Soc. of Fund Raising Execs. (past v.p., charter mem. San Diego Chpt.), Agency Execs. Assn. S.D., Univ. Mo. Alumni Assn. (mem. Nat. Alumni Board 14 yrs.), US Navy League, Am. Legion, San Diego P.R. Club (past pres.), Kiwanis (La Jolla Club past pres., past lt. gov. div. #21 Cal-Nev-Hawaii Dist.); civic bds: Gillispie Sch. and Child Care Assn., La Jolla (pres. bd. dirs.), Woodlands North HOA (pres.), Kentucky Col., United Way Speakers Bureau, San Diego YMCA, San Diego Padres Action Team; (past): Citizens Advy. Council La Jolla H.S. (past chmn.), La Jolla Bronco Boys Baseball League (past pres.), La Jolla Youth Little League (coach 12 yrs.); mil: enlisted USN 1943-46 (incl. overseas duty); Republican; Presbyterian; rec: tennis, spectator sports, walking, theatre. Ofc: Community Campership Council 7510 Clairemont Mesa Blvd Ste 208 San Diego 92111

GALMAN, HERBERT, company president; b. Feb. 28, 1921, Philadelphia, Pa.; s. Lewis and Fanny (Schneyer) G.; m. Elayne Velma Goodman, Dec. 14, 1947; children: Steve b. 1953, Linda b. 1955; edn: BSEE, Drexel Univ. 1943; MSEE, Univ. Pa. 1951. Career: co-owner, chief engr. Voltron Products, Pasadena 1957-66; chief engr. Kratos 1966-69; owner, pres. Arga Controls Inc. 1969–; mem: Precision Measurement Assn. (sr.mem., past pres.); inventor expanded scale voltmeter (1947, 52), AC voltage standard (1962); mil: tech. sgt. AUS 1944-45; Democrat; Jewish; rec: bowling. Res: 1612 N Altadena Dr Pasadena 91107

GAMBLE, LARRY WARD, radio station owner, marketing consultant, advertising executive; b. Feb. 1, 1943, Postville, Iowa; s. Adrian Ward and Arlene Isadore G.; m. Sylvia Ann, June 12, 1964; children: Robert Lawrence b. 1970, Johannes Sanger b. 1973; edn: AA, Modesto Jr. Coll. 1964; BA, Fresno St. Coll. 1966, MA, CSU Fresno, 1968; postgrad. studies Western Mich. Univ., 1973; cert., N.Y. Sch. Design, 1974. Career: asst. prof. theatre arts Kalamazoo Coll. 1969-74; artist-in-residence Western Mich. Univ., 1975; asst. prof. performing arts Coll. Santa Fe, 1974-76; account exec. KMJ-KSEE TV, Ch. 24, 1977-80; dir. mktg. Pappas Teleproductions, 1980-83; pres., owner KAAT-FM Radio, Oakhurst 1982–; pres., owner KTNS-AM Radio, Oakhurst 1988–; pres., creative dir., owner Larry Gamble Public Relations, 1985–; exec. secty., treas. Calif. Sierra Corp. 1980-86, CEO 1988–; awards: Nat. Silver Medal, Am. Advtg. Fedn. 1983, Golden Oaks awards Fresno Advt. Fedn., Man of Yr., Lions Club of the Sierra 1992, Sierra Mountaineer Days Honored Citizen, Ea. Madera Co. C. of C. 1993; mem: Am. Advtg. Fedn. (gov. Dist. XIV Calif./Nev. 1983-84), Fresno Advtg. Fedn., Toastmasters; civic: mem. Clovis Downtown Steering Com. and founding bd. B.O.O.T. (Bus. Org. of Old Town, Clovis); Democrat; Presbyterian; rec: real estate investments, historic renovation, photog. Res: 2179 Rall Ave Clovis 93611 Ofc: Fifth Avenue Profl. Complex, 621 5th Ave Clovis 93612

GAMMEL, EDWARD O., neurological surgeon; b. Aug. 2, 1930, Danville, Ill.; s. Gordon and Dot G.; m. Patricia Martin, Dec. 26, 1955; children: Susan b. 1956, Leslie b. 1960, Edward, Jr. b. 1962; edn: BA, DePaul Univ., 1952; MD, Howard Med. Sch., 1956. Career: med. intern Seaside Mem. Hosp., Long Beach 1956-57; gen. resident Merced County Gen. Hosp., 1957-58; neurological surgery resident Long Beach Vet. Hosp., 1960-64; pvt. practice neurol. surgery, Sacramento 1964–; clin. instr. neurol. surg. UC Davis, 1969–; mem. AMA, CMA, Sacto. Med. Soc., Congress Neurological Surgery; mil: capt. USAF 1958-60; rec: tennis. Ofc: Gammel & Leigh Medical Corp. 3644 Mission Ave Carmichael 95608

GANGWERE, HEATHER HENDRY, teacher, foreign language and English as a second language; b. April 11, 1964, Orange, Calif.; d. James Hendry (dec.) and Phila Margaret (Hurter) Acuff; m. Walt Lewis Gangwere, Nov. 22, 1986; edn: BA, Univ. of Redlands, Redlands, Calif. 1982-86; career: tchr., Leland H.S., San Jose, Calif. 1988–; chair, foreign lang. dept., Leland H.S. 1991–; dir. of student exchange, Pacific Neighbors, San Jose 1991–; awards: listed in Who's Who of Am. Univ. & Colls., Univ. of Redlands 1985-86, Outstanding Young Women of Am. 1987, Who's Who in the West 1989, Who's Who of Am. Tchrs. 1992; mem: Pacific Neighbors/Sister Cities Internat. 1990–; Redlands Admissions Assistance Program 1990–; Crossroads Bible Ch. Ofc: Leland High School 6677 Camden Ave. San Jose 95120

GANIERE, ROBERT C., corporate financial executive; b. Oct. 14, 1936, Cleveland, Ohio; s. Harold Francis and Elizabeth V. (Gregor) G.; m. Mary Ann Henderson, July 16, 1955; children: Mary b. 1956, Susan b. 1958, Elizabeth b. 1965, Christopher b. 1967, James b. 1972, David b. 1973, Catherine b. 1975,

Sarah b. 1978, Rachel b. 1980; edn: BBA acctg., Cleveland State Univ., 1964. Career: staff acct. Performed Line Products, Cleveland, O. 1962; Givelber & Givelber, 1963; Haskins & Sells, 1964; staff acct. to mgr. of tax dept. Harris Kerr Forster & Co., Los Angeles 1964-67; c.f.o. Dr. R.F. Beauchamp et al, Newport Beach and Beauchamp Western Group of Cos., 1967–; dir., sec.-treas. Dental Finance, N.B. 1968–; founder, dir., v.p. Independent Indemnity (Calif. ins. co.), Newport Beach 1973–; pres., dir. Midlands Co., Newport Beach 1981-87, sec.-treas. 1987–; founder., dir., sec.-treas. Founders Leasing Co., N.B. 1982–, Western Dental Services Inc., N.B. 1984–; dir., sec.-treas. Video Leasing Co., Anaheim 1982–; dir. North Am. Video Corp. (NAVCO), Anaheim 1988–; active Boy Scouts, Huntington Beach (coms., asst. scout master, scout master 1979-87); Ch. of Jesus Christ of Latter Day Saints; rec: scouting, hiking, camping, snorkling, economic theory. Ofc: Western Dental Services Inc. 300 Plaza Alicante Ste 800 Garden Grove 92640

GANS, ERIC L., educator; b. Aug. 21, 1941, New York; s. Irving and Pearl (Fintell) G.; m. Michele Hausser, Sept. 17, 1969 (div. 1977); m. Monique Roy, Oct. 15, 1977; 1 son, Georges b. 1970; edn: BA, Columbia Univ. 1960; MA, Johns Hopkins Univ. 1961; PhD, 1966. Career: instr. St. Univ. N.Y. Coll. at Fredonia 1965-67; asst. prof. Ind. Univ., Bloomington 1967-69; asst. prof., assoc. prof., prof. UCLA 1969–; awards: Acad. Francaise Prix de la Langue Francaise 1977, Edn. Ministry Palmes Acad. 1983; author: Musset et Le Drame Tragique, 1974, Essais D'Esthetique Paradoxale, 1977, Origin of Language, 1981, End of Culture, 1985, Science and Faith, 1990, Originary Thinking, 1993; rec: micro computer programming, running. Ofc:Dept. of French Univ. Calif. 405 Hilgard Ave Los Angeles 90095-1550

GANS, ROBERT A., investment company president; b. July 16, 1941, Port Chester, N.Y.; s. Robt. Altha, Jr. and June (Maule) G.; m. Joyce E., June 17, 1978; children: David b. 1969, Hollis b. 1969, Michael b. 1979, Brian b. 1981; edn: Principia Upper Sch., 1959; BA, Stanford Univ. 1963, MBA, 1968; lic. Real Estate Broker; Reg. Prin., NASD; Cert. Property Mgr. (CPM). Career: chief fin. ofcr. Basile Corp., Douglasville, Pa. 1970-73; treas. Index Systems Inc., Cambridge, Mass. 1973-75; fiscal analyst San Diego Co., Calif. 1975-77; pres./dir. Windsor Jewels U.S.A. Inc. 1977-80; chief fin. ofcr./dir. Data Mgmt. Labs. Inc., San Jose 1980-82; CFO Selanar Corp., Santa Clara 1982-83; pres./dir. Gans Investment Corp., Beverly Hills 1983-87; pres./dir. Robt. Gans and Assocs., Julian, Calif. 1987–; mem: Univ. Housing Gp. (pres.), Univ. Legislature, Inst. Real Estate Mgmt., Internat. Assn. Fin. Planners, Los Angeles Bd. Realtors, Apartment Owners Assn. of L.A.; civic: Rotary Intl. 1988-90, YMCA Indian Guides (chief), AYSO Soccer (coach), Toastmasters (pres.), PTA, Back Country Basketball Inc. (pres.), Intermountain Park and Recreation Inc. (exec. v.p.); mil: capt. USMC 1963-66, 3 Purple Hearts, Bronze Star w/Combat V, Vietnam; rec: jogging, backgammon, U.S. hist. Res: Julian 92036 Ofc: Robert Gans and Associates PO Box 520 Julian 92036

GARBER, CHESTER STANTON, businessman, lawyer; b. Nov. 28, 1943, Fresno; s. Chester and Virginia Lee (Trimmer) G.; m. Emilia Ting, MD, June 20, 1981; edn: BA, Univ. of San Francisco 1967; MA, 1968; JD, S.F. Law Sch. 1971; admitted Calif. State Bar; ins. lic.- life, disability; FAA lic. commercial pilot (multi engine and instrument ratings), cert. flight instr. single & multi engine airplane and instrument. Career: past pres. and c.e.o. John's Italian Restaurants Inc., Garmah Investments Co. Inc., Maurlee Investment Co. Inc., Stage Lounges Inc., 418 Geary Corp.; current pres., chmn. bd. and CEO, Golden Valley Aero Inc.; asst. treas. Emilia C. Ting, MD, Inc. (lic. med. corp.); retired; mem: Calif. State Bar, Aircraft Owners & Pilots Assn., NASD, Nat. Assn. Aircraft Appraisers (cert. aircraft appraiser); nationally publ. profl. wildlife photographer; mil: capt. Spl. Forces, US Army, silver, bronze stars, DSC, Purple Heart (4); rec: gardening, firearms, computers. Ofc: C.S. Garber & Associates 5746 E Shields Ave #104 Fresno 93727-7820

GARCIA, MICHAEL JOSEPH, business executive; b. July 23, 1949, Alameda; s. Manuel Olivera and Mary (Gonzales) G.; m. Patti Garcia, July 22, 1972; children: Michael b. 1977, Jennifer b. 1978; edn: grad. Ofcr.'s Prep. Acad., Squadron Ofcr. Sch., Air Command and Staff Coll. USAF; BS in math./BS in Econs., UC Berkeley, 1971; cert. employee benefit splst., Wharton Sch. of Bus., 1987. Career: staff mgr. acctg. (computer ops., proj. mgmt., billing and collection) Pacific Bell, San Francisco 1971-83, staff dir. benefit adminstrn., 1983-87, dir. financial mgmt. 1987-88, exec. dir. 1988–; v.chmn. bd. dirs. Contra Costa Health Plan (1985–), bd. dirs. Western Medical Rev. (1986–), bd. dirs. Golden Carousel Inc. (1987–); mem: Nat. Guard Assn., Am. Mgmt. Assn., Internat. Found. of Employee Benefits; civic: mem. local Sch. Board; mil: lt. col. USAF, logistics group cmdr. Calif. Air Nat. Guard 1967–, former comdr. 561st AF Band, decorated AF Commendn. Medal, Presdl. Medal of Merit; Democrat; R. Cath.; rec: golf. Address: Blackhawk 94506

GARCIA, NICOLAS M., business owner; b. Oct. 28, 1937, San Angelo, Tex.; s. Nicolas W. and Dahlia (Ortega) G.; m. Sally Marie Villa, Sept. 29, 1956; children: Pamela Marie b. 1957, Theresa Ann b. 1959, Nicolas M. Jr. b. 1962; edn: AA, Calif. Coll. of Arts & Crafts, 1962; cert. bus. mgmt., American River Coll., 1976. Career: mktg. Bell Distbg. Co., Sacto. 1967-77; ptnr. Spectrum Sales,

1977-78; dir. of tribal devel. Calif. Tribal Chmns. Assn. Sacto. 1978-80, dir. of planning Sacto. Indian Ctr. 1980-81, author funded proposals for Indian Child Welfare 1979, Career Devel. Pgm. 1981; owner/c.e.o. New Dimension Carpet Maint., Sacto. 1981-89; point of sale mktg. specialist Youngs Market Co. Sacto. Div., 1990-93; pres. Tactile Signage of Superior CA 1993–; awards: appreciation Sacto. Employment & Tng. Agy. 1986, Private Industry Council Sacto. 1987; civic: Hispanic C.of C. (bd. 1985-87), Mex.-Am. Alcoholism Pgm. (bd. 1983-85), Sacto. Alliance for the Mentally Ill (bd. 1989–), Sacto. Area Mayors Com. On Disability Issues; publ: (brochure) Sacto. Indian Center 1981; mil: seaman USCG 1956-60; Republican; Unity; rec: reading, fishing. Res: 6360 Parkcreek Circle Citrus Heights 95621

GARCIA, SERAFIN MONTEALTO, physician; b. Nov. 12, 1943, Quezon, Philippines, nat. 1984; s. Zacarias and Roberta (Montealto) G.; m. Zenaida, Aug. 14, 1966; children: John b. 1969, Linda b. 1973, Kim b. 1976; edn: med. tech. Western Reserve Univ. 1963; BS med. tech., Columbia Union Coll. 1969; MD, Loma Linda Univ. 1973; diplomate internal med. Calif. Career: solo practice int. and pulmonary med., Glendale 1976–; chmn., pres. San Gabriel Valley Med. Investment Inc. (managing gen. partner Covina Valley Comm. Hosp.) 1979–; dir. pulmonary dept. Covina Comm. Hosp. 1979–, chmn. and pres. of Thompson Mem. Med. Ctr., Burbank, 1992-1994; Seventh Day Adventist; Ofc: 1560 E Chevy Chase Dr N Glendale 91206

GARDNER, FREDERICK BOYCE, library director; b. Mar. 12, 1942, Hopkinsville, Ky.; s. Boyce and Alleen Louise (Brown) G.; edn: BA, Univ. Ky., 1964; MA, Ind. Univ., 1966; postgrad. City Univ. N.Y., 1970-71, CSU Northridge, 1973-76, UCLA. 1982-85. Career: head librarian Univ. Ky. Hopkinsville Community Coll., 1966-69; head, reader's svs. Manhattan Community Coll. CUNY, N.Y.C., 1969-71; reference librarian Calif. Inst. Arts, Valencia 1971-74, head public services, 1974-85, dir. computer services, 1984-86, acting dir. 1987, dean 1988–; cons. Total Interlibrary Exchange, Ventura 1984-85, v.p. 1980-81, pres. 1981-82, chmn. tech. task force 1983-88; exec. bd. Calif. Private Academic Libraries 1988–, chmn. exec. bd. 1990; Calif. Library Networking Task Force 1990-95; mem: Santa Clarita Interlibrary Network (pres. 1989–), Calif. Conf. on Networking (del. 1985), Am. Library Assn., Calif. Library Assn., Performing Arts Libraries Network of Greater Los Angeles (chmn. 1990); mil: capt. USAF 1968-69; rec: music, computer games, hiking, camping. Ofc: Calif. Institute of the Arts, 24700 McBean Pkwy Valencia 91355

GARDNER, NORD ARLING, executive director university relations, management consultant; b. Aug. 10, 1923, Afton, Wyo.; s. Arling A. and Ruth (Lee) G.; m. Thora Marie Stephen, Mar. 24, 1945; children: Randall Nord, Scott Stephen, Craig Robert, Laurie Lee; 7 grandchildren; edn: BA, Univ. Wyo. 1945; MS, CSU Hayward 1972; MPA, 1975; postgrad. Univ. Chgo., Univ. Mich., UC Berkeley. Career: Commnd. 2d.lt., advanced through grades to lt. col. US Army, 1942-66, ret. 1966, (Army Commendn. medal); personnel analyst Univ. Hosp. UC San Diego 1966-8; coord. manpower Univ. UC Berkeley 1968-75; univ. tng. ofcr. San Francisco State Univ. 1975-80, personnel mgr. 1976-80; exec. dir. CRDC Maintenance Tng. Corp. (non-profit), S.F. 1980-85; founder/gen. mgr. Vericlean Janitorial Service, Oakland 1984-86; bus. developer East Bay Asian Local Devel. Corp. 1983-85; pres. Indochinese Community Ent. USA Ltd. 1985-87; v.p./sec. LAO Internat. Comm. Devel. Corp. 1988-90; ptnr. Oi Kit Building Maint. Service 1988-90; ops. mgr. Phimmason's Internat. Import-Export 1988-89; sec. bd. dirs. New Ideas New Imports Inc., 1989–; adminstrv. asst. to chancellor International Pacific Univ., San Ramon 1990; dir. university relations, International Pacific Univ., 1991-94, exec. dir Internat. Pacific Inst. 1994–; bus. mgmt. and devel. cons. 1987–; family counselor 1988–; pres./dir. Sandor Assocs. Mgmt. Cons., Pleasant Hill 1973-85, 91–; dir. U.S. Devel.-Educational Foundation Group, 1991–; instr. Japanese, psychol. courses, 1977-88; mem. advy. council S.F. Comm. Coll. Dist.; mem: Retired Ofcrs. Assn., Army Intelligence Corps Veterans (charter), Am. Soc. Tng. and Devel., No. Calif. Human Rels. Council, Am. Assn. Univ. Adminstrs., Internat. Personnel Mgrs. Assn., Coll. and Univ. Personnel Assn. (W. Coast rep.), Am. Legion; clubs: Commonwealth of Calif., UCB Faculty, University (SF); listed nat., internat. biographical ref. books; author: To Gather Stones, 1978; Republican. Res: 2995 Bonnie Ln Pleasant Hill 94523-4547

GARDNER, ROBERT ALEXANDER, career management counselor; b. Sept. 16, 1944, Berkeley; s. Robert Alexander and Eleanor (Ambrose) G.; m. Alexandra "Sandie" Ross, Mar. 22, 1987; edn: BA, UC Berkeley 1967, MA, CSU Chico 1974, MS, SFSU 1992; nat. cert. counselor, nat. cert. career counselor, reg. prof. career counselor. Career: placement counselor Sonoma Co. Ofc. of Edn., Santa Rosa 1975-76; personnel ofcr. Wells Fargo Bank, San Francisco 1977-80; dir. personnel Transam. Airlines, Oakland 1980-84; human resource devel. cons. and career managementcounselor, Gardner Assocs., Oakland 1983–; instr. Armstrong Coll. Bus. and Mgmt. Div., 1978-80, UC Berkeley Ext., 1980–; career counselor (volunteer) Forty Plus of No. Calif., Oakland 1988-93; mem: Career Planning and Adult Devel. Network, Calif. Career Development Assn., Am. Assn. for Counseling and Devel., Calif. Assn. for Counseling and Devel., Internat. Assn. of Career Mgmt. Professionals (IACMP), Rotary Internat., UC Alumni Assn.; publs: The National Review Magazine: A Survey from 1955 to

1973 (CSU Chico 1974); Time Management (Telelearning Systems, Inc. S.F., 1983); Achieving Effective Supervision (UCB, 1984, Revised edit. 1989); Managing Personnel Adminstrn. Effectively (UCB, 1986); Career Counseling: Matching Yourself To A Career (UCB, 1987); mil: 1st lt. AUS Intel. 1970-71, Bronze Star, Cross of Gal. w/star cluster, Rep. of Vietnam Service medals; Republican; Congregational; rec: collect and study antique Chinese Snuff Bottles. Res: 42 Aronia Ln Novato 94945 Ofc: Gardner Associates 3873 Piedmont Ave Ste 12 Oakland 94611

GARDNER, WILFORD ROBERT, physicist; b. Oct. 19, 1925, Logan, Utah; s. Robert and Nellie (Barker) G.; m. Marjorie Louise Cole, June 9, 1949; children: Patricia b. 1956, Robert b. 1958, Caroline b. 1960; edn: BS physics, Utah St. Univ. 1949; MS, Iowa St. Univ. 1951; PhD, 1953. Career: physicist U.S. Salinity Lab., Riverside 1953-66; prof. Univ. Wis., Madison 1966-80; prof., chair Univ. Ariz., Tucson 1980-86; dean natural resources UC Berkeley 1987–; mem: Nat. Acad. Scis., Soil Sci. Soc. Am. (pres. 1989-90); author: Soil Physics (1973); mil: AUS Corps Engrs. 1943-46; Mormon. Ofc: Univ. of Calif. 101 Giannini Hall Berkeley 94720

GARFIELD, HOWARD M., lawyer; b. Aug. 16, 1942, N.Y.C.; s. Jack Garfield and Pearl (Levine) Shaw; m. Elizabeth R. Lehmann, Oct. 23, 1978 (div. Dec. 1991); 1 dau. Mackenzie b. 1985; edn: Columbia Univ., 1960-61; AB (gt. distinction and hons. in humanities), Stanford Univ., 1964; JD (cum laude), Harvard Univ., 1968; admitted bar: Calif. 1968. Career: atty., assoc. Pacht, Ross, Warne, Bernhard & Sears, Los Angeles 1968-70; Ambrose & Malat, Beverly Hills, 1970-71; ptnr. law firm Garrett, Garfield & Bourdette, Santa Monica 1971-78; of counsel Goldstein & Phillips, San Francisco 1978-79; atty., assoc. Long & Levit, S.F., 1978-80, ptnr. 1980–, mng. ptnr. 1983-92; adj. prof. Golden Gate Law Sch., 1979; awards: Phi Beta Kappa 1963, Woodrow Wilson fellow 1964, Danforth fellow 1964; mem: State Bar of Calif. 1968–, Internat. Assn. of Defense Counsel 1986–, Defense Research Inst. 1986–, Bar Assn. of S.F. 1980–, Am. Bar Assn. 1986–, Am. Arbitration Assn. (cert. arbitrator 1990–); civic: Mill Valley Parks & Rec. Commn. (commr. 1990–); club: Scott Valley Swim & Tennis (Mill Valley 1980–); coauthor book: Corporate Directors and Officers Liability, Insurance and Risk Mgmt. (1989), numerous articles (1980–); Democrat; Jewish; rec: opera, Italy, travel. Ofc: Long & Levit 101 California St Ste 2300 San Francisco 94111

GARLAND, G(ARFIELD) GARRETT, sales executive; b. Dec. 17, 1945, Lakewood, Oh.; s. Garfield George and Lois Marie (Calavan) G.; edn: BA, Univ. Colorado, Boulder 1974. Career: broker Marcus & Millichap, Newport Beach, Calif. 1982-84; v.p. Pacific Coast Federal, Encino 1984-85; dir. acquisitions Prudential Investment Fund, L.A. 1985-86; v.p. A.S.I.A., Los Angeles, Tokyo, 1986-89; senior account exec. Lojack Corp., L.A. 1989–; honors: U.S. Ski Team mem. 1966-67; mem: PGA of Am., World Affairs Council 1990–, L.I.F.E. Found., Am. Legion, V.F.W., Nat. Trust for Hist. Preserv.; mil: capt. US Army 1967-71; Methodist; rec: golf, reading, snow skiing. Res: 1202 La Paloma Glen Escondido 92026 Ofc: Lojack Corp., 9911 Pico Blvd Ste 1000 Los Angeles 90035

GARRETT, DUANE DAVID, accountant, hospitality executive; b. March 28, 1952, New York; s. Gloria Lynn Magliana; m. Chahla, Nov. 10, 1977 (div. 1986); edn: BBA, St.Univ. N.Y. 1989; MBA, West Coast Univ. 1990. Career: gen. mgr. Riese Orgn., N.Y.C. 1974-77; Burger King Corp., L.A. 1977-83; staff acct. Baar Accountancy Corp., Encino 1983-85; comptroller Playboy Club Hollywood 1985-86; Mayfair Hotel, L.A. 1986-87; adminstr., employee stock plan Litton Industries Inc., Beverly Hills 1987–; cons. No. Star Production Co., Beverly Hills 1985-89; Video Butler Enterprises, Van Nuys 1984-86; auditor Bank of Am., L.A. 1987; Advy. Bd. Restaurant Bus. Mag. 1985-89; mem: Republican Party of Calif., Calif. St. Womens Center (publicity chmn.), Nat. Assn. Female Execs., Internat. Student Orgn.; Republican; Episcopalian; rec: computers, antique book collecting. Res: 15353 Weddington St C102 Van Nuys 91411 Ofc: Litton Industries Inc. 360 N Crescent Dr Beverly Hills 90210

GARRETT, RICHARD MARVIN, chemical engineer, executive; b. June 30, 1921, Lakewood, Ohio; s. Harold B. and Lorraine (Robison) G.; m. Bernice Stewart, Aug., 1951 (div. 1978); children: William b. 1953, Diana b. 1955, Sheryl b. 1958, Richard b. 1963; edn: BSChE, Ohio St. Univ. 1943; naval ofcr. indoctrination, Princeton Univ. 1944; Univ. Chgo. Grad. Sch. 1946; MBA, UC Berkeley 1948. Career: chemical engr. Rohm & Haas, Bristol, Pa. 1943-44; sales Taylor Instruments 1948-52; ptnr. Silver Plastic Co., El Segundo 1952-54; Chem Nickel Co., South Gate 1952-53; ptnr., engr. Carbon Wool Corp., Ojai 1953; pres. Margar Co., Manhattan Beach 1954–; pres. L.A. Council of Engring. Soc. 1960; mem: Am. Inst. Chem. Engrs. (chmn. So. Calif. sect. 1962), Am. Cetacean Soc., Internat. Brotherhood of Magicians, Magic Castle, Checkered Flag Club, Nat. Air-racing Group; articles pub. in profl. jours., 1964-85; mil: lt.j.g. USNR 1944-46; rec: tennis, bicycling, travel. Res: 424 7th St Manhattan Beach 90266 Ofc: Margar Co. Box 3253 Manhattan Beach 90266

GARRIO, ROCCO ROBERT, corporate president; b. Jan. 10, 1949, New York City, N.Y.; s. Anthony Joseph Garrio and Julia (Mochinal) Cragnotti; m. Beth Ann Nurmi, 1973 (div. 1980); children: Nicole b. 1979; m.2d. Vanetta Gale

Lindsay, July 4, 1981 (div. 1993); children: Anthony b. 1982; edn: Bronx Comm. Coll. (N.Y.) 1966-69; El Camino Coll., Torrance 1976-77. Career: group ldr. Revlon Research Ctr., Bronx, N.Y. 1966-71; chemist Azoplate, div. Am. Hoechst, Murray Hill, N.J. 1972-75, tech. sales, Los Angeles 1975-79; tech. sales Richardson, L.A. 1979-80; tech. sales Howson Algrahy, L.A. 1980-81, dist. mgr. 1981-82; branch mgr. Polychrome Corp., L.A. 1982-84; branch mgr. R&P, Inc., L.A. 1984-86; pres. Distribution West, Inc. 1986–; awards: top national salesman Azoplate (1977, 78), mgr. highest sales to quota Polychrome (1983); mem. Orange Co. Litho Club, 1988–; Republican; R.Cath.; rec: target shooting, fishing. Ofc: Distribution West 1895 W Commonwealth #E Fullerton 92633

GARRISON, BETTY BERNHARDT, mathematics professor; b. July 1, 1932, Danbury, Ohio; d. Philip Arthur and Reva Esther (Meter) Bernhardt; m. Robert Edward Kvarda, Sept. 28, 1957 (div. 1964); m. John Dresser Garrison, Jan. 17, 1968; 1 son, John Christopher b. 1969; edn: BA, BS in edn., Bowling Green State Univ., 1954; MA, Ohio State Univ., 1956; PhD, Oregon State Univ., 1962. Career: tchg. asst. Ohio State Univ., Columbus 1954-56; instr. Ohio Univ., Athens 1956-57; San Diego State Univ., 1957-59; tchg. asst. Oregon State Univ., Corvallis 1959-60; asst. prof. San Diego State Univ., 1962-66, assoc. prof. 1966-69, prof. mathematics 1969–; reviewer: Mathematical Reviews, Ann Arbor, Mich. 1966–, Zentralblatt fur Mathematik, Berlin, Ger. 1966–; awards: NSF fellow 1960-62; mem: Am. Math. Soc. 1965–, Math. Assn. of Am. 1965–; pub. articles (1981, 90). Ofc: Dept. Math. Scis. San Diego State University, San Diego 92182

GARRISON, R. LEONARD, JR., shopping center developer, rancher; b. Sept. 7, 1937, Ontario, Oreg.; s. Ray Leonard and Alma Theresa (Sandwick) G.; m. Linda Bridgman, June 26, 1966; children: Holly b. 1969, Wendy b. 1969, Cindy b. 1971, Katy b. 1980; edn: BS, Oreg. St. Univ. Corvallis 1959; MBA, UC Berkeley 1963. Career: developer Desmond Mactavish Assoc., San Francisco 1963-66; pres. Gen. Exploration Devel. 1970; Garrison Pacific Properties, San Rafael 1971–; owner Tulana Farms, Chilquia, Oreg. 1988–; ptnr. Austex Oil & Gas, San Francisco 1980–; dir. Calif. Bus. Properties 1980–; honors: Alpha Zeta, Calif. Real Estate Assn. Willamen Found. fellowship 1963, Sears Roebuck scholarship 1959; mem: Internat. Council Shopping Centers (trustee 1982-88, v.p. 1986-88), Nature Conservancy, Tulana Wildlife Found., Univ. Club San Francisco, Found. N. Am. Wild Sheep, Safari Club Internat., Ducks Unlimited, Calif. Waterfowl, Calif. Trout; articles pub. on shopping ctrs., 1966-; inventor: boat loader, 1978; mil: lt. USN 1959-63; Republican; Methodist; rec: skiing, big game hunting, travel. Res: 55 Toussin Ross Ofc: Garrison Pacific Properties 1050 Northgate Dr Ste 285 San Rafael 94903

GARRISON, THOMAS S., editor; b. Jan. 18, 1952, Bakersfield; s. Thomas and Nell (Chinnis) G.; m. Lorraine D. Irwin, June 24, 1974 (div. 1980); m. Deborah A. Looker, March 8, 1982; edn: BA magna cum laude, political sci., CSU Bakersfield 1974; MA political sci., UC Davis 1976; UC Santa Barbara 1980. Career: coord. The Gathering Place, Santa Barbara 1981; editorial dir. Current World Leaders 1981–; Annual Directory of World Leaders 1988-91; editorial dir. Guide To Political Videos 1993–; cert. microcomposer ops. Autologic Inc., Newbury Park 1982; awards: UCSB Acad. Senate grant 1979, Instructional Devel. grant 1978, CSU Pelletier Found. scholarship (1972, 73), Unitarian Universalist scholarship 1972; mem: Am. Political Sci. Assn., S.B. Co. Peace & Freedom Party Central Com. (chmn. 1988-94), Socialist Party USA, S.B. Rental Housing Mediation Task Force (v.chmn., secty. 1984-86), War Registers League, S.Coast Info. Project (bd. dirs. 1984-86), ACLU; writer The Socialist mag. (1984-87), Left Out mag. (1987-93), adv. Bd. Mem. ABC POL SCI 1993-96; Socialist; rec: table tennis. Ofc: International Academy 800 Garden St Ste D Santa Barbara 93101

GARSKE, DAVID JOSEPH, title company president; b. Nov. 11, 1952, Santa Clara; s. Joseph Edward and Shirley Anne (Schwab) G.; m. Carla Suzanne Harris, June 14, 1975; children: Lauren Enid b. 1978, Karl David b. 1980; edn: AS, Coll. of Sequoias 1972; BS political sci., Univ. Santa Clara 1974. Career: Kings Co. Title Co., Hanford 1974-86, chmn. bd., pres., mgr. 1986–; asst. v.p. & sec., signatory First Am. Title Ins. Co., Santa Ana 1989–; honors: coll. mens student body pres. (1972), Alpha Gamma Sigma (1971-2), Circle K Club coll. div. Kiwanis (sec. 1972), Hanford H.S. Key Club (1970), Calif. Scholarship Fedn. (life); mem: Calif. Escrow Assn. (cert. 1983, state dir. 1984), Central Valley Escrow Assn. (pres. 1984), Kings County Trade Club, Newman Club (pres. 1969), Forensics Club (pres. 1970), Nat. Fedn. of Indep. Bus., Better Bus. Bureau, Kings Co. Bd. Realtors, Bldg. Industry Assn., Calif. Land Title Assn., Am. Land Title Assn., Am. Escrow Assn.; civic: Hanford C.of C. (amb.), Boy Scouts Am./Mt. Whitney Council (co-ch. BSA Friends Breakfast 1989), Kings Co. YMCA, Land Sharks Youth Soccer (coach), Kings Hanford Kiwanis (bd., div. sec. 1991-92, recipient distinguished pres. award 1989-90, distinguished sec. award 1990-91); musical compositions, 1988-; R.Cath.; avocation: composing. Ofc: Kings County Title Co. 1479 W Lacey Blvd Hanford 93230

GARST, J. F., JR., newspaper publisher; b. Sept. 28, 1932, Garden City, Kans.; s. J. F., Sr. and Irene (Morgan) G.; m. Peggy E.M. Stalcup, May 25, 1952; children: Jeannine b. 1953, Jay b. 1956; edn: Masters equiv. USC Ext. classes 1968-73. Career: linotype opr. Freedom Newspapers, Santa Ana, Calif./Colo. Springs,

1947-54; Los Angeles Times, L.A. 1954-68; prodn. mgmt. L.A. Times satellite Costa Mesa facility, 1968-75, cons. 1974-75; owner/pub. The Kourier, Willow Creek 1974–; guest lectr. journ. various instns. incl. Humboldt St. Univ.; dir. Cypress (Calif.) Nazarene Chr. Sch. 1957-60; recipient commendations for comm. svc. schools, Kiwanis and Lions Clubs, others; civic: Trinity County Fair Assn. (bd. 1988–), trustee Trinity Union H. S. (bd. 1993–), Trinity Co. Gen. Hosp. (bd. 1995–); invention: Universal Bell Code System for computer typesetting, 1970; Prot.; rec: ranching. Res: Burnt Ranch Ofc: The Kourier Box 355 Willow Creek 95573

GARTNER, HAROLD HENRY, III, lawyer; b. June 23, 1948, Los Angeles; s. Harold H. and Frances Mildred (Evans) G.; m. Denise Young, June 7, 1975; children: Patrick Christopher b. 1977, Matthew Alexander b. 1982; edn: Pasadena City Coll. 1966-67; Geo. Williams Coll. 1967-68; CSU Los Angeles 1968-69; JD, cum laude, Loyola Univ. Sch. of Law 1972. Career: atty., assoc. Hitt, Murray & Caffray, Long Beach 1972; deputy city atty. City of Los Angeles, 1972-73; atty., assoc. Patterson, Ritner, Lockwood, Zanghi & Gartner (and predecessor firm) Los Angeles, Ventura, San Bernardino, and Bakersfield, 1973-79, ptnr. 1979–, mng. ptnr. 1991–; instr. of law Ventura Coll. of Law 1981–; honors: Am. Jurisprudence Award (Trusts & Equity 1971), St. Thomas More Law Honor Soc. (bd. dirs. 1971-72), Law Review; mem: Am., Calif., Ventura Co. bar assns.: Ventura Co. Trial Lawyers Assn., Assn. of So. Calif. Defense Counsel, Nat. Assn. Defense Counsel, Direct Relief Internat. (bd. trustees); club: Pacific Corinthian Yacht; Republican; rec: sailing, scuba diving, skiing. Res: 6900 Via Alba Camarillo 93012 Ofc: Patterson, Ritner, Lockwood, Zanghi & Gartner, 3580 Wilshire Blvd., Suite 900, Los Angeles 90010

GARVEY, BARBARA HARMAN, clothing design executive, publisher; b. Nov. 10, 1934, Champaign, Ill.; d. Harry Jones and Helen Betty (Rosenblatt) H.; m. Albert Garvey; children: Megan, Samantha; edn: BA, Oberlin Coll., 1956. Career: systems svc. rep. IBM, Chgo., 1956-59; artist's agent Al Garvey Designs, Fairfax, 1966-74; ptnr. Folkwear, Forestville, 1975-79; pres. Folkwear Inc., San Rafael, 1979-89; public relations, Pinta Communications, San Anselmo 1992–; marketing, Master Craftsman Source, San Anselmo 1994–; pres. Bay Area Argentine Tango Assn. (non-profit Calif. corp.) 1994–; bd. trustees Museum of Vintage Fashion 1990–; Democrat; rec: travel, Argentine tango. Res: 281 Scenic Rd Fairfax 94930 Ofc: Pinta Communications 524 San Anselmo Ave #104 San Anselmo 94960

GARVIN, PAMELA ANN, lawyer; b. April 21, 1957, Nashville, Tenn.; d. Samuel and Rita (Abramson) Rotenberg; m. Glenn Bradley Garvin, Aug. 9, 1981; edn: BA, USC, 1978; JD, Southwestern Univ., 1981; LLM, Georgetown Univ. Law Center, 1983; admitted St. Bar Calif. 1985. Career: assoc. atty. Malley, Scott, Koffman & Heston, Beverly Hills 1985-87; Reish & Luftman, Los Angeles 1987-88; sole practice, Los Angeles 1988–; mem: L.A. Co. Bar Assn., Beverly Hills Bar Assn., Women Lawyers Assn., Nat. Inst. Pension Adminstrs., Western Pension Conf., Women in Bus., Nat. Assn. of Women Bus. Owners, Amer. Soc. of Pension Actuaries. Ofc: 1801 Century Park E 24th Floor Los Angeles 90067 and 2660 Townsgate Rd., Ste 760, Westlake Village, CA 91361

GARWOOD, VICTOR P(AUL), professor emeritus audiology and otolaryngology; b. Sept. 13, 1917, Detroit, Mich.; s. Paul J. Schultz and Helen Elizabeth Garwood; m. Dorothy Ann Olson, Mar. 13, 1942; children: Don b. 1950, Martha b. 1955; edn: BA, Univ. of Mich., 1939, MS, 1948, PhD, 1952; lic. audiologist & speech pathologist, 1952, psychologist, 1954. Career: prod. mgr. Bohn Alum. & Brass Corp., Detroit 1942-46; chief exam. div. speech & hearing clinic Univ. Mich., Ann Arbor 1947-50; asst., assoc., full prof. Univ. So. Calif., Los Angeles 1950-88, prof. emeritus audiology and otolaryngology 1988–; mem. USC Retired Faculty Assn. 1988– (pres. 1990-92, treas. 1993-95), USC Emiriti Council 1990–, sr. audiologist L.A. Unified Sch. Dist., 1972-76; speech pathologist and audiol. cons. Calif. Dept. Hlth. Serv., L.A. 1968-87; audiol. cons. Childrens Hosp., L.A. 1964-86; mem., chmn. H.A.D. Adv. Com., Dept. Cons. Affairs, Sacto. 1971-79; honors: univ. scholar Univ. of Mich. (1949-50), research fellow NINDB (NIH) L.A. and Evanston, Ill. (1958-59, 1960-63); mem: Am. Sp. & Hearing Assn. (fellow 1960, life mem. 1982), Sigma Xi (life mem. 1958), Acoust. Soc. Am. (life mem. 1960), Am. Psyc. Assn. (life mem. 1952), Calif. Sp. & Hearing Assn. (life mem. 1950, honors of assn. 1985), Calif. Assn. of Sp. & Hearing Pvt. Practice (honors of assn. 1985); civic: Eagle Scout Nat. Assn. 1985-, profl. advy. com. L.A. Co. Welfare Planning Council 1966-68; Area Agency on Aging Advy. Council, L.A. County Com. on Health & Long Term Care 1995–; publs: author book chapts. in 4 med. books, 1979-88, 25+ jour. articles, 1952-88, mem. edn. advy. bd. Jour. of Auditory Research, 1976-89; rec: off-road driving, photography. Res: 1240 Chautauqua Blvd Pacific Palisades 90272 Ofc: Univ. So. California, Retired Faculty Assn., Emeriti Ctr., GER 220, Los Angeles, CA 90089-0191

GARZOLI, JOHN H., fine art dealer; b. Nov. 23, 1940, San Francisco; s. Henry John and Evelyn Virginia (Dapello) Garzoli (parents 5th generation San Franciscans). Career: fine art dealer, splst. American 19th and 20th Century art, San Francisco 1960s–, Fine Arts cons. Calif. State Senate, active in Capitol restoration project and in formation of Capitol Historic Commn. (restoration and art projects in Sacto. and statewide); civic: Oakland Art Mus., San Francisco museums, Calif. Hist. Soc., Am. Conservatory Theatre, S.F. Ballet Assn., S.F. Symphony Assn., S.F. Zoological Soc. (hon. mem.); advisor Smithsonian Instn.; lender, advisor to 100+ nat. touring art exhibits; mil: USMC, ret.; rec: boating, fishing, tennis. Ofc: Garzoli Gallery 930 B Street San Rafael 94901

GATTI, ALESSANDRO CARLO, company president; b. Aug. 12, 1959, Milan, Italy; s. Idor and Silvana (Schieppati) G.; edn: BS hons., Kings Coll. 1983; MS, Yale Univ. 1985. Career: mktg. analyst, product planner Olivetti, Cupertino 1985-90; business mgr. Conner Peripherals, 1990-91 dir. internat. mktg. Fujitsu Personal Systems, Inc. 1991-93; pres. Cresta Systems, Inc. 1993–; mem. IEE; clubs: St. Moritz Tobogganing, Royal Automobile (London). Address: San Francisco

GAULTNEY, STEPHEN GLENN, business owner, investor; b. Feb. 26, 1947, Alameda; s. James O. and Freida R. (Hammond) G.; m. Ellene, Jan. 9, 1970; children: Jennifer b. 1971; edn: BA zool., Humboldt State Univ. 1969. Career: owner Steve Gaultney Investments (real estate devel. co.); store dir./opr. Big J Foods Inc. dba Hagstroms Supermarket, Petaluma; dir. Big J Foods Inc 1970–, v.p. 1985–; advy. bd. Big T Supermarkets 1978–; apptd. City of Petaluma Housing Allocation Bd. (1977), Downtown Design Com. (1985); trustee Petaluma Valley Hosp. Found. (1978-85); mem. Petaluma C.of C. (dir. 1978-83, pres. 1983-84), Petaluma Rotary Club, No. Calif. Grocers Assn. (chmn. bd. of dir. 1994-95, dir. 1988–, pres. Coastal NCGA 1990-91); Republican; Baptist. Res: 913 B St Petaluma 94952 Ofc: Hagstroms Supermarket 200 Douglas St Petaluma 94952

GAYLORD, ROBERTA IRENE, speech pathologist; b. Jan. 18, 1922, Detroit, Mich.; d. Lloyd Rutherford and H. Irene (Slagel) Worden; mother, Irene Worden, author, rec'd. internat. Mark Twain award for book 'Our Falling Image'; m. Richard Cody Marsh, July 5, 1941; m.2d Harold Bernard Gaylord, Apr. 5, 1957; 1 dau. Sandra b. 1944; edn: BA, CSU San Jose 1969, MA in edn., 1973. Career: prod., writer commentator "Star's Stairway Radio Show" (stage show revs. & celebrity interviews) Sta. KWKW, Pasadena 1949-54; v.p./co-owner Gaylord Constrn. Co., 1963-67; language, speech and hearing splst. Moreland Sch. Dist., Campbell 1969-82; cons. 1982-83; recipient V.F.W. Voice of Democracy award; mem: Calif. Speech-Lang.-Hearing Assn. (nominating com. 1976), Santa Clara Co. Speech-Hearing Assn. (Hosp. Com. chair 1974, sec. 1975, legis. chair 1976), CTA (life), Calif. Retired Teachers Assn. (El Dorado Co. Div. No. 73 Area III, v.p. 1992-93), Res. Svc. (I.P.S.) chair, Am. Fedn. TV Radio Artists, AAUW (legis. chair 1985-6, sec. 1987-89), Sigma Alpha Eta, Pi Lambda Theta (chair Hosp. com. 1983, Newsletter ed. 1983-85), Internat. Platform Assn. (authors' com. 1983, 84), People to People Internat. (secty. 1983-85); publs: TORP Pgm., research in sp. pathol. (1978-79); Republican; rec: travel, dancing, bridge. Res: 3312 Sudbury Rd (POB 1067) Cameron Park 95682

GAYNOR, JOSEPH, international business and technology consultant; b. Nov. 15, 1925, N.Y.C.; s. Morris and Rebecca (Schnapper) G.; m. Elaine Bauer, Aug. 19, 1951; children: Barbara Lynne, Martin Scott, Paul David, Andrew Douglas; edn: BChE, Polytechnic Inst. of Brooklyn, 1950; MS ChE, Case Western Reserve Univ., 1952, PhD phys. chem., 1955, grad. bus. adminstrn. courses. Career: mgr. info. mats. & processes, General Electric Co., Res. & Devel. Ctr., 1955-66; v.p./res. bus. equip. gp. and mgr. mats. R&D, Bell and Howell Co. Central Research Labs., 1966-72; mgr. commercial devel. and mem. Pres.'s Office, Horizons Research Inc., 1972-73; pres. Innovative Technology Assocs., 1973–, proposals, and project mgmt. in U.S., Europe and Japan; honors: Phi Lambda Upsilon, Tau Beta Pi, Alpha Chi Sigma, Sigma Xi, recipient IR-100 Awards (2), Plenary lectr. Internat. Photographic Sci. Congress, Moscow 1970, keynote spkr. US Treasury Dept. ann. conf. on security documents; appt. NAS Materials Advy. Bd. currency study com.; tech. advy. bd. Delphax Corp.; mgmt. advy. bd. Chemical Week; chem. engring. product resrch. panel, editl. bd. Photographic Science and Engineering Jour. and Jour. of Applied Photographic Engring.; guest editor Jour. of Imaging Technology 1988-89; sci. advy. bd. Lehigh Press; mem: AAAS (fellow), ACS, SPSE (senior mem., fellow), AIChE (fellow), SID, SPIE, Internat. Photochemistry Soc., Internat. Soc. for Photobiology; author: Patents (40), publs. (35+), papers presented (40+), editor Proceedings, 1st, 3d Intl. Cong. on Advances in Non-Impact Printing Technologies, (book in progress) Electronic Imaging-Technologies and Applications (Marcel Dekker Inc.). Res: 108 La Brea St Oxnard 93035 Ph: 805/984-2979

GECK, DUANE MICHAEL, lawyer; b. Aug. 4, 1959, Bismarck, N.D.; s. Douglas Michael and MariAnne (Wolberg) G.; m. Theresa Marie Deily, Aug. 8, 1987; children: Kevin b. 1988, Richard, b. 1991, Michelle, b. 1994; edn: BA, Colgate Univ. 1981; JD, Duke Univ. Sch. Law 1984. Career: atty. Severson & Werson, San Francisco 1984–, shareholder 1992–; mem: S.F. Bar Assn. (comml. law sect.), Am. Bar Assn.; Cath. Ofc: Severson & Werson 1 Embarcadero Center 25th Floor San Francisco 94111

GEE, DELBERT CALVIN, lawyer; b. July 29, 1955, Oakland; s. Stanley Hung and Amy (Sung) G.; m. Doris Louise Wong, Jan. 29, 1983; edn: BA, UC Davis 1977; JD, Santa Clara Univ. 1979; admitted St. Bar Calif. (1980). Career: Deputy Dist. Atty., Ventura 1980-82; atty. Hassard Bonnington Rogers &

Huber, S.F. 1982-87; Bronson Bronson & McKinnon 1987-1989, Sturgeon, Keller, Phillips and Gee, S.F. 1989–; mem: Bar Assn. S.F., Alameda Co. Bar Assn., Asian Am. Bar Assn., Wa Sung Service Club, Oakland Chinatown C.of C.; civic: Rotary Club of S.F., Fisherman's Wharf; Democrat; Prot.; rec: athletics, national affairs. Ofc: Sturgeon, Keller, Phillips and Gee, 388 Market St. Ste 670, San Francisco 94111

GEE, NANCY ANN, lawyer; b. June 30, 1953, Albuquerque, NM; d. Henry W. and Eudora M. (Ma) G.; edn: BS, UC Davis 1975; JD, Univ. of Santa Clara 1978. Career: lab. asst. NASA Ames Research Ctr.; atty. assoc. William K. Wilburn, a profl. corp.; currently, atty. at law sole practice, Mountain View; honors: Calif. State Scholar; mem: Chinese Am. Citizens Alliance (pres. Peninsula Lodge 1980, 81) Grand Lodge (spl. asst. to pres. on women affairs 1981, first woman elected to Grand exec. bd. 1983, Grand First V.P. 1993–), Santa Clara Co. Bar Assn., Mountain View C.of C. (dir., pres. 1990-91), Asian Pacific Bar Assn. of So. Bay Area; rec: photog., music. Res: 891 Cascade Dr Sunnyvale 94087 Ofc: Nancy Ann Gee, Atty., 774 W Dana St Mountain View 94041

GEESMAN, JOHN LEONARD, investment banker; b. May 6, 1951, Long Beach; s. James Woodrow and Junne (Wallen) G.; m. Kathryn Burkett Dickson, Dec. 31, 1984; edn: BA, Yale Coll. 1973; JD, UC Berkeley Boalt Hall 1976; admitted St. Bar Calif. 1977. Career: atty., energy policy cons., San Francisco 1976-78; spl. advisor Calif. Energy Commn., Sacto. 1978-79, exec. dir. 1979-83; assoc. First Boston Corp., N.Y.C. 1983-84; San Francisco 1984-85; v.p. Rauscher Pierce Refsnes Inc. 1985-91, managing dir. 1991–, western regional mgr. 1995–; author Deceptive Packaging: A Close Look at Calif. Dept. of Consumer Affairs, 1974; Democrat; rec: backpacking, cross country skiing. Res: 111 Bear Ridge Trail Orinda 94563 Ofc: Rauscher Pierce Refsnes Inc. One Market Plaza 1100 Stewart St San Francisco 94105

GEFFEN, DAVID I., optometrist; b. Sept. 1, 1955, Portland, Oreg.; s. Herbert Wolf and Ruth Estelle (Pearl) G.; m. Sylvia Helen Fischer, July 22, 1979; children: Brian b. 1984, Michele b. 1987, Nicole b. 1991; edn: BA, UCLA, 1977; BS, UC Berkeley, 1980, OD, 1982. Career: pvt. practice optometry, La Jolla 1982–; clin. investigator Bausch & Lomb, Rochester, N.Y. 1983-, Polymer Tech., Boston, Mass. 1987-, Ciba Geigy, Atlanta, Ga. 1987-, Allergan Pharmaceutical, Irvine 1985-; speaker Bausch & Lomb 1988, Nat. Speakers Bur. 1988–, speaker Summit Tech. 1994–; awards: Bausch & Lomb recognition award 1988; mem: Am. Optometric Assn. (contact lens sect. and low vision section), Calif. Optometric Assn., San Diego Co. Optometric Assn., Jewish Comm. Center La Jolla (bd. 1986-), Guardians of S.D. (bd. 1985-88); Republican; Jewish; rec: golf, softball, basketball. Res: 8327 Caminito Helecho La Jolla 92037 Ofc: 6523 La Jolla Blvd La Jolla 92037

GEISE, HARRY FREMONT, meteorologist (ret.); b. Jan. 8, 1920, Oak Park, Ill.; s. Harry and Rosalind (Muser) G.; children: Marian Apgar b. 1955, Gloria Peterson b. 1943, triplets: Barry, Gary, Harry b. 1976; edn: Univ. of Chgo. 1938-39; Meteorologist Svc. Sch., Lakehurst, NJ 1943-44; Calif. Comm. Colls. tchg. credential (first recipient Calif. tchg. cred. for eminence in field) 1964. Career: pvt. weather svc., Chgo. 1937–; chief meteorologist Kingsbury Ord., 1943; meteorol. radio sta. WLS and Prarie Farmer newspaper 1941, 42, 46; assoc. Dr. Irving P. Krick, meteorol. cons. 1947-49; media dir., dir. Pac. div. 1955-59; Army Air Corps. research, developed new temperature forecasting technique, Calif. Inst. of Tech. and Am. Inst. Aerological Research 1948-49; cond. weather and travel shows: WBKB- TV, Chgo,; radio sta. WOPA, Oak Park, Ill., 1950-51; pvt. weather svc. 1954; staff meteorol., San Jose Mercury and News: radio KSJO, KNTV, San Jose; KHUB, Watsonville; KGO-TV, S.F.; cond. 'The Weather and You' series, Columbia Pac. radio network 1956-58; Panorama Pac. Weather Show, KNXT- TV, CBS, L.A. 1957-58; prod. over 70 daily radio pgms. in U.S. 1959; est. Weather Center for CBS, NY (demonstrated forecasts 2 yrs. in advance), WCBS-TV 1966-67; pvt. weather svc., incl. commercial accts. and radio sta. 1962-81, produced over 100,000 radio, TV & trade shows and made over 1 million forecasts; Nat. Defense Exec. Reservist 1968-75; instr. meteorol.: Santa Rosa Jr. Coll. 1964-66; Sonoma State Coll. 1967-68; issued first week in advance forecasts to pub., also first month in advance and first year or more in advance; recognized relationship between specified solar emissions and maj. changes in earth weathel pattern 1956; initiated thunderstorrn warning sys. using radio static known as Sferics (lst discovered in 1936), which became model for US Ord. plants 1942; Calif. 1st tchg. cred. based on outstanding eminence in meteorol. 1964; discovered a relationship between a particular weather type and rash type tomado outbreaks in Midwest, US 1965; origin. transatlantic weather radio pgm. from Geneva, London and Paris to Calif., Dec. 1965-77. Awards: Am. Legion Outstanding Student (1934), US Navy Outstanding War Bond Sales (1944), Calif. Assembly Resolution No. 678 (1972). Author: USA: Voice of America 1968; sev. TV films, arts. publ. in newspapers, mags., trade and profl. journals, num. radio and TV stations.; spkr. on environrnental problems to Rotary clubs, Chambers of Commerce, AAUW, Commonwealth Club of Calif., CBS bdcsts.; life foreign mem. Royal Meteorological Soc.; mil: Aerologist, USMC, 1943-45, WWII; rec: world travel, writing, reading. Res: 4585 Brighton Pl Santa Maria 93455 (also) 49-975 Avenida Obregon La Quinta 92253

GELFAND, JULIA MAUREEN, applied sciences librarian; b. Sept. 26, 1954, Cleveland, Oh.; d. Lawrence Emerson and Miriam (Ifland) Gelfand; m. David B. Lang, Apr. 30, 1995; edn: AB, Goucher Coll., 1975; MLS and MA in hist., Case Western Reserve, 1977. Career: reference librarian Penrose Library, Univ. Denver Lib., Denver 1977-81; reference librarian and bibliographer Univ. Calif. Irvine, 1981-87, applied scis. librarian 1987–; awards: Thos. J. Watson fellow Thos. J. Watson Found., Providence, R.I. (1975-76), Fulbright Prof. Librarian Award, Imperial College, London 1982-83; mem: Am. Lib. Assn. 1976-, Calif. Assn. Research Libraries 1981-, Soc. of Scholarly Publishing 1988-, No. Am. Cartographic Info Systems 1989-, W. Assn. of Map Libraries 1981-, Am. Soc. Engring. Edn. 1987-; civic: Am. Jewish Com. Orange Co. (bd.), Jewish Fedn. O.C., CASA O.C. (Ct. Apptd. Spl. Advocates); publs: num. articles, book revs. in acad. librarianship, 1977-; Democrat; Jewish. Res: 22 Schubert Ct Irvine 92715 Ofc: Science Library Univ. Calif. Irvine 92713-9556

GELMAN, GLENN M., accountancy firm president; b. April 28, 1954, Brooklyn, NY; s. Irving and Rochelle (Smola) G.; m. Bernice, Dec. 25, 1982; children: Rebecca b. 1981 (step), Lisa b. 1983, Elana b. 1984, Joshua b. 1986; edn: BS, New York Univ. 1975; MS, in progress, Golden Gate; CPA, NY 1978. Career: audit supvr. Coopers & Lybrand, NYC, NY; audit mgr. Newport Beach CPA firm; pres. Glenn M. Gelman & Assocs., Irvine; mem: Am. Inst. CPAs, NY, Calif. Socs. CPAs; Temple Beth Shalom (cantor). Res: 4921 Corkwood Irvine 92715 Ofc: Glenn M. Gelman and Associates, An Accountancy Corp., 2600 Michelson Dr Irvine 92715

GENO, RICHARD EARL, life insurance agency manager; b. Mar. 20, 1942, Oakland; s. Claude Earl (dec.) and Florence Jacqueline Geno (dec.); children: Jennifer b. 1965, Deborah b. 1967, Kristin b. 1968, Richard II b. 1969, Lauren b. 1976, Jodi b. 1978, Stephanie b. 1980; edn: BS, UC Berkeley, 1964; MS, The American Coll., 1979, CLU 1970, ChFC 1982, CFP 1983. Career: agent College Life Ins. Co. 1964-74; general agent 1974-82; pres. Richard E. Geno & Assoc. Ins. Svcs., Inc., San Jose 1979-82; general mgr. The Principal Fin. Group 1982–; awards: Jack Richter Memorial Award, Underwriter of Yr. San Jose Life Underws. Assn. 1980, Million Dollar Round Table 1965–, College Life Ins. Co. sales leader (1972, 76, 78) and #1 Agency (1978, 80, 81, 82); mem: Nat. Assn. Life Underws., San Jose Life Underwriters Assn. (dir. 1989-93, 1995-, pres. 1991-92), Am. Soc. of CLUs, CLU/San Jose (dir. 1981-88, pres. 1986-87), San Jose Gen. Agents and Mgr. Assn. (dir. 1975-91, pres. 1980-81, 87-88), Leading Life Ins. Producers of No. Calif. (dir. 1978-80, pres. 1979), Peninsula Life Underwriters (dir. 1971-72); Republican; R.Cath.; rec: tennis, Chinese culture, reading, bridge. Res: 21449 Toll Gate Rd Saratoga 95070 Ofc: The Geno Building 1042 W Hedding Ste 200 San Jose 95126

GENTRY, ROBERT WILTON, physician-surgeon; b. April 11, 1916, Springfield, Mo.; s. Charles Burt Gentry and Kathelene Moore; m. Priscilla Moerdyke, June 21, 1942; m. 2d. Marion P. Mulroney, Sept. 25, 1977; children: Perry Charles, Priscilla Jo; edn: BS, Univ. Conn.; Cornell Univ., 1937; MD, Harvard Med. Sch. 1942; MS surgery, Univ. Minn. 1947; cert. Am. Bd. Surgery 1949; vis. com., bd. trustees Harvard Univ. Med. Sch. 1972-78; mem: L.A. Co. Med. Assn., CMA, AMA (advy. com. motion picture & t.v.), A.C.S. (Fellow), Pan Pacific Surgical Assn., Trudeau Soc., Cavalcade of Health & Med. Progress (pres. L.A. 1956), Harvard Univ. Med. Alumni Assn. (dir. 1980-81, chapt. pres. L.A. 1955-57); clubs: Harvard/L.A. (pres. 1975-76), Valley Hunt, University (Pasadena); num. articles pub. in med. jours.; mil: Medical Adminstrv. Corps 1941-44; Prot.; rec: Tennessee Walking Horses, avocado grower. Address: Sun Valley 91352

GEORGIADES, GABRIEL GEORGE, aerospace engineer, educator; b. Nov. 23, 1956, Amarousion, Greece; s. George Gabriel and Evanthia Spyrou (Ioannou) G.; edn: BA in physics (cum laude), Jacksonville Univ., 1979; B.aerospace engring., Ga. Inst. of Tech., 1979; MS aerospace engring., Pa. State Univ., 1982; lic. E.I.T., Ga. 1979. Career: structural engr. Piper Aircraft Corp., Lockhaven, Pa. 1979-80; prof. aircraft structrue Embry-Riddle Aeronautical Univ., Prescott, Az. 1982-85; prof. aerospace engring. Cal State Polytechnic Univ., Pomona 1985–; cons. Naval Weapons Ctr., China Lake, 1985–, Lockheed Aircraft Svc. Co., Ontario, 1991–, Field Svc. & Maintenance Co., N. Palm Springs, 1991–, Wyle Labs, El Segundo 1992–; awards: cert. achiev. NATO, Belgium 1974, C.W. Brownfield Meml. Award US Jaycees, Lockhaven, Pa. 1980, Disting. svc. AIAA-ERAU, Prescott, Az. 1985, Disting. svc. SHSE, Pomona 1991, listed Who's Who in the West 1992; mem: Am. Inst. of Aero. & Astro. (1976–, v.ch. edn. AIAA-SGV 1988–), Sigma Gamma Tau 1979–, Aerospace Edn. Assn. 1991–, Aerial Phenomena Research Org. 1976–; civic: Minority Engring. Pgm., Pomona (advisor 1987–), Math. Engring. Sci. Achiev., Claremont (advy. bd. 1988–), Soc. Hispanics in Sci. & Engring., Pomona (faculty advisor 1989–); author: Aerospace Structures Lab Manual (1988); Greek Orthodox; rec: reading, photography, music. Ofc: Aerospace Eng. Dept. Cal Poly Pomona 3801 W Temple Ave Pomona 91768

GERATY, LAWRENCE THOMAS, university president; b. Apr. 21, 1940, St. Helena, Calif.; s. Thomas Sinclair and Hazel Mae (McVicker) G.; m. Gillian Anne Keough, Aug. 5, 1962; children: Julie b. 1965, Brent b. 1967; edn: BA,

Pacific Union Coll., 1962; MA, Andrews Univ. 1963, BD, 1965; PhD, Harvard Univ., 1972. Career: minister SE Calif. Conf. of SDA, Santa Ana, Calif. 1965-66; tchg. fellow Harvard Univ., Cambridge, Mass. 1971-72; asst./assoc. prof. Andrews Univ., Berrien Springs, Mich. 1972-85; pres. Atlantic Union Coll., So. Lancaster, Mass. 1985-93; pres. La Sierra Univ., Riverside, Calif. 1993–; Fulbright fellow U.S. Govt., Jerusalem, Israel 1970-71; dir. Hesban Expedition, Tell Hesban, Jordan 1973-78; v.p. Am. Ctr. of Oriental Res., Amman, Jordan 1980–; dir. Madaba Plains Project, Amman, Jordan 1984–;awards: Teacher of Yr. Andrews Univ. 1985, Atlantic Union Coll. 1986; mem.: Am. Oriental Soc. 1972–, Archaeological Inst. of Am. (councilor 1980–), Am. Schools of Oriental Res. (trustee 1980–), Soc. of Biblical Lit. (pres. midwest region 1986-88), assn. of Adventist Coll. & Univ. Presidents (pres. 1991-92), Thayer Symphony Orch., Lancaster, Mass. (dir. 1986-93), Clinton, Mass. C.of C. (dir. 1989-92); author: 70 pub. articles, 1972–; editor: 12 books on archaeology, 1975–; Independent; Seventh-day Adventist; rec: hiking, reading, stamp collecting. Res: 16658 Rocky Creek Drive Riverside 92503 Ofc: La Sierra University 4700 Pierce St Riverside 92505

GERBER, BARRY ELDON, data processing executive, consultant, technical editor; b. May 12, 1942, Los Angeles; s. Harry and Elsie (Lubin) G.; m. Jane Bernette Margo, June 7, 1962; children: Margot, Karl, Georg; edn: BA, UCLA, 1964, MA, 1966, CPil, 1972. Career: prof. CSU Fullerton, 1968-77; dep. dir. Community Cancer Control, Los Angeles 1977-82; research assoc. Neuropsychiatric Inst. UCLA, 1982-83; v.p. info. systems Zenith Ins., Encino 1983-85; adminstrv. dir. Social Sci. Computing UCLA, 1985–; dir High Performance Computing Ctr. Univ. of Guadalajara, Mexico 1993–; technical editor mag., Network Computing, 1990–; writer, cons. in field; contbg. editor mag. PC Week, 1988-90. Res: Van Nuys Ofc: UCLA Social Sciences Computing 2121 Bunche Hall Los Angeles 90024

GERBRACHT, BOB (ROBERT) THOMAS, portrait artist and teacher; b. June 23, 1924, Erie, Pa.; s. Earl John and Lula Mary (Chapman) G.; m. Delia Marie Paz, Nov. 27, 1952; children: Mark b. 1954, Elizabeth b. 1956, Catherine b. 1967; edn: BFA, Yale Univ., 1951; MFA, USC, 1952. Career: art and art history tchr. Wm. S. Hart Jr.-Sr. High Sch., Newhall 1954-56; artist in stained glass Cummings Studio, San Francisco 1956-58; art tchr. McKinley Jr. High Sch., Redwood City 1958-60; arts & crafts tchr. Castro Jr. High Sch., San Jose 1960-79; portrait painter, teacher, self-employed, San Jose, San Francisco, 1979–; art instr. Coll. of Notre Dame, Belmont 1958-60, Notre Dame Novitiate, Saratoga 1968, San Jose City Coll. 1968-71, West Valley Coll., Saratoga 1976-79, Univ. Calif. Santa Cruz 1979, 80, 81, conducted workshops CA, NV, NM, CO, WI, VT, SC, FL, WA, MA, and Mexico 1981–; awards incl. Best of Show- San Jose Art League (1983, 84), Pastel Soc. of West Coast, Sacto. 1988, Soc. of Western Artists, S.F. (1982, 90), Best Portrait, Soc. We. Artists, S.F. 1985, Am. Artist Achievement Award for Tchr. of Pastels 1993; mem: Pastel Soc. of Am. 1978–,Pastel Soc. of West Coast (advisor 1980–), Soc. We. Artists (trustee 1986–), Calif. Pastel Soc. (advisor 1991–); commissions: (oil painting portrait) Mr. Austen Warburton, 1991, Rev. Cecil Williams, 1991; represented in collections: Triton Mus., Santa Clara, Glide Church, S.F.; articles in Am. Artist Mag. (1981, 85, 92, 93), Today's Art & Graphics, 1982, The Art and Antique Collector, 1984, U.S. ART, 1989, Profile mag. of Am. Portrait Soc., 1984; mil: T5 US Army 1943-46; Glide Ch. S.F. Res: 1301 Blue Oak Ct Pinole 94564

GERINGER, SUSAN D., university professor, b. Dec. 23, 1954, Madera, Calif.; d. Gaston D. and Betty L. (Crane) Ownbey; m. Steven A. Geringer, Aug. 8, 1975; children: Steven b. 1979, Alexandra b. 1986; edn: BA, Calif. State Univ., Sacto., 1976-78; MA, Calif. State Univ., 1980-84; post-grad. work, N.Y. Univ., 1993. Career: retail exec. Macy's, S.F., Calif., 1978-80; div. chairperson Bauder Coll., Sacto., Calif., 1980-81; instr. Am. Riv. Coll., Sacto., 1982-86; prof. Calif. State Univ., Sacto., 1986-92; retail cons. self-employed, Madera, Calif., 1988–; instr. Calif. State Univ., Fresno, 1992–; expert witness, TASA, Mass., 1991–; awards: Outstanding Alumni, Calif. State Univ., Sacto., 1981; tchg. fellowship, N.Y. Univ. NY, NY, 1989; nat. scholarship, Phi Mu Sor., Atlanta, Ga., 1989; scholarship, NCD-CHEA, Sacto., Calif., 1989; membership, Kappa Omicron NU, Nat. Honor Soc., 1989–;mem: Internat. Textile & Apparel Assn. 1983–, Am. Collegiate Retail Assn. 1989–, The Fashion Group Internat. (S.F. chpt.) 1987–, Costume Soc. 1989–, Am. Assn. of Univ. Women, Madera, Calif.; civic bds: LARCS, Sacto., 1984-87; Children's Receiving Home, 1985-87; Legal Auxiliary, Sacto., 1984-91; pres., C.S.U.S. Home Econ. Alumni, Sacto., 1987-89; author: textbook, Fashion: Color, Line & Design, 1986; co-author, textbook, History of 20th Century Costume, 1993; presenter, prof. confs., 1991-92; rec: skiing, golf, quilting, racquetball. Ofc: P.O. Box 207 Madera 93639

GERMAN, WILLIAM, newspaper editor; b. Jan. 4, 1919, N.Y.C.; s. Sam and Celia (Norack) G.; m. Gertrude Pasenkoff, Oct. 12, 1940; children: David b. 1944, Ellen b. 1947, Stephen b. 1953; edn: BA, Bklyn. Coll. 1939; MS, Columbia Univ. 1940. Career: reporter, asst. foreign ed., chief copy desk San Francisco Chronicle 1940-43, chief copy desk 1945-49, news editor 1950-60, exec. news ed. 1960-77, also ed. Chronicle Foreign Service 1960-80, executive editor 1982-93, editor 1993–, mng. ed. KQED Newspaper of the Air 1968, moderator KQED, Profile Bay Area, S.F. 1969-70; lectr. UC Berkeley 1946-47,

1968-70; selection bd. Nieman Found. Harvard 1959-60; cons. Ford Found. on t.v. news projects 1969; juror Pulitzer Prize in Journalism (1986, 87); editor (literary collection) The Chronicle Reader; awards: Nieman fellow Harvard Univ. (1949-50); mem. Am. Soc. Newspaper Editors, AP Mng. Editors Assn., Com. on Fgn. Relations, World Affairs Council (bd. trustees 1980-92); clubs: Commonwealth Club of Calif. (pres. 1995); mil: AUS 1943-45. Ofc: San Francisco Chronicle 901 Mission St San Francisco 94103

GERSHEN, JAY ALAN, professor of dentistry; b. Apr. 9, 1946, Bronx, NY; s. Julius and Vera (Sherman) G.; m. Arleen Yvonne Corman, July 3, 1971; children: Valari B. b. 1983, Jenna R. b. 1988; edn: BA, psychol., SUNY at Buffalo 1968; DDS, Univ. of Maryland 1972; gen. dentistry internship Eastman Dental Ctr., Rochester, NY 1972-73; postdoctoral prog. in pediatric dentistry, UCLA Sch. of Dentistry 1973-75; postdoctoral scholarship in child psychiatry Neuropsychiatric Inst., UCLA 1974-75; PhD, edn., Sch. of Edn., UCLA 1976; state dental lic.: Maryland and NY 1971–, Mass., Ill., DC, Ohio, Pa., N.J., Conn. 1977–, Calif. 1983–. Career: p.t. assoc., pvt. practice gen. dentistry, Rochester, NY 1972-73; p.t. assoc. in dentistry, UCLA Sch. of Dentistry 1975-76; faculty, UCLA Sch. of Dentistry 1976–, asst. prof. pediatric dentistry 1976-79, assoc. prof. 1979-83, prof., Sect. of Public Health Dentistry 1983–; dir. Mobile Dental Clinic 1976-82, faculty Group Dental Practice for Children 1976-85, assoc. dean for Policy & Prog. Devel. 1983-84, dir. Dental Care Evaluation Consultants 1984-92, acting coord. Robert Wood Johnson Dental Scholars Prog. 1988-89, chair Section of Public Health Dentistry 1988–, mem. Academic Coord. Com 1988–, chair Ad Hoc Com to develop a dental plan for Sch. of Dentistry 1993–; mem. doctoral coms. Dept. of Edn. and Dept. of Psychology, Univ. of Calif. 1977–; mem. Health Scis. Com., Ofc. of the Pres., Univ. of Calif. 1992– (chair 1993–), Com. on Faculty Welfare, L.A. Campus 1994–; bd. dirs. Am. Fund for Dental Health 1993– (editl. review com. 1994–); health policy fellow, Full Com. on Energy and Commerce, U.S. House of Reps., W.D.C. 1982-83; cons. and evaluator of dental care progs.: Congl. Ofc. of Technology Assessment, Fed. Trade Commn., L.A. Co. Dept. of Health Svs., Calif. Dept. of Corporations (1979–), Blue Cross of Calif., Gen. Motors/United Workers and several union trust funds, others; frequent speaker to profl. orgns.; research work on dental edn., health svs. and behavioral scis., dental delivery systems, third party financing and their effect on the quality of dental care; honors: Nat. Inst. of Dental Res. predoctoral res. fellowship, Johns Hopkins Univ. Sch. of Public Health 1970, NIH postdoctoral res. fellowship UCLA Sch. of Dentistry 1974-76, Mobile Dental Clinic Faculty award, UCLA Sch. of Dentistry 1977, Robert Wood Johnson Health Policy fellowship, Inst. of Medicine of Nat. Acad. of Scis. 1982-83, listed Who's Who in Frontier Sci. & Tech. 1984, appt. affiliate mem. Grad. Sch. of Edn., UCLA 1984-88, Omicron Kappa Upsilon 1990, Awards for Svc., Am. Assn. of Dental Schs. 1990, 1993, Am. Assn. for Dental Res. 1991; grantee, co-prin. investigator: Am. Fund for Dental Health 1978-80, Fed. Trade Commn. 1981-85, The Robert Wood Johnson Found. 1994–; mem: Am. Assn. of Dental Schools, Sect. on Behavioral Scis. (chair, 1981-83), Sect. on Comm. and Preventive Dentistry, Sect. on Ednl. Res., Devel. and Curriculum (chair, Council of Sects. Adminstrv. Bd. 1984-86; v.p. Council of Sections 1987-90, pres. 1990-92; legis. advy. com. 1987–; past mem. num. other coms.), Am. Assn. of Public Health Dentistry (work group for oral health policy 1994–), Am. Dental Assn., Calif. Dental Assn., We. L.A. Dental Soc., Am. Public Health Assn. (Dental Health Sect.), Assn. for Health Svs. Res., Assn. of Behavioral Scientists and Dental Res., Internat. (Am.) Assn. for Dental Res. (Behavioral Scis. and Health Svs. Res. Group), Research!America (com. on public affairs 1991–); editl reviewer: Jour. of Dental Edn. 1977-78, 84–, Jour. of Am. Dental Assn. 1991–; grant reviewer NIH Nat. Inst. for Dental Res. 1983, Am. Fund for Dental Health 1984, 87; referee, Jour. of Public Health Dentistry 1988–; editl bd., UCLA Dentistry Mag. 1992–; Congressional testimony, 102nd Congress, pub. 1991, author: instruction manual, 1976, encyclopedia entry, Encyclopedia of Ednl. Res., 5th edit., 1982, num. pub. policy papers; co-author: 4 Teacher's Manuals, 1980, 4 instructional videotapes, 1980; contbg. author: 14 abstracts and 27 articles to profl. jours, 1974–; Democrat; Jewish. Ofc: UCLA School of Dentistry 10833 Le Conte Ave Los Angeles 90024-1668

GERTH, DONALD R., university president; b. Dec. 4, 1928, Chgo.; s. George and Madeleine Agnes (Canavan) G.; m. Beverly Jean Hollman, Oct. 15, 1955; children: Annette Schofield, Deborah Hougham; edn: AB liberal arts, Univ. Chgo. 1947, AM polit. sci. 1951, PhD polit. sci. 1963. Career: Govt. Pub. Service, CSU Chico, 1968-70; assoc. v.p. acad. affairs Univ. of Skopie, Yugoslavia 1969-70; prof. political sci., dir. internat. programs CSU Chico, 1964-76, also v.p. acad. affairs 1970-76; univ. pres. and prof. political sci. CSU Dominguez Hills, 1976-84; prof., univ. pres. CSU Sacramento, 1984–; appt. Commn. of the Californias (del., edn. com.); mem: Internat. Assn. Univ. Presidents (chair N.Am. Council and pres.-elect), Calif. State Univs. Admissions Advy. Council (chair), AASCU (bd. dirs.), Advy. Bd. Inst. of Internat. Edn.; civic: Sacto. C.of C., United Way of Gr. Sacto. (bd., chair-elect), Sacramento Club (bd.), Port of Sacramento (commodore); author, ed.: An Invisible Giant, 1971, coauthor monograph: The Learning Society, 1969; contbg. ed. Edn. for the Public Service, 1970, Papers on the Ombudsman in Higher Edn., 1979; mil: capt. USAF 1952-56; Democrat; Episcopalian; rec: tennis, skiing, reading. Ofc: California State University 6000 J St Sacramento 95819-6022

GEST, HOWARD D., lawyer; b. Jan. 25, 1952, Bergenfield, N.J.; m. Lucy Acevedo; 1 son, Aaron b. 1984; edn: AB econ., UC Berkeley 1974; JD, UCSF Hastings Coll. Law 1977. Career: asst. U.S. atty. U.S. Atty. Central Dist. Calif., Los Angeles 1978-83; ptnr. Sidley & Austin 1986–. Ofc: Sidley & Austin 555 W. Fifth St, Ste 4000, Los Angeles, CA 90013-1010

GIANNINI, DANTE HENRY, lawyer; b. Jan. 16, 1952, San Jose; s. Dante Henry and Eletta Maria (Baldacci) G.; m. Alena Margarita Rodriguez, May 26, 1977; children: Dante b. 1980, Jessica b. 1985; edn: BS acctg., Univ. Santa Clara 1974; JD magna cum laude, 1979. Career: staff acct. Price Waterhouse, San Jose 1974-76; atty. Berliner Cohen & Blagini 1977-85; ptnr. Price Waterhouse 1986–. Ofc: Price Waterhouse 150 Alamden Blvd Ste 1200 San Jose 95113

GIBBONS, JAMES FRANKLIN, university professor and administrator; b. Sept. 19, 1931, Leavenworth, Kans.; s. Clifford Hugh and Mary Jewel (Petty) G.; m. Mary Lynn Krywick, Mar. 19, 1954; children: Robert b. 1958, Laura and Sarah b. 1961; edn: BS, Northwestern Univ. 1953; PhD, Stanford Univ. 1956. Career: faculty, elec. engring., Stanford Univ. 1957–, prof. of elec. engring. 1964–, dean, Sch. of Engring. 1984–; bd. dirs.: Lockheed Corp. 1985–, Raychem Inc., Centigram, Cisco Systems, El Paso Gas; bd. mem. and/or scientific adv. for 3 start-up ventures; cons. to semiconductor electronics industry 1957–; mem. U.S. (Nat. Acad. of Scis.) Scientific Team for Exchanges on Ion Implementation and Beam Processing (Japan, 1971, PRC, 1976, USSR, 1977, 79, Australia 1981); panel mem. President's Sci. Advy. Com. (during Nixon, Reagan and Bush adminstrns.); expert witness on solar energy, U.S. House of Reps. Com. on Sci. and Tech. 1977; mem. U.S.-Japan Joint High Level Advy. Panel 1989–; chmn. advy. panel, Congl. Ofc. of Technology Assessment study, U.S. Energy Efficiency: Past Trends and Future Opportunities 1991, awards: Eshbach award Northwestern Univ. 1953, elected to Tau Beta Pi, Eta Kappa Nu, Sigma Xi 1956, We. Elec. Fund award for Excellence in Tchg. 1971, No. Calif. Solar Energy Assn. award for Outstanding Achievement 1975, Tau Beta Pi award for Outstanding Undergrad. Engring. Tchg. 1976, IEEE Jack A. Morton award 1980, Texas Instruments Founders' Prize 1982, named Reid Weaver Dennis Prof. of Elec. Engring., Stanford Univ. 1983, Frederick Emmons Terman Prof. and Dean, Sch. of Engring. 1984, IEEE Edn. Medal 1985, Outstanding Alumni award Northwestern Univ. 1985, Electrochem. Soc. award in Solid State Sci. & Tech. 1989, IEEE Electron Devices Soc. Rappaport award 1990; mem: IEEE (fellow, 1971–), Nat. Acad. of Engring. 1974– (mem. governing council 1989–), Nat. Acad. of Scis. 1985– (mem. NAE/NAS Manufacturing Forum 1989–, NAS/NRC Com. on Sci., Tech. and Econ. Policy 1989–), Royal Swedish Acad. of Scis. (elected 1985), White House Sci. Council Panel on Semiconductors (SEMATECH, 1987), Norwegian Acad. of Tech. Svs. (elected 1988), Am. Acad. of Arts & Scis. (fellow, 1989–); assoc. editor, IEEE Transactions on Electron Devices, 1964-70; editor, McGraw-Hill, Fundamentals of Electronic Science 1970-78; author or co-author: 4 textbooks in semiconductor electronics, 4 res. monographs on ion implantation and beam processing of semiconductors, 279 papers on semiconductor device analysis, process physics and solar energy; rec: playing trombone. Res: 320 Tennyson Ave Palo Alto 94301 Ofc: Stanford University Terman 214 Stanford 94305

GIBSON, VIRGINIA L., lawyer; b. March 5, 1946, Independence, Mo.; d. Jim C. and Margaret I. (Baird) Finck; edn: BA, UC Berkeley 1972; JD, UCSF 1977; admitted St. Bar Calif. (1981). Career: atty., assoc. Pillsbury Madison Sutro, San Francisco 1980-83; ptnr. Chickering & Gregory 1983-85; ptnr. Baker & McKenzie 1985–; mem: Am. Bar Assn. (employee benefits subcom. tax sect.), Calif. Bar Assn. (exec. com. tax sect. 1985-88), S.F. Bar Assn. (internat. and comparative law, taxation sects.), Western Pension and Benefits Conf. (pres. S.F. chpt. 1989-91, chmn. program com. 1986-88, steering com. 1988-91), Internat. Found. Employee Benefit Plans. Ofc: Baker & McKenzie 2 Embarcadero Center Ste 2400 San Francisco 94111

GIDDINGS, DAVID WIGHT, company executive; b. Feb. 5, 1954, Lynwood; s.Edwin and Manya (Koshko) G.; edn: CSU Fullerton, 1972-78. Career: pres. D.W. Giddings Co., Inc., Downey 1972-85; dir. Elsinore Aerospace Services, Inc., Downey 1982-90; owner Jet Set Enterprises, Laguna Niguel 1983–; mem: BBB of the Southland, Window Coverings Assn. of America; Nat. Decorating Products Assn.; rec: computers, electronics. Address: Jet Set Enterprises 26 Newcastle Ln Laguna Niguel 92677

GIDDINGS, MANYA KOSHKO, corporate executive, entrepreneur; b. Sept. 21, 1922, Kansas City, Kans.; d. Stefan and Mehelena (Zybko) Koshko; m. Edwin Wight Giddings, July 12, 1948 (dec. Apr. 15, 1980); children: David Wight b. 1954; edn: AA, Cerritos Coll., 1967, BS, CSU Fullerton, 1970. Career: secty. North American Aviation, Kansas City, Kans. 1941-43; TransWorld Airlines, 1943-48; exec. v.p., pres., chmn. bd. and chief exec. ofcr. Elsinore Aerospace Services Inc., Downey 1971-90 (sold co. to Air/Lyon); v.p. finance, co-owner, director, M & G Fire Equipment, Inc., Bonner Springs, KS 1992–; honors: finalist Arthur Anderson Inc. magazine Entrepreneur of Yr., L.A. (1988), mag. cover feature Airline Executive Mag., Atlanta, Ga. (1988), listed in Who's Who of Am. Women; Republican; R.Cath.; rec: writing, gardening. Res: 42 South Peak Dr Laguna Niguel CA 92677-2903

GIDEON-HAWKE, PAMELA LAWRENCE, fine arts gallery owner; b. Aug. 23, 1945, N.Y.C.; d. Lawrence Ian Verry and Lily S. (Stein) Gordon; m. Jarrett Redstone, June 27, 1964; 1 child, Justin Craig Hawke; graduate West Point 1993. Career: owner Gideon Gallery Ltd., Los Angeles 1975–; named friend of design industry Designers West Mag. 1987; listed 2000 Notable Am. Women 1995, Disting. Women of so. Nevada 1995; mem. Am. Soc. Interior Designers (publicist), Internat. Soc. Interior Designers (trade liaison 1986-88), Network Exec. Women in Hosp. (exec. v.p. L.A. chpt., programming chair 1995; pres. Las Vegas chpt. 1994, 95), Internat. Furnishings and Design Assn. (program chair). Ofc: Gideon Gallery Ltd. 8748 Melrose Ave Los Angeles 90069 and 8121 Lake Hills Dr Las Vegas 89103

GIFFORD, JERRI JACKLYN, director student financial services; b. Aug. 13, 1946, Grand Island, Nebr.; d. Vernon Henry and Loretta Mae (Loewen) Koenig; m. Gary Donald Gifford, June 25, 1967; children: Shauna b. 1970, Chip b. 1972; edn: diploma, Lodi Acad., Lodi, Calif., 1964; BS, Andrews Univ., Berrien Springs, Mich.; MA, Loma Linda Univ., Riverside, Calif., 1981; career: tchr. SPA, Escondido, Calif., 1975-79; tchr. Hawaiian Mission Ac., Honolulu, Hawaii, 1979-81; tchr. Southwestern Adv. Coll., Keene, N.C., 1981-85; computer broker Strata Marketing, Santa Cruz, Calif., 1986-88; student finance dir. Pacific Union Coll., Angwin, Calif., 1988–; cons., tchg., Pacific Union Coll.; mem: CASFAA 1988–, WASFAA 1988–, NASFAA 1988–, WACUBO 1991–; Seventh-Day Adventist; rec: reading, travel.

GILB, CORINNE LATHROP, educator; b. Feb. 19, 1925, Lethbridge, Canada; d. Glen Hutchison and Vera (Passey) Lathrop; m. Tyrell T. Gilb, Aug. 18, 1945; children: Lesley b. 1946, Tyra b. 1955; edn: BA, Univ. Wash. Seattle 1946; MA, UC Berkeley 1951; PhD, Radcliffe Harvard 1957. Career: head oral history project UC Berkeley 1950-57; lectr. Mills Coll., Oakland 1957-61; prof. humanities San Francisco St. Univ. 1964-68; research assoc. UC Berkeley 1956-68; dir. planning dept. City of Detroit, Mich. 1979-85; prof. history Wayne St. Univ. 1968-94, dir. urban studies program 1976-85; vis. scholar Stanford Univ., fall 1993; spl. cons. Calif. Legislature Assembly Com. on Revenue & Taxation 1964; honors: Phi Beta Kappa, Guggenheim fellow 1967-68; rep. of Internat. Organization for Unification of Terminological Neologisms, to U.N. non-governmental organizations; mem: Am. Historical Assn., Internat. Soc. for Comparative Study of Civilizations (first v.p. 1995-98, 5 terms on exec. council), Am. Planning Assn., Commonwealth Club, World Affairs Council, Women's Faculty Club, and num. others; author: Hidden Hierarchies, 1966, 76, 40+ book reviews, book chpts. and articles, 1957–; Presbyterian; rec: travel, gardening, swimming. Res: 19 Selby Lane Atherton 94027

GILBERT, JARVEY, physician; b. Oct. 14, 1917, Mpls.; s. Nathan and Betty (Rosenthal) G.; m. Sarah E. Seligman, Sept. 26, 1948; children: Jean Seager b. 1950, Deborah Ross b. 1955, Laura Gilbert b. 1953; edn: BS, Univ. Minn. 1940; MB, 1942; MD, 1943. Career: city councilman City of Burbank 1967-75, Mayor 1970-71, mem. sch. bd. 1981-85; mem: So. Calif. Assn. Govts. 1971 (pres. 1975); author Prescriptions for Living, 1971; capt. USPHS 1953-55; Jewish; rec: golf. Res: 828 Grinnell Burbank 91501

GILBERT, JO, clinical and forensic psychologist; b. July 25, 1949, Los Angeles; d. Joseph Raymond and Rochelle Rose (Burdman) Gilbert; m. Christopher Leroy Smale, MD, Dec. 19, 1969, div.; son, Branden b. 1974; edn: BA in psych., cum laude, UCLA, 1972; minor in anthropology, Univ. Houston, 1971-72; grad. psych. pgm., A.B.D., William Marsh Rice Univ., Houston 1972-77; PhD clin. psych., Calif. Sch. Profl. Psychology, Fresno 1980; forensic psych. cert., 2-yr post-doc. tng. Forensic Psychology Inst. C.S.P.P., Berkeley 1983-85; lic. clin. psychologist, Calif. 1982. Career: psychol. intern, counselor Olive Street Bridge, Fresno County drug abuse prevention & treatment agy., 1978-80; reg. psychologist pgm. for serious youth offenders, Project Fresno Pride, 1980-82; clinical psychologist pvt. group practice Fox, Pick & Assocs., Napa 1982-85, clinical and forensic solo practice, 1985–; ptnr. Napa-Solano Psychotherapy Services, Inc. 1993–; mem. County List of Court Apptd. Psychologists (Yolo, Sacto., Napa, Solano); Keyhea certification hearing ofcr. Solano Co. 1987-93; qualified Medical Evaluator 1992–; adj. faculty Univ. San Francisco 1987-88; v. chair bd. dirs. Catholic Social Svs. 1983-87; awards: full tuition scholar Rice Univ. 1972-75, Silver Psi award Calif. Psychol. Assn. 1992; mem: Am. Psychol. Assn. (Divs. 31 & 41), Nat. Reg. Health Svc. Providers 1983–, Calif. Psychol. Assn. (chair div. of profl. practice 1989, div. rep. to CSPA Bd. 1990-93, sec.-elect 1993, sec. 1994-95, mem. Exec. Council), Mental Hlth. Advy. Bd. Fresno 1980-82, Napa Valley Psychol. Assn. (pres. 1985), No. Calif. Council Psychol. Assns. (pres. 1984), Soc. for Personality Assessment, Napa County Mental Health Advy. Bd. 1989-91; frequent spkr. profl. seminars and meetings, and local radio; Democrat; Jewish; rec: music, literature. Ofc: 1040 Main St Ste 207A Napa 94559

GILBERT, STEVEN EDWARD, professor of music; b. Apr. 20, 1943, Brooklyn, N.Y.; s. Milton and Sylvia Ruth (Meyerson) G.; m. Patricia Jean King, May 28, 1977 (div. Jan. 14, 1994); children: Jonathan b. 1981, Matthew b. 1989; edn: BA, CUNY/Brooklyn Coll., 1964; MM, Yale Univ., 1967, MPhil, 1969, PhD, 1970. Career: asst. to full prof. dept. of music CSU Fresno, 1970–; ptnr. JAJ Properties, Reno, Nev. 1988–; recipient Student Composers Awards,

Broadcast Music Inc., N.Y. (1964, 66, 67); mem: College Music Soc. (1971–, Life), Am. Musicol. Soc. 1969–, Soc. for Music Theory 1977–, Sonneck Soc. 1980–, Nat. Assn. of Scholars 1990–, Yale Club of San Joaquin Valley (pres. 1979-82, 85-86), Porsche Club of Am. (local pres. 1985-86); author: The Music of Gershwin, 1995, coauthor: Intro. to Schenkerian Analysis, 1982, contbr. articles in The Musical Quarterly, J. of Music Theory, Perspectives of New Music, Grove's Dictionaries of Music, The World Book Ency., reviews The Fresno Bee; Republican; Jewish; rec: automobiles, stock trading. Res: 7567 N Angus, Fresno 93720 Ofc: Dept. Music Calif. State Univ., Fresno 93740-0077

GILBERT, THOMAS ANGUS, realtor; b. Aug. 5, 1948, Pensacola, Fla.; s. Randall DeWayne and Catherine (Allan) G.; m. Teresita Lee, July 1, 1970 (div. 1981); m. Lilia Rey, Nov. 27, 1987; children: Rowelina b. 1968, Kenneth b. 1971; edn: BA in bus. adminstrn., BA adminstrn. of justice, Columbia Coll., 1979; MBA, National Univ., San Diego 1990. Career: SKC, SKCS USS Voge FF-1047, Jacksonville, Fla. 1980-82; SKCS USS Platte AO-186, Norfolk, Va. 1982-84; SKCS, CWO2, SC, USN FCDSSSA Dam Neck, Virginia Beach, Va. 1984-85; CWO2, SC, USN NAVSUP Corps Sch., Athens, Ga. 1985; USS Nimitz CVN-68, Bremerton, Wash. 1986-88; supply analyst CACI Inc. Federal, San Diego 1989–; honors: Outstanding Young Men of Am. (1980), Who's Who in West (1989); mem: Retired Ofcrs. Orgn., Columbia Coll. Alumni, Am. Legion; mil: CWO2 USN 1967-88; Republican (exec. com. Lake County FL 1972-74); Catholic. Res: 2081 Crosscreek Rd Chula Vista 91913-2381 Ofc: Century 21 Teamwork 5034 Bonita Rd Ste E, Bonita 91902

GILE, BARRIE AVERILL, financial planner; b. Dec. 18, 1938, Waltham, Mass.; s. Harold R. and Geraldine (Olmstead) G.; div.; 1 son: Jason B., b. 1961; edn: Bowdoin Coll. 1956-57; BA, Boston Univ. 1961; reg. fin. planner (RFP), Internat. Assn. Reg. Fin. Planners 1984; certified investment specialist (CIS) 1993, Internat. Assn Profl. Fin. Cons. (RFC) 1994, Internat. Assn. for Fin. Planning 1995. Career: sales mgr. P.F. Collier, Inc., Hartford, Conn., Springfield and Boston, Mass. 1961-65; sales rep. Prudential Ins. Co. of Am., Salem & Gloucester, Mass. 1965-68; sales mgr., sales rep. Mass. Mutual Life Ins. Co., Boston, Los Angeles and Long Beach 1969-95; reg. fin. planner MML Investors Services, Inc., Long Beach 1984-88; Shearwater Securities Corp., Manhattan Beach and Concord. Ca. 1988-89; Portfolio Asset Management, El Paso, Tx. and Manhattan Beach, Ca. 1990-93; EDI Fin., Inc., Dallas, Tx. and San Pedro, Calif. 1994-95; cons. Am. Fedn. of Tchrs., ABC Unified Sch. Dist., Cerritos 1981-95; recipient NALU awards: Life and Qualifying mem. Million Dollar Round Table 1982-95, Nat. Sales Achiev. Award 1981-95, Nat. Quality Award 1967-68, 1981-93; mem: Nat. Assn. Life Underwriters, Internat. Assn. Reg. Fin. Planners, Internat. Assn. Profl. Fin. Cons., Spectrum Athletic Club, Amnesty Internat., Greenpeace, Cabrillo Beach Yacht Club; rec: collect music CDs & records, sports. Res: 320 W 19th Townhouse 3 San Pedro 90731 Ofc: 100 Oceangate Ste 1400 Long Beach 90802

GILES, WAYMON KEITH, produce company executive; b. Jan. 27, 1963, Vandenburg AFB; s. Waymon Deadrick and Virginia Mae (Slade) G.; m. Laura Kay Lamb, Aug. 15, 1981; children: Candice, Cassandra; legal guardians: Rosalind and Beatriz Guillen. Career: warehouser Antelope Valley Produce, Lancaster 1978-79, sales 1979-80, asst. mgr. 1984-89, jr. v.p. 1989–; awards: PTA, 1981, goodwill amb. Small World Adventure, 1989; lic. foster parent 1991–; Republican; Assemblies of God (named Father of Yr. 1989, comdr. Royal Rangers 1983-86, coord. Missionettes 1986-92, Bible quiz coach and youth sponsor 1992–, elected deacon, ch. bd. First Assembly of God Ch., Lancaster 1993-96); rec: golf. Ofc: 206 W. Nugent Lancaster 93534

GILKESON, FILLMORE BOLLING, navy officer, retired; b. Oct. 27, 1915, Bluefield, W.Va.; s. William Eskridge and Elizabeth Burrell (Jones) G.; m. Elizabeth Jeannette Graham, Feb. 17, 1942; children: Ellen b. 1943, Patricia b. 1947; edn: BS naval engring., U.S. Naval Acad. Annapolis 1937; BS aero. engring. USN Postgrad. Sch. 1948; Calif. Inst. Tech. Pasadena 1949. Career: midshipman U.S. Naval Acad., Annapolis, Md. 1933-37, ensign to lt.comdr. USN 1937-43, comdr. 1945, capt. 1955, rear admiral 1965, ret. 1975; mem: Golden Eagle Club S.D. Co. (bd. dirs. 1983-85, 1989), U.S. Naval Acad. Alumni Assn. (chpt. pres. 1977-79), Regional Employment & Tng. Consortium (bd. dirs. 1976-89), ARC (bd. dirs. 1986-89); mil: rear admiral USN 1965-75; Republican; Episcopalian; rec: golf, hunting. Res: 1770 Avenida del Mundo Coronado 92118

GILL, JOHN STILLMAN, clergyman, educator; b. Jan. 2, 1917, San Diego; s. Louis John and Mildred Elizabeth (Stillman) G.; edn: BA, CSU San Diego 1938; MA, UCLA 1961; DD, Ch. Div. Sch. of Pacific 1978. Career: instr. math. and history Bonita Sch. 1940-42; stress analyst Consolidated Air Co., San Diego 1942; instr. math. and history Harvard Sch., Studio City 1942-86, sch. chaplain 1947-78, senior chaplain 1978-86; assoc. rector Saint Marks Ch., Los Olivos 1986–; canon Diocese of Los Angeles 1977–, chmn. examining chaplains Diocese of Los Angeles 1951-74, chaplain to bishop 1973-86; Los Angeles Mayor's Advy. Com. 1964-72; honors: Lambda Delta Lambda, Kappa Delta Pi, Coll. of Arms hon. arms (1952); mem: Hospitaler Order St. John of Jerusalem (prelate), Hospitaler Order of St. Lazarus of Jerusalem, Calif. Hist. Soc., Am. Philatelic Soc., Heraldry Soc., Sierra Club, Nature Conservancy; designer

stained glass St. Saviours Chapel Harvard Sch. (1962); D;; Episcopalian; rec: philately, heraldry. Address: Box 719 Los Olivos 93441

GILL, KEITH HUBERT, lawyer; b. May 31, 1929, Pocatello, Ida.; s. Hubert Samuel and Myrtle Frances (Olsen) G.; m. Glenna Jean Lowery, June 16, 1956; children: Suzanne b. 1963, Gina b. 1965; edn: BA, Idaho St. Univ. 1952; MBA, UCLA 1964; JD, USC 1968; admitted St. Bar Calif. 1969, Fed. Bar 1969. Career: sect. chief adminstrn. I.R.S., Los Angeles 1964-68; ptnr., atty. Kadison Pfaelzer 1969-80; of counsel Mitchell Silberberg 1980-81; prin. Rooi Pollock et al 1981-85; atty. sole practice, Woodland Hills 1985–; judge pro tem Los Angeles Municipal Ct. 1975-; mem: San Fernando Valley Bar Assn. (state bar del. Van Nuys 1987-88), L.A. Co. Bar Assn. (del. 1975-81); honors: USC Law Rev. assoc. ed. 1967-68; Republican; Mormon. Ofc: 21550 Oxnard St Ste 300 Woodland Hills 91367

GILLIES, PATRICIA ANN, public health biologist (retired); b. Sept. 23, 1929, Berkeley; d. William W. and Barbara A. (Weddle) Myers; m. Robert W. Gillies, Sept. 17, 1948 (div. Dec. 1968); children: Catherine I. Lindsey b. 1949, Coila L. McGowan b. 1960; edn: AB, CSU Fresno, 1954, MA, 1961. Career: tchr. Parlier Unified Sch. Dist., Parlier 1955-56; insp. US Dept. Agriculture, Fresno 1956-58; tchg. asst. CSU Fresno, 1958-59; public health biologist State of Calif., 1959-94 (ret.); dir. Consolidated Mosquito Abatement Dist., 1974–; mem: Calif. Mosquito & Vector Control Assn. (1963–, regional rep. 1992–), Soc. for Vector Ecologists 1972–, Am. Mosquito Control Assn. 1963–; contbr. to profl. jours. incl. Jour. Economics Entomology, Proc. - Am. Mosquito Control Assn., Calif. Mosquito & Vector Control Assn., Utah Mosquito Abatement Assn.; Democrat; Episcopalian. Res: 7060 E Butler Fresno 93727

GILLIGAN, DOREEN ELAINE, real estate broker, ret.; b. Canada, naturalized U.S. citizen 1958; d. Neil and Ada (Rothwell) McArthur; m. Timothy Gilligan, Oct. 18, 1952. Career: var. pos. Bank of Toronto, Vancouver BC; Lansdown Race Track, Vancouver; bank ofcr. Bank of Am.; American City Bank; real estate broker and owner interior improvement co., Westwood; ret.; mem: Women's Nat. Book Assn., Santa Monica Hist. Soc., UCLA Alumni Assn., YMCA (health & phys. edn. com.), Twilite Hikers; rec: camping, hiking, travel. Res: 1815 Butler Ave Ste 106 Los Angeles 90025

GILMAN, NELSON J., library director; b. Mar. 30, 1938, Los Angeles; s. Louis L. and Alice (Cohen) G.; m. Virginia L. Ford, May 27, 1961; m. 2d. Lelde B. Patvalds, Nov. 23, 1970; children: Justine C. b. 1963, Seth F. b. 1966; edn: BS, USC, 1959, MS, 1960; MLS, UC Berkeley, 1964. Career: tchr. math. dept. Pasadena H.S., 1960-61, Tamalpais H.S., Mill Valley 1962-63; library adminstrv. intern UCLA Lib., 1964-65, asst. to the Univ. Librarian (in chg. lib. bldg. & plnng.) UCLA, 1965-66, asst. to the Biomedical Librarian, UCLA 1966-67, asst. biomed. librarian UCLA Biomed. Lib., 1967-69, assoc. dir. Pacific S.W. Reg. Medical Lib. Svc. UCLA Biomedical Library 1969-71; dir. L.A. Co./USC Medical Ctr. Libraries, L.A. 1974-79; assoc. dir. Devel. & Demonstration Ctr. in Contg. Edn. for Health Professionals, USC Sch. of Medicine, 1981–, asst. prof. dept. med. edn. USC Sch. of Medicine, 1971–, dir. USC Norris Medical Library 1971–, dir. USC Health Sciences Library System 1984–, USC assoc. dean for libraries & dir. of planning for the Teaching Lib. 1989-90, USC interim dir. Central Library System 1990-91; mem: Am. Lib. Assn., Am. Soc. for Info. Sci., Assn. of Acad. Health Scis. Lib. Dirs. (bd. 1980-83), Med. Lib. Assn. (bd. 1977-79), Special Lib. Assn.; publs: 16+ profl. jour. articles; mil: pfc USAR 1961-67; Democrat; Jewish; rec: gardening. Res: 615 22nd St Santa Monica 90402

GILMAN, RICHARD CARLETON, educator; b. July 28, 1923, Cambridge, Mass.; s. George Phillips Brooks and Karen Elise (Theller) G.; m. Lucille Young, Aug. 28, 1948 (dec. June 1978), m. Sarah Gale, Dec. 28, 1984 (dec. July 1986); children: Marsha, Bradley Morris, Brian Potter, Blair Tucker; edn: BA, Dartmouth, 1944; New Coll. Univ. London, England 1947-48; PhD, (Borden Parker Bowne fellow philosophy) Boston Univ. 1952; LHD, 1969; LLD, Pomona Coll., 1966; USC, 1968; Coll. Idaho 1968; Occidental Coll., 1988; LHD, Chapman Coll. 1984. Career: tchg. fellow religion Dartmouth 1948; mem. faculty Colby Coll. 1950-56, assoc. prof. philosophy 1955-56; exec. dir. Nat. Council Religion Higher Edn., New Haven 1956-60; dean coll., prof. philosophy Carleton Coll. 1960-65; pres. Occidental Coll. 1965-88, pres. emeritus 1988–, Southwest Mus. Mng. Trustee 1994–; bd. dirs. Indep. Colls. So. Calif., Assn. Indep. Calif. Colls. and Univs., L.A. World Affairs Council; apptd. Interngovtl. Advy. Council on Edn. 1980-82, Calif. Student Aid Commn.; mem: Nat. Council Ind. Colls. and Univs. (policy plng. commn.), Am. Council on Edn. (past dir.), Assn. Am. Colls., Council for Fin. Aid to Edn., Council on Postsecondary Edn., Indep. Coll. Funds Am., Nat. Collegiate Athletic Assn. President's Commn.; honors: Fellow Nat. Values in Higher Edn., Phi Beta Kappa; mem: Newcomen Soc.; club: California (L.A.), Twilight (Pasadena); mil: USNR 1944-46; Res: 131 Annandale Rd Pasadena 91105

GILMARTIN, PLATT JAY, paint company executive; b. Oct. 20, 1952, Morristown, N.J.; s. Thomas Joseph and Ethel Louise (Cooper) G.; m. Kathleen Marie Hall, Jan. 25, 1979; children: Courtney Elizabeth b. 1985, Caitlin Marie b. 1989; edn: BS (summa cum laude), Cook Coll., Rutgers Univ., 1974, Rutgers

Grad. sch. of Edn. 1983; grad. mgmt. coursework Claremont Grad. Sch., 1985-86; N.J. tchr. credential, sci. K-12 and FFA Vocational Agriculture 1974. Career: served to capt. US Air Force 1974-79, sq. comdr. Wichita Falls, Tx. 1975-76, det. comdr. Ft. Leonard Wood, Mo. 1977-78, tech. instr. 1977-78, commendn. medal 1976, meritorious service 1978; gen. mgr. J.L. Armitage Co., Newark, N.J. 1980-83; ops. mgr. Tnemec Co. Inc., Compton 1984-90; sr. sales rep. Unocal Chemicals, La Mirada 1991; territory mgr. Ashland Chemical Inc., Orange 1992; plant supt. Con-Lux Coatings, Inc. 1993–; honors: Alpha Tau Alpha 1974, Arnold Air Soc. 1974; mem: L.A. Soc. for Coatings Technology (mfg. com. 1984-92), So. Calif. Paint & Coatings Assn.; Republican; R.Cath.; rec: reading, running, biking, sailing, swimming, equestrian. Res: 209 Eastham Rd Pt Pleasant, NJ 08742

GILSDORF, LEROY GUIDO, financial consultant, tax preparer, retired county government official; b. March 13, 1930, Lawrence, Nebr.; s. George Henry and Jeanette Lena (L'Heureux) G.; m. Jennie Joan Hyde, June 11, 1955; children: Jane b. 1956, Gail b. 1963; edn: Univ. Nebr. 1952-54; Hastings Coll. 1955-56; UC Stanislaus 1961-63. Career: delinquent accounts mgr. Merced Co., 1957-58, hosp. office mgr. 1958-62, asst. auditor-controller 1962-75, Merced Co. auditor controller and recorder R&R, 1976-90, ret.; fin. cons., tax preparer, 1990–; treas. MCMC Hosp. Found.; awards: Toastmaster of Year (Distr. 33), Disting. Toastmaster 1985, Merced Co. Employee of Yr. 1971, Govt. Fin. Ofcr. Assn. Cert. of Conformance 1985; mem: Co. Recorders Assn. of Calif. (pres. 1980-81), Co. Auditors Assn. of Calif. (pres. 1987), K.C. (past grand knight, past dist. dep.), Toastmasters (past pres., area gov.), Merco Credit Union (past pres.); mem. and past pres. Our Lady of Mercy Sch. Bd.; club: Merced G&C; mil: clk. 2/c USN 1948-52; Democrat; R.Cath. (Fresno Dioceses fin. com.); rec: woodworking, philately, golf. Res: 2302 E Lakeside Dr Merced 95340 Ofc: 2302 E Lakeside Dr Merced 95340

GILWEE, JON D., healthcare executive; b. Aug. 21, 1952, Long Beach; m. Bernadette, April 4, 1981; edn: BA political sci., UCLA 1976. Career: campaign coordinator Winner Wagner & Assocs., L.A. 1976; account exec. Johnson & Higgins, L.A. 1976-79; asst. exec. dir. Orange Co. Med. Assn., Orange 1979-84; vice-pres. Government Relations, Hosp. Council of So. Calif., Los Angeles 1984-95; v.p. Orange Co. Ofc., Healthcare Assn. of So. Calif. 1995–; advy bd L.A. Alzheimer's Assn. 1994-95; bd. dirs. Calif. Health Decisions 1985–; trustee Orange Co. Poison Prevention Found. 1985-92; bd. dirs. Orange Co. Perinatal Council, Santa Ana 1984-85; honors: Orange Co. Health Planning Council Leadership award (1984-85); mem: UCLA Govt. Relations Steering Com., Am. Coll. Healthcare Execs., Healthcare Execs. of So. Calif., Orange County Public Affairs Assn.UCLA Alumni Assn., Friends of UCLA Rowing, United Way Orange Co. Healthcare Council, Delta Sigma Phi; rec: skiing, photog., gardening. Res: 1318 Frances Ave Fullerton 92631 Ofc: Healthcare Assn of So Calif 2020 E First St Ste 509 Santa Ana 92705

GIN, PETER, senior risk control consultant - casualty; b. Oct. 30, 1959, Chgo.; s. John Poi Lok and Lin Mei (Wong) G.; m. Sally, Apr. 23, 1988; edn: BA in health & safety, CSU Los Angeles, 1982, MA in edn., 1983, MA in health & safety, 1987; cert. safety splst. World Safety Orgn. 1987. Career: student worker L.A. County, 1980-83; loss control rep. Chubb Group of Ins., L.A. 1983-84; safety tng. adminstr. Hughes Aircraft Co., El Segundo 1984-87; safety program coord. Vons Cos., Inc. El Monte 1987-88; safety engr. Calif. Indemnity Ins. Co., Burbank 1988-89; senior risk control cons. - casualty, Alexander & Alexander of California, Inc., L.A. 1990–; mem: World Safety Orgn., Am. Soc. of Safety Engrs., Nat. Safety Mgmt. Soc., Nat. Fire Protection Assn., So. Calif. Industrial Safety Soc., Soc. of Fire Protection Engrs., Pi Lambda Theta; MA thesis: Van Pooling, 1987; Democrat; First Chinese Baptist Ch., Walnut Br. (camp dir. 1981–); rec: swimming. Res: 21035 Northview Dr Walnut 91789 Ofc: Alexander & Alexander of California, Inc. 55 S Lake Ave Pasadena 91101

GINALSKI, MARK, lawyer; b. Aug. 25, 1959, Fall River, Mass.; s. William and Kathleen (Collins) G.; m. Diana Maureen Mogerman, June 16, 1984; edn: BS, Ariz. St.Univ. 1983; JD, Univ. San Francisco 1986; admitted St. Bar Calif., Distr. of Columbia Bar, U.S. Tax Ct. Career: law clk. Thelen Marrin Johnson & Bridges, San Francisco 1984-86; Case & Lynch, Honolulu, Hawaii 1985; atty., assoc. Fisher & Hurst, San Francisco 1986-87; Sternberg Eggers Kidder & Fox, San Diego 1988; Wright Robinson McCammon Osthimer & Tatum, San Francisco 1988-92, Pandell, Novich & Borsuk 1992-93, Vogl & Meredith 1993–; awards: Ariz. St. Univ. Academic Scholar 1978-83, Univ. S.F. McAullife scholar 1986; mem: Marin Co. Bar Assn., San Francisco Bar Assn., Dist. of Columbia Bar Assn., World Affairs Council, SPUR, Marin Conservation League, Tiburon Design Review Bd. 1987-92, Tiburon Planning Commn. 1992-94, Tiburon Town Council 1994– (vice mayor); Democrat; R.Cath.; rec: sailing. Res: 1828 Vistazo West, Tiburon 94920 Ofc: Vogl & Meredith, 456 Montgomery St., Ste 2000, San Francisco, CA 94104

GINOZA, HELEN KAZUE, educational psychologist; b. March 3, 1938, Kohala, Hawaii; m. Hideo Ginoza, July 31, 1960; children: Kimi Anne b. 1961, Asa Joel b. 1962, Mori Michael b. 1964; edn: BA psychology, Bethany Nazarene Coll. 1965; MS counseling, CSU Los Angeles, 1974; lic. ednl. psychologist 1984.

Career: sch. psychologist Rowland Heights Unified Sch. Dist., Rowland Heights 1974-76; Charter Oak Unified Sch. Dist., Covina 1976-77; Chino Unified Sch. Dist., Chino 1977-88; Moreno Valley Unified Sch. Dist., Moreno Valley 1988–; honors: Phi Delta Lambda, Kappa Delta Pi, Delta Kappa Gamma, Calif. Assn. Neurologically Handicapped Children (Pomona Chapt.) Pres.'s award 1986, Calif. Assn. Sch. Psychologists Outstanding Psychologist award 1988, LDA-CA State Award of the Year 1994; mem: Learning Disabilities Assn. of Calif. (state sec. 1988-89, state v.p. 1989-90, pres. Riverside chpt. 1992-94), SE Co. Sch. Psychologists Assn., Riverside Co. Sch. Psychol. Assn., Council for Exceptional Children, Calif. Assn. Sch. Psychologists, YWCA, Pomona Valley Art Assn., San Gabriel Valley Japanese Christian Ch. (edn. deaconess 1987), Inland Empire Japanese Christian Ch., Pomona CANHC-ACLD (pres. 1984-86); editor newsletters: Chino USD Special Edn., 1980-85, Pomona CANHC-ACLD, 1980-86, So. East Co. Sch. Psy. Assn., 1988-90, Riverside LDA-CA, 1988–; Republican; Prot.; rec: drawing, painting, gardening. Ofc: Moreno Valley Unified School District 25634 Alessandro Blvd Moreno Valley 92553

GINSBURG, DAVID RICHARD, television production company executive; b. Jan. 20, 1951, Los Angeles; s. Bearl L and Bernice (Tishkoff) G.; m. Dena Rose Hibshman, June 25, 1972; children: Lev b. 1977, Lauren b. 1978; edn: BA summa cum laude, UCLA 1972; JD, 1976; admitted St. Bar Calif. 1976, Hawaii 1977, U.S. Supreme Ct. 1980. Career: law clk. U.S. Ct. Appeals 9th Circuit, Honolulu, Hawaii 1976-77; atty. Kaplan Livingston Goodwin Berkowitz & Selvin, Los Angeles 1977-81; atty., lectr. UCLA Sch. Law 1980-82; judge pro tem Los Angeles Municipal Ct., Small Claims Div. 1982-84; ptnr. Sidley & Austin 1982-86, of counsel 1986-88; chmn., pres. Citadel Entertainment 1986–; ed., instr. UCLA Ext. 1980; lectr. UCLA Sch. Law 1980-82; chmn. UCLA Entertainment Symposium Advy. Com. 1983-85; honors: Phi Beta Kappa, N. Hollywood H.S. Valedictorian 1968, MIT Danforth Found. fellow 1972, UCLA Sch. Law Ed. in Chief Law Review 1976, Nathan Burkan Memorial Competition 1st prize 1975; mem: L.A. Copyright Soc., Acad. TV Arts & Scis., Nat. Acad. Cable Programming; article pub. profl. jour., 1975, exec. producer over 30 t.v. movies; Democrat; Jewish. Ofc: Citadel Entertainment 11340 W Olympic Blvd Ste 100 Los Angeles 90064

GIOVACCHINI, JAMES ANDREW, physician, surgeon; b. Aug. 22, 1919, Del Rey; s. Amerigo and Jane (Mencarini) G.; m. Norma Kathryn Kealy, Sept. 23, 1944 (dec.); children: James, Thomas, Robert; edn: BS, Univ. Santa Clara 1941; MD, Creighton Med. Sch. 1944. Roman Catholic. Res: 2221 7th St Sanger 93657 Ofc: 621 O St Sanger 93657

GIRAMONTI, ADRIANA AURORA, chef; b. May 24, 1929, Rome, Italy, nat. US cit. 1961; d. Umberto and Clotilde (Pascale) Silvestri; m. Frank Giramonti, July 7, 1960 (div. Oct. 1988); children: Piero b. 1964, Roberto b. 1967; edn: Armando Diaz Coll. (Italy) 1944; shorthand/ typist, Berlitz Sch. 1952. Career: bkpg. helper, cashier First Class Ristorante Roma 1949-53; pvt., personal secty. Dr. Claudi Roma 1953-56; practical nurse, cook Serra Sanitarium Millbrae 1956; rubber pillow making factory 1957-58; waitress Little Joe Restaurant S.F. 1958-77; chief owner, pres. Giramonti Restaurant Inc. dba Giramonti Rest. in Mill Valley and Adriana Rest. in San Rafael; demonstration classes Macy's S.F. 1984-85, La Cordon Rouge Sausalito 1983, Loni Khun Cooking Tour 1983-84, Culinary Carnival 1984-85; chef demo. on CBS-TV "Good Morning Bay Area, 1987, 88, 89; guest master chef demo. for Italian Festival, Fishermans Wharf, S.F. benefit for problem children, 1988; ABC-TV Ch. 7 guest "Star-Athon 89" and United Cerebral Palsy, 1985; honors: Diploma and Medal (Great Chefs of S.F. 1984), Italian Chef of A.M. San Francisco ABC (1983, 84, 85, 86), Gourmet Mag., Pacific Sun of Marin; publs: Great Chefs of S.F. (from the PBS nat. TV series, Avon Books NY 1983); R.Cath.; rec: dressmaking, artist- hand painted ceramic decorative & serving platters. Ofc: Giramonti Restaurant Inc. 999 Anderson Dr San Rafael 94901

GIRGA, BARBARA ANN, psychotherapist/college counselor, hypnotherapist, alcohol/drug counselor; b. Oct. 11, 1937, Rayland, Ohio; d. C. Virgil and Marjorie T. (Diehl) Fisher; children: Susan b. 1963, Robert b. 1966; edn: AA, Bakersfield Coll., 1973; BA, CSU Bakersfield, 1978; MA, 1986; CAC, UCSB, Ky. Christian Coll., 1956. Career: supr. CSU Bakerfield 1975-78; editor Bakersfield Chamber of Commerce publs., 1977-79; diet counselor Nutra-Systems 1980-81; mgr. Water Assn. Kern Co. 1976-81; analyst Occidental Petroleum 1981-86; pvt. practice Bakersfield Counseling Group 1987-90; clin. therapist Haven Counseling Center 1986-88; Charter Hosp. 1988–; counselor Bakersfield Coll. 1986–; seminar leader 1976–; workshop instr. 1987–; honors: Chi Sigma Iota 1986, Employee of Year 1978, Employee Performance Bonus 1982; mem: CAMFT, AAMFT, AACD, Am. Businesswomen's Assn. (secty. 1977), CAPH (secty. 1977-79); civic: Jr. League Saturday Adventurers (dir. 1978), C.of C.; poems pub. (Opheus 1979); Calvary Bible Ch.; rec: skiing, reading, writing. Res: 2401 San Ramon Ct. Bakersfield 93304 Ofc: 930 Truxtun Ave Ste 210 Bakersfield 93301

GIROD, ERWIN ERNEST, physician; b. Oct. 1, 1944, Los Angeles; s. Dudley L. and Rena M. (Hudson) G.; m. Jill Johnson, Dec. 16, 1967; children: Jeffrey b. 1973, Janette b. 1975; edn: BA (honors), CSU Los Angeles, 1966; MD, UC Irvine, 1970; Calif. Coll. Med.; Dipl. Am. Bd. Internal Med. (1973, Recert.

1980). Career: med. intern L.A.Co.-USC Med. Ctr., 1970-71, resident in internal medicine, 1971-73; US Naval Regional Med. Center, San Diego, 1973-75; ward med. ofcr. Med. Intensive Care Unit, adminstr. Acute Care Areas, asst. clin. prof. med. UC San Diego Sch. Med.; asst. prof. med. Loma Linda Univ. Sch. Med. 1978-80; chief gen. med. section 1978-80, asst. chief med. service 1979-80, VA Hosp. Loma Linda; pvt. practice 1981–; med. staff Huntington Mem. Hosp., 1981–, chmn. Internal Med. Clinic 1984-85; St. Luke Med. Ctr., 1982–, chmn. Utilization Rev. Com. 1989-91, chmn. I.P.A. Util. Rev. Com. 1989–, bd. dirs. St. Luke Hosp. Med. Group; asso. Methodist Hosp. of So. Calif., Arcadia, 1986–, staff phys. Chemical Dependency Recovery Ctr.; Community Lecture Series: Meth. Hosp., and St. Luke Med. Ctr., 1987–; Humanitarian service: asst. prof. med. Punjab Univ., India, and co-dir. intensive care unit Christian Med. Coll. and Brown Memorial Hosp., Ludhiana, Punjab, India 1976-77, Overseas Missionary Fellowship, med. advisor to SW Region-U.S.A., 1988-92; honors: Ephebian Soc. L.A. 1962–, Math. award 1962, Alpha Gamma Omega Frat. (1964–, Delta Chpt. pres. 1965-66, Alumni sponsor 1966–, Legion of Honor 1989–, Microbiol. award 1966, Phi Kappa Phi Hon. Soc. 1967–, Admiral Stitt Award for physician who contbd. most to med. edn. from the intern classes at Naval Regional Med. Ctr., S.D. (1973-4, 1974-5); biog. listings: Internat. Register of Profiles, Internat. Book of Honor, Dict. Internat. Biography, 5000 Personalities of World, Men of Achiev., Dir. of Disting. Americans, Personalities of Am., Comm. Leaders of Am., 1990; Internat. Who's Who of Intellectuals, Internat. Dir. of Disting. Leadership, 1991, Internat. Biographical Assn. (life fellow 1993–); Fellow Am. Coll. Physicians 1980, mem. Calif. Med. Assn., Christian Med.-Dental Soc.; civic: Pasadena Mayor's Prayer Breakfast Com. 1986, 87, Upper Hastings Ranch Assn. (block capt. 1984–), publs. in profl. jours.; mil: lt. cmdr. USNR, active duty 1973-75; Republican; Congregational; rec: swimming, music, roses. res: 1195 Coronet Ave Pasadena 91107

GIRSH, FAYE JOAN, psychologist; b. May 5, 1933, Philadelphia, Pa.; d. Jack and Rose (Rosenberg) Girsh; m. Leon I. Goldberg Feb. 2, 1958 (div. 1978); children: Mark b. 1958, Claudia Otee b. 1960; edn: BA, Temple Univ. 1954; MA, Boston Univ. 1955; EdD, Harvard Univ. 1962; lic. clin. and forensic psychologist 1978. Career: research asst. Harvard Univ., Cambridge, Mass. 1956-57; clin. intern Mass. Mental Health, Boston 1957-58; research psychologist NIMH, Bethesda, Md. 1958-61; instr. psychiatry Emory Univ., Atlanta, Ga. 1961-62; psychology faculty Morehouse Coll. 1965-74; vis. prof. Kyoto Inst. Tech., Japan 1972-73; research assoc. Univ. Chgo. 1974-78; assoc. prof. U.S. Internat. Univ., San Diego 1978-79; clin. psychologist Psychiatry and Law Center 1979-81; adj. faculty Calif. Sch. Profl. Psychology 1980–; honors: Psi Chi, Nat. Inst. Drug Abuse grantee 1970; mem: Hemlock Soc. S.D. (pres. 1988–), Nat. Hemlock Soc. (bd. mem.), Acad. S.D. Psychologists, ACLU (So. Calif., S.D.), Nat. Soc. Psychology in Addictions (pres. 1977-79), Harvard Club S.D. (bd. mem. 1980–), Soc. Profls. in Dispute Resol. (bd. mem. 1987–), Am. Psychological Assn.; 40+ articles and chapters pub. in med. and legal jours.; Democrat; Jewish; rec: travel, play reading. Res: 400 Prospect St #5B La Jolla 92037 Ofc: 401 West A St Ste 1200 San Diego 92101

GISS, JUDITH ELAINE KRIENKE (Mrs. Kenneth A. Giss), real estate broker; b. July 7, 1947, Hawthorne, Calif.; d. Oliver Kenneth and Carol Belle (Manikowski) Krienke; m. Kenneth Arnold Giss, Nov. 24, 1967; edn: att. Az. State Univ., Tempe 1965-67; AA, El Camino Coll., Torrance, 1970; MBA, CSU Dominguez Hills, 1977; Calif. lic. R.E. Broker 1967, Property Mgr. Career: real estate broker O.K. Krienke Realty, 1967–; ptnr. G & G Consultants, ptnr. G & G Schools, R.E. Sch., 1978–; awards: outstanding Jaycett Manhattan Beach Jaycees 1971; mem: Nat. Assn. Realtors 1967–, Calif. Assn. Realtors 1967–, South Bay Bd. of Realtors 1967–, Nat. Assn. R.E. Appraisers 1987-93, Nat. Notary Assn. 1978-91, Manhattan Beach C.of C., Alumni Assn. Ariz. St. Univ. (life), Alumni Assn. CSUDH, Nat. Soc. Colonial Dames of XVII Century (ct, v.p., sec., historian Jared Eliot Chpt.); civic: Soroptimist Internat., M.B. (1976–, pres. 1977), Sister City Manhattan Beach 1980–, Friends Manhattan Beach Library 1976–, Pioneer 8's of Redondo Beach (1991–), Soc. for Preserv. of Magical Arts/ Magic Castle 1974–, Soc. for Preserv. of Variety Arts 1980–, Girl Scouts Am., Dolphin Jr. Fed. Womens Club 1967-77, Dutch Club Neerlandia Inc. of Westchester 1987–, Commonwealth Club of Torrance 1988–, M.B. Comm. Ch., M.B. Hist. Soc., Western Stars Redondo Bch. 1990–, Britannia Club 1985–, Internat. Platform Assn. 1990-94, Beach Cities Symphony (1990–, patron), Friends of Banning Park 1990–, Hist. Soc. of Centinela Valley 1989–; rec: travel, historical homes, comm. svc. Res: 1609 9th St Manhattan Beach 90266 Ofc: 1716 Manhattan Beach Blvd Manhattan Beach 90266

GITLIN, TODD, author, professor of sociology; b. Jan. 6, 1943, N.Y., N.Y.; s. Max Gitlin and Dorothy (Siegel) Renik; edn: BA, Harvard Univ., 1963; MA, Univ. Mich., 1966; PhD, UC Berkeley, 1977. Career: prof. sociology and director mass communications pgm. UC Berkeley, 1978–; author: Busy Being Born, 1974, The Whole World Is Watching, 1980, Inside Prime Time, 1983, The Sixties: Years of Hope, Days of Rage, 1987, The Murder of Albert Einstein, 1992, The Twilight of Common Dreams: Why America is Wracked by Culture Wars, 1995; editor: Watching Television, 1987; coauthor: Uptown: Poor Whites In Chicago, 1970.

GITNICK, GARY LEE, physician; b. Mar. 13, 1939, Omaha, Nebr.; s. Nathan Gitnick and Ann (Tretiak) Hahn; m. Cherna Lee Schrager, June 21, 1963; children: Neil b. 1967, Kimberly b. 1969, Jill b. 1971, Tracy b. 1973; edn: BS, Univ. of Chgo., 1960, MD, 1963. Career: intern internal medicine Osler Medical Service, Balt., Md. 1963-64; fellow int. medicine Johns Hopkins Hosp., Balt. 1963-64; resident int. med. Mayo Clinic, Rochester 1964-65, resident gastroenterology, 1967-69; project/ med. officer NIH, Bethesda, Md. 1965-67; prof. of medicine UCLA Sch. of Medicine, Los Angeles 1969–, dir. div. gastro res. labs 1979–, med. dir. UCLA Health Care Program 1985–, chief of staff UCLA Medical Ctr., 1990-92; chief div. digestive diseases, UCLA Sch. of Medicine 1993–; awards: J. Arnold Bargan Award 1969, special appreciation United Liver Assn., L.A. 1988, Special Paul Harris Fellow Rotary Intl., L.A. 1988, award of merit Los Angeles Mayor 1990, Rotarian of Yr. Westwood Village Rotary 1991; pres. Fulfillment Fund 1977–; trustee The Harvard-Westlake Sch.; trustee LEARN 1991–; mem: United Liver Assn. (bd. dirs., chair sci. advy. bd. 1982–), Rotary Intl. (1984–); editor 45+ books: Principles & Practice of Gastro (1988), IBD: Diagnosis & Treatment (1991), Diseases of the Liver & Biliary Tract (1991), The Business of Medicine (1991); mil: lt. col. USPHS 1965-68. Res: 17321 Rancho St Encino 91316 Ofc: Gary Gitnick M.D. 924 Westwood Blvd Ste 515 Los Angeles 90024-7018

GITTLEMAN, ARTHUR PAUL, educator; b. Oct. 7, 1941, N.Y., N.Y.; s. Morris and Clara (Konefsky) G.; m. Carole Anne McGee, July 30, 1966 (div. Jan. 1985); m. Charlotte Marie Singleton, June 1, 1986; 1 dau., Amanda b. 1985; edn: BA, UCLA, 1962, MA, 1965, PhD, 1969 Career: asst. prof. math. dept. CSU Long Beach, 1966-70, assoc. prof., 1970-75, prof. 1975-88, dept. chair 1978-83, prof. computer engring., computer sci. dept., 1988–; mem. Assn. for Computing Machinery 1975–, Mathematical Assn. of Am. 1963–, Inst. Electrical and Electronic Engrs. 1990–; author: History of Mathematics 1975; rec: running, piano. Res: 6572 Montoya Circle Huntington Beach 92647 Ofc: Calif. State Univ., Long Beach 90840

GIUMARRA, JOHN GEORGE, JR., agricultural and wine industry executive; b. Oct. 13, 1940, Los Angeles; s. John George and Florence (Respoli) G.; m. Pamela Presley, Sept. 11, 1965; children: John, III b. 1968, Randall b. 1972, Juliana b. 1975, Joseph b. 1978, Jillian b. 1981; edn: BS, UC Berkeley 1962; LLD, Stanford Sch. of Law 1965; admitted Calif. State Bar 1965. Career: atty. law firm Rutan & Tucker, Santa Ana 1966-67; prin. and v.p. Giumarra Vineyards Corp. (largest grower of table grapes in USA) since 1967–, and opr./owner of winery (12th largest in state); negotiated first major collective bargaining agreement between grape growers of Calif. and Cesar Chavez of United Farm Workers; active in drafting and enacting the Agri. Labor Relations Act; mem. var. wine tasting panels incl. LA Times Home Mag. panel; honors: book rev. editor Stanford Law Rev., award for excellence in legal writing 1965; mem: Calif. Grape & Tree Fruit League (bd. chmn. 1982), Wine Inst. of Calif. (bd.), Winegrower of Calif., Calif. Table Grape Commn.; trustee Gr. Bakersfield Meml. Hosp.; chmn. fundraising event for CSUB Athletic Found.; frequent speaker (1967–) produce and wine conventions and meetings nat. on agricultural wine, labor rels., mktg., fin. topics; Republican; R.Cath.; rec: golf, tennis, sailing. Res: 4224 Country Club Dr Bakersfield 93306 Ofc: Giumarra Vineyards PO Bin 1969 Bakersfield 93303

GIVANT, PHILIP JOACHIM, educator, real estate investment company president; b. Dec. 5, 1935, Mannheim, Germany, nat. US cit. 1940; s. Paul and Irmy (Dinse) G.; m. Kathleen Joan Porter, 1960; children: Philip Paul b. 1963, Julie Kathleen b. 1965, Laura Grace b. 1968; edn: BA, CSU San Francisco 1957, MA, 1960. Career: math. prof. San Francisco State Univ. 1958-60, American River Coll. (Sacto.) 1960–; pres. Grove Ents. Real Estate Investment Co. 1961–; mem. Calif. Community Colls. (CCC) Academic Senate (v.p. 1974-77), Am. River Coll. Acad. Senate (pres. 1966-69), State Chancellor's com. on the Academic Calendar 1977-79; awards: spl. commendn. CCC Academic Senate, spl. human rights award for InterCultural Affairs, CCC 1977, human rights award Fair Housing Commn. Sacto. Co. 1985, named Blues Promoter of the Year, Nat. Blues Found., Memphis 1987, recipient 1st critical achievement award Sacramento Music Awards Acad. 1992; mem. CCC Faculty Assn. 1966–, Am. Soc. for Psychical Res. 1965–, Nat. Blues Found. Memphis (nat. advy. com.), Sacto. Blues Soc. (charter 1980–), Lake Tahoe Keys Homeowners Assn., Sea Ranch Homeowners Assn., Klamath River Country Estates Homeowners Assn., NAACP (life); works: founder/pres. & prod. Sacto. Blues Festival Inc. 1976–; prod. weekly music pgm. "Blues with Phil" on Public Radio St. KVMR, Nevada City; prod. musical festival Folsom State Prison 1979-81, Vacaville State Prison 1985; rec: tennis, music, boating. Address: Grove Enterprises 3809 Garfield Ave Carmichael 95608

GLAD, DAIN STURGIS, retired aerospace engineer; b. Sept. 17, 1932, Santa Monica; s. Alma Emanuel and Maude La Verne (Morby) G.; m. Betty Alexandra Shainoff, Sept. 12, 1954 (dec. 1974); 1 dau. Dana Elizabeth; m. 2d. Carolyn Elizabeth Giffen, June 8, 1979; edn: BS engring., UCLA, 1954; MSEE, USC, 1963; Reg. Profl. Engr., Calif. Career: electronic engr. Clary Corp., San Gabriel 1957-58; engr. Aerojet ElectroSystems Co., Azusa, 1958-72; missile systems div. Rockwell Internat., Anaheim 1973-75; Aerojet Electrosystems,

Azusa 1975-84; support systems div. Hughes Aircraft Co., 1984-90; Electro-Optics Ctr., Rockwell Internat. Corp., Anaheim 1990-94; cons., 1994-; mem: IEEE; tech. papers in profl. jours. and proc.; mil: lt. j.g. USN 1954-57. Res: 1701 Marengo Ave South Pasadena 91030

GLAD, SUZANNE LOCKLEY, retired museum administrator; b. Oct. 2, 1929, Rochester, N.Y.; d. Alfred Allen and Lucille A. (Watson) Lockley; m. Edward Newman Glad, Nov. 7, 1953; children: Amy b. 1957, Lisanne b. 1959, William b. 1960; edn: BA, Sweet Briar 1951; MA, Columbia Univ. 1952. Career: exec. dir. Assn. N.Y.St. Young Republicans, N.Y.C. 1953-57; Dolphin Group, L.A. 1974-82; scheduling secty. Office of the Governor, Sacto. 1983-87; dep. dir. ext. affairs Calif. Museum Sci. & Industry, Los Angeles 1988-94; honors: Phi Beta Kappa; mem: Assistance League of Flintridge, Flintridge Guild of Children Hosp., Sweet Briar Alumnae (past pres.); Republican; Episcopalian; rec: gardening. Res: 480 S Orange Grove Blvd Pasadena 91105

GLANCY, DOROTHY JEAN, law professor; b. Sept. 24, 1944, Glendale; d. Walter Perry and Elva T. (Douglass) Glancy; m. Jon Tobias Anderson, June 8, 1979; BA, Wellesley Coll., 1967; JD, Harvard Law Sch., 1970; admitted bar: Dist. Col. 1971, Calif. 1976. Career: atty., assoc. Hogan & Hartson, Wash. DC 1971-73; counsel U.S. Senate Judiciary subcom. on constnl. rights, 1973-74; Harvard fellow, Cambridge 1974-75; prof. of law Santa Clara (Calif.) Univ. Sch. of Law, 1975-82, 1984-; asst. gen. counsel U.S. Dept. Agriculture, Wash. DC 1982-83; cons. Commn. of Fed. Paperwork, Wash. DC 1976; dir. Summer Law Study Pgm. in Hong Kong, 1985-; advisor Restatement, Third, Property: Servitudes 1986-; honors: Phi Beta Kappa 1966, Stevens Traveling Fellow Wellesley Coll. 1970-71, Harvard Univ. fellow in law & humanities, Cambridge 1974-75, Inst. on Law & Ethics, Williamstown, Mass. 1977; mem: ABA, Am. Law Inst., Calif. Women Lawyers, Soc. of Am. Law Tchrs.; contbr. articles profl. jours.; Democrat; rec: gardening, travel. Res: San Francisco 94118

GLASER, BOBBY G., lawyer, political consultant; b. Juy 23, 1954, Anaconda, Mont.; s. Wm. Otto and Lavene Carole G.; edn: BA in sociol. (distinction), San Diego St. Univ., 1979; JD, Calif. Western Sch. of Law, 1982; admitted Calif. St. Bar 1982. Career: atty./prin., La Jolla, spec. in pub. interest law and small bus. law; political cons. The La Jolla Group, spec. in grassroot politcs for Democratic and Environmental clients in San Diego Co., involved in San Diego Clean Air Initiative, Calif. Parks and Wildlife Initiative, candidate for San Diego City Council Dist. 6 (1987); dir. Jeri-Glo Innovations Inc.; mem. bar assns., SDSU Young Alumni (bd.); civic bds: Citizens Advy. Com. on Growth and Devel., San Diegans for Managed Growth, San Diegans for Clean Air, San Diegans for Parks and Wildlife, Pacific Beach Plng. Com., Marian Bear Natural Park Rec. Council (chmn.), Beach Coalition for Farnum (mem., legal counsel), Foothills for Managed Growth (mem., legal counsel); awards: Durfee 1986, Roger J. Traynor Moot Court Team Calif. W. Sch. Law, Am. Jurisprudence 1980, assoc. student pres. San Diego Mesa Coll. 1976, Nat. Honor Soc., BSA Order of Arrow, Eagle Scout, Explorers Post 210 (founder, pres.). Res: 4416 34th St San Diego 92116 Ofc: The La Jolla Group 1150 Silverado San Diego 92037

GLASER, RUTH BONNIE, psychologist; b. May 11, 1937, Tenafly, N.J.; d. John Henry and Ruth Louise (Ferris) Thompson; m. Donald Glaser, Nov. 28, 1960 (div.); children: Louise b. 1964, William b. 1965; edn: BA, UC Berkeley 1969; MA, 1975; PhD, 1976. Career: pvt. practice psychology, Berkeley 1976-; psychologist UC Berkeley 1976-89; dean of students, bd. dirs. S.F. Inst. Psychoanalytic Psychol. and Psychoanalysis, San Francisco 1984-94; clin. faculty Children's Hosp., San Francisco 1979-; researcher UC Berkeley Psychology dept. 1988-, instr. 1980; mem: Am. Psychology Assn.; editor: Ruby: An Ordinary Woman (Faber and Faber, Boston, 1995). Res: 1140 Grizzly Peak Blvd Berkeley 94708 Ofc: 3036 Regent Berkeley 94705

GLASKY, ALVIN JERALD, medical research scientist; b. June 16, 1933, Chicago, Ill.; s. Oscar and Bessie (Akwa) G.; m. Rosalie Hanfling, Aug. 25, 1957; children: Michelle b. 1959, Karen b. 1960, Mark b. 1961, Ira b. 1970; edn: BS pharm., Univ. Ill. 1954; PhD biochem., 1958. Career: dir. biochem. research Michael Reese Hosp., Chgo., Ill. 1959-61; research pharmacology Abbott Labs., N. Chgo., Ill. 1961-66; v.p. research ICN Pharm., Burbank 1966-68; CEO Newport Pharm., Newport Beach 1968-86; exec. dir. Am. Social Health Assn., Palo Alto 1986-87; CEO Advanced Immuno-Therapeutics, Irvine 1987-; lectr. USC, L.A.; UCSD, La Jolla; awards: NSF internat. fellow 1958-59; mem: AAAS, Am. Pharm. Assn., Calif. Pharm. Assn., Am. Soc. Microbiology, Am. Chem. Soc.; articles pub. in profl. jours.; Republican (Rep. Nat. Com.); Jewish; rec: aerobics, tennis, swimming. Res: 9902 Brier Ln Santa Ana 92705 Ofc: Advanced Immuno-Therapeutics 1582 Deere Ave Irvine 92714

GLASRUD, BRUCE ALDEN, historian; b. Sept. 20, 1940, Plainview, Minn.; s. Leslie E. and Margaret (Rud) G.; m. Evelyn Pearlene Vestal, Oct. 17, 1964; edn: BA, Luther Coll., 1962; MA, Eastern New Mexico Univ., 1963; PhD, Texas Tech. Univ., Lubbock 1969. Career: instr. history Texas Lutheran Coll., Seguin, Tx. 1964-65; asst. prof. CSU Hayward, Calif. 1968-73, assoc. prof. 1973-78, prof. of history 1978-, chair history dept. 1977-81, 84-86, 92-93; trustee Res. Found., CSUH 1977-81, pres. bd. dirs. Faculty Club CSUH 1978-

79, sec., exec. com. CSU Academic Senate, Long Beach 1986-87, dir. University Union 1989-91, v.ch. bd. dirs. CSUH Found. 1991-93; awards: best lectr. CSU Hayward (1972), NEH grantee (1981), MPPPA stipend CSUH (1987, 90), profl. res. leave CSUH 1990-91, distinguished service award Luther Coll. 1992, Outstanding Professor of the Year, 1993 CSUH; mem: Texas State Hist. Assn. 1972-, Western History Assn. 1974-, Immigration Hist. Soc. 1988-, Am. Scandinavian Found. 1989-, Calif. Faculty Assn. (1968-, pres. 1985-87); civic: Greenpeace, ACLU, Amnesty Internat., So. Poverty Law Ctr., NAACP; coauthor: Promises to Keep (1972), The Northwest Mosaic (1977), Race Relations in British No. Am. (1981), numerous scholarly jour. articles and book revs.; Democrat; Lutheran; rec: research, writing. Res: 5030 Seaview Ave Castro Valley 94546 Ofc: Calif. State Univ., Hayward 94542

GLASSETT, TIM SCOTT, lawyer; b. March 29, 1956, Salt Lake City; s. Joseph M. and Mildred Joleen (Ames) G.; m. Janet Rankin, July 11, 1987; 2 sons, Ryan b. 1988, Trevor b. 1989; edn: BS cum laude, Univ. Utah 1978; MBA, 1981; JD, 1981; admitted St. Bar Calif. (1981). Career: atty., assoc. Adams Duque & Hazeltine, Los Angeles 1981-85; corp. counsel H.F. Ahmanson & Co. 1985-86, v.p., corp. counsel 1986, sr. v.p., corp. counsel, asst. secty., Irwindale 1987-, asst. gen. counsel 1993-; tchg. asst. legal writing Univ. Utah 1980-81, quantitative analysis 1980-81; honors: Order of Coif, William H. Leary scholar Univ. Utah (1981); mem: Am. Bar Assn., Sigma Chi; sr. ed. Utah Law Review, 1980-81, staff, 1979-80; Republican; Mormon. Ofc: H.F. Ahmanson & Co. 4900 Rivergrade Rd Irwindale 91706

GLEBERMAN, FRANK MARTIN, financial services company principal; b. Jan. 26, 1938, Cincinnati, Ohio; s. M. Fernando and Betty (McKim) G.; edn: USC Sch. of Business, 1955-60; Chartered Life Underwriter (CLU) Am. Coll. (1969), Cert. Fin. Planner (CFP), Coll. Fin. Plng. (1985). Career: asst. advt. mgr. Carnation Co. 1961-62; life ins. agent New York Life Ins. Co., 1962-66, asst. mgr. 1966-70, supt. So. Pacific Region, 1971-74, gen. mgr. 1970-71, 1974-78; asst. gen. agent Mass. Mutual Life, 1978-80; prin. Mfrs. Fin. Services, Los Angeles 1981-; prin. Century Benefits Group, Los Angeles 1986-; CEO, The Gleberman Group 1986-; dir: LAACO Ltd., Westways Inc., Western Mayflower Moving & Storage, Modern Mayflower Moving & Storage, Great American Moving & Storage, All Continents Travel, Lorentine Corp.; gen. mgmt. cons., writer, lectr. fin. plnng. & ins. seminars; chmn. L.A. Unified Sch. Dist. underutilized sch. sites com.; honors: resolutions: L.A. City Council 1973, 95, L.A. Co. Bd. Suprs. (1973, 88, 95), Calif. St. Senate, Calif. St. Assembly and U.S. House of Representatives 1995; named KNX Radio Citizen of Week 1977; mem: Nat. Assn. Life Underwrs., Am. Soc. CLU, Internat. Assn. Fin. Plng., Nat. Assn. Securities Dealers (chmn. Fin. Planning Study Group); civic: Crittendon Foun. (dir.) Nat. Assn. for People w. Disabilities (past pres.), L.A. Co. Easter Seal Soc. (past pres., chmn.), L.A. Jr. C.of C. (past pres., chmn., pres. Charity Found.), L.A. Area C.of C. (past dir.), Marina del Rey C.of C. (pres. 1993-94, chmn. of bd. 1995), Commerce Assocs. USC (past pres., chmn.), USC Assocs. (life), L.A. Civic Light Opera Assn. (past dir.), L.A.P.D. Comm. Adv. Com., L.A. Co. Sheriff's Dept. Comm. Adv. Com., L.A. Open Golf Tournament Advy. Com. (past v.chmn.), Glen Campbell-LA Open Golf Found. (past pres.); clubs: Calif. Yacht (commodore), Riviera CC, L.A. Athletic, Riviera Tennis; mil: E5 USCGR; Republican; R.Cath.; rec: sail, ski, travel, photog., writing. Res: 4314 Glencoe Ave Marina del Rey 90292 Ofc: Manufacturers Financial Services 3007 Washington Blvd Marina del Rey 90292

GLENN, BELINDA DEANNE, construction engineer; b. June 27, 1963, Garden City, Kans.; d. Everett Lee and Karin Kaye (Coerber) G.; edn: BS in constrn. sci., Kansas State Univ., 1986. Career: surveyor Coleman Indsl. Constrn., Wichita, Kans. 1986-87; field engr. Herzog Contracting Corp., Los Angeles 1987-89, project engr. Herzog Contracting Corp., Long Beach 1989-90, project engr. Herzog Contracting Corp., Sacramento 1990-92; asst. constrn. engr. Sacramento Regional Transit Dist., Sacramento 1992-; honors: listed Who's Who of Am. Women 1991-92, Who's Who in West 1992-93, Who's Who in Sci. & Engring. 1992-93; mem: Nat. Assn. Female Execs. 1989-, Kans. State Univ. Alumni Assn. 1986-. Res: P.O. Box 1038 Gridley 95948-1038 Ofc: Sacramento Regional Transit Dist. 2811 O St Sacramento 95816

GLENN, JOHN WILEY, transit district president; b. Dec. 2, 1927, Puxico, Mo.; s. Charles Thomas and Minnie Elizabeth (Hodge) G.; m. Betty Berry, June 30, 1951; children: John b. 1955, Sharon b. 1962, Karen b. 1966; edn: BS mktg., S.E. Mo. State Univ. 1952. Career: chmn., c.e.o. John Glenn Adjusters and Administrators, Inc., offices in Los Angeles, Oakland, San Rafael, and San Jose, 1966-; v.p. S.F. Bay Area Rapid Transit Dist. (BART) 1978, 85, pres. 1981, 88; dir. Royal Nufoam Corp. 1968-77; organizer and dir. Civic Bank of Commerce, in Oakland, Walnut Creek, San Leandro, Concord, Fremont, Rossmoor, 1984-; trustee Holy Family Coll. 1983-86, Ohlone Coll. Found. 1986; honors: S.E. Missouri State Univ. alumni merit award and Hall of Fame (1986, 89); mem: Calif. Assn. Independent Ins. Adjusters (pres. 1979-80), East Bay Adjusters Assn. (pres. 1970), Am. Public Transit Assn. (bd. dirs. 1981-), Central Coast Claims Assn.; Democrat; United Methodist; rec: gardening, photog., travel. Res: 36601 Cuenca Ct Fremont 94536 Ofc: John Glenn Adjusters & Administrators, Inc. 2201 Broadway Ste 308 Oakland 94612

GLORIG, ARAM, physician; b. June 8, 1906, Manchester, Eng.; US citizen; s. Aram and Beatrice (Allen) G.; div.; children: Patricia b. 1947, Deborah b. 1951; edn: BS, Atlantic Union Coll. 1931; MD, Loma Linda Univ. 1938. Career: intern Lawrence Meml. Hosp., New London, Conn. 1937-8, res. Willard Parker Hosp., NYC 1939-40, Henrietta Egleston Hosp., Atlanta, Ga. 1940-1; major US Army M.C., chief, ENT, various hosps. Iceland, Eng., Ger., 1942-46; dir. Audiology and Speech Correction Ctr., Walter Reed Army Med. Ctr./ and dir. Tech. Resrch in Hearing Dept. of Army/ and chief, Audiol. and Speech Correction, VA, Wash DC 1947-53; dir. of resrch. The Los Angeles Found. of Otology, and Noise Resrch. Ctr., 1953-64; dir. Callier Ctr. for Communication Disorders, 1964-77, Dir. Emeritus 1977–; cons. industrial and forensic otology House Ear Clinic, Inc., L.A. 1977–, assoc. dir. res. House Ear Inst., L.A. 1977–; teaching, num. med. instns., univs. 1949–; Dean Emeritus, Univ. of Texas, Dallas, 1977–; Calif. lic. Provider Cont. Edn. for RNs, 1981-3; mem: Acoustical Soc. of Am. (Fellow), Am. Acad. Opthalmol. and Otolaryngol. (Fellow), AAAS, Am. Auditory Soc. (founding pres. 1972), Am. Indsl. Hygiene Assn. (past pres. No Tex. Sect.), Am. Laryngol., Rhinol., Otol. Soc. Inc. (Fellow), AMA, Am. Otol. Soc. (Fellow), Am. Speech and Hearing Assn. (Fellow, life), Royal Soc. of Med., etc.; awards: Ignacio Berraquer 1968, Citizenship, WFAA 1969, Am. Acad. of Ophthal. and Otol. 1971, Amplifon Center for Resrch. Study, Milan, Italy 1979, Carhart Meml., Am. Auditory Soc. 1979, Mem. of Honor, XV Intl. Cong. of Audiol., Krakow, Poland 1980; author four books, num. med. arts.; Republican; Prot.; rec: golf, sailing. Res: 9941 Westhaven Cir Westminster 92683 Ofc: House Ear Clinic 2100 W Third St Los Angeles 90057

GLOVER, JAMES THOMAS, financial executive; b. Feb. 23, 1950, Petaluma; s. Arthur Raymond and Minnie (Beaver) G.; m. Kathleen Elizabeth Miller, June 17, 1978; children: Makenzie Terrill b. 1979, Matthew Tyson b. 1982; edn: AA, Chaffey Coll. 1971; BS acctg., Calif. Polytechnic St. Univ., Pomona 1974; MBA, Pepperdine Univ. 1982; C.P.A. Calif. 1976. Career: Artco Engring., Cucamonga 1971-74; mgr. Peat Marwick Mitchell, Newport Beach 1974-80; mgr. western region oil and gas acctg. Aminoil USA/R.J. Reynolds Inc., Huntington Beach 1980-83; controller, corp. acctg., Beckman Instruments, Fullerton 1983-86; sr. dir. fin. planning and analysis Allergan Inc., Irvine 1986-89; v.p., controller Beckman Instruments Diagnostic Systems Group, Brea 1989-93; v.p. & controller Beckman Instruments, Inc. 1993–; mem: Fin. Execs. Inst., Am. Inst. C.P.A., Calif. Soc. C.P.A., YMCA (group leader); mil: s.sgt. Calif. Army Nat. Guard 1970-76; Republican; R.Cath.; rec: golf, sailing. Ofc: Beckman Instruments Inc 2500 Harbor Blvd PO Box 3100 Fullerton 92634-3100

GLUSKER, PETER, physician; b. Sept. 3, 1936, NY, NY; s. David S. and Anita (Brenner) G.; m. Gretchen Knapp, June, 1959 (div. 1964); edn: Reed Coll. 1954-57; BA, UC Berkeley 1959; MA, MD, PhD, Univ. Okla. 1970, 1974, 1975; cert. Am. Bd. Psychiatry & Neurology 1981. Career: physician pvt. practice, Fort Bragg 1978–, med. staff Mendocino Coast Dist. Hosp.; Fellow Am. Acad. Neurology, mem. Soc. for Neurosci., Am. EEG Soc., Am. Assn. Electrodiag. & Electroencepholography, Am. Heart Assn. and Stroke Council; works: poems (1970-); rec: bicycling, hiking, kayaking. Ofc: 442 N McPherson St POB 1639 Fort Bragg 95437

GLYNN, JAMES A., writer, professor of sociology; b. Sept. 10, 1941, Brooklyn; s. James A. and Muriel Marie (Lewis) G.; m. Marie Janet Gates, Dec. 17, 1966 (div. Apr. 27, 1995); 1 son, David b. 1972; edn: AA, Foothill Coll., 1962; BA, San Jose State Univ., 1964, MA, 1966. Career: prof. sociology Bakersfield Coll., Bakersfield 1966–; adj. prof. CSU Bakersfield, 1988–; adj. prof. CSU Fresno 1968-69, Chapman Univ., Orange 1970-71; text reviewer and consulting editor for several book cos.; awards: Innovator of Yr. League for Innovation for Comm. Colls., St. Louis, Mo. 1989, Pres.'s Award for textbook author Bakersfield Coll. 1989, Innovator of Yr. Kern Comm. Coll. Dist. 1992; mem: Calif. Academic Senate (Bakersfield Coll. pres. 1975-94, state del. 1980-90, Calif. Great Teachers Seminar, Santa Barbara 1990), Faculty Assn. for Calif. Comm. Colls. Sacto. (Council 1987–), Am. Sociol. Assn. 1965–, Calif. Sociol. Assn. (exec. dir. 1993–, pres. 1992-93, treas. 1990-91), Pacific Sociol. Assn. 1980– (mem. commn. on teaching 1994-97), Textbook Authors Assn. 1986–, Kern Comm. Coll. Fedn. of Tchrs. (founder 1976), Worldwatch Inst., Pop. Ref. Bureau, World Future Soc.; civic: Reading Is Fundamental (vol. 1979-81), Kern Coun. for Civic Unity (sec. 1968-70); author: Focus on Sociology, 1994, Guide to Human Services (Bakersfield: Bakersfield Coll. 1993), Understanding Racial and Ethnic Groups (Bakersfield: Fairway House, 1992), Guide to Social Psychology, 1991, Hands On: User's Manual for Data Processing, 1986, (with Elbert W. Stewart) Intro. to Sociology (McGraw-Hill Book Co., 1985, prev. editions 1971, 75, 79, internat. ed. pub. 1986, Portuguese lang. ed. 1978; Spanish lang. ed. 1977), contbg. author: Using Humor to Teach Sociology (Am. Sociol. Assn., 1988), author: Writing Across the Curriculum Using Sociological Concepts (Fairway House, 1983), Studying Sociology, 1979, (with Gregory L. Goodwin) New Directions for Community Colleges (S.F., Jossey-Bass, 1977); Democrat. Res: 4512 Panorama Dr Bakersfield 93306-1354 Ofc: Bakersfield College Bakersfield 93305-1299

GO, HENRY, physician; b. Dec. 28, 1933, Courtland, Calif.; s. Wah Yoo Go and Hoon Moy Chan; m. Patricia Louise Rigg, 1961; children: Rosemary b. 1962, Adrienne b. 1963; edn: AA, UC Berkeley 1955; MD, UCLA 1959; lic. physician, Calif. 1960; cert. Am. Bd. of Family Practice 1975, recert. 1987, 93. Career: intern L.A. Co. Hosp., Loma Linda/USC 1959-60; resident in surgery Cedars of Lebanon (Cedars-Sinai) Med. Ctr. 1960-61; family physician, The Doctor's Office, Courtland Calif. (current); mem. med. staff Methodist Hosp., Univ. Med. Ctr.; courtesy staff Mercy Hosp., Sutter Hosps.; clin. prof. family practice UC Davis 1992–; awards: Golden Stethoscope award, Sacramento-El Dorado Med. Soc. 1973, Frederick Plessner Award, CMA 1990; mem: AMA, CMA 1972- (com. on rural health 1972, alternate delegate 1974-78), Calif. Med. Bd. 1977- (mem. 2nd dist med. quality review com. 1977-82, com. chmn. 1977-78), Sacramento-El Dorado Med. Soc. 1967- (bd. dirs. 1971-74, treas. 1974, exec. com. 1974, dists. com. 1978, profl. conduct & ethics 1976-77, fin. com. 1974, hosp. affairs 1974, profl. liability com. 1974, profl. liability review 1973, cont. med. edn. com. 1973, disaster radio com. 1972-83, public health com. 1972-74, chmn. Golden Empire health planning council 1973, mem. 1972, mal-practice ins. review 1972, 73, physician procurement com. 1972, reg. med. prog. 1972, chmn. rural health com. 1973, mem. 1971, 72, emergency care com. 1970, post-grad. edn. com. 1967, 69);contbr. article to profl. jour., 1994; Republican; Lutheran. Ofc: PO Box 338 Courtland 95615

GOBAR, ALFRED JULIAN, economic consultant, educator; b. July 12, 1932, Lucerne Valley; s. Julian Smith and Hilda (Millbank) G.; m. Sally Ann Randall, June 17, 1957; children: Wendy Lee, Curtis Julian, Joseph Julian; edn: BA in econs., Whittier Coll., 1953, MA in history, 1955; postgrad. Claremont Grad. Sch., 1953-54; PhD in econs., USC, 1963. Career: asst. to the pres. Microdot Inc., Pasadena 1953-57; regional sales mgr. Sutorbilt Corp., Los Angeles 1957-59; market res. assoc. Beckman Instruments Inc., Fullerton 1959-64; senior mktg. cons. Western Mgmt. Consultants Inc., Phoenix, Az. and Los Angeles, 1964-66; ptnr., prin., chmn. bd. Darley/Gobar Assocs. Inc., 1966-73; pres., chmn. bd. Alfred Gobar Assocs. Inc., Brea 1973-91; pres. and chmn. bd. AJGA, Inc. 1991–; asst. prof. finance USC, 1963-64; assoc. prof. bus. CSU Los Angeles, 1963-68, 70-79, assoc. prof. CSU Fullerton, 1968-69; mktg., fin. adviser 1957–; dir. Quaker City Fed. Savings & Loan Assn., Whittier 1992–; bd. trustees Whittier Coll., 1992–; honors: Lambda Alpha (hon. land econs. frat.); mem. Am. Soc. Real Estate Counselors, Urban Land Inst.; public speaker seminars and convs.; pub. articles in field. Res: 1100 W Valencia Mesa Dr Fullerton 92633 Ofc: 721 W Kimberly Ave Placentia 92670

GODAGER, JANE ANN, psychiatric social worker; b. Nov. 29, 1943, Blue River, Wis.; d. Roy and Elmyra Marie (Hood) Godager; edn: BA, Univ. Wis., Madison 1965; MSW, Fla. State Univ., Tallahassee, 1969; Calif. Lic. Clin. Soc. Worker; Acad. Cert. Soc. Worker, NASW; Bd. Cert. Diplomate in soc. work Am. Bd. BCD's. Career: social worker Dept. Corrections, Wis. 1965-71; State Dept. of Mental Health, Calif. 1972-85; Mental Health Dept., Riverside 1985-86; mental health counselor Superior Court, San Bernardino 1986–; mem. advy. bd. Sch. of Soc. Work, CSU San Bernardino; mem. Kappa Kappa Gamma Alumnae, Nat. Assn. of Soc. Workers; rec: reading, travel. Ofc: MHC/ Superior Ct. 700 E Gilbert Bldg, One, San Bernardino 92415-0920

GOEBEL-D'ESMOND, GRACE B., physician; b. Feb. 3, 1919, Boynton, Pa.; d. Christian H. and Mary Edna (Keim) Baker; m. James L. Goebel, M.D., urologist, Sept. 1, 1940, dec. 1983; children: Camille A. Goebel-Lennon b. 1951, James Baker Goebel b. 1953; m. Col. Adrian A. D'Esmond, Ret., June 28, 1986; edn: AB, Manchester Coll., 1939; MD, Univ. Chgo. Sch. of Med., 1943; MPH, UC Berkeley, 1965; Cert. Am. Bd. of Pediatrics 1948. Career: intern Cook Co. Hosp., Chgo. 1943-44; preceptor Rees-Stealy Clinic, San Diego 1944-46; pediatric resident, resident in communicable disease Children's Hosp., San Francisco 1946-48; pvt. practice pediatrician Mill Valley, 1948-62; clinician, medical cons. San Francisco Dept. Pub. Health 1962-64, dist. med. ofcr. 1965-66; pub. health med. ofcr. III Calif. St. Dept. Pub. Health, Berkeley 1966-84; elected ofcl., bd. dirs. Marin Hosp. Dist., Marin Co. 1984-88; apptd. mem. bd. dirs. Marin Gen. Hosp. 1985-92 (2 terms); mem: Acad. of Pediatrics 1948–, No. Calif. Pub. Health Assn. 1965–, Marin Med. Soc. 1948–, Physicians for Soc. Responsibility; club: Meadow (Fairfax); Republican; Presbyterian. Res/Ofc: Box 995 Ross 94957

GOFF, THOMAS MICHAEL, real estate consulting firm executive; b. April 30, 1948, Elgin, Ill.; s. Walter Earl, Jr. and Jeanne Marie (Blanchard) G.; m. Gerrianne M. Ringlespaugh, July 28, 1970; 1 dau., Kristen b. 1981; edn: BS, Univ. of Ill. 1974; MBA, Mich. State Univ. 1976. Career: senior prin. Laventhol & Horwath, Los Angeles 1976-90; exec. Robert Charles Lesser & Co., Beverly Hills 1990–; instr. Mich. State Univ. 1974-76; bd. advisors Hotel Sch. at Calif. Polytechnic Univ., Pomona 1991–; mem. bd. dirs: Small Luxury Hotels & Resorts Assn. (treas. 1987-89), L.A. Visitors & Convention Bureau, Calif. Hotel & Motel Assn., San Gabriel Country Club; mil: 1st lt., U.S. Army 1969-72; Republican; rec: golf. Ofc: Robert Charles Lesser & Co. 11111 Santa Monica Blvd Ste 1800 Los Angeles 90025

GOGOLIN, MARILYN TOMPKINS, educational executive; b. Feb. 25, 1946, Pomona; d. Roy Merle and Dorothy (Davidson) Tompkins; m. Robert Elton Gogolin, Mar. 29, 1969; edn: BA, Univ. LaVerne 1967; MA, Univ. Redlands 1968; MS, CSU Fullerton 1976; Univ. Wash. Seattle 1968-69.

Career: speech pathologist Casa Colina Hosp. Rehab. Medicine, Pomona 1969-71; diagnostic tchr. L.A. Co. Office Edn., Downey 1971-72, program splst. 1972-74, program mgr. 1974-76, organizational behavior mgmt. cons. 1976-79, dir. administrative affairs and asst. to supt. 1979-; exec. dir. Co. Sch. Bds. Assn., Los Angeles 1979-; cons. sch. dists. and profl. assns. 1976-; awards: Univ. LaVerne Sarafin 1967, Univ. Wash. Doctoral Fellowship 1968-69, PTA Hon. Service 1985, 86, Outstanding Young Women in Am. 1977, Who's Who in West, Who's Who Am. Women, Who's Who Emerging Leaders; mem: Am. Ednl. Research Assn., Am. Speech & Hearing Assn., Calif. Speech & Hearing Assn., Am. Mgmt. Assn., Kidney Found. of Desert (founding patron), Turtle Rock Glen Homeowners (pres. 1988, v.p. 1987); club: Silver Sands Racquet (pres. 1991); Baptist; rec: travel, tennis. Res: 15 Sweetwater Irvine 92715 Ofc: Los Angeles County Office of Education 9300 E Imperial Hwy Downey 90242

GOKA, RICHARD S., physician; b. June 7, 1947, Santa Monica, Calif.; s. Robert K. and Miwako (Tanaka) G.; m. Benecian Hong, Mar. 31, 1978; children: Kimberly N. b. 1983, K. Robert b. 1988; edn: BS, biology, Calif. State Univ., Hayward 1973; MD, Univ. Autonoma de Guadalajara Sch. of Med., Jalisco, Mex. 1977; Rutgers Med. Sch. Coll. of Medicine & Dentistry, N.J., Fifth Pathway Prog. St. Joseph's Hosp., Paterson, NJ 1977-78; internship Univ. of Utah Coll. of Medicine 1978-79, residency, physical medicine and rehab. 1978-81; lic. physician NY 1978, Utah 1979, Calif. 1980, DEA 1979; cert. Am. Bd. of Physical Medicine & Rehab. 1982, Am. Bd. of Pain Mgmt. 1990; cert. Case Manager 1993. Career: clin. instr. Univ. of Utah Coll. of Medicine 1981-88; med. dir. Holy Cross Hosp. Quinney Rehab. Ctr., Salt Lake City, UT 1982-89; med. dir. Leon S. Peters Rehab. Ctr., Fresno, Calif. 1989-92, out patient med. dir. 1992-94; med. dir. Western States Adminstrs./Q.C. Med., Fresno 1990-95; med. cons. Learning Services, Gilroy, Calif. 1990-94, Pacific Review Svs., Cypress, Calif. 1991-94; cons. CAPP Care, Irvine 1994-; Med. Review Inst., Salt Lake City 1992-, Meridian Neurocare, Fresno 1991- (acting med. dir. 1994), Mutual of Omaha 1994-, Personal Health Care, Irvine 1994- Revendell Children & Youth Ctr. 1987-88, Sandy Reg. Rehab. & Convalescent Ctr. 1987-89, Pain Clinic, Div. of Behavioral Medicine, Univ. of Utah Coll. of Medicine 1981-82; med. dir. Villa Serena, Magna, Utah 1987-89; hosp. staff: Holy Cross Hosp., Salt Lake City 1981-89, Univ. of Utah Med. Ctr. 1981-88, Fresno Comm. Hosp. 1989-, Clovis Hosp. 1989-, Sierra Hosp. 1989-, Valley Med. Ctr., Fresno 1990-92, St. Agnes Med. Ctr., Fresno 1990-, San Joaquin Rehab. Hosp. 1991-; vis. prof. Univ. Autonoma de Guadalajara 1985; vis. faculty Emory Univ. 1985, 86; mem: Am. Subacute Care Assn. (pres., 1993-94, bd. dirs. 1993-95); Nat. Subacute Care Assn. (bd. dirs. 1995-); Am. Acad. of Physical Medicine & Rehab. (fellow 1981-, mem. sect. of brain injury rehab. 1988-, chair task force, subacute rehab. 1993), Am. Assn. of Electrodiagnosis & Electromyography 1982-, Am. Congress of Rehab. Medicine 1981- (membership com 1989-92, public relations & mktg. com 1990, interdisciplinary special interest group on brain injury 1986-, chmn. membership com. 1987-93, minor brain injury, ethics & mgmg. of persistent veg. state 1987-92, post-acute com. 1989-93, inpatients 1991-93, profl. edn. 1989-, case mgmt./reimbursement com. 1988-), AMA 1980-, Am. Paraplegia Soc. 1991-, Am. Spinal Injury Assn. 1984-, CMA 1989-, Case Mgmt. Soc. of Am. 1991- (No. Calif. 1992-), Fresno-Madera Co. Med. Soc. 1990-, Internat. Med. Soc. of Paraplegia 1981-, Internat Rehab. Med. Assn. 1982-; num. TV and radio interviews, 1985-; author or co-author: 12+ articles pub. in profl. jours., 1981-, num. sci. presentations 1981-; creator: video tapes, 1981, 4 motion pictures (with Robert Watanabe, MD); Protestant; rec: fishing, skiing. Res: PO Box 14089 Fresno 93650 Ofc: 5740 N Palm Fresno 93704

GOLD, RUSSELL STUART, psychologist; b. Jan. 7, 1949, Chicago, Ill.; s. Irving Louis and Victoria (Saltzman) G.; m. Andrea, Aug. 1, 1982; children: Celia b. 1983, Seth b. 1988, Kristen b. 1970, Kristopher b. 1974; edn: AB, Univ. Ill. Champaign 1970; MA, Northwestern Univ. 1973; PhD, Calif. Sch. Profl. Psychology 1978; lic. psychologist 1979. Career: pvt. practice psychology, San Diego 1979-; adj. clinical supr. Mercy Hosp. And Med. Ctr. 1980-; police psychologist San Diego Co. 1985-89, San Diego Police Dept. 1990-; dir. Child Custody & Family Research Ctr. 1988-; Family Court Case Consultation Team 1992-; mem: Acad. San Diego Psychologists (pres., secty. 1979-), Am. Psychological Assn., Calif. St. Psychological Assn.; Jewish. Ofc: 4060 4th Ave Ste 615 San Diego 92103

GOLDBERG, FRED SELLMANN, advertising agency executive; b. Jan. 22, 1941, Chgo.; s. Sydney Norman and Birdie (Cohen) G.; m. Jerrilyn Toby Tager, Apr. 12, 1941; children: Robin b. 1965, Susanne b. 1968; edn: BS, Univ. Vermont, 1962; MBA, New York Univ., 1964. Career: mktg. research mgr. P. Ballantine & Sons, Newark, N.J. 1964-67; senior v.p., mgmt. supr. Young & Rubicam, N.Y.C., 1967-78, senior v.p. and gen. mgr. Young & Rubicam, Los Angeles 1978-82; exec. v.p., gen. mgr. Chiat Day Inc., San Francisco 1982-85, c.o.o. Chiat Day Inc., Los Angeles 1985-87, pres. and c.e.o. Chiat-Day San Francisco and v. chmn. Chiat-Day Advt., Inc., L.A. 1987-90; founder, pres. and c.e.o. Goldberg Moser O'Neill Advertising, San Francisco 1990-; Republican; Jewish; rec: tennis, music, running. Res: 154 Santa Rosa Ave Sausalito 94965-2035 Ofc: Goldberg Moser O'Neill, 77 Maiden Ln San Francisco 94108

GOLDBERG, HERB, psychologist; b. July 14, 1937, Berlin, Germany; s. Jacob and Ella (Nagler) G.; 1 dau., Amy Elisabeth b. 1981; edn: BA cum laude, City Univ. N.Y. 1958; PhD, Adelphi Univ., N.Y. 1963. Career: prof. psychology CSU Los Angeles 1965-; pvt. practice psychotherapy, Westwood 1966-; honors: Phi Beta Kappa; mem: Am. Psychological Assn.; author: w. George Bach, Creative Aggression, 1974; Hazards of Being Male, 1976; w. Robert Lewis, Money Madness, 1978; New Male, 1979; New Male-Female Relationships, 1983; Inner Male, 1987; What Men Really Want, 1991. Ofc: 1100 Glendon Ave #939 Los Angeles 90024

GOLDBERG, LEONARD, motion picture studio president and independent producer; b. Jan. 24, 1934, Brooklyn, NY; s. Wm. and Jean (Smith) G.; m. Wendy Howard, Nov. 26, 1972; dau. Amanda Erin b. 1974; edn: BS in econs., Univ. Pa., Wharton Sch. Career: research dept. ABC-TV, NY, 1956-57; NBC, 1957-61; bdcstg. coordinator BBD&O, 1961-63; mgr. program devel. ABC-TV 1963-64, v.p. daytime programming 1964-66, v.p. network programming 1966-69; v.p. prodn. Screen Gems (now Columbia), Los Angeles 1969-72; co-owner Spelling/Goldberg Prodn.; pres. Leonard Goldberg Co., 1972-; pres. Mandy Films; pres./c.o.o. 20th Century Fox Film Corp. 1986-; bd. dirs. Spectrovision; guest lectr. Beverly Hills H.S. 1986-89; awards: Peabody Award for "Brian's Song" 1984, Film Advy. Bd., excellence, "Something About Amelia" 1984, Emmy nomination for "Family" 1984, Emmy Award for "Something About Amelia" 1984, Humanitarian Award NCCJ 1987, Image Award NAACP 1987; mem: Acad. Motion Picture Arts & Scis., Hollywood Radio & TV Soc.; civic: Cedars Sinai Med. Ctr. (bd. dirs.); works: network executive: created the form for TV Movies of the Week; exec. producer: TV series: The Rookies, Charlie's Angels, Starsky & Hutch, Family, Hart to Hart, Fantasy Island, SWAT, T.J. Hooker, The Cavanaughs; motion pictures: Baby Blue Marine, California Split, Bad News Bears in Breaking Training, Wargames, Spacecamp, Sleeping With The Enemy, The Distinguished Gentleman; movies for TV: 40 including Something About Amelia, The Boy in the Plastic Bubble, Alex-Life of a Child; rec: tennis, ski, swim. Ofc: Mandy Films, Inc. Lantana Ctr 3000 W Olympic Blvd Bldg 4 Ste 1200 Santa Monica 90404

GOLDBERG, MARK ARTHUR, neuropharmacologist; b. Sept. 4, 1934, N.Y., N.Y.; s. Jacob and Bertha (Gruslausky) G.; widower, 1982; 1 son, Jonathan Lee b. 1971. edn: BS, Columbia Univ., 1955; PhD, Univ. Chicago, 1959, MD, 1962. Career: resident neurology N.Y. Neurolog. Inst., 1963-66; asst. prof. neurology Columbia Univ., 1968-71; prof. neurology and pharmacology, UCLA, Los Angeles, 1971-, chair dept. neurology UCLA/Harbor Med. Ctr., Torrance 1977-; mem: Am. Neurol. Assn. (Fellow), Am. Acad. of Neurology (Fellow), Am. Soc. for Neurochemistry, L.A. Soc. for Neurology (pres.); author numerous book chapters and articles on neuropharmacology; mil: capt. US Army 1966-68. Ofc: UCLA/Harbor Medical Center, 1000 W Carson St Torrance 90509

GOLDBERG, MITCHEL ROY, federal bankruptcy judge; b. March 12, 1943, Denver, Colo.; s. Alvin and Ruby (Soffen) G.; m. Janice Ellen Jacobs, Aug. 23, 1964; children: Andrea b. 1969,, Shani b. 1972; edn: BA, Univ. Colo. 1965; JD, 1968. Career: atty. Rosen & Goldberg, Santa Ana 1971-81; Mitchel R. Goldberg, A Profl. Corp. 1981-88; judge U.S. Bankruptcy Ct., Central Dist. Calif. 1988-; mem: Temple Beth Tikvah (religious practice v.p. 1987-88, pres. 1989-91); mil: capt. AUS 1969-71; Jewish. Ofc: U.S. Bankruptcy Court 699 N Arrowhead Ste 200 San Bernardino 92401

GOLDBERG, URIEL CHAIM, research engineer; b. March 16, 1951, Haifa, Israel; nat. 1982; s. Nathan Goldberg and Eva (Neufeld) Bansky; edn: BS aeronautical engring., Israel Inst. Tech. 1976; MS, Case Inst. Tech. 1979; PhD, 1984. Career: engr. Gen. Electric Aircraft Engine Group, Lynn, Mass. 1979-80; sr. scientist Avco Systems, Wilmington, Mass. 1983-84; tech. staff Rockwell Sci. Center, Thousand Oaks 1984-; mem: Am. Soc. Mechanical Engineers; articles pub. in tech. jours., 1984-95; rec: classical music, chess. Ofc: Rockwell Science Center 1049 Camino Dos Rios Thousand Oaks 91360

GOLDEN, JOHN JACOB, optometrist; b. Oct. 18, 1935, Toronto, Canada; nat. 1944; s. Michael Wolfe and Lillian (Goldstein) G.; m. Linda, June 28, 1991; edn: BS magna cum laude, City Coll. N.Y.; OD, Ill. Coll. Optometry. Career: pres. Ill. Coll. Optometry, Phi Theta Upsilon 1959-61, student body 1960-61; mem. Calif. Optometric Assn. Sacto. 1961-; Am. Optometric Assn., St. Louis, Mo. 1961-; mil: AUS 1954-56; Republican; Jewish; rec: astro photog., tennis. Res: 4112 Oak Hollow Rd Calabasas 91302 Ofc: 20812 Ventura Blvd., Ste 106, Woodland Hills, CA 91364

GOLDFARB, I. JAY, accounting firm executive; b. Mar. 8, 1933, N.Y.C.; s. Joseph and Fay Esther (Hirschhorn) G.; m. Arlene Storch, May 8, 1955; children: Meryl Lori, David; edn: BA in econs., Queen's Coll., N.Y. 1955; CPA, N.Y. 1962, Calif. 1972. Career: staff acct. T.D. Davidson & Co., CPAs, N.Y.C. 1957-59; ptnr. Rashba & Pokart, CPAs 1959-65; chief fin. ofcr. Fabrics by Joyce Inc. 1965-66; ptnr. Clarence Rainess & Co. CPAs 1966-71, co-executive ptnr. 1971-75; senior ptnr. Joseph S. Herbert & Co. CPAs, L.A., Calif. 1975-78; mng. ptnr. Goldfarb, Whitman & Cohen CPAs, L.A. 1978-; dir: Sam & Libby Inc.,

NY, NY 1992–, Jalotte Inc. 1995–; awarded "Spirit of Life" City of Hope 1990; mem. Am. Inst. of CPAs 1962–, N.Y. State Soc. of CPAs 1962–, Calif. State Soc. CPAs 1972–; civic: City of Hope Profls. & Fin. Assocs. (pres. 1974-76, dinner chmn. 1977-79), City of Hope Bd. of Govs. 1993–, Boys & Girls Club San Fernando Valley/Pacoima (v.p. 1989, treas. 1990), United Jewish Welfare Fund (major gift com. 1987–); mil: 1st lt. USAF 1955-57; Stephen J. Weiss Temple; rec: golf, bridge. Ofc: Goldfarb, Whitman & Cohen, CPAs 12233 W Olympic Blvd Ste 210 Los Angeles 90064

GOLDHAMMER, ALAN, state bar court judge; b. Nov. 30, 1942, Cleveland, Ohio; s. Leonard and Rose (Brenner) G.; m. Renee Phyllis Kurman, June 5, 1966; children: Jesse b. 1967, Brenda b. 1971, Seth b. 1974; edn: BA, UCLA 1963; JD, Harvard Law Sch. 1966; admitted St. Bar Calif. 1967. Career: vol. U.S. Peace Corps, Recuy, Peru 1966-67; staff atty. Legal Aid Found. Los Angeles 1967-68, dir. major case devel. 1968-69; ptnr. Goldhammer & Horowitz 1969-72; Goldhammer & Kaufman 1972-74; hearing examiner Office of Hearings & Appeals, Social Security Adminstrn., Oakland 1974-77, adminstrv. law judge 1977-89; appointed by Calif. Supreme Ct. to a six yr. term on the newly created State Bar Ct. lectr. Nat. Judicial Coll., Reno, Nev. 1980, and St. Louis, Mo. 1992; faculty John F. Kennedy Sch. Law, Walnut Creek 1984-85; co-chair, contg. judicial edn. com. Office of Hearings & Appeals 1987-89; honors: Ten Years Extraordinary Achievement Promoting Fostering & Implementing Cont. Judicial Edn. 1988; mem: Calif. Judges Assn., Am. Bar Assn.; articles pub. in profl. jours.; Democrat; Jewish; rec: running. Ofc: Office of State Bar Court 100 Van Ness Ave, 28th Pl., San Francisco 94102-5238

GOLDING, SUSAN, mayor; b. Aug. 18, 1945, Muskogee, Okla.; d. Brage and Hinda Fay (Wolf) G.; children: Samuel b. 1971, Vanessa b. 1974; edn: Cert. Pratique De Langue Francaise, Univ. of Paris, 1965; BA Govt. & Internat. Relations, Carleton Coll., 1966; MA Romance Philology, Columbia Univ., 1974. Career: assoc. ed. Jour. of Internat. Affairs of Columbia Univ.; PhD tchg. fellow Emory Univ.; coll. instr. San Diego College Dist.; assoc. pub./gen. mgr. The News Press Group, San Diego -1980; elected San Diego City Council, 1981-83; dep. state secty. of bus., transp., housing State of Calif., Sacto. 1983-84; elected County Bd. of Supervisors, Dist. 3, San Diego 1984-92, v. ch. 1988, bd. chmn. 1989; elected mayor, City of San Diego 1992-; advy. bd. U.S. Conf. of Mayors 1994-, chair, Conf. com. on mil. base reuse 1994-; chair Governor's Calif. Mil. Base Reuse Task Force 1994; founder Calif. "Big 10" (org. of mayors of 10 largest cities) 1993; founder Internat. Trade Commn. S.D. 1985, chair Alcohol & Drug Prevention Task Force 1987-88, chair Earthquake Preparedness Com. Disaster Council 1986–; awards: Catalyst of Change Award, Greater S.D. C.of C. 1994, Women Who Mean Bus. Award, S.D. Bus. Jour. 1994, Internat. Citizen Award, World Affairs Council of S.D. 1994, named One of Ten Outstanding Repub. Co. Officials in U.S., Repub. Nat. Com., Disting. Achiev. Award Carleton Coll. 1991, Woman of Achiev. Soroptomists Internat. S.D. 1988, listed Am.'s 2,000 Most Notable Women, Who's Who of Emerging Leaders in Am.; Republican (State Central Com.), chair Local Elected Ofcls. 1987–); rec: languages, theater & arts, scuba. Ofc: Mayor, City of San Diego City Adminstrn Bldg 202 C St San Diego 92101

GOLDSMITH, DENNIS GORDON, artist-engraver; b. July 20, 1931, London, England, naturalized 1966; s. Wm. James and Florence Agnes (Chick) G.; m. Gladys Sewell, Dec. 2, 1952 (div. 1977); children: Rebecca b. 1957, Mark b. 1960, Graham b. 1962, Paul b. 1964 (dec. 1977); m. Gloria Lieberman, July 10, 1978; edn: cert. commercial engraving, London Central Sch. of Arts & Crafts. Career: apprentice William Day, Ltd., London, U.K. 1947-52, journeyman 1954-55; W.R. Royal & Sons, Ltd. 1955-56; Springer Engraving Co., Vancouver, Canada 1956-60; master hand engraver Marier Engraving Co., San Francisco, Calif. 1960–; honors: assoc. certif. Royal Soc. of Arts (RSA) London (1955), recipient nat. awards: Best of yr. letterhead Crane Co. (1967), Best of show and cert. of excellence for engraved letterhead Engraved Stationer's & Mfrs. Assn. (1980); mem: Soc. Lithographic Artists & Designers U.K. (1950-56), Engravers Union S.F. (1960-67), Graphic Communications Union/ W. states (1967–, del., exec. bd. and pension fund trustee); club: Marin Rod & Gun; author: Stds. for Apprentice for Calif. Dept. of Indsl. Rels. for Engraved Stationery Indus. (1968); contbg. author/editor text & manual in field (in progress); mil: cartographic draughtsman British Army 1952-54; Episcopalian; rec: bibliophile, horticulturist, cyclist. Res: 10 Hazel Ct San Rafael 94901 Ofc: Marier Engraving Co. 1073 Howard St San Francisco 94103

GOLDSTONE, JERRY, vascular surgeon, educator; b. Nov. 18, 1940, Ontario, Oreg.; s. Ralph and Annette Lee (Rogoway) G.; m. Linda F. Kay, July 7, 1962; children: Adam E. b. 1969, Lara E. b. 1971, Stefan G. b. 1973; edn: Univ. Wash., Seattle 1958-61; BS (by reciprocity) Univ. Oregon, Eugene; MD (cum laude) Univ. Oregon Med. Sch., Portland 1965; lic. Calif. BME 1966. Career: asst. prof. surgery UC San Francisco, 1972-78, assoc. prof. surg. 1978-80; prof. surgery Univ. Ariz., Tucson 1980-84; prof. surgery UC San Francisco, 1984–, medical director Cardiovasc. Special Care Unit 1986–, v.chmn. dept. of surgery and chief div. vascular surgery, 1987–; cons. Letterman Army Med. Ctr., S.F. 1984–, director STAMP Prog. VA Med. Ctr., S.F. 1984–, cons. David Grant USAF Med. Ctr., Travis AFB, 1985–; awards: clin. investigator VA Med. Ctr.

S.F. 1973-76, Outstanding Tchr. nom. Sch. of Med. UCSF 1974, Dean's list, Excellence in Tchg., Univ. Ariz., Tucson 1982, Annual Gore lectr. Royal Australian Coll. of Surgeons, Sydney, Aus. 1985, Harvey Lozman Memorial lectr. Beth Israel Med. Ctr., N.Y.C. 1986; mem: Internat. Soc. for Cardiovascular Surgery (secty., mem. exec. council, 1989-93, pres. elect 1994), Vascular Surgery Biology Club (sec. treas. 1989-93), Soc. for Vascular Surgery (p.r. com. 1988-90), Am. Coll. Surgeons (surgical forum com. 1989–), Western Vascular Soc. (founding mem. 1984–, pres.-elect 1994), Assn. Of Internat. Vascular Surgeons (1983–, pres. 1991); Sierra Club (S.F.); author med. book chapters, 1971–, med. jour. articles, 1965–, editor book series: Perspectives in Vascular Surgery, 1989–; mil: capt. USAR 1966-75; rec: sports, travel, nature. Ofc: UCSF 505 Parnassus Rm M-488 San Francisco 94143-0222

GOLDSTRAND, DENNIS JOSEPH, financial and estate planning executive; b. July 12, 1952, Oakland; s. Joseph N. and Frances M. G.; m. Judy A. Goldstrand; edn: BSBA, CSU Chico 1975; Chartered Life Underwriter (CLU) 1986, Chartered Fin. Cons. (ChFC) 1988. Career: asst. mgr. Household Fin. Corp. 1975-76; reg. rep. Equitable Fin. Svcs. 1976-79, dist. mgr. 1979-85; ptnr. Goldstrand & Small Ins. & Financial Svcs. 1986-89; owner, Goldstrand Financial and Insurance Services 1989–; honors: recipient Life Underwriter of Yr. Award, Stockton Assn. Life Underwriters 1994, Million Dollar Round Table 1984-86, 93, 94, 95, nat. champion Equitable Fin. Svcs. 1982; mem: Am. Soc. CLU and ChFC (pres. Stockton Chpt. 1989-90), Stockton Assn. Life Underwriters (pres. 1990-91, guest spkr. 1986, chair ethics com. 1993-94), NALU PAC, Calif. Assn. Life Underwriters (trustee 1995-96), Stockton Estate Planning Council (bd.), Rotary (North Stockton), Greater Stockton C.of C., mem. Univ. of the Pacific Endowment Devel. Com., United Way of San Joaquin County Endowment Found. Inc. (bd., pres. 1994); publs: feature articles in Life Insurance Selling mag., 1986, 8/88; Republican; rec: tennis, golf. Res: 9215 Stony Creek Ln Stockton 95219 Ofc: Goldstrand Financial and Insurance Services 5250 Claremont Ave Ste 230 Stockton 95207

GONICK, JERRY G., lawyer; b. Oct. 13, 1936, New York; s. Max and Gussie G.; m. Barbara May Kaplan, June 22, 1962 (div. 1978); m. Susan Berch, Feb. 10, 1979; edn: BS, Rensellaer Polytech. Inst. 1959; MS, George Wash. Univ. 1963; MBA, Calif. Lutheran Coll. 1975; JD, San Fernando Coll. Law 1979; LL.M, Univ. San Diego 1984; admitted Wash. D.C. Bar 1987, Calif. 1980. Career: advy. scientist IBM, Westlake Village 1964-78; pres. Voyager Systems 1978-83; atty., ptnr. Friedman, Jay & Cramer, San Diego 1984-86; Robinson & Gonick 1986-90; prin. Jerry G. Gonick, Atty. at Law, 1990–; awards: Univ. San Diego Grad. Research Fellow (1983-84); mem: Univ. San Diego Grad. Tax Program (advy. bd. 1987–), Am. Arbitration Assn. (bus. panel 1985–), IEEE, Am. Bar Assn.; publs: 4 articles in profl. jours., 1986-93; rec: racquetball. Ofc: 610 West Ash Street Ste 1610 San Diego 92101

GONSALVES, MARIANNE ETHEL, nurse epidemiologist/practitioner, cancer program administrator, consultant; b. Jan. 10, 1954, Santa Monica; d. Henry Charles and Theodora Axenty Griswold; edn: BS nursing, CSU Long Beach 1978; MS, currently. Career: clin. instr. nursing CSU Long Beach 1982-83; home IV therapy nurse pvt. practice, Long Beach 1985-87; adult nurse practitioner oncology pvt. practice 1984-87; adminstr., nurse mgr. UC Irvine Cancer Center, Orange 1987-89, nurse epidemiologist USC Cancer Res., Los Angeles 1985-95, and coordinator Adult Oncology Nurse Practitioner Pgm. 1990-92; dir. oncology program Western Med. Ctr., Santa Ana 1992–94; adult nurse practitioner, pvt. practice, Fountain Valley 1995-; ednl. cons. UCSD Med. Center 1989-90; nursing cons. and lectr.; breast health facilitator Am. Cancer Soc.; honors: Lane Adams award 1993-94, Orange Co. Oncology Nursing Soc. Pres. award 1989, Internat. Assn. Bus. Communicators Bronze Quill Hon. 1985, Sigma Theta Tau 1983, Am. Cancer Soc. Vol. of Year 1988, 1993-94, Edn. Dept. Vol. of Year 1987; mem: Oncology Nursing Soc., Am. Cancer Soc., Calif. Coalition of Nurse Practitioners, Pageant of Masters (vol.); audiovisual productions for healthcare, 1985–, co-inventor home pro infusion pump, 1984, adult oncology nurse practitioner program CSU Long Beach 1989; Republican; Christian; rec: travel, cooking, exercising. Res: 2457 N Heliotrope Dr Santa Ana 92706 Ofc: 11160 Warner Ave Ste 313 Fountain Valley 92708

GONZALEZ, CESAR AUGUSTO (aka Gonzalez-T.,Cesar A.), educator, writer; b. Jan. 17, 1931, Los Angeles; s. Jose Andalon and Camerina (Trujillo) G.; m. Bette L. Beattie, Aug. 30, 1969; edn: BA, Gonzaga Univ., 1953, MA, licentiate in philosophy, 1954; MST, licentiate in sacred theology, Univ. Santa Clara, 1961; postgrad., sociology, UCLA, 1962-65. Career: tchr. Instituto Regional Mexico, Chihuahua, Mex. 1954-57; community devel. specialist Centro Laboral Mexico, Mexico D.F., 1965-68; supr. A.B.C. Headstart, East L.A., Calif. 1968-69; employment counselor Operation SER, San Diego 1969-70; prof. and dept. chair Chicano studies, San Diego Mesa Coll., 1970–; founding chair Raza Consortium, 1971-72; cons. Chicano Fedn. of San Diego County Inc., 1987-89; author book of poetry: Unwinding the Silence (1987), editor, contbr. book of lit. criticism: Rudolfo A. Anaya: Focus on Criticism (1990), coeditor: English Grammar and Comp. (1978, 79), contbr. poetry, short fiction and lit. criticism to scholarly journals, mags., newspapers and anthologies; ed., assoc. ed. literary journals, 1976-: Revista Apple, Ariz. State Univ., Tempe 1991,

Sequoya, Santa Ana, Calif. (1990–), Fragmentos de Barro, San Diego (1976–); founding bd. dirs. Mex.-Am. Advy. Com. to L.A. Bd. of Edn., 1969; awards: Fulbright-Hays fellow, Peru 1982, NEH fellow, UCSB 1984, comm. svc. award Chicano Fedn. San Diego Inc. 1982, outstanding tchr. San Diego Mesa Coll. 1985, 95, outstanding tchr. and scholar Concilio of Chicano Studies for San Diego, Imperial Valley and Baja, Calif. 1990, tchg. excellence award Nat. Inst. for Staff and Orgn. Devel. 1993, Cesar Chavez Social Justice Award 1994, Latina-Latino Indigenous People Coalition award 1995, Special Congressional Recognition (Congressman Bob Filner) 1995; mem: Am. Fedn. of Tchrs. 1970–, Nat. Assn. of Chicano Studies 1988–, La Raza Faculty Assn. 1970–, Centro Cultural de la Raza (1972–, past bd. mem.), Poets and Writers 1990–, Assn. Internacional de Hispanistas 1991–; Democrat; R.Cath.; rec: travel, reading, music. Ofc: Chicano Studies Dept. San Diego Mesa College 7250 Mesa College Dr San Diego 92111 Ph: 619/627-2751

GONZALEZ, CHARLES, lithography company owner; b. July 24, 1941, Los Angeles; s. Edward and Rosemary (Rodriguez) G.; m. Sylvia; children: Charles b. 1965, Patricia b. 1966, Christina b. 1972, Brian b. 1976; edn: cert. in printing, L.A. Trade-Tech, 2 yrs. Career: pres. Castle Litho, Los Angeles 1968–; mem. advy. com. Trade Tech L.A. 1979; Democrat; Cath.; rec: Kenpo (3d degree black belt 1976-89). Res: 5320 Davidson Dr Whittier 90601 Ofc: Castle Litho 5925 East Washington Blvd City of Commerce 90040

GOOD, JAMES EDWARD, lawyer; b. Sept. 7, 1930, Chicago, Ill.; s. James Edward and Evelyn Ann (Jeresek) G.; m. Frances Mary Rick, June 26, 1954 (div. 1988); m. Sylvia Ann Jordan, March 3, 1989; children: Cynthia b. 1955, Mark b. 1956, James b. 1957, Alison b. 1960; edn: BS commerce, Univ. Notre Dame 1952; JD, Univ. Minn. 1955; admitted St. Bar Calif. 1965, Minn. 1955. Career: atty. Cargill Inc., Mpls. 1959-64; Kaiser Industries Corp., Oakland 1964-79; ptnr. Gresham Varner Savage Nolan & Tilden, San Bernardino 1979–; honors: Order of Coif; mem: Calif. Mining Assn. (pres. 1985-87, exec. com. 1989-91); article pub. in profl. jour., 1988; mil: capt. USMC 1955-59; Republican. Ofc: Gresham Varner Savage 600 N Arrowhead Ave Ste 300 San Bernardino 92401

GOODCHILD, JACK, lawyer; b. July 16, 1950, Antwerp, Belgium; nat. 1956; s. Abraham and Sonja (Mirman) Gutkin; m. Carrie Kramer, Nov. 22, 1981; children: Adam b. 1984, Sarah b. 1985; edn: BA cum laude, St. Univ. N.Y. 1971; JD, 1974; admitted St. Bar Calif. 1975. Career: atty. Schermer & Rand, PLC, Sherman Oaks 1976-81; atty., v.p. Rand & Goodchild, P.L.C., 1981-89; pres. Jack Goodchild P.L.C., Van Nuys 1989–; advr. to Assemblyman Burt Margolin on worker's comp. reform 1989-94; judge pro tem Workers Compensation Appeals Bd. 1986–; splst. Workers Compensation 1981–; speaker, Insurance Edn. Assn.; mem: ABA, L.A. Bar Assn., Calif. Trial Lawyers Assn., L.A. Trial Lawyers Assn.; Democrat; Jewish. Address: Woodland Hills 91364

GOODHEAD, BERNARD, physician-surgeon; b. Oct. 20, 1934, Derby, England; nat. 1975; s. Arthur Reginald and Starletta (Goshawk) G.; m. Susan Richards, March 3, 1963 (div. 1977); m. Arlene Johnson, March 19, 1978; children: Deborah b. 1970, Sheryl b. 1971; edn: BS, Birmingham Univ. England 1958; LRCP, MRCS, London, England 1958; MS, McGill Univ. Canada 1968. Career: intern, England 1958-65; resident 1967-69; fellow Long Beach Heart Assn., Harbor Gen. Hosp., Torrance 1965-66; res. fellow Royal Victims Hosp., Montreal, Canada 1966-67; chief resident dept. surgery Bexar Co. Hosp., Univ. Tx. Med.Sch., San Antonio 1969-71; pvt. practice, Houston and San Antonio, Tx. 1971-73; San Diego 1973–; mem: San Diego Med. Soc., CMA, Soc. Gen. Surgeons San Diego, Southwestern Surgical Congress, A.C.P., English Coll. Surgeons, Pan Pacific Surgical Assn., Internat. Coll. Surgeons, Internat. Soc. Surgeons, FRCS, FACS, FICS; 27 articles pub. in sci. jours.; rec: travel. Res/Ofc: 1395 Park Row La Jolla 92037 Tel: 619/454-3636

GOODMAN, JULIEN MAX, general surgeon, retired; b. Jan. 1, 1913, Cleveland, Ohio; s. Max P. and Julie Elizabeth (Bamberger) G.; m. Margaret Muriel Wolfe, Aug. 28, 1947; son, Larry Jay b. 1949; edn: MD, Ohio State Univ., 1937; cert. Am. Bd. Surgery 1955. Career: intern Mt. Sinai Hosp., Cleveland, Ohio 1937-38; resident Royal Hosp., N.Y.C. 1938-40; resident in surgery Ohio State Univ. Hosp., 1945-50; chief of surgery Mt. St. Mary Hosp., Nelsonville, Ohio 1950-55; pvt. surgical practice, Castro Valley, Calif. 1955-84; surgical cons. CSU Hayward, 1970–; bd. dirs. Eden Med. Ctr., Castro Valley 1982–; bd. trustees Calif. Assn. of Hosps. & Health Systems, 1989; appt. Calif. Med. Quality Rev. Com., Dist. 5, 1984–, cons. and commr. Alameda Co. Health Care Svs. Commn. 1963-75, mem. Alameda Co. Emergency Med. Care Com. 1985–; awards: 2-yr honors in biology CWR Univ. 1933; mem: Alameda Contra Costa Med. Assn. (pres. 1975-76, bull. ed. 1975-76, 79-), Calif. Med. Assn. (surveyor for hosp. accreditation 1979-, bd. PAC, commr. BMQA 1972-, exam. coms.), Am. Trauma Soc. (founding mem. 1974-), Fellow Am. Coll. Surgeons (No. Calif. Chpt. trauma com. 1970-80), S.F. Surgical Soc., East Bay Surgical Soc., Pan-Pacific Surg. Assn., So. Alameda Surg. Soc., SW Surgical Congress (fellow), Calif. Acad. Med.; lodge: Tri Square Masonic (treas. 1959-65); author: (hist. biography) M.D.P.O.W. (1973), 22+ articles in med. jours., contbg. author (book) Clinical Anatomy (Lange Apleton, 1988); mil: served to maj. US Army Med. Corps 1940-46,

ward surgeon Army Med. Corps, McKinley Station Hosp., Rizal, Philippines 1941-42, Japanese prisoner of war 1942-45; Republican; Lutheran; rec: sailing, swimming, golf. Res: 2404 Mikemary Ct Castro Valley 94546

GOODMAN, MAX A., law professor, lawyer; b. May 24, 1924, Chicago, Ill.; s. Sam and Nettie (Abramowitz) G.; m. Marlyene Monkarsh, June 2, 1946; children: Jan b. 1949, Lauren b. 1951, Melanie b. 1954; edn: AA, Herzl Jr. Coll. 1943; Northwestern Univ. Law Sch. 1946-47; JD, Loyola Univ. Law Sch. 1948; admitted St. Bar Calif. (1948). Career: sole practice, Los Angeles 1948-53; ptnr. Goodman Hirschberg & King 1953-81; prof. law Southwestern Univ. Sch. Law 1966–; mediator L.A. Co. Superior Ct 1985-; awards: Spencer Brandeis Family Law Service award 1988, Irwin R. Buchalter Prof.(1988; mem: Am. Acad. Matrimonial Lawyers (fellow), L.A. Co. Bar Assn. (exec. com. family law sect., past chair); ed. Family Law Symposium Handbook, 1974-, cons. Calif. Family Law Service, 1985, articles pub. in profl. jours.,(1970-; mil: cpl. AUS 1943-45; Democrat; Jewish; rec: contract bridge. Ofc: Southwestern University 675 Westmoreland Ave Los Angeles 90005

GOODMAN, STEPHEN KENT, composer, conductor, arranger; b. Aug. 12, 1949, Glendale; s. Kent and Naoma (Noble) G.; m. Elizabeth Anne Blankinship, July 4, 1976 (div. 1982); m. Kelly Kay Ebinger, Apr. 30, 1984 (div. 1994); edn: USC, 1968, Calif. Inst. of the Arts 1971-72, Grove Sch. of Music, L.A. 1981-82. Career: profl. conducting debut as "World's Youngest Composer/Condr. of Marches" N.Y.C., July 13, 1966; pioneer work in sonic sculpture 1975-83; recording studio and commercial musical cons., condr., composer, arranger Harlequin Studios, Northridge, Calif. 1979-84; musical compositions rep. by various publishers 1973–; newspaper editor, West Coast Rag, 1991-92; writer articles dealing with music & culture, 1982–; honoree, N.Dak. state recognition 1989; mem: ASCAP (elected 1973 for film score "Maxie"; recipient 3 consecutive awards for ragtime compositions), Christian Instrumental Directors Assn. 1992–, Windjammers Internat. 1990, Maple Leaf Club (Grass Valley), Bohemia Ragtime Soc. (Boulder, Co.); Christian; rec: hunting, scuba diving. Ofc: PO Box 5459 Fresno 93755-5459

GOODMAN, TERENCE JAMES, actor, director, playwright; b. Nov. 29, 1950, Fort Dodge, Iowa; s. Wayne (Connie) Alva and Helen Loretta (O'Connor) G.; m. Catherine Amy Jackson, May 4, 1992; edn: BFA in theatre arts, Ark. State Univ., 1973; MFA theatre arts, Utah State Univ., 1990, profl. tng. with HB Studio NY, NY 1973, Michael Shurtleff, NY, NY 1974, Charles Conrad, L.A. 1976-77. Career: equity actor profl. theatre 1973-: selected roles include: King of Hearts "Alice in Wonderland" Prince Street Players, N.Y. 1973-74, Charlie "Oh, Lady Lady" Off-Broadway 1974, Smokey "Damn Yankees" (revival) Broadway Nat. Tour 1974, Annas "Jesus Christ Superstar" Broadway Nat. Tour 1975, Judas "Godspell" Off-Broadway 1975, Charlie "Queen of the Soaps" Internat. City Theatre, Los Angeles 1990, also numerous stage appearances in stock, semi and non-profl. theater 1971–; feature films include: (star) "Ode to Billy Joe" Warner Bros. 1975, "Who Done It" Dody Dayton Prodns. 1984, (featured) "Ninja III The Domination" Cannon Prodns. 1985, "Ruthless People" Walt Disney 1986, "Camp Beverly Hills" Touchstone 1988; profl. T.V., 1976–, guest star "Laverne and Shirley" ABC 1978, "The Brothers Wright" NBC 1978, principle "Newhart" CBS 1983, semi-regular "Young and the Restless" CBS 1984, series regular "Days of Our Lives" NBC 1985-86, guest star "Hill Street Blues" NBC 1986, "Perfect Strangers" ABC 1987, featured "Knots Landing" ABC 1987, "American River" NBC 1989; nat. commercials incl. AT&T, Denny's Restaurants, Volvo, Long John Silver, Kubota Lawn Mowers, Warner Books, Michelob, RC Cola, 1976–; director "A Lovely Sunday for Creve Coeur" 1989 (meritorious achiev. award for direction, ACT/Am. Coll. Theater Fest., 1990) "Broadway Bound" 1990, Utah State Theatre, Logan; author (optioned written works): "The Times of Danny Bailey" (screenplay, 1978, rev. 80, 82, 83, 85, 91), "Lost in the Sky" (play, 1989), "Puppetman" (screenplay, 1984), "A Mother's Love" (play, in progress); R.Cath.; rec: Mark Twain historian, skiing. Res/Ofc: 455 W 35th St #1 New York NY 10001

GOODWINE, JAMES K., JR., aviation consultant; b. Mar. 9, 1930, Evanson, Ill.; s. James K. and Janet B. (Dyer) G.; m. Helen L. Murray, June 6, 1959; children: Kathryn b. 1960, Robert b. 1962; edn: BSME, Purdue Univ., 1952, MSME, 1956, PhD, 1960. Career: research asst. Purdue Univ., 1954-57, instr. 1957-58; research engr. Chevron Research Co., Richmond, Calif. 1959-67; staff engr. United Airlines Co., San Francisco 1967-70, mgr. powerplant engring. 1970-79, mgr. new aircraft and operational engring. 1979-82, dir. engine tech. svs. 1982-87, actg. v.p. tech. svs. 1987, mgr. new technology 1987-89; consultant Aviation Mgmt. Systems, Concord, Mass. also Michael Goldfarb Assocs., Wash. D.C., 1989–; recipient Spl. Recognition Award United Airlines, Chgo. 1978; mem.: Soc. Automotive Engrs. (1959–, sect. chair 1976-77), Sigma Xi 1959–; clubs: Commonwealth (S.F.), Early Ford V-8 San Leandro (pres. regional gp. 1981-82); inventor: Detergent Lube Comp. (Pat. #3405065, 1968), Method of Oper. & Lube (Pat. #3426738, 1969); publs: 8+ tech. papers; mil: cpl. US Army 1952-54; Republican; Prot.; rec: early Ford V-8, collector antique toys. Res: 1423 Enchanted Way San Mateo 94402

GOODYEAR, NELSON, educator, design engineer; b. Jan. 12, 1912, NYC; s. Nelson, Sr. and Katherine G.; m. Barbara H., March 1945; children: Charles, Lydia, Katherine; m. 2d, June, May 1956; son, Lawrence; m. Virginia, May 9, 1972; edn: BA in languages, and MA in secondary edn., Columbia Univ., 1933, 1950; PhD, Calif. Christian Univ., 1972; pub. adminstrn., Yale. Career: private sch. tchr. and bus. mgr., 1934-39; insp. defense industries, 1939-44; industrial engr., cons. US War Dept., Venezuela "Aeropostal" airlines, Canadian textile, leather & processing industries; technical writer, 1950-72; prof. of industrial mgmt. Syracuse Univ. 1947-50, USC 1950-52; v.pres. and dean Calif. Christian Univ., 1972-81; real estate investor, mgr. 1970–; honors: Sigma Iota Epsilon, rec'd 87 war prodn. suggestion awards from Pratt & Whitney and Brewster Aeronautical Corp. 1939-43; mem: SAIE, AAUP, Inst. of Human Engineering Scis., Psi Upsilon Frat.; inventions: rubber tire drafting aid for H.S. students and designers, a tool and hardware rack, an electro-mech. recusitator (devel. for USN Bur. of Aero. Spl. Devices Div.), low-cost microfilming sys., Office Organizer (U.S. Pat. 1987), others; mil: seaman USN 1943-45; rec: swimming, chess, bridge, fencing coach. Res: 15111 Bushard Sp23 Westminster 92683

GORBIS, BORIS ZINOVJEVICH, lawyer; b. Aug. 29, 1950, Odessa, USSR, nat. US cit. 1985; s. Zinovy R. and Nelli (Goldenstein) G.; m. Eda Jacobashvili, Nov. 29, 1981; children: Andrew Rafael b. 1985, Alexander Ariel b. 1992; edn: BS, Odessa Inst. Tech. 1969; MA, Univ. Odessa 1972; JD, UC Berkeley 1980; admitted to bar Calif. 1980. Career: immigrated to US 1975; pres. RETTCO 1976-80; atty., assoc. Graham & James, Los Angeles 1980-82; founding atty. Law Offices of Gorbis & Liberty, Los Angeles, San Francisco, Moscow (Russia), Kiev (Ukraine), 1982–; vis. prof. Stanford Univ. 1976; bd. dirs. Am. Jewish Congress, S.F. 1976, Westside JCC, L.A. 1982-84; bd. dirs., exec. com. Los Angeles Jewish Comm. Relations Council 1991–; bd. dirs. Wilstein Inst. Jewish Policy Studies 1991–; vis. prof. Odessa Univ. Sch. of Law 1992; mem: ABA, Calif. Bar Assn. 1980–, Calif. Trial Lawyers Assn., LA Trial Lawyers Assn., past pres. (2 terms) Internat. Law Soc. of Boalt Hall 1977-79; civic: New Times, Guardians; Republican (Repub. Senatl. Inner Circle, Russian Repub. Club, fin. bd.); publs. (5) in psycholinguistics and gen. theory of communication; rec: pol. and advt. button collector, New Americans contbn. to Am. culture. Res: 1201 Delresto Dr Beverly Hills 90210

GORDON, CLAUDE EUGENE, musician; b. Apr. 5, 1916, Helena, Mont.; s. James Austin and Nellie G. (Elge) G.; m. Genevieve Alice Pentecost, Apr. 19, 1936 (dec. 1988); 2 sons: Gary Anthony, Steven Robert; m. Patricia J. Kasarda, Sept. 22, 1990; (hon.) MusD in music and letters, La Sierra Univ., Riverside 1992. Career: trumpeter NBC, CBS, motion pictures, Los Angeles 1937-69; first trumpet big bands, stage shows, hotels, 1937-44, CBS, Hollywood 1944-56; orchestra leader, Los Angeles and nat. tours, 1950-69; conductor TV mus., stage shows for stars, Los Angeles, Las Vegas, Reno, 1960-69; lectr., instr. in clinics Mich. Univ., No. Ill. Univ., Fla. State Univ., No. Texas State Univ., others, 1970-87; instr. Claude Gordon Internat. Brass Camp, La Sierra Univ., Riverside; author: Brass Playing Is No Harder Than Deep Breathing, The Physical Approach to Elementary Brass Playing, Systematic Approach to Daily Practice, Daily Trumpet Routines, Tongue Level Exercises, 30 Velocity Studies; annotator: Arban Complete Method, 1982 (all Carl Fischer publications); instrument designer: CG Benge trumpet, 1960, CG Personal mouthpiece for trumpet, cornet and flugel horn, 1974, Claude Gordon Selmer trumpet, 1977; rec: pvt. pilot. Ofc: CG Music Enterprises PO Box 546 Big Bear Lake 92315-0546

GORDON, DAVID ELIOT, lawyer; b. March 8, 1949, Santa Monica; s. Sam and Sadie (Wahl) G.; m. Mary Debora Lane, March 5, 1978; edn: BA, Harvard Univ. 1969; JD, 1972; admitted St. Bar Calif. 1973. Career: ptnr. O'Melveny & Myers, Los Angeles 1972–; mem: Am. Bar Assn. L.A. Co. Bar Assn. (tax sect.); num. articles on employee benefits pub. in profl. jours.; rec: squash. Ofc: O'Melveny & Myers 400 S Hope St Ste 1500 Los Angeles 90071-2899

GORDON, HELEN HEIGHTSMAN, writer, English professor; b. Sept. 7, 1932, Salt Lake City; d. Fred C. and Florence (Hale) H.; m. Norman C. Winn, Aug. 10, 1950 (div. Sept. 1972); children: Bruce b. 1954, Brent b. 1957, Holly b. 1959; m. Clifton B. Gordon, Feb. 17, 1974; edn: BA in English, CSU Sacramento, 1964, MA, 1967; EdD, Nova Univ., Ft. Lauderdale, 1979. Career: assoc. prof. English, Porterville Coll., 1967-74; prof. English, Bakersfield Coll., 1974–; mem. and contbr. to jour., English Council of Calif. 2-yr. Colls., 1979–, dir. Region V, 1990-92; presenter at confs.: English Council of Calif. 1991, also at Western Coll. Reading & Learning Assn., Calif. Assn. Tchrs. of English, SW Reg. English Tchrs. Conf., Calif. Tchrs. of English as a Second Language, Nat. Assn. of Developmental Educators and Assn. of Calif. Colls. Tutorial & Learning Assistance; awards: honors pgm. Univ. Utah, S.L.C. 1960, 61, outstanding educator Porterville Coll. 1972, 73, Am. Assn. of Women in Comm. and Jr. Colls. nat. leaders conf. 1983, 85 also Service to Women reg. award, Bakersfield 1991, guest mem. editorial bd. Bakersfield Californian 1988, L.W.V. Calif. distinctive feature writing 1990; mem.: NEA (1967-life), Nat. Council of Tchrs. of English 1967–, Am. Assn. of Women in Comm. & Jr. Colls. (1983–, chapt. pres. 1989), Textbook Authors Assn. 1987–, AAUW, L.W.V. Bakersfield (pres. 1981-83, 89-90); author textbooks: From Copying To Creating (1981, 85), Wordforms: I, II (1985, 90), Developing College Writing (1989), Interplay:

Sentences In Context (1991), 20+ articles and resrch. reports; Democrat; Unitarian (Fellowship of Kern Co. pres. 1975-77); rec: bowling, tennis, reading, films, discussion groups. Res: 6400 Westlake Dr Bakersfield 93308-6519 Ofc: English Dept. Bakersfield College, 1801 Panorama Dr Bakersfield 93305

GORDON, JEFFREY LAWRENCE, telephone company marketing executive; b. Aug. 30, 1956, Cleveland, Ohio; s. Gerald N. and Myrna B. (Meister) G.; m. Constance, Sept. 14, 1986; edn: BA, San Diego St. Univ. 1978; MA, Claremont Grad. Sch. 1981. Career: CATV consultant Coral Group, Manhattan Beach 1981-82; telecomms. cons./pres. J&L Gordon & Assoc., Santa Monica 1982-84; staff mgr. Pacific Bell, San Francisco 1984-86, dir. product mktg. 1986, dir. bus. market strategy 1986-87, district sales mgr. 1987-90, v.p. public sector Bay region Pacific Bell, 1991, dir. process re-engring., marketing/sales 1992-94, quality re-engring. 1994–; fellow Coro Found., St. Louis, Mo. 1979-80; cons. CATV 1982-84; awards: Pacific Bell Marketing Leader 1985, Outstanding Young Men in Am.; mem. Jewish Community Rels. Com. East Bay.; contbr. articles to profl. jours.; Democrat; Jewish; rec: books, films. Ofc: Pacific Bell 2600 Camino Ramon Rm 2E104 San Ramon 94583

GORDON, JERRY A., university administrator; b. April 27, 1939, Rochester, N.Y.; s. Philip R. and Grace (Itkin) G.; m. Susan Gerring, June 24, 1962; children: Julie b. 1968, Lili b. 1970; edn: BS, Ithaca Coll. 1962; MS, Syracuse Univ. 1966; EdD, SUNY at Buffalo, 1979. Career: dir. media service Westhill Schs., Syracuse, N.Y. 1965-66; instr. St. Univ. N.Y., Fredonia 1966-69; assoc. prof. Alfred St. Coll., N.Y. 1969-82; dir. media resources UC Riverside 1982-94, dir. of distance learning and instrtional devel. 1994–; mem: Directors of Ednl. Meda/Calif. Higher Edn. (past pres., co-founder), Internat. TV Assn., Assn. Ednl. Comms. & Tech., Consortium of Coll. & Univ. Media Centers; Democrat; Jewish; rec: travel. Res: 375 Two Trees Rd Riverside 92507-3225 Ofc: Univ. of Calif. Riverside 92521

GORDON, KENNETH LEE, physician, ophthalmologist; b. June 1, 1948; s. Arnold J. and Claire (Levine) G.; m. Debra Chernoff, June 18, 1978; children: Michael b. 1979, Dara b. 1981, David b. 1986; edn: BS, Univ. Oreg. 1970; MD, Tulane Univ. Sch. Medicine 1974. Career: ophthalmologist, founder/dir. Beverly Hills Eye Inst., Beverly Hills 1979–; chief ophth. Beverly Hills Med. Center 1984–; mem: A.C.S. (fellow), Am. Coll. Eye Surgeons (fellow), Contact Lens Assn. of Ophthalmologists, L.A. Co. Med. Assn., Beverly Hills C.of C.; Republican; Jewish; rec: sports, history. Ofc: 2080 Century Park East #800, Los Angeles, CA 90067

GORDON, MARILYN, clinical hypnotherapist, author, teacher; b. Dec. 11, 1940, Chgo.; d. Harold David and Gertrude (Goldman) Goldberg; div., 1 child, Dana b. 1964; edn: BA in English, Univ. Mich., 1962; grad. studies Univ. Calif. Berkeley; counseling psych. JFK Univ., Orinda; cert. clinical hypnotherapist, 1974. Career: sch. tchr., English lang. & lit., Chgo. Bd. of Edn., Ill. 1965-69; tchr. lang. arts, yoga, Evelyn Wood, Marin County, Calif. 1970-89; clin. hypnotherapist, pvt. practice, 1974–, tchr., writer, tnr., consultant; honors: Phi Beta Kappa 1962, Phi Kappa Phi 1962, Pi Lambda Theta 1962; mem. Am. Council of Hypnotist Examiners 1987–, Nat. Guild of Hypnotists 1989–; author: Healing is Remembering Who You Are (1990), Manual for Transformational Healing with Hypnotherapy (1993); contr. author: Journal of Hypnotism (1992, 93); speaker Internat. Hypnotherapy Conf. 1990-93; audio video tapes, radio and tv appearances; rec: yoga, meditation. Ofc: PO Box 10795 Oakland 94610

GORDON, RUTH VIDA, structural engineer; b. Sept. 19, 1926, Seattle; d. Solomon Alexander and Leah (Yoffe) Gordon; m. Michael Herbert Schnapp, Sept. 28, 1949; children: Madeline Ruth b. 1954, Marcia Lea b. 1955, Michael Gordon b. 1957; edn: BS, Stanford Univ., 1948, MS, 1949; Calif. lic. Civil Engr. 1953, Structural Engr. 1959 (first woman). Career: structural designer Isadore Thompson, Consulting Engr., San Francisco 1950-51; K. P. Norrie, Cons. Engr., Spokane, Wash. 1951; Bechtel Corp., San Francisco 1951-53; civil engr. CAL-TRANS, S.F. 1953-54; struct. designer Russell Fuller, Cons. Engr., S.F. 1954; Western Knapp Engring. Corp., S.F. 1954-55; struct. engring. assoc. struct. safety sect. Calif. State Architect, S.F. 1956-57, senior struct. designer 1957-59 (first woman), senior struct. engr. 1959-76 (first woman), dist. struct. engr. 1976-86 (first woman); pres. Pegasus Engring. Inc., 1984–; appt. Yacht Harbor Advy. Com., S.F. Rec. & Park Dept. 1986-88, advy. com. master plan S.F. Unified Sch. Dist. 1971-72, engr. mem. of advy. panel Calif. Bd. Archtl. Examiners examination revision project 1979-81; awards: Margaret Byrne undergrad. scholar 1943-45, Wing and Garland scholar C.E. Stanford Univ. Grad. Sch. (1st woman recipient 1948-49), woman of achiev. Union Sq. BPW (1975, 82), outstanding svc. Soc. Women Engrs. Golden Gate (1979, 84), Calif. Fedn. of BPW Top Hat Award 1978-79, Working Woman Mag. achiev. 1983, Calif. Dept. Gen. Svs. profl. proficiency 1984, Inducted into Calif. Fedn. of Bus. and Profl. Women BPW Hall of Fame in recogn. of outstanding achiev. field of sci. 1992, Tau Beta Pi Engring. Soc. Eminent Engr. Award 1995; mem: Struct. Engrs. Assn. No. Calif. (first woman mem. 1953, legis. com. chair 1978-79, del. Calif. Legis. Coun. 1978-79, dir. 1984-86), SF Bay Area Engring. Coun. (dir. 1977-79, first woman pres. 1982-83), Nat. Soc. of Women Engrs. (affirmative action coord. 1979-80, Golden Gate sect. pres. 1978-79, nat. conv. v.ch. 1979, affirmative action chair 1979-80, 84–),

ASCE, Math/Sci. Network Coun., Assn. for Women in Sci.; clubs: Union Square BPW, Golden Gate Yacht (sail fleet capt. 1987-88, dir. 1991-93), S.F. Yacht (Aux.), Yacht Racing Assn. S.F. Bay (cert. race ofcr.), US Sailing Assn. (sr. judge, race mgmt. com., sr. race ofcr., N. CA & NV race ofcr.); Democrat (S.F. Dem. Women's Forum, dir. 1976-78, 79-81, 82-83, 85-87, 91-92); rec: sailing, knitting, reading, puzzles. Res: 726-23rd Ave San Francisco 94121 Ofc: Pegasus Engineering, Inc. PO Box 210425 San Francisco 94121-0425

GORELICK, ELLEN CATHERINE, museum director-curator, artist, art history educator, civic volunteer; b. Jan. 2, 1946, Chicago, Ill.; d. Martin Francis and Doris Harriet (Adams) Heckmann; m. Walter Lee Gorelick, Dec. 19, 1970; edn: AA cum laude, Coll. of Sequoias 1966; BA cum laude, CSU Fresno 1979; MA, 1982; Career: book div. correspondent Time Inc., Chgo., Ill. 1964-68; accounts receivable supr. Tab Products Co., San Francisco 1968-69; exec.secty. Foremost McKesson Inc., San Francisco 1969-71; McCarthy Land Co., Visalia 1972-74; adminstrv. dir. Creative Center for Handicapped 1979-80; curator Tulare Hist. Museum, Tulare 1984-87; adj. faculty Coll. of Sequoias, Visalia 1985–; dir.-curator Tulare Hist. Museum 1994–; civic bds: Tulare-Kings Regional Arts Council (pres. 1989-90), Tulare County Art League (pres. 1977-78), Leadership Tulare (CORE com. 1991-93, Alumni chair 1992-93), Tulare Co. Univ. Calif. Campus Expansion Task Force, Visalia 1988-91, Tulare City Sch. Dist. Classrooms for Kids Campaign (co-chair 1989), Tulare City Historical Soc. Long Range Planning Com. 1991–, Tulare Co. Sym. Assn. (1992–, sec. 1993–), "Taste Treats in Tulare" Fundraiser (co-chair 1991), City of Tulare Community Improvement Com. 1992–; honors: Phi Kappa Phi, Alpha Gamma Sigma, Soroptimist Internat. of Tulare Women of Distinction Award 1994, appreciation awards: City of Tulare 1989, Tulare County Bd. Suprs. 1991, Tulare Dist. Hosp. 1991, Tulare Board of Realtors 1990, named Artist of Year Tulare Palette Club 1985, Tulare Co. Reg. Arts Council 1988, Outstanding Young Women of Am. 1979; mem: Les Petits Amis (pres. 1988-89), Valley Oak Garden Club, Tulare Co. Womens Symphony League, Acorn Garden Club (pres. 1981-82), Lawyers Wives of Tulare Co. (pres. 1979-89), Tulare Palette Club (pres. 1984-85); artist intaglio print, The Dream (Best of Show Tulare Co. Art League 1983); Tulare Co. Fair Ball Jar Award 1993; Democrat; R.Cath.; rec: photog., cooking. Res: 433 E Chevy Chase Dr Tulare 93274 Ofc: College of the Sequoias 915 S Mooney Blvd Visalia 93277

GORELICK, WALTER LEE, judge; b. Mar. 30, 1945, Los Angeles; s. Leon and Dr. Molly C. (Chernow) G.; m. Ellen, Dec. 19, 1970; edn: BA, UC Los Angeles, 1967; JD, Golden Gate Univ., 1970; cert. specialist criminal law (1977). Career: deputy public defender, asst. pub. defender, chief pub. defender Public Defender's Office of Tulare County, Visalia 1971-80; judge Tulare-Pixley Municipal Court, 1980–; faculty Calif. Judicial Coll., 1983; U.S. advisor Asian Legal Research Inst., Japan 1978-80; Drug Abuse Advy. Bd. to Tulare County Board of Suprs. 1978-87; honors: Outstanding Young Men Am. 1981, Who's Who in Am. Law (1st, 2d edits); civic: Greater Tulare C.of C. 1981–, U.S. Constitution Bicentennial Com. of Tulare 1987-88, Tulare Dist. Hosp. Found. (bd. 1987–), Tulare City Historical Soc. (charter 1984–); author/editor 5 books: The Rights of Victims and Witnesses under California Law (1995, 1st edit.), Summary of California Evidence and Trial Cases (1994, 1st edit.), Preliminary Hearing Courtroom Handbook (1986, 2nd edit. 1993), Summary of Calif. Driving Under the Influence of Alcohol Cases (1992, 4th edit.), Narcotics Law Manual (1988, rev. 1991), numerous articles on criminal law; rec: current events, gardening, collect stamps, rocks, fruit box labels. Res: 433 E Chevy Chase Dr Tulare 93274 Ofc: Tulare-Pixley Municipal Court 425 E Kern Ave Tulare 93274

GORMAN, RUSSELL WILLIAM, marketing professional, retired naval officer; b. Aug. 17, 1927, Glen Ridge, N.J.; s. Wm. Francis and Emily (Weldon) G.; m. Eriko Deguchi, Jun. 19, 1956; edn: BS marine transp., U.S. Merchant Marine Acad., Kings Point, L.I. 1949; lic. chief mate. Career: 2d mate Moore McCormack Lines, N.Y.C. 1949-53; dir. shipboard adminstrn. US Navy - MSTS Yokosuka, Japan 1953-57; tng. coord. Chevron Shipping Co., San Francisco 1957-77; mgr. orgn. & adminstrn. Utah Internat., S.F. 1977-84; pres. Lumier Inc., S.F. 1984-85; v.p. J. Perry Assocs., Concord 1985-87; pres. Market Development Assocs., Danville 1987–; served to RADM USNR (ret.) 1949-87: USN with Mil. Sea Transp. Service in Japan and Okinawa 1953-57; Dep. Cdr. Mil. Sealift Command 1983 Reserve dir. ops. on staff of the Cdr. Military Sealift Command, W.D.C. 1980-87, also served as COMSC Exercise Dir., active duty Dir. Joint Control Group Ocean Venture '84, MSC Pgm. monitor, NR Merchant Marine monitor, and mem. of Chief of Naval Reserve Flag Component; decorated Legion of Merit 1986, 1987, Navy Commendn. Medal 1978, various Area Service Awards, Merchant Marine Awards (2), CNO Merit Cert. for contributions. in Sea Power Pgm. (6); mem. Calif. Maritime Acad. curriculum advy. bd. 1973-84, cont. edn. advy. bd. 1974-85; mem: Naval Reserve Assn. (life, Polaris Chpt. pres. 1975-76, nat. v.p. membership 1988-89), Reserve Officers Assn. (Chpt. 8 v.p. Navy 1978–, chmn. mem. com. Calif. 1988, nat. chmn. Naval Affairs 1988, Nat. V.P. Navy 1992-93, Chmn. Long Range Planning 1993-95), Am. Soc. of Naval Engrs. (Golden Gate Sect. dir. 1975-78, 79-88), Navy League of U.S. (v.p. reserve affairs Oakland Council 1976–, S.F. Council com. 1973–, Pacific Cent. Region v.p. Navy Liaison 1987–), No. Calif. Com. for Support of the Guard & Reserve 1982–,

Naval Inst. Assoc. 1977–, Naval Order 1981–, US Merchant Marine Acad. Alumni Assn. (W. region gov. 1961-66, nat. v.p. 1967-71), S.F. Jr. C.of C. (exec. v.p. 1963-64), Am. Inst. of Merchant Shipping 1971-73, Am. Arbitration Assn., Bay Area Marine Inst. (dir. 1976-84), Am. Soc. for Tng. & Devel. 1969-75, Nat. Wildlife Assn. 1974-85, Assn. of Naval Aviation, Tailhook Assn., Naval Helicopter Assn.; civic: United Way of Bay Area (loaned exec. 1964, 65, 74, coord. Chevron Shipping 1969-75, Std. Oil Co. of Calif. 1976, Utah Intl. 1977-83, recipient Honor Award 5t.), Citizens Com. for Recycling of Solid Waste Contra Costa Co. 1972-74, Danville South HOA (bd. 1969-79), Woodview Devel. Archtl. Control Com. (chmn. 1983–); Republican (Presdl. election area chmn. 1964, 68, Presdl. Task Force 1982–, state coord. Vets. Coalition liaison Californians for Bush 1988, campaign spkr. for Sen. Pete Wilson 1988), Secty. of the Navy Adv. Bd. Naval Hist. 1990-93, Secty. of Defense Adv. Com. on Hist.-Naval Subcom. 1994–, Secty. of the Interior Adv. Commn. for S.F. Nat. Maritime Hist. Park (mem. 1991–, v.chmn. 1994); United Methodist; rec: wood working, gardening. Address: 46 Willowview Ct Danville 94526

GORNEY-LUCERO, MARY JO, nursing educator; b. Nov. 18, 1947, Harbor Beach, Mich.; d. Alice Rose Gorney; m. Jeffrey Fadiman, Jan. 7, 1978; edn: RN, St. Marys Sch. Nursing 1968; BA, Mich. St. Univ. 1971; MS, Univ. Mich. 1975; PhD, 1985. Career: assoc. prof. San Jose St. Univ. 1981-86; pres. Calif. Nurses Assn., Region 10, Santa Clara 1988-92; cons. Bd. Reg. Nursing, Sacto. 1985-93; adj. research prof. Stanford Univ., Palo Alto 1986-88, prof. 1986–; cons. San Jose Hosp. 1987-88, v.p. Bd. of Registered Nursing, Calif. 1994– honors: Sigma Theta Tau, San Jose St. Univ. Merit. Performance 1986, 88, Alpha Gamma Leadership 1987, Who's Who in Am. Nursing. 1986-95; mem: Calif. Nurses Assn., Am. Nurses Assn.; co-author Nursing Research, 1986, 1994 articles pub. in profl. jours., 1980-81. Ofc: San Jose State University HB420 San Jose 95192-0057

GOSSELIN, EDWARD ALBERIC, historian; b. Feb. 12, 1943, Rutland, Vt.; s. Alberic William and Marie Helen (L'Ange) G.; m. Claudia Isabel Hoffer, July 11, 1970; children: Elisabeth b. 1979, David b. 1982; edn: BA, Yale Univ., 1965; MA, Columbia Univ., 1966, PhD, 1973; auditeur Coll. de France, Paris, 1976. Career: lectr. Brooklyn Coll., 1966-68; asst. prof. CSU Long Beach, 1969-73, assoc. prof. 1973-79, prof. 1979–, chair history dept. 1986-93; editor The History Teacher, 1986–; awards: Fulbright fellow, Paris, Fr. 1968-69, NEH fellow, CSULB (1973-74, 80-81), NEH fellow, Univ. Chgo. 1977-78; mem: Soc. for History Edn. (exec. mem. 1986–), Societe Internat. de Didactiques de l'Histoire (editl. advy. bd. 1991–), Am. Hist. Assn. 1975–; author: King's Progress to Jerusalem, 1976, (book translator) Giordano Bruno's Ash Wednesday Supper, 1584 (1994), numerous jour. articles and revs., 1970–; Democrat; R.Cath.; rec: music -clarinet. Ofc: Dept. History Calif. State Univ., Long Beach 90840-1601

GOTHOLD, STUART E., Los Angeles County superintendent of schools (retired); b. Sept. 20, 1935, Los Angeles; s. Hubert Eugene and Adelaide Louise (Erickson) G.; m. Jane Ruth Soderberg, July 15, 1955; Jon b. 1956, Susan b. 1958, Eric b. 1967, Ruth b. 1970; edn: BA, Whittier Coll. 1956; MA, 1961; Ed.D, USC 1974. Career: tchr. El Rancho Unfied Sch. Dist., Pico Rivera 1956-61, prin. jr. h.s. 1961-66; curriculum cons. Los Angeles Co. Schs., Downey 1966-69; asst. supt. So. Whittier Sch. Dist., Whittier 1969-71, supt. 1971-77; asst. supt., chief deputy Los Angeles Co. Schs., Downey 1977-80, supt. 1980-94; asst. dean/clin. prof. Sch. of Edn., USC 1994–; adj. prof. Whittier Coll. 1975–; adj. instr. USC, Los Angeles; bd. mem. Nat. Center Fgn. Language, W.D.C. 1987–; advy. bd. mem. Nat. Computer Systems, Des Moines, Iowa 1988; awards: Delta Epsilon lectr. 1984, Whittier Coll. hon. LL.D 1988; mem: Calif. Assn. Co. Supts. (pres. 1980-81), Delta Epsilon (pres. 1982-83), Am. Assn. Sch. Adminstrs., Assn. Calif. Sch. Adminstrs., Rotary Internat.; author: Decisions: A Health Curriculum, 1971, Inquiry, A Way of Tchg. and Way of Learning, 1971; Republican; R.Cath.; rec: tennis, hiking, fishing, choral singing. Res: 10121 Pounds Ave Whittier 90603

GOTZMER, SHIRLEY ELIZABETH, manufacturer's representative, piano teacher; b. Jan 6, 1930, Chgo.; d. Carter Arno and Margaret L. (Schultz) Rehoff; m. John Degenar; m. Bruno Gotzmer, Jan. 19, 1980; children: Lynnette b. 1949, Michele b. 1958, Robert b. 1959, Tamara b. 1963; edn: music major, Carthage Coll., Ill. 1947-49; sociology degree 1972; spl. courses Ohlone Coll., Univ. Calif., CSU Hayward, John F. Kennedy Univ., (pub. adminstrn.) Anthony Sch. R.E., C.L. Williams; lic. insurance agt. 1984. Career: piano teacher own music studio, 1961–; buyer II, Contra Costa Co., 1979-81; founder, owner Gotzmer Enterprises 1981–, mfr.'s rep., devel. software programs; former buyer City of Concord (6 yrs), adminstrv. asst. to chief engr. Alameda Co. Water Dist. (3 yrs), exec. secty. Kaiser Steel and Kaiser Aluminum Chem. Co. (12 yrs); mem: Calif. Assn. Public Purch. Ofcrs. Inc. (secty. 1985–), Nat. Assn. Purch. Mgrs. No. Calif. 1973-79, civic: 700 Club (prayer counseling), Toastmasters, Homeowners Assn.; clubs: Sons of Norway, Flying Club of No. Calif. (emergency task force 1988-91), Benicia Golf Assn., Yacht Club; author technical books, var. manuals, geneology source book, composer and playwright; rec: golf, music, people, study, blues/jazz, travel. Res: 151 Mt Kennedy Dr Martinez 94553 Ofc: Contra Costa County 1220 Morello Ave Ste 101 Martinez 94553

GOUGH, AIDAN RICHARD, professor of law; b. May 22, 1934, Los Angeles; s. James Albert and Marian (Ford) G.; children: Michael James Tod b. 1956, Thomas Aidan b. 1965; edn: BA, Stanford Univ. 1956; MA, 1957; JD, Santa Clara Univ. 1962; LL.M, Harvard Univ. 1966; admitted St. Bar Calif. 1963, Supreme Ct. U.S. 1966. Career: dep. juvenile probation ofcr. Co. Santa Clara 1956-60; prof. law Santa Clara Univ. 1962–; exec. dir. govs. commn. on family St. of Calif., Sact. 1965; vis. prof. law Stanford Univ. 1971; acad. visitor, vis. prof. London Sch. Econ. and Political Sci., London 1973;adv. and spl. counsel for emergency svs., Co. of Santa Cruz 1989–, cons. emergency and legal medicine and pre-hosp. care San Francisco Gen. Hosp. Med. Center and Stanford Univ. Hosp. 1978–; dir. Lifeguard HMO, San Jose 1982-92; reporter Nat. Joint Commn. Juvenile Justice Standards, N.Y.C. 1970-76; awards: Nat. Emergency Nursing Disting. Service 1987, Ford Found. Fellowship 1965-66; mem: Am. Bar Assn., Nat. Health Lawyers Assn., Nat. Council Juvenile & Family Ct. Judges, Am. Coll. Legal Medicine, Santa Clara Co. Bar Assn., Univ. Golf Club Santa Clara; co-author, ed. Beyond Control, 1977, author Juvenile Justice Standards Relating to Non-Criminal Misbehavior, 1977, 38 articles pub. in profl. jours.; Republican; R.Cath.; rec: golf, fly fishing, bird watching. Ofc: Santa Clara University School of Law Santa Clara 95053

GOUGH, HARRISON GOULD, psychologist, professor emeritus; b. Feb. 25, 1921, Buffalo, Minn.; s. Harry Betzer and Aelfreda (Gould) G.; m. Kathryn Whittier, Jan. 23, 1943; 1 dau. Jane Kathryn b. 1950; edn: BA, summa cum laude, Univ. Minn. 1942, MA, 1947, PhD, 1949. Career: asst. prof. psychol. Univ. Minn. 1948-49; prof. psychol. and res. psychol. UC Berkeley 1949-86, prof. emeritus 1986–, chmn. psychol. dept. 1967-72, dir. Inst. of Personality Assessment and Research 1973-83; cons. clinical psychologist Veterans Adminstrn., 1950–, U.S. Army, 1987–; dir. Consulting Psychologists Press 1956–; appt. Res. Advy. Com. Calif. Dept. of Corrections, 1958-64; Res. advy. com. Calif. Dept. of Mental Hygiene, 1964-69; Gov.'s Advy. Com. on Mental Health 1968-72; Citizen's Advy. Council Calif. Dept. of Mental Health 1969-72; Clin. projects res. review com. NIMH, 1968-72; awards: Social Sci. Res. Council demobilization fellowship 1946-47, Fulbright Res. Fellow (1958-59, 1965-66), Guggenheim Found. Fellow 1965-66, Univ. of Calif. Berkeley Citation 1986, Bruno Klopfer Disting. Contbn. Award, Soc. for Personality Assessment 1987, Phi Beta Kappa; mem: Am. Psychol. Assn. (Fellow), Internat. Assn. for Cross-Cultural Psychology (Fellow), Soc. for Personality Assessment (Fellow), Calif. State Psychol. Assn. (pres. 1961), Commonwealth Club S.F., Soc. of Mayflower Descendants; author: the Adject. Check List, the Calif. Psychological Inv. and other psychol. tests, 200+ res. papers and monographs on topics of psychol. assessment, perception, cognition and psychodiagnostics, editorial affil. 10 American and fgn. psychol. jours.; mil: 1st lt. US Army 1942-46; Protestant. Res: POB 909 Pebble Beach 93953 Ofc: Dept. Psychology Univ. California Berkeley 94720

GOULIAN, MEHRAN, physician, scientist, educator; b. Dec. 31, 1929, Weehawken, NJ; s. Dicran and Shamiram (Mzrakjian) G.; m. Susan Ann Hook, Aug. 5, 1961; children: Eric, b. 1963; Mark, b. 1964; Jonathan, b. 1968; edn: MD, Columbia Univ., Coll. of Phys. & Surgeons, N.Y. 1954; AB, Columbia Coll., N.Y. 1950; career: fellow in medicine (hematology), Yale Univ. of Med., New Haven, CT 1959-60; res. fellow in medicine (hematology), Mass. General Hosp./Harvard Med. Sch., Cambridge, MA 1960, 1962-63; instr. in medicine, Mass. Gen. Hosp./Harvard Med. Sch. 1963-65; fellow in biochemistry, Stanford Univ. 1965-67; assoc. prof. of medicine, Univ. Chicago 1967-70; dir. Div. of Hem./Onc., Univ. Calif. San Diego, La Jolla 1970-78; prof. of medicine, Univ. Calif. San Diego 1970–; editorial bd., Jour. of Biological Chemistry 1983-89, 1990-92; awards: Phi Beta Kappa, Columbia Coll., N.Y. 1950; Alpha Omega Alpha, Columbia Univ. Coll. of Phys. & Surgeons, N.Y. 1953; mem: Am. Soc. of Biochem. & Molecular Biology; Am. Soc. for Clin. Investigation; Am. Soc. of Hematology; Assn. of Am. Phys.; author: 75 pub. works; mil: sr. asst. surgeon, USPHS 1955-57; rec: music; photography; res: 8433 Prestwick Dr., La Jolla 92037. Ofc: Univ. of Calif., San Diego, Dept. of Medicine (0613-G), La Jolla 92093-0613

GRABER-PASTRONE, SYLVIA LUJEAN, criminal defense trial lawyer; b. April 14, 1952, Freeman, S.Dak.; d. Arnold Erwin and Ella May (Bell) Graber; edn: BA, Bethel Coll. 1974; JD, Pepperdine Univ. Sch. Law 1977; admitted St. Bar Calif. 1977. Career: dep. pub. defender Riverside Co. Pub. Defenders Ofc. 1977–; mem: Am. Bar Assn., Calif. Attys. for Criminal Justice, Calif. Pub. Defenders Assn., Calif. St. Bar Assn., Nat. Assn. Criminal Defense Lawyers; Democrat; Mennonite. Ofc: Riverside Public Defenders Office 4200 Orange St Riverside 92501

GRADDY, ELIZABETH A., economist; b. Sept. 25, 1950, Harrisburg, Ark.; d. Henry T. and Catherine E. (Burrow) Graddy; m. Glen A. Reed; children: Acacia b. 1981, Alexandra b. 1987; edn: BA higest hons., Memphis St.Univ. 1974; PhD, Carnegie Mellon Univ. 1984. Career: asst. prof. USC, Los Angeles 1984-90, assoc. prof. 1990–, Vice Dean, Sch. of Public Admin. 1994–; awards: Sigma Xi, U.S. Dept. HEW doctoral fellow 1978-81; mem: Am. Econ. Assn., Assn. Pub. Policy Analysis & Mgmt., Inst. Mgmt. Sci., Western Econ. Assn.; 16 articles pub. Ofc: Univ. of So. Calif., VKC 363, Los Angeles 90089-0041

GRAFFT, WILLIAM DAVIS, superintendent of schools; b. Dec. 9, 1929, Ventura; s. Clark Francis and Aileen (Willard) G.; m. Marilyn, June 16, 1951; children: Katherine b. 1957, Paul b. 1959; edn: AB, UC Berkeley 1951; MA, 1959; Ed.D, 1966. Career: v.p., tchr., Oakland 1955-64; prin. Maxwell Park Sch. 1964-65; Ralph J. Bunche Sch. 1965-68; Glorietta Sch., Orinda 1968-70; asst. supt. Orinda Union Sch. Dist. 1970-78; supt. Mountain View Sch. Dist., Mountain View 1978-92; instr. UC Berkeley 1966-68; S.F. St. Univ. 1966-68; St. Mary's Coll., Moraga 1968; bd. mem. Whitney Edn. Found., Los Altos 1983-87; honors: St. Dept. Edn. Calif. Disting. Sch. 1985-86, 86-87, UC Berkeley Scaife scholar 1947-51; mem: Assn. Calif. Sch. Aminstrs. (chpt. pres.), Individualized Instn. Assn., Phi Delta Kappa, Assn. Supervision & Curricular Devel., Nat. Edn. Assn., Mountain View Rotary, YMCA (Mountain View), Sunnyvale Life Inc., Release to Renew (Orinda); articles pub. in profl. jours., 1968-87, dissertation 1966; mil: lt. comdr. USN 1952-55; Democrat; Presbyterian; rec: tennis. Res: 313 Lester Ct. Santa Clara 95051

GRAHAM, ROBERT GREGORY, contracts manager; b. May 7, 1958, Pasadena; s. Robert Atwood and Victoria Marie (Gallo) G.; m. Jeanne Marie Copeland; edn: BA in pol. sci., Whittier Coll., 1983; MPA, USC, 1985; certified profl. contracts mgr. (CPCM) NCMA, 1990. Career: sgt., E4, US Air Force, 1976-82: target intelligence March AFB, Calif. 1976-79, spl. intell. ops. Frankfurt, W.Ger. 1979-82, AF Commendn. medal 1980; weapons research US Navy, Naval Weapons Ctr., China Lake, Calif. 1985-87; weapons acquisition US Navy, Wash. DC 1987-89; satellite acquisition USAF, Los Angeles AFB, Calif. 1989–; Presdl. mgmt. intern USN, China Lake 1985-86, mem. Presdl. Transition Team, Bush Adminstrn., Wash. DC 1989; coord. Combined Fed. Campaign 1988, cabinet mem. Combined Fed. Campaign 1993-95); awards: hon. mem. Va. Young Repub. Fedn., chmn.'s award YR Nat. Fedn. Wash. DC 1988, outstanding coll. Repub. Whittier Coll. Republicans 1983, Milton Friedman Econ. Freedom Essay award Freedom Found. 1983/84, arms control disarmament essay award Arms Control Assn., L.A. 1985; mem: L.A. Area Conservative Network (chmn. 1988–, spl. events vol. nat.), Acad. of Political Sci. (life 1982–), Ctr. for the Study of the Presidency 1982–, Phi Sigma Alpha 1983, Nat. Contract Mgmt. Assn., William Penn Soc. 1982–; author: No Turning Back on This Road, 1986, Rebels, 1983; Republican (Repub. Nat. Com. 1984–, spl. events vol. 1985–); Cath. Ofc: SSD/PKVSI PO Box 92960 Los Angeles AFB Los Angeles 90009-2960

GRAHAM, ROBERT KLARK, optical manufacturer; b. June 9, 1906, Harbor Springs, Mich.; s. Frank Archie, DDS, and Ellen Fern (Klark) G.; m.Marta Everton, MD, Oct. 15, 1960; children: David b. 1935, Gregory b. 1937, Robin b. 1941, Janis b. 1947, Robert Jr. b. 1950, G. Wesley b. 1955, Marcia b. 1966, Christie b. 1969; edn: AB, Mich. St. Univ. 1933; BS, Ohio St. Univ. 1937. Career: with Bausch & Lomb Optical Co., Rochester, NY 1937-40; western mgr. Univis Lens Co., Dayton, Oh. 1940-44, asst. sales mgr., sales mgr. 1945-46; v.p./dir. Research Plastic Optics Co. 1946-48; founder/pres./bd. chmn. Armorlite Inc. 1947-78, in Pasadena 1947-48, Burbank 1948-73, San Marcos 1973-78; Graham Internat. Inc., Carlsbad 1978–; cons. 3M Co., 1978; dir: Orange City Bank 1978-80, Advanced Concepts Technology; lectr., optics, Loma Linda Univ.; honors: Nat. Eye Res. Found. citation "The man who made it safe to wear glasses" 1966, Frederik Wilhelm Herschel Gold Medal, Ger. 1958, Sigma Xi 1981; mem: life fellow AAAS, Intra-Sci. Res. Found. (dir., v.p.), Inst. for Res. on Morality (dir.), Mensa, Am. Inst. Physics Profls., Optical Soc. of Am., Am. Acad. of Optometry, Found. for the Advancement of Man (founder, trustee), Rotary; co-founder (w/Hermann J. Muller) Repository for Germinal Choice;O.D., Ohio State U. 1987, Doctor of Optical Science (Honoris Causa), Louis Pasteur Found., 1987; dist. alumnus, Ohio State U., 1987; author: The Evolution of Corneal Contact Lenses; The Future of Man; Five Changepoints of Intelligence; articles in Optical Jour., other sci. jours.; inventor: variable focus lens (US Pat. 2,269,905), corneal hybrid lens (US Pat. 4,166,255); directed devel. of hard resin lenses; Republican; Prot.; rec: farming, eugenics. Res: 3024 Sycamore Ln Escondido 92025 Ofc: Graham International Inc. 2141 Palomar Airport Rd Ste 300 Carlsbad 92009

GRAHAM, ROGER JOHN, professor of journalism and photography; b. Feb. 16, Phila.; s. Wm. K. and Peggy E. (Owens) G.; m. Debbie Kenyon, Dec. 28, 1991; children (by previous marriage): John b. 1968, Robb b. 1972; edn: AA, Los Angeles Valley Coll., 1961; BA, Fresno State Coll., 1962; MA, CSU Fresno, 1967; ABD, UCLA, 1976; Credentials: Elem., Secondary, Junior Coll., Counseling, Comm. Coll. Adminstrn. Career: newspaper staff Turlock Jour. 1962; Fresno Guide 1963; tchr. Riverdale Sch. 1964; Raisin City Sch. 1965; tchr., counselor State Prison, Jamestown 1966; tchr. Kirk Sch. 1966; tchr. trainer UCLA Western Center; prof. journalism and photog. Los Angeles Valley Coll. 1968–, dept. chair Journalism, Photography, and Media Arts, 1990–; vis. prof. Calif. Lutheran Coll. 1974, Pepperdine Univ. 1976, Internat. Edn. Prof., Spain, Summer 1990; awards: NEH Scholar 1981, L.A. Mayors outstanding citizen 1974, UCLA extraordinary svc. 1971, outstanding young men Am. 1971, Nat. Dedication Journalism (1972, 76); mem: Calif. Journalism Assn. Comm. Colls. (pres. 1972), Nat. Comm. Coll. Journalism Assn. (pres. 1978), Sigma Delta Xi, Phi Delta Kappa, Pi Lambda Theta; civic: Am. Legion, YMCA, Hayden's Com. on Schs., Democratic Club Pac. Palisades (pres. 1992), Sons of the Desert 1994;

author: Observations on the Mass Media 1976, and articles in The Journalist 1971-76; photo illustrator: The San Fernando Valley 1980; mil: USN 1957; Democrat; rec: hiking, photog. Res: 6516 Riggs Pl Los Angeles 90045 Ofc: LA Valley College 5800 Fulton Ave Van Nuys 91401

GRAMMATER, RUDOLF DIMITRI, retired construction executive; b. Nov. 29, 1910, Detroit; s. D.M. and Amelia (Busse) G.; m. Fredricka W. Cook, Aug. 18, 1943; 1 son, Douglas; edn: Pace Coll. 1928-32; LLB, Lincoln Univ., 1937; CPA, Calif.; admitted bar: Calif. 1938. Career: with Bechtel Corp., San Francisco, 1941-73, treas., v.p., 1955-62, v.p., 1962-71, dir. 1960-73, cons., 1973, v.p., dir. subsidiaries, 1955-71; mem.: Am. Inst. CPAs, Calif. Soc. CPAs, ABA, State Bar of Calif.; club: Menlo CC. Res: 50 Mounds Rd Apt 302 San Mateo 94402

GRANGER, CLIVE WILLIAM JOHN, econometrician; b. Sept. 4, 1934, Swansea, U.K.; s. Edward John and Evelyn Agnes (Hessey) G.; m. Patricia, May 14, 1960; children: Mark b. 1964, Claire b. 1968; edn: BA in math., Univ. Nottingham, England 1955, PhD, 1959, DSc, 1992. Career: lectr. Univ. of Nottingham 1956-63, prof. of statistics 1966-74; prof. economics UC San Diego, 1974–; Chancellor's Assoc. Chair 1994–; awards: Commonwealth fellow Harkness Found.(1959-60, fellow Econometric Soc. 1975, Guggenheim Fellow 1988, Fellow, Am. Acad. of Arts and Sciences; rec: walking, swimming, travel. Ofc: Univ. Calif. San Diego, Economics Dept., D-0508, La Jolla 92093

GRANLUND, THOMAS ARTHUR, management consultant; b. Mar. 1, 1951, Spokane, Wash.; s. William Arthur and Louise (Urie) G.; m. Jean MacRae Melvin, May 25, 1974 (div. 1991); edn: BA, Wash. State Univ., Pullman 1973, MBA, Gonzaga Univ., Spokane 1982. Career: 1st lt., B-52 navigator US Air Force, Fairchild AFB, Wash. 1973-78; adminstrv. mgr. Lockheed, Burbank, Ca. 1978-91; mgmt. cons., 1991–; honors: listed Who's Who in West (1992); Who's Who in the World mem. Wash. State Univ. Alumni Assn. (1990–); coauthor 2 screenplays: Identities (1988), Flash (1989). Res: 20924 West Ben Ct Santa Clarita 91350

GRANOFF, DAN M., physician, pharmaceutical company executive, research scientist; b. Jan. 22, 1944, NY, NY; s. N. Henry and Jeanette (Trum) G.; m. Alice Baghdassarian, Feb. 15, 1971 (div. 1986); children: Jeffrey b 1972, Jonathan b. 1972; edn: AB, Johns Hopkins, Baltimore, Md., 1965, MD 1968; pediatric internship 1968-69, Phila. Children's Hospital, Phila.; pediatric residency 1969-71 Johns Hopkins; fellowship, infectious diseases Case Western Reserve, Cleveland, Ohio 1973-75. Career: asst. chief pediatrics Valley Med. Ctr., Fresno, Calif. 1975-79; assoc. prof. Wash Univ. Sch. of Medicine, St. Louis, Mo. 1980-85, prof. of pediatrics 1985-93; dir. Div. of Pediatric Infectious Diseases, St. Louis Hosp. and Wash. Univ., St Louis, Mo. 1980-93; res. scientist Children's Hosp. Oakland Res. Inst., Oakland Calif. 1993–; exec. dir. Biocine Clin. Res., Chiron Corp., Emeryville, Calif. 1993-95; v.p. scientific affairs, Chiron Biocine 1995-; cons. Inst. of Medicine, Nat. Acad. of Scis., Res. Grants Prog., W.D.C. 1984-90; honors: Alpha Omega Alpha; mem: Am. Soc. of Clin. Investigation 1989–, Infectious Diseases Soc. of Am. (fellow), Soc. of Pediatric Res., Am. Acad. of Pediatrics (fellow, infectious diseases com. 1991-93), Am. Pediatric Soc., Am. Acad. of Microbiology (fellow); author/co-author: 100+ res. articles in peer-reviewed scientific jours.; editor (res. jour.): Pediatric Research, 1988-92; co-editor (book): Development and Clinical Uses of Haemophilus b Conjugate Vaccines, 1994; mil: maj. USAF 1973 75. Ofc: Chiron Corp. 4560 Horton St Emeryville 94608

GRANT, DAVID BROWNE, manufacturing company executive; b. Apr. 21, 1915, Sharonville, Ohio; s. David J. and Catherine Emma (Browne) G.; m. Elizabeth A. Connolly, May 17, 1942 (dec.); children: Ann b. 1943, Bonnie b. 1944, David b. 1947, Susan b. 1949, Mary b. 1951, James b. 1953, Patricia b. 1958; edn: BA cum laude, Colgate Univ., 1936; LLB, Yale Univ. Sch. of Law, 1939; admitted Mich. State Bar 1939. Career: atty. Law Offices Eddie Bryant/Vandeveer Haggerty, Detroit 1939-41; sales rep., reg. mgr. Mich., Empire Tool Co., Detroit 1941-42; sales rep. Stone Tool Co., LA 1945-47, pres. 1948-52; owner/pres. Tool Electrolizing Co., LA 1947-50; bd. chmn./pres. Electrolizing, Inc. 1950–; honors: Phi Beta Kappa 1936; mem: Am. Soc. Metals, Am. Rocket Soc., Inst. Aero & Astro., Phi Gamma Delta Frat.; clubs: Jonathan, Newport Beach CC, Braemar CC; mil: lt. USNR 1942-47; Republican; Catholic (St. Timothy's Lector Soc., W.L.A. 1964-84, Our Lady Queen of Angels Ch. N.B. Ushers' Soc. 1984–); rec: golf, swim. Res/Ofc: 3 Northampton Ct Newport Beach 92660

GRANT, LORRAINE DENISE, journalist; b. Oct. 29, 1965, Vallejo, Calif.; d. Charles Edward and Edna Joann (Morris) Grant; edn: diploma, Vallejo Sr. H.S., Vallejo, Calif.; Solano Coll., Suisun, Calif.; BA in journalism, San Jose State Coll., San Jose, Calif. Career: chief managing ed., Buffalo Soldier Newsmagazine, San Jose, 1990-92; managing ed., Exodus Newsmagazine, San Jose, 1993–; comms. chairperson, NAACP, San Jose, 1993–; rec: writing poetry, reading, cooking, shopping, listening to music.

GRANVILLE, RONALD VINCENT, real estate investment executive; b. Oct. 23, 1952, San Francisco; s. Joseph James and Margaret Mary (Walsh) G.; m. Catherine Anne Alich, Oct. 26, 1974; children: Jennifer b. 1979, Lauren b. 1984;

edn: BA, UC Berkeley 1974; Cert. Property Mgr. (CPM) 1979. Career: pres. Woodmont Cos., Belmont 1974–; faculty Coll. of San Mateo 1978-85; mem: Calif. Housing Council (pres. 1989, dir. 1986–), Tri Co. Apartment Assn. (pres. 1985-86, dir. 1980-88, trustee 1983–), Inst. Real Estate Mgmt. (S.F. chpt. dir., v.p. 1987-89), San Mateo Co. Devel. Assn., Urban Land Inst.; Republican; rec: bicycling, jogging. Ofc: Woodmont Cos. 1050 Ralston Ave Belmont 94002

GRASS, ALAN BRIAN, lawyer; b. Dec. 13, 1942, Detroit, Mich.; s. Morton M. and Toba (Davidson) G.; m. Julie C. Grass, May 27, 1978; children: Benjamin b. 1980, Jonathan b. 1982; edn: BA, Univ. Mich. 1964; JD, Harvard Law Sch. 1967; admitted St. Bar Calif. 1980, St. Bar Mich. 1968. Career: atty. Bizer Sommers & Gordon, Detroit, Mich. 1968-72; ptnr. Schlussel Lifton 1972-76; Goldstein Serlin & Grass, Southfield, Mich. 1976-79; atty. Brent & Herzog, Los Angeles 1979-81, of counsel, Memel, Jacobs, & Ellsworth 1981-87, of counsel, Agapay, Levyn & Halling, 1991–; assoc. prof. law Whittier Coll. Sch. of Law 1983-87, prof., Univ. of So. Calif., Sch. of Accounting 1990–; of counsel Hirschtick Chenen Lemon & Curtis, Los Angeles and Marina del Rey 1987-91; assoc. prof. Whittier Coll. Sch. of Law, 1983-87; panelist Calif. Cont. Edn. of Bar 1982-84; mem: Am. Bar Assn., L.A. Co. Bar Assn., Beverly Hills Bar Assn., Temple Isaiah (bd. trustees 1988-93); Democrat; Jewish; rec: sports, music. Ofc: 10801 Natl. Blvd., Ste 400, Los Angeles, CA 90064

GRASSMAN, CURTIS EDWIN, university administrator; b. Dec. 7, 1942, Kearny, N.J.; s. Elmer Edward and Eunice (Wagner) G.; m. Marilyn Claire Morris, Dec. 17, 1966; children: Colin b. 1971, Carina b. 1980; edn: BA cum laude, Rutgers Univ. 1965; MA, UCLA 1966; PhD, 1970. Career: tchg. fellow UCLA 1966-69; lectr. hist. CSU 1968-72, UC Riverside 1972-77; ombudsman 1975-81, adminstv. dean 1980–; pres. Co. Bd. Edn., Riverside 1990-91, mem. 1986–; cons. UC Riverside 1986-90; chmn. City Parks Commn. Riverside 1980-86; pres. City Hist. Bd. 1979; honors: Phi Beta Kappa pres. 1985; mem: Riverside Downtown Assn., Calif. Sch. Bd. Assn., Acad. Booster Club North H.S. (pres. 1987-88); edn. and history articles pub. in profl. jours., 1972-88; mil: capt. USAR 1970-76; Democrat; Presbyterian; rec: classic car collecting. Res: 2980 Locust St Riverside 92501 Ofc: Univ. of Calif. UCR Extension CenterRiverside 92521

GRATER, MARGARET KAY, educator; b. July 12, 1942, Cedar City, Utah; d. Russell K. and Evelyn P. Grater; edn: BA, CSU Long Beach 1966; MA, CSU Fresno 1972; PhD, Univ. So. Carolina, 1975. Career: tchr. St. Mary's Jr. H.S., Augusta, Ga 1966-67, Adult Edn. Ctr., Camp Darby, Italy 1967, Woodlake H.S., Woodlake, Calif. 1968-69; staff devel. coord. Fresno Unif. Sch. Dist. 1971-73, 1975; instr., coord. Model Schs. Proj., Univ. S. Carolina 1973-75; prin. Norwalk, La Mirada Unif. Sch. Dist. 1975-80; coord. L.A. Co. Ednl. Resource Consortium (LACERC), L.A. Co. Supt. of Schs. Ofc., Downey 1980-84; cons., Mgmt. Devel. Ctr., L.A. Co. Ofc. of Edn. 1984-92; mgmt. cons. Center for District Leadership, 1992–; pres. Grater & Assocs., Leaders in Excellence Cons. Firm 1986–; instr. sch. adminstrn., CSU Fullerton Grad. Sch. 1980–; instr. ext. classes CSU Fresno, Pepperdine Univ., UC Santa Cruz 1968-78; cons. var. states, dists. 1968–; honors: merit awards, Assn. of Calif. Sch. Adminstrs., Norwalk La Mirada Adminstrn. Assn., Am. Red Cross/Europe 10-Year Svc. Award; mem: CSU Fullerton Educ. Adminstr. Adv. Bd. 1980–, Assn. of Calif. Sch. Adminstrs. (reg. v.p. 1980-82, reg. dir. 82-85, profl. stds. chair 85–) ALA-COSA (charter v.p. pgms. 1982–, pres. 1984, pres. elect 1992), Norwalk La Mirada Adminstrn. Assn. (pres. 1978-79), L.A. C.of C. (Edn. Com. 1980–), Assn. of Supvn. & Curriculum Devel. 1977–, Phi Delta Kappa (CSUF chpt. v.p. mem. 1986-87), CSUF Partnership Acad. 1982–, La Mirada Coord. Council (parliamentarian 1975-80), Dist. PTA 1975-80; co-author Task Force Report to Calif. Commn. for Tchr. Licensing (1981), Tchr. Preservice & Inservice (1982); Presbyterian; rec: tennis, music, art, writing. Res: 918 Magnolia Ave Placentia 92670 Ofc: Los Angeles Supt. o Schools, 9300 Imperial Hwy Downey 90242

GRAY, IONE YOUNG, lawyer, author, lecturer; b. June 15, 1947, Fort Worth, Tx.; d. Earle Francis and Ione Caddie (Young) Gray; edn: BA, Rice Univ., 1968; JD, Columbia Univ., 1971; admitted bar: Ga., Ill., Calif.; lic. R.E. Broker, Calif. 1976. Career: atty. Paul Weiss Rifkind Wharton & Garrison, NYC 1971; Hansell Post Brandon & Dorsey, Atlanta 1973; legal counsel (highest ranking woman) Caterpillar Tractor Co., Peoria, Ill. 1974; division counsel (highest ranking woman) Whittaker Corp., Los Angeles 1975; division counsel (highest ranking woman) The Colwell Co., L.A. 1976; atty. Law Offices of Ione Young Gray, L.A. 1977–; author: Buy Property Without Cash (1980), Foreclosure Purchasing For Profit (1982), Riches in R.E.O. Investing (1986); guest lectr. UCLA Business Sch., 1982–; show host (t.v.) Riches in Real Estate, 1983–, (radio) Profits in Real Estate, 1984–; mem. State Bar Assns. Ga., Ill., Calif., Women in Business (L.A.). Ofc: 2040 Ave of the Stars Ste 400 Los Angeles 90067

GRAY, JAN CHARLES, lawyer, executive; b. June 15, 1947, Des Moines, Iowa; s. Charles Donald and Mary C. Gray; children: Charles Jan b. Feb. 3, 1990; BA econ., UC Berkeley 1969; JD, Harvard Law Sch. 1972; MBA, Pepperdine Univ. 1986; admitted bar Calif. 1972, D.C. 1974, Wyoming 1992; lic. R.E. broker 1973. Career: atty., assoc. Halstead, Baker & Sterling, L.A. 1972-75; senior v.p., gen. counsel and secty. Ralphs Grocery Co., L.A. 1975–;

real estate broker, L.A. 1973–; owner American Presidents Resorts, opr.: All American Inn: Custer, American Presidents Cabins & Camp, American Presidents Motel, Custer Motel, French Creek Motel , Custer, S.Dak., All American: Glenrock, Glenrock Motel , Glenrock, Wyo., Big Bear Cabins: Lakeside , Big Bear, Calif.; pres. and c.o.o. Mt. Rushmore Bdcstg. Inc., Radio Station KFCR, Custer, S.Dak.; KZMX, Hot Springs, S.Dak.; KGOS/KERM, Torrington, WY; KRAL/KIQZ, Rawlins, WY; KQLT-FM, Casper, WY; judge pro tem L.A. Municipal Ct. 1977-85; instr. bus. UCLA 1976-85, MBA pgm. Pepperdine Univ. 1983-85; arbitrator, Am. Arb. Assn., 1977–; honors: Phi Beta Kappa, recipient So. Calif. Grocers Assn. award for outstanding contbns. to food industry 1982, Cal-Nev Soft Drink Assn. appreciation award for No on 11 campaign 1983; civic bds: South Bay Univ. Coll. Law, (bd. trustees 1978-79), Southwestern Univ. Sch. of Law (bd. vis. 1983–), L.A. City Employees Ret. System Commn. 1993–, L.A. County Pvt. Industry Council (1982–, exec. com. 1984–, chmn. econ. devel. task force 1986–, chair mktg. com. 1991–), M.L.K. Jr. Gen. Hosp. Auth. 1984–, Aviation Commn. (1986-92, chair 1990-91), L.A. Crime Prevention Advy. Council 1986–, Angelus Plaza Advy. Bd. 1983-85, RecyCAL of So. Calif. (bd. dirs. 1983-90), Santa Monica Hosp. (bd. trustees 1986-91; advy. bd. 1991–); mem. L.A. Co. Democratic Central Com. 1980-90, del. Dem. Nat. Conv. 1980; mem: ABA, Calif. Bar Assn. (conv. del. 1976-81), L.A. Co. Bar Assn. (bd. trustees 1991-93, exec. com. Corp Law Depts. Sect. 1975-76, 79–, chair 1989-90, exec. com. Barristers Sect. 1974-75, 79-81, Judicial Eval. Com. 1993–, Nom. Com. 1994), San Fernando Valley Bar Assn. (chmn. Real Prop. Sect. 1975-77), L.A. Pub. Affairs Officers Assn., L.A. World Affairs Council, Calif. Retailers Assn. (supermkt. com. 1977–), Food Mktg. Inst. (govt. relations com.), Lawyers & Economists (chair 1994–), Benefits Council 1993–, So. Calif. Business Assn. (chair 1991–, bd. 1981–, exec. com. 1982–, sec. 1986–), Town Hall Calif., Univ. Calif. Alumni Assn., Ephebian Soc.; clubs: L.A. Athletic, Harvard of So. Calif.; contbg. author: Life or Death: Who Controls? (Springer Pub. 1976); legal jour. articles; mil: USAR; R.Cath.; rec: tennis, travel. Res: 2793 Creston Dr L.A. 90068 Ofc: Ralphs Grocery Co. PO Box 54143 Los Angeles 90054

GRAY, ROBERT M., professor and vice chair of electrical engineering; b. Nov. 1, 1943, San Diego; s. Augustine Heard and Elizabeth Dubois (Jordan) G.; m. Arlene Francis Ericson; children: Timothy b. 1965, Lori b. 1967; edn: BS, MS, Mass. Inst. Tech., 1966; PhD, USC, 1969. Career: prof. elec. engring. Stanford Univ., 1969–, v.chmn. Dept. Of Elect. Engring. 1993–, dir. Information Systems Laboratory 1981-87; awards: 1976 paper prize IEEE Info. Theory Gp. 1976, 1983 ASSP Sr. Award IEEE ASSP Soc. 1984, IEEE Centennial Medal 1984, Society Award, SP Soc. 1993; Fellow Inst. of Electrical & Electronics Engrs. (1980, mem. 1969–), IEEE Info. Theory Gp. (bd. govs. 1974-80, 84-87, editor in chief IEEE Transactions in Info. Theory 1980-83, co-chair IEEE Internat. Symp. on Information Theory, Sa Antonio, Tx. 1993), Inst. of Math. Statistics (1974–, fellow 1992–), AAAS 1972–, Classification Soc. of N.Am. 1989–, Am. Math. Soc. 1990–; civic: La Honda Fire Brigade (fireman 1970-80, pres. 71-72); co-author: Random Processes, 1986, Vector Quantization & Signal Compression, 1992, Fourier Transforms, 1995; author: Probability, Random Processes, and Ergodic Properties,(1988, Source Coding Theory, 1990, Entropy and Info. Theory, 1990, 100+ tech. articles; rec: hiking, guilded age history. Ofc: E.E. Dept. Stanford Univ. 127 Durand Stanford 94305-4055

GRECU, EUGENE OVIDIU, physician; b. Feb. 24, 1941, Cimpia-Turzii, Romania; s. Eugen G. and Cornelia (Olteanu) G.; m. Kirsten R. Hammarstrand, Oct. 5, 1988; edn: Baccalaureate, H.S., Cluj, Romania 1957; MD, Med. Sch., Cluj, Romania 1964, PhD, endocrinology, Romania 1972. Career: endocrinologist Clinica de Endocrinologie, Cluj, Romania 1967-73; staff physician U.S. Army Hosp. (120th), Nuremberg, Germany 1973-74; chief med. ofcr. VA OPC, Sacramento, Calif. 1978-91; sr. investigator Aoki Diabetes Res. Inst., Sacramento 1991–; assoc. prof. internal medicine UC Davis Sch. of Medicine 1978-94; awards: VFW Dept. of Calif., VA. Employee of Yr. award 1983, State of Calif. Golden Seal award 1987, 89, 90; mem: Am. Fedn. for Clin. Res. 1978–, Am. Coll. of Physicians 1980–, Am. Endocrine Soc. 1980–, Am. Diabetes Assn. 1984- (dir., Sacto. 1980-83); author: 25+ scientific papers pub. in profl. jours., 1964–; Independent; Catholic; rec: tennis, reading, classical music. Ofc: Aoki Diabetes Research Institute 3100 O St Sacramento 95816 Tel: 916/455-2374

GREEN, HILTON A., motion picture producer; b. Mar. 3, 1929, Hollywood; s. Alfred E. and Vivian (Reed) G.; m. Helen Harker, June 6, 1952; children: Wendolyn b. 1954, Bradley b. 1958, Pamela b. 1960; edn: BS, USC, 1952. Career: executive v.p. Universal City Studios, 1968-82; producer H & H Green Productions, Pasadena 1982–; recipient USC Merit Award, L.A. 1982; mem. USC Bd. trustees 1990–; mem. Gen. Alumni Assn. USC (pres. 1991-92); club: Annandale Golf (Pasadena); mil: cpl. US Army 1952-54; Republican; R.Cath.; rec: golf, tennis. Res: 1134 Glen Oaks Blvd Pasadena 91105

GREEN, THERESA DIANE, social worker; b. Oct. 10, 1939, Port Angeles, Wash.; d. Walter Arnold and Edna Katherine (Lanich) Vickery; m. Sept. 5, 1964 (div. June 1983); children: Darrin Scott, Brian Allen; edn: BS in Psychology, Wash. State Univ., 1961; MSW, Univ. Denver, 1969; diplomate in Clin. Soc. Work, 1988. Career: child welfare worker Spokane County State Dept. Pub.

Assistance, Wash., 1962-64, State Dept. Pub. Assistance, Colfax, Wash., 1970-72; asst. prof. social work Wash. State Univ., Pullman, 1970-76; diagnostic intake worker, Whitman County Mental health, Pullman, 1974-76; child abuse psychiat. social worker, Humboldt Child Care Council, Eureka, 1978-84; pvt. practice in social work, Arcata, 1984–; cons. Hoffman Inst., San Francisco, 1984-86, Humboldt and Del Norte Counties, Eureka, 1985–, State Dept. Alcoholism Prevention, 1986-, Rural Human Services Domestic Violence Program Services to Children, 1986-88, Therapist to Child Victims of Domestic Violence; child abuse tnr. Inst. for the Advancement of Human Behavior; recipient Redwood Bdcstg. Heroism award 1982; named Outstanding Faculty Mem. of Yr. Wash. State Univ. 1974; mem. Nat. Assn. Social Workers (cert.), Acad. Cert. Social Workers, Women Against Pornography, Serious Legis. Against Molesters, Psi Chi; Democrat; rec: art, music, creative visualization. Address: 1179 Stromberg Ave Arcata 95521

GREENBERG, MYRON SILVER, lawyer; b. Oct. 17, 1945, Los Angeles; s. Earl W. and Geri (Silver) G.; m. Shlomit Gross, Aug. 23, 1985; children: David b. 1972, Amy b. 1975, Sophie b. 1989, Benjamin b. 1992; edn: BS in bus. adm., UCLA 1967, JD, 1970; admitted Calif. State Bar 1971; CPA, Calif. 1972; certified tax splst., Calif. Bd. Legal Spec. 1977; admitted to US Dist. Ct. (Central) Calif. 1971, US Tax Ct. 1978. Career: staff acct. Touche Ross & Co., Los Angeles 1970-71; assoc. Kaplan, Livingston, Goodwin, Berkowitz & Selvin, Beverly Hills 1971-74; ptnr. Dinkelspiel, Pelavin, Steefel & Levitt, S.F. 1975-80; ptnr. Steefel, Levitt & Weiss, S.F. 1981-82; atty. prin., Larkspur 1982–; profl. lectr. Golden Gate Univ.; lectr. UC Berkeley Ext. 1989–, advy. bd. Certificate Pgm. in Personal Financial Planning, UCB Ext. 1991–; planning com. Real Estate Tax Inst., Calif. Cont. Edn. of the Bar (CEB); honors: bd. editors UCLA Law Review; mem: ABA, Calif. Bar Assn., Marin County Bar Assn. (bd. dir. 1994–), L.A. County Bar Assn., Am. Inst. CPAs; civic: Am. Heart Assn. (bd. dirs., pres. Marin County chpt. 1983-90), Am. Technion Soc. (bd. dirs. No. Calif. chpt.), Larkspur C.of C. (bd. dirs.), San Anselmo Planning Commn. 1976-77, Marin Opera (bd. dirs. 1989-90); author: California Attorney's Guide to Professional Corporations, 1977, 1979; Democrat; Jewish. Ofc: Myron S. Greenberg, APC, 700 Larkspur Landing Circle Ste 205 Larkspur 94939

GREENFIELD, LAWRENCE RICHARD, lawyer, political consultant, businessman; b. Jan. 29, 1962, Long Beach; edn: AB (Class Valedictory Speaker), UC Berkeley, 1983; JD, Georgetown Univ. Law Ctr., 1986; admitted bar: Calif. 1987. Career: pvt. practice atty. at law, Sherman Oaks 1987–; pub. lectr. and political commentator 1986–, indep. political consultant/prin.; radio talk show host KIEV-AM Radio 1987, Glendale 1988; advy. cons. U.S. Congress, Wash. DC 1988–; mem: Calif. Young Lawyers Assn. (bd. 1989-92), L.A. World Affairs Council, Town Hall of Calif., B'nai B'rith Entertainment Lodge (Hywd.); internat. travels in Afghanistan, So. Africa, Namibia, Israel-West Bank, Central Am., Asia, 1986-. Ofc: 14755 Ventura Blvd Ste 1620 Sherman Oaks 91403 Ph: (310)277-4986

GREENHALL, CHARLES AUGUST, mathematician; b. May 5, 1939, N.Y.C.; s. A Frank and Miriam (Housman) G.; edn: BA, Pomona Coll., 1961; PhD, Caltech, 1966. Career: research assoc. Jet Propulsion Lab., Pasadena 1966-68; asst. prof. Univ. So. Calif., 1968-73; consultant, contr. Jet Propulsion Lab., 1973-77, mem. tech. staff, 1977–; awards: NASA monetary award 1990; mem. Am. Math. Soc., Math. Assn. of Am., Soc. for Indsl. and Applied Math., Inst. of Electrical and Electronic Engrs.; inventor: Frequency Stability Measurement (pat. 1989); Republican; Res: 1836 Hanscom Dr South Pasadena 91030 Ofc: Jet Propulsion Laboratory, 298-100, 4800 Oak Grove Dr Pasadena 91109

GREENLEAF, JOHN EDWARD, research scientist; b. Sept. 18, 1932, Joliet, Ill.; s. John Simon and Julia Clara (Flint) G.; m. Carol Lou Johnson, Aug. 28, 1960; edn: BS phys. edn., Univ. Ill., 1955; MA phys. edn., New Mexico Highlands Univ., Las Vegas, N.M. 1956; MS and PhD physiology, Univ. Ill., 1962, 63. Career: tchg. asst. N.M.H.U. 1956 and dir. recreation town of Las Vegas, N.M.1955-56; tchg. asst. Univ. Ill., Urbana 1957-62, NSF summer fellow 1962, NIH pre-doctoral fellow 1962-63; res. physiologist Life Scis., NASA-Ames Res. Ctr., Moffett Field, Calif. 1963-66, 1967–; adj. prof. Biology Dept., San Francisco State Univ., 1988–; grad. faculty Univ. No. Colo., Greeley, 1974–; Swedish Med. Res. Council sr. post-doctoral fellow at Karolinska Inst., Stockholm 1966-67; Nat. Acad. of Scis. exchange fellow 1973, 74, 77, 89, and NIH exchange fellow 1980, at Polish Acad. of Scis. Lab. of Applied Physiology, Warsaw; honors: Sigma Xi, Phi Epsilon Kappa; mem: Aerospace Med. Assn. (fellow), Am. Coll. of Sports Med. (fellow, bd. trustees 1984-87), Am. Acad. of Phys. Edn. (assoc. fellow), Am. Physiol. Soc., Am. Soc. for Gravitational and Space Biology; editl bds.: Jour. Applied Physiol. 1976-78, 1989–, Aviation Space Env. Med. 1985-94; co-editor Internat. Jour. of Biometeorology 1966-75; res. cons. The Coca-Cola Co., 1970-75, USMC 1982; nutrition cons. Shaklee Corp.: China Everest Expedition 1981-82, Voyager circumnav. flt. 1986, and Daedalus flt. 1987; inventions: new sys. for bathing bedridden patients, thermistor holder for skin-temp. measurements (pat. 1976), sweat collection capsule (pat. 1980); publs: 300+ abstracts, tech. and profl. jour. articles, 1963–; Republican; Prot.; rec: tennis, gardening. Res: 12391 Farr Ranch Ct Saratoga 95070 Ofc: NASA Ames Research Ctr Moffett Field 94035-1000

GREENLY, DAVID IRWIN, physician; b. June 29, 1942, Los Angeles, Calif.; s. Seymour Elliot and Ethel (Hurwitz) G.; m. Susan C., June 8, 1968; 1 son Michael David b. 1979; edn: BA, econ., UC Berkeley 1963; MD, Univ. of Ohio, Cincinnati 1967; med. lic. Calif., N.M., Va., Ohio; cert. Am. Bd. of Emergency Medicine 1981, recert. 1989. Career: rotating internship Alameda Co. Med. Insts., Highland Hosp., Oakland 1967-68; gen. practice residency Contra Costa Co. Med. Insts., Merrithew Hosp., Martinez 1972-73; cardio-pulmonary preceptorship Calif. Pacific Med. Ctr., S.F. 1971; emergency ward/intensive care preceptorship Mass. Gen. Hosp./Harvard Med. Sch. 1971; dir. emergency svs., chmn. dept. clin. svs., exec. com., med. exec. bd. Alta Bates Med. Ctr., Berkeley; clin. attending staff Mission Emergency Svs., S.F. Gen. Hosp., UCSF, Stanford Med. Ctr. and Contra Costa Co. Merrithew Hosp., Martinez ; assoc. chief emergency svs. Highland Alameda Co. Hosp., Oakland; clin. instr. surgery Stanford Univ. Sch. Medicine, UCSF Sch. Medicine; awards: AMA Physician's Recognition award, CMA Cont. Med. Edn. award; mem: Am. Coll. of Emergency Physicians (fellow, charter mem.), Am. Bd. of Emergency Medicine (oral examiner); asst. chief clin. svs., Direct Relief Found. Hosps., Nairobi, Kenya; vol., rural clinics, Thomas Dooley Found., Katmandu, Nepal; mil: capt. USAF 1968-70. Res: PO Box 7080 Corte Madera 94976-7080 Ofc: Health Resource Options 34 Forrest St Mill Valley 94976

GREENSPAN, BERNARD, professor of mathematics emeritus; b. Dec. 17, 1914, N.Y., N.Y.; s. Harry and Yetta (Siegel) G.; m. Beatrice Meltzer, Aug. 26, 1939; children: Valerie b. 1942, Ellen b. 1949; edn: BS (cum laude), Brooklyn Coll., Brooklyn, NY 1935; MA, Brooklyn Coll. 1936; postgrad. work, Columbia Univ. 1936-38; UC Berkeley 1958-59, Rensselaer Poly. 1960; PhD, Rutgers Univ., New Brunswick, N.J. 1958. Career: instr. math., Brooklyn Coll. 1935-44; instr. math., Polytechnic Inst., Brooklyn, NY 1943-44; instr. math., Drew Univ., Madison, N.J. 1944-47, asst. prof. math. 1947-58, assoc. prof. math. 1958-59, prof. math. 1959-81 (chmn. 1959-75), prof. Emeritus 1981–; lectr. & cons., Bell Telephone Labs., Whippany, N.J. 1953-58; dir. Inservice Math. Inst., NSF, Drew Univ. 1961-75; dir. Math. Summer Inst., NSF, Drew Univ. 1962-74; reader (table leader 1972), Advanced Placement Exams, Ednl. Testing Svc., Princeton, N.J. 1966-72; vis. prof., Univ. of Santa Clara 1961; vis. prof., Rutgers Univ. 1971; awards: medalist, math., Brooklyn Coll., Brooklyn, NY 1935, 36; NSF Fellowship, UC Berkeley 1958-59; mem: Sigma Xi, Pi Mu Epsilon, Sigma Phi; mem: Am. Math. Soc. 1961–; Math. Assn. of Am. (past chmn N.J. Section) 1961–; Am. Assn. of Univ. Professors 1947-81; Math. Teachers of N.J. 1947-81; Math. Assn. of Am., No. Calif. Section 1981–; author: mimeographed notes in the Theory of Equations, 1947; article in profl. jour., 1959; over 12 book reviews; Independent; rec: bridge, chess. Res: 9164 Tangerine St. San Ramon 94583

GREENWOOD, JAMES RICHARD, educator, laboratory director; b. Sept. 14, 1945, Riverside; s. Nathaniel and Sara (Berkovich) G.; m. Sydney Maureen Harvey, Jan. 16, 1978; edn: BA, UC Riverside 1967; MPH, UCLA 1975; PhD, 1978. Career: lab. dir. Health Care Agency, Orange Co. 1979–, asst. div. mgr. Communicable Diseases 1987–, dir., Office of Environment, Health & Safety, UCLA 1994–; adj. assoc. prof. UCLA Pub. Health 1979–; adj. asst. prof. UC Irvine 1988–; sci. advisor U.S. Food & Drug, Los Angeles 1980–; cons. Cigna Med. Corp. 1986–; adj. asst. prof. UC Irvine 1987–; honors: Delta Omega; mem: Sigma Xi, Am. Soc. Microbiology, Calif. STD Control Assn., Rotary Internat., March of Dimes (v.chair health advy.), Am. Lung Assn.; 40 papers pub. in sci. jours., 13 book chpts. (1975-), patent for low protein peptone medium, 1984; rec: gardening, music. Ofc: Univ. of Calif. at Los Angeles, 405 Hilgard Ave, Los Angeles, CA 90024

GREGO, PETER, professor of theatre arts, director; b. May 29, 1949, Pittsburgh, Pa.; s. William Joseph, Sr. and Veronica Margaret (Zamulovich) G.; m. Barbara Cavalier, May 1977 (div. Aug. 1991); edn: BFA, Carnegie Mellon Univ., 1972, MFA, 1973. Career: instr. Penn State Univ., New Kensington, Pa. 1973-76; instr., coord. acting pgm. Florida Sch. of Arts, Palatka, Fla. 1976-78; prof. CSU Bakersfield, 1978-84, CSU Northridge, 1984–; director: International City Theatre, Los Angeles 1988-92, Laguna Playhouse 1991, Producers Club, NY, NY 1991, Santa Paula (Calif.) Theatre 1990; awards: Drama-Logue Award, L.A. 1990, best play Arrow Rock Lyceum Theatre, Arrow Rock, Mo. 1991; mem.: Soc. of Stage Dirs. & Choreographers 1988–, Dramatists Guild 1991–; author (play): From Dust Thou Art (1983). Res: 5018 Cartwright Ave North Hollywood 91601

GREGORY, CALVIN LUTHER, insurance agent, educator, counselor; b. Jan. 11, 1942, Bronx, NY; s. Jacob and Ruth (Cherchian) G.; m. Rachel Anna Carver, Feb. 14, 1970, div. 1977; 2 daus: Debby Lynn, Trixy Sue; m. 2d. Carla Deaver, June 30, 1979; edn: AA, L.A. City Coll.; BA, CSU Los Angeles 1964; M.Div., Fuller Theol. Sem. 1968; M.Re.Edn., Southwestern Sem. 1969; D.D., Otay Mesa Coll, San Diego 1982; PhD in religion, Universal Life Ch., Inc. 1982; Ordained minister Am. Baptist Conv. L.A. 1970; real estate lic., Calif. 1969; Notary Public, Calif. 1969. Career: USAF Chaplain, Edwards AFB 1970; pastor First Baptist Ch., Boron, CA 1971; ins. agent Prudential Life Ins. Co., Ventura 1972; mgr. Prudential Ins. Co., Thousand Oaks 1973; casualty ins. agent Allstate Ins. Co., Thousand Oaks 1974; pres. Ins. Agcy. Placement Svc., Thousand Oaks 1975–; counselor Wilshire Presbyterian Ch., Los Angeles, fmr. hd. youth minister, 1974; tchr. polit. sci. Maranatha High Sch., Rosemead;

investor/owner apt. bldgs. and real property 1974–; profl. awards: WLRT and Pres.'s citation Prudential 1972, Top-20 sales Southwestern Co. 1967; mem. Forensic Club CSULA 1963, Apartment Assn. L.A. 1975–; Republican; rec: travel, video tapes, jogging. Res: 3307 Big Cloud Circle Thousand Oaks 91360 Ofc: Insurance Agency Placement Service, POB 4407 Thousand Oaks 91359

GREIFINGER, DAVID ROSS, lawyer; b. June 25, 1957, Los Angeles; s. Carl and Phyllis (Stoliar) G.; edn: BS physics, UCLA 1979; JD, Loyola Law Sch. 1982; admitted St. Bar Calif. 1982. Career: atty. sole practice, L.A. 1982–; bd. dirs. Athletics Congress, Indianapolis, Ind. 1980-92, 1994–; v.p. Santa Monica Track Club 1982–, chief legal counsel 1982–; honors: Loyola Law Rev. staff, editor 1981, 82, St. Thomas Moore Law Hon. Soc. 1981, 82; rec: long distance running. Ofc: 1801 Ocean Park Blvd Ste 201 Santa Monica 90405

GRENIER, JUDSON A., JR., educator; b. March 6, 1930, Idpls.; s. Judson A. and Beatrice Olivia (Bjeldanes) G.; m. Nancy Hicks, Aug. 9, 1954; children: Karen b. 1956, Eric b. 1958, Jonathan b. 1961, Caddie b. 1962; edn: BA, Univ. Minn. 1951; MA, UC Berkeley 1952; PhD, hist., UCLA 1965. Career: tchg. asst. UC Berkeley 1951-52; analyst IPS U.S. Dept. of State, Wash. D.C. 1952; reporter Los Angeles Mirror-News, 1957, 58; instr. El Camino Coll., Torrance 1956-65; vis. lectr. UCLA 1965-66; prof. history CSU Dominguez Hills, Carson 1966–; mem. CSU Academic Senate 1974-83, secty. 1976-78, v.chmn. 1979-80; dir. CSU Oral History Project 1986-89; cons. El Pueblo St. Historic Park L.A. 1980-83, cities of Gardena, Torrance, Redondo Beach 1980-87, L.A. County Dept. of Edn. 1979-81; awards: distinguished prof. CSU Dominguez Hills 1974, disting. community service CSUDH 1987, Nat. Endowment Humanties travel fellow 1984, Huntington-Haynes Fellow 1985, Pflueger Regional History Award, Newberry Library Fellow 1991, research assoc. L.A. County Mus. of Natural Hist. 1977–; mem: Hist. Soc. So. Calif. (v.p. 1981-83), Am. Hist. Assn., Los Angeles 200 (hist. and edn. com. 1978-81), Manhattan Beach Hist. Com., L.A. Bicentennial Com. (hist. team 1973-76); editl. bd. Calif. History 1988–; author: Calif. Legacy: Watson-Dominguez Family, 1987, ed. The Rancho San Pedro, 1983, Guide to Historic Places in Los Angeles, 1978, 83, coauthor History of Calif. State Univ., 1981, num. articles in Calif. hist. jours.; mil: ASA 1952-55; rec: writing, tennis, photog. Res: 587 33rd St Manhattan Beach 90266 Ofc: Calif. State Univ. Dominguez Hills 1000 E Victoria Carson 90747

GRETZKY, WAYNE, professional hockey player; b. Brantford, Ont., Can., Jan. 26, 1961; s. Walter and Phyllis G.; m. Janet Jones, July 16, 1988; children: Paulina, Ty Robert, Trevor Douglas. Career: center Peterborough Petes, Jr. Ontario Hockey Assn., 1977-78; Sault St. Marie Greyhounds 1977-78; Indpls. Racers, World Hockey Assn. 1978-79; Edmonton Oilers (Alta., Can.), NHL 1979-88; Los Angeles Kings, NHL 1988–; awards: Player NHL All- Star Game 1980-92, named Rookie of Yr. World Hockey Assn. 1979, Hart Trophy for Most Valuable Player NHL (1980-87, 89), Sportsman of Yr. Sports Illus. 1982, recipient Lady Byng Meml. trophy NHL (1980, 91, 92), Art Ross Meml. trophy NHL (1981-87, 90, 91), Conn Smythe trophy (1985, 88), holder NHL career scoring record. Ofc: c/o Los Angeles Kings The Forum 3900 W Manchester Blvd Inglewood 90306

GRGICH, LAURA LYNN, registered nurse; b. Feb. 6, 1955, Vallejo; d. John Emerson and Gloria Joyce-Margaret (O'Gara) Messing; m. Mark Steven Grgich, Feb. 26, 1983; children: Jordan Daniel b. 1983, Aaron Andrew b. 1985, Rachel Elizabeth-Joyce b. 1987, John Steven b. 1990; edn: RN, Coll. San Mateo 1982; med. asst., Bryman Sch. 1977-78. Career: sales Sears & Roebuck, San Mateo 1974-75, security 1975-77; police cadet, San Mateo P.D. 1975-77; med. asst. Meba Clinic, San Francisco 1977-78; phlebotomist Seton Med., Daly City 1978-82, reg. nurse 1982–; reg. nurse, med. adv. Kaiser Permanente, South San Francisco 1990-92; awards: S.S.F. H.S. Pres.'s Physical Fitness 1973; Democrat; Agnostic. Res: 83 Irving St South San Francisco 94080

GRIFFIN, DEBRA KATHLEEN, senior systems analyst; b. Feb. 25, 1954, Corona; d. Laurence Ronald and Mary Louise (Buckley) Seaward; m. William Kirk Griffin, Mar. 24, 1973; 1 son, Jason Ryan b. 1978; edn: AA in bus. (4.0, honors), Diablo Valley Coll., 1990; BS in info. sys. mgmt. (3.86 g.p.a., dean's list), Univ. San Francisco, 1991; Carnegie Mellon Univ. Adv. Technology Inst. (4.0), 1993. Career: staff clk. Pacific Telephone, Los Angeles, 1973-76, service rep., 1976-80, business office mgr. 1980-83; planner Pacific Bell, San Ramon, 1983-86, assoc. systems analyst 1986-88, senior systems analyst 1988–, cons. tchr. 1991–; awards: Pacific Bell-Ebbon's Eagle 1982, Quality Circle 1986-89, Quality Excellence Award 1989; civic: Pacific Choral Co. (exec.v.p. 1990–), Crescenta Valley Alumni Chorale (pres. 1979-83), Canyon Creek Little League San Ramon (chief scorekeeper 1984-91); author/prod. musical show script: America -A Family Musical, 1991; performances (voice & dance): Circle Star Theater (San Carlos), Oakland Coliseum, Candlestick Park (S.F.), Oakland Paramount Theater, Blackhawk Plaza, Disneyland; Republican; Prot.; rec: music - voice/piano, baseball. Ofc: Pacific Bell 2600 Camino Ramon MC 3E700B San Ramon 94583

GRIFFIN, JAMES CLYDE, trucker, political activist; b. Oct. 1, 1937, Tenn.; s. Dewey Sampson and Osa Nelson (Akers) G.; div.; 3 daus.; Career: with Milne Truck Lines, Inc. Whittier, 28 years, now employee Consolidated Freightway,

Mira Loma; records 3,200,000+ miles of accident free driving; awards: Truck Driving Roadeos: Heavy-Semi: Calif. State Roadeo 1st Place (1981, 83, 89), L.A. Area Roadeo 1st Place (1978, 79, 81, 82, 83, 89); Calif. Trucking Assn. driver of mo. (7/81, 8/83), KLAC Radio trucker of week (4/74), appreciation Norwalk Sr. Citizens Ctr.; nominated Hiway Goodwill Amb. Road Team Am. Trucking Assn. 1987, "Hiway Heroes" Goodyear Tire & Rubber Co. 1988, Citizen of Yr. Norwalk (6t nominee 1975-80); recipient nat. t.v. publicity as a spokesman for Indep. truckers during fuel shortage of 1973; listed Who's Who in West 1985, Personalities of Am. 1985, Internat. Who's Who of Intellectuals (9th ed.), Almanac-Information Please (1990, 91, 92), Who's Who in Calif. 1988-94, others; civic: Norwalk Citizens Action Council (3-term chmn. 6 yrs.), Assem. Bruce Young Advy. Panel (past), Calif. Dept. Motor Vehicles Advy. Panel 1976-80; mem: Norwalk C.of C., Jurupa C.of C., Moose, Elks, Norwalk Rod & Gun Club, Nat. Rifle Assn; American Indep. Party: elected state chmn. 1993-94, st. exec. com., past chmn. cent. com., candidate for Congress 33rd C.D. 1974, cand. for US Senate 1980, cand. for gov. Calif. 1982, cand. for lt. gov. Calif. 1986, nat. cand. for US Pres. 1988; rec: golf, politics, truck roadeos. Res: 5069 Bain St Mira Loma 91752

GRIFFIN, JAMES RAY, aerospace systems engineer; b. Mar. 30, 1943, Vancouver, Wash.; s. William (dec. 1994) and Esther (Joy) G.; m. Deanna Turek, No 23, 1962; children: Scott b. 1963 (dec. 1984), JoAnn b. 1968, Paul b. 1974, Ellen b. 1979; edn: AA, Riverside City Coll., 1975; BS in E.E., CSU-Long Beach, 1990. Career: tech. Rockwell Internat., Anaheim 1962-69; assoc. test engr. Calif. Computer Products, Anaheim 1969-77; R & D tech. McDonnell Douglas Corp., Long Beach 1977–, electrical engr., data acquisition systems engring. for flt. test aircraft (MD11), 1988-94, aircraft ice detection systems design and devel. 1994-; Democrat; rec: travel, music, camping. Res: 1142 Azalea Circle Corona 91720 Ofc: McDonnell Douglas Corp. 3855 Lakewood Blvd Long Beach 90846

GRIFFIN, MARY ELIZABETH, county supervisor; b. May 24, 1932, Yuba City; d. Zacharias Walters and Mary (Nickerson) Wilson; m. Donald F. Griffin, Sept. 6, 1958 (dec. Nov. 1988); children: John, Mimi, Zachary; m. Walter F. Ramseur, Jan. 26, 1991; edn: AA, Yuba Coll., 1952; AB cum laude, Chico St. Coll., 1954; postgrad. studies CSU Sacto. 1956, San Francisco St. Univ. 1957-58. Career: assoc. prof. edn. San Francisco State, 1957-59; co. ofcr. Griffin Metal Prod., S.F. v.p. 1960-63, sec. treas. 1963-80, pres. 1980-90; tchr. South San Francisco Unified Sch. Dist., 1973-87; elected Millbrae City Council 1976-87, mayor 1980-81, 84-85, chair No. San Mateo Council of Cities (1978-79), pres. Peninsula Div. League of Calif. Cities (1982-83); elected San Mateo County Bd. Suprs., Redwood City 1987-96, pres. bd. suprs. 1989-90, 93-94; chair San Mateo Co. General Hosp. 1993-94; mem.: Metropolitan Transportation Commn. 1993–, Assn. of Bay Area Govts. (pres. 1991-93, v.p. 1988-91); honors: appreciation Cub Scouts of Am., Millbrae 1969, 70, 71, hon. service Calif. Congress PTA, Millbrae 1973, woman of yr. Calif. Fedn. of Women's Clubs, Millbrae 1980; mem: Soroptimist Internat. (woman of distinc. Millbrae/San Bruno 1989), AAUW; Democrat; Presbyterian. Res: 25 Mullins Ct Millbrae 94030 Ofc: County of San Mateo 401 Marshall St Redwood City 94063

GRIFFIN, MERV E(DWARD), television performer/producer, executive; b. July 6, 1925, San Mateo; s. Merv E., Sr. and Rita Elizabeth (Robinson) G.; m. Julann Elizabeth Wright, May 18, 1958, div. 1976; children: Anthony Patrick b. 1959; edn: San Mateo Coll. 1942-44; L.H.D., Emerson Coll. 1981. Career: performer Merv Griffin Show radio sta. KFRC, San Francisco, 1945-48; vocalist Freddy Martin's Orch., 1948-52; contract player, star So This is Love, Warner Bros., 1953-55; TV master of ceremonies Game Shows 1958-62, Merv Griffin Show, NBC-TV, 1962-63, Westinghouse Bdcstg. Co., 1965-69, CBS-TV, 1969-72, Metro Media Prodns., syndicated TV, 1972-86; CEO Merv Griffin Ents. (unit of Sony Corp.), currently producing: Jeopardy, Wheel of Fortune; chmn. bd. Merv Griffin Prodns., Beverly Hills; chmn. Resorts Internat., Atlantic City and the Bahamas; trustee Dr. Armand Hammer United World Coll. of Am. S.W.; owner 6 radio stas. 1965–, Teleview Racing Patrol Inc., Miami, Fla., Video Racing Patrol Inc., Seattle, Beverly Hilton Hotel, Beverly Hills; Deerfield Hilton, Boca Raton, Fla.; honors: 10 Emmy awards, Medal of Paris; mem. Bohemian Club (S.F.). Ofc: The Griffin Group 9860 Wilshire Blvd Beverly Hills 90210-3115 and The Griffin Group 780 Third Ave New York NY 10017

GRIFFITH, DAVID MARTIN, architect, civil engineer; b. July 1, 1955, Portland, Oreg.; s. Norman Nelson and Alice Sigrid (Egeland) G.; m. Elizabeth Ellen Turner, June 18, 1977 (div. 1985); m. Jeanine Lynn Bascom, June 30, 1985 (div. 1994); children: Ian Conley b. 1971, Matthew David b. 1986; edn: Whitworth Coll. 1973-75; BA, Harvard Coll. 1977; reg. civil engr. Calif. and Oreg. 1982; lic. architect 1992. Career: draftsman G.R. Everhard & Assoc., Magalia 1978-79; draftsman, civil engr. McCain Assoc., Chico 1979-82; prin., engr. and architect, Griffith & Assoc. 1982–; mem: Structural Engrs. Assn. Central Calif., Bidwell Presbyterian Ch.; Republican; Presbyterian. Ofc: Griffith & Associates 202 Design Arts Bldg 25 Main St Chico 95928

GRIFFITH, J. GORDON, real estate executive; b. Dec. 16, 1934, Council Bluffs, Iowa; s. Frank L. and Geneva (Seitz) G.; children: Stephen J. b. 1950, Jessica Geneva b. 1979; edn: BS, Iowa State Univ., 1956. Career: pres.

Centurion Real Estate and Investment Corp., Newport Beach 1973–; dir. Bio-Trends Internat., Sacto. 1983–; mem.: Building INd. Assn. 1988–; mil: 2d lt. USAF 1954-55; Republican; Prot.; rec: golf, skiing. Ofc: Centurion R.E. & Investment Corp. 2043 Westcliff Drive Ste 201 Newport Beach 92660

GRIFFITH, JOHN CHADWICK, JR., lawyer; b. Bern, Switz.; s. John Chadwick and Jane Ann (Berg) G.; edn: BA, Boston Univ., 1980; JD, Univ. Va., 1985, MA, 1995; admitted bar: Ariz. 1986, Calif. 1988, Hawaii 1993. Career: atty., assoc. Winston & Strawn, Phoenix, Az. 1985-88, Graham & James, Los Angeles 1988-93; general counsel The Mitsui Trust & Banking Co., Ltd. Tokyo, Japan 1993–; honors: editor Va. Jour. Internat. Law (1984-85), Pi Sigma Alpha, Psi Chi, Phi Theta Kappa; mem: ABA, Ariz. State Bar Assn., Calif. State Bar Assn., Hawaii State Bar Assn. Res: 35 Vistawood Way San Rafael 94901 Ofc: The Mitsui Trust & Banking Co., Ltd. 2-1-1 Nihonbashi Muromachi, Chuo-Ku Tokyo 103 Japan

GRIFFITH, LADD RAY, retired research company executive; b. Nov. 21, 1930, Cory, Colo.; s. William Roy and Ida Geneva (Williams) G.; m. Jeanne Maryly Hoffman, Feb. 6, 1955; children: Dina b. 1957, Julie b. 1960, David b. 1965; edn: BA chem., Univ. Colo. 1952; PhD, UC Berkeley 1957. Career: mgr. product devel. Chevron Research Co., Richmond 1972-77, mgr. bus. planning Chevron Chemical Co., San Francisco 1977-79; mgr. planning analysis Oronite Additives 1979-81; Chevron Ag. Chem. 1981-84, mgr. inventive res. Chevron Ag. Chem. Res., Richmond 1984-86, dir. res. Chevron Chem. Co. 1986-90; honors: Phi Beta Kappa, Sigma Xi, Phi Lambda Upsilon; research papers pub. on hydrocarbon fuel cells (1959-62); Democrat; Unitarian; rec: skiing (water, snow). Res: 852 Gelston Place El Cerrito 94530

GRIFFITHS, BARBARA GAYLE, physician; b. Dec. 30, 1955, Valley Forge, Pa.; d. Cadvan Owen Griffiths, MD, JD and Barbara Frances (Williams) Griffiths; edn: BA, Mills Coll., Oakland 1978; diplome moyen, Univ. of Paris, Sorbonne 1977; MPH, UC Berkeley 1979; MD, Universidad Central Del Este, Dominican Republic 1982; med. lic. Calif. 1985; bd. eligible: Occupational, Environ. and Preventive Medicine. Career: internship Hosp. of St. Raphael and Yale-New Haven Hosp., New Haven, Ct. 1983-84; fellowship in med. edn. UCSF 1984-86; fellowship residency in diagnostic radiology UCSF and UC Davis 1986-89; plastic & reconstructive surgery, Cadvan Owen Griffiths, MD, Jr., L.A. 1979-83; urgent care physician Med. Clinic of Sacto. 1989-92; lead physician, Folsom Clinic, Readicare Indsl. Med. Clinics, Sacto. 1989-94; site dir. Am. Health Med. Clinic, Sacto. 1995–; awards: acad. scholarship Mills Coll. 1974-78, Achievement Award (electron microscopy) Lawrence Berkeley Labs. 1978, Federal Traineeship award UC Berkeley 1978-79, Acad. Senate Grant, UCSF 1985-86; mem. Am Coll. of Occupational & Environmental Medicine, We. Occupational Med. Assn., Nat. Assn. of Female Execs.; contbr. 3 articles to sci. jours., 1987-89; illustrator; artist, watercolor painting: group exhibit Sacto. Fine Arts Gallery, 1992, rec: painting, tennis, skiing, scuba diving, horticulture. Ofc: 6000 Fairway Dr Ste 1 Rocklin 95677

GRIMES, RITA CHARLOTTE, publisher; b. May 29, 1923, San Francisco; d. Francesco Vincenzo and Charlotte (Philipsborn) Forzano; m. Philip Stanford Grimes, Dec. 26, 1947; children: Christine Marie b. 1952, Sandra Louise b. 1954; edn: grad., Riverside Bus. Coll. 1941; student, UCLA 1944-45; UC Berkeley 1946-47; Schaefer Sch. of Design, San Francisco 1947. mgr. personal/fin. affairs for retired naval ofcr., 1978; exec. dir. The Occidental Pub. Co., 1978; coord. The American Lives Endowment, 1980; exec. secty. for dir. Health Orgn. Bus. Systems, 1981; cons. Linwood Realty and Fin. Services, 1982; owner/dir. Medical Records Pub. Co., Stanford 1983–, founder/dir. Portola Valley Community Center, publish, design and edit Portola Valley Sch. Dist. newspaper; awards: for "Action in Education" Nat. Sch. Boards Assn., Calif. Gubnatl. Proclamation dedicating October as "Talk About Prescription Month" 1990 on behalf of the Nat. Council on Patient Information and Edn. 1990; mem: Internat. Union for Health Edn. (del. XIII World Conf. on Health Edn., Houston, Tex. 1988, Certified participant Inter-Am. Symp. on Health Edn., Rio De Janiero 1990, Nat. Council on Patient Info. and Edn. (S.F. Health Dept. rep. to Calif. Medication Edn. Coalition & Seniors Regional Pgm., Sacto. 1988); active P.V. PTA (dir.), No. Calif. Kidney Found. (dir.), Palo Alto Acad. of Art (dir.), KRON-TV Viewer Advy. Council 1985–, TV panelist on prescription drugs KCRA-Sacto. 1988; publs: The Medical and Dental Record Book (listed in Directory of Prescription Drug Info. & Edn. Pgms. & Resources of the Nat. Council on Patient Infor. & Edn., also a permanent item in NCPIE's Food & Drug Adminstrn. Inventory of Resources); research: Cinabar in Calif., mineral water domestic and fgn., alcohol and drug rehab.; Democrat; R.Cath.; rec: edn., travel, horses, design. Res: 1301 Crossgates Ln Almaden Valley San Jose 95120 Ofc: Medical Records Publishing Co. PO Box 8545 Stanford 94309-8545

GRIMM, LUCIEEN CHARLOTTE, fashion designer; b. Apr. 28, 1921, Berlin, Ger.; nat. USA 1962; d. Fritz George and Marie Charlotte (Mietz) Henschel; edn: attended Victoria Oberlyzeum (Berlin) 1931-36, stu. Coll. Fashion Design (Ger.) 1936-69. Career: fashion designer, Germany, 1940-52; fashion designer of Antiguelaces, bridal gowns, dresses, Los Angeles 1952–, business owner, Lucieen, L.A.; honors: listed as Fashion Designer of Berlin, 1952; mem. Art Guild (Berlin); Prot. Res: 752 S Wilton Place Apt 1 Los Angeles 90005 Ofc: Lucieen, 225 N Larchmont Blvd Los Angeles 90004

GRIMSHAW, CHARLES EDWARD, biochemist; b. Sept. 7, 1953, Hartford, Conn.; s. Edward Chapman and Margaret (Brouwer) Coholan G.; m. Margaret Louisa M., Aug. 6, 1977; children: Charles S. b. 1980, Adam C. b. 1983, Matthew A. b. 1989; edn: BS, UC Berkeley 1975; PhD, Univ. Wis. 1979. Career: NIH postdoctoral fellow Dept. of Chemistry, Harvard Univ., Cambridge, Mass. 1979-81; asst. mem. Scripps Clinic and Res. Found., La Jolla 1982–; lectr. UCSD 1983–; faculty Research Inst. of Scripps Clinic, La Jolla 1989–; honors: Sigma Xi, Phi Beta Kappa, Lambda Chi Alpha; mem: Am. Chem. Soc., Am. Soc. Biochem. & Molecular Biology, AAAS, BSA (cubmaster 1986–); res. articles pub. in profl. jours. (1984–); Democrat; Methodist; rec: woodworking, camping, backpacking. Ofc: Scripps Clinic & Research Found. Dept. of Biochemistry BCR-7 10666 N Torrey Pines Rd La Jolla 92037

GRISSOM, LEE ALAN, state official; b. Sept. 7, 1942, Pensacola, Fla.; s. Levi Aaron and Virginia Sue (Olinger) G.; m. Sharon Kay Hasty, May 14, 1966; children: David, Jonathan, Matthew, Andrew; edn: BA pub. adminstrn., San Diego St. Univ. 1965; MA city planning, 1971. Career: sr. res. assoc. Western Behavioral Scis. Inst., La Jolla 1965-73; mgr. planning div. Greater San Diego C.of C., 1973-74, gen. mgr. 1974-75, pres. and chief ops. ofcr. 1975-92; dir. Governor's Ofc. Of Planning & Res. and Governor's Sr. Adv. For Econ. Dev. 1992–; exec. dir. Governor's Council of Econ. Adv. 1992–; mem. Calif. Council on Defense Ind. Conv. 1992–, Calif. Housing Finance Agency 1993–, Governor's Cabinet 1993–, bd. dirs. Econ. Devel. Corp. San Diego 1976; bd. trustees Cal State Univ. 1984-90; awards: SDSU Alumnus of Yr. 1987, Jaycees Outstanding Young Man, San Diego 1976, Calif. 1977, U.S. 1978; club: San Diego Rotary; contbr. 50+ articles and research papers (1965-73); mil: USAR; Republican; rec: jogging. Ofc: 1400 10th St Sacramento 95814

GROFER, TED (EDWARD JOSEPH), marketing executive, publisher; b. Sept. 20, 1934, Cinti.; s. Edward Joseph and Margaret Mary (McGinley) G.; m. Mary Janet Procissi, Aug. 18, 1962; children: Catherine Mary, Laura Marie, Daniel McGinley; edn: BA, Univ. Cincinnati, 1957; MA, Univ. Iowa, 1959; computer mgmt., National Univ., San Diego 1987. Career: asst. dir. pub. relations Champion Paper, Hamilton, Oh. 1959-61; mktg. dir. The Jam Handy Org., Detroit, Mich. 1961-69; dir. of promo. & res. The Detroit News,1969-74; v.p and publ. The Desert Sun, Palm Springs 1974-80; pres. Ted Grofer Associates, 1980-88; publisher Desert Community Newspapers, Palm Desert 1981-85; gen. ptnr. The Graphic Arts Ctr., Cathedral City 1985-89; pres. TGA Publishing, Palm Springs 1989–; exec. dir. Palm Springs Main Street org., 1990-92, Palm Springs NOW, 1990-92; Downtown Bus. Improvement Dist. P.S., 1990-92; v.p. marketing/sales Mark Palmer Design 1993–; vice chair exec. com. Catholic Charities of Diocese San Bernardino 1991–; mem: Rotary P.S. (treas. Dist. 5330, pres. elect bd. dir. 1987–, Sun-Up, editor 1987-89, social chair 1990–), The Palm Springs (P.S.), Pi Kappa Alpha Frat., Memphis, Tenn. (nat. v.p. 1982-86); publs: res. newspaper mkt. analysis, 1980-89, mktg. presentation "The Palm Springs ADI", 1992; Republican; R.Cath. (parish coun. 1988–); rec: rv-ing, dancing, computers. Res: 584 Fern Canyon Palm Springs 92264 Ofc: Mark Palmer Design 75-140 St. Charles Pl Palm Desert 92211-9044

GROLLMAN, JULIUS HARRY, JR., cardiovascular and interventional radiologist; b. Nov. 26, 1934, Los Angeles; s. Julius Harry and Alice Carolyn (Greenlee) G.; m. Alexa, March 20, 1959; children: Carolyn b. 1960, David b. 1962, Elizabeth b. 1965; edn: BA, Occidental Coll. L.A.; MD, UCLA; cert. Am. Bd. Radiology 1965; Career: chief cardiovascular radiology Walter Reed Army Hosp., Wash. D.C. 1965-67; to prof. Dept. Radiological Sci., UCLA Sch. of Medicine, 1967-78; chief cardiovascular radiology Little Company of Mary Hosp., Torrance 1978–; cons. VA Hosp. L.A. 1967-90; cons. Martin Luther King/Drew Medical Ctr. 1984–; Walter Reed Army Inst. Pathology, Wash. D.C. 1965-67; clin. prof. radiology UCLA 1978–; mem: Am. Coll. Radiology (fellow), We. Angiography Soc. (pres. 1977), N. Am. Soc. Cardiac Imaging (pres. 1991-92), Soc. Cardiac Angiography & Interventions (fellow, trustee), Soc. Cardiovascular and Interventional Radiology (fellow), RSNA, AMA, ARRS, STR, LARS, CRS; civic: Los Angeles Mandolin Orch.; author 8 med. book chapters, 100+ res. papers 1964–; mil: capt. USAR 1965-67 Army Commendn. medal; Republican; Presbyterian; rec: music, sailing, hunting. Res: 448 27th St Manhattan Beach 90266 Ofc: Little Company of Mary Hospital, 4101 Torrance Blvd Torrance 90503

GRONSKE, MYRTLE J., shopping center owner; b. Jan. 27, 1927, Sedro Wooley, Wash.; d. Ole P. and Anna (Howen) Gronske. Career: bookkeeper Sanford Nash, Tacoma, Wash. 1946-48; Grendahls Acctg. Services, 1948-50; hd. acctg. dept. Forrester Realty & Mortgage Co., 1950-68; owner Oakwood Motor Lodge, and The Flame Restaurant, Tacoma 1968-76; owner The Chinowth House Restaurant, Visalia 1978-93, also Crepe Myrtle Cottages, 1985–, 1/2 owner Mineral King Plaza Shopping Center, Visalia 1984–, 1/2 owner in redevel. proj. The Old Bakery Plaza 1988–; honors: rec'd City of Visalia Beautification awards for The Chinowth House (1985, 1986, 1990) and

The Mineral King Plaza Shopping Center (1986, 1990); Republican; Prot. Res: 700 S Linwood Ave Visalia 93277

GRONSKY, RONALD, materials scientist; b. July 9, 1950, Pittsburgh, Pa.; s. Andrew John and Veronia Rosalia (Sefcik) G.; m. Andrea Jean Hritz, Dec. 20, 1970; children: Kristin b. 1973, Damian b. 1976, Stefan b. 1979, Ryan b. 1983; edn: BS, Univ. Pittsburgh 1972; MS, UC Berkeley 1974; PhD, 1977. Career: prin. investigator Lawrence Berkeley Lab., Berkeley 1979–; assoc. prof. UC Berkeley 1982-88, prof. 1988–, chair Dept. Materials Sci. and Mineral Engring., 1990–, dep. assoc. lab. dir. Lawrence Berkeley Lab. 1988-89; awards: TMS AIME R.L. Hardy Gold Medal 1979, EMSA Burton Medal 1983, Sci. Digest 100 Brightest Scientists Under 40 (1984), ASM Bradley Stoughton award 1985, Disting. Alumni Univ. Pittsburgh 1995; mem: Electron Microscopy Soc. of Am., Minerals Metals & Materials Soc., Am. Soc. for Metals Internat., AAAS, ASM Internat. (fellow), Microbeam Analysis Soc., Materials Res. Soc., Sigma Xi; editor: High Voltage Electron Microscopy, 1983, Images of Materials, 1989, contbr. 200+ articles to tech. jours. Ofc: Dept. Materials Science and Mineral Engring., Univ. California, Berkeley 94720-1760

GROSS, ROBERT ALLEN, insurance broker; b. Sept. 19, 1943, San Luis Obispo; s. Karl Randolph and Mary Ethel (Thomas) G.; m. Machelle Louise Knapp, Aug. 19, 1979 (div. 1985); dau., Elizabeth b. 1980; edn: undergrad. Menlo Coll. 1961-63, Coll. of William & Mary 1967, BS in mktg. Woodbury Univ., 1972. Career: president Haywood, Chapman & Kirby, Los Angeles 1972–, served as corp. sec. and in chg. of producers and personnel, 1972-92, pres. and C.E.O., 1992–; mem: We. Assn. of Ins. Brokers, S.F. 1972–; club: San Gabriel CC, San Gabriel (pres. 1988-89, bd. 1985-89, 6 time club champion 1971, 73, 74, 76, 78, 85); mil: s.sgt. USAF 1967-71; Republican; Prot.; rec: golf, skiing. Ofc: Haywood Chapman & Kirby PO Box 7000 Los Angeles 90022

GROSSBARD, JILL LAURIE, manager, human resources; b. Oct. 3, 1953, New Rochelle, N.Y.; d. David Daniel and Judith (Shapiro) Grossbard; edn: BS summa cum laude, Syracuse Univ. 1975; MS, USC, 1977. Career: admissions counselor Whittier Coll., Whittier, Calif. 1977-78; residence dir. Syracuse Univ., N.Y. 1978-80; tng. coordinator Pepsi-Cola Co., Purchase, N.Y. 1981-82; human resources splst. Mattel Toys, Hawthorne, Calif. 1982-84, mgr. human resources 1984-86, dir. human resources 1986-91; honors: Who's Who Among Young Am. Profls. 1989, 1993, Who's Who of Women Execs. 1990; mem: Leadership Calif. Alumni Assn., Soc. for Human Resource Mgmt., Am. Compensation Assn.; rec: tennis, skiing, running. Ofc: Atlantic Richfield Co., 300 Oceangate, Long Beach, CA 90802

GROSSER, MORTON, consultant, author; b. Dec. 25, 1931, Phila.; s. Albert Jay and Esther (Mendelstein) G.; m. Janet Zachs, June 28, 1953; son, Adam b. 1961; edn: BS, M.I.T., 1953, MS, 1954; PhD, Stanford Univ., 1961; reg. rep., fin. prin. NASD 1985; Career: design engr. Clevite Transistor, Waltham, Mass. 1955-57; dir. of publication Boeing Corp., Seattle 1964-65; mng. dir. L.H. Alton & Co., San Francisco 1984-87; mgmt. and technology cons./ prin., Menlo Park 1966-83, 87–; dir: L.H. Alton & Co. 1984-87, I-Flow Corp., Torrance 1985-87, Lazer-Tron, Inc., Pleasanton 1994-95; awards: Coats & Clark Fellow, M.I.T. 1954, Ford Found. fellow Stanford Univ. 1960, NIH postdoctoral fellow UCLA Med. Ctr. 1961-62, Stegner Creative Writing fellow Stanford 1963-64, Commonwealth Club Medal for Literary Excellence 1991; assoc. fellow, Am. Inst. Aero. & Astro.; Fellow Am. Soc. Mech. Engrs.; mem: Assn. for Computing Machinery, Soc. of Automotive Engrs., The Authors Guild; author 8 books: The Discovery of Neptune, 1962, The Hobby Shop, 1967, The Snake Horn, 1973, novel, Diesel: The Man & The Engine, 1978, Gossamer Odyssey, 1981, On Gossamer Wings, 1982, novel, The Fabulous Fifty, 1990, co-edit. 100 Inventions That Shaped History, 1993; contbr. articles, fiction and poetry in The Atlantic, Harper's, Holidays, Industrial Design, Natural History, The New Yorker, The Sat. Evening Post, Stanford Mag., Technology Rev., The Whole Earth Catalog, The Writer, 1964–; jour. articles in Artibus Asiae, Isis, Jour. of Asian Studies, Artificial Organs, Jour. of the Astronomical Soc. of The Pacific, Jour. of the Franklin Inst., Jour. of Rehabilitation Research and Devel., Proc. of the Plastic Surg. Research Coun. Restorative Neurology & Neuroscience, 1963–; ed. tech. jour. Boeing Sci. Labs. Rev., 1964-65; patentee (3), co-inventor Microelectronic Axon Processor (pat. 1986); Presbyterian; rec: weight tng., model bldg. Ofc: MG Consulting, 1016 Lemon St Menlo Park 94025

GROSSMAN, PAUL, lawyer; b. Aug. 26, 1939, Palo Alto; s. Maurice and Mollie (Froman) G.; m. Margaret Douglas Gregg, Dec. 28, 1966; children: Paul Douglas b. 1969, Elizabeth Dillon b. 1971; edn: BA, Amherst Coll. 1961; JD, Yale Law Sch. 1964. Career: assoc. atty. Paul Hastings Janofsky & Walker, Los Angeles 1964-71; ptnr. 1971–; chmn. employment law dept. 1978-85, 1988–; nat. chmn. equal opportunities law com. Defense Research Inst. 1978-80; pres. Legal Aid Found. L.A. 1982-83; gen. counsel Calif. Employment Law Council 1984–; awards: MALDEF Civil Rights award 1978; mem: Am. Bar Assn. (labor and employment law sect.); Chancery Club, Twilight Club, Calif. Club, Valley Hunt Club; co-author Employment Discrimination Law (1976, 79, 82, 83, 84, 85, 87, 89); rec: tennis, skiing, photog. Ofc: Paul Hastings Janofsky & Walker 555 S Flower St Los Angeles 90071

GROSSMAN, REGINA VALDEZ, computer systems analyst, psychotherapist; b. Apr. 29, 1946, Oakland; d. Robert K. and Louisa (Valdez) Mitchell; m. Dr. Stephen Grossman, July 26, 1972; edn: MSW, UC Berkeley 1971; Postmasters cert. in Comm. Mental Health, 1973; MPH, 1973; JD, UCLA Sch. of Law 1980; MCS in computer sci., Univ. San Francisco, 1989; Lic. Clin. Soc. Wkr. (LCSW) Calif. 1974. Career: soc. wkr, staff Children's Hosp. of Oakland 1973-74; Stanford Univ. Med. Ctr. 1974-76; dir. soc. work Kaiser Hosp., South S.F. 1981-83; computer pgmr. Control Data Corp. 1985; computer systems analyst Lockheed 1985-87; software designer Tandem Computers 1987; cons. to legal profession re psycho-social aspects of family law; pvt. practice 1983–; past adminstrv. research for Judge C. Reynoso (former Calif. Supreme Ct. Justice); UCLA judicial extern in Marin Co. Superior Ct.; honors: Upsilon Pi Epsilon (comp. sc. hon. soc.), Calif. State Fellow (1964); mem. Profl. Connections for Women (Palo Alto); rec: computers, photography, sports. Res: POB 7315 Menlo Park 94026-7315

GROSSMAN, SEYMOUR, gastroenterologist; b. July 5, 1933, Newark, N.J.; s. Abraham and Sally G. (Pilchman) G.; m. Bonnie Simon, June 26, 1955; children: Michael b. 1958, Deborah b. 1960; edn: attended M.I.T., Cambridge, Mass. 1950-53; MD, NY Univ. Coll. of Medicine 1957; med. internship/residency Metropolitan Gen. Hosp. (Case Western Reserve), Cleveland, Ohio 1957-61; fellowship in gastroenterology Cornell Univ. Med. Coll., NY, NY 1961-63. Career: pvt. practice, White Plains, NY 1963-65; physician Kaiser Permanente, Oakland, Calif. 1965-67; asst. chief gastroenterology, maj. to lt. col., U.S. Army, Brooke Army Med. Ctr., San Antonio, Tx. 1967-69; chief, gastroenterology Kaiser Permanente, Oakland 1969–; clin. prof. medicine UCSF Sch. of Medicine, San Francisco 1984–; awards: cancer research grant Nat. Cancer Inst. (NIH), Bethesda, Md. 1984-87; mem. Am. Gastroenterological Assn. 1965–, Am. Soc. for Gastrointestinal Endoscopy 1966–; life mem. Am. Civil Liberties Union Found. of N. Calif. 1978–; author: res. studies and review article on colon cancer screening pub. in profl. jours., 1988, 89, 92; Democrat; Jewish; rec: jazz piano, skiing. Ofc: Kaiser Permanente 280 W MacArthur Blvd Oakland 94611

GROVES-FREEMAN, JAN LYNN, attorney; b. Feb. 10, 1956, Inglewood; d. Leonard V. and Dorothy Ruth (Bergemann) Groves; m. Thomas Bond Freeman, May 25, 1985; edn: BBA, Univ. Redlands 1989; JD, Western State Univ. of Law 1994. Career: mktg. publs. coordinator Topaz Inc., San Diego 1982-84; controller Fisher Nielsen & Thurber 1984-89; accountant City of Carlsbad, Calif. 1989-91; law clerk Murphey Law Offices, Carlsbad, Calif. 1991-92, Law Ofc. of Michael Pines, Carlsbad 1992-93; prof. Watterson Coll. Pacific, Vista, Calif. 1993-94; appointed city mem. Child Care Task Force, Carlsbad 1987-88; honors: Nat. Dean's List 1993. Res: 6428 La Garza Ct Carlsbad 92009

GRUBB, WILLIAM FRANCIS X., consumer software executive, marketing executive; b. Aug. 11, 1944, New York; s. William Martin and Eileen F. (Donnelly) G.; m. Eileen B. O'Leary, April 4, 1964; children: Catherine E., William M., Kerri A., Christopher M.; edn: BA, Fordham Univ. 1966; MBA, Seton Hall Univ. 1972. Career: mtkg. and sales exec. Black & Decker, Towson, Md. 1968-79; v.p. mktg. Atari, Sunnyvale 1979-81; chmn., pres. New West Mktg., Mountain View 1981; pres., CEO, chmn. Imagic, Los Gatos 1981-84; exec. v.p. Dataspeed 1984-85; pres. Axlon Inc. 1985-86; exec. v.p., gen. mgr., Worlds of Wonder Inc., Freemont 1986-87; pres., chief exec. The Complete PC, San Jose 1987-93, pres., CEO ICTV 1994–. Res: 12421 Frederickburg Dr Saratoga 95070 Ofc: 14600 Winchester Blvd., Los Gatos, CA 95030

GRUBE, STANLEY MORRIS, corporate executive; b. Sept. 18, 1938, Cooperburg, Pa.; s. Earl S. and Ruth Naomi (Greasemer) G.; m. Betty Hurst, Nov. 22, 1958; children: Gregory W. b. 1959, Douglas E. b. 1961; edn: MBA, George Washington Univ. 1966. Career: adminstrv. and exec. dir. Corona Comm. Hosp., Corona 1966-82; pres., CEO Versacare 1982–; advy. council Loma Linda Univ. 1988–; Riverside Co. Med. Indigent Adults Funding Task Force 1985–; Riverside Emergency Med. Care Com. 1984–; oral examiner Am. Healthcare Execs., Chgo., Ill. 1974–; Hosp. Council So. Calif. Payors Rels. Com., L.A. 1988–; awards: Corona C.of C. Outstanding Citizen of Year 1986, Corona Jaycees Disting. Service 1971; mem: Assn. of Hospitals (pres. 1975-82), Am. Coll. Healthcare Execs. (fellow), Corona Group (pres. 1985–), Corona Norco Unified Sch. Dist. (year-round task force pres. 1987), Inland Cos. Health Systems Agency (bd. trust, treas. 1976-84), Corona SDA Ch. (bd. dirs.), Rotary (pres. 1971-72), Corona Airport Advy. Council (chmn.), YMCA (bd. trustees 1976–), Am. Heart Assn. (bd. trustees 1989–); reports pub. (1966, 74); Republican; SDA; rec: flying. Ofc: Versacare Inc. 702 S Washburn Corona 91720

GRUBER, HOWARD S., physician, pediatrician; b. July 13, 1937, NY, NY; s. Hyman and Esther (Reisenfeld) G.; m. Alice J. Schrader, Dec. 31, 1939; children: Stephanie Gruber Fried b. 1966, Amy b. 1967, Craig b. 1973; edn: AB, Columbia Coll., NY, NY 1958; MD, Albert Einstein Coll. of Medicine, NY, NY 1962; fellow, Am. Bd. of Pediatrics 1967. Career: intern, resident Univ. Hosps., Cleveland, Ohio 1962-64; sr. resident NY Hosp.-Cornell Med. Ctr., NY, NY 1964-65; fellow in newborn medicine Case Western Univ. Sch. of Medicine, Cleveland, Ohio 1967-69; pediatrician, mng. ptnr. Berkeley Pediatric Med. Group, Berkeley, Calif. 1969–; acting attending staff Alta Bates Hosp., Berkeley

and Children's Hosp., Oakland 1970–; clinical faculty UC Berkeley 1971–; awards: Disting. Teaching award, UC Berkeley 1981, 84, 85, Outstanding Attending Award of the Yr., Children's Hosp., Oakland 1985; mem: Am. Acad. of Pediatrics 1967–, CMA 1969–, Alameda-Contra Costa Med. Assn. 1969–; mil: capt. U.S. Army 1965-67. Ofc: Berkeley Pediatric Medical Group 1650 Walnut St Berkeley 94709 Tel: 510/848-2566

GRUEN, CLAUDE, urban economist; b. Aug. 17, 1931, Bonn; came to U.S., 1938; s. Walter and Elsbet (Bronne) G.; m. Nina Jaffe, Sept. 11, 1960; children: Les, Dale, Adam, Joshua, Aaron; edn: BBA, Univ. Cincinnati, 1954, MA, 1962, PhD in econs., 1964. Career: faculty Xavier Univ., Cinti. 1963-64, Univ. Calif., Berkeley 1964-70; economist Arthur D. Little Inc., San Francisco 1964-70; pres., prin. economist Gruen Gruen & Associates, 1970–, cons. municipal and county govts., pub. and pvt. agencies, and commercial developers; mkt., investment and fiscal analysis for major downtown devel. projects in Dayton and Cleveland, Ohio, Scottsdale, Ariz., Medford and Portland, Oreg., Calif. cities of Santa Maria, Chula Vista, Mountain View, Palo Alto, and Pleasanton; frequent testimony on housing and zoning policy, expert witness on real estate litigation in Municipal and Superior Cts. and in No. Dist. Fed. Ct.; condr. fiscal impact studies for many Calif. cities; dir. RREEF America (REIT) 1994–; mem: Real Estate and Urban Economics Assn., Lambda Alpha Hon. We. Regional Sci. Assocs., Urban Land Inst. (urban devel. and mixed-use coun.); contbg. editor The Instnl. Real Estate Letter; contbr. articles in profl. jours. Ofc: 564 Howard St San Francisco 94105-3002 Tel: 415/433-7598

GRUENWALD, GEORGE HENRY, new products management consultant; b. April 23, 1922, Chicago, Ill.; s. Arthur Frank and Helen (Duke) G.; m. Corrine Rae Linn, Aug. 16, 1947; children: Helen Marie, Paul Arthur; edn: BS journalism, Northwestern Univ. 1947; asst. to pres. Uarco Inc., Chgo., Ill. 1947-49; creative dir., mgr. merchandising aids, Willys Overland Motors Inc., Toledo 1949-51; new products, brand and advt. mgr. Toni Co., Chgo. 1951-53; v.p. creative dir., account supr. E.H. Weiss Agency 1953-55; exec. v.p., supr. mgmt. North Advt. 1955-71; pres., treas., dir. Pilot Products 1963-71; pres., dir. Advance Brands Inc. 1963-71; exec. v.p., dir. Campbell Mithun Inc., Minneapolis and Chgo. & branch offices 1971-72, pres., dir. 1972-79, chmn., dir. 1979-81, CEO, dir. 1981-83, chief creative ofcr., dir. 1983-84; v.chmn., dir. Ted Bates Worldwide, N.Y.C. 1979-80; mgmt. cons. new products 1984–; ed. in chief Oldsmobile Rocket Circle mag., 1956-64, Hudson Family mag., 1955, author New Product Devel. What Really Works, 1985, Guide to New Product Devel. Checklists - from Mission to Market, 1991, New Product Devel. video, 1989, New Products Seven Steps to Success video, 1988, New Product Devel. - Responding to Market Demand, 1992 (2nd ed.), 1996 (3rd ed.) expert columnist Mktg. News, 1988-, contbr. articles to profl. jours., creator num. packaged consumer products; awards: Hermes award 1963. Ednl. T.V. awards 1969, 71, 86; mem: Chgo. Pub. T.V. Assn. (trustee 1969-73), Minneapolis Soc. Fine Arts (trustee 1975-83), Linus Pauling Inst. Sci. & Medicine (trustee 1984-92, 95–, adv. 1992-95); Northwestern Univ. Alumni Fund Council Chgo. (chmn. v.p., chmn. class reps. 1965-68), Twin Cities Pub. T.V. Corp. (trustee, chmn., pres., CEO 1971-84), Minn. Pub. Radio Inc. (trustee 1973-77, v.chair 1974-75), Pub. Bdcstg. Service (bd. dirs., exec. com. 1978-86, 1988-94, comm. advy. com. 1993–), St. Paul Chamber Orchestra (bd. 1982-84), San Diego Chamber Orch. (bd. 1986-88), San Diego St. Univ. Pub. Bdcstg. (com. advy. bd. 1986-), Ednl. T.V. awards Club, Am. Assn. Advt. Agencies (mgnt. com. 1976-84), Am. Inst. Wine & Food (bd. dirs. 1985-92), Nat. Soc. Profl. Engrs., Nat. Soc. Profl. Journalists, Internat. Assn. Cooking Profls.; mil: USAAF 1943-45. Ofc: POB 1696 Rancho Santa Fe 92067-1696

GRUENWALD, OSKAR, research institute executive, consultant; b. Oct. 5, 1941, Yugoslavia, came to U.S., 1961; s. Oskar and Vera (Wolf) G.; edn: AA, Pasadena City Coll., 1964; BA, UC Berkeley, 1966; MA, Claremont Grad. Sch., 1967, PhD, 1972; Calif. life std. tchg. credential. Career: internat. economist U.S. Treasury Dept., W.D.C., 1967-68; vis. res. assoc. Univ. Erlangen, Nurnberg, Germany 1971-72; lectr. Pepperdine Univ., Malibu, Calif. 1972-73, Santa Monica Coll. 1973-76; independent res., writer, Santa Monica, 1976-83; founder and pres. Inst. for Interdisciplinary Research, 1983–; guest lectr. internat., 1976–; research assoc. Ctr. for Russian and East European Studies, Univ. Ill., Champaign, Urbana, summers 1976, 79; cons. Inst. for Advanced Philosophic Research, Boulder, Colo. 1977–, Com. to Aid Democratic Dissidents in Yugoslavia, W.D.C., 1980–; pub. research, Syndicated, Claremont, Calif. 1982–, Freedom House Exchange, N.Y.C., 1985–; awards: Templeton Award for best publ. paper on sci. and religion 1992, NEH Summer Seminar on Political Cultures, Univ. Calif. 1989, Ludwig Vogelstein Found. grantee 1976-77; mem. Am. Polit. Sci. Assn. 1969-93, Am. Philos. Assn., Am. Assn. for Advancement Slavic Studies (cons. Slavic Rev. 1986–), Am. Sci. Affiliation, Inst. for Study Internat. Problems (bd. 1988–), Internat. Christian Studies Assn. (founder, pres. 1983–, ed. newsletter 1983–), Delta Tau Kappa; author: The Yugoslav Search for Man (1983); co-editor: Human Rights in Yugoslavia (1986); founder, ed. J. Interdisciplinary Studies: Internat. J. Interdisciplinary and Interfaith Dialogue (1989–). Ofc: Inst. Interdisciplinary Research, 2828 3d St Ste 11 Santa Monica 90405 Tel: 310/396-0517

GRUNER, RICHARD STEVEN, professor of law; b. March 10, 1953, Frankfort, Germany; s. George F. and Irene L. (Obermiller) G.; m. Marie Helen Beall, July 29, 1978; children: Helen Irene b. 1985, Elizabeth Diane b. 1987; edn: BS, Caltech (Pasadena) 1975; JD, USC Law Center 1978; LLM, Columbia Law Sch. (New York) 1982. Career: staff attorney IBM Corp., New York, N.Y. 1978-83; prof. of law Whittier Coll. Sch. of Law, Los Angeles 1983–; mem: New York Bar, Calif. Bar; author articles on expert computer systems in law, 1983–, articles on corp. crime and sentencing, 1985–. Ofc: Whittier College School of Law 5353 W Third St Los Angeles 90020

GRZANKA, LEONARD G., writer; b. Dec. 11, 1947, Ludlow, Mass.; s. Stanley Simon and Claire (Rozkuszka) G.; m. Jannette Donnenwirth, Sept. 3, 1982 (div. 1987); edn: BA, Univ. of Mass. 1972; MA, Harvard Univ., 1974. Career: sales promotion writer Tymshare Transaction Svs., Fremont 1981-82; acct. exec. Strayton Corp., Santa Clara 1981-82; mng. ed. Portable Computer Mag., San Francisco 1982-84; No. Calif. Bureau Chief Digital News; columnist California Farmer Mag., S.F. 1984-87, VAR Mag. (W. Coast edit.) and PC Companion Mag., Camden Communications, 1985-87; prin. Grzanka Associates, San Francisco 1984–; lectr. Golden Gate Univ. 1985-87; contbg. ed. Silicon Valley Mag. 1982-85; battery prog. cons. Electric Power Res. Inst. & U.S. Advanced Battery Consortium from Bevilacqua, Knight, Inc. 1991–; honors: Phi Beta Kappa 1972, Phi Kappa Phi 1972, Danforth Fellow 1972-74, Japan-US Friendship Commn. Literary Translation Award 1982; mem: Harvard Club of S.F., Press Club S.F. (admissions com.), Calif. Hist. Soc.; author Neither Heaven Nor Hell, 1978; edit. Master Pieces of Contemporary Japanese Crafts, 1977; contbr. Manajo: The Chinese Preface in Kokinshu: A Collection of Poems Ancient & Modern (Princeton 1984); mil: sgt. USAF Pararescue, Sr. Jumpmaster, Vietnam Svc.; Democrat; R.Cath.; rec: writing. Res: 2909 Madison St Alameda 94501-5426

GUENTHER, ROBERT STANLEY, II, private investment manager; b. Sept. 29, 1950, Orange, Calif.; s. Robert Stanley G. and Fanny (Neuman) Shaw; edn: BA in psych. and sociol., Univ. Calif. Santa Barbara, 1975. Career: investor, Templeton, Calif. 1971–; lodge: Moose, Santa Margarita 1986–; rec: collecting. Res: 7245 El Pomar Dr Templeton 93465

GUGGENHEIM, WOLF Z., physician, internist; b. Mar. 28, 1932, Western Europe; s. Willy and Betty (Schlesinger) G.; m. Vivian ; children: Arye b. 1967, Achiezer b. 1972, Shlomo b. 1984, Sharona b. 1985, Willy b. 1989; edn: MD, Univ. of Zurich 1959; lic. MD, Switzerland (1959), NY (1964), Calif. (1966). Career: postdoc. research fellow Univ. Zurich Med. Sch. 1959-60; intern State Univ. New York, Glensfalls Gen. Hosp. 1960-1; res. physician, internal med. N.Y. Polyclinic Hosp. Med. Ctr. 1961-3; sr. res./NIH Fellow Joslin Diabetes Ctr., Harvard Med. Sch. 1963-4; physician/internist, solo pvt. practice 1964–; instr., asst. prof. Internal Med., N.Y. Med. Coll. 1964-67; prof. of medicine (Distinguished Professorship) Touro Coll. 1975-78; recipient Klaus Found. Postgrad. Merit Scholarship 1959-60; mem: Am. Diabetes Assoc., So. Calif. affil.; Graduate Council, Univ. of Zurich; mil: capt., inf./field intell., I.D.F.; rec: classical music, swimming. Ofc: 804 Venice Blvd Venice 90291

GUILFORD, ANDREW JOHN, lawyer; b. Nov. 28, 1950, Santa Monica; s. Howard Owens and Elsie Jennette (Hargreaves) G.; m. Loreen Gogain, Dec. 22, 1973; children: Colleen Catherine b. 1979, Amanda Joy b. 1981; edn: AB, summa cum laude, UC Los Angeles 1972, JD, 1975; admitted Calif. St. Bar 1975. Career: atty., assoc. Sheppard, Mullin, Richter & Hampton, Los Angeles and Newport Beach, –; ptnr. 1983–; lectr. Calif. Cont. Edn. of Bar 1978–; The Rutter Group 1983–, Hastings Ctr. for Advocacy, S.F. 1988; Superior Ct. judge pro tem and arbitrator 1983–; A.A.A. Large, Complex Case Program arbitrator 1993–; awards: fellow Am. Coll. of Trial Lawyers, fellow Am. Bar Assn., winner Poverty Law Ctr. Outstanding Service Award 1991, co-winner State Bar President's Pro Bono Service Award, UC Regents Scholar 1968, UCLA Alumni Assn. Scholar 1968, Phi Beta Kappa 1972, Pi Gamma Mu; mem: Am. Bar Assn., Assn. of Bus. Trial Lawyers, Federal Bar Assn., Calif. Bar Assn. (chmn. delegation to st. conv. 1986, 87), Commn. on the Future of the State Bar 1993-, Orange Co. Bar Assn. (chmn. Bus. Litigation Sect. 1983, bd. dirs. 1985-87, ofcr. 1988-90, pres. 1991, chmn. Law and Motion Com. 1982, chmn. Standing Com. for Trial Court Delay Reduction 1987-93, Public Law Center (bd. 1990–), Ninth Cir. Judicial Conf. delegate 1990-93, Constnl. Rights Found. (bd. 1990), UCLA Law Alumni Assn. (bd. 1992-95), Baroque Music Festival (bd. 1992–), Phi Beta Kappa Alumni Assn. (ofcr. 1978-84), Amicus Publico, Center 500, Sigma Pi; publs: UCLA Law Rev. 1975, Calif. CEB; Republican; Episcopal (subdeacon, warden, del. 1976–); rec: theater, photog., sports, poetry, garden. Res: 23 Via Terracaleta Coto De Caza 92679 Ofc: Sheppard, Mullin, Richter & Hampton, 4695 MacArthur Ct 7th Flr Newport Beach 92660

GUISE, STEVEN LEE, lawyer; b. December 10, 1946, Harrisburg, Pa.; s. Richard Christian and Lois Marie (Harbold) G.; m. Sara Simpson McWilliams, Oct. 21, 1972; 1 dau., Elizabeth b. 1985; edn: BA, Univ. Mich. 1968; JD, Vanderbilt Univ. 1971; LL.M, Georgetown Univ. 1976; admitted St. Bar Calif. 1978. Career: law clerk Mich. Ct. of Appeals, Lansing, Mich. 1971-72; atty. Interstate Commerce Commn., Wash. D.C. 1972-77; atty., assoc. Shahin Wawro

& Lorimer, Los Angeles 1978-79, ptnr. 1979-81; ptnr. Fulop & Hardee, Beverly Hills 1981-83; of counsel Munger Tolles & Olson, Los Angeles 1985, ptnr. 1986–; mem: Am. Bar Assn. (employee benefits com. of taxation sect. 1988-), L.A. Co. Bar Assn. (employee benefits subsect. of taxation sect., chmn. 1990-91), St. Bar of Calif. (empl. benefits com. of taxation chmn. 1991-92); Republican; Episcopalian. Ofc: Munger Tolles & Olson 355 S Grand Ave 35th Floor Los Angeles 90071

GUNER, OSMAN FATIH, physical-organic chemist; b. Feb. 25, 1956, Manisa, Turkey; s. Ahmet Tarik and Ayse Nurcan (Guneysu) G.; m. Nazli Rukiye Erbay, Apr. 23, 1982; children: Kurt b. 1987, Sibel b. 1990; edn: BS chemistry, Middle East Tech. Univ., Ankara, Turkey 1979, MS organic chem., 1981; PhD phys. org. chem., Va. Commonwealth Univ., Richmond, Va. 1986. Career: postdoctoral fellow Univ. Alabama, Birmingham 1987-89; sr. applications scientist Molecular Design Ltd., San Leandro 1989-93; sr. scientist MDL Information Systems, Inc., San Leandro 1993–; mem: Am. Inst. of Chemists (Fellow), Am. Chem. Soc. 1985–, US Chess Fedn.; lodge: Strict Observance (Richmond, Va.); contbr. articles in J. Am. Chem. Soc., J. Org. Chem., J. Chem. Inf. Computer Sci. 1987–; rec: chess, volleyball, golf. Ofc: MDL Information Systems, Inc. 14600 Catalina Street San Leandro 94577

GUNTHER, GERALD, legal educator, writer, biographer; b. Usingen, Taunus, Ger., 1927; s. Otto and Minna (Floersheim) Gutenstein; married, two children; edn: AB, Brooklyn Coll., 1949; MA, pub. law and govt., Columbia Univ., 1950; LLB (JD), Harvard Law Sch., 1953; LL.D (hon.), Ill. Inst. of Tech. 1987; LL.D. (hon.) Brooklyn Law Sch., 1990; LL.D. (hon.) Brooklyn Coll. of the City Univ. of N.Y., 1990; LL.D. (hon.) Duquesne Univ. 1995. Career: instr. polit. sci. and constnl. law Bklyn. Coll. and City Coll. N.Y., 1949-50, 51; editor Harvard Law Rev. 1951-53, Note ed. 1952-53 (Sears Prize 1951, 1952); law clk. Judge Learned Hand, U.S. Ct. Appeals 2d Cir. 1953-54, Chief Justice Earl Warren, U.S. Supreme Ct., 1954-55; atty., assoc. Cleary, Gottlieb, Friendly & Hamilton, NY 1953, 54, 55-56; assoc. prof., prof. of law Columbia Univ. Sch. of Law, 1956-62; prof. constnl. law Stanford Univ. Law Sch. 1962–, William Nelson Cromwell Prof. of Law, 1972–; vis. prof. Columbia Grad. Faculties summers 1962, 64, Harvard Law Sch. 1972-73, Brooklyn Law Sch. 1993, faculty Salzburg Seminars summer 1976, chair 1988, Peking Univ., PRC, summer 1986, Ariz. St. Univ. 1994, Lewis & Clark Coll. 1994; awards: disting. alumnus Bklyn. Coll. 1961, Guggenheim fellow 1962-63, Ford Comparative Law fellow in Europe 1966-67, fellow Ctr. for Adv. Study in Behavorial Scis. 1969-70, Nat. Endowment for Humanities sr. fellow 1980-81 and Constnl. Bicentennial fellow 1985-86, Fed. Bar Council honoree Learned Hand Medal for excellence in Fed. Jurisprudence 1988, selected as best qualified choice for U.S. Supreme Ct. in nat. poll N.Y. Law Jour. 1987; elected mem. Am. Acad. Arts & Scis. (fellow 1973), Am. Law Inst. 1974, Am. Philosophical Soc. 1981; author: Learned Hand: The Man and the Judge, 1994; editor or prin. author textbooks (and multiple editions), num. articles and book revs. in legal and other publs. Ofc: Law Sch. Stanford University Stanford 94305

GUNTHER, RICHARD EDWARD, educator; b. Mar. 1, 1946, Long Beach; s. Joseph Richard and Evelyn Alice (Balsiger) G.; m. Suzanne Hirshberg, July 10, 1976; children: Lisa b. 1987; edn: BA, USC, 1968; MS, UC Los Angeles, 1970, PhD, 1976. Career: research asst. UC Los Angeles, 1968-71; asst. prof., assoc. prof., prof., dept. chair, of mgmt. sci. CSU Northridge, 1971–; cons. City of Simi Valley, 1984, Southern Calif. Gas Co., 1986-87, Pacific Info Tech, Chatsworth 1987; honors: Beta Gamma Sigma 1970, Calif. St. graduate fellow 1968, merit award CSUN 1989; mem. The Inst. of Mgmt. Sci., So. Calif. chpt. (pres. 1983); civic: Conejo Free Clinic, Thousand Oaks (bd. 1981-, pres. 1988-90); contbg. editor, Maximum Performance: Complete Guide to Practical Business Management (Dow-Jones, 1990); Democrat; Baptist; rec: genealogy, computers, coins, golf. Res: 3337 Prairie Ct Newbury Park 91320 Ofc: Dept. Mgmt. Sci. Calif. State Univ. Northridge 91330

GUPTA, DINESH CHANDRA, manufacturing company executive; b. June 25, 1937, Meerut, India, nat. 1985; s. Faqir Chand and Manorma (Jain) G.; m. Vijay Rastogi, Dec.23, 1963; 1 child, Anju b. 1970; edn: BS, Meerut (India) Coll., 1955, MS in math., 1957; BSEE, Indian Inst. of Sci.,Bangalore, India 1960; MSEE, Carnegie-Mellon Univ., 1961. Career: research asst. Carnegie Inst. of Tech., Pittsburgh, Pa. 1960-61; mem. tech. staff Texas Instruments Inc., Dallas 1961-65; senior engr. GTE Labs. Inc., Bayside, N.Y. 1965-72; mng. dir. Superior Electronic Systems Ltd., Bombay, India 1972-77; senior engr. Unitrode Corp., Watertown, Mass. 1977-79; ops. mgr. Siliconix, Inc. Santa Clara 1979-90; dir. of technology SEH America, Inc., San Jose 1990–; chmn. biennial Internat. Symposium on Semiconductor Processing; advy. editor Solid State Technology; mem: Am. Soc. Testing & Materials (fellow, chmn. Com. F1.06, Profl. Award of Merit 1986), IEEE (senior), The Electrochemical Soc.; 4 Patents; contbr. 30+ tech. publs., editor 4 books: Silicon Processing, Semiconductor Processing, Emerging Semiconductor Technology, Semiconductor Fabrication: Technology & Metrology; rec: bridge, tennis. Res: 3103 N.E. 115th Circle Vancouver WA 98686-3948 Ofc: SEH America, Inc. 1737 N First St San Jose 95112

GUR-ARIEH, CHAIM, flavor manufacturing company president; b. July 26, 1934, Istanbul, Turkey; nat. 1968; s. Leon and Esther (Levy) Mizrahi; m. Elisheva Gilon, Sept. 15, 1974; 1 child, Sivan b. 1978; edn: BS, Technion Israel Inst. 1960; MS, PhD, Univ. Ill. 1963. Career: project leader Quaker Oats Co., Barrington, Ill. 1963-65; scientist United Technology Center, Sunnyvale 1965-67; asst. dir. of research Del Monte Corp., Walnut Creek 1967-75; pres., founder Food Devel. Corp., Oakland 1975–; Calif. Brands Flavors & Frangrances Inc. 1975–. Ofc: California Brands Flavors, Inc. 411 Pendleton Way Oakland 94621

GURASH, JOHN THOMAS, insurance company executive; b. Nov. 25, 1910, Oakland; s. Nicholas and Katherine (Restovic) G.; m. Katherine M. Mills, Feb. 4, 1934; 1 son, John Nicholas b. 1939; edn: law, Loyola Univ., L.A. 1936-39. Career: underwriting mgr. Am. Surety Co. of New York, 1930-44; v.p. and dir. Pacific Employers Ins. Co., 1944-53; pres. and organizer, dir. Meritplan Ins. Co. (1st co. to offer direct bill ins. through indep. agents), also exec. v.p. Teachers Ins. Underwriters, 1953-59; v.p. Insurance Co. of North America, 1966-70, dir. 1965-80; exec. v.p. INA Corp., 1968-69, pres. 1969-74, chmn. bd. and CEO 1969-75, chmn. exec. com. 1975-77, dir. 1968-82; dir. Household Finance Corp., 1974-81; chmn. bd. Household Internat. Inc., 1982-83, chmn. exec. com. 1983-84, dir. 1981-84; CEO Purex Industries Inc., 1984-86, chmn. bd. 1984-89, dir. 1974-89; chmn. bd. and dir. CertainTeed Corp. 1978-92, Horace Mann Educators Corp. 1989–, Saint-Gobain Corp. 1991-92 (chmn. emeritus, dir. 1992–); dir.: Weingart Found. 1972–, Pic 'N' Save Corp., 1984-90, Norton Co., 1990-92; awards: Gold Medal Netherlands Soc., Phila. 1971, Am. Jewish Com. 1971, John Wanamaker 1972, NCCJ nat. human relations award 1973, Sourin award Cath. Philopatrian Literary Inst. 1973, Chevalier French Legion of Honor 1975; mem.: Pa. Soc., Newcomen Soc. N. Am., Kts. of Malta, L.A. World Affairs Council; clubs: California, Pine Valley GC, Los Angeles CC, Annandale GC, 100 Club, The Valley Hunt; author (book) The Report of the Archdiocesan Advy. Com. on Fin. Crisis of Cath. Schs. in Phila. and Surrounding Counties, 1972; rec: golf, reading. Res: 456 S Orange Grove Blvd Pasadena 91105 Ofc: 1000 Wilshire Blvd Ste 610 Los Angeles 90017

GUTHRIE, JAMES WILLIAMS, professor of education; b. Aug. 28, 1936, Chicago, Ill.; s. James Williams and Florence Pearl (Harvey) G.; children: Sarah b. 1962, James Jr. b. 1965, Shannon b. 1966, Kyle b. 1980; edn: BA, Stanford Univ. 1958; MA, 1960; PhD, 1968; post doctoral, Harvard Univ. 1971. Career: tchr. Palo Alto Unified Sch. Dist., 1961-64; asst. dir. Carnegie Sch. Bd. Studies, Stanford 1964-66; spl. asst. Dept. of HEW, Wash. D.C. 1966-67; asst. prof. UC Berkeley 1967-71; dep. dir. N.Y. State Edn. Commn., N.Y.C. 1971-72; assoc. prof. UC Berkeley 1972-78, prof. 1978–; ed. Ednl. Evaluation & Policy Analysis, WDC 1986–; awards: James B. DeGolyer Hons. Fellowship (1956-58), Alfred North Whitehead postdoctoral fellowship 1969-70, Irving R. Melbo disting. vis. prof. 1986-87; mem: Phi Delta Kappa, Am. Edn. Research Assn., YMCA (pres. 1983-88); Episcopalian; rec: hiking. Ofc: Univ. of Calif. Policy Analysis for California Education School of Education Berkeley 94720

GUTIERREZ, OLGA, psychiatrist, consultant, educator; b. Dec. 29, 1929, Buenos Aires, Argentina; d. Gabriel and Soledad (Garcia Bueno) G.; granddau. of Jose San Roman, Dean of Sch. of Medicine, Spain; widow; 1 son, Luis Eduardo, b. 1961; edn: PhD in biochem., Univ. Buenos Aires, 1954; Immunologist, Inst. Pasteur, Paris 1959; MD, Univ. of Buenos Aires, 1967; Diplomate Am. Bd. Psychiatry and Neurology 1987; Diplomate Am. Bd. Child and Adolescent Psychiatry 1989; Diplomate Am. Bd. in Forensic Psychiatry 1994. Career: ednl. asst. Univ. Buenos Aires, 1953-58; res. fellow, Inst. Pasteur, Paris, 1958-60; ednl. chief and res. assoc. Univ. Buenos Aires, 1960-70; res. fellow Superior Council of Biol. Resrch, Madrid, Spain 1970-71; res. fellow, Reproductive Biol., OB-Gyn, USC, 1971-74; pvt. practice of medicine, Buenos Aires, 1975-77; adult psychiatry L.A. Co./USC Med. Ctr., 1978, child and adolescent psychiatry, L.A. Co./USC Med. Ctr., 1982, forensic psychiatry Dept. Psychiatry, Inst. of Psychiat., Law and Behavioral Scis., USC, 1985; currently staff psychiatrist L.A. Co. Dept. of Mental Health, and staff child psychiatrist and adolescent psychiatrist USC-LAC Child Guidance Clinic; consultant; awards: Univ. of Buenos Aires Golden Medal 1952, Faculty of Medicine Award 1954, Acad. of Med. Award 1966, Junior Chamber Award 1966, AMA Award 1988; mem: Soc. of Chem. of Uruguay (corres. mem.), Acad. of Pharm. and Biochem. (Arg.), Microbiol. and Immunol. Assn., AMA, Biochem. Assn., Salerni Coll. USC, Am. Acad. of Child and Adolescent Psychiatry, Am. Acad. of Psychiatry and Law, Am. Bd. of Forensic Examiners; publs: num. sci. articles rel. to medicine; guest appearances on t.v. and radio re psychiatric issues; rec: sports, swimming, sailing, tennis, music, cinema, theatre, travel. Res: 101 California Ave Apt 507 Santa Monica 90403 Ofc: 3787 S Vermont Blvd Los Angeles 90007

GUTNER, KIM ALLISON, physician, child psychiatrist; b. Jan. 12, 1956, Chicago, Ill.; d. Kenneth Howard and Lynnette (Nelson) Gutner; m. Russell Alan Davis, June 10, 1984; children: 2 daughters b. 1990, 1993; edn: BA biology, summa cum laude, UC Santa Barbara, 1979; MD, Yale Univ., 1984; lic. physician N.Y., Calif. Colo. Career: psychiatry resident N.Y. Hosp.- Cornell, White Plains, N.Y. 1984-87; child psychiatry fellow UC San Diego, 1987-89; med. dir. Family Development and Learning Center, Solana Beach 1989-90; attdg. physician Southwood Psychiatric Hosp., Chula Vista 1988-90; courtesy

CPC San Luis Rey Hosp.; Charter/API Hosp.; full time solo pvt. practice, Del Mar; adminstrv. asst. Planned Parenthood, S.B. 1980; honors: UCSB dean's hons. list 1974-79; mem: Am. Psychiatric Assn., Am. Acad. Child & Adolescent Psychiatry, Am. Med. Soc. Alcoholism & Drug Dependencies, San Diego Psychiatric Soc.; 2 research articles pub., 1984, 85; rec: skiing, swimming, travel. Ofc:240 9th Street Del Mar 92014

GYEMANT, ROBERT ERNEST, lawyer; b. Jan. 17, 1944, Managua, Nicaragua, naturalized 1954; s. Emery and Magda (Von Rechnitz) G.; m. Sally Bartch Libhart, 1992; children: Emily b. 1993; children from prev. m: Robert, Jr. b. 1971, Anne Elizabeth b. 1972;; edn: AB, UCLA, 1965; JD, Boalt Hall UCB, 1968; C.P.A., Calif. 1968; admitted bar: Calif. 1969, N.Y. 1981; cert. criminal splst. State Bar Calif. 1988-93. Career: lawyer, assoc. Orrick Herrington Rowley & Sutcliffe, San Francisco 1968-70; ptnr. Skornia Rosenblum & Gyemant, 1970-74; prin. R.E. Gyemant, APC, 1974–; prin. Niesar, Cecchini & Gyemant, 1987-89; of counsel to Sullivan, Roche & Johnson 1989-90; prin. McCarthy Gyemant & Bobbits, San Francisco and Pasadena, 1992–; appt. Hon. Vice-Consul Republic of Costa Rica, 1980–; mem: Am. Inst. CPAs, Calif. Soc. CPAs, San Francisco Bar Assn. (ethics com. 1987–), Calif. Trial Lawyers Assn., State Bar of Calif., Assn. of Defense Counsel, N.Y. State Bar, St. Thomas More Soc.; trustee Fr. Am. Bilingual Sch. 1976-79; clubs: World Trade (S.F.), N.Y. Athletic, Racquet & Tennis (N.Y.); contbr. Calif. Law Rev. (1968); Republican (alt. del. Rep. Nat. Conv. 1992); Episcopalian. Ofc: McCarthy Gyemant & Bobbits, P.C. 332 Pine St 7th Fl San Francisco 94104; 350 W Colorado Blvd 2d Fl Pasadena 91105

HAAS, NEIL B., psychiatrist; b. Feb. 27, 1941, Detroit, Mich.; s. Abraham Haas and Florence N. (Pearlman) (Haas) Burrows; m. Rowena Marie Randall, June 10, 1965; 1 son, Jeremy b. 1971; edn: Univ. Mich. 1958-61; MD, Univ. Mich. Med. Sch. 1965; MS social psychiatry, UCLA 1972. Career: psychiatry resident UCLA 1968-71; pvt. practice psychiatry, Los Angeles 1971–; asst. clin. prof. UCLA 1974–; psychiatrist Sepulveda VA Hosp. 1973–; co-investigator Naltrexone Project, 1974-84; psychiatry cons. Found. Jr. Blind, Los Angeles 1971-86; commr. Los Angeles Co. Narcotics & Dangerous Drugs Commn. 1984–; attdg. chief Cedars Sinai Chemical Dependancy 1989; mem: So. Calif. Psychiatric Soc. (ethics com. 1986–), Am. Psychiatric Assn., Calif. Soc. for the Treatment of Alcohol & Other Drug Dependencies, Am. Soc. Addiction Medicine; mil: lt. USN 1966-68. Ofc: 1800 Fairburn Los Angeles 90025

HAAS, RICHARD, lawyer; b. Sept. 1, 1924, Glens Falls, N.Y.; s. Marc and Henrietta (Vogelsanger) H.; m. Dorothy J. Walz, Aug. 2, 1946; children: Eric, Marco, Gregory; edn: BA, UCLA 1946; LLB, UC Berkeley 1950; admitted St. Bar Calif. 1951, U.S. Dist. Ct. Calif. 1951, U.S. Supreme Ct. 1970. Career: ptnr. Brobeck Phleger & Harrison, San Francisco 1959-79;mem. Lasky Haas Cohler & Munter 1979-94; honors: Order of Coif, Kappa Sigma; mem: Am. Coll. Trial Lawyers (fellow), Claremont Country Club, Berkeley Tennis Club; mil: lt. USNR 1941-46. Res: 2901 Forest Ave Berkeley 94705 Ofc: Lasky Haas & Cohler 505 Sansome St 12th Floor San Francisco 94111

HAAS, ROBERT DOUGLAS, apparel manufacturing company executive; b. Apr. 3, 1942, San Francisco; s. Walter A. Jr. and Evelyn (Danzig) H.; m. Colleen Gershon, Jan. 27, 1974; 1 child, Elise Kimberly; edn: BA, UC Berkeley 1964; MBA, Harvard Univ. 1968. Career: Peace Corps, Ivory Coast 1964-66; assoc., McKinsey and Co. 1969-72; Levi Strauss & Co., San Francisco 1973-: sr. v.p. corp. planning and policy 1978-80, pres. new bus. group 1980, pres. operating groups 1980-81, exec. v.p., chief operating officer 1981-84, pres., chief exec. officer 1984-89, CEO, chmn. bd. 1989–; dir. Levi Strauss Associates Inc. 1985–; pres. Levi Strauss Found.; Hon. trustee Brookings Institution; Hon. dir. San Francisco AIDS Found.; trustee Ford Found.; honors: Class Valedictorian, UC Berkeley 1964; Phi Beta Kappa 1964–; Baker Scholar, Harvard Grad. Sch. of Bus. 1968; White House Fellow 1968-69; mem: Am. Apparel Mfrs. Assn. (bd. dirs.), Bay Area Council (bd. dirs.), Meyer Friedman Inst. (bd. dirs.), No. Am. Exec. Com. of the Trilateral Commission, The Conference Bd., Council on Foreign Relations, Calif. Business Roundtable. Ofc: Levi Strauss & Co PO Box 7215 San Francisco 94120

HABER, JUDY A., microbiologist; b. April 9, 1944, Buffalo, N.Y.; d. Manuel and Edith Rose (Feldstein) Haber; m. Jack E. Cain, March 31, 1979; 1 dau., Darcy b. 1985; edn: BA, St. Univ. N.Y. at Buffalo 1965; MA, 1968; PhD, UCSF Med. Center 1971; dipl. Am. Bd. Med. Microbiology 1977. Career: postdoctoral studies Calif. St. Dept. Health, Berkeley 1972-74; supr. microbiology and serology depts. Smith Kline Lab., Burlingame 1974-75; dir. microbiology lab. Valley Med. Center, Fresno 1976–; asst. clin. prof. UCSF 1977–; adj. prof. CSU Fresno 1977-85; cons. Mercy Hosp., Bakersfield 1987-92; expert witness 1977-85; cons. Baxter Micro Scan, Sacto. 1989; honors: Phi Beta Kappa; mem: No. Calif. Am. Soc. for Microbiology (treas. 1987-91, councilor 1993-95), Nat. Am. Soc. for Microbiology 1972– (council 1993-95), Fresno ASM Workshop Com. (chair 1977-87), Pure Culture Soc. (bd. dirs. 1983), Fresno Reg. Microbiology Group, chair 1994–, Fresno MacIntosh User Group, treas. 1994, pres. 1995, Sierra Club; 11 articles pub. in sci. jours., 1964-94. Res: 468 E Sample Ave Fresno 93710 Ofc: Valley Medical Center Laboratory 445 S Cedar Ave Fresno 93702

HABERFELD, STEPHEN EMIL, lawyer/magistrate, judge; b. July 18, 1944, Baltimore, Md.; s. Alfons and Felicia (Spirer) H.; m. Sharon Burton, Aug. 3, 1969; 1 dau., Meredith Allison b. 1973; edn: AB (valedictorian), UCLA 1965; MPA, Princeton Univ. 1967; JD, Harvard Law Sch. 1970. Career: law clerk to Hon. Leonard P. Moore, U.S. Ct. of Appeals, 2d Cir. 1970-71; Asst. Watergate Special Prosecutor, 1973-75; lawyer pvt. practice, 1971, arbitrator Am. Arb. Assn. 1972; referee, receiver Los Angeles Superior Ct., 1984, U.S. Magistrate Judge (p.t.) 1988-92; judge pro tem L.A. Municipal Ct. 1987, L.A. Superior Ct. 1988; adj. prof. Pepperdine Law Sch. 1979-86, 90; honors: Phi Beta Kappa, Regents Scholar 1965, article editor Harvard J. of Legislation 1969; mem: L.A. Co. Bar Assn., Malibu Ballet Soc. (pres. 1985-87), Pt. Dume Comm. Assn. (dir. 1982-86), Malibu C.of C. (dir. 1978-82), 1939 Club (dir. 1978), L.A.Co. Mus. of Art; pub. article law jour., 1969; co-author: treatise, 1992; mil: AUS 1967-69. Res: 29221 Sea Lion Place Malibu 90265 Ofc: Haberfeld & Haberfeld 8224 Blackburn Ave Ste 100 Los Angeles 90048

HACKBARTH, DOROTHY ALICE, educational consultant; b. Apr. 21, 1921, Naperville, Ill.; d. Walter Dewey and Nellie Louise (Staffeldt) Eichelberger; m. Charles Alfred Hackbarth, Oct. 24, 1942; children: Christofer Lee b. 1944, Cathleen b. 1948, Timothy Scott b. 1952; edn: BA, UC Berkeley, 1964, gen. sec. lifetime tchg. credential, 1965. Career: secty. Lucien Lelong, Chicago 1942-43; telephone opr. Hinsdale (Ill.) Bell Tel. Co., 1943-44; dress designer, self-empl., 1947-55; tchr. Oakland (Calif.) Unified Sch. Dist., 1965-66, tchr. Berkeley Unified Sch. Dist. 1966-78, chair fgn. lang. dept. 1969-74; pres. UNA/USA, A1. Chapter, Oakland 1969-72; chair Nor Cal Coun. 1971-73; pres., founder and CEO Unesco Assn./USA, Inc. Oakland 1971–, UNA/USA Newsletter editor 1972–; awards: fellow Unesco, Paris, France 1971, Berkeleyans for Acad. Excellence tchg. award 1977, Calif. PTA cont. edn. scholar UC Berkeley 1977; mem: Cal Alumni Assn. (1964–, life), Berkeley /Oakland /Piedmont Alumni Club 1991; pub. articles: Patramoine Mondial (1979), Philosophy of Edn.: Teaching Values (1988); Indep.; rec: fgn. lang. study, problem-solving, all kinds of mental exercise, travel, people. Res/Ofc: Unesco Assn./USA, Inc. 5815 Lawton Ave Oakland 94618-1510

HACKETT, GERALD EDWARD, JR., university veterinarian, professor of animal and veterinary science; b. Aug. 17, 1947, St. James, Minn.; s. Gerald Edward and Frances Claire (Kruck) H.; m. Nancy Kathleen Kratzer, Sept. 7, 1968; children: Liberty Anne b. 1975, Gerald Edward b. 1977, Richard Patrick b. 1982, James Henry b. 1986; edn: BS in animal sci., Univ. Minn., 1972, BS vet. sci., 1976, DVM, 1978, MS, 1979. Career: veterinary clinician Ridgeland Vet. Svs., Ridgeland, Wis. 1978-79; St. James Vet. Clinic, St. James, Minn. 1979-80; univ. veterinarian and prof. animal sci. Calif. St. Polytechnic Univ. Pomona, 1980–, dir. of equine research 1986-94; indep. consulting vet., 1985–; contract vet. Am. Horse Show Assn., Columbus, Oh. 1982-87, 89–; vis. scientist Louisiana St. Univ., Baton Rouge, 1987-88; instr. UC Riverside Ext. 1985, 86, 87, Chino Park & Rec. Dept. 1989-90; ag advy. bd. Don Lugo H.S., Chino 1986-89; honors: Phi Kappa Phi, Gamma Sigma Delta (mem. 1972, merit awards 1986, 87, 91), CalPoly profl. promise and performance awards (1986, 87); mem: Am. Vet. Med. Assn., Calif. VMA (del. and equine com. chair), So. Calif. VMA (trustee, treas. 1986-87, 1991, Equine chpt. pres. 1983-85, 1989-90, pres. 1994), AAEP, AAVP, AALAS, ASLAP, AAVN, Kiwanis Internat. (pres. Chino Club 1991); publs: contbr. sci. jour. articles and research papers, research grantsman, 1986, 88, 90, writer/actor/prod. video tapes on equine health care and mgmt., 1985, 86; Democrat; rec: outdoors, horses, clay targets, fishing. Res: 6165 Chino Ave Chino 91710 Ofc: Cal Poly, Pomona Vet Clinic 3801 West Temple Ave Pomona 91768

HADCOCK, MARY MARGARET, physician and surgeon; b. July 2, 1954, Conrad, Montana; d. Alfonse Frederick and Margaret Frances (Salansky) Wurth; m. William E. Hadcock, Jr., MD, June 26, 1976; children: Elisabeth b. 1984, Billy b. 1987, Michael b. 1989; edn: BA, biology, Carroll Coll., Helena, Mont. 1976; MD, Loyola Univ. of Chgo. 1979; cert. Am. Bd. of Surgery 1986. Career: internship and residence, categorical surgical, Loyola Univ. Affiliated Hosps. 1979-83; pvt. practice, surgeon, Fresno, Calif. 1984–; bd. dirs. Fresno Surgery Ctr. 1992-93, 93-94; mem. credentials com. Fresno Surgery Ctr. 1993, 94; pres. Fresno Surgical Soc. 1992-93 (v.p. 1991-92, sec./treas. 1990-91); past chief of staff and dept. of surgery chmn. Sierra Comm. Hosp.; past dept. of surgery chmn. Fresno Comm. Hosp.; lectr., num. hospitals and civic organizations 1986–; fellow, Am. Coll. of Surgeons; mem: C.B. Puestow Surgical Soc., AMA, CMA, Fresno-Madera Med. Assn., Assn. of Women Surgeons, Fresno-Madera Med. Women's Assn., Am. Med. Women's Assn.; contbr. articles to profl. jours., 1980-83; sr. honors thesis pub. 1976; Roman Catholic; rec: piano, opera, racquetball, skiing. Address: Fresno 93711

HADDAD, LOUIS NICHOLAS, paralegal; b. Sept. 3, 1923, Beggs, Okla.; s. Abraham and Tammam (Lelo) H.; m. Jacqueline Pratali, Sept. 22, 1945 (div. 1952); children: Carole b. 1948, Shirley b. 1950, Charles b. 1951; m. Martha Maria Laengst, Dec. 31, 1954; children: Sheila, Stephanie. Career: prop. Haddad's Cafe, Corpus Christi, Tex. 1946-50; ptnr. Haddad Bros. Wholesalers, Lancaster, Calif. 1956-57; reg. v.p. Nulite Corp., N.J. 1957-59; owner Camptown West Motor Home, Seaside, Calif. 1960-79; co-owner Monterey Bay Tribune, 1983-89; City of Seaside plng. commr. 1962-64, councilman 1964-66, 78-80, mayor 1966-72; bd. dirs. Assn. of Monterey Bay Area Govts., Alliance on Aging; chmn. Calif. Council on Criminal Justice 1971-72, chmn. Laguna Grande Agy., Seaside Co. Sanitation Dist., chmn. Monterey Overall Econ. Devel. Com., v.chmn. So. Monterey Bay Water Pollution Control Agy., Monterey Co. Local Agys. Formation Commn.; bd. dirs. Monterey Peninsula Water Mgmt. Dist. 1993–; mem: Seaside C.of C. (dir.), Am. Judicature Soc., Navy League, Assn. U.S. Army, NCO Assn. Am. (hon.), Am. Legion, VFW; mil: served to capt. 1940-46, AUS 1950-55; Republican; Cath.; rec: golf. Res/Ofc: 5 Deer Stalker Path Monterey 93940-6311

HADDAD, WISAM BOULOS, surgeon; b. Mar. 4, 1954, Amman, Jordan, nat. USA 1985; s. Boulos Somail and Tamam M. (Hawatmeh) H.; m. Rozanne, June 12, 1977; children: Angie b. 1980, Laila b. 1982, Laura b. 1985; edn: BS, acad. distinction, Andrews Univ. 1976; MD, Loma Linda Univ. 1979; lic. phys. Calif. 1981; bd. cert. Am. Bd. of Surgery 1986. Career: gen. surgical resident Loma Linda Univ., 1980-85; asst. prof. of surgery Loma Linda Univ., 1988–; attdg. surgeon Riverside General Hosp., University Medical Center; instr. in surg. Loma Linda Univ. 1985; honors: Who's Who Among Students in Am. Univs. and Colls. 1975-76, Alpha Omega Alpha, LLU Sch. of Med. Alumni Assn. medal for Distinction in Quest of Excellence 1979, President of Soc. of LLU Surgeons 1992–, AMA Physicians Recogn. Award 1989, 92; mem: AMA, CMA, Am. Coll. of Surgeons (fellow); publs: Am. J. of Surgery, 1985, Am. J. of Diseases of Children, 1986, Univ. Surgeon, 1986, Complications in Surgery, 1991, The AIDS Reader, 1993 papers presented Tri-County Surg. Soc. of So. Calif. Annual Clinic Day, 1984-94; Seventh Day Adventist; rec: gardening, travel, camping, fishing. Res: 969 Talcey Terrace Riverside 92506 Ofc: Beaver Medical Clinic 2 West Fern Ave Redlands 92373

HADDIX, CHARLES E., legislative and regulatory consultant; b Nov. 23, 1915, Astoria, Oreg.; s. Charles and Mattie (Wilson) H.; m. Betty Lee Wylie, Aug. 22, 1948; children: Bruce W., b. 1951, Anne C., b. 1953, C. Brian, b. 1955; edn: Grad. US Maritime Officers Sch., 1943; grad. traffic mgmt. courses, Golden Gate Univ. 1948-51, spl. courses UC San Francisco 1952. Career: national sales mgr. Radio Station KLX, Oakland, 1953-55; West Coast mgr. Forjoe & Co., AM-TV sales rep., 1955-60; v.p. Calif. Spot Sales, Radio California 1958-60; v.p. Radio Station KLIP, Fowler, Ca. 1961-63; medical sales rep. Ives Labs. Inc., Sanger 1964-73; state govt. relations cons. Marion Laboratories Inc., 1973–; Calif. Legislative Advocate 1968-85, Ariz., Nev., N.M., Oreg., Wash., 1975; field cons. U.S. Sen. Alan Cranston 1987-90; Calif. State Forum on Refugee Affairs 1983–, state chair 1988, chair Cent. Calif. Forum 1987-88; appt. Calif. Advy. Council on Refugee Assistance and Services 1988-90, commr. Fresno Co. Econ. Opportunities Commn. 1992-93; refugee coord. Dooley for Congress campaign 1990; dir. Laotian C.of C. of America 1992-93; CEO central Calif. chpt. Am. Merchant Marine Veterans 1994–; field cons. Calif. State Senator Rose Ann Vuich 1991-92; refugee coord. Dooley for Congress campaign 1990; Bustamente for Assembly campaign 1993; mem. Clinton Presdl. Transition Planning Found. 1993, U.S. Senate Staff Club 1987-90, Clinton/Gore Nat. Steering Com. 1995; field cons. Senator Jim Costa 1995; mem: U.S. Naval Inst., Oreg. Hist. Soc., Manuscript Soc., Clatsop Co. Hist. Soc., Columbia River Maritime Mus., Commonwealth Club of Calif. (S.F.); author: Reminiscenses of an Old Astoria House, 1992, River Travel Memories on the Columbia, 1992, An Adventure in Dredging, 1993; mil: U.S. Merchant Marine 1939-41, USCG 1942-45, Marina Mercante Nat., Rep. of Panama 1945. Address: 3218 North McCall, Sanger 93657

HADGES, THOMAS RICHARD, media consultant; b. Mar. 13, 1948, Brockton, Mass.; s. Samuel Charles and Ethel Toli (Prifti) H.; m. Beth Evelyn Rastad, Oct. 22, 1988; edn: BA in biology (magna cum laude), Tufts Univ., 1969; att. Harvard Sch. Dental Med. 1969-71. Career: radio announcer Sta. WOKW, Brockton 1965-67, Sta. WTBS-FM, MIT, Cambridge 1966-68; announcer, program dir. Sta. WTUR, Medford, Mass. 1967-69; announcer Concert Network, Sta. WBCN-FM, Boston 1968-78, program dir. 1977-78; program dir. Sta. WCOZ-FM, Blair Bdcstg., Boston 1978-80, Sta. KLOS-FM, ABC, Los Angeles 1980-85; pres. Pollack/Hadges Ents., 1985-89; sr. programming advisor Pollack Media Group, Pacific Palisades 1985-89, pres. 1989–; honors: Phi Beta Kappa (1969), program dir. of year Los Angeles Times (1981); rec: jogging, electronics. Ofc: Pollack Media Group 984 Monument St Ste 105 Pacific Palisades 90272

HAERLE, PAUL R., judge; b. Jan. 10, 1932, Portland, Oreg.; s. George William and Grace (Soden) H.; m. Susan Wagner, May 30, 1953 (div. 1973); children: Karen b. 1956, David b. 1959; m. Michele A. Monson, June 1, 1991; edn: BA, Yale Univ. 1953; JD, Mich. Univ. 1956; admitted St. Bar Calif. 1956. Career: atty., assoc. Thelen, Marrin, Johnson & Bridges, San Francisco 1956-64, ptnr. 1965-67, 1969-94; assoc. justice Calif. Court of Appeal (conf. 8/8/94) 1994–; appointments secty. Gov. Ronald Reagan, Sacto. 1967-69; secty. Republican St. Central Com. of Calif. 1969-73, v.chmn. 1973-75, chmn. 1975-77, No. Calif. chmn. Com. to Re-elect Gov. Reagan 1970; honors: Order of Coif; Fellow Am. Coll. Trial Lawyers; mem: Am. Bar Assn., Calif. Judges Assn., Yale Club of San Francisco, Tiburon Peninsula Club; comments and articles pub. in profl. jours., 1955-56, ed. Mich. Law Review, 1955-56; Republican; Prot.; rec: tennis, hiking, travel. Res: 62 Red Hill Circle Tiburon 94920 Ofc: Court of Appeal First District, Marathon Plaza, South Tower, Rm 600, 303 Second St San Francisco 94107

HAFFORD, DAVID GORDON, retired insurance brokerage president; b. Oct. 18, 1924, San Francisco; s. Samuel John and Ethel Lucille (Turner) H.; m. Doris Kristine Smith, Sept. 3, 1948 (dec. 1974); m. 2d. Thelma May Busick, Jan 17, 1976; children: Linda b. 1950, Eddie b. 1954, Douglas b. 1956; edn: UC Berkeley 1946-49; UCLA 1954; BS, Golden Gate Univ. 1955; reg. Am. Inst. Property & Casualty Underwriters 1955. Career: underwriter Phoenix Ins. Co., San Francisco 1949-53, mgr. fire dept., Los Angeles 1954-55, multiple spl. agent, San Diego 1955-57; account exec. Willis H. Fletcher Co. 1957-66; pres. Snapp Ins. Agency, El Cajon 1966-91; cons., property and casualty ins. (current); lectr. S. D. City Coll. 1955-66; Calif. Western Univ. 1957-59; asst. prof. San Diego St. Univ. 1964-75; mem: CPCU (pres. San Diego chpt. 1964, 70), El Cajon Rotary (pres. 1973-74), El Cajon C.of C. (pres. 1976-77, chmn. air show com. 1972-75); mil: USNR 1943-52; Republican; rec: flying, fishing. Res: 1069 Rippey St El Cajon 92020

HAGENBUCH, JOHN JACOB, investment banker; b. May 31, 1951, Park Forest, Ill.; s. David Brown and Jean Iline (Reeves) H.; m. Christy A. Nichols; children: Henry, Hunter, Hilary, Hunter Scott, Will; edn: AB (magna cum laude), Princeton Univ., 1974; MBA, Stanford Univ., 1978. Career: assoc. Salomon Bros., N.Y.C., partner 1980-84, v.p., San Francisco, 1980-85; gen. ptnr. Hellman & Friedman, 1985-93; owner John J. Hagenbuch & Co. 1993–; gen. ptnr. M&H Realty Partners, L.P. 1993–; bd. dirs. AOFII, Inc., StoryFirst Communications Inc.; trustee Town Sch. for Boys, The William Donner Found.; mem. bd. govs. San Francisco Symphony; clubs: Burlingame CC, Pacific-Union, California Tennis, Menlo Circus Club, Villa Taverna. Ofc: M&H Realty Partners 353 Sacramento St San Francisco 94111 Tel: 415/693-9000

HAHN, ERWIN LOUIS, professor of physics emeritus; b. June 9, 1921, Sharon, Pa.; s. Israel and Mary (Weiss) H.; m. Marian Ethel Failing, Apr. 8, 1944 (dec. Sept. 28, 1978); children: David b. 1945, Deborah b. 1949, Katherine b. 1955; m. Natalie Woodford Thompson Hodgson, Apr. 12, 1980; stepchildren: Welles b. 1958, Elisabeth b. 1960; edn: BS, Juniata Coll., Huntingdon, Pa. 1943; MS, Univ. Ill., 1948, PhD, 1949. Career: asst. in physics Purdue Univ., 1943-44; resrch. assoc. Univ. of Ill., 1950; instr. Stanford Univ. 1950-52, Nat. Research Council fellow at Stanford 1950-51, cons. Office of Naval Res. 1950-52; assoc. Columbia Univ., and res. physicist IBM Watson Scientific Computing Lab., 1952-55; cons. US AEC, 1955–; asst. assoc., prof. dept. physics Univ. Calif., Berkeley 1955-91; assoc. res. prof. Miller Inst. for Basic Research UCB, 1958-59, res. prof. (1966-67, 1985-86), prof. emeritus 1991–; awards: NRC fellow Stanford Univ. 1950-51, Guggenheim Fellow Oxford Univ., Eng. (1961-66 1969-70), Canadian Research Coun. traveling lectr. series 1964, Hon. D.Sc. Juniata Coll. 1966, Buckley Prize in solid state physics Am. Physical Soc. 1971, 1971 Prize of Intl. Soc. of Magnetic Resonance, Fgn. mem: Royal Instn. of G.B. 1971, Hon. D.Sc. Purdue Univ. 1975, Alexander von Humboldt Award of German Fed. Govt. at Max-Planck Inst., Heidelberg 1976-77, Japanese Phys. Soc. traveling lectr. series 1977, 66th Ann. Faculty Resrch. Lectrship UCB 1979, fgn. assoc. mem. Slovenian Acad. Scis. 1981, hon. mem. Brasenose Coll., Oxford, Eng. 1982; co-winner Wolf Found. Prize in Physics 1983-84, Calif. Inventors Hall of Fame 1984; Dept. Energy Award for sustained res. on NMR with DC Squids 1986; vis. Eastman Prof. Balliol Coll., Cherwell-Simon Lectr., Oxford 1988-89; citation UC Berkeley 1991; fgn. assoc. French Acad. Scis. 1992; co-recipient Comstock Prize, U.S. Nat Acad. of Sci. 1993, Alexander von Humboldt Award 1994; apptd. spl. cons. USN 1959, advy. panel to Nat. Bur. Stds. Radio Std. Div. 1961-64, NAS/NRC com. on basic resrch., advr. to US Army Res. Office, Durham 1967-69; mem. Am. Physical Soc. (Fellow, exec. com. div. solid state physics 1967-69), Sigma Xi, Am. Acad. Arts and Scis. (Fellow), Nat. Acad. Scis.; coauthor: Nuclear Quadrupole Resonance Spectroscopy (1958) with T.P. Das; mil: tech. mate US Naval Reserve, WWII, 1944-46; rec: violin, chamber music. Res: 69 Stevenson Ave Berkeley 94708 Ofc: Physics Dept Univ. Calif., Berkeley 94720-7300

HAILE, LAWRENCE BARCLAY, lawyer; b. Feb. 19, 1938, Atlanta, Ga.; m. Ann Springer McCauley, Mar. 28, 1984 (dec. 1994); children: Gretchen, Eric, Scott; edn: BA in econs., Univ. Texas, 1958, LLB, 1961; admitted bar: Tex. 1961, Calif. 1962, U.S. Supreme Ct. Career: law clk. to fed. judge Joseph M. Ingraham, Houston 1961-62; pvt. practice law San Francisco 1962-67, Los Angeles 1967–, instr UCLA Civil Trial Clinics 1974, 76; lectr. Calif. Cont. Edn. of Bar 1973-74, 80–; nat. panel arbitrators Am. Arb. Assn. 1965–; honors: assoc. editor Texas Law Rev., 1960-61, Phi Delta Phi, Delta Sigma Rho; mem: Calif. Bar Assn., Texas Bar Assn., Internat. Assn. Property Ins. Counsel (founding, pres. 1980); clubs: Vintage Auto Racing Assn. (dir.), Vintage Motorsports Council (pres.). Ofc: Haile & Simon 12304 Santa Monica Blvd Ste 300 Los Angeles 90025

HAINES, RICHARD FOSTER, research scientist, author; b. May 19, 1937, Seattle, Wash.; s. Donald Hutchinson and Claudia May (Bennett) H.; m. Carol Taylor, June 17, 1961; children: Cynthia Lynn b. 1965, Laura Anne b. 1970;

edn: BA psychology, Pacific Lutheran Coll., 1960; MA and PhD, exptl. psych., Mich. St. Univ. 1962, 1964. Career: naval architect draftsman W.C. Nickum & Sons, Seattle 1962; weights and balances Boeing Airplane Co., 1957; grad. tchg. fellow Mich. State Univ., E. Lansing 1962-63, res. fellow 1963-64; post doctoral res. assoc. Nat. Res. Council, Ames Res. Ctr., NASA 1964-67, res. scientist NASA Ames Res. Ctr., Moffett Field, Calif. 1967-86, chief space human factors 1986-88, ret.; res. scientist Res. Inst. for Advanced Computer Sci. 1988-90, RECOM Technologies, Inc. 1991–; awards: Pacific Lutheran Univ. Alumnus of Yr. 1972, 5 awards NASA (1976, 84, 88, 89), presentation AIAA conf. 1986, speaker's certif. Essilor Intl. 1989; mem: Soc. Automotive Engrs., Aerospace Med. Assn. (assoc. fellow), Joint USA-CIS Aerial Anomaly Fedn. (American dir. and co-founder, 1991), Sigma Xi; civic: Palo Alto Comm. on Youth Activities; author: Observing UFOs (Nelson Hall 1979), UFO Phenomena & Behavioral Scientist (Scarecrow Press, 1980), Melbourne Episode (LDA Press, 1987), Advanced Aerial Devices Reported During the Korean War (LDA Press, 1990), Night Flying (TAB Books, McGraw-Hill) with Courtney Flatau, 1992, Project Delta - A Study of Multiple UFO (LDA Press, 1994), 60+ articles pub. in sci. jours.; inventor, 4 patents for optical devices, vision tester, info. layout device; Republican; Christian; rec: UFO studies, photog., writing. Res: 325 Langton Ave Los Altos 94022 Ofc: N269-4 RECOM Technologies, Inc. Ames Research Center NASA Moffett Field 94035

HAINING, JEANE MARIE, psychologist; b. May 2, 1952, Camden, N.J.; d. Lester Edward and Adina (Rahn) Haining; edn: BA, psychol., CSU Northridge, 1975, MS, recreation therapy, 1982; MA, psychol., Pepperdine Univ., 1979; PhD, clin. psychol., Calif. Sch. Profl. Psych., 1985; cred. in pupil personnel svs., sch. psychol. 1979; Calif. lic. ednl. psychologist 1982, lic. clin. psychologist 1987. Career: crisis counselor CSU Northridge 1973-74; recreation therapist fieldwork Camarillo St. Hosp. 1974; recreation therapist intern UCLA Neuropsychiatric Inst., 1975-76; tchr./recreation therapist New Horizons Sch. for Mentally Retarded, Sepulveda 1976-79; sch. psychologist Rialto Unified Sch. Dist., 1979-82; clin. psych. intern Fuller Psychol. Ctr., Pasadena 1984-85; examiner Calif. Bd. of Behavioral Sci. Examiners 1985; clin. psychologist and intermittent actg. chief psychol. svs. Terminal Island Fed. Prison, 1985-86; community mental health psychologist Sybil Brand Inst., forensic outpatient unit L.A. Co. Dept. Mental Health, 1987-89, also inservice tng. for L.A. Co. Sheriff's Dept.; clinical psychologist Calif. Dept. of Corrections, Parole Outpatient Clinic, 1990–, Mary Magdalene Project, Commerce 1992–; postdoctoral internship O. Carl Simonton Cancer Ctr., Pacific Palisades 1992-93, clin. psychologist 1993–; examiner, ednl. psych., Calif. Bd. Beh. Sci. Examiners, Sacto. 1985; mem. U.S. Dist. Ct., Cent. Dist. of Calif., Psychiatric Panel 1989–, Juvenile Dependency Ct. 730 Evidence Code Experts Panel 1992–, Superior Ct. Psychiatric-Psychol. Panel: Juvenile 1992–, Superior Ct. Psychiatric-Psychol. Panel: Adult 1992–; advy. bd. for mentally disordered Camarillo St. Hosp. 1994–; recipient award outstanding achiev. W. Psych. Conf. for Undergrad. Research, Santa Clara 1974, listed Who's Who in Calif. 1989–; mem. L.A. Psych. Assn., Forensic Mental Health Assn. Calif.; PhD diss: Schizophrenic patients decision-making process in regard to medication treatment compliance, 1985; Democrat; Lutheran; rec: skiing (capt. CSU Northridge/So. Calif. Intercollegiate Ski Race Assn. 1975, women's team won 2d pl. overall, and placed within top ten in Individual Womens Championship Races), skating, tennis, racquetball, rock climbing, piano.

HAISCH, BERNHARD MICHAEL, astronomer; b. Aug. 23, 1949, Stuttgart-Bad Canstatt, Germany; s. Friedrich Wilhelm and Gertrud Paula (Dammbacher) H.; m. Pamela S. Eakins, July 29, 1977 (div. 1986); children: Katherine Stuart, Christopher Taylor; m. Marsha A. Sims, Aug. 23, 1986; edn: St. Meinrad Coll., Ind. 1967-68; BS in astrophysics (w/high distinction), Indiana Univ., 1971; PhD astronomy, Univ. Wis., Madison 1975. Career: res. assoc. Jt. Inst. Lab. Astrophysics, Univ. Colo., 1975-77, 78-79; vis. scientist The Astronomical Inst., Utrecht, The Netherlands 1977-78; res. scientist Lockheed Palo Alto Research Lab., 1979-83, staff scientist 1983–; dep. dir. Ctr. for EUV Astrophysics, Univ. Calif. Berkeley 1992-94; vis. fellow Max-Planck Institut fur Extraterr. Physik, Garching, Germany 1991-94; guest investigator programs: Internat. Ultraviolet Explorer, Einstein Obs., ROSAT Obs., EUVE Obs., ASCA (Astro-D), 1980–; managing ed. Jour. of Sci. Exploration 1988–; assoc. ed. Astrophysical Jour. 1993–; mem: NASA rev. coms.; mem: Internat. Astronomical Union (co-chmn. Colloquium No. 104: Solar and Stellar Flares, Stanford Univ. 1988; co-chmn. Colloquium No. 152 Astrophysics in the EUV, UC Berkeley 1995), Am. Astronomical Soc., Royal Astron. Soc. (fellow), Am. Inst. Aero. and Astro. (assoc. fellow), European Astron. Soc., Phi Beta Kappa, Sigma Xi, Phi Kappa Phi, Commonwealth Club of Calif.; invention: Anchor Bolt Extractor (US Pat. No. 4,941,252); publs: 90+ papers in sci. jours., (book) Solar and Stellar Flares, with Rodono (Kluwer Acad. Press, 1989), editorial bd.: Solar Physics 1992-95; fgn. languages: speak German, read Dutch, French, Latin; rec: Tae Kwon Do, internat. folk dance, downhill skiing, songwriting. Ofc: Lockheed (91-30, Bldg 252) 3251 Hanover St Palo Alto 94304 Tel: 415/424-3268

HAISLEY, FAY BEVERLEY, academic dean; b. Feb. 20, 1933, Sydney, Australia; came to U.S., 1971; d. Reginald Charles and Edna Irene (Kidd) Sambrook; m. Ian George Haisley, May 11, 1963, div. 1973; edn: BA, Univ. Papua, New Guinea, Port Moresby 1970; MEd (honors) Univ. Oregon, 1971,

PhD, 1973; cert. elementary tchr., spl. edn., Oreg., New South Wales, Australia. Career: tchr., principal Dept. Edn., Australia 1952-70; prin., lectr. Dept. Edn., Port Moresby, Papua, New Guiinea 1969-70; lectr. early childhood UC Santa Barbara, 1973-75; asst. prof., assoc. prof. learning disabilities and elem. edn. Univ. Oreg., Eugene 1975-80, assoc. dean, tchr. edn., 1981-84; dean Sch. of Edn. Univ. of Pacific, Stockton 1984–, dir. dean's grant 1977-83; commr. Calif. Commn. on Tchr. Credentialling, 1985-87; dir. spl. project Am. Nepalese Edn. Found., Eugene, Oreg. 1982-84; dir. doctoral dept. edn. program Univ. Guam, 1983-84; dir. Far West Educational Labs 1986–; Bd. of Examiners NCATE, 1989–; awards: grantee U.S. Office Edn. 1979-82, Nat. Inst. Edn. 1981, Oregon State Dept. Edn. 1978; mem. Phi Delta Kappa, Am. Ednl. Research Assn., Assn. Tchr. Educators, Am. Assn. Colls. Tchr. Edn., Calif. Assn. Tchr. Educators (pres. 1988-89), Calif. Assn. for Colls. of Tchr. Edn. (pres. 1991-93); contbr. articles to profl. jours.; Anglican. Ofc: Univ. of the Pacific Sch. Edn. Pacific Ave Stockton 95211

HAKIM, HOSNY F., civil engineer, structural design; b. March 1, 1946, El Maragha, Egypt, nat. US cit. 1983; s. Fawzy H. and Thoria (Ghali) H.; m. Soad, July 20, 1975; children: Marian Grace b. 1981, Rose Mary b. 1982; edn: BS, Univ. of Alexandria 1968; MS, Univ. of Toronto 1977; Reg. Profl. Engr., Wash. 1984, Calif. 1985; gen. engring. contractor, Calif. 1985. Career: research asst. Univ. of Toronto, Canada 1975-77; designer office of Jame Ruderman, NYC 1977-79; engr. Geiger Berger Assn., NY 1978-79; design engr. Ebasco Svcs. Inc., NY 1979-81, Wash. 1981-84; pres. Pacific H H Developers, Inc., Glendale 1984-88; prin. Hakim Engring. Svcs., Torrance 1988–; tchg. asst. Univ. of Toronto 1975-77; tchg. asst. Univ. of Alexandria, Egypt 1968-75; awards: fellowship Univ. of Toronto 1975-76, scholarship Univ. of Alexandria 1963-68; mem. Am. Soc. Civil Engrs., Am. Concrete Inst.; publs: Automated Design of Rigid Steel Frames, Canadian Soc. of Civil Engrs., Conf. Montreal 1977; Christian. Ofc: Hakim Engineering Services, 22907 Marjorie Ave Torrance 90505

HALBERG, FRANCINE ERNA, physician; b. June 28, 1952, Minneapolis, Minn.; d. Franz and Erna Halberg; edn: BS, Stanford Univ. 1974; MD, Cornell Univ. 1978; cert. Am. Bd. Internal Medicine 1981, Radiation Oncology 1984. Career: faculty Stanford Univ. 1984-85; faculty UC San Francisco 1985-91, clin. faculty 1991–; radiation oncologist Marin Cancer Inst., Greenbrae 1991–; com. mem. FDA Radiologic Device Panel 1994-98; honors: President's Cancer Panel, Commn. for Breast Cancer 1993, mem. NIH Consensus Devel. Conf. in Treatment of Early Stage Breast Cancer; listed in Best Doctors in Am. (top 1% of U.S. doctors); mem: Am. Soc. for Therapeutic Radiology Oncology 1984- (bd. dirs. 1994-98), Am. Soc. for Clinical Oncology (public issues com. 1994-98), Am. Coll. Radiology (breast cancer treatment appropriateness task force), CMA, AMA, Radiation Research, Am. Cancer Soc. (Marin Co. bd. dirs. 1993-96); author: 33 pub. peer review articles; mil: lt.-03 USPHS 1978-81; rec: sports. Res: 24 Old Landing Rd Tiburon 94920

HALBREICH, DAVID M., lawyer; b. July 24, 1958, New York; s. Lester and Shirley (Scheller) H.; m. Rebecca Fletcher Gale, Aug. 4, 1989; edn: BA, St. Univ. N.Y. 1980; JD, George Washington Univ. 1983. Career: atty. Dutton & Overman, Wash. D.C. 1983-85; Anderson Baker Kill & Olick 1985-88; Brobeck Phleger & Harrison, S.F. and L.A. 1988–; honors: Phi Beta Kappa, Pi Sigma Alpha; mem: Am. Bar Assn.; rec: sailing, skiing, bicycling. Res: 3071 Hutton Dr Beverly Hills 90210 Ofc: Brobeck Phleger & Harrison 550 S Hope St Ste 2300 Los Angeles 90071

HALET, GLORIA, freelance designer; b. Aug. 15, 1945, NY, NY; d. Sam and Pearl (Simon) Cohen; m. Robert M. Halet, Mar. 10, 1974 (div. 1991); children: Sander b. 1974; edn: AA, N.Y. Univ. 1965; cert. of completion, Julliard Sch. of Design, NY 1967; reg. nurse, UCLA 1970; flight attendant tng., Am. Airlines, Burbank, Calif. 1970-71. Career: flight attendant Pan Am. Airlines, NY, NY 1971-82; flight attendant trainer Pan Am Airlines, L.A. 1978-82; designer/ studio owner, Santa Monica 1982–; customer svc. vol. Humana Hosp., West Hills, Calif. 1982-84; vol. arts & crafts tchr. Aviva House, Hollywood 1986–; vol. rehab. asst. Cedars Sinai Hosp., L.A. 1987-89; advocate Westside Ctr. of Indep. Living, W. L.A. 1991–; vol. restorer/docent Museum of Flying, Santa Monica 1993–; awards: B'nai B'rith fundraising award, L.A. 1986, 2nd place-decorations, Single Mariners, Newport Beach 1993; Toastmaster of Yr., Toastmasters Internat., L.A. 1991, Competent Toastmaster 1992, Backbone award 1994; mem: B'nai B'rith (past pres.) 1986–, Toastmasters Internat. (treas. 1990–), Single Mariners (v.p. public relations 1992–), Am. Cancer Soc. (lectr. 1992–), League of Women Voters L.A. 1987–, Del Rey Toastmasters 1990–, Windjammers Yacht Club, Marina del Rey 1990–; prod. videotape, Total Hip Joint Replacement, 1989, pamphlet designer, Orbitron, Inc. 1990, researcher (booklet) West Hollywood Access Guide, 1990, co-author (pamphlet) 12-Step Stop Smoking Program, 1991; Democrat; Jewish; rec: making collages, jigsaw puzzles, knitting, gardening. Ofc: SIPRA 1800 S Robertson Blvd #388 Los Angeles 90035

HALL, ADRIENNE A., international marketing and communications company executive; b. Los Angeles; d. Arthur E. and Adelina P. Kosches; m. Maurice Arthur Hall; children: Adam, Todd, Stefanie, Victoria; edn: BA, UCLA; mgmt. seminars Harvard Univ. Bus. Sch., Univ. Chgo. Bus. Sch., MIT Sloan Sch.

Mgmt. Career: founder, chmn. bd. Hall & Levine Advt., Los Angeles 1965-80 (first advt. agy. headed by women); v. chmn. bd. Eisaman, Johns & Laws Advt. Inc., 1980-94, L.A., Houston, Chgo. N.Y.; pres./CEO, The Hall Group 1994–; founder, chair exec. com. Women Incorporated 1995 (largest org. of women entrepreneurs and bus. owners in nation); dir: Calif. Mfrs. Assn. Service Corp. 1989–, Calif. Life Ins. Co. 1978-82, Calif. Life Corp., Exec. Service Corps, United Way, Am. Red Cross, The Shelter Partnership, Am. Women for Econ. Devel.; trustee: UCLA Found. Bd. 1980–, Nat. Health Found.; regent Loyola Marymount Univ. 1982–; guest lectr. MBA Pgm. UCLA, USC Grad. Sch. Bus., Rice Univ., Lockheed Mgmt. Assn., various instns. nat.; mem: Am. Assn. Advt. Agys. (dir. 1986-89, chmn. bd. govs. we. reg. 1984-85), We. States Advt. Agys. Assn. (pres. 1972), L.A. Advt. Club (pres. 1977), Hollywood Radio & TV Soc. (dir.), Advt. Indus. Emergency Fund (founder), Nat. Advt. Rev. Bd. 1986-90, L.A. Area C.of C. (dir. 1985-92), The 2000 Partnership, Rotary Internat. (LA 5); Leadership America (nat. advy. bd.), Nat. Womens Econ. Alliance, The Com. of 200 (founder, 1st we. chair), Internat. Women's Forum (founder), Town Hall of Calif. (gov.), L.A. County Commn., Music and the Performing arts (commnr.); rec: politics, collect primitive and folk art. Res: 1131 San Ysidro Dr Beverly Hills 90210 Ofc: The Hall Group.

HALL, CARLYLE WASHINGTON, lawyer; b. Feb. 6, 1943, New York; s. Carlyle Washington and Anzonette M. (Asmussen) H.; m. Wendy Stone, Aug. 26, 1964 (div. 1972); m. Joanne Jackson, Dec. 31, 976; children: Carlyle W. b. 1969, Christopher Jackson b. 1977, Andrew Jackson b. 1980; edn: BA, Yale Coll. 1963; JD, Harvard Law Sch. 1966. Career: law tchr. Internat. Legal Center, Sudan and Uganda 1966-69; assoc. atty. O'Melveny & Myers, Los Angeles 1969-71; exec. dir. Center for Law in Pub. Interest 1971-88; ptnr. Hall & Phillips 1988; awards: Durfee Found. award 1983; Democrat; Methodist. Ofc: 10951 W Pico Blvd Los Angeles 90064

HALL, DAVID STANLEY, consultant in aviation safety; b. Jan. 12, 1935, Oak Park, Ill.; s. Clifford Francis and Alice Elizabeth (Brandenburger) H.; m. Arlene Denzler, June 7, 1957 (div. 1983); children: Sheridan b. 1958, D. Michael b. 1960, Tina b. 1964; m. LaNette Vinson, July 21, 1983 (div. 1991); m. Roseann Hannon, PhD, July 31, 1992; edn: BSEE, Ill. Inst. of Tech., 1957; MS in sys. mgmt., USC, 1972; Calif. reg. profl. engr., safety. Career: Lt., naval aviator USN, 1957-62; flight test engr. Lockheed-Calif. Co., Burbank 1962-66; sr. flt. test engr. Garrett/ AiResearch Mfg. Co. of Ariz., 1967-69; cons. in mishap investigation and prevention, 1969–; f.t. faculty Univ. So. Calif. Inst. of Aerospace Safety and Mgmt., 1969-72, guest lectr. in aviation safety USC 1972-73; lectr. and faculty assoc. Ariz. State Univ., 1973-86; product safety splst. Garrett/AiResearch Mfg. Co. of Ariz., 1973-78; supr. engring. flt. test 1976-77; dir. res. Crash Research Inst., Robertson Research Inc., 1979-83; faculty Internat. Ctr. for Safety Edn., Tempe, Az. 1981-93, and Internat. Ctr. for Aviation Safety, San Diego, 1986–; mem: Tau Beta Pi, Mensa, Am. Inst. Aero. and Astro., System Safety Soc., Soc. of Automotive Engrs., Internat. Soc. of Air Safety Investigators (fellow, past pres. L.A. chpt., gen. chmn. 2d, 16th internat. sems., past chmn. bd. of awards); publs. in field. Res: 2111 Lido Circle Stockton 95207 Tel: 209/474-7421

HALL, DONN (DONALD) BRYANT, architect; b .Feb. 12, 1938, Pasadena; s. Bryant Goodridge Hall and Margaret Elizabeth (Zienz) Waldron; m. Janet Kay Simonin, April 29, 1961 (div. 1979); m. Shelley K. Christie, June 4, 1983; children: Nicole b. 1962, Jordan Rachel b. 1986, Kayla Jaqlyn b. 1991, Hunter Goodridge b. 1992; edn: AA, Orange Coast Coll. 1967; B.Arch., Calif. St. Polytech. Univ. 1971. Career: project architect D. Salerno & Assoc., San Diego 1971-73; prin. project architect Gieldert Hall & Assoc., El Cajon 1973-74; arch. cons. R. Lancaster & Assoc., Oman, Arabia 1980; A. Strotz & Assoc., Kuwait 1981-82; architect, prin. Donn Hall Architect, Imperial Beach 1982–; elected city councilman, Imperial Beach 1994–; solar engery cons. Ways & Means Com. Calif. St. Assembly 1975; instr. Healds Engring. Coll., San Francisco 1978; awards: Newport Balboa S&L Arch. Design, Orange Coast Coll. Found., So. Calif. Edison, Calif. St. Polytech. Deans Hon. List 1970-71, Pres. Hon. List 1971; civic bds: Imperial Beach Community Clinic (v.chmn. bd. of dirs.), Imperial Beach Planning Commission (chmn. 1985-87), Imperial Beach Zoning Ordinance Advy. Com. (chmn.), Imperial Beach Arch. Design Review Advy. Com. (chmn. 1984-85), Kiwanis Internat., Imperial Beach Boys & Girls Club (advy. bd. 1988–), Americas Cup Task Force, San Diego Metropolitan Transit Devel. Bd. (bd. dirs. 1995–); architect: residential and commercial projects, Calif. & Mexico 1984-94, Republican; Christian; rec: ocean sailing. Res: 1352 Seacoast Dr Imperial Beach 91932 Ofc: Donn Hall Architect 143 Palm Ave The Tower Imperial Beach 91932

HALL, ELINOR CAROLINE, health administrator; b. March 1, 1949, Hamilton, Ohio; d. James Byron and Elizabeth (Cushman) H.; m. Kenneth Gustav Venzke, Sept. 25, 1982; children: Daniel b. 1983, Charles b. 1987; edn: BA, UC Santa Cruz 1972; MPH, Univ. of Mich. 1974. Career: health planner Midcoast Health Systems, Salinas 1974-76; analyst County of Santa Cruz 1976-79, admin. County Health Services Agency 1979–; fellow Public Health Leadership Inst. 1993; bd. dirs. Santa Cruz Comm. Credit Union, Santa Cruz 1989-90; mem: Calif. Health Execs. Assn., State Breast Cancer Control Council,

Assn. of Bay Area Health Officials, Am. Public Health Assn., Medical Care Orgn. Alumni, Handgun Control Inc., Food First; rec: gardening.

HALL, HUGH A., retired home furnishings industry leader, civic volunteer; b. Sept. 23, 1926, Durham, N.C.; s. Hugh A. and Grace Mildred (Hartz) H.; m. V. Elaine Hakala (dec. Jan. 23, 1989); children: Stephen L. and Linda Eileen; m. Bonnie Oglesby, Oct. 1990; children by marriage, nee Oglesby: Jeffrey, Terri Lynn (Mrs. Hartman), Karen Michele (Mrs. Dunn), Charles Stanley. Career: owner, ptnr. automotive and indsl. parts & supply cos. in San Diego County, 1950s; pres. Highway Devel. Assn. San Diego Co., 1960s, com. chmn. Try San Diego Co. First, co-chair S.D. Citizens for Better Bus Service, chmn. S.D. Stadium campaign (C.of C.), celebration dir. year-long 200th Anniversary San Diego; exec. dir. U.S. Bicentennial, 1970s; owner, pres. San Diego Rattan, 1974-90; pres. Morena Home Furnishings Dist.; mem., pres. San Diego Co. Home Furnishings Assn.; awards: outstanding svc. U.S. Govt., Calif. Gov.'s nominee for outstanding citizenship 1967, nat. award Outstanding Retailer of Year; mem. San Diego C.of C. (past v.p., dir., Chmn. of Year Award-3), Mission Valley YMCA (bd. 1980–), San Diego Zool. Soc., Nat. Historic Preservation Trust, Scripps Inst. of Oceanography Assocs., S.D. Symphony Assn.; club: Stardust CC; mil: USN 1944-46; rec: swimming, golf, music. Res: 6047 Cirrus St San Diego 92110

HALL, JOSEPHINE WEISSMAN, physician-surgeon, educator; b. Dec. 29, 1937, N.Y.C.; d. Jacob Eliah and Sonia (Litsky) Weissman; m. Jearld Wayne Hall, Dec. 20, 1970; children: Michael b. 1965, Gillian b. 1967, James b. 1972, Jesse b. 1973, Cameron b. 1975; edn: BA, Swarthmore Coll., 1959; MD, Chgo. Med. Sch., 1963. Career: physician, Wash. D.C. 1968-70; Tufts Delta Health Ctr., Mound Bayou, Miss. 1970; Ross Loos Med. Ctr., Los Angeles 1970-72; clin. assoc. prof. OB-Gyn, USC Sch. of Medicine, L.A. 1970-89, full clin. prof. OB-Gyn, 1989–; bd. govs. The Chicago Med. Sch., 1991–; mem: Am. Coll. Obstets. & Gynecol., Am. Fertility & Sterility Soc., Assn. Laparoscopists; civic: Nat. Charity League, Glendale; rec: dressage horseback riding. Ofc: 1910 W Glenoaks Blvd Glendale 91201

HALL, MICHAEL W., lawyer, author; b. Oct. 25, 1952, Murfreesboro, Tenn.; s. William F. and Louise (Beasley) H.; edn: BS, Middle Tenn. St. Univ. 1975; JD, Vanderbilt Univ. 1980; admitted St. Bar Calif. 1983, St. Bar Fla. 1980. Career: assoc. atty. Henderson Franklin Starnes & Holt, Ft. Myers, Fla. 1980-83; Wilson Sonsini Goodrich & Rosati, Palo Alto 1984-85; ptnr. Tomlinson, Zisko, Morosoli & Maser, 1985-90; Law Offices of Michael W. Hall, 1990–; mem: Calif. Young Lawyers Assn. (bd. dirs. 1985-89), Santa Cruz Bluegrass Soc. (dir. 1990–, pres. 1991-92), We. Bluegrass Assocs. (pres. 1995–); contbg. edit. The Bluegrass Chronicle, 1995–; contbr. Calif. Secured Transactions, 1987, Advising Calif. Partnerships (2d. ed. 1988). Law Offices of Michael W. Hall 666 College Ave Palo Alto 94306

HALL, RICHARD DENNIS, freelance writer; b. Apr. 12, 1935, Troy, N.Y.; s. Dennis John and Clara Eleanor (Hanson) H.; m. Joyce Ann Huntington, June 7, 1957; children: Brian Huntington b. 1959, Roger Hanson b. 1961; edn: BS, Boston Univ., 1957. Career: gen. assignment reporter Worcester (Mass.) Telegram and Evening Gazette, 1957-60; city hall reporter and columnist Springfield (Mass.) Union, 1960-65; reporter Fresno (Calif.) Bee, 1965-77, agriculture and water reporter 1977-79, Washington corr. McClatchy Newspapers, W.D.C., 1979-83, agribus. writer Fresno Bee, Fresno 1983-91; freelance writer, agribus. and internat. trade, Hanford, Calif. 1991–; awards: invited guest Agribus. Sem., Taiwan, 1983, Ninth Ann. Conf. European and Am. Journalists, Maastricht, Netherlands, 1985; helped establish comm. sys. for farmers in Armenia through Volunteers for Overseas Coop. Assistance, 1993; mem: Western Hist. Club Garden of the Sun Corral 1987-94, Nature Conservancy 1984–; author: Fresno County in the 20th Century, 1987, Hanford Hometown America, 1991; mil: sp3c Army N.G. 1957-63; rec: bird watching, baking bread. Res/Ofc: 1978 Mulberry Dr Hanford 93230

HALLADAY, KAREN SUE, educator, real estate broker, financial planner; b. July 26, 1943, Stockton; d. Dr. Louis, Jr. and Eleanor Sue (Sandberg) Jaques Keene; m. Wayne Halladay, Feb. 4, 1967; edn: BA, 1965 and MA, 1967, highest honors, CSU San Jose; postgrad. work in ednl. psych. and community mental health, UC Berkeley 1970-76; Calif. Std. Elem. tchg. cred., Calif. Comm. Colls. instr., counselor creds.; Calif. lic. R.E. broker; reg. rep. NASD, Cert. Fin. Planner, life/disability ins. agent, 1984-90; Cert. Residential Splst., NAR 1988–. Career: elementary sch. tchr. Lompoc Unified Sch. District, 1967-70; instr. Alan Han Jr. Coll., Santa Maria 1968-70; coll. instr./ supr. student teachers, St. Marys Coll., Moraga 1974-76; R.E. agent, Walnut Creek 1977-81; realtor/prin. Halladay & Assocs., Concord 1982-83; fin. planner 1984-90; broker Security Pacific Real Estate, Walnut Creek 1984-94; account exec. WZW Financial Services; Southmark Financial Svcs. 1984-86; Pvt. Securities Network, Skaife, 1989-90; mem: Am. Arbitration Assn. (arb.), Nat. Assn. Realtors (profl. stds. com. 1993), Calif. Assn. Realtors (state dir. 1987–, MLS com. 1987–, MLS dist. chair 1989-90, computer com. 1989, PAC 1990, MLS com. state v.chair 1991, Profl. Stds. com. 1991–, v.chair 1992, MLS com. state chair 1994), Contra Costa Bd. of Realtors (first woman MLS pres. 1988, v.p. & c.f.o. 1989-90, bylaws

com. chair 1989-90, pres. MLS 1991, Assn. pres.-elect 1992, Assn. pres. 1993, immed. past pres. 1994 profl. stds. panel 1981-84, 88, chair ethics com. 1985, mediator 1987, chair Realtor/title co. relations com., dir. MLS 1986, instr. 1989), Conflict Resolution Panel Contra Costa (bd. 1987, chair election com.), Alamo Improvement Assn. (zoning com. 1989), Structural Com. East Bay Regional Data (structure com. chair 1991); Democrat; Episcopalian; rec: kite flying, swimming, bread baking, writing poetry, ethnic cooking. Res: 2365 Hagen Oaks Dr Alamo 94507 Ofc: Pacific Union Residential Brokerage 601 Sycamore Valley Rd West, Danville 94526

HALLER, HOWARD EDWARD, real estate developer, entertainment company executive; b. March 30, 1947, Baltimore, Md.; s. Howard Earl and Clemence Anne (Young) H.; m. Terri Lynne Koster, June 20, 1969; children: Jennifer b. 1970, Justin b. 1973, Jason b. 1979; edn: USC 1968-75; BA, CSU Northridge 1970; MA mgmt., Univ. Redlands; lic. real estate broker Calif., lic. gen. contractor Calif., lic. commercial pilot. Career: reg. mgr. U.S. Leasing Corp., Los Angeles 1973-78; Chemical Bank of N.Y., Santa Monica 1976-77; v.p. Patagonia Corp., Phoenix, Ariz. 1977; pres. and c.e.o. Haller Koster & Haller Corp., Woodland Hills 1977-90; sr. v.p., c.o.o. IFC Capital Corp., Beverly Hills 1977-88; sr. v.p., reg. gen. mgr. United Artists Entertainment, Woodland Hills 1988-91; pres. and c.e.o. Rebel Productions, Hollywood 1991–; prof. CSU Northridge 1980–; Pierce Coll., Woodland Hills 1987–; dir. Rebel Productions, Hollywood 1968–; Ed Haller & Sons Constrn., Woodland Hills 1968–; awards: BSA varsity land coach of year (1987, 88); mem: AFTRA, Writers Guild of Am. (West), Nat. Realtors Assn., Urban Planning Inst., Builders Ind. Assn., Motion Picture Pioneers, Nat. Eagle Scouts Assn. (life), CSU Northridge Trust Fund (trustee, v.p., past pres.), USC Cinema TV Alumni Assn. (life), CSU Northridge Alumni Assn. (dir., past pres., v.p.), Am. Legion, BSA, AYSO Soccer; screenwriter: TV screenplay, Paper Chase: Real World 101 (1978), feature films, White Lies (1987), Debt of Honor (1991); mil: capt. USAF 1968-70; Republican. Ofc: 23271 Ventura Blvd Woodland Hills 91364

HALLETT, DEAN CHARLES, entertainment company executive; b. June 9, 1958, Encino; s. William Charles and Sally (Lane) H.; m. Kelli Lynn Frisinger, July 2, 1983; children: Drew b. 1989, Makenzie b. 1991; edn: BBA (cum laude), USC, 1980; CPA, Calif. Bd. Acctncy. Career: sr. audit mgr. Ernst & Whinney, Los Angeles 1980-88, exchange visitor Ernst & Whinney, London, Eng. 1986-87, campus recruiting coord., USC, 1985-88; group controller Anthony Industries, Inc. 1988-90; mgr. corp. mgmt. audit Walt Disney Co., Burbank 1990-91, dir. of fin. Buena Vista Pictures Mktg. (div. Walt Disney Studios), 1991-94, v.p. fin. & adminstrn. 1994–; Republican; rec: skiing, golf. Ofc: Walt Disney Co. 500 S Buena Vista St Burbank 91521-1274

HALLINAN, VIVIAN MOORE, peace activist; b. Oct. 21, 1910, San Francisco; d. Edward Frances and Katherine Rose (Lagomarsino) Moore; m. Vincent Hallinan, Sept. 23, 1932; children: Patrick b. 1934, Terence b. 1936, Michael b. 1939, Matthew b. 1940, Conn b. 1942, Daniel b. 1948; edn: stu. UC Berkeley 3 yrs. Career: investor, apartment mgmt. bus., San Francisco 1933–, bought downtown apartment bldgs. in need of renovation and furnishing, active apt. mgmt. until 1984, semi-ret.; honors: recogn. U.S. Peace Council 1957, outstanding woman of yr. Sun Reporter 1964, outstanding older women in S.F. Older Women League 1983, recogn. for peace activities and work in civil rights Cong. Barbara Boxer and Cong. Ronald Dellums 1984, Gray Panthers 1985, Central Amer. Refugee 1985, M.L. King, Jr. Humanitarian Award 1987, Fifth Annual Age & Youth Award 1988, honoree Nicaraguan Govt. 1988, Veterans Abraham Lincoln Brigade 1989, Eleanor Roosevelt Humanitarian Award of Democratic Womens Forum 1990; civic: chair Comm. Chest Fund Drive, Ross 1947, chair Red Cross Home Nsg. Pgm., Marin Co. 1947, West coast chair `Women for Wallace' for U.S. Pres. Progressive Party ticket 1948, campaigned nat. for Vincent Hallinan for U.S. Pres. Progressive Party ticket 1952, active in Civil Rights Movement w/ Coretta and Martin Luther King, Jr. 1960s, nat. organizer the `Jeannette Rankin Brigade' to protest Vietnam War 1967, mem. del. to meet with peace negotiating teams in Paris rep. U.S., N. Vietnam, and Viet Cong 1968, organized El Salvador's Childrens Relief Pgm. 1983, founded/dir. Project Nat. Interest, orgn. vs. mil. intervention in Central Am. 1984, mem. Womens Internat. League for Peace and Freedom (S.F. pres. 1974-78, 1981-84), Womens Political Caucus, Womens Democrat Club; apptd. San Francisco Human Rights Commn., 1990; publs: book on apt. house ops. (1939), My Wild Irish Rogues (Doubleday, 1952), num. political pamphlets; Democrat; rec: contemporary politics and social injustice. Res: 1080 Chestnut San Francisco 94109 Ofc: Bally Hallinan, Downtown Apartments 535 Geary St Ste 914 San Francisco 94102

HALLORAN, JAMES VINCENT, III, technical writer; b. May 12, 1942, Greenwich, Conn.; s. Dr. James Vincent and Rita Lucy (Keator) H.; m. Barbara Sharon Case, Sept. 7, 1974; edn: BME, Catholic Univ. of Am., 1964; MBA, Univ. Chicago, 1973. Career: mktg. rep. Rockwell Internat. Corp., El Segundo 1973-76, bus. area mgr. 1976-80, mgr. of bus. analysis 1980-84; dir. of mktg. H. Silver and Assocs. Inc., Los Angeles 1984-90; program mgr. Technology Training Corp., Torrance 1990-91; prin. Business Information & Analysis, Redondo Beach 1991-94; mgr. of special projects, Wyle Labs., El Segundo 1994–; bd. dirs. Curtiss-Wright Hist. Assn./Project Tomahawk, 1994–; mem:

Redondo Beach Housing Advy. Appeals Bd. 1985-89, Citizens Advy. Bd. for South Bay Union H.S. Dist. 1983; mil: capt. USAF 1964-68, master team chief award SAC, Grand Forks AFB, N.D. 1966; Libertarian; rec: cycling, photography, body surfing. Res: 612 S Gertruda Ave Redondo Beach 90277

HALLUIN, ALBERT PRICE, lawyer; b. Nov. 8, 1939, Wash. D.C.; s. William Ord and Martha (Blundon) H.; (div.); children: Marcus A. b. 1964, Russell P. b. 1968; edn: AA, Montgomery Jr. Coll. 1961; BA, La. St. Univ. 1964; JD, Univ. Baltimore 1969; admitted bar: Md. 1970, N.Y. 1985, Calif. 1991, U.S. Patent and Trademark Office 1969, US Supreme Ct. 1976, US Ct. Appeal Fed. Cir. 1982, US Dist. Ct. No. Dist. Calif. 1986. Career: patent examiner US Patent and Trademark Office, Arlington, Va. 1965-69; assoc. atty. Jones, Tullar & Cooper 1969-71; sr. patent atty. CPC Internat. Inc., Englewood Cliffs, NJ 1971-76; counsel Exxon Res. and Engring. Co., Florham Park 1976-83; v.p., chief intellectual property counsel Cetus Corp., Emeryville 1983-90; partner Fliesler, Dubb, Meyer & Lovejoy, San Francisco 1990-92; partner Limbach & Limbach, San Francisco 1992-94; partner Pennie & Edmonds, Menlo Park 1994-; mem: Am Intellectual Property Law Assn. (chmn. chem. practice com 1981-83, secty. 1984-85, bd. dir. 1985-88, chmn. biotechnology com. 1990-92), N.J. Patent Law Assn. (treas. 1982-83), Am. Bar Assn., Licensing Exec. Soc.; civic: BSA (chmn. troop com., asst. scoutmaster 1977-83); author: U.S. patentee: 7 in catalysis, 2 in biotechnology; songwriter "Uncertain" (1959), publ. articles: 1990 European Harvard Mouse (Biotechnology Law Report 1990), Patent Battles May Give Way To Cross-Licensing in the 90's (Bioworld 1991), Practice After Amgen and Scripps: The New Biotechnology Practice (Biotechnology Law Report 1991),Enforcement of Biotechnology Patent Rights (W. Coast Biotechnology Patent Conf. Workbook 1/91), Scope of Biotechnology Patent Rights (Chemistry and the Law 8/91), Courts Might Be Locking Up Cures (San Francisco Examiner 2/12/92), The Cure Has A Disease (Am. Chem. Soc. 1992); Republican; Episcopalian; rec: music, backpacking. Ofc: Pennie & Edmonds 2730 Sand Hill Road Menlo Park 94025 Tel: 415/854-3660 FAX: 415/854-3694

HALM, D. RAY, university president; b. Jan. 26, 1941, Portland, Ore.; s. Ralph L. and Anne Edna H.; m. Darlene Ann Bjerke; children: Heather b. 1966, Shawne b. 1969; edn: AA, Concordia Coll., St. Paul, Minn. 1961; BS, Concordia Coll., Seward, Nebr. 1963; MA, Ball State Univ., Muncie, Ind. 1966; EdD, Pepperdine Univ., L.A. 1986; DD, Concordia Seminary, St. Louis, Mo. 1987. Career: English tchr. Concordia LHS, Ft. Wayne, Ind. 1963-66; English tchr. & asst. principal Concordia LHS, Seward, Nebr. 1966-71; principal Milwaukee LHS, Milwaukee, Wis., 1971-77; pastor Cross View Lutheran Ch., Edina, Minn. 1978-80; pres. Concordia Univ., Irvine, Calif. 1980-; v.p. Bd. for Higher Edn., St. Louis, Mo. 1975-80; v.p. Concordia Univ. Sys., St. Louis, Mo. 1992-; chair Presdl. Advy. Council, St. Louis, Mo. 1992-; co-dir. Concordia Univ. Sys. Strategic Initiatives, St. Louis, Mo. 1993-; listed Who's Who Worldwide; author, articles: Cycle of Discipline/Ministry, 1974, A Lutheran Perspective for the Third Wave, 1982, The Creation of a Private Religious College, 1955-85, pub. 1988; author: BHE Report #601, 1979; mem. Lutheran Ch.-Missouri Synod. Ofc: Concordia University 1530 Concordia West Irvine 92715

HALSETH, JAMES A., university adminstrator; b. Aug. 19, 1940, Pine City, Minn.; s. Allwyn Yvone and Esther Clarice (Raymond) Halseth; m. Mary Elizabeth Rossi, June 10, 1965; edn: Luther Coll., Decorah, Ia. 1958-59; BA, Concordia Coll., Moorhead, Minn. 1962; MA, Ea. N.M. Univ. 1963; PhD, Texas Tech Univ. 1973. Career: tchg. fellow, Ea. N. Mex. Univ., history, 1962-63, political science, 1963; tchg. asst., history, Texas Tech Univ. 1963-65; instr. of history, San Antonio Coll. 1965-66; instr. of hist., Pacific Lutheran Univ. 1966-68; part-time instr. of hist., Texas Tech Univ. 1968-69; asst. prof. of hist., Moorhead State Univ., Minn. 1971; asst. prof. of hist., Pacific Lutheran Univ. 1970-75, assoc. prof. of hist. 1975-80, prof. of hist. 1980-81; prof. of hist., Texas Lutheran Univ. 1981-86; prof. of hist., Calif. Lutheran Univ. 1986-; chairman, div. of social sciences, Pacific Lutheran Univ., Tacoma, Wash. 1975-81; v.p. for academic affairs and dean, Texas Lutheran Univ. 1981-86; CEO, Texas Lutheran Univ. 1983; v.p. for academic affairs and dean, Calif. Lutheran Univ. 1986-; provost, Calif. Lutheran Univ. 1990-; program devel. for Title I Agency, Olympia, Wash., Tacoma Comm. Coll., Bellevue Comm. Coll., and Pierce County Library System 1971-81; grants-manship workshop, Bethany Coll. Devel. Office 1984; Mid-Tex. Consortium for Internat. Edn. and Programs 1984-85; bd. mem., Luth. Inst. for Religious Studies Program, Amer. Luth. Ch., Luth. Ch. in Amer. 1983-85; advy. mem., Seguin Ret. Sr. Vol. Program 1981-85; program devel., Guadalupe Valley Comm. Hosp., Warm Springs Rehab. Hosp., McKenna Mem. Hosp. 1983-85; awards: Pi Gamma Mu (Nat. Social Sci. Hon. Soc.) 1962; Silver Key (Univ. Honors Assoc.), Ea. N.M. Univ. 1963; Univ. Fellowship Award, Tx. Tech Univ. 1968; fellowship award, Nat. Seminar for Hist. Adminstrs., Williamsburg, Va. 1965; Faculty Fellowship Award, Amer. Luth. Ch. 1968; mem: Amer. Scandinavian Found. 1986-90, Amer. Assn. of Univ. Professors, Orgn. of Amer. Historians, We. Hist. Assn., We. Social Sci. Assn., Growth Policy Assn. of Pierce Co., Wash., So. Hist. Assn., Pacific NW Hist. Assn., Nat. Trust for Hist. Preservation, Nat. Mgmt. Assistance Assn., Nat. Luth. Deans Conf., Am. Assn. of State and Local Hist., Luth. Edn. Conf. of N. Am., So. Calif. Consortium of Academic Deans, Assn. of

Luth. Faculties, Indep. Colls. and Univs. of Tx., Comm. Leaders Club, Thousand Oaks, Special Collections in NW Hist., Pacific Luth. Univ. Lib. (dir., 1972-80), Luth. Inst. for Theol. Studies (bd. mem. 1982-86), Tx. Luth. Coll. (devel. bd. 1981-86, bd. of regents advy. mem. 1981-86), Calif. Luth. Univ.(bd. of regents advy. mem.); coauthor: The Northwest Mosaic: Minority Conflicts in Pacific Northwest History, 1977; numerous scholarly jour. articles and book revs. Res: 1190 Monte Sereno Drive, Thousand Oaks 91360 Ofc: California Lutheran University, 60 W. Olsen Road, Thousand Oaks 91360-2787

HALSTEAD, LESTER MARK, educational psychologist, administrator; b. June 15, 1927, San Pedro; s. Levi L. and Luty June (Newcomer H.; m. Eleanor Grace, Sept. 25, 1949; children: Lester Mark, Jr. b. 1950, Michael Lee b. 1951, Edward Frank b. 1953, Richard Paul b. 1954, Thomas Alexander b. 1955; edn: BS in psych., Brigham Young Univ., Provo, Utah, 1960; MS in clin. psych., Univ. Utah, S.L.C., 1963; PhD in Edn., USC, 1976; lic. Ednl. Psychologist, Calif., 1980. Career: lic. engr. US Merchant Marines, South Pacific, 1944-46; croupier Tropicana Hotel, Las Vegas, Nev., 1957-60; chief psychologist Clark County Juvenile Ct., Las Vegas, 1963-70; sch. psychologist Clark County Sch. Dist., 1963-66; adminstrv. psychologist Baldwin Park Sch. Dist., Calif., 1970-; instr. Parent Guidance, 1975-85; asst. prof. Inst. Counseling/Guidance, Pepperdine Univ., 1977-83; dir. Parent Support Group, Baldwin Park 1975-89, Huntington Beach 1976-89; dir. Perceptual Res. Ctr., Las Vegas, 1957-60; awards: Delta Epsilon 1976-; Internat. Sch. Psychologists Assn. disting. lectr.: Univ. South Hampton, Eng. 1983, Interlaken, Switz. 1987, Europe 1985-87; mem: EDCAL, 1970-; BPOSA, 1970-; Baldwin Park Boys Club Sponsor, 1989-; author: A Tri-Dimensional Theory of Personality, 1980; A Diversified Treatment Model, 1988; Republican (Presdl. Task Force 1987-); LDS Ch.; rec: golf, sailing, skiing, hunting, fishing, research. Res: 5642 Kern Dr. Huntington Beach 92649 Ofc: 4600 Bogart St. Baldwin Park 91706

HALTERMAN, HAROLD LELAND, counsel; b. Oct. 11, 1950, Vallejo; s. Harold Prescott and Lorraine Edna (Lowery) H.; m. T. Roberta Brooks, Jan. 7, 1978 (div. 1989); son, Alexander Cheff b. 1980, stepson, Joshua Lawrence b. 1969; m. 2d. Margaret M. Russell, June 23, 1991; edn: BA, UC Berkeley 1974; JD, UC Berkeley Boalt Hall 1979. Career: adminstrv. aide U.S. Rep. Ronald V. Dellums, Oakland 1971-79, dist. counsel 1979-92, dist. dir. and general counsel 1993-94; gen. counsel to U.S. Rep. Ronald V. Dellums and counsel U.S. House National Security Com. 1994-95; legal ofcr. Internat. Commn. Jurists, Geneva, Switzerland 1978; exec. bd., central com. mem. Calif. Democratic Party 1986-94; awards: Lions Club 1967, Outstanding Young Men Am. 1976, 81; mem: UC and Boalt Hall Alumni Assn., Nat. Lawyers Guild, Surviving 80's Inc. (chair, pres. 1979-93), ACLU No. Calif. (bd. ch. 1988-91), Central Com. for Conscientious Objectors (council 1976-79), Human Rights Advocates, Calif. Alumni Assn., Alameda Co. Democratic Lawyers Club, Amnesty Internat., Mayors Advy. Com. Berkeley (ch. 1979-81), Berkeley Citizens Action (ch. 1974-76); author Defense Sense, 1983, wine columnist San Francisco Bay Guardian, 1981-85; Democrat. Ofc: U.S. Representative Ronald V. Dellums 1301 Clay St Ste 1000N Oakland 94612 and House National Security Committee 2120 Rayburn Washington DC 20515

HALVERSON, ODA SIGRID, licensed acupuncturist; b. Oct. 28, 1937, Hamburg, Germany; nat. U.S. 1966; d. Walter and Leokadya R. (Zaworski) Parian; m. David R. Halverson, Sept. 14, 1968 (div. 1984); children: Leif b. 1973; edn: BA CSU Dominguez, L.A. 1980, MA, CSU 1982; PhD of Chinese Medicine, Internat. Coll., L.A. 1984; MS, SAMRA Univ., L.A. 1987; lic. med. acupuncture, Med. Bd. of Calif.; diplomate in acupuncture, NCCA. Career: secty. Im & Export, Hamburg, Germany 1955-59, L.A. 1961-66; exec. secty. Ducommun, L.A. 1966-68; herbologist, self-employed, L.A. 1980-88; lic. acupuncturist, pvt. practice, Torrance 1988-; lectr. Internat. Med. Orgn., Germany 1984; tchr. Dept. of Aging, L.A. 1990-; mem: Oriental Healing Arts Inst. 1976-, Calif. Acupuncture Assn. 1988-; creator of course in biology of cancer, Am. Cancer Soc., L.A. 1981; author: pub. article, Coronary Heart Disease 1984; interested in Buddhism; rec: reading, nature walks, discussion groups. Ofc: Oda S. Halverson PhD LAc, 3655 Lomita Blvd #412 Torrance 90505

HALVERSTADT, JONATHAN SCOTT, actor and seminar leader; b. Oct. 21, 1952, Fresno; s. Lee W. and Dorothy (Weller) H.; edn: BA, Fresno Pacific Coll. 1977; MS Counseling, Calif. State Univ., Fresno 1993; Career: social svs. staff Cedar Vista Psychiatric Hosp., Fresno 1994-; counseling intern supervised by Nancy Stark, MFCC, Fresno 1994-; owner, Jonathan Scott Productions, Fresno 1978-; owner, Dreikurs Relationship Ctr., Fresno,1988-91; owner Jonathan Scott & Assoc., Fresno 1990-; exec. editor, Am Magazine, Fresno,1989; announcer, KMJ/KNAX, Fresno 1980-82; announcer, KFIG-FM, Fresno 1979-80; workshop & seminar leader, 1984-;freelance copy writer, 1980-; musical performer & guest speaker US and Scandinavia, 1970-77; ski inst., Sierra Summit 1982-87; asst. inst., Small World Presch. 1974-75; author: Today, Tyndale House Pub., 1974; Communication By Candlelight, Family Life Today, Gospel Light Pub., 1975; Tears Of Your Heart, So Many Songs About Jesus, Gospel Pub. House, 1979; recorded compositions: Mush, orig. music by Jonathan M. Scott, 1977; Tears Of Your Heart, So Many Songs About Jesus, Melody Records, 1977; She Told Me, Valley Grown, KYNO Records, 1978; Help Me Lord, This Is Love,

Gabriel Records, 1979; syndicated radio prods: Serve It With Love; Tax Tips with Jack Vance; With Wine and You; Fitness Finesse; tv perf: played Barry Parker on General Hospital, 1985; num. app. Days Of Our Lives, Young And The Restless, and Capitol, 1983-1987; host, Central Calif. Easter Seal Soc. Telethon; nat. and reg. commercials: Reebok, Toyota, General Foods, NBC-TV, CBS-TV, Norwest Banks, We Are Sportswear, GMC Trucks, plus num. indsl. voice over and on-camera exp.; radio exp: morning news anchor/talk show host, KMJ; on-air pers., KNAX/Fresno, KFIG/Fresno, KFYE/Fresno, KBIF/Fresno, KOAD/Lemoore; mem: nat. bd. dir., Am. Fed. of TV and Radio Artists 1986-1992; v.p. and chmn. nom. and publicity, Easter Seal Soc. of Central Calif.; pres., Hidden Gardens Cond. Assn.; Nat. Assn. of Rehab. Prof.; Prof. Ski Inst. Assn.; Screen Actors Guild; Am. Fed. of Musicians; Internat. Brotherhood of Elect. Workers, Am. Counseling Assn., Calif. Assn. of Marriage Family Therapists; Methodist; rec: bicycling, backpacking, gourmet cooking, skiiing, scuba diving. Ofc: Jonathan Scott & Assoc., P.O. Box 16172 Fresno 93755

HALVORSEN, ROBERT ALFRED, JR., physician; b. Oct. 12, 1948, NY, NY; s. Robert Alfred and Dorothy Deeble (Stalcup) H.; edn: BS, chem., Univ. Miami, Coral Gables, Fla. 1970, MD, 1974; internship St. Mary's Med. Ctr., Long Beach, Calif. 1974-75; residency, radiology, Univ. of Tex., San Antonio 1977-80; mini-MBA, health care mgmt., Coll. of St. Thomas, Minneapolis, Minn. 1990; chiefs of clin. svc. course, health care mgmt., Harvard Sch. of Public Health, Boston, Mass. 1991; med. lic. Calif. 1975, Texas 1979, N.C. 1980, Minn. 1987; cert. Am. Bd. of Radiology 1980. Career: clin. instr. radiology Univ. of Tex., San Antonio 1980; fellow, abdominal imaging, Duke Univ. Med. Ctr., Durham, NC 1980-81; asst. prof. radiology Duke Univ. 1981-85, assoc. prof. 1985-87; assoc. prof. radiology Univ. of Minn., Minneapolis 1987-90; prof. & vice chmn. radiology UCSF 1990–; chief, dept. of radiology, S.F. Gen. Hosp. 1990–; prof. of medicine, UCSF 1993–; exec. com. dept. radiology, UCSF 1990–, radiology residency tchg. com. 1991-93, promotions com. 1991–, postgrad. edn. com. 1991-93, ad hoc com. review 1994; mem. S.F. Gen. Hosp. exec. com. 1990–, vice chair exec. com., clin. practice group 1993–, finance com. 1994-95, chair search coms. 1993-94, patient referral task force 1994, steering com. clin. practice orgn. planning task force 1992–; chair steering com. Dept. Public Health Info. Sys. Implementation; mem. oversight com., Dept. Public Health Info. Sys.; cons. sci. advy. bd. Voxel Inc., Laguna Hills, CA 1993–; vis. prof. Univ. Colo. 1986, Univ. N.C., Chapel Hill 1988, Mayo Clinic, Rochester, MN 1990, Med. Coll. Wis. 1991, Univ. Medicine and Dentistry of N.J. 1991, 93, Henry Ford Hosp., Detroit, Mich. 1991; awards: med. student rep. to Fla. St. Legislature 1974, President's Club, Univ. of Minn. 1988, Roscoe E. Miller award, Soc. Gastrointestinal Radiologists 1989, Mentor award Univ. of Minn. Med. Sch. Class of 1989; Cum Laude award Soc. of Computed Body Tomography 1990; Departmental Achievement award S.F. Gen. Hosp. 1992, 11 sci. exhibit awards from profl. societies 1981-92; mem: Radiological Soc. of N. Am. 1978–, Assn. of Univ. Radiologists 1980- (exec. com. 1987–, sci. exhibit award com. 1992, chair 1993; chair-Stauffer award com. 1992-94, nominating com. 1995), Am. Coll. of Radiology 1981–, AMA 1981–, Am. Roentgen Ray Soc. 1982–, Soc. of Gastrointestinal Radiologists 1986- (sci. prog. com. 1990-91, 95, cannon lecture com. 1990-93, membership com. 1994), Soc. of Computed Body Tomography/Magnetic Resonance 1989- (chair standards com. 1993-95), Soc. of Cancer Imaging 1992–, Soc. of Emergency Radiology 1993– (membership com. 1994, chair prog. com. 1995–, prog. dir.: nat. meeting 1995), Am. Coll. of Radiology (fellow 1994), San Francisco Med. Soc. (AIDS task force 1991–, public health task force 1992–, membership com. 1993–); club: Sausalito Yacht; jour. reviewer for Investigative Radiology 1987–, Am. Review of Respiratory Disease 1988–, Am. Jour. of Roentgenology 1989–, Investigative Radiology (editl. bd.) 1990–, Am. Jour. of Gastroenterology 1993–, Physician Exec., Jour of Mgmt. 1994–, New England Jour. of Medicine 1995–; prin. investigator, num. res. grants 1984–; author or co-author: 17 book chpts., 1984-93, 2 book reviews, 1989, 30+ sci. abstracts, 4 med. edn. courses (non-print media), num. sci. papers, lectures and presentations, 1981–, contbr. 90+ articles to sci. jours., 1984–; Republican; rec: sailing (recreational and competitive), house renovation, radiology. Res: 37 Mountain View Rd Fairfax Ofc: Dept Radiology San Francisco General Hospital 1001 Potrero Ave San Francisco 94930

HAMBRICK, HAROLD E., public relations executive; b. Feb. 17, 1943, New Orleans, La.; s. Harold E. and Mary Ellen (Clark) H.; children: Jefferey, Tyra; edn: BS, Pepperdine Univ., 1976; grad. cert. public relations, UCLA, 1988. Career: office mgr. Watts Health Found., Los Angeles 1967-68; acctg., office mgr. New Communicators Inc., Hollywood 1968-69; sr. acct. Watts Health Found., 1969-75; exec. dir. Western Assn. of Comm. Health Center, 1975-83; v.p. corp. communications Watts Health Found., 1983–; pres. Watts Credit Union 1987–, pres. Black Health Leadership Council, Inc. 1982–, pres. Calif. Black Health Network 1989-91; honors: Assemblyman Curtis Tucker Sr. Health & Human Service Award 1990, Outstanding Young Men of Am. 1978, Danforth Found. `I Dare You' Honor Roll 1961; mem. Gr. Los Angeles Press Club; AME; rec: model ships, photog., videography. Address: Los Angeles

HAMDANI, HASAN JAHANGIR, scholar, poet, executive; b. Dec. 12, 1940, Ludhyana, Punjab; nat. 1974; s. Nazar Husain and Shahjahan Begum (Bokhari) H.; m. Sohab Maqbool Zaidi, Aug. 26, 1979; children: Ehsan b. 1981, Asma b.

1983, Eban b. 1986; edn: BA hons., Govt. Coll. 1959; MA literature, Punjab Univ. Pakistan 1981; UC Berkeley 1968-73. Career: cultural affairs splst. U.S.Info. Service, Lahore, Pakistan 1961-63; research fellow McGill Univ., Montreal, Canada 1963-68; lectr., research UC Berkeley 1968-73; chmn. Avila Imports 1973-78; pres. Worldwide Productions, Lafayette 1978-87; pres. University Systems Inc., Milpitas 1988-90; c.e.o. California Allied Technologies 1990–; chief research ofcr. Dept. Linguistics, Lahore, Pakistan 1960-62; awards: H.S. most outstanding student 1955, Govt. Coll. debating medal 1959, Pak Canadian Guide literature laureate 1966, UC Berkeley best master of ceremonies 1969, Council of Middle Eastern Affairs best services 1982; mem: Commonwealth Club San Francisco, Council Internat. Affairs, Movie Theatre Owners Assn., Council Muslim Assn. (chmn. 1984-90), Literary Guild Calif. (pres. 1980-84), Pakistan Assn. (pres. 1975-78), Pakistan Canadian Friendship Club (chmn. 1965-68); author A Course in Urdu (1968), A News Paper Wordcount (1969), ed. poetry anthology Mehfil (1969), author A Newspaper Reader (1970); Republican; Muslim; rec: philately, numismatics, community service. Res: PO Box 7523 Berkeley 94707

HAMERSLOUGH, WALTER SCOTT, university professor; b. Dec. 15, 1935, Needles, Calif.; s. Walter Kenneth and Frances (Brown) H.; m. V. Darlene Berdan, Dec. 17. 1961; children: K. Scott b. 1963, Rhonda b. 1965; edn: AA, L.A. City Coll., 1955; BS, La Sierra Univ., Riverside, Calif., 1958; MA, Univ. of Redlands, Redlands, Calif., 1964; EdD, Univ. of Oregon, Eugene, 1971. Career: 7-8th grade tchr. Fairview Elem., San Bernardino, Calif., 1959-61; H.S. tchr. Loma Linda Acad., Loma Linda, Calif., 1961-64; prof. La Sierra Univ., Riverside, Calif., 1964–; prof. and chair, dept. of health & phys. edn. La Sierra Univ., 1973–;cons. YMCA, 1970; lectr. Azusa Pacific Coll., 1973; bd. mem./v.p. Alvord Pony League, Riverside, 1976-77; awards: listed in Who's Who in Calif. 1982, 84, Who's Who in the West,1983-94, Who's Who in Religion 1985, Who's Who in Am. Edn. 1994; recipient, Zapara Tchg. Award, Gen. Conf., SDA, Wash., DC 1989, Alumnus of the Year, La Sierra Univ. 1990; mem: Am. Alliance for HPERD 1963–; res. chair, v.p., state rep., Calif. Assn. for HPERD, 1963–; bd. mem. We. Coll. PE Soc. 1963–;mem: Phi Epsilon Kappa Frat. 1970, Am. Coll. of Sports Medicine 1980; pres., exec. dir. SDA-HPERA 1983–; civic: SDA Ch., Riverside, Calif.: SS sponsor 1972-79, SS coord. 1981-83, superintendent 1972-88, elder 1972–; sch. bd. mem. La Sierra Acad., Riverside, Calif.; coauthor, book, Swim for Child with Impairments, 1977; contbg. author (books): Study Guide/Happiness Homemade, 1975, Christ in the Classroom, Vol. 10, 1994; 2 pub. articles on sch. sports competition; Republican; Seventh-day Adventist; rec: gardening, reading, tennis, golf. Res: 5133 Harcourt Circle Riverside 92505. Ofc: La Sierra Univ. Riverside 92515

HAMILL, RICHARD DAVID, medical products company executive; b. Jan. 5, 1939, Visalia; s. Edward Charles and Elizabeth (Scheidt) H.; m. Mary Lucinda Kilbourne, Aug. 26, 1961; children: Lucinda b. 1963, Pamela b. 1965, Edward b. 1967, Stephanie b. 1971; edn: BS, Univ. Utah 1960; PhD, 1965; reg. pharmacist Calif., Utah. Career: res. pharmacist Miles Labs., Elkhart, Ind. 1965-66; asst. to sr.v.p. res. and devel. Baxter Labs., Deerfield, Ill. 1966-68, dir. res. adminstrn. 1968-70, dir. quality control Hyland div., Costa Mesa 1970-74, dir. product assurance, Deerfield, Ill. 1974-76; dir. corp. compliance G.D. Searle & Co., Skokie, Ill. 1976-79; pres. Hamill Assoc., Northbrook, Ill. 1979-83; chmn., c.e.o., pres., Hycor Biomed. Inc., Irvine 1983–; Republican; Christian; rec: pvt. pilot. Res: 22686 Ledana Mission Viejo 92691 Ofc: Hycor Biomedical Inc. 18800 Von Karman Irvine 92715

HAMILTON, WILLIAM K., physician (retired); b. Dec. 15, 1922, Guthrie Center, Iowa; s. Orren G. and Marie (Moberly) H.; m. Shyrlee Cole, July 14, 1946; children: Douglas b. 1950, Deborah b. 1952; edn: BA, Univ. of Iowa, Iowa City 1943, MD, 1946. Career: instr. to prof. Univ. of Iowa Coll. of Medicine 1951-67, dept. chair, anesthesia 1958-67; prof. & chair, Dept. of Anesthesia, UC San Francisco 1967-83; vice dean Sch. of Medicine, UC S.F. 1983-92, prof. emeritus 1992; dir., pres. Am. Bd. of Anesthesiology 1962-74; pres. Univ. Anesthesiologist Soc. of Academic Chairs; internat. lecturer; awards: Teaching Awards, Univ. of Iowa 1965, William Hamilton Disting. Professorship, UC S.F. 1993; mem. Am. Soc. of Anesthesiologists 1951–, Calif. Soc. of Anesthesiologists 1967–; past mem. AMA, CMA; author: num. book chapters, res. reports, invited lectures, 100+ scientific articles; mil: capt. M.C., U.S. Army 1943-46, 1947-49; Independent; Presbyterian; rec: golf, woodworking, travel. Res: 1115 South Eliseo Greenbrae 94904 and 6463 Stone Bridge Rd Santa Rosa 95409

HAMLIN, CARL TED, gemologist-jeweler; b. Jan. 2, 1939.; s. Carl Cecil and Clara Savanna (Anderson) H.; 2 children: Jay Thomas b. 1957, Garrett Carl b. 1968; edn: San Diego Coll. 1964; tchr. cred., CSU San Diego 1974; cert. GIA, Gemological Inst. of Am. 1971. Career: owner/opr. manufacturing jewelry firm, Hamlin's Mfg. Jewelers, El Cajon, Calif. 1969–; lectr., tchr., gemcutter and master jeweler; awards: for jewelry designs num. shows 1973-78; mem: Retail Jewelers of Am., Calif. Retail Jewelers Assn., San Diego Gemological Soc.; publs: num. gemological and jewelry technical articles 1973-85, research in field of gemology, goldsmithing and lapidary arts; mil: USAF 1956-60; Republican; Prot.; rec: travel. Ofc: Hamlin's Manufacturing Jewelers 2234 Fletcher Pkwy El Cajon 92020

HAMM, WILLIAM GILES, banking executive; b. Dec. 29, 1942, W.D.C.; s. John Edwin and Letty Belle (Wills) H.; m. Kathleen Ann Kelley, Sept. 5, 1970; children: Giles b. 1975; edn: AB (magna cum laude) Dartmouth Coll., 1964; MA econs., Univ. Mich., 1966, PhD econs., 1969. Career: budget examiner Bur. of the Budget, W.D.C. 1969-72, chief HUD Br. Ofc. of Mgmt. & Budget, 1972-76, dep. assoc. director 1976-77; legislative analyst Cali Legislature, Sacramento 1977-86; v.p. World Savings, Oakland 1986-91; sr. v.p. Federal Home Loan Bank of San Francisco, 1991-92, exec. v.p. and c.o.o. 1992–; awards: Colby Govt. Prize, Dartmouth 1964, Phi Beta Kappa 1964, Wm. A Jump Award for exemplary svc. US Govt. 1972; mem: Am. Economics Assn. 1964–, Nat. Acad. of Pub. Adminstrn. (fellow 1983–), Council for Excellence in Govt. (prin. 1986–), Western Legislative Fiscal Officers (pres. 1984-85), Deans Advy. Coun. UC Davis (1983-93); mem. bd. vis. Inst. for Policy Studies, Duke Univ. (1986-90); rec: skiing, hiking, bridge, cooking, pers. computers, gardening. Res: 858 Mountain View Dr Lafayette 94549-4214 Ofc: FHL Bank-S.F. 600 California St San Francisco 94108

HAMMER, JOSEPH KEITH, company executive; b. Dec. 4, 1953, Los Angeles; s. Morris Keith and Marjory Carol H.; m. Ada Kathleen Haas, Sept. 6, 1980; children: Joseph, Jr. b. 1982, John Henry b. 1986; edn: AA, Long Beach City Coll., 1974; BS, CSU Los Angeles, 1977; career: non-profit orgn. exec. Long Beach Area Council BSA, 1977-78; dispatcher Long Beach Police Dept., 1978-79; agt. N.Y. Life Ins. Co., Los Angeles 1979-81; v.p. American Typewriter Inc., Westminster 1981-88; coordinator Edgemont Sales 1988-92; ops. mgr. Arrowhead Business Machines, 1992–; mem: So. Calif. Office Machine Dealers Assn. (treas. 1986-88, newsletter ed. 1988–), Downtown Long Beach Assocs. (dir. 1984-87), Long Beach C.of C., Westminster C.of C., Nat. Rifle Assn. (life), All States Masonic Lodge (Past Master, newsletter ed. 1985-86), L.B. Scottish Rite (32 deg.), L.B. Lions (sec. 1984-86), Westminster Lions (pres. 1988-89), Los Alamitos Rotary (dir. 1991-92); Eagle Scout, var. pos. in scouting L.B. & Westminster; contbr. articles in trade jours.; Republican; Christian; rec: trophy hunter, knifemaker.

HAMMERBACK, JOHN CLARK, professor of communication; b. Oct. 6, 1938, San Francisco; s. William Joseph and Susan (Rigik) H.; m. Jean Melton, Aug. 29, 1965; children: Kristen b. 1969, Karen b. 1972; edn: BA, San Francisco St. Coll., 1962; MA, Univ. Oklahoma, 1965; PhD, Indiana Univ., 1970. Career: tchg. asst. Univ. Oklahoma, Norman 1963-65, Indiana Univ., Bloomington 1965-68; prof. comm. CSU Hayward, Calif. 1968–, chair 1971-77, asst. v.p. CSUH 1989-91, assoc. dean 1993–; assoc. editor Western Jour. of Communication 1979-81, 84-86, 90–; editorial bd. Internat. and Intercultural Communication Annual, vol. 20; dir. Hayward Conf. in Rhetorical Criticism, 1988-93; Faculty Affirmative Action ofcr. CSUH 1987-89; mem. bd. dirs. Community Counseling and Edn. Ctr., Fremont 1989-93; awards: outstanding lectr. CSUH 1971, exceptional merit CSUH 1984, listed Dir. of Am. Scholars, Who's Who in the West; mem: Western Communication Assn. (1968–, pres. 1983-84), Speech Comm. Assn. (1963–, chair pub. address div. 1993), Rhetoric Soc. of Am. 1985–, Calif. Speech Comm. Assn. 1975–, Execs. Club WS (pres. 1991-92); coauthor: In Search of Justice, 1987, War of Words, 1985, author 25+ articles and chapters in books (1971–), 7 book revs. (1967–), 25+ conv. papers (1969–); mil: A2c USN Reserve 1962-68; Prot.; rec: tennis. Res: 203 Fisalia Ct Fremont 94539 Ofc: Speech Comm. Dept. Calif. State Univ., Hayward 94542

HAMMOND, CHARLES EDGAR, data processing executive; b. Dec. 24, 1943, Kellogg, Ida.; s. Charles Wm. and Irene Elizabeth (Hoffman) H.; m. Jennifer Giard, Aug. 12, 1967; children: Christa b. 1973, Robert b. 1976; edn: BBA, Wash. St. Univ. 1967; MBA, Golden Gate Univ. 1973. Career: pgmr./analyst Boeing Airplane Co., Seattle 1967-68; pgmr./analyst Chevron Corp., San Francisco 1969–, div. mgr. Technology Svs., Chevron Information Technology Co., San Ramon 1986–; recipient award of merit Calif. Dept. Rehab. 1981; mem. advy. com. Computer Sci. Re-entry Pgm., UCB 1983–; mem. Alumni Beta Theta Pi Frat.; rec: outdoor activities. Ofc: Chevron Information Technology Co. PO Box 5031 San Ramon 94583

HAMMOND, LOUISE MARIE, photographer; b. July 16, 1934, Oakland (3d gen. Californian); d. Amiel John and Louise Agnes (Grewe) Figrouid; m. 1957-1982; edn: cert. in ornithology Cornell Univ., 1980. Career: photographer prin. Hammond Photography, Oakland 1968-: credits include American Forests, Ariz. Highways, Givaudanian, Horticulture, Westways, Wildlife, and other magazines, Flying Spur Yosemite Calendars (14+ yrs.), postcards, photograph in 1990 Yosemite Renaissance V Centennial Art Competition, B/W salon prints in num. pvt. collections; sales brochure designer Forum Travel, and tour leader in Kenya, Tanzania and Seychelles; acct. Lybrand, Ross Bros. & Montgomery, Oakland 1970-72; bus. mgr. and telethon co-ord. Easter Seal Soc., 1972-78; property and leasing mgr. Broadway Webster Med. Bldg., Summit Med. Bldg., 1978-89; awards: Who's Who In Photography, Nikon Award of Excellence 1983, runner-up Wildlife Photographer of Yr. London; bd. trustees Western Aerospace Mus. 1982-89, secty.-treas. 1982-85, treas. 1985-87; mem: Internat. Freelance Photographers Orgn., Calif. Alumni Assn., Epiphyllum Soc. of Am., Orchid Soc. of Am., Orchid Soc. of Calif., Oakland Art Assn., num. conserv. orgns.; 2 books in progress: culture of epiphytic plants, and photo study of

Southwest Canyonlands; Republican; Roman Catholic; rec: hiking, snorkeling, gardening, oil and pastel artist, travel. Address: PO Box 11332 Oakland 94611

HAMMOND, R. PHILIP, research scientist, engineer; b. May 28, 1916, Creston, Iowa; s. Robert Hugh and Helen (Williams) H.; m. C. Vivienne Fox (dec. 1987); edn: BS chem. engring., Univ. So. Calif.; PhD physical chem., Univ. Chgo.; reg. profl. engr. Calif., Ill. Career: chief chemist Lindsey Chem. Co., West Chgo, Ill.; group leader Los Alamos Sci. Lab., Los Alamos; program dir. Oak Ridge Nat. Lab., Oak Ridge, Tenn.; sr. scientist R&D Assoc., Marina del Rey; adj. prof. engring. UCLA; design team leader Large Desalination Project, Met. Water Dist. of So. Calif.; cons. engr., Santa Monica; mem U.S. delegation to Internat. Conf. on Peaceful Uses of Atomic Energy 1955, 60, 65; U.S. del. to USSR Desalination Exchange 1964; U.S. study team Mexico Desalination Project; U.S. del. to Internat. Atomic Energy Agency; honors: Sigma Xi; mem: Am. Nuclear Soc.; 100 papers pub. in tech. jours.; 25 patents; mil: USCG Aux.; Prot.; rec: sailing, cabinet making, painting. Ofc: POB 1735 Santa Monica 90406

HAMPTON, WADE PAUL, JR., insurance company executive; b. Oct. 10, 1946, Santa Rosa; s. Wade Paul and Isabel Kay (Burt) H.; m. Marilyn S. Scott, March 15, 1970 (div. 1975); m. Betty Annett Stornetta, Aug. 30, 1982; children: Heather b. 1983, Patrick b. 1985, Mathew b. 1989; Career: ins. agent Farmers Ins. Group, Santa Rosa 1969-80, dist. mgr., Fresno 1981–, trainer, tchr. 1982–; awards: Farmers Ins. Group topper club (1971-76), life masters club (1972-84), comml. master club (1974-87), comml. round table (1987), Blue Max (1984), Wall of Fame (1987); mem: Fresno Lions, Santa Rosa 20-30 Club (bd. mem.), Jaycees (bd.mem.); mil: E-5 AUS 1966-68; Republican; Presbyterian; rec: automobile collecting. Res: 2588 W Scott Fresno 93711 Ofc: Farmers Insurance 3435 W Shaw Ste 101 Fresno 93711

HAMPTON-WAGENER, JOHANN, psychotherapist; b. June 6, 1941, Ber le Tang, France; s. Hermann Bernard and Martha (Du Bois) Wagener; children: Mark b. 1961, Christine b. 1962, Traci Lee b. 1965, Devon b. 1974, Aaron b. 1981; edn: BS, CSU Dominguez Hills 1981; MS, USC, 1985; postgrad. Calif. Coast Univ.; reg. psychological asst., 1988. Career: Calif. 1963-73; security dir. Am. Protection Systems (airport sec. svcs. for 24 carriers), LAX 1973-75; family therapist Charter Pacific Hosp., 1975-81, Vista Recovery Center 1981-84; assoc. dir. Peninsula Counseling Inc., Redondo Beach 1981-88; program dir. Advanced Recovery Inst. (ARI), 1984-88; primary therapist/program dir. Vista Recovery Centers, Anaheim 1988–; reg. psychol. asst. Flynn Gelbart Kodimer and Assocs., Comprehensive Psychol. Services, Redondo Beach 1988–, in chg. alcohol/chem. dependency pgms.; honors: Psi Chi, listed Who's Who Am. Univs. and Colls. (1981); mem: Internat. Council on Alcohol and Addictions, Am. Psychol. Assn., Am. Psychol. Soc. (student affil.), Am. Coll. of Addiction Treatment Adminstrs., Assn. for Transpersonal Psych., Calif. Personnel and Guidance Assn., Nat. Assn. on Sexual Addiction Problems Inc., Southbay Coalition for Alternatives to Domestic Violence, Californians Preventing Violence, Alliance for the Formerly Abused (bd.), Calif. Assn. of Marriage and Family Therapists, ALMACA, Am. Coll. of Addiction Treatment Adminstrs., ACLU, USC Alumni Assn., CSUDH Alumni Assn.; Democrat; R.Cath.; rec: fitness. Res: 5 Ponderosa Ln Rolling Hills Estates Ofc: PO Box 530 Redondo Beach 90277-0530

HANCOCK, EMILY STONE, psychologist; b. Nov. 18, 1945, Syracuse, N.Y.; d. Theodore McLennan and Eleanor Sackett (Stone) H.; m. Philip Yenawine, Aug. 28, 1965 (div. 1970); 1 son, Tad; edn: BA, Syracuse Univ., 1971; MSW, Boston Univ., 1974; EdD, Harvard Univ., 1981; Lic. Clinical Social Worker (LCSW), Mass., Calif. Career: clin. social worker Children's Hosp., Boston 1974-77; pvt. practice Mass., Calif., 1976–; co-founder, therapist Divorce Resource Ctr., Cambridge 1976-78; tchg. fellow Harvard 1978-79; counselor Alameda Co. Superior Ct., Oakland 1982–; screening coord. dept. pediatrics, UC San Francisco, 1982-85; faculty Ctr. for Psychological Studies, Albany 1982–; chair Askwith Symp. and Colloquia, Cambridge 1979, editor Harvard Ednl. Rev. 1979-81, fellow HEW 1972-74, fellow Danforth Found. 1978-80, fellow NIMH 1981-82; awards: grantee Radcliffe Coll. (1978, 80), Woodrow Wilson Found. 1980, Phi Beta Kappa, Phi Kappa Phi; mem: Am. Psychol. Assn., Acad. Cert. Soc. Workers; author: The Girl Within (1989), articles in profl. jours.; rec: music. Res/Ofc: 1230 Glen Ave Berkeley 94708-1841 Ph: 510/540-5510

HANCOCK, JACK LOGAN, retired telecommunications executive and retired military officer; b. April 30, 1930, Welch, West Va.; s. Everette W. and Gladys (Gay) H.; m. Patricia R., Oct. 15, 1955; children: Jack b. 1958 (dec.), Kevin b. 1959, Jeffrey b. 1961, Annemarie b. 1963, Natalie b. 1966, Patrick b. 1968; edn: BA, W. Va. Univ. 1952; MBA, George Washington Univ. 1961. Career: maj. gen. (ret.) US Army 1952-78; sr. v.p. Chemical Bank, N.Y.C. 1978-82; exec. v.p. Wells Fargo Bank, San Francisco 1982-87; v.p. Pacific Bell 1987-93 (ret.); mem: IEEE, Assn. Computer Machinery, Armed Forces Comm. Electronic Assn., Center for Excellence in Govt.; club: The Family (S.F.); Republican; R.Cath. Res: 936 Natchez Ct Walnut Creek 94598

HAND, TERRY LEE, plastic surgeon; b. Oct. 31, 1942, Sunburry, Pa.; s. Leon Russell and Izora (Yeager) H.; m. Lisa, July 10, 1982; children: Tiffany b. 1966, Sara b. 1968, Brianna b. 1986, Christina b. 1987; edn: BA, Susquehanna Univ.

1964; MS, Univ. of Mo. 1966; MD, Temple Univ. Sch. of Med. 1970; UC Davis Sch. of Med. 1976-81: Diplomate Am. Bd. of Plastic and Reconstruction Surgery. Career: pvt. practice plastic surgery; asst. clin. prof. plastic surgery UC Davis; clin. attending plastic surgery V.A. Hosp., Martinez; awards: Babcock Surgical Soc. award 1970; mem: CMA, MMS, AMA, ASPRS; rec: art, ski. Res: 32 Estates Ct San Rafael 94901 Ofc: Terry L Hand MD 900 So Elieso Ste 103 Greenbrae 94904

HANDLERY, PAUL ROBERT, hotel executive; b. Apr. 8, 1920, St. Helena; s. Harry and Rose Helen (Braun) H.; m. Ardyce Arlene Lundquist, June 1, 1945; children: Barbara Kim (Mrs. David R. Metcalf) b. 1947, Michael Kent b. 1951, Nancy Liane b. 1953, Jon Steven b. 1956, Lane Ardyce b. 1960; edn: AA, UC Berkeley, 1940; BS (honors) Cornell Univ., 1943; cert. hotel adminstr. Career: vice pres. Handlery Hotels Inc., San Francisco 1946-63, pres. 1963-86, chmn. and CEO, 1986–; dir. Civic Bank of Commerce; awards: Men of Distinction, Innkeeping Mag. 1963, Hospitality Mag. Hall of Fame 1966, Pacific Hotel-Motel News Man of Year 1970, Nat. Jewish Hosp. Man of Year, Denver 1973, Hon. LLD, GGU, 1991, CH&MA Hall of Fame 1991, Hon. Regent John F. Kennedy Univ., Orinda, USF Presidents Medallion 1993, Peter Goldman Award of Excellence 1993, AHMA Ednl. Inst. "CHA Emeritus" 1995; mem. advy. bds. of Hotel and Restaurant Sch., Cal Poly Pomona, Golden Gate Univ., Univ. San Francisco, (bd. past chmn.) City Coll. S.F., Cornell Univ. Council; mem: S.F. Conv. and Visitors Bur. (bd. mem., past pres.), American Hotel and Motel Assn. (pres. 1974, chmn. bd. 1975, v.chair Allied Member com., chmn. liaison com. w. Internat. Hotel Assn. (bd. dirs.), Ambassador Ednl. Inst.), American Hotel Found. (hon. chmn. for life, past pres., trustee), Calif. Hotel and Motel Assn. (past pres., dir. emeritus), Hotel Employers Assn. S.F. (past pres.), Hotel & Restaurant Found. (pres.), East Bay Hotel Assn. (past pres.), Cornell Soc. of Hotelmen; civic: Salvation Army Advy. Bd. (past chmn.), No. Calif. Chpt. Leukemia Soc. Am. (trustee, past pres.), Union Square Assn. (dir., past pres.); clubs: Commonwealth (S.F.), Bermuda Dunes CC, Stardust CC, Moraga CC; mil: capt. US Army; rec: spectator sports. Res: 766 Augusta Dr Moraga 94556 Ofc: Handlery Hotels, Inc. 180 Geary Ste 700 San Francisco 94108

HANEY, FREDERICK MARION, venture capitalist; b. Mar. 5, 1941, Columbus, Ohio; s. George Edward and Margaret Ann (Marion) H.; m. Barbara Breig, June 8, 1963; children: Karen b. 1967, Bradford b. 1969; edn: BA, Ohio Wesleyan Univ. 1963; MS math., Colo. St. Univ. 1965; PhD, Carnegie-Mellon, 1968. Career: product devel. mgr. Scientific Data Systems, El Segundo 1968-70; strategy mgr. Xerox Corp., El Segundo 1970-75; mgr. Computer Scis. Corp., El Segundo 1975-77; mgr. strategic plnng. Xerox Corp. 1977-80; strategic plan-ning/gen. mgmt. TRW, Redondo Beach 1980-83; venture capital mgr. 3i Ventures, Newport Beach 1983-91; pres. Venture Management, 1991–; gen. ptnr. Calif. Technology Fund 1994–; dir: IC Sensors, Milpitas 1988-94, Evernet Inc., L.A. 1989-92, Adaptive Solutions Inc., Portland 1991–, FRS Inc., Sacramento 1985-93; Mykotronx, Torrance 1993–; Silicon Power Corp., Long Beach 1985-92, Electronic Mapping, Pasadena 1995–, Design Intent, Dana Point 1995–; chmn. of bd. dirs. Pepgen, Inc., Huntington Beach 1993–; co-founder Technology Bank, Torrance; honors: Omicron Delta Kappa 1963, Balfour Award, Sigma Chi 1963; appt. bds: USC Entrepreneurial Prog. (advy. bd. 1987–), UCI Accelerate Program (dir. 1991–), Ohio Wesleyan Univ. (Assoc. 1984–); chmn. Orange Co. Project 2010 Defense Conversion Task Force; mem: Nat. Assn. of Venture Capitalists, We. Assn. of Venture Capitalists, Orange County Venture Capital Assn.; civic: Project Mexico, Rolling Hills, Ca. 1977–, Palos Verdes Estates Coastline Com. (chair 1974-75); clubs: P.V. Golf, P.V. Tennis; publs: 7+ tech. articles, 1968-73, 50+ public speaking engagements on venture capital and new bus. startups; Republican; Presbyterian; rec: golf, tennis, sportfishing. Res: 3433 Paseo Del Campo Palos Verdes Estates 90274

HANKINS, HESTERLY G., III, computer systems scientist, educator; b. Sept. 5, 1950, Sallisaw, Okla.; s. Hesterly G., II and Ruth Faye (Jackson) H.; edn: attended Ventura Coll. 1970, Antelope Valley Coll. 1977, La Verne Univ. 1987; BA in sociology, UC Santa Barbara, 1972, Scholars Program, UCSB, 1970; MBA mgmt. info. sys., UCLA, 1974; postgrad. telecomms., Golden Gate Univ., 1985-86; Calif. Comm. Colls. tchr., college supr., chief adminstr. creds. Career: applications pgmr. Xerox Corp., Marina del Rey 1979-80; computer pgmr. engring. div. Naval Base, Port Hueneme, 1981-84; spl. asst. ceo NAS Moffet Field 1984-85; computer analyst Pacific Missile Test Ctr., Point Mugu 1985-88; MIS specialist Defense Contract Administrv. Svs. Reg., El Segundo 1988–; instr. Ventura Coll., Golden Gate Univ., Chapman Coll., De Anza Coll., National Univ., L.A. 1988–, CORE; SCAS National Univ. faculty; adj. lectr. West Coast Univ. 1987; awards: 20th Century Onyx Scholar 1968, UCSB Dean's List 1971. Alpha Kappa Psi (life, sec. 1973-74), Outstanding Young Men of Am., Montgomery, Ala. Jaycees 1980, SMART beneficial suggestion awards-NSWSES 1984, suggestion awards PMTC (Pt. Hueneme 1988, Pt. Mugu, DCMDW, El Segundo), Arthur Young nominee for Entrepreneur of Year 1987, Pt. Hueneme, outstanding perf. award Weapons Support Directorate CAMAIR, PMTC, Pt. Mugu 1988, Spl. Act Award Def. Contract Adminstrn. Svs. Reg. 1989, profl. appreciation letters (3), listed Who's Who in the World 11th edit., Who's Who in the West 1993 (21st, 22nd, 23rd & 24th edits.), Who's Who in Calif. 1990-95, Internat. Leaders of Achiev. (1st edit.) 1988, Men of

Achievement, Am. Men & Women of Sci., Who's Who in Sci. & Engring., Who's Who in Finance & Industry, Who's Who in Black Am., Internat. Directory of Disting. Leadership (5th edit.), Am. Biographical Inst. (res. fellow, recipient world lifetime achievement award), others; mem: Assn. for Computing Machinery 1974, Grad. Students of Mgmt. Alumni 1974, IEEE Computer Soc., Fed. Mgrs. Assn., Intergovtl. Council on Technology of Information Processing, Internat. Platform Assn./Am. Lyceum Assn., Nat. Assn. Accountants, Calif. Assn. Accountants; civic: City of Oxnard Comm. Relations Bd. 1984, YWCA Benefit Rodeo Assn. (vol. 1975-76), ANRC Blood Donor Campaign 1973, Combined Fed Campaign (Key Person 1978, honors); mem. Palm Springs Tennis Club (P.S.), El Dorado Ranch Estates (San Felipe); author: Campus Computer, 1986, Satellites & Teleconferencing, Network Planning, 1986, Quotations, 1992, Living Expressions and Quotes of Notables, 1993, Idea Bank, 1993, Product Rating System, 1993, Jobs of the Future Year 2000, Training Base Model, 1993, My Bio, A Decision Tree for Preventive Health, 1994, Sound Seal/Shield (c. 1994), A Review of Electronic Meetings Technical Alternatives and Social Choices in Telecommunication; mem. U.S. Presdl. Task Force (Medal of Merit 1990); United Methodist (parish & ch. rels. 1987-88); rec: chess, reading, jogging. Res: 3700 S Sepulveda Blvd West Los Angeles 90034-6851 Ofc: 9920 La Cienega Blvd Inglewood 90301

HANNON, TIMOTHY PATRICK, lawyer; b. Nov. 29, 1948, Culver City; s. Justin Aloysius and Ann Elizabeth (Ford) H.; m. Patricia Ann, May 1, 1976; children: Sean Patrick b. 1978, James Patrick b. 1980; edn: Wien Univ., Vienna, 1968-69; BA, JD (cum laude), Santa Clara Univ., 1970; Naval War Coll. 1988; admitted bar: Calif. (1974). Career: atty., assoc. Alvan Fisher, Banning 1975; atty., ptnr. Moerdyke & Hannon, Palo Alto 1975-84; atty. Atwood, Hurst, Knox & Anderson, San Jose 1984-86; sole practice atty., Campbell 1986–; instr. Lincoln Univ., San Jose 1988–, De Anza Jr. Coll. 1987–, San Jose St. Univ. 1983-86, UC Santa Cruz 1981; awards: Calif. scholarship 1966-70, Santa Clara Univ. Law Sch. scholar 1971-74, U.S. Govt. Jr. Fulbright 1968-69; mem. Santa Clara Univ. Law Alumni (bd. 1979-84, pres. 1984-86), Santa Clara Univ. Nat. Alumni, Nat. Alumni Exec. Com., Menlo Park Housing Commn., Kiwanis San Jose (bd. dirs. 1991-93), Kiwanis Palo Alto (bd. dirs. 1977-79), Naval Reserve Assn.; 3 articles pub. in profl. jours., 1979, 81; editor Navy Legal Handbook, 1992-93; mil: comdr. USNR 1978–, sp6 Army/Calif. Nat. Guard 1970-76, Navy Achievement Medal 1986, Naval Reserve OAG atty., CINCPACFLT, Pearl Harbor 1993-95; Republican; R.Cath.; rec: sailing, trains. Res: 806 Buckwood Ct San Jose 95120 Ofc: 1901 S Bascom Ave Ste 1440 Campbell 95008

HANOWELL, ERNEST GODDIN, physician-internist; b. Jan. 31, 1920, Newport News, Va.; s. George Frederick and Ruby Augustine (Goddin) H.; m. Para Jean Hall, June 10, 1945; children: Ernest D., Deborah J. Hanowell Orick, Leland H., Dee P. Hanowell Martinmaas, Robert G.; edn: AB, George Wash. Univ., 1945, MD, 1948; postgrad. Nat. Heart Inst. 1959-61, Tufts Univ. 1960-61, Johns Hopkins 1961-62; diplomate Am. Bd. Internal Medicine. Career: intern, USPHS Hosp., Norfolk, Va. 1948-49; resident internal medicine USPHS Hosp., Seattle 1952-55; chief medicine USPHS Hosp., Ft. Worth 1955-57; dep. chief medicine USPHS Hosp., Boston 1957-59; cons. chest disease Phila. Gen. Hosp. 1960-61; clin. asst. Tufts Med. Sch., and lectr. medicine Hahnemann Med. Coll. 1960-61; asst. prof. Univ. Md. Med. Sch. 1961-64; instr. Univ. Tenn. Med. Sch. 1964-65; chief medicine USPHS Hosp., Memphis 1964-65, Monterey County Gen. Hosp. 1969-70; attdg. staff Cardiac Clinic, Stanford Univ. Med. Sch. 1967-69; med. staff Kaiser Permanente Med. Group, Sacramento 1971-87, ret.; asst. clin. prof. Sch. Med., UC Davis 1973-81; Fellow ACP, Fellow Am. Coll. Chest Diseases, mem. AMA, TB and Health Assn., Crocker Art Mus. Assn., Phi Chi, Salinas School Board (1967-69); Am. Heart Assn. (bd. dirs.); clubs: Commonwealth (S.F.), Comstock (Sacto.); mil: U.S. Army 1943-46. Res: 1158 Racquet Club Dr Auburn 95603

HANRETTA, ALLAN GENE, physician, psychiatrist; b. June 24, 1930, Galveston, Tx.; s. Aloysius Thomas and Genevieve M. (Feeney) H.; m. Carolyn Jean Jacobs, Sept. 4, 1954; children: Allan Thomas b. 1955, Mark Daniel b. 1956, Patrice Marie b. 1960; edn: BS pharm., Univ. Tx. Austin 1952; BA arts and sci., 1957, MD, Univ. Tx. Med. Branch Galveston 1959; lic. physician and surgeon Calif. 1960. Career: pvt. practice psychiatry, Santa Barbara 1964-83; chief of staff Dani's Psychiatric Hosp. 1968-71; outpatient psychiatrist Santa Barbara Co. Mental Health 1964; night med. duty ofcr. Camarillo St. Hosp. 1974; outpatient psychiatrist VA Clinic 1983; awards: Santa Barbara Pharm. Assn. Contbn. to Profession of Pharmacy 1975; mem: Santa Barbara Psychiatric Soc. (pres. 1969-71), Am. Psychiatric Assn., AMA, Am. EEG Soc., So. Calif. Psychiatric Assn.; 4 articles pub. in profl. jours., 1963, 64; mil: lt.j.g. USN 1952-54; Cath.; rec: chess, sailing, flying. Res: 3728 Calle Cita Santa Barbara 93105

HANSEN, CHRISTINE M., pharmacist; b. Dec. 26, 1954, Inglewood; d. Dr. Oluf Steffen (M.D.) and Betty Jane (Henderson) Hansen; edn: Golden West Jr. Coll. 1972-75, PharmD, USC, 1979; AA in music, Golden West Coll., Huntington Beach 1993 Career: pharmacy intern Long Beach VA Hosp., Long Beach, summer 1978; clin. pharmacist Cottage Hosp., Santa Barbara, 1979-87, also instr. nsg. edn. in pharmacology at hosp. and coord. of the Drug of the Week pgm. to keep nurses current; instr. public awareness in poison information; piano tchr.; creative: performing classical pianist retirement homes 1975–; fashion modeling and film work, La Belle Agy. and John Robert Powers; watercolor painter, local exhibits; editor/writer, newsletter: Our Generation; creator/writer, comic strip: Philippe (in process); rec: swimming, singing, piano, humor. Res: 16924 Edgewater Huntington Beach 92649

HANSEN, DON CURTIS, envelope manufacturing executive; b. March 13, 1929, Marinette, Wis.; s. Curtis Albert and Dagmar Anne H.; m. Joan Crant, Nov. 9, 1973; edn: bus. admin., Carroll Coll. 1952. Career: purchasing agent Prescott/ Sterling, Menominee, Mich. 1954-62; mfrs. rep. Don C. Hansen Assoc., Phoenix, Ariz. 1962-63; salesmgr. Karolton Envelope Co., San Francisco 1964-72; pres., owner San Francisco Envelope, San Francisco 1972-79; owner Curtis Swann Cards, San Francisco 1977-79; pres., owner Don C. Hansen Inc. dba The Envelope Co., San Francisco 1979–; mem: Printing Industries of No. Calif. (dir. 1980–), Envelope Printing Specialists Assn. NY, NY (pres. 1983-84, dir. 1983–), S.F. Litho & Craftsmans Club, Printing Industries of No. Calif., Envelope Mfrs. Assn. Am., Masons, Ahmed Shrine; clubs: Wing Point CC (Bainbridge Island, Wn.) Harbor Point Tennis, S.F. Tennis (bd. govs. 1988-91); mil: pfc US Army 1952-54; Republican; rec: golf, tennis, skiing, bridge. Ofc: The Envelope Co. 2857 Cypress St Oakland 94608-4011

HANSON, DONALD HARLAN, county road superintendent; b. Mar. 6, 1937, Harlowton, Mont.; s. George C. and Myrtle T. (Carlson) H.; m. Mary L. Roman, July 16, 1955; children: Pamela b. 1958, Scott b. 1962; edn: grad. Helena (Mont.) H.S. 1955, Hwy. engring. ICS (corresp.) 1964. Career: engring. aide Montana Hwy. Dept., Helena 1956-59; engr. roads dept. San Diego County, 1959–, Division Road supt., 1978–; mil: s/sgt. E6 Nat. Guard 1954-63; Republican; Lutheran; rec: camping, rosarian. Ofc: San Diego County, 1600 Descanso Ave San Marcos 92069

HANSON, GARY A., lawyer, legal educator; b. Sept. 30, 1954, Santa Fe, N.Mex.; s. Norman A. and Mary Gene (Moore) Garrison H.; m. Tracey J. Tannen, March 11, 1982; children: Paul b. 1987, Carly b. 1989, Sean b. 1992; edn: BS magna cum laude, Univ. Utah 1976; JD, Pepperdine Univ. Sch. Law 1980. Career: atty. sole practice, Westlake Village 1980-82; assoc. gen. counsel Pepperdine Univ., Malibu 1982-83, actg. gen. counsel 1983-84, univ. gen. counsel 1984, also adj. prof. of law 1982, lectr. bus. law Seaver Coll. 1986; atty. pro bono San Fernando Valley Christian Sch., L.A. 1982-83; cons. West Pub. Co. 1988; awards: San Diego Christian Found. pres.'s award 1984, Am. Bd. Trial Advocates Excellence Preparation for Trial 1980; mem: Am. Bar Assn., L.A. Co. Bar Assn., Nat. Assn. Coll. & Univ. Attys., Pro Bono Estate Advy. Service; article pub. in profl. jour., 1989; Republican; Christian. Ofc: Pepperdine University Malibu 90263

HANSON, JOHN FRANCIS, JR., lawyer; b. Oct. 1, 1914, Alameda; s. John Francis and Emily (Jost) H.; m. Virginia Lillian Jones, April 18, 1943; edn: BA, Stanford Univ. 1935; JD, Stanford Law Sch. 1938. Career: claims adjuster Hartford Ins., Oakland 1938-41; ptnr., atty., Alameda 1945-77; sole practice, Alameda 1977; v.p. Alameda Coupon 1960; mem: Alameda Kiwanis, Alameda Elks, Native Sons Golden West, Am. Legion, Reserve Ofcrs. Assn., Navy League; mil: col. AUS 1941-45; Republican; Christian; rec: travel. Res: 1810 Central Ave #207 Alameda 94501

HANSON, LARRY KEITH, manufacturing company executive; b. Aug. 14, 1932, Hawkins, Wis.; s. Harold and Clara Pauline (Lund) H.; m. Patricia Rosalie Sammarco, Aug. 6, 1955; children: Larry b. 1956, John b. 1957, James b. 1963; edn: BS, U.S. Merchant Marine Acad. Career: devel. engr. Curtiss Wright Corp., Woodridge, N.J. 1955-58; sales engr. Gits Bros. Mfg. Co., Chgo., Ill. 1958-66; sales mgr. Aeroquip Corp., Jackson, Mich. 1966-70; exec. v.p. Furon Co., Laguna Niguel 1970–; mng. dir. Merkel Co., Hamburg, Germany; mem: Soc. Automotive Engrs., Am. Soc. Mfg. Engrs.; 6 patents in field; mil: ensign USNR 1955-57; rec: drawing, fly fishing. Ofc: Furon Co. 29982 Ivy Glenn Dr Laguna Niguel 92677

HANSON, RAYMOND LESTER, lawyer, retired; b. Nov. 2, 1912, San Francisco; s. Raymond Osborne and Hilda Frances (Beavis) H.; m. Eleanor E. Quandt, June 15, 1935; children: Eleanor Lynne b. 1936, Christine b. 1939; edn: BA, Stanford Univ. 1933; JD, UCSF Hastings Coll. Law 1936; LL.D hon., Whitworth Coll. 1977; LHD hon., Coll. Idaho 1980; admitted St. Bar Calif. (1936), U.S. Supreme Ct. (1956). Career: ptnr. Hanson Bridgett Marcus Vlahos & Rudy, S.F. 1957; vol advy. com. atty. gen. Calif. 1972-84, asst. dist. atty. City and Co. of S.F. 1937-38; columnist, lectr. trusts and estate planning; elder, trustee Calvary Presbyterian Ch., S.F. 1939-41; ruling elder United Presbyterian Ch. U.S.A. 1939-75; pres. bd. of ch. extension Presbytery of S.F. 1946-49, moderator 1953; justice Permanent Jud. Commn. Supreme Ct. of demonination 1952-61; chmn. bd. San Francisco Theological Semi. 1974-84; chmn., mem. worship and music com. First Presbyterian Ch. of San Mateo 1959-64; past pres., secty. Pacific Med. Center Inc.; past pres. No. Calif. Presbyterian Homes Inc.; past chmn. bd., dir. S.F. Met. YMCA; pres., bd. dirs. Goodwill Industries S.F. 1972-73; bd. dirs. UCSF Hastings Coll. Law; mem. assoc. bd. S.F. Council BSA; pres. Fellowship Forum, Palo Alto 1987; advy. bd. Golden Gate Univ.

Center for tax Studies; Univ. Calif. Alumni Council 1970-71; trustee Oreg. Shakespeare Festival 1982–; recipient outstanding & disting. svc. award UC Hastings Coll. Law (1975); mem: Am. Coll. Probate Counsel (fellow, chmn. subcom. adminstrn. estates uniform probate code com. 1972), Am. Judicature Soc., Nat. Assn. Coll. & Univ. Attys., Lawyers Club S.F., S.F. Estate Planning Council, Am. Bar Assn. (st. chmn. com. on charitable trusts 1972), Calif. Bar Assn. (chmn. com. on conf. resolution 1967-69), S.F. Bar Assn. (past dir., past chmn. estate and trust law sect., chmn. publs. com. 1969-70), Am. Assn. Homes for Aging, Internat. Acad. Estate and Trust Law (academician), Kiwanis Internat. (past chmn. boys and girls work com. Calif.-Nev.-Hawaii Dist., past pres. S.F.); mil: lt. USNR 1943-46. Address: Sequoias 501 Portola Rd (POB 8062) Portola Valley 94028

HARDCASTLE, ROBERT TAYLOR, management and insolvency consultant; b. Jan. 28, 1952, San Francisco; s. Robt. Leon and Marjorie Pearl (Bryson) H.; m. Karen C. Welch, June 23, 1990; children: Heather b. 1976, Barrett b. 1979, Greysen b. 1983; edn: AA, Bakersfield Coll. 1972; BS, CSU Bakersfield, 1974; MBA, Claremont Grad. Sch., 1984. Career: constrn. ind. exec. 1976-85; owner Bottom Line Management Technologies Co., Bakersfield 1986–, also Atlanta 1991–; mem: Am. Mgmt. Assn., Nat. Fire Protection Assn., Am. Fire Sprinkler Assn., Kern Co. Builders Exchange, Kern Co. Contractors Assn. (founding dir.), Cal-State Bakersfield Alumni Assn.; developer: Finally a computer bus. program; contbr. articles various mags. and industry publs.; Republican (Co. Central Com.); R.Cath.; rec: skiing, baseball. Ofc: 4909 Stockdale Hwy Ste 355 Bakersfield 93309-2637

HARDIE, GEORGE GRAHAM, gaming club executive; b. Aug. 19, 1933, Cleveland, Ohio; s. Wm. M., Jr. and Helen (Graham) H.; m. Paula Daniel (div.); children: George, Jr. b. 1967, Jennifer b. 1970; ed. pub. schs. N.Y. and Mass. Career: sales dept. of family candy bus., Hardie Bros., Pittsburgh, Pa.; various mgmt. pos., then owner direct sales agys.; purchased first standardbred horse, 1963, driving, tng. and racing harness horses, 1963–; cons. expert on gaming and racing issues, cons. greyhound racing proposal for State of Hawaii; founder pub. relations and advt. agy. (spec. in initiative qualification and campaign mgmt.) 1973, agy. merged with Profile Inc., 1978–, owner/mgr. Hardie Group, Inc. involved in bus. devel. and acquisitions, gaming cons. and evaluations; owner Emerald Meadows Ranch, Inc., thoroughbred horse farm, 1989–; owner/mgr. Profile Communications, Inc. 1990–; owner/mgr Hardie's Nut Kettle, Inc., gourmet treats and gifts, 1990–; founder and mng. ptnr. Bicycle Club Casino (world's largest card casino), Bell Gardens 1981-94; recipient Resolutions of commendn. for community service U.S. Cong. Matthew G. Martinez, L.A. Co. Supr. Ed Edelman, Calif. St. Sen. Art Torres, L.A. Dist. Atty. Ira Reiner, and Calif. St. Assemblywoman Gloria Molina; mem: Calif. Harness Drivers Guild (3t pres.), Western Standardbred Assn. (dir.), Golden State Greyhound Assn. (organizer, pres. 1973); civic: elected City Council Cathedral City (mayor 1988-90, mayor pro-tem 1990-91), active Bell Gardens C.of C. (pres. 1986); works: placed initiative to legalize greyhound betting on Calif. 1976 statewide ballot (defeated), won case Hardie vs. Eu in Calif. State Supreme Ct. which established the right to circulate initiatives in Calif. without fin. restrictions 1976, was campaign mgr. for Bell Gardens card club issue (passed 1980). Ofc: Bell Gardens Bicycle Club, 7301 Eastern Ave Bell Gardens 90201

HARDIN, JEFFREY M., physician; b. Dec. 12, 1961, Long Beach, Calif.; s. George Robert and Wilma Eileen (Pfund) H.; m. Susan Hope Goldner, Aug. 8, 1990 (div. 1994); edn: BA, Calif. State Univ., Fullerton 1984; MD, USUHS, Bethesda, Md. 1988. Career: intern Naval Hosp., San Diego 1988-89; battalion surgeon First Marine Div., Camp Pendleton 1989-91; internal medicine resident Naval Hosp., Oakland 1991-94, training ofcr. 1994–; chief resident Internal Med. Residency, Oakland 1993-94, training ofcr. 1994–; awards: U.S. Navy Achievement Medals, Camp Pendleton 1991, Oakland 1994; Governor's award, Am. Coll. Physicians (Navy chpt.) 1994; mem: Assn. of Mil. Surgeons of U.S. 1984–, AMA 1988–, Undersea and Hyperbaric Med. Soc. 1990–, Am. Coll. of Physicians 1991–; author: scientific abstract, 1992; mil: lt. comdr. USN 1984–; Democrat; Roman Catholic; rec: guitar, backpacking, tennis. Res: 605 Canyon Oaks Dr #A Oakland 94605

HARDING, JOANNA SAVAGE (SAVICH), Olympic athlete, fencing school founder, real estate broker; b. Apr. 30, Detroit, Mich.; d. George Thomas and Gizella D'Aguillar (Vojner) Savich; m. Bela de Tuscan, May 9, 1931; m. 2d. Cyril R.B. Harding, Jan. 1, 1947 (dec.); children: Joanna Candice and George Thomas Harding; edn: Detroit Sch. of Arts and Crafts 1926-29, Rhode Is. Sch. of Design 1929-30, pvt. stu. portrait painting w/John Hubbard Rich; Santelli Sch. of Fencing 1932-36. Career: co-founder Salle de Tuscan Sch. of Fencing and Club (world's largest Salle d'armes), Detroit 1930-43; US Nat. Champion Women's Foil 1936 and capt. US Womens Olympic Fencing Team (voted Most Beautiful Olympian, Olympic Games Berlin) 1936; fencing tchr. Wayne Univ. and the Cranbrook Sch., Bloomfield Hills, Mich. 1934-36; choreographer and performer in a fencing ballet for full-year run at the Palladium, London 1938-39; World Profl. Champion Women's Foil 1939; fencing exhibs. in prin. cities Europe and Balkan countries 1939-40 (on last convoy lv. France during German invasion WWII); entertainer featured act, fencing and dancing, Broadway musicals incl. Keep Off the Grass, others, NYC 1941-43; USO Sports Unit entertainer Armed Forces in Pacific 1944-45; fencing tchr. 20th Century-Fox Studios, Agnes Moorhead Sch. of Drama, movie double for stars in fencing scenes 1957-62; real estate broker, Hollywood 1945-, dba Peerless Investment Co. 1957-, incorporated, v.p. 1975-; mem. 1984 Olympic Speakers Bureau; first female fencer to wear trousers, subject of Paul Gallico column in the N.Y. News headlined "Pants is for Guys" w/3-col. cartoon; cited in Ency. Britannica (1941 supplement), and Black's Hist. of Aviation as the first person to lift off ground in a heavier-than-air machine using only her own power; first woman cmdr. LA Power Squadron 1988-89. Address: 7454 Hillside Ave Los Angeles 90046

HARDT, JAMES V., research psychologist; b. Feb. 10, 1945, Red Wing, Minn.; s. Dr. Victor Henry and Rosella Margaret (Dille) H.; edn: BS physics, Carnegie Inst. of Tech., 1967; MS psychology, Carnegie-Mellon Univ., 1969, PhD psychology/ psychophysiology, 1974; postdoctoral UC San Francisco -Langley Porter Neuropsychiatric Inst., 1974-77. Career: computer pgmmr. Computer Center, Carnegie Inst. of Tech., 1965, 66; systems analyst, instr. psychology, Carnegie-Mellon Univ., 1968-71; pre-doc. fellow UCSF Langley Porter Neuropsychiatric Inst., 1971-72, res. assoc. 1973-74, NIMH postdoc. fellow w/Dr. Joe Kamiya, 1976-77: pgmr. EEG Systems Lab. Langley Porter Inst. 1974-76, res. assoc. on alpha EEG feedback 1976-77, asst. res. psychologist UCSF Brain Wave Group/Human Devel., 1977-79; asst. adj. prof. med. psychology Langley Porter Inst., 1979-90; asst. adj. prof. med. psychology and dir. UCSF Brain Wave Group 1979-90; founder, chmn. & pres. Biocybernaut Institute, Inc. 1983-; co-founder, bd. dir., v.p. res. & devel. MindCenter Corp., Palo Alto, 1984-91; awards: NIMH Fellow 1976-77, NIMH investigator, grantee "Anxiety & Aging: Intervention with EEG Alpha Feedback 1979-82, Maco Stewart Scholarship and Research Fund 1979-83, Fetzer Found.; Long Term Tng. in EEG Feedback 1976-88, John E. Wertin Fund 1981, Joseph H. Akerman Fund 1981; mem: AAAS, Am. Psychol. Assn., Assn. for Applied Psychophysiology and Biofeedback, Biofeedback Soc. Calif., Soc. for Psychophysiol. Res., Soc. for the Study of Neuronal Regulation; publs: res. papers, num. profl. jour. articles in field; Democrat; Lutheran; hobby: classic cars of the '60s (mem. Pontiac Oakland Club). Res: 1052 Rhode Island St San Francisco 94107

HARDY, CHARLES EXTER, III, clergyman; b. Dec. 22, 1960, Atlanta, Ga.; s. Charles Exter, Jr. and Loretta (Westmoreland) H.; m. Claudia Gail Barton, Jan. 11, 1986; children: Lauren Nicole b. 1989, "Chase" Charles Exter, IV b. 1991; edn: BS in agric., Univ. Tenn., Knoxville 1982; MDiv, Golden Gate Baptist Theol. Sem., Mill Valley 1987; ordained minister First Baptist Ch., Winters, Calif., 1987; currently pursuing Masters of marriage, family & child counseling, Calif. State Univ., Sacramento. Career: youth minister Rollingwood Baptist Ch., San Pablo, Calif. 1983-84; minister to the deaf El Camino Baptist Ch., Sacto. 1984; asst. youth pastor Narwee Baptist Ch., Australia 1985; asst. pastor First Baptist Ch., El Sobrante, Calif. 1986-87; pastor First Baptist Ch., Winters 1987-90, First Southern Baptist Ch., Davis 1991-; seminar ldr. So. Baptist, Ga., Calif., Ida., 1982-, mem. mission team to Indonesia 1986, Jamaica 1988, Ecuador 1990; led mission team Argentina 1992, mission to Kenya 1994; mem. nominating com. Sacto. Baptist Assn., 1991-94, moderator 1994-; mem. Winters Ministerial Assn. (pres. 1989-90); listed Outstanding Young Men of Am. (ann., 1984-90), Who's Who in West 1991; author (drama): Cheap Show, 1990; rec: photography. Res: 2650 Belmont Dr Davis 95616 Ofc: First Southern Baptist Church, 770 Pole Line Rd Davis 95616

HARDY, LEROY CLYDE, professor of political science; b. March 29, 1927, Welch, Okla.; s. Howard Lee and Pearl Irene (Headley) H.; edn: BA, UC Santa Barbara 1949; PhD, UCLA 1955. Career: tchg. asst. UCLA 1950-52; instr. Long Beach St. Coll. 1953-55, asst. prof. 1956-59, assoc. prof. 1959-63, prof. 1963-93; CSU Long Beach 1963; sr. research assoc. Rose Inst., Claremont McKenna Coll., Claremont 1988-94; cons. St. Assembly, Sacto. 1960-61; Calif. Gov. 1964-65; Congressional Delegation, Wash. D.C. 1965, 67, 69-73, 80-82; mem: Am. Political Sci. Assn., So. Political Sci. Assn., Midwestern Political Sci. Assn., Western Political Sci. Assn., Sigma Pi, Pi Sigma Alpha, Phi Alpha Theta; author: Calif. Govt. (1963, 66, 70, 73), Politics of Calif., 1968, Reapportionment in U.S., 1981, Redistricting in the 1980's. U.S., 1992, Bibliography on Representation and Redistricting, 1993, Golden Betrayal: Erosion of Representation and Loss of Legitimacy in California 1850-1994 (pub. 1994), articles pub. in profl. jours., 1970-77; mil: USN 1945-46; Democrat; Methodist; rec: philately. Res: 1800 Fanwood Ave Long Beach 90815-4511

HARDY, LYNN PERRI HERON, resource specialist, school district consultant; b. Dec. 9, 1958, Chico; d. Charlie Earnest and Carol Jane (Voyles) Heron; edn: BS, Brigham Young Univ. 1982; MA, CSU Fresno 1989. Career: preschool tchr., Redding 1978-79; resource splst. Uintah Sch.Dist., Vernal, Utah 1982-84; El Nido Sch. Dist. 1984-87; Oakley Union Sch. Dist. 1987-91, collaborative cons. 1989-91; wife and mother 1991-; resource splst. Susanville Sch. Dist. 1992-93, Preschool Inst. 1994-; mem. Contra Costa County Supt. of Schs. quality review team 1984-87, mem. Adminstrv. Council, 87-91, staff devel. com. Spl. Edn. Local Plan Area, 87-91, Marching Band Auxiliary advisor 88-91; awards: Bus. Profl. Womens Club scholarship 1977; mem: Council for Exceptional Children, Council for Learning Disabilities, Calif. Assn. Resource Splsts.,

Performing Arts Guild, Concerts Guild, LDS Relief Soc., Uintah Comm. Performing Arts; author: (play) We the Children of Am., 1987, spl. edn. program, 1989, editl. LDS Ch. News, 1988; Republican; Mormon; rec: piano, tchg. Res: 3319 Adams Lane Redding 96002

HARDY, T. NORMAN, manufacturing executive; b. June 2, 1946, Fresno; s. Fred A. and Hazel L. (Swartz) H.; m. Marilyn Jensen, 1968 (div.); edn: BS, UC Berkeley 1964. Career: pilot U.S. Navy 1968-72; various engring positions with Systron Donner, Concord 1972-79; quality assurance mgr. Honeywell, Santa Barbara 1980-83; production mgr. Honeywell/Watkins-Johnson, Santa Barbara 1983-88; pres. Diablo Industries, San Jose 1988-90; product line mgr. Litton, Santa Clara, 1990-; con. Systron Donner, Concord 1979; awarded: Special Achievement award, Honeywell (1986); mem. UCB Alumni, Mensa, Sierra Club (life), E Clampus Vitus, Elks Lodge (Lompoc and Santa Clara), co-inventor waveguide variable length line (patent 1985); mil: lt. U.S. Navy, 1968-72; Democrat; rec: golf, photography, travel, bridge, ballroom dancing, music (piano, guitar, vocal). Res: 4271 N First St #116 San Jose 95134 Ofc: Litton Solid State 3251 Olcott St Santa Clara 95054

HARKEY, VERNA RAE, piano teacher; b. Nov. 20, 1928, Fort Worth, Tx.; d. Verne and Rachel I. (Beam) Morrill; m. Kenneth Harkey, Sept. 21, 1951; children: Karl b. 1956, Kevin b. 1958; edn: BA, George Pepperdine 1950. Career: piano tchr. 1950-; mem., past pres. Mu Phi Epsilon, charter mem./charter pres. Long Beach Alumnae Chpt.; mem. Ebell Club, Music Tchrs. Assn. Calif., Music Tchrs. Nat. Assn., Long Beach Musical Arts Club; civic: Crippled Childrens Soc. L.B.; Republican; Prot.; rec: home econs. Address: 2243 Canehill Ave Long Beach 90815

HARKINS, CRAIG, consultant, public speaker; b. May 1, 1936, Boston; s. Edwin Craig and Shirley Nadine (Pike) H.; div.; children: Daniel b. 1962, Sean b. 1964, Lance b. 1968, Angelika b. 1991; edn: BA, Colby Coll., 1958; MA English, N.Y. Univ., 1959; dipl. in comm. arts, Columbia Univ., 1963; PhD comm., Rensselaer Polytechnic Inst., 1978. Career: reporter photographer St. Petersburg (Fla.) Evening Independent 1960-61; communication mgr. IBM, San Jose 1961-82; cons. prin./v.p. Hamlin Harkins Ltd. (full-service consulting firm), San Jose 1982-; lectr., pub. speaker rep. by The Speakers Guild, Sandwich, Mass.; adj. faculty Univ. S.F., 1984-, Evergreen Valley Coll., 1982-84, instr. Rennselaer Polytech. Inst., 1976-78; awards: Sigma Tau Chi 1980, Cindy award for IBM tng. film "Little Things" Info. Film Prod. Assn., L.A. 1975, Golden Eagle Council on Int. Ex., NY, NY 1975, 5 performance awards IBM; mem.: Internat. Comm. Assn. 1965-, IEEE Profl. Comm. Soc. (adminstrv. com. 1972-, nat. secty. 1973-76, 78-80, editl. bd. IEEE Spectrum 1974-75), Profl. and Tech. Cons. Assn., Peninsula Mktg. Assn.; civic: United Way Santa Clara Co. (chmn. mkt. res. com.); coauthor with Daniel L. Plung: A Guide for Writing Better Technical Papers (John Wiley & Sons 1982); founder/ed. The Campaigner, a Marine Corps newspaper (rated best in USMCR 1963); prod. or co-prod. 7 award-winning IBM films; mil: cpl. USMCR 1961-66; Democrat; R.Cath.; rec: hockey, poetry, swimming. Res: 1301 Mariposa Ave San Jose 95126 Ofc: Hamlin Harkins, Ltd. 1611 The Alameda San Jose 95126-2202

HARLEY, ROBISON DOOLING, JR., lawyer; b. July 6, 1946, Ancon (C.Z.) Panama; s. Robison Dooling and Loyde Hazel (Gouchenauer) H.; m. Suzanne P. Bendel, Aug. 8, 1975; children: Arianne Erin, b. 1980, Lauren Loyde b. 1982; edn: BA, Brown Univ. 1968; JD, Temple Univ. 1971; LLM in crim. law, Univ. of San Diego 1984; cert. crim. law splst. Calif. St. Bar (1981, recert. 1986, 91), cert. crim. trial advocate Nat. Bd. Trial Advocates (1982, recert. 1987, 92); admitted bar: New Jersey, Pa., Dist. of Columbia, Calif., U.S. Supreme Ct., U.S. Ct. of Mil. Appeals, U.S. Circuit Ct. Appeals (3d., 9th Cir.), U.S. Dist. Cts. N.J., Pa. (E. Dist.), Calif. (Cent., So. Dists.). Career: judge advocate (trial counsel, def. counsel, mil. judge, asst. staff judge adv.) USMC, 1971-75; asst. agency dir. Safeco Title Ins. Co., Panorama City 1975-77; crim. defense atty. and ptnr. law firm of Cohen, Stokke & Davis, Santa Ana 1977-85; sole practitioner, Santa Ana 1985-; instr. Orange Co. Coll. of Trial Advocacy, Orange Co. Bar Assn., Univ. Calif. paralegal pgm.; instr. trial advocacy tng. pgms. for fed. govt., USN, USAF, USCG, USMC; judge pro tem Superior and Muni. Cts., Orange Co.; mem: Am., Calif., Pa., N.J. and D.C. bar assns., Calif. Attys. for Crim. Justice, Calif. Pub. Defenders Assn., Nat. Assn. of Crim. Def. Lawyers, Orange Co. Bar Assn. (Judiciary Com., Adminstrn. of Justice Com., Criminal Law Sect.), O.C. Trial Lawyers Assn., Assn. of Trial Lawyers of Am., Calif. Trial Lawyers; bd. dirs. Legal Aid Soc. of O.C.; reported cases: People v. Orduno (1978) 80 Cal. App3d. 738, 145 Cal. Rptr. 806; Andrus v. Municipal Ct. (1983) 143 Cal. App3d. 1041, 192 Cal. Rptr. 341; People v. Brown (1984) 152 Cal. App3d. 674, 199 Cal. Rptr. 680; People v. Henderson (1985) 163 Cal. App3d. 1001, 209 Cal. Rptr. 883; People v. Marsh (1985) 175 Cal. App3d. 987, 221 Cal. Rptr. 311; People v. Bas (1987) 194 Cal. App3d. 878,241 Cal. Rptr. 299; Inre Monigold (1988) 205 Cal. App3d. 1224, 253 Cal. Rptr. 120; People v. Eiler (1991) 231 Cal. App3d. 288, 282 Cal. Rptr. 252; People v. Autry (1991) 232 Cal. App3d. 365, 283 Cal. Rptr. 417; People v. Gentry (1991) 234 Cal. App3d. 131, 285, Cal. Rptr. 591; People v. Henandez (1992) 9 Cal. App4. 438, 11 Cal. Rptr.2 739; People v. Rhoden (1989) 216 Cal. App3d 1242, 265 Rptr. 355; trial counsel People v. Balcom (1994) 7 Cal4 414; mil: lt.col. USMC(R), asst. regl. defense counsel USMC, recipient 23 congratulations cert. from Marine Corps Commandant and commend. from the Comdg. Gen.; Republican; Prot.; rec: sports, phys. fitness. Res: 31211 Paseo Miraloma San Juan Capistrano 92675 Ofc: Law Office of Robison D. Harley 825 N Ross St Santa Ana 92701

HARMAN, JANE LAKES, lawyer, former congresswoman; b. N.Y.C., June 28, 1945; d. A. N. and Lucille (Geier) Lakes; m. Sidney Harman, Aug. 30, 1980; children: Brian Lakes, Hilary Lakes, Daniel Gaer, Justine Leigh; edn: BA, Smith Coll., 1966; JD, Harvard U., 1969; Bar: D.C. 1969, U.S. Ct. Appeals (D.C. cir.) 1972, U.S. Supreme Ct. 1975. Career: spl. asst. Commn. of Chs. on Internat. Affairs, Geneva, Switzerland, 1969-70; assoc. Surrey & Morse, Washington, 1970-72; chief legis. asst. Senator John V. Tunney, Washington, 1972-73; chief counsel, staff dir. Subcom. on Rep. Citizen Interests, Com. on Judiciary, Washington, 1973-75; adj. prof. Georgetown Law Ctr., Washington, 1974-75; chief counsel, staff dir. Subcom. on Constl. Rights, Com. on Judiciary, Washington, 1975-77, dep. sec. to cabinet The White House, Washington, 1977-78; spl. counsel Dept. Def., Washington, 1979; ptnr. Manatt, Phelps, Rothenberg & Tunney, Washington, 1979-82; Surrey & Morse, Washington, 1982-86; of counsel Jones, Day, Reavis & Pogue, Washington, 1987-92; mem. 103rd Congress from 36th Calif. dist., 1992-94; mem. vis. coms. Harvard Law Sch., 1976-82, Kennedy Sch. Govt., 1990–. Counsel Dem. Platform Com., Washington, 1984; vice-chmn. Ctr. for Nat. Policy, Washington, 1981-90; chmn. Dem. Nat. Com. Nat. Lawyers' Council, Washington, 1986-90; mem: Phi Beta Kappa; Democrat. Ofc: 325 Cannon House Office Bldg. Washington DC 20515 also: Ste 960 5200 W Century Blvd Los Angeles CA 90045 also: 3031 Torrance Blvd Torrance CA 90503

HARMSEN, MARK SPAULDING, congressional aide; b. April 28, 1956, Pasadena; s. Tyrus George and Lois M. (Spaulding) H.; edn: AA, Pasadena City Coll. 1976; BSBA, San Diego St. Univ. 1978. Career: research dir. Republican Assoc., Glendale 1979-85; district representative U.S. Congressman David Dreier, Covina 1985–; civic: Pasadena Tournament of Roses Assn. Res: 1300 Medford Rd Pasadena 91107 Ofc: U.S. Congressman David Dreier 112 N Second Ave Covina 91723

HAROUN, ANSAR M., forensic psychiatrist; b. 1947 in Pakistan, raised in Italy and England; m. Nasra Haroun, M.D. (child psychiatrist) 1977; edn: pre-med., Christ's Hosp., Sussex, England; med. edn. Univ. of London at St. Thomas' Hosp. & King Edward Med. Coll.; M.Med. Sci., Medical Sch. Nottingham, Eng. 1979; ABPN bd. certified psychiatry 1985, bd. cert. child and adolescent psychiatry 1989. Career: community physician Med. Sch., Nottingham, Eng. 1976-79; psychiatrist Yale Med. Sch., 1980-85; pediatric psychiatrist Columbia Univ. Coll. of Physicians & Surgeons, N.Y. 1985-87; forensic psychiatrist Superior Ct. Calif., San Diego 1987–; asst. clin. prof. psychiatry and pediatrics, dir. of forensic psychiatry UCSD Sch. of Med., San Diego; adj. prof. Univ. San Diego Sch. of Law; awards: Royal, Religious & Ancient Found. of Christ's Hosp. scholarship, Roosevelt Scholar, Ciba award Royal Soc. of Med. (London), elected Yale Univ. Med. Sch. Council, elected Univ. Nottingham Senate, bd. Faculty of Med., and bd. Postgrad. Studies, tutor Lenton Hall; Fellow Royal Soc. of Health (London), mem: Am. Acad. Psychiatry and Law, Am. Psychiatric Assn., Am. Soc. Law & Medicine, Am. Coll. of Utilization Rev. Physician, Am. Coll. Forensic Psychiatry; author: Insomnia & Depression in General Practice, 1979; Clinical Guidelines for Involuntary Outpatient Treatment, 1990; mil: major M.C. US Army 1984–; rec: polemics, rhetoric, ethics, the boundary between `mad' and `bad'. Ofc: Superior Ct. of Calif. Forensic Psychiatry Clinic, Rm 1003, County Courthouse San Diego 92101-3814 Ph: 619/531-3047

HARPER, JON KURT-PATRICK, educator, educational technology futurist; b. Sept. 12, 1953, Baltimore, Md.; s. Cdr. William Waldo Harper, USN and Billie Jean (Jones) Aicklen; children: Ashley, Richard, Jon; edn: George August Univ., Goettingen, Ger. 1976-77, BA in German, UC Riverside, 1977; EdD, Univ. La Verne, 1990. Career: adminstrv. asst. Univ. of Calif. Study Center, Goettingen, Ger. 1976-77; tchr. St. John Bosco High Sch., Bellflower 1977-79; product line mgr. E.F. Hutton & Co. Inc., Torrance 1979-81; dean of students Don Bosco Tech. Inst., Rosemead 1982-85, dir. pub. affairs and planning 1985-86; Perris Union H.S. Dist. projects splst. 1986-89, projects coordinator, 1989-91; v. prin. Perris High Sch., 1991; coordinator projects and evaluation Apple Valley Unified Sch. Dist., 1991-93; dist. ednl. tech. Snowline Jt. Unified Sch. Dist. 1993–; exec. dir. Excelsior Acad. Charter Sch., Snowline JUSD 1994–; dir. Essential Techlogies Inc., Long Beach 1989-92; cons. Info. Systems Plus, Wrightwood 1987-90; systems opr. Compuserv Educators Forum 1987–; mem: World Future Soc., Assn. Calif. Sch. Adminstrs., Calif. Assn. Sch. Bus. Officials, Masons, DeMolay, Phi Beta Kappa; 3 articles pub. in profl. jours. (1986-87); author: book, Blue Ridge (1994); Republican; R.Cath.; rec: sailing, travel, skiing, target shooting. Res: 12272 Hitching Post Dr Victorville Ofc: Snowline JUSD, PO Box 296000, Phelan 92329

HARPER, SHARYNE RAE, health services financial executive; b. Nov. 10, 1946, Crescent City; d. Joseph Fairchilds Hostler and Sylvia (Stewart) White; m. Richard James Harper; children: Michele b. 1964, Lisa b. 1966; edn: AA hons.,

Coll. of Redwoods 1974; BS, Humboldt St. Univ. 1976; MBA, 1989. Career: tax preparer, mgr. EBS Tax Service Inc., Eureka 1972; H&R Block 1970-72; fin. ofcr., asst. dir. United Indian Health Services Inc., Trinidad 1973–; mem: Calif. Employers Council (exec. bd., treas., fin. com., reg. v.p., legis. com.), Redwood Empire Personnel Mgrs. Assn., Employers Advy. Council (vice chair, pres., sec.); civic: Clarke Memorial Mus., 4-H Cutten & Ferndale, PTA Eureka, No. Calif. Indian Devel. Council (vol.), Calif. State Schools Book Rev. Com. Grades K-6 (vol.); publs: booklet (1989); mem Faith Center Foursquare Ch.; rec: needlepoint, bowling, scuba, flying, reading. Ofc: United Indian Health Services POB 420 Trinidad 95570

HARRACH, ROBERT JAMES, research physicist; b. March 30, 1937, Holyoke, Colo.; s. Elmer and Esther Viola (Simmerman) Roberts H.; m. Caroline Nadine Ginther, Sept. 9, 1962; children: David b. 1967, Ben b. 1969; edn: BA physics, Dartmouth Coll. 1960; MS, Univ. Colo. Boulder 1962; PhD, 1965. Career: research physicist Nat. Bureau of Standards, Boulder, Colo. 1961-66; lectr. UC Davis Dept. Applied Sci., Livermore 1969-74; vis. assoc. prof. Dartmouth Coll. Physics Dept., Hanover, N.H. 1978-79; sr. physicist Lawrence Livermore Nat. Lab., Livermore 1966–; mem: Am. Physical Soc., Am. Assn. Physics Tchrs.; author: 60+ research reports and papers pub. in sci. jours., 1966–, thesis pub., 1965; rec: photog., sports. Res: 255 Kottinger Dr Pleasanton 94566 Ofc: Lawrence Livermore National Laboratories POB 808 L-629 Livermore 94550

HARRIMAN, JOHN HOWLAND, lawyer; b. April 14, 1920, Buffalo, N.Y.; s. Lewis Gildersleeve and Grace (Bastine) H.; m. Barbara Ann Brunmark, June 12, 1943; children: Walter b. 1945, Constance b. 1948, John, Jr. b. 1954; edn: BA, Dartmouth Coll. 1942; JD, Stanford Univ. 1949. Career: atty., assoc. Lawler Felix & Hall, Los Angeles 1949-55; asst. v.p., v.p. Security Pacific Nat. Bank 1955-72, sr. v.p. 1972-85; secty. Security Pacific Corp. 1971-85; exec. dir. Calif. Republican Party, Burbank 1985-86; chmn. bd. Master Metal Works, S. El Monte 1989; mem: Town Hall Calif., L.A. Fgn. Affairs Council, Calif. Club L.A., Beach Club Santa Monica; mil: capt. USAF 1943-46; Republican; Episcopalian. Res: 245 S Plymouth Blvd Los Angeles 90004

HARRINGTON, EUNICE PETERS, educator; b. Middletown, Conn.; d. Wm. J. and Eunice S. (Lowery) Peters; 1 dau. Lisa Beth b. 1965; edn: BA, Whittier Coll. 1951; MA, Azusa Pacific Univ. 1978; PhD, Pacific Western Univ., 1990; Calif. Std. Tchg. creds., reading specialist 1978. Career: educator 35 yrs., tchr. USAF in England, US Army in West Ger. and U.S., currently pub. sch. tchr. San Gabriel Sch. Dist.; owner/dir. Harrington Reading Lab, Azusa 1978–; recipient appreciation awards, Azusa H.S. (1981), Dalton Sch. (1976-77), Leukemia Soc. Am. (1976), LA County Heart Assn. (1970), Americanism Award, VFW Post 8070 (1972); civic: East San Gabriel Valley Regl. Occupational Pgm. (v.chmn.), City of Azusa Parks and Rec. Dept. (commnr.), Azusa Pac. Univ. (Comm. Advy. Council), Azusa U. Sch. Dist. (bd. govs. 1981–, past pres.); publs: handbook for parents of children entering Kindergarten; rec: music, creative arts. Address: Harrington Reading Lab 230 Viewcrest Dr Azusa 91702

HARRINGTON, HANNAH KARAJIAN, professor; b. Dec. 25, 1958, Berkeley, Calif.; d. Samuel Levon and Constance Maggie (Moore) Karajian; m. William James Harrington, June 20, 1981; edn: BA, Biblical studies, Patten College, Oakland, Calif., 1978; B. Music, S.F. Conservatory of Music, 1982; MA, Near Eastern studies, UC Berkeley, 1985; PhD, Near Eastern studies, UC Berkeley, 1992; Career: instr. of Modern Hebrew, Patten Acad., Oakland 1978–; instr. of Old Testament & Hebrew, Patten Coll., Oakland 1983-89; Modern Hebrew grad. student instr., UC Berkeley 1986-91; asst. prof. of Old Testament & Hebrew, Patten Coll. 1989–; instr. of post-Biblical Hebrew texts, UC Berkeley 1993; adjunct prof. of Old Testament, Fuller Theological Sem. 1993–; chair, Biblical Studies Div., Patten College 1989–; awards: scholarship, Patten Coll. 1974; Nat. Endowment for Humanities grants, Brown Univ. 1988, Brandeis Univ. 1993, Univ. of Calif. Berkeley 1994; listed Who's Who in Humanities 1992, Who's Who in Religion 1992-93; mem: Soc. of Biblical Lit.; steering com., Soc. of Biblical Lit., History & Lit. of Early Rabbinic Judaism Section; cellist, Modesto Symphony, Modesto, Calif. 1981–; author: Impurity Systems of Qumran and the Rabbis: Biblical Foundations, 1993; Democrat; Christian Evangelical. Res: 2479 Coolidge Ave. Oakland 94601. Ofc: Patten College 2433 Coolidge Ave. Oakland 94601

HARRIS, CYNTHIA VIOLA, educator; b. Aug. 18, 1948, San Francisco; d. Gilbert and Mary Lee Harris; edn: BA and MA, San Francisco State Univ.; EdD, Nova Univ. Career: tchr. Oakland Public Schs. 1971-80, sch. principal 1980-86, staff devel. and mentor tchr. pgm. coordinator 1986-91, coordinator recruitment, employee support & marketing 1991-93; adminstr. Community Affairs, Superintendent's Office, Oakland Public Schools 1993–; cons. CSU Hayward 1987-88, Kids on Job 1988; honors: "Just Say No" award Within You, Oakland 1988, Networker award Capwell's, Oakland 1985; mem. Assn. Calif. Sch. Adminstrs. (mem. chair 1986-89), Phi Delta Kappa; commr. Self Esteem Alameda Co., 1988; mem. Marcus Foster, Oakland (com. 1983-88); author 3 manuals: Peer Tutoring Expansion, 1985; Self-Esteem For You & Your Students, 1987; Parents as Partners, 1988; Democrat; Pentecostal; rec: fitness, public speaking, travel. Ofc: Oakland Public Schools 1025 Second Ave St Rm 320 Oakland 94804

HARRIS, DAVID JACK, artist; b. Jan. 6, 1948, San Mateo; s. Jack McAllister and Audrey (Fegley) H.; edn: att. San Francisco Art Inst. 1960-66; BA in art (cum laude), San Francisco State Univ., 1971, MA art, 1976; sec. tchg. cred., 1972. Career: art gallery director Galerie De Tours, San Francisco, 1971-72; substitute tchr. high schs. San Francisco, Sequoia, San Mateo, 1973-80; art instr. Chabot Comm. Coll., 1976-81; pres. and owner David Harris Associates, Belmont, Calif., commercial & residential interiors 1978-82, freelance fine artist 1982–; founder, art director and ptnr. Fine Art Publishing, Belmont 1988–; v.p. Coastal Arts League Museum, Half Moon Bay; work in permanent collections Stanford Univ., First Am. Title Guaranty Co., Spieker Ptnrs. Uoysys, Cannell and Chaffin (L.A.), Caesar's Palace (Las Vegas), Internat. Red Cross, Litton Inds., Verilink, Foothill Bank (Los Altos), Chartered Bank of London (S.F.), N.Central Wash. Mus., Sheraton Grande (L.A.), Old England Inn (Victoria, B.C.), Walt Disney, Lawry's Restaurant, L.A., others; exhibitions: 30+ group and solo exh. 1970-85, one-man shows: Eva Cohon Gal. Chgo. 1986, 88, 90, North Central Washington Mus., Wenatchee 1987, Metro Contemporary Gal., San Mateo 1989, A Gallery, Palm Desert 1989, Five Feet Gal., Laguna Beach 1989, Souder Gal., Burlingame 1990, Robert Wright Gal., Escondido 1990, Coastal Art Mus., Half Moon Bay 1991, The Cannery, S.F. 1991, Maturango Mus., Ridgecrest 1992, Collabrations 94 Santa Fe, NM; publs: Art in Am., Palm Springs Life, Artist Mag., West Art, Confluence Mag., Kiosk, Signature Mag., Southwest Art, Antiques and Fine Art, Artweek, Valley Mag. (1989), San Mateo Times, Wenatchee Times. Ofc: 427 Casa Del Mar Half Moon Bay 94019 Tel: 415/593-4796

HARRIS, GODFREY, consultant, international travel association executive director; b. June 11, 1937, London, England, came to U.S. 1939, naturalized 1945; s. Alfred and Victoria H.; m. Linda Berkowitz, Dec. 21, 1958 (div. 1982); children: Gregrey, Kennith, Mark; edn: BA (gt. distinction) Stanford Univ., 1958; MA (disting. mil. grad.) UCLA, 1960. Career: lectr. Rutgers Univ. 1960-61; Foreign Service ofcr. U.S. State Dept., W.D.C., Bonn, Ger., London, Eng., 1962-65, mgmt. analyst Office Mgmt. and Budget, W.D.C., 1965-67; spl. asst. to pres. IOS Devel. Co., Geneva 1967-68; pres. Harris/Ragan Mgmt. Group, Los Angeles 1968–; founder, editor Almanac of World Leaders, 1957-62, Consultants Directory, 1975-76; exec. dir. Soc. of Internat. Travel Reps., 1992–; former west coast rep. Panamanian Export Promo. and Investment Devel. Ctr.; mem: Am. Acad. Consultants (fellow), Assn. Mgmt. Consultants, Stanford Univ. Alumni Assn., London Chamber of Commerce & Industry (mem. secty.), L.A. World Affairs Council, Town Hall Calif., mem. advy. com. on gifted children Santa Monica Unified Sch. Dist. (chair 1978-79); author: (pub. Fgn. Policy Assn. of Panama): Panama's Position, 1973, The Panamanian Perspective, 1987; (pub. The Americas Group): Commercial Translations Promoting International Tourism, 1986, The Ultimate Black Book 1988, Invasion, 1990, The Fascination of Ivory, 1991, Talk Is Cheap, 1991, Mapping Russia & Its Neighbors, 1993, Power Buying, 1993, European Union Handbook & Business Titles, 1995, How To Generate Word of Mouth Advertising, 1995, other books and monographs. Ofc: 9200 Sunset Blvd Ste 404 Los Angeles 90069

HARRIS, HARRY GEORGE, professor of management and senior fellow; b. Oct. 25, 1935, Corcoran; s. George Harry and Athanasia G. (Stasinopoulos) H.; edn: AB, hons., UC Berkeley 1957; MA, UC Berkeley 1963; MPA, Harvard Univ. 1967; PhD, 1970, Harvard Univ. Career: exec. asst. Office of Secty. of Defense, Wash. D.C. 1964-66; course dir. Air Force Acad., Colorado Springs 1969-71; dir. Office of Secty. of Defense, Wash. D.C. 1971-76; senior profl. staff White House 1976-77; v.p. Nat. Alliance of Bus. 1977-79; prof. mgmt. CSU, Fresno 1980–; cons. U.S. Info. Agency, Wash. D.C., UNDP, N.Y., NY; honors: Presdl. of the U.S. citation 1977, Office Secty. of Defense Legion of Merit 1975, Acad. of Econ. Medal 1986; mem: Phi Beta Kappa, Acad. Mgmt., Inter Univ. Seminar on Armed Forces & Soc. (fellow), Pan-Pacific Bus. Assn. (founding mem.), Acad. Internat. Bus.; Republican; Eastern Orthodox; rec: sailing, tennis. Ofc: Univ of California Educational Research Center Fresno 93710-6002

HARRIS, JEFFREY SAUL, physician executive; b. Mar. 13, 1949, Pittsburgh, Pa.; s. Aaron Wexler and Janet Mary (Szerlip) Wexler Harris; m. Mary Virginia Anderson, Jan. 2, 1981; children: Sarah b. 1982, Noah b. 1985, Susannah b. 1988; stepchildren: Dominic b. 1973, T. Howard b. 1975; edn: BS, molecular biophysics and biochem., Yale Univ. 1971; MD, Univ. of New Mexico 1975; MPH, med. care orgn., Univ. of Michigan 1982; MBA, gen. mgmt., Vanderbilt Univ. 1988; cert. Nat. Bd. Med. Examiners 1975; bd. cert. in occupational and preventive medicine, emergency medicine and med. quality. Career: gen. med. ofcr. SE Alaska Health Ctr., Juneau 1976-78; clin. dir. SE Alaska Reg. Health Corp., Juneau 1978-79; emergency physician Providence Hosp., Anchorage, Alaska, Alaska Hosp. & Med. Ctr., Anchorage, Sumner Mem. Hosp., Gallatin, Tenn., St. Thomas Hosp., Nashville, Tenn. 1979-83; pres. Harris Assocs., Nashville, Tenn. 1979-; asst. to the commr. Tenn. Dept. of Health and Environment, Nashville 1980-83; dir. health care mgmt. Northern Telecom, Nashville 1983-88; prin. Harris, Dibble & Makens, Inc., Nashville 1988-90; med. dir. Aetna Health Plans of Tenn., Nashville 1990-91; dir. R&D to nat. practice leader Alexander and Alexander Cons. Group, San Francisco, Calif. 1991-94; chief prevention, health and disability ofcr. Industrial Indemnity, San Francisco 1994-; asst. clin. prof. Duke Univ. 1984-89, Med. Coll. of Wisconsin 1985-; assoc. clin. prof. UC San Francisco 1994-; dir. Am. Coll. Occupational & Environmental Medicine, Arlington Hts., Ill. 1992-; dir. Filoli Info. Sys., Palo Alto 1994-; editorial bds.: Am. Jour. of Health Promotion, Occupational and Environmental Medicine Report; editl. reviewer: JAMA, Am. Jour. of Public Health, Jour. of Occupational and Environmental Medicine; awards: Dean's Award for Academic Excellence, Owen Grad. Sch. of Mgmt., Governor's Health Promotion awards, Tenn. and N.C. 1985, 86, 88, Secretary's Award for Excellence in Health Promotion, U.S.D.H.H.S. 1986, Dedicated Svc. Award, Tenn. Coll. Occupational Medicine 1988, Membership Award, Am. Coll. of Emergency Physicians 1989-90, listed Who's Who Worldwide 1993, Presidential Award, Am. Coll. of Emergency Physicians 1995; mem: Am. Acad. of Family Practice (fellow 1973-); Am. Coll. of Occupational and Environmental Medicine (fellow, dir., com. chair 1982-), Am. Coll. of Preventive Medicine (fellow 1983-), Am. Coll. of Med. Quality (fellow 1988-), Am. Bd. of Emergency Physicians (fellow 1989-), MENSA, Beta Gamma Sigma; co-author: The OEM Occupational Health and Safety Manual, 1992; co-editor and author (books): Managing Employee Health Care Costs, 1992, Health Promotion in the Workplace (Wiley, 1984; 2d edit. 1993); author: Strategic Health Management (Jossey-Bass Publishers., 1994); contbg. author: 55+ articles to profl. jours., num. chapters/articles in books, manuals and handbooks, 5 videotapes, 1971-; num. presentations and reports in field, 1981-; mil: surgeon, USPHS 1973, inactive reserve 1975-; rec: skiing, music performance, running, art, sci. fiction, writing. Res: 386 Richardson Way Mill Valley 94941 Ofc: Industrial Indemnity 255 California St San Francisco 94111

HARRIS, MICHAEL DAVID, journalist; b. Feb. 11, 1950, Phila., Pa.; s. Morton Louis and Jane (Kirby) H.; edn: BA, Temple Univ., Phila., Pa. 1973; Calif. State, L.A., 1976-79. Career: reporter/ed., Progress Newspapers, Alhambra, Calif. 1977-78; reporter/ed., City News Svc., L.A. 1978-81; reporter/ed., UPI, L.A. 1981-90; ed., KFWB-AM, L.A. 1985-94; reporter, L.A. Daily Jour., L.A. 1991–; listed in Who's Who in the West, 1992; author: screenplay, Special Circumstances, 1992; rec: reading, writing, physical fitness, music. Ofc: Daily Journal Corp. 915 E. First St. L.A. 90012

HARRIS, ROBERT L., utility company vice president; b. March 4, 1944, Arkadelphia, Kans.; s. Benjamin F. and Lucy (Luster) H.; m. Glenda Newell, March 17, 1984; children: Anthony b. 1964, Regina b. 1966, Brittany b. 1986, Phillip b. 1989; edn: AA, Merritt Coll. 1963; BA, S.F. St. Univ. 1965; JD, UC Berkeley 1972; AMP, Harvard Bus. Sch. 1988. Career: probation ofcr. Alameda Co., Oakland 1965-69; atty. Pacific Gas & Electricity Co., S.F. 1972-89, div. mgr., Oakland 1989; corp. mem. Blue Shield Calif., S.F.1979; honors: Kappa Alpha Psi (nat. pres. 1991-95), Nat. Bus. Assn. C. Francis Stratford award 1988, NAACP W. Robert Ming 1986, Calif. Assn. Black Law Loren Miller; mem: Nat. Bar Inst., Am. Bar Assn., Nat. Bar Assn. (pres. 1979-80), Charles Houston Bar Assn., NAACP; articles pub. in profl. jours.; rec: fishing. Res: 4082 Sequoyah Rd Oakland 94605 Ofc: Pacific Gas & Electric 77 Beale St San Francisco 94106

HARRIS, ROBERT NORMAN, advertising and communications executive, educator; b. Feb. 11, 1920, St. Paul, Minn.; s. Nathan and Esther (Roberts) H.; m. Paula Nidorf, May 2, 1992; children: Claudia b. 1943, Robert b. 1945, Randolph b. 1951; edn: BA, Univ. Minn. 1940. Career: founder Toni Co. (div. of Gillette Co)., Chgo., Ill. 1940-55; exec.v.p., ptnr. Lee King & Ptnrs. 1955-60; exec. v.p. Allen B. Wrisley (div. Purex Ltd.) 1960-62; exec. v.p., ptnr. North Advertising. 1962-72; pres. Westbrook Harris Inc. 1973-77; corp. exec. v.p. Creamer Inc. 1977-81; pres. Harris Creative Group, Chgo. and San Jose 1981; prof. advt. and mass comms. San Jose St. Univ. 1983; dir. Samaritan Family Practice Med. Group Inc. 1982; founder Falcon Comm., Los Angeles 1968-81; ptnr. Harriscope Bdcstg. Inc. 1962-79; mem: Nat. Acad. T.V. Arts & Scis., Am. Mktg. Assn., Am. Advt. Fedn., Am. Assn. Advt. Agencies, Sons in Retirement (dir. 1985-87), Am. Legion; author Handbook for Advt. Account Execs., 1962; mil: USNR 1942-45; Republican; Jewish; rec: tchg., golf, walking. Res: 7220 Via Sendero San Jose 95135-1340

HARRIS, SIDNEY EUGENE, dean; b. July 21, 1949, Atlanta, Ga.; s. Nathaniel and Marion (Johnson) H.; m. Mary Styles, July 24, 1971; children: Savaria b. 1980; edn: BA, math., Morehouse Coll., Atlanta, Ga. 1971; MS, ops. res., Cornell Univ. 1975, PhD, 1976. Career: enlisted U.S. Coast Guard 1971; tchg. fellow in math, Cornell Univ. and Bell Tel. Labs. cooperative res. fellow, 1972-76; tech. staff Ops. Res. Dept., Bell Tel. Labs. 1973-78; asst. prof. to assoc. prof. and dir. of res. Coll. of Bus. Adminstrn., Georgia St. Univ. 1978-87; prof. of mgmt. Peter F. Drucker Mgmt. Ctr., Claremont Grad. Sch. 1987, appt. chair of Mgmt. Prog. 1990, dean 1991–; summer sabbatical Nanyang Technological Univ., Singapore 1991; cons. to sr. mgmt.: U.S. Govt. agys., ServiceMaster, Coca-Cola, Xerox Corp., IBM, Hewlett Packard, BellSouth, Landmarks Group, AT&T, Golden St. Mutual Life Ins. Co., Equifax Svs.; participant exec. edn. progs. by The Young President's Orgn., Nanyang Technological Univ., Xerox Corp., IBM, Ga. Power Co., Life Ofc. Mgmt. Assn.; cons. on adminstrv. svs. to Council of Presidents, Atlanta Univ. Ctr. 1977-82; bd. dirs.: Family Savings Bank, L.A. 1988– (chair, audit com.), Property Security Investments, Inc., L.A. (audit com., compensation com.), ServiceMaster Com., Chgo.; bd. of govs. Peter F. Drucker Non-profit Found.;

bd. trustees Menlo Coll., Calif.; mem. num. standing faculty and administrv. governance coms. Claremont Grad. Sch. 1987–; administrv. rep. Claremont Grad. School's. Bd. of Fellows Academic Affairs Com.; awards: Disting. Svc. award Nat. Computer Conf. Com. Bd. 1985, Sigma Xi, Beta Gamma Sigma, listed Men of Achievement, Who's Who in World, Who's Who in Calif.; res. grantee NSF and several major corporations; author/contbg. author: num. books, monographs, 40+ pub. articles. Ofc: Peter F. Drucker Management Center, Claremont Graduate School Claremont 91711

HARRIS, STEPHEN L., humanities professor, author; b. Feb. 5, 1937, Aberdeen, Wash.; s. Glenn E. and Ruby O. (Bell) H.; m. 1965-1985, 2 sons, Geoffrey Edwin b. 1971, Jason Marc b. 1973; edn: BA, Univ. Puget Sound, 1959; MA, Cornell Univ., 1961, PhD, 1964. Career: asst. prof. Wash. State Univ., Pullman 1964-65; asst. prof. Calif. State Univ., Sacramento 1965-70, assoc. prof. 1970-74, prof. humanities 1974–, and dept. chair 1972-76, 1992–; author: Classical Mythology: Images and Insights, 1995, Agents of Chaos, 1990, Understanding the Bible, 3d. ed., 1992, The New Testament: A Student's Intro., 2nd edit. 1995, Fire Mountains of the West, 1988, Fire and Ice: The Cascade Volcanoes, 1976, Touchstones: Classic Readings in the Humanities, 1990; writer, columnist Am. West (mag.), 1983-89, reviewer Nev. Historical Quarterly, 1989–, Ore. Historical Quarterly, 1991–, contbr. Columbia Mag., Tacoma, Wash., 1989–; awards: Crown-Zellerbach, Univ. Puget Sound 1957-59, Woodrow Wilson fellow Cornell Univ. 1960-61, Annual Faculty Research Award CSUS 1981-82; Fellow Westar Inst.-Jesus Sem. 1986–, mem: Volcanological Assn. of Sacto. 1988–, Soc. of Biblical Literature (SBL) 1994–; rec: mountain climbing in Cascade Range. Ofc: Humanities and Religious Studies Dept. Calif. State Univ., Sacramento 95819-6083

HARRISON, EDWARD WILLIAM, chief of police; b. Aug. 23, 1947, Omaha, Neb.; s. John Irving and Delores Gladys (Horne) H.; m. Tanis L. Hamilton, May 15, 1965 (div. 1973); children: Renaye b. 1965, Stacy b. 1969; m.2d. Gerry H., Aug. 3, 1991; edn: AA, Pasadena City Coll. 1973; CSU Los Angeles 1976; MPA, Univ. Laverne 1984. Career: custodian supr. Pasadena City Coll. 1966-75, peace ofcr. 1975-77; sgt. CSU Long Beach 1977-86; lt. CSU San Bernardino 1986-87, chief of police 1987–; awards: Inland Empire POA Leadership 1988, Gov. Deukmejian Community 1988; mem: Calif. Peace Ofcrs. Assn., Internat. Assn. Campus Law Enforcement Adminstrs., Internat. Assn. of Chiefs of Police, Kiwanis Internat., Inland Empire POA; rec: tennis, jogging. Ofc: California State University 5500 University Parkway San Bernardino 92407

HARRISON, HAZEL CLAYTON, writer; b. Nov. 11, 1948, Camilla, Ga.; d. Morris E. and Dorothy Jean (Keaton) Clayton; m. Terry R. Harrison, Aug. 31, 1985; children: Angela b. 1969, Elias b. 1989; edn: BS, Kent St. Univ. 1971; M.Edn., 1972. Career: tchr. Robinson Jr. H.S., Akron, Ohio 1972; counselor Nashville Tech. Inst., Tenn. 1974-76; mktg. splst. Minn. St. Dept. Edn., Mpls. 1977-78; mgr. Control Data Corp. 1978-82; mktg. analyst Xerox Corp., El Segundo 1982-84; tng. cons. Word Write Tng. Systems, Manhattan Beach 1984–; bd. dirs.. Guild Press, Mpls., Minn. 1979–; awards: Internat. Black Writers & Artists outstanding achievement 1989, Xerox Corp. outstanding achievement plaque 1988; mem: Soc. Tech. Com., Assoc. for Tng. & Devel., Internat. Black Writers & Artists (pres.); ed. On Being Black (1981), co-author: A Most Defiant Act (1985), ed. Bearers of Blackness (1987); author: Winter in L.A. (1992); Democrat; Baptist; rec: creative writing. Res: 636 Del Monte St Pasadena 91103 Ofc: WordWrite 686 S Arroyo Pkwy Ste 219 Pasadena 9115

HARRY, PHILLIP BROOKS, composer, playwright; b. Aug. 24, 1947, Hollywood; s. Kenneth James and Elizabeth Marian (Brooks) H.; edn: AA, Pasadena City Coll., 1967; BA, and MA, Occidental Coll., 1969, 71. Career: original dir. PCC Singers, Pasadena City Coll. 1965-67; pres. Foothill Assn. of Am. Baptist Youth Fellowship of So. Calif. 1965; worship coord. Pasadena Ecumenical Youth Council 1965-66; accompanist Oxy Glee Clubs, Occidental Coll. 1969-71, "Spirit", Pasadena (U.S. Premiere, 1974), "If My People...", Bel Air (U.S. premiere, 1976), Jimmy Owen's "If My People...", (U.S. tour 1976-78), Jimmi Irving's "Gospel Ministry of Music", (So. Central L.A. concert tour 1978-80); arranger: "Sawing a Woman in Half" (for "Trademarks" barbershop quartet 1965, on file with SPEBQSA, L.A. & S.D.), "The Sands of Time", 1966, "Jesus, I am Resting", 1968, "I am His and He is Mine", 1970; composer: "Concerto for Two Pianos" 1967, "Luxuriant" (tone poem 1970); composer film score: "Houses of Worship" USIA 1972, cantata: Psalm "25" (1976, revised 1984), Ps. "57-Omega" (1980, revised 1994), Ps. "104-entering into eternity" (1988, revised 1992); dramatist "Feudin' Folks" GALTA 1986; awards: PCC Choir award 1965, Music Council Scholarship award 1966, first place Annual Music Comp. ABYF of So. Calif. at Univ. of Redlands: solo (instrumental), accompanist (vocal and instrumental) 1967, PCC Faculty award 1967, Alpha Gamma Sigma 1967, west coast premiere performance of "Volumina" for organ at Occidental Coll. reviewed L.A. Times "virtuosic" and by composer G.Ligeti "wonderful" 1970, nat. finalist "Psalm 27-The Lord is my Light", Broadcast Music Inc., N.Y./Composers Guild S.Calif., USC 1971; mem: The Planetary Soc., ACLU, People for Amer. Way, Evangelicals Together, Americans United for Separation of Ch. and State, Human Rights Campaign Fund; Democrat; Am. Baptist; rec: gardening, movie buff. Res: 5139 E Sereno Dr Temple City 91780-3040

HARSANYI, JOHN C., economist, emeritus professor, Nobel Prize winner; b. Hungary; emeritus prof. UC Berkeley; awarded the Nobel Memorial Prize in Economic Science (with John C. Nash and Reinhard Selten) for their work in game theory, 1994.*

HART, ARCHIBALD DANIEL, professor of psychology; b. Apr. 27, 1932, Kimberly, Cape, So. Africa; nat. 1984; s. Daniel Henry Hart and Gertrude (Smith) Ausker; m. Kathleen, Dec. 4, 1954; children: Catherine b. 1957, Sharon b. 1960, Sylvia b. 1963; edn: M.I.C.E., Inst. of Civil Engrs., London, UK 1954; BSc (with honors), Univ. of So. Africa, Pretoria 1965; MSc, Univ. of Natal, Pietermaritzburg, S. Africa 1966, PhD, 1969; lic. psychologist, St. of Calif. Psychol. Examining Comm. 1976; cert. biofeedback practitioner, Biofeedback Soc. Calif. and Am. Feedback Soc.; cert. health svc. provider, Council for Nat. Reg. of Health Svc. Providers. Career: pupil/engr. Springs Council, So. Africa 1949-54; civil engr. Pietermaritzburg Council, So. Africa 1954-70; post-doctoral fellow, Fuller Grad. Sch. of Psychol., Pasadena, 1971; pvt. practice clin. psychol., So. Africa 1972-73; prof. of psychol. Fuller Sch. of Psychol. 1973–; dean Grad. Sch. Psychol., Fuller Theol. Sem. 1982–; honors: first recipient of Weyerhaeuser Award for Faculty Excellence, Fuller Theol. Sem. 1978, Golden Medallion Award finalist book Counseling the Depressed; mem. Am. Psychol. Assn., Biofeedback Soc. of Calif. (bd. dirs. 1977-81, pres. 1980-81), Calif. State Psychol. Assn. (chmn. biofeedback com. 1975-78), Pasadena Area Psychol. Assn. (pres. 1976); author: 17 books on stress, depression and anxiety including Adrenaline and Stress, 1986, Rev. 1995, Dark Clouds, Silver Linings, 1993, The Sexual Man, 1994, contbr. 10+ chpts. in books, 48 articles to profl. jours., num. profl. papers; rec: jewelry making, photography, video production, electronics. Ofc: Fuller Theological Seminary Grad Sch of Psychology 180 N Oakland Ave Pasadena 91182

HART, FRANK JAMES, engineering manager; b. May 8, 1947, San Francisco; s. Frank Hjalmer and Naomi June (Hockett) H.; m. June Ellen Peters, Apr. 28, 1973; children: Bret b. 1981, Katy b. 1989; edn: AS in E.T., Mission Coll., Santa Clara 1980; BSE in comp. sci., San Jose State Univ., 1985. Career: field service engr. Wang Labs., San Mateo 1972-74; applications engr. Signetics, Sunnyvale 1974-86; senior applications engr. Fairchild Semiconductor, Palo Alto 1986-87; systems engr. Intergraph APD, Palo Alto 1987-93; engring. mgr. NEC Electronics, Mt. View 1993–; inventor: Interactive Surveillance Device (pat. pending), Infrared Tracking Device (pat. 1994), Interactive Display Devices (pat. 1990); pub. articles on RISC Processors, Interface Techniques (1988, 89, 90, 92); rec: gardening, beer brewing, fishing. Ofc: NEC Electronics 475 Ellis St (MV4581) Mt. View 94039

HART, MAURICE ARTHUR, lawyer; b. Dec. 22, 1927, New York; s. Larry and Irene (Levy) H.; m. Elynor Wayne, Nov. 12, 1950; children: Jana, Melissa; edn: BS, USC, 1950, JD, 1963; admitted St. Bar Calif. 1963. Career: v.p. Hollywood Plastics 1955-63; atty. pvt. practice, Los Angeles 1963; prin. Hart & Leonard, Los Angeles 1968-85, Hart & Hart 1985; judge pro tem Los Angeles Municipal Ct.; spl. master St. Bar Calif., mem. franchise legislation com.; mem. of exec. com. Bd. of Governors, City of Hope; pres. Leo Baeck Temple 1979-81; mil: AUS 1946-48. Address: 1925 Century Park E, Los Angeles 90067

HARTER, PAUL ROBERT, lawyer; b. Oct. 11, 1957, Vallejo; s. Melvin Manuel and Raymonde Lucette (Larpin) H.; m. Lisa Marie Cummings, Sept. 9, 1989; edn: BA summa cum laude, Yale Univ. 1979; JD cum laude, Harvard Law Sch. 1983; admitted St. Bars Calif. 1983, N.Y. 1984. Career: assoc. atty. Baker & McKenzie, N.Y.C. 1983-84; Gibson Dunn & Crutcher, Los Angeles 1984-89, Gibson Dunn & Crutcher, London 1989–; mem: Am. Bar Assn., Los Angeles Co. Bar Assn. Ofc: Gibson Dunn & Crutcher 30-35 Pall Mall London SW1Y 5LP England

HARTMAN, MARGARET J., university administrator, educator; b. Nov. 10, 1943, Columbus, Ohio; s. Herbert J. and Amabelle (Haller) H.; edn: BS, Calif. Polytech. Univ. 1966; MA, Oreg. St. Univ. 1968; PhD, 1970. Career: prof. biology CSU Los Angeles 1970, chair biology 1977-81, asst. v.p. 1981-87, assoc. v.p. 1987, provost and v.p. 1994–; chmn. of bd. Pat Brown Inst. 1987; honors: Phi Kappa Phi (pres. 1987-88, secty. 1988-89), NIH Extramural Assoc. 1983; mem: So. Calif. Acad. Scis., AAAS, Entomological Soc. Am., Sigma Xi; 10 articles pub. in profl. jours. Ofc: California State University 5151 State University Dr Los Angeles 90032

HARTWICK, THOMAS STANLEY, aerospace company executive; b. Mar. 19, 1934, Vandalia, Ill.; s. Wm. Arthur and Berniece Elizabeth (Daniels) H.; m. Alberta Elaine Lind, June 10, 1961; children: Glynis, Jeffrey, Thomas; edn: BS, Univ. Ill., Urbana 1956; MS, UCLA, 1958; PhD, USC, 1969. Career: mem. tech. staff Hughes Aircraft Co., Culver City 1956-61; asst. dir. The Electronics Res. Lab. The Aerospace Corp., El Segundo 1961-79; laboratories mgr. Hughes Aircraft Co., El Segundo 1979-83; microelectronics ctr. mgr. TRW Inc., Redondo Beach 1983-89, prog. mgr. 1989–; dir. Laser Technology Inc., Hollywood 1968-95; consulting mem. Advy. Group Electron Devices, US DoD, Wash. DC 1977, chmn. WGC DoD Advy. Group on Electron Devices, 1988; mem. Japan/US Tech. Assessment Team, Wash. DC 1984; advy. coms. CSU

Long Beach 1983-85, Univ. Colo. (opto-electronics) Boulder 1986-87; tech. advy. bd. U.S. Army Res. Labs. 1993–; awards: univ. visiting physicist Am. Physical Soc., Calif. 1974; mem: Am. Physical Soc. 1958, Optical Soc. of Am. 1973, Am. Def. Preparedness Assn. (w.coast com. 1986); civic: United Way L.A. (exec. assist. 1987), Peninsula Symph. Assn. P.V., coach youth sports P.V.E. 1972-77; invention: Far Infra Red Laser (pat. 1975); publs: 30+ tech. papers, 1961-78, editor: Far IR Technology, SPIE Vol. 105, 1978, tech. proceedings Competitive Strategies, 1985; rec: pianist. Ofc: TRW Inc. One Space Park Redondo Beach 90278

HARUDA, FRED DAVID, neurologist; b. Mar. 16, 1950, N.Y.C.; s. Joseph Stanley and Iva Fern (Lindstrom) H.; m. Alexandria S. Francis, PhD, May 28, 1983; children: Ashleigh b. 1985; edn: BA in biology (cum laude) Whitman Coll., 1972; MD, MS path., Univ. of Chgo., Pritzker Sch. of Med., 1976; bd. cert. pediatrics Am. Bd. Peds. 1984, neurology, child neurology Am. Bd. Psychiatry and Neuro. 1986, EEG, Am. Bd. of EEG and Neurophysiology 1988. Career: pediatric intern, resident Johns Hopkins Hosp., Balt. 1976-78; child and adult neurology fellow Columbia Univ. Coll. of Physicians and Surgeons, 1978-81; physician, owner Fred Haruda MD, Salinas, 1981-89, Central Coast Neurological Associates, Salinas, 1989–; clin. instr. UC San Francisco Sch. of Med., 1981-86, asst. clin. prof. 1986–; attdg. physician Salinas Valley Meml. Hosp., Salinas 1981–, cons. San Andreas Reg. Ctr., Salinas 1981–, Calif. Children's Svs., Sacto. 1981–, cons. neurologist Natividad Med. Ctr., Salinas 1981–, Mee Meml. Hosp., King City 1988–; med. advy. bd. Monterey Bay Multiple Sclerosis Soc., 1981–; awards: Phi Beta Kappa 1972, Sigma Xi (assoc. 1975, mem. 1991–), summer res. award March of Dimes 1975, Physician's recogn. award AMA, Chgo. (1983, 90); examiner child neurology Am. Bd. Psychiatry and Neurol., Evanston, Ill. 1980; mem: AMA, CMA, Monterey Co. Med. Assn. 1981–, Am. Acad. of Peds. (fellow), Am. Acad. Neurology (EEG, 1981–), Am. Electroencephalographic Soc., Am. Epilepsy Soc., Child Neurol. Soc., Internat. Child Neurol. Soc., Sigma Xi, Am. Acad. of Clin. Neurophysiology, Am. Med. EEG Soc., Am. Assn. Adv. of Sci., NY Acad. Sci.; civic: Boy Scouts Am. (district chmn.), Eagle Scout, Salinas; Elks Lodge (614); author 3 chapters in med. texts, numerous profl. jour. articles and sci. presentations; Indep.; Christian; rec: writing, golf, skiing, fishing.

HARVEY, ELAINE LOUISE, artist; b. Mar. 1, 1936, Riverside; d. Edgar Arthur and Emma Lou (Shull) Siervogel; m. Stuart Herbert Harvey, June 16, 1957; children: Kathleen b. 1959, Laurel b. 1961, Mark b. 1964; edn: BA, San Diego State Univ., 1957, Calif. Gen. Std. elem. tchg. credential, 1957. Career: elem. tchr. Cajon Valley Schs., El Cajon 1957-58; watermedia artist, 1975–; art lectr. and demonstrator, art groups in various cities, 1982–, tchr. art seminars 1985–; instr. art Athenaeum Sch. of Music & Arts, 1990–; juror art shows 1985–; trustee San Diego Mus. of Art, 1986; exhibition dir. Nat. Watercolor Soc., Calif. 1988; awards incl. silver San Diego Watercolor Soc. 1986, First Jurors Award S.D. Watercolor Soc. internat. exh., Calif. 1986, Winsor Newton Award Midwest Watercolor Soc., Wis. 1985, Creative Connections award Rocky Mountain Nat. Exh., Colo. 1986, Martha T. McKinnon Memorial Am. Watercolor Soc. 1985, Arjomari/Arches/Rives award Watercolor West, Calif. 1990; mem: Allied Artists of Am. 1989–, Nat. Watercolor Soc. (1986–, dir. 1986, 87, juror 1988), Rocky Mtn. Nat. Watermedia Soc. 1986–, Watercolor West (1985–, dir. 1986-87, 94–), West Coast Watercolor Soc. (1988–, pres. 1992–), San Diego Watercolor Soc. (pres. 1980-81), S.D. Mus. of Art Artists Guild (pres. 1986, dir.); publs: cover picture & article, The Artists Mag., 1987, contbr. paintings & text (book) The New Spirit of Watercolor, 1989, (book) Splash, 1991, Splash II, 1993, Watermedia Techniques for Releasing the Creative Spirit, 1992, editor (books): Palate to Palette, 1987, The Artist's Touch, 1994, Collage Techniques, 1994; Methodist; rec: choral director. Res/Studio: 1602 Sunburst Dr El Cajon 92021

HARVEY, JAMES GERALD, educational consultant; b. July 15, 1934, California, Mo.; s. William Walter and Exie Marie (Lindley) H; edn. BA, Amherst Coll., 1956; MA., Harvard Univ., 1958; MEdn., Harvard, Univ., 1962. Career: asst. to the dean, Grad. Sch. of Edn. Harvard Univ. 1962-66; dir. of admissions and fin. aid, Grad. Sch. of Edn. Harvard Univ. 1966-69; dir. of counseling, UC, Irvine, 1970-72; ednl. cons., Ednl. Counseling, Los Angeles, Calif., 1972–; honors: Mayo-Smith Fellow in Coll. Admissions, Amherst Coll. 1956-57; Amherst Meml. Fellow , Harvard Univ. 1957-58; UCLA Adminstrv. Fellow 1969-70; mem.: Amer. Ednl. Res. Assn., Nat. Council for Measurement in Edn., Amer. Counseling Assn.; author: ednl. materials, HARVOCAB Vocabulary Program, 1985–; mil: first lt., USAF 1958-61. Res: 1845 Glendon Ave., Los Angeles 90025 Ofc: Educational Counseling, 1845 Glendon Ave., Los Angeles 90025

HARVEY, JAMES ROSS, finance company executive; b. Los Angeles, Aug. 20, 1934; s. James Ernest and Loretta Rerniece (Ross) H.; m. Charlene Coakley. July 22, 1971; children: Kjersten Ann, Kristina Ross; edn: B.S. in Engring., Princeton Univ. 1956; MBA Univ. Calif., Berkeley 1963. Career: engr. Chevron Corp., San Francisco, 1956-61; acct. Touche Ross, San Francisco, 1963-64; chmn. bd. Transamerica Corp., San Francisco 1965–; bd. dirs.: Airtouch Communications, McKesson Corp., Charles Schwab Corp.; mil: AUS 1958-59;

mem: Bohemian Club, Pacific-Union Club, The Fly Fishers Club, London; rec: fly fishing, ranching, tennis.. Ofc: Transamerica Corp 600 Montgomery St San Francisco CA 94111-2702

HARVEY, MARC SEAN, lawyer, consultant; b. May 4, 1960, NY, NY; s. M. Eugene and Coleen (Jones) H.; edn: BA (high hons., Dean's list), So. Illinois Univ., 1980; JD (top 10%), Southwestern Univ., 1983; MBA (pending), Loyola Marymount Univ.; admitted bar: Calif. 1984, Mo. 1985, US Tax Ct. 1985, US Supreme Ct. 1988. Career: counsel US Small Bus. Adminstrn., Los Angeles 1982-83; counsel enforcement div. U.S. SEC, Los Angeles 1983-84; counsel State Farm Ins. Co., L.A. 1984-85; counsel 20th Century Ins. Co., Woodland Hills 1985-86; sole law practice, Encino 1986–; judge pro tem Culver Municipal Ct., 1991–; awards: 1st pl. essay Vets. Fgn. Wars, Collinsville, Ill. 1976, acad. scholar So. Ill. Univ. 1979-80, Nat. Hon. Soc. 1975-77; mem: Am. Bar Assn., L.A. Co. Bar Assn., SAG, AFTRA; Republican: charter/trustee Presdl. Task Force 1981–, Nat. Senatl Com. 1983–, Victory Fund spons. 1984–, Senatl. Inner Circle 1988–, Congl. Leadership Council 1987–; rec: history, travel, art collector. Law Offices of Marc S. Harvey, 16530 Ventura Blvd Penthouse Ste Encino 91436

HARVEY, PATRICIA JEAN, educator; b. Oct. 27, 1931, Newman, Calif.; d. Willard Monroe and Marjorie (Greenlee) Clougher; m. Richard Blake Harvey, Aug. 29, 1965; children: G. Scott Floden, Timothy P. Harvey, Lou D. De Lorca; edn: BA, Whittier Coll., 1966, MA, 1971. Career: resource specialist Monte Vista High Sch. and Whittier High Sch., 1977–, dept. chair spl. edn. Whittier High Sch. 1982–; co-dir. and founder The Learning Advantage Ctr.; civic: Whittier Fair Housing Com. 1972, Women's Aux. Whittier Coll. (pres. 1972-73, sec. 1971-72); mem. Docian Soc. Whittier Coll. (pres. 1965-66); publs: (tchrs. manual) The Dynamics of Calif. Govt. and Politics (1970, 1990), coauthor: Meeting The Needs of Special High School Students in Regular Education Classrooms (1988); Democrat; Episcopalian. Res: 424 Avocado Crest Rd La Habra Heights 90631 Ofc: The Learning Advantage Ctr 13710 Whittier Blvd Whittier 90605

HARVEY, PAUL W., electronics consultant; b. Aug. 12, 1957; edn: BSEE, M.I.T., 1979. Career: integrated circuit design engr. Harris Semiconductor, Melbourne, Fla. 1979-81; senior IC design engr. Advanced Micro Devices, Sunnyvale, Calif. 1981-85; senior cons. Logical Consulting, Palo Alto 1985-86; owner Integrated Circuit Design Consulting, Santa Clara 1986–, cons. clients incl. Synopsys, Intel, Fujitsu Micro, Gazelle Micro, Watkins Johnson, Kaiser Electronics, Raynet, Logical Svs., Kodak Berkeley Research, Nara; mem. IEEE, Profl. and Tech. Consultants Assn.; co-inventor 22V10 PAL output (pat. no. 4717912). Ofc: Integrated Circuit Design Consulting, 1556 Halford Ave Ste 310 Santa Clara 95051

HARVEY, RICHARD BLAKE, professor of political science; b. Nov. 28, 1930, Los Angeles; s. George Blackstone and Clara Ethel (Conway) H.; m. Patricia Jean Clougher, Aug. 29, 1965; 1 son, Timothy Patrick b. 1968; edn: BA, Occidental Coll. 1952; MA, UCLA 1954; PhD, 1959. Career: tchg. asst. UCLA 1954-57; legislative intern Calif. State Assembly, Sacto. 1957-58; instr. asst., assoc. prof., 1960-70, prof. political sci. Whittier Coll. 1970, dean acad. affairs 1970-80, dept. chair polit. sci. 1984-87; co-host Falcon pgm. L.A. Cable-TV 1986-87; honors: Pi Sigma Alpha, Haynes Found. grants 1961, 68; mem: Am. Political Sci. Assn., Western Political Sci. Assn., Newomen Soc. N. Am., Univ. Club Whittier (pres. 1978); author: Dynamics of Calif. Govt. & Politics (1970, 85, 90), Earl Warren Gov. of Calif., 1969, articles and book reviews pub.; Democrat; Presbyterian; rec: racquetball, avocado growing. Res: 424 Avocado Crest Rd La Habra Heights 90631 Ofc: Whittier College Dept. of Political Science Whittier 90608

HARWICH, MATHEW VIVIAL, insurance agent and musician; b. June 12, 1919, Redlands, Calif.; s. Joseph and Minnie Faye (Vivial) H.; m. Mary Marlene de la Cueva, Nov. 3, 1946; children: Gregory b. 1947, David b. 1955, Mark b. 1965; edn: Hollywood H.S., L.A. City Coll.; graduate Lumbleau Sch. of Real Estate and Anthony Sch. of Ins. Career: gen. ins. agent Allstate Ins. Co., Pomona 1955–; profl. trombonist with the Glentones (full size dance band in Glendora) 1979–; real estate broker Harmark Ins. Co., Hollywood 1945-55; awards with Allstate Ins. Co.: honor ring, disting. service; mil: Disabled American Vet; Purple Heart awarded due to wounds received on Attu (Aleutian Islands), 1943; sgt. AUS 1941-45; Inf. Badge for Aleutians, Leyte Is. (Philippines) and Okinawa; later entered Korean conflict; Republican; R.Cath.; rec: music, model building. Res: 1714 N Vallejo Way Upland 91784 Ofc: Allstate Insurance Co. 504 W Baseline Ste C Glendora 91740

HASAN, WAQAR, computer scientist; b. Apr. 1, 1963, Jalaun, India; s. Amir and Fatima (Ali) H.; m. Shirin, June 25, 1990; edn: BS, Computer Sci., IIT, Kanpur, India, 1984; MS, Computer Sci., Stanford Univ., Stanford, Calif., 1988. Career: M.T.S., Hewlett Packard Labs., Palo Alto, Calif., 1988–; mem: ACM, 1989–; author: numerous publ. tech. articles on the design and implementation of database languages. Ofc: Hewlett Packard 1501 Page Mill Rd. 3U Palo Alto 94304-0969

HASENKAMP, BRUCE HENRY, foundation executive; b. May 12, 1938, Brooklyn, N.Y.; s. Henry Ernst H. and Ruth Frances (Hoyer) Savage; m. Inta Sarma Macs, May 13, 1973; 1 son, Peter b. 1976; edn: BA, Dartmouth Coll. 1960; JD, Stanford Univ. 1963. Career: atty. Simpson Thacher & Bartlett, N.Y.C. 1963-68; asst. dean Stanford Law Sch. 1968-73; dir. Pres. Commn. on White House Fellowships, Wash. D.C. 1974-77; dir. pub. affairs Shaklee Corp., San Francisco 1978-82; exec. v.p. Hannaford Co. 1983-85; v.p. The Asia Found. 1985-86; v.p. Hosp. Council of No. Calif., San Mateo 1986-89; exec. dir. St. Francis Found. 1989–; bd. dirs. Federation of St. Med. Bds. of U.S., 1993, mem. editl. bd. 1989; bd. dirs. Nat. Commn. on Certification of Physician Assistants, Inc. 1990; dir. Pub. Affairs Council, Wash. D.C. 1988-89; mem. Med. Board of Calif., Sacto. 1987; dept. Calif. Roundtable, San Francisco 1980-82; dir. Council of Better Bus. Bureaus, Wash. D.C. 1980-84; honors: Order of Golden Heart, Sigma Phi Epsilon, Stanford Law Sch. Bd. of Visitors 1966-68, Hastings Coll. of Law Bd. of Visitors 1968-69; mem: Hillsborough City Sch. Dist. (bd. trustees 1985-93, past pres.), Commonwealth Club Calif. (treas., gov. 1980-86), World Affairs Council (dir 1980-87), Sigma Phi Epsilon Frat. (bd. dirs. 1973-87, 91-93; nat. pres. 1991-93; mil: 1st lt. AUS 1964-66, USAR 1960-66; Republican; Anglican; rec: collecting antique Korean ceramics. Res: 2435 Skyfarm Dr Hillsborough 94010 Ofc: Saint Francis Foundation 900 Hyde St Ste 1208 San Francisco 94109

HASHIMOTO, FRANCES KAZUKO, food products executive, civic activist; b. Aug. 26, 1943, Poston, Ariz.; d. Koroku and Haru (Kataoka) H.; m. Joel Lawrence Friedman, Jan. 22, 1972; children: Bryan b. 1976, Ryan b. 1978; edn: BS, USC 1966; tchg. credential Calif. (1966). Career: elem. tchr. Los Angeles Unified Sch. Dist., 1966-70; pres. Mikawaya Inc. 1970–; dir. Japanese Am. Cultural Comm. Center 1980–; awards: Little Tokyo Service Center comm. service (1987); mem: Little Tokyo Bus. Assn. (dir. 1974–, v.p. 1978-85, pres. 1994–), Japanese Village Plaza Merchants Assn. (pres. 1987-88), Japanese C.of C. (dir., v.p. 1990-93), Los Angeles C.of C., Pvt. Industry Council (treas. 1985-88); civic: Little Tokyo Centennial Com. (chmn. 1983-84), Nisei Week Japanese Festival (dir., gen. chmn. 1982, 1990), Mayor's Little Tokyo Community Devel. Advy. Com. 1980– (vice chmn. 1988), Mayor's Task Force on Central City East, L.A. City Human Relations Commn.; Republican; Buddhist; rec: target shooting. Ofc: Mikawaya 800 E 4th St Los Angeles 90013

HASKELL, ERIC TODD, educator, museum director; b. Oct. 2, 1950, Marysville, Calif.; s. Coburn and Joanne Dale (Taverner) H.; m. Danielle Floquet, July 7, 1973; children: Olivia Hanna b. 1975, Jean-Christophe b. 1978; edn: Baccalaureate (Lettres) Univ. of Paris, Fr. 1971; BA (cum laude) Pomona Coll., Claremont 1973; MA, UC Irvine, 1975, PhD, 1979. Career: tchg. asst. in French, UC Irvine, 1974-77, tchg. assoc. humanities, 1977-78; lectr. in French, Scripps Coll., Claremont 1978, asst. prof. of French, 1979-85, assoc. prof. French and humanities, 1985-93, prof. of French and humanities 1993–, chair French dept. 1985-90, dir. Clark Humanities Mus., 1984–; curator The Fleming Lecture Series, 1988-90; curator 6 exhs., co-curator Personal Edens: The Gardens and Film Sets of Florence Yoch (The Huntington Gallery 1992); internat. lectr. 100+, various univs. and art museums incl. L.A. Co. Mus. of Art, Stanford, Duke, Harvard, Univ. Calif., Univs. of Amsterdam, Zurich, Paris and Tunisia; awards: research and exhibition grantee Mellon Found. 1981, list of nat. lectrs. Garden Club of Am., NY, NY 1991; mem: Decorative Arts Study Ctr. (Curatorial Bd. 1987–), Assn. for Interdisciplinary 19th Century Studies (treas. 1986-88), Philol. Assn. of Pacific Coast (Literature and the Other Arts presiding ofcr. 1983, 87), Claremont Heritage (bd. 1989-90), Rancho Los Alamitos (dir. 1992–), Banning Residence Mus. Found. (dir. 1992–), Modern Language Assn. of Am., Internat. Assn. for Word and Image Studies, Interdisciplinary 19th Century Studies, 19th Century French Studies, Assn. des Vieilles Maison Francaises; publs: (exh. cats.) Transcending Mimesis: The French Illustrated Book (1982), scholarly articles on Baudelaire, Flaubert, Nerval, Rimbaud and Huysmans and French garden history (1970–). Ofc: Scripps College, 1030 Columbia St., Claremont 91711-3948

HASSID, SAMI, architect, professor emeritus; b. Apr. 19, 1912, Cairo, Egypt, nat. 1962; s. Joseph and Isabelle (Israel) H.; m. Juliette Mizrahi, June 29, 1941; children: Fred b. 1943, Muriel b. 1950; edn: diploma w/distinction, Sch. of Engring., Giza 1932; BA, honors in arch., Univ. London, Eng. 1935; M.Arch. Univ. Cairo, 1943; PhD in arch., Harvard Univ., 1956; reg. architect Calif. (1958). Career: prin. architectural office, Cairo, Egypt 1932-57, Berkeley, Calif. 1957-86; designer Office of Ali Labib Gabr, Cairo 1935-47; architect numerous bldgs., 1939-70; tchr. Technical Sch., Alexandria, Egypt 1932-34; lectr., asst. prof. Univ. of Cairo, Giza 1934-56; prof. Univ. of Einshams, Cairo 1957; lectr., prof. Univ. Calif., Berkeley 1957-79, emeritus 1979–, assoc. dean 1977-83, asst. to vice chancellor UCB 1980-85, dir. campus planning UCB 1983-84; awards: prizes archtl. competitions, Cairo (1933-63), Fulbright travel-study grantee (1954-56), 1st prize- Hqtrs. A.I.A., San Francisco 1963), Berkeley Citation UCB (1981, 85), Fellow (FAIA,E) Am. Inst. Arch. (1985–), mem. Royal Inst. British Arch. (cert. 1935–), Nat. Soc. Historic Preserv., AARP; author books on Minarets; Specifications; Construction (1939, 1940, 1954), PhD Thesis: Rural Housing (1956); pub. articles on design criteria, edn., life safety, campus plng. (1960-85); Democrat; Reform Jewish (past pres., trustee Cong. Beth El 1968-80, v.p. East Bay Syn. Council 1970-71); rec: research, writing, travel. Res: 2851 Rockridge Dr Pleasant Hill 94523

HASTINGS, ROBERT PUSEY, lawyer; b. May 23, 1910, Los Angeles; s. Hill (M.D.) and Mary Garvin (Brown) H.; m. Susan S. Schriber, July 9, 1938 (dec.);children: Susan Hastings Mallory; edn: BA, Yale Univ. 1929; LL.B, Harvard Law Sch. 1933; State Bar Calif. 1936. Career: counsel Motion Picture div. Office Coord. Inter-Am. Affairs 1942-43; ptnr. firm Paul, Hastings, Janofsky & Walker 1946-81, counsel, 1981–; chmn. Calif. campaign USO 1956-57; pres., chmn. bd. LA Civic Light Opera Assn., 1959-65, trustee 1939-79; trustee Calif. Light Opera Assn. 1979; secty., trustee Music Center Operating Co. 1961-65; trustee Harvey Mudd Coll. Sci. and Engring. 1956–, v.chmn. bd. 1956-80; chmn. Thacher Sch. 1965-70, trustee 1938-73; trustee Friends of Claremont Colls. 1970–, pres. 1973-75; trustee Friends Huntington Library and Art Gallery; bd. overseers Huntington Library and Art Gallery; trustee Winston Churchill Found. U.S. 1964–, Miss Porter's Sch. 1969-73; mem: LA Co. Bar Assns., So. Calif. Harvard Law Sch. Assn. (trustee, chmn. 1967-69), Delta Kappa Epsilon; Republican; Episcopalian (vestryman 1968-69, 72-73); civic clubs: Chancery (L.A.), California (L.A.), Valley Hunt, Sunset (L.A.) (past secty., pres. 1970-71), Zamorano (literary), Lincoln (L.A.), Brit. United Svs. (L.A.), Grolier (N.Y.C.); mil: lt. USNR, 1943-45, decorated Bronze Star w/clasp, Pacific Theater ribbon w/3 clasps, Philippine Liberation w/1 clasp, Am. theater ribbon; Hon. Order British Empire; Republican; Episcopalian; rec: book collecting. Ofc: Paul, Hastings, Janofsky & Walker 555 So Flower St Los Angeles 90071

HATAI, THOMAS HENRY, marketing executive; b. Dec. 27, 1937, Tokyo; came to U.S., 1951; s. Isamu Herbert and Kiyoko (Kume) H.; m. Geraldine (div. 1978); 1 son, Dickson Y. b. Jan. 19, 1970; edn: BS, Woodbury Coll., 1965; supr. internat. dept. Union Bank, Los Angeles 1964-66; sales rep. United Airlines, Los Angeles 1966-69; v.p. far east Travel Systems Internat., Oakbrook, Ill. 1969-75; pres. Hatai Internat., Los Angeles 1975-78; pres., CEO, Pace Mktg. Inc., La Habra, Calif., 1978–; pres. D.B.H. Global Ltd., 1983–; v. chmn. and CEO, Yamano Cosmetics Inc. 1991–; pres. Yamano Products, Inc. d.b.a (AVEC) 1992–; dir. Grand Five Corp., Bankok, Thailand 1992–; mem. United Internat. Club (bd. dirs. 1969 Japan), US Chamber of Commerce; illustrator: The Marty Story 1954, The St. Meinrad Story 1954; Republican. Res: 8544 Buena Tierra Pl Buena Park 90621 Ofc: D.B.H. Global Ltd. 1251-C S Beach Blvd La Habra 90631

HATCH, EDWARD IRVING, gemologist, investor; b. Apr. 25, 1929, Nashville, Tenn.; s. Rufus James and Marion Louise (Jennings) H.; m. Irene Tanaka, Dec. 6, 1955; edn: AA, San Diego Mesa Coll. 1974; AB, CSU San Diego 1976; cert. gemologist Gemol. Inst. Am. 1969. Career: served to ATCS, US Navy 1947-72, ret., decorated Air medal, merit. unit commendn. 4 bronze stars, Korean Service; jewelry industry investor and rental co. prop., 1972–; recipient recogn. award for saving trees in Tecolote Canyon, City Councilman Bruce Henderson 1989, Victory '88 disting. vol. svc. Calif. Repub. Party 1989, vol. svc. award City Councilwoman Judy McCarty; mem: San Diego Co. Apartment Assn. (Owner Operator Council 1990-91); civic: Japanese Am. Cosmopolitan Assn. (pres. Br. One 1955-56), Phi Kappa Phi 1976, Privately Owned Canyons and Environs Com. (founding bd., chmn. 1985-88), Tecolote Canyon Rim Owners Protective Assn. (sec. 1986), S.D. Sato Matsutoyo-Kai Koen-Kai (treas. 1986-88), Tecolote Canyon Citizens' Advy. Com. appt. by Councilman Bruce Henderson 1989–, Nat. Model Railroad Assn. 1991, Fleet Reserve Assn. (Branch 312 v.p. 1992-93, pres. 1993-94); invention: coaxial R.F. Relay and Power Switch Tester, used by USN for electronic maint. 1955-56; Republican (del. S.D. Co. Repub. Party Conv. 1988, precinct chair 78th A.D. 1988-89); R.Cath.; rec: mountaineering, garden, gemological test equip. design, computer pgmmg, model railroad design and construction. Res: 4442 Bertha St San Diego 92117-3803

HATCH, ROBERT FRED, executive; b. Aug. 27, 1934, Chicago; s. Lester Warren and Mabel Dorothy Christina (Fulton) H.; m. Sandra Karen Thunander, Dec. 24, 1964; children: Hilary Joy b. 1969, Holly Christina b. 1972, Heather Daisy b. 1975; edn: BA, Valparaiso Univ., 1958, JD, Northwestern Univ. Sch. of Law, Chgo. 1960. Career: atty. law firm Tenney Sherman Bentley & Guthrie, Chgo. 1960-66; stockbroker White Weld & Co. Inc., Chgo. and Los Angeles, 1966-70; real estate devel., George Elkins & Co., Beverly Hills 1970-72; Donald Bren & Co., Sherman Oaks 1973; owner Robert F. Hatch Inc., L.A. 1973-77; v.p. and dir. real estate mgmt. George Elkins & Co., Beverly Hills 1978-79; pres. Filtration Systems Inc., Hawthorne 1979-80; ptnr. Cambrian Energy Systems, Los Angeles 1980–; elected State Senator 19th dist. Ill., Chgo. 1962-66, elected Republican Party 19th ward chmn., Chgo. 1964-66, del. Republican Nat. Conv., Kansas City, Kans. 1976; appt. Pres. Reagan's Commn. on Housing, W.D.C. 1982; club: Riviera Tennis 1986–; mil: sp3c US Army 1954-55; Republican; Presbyterian; rec: genealogy, history, travel, tennis. Res: 125 N Layton Dr Los Angeles 90049 Ofc: Cambrian Energy Systems 629 S Grand Ste 2420 Los Angeles 90017

HATFIELD, DALE CHARLES, bank insurance executive; b. May 26, 1931, Springfield, Ill.; s. C. Ray and Gladys (Shumate) H.; m. Lura Ann Northrop, 1958; children: Dana b. 1960, Dean b. 1962, Dianne b. 1968; edn: BS, Bradley Univ. 1953; MBA, Univ. Denver 1963. Career: research mgr. Boise Cascade Corp., Boise, Ida. 1963-67; v.p. Bank of California, Los Angeles, San Francisco

1967-87; v.p. Calif. Bankers Assn. 1987; pres./dir. Calif. Bankers Insurance Services Inc. 1988; dir: BancInsure Inc., Okla. City; faculty The School for Bank Adminstrn. B.A.I. 1983; American Bankers Assn. faculty chmn. Risk Mgmt. Seminars 1977-78, dir. Ins. and Protection Div. ABA 1976-78, chmn. Ins. Com. ABA 1976; Calif. Bankers Assn. chmn. Emergency Planning Task Force CBA 1981-85, chmn. Ins. Com. CBA 1978-80; appt. Gov's Task Force on Earthquake Preparedness 1980-86, Calif. State Fin. and Monetary Svs. Com. 1981-85; mem. Orinda Assn. (pres. 1975, dir. 1974-76), Masons, Commonwealth Club Calif., Moraga Country Club; publs: Guidelines for Disaster Planning (CBA 1982); mil: 1st lt. USAF; Republican; Presbyterian (Elder). Res: 29 Cedar Ln Orinda 94563

HAUCK, DENNIS WILLIAM, author, magazine editor, software systems engineer, mathematics consultant; b. Apr. 8, 1945, Hammond, Ind.; s. Floyd Wm. and Wilma (Frey) H.; edn: AA, Indiana Univ., 1969; postgrad., Univ. Innsbruck, Austria, 1970; cand. phil., math., Univ. Vienna, 1973. Career: systems analyst Trans Am. Corp., East Chicago, Ind. 1973-75; research supr. U.S. Gypsum Co., 1975-79; elec. engr. Howmet Turbine, Reno, Nev. 1979-80; engring. mgr. EPCO, 1980-81; project engr. Campbell Soup Co., Sacto. 1981-83; process mgr. Odenberg Inc., 1983–; freelance writer, 1972–; cons. math. GSW Inc., Phoenix 1977–; editor Jour. of Ufology, 1975-77, Mufon Jour., 1976–, four mags. 1976-78; appeared in film documentary Mysteries of the Gods, 1978; speaker Internat. Conf. on UFO's, Acapulco, Mex. 1978; mem: Inst. Transpersonal Psychology, Green Peace; author (books): Secret of the Emerald Tablet (translation from German, Holmes Pub. 1993), William Shatner: A Bio-Bibliography (Greenwood Press 1993), The Nat'l Directory of Haunted Places (Athanor Press 1994), Captain Quirk: The Unauthorized Biography of William Shatner (Kensington Pub. 1995). Res: 5550 Franklin Blvd Apt 101 Sacramento 95820

HAUSE, DONALD WILLIAMS, plastic and reconstructive surgeon; b. Sept. 25, 1960, Sacramento, Calif.; s. Donald Phillip and Verde Belle (Williams) H.; m. Lisa Ann Saillant, Dec. 19, 1992; edn: BS, Univ. of Southern Calif. 1982; MD, Baylor Coll. of Medicine, Houston, Tx. 1986. Career: plastic and reconstructive surgeon, pvt. practice, Sacto. Res: 1655 El Nido Way Sacramento 95864 Ofc: Donald W. Hause, M.D. 3941 J Street #360 Sacramento 95819

HAUSMAN, ARTHUR HERBERT, corporate board director; b. Nov. 24, 1923, Chicago, Ill.; s. Samuel Louis and Sarah Elin H.; m. Helen Mandelowitz, May 19, 1946; children: Susan (dec.), Kenneth b. 1954, Catherine b. 1959; edn: BSEE, Univ. Tx. 1944; MS, Harvard Univ. 1948; reg. profl. engr. D.C. (1988). Career: electronics engr. Engring. Research Assn., St. Paul, Minn. 1946-47; supr., electronics scientist U.S. Govt., Wash. D.C. 1948-60; v.p., dir. of research Ampex, Redwood City 1960-63, v.p. ops. 1963-65, group v.p. 1965-67, exec. v.p. 1967-71, pres., CEO 1971-81, pres., CEO, chmn. bd. 1981-83, chmn. 1983-88; awards: U.S. Govt. Dept. of Defense merit. civilian service (1960); mem: IEEE, Pres. Export Council (export adminstrn. subcom. chmn. 1985-89), MIT Dept. Math Visiting Com., Cosmos Club; articles pub. in tech. jours. (1949-54), patentee in field (1950-65), moderator NATO Conf. 1975; mil: lt.j.g. USNR 1944-50; Republican; rec: amateur radio. Address: Atherton 94027

HAVARD, JOHN FRANCIS, mining consultant; b. Mar. 15, 1909, Helena, Mont.; s. Francis Thompson and Margaret Eliza (Raleigh) H.; m. Faith Hartley, Aug. 19, 1943 (dec. May 11, 1991); children: David b. 1944, Edith Ann b. 1946, John b. 1949, Patrick b. 1953; edn: Montana Sch. of Mines, Butte 1929-32; PhB in geology, Univ. Wis., Madison 1934; PhM and BS in mining engring., 1935, Engr. of Mines, 1943; reg. geologist, engr. various states. Career: engr., works mgr., chief engr. mines U.S. Gypsum Co., Chgo. 1935-52; v.p. Fibreboard Corp., San Francisco 1953-62; v.p. Kaiser Engineers, Oakland 1963-74, senior v.p. 1975-79; indep. cons., Nevada City, Calif. 1980–; appt. U.S. Nat. Com. on Geology, W.D.C., 1975-79; awards: Hardinge Award AIME, NY, NY 1982, distinguished service Univ. Wis. 1986; mem.: Soc. for Mining Metallurgy and Exploration (1935–, past pres., Distinguished Mem., Littleton, Co. 1977), AIME (1935–, past dir., Hon. Mem., N.Y.C. 1984), AAAS (1965–, Fellow), Soc. of Economic Geologists 1948–; numerous pub. tech. papers; Republican; Episcopalian; rec: reading. Res: 181552 Augustine Rd Nevada City 95959

HAVAS, THOMAS TAMAS, data processing executive, civil engineer; b. Feb. 21, 1937, Budapest, Hungary; nat. 1980; m. Bernadette Simone, Feb. 20, 1969; 1 son, Thomas G. b. 1973; edn: BS, Mt. Allison Univ. 1961; reg. profl. engr. Ontario (1969). Career: systems engr. G.E. Corp., Phoenix, Ariz. and Toronto, Canada 1966-69; RCA Corp., Palo Alto and Cinnaminson, N.J. 1969-71; simulation splst. Bechtel Power Corp., San Francisco 1972-75, scheduling splst., 1975-80, mgr. Bechtel Espana, Madrid, Spain 1980-84, engring. product specialist Bechtel Power Corp., San Francisco 1984-89; product support dir. Bechtel Software Inc./R&D, 1989–; instr. Mt. Allison Univ., Sackville 1960-61; N.S. Tech. Coll., Halifax 1961-63; awards: Mt. Allison Univ. scholarships 1957-61; mem: Project Mgmt. Inst., Am. Assn. Cost Engrs., IEEE (Computer Soc.), Assn. Profl. Engrs. of Ontario, Am. Assn. Artificial Intelligence; 3 papers pub. in tech. jours., 1963, 88, 95; rec: private pilot, chess, travel. Res: 65 Hickory Ct Danville 94506 Ofc: Bechtel Corp. POB 193965 San Francisco 94119

HAVENS, CARL BRADFORD, research scientist, ret.; b. May 30, 1918, Hope, Mich.; s. Boyd L. and Mary Ada (Gransden) H.; m. Grace Jeannette Cummins; children: David C., b. 1939; Sandra J., b. 1944; Paul L., b. 1946; edn: BSCE, Internat. Coll. 1943; Univ. Mich. 1944-45; Mich. St. Univ. 1946-47. Career: group leader Dow Chemical Co., Midland, Mich. 1949-57, production supr., Bay City, Mich. 1957-58, res. mgr., Cleveland, Ohio 1958-64, Findlay, Ohio 1964-66, Fresno 1966-76, res. scientist, Granville, Ohio 1976-86; awards: Dow award 1981, Hall of Fame 1982; mem: Am. Chem. Soc., Soc. Plastics Engrs.; 55 U.S. and fgn. patents held (1942-88), 5 papers pub. in sci. jours.; Republican; Presbyterian; rec: skiing, skating, surfing. Address: Fresno 93710

HAVLICEK, MARY JANE DYKSTRA, environmental consultant; b. Nov. 11, 1941, Muskegon, Mich.; d. Carl Sheffield and Viola Rose (Kleyn) Dykstra; m. Stephen Charles Havlicek, Aug.; 26, 1961; children: Lani b. 1972, Malia b. 1974, John b. 1979; edn: BA, Hope Coll. 1963; MS chemistry, Ohio St. Univ. 1965; PhD, Univ. Hawaii 1970. Career: chemistry instr. Detroit Inst. Tech., Mich. 1965-67; chemist Vinings Chemical Co., Marietta, Ga. 1977; asst. prof. chemistry Floyd Jr. Coll., Rome, Ga. 1977-79; assoc. prof. chemistry CSU San Francisco 1980-81, CSU Sonoma, Rohnert Park 1981-82; chemist Ark Distributing, Martinez 1982-83; dir. analytical services Herguth Petroleum Lab., Vallejo 1983-84; pres. Coast-to-Coast Analytical Services, San Luis Obispo 1984–, Goleta 1986–, dir., San Luis Obispo 1984–, Santa Barbara 1986–; environmental cons. Environmental Project Mgmt., Camarillo 1994–; instr. UCSB 1988–; guest speaker, instr. Tri Counties Water Pollution Control Fedn. 1985–; awards: Inc. Mag. 500 (1988), Reed City H.S. Salutatorian (1959); mem: Am. Chem. Soc., Assn. Analytical Chemists, Inc. Council of Growing Cos., Am. Council Indep. Labs., Air Pollution Control Assn., Sigma Iota Pi, Am. Cancer Soc., Am. Assn. Univ. Women (secty. 1975), Am. Lung Assn., N. Minn. Reg. Sci. Fair (chmn., dir. 1971); staff Am. Chem. Soc. publ. Vortex, 1981-84, author Organic Chemistry Lab., 1966; Methodist. Ofc: Coast-to-Coast Analytical Services 141 Suburban Rd San Luis Obispo 93401; Environmental Project Management 335 E Highland Hills Dr Camarillo 93010

HAWKES, GLENN ROGERS, psychology educator; b. Apr. 29, 1919, Preston, Idaho; s. William and Rae (Rogers) H.; m. Yvonne Merrill, Dec. 18, 1941; children: Kristen, William Ray, Gregory Merrill, Laura; edn: BS in psychology, Utah State Univ., 1946, MS psych., 1947; PhD psych., Cornell Univ., 1950. Career: asst., assoc., full prof. child devel. and psychology Iowa State Univ., Ames 1950-66, chmn. dept. child devel., 1954-66; research psychologist, prof. human devel. Univ. Calif., Davis 1966-89, assoc. dean applied economics and behavioral scis. 1966-83, prof. emeritus 1990–, academic coord. Hubert Humphrey Fellowship Program, 1990–, prof. behavioral scis. dept. family practice Sch. Medicine, chmn. teaching dev. 1970-72, chmn. dept. applied behavioral scis. 1982-86; vis. scholar Univ. Hawaii 1972-73, Univ. London 1970, 80, 86; bd. dirs. Creative Playthings Inc. 1962-66; awards: research grantee pvt. foundations and govt. bodies, Iowa State Univ. Faculty Citation 1965, Outstanding Service cit. Iowa Soc. Crippled Children and Adults 1965, cit. Dept. Child Devel. 1980, Coll. Agrl. and Environmental Scis. 1983, named Hon. Lt. Gov. Oklahoma 1966; author: w/Pease, Behavior and Development from 5 to 12 (1962), w/ Frost, The Disadvantaged Child: Issues and Innovations (1966, 2d edit. 1970), w/ Schultz and Baird, Lifestyles and Consumer Behavior of Older Americans (1979), w/ Nicola and Fish, Young Marrieds: The Dual Career Approach (1984), contbr. numerous articles in profl. jours.; mil: US Army 1941-45. Res: 1114 Purdue Dr Davis 95616-1736 Ofc: University California Dept. Applied Beh. Scis. Internat. House 10 College Park Davis 95616

HAWKINS, AVERILL ERIC, retired insurance agent, retired military officer; b. Dec. 7, 1936, Dinuba, Calif.; s. Averill Evans and Irene Ellen (Schonher) H.; m. Barbara Steele, Apr. 3, 1955; children: Christopher Averill b. 1957, Darren Carl b. 1959; 3 granddaus.: Sarah Elizabeth b. 1988, Brittany Michelle b. 1990, Rebecca Nichole b. 1992; edn: AA, eng., Reedley Coll. 1956; BS, Univ. of St. of N.Y., 1987; CLU, Am. Coll. of Chartered Life Underwriters 1972. Career: life & health insurance agt. 1962-90; instr. Life Underwriters Assn., 1965-66; dir. Sierra Masonic Family Club 1983–; awards: Hall of Fame 1966-82, Sower Club 1967-79, Nat. Sales Achievement 1973-81, Nat. Quality Awd. 1967-88, Centurion Club 1976, Sower Round Table 1975, 76, 78, Actuaries Honor Roll 1974-87, Masonic Light Award 1982; former mem: Fresno Life Underwriters Assn. (dir. 1972/3), Calif. Assn. Life Underwriters, Nat. Life Underwriters Assn., Fresno Chp. CLUs, Nat. Assn. CLUs; mem: Nat. Guard Assn. of Calif., Nat. Guard Assn. of the US; orgns: Kiwanis (pres. 1964, lt. gov. 1970/1); Masons; Dinuba Plnng. Commn., Dinuba Indsl. Plnng. Commn. (v.chmn. 1972/3); C.of C.; publs: arts. in company mag.; mil: promoted through ranks to maj. gen. Army Nat. Guard, 1989, decorated Army Disting. Svc. Medal, Legion of Merit, Merit Service (5), Calif. Medal of Merit, Gov's unit cit., merit unit cit., Good Conduct; Republican; Presbyterian (elder); rec: motorcycle touring, tennis. Address: 1625 Cass #38 Cayucos 93430

HAWKINS, MARGARET ALLEN, real estate broker (retired), interior designer (retired); b. Oct. 8, 1920, El Centro; d. Paul Verne and Clementine Celeste (Hopking) Allen; m. Charles John Hawkins, Nov. 29, 1941; children: Charles John b. 1944, Johanna b. 1948; edn: B.Edn., UCLA 1942. Career: tchr.

Los Angeles City Schs. 1942-43, 1946-47; Minneapolis Schs. 1955-60; interior decorator 1960-66; Theo. Hofstatter & Co., N.Y. 1966-73; Margaret Hawkins, Inc. 1973-76; real estate agent Rand & Stewart, Rancho Santa Fe 1978-79; real estate agent and broker Rancho Santa Fe Properties 1979-80; broker, mng. dir. Fairbanks Ranch 1980-84; pres. RSF Properties 1979; mem: UCLA Alumni Assn., Kappa Alpha Theta; Republican; Protestant; rec: oil painting. Res: 4125 Hermosa Way San Diego 92103-1212

HAWKINS, RICHARD MICHAEL, lawyer; b. July 23, 1949, Nevada City; s. Robert Augustus and Virginia June (Hawke) H.; m. Linda Lee Chapman, Sept. 27, 1975; children: Alexandra Michelle; edn: BS, UC Davis, 1971; JD, Hastings Law Coll., 1974; LLM, McGeorge Univ., 1983; Cert. Specialist in estate planning, trust & probate law, State Bar of Calif. Bd. of Legal Specialization. Career: atty., assoc. Larue & Francis, Nevada City 1973-76; ptnr. Larue Roach & Hawkins 1977-78; Berliner Spiller & Hawkins 1978-81; prin. Richard M. Hawkins, Grass Valley 1981–; honors: Phi Kappa Phi, Thurston Hon. Soc., Order of Coif, Kraft Scholarship Prize (1967), Am. Jurisprudence awards (1973-74); mem: Am. Bar Assn., Calif. Bar Assn., 49er Fire Dist. (bd. dirs. 1978-83, fire chief 1983-89); Republican; R.Cath.; rec: running, skiing. Res: 14762 Banner Quaker Hill Rd Nevada City 95959 Ofc: 10563 Brunswick Rd Ste 2 Grass Valley 95945

HAWKINS, ROBERT L., JR., physician; b. Aug. 24, 1952, Richmond, Calif.; s. Robert L. Hawkins, Sr. and Dorthy (Harris) H.; m. Martha, June 18, 1983; children: Matthew b. 1991, Andrew b. 1992; edn: BS, Biological Sci., UC Irvine 1978, BA, Physical Sci. 1978; MD, UCLA Sch. of Medicine 1982. Career: intern Univ. of Ariz., Tucson 1982-83, resident 1983-87; fellow Univ. of Tex., Houston 1987-88; physician, pvt. practice, Carmichael, Calif. 1988–; awards: cancer research, Am. Coll. of Surgeons, Tucson, Ariz. 1987; mem: Am. Soc. of Colon & Rectal Surgeons 1988–, SAGES 1990–, Am. Coll. of Surgeons (fellow 1991–), Am. Coll. Physician Executives 1992–; Republican. Ofc: 6620 Coyle Ave #316 Carmichael 95608 Tel: 916/863-7671

HAWKYARD, EDGAR WILLIAM, lawyer; b. Jan. 16, 1960, Vallejo; s. William Leo and Maria Teresa (Aguirre) H.; m. Maria Luz Torrico, June 22, 1991; edn: BA, Univ. Santa Clara 1982; JD, Univ. Pacific McGeorge Sch. Law 1986. Career: intern Calif. C.of C., Sacto. 1984-85; law clk. Law Offices Anthony I. Picciano 1985-87; trainee Peace Corps, Costa Rica 1987; atty., assoc. Bennett Samuelsen Reynolds & Allard, Oakland 1987-91; assoc. atty. Imai, Tadlock & Keeney, S.F. 1992-95; atty., assoc. Law Ofcs. of James A. Alexander 1995–; mem: San Francisco Bar Assn., Commonwealth Club, Pan-Am. Soc., World Affairs Council No. Calif., Federalist Soc., Acton Soc.; Republican; Catholic; rec: basketball, tennis. Ofc: Law Offices of James A. Alexander 101 Ygnacio Valley Rd Walnut Creek 94596

HAWTHORNE, DONALD BRUCE, healthcare industry executive; b. Dec. 31, 1955, Los Angeles; s. Donald Claire and Elene Ruth (Roussey) H.; m. Dianne M. Ritter, Oct. 7, 1989; edn: BS, Harvey Mudd Coll. 1977, MBA, Stanford Univ. 1981. Career: financial plnnr. Westinghouse Electric Corp., Sunnyvale 1978-79; summer intern Morgan Guaranty Trust Co., NY, NY 1980; summer cons. Arabian- Am. Oil Co., Dhahran, Saudi Arabia 1981; sr. finl. analyst treasury dept. Atlantic Richfield Co., Los Angeles 1981-83; sr. finl. analyst corp. plnng. Syntex Corp, Palo Alto 1983-84, finl. plnng. mgr., controller Syntex Corp. Ophthalmics Div., Phoenix, Ariz. 1984-85; mgr. fin. and adminstrn. Genelabs Inc., Redwood City 1985-87, dir. fin. 1987-89, chief fin. ofcr. 1989-90; v.p. fin. and adminstrn. and c.f.o. Oclassen Pharmaceuticals Inc., San Rafael 1990; v.p. fin. and c.f.o. Biocircuits Corp., Sunnyvale 1991–; honors: Calif. State Scholar 1973-77, ARCS (Achievement Rewards for Coll. Scientists) scholar 1976-77, Dean's List distinction, Harvey Mudd Coll. Student Body Pres. 1976-77, Pi Sigma Alpha 1977, scholarship awards Stanford Bus. Sch. 1979-81, Who's Who Among Students in Am. Univs. and Colls. 1976-77, Who's Who in the West 1990; mem: Harvey Mudd Coll. Alumni Assn. (bd. govs. 1981-1987, bd. govs. treas. 1982-3, v.p. 1983-4, pres. 1984-6), Stanford Bus. Sch. Alumni Assn., Assn. of Bioscience Financial Ofcrs.(No. Calif. Bd. 1991–, co-chmn. Nat. Conf. 1992, chmn. Nat. Conf. 1993); bd. trustees Harvey Mudd Coll. 1986-89; Republican (Calif. Rep. Assembly Peninsula chpt. bd. 1987-88, treas. 1988, 11th Senate Dist. dir. 1988-89); R.Cath. Res: 260 Windsor Dr San Carlos 94070 Ofc: Biocircuits Corporation, 1324 Chesapeake Terrace Sunnyvale 94089

HAXTON, RONALD SCOTT, physician, pediatrician; b. Mar. 15, 1942, Los Angeles; s. Alexander Scott and Jacqueline (Adams) H.; m. Betty Jane Glenn, Aug. 7, 1971; edn: BA, Whittier Coll. 1963; MD, Univ. Calif. 1967. Career: intern USC Med. Center, Los Angeles 1967-68; resident, pediatrics UC Irvine 1970-72; pediatrician pvt. practice, Mission Viejo 1972–; mil: lt. USN 1968-70; Independent; rec: gardening, reading. Res: 27771 Horseshoe Bend San Juan Capistrano 92675-1522 Ofc: 27800 Medical Center Rd Ste 204 Mission Viejo 92691-6408

HAYCRAFT, CHARLES LEROY, data systems company president; b. June 23, 1939, Witt, Ill.; s. Worth and Ruby (Meyer) H.; m. Karen Georgia Maxwell, Nov. 16, 1963; edn: CE, Univ. Ill. 1958; BS, So. Ill. Univ. Carbondale 1964;

MS, So. Ill. Univ. Edwardsville 1969; MBA, 1978. Career: sales exec. Ruben H. Donnelly, St. Louis, Mo. 1965-67; Lin Broadcasting 1967-69; dir. sales MSI Data Corp., Costa Mesa 1969-77; v.p. mktg. Azur Data Inc., Newport Beach 1977-80; pres. N. Am. Micronics Inc., San Clemente 1980-85; Venture Data Systems Inc., Irvine 1985–; sales exec. Bemis Corp., St. Louis, Mo. 1964-65; awards: MSI Data Corp. mgr. of year (1975), Azur Data Corp. mgr. of year (1979); mem: Lions, SIU Parachute Club (pres. 1960-64); mil: SP-4 AUS 1959-60; Republican; Presbyterian; rec: running. Res: 2314 Plaza Ala Playa San Clemente 92672 Ofc: Venture Data Systems, Inc. 800 S El Camino Real Ste 213 San Clemente 92672

HAYES, CLAUDE QUINTEN CHRISTOPHER, science and technology consultant, executive; b. Nov. 15, 1945, N.Y.C.; s. Claude and Celestine (Stanley) H.; edn: BA chemistry and geol. scis., Columbia Univ., 1971, MBA pgm. internat. bus. 1972-73; New York Law Sch. 1973-75; patent law rev. Practicing Law Inst., 1975; JD, Western State Law Sch., 1978; Calif. Comm. Colls. life instr. in chemistry, geophysics, phys. geography, earth sci., phys. sci., geology, law, bus. and law 1976, C.C.C. life supr. cert. 1979. Career: tech. writer Burroughs Corp., San Diego 1978-79; senior systems analyst Gen. Dynamics Convair, 1979-80, advanced mfg. technologist, senior engr. 1980-81; scientist consultant 1979–; govt. contr., cons. USN, 1982, U.S. DoD, 1986–, contr. to DNA, NOSC, DARPA, SDIO, USAF, and US Army, 1988–; faculty San Diego Community Coll. Dist. 1976-82, 85-90; instr. phys. scis. National Univ., San Diego 1980-81; instr. bus. law, earth scis. Miramar Coll., 1978-82 (studentbody Tchr. of Yr. 1982); recipient N.Y.C. citizenship award for sci. activity 1959; patents: Composite Fabric Endothermic Electronic Component Cooling (1984), 3 patents at Gen. Dynamics (1981), patents pending re Aggregate Suspended Particle Electric Charge Collector (1990, 91); mem.: AAAS, Am. Inst. Aero. & Astro. (senior mem.), N.Y. Acad. Scis., Am. Chem. Soc.; R.Cath.; rec: travel, boating, music, films, technology, people. Res/Ofc: 3737 Third Ave #308 San Diego 92103 Tel:619/299-2267

HAYES, GREGORY MICHAEL, school teacher/coach; b. Dec. 28, 1954, Queens, N.Y.; s. John Aloysius, III, and Patricia Marie (Kennedy) H.; m. Jan Marie McGlothlin, Aug. 4, 1990; children: Megan Kimberly b. June 9, 1992, Kara Marie b. Oct. 19, 1994; edn: BA in history, UCLA, 1977, MEd, 1980. Career: grad. asst. men's basketball coach UCLA 1977-79, asst. women's basketball coach UCLA, 1979-81; substitute tchr. Placentia Unified Sch. Dist., 1980-82; teacher/coach Wm. S. Hart Sch. Dist., Santa Clarita 1982–; Canyon High Sch. asst. track coach 1982-89, varsity boys basketball coach 1982–, varsity girls softball coach 1991–, Staying Alive advisor 1988–, substance abuse chair 1986-90, social studies dept chairperson 1994-95; basketball coach Athletes In Action -USA, summers 1984-85; nat. shot doctor Shot Doctor Basketball, USA, Raleigh, N.C. 1986–; NCAA Volleyball line judge 1987-90; awards: Canyon High Sch. most inspirational tchr., coach of yr. 1986, 1987, listed Outstanding Young Men of Am. 1989, listed Who's Who in the West 1991, "All-Star Coach" Daily News Bernie Milligan All-Star Softball Game, Northridge, Calif. 1991; mem. So. Calif. Interscholastic Basketball Coaches Assn. (pres. 1990-92), Fellowship of Christian Athletes (mem., camp coach 1981–), Calif. Tchrs. Assn. 1988–, Canyon Theatre Guild (mem., actor 1988–); civic: L.A. Olympic Sports Fest. (vol. summer 1991), Grace Baptist Ch. Orchestra, Newhall 1991–; pub. articles in SCIBCA Coaches Notebook (1989, 91, 94); Christian; rec: acting, trumpet, sports, reading, bicycling, family activities. Ofc: Canyon High School 19300 W Nadal St Canyon Country 91351

HAYNES, EDITH MAE, college administrator; b. Jan. 23, 1934, Marshfield, Mo.; d. Marion Manning and Delphia Bernice (Richerson) McGaughey; m. Clifford Elmer Gantner, June 12, 1949 (div. 1960); children: Deborah b. 1950, Patti b. 1953, Barbi b. 1956, Clifford b. 1958; edn: D.C., Cleveland Chiropractic Coll., Kansas City, Mo.; lic. D.C., Calif., 1983. Career: purch. agent, Kansas City, Mo.; secty. Cleveland Chiropractic Coll., K.C., Mo., transferred to Los Angeles, 1977–, as gen. office, subsequently dir. admissions, dir. postgrad. edn., dir. of devel./alumni affairs, administrv. asst. to the president; mem: Internat. Chiropractors Assn., Am. Chiropractic Assn., Calif. Chiropractic Assn., Am. Public Health Assn., Nat. Assn. of Fund Raising Executives, Int. Notary Assn., Sigma Chi Psi, Delta Tau Alpha; rec: reading, travel. Res: PO Box 9217 Glendale 91226-9217 Ofc: Cleveland Chiropractic College, 590 N Vermont Ave Los Angeles 90004

HAYWARD, FREDRIC MARK, men's rights activist, association executive; b. July 10, 1946, N.Y.C.; s. Irving Michael and Mildred (Feingold) H.; m. Ingeborg Beck, Aug. 18, 1971 (div. Aug. 1974); children: Kil R., b. 1981; KJ, b. 1994; edn: BA, Brandeis Univ., 1967; MA, Fletcher Sch. of Law & Diplomacy, 1968, MALD, 1969. Career: sales JNSIII, Paris, France 1965; satellite research TRW Systems, Redondo Beach 1966; diplomatic svc. US State Dept., Bangkok, Thailand 1968; tchr. Concord Pub. Sch., Concord, Mass. 1969-77; exec. director Men's Rights, Inc., Newton, Mass. 1977–; writer and lectr., Sacramento, Calif. 1977–: articles in newspapers, mags. and jours., and 3 anthologies: Male/Female Roles, 1983, Men Freeing Men, 1985, To Be A Man, 1991; num. lectures and workshops various univs., groups and confs.; frequent guest appearances on local, nat. and fgn. t.v. and radio shows; host and producer weekly TV talk show, The

SacraMENshow; contbg. writer Spectator, Berkeley 1988–, contbg. editor Liberator, Forest Lake, Minn. 1988-89; mem. advy. bd. Ctr. for Men's Studies, Berkeley 1988-94; bd. dirs. Men Internat., Mpls. 1982-86, Nat. Congress for Men and Children, W.D.C. 1981-90; awards: fellow Fletcher Sch. of Law & Diplomacy 1967-69, vis. lectr. Tufts Univ. 1979, fellow Warren Farrell Found., Leucadia, Calif. 1989, The Golden State Award 1993, Nat. Coalition of Free Men Annual Award for Excellence 1993; mem: Nat. Congress for Men and Children (1981–, bd. 1981-90), Sacramento Valley Men's Council 1992–, AFTRA 1979–; Jewish; rec: guitar, tennis. Ofc: Mr. Inc., PO Box 163180 Sacramento 95816

HAZE, NEALA JEAN, educator, dance/movement therapist; b. Sept. 27, 1947, Kirksville, Mo.; d. Neal James Haze and Garnet Irene (Reitz) Firth; edn: Western St. Coll. 1965-66; Univ. Colo. 1966-67; BS, Colo. St. Univ. 1969; MA, dance, Mills Coll. 1974: MA, counseling psychol., National Univ. 1992. Career: dance and movement therapist Clausen House, Oakland 1974-82; adj. faculty: dance and movement therapist, internship supr. J.F.K. Univ., Orinda 1980–, and The Inst. of Trans. Psychol., Aptos 1993–; lectr./coord. Graduate Pgm. in Dance/Movement Therapy, CSU Hayward 1983-92; founder, dir. Authentic Movement Inst., Oakland 1992–; awards: CSU Hayward Affirmative Action grant 1985, 87; mem: Am. Dance Therapy Assn., Calif. Dance Educators Assn., Am. Assn. Univ. Women, Womens Council CSU; publs: fine arts curriculum, 1979-80, coauthor: Clausen House program manual, 1978, Interview Janet Adler, 1993, The Authentic Movement Institute Opens, The Moving Journal, 1994, Authentic Movement: Origins and Theory, Berlin, 1994; Democrat; rec: eastern studies, gardening.

HEADDING, SALLY (LILLIAN SUSAN), author and forensic clairvoyant; b. Jan. 1, 1944, Milw.; d. David Morton and Mary Davis (Berry) Coleman; m. James K. Hill (div. 1976); children: Amy Denise; m. John Murray Headding (div. 1987); edn: BA sociology (GPA 4.0) Univ. Nev., 1975; MA urban affairs, Univ. of Pacific, 1976; cert. Am. Assn. of Profl. Psychics. Career: served in US Women's Army Corps, spl. assignment to G-2 USAPIC, hon. disch. 1963; asst. buyer/jr. exec. tng. pgm. Gimbels, Milw. 1964-65; new store set-up/ops. mgr. Frandisco Corp. of N.Y., 1966-67; store mgr., actg. reg. mgr. Anita Shops (clothing chain), Los Angeles, 1968-69; store mgr., buyer Clothes Closet, (clothing chain), Sunnyvale 1970; human resources devel. Tehachapi State Prison Early Out Parole Pgm., St. Calif., 1971; orgn. co-founder and bd. Community Action Against Rape, Las Vegas, NV 1972-75; owner/opr. Lillian Headding Interiors (commercial medical design), Pittsburg, Calif. 1977-88; mfrs. sales rep. JG West, San Francisco 1989-91; appt. family svs. advy. com. Contra Costa Co. Bd. of Suprs., 1986, numerous city commns., 1976-86; works with police depts. as clairvoyant; recipient commendns. Nevada State Gov., Las Vegas Metro P.D., N.Las Vegas P.D. (1973-74); mem. Calif. Writer's Club (Walnut Creek chpt. pres. 1987-88), Philippine, Hawaiian, and Am. Black Belter's Assn. (life 1973), Am. Assn. of University Women, People for the Ethical Treatment of Animals, Am. Assn. of Profl. Psychics; author, as Sally Davis (novels) Willows End (1988), When Gods Fall (1992), short stories and poetry; Democrat; Jewish. Res: 5333 Park Highlands Blvd #33 Concord 94521

HEADLEE, ROLLAND DOCKERAY, bank founder, business consultant; b. Aug. 27, 1916, Los Angeles; s. Jesse William and Cleora (Dockeray) H.; desc. Thomas Wight, English emigrant to Mass. 1634; stu. UCLA; m. Alzora Burgett, May 13, 1939; children: Linda Ann (Pohl), b. 1946. Career: asst. mgr. Finance Assocs. 1946-59; fin. & bus. cons. R.D. Headlee & Assocs. 1959–; acct. exec. and cons. Walter E. Heller & Co. 1962-65; exec. v.p. Genrus Engring. Corp. 1965-67; exec. dir. Town Hall of California, 1967-1987; cons. 1987–; dir.: Am. Internat. Bank, Mfrs. Assocs., Starfire Engring. Co., (past) Genuss Engring., Jolie Cosmetics; nat. radio pgm. moderator Town Hall on the Air; guest lectr. USC Sch. Engring. 1977, 78; tchr. Comparative Religions 1954-69; honored by formal resolutions US Senate 92d & 95th Sessions, US Cong. 91st Session, Calif. State Assembly (1971, 76), City of Los Angeles 1971; mem: Town Hall (life), Mensa Internat., L.A. World Affairs Council, US Power Squadron, US Coast Guard Aux. (flotilla cmdr.), Commonwealth Club, Newcomen Soc., Com. on Foreign Relations (advy. bd. L.A.), BSA, Oceanic Soc.; editor 11 anthologies re 20+ subjects; guest writer various trade publs.; mil: served to 1st lt. Adj. Gen. Dept. AUS 1943-46, lt.(jg) USCGR post-WWII; Republican; Methodist (adult supt., v.chmn. bd.); rec: skiing, gem/mineral collector, sailing, equestrian. Res: 8064 El Manor Ave Los Angeles 90045 Ofc: Town Hall, R.D. Headlee Associates 523 W Sixth St Ste 232 Los Angeles 90014

HEARNE, JAMES DIXON, professor of education, educational consultant; b. Mar. 17, 1948, Monroe, La.; s. Henry Drew and Wilda Elise (Spillers) H.; edn: BA (magna cum laude), Univ. of St. Thomas, Houston 1972; MA, Pepperdine Univ., 1977; PhD, Claremont Grad. Sch., 1984. Career: tchr., special edn. resource specialist Chino Unified Sch. Dist., Diocese of Orange, 1976-84; instr. in edn. Claremont Graduate Sch., 1984-87; CSU Pomona and CSU San Bernardino, 1987-88; prof. of edn. Whittier Coll., 1988–; ednl. cons., L.A., 1978–; honors: Delta Epsilon Sigma 1974, Phi Alpha Theta 1974, Phi Delta Kappa, Mentor Teacher Corona-Norco Sch. Dist., Teacher of Yr. Compton Unif. Sch. Dist. 1978, 79; mem: Calif. Credential Counselors Assn., Calif. Assn. for Neurologically Handicapped children (state dir. 1985-87), Council for Learning Disabilities (editl. bd. 1984–), Calif. Assn. for Children with Learning Disabilities (editor, state dir. 1985-87), Community Advy. Council Ontario (bd. 1984–); civic: elections supr. L.A. County Registrar of Voters 1978-85; coauthor (textbook) Critical Pedagogy in Special Education, 1990; contbr. 25+ articles in profl. jours. in regular and spl. edn., and field of reading; Republican; R.Cath.; avocation: writer children's stories, lectr. schs. and workshops on topics of literacy, learning disabilities, and critical pedagogy. Res: 2251 Hummingbird Pl Pomona 91767

HEARNE, JOHN Q., business owner, lawyer; b. June 10, 1948, San Francisco; s. John Patrick and Genevieve (Carolan); m. Elizabeth Michaels; children: Jennifer b. 1970; Brendan b. 1979; Megan b. 1983; edn: BA (summa cum laude), UCLA, 1970; JD, Stanford, 1973; admitted bar: Dist. of Col., Calif. Career: owner and chmn. bd. Point Communications Co. 1988–; owner and chmn., Point Broadcasting Co. 1994–; owner and chmn. Gold Coast Broadcasting Co. 1994–; owner Santa Monica Broadcasting Inc. 1976-87; atty. Fisher Wayland Cooper & Leader, assoc. 1977-82, ptnr. 1982-89, of counsel 1990–; honors: Woodrow Wilson Nat. Fellowship 1970, Phi Beta Kappa 1970; mem: Fed. Communications Bar Assn. (chair, numerous coms.), Calif., Dist. of Col., and L.A. Bar Assns., So. Calif. Bdcstrs. Assn., Cellular Telecomms. Industry Assn. (bd. dirs. 1990-94), Surfrider Found., Malibu Surfing Assn., Rotary Club Santa Monica; contbr. articles in communication trade jours.; rec: surfing, swimming, skiing. Ofc: 100 Wilshire Blvd, Suite 1000 Santa Monica 90401

HEARST, RANDOLPH APPERSON, publishing company executive; b. Dec. 2, 1915, NYC; s. William Randolph and Millicent (Willson) H.; m. Catherine Campbell, Jan. 12, 1938, div. 1982; children: Catherine; Virginia; Patricia; Anne; Victoria; m. 2d. Maria C. Scruggs, May 2, 1982, div. 1986; m. Veronica deUribe, July 5, 1987; edn: student, Harvard 1933-34. Career: asst. to ed. Atlanta Georgian 1939-40; asst. to pub. San Francisco Call-Bulletin 1940-44, exec. ed. 1947-49, pub. 1950-53; pres./ dir./ CEO Hearst Consol. Publs., Inc. and Hearst Publ. Co. Inc. 1961-64; chmn. exec. com. The Hearst Corp. 1965-73, chmn. bd. 1973–, dir. 1965–, pres. San Francisco Examiner 1972–; trustee Hearst Found.; clubs: Piedmont Driving (Atlanta), Burlingame CC, Pacific Union; mil: capt. USAAF Air Transport Command 1943-45; Cath. Ofc: 110 5th St San Francisco 94103, and 959 Eighth Ave New York City 10019

HEARST, ROSALIE MAY WYNN, philanthropist/foundation executive; b. Mar. 7, Oklahoma City, Okla.; d. Mathis O. and Audell Bertha (Clary) Wynn; m. George Randolph Hearst, Sr. July 16, 1958; edn: Okla. City Coll., UCLA. Career: Hearst representative U.S. Senate Youth Program; pres. George Randolph Hearst Memorial Found. for Diabetic Edn.; pres. Rosalie Hearst Ednl. Found.; bd. mem. Elvirita Lewis Found.; life mem: Eisenhower Med. Ctr., Pathfinders, Tiempo de Los Ninos, Desert Hosp. Aux., Desert Press Club, College of the Desert Aux., Internat. Orphans; board mem. Pathfinder's Ranch Boys Club; former bd. mem: Friends of Cultural Ctr. of Coll. of the Desert, Joslin Diabetes Found., nat. Assistance League of the Desert, Children's Village USA, Opera Guild, Braille Aux. of the Desert, Warner Guidance Ctr. for Emotionally Disturbed Children, Palm Springs Opera Guild; trustee emeritus: The Bob Hope Cultural Ctr.; coordinator Officers Wives Volunteer Services Dibble Gen. Hosp., Palo Alto; coord. Am. Womens Vol. Services Sawtelle Hosp. L.A.; created Rosalie and George Hearst Fellowship in Ophthalmology UC Berkeley; honors include George and Rosalie Hearst named Man & Woman of Yr. City of Hope 1971, lifetime achiev. in comm. svc. Palm Springs Womens Press Club 1987, distinguished woman Northwood Univ. 1988. Res: 550 Camino del Sur Palm Springs 92262

HEATH, DONALD WAYNE, estate planning specialist; b. June 2, 1942, Wendover, Utah; s. Earl Charles and Violet (Susich) H.; m. Barbara Lyn Beesley, Aug. 11, 1963 (div. Nov. 2, 1979); m. 2d. Laurie Jean Lichter Feb. 28, 1981; children: Jeffery b. 1965, Christian b. 1968, Jill b. 1970, Michele b. 1983, Adam b. 1988, Jason b. 1990; edn: BA, bus. adminstrn., Univ. of Nevada, Reno, 1964; CLU, Am. Coll., Pa., 1972; ChFC, Am. Coll., Pa., 1984; LUTCF, Wash. DC, 1988; C.F.P., Inst. of Cert. Financial Planners, Denver, Colo. 1994. Career: adjunct prof., Univ. of Nevada 1974-80; commr. of ins., State of Nevada 1979-81; sales mgr., NY Life Ins. Co. 1981-83; field v.p., Integrated Resources 1983-84; securities wholesaler, Angeles Corp. 1984-85; v.p., sales, Ins. Office of Am., Inc. 1985; instr., Univ. of the Pacific 1986-87; instr., San Joaquin Delta Coll. 1987-88; reg. v.p., Capstone Fin. Svc., Inc. 1987-88; reg. marketing dir., Ameritas Variable Life Ins. Co. 1988-91; pres., CEO, Heath Fin. Dynamics Corp. 1985-93; estate & bus. ins. splst., Merrill Lynch, San Diego 1992–; awards: listed Who's Who Among Students in Am. Universities & Colleges 1964, Who's Who in Outstanding Young Men of Am., Jaycees 1972, Who's Who in the West 1991; mem: area gov./club pres., Toastmasters Internat., Reno 1970-77; pres., Univ. of Nevada Alumni Assn. 1976, 1983-86; mem, Rotary Internat. 1977-88; comm. chmn., Greater Reno C.of C. 1977-78; comm. chmn., Calif. Assn. of Life Underwriters 1987-88; mem: Nat. Assn. of Ins. Commrs., Passe Club, "Million Dollar Round Table", "Court of the Table", Am. Soc. of CLU & ChFC, Internat. Assn. for Fin. Planning, Nat. Assn. of Life Underwriters, Nat. Assn. of Securities Dealers, Advance Life Underwriting Assn., WDC 1994; mil: capt., US Army 1965-70; rec: fishing, camping. Ofc: Merrill Lynch 2400 Imperial Bank Tower 701 B St. San Diego 92101

HEAVENSTON, DEBRA BELZER, college personnel administrator; b. Aug. 31, 1953, Chgo.; d. Charles Henry and Joanne Ruth (Franz) Belzer; m. Wilson Palmer Heavenston, Mar. 9, 1985; edn: BA, Univ. La Verne, 1988. Career: office mgr. Century 21 Moulton Realtors, Pasadena; asst. Lewis Homes/Republic Management, Upland 1978-80; adminstrv. asst., office mgr. Coll. Osteopathic Medicine of the Pacific, Pomona 1980-83; staff acct. Harvey Mudd Coll., Claremont 1984-87, personnel adminstr. 1987–; mem. Coll. and Univ. Personnel Assn.; rec: int. design. Ofc: Harvey Mudd College 301 E Twelfth St Claremont 91711

HECK, OTTO LUDWIG, manufacturing company executive; b. Aug. 10, 1920, Germany, nat. US cit. 1943; s. Ludwig and Hedwig Clementine H.; m. Barbara, May 31, 1942; 1 dau. Susanne b. 1947. Career: mgr. customer svc. Angelus Sanitary Can Machine Co., 1960–, v.p. Customer Svc. 1969–, v.p. ops. 1978–, exec. v.p./secty. 1980–, pres./chief ops. 1983-87, chmn./CEO 1987–; dir: Angelus Sanitary Can Machine Co., Angelus Export Co., dir./pres. Angelus Corp. Internat., dir./sec.treas. Henry L. Guenther Found.; mem: Food Industries Internat. Trade Council (dir.), Nat. Assn. of Mfrs., Food Processing Mach. & Suppliers Assn., Old Guard Soc. (FPM & SA), The Presidents Assn., Master Brewers Assn. of Am., U.S. Brewers Assn. (Beer Inst.), The Packaging Inst. of USA, Fgn. Trade Assn. of So. Calif.; mem. U.S. C.of C., Calif. C.of C., Vernon C.of C., 552 Club of Hoag Hosp., Masons, Balboa Bay Club, B.P.O.E.; mil: T5 US Army Engrs. 1943-46, decorated Presdl. Citation, Am. Theatre rib., ETO rib. w/clusters, Victory rib., Expert Rifleman, Good Conduct medal; Republican; Prot.; rec: golf, stamp collection; ofc: Angelus Sanitary Can Machine Co 4900 Pacific Blvd Los Angeles 90058

HEDBERG, THOMAS MICHAEL, psychotherapist, author, cleric; b. Dec. 21, 1938, Los Angeles; s. Robert Bernard and Catherine Meriam (Nolan) H.; edn: BSC, Univ. Santa Clara 1960; MRE, relig. edn., Pontifical Josephinum 1970; MA, Loyola Univ. 1976; PhD, Sierra Univ. 1988; ordained Salesian priest (S.D.B.) 1971; Reg. Poetry Therapist (RPT) 1993. Career: editor, author, poet The Literary G.H.Q. 1964-66; currently sr. psychotherapist and chmn. med. edn. com., Psychiatric Behavioral Health Prog.; supr.psychiatric progs., Daniel Freeman Marina Hosp.; also pvt. practice, So. Calif.; U.S.A. presenter from Nat. Assn. for Poetry Therapy at Internat. Conf. on Creative Arts in Psychotherapy, Edn. and Medicine, St. Petersburg, Russia 1994; bd. dirs. co-chair Center for Sacred Psychology 1983–; bd. dirs. Nat. Assn. of Poetry Therapists 1995– (chair, edn. com.); mem: (YES) Youth Encounter Spirit Inc. (chmn., founder, bd. dirs. 1971), Analytical Psychology Club-C.G. Jung Inst. of L.A. (bd. dirs. 1986), St. Josephs Renewal Center (bd. dirs. 1977-87, v.p. bd. dirs. 1979-83); co-author: Coming Home (Paulist Press 1986), At a Dream Workshop (ibid 1987), case study: Catholicism and Jungian Psychology (Falcon Press 1988), first "Code of Ethics for Spiritual Directors" in U.S. (1990); Catholic; spl. interest: reading med. and legal mysteries, mythology, fairytales, Jungian psychology; rec: swimming, walking, racquetball, tennis, paddle tennis, biking, traveling to study fgn. cultures, music, poetry, book stores. Res: 833 21 St Santa Monica 90403 Ofc: Center for Sacred Psychology POB 643 Gateway Station Culver City 90232

HEINE, LYMAN H., university professor; b. June 18, 1940, Fremont, Nebr.; s. Lyman H. and Ceola Catherine (Edinger) H.; m. Ardis M.; edn: BA, Johns Hopkins Univ. 1962; MA, Univ. Neb. 1966; PhD, 1970. Career: prof. political sci. CSU Fresno 1968; awards: CSU Bd. Trustees 1987-89, 1989-91. Ofc: California State University Dept. of Political Science Fresno 93740

HEINRICH, MILTON ROLLIN, biochemist; b. Nov. 25, 1919, Linton, N.Dak.; s. Fred and Emma (Becker) H.; m. Ramona G. Cavanagh, May 31, 1966; edn: AB, Univ. S.Dak., Vermillion 1941; MS, Univ. of Iowa, 1942, PhD, 1944. Career: NIH postdoc. fellow Univ. Pa., Phila. 1947-49; research assoc. Amherst Coll., 1949-57; NIH senior postdoc. fellow UC Berkeley, 1958-60; asst. prof. biochemistry Univ. So. Calif., Los Angeles 1960-63; branch chief, project scientist NASA, Ames Research Ctr., Moffett Field, 1963-85; cons. Lockheed Missiles & Space, Sunnyvale 1985–; pres. Zerog Corp., Los Altos Hills 1985-91; honors: Phi Beta Kappa, Sigma Xi, Phi Lambda Upsilon, Cosmos Group award NASA 1981, 1984, Space Station Group award NASA 1984, Fellow Explorers Club (NY); mem.: Am. Soc. Biochem. & Molecular Biology 1958–, Am. Chemical Soc. 1942–, Am. Soc. Gravitational & Space Biology 1987–; author numerous book chapters and research papers; editor: Extreme Environments (1976), co-editor: Cosmos 1129 Mission, Plants & Radiation (1981), Cosmos 1129 Mission, Rat Expts. (1981); mil: ltjg USNR 1944-47; rec: travel, photography. Res: 27200 Deer Springs Way Los Altos Hills 94022

HEINZE, RUTH-INGE, researcher, author, motivator; b. Nov. 4, 1919, Berlin, Germany, naturalized U.S. citizen 1962; d. Otto Albert and Louise Auguste (Preschel) Heinze; edn: BA, UC Berkeley, 1969, MA, 1971, PhD, 1974. Career: lectr. Mills Coll., Oakland 1974; res. assoc. UC Berkeley, 1974–; staff research asst. Univ. Calif., San Francisco 1975; res. fellow Inst. of Southeast Asian Studies, Singapore 1978-79; prof. Calif. Inst. of Integral Studies, S.F. 1984–, prof. Saybrook Inst., S.F. 1985–; producer Universal Dialogue, Berkeley 1979–; nat. dir. Independent Scholars of Asia, 1981–; dir. Oakland Asian Cultural Ctr., 1987-93; awards: grantee UCB 1969-73, travel grantee Am. Inst. of Indian

Studies, W.D.C. (1975, 78), Fulbright-Hays res. grantee, Singapore 1978-79; mem: Assn. for Asian Studies 1974–, Internat. Assn. for the Study of Traditional Asian Medicine 1988–, Parapsychology Res. Group 1984–, Calif. Soc. for Psychical Study 1984–, Spiritual Emergency Network 1984–, Nat. Pictographic Soc. 1989–, Spiritual Emergency Network 1990–, Nat. Coalition of Independent Scholars 1994–, Internat. Soc. for the Study of Subtle Energies & Energy Medicine 1994–, Internat. Soc. for Shamanic Res. 1993–; author: Visions to Live By, 1994, Shamans of the 20th Century, 1991, Trance & Healing in SEA Today, 1988, Tham Khwan-How to Contain the Essence of Life, 1982; editor (book) Proceedings of the Internat. Conf. on the Study of Shamanism & Alt. Modes of Healing, 1984-95; rec: use of sound in healing, acupuncture, Chinese herbal medicine, Reiki. Res: 2321 Russell St #3A Berkeley 94705-1959

HELMBOLD, WILLIAM ROSS, lawyer, educator; b. March 17, 1947, Cincinnati.; s. Wm. Wallace and Muriel Mary (Washington) H.; m. Nancy, Jan. 7, 1968; son, Jonathan b. 1970; edn: BS cum laude, Calif. Lutheran Univ. 1972; JD, Calif. Western Sch. Law 1975; admitted Bar: Calif. 1976, US Dist. Cts. Calif. so. dist. 1977, cent. dist. 1982, US Supreme Ct. 1980. Career: dep. pub. defender Ventura Co. Pub. Defenders Office 1977-80; pvt. practice atty. prin., offices in Ventura, Victorville and Westlake Village, 1980-93, Redding 1995–; prof. dept. of grad. studies (MBA) Calif. Lutheran Univ., 1977-88; judge pro tem Ventura Co. Municipal and Superior Cts. 1980-93; awards: Ventura Co. Legal Sectys. Assn. Boss of Year award 1980, Outstanding Trial Atty. Ventura Co. Pub. Defenders Office 1977-80, Calif. Western Sch. Law Internat. Law Jour. 1973-75, Calif. Luth. Univ. Dept. Mgmt. and Econ. outstanding departmental student graduate award 1972, listed Who's Who in Am. Law 1989-95, Who's Who in The World 1991-95, Who's Who in Calif. 1989-96, Who's Who in Am. Edn. 1991-95; mem: Am. Bar Assn., Ventura Co. Bar Assn., Ventura Co. Criminal Defense Bar Assn. (bd. 1984-85, 87-92), ALS Soc. Ventura Co. (founding trustee; pres. 1989-92), Ventura Co. Lawyer Referral Service; works: Mark F. v. Superior Ct. Calif., 234 Calif. Reporter 388 (1987) changed juvenile law in Calif. regarding drunk driving cases; mil: s/sgt. USAF 1967-71; Republican; Prot.; rec: golf. Ofc: Law Office Ross Helmbold 1721 Court St Redding 96001

HELSPER, JAMES THOMAS, surgeon, medical researcher, educator; b. Mar. 29, 1924, Mpls.; s. Salvius John and Gretchen Louise (Gleissner) H.; m. 2d. Carolyn Harrison, Dec. 26, 1975; children: James Thomas, Jr. b. 1955, Richard Scott b. 1957, Paige Carla b. 1961, Brian Harrison b. 1981; edn: BS, St. Vincent Coll., Latrobe, Pa. 1945; MD, Jefferson Med. Coll. 1947; grad. stu. Univ. of Penn. 1949-50. Career: med. intern Medical Ctr., Jersey City 1947-48, internal medicine resident 1948-49; surgery resident US Naval Hosp. Portsmouth, Va. 1951-52, Queens Hosp. N.Y.C. 1952-53, Memorial Ctr. for Cancer N.Y.C. 1953-57; former asst. clin. prof. surgery, Loma Linda Univ. Sch. of Medicine; emeritus assoc. clin. prof. tumor surgery, USC Sch. of Medicine, Los Angeles; attdg. surgeon L.A. County/USC Med. Ctr., chief surgical tng. service Huntington Memorial Hosp. 1962–, Kenneth Norris Jr. Cancer Hosp.; Huntington Med. Research Insts. 1982–; mem: Am. Cancer Soc. (bd. dirs. Calif. div. 1967–, pres. L.A. County Unit 1970-71), AMA, Calif. Med. Assn. (cancer com.), L.A. Co. Med. Soc. (com. on cancer), Pasadena Med. Soc., L.A. Surgical Soc., Am. Soc. Clin. Oncology, Soc. Surgical Oncology, Soc. Head & Neck Surgeons (pres. 1988-89), Am. Radium Soc., Am. Coll. Surgeons, Pan-Pacific Surgical Assn., Flying Physicians Assn.; mem. internat. sci. advy. com. UICC; research: devel. Stoma Button (named for author) for laryngectomy patients; contbr. numerous articals in med. jours., article in Aero mag. (9/77); mil: capt. USNR-Ret. 1984, Active (1943-45, 1950-52); Republican; R.Cath.; rec: flying, photography. Res: 580 Arbor St Pasadena 91105 Ofc: 50 Bellefontaine St Pasadena 91105

HEM, JOHN DAVID, research chemist; b. May 14, 1916, Starkweather, N.Dak.; s. Hans Neilius and Josephine Augusta (Larsen) H.; m. Ruth Evans, Mar. 11, 1945 (dec. May 1987); children: John D. b. 1948, Michael b. 1949; edn: undergrad. Minot St. Univ. 1932-36, N.Dak. State Univ. 1937-38, Iowa State Univ. 1938; BS chemistry, George Washington Univ., W.D.C. 1940; Career: chemist Water Resources Div., US Geological Survey, 1940–; analytical chemist in Safford, Az. (1940-42, 43-45), Roswell, N.M. 1942-43, Albuquerque 1945-47, dist. chemist in Albuquerque 1948-53, res. chemist in Denver, Colo. 1953-63, in Menlo Park, Calif. 1963–; instr. in-house tng. facility USGS, Denver 1970-80, research advisor Water Research Com., USGS, Menlo Park (1974-79, 84–); awards: US Interior Dept. meritorious service, distinguished service 1976, 80, Nat. Water Well Assn. science award 1986, O.E. Meinzer award Geologic Soc. Am., Boulder 1990, Special award Internat. Assn. of Geochem. & Cosmochem. 1992; mem: Am. Chemical Soc. (50-yr. mem.), Am. Geophysical Union 1945–, Geochemical Soc.(1951–, Am. Water Works Assn. 1952–, Soc. for Geochemistry and Health 1975–; author: Study & Interpretation of the Chemical Characteristics of Natural Water (1959, 2d ed. 1970, 3d ed. 1985), 100+ book chapters and articles on water chemistry. 1945–; Democrat; Lutheran (coun. mem., chmn. Holy Shepherd Luth., Lakewood, Colo. 1957-60, coun. Grace Luth. Ch., Palo Alto, Ca. 1975-77; rec: singing choral music. Res: 3349 Saint Michael Ct Palo Alto 94306 Ofc: USGS 345 Middlefield MS427 Menlo Park 94025

HEMMINGS, PETER WILLIAM, opera company executive; b. Apr. 10, 1934, London, England; s. William and Rosalind Alice Mary (Jones) H.; m. Jane Frances Kearnes, May 19, 1962; children: William b. 1965, Lucy b. 1966, Emma b. 1969, Rupert b. 1970, Sophie b. 1973; edn: undergrad. Mill Hill Sch., London 1947-52; MA, classics, Gonville and Caius Coll., Cambridge, 1957. Career: clk. Harold Holt Ltd., London 1957-59; first general mgr. New Opera Company, Sadler's Wells Theatre, London, 1957-65, personal asst. to gen. mgr. then repertory and planning mgr. Sadlers Wells Opera, 1959-65; gen. adminstr. Scottish Opera, Glasgow 1962-77, spearhd. reopening Glasgow's Theatre Royal 1975; gen. mgr. Australian Opera, Sydney 1977-79; mng. director London Symphony Orch., London 1980-84; gen. director Los Angeles Music Center Opera, L.A. 1984–; gen. cons. Compton Verney Opera Project, Eng. 1988–; bd. mem. Sadlers Wells Assn., W.D.C. 1988 (pres. 1994–), Royal Acad. of Music, London 1981–, Opera America, W.D.C. 1989–; v.p. Opera America 1993-95; honors: pres. Univ. Opera Group, Cambridge 1956-57, Hon. LL.D., Strathclyde Univ., Glasgow 1978, Fellow Royal Scottish Acad. of Music, Glasgow 1978, Hon. Fellow Royal Acad. of Music, London 1992; club: Garrick (London); works: bdcstr. Digital Planet, Calif., 1992; mil: lt. Royal Signals, 1952-54; Anglican. Res: 775 S Madison Ave Pasadena 91106 Ofc: Los Angeles Music Center Opera, 135 N Grand Ave Los Angeles 90012

HEMPY, MARIE WILLETT, real estate broker; b. May 2, 1930, Chicago, Ill.; d. William Arthur and Florence Amelia (Baehler) Willett; m. William Daniel Hempy, Nov. 12, 1955 (div. 1979); children: Daniel Willett b. 1956, David William b. 1958, Robert Michael b. 1961; edn: BA cum laude, UCSB 1952; MA, UCLA 1953. Career: producer, writer McClatchy Bdcstg., Sacto. 1953-56; co-owner RAMA World Silk Screens, Riverside 1970-74; instr. Riverside Comm. Coll. 1974-77; sales agt. Hallmark West Realty 1977-81; co-owner Shelter West Realty 1981-88, broker 1988–; pres. and gen. mgr. Cal-I 1988–; Sunhaven Escrow Inc. 1988–; bd. dirs. Riverside Community Coll. Dist. Devel. Corp. 1987–, pres. 1991-92; awards: Hallmark West Realty Sales Person of Year (1978-80), Shelter West Realty Sales Person of Year (1982, 84, 85), Riverside Area Bd. Realtors Top 10 Sales (1985, 87); mem: Calif. Assn. Realtors, Nat. Assn. Realtors, Mensa, Soroptimist Internat. Riverside (past pres.), Riverside Community Players, Riverside Art Alliance, Riverside Folk Song Soc., Why Nots. Actor's Co., Riverside Inter-Ch. Drama Group; Prot.; rec: photog., travel. Res: 1453 Tiger Tail Dr Riverside 92506 Ofc: Shelter West Realty 5885 Brockton Riverside 92506

HENDERSON, ROBBE LYNN, educator, psychometrician; b. Nov. 19, 1946, Chgo.; d. Robert Ogden Henderson, Edward (stepf.) and Irene Delores (Parks) Foster; edn: BA, We. Mich. Univ., 1969; MEd, Univ. Ill. Urbana 1972, PhD, 1982. Career: Spanish tchr. H.S., Chgo. (Ill.) Bd. of Edn., 1969-71, Bilingual tchr., 1971-73; reg. supr. Ill. Ofc. of Edn., Chgo., 1973-80; dir. of research Garfield Park Mental Health, Chgo., 1980-81; dir. curriculum devel. City Colleges Chgo., 1981-82; asst., assoc. prof. Western Ill. Univ., Macomb, 1982-86; vis. prof. Univ. Calif. Riverside, 1986-87; adj. prof. Univ. of San Diego, 1987-88; assoc. prof. CSU Dominguez Hills, Carson, Calif. 1988-92, full tenured prof. 1992- (coord. ed. adm. prog 1993–), elected chair, Grad. Dept. of Edn. and coord. Edn. Adminstrn. Prog. 1995–; cons. to West Indies Edn., Jamaica, W.I., 1970; liaison to Ministry of Edn., Toronto, Can. 1974; cons. Dillingham Assoc., Chgo., 1974-86; cons. U.S. Dept. of Labor, assigned to Spain, N.Africa, Canary Is., 1979-80; cons. U.S. Dept. Edn., 1976–; evaluator Rockford (Ill.) Sch. Dist., 1975–; awards: Spelling Bee champion Chicago Daily News 1956, singer Morris Sachs TV Amateur, Chgo. 1958, legislative scholar State of Ill. 1960, Sweetheart Alpha Sphinxmen Champaign 1964, Sweetheart Kappa Scrollers Champaign 1965, v.p. Assn. Women Students WMU 1967-69, Homecoming Queen Court WMU 1968, Who's Who Am. Colls. & Univs. 1969, Minority Grad. Fellow Univ. Ill., Urbana 1970-72, outstanding svc. Crete-Monee Sch., Ill. 1974, regl. supt.'s award Kankakee (Ill.) Schs. 1975, Minority Fellow Univ. Ill. 1978-80, Phi Delta Kappa 1978, Order of Omega WIU-Students 1983, Edn. Profl. Leadership Fellows, W.D.C. 1984, outstanding tchr. WIU Student Body 1984, outstanding black faculty WIU -APHIA 1986, IMAGES Award Profl. 1987, tchg. award City Colls. San Diego (summer 87, 88), AA res. grantee CSUDH 1988-92, Academic Senate CSU Dominguez Hills (v.p. 1990-92, parliamentarian 92-94) and GWE or GWAR Sch. of Edn. rep. 1994-95, Lyle E. Gibson Disting. Tchr. of Year 1992-93, Phi Delta Kappa del. 1994-95 (Leadership Inst. 1995, v.p. membership 1995-96); mem: AERA, NABE, TESOL, ASCD, CAPEA; journal reviewer, CAPEA Jour. 1994–; publs: translator (Children's Sci. series) "Now You Know" Ency. Brit. (1972), jour. article NABE (1986). Ofc: Calif. State Univ. Dominguez Hills HFA B-104 School of Education Carson 90747

HENDLER, GORDON LEE, curator; b. Dec. 11, 1946, New York; s. Jack and Charlotte (Weinstein) H.; edn: BA, Rutgers Univ. 1968; PhD, Univ. Conn. 1973. Career: dir. Galeta Marine Lab. Smithsonian Inst., Panama 1976-78; supr. Smithsonian Oceanographic Sorting Center, Wash., D.C. 1978-85; assoc. curator Los Angeles Co. Nat. Hist. Museum, 1985-88; head. sect. of intertebrates, Natural History Museum 1988; advisor Diseases of Aquatic Organisms 1987; awards: LACM Dirs. Prize 1986-87; mem: AAAS, Am. Soc. Zoologists, WSN, ESA; num. research articles pub. in sci. jours. Ofc: Natural History Museum 900 Exposition Blvd Los Angeles 90007

HENDRICKSON, THOMAS ROY, architect; b. Sept. 29, 1951, Seattle, Wash.; s. Laurie John and Rose Josephine (Helina) H.; m. Lana Shull, Jan. 12, 1973; children: Aaron b. 1973, Charity b. 1975, Melody b. 1976; edn: BA environmental design, Univ. Wash. 1973; reg. arch. Wash., Calif. 1984. Career: designer Olympic Assoc. Seattle & Richland, Wash. (nuclear projects incl. fusion reactor planning) 1978-82; project arch. Ehrlich-Rominger Archs. Los Altos (hi-tech micro-electronics projects in Calif., NY, Mass.) 1982-86; project arch. George Miers & Assocs. (Novato City Hall, Park Place rental condominiums), S.F. 1986-87; assoc. McLellan & Copenhagen, Cupertino, Calif. & Seattle, Wash. (Fred Hutchinson Cancer Res. Ctr., Univ. Sci. Facilities, Lifescan, UCLA Chem/Bio, Biotech. Projects), 1987–; honors: Seattle Times Open House 1981; mem: Am. Inst. Archs. (contg. edn. com. 1985), Bay Vista Town Homes Assn. (dir., v.p.); Solar Master Conserver Wash. State 1981; US Solar Demo. Proj. 1976, Lab of the Yr. 1994; Christian; rec: internat. travel, skiing. Res: 142 Shooting Star Isle Foster City 94404 Ofc: McLellan & Copenhagen, 10051 Pasadena Ave Cupertino 95014

HENEBRY, JOHN PAUL, JR., private investigator; b. Feb. 1, 1964, Los Angeles s. John P. and La Verne M. (Phillips) H.; m. Holly Schaefer; edn: MS bus. entrepreneurship (cum laude, Phi Kappa Psi), USC. Career: v.p. mktg. Pacific Inspections, Inc. (insurance inspections and investigations) Los Angeles; pres. Commercial Concepts Inc. (comml. prodn. co.); mem. World Assn. of Detectives; mem. So. Calif. Underwriters Assn.; clubs: Assoc. Reporting Cos of Am. (pres. 1994), L.A. Athletic, Hollywood Magic Castle (life), Blue Goose Calif. Pond; Republican; R.Cath. Res: 26700 Indian Peak Rd Rancho Palos Verdes 90274 Ofc: Pacific Inspections, Inc. 1212 N Vermont Ave Los Angeles 90029

HENRIKSEN, THOMAS HOLLINGER, educator, administrator; b. Nov. 16, 1939, Detroit; s. Paul and Irene (Hollinger) H.; m. Margaret Mary Mueller, Sept. 9, 1968; children: Heather Anne, Damien Paul; edn: BA, Va. Mil. Inst., 1962; MA, PhD, Mich. State Univ., 1966, 1969. Career: asst. prof. State Univ. N.Y., Plattsburgh, 1969-73, assoc. prof. 1973-79, prof. 1979-80; Peace fellow Hoover Instn. on War, Revolution and Peace, Stanford Univ., 1979-80, research fellow 1980-82, assoc. dir. 1983–, senior res. fellow 1982-86, senior fellow 1986–; exec. secty. Nat. Fellows Program 1984–; appt. Pres.'s Commn. on White House Fellows 1987–; trustee George Marshall Found. 1993–; mem. U.S. Army Sci. Bd. 1984-90; author: The New World Order: War, Peace, and Military Preparedness, 1992, Mozambique's War of Independence, 1964-74 (1983); coauthor: The Struggle for Zimbabwe: Battle in the Bush, 1981; contbg. editor: Soviet and Chinese Aid to African Nations, 1980, Communist Powers in Sub-Saharan Africa, 1981, One Korea? Challenges and Prospects for Reunification, 1994; contbr. articles to profl. jours.; mil: lt. AUS 1963-65. Res: 177 Lundy Ln Palo Alto 94306 Ofc: Hoover Institution, Stanford University, Stanford 94305

HENSEL, JEFFREY, geologist; b. Nov. 15, 1962, Detroit; s. Manfred Karl and Liane Bertha (Frueck) H.; m. Kimberly Ann Habel, Sept. 6, 1986; children: Rachael, b. 1990; Kayla, b. 1993; edn: BS geology, Wayne State Univ., 1984; MS environmental studies, CSU Fullerton, 1992; reg. geologist Calif., Ky. and Wy., reg. environmental assessor Cal-EPA, 1990. Career: geologist GMC Associates, Inc. Northville, Mich. 1985-86; BCL Associates, Inc. Huntington Beach 1986-89; Radian Corp., Irvine 1989–; awards: indsl. arts, State of Mich. 1980; mem: Nat. Water Well Assn. 1989–, Ducks Unlimited 1981–; publs: tech. abstracts (1982, 83, 84, 92); Republican; R.Cath.; rec: softball. Ofc: Radian Corp. 16845 Von Karman Ave Ste 100 Irvine 92714

HENSTELL, HENRY H., physician, medical consultant; b. Jan. 27, 1909, New York; s. Raphael H. and Frances (Turner) H.; m. Harriet J. Jares, Feb. 5, 1974; children: Bruce b. 1944, Lisa b. 1950; edn: BS, Yale Univ. 1930; MD, Yale Sch. Medicine 1933. Career: pvt. practice medicine, hematology, Los Angeles 1938-88; cons. internal medicine and hematology 1938; chief hematology clinic Cedars Lebanon Hosp. 1938-62; instr. USC, Los Angeles 1939-41; Coll. Med. Evangelists 1939-41; asst. clin. prof. medicine USC Med. Sch. 1944-68; founder Hematology Clinic, Cedars Lebanon Hosp. 1938; co-founder ARC Blood Donor System 1940; created and ran Blood Bank for Israel 1948; awards: Tufts Med. Sch. Charlton fellow 1937-38; mem: A.C.P. (fellow), Am. Soc. Hematology (founding mem.), Internat. Soc. Hematology (founding mem.), Leukemia Soc. Am. (founding mem. western branch 1967); 50+ research papers pub. in med. jours., 1938-75; mil: enlisted AUS, 1939, served to capt. AUS MC, hon. discharge for physical disability, 1945; Democrat; Jewish; rec: electronics, mechanics, travel. Address: 10131 Angelo Circle Beverly Hills, CA 90210

HEPLER, MARTIN EUGENE, management analyst/consultant; b. Oct. 4, 1949, Lancaster, Pa.; s. James Painter and Janet Marie (Hess) H.; m. Rose Ann Baldo, Apr. 14, 1990; edn: AA, Miramar Coll. 1977; BS, San Diego St. Univ., 1980, MPA, 1983; grad. indsl. engring. tech. Career: prodn. mgr. Cerebronic Inc., San Diego 1973-74; aircraft engine tech. Naval Air Rework Facility, San Diego 1974-80, indsl. engring. tech. 1980-83, pgm. coord. 1983-85, internal cons. 1985-86, Total Quality Mgr. 1986-90, TQM dir. General Dynamic Space Systems Div., 1990-91; Total Quality Mgr. NAS Miramar; mgmt. cons./pres. Brenman Assocs., San Diego 1984–, instr. UCSD 1991–; bd. dirs. Clairemont Friendship, S.D. 1978-80; honors: Phi Alpha Alpha 1983, Meritorious Civilian Service Award

1993; mem: Deming Users Group (pres. 1984–), Western Criminology Soc. (life), Internat. Assn. of Quality Circles (S.D. chpt. dir.), V.F.W. (life), Nat. Riflemans Assn.; civic: Zoo Soc. S.D. 1979–, Heart Assn. (instr. 1976–); publ: Internat. Assn. of Quality Circle Transactions 1984; mil: USNR-R AFCM (AW) 1968–; Democrat; R.Cath.; rec: scuba, waterski, run. Ofc: Brenman Assocs. Consultants International 14560 Vintage Dr San Diego 92129

HERGERT, MICHAEL L., professor of management; b. Nov. 17, 1954, Oakland; s. Harvey L. and Catherine (Monahan) H.; m. Robin Leslie Browne, May 29, 1982; 1 dau., Stephanie b. 1986; edn: BA, Kalamazoo Coll. 1976; MA, Harvard Univ. 1983; PhD, Harvard Univ. 1983. Career: cons. DRI, Lexington, Mass. 1976-79; McKinsey & Co., Duesseldorf, Germany 1979; prof. Insead, Fountainebleau, France 1983-85; San Diego St. Univ. 1985; coauthor: Surviving Merger & Acquisition, 1988, 20+ articles pub. in scholarly jours. Res: 22 Port Royale Rd Coronado 92118

HERLIHY, JOHN FRANCIS, judge; b. Dec. 17, 1949, Atlanta, Ga.; s. James Thomas and Helen Marie (Savoie) H.; m. Mary Ann M. LaPorta, Sept. 4, 1971; children: Shannon b. 1977, Jennifer b. 1980; edn: BA w. distinction, San Jose St. Univ. 1971; JD, UCSF Hastings Coll. of Law 1974. Career: atty. Hansen & Herlihy, Los Altos 1974-76; dept. dist. atty. Santa Clara Co. Dist. Attys. Office, San Jose 1976-80; ct. commr. Santa Clara Co. Mcpl. Ct. 1980-83, judge 1983–; instr. Santa Clara Univ. Law Sch. 1984–; Hastings Trial Advocacy Coll., S.F. 1979, 81; Foothill Coll., Los Altos 1975-80; presiding judge Santa Clara Co. Mcpl. Ct. 1986-87; awards: Santa Clara Univ. Contbn. to Trial Advocacy, Calif. Parol Probation & Correctional Ofcrs. Contbn. 1987, Hastings Coll. Quarterly editl. assoc. 1973, Moot Ct. Competition winner 1973; mem: St. Thomas More Soc. (past v.p.), Calif. Judges Assn., Sentencing Alternative Program (bd. dirs., 1st pres. and chmn., pres. 1989-90), Kenna Club Santa Clara Univ., San Jose Hist. Museum (former bd. dirs.), Friends of Cupertino Library, Santa Clara Co. Law Library (former bd. trustees), Justice Systems Advy. Bd., Mayor of San Jose-Gang Task force 1991–, San Jose Conservation Corps 1995–; num. articles pub. in profl. jours., 1973–; mil: capt. Calif. Army Nat. Guard 1980-85; Cath.; rec: skiing, tennis, gardening. Ofc: Santa Clara County Superior Court 191 N First St San Jose 95113

HERMAN, MICHAEL ALAN, musician, music educator, entertainment executive; b. Jan. 11, 1945, Davenport, Iowa; s. William Watt and Leona Lillian (Markovitch) H.; m. Willitte Hisami Ishii, Nov. 23, 1980; edn: Univ. Iowa, 1963-67. Career: bdcstr. host WSUI Radio/TV, Univ. of Iowa, Iowa City, 1964-65; freelance musician, folk and blues, nat. 1965–; guitar tchr., Oakland, Calif. 1973–; owner, entertainment coord., producer Redwood Music, Oakland 1973-92, Topaz Productions, 1992–; entertainment chmn. Mill Valley Fall Arts Fest., Mill Valley 1980–; entertainment coord. San Francisco Folk Music Club, S.F. 1980-85; educator "Blues in the Schools" program 1986–; entertainment cons. Mississippi Valley Blues Soc., Davenport, Ia. 1989–; awards: scholarship Am. Conservatory Theatre, S.F. 1970, cert. merit Nat. Traditional Country Music Found., Council Bluffs, Ia. 1986-88, hon. mention Am. Song Fest., L.A. 1986; mem: Mississippi Valley Blues Soc. 1988–, Quad Cities Friends of the Heritage Arts 1989–, Freedom Song Network (musician, orgnzr., arranger 1986–); civic vol. Helping Hands Proj., S.F. 1990–; Bread & Roses, Mill Valley 1992–; publs: musician, songwriter, arranger, prod. (audio cassette albums): Everyday Living, 1989, Cow-Cow Boogie, 1992, Blues Alive!, 1992; songwriter (songs): Rock Island, 1975, Truckstop Blues, 1986, Phantom of the Jukebox, 1987, Rocket to Chicago, 1989, Man Or Mouse, 1989, New Crossroads, 1989, Abuser's Test, 1990, Blues for Satchell Paige, 1990, Black Drawers, 1990, Hero's Blues, 1991, Give Me A Granma Every Time, 1991, The Great Flood of '93, 1993; composer (video soundtrack): How Not To Get Elected, 1990, Christmas In April, 1991; arranger musical score, performer (play) Smokin', 1990, arranger musical score, composer, performer (play) El Paso Blue, 1994, musical dir., performer (play) El Paso Blue, 1995; Democrat; rec: fishing, rock hounding, collect guitars, walking, reading. Res: 3416 Coolidge Ave Oakland 94602-3202 Ofc: Topaz Productions PO Box 2725 Oakland 94602

HERNANDEZ, JO FARB, museum and curatorial consultant; b. Nov. 20, 1952, Chgo.; d. Leonard and Leanora (Kohn) Farb; m. Sam Hernandez, Sept. 5, 1976; 1 dau. Larissa Anne b. 1988; edn: BA polit. sci./French (with honors), Univ. Wis., 1974; MA in folklore, UCLA, 1975; cert. museum mgmt. UC Berkeley, 1981. Career: registr. Mus. of Cultural History, L.A. 1974-75; Rockefeller fellow Dallas Mus. of Fine Art, Dallas, Tx. 1976-77; asst. dir. Triton Mus. of Art, Santa Clara, Calif. 1977, dir. 1978-85; dir. Monterey Peninsula Mus. of Art, 1985-93; cons. curator Monterey Peninsula of Art 1994-95; museum and curatorial cons. 1994–; lectr. various museums and univs. internat., 1975–; grants panelist U.S.I.A., W.D.C. 1992, Calif. Arts Council, Sacto. 1983-86, 88-90, 92; museum assessment surveyor Am. Assn. of Museums, W.D.C. 1990–; exec. com. We. Museums Conf. (1989-91, pgm. chair L.A., 1990); awards: Golden Eagle C.I.N.E., W.D.C. 1992, Ralph C. Altman Award Mus. of Cultural History UCLA 1975, special exhibitions NEA, W.D.C. 1984-93, gen. op. support, conservation awards Inst. of Mus. Svs., W.D.C. 1985, 86, 91, 92, Leader of the Decade-Arts Leadership Monterey Peninsula 1992, guest on various TV and radio programs; mem.: Calif. Assn. of Museums (v.p. 1985-91, pres.

1991-92), Artable 1986–, Am. Assn. of Museums 1977– (mus. assessment prog. surveyor 1990, 94; nat. prog. com. 1992-93); reader Columbia Univ. Press 1994; art historian, videos, Monterey Peninsula Mus. of Art, Mendocino Co. Mus.; author: The Day of The Dead: Tradition & Change in Contemporary Mexico, 1979, Mexican Indian Dance Masks, 1982, Three from the Northern Island: Contemporary Sculpture from Hokkaido, 1984, Crime & Punishment: Reflections of Violence in Contemporary Art, 1984, Mark Walker: From Old Timer to New Timer, 1989, Jeremy Anderson: The Critical Link/A Quiet Revolution, 1995; co-author: New Furnishings, 1985; intro., editor 20 books including Colors & Impressions: E. Charlton Fortune, 1989, The Expressive Sculpture of Alvin Light, 1990, The Quiet Eye: Pottery of Shoji Hamada & Bernard Leach, 1990, Alan Shepp: The Language of Stone, 1991. Ofc: 345 White Rd Watsonville 95076

HERNANDEZ, LEOPOLDO HERNANDO, lawyer; b. Apr. 6, 1947, Havana, Cuba, nat. 1985; s. Ruben Aurelio Hernandez and Elena Antonia (Ramos) Ledon; m. Alita Marie Lewis, Apr. 10, 1982; children: Alice Marie b. 1987, Lucy Ellen b. 1988; edn: BS, Woodbury Univ., 1974, JD, Univ. West L.A., 1982; admitted bar Calif. 1982. Career: claims examiner Blue Cross of So. Calif., Los Angeles 1969-74, med. underwriter 1974-76, mktg. rep. 1976-82; lawyer pvt. practice, Santa Monica 1982–; mem: ABA, Cuban Am. Bar Assn., L.A. Co. Bar Assn., Calif. App. Attys. Assn.; Democrat; Cath.; rec: camping, RVing. Law Ofcs. Leo Hernandez, 3330 Pico Blvd Ste 2308 Santa Monica 90405

HERRICK, ALBERT WILLIAM, investor, retired; b. Mar. 4, 1906, Liecester, Eng., nat. US cit. 1930; s. Thomas and Harriet Ada (Smith) H.; m. Marian, Apr. 28, 1960; edn: Pasadena City Coll. 1940-48. Career: chemist's asst. Colonial Dames Cosmetics 1924-26; mgr. North East Svc. 1926-30; owner, mgr. H&H Automotive Los Angeles 1930-69, H&H Hardware 1940-69; rancher Tulare County 1969-80; real estate investor 1975-90; honors: Merit Award (Texaco 1965); mem: Rotary, Masons (master mason 50 yrs., Golden Veteran Pin 1986), Kiwanis, Exeter Meml. Hosp. Assn.; trustee First Presbyterian Ch. of Exeter 1972-75; inventor several mechanical devices; Republican; Baptist; rec: travel, woodworking. Res: 2193 W Visalia Rd Exeter 93221

HERRICK, SONJA JANE, healthcare executive; b. March 30, 1949, Willits; d. Clifton Eugene and Eleanor Jane (Steinmeyer) Snider; m. Greg Herrick, May 18, 1986; Career: dir. data processing Simi Valley Adventist Hosp., Simi Valley 1977-79; ops. mgr. St.Joseph Med. Center, Burbank 1979-82; data center mgr. St. Johns Hosp., Santa Monica 1982-85; dir. data processing St. Josephs Hosp., Orange 1985-88, contract dir. 1988-89; indep. contractor, Healthcare Finance, Los Angeles 1989–; asst. personnel dir. Simi Valley Adventist Hosp. 1973-77, nse. staffing schedule 1970-73; mem: HFMA. Res: POB 9459 Glendale 91226

HERRICK, WILLIAM JAMES, motel chain executive; b. Jan. 29, 1927, Carthage, S.D.; s. William C. and Ellen M. (Finley) H.; m. Donna, June 6, 1953; children: Kathleen b. 1954, Joan b. 1955, Leann b. 1957, William C. b. 1959, Susan b. 1960, Joseph b. 1962; edn: AA, L.A. City Coll. 1950; CSC Los Angeles 1952. Career: v.p. Citizens Bank, Los Angeles 1948-64; Crocker Bank 1964-69; founder/pres. two motel chains: Calif. 6 Motels, Hacienda Heights 1969-83; Economy Inns of America, Del Mar 1983–; founder Landmark Bank, La Habra 1979; founder Capital Bank, Carlsbad 1986–; mil: s.sgt. USAF 1945-46; Republican; R.Cath.; rec: golf, horse racing. Res: POB 1743 Rancho Santa Fe 92067 Ofc: Economy Inns 755 Raintree Carlsbad 92009

HERRING, BERNARD DUANE, medical doctor; b. Jan. 27, 1929, Massilon, Ohio; s. James and Eva H.; m. Odessa Mae Appling, Sept. 6, 1950; children: Kevin b. 1954, Bernard b. 1956, Terez b. 1960, Sean b. 1965; edn: BS (magna cum laude), Kent State Univ., Kent, Ohio 1952; MD, Univ. of Cincinnati Med. Sch. 1956; LLB, LaSalle Univ., Chgo., Ill. 1965; cert. Am. Bd. of Family Medicine 1979-94, Bd. of Geriatric Medicine 1994. Career: intern San Francisco Hosp. 1956-57; resident in medicine Crile Veterans Hosp., Cleveland, Ohio 1957-58, Brooklyn Veterans Hosp., Brooklyn, Ohio 1958-59; med. staff Merritt Hosp. and Summit North Hosps., Oakland 1966–; asst. clin. prof. UCSF Med. Sch. 1979–; R.E. broker, Oakland 1988; pres. Sunshine Vitamin Co., Oakland 1980; honors: Phi Beta Kappa 1952, listed in Who's Who in West 1977–, Who's Who Among Black Americans 1977–; mem: Am. Diabetes Assn. 1992–, Am. Coll. of Legal Medicine (fellow 1963-), Am. Soc. of Internal Medicine 1980–, ASCAP (publisher, songwriter) 1984–; author: med. magazine articles on Pernicious Anemia in Blacks, 1963, Kaposi Sarcoma, 1963, Male Baldness Pattern, 1985, music to num. songs 1980–; Watchtower Bible Tract Soc.; rec: music, gold mining. Ofc: Rumford Clinic 2960 Sacramento St Berkeley 94702

HERRON, SANDRA WHITACRE, psychotherapist, speech pathologist; b. July 1, 1935, Calumet, Mich.; d. Ahti John and Inga Aurora Minerva (Savela) Jaaskelainen; m. James Herron, Oct. 30, 1982; children: Lisa b. 1956, Lance b. 1958, Leslee b. 1961; edn: BA, Whittier Coll. 1956; MA, CSU Fullerton 1969; MA, Sierra Univ. Santa Monica 1984; PhD, Sierra Univ., 1989. Career: psychotherapist New Hope Counseling Svcs., Tustin 1984–, and Crystal Cathedral Counseling Ctr., Garden Grove; fmr speech therapist Magnolia Sch. Dist., Anaheim 1970-91; speaker at seminars 1982–; honors: La Mirada Bus. & Profl.

Womens Assn. Outstanding Women of Year (1971); mem: CTA, NEA, CSHA, CAMFT, CAPS; article pub. in profl. jour. (1986); rec: photog. Ofc: New Hope Counseling Center, 17821 E. 17th St. Ste. 190, Tustin 92680 and Crystal Cathedral Counseling Center, 12141 Lewis, Garden Grove 92640 Ph: 714/971-4222

HERSHBERGER, JOHN DOUGLAS, lawyer; b. Jan. 12, 1958, Inglewood, Calif.; s. John Howard and Mary Catherine (Berkstresser) H.; m. Kristine M. Lind, Dec. 30, 1983; children: Laura Marie b. 1986, John Patrick b. 1992; edn: BA in hist. (summa cum laude), UCLA, 1979; JD (cum laude), Georgetown Univ. Sch. of Law, 1983; admitted bar: Calif. 1984, D.C. 1994, U.S. Supreme Ct. Career: clerkship to Hon. Wm. P. Gray, U.S. District Ct., cent. dist. Calif., 1983-84; atty. law firm McKittrick, Jackson, et al, Newport Beach 1984-86; Baker & McKenzie, San Diego 1986-90; John D. Hershberger, A.P.C., San Diego 1990–; honors: Phi Beta Kappa; mem: Am. Bar Assn. (litigation sect.), Calif. St. Bar Assn., L.A. Co. Bar Assn., Orange Co. Bar Assn., San Diego Co. Bar Assn., D.C. Bar Assn.; Republican; Cath.; rec: computer technologies. Res: 14479 Rutledge Sq San Diego 92128 Ofc: John D. Hershberger, APC 550 West "C" St Ste 620 San Diego 92101

HERST, DOUGLAS JULIAN, lighting company executive; b. June 21, 1943, San Francisco; s. Samuel Bernard and Claire (Beer) H.; m. Carolen Landis, March 20, 1966; children: Chad b. 1973; edn: BS, UC Berkeley 1965. Career: sales Peerless Electric, Berkeley 1965-69, sales mgr. 1969-72, v.p. 1972-74; pres. Peerless Lighting 1974–, dir. 1970–; awards: Govs. Award Calif. New Product Competition, 1985; mem: Young Pres. Orgn., Illumination Engring. Soc. (pres. Golden Gate chp. 1977-78); article pub. in tech. jour., patents held in lighting, 1981–; rec: running, bicycling, swimming. Ofc: Peerless Lighting POB 2556 Berkeley 94702

HERST, PERRY STERN, JR., real estate executive; b. Sept. 18, 1929, Chgo.; s. Perry Stern and Gertrude (Browarsky) H.; children: Perry III, b. 1964; Craig, b. 1966; m. Angela Edge; edn: BA, Brown Univ. 1951; MBA, Harvard Grad. Sch. 1953. Career: loan ofcr. Equitable Finance Corp., Chgo. 1957; R.E. leasing & devel. broker Arthur Rubloff & Co., Chgo. 1958-64; v.p. Tishman-Gateway Inc., Chgo. 1964-68; senior v.p. Tishman Realty & Constrn. Co., Inc., Los Angeles 1968-77; pres./CEO Tishman West Mgmt. Corp., 1977-88, bd. chmn./CEO Tishman West Companies, 1988-93; chmn. emeritus Tishman Internat. Companies 1994; awards: Humanitarian award NCCJ 1976; Civic Achiev. Awd., The Am. Jewish Com. 1979; mem: Lamda Alpha; Urban Land Inst.; L.A. area C.of C. (Long Range Plng. Com.); Los Angeles Mayor's Economic Council; Nat. Conf. of Christians & Jews; The Am. Jewish Com.; Jr. Achiev. of So. Calif.; UCLA Chancellor Assocs.; mil: lt. sr. grade USN 1954-56; Republican; Jewish; rec: fishing, hunting, tennis. Res: Rancho Santa Fe Ofc: Tishman International Companies 10900 Wilshire Blvd Ste 510 Los Angeles 90024

HERTWECK, E. ROMAYNE, educator; b. July 24, 1928, Springfield, Mo.; s. Garnett P. and Gladys (Chowning) H.; m. Alma Louise Street, Dec. 16, 1955, 1 son: William Scott, b. 1970; edn: BA, Augustana Coll. 1962; MA, Pepperdine Coll. 1963; EdD, Ariz. State Univ. 1966; PhD, US Internat. Univ. 1978. Career: night ed. Rock Island Argus Newspaper, Ill. 1961-62; grad. tchg. asst. Pepperdine Coll., Los Angeles 1963; counselor, VA, Ariz. State Univ., Tempe, Ariz. 1964; assoc. dir. conciliation ct. Miracopa Co. Superior Ct., Phoenix, Ariz. 1965; instr. Phoenix Coll. 1966; prof. psychol. Mira Costa Coll., Oceanside, Calif. 1967–, dept. chmn. Psychol. Counseling 1973-75, Behavioral Sci. 1976-82, 87-88, 90-91, mem. Academic Senate Council 1968-70, 1985-87, 89-91; prof. psych. World Campus Afloat, S.S. Ryndam, spring 1970; p.t. instr. edn. dept. Univ. of San Diego 1968-69; instr. Chapman Coll. Residence Ctr., Camp Pendleton 1969-78; p.t. lectr. dept. of bus. adminstrn. San Diego State Univ. 1980-84; Sch. of Human Behavior US Internat. Univ. 1984-89; pres. El Camino Preschools, Inc., Oceanside 1985–; bd. dirs. Christian Counseling Ctr., Oceanside 1970-82; civic bds: City of Oceanside Child Care Task Force, 1991–, Oceanside Community Relations Commn., 1991- (vice chmn. 1994); Oceanside California Healthy Cities Project 1993–; mem: Am. Psychol. Assn., We. Psychol. Assn., North San Diego Co. Psychol. Assn., Am. Personnel & Guidance Assn., Phi Delta Kappa, Kappa Delta Pi, Psi Chi, Kiwanis, Carlsbad Club, Republican; Prot.; rec: travel, golf, photog. Res: 2024 Oceanview Rd Oceanside Ofc: Mira Costa College, Oceanside.

HERWIG, KARL R., physician, medical educator; b. Nov. 12, 1935, Philadelphia, Pa.; s. Louis and Elizabeth Francis (Myers) H.; m. Barbara Kay Bosscher, Oct. 26, 1963; children: Susan Elizabeth b. 1964, K. Robert b. 1966; edn: BS, Ursinus Coll. 1957; MD, Jefferson Med. Coll. 1961; cert. Am. Bd. Urology 1971. Career: intern, resident Univ. Mich., Ann Arbor 1961-67; staff urologist N.N.M.C., Bethesda, Md. 1967-69; faculty Univ. Mich., Ann Arbor 1969-73; head div. urology Scripps Clinic, La Jolla 1977–; clin. assoc. prof. UCSD 1977–; assoc. prof. Univ. Mich. 1969-77; honors: Alpha Omega Alpha; mem: A.C.S., Am. Urological Assn., Central Surgical, Am. Assn. Endocrine Surgery, AMA, Rotary Del Mar; 42 articles pub. in med. jours. (1966–), 5 book chpts. pub. (1966–); mil: cmdr. USNR 1967-69; Republican; Presbyterian; rec: golf, gardening. Res: Box 2076 Rancho Santa Fe 92067 Ofc: Scripps Clinic 10666 N Torrey Pines La Jolla 92037

HERZBERG, DOROTHY CREWS, teacher; b. July 8, 1935, New York; d. Floyd Houston and Julia (Lesser) Crews; m. Hershel Zelig Herzberg, May 22, 1962 (div. 1988); children: Samuel b. 1964, Laura b. 1966, Dan b. 1968; edn: BA, Brown Univ. 1957; MA, Stanford Univ. 1964; JD, S.F. Law Sch. 1976. Career: tchr. Mission Adult Sch., S.F. 1965-66; Peace Corps, Nigeria 1961-63; investigator Family Support Bureau Dist. Atty., S.F. 1978-80; dept. adminstr. Dean Witter Reynolds 1980-83; tchr. S.F. Sch. Dist. 1985-87; revenue ofcr. IRS 1987-89; tchr. West Contra Costa Sch. Dist., 1991–; honors: Who's Who Am. Women, Who's Who in West; mem: First Unitarian Ch. Berkeley (choir), Miraloma Improvement Club (bd. 1976-88, pres. 1980-81, ed. newsletter 1976-82); Democrat; Unitarian; rec: swimming. Res: 1006 Richmond St., El Cerrito 94530

HESSE, CHRISTIAN AUGUST, minerals industry consultant; b. June 20, 1925, Chemnitz, Saxony, Germany; s. William Albert (Canadian mining geologist, discoverer of Mt. Wright, Quebec, iron ore deposits) and Anna Gunhilda (Baumann) H.; mat. grandfather, Supreme Ct. Justice, Norway; m. Brenda Nora Rigby, Nov. 4, 1964; children: Robin "Rob" Christian b. 1968, Bruce William b. 1969; edn: B. Applied Sci. (hons.), Univ. of Toronto, 1948; Chartered Engineer (U.K.); Registered Profl. Engr. (ON Can.). Career: mining engring., tunneling, mine ops., exploration, constrn. and engring. mgmt. with various cos. U.S. and Canada, 1948-63; shaft and mine supt. Allan Potash Proj., U.S. Borax & Chem. Corp., Saskatchewan, Can. 1964, through design & constrn. phases, becoming ops. mgr. 1969; loaned to parent co. (London) as mng. dir. and proj. mgr. for Yorkshire Potash Ltd., Yorkshire, Eng. 1970-71; pres. and gen. mgr. APM Operators, Ltd. 1974, later chief engr. U.S. Borax & Chem. Corp., Los Angeles 1974-77, v.p. engring. and mining devel. 1978-90, v.p. and project mgr. Quartz Hill molybdenum mining proj. near Ketchikan, Ak. 1981-90, v.p. in charge Trinity Silver Mine jt. venture, Nev. 1987-90; recipient scholarship awards: Sault Daily Star (1944), Women's Mining Assn. (1945); mem: Canadian Inst. Mining & Metallurgy, Montreal (life), Soc. for Mining, Metallurgy & Exploration (Am. Inst. Mining Engrs.), Inst. Mining & Metallurgy, London (Fellow), Assn. Profl. Engrs. of Ontario, Can., Prospectors & Developers Assn. of Canada, Northwest Mining Assn., Alaska Miners Assn.; club: Los Angeles Tennis; mil: Canadian Ofcrs. Tng. Corps 1944-45; Lutheran; rec: skiing, tennis. Res: Hollywood Hills 90068-1629

HESSELTINE, WALLY G., lawyer; b. July 22, 1943, Chico; s. Waldo L. and Margaret E. (Ruppert) H.; m. Lynn E. Capachi, Aug. 21, 1966; children: Michele A. b. 1971, Stephen M. b. 1972; edn: BS, USC 1966; JD, Golden Gate Univ. 1969; admitted St. Bar Calif. 1970. Career: dep. dist. atty. San Bernardino Co. Dist. Atty. 1970-73; atty., assoc. Malott Pedder & Stover, Lafayette 1973-76; ptnr. Malott Pedder Stover & Hesseltine 1976; mem: Calif. Attys. for Criminal Justice; Republican; SDA; rec: running, skiing, reading. Ofc: Pedder Stover Hesseltine & Walker 3445 Golden Gate Way POB 479 Lafayette 94549-0479

HESTER, DOUGLAS A., financial executive; b. Oct. 31, 1951; m. Clarice A. Strebig RN; children: Jonathan b. 1981, Jameson b. 1983, Jacqueline b. 1987; edn: AB, UCLA, 1974; MBA, USC, 1977, MSBA, 1981; CPA, Calif., 1981. Career: summer intern Ernst & Ernst, L.A. 1976; staff acct. Touche Ross & Co., 1977-79; loan ofcr. First Interstate Mortgage Co., San Diego 1983-84, asst. v.p. 1985-87, v.p. 1987-89; v.p./office mgr. Northland Fin. Co., San Diego 1989-92; pres. Scripps Realty Advisors 1992–; grad. tchg. asst. in acctg. USC, 1974-76, instr. 1976-77, lectr. 1977-83, asst. dean Sch. of Acctg., USC, 1979-83, substitute lectr. USC's CMA Review Pgm., faculty adv. for Beta Alpha Psi and Acctg. Soc., guest lectr. numerous acctg. and fin. courses; cons. Financial Appraisals Inc., L.A. 1981, Weyerhaeuser Mortgage 1993, Wells Fargo 1993; awards: coll. scholarship Wedbush Noble Cook Inc., Beta Alpha Psi (1975, pres. Iota chpt. 1976), Fellowship Org. for Res. & Knowledge Award 1977, Beta Gamma Sigma 1977, top grad. in class USC Grad. Sch. Bus. Adminstrn. (1977, 81), USC Acctg. Dept. Chairman's Award 1978, founder Acctg. Soc. USC 1979, Alpha Kappa Psi hon. faculty mem. 1982; mem: Am. Inst. CPAs, Calif. Soc. CPAs, Am. Finance Assn., Building Ind. Assn., Mortgage Bankers Assn. Calif., San Diego Mortgage Bankers Assns., USC Gen. Alumni Assn., USC MBA Alumni, The Accounting Circle USC (bd., pres. 1977, sec. 79-82), Commerce Assocs. USC, UCLA Gen. Alumni Assn., Loyola Marymount Alumni Assn., Alpha Delta Gamma; publs: contbr. Meigs and Mosich Financial Acctg. textbook series, jour. articles and papers in field. Res: 10274 Rue Cannes San Diego 92131

HETZEL, MELVYN LEE, banking automation executive; b. July 29, 1939, Los Angeles; s. Myron Walton and Edith Kirstine (Coats) H.; m. Maureen Curtin, Aug. 10, 1968; children: Kirsten b. 1975, Ryle b. 1976; edn: BA, Stanford Univ. 1961; MPA, George Washington Univ. 1964. Career: mgr. I.R.S., San Francisco 1970-71; Bank of America 1971-92; CFO, St. Vincent de Paul Society 1992–; curriculum cons. Univ. San Francisco 1984-86; tchr. U.S. Dept. of Agri. Coll., Wash. D.C. 1967-70; awards: U.S. Presdl. citation (1967), Bank of Am. exceptional performance (1984, 85, 88, 89); St. Vincent de Paul Soc. (treas., dir.), CASE Users Group (secty., dir. 1989), Am. Soc. Pub. Adminstrn. (ed. 1966-69), S.F. Press Club, Young Republicans; author: Project Management Process, 1990; Systems Devel. Process, 1982; numerous profl. papers on automation, 1984-89. Res: 65 Shore View Terrace San Francisco 94121

HEUSCHELE, WERNER PAUL, veterinary virology, research director; b. Aug. 28, 1929, Ludwigsburg, Germany, naturalized U.S., 1951; s. Karl August and Margarete Anna (Wagner) H.; m. 4th, Carolyn Rene Bredeson, Jan. 1, 1983; children: Eric b. 1954, Mark b. 1960 (dec. 1994), Jennifer b. 1960; edn: undergrad. San Diego State, 1947-50, BA zoology (hons.) UC Davis, 1952, DVM, 1956; tng. res. vet. pathology Armed Forces Inst. of Path., W.D.C., 1965-66; PhD vet. sci., med. microbiology, virology, Univ. Wis., 1969. Career: veterinarian, mgr. Zoo Hosp. and Labs., San Diego Zoo, 1956-61; res. veterinarian Plum Island Animal Dis. Lab., ARS, USDA, N.Y., 1961-70; assoc. prof. microbiology Coll. Vet. Med. Kansas State Univ., Manhattan 1970-71; hd. virology Jensen-Salsbery Labs., Div. Richardson-Merrill Inc., Kansas City, Ks. 1971-76; assoc. prof. dept. vet. preventive medicine Ohio State Univ., Columbus 1976-78, prof. 1978-81, chmn. dept. grad. com. 1979-81; hd. microbiology /virology, res. dept. San Diego Zoo, Calif. 1981-86, dir. res. Ctr. for Reprodn. Endangered Species, 1986–; awards: Phi Zeta (1956, chapt. pres. 81-82), Hutchinson Scholar UC Davis 1956, cons. animal hlth. Smithsonian Inst. 1967-68, San Diego Jaycee's Outstanding Young Men 1960, res. assoc. UC Davis Sch. Vet. Med. 1960, rev. panel AVMA Colloquium Purdue Univ. 1971, Sigma Xi 1979, F.K. Ramsey Lectr. Iowa State Univ. 1991, UC Davis Sch. Vet. Med. Alumni Achiev. Award 1991; trustee Columbus (OH) Zoo Assn. (trustee of yr. 1978), Life Mem. Award, Am. Assn. of Zoo Vets. 1993; tech. and sci. cons. various corps., nat. and fgn. govts.; mem: N.A.S., NRC, Com. Bovine TB Eradication, Panel on Animal Hlth. & Vet. Med., Bd. on Agric., Am. Assn. of Zoo Veterinarians (founding, charter mem., chmn. 1958-59, sec. treas. 1960-61, com. ch. 1982-85), San Diego Biomed. Res. Inst. (v.p. 1959-60, bd. 59-61), Wildlife Disease Assn. (coun. 1981-84, v.p. 85-87), Am. Vet. Med. Assn., Conf. of Res. Workers in Animal Diseases, US Animal Hlth. Assn. (coms.), Am. Assn. Vet. Lab. Diagnosticians, Am. Coll. Vet. Microbiologists (bd. govs. 1984-87), Am. Assn. Wildlife Vets., Am. Assn. of Zool. Parks and Aquariums (animal hlth. com.), Intl. Union for Conserv. of Nature/Vet. Specialist Gp., Conserv. Breeding Specialist Gp. (species survival commn.), Conservation Internat., Nat. Wildlife Fedn., Kiwanis Intl./Balboa Pk. (pres. 1989-90); author 17+ med. books and book chapts., 126+ sci. jour. articles and abstracts; Democrat; rec: music, painting. Ofc: San Diego Zoo, CRES, PO Box 551 San Diego 92112-0551

HEYCK, THEODORE DALY, lawyer; b. Apr. 17, 1941, Houston, Tx.; s. Theodore Richard and Gertrude Paine (Daly) H.; edn: AB, Brown Univ. 1963; LLB, Georgetown Univ. Law Center 1963-65, 71-72; N.Y. Law Sch. 1979; MFA, Drama Centre, London 1967; admitted bar: New York, Calif., U.S. Supreme Ct., U.S. Ct. Appeal (9th cir., 2d cir.), Fed. Dist. Cts. N.Y. (No. dist., So. dist., East dist., West dist.) and Calif. (So. dist., Cent. dist.). Career: self-empl. entertainment industry, 1967-79; paralegal Dist. Atty. Kings Co., Bklyn. 1975-79, asst. dist. atty. 1979-85; dep. city atty. City of Los Angeles, 1985–; mem: Screen Actors Guild, Actors Equity Assn., Nat. Acad. TV Arts & Scis., ABA, Brooklyn Bar Assn., Los Angeles Co. Bar Assn., Am. Trial Lawyers Assn., N.Y. Trial Lawyers Assn., Federal Bar Council; listed Who's Who in Am. Law, Who's Who in Am., Who's Who in West, Who's Who in World; Res: 2106 Live Oak Dr East, Los Angeles 90068 Ofc: City Attorney 200 N Main St 17th Flr Los Angeles 90012

HEYER, CAROL ANN, artist, illustrator, writer; b. Feb. 2, 1950, Cuero, Tex.; d. William Jerome and Merlyn Mary (Hutson) Heyer; edn: BA, Calif. Lutheran Univ., 1974. Career: freelance artist various cos., Thousand Oaks 1974-79; computer artist Image Resource, Westlake Village 1979-81; staff writer, artist Lynn-Davis Prodns., Westlake Village 1981-87; art director Northwind Studios Internat., Camarillo 1988-89; illustrator, prin. Touchmark, Thousand Oaks 1989–; cons. art dir., writer Lynn-Wenger Prodns. 1987-89; illustrator children's books: A Star in the Pasture, 1988, The Dream Stealer, 1989, The Golden Easter Egg, 1989, Prancer, 1989, All Things Bright and Beautiful, Rapunzel, The Gift of the Magi, 1994, Dinosaurs, 1994, The Christmas Carol, 1995; book covers for Disney Hyperion; poster for Hollywood Bowl concert, Motion Picture and Television Fund; novel cover for TSR, Books "The Road West", interior full page/full color, TSR, Books "Legend and Lore"; interior illustration for Science Fiction Age; magazine cover art for Dragon mag., Dungeon mag., Aboriginal Science Fiction mag., and The McCone Files (mystery); cover illustration for Steve Jackson Games "Gurps Fantasy Bestiary and num. others; puzzle for F.X. Schmid USA; writer/illustrator: The Easter Story, 1989, Beauty and the Beast, 1989, featured in "The Artist's Market" a Writer's Digest Book, 1990, The Christmas Story, Excalibur, Robin Hood; co-author (screenplay) Thunder Run, 1986; writer, Disney Ednl. Productions; awards: Print's Reg. Design Annual 1992, Literature 1992, Magazine Merit 1988, 92, Aboriginal Sci Fiction Mag. (Best Art, First Pl.), Soc. of Illustrators Cert. of Merit 1990, 91, 92, Cert. of Excellence (2) Calif. Lutheran Univ., featured in The Worlds of TSR (book of fantasy artists); featured in front page newspaper articles: The Daily News and The News Chronicle, featured in "The Artist Mag.", L.A. Times, Daily News, News Chronicle, represented by "Every Picture Tells a Story" (gallery of art from children's books), "Worlds of Wonder" (art from sci. fiction and fantasy illustrations), listed Who's Who in California, Who's Who In the West, Contemporary Authors, All About the Author; mem: Soc. of Children's Book Writers (judge for 1990 Mag. Merit Award), Assn. of Sci. Fiction and Fantasy Artists (Chesley Award nom. 1989, 90, featured in "The Artist's" mag.), Soc. of Illustrators, Westlake Village Art Guild (family liturgy com.). Address: Touchmark, 925 Ave De Los Arboles Thousand Oaks 91360

HEYMAN, IRA MICHAEL, university chancellor; b. May 30, 1930, NYC; s. Harold Albert and Judith (Sobel) H.; m. Therese Thau, Dec. 17, 1950; children: Stephen Thomas b. 1961, James Nathaniel b. 1963; edn: AB govt. Dartmouth Coll. 1951; JD, Yale Law Sch. 1956; admitted bar: NY 1956, Calif. 1961. Career: legislative asst. Sen. Irving M. Ives, WDC 1950-51; atty., assoc. Carter, Ledyard and Milburn, NYC 1956-57; law clerk Chief Judge Charles E. Clark, Ct. of Appeals (2d Circuit) New Haven, CT 1957-58; chief law clerk Chief Justice Earl Warren, US Supreme Ct.1958-59; acctg. assoc. prof. law, UC Berkeley, 1959-61, prof. of law 1961–, vice chancellor 1974-80, chancellor Univ. of Calif., Berkeley, 1980–; vis. prof. Yale Law Sch. 1963-64, Stanford Law Sch. 1971-72; trustee Dartmouth Coll., 1982–; dir. PG&E, S.F. 1985–; govt. planning and zoning cons. Virgin Islands 1975-76, Am. Samoa 1973-74, County of Kauai, HI 1972-73, Tahoe Reg. Plng. Agy. 1970-75, S.F. Bay Conserv. and Devel. Commn. 1968-70; appt. U.S. Commn. on Civil Rights (sec. Calif. advy. com. 1962-67), City of Berkeley Human Rels. & Welfare Commn. (chmn. 1966-68); honors: review ed. Yale Law Jour. 1956, LLD (hon) Univ. Pacific 1981, LHD (hon) Hebrew Union Coll. 1984, Chevalier de la Legion d'Honneur, France 1985, LLD (hon) Univ. Maryland 1986; mem: Nat. Collegiate Athletic Assn. (div. I subcom. chmn. NCAA Presidents Commn. 1986-88), Nat. Assn. State Univs. and Land-Grant Colls. (exec. com. chair 1986, subcom. audit & fin. 1987–, com. on legal affairs 1988–), Am. Council on Edn. (bd. 1984-85); num. jour. articles, papers and legal documents in areas of civil rights, constnl. law, land plng., metro. govt., housing, environmental law and mgmt., affirmative action; mil: 1st lt. USMC 1951-53, capt. USMCR 1953-58; Democrat; rec: tennis, opera. Office of the Chancellor Univ. of Calif. Sch. of Law Berkeley 94720

HEYWOOD, ROBERT GILMOUR, lawyer; b. May 18, 1949, Berkeley; s. Warren Zimri and Jean (Reinecke) H.; m. Carolyn Cox, June 10, 1972; children: Karen, Laura, John; edn: BA distinction, Stanford Univ. 1971; MA, UC Berkeley 1972; JD cum laude, Santa Clara Univ. 1975; admitted St. Bar Calif. 1975, U.S. Dist. Ct. No. and Eastern Dists. 1975, U.S. Ct. Appeals 9th Circuit 1976, U.S. Supreme Ct 1979. Career: Hanna Brophy MacLean McAleer & Jensen, Oakland 1976; instr. Santa Clara Univ. 1975-77; faculty center for trial and appellate adv. UC Hastings Coll. of Law, San Francisco 1983; adj. prof. law UC Hastings Coll. of Law 1982-86; judge pro tem, arbitrator Alameda Co. Superior Ct., faculty, Stanford Univ. Law School Advocacy Skills Workshop 1994–, faculty, Univ. of S.F. Law School Intensive Advocacy Workshop 1995–; mem: Alameda Co. Legal Aid Soc.(bd. dirs. 1978-85), Am. Bar Assn., Calif. Bar Assn. (panelist and author Cont. Edn. Bar), Alameda Co. Bar Assn., Assn. Defense Counsel, Calif. Compensation Defense Attys. Assn., Pres. Oakland East Bay Symphony; editor Law Review; Ofc: Hanna Brophy et al 155 Grand Ave Ste 600 Oakland 94612

HIATT, ROBERT ALLAN, epidemiologist; b. Jan. 28, 1943, Boston, Mass.; s. Ralph Ellis and Elloise (Kunz) H.; m. June Hemmons Nelson, Mar. 25, 1972; children: Jesse b. 1974; edn: BA, zoology, Univ. of Mich., Ann Arbor 1964; MD, Univ. of Mich. Med. Sch. 1968; internship San Francisco Gen. Hosp. 1968-69; residency USPHS Hosp., S.F. 1969-71; MPH, epidemiology, Univ. of Calif. Sch. of Public Health, Berkeley 1972, PhD, epidemiology 1980; med. lic. Calif., Mich.; eligible Am. Bd. of Internal Medicine 1971. Career: field project (Mexico) res. asst. George Williams Hooper Found., UC San Francisco 1971; res. assoc. (Ethiopia) 1972-73; clin. instr. medicine UC Med. Sch., S.F. and dir. Employee Health Svc., S.F. Gen. Hosp. 1974; physician Berkeley and Hayward Ind. Med. Groups 1974, 1976-81; epidemic Intelligence Svc. Tng. Course, Ctr. for Disease Control, Atlanta, GA 1974; chief parasitology sect. San Juan Labs. Ctr. for Disease Control, USPHS, Puerto Rico 1974-76; dep. project ofcr. Egyptian-Am. Bilharzia Control Project, Cairo, Egypt 1975-76; temp. adv. WHO, Geneva, Switzerland 1976, West Indies 1979; epidemiologist Kaiser Permanente Med. Care Prog., Oakland, CA 1977-84; cons. Kaiser Aluminum & Chem. Corp., Oakland 1980-81; lectr. dept. of epidemiology and internat. health Sch. of Medicine, UC San Francisco 1980–; lectr. dept. of biomed. & environ. health scis. Sch. of Public Health, UC Berkeley 1981–; physician, internal medicine Berkeley Family Practice Med. Group, Berkeley 1981-86; mem. central res. com. Kaiser Found. Res. Inst. 1982–; sci. advy. com. S.F.-Bay Area Chpt. Nat. Found. for Ileitis and Colitis 1984-87; sr. epidemiologist Div. of Res., The Permanente Med. Group 1985-91, asst. dir. 1991–; mem. reg. AIDS com. Kaiser Permanente Med. Care Prog., No. Calif. region 1987–, and VDT advy. com. 1988-90; mem. overview com. Mammography Screening Task Forces, Cancer Coalition of Calif. 1987-89; assoc. dir. for detection, prevention and edn. No. Calif. Cancer Ctr. 1988-93; steering com Bay Area Cancer Coalition 1988–; com. for protection of human subjects, UC Berkeley 1991-93; dir. of prevention scis. No. Calif. Cancer Ctr. 1993–; bd. dirs., chmn. of policy com. Am. Coll. of Epidemiology 1993- (fellow 1986); mem. breast cancer task force Kaiser Permanente Med. Care Prog. 1993–; chair strategic planning group, Div. of Res., Kaiser Permanente Med. Care Prog. 1993-94; mem. res. & devel. tech. advy. com, Kaiser Permanente Central Ofc. 1993-94; reviewer for profl. jours., 1988-94 incl. Am. Jour. of Epidemiology (assoc. ed. 1993–), Annals of Internal Medicine, British Jour. of Cancer, Cancer, Cancer Causes and Control, Cancer Res., Epidemiology, Internat. Jour. of Cancer, Jour. of AMA, Jour. of Nat. Cancer Inst., Preventive Medicine, Surgeon General's Report 1990: The Health

Benefits of Smoking Cessation; internat. speaker and lectr. 1975–; honors: Victor Vaughn Med. Hist. Soc., Univ. of Mich. Med. Sch. 1967-68, HEW Children's Bureau Fellowship, Belgrade, Yugoslavia 1968; fellow Am. Coll. of Preventive Medicine 1974; mem: Alameda-Contra Costa Med. Assn. 1977–, Am. Epidemiological Soc. 1991–, Am. Occupational Med. Assn. 1978-82, Am. Publ. Health Assn. 1974–, Am. Soc. of Preventive Oncology 1987–, CMA 1977–, Am. Soc. of Tropical Medicine and Hygiene 1976-83, Soc. for Epidemiological Res. 1975–, Royal Soc. of Tropical Medicine and Hygiene (fellow, 1974-82); author or co-author 70+ pub. jour. articles, num. pub. abstracts and letters, 1967–, over 50 scientific presentations in U.S., Can. France, Sweden, Venezuela, 1975–; mil: USPHS Commd. Corps, 1968-76. Ofc: Division of Research, Kaiser Permanente 3505 Broadway Oakland 94611-5714

HIBBEN, JOSEPH WEST, investment banker; b. May 31, 1909, Lakewood, Ohio; s. Fred Martin and Lucy Calvert (West) H.; m. Ingrid Bridget Haut, Feb. 17, 1980; children: Barry Joseph, Bonnie Elizabeth; edn: BA, Princeton Univ. 1931; MBA, Harvard Univ. 1933. Career: ptnr. Kidder Peabody & Co., N.Y.C. 1938-72; pres. Exec. Club, Chicago., Ill. 1965-68; mayor Glenview, Ill. 1967-70; pres. San Diego Comm. Found. 1980-83; dir. La Jolla Museum 1972–; pres. San Diego Museum of Art 1986-90, 1992-93; dir.: Thomas Industries, Louisville, Ky. 1956-89, Parker Hannifin Inc., Cleveland. 1972-84, North Carolina Natural Gas, Fayetteville, N.C. 1959-81, Fin. Fedn., L.A. 1959-79; trustee and treas. Univ. Calif. San Diego 1993-95; awards: Distinguished La Jollan award Rotary and San Diego Community Foundation 1987, 1991 Leonardo da Vinci Award for extraordinary leadership to the arts in Calif., Calif. Confedn. of the Arts (11/91); mem. Com. of 100 (dir.), San Diego Opera (fin. v.p., trustee); clubs: University (S.D.), Monterey CC, La Jolla CC, La Jolla Beach & Tennis, Union League Club; Republican; Presbyterian; rec: flying, golf. Res: 7247 Encilia Dr La Jolla 92037 Ofc: 1205 Prospect St Ste 500 La Jolla 92037

HICKERSON, GLENN LINDSEY, aircraft leasing company marketing executive; b. Aug. 22, 1937, Burbank; s. Ralph Millard and Sarah (Lindsey) H.; m. Jane Fortune, Feb. 24, 1973; edn: BA, Claremont McKenna Coll., 1959; MBA, NYU Stern Grad. Sch. Bus. Administrn., 1960. Career: exec. asst. Douglas Aircraft Co., Santa Monica 1962-63, sec. treas. Douglas Fin. Corp., 1964-67; exec. asst. to pres. Universal Airlines, Detroit, Mich. 1967-68, v.p./treas. 1969-72; group v.p. Marriott Corp., W.D.C. 1972-76; v.p. sales Lockheed Calif. Co., Burbank 1976-83; v.p. mktg. Douglas Aircraft Co., Long Beach 1983-89; mng. dir. GPA Asia Pacific Inc., Los Angeles 1989-90; exec. v.p. mktg. GATX Air, San Francisco 1990–; award: H.B. Earhart Found. fellow 1961; mem.: bd. govs. Keck Ctr. for Internat. Strategic Studies, 1988–; club: Pacific Union S.F., Wing's NY, 1969–; mil: ltjg USCG Res. 1960-62; Republican; Methodist; rec: sailing. Res: 3225 Jackson St San Francisco 94118 Ofc: GATX Air 4 Embarcadero Ctr Ste 2200 San Francisco 94111

HICKERSON, MARK, college history/political science instructor; b. Jan. 11, 1955, Buffalo, N.Y.; s. George and Dolores Carolina (Johnson) H.; edn: AA, Mt. San Antonio Coll. 1978; BA, CSU Fullerton 1980; MA, 1986. Career: substitute tchr. Walnut, Rowland, Ontario & Cucamonga sch. dists., 1981-83, 85-88; grad. asst. CSUF History Dept. 1983-85; instr. Mt. San Antonio Coll., Walnut 1989–, Riverside Comm. Coll. 1993–; awards: Bank of America achievement 1973, Mt. SAC Student of Distinction 1977-78, Alpha Gamma Sigma State Honors 1978, CSUF James Jordan Award 1984, William Langsdorf Award 1985, Phi Kappa Phi Scholarship Award 1984, Giles T. Brown Outstanding Thesis Hon. Mention 1987, The Californian's semi-annual History Award 1990; mem: Nat. Hon. Soc., Nat. Soc. for Student Leaders, Phi Alpha Theta & Phi Kappa Phi Hon. Soc., Soc. Historians Am. Fgn. Rels., Acad. Political Sci., Amnesty Internat., Arms Control Assn.; 4 articles pub. in profl. jours., 1983–; mil: cpl. USMC 1974-76, merit. promotions, Good Conduct Rib.; Democrat; rec: tennis, jogging, basketball. Res: 826 E Dunes St Ontario 91761

HICKEY, MICHAEL JOHN, manufacturing and distribution company president; b. June 19, 1948, San Gabriel; s. Francis Joseph, Jr. and Marian Ann (McCain) H.; m. Katherine Margaret Saltzer, July 22, 1972; children: Erin and Erika (twins) b. 1976; edn: mech. engring., Cal Poly Pomona 1968; mgmt. devel., Cal Tech, 1974; AA, Orange Coast Coll., 1976. Career: owner/opr. M.J.H. Mfg., Arcadia 1962-82; owner/opr. Marine Ecological Systems (marine research and comml. fishing vessel), Costa Mesa 1975-80; prod. M.E.S. Film Prodn. Co., Costa Mesa 1976-82; pres. and c.e.o. Newport Fastener Co. Inc., Anaheim 1982–; ptnr. M&M Mfg. Co., Riverside, 1988–; ptnr. Newport Architectural Products, Newport Beach, 1988–; guest instr. Const. Apprentice Pgm., So. Calif. 1974-80; dir. A.C.S. Edn. Pgm., Orange Co. 1977-79; guest spkr. Roofing Contr. Assn. So. Calif. 1970–, Am. Cetacean Soc., Orange Co. 1975-80; awards: Disneyland (sponsored) community service award Anaheim 1979, leadership Am. Cetacean Soc. O.C. 1979, Orange Co. Fair best film - non-theatrical 1979 and best profl. film 1980; mem: Nat. Roofing Conrtrs. Assn., We. States Roofing Contrs. Assn., Anaheim C.of C., Constrn. Specifiers Inst.; civic: Whalewatch edn. pgm. Newport Beach (founding dir. 1977-79), Am. Cetacean Soc. (O.C. dir. 1976-79), La Habra Comm. Theatre (actor, dir. 1988-91), Gr. L.A. Childrens' Theatre Long Beach/ Orange Co., Irvine Civic Light Opera (staff 1990–), Stagelight Family Prodns. (staff 1991–); publs: scripts, tech. manuals, contbr.

articles to trade jours., travel mags. (1978–); 16mm films: Six Days At La Paz (prod./dir. 1979), Clay Tile - The Jewel of Roofing (writer/dir. 1980); stage plays: Dracula (prod. 1989), Best Christmas Pageant Ever (prod. 1989), Annie (actor 1987), Sound of Music (actor 1988), stage mgr.- Peter Pan (1989), Music Man (1989), Mary Poppins (1990), Oliver (1991); Democrat; R.Cath.; rec: theatre arts, film, boating, big game fishing. Res: 27 Sycamore Creek Irvine 92715-3428 Ofc: Newport Fastener Co., Inc. 1300 E Gene Autry Way Anaheim 92805

HICKMAN, DAVID FRANCIS, food distribution company marketing executive; b. July 26, 1947, Flint, Mich.; s. Clarence Joseph and Rejeania Emeline (Nickerson) H.; m. Laura Elizabeth Agness, Jan. 27, 1971; edn: BS, Purdue Univ., 1970; MA, Indiana No. Univ., 1978. Career: dept. Armour & Co., Balt. 1970-72, dist. sales mgr., Nashua, N.H. 1972-74; region sales mgr. Pittsburgh, Pa. 1974-75; nat. sales mgr. La Choy Food Products, Archibold, Oh. 1975-85; mktg. mgr. Hunt-Wesson, Inc., Fullerton, Calif. 1985–; recipient internat. sales and mktg. award Beatrice Foods Co., Chgo. 1985; Republican; Congregationalist; rec: computers, travel, reading. Res: 2455 Via La Mesa Chino Hills 91709 Ofc: Hunt-Wesson, Inc. 1645 W Valencia Dr Ste 653 Fullerton 92633-3899

HICKS, FRANK ENOCHS, JR., pharmacist; b. Sept. 27, 1930, Stockton; s. Frank Enochs and Celia Agnes (Woods) H.; m. Patricia Olive Johnsen, July 1, 1956; children: Jane b. 1958, Daniel b. 1959, John b. 1963; edn: AA, Stockton Coll. 1950; BS pharm., UCSF Sch. Pharm. 1953; reg. pharmacist Calif. 1953. Career: mgr. Cliffords Plaza Pharm., Sunnyvale 1956-60; Cliffords Rancho Pharm., Los Altos 1960-62; pharmacist Weaverville Drug Store, Weaverville 1962-67, owner 1967–; preceptor Calif. St. Bd. Pharmacy 1988; honors: Rainbow Girls Grand Cross of Color 1977, Masons Hiram award 1988, Rotary Internat. Paul Harris fellow 1984, Who's Who in W., Trinity Co. Citizen of Year 1978, Phi Delta Chi; mem: Weaverville C.of C., Trinity Co. C.of C., Allied Masonic Degrees, Order of Eastern Star, Korean War Vets. Assn., Vets. of Foreign Wars, Rotary Club Weaverville (pres. 1964), Masons (Master 1972), Ben Ali Temple Shriners, Weaverville Joss House Assn. (chmn. 1983–); mil: 1st lt. AUS 1954-56; Republican; Congregational; rec: piano, numismatics. 219 Court St Weaverville 96093 Ofc: Weaverville Drug Store 219 Main St Weaverville 96093

HICKS, PATRICIA JOHNSEN, author; b. Jan. 15, 1931, Alameda, Calif.; d. Gudmund and Helen Ramona (Warhurst) Johnsen; m. Frank E. Hicks, Jr., July 1, 1956; children: Jane b. 1958, Daniel b. 1959, John b. 1963; edn: AA, Stockton (Calif.) Coll. 1950; BA, UC Berkeley 1952, grad. sch. 1952-53; gen. elementary tchg. cred. 1953. Career: elem. tchr. Oakland Public Schs. 1953-56, Los Altos Sch. Dist. 1956-58; founder, tchr., dir. Weaverville Parent Nursery Sch. 1962-70; adult edn. instr. Trinity H.S., Weaverville 1962-70; researcher (p.t.) Weaverville Drug Store 1966-95, buyer 1972–; researcher, I Collect Facts, Weaverville 1974–; piano accompanist Trinity H.S. 1978-83, Weaverville Elem. Sch. 1981-82; mgr. Weaverville Drug Store 1986–; dir., life mem. Weaverville Joss House Assn. 1983–; awards: Grand Cross of Color, Rainbow Girls 1976, Silver Beaver, BSA-Mt. Lassen Area Council 1979, Woman of Yr., Weaverville Bus. & Profl. Women's Club 1983, Citizen of Yr., Trinity Co. 1985, Most Honored Mem., Weaverville Joss House Assn. 1988, profiled in RECORD-SEARCHLIGHT, Redding 1989; mem: Trinity Co. Historical Soc. 1962–, Girl Scouts USA (life mem. 1966–, jr. ldr. 1967-70, dir. Sierra-Cascade Girl Scout Council 1979-83), BSA (Troop 55 com. 1970–, chmn. 1977-80, den ldr. 1970-73, merit badge counselor 1970–, Eagle Scout adv. 1976-86), Daughters of the Nile 1976–, St. John's Chpt. 14, Order of Eastern Star (organist 1995-96), Four Counties Rose Soc., Redding (pres. 1972-74); TV monologue on pruning roses, 1973; author: (books) Stories of a Gold Miner 1989, 92, Weaverville, Trinity County, CA 1990, 94, The Mountain Cookbook, 1991, Weaverville, A Jewel of a Town, 1993, contbr. article to Am. Rose Annual, 1972, columns and articles to Trinity Jour., Weaverville 1974–; Republican; Congregational/UCC (deaconess for life, Trinity Congregational Ch. 1968, subs. organist 1963–); rec: collecting facts, cooking, sewing, embroidery, quilting, gardening, photog., music, genealogy. Res: 219 Court St Box 370 Weaverville 96093-0370 Ofc: Weaverville Drug Store 219 Main St Box 370 Weaverville 96093-0370

HIGDON, BERNICE COWAN, civic volunteer, retired teacher; b. Feb. 26., 1918, Sylva, N.Caro.; d. Royston Duffield and Margaret Cordelia (Hall) Cowan; m. Roscoe John Higdon, Aug. 12, 1945; children: Ronald Keith, Rodrick Knox, Krista Dean; edn: BS, We. Carolina Univ., 1941; tchr. cert., So. Oreg. Coll., 1967; Chapman Coll., 1971; Calif. St. life tchg. cred. Career: sch. principal, tchr. Dorsey Sch., Bryson City, N.C., 1941-42; expeditor Glenn L. Martin Aircraft Co., Baltimore 1942-45; tchr. elem. sch. Seneca, S.C., 1945-46, Piedmont, S.C., 1946-47, Columbia, S.C., 1950-51, Manteca, Calif. 1967-68; kindergarten tchr. First Baptist Ch., Medford, Oreg. 1965-67; tchr. elem. sch. Marysville (Calif.) Unified Sch. Dist., 1968-83; tchr. Headstart, Manteca 1968; recipient appreciation Marysville Unif. Sch. Dist. 1983; mem: Calif. Ret. Tchrs. Assn., Nat. Ret. Tchrs. Assn., AAUW, AARP, Sutter Hist. Soc.; civic bds: Fremont Med. Ctr. Auxiliary Volunteers, Yuba City 1984-94, Christian Assistance Network, Yuba City (bd. 1984-85), Youth Service Bur. Yuba City (past counselor), Girl Scouts Am. Medford, Oreg. (troop ldr. 1962-63); Evangelical Free Ch. (deaconess, past S.S. tchr.). Res: 1264 Charlotte Ave Yuba City 95991

HIGGINBOTHAM, LLOYD WILLIAM, professional association executive director; b. Nov. 24, 1934, Smithfield, Pa.; s. Clarence John and Nannie Mae (Piper) H.; m. Genevieve Law, Oct. 17, 1954 (div.); m. Mary Bannaian, July 23, 1966; children: Mark William b. 1958, Samuel Lloyd b. 1967. Career: pres. Higginbotham Research, Cleve. 1953-64; pres. Lloyd Higginbotham Assoc., Canoga Park, Calif. 1970–; founder, pres. & CEO: Enhance Engring. Edn. Found. Inc., Engineers of the World, Inc., and Engineer's Councils Inc. 1994–; exec. dir. Inst. for the Advancement of Engring., Woodland Hills 1984-93, exec. mgr. Los Angeles Council of Engrs. & Scientists, L.A. 1984-93; awards: comm. svc. Mayor City of Downey 1974, NASA Space Shuttle technology transfer award 1980, commendn. Calif. Legislature 1983, numerous profl. awards include Soc. of Carbide and Tool Engrs. (chmn's award 1974), Soc. of Mfg. Engrs.- individual contbns. to industry, edn. and govt. 1978, 79, 80, mgmt. award 1982, disting. engring. interprofessional relations award 1989, Nat. Soc. Profl. Engrs./ Calif. Soc. Profl. Engrs. engring. achiev., mgmt. skills 1983, outstanding contbn. to engring. and sci. community 1986, distinguished interprofl. engring. relations award 1987, William B. Johnson Internat. Interprofessional Founders Memorial Award, SFVEC 1992; mem: N.Y. Acad. Scis. 1989, Inst. for Advance. Engring. (Fellow 1982, Coll. of Fellows, mgr. currently), Soc. of Carbide and Tool Engrs. (1967–, exec. bd., chapt. chmn. 1974-76), Sales and Mktg. Assn. L.A. (founding mem., ofcr. 1967–), Toastmasters Salesmasters 999 L.A. 1966–, Soc. Mfg. Engrs. (1977–, western reg. ofcr.), S.F.V. Engrs. Joint Council (1977, pres. 1981-82, 92-94, permanent pres. & CEO, steering com., advy. council), L.A. Council Engrs. and Scientists (del. from SME 1977–), Am. Soc. Assn. Execs., L.A. Area C.of C., Town Hall of Calif., Coll. and Univ. Mfg. Engring. Council (founding charter mem. 1979), Computer and Automated Systems Assn. (founding chmn. L.A. chpt. 249, 1978), F&AM Zenith Lodge (Van Nuys); Republican; Prot.; rec: boating, golf, spectator sports. Res: 24300 Calvert St Woodland Hills 91367 Ofc: POB 5012 Woodland Hills 91365

HIGGINS, K. MILTON, pastor, Baptist foundation executive; b. Dec. 31, 1936, Kosse, Tx.; s. Leland Alonza and Ida Florine (Ray) H.; m. Jarrene S. Pearce, Feb. 1, 1958; children: Kathrine E. Cruise b. 1959, K. Milton, Jr. b. 1960, Janneth G. Russell b. 1964; edn: BA, Baylor Univ., 1959; BD, Golden Gate Baptist Sem., 1962, DMin, 1973; ordained to ministry So. Baptist Ch., 1959. Career: music dir. East Waco Baptist Chapel, Waco, Tx. 1955-57; music, youth dir. Bosqueville Baptist Ch. 1957-59; First Baptist Ch., Gilroy, Calif. 1959-60; pastor First Baptist Ch., Hilmar, Calif. 1960-62; Hillsdale Blvd. Baptist Ch., Sacramento 1962-69; First Southern Baptist Ch., San Mateo 1969-77; First Southern Baptist Ch., Seaside 1977-79; Richland Baptist Ch., Richland, Wash. 1979-84; director Calif. Plan of Ch. Finance, Fresno 1984-91, exec. v.p. Calif. Baptist Found., 1991–, 1st v.p. Calif. Southern Baptist Convention 1973-74, bd. mem. Golden Gate Baptist Theol. Seminary (Alumni Assn. Bd.), Mill Valley; bd. mem. various com. Southern Baptist Convention and Calif. Southern Baptist Convention (commr. Stewardship Commn. 1994); listed Outstanding Young Men Am. 1971, Who's Who in West 1975–, Who's Who in Religion 1980–, Who's Who in Am. 1984–, Who's Who in Finance 1989–; mem. Assn. of Baptist Found. Execs. 1984–; contbr. articles in num. jours. 1975–, "Tieing Up Loose Ends of Life" 1992; Republican; rec: golf, gardening, fishing, hunting. Res: 945 W Alamos Fresno 93705 Ofc: Calif. Baptist Foundation 7120 N Whitney Ave #105 Fresno 93720

HIGHTOWER, CAROL ANN, advertising company executive; b. Sept. 22, 1950, Hanford, Calif.; d. Russell Malcolm and Carolyn Elizabeth (Brothers) Hightower; edn: AA, West Hills Coll., Coalinga, Calif. 1970; BA, Fresno State 1972, MA, advt., Calif. State Univ., Fullerton 1977. Career: reporter KFRE TV, Fresno, Calif. 1970-72; P.R. dir. Kings Co. YMCA, Hanford, Calif. 1968-70, Central Valley YMCA, Fresno 1971-73, Anaheim C.of C. 1973-74; freelance work, Orange Co. 1974-75; pres. Tower Advt., Costa Mesa 1975–; listed Who's Who in Leading Executives, Who's Who in Am.; mem.: Sigma Delta Chi 1972-84, PAWS; author: currently writing 2 books in field; Republican; Baptist; rec: dogs, boating, swimming, reading. Ofc: Tower Advertising 3151 Airway Bldg I #2 Costa Mesa 92626

HILDEBRAND, FRANCES L., computer technologies executive, consultant, civic leader; b. Sept. 30, 1943, San Francisco; d. Daniel and Matilda (Wellington) Hildebrand; edn: Barnard Coll.; BS, UC Berkeley 1966; adv. profl. seminars Stanford, MIT. Career: staff Standards/Disaster Recovery, San Francisco 1977; dist. mgr. Buena Park Computer Ctr., Buena Park 1978-80; hardware, asset mgmt., site planning, Pacific Bell, San Francisco 1980-85, dist. mgr. Future Technologies Architecture, Pacific Bell 1986-88, staff dir. Systems Technology Dist., 1988-89, dir. hardware, asset mgmt., operational support, 1989-94; owner Hildebrand Consulting 1994–; advy. com. JFK Univ. graduate pgm. in data proc. 1985, instr., data proc., UCB Ext. 1984; honors: Phi Beta Kappa 1966; civic: Ctr. for Elderly, Suicide Prevention and Grief Related Services (bd.), Commonwealth Club, World Affairs Coun., Grand Prix Assn. (past patron), Nob Hill Assn.; rec: writing, current events. Address: 1177 California St #722 San Francisco 94108

HILEMAN, RALPH ARMS, consultant; b. Oct. 25, 1931, Detroit, Mich.; s. W. Ralph and Esther Elizabeth (Arms) H.; m. Beatrice Ackley, Feb. 17, 1950;

children: Don b. 1955, Catherine b. 1957, Lawrence b. 1961, Raymond b. 1963; edn: BS physics, Univ. Mich. 1952; Univ. Minn. 1957-58; Calif. Western Univ. 1960-62; MBA mktg., UCLA 1976. Career: consultant computer networks; pres. Advanced Combat Systems Internat., dir. Navy Programs, QuesTech Tactical Systems Group; v.p. bus. devel. DRS of Calif., Tustin, dir. bus. devel. we. region; program mgr. Litton Data Systems, Van Nuys; dir. army and intelligence programs Univac (div. Sperry Rand Corp.); engr. Norden Labs., White Plains, N.Y.; honors: Phi Eta Sigma; mem: IEEE (sr.), Navy League, Am. Soc. of Naval Engrs., Am. Radio Relay League; co-inventor data processing system; mil: E-4 AUS 1953-55; Republican; rec: amateur radio, photog. Address: 14176 Grande Vista Ave Lake Mathews 92570

HILGER, FREDERICK LEE, JR., lawyer, financial and real estate executive; b. Feb. 17, 1946, Dallas; s. Frederick Lee Sr. and Maryann Taylor (Ayers) H.; m. Terri Lynn Wilson, May 13, 1984 (div. 1990); children: Matthew Charles, Kristen Leigh; edn: BA, Univ. of the Pacific, 1967; JD, UC Berkeley, 1970; admitted bar: Calif. 1971. Career: sr. tax acct. Touche Ross and Co., San Francisco 1971-73; atty. F.L. Hilger Profl. Corp., Eureka 1973-75; mng. ptnr. Moses Lake Farms, Wash. 1975-78; sr. cons. Sites and Co. Inc., Seattle 1978-79; v.p. ops. mgmt. U.S. Cruises Inc., Seattle 1980-83; pres. and c.f.o. First Nat. Bank, Chico, Calif. 1984-86; pres. and c.e.o. FreeHill Corp., San Marcos 1986–; awards: Outstanding banker Am. Bankers Assn., First Nat. Bank (1984, 1985); mem: Am. Bar Assn., Calif. Bar Assn., San Diego County Bar Assn.; clubs: Olympic (S.F.), Shadowridge Golf; Republican; Presbyterian. Ofc: Freehill Corp. PO Box 1808 San Marcos 92079-1808

HILL, ALICE LORRAINE, researcher, educator; b. Jan. 15, 1935, Moore, Okla.; d. Robert Edward Hill (Kingfisher '89er) and Alma Alice (Fraysher) H.; children: Debra Hrboka b. 1952, Pamela Spangler b. 1955, Eric Shiver b. 1960, Lorraine Smith b. 1965; edn: grad., Patricia Stevens Modeling Sch., Orlando, Fla. 1963; student, Draughton Sch. Bus., Oklahoma City 1968-69, Troy State Univ. 1970-71, Ventura Coll. 1974; AA in gen. edn., Rose Coll., Midwest City, Okla.; BS in bus. and acctg., Central State Univ. 1977; student, Univ. Okla. 1977-78; earned 4 masters degree-equivalents in acctg., bus., real estate and computer sci.; accredited tchr. Calif.; ordained minister Gospel Ministry, 1982; lic. realtor. Career: former model; with L.A. Unified Sch. Dist.; Gravity Drop & Dead Bolt Lock Inc., Oxnard, Calif. 1993; founder A. Hill & Assocs. 1993–; co-producer "Americana 2000" internat. edn. project 1994–; co-founder (with E. Shafenberg) Laws of Moses Common Law Legal Assn., Kingfisher, Okla.; honors: lifetime Calif. State comm. coll. tchg. credentials, hon. scholarship Okla. Univ. 1977-78, recognized by the Nat. Registry for patriotic poems, known as "The Oklahoma Poet", listed Who's Who of Intellectuals, Internat. Biographical Inst. and others, named Most Admired Woman of Decade and appt. gov. (life) Am. Biographical Inst.; mem: Nat. Assn. Female Executors 1995–, Internat. Platform Assn., United Teachers. of L.A., NEA, English Fellowship; author: America, We Love You (poem printed in Congressional Record 1975), num. other poems and songs; Independent; Israelite. Res: 1646 Lime Ave Oxnard 93033-6897 Ofc: A. Hill & Assocs PO Box 6605 Oxnard 93031-6605

HILL, FRANKLYN CHAPMAN, JR., physician; b. Dec. 31, 1926, Wash., D.C.; s. Franklyn Chapman Hill, Sr. and Alice Rose (Bowen) H.; m. Martha Jean Roberts, July 19, 1959; children: Elizabeth b. 1960, Anne b. 1962, Martha b. 1964, Sarah b. 1966; edn: BS, Franklin & Marshall, Lancaster, Pa. 1946; MD, Jefferson Med. Coll., Phila., Pa. 1950. Career: residency tng. Highland Co. Hosp., Oakland, Calif. 1953-55, VA Hosp., San Francisco 1955-56, Jefferson Med. Coll., Phila., Pa. 1956-57, Stanford Univ. Hosp. 1957-59; physician, pvt. practice, Oakland, Calif. 1959–; mem: AMA 1950–, CMA 1959–, ACCMA 1959–, Am. Acad. of Neurology 1962–, San Francisco Neurologist Soc. 1958–; mil: comdr. USNR 1944-ret.; Republican; rec: fly fishing, tennis, golf. Ofc: 419 30th St Oakland 94609 Tel: 510/832-0331

HILL, LORIE ELIZABETH, psychotherapist; b. Oct. 21, 1946, Buffalo, NY; d. Graham and Elizabeth Helen (Salm) H.; edn: Univ. of Manchester, Eng. 1966-67; BA, Grinnell Coll. 1968; MA, Univ. Wis. 1970; MA, CSU Sonoma 1974; PhD, Wright Inst. 1980. Career: English instr. Univ. of Mo. 1970-71; adminstr./supr. Antioch- West & Ctr. for Independent Living, Berkeley 1975-77; dir. of tng. Ctr. for Edn. & Mental Health, S.F. 1977-80; exec. dir. 1980-81; instr. MA pgm. in psychol. John F. Kennedy Univ., Orinda 1994–; psychotherapist, pvt. practice, Berkeley and Oakland, 1981–; speaker on cross-cultural psychology; civic: Psychotherapists for Soc. Responsibility (founding mem.), Nat. Abortion Rights Action League, Nat. Orgn. Women, Big Brothers & Big Sisters of the East Bay (psychologist 1986-88), City of Oakland Youth Skills Devel. Pgm. (vol. instr.); Rainbow Coalition for Jesse Jackson's Pres. Campaign, Ron Dellums Reelection Com., Mental Health Profls. Against Racism (founding mem.); campaign to elect Keith Carson Alameda Co. Supr., Social Action Chair Alameda Co. Psychol. Assn. 1992-95, co-chair Cultural Diversity for Calif. Psychol. Assn. 1993-95, co-chair of social issues, Calif. Psychol. Assn., founder and chair Psychotherapists Against Violence (teach violence prevention and unlearning racism), and trainer for trainers at 3rd Internat. Conflict Resolution Conf., St. Petersburg, Russia; rec: sports, travel, reading. Ofc: 3955 Shattuck Ave Berkeley 94705

HILL, LOWELL STANLEY, designer, business owner; b. Feb. 5, 1934, Fort Sheridan, Ill.; s. Jack and Velma Opal (Borton) H.; m. Barbara Matilde Suarez, Nov. 9, 1957; children: Lowell b. 1958, Velma b. 1959, Barbara b. 1961, Sandra b. 1962, Stanley b. 1964; edn: Univ. of Mo. 1953-56; Chaffey Coll. 1959; AA, Mt. San Antonio Coll. 1962, tchrs. creds. 1967. Career: illustrator US Army, Ft. Leonard Wood, Mo. 1953-56; mgr. Stout Sign Co., Long Beach 1957-58; lead man Circuit Bd. Div. Gen. Dynamics, Pomona 1959-63; tech. advr./ store mgr. E.W. Dorn Co., Gardena 1963-70; tchr. Los Angeles Trade Tech. Coll., L.A. 1966-68; owner/ designer/ cons. Lowell S. Hill Enterprises, Ontario 1970–; guest spkr.: Cal Poly Univ., Pomona; Mt. San Antonio Coll., Walnut; Foundation Sch., Montebello; moderator and featured spkr. Screen Printing Internat. Convention, L.A. 1984; guest technical trainee Zurich Bolting Mfg. Co., Switz. 1975; honors: hon. chief Nez Perce Nation (1970); mem: Screen Printing Internat., Nat. Small Bus. Assn., Calif. Assn. Indep. Bus., U.S. C.of C., Rancho Cucamonga C.of C.; civic: L.A. Trade Tech. Coll. trade advy com., Am. Indian Week (v.p 1968–), Boy Scouts of Am. (ldr. 1972-75); research: European methods as applied to design, mfg. of screen printing rel. prods.; original designs of metal frames; first to import the Swiss Harlacher screen stretcher to U.S., 1980; mil: sgt. E-5 AUS 1953-56, Army Champion Pistol Team 1955; Republican; R.Cath.; rec: target shooting, hunting, archery. Res: 775 W 24th St Upland 91784 Ofc: Lowell S. Hill Enterprises, 8555 Red Oak St Rancho Cucamonga 91729

HILL, MARTIN ROY, journalist; b. Jan. 2, 1954, Long Beach; s. Martin Raymond and Sophie Wanda (Bralski) H.; m. Winke Self, May 18, 1984; edn: AA, El Camino Coll., 1975; BA in journ., CSU Dominguez Hills, 1977. Career: assoc. editor The Weekly Journal, CSUDH, 1975-77; news editor Beach Cities Newspapers, Hermosa Beach 1977-78; staff writer The Desert Sun, Palm Springs 1978-81; editor Today Mag., Palm Desert 1981-82; staff writer San Diego Log, San Diego 1982-83; senior editor San Diego Magazine, 1983, 90, freelance writer 1990-93, editor San Diego Business Journal 1993–; awards: Who's Who in Poetry in Am. Colls. and Univs. 1975, Outstanding Young Men Am. 1977, best news story, best news photo, best editiorial P.S. Desert Press Club 1980, achiev. award Evening News Assn. 1981 Best news feature, Best business writing San Diego Press Club 1984, Best news feature, Best of show S.D. Press Club 1986, 1st pl. magazines, S.D. Co. Med. Soc. Media/Health Awards 1985, 88, William Allen White Awards for investigative reporting City and Regional Mag. Assn. 1986, 88, best feature writing, best editorial Soc. Profl. Journalists S.D. Chpt. 1987, 88, 1st pl. media award for legal issues, mag., S.D. Co. Bar Assn. 1987; mem: Soc. Profl. Journalists, S.D. Press Club; mil: p.o. USCGR 1973-80, USNR 1983-86; rec: animals/ wildlife, computers. Ofc: San Diego Business Journal, 4909 Murphy Canyon Rd., Ste 200, San Diego 92123

HILSINGER, RAYMOND LOUIS, JR., otolaryngologist - head & neck surgeon; b. Aug. 24, 1936, Cincinnati, Ohio; s. Raymond Louis and Angelese Clarisa (Hays) H.; m. Cristine Astrid Bjork; children: Daniel b. 1986, Elise b. 1991; edn: BA, Dartmouth Coll., Hanover, NH; MD, Univ. of Cincinnati, Ohio 1964; rotating internship, Phil. Gen. Hosp. 1964-65; general surgery, Hahnemann Med. Coll. and Hosp., Phil., PA 1965-66; otolaryngology, Eye and Ear Hosp., Univ. of Pittsburgh, PA 1966-69; med. lic. Arizona, Calif., PA; cert., Am. Bd. of Otolaryngology 1970. Career: dept. of otolaryngology, USAF, Sheppard Reg. Hosp., Wichita Falls, TX 1969-71; chief, dept. of otolaryngology 1970-71; dept. of head & neck surgery Kaiser Permanente Med. Ctr., Oakland 1971–, dir. otolaryngology-head & neck surgery residency tng. prog. 1972–, chief, dept. of head & neck surgery 1985–; cons. staff VA Med. Ctr., Martinez, Calif. 1976–; courtesy staff Kaiser Permanente, San Francisco 1976–; bd. dirs. Bay Area Tumor Inst. 1985–; mem. Kaiser Permanente Med. Ctr., Oakland, prog. dirs. com. 1987–, quality assurance com. 1985–, operating rm. com. 1985–, exec. com. 1985–, tumor bd. com. 1977–, profl. edn. com. 1975–, resident com. 1972–, acting chmn. East Bay Head & Neck Tumor Conf. 1989–, steering com. chmn. East Bay Head & Neck Pretreatment Conf. 1989–; chiefs of otolaryngology com. Kaiser Permanente Med. Ctrs. No. Calif. Region 1985- (chmn, chiefs. of otolaryngology com. 1985-87); mem. We. Head & Neck Cooperative Study Group 1989–; reviewer Otolaryngology-Head & Neck Surgery Exec. Com. 1988–; reviewer Annals of Otology, Rhinology and Laryngology 1984–; honors: Honor Award, Am. Acad. of Otolaryngology Head & Neck Surgery 1986, Thaddeus Seymour Award, Dartmouth Co.. 1958; mem: Soc. of Univ. Otolaryngologists-Head & Neck Surgeons 1991–, Assn. of Academic Depts. of Otolaryngology 1989–, Am. Soc. for Head & Neck Surgery (fellow 1989–), Pan Am. Assn. of Oto-Rhino-Laryngology Head & Neck Surgery 1988–, Pacific Coast Oto-Ophthalmological Soc. 1987- (councillor-at-large, otolaryngology 1990–), Am. Laryngological, Rhinological and Otological Soc. (The Triological Soc.; fellow 1985–), Am. Acad. of Otolaryngology-Head & Neck Surgery (fellow 1985–, med. informatics com. 1992–, plastic & reconstructive surgery com. 1991–, gov. 1989–), Am. Coll. of Surgeons (fellow 1972–, com. of applications., Dist. #2 1982–, prog. co-chmn. No. Calif. chpt. otolaryngology sect. 1986-87, prog. chmn. 1987-89), No. Calif. Kaiser Permanente Head & Neck Surgery Soc. (1971–, pres. 1975-76), Alameda-Contra Costa Co. Med. Assn., AMA, CMA, Calif. Assn. of Laryngectomies (exec. com. 1987–), Am. Acad. of Ophthalmology and Otolaryngology (fellow 1971-82), Am. Council of Otolaryngology 1970-81, Easter Seal Soc. of

Alameda Co. (profl.-med. advy. com. 1984–); author/co-author: 30+ scientific articles pub. in profl. jours., 1970–, num. scientific presentations, 1969–; mil: maj., USAF 1969-71. Ofc: Dept. Head & Neck Surgery Kaiser Permanente Medical Ctr Oakland 94611

HILTON, WILLIAM BARRON, hotel executive; b. Oct. 23, 1927, Dallas, Tx.; s. Conrad Nicholson and Mary Barron H.; m. Marilyn June Hawley, Chgo., June 20, 1947; children: William Barron, Jr., b. 1948, Hawley Anne, b. 1949, Stephen Michael, b. 1950, David Alan, b. 1952, Sharon Constance, b. 1953, Richard Howard, b. 1955, Daniel Kevin, b. 1962, Ronald Jeffrey, b. 1963. Career: founder, gen. ptnr. Vita-Pakt Citrus Products Co., 1946; v.p./ dir. Hilton Hotels Corp., 1954-66, pres./CEO, chmn./ pres./ c.e.o. 1979–; pres. San Diego Chargers Ltd., 1961-66; pres. Am. Football League, 1965; dir. Mfrs. Hanover Trust Co. 1970–, dir. Conrad N. Hilton Found.; trustee City of Hope; honors: Hon. Dr. of Humane Letters, Univ. of Houston 1986, Hotel Man of Year, Penn State Univ. 1969; mem: LA World Affairs Council, Chevalier Confrerie de la Chaine des Rotisseurs, Magistral Knights Sovereign Mil. Order of Malta, Pres. Council of EAA Fedn.; clubs: Bel Air CC, Los Angeles CC, Morningside CC, Thunderbird CC, Bel-Air Bay; mil: photog. mate USN, 1946; rec: soaring, flying, photog., hunting & fishing. Res: 1060 Brooklawn Dr Holmby Hills 90024 Ofc: Hilton Hotels Corp. 9336 Civic Center Dr Beverly Hills 90210

HINCKLEY, GREGORY KEITH, financial executive; b. Oct. 3, 1946, San Francisco; s. Homer Clair and Josephine F. (Gerrick) H.; m. Mary Chomenko, Feb. 14, 1987; children: Blake b. 1987, Allison b. 1989; edn: BA physics, Claremont McKenna Coll., 1968; MS physics, UC San Diego, 1970; MBA, Harvard Univ., 1972; CPA, Ill., 1977. Career: 2d v.p. Continental Bank, Chgo. 1972-78; dir. finance Itel Corp., San Francisco 1978-79; group controller Raychem Corp., Menlo Park 1979-83; v.p. fin. Bio-Rad Laboratories, Hercules 1983-88; sr.v.p. fin. Crowley Maritime Corp., Oakland 1988-91; v.p. fin. VLSI Technology Inc., San Jose 1992–; dir: Escagenetics Corp., San Bruno 1983-90, Advanced Molecular Systems, Vallejo 1989–, Compass Design Automation Inc., San Jose 1993–, OEC Med. Systems Inc., Salt Lake City 1995–; awards: Woods Hole Oceanographic Inst. fellow 1967, Fulbright scholar Nottingham Univ., England 1968-69; mem: Am. Inst. CPAs 1977–, Financial Execs. Inst., Am. Diabetes Assn. No. Calif. (dir. 1985-87). Res: 26201 Catherine Ct Los Altos Hills 94022

HINDERSCHEID, ROBERT EDMUND, accountant; b. Jan. 4, 1934, Youngstown, Ohio; s. Edmund Anthony and Agnes Elizabeth (Welsch) H.; m. Judith Ann Labbe, Sept. 3, 1955 (div. 1982); children: Robert b. 1956, James b. 1957, Nancy b. 1958, David b. 1959, Ann b. 1961, William b. 1963; m. Helen Louise Hensley, Jan. 16, 1982; edn: BSBA, Univ. Notre Dame, 1955. Career: acctg. staff Firestone Tire & Rubber Corp., Akron, Oh. 1955-56, acctg. mgr. Firestone, Salinas, Calif. 1966-76, personnel staff 1976-82; controller McCormick/Schilling Co., 1982-85; gen. acctg. mgr. Radionics Inc., 1985; recipient outstanding achiev. of yr. United Way Salinas 1976, 1986; mem. Nat. Assn. of Accts., Notre Dame Club of Mont. Peninsula, Elks Lodge; civic: United Way of Salinas Valley (bd. dirs. 1980-87), Sacred Heart Ch. (Pastoral Council pres. 1988-90, Internat. Fest. chmn. 1989, fin. com. 1988, Eucharistic Minister 1987); Republican; Cath.; rec: golf, charities, grandchildren, ch. activities. Res: 150 Kern St #89 Salinas 93905

HINDIN, RUSSELL, investment banker; b. March 11, 1946, Los Angeles; s. Irving and Alice (Jacobson) H.; children: Trevor Russell, Devin Alyce; edn: BS internat. fin., USC 1969. Career: loan ofcr. Union Bank, San Francisco 1969-72; branch mgr. Crocker Bank Leasing 1972-74; dist. mgr. Bank of Calif., Los Angeles 1974-75; dist. mgr. Chemical Bank Leasing 1975-76; v.p. A.M. Gelber & Co. 1976-79; mng. dir. Hindin/Owen/Engelke Inc. 1979–; dir. Turnaround Mgmt. Assn. 1992, 93; contbr. articles on fin. to profl. jours.; mem: Western Assn. Equipment Lessors (dir. 1974-75), Commerce Assocs., Assn. Corp. Growth (dir. 1989); mil: tech. sgt. USAF 1967-73; rec: tennis. Ofc: Hindin Owen Engelke Inc. 10920 Wilshire Blvd Los Angeles 90024-6516

HINKLE, JAMES ROBERT, II, dentist; b. Sept. 26, 1948, Iowa City; s. James R. and Jean (Sankot) H.; m. Randi Carlson, Aug. 6, 1985; 1 son, James R., III, 1 dau., JoCarlson; edn: BS, US Naval Acad., 1970; DDS, Georgetown Univ., 1981. Career: gen. dentist pvt. practice, Alameda Calif., 1982; Fellow Acad. Gen. Dentistry, mem. Craniomandibular Inst., US Naval Acad. Alumni Inst. (life), Navy League; mil: lt. jg USN 1970-75; Republican; Presbyterian; rec: sailboat racing, computers. Res: 607 Harbor Rd Alameda 94501 Ofc: James R. Hinkle DDS 2229 Santa Clara Ave Ste D Alameda 99501

HINMAN, HARVEY DEFOREST, lawyer; b. May 7, 1940, Binghamton, N.Y.; s. George Lyon and Barbara (Davidge) H.; mm. Margaret Snyder, June 23, 1962; children: George, Sarah, Marguerite; edn: BA, Brown Univ. 1962; JD, Cornell Univ. 1965; admitted St. Bar Calif. 1966. Career: atty., assoc. Pillsbury Madison & Sutro, San Francisco 1965-72, ptnr. 1973-93; v.p. and gen. counsel Chevron Corp. 1993–; bd. dirs., secty. Holbrook Palmer Park Found. 1977-86; bd. dirs. Phillips Brooks Sch. 1978-84, pres. 1982-84; bd. trustees Castillija Sch. 1988-92; bd. govs. Filoli Center 1988–, pres. 1993–; bd. dirs. Legal Aid Soc. of San Francisco 1995–; mem: Am. Bar found. (fellow), Am. Bar Assn., S.F. Bar Assn.

HIRAMATSU, MIKA, pediatrician; b. Oct. 26, 1963, Stanford, Calif.; m. John W. Duey, Oct. 6, 1990; edn: BS, UC Berkeley 1985; MD, UC San Francisco 1989. Career: resident physician Children's Hosp., Oakland 1989-92; physician Castro Valley Pediatrics 1992–; staff attending physician Children's Hosp., Oakland 1992–; awards: Phi Beta Kappa, UC Berkeley Regents & Alumni Scholar 1981-85, Children's Hosp., Oakland Higashino award for Clin. Excellence 1992; mem: Am. Acad. of Pediatrics (cand. fellow) 1992–, Japanese Am. Citizens League 1984–; rec: piano, violin, singing. Ofc: Castro Valley Pediatrics 20101B Lake Chabot Rd Castro Valley 94546 Tel: 510/581-1446

HIRASUNA, ALAN RYO, research and development company executive; b. Sept. 27, 1939, Fresno; s. Fred Yoshio and Setsu H.; m. Diana Woods, Aug. 1963; m. 2d. Teresa, Feb. 22, 1986; 1 son, Brian b. 1964; edn: BS, UC Berkeley 1962; MS, USC, 1969; reg. profl. engr. Calif. 1965. Career: refinery engr. Chevron, El Segundo 1962-64; research engr. N. Am. Rockwell, Downey 1964; program engr. Ford Aerospace, Newport Beach 1964-71; v.p. L'Garde Inc., Tustin 1971–, dir. 1971–; AASRC, Prospect Park, Pa. dir. 1984–; awards: Geothermal Resources Council Best Paper 1980; mem: Am. Chemical Soc. (rubber div.), ASME, Soc. Petroleum Engrs., Am. Defense Preparedness Assn., Tustin Comm. Found. (dir. 1995–), Tustin C.of C. (ambassador 1988–), Tustin Sr. Center Sr. Task Force; 3 patents, 1981-86, 35+ reports and papers pub. in tech. jours., 1975–; rec: woodworking. Res: Newport Beach

HIRATA, HENRY MINORU, civil engineer/public works director; b. March 29, 1937, Stockton; s. Roy Ko and Toshiye (Teranishi) H.; m. ALice Nasuko, July 17, 1939; children: Lori b. 1967, Karen b. 1969; edn: AA, Stockton Jr. Coll. 1961; BSCE, Univ. of Pacific 1964. Career: asst. civil engr. San Joaquin County Dept. of Public Works, Stockton 1964-74, assoc. civil engr. 1974-75, senior civil engr. 1975-78, prin. civil engr. 1978, dep. dir. 1978-83, dept. public works director, 1983–, San Joaquin County, FHWA Region 9 county engr. advisor; awards: Stockton Buddhist Temple Parents of Year 1980, Univ. Pacific Alumni fellow 1983, San Joaquin Engrs. Council Engr. of Year 1985, Univ. of Pacific Disting. Alumni award-Public Service 1994, United Way Hall of Fame Volunteer; mem: Japanese Am. Citizen League, Stockton Buddhist Temple, Am. Pub. Works Assn., Calif. Assn. County Engrs. (dir., past pres.), Nat. Assn. County Engrs. (research dir.), Univ. Pacific Alumni Assn., Inst. Transp. Engrs., Calif. Soc. Profl. Engrs., Nat. Soc. Profl. Engrs., Calif. Central Valley Flood Control Assn. (dir.), Calif. Assn. Flood Control Agencies, Rotary, Young Adult Buddhist Assn., ASCE, Pacific Athletic Found.; mil: AUS 1957-58; Buddhist; rec: basketball, sports, home improvements. Res: 5247 Shippee Ln Stockton 95212 Ofc: San Joaquin County Dept. of Public Works POB 1810 Stockton 95201

HIRAYAMA, YASUMASA, architect; b. Aug. 30, 1938, Kumamoto, Japan; s. Kazuyoshi and Nobuko (Tanaka) H.; m. Hiroko Matsumoto, May 29, 1971; children: Yukari b. 1971, Bertrand b. 1972, Emiko b. 1974; edn: BS arch., Tokai Univ. Japan 1962; BA arch., USC 1968. Career: staff W. Skinner 1968-69; job capt., architectural sr. draftsman Langdon & Wilson, Los Angeles 1969-73; project architect Esco Internat., Guam 1973-75; sr. draftsman Gin Wong & Assoc. 1975; job capt., sr. archtl. draftsman Maxwell Starkman & Assocs., Los Angeles 1975-76; William Pereira & Assocs. 1976; architect coordinator Genslera Assocs. 1976-78; architect Albert C. Martin 1978-86; The Ralph M. Parsons Co., Pasadena 1987; mem: AIA, Japanese Am. Citizen League, Japanese Am. Cultural & Comm. Center, Hollywood Japanese Cultural Inst., Japanese Sch. C.U.; Democrat; Buddhist; rec: golf, fishing. Res: 10132 Woodman Ave Mission Hills 91345 Ofc: Ralph M. Parsons Co. 100 W Walnut St Pasadena 91124 or Parson Engineers Ldt PO Box 9912 Ahmadi 61008, Kuwait

HIRSCH, RICHARD GARY, lawyer; b. June 15, 1940, Los Angeles; s. Charles and Billie (Leopold) H.; m. Claire Renee Recsei, March 25, 1967; 1 dau., Nicole b. 1967; edn: BA, UCLA 1963; JD, UC Berkeley Boalt Hall 1965. Career: intern Calif. St. Legislature 1965-66; dep. dist. atty. Los Angeles Dist. Attys. Office 1967-71; ptnr. Nasatir Sherman & Hirsch 1971-83; Nasatir, Hirsch & Podberesky, Santa Monica 1983–; judge pro tem Beverly Hills Municipal Ct.; chair Greek Theatre Advy. Com., L.A. 1976-79; field rep. Com. to Re-elect Gov. Brown 1966; awards: spl. merit Criminal Cts. Bar Assn. 1988, merit resolution L.A. City Council 1984; mem: Calif. Attys. for Criminal Justice (pres. 1987-88), Criminal Cts. Bar Assn. (pres. 1980), Beverly Hills Bar Assn. (bd. trustees 1984), Am. Bd. of Criminal Lawyers (fellow), L.A. Olympic Organizing Com., Santa Monica Museum of Art (pres. 1987-91), KCET Pub. T.V. (advy. com.); coauthor: Criminal Law, Practice and Procedure, Calif. CEB, Univ. Calif., 1986, 94, pub. law rev. article, 1971; mil: lt. AUS 1961-62. Ofc: Nasatir, Hirsch & Podberesky 2115 Main St Santa Monica 90405

HITCHCOCK, VERNON THOMAS, lawyer; b. Feb. 21, 1919, Selma, Ind.; s. Lucian Elmer and Loda Alice (King) H.; m. Betty K. Orr, May 24, 1949; children: Brenda, b. 1950; Linda, b. 1953; Nancy, b. 1955; Debra, b. 1957; Randolph, b. 1960; edn: BS, agric., Purdue Univ. 1940; JD, Stanford Univ. 1953; admitted Calif. Bar, U.S. Supreme Ct. Career: naval aviator, USNR, US & Pacific 1941-45; airline pilot Southwest Airways, S.F. 1946; airline pilot TWA, Kansas City, Mo. & San Francisco, Calif. 1947-51; atty. at law., pvt. practice, Healdsburg 1954-55; dep. Atty. Gen., State of Calif., Sacto. 1956; dep. County

Counsel, Sonoma County, Santa Rosa 1957-65; exec. dir. Libyan Aviation Co., Tripoli, Libya 1966-67; Legal Counsel Sonoma Co. Schs., Santa Rosa 1967-82; pvt. practice, law 1982-83; ptnr., farm mgr. GHJ Farms 1975-86; orginator of Freedom Under Law pgm. for tchg. jr. and sr. high sch. students about Am. law; mem: Reserve Ofcrs. Assn., US; Commonwealth Club, Calif., Naval Order of US, Quiet Birdmen, Ind. Order of Odd Fellows, Am. Security Council, Alpha Zeta, Purdue chpt., Indiana 4-H Club; author novel: The Airline to Infinity; mil: comdr. USNR 1941-69; Republican; Episcopalian; rec: trumpet (mem. Las Gallinas Valley Sanitary Dist. Non-Marching Band, Terra Linda), ham radio operator, KB6UOJ.

HOAGE, W(ILLIAM) GRANT, project engineering manager; b. Apr. 12, 1923, Butte, Mont.; s. William Grant and Lyra Evalena (Sanborn) H.; m. Edith Rae Maple; children: Mark Steven, Carol Frances; edn: BA, Occidental Coll., 1949; MHA, Washington Univ., St. Louis, Mo. 1951. Career: safety analyst Douglas Aircraft, El Segundo 1951-59; hosp./clinic adminstr. West Covina Hosp. and Med. Clinic, 1959-60; quality control analyst North American Aviation, Downey and Anaheim, 1960-71; regional med. planner UC Irvine, 1971-73; project engring. mgr. Rockwell Internat., Downey 1973–; cons. H.A. Price Assocs., Orange 1970, Northrop Services, Chgo., 1971; civic: Rockwell Employees Donate-Once (bd. 1987–), Orange County Health Planning Council (v.p., chmn. HMO, emergency svs. and facilities review coms. 1971-75), Hoag Memorial Hosp. Presbyn. Assn., Newport Beach (1964–, pres. 1974-84, mem. health ethics com. 1995–); lodge: Masons; mil: cpl. Army Air Corps 1942-45; Republican; Presbyterian. Res: 1617 N Shaffer St Orange 92667

HOANG, KIM-THOA T., lawyer; b. Saigon, Vietnam; edn: BA, Univ. Rennes France 1980; JD, Calif. Western Sch. Law 1987; admitted St. Bar Calif. 1987. Career: dep. city atty., San Diego City Atty. Office, Criminal div. 1987-89; research atty., San Diego Superior Court 1989-91; dep. dist. atty., San Diego County Dist. Attorney's Ofc. 1991–. Ofc: District Atty San Diego County 220 W Broadway San Diego 92101

HOARE, TYLER JAMES, sculptor, printmaker; b. June 5, 1940, Joplin, Mo.; s. Melvin James and Dorotha (Beadle) H.; m. Kathy Joyce Quinn, Mar. 9, 1963; dau., Janet Elane Orr b. 1964; edn: stu., sculpture, Univ. Colo. 1959, Sculpture Ctr., N.Y.C. 1960-61, Calif. Coll. Arts and Crafts 1966; BFA, Univ. Kansas, 1963. Career: sculptor and printmaker, Berkeley, 1965–; instr. UC Berkeley, Ext. 1973, 74; guest lectr. art depts. various univs. and colls., 1972–; exhibits internat. incl. San Francisco Mus. of Art, Cinti. Art Mus., Oakland Mus., Library of Congress, L.A. Co. Mus. Art, Pratt Graphics Center, N.Y., Pasadena Art Mus.; in permanent public collections: USIA, SUNY, Oakland Mus.; one man shows, 1964–, incl. UC Berkeley, Derby Gal., Berkeley, Lucien Labaud Gal., S.F. 1966, Free Univ. of Berkeley Gal., Frederic Hobb's S.F. Art Ctr. 1967, Green Gal., S.F. 1968, St. Mary's Coll. Art Gal., Moraga 1969, John Bolles Gal., S.F. (1969, 71, 74), Univ. Lancaster (Eng.), Camberwell Sch. Art, London, England 1971, SUNY, Albany, Atherton Gal., Menlo Park, Ca. 1972, Chabot Coll. Art Gal., Hayward, Stanford Univ., Richmond (Ca.) Art Ctr. 1973, CSU Hayward, Olive Hyde Art Ctr., Fremont 1974, Daly City Civic Ctr., San Mateo Arts Coun., County of San Mateo Hall of Justice 1975, Purdue Univ. Gallery 1 (1976), Spiva Art Ctr. Mo. So. State Coll. 1977, Manner of Speaking, S.F., Stuart Gal., Berkeley 1978, Studio 718, S.F. "Xerox Art 1970-1980" (1980), Geotrope Gal., Berkeley 1981, Studio Nine, Benicia, Marin Co. Civic Ctr., San Rafael 1982, Solano Comm. Coll. Art Gal. 1983, Oakland Art Assn. Gal. 1986, 1975 to 1993 Sculpture on the S.F. Bay, Six WWI Airplanes and Six Ships on the Bay 1988, Coastal Art League Mus., Half Moon Bay 1989; 1993 exhibits: Reverence in Wood, Univ. Art Gallery CSU Hayward;Sculpture & Sculptors Drawings ACCI Gallery; Ctr. for the Visual Arts, Oakland; ArtPool, Art Res. Ctr., Budapest; Steering Wheel West Art Gallery, S.F.; Photocopier Art, Ace Art , Winnipeg; Crossing Borders, Irvine Arts Ctr.; Campbell Hall U.C. Berkeley; The Univ. of Texas at Dallas; 10,000 Humans Edicions, Barcelona; Linked Dogma, Culver City; Monroe Com. Coll., Rochester NY; Hockey 100, Calgary; Kings & Queens, Fresno Art Museum; Museu de Arte de Goiania, Brasil; Luther Coll., Decora, Ia.; Corridor Gallery, Texas Tech. Univ.; Centre d'Art de Baie, Saint-Paul Quebec; AUA Gallery, Lebanon, NH; Artists Book-Works, Chicago; Les Vraie Folies Bergeres, Paris; Arlington Art Ctr., Arlington, Va.; Barrett Art Gallery, Utica College; Trip to Paris with the Maestro & Alice & Kathy (1993); videos,films, local and nat. radio and TV shows incl. Bill Moyers PBS "Creativity"; awards incl. Hon. Master Painting, Acad. Italia and dipl. of merit Univ. Delle Arti (Italy), Age of Enlightenment, T.M. Berkeley World Plan Ctr., 4th Ann. Bay Area Graphics competition DeAnza Coll., "Focuserie" Nat. Photog. Exh., Eire, Pa., 32nd Ann. San Francisco Art Fest.; mem. Richmond Art Ctr., L.A. Print Soc., Nat. Soc. Lit. and the Arts, Metal Arts Guild (S.F.), Oakland Mus. Assn., S.F. Art Inst., S.F. Mus. Art, Ctr. for the Visual Arts, Pro Arts (Oakland). Res: 30 Menlo Pl Berkeley 94707

HOBBS, FRANKLIN DEAN, III, lawyer; b. May 30, 1952, Huntington Park; s. Franklin Dean and Bette Jane (Little) H.; m. Barbara Victoria Shevlin, March 6, 1987; children: Matthew Martin Howley b. 1981, Lauren Anne Howley b. 1983, Rebecca Ellen b. 1988, Franklin Dean IV b. 1989; edn: BA, Claremont McKenna Coll. 1974; JD, UCLA Sch. Law 1977. Career: atty., assoc. Rutter &

Ebbert, Los Angeles 1977-81; Rutter Ebbert & O'Sullivan 1981-82, atty. 1983-84, Rutter O'Sullivan Greene & Hobbs 1984; Republican; Episcopalian. Res: 311 S Lucerne Blvd Los Angeles 90020 Ofc: Rutter O'Sullivan Greene & Hobbs 1900 Ave of Stars Los Angeles 90067

HOBBS, MARCIA L., investment company president; b. June 23, 1947, Los Angeles; d. William Albert and Elizabeth Anne (Johnson) Wilson; m. Jeffrey M. Hobbs, March 26, 1967 (div. 1984); children: Christian b. 1970, Nicholas b. 1972, Jeffrey b. 1973; edn: UCLA 1965-67; UC Berkeley 1967-68. Career: pres. Greater Los Angeles Zoo Assn., 1978-87; San Vicente Investments Inc. 1987–; commr. Calif. St. Dept. of Parks & Recreation 1984–; mem. Calif. Tourism Corp. 1983–; pub. mem. Nat. Petroleum Action Council, Wash. D.C. 1986-92; civic bds: Loyola Marymount Univ. Bd. Regents, Nat. Com. on U.S.-China Rels., Bd. Regents Childrens Hosp. L.A., Am. Women for Internat. Understanding, Rose Inst. of Claremont Mc Kenna Coll., L.A. (trusteeship), State Park Partners (pres.); Republican. Ofc: San Vicente Investments, Inc. 10475 Bellagio Rd Los Angeles 90077

HOBBS, MICHAEL STEVEN, corporate executive, real estate lawyer; b. June 24, 1949, Phoenix, Ariz.; s. Robert Stinson and Genevieve Lucille (Herbella) H.; m. Lori Ann Jemelian, Sept. 14, 1985; children: Brian b. 1987, Steven b. 1990; edn: BA, Pepperdine Univ. 1977; MBA, Loyola Marymount Univ. 1979; JD, Univ. West L.A. Law Sch. 1983; admitted bar: Calif. 1984. Career: regional mgr. Collins Food, Los Angeles 1969-85; v.p. ops. Am. Golf., Santa Monica 1985-88; dir. of real estate Sizzler Internat., Inc., Los Angeles 1988–; adj. prof. bus. law National Univ. 1991–; honors: Am. Jurisprudence award 1980, Traynor Tournament Moot Ct. 1982, Univ. West L.A. Dean's List 1981; mem: Am. Bar Assn., Assn. Trial Lawyers, Nat. Assn. Real Estate Execs. (past pres. Los Angeles chapt.); Republican; Christian; rec: photog., motorcycling, flying. Ofc: Sizzler International, Inc. 12655 W Jefferson Blvd Los Angeles 90066

HOBDY, FRANCES LEAP (RADER), real estate broker; b. Mar. 1, 1920, Fresno; d. Edward Gerald and Emma (Tittle) L.; m. Robert J. Rader, Jan. 19, 1943 (dec.); m. Morris M. Hobdy, May 27, 1972 (dec.); children: Robert Rader, Jr. b. 1944, Judith Rader b. 1948; edn: Coll. of William & Mary 1968-69; AA, Palomar Coll. 1976; BA, Newport Univ. 1979; desig: GRI (Graduate Realtors Inst.), Calif. Assn. of Realtors; CRS (Cert Residential Splst.), CRB (Cert RE Brokerage), Nat. Assn. of Realtors. Career: legal secty. Hatchett & Ford, Hampton, Va. 1961-67; realtor assoc. Denny Realty, Escondido 1973-75; broker assoc. Mark, Realtors, Escondido 1975-78; owner/broker Hobdy, Realtors, Escondido 1978–; dir. Fowble & Assocs., San Diego 1974–; trustee BORPAC, 1986-90; honors: resolution Calif. State Legislature 1983, appreciation Fifth Supervisorial Dist. 1983, Escondido Bd. of Realtors Realtor of Yr. 1986 and Special Appreciation Award- Mediator (1985, 89, 90), listed Who's Who in Fin. & Ind., Who's Who of Am. Women, Who's Who in Real Estate in Am., Book of Honor, Grand Amb. of Achiev. Intl., Directory of Distinguished Americans; mem: Escondido Bd. of Realtors (past pres., dir., mediator 1985–), Calif. Assn. of Realtors, Nat. Assn. Realtors, Nat. Mktg. Inst.; civic: Escondido C.of C., Zool. Soc. of San Diego, Smithsonian Assocs., San Diego Opera, Golden Wives Club, Meadowlark CC; Republican; Prot.; rec: exercise, computer. Ofc: Hobdy Realtors 10142 Lake Meadow Ln Escondido 92026

HOBERG, MICHAEL DEAN, management analyst, educator; b. Feb. 27, 1955, Pipestone, Minn.; s. Dennis Edwin and Beverly Ann (Voss) H.; divorced; 1 child. Heather b. 1982; m. Janet Lee Freeman, Mar. 5, 1995; edn: BS in Park Adminstrn., Calif. State Univ., Sacramento, 1977; MPA, Calif. State Univ., Turlock, 1982; grad., Law Enforcement Mgmt. Ctr., Stanton, Calif., 1988; PhD In Pub. Adminstrn., Greenwich Univ., 1993; grad. Christian Writers Guild, 1994. Career: ranger-naturalist Nat. Park Svc., Three Rivers, Calif., 1977; park ranger San Joaquin County, Stockton, Calif., 1977-82; park ranger State of Calif., Perris, 1982-83; park svs. specialist, San Joaquin Co., Stockton 1983-86, mgmt. analyst, 1986–; adj. instr. Delta Coll., Stockton, 1987-90; dir. Hoberg Mgmt. and Consulting, Stockton, 1987–; awards: recipient Cert. of Appreciation Calif. Peace Officers Assn., 1994, Sacramento Athletic Hall of Fame, Sacto. C.of C. 1977, Fencing Champion foil No. Calif. Intercollegiate Athletic Conf., 1977; mem. AAUP 1994–, ASPA 1994–, Acad. Criminal Justice Scis. 1994– (student affairs com. 1993-94), U.S. Fencing Assn. (9th pl. Nat. Championships award 1988), Stockton Asparagus Festival (com. mem. 1985); author: articles in Calif. Peace Ofcr. and Baptist Herald, 1994, dissertation "Quantifiable Indicators", 1993; Democrat; Baptist (mem. Quail Lakes Baptist Ch., Stockton 1986–); rec: fencing. Res: 2209 Meadow Ave Stockton 95207 Ofc: San Joaquin County Sheriff's Office 7000 S Canlis Blvd French Camp 95231

HOCH, SALLIE O'NEIL, biologist; b. Feb. 15, 1941, Mineola, N.Y.; d. Thomas F. and Mary (Robinson) O'Neil; m. James A. Hoch, May 17, 1969; children: James A., Jr. b. 1970, Patrick E. b. 1973; edn: St. Mary's Coll., Notre Dame, 1958-60; BS (magna cum laude) St. Bonaventure Univ., Olean, N.Y., 1964; MS, and PhD, Univ. Ill., Urbana, 1966, 1969. Career: postdoctoral fellow Scripps Clinic and Research Found., La Jolla, Calif. 1969-71, asst., assoc. 1971-77, asst. member 1978-83; principal scientist The Agouron Inst., La Jolla 1983–, and sr. scientist Agouron Pharmaceuticals Inc., 1984-93; mem. Arthritis Found.

Research Com. 1989-90; mem. NIH Special Review Coms. 1981, 90, 93, 95; ad hoc grant reviewer NIH, NSF, Lupus Found. of Am.; awards: NIH predoctoral fellow, 1966-68, Am. Cancer Soc. postdoctoral fellow, 1969-71, NIH res. career devel. award, 1975-80, res. grantee NIH, NSF, Lupus Found. of Am., 1971–; mem: Am. Coll. of Rheumatology, Am. Soc. for Cell Biology, Am. Soc. for Microbiology, Am. Soc. for Biochem. and Molecular Biology, Soc. of Sigma Xi; publs: 60+ research publs., 1968–, current ad hoc reviewer 15 sci. jours.; R.Cath. Res: 1054 Havenhurst Dr La Jolla 92037 Ofc: The Agouron Institute 505 Coast Blvd S La Jolla 92037

HOCKNEY, DAVID, artist; b. Bradford, Yorkshire, Eng., July 9, 1937; s. Kenneth and Laura H.; edn: Bradford Coll. Art, 1953-57; Royal Coll. Art, London 1959-62; D (hon.), Royal Coll. Art, London 1992; hon. degree, Univ. Aberdeen 1988, Royal Coll. Art. London 1992. Career: lectr. Univ. Iowa 1964; lectr. Univ. Colo. 1965; lectr. Univ. Calif., Berkeley 1967; lectr. UCLA 1966, hon. chair of drawing 1980; One-man shows: Kasmin Gallery 1963-89, Mus. Modern Art, N.Y.C. (1964, 68), Stedelijk Mus., Amsterdam, Netherlands 1966, Whitechapel Gallery, London 1970, Andre Emmench Gallery, N.Y.C. 1972–, Musee des Arts Decoratifs, Paris 1974, Museo Tamayo, Mexico City 1984, L.A. Louver. Calif. (1986, 89-90), Nishimura Gallery, Tokyo (1986, 89), Md. Mus. Art 1988, L.A. Co. Mus. Art 1988, Tate Gallery, London (1988, 92), others; designer: Rake's Progress, Glyndebourne, Eng. 1975; sets for Magic flute, Glyndebourne 1978, Parade Triple Bill, Stravinsky Triple Bill, Md. Opera House 1980-81, Tristan und Isolde, Los Angeles Music Ctr. Opera 1987; Turandot, Lyric Opera, Chgo. 1992–, San Francisco Opera 1993, Die Frau Ohne Schatten, Covent Garden, London 1992, L.A. Music Cir. Opera 1993; author: David Hockney by David Hockney 1976, David Hockney: Travels with Pen, Pencil and Ink 1978, Paper Pools 1980, David Hockney Photographs 1982, Cameraworks 1983, David Hockney: A Retrospective 1988, Hockney Paints the Stage 1984, That's The Way I See It 1993; illustrator: Six Fairy Tales of the Brothers Grimm 1969, The Blue Guitar 1977, Hockney's Alphabet 1991; awards: Guinness award and 1st prize for etching 1961, Gold medal Royal Coll. Art 1962, Graphic prize Paris Biennale 1963, 1st prize 8th Internat. exhbn. Drawings Lugano, Italy 1964, 1st prize John Moores Exhbn., Liverpool, Eng. 1967, German award of Excellence 1983, 1st prize Internat. Ctr. of Photog., N.Y. 1985, Kodak photog. book award for Camera works 1984, Praemium Imperiale Japan Art Assn. 1989. Ofc: 7508 Santa Monica Blvd West Hollywood 90046-6407

HODES, ABRAM, pediatrician; b. Mar. 2, 1922; s. Samuel and Rachel (Gross) H.; m. Mildred Rose Berzosky, June 22, 1947; children: Alan b. 1949, Jay b. 1951; edn: BS, Penn. State Coll., 1942 (Phi Beta Kappa 1942); BM, Northwestern Univ. Med. Sch., 1945, MD, 1946; bd. cert. Am. Bd. Peds. 1951, diplomate Am. Acad. Pediatrics 1958. Career: sch. pub. health physician San Bernardino County Health Dept., 1950; pvt. practice peds., San Bernardino 1950-89, pediatric staff San Bernardino County Hosp. 1950-87; honoree, named Staff Doctor of Yr. San Bernardino Community Hosp. 1989; mem: San Bdo. County Med. Soc. 1950–, Calif. Med. Assn. (ret.), AMA (ret.), L.A. Pediatric Soc., Hinterland Pediatric Soc., B'nai B'rith (San Bdo. pres. 1991-95), Elks, Optimist (life), Jewish War Veterans; mil: 1st lt. US Army; Republican; Jewish; rec: violin, medical book collector. Res: 604 E Avery St San Bernardino 92404

HODGIN, DAVID T., recreational parks management executive; b. June 8, 1932; s. David Reid and Elva Timberlake (Twamley) H.; m. Claire Evelyn Arnold, July 19, 1953; children: David Arnold, Kathryn Anne, Elizabeth Claire, Amanda Claudia; edn: Wesleyan Univ. 1950-51, BA econ., UC Santa Barbara, 1954; BFT internat. mgmt., Am. Grad. Sch. for Internat. Mgmt., Phoenix 1961; N.Y. Univ. Grad. Sch. of Bus. 1963-65; Cert. Plant Opr. (CPO). Career: asst. to v.p. International Paul Hardeman, Inc. Stanton, Calif. 1961; dir. adminstrn. Paul Hardeman S.A., Buenos Aires, Arg. 1962-63; office svs. supr. Owens Corning Fiberglas Corp., NY, NY 1964-65; v.p. adminstrn. Fibraglas S.A., Bogota, Col. 1965-67; bus. analyst Owens Corning Fiberglas Corp., Toledo, Oh. 1967-68; pres. Daire Assocs., Walnut Creek, Calif. 1968-78; pres. Am. Powerwash Corp., Concord 1969-78; v.p./gen. mgr. Sunset Recreation Inc., Menlo Park 1973-77; sr. cons. Leisure Mgmt. Consultants Inc., Concord 1975-77; pres. Pathfinder Cos., Scotts Valley 1977-89, chmn. bd. 1989–; pres. American Holiday Resorts Inc., 1983–; chmn./ceo Calif. Microelectronic Systems Inc. 1989-91; dir: Evergreen Holding Co. Ltd. 1986–, Conifer Reinsurance Ltd. 1987-93; mem: Calif. Travel Parks Assn. (pres. 1974-75), Nat. Campground Owners Assn. (v.p. 1976-78, pres. 1978-80); advisor Small Bus. Edn. Pgm. Cabrillo Coll. 1984-89; appt. Calif. Senate and Assembly Select Com. on Small Business, Sacto. 1982–, U.S. Small Bus. Adminstrn. Advy. Council, San Francisco (dist. chmn. 1983-87), Calif. State Conf. on Small Bus., Sacto. (pres. 1986-88); active Calif. Small Bus. Assn., Sacto. (pres. 1988-93), Nat. Small Bus. United, Wash. D.C. (trustee 1989–); mil: 1st lt. US Army, Civil Affairs and Mil. Govt., Active 1954-56. Ofc: #2 Blue Hill Scotts Valley 95066-3638

HODGSON, FRANK MILTON, school administrator; b. Feb. 3, 1924, Glendale; s. Christopher Thomas and Freda (Wilson) H.; m. Virginia Dollard, June 21, 1949; children: Lisa b. 1956, Lynn b. 1959; edn: BA, UC Santa Barbara 1948; MS, USC 1949; EdD, 1953; tchg. & admin. credentials Calif. (1949-53). Career: trng. tchr. Los Angeles Unif. Sch. Dist. 1949-53; asst. prin./coordinator research 1954-64; adminstv. coordinator 1965-66; asst. supr. inst. services 1967-70; dep. area adminstr. 1971-84; arbitrator: NYSE, Pac. Stock Exch. AAA, NASD, MSRB, 1988–; personnel commn. Santa Monica Unif. Sch. Dist.; adj. prof. USC, CSU San Diego, CSU Los Angeles, CSU Northridge 1953-76; cons. math. & social studies publs., Holt Rinehart Winston (1962-68); awards: Los Angeles City Council Resolution (1984), Who's Who in Am. Edn. (1966), recipient ten comm. service awards; mem: Chi Alpha Delta (pres. 1948), Phi Delta Kappa; civic: Los Angeles Grand Jury Service (1985-86), Personnel Commnr. (1985); contbr. articles in ednl. jours: Exceptional Children (1/64), Social Studies (11/56), Los Angeles Sch. Jour. (1/56), Sch. and Society (9/54); mil: sgt. AUS 1943-46; Indep.; Prot.; rec: swimming, travel. Address: Santa Monica 90403

HOELTER, JAMES EDWARD, international shipping industry executive; b. June 26, 1939, Milwaukee, Wis.; s. Edward H. and Suzanne E. (Grabill) H.; m. Virginia Smith, June 30, 1962; children: Christine, Elizabeth, James; BBA fin., Univ. Wis. 1961; MBA, Harvard Univ. 1965. Career: mktg. analyst corp. staff Ford Motor Co., Dearborn, Mich. 1965-66; zone mgr. Lincoln Mercury (div. Ford Motor Co.), Oakland 1966-70; CFO, Medimation, Ft. Worth 1970-71; dir. fin. leasing Itel Corp. (container div.), San Francisco 1971-75; v.p. N. Am. Trans Ocean Ltd. 1976-78; pres., co-founder Intermodal Equipment Assocs. 1979-87; bd. chmn. and CEO, Textainer Equipment Mgmt., Netherlands Antilles 1987-93; pres., CEO,Textainer Group Holdings Ltd., Bermuda 1993–; bd. dirs. Textainer Ltd., Bermuda, Holmac Holdings Inc., San Francisco, Textainer Capital Corp.; bd. of visitors Univ. of Wisconsin Sch. of Bus. 1994–; lectr. grad. sch. mgmt. Golden Gate Univ. 1977-78; mem: Piedmont Campfire Girls (dir. sustaining membership Piedmont 1973-76, BSA (com. chair recruiting 1979-85), Convalescent Hosp. Ministry-Alameda Co. (bd. overseers 1981-86, 90–), World Trade Club, Bankers Club, Chi Psi; co-author: Optical Scanning for Businessman, 1965; mil: 1st lt. AUS 1961-63; Republican; Episcopalian; rec: sailing, skiing, fly fishing. Address: Piedmont 94611

HOFFMAN, CHARLES LOUIS, physician; b. May 10, 1925, Dayton, Ohio; s. Hugh Holland and Ruth Louise (Thiele) H.; m. Nancy Adele Fahrendorf, June 14, 1947; children: Thomas C., Mary Lynne Hoffman Lamb, Lori Hoffman Brustkern, William Edward; edn: student, v.p. freshman class, Univ. of Dayton 1943; AB, Oberlin Coll. 1945; MD, St. Louis Univ. 1949. Career: med. intern U.S. Marine Hosp., Baltimore 1949-50; chief op. dept. U.S. Marine Hosp., Kirkwood, Mo. 1950-51; chief med. ofcr. 2nd Coast Guard Dist., St. Louis 1951; resident internal medicine U.S. Marine Hosp., San Francisco 1951-53, chief resident internal medicine 1953-54, asst. chief internal medicine 1954-55; pvt. practice internal medicine Marin County, Calif. 1955-92; cons. internal medicine and pulmonology Neumiller Hosp., Tamal, Calif. 1957-83; active staff Marin Gen. Hosp. 1955-93; chief of med. staff Ross (Calif.) Gen. Hosp. 1969; exec. com.. Ross Gen. Hosp. 1968-71, 82-88; co-founder Med. Insurance Exchange of Calif. 1975; med. dir. Aldersly Danish Home, San Rafael 1987-92; med. dir. Rafael Conv. Hosp. 1987–; med. cons. & med. coord. Regional Cancer Found., S.F. 1993–; awards: Man of Yr. in the Healing Arts, BPOE, San Rafael 1976, knighted by sovereign order of St. John of Jerusalem (Knights of Malta) 1992; fellow: AMA, CMA; mem: Calif. Soc. Internal Medicine (bd. dirs. 1976-79), Marin Med. Soc. (pres. 1975-76, bd. dirs. 1966-69, 74-77, 88–), Calif. Acad. of Medicine, Serra Club of Marin (pres. 1961), Richardson Bay Yacht Club, BPOE, Gen. Soc. Mayflower Descendants, Calif. Soc. Mayflower Descendants, Internat. Med. Assn. of Lourdes; mil: USNR 1943-46, lt. comdr. USPHS 1948-55; Republican; Roman Catholic; rec: tennis, swimming, scuba diving, bridge, backgammon. Res: 48 Junipero Serra Ave San Rafael 94901-2320

HOFFMAN, DARLEANE CHRISTIAN, educator; b. Nov. 8, 1926, Terril, Ia.; d. Carl Benjamin and Elverna (Kuhlman) Christian; m. Marvin M. Hoffman, Dec. 26, 1951; childen: Maureane R. and Daryl K.; edn: BS, and PhD, Iowa St. Univ., 1948, 1951. Career: chemist Oak Ridge Nat. Lab., 1952-53; staff mem. radiochemistry group Los Alamos Sci. Lab., 1953-71, assoc. group ldr. 1971-79, div. ldr. chemistry -nuclear div. 1979-82, isotope and nuclear chemistry div. 1982-84; prof. chemistry UC Berkeley, faculty sr. scientist Lawrence Berkeley Lab., 1984-91; prof. emeritus, prof. grad. school 1994–, dir. G.T. Seaborg Inst. for Transactinium Science, Livermore 1991–; mem. internat. coms. for internat. confs. on nuclear & radiochemistry Brighton, Eng. 1988, Beijing, China 1986, Lindau, W.Ger. 1984; awards: sr. NSF postdoc. fellow Oslo, Norway 1964-65, Am. Chem. Soc. John Dustin Clark Award for merit. svc. to chemistry in N.Mex. 1978, Iowa St. Univ. Coll. of Scis. and Humanities Alumni merit cit. 1978, Guggenheim fellow for study of mechanisms of nuclear fission 1978-79, Am. Chem. Soc. award for nuclear chemistry 1983, Iowa St. Univ. Alumni Assn. disting. achiev. cit. 1986, JSPS fellow 1987, ACS Garvan Medal 1990; mem: Am. Chem. Soc. (exec. com. mem. at large 1987–), Nat. Acad. of Scis. (com. chair 1982-84), IUPAC Commn. on Radiochem. & Nuclear Techniques 1984-93 (sec., chair), Am. Inst. of Chemists (fellow, pres. N.Mex. Inst. 1976-78), Am. Physical Soc. (fellow), Am. Nuclear Soc. (co-chair internat. conf. Hawaii 1987), AAAS (fellow, 1995), Am. Women in Sci., Sigma Xi, Phi Kappa Phi, Iota Sigma Pi, Pi Mu Epsilon, Sigma Delta Epsilon; Res: 2277 Manzanita Dr Oakland 94611 Ofc: Nuclear Sci. Div. Lawrence Berkeley Lab. MS 70A/3307 Univ. California, Berkeley 94720

HOFFMAN, MARVIN, computer professional resource and testing company president; b. July 27, 1933, Wauwatosa, Wis.; s. Sam and Anna (Cohen) H.; m. F. Evelyn Lazar, Sept. 28, 1955; children: Loren b. 1959, Darryl b. 1960; edn: BA math., CSU Northridge 1962; postgrad. wk., CSU and UCLA; Life Tchg. Credential Bus. Data Processing. Career: systems supr. North Am. Rockwell 1961-66; dir. 6000 Software Devel., Control Data Corp. 1966-69; dir. software devel. Ampex Corp. 1969-72; mgr. software devel. F&M Systems Co. 1972-73; dir. R&D Div. Computer Machinery Corp. 1973-76; founder/pres./bd. chmn. XXCAL, Inc. (multi-branch data processing consulting and human resource co.), Los Angeles 1976–; dir: Rainbow Technologies Inc., Interactive Classrooms Inc.; instr., and mem. adv. com. L.A. City Coll.; bd. mem., pres. L.A. City Coll. Found.; honors: Alpha Gamma Sigma 1958; mem: West LA C.of C., So/Cal/Ten; mil: AG2 USN 1952-56, Korean, Far East Campaign, Good Conduct; Democrat; Jewish; rec: skiing, fishing, jogging. Res: 2423 S Beverly Dr Los Angeles 90034 Ofc: XXCAL, Inc. 11500 Olympic Blvd Ste 459 Los Angeles 90064

HOFFMAN, MERRILL LELAND, security company president, consultant; b. Nov. 22, 1934, Clinton, Mass.; s. Frank Albert and Grace Elizabeth (Quittmeyer) H.; m. Arlene Rita Witkowski, June 12, 1954 (dec. 1992); children: Linda Marie (Rogers) b. 1954, Glenn Albert b. 1956; m. Paulette Rita Cingolani, Feb. 26, 1994; stepchildren: David Cingolani, Paul Cingolani, Jill Cingolani; edn: grad. South Lancaster (Mass.) Acad., 1952; reg. locksmith. Career: sr. chief petty officer U.S. Navy 1952-72, Navy Achievement Medal 1971; pres. Santa Barbara Locksmiths Inc., Santa Barbara, Calif. 1972, cons. local law enforcement agys. 1981, design custom systems for other security cos. 1981; instr., contract tng. for company supplying personnel for US Embassy work; instr. vocat. sch. Santa Barbara; awards: YMCA, S.B. 1985, recipient appreciation awards numerous orgns.; mem: Am. Soc. for Industrial Security (S.B. chapt. past pres., exec. bd. 1980), Associated Locksmiths of Am. 1978, Calif. Locksmiths Assn. 1976, Safe and Vault Technician Assn. 1986, Am. Mensa, Santa Barbara C.of C., Rotary Club S.B. (bd., pres. 1990-91), S.B. Shrine Club (bd., past pres. 1988), Channel Islands YMCA (exec. bd. 1993–), Adventures in Caring (exec. bd. 1993–); contbr. tech. safe articles in industry publs.; Republican; rec: world travel. Res: 5030 Rhoads Ave Santa Barbara 93111 Ofc: Santa Barbara Locksmiths, Inc. 636 Santa Barbara St Santa Barbara 93101

HOFFMAN, MICHAEL JEROME, humanities educator, writer; b. Mar. 13, 1939, Phila.; s. Nathan P. and Sara (Perlman) H.; m. Margaret Boegeman, Dec. 27, 1988; children: Cynthia, Matthew; edn: BA, Univ. Pa., 1959, MA, 1960, PhD, 1963. Career: instr. Washington Coll., Chestertown, Md. 1962-64; asst. prof. Univ. Pa., Phila., 1964-67; asst. prof. and prof. UC Davis, 1967–, asst. vice chancellor acad. affairs, 1976-83, chmn. English dept. 1984-89, coordinator of writing programs, 1991-95, graduate advisor 1995–; dir. Humanities Inst., Davis 1987-91; chair jt. projects steering com. Univ. Calif./Calif. State Univs., 1976-87; chair advy. bd. Calif. Acad. Partnership Pgm., 1985-87; dir. Calif. Humanities Project, 1985-91; author: The Development of Abstractionism in the Writings of Gertrude Stein, 1965, The Buddy System, 1971, The Subversive Vision, 1972, Gertrude Stein, 1976, Critical Essays on Gertrude Stein, 1986, Essentials of the Theory of Fiction, 1988, Critical Essays on America Modernism, 1992; mem. Modern Language Assn.; mil: USAR 1957-61, Nat. Defense Edn. Act lecture US Govt., 1959-62; Democrat; Jewish; rec: tennis. Res: 4417 San Marino Dr Davis 95616-5012 Ofc: Univ. Calif. Dept. English, Davis 95616 Tel: 916/752-2268

HOFFMAN, PAUL RODERIC, bank executive; b. Oct. 18, 1941, Columbus, Ohio; s. George Martin and Hazel Marie (Hazelett) H.; m. Cheryl, Apr. 7, 1969; edn: grad. Marion Harding H.S., Marion, Ohio 1959. Career: served to major US Marine Corps 1959-84: supply officer 1st FSR, MCB Camp Pendleton 1969-75, supply analyst 1975-76; supply officer Camp Garcia, Vieques, P.R. 1976-77; logistics officer 9th Marine Corps, Shawnee, Ks. 1977-80; contracting officer 29 Palms 1980-84, decorated Navy Achiev. (USMC Combat V 1971, USMC 1977), Navy Commendn. (USMC 1984); asst. v.p. First Community Bank (Bank of Yucca Valley), Yucca Valley 1985–; awards: military mgr. of year Fed. Mgrs. ASSC 29 Palms 1984, Yucca Valley C.of C. Citizen of Year 1986, Yucca Valley Hon. Mayor 1986-87, Business of Yr. Mgr. 1991, Hon. Judge, 29 Palms 1991, Freedom Found. Honor certificate and Honor Medal (1966, 1984), People Helping People award United Way 1992; civic: 29 Palms C.of C. (pres. 1992-93), Joshua Tree Rotary (pres. 1992-93), Tri Valley Little League (pres. 1984-91), Youth Action Com. (chmn. 1987–), Save our Park Com. (chmn. 1988–), United Way Y.V. 1986-87, Joshua Tree C.of C. (treas. 1988-89), Elk Lodge 2314 (Citizen of Yr. 1988-89), Municipal Advy. Yucca Valley 1984–, treas. Old Schoolhouse Project 1991–; rec: youth baseball. Res: 58242 Delano Trail Yucca Valley 92284 Ofc: First Community Bank 7272 Joshua Ln Yucca Valley 92284

HOFFMANN, JON ARNOLD, professor of aeronautical engineering; b. Jan. 13, 1942, Wausau, Wis.; s. Arnold D. and Rita J. (Haas) H.; m. Carol Rae Frye, Sept. 21, 1973; edn: BSME, Univ. Wis., Madison 1964, MSME, 1966; reg. profl. engr. Calif. 1989. Career: prof. aeronautical engring., Calif. State Polytechnic Univ., San Luis Obispo 1968–; grantee NSF 1970, NASA (prin. investigator, NASA, Edwards AFB 1981-83, Moffett Field 1979-86, 1987, 87-89); recipient merit. performance and profl. promise awards Cal Poly 1985, 86;

mem.: ASME 1986–; publs: 15+ articles in sci. jours. of AIAA, ASME, NASA. Ofc: Calif. State Polytechnic Univ., Dept. Aero. Engr., San Luis Obispo 93407

HOFFMEISTER, GERHART, educator; b. Dec. 17, 1936, Giessen, Germany; s. Johannes Emil and Inge (Johannsen) H.; m. Margaret von Poletika, May 28, 1966 (div. Dec. 1988): 1 son, George A. b. 1967; edn: Bacc., Univ. of Bonn, W.Ger., 1963; Teachers Trng. Coll., Cologne, 1966; PhD, Univ. Maryland, 1970. Career: sch. tchr., Cologne, Germany 1964-66; instr. Univ. Maryland, College Park, Md. 1966-70; asst. prof. Univ. Wisconsin, Milw. 1970-74; assoc. prof. Wayne State Univ., Detroit, Mich. 1974-75; assoc. prof. Univ. Calif. Santa Barbara, 1975-79, full prof. of German & comparative literature, 1979–; awards: DAAD stipend German Acad. Exchange Service of Bonn (1962-63, London), grantee Am. Philosophical Soc., Phila. 1974; mem.: Am. Assn. of Tchrs. of German 1970–, Modern Language Assn. Am. 1970–, Goethe Soc. N.Am. 1980–, Pacific Coast Philol. Assn. 1976–; coauthor: Germany 2000 Years vol. III (1986), book editor: Goethe in Italy (1988), French Revolution (1989), European Romanticism (1991); rec: swimming, tennis. Res: 117 Calle Alamo Santa Barbara 93105 Ofc: Univ. Calif., Santa Barbara 93106

HOKAJ, RICHARD RAE, data communications company executive; b. Oct. 6, 1944, Pittsburgh, Pa.; s. Ignatius P. and Alfreda (Paulson) H.; m. Christine Denise Gaca, July 8, 1967; children: Brigitte Lea b. 1969, Heidi Holly b. 1972, Heather Joy b. 1974; edn: BA math., Washington & Jefferson, 1966; Dipl. Comp.Sci., Edinburgh Univ., Scotland, 1967. Career: staff supr. AT&T, Phila., Pa. and WDC, 1970-73; engr. GEISCO, Cleveland, Rockville, Md., London, Amsterdam, 1973-81; dir., customer supt. American Satellite Co., Rockville, Md., 1981; v.p./quality assurance and customer supt. United Info. Svc., also v.p./ops UNINET, Kansas City, Mo., 1982-86; indep. cons., 1986-87; v.p. network services INFONET, El Segundo, Calif., 1987-92, v.p./gen. mgr. Enterprise Systems, Infonet 1992–; awards: Disting. military grad. Washington & Jefferson 1966, Rotary Found. fellow Edinburgh Univ. 1966-67, Infonet Pres.'s Club 1989 and Outstanding performance award 1989-90; Delta Tau Delta frat. (treas. 1964-65); civic: Am. Diabetes Assn., Juvenile Diabetes Found. (treas. 1984-87); club: North Ranch CC (Westlake Village); mil: capt. US Army 1967-70, Bronze star Qui Nhon, Vietnam 1970; Republican; R.Cath.; rec: golf, bridge, church choir. Res: 3300 Blue Ridge Ct Westlake Village 91362 Ofc: 2100 E Grand Ave El Segundo 90245

HOKANSON, CARL GUSTAF, multinational corporation executive; b. Mar. 9, 1937, Los Angeles; s. Carl Gustaf and Blanche M. H.; m. Mercedes Lasarte (internationally known artist) June 14, 1969; children:, Christer G.; edn: BA in math., Brown Univ., 1959; MBA with distinction, Harvard, 1970 (Student Body Pres.). Career: v.p. mktg. C.G. Hokanson Co. Inc., Los Angeles and Santa Ana, 1960-66; v.p. mktg. and contracts Transp. Support Div., Lear Siegler, Inc. 1966-68; with Lear Siegler Corporate HQ 1970-77 as: v.p. admin., systems & services (military) group 1970-71; v.p. adminstrn., climate control & housing group 1971-73; corp. workout dir. 1973-75; v.p. fin./cfo and dir. S.W. Properties, Inc., 1974-75; pres./ceo LSI Internat., 1975-77; owner Hokanair GmbH & Co., Ger. 1971-84; pres. Carl G. Hokanson & Assoc., Inc. 1978–; pres./ceo/dir. Volpar Aircraft Corp. 1985-87; pres./coo Gibraltar Financial Corp. 1990-91; pres. Environmental Container Corp. 1993-94; Boards: C.G. Hokanson Co. Inc. 1963-66; Valley Community Hosp. 1972-73; Olympic Internat. Inc. 1973-74; Erma Maschinen and Waffen Fabrik, GmbH (Ger.) 1973-77; Central de Industria, S.A. (Mex.) 1975-77; No-Sag, S.A., Venezuela and Farfisa Sp.A.(Italy), 1974-77; Arbitrator Am. Arb. Assn.; Life mem. Air Force Assn.; Town Hall of Calif.; Bel Air Country Club. Address: Encino

HOLCOMB, WILLIAM WINFIELD, lawyer; b. May 10, 1948, Berkeley; s. William Robert and Pearl Lois (Pennington) Holcomb; m. Deborah Lynn Geffner, July 31, 1983; 1 dau., Jesse A. b. 1985; edn: BA, Dartmouth Coll. 1970; JD, Benjamin N. Cardozo Sch. Law 1980; LL.M, N.Y. Univ. 1984; admitted St. Bar Calif. Career: performing artist James Cunningham and Acme Dance Company, N.Y.C. 1970-75; exec. dir. Pentacle Dance Mgmt. 1975-77; atty. Fulop Rolston Burns & McKittrick, Beverly Hills 1980-81; Fulop & Hardee 1981-82; Burns & Resnick 1982-83; DeCastro West Chodorow & Burns, L.A. 1984-86; Tyre Kamins Katz & Granof 1986; mem: L.A. Co. Bar Assn., Beverly Hills Bar Assn. Ofc: Tyre Kamins Katz & Granof 1840 Century Park E Ste 800 Los Angeles 90067

HOLDAWAY, GEORGE HARMER, retired aerospace engineer; b. Oct. 10, 1921, Ogden, Utah; s. Hugh and Pearl (Harmer) H.; m. Lorna Lee, Sept. 4, 1945; children: Larry b. 1949, Sheryl b. 1950, Steven b. 1954, George Lee b. 1956; edn: BS in engring., Univ. Utah, 1944; MS engring. sci., Stanford Univ. 1956. Career: aero research project engr. NACA and NASA Ames Research Center (ARC), Moffett Field 1944-66, staff asst. Director's Staff 1966-71, chief Facilities Planning Office 1971-80, retired govt. service 1980; re-employed Annuitant, NASA ARC, asst. to Dir. of Research Support 1980-81, currently ret.; awards: NASA Group Achiev., Lifting Body Research Team (1970), NASA Spl. Achiev. (1973), BSA Silver Beaver (1976); mem: AIAA (assoc. fellow 1964), Planetary Soc. (Charter), Internat. Right of Way Assn. (chmn. property mgmt. 1977-78), AAAS; civic: leader Boy Scouts Am. 1948- (exec. bd. Stanford Area BSA

Council 1961-87, chmn. Scouting for the Handicapped 1974-87, Advy. Board 1988–); mil: lt. jg USNR 1944-46, American, Victory medals; Republican; Ch. of Jesus Christ of L.D.S. (f.t. missionary in N.C. 1989, officiator in Oakland Temple 1991–; pres. of Sequoia Group, Menlo Park Stake 1995–); rec: water ski, tennis, astronomy. Res: 3861 Grove Ct Palo Alto 94303-4554

HOLDER, GEORGE H., company executive; b. June 24, 1936, Lafayette, Ind.; s. George A. and Carolyn J. (Switzer) H.; m. Suzanne L. Lamb, Nov. 27, 1976; edn: BS in ag., Purdue Univ., 1957. Career: asst. advt. mgr. Nat. Livestock Producer mag., Chgo. 1960-63; sales rep., advt. mgr., sales mgr. product mgr., mktg. mgr., country mgr. for Thailand, all with Elanco Products Co. div. Eli Lilly and Co., 1963-80; v.p. mktg. Syntex Agribusiness, 1980-83, v.p./gen. mgr. Syntex Agribusiness USA 1984-85, pres. 1985-95, and v.p. Syntex Corp.; pres. Agritek Bio Ingredients Corp. 1995–; past chmn. bd. dirs. Animal Health Inst.; chmn., bd. dirs. Calif. 4-H Found.; mil: 1st lt. US Army Arty. 1957-59, Korean Service. Address: Menlo Park 94025

HOLGATE, GEORGE JACKSON, university president; b. Feb. 19, 1933, Lakewood, Ohio; s. George Curtis and Melba (Klein) H.; 1 dau. Leigh M.; edn: BM, Baldwin-Wallace Coll. 1953; MS, Univ. So. Calif. 1955, EdD, 1962; PhD, Riverside Univ. 1970, LLD. Career: exec. v.p. Sierra Found., 1953-56; tchr. Oxnard High Sch. and Ventura Coll., 1956-62; campus coord. Congo Polytech. Inst., 1962-64; pres. Riverside Univ., 1965; dir: Pacific Orient Bank; Lincoln Gen. Corp. 1972-77; music conductor Ojai Festival, 1958, Ventura Co. Concert Chorale and Chamber Singers, 1956-60, Ventura Bach Festival, 1958, Columbia Orch. 1960; recipient US Jr. C.of C. disting. svc. award 1962; mem. bd. dirs: Riverside Sym. Orch., Riverside Opera Assn., Calif. Assn. for Pvt. Edn., Calif. Council of Business Schs., Lincoln Charitable Trust, US Coast Guard Found.; mem. Phi Mu Alpha Sinfonia, Phi Delta Kappa, Sigma Phi Epsilon, Delta Epsilon; mil: flotilla comdr. USCG Aux. 1983-1985, div. capt. 1985-1987; Democratic State Central Com. of Calif. and Dem. nominee for Cong. 1962; rec: music, fishing, sailing, flying. Ofc: PO Box 1084 Pomona 91769

HOLL, P. EDWARD, securities company executive; b. July 7, 1959, Munich, W. Germany; s. Richard A. and Ingrid F. (Gerhardt) H.; edn: BA, Occidental Coll., 1982; CEP, Inst. D'Etudes, Politiques de Paris, France 1980; MBA, UCLA, 1988. Career: arrival supr. Air New Zealand, Los Angeles 1981-83; v.p. Bateman Eichler 1983-89; sr. v.p./inv. mgmt. group Paine Webber Inc., L.A. 1989-90; sr. v.p. Shearson Lehman Brothers, 1990-93; pres. Capital Markets Research Co. 1993–; pres. Holl & Co. 1994–; dir: CDB Corp., Wilmington, N.C. 1988-90, Eurocapital Ltd., Luxembourg 1985–; honors: Duke of Edinburgh Gold Medal of govt. Canada, Ont. 1978; mem: ATO Frat.; club: L.A. Athletic; author chapt. in book: Performance Measurement, 1989, contbr. articles to bus. & inv. jours.; mil: lt. Canadian Cadet Corps 1974-78; rec: windsurfing. Res: 17 Escalon Dr Mill Valley 94941

HOLLAND, ELIZABETH, artist; b. July 23, 1913, Detroit; d. Edward Morton Holland and Elsie (Nicols) Brady; m. George Edgar Naylon, Jr., July 20, 1934 (div. 1939); m. 2d, Gene Winans McDaniel, Dec. 29, 1940 (div. 1968); children: Gene Ross b. 1945, Lauralyn b. 1947; edn: student Grand Central Sch. Art, 1930-31, Sarah Lawrence Coll., 1932-33, Ecoles d'arts Americaines, Fountainebleau, France 1932-33. Career: artist, painter, 1929–; tchr. landscape in oils, acrylics and color theory Marin Art and Garden Center, Ross, Calif. 1968–, teach 3 classes weekly in own studio in Bolinas, tchr Napa Valley Art Assn. 1967-95, Tiburon Peninsula Club 1977, summer classes St. Mary's Art Ctr., Virginia City, Nev.; tutor in computer and computer painting: "Landscapes, Portraits, etc.", 1995–; owner "Off-Beat Cards" (original cards painted on computer), 1995–; currently profl. group instr. in a new encaustic technique, 1989; showed new technique in preview exh. St. Paul's Gallery, Virginia City, Nev. 1990; one-man shows Casa de Manana, La Jolla 1941, Nevada Art Gal., Reno 1965, St. Mary's Art Gal., Virginia City, Nev. 1966-68, Depot Gal., Yountville 1968, Torrance Gal., San Anselmo 1969, Kaiser Found. 1974; group shows include Oakland Anns, Marin Soc. Artists Shows, Soc. Western Artists Shows, Winblad Gal. S.F., Town and Country Gal., Palo Alto, Gold Hill Gal., Round Hill Mall, Zephyr Cove, Nev., St. Mary's Art Gal., Virginia City, Nev., Rosicrucian Gal., San Jose, Brandy Buck Gal.; represented in permanent collection Artists Studio, Bolinas; exhibited in Bolinas Museum 1993, West Marin Seniors Show, Pt. Reyes Station 1993, and Mainly Marin, Larkspur 1993; producer, dir. Emigrant Trail Show, Nev. and Calif., 1973-74; Bolinas "Stagecoach Barn Annuals" 1993-94; awards include Purchase award St. Mary's in Mountains 1968, awards Nevada Heritage Shows; mem: Marin Soc. Artists (juror); Republican; Episcopalian. Res: Box 147-190 Horseshoe Hill Road Bolinas 94924

HOLLAND, PAUL MICHAEL, scientist; b. Nov. 18, 1947, Ames, Iowa; s. Erick Martin and Sarah Beatrice (Nelson) H.; m. Cynthia Elma White, Aug. 24, 1974; children: Katherine b. 1981, Jennifer b. 1983; edn: BA chem., Colo. Coll. 1969; MS oceanography, Old Dominion Univ. 1974; PhD physical chemistry, Univ. Colo. 1980. Career: chemist Nat. Bureau of Standards, Boulder 1969-70; tchg. asst. Univ. Colo. 1975-76, research asst. 1976-80; research chemist Proctor & Gamble Co., Cincinnati, Ohio 1980-87; sr. scientist, dir. Gen. Research Corp.,

Santa Barbara 1987–; honors: Phi Lambda Upsilon, Sigma Xi; mem: Am. Chem. Soc., Am. Physical Soc., Colo. Coll. Alumni Assn. (metro area chmn. 1986-87); 90+ articles and papers pub. in sci. jours., 10 book chpts. pub., ed. Cationic Surfactants: Physical Chemistry, 1990, ed. Mixed Surfactant Systems, 1992; author Tables of Collision Integrals & Second Virial Coefficients for (m,6,8) Potential, 1974; mil: USN 1970-74. Res: 5552 Cathedral Oaks Rd Santa Barbara 93111 Ofc: General Research Corp. POB 6770 Santa Barbara 93160

HOLLEY, ELIZABETH SHELBY, educational therapist; b. Dec. 4, 1926, Lennox; d. Guy Sheldon and Bessie Edna (Humphreys) Bedwell; m. Erwin Dale Thomson, April 26, 1943 (dec. 1963); m. Kenneth Gunnar Holley, April 9, 1963; children: Edward b. 1944, Evonne b. 1946, Fiona b. 1949, Luana b. 1950, Raymond b. 1952, Jean b. 1964, Kevin b. 1967; edn: BA, Calif. St. Coll. 1961; MA, 1963; lic. marriage family and child counsellor (1965). Career: ednl. therapist Frostig Center, L.A. 1961-64; W. Valley Center, Canoga Park 1964-81; dir. Studio for Acad. Achievement, Sherman Oaks 1981-87; vol. U.S. Peace Corps, Spaldings, Jamaica 1987; vol. Juvenile Justice, Van Nuys 1984-87; awards: Assn. Ednl. Therapists Plaque 1985, Juvenile Justice Cert. 1986, U.S. Peace Corps Beyond War award 1988; mem: Assn. Ednl. Therapists (bd. mem. 1979-87, 91-95), Orton Dyslexia Soc. (exec. bd. 1979-87), Church of Inner Light; author: A Practical Parents' Handbook for Teaching Children with Learning Disabilities (copyright 1994); Democrat; Res: 5656 Manton Ave Woodland Hills 91367

HOLLINGSWORTH, PRISCILLA MARIE, lawyer; b. March 14, 1956, Schenectady, N.Y.; d. Jack Waring and Nancy Lee (Harris) Hollingsworth; m. Daryl Ronald Herzog, June 6, 1987; edn: BA, Union Coll. 1979; JD, Franklin Pierce Law Center 1983; admitted St. Bar Calif. (1984). Career: researcher, writer N.M. Pub. Defender, Santa Fe 1983; atty. Riverside Co. Dist. Atty., Riverside 1984-85; Orange Co. Pub. Defender 1984, 1985-88; atty. Santa Barbara Co. Pub. Defender, Santa Maria 1988; tchg. asst. Torts Law Sch. 1981-82; Constitutional Law Sch. 1982-83; research asst. Civil Rights Law Sch. 1982-83; mem: No. S.B. Co. Bar Assn. (v.p. 1988-91, sec./treas. 1991-93), Am. Bar Assn., Am. Trial Lawyers Assn., Calif. Attys. for Criminal Justice, Calif. Pub. Defenders Assn., No. S.B. Co. Women Lawyers, Central Coast Trial Lawyers Assn., S. San Luis Obispo Co. Quilters Guild, Kiwanis 1992–; researcher and writer of 2 manuals (1982, 83); Democrat; Methodist; rec: quilting, needlepoint, photog. Ofc: Public Defender 312-P East Cook St Santa Maria 93454

HOLLISTER, ARTHUR CLAIR, II, consulting medical epidemiologist; b. May 9, 1918, New Orleans, La.; s. Arthur Clair and Cora Preston (Odom) H.; m. Olivia Corinna Ewing, Aug. 2, 1942; children: Arthur Clair III b. 1945, Olivia Corinna b. 1950; edn: BS, Tulane Univ. 1938; MD, 1941; MPH, Johns Hopkins Univ. 1948; cert. Am. Bd. Preventive Medicine & Public Health (1950). Career: med intern So. Baptist Hosp., New Orleans, La. 1941-42; pub. health med. ofcr. Calif. St. Health Dept., S.F. and Berkeley 1946-47; chief bureau of acute communicable disease, Berkeley 1948-58, asst. chief div. of research 1959-64, chief div. of alcoholism 1964-69, chief health intelligence 1969-73, chief health manpwer sect., Sacto. 1973-74, med. cons. occupational health, Berkeley 1974-77, chief hosp. infection control 1977-83; ret. 1983; consulting epidemiologist, 1983–; lect. UC Berkeley 1950-74; UCLA Sch. of Pub. Health, L.A. 1952-85; cons. USPHS Ctr. for Disease Control, Atlanta, Ga. 1950-63; Bureau St. Services, Wash. D.C. 1963-68; mem. Study Sections of Div. Research Grants, NIH, 1960-73; honors: Delta Omega; mem: Am. Epidemiological Soc. (Fellow), Alameda Co. Med.Soc., Contra Costa Med. Soc., CMA, Am. Pub. Health Assn. (Fellow, chair epidemiology sect. 1954-58, govng. council 1956-60; APHA Western br. pres. 1960), Am. Coll. Preventive Medicine (Fellow), Am. Coll. Epidemiology (Fellow), No. Calif. Pub. Health Assn. (pres. 1950), Samaritan Counseling Ctr. of Contra Costa (bd. 1982-89), Diablo Valley Masterworks Chorale (bd. 1985-87); 20+ papers pub. in profl. jours. (1968-85); mil: served 1st lt. to major USAAF 1942-46; served to col. USPHS Commissioned Reserve Corps 1956-80, senior surgeon 1956-66, medical dir. 1966-80; Democrat; Episcopalian (vestryman 2t); rec: piano, classical, jazz. Res/Ofc: 14 Boies Ct Pleasant Hill 94523 Ph: 510/944-1872

HOLLY, EDWIN E., motion picture production company executive; b. Oct. 3, 1926, Elizabethton, Tenn.; s. Earl H. and Rada C. (Jordan) H.; m. Patricia R. Motschman, Oct. 2, 1976; children: Patrice Katz, Amy Weber; edn: BS, Univ. Tenn., 1949; C.P.A., Calif. Career: staff auditor Lybrand, Ross Bros. & Montgomery, CPAs, N.Y.C. 1949-52; asst. corp. controller CBS, N.Y.C. 1952-54; v.p. adminstrn. and fin. Desilu Prodns. Inc., Hollywood 1954-67; v.p. studio facilities Paramount Pictures Corp., Hollywood 1967-69; dir. fin. William Morris Agency, Beverly Hills 1969-75; pres. First Artists Prodn. Co. Ltd., Sherman Oaks 1975-83; cons. entertainment industry, 1983; mem. Calif. Soc. CPAs; mil: US Army 1944-46. Ofc: 29204 Village Camarillo 93012

HOLT, LARRY R., telecommunications company executive; b. May 14, 1948, Ft. Worth, Tx.; s. Robert V. and Anna M. Holt; m. Diane L., May 29, 1970; children: Amy b. 1973, Wendy b. 1976, Andy b. 1984; edn: BS mech. engring., Okla. State Univ., Stillwater, Okla. 1970; Exec. MBA, Carnegie Mellon Univ., Pittsburgh, Pa. 1985. Career: with Southwestern Bell 1970-81; joined AT&T in 1981 as div. mgr.-edn. Services Div. (N.J.), div. mgr.-Nat. Tech. Support Ops.

(Colo.), dir. sales ops. and planning General Business Systems Sales & Svc. 1988, currently nat. v.p. AT&T Global Bus. Comms. Systems, SW Region; bd. dirs.: Univ. of Calif.-Irvine, Pacific Symphony Assn.; mem. exec. com. Sales & Svc. Div., AT&T GBCS; mem: HISPA, Mission Viejo Little League Assn., Telephone Pioneers. Ofc: AT&T 8001 Irvine Center Drive Irvine 92718

HOLTEN, VIRGINIA LOIS, educator, college president; b. Mar. 29, 1938, McKeesport, Pa.; d. Albert J. and Virginia Kathryn (Minnick (Zewe); m. Darold D. Holten, Dec. 29, 1962; 1 dau. Peggy b. 1967; edn: BA, Carlow Coll., Pittsburgh, Pa. 1960; MS, Univ. N. Dakota, Grand Forks, 1962, PhD, 1965; diploma, Management, Glasgow, Scotland 1975. Career: faculty mem. Riverside Comm. Coll., Riverside, Calif. 1969-78, div. dean 1978-82; v.p. instruction, Victor Valley Coll., Victorville, Calif. 1982-86; pres. Lassen Coll., Susanville, Calif. 1986-90; pres. Solano College, Suisun, Calif. 1990–; awards: Sioux award, Univ. N. Dakota 1990; mem: Calif. Comm. Colls. CEO's 1986–, Rotary Internat. 1990–, Solano Work Services (bd. dirs. 1990–), Goodwill Industries (bd. dirs. 1992–), Chapman Centers Advy. (bd dirs. 1992–); author: scientific articles pub. in Biochemistry, 1962-72; Democrat; rec: jogging, wine tasting. Res: 2615 Piedmont Dr Riverside 92506

HOLZBOG, THOMAS JERALD, architect-planner; b. Oct. 25, 1933, Milwaukee; s. Walter Charles and Dorothy (Van Holten) H.; m. Wendy Anne Wilson, June 12, 1958 (div.); children: Jessica Jane b. 1963, Arabella Laura b. 1966; edn: BA, Yale, 1960; MArch, Harvard, 1968; Reg. Arch. (AIA), Landscape Arch. (ASLA) and qualified Planner (AICP). Career: pvt. practice, pres. T.J. Holzbog-Architects, Los Angeles and Boston, 1967; apprenticeships: I.M. Pei & Ptnrs., NYC; Sir Denys Lasdun & Ptnrs., London, Eng.; Sir Leslie Martin, Cambridge, Eng.; Candilis, Josic & Woods, Paris, Fr.; Paul Rudolph, New Haven, Conn.; Walter C. Holzbog, Wis.; design instr., lectr. Harvard, Columbia, Pratt, R.I. Sch. of Design, Tufts, Cal Poly, UCLA, and vis. critic other univs.; speaker numerous symposiums, panels, pvt. functions and on radio and t.v.; awards: Scarab, Fulbright Scholar - Paris, Fr., Agnus T. Hopper Fellow-Yale, Exchange Pgm.-Edinburgh Univ., Scotland; mem: Am. Inst. Arch., Am. Inst. Cert. Planners, Am. Soc. Landscape Arch., Architl. Assn. (U.K.), Nat. Inst. of Architl. Edn., Sigma Chi Frat.; mil: capt. AUS, mem. U.S. Armed Svs. All-Star Track Team; Indep.; Prot. Res/Ofc: 1301 Warnall Ave Los Angeles 90024

HOLZER, THOMAS LEQUEAR, geologist; b. June 26, 1944, Lafayette, Ind.; s. Oswald Alois and Ruth Alice (Lequear) H.; children: Holly b. 1970, Elizabeth b. 1972; edn: BSE (cum laude), Princeton Univ., 1965; MS, Stanford Univ., 1966, PhD, 1970. Career: asst. prof. geology Univ. Conn., Storrs, Ct. 1970-75; adj. environmentalist Griswold & Fuss, Manchester Ct. 1973-75; geologist US Geol. Survey, Menlo Park, Calif. 1975-82, 1984-88, 1993–, branch chief 1989-93, asst. dir. for research USGS, Reston, Va. 1982-84; recipient USGS awards for superior service 1980, public svc. 1991; mem.: Geol. Soc. Am. 1967– (Fellow, chairperson Engring. Geology Div. 1989; councilor 1995-97), Am. Geophysical Union 1968–, Assn. Ground Water Scientists and Engineers 1973–, AAAS 1968–, Sigma Xi 1965–; Foothills Tennis & Swim Club Palo Alto (pres. 1988-89); publs: numerous sci. articles, 1970–, book editor, Man-induced Land Subsidence, 1984; Republican; Presbyterian; rec: tennis. Res: PO Box 851 Palo Alto 94302 Ofc: US Geological Survey 345 Middlefield Rd MS977 Menlo Park 94025

HOLZGANG, DAVID ALLAN, computer consultant, author; b. Oct. 6, 1941, Los Angeles; s. Albert Otto and Marianne J. (Kane) H.; edn: BA, UCLA 1964; MBA, 1974. Career: systems analyst Penn Corp Fin., Santa Monica 1974-77; dir. adminstrn., Petersen Publishing, L.A. 1977-81; v.p. systems Haney Group, Woodland Hills 1981-85; mng. gen. ptnr. Cheshire Group, Chatsworth, Calif. 1983-88, S.F. 1988-90, Sebastopol, Calif. 1990–; sr. cons. Denver Group, L.A. 1986; cons. Kennedy Center, Wash. D.C. 1988; mem: SPS Assn. (Redbook Task Force chmn. 1989); author: Understanding PostScript, 3rd edit., 1992, Welcome to...Computer Graphics, 1993, Word Perfect 6.0 Tips and Techniques, 1994, Teach Yourself...Visual C++, 1994; rec: flying, spinning sailing. Ofc: Cheshire Group 321 S Main St Ste 36 Sebastopol 95472

HOLZMAN, BETH FRANCES, legal writer; b. June 3, 1954, San Francisco; d. Robert Ellis and Evelyn (Siegel) Holzman; 1 dau., Shevona K. b. 1978; edn: BA, UC Berkeley 1975; JD summa cum laude, Univ. Santa Clara 1982; admitted St. Bar Calif. (1982), U.S. Dist. Ct. No.Dist., Eastern Dist. (inactive status). Career: law extern Justice Matthew Tobriner Calif. Supreme Ct., San Francisco 1981, staff atty. Justice Allen Broussard, 1982-83; staff legal writer and coordinating legal editor (criminal law) Matthew Bender & Co., Oakland 1983-95; adj. faculty, Santa Clara Univ. Sch. of Law 1995–; speaker on criminal law topics, 1994–; indep. contractor, author and edit. of California Criminal Defense Practice Reporter (Matthew Bender & Co., pub.), 1995–; editor/author: num. articles and publications (Matthew Bender & Co.); awards: Am. Jurisprudence 1980-81. Ofc: contact 415/665-1829

HOM, FREDERICK GOR, physician; b. Oct. 12, 1949, China (nat. 1955); s. Woo and Mary (Cheung) H.; m. Nancy Ruth Benbasset, Jan. 9, 1977; children: Gregory b. 1980, Sharon b. 1984, Rebecca b. 1986; edn: AB, UC Berkeley 1971; MD, George Washington Univ., W.D.C. 1975. Career: intern, resident in internal medicine, UCLA San Fernando Valley Med. Ctr., Sepulveda, CA 1975-78; fellow, endocrinology, Univ. of Wash., Seattle 1978-81; staff physician Kaiser Permanente, Fremont 1981–; clin. instr. Stanford Univ. 1981-84; chief, pharmacy & therapeutics Kaiser, Fremont 1992–; mem: Am. Coll. of Physicians 1976–, Alameda Co. Contra Costa Med. Assn. 1984–, The Endocrine Soc. 1992–; author: pub. articles, 1980-83; Democrat; rec: computers. Ofc: Kaiser 39400 Paseo Padre Pkwy Fremont 94538

HOM, SHERMAN SIU MING, molecular geneticist; b. June 7, 1952, Hong Kong; nat. 1978; s. Git Suey and Wai Kam (Choi) H.; m. Judith Hiti, June 25, 1973 (div. 1976); m. Anne Conyers, Aug. 6, 1976; edn: BA, UCSD 1975; PhD, UC Davis 1983; postdoctoral fellow, The Johns Hopkins Univ. 1982-85. Career: sr. scientist Henkel Research Corp., Santa Rosa 1985-91; information scientist Cognis, Inc. 1991-92; pres. New South Internat. 1992–; genetics instr. Am. Univ. of the Carribean, Sch. of Medicine (fall 1995); mem: Am. Soc. Microbiology, Soc. Indsl. Microbiology, Soka Gakkai Internat.-USA; num. articles pub. in sci. and profl. jours., patent; Democrat; rec: volleyball, weight training. Res: 1237 St Francis Rd Santa Rosa 95409

HONE, MICHAEL, law professor; b. June 21, 1937, San Francisco; s. Leo B. and Hazel (Curran) H.; children: Michael b. 1965, Elizabeth b. 1965; edn: BS, and JD, UC Berkeley, 1959, 63. Career: v.p. Continental Capital, San Francisco 1969-75; prof. of law Univ. San Francisco, 1975; pres. HMS Capital Ltd., S.F. 1982-88, ptnr. HMS Capital, Menlo Park 1987; dir: Matrix Integrated Systems, Richmond, 1989, Dynamic Materials, Louisville, Colo. 1984; honors: Order of Coif (1963); mem: Barristers Club S.F. (pres. 1970), Calif. Young Lawyers (pres. 1973-4), Western Assn. Venture Capitalists (v.p. 1973); editor: Advising Calif. Nonprofit Corporations, 1984, reporter: ABA model nonprofit corp. act, 1987, Calif. nonprofit corp. law, 1979; mil: E5 AUS 1956. Ofc: USF Law School, Ignatian Heights San Francisco 94117-1080

HONG, SU-DON, company president; b. June 23, 1941, Taiwan, R.O.C., nat. 1985; s. Tien-Shern and Tze (Lee) H.; m. Grace Wang, Jan. 30, 1971; children: Emily b. 1975, Jennifer b. 1976; edn: BS, Nt. Taiwan Univ., 1966; MS, Univ. of Waterloo, Ont., Can. 1970; PhD polymer sci., Univ. of Mass., Amherst 1975. Career: res. assoc. Univ. Calif., Berkeley 1976-77; sr. scientist Jet Propulsion Lab., Pasadena 1977-78, technical group ldr. 1978-85; pres. Sida Corp., Monterey Park 1985–; cons. JPL, 1986; recipient 6 achiev. awards NASA, Wash. D.C. (1978, 79, 80, 81, 82, 83); mem: Sigma Xi, Am. Physical Soc., Am. Chemical Soc.; inventions: Broad Band Optical Radiation Dector (1981), Double Beam Optical Method and apparatus for measuring thermal diffusion (1981); pub. sci. articles (1972-86); Democrat; rec: music, bridge. Res: 10551 E Danbury St Temple City 91780 Ofc: Sida Corporation 1055 Corporate Center Dr Ste 510 Monterey 91754

HOPE, GERRI DANETTE, telecommunications officer.; b. Feb. 28, 1956, McClellan AFB (Sacto.) Calif.; d. Albert Gerald and Beulah Rae (Bane) Hope; edn: assoc. of sci., Sierra Coll., Rocklin, Calif. 1977; misc. other credits, Okla. State Univ. 1977-79, Sacto. State Univ. 1980; career: instructional asst. II, San Juan Sch. Dist., Carmichael, Calif. 1979-82; telecomms. supr., Delta Dental Svc., San Francisco 1982-85; telecomms. coord., Farmers Savings, Davis, Calif. 1985-87; telecomms. ofcr., Sacto. Savings Bank, Sacto., Calif. 1987-95; telecommns. analyst II, State of Calif. Dept. of Insurance 1995–; owner, custom label designer GDH Enterprises 1993–; awards: Outstanding Service Award, Sacto. Savings 1990, 91, 93, 94; advy. panel, Telcom Div., Golden Gate Univ., Sacto. 1992, 93, 94, 95; mem: TCA (Telecomms. Assn.; v.p. 1993, asst. v.p. 1990-95, programs com. 1995–), Am. Philatelic Soc. 1991-95; Sacto. Philatelic Assn. 1991-95; Errors, Freaks & Oddities Philatelic Collectors 1991-95; Nat. Assn. of Female Executives 1992-95, Internat. Platform Assn. 1994-95; Republican; Born Again Christian, non-denominational; rec: computers, ceramic Christmas ornaments, reading, cats, animal behavior, philately, Christian Ministry, lectr. in telecomms, toll fraud prevention and awareness. Ofc: GDH Enterprises P.O. Box 838 Elverta 95626-0838

HOPE, KATYA MICHELE, psychotherapist; b. April 2, 1947, Washington, D.C.; d. Roger and Jacqueline Henrietta (Firpo) Hope; m. Jay Marx, July 7, 1977; children: Elena b. 1978, Daniel b. 1988; edn: BA, Mills Coll. 1969; MSW, San Francisco St. Univ. 1975; lic. clin. social worker 1978, marriage family and child counselor 1977, Bd. cert. Diplomate in Clin. Soc. Work 1988. Career: co-dir., co-founder Safari Sch., Berkeley 1970-75; dir. family therapy New Bridge Found. 1975-77; pvt. practice psychotherapy 1977; adj. prof., grad. clin. psychology, John F. Kennedy Univ., Orinda 1978; cons. and speaker; mem: Assn. Family Therapists of No. Calif., Calif. Assn. Marriage & Family Therapists, Assn. of Play Therapy (supervisor), co-founder Ctr. for Shared States, No. Calif. Sandplay Therapists; Unitarian. Address; 1821 Delaware St Berkeley 94703

HOPKINS, CECILIA ANN, college administrator; b. Feb. 17, 1922, Havre, Mont.; d. Kost L. and Mary (Manaras) Sofos; m. Henry E. Hopkins, Sept. 7, 1944; edn: BS, Mont. State Coll. 1944; MS, San Francisco St. Coll. 1958, 2d. MA, 1967; adv. admin. educ., Stanford Univ. 1958-60; PhD, Calif. Western Univ. 1977. Career: business tchr. Havre H.S., 1942-44; secty. George P.

Gorham Real Estate, 1944-45; escrow secty. Fox & Carskadon Realtors, 1945-50; escrow ofcr. Calif. Pacific Title Ins. Co. 1950-57; bus. tchr. Westmoor H.S., 1957-58; instr. Coll. of San Mateo, 1958- (ret.), chair Real Estate Dept. 1963-76, dir. Div. of Business 1976-86, post-retirement dir. real estate dept. 1986-91; cons. Calif. State Dept. Real Estate, Sacto.; chair Calif. Comm. Colls. (CCC) Advy. Commn. 1971-72, mem. advy. coms.: CCC Chancellor 1976–, CCC Real Estate Edn. Endowment Fund 1977, proj. dir. Career Awareness Consortium Com. 1976–; dir. emeritus No. REEA; appt. Calif. State Dept. of R.E. Commnrs. Advy. Com. for Edn. and Res. 1983–; awards: San Mateo-Burlingame Bd. of Realtors Commendation for 30 Yrs. Svc. to Membership, RECI (Real Estate Cert. Inst.) Award, REEA Nat. Award emeritus 1993, Calif. Assn. of Realtors 1982; RECI Geo. Thuss Award 1982, 86; CBEA (Calif. Bus. Education) Commendn. for devel. real estate curriculum and devotion to bus. edn. 1978; Soroptimist Intl. (San Mateo - Burlingame) Woman of Achievement 1979; mem: Delta Pi Epsilon (nat. historian 1967-68, nat. sec. 1968-69), Real Estate Tchrs. Assn. (Calif. state pres. 1964-65, hon. dir. 1965–, Hon. dir. emeritus N. REEA), San Francisco State Coll. Counseling and Guidance Alumni Assn., Calif. Bus. Tchrs. Assn., Alpha Gamma Delta, Theta Alpha Delta, Phi Lambda Theta, AAUW; coauthor: Calif. Real Estate Principles (John Wiley & Sons 1980); rec: travel, antiques, hiking. Res: 504 Colgate Way San Mateo 94402 Ofc: College of San Mateo 1700 W Hilldale Blvd San Mateo 94402

HOPKINS, HENRY TYLER, art museum director, professor; b. Aug. 14, 1928, Idaho Falls, Idaho; s. Talcott T. and Zoe (Erbe) H.; children: Victoria b. 1955, John b. 1958, Christopher b. 1965; edn: BA, art edn., Sch. of the Art Inst. of Chgo. 1952, MA, 1954; post-grad. work, art history UCLA 1957-60. Career: tchg. asst. art edn., theory and art history, UCLA 1957-60; tchr. univ. extension courses in art history 1957-68; dir. Huysman Gallery, L.A. 1960-61; asst. head curator of modern art L.A. Co. Mus. of Art 1961-63, head of edn. 1963-65, head of mus. progs. 1965, head curator of exhbns. and pubs. 1965-68; dir. Fort Worth Art Mus., Tx. 1968-73; dir. San Francisco Mus. of Modern Art 1974-86; dir. Frederick R. Weisman Art Found., L.A. 1968-91; prof., chmn. art dept. UCLA 1991–; dir. UCLA Wight Art Gallery 1991–; dir. UCLA/Armand Hammer Mus. of Art and Cultural Ctr. 1994–; internat. lectr. on Calif. contemporary art; art exhbn. juror in 36 states; art critic; panelist: Nat. Endowment for the Arts (chmn. mus. policy panel 1979-83), Nat. Endowment for the Humanities 1976-77; trustee Art Assn. of Am. (1975-77, pres. 1978), Assn. of Art Mus. Directors (v.p. 1984, pres. 1985); advy. bd. trustees: Univ. of Okla. Art Div., San Francisco Airport, Moscone Convention Ctr. art commn., Houston Mus. of Contemporary Art, Internat. Sculpture Ctr., W.D.C.; honors: knighted with the Order of Leopold, Govt. of Belgium 1982, St. of Calif. Commendation for Svc. 1985, City of S.F. Commendation for Svc. 1986, hon. PhD: Calif. Coll. of Arts & Crafts, Oakland 1983, S.F. Art Inst. 1985, Special Internat. Art Award for Svc., Art L.A. 1991, listed Who's Who in Am., Who's Who in Am. Art; mem: We. Assn. of Art Museums (pres. 1976-77), Assn. of Art Mus. Directors (1984-85), L.A. Bd. for the Municipal Art Gallery (1st v.p.), L.A. Art Fair (co-chair 1987), Calif./Internat. Arts Found., Beyond Baroque Poetry Ctr., Santa Monica Coll. of Art, Design and Arch.; author: California Painting and Sculpture: The Modern Era, 1976, Clyfford Still, 1976, Fifty West Coast Artists, 1982, California Painters: New Work, 1989; art entries for Funk & Wagnall Encyclopedia Yearbook, 1976-80, contbr. The Dictionary of Art, essays to catalogues on num. artists, jour. articles. Ofc: UCLA/Hammer Museum 10899 Wilshire Blvd Los Angeles 90024

HOPKINS, PATRICIA MARGARET, college professor; b. June 6, 1939, Ilford, England; nat. 1964; d. Edward George and Freda Miriam (Farrant) Berg; m. McMillen Hopkins, March 5, 1960 (div. 1980); children: Craig Edward b. 1963, Keith Bryan b. 1968; edn: AA hons., Fullerton Jr. Coll. 1967; BA hons., CSU Fullerton 1971; MBA, 1972; PhD, Claremont Grad. 1977. Career: secty. Leonard Bloch & Co., London, England 1957-58; credit analyst Getty Oil, Los Angeles 1958-63; statistician Rockwell, Anaheim 1965-69; dept. chair, prof. Calif. St. Polytech. Univ., Pomona 1975; honors: CSU Fullerton Outstanding Grad. 1971, Calif. St. Polytech. Univ. (Pomona) Outstanding Educator 1984, and Outstanding Prof. 1992-93, Alpha Gamma Sigma, Beta Gamma Sigma, Phi Kappa Phi, Mu Kappa Tau, Golden; mem: Acad. Mktg. Sci. (editl. bd. 1976), Am. Mktg. Assn., Western Mktg. Educator Assn. (dir. 1972), Pi Sigma Epsilon, Womens Council of St. Univs., City of Hope, Calif. Polytech. Womens Club, Womens Forum, NOW; Democrat; rec: travel. Res: 16326 Santa Bianca Hacienda Heights 91745 Ofc: California State Polytechnic University 3801 Temple Pomona 91768

HOPPING, RICHARD LEE, college president; b. July 26, 1928, Dayton, Ohio; s. Lavon Lee and Dorothy Marie (Anderson) H.; m. Patricia Louise Vance, June 30, 1951; children: Ronald L. b. 1952, Debra L. b. 1954, Jerrold A. b. 1956; edn: attended Univ. of Dayton; BS. OD, DOS, Southern Coll. of Optometry; post grad. study Indiana Univ., Div. of Optometry and Ohio State Univ., Coll. of Optometry; management devel. seminar, Hillsdale Coll. Career: pres. Southern Calif. Coll. of Optometry, 1973–; chmn. profl. enhancement advy. com. Am. Optometric Ass.. 1982–, chmn. industry relations com. 1989–, cons. communications ctr. exec. com. 1989–, chmn. nat. ednl. summit conf. 1992; chief coord./cons. pathways in optometry prog. Am. Optometric Assn. and

Allergan, Inc. 1989–; chmn. OD of yr. com. Calif. Optometric Assn. 1990-91, mem. academic relations com. 1990–; honors: Beta Sigma Kappa, Sigma Alpha Sigma (secty. treas.), Outstanding Optimist of yr. award Dayton View Optimist Club, One of Ohio's Ten Outstanding Young Men of Yr. 1960, Outstanding Young Man of Yr. award Dayton Jr. C.of C. 1960, Optometrist of Yr.: Ohio St. Optometric Assn. 1962, Calif. Optometric Assn. 1988, Am. Optometric Assn. 1988, fellow Am. Public Health Assn. 1967, fellow Am. Acad. of Optometry, hon. Doctor of Ocular Sci., So. Coll. of Optometry, Memphis, Tenn. 1972, Disting. Achievement award Am. Public Health Assn. Vision Care Sect. 1984, Orange Co. Retinitis Pigmentosa Award of Excellence in the field of low vision care 1988, commissioned Hon. Kentucky Colonel 1989, Dr. Raymond I. Myers award Am. Optometric Student Assn. 1990, Award of Excellence, VisionAmerica 1991, Disting. Service award Am. Optometric Assn. 1993, hon. Doctor of Sci., State Univ. of N.Y. 1995; hon. mem: Omega Epsilon Phi, Optometric Ext. Prog. Found., Ohio St. Univ. Alumni Assn., So. Calif. Coll. of Optometry Alumni Assn., Hawaii Optometric Assn., Ohio Optometric Ass.; mem: Nat. Academies of Practice 1983–, Am. Optometric Found. (life) 1983–, Am. Optometric Student Assn. (life) 1990–; civic: Boy Scouts of Am (mem. advy. com. Orange Co. Council 1979–), Orange Co. Public T.V. KOCE Channel 50 (advy. com. 1981–), YWCA of No. Orange Co. (advy. council 1984–), Better Vision Inst. (nat. spokesperson 1988–), Res: 2741 Anacapa Place Fullerton 92635 Ofc: Southern California College of Optometry 2575 Yorba Linda Blvd Fullerton 92631

HORN, STEPHEN, congressman, educator; b. May 31, 1931, Gilroy; s. John Stephen and Isabelle (McCaffrey) H.; m. Nini, Sept. 4, 1954; children: Marcia Karen (Yavitz) b. 1955, John Stephen b. 1960; edn: AB w/gr. distinction, Stanford 1953; MPA, Harvard 1955; PhD, Stanford 1958. Career: Congl. fellow of Am. Political Sci. Assn. 1958-59; adminstrv. asst. US Secty. of Labor James P. Mitchell 1959-60; legis. asst. Sen. Thomas H. Kuchel 1960-66; senior fellow The Brookings Inst., Wash. DC 1966-69; dean grad. studies and res. The American Univ., Wash DC 1969-70; pres. Calif. State Univ. Long Beach 1970-88, trustee, prof. political sci., 1988-92; mem. 103rd Congress from 38th Dist., Calif. 1992–; commr. US Commn. Civil Rights (1969-82, v.chair 1969-80), Nat. Inst. of Corrections advy. bd. (1971-88, chair 1984-87); honors: Phi Beta Kappa 1953, adminstrv. fellow 1954-55 and fellow 1966-67, Inst. of Politics, Harvard Univ., Nat. Acad. of Pub. Adm. 1986; mem: Am. Assn. of State Colls. and Univs. (chmn. 1985-86), Am. Council on Edn. (bd. dirs., mem. Commn. on Nat. Challenges in Higher Edn.), Long Beach C.of C. (dir.-at-large, v.chmn. exec. council 1985-88), FHP Found. (bd. dirs. 1985, v.p. 1986); author The Cabinet and Congress, 1960, Unused Power: The Work of The Senate Committee on Appropriations, 1970; coauthor (w/ Edmund Beard) Congressional Ethics: The View From The House, 1975; mil: E-7 USAR Intel. Reserve, 1954-62; Republican. Res: 3944 Pine Ave Long Beach 90807 Ofc: U.S. House of Representatives 129 Cannon Washington DC 20515

HORNAK, THOMAS, electronics research executive; b. Oct. 14, 1924, Bratislava, Czechoslovakia; nat. 1974; s. Stephan and Elisabeth (Meer) H.; m. Vera Lautner, March 15, 1958; 1 son, Tom b. 1962; edn: BSEE, Slovak Tech. Univ. Bratislava Czechoslovakia 1946; MSEE, 1947; PhD, Czech. Tech. Univ. Prague 1966. Career: section mgr. Tesla Research, Prague, Czechoslovakia 1947-61; head advisor Computer Research Inst. 1962-68; tech. staff Hewlett Packard Labs., Palo Alto 1968-73, dept. mgr. 1973-92, prin. lab. scientist 1992–; vis. prof. Czecholslovakia Tech. Univ., Prague 1952-56; mem: IEEE (fellow); 43 patents held in electronics, 48 articles pub. in electronics. Ofc: Hewlett Packard PO Box 10350 Palo Alto 94303

HORNER, LELAND JOHN, city manager; b. March 18, 1933, Pasadena; s. Clealand Archie Shell and Olga Ida (Hokenson) H.; m. Dorothy Jean Cannon, Feb. 1, 1959; children: Cyndi b. 1961, Scott b. 1963, Amy b. 1966, David b. 1968; edn: AB, San Jose St. Univ.; MPA, USC. Career: asst. adminstv. ofcr. City of Gardena 1962-69; asst. city mgr. City of Ventura 1969-73; city adminstr. City of Millbrae 1973-78; city mgr. City of Livermore 1978–; mem: Livermore Rotary Club (pres. 1992-93), Livermore C.of C., Our Saviors Lutheran Ch. (bd. elders 1987–), El Camino Kiwanis (pres. 1968), Alameda City Mgmt. Assn. (chmn. 1983-84); mil: USN 1952-56. Ofc: City of Livermore 1052 S Livermore Ave Livermore 94550

HOROWITZ, BEN, medical center executive; b. Mar. 19, 1914, N.Y.C.; s. Saul and Sonia (Meringoff) H.; m. Beverly Lichtman, 2 children, Zachary b. 1953, Jody b. 1955; edn: BA, Brooklyn Coll., 1940; LLB, St. Lawrence Univ., 1935; New Sch. for Social Research, N.Y., 1942; admitted bar, 1941. Career: director New York Fedn. of Jewish Philanthropies, 1940-45; eastern reg. dir. City of Hope Nat. Medical Ctr., Los Angeles 1945-50, nat. exec. secty. City of Hope, 1950-53, exec. director 1953-85, bd. dir. 1980–, general v.p. 1985-: formulated the role of City of Hope as a pilot ctr. in medicine, science and humanitarianism, and author City of Hope "Torchbearers Creed" 1959; awards: City of Hope nat. awards: Spirit of Life, Gallery of Achiev. (1970, 74), profl. of year Nat. Soc. of Fund Raisers/ So. Calif. 1977, Ben Horowitz Chair in Research estab. at City of Hope 1981, L.A. city street named in his honor 1986; mem: bds. Beckman Research Inst. 1980–, Hope for Hearing Found., UCLA (v.p. 1972–),

Forte Found. 1987-92, Leo Baeck Temple (1964-67, 86-89), Church-Temple Corp. for Homeless 1988-93, Westwood Property Owners Assn. (bd. 1991–); appt. Calif. Gov.'s Task Force on Flood Relief (1969-74). Res: 221 Conway Ave Los Angeles 90024 Ofc: City of Hope, 208 West 8th St Los Angeles 90014

HOROWITZ, DAVID CHARLES, consumer correspondent; b. June 30, 1937, NY, NY; s. Max Leo and Dorothy (Lippman) H.; m. Suzanne E. McCambridge, 1973; 2 daus.; edn: BA, hons. journ., Bradley Univ. 1959; MSJ, Northwestern Univ. 1960; CBS Fellow, Columbia Univ. 1962-63. Career: editor-in-chief Tazewell Co. (Ill.) Newspaper, 1956; reporter Peoria (Ill.) Journ. Star, 1957-60; reporter, columnist Lerner Newspapers and Chgo. City News Bureau, 1959-60; newscaster KRNT Radio-TV, Des Moines 1960-62; news writer/ prod. ABC Radio Network, NYC 1963; Far East corr. NBC News, 1963-64; pub. affairs dir. WMCA, NYC 1964-66; corr.-edn. ed., Consumer Ombudsman, KNBC News Action Reporter, L.A. 1966-93; reporter KCBS "Fight Back!" L.A. 1993–; concumer reporter CNBC 1989–; spl. features: Consumer Guideline, Of Consumer Interest, Consumer Close/Up; nat. syndicated pgm. David Horowitz Consumer Buyline, Fight Back! with David Horowitz; worldwide Apollo 15 splashdown, 1971; Calif. earthquake 2/9/71; Dem. Conv. 1972; host/exec. prod./dir. of home videotape: The Baby Safe Home (distbd. Embassy-McGraw Hill); synd. columnist Creators Synd. 1989–; Western Internat. Synd. 1989–; synd. TV show Fightback! David Horowitz; host/exec. prod./dir. of home videotape: The Baby Safe Home (Embassy-McGraw Hill); exec. prod. CBS-TV Aftersch. Spl. "Frog Girl: The Jenifer Graham Story" (Genesis Animal Rights Award 1990); host, exec. prod. "Best Defense" TV Special 1993; exec. prod. feature TV movie "Tears of Joy, Tears of Sorrow" (disting. svc. award, Ill. Bdcstrs. Assn.; 1st place award UPI Bdcstrs. Assn.); author 7 books: Fight Back and Don't Get Ripped Off, 1979,The Business of Business, 1989; Fight Back! Health Guides, 1993; FightBack! At Work, 1994; advr. UCLA publs.; pres. Fight Back! Found. for Consumer Edn., 1988–; Consumer Commentator CNBC-TV 1990–; synd. Fightback Radio Reports, The Entertainment Networks, 1989–; pres. Medill Sch. of Journalism, So. Calif. Chpt., 1990–; awards: Nat. Radio-TV Daily Award 1963, Emmy for consumer ombudsman KNBC Newsservice, Emmy awards for comsumer reporting (1973, 75, 77, 2 in 1982, 83, 89, 90, 91, 92, 93, 94, 95), resolutions LA City, LA Co., State of Calif. 1979, City of Hope spirit of life award 1979, US Postal Insps. 1981, Vista Del Mar, Jewish Fedn. Council 1981, media award Nat. Soc. of Consumer Affairs Profls. 1982, Calif. State disting. citizen 1982, US Consumer Product Safety Commn. 1982, Calif. Consumer Affairs Assn. 1982, Humane Soc. of the US, LA Press Club, LA Co. Commn. on Alcoholism, Work Tng. Pgm. for Devel. Disabled Young Adults, Golden Mike Award 1986, 95, Excellence in Journalism award of Nat. Assn. for Home Care 1992, Northwestern Univ. Distinguished Alumni Award 1994; frequent TV talk show guest; feature subject in Time Mag. (1/4/82), TV Guide (5/15/82); mem. Child Passenger Safety Assn.; bd. mem: Nat. Bdcst. Edn. Conf., Am. Cancer Soc. Calif. Div., LA Jewish Home for Aged, The Silent Network, The Young Musicians Found. Inc.; advy. bd. S.H.A.R.E., Inc.; patron LA Co. Art Mus.; mem: AFTRA, SAG, W.G.A., BMI, ASCAP, Acad. TV Arts and Scis., Internat. Radio-TV Soc., Radio-TV News Dirs. Assn., Nat. Edn. Writers Assn., The Guardians, Sigma Delta Chi, Phi Delta Kappa, Overseas Press Club of Am., Friars Club; mil: USNR 1954-62. Ofc: PO Box 49915 Los Angeles 90049

HOROWITZ, ZACHARY I., music industry executive; b. Apr. 27, 1953, N.Y.C.; s. Ben and Beverly (Lichtman) H.; m. Dr. Barbara Natterson; edn: BA (summa cum laude) Claremont Mens Coll., 1975; JD, Stanford Univ., 1978; admitted bar: Calif., 1978. Career: atty., assoc. Kaplan, Livingston, Goodwin, Berkowitz & Selvin, Beverly Hills 1978; senior atty. CBS Records, Los Angeles 1978-80, dir. bus. affairs West Coast, 1980-83; v.p., senior v.p. bus. and legal affairs MCA Music Entertainment Group, Universal City 1983-88; exec. v.p. MCA Music Entertainment Group, 1989–; operating com. Motown Record Company L.P. 1988-93; bd. dirs. MCA Victor Japan 1991–; bd. dirs. Record Industry Assn. Am. 1989–; bd. dirs. City of Hope 1989–, Music Industry Chpt. v.chmn. 1985-86, chmn. major gifts com. 1986-89, pres. 1990–, chmn. 1993–; honors: bd. of editors Stanford Law Rev. 1977-78. Ofc: MCA Records, Inc. 70 Universal City Plaza Universal City 91608

HORTON, JACK K., utility company executive; b. June 27, 1916, Stanton, Nebr.; s. Virgil L. and Edna L. (King) H.; m. Betty Lou Magee, July 15, 1937; children: Judy b. 1944, Sally b. 1948, Harold b. 1952; edn: BA, Stanford Univ. 1936; LLB, Oakland Coll. Law 1941; admitted bar Calif. 1941. Career: Shell Oil Co. Treasury Dept. 1937-42; pvt. law practice, San Francisco 1942-43; atty. Standard Oil Co. 1943-44; secty., legal counsel Coast Cos. Gas & Electric Co. 1944-51, pres. 1951-54; v.p. Pacific Gas & Electric Co. 1954-59; pres. So. Calif. Edison Co., Rosemead 1959-68, CEO 1965, chmn. bd. 1968-80, chmn. exec. com. 1980-89; trustee USC; mem: State Bar Calif. Bus. Council; clubs: Bohemian, Calif., Los Angeles Country, Cypress Point. Ofc: So Calif Edison Co 2244 Walnut Grove Ave Rosemead 91770

HORTON, MARVIN RICHARD, rocket engineer, mechanical engineering consultant; b. Oct. 15, 1935, San Jose; s. Jack Brown and Lillian (Weigant) H.; m. Inge Schaefer, Mar. 31, 1967; children: Bertina b. 1967, Kimberly b. 1971; edn: BSME, CalPoly S.L.O., 1959; reg. profl. engr., mech. (No. M24370) Calif.

1986. Career: hydraulic engr. Army Corps of Engrs., Sausalito 1960-62; mech. engr. Finnish State R.R., Hyvinkaa, Finland 1962-63; constrn. engr. Army Corps Engrs., military sites in Turkey 1964-65; mech. engr. Morrison-Knudsen (BMKF), Milano, Itlay 1966-67; project mgr. Tamimi & Fouad Contrs., Dammam, Saudi Arabia 1968-69; chief field engr. H.K. Ferguson, Butte, Mont. 1970; nuclear q.c. engr. Bechtel Power Corp., San Francisco 1971-75; R&D engr. Selkirk Metalbestos, Belmont 1975-85; cons. engr. prin. Horton Engineering Co., 1985–; mech. (rocket) engr. PACAM, Redwood City 1988–; devel. engr. Univ. of Calif. Berkeley 1992–; honors: recogn. Robotics Dept. Stanford Univ. 1982; mem: ASME, NSPE, AIAA, Nat. Space Soc., Planetary Soc., AAAS, Space Studies Inst., Film Arts Found. 1975; prod. 3 short films: Live Steam, 1963, A Day At Neothakikar (Israel, 1966), The Hill, 1971; mil: E4 USAR 1960-65; Democrat; Lutheran; rec: skiing. Res: 2363 44th Ave San Francisco 94116 Lab: Horton Engineering Co. 108 Murlagan Ave Mountain View 94043

HORTON, MICHAEL LYNN, mortgage banker; b. Oct. 19, 1961, Pasadena, Calif.; s. Jerry Stanley and Mary Louise H.; edn: BA econs., Claremont McKenna Coll. 1983; realtor Calif. 1986. Career: ops. mgr. I.W.S. Pasadena 1977-78; exec. asst. to pres. Harris Constrn. Co. La Verne 1979-80; founder NBB Svcs. 1980; sr. mortgage banker, regional mgr. Sycamore Financial Group, Rancho Cucamonga 1984-87; pres. Boulder Fin. Corp., Rancho Cucamonga 1988–; pres. MCM Publishing Group 1992–; CEO, pres. Sandstone Realty Group, Inc. 1995–; instr. mortgage finance workshop; honors: life mem. CSF, Outstanding Student of Yr. (Chaffey Comm. Coll. econ. dept. 1980), Calvin G. Justice Meml. Scholar 1980, Doris D. Lepper Meml. Scholar 1981, Outstanding Bus. Student (Chaffey 1981), Dean's List (Chaffey, Claremont Men's Coll.), acad. scholarship (Claremont McKenna 1981), Calif. State Scholar 1981; mem: L.A. World Affairs Coun., West End Executive Assn.; author: A Real Estate Professional's Reference Guide to Mortgage Finance 1985, Money Talks (newsletter); Republican (Calif. Central Com. 1981-91, Pete Wilson nominee to Repub. Senatorial Inner Circle 1985); rec: basketball, racquetball, tennis, water sports. Ofc: Boulder Financial Corp., 9121 Haven Ave Ste 150 Rancho Cucamonga 91730

HORWIN, LEONARD, lawyer; b. Jan. 2, 1913, Chgo.; s. Joseph and Jeanette H.; m. Ursula Helene Donig, Oct. 15, 1939; children: Noel S. b. 1940, Leonora Marie b. 1947; edn: BA (honors) UCLA, 1933; LLB (cum laude) Yale Law Sch., 1936; Career: atty., assoc. pioneer law firm Lawler, Felix and Hall, 1936-39; ptnr. (Jack W.) Hardy and Horwin, attys. for L.A. Examiner, Sterling Elec. Motors, others, 1939-42; ptnr. Witkin-Horwin Review Course on Calif. Law, 1939-42; lectr. labor law, USC Law Sch., 1941; counsel Bd. of Econ. Warfare and mem. program adjustment com. and alt. mem. requirements com. War Prodn. Bd., 1942-43; attache U.S. Emb., Madrid, Spain 1943-47; American rep. in Spain, Allied Control Council for Ger., 1945-47; lectr. (in Spanish lang.) on Am. constl. law, Am. Cultural Inst., Madrid, 1945; lectr., fgn. affairs, Town Hall of Calif., other civic groups, 1949; pvt. law practice, 1950–; elected Beverly Hills City Council, 1962, mayor pro tem 1963, mayor 1964, chmn. com. on municipal ct. reorganization League of Calif. Cities, 1963-65; dir. So. Calif. Rapid Transit Dist., 1964-66; com. chmn. Transp. Com. L.A. Goals Council, 1966-70; chmn. Beverly Hills Rent Control Adjustment Com., 1980; publs: numerous articles on legal subjects, ed. Yale Law Jour. 1934-35; awards: Yale Univ. Israel H. Peres Prize for legal writing 1934-35, Yale Univ. Edward D. Robbins Mem. Prize 1935-36; author: Insight and Foresight, 14 vols., Dawn Publications Ltd. 1991; Jewish; rec: community projects, hunting, riding, skiing; res: 434 El Camino Dr Beverly Hills; ofc: 121 S Beverly Dr Beverly Hills 90212

HORWITZ, BRUCE ALEX, physician (pediatrics)/mortgage banker; b. Sept. 2, 1937, Oakland, Calif.; s. Harry H. and Esther (Mintz) H.; m. Jacquelyn Faye Sigoloff, Dec. 17, 1961; children: Cynthia b. 1963, Joel b. 1965; edn: attended UC Berkeley 1955-58; MD, Washington Univ., St. Louis, Mo. 1962; cert. Am. Bd. of Pediatrics 1967. Career: pediatrics intern Univ. of Rochester 1962-63; pediatrics residency Univ. of Rochester 1963-64, Children's Hosp. Oakland, Calif. 1964-65; staff pediatrics U.S. Army, Ft. Belvoir, VA 1965-67; pvt. practice Oakland 1967-; mortgage banker BARK Inc., San Leandro 1980-; bd. mem. Hill Physicians-IPA, San Ramon 1991-94; team physician Oakland Athletics Baseball, Oakland 1973-83; chief pediatrics Samuel Merritt Hosp., Oakland 1977-83; awards: Pacific Coast Conf. Athletic Scholar award 1958; fellow Am. Acad. of Pediatrics 1967-; mil: capt. U.S. Army 1965-67; Independent; Jewish; rec: marathon running, biking. Ofc: 411 30th St #212 Oakland 94609

HOSANG, ROBERT ANTHONY, physician; b. Apr. 6, 1950, Kingston, Jamaica; s. Hugh Anthony and Iris (Shim) H.; m. Joyce Yap, Oct. 20, 1984; edn: MBBS, Univ. of the West Indies, Mona, Jamaica 1976; MPH, UC Berkeley 1985; MBA, UC Berkeley 1995. Career: lectr. Univ. of West Indies 1980-84; sr. physician Kaiser Permanente, Hayward 1986-93; lectr. UC Berkeley 1989–; fellow, Am. Coll. of Obstetrics & Gynecology 1983–; rec: music, dance, fishing. Ofc: Hayward 94545

HOSIE, STANLEY WILLIAM, S.M., theologian, foundation executive, writer; b. Apr. 28, 1922, Lismore, New South Wales, Australia; s. Stanley James and Catherine Clare (Chisholm) H.; edn: BA, Univ. Queensland, Brisbane 1945; M.Theol. Catholic Univ., W.D.C., 1947, MA, 1948; Soc. of Mary. Career: dean of studies Marist Coll., Lismore 1949-57; pres., founder Chanel Coll., Geelong, Victoria, Australia 1958-62; writer-in-residence Casa Generalitia Societatis Mariae, Rome 1963-66; exec. dir. The Found. for the Peoples of the South Pacific Inc., N.Y.C. 1966–; theologian for Conf. of Pacific Catholic Bishops, 2d Vatican Council, Rome 1963-65; dir. Am. Council for Voluntary Internat. Action (Interaction), N.Y.C. 1968–, treas. 1983-84; dir. Private Agencies Collaborating Together, 1977-90; apptd. Presdl. Advy. Com. on Voluntary Fgn. Aid, 1988-93; author: The Swiss Conspiracy, 1976, The Boomerang Conspiracy, 1978, (biography) Anonymous Apostle, 1966, also numerous screenplays; awards: best article Vatican II, Nat. Cath. Periodicals Assn. 1964; mem: Writers Guild Am. East, Soc. des Oceanistes, Australian Coll. Edn.; Democrat; R.Cath.; rec: tennis, swimming. Res: 723 Palisades Bch Rd Santa Monica 90402 Ofc: Counterpart Foundation 910 Seventeenth St #328 Washington DC 20006

HOTCHNER, BRADLEY ROSS, physician, orthopedic surgeon; b. Aug. 22, 1955, St. Louis, Mos.; s. Selwyn Ross and Beverly June (Novack) H.; m. Cynthia Ann Huckelberry, June 7, 1986; edn: BS (honors), Univ. of Wisc., 1977; MD, St. Louis Univ. 1981, Orthopedic Surg., 1986. Career: intern, general surg. St. Louis Univ., Mo. 1981-82, resident orthopedic surg. 1982-86; fellowship, knee & shoulder, Dr. Robt. Jackson, Toronto, Can. 1990, A-O, Basel, Switz. & West Berlin, W.Ger. 1990, hip & knee joint replacement, Dr. Wayne Pagrosky, Chgo. 1990; staff surg. Palm Springs Med. Ctr. 1986; staff surgeon San Bernardino Co. Hosp. 1987–; asst. clinical prof. orthopedic surgery Loma Linda Univ. 1987–; mem. honor societies: Phi Eta Sigma, Phi Kappa Phi, Phi Beta Kappa. Ofc: San Bernardino Orthopedic Medical Group 780 E Gilbert San Bernardino 92404

HOTTI, CRAIG RICHARD, video producer; b. Sept. 12, 1964, Burnaby, Canada; nat. 1988; s. Allan Robert and Margaret (Nicol) H.; m. Kimberly Dawn Platz, June 23, 1986; edn: BA broacast journalism and internat. rels., USC 1986. Carer: newswriter CBS, Los Angeles 1986; video producer Brewster Video, Long Beach 1986-87; self-employed video producer, Pacoima 1987–; mem: Internat. T.V. Assn. (bd. dirs. L.A.), Assn. Visual Com. (awards judge), Internat. Teleproduction Soc. (awards judge); Democrat; rec: writing, bicycling, volunteer work.Res: 11388 Dronfield Terr Pacoima 91331

HOUCK, LAURIE GERALD, research plant pathologist; b. Aug. 13, 1928, Tucson, Ariz.; s. Gerald Wesley and Laura Lee (Baker) H.; m. Marlene Moore, Sept. 20, 1958 (dec. 1970); m. Margaret Victoria Evers, July 28, 1979; children: Lorna Jeanne b. 1959, Marlys Lee b. 1961; edn: BS, Univ. Ariz. 1952; MS, 1954; PhD, Oreg. St. Univ. 1962. Career: research plant physiologist U.S. Dept. of Agri., Phoenix, Ariz. 1954-55; asst. horticulturalist Univ. Ariz., Mesa 1956-57; research plant pathologist U.S. Dept. Agri., Pomona 1962-73, Riverside 1973-77, Fresno 1977; p.t. lectr. Calif. St. Polytech. Univ., Pomona 1963, 64, 66; awards: Univ. Ariz. Johnson Wax fellow (1953-54); mem: Toastmasters (v.p., past pres.), Am. Soc. Phytopathology, Am. Soc. Horitcultural Sci., Council for Agri. Sci. & Tech., Food Distribution Research Soc.; 40+ articles pub. in profl. jours., 3 book chpts. pub. (1965, 92, 94); mil: pfc AUS 1946-48; Democrat; Unitarian Universalist; rec: gardening, hiking. Res: 1758 S Waldby Ave Fresno 93727 Ofc: U.S. Dept. of Agriculture 2021 S Peach Ave Fresno 93727

HOUSER, JOE JAMES, insurance broker; b. April 17, 1916, Udall, Kansas; s. John Jefferson and Elsie Mae (Effner) H.; m. Sherry Lindberg, July 10, 1978; children: Joe James II b. 1946, Jeffrey Jay b. 1948; edn: var. studies USC, UCLA 1941-46. Career: asst. buyer Bullocks, Los Angeles 1938-41; supvr. North American Aviation, L.A. 1941-46; v.p. J.E. Wells Co.Inc., L.A. 1946-57; pres., owner Houser Ins. Agency, L.A. 1957–; fmr. dir. Insurance Brokers Assn.; recipient service awards: L.A. City and County (1968, 1970), Boys Club of Am. medallion award 1975, Goodwill Industries 1990, LA Elks Lodge (1957, 67, 74), Wilshire C.of C. 1968), Beverly Hills Shrine Club (1964, 67), Elks Roses for the Living 1980, Hyatt House Comm. award 1977; mem. Independent Ins. Agents & Brokers Assn.; life mem: US Navy League, F&AM Masons, L.A. Commandery Knights Templar, L.A. Scottish Rite, Beverly Hills Shrine Club, Al Malaikah Temple of the Shrine, L.A. Elks Lodge (advisor, past pres., past dist. dep. grand exalted ruler), Elks of L.A. Found. (gov.); civic: L.A. Conservancy, Boys and Girls Club Hollywood (dir.), Boys and Girls Club Am./L.A. Co. Area Council (past chmn.), Baja Club of Hollywood (pres.), L.A./ Bombay Sister City Affil. (pres., dir.), Goodwill Inds. So. Calif. (dir.), U.S.O./L.A. Area (past dir.), Wilshire C.of C. (past pres.), Wilshire Rotary Club (past dir.), L.A. Royal Arch Masons, Trojan Shrine Club, L.A. Philanthropic Found., Am. Film Inst.; Republican Presidential Task Force. Res: 11039 Wrightwood Pl Studio City 91604 Ph 213/877-6657

HOUSTON, ELIZABETH REECE, educator, consultant; b. June 19, 1935, Birmingham, Ala.; d. Reuben Cleveland and Beulah Elizabeth (Reece) Manasco; edn: BSc, Univ. Texas, Austin 1956; MEdn, Boston Coll., 1969. Career: tchr. Ridgefield (Ct.) Pub. Schs., 1962-63; Northampton (Mass.) Pub. Schs., 1972-73; dir. Jack Douglas Vocat. Ctr., San Jose, Calif. 1974-76; tchr. Santa Clara County Office of Edn., San Jose 1976-80, behavioral specialist 1980-82, staff devel. coordinator 1982-86; instr. CSU San Jose, 1980-86; instr. UC Santa Cruz, 1982-84; director Alternative Schools, Santa Clara Co. Office of

Edn., San Jose 1986-94; instr. Santa Clara Univ. 1992–; awards: Pres.'s award Soc. of Photo-Optical Engrs. 1979, Sch. Bd. Assn., San Jose 1985, svc. to youth Juvenile Ct. Sch. Adminstrs. of Calif. (1989, 90, 91, 92), Outstanding Educator award Santa Clara Univ. 1992; mem: Juvenile Ct. Sch. Adminstrs. (chair 1986-94), Council of Exceptional Children 1976-92, Assn. for Supervision and Curriculum Devel. 1982-94, Assn. of Calif. Sch. Adminstrs. 1982-92; civic: Sudbury (Mass.) Public Health Nurses (dir. 1970-72), Eastfield Ming Quong, Los Gatos (dir. 1978-86), Santa Clara Co. Justice System Adv. Bd. 1989-94; author book chapt., Learning Disabilities, 1992, manuals: Behavior Mgmt. for Bus Drivers, 1980, Classroom Mgmt., 1983, Synergistic Learning, 1986. Res: 12150 Country Squire Ln Saratoga 95070 Ofc: Santa Clara County Office of Education, 100 Skyport Dr Santa Clara 95110

HOUX, MARY ANNE, businesswoman, county official; b. Kans. City, Mo.; d. Rial Richardson and Geraldine Marie (McHale) Oglevie; m. Phillip Clark Houx, May 12, 1962 (dec.); 1 son, Clark Oglevie b. 1966; edn: BS edn., Univ. Kans., 1954. Career: sch. tchr. in Mo., Kans., Mich., Calif.; midwest dir. C.A.R.E., Inc., Kansas City, Mo. 1960-63; owner Houx Investments, Chico 1974-93; elected Chico Unified bd. of trustees 1977-90 (pres. 1979-81); elected Chico City Council 1990-91; apptd. to Butte County Board of Supervisors, June 1991, elected Nov. 1992 (chair 1993), elected June 1994; Calif. Sch. Bds. Assn. (pres. 1987-88); awards: Athena Award 1992; mem. Chico State University Assoc. (pres. 1983-85), Chico State Faculty Wives (pres. 1969-70), Chico C.of C., Commonwealth Club of Calif., Cosmos Club; Republican; R.Cath. Ofc: PO Box 1087 Chico 95927

HOVERLAND, HAL, professor of accounting emeritus; b. May 13, 1928, Boston, Mass.; s. Arthur Reed and Bertha Mae (McCrary) H.; edn: BS, Miami Univ. 1951; MS, Univ. Ill. 1954; PhD, Univ. Mich. 1963. Career: auditor, indsl. engr. Proctor & Gamble, Cincinnati, Ohio 1951-53, 1954-55; prof. San Jose St. Univ. 1959-63; Univ. Aix Marseille, Aix en Provence, France 1970-71; Naval Postgrad. Sch., Monterey 1963-72; dean sch. of bus. CSU, San Bernardino 1972-86, prof. 1986-92; mem: Am. Acctg. Assn.; co-ed. Crisis Mgmt. in Higher Edn., 1986, articles pub. in profl. jours., 1965-88; mil: airman 2d. USN 1946-48; rec: fishing, backpacking. Ofc: California State University 5500 University Parkway San Bernardino 92407

HOWARD, DAVID JOHN, fine art dealer, art consultant; b. Aug. 9, 1947, New Rochelle, N.Y.; s. Lee and Eleanor Francis (Leibowitz) H.; m. Kathy Evers 1992; edn: AA, Mich. St. Univ. 1967; BA hons., Univ. Fla. 1969. Career: tchr. Atlanta City Schs., Ga. 1969-70; asst. dir. Homestead Family 1970-71; toymaker David Howard Fine Toys, Oakland 1971-74; dealer David Howard, Boulder, Colo. 1974-77, owner 1977-81; regional sales mgr. W. Graham Arader III, King of Prussia, Pa. 1981-83, nat. sales mgr., San Francisco 1983-88; fine art dealer David Howard Fine Art, San Francisco and Mill Valley 1988–; pres. Holloway-Howard Fine Art, San Francisco 1990-91; owner David Howard Fine Art, Mill Valley 1991–; cons. Hellman & Friedman, San Francisco 1988–; cons. W. Garaham Arader III, S.F. 1993-94; mem: Calif. Map Soc. (v.p. 1985-86), Oakland Art Mus., Laguna Art Mus., Hist. Collections Com., L.A. County Art Mus., de Young Art Mus.; honors: biog. listing Who's Who in West 1989-90; publs: art catalogues, 1983, 85, articles in profl. jours., 1985–; Democrat; Jewish; rec: golf, sports, history. Address: 11 Somerset Dr Mill Valley 94941

HOWARD, MURRAY, manufacturing, real estate, property management executive, farmer, rancher; b. July 25, 1914, Los Angeles; s. George A. J. and Mabel (Murray) Howard; edn: BS, UCLA, 1939; C.P.A., Calif. Career: mgr. budget control dept. Lockheed Aircraft 1939-45; pres., chmn. bd. Stanley Foundries, Inc. 1945-59, Howard Machine Products, Inc. 1959–, Murray Howard Realty, Inc. 1959–, Murray Howard Devel., Inc. 1969–, Howard Oceanography, Inc. 1967–, Ranch Sales, Inc. 1968–, Murray Howard Investment Corp. 1961–; owner, gen. mgr. Greenhorn Ranch Co., Greenhorn Creek Guest Ranch, Spring Garden, Calif.; pres., chmn. bd. Murray Howard Cattle Co., Prineville, Oreg.; dir. Airshippers Publ. Corp., La Brea Realty & Devel. Co., Shur-Lok Corp.; apptd. mem. Gov. Calif. Minority Commn.; mem. Nat. Assn. Cost Accts. (dir., v.p.), Nat. Assn. Mfrs. (dir.). Ofc: 4676 Admiralty Way Ste 300 Marina Del Rey 90292-6695

HOWATT, HELEN CLARE, library director; b. Apr. 5, 1927, San Francisco; d. Edward Bell and Helen Margaret (Kenney) H.; edn: BA, Holy Name Coll., 1949; MS in library sci., USC, 1972; joined Order Sisters of the Holy Names, R. Catholic Ch., 1945; cert. advanced studies Inst. Sch. Librarians, Our Lady of the Lake Univ., San Antonio 1966; Calif. (life) tchg. and special services credentials. Career: principal St. Monica Sch., Santa Monica 1957-60, St. Mary Sch., Los Angeles 1960-63; tchr. jr. high sch. St. Augustine Sch., Oakland 1964-69; jr. high math tchr. St. Monica Sch., San Francisco 1969-71, St. Cecilia Sch., San Francisco 1971-77; library dir. Holy Names Coll., Oakland 1977-94; activities dir. Collins Ctr., Sr. Services 1994–; awards: NSF grantee 1966, NDEA grantee 1966; mem. Cath. Library Assn. (chair No. Calif. elem. schs. 1971-72), Calif. Library Assn., Am. Library Assn., Assn. Coll. and Research Libraries; publs: contbr. math. curriculum San Francisco Unified Sch. Dist., Cum Notis Variorum (publ. Music Library, UCB), articles in Catholic Library World, 1987. Address: 2550 18th Ave San Francisco 94116

HOWELL, FRANCIS VERNON, oral pathologist; b. Jan. 12, 1923, Salt Lake City, Utah; s. Vernon W. and Grace McClelland (Davis) H.; m. Margaret L. Pence, July 21, 1951; children: Ruth b. 1952, Susan b. 1954, Amy b. 1960, John b. 1963; edn: BA, Stanford Univ. 1948; DDS, Univ. Pacific 1950; MS pathology, Univ. Oreg. Med. Sch. 1956; diplomate Am. Bd. Oral Pathology (1956). Career: assoc. prof. Univ. Oreg., Portland 1952-56; USC Med. and Dental Sch., Los Angeles 1956-68; UCSD Med. Sch. 1968-88; founder Oral Pathology Service, San Diego 1956-88; Oral Pathology Div., La Jolla 1988; oral medicine chmn. Scripps Clinic 1978-87; honors: Sigma Xi; mem: Am. Coll. Dentists (fellow), Am. Dental Assn. (life), Am. Acad. Oral Pathology (pres. 1968), Am. Soc. Clin. Pathologists, Internat. Assn. Dental Research, Friends of UCSD Library (pres. 1987-89); 7 book chpts. pub. and 48 articles pub. in sci. jours.; mil: sgt. AUS 1942-46; Republican; Episcopalian; rec: antique book collecting. Res: Box 1839 La Jolla 92038

HOWELL, RICHARD JAMES, aerospace engineer; b. Jan. 9, 1935, San Bernardino; s. Weldon Olin and Barbara May (Mulligan) H.; div.; 1 son, Wesley, b. 1958; edn: AA, Mt. San Antonio Coll. 1965; BS, mech. eng., West Coast Univ. 1974, BS, elec. eng., 1974, 1 yr. postgrad work at Cal Poly, Pomona in mech. eng. 1981; granted life time Secret clearance by US DOD Chief Mil. Tribunal, Wash. DC, 1984. Career: elec. engr. General Dynamics, Pomona 1959-73; elec. engr. USN, Corona 1974-75: uncovered and reported flaws in the USN AN/DSM-75 test equipt. (used to verify flt. worthiness of navy's prin. surface-to-air missile) as reported in NBC-TV documentary 3/75 w. the late Don Harris chief NBC Network News (killed in Georgetown, Guyana, 1978, along w. US Congressman Ryan); elec. engr. Metron Corp., Upland 1975-78; sys. analyst Chemsult A.G., Dhahran, Saudi Arabia 1978-79; lead engr./sr. mem. tech. staff TRW Inc. Ballistic Missiles Div., Norton AFB, San Bernardino 1980–, prin. systems design engr. for the Peacekeeper (MX) Missile guidance and control sect., automatic test equipt. for 3d gen. gyroscopes, specific force integration receivers, missile electronic computer assemblies, inertial measurement units and missile guidance and control sets; pres. Howell Eng. Co., Bryn Mawr 1963–; awards: for service asst. football coach, City of Chino Pop Warner Football Assn. 1969; mem: Soc. of Automotive Engrs., IEEE, Am. Soc. Mech. Engrs., The Fibonacci Assn., Assn. of Old Crows, Harley Owners Gp., H.O.G. San Bdo., Am. Motorcyclists Assn., Nat. DeSoto Club, San Bdo. Co. Mus. Assn., Am. Brotherhood Aimed towards Edn., Chrysler Perf. Parts Assn., Calif. Astrology Assn.; donor of ancient Arabian antiquities to San Bdo. Co. Mus., UCLA Dept. of Geology, and Big Bear Valley Hist. Soc.; author: Automotive Engine Piston, Connecting Rod, and Crank Dynamics; Engineering Notes on Piston Displacement Motion, Displacement Motion Velocity, Displacement Motion Acceleration; num. original works on math. & engring. mathematics; exposé on corruption and incompetence in USN fleet missile systems analysis and testing during 1974-76; mil: sgt. USAF 1955-59, GCM, Nat. Defense Svc., AF Longevity Svc.; Republican (state, nat. party, Nat. Fedn. Rep. Women, Nat. Rep. Senatl. Com.); Presbyterian; rec: high performance big block Pontiac wedge, Oldsmobile wedge and Chrysler Corp. Hemi Automotive engineering, theater pipe organ, power lifting, hist. of U.S. steam locomotives. Res: 1125-6B Pine Ave Redlands 92373 Ofc: TRW, Inc., SB2/1052 606 E Mill St San Bernardino 92408

HOWELL, RUTH MARGARET, state social services licensing program analyst; b. Sept. 22, 1932, San Diego; d. Vernon Wilford and Grace McClellan (Davis) H.; m. James McClellan, Dec. 27, 1964 (dec. 1979); son, Jason b. 1968; edn: BA, San Diego St. Univ., 1955; MSW, USC Sch. of Soc. Work, 1962; soc. work supvn., USC, 1965. Career: group work splst. Special Service for Groups, 1960-61; comm. orgn. soc. wkr. S.Cent. Area Welfare Planning Council, L.A. 1961-62; group soc. worker Avalon Comm. Ctr., L.A. 1962-63; child welfare supr. Dept. Pub. Soc. Svs., L.A. Co. 1963-68; psychiatric soc. worker St. Dept. Soc. Welfare, Community Svs. Div. L.A. 1969-72, 1973-76; exec. dir. L.A. Area chpt. Nat. Assn. of Soc. Workers 1972-73;p.t. instr. CSU Los Angeles, 1970-76; mgr. home svcs. div. Harbor Regional Ctr. for Developmentally Disabled, Torrance 1976-77; licensing pgm. analyst State Dept. of Soc. Svs., Community Care Licensing Div., San Diego 1977-91 (ret.); cons./ staff devel. comm. care facilities and pvt. bus. Ruth M. Howell & Assoc. 1991–; rec: golf, walking, swimming, theatre, reading. Res/Ofc: 7303 Calle De Fuente, Rancho La Costa, Carlsbad 92009-7608 Tel: 619/436-3550

HOXSIE, ROBERT MICHAEL, general contractor; b. April 19, 1955, Long Beach; s. Robert Devillo and Loretta Louise (Guglilmano) H.; m. Julie Ann Larson, July 6, 1975; children: Jennifer b. 1976, Casey b. 1978, Lauren b. 1982; edn: Huntington Beach H.S. 1969-73. Career: carpenter 1973-86; mem: ARC (advisor, disaster action team chmn. 1990–), Huntington Valley Boys & Girls Club (dir. 1987–), Fountain Valley Republican Assembly (pres. 1988), Fountain Valley Disaster Preparedness Com. 1988–, Internat. Conf. of Bldg. Ofcrs., Fountain Valley Hist. Soc. (chmn. 1986), Fountain Valley C.of C., Ontario Parks & Recreation (commr. 1982-86); artistic dir., CATS; Republican; Lutheran; rec: rock climbing, off road racing, politics. Res: 10188 Falcon Ave Fountain Valley 92708-7457

HOYE, WALTER BRISCO, consultant, retired community college district administrator; b. May 19, 1930, Lena, Miss.; s. William H. and LouBertha

(Stewart) H.; m. Vida M. Pickens, Aug. 28, 1954; children: Walter B. II, JoAnn M.; edn: BA, Wayne State Univ., 1953. Career: sports, and auto editor Detroit Tribune, 1958-65; sports editor Mich. Chronicle, 1965-68; assoc. dir. pub. relations San Diego Chargers Football Co., 1968-76; media liason NFL, 1972-75; staff ofcr. San Diego Coll. Dist., 1976-92: community services ofcr. 1976-78, placement ofcr./adminstrv. asst. 1982-83, supr. Placement and Program Support 1983-89, supr. Program Support Services 1989-92, ret.; indep. consultant, 1992–; honors: San Diego County citizen of month 5/79, award of merit United Way 1974; mem: Am. Personnel and Guidance Assn., San Diego Career Guidance Assn., Nat. Mgmt. Assn., Assn. Calif. Community Coll. Adminstrs., Calif. Community Coll. Placement Assn., Internat. Assn. of Auditorium Mgrs.; civic: Am. Red Cross San Diego County (bd.), San Diego Conv. and Tourist Bur., Joint Ctr. Political Studies, San Diego Urban League, Neighborhood Housing Assn., Public Access TV. Res: 6959 Ridge Manor Ave San Diego 92120-3146

HOYT, GEORGE WASHINGTON, newspaper publishing company president; b. Mar. 26, 1936, Portland, Ore.; s. George W. and Isabell (Murray) H.; m. Joanne, Sept. 1, 1960 (div. 1980); m. Colleen, Apr. 24, 1982; children: Brian Scott b. 1963, Mark b. 1965; edn: BA, Willamette Univ., 1958; MBA, Univ. Oreg., 1963; OPM pgm. Harvard Bus. Sch., 1989. Career: gen. mgr. Times Publications, Beaverton, Oreg. 1963-71; pres./pub. Pioneer Press, Wilmette, Ill. 1971-78; pub./v.p. Washington Star, W.D.C. 1978-81; prodn. dir. Time Inc., N.Y. 1981-85; pres. and c.o.o. Lesher Communications, Inc. Walnut Creek, Calif. 1985-91; pres. San Gabriel Valley Publishing Co., West Covina 1992–; instr. advt., pub. rels. Pacific Univ., Forest Grove, Oreg. 1964-66; mem. Suburban Newspapers of Am. (pres. 1978-79), Calif. Newspaper Publishers Assn. (dir. 1986-88, 1992–); civic bds: San Gabriel Valley Consortium of Commerce & Cities (treas. 1992-93), Contra Costa Taxpayers Assn. (exec. com. 1986–), Contra Costa Co. Exec. Council 1988–, Willamette Univ. (trustee 1989–), United Way Campaign Contra Costa (chmn. 1991-92), Nat. Capital Council BSA (dir. 1980-81), Cultural Alliance W.D.C. (pres. 1981), Federal City Council W.D.C. (exec. com. 1979-81), Greater W.D.C. Board of Trade (exec. com. 1979-81), Found. for Creative Space W.D.C. (dir. 1980-81); author (newspaper tabloid sect.) Vietnam & Cambodia (1988); mil: E5 sgt. AUS 1958-59; Republican. Res: 216 Lone Hill Rd Glendora 91740 Ofc: San Gabriel Valley Publishing Co. 1210 Azusa Canyon Rd West Covina 91790

HOYT, JACK W., educator; b. Oct. 19, 1922, Chgo.; s. Claire A. and Fleta (Wheeler) H.; m. Helen Erickson, Dec. 27, 1945; children: John b. 1948, Katheryn b. 1952, Annette b. 1959, Denise b. 1964; edn: BS, Ill. Inst. of Tech. 1944; MS, UCLA 1952, PhD 1962. Career: engr. Nat. Advis. Com. on Aeronautics, Cleveland, Oh. 1944-48; engr. Naval Ocean Systems Center, San Diego 1948-79; prof. mech. engring. US Naval Acad., Annapolis 1976-77, Rutgers Univ. 1979-81, CSU San Diego 1981–; honors: Freeman Scholar, ASME (1971), Gilbert Curl Award, USN (1975); mem: ASME, NY Acad. of Scis., Soc. of Naval Architects and Marine Engrs.; numerous tech. papers in field of hydrodynamics; rec: jogging, woodwork, stamps. Res: 4694 Lisann St San Diego 92117 Ofc: San Diego State University, San Diego 92182-0191

HSU, CHIEH SU, engineering professor; b. May 27, 1922, Soochow, Kiangsu, China, naturalized U.S., 1961; s. Chung Yu and Yong Feng (Wu) H.; m. Helen Yung-Feng Tse, Mar. 28, 1953; children: Raymond b. 1954, Katherine b. 1960; edn: grad. Nat. Inst. of Technology, Chungking, China 1945; MS, Stanford Univ., 1948, PhD, 1950. Career: engr. Shanghai Naval Dockyard and Engineering Works, Shanghai, China 1946-47; res. asst. Stanford Univ., Calif. 1948-51; engr. IBM Corp., Poughkeepsie, N.Y. 1951-55; assoc. prof. Univ. of Toledo, Ohio 1955-58; assoc. prof. UC Berkeley, Calif. 1958-64, prof. engring. 1964–, chair div. applied mechanics, 1969-70; tech. editor J. of Applied Mechanics, 1976-82; assoc. ed. 8 profl. journals, 1971–; appt. US Nat. Com. on Theoretical and Applied Mechanics, NAS, 1985-89; sci. advy. bd. Alexander von Humboldt Found., Germany 1985–; awards: Westinghouse Postgrad. fellow Stanford Univ. 1948-50, John Simon Guggenheim fellow, N.Y., N.Y. 1964-65, Miller Res. Prof., UC Berkeley 1973-74, centennial award ASME 1980, Alexander von Humboldt Sr. U.S. Scientist Award 1986; mem: ASME (Fellow 1977), Am. Acad. of Mechanics (Fellow 1980), U.S. Nat. Acad. of Engring. (elected mem. 1988), Academia Sinica R.O.C. (elected mem. 1990); author: Cell-to-Cell Mapping (1987), 106+ sci. papers (1951–). Ofc: Dept. Mech. Engring. Univ. California, Berkeley 94720-1740

HSU, SHU-DEAN, hematologist-oncologist; b. Feb. 21, 1943, Chiba, Japan, came to U.S. 1972; parents: Tetzu and Takako (Koo) Minoyama; m. San-San Hsu, Mar. 3, 1973; children: Deborah Te-Lan, Peter Jie-Te; edn: MD, Taipei Med. Coll., Taiwan 1968; diplomate Am. Bd. Internal Medicine, Am. Bd. Hematology, Am. Bd. Med. Oncology. Career: asst. in medicine Mt. Sinai Sch. Med., N.Y.C., 1975-77; asst. instr. medicine Univ. Texas, Galveston, 1977-78; lectr. Texas A&M Univ., also chief hematology and oncology VA Med. Ctr., Temple, Tx., 1978-80; asst. prof. medicine Univ. Ark., Little Rock, 1980-83; pvt. practice splst. hematology-oncology Visalia Med. Clinic, Visalia, Calif. 1983–; Fellow ACP, mem. N.Y. Acad. Scis., Am. Soc. Clin. Oncology, Am. Soc. Hematology, Calif. Med. Assn., Tulare County Med. Soc.; club: Visalia Racquet. Res: 3500 W Hyde Visalia 93291 Ofc: Visalia Medical Clinic 5400 W Hillsdale Visalia 93291

HSU-WINGES, CHARLENE, ophthalmologist, hospital chief of quality; b. May 12, 1948; d. Henry E. and Joan (Pao) Hsu; m. Jerry L. Winges, Aug. 25, 1973; children: Kimberly b. 1979, Kristin b. 1981; edn: AB, Stanford Univ., 1970; MD, Tufts Univ., 1976. Career: pediatrics intern Childrens Hosp., Los Angeles 1976-77; resident ophth., Pacific Medical Center, 1977-80; fellow pediatric ophth. Univ. Calif. San Francisco 1980-81; sr. physician Permanente Med. Group No. Calif., San Francisco 1981; asst. clin. prof. ophth. UC San Francisco 1983; clin. research Smith Kettlewell Eye Research Found. 1988-89; awards: Alpha Omega Alpha 1976, Janet Glasgow Award Am. Womens Med. Assn. 1976; Fellow Am. Acad. Ophth. 1981, mem. Am. Assn. Ped. Ophth. & Strabismus, Internat. Strabismol. Assn., San Mateo Co. Med. Soc.; civic: Stanford Univ. Cap & Gown (bd. 1992-95), Enterprise for High Sch. Students S.F. (bd. 1986-88); research papers: Photorefractive Screening of Infants, 1988, Devel. of monocular & binocular visual acuity, 1989; rec: bicycling, skiing. Res: Hillsborough 94010 Ofc: 1200 El Camino Real South San Francisco 94080

HU, GENDA JAMES, microelectronics device physicist; b. Jan. 20, 1952, Taipei, Taiwan, R.O.C.; s. Su-Hung and Chang-Chi (Wan) H.; m. Wen-ming Shen, July 23, 1977; children: An-swol b. 1980, An-yen b. 1982; edn: BSE, National Cheng Kung Univ. 1973; MS, Princeton Univ. 1977, PhD, 1979. Career: research staff mem. IBM T.J. Watson Research Ctr., Yorktown Hts., NY 1979-83; Xerox Palo Alto Research Ctr. 1983-84, proj. mgr. device design and simulation 1984; dept. mgr., dir. device engineering Sierra Semiconductor Corp., San Jose 1984-90; dir. non-volatile technology Cypress Semiconductor Corp., San Jose 1990–; honors: Invention Achievement Award (IBM 1983), Spl. Recogn. Award (Xerox PARC 1984); mem: IEEE (fellow); publs: 20+ articles in tech. jours. and confs.; 1 US patent issued 1984; Republican; rec: sports, music. Res: 776 Carlisle Way Sunnyvale 94087 Ofc: Cypress Semiconductor Corp. 3901 N First St San Jose 95134

HU, STEVE SENG-CHIU, research executive/college president; b. Mar. 16, 1922, Yangchou, Kiangsu Province, China; s. Yubin and Shuchang (Lee) H.; m. Lily Li-wan Liu; children: April b. 1962, Yendo b. 1963, Victor b. 1964; edn: BS, Chiao-Tung Univ., Shanghai 1939; MS, Rensselaer Polytech. Inst. 1940; DSc, Mass. Inst. of Tech. 1942. Career: tech dir. Douglas Aircraft's China Aircraft/China Motor Pgms., Calif. & N.J. 1943-48; tech. dir. Kelley Eng. Co., N.Y. & Ariz. 1949-54; sys. engr./meteorological spec. RCA Corp., Ariz. 1955-58; cons. gas dynamics Aerojet Gen. Corp. 1958-59; research scientist Jet Propulsion Lab., Calif. Inst. Tech. 1960-61; tech. dir. Northrop Corp. & Northrop Space Labs., Ala. 1961-72; pres. Univ. of Am. United Research Inst., and Am. Technical Coll., Calif. & Taiwan 1973–; dir. Century Research Inc., Gardena 1973–; nat. dir./exec. v.p. Am. Astronautical Soc., Wash. DC 1963-71; ed. AAS Proceedings of Missiles & Aerospace Vehicle Scis.; prof., part-time, Univ. Ariz. 1957-58, USC 1959-63, 1968-71, Univ. of Ala. 1963-68, Auburn Univ. 1964-66, CSU 1968-71; awards: Salisbury Prize & Sloan Prize, M.I.T. 1942; Merit Cert. & cash award, Commn. of Aeronautical Affairs, Repub. of China 1945; Merit Cert. & cash award for sci. achiev. & dynamic leadership, Northrop/NASA Space Labs. 1966; mem: Am. Astronautical Soc., Inst. of Aeronautics & Astronautics; Nat. Assn. of Tech. Schs.; works: tech. dir. Northrop/NASA Electronic Guidance Sys. for Lunar Landing Vehicle Pgms. 1963-68; author: Theory of Guidance/Control and Optimization of Tactical/Strategic Missiles and Aerospace Vehicles, pub. Univ. of Ala./Century Research Inc. 1969, 73; rec: opera music, dancing, travel. Res: 6491 Saddle Dr. Long Beach 90815 Ofc: Century Research Bldg. 16935 S Vermont Ave Gardena 90247

HUANG, AILEEN BING, acupuncture doctor, professor of Chinese medicine; b. Nov. 9, 1950, Nanjing City, China; d. Bing GuoHuang and Min Zhang; m. Robins Honggui Zhang, July 28, 1977; children: Jenny Y. Zhang b. 1979; edn: OMD, Beijing Univ. of Traditional Chinese Medicine, Beijing, China 1975; adv. training in acupuncture theory, Nanjing Coll. of Traditional Chinese Medicine, Nanjing; MS, Found. for Internat. Services, Inc., Wash. 1992; lic. acupuncturist Calif. 1992. Career:acupuncture doctor and internist of Chinese medicine Xishan Hosp., Beijing 1975-82; acupuncture doctor in charge, Internat. Acupuncture Ctr., Beijing 1982-90; guest acupuncturist and prof., Egypt Acupuncture Soc., Cairo, Egypt 1990-91; v.p. Tran-America Acad. of Chinese Medicine, Albany, Calif. 1991–; assoc. prof. Acad. of Chinese Culture and Health Sci., Oakland 1992–; mem: Internat. Red Cross Assn. 1984–, Calif. Certified Acupuncturists Assn. 1993–; author: journal articles in China Acupuncture Jour. 1989, 90, Beijing Labor Jour. 1990. Res: 1160 6th Street Albany 94710 Ofc: Tran-America Academy of Chinese Medicine 1284 Solano Ave Albany 94706

HUBBARD, CHARLES RONALD, corporate programs executive; b. Feb. 4, 1933, Weaver, Ala.; s. John Duncan and Athy Pauline (Lusk) H.; m. Betty McKleroy, Dec. 29, 1951; 1 son: Charles Ronald II, b. 1957; edn: BSEE, Univ. of Ala. 1960. Career: engr./ mktg. & pgm. mgr. Sperry Corp., Huntsville, Ala., 1960-71; sect. head 1971-74; sr. staff engr. Honeywell, Inc., Clearwater, Fla. 1974-76, mgr. 1976-79; chief engr., Honeywell, Inc., West Covina, Calif. 1979-82, assoc. dir. engring. 1982-84, assoc. dir. Advanced Systems 1984-88, v.p. govt. systems div. Integrated Inference Machines, Anaheim, 1988-91; pres. Synergy Computer Systems, Anaheim 1991–; dir. S&H Office Supplies, Huntsville, Ala. 1972-74; awards: recipient Outstanding Fellow Award, Univ. of

Ala. Dept. of Electrical Engring.; mem: IEEE (Govt. Rels. Com.,sect. chmn.); publs: Saturn V/ Apollo and Beyond, Am. Astronautical Soc., 1967; mil: USAF 1953-57; Methodist; rec: jogging, golf. Res: 5460 Willowick Cir Anaheim 92807

HUBBARD, ERIC RODNEY, podiatrist; b. Oct. 11, 1943, Palm Springs; s. Clinton George and Edyth Victoria (Kaneen) H.; m. Millie; children: Corey, Susan, Sean, Heather, Nicole; edn: Brigham Young Univ., Univ. Long Beach; MS, cum laude, Pepperdine Univ., 1977; DPM, Calif. Coll. Podiatric Med.; lic. in podiatry Calif., Ida., Nev.; cert. Am. Bd. Podiat. Surgery, Am. Bd. Podiat. Orthopedics. Career: ins. cons. Aetna, Travelers, Bankers Life, The Equitable; clin. instr. USC County Hosp., Calif. Coll. Podiatric Medicine (bd. of trustees); podiatrist pvt. practice, Long Beach; mem. Am. Bd. Quality Assur. and Utilization Rev., pres. podiatry div. 1989-90; honors: Hon. Dr. of Science Calif. Coll. of Podiatric Medicine, Podiatrist of Year Calif. Podiat. Med. Assn. (1984), elected nat. pres. Am. Podiat. Med. Assn. (1989-91); mem: Am. Coll. Foot Surgeons (Fellow), Am. Coll. Foot Orthopedists (Fellow), Nat. Academies of Practice, Harbor Soc., Calif. Podiat. Med. Assn. (past pres., PAC), Am. Podiat. Med. Assn. (pres. 1989-90, bd. trustees hosp. com., PAC), C.C.P.M. Alumni Assn. and Pierce Nelson Soc., Am. Coll. Sports Med.; contbr. articles in med. jours. Ofc: 2333 Pacific Ave Long Beach 90806

HUBBELL, FLOYD ALLAN, physician, medical educator; b. Nov. 13, 1948, Waco, Tx.; s. Floyd E. and Margaret (Fraser) H.; m. Nancy, May 23, 1975; 1 son, Andrew b. 1985; edn: BA, Baylor Univ. Waco Tx. 1971; MD, Baylor Med. Houston Tx. 1974; MSPH, UCLA 1983. Career: faculty UC Irvine 1979–; chief, Div. of Internal Medicine and Primary Care, UC Irvine 1992–, dir. Ctr. for Health Policy and Res., UC Irvine 1993–; honors: UC Irvine Outstanding Faculty 1983, Faculty of Year 1987, Baylor Med. Excellence in Comm. Med. 1974; mem: Am. Fedn. Clin. Research, A.C.P. (fellow), Am. Pub. Health Assn., Soc. Gen. Internal Med.; 50 articles pub. in med. jours., 1979-95; Democrat. Ofc: Univ. of California, Irvine 92717-5800

HUCKABEE, PHYLLIS, gas industry professional; b. Aug. 11, 1963, Andrews, Tx.; d. Tommie Jack and Sylvia (Wingo) H.; edn: BBA in fin., Texas Tech. Univ., Lubbock 1984, MBA, 1986. Career: loan escrow clk. First Federal Savings, Lubbock, Tx. 1984; mgmt. tng. pgm. El Paso (Tx.) Natural Gas, 1986-87, analyst rate dept. 1987-88, specialist, then representative Calif. Affairs, San Francisco, 1988-92; asst. dir. Cambridge Energy Research Associates, Oakland 1992-93; regulatory rels. mgr. So. Calif. Gas Co., San Francisco 1994–; adj. faculty mem. Univ of Phoenix N. Calif. 1994–; mem: Women Energy Assocs. (bd. 1990-), Pacific Coast Gas Assn., Internat. Assn. for Energy Economics (1990-93), Berkeley Architectural Heritage Assn., The Daguerreian Soc.; civic: Performing Arts Workshop, S.F. (bd. 1990-92, advy. bd. 1992–), El Paso Comm. Concerts Assn. (bd. 1988), Business Volunteers for the Arts S.F. 1989, volunteer E. Bay Habitat for Humanity; Democrat; Methodist; rec: photography. Res: 1721 McGee Ave Berkeley 94703 Ofc: Southern Calif. Gas Co. 601 Van Ness Ave Ste 2014 San Francisco 94102

HUDNUT, F. VERNON, retired engineer; b. June 25, 1936, Portland, Oreg.; s. Forrest V. and Evelyn May (Lytle) H.; m. Sophie Kwiatkowski, June 16, 1968; children: Steven b. 1970, David b. 1972; edn: BSME, Oregon St. Univ., Corvallis 1958; MS, Univ. Utah, S.L.C., 1965; reg. profl. engr. Calif. (1975–). Career: test engr., project engr. USAF FlightTest Center, Edwards AFB 1958-66; sr. engr. Northrop Corp., Hawthorne 1966-70; cons., Hawthorne 1970-71; gen. engr. Naval Weapons Center, China Lake 1971-78; materials engr., aerospace engr., AFPRO/LMSC, Sunnyvale 1978-87; resident SRM & QA rep., Hubble Space Telescope, NASA/MSFC Resident Office 1987-90; resident assurance mgr., Space Station, NASA/LeRC Resident Office, 1990-95; awards: Univ. Utah Tchg. Assistantship 1964-65, Thesis grant 1965; mem: ASME, NSPE, CSPE, BSA (com. chmn. 1986-88), Masons, Sr. DeMolay (Legion of Honor; Chevalier; PMC; RD; BHK; Advy. Coun. 1960-66; chapt. advr. 1961-62); author Computer Registration (1965), tech. papers pub. (1962–); Republican; Eastern Orthodox Christian; rec: ferroequinology, model railroads. Res: 19971 Lindenbrook Ln Cupertino 95014

HUDSON, CHRISTOPHER JOHN, publisher; b. June 8, 1948, Watford, England, came to U.S. 1971; s. Joseph Edward and Gladys Jenny Patricia (Madgwick) H.; m. Lois Jeanne Lyons, June 16, 1979; children: Thomas b. 1959, Ellen b. 1960, Ronald b. 1964, Timothy b. 1966; edn: BA (hons.), Cambridge Univ., 1969, MA (hons.), 1972. Career: promotion mgr. Prentice-Hall Internat., Hemel Hempstead, U.K. 1969-70, area mgr. (U.K., France) 1970-71, mktg. mgr./ dir. mktg./ asst. v.p., Englewood Cliffs, N.J. 1971-76; group internat. dir. ITT Publishing, N.Y., N.Y. 1976-77; pres. Focal Press Inc., N.Y.C., mem. bd. Focal Press Ltd., London, Eng. 1977-82; publisher (journal) Aperture, and v.p. Aperture Found., 1983-86; head of publs. J. Paul Getty Trust, Los Angeles 1986–, pub. J. Paul Getty Museum Jour., 1986–; awards: distinction, merit awards Am. Assn. of Museums (1987, 88, 93), book & journal awards Assn. of Am. Univ. Presses N.Y. (1989, 90, 92, 93),Excellence in Pub. award Assn. of Am. Pubs. 1992, merit award Bookbuilders West, S.F. (1990, 91, 93), publs. award Am. Fedn. of the Arts (1990, 91), we. book award Rounce & Coffin Club (1992,93); mem: Internat. Publishers Assn. 1987–, Internat. Assn.

Scholarly Publishers 1988–, US Museums Pub. Group N.Y. (chmn. 1989–),Internat. Assn. of Mus. Publ. Frankfurt, Ger. (steering com. 1989–, chmn 1992-94), Assn. of Am. Publishers N.Y. (trade with Ea. Europe com. 1976-79, intl. fairs com. 1986-88), Hellenic Soc. (London, 1967–), Oxford & Cambridge Club (London), Nat. Heritage Village Kioni, Greece (advy. council 1991–); author: Guide to International Book Fairs, 1976; rec: rural preservation projects in Europe & U.S. Ofc: J. Paul Getty Museum 17985 PCH Malibu 90265

HUDSON, WALTER WARREN, financial executive, consultant; b. March 13, 1922, Cincinnati, Ohio; s. Earl Osborn and Elizabeht Bell (Brust) H.; m. Cora Lee Brown, May 7, 1948; children: Claudia b. 1951, Jeffrey b. 1956, Melanie b. 1965; edn: Ohio Wesleyan Univ. 1940-43; BS, UCLA 1947; Univ. Mich. 1953-58; cert., USC 1972. Career: asst. gen. mgr. Ford Motor Co., Dearborn, Mich. 1948-62; asst. treas. Hughes Aircraft Co., Culver City 1962-75; self-employed Land Development, Marina Del Rey 1975-80; pres. Internat. Tungston Inc., Carson City, Nev. 1980-83; pres., dir. Melcor Resources Inc., Century City 1983-88; ICC Corp., Palos Verdes 1986–; Purple Mountain Resources, Canoga Park 1987–; guest lectr. USC Grad. Sch. Bus., 1966-74; cons. Doxxon 1985–; bd. mem. USC Grad. Sch. Bus. Adminstrn. 1970-74; awards: Nat. Secretaries Assn. boss of year (1970); mem: Los Angeles Co. Small Craft Harbor (mediator 1972-74), Marina Del Rey C.of C. (pres. 1973-75); mil: 1st lt. AUS 1943-47; rec: sailing. Address: San Pedro 90731

HUEBNER, KURT BENOIT, lawyer; Feb. 17, 1955, Hammond, Ind.; s. Paul Brian and Carol Ann (Lindholm) H.; edn: BA, Butler Univ. 1976; JD, Ind. Univ. Sch. Law 1979; admitted Bar Calif. (1982), Ind. (1979), US Supreme Ct. (1983). Career: chief dep. court reporter Ind. Cts. of Appeal, Indianapolis 1979-81; atty., assoc. Severson Werson Berke & Melchior, Los Angeles 1981-82; Parker, Milliken, Clark & O'Hara 1982-84; Wyman Bautzer Rothman Kuchel & Silbert 1984; Reavis & McGrath 1985; Pachter Gold & Schaffer 1985-86; Law Office of Kurt B. Huebner, 1986-91; Law Offices of Arnold Laub, 1991-94; atty. Brayton, Grisvold & Harley 1994–; awards: Top 10 Student award Butler Univ. 1976; mem: Calif. St. Bar Assn., Ind. St. Bar Assn.; Democrat. Ofc: Brayton, Gisvold & Harley PO Box 2109 Novato 94948 Tel: 415/898-1555 Fax 415/898-1247

HUEN, FLOYD TAK-FAY, physician, medical director; b. May 27, 1947, Tsingtao, China; s. Tak Ping and Lai Keen (Tong) H.; m. Jean Quan, Sept. 20, 1970; children: William b. 1977, Lailan b. 1982; edn: BA (with honors), UC Berkeley 1969, MA course work, sociology 1971; MD, Albert Einstein Coll. Medicine, NY, NY 1974; MBA, Univ. of So. Florida, Tampa 1994; lic. physician and surgeon, Calif. Med. Bd. 1979; diplomate, Am. Bd. of Internal Medicine 1987. Career: Asian-Am. studies coord. UC Berkeley 1969-70, vice pres. ASUC 1969-70, faculty instr. Asian-Am. studies 1970-71; pediatric intern Beth Israel Hosp., N.Y.C. 1974-75; pvt. practice of medicine, Hayward, Calif. 1979-83; public health physician, Dept. of Public Health, San Francisco 1981-83; resident and faculty, internal medicine Highland Hosp., Oakland 1983-87, transitional prog. dir. 1987-90; med. dir. Alameda County Med. Ctr., Oakland 1987–; attending staff, internal medicine Highland Hosp., Oakland 1987-89; co-dir. (med.) Highview Neuro-Rehab. Unit, Oakland 1993–; bd. dirs. UC Berkeley Comm. Health 1992-93; bd. dirs. E. Oakland Fighting Back, Oakland 1991-93; Planning; bd. mem. Public Hosp. R.W. Johnson Grant for Quality Assurance, Berkeley 1990-92; honors: Ford Found. Fellowship, UC Berkeley 1969-71, Honor Soc., Univ. of So. Fla. MBA Prog. 1993-94; mem: Calif. Physicians Alliance (steering com. 1989-92), Alameda Co. Vote Health Coalition (steering com. 1984–), Calif. Health Access Coalition (founder 1987), Am. Coll. of Physician Execs. 1987-92; Physicians for Nat. Health Prog. (founding mem. 1987), Orgn. of Chinese Americans, Oakland. Ofc: Alameda County Medical Center 1411 E 31st St Oakland 94602

HUESTIS, DAVID LEE, physicist; b. Dec. 20, 1946, St. Paul, Minn.; s. William D. and Dorothy M. (Fuller) H.; m. Wray Hughes, June 2, 1968; edn: BA chem./math., Macalester Coll. 1968; MS chem., Caltech Pasadena 1969; PhD, 1973. Career: fellow applied physics Caltech, Pasadena 1972; fellow physics SRI Internat., Menlo Park 1973, physicist 1973-77, asst. program mgr. 1977-80, program mgr. 1980-88, assoc. dir. molecular physics lab. 1988–; vis. lectr. chem. Stanford Univ. 1978; honors: Phi Beta Kappa, NSF predoctoral fellow 1968-72, Woodrow Wilson Found. hon. fellow 1968-69; Fellow Am. Physical Soc.; mem: Am. Geophysics Union, Gaseous Elec. Conf. (treas. 1984-90), Comm. AUS Basic Sci. Research Nat. Res. Council 1986-88; publs: 69+ articles in profl. jours., 1971, 161+ tech. papers presented, 1969–, 2 book chpts., 1982, 84, edit. Elec. & Atomic Collisions, 1985; patentee: noble gas halogen transfer laser, 1981, simulated echo image processing and pattern recognition, 1993. Ofc: SRI International Molecular Physics Laboratory Menlo Park 94025

HUFFINGTON, MICHAEL former congressman; b. Dallas, 1947; s. Roy M. Huffington; m. Arianna; 2 children; edn: BS engring., Stanford Univ., BA economics, MBA Harvard Univ., Cambridge, Mass.. Career: chmn. Crest Films, Santa Barbara; chmn. Roy M. Huffington, Inc.; deputy asst. Sec. of Defense for Negotiations Policy 1986-87; mem. 103rd Congress from 22d Calif. Dist. 1993-94; Republican cand. for U.S. Senate 1994; bd. dir. Overseers L.A. Music Ctr.; bd. trustees Univ. Calif. Santa Barbara Found.; bd. dir. Santa Barbara Zoological Found.; Republican.*

HUFFMAN, JAMES GARLEN, university public safety director; b. Nov. 19, 1949, Carmel; s. Joseph Garlen and Margaret M. (Davis) H.; m. Paula Jean Schlegel, Aug. 21, 1971; children: Jennifer b. 1973, Hollie b. 1975, Heidi b. 1978; edn: AS, Mt. San Antonio Coll., 1975; BA, Univ. Redlands, 1977; MS, Pepperdine Univ., 1986. Career: dep. sheriff Los Angeles Co. Sheriff 1973-80, San Joaquin Co. Sheriff, Stockton 1980-82; instr., police sgt. San Joaquin Delta Comm. Coll., Stockton 1982-86; dir. Delta Coll. Peace Officer Acad., 1983-84; dep. dir. dept. pub. safety Pepperdine Univ., Malibu 1986-89, dir. 1989–; honors: Nat. Security Inst. Who's Who (1989); mem: So. Calif. Campus Police & Security Assn., Calif. Peace Ofcrs. Assn., Internat. Assn. Chiefs of Police, Internat. Assn. Campus Law Enforcement Adminstrs.; mil: helicopter pilot, chief warrant ofcr. US Army 1968-70, decorated Air Medal, 19 awards Vietnam, mem. Nat. Guard 1980-85; Republican; Presbyterian; rec: fishing. Ofc: Pepperdine Univ. Dept. Public Safety 24255 Pacific Coast Hwy Malibu 90263

HUFSTEDLER, SETH MARTIN, lawyer; b. Sept. 20, 1922, Dewar, Okla.; s. Seth Martin and Myrtle (Younts) H.; m. Shirley Ann Mount, Aug. 16, 1949; 1 son, Steven; edn: BA magna cum laude, USC, 1944; LLB, Stanford Univ., 1949; admitted St. Bar Calif. 1950. Career: assoc. Lillick Geary & McHose 1950-51; Charles E. Beardsley 1951-53; ptnr. Beardsley Hufstedler & Kemble 1953-81, Hufstedler Miller Kaus & Beardsley 1981-90, Hufstedler & Kaus 1990-95, Morrison & Foerster 1995–; legis. ed. Stanford Univ. Law Review 1948-49; secty. United Way Regional Planning Council 1971-75; co-chmn. Pub. Commn. Co. Govt. L.A. 1975-76; trustee AEFC Pension Fund 1978-82; mem. Calif.Citizens Commn. on Tort Reform 1976-77, Calif. Jud. Council 1977-78; bd. visitors Stanford Law Sch., chmn. 1972-73; honors: Order of Coif, Phi Beta Kappa, Shattuck Price Meml. Award, L.A. Co. Bar Assn. 1976; mem: Am. Bar Assn. (chmn action com. to reduce ct. costs and delay 1979-81, mem. council sr. bar div. 1986, chmn., 1987-88), L.A. Co. Bar Assn. (trustee 1963-65, 1966-70, pres. 1969-70), St. Bar Calif. (bd. govs. 1971-74, pres. 1973-74), Am.Judicature Soc., Am. Law Inst., Am. Coll. Trial Lawyers, Am. Bar Found. (bd. govs. 1975-86, pres. 1982-84), Chancery Club (pres. 1974-75); mil: served to lt.j.g. USNR 1943-46. Address: 555 W 5th St 35th Flr Los Angeles 90013-1024

HUGHES, AUTHOR E., university president, executive; b. Nov. 4, 1929, Hoopeston, Ill.; s. Author E. and Nora (Cleveland) H.; m. Marjorie Ann Herman, Aug. 21, 1956; children: James b. 1957, Timothy b. 1959, John b. 1964, Susan b. 1968; edn: BS, bus. edn., Eastern Ill. Univ., Charleston, Ill. 1951; MA, bus. edn., Northern Colo. Univ., Greely, Colo. 1954; PhD, bus. adminstrn., Univ. of Iowa, Iowa City 1960. Career: instr. Eastern Illinois Univ., Charleston 1954-56; bus. prof. No. Ariz. Univ., Flagstaff 1961-66, dean, Business Sch., No. Ariz. Univ., Flagstaff 1966-69, v.p./provost, 1969-71; pres. Univ. of San Diego 1971-95; chmn. Energy 2000, San Diego 1980–; dir. Calif. First/Union Bank, San Francisco 1986-92; trustee The Whittier Inst. 1992–; commr. Commn. on Improving Life Through Service, Sacramento. 1994–; awards: Disting. Alumnus, Ea. Ill. Univ. 1976, Headliner of Yr., San Diego Press Club 1978, hon. degrees: Chapman Coll. 1983, Dominican Coll. 1993, co-recipient Outstanding Citizen award, Catholic Comm., S.D. 1986, Internat. Citizen award, World Affairs Council, S.D. 1992; mem.: Assn. of Indep. Calif. Colls. & Univs. (past pres. 1975-81), Assn. of Catholic Colls. & Univs. (past chair bd. dirs. 1987-93), Nat. Assn. of Indep. Colls. & Univs. (past chair bd. dirs. 1990-93), Thomas Ackerman Found. (dir.) 1992–; Am. Council on Edn. (dir.) 1993-95, Knights of the Holy Sepulchre 1974–, San Diego C.of C. (past v.p.) 1976-95, United Way/CHAD (chmn. 1976, 90), Am. Cancer Soc. (dir.) 1985-95; Republican; Catholic; rec: sailing, tennis. Ofc: University of San Diego 5998 Alcala Park San Diego 92110

HUGHES, CHARLES WILSON, university purchasing executive; b. May 3, 1946, Greenville, Ky.; s. Clifton J. and Christine Vive (Critzer) H.; m. Daniele Kay Martin, Oct. 6, 1973; children: Charles b. 1975, Jennifer b. 1977; edn: BS, Univ. of Tenn., Martin 1967; JD, Univ. Tenn., Knoxville 1971; admitted bar: Tenn. 1971. Career: served to Major US Army (Ret.) 1971-91, meritorious svc. awards 1975, 81, 83, 91: logistics ofcr. Pusan Garrison, Korea 1973-75; chief contract ops. Def. Plant Office, Woodland Hills, Calif. 1976-81; dir. indsl. ops. Wuerzburg MILCOM, Ger. 1981-83; chief ops. Program Mgr. Tank Sys., Warren, Mich. 1983-86; chief contract adminstrn. Def. Contract Adminstrn. Svs., El Segundo, Calif. 1986-90; dir. purchasing CSU Long Beach 1991–, guest lectr. CSULB 1992; indep. cons. Hughes Assocs., Garden Grove 1987–; awards: merit BSA El Capitan Dist., Garden Grove 1989, silver beaver BSA Orange County 1989, achiev. Junior Achievement, Costa Mesa 1981, achiev. Am. Logistics Assn. Ft. Lee, Va. 1973, 75; mem.: Calif. Assn. Pub. Purchasing Ofcls. 1991–, Nat. Assn. Ednl. Buyers 1991–, Nat. Contract Mgmt. Assn. (1976–, v.p. 1977-78), Marne Assn. 1981–, Retired Ofcrs. Assn. 1991–, Masons (Kts. of Malta), DCAS Computer Users Gp., El Segundo (pres. 1986-88); scoutmaster BSA Troop 147, Garden Grove 1987-92, dist. commr. Orange County 1988-90; publs: articles in trade and profl. jours. (1967–), editor Collection of Poems (1976); Republican; Baptist; rec: stamps and coins, tennis, golf. Res: 10072 Roselee Dr Garden Grove 92640-1826 Ofc: CSU Long Beach 1250 Bellflower Blvd Long Beach 90840-0123

HUGHES, JUDITH MARKHAM, professor of history; b. Feb. 20, 1941, N.Y.C.; d. Sanford H. and Sylvia (Kovner) Markham; m. H. Stuart Hughes,

Mar. 26, 1964; 1 son, David; edn: BA (high hons.), Swarthmore Coll., 1962; MA, Harvard Univ., 1963, PhD, 1970. Career: tchg. fellow Harvard Univ. 1965-66, 67-70, asst. prof. social studies, 1970-75; assoc. prof. UC San Diego, 1975-84, prof. history, 1984–; awards: Phi Beta Kappa 1962, Woodrow Wilson fellow 1962-63, Harvard Univ. tuition scholar 1963-64, West European Studies fellow 1972-73, NEH fellow 1974; mem.: Am. Hist. Assn., N.Am. Conf. on British Studies, Group for Use of Psychology in History, We. Assn. of Women Historians (article prize com. 1985), Am. Psychoanalytic Assn. (affiliate mem.); author: To the Maginot Line: The Politics of French Military Preparation in the 1920's (Harvard Univ. Press, 1971), Emotion and High Politics: Personal Relations at the Summit in Late 19th C. Brit. and Ger. (UC Press, 1983), Reshaping the Psychoanalytic Domain: The Work of Melanie Klein, W.R.D. Fairbairn, and D.W. Winnicott (UC Press, 1989), From Freud's Consulting Room: The Unconscious in a Scientific Age (Harvard Univ. Press 1994) Res: 8531 Ave de las Ondas La Jolla 92037 Ofc: UCSD Dept. History, 0104, 9500 Gilman Dr La Jolla 92093-0104 Ph: 619/534-1996

HUGHES, WAYNE PHILO, JR., teacher; b. May 30, 1930, Charleston, Ill.; s. Wayne Philo and Nancy Gay (Case) H.; m. Joan Cavins Hughes; children: Gwendolyn b. 1957, Margaret b. 1958, Nancy Lee b. 1964; edn: BS, USNA 1952; MS, USNPS 1962. Career: ofcr. USN 1952-83; prof. U.S. Naval Postgrad. Sch., Monterey 1983; cons. in tactics and tech. 1983-89; honors: Sigma Xi, Naval Inst. Prize Essay 1963, 86, Disting. Mil. Ops. 1989; mem: Mil. Ops. Research Soc. (pres. 1972-76, 1983-88), Mil. Conflict Inst. (bd. dirs. 1983-89); author: Fleet Tactics: Theory & Practice, 1986, Naval Tactics (in Encyclopedia Britannica); ed. Mil. Modeling, 1984; mil: capt. USN 1952-83; Republican; Presbyterian. Res: 705 Walnut St Pacific Grove 93950 Ofc: U.S. Naval Postgraduate School Monterey 93943

HUGHES-KASSAR, LYNN M., chief financial officer, secretary/treasurer; b. Feb. 23, 1945, Cleveland, Oh.; d., Clarence T. (dec. 1948) and Mary M. (Jewel) Hughes; m. Denis Filbey, July 4, 1965 (dec.); m. Bruce L. Johnson, Mar. 17, 1971 (widowed Dec. 23, 1978); m. Wayne L. Kassar, Aug. 23, 1980; children: Daniel b. 1966, Charles b. 1967; stepchildren: Anna, Emily b. 1962; edn: AA, De Anza, Cupertino, Calif. 1978; BA, bus. economics, UC Santa Cruz 1987. Career: asst. treas. Citizens Financial Corp., Cleveland, Ohio 1973-76; accounting mgr., Tymshare, Cupertino 1978-80; accounting mgr., Shugart Assoc., Sunnyvale 1980-82; accounting mgr., ESL, Inc., Sunnyvale 1983-85; accounting mgr., Pacific We. Bank, San Jose 1987-90; CFO, Traveling Sch., Inc., Santa Cruz 1986–, bd. of trustees 1990–, treas. 1990–; Methodist; rec: reading, spending time with grandchildren. Res: P.O. Box 1491 Aptos 95001. Ofc: Traveling School, Inc. 819-1/2 Pacific Ave. #2 Santa Cruz 95060

HUHNDORF, SUSAN KOURA, advertising executive; b. April 27, 1954, Tokyo, Japan; nat. 1966; d. Tony and Alice (Yamane) Koura; m. Michael Stanley, March 18, 1978; edn: BS summa cum laude, UCLA 1976. Career: account exec. Competitive Edge, Costa Mesa 1978-81; Harte-Hanks Direct Mktg., Garden Grove 1981; Della Femina Travisano, Los Angeles 1982-84; account supr. Keye Donna Pearlstein 1984-87; Chiat Day 1987-88; v.p., mgmt. supr. Livingston & Keye 1988-90; advt. mgr. Amati Div., Mazda Motors of Am., 1991-92; principal Huhndorf & Assocs. 1992–; honors: Phi Beta Kappa, Gold EFFIE award for advertising effectiveness; mem: Los Angeles Ad. Club; Republican; rec: art collecting, skiing. Address: Huhndorf & Associates 2221 Bowman Ave Tustin 92680

HUI, HELEN Y. H., lawyer; b. Jan. 3, 1944, Hong Kong; d. Lap Sam and Shuk Han (Cheng) Hui; m. Gordon Lew, July 12, 1969; 1 dau., Beverly b. 1979; edn: BA, Smith Coll. 1967; MSW, UC Berkeley 1970; JD, UCSF Hastings Coll. Law 1974; admitted Calif. Supreme Ct. 1975; splst. in immigration and nationality law cert. by St. Bar of Calif. Career: intern ACLU, San Francisco 1973; atty., assoc. Hardesty & Lau 1973-77; ptnr. Law Office Lau & Lee 1977-79; Law Office Lee & Hui 1979-88; prin. Law Office Helen Y.H. Hui 1988–; dir., ofcr. East-West Pub. Co. Inc. 1968; pres. Northeast Med. Service 1982-88; Chinatown Comm. Childrens Center 1984-88; dir. Childcare Law Center 1987-88; awards: pro bono svs. awards from St. Bar of Calif., Bar Assn. of S.F. and Asian Am. Bar Assn.; mem: Am. Bar Assn., Am. Immigration Lawyers Assn. (pres. No. Calif. chpt. 1992-93; ed. Key Issues in Immigration Law, 1992), Bar Assn. S.F., Asian Am. Bar Assn. of Greater Bay Area, Nat. Asian Pacific Am. Bar Assn., Queen's Bench (life), Lions; civic: East/West Pub. Co., S.F. (ofcr. & dir. 1968–), Chinese Newcomers Svc. Ctr., S.F. (dir. 1977-83, 94–), Self-Help for the Elderly, S.F. (ofcr. & dir., then advy. bd. mem. 1977–), Chinese Culture Found., S.F. (dir., chair of bd. 1987–), Orgn. of Chinese Ams. (gen. counsel, S.F. Bay Chpt. 1990–), State Bar of Calif. (commnr. Immigration Law Advy. Commn. 1991-94), World Affairs Council (citizen advy. bd. 1994–), Angel Island Immigration Station Found. (dir. 1994–); speaker and panelist on mun. comm. svc. forums, radio & TV progrs. for PBS, churches and non-profit orgns.; rec: classical music. Ofc: 456 Montgomery St Ste 700 San Francisco 94104-1240

HUIGENS, DANIEL DEAN, dentist; b. May 16, 1953, Osmond, Nebr.; s. Dean Phillip and Myrtle Ellen (White) H.; m. Linda, May 29, 1982 (div.); 1 son Matthew b. 1988; edn: BA, Univ. of LaVerne, 1975; BS, Univ. Okla., 1979,

DDS, Univ. Okla., 1986. Career: emergency medical tech San Dimas Community Hosp., 1975-77; physician's assoc. Muskegee Bone & Joint Clinic, Muskegee, Okla. 1979-82; dentist pvt. practice, La Verne, Calif. 1986; honors: Omicron Kappa Upsilon, OKU Honor Soc.; mem: ADA, Calif. Dental Assn., Tri-County Dental Assn., Acad. of Gen. Dentistry, Humane Soc. of U.S., La Verne C.of C., Pomona Valley Amateur Astronomers Assn.; original research pub. Am. Biology Tchr. Jour., 1976; private pilot; rec: oil painting, piano, stainged glass work, sports. Res: 2982 Gayridge Pomona 91767 Ofc: Dr. Huigens 2187 Foothill Blvd La Verne 91750

HUMPHREY, JO ANN, nurse, educator, administrator, executive; b. July 29, 1937, Missoula, Mont.; d. Henry Albert and Wanda Alene (Anderson) Dray; m. John Francis Humphrey; children: Robb b. 1961, Rand b. 1969; grandchildren: Joshua b. 1991, Dalton b. 1991, Kaitlyn b. 1993; edn: BSN, R.N., Columbia Univ., 1960; MS in nsg. edn., Univ. of Wash., 1969; clin. psychology, U.S. International Univ. Career: faculty, Brigham Young Univ., Provo, Utah; faculty, San Diego St. Univ., dir. nursing, Heartland Comm. Hosp., S.D.; consultant Coordinating Council for Edn. in Health Sciences for San Diego and Imperial Counties; instr. Southwestern Comm. Coll.; founding mem., exec. dir. Assn. for Holistic Health, San Diego; researcher Cassel Psychology Center, Chula Vista and NCRD and Naval Research Center, San Diego; official guest for health care & edn. of govts. of Japan, China, Taiwan, Korea, Philippines, Singapore; current: adminstr. Acad. for Holistic Edn., S.D.; chief exec. ofcr. Custom Box and Packaging Corp., S.D. (founded, 1959); mem. San Diego Co. Self-Esteem Task Force, S.D. Nurses' Assn. (chair by laws comm.), Columbia Univ. Alumni Assn., BYU Alumni Assn., Univ. Wash. Alumni Assn.; listed Who's Who in Calif., 1991, Who's Who in Psychophysiology; publs: Holistic Health... What Is It? and The Holistic Health Practitioner... What Standards Set Him Apart?; Autogenics for Execs: Wellness Attainment with Diagnostic Assessment and Autogenics for Neuro Self Regulation; civic: vol. hostess, S.D. Mormon Temple tours; tchr. S.E. Asian refugees; poll worker; Republican; Ch. of Jesus Christ of Latter-day Saints; rec: modeling, piano, reading, computers. Res: 8263 Camino Del Oro #272 La Jolla 92037 Ofc: Custom Packaging Corp. 4748 Old Cliffs Rd San Diego 92037

HUND, DIANNA LEE, medical sales company president; b. Jan. 24, 1951, Oceanside; d. Charley Ray Lee and Dorothy (Eaton) Gosnell; m. T. Kent Prater, 1972 (div. 1981); m.2d. Robert Anthony Hund, June 22, 1986; 1 child: Tiana Renee Hund. Career: sales rep.: Johnson & Johnson, New Brunswick, N.J. 1977-79, Diatek, San Diego 1979-81, Kimberly-Clark, Roswell, Ga. 1981-83; sales trainer Nice-Pak, Orangeburg, N.Y. 1983-86; pres. Kare Medical Sales, Costa Mesa 1986–; awards: Rep. of the Yr. Johnson & Johnson 1978, named Rep. of the Yr. Medical Product Sales mag. 1988; mem: Internat. Assn. of Hosp. Central Svc. Mgmt., Health Industry Rep. Assn.; Republican; Lutheran. Ofc: Kare Medical Sales 15011 Mammoth Lake Forest CA 95630

HUNG, MARGUERITE MEI-YU, acupuncturist; b. Apr. 20, 1941, Tao-Yuan, Taiwan, nat. 1988; d. Ping Yueh and Tui (Huang) Hung; m. Wen-Fun Kay Burns, Feb. 15, 1968, div. 1981; children: Jean Kay b. 1969, Janine Kay b. 1970, Joyce Kay b. 1971; m. 2d. Richard David Blaine, Feb. 20, 1987; edn: OMD, Calif. Acupuncture Coll., 1985; cert. acupuncturist 1987; Diplomate in Acupuncture, Nat. Commn. for Certification of Acupuncturists (NCCA) 1991. Career: Dr. of Chinese medicine/acupuncturist Taipei Acupuncture & Moxibustion Clinic Ctr., Taiwan 1973-78; Hunan-Yale Acupuncture Clinic, 1978-79; Tri-Service Gen. Hosp., 1978-79; Shanghai Acupuncture Inst., Chula Vista, Calif. 1980-86; prin. Dr. Hung's Chinese Acupuncture Clinic, Chula Vista 1987–, also practice Office of Dr. Charles C. Lai, Brawley (Saturdays) and Alternative Health Care Inc., Vista (Mondays); pres. Acupuncture Inst. for an Addiction-Free Life (non-profit statewide org.) 1990–; com. mem. State of Calif. Medical Bd. Acupuncture Com., 1992–; awards: Acupuncturist of the Yr., Am. Assn. of Acupuncture and Oriental Med. 1994; mem: Acupuncture Res. Ctr., Chinese Acupuncture Sci. Res. Found., Calif. Certified Acupuncturists Assn., Acupuncture Medicine Assn. of So. Calif. (v.p. 1991–, v.chair Council 1991-92), Am. Assn. of Acupuncture and Oriental Medicine (nat. bd. dirs. 1991-93, v.chair Chemical Dependency Task Force 1991–, v.p. 1993-94), Calif. Med. Bd. (Acupuncture Com.); Res: 3963 Broadlawn St San Diego 92111 Ofc: Dr. Hung's Chinese Acupuncture Clinic 236 F St Chula Vista 91910

HUNG, SAMMY TUNG-CHUEN, doctor; b. Jan. 12, 1945, Swatow, China (nat. 1970); s. Phillip H. and Shou-Mui (Wong) H.; m. Patty, Aug. 22, 1970 (div. 1988); children: Erick, Kevin, David, Mailee; edn: BA, Amherst Coll., Amherst, Mass. 1968; PhD, UC Berkeley 1972; MD, UC San Francisco 1976. Career: medical dir. pulmonary services St. Rose Hosp., Hayward, Calif. 1981–; honors: Phi Beta Kappa 1968; mem: Am. Thoracic Soc. 1979–, Am. Coll. of Chest Physicians 1980-(fellow 1983); rec: classical music, backpacking. Ofc: 27001 Calaroga Ave #4 Hayward 94545

HUNTER, DUNCAN LEE, congressman; b. May 31, 1948, Riverside, Calif.; m. Lynne Layh, 1973; children: Robert Samuel, Duncan Duane; edn: JD, Western State Univ. 1976; admitted to bar Calif. 1976. Career: practiced in San Diego; mem. 97th Congress from 42nd Dist. Calif., 98-102nd Congresses from 45th Dist. Calif., 103-104th Congresses from 52nd Dist. Calif.; mem. Armed Svcs. com., subcom. mil. installations, facilities, research, tech., House Rep. research com.; mem. Navy League; mil: U.S. Army 1969-71, Vietnam; decorated Air Medal, Bronze Star; Republican; Baptist.*

HUNTER, JAMES GALBRAITH, JR., lawyer; b. Jan. 6, 1942, Phila.; s. James Galbraith and Emma Margaret (Jehl) H.; m. Pamela Ann (Trott), July 18, 1969 (div.); children: James b. 1973, Catherine b. 1978; m. 2d. Nancy (Scheurwater) H., June 21, 1993; edn: BS in eng. sci., Case Inst. of Tech. 1965; JD, Univ. Chgo. 1967; admitted to Ill. State Bar 1967, Calif. State Bar 1980, US Supreme Ct. 1979, US Cts. of Appeals for the 7th (1967), 4th (1978), 9th (1978), 5th (1982) and Federal 1982 Circuits, US Claims Ct. 1976, US Dist. Cts. Ill. (No., 1967, Central, 1980) and Calif. (So., 1980, Cent., 1980, and No., 1982). Career: atty. ptnr. Hedlund, Hunter & Lynch, Chgo. 1976-82; Latham & Watkins, Hedlund, Hunter & Lynch, 1982-84; ptnr. Latham & Watkins, Los Angeles 1982–, and Chgo. 1984–; mem. ABA, Chgo. Bar Assn., Calif. St. Bar Assn., L.A. Cty. Bar Assn., Metropolitan Club, Chgo. Athletic Assn.; honors: exec. editor Univ. Chgo. Law Rev. 1966-67; mil: lt. USNR 1968-70, Navy Commendn. with combat distg. device, Vietnamese Cross of Gall. with Palm, Vietnam Service, Vietnam Campaign, Nat. Def. Service medals. Ofcs: Latham & Watkins, 633 West Fifth St Los Angeles 90071; 5800 Sears Tower Chicago IL 60606

HURLEY, JAMES WILLIAM, financial executive; b. July 4, 1939, St. Cloud, Minn.; s. James Warren and Margaret Caroline (Kapphahn) H.; m. Kathleen Ann Krol, Aug. 26, 1978; children: Rory b. 1982, Jill b. 1984; edn: BS, So. Ill. Univ., 1967; MBA, Northwestern Univ., 1974; C.P.A., Ill. Career: senior auditor Arthur Andersen & Co., Chgo. 1968-72; mgr. taxes Oak Industries Inc., Crystal Lake, Ill. 1972-74; asst. treas. Trans Union Corp., Lincolnshire, Ill. 1974-82; dir. of finance Comdial Technology, Sunnyvale, Calif. 1982-85; dir. fin. reporting DFS Group Ltd., San Francisco 1985-87; consulting prin., Fremont 1987-88; controller KTI Chemicals Inc., Sunnyvale 1988-92; v.p. finance, CFO, Startech Semiconductor, Inc., Sunnyvale 1993–; mem. Calif. Soc. CPA. Res: 194 Viento Dr Fremont 94536 Ofc: Startech Semiconductor, Inc. 1219 Bordeaux Drive Sunnyvale 94089

HURST, DEBORAH physician; b. May 9, 1946, Wash. DC; d. Willard and Frances (Wison) H.; m. Stephen M. Senter, June 14, 1970; children: Carlin b. 1977, Daniel b. 1981; edn: BA, Radcliffe/Harvard, Cambridge, Mass. 1968; MD, Med. Coll. of Penn., Phila. 1974. Career: intern/resident Bellevue/NYU Hosp., 1974-76; ambulatory fellow Bellevue Hosp. 1976-77; pediatric hematology/oncology fellow Bellevue/NYU Hosp. 1977-79, Columbia Presbyterian Med. Ctr. 1979-80; staff hematologist Children's Hosp. Oakland 1980-92; med. dir. Bayer Corp., Berkeley 1992–; mem: Am. Assn. of Pediatrics 1978–, Bd. of Pediatric Hematology-Oncology 1982–, Nat. Hemophilia Found. 1985–, Am. Soc. of Hematology 1984–, AAAS 1990–, Internat. Soc. of Thrombosis and Hemostasis (ISTH); contbr. articles pub. in med. jours., clin. res. on sickle cell, thalessemia and hemophilia. Ofc: Bayer Corporation 4th & Parker St Berkeley 94701

HUSSAIN, ANJUM, light manufacturing company owner; b. Aug. 12, 1962, Hyderabad, India; nat. 1985; s. Amjad and Syeada (Fatima) H.; edn: BA in management, San Jose 1989. Career: quality engr. Karkar Electronics, S.F., Calif. 1983-87; quality engr. Opcom, San Jose 1987-88; quality engr. Lasersonics, San Jose 1988-89; founder/owner, International Computer Systems Printing, Stockton 1990–; chmn Am. Soc. for Quality Control #0604, S.F.; awards: Business of Year award, Mexican-American Chamber of Commerce, Stockton 1993; New Horizon of Year award, American Black Chamber, Stockton 1993; sr. mem. Am. Soc. for Quality Control, 1990-93; mem: Kiwanis 1993–, Greater C.of C. 1993–, Mexican-Am. C.of C. 1993–, African Am. C. of C. 1993–; editor, Health Awareness articles, 1993; publisher, health newsletter on Alcohol and Drug Prevention, 1993; Dawoodi Bohra Society. Res: 3011 Estate Dr Stockton 95209

HUTCHESON, LYNDA LOU, company executive; b. Nov. 26, 1936, Clovis, N.M.; d. John S. and Iva (Neff) Weber; m. Jerry D. Hutcheson, Mar. 9, 1953; children: Gerald b. 1954, Lisa Marie (Shufelt) b. 1956, Vicki Lynn (Verducci) b. 1957; edn: spl. courses Foothill Coll. Career: ofc. mgr., adminstrv. asst., office publications methods analyst, Technical Ventures, 1976-81; co-founder/v.p. adminstrn. VLSI Research Inc., 1981–, bd. dirs. 1983–; Republican; Presbyterian; rec: interior design, gardening, tennis. Res: 5950 Vista Loop San Jose 95124 Ofc: VLSI Research Inc 1754 Technology Dr Ste 117 San Jose 95110

HUTCHINSON, NANCY ANNE, educator; b. May 3, 1947, Peoria, Ill.; d. E. John and Alvina K. (Zeeck) Richardson; m. Bennett Buckley; children: Amy Ann; edn: BA, Illinois State Univ., 1969; MA, Abilene Christian Univ., 1975. Career: director Call for Help, Abilene, Tx. 1975-78; Methodist Service Ctr., 1978-79; social worker Brentwood Day Care, Austin, Tx. 1979-80; tchr. Cooper High Sch., Abilene, Tx. 1980-90; vis. prof. communication, Pepperdine Univ., Malibu 1990–; honors: Phi Delta Kappa, Delta Kappa Gamma, listed. Who's Who Am. Tchrs. 1992, Who's Who Am. Women 1993, Who's Who in West 1992; mem. AAUW, Junior League Abilene, Tx. 1974–; publs: articles in scholarly jours. (1983, 85); Democrat; Methodist. Res: 24303 Baxter Dr Malibu 90265

HUTCHINSON, WILLIAM KINSEY, III, aircraft company executive producer; b. Apr. 27, 1953, Carlisle, Pa.; s. Wm. Kinsey, II and Lois Ann (Lackey) H.; edn: att. Volkschochschule, Karlsruhe, W. Ger. 1973; BFA, Calif. Inst. of Arts, 1977; MBA, Pepperdine Univ., 1988. Career: travel cons. AAA, Washington, DC 1973-74; park attraction ops., Disneyland, Anaheim 1975-78; sales rep. United Airlines, L.A. 1978-84; mgr., media services. McDonnell Douglas, Long Beach 1984-, chmn. Engring. Master Schedules Com. 1987-89, mem. Mgmt. Control Systems Rev. Com. 1984-89, mem. Mgmt. Schedule & Control Sys. Com. 1988; prodn. asst. KABC-TV, L.A. 1975, Walt Disney Prodns., Burbank 1976; mem: AFI, Assn. of MBA Execs. 1988-89, Filmex 1974-85, McDonnell Douglas Mgmt. Club 1984; Republican; Anglican/Rel. Sci.; rec: travel, photog., cycling. Res: 10402 Sande St Cypress 90630 Ofc: McDonnell Douglas Aerospace 1510 Hughes Way Long Beach 90810-1870

HUTCHISON, JOHN WILLIAM, software corporation president; b. Aug. 4, 1938, Long Beach; s. John and Margaret (Marshall) H.; m. Elaine W., Sept. 21, 1964; edn: BSBA, Long Beach St. Univ. 1966; MBA, Pepperdine Univ. 1986. Career: chief data processing City of Long Beach 1960-75; exec. v.p. Tone Software Corp., Anaheim 1975-86, pres. 1986–; awards: CDP; Republican; rec: flying. Res: 1477 Bryant Dr W, Long Beach 90804 Ofc: 1735 S Brookhurst Anaheim 92804

HUTCHISON, MICHAEL MERCIER, economist, educator; b. March 2, 1953, Oakland; s. John Ralph and Agatha Emma (Mercier) H.; m. Greta, July 18, 1981; children: Erik b. 1984, Emma b. 1988; edn: BA, UC Santa Cruz; PhD, Univ. Oreg., Eugene. Career: lectr. UC Berkeley 1985; economist Fed. Reserve Bank S.F. 1983-85, vis. scholar 1985; prof. of economics UC Santa Cruz 1985–; vis. scholar Bank of Japan, 1993-94, Reserve Bank of New Zealand, 1994-95; mem: Am. Econ. Assn.; num. articles pub. in profl. jours.; rec: skiing, travel. Res: 309 Dickens Way Santa Cruz 95064 Ofc: Univ. California Crown College Santa Cruz 95064

HUTT, LAURENCE J., lawyer; b. Dec. 15, 1950, New York; s. George Joseph and Miriam Marta (Cohen) H.; children: Marcie b. 1982, Ethan b. 1983, Amanda b. 1985, Denver b. 1987; edn: BA hist., Univ. Pa. Phila. 1972; JD, Stanford Univ. 1975. Career: atty., assoc. Kadison Pfaelzer Woodard Quinn & Rossi, Los Angeles 1976-82, ptnr. 1982-87; prin. Quinn Kully & Morrow 1987–; honors: Phi Beta Kappa, Order of Coif; mem: State Bar of Calif. (exec. com. of conf. of delegates, dist. 7, 1992–), Am. Bar Assn., Assn. Bus. Trial Lawyers, L.A. Co. Bar Assn. (st. bar del. exec. com. 1986-92, del ofcr. 1989-92, chair superior cts. subcom. 1988-89, v.chair st. cts. com. 1989-90, bench and bar com. 1989-93, judicial systems com. 1988); rec: theatre, wine tasting. Ofc: Quinn Kully & Morrow 520 S Grand Ave 8th Flr Los Angeles 90071

HUYSER, ROBERT ERNEST, executive, retired air force general; b. June 14, 1924, Paonia, Colo.; s. Wm. and Alma Madline (Davis) H.; m. Wanda, Nov. 15, 1942; children: Cheryl b. 1944, Christine b. 1956; edn: courses, Ouachita Baptist Coll. 1944, Modesto Jr. Coll. 1949; AA, So. Miss. Univ. 1955; grad. Air War Coll. 1963; Hon. Dr. of Laws, Univ. of Akron. Career: served to Gen. US Air Force 1943-1981: drafted buck pvt. Army Med. Corps 1943; transferred to Army Air Corps aviation cadet pgm., earned pilot wings and commd. 2d lt. Sept. 1944, command pilot (10,000 hours piloting aircraft from open cockpit to 3 times speed of sound, flew propeller, turbo prop and jet planes: trainers, airlift, fighters, tankers and bombers) combat missions in WWII, Korea and Vietnam; aircraft cmdr. to wing cmdr. S.A.C. 26 yrs., cmdr. 449th Bombardment Wing, Kincheloe AFB, Mich. 1966-68, dir. comand control/dep. chief of staff ops., Hqs. SAC, Offutt AFB, Neb. 1968-70, then dir. ops. plans/chief Single Integrated Operational Plans Div., Jt. Strategic Target Plnng. Staff, Hqs. SAC 1970-72; dep. chief of staff, plans and ops. Hqs. USAF, WDC 1972-75; named 4-Star General USAF, 1975 (highest rank in peacetime, 1st draftee to achieve 4-Star Gen. rank USAF); dep. cmdr. in chief U.S. European Command (under Gen. Alexander Haig), Stuttgart-Vaihingen, Ger. 1975-79; cmdr. in chief Military Airlift Command, Scott AFB, Ill. 1979-81, ret. 1981; advisor govts. on nat. defense systems, respons. for US fgn. mil. sales pgms. in 44+ countries in Europe, Middle East and Africa; personal presdl. envoy of Pres. Carter to Iran during final 31 days of the Shah's reign, Jan. 79; decorated Defence Disting. Service Medal (2), Legion of Merit, Bronze Star, Air Medal, Joint Svc. and Army Commendn. medals, AF Commendn. w/2 o.l.c., Presdl. Unit Citation emblem; awards from Republic of Korea and Fed. Republic Ger., 26 ribbons; currently pres./CEO, Four Star Ents. Inc., cons. Boeing Co.; Proclamations from 22 State Governors of for dedicated and superior svc. to country on retirement from active duty (7/1/81), letters from US Senators and Congressmen and num. city Mayors; premier Nat. Def. Transp. Assn. DoD award 1981, Silver Beaver award BSA, Geo. Washington honor medal Freedoms Found. Valley Forge 1982, Tennessee Ernie Ford award 1983, first living person to be inducted into the Airlift/Tanker Hall of Fame 1994; mem: No. Calif. Aero Club, Airlift Assn. (bd. chmn.), War Coll. Found. (trustee advy. bd.), Airmans Mem. Found. (bd. dirs.), Rotary, World Affairs Council, A.F. Assn.; mem. advy. bds: San Jose State Univ., San Francisco Univ., Air Univ., nat. chmn. What's Good with America (patriotism pgm.); BSA Nat. Council (exec. bd.), Santa Clara Co. Scout Council (pres. 1983-84); author: Mission to Tehran (Harper and Row; Andre Deutsch, U.K., Ger., Italy); Republican; Prot.; rec: golf, fishing. Res: 6191 McAbee Rd San Jose 95120

HWANG, HENRY Y., bank chairman, president and chief executive officer; b. Nov. 28,1929, Shanghai, China; nat. 1962: s. Jin Yu- and Ai Tseng(Chao)H; m. Dorothy Huang; June 11, 1955; children: David Henry b. 1957, Margery Anne b. 1961, Grace Elizabeth b. 1962; edn: Univ. Shanghai 1949; Nat. Taiwan Univ. 1950; BA internat. rels., Linfield Coll. 1951; grad. studies internat. rels. and acctg., USC 1955; C.P.A. Calif. 1960; LLD(hon.) Linfield Coll., 1988. Career: pres. Henry Hwang & Co. CPA, Los Angeles 1960-76; Hwang & Chuang Accountancy Corp. 976-78; chmn., pres., ceo, Far East Nat. Bank 1974–; chmn. Far East Internat. Trading Corp.; Sr. Advisor Four Earth Investment Corp.; Chmn Far East Capital Corp; served as vice chmn. bd. of fellows and currently mem. bd. of Claremont Univ. Ctr. & Grad. Sch.; mem. bd of Visitors at Peter Drucker Center for Mgmt.; advy. com. to White House on U.S. Trade Negotiations, WDC 1984-87; mem. regional commrs. advy. council to Dept. of Justice 1984; chmn. bd. trustees Calif.-Bicentennial Found. for U.S. Constitution, LA 1988; advy. bd. Immigration Services and U.S. Small Bus. Assn.; appt. by U.S. Secty. of Commerce to Minority Enterprise Devel. Advy. Council 1989–; bd mem. Huntington Memorial Hosp, Japan American Symph Assn. of LA, City Club; past pres. and current chmn Nat. Assn. of Chinese Am. Bankers, 1993; awards: Execs. Mag. exec. of yr. 1986, U.S. Small Bus. Administrn., fin. advocate of yr. 1986, Asian Bus. League businessman of yr. 1986, L.A. C. of C. Medici award 1987, Black Businessmen Assn. banking and fin. award 1988; Merrill Lynch/Ernst & Young,Entrep. of yr. 1991, Asian Bus. Assoc. Businessman of Yr. 1993; mem: Nat Bankers Assn.(v chmn 1988), Am. Bankers Assn., Calif. Bankers Assn., Am. Inst. C.P.A., Calif. Soc. C.P.A., Indep. Bankers Assn.; Calif. Bankers Insurance Services, Inc.; Am. Bankers Assn., Govt. Rels Council; civic bds: Pacific Asia Museum (trustee 1987), United Way (dir. 1984-88), L.A. Olympic Orgn. Com. Advy. Bd. 1984, Catholic Charities (bd.) 1989-94, Metropolitan YMCA (bd.), co-pub. Complete Guide to Fgn. Investment in China (1987), The U.S. Constitution (1987);Republican; rec: golf, swimming, singing. Ofc. Far East National Bank Two Calif Plaza 350 S Grand Ave Ste 4100 Los Angeles 90071

HYATT, WALTER JONES, engineer, consultant-marketing, exhibits, models; b. Feb. 2, 1918, Greensboro, N.C.; s. Frederick Carlyle and Myrtle Anna (Cook) H.; m. Mary A. Malloy, July 18, 1942; children: Mary Valerie b. 1945, Catherine Maureen b. 1948; edn: BS, Univ. of St. Louis Parks Sch. of Aeronautical Engring., 1938; postgrad. Cal Tech, 1942-43. Career: engr. Curtiss-Wright Corp., St. Louis 1938-39; engr. field supr. Lockheed Aircraft Corp., 1939-46, instr. Lockheed Tng. Pgm. Burbank H.S., Burbank Night Sch., 1943-45; nat. sales mgr. Jackson Chem. Co. of Calif., 1947-50; div. mgr. Pac. Airmotive Corp., Kansas City, 1950-51; sales engr. Adel Precision Prods. 1950-57; est. W.J. Hyatt Co. (mfrs.) 1957-66, pres., prin. 1966–; est. Aqualite Corp. 1958; ptnr. W.J. Hyatt & Assocs., Beverly Hills 1966–; v.p. Penwal Industries, Chino 1981–; pres. Air Hydraulics Control, Canoga Park 1981-87; dir: Hi-Temp Insulation, Camarillo 1972–, Insulfab, Camarillo 1972–; tech. writer Aero Publs. 1943-45; ptnr. Struc. Engring. Serv. for Architects 1946; publs: War Prodn. Council Inspection Handbook, sect. of "Aviation Thesaurus", "Propeller Design and Simplified Stress Analysis"; co-ord. aviation and Lockheed rep. Micro-Inch Finish Stds. for aircraft ind., 1943, estab. X-ray and Magnetic Design Stds. for Design Manual and USAF Design Handbook, 1944, devel. procedures and orgn. of Maint. Trouble Reports for all aircraft (adopted); Patents: synthetic rubber compound for rotating seals, 1943, 3-way auto rear view safety mirror; awards: man of yr. Kansas City C.of C. 1950; past dir. L.A. C.of C. (mfg. gp.), Aircraft Distbrs. and Mfrs. Assn. 1950; mem: Air Force League, Navy League, Assn. of U.S. Army, Magic Castle (Hollywood); mil: field serv. USAF and USN, WWII; R.Cath.; rec: gardening, woodworking. Res: 630 N Foothill Rd Beverly Hills 90210 Ofc: PO Box 943 Beverly Hills 90213

HYMAN, EDWARD J., forensic and clinical psychologist, information scientist; b. Oct. 25, 1947, Roslyn, N.Y.; s. Herbert H. and Edith (Tannenbaum) H.; m. Deborah Anne McDonald, May 1, 1986; children: Cameron Scott, Devon Edward; edn: AB, Columbia Univ. 1969; grad. studies, Harvard Univ. 1970; C.Phil., UC Berkeley 1974; PhD 1975; lic. psychologist Calif. 1978. Career: lectr. UC Berkeley 1976-78; asst. dean 1978-79; asst. prof. Univ. San Francisco 1979-81; assoc. prof. Center Social Research, Berkeley 1981-86, prof. 1986–, sci. dir. 1981–; coord. UC Berkeley Ctr.Participant Edn. 1970-72; jr. fellow Center for Social Res. 1974-75; psychology intern Health Services Agency, Santa Cruz 1973-74; regents fellow UC Berkeley 1974-75; awards: Univ. San Francisco Disting. Researcher 1980; mem: Am. Child Abuse Prevention Soc. (trustee), Am. Psychol. Assn., Calif. Psychol. Assn., Am. Coll. of Forensic Psychol., Soc. for Personality Assessment, Internat. Soc. Political Psychol., Am. Orthopsychiatric Assn., Soc. Personality & Social Psychol., Assn. for Info. & Decision Scis., AAAS, Commonwealth Club; contbr. book Life Stress (1985), Marcuse: Critical Theory and Promise of Utopia (1986, 88); rec: running, hiking, sailing. Res: 1315 Star Route Sausalito 94965 Ofc: Center for Social Research 2709 Alcatraz Ave Berkeley 94705

HYNES, WILLIAM MARTIN, II, communications company executive; b. Sept. 6, 1942, NY, NY; s. Wm. Martin and Norita Maria (Casey) H.; m. Elizabeth Cline, July 3, 1963; m. 2d. Elizabeth J Multer, Dec. 7, 1975; children: Shannon b. 1968, William b. 1978, Brian b. 1980, Casey b. 1983; edn: history major Farleigh Dickinson, 1963. Career: empl. AT&T, New York 1960-65; mgr. telecommunications ABC T.V., N.Y. 1965-78, dir. telecomms. 1978-85; exec. v.p. and c.o.o. Wold Communications, Los Angeles 1985-88; chief ops. ofcr. Stars West, 1988-91; pres. Pacific Syndication, 1991–; instr. New School, N.Y. 1985; awards: Emmy award NATAS 1984; mil: E5 AUS 1966-68; Republican; R.Cath.; rec: running/triathalon. Ofc: Pacific Syndication, 2829 W Burbank Blvd Burbank 91505

IACONO, JAMES MICHAEL, research center director; b. Dec. 11, 1925, Chgo., Ill.; s. Joseph and Angelina (Cutaia) I.; children: Lynn, Joseph, Michael, Rosemary; edn: BS, Loyola Univ., Chgo. 1950; MS, Univ. of Ill. 1952, PhD 1954. Career: chief, Lipid Nutrition Lab Nutrition Inst., ARS, USDA, Beltsville, Md. 1970-75, dep. asst. admin., National Pgm. ARS, USDA, WDC 1975-77, assoc. adminstr. Office of Human Nutrition 1978-82, dir. Western Human Nutrition Res. Ctr., ARS, USDA, San Francisco 1982-94; adj. prof. nutrition UCLA 1987–; award: res. career devel. award Nat. Inst. of Health 1964-70; mem: Am. Inst. of Nutr., Am. Soc. of Clinical Nutr., Am. Oil Chemists Soc., Am. Heart Assn. (fellow), Am. Inst. of Chemists (fellow); author 120+ chapters in books, res. & technical papers in fields of nutrition and biochemistry, lipids; mil: served U.S. Army 1944-46. Res: 480-1 Pointe Pacific Dr Daly City 94014 Ofc: Western Human Nutrition Research Center, USDA-ARS POB 29997 San Francisco 94129

IAMELE, RICHARD THOMAS, law librarian; b. Jan. 29, 1942, Newark, N.J.; s. Armando Anthony and Evelyn (Coladonato) I.; m. Marilyn Ann Berutto, Aug. 21, 1965; children: Thomas b. 1966, Ann Marie b. 1968; edn: BA, Loyola Univ., 1963, MSLS, USC, 1967, JD, Southwestern Univ. Sch. of Law, 1976; admitted bar: Calif., 1977. Career: cataloger Univ. So. Calif., L.A. 1967-71; asst. cataloger L.A. County Law Library, 1971-77, asst. reference librarian 1977-78, asst. librarian 1978-80, library director 1980–; mem: Am. Bar Assn. 1980–, Calif. State Bar 1977–, Calif. Library Assn. 1980–, Am. Assn. of Law Libraries 1971–, Coun. of Calif. County Law Librarians 1980–, So. Calif. Assn. of Law Libraries 1971–. Ofc: L.A. Co. Law Library 301 W First St Los Angeles 90012

IBA, SHOZO, physician, radiologist, retired; b. Nov. 10, 1918, Los Angeles; s. Kennosuke and Sumie (Misumi) I.; m. Margaret; children: Nadine S. b. 1955, Diane A. b. 1956, Lynn E. b. 1957, Mylene M. b. 1958, Wayne S. b. 1959, Elaine M. b. 1961; edn: AB, USC 1940; MS, 1941; MD, Boston Univ. Sch. Med. 1945; cert. Am. Bd. Radiology (1952). Career: intern Mt. Auburn Hosp., Cambridge Hosp., Mass. 1944-45; USPHS, N.Y. St. Hosp., Ray Brook, N.Y. 1946, staff 1947; resident, radiology City Hosp., Cleveland, Ohio 1948-51, asst. radiologist 1952; demonstrator, instr. Western Reserve Med. Sch. 1952; staff L.A. County Harbor Gen. Hosp., 1953-60; staff L.A. County Long Beach General Hos. 1953-61; awards: Rotary Club Internat. award; civic: Rotary Club (Huntington Park 1956-71), Civil Defense Com.; Republican; Prot. Address: Shozo Iba MD 27787 Rota Mission Viejo 92692

IBBETSON, EDWIN THORNTON, development company president; b. Apr. 17, 1923, Los Angeles; s. Robert Edwin and Ann E. (Thornton) Ibbetson; m. Harriett Alice Hudson, Dec. 28, 1947; children: Elizabeth Ann (Mrs. Phillip Hitchcock), Douglas Hudson, Gregory Bruce, Timothy Edwin, Julia Katherine (Mrs. Martin Zilinskas), Erika Alice (Mrs. Brian White). Career: with Union Devel. Co., Cerritos 1944, pres. 1961–; partner Paramount Constrn., Cerritos 1948; v.p. Valley Properties Inc., Imperial Valley 1962-95; pres. Union Farms Inc., Cerritos 1962-81; chmn. bd. dirs. Dutch Village Bowling Ctr. Inc., Lakewood 1965-86; ptnr. Ibbetson-Marsh Realtors 1975; vice chmn. bd. Equitable Svg.& Loan Assn. 1977-85; bd. dirs.(chmn. 1977-79) Garden State Bank 1974-79; gen. ptnr. Future Energy, 1980–; bd. dirs. Metropolitan Water Dist. So. Calif., 1959, bd. sec. 1979-82, bd. chmn. 1983-86, gov. apptd. mem. Colo. River Board of Calif. 1986; chmn. Bellflower Water Devel. Com. 1965; chmn. Los Angeles County Real Estate Advy. Com. 1974; bd. dirs. Armed Services YMCA, Long Beach 1962-72; trustee St. Mary's Hosp., Long Beach, chmn. 1994-96; honors: Young man of year Bellflower Jaycees 1959, Hon. Pres. for Life, CAR 1980, realtor of year Bellflower Dist. Bd. Realtors 1962, 67, 71, Bellflower Kiwanis man of year 1983, Long Beach City Coll. Hall of Fame 1983; mem: Am. Soc. Real Estate Counselors (pres. 1977), Calif. Assn. Realtors (treas. 1972-79, dir.), Internat. Real Estate Fedn., Nat. Assn. Realtors (dir.), Nat. Inst. Real Estate Brokers (cert. comml. investment mem.), Inst. Real Estate Mgmt. (CPM, cert. property mgr.), Urban Land Inst., Rancho Los Cerritos Bd. Realtors (1949, pres. 1961), Calif. Water Resources Assn. (v.p. 1985), Central Basin Mcpl. Water Dist. (dir.), Calif. Real Estate PAC, Internat. Council Shopping Centers; clubs: Elks, Kiwanis (pres. 1958), Internat. Traders, So. Calif. Tuna, Long Beach (sec. 1988, pres. 1995), Tuna Club at Avalon 1991; mil: USNR 1943-46; Cath. Ofc: 16550 Bloomfield Ave Cerritos 90703

IBBETSON, GREGORY BRUCE, real estate executive; b. Nov. 7, 1951, Long Beach; s. Edwin Thornton and Harriett Alice (Hudson) I.; m. Trudy, Sept. 11, 1971; children: Gregory B. b. 1973, Eric b. 1976; edn: AA, Long Beach City Coll. 1976; BA, CSU Dominguez Hills 1978; Lic. Real Estate Broker, Calif. 1981. Career: air traffic controller USAF 1970-73; maintenance crew Union Devel. Co. 1973-74, property mgr. 1974–; dir. Union Devel. Co. 1976; dir., v.p.

Dutch Village Bowl 1980-90; secty. Union Devel. of Hawaii Inc. 1985–; honors: Hon. Svc. Award, Bellflower Unif. Sch. Dist. 1984; Realtor of the Year, Rancho Los Cerritos Bd. Realtors 1985; Referee of the Year, AYSO 1982; mem: Calif. Assn. of Realtors (chmn. Pension & Retirement 1986, chmn. Policy Com. 1989), Rancho Los Cerritos Bd. Realtors (treas. 1984, pres. elec. 1985, pres. 1986), Am. Soc. of R.E. Counselors, Bellflower Kiwanis, AYSO (referee), Lambda Alpha, SPMA, Washington Elem. School Site Council (chmn. 1985-86), Bellflower School Site Council (chmn. 1987-89), CSU Dominguez Hills Economic Club (charter pres.), youth coach Image Surf Club/Huntington High Sch. Beach; mil: E-3 USAF, decorated Fgn. Conflict, Marksmanship; Republican; rec: surfing, swimming, photog. Ofc: Union Development Co Inc.16550 Bloomfield Cerritos 90703

ICE, MARIE ANN, educator; b. Jan. 18, 1938, Wiley, Colo.; d. Irvan Oliver and Jennie Elizabeth (Parrish) Ice; edn: BA, Univ. No. Colorado, 1967, MA, 1971; PhD, Univ. Mo., Columbia 1983. Career: instr. Arapahoe Sch. Dist., Littleton, Colo. 1967-70; instr. and supr. Central Missouri State Univ., Warrensburg, Mo. 1973-80; asst. prof. and dir. elem. edn., Marymount Coll., Salina, Kans. 1983-85; prof. CSU Bakersfield, Calif. 1986–, Reading Pgm. coord. 1986-91; awards: postdoc. tng. in child language pgm. Univ. of Kansas 1985-86; mem. Internat. Reading Assn. 1983–, Nat. Reading Conf. 1986–, Nat. Coun. of Tchrs. of English 1983–, Kern Reading Assn. (treas., v.p., pres. 1990–); publs: articles on Children's Generated Stories (1980–), coauthor: CBEST Test Preparation Guide (in press), co-editor (texts) Reading: The Blending of Theory & Practice, I, II (1990, 91); Republican; Lutheran; rec: reading. Res: 3508 Sweetbriar Way Bakersfield 93311 Ofc: Calif. State Univ. Bakersfield, 9001 Stockdale Hwy Bakersfield 93311-1099

IERARDI, STEPHEN JOHN, physician; b. July 5, 1960, Honolulu; s. Ernest J. and Roberta (Hackett) I.; m. Erica Ewing, May 28, 1989; children: Daphne Alexandra b. 1991, Weston Eric b. 1995; edn: BA biology (cum laude), Williams Coll., 1982, MD, Univ. Rochester Sch. of Med. & Dentistry, 1986; Diplomate and Fellow Am. Bd. of Family Practice 1989–. Career: resident, chief resident UC Irvine Medical Ctr., Orange (1986-88, 88-89); physician, Saddleback Family Medicine, Laguna Hills 1989–, ptnr. 1991–; chair Dept. of Family Med., Saddleback Memorial Med. Ctr. 1993–; awards: Nat. Merit Scholar 1978, Gannett Publishing scholastic achiev. scholar 1978, UCI Care Awards (1986, 87, 88); mem. Calif. Acad. of Family Physicians, Am. Acad. of Family Physicians; rec: surfing, sailing, skiing. Ofc: Saddleback Family Medicine 23961 Calle de la Magdalena Ste 334 Laguna Hills 92653

IKEDA, CLYDE JUNICHI, plastic surgeon; b. July 1, 1951, Kobe, Japan; s. Paul and Kazu I.; edn: BA (hons. in English, outstanding acad. performance), SUNY, Binghamton, NY 1973; pre-med. CUNY and CCNY, Queens, NY 1975; MD, N.Y. Med. Coll., Valhalla, NY 1979. Career: research asst. N.Y. Medical Coll., 1973-75; clerkship orthopedic surg. Indian Health Service, Alaska 1977; researcher Tokyo Med. Coll., Pheriche, Nepal 1979; research asso. dept. dermatology UC Med. Ctr., San Francisco 1987–; dir. Bothin Burn Unit and dir. Wound Healing Ctr., St. Francis Hosp., S.F. 1987–; mem: AMA, Am. Soc. Plastic and Reconstructive Surgery, CMA, S.F. Med. Soc., Calif. Soc. of Plastic Surgeons; contbr. numerous med. jour. articles; rec: Black-belt Kendo, photography, poetry reading. Ofc: Clyde Ikeda, MD, 1199 Bush St Suite 640 San Francisco 94109

IKEGAWA, SHIRO, artist; b. July 15, 1933, Tokyo, Japan; came to the U.S., 1956; s. Fujinori and Sumie (Matsuki) I.; div. 1979, 1 child, Jima b. 1967; edn: Tokyo Univ. of Arts; MFA, Otis Art Inst. of L.A., 1961. Career: asst. prof. of art Pasadena City Coll. 1961-67, CSU Los Angeles 1967-76; prof. art Otis Art Inst. of Parsons Sch. of Design, 1979-85, chair printmaking dept.; guest prof. Chouinard Art Sch. 1968-71, Otis Art Inst. 1967, CSU San Francisco 1972, UC Berkeley 1973, Vancouver (B.C.) Sch. of Art 1974, UC Irvine 1974-75, CSU Dominguez Hills 1985; vis. prof. Claremont Grad. Sch. 1987, UC Davis 1989; artist in residence for Detroit Nat. Print Symp., Cranbrook Acad. of Art, Mich. 1980; lectr. univs., colls. and art assns. nat., 1960s–; commissioned works include Two Edition Etchings, L.A. County Mus. of Art (1973), Prints Commn. on Intl. Multiple Exh. in Tokyo, Normura Display Co. Ltd. (1973), 32 Feet Color Etching "Tale of Genji" L.A. Times (1973); awarded num. art prizes 1960–; grantee: Otis Art Inst. Found. 1960, CSULA Found. 1968-72, NEA fellow printmaking 1974, Ford Found. Faculty Enrichment 1977, 1980, NEA fellow for conceptual art and performance art 1981; One-person exhibits incl. Comara Gal., L.A. (1961, 63, 64, 65, 68), Crocker Art Mus., Sacto. (1965), Container Corp. Am., Chgo. (1966), Idaho State Univ., Pocatello, Id. (1966), Santa Barbara Mus. of Art (1966), Beni Gal., Kyoto, Japan (1967), Univ. Idaho, Moscow (1967), Comsky Gal., L.A. (1979), Long Beach Mus. Art (1971), Univ. Colo., Boulder (1972), UC Irvine (1976), Retrospective show Santa Monica High Sch. (1979), Pasadena City Coll. (1979), L.A. Inst. Contemporary Art (1980), Fine Arts Gal., Laguna Beach (1983), CSULA (1983), Shinno Gal., L.A. (1984), No. Ariz. Univ., Flagstaff (1985), Soker-Kaseman Gal., S.F. (1985), Monterey Bay Gal. (1987), So. Oregon Coll., Ashland (1987); participant numerous competitive and invitational annuals and group exhibitions. Res: 323 E Altadena Dr Altadena 91001

ILFELD, FREDERIC WILLIAM, JR., psychiatrist; b. Dec. 19, 1940, Los Angeles, Calif.; s. Frederic William and Barbara (Squire) I.; children: Brian b. 1966, Jeffrey b. 1969, Benjamin b. 1981; edn: BA (magna cum laude with high honors), Yale Univ. 1962; MD, Harvard Univ. 1966; MA, sociology, Stanford Univ. 1969; med. lic. Calif.; cert. Am. Bd. of Psychiatry & Neurology. Career: rotating internship S.F. Gen. Hosp. 1966-67; resident in psychiatry Stanford Sch. Medicine 1967-70; res. psychiatrist Lab. of Socio-environmental Studies, Nat. Inst. Mental Health 1970-72; staff psychiatrist UC Davis-Sacto. Med. Ctr. 1972-73, chief of psychiatric crisis team 1973-74; pvt. practice of psychiatry Alhambra Psychotherapy Ctr., Sacto. 1974–; cons. Yolo Co. Mental Health Svs., Calif. State Univ. Sacto. Health Svs. 1978-80, UC Davis Student Health & Counseling Ctr. 1986-87; assoc. clin. prof. psychiatry UC Davis Sch. Medicine; honors: Sigma Xi 1962, Pawlowski Peace Prize 1974, res. grantee Ctr. for Epidemiology, Nat. Inst. of Mental Health 1976-78, res. grantee Roche Labs. 1979, Outstanding Tchr. vol. clin. faculty UC Davis Sch. Medicine 1986-87; mem: Am. Psychiatric Assn. (fellow 1979–), Sacto. Psychiatric Soc. (pres. 1986), Central Calif. Psychiatric Soc. CMA, No. Calif. Group Psychotherapy Assn. (council mem. 1992), Sacto. Co. Med. Soc., Sigma Xi, Aesculapian Club (Harvard Med. Sch.), Jewish Fedn., Sacto. (bd. trustees); author: Social Nudism in America (Coll. & Univ. Press, 1964), Violence and the Struggle for Existence (Little, Brown & Co., 1970), contbr. num. articles to profl. jours., 1969-82; mil: lt. comdr., USPHS 1967-72; Democrat; Jewish; rec: skiing, kayaking, mountain biking. Ofc: 4300 Auburn Blvd #205 Sacramento 95841

ILIFF, WILLIAM BENNETT, dentist; b. Feb. 16, 1958, Sacramento; s. Robert John and Patricia Ann (Cutting) I.; m. Nina Locke, May 21, 1983; 1 dau., Katherine b. 1985; edn: AA, Sacto. City Coll. 1978; BS, UCLA 1980; DDS, 1984. Career: resident Denver Gen. Hosp., Denver, Colo. 1984-85; pvt. practice, Sacto. 1985–; postgrad. resident Denver Gen. Hosp. 1984-85; vis. lectr. Sacto. City Coll. 1986-87; honors: Phi Kappa Psi, Delta Sigma Delta, Sacto. City Coll. Dean's List 1977, 78, UCLA Sch. Dentistry Treatment of Handicapped Patient award 1984, Bausch & Lomb Sci. Medal of Hon. 1976; mem: Sacto. Dist. Dental Soc. (chair dental care com. 1988), Calif. Dental Assn., ADA, Acad. Gen. Dentistry, Christian Brothers Alumni Assn.; pub. article in profl. jour., 1985; Republican; Cath.; rec: baseball, woodwork, history. Ofc: 5340 Elvas Ave Ste 400 Sacramento 95819

ILLING, LILLIAN BAKER, real estate broker; b. April 29, 1922, Bronx, NY; d. William C. and Esther (Berman) Ulrich; m. 1st Frank Baker, Feb. 17, 1945, div. June 17, 1955, 2d. Hans Illing, PhD, April 19, 1962 (dec. Feb. 16, 1987); 1 son, Theodore Lloyd Baker b. 1952; edn: Los Angeles City Coll. 1939-42. Career: indep. insurance agent, 1952-91, and real estate broker, owner Advisory Mortgage Loan Svc., Los Angeles 1962–; Shaklee distbr.; mem. Pacific Beach Toastmasters (adm. v.p. 1989-90); civic: vol. Santa Monica Westside Hotline 1980-91, Crime Prevention splst. 1982–; past mem. Wilhelm Furtwangler Soc. (recording secty. 1978-85); Democrat; Baptist; rec: piano (performed w/ LACC orch. 1941), artist (oil painting). Address: Advisory Mortgage Loan Service, 6112 W 77th St Los Angeles 90045

IMANA, JORGE GARRON, artist; b. Sucre, Bolivia, Sept. 20, 1930; nat. 1974; s. Juan S. and Lola (Garron) I.; m. Cristina I.; children: George, Ivan; edn: grad. Fine Arts Acad., Univ. San Francisco Xavier 1950; cert. Nat. Sch. for Tchrs., Bolivia 1952. Career: prof. art Nat. Sch. Tchrs., Sucre 1954-56; prof. biology Padilla Coll., Sucre 1956-60; head dept. art Inst. Normal Simon Bolivar, La Paz, Bolivia 1961-62; owner/mgr. The Artists Showroom, San Diego 1973–; Over 86 one-man shows of paintings in U.S., S. Am. and Europe, 1952–; including: Gallery Banet, La Paz, 1965, Artists Showroom, San Diego (1964, 66, 68, 74, 76, 77), San Diego Art Inst. (1966, 68, 72, 73), Contrast Gallery, Chula Vista, Calif. 1966, Central Public Library, San Diego 1969, Universidad de Zulia, Maracaibo, Venezuela 1969, Spanish Village Art Center, San Diego (1974, 75, 76), La Jolla Art Assn. Gallery (1969, 72-88), Internat. Gallery, Washington 1976, Galeria de Arte L'Atelier, La Paz 1977, Museo Nacional, La Paz 1987, Casa del Arte, La Jolla, Calif. 1987, Museo Nacional, La Paz, Bolivia 1988; num. group shows incl: Fine Arts Gallery, San Diego 1964, Mus. of Modern Art, Paris 1973, exhib. in galleries of Budapest (Hungary) 1975, Moscow (USSR) 1975, Warsaw (Poland) 1976; permanent collections: Museo Nacional, La Paz, Bolivia, Museo de la Universidad de Potosi, Bolivia, Muse Nacional de Bogota, Colombia, S. Am., Ministerio de Edn., Managua, Nicaragua, Bolivian embassy, Moscow and Washington, pvt. collections in U.S., Europe and Latin Am.; num. murals incl: Colegio Padilla, Sucre, Bolivia 1958, Colegio Junin, Sucre, Bolivia 1959, Sindicato de Construccion Civil, Lima, Peru 1960. Hon. consul of Bolivia, So Calif. 1969-73. Served to lt. Bolivian Army 1953; awards: Mcpl. award Sucre, Bolivia. 1958; mem: San Diego Art Inst., San Diego Watercolor Soc., Internat. Fine Arts Guild, La Jolla Art Assn. Res: 3357 Caminito Gandara La Jolla 92037-2907

IMBRECHT, CHARLES RICHARD, lawyer; b. Feb. 4, 1949, Ventura; s. Earl Richard and Hazel Victoria (Berg) I.; m. Alida Margit Bergseid, Sept. 23, 1979; children: Erica b. 1987, Emily b. 1991; edn: BA, Occidental Coll. 1971; JD, Loyola Univ. 1974. Career: atty., advisor U.S. Interstate Commerce Commn., Wash. D.C. 1974-75; ptnr. Robinson Melikian Imbrecht & Weems,

Ventura 1975-80; assemblyman Calif. Legislature, Sacto. 1976-82; chmn. Calif. Energy Commn. 1983–; govs. energy advisor St. Calif., Sacto. 1983–; state liaison Nuclear Regulatory Commn., Wash. D.C. 1883–; bd. dirs. Calif. Alternative Energy Source Fin. Authority, Sacto. 1983–; awards: Occidental Coll. Richter fellow 1970, Calif. Jr. C.of C. Outstading Young Man of Calif. 1981, Nat. Soc. Profl. Engrs. Outstanding Pub. Servant 1984; mem Electric Power Res. Inst. advy. council 1991–; appt. by U.S. Environmental Protection Agency to nat. advy. council on 1990 Federal Clean Air Act, 1991–; appt. co-chmn. U.S. Alternative Fuels Council by U.S. Dept. Energy,. 1990-92; mem: Western Interstate Energy Bd. (chmn. 1986-88), Nat. Assn. St. Energy Officals (bd. dirs.), Assn. Profl. Energy Mgrs., Ventura Co. Bar Assn., Calif. St. Bar Assn., Ventural Co. Republican Central Com., Calif. St. Republican Central Com.; Republican; Lutheran; rec: swimming, scuba diving. Res: 4230 Euclid Ave Sacramento 95822 Ofc: California Energy Commission 1516 9th St MS 31 Sacramento 95814

IMHOFF, MYRTLE MARY ANN, retired educator; b. Oct. 7, 1910, St. Louis, Mo.; d. Clyde C., Sr. and Laura E. (Asmuth) Imhoff; edn: BA, edn. and music, Harris Tchrs. Coll., St. Louis 1931; MA, psych., St. Louis Univ. 1935; PhD, edn. and psych., Washington Univ., St. Louis 1952. Career: estab. and taught Kindergarten, Crystal City, Mo. 1932-34; elem. tchr. St. Louis, Mo. Public Schs., 1934-44; fed. personnel and field rep. Navy Civilian Dept., Civil Service, Wash. DC 1945-46; tchr. Normal Univ., Ill. 1946-47; dir. edn. Brentwood, Mo. Pub. Schs. 1947-48; assoc. prof. Adams State Coll., Alamosa, Colo. 1948-50; lectr. in edn. Wash. Univ. 1952-53; splst. Early Elem. Edn. and generalist Elem. Edn., US Office of Edn., Wash. DC 1958-59, UNESCO curriculum expt./adv. to Ministry of Edn., Thailand 1959-60; prof. edn. CSU Fullerton 1960-68, CSU Los Angeles 1968–, ret.; acad. cons. pvt. sch.; del. regional and nat. ednl. confs., 1960s; Fulbright adv. CSUF 1967-68, advy. bd. World Explorers Pgm. 1965–, adv. Best Books 1971-73, past cons. Coronet Instl. Films, Ednl. Testing Service; awards: Jesse K. Bar hon. fellow, Heerman fellow, McMillan scholar, 1950-52; mem: Kappa Delta Pi, Am. Orthopsychiat. Assn.; past mem. Am. Psychol. Assn., Internat. Council Psychologists, Am. Acad. Pol. and Social Sci., Am. Edn. Res. Assn., Nat. Soc. for Study of Edn., US Com. for Early Childhood Edn., CTA Inst. for Tchg., NEA, Am. Mus. Natural Hist., Day Care and Child Dev. Council Am., World Affairs Council O.C.; author text: Early Elementary Edn., Apppleton Century Croftts 1959, num. reports, articles in ednl. jours.; Republican; Prot.; rec: music, swim. Res: 1824 Arlington, El Cerrito 94530

IMWINKELRIED, EDWARD JOHN, law professor; b. Sept. 19, 1946, San Francisco; s. John Joseph and Enes Rose (Gianelli) I.; m. Cynthia Marie Clark, Dec. 30, 1978; children: Marie b. 1983, Kenneth b. 1985; edn: BA, Univ. San Francisco 1967; JD, 1969. Career: consumer atty. San Francisco Neighborhood Legal Assistance Found., San Francisco 1970; capt., judge advocate generals corps AUS 1970-74; prof. of law Univ. San Diego 1974-79; Wash. Univ., St. Louis, Mo. 1979-85; UC Davis 1985–; awards: Nat, Coll. Dist. Attys. Disting. Faculty 1978, Nat. Assn. Criminal Defense Lawyers Pres.'s award 1983; mem: Am. Acad. Forensic Scis., Am. Bar Assn., Nat. Assn. Criminal Defense Lawyers; coauthor: Dynamics of Trial Practice, 2d edit., 1995, Calif. Evidentiary Founds., 2d edit., 1995, Scientific Evidence, 2d edit., 1993, author Uncharged Misconduct Evidence, 1984; mil: capt. AUS 1970-74; Democrat; Cath.; rec: jogging. Res: 2204 Shenandoah Pl Davis 95616 Ofc: University of California School of Law Davis 95616-5201

INAMA, CHRISTOPHER R., lawyer; b. April 4, 1952, Burbank; s. Leo H. Inama and Jeanne M. (Bauer) Truax; m. Monica L. Medina (div.); m. Colleen J. Deal, Dec. 30, 1986; edn: BA political sci., UCSB 1974; JD, UCSF Hastings Coll. of Law 1977; admitted St. Bar Calif. 1977. Career: atty. sole practice, San Carlos 1977–; chief of security San Francisco Giants, 1989–; mem: Calif. St. Bar Assn., San Mateo Co. Bar Assn., San Mateo Co. Pvt. Defender Program, Native Sons Golden West (1st v.p. 1989), Hastings Alumni Assn., UCSB Alumni Assn., Sigma Pi; contbr. Drunk Driving: Trial Source Book, 1985; mil: U.S. Coast Guard Reserve 1987; Libertarian; Cath. Ofc: C.R. Inama 790 Laurel St San Carlos 94070

INCORVAIA, JOEL LEE, lawyer; b. March 12, 1954, Whittier; s. Joseph Vincent and Nellie Nancy (Tenenblum) I.; m. Cynthia Diane Pedersen, Sept. 28, 1980; children: Meghan b. 1983, Kirsten b. 1986, Joseph b. 1991; edn: BA, UCSB 1976; JD, Univ. San Diego 1979; admitted St. Bar Calif. (1979). Career: atty., ptnr. Incorvaia and Glancy, San Diego 1979–; mem: San Diego Bar Assn. (chmn. real property com. 1984), San Diego Co. Trial Lawyers Assn., Mortgage Bankers Assn. Am., Bldg. Industry Assn.; article pub. in profl. jour. (1979); Presbyterian; rec: golf, jogging. Ofc: Incorvaia & Glancy 12626 High Bluff Pl #325 San Diego 92130

INFANTE, DONALD RICHARD, electronics executive, major general (retired); b. Youngstown, Ohio, May 2, 1937; s. Michael and Fannie Susan (Felice) I.; m. Norma Jean Barchie, May 9, 1959; children: Dean Michael, Renee Louise; edn: BS Youngstown State Univ. 1958; D Mil. Sci. 1986; MS Ops. Res. Rensselaer Polytechnic Inst. 1969. Career: commd. 2d lt. U.S. Army 1959, advanced through grades to maj gen. 1986, num. mgmt. positions, 1959-

79; commanding ofcr. 69th Air Def. Brigade U.S. Army, Wurzberg, Fed. Republic Germany 1979- 82; dep., comdg. gen. 32nd Army Air Def. Commd. U.S. Army, Darmstadt, Fed. Republic Germany 1982-83; proj. mgr. Patriot Proj. Ofc. U.S Army, Redstone Arsenal, Ala. 1983-85, proj. mgr. Air Def. Proj. Ofc. 1985; comdg. gen. U.S. Army, Fort Bliss, El Paso, Tex. 1985-89 (ret.); asst. div. mgr. defense electronics systems Hughes Aircraft Co., Fullerton, Calif. 1989-93, div. mgr. 1993–; bd. dirs. U K Systems Ltd., London; mem. Hughes Aircraft Air Def. Adv. Council., Westchester, Calif., 1990–; mem: Pres. Kilmer PTA, Vienna, Va., 1970-73, Fairfax County Parents of Spl. Children's Assn., Fairfax, Va., 1972-73; bd. dirs. Armed Svs. YMCA, Fort Bliss, 1985-89; awards: Decorated Legion of Merit, U.S. Army (1975, 79), Disting. Svc. medal Pentagon, Washington 1989; recipient Vol. of Yr. award Nat. Armed Svs. YMCA Chgo. 1988, Key to City awards Youngstown City Council. 1989, El Paso City Council. 1989; mem: VFW, Def. Preparedness Assn., Assn. of U.S. Army (Cert. achievement 1989); contbr. articles to profl. jours.; Republican; R. Cath. Res: 7720 E Doheny Ct Anaheim 92808-2100 Ofc: Hughes Aircraft Co. PO Box 3310 Bldg. 676/D313 Fullerton 92634-3310

INGERSOLL, ANDREW PERRY, planetary science educator; b. Chgo., Jan. 2, 1940; s. Jeremiah Crary and Minneola (Perry) I.; m. Sarah Morin, Aug. 27, 1961; children: Jeremiah, Ruth Ingersoll Wood, Marion, Minneola, George; edn: BA Amherst Coll. 1960; PhD Harvard U. 1965. Career: res. fellow Harvard Univ., Cambridge, MA 1965-66; mem. staff summer study prog. Woods Hole (Mass.) Oceanographic Inst. (1965, 70-73, 1976, 80, 92); asst. prof. Calif. Inst. Tech., Pasadena 1966-71, assoc. prof. 1971-76, prof. 1976–; prin. investigator Pioneer Saturn Infrared Radiometer Team, NASA; mem. Voyager Imaging Team, NASA, Cassini Imaging Team; interdisciplinary scientist, Mars Observer Project, Galileo Project, NASA; bd. trustee Poly. Sch., Pasadena; AAAS (fellow), Am. Geophys. Union (fellow); mem. Am. Astron. Soc. (vice chmn. div. planetary sci. 1988-89, chmn. 1989-90). Ofc: Calif. Inst. Tech 170-25 Pasadena CA 91125

INGERSOLL, JOHN GREGORY, physicist, energy specialist, educator; b. Athens, Greece, July 25, 1948; came to U.S. 1971; s. Gregory and Catherine (Astetis) I., m. Sally Lynn Roberts, Apr. 7, 1984; edn: BS Nat. Tech. Univ. Athens, 1970; MS Syracuse Univ. 1973; PhD Univ. Calif., Berkeley. 1978. Career: instr. physics Univ. Calif. 1974-75; res. asst. Lawrence Berkeley Lab. 1975-77, from asst. res. prof. to assoc. res. prof. Lawrence Berkeley Lab. 1978-82; sr. staff scientist Hughes Aircraft Co., Los Angeles 1983–; staff mem., adv. USN Energy Office, Washington 1988–; cons. Calif. Energy Commn., Sacramento 1981-82; U.S. Dept. Energy, Washington 1981-83; Bldg. Industry, N.Y. and Calif. 1982–; prin. investigator Energy Tech. Group UCLA 1983–; mem. tech. team for devel. of a comml. passenger electric vehicle GM 1990–; awards: Recipient 2d Pl. award Edison Electric Inst., Gen. Motors, and Dept. Energy 1993; fellow Democritus Nuclear Res. Ctr., Athens 1970, Syracuse Univ. 1972, Rockefeller Found. 1974; mem: Rep. Profl. Task Force, Calif., 1981-83, mem. GM team (tasked with develop., prod., mktg. of passenger electric vehicle); contbr. 70+ articles on nuclear sci., renewable energy sources, indoor air quality, efficient utilization of energy in bldgs., passive solar systems and solar elec. energy to profl. jours.; contbg. author to 3 books on energy mgmt. in bldgs.; patentee heat pipe devels., non- freon low power air conditioner for electric vehicles and busses; mil: lt. USNR; Presbyterian. Res: 21315 Lighthill Dr Topanga 90290-9715 Ofc: Hughes Aircraft Co. PO Box 902 El Segundo 90245-0902

INGHAM, GEORGE JOSEPH, dentist; b. May 11, 1958, King City; s. George Raymond and Alvira Josephine (Sala) I.; edn: BA summa cum laude, CSU Fresno 1980; DDS, UCSF Sch. Dentistry 1984. Career: pvt. practice gen. dentistry, Greenfield 1985–; honors: Omicron Kappa Upsilon; mem: ADA, Calif. Dental Assn., Monterey Bay Dental Soc., Greenfield Rotary (sec. 1987-89, v.p. 1989-90, pres. 1990-91, 95); rec: wt.lifting, bowling, Spanish, French, softball, sports. Ofc: POB 2448 847 Oak Ave Greenfield 93927

INNIS, DONALD ALWYN, architect; b. Sept. 17, 1931, Olean, N.Y.; s. Alwyn Osman and Greta (Matson) I.; brothers: Jack, Donald, and W. Joe Innis (artist, known internat.); edn: Univ. Ill. 1949-51, Univ. Ariz. 1950; BArch (summa cum laude), UC Berkeley, 1961; m. Virginia Maples, July 5, 1962; children: Christina b. 1966 (BA UCB 1988, MFA in film prodn. Cal Arts, Valencia 1991, prodn. coord. ABC-TV "America's Funniest Home Video TV Show in Am." 1990, apprentice film editor "JFK"), Donald Jr. b. 1967, Cynthia b. 1969 (artist, sculptor, BA magna cum laude, UC Berkeley, 1991); Career: chief design architect Paderewski Dean & Assoc., San Diego 1961-65; prin. architect Donald Innis & Assoc. 1965-67; pres. Innis Tennebaum 1967–; bd. dirs. Fin. Fed. Credit Union 1989–; bd. dirs. Float, Inc. 1992–; speaker Univ. Hawaii conf. on Large Floating Sturctures (4/91), S.D. Fine Art Mus. on "Future of San Diego" (91); proposed concept of floating airports offshore (1970s–), full page story in San Diego Union newspaper edn. dept. sect. Quest for Learning, 6/24/91; designer San Diego Lindburgh air terminal (1964), architect Flower Hill Shopping Center (1979), Broadway Pier (1975), San Diego Embarcadero (1975, 83); honors: Phi Beta Kappa; mem: Am. Soc. Mil. Engrs. (sustaining), Nat. Arch. Registration Bd., Soc. Am. Reg. Architects, Central City Assn. (bd. dirs. 1976–), San Diego Yacht Club; mil: ACS 1956-58; Republican; rec: sailing. Ofc: Innis Tennebaum 1400 5th Ave Ste 400 San Diego 92101

IRELAND, JERRY MEADE, marketing executive; b. Oct. 19, 1944, Cody, Wyo.; s. Earl Strawn and Mary Mildred (Warren) I.; m. Corinda Miriam Barbour, April 14, 1979; 1 son, Fraser b. 1981; edn: BS, Tufts Univ. 1966; MBA, Stanford Univ. 1971. Career: asst brand mgr. Clorox Co., Oakland 1971-74; product mgr. Holubar Mountaineering, Boulder, Colo. 1975; mktg. cons., Oakland 1976-77; account supr. Hoefer Dieterich & Brown, San Francisco 1977-79; gen. mgr. Levi Strauss & Co. 1979-87; dir. Landor Assoc. 1988-90; mgr. new bus. devel., Pacific Bell 1992–; awards: Direct Mktg. Assn. Echo 1987; article pub. in profl. jour., 1987; mil: 1st lt. AUS 1966-69; Episcopalian; rec: backpacking. Address: Orinda 94563

IRELAND, MARILYN JEAN, law professor; b. March 4, 1943, Mariemount, Ohio; d. Carl Mathew and Fern Alta (Helfrich) Schleue; children: Tera b. 1968, Deron b. 1970; edn: Univ. Va. 1964-66; BA, Miami Univ. 1966; JD, Univ. Chgo. 1969; admitted St. Bars. Ill. (1969), Mo. (1975). Career: atty. Friedmen & Koven, Chgo., Ill. 1969-71; Fortas & Koven, Wash. D.C. 1970-71; asst. prof. law Wash. Univ., St. Louis, Mo. 1971-78, assoc. dean 1972-74; assoc. prof. law Calif. Western Law Sch., San Diego 1979-81, prof. law 1981–; vis. prof. law Univ. San Diego 1989-90; instr. San Diego St. Univ. 1988-90, 93; honors: Order of Coif, Phi Beta Kappa, Susan B. Anthony Woman of Yr., San Diego 1990; past chair and mem: AALS (sect. of women law tchrs.), Fed. Women Lawyers Judicial Selection Panel; bd. dirs. and treas., Diversionary Theatre 1994–; contbr. to legal periodicals. Res: 2004 Cardinal Dr San Diego 92123 Ofc: California Western School of Law 340 Cedar St San Diego 92123

IRELL, LAWRENCE ELLIOTT, lawyer; b. Mar. 23, 1912, Boston, Mass.; s. Hyman and Bessie (Shain) Israel; m. Elaine Smith, 1939; children: Stephen Charles b. 1942, Eugene Harvey b. 1945, Lauren Catherine b. 1946; edn: BA, UC Los Angeles 1932; LLB, USC Law Sch. 1935; LLM, Harvard Law Sch. 1936; admitted Calif. bar (1936). Career: senior ptnr. Law Firm of Irell & Manella, Los Angeles 1949-93 (ret.); instr., income taxation of trusts and estates, USC Law Center 1951-54, lectr. USC Tax Inst. 1950, 55, 59, 61, 64; honors: USC Alumni Award Scholastic Honors 1935, Order of the Coif, editl. bd. Law Rev. 1933-35, recipient UCLA Alumni Assn. Edward A. Dickson Alumnus of Year achieve. award 1979 and UCLA Alumni Profl. achieve. award 1971, Am. Jewish Com. Human Relations Award, L.A. Chpt. 1978; mem: ABA (Sect. of Taxation 1949, Corp., Banking & Bus. Law Sect. 1963), Beverly Hills Bar Assn. (bd. govs. 1963-72, pres. 1969, del. annual conf. state bar 1960, 62-68, 70-71, 74, chmn. taxation com. 1954-60), L.A. County Bar Assn. (bd. trustees 1971-72), Harvard Law Sch. Assn. (Nat. Council 1964-65), UCLA Found. Bd. Trustees (1967–, chmn. 1975-78, pres. 1971-75, gen. counsel 1967-71, chmn. grants & allocations com. 1978-85, dir. Charitable Fund 1978, chmn. 1978-80), UCLA Bd. Visitors (founding chair 1990-92), UCLA Chancellor's Assocs. (life), UCLA Order of Blue Shield Soc. (life); civic: Jewish Fedn. Council of Gr. L.A. (dir. 1938-41, 48-54, 58-66, 67-73, 75–, pres. 1980-82, pres. Jr. Div. 1937-41), Jewish Comm. Found. of Jewish Fedn. L.A. (pres. 1967-69, trustee 1964–), Council of Jewish Fedns. Inc. (dir. 1960-84, nat. v.p. 1967-70, 82-84, chmn. W. Reg. 1966-79), Am. Jewish Com. (nat. exec. council 1972-76, exec. bd. So. Calif. Chpt. 1967-82, 89-91, v. chmn. 1980-82), Constl. Rights Found. (dir. 1969-73), Hope for Hearing Research Found. (trustee 1959–), Metro. Rec. & Youth Services Plnng. Council (pres. 1963-66, dir. 1969-73), Jewish Ctrs. Assn. L.A. (pres. 1956-59, dir. 1943–), Nat. Jewish Welfare Bd. (dir. 1953-64, pres. W. Reg. 1953-55), Reiss-Davis Child Study Ctr. (dir. 1951-58, v.p. 1955-58), United Way (chmn. L.A. West div. 1966-67), United Way (corp. bd. dirs. 1987, corp. exec. com. 1987). Ofc: 1800 Ave of the Stars Ste 900 Los Angeles 90067-4201

IRICK, ROBERT LEE, educational and business executive; b. Aug. 14, 1930, Competition, Mo.; s. Melvin Hollege and Delphia Ruth (Handley) Irick Tyre; edn: BA, Southwest Mo. State Univ. 1955; cert. Yale Ins. of F.E. Languages, 1951-52; MA, Harvard Univ. 1958, PhD, 1971; Cert, Stanford Univ. 1978. Career: v.p., mng. dir. Chinese Materials and Research Aids Service Ctr. Inc., Taipei 1964-74; gen. mgr. Taiwan Enterprises Co. Ltd., Taipei 1970-88; res. dir. Calif. State Internat. Programs, Taipei 1966-91; resident facilitator Friends World Program, Long Island Univ., 1989-95; adv. Govt. Information Ofc., Exec. Yuan, Republic of China 1993–; columnist China News, Taipei 1993–; bd. dirs. Found. for Scholarly Exchange 1992-; pres. Chinese Materials Center, Hong Kong 1978-88; pres. Chinese Materials Center Publications, San Francisco 1982-93; pres. and gen. mgr. Chinese Materials Center, Taipei 1988-93; rep. The Hannaford Co. Inc. 1983-89; v.p. Sen Bin Chemical Industries Corp. 1985-88; v.p. Consul Chemical Industries Corp., 1988–; instr. Yale Univ. 1957; adj. prof., assoc. prof., prof. Nat. Chengchi Univ. 1976-79, Nat. Chengkung Univ. 1974-75, adj. prof. Nat. Taiwan Univ. 1982-83; advisor and mem. Chinese Nat. Fedn. of Industries, Nat. Anti-Counterfeiting Com. 1985-89, Intellectual Property Protection Com. 1989–, Internat. Affairs Com. 1994–; secty. Advy. Bd. Sino-Am. Comm. Workshop on Cooperation in Scis. and Humanities, Taipei 1965-71; hon. dir. World-Wide Ethical Soc. 1981–; honors: Boys Nation, Lebanon H. Sch. No. 1 grad., Debate Letter 1951, Who's Who Among Students in Am. Colls. and Univs. 1955, Internat. Who's Who in Edn., Men of Achievement, Who's Who in World, Internat. Directory of Scholars & Splsts. in Third World, Who's Who in Library and Info. Services, Directory of Am.

Scholars, Internat. Book of Honor; mem: General Soc. of Mayflower Descendants, Sons of Am. Revolution, Am. C.of C. (bd. govs., chmn. intellectual prop. & licensing, chmn. APCAC liaison com.), Asia-Pacific Council of Am. Chambers of Commerce (chmn. 1992-93, v. chmn. intellectual prop. com. 1990-92), Harvard Club of Taipei (past pres.), Am. Univ. Club Taipei (dir.), Internat. House of Taipei (dir.), Amvets Free China Post 1 (1st v. comdr.), Republicans Abroad/ Taiwan (sr. advisor), Assn. for Asian Studies Inc., Ann Arbor (Com. on East Asian Libraries), Chinese Language Tchrs. Assn., Kappa Alpha Order No. 1, Pres.'s Club Southwest Mo. State Univ. (1950-51), Smithsonian Assn.; num. publs. incl. 50th Annual edition SMSU Ozarko; mil: t/sgt. USAF 1951-55, Commendn.; Republican; Seventh-Day Adventist; rec: collect cookbooks. Res: 335 Shields St San Francisco 94132

IRWIN, CHARLES EDWIN, JR., physician; b. Dec. 15, 1945, Medford, Mass.; s. Charles Edwin and Molly Esther (Rosenberg) I.; m. Nancie Noe Kester, Apr. 21, 1979; 1 son, Seth Charles b. 1988; edn: BS, Hobart Coll. 1967; BMS, Dartmouth Med. Sch. 1969; MD, UCSF 1971. Career: intern, resident UCSF Med. Center 1971-74, clin. scholar 1974-77, asst. prof. pediatrics 1977-84, assoc. prof. 1984-90, prof. of pediatrics 1990–, dir. div. of adolescent medicine 1980–, dir. Nat. Adolescent Health Info. Ctr. 1994–; vis. prof. Univ. Gothenberg 1988; editorial bd. Jour. Adolescent Health 1980–; editorial bd. Pediatrician 1984–; awards: Soc. Adolescent Medicine Disting. Scholar 1984, Nat. Center Youth Law Disting. Researcher 1988; mem: Soc. Adolescent Medicine (exec. com. 1985-88), Am. Acad. Pediatrics (exec. com., sect. adolescent health 1982-85), Soc. Pediatric Research, Soc. Research Child Devel., Am. Pediatric Soc., Am. Bd. Pediatrics (chair, sub board adolescent medicine); ed. Adolescent Social Behavior & Health 1988; assoc. ed. Pediatrics (Rudolph 1991); Prot.; rec: skiing. Res: 401 Vermont Ave Berkeley 94707 Ofc: University of California Medical Center 400 Parnassus Ave San Francisco 94143

ISENBERG, DAVID EVIN, lawyer; b. June 21, 1960, Los Angeles; s. Edwin and Susan Gay (Ehrenberg) I.; edn: BA, UCLA 1983; JD, UCLA Law Sch. 1986; admitted St. Bar Calif. 1986. Career: atty., assoc. Sheppard Mullin Richter & Hampton, Los Angeles 1986–; mem: Am. Bar Assn., L.A. Co. Bar Assn., Fin. Lawyers Conf., L.A. Athletic Club. Ofc: Sheppard Mullin Richter & Hampton 333 S Hope St 48th Floor Los Angeles 90071

ISHII, ROBERT FRANK, real estate development executive; b. Aug. 26, 1956, Albuquerque, N.M.; s. Edward Frank and Rose K. (Matsunami) I.; m. Donna Marie Chun, Aug. 15, 1981; children: Taylor b. 1986, Spenser b. 1989, Chase b. 1991, Larson b. 1993; edn: BSBA, Univ. Neb. 1982. Career: asst. treas. Centennial Beneficial Corp., Orange 1984-87; exec. v.p., chief operating ofcr. Centennial Group, Inc., Orange 1984-94; exec. v.p., chief operating ofcr. Centennial Corp. 1993-94; asst. dir. Cathedral Mortgage Co., Costa Mesa 1983-84; auditor Avco Corp., Newport Beach 1982-83; branch mgr. Avco Fin. Service, Omaha, Neb. and Council Bluffs, Iowa 1978-82; awards: Pres. Nixon letter of commend. 1974; Christian. Ofc: 22751 Corralejo Mission Viejo 92692-1321

ISHII, ROY T., physician, pediatrician; b. Mar. 29, 1942, Honolulu, Hawaii; s. Cyrus K. and Bessie A. (Tanimoto) I.; m. Gayle F. Fink, Mar. 17, 1973; children: Nichole b. 1979, Andrea b. 1980; edn: BS, Purdue Univ. 1964; MD, UCSF 1968. Career: Lodi Pediatrics, Lodi; mem at large Am. Acad. Pediatrics 1988-89; mem: CMA, AMA; mil: major USAF 1971-73; Republican; Baptist; rec: painting, gardening, fishing, golf. Res: 1224 Midvale Rd Lodi 95240 Ofc: Lodi Pediatrics 900 S Fairmont Ave Ste A Lodi 95240

ISHLER, MICHAEL WILLIAM, structural engineer; b. Dec. 21, 1952, Cleveland; s. William Edward and Elizabeth (Swift) I.; m. Kathleen Ann Abell, Sept. 6, 1975; children: Stephanie Ann, Matthew Scott; edn: BArch, Univ. Cinti., 1977, MS, 1979; SM, M.I.T. 1981. Career: senior engr. Owens Corning Fiberglas, Toledo and Granville, Ohio, 1981-86; assoc. Ove Arup & Ptnrs., London, England 1987-88, L.A., Calif. 1988-93; Ishler Design & Engineering Assocs. 1993–; mem: ASCE (Toledo chpt. sec. treas. 1983-85, Outstanding Engr. 1985), Structural Engrs. So. Calif., Alpha Rho Chi; inventor Double hexagonal mesh air supported fabric roof structure (1985), Parallel compression ring fabric roof structure (1986); Christian. Res: 2314 Pearl St Santa Monica 90405

ISPAHANI, AHMED S., professor of economics; b. Jan. 11, 1935; edn: BA econ., Univ. Karachi Pakistan 1959; MA, USC, 1962; PhD, USC, 1965. Career: asst. prof. econn. Univ. Laverne 1964–; econ. advisor govt. of Iran, Central Bank of Iran, Teheran 1968-69; assoc. prof. econ. Univ. Laverne 1969-71; economist Battelle Labs., Columbus Ohio and Teheran 1971-72; head of research and project devel. Govt. of Iran 1972-76; mem: Am. Econ. Assn. Ofc: School of Business/Economics University of Laverne 1950 3rd St Laverne 91750

IVERSON, LEIGH I. G., cardiothoracic surgeon; b. June 3, 1941, LaCrosse, Wis.; s. Carl H. and Esther E. (Larson) I.; m. Mary E. Bachman, April 25, 1970; children: Leisel b. 1973, Rachael b. 1976, Sarah b. 1979; edn: BA, St. Olaf Coll. 1963; MD, Univ. Wis. 1967; lic. Bd. Thoracic Surgery 1976. Career: cardiothoracic surgeon, Oakland 1975–; mem: Am. Coll. of Surgeons, Am. Coll. Cardiology, Am. Assn. for Thoracic Surgery, Soc. Thoracic Surgeons, Western

Thoracic Surgical Assn., Denton A. Cooley Cardiovascular Surgical Soc.; contbr. articles in J. Heart Transpl., Amer. J. Surg., Ann. Thor. Surg., J. Thor. & Cardiovasc. Surg., 1977. Res: 326 El Cerrito Ave Piedmont 94611 Ofc: 365 Hawthorne Ave Ste 301 Oakland 94609

IWASAKI, RONALD SEIJI, insurance claims manager; b. Dec. 10, 1947, Los Angeles; s. Joe Sotowo and Helen Tomiko (Yamaura) I.; m. Elaine Ida Mandel, Jan. 4, 1982; edn: BA in hist., CSU Long Beach, 1970; gen. ins. pgm. Ins. Inst. of Am., 1986; legal principles, Am. Ednl. Inst., 1990; desig: Assoc. in Claims, Ins. Inst. of Am., 1990, Grad. in Claims Adminstrn., Farmers Ins., 1990. Career: mgmt. trainee Goodyear Tire & Rubber Co. 1972, retail sails mgr. Goodyear Service Center, Wilmington 1972-73, store mgr. 1973-76, Goodyear Service Center, Wilmington and Los Angeles; claims trainee, field claims rep., sr. field claims rep. Farmers Ins. Group, Pasadena 1976-80, br. claims supr., cons. instr. 1980-82; br. claims mgr. Farmers Ins. Group, Long Beach 1982–, special claims mgr. 1991–; awards: sales achievement Goodyear Tire & Rubber Co. (1973, 74, 75), recipient profl. awards Farmers Ins. (1985, 86, 88, 90, 93, 94); honors: listed Who's Who in Fin. and Industry 1996, Who's Who Among Asian Americans 1994, Internat. Directory of Disting. Leadership 1990, Community Leaders of Am. 1991; mem: Japanese Am. Nat. Museum 1993; Republican; rec: reading, music, fishing, dancing, biking, Civil War buff. Ofc: Farmers Insurance Group PO Box 4748 Long Beach 90804

JACKS, BRIAN PAUL, physician, psychiatrist; b. May 23, 1943, Regina, Sask., Canada; came to U.S. 1968; s. Dr. Nathan Benjamin and Ida (Nathanson) J.; m. Carole Ann Marks, June 1968 (div. 1973); children: Erica b. 1974; m. Brooke Ann Foland, Nov. 14, 1976 (div. 1992); m. Nicole T. Jones, Apr. 11, 1993; edn: MD, Univ. Toronto, 1967; Canadian Med. Bds. 1967, Calif. Med. Bds. 1968, Am. Bd. Psychiatry and Neurology, Adult 1974, Child/ Adolescent 76. Career: intern Vancouver (B.C.) Gen. Hosp., 1967-68; resident gen. psychiatry, L.A. County- Univ. So. Calif. Med. Ctr., L.A. 1968-70, child psychiatry, 1970-72, chief resident child psychiatry 1971-72; asst. dir. child/adol. psychiatry outpatient svs. LAC-USC Med. Ctr., 1972-76, ward chief long-term adol. inpatient svs., 1976-79; also faculty USC Sch. of Med. 1972–, assoc. clin. prof. psychiatry USC, 1976–; pvt. practice f.t., 1979–; expert witness Calif. State Bar Assn., 1980–; indep. med. examiner Calif. St. Dept. Indsl. Relations, 1981–, qualified med. evaluator (QME), Div. of Workers' Compensation, examiner Nat. Bds. in Child/Adol. Psychiatry, 1991–; mem: Am. Acad. Child Psychiatry (Fellow 1979), Am. Psychiatric Assn., Am. Soc. Adol. Psychiatry, So. Calif. Psychiatric Soc. (chmn. com. child/adol. psychiat. 1988), So. Calif. Soc. for Child Psychiatry (com. peer rev. 1985-89, exec. coun., pres. 1982-83), So. Calif. Soc. for Adolescent Psychiatry (exec. com. pres. 1983-84), USC Psychiatric Alumni in Cont. Edn., Calif. Soc. Indsl. Medicine, AMA; lectr. on behavioral modification before numerous groups incl. child and sch. psychologists, student nurses, sch. teachers, sch. and drug counselors, social workers, police and probation ofcrs., students and parents; contbr. chapters in med. books. Ofc: 462 N Linden Ste 254 Beverly Hills 90212 also 5500 Telegraph Rd #175 Ventura 93003

JACKSON, CYNTHIA LEE, lawyer; b. May 6, 1954, Houston, Tx.; d. Richard H. and Bobbette Lorraine (Burke) Jackson; m. Guy Tolomeo, Dec. 31, 1994; children: Richard b. 1986, Matthew Raymond b. 1988, Madeline b. 1989, Sebastian b. 1994; edn: BA w. hons., Stanford Univ. 1976; JD w. hons., Univ. Tx. Law Sch. Austin 1979. Career: atty. Morrison & Foerster, San Francisco 1979-83; ptnr. Heller Ehrman et al 1983–. Ofc: Heller Ehrman et al 525 University Ave Palo Alto 94301

JACKSON, DURWARD P., educator; b. April 12, 1940, Hartsville, S.C.; s. Erby L. and Sue (Duffee) J.; m. Sandra Wright, Sept. 27, 1967 (div. 1976); m. Alice Renfroe, June 8, 1984; edn: BS aerospace engring., Univ. Ariz. 1964; MS engring. adminstrn., Univ. Utah 1969; MBA, Golden Gate Univ. 1978; PhD, Claremont Grad. Sch. 1983. Career: cons. Touche Ross & Co., Denver, Colo. 1969-71; owner, cons. DataPhase Inc., Park City, Utah 1971-76; computer splst. USAF, Edwards AFB 1976-81; indep. cons. 1981–; prof. CSU Los Angeles 1981–; dir. Atelope Valley E. Kern Water Agency, Quartz Hill 1984; lectr. Sinopec, Liaoyang, China 1987; mil: capt. USAF 1961-68; Republican; rec: skiing, travel. Ofc: Dept. Information Systems, California State University Los Angeles 90032

JACKSON, JEWEL A., state youth correctional program manager, retired; b. June 3, 1942, Shreveport, La.; d. Willie Burghardt and Bernice Jewel (Mayberry) Norton; m. Edward James Norman, May 17, 1961 (div. 1968); children: Steven, June Kelly; m. Wilbert Jackson, Apr. 6, 1969; children: Michael, Anthony. Career: with Calif. Youth Authority, 1965–, group supr., San Andreas and Santa Rosa, 1965-67, youth counselor, Ventura 1967-78, senior youth counselor, Stockton 1978-81, treatment team supr., program mgr., Whittier and Ione, 1981-91; owner/exec. dir. Valley Paralegal Services, Stockton 1992–; mem. Stockton Women's Network 1993–; past mem: Women in Crim. Justice (co-chair 1974-76), Assn. Black Correctional Workers (chpt. v.p. 1979, newsletter editor 1978-80); rec: equestrienne, literature, writing poetry and short stories, designing clothes. Res: 2416 Hall Ave Stockton 95205

JACKSON, JOHN HOWARD, physician; b. June 30, 1951, Columbia, Mo.; s. Albert Howard and Jeanette Elizabeth (Hennessee) J.; m. Annette Yangwon Park, June 14, 1975; children: Rebecca b. 1981, Elizabeth b. 1984; edn: BS chemistry, UCLA 1972; MD, George Washington Univ. 1980. Career: intern, resident, internal medicine UCLA 1980-83; pvt. practice, Crescent City Internal Medicine, Crescent City 1983-93, Santa Cruz Medical Clinic 1993–; med. dir. internal medicine Seaside Hosp. 1984-85, med. dir. cardiopulmonary dept. 1985-90; chief med. staff Sutter Coast Hosp. 1985-87, 1990-92; chmn. profl. review com. Seaside Hosp. 1984-85; honors: Alpha Omega Alpha; mem: F.A.C.P., Rotary; Republican; Christian; rec: flying, genealogy, archaeology. Res: 2621 Willowbrook Lane #105 Aptos 95003 Ofc: Santa Cruz Medical Clinic 2025 Soquel Avenue Santa Cruz 95062

JACKSON, JOSEPH BRIAN, physician; b. Dec. 23, 1946, Brunswick, Ga.; s. Joseph A. and Maxine (Ross) J.; m. Cathleen Ann Goddard, Feb. 12, 1969 (div. 1981); children: Tracy Rene b. 1972, Brian Eric b. 1975; edn: BS chem., San Diego State Univ., 1969; MD, Loma Linda Univ., 1973. Career: criminalist San Bernardino Sheriffs Crime Lab, San Bdo., 1969-70; intern Santa Clara Valley Med. Ctr., San Jose 1973-74; emergency physician Sharp Cabrillo Hosp., San Diego 1975-82, dep. director emergency svs. 1980-82; medical dir. East County Community Clinic, El Cajon 1982-91; pvt. family practice, San Diego, 1984-88, Ramona, 1991-92; staff physician Logan Heights Family Health Ctr., San Diego 1991-93; chief adult med. Logan Heights Family Health Ctr. 1992–; honors: Nat. Merit Scholar 1964; mem. Am. Coll. of Emergency Physicians 1975-82; rec: art, music. Ofc: 1809 National Ave San Diego 92113

JACKSON, MICHELE CHICKERELLA, lawyer; b. Jan. 17, 1954, Redwood City; d. Joseph Anthony and Enessa (Mandy) Chickerella; m. Warren Bruce Jackson, Aug. 14, 1976; children: Olivia Rose, Kirk Geoffrey; edn: BA hons., econ., Stanford Univ. 1976; JD cum laude, Univ. San Francisco 1979; admitted U.S. Supreme Ct. 1988, Ct. Appeals 9th Circuit 1981, U.S. Dist. Ct. No. Dist. 1979, Central Dist. 1985, St. Bar Calif. 1979. Career: extern Hon. Wiley Manuel, Calif. Supreme Ct., San Francisco 1978; atty., assoc. Furth Fahrner Bluemle & Mason 1980-86, ptnr. Furth, Fahrner & Mason 1987–; awards: St. Bar Calif. Bd. Govs. award 1984; mem: San Francisco Bar Assn.; Am. Bar Assn.; rec: hiking, travel. Ofc: Furth Fahrner & Mason 201 Sansome Ste 1000 San Francisco 94104

JACKSON, ROBERT CHARLES, research engineer, teacher, manufacturer, writer's mentor; b. Sept. 17, 1911, Lima, Oh.; s. Earl Arthur and Letha Mary (Sprague) J.; Gr. Grandfather invented "Neats Foot Oil"; m. Katharine Adams, 1934 (dec. Nov. 22, 1986); children: Marjorie Ellen b. 1938, Lawrence Adam b. 1942; edn: BSEE, Purdue Univ., 1933; tchg. cred., Redlands Univ. 1939; grad. study in edn., USC, 1945. Career: tchr. jr. high sch. and adult edn. Riverside and San Bernardino pub. schs. 1939-42; research engr., torpedo water entry res., CalTech, 1943-45; ptnr. De Vel Industries (devel. and mfd. first Elec. Constrn. Kit; 1st Transparent Lid for comml. ice cream cabinet displays), Pasadena 1946-50; ops. mgr. navy pgm. Submarine Albacore Hydrodynamics Pgm., CalTech, 1950-53; sales mgr. Multiband Ham Antenna, Antenna Engring. Corp., Los Angeles 1954-55; tech. splst., Mark 46 Torpedo, Snap 8 space power plant, Aerojet Gen. Corp., Azusa, 1955-68; pres./gen. mgr. Dynafoam, Inc. (foamed aluminum machine shop) Azusa and Pasadena, 1969–; cons. engr.; awards: Office of Sci. Res. & Devel., WWII 1945, Ramona Radio Club HAM of Yr. 1961, AerojetToastmasters Effective Communicator award 1964; mem: NEA/Calif. Tchrs. Assn. 1939-42, Armed Forces Comms. & Electronic Assn. 1960; civic: BSA (scoutmaster 1935-38), Pasadena Lions Club 1943-46, Toastmasters Intl. 1947-75 (then Pastmasters); former radio amateur K6GWH (Gee Whillakers Hallelujah); publs: tech. papers and reports in field; rec: flowers. Res: 1150 S El Molino Ave Pasadena 91106

JACOBS, CHARLOTTE D., physician, associate professor of medicine, dean of medical education; b. Jan. 27, 1946, Oakridge, Tenn.; d. George and Lucille De Crops; edn: BA, Univ. of Rochester, Rochester, NY 1968; MD, Wash. Univ., St. Louis, Mo. 1972. Career: dir. Oncology Day Care Ctr., Stanford Medical Sch., 1977-90; dean of edns., Stanford Med. Sch. 1990–, assoc. prof. of medicine 1992–; awards: Kaiser Award for outstanding contributions to med. edn., Stanford Univ. Med. Sch. 1986, Rambar Award for excellence in patient care 1990, Kaiser Award for excellence in teaching 1991; Hofsommer Award for academic achievement, Wash. Univ. Med. Sch. 1993; mem: Physicians for Social Responsibility 1990–, Am. Soc. Head and Neck Surgery 1990–, Am. Ednl. Res. Assn. 1992–, Am. Soc. of Clinical Oncology (exec. bd.) 1992-95; author: over 60 papers pub. on head and neck cancer; editor: several books on head and neck cancer. Address: Stanford

JACOBS, HERBERT HOWARD, investor, executive, developer; b. March 23, 1923, Freeport, N.Y.; s. Murray Lawrence and Anna (Deutsch) J.; m. Blanche Goldman, Jan. 26, 1947; children: Lynne b. 1949, Janis b. 1954, Neil b. 1956, Nancy b. 1958; edn: BSChE, Cornell Univ. 1944; MS engring., Columbia Univ. 1947; PhD, 1955. Career: assoc. Dunlap & Assoc. Inc., N.Y.C. 1949-53, v.p. 1956-62; asst. prof. Columbia Univ., NYC 1953-56; v.p. Hallmark Cards Inc., Kansas City, Mo. 1962-72; pres. April House Inc., Lenexa, Kans. 1972-77; Jacobs Co., La Jolla 1977–; dir. Am. Greetings Corp., Cleveland, Ohio 1982–;

cons. Surgeon Gen. U.S., Bethesda, Md. 1956-63; vis. prof. Waseda Univ., Tokyo, Japan 1958; mem: Ops. Res. Soc. Am. (fellow, founding mem., awarded Lanchester Prize 1956), Inst. Mgmt. Sci. (founding mem.), Joint Engring. Soc. (accred. com. 1966-72), Midwest Res. Inst. (trustee, exec. com. 1965-72); mil: lt.j.g. USNR 1943-46. Res: 1708 Caminito Ardiente La Jolla 92037

JACOBSEN, (ARTHUR) EDWARD, real estate broker; b. Aug. 30, 1921, Missoula, Mont.; s. Arthur Daniel and Ruth Frazier (Davis) J.; m. Dorothy Eleanor Bohn, June 28, 1947; children: Alan b. 1942, Karen b. 1944, Stephen b. 1952, Kristen b. 1957; edn: BA bus. adm., Univ. Redlands, 1943; Calif. lic. R.E. agt. 1950-52, broker 1952–. Career: fed. civil svc. appraiser props. & VA constrn., O.P.A., San Bernardino 1945-50; owner Ed Jacobsen Realtor (commercial, industrial, single fam. brokerage, with 4 br. offices in past) San Bernardino 1950–, involved in land devel., gen. real estate sales, subdivs., comml. sales and leases, prin. in 700+ real props. San Bdo. area; real estate cons. San Bdo. County Schs., Bank Am. Trust Dept. L.A., Univ. Redlands, others; appt. Calif. R.E. subdiv. activities advy. commn. 1967, Hwy. Commn. Air Space Com. 1974-78, bd. dirs. Regional Devel. Commn. 1965-67; mem. Calif. Assn. Realtors (dir. 1951, dir.-at-lg. 1965-67, dir. for life 1968, v.p. 1963, hon. pres. 1983, PAC chair 1985), San Bdo. Valley Bd. Realtors (dir. 12 yrs., pres. 1959, Realtor of Yr. 1957, 69, hon. life mem. 1974, citizen of yr. 1980), San Bdo. Exec. Assn. (charter, bd.), San Bdo. C.of C. (dir. 10 yrs., pres. 1966-67), Rotary San Bdo. (dir. 7 yrs., pres. 1985-86); civic: bd. trustees Del Rosa Sch. (1952-54), chmn. Am. Red Cross Fund Emergency Cpgn. 1968, chmn. San Bdo. Valley Coll. Fund Cpgn. to Build Crafton Hills Coll., bd. of councillors CSU San Bdo. Sch. of Bus., R.E. advy. com. UC Riverside; club: Arrowhead CC; Congregational; rec: golf, travel. Address: PO Box 23097 San Bernardino 92406

JACOBSON, ALBERT HERMAN, JR., educator, industrial and systems engineer; b. Oct. 27, 1917, St. Paul, Minn.; s. Albert Herman and Gertrude (Anderson) J.; m. Elaine Virginia Swanson, June 10, 1960; children: Keith b. 1962, Paul b. 1965; edn: BS indsl. eng. (cum laude), Yale Univ. 1939; SM bus. & engring. admin., MIT, 1952; MS applied physics, Univ. Rochester, 1954; PhD mgmt. engring., Stanford Univ. 1976; reg. profl. engr. Calif. Career: personnel asst. Yale Univ., New Haven, Conn. 1939-40; indsl. engr. RCA, Camden, N.J. 1940-43; electronics prodn. ofcr. BUORD, USN 1943-44; res. insp. of naval material Colonial Radio (Sylvania) 1944-45; naval insp. of ordnance Eastman Kodak Co. 1945-46; chief engr./dir. quality control Naval Ordnance Office, Rochester, N.Y. 1946-57; staff engr., Space Satellite Prog., Eastman Kodak Co. 1957-59; assoc. dean Coll. Engring. & Arch., Penn State Univ., Univ. Park, Pa. 1959-61; v.p., gen. mgr. to pres. Knapic Electro-Physics Co., Palo Alto 1961-62; prof. Coll. of Engring. San Jose State Univ. 1962–; co-founder and coord. Cybernetic Systems grad. pgm. 1968–; indep. cons. Lockheed, Motorola, Santa Fe RR, 20th Century Fox, Aluminium Corp., Banner Container, Sci. Mgmt. Corp., No. Telecom, others, 1962–; honors: Tau Beta Pi, Sigma Xi, MIT Alfred P. Sloan fellowship in exec. devel. 1951-52, Stanford Univ. NSF fellow 1965-66, Eagle Scout 1931, Scouter's Key & Award of Merit BSA Stanford Council 1976; mem: Am. Soc. Engring. Edn., Inst. Indsl. Engrs., Am. Production & Inventory Control Soc. (bd. 1975–), Masons; civic: YMCA (pres. N.Y. state Young Adults Council 1954-55), Mountain View City Personnel Commn. (chmn. 1968-78), Boy Scouts Am. scoutmaster and mem. Council Stanford Area 1970-83, Campus Lutheran Council San Jose State Univ. (chmn. 1981-86), Santa Clara Valley Luth. Parish Council 1991–; publs: Mil. & Civilian Personnel in Naval Adminstrn., 1952, pub. monograph, 1954, R.R. Consolidations & Transp. Policy, 1976, editor: Design & Engring. of Prodn. Systems, 1984; jour. articles; mil: LCDR USNR 1943-46, commendn.; rec: music (orchestra and choir), photog., swimming, tennis, skiing. Res: 1864 Lime Tree Ln Mountain View CA 94040

JACOBSON, EDWIN JAMES, physician; b. June 27, 1947, Chgo.; s. Edwin Julius and Rose Josephine (Jirinec) J.; m. Martha, May 29, 1977; children: Emily b. 1986; edn: MD, UCLA, 1976. Career: medical resident UCLA, Los Angeles 1976-79, chief med. res. 1981-82, attdg. physician, assoc. clin. prof. medicine 1982–; honors: Alpha Omega Alpha (1976); author: Clinical Decisions (1987), Il Processo Nella Diagnosc Medica (1992), 22+ articles (1972–). Ofc: 100 UCLA Medical Plaza H690 Los Angeles 90024

JACOBSON, ERIC MICHAEL, physician; b. April 3, 1947, Milwaukee, Wis.; s. Phillip Gordon and Charlotte (Shapiro) J.; m. Cheryl Sward, Jan. 7, 1978; children: Lauren b. 1984, Sarah b. 1986; edn: BS, Marquette Univ. 1968; MD, Med. Coll. Wisc., 1972. Career: intern Riverside Gen. Hosp., Loma Linda Univ., 1972-73, resident Brown Univ., 1973-76; coordinator/dir. OP Svs. Mental Health Svs. of S.E. Vt., Bellows Falls, Vt. 1976-78; dir. Behavioral Medicine Ctr., Community Hosp. Monterey Peninsula, Monterey, Calif. 1978–; tchg. fellow Brown Univ., Providence, R.I. 1975-76; adj. asst. prof. clin. psychiatry Dartmouth Univ., Hanover, N.H. 1977-78; mem: AMA, Calif. Med. Assn. (chmn. com. on mental health 1989-91, delegate 1991-96), Fellow Am. Psychiatric Assn., Am. Assn. Gen. Hosp. Psychiatrists (councellor 1992-95), Monterey Co. Med. Soc. (pres. 1994-96), No. Calif. Psychiatric Soc. (past pres. Central Coast Counties Chpt.), Alliance for Mentally Ill; contbr. med. jour. articles. Ofc: Behavioral Medicine Center Community Hospital of Monterey Peninsula POB HH Monterey 93942

JACOBSON, JODY ELLEN, pharmacist; b. May 2, 1955, Boston, Mass.; d. Stanley Irwin and Marcia Grace Jacobson; edn: BS pharm., Univ. Ariz. Tucson 1977; Cornell Univ. 1972; lic. pharmacist Calif. 1977, Ariz. 1977. Career: pharmacist UCLA Med. Center, Los Angeles 1979-94; sr. pharmacist UCI Med. Ctr 1994–; asst. clin. prof., UCLA and UCSF 1995–; recipient UCLA Special Achievement Award (1989, 90, 92); mem: Calif. Soc. Hosp. Pharmacists (legis. com. 1993, 94, , seminar mgmt. team, cont. edn. com. 1986, 88, 92, 93), So. Calif. Soc. Hosp. Pharmacists (pres. elect 1995, delegate 1989–, treas. 1994), Anti-Defamation League (nat. v.chair leadership com. 1987-90, L.A. bd. and exec. com., Forum chair 1984-86), Jewish Comm. Relations Com. 1984–, Jewish Fedn. (we. region bd. 1980, community rels. com. bd. 84–, chair 87-89), Westside Jewish Comm. Center (bd. 1987-89), Jewish Family Service of Santa Monica (v.p., bd. 1991-94, pres. 1995), New Leaders Project 1992, L.A. Co. Mus. of Art; Republican; Jewish; rec: skiing, travel. Ofc: UCLA Center for Health Services A7222 Westwood 90024

JACOBSON, RAYMOND EARL, electronics company executive; b. May 25, 1922, St. Paul, Minn.; s. Albert H. and Gertrude W. (Anderson) J.; m. Margaret Maxine Meadows, Dec. 22, 1959 (div. 1986); children: Michael David, Karl Raymond, Christopher Eric; edn: BE (high hons.) Yale Univ., 1944; MBA (distinction) Harvard Univ., 1948; BA (Rhodes Scholar) Oxford Univ., 1950, MA, 1954. Career: asst. to gen. mgr. PRD Electronics Inc., Bklyn. 1951-55; sales mgr. Curtiss-Wright Electronics Div., Carlstadt, N.J. 1955-57; dir. mktg. TRW Computers Co., L.A. 1957-60; v.p. ops. Electro-Sci. Investors, Dallas 1960-63; pres. Whitehall Electronics Inc., Dallas 1961-63, dir. 1961-63; chmn. bd. Gen. Electronic Control Inc., Mpls. 1961-63, Staco Inc., Dayton, Ohio 1961-63; pres. Maxson Electronics Corp., Great River, N.Y. 1963-64; pres. Jacobson Assocs., San Jose, Calif. 1964-67; co-founder, pres., chmn. bd., CEO Anderson Jacobson Inc., San Jose 1967-88; also: chmn. Anderson Jacobson, S.A., Paris 1974-88; mng. dir. Anderson Jacobson Ltd., London 1975-85, chmn. Anderson Jacobson Canada Ltd., Toronto 1976-85, chmn. Anderson Jacobson, GmbH, Cologne 1978-83; chmn. CXR Corp., San Jose 1988-93; dir: Tamar Electronics Inc., L.A., Rawco Instruments Inc., Dallas 1960-63; lectr. engring. UCLA, 1958-60; mem. underwriting Lloyd's London, 1975–; Eagle Scout 1934, BSA committeeman 1969-81; mem. Sigma Xi, Tau Beta Pi, Assn. Am. Rhodes Scholars, Harvard Bus. Sch. Assn., Courtside Tennis Club; Republican; Lutheran. Res: 1247 Montcourse Lane San Jose 95131-2420

JACOBSON, STEVE EVAN, studio executive; b. May 8, 1955, St. Louis, Mo.; s. Leonard and June Annette (Groff) J.; children: Matthew b. 1989, Cameron b. 1990; edn: BA cinema, Univ. of So. Calif., 1977. Career: producer, writer Walt Disney Prodns., Burbank 1978-79; freelance producer/writer, 1978-80; writer/producer on-air promotion NBC, Burbank 1980-83, mgr. on-air promotion, NBC, Burbank 1983-88; v.p. on-air promotion CBS, L.A., 1988-93; pres. Pittard/Sullivan/Fitzgerald, L.A. 1993–; awards: bronze Bdcst. Designers Assn., L.A. (1988, 1990), finalist Internat. Film & TV Fest., N.Y. 1988, distinction Promotion Mktg. Assn. of Am., N.Y. 1990, listed Who's Who Among Young Americans 1991, Who's Who in the West 1992; mem. Bdcst. Promotion and Mktg. Execs. 1989–, USC Cinema-TV Alumni Assn. 1982–; exec. producer TV show: Crimetime After Primetime (preview 1991), co-producer, co-writer movie: Junior High School, 1978; rec: camping, music, racquetball, baseball.

JACQUES, CLAUDE, advertising agency creative director; b. Sept. 17, 1949, Quebec, Canada; s. Alfred and Francoise (Roux) J.; m. Mary Danaher Manilla, Oct. 11, 1975; children: Alessandra Manilla b. 1985, Giovanna Manilla b. 1991; edn: BA design, Cegep de Trois Rivieres Quebec 1970; BA design, Art Center Coll. Design 1973. Career: art dir. Young & Rubican, Los Angeles 1973-77; v.p., sr. art dir. Grey Advt. 1977-83; creative dir., sr. v.p. Foote Cone & Belding, San Francisco 1983–; awards: London Film Festival Gold Medal 1992, Clio (1987, 88, 90, 91), Comm. Arts award 1974-85; rec: photog., running, wine collecting. Address: Greenbrae 94904

JACQUES, KENNETH BORDEN, orthopaedic surgeon; b. Dec. 27, 1911, St. Johnsbury, Vt.; s. Frank Bismark and Laura Gertrude (Fessenden) J.; m. Elizabeth Matheson, June 15, 1940; m. 2d. Barbara Johnson Ferguson, Apr. 27, 1984; children: Elizabeth b. 1942, Heather b. 1944; edn: BA, Dartmouth, 1933; MD, CM, McGill Univ., Montreal 1937. Career: asst. residencies, path. Deaconess Hosp., Boston 1937-38, surgery, Montreal Gen. Hosp. 1938-39, med. Royal Victoria Hosp., Montreal 1939-40, neurosurg. Neurological Inst. Montreal 1940; res., surgery, Univ. Alberta Hosp., 1940-41; physician Weyerhauser Timber Co., Longview, Wash. 1941-42; resident, ortho., Orthopaedic Hosp., Los Angeles 1942-43; major Med. Corps US Army Air Corps 1943-46; orthopaedic surgeon private practice, Calif. 1946–; honors: med. staff pres. Hollywood Presbyterian Hosp. 1968-69, honoree McGill Grad. Soc. L.A. 1987 and Orthopaedic Hosp. L.A. 1987; mem: AMA, Calif. Med. Assn., L.A. Co. Med. Soc., Fellow Internat. Coll. Surgeons (So. Calif. sect. pres. 1981-82), Fellow Am. Coll. Surgeons, Am. Acad. Ortho. Surg., McGill Grad. Soc. (pres. 1952, 1990-91, v.p. 1981), Rotary Club; numerous illustrated lectures on orthopaedic surgery posterior lumbar interbody fusion, cerebral palsy, total hip replacement 1947-87; Republican; Prot. Bible Ch. (elder 1954-64); rec: skiing, hiking, bicy-

cling, photog., Bible study. Res: 5759 Valley Oak Dr Los Angeles 90068 Ofc: Jacques Orthopaedic, 5759 Valley Oak Dr Los Angeles 90068

JAFFE, JAN PAYNTER, marketing consultant; b. Sept. 23, 1944, Chicago, Ill.; d. Gilman Caldwell and Helen (Hepner) Paynter; m. Harris S. Jaffe, June 19, 1965 (div. 1969); edn: BA, Univ. Chgo. 1964; MBA, Univ. Chgo. Sch. Bus. 1966; MA, New Sch. Social Research 1987. Career: v.p., dir. mktg. and research Tatham Laird & Kudner, N.Y.C. 1966-73; v.p., dir. mktg. Smith Greenland 1973; v.p., assoc. research dir. McCann Erickson 1973-79; group product mgr. Airwick, Carlstadt, N.J. 1979; sr. v.p., dir. mktg. Backer & Spielvogel, N.Y.C. 1979-87; exec. v.p., ptnr. Bayer Bess Vanderwarker, Chgo., Ill. 1987-88; pres. Jan Jaffe & Assoc., Aptos, Calif. 1988–. Ofc: Jan Jaffe & Associates, Inc. 900 Day Valley Aptos 95003

JAGELS, GEORGE DANIEL, investments company executive; b. Aug. 8, 1908, Mountain View; s. Henry Richard Jagels and Jeanette (Hoffman) (Jagels) Bill; m. Margaret Melissa Foley, Dec. 7, 1946; children: Edward b. 1949, George, Jr. b. 1950,, Jeffrey b. 1954, Jean Elise Vaughn b. 1957; edn: BA, Stanford Univ. 1929; JD, Harvard Univ. 1932; LLD, Claremont Grad. Sch. 1971. Career: atty., assoc., ptnr Gibson Dunn & Crutcher, Los Angeles 1932-47; pres. Investment Operating Corp., 1947–, gen. ptnr. Woodland Farms Ltd., Pasadena 1947–; bd. dir. Santa Anita Consolidated, 1968-89; mem: Claremont Univ. (fellow 1959–), Caltech Assocs. (past pres., emeritus dir. 1972–), L.S.B. Leakey Found. (dir., chmn. bd. 1970-83, life trustee), Friends of Huntington Library (bd. of fellows 1970-76, bd. of overseers 1973–); clubs: California, Bohemian; mil: comdr. USNR 1942-46; Republican; Episcopalian; rec: travel, hunting. Res: 2134 Oak Knoll Ave San Marino 91108 Ofc: Woodland Farms Ltd. 301 North Lake Ave Ste 10-A Pasadena 91101

JAGOE, THOMAS ANTHONY, photojournalist, editor, assistant director of photography; b. Oct. 12, 1955, Bridgeport, Conn.; s. Donald Howard and Joan Treasea (D'Andrea) J.; m. Linda Michelle Swartz, Feb. 11, 1984; son, Aaron Jesse b. 1986; edn: AA, cum laude, L.A. Valley Coll., 1976; BA, CSU Northridge, 1980. Career: mgr./lab tech. The Darkroom Workshop Custom Lab, Northridge 1975-80; photojournalist The Daily News, L.A., Woodland Hills 1980-91; photo editor The Daily News, L.A., 199194, asst. dir. of photography 1994–; instr. CSUN 1986–, UCLA 1986–; numerous photog. awards include: Forest Lawn Press Photogs. Competition Sweepstakes Award (1981, 82, 85, 88), 1st pl. news Calif. State Fair (1982, 83), Gr. L.A. Press Photogs. Assn. Photographer of Yr. (1982), 1st place awards (news 1982, fire photo 1985, animal photo 1988) and L.A. Dodgers Andy Castle Award (1987 and 1989), Gr. L.A. Press Club 1st pl. (news & feature 1983, sports 1984), Valley Press Club 1st pl. (feature photo page 1984, 85), 2d pl. portrait/personality award in The Pictures of the Yr. competition Nat. Press Photographers Assn. (1985), others; mem. Nat. Press Photogs. Assn., PPA Gr. L.A. (past dir.); Republican; R.Cath.; rec: reading, fishing, camping, gardening, music, comic collecting. Res: 27639 N Renwick Ct Saugus 91350 Ofc: The Daily News, L.A. 21221 Oxnard St Woodland Hills

JAKEL, OTTO WILLIAM (Sir Otto W. Jakel), mechanical-electrical engineer, retired; b. May 20, 1915, Los Angeles; s. Otto Karl and Freda Sofa (Sommers) J.; m. Gwyneth K. Smith, Sept. 21, 1940 (dec. Sept. 30, 1967); children: William K. b. 1942, Margaret K. b. 1945, Gwyneth P. b. 1953; m. Alice M. Moore (Lady Alice), May 17, 1973; edn: BS, Calif. Maritime Acad., 1935; BSE, UC Berkeley, 1941; lic. Unrestricted 3d Mate 1935, reg. profl. mech. engr./elec. engr., Calif. 1945. Career: supr. Underwater Sound Installations on Naval Vessels, Mare Island, N.Y. 1941-46; research engr. U.S. Dept. Agric., Albany, Ca. 1946-48; radio engr. Mare Island Naval Shore Station, 1948-50; senior project engr. Colgate Palmolive Co., Berkeley 1951-78; mem. engring. advy. bd. S.F. City Coll.; instr. Contra Costa Coll.; honors: Tau Beta Pi, Eta Kappa Nu, Kt. Order of St. George awarded by Prince Albert Habsburg-Hohenburg of Austria (June 5, 1990); scoutmaster BSA Troop #104 El Cerrito, skipper El Cerrito Sea Scout Ship #108 BSA 1955-60; mem. US Coast Guard Aux. (life, instr. and past comdr. Flotilla 21), Masons, Shriners (past pres.), Moose; clubs: Pt. San Pablo Yacht (commodore 1975), Sportsmens; Democrat; Episcopalian; rec: boating, garden, camping, dancing, computers, model RR, travel. Res: 7543 Terrace Dr El Cerrito 94530

JAMES, BERT ALAN, architect; b. April 24, 1955, San Fernando; s. Charles Wendel and Elsie (Fred) J.; edn: BA, Calif. Polytechnic Univ. S.L.O., 1978; reg. architect Calif. 1983, cert. project architect NCARB. Career: designer, draftsman Froelich & Kow Architects, Beverly Hills 1978-79; designer, draftsman Howard R. Lanes Assoc., Woodland Hills 1979-80; project mgr. Nash Brown Assoc., Bakersfield 1980-81; project mgr. Roger Grulke Architects, Bakersfield 1981-82; project architect KSA Group Architects, Bakersfield 1982-85; project architect Milazzo & Assoc., Bakersfield 1985-92; principle Bert A. James Architect 1993–; mem: Am. Inst. Architects (corp. mem., dir. 1992-93), Kern County Officials Assn. (football referee 1983–), Kiwanis Club of Westchester; rec: golf, photog. Res/Ofc: Bert A. James Architect 3612 Sampson Ct Unit C Bakersfield 93309

JAMES, HOWARD PHILLIP, lawyer; b. April 27, 1948, Philadelphia, Pa.; s. Edwin Clarke and Doris Edith (Zeising) J.; edn: BA, Trinity Coll. 1970; JD, Univ. Pa. Phila. 1974; admitted St. Bar Conn. 1974. Career: mgmt. analyst Girard Bank, Phila., Pa. 1970-71; atty., assoc. Day Berry & Howard, Hartford, Conn. 1974-80; sr. counsel Thomas J. Lipton Inc., Englewood Cliffs, N.J. 1980-86; assoc. gen. counsel Hitachi Am. Ltd., Brisbane, Calif. 1986–; mem: Am. Bar Assn., San Francisco Bar Assn., Calif. Heritage Counsel, S.F. Museum of Modern Art, Housatonic Boat Club; mil: USAR 1970-76; Republican; Episcopalian; rec: sailing. Res: 1880 Jackson St #203 San Francisco 94109 Ofc: Hitachi America Ltd 2000 Sierra Point Parkway Brisbane 94005

JANOS, GREGORY GEORGE, physician; b. Aug. 6, 1949, Charleston, W. Va.; s. George Alexander and Margaret (Zaharis) J.; m. Kathlyn Rae Lamoure, Aug. 22, 1976 (div. 1993); m. 2d. Lauri Ann Anderson, July 24, 1994; children: Nicholas b. 1977, Andrew b. 1980; edn: BS, UC Berkeley 1971; MD, UC Irvine 1975. Career: asst. prof. UC Davis 1981-83; pediatric cardiologist, pvt. practice, Sacramento 1983–; honors: Alpha Omega Alpha 1975, Senior Award, UC Irvine 1975; rec: fly fishing, woodworking. Ofc: 5609 J St Sacramento 95819

JANTZEN, J(OHN) MARC, professor and dean emeritus; b. July 30, 1908, Hillsboro, Kans.; s. John D. and Louise (Janzen) J.; m. Ruth Patton, June 9, 1935; children: John Marc, Myron Patton, Karen Louise; edn: AB, Bethel Coll., Newton, Kans., 1934; AM, Univ. Kans., 1937, PhD, 1940. Career: elementary sch. tchr. Marion County, Kans. 1927-30, Hillsboro, Kans. 1930-31; high sch. tchr. 1934-36; instr. Sch. of Edn. Univ. Kans., 1936-40; asst. prof. Sch. of Edn., Univ. of Pacific, Stockton 1940-42, assoc. prof., 1942-44, prof. 1944-78, prof. emeritus, 1978–, dean. Sch. of Edn., 1944-74, emeritus 1974–, dir. summer sessions, 1940-72; bd. dirs. Educational Travel Inst., 1965-90, ldr. 13 fgn. ednl. seminars; past chmn. Commn. for Equal Opportunities in Edn., Calif. Dept. Edn. 1959-69; mem. Nat. Council for Accreditation Tchr. Edn. 1969-72; mem. (past chmn) Calif. Tchrs. Assn. Commn. for Tchr. Edn. 1956-62; honors: Phi Delta Kappa (mem. Internat. Bd. 1966-68), hon. service award Calif. Congress of Parents and Tchrs. 1982, Paul Harris fellow Rotary Found. 1980; mem: Am. Edn. Research Assn., Calif. Edn. Research Assn. (past pres. 1954-55), Calif. Council for Edn. Tchrs., Calif. Assn. of Colls. For Tchr. Edn. 1975-85), Nat. Edn. Assn., Rotary; Methodist. Res: 117 W Euclid Ave Stockton 95204

JAPRA, ROMESH KUMAR, cardiologist; b. Jan. 3, 1950, Phagwara, India; s. Sadhu Ram and Shama (Wati) J.; m. Sunita Mehta, Oct. 21, 1977; children: Ratika b. 1979, Deepa b. 1982, Jay b. 1989; edn: MD and rotating internship All India Inst. of Med. Sci., New Delhi 1972; med. internship Maimonides Med. Ctr., Elmhurst, NY 1973-74; chief/med. residency Mt. Sinai Med. Ctr., Elmhurst, NY 1974-76; cardiology fellow Cleveland Clinic, Ohio 1976-78; diplomate Am. Bd. of Internal Medicine 1977–, Am. Bd. of Internal Medicine in Cardiovascular Diseases 1978–. Career: attending staff Kaiser, L.A. 1978-79; pres. Pacific Cardiology Assn., Fremont 1979–; chief of staff Wash. Hosp., Fremont 1993-94; co-dir. Wash. Out-Patient Cath. Lab., Fremont 1992-94; bd. dirs. Tri-City Chpt. Am. Heart Assn., Fremont 1992–; sec./treas. med. staff Wash. Hosp., Fremont 1991-92, chief of medicine 1987-89; awards: Best Immigrant award Internat. Inst. of East Bay, Oakland, Calif. 1987, Pride of India Gold Medal, NRI Inst., New Delhi/NY 1991; mem: AMA, Am. Coll. of Cardiology (fellow 1980–), Am. Soc. of Cardiovascular Interventionists (fellow 1991), Fedn. of Indo-Am. Assns. (chmn. FIA of No. Calif. 1993–, pres. 1988-93, v.p. Pacific Region Nat. FIA 1990–); commr. Meritorious Award Commn. (apptd. by Pres. Bush 1990-93); convener Festival of India 1st & 2nd, 1993-94; primary investigator, 3 clin. trials: 14 K Angioplasty Balloon, 1992, Spirit Angioplasty Balloon, 1993, ERGOS Pulse Generator (Pacemaker), 1992-93; Republican; Hindu; rec: tennis, community work, publishing, mountaineering. Ofc: 1900 Mowry Ave Ste 201 Fremont 94538

JASON, ROBERT MAXWELL, lawyer; b. March 4, 1956, New York; s. Harold Arch and Adele Shirley (Harris) J.; m. Judith Mia Noodleman, Aug. 10, 1980; children: Jennifer b. 1985, Michael b. 1989, Jonathan b. 1993; edn: BA, Harvard Coll. 1978; JD, Harvard Law Sch. 1981. Career: atty., assoc. O'Melveny & Myers, Los Angeles 1981-84; ptnr. Hill Wynne Troop & Meisinger 1984–; honors: ed. Harvard Law Review 1979-81; mem: Los Angeles Child Guidance Clinic (exec. com. 1994-95), Toychest of Hope L.A. (treas. 1988-89). Ofc: Hill Wynne Troop & Meisinger 10940 Wilshire Blvd 90024

JAWAD (DJAWAD), SAID T., paralegal; b. Feb. 27, 1969, Kandahar, Afghanistan; came to U.S. 1986; s. Prof. Mir. Hussain Shah and Zakia D.; m. Shamim Rahman, Nov. 16, 1986; edn: student, Kabul Univ., 1980; postgrad. studies Wilhelms Univ., Muenster, Germany 1985; cert. Long Island Univ., 1986. Career: paralegal Lehnardt & Bauman, NY, NY 1987; Dewey, Ballantine, NY, NY 1988; Steefel, Levitt & Weiss, San Francisco 1989–; dir. Afghanistan Cultural Soc.; mem. Council of Fgn. Affairs, Internat. Soc. for Human Rights; ed. weekly newspaper, OMAID; author: 300+ articles pub. in U.S., Can., Germany, Afghanistan incl. The Inter Service Intelligence Services of Pakistan and the Afghan Resistance, The United States and the Afghan Resistance, Fundamentalism in Central Asia, Modern Dictatorship; Dictatorship of Future, Future of Dictatorship; Occupation of Wakhan: Soviet

expansion to the South; fluent in French, German, English and Farsi langs. Res: 4279 Merced Cir Antioch 94509 Ofc: Steefel, Levitt & Weiss One Embarcadero Center San Francisco 95111

JAY, DAVID J., computer software engineering consultant; b. Dec. 7, 1925, Gdansk, Poland, nat. 1944; s. Mendel and Gladys Gitta (Zalc) Jakubowicz; m. Shirley Anne Shapiro, Sept. 7, 1947; children: Melvin b. 1948, Evelyn Deborah b. 1950; edn: BS, Wayne State Univ., 1948; MS, Univ. Mich., 1949; grad. work Univ. Cinti. 1951-53, Univ. Mich. 1956-57, M.I.T. 1957; reg. profl. engr. Calif., Mich., Ohio. Career: instr. Univ. Detroit, 1948-51; supr. man-made diamonds, Gen. Electric Co., Detroit 1951-52; asst. to v.p. engring. Ford Motor Co., Dearborn 1952-63; project mgr. Apollo Environmental Control Radiators, N. Am. Rockwell, Downey 1963-68; staff to v.p. corp. planning Aerospace Corp., El Segundo 1968-70; pres. Profl. Bus. Mgmt. Inc., 1970-79; pres.. Jay Consulting Enterprises, Inc., 1979–; mem. Tau Beta Pi (nat. dir. alumni affairs 1972-73, sec.treas. 1972-75, pres. Detroit Alumnus chpt. 1962-63, pres. So. Calif. Alumnus 1963-70), Fellow Inst. for Adv. of Engring., Inst. of Mgmt. Sci. (sect. chmn. 1961-62), Western Greenhouse Vegetable Growers Assn., American Contract Bridge League (life master); club: Long Beach Yacht; works: 3 U.S. patents, 10 tech. papers; mil: ETM 3/c USN 1944-46; Jewish, pres. Temple Beth David; rec: bridge, yachting. Res: 13441 Roane Circle Santa Ana 92705 Ofc: 13882 Newport Ave Ste E Tustin 92680

JAYMES, DOROTHY LEE, municipal administrator, union trustee; b. Mar. 10, 1934, New Orleans, La.; d. Hampton Moten and Dr. Beulah Mae (Houston) Jones; div. Herbert Harrison; m. 2d Charles Royal Jaymes, June 1968 (dec. 1985); children: Brenda J. Perkins, Beulah M. Winfield (RN), Mary P.H. Offray, B.J. Harrison (M.Sgt.); edn: Heald Bus. Coll., S.F. 1966-72; Patten Bible Coll., Oakland 1978-80; BS, Univ. San Francisco, 1983; Career: owner, tchr. Clabon Kindergarten, New Orleans 1960-62; owner, whlse. retail furniture & appliance store, New Orleans, LA 1960-65; mgr., supr. municipal handicapped pgm. San Francisco, 1978-90; mgr. and adminstr. dept city planning San Francisco, 1990-92; physical plant mgr., City Planning, San Francisco 1992–; trustee and ofcr. Local 790 SEIU, AFL/CIO, San Francisco 1983–; shop steward/counselor Local 790, (1977–); del. S.F. Labor Counsel 1983–; del. S.F. Organizing Proj. 1983-90; chapter pres. 949 Presidio Muni/PUC, S.F. 1983-90; advy. bd. RTA Transit Auth. Oakland 1982-90; awards: service AMICAE/Zeta Phi Beta, S.F. 1981-82, civic leadership Third Baptist Ch. S.F. 1986, dean's award Patten Bible Coll. 1980, unionist of year Local 790 (1989), leadership Muni Elderly & Handicapped S.F. 1990, achiev. recogn. Univ. S.F. and poster honoree in Civic Ctr. BART Sta. and Train (3 mos. 1983); biog. listings incl. Who's Who Profl. Human Services, Nat. Ref. Inst. 1991, hon. mem., Who's Who Registry Worldwide 1992, Pres Inaugurration 1993, chtr. mem., Amer. For Change, presdl. task force 1993, books & awards of Marquis Who's Who Publs., Am. Biog. Inst., Internat. Biog. Ctr.; mem. O.E.S. (worthy matron 1953-60, grand dep. 1959-60, instr. 1967–), Nat. Women League Voters, Commonwealth Club (S.F.), Golden Gate Nat. Park Assns., HERE; Democrat (registrar, nat. fund raiser 1980–); Baptist; rec: sports, fishing, music, movies, dancing, singing. Res: 1665 Golden Gate Ave #12 San Francisco 94115 Ofc: 450 McAllister St 5th Fl., San Francisco 94102

JEEWANJEE, ZAIN A., business owner; b. June 13, 1955, Nairobi, Kenya; nat. 1988; s. Akbar Ali Jeewanjee and Batool (Tapal) J.; m. Farzana Zain Subzwari, Sept. 9, 1979; children: Zainab b. 1981, Zubair b. 1984, son b. 1994; edn: A Level, Karachi Grammar Sch., 1972; MBA, Karachi Bus. Coll. Pakistan 1976. Career: owner, mgr. Shaft Clothing, Karachi, Pakistan 1973-83; acct. Darton Inc., Los Gatos 1983-86; sales Macys, San Jose and Nordstrom, Palo Alto 1985-86; fin. cons. BMA Fin. Group, San Jose 1985–; ptnr. Jeewanjee & Hall, San Jose 1989–; owner Zain Jeewanjee, Inc.; awards: Penn. Mutual pres. award 1986, Royal Blue 1986-88, Nordstrom salesman 1986, PESS comm. service 1979, Pakistan C.of C. citizen of year 1982; mem: Pakistan Engrs. & Sci. Assn. (secty. 1988-90), Mensa, Jr. Lions Club Karachi (pres. 1978), Rotary Club Karachi; author: America in the Eyes of a Foreigner; Pakistan Peoples Party; Islam; rec: swimming, squash, chess. Res: 6209 Meridian Ave San Jose 95120-4916 Ofc: 337 South Monroe San Jose 95128

JEFFERSON-BRAMHALL, RONA LEE, tax preparer, executrix of estates; b. Nov. 26, 1900, Salisbury, Tenn.; d. John Thomas and Margaret Ann (Moore) Tice; m. William Tanner, Feb. 22, 1922; 1 dau. Colette b. 1924; m. Ray Carlton Bramhall, Dec. 24, 1982; edn: Univ. So. Calif. 1937-40; enrolled agent IRS 1978; reg. parliamentarian. Career: clerk Census Bureau Wash. DC 1941; clerk, editor Safety Sun, Corps of Engrs., L.A. 1942-49; USAF clerk, prodn. splst, indsl. splst. contractor plants Hawthorne, Inglewood, Culver City 1950-70; income tax preparer, executrix self-empl. 1960–; listed Internat. Directory of Disting. Leadership, 2000 Notable Am. Women, 5000 Personalities of World, World Who's Who of Women, Internat. Who's Who of Intellectuals, Personalities of Am.; mem: L.A. World Affairs Council, Scripps Clinic and Research Found., Nat. and Calif. Assn. Parliamentarians (state treas.), Internat. Toastmistress Club (all local ofcs., reg. treas.), Order of Eastern Star (Worthy Matron 1970, So. Coast Assn. pres. 1988, Belles & Bldrs. of So. Calif. pres. 1979, Grand Rep. Ky. 1984-85), Order of White Shrine of Jerusalem (WHP 1989-90), Am. Biog. Inst. Res. Assn. (life dep. gov.), Sierra Club, Viennese 200

Club (secty., treas., pres.); Prot.; rec: stamps, dancing, travel. Res: 5537 Littlebow Rd Palos Verdes 90275

JEFFERY, JAMES NELS, state emergency services official; b. May 16, 1944, Torrance; s. Daryl Fredrick and Mildred Evelyn (Sogard) J.; edn: AA, Long Beach City Coll., 1964; CSU Long Beach 1964-65, CSU Sacramento 1979-80. Career: firefighter, capt. Los Angeles Fire Dept., 1965-87; dir. Long Beach Search & Rescue Unit, 1968–; asst. chief fire div. Calif. Office Emergency Services, Riverside 1987–; rep. Firescope Communications, Riv. 1979–, coauthor Emergency Plans; awards: disting. service Long Beach Jaycees 1977, comm. service Long Beach Fire Dept. 1978, Silver Beaver BSA 1983, commendn. Mayor of Los Angeles 1985; mem: Calif. State Firemens Assn., Nat. Coordinating Council on Emergency Mgmt., So. Calif. Assn. Foresters and Fire Wardens, L.A. Fire Fighters Assn., Lions, Elks, Nat. Eagle Scout Assn.; civic: Boy Scouts Am., L.B. (chmn. service com. 1979-81, tng. com. 1982–), L.B. Community Epilepsy Clinic (bd. 1971-72); Republican; Lutheran. Res: 3916 Cerritos Ave Long Beach 90807 Office Emergency Fire Services PO Box 92257 Long Beach 90809-2257

JEFFREY, HELENE BARBARA, business owner, civic activist; b. Fresno; d. A. and N. Yeretzian; m. John A. Jeffrey; children: John, Jody; edn: psych., UC Berkeley ext. Career: owner Calif. Equipment & Fixture Co., Oakland 1965-85; govt. installation of refrigeration and air conditioning for U.S. Army, Navy, Air Force; music cons., owner Orinda Music, Orinda 1972–; civic: Pro America, Farm Animal Reform Movement, PETA/People for Ethical Treatment of Animals, In Defense of Animals, Humane Soc. of U.S., Contra Costa County SPCA; Republican (listed in charter issue Republican Party Who's Who 1991, also 1992 edit); mem. Repub. Nat. Com., Geo. Bush Presdl. Task Force life mem. and Honor Roll, also Wall of Honor on West wall of courtyard The White House, U.S. Senatorial Club preferred mem., Repub. Senatorial Inner Circle, Ronald Reagan Presdl. Found. sustaining sponsor, Library sponsor, nom. Presdl. Round Table 1990, Repub. Legion of Merit 1992, at-lg. del. 1992, Repub. Platform Planning Com. (recipient V.P. commendation 1992), Repub. Order of Merit 1994, Founders Wall and Eternal Flame 1994 (name placed on base of Eternal Flame in honor of Ronald Reagan), recipient Young America's Found. 1995 Conservative Leadership award, Heritage Found. 1995 Cert. of Active Membership, Veterans of Fgn. Wars of the U.S. 1995 Cert. of Appreciation. Ofc: Orinda Music, Orinda 94563

JELLEY, JOSEPH G., company president; b. Apr. 19, 1937, Blairsville, Pa.; s. Joseph G. and E. (Freidline) J.; m. Patricia A. Tremellen, July 29, 1982; children: Joseph b. 1957, James b. 1959, Joanna b. 1961, John b. 1962; edn: BS, cum laude, Tri- State Univ. 1957; GRI, Calif. 1978; Cert. Residential Splst., Nat. Assn. Realtors 1979; cert. R.E. broker, mgr., N.A.R. 1980. Career: sales mgr. Robert Hall Co., NY 1962-64; mdsg. supt. Sears Roebuck & Co., NY 1964-70; midwest dist. sales mgr. Melville Shoe Co., Foxmoor Div., NY 1971-74; senior reg. v.p. V.E. Howard & Co., Del Mar 1975-76; founder/pres. Western State Pacific Pines Corp., Del Mar 1976–; pres. Del Mar Mortgage Co. Inc., Del Mar 1978–; profl. lectr. and cons. in fin., mktg., and mgmt.; recipient numerous corp. awards; mem: Nat. Assn. Realtors, Calif. Assn. Realtors, Internat. Assn. R.E. Appraisers (senior); contbr. numerous articles on fin. and real estate, San Diego Co. newspapers, periodicals; rec: creative design, writing. Res: 13635 Pine Needles Dr, Del Mar 92014

JELLOIAN, CHARLES H., company executive; b. Dec. 20, 1959, Hollywood, Calif.; s. Hackadoor and Ardella (Bestigian) J.; m. Linda Marie Webber, Apr. 27, 1985; children: Christopher Charles b. 1994; edn: BA, journalism (minor in pol. sci.), Calif. State Univ., Northridge 1983. Career: exec. asst. Senator Newton Russell, Glendale, Calif. 1984-89; exec. dir. Ronald Reagan Presidential Found., Los Angeles 1989-92; v.p. Western Waste Industries, Torrance 1992–; trustee Western Diocese Endowment Bd., Los Angeles 1992–; commissioner Bd. of Transportation, Los Angeles 1993–; awards: Ferdinand Mendenhall Outstanding Scholarship 1979, Outstanding Young Men of Am. 1986; mem. Republican Nat. Com. Address: Northridge 91327

JEN, JOSEPH JWU-SHAN, educator, academic administrator; b. May 8, 1939, Chun King, China; nat. 1977; s. H.C. and Lucia (Chang) J.; m. Salina Fond, Sept. 4, 1965; children: Joanne b. 1967, Jeffrey b. 1973; edn: BS, National Taiwan Univ., Taipei, Taiwan, ROC 1960; MS, Wash. State Univ., Pullman, Wash. 1964; PhD, UC Berkeley 1969; MBA, So. Ill. Univ., Edwardsville, Ill. 1986. Career: res. food tech. U.S. Dept. Agric., Beltsville, Md. 1975-76; asst. prof., assoc. prof., prof. Clemson Univ., Clemson, S.C. 1969-79; prof. Mich. St. Univ., East Lansing 1979-80; dir. res. Campbell Soup Co., Camden, N.J. 1980-86; div. chair, food sci. tech. Univ. of Georgia, Athens 1986-92; dean coll. of agric. Calif. Polytechnic St. Univ., San Luis Obispo 1992–; cons. United Nations, N.Y. 1985-89; dir. Calif. Dairy Res. Bd., Davis, 1992–; dir. Cal Poly Found., San Luis Obispo 1992–; awards: Certificates of Merit, Ministry of Econ. Affairs, ROC, Taiwan, China 1980, Ministry of Agric. 1988; mem: Inst. of Food Technologists 1965- (fellow 1992), Chinese Am. Food Soc. 1976- (past pres.), Rotary Internat.; editor, books: Chemistry & Function of Pectin, 1986, Quality Factors of Fruits and Vegetables, 1989; author: over 75 articles pub. in profl.

jours.; rec: philately. Res: 1572 Cordova Drive San Luis Obispo 93405 Ofc: Calif. Polytechnic State Univ. College of Agriculture, San Luis Obispo 93407

JENDEN, DONALD J., educator, pharmacologist; b. Sept. 1, 1926, Horsham, Sussex, England; nat. U.S. cit. 1958; s. Wm. Herbert and Kathleen Mary (Harris) J.; m. 1950, 3 children; edn: scholarship, chem. & physics, Westminster Med. Sch., Univ. of London, 1944; BSc in physiology (first class), Kings Coll. London, 1947; MB, BS, distinction in pathology, pharmacology & therapeutics, medicine, surgery & gyn./ob. (Univ. Gold Medal), Westminster Med. Sch., Univ. of London, 1950. Career: awards: NSF sr. postdoctoral fellow/hon. res. assoc. dept. biophysics Univ. Coll., London, 1961-62, Hon. PhD in pharmaceutical chemistry Univ. Uppsala, Sweden, 1980, Fulbright short-term sr. scholar Australia, 1983, Wellcome Vis. Prof. Univ. Alabama, 1984. Career: lectr. in pharmacology UC Med. Ctr., San Francisco 1950-51, USPHS postdoc. fellow 1951-53, asst. prof. pharmacology 1952-53; asst. prof. UCLA, 1953-56, assoc. prof. 1956-60, prof. pharmacology 1960–, actg. dept. chmn. 1956-57, dept. chmn. pharmacology UCLA Sch. of Med. 1968-89; mem. The Brain Research Inst., UCLA, 1961–, prof. biomathematics UCLA 1967–; lt. Med. Corps USNR, assigned to Naval Med. Res. Inst., Bethesda, Md. 1954-56; cons. govt. agys. NIH, NIMH, Los Alamos Sci. Lab., Nat. Inst. on Aging (chmn. aging rev. com. 1985-87), others; mem. nat. sci. advy. com. Am. Fedn. for Aging Research 1985–; mem: AAAS, Am. Chem. Soc. Div. of Medicinal Chemistry, Am. Coll. Neuropsychopharmacology (Fellow), Am. Physiol. Soc., Am. Soc. for Mass Spectrometry, Am. Soc. for Med. Sch. Pharmacology, Am. Soc. of Neurochemistry, Am. Soc. for Pharmacology & Exptl. Therapeutics, Assn. for Med. Sch. Pharmacology, NY Acad. of Sci., The Physiol. Soc. (London), Soc. for Neurosci., West Coast Coll. of Biol. Psychiatry (charter fellow), We. Pharmacology Soc. (pres. 1970); mem. editl. bds. Alzheimer Disease and Associated Disorders an Intl. J., Life Scis., Neurobiology of Aging, Neuropsychopharmacology, Research Comms. in Chemical Pathology and Pharmacology, Substance and Alcohol Actions/Misuse; contbr. 400+ sci. publs. Res: 3814 Castlerock Rd Malibu 90265

JENINGS, HUGH STANLEY ("CASEY"), retired investment banker; b. Feb. 17, 1921, Buffalo, N.Y.; s. George William and Anita Mabel (Jones) J.; m. Barbara Lou Ehler, Feb. 28, 1945; children: Kathryn Anita, Leslie Gayle, George Wm. IV, Hugh Stanley, John Kirkley, Andrew Cray; edn: Monmouth Coll. 1941-42, Colo. Coll. Navy V-12 Unit 1944-45, Occidental Coll. 1945-47; BA, Univ. Colo., 1949. Career: reporter Denver Post 1947; advance man for Gov. Thornton 1948; tchr. Sullivan Sch. Dist., Denver, Colo. 1948-50; draftsman Douglas Aircraft, Santa Monica 1949-50; reg. rep. J.A. Hoyle & Co., Los Angeles 1951-60; Paine Webber 1960-68; awards: J.A. Hogle Top Producer 1958, 59, Paine Webber Top Ten Producers 1966, 67, Remember Oxy When Reunion chmn. 1982, Kappa Sigma Alumni Man of Year 1988, Colo. Coll. V-12 50 Yr. Reunion chmn. 1995; mem: Mt. San Antonio Coll. Relays (dir. 1982), Corp. One (dir. pub. rels.), Kappa Sigma So. Calif. Alumni Assn. (dir. 1980), Nixon for Pres. Club; book pub. "Year", pictorial history of world, 1950-54; mil: USN 1942-45; Republican; Cath.; rec: golf. Address: Mergers Acquisitions Underwritings Pres. 648 S San Antonio Dr Covina 91723

JENKINS, THOMAS M., judge; b. Mar. 7, 1921, Benton, Ill.; s. Thomas M. and Ruby (Lasley) J.; m. Anne Oakhill, July 13, 1944; children: Thomas Mark, III b. 1949, Jo Anne b. 1950, Dirk b. 1954; edn: B.Ed., Chgo. State Univ. 1943; LLD, UC Hastings 1949. Career: atty. Hanson, Bridgett, Marcus & Jenkins, 1950-75; judge Superior Ct., State of Calif., Co. of San Mateo, 1975-90; elected mayor and councilman City of San Carlos, 1962-74; bd. dirs. League of Calif. Cities, 1970-74; mem: Gov.'s Hosp. Advy. Council 1963-67; chmn. bd. Calif. Ctr. for Judicial Edn. 1982-90, Calif. Judicial Council 1972-76, Calif. Judges Assn. (exec. bd. 1979-83), State Bar of Calif. (v.p., bd. govs. 1969-72, chmn. Conf. of Dels. 1967), Am. Bar Assn. (Ho. Dels. 1959-64); civic: Peninsula Comm. Found. (chmn. bd. 1985–), Mills-Peninsula Hosp. Senior Care Pgms. (chmn., bd. 1985-90), Friends Svs. for Aging, Phila. (advy. bd. 1984-88), Living at Home Pgm., N.Y. (advy. bd. 1985-89), United Way of Calif. (pres. bd. 1976-77), Am. Assn. of Homes for the Aging (pres. 1966-67, bd. 1962-68), No. Calif. Presbyn. Homes (bd., chmn., 1977-95), S.F. Assn. for Mental Health (bd. 1971-76), S.F. Services for Seniors (bd. chmn. 1991-95), Campfire Girls (v.chmn., nat. bd. dirs. 1962-66); Democrat; Prot. Res: 711 Terrace Rd San Carlos 94070 Ofc: Judicial Arbitration & Mediation Services Two Embarcadero San Francisco 94111

JENNINGS, PAUL C., college acting vice president for business and finance; b. May 21, 1936, Brigham City, Utah; s. Robert W. and Elva (Simonsen) J.; m. Barbara Morgan (div. 1981); children: Kathryn b. 1962, Margaret b. 1963; m. 2d. Millicent M. Sivers, Aug. 28, 1981; edn: BS, Colo. State Univ., Ft. Collins, Colo. 1958; MS, Calif. Inst. of Technology, Pasadena, Calif. 1960, PhD, 1963. Career: teaching staff U.S. Air Force Acad., Colorado 1963-66; asst. prof. Calif. Inst. of Tech. 1966-68, assoc. prof. 1968-72, prof. civil engring. 1972, chmn Engring & Applied Sci. Div. 1985-89, v.p. and provost 1989-95, acting v.p. for bus. and finance 1995–; cons. on seismic design for offshore drilling platforms, Exxon Corp. 1970-86; mem. NAE-NRC Comm. on Seismology 1979-82, engring. panel NAS Comm. on Alaska Earthquake (co-editor pub. report 1972); Governor's Bd. of Inquiry on 1989 Loma Prieta earthquake; honors: Erskine Fellow, Univ. of

Canterbury, New Zealand 1970-85; fellow Am. Assn. for the Advancement of Sci.; Walter Huber Research Prize, Am. Soc. of Civil Engrs. 1973; listed Am. Men and Women of Sci., Who's Who in Engring.; Colo. State Univ. Honor Alumnus 1980; Achievement in Academia, Colo. State Univ. 1992; Nathan M. Newmark Medal, Am. Soc. of Civil Engrs. 1992; mem: Seismological Soc. of Am. (pres. 1980), Earthquake Engring. Res. Inst. (pres. 1981-91), Sm. Soc. of Civil Engrs., Am. Geophysical Union, Am. Soc. for Engring. Edn.; editor (2 books): The San Fernando Earthquake, 1971, Earthquake Engineering & Hazard Reduction in China, 1980; co-author (book): Earthquake Design Criteria, 1987; author: over 80 tech. articles on earthquake engring. and the dynamics of structure. Res: 640 South Grand Ave Pasadena 91105 Ofc: California Institute of Technology Mail Code 212-31 Pasadena 91125

JENSEN, DEBORAH ANN, wedding photographer; b. Dec. 21, 1952, Santa Rosa, 4th gen. Californian; d. David Laurens and Barbara Evelyn (Hackler) Jordan; great grandparents migrated west from Ohio by wagon train in 1874 on the Oregon Trail, settled in Calif. 1870s; m. William Hans Jensen II; children: Natalie, Trudie, Erik; edn: AA in bus. & photography, Mesa Jr. Coll., San Diego, 1973; pvt. studies in piano, 1963-77. Career: metal sculptress, works in Hallmark and other gift stores (12+ states) 1973-76; piano tchr. self-empl. 1976-77; videographer, photographer, florist, pianist Wedding Chapel San Diego, 1977-82; freelance wedding photographer, San Diego, Sacramento, and Auburn area, 1977–; profl. keyboard artist for weddings, 1977-82; Weight Watcher's group leader., photographer, videographer, San Diego, 1987-89, staff instr. photography, 1985–; design & mfr. custom wedding frames for photos, 1991–; listed Who's Who of La Jolla 1988-9; mem. Bridal Mart of Am. (assoc. 1990–); Christian Ch. (pianist 1975-91);profl. soft sculpture, mtr. clocks (Sacramento area crafts store 1991-93); rec: piano, walking (long distance), general photog., painting. Res: Rocklin 95677

JENSEN, GERALD RANDOLPH, editor, graphic artist; b. Aug. 12, 1924, Kalispell, Montana; s. Hans Clemen and Mabel E. (Everson) J.; m. Helen Levine, Dec. 11, 1943; children: Marjorie, b. 1955; edn: G.Th., Life Coll. 1945; Litt.D., Internat. Acad. 1970; MA, Union Univ. 1976; PhD, 1978. Career: regional and nat. dir. Youth & Christian Edn., Internat. Ch. Foursquare Gospel, Los Angeles 1946-54; dir. San Francisco area Youth for Christ 1955-60; v.p. Sacred Records, Whittier 1960-63; dir./ed. internat. publications Full Gospel Businessmen's Fellowship 1963-69, 1985–; pres. Triangle Productions, Burbank 1970-79; pres. Claiborne/ Jensen Advtsg. 1980-82; pres. Jerry Jensen & Assocs., Santa Fe Springs 1982-85; bd. dirs.: High Adventure Ministries (Van Nuys), Found. for Airborne Relief (Long Beach), Ambassadors of Aid (Vancouver, B.C., Canada), Friends in the West (Seattle, Wash.), Internat. Bible Inst. (Santa Fe Springs), Outreach Korea (Torrance); publs. dir. World Missionary Assistance Plan; Wings of Healing; Total Health Mag.; Am. Bible Soc.; Revival Fires; The Methodist Hour; Jimmy Snow Evangelistic Assocs., Nashville, Tenn.; awards: design, Dynamic Graphics 1961, Christian Edn. award Internat. Bible Inst. 1980, spl. service award Golden State Univ. 1983; founder/editor Acts Mag., Voice Mag. (Asian, Scandinavian, European and Spanish editions) FGBMFI, 1977–; youth mags.: Vision, Young America, Today's Youth, Campus, View, Charisma Digest; Republican; Prot.; rec: art collection, golf, travel. Res: 5772 Garden Grove Blvd #482 Westminster 92683 Ofc: Full Gospel Business Men's Fellowship Internat. 3150 Bear St Costa Mesa 92626

JENSEN, JOHN PAUL, JR., engineering executive, consultant; b. Feb. 27, 1917, Sioux City, Iowa; s. John Paul and Bertha (Jorgensen) J.; m. Judith Karker, Nov. 1, 1981; edn: Iowa State Univ. 1937-38; Morningside Coll. 1939-40. Career: vol. Royal Canadian Air Force prior to Pearl Harbor, 1940-41; served in U.S. Air Force 1941-45 with 6th Photogrammetry Sq., aerial maps and bomb charts in 35 countries; consulting engr., v.p. Thermodynamics Universal, Inc., (predecessor co., Communications Cons., Inc.), Burlingame; pres. Chloro-Guard Electronics of Ariz.; sales & advtg. dir. Seagrams Distillery, San Francisco; builder, owner John's Back Bay, Lodi 1976-83; indep. cons. 1984–; Sunworks Solar Electronics Inc. 1984; Nat. Micro Systems Inc. 1984; dir. Consumer Credit Union; mem: Lions Internat., Delta Tau Delta , Lodi C. of C. 1977-83, Woodbridge Golf & Country Club; Republican; Worldwide Ch. of God. Address: POB 810 Pine Grove 95665-0810

JENSEN, MARGARET THERESA, rancher, business owner, activist for the homeless and underpriveleged children; b. Mar. 19, 1939, Princeton, Wis.; d. Joseph and Margaret (Clark) Hoppa; children: Linda b. 1960, Theresa b. 1961, Michael b. 1962; desig: Assoc. in Risk Mgmt. (ARM), Chartered Property Casualty Underwriter (CPCU) Ins. Inst. of Am., 1980, 81. Career: secty. Russell Moccasin Co., Berlin, Wis. 1957-60; distbn. mgr. Milwaukee Journal & Sentinel, Berlin, Wis. 1963-65; secty. NML Ins., Berlin, Wis. 1962-68; NML broker's asst. The Walker Agy., Berlin, Wis., 1968-76; service rep. Flinn, Gray & Herterich, Palo Alto, Calif. 1976-77; broker's asst. Robert N. Burmeister, Menlo Park 1977-78; underwriter Boring-R-G-V, Redwood City 1978; insurance coord. Lockheed Missiles & Space Co., Sunnyvale 1979-86; employee benefits adminstr. Lockheed Technical Ops. Co., Inc., Sunnyvale 1987-88; owner/mgr. Jensen's Pick & Shovel Ranch, Angels Camp, 1989–; sponsor, activist for the homeless; honors: E.H. Schraeder Mem. Award, Milw. Jour.

1967, appreciation for outstanding leadership in youth devel. Lockheed Mgmt. Assn. 1987, recipient 15 Productivity Improvement awards-multi-mil. $ cost savings, and Lockheed Employee of Month (4t), Personality of Yr. 1991; dep. gov. Am. Biographical Inst. Res. Assn., mem. Am. Biog. Inst. advy. bd., ABI Woman of Yr. 1990, recognition for disting. svc. to comm. & nation by Historical Preservations of Am., Most Admired Woman of Decade 1993, listed Who's Who in Calif., World Who's Who of Women, 2000 Notable Am. Women, 5000 Personalities of World, 2000 Women of Achiev., Dict. Intl. Biography, Intl. Leaders in Achiev., Dict. Intl. Biography, Intl. Dir. Distinguished Leadership, Who's Who Intellectuals, Personalities Am., Comm. Leaders Am., Men & Women of Distinction, mem: Chartered Prop. Cas. Underw. Soc. (sponsor CPCU Candidate devel. No. Calif. 1982-88), Risk Ins. Mgmt. Soc. (dir. & secty. 1980–), Nat. Mgmt. Soc.1979–, Am. Quarter Horse Assn.1989–, Calif. Farm Bur. Fedn. 1990–, We. Mining Council 1988–, Gold Prospectors Assn. of Am. 1989–, Calaveras Co. C.of C. 1990–, Tuolumne Co. Visitors Bur. 1990–, Calif. Hist. Soc. 1990–, Columbia (Calif.) C.of C. 1992–, Calif. Travel Parks Assn. 1992–, Calaveras Lodging & Visitors Assn. 1992–, Berlin (Wis.) Alumni Assn. 1957–, Don Pedro Homeowners Assn. (LaGrange) 1979–, Peninsula Academies Palo Alto (mentor 1987), Murphys (Calif.) Bus. Assn. 1992–, Nat. Trust for Hist. Preservation 1993–; R.Cath.; rec: designed & blt. energy efficient home, collect antiques, photog., gold prospecting, roller skating, crafts. Res: 4977 Parrots Ferry Rd (POB 1141) Angels Camp 95222

JENSEN, NANCY BLANCHE, minister, artist, poet, civic activist; b. Oct. 14, 1937, Great Falls, Mont.; d. Antone R. (Count Sir Anthony Rudolph Strocki) and Evalyn Pearl (Fuller) Strosky; m. William Melvin Jensen, May 18, 1970; children: Michael J. Pope b. 1958; edn: John C. Fremont H.S., L.A. 1955; Calif. lic. collector, 1984–. Works: poet; artist in oils and acrylics; poems pub. in poetry anthologies: Our Western World Most Beautiful Poems 1984, Our Worlds Most Beloved Poems (1984), American Anthology 1985-88, Words of Praise, ed. John Frosts 1987, Best Poems of Today 1987, Favorite Poets 1988; chair Patriotic T-Shirts (given free to sch. children) for Bear Valley Elem. Sch. and Glen Martin Sch.; awards: Nat. Lib. of Poets "Editor Choice Award", Best Poems of 1995, read poem "Power of Peace" at U.N. (8/24/93), Citizen of Year Citizens Com. for Right to Bear Arms (1989, 91), golden poet Am. Poetry Press, Santa Cruz (1988, 89), Who's Who in Poetry, golden poet, silver poet awards World of Poetry, Sacto. (1986, 87, 88, 89, 90, 91), best new poet Best Poems of Today 1987; correspondent and writer num. letters on local and nat. issues to the U.S. Pres. and other elected govt. officials 1970–; mem. Am. Legion Aux. (exec. bd., historian, legis. chair 1989-91), V.F.W. Ladies Aux. Post 7379 (1990–), Nat. Mus. of Women in the Arts (charter mem.), Nat. Rifle Assn., Bear Valley Charcoal Burners - Black Powder Club 1990–, Bear Valley HOA, Big Bear Hist. Soc., Elks; Republican (Presdl. Order of Merit 1991, listed Repub. Who's Who 1991, U.S. Senatl. Club 1990–, Presdl. Commn. 1992–, Nat. Poetry Soc. 1994–, Internat. Poetry Soc. 1994–; Christian; rec: gardening, walking, fishing. Res: POB 1592 Big Bear City 92314

JENSEN, WILLIAM HANS, II, entrepreneur, wedding consultant/photographer (owner/ptnr. w/wife), lawn care company owner; b. Dec. 17, 1955, on the family farm in Webster City, Ia.; s. William and Phyllis (director Dietetics, Sharps Mem. Hosp., San Diego, 30 yrs.) Jensen; m. Deborah Ann Jordan (profl. pianist and photographer); children: Natalie, Trudie, Erik; edn: grad. Madison H.S. 1974, photography courses Consumes City Coll. 1982, and private lessons from profl. photographers. Career: videographer, 1983-89; wedding photographer 1984–; mem: Bridal Mart of Am., Christian Minister, RV Club mem.; rec: traveling, reading and hiking/nature photography.

JESSER, FRANKLIN WAYNE, logistician; b. July 19, 1931, Oakland; s. George H. and Margaret J. (Buie) J.; m. Betty Smith, Sept. 10, 1955; children: Franklin Jr. b. 1956, Sally b. 1959, Karen b. 1961; edn: AA, Diablo Valley Coll. 1955; BA, CSU San Francisco 1957; MS, Air Force Inst. Tech. 1972; Calif. Secondary tchg. cred. (1958). Career: tchr. Folsom H.S. 1958-60; logistics splst. civil service, USAF, McClellan AFB 1960-82, asst. dep. pgm. mgr. logistics, Los Angeles A.F. Sta. 1982-86, ret. 1986; recipient USAF awards- Superior Performance Rating (1968), Outstanding Performance Rating (1979), Outstanding Career Service (1986); subst. tchr., Grant, Roseville and Folsom Cordova High Sch. Dists., 1986-87; eve. instr. intro. to logistics Am. River Coll. 1974-81; mem: Soc. Logistics Engrs. (chpt. chmn.), McClellan Mgmt. Soc. (pres.), Alpha Mu Gamma, Sigma Iota Epsilon, AARP, NARFE, V.F.W., Am. Legion; thesis: Inspection and Acceptance of Contractor-Prepared Engring. Data (1972); contbr. article Good Enough for Govt. Work, A.F. Jour. of Logistics (1985) and essay My Most Precious Freedom, Am. Legion Mag. (1987); mil: electronic tech., p.o. 3/c USN 1949-53; Presbyterian (elder/deacon); rec: acting, singing. Address: Rocklin 95677

JEW, WING, psychologist, retired school district administrator; b. March 31, 1929, Stockton; s. Fook and Gin (Shee) J.; m. Doris Ann Quan, June 17, 1951; children: Christine b. 1952, Kathleen b. 1953, Andy b. 1968; edn: BA, Univ. of Pacific 1957; MA, 1963; Ed.D, 1970; lic. psychologist Bd. Med. Quality Assurance 1973. Career: tchr. Stockton Unified Schs., Stockton 1955-64; counselor 1964-69, sch. psychologist 1969-81, adminstr. 1981-89; psychologist, pvt.

practice 1989–; vis. prof. Univ. of Pacific 1974-77; mem: Phi Delta Kappa, Assn. Calif. Sch. Adminstrs., Chinese Culture Soc. (bd. dirs. 1988), Stockton Cathay Club; co-author: Going Places with Your Personality, 1971, My Job Application File, 1975, Janus Job Planner, 1976, Job Interview (kit), 1976, Using the Want Ads., 1977; Democrat; Methodist; rec: photog. Res: 3612 Harpers Ferry Dr Stockton 95209 Ofc:Delta Center 2087 Grand Canal Blvd Ste 12 Stockton 95207

JEWELL, JOHN HUTTSELL, librarian; b. May 13, 1940, Kansas City, Mo.; s. Jack Huttsell and Corrinne Elizabeth (Fye) J.; m. Carol Thompson, June 16, 1961; 1 dau: Teresa Elizabeth, b. 1972; edn: BA, Univ. of Ks. 1961; MA, Univ. of Denver 1969. Career: dir. WTTV, Bloomington, Ind. 1962-64; intern, Fresno Co. Free Library 1967-69; science librarian 1970-76; coord. reference svcs. 1976-82; principal librarian reference svcs. 1982-1986; library microsystems splst. Calif. State Library 1986-90, head, State Info. and Reference Ctr. 1990-92; asst. dir. for info. svs., Calif. Research Bureau 1992–; honors: Phi Beta Kappa; Beta Phi Mu; mem: Calif. Alliance of Info. & Referral Svcs.; Spl. Libraries Assn.; Am. & Calif. Library Assns. Res: 3015 Grinnel Place, Davis 95616 Ofc: California State Library, Calif. Research Bureau 900 N St Ste 300 Sacramento 95814

JEWETT, DON LEE, research director; b. Jan. 28, 1931, Eureka, Calif.; edn: AB, San Francisco State 1953; AB, UC Berkeley 1956; MD, UC San Francisco 1960; D.Phil., Oxford Univ., England 1963; lic. physician and surgeon Calif. 1961–; bd. eligible, orthopaedic surgery 1975. Career: internship Kaiser Found. Hosp., S.F. 1960-61; postdoctoral fellow, NIH: Oxford Univ.-Physiol. Dept. 1961-63, Yale Univ.-Psychol. Dept. 1963-64; asst. prof. UCSF Dept. Physiol. 1964-66, Depts. Physiol. & Neurosurgery 1966-72; clin. instr. UCSF Dept. Orthopaedic Surgery 1972-75, assoc. prof. 1975-89, prof. 1990-91, prof. emeritus 1991–; med. staff UCSF 1975-91, med. dir. Dept. Physical & Occupational Therapy 1981-91; res. dir. Abratech Corp., Sausalito, Calif. 1991–; co-author (textbook): Basic Concepts of Neuronal Function (Little, Brown & Co., 1984); contbg. author: num. books and multi-level textbooks, 1972-93, 75+ articles to profl. jours., 1960–. Ofc: Abratech Corporation 475 Gate Five Rd #255 Sausalito 94965

JEZYCKI, CHARLES WOJCIECH STANISLAW, chief operating officer; b. Sept. 5, 1936, Warsaw, Poland; nat. 1957; s. Karol P. and Wanda Cecylia (Krzyzanowska) J.; m. Helen Marie Flaherty, July 9, 1961 (div. 1986); m. Barbara L. Wascom Oct. 7, 1989; children: Charles b. 1962, Camille b. 1963, Charles David b. 1964, Stefan b. 1967, Craig b. 1968, Patrick b. 1968, Jennifer b. 1971; edn: BS, Univ. S.F. 1956; MBA, S.F. St. Univ. 1980; tchg. credential 1980. Career: personnel rep. St. Compensation Ins., S.F. 1959-65; personnel and. pub. rels. dir. Queen of Valley Hosp., Napa 1965-68, asst. adminstr. 1968-85, v.p. 1985-88; pres. Exec. Mgmt. Consulting Group 1988–; realtor Vintage Properties, 1991-93; dir. of human resources and C.O.O., Peninsula Blood Bank, Burlingame 1993–; honors: Calif Soccer Assn. Hall of Fame 1989, League Official of the Year awarded by Soccer Magic, Calif. monthly soccer publ. 1989, Calif. Legislature resolution 1988, Who's Who in West, Outstanding Young Men Am.; mem: Napa C.of C. (pres., bd.), Ambassadors (pres.), San Mateo C. of C. Ambassadors 1995–, Napa Co. Emergency Med. Care Com. (chmn., bd. mem.), N. Bay Hosp. Conf. (pres., bd. mem.), Leadership Napa Valley (bd., mem. selection com.), Am. Coll. Healthcare Execs., Am. Assn. of Blood Banks 1993–, Calif. Blood Bank Soc. 1993–, Calif. Soccer Assn. (v.chmn. 1987-91, exec. bd. 1988-95), U.S. Army Med. Command-Japan Assn. 1991–, Napa Sr. Soccer League (chmn. select com., coaching adminstr., pres., 1981-88), N. Bay Soccer League (pres. 1985-92), Edinburgh Academy Academicals, Scotland 1956–, Napa City Civil Service Commn. (chmn. 1969-78), Kiwanis, Napa Ambassadors Club (pres.); 2 articles pub. in med. jours., 1972, 73; articles pub. on soccer Napa Register (1965–) and Soccer Magic (1990–); mil: E-4 AUS 1956-59; Republican; R.Cath.; rec: backpacking, skiing, soccer. Res: 10 Riviera Circle Redwood Shores 94065 Ofc: Peninsula Blood Bank 1791 El Camino Real Burlingame 94010

JINADU, BABATUNDE ADEGBITE, physician/county public health official; b. Mar. 17, 1945, Lagos, Nigeria, nat. U.S. cit. 1987; s. The Hon. Mr. Justice Yaya Abiodun Jinadu and Amudat (Salako) Dabiri; m. Linda Adele Warren, June 18, 1977; children: Laide b. 1978, Babalola b. 1981; edn: BS (cum laude) Central St. Univ., Wilberforce, Oh. 1970-72; MD, Columbia Univ. P&S, NY, NY 1972-76; MPH, UC Berkeley, 1979-80; bd. cert. Am. Bd. Pediatrics (1982). Career: health ofcr., dir. pub. health Kern Co. Health Dept., Bakersfield 1988–; asst. clin. prof. pediatrics, USC, 1981-82, also attdg. phys. Childrens Hosp., Los Angeles; attdg. physician Bronx Lebanon Hosp., NY, NY 1980-81, also asst. clin. prof. peds. Albert Einstein Coll. of Med. 1980-82; honors: Dean's List Central St. Univ. (1970), Beta Beta Beta (1971); mem: Kern Co. Med. Soc., Calif. Med. Soc., Am. Pub. Health Assn., Ambulatory Ped. Assn., L.A. Peds. Soc., Calif. Conf. of Local Health Ofcrs., Cancer Registry Advy. Bd. (1986–), Kiwanis Internat. Res: 4305 Player Ct Bakersfield 93306

JOBS, STEVEN PAUL, computer corporation executive; b 1955; adopted s. Paul J. and Clara J. (Jobs); m. Laureen Powell, Mar. 18, 1991; edn: Reed Coll. Career: Hewlett Packard, Palo Alto; designer video games Atari, Inc. 1974; co-founder, chmn. bd., Apple Computer, Cupertino 1975-85, co-designer (with Stephen Wozniak) Apple I computer; pres. NeXT, Inc., Redwood City 1985–; Ofc: NeXT Inc. 900 Chesapeake Dr Redwood City 94063

JOECK, NEIL ARCHIBALD, international political analyst; b. Feb. 16, 1950, Montreal, Canada; s. Werner F. and Nancy (Archibald) J.; m. Melinda Erickson, Sept. 16, 1972; children: Morgan b. 1981, Graeme b. 1983; edn: BA, UC Santa Cruz 1973; MA, Carleton Univ. Canada 1976; MA, UCLA 1980; PhD, 1986. Career: vol. Vols. in Asia, Stanford 1970; adminstrv. asst. UC Berkeley 1976-78; lectr., researcher Center for Internat. & Strategic Affairs UCLA 1979-86; res. fellow Inst. on Global Conflict & Cooperation, UCSD, La Jolla 1986-87; internat. political analyst Lawrence Livermore Nat. Lab., Livermore 1987–; cons. War & Peace in Nuclear Age, Boston 1986; tchr. Chinese Acad. of Social Sci., Beijing, China 1987; advisor Nuclear Suppliers Research Project, Monterey Inst. Internat. Studies 1988-89; awards: UCLA Graham fellowship 1984, UCSD IGCC fellowship 1985-87, Bank of Am. Gimbel fellowship 1983; author, ed. Strategic Consequences of Nuclear Proliferation in S. Asia (1986), ed. Arms Control & Internat. Security (1984), monograph Comprehensive Test Ban (1986), articles and editorial pub.; Democrat; rec: travel, 20th century American fiction, detective fiction. Ofc: LLNL L-389 POB 808 Livermore 94550

JOHANSON, DONALD CARL, physical anthropologist; b. June 28, 1943, Chicago; s. Carl Torsten and Sally Eugenia (Johnson) Johanson; m. Lenora Carey, 1988; edn: BA, Univ. Ill. 1966; MA, Univ. Chgo. 1970; PhD, 1974; DS hon., John Carroll Univ. 1979; DS hon., Coll. of Wooster 1985. Career: dept. physical anthropology Cleveland Museum of Natural Hist. 1972-81, curator 1974-81, adj. prof. Case Western Reserve Univ. 1978-81; Kent St. Univ. 1978-81; pres. and founder Inst. Human Origins 1981; adj. prof. antrhopology Stanford Univ. 1983; grantee Wenner-Gren Found., NSF, L.S.B. Leakey Found., Cleveland Found., George Gund Found., Roush Found., Nat. Geog. Soc.; awards: Golden Plate Am. Acad. Achievement 1976, Jared Potter Kirtland, Cleveland Museum of Natural History 1979, Profl. Achievement Univ. Chgo. 1980, Gold Mercury Internat. (ad personem 1982), Humanist Laureate Acad. Humanism 1983, Disting. Service Am. Humanist Assn. 1983, Alumni Achievement award Univ. Ill. 1995; mem: AAAS (fellow), Calif. Acad. Sci., Rochester Museum, Centro Studi Richerche Ligabue, Explorers Club (hon. dir.), Fellow Royal Geographical Soc., Founders Council, Chgo. Field Art Museum of Natural History (hon.), Am. Assn. Phys. Anthropologists, Am. Assn. Africanists Archeologists, Internat. Assn. Dental Research, Internat. Assn. Human Biologists, Assn. Internat. Pour "Etude de Paleontologie Humaine, Soc. de l'Anthropologie de Paris, Soc. Vertbrate Paleontology, Soc. for Study of Human Biol., Museum Nat. d'Histoire Naturelle de Paris (correspondent), Nat. Center Sci. Edn. (supporting scientist); author: (with M.A. Edey) Lucy: The Beginnings of Humankind (1982, Am. Book Award), Blueprints: Solving the Mystery of Evolution, 1989, (with James Shreeve) Lucy's Child: Discovering A Human Ancestor, 1989, (with Kevin O'Farrell) Journey From the Dawn, 1990, (with Lenora Johanson and Blake Edgar) Ancestors: In Search of Human Origins, 1994 (nominated for Emmy Award), contbr. num. sci. articles, papers and reviews; host and narrator: 3-pt. PBS NOVA series, In Search of Human Origins, 1994, PBS Nature series, 1982; films produced: The First Family, 1981, Lucy in Disguise, 1982. Address: 1288 Ninth St Berkeley 94710

JOHANSON, JERRY RAY, consulting engineer; b. Aug. 29, 1937, Salt Lake City, Utah; s. Albert F. and Elizabeth (Cox) J.; m. Harlean Shepherd, July 12, 1957; children: Kerry b. 1959, Bryan b. 1961, Michael b. 1963, Cynthia b. 1966, Elizabeth b. 1969; edn: BSME, Univ. Utah 1959; PhD mechanical engring., 1962; reg. profl. engr. Mass. and Calif. Career: sr. technologist U.S. Steel, Monrowville, Pa. 1962-66; pres. Jenike & Johanson, San Luis Obispo 1966-85; J.R. Johanson Inc. 1985–; awards: ASME Henery Hess award 1966; mem: ASME, AICHE, IBA; publs: 120+ tech. papers re Bulk Solids Handling, 1963, patents in field (7 fgn. and 14 U.S. pats.); Republican; Mormon; rec: piano, organ, vocal, fishing. Ofc: JR Johanson Inc. 712 Fiero Ln #37 San Luis Obispo 93401

JOHARI, SHYAM, computer consultant; b. June 30, 1948, Jodhpur, India; s. Mohan L. and Gauri D. (Taparia) J.; m. Kamala Baheti, Nov. 22, 1972; children: Priti, Umesh; edn: BS. Univ. Jodhpur 1965; MS, 1967; MS, Univ. Ill. 1969; PhD, 1975. Career: sr. systems analyst western area devel. center Burroughs Corp., Irvine 1975-77, sr. splst. internat. group, Detroit 1977-80, mktg. splst. 1980-82, asst. to v.p. quality 1982-84, mgr. data comms. fin. systems group 1984-86; sr. cons. Joseph & Cogan Assocs. (subsid. Unisys Corp.), Naperville, Ill. 1986-87; mgr. performance group Tandem Computers Inc., Cupertino 1987–; assoc. editor Performance Evaluation Rev. (ACM Sigmetrics) 1987–; mem: Assn. Computing Machinery, IEEE (computer soc.), Computer Measurement Group; Hindu. Res: 3181 Heritage Valley Dr San Jose 95148 Ofc: Tandem Computer, Inc. 19333 Vallco Pkwy, LOC 252-10 Cupertino 95014

JOHN, MADHU JOSEPH, radiation oncologist; b. Dec. 7, 1946, India; s. Joseph C. and Rachel (Thomas) J.; m. Shama Mathai; children: Nithya b. 1979, Neha b. 1982; edn: M.B.B.S., Christian Med. Coll., Ludhiana, India 1970; intern (rotating) Brown Mem. Hosp., Ludhiana, India 1970-71, St. Agnes Hosp., Baltimore, Md. 1972; residency Memorial Sloan-Kettering, NY, NY 1973-75;

med. lic. N.Y., Maine, Calif.; Diplomate Am. Bd. of Radiology-Therapeutic Radiology, 1979. Career: instr. & asst. prof. N.Y. Med. Coll., NY, NY 1977-79; assoc. radiation oncologist Fresno Comm. Hosp. and Med. Ctr., Fresno, Calif. 1980-89; asst. clin. prof. UCSF 1980-90; med. dir. Kaweah Delta Cancer Care Ctr., Visalia 1990–; med. dir. The Cancer Ctr. at St. Agnes Med. Ctr., Fresno 1993–; assoc. clin. prof. UCSF 1991–; adv. Kaweah Delta Dist. Hosp. Tumor Bd. and St. Agnes Med. Ctr. Tumor Bd. 1990–; lectr./instr.: Tulare Co. Med. Soc., Coll. of Sequoias, Visalia; instr. resident clinics, UCSF 19809–; lectr. N.Y. Med. Coll. 1977-79; Mem. Sloan-Kettering Cancer Ctr. 1973-75; honors: named in Best Doctors in the U.S.A. 1994-95; mem: Am. Coll. of Radiology, AMA, Am. Soc. of Clin. Oncology, Am. Soc. of Therapeutic Radiology and Oncology, CMA, Fresno-Madera Med. Soc., Tulare Co. Med. Soc., We. Assn. of Gynecology Oncology, Assn. of Clin. Faculty, UCSF; No. Calif. Oncology Group (gyn. com.), Radiation Therapy Oncology Group (gastrointestinal com. gyn. com.) San Joaquin Valley Comm. Clin. Oncology Prog., Southwestern Oncology Group, Nat. Surgical Adjuvant Breast and Bowel Project, Univ. of Rochester Cancer Ctr., Central Calif. Cancer Res. Group (prin. investigator); editor and author of 8 chpts., textbook: Chemoradiation: An Integrated Approach to Cancer Therapy (Lea & Febiger, Phila. 1993); contbr. 27 articles to sci. jours, 28 abstracts, 4 textbook chapters, num. sci. presentations, clin. res. projects, 1975–. Ofc: 7130 N Millbrook #112 Fresno 93720

JOHN, WALTER, JR., physicist; b. Feb. 16, 1924, Newkirk, Okla.; s. Walter and Carrie (Hollingsworth) J.; m. Carol Salin, Jan. 22, 1954; children: Kenneth, Laura, Claudia, Leslie; edn: BS, Calif. Inst. Tech. 1950; PhD, UC Berkeley 1955. Career: instr. Univ. of Ill. 1955-58; sr. physicist Lawrence Livermore Nat. Labs., Livermore 1958-71; prof. Calif. State Coll., Turlock 1971-74; res. scientist Calif. Dept. of Health Services, Berkeley 1974-92; vis. scholar UC Berkeley 1993–; dir. Am. Assn. for Aerosol Res. 1987-92; ed. bd. Aerosol Sci. Tech. 1988-92; ed. bd. Applied Occupational and Environmental Hygiene 1989–; ed. bd. Jour. Aerosol Sci. 1994–; Fellow, Am. Physical Soc.; mem: Am. Conference Gov. Indsl. Hygienists, Am. Assn. of Physics Tchrs., Sigma Xi, Tau Beta Pi; author 90+ articles in books and profl. jours. on nuclear physics, x-rays, aerosols and air pollution; mil: served U.S. Army, 1943-46. Res: 195 Grover Ln Walnut Creek 94596

JOHNSON, BRUCE, television producer, screenwriter; b. July 7, 1939, Oakland; s. Robert Steele and Edith Kristene (Pederson) J.; m. Kathleen Ross, Nov. 5, 1966; children: Jonathan Alan, Grant Fitzgerald; edn: S.F. City Coll. 1958-60, BA, USC, 1962. Career: producer and head writer television shows: Gomer Pyle 1967-68, Jim Nabors Hour 1969-71, Arnie 1971-72, The Little People 1972-73, The New Temperature's Rising Show 1973-74, Sierra 1974-75, Excuse My French (Canada) 1975-76, Alice 1976-77, Blansky's Beauties 1977, Quark 1977-78, Angie 1978-79, Mork and Mindy 1978-82, Webster 1982-89, The People Next Door 1989, Doghouse 1990-91; Flesh 'N Blood 1991-92; Hangin' with Mr. Cooper 1992-93; numerous movies of the week and pilots for TV; awards: People's Choice best t.v. show award for Mork and Mindy (1979), Photoplay mag. best evening t.v. show (1979), Emmy nomination for best comedy series (1979); mem: Writers Guild Am.-West, Producers Guild Am., Caucus for Prods. Writers and Dirs.; mil: USAF Reserve 1962-68.

JOHNSON, BURELL CARVER, manufacturing and marketing executive, retired; b. Aug. 10, 1924, Bessemer, Ala.; s. Burell Carver and Bertha Mae (Waldrop) Loveless J.; m. Ada L. (Sherry) Calhoun, Dec. 9, 1944 (div. 1982); children: Gaylen Denise b. 1956, Heide Carol b. 1963; edn: BS, USC 1951. Career: med. sales rep. Chemetron Corp., Nat. Cylinder Gas div., Los Angeles 1951-55, asst. dist. mgr. 1955-58, dist. mgr., San Leandro 1958-67; v.p., gen. mgr. Puritan Bennett Aero Systems Co., El Segundo 1967-90, ret.; mem: Aviation Distbrs., Mfrs. Assn. (past pres.), Nat. Bus. Aircraft Assn., Aircraft Owners & Pilots Assn., City of Palos Verdes Estates (mayor 1978-80, city council 1976-78), Masons (Past Master), Scottish Rite, Shriner; mil: 2d. lt. USMC 1942-46; Republican; Prot.; rec: flying, golf, photog. Res: 32759 Seagate Dr Rancho Palos Verdes 90275 Ofc: Puritan Bennett Aero Systems Co. El Segundo 90245

JOHNSON, CHERYL LEE, lawyer; b. June 9, 1950, Burlington, Wash.; d. Jean Carolyn (Wick) Johnson; m. Richard Graham Maloney, 1976 (div. 1981); m. Marc Marmaro, July 11, 1981; 2 daus.: Ashley b. 1983, Morgan b. 1991; edn: BA magna cum laude, Barnard Coll.1971; M.Ed, Harvard Grad. Sch. Edn. 1972; JD, Columbia Sch. Law 1975. Career: ptnr., assoc. atty. Morrison & Foerster, San Francisco and Los Angeles 1975-83; v.p., sr. mng. counsel Crocker Nat. Bank, L.a. 1983-86; ptnr. Graham & James 1986–; honors: Columbia Law Sch. Law Review 1974-75, Harlan Fiske Stone scholar 1974-75; mem: Am. Bar Assn., Women Lawyers Assn., Fin. Lawyer Conf., Los Feliz Sch. Parents Ogn. (pres. 1986-87), Pilgrim Sch. Parents Orgn. (pres. 1989-90, 92-93); 3 articles pub. in profl. jours., 1975-78; editor-in-chief, California Antitrust Law, 1992. Ofc: Graham & James 801 S Figueroa 33d Floor Los Angeles 90071

JOHNSON, DANIEL LEE, SR., state transportation agency administrator; b. July 6, 1936, Yuba City; s. John Clem Johnson and Virginia Nellie (Hammons) Clark; m. Myra Jeanne Vetter, Mar. 13, 1955 (div. 1966); children: Daniel, Jr. b. 1955, John Ora b. 1958 (dec.), Michael b. 1959, Theodore b. 1963; m. Loretta Faye McMullen, Mar. 3, 1968 (div. 1972); m. Carolyn Ann Nelson, Oct. 12,

1974 (div. 1992); m. Sandra M. Compson, Feb. 14, 1995; edn: grad. Yuba City H.S., 1954, att. Yuba Coll., 1955-71, cert. UC Davis, 1974. Career: sales Standard Oil, Grass Valley 1956-57; freelance artist, 1953-89; draftsman Calif. Div. Highways, Marysville 1956-71; police ofcr. Yuba City Police Dept. 1961-71; graphic artist Caltrans, Marysville 1971-79, sr. delineator 1979-91, adminstr. 1991–; recipient Caltrans 25-Year award, Sacto. 1981, Dist. director award, Marysville 1987, Affirmative Action award 1988, Sustained Superior Accomplishment award, Caltrans, Sacto. 1990, winner First Award in Publicity Competition, Calif./Nev. Moose Assn. Inc. (1980, 89, 90, 91, 92), Moose of Yr. award 1990-92, Comm. Svc. award Cal/Nev. Moose Assn. 1990, nat. Shining Star award nominee 1990-91, 1st Pl. Internat. Publicity Award 1993, Shining Star Award Moose Internat. Editor of Yr. 1993, listed Who's Who in West 1992-93, Who's Who in California 1993, 94, 95, 96, Dictionary of Internat. Biographies 1993; chmn. Caltrans Disabled Advy. Com. 1981-88; mem: Am. Red Cross, Yuba City (instr. 1974-84), Am. Legion 1988–, E. Clampus Vitus 1972–, Nat. Rifle Assn. (1974–, charter founder 2nd amendment task force 1993, life mem.), Citizens Right to Keep Arms (1986–, Citizen of Yr. 1989, 90, 91, 92), Dist. 3 Quarter Century Club (1981–, dir. 1985-87), Loyal Order of Moose Lodge No.1204 Yuba City (1969–, Moose Call bulletin editor 1971-94, 1st Pl. Internat. Bulletin Award and 2d Pl. Internat. Award for Editl. Excellence, L.O.O.M. 1990, 92, publicity dir. 1977-94, gov. 1982-83), Moose Internat. Calif./Nev. (publicity ofcr. 1990–, dep. dir. dept. public relations 1995–), Legion of the Moose (1978–, Fellowship Degree 1989, Pilgrim Degree of Merit 1995, mem. 25 Club in Membership-75 Div., pres. North State High Degree Council (Moose Internat.) 1995-96); inventor: rubber powered boats, Johnson's Marina Boat Regatta (1981-87); mil: p.o. 3c USN 1953-61; Republican; Methodist; rec: hunting, fishing, boating, radio control modeling. Ofc: Caltrans PO Box 911 Marysville 95901

JOHNSON, DAVID ARTHUR, corporate executive; b. Apr. 23, 1946, Yankton, S.Dak.; s. Arthur Wm. and Dagny S. (Olson) J.; m. Marilyn Lee Bessey, Apr. 11, 1970; children: Allan David b. 1974, Michael Paul b. 1977; edn: AA in psych., Pasadena Comm. Coll., 1966; BS personnel mgmt., CSU Los Angeles, 1972, BS in acctg., 1978. Career: adjuster Morris Plan, Alhambra 1968-70; office mgr. Hussmann Refrig., Vernon 1972-74; acctg. mgr. Bell & Howell, Pasadena 1975-80; controller Carter Automotive, Commerce 1981-86; bd. dir., exec. v.p., gen. mgr. LAWI/CSA Consolidators Inc., City of Commerce 1987–; civic: singer, soloist community functions, mem. Occidental Coll. Comm. Choir (1986-87), Contact Helpline 24-hr. crisis prevention svc. (mem., counselor, bd. dirs. 1987-88); mil: E3 USNR 1967-73, Vietnam vet. active duty 1967-68; Lutheran (ch. treas. 1983-86). Ofc: LAWI/CSA Consolidators 2043 Ross St Vernon 90058

JOHNSON, DAVID DEAN BRIAN, structural engineer; b. Feb. 7, 1956, North Hollywood; s. Charles Walton and Marcia Miriam (Baile) J.; 4th generation Los Angelonian, great-great grandson of San Fernando Valley pioneers Neils and Ann Wilden Johnson; edn: BS, CSU Northridge 1980; grad. studies, UCLA 1986–; Calif. Reg. Profl. Engr.- civil (#34859, 1982), structural (#3032, 1988). Career: design draftsman Aircraft Component Repair Co., Sun Valley 1977-79; struct. designer/ draftsman John Chan & Assoc., Struct. Engrs., Van Nuys 1979-80; mgr. Calif. Div., KPFF Consulting Engrs., Santa Monica 1980-90; pres. David D.B. Johnson, Structural Engrs., Santa Monica 1990–; mem: Am. Soc. Civil Engrs., Structural Engring. Assn. of So. Calif., Am. Concrete Inst., Earthquake Engring. Research Inst.; Libertarian; Methodist; rec: golf, running, wine tasting. Res: 120 Pico Blvd #409 Santa Monica 90405

JOHNSON, DONNA, religious order financial officer; b. Sept. 11, 1931, Stockton; d. Ralph Wesley and Elizabeth Louise (Pucci) Johnson; edn: BA, CSU Fullerton 1976; MSA, Univ. Notre Dame 1982; religious sister Dominican Sisters of MSJ. Career: bus. tchr. St. Elizabeth H.S., Oakland 1963-65; treas. St. Catherines Military Sch., Anaheim 1965-75; dir. devel. Immaculate Conception Academy, San Francisco 1975-86; treas. gen. Dominican Sisters of MSJ, Fremont 1986–; treas. Queen of Holy Rosary Coll., Fremont 1986–; dir. St. Catherines Mil. Sch., Anaheim 1986–; trustee Reta Trust, San Francisco 1986-90; mem: Conf. of Religious Treas. (secty., treas.), Nat. Assn. Treas. of Religious Insts.; Democrat; R.Cath.; rec: sailing. Res: 43326 Mission Blvd Fremont 94539 Ofc: POB 3908 Fremont 94539

JOHNSON, DOROTHY MYERS, jeweler, accountant, retired; b. Sept. 27, 1917, Magna, Utah; d. Gilbert Yost and Elizabeth (Kitchen) Myers; m. Harvey Kenneth Johnson, Apr. 7, 1944 (div. 1956); edn: grad. University H.S., Oakland 1935. Career: office staff Brisacher Advertising, San Francisco 1935-42; cost acct. Jones & King, Hayward 1942-43; co-owner Johnson Jewelers, Oakland 1944-56; ptnr. Parker & Johnson Jewelers, Hollister 1947-56; staff acctg. Margaret Axell, P.A., San Rafael 1956-79; honors: biog. listings in Two Thousand Notable Am. Women (2d edit.), The Inner Circle of Women 1990, Internat. Dir. of Disting. Leadership (3d edit.), Hall of Fame, Five Thousand Personalities of World 1991; clubs: Internat. Platform Assn., Eastern Star, White Shrine of Jerusalem, Newcomers Club, var. senior orgns., Paradise; past mem. Bus. & Profl. Women; Republican; Prot.; rec: sci. studies, fin., politics. Res: PO Box 1536 Paradise 95967

JOHNSON, EINAR WILLIAM, lawyer; b. Apr. 6, 1955, Fontana; s. Carl Wilbur and Judith Priscilla (Orcutt) J.; m. Cynthia, Oct. 9, 1976; children: Brian b. 1977 (dec.), Carl b. 1979, Gregory b. 1980, Christopher b. 1983, Shaun b. 1986, Bradford b. 1989; edn: BA in speech comm., Brigham Young Univ., 1980; JD, J. Reuben Clark Law Sch., Provo, Ut. 1983; admitted Calif. Bar, 1983. Career: asst. debate coach BYU, Provo 1979-80; fin. com. Jed Richardson for Congress, Provo 1980; sales mgr. Ortho Mattress, Orem, Ut. 1979, 81; law clk. Acret & Perrochet, Los Angeles 1982; judicial clerkship U.S. Courts-Hon. A. Sherman Christensen, Salt Lake City 1983-84; litigation atty. law firm Smith & Hilbig, Torrance, 1984-89, litigation ptnr. 1990-93; founder, law firm Johnson and Associates 1993–; honors: outstanding varsity debater BYU (1974, 80), Am. Jurisprudence awards Bancroft-Whitney 1981, Dean's Cup for top oralist 1982, Am. Inn of Court I, Provo, editor Moot Ct. pgm. J. Reuben Clark Law Sch., and Nat. Moot Ct. Team 1982-83, Nat. Order of Barristers 1983, A.H. Christensen Award for Advocacy 1983; mem: ABA, Calif. State Bar, L.A. Co. Bar Assn., Assn. of Trial Lawyers of Am., Internat. Platform Assn.; publs: law rev. comment, 1982, award winning thesis, 1983, award winning oratory, 1969-80, incl. John Baker's Last Race, 1977; Republican (dist. ofcr., state del. Utah Rep. Conv. 1978); Ch. of Jesus Christ of Latter Day Saints (Colorado Mission, Denver 1974-76, Sunday Sch. tchr., L.A. 1986-89, stake high counselor 1989–, Bishop's counselor 1992-93, Elders Quorum Pres. 1993–); rec: photography, guitar, auto restoration, fishing, boating. Res: 211 Via La Soledad Redondo Beach 90277 Ofc: Smith & Hilbig 21515 Hawthorne Blvd Torrance 90503 Tel: 213/540-9111

JOHNSON, FORDYCE, physician; b. Dec. 6, 1904, Fargo, N.D.; s. Johan and Mary Anne (Bentson) J.; m. Astrid Ann Erickson, May 28, 1933; children: Karen b. 1939, Kirsten b. 1941,, Gregory b. 1946; edn: Univ. Puget Sound 1923-26; BS, Univ. Oreg. Med. Sch. Portland 1930; MD, 1930. Career: pvt. practice ear nose throat, head neck surgery, Wash. D.C. 1935-38; Med. Profl. Building, Tacoma, Wash. 1938-42; pvt. practice, Pasadena 1946-80; ret.; asst. prof. USC Med. Sch., 1946-80; UC San Diego, 1984–; chief civil defense med., Pasadena 1947-67; awards: Pasadena C.of C. Merit. Service (1960); mem: Pasadena Med. Bd. (pres. 1954), Pacific Coast Otolaryngology-Ophthalmology Soc. (bd. dirs. 1960-62), E. Pasadena Kiwanis (bd. dirs. 1952-60), Pasadena C.of C. (v.p. 1960), Am. Acad. Otolaryngology- Allergy (pres. 1980); 32 papers pub. in med. jours. (1938-72), 3 texts. pub. (1976-80); mil: major AUS MC 1942-46; Republican; Prot.; rec: teaching. Res: Fordyce Johnson M.D. 3890 Nobel Dr Ste 901 San Diego 92122 Tel: 619/597-8109

JOHNSON, FRED IRVING, government health services executive; b. June 5, 1947, Monrovia; s. Floyd Charles and Frances Elizabeth (Shepherd) J.; children: Erik Daniel b. 1976, Heather Leah b. 1978; edn: student, Drury Coll. 1968; AA, Citrus Coll. 1972; BA, CSU Fullerton 1975; MPA, Univ. of San Francisco 1990. Career: credit mgr. Dial Fin. Corp., Los Angeles 1968-69; mgr. electronic systems Instrumentation Div., Kenney Engring. Corp., Monrovia 1970-74; staff acct./auditor Shasta Co., Auditor-Controller's Office 1975-78, mental health adminstr. Dept. Mental Health 1978-79, dep. health svcs. adminstr. Dept. Health Svcs. 1979-82, dept. dir. Health Svcs. Agency 1982, acting dir. 1982-83, dir. 1983-87. hosp. adminstr./controller Shasta Gen. Hosp. 1982-83; director health/med. svcs. Placer County, Health Dept. 1987–; mem. Shasta Co. coms.: Cabinet Advy., Budget Planning, chmn. Staff Advy., secty. Health Svcs. Advy., Legislative, Mgmt. Council, Health Ins.; honors: Resolution, Calif. State Senate 1987, merit award Shasta Co. Bd. Suprs. 1986, appreciation, Private Industry Council 1986, Junction Sch. Dist. 1986, Soroptimist Internat. Redding 1985, Shasta Co. Chem. People 1985, Calif. State Advy. Bd. Drug Programs 1984; mem: Calif. Hosp. Assn., County Suprs. Assn. Calif., County Health Care Execs. Assn. (past pres.), Calif. Conf. Local Mental Health Dirs. (exec. bd., var. coms.), Calif. Assn. Co. Alcohol Pgm. Adminstrs., Calif. Assn. Co. Drug. Pgm. Adminstrs., Forensic Assn. Calif., Am. Mgmt. Assn., Healthcare Fin. Mgmt. Assn., Calif. Assn. Pub. Hosps., Shasta Co. Econ. Devel. Task Force, Shasta Co. Inter-Hosp. Advy. Bd., Am. Sch. Bds. Assn., Calif. Sch. Bds. Assn., Shasta Co. Trustee's Assn., Shasta Co. Employee's Fed. Credit Union (credit com.), Placer Health & Welfare Functional Group (chair); civic: S.P.C.A. (v.chair), Rotary (team capt. health svcs.), Palo Cedro Youth Soccer (coach), Cow Creek 4-H Club, Juction Elem. Sch. Dist. (trustee, 3-term pres. 1976-86), IRS Vol. Income Tax Pgm., Lions; mil: E-5 AUS 1965-68, chief personnel splst Batt. Hq.; Republican; Prot.. Res: 8833 Garden Glen Way Sacramento 95826Ofc: Office of Statewide Health Planning and Development 1600 Ninth St Rm 450 Sacramento 95814

JOHNSON, HAROLD, judge; b. Oct. 8, 1928, Syracuse, NY; s. Harold Oscar and Elizabeth Lulu (Kittell) J.; m. Kay Reilly Blair, June 24, 1950; children: Michael b. 1952, Kevin b. 1954, Kristin b. 1958, Linda b. 1963; edn: undergrad. Syracuse Univ. 1945-46; BS pol. sci., Northwestern Univ. 1951; Calif. tchr. credential, UC Los Angeles 1954; JD, Southwestern Univ. Law Sch. 1961; admitted Calif. State Bar 1963. Career: mgmt. trainee Provident Mutual Life Ins. Co. 1951-52; tchr. Simi Valley Unified Sch. Dist. 1954-56, 1960-61; staff asst. mat. & contracts adminstrn. depts. No. Am. Aviation Inc. 1956-60, 61-63; deputy dist. atty. San Luis Obispo County 1963-64, 1965-66; assoc. Muller & Woolpert, San Luis Obispo 1964-65; city atty. City of San Luis Obispo 1966-71; justice court judge S.L.O. County 1971-75, judge San Luis Obispo County

Municipal Ct. 1975-91; instr. bus. law Cuesta Coll. 1964-66; instr. legal aspects of real estate Univ. Calif. Ext. 1964-65; mem. Calif. Judges Assn., Phi Alpha Delta legal frat., Rotary, Zeta Psi frat.; wks: Radio actor, Stations WFBL and WSYR, Syracuse, NY 1937-43; mil: ET3 USN 1946-49 WWII Victory Medal; Republican; Prot.; rec: tennis, bowling. Res: 1567 Bee Canyon Rd., Arroyo Grande 93420 Ofc: SLO County Municipal Court, County Government Center, 1050 Monterey St Rm 220 San Luis Obispo 93408

JOHNSON, HERBERT EARL, physician; b. Dec. 28, 1937, Belzoni, Miss.; s. T.V. and Josie Lou (Gardner) J.; m. Judith Dale Stewart, Dec. 27, 1960; children: Herbert b. 1962, Angela b. 1963, Stewart b. 1968; edn: BS, Mich. St. Univ., 1958; MD, Wayne St. Univ., 1963; cert. Am. Bd. Physicial Medicine & Rehab. (1971). Career: intern Harper Hosp., Detroit, Mich. 1963-64; resident Letterman Hosp., San Francisco 1964-65; resident, physiatrist Rehab. Inst., Detroit, Mich. 1967-70; med. dir. Casa Colina Hosp., Pomona 1970-82, chief of staff 1980-82; physiatrist Kaiser-Permanente, Fontana 1982-88; chief physical med. and med. rehab. Kaiser Permanente, Riverside 1988–; bd. dirs. So. Calif. Permanente Med. Group, Pasadena 1988-95; clin. instr. Wayne St. Univ., Detroit 1969-70; clin. prof. UC Irvine, Orange 1971; mem: Calif. Soc. Phys. Med. & Rehab. (v.p. 1988-89), Riverside Co. Med. Soc., Calif. Med. Assn., Inst. Religion & Wholeness (pres. bd. dirs. 1981-83); mil: capt. AUS Med. Corps 1964-67; Republican; Cath., Our Lady of Assumption; rec: golf, tennis, backgammon. Res: 2342 Coalinga Ct Claremont 91711 Ofc: Kaiser-Permanente Medical Center 10800 Magnolia Riverside 92505

JOHNSON, JOY L., clinical social worker; b. June 13, 1945, Oakland; d. Bishop La Far Benjamin and Julia (Robinson) J.; son, L. Aaron Smith b. 1979; m. Gabriel B. Donaldson, Jr., 1988; edn: BA sociology, San Francisco St. Univ., 1968, MSW, 1973; Lic. Clin. Social Wkr., 1975. Career: private practice, Oakland 1975–; asst. clin. prof. dept. psychiat. UC Med. Sch., San Francisco 1977-81; clin. social worker Permanente Med. Group, S.F., Richmond, 1981-94; awards: NIMH Fellow Mt. Zion Hosp., S.F. 1973-75; mem: Bay Area Black Soc. Wkrs. 1973–, NASW, BCD; Pentecostal; rec: reading. Ofc: 465 34th Street Oakland 94609

JOHNSON, KEITH WHITAKER, economist, artist; b. March 13, 1912, Avant, Okla.; s. Bertram and Elizabeth (Whitaker) J.; m. Lupe De Osma, Sept. 9, 1936; 1 son, Keith O. b. 1938; edn: BA, Univ. Kans. 1934; Cornell Univ. 1934-35; MA, Duke Univ. 1937; PhD, 1944. Career: actg. prof. Doane Coll., Crete, Neb. 1938-40; instr. Franklin & Marshall Coll., Lancaster, Pa. 1940-42; econ., statistician U.S. Govt., Wash. D.C. 1942-47, Dallas, Tx. 1952-54; asst. prof. Univ. N.M., Albuquerque 1947-48; economist Fed. Reserve Bank, Dallas, Tx. 1948-52; Pacific Gas & Elec., San Francisco 1954-77; cons. Civilian Defense Adminstrn., Waco and Dallas, Tx. 1953-54; Bay Area Council, San Francisco 1955-60; Business Council, Wash. D.C. 1956-70; U.S. C.of C. 1969-71; San Francisco C.of C. 1974-76; mem: World Future Soc., AAAS, Am. Econ. Assn., Smithsonian Inst., Metro. Museum of Art N.Y., Santa Barbara Museum of Art, Am. Humanist Assn.; author: Survival of West, World Energy Use; articles pub. in bus. jours. (1942-76), patentee in field (1947-59), artist/painter (1982-89); rec: chess. Res: 1731 Las Tunas Rd Santa Barbara 93103

JOHNSON, LEDENE CORDA, quality manager; b. Feb. 19, 1952, San Jose; d. James Guy and Martha Jane (Myers) Corda; m. Charles Glenn Johnson, Nov. 7, 1981; edn: BSBA, Univ. Redlands 1980. Career: receptionist IBM, San Jose 1974-76, secty. 1976-80, mktg. rep. IBM, San Francisco 1980-83, systems engr., Palo Alto 1983-87, mgr. First Line, IBM, S.F. 1987-89, quality mgr. 199095, JAD facilitator 1995–; mem. Internat. Tng. in Comm., S.F. 1988-90; career counselor Alumnae Resources 1988-94; mem: Woman's Aglow Fellowship (area bd. treas.), Bay Area Profl. Network, Commonwealth Club Calif. 1980-93, Campfire Inc. (bd. 1988-90), Am. Soc. of Quality Control (ASQC) 1990–; Republican; Christian; rec: gardening, golf. Ofc: IBM/ISSC 221 Main St Ste 1650 San Francisco 94105

JOHNSON, LEONIDAS ALEXANDER, optometrist; b. Jan. 16, 1959, Chgo.; s. Rev. Leon and Dolores J.; m. Crystal D. Ellington, June 23, 1990; edn: BA biology, Ill. Wesleyan Univ., 1977-81; BS visual sci., So. Calif. Coll. Optometry, 1983, OD, 1985; stu. Talbot Sch. of Theology, La Mirada 1991–; Calif. reg. optometrist, 1985. Career: optometrist: Larry Gotlieb, OD Inc., Redondo Beach 1985-86; James Moses O.D., Inglewood 1986-87; Eyecare USA, Montclair 1987-89, mem. quality assurance com. 1988-89; Pearle Visioncare, Brea 1989-94; Watts Health Found., Inc., Los Angeles 1994–; Reginald Sampson, M.D., Montebello 1994–; clin. investigator, The Ocular Hypertension Treatment Study (OHTS) 1994–; honors: Optometric recogn. award Pearle Inc. 1990, Outstanding Young Men of Am. 1986, listed The Soc. of Distinguished Am. High Sch. Students 1977, Who's Who in the West (23d); mem. Am. Acad. of Optometry (fellow 1993–), Am. Optometric Assn. 1982–, Calif. Optometric Assn. 1986–, Nat. Optometric Assn. (v.p. So. Calif. chpt. 1993); pub. article in peer rev. jour., 1985; Friendship Baptist Ch., Yorba Linda (trustee 1987-89, deacon 1987–). Res: PO Box 4434 Diamond Bar 91765 Ofc: Watts Health Center 10300 S Compton Ave Los Angeles 90002

JOHNSON, MARIAN ILENE, educator; b. Oct. 3, 1929, Hawarden, Iowa; d. Henry Richard and Wilhelmina Anna (Schmidt) Stoltenberg; m. Paul Irving Jones, June 14, 1958 (dec. Feb. 26, 1985); m. William Andrew Johnson, Oct. 3, 1991; edn: BA, Univ. LaVerne, 1959; MA, Claremont Grad. Sch., 1962; PhD, Ariz. State Univ., Tempe 1971. Career: elementary sch. tchr. pub. schs. Cherokee, Iowa 1949-52, Sioux City, Ia. 1952-56, Ontario, Calif. 1956-61, Belvedere-Tiburon, Calif. 1962-65, Columbia, Calif. 1965-68; prof. of edn. Calif. State Univ. Chico, 1972-91, also supr. of student tchrs., Center coord. Dept. of Edn.; honors: Phi Delta Kappa 1976-92, Delta Kappa Gamma 1985-92, listed Who's Who- in the World, in Am. Edn., in Am., in the West, of Am. Women; mem. Internat. Reading Assn. 1972-92, AAUW 1985-91; rec: travel. Res: 26437 S Lakewood Dr Sun Lakes Az 85248

JOHNSON, PHILIP LESLIE, lawyer; b. Jan. 24, 1939, Beloit, Wis.; s. Philip James and Christabel (Williams) J.; m. Kathleen, May 12, 1979; children: Celeste b. 1984, Nicole b. 1990; edn: AB, Princeton Univ. 1961; JD, USC 1973. Career: pilot US Marine Corps 1961-70; atty., assoc. Tucker & Coddington, 1973-78; ptnr. Engstrom, Lipscomb & Lack, Los Angeles 1978-92; of counsel Lillick & Charles, Long Beach 1993–; lectr. Calif. Cont. Edn. of Bar (CEB) 1990–; speaker So. Methodist Univ. Air Law Symp. 1986, 1993; lectr. USC Inst. on Safety & System Mgmt.; mem: Calif. State Bar Assn., LA Co. Bar Assn.; mil: Col.(Ret.) USMC 1961-70, Reserve 1970-92; rec: flying, skiing. Res: 5340 Valley View Rd Rancho Palos Verdes 90275 Ofc: Lillick & Charles One World Trade Center #950 Long Beach 90831

JOHNSON, RICHARD LLOYD, physician; b. Feb. 16, 1918, Weaverville, Calif.; s. Lloyd Godfrey and Elizabeth Avis (Henderson) J.; m. Claire Wheeler Morgan; children: Elizabeth, Ellen, Victoria, Caroline; edn: AB, UC Berkeley, 1939; MD, UC San Francisco, 1942. Career: intern Sacto. Co. Hosp. 1942-43; resident internal med. Milwaukee Co. Hosp., Wis. 1946-48; solo practice physician-internist, Sacramento 1949-88, med. dir. Pub. Health Div., Sacto. Co. Health Dept. 1988-93 (ret.); chief dept. of med. 1965, 1975-76, pres. of staff 1966, Sutter Comm. Hosps.; chief dept. of med. 1960, Mercy Gen. Hosp.; appt. White House Conf. on Aging 1961, 81, Gov.'s Advy. Com. on Aging 1958-65, Calif. St. Bd. of Med. Examiners 1965-69; mem. AMA (alt. del. 1985-89), CMA (del. 1977-92), Sacto. Co. Med. Soc. (pres. 1978, editor 1955, 79-93), Sacto. Soc. Int. Med. (pres. 1975), Calif. Soc. Int. Med. (pres. 1980), Masons, Scottish Rite, SAR; mil: capt. US Army M.C. 1943-46; Episcopalian; rec: genealogy, Calif. history. Res: 443 10th St Colusa 95932-2216

JOHNSON, ROYCE H., physician, medical educator; b. April 28, 1944, Pasadena; children: Bradley b. 1975, Kimberley b. 1979, Stephanie b. 1989, Jacqueline b. 1992; edn: BA, UCSB 1966; MD, UC Irvine 1970. Career: chief, infectious disease Kern Med. Center, Bakersfield 1975–; asst. prof. medicine UCLA 1976, assoc. prof. medicine 1983, prof. medicine 1990–; vice chmn. medicine Kern Med. Center 1978–; awards: Rotary Paul Harris fellow 1984; A.C.P. (fellow); Infectious Disease Soc. Am. (fellow). Ofc: 1830 Flower St Bakersfield 93305

JOHNSON, WILLIAM HARRY, international management consultant; b. Oct. 1, 1941, Ridley Park, Pa.; s. Harry Brown and Florence (Round) J.; m. Anna Marie Castellanos, Oct. 19, 1984; edn: BS, Drexel Univ., 1963, MBA, 1967; mfg. methods engr., N.J. Career: mgmt. exec. DuPont Co., Wilmington, Del. 1963-69; bus. analysis mgr. Imperial Chemical Inds., 1970-76; fin. analysis and acquisitions Fluor/Daniel Corp., Irvine, Calif. 1976-78; fin. analysis mgr. Alexander Proudfoot, Chgo. 1978-79; exec. v.p. and c.f.o. Sego Internat., Niagara Falls, Ontario, Can. 1980-82; exec. v.p./gen. mgr. Science Mgmt. Corp., Basking Ridge, N.J. 1982-87; exec. mgr. McDonnell Douglas, Long Beach, Calif. 1987–; dir: Drexel Univ. Alumni Assn. 1991–, Clariton (Pa.) Recycling Assn. Inc. 1990–, Madden Associates, Buffalo Grove, Ill. 1990–, KABB Inc., El Segundo, Ca. 1987–, SEGO Internat., Niagara Falls Ontario, Can. 1980–, Penn Bus. Resources, Santa Ana, Ca. 1982–; awards: MDC extraordinary achiev. McDonnell Douglas 1990, MDC productivity award 1988, chmn.'s productivity award Sci. Mgmt. Corp. 1986, Presdl. Achiev. award Republican Nat. Com., W.D.C. 1988, bd. dirs. outstanding achiev. SEGO Internat. 1981; mem: Inst. of Indsl. Engrs. 1973–, Am. Mgmt. Assn. 1970–, Nat. Productivity Assn. of Canada 1980–, Nat. Assn. of Accts. 1965–, Nat. Petroleum Refinery Assn. 1980–, Am. Mktg. Assn. 1965–, Internat. Productivity Org. 1978–, Dewar's Highlander Clan (Glasgow, Scot.), Lions Club of Kowloon (cent. H.K.), El Segundo (Ca.) Residents Assn.; author: Explosives Distributors (1967), pamphlet: Work Order Guide (1980), articles (1984, 86); Republican (Nat. Com.); Presbyterian; rec: dogs, internat. travel, tennis, swimming, volunteer work. Res: 807 Hillcrest St El Segundo 90245 Ofc: McDonnell Douglas 4060 Lakewood Blvd Long Beach 90801

JOHNSTON, CHARLES LELAND, III, investments executive; b. Oct. 10, 1946, Los Angeles; s. Charles L., Jr., MD, and Evelyn (Dorthy (Apel) J.; m. Judith Sumner Pratt, June 18, 1969 (div. Dec. 1972); m. Lisa Cumilla Peacock, June 12, 1982 (div. June 12, 1994); children: Sarah Marie b. 1969, Tanya Simone b. 1984; edn: AA, New Mexico Mil. Inst. 1966; BA, Univ. Ariz. 1969; BS internat. mgmt., Am. Grad. Sch. Internat. Mgmt. 1970. Career: export sales mgr. Sunkist Growers, Ontario 1970-81; v.p. mktg. and sales Continental Flavors & Frangrances, Brea 1981-82; v.p. investments Dean Witter Reynolds, Napa 1982–; dir. Sunkist Soft Drinks Inc., Atlanta, Ga. 1978-81; owner Johnston Vineyards; Helena View Winery; mem: Napa Valley Opera House Inc. (past pres., exec. com., bd. 1988–), Napa Valley Grape Growers Assn., Sierra Club, Napa Valley Wine Library Assn., Am. Enology Assn., San Francisco Com. Fgn. Rels., Napa Valley Symphony Assn., Calistoga C.of C., World Affairs Council No. Calif., Commonwealth Club S.F., Calif. Certified Organic Farmer; Republican; rec: wine grape growing. Res: PO Box 658 Napa 94559 Ofc: POB 3440 Napa 94558

JOHNSTON, PAMELA MC EVOY, psychologist; b. Mar. 8, 1937, Forest Hills, N.Y.; d. Renny T. and Pamela Shipley (Sweeny) McEvoy; widow of Percy H. "Duke" Johnston; children by previous marriage: Michael B. Anderson, Jeffery A. Thomas, Candy A. Watts, Kenneth L. Anderson; edn: BA, Univ. La Verne, 1978, MS, 1980; PhD, U.S. Internat. Univ., 1982. Career: instr. psychology, sociology, Allan Hancock Coll., Santa Maria 1977-78; mental health asst. Santa Barbara City Alcoholism Dept., 1977-78; gen. mgr. Professional Suites, San Diego 1978-81; therapist Chula Vista Community Counseling Ctr., San Diego 1978-85, staff pres. 1978; research asst. USIU, 1979-82; research coord. Military Family Research Ctr., San Diego 1981-82; assoc. dir. Acad. Assoc. Psychotherapists, 1982-86; private practice, San Diego 1982-93, Santa Maria 1993–; instr. psychology Mesa Coll., San Diego 1989-90; awards: Calif. State scholar 1976-77, State fellow 1979, 80, 81, 82; mem: Am. Psychol. Assn., Am. Assn. Marriage and Family Therapists, Calif. Assn. Marriage and Family Therapists, San Diego County Mental Health Assn. (bd. 1978-80), Rotary Internat. of Borrego Springs 1989–, Women's Internat. Ctr. (bd. 1984–), North County InterFaith Council (bd. 1990-92); Republican; R.Cath.; Res: PO Box 1198 Borrego Springs 92004 Tel: 619/767-5224

JOHNSTON, ROBERT, certified public accountant; b. April 3, 1932, Los Angeles; s. James and Helen A. (Mills) J.; m. Virginia E., June 26, 1947; children: Donald E. b. 1949, Kent E. b. 1952, Ronald E. b. 1961; edn: BS, UCLA 1948; MA, tax., Golden St. Univ. 1975; C.P.A. Calif. 1965. Career: tax dept. Deloitte Haskins & Sells; tax auditor St. of Calif., L.A.; prin. Robert Johnson CPA, (acctg. firm), Long Beach; awards: So. Calif. Tax Conf. Outstanding Leadership 1973-74, Nat. Soc. Pub. Accts., Nat. Editl. award 1980, Execellence in Writing; mem: AICPA, Calif. Soc. C.P.A., Long Beach Estate Planning & Trust Council, Calif. St. Bd. Accountancy (past v.p.), Soc. Calif. Accts. (past pres.), Lynwood C.of C. (past v.p.), Elks, Vets. of Fgn. Wars, Am. Legion; mil: USN; Republican; Presbyterian; rec: golf, boating. Res: 1 Third Pl Unit 802 Long Beach 90802 Ofc: 3636 No Long Beach Blvd Long Beach 90807-4006

JOHNSTONE, IAIN MURRAY, statistician, educator, consultant; b. Dec. 10, 1956, Melbourne, Australia; s. Samuel Thomas Murray and Pamela Beatrice (Kriegel) J.; edn: BS hons., Australian Nat. Univ. Canberra 1978; MS, 1979; PhD, Cornell Univ. 1981. Career: asst., assoc. prof. statistics Stanford Univ. 1981–; assoc. prof. biostats. Stanford Univ. Med. Sch. 1989–; prof. statistics and biostatistics, Stanford Univ. Med. Sch. 1992–, statistics dept. chair 1994–; assoc. editor Annals of Statistics 1987-91; contbr. articles to profl. jours.; awards: Alfred P. Sloan Research fellow, 1988-90, Presdl. Young Investigator NSF, 1985-92; mem: Royal Statistics Soc. (fellow), Inst. Math. Statistics (fellow, program secty.), Am. Statistical Assn., Am. Math. Soc., AAAS. Ofc: Stanford Univ. Dept. Statistics Sequoia Hall Stanford 94305-4065

JOLLEY, DONAL CLARK, artist-painter; b. Oct. 20, 1933, Zion National Park, Utah; s. Donal Jones and Nora (Crawford) J.; m. Virginia Elizabeth Harrison, Nov. 14, 1970 (dec. 1994); children: Karen b. 1960, Donal b. 1962, Keith b. 1965; edn: BS, Brigham Young Univ., Provo 1959. Career: served to sp4, illustrator, US Army, Germany 1956-57; illustrator Spacetech Lab., Redondo Beach, Calif. 1960-61; illustrator The Aerospace Corp., San Bernardino 1961-71; art instr. San Bdo. Valley Coll., 1973-77; awards: 3rd, Watercolor West, Redlands 1975; Nat. Watercolor Soc. Members cash award, L.A. 1980, 3rd, NWS Members 1992; Am. Indian and Cowboy Artists Assn.-gold medal/watercolor, L.A. 1990, bronze/watercolor 1992, gold medal/watercolor 1994, Best of Show Eagle Feather award 1994; mem. Nat. Watercolor Soc. 1975–, Am. Indian and Cowboy Artists 1990–, Watercolor West 1970–. Res: PO Box 156 Rim Forest 92378

JONES, CHARLIE, television sportscaster; b. Nov. 9, 1930, Ft. Smith, Ark.; s. Ira Fulton and Mary Virginia (Norris) J.; m. Ann, June 16, 1954; children: Chuck b. 1958, Julie b. 1963; edn: undergrad., USC; JD, Univ. of Ark. Law Sch. 1953. Career: sports dir., then station mgr. KFPW, Fort Smith, Ark. 1955-60, dir. t.v. and radio, AFL Dallas Texans 1960, began network bdcstg. with ABC-TV (3 AFL Championship Games) ABC's Wide World of Sports, and sports dir. WFAA-TV, 1960-65; sportscaster NBC-TV, 1965–; play-by-play broadcaster Colorado Rockies TV network 1993–; NBC Host-Announcer for 1986 World Cup Soccer, Mexico City (largest internat. sports event ever); NBC Track and Field announcer 1988 Olympic Games, Seoul, Korea; NBC Swimming and Diving announcer 1992 Olympic Games, Barcelona, Spain; TV broadcast firsts include: Super Bowl I, first AFL nationally televised game, first NBC

SportsWorld, first World Cup Gymnastics, first World Cup Marathon, first World Championships of Track and Field, and first Senior Skins Game; actor (1951–) in over 30 t.v. series incl. Ironside, McMillan, Colombo, The Dick Van Dyke Show, Rich Man-Poor Man, and in 12+ Movies of the Week; motion pictures: Personal Best, Return of the Killer Tomatoes, and Killer Tomatoes Strike Back; hosted t.v. series "Almost Anything Goes" and sports-game show "Pro-Fan;" honors: Emmy award 1973 as writer/prod. and host of documentary "Is Winning The Name of the Game?"; Cine Golden Eagle 1982, bronze medal, N.Y. Film & TV Festival 1982, Freedom Found. Award for PBS series "The American Frontier" (co-prod., co-wrote, co-host w/Merlin Olsen, 1982); Toastmasters Intl. Speech Champion 1957; awarded Headliner of Yr. for outstanding contbns. in field of TV, San Diego Press Club 1986, Univ. of Ark. disting. alumnus 1989; mem. Confrerie Des Chevaliers du Tastevin; mil: 1st lt. USAF 1953-55; Christian; rec: golf. Address: Charlie Jones Associates, Inc. 8080 El Paseo Grande La Jolla 92037

JONES, CLEON BOYD, research engineer; b. Nov. 9, 1961, Norwalk; s. Cleon Earl and Marjorie Helen (McDade) J.; edn: BS in math., Biola Univ., 1983. Career: research librarian Christian Research Inst., San Juan Capistrano 1981-84; flight control engr. Leading Systems Inc., Irvine 1984-90; research engr. Dynamic Research Inc., Torrance 1990–; awards: NASA Group Achievement Award, Pilot Project Team 1994; Republican. Res: 12464 Fallcreek Lane Cerritos 90701

JONES, EDWARD GEORGE, university professor; b. March 26, 1939, Upper Hutt, New Zealand; nat. 1978; s. Frank Ian and Theresa Agnes (Riordan) J.; m. Elizabeth Suzanne Oldham, April 27, 1963; children: Philippa b. 1966, Christopher b. 1969; edn: MD, Univ. Otago N.Z. 1962; PhD, Oxford Univ. England 1968. Career: lectr., assoc. prof. Univ. of Otago, N.Z. 1964-71; Nuffield Dominions demonstrator Oxford Univ., England 1966-68; lectr. Balliol Coll. 1967-68; assoc. prof., prof. Wash. Univ. Sch. Medicine, St. Louis, Mo. 1972-84; prof., chmn. UC Irvine Coll. of Medicine 1984–; dir neural systems lab. Inst. for Physical & Chem. Research, Japan 1988–; ed., assoc. ed. of sci. jours. 1975–; awards: Anatomical Soc. Great Britain & Ireland Symington Prize 1969), Oxford Univ. Rolleston Prize 1969, Am. Assn. Anatomists Cajal Medal 1989; mem: Soc. Neurosci., Am. Assn. Anatomists, AAAS, Anatomical Soc. Great Britain & Ireland; author: Thalamus & Basal Telencephalon, 1982, The Thalamus, 1985, Structural Basis of Neurobiology, co-ed. book series: Cerebral Cortex, 1984, 250+ articles pub. in sci. and hist. jours., 1965; Democrat; rec: carpentry. Ofc: UCI California College of Medicine Dept. Anatomy & Neurobiology, Irvine 92717

JONES, IDA MAE, law professor; b. Aug. 18, 1953, Omaha, Nebr.; d. Jonathan and Mary (Cooper) Jones; m. Harry Edward Williams, Aug. 16, 1977 (div. 1981); children: Kenneth b. 1973, Eugene b. 1974, Kamali b. 1979, Jamilla b. 1981; edn: BA sociology, Creighton Univ. 1974; JD, N.Y. Univ. 1977. Career: law clk. HEW, N.Y.C. 1976-77; assoc. appellate counsel Legal Aid Criminal Appeals 1977-79; staff atty. Legal Aid Soc., Omaha, Neb. 1979-81; sole practice, Omaha, Neb. 1981-87; asst. prof. Univ. Neb., Omaha 1981-86, assoc. prof. 1986-87; prof. CSU, Fresno 1987–; bd. dirs PILCO, Omaha 1981-84; advy. bd. Child Saving Inst. 1981-87; Center Stage 1985-86; bd. dirs. Gt. Plains Black Museum 1984-85; cons., tchr. Fairfax Lecturn, Fresno 1987; Valley Bus. Center 1989; awards: LaFern Williams Center Outstanding Performance 1986, Child Saving Inst. Adoptive Family of Year 1987, CSU Fresno Merit. Performance & Profl. Promise 1988, and Faculty Award for Ednl. Innovation 1991; mem: Western Bus. Law Assn. (program chair 1989-90, pres. 1992-93), Neb. Bar Assn., Calif. Bar Assn., Am. Bus. Law Assn.; author: instructors man. (Corley Shedd & Roberts 1989), articles pub. in profl. jours.; co-author: textbook (McGraw Hill, 1994); Democrat; Baptist; rec: piano playing, writing, computers. Res: 5382 N Angus Fresno 93710 Ofc: Calif. State Univ. School of Business Dept. of Finance and Business Law Fresno 93740

JONES, JOANNA PATRICIA, educator; b. Dec. 23, 1935, Chicago, Ill.; s. John Howard and O'Deal Pauline (Dammann) Fear Payne; children: Glenn b. 1956, Randy b. 1957, Diana b. 1961, Bonnie b. 1962, Paula b. 1966; edn: BA, BMTS 1958; BS, Pacific Oaks Coll. 1960; MS, 1962; MA, Claremont Grad. Sch. 1968; PhD, 1981. Career: head tchr. Pacific Oaks, Pasadena 1960-65; tchr., dir. Head Start, Claremont 1965-68; itenerant tchr. Chico St. Univ. 1968-69; edn. dir. Orange Co. Head Start, Santa Ana 1969-71; prof. Mt. Sac Coll., Walnut 1969-71; prof. Chaffey Coll., Alta Loma 1971–; currently staff devel. dir., Chaffey Coll.; coordinator child devel. dept. 1975-76, 1987-89; cons., Alta Loma 1975; trainer Head Start, East L.A. 1975-85; cons. Farwest Lab., San Francisco 1969-78; advisor Student Govt., Alta Loma 1982-86; secty. Faculty Senate Chaffey Coll. 1988-89; awards: Barbara Greenwood scholarship 1962, Claremont Grad. Sch. staff intern 1966-68) Pi Lambda Theta, Faculty of Year 1984, 85, Faculty Senate Cert. Appreciation 1984; mem: Assn. Prevention Child Abuse (bd. 1982), Assn. Childhood Edn. Internat., Nat. Assn. Edn. Young Children, Internat. Play Assn., Cultural Arts Com., Ganesha Hills Assn.; articles and papers pub. in profl. jours., 1983, inventor Luv bats, 1981; rec: doll collecting. Ofc: Chaffey College 5885 N Haven Alta Loma 91701

JONES, LOUIS WORTH, management analyst, journalist, retired; b. Jan. 8, 1908, St. Louis, Mo.; s. Ed C. and Vida Pearl (Wrather) J.; m. Pauline Marie Ernest, May 24, 1947; children: David Worth b. 1948, Roger Louis b. 1949, Ethan Ernest b. 1956, Faye b. 1932, Arthur Carlyle b. 1936; edn: Washington Univ. (Honor Soc. scholarship) 1925-27. Career: trainee, adminstrv. ofcr. Farm Security Adminstn., US Dept. Agric., Wash. DC 1934-46; mgmt. analyst War Assets Adminstrn., San Francisco 1946-48; mgmt. analyst US AEC, Los Alamos, N.Mex. 1948-50; mgmt. analyst USN Radiological Defense Lab., S.F. 1950-68; editor and publisher Lou Jones Newsletter, 1959-70;trustee emeritus The World Univ., Hqtrs. Benson, Ariz.; honors: Nat. Honor Soc., 1925; former mem. Am. Soc. for Pub. Admin., Western Govtl. Research Assn., Nat. Assn. of Intergroup Rels. Ofcls., Internat. Platform Assn.; civic: vol. alt. Civil Def. coord. San Mateo Co. 1957-58; mem: AARP, Nat. Assn. of Retired Fed. Employees (NARFE); former mem: Mid-Peninsula Council for Civic Unity (pres. 1959-60), Bi-County Commn. on Human Relations, Intergroup Relations Assn. of No. Calif. (founder and past dir.), Humanist Community of the Peninsula (co-founder); author scripts, Meet Mary Wollstonecraft (c. 1977), Meet Alexander Meiklejohn (c. 1978), lecture "Free Speech: The Great Deception" (c. 1987); Unitarian-Universalist (trustee 1958, mem. of year 1977); rec: music (piano), photog. Res: 511 Verano Ct San Mateo 94402

JONES, MICHAEL OWEN, professor; b. Oct. 11, 1942, Wichita, KS; s. Woodrow Owen and Anne Elizabeth (Blackford) J.; m. Jane Dicker, Aug. 1, 1964; children: David 1967; edn: BA Univ. Kansas, Lawrence, Kans. 1964; MA, Indiana Univ., Bloomington, Ind. 1966; PhD, Indiana Univ. 1970. Career: prof., Univ. Calif., Los Angeles 1968–; dir. Folklore and Mythology Ctr., Univ. Calif., L.A. 1984-91; awards: fellowship, Woodrow Wilson 1968; fellowship, Younger Humanist, UCLA 1971; grant, Nat. Endowment for the Humanities, W.D.C. 1983; fellow, Am. Folklore Soc., W.D.C. 1986; fellow, Soc. for Applied Anthropology 1989; fellow, Folklore Fellows, Finnish Acad. of Sci. and Letters, Helsinki 1990; mem: Am. Folklore Soc. 1968–, Calif. Folklore Soc. 1966–, Soc. for Applied Anthropology 1985–, Acad. of Mgmt. 1986–, Orgn. Development Network 1983–; author: Why Faith Healing?, 1972; The Handmade Object and Its Maker, 1975; Exploring Folk Art, 1987; Craftsman of the Cumberlands, 1988; co-author: People Studying People, 1980, Folkloristics, 1995; co-editor: Foodways and Eating Habits, 1981; Inside Organizations, 1988; editor: The World of the Kalevala, 1987; Putting Folklore to Use, 1994; rec: collecting and restoring classic cars. Ofc: Folklore and Mythology, 1037 Public Policy Bldg University of California Los Angeles 90095-1459

JONES, MILTON WAKEFIELD, publisher; b. April 18, 1930, Burbank; s. Franklin M. and Lydia (Sinclair) J.; m. Rita Strong, May 4, 1959; 1 son, Franklin Wayne; edn: AA, USC 1952; BS. Career: v.p. mktg. Sav Ink Co., Newport Beach 1956-58; account exec. KDES Radio, Palm Springs 1958-60; pres. Milton W. Jones Advt. & Pub. Rels. Agency 1960–; Desert Publs. Inc., Palm Springs 1965–; Riverside Color Press Inc.; Olman Travel Service 1979-84; pres. Vista Comms. (KPSL radio) 1987–; Airport Displays Ltd. 1972–; Pub: Palm Springs Life Mag. 1965–; Wheeler Bus. Letter 1969-77; San Francisco Mag. 1973-79; Guest Life, Orange Co.; Rocky Mountain, N.M., Carmel, Monterey 1978–; Orange Co. Mag. 1987–; Official Guide to Houston 1994; mem: Desert Press (pres. 1965). Res: 422 Farrell Dr Palm Springs 92262 206 Abalone Ave Balboa Island 92662 Ofc: 303 N Indian Ave Palm Springs 92262

JONES, RANDY KANE, lawyer; b. Oct. 25, 1957, Jacksonville, N.C.; s. Henry and Julia Mae (Saunders) J.; 1 child, Randy b. 1980; edn: BA political sci., Univ. N.C. 1979; JD, Univ. N.C. Law Sch. 1982; admitted bars Calif. 1987, N.C. 1983. Career: atty. USN, San Diego 1982-86; asst. U.S. Atty. Dept. Justice, San Diego 1987–; awards: Naval Legal Service Defense Lawyer of Quarter 1985; mem: Nat. Bar Assn. (regional dir. 1991-93, v.p. 1993-95), Fed. Bar Assn., Am. Bar Assn., N.C. Bar Assn., San Diego Co. Bar Assn., Calif. Assn. Black Lawyers, Christian Fellowship Congregational Ch. (chair young adults 1986), Earl B. Gilliam Bar Assn. (parliamentarian 1989, pres. 1990), NAACP, San Diego Crime Victims Fund (bd.), Voices for Children (bd.); mil: comdr. USNR 1983; Democrat; Methodist; rec: basketball, music, singing. Ofc: 880 Front St Rm 6293San Diego 92101

JONES, ROBERT RICHARD, financial/insurance consultant, educator; b. Canton, Oh.; s. Robert Hall and Clara M. (Channell) J.; children: Melinda Lou, Christopher; edn: BA, UC Los Angeles, 1951; cert.: Asian Studies Inst., N.Y.C. 1952-53; MA, New York Univ., 1962; postgrad. Univ. of Pa. Wharton Sch. of Bus., cert.: Fin. Mgmt. and Control, 1974; Chartered Life Underwriter (CLU), American Coll., 1978; Doctorate, Golden Gate Univ., 1991. Career: Western field news reporter, info. ofcr., special events reporter/producer, US Dept. of State, Internat. Information Adminstrn., news corr. United Nations, Voice of America, NYC, 1948-53; Mktg. Div. NY Life Ins. Co., NYC, 1953-66; faculty St. John's Univ. Grad. Sch. Bus., NY, NY, 1960-63; asst. v.p. Gulf Life Ins. Co., Jacksonville, Fla. 1966-68, v.p. sales Mutual Funds 1967, pres. and ceo Fla. Growth Mutual Fund, Jacksonville 1968-69; a.v.p., PALIC, dir. manpower devel. Aetna Variable Annuity Life, Wash. DC, Hartford, Conn., 1969-72; nat. dir. specialized mktg. Hartford Variable Annuity Life, Hartford Ins. Gp. (subs. ITT), Hartford, Conn. 1972-78, planned & devel. internat. jt. venture with

ITT/Brazil, 1975; cons. Robert R. Jones and Assocs., San Francisco, Burlingame 1978–, senior ins. cons. Stanford Research Inst. Int'l (SRI), Fin. Industries Center, Internat. Mgmt. & Econs. Gp., Menlo Park 1982–; research/ expert testimony for ins. litigation, Tech. Advy. Service for Attys. (TASA), 1983-95; prof., grad. sch. of bus. Coll. of Notre Dame, Belmont, 1986–; instr. bus. management and insurance, Calif. Comm. Colleges; instr. prelicensing and continuing edn., State of California; honors: Tau Kappa Alpha (speech hon.), Phi Mu Alpha Sinfonia (professional music hon.), Debate and Oratory Champion Wittenberg Univ., State of Ohio Original Oratory award, J.N. Flint, and NBC Radio Scholar, UCLA, Lifetime Theater Award for Outstanding Contbns. to University Theater, UCLA, nat. Award of Excellence, Life Advertisers Assn., AETNA-PALIC $25,000 Corporate Growth Award, ITT Internat. Sales Achiev. Award 1973, Disting. Service Award 1984 and Leadership Award 1985 Internat. Assn. for Fin. Planning S.F.; mem: N.Y. Univ. Alumni Assn. (past NYC pres.), Parents Without Partners (internat. pres., hon. life mem.), UCLA Alumni Assn. NYC (past pres.), Hartford Arts Council (dir.), Old First Concerts, S.F. (bd. dirs.), Internat. Assn. for Fin. Plng. S.F. (pres. 1984-85, chmn. 1985-86), Am. Soc. CLU/ChFC (nat. bd. dirs. p.r. com. 1986, Peninsula Calif. Chpt. pres. 1986-87), Nat. Assn. Life Underwrs.; Caminar Mental Health Pgms. San Mateo Co., Calif. (bd. dirs. 1984-86), Safe Rides, San Mateo Co. (adult monitor), mediator San Mateo County Mediation Svc. 1990–, appt. commr. City of Burlingame Senior Commn. 1991–; publs: "Administrative Variables in the California Multi-level Penal System," "Childhood Mental Illness: The Search for Answers to Childhood Autism," num. articles and studies; legal cons. "Materiality of Applicant's Misrepresentation in Application for Life and Health Insurance" pub. in Am. Jurisprudence; mil: USN Comms. Div. 1943-46, decorated Am. Campaign, Victory, Euro. Mideast & African Campaign medals, Armed Forces Network (AFN), 1946-51 (USNR); rec: pvt. pilot, Classic Car Assn., Jaguar XKE. Address: POB 489 Burlingame 94011-0489

JORDAN, DANNY JOSEPH, certified public accountant; b. Jan. 15, 1948, Detroit, Mich.; s. Homer Augustine and Gertrude Jean (Nuttle) J.; m. Rita Rosina Slagel, Dec. 28, 1973; edn: BS. accounting., Sacto. State Univ. 1971; MBA fin., UC Berkeley 1977; C.P.A. Calif. 1973. Career: sr. auditor Arthur Anderson & Co., San Francisco 1971-73; asst. controller Central Banking System, Oakland 1973-74; controller Pacific Union Assurance Co., S.F. 1974-77, West Coast Life Ins. Co. 1977-78; CFO L.K. Lloyd & Assoc. 1978-80; supr., mgr. Greene Nakahara & Arnold, Oakland 1980-85, ptnr. 1985; owner Dan Jordan CPA, Mill Valley 1985-86; ptnr. Jordan & Decker 1986–; dir. Coast Furniture Co., Oakland 1987–, Calif. No. Consumer Fin. Services 1988–; adminstrv. com. mem. Calif. Soc. CPA's Group Ins. Trust, Redwood City 1980–; awards: Calif. Soc. CPA Top Accounting. Student 1971; mem: Am. Inst. CPA, Calif. Soc. CPA, Nat. Assn. Accountants, Am. Mgmt. Assn.; author: article pub. in profl. jour. 1984, developer computer program 1988; mil: USCGR 1967-72; Republican; rec: tennis. Ofc: Jordan & Decker POB 1755 Mill Valley 94942

JORDAN, FRANK M., mayor; b. San Francisco, Calif.; three sons: Jim, Frank J. Jordan, and Thomas. Career: chief of police, San Francisco 1986-90; mayor City of San Francisco 1992–. Ofc: Office of Mayor 200 City Hall 400 Van Ness Ave San Francisco 94102*

JORDAN, JAMES HERBERT, marketing executive, writer; b. July 22, 1946, Pittsburg; s. John Frederick and Ruby Loraine (Robinson) J.; m. Teri Bridgman, June 11, 1966; children: Jonni Ann b. 1969, Randi b. 1972; edn: att. San Franciso State Univ. 1964-68, Las Positas Coll., Livermore 1990-91. Career: exec. editor Western Ski Time Mag., San Francisco 1968-71; editor Sunset Mag., Menlo Park 1971-75; mng. editor Home Mag., Palo Alto 1975-76; editor Colorado Mag., Denver 1976; mktg. dir. Multiple Allied Svs., Hayward, Calif. 1977–; prin., writer Jordan/Garvine Advt., Pleasanton 1986-88; prin. Jordan's Village Books, Castro Valley 1980–; author: Exploding the Franchising Myth 1990; contbg. editor to numerous books; editor: Elementary Education Language Primer 1989, Whiplash Mgmt. and Treatment 1991; recipient Calif. Mag. Assn. annual magazine award 1975; civic: Citizens Against Redevel. Pleasanton (chmn. 1975), P.A.S.S. Soccer League, Pleasanton (ofcr. 1978); mem. San Francisco Advt. Club, Castro Village Merchants Assn. (bd. 1991–); Republican; Prot.; rec: mosaic designer and builder, mosaic restorations. Res: 7882 Marigold Ct Pleasanton 94588 Ofc: Multiple Allied Services Inc. 3157 Corporate Pl Hayward 94545

JORDAN, THOMAS VINCENT, professor of advertising; b. Aug. 8, 1941, Washington, D.C.; s. Vincent Joseph and Elizabeth Jean (Quinlan) J.; m. Barbara S. Faulkner, Dec. 14, 1941 (div. 1987); children: Shannon Ann b. 1970; edn: AA, San Francisco City Coll. 1968; BA creative writing, San Francisco St. Univ. 1970; MA, 1971. Career: pub. rels. rep. United Airlines, S.F. and Chgo., IL 1968-73; copywriter Leo Burnett Co., Chgo., Ill. 1973-76; mgr. comms., Honeywell Info. Systems, Phoenix, Ariz. 1978-85; adj. prof. advt. Ariz. St. Univ., Tempe 1979-86; assoc. prof. advt. San Jose St. Univ. 1987–; acad. senate 1993–, mktg. comm. cons., Phoenix, Ariz. and San Jose 1984–; chmn. Santa Clara Cultural Advy. Commn. 1991–; awards: United Airlines Pres. award 1973, City of Chgo. Hon. Librarian 1975, Honeywell Info. Systems Merchandiser of Year 1978, Ariz. Alliance of Bus. Commend. 1983, B/PAA Nat. Winner 1989;

v.p. univ. relations: Bus. Mktng. Assn. (Internat. Speakers Bureau); mem. Calif. Faculty Assn. (treas.), Mensa (pub. rels. 1978-79), World Future Soc., ACLU; author: Carrion Comfort 1971; newsletter editor: Cargolines 1972-76; profl. jour. articles include: A Guide to Mktg. Comms., Cut Copy vs. Cute Copy, The Plastic Package Paradigm, Radio in 3 Easy Steps, How to Get Press, An Exemplary Internship Program, A Perennially Successful Live Case Proj., The Marketing Comms. Course; mil: airman 1c USAF 1959-63; Libertarian; Humanist; rec: writing, hiking, travel. Res: 1700 Civic Center Dr #602 Santa Clara 95050 Ofc: San Jose State Univ. 1 Washington Sq. San Jose 95192-0055

JORGENSEN, IVER LORENZ, seed company executive (retired); b. Sept. 26, 1924, Des Moines, Iowa; s. Hans Peter and Petra (Pedersen) J.; m. Lis Tove Petersen, July 1, 1951; children: Karen b. 1952, Susan b. 1958, Hans b. 1963; edn: Grand View 1942-43, 1946-47; BS, Iowa St. Coll. 1949; MS, Univ. Nebr. 1952. Career: horticulturist, sales Northrup King Co., Mpls. 1951-81, plant breeding and vegetable production mgr., Gilroy 1975, procurement mgr. vegetable seed div. 1985-90; dir. All-Am. Selection, Downers Grove, Ill. 1974-78, pres. 1979-80; mem: Am. Soc. Horticultural Sci.; num. plant breeding developments incl. Beans Sprite 1961, Green Isle 1967, Green Genes 1976, Triumph 1977, Carrot Gold King 1972; mil: staff sgt. USAF 1943-46; Republican; Lutheran; rec: golf, travel, gardening. Res: 7250 Miller Gilroy 95020

JORGENSEN, JUDITH ANN, psychiatrist, educator; b. Aug. 31, 1941, Parris Island, S.D.; d. George Emil Jorgensen (dec.) and Margaret Georgia (Jorgensen) Prunk dec.); m. Ronald F. Crown, M.D., July 11, 1970; edn: BA, Stanford Univ., 1963, MD, UCLA, 1968, cert. psychiatry residency, San Diego County Mental Health Services, 1973; bd. certified Psychiatry and Neurology, 1977; diplomate Am. Bd. Sexology. Career: gen. medical physician San Diego Co. Mental Health Services, 1969-70, staff psychiatrist Dept. of Profl. Edn. 1973-76, Children and Adolescent Div. 1973-78; psychiatric cons. San Diego City Coll., 1973-78, 85-86; staff psychiatrist San Diego St. Univ., 1985-87; pvt. practice prin., 1973–; clin. faculty Dept. of Psychiatry UCSD 1976–, asst. clin. prof. of psychiatry 1978-91, assoc. prof. psychiatry 1991–; consulting staff: University Hosp., Southwood Mental Health Ctr., Vista Hill Hosp., past staff Hillside Hosp. 1972-87; honors: CMA cont. edn. cert. 1972-96, AMA Physician's Recognition 1974-96; mem: Calif. Med. Assn., San Diego Co. Med. Soc. (credentials chair 1982-83), Am. Psychiatric Assn., San Diego Psychiatric Soc. (mem. chair 1976-78, v.p. 1978-80, fed. legis. rep. 1984-87, fellowship com. 1989–), Am. Soc. for Adolescent Psychiatry, San Diego Soc. for Adolescent Psychiatry (pres. 1981-82), AASECT (cert. sex therapist), Soc. for the Sci. Study of Sex, San Diego Soc. for Sex Therapy and Edn., Am. Med. Womens Assn., Assn. for Women in Sci., NOW, ZLAC Rowing Club; publs: Psychiatric Treatment of Severely Burned Adults, Psychosomatics J. (Nov-Dec 1973), contbr. book chpt. in Current Psychiatric Therapies (ed. Jules Massermann, 1975); rec: skiing, tennis, riding, mosaics. Ofc: 470 Nautilus St Ste 211 La Jolla 92037

JOSEPH, JACK MICHAEL, municipal government executive; b. Aug. 5, 1948, San Francisco; s. Daniel Morris and Adelyne May (Barr) J.; m. Anamaria Fidani; edn: BA, UCLA 1972; MA, Univ. Notre Dame 1973. Career: adminstv. analyst City of Garden Grove 1974-78; adminstv. asst. City of Cerritos 1978-86; asst. city mgr. City of Cudahy 1986-89; city mgr. City of Cudahy 1989–; Republican; R.Cath.; rec: baseball. Ofc: City of Cudahy 5220 Santa Ana St Cudahy 90201

JOSEPH, JAMES, marine scientist; b. Oct. 28, 1930, Los Angeles; s. Paul B. and Julia (Shaddy) J.; m. Patricia Duffy, Aug. 31, 1958; children: Jerold b. 1961, Michael b. 1964; edn: BS, and MS, Humboldt St. Univ., 1956, 1958; PhD, Univ. of Wash., 1968. Career: asst. scientist in chg. Manta, Ecuador 1958-60; prin. scientist Tuna Commn., 1961-68; dir. Inter-American Tropical Tuna Commn., Scripps Instn. of Oceanography, La Jolla 1969–; dir. Porpoise Res. Found., San Diego; dir. San Diego Oceans Found.; affil. prof. Univ. of Wash.; vis. fellow Ministry of Agri., N.Z. 1975-76; advr. in marine service and fisheries R&D to govts. and nat., internat. orgns.; awards: Nautilus award Marine Technol. Soc., David H. Wallace award Portuguese Hist. Soc., Hon. Dr. L'Universite de Bretagne, Sigma Xi; mem. AIFRB, AAAS; author 2 books, 85+ sci. pubs.; mil: s/sgt. AUS Korea 1952-54. Res: 2790 Palomino Circle La Jolla 92037 Ofc: Inter-American Tropical Tuna Commission, c/o Scripps Instn. of Oceanography, La Jolla 92093

JOSEPHSON, DAVID LANE, engineer; b. June 17, 1956, New Haven, Ct.; s. Stanley Davis and Carolyn Virginia (Buck) J.; edn: elect. engring., UC Berkeley, 1975-79. Career: chief engr. KALX-FM Radio, Berkeley 1975-79; systems engr. High Life Helicopters, Puyallup, Wash. 1979-81; systems engr. EG&G Geometrics, Sunnyvale, Calif. 1981-85, dir. China Op., Beijing, China 1985-87, mgr. Military Div., Sunnyvale, Calif. 1987-90; owner Josephson Engineering, San Jose 1990–, mfg. microphones and acoustic equipment, cons. pvt. cos. and govt. agys. nat. and internat., 1980–; mem. Audio Engineering Soc. (1974–, chapt. bd.); num. inventions in field of microphones and acoustics; Democrat; rec: aviation, music, civics. Res: 3729 Corkerhill Way San Jose 95121 Ofc: Josephson Engineering, 2502B John Montgomery Dr San Jose 95148

JUBERG, RICHARD KENT, mathematician, professor emeritus; b. May 14, 1929, Cooperstown, N.Dak.; s. Palmer and Hattie Noreen (Nelson) J.; m. Janet Elisabeth Witchell, Mar. 17, 1956 (div. 1984); children: Alison b. 1961, Kevin b. 1963, Hilary b. 1964, Ian b. 1972; m. Sandra Jean Vakerics, July 8, 1989; edn: BS, Univ. Minn., 1952, PhD, 1958. Career: temp. mem. math. studies and res. Courant Inst. of Math. Scis., New York Univ., N.Y.C. 1957-58; instr., asst. prof. Univ. Minn., Mpls. 1958-65; science faculty fellow NSF, Univ. di Pisa, Italy 1965-66; assoc. prof. UC Irvine 1966-72; vis./assoc. prof. Univ. of Sussex, England 1972-73; prof. UC Irvine, 1974-91, prof. emeritus 1991–; vis. prof. Univ. of Goteborg, Sweden 1981; awards: Tau Beta Pi 1953, temporary mem. Courant Inst. Math. Scis. NYU 1957-58, NSF fellow, Italy 1965-66; mem. Am. Math. Soc. 1958–; contbr. res. articles to profl. jours.; mil: p.o.3c USN 1946-48; Democrat; rec: bird watching. Res: 9356-D Mesa Verde Dr Montclair 91763 Ofc: Math. Dept. Univ. of California Irvine 92717

JUDD, RALPH WAVERLY, writer, lecturer, publisher; b. April 22, 1930, Zillah, Wa.; s. Van Evrie and Theona Ruth (Stanhope) J.; edn: Harvard Coll. 1947-49; BS, US Coast Guard Acad. 1954; MBA, George Washington Univ. 1964; PhD communications, Clayton Univ., 1988. Career: served to cmdr. US Coast Guard 1949-72: airborne ice observer, USCG, Arctic & Antarctic, 1955-57; chief Physics Sect. USCG Acad., New London, Conn. 1962-63; cmdg. ofcr. USCGC Comanche, San Francisco 1964-66, Loran Station, Con Son, Vietnam 1966-67; chief resale systems USCG Hqtrs., W.D.C. 1967-71; cmdg. ofcr. USCGC Rockaway, NY, NY 1971-72, ret.; decorated Command-at-Sea Insignia 1964, CG Unit Commendn. 1966, Combat Action rib. 1966; cross-country coach USCG Acad. 1959-61, writer num. Coast Guard publs. (1960-71), contbr. var. magazines and newspapers, author/pub. (book) Drag Gags, 4 unpub. books on hist. of entertainment (1968-87); awards: cert. of merit Nat. Honor Soc. 1947, Harvard Nat. Scholar 1947, Lifetime Achiev. Golden Academy Award, decorated Republic of Vietnam Civic Action Medal 1st Class, Republic of Vietnam Gallantry Cross with Palm, Pres. Clinton Roll-of-Honor Medal, listed Who's Who in US Writers, Editors & Poets, Internat. Who's Who of Intellectuals; mem: Comedy/Humor Writers Assn., Nat. Writers Union, Nat. Writers Club, ACLU, AARP, S.F. YMCA, Coast Guard Combat Veterans Assn.; clubs: Playboy, S.F. Arts Democratic Club; Democrat (Dem. Nat. Com.), Harvard Club at the Nat. Press Club; Christian; rec: collect special interest movie stills, posters & stage photos, swim. Address: 1330 Bush St Apt. 4H San Francisco 94109

JUDGE, GEORGE GARRETT, professor of econometrics; b. May 2, 1925, Carlisle, Ky.; s. William Everett and Etna (Perkins) J.; m. Sue D., Mar. 17, 1950 (div. Mar. 1976); children: Lisa b. 1953, Laura b. 1956; m. Margaret C., Oct. 8, 1976; edn: BS, Univ. Ky., 1948, MS, Iowa State Univ., 1949, PhD, Iowa State Univ., 1952. Career: asst. prof. Univ. Conn., Storrs 1951-55; prof. Oklahoma State Univ., Stillwater 1955-58; vis. prof. Yale Univ., 1958-59; prof. Univ. Illinois, Urbana 1959-86; prof. UC Berkeley, 1986- mem. Econometric Soc. 1951- Am. Statistical Assn. 1960–; author: Theory and Practice of Econometrics 1980, 85, Introduction to Econometrics 1982, 88, Inference in Econometrics 1978, 86, Spatial Equilibrum 1971; tech. sgt. USAF 1943-45; rec: golf, sailing. Ofc: Univ. California, 207 Giannini Hall Berkeley 94720

JUDSON, PHILIP LIVINGSTON, lawyer; b. Oct. 25, 1941, Palo Alto; s. Philip MacGregor and Elizabeth Stuart (Peck) J.; m. Dorothy Louisa Lebohner, Sept. 6, 1963; children: Wendy Patricia, Philip Lebohner, Michael Lee; edn: BA, Stanford Univ. 1963; JD, UC Hastings Coll. Law 1969; admitted St. Bar Calif. 1970, U.S. Dist. Ct. No. Dist. 1970, U.S. Ct. Appeals 9th Circuit 1970, U.S. Dist. Ct. Cent. Dist. 1984, U.S. Dist. Ct. Ea. Dist. 1985, U.S. Supreme Ct. 1987, Dist. of Columbia Bar 1988, U.S. Dist. Ct. So. Dist. Calif. 1989. Career: atty., assoc. Pillsbury Madison & Sutro, San Francisco 1969-76, ptnr. 1977–; lectr. Practising Law Inst.; pres. St. Mark's Sch., San Rafael 1983-85, founding mem., trustee 1980-86; trustee Marin Acad. 1985-91; honors: Order of Coif, Phi Delta Theta; mem: Am. Bar Assn. (antitrust and litigation sects.), San Francisco Bar Assn.; mil: served to 1st lt. AUS 1963-65; Republican; Episcopalian. Res: 19 Byron Circle Mill Valley 94941 Ofc: Pillsbury Madison & Sutro 225 Bush St POB 7880 San Francisco 94120

JUDSON, WALTER WORTH, manufacturer; b. May 7, 1941, Glendale, Calif.; s. Horace and Blanche (Worth) J.; m. Karen Sauder, 1962; children: Lisa b. 1962, William b. 1965, David b. 1969; edn: BA, USC, 1962. Career: staff The Judson Studios (bus. founded in Los Angeles 1897), 1962–, pres. 1978–; pres. Judson/Voorhees Inc. 1991; lectr. Univ. Pepperdine, CSU Fullerton, 1978; profl. affiliate Am. Inst. of Architects; mem: Stained Glass Assn. of America (pres. 1988-90), Interfaith Forum on Religion, Art and Architecture, Rotary Intl.; author: Introduction to Stained Glass; R.Cath.; rec: travel, fitness. Ofc: The Judson Studios 200 S Ave 66 Los Angeles 90042

JULIEN, RICHARD EDWARD HALE, JR., lawyer; b. July 24, 1939, San Francisco; s. Richard Edward Hale and Sophie (Hill) J.; m. Victoria Ford, Sept. 7, 1963 (div. 1986); children: Sophie b. 1964, Richard b. 1966; edn: BS, MIT 1960; JD, Boalt Hall Sch. Law UC Berkeley 1963; admitted St. Bar Calif. (1964). Career: assoc. atty. Kelso Cotton & Ernst, S.F. 1964-67; sole practitioner, pvt. practice 1967-74; ptnr. Julien & Julien 1974-78; Layman Julien &

Lempert 1978-81; pres. Richard Julien Profl. Corp. 1981–; lectr. var. profl. programs; honors: mem. Am. Law Inst., Am. Coll. Tax Counsel, life fellow Am. Bar Found.; mem: Am. Bar Assn., Calif. St. Bar Assn., S.F. Bar Assn.; elected Town Council, Ross 1984-88, mayor 1986-88; mem. Soc. Calif. Pioneers, Phi Delta Theta; clubs: St. Francis Yacht, University; contbr. articles to legal jours.; Republican; R.Cath.; rec: restoration of family ranch. Ofc: 200 Montgomery St., Ste 393 San Francisco 94104

JULIUS, EDWARD HOWARD, college professor; b. May 14, 1952, Boston, Mass.; s. Nathan and Eleanor Frances (Marshall) J.; m. Marion R. Valdez, Aug. 22, 1981; children: Marina b. 1982, Alexandra b. 1986; edn: BA bus. adminstrn., Rutgers Univ. 1974; MS acctg., Univ. Pa. 1975; CPA Ill. 1977. Career: asst. prof. acctg. Chgo. St. Univ., Ill. 1975-77; CSU Northridge 1978-81; asst. prof., assoc. prof., prof. acctg. Calif. Lutheran Univ., Thousand Oaks 1981–; awards: CSU Merit. Performance 1989, CLU Excellence in Tchg. 1988; mem: Ill. C.P.A. Soc., Am. Acctg. Assn., Comm. Leaders Club, Wharton Club So. Calif.; author num. textbook ancillaries, One-A-Day crossword vols. 1-6 (1975-81), articles pub. in profl. jours., 1987, 89, Rapid Math Tricks and Tips, 1992, Rapid Math in 10 Days, 1994, Arithmetricks, 1995; Republican; Jewish; rec: crossword puzzle constructor. Res: 22009 Vincennes St Chatsworth 91311 Ofc: California Lutheran University School of Business 60 Olsen Rd Thousand Oaks 91360

JUNAK, STEVEN A., botanist; b. April 25, 1949, Chicago, Ill.; s. Walter J. and Josephine H. J.; edn: BA, UCSB 1972; MA, 1987. Career: instr. botany Santa Barbara Comm. Coll. 1975-81, 1984-85; herbarium botanist Santa Barbara Botanic Garden 1976-87, herbarium curator 1987–; honors: Sigma Xi, listed Who's Who in the West; mem: Linnean Soc. London (fellow), Am. Soc. Plant Taxonomists, Calif. Botanical Soc. (2nd v.p. 1992-93), So. Calif. Botanists; co-author books on the flora of Santa Cruz and Santa Barbara Is.; 15+ articles pub. in profl. jours. (1980–); Democrat; rec: photog., travel, historical research, aerobic exercise, hiking. Ofc: Santa Barbara Botanic Garden 1212 Mission Canyon Rd Santa Barbara 93105

JUNCKER, JUDITH DIANNE, psychotherapist, artist; b. Nov. 18, 1942, Montgomery, Ala.; d. Walter Eugene and Mary Juette (Singleton) Graddy; m. Phillip Bailey, Sept. 9, 1960 (dec.); m. 2d. Rodney Juncker, Aug. 31, 1968; children: Rick b. 1965, Jeff b. 1970; edn: BA, S.F. State Univ., 1968; MA, Am. Acad. Family Studies, 1981; lic. Marriage Family Counselor, lic. Clin. Hypnotherapist, Calif. 1981. Career: NIMH grantee, res. asst. San Francisco St. Univ. 1968-70, Stanford Univ. 1969-70, Harvard Univ. Grad. Sch. of Edn. 1973-77; social work asst. Met. State Hosp., Waltham, Mass. 1971-72; partners' group facilitator Veteran Outreach, San Jose 1979-80; pvt. practice ONTOS, 1981-87, Adult & Child Therapy Ctr. 1987–; cons. various univs. and instns., 1980–; lectr. CSU San Jose 1986-87; adj. faculty Santa Clara Univ. 1989-90; mem: Am. Assn. of Marriage & Family Therapist, Calif. Assn. Marriage & Family Therapist; civic: Center for Living with Dying, S.J. (group facilitator 1979-85, outstanding volunteer award 1980, 81, 82, 83), ARIS Project, S.J. (group facilitator 1985–, team. ldr. for People with HIV Disease, mem. Client Svs. Com. 1990–); artist mixed media, works in pvt. collections; Democrat; Prot. Ofc: Adult & Child Therapy Center 1190 S Bascom Ste 216 San Jose 95128

JUNG, CHAI HWAN, company president; b. Jan. 16, 1947, Korea; s. Doo Keun and Mi Ja (Lee) J.; m. Hyon Sook, Apr. 8, 1976; children: Hana Jung b. 1977, James b. 1979; edn: BA, Korea Univ., 1973; grad. Anthony Sch. of Real Estate, 1981; Calif. R.E. broker 1981. Career: mgr. Korea Exchange Bank, 1973-80; dir. Namsan Corp., Korea 1979-81; real estate broker United Business Investment, Los Angeles 1982-84; spl. agent Northwestern Mutual Life Ins. Co., 1982-87; gen. agent Western State Life Ins., 1987–; pres. Joy Toy Co., 1985–; pres. AAlum Internat. Co.; honors: appreciation Korean Consulate General 1986, Korean Ministry of Edn. 1987, Northwestern Mutual Life diamond club 1985, Western State Life 30-30 Club and Elite Club 1987, 88, Nat. Sales achiev. award 1985, 86; mem: Cert. Life Underwriter Assn., Profl. Salesman Assn. USA; civic: Korean School Assn. (pres. 1987, 1988), Korea Univ. Alumni Assn. of So. Calif. (gen. sec. 1986, v.p. 1989, pres. Tae Kwon Do Team), PIOPICO Library Support Team (dir.), Korean Eastern Church School (pres. 1983-90); elder Korean Eastern Presbyn. Ch. 1992; publs: 30+ essays in Korea Times, Korean Street Jour.; Democrat; Christian; rec: travel, golf. Res: 136 Fremont Place W Los Angeles 90005 Ofc: Joy Toy Co./AAlum Trading Co. 1110 E 14th St Los Angeles 90021

KADING, KEITH GORDON, school principal; b. May 3, 1935, Sioux City, Iowa; s. Ralph C. and Bernice E. K.; m. Gayle, Dec. 4, 1956; children: Kelly b. 1958, Kevin b. 1961, Kent b. 1962; edn: BS, Morningside Coll. 1957; MA, Sacto. St. Univ. 1970. Career: instr. Theo Judah Elementary Sch. 1957-58; chair math. dept. Folsom H.S. 1958-65; vice principal Folsom-Cordova Unified Sch. Dist., Folsom 1965-67, dir. research and testing 1967-69, principal 1969-73, Rancho Cordova 1973-95 (ret.); v.p. Calif. Math. Council 1982-84; mem. Instrn. Materiel Evaluation Panel (math.) St. of Calif., and chair St. Quality Review Team; chair Western Assn. of Schs. and Colls. Evaluation Team; mem: Assn. Calif. Sch. Adminstrs., Rancho Cordova Kiwanis (pres.), Toastmasters Internat.; Republican; Lutheran; rec: sports, camping. Ofc: Folsom-Cordova Unified School District 125 E Bidwell Folsom 95630

KADRI, TARIQ RASHID, lawyer; b. Nov. 17, 1949, Altadena; s. Syed Sirajuddin and Frema Sara (Fenton) K.; m. Maxine Jellie, Jan. 1, 1988; 1 son, Sharif b. 1988, 1 dau., Aden b. 1990; edn: BA, UC Berkeley 1972; JD, Georgetown Univ. 1976. Career: legal analyst Congressional Research Service, Am. law div., Wash. D.C. 1973-76; atty., assoc. Shahin Wawro & Lorimer, Los Angeles 1976-78; secty., gen. counsel Oasis Petroleum, Culver City 1978-83; pres. Triad Am. Internat., Santa Barbara 1983-86; dir. Triad Am. and Triad Energy Corps., Salt Lake City, Utah 1983-86; pres., bd. dirs. Concrete Tech. Corp., Santa Barbara 1985-86; dir. Am. Barrick Resources Corp. 1986; dir. Arlington Investments Ltd., Nassau, Bahamas 1983-89; pres., dir. Kadri & Assocs. Inc., Montecito 1988–; mem: Am. Bar Assn., Calif. Bar Assn. Address: Montecito 93108

KAGEMOTO, HARO, filmmaker/printmaker; b. Jan. 9, 1952, Tokyo, Japan, naturalized U.S. cit. 1962; s. Herbert Yoshito and Nobuye Shirley (Furukawa) Kagemoto; m. Patricia Mae Jow, Sept. 21, 1991; children: Kenya b. 1982; edn: profl. cert. Sch. of Modern Photography, N.J. 1972; BFA, Univ. Hawaii, 1977; MFA, SUNY, New Paltz, 1979. Career: vis. artist UC Berkeley Ext., San Francisco 1980-82; vis. lectr. San Francisco State Univ., 1983; prodn. mgr. Wonderland Prodns., S.F. 1983-91, director, 1991–; mem. Am. Film Inst. 1987–, San Francisco Mus. of Modern Art 1994–; author: (poetry collection) Orion's Winter, 1972-75, (short story) Daruma 1976; rec: guitar, reading. Res: 2806 Truman Ave Oakland 94605-4847

KAGEMOTO, PATRICIA JOW, artist/printmaker; b. Feb. 20, 1952, N.Y.C.; d. Tong Fook and Toy Kuen (Lee) Jow; m. Haro Kagemoto, Sept. 21, 1991; edn: Syracuse Univ. Sch. of Art, 1970-71, Hunter Coll., N.Y.C. 1971-72; BFA, SUNY, New Paltz, 1975. Career: printmaking workshop asst. SUNY at New Paltz, N.Y. 1974-75, printshop asst. 1975; arts and crafts tchr. Neighborhood Service Orgn., Poughkeepsie, N.Y. 1976; printmaking instr. and adminstrv. asst. Communications Village Ltd., Kingston, N.Y. 1977-79, printmaking cons. 1975-84; exhibition auditor N.Y. State Council on the Arts, N.Y.C. 1984-87; gallery asst. Watermark/ Cargo Gallery, Kingston, N.Y. 1988-91; vis. artist N.Y. State Summer Sch. of the Visual Arts, Fredonia, N.Y. 1978; vis. artist SUNY at New Paltz 1983-84; cons. printer The Printmaking Workshop, N.Y.C. 1984; children's printmaking workshop dir. The Woodstock (N.Y.) Library 1989; awards: spl. award in graphics Gallery North, Setauket, N.Y. 1974, America The Beautiful Fund grantee N.Y.C. 1976, 1st and 2d pl. in graphics Catskill Art Soc., Hurleyville, N.Y. 1983, Alumni Printmakers' Invitational SUNY, New Paltz 1984, Ulster County Decentralization grantee N.Y. State Council on the Arts, Woodstock 1989; rec: cats, sewing, gardening. Ofc: Pat Jow Kagemoto 2806 Truman Ave Oakland 94605-4847

KAGIWADA, REYNOLD SHIGERU, engineer; b. July 8, 1938, Los Angeles; s. Harry Yoshifusa and Helen Kinue (Imura) K.; m. Harriet Hatsune Natsuyama, Aug. 19, 1961; children: Julia b. 1968, Conan b. 1969; edn: BS physics, UCLA, 1960, MS physics, 1962, PhD physics, 1966. Career: asst. prof. in residence, UC Los Angeles, 1966-69; asst. prof. USC, 1969-72; engr. TRW, Redondo Beach, 1972-: sect. head, MTS, dept. mgr.; sr. scientist 1972-83, lab. mgr. 1984-87, project mgr. 1987-88, MIMIC chief scientist 1988-89, asst. pgm. mgr. 1989-90, advanced technology mgr. 1989–; awards: Gold medal Ramo Technology Award, TRW 1985, ESG Chmn's. award for Innovation 1991, Sigma Pi Sigma 1960–, Sigma Xi 1967–; mem: IEEE 1972– (Fellow 1989), IEEE Ultrasonic Ferroelectric Freq. Control (sec. treas. 1984-86), IEEE Microwave Theory & Techniques Soc. (v.p. 1991, pres. 1992), Assn. of Old Crows 1980–; author, inventor (9 patents), 44+ publs. and 13 tech. paper presentations; Democrat; Methodist; rec: fishing, biking. Res: 3117 Malcolm Ave Los Angeles 90034 Ofc: TRW, MS M5/1470, One Space Park Redondo Beach 90278

KAHAN, JAMES PAUL, psychologist; b. Oct. 15, 1942, New York; s. Robert Helmen and Janet Rieders (Pressman) K.; m. Edith Jane Lester, Dec. 27, 1970 (div. 1983); m. 2d. Elaine Marie Engman, June 29, 1984; children: Rebecca b. 1978, Emily b. 1988; edn: BA, Reed Coll. 1964; MA, Univ. N.C. Chapel Hill 1966; PhD, 1968; lic. psychologist Calif. 1975. Career: N.S.F postdoctoral fellow, Univ. de Provence, Aix-eu-Province, France 1968-69; asst. prof., assoc. prof. USC, Dept. Psychology, Los Angeles 1970-80; fellow Netherlands Inst. Advanced Study, Wassenaar, Netherlands 1977-78, 1994-95; vis. prof. Univ. Haifa, Israel 1980-81; sr. scientist RAND Corp., Santa Monica 1981–; prof. RAND Grad. Sch. 1983–; awards: NSF/NATO postdoctoral fellow 1968-69; mem: Am. Psychological Soc. (fellow), Soc. for the Psychological Study of Social Issues (fellow); author: 90+ books and articles pub. in profl. jours. 1965–; rec: folk dancing, folk music, volleyball. Res: Pacific Palisades Ofc: The RAND Corp 1700 Main St Santa Monica 90407-2138

KAHAN, WILLIAM M., professor of mathematics and computer science; b. June 5, 1933, Toronto, Ont., Canada; s. Myer and Gertrude (Rosenthal) K.; m. Sheila Kay Strauss, Sept. 1954; children: Ari b. 1962, Simon b. 1964; edn: BA, Univ. Toronto, 1954, MA, 1956, PhD, 1958. Career: lectr. Univ. Toronto, 1954-58, asst. prof., prof. 1960-68; prof. UC Berkeley, 1969–; postdoctoral fellow Cambridge Univ., Eng. 1958-60; vis. assoc. prof. Stanford Univ., 1966; vis. res. scientist IBM Research, Yorktown Heights, N.Y. 1972-73; cons. IBM, New York, Austin, Tx. 1967, 1984–; cons. Hewlett-Packard, Corvallis, Oreg. 1974-85, Intel, Santa Clara, Ca. 1977–; awards: 1st G.E. Forsythe Award, Assn. for Computing Machinery, N.Y. 1972 and A.M. Turing Award, ACM, N.Y. 1989, Lin. Algebra Paper Award, Soc. for Industrial & Applied Math. 1990; mem: Am. Math. Soc. 1955–, Assn. for Computing Machinery (1961–, fellow 1994), Soc. for Indsl. & Appl. Math. 1965–, IEEE Computer Soc. (1989–, com. stds. #754 & 854 for computer arithmetic 1985, 89); co-inventor: Floating-point co-processor INTEL 8087 (1980); publs: num. res. papers on numerical computation (1961–); Jewish; rec: repairing old appliances, autos, etc. Ofc: E.E. & C.S. Dept. Univ. Calif., Evans Hall, Berkeley 94720

KAHL, ARTHUR GLENN, commercial photographer; b. May 20, 1937, Los Angeles; s. Art George and Kathryn (Drees) K.; m. Mary Louise Johnson, June 18, 1960; children: Steven b. 1962, Scott b. 1965, Sharon b. 1967, Tim b. 1970; edn: Pasadena City Coll. 1955-57. Career: pub. rels. photographer Photography Inc., L.A. 1957-58; photographer Manteca Bulletin, Manteca 1960-64; ed. Daily Press, Victorville 1965-67; ed., reporter San Bernardino Co. News Service 1968-69; ed., Manteca Bulletin 1969-75; owner, operator Kahl Photography Inc., Manteca 1975–; p.t. tchr. E. Union H.S. 1988-89; awards: Manteca Bulletin Best Front Page 1971, Rotary Govs. award 1982; mem: Manteca Rotary, Profl. Photographers of Am., Manteca Toastmasters (organizing pres. 1969); columnist Mantecca News, 1979-81; mil: AUS 1958-60, USAR 1960-64; Republican; Cath. Ofc: Kahl Photography Inc. 300 E Yosemite Manteca 95336

KAIN, MICHAEL EDWARD, accounting and finance executive; b. March 15, 1955, Los Angeles; s. Edward Michael K. and Wyla Jean (Hellback) Stevenson; m. Rebecca Anne Crummel, Apr. 21, 1984, div. Dec. 28, 1991; edn: UC San Diego, 1973-75; BS in bus., USC, 1978; CSU Long Beach, 1981-82. Career: asst. mgr. food service Marineland, Palos Verdes 1973-75; staff acct. Garrett Corp./Signal, Los Angeles 1979; staff acct. Ace Industries Textron, Santa Fe Springs 1980, acctg. supr. 1981-82, asst. controller 1983-86, controller 1987–; honors: Revelle Coll. Provosts hon. list (1974); mem: Nat. Mgmt. Assn., Tarbell Real Estate; rec: skiing, tennis, home renovation. Res: 5632 Oak Dr La Palma 90623

KALIFON, DAVID, lawyer, physician; b. Feb. 18, 1946, New York; s. Sam and Rose(Ballon) K.; m. Elizabeth Ann Walker, July 30, 1988; children: Micole b. 1973; edn: BA Rutgers Coll. 1967; MD Cornell Univ. 1971; JD, UCLA 1988; lic. physician Calif. 1972, admitted St. Bar Calif. 1988, D.C. Bar 1989. Career: intern and resident, internal medicine, UCLA Hosp. and Clinics 1971-73; resident, emergency med. USC, Los Angeles County General Hosp. 1973-75; emergency physician Valley Presbyterian Hosp., Van Nuys 1971-90, dept. chair and mem. Medical Exec. Com.; instr. L.A. Co. Paramedic Training Ctr., 1975; clinical asst. prof. Emergency Med. Ctr., UCLA Hospital 1978-85; assoc., principal Hirschtick Chenen, Marina del Rey 1988-93; of counsel Jeffer, Mangels, Butler & Marmaro, Los Angeles 1993–; honors: Phi Beta Kappa, Alpha Omega Alpha, Henry Rutgers scholar 1966, UCLA Law Review 1986; mem: Am. Coll. Emergency Physicians (fellow; former dir., councilor, ho. del. Calif. chpt.); gen. counsel Calif. chpt. 1989–; Medicolegal Com. chair 1990-93), Am. Coll. of Emergency Physicians and Coll. of Legal Med. (fellow), Calif. Med. Assn. (adv. panel on Emergency Med.), Am. Bd. of Emergency Med. (diplomate 1980–), Calif. Bar Assn., Calif. Soc. for Healthcare Attorneys; edit. Emergency Med. Reports Legal Bulletin, reviewer Annals of Emergency Med., examiner Am. Bd. of Emergency Med. 1983-93; articles pub. in profl. jours., 1989; rec: travel, collecting antique maps. Ofc: Jeffer, Mangels, Butler & Marmaro 2121 Ave of the Stars 10th Fl Los Angeles 90067

KALLENBERG, JOHN KENNETH, librarian; b. June 10, 1942, Anderson, Ind.; s. Herbert August and Helen Elizabeth (Suttles) K.; m. Ruth Ann Barrett, Aug. 19, 1965; children: Jennifer Ann, Gergory John; edn: AB, Ind. Univ. 1964, MLS, 1969. Career: Reader's adv. Fresno County Library, 1965-67, librarian Fig Garden branch, 1967-70, county librarian, 1976–; asst. dir. Santa Barbara Public Library, 1970-76; chmn. advy. council, bd. dirs. Calif. Auth. for Systems and Services, 1978-80; mem: Calif. Lib. Svs. Bd. 1990– (v.p. 1992-95), ALA, Calif. Library Assn. (adminstrv. council 1975-77, 1984-85, v.p. 1986, pres. 1987), Am. Soc. Public Adminstrn., Calif. County Librarians Assn. (pres. 1977), Kiwanis (treas. 1974-75, v.p. 1975-76 North Santa Barbara, dir. Fresno 1977-78, 79-80, v.p. 1980-81, pres. 1981-82, lt. gov. 1991-92); Presbyterian. Ofc: Fresno County Free Library 2420 Mariposa St Fresno 93721

KALLGREN, EDWARD EUGENE, lawyer; b. May 22, 1928, San Francisco; s. Edward H. and Florence E. (Campbell) K.; m. Joyce Elaine Kislitzin, Feb. 8, 1953; children: Virginia Elaine b. 1961, Charles Edward b. 1964; edn: AB, UC Berkeley, 1951, JD, Boalt Hall, 1954. Career: atty., ptnr. Brobeck, Phleger & Harrison, San Francisco 1954-93, of counsel 1993–; dir: Olivet Memorial Park, Colma 1970–, pres. 1992–; trustee Lawyers Com. for Civil Rights Under Law, Wash. DC 1986–; mem: ABA (mem. House of Dels. 1986–), Calif. Bar Assn. (mem. bd. govs. 1989-92), Bar Assn. of San Francisco (dir. 1984-88, pres. 1988), S.F. Lawyers Com. for Urban Affairs (founding dir. 1968-86, co-chair 1984-86); civic: elected Berkeley City Council 1971-75, Berkeley Democratic Club (past pres., dir. 1975-85), Planned Parenthood Alameda/S.F. (dir., v.p., treas. 1984-90); mil: sgt. USMC 1945-48; Democrat. Res: 28 Hillcrest Rd Berkeley 94705 Ofc: Brobeck, Phleger & Harrison Spear Street Tower One Market Plaza San Francisco 94105

KALLSHIAN, HARRY C., civic activist, former public utility executive; b. June 18, 1913, Troy, N.Y.; s. Misak and Vaheda (Manoogian) K.; m. Margaret Opp, Oct. 22, 1948; children: Terri b. 1950, Jan b. 1954, Katie b. 1956; edn: BA, Occidental Coll., 1935; MBA (honors), Stanford Univ., 1940. Career: gen. acctg. mgr. Pacific Telephone Co., San Jose 1961-63, asst. controller Pacific Tel., San Francisco 1963-69, asst. v.p. ops., S.F. 1969-73, area v.p., San Jose 1973-78, ret.; cons., comm. affairs, AT&T 1978-80; adj. prof. San Jose St. Univ. Sch. of Bus., 1973-78; honors: Phi Beta Kappa (1935); elected mayor City of Los Altos 1980-81, 84-85; current civic bds: Santa Clara Co. Transp. Commn., City of San Jose Infra-Structure Com., San Jose St. Univ. Sch. of Edn. (advy. bd.), San Jose Rotary Club (pres. 1987-88), San Jose C.of C. (chmn. 1978-79); former: Santa Clara Co. Bd. of Edn. (pres. 1974-75), Santa Clara Co. Mfg. Group (past v.p.), Public TV (chmn. Found. Fin. Com. KTEH Ch. 54; PBS nat. audit com., human resources com.), Private Post Secondary Edn. Commn. Calif.; mil: lt. USN 1942-46, P.T. Boat ofcr., Naval Intell., No. Africa, Middle East and So. Pac. (fluent in Turkish, loaned to Brit. Navy torpedo boat commando raids on Ger. held islands in the Agean 1943-44, POW in Turkey 3 mos.); Republican; Presbyterian (trustee, elder); rec: golf, garden, local politics. Res: 59 Alma Ct Los Altos 94022

KALM, BERTHA EVELYN, business educator, adventurer; b. Oct. 9, 1914, Calif.; d. Charles and Amanda (Sodergren) Kalm; edn: AA, San Bernardino Jr. Coll., 1933; AB, San Jose State Coll., 1936; gen. secondary tchg. credential, USC, 1939. Career: tchr. Aromas Elem. Sch., Calif. 1936-38; business tchr. Colton High Sch., 1939-40; L.A. City Sch. System, 1942-72: instr. business edn. Manual Arts High Sch. 1944-55, also grade counselor 6+ yrs., instr. bus. edn. Hollywood High Sch. 1963-72, also work experience coord. 7+ yrs.; office work, Los Angeles, 1940-42, 1955-57, US Govt., W.D.C., 1957-58; mem: Calif. Retired Tchrs. Assn. 1973–, Nat. Retired Tchrs. Assn. 1974–, Theta Alpha Delta (bus. tchrs. frat. 1947–); club: Los Angeles Breakfast; Republican; Prot.; avocation: adventure travel: on sabbatical lv. bought & drove auto through Europe (12,000 mi.), then sailed to Greece, Egypt, Jerusalem, Beirut, Paris, and home to L.A. 1952, air and land trips through Central Am., South Am. and Brasilia, Africa, Sicily, Corsica and Portugal 1967-68. Res: PO Box 481202 Los Angeles 90048

KALT, HOWARD M., public relations consultant; b. June 11, 1943, Racine, Wis.; s. Nat and Fay (Schwartz) K.; m. Barbara Lee Schowalter, Feb. 2, 1963; children: Jennifer b. 1964, Jeffrey b. 1968; edn: BS journalism, Univ. Wis. 1964. Career: writer Wis. State Journal 1963-64; v.p. Gardner Jones & Co., Chgo. 1964-74; v.p. comm. Fred S. James & Co., Chgo. 1974-75; comm. mgr. Marmon Group 1975-76; v.p. Ruder & Finn Inc., San Francisco 1976-77; Hoefer Amidei Assoc. 1977-79; v.p comm. ISU Cos. 1979-82; prin. Kalt Rosen & Assoc. 1982–; instr. Golden Gate Univ. 1987-89; mem: The Family, Pub. Rels. Soc. S.F. (former dir., pres.), Internat. Assn. Bus. Comms. (chpt. pres. 1974); Jewish. Ofc: Kalt Rosen & Associates 220 Montgomery St San Francisco 94104

KALVINSKAS, JOHN JOSEPH, chemical engineer; b. Jan. 14, 1927, Phila.; s. Anthony and Anna (Slezute) K.; m. Louanne Marie Adams, Sept. 3, 1955; 1 child, Adrian b. 1965; edn: BS chem. engring., M.I.T., 1951, MSCE, 1952; PhD chem. engring., Calif. Inst. Tech., 1959. Career: chem. engr. DuPont, Gibbstown, N.J. 1952-55, 59-60; supr., mgr., dir. Rockwell Internat., El Segundo 1960-70; pres. Resource Dynamics Corp., L.A. 1970-74; corporate resrch. dir. Monogram Industries Inc., L.A. 1972; proj. mgr. Holmes & Narver Inc., Anaheim 1974; supr., project mgr., mem. tech. staff Jet Propulsion Lab., Pasadena 1974–; cons. Rockwell Internat., 1972-73, Kinetics Technology Internat., Pasa. 1982-83; awards: Stauffer Found. tchg. fellow CalTech 1957-58, Sigma Xi 1956, 59, Kappa Kappa Sigma 1950, NASA recogn. awards (8) 1975-85; mem: N.Y. Acad. Scis. 1980–, Am. Inst. Chem. Engrs. 1953–, Am. Chem. Soc. 1953–, Town Hall of Calif., MIT Club So. Calif.; inventor, 8 patents chem. engring. appls. 1958-85; coauthor: Nuclear Rocket Propulsion (1962); publs. in field propulsion, energy, env. engring. 1960-87; mil: electronic techn. mate 2/c USN 1944-46; Republican; R.Cath.; rec: jogging. Res: 316 Pasadena Ave #3 South Pasadena 91030 Ofc: JPL, 4800 Oak Grove Dr Pasadena 91109

KAM, JAMES T.K., scientist, engineer; b. July 29, 1945, Hong Kong; nat. 1987; s. Nai Fai and Big Chun (Au) K.; m. Winna M. Wong, June 9, 1974; children: Kelvin b. 1975, Theresa b. 1978; edn: BS, Univ. Manitoba 1970; PhD, UC Berkeley 1974; reg. profl. engr. Calif. 1979. Career: research assoc. UC Davis 1974-75; project hydrologist Internat. Engring., San Francisco 1975-79; sr. hydrologist Sci. Applications Inc., San Leandro 1979-81; staff engr. Davy McKee Corp., San Ramon 1981-85; prin. engr. Morrison Knudsen, San Francisco 1985–; p.t. tchr. UC Davis 1974-75; cons. 1985–; honors: Am. Men & Women of Sci. 1987; mem: ASCE, Assn. Groundwater Scientists & Engrs., Sigma Xi, Lions (dir. S.F. 1984-86), Chi-Kung Health Exercise Club (pres. 1985-87); contbg. author (book) Computer Methods for the 80's in the Mineral Industry, 1979; Republican; R.Cath.; rec: golf, tennis, marathon and triathlon. Res: 2430 35th Ave San Francisco 94116 Ofc: Morrison Knudsen 180 Howard St San Francisco 94105

KAMPER, MICHAEL JAY, plastic surgeon; b. July 14, 1939, Chicago, Ill.; s. Abraham A. and Fannie K.; m. Carole E. Goldfein, Feb. 22, 1970; 1 son, David b. 1973; edn: BS, Univ. Ariz. Tucson 1961; MD, UCSF 1965. Career: pvt. practice plastic surgery, Huntington Beach 1974–; secty., treas. Orange Co. Plastic Surgery Soc. 1987-89; chief, dept. surgery Humana Hosp., Huntington Beach 1984-85; mem: Am. Coll. Surgeons, (fellow), AMA, CMA, Am. Soc. Plastic Surgeons, Calif. Soc. Plastic Surgeons, Orange Co. Soc. Plastic Surgeons (v.p. 1989-91, pres. 1991-93), Am. Cancer Soc., Harbor Reform Temple (pres. 1984-85); article pub. in med. jour., 1972; mil: major AUS Med. Corps 1970-72; rec: metal sculpture, bicycle riding. Ofc: 17742 Beach Blvd 335 Huntington Beach 92647

KAN, HENRY, insurance and financial planning specialist; b. Oct. 10, 1921, China, nat. US cit. 1975; s. Sing-Yuek and Wai-Sing (Li) K.; m. Linda, May 5, 1951; children: Grace b. 1952, John b. 1954; edn: BS, Nat. Sun Yat-Sen and Wu-Han Univ., 1945; MS mech. engring., City Univ. of NY, 1967; MBA, Golden Gate Univ., 1976; Reg. Profl. Engr., Calif. 1972. Career: asst. to v.p., dist. chief engr. Taiwan Sugar Corp., Taiwan 1946-67; adminstrv. mgr. Foremost Dairies Ltd., Taiwan 1967-69; proj. eng. supvr. Bechtel Inc., San Francisco, Petroleum and Nuclear Projects 1969-85; agent and reg. rep. Prudential Ins. Co. of America, 1987-88; pres. Kans Enterprise 1989–; Congo Sugar Refinery Revamping & Op. 1961; Singapore Sugar Refinery Construction Proposal 1965; productivity studies, India & Japan 1965; citations: excellent achiev. and awards, Ministry of Economic Affairs, ROC 1956; Taiwan Sugar Corp., Taiwan 1965, Bechtel Inc., San Francisco 1980; listed: Who's Who in the west 1980, Men of Achievement 1982, Dict. of Internat. Biog. 1982, Personalities of Am. 1985; mem: Am. Soc. Mech. Engrs.; publs: contb. ed., Taiwan Sugar Hand Book; mil: lt. reserve ofcr. Chinese Army 1941-45; Republican; Christian; rec: philately, gardening, travel, swimming, boating. Res: 40 Moss Wood Ct Danville 94506

KANE, MARY KAY, college dean and professor of law; b. Nov. 14, 1946, Detroit, Mich.; d. John Francis and Frances (Roberts) Kane; m. Ronan Eugene Degran, Feb. 7, 1987 (dec. Oct. 10, 1987); edn: BA, Univ. of Mich., Ann Arbor, 1968, JD, 1971. Career: res. assoc. Univ. of Mich. Law Sch., Ann Arbor, 1971-72; res. assoc. Harvard Univ. Law Sch., Cambridge, Mass., 1972-74; asst. prof. of law SUNY at Buffalo Law Sch., Buffalo, NY, 1974-77; prof. of law Hastings Coll. of the Law, San Francisco, Calif., 1977-93, dean, 1993–; assoc. reporter Complex Litigation Project, Am. Law Inst., Phila., Pa. 1989-93; mem.: Assn. of Am. Law Schools (exec. com. 1990-93), Am. Bar Assn. (bar admissions com. 1993–), Am. Law Inst. (advy. com., Restatement 3d Torts: Apportionment 1993–), ABA/AALS Commn. of Financing Legal Edn. 1993–; author: Nutshell on Civil Procedure, 1992; 16 pub. articles, 1975–; co-author: Federal Practice & Procedure (8 volumes), 1983-93, Hornbook on Civil Procedure, 1993. Res: 8 Admiral Drive #421 Emeryville 94608 Ofc: Hastings College of the Law 200 McAllister St San Francisco 94102

KANE, SARAH R., company president; b. Dec. 10, 1918, Eclectic, Ala.; d. Henry Clay and Una Mae (Sanford) Rouse; children: Kimberlin J., II b. 1942, Tracy Peyton b. 1947, Sanford M. b. 1949, Courtney E. b. 1951; edn: Daisy Currie Bus. Coll., 1938, Valley Coll., San Bernardino. Career: exec. secty. Alabama State Bd. of Health, 1938-41; adminstrv. asst. and secty. to chmn. Dept. Orthopaedic Surgery, Wilford Hall Teaching Hosp., San Antonio, Tex. 1958-62; supr. Welcome Wagon Internat., 1966-67; pres. REA Associates, Inc. dba Redlands Employment & Temporary Services, Redlands 1971-92; awards: public relations award Calif. Assn. of Personnel Consultants 1978-79, various civic awards- Lions Club, Rotarians, Kiwanis, Soroptimist, 1972-82; mem: Calif. Assn. of Personnel Consultants. (state dir.), CAPC Inland Empire (chpt. pres. 1978, 81-82), Riverside, San Bernardino and Redlands Chambers of Commerce, Sunrise Rotary Club; anchorperson tv documentary: The Professional Edge on How to Get a Job (1982); Republican; Sci. of Mind (pres. bd. trustees); rec: bridge, sewing, walking. Res: 925 Evergreen Ct Redlands 92374

KANN, MARK E., educator, administrator, author; b. Feb. 24, 1947, Chgo.; s. Sam N. and Ann E. K.; m. Kathy E. Michael, Feb. 13, 1969; children: Simon b. 1973; edn: BA, Univ. Wis., Madison 1968, MA, 1972, PhD, 1975. Career: prof. Univ. So. Calif., L.A. 1975–, assoc. dean 1990-93; v.p. Jefferson Center For Character Educ., Pasadena 1991-93; author: On The Man Question (1991), Middle Class Radicalism in Santa Monica (1986), The American Left (1982). Ofc: USC Dept of Political Science University Park Los Angeles 90089-0044

KAO, PHILIP MIN-SHIEN, systems administrator; b. Dec. 16, 1963, Los Angeles, Calif.; s. Donald and Jennie (Chen) K.; m. Lori Suzanne Wilson, June 25, 1989; edn: BA, Chemistry, UC San Diego 1985. Career: student engr., Hughes Aircraft Co., Fullerton, Calif. 1983-85; res. asst., Hybritech, Inc., San Diego 1986; res. assoc./technical, SIBIA, La Jolla 1986-90; analytical chemist, Alliance Pharmaceuticals, S.D. 1990-91; programmer/analyst, Ligand Pharmaceuticals, S.D. 1991-92, microcomputer coordinator 1992-94, systems administr. 1994; software cons. Artecon Inc., Carlsbad 1994–; honors: listed Who's Who in the West (23rd-25th edits.) Who's Who In California (23rd., 24th edit.); mem. Am. Assn. of Clinical Chemists 1991-94, Am. Chem. Soc. 1981–, AAAS 1990-95, Mathematical Assn. of Am. 1991-94; Villarrica Homeowners

Assn. (treas.1991-94, pres. 1994-95), listed Who's Who in the World 1995; co-author: presentations, Amer. Chem. Soc., 1988, 89; publ. article in Jour. of Infectious Diseases, 1990; second author, publ. articles in Analytical Biochemistry 1989, Bioconjugate Chemistry 1990. Ofc: Artecon Inc. 6305 El Camino Real Carlsbad 92009

KAPLAN, JOSEPH M., safety council president; b. May 29, 1914, Cleveland, Ohio; s. Edward and Mamie (Krislove) K; m. Henrietta Lurie Kaplan, Mar. 30, 1941; children: Paul Dana, Drew Alan; edn: AB, UCLA 1931-35; masters cert., Harvard, Cambridge, MA 1937-38; instit. of organization mgmt., Univ. of Santa Clara, San Jose 1960-82. Career: dir., So. Calif. War Manpower Conservation Pgm. prior to WWII service; Greater Los Angeles Chapt. Nat. Safety Council, 1939-1979, pres. 1979–; cons. to White House Conf. on Traffic Safety; bd. dirs. March of Dimes; honors: 1st safety exec. designated Chartered Assn. Exec. (CAE), Am. Soc. of Assn. Execs.; recipient Key Award 1974 Outstanding Local Assn. Exec. in the nation; Award of Honor by Assn. of Safety Councils 1973, named Assn. Exec. of Yr. by So. Calif. Soc. of Assn. Execs. 1979; bd. mem. Nat. Safety Council; mem. Am. Soc. of Assn. Exec., Am. Soc. of Safety Engrs., Inst. of Traffic Engrs., Nat. Assn. of Exposition Mgrs., So. Calif. Industrial Safety Soc., Calif. Assn. of Safety Councils, Veterans of Safety Internat. (pres. 1976), Rotary Intl.; mil: US Army during WWII. Ofc: National Safety Council Greater Los Angeles 3450 Wilshire Blvd Ste 700 Los Angeles 90010

KAPLAN, JULIUS DAVID, administrator, professor, art historian; b. July 22, 1941, Nashville, Tenn.; s. Abraham Morris and Ada Sarah (Berlin) K.; m. Robin Lillian Reiser, March 1, 1970; edn: BA, Wesleyan Univ. 1963; MA, Columbia Univ. 1965; PhD, 1972. Career: asst. prof. Colby Coll, Waterville, Me. 1966; UCLA 1969-77; assoc. prof., prof. CSU San Bernardino 1977–, chair art dept. 1979-84, assoc. dean grad. programs 1986-89, dean grad. studies research and faculty devel. 1989–; advy. bd., GRE (Grad. Record Exam) and TOEFL (Test of English as a Fgn. Lang.) 1994-98; grad. fellowship advy. com. Calif. Student Aid Commn., Sacto. 1988-90; honors: Phi Kappa Phi, San Bernardino C.of C. Excellence in Tchg. 1987, Calif. Arts Council grant 1981-89; mem: Coll. Art Assn., Art Historians of So. Calif., Calif. Faculty Assn., L.A. Co. Museum of Art, L.A. Music Center Opera League; author Gustave Moreau 1982, 2 articles pub. in profl. jours., 1966, 70, exhibitions and exhibition catalogue, 1974-89; Democrat; Jewish; rec: music, travel. Res: 1719 Redwood Way Upland 91784 Ofc: Calif. State Univ. 5500 Univ. Parkway San Bernardino 92407

KAPLAN, MICHAEL ALLEN, lawyer; b. May 16, 1942, New York; children: Kira Anna b. 1975; edn: BA, Alfred Univ. 1964; JD, Albany Law Sch. 1967; admitted St. Bars Calif. 1970, N.Y. 1968. Career: atty. pvt. practice, N.Y.C. 1968, La Jolla 1971-80, San Diego 1980–; mem: N.Y. St. Bar Assn., Calif. St. Bar Assn., S.D. Co. Bar Assn., S.D. Trial Lawyers Assn., Vol. Lawyers Assn., Golden Triangle C.of C.; mil: capt. JAG/AVS 1968-70, bronze star w/oak leaf cluster; rec: tennis. Ofc: 3232 Governor Dr Ste A San Diego 92122

KAPLOWITZ, RICHARD ALLEN, academic dean; b. Dec. 12, 1940, Bklyn.; s. Joseph and Sonya (Taub) K.; m. Lisette Feldstein, Dec. 22, 1964 (div. Oct. 1990); children: David, Robert; edn: BA, Bklyn. Coll., 1961; MA, Columbia Univ., 1962; EdD, Harvard Univ., 1970. Career: tchr. schools in New York and France, 1962-67; founding dir. Weekend Coll., C.W. Post Univ., Greenvale, N.Y. 1970-72; dean continuing edn. Merrimack Coll., North Andover, Mass. 1974-80; dir. human resource devel. Raytheon Co., Andover, Mass. 1980-82; pres. Teem Inc., Andover 1982-90; dean New England Inst., Boston 1985-87, chair grad. div. Notre Dame Coll., Manchester, N.H. 1988-90; v.p. enrollment mgmt. Pacific Grad. Sch. Psychology, Palo Alto, Calif. 1990–; mem. bd. overseers Lawrence Gen. Hosp. 1980-90, Gr. Lawrence Mental Hlth. and Retardation Bd. (pres. 1977-79); mem: Assn. Cont. Higher Edn. (bd. 1979-82), Leadership Palo Alto 1994-95; author: Selecting Academic Administrators, 1973, Selecting Coll. and Univ. Personnel: The Quest and the Questions, 1988; contbr. articles to profl. jours.; Jewish; rec: flying. Res: 181 El Carmelo Palo Alto 94306 Ofc: Pacific Graduate School of Psychology 935 E Meadow Palo Alto 94303

KARABENSH, JEROLD KENT, healthcare marketing executive; b. Dec. 10, 1934, Milwaukee, Wis.; s. Fred August and Blanche (Shavzin) K.; m. Delores Ann Prosen, May 28, 1960; children: David b. 1961, Joseph b. 1963, Catherine b. 1964; edn: BS pharm., Univ. Wis. 1957; MBA mktg., 1960; reg. pharmacist Wis. (1959), Calif. (1961). Career: mktg. research mgr. Riker Labs., Northridge 1961-63, mktg. planning mgr. 1963-67, mktg. dir. 1967-71; v.p. mktg. Profl. Exchange, Cresskill, N.J. 1971-74; pres. Health Care Marketing Service, Los Altos 1974–; bd. vis. Univ. Wis. Sch. of Pharmacy, Madison 1988–; bd. dirs. Jews for Jesus, S.F. 1989–; dir. publications com. Kappa Psi, Oklahoma City 1989–; mem: Pharmaceutical Market Research Group (past pres.), Med. Mktg. Assn. (past pres.), Pharmaceutical Adv. Council, Mid-west Pharm. Advt. Club, Am. Pharmaceutical Assn., Calif. Pharmaceutical Assn., This Side of Hill Players (bd. mem. 1987–); article pub. in med. jour. (1989); mil: 1st lt. AUS MC 1957-65; Republican; Christian. Res: Box 639 Moss Beach 94038 Ofc: Health Care Marketing Services Box AP Los Altos 94023

KARAS, SAM P., county supervisor; b. Feb. 7, 1922, Chgo.; s. Peter and Penelope Ann (Falles) K.; m. Edith J. James, June 17, 1944; children: Penelope b. 1945, Judith b. 1947, Rachel b. 1953; edn: grad. Jones Commercial H.S., Chgo. Career: elected supr. dist. 4 Monterey County Bd. Suprs., 1985–, chair 1986, elected 5th Dist. 1993–; appt. to Calif. Coastal Commn. 1994–; mem: CSAC (st. bd. dirs. 1987-88), Nat. Assn. Co. Suprs. (1986-87), LAFCO, Pacific Grove C.of C., Seaside C.of C., Monterey Peninsula C.of C., Citizens League of Progress, L.W.V., NAACP; voted one of 10 most influential individuals Monterey Co., 1987; mil: 1st lt US Army 1942-45; Democrat; Greek Orthodox; rec: theatre. Ofc: Monterey County 1200 Aguajito Rd Monterey 93940

KARDOS, GARY G., physician, nephrology; b. May 23, 1936, Budapest, Hungary; nat. 1952; s. Leslie and Magdolna (Pasternak) K.; m. Zeeva Zaretsky, June 12, 1961; children: Leslie S. b. 1963, Kate D. b. 1966; edn: BA, UCLA 1957; MD, UCSF 1961; lic. physician and surgeon Calif. Career: pvt. practice medicine and nephrology, San Francisco 1967–; assoc. clin. prof. medicine UCSF 1978–, asst. prof. 1969-78, instr. 1967-69; mem: San Francisco Med. Soc., CMA, AMA, Am. Soc. Nephrology, Internat. Soc. Nephrology, Am. Soc. Internal Medicine, Calif. Soc. Internal Medicine; 2 articles pub. in med. jours. 1969, 88; mil: capt. AUS 1965-67; Jewish; rec: writing, photog.

KARNES, BARRY GORDON, project engineer; b. Oct. 3, 1958, San Jose; s. Gordon Milton and Alma Faye (Pendleton) K.; m. Dawna, June 13, 1981; children: Joshua b. 1988, Caleb b. 1992; edn: BSME, San Jose St. Univ. 1980; reg. profl. engr. (1984). Career: sr. project engr. Underwriters Labs., Santa Clara 1980–; dir. Burbank Sanitary Dist., San Jose 1988-90, pres. 1990–; awards: Underwriters Labs. Profl. Engrs. (1988); Republican; Prot.; rec: pvt. pilot. Ofc: Underwriters Laboratories 1655 Scott Blvd Santa Clara 95050

KARWELIS, DONALD CHARLES, artist; b. Sept. 19, 1934, Rockford, Ill.; s. Charles William and Lucille Ann (Pujdak) K.; children: Jean b. 1962, Kevin b. 1964; edn: undergrad. Riverside City Coll., 1966-68; BA, UC Irvine, 1968, MFA (summa cum laude), 1971. Career: instr. UC Irvine 1969-71, Riverside City Coll. 1971-72, So. Calif. Art Inst., Laguna Beach 1978-82, Saddleback Coll., Irvine 1979-80; lectr. UC Irvine, 1986-87; lectr. art history Fullerton Coll., UC Irvine 1993–; One-man shows: Kirk de Gooyer Gal., L.A. 1984, Irvine Fine Arts Ctr. 1986, LJ Gal., Newport Beach 1989, Interior Designer's Inst., Newport Beach 1991, Lithuanian Art Mus., Vilnius 1991, Orange Co. Ctr. for Contemporary Art 1992, Antoinette A. Sullivan Gallery 1992; group exhibits: Marilyn Pink Master Prints & Drawings, L.A. 1988, Lithuanian Art Mus., Lithuanian World Ctr. 1990, Irvine Fine Arts Ctr. 1990, Sata Fine Art, Costa Mesa 1991, The Works Gallery, Long Beach 1991, Fullerton Coll. 1991, Newport Harbor Art Museum 1992; represented in permanent collections of L.A. County Mus. Art, Newport Harbor Art Mus., Laguna Art Mus., Atlantic Richfield Corp., L.A., Calif. Canadian Bank, L.A.; awards: research grantee Nat. Def. Edn. Act 1970, fellow Nat. Endowment for Arts 1976-77; publ.: Artweek 1987; mil: sgt. USMC 1954-57; Democrat; R.Cath.; rec: cultural anthropology, R.R. ops. Studio: 17891 Allegheny Dr Santa Ana 92705

KASARI, LEONARD SAMUEL, concrete consultant, quality control professional; b. Sept. 22, 1924, Los Angeles; s. Kustaa Adolph and Impi (Sikio) K.; m. Elizabeth P. Keplinger, Aug. 25, 1956; children: Lorraine Carol, Lance Eric; edn: Compton Coll. 1942-43, UCLA 1964-70; reg. Profl. Engr. Calif. Career: gen. constrn. Los Angeles area 1946-61; supr. inspection svc. Osborne Labs., Los Angeles 1961-64; mgr. customer svc. Lightweight Processing, 1965-77; dir. tech. svc. Crestlite Aggregates, San Clemente 1977-78; quality control mgr. Standard Concrete, Santa Ana 1978-92; honors: Hon. Life mem. Calif. PTA 1983, Sam Hobbs Service Award ACI-So. Calif. 1992; mem. Am. Concrete Inst., So. Calif. Structural Engrs. Assn.; civic: Torrance YMCA (bd. mgrs. 1970–, camp dir. High Sierras 1969-80); mil: USN 1943-46; Democrat; Lutheran. Res/Ofc: 2450 W 233 St Torrance 90501

KASKEL, NEAL T., mergers and acquisitions executive; b. Oct. 6, 1943, Buffalo, N.Y.; s. David and Bertha (Perlmuter) K.; m. Geraldine Slutsky, Apr. 3, 1966; children: Amy b. 1970, Robert b. 1973; edn: BS, DePaul Univ., 1966; MBA, Northwestern Univ., 1972. Career: mktg. resrch. analyst D'Arcy Advt., Chgo. 1966-67; mktg. resrch. supr. Foote, Cone & Belding, Chgo. 1967-72; mgr. mktg. resrch. Armour-Dial, Phoenix, Ariz. 1972-74, Hunt-Wesson, Fullerton, Calif. 1974-79; dir. mktg. svs. FHP, Fountain Valley 1979-81; mktg. mgr. Smith Internat., Irvine 1981-83; v.p. The Geneva Cos., Irvine 1983–; adj. prof. CSU Fullerton, also CSU Long Beach, 1975-90, Univ. of La Verne, 1990–, Univ. of Phoenix, Fountain Valley 1990–; mil: lt. USNR 1966-72; Democrat; Jewish (Jewish Fedn. of Orange Co. bd. 1983–, treas. 91-93); rec: tennis, travel. Ofc: The Geneva Cos. 5 Park Plaza Irvine 92714

KASTL, ALBERT JOSEPH., psychologist; b. June 25, 1939, NY, NY; s. Albert and Emmy (Kannengeisser) K.; m. Donna Old, June 10, 1977, div. 1988; dau. Alison Joy b. 1978; edn: BA cum laude (spl. honors psych.), CUNY, N.Y. 1961; MS, Yale Univ., 1963, PhD, 1965. Career: postdoctoral fellow Mt. Zion Hosp., San Francisco 1967-68; staff psychologist Pacific Med. Ctr., S.F. 1968-70; pvt. practice, Santa Rosa 1972–, qualified forensic psych. expert witness civil and crim. cases Superior Cts.; faculty Calif. Sch. Profl. Psychology, S.F. 1974-76; dir. Health Plan of the Redwoods, Santa Rosa; peer claims reviewer Redwood Health Found. (MediCal pilot proj. for Sonoma, Mendocino, and Lake Counties), 1982; oral commr. Psych. Examining Com. Calif. BMQA, 1986–; honors: Phi Beta Kappa 1961, Carnegie Found. tchg. fellow 1962, NSF fellow 1961-63, VA tng. fellow 1963-65, USPHS post-doc. fellow 1967-68; mem: Redwood Psychol. Assn. S.R. (pres. 3t), Am. Psychol. Assn., W. Psychol. Assn., Calif. Psychol. Assn., Nat. Acad. Neuropsychology; co-author: Journey Back: Escaping the Drug Trap, 1975, contbr. numerous articles to profl. jours.; mil: capt. AUS 1965-67; Republican; Prot.; rec: piano, chamber music, jogging. Res: 115 Alderbrook Dr Santa Rosa 95405 Ofc: 114 Sotoyome St Santa Rosa 95405

KATHOL, ANTHONY LOUIS, asset management company executive; b. June 12, 1964, San Diego; s. Cletus Louis and Regina Antoinette (Ellrott) K.; m. Kathleen Marie Moore, Jan. 23, 1988; children: Nicole Kathleen b. 1989, Natalie Antoinette b. 1992, Holly Rose b. 1993; edn: BS, Univ. So. Calif., 1986; MBA, Univ. San Diego, 1988. Career: fin. and budget coord. Atcheson Topeka & Santa Fe Railway, Brea 1988-89; fin. and budget coord. Catellus Devel. Corp., Anaheim 1989-92, mgr. fin. analysis, 1992-93, mgr. leasing at the Pacific Design Ctr. 1994-95, dir. of finance 1995–; awards: Calif. Building Ind. Assn. fellow, USC 1986, Univ. San Diego fellow econ., mktg. (1987, 88), employee of yr. Catellus Devel. Corp., S.F. 1991; mem. Kts. of Col. (chpt. fin. sec. 1989-90), Future Bus. Leaders of Am. (So. Calif. judge 1991, 92, 94); Republican; R.Cath.; rec: reading, basketball, gardening. Res: 3805 Maxon Ln Chino 91710 Ofc: Pacific Design Ctr 8687 Melrose Ave M-60 West Hollywood 90069

KATO, MINOBU, financial executive; b. April 28, 1953, Kariya, Japan; s. Hiroyoshi and Yoshie (Taguchi) K.; m. Tomoko Fujita, April 29, 1983; chldren: Naoki b. 1988, Yusuke b. 1990; edn: BS, Shiga Univ. Career: staff acct. Makita Electric Works Ltd., Anjyo, Japan 1977-82; fin. dir. Makita USA Inc., La Mirada 1982-94; chief financial ofcr. Makita USA Inc., La Mirada 1994–; Buddhism; rec: backpacking. Ofc: Makita USA, Inc. 14930 Northam St La Mirada 90638

KATZ, KENT DOUGLAS, medical researcher, gastroenterologist; b. Dec. 10, 1954, Twin Falls, Ida.; s. Benjamin Edward and Gloria Elaine (Emery) K.; edn: BS, Univ. Utah, 1977; MD, Univ. Wash., 1981. Career: med. resident May Clinic, Rochester, Minn. 1981-84, research fellow 1984-85; gastroenterology fellow UC Irvine, 1985-87, research fellow 1987-88, asst. prof. of med. UCI, 1988; staff physician Long Beach Veterans Adminstrn. Med. Ctr., 1988–; awards: research fellow NIH 1984, UCI 1987; mem. AMA, Am. Coll. Physicians; contbr. med. jour. article, 1988; Latter Day Saints; rec: astronomy, scuba, swimming. Ofc: Long Beach VA Medical Ctr. Long Beach 90822

KATZ, MARTY, producer, motion picture and television production executive, consultant; b. Sept. 2, 1947, Landsburg, Fed. Rep. Germany; m. Campbell Hull; edn: UCLA; Univ. Md. Career: dir. film production ABC Circle Films, LA 1971-76; exec. v.p. production Quinn Martin Productions, LA 1976-77; production TV movies 1977-78; production cons., writer, producer Paramount Pictures Corp., Hollywood 1978-80; indep. producer Marty Katz Productions, LA 1980-85; exec. v.p. motion picture and TV productions Walt Disney Studio, Burbank 1985-92; producer Marty Katz Productions/ Disney Studios 1992–; supr. production 50+ TV movies that earned 25 Emmy awards; feature producer: Heart Like A Wheel, Lost In America, Man of the House, Mr. Wrong; mil: 1st. lt. US Army, Combat Pictorial Unit director, Vietnam, Bronze star. Ofc: Walt Disney Pictures 500 S. Buena Vista St. Burbank 91521

KATZ, RICHARD DANNY, member, California Legislative Assembly, 39th District; b. Aug. 16, 1950, LA., Calif.; s. Julius and Lillian (Ochacher) K.; m. Gini Barrett, Apr. 12, 1987; edn: BA, Calif. State Univ., San Diego, 1982. Career: graphics artist/printer, self-employed, Sepulveda, Calif.; mem. Calif. Legislative Assembly, 39th Dist., 1980–; chair Assembly Transp. Com., 1985–; mem. Televising the Assembly and Info. Tech. Com.; mem. Governmental Organization Com.; mem. Assembly Water, Parks & Wildlife Com.; awards: Legislator of the Year: Calif. Assn. of Independent Businesses 1983, The Victims Legal Assistance Council 1987, The Affiliated Committees on Aging 1987, Calif. Assn. of the Physically Handicapped 1987, Nat. Council of Alcoholism & Drug Dependence 1992, League of Calif. Cities 1992; Crimefighter of the Year, Assn. for L.A. Deputy Sheriffs 1992; mem: Advy. Bd Am. Jewish Com., 1980–; bd. dir. Nat. Defenders of Wildlife 1989-93; mem. Valley Industry/Commerce Assn. 1980–, Foothill Police Activity League 1986–; advy. bd. Valley Interfaith Council 1988–; bd. dir. Boys & Girls Club of San Fernando Valley 1985–; author, Calif. legislation: Taxpayers Bill of Rights, Paperwork Reduction Act, Bad Check Law, Regulatory Fairness Act, Computer Education Act of 1983, Children's Poison Prevention Act, legislation to permit market-based water transfers, Proposition 111 (Calif. transp. funding blueprint approved by Calif. voters in June, 1990), Safe Streets Act of 1994, Smog Check Program; Democrat; Jewish; rec: basketball, hiking, horseback riding, country & western music. Ofc: 9140 Van Nuys Blvd. No. 109 Panorama City 91402

KATZBERG, RICHARD WIER, radiologist; b. Oct. 23, 1945, Valdosta, Ga.; s. Arthur Joseph and Mary Frances (Wier) K.; children: Jenna b. 1974, Kimberly b. 1977, Richard b. 1982; edn: BS, Duke Univ. 1967; MBA, Univ. of So. Carolina, Columbia, S.C. 1969; MD, Med. Univ. of So. Carolina, Charleston, S.C. 1973; med. lic. N.Y. 1975, Tx. 1978, Mass. 1979, Ore. 1989, Calif. 1991; diplomate Am. Bd. Radiology 1977. Career: intern, resident in radiology Univ. of Rochester Sch. Medicine, NY 1973-77; maj. USAF, Lackland AFB, Tx. 1977-79; res. fellow, instr. in radiology Harvard Med. Sch., Boston, Mass. 1979-81; asst. prof. radiology Univ. of Rochester 1981-84, assoc. prof. 1984-89; clin. and res. assoc. orthodontics, Eastman Dental Ctr., Rochester, NY 1983-89; dir. radiological res. Univ. of Rochester Med. Ctr. 1986-88, dir. dept. radiology magnetic resonance clin. imaging ctr. 1987-89; prof. and chair radiology Ore. Health Scis. Univ., Portland, Ore. 1989-91; prof. and chair radiology UC Davis 1991–; mem. diagnostic imaging bd. sci. advs., Sterling-Winthrop Inc. 1992-94, FDA med. imaging drugs. advy. com. 1993–; mem. UC Davis and UC Davis Med. Ctr. clin. chairs com 1991–, clin progs. adminstrv. advy. com. 1991–, council of deans & dept. chairs 1991–, med. staff exec. com. 1991–, VA dean's com. 1991–, UCD nuclear magnetic resonance facility advy. bd., UCDMC Transition Sys., Inc. com. 1991–, UCD grad. group in comparative pathology 1992–, Tower II bldg. com. 1992–, UCDMC advy. com. for C.O.O. 1993–; UCDMC capitated income com. 1994–; UCDMC info. sys. com. 1994–, Med. Sch. clin. compensation plan implementation com. 1994–; internat. speaker, lectr., tchr. 1985–; awards: Beta Gamma Sigma Mgmt. Honor Soc. 1969, Alpha Omega Alpha 1973, Assn. of Univ. Radiologist's Resident Gold Medal award for res. 1977 and Stauffer award 1986, James P. Wilmot Disting. Asst. Prof. 1981-83, Sigma Xi 1985-87, hon. mem. dept. orthodontics Eastman Dental Ctr. 1986–, num. res. and reviewer awards from profl. jours. 1986, 87, 88, 89, 90, 91, recipient NIH res. grant 1987-91, 11 awards for clin. trials/animal studies 1987-94; mem: Assn. of Univ. Radiologists (pres. 1994-95, exec. com. 1990–, pres. elect 1993-94, sec./treas. 1992-93, ad hoc publs. com. 1992–, subcom. for annual meeting support 1992–, fin. com. 1992-94, chmn. membership com. 1992-94), CMA (sci. advy. panel on radiology 1991–), No. Calif. Radiological Soc. 1991–, Soc. of Chairs of Acad. Radiology Depts. 1990–, Am. Coll. Radiology 1989–, Soc. of Magnetic Resonance in Medicine 1987–, Am. Roentgen Ray Soc. 1987–, Soc. of Uroradiology 1983– (ad hoc com. on core curriculum 1992-94), Farrar/Norgaard Soc. (charter mem. 1981–), Radiological Soc. of N. Am. 1977–; editor: Jour. of Craniomandibular Practice 1985–, Radiology 1988–, Advances in Clin. Radiology, Academic Radiology 1989– (editl. exec. com. 1988–); guest reviewer Am. Jour. Roentgenology 1986–, Jour. of Oral and Maxillofacial Surgery 1988–, Acta Radiologica 1988–; editor The Contrast Media Manual (Williams & Wilkins 1991, Japanese lang. translation 1994); contbg. author/editor: 5 books, include. Diagnosis of the Temporomandibular Joint (W.B. Saunders 1993), 15 book chpts., 1980–; contbr. 118 original articles and 60 abstracts to sci./med. jours. and publications, 1975–; mil: maj. USAF 1977-79; rec: tennis (ranked 20th in 45-yr.-old men's singles No. Calif. 1993/94). Res: 1748 Haggin Grove Way

KAUFLIN, ANTHONY CHARLES, academic librarian, bookstore owner; b. May 21, 1933, Dayton, Ohio; s. Anthony Charles and Cecelia Theresa (Kuhn) K.; m. Leona, July 21, 1973; edn: BA, Univ. of Dayton, 1955; MLS, St. John's Univ., Jamaica, NY 1965. Career: tchr./librarian Chaminade High Sch., Mineola, NY 1955-61, and Dayton, Ohio 1961-62; St. Joseph H.S., Cleveland, Ohio 1962-65; Cathedral Latin Sch., Cleveland 1965-72; librarian Calif. Sch. Professional Psychology, San Diego 1973-78; librarian p.t. Grossmont Coll., El Cajon 1973–; owner Bookstore Cooperative, San Diego 1978–; mem. Nat. Assn. of College Stores; civic: Community Advy. Bd. Encinitas 1987, Heartland Human Relations Assn., La Mesa (bd. 1974-86, pres. 1985-86, recipient Annual award 1983), Leucadia-Encinitas Town Council (v.p., bd. 1985), Leucadia-Encinitas C.of C.; Democrat; Christian; rec: music, reading, travel. Res: 928 Cornish Dr Encinitas 92024 Ofc: Bookstore Cooperative 6212 Ferris Sq San Diego 92121

KAUFMAN, CARY STEVEN, surgeon; b. Jan. 5, 1948, Los Angeles; s. Carl and Betty K.; m. Leslie; children: Casey b. 1975, Lauren b. 1979, Amanda b. 1983; edn: BS chem., cum laude, UCLA 1969; MD, UCLA Sch. of Med. 1973; Diplomate Am. Bd. Surgery 1981, recert. 1989; MD lic. Wash., Calif., 1975. Career: surg. resident Univ. of Wash. 1973-75, Harbor/UCLA Med. Ctr. 1975-79; gen. and vascular surgeon pvt. practice, Long Beach 1979–; att. surgeon Long Beach Memorial Hosp. 1979–, chief gen./vasc. surg. 1988-90; bd. Memorial Cancer Inst., 1989-94; clin. asst. prof. surg. UCLA 1979–; researcher Nat. Surg. Adjuvant Breast Proj. 1988–; Fellow Am. Coll. of Surgeons, Fellow Internat. Coll. of Surgeons; mem: Long Beach Surgical Soc., Calif. Med. Assn., L.A. Co. Med. Assn., L.A. Surg. Soc., Am. Cancer Soc. Bd. 1984-87, med. advisor Reach for Recovery Pgm. 1981–; contbr. med. journals. Ofc: Cary S. Kaufman MD 2940 Squalicum Pkwy #100 Bellingham WA 98225

KAUNE, JAMES E., marine engineering executive; b. Mar. 4, 1927, Santa Fe, N.Mex.; s. Henry Eugene and Lucile (Carter) K.; m. Pauline Stamatos, June 24, 1956; children: Bradford Scott, Audrey Lynn, Jason Douglas; edn: BS engring., US Naval Acad., 1950; Naval Engr., naval architecture and marine engring., M.I.T., 1955; BS metallurg. engring., Carnegie Inst. Tech., 1960. Career: commd. ensign US Navy 1950, advanced through grades to capt., 1970, asst. gunnery ofcr. USS Floyd B. Parks 1950-52, project ofcr. USS Gyatt, Boston

Naval Shipyard 1955-57, main propulsion ofcr. USS Tarawa 1957-58, asst. planning ofcr. Her Majesty's Canadian Dockyard, Halifax, Nova Scotia 1960-62, repair ofcr. USS Cadmus 1962-64, fleet maintenence ofcr. Naval Boiler and Turbine Lab., design supt. (responsible all ship repair and modernization design plans) Philadelphia Naval Shipyard, 1964-68, project mgr. USS Midway conversion project, Hunters Point Naval Shipyard, San Francisco 1968-71, material staff ofcr., maintenance mgr. all aircraft carriers in Atlantic Fleet, Norfolk, Va. 1971-74, prodn. ofcr. (responsible all ship and waterfront prodn.) Phila. Naval Shipyard 1974-77, comdg. ofcr. Long Beach (Calif.) Naval Shipyard 1977-80; industrial mgr. Am. Metal Bearing Co., Garden Grove 1979-80; gen. mgr. Todd Shipyards Corp., S.F. Div. 1980-83; v.p. engring. and planning Port Richmond Shipyard Inc., Richmond 1983-84; v.p. engring. and mktg. Service Engineering Co., San Francisco 1984-93; CEO, Am. Modular Power Systems 1993–; mem: Am. Soc. Naval Engrs., US Naval Inst., Am. Soc. Metals, Masons; contbr. articles to profl. jours.; Episcopalian. Res: 403 Camino Sobrante Orinda 94563 Ofc: AMPS 165 Bovet Rd Ste 150 San Mateo 94402

KAUR, SWARAJ, biochemist; b. Jan. 30, 1955, Lucknow, U.P., India; d. Kartar Singh and Joginder Kaur; m. Timothy Alan Guetling, July 14, 1991; children: Swaim b. 1992; edn: BS, Lucknow Univ., 1973, MS, 1975, PhD, 1981; MBA, National Univ., San Diego, 1989. Career: jr.and sr. research fellow King George's Med. Coll., Lucknow U.P. India 1978-84; postdoc. res. toxicologist Univ. Calif., Riverside 1984-86; sr. project scientist Alpha Therapeutic Corp., Los Angeles 1986-88, prin. scientist 1988-91, sr. prin. scientist 1992-93, assoc. dir. 1993-94, dir. 1994–; awards: jr. and sr. res. fellowship Council of Scientific & Industrial Res., New Delhi (1976-78, 1978-80), sr. res. fellowship, res. associateship Indian Council of Med. Res., New Delhi (1980-81, 1982-84), postdoc. res. UC Riverside (1984-86), Golden State Award 1993, Award of Honor 1993, Who's Who In California 23rd, 24th edits.; mem. Sigma Xi, Internat. Biographical Assn.; publs: jour. articles and presentations sci. meetings; rec: shopping, singing, aerobics, sightseeing. Res: 10395 Vernon Ave Montclair 91763 Ofc: Alpha Therapeutic Corp.5555 Valley Blvd Los Angeles 90032

KAYE, "SANDY"ALEX ROBERT, manufacturing and marketing company executive; b. Dec. 24, 1936, New York; s. Saul and Vilma Kaye; m. Farida Karoon, June 27, 1954; 1 dau., Lorie; edn: Bx. H.S. of Sci.; BBS, CCNY, 1958. Career: div. mgr. Sears Roebuck & Co. 1956-58; v.p., branch mgr. Field Enterprises Edn. Corp., San Mateo 1958-76; pres., chmn. bd. Energy Assoc., Latham, N.Y. 1966-67, Land N'Sea Craft Inc., San Jose 1969-74, Porta-Bote Internat., Menlo Park 1974–; cons. mktg. to industry; chmn. bd., mem. sales ethics com. San Francisco Better Bus. Bureau 1968-69; awards: Fisher Body Craftsmans Guild award Gen. Motors (1951), Soc. Automotive Engrs. award CCNY (1955), Mahareshi award City of Palo Alto (1978); mem: Am. Boat & Yacht Council, San Mateo Better Bus. Bureau (bd. dirs. 1971-72), Big Brothers Orgn., Commonwealth Club.

KAYE, BRIAN R., physician; b. Dec. 13, 1957, Detroit, Mich.; s. Ronald Lee and Tobye Faye (Davidson) K.; m. Fran Alice Tannenbaum, Apr. 30, 1983; children: Naomi Shoshana b. 1987, Joshua Hillel b. 1990; edn: AB (summa cum laude), Princeton Univ. 1979; MD, Baylor Coll. of Medicine, Houston, Tx. 1983; internal medicine residency, Santa Clara Valley Med. Ctr., San Jose 1983-86; rheumatology fellowship, Stanford Univ. 1986-88. Career: physician East Bay Rheumatology Med. Group, Oakland and San Leandro 1988-90; physician Arthritis Ctr. Med. Group, Berkeley and Orinda 1991–; asst. clin. prof. of medicine UCSF 1989–; clin. asst. prof. of medicine Stanford Univ. 1992–; Wexner Heritage Found. Fellowship 1995-97; mem: Am. Coll. of Physicians (fellow 1991–), Am. Coll. of Rheumatology (fellow 1986–), AMA 1979–, CMA 1983–, No. Calif. Rheumatism Assn. (pres. 1994–), Princeton Univ. Alumni Assn. (mem. schools com.), Beth Jacob Congregation, Oakland (mem. bd. dirs.; chair, youth com.; chair, adult edn. com.); author: 11 articles pub. in med. jours., 7 med. textbook chpts.; rec: genealogy, calligraphy, philately, reading. Ofc: 3010 Colby St Ste 118 Berkeley 94705

KAYE, JEFFREY KENNETH, broadcast journalist/producer; b. Jan. 14, 1950, London, Eng., naturalized 1968; s. Harry and Rebecca (Richtiger) K.; m. Deborah, June 21, 1970; children: Sara b. 1983, Sophie b. 1990; edn: UCLA, 1967-71. Career: freelance journalist, L.A. 1974-80; reporter/prod. KCET-TV, Los Angeles 1980–, also correspondent MacNeil/Lehrer Newshour (PBS), NY, NY 1985–; awards: 6 L.A. Area Emmys, Acad. TV Arts & Scis. (1977, 82, 84, 88, 91, 92), 4 Golden Mikes Radio/TV News Assn. of So. Calif. (1980, 81, 82, 92), nat. Emmy nominee (1987, 88,94), Nat. Media Owl Awrd, Retirement Res. Found., Chgo. 1987, Red ribbon Am. Film & Video Fest., NY 1987; mem. Sigma Delta Chi, Investigative Reporters & Editors; contbr. news articles Washington Post, 1978-80, L.A. Mag., 1975-78, New West Mag., 1978-80. Ofc: KCET-TV, 4401 Sunset Blvd Los Angeles 90027

KAYE, RONALD LEE, physician; b. Apr. 15, 1932, Toledo, Ohio; s. Philip and Gertrude (Berman) K.; m. Tobye Fay Davidson, June 19, 1955; children: Brian b. 1957, Todd b. 1959, Douglas b. 1961, Jeffrey b. 1965; edn: BA, and MD, Univ. Mich., Ann Arbor, 1953, 1957. Career: rheumatologist, dir. of medical edn., Palo Alto Medical Clinic, 1963–; honors: Soc. of Sigma Xi (Mayo

Clinic, and Stanford), disting. service award Nat. Arthritis Found. 1973; mem: Am. Soc. of Clin. Rheumatology (1973–, past pres.), Am. Med. Assn. (sci. bd. 1963–), Sino-Judaic Inst. (exec. bd. 1973–), U.S. China Ednl. Inst. (exec. bd. 1973–), B'nai Brith; author: Katz's "Textbook of Rheumatology" (1989), 50+ journal articles; mil: capt. USAF 1959-66; Jewish; rec: philately, mineral collection, travel. Res: 2108 Bellview Dr Palo Alto 94303 Ofc: Palo Alto Medical Clinic 300 Homer Ave Palo Alto 94301

KAZAN, BENJAMIN, display technology consultant; b. May 8, 1917, New York; s. Abraham Eli and Esther (Bookbinder) K.; m. Gerda Bloch, Nov. 4, 1988; 1 son, David b. 1952; edn: BS physics, Calif. Inst. Tech. 1938; MA, Columbia Univ. 1940; PhD, Tech. Univ. Munich W. Germany 1961. Career: radio engr. Dept. of Defense, Ft. Monmouth, N.J. 1940-50; research engr. RCA Labs., Princeton, N.J. 1950-58; head solid state display group Hughes Research Lab., Malibu 1958-61; head imaging sect. Electro-Optical Systems, Pasadena 1961-68; head exploratory display group T.J.Watson Research Center, Yorktown Heights, N.Y. 1968-74; prin. scientist Xerox Research Center, Palo Alto 1974-85; cons., Los Altos 1985–; Advy. Group on Electron Devices of Defense Dept., Wash. D.C. 1973-82; adj. prof. Univ. R.I., Kingston 1970-74; awards: Am. Roentgen Ray Soc. Silver Medal 1957; mem: IEEE (fellow), Soc. Info. Display (fellow), Am. Physical Soc., Tau Beta Pi, Sigma Xi; coauthor: Electronic Image Storage, 1968, Storage Tubes, 1952; editor book series Advances in Image Pickup & Display, 1974-84; assoc. editor book series Advances in Imaging and Electron Physics, 1984–; 90+ inventions; rec: violin. Res: 557 Tyndall St Los Altos 94022 Ofc: Xerox Research Corp. 3333 Coyote Hill Rd Palo Alto 94304

KEARNEY, PAUL LOUIS, aerospace contracts executive; b. Nov. 20, 1934, Philadelphia, Pa.; s. Louis Edward and Eunice Mary (Caffery) K.; m. Mary Margaret Dahm, July 27, 1957; children: Michael b. 1958, Kathryn b. 1959, Timothy b. 1960, Margaret b. 1963, Joseph b. 1967; edn: BS physics, Univ. Notre Dame 1956, JD, Loyola Law Sch. 1966; admitted St. Bars Ill. 1967, Wis. 1968. Career: Grumman Corp., Bethpage, N.Y. 1969-73; mgr. contracts AiResearch Mfg. Co., Torrance 1973-87; dir. contracts Garrett Corp., Los Angeles 1985-87; Allied Signal Aerospace, Torrance 1987–; mem: Proprietary Industries Assn. (dir. 1987–, treas. 1994–), NCMA (bd. advisors S. Bay chpt. 1982-87), Notre Dame Club L.A., LACMA; mil: lt. USN 1956-59; Republican; R.Cath.; rec: travel, running. Res: 28435 Covecrest Dr Rancho Palos Verdes 90275 Ofc: AlliedSignal Aerospace 2525 W 190th St Torrance 90509

KEARNEY, REX THOMAS, JR., lawyer; b. May 9, 1938, Modesto; s. Rex Thomas and Esther Sterling (Weeks) K.; edn: BS, UC Berkeley 1962; LLB, Hastings Coll. of Law 1966; admitted Calif. Bar 1966. Career: deputy dist. atty. Sacramento County, 1967-68; atty., assoc. McDonald & Donahue 1968-74; sr. ptnr. Ingoglia, Marskey & Kearney, Lobner & Bull, Sacto. 1974–; instr. Assn. of Trial Lawyers of Am., Trial Coll. (2 yrs.), Calif. Cont. Edn. of the Bar 1984–; mem: Phi Delta Phi, Am. Bar Assn., Am. Bd. of Trial Advocates (Advocate), Calif. Bar Assn., Sacto. Co. Bar Assn., Def. Res. Inst., No. Calif. Assn. of Def. Counsel; mil: AUS 1957-60; Republican; rec: automobile racing CSRG, tennis. Ofc: Ingoglia, Marskey, Kearney, Lobner & Bull, 740 University Ave Ste 100 Sacramento 95825

KEEFFE, SUSAN DEVORE, educator, administrator; b. May 20, 1944, Hastings, Nebr.; d. Richard Geo. and Kathryn DeVore (King) Van Buskirk; m. Philip Lewis Keeffe, Jan. 28, 1966 (div. 1975); children: Darren b. 1970, Kathleen b. 1972; edn: BA in advt., San Jose St. Univ., 1966; MS spl. edn., Dominican Coll., San Rafael 1979; EdD, Univ. San Francisco, 1986. Career: educator, West Contra Costa Co. Unified Sch. Dist., 1975–, subst. tchr. 1975, Home tchr. 1976, tchr. 3rd/4th gr. 1977, special edn., transitional edn. pgm., 1986-95, program splst. 1995–, summer sch. tchg. 1978-88, summer sch. prin. Richmond High Sch. 1985, Castro Elem. 1986, hd. summer sch. principal Richmond Unified Sch. Dist., 1987; p.t. faculty Sch. of Edn., St. Mary's Coll., Moraga 1989–; Program Quality Review reviewer for Contra Costa Co.; honors: nominee and finalist Richmond USD Education Fund teaching excellence award 1991; mem. Seaview Sch. Program Quality Rev. Leadership Team, and v.chair Seaview Sch. School Site Council, 1990-91; mem. bd. Richmond U.S.D. Comm. Advy. Com. for Special Edn. (past pres., sec. 1983-85); awards: CANHC scholar (1976, 78), CTA scholar 1984, CTIIP grantee (1985, 87), mentor tchr. (1987/88, 89/90, 91/92, 93/94), State Dept. Edn. exemplary spl. edn. technology pgm. nominee, CANHC educator of yr. 1987, Richmond USD tchr. of yr. 1988; mem. CANHC/ACLD (past pres. West Contra Costa Chpt.), Phi Delta Kappa, Delta Kappa Gamma (past pres.); civic: Chelsea By-The-Bay HOA (pres. 1988-90, bd. v.p. 90-93), Friends of the Red-Tail Hawk (sec. 1989); contbr. 5+ articles in acad. and profl. jours.; Democrat; Unitarian; rec: camping, tropical birds, computers. Ofc: Pupil Personnel Services Ctr 2465 Dolan Way San Pablo 94806

KEELER, GEORGE ROBERT, journalism professor; b. May 1, 1954, Pomona; s. Robert Lee and Lucille Mae (Sarafian) K.; edn: BA, Univ. La Verne, MAT, 1979; PhD, USC, 1990. Career: ed. in chief La Verne Mag. 1976-77; editl. asst. Messenger Mag., Elgin, Ill. 1977-78; chmn. commns. dept. and assoc. prof. journalism Univ. La Verne 1978–; senior adv. The Thalians Mag., Beverly Hills 1982, 83, writing coach, consultant; awards: Victor DeRose, Paul M. Hinkhouse award Religious Pub. Relations Council 1977, Silver Crown Columbia Univ.

1985, medalist Columbia Scholastic Press Assn. (1982, 83, 85), 7 All-Am. awards Assoc. Collegiate Press (1979-86), Univ. La Verne student svc./humanities scholar 1977, life mem. Calif. Scholastic Fedn.; bd. mem: Sigma Delta Chi, Soc. Profl. Journalists (dir. L.A. chpt. 1986, Mark of Excellence award), L.A. Press Club; civic: Citizens for Environmental Land Protection (founder), Community Assn. for a Responsible Environment (founder), L.A. Co. Marshall Canyon Mounted Assistance (Mountain Bike Unit founder); Ch. of the Brethren (worship/witness commn. chmn. 1984-86); contbg. writer: History of the Am.-Armenian Internat. Coll.: Promise and Reality (1987); Inquiry Into Who Should Have the Final Authority Over What Is Printed in a Campus Newspaper (1981); numerous profl. jour. articles; rec: white water river kayaking guide, mtn. biking, wedding and magazine photog., trumpet. Res: 381 Baseline Rd Claremont 91711 Ofc: University of La Verne 1950 Third St La Verne 91750

KEELER, RICHARD LEE, college executive assistant; b. July 19, 1958, Pomona; s. Robert Lee and Lucille Mae (Sarafian) K.; edn: BA, magna cum laude Univ. of La Verne 1980, MA, Univ. of La Verne 1983; MA, Univ. Calif., Berkeley 1989. Career: publicity coord. Univ. of La Verne, 1980-81; gen. assignment reporter Claremont Courier newspaper, Claremont 1981-82; assoc. dir. communications, Nat. Energy Research & Info. Inst. (editor, Cogeneration World Mag., Energy Report), Univ. of La Verne, 1983-86, instr. Journalism and Communications, 1985-86; asst. to pres., acting campus dean, Colo. Mtn. Coll., Leadville campus, 1986, Spring Valley Campus 1987; exec. asst. to the Chancellor, Peralta Colls., 1987-88; acct. exec. So. Calif. Edison 1990-94; appointed deputy dir. Office of Strategic Tech., State of Calif. Trade & Commerce Agency 1994–; honors: cert. Creativity 1984 Contest, Cogeneration World Mag., listed Who's Who in Am. Colls. and Univs. 1980; Republican. Res: 381 Baseline Rd Claremont 91711

KEELER, RONALD FRANKLIN, federal credit union president; b. June 11, 1938, Great Bend, Kans.; s. Ray A. and Lelamae (Hartmetz) K.; m. Diana Marie Tuggle, Feb. 1, 1963; children: Jana b. 1957, Rick b. 1959, Sheri b. 1963, Lance b. 1967; edn: BS bus., Univ. Kans., 1960; JD, UCLA, 1963; admitted bar: Calif. 1963. Career: atty. Atlantic Richfield Co., Los Angeles 1964-67; Am. Potash & Chem. Corp. 1967-68; assoc. counsel Lockheed California Co., Burbank 1968-77, asst. div. counsel 1977-82, pres. Lockheed Federal Credit Union 1982–; dir: Wescorp. Inc. (1989–, chmn. bd. 1994–), USERS Inc., Valley Forge, Pa. (1986–, chmn. bd. 1988–), CU Mortgage Corp., Pomona (1989–, chmn. 1992, CU Task Force Com. 1986–), dir. Nat. Assn. of Federal Credit Unions 1992–; honors: Sigma Chi, Alpha Kappa Psi, Phi Delta Phi; mem: L.A. Co. Bar Assn.; Republican; Presbyterian; rec: camping. Res: 5838 Beckford Ave Tarzana 91356 Ofc: Lockheed Federal Credit Union 2340 Hollywood Way Burbank 91510

KEENAN, JOHN PAUL, physician; b. Mar. 9, 1943, Newton, Mass.; m. Pamela Joanne Beam, Aug. 28, 1964; children: Catherine b. 1966, Michael b. 1967, Mary Louise b. 1970, Cynthia b. 1972, Elizabeth b. 1976, Paula b. 1979, Sean Patrick b. 1982; edn: BS, Loyola Univ. L.A., 1964; MD, Marquette Sch. of Med., 1968; med. lic. Calif., Mass., Hawaii. Career: intern Orange Co. Med. Ctr., 1968-69; resident Univ. Hosps. of Cleveland, 1973-76; fellow in glaucoma George Wash. Univ. Med. ctr., Wash. DC 1976-77; pvt. practice San Pasqual Ophthalmology Med. Group Inc., Escondido current; Fellow Internat. Coll. Surgeons, Am. Coll. Surgeons, Am. Acad. Ophthalmology and Otolaryngology; mem. AMA, Am. Soc. Cataract and Refractive Surgery, Calif. Assn. Ophth., CMA, Internat. Soc. Refractive Keratoplasty, Pan Am. Assn. Ophth., San Diego Co. Med. Soc.; contbr. med. jour. article, 1978; mil: flt. surgeon/lt. cdr. M.C. USNR 1969-73. Ofc: 700 West El Norte Parkway Escondido 92026

KEENAN, RETHA VORNHOLT, registered nurse, educator, consultant; b. Aug. 15, 1934, Solon, Iowa; d. Charles E. and Helen M. (Konicek) Vornholt; m. Roy V. Keenan, Jan. 5, 1980; 2 sons (nee Iverson): Scott b. 1959, Craig b. 1961; edn: BS in nsg., Univ. of Iowa 1955; MS in nsg. CSU Long Beach 1979; cert. nurse practitioner, mental health, CSULB, 1979; R.N., Calif. Career: mental health cons. Inter-City Home Health Agency, Los Angeles 1979-80; instr. mental health nsg. Los Angeles City Coll. 1980-81, El Camino Coll., Torrance 1981-86, Mt. St. Mary's Coll. 1986, West Los Angeles Coll., Culver City 1981-87; Commencement speaker 1984, 85, 86, 87; public health nurse City of Long Beach 1994–; awards: NIMH grant for grad. study 1977-78, Phi Kappa Phi 1977, Sigma Theta Tau 1985; mem: Am. Nurses Assn. (Coun. Psychiat. and Mental Health Nsg. 1984-90), Calif. Nurses Assn., Delta Zeta Sor., Assistance League of San Pedro, Palos Verdes; major contbg. author: Am. Jour. of Nsg. Question & Answer Book for State Bd. Rev., pub. 1983, rev. 1985, 1987, Nursing Care Planning Guide for Adults, 1987, Nursing Care Planning Guide for Children, 1987, Nursing Care Planning Guide for Psychiatric and Mental Health Nursing, 1988, Critically Ill Adults: Nursing Care Planning Guides, 1988; Republican; Lutheran; rec: travel, writing. Res: 27849 Longhill Dr Rancho Palos Verdes 90275

KEENEY, EDMUND LUDLOW, Scripps Clinic president emeritus; b. Aug. 1908, Shelbyville, Ind.; s. Bayard G. and Ethel (Adams) K.; m. Esther Cox Loney Wight, Mar. 14, 1950; children: Edmund L. Jr., Eleanor (Smith); edn: AB, Ind. Univ. 1930; MD, Johns Hopkins Univ. 1934; diplomate Am. Bd. of Internal Med., subsplty. allergy. Career: intern Johns Hopkins Hosp., 1934-35,

med. resident 1935-36, instr. in medicine 1940-48; pvt. medical practice, splst. in allergy, San Diego 1948-55; pres./director Scripps Clinic and Research Found., La Jolla 1955-77, pres. emeritus 1977–; dir. research on fungus infections Ofc. of Sci. Research and Devel., cons. U.S. Navy 1948-64; bd. trustees Univ. San Diego 1974–; honors: Phi Beta Kappa, Alpha Omega Alpha, Beta Theta Pi; mem: AMA (1938–, secty. Sect. on Allergy 1964-65), Fellow Am. Acad. of Allergy (1940–, pres. 1963-64, editl. bd. Journ. of Allergy), Allergy Found. of Amer. (dir.), Am. Soc. for Clin. Investigation 1945–, Fellow Am. Coll. of Phys. 1946–, Western Soc. for Clin. Research 1948–, Western Assn. of Phys. 1955–, Calif. Med. Assn. (sci. bd. dirs.), Rotary, Eldorado Country Club; author: Practical Medical Mycology (Charles C. Thomas, 1955), contbr. num. articles re allergy, immunology, mycology to profl. jours.; Republican; Presbyterian; rec: golf, fishing, swim. Res: 338 Via del Norte La Jolla Ofc: 10666 N Torrey Pines Rd La Jolla 92037

KEESLAR, OREON, author, retired educator and public school administrator; b. Dec. 19, 1907, Orland, Ind.; s. Glenn Leroy and Janette (Gillis) K.; m. Julia May Hackett, Feb. 22, 1936 (dec. Feb. 1988); children: Peter b. 1939, Daniel b. 1944, Mary Judith b. 1947; edn: 2-yr. Normal Dipl., Manchester Coll., 1934; BS edn., Ohio St. Univ., 1938, MA sci. edn. 1939; PhD sci. edn., Univ. of Mich., 1945. Career: 1-room rural tchr. Sand Hill Sch., Angola, Ind. 1929-34, jr. high tchr. Angola Pub. Schs., 1934-37; also scoutmaster and dist. commr. Boy Scouts Am., Anthony Wayne Area Council, 1930-37; university high sch. science tchr. Ohio St. Univ., Columbus 1938-40, Univ. of Mich., Ann Arbor 1940-43; tchr. Plymouth H.S., Plymouth, Mich. 1943-44; Lt. US Naval Reserve 1944-49, ofcr. in chg. rating exams Pensacola Naval Air Base, 1944-46; dir. A-V (audio-visual) edn. and H.S. curriculum coord. Kern County Schs., Bakersfield, Calif. 1946-54; dir. edn. Inyo County Schs., Independence 1954-55; H.S. curriculum coord. Santa Clara County Schs., San Jose 1955-73; instr. A-V, Fresno St. Coll. and UCSB, Ext. courses, 1947-50, on-campus Fresno State, summer 1949; vis. prof. UCLA, 6 summers 1950-55, San Jose St. Coll., summer 1960; active num. tchr. organizations 1954-73, ofcr. and bd. mem. Calif. Sch. Suprs. Assn. (state secty. 1949-50), San Joaquin Valley A-V Assn. Bksfld. (pres. 1947-48), Nat. Science Tchrs. Assn. (chmn. conv. plng. com. Chgo. 1961), past sec.-treas. 8 tchr. orgns. (Math; Sci.; Soc. Studies; Fgn. Languages; HS Librarians; English; Sci. Fair; Jt. Council/Math & Sci.) San Jose, Santa Clara Co., 1954-73; honors: French horn player chosen to rep. the Steuben County Schs. Orch. (NE Ind.) in Dr. Joseph E. Maddy's First National H.S. Orch. (Detroit) made up of 225 of best student musicians nat. 1926; Phi Kappa Phi (1943), Phi Delta Kappa 1937-70, science fair award of honor Calif. Acad. of Sci., San Francisco 1973; civic: Photog. Soc. of Am. 1975–, Gold Rush Chapt. P.S.A. (dir. at lg. 1989-92), Placer Camera Club (Auburn, Calif.), Audubon Soc., Nature Conservancy, Wilderness Soc., Sierra Club, others; author: Financial Aids for Higher Education (coauthor, Judy Keeslar Santamaria) (pub. biennially 1963-94, now 800-page book in 16th edit.), series of articles in Science Education J. 1945-50, book chapt. in Film And Education 1948; Democrat; Prot.; rec: photog., cabinetry, bookbinding, fiction writing, travel. Res: 736 Auburn Ravine Road #635 Auburn 95603

KEHL, ROBERT SCOTT, family practice physician; b. Oct. 20, 1961, Pittsburgh, Pa.; s. Jack Robert and Louise Claudette (Warner) K.; m. Martha Verran Jones, Oct. 1, 1983; children: Sarah b. 1990, Anna b. 1991; edn: BS, biol. scis., UC Davis 1983; MD, Med. Coll. of Va., Richmond 1988; family medicine resident, Univ. of Wisconsin, Madison 1991; diplomate, Am. Acad. of Family Practice 1991–. Career: family physician Palo Alto Med. Found.-Fremont, Fremont, Calif. 1991–; patient edn. com. Palo Alto Med. Found., Palo Alto 1992–; family practice com. Wash. Hosp., Fremont 1992–, ICU com. 1992–; honors: Outstanding Sr., UC Davis 1983, Alpha Omega Alpha 1987; mem: Christian Med. Soc. 1988–, AMA 1991–, Am. Acad. of Family Practice 1991–; vol. physician Rotacare Health Clinic, Fremont 1991–; Republican; Presbyterian (mem. Centerville Presbyn. Ch.); rec: softball, golf, hiking, fishing, travel. Ofc: 39500 Liberty St Fremont 94538

KEHLER, DOROTHEA FAITH, humanities professor; b. Apr. 21, 1936, N.Y.C.; d. Nathan and Minnie (Coopersmith) Gutwill; widowed; children: Paul Dolid b. 1957, Eve Boyd b. 1959, Jessica Kehler b. 1971, Edward Kehler b. 1973; edn: BA, City Coll. N.Y., 1956; MA, Ohio Univ., 1967, PhD Eng. lit., 1969. Career: instr. MacMurray Coll., Jacksonville, Ill. 1964-65; instr. Ohio Univ., Athens, Oh. 1965-66, teaching fellow 1966-68; lectr. San Diego State Univ., 1969-70, asst. prof. 1970-88, prof. dept. English, 1988–; awards: summer fellow NEH, Harvard Univ. 1983, travel grantee Folger Libr. Inst., W.D.C. 1988, merit. performance and profl. promise SDSU 1988, res., scholarship and creative activity SDSU 1990, English Dept.'s most influential professor tchg. award SDSU 1991; mem: Modern Language Assn. of Am. 1970–, Shakespeare Assn. of Am. 1983–, Internat. Shakespeare Assn. 1984–, Rocky Mountain Modern Language Assn. 1984–, Southeastern Renaissance Conf. 1986–, Philological Assn. of Pacific Coast 1986–, Renaissance Conf. of So. Calif. 1990–; author: Problems in Literary Research (3 revised edits. 1975, 81, 87); editor anthology: In Another Country: Feminist Perspectives on Renaissance Drama, 1991; pub. articles in Shakespeare-Jahrbuch, Upstart Crow, Renaissance Papers, other jours.; Democrat; rec: piano, travel, theatre, movies. Ofc: English Dept. San Diego State University, San Diego 92182-8140

KEHOE, VINCENT JEFFRÉ-ROUX, photographer, author, cosmetic company executive; b. Sept. 12, 1921, Brooklyn, N.Y.; s. John James and Bertha Florence (Roux) K.; m. Gena Irene Marino, Nov. 2, 1966; edn: MIT 1940-41; Lowell Tech. Inst. 1941-42; Boston Univ. 1942; BFA motion picture and t.v. production, Columbia Univ. 1957. Career: dir. make-up dept. CBS T.V., N.Y.C. 1948-49; NBC Hallmark Hall of Fame series 1951-53; make-up artist in charge of make-up for num. film., t.v. and stage productions 1942–; dir. make-up Turner Hall Corp. 1959-61; Internat. Beauty Show 1962-66; pres., dir. research Research Council of Make-up Artists Inc., L.A. 1963–; chief press ofcr. Spanish Pavilion, N.Y. Worlds Fair 1965; freelance photographer 1956-;awards: Torch Award Council of 13 Original States 1979; mem: Co. Mil. Historians (fellow), Soc. Preservation Colonial Culture (life curator), Tenth Foot Royal Lincolnshire Regimental Assn. (life, Hon. Col. 1968), Soc. Motion Picture & T.V. Engrs. (life), Acad. T.V. Arts & Scis., Soc. Army Hist. Research (life), British Ofcrs. Club New England (life), Tenth Mountain Div. Assn. (life), 70th Infantry Div. Assn. (life), DAV (life), NRA (life); contbr. photographs to num. mags. incl. Time, Life, Sports Illustrated, Argosy, Popular Photog.; author: The Technique of Film & T.V. Make-up for Color, 1970, The Make-up Artist in Beauty Salon, 1969, We Were There: April 19, 1775 (1975), The Military Guide, 1975, 2nd Edit., 1993, The Technique of the Profl. Make-Up Artist, 1985, 2nd Edit., 1995, numerous other books; mil: AUS, Bronze Star, Purple Heart, C.I.B. Address: POB 850 Somis 93066

KEIL, RONALD LEE, pharmacist; b. July 18, 1945, Oakland; s. Ralph Leo Keil and Josephine Lorraine (Swan) Holby; m. Joan Ryniewicz, June 22, 1968 (div. 1982); m. Cathy Kuenzinger, Sept. 19, 1987; children: Leslie b. 1979; edn: B.Pharm., Univ. Colo. Boulder 1975; reg. pharmacist Calif. 1975. Career: pharmacist Villages Pharm., San Jose 1975–, pres. 1980–; adj. prof. Univ. Pacific, Stockton 1984–; mem. Bd. Med. Quality Review, San Mateo 1989-92; honors: Univ. Pacific Preceptor of Year 1987; mem: Calif. Pharm. Assn. (pres. 1994, trustee 1988-91), Am. Cancer Soc., Santa Clara Co. Unit (dir. 1978-93), Santa Clara Pharmacists Assn. (past pres.), Am. Pharm. Assn., Am. Coll. Apothecaries (fellow), Nat. Assn. of Retail Druggists, Rotary (pres. 1981); mil: USN 1966-70; Republican; Cath.; rec: water skiing, boating, swimming. Res: 3758 Rosemar Ave San Jose 95127 Ofc: The Villages Pharmacy 2925 The Villages Parkway San Jose 95135

KEISTER, JEAN CLARE, lawyer; b. Aug. 28, 1931, Warren, Ohio; d. John R. and Anna (Brennan) Keister; child: John b. 1954 (dec. 1975); edn: JD and LLB, Southwestern Sch. of Law, L.A. 1966; admitted bar: Calif. 1967, US Supreme Ct. 1972. Career: atty., solo law practice, Los Angeles, Burbank, Lancaster, 1967–; atty. Bezaire, Bezaire, Bezaire & Bezaire, APC, San Marino 1988-89; legal writer Gilbert Law Summaries, L.A. 1967; instr. Glendale Coll., Glendale 1968; mem. Burbank Bar Assn. (1986–, secr. 1993), Glendale Bar Assn. 1987, Antelope Valley Bar Assn. 1990–, Burbank C.of C., Themis Soc. 1989–; write prose and poetry, recipient Golden Poet Award, World of Poetry anthology (1988, 89, 91). Law Offices of Jean Clare Keister, 1321 W Burbank Blvd Burbank 91506

KELISKY, MAURY DAVID, physician; b. May 17, 1923, Chgo.; s. Sam L. and Sadie (Aronoff) K.; m. Dana D. Kleinberg, June 29, 1957; children: Monique b. 1958, Gregory b. 1960, Peddie b. 1961; edn: BS, Univ. Tex., 1951, MD, 1955. Career: intern Phila. Gen. Hosp., 1955-56; resident Bronx VA Hosp., NYC 1956-57; resident Stanford Service, S.F. Gen. Hosp. 1957-58; chief med. resident Mount Zion Hosp., San Francisco 1958-59, asst. chief dept. med. 1959; pvt. practice physician, 1959–; honors: Alpha Omega Alpha; mil: sgt. US Army 1941-45; Republican; Jewish; rec: fishing, building, gardening. Res: 70 San Andreas Way San Francisco 94127 Ofc: 2186 Geary Blvd Ste 210 San Francisco 94115

KELLEHER, MATTHEW DENNIS, professor of mechanical engineering; b. Feb. 1, 1939, Flushing, N.Y.; s. James Finbar and Mary Florence (Fitzgerald) K.; m. Jean Esther Jolliffe, May 31, 1969; children: Genevieve b. 1977, Veronica b. 1980; edn: BS engr. sci., Univ. of Notre Dame, 1961, MS in M.E., 1963, PhD in M.E., 1966; reg. profl. engr. Calif. 1973. Career: asst. prof. Univ. of Notre Dame, 1965-66; Ford Found. fellow Dartmouth Coll., 1966-67; assoc. scientist AVCO Res. Lab., Everett, Mass. summer 1967; faculty Naval Postgrad. Sch., Monterey, Calif. 1967–, asst. prof. 1967-72, assoc. prof. 1972-82, prof. mech. engring. 1982–, and dept. chmn. 1992–; cons. Livermore Nat. Lab. 1985-88, Apple Computer Inc., Cupertino 1984; awards: grad. fellow NSF 1963-64, Ford Found. fellow 1966-67, NASA & Am. Soc. for Engr. Edn. fellow 1970, 71, vis. prof. Univ. Notre Dame 1987, senior acad. vis. Oxford Univ., England (1988-89), Sigma Xi 1965–; Fellow ASME 1965–; civic: Lower Carmel Valley advy. com. to Monterey County Planning Commn. 1981-87 (chair 83-86); author chapt. in book: Diffusion of Turbulent Bouyant Jets 1984, 40+ tech. papers 1964–; R.Cath. Res: 25000 Outlook Dr Carmel 93923 Ofc: Naval Postgraduate Sch. Mechanical Engineering Dept., ME/KK, Monterey 93943

KELLER, J. WESLEY, credit union executive; b. Jan. 6, 1958, Jonesboro, Ark.; s. Norman Grady and Norma Lee (Ridgeway) Patrick; m. Patricia Maria Delavan, July 7, 1979; edn: undergrad. Univ. of Miss. 1976-78; BS bus. adm. & mgt., Redlands Univ., 1990; MBA, Redlands Univ., 1995. Career: senior collec-tor Rockwell Fed. Credit Union, Downey 1978-79; acct. Lucky Fed. Credit Union, Buena Park 1979-84; pres./CEO Long Beach State Employee Credit Union, 1984–; mem: Calif. Credit Union League (regulatory rev. bd. 1986-87, bd. govs. treas. Long Beach Chpt. 1985), Credit Union Exec. Soc., So. Calif. Credit Union Mgrs. Assn.,bd. dirs. Nat. Assn. State Chartered Credit Unions 1991–, Kiwanis Intl.; Republican; Baptist; rec: photog., skiing, woodworking. Ofc: Long Beach State Employees Credit Union 3840 Long Beach Blvd Long Beach 90807

KELLER, JOHN FRANCIS, management consultant, municipal official; b. Feb. 5, 1925, Mt. Horeb, Wisconsin; s. Francis S. and Elizabeth (Meier) K.; m. Barbara Dawn Mabbott, Feb. 18, 1950; children: Thomas b. 1951, Patricia b. 1952, David b. 1954, Daniel b. 1954, John J. b. 1963; edn: BBA, Univ. of Wisconsin, 1949; MBA, Univ. of Chicago, 1963; SEP, Stanford Univ., 1978; cert. CPA, Wis., Ill. 1959. Career: mgr. acctg. Miller Brewing Co., Milw., 1950-58; controller Maremont corp., Chicago, Ill. 1958-68; v.p. fin. Heublin Inc., St. Paul and San Francisco 1968-80, group v.p. Heublein Wine Group, c.e.o. 1980-84; pres. ISC Wines of Calif., San Francisco 1983-84; admin. dir. Calif. Wine Mktg. Order 1984-85; mgmt. cons. J.F. Keller & Assoc. 1985–; councilman Hillsborough, Calif. 1982–, mayor Hillsborough 1988-90; asst. prof. CSU Hayward grad. sch. 1979-82; adjunct prof. Golden Gate Univ. grad. sch. of bus. 1983-86; awards: 25-Year award Nat. Assn. Accts., S.F. 1989, distinguished alumni Univ. of Wis. 1990; mem: Calif. Soc. of CPA's 1972–, Wis. Soc. of CPA's 1958–, Serra Club of San Mateo 1987–, Kts. of Col. 1954–, Order of Malta 1989–, Order of Holy Sepulchure 1990–; mem. (ret.) Nat. Assn. of Accts. 1954–, Financial Execs. Inst. 1972–; civic bds: Alemany Scholarship Found. (dir. 1983–, pres. 1990-92), Cath. Archdiocese Edn. Development Council 1989–, Seton Med. Ctr. and Seton Health Svs. Found. (bd. dirs. 1988–), Daughters of Charity Nat. Health System (audit com. 1989–), Lesley Found. (dir., treas. 1987–), Univ. Wisconsin Found. (exec. com.), Univ. Chicago Found., Justice & Peace Commn. S.F. Cath. Archdiocese (1986–, coord. conf. on Economic Justice - Religion, Business and the Poor, 1989), Specialty Wine Services, Inc. (dir., ofcr.); mil: paratrooper, lt. U.S. Army, 1944-51; Republican; R.Cath. (40th Anniversary com. St. Anthony's Kitchens 1989); rec: golf, charity work, travel. Res: 785 Tournament Dr Hillsborough 94010

KELLER, LYNN ROBIN, educator; b. Oct. 25, 1952, Pasadena; d. Robert Phillips and Colleen Ann (Putnam) K.; m. Dr. Henry Mark McMillan, Oct. 11, 1987; edn: BA, MBA, and PhD, UCLA, 1974, 1976, 1982. Career: asst. prof. UC Irvine Grad. Sch. Mgmt., 1982-89, assoc. prof. 1989–; assoc. pgm. dir. Nat. Science Found., WDC 1989-90, pgm. dir. 1990-91; vis. scholar UCLA 1993-94; vis. asst. res. prof. Duke Univ., Durham, N.C. 1987; dept. editor and contbr. to: Management Science, assoc. ed. and contbr. to: J. of Risk & Uncertainty, Information & Decision Technologies; contbr. articles to Risk Analysis, Organizational Behavior & Human Decision Processes, other profl. jours.; honors: Beta Gamma Sigma 1976, outstanding grad. UCLA 1982, excellence in tchg. UCI Grad. Sch. of Mgmt. (1982-83, 1985-86); mem: Operations Research Soc. of Am., (council mem. spl. interest group on decision analysis 1986-89), The Inst. of Mgmt. Sci. (v.p. finance 1993-96, council 1991-93), Alpha Phi Internat. Frat. Inc. (UCLA collegiate pres. and rep. to internat. exec. bd. 1973-74, frat. advisor UCLA 1970s, UCI 1988-89). Ofc: Graduate School Mgmt. Univ. Calif. Irvine 92717-3125

KELLER, SHARON PILLSBURY, speech pathologist, educator; b. Sept. 28, 1935, Los Angeles; d. Edward Gardner and Iris Noriene (Hager) Pillsbury; m Clarence Stanley Keller (dec. 1982); children: Jann Kathleen b. 1956, Jennifer Beth b. 1959, Lauren Elaine b. 1962; edn: AA, Chaffey Comm. Coll. 1971; BA, Univ. La Verne 1978, MS in comm. disorders, 1983; cert. clin. competence sp.-lang. pathologist, ASHA lic. sch. audiometrist (1983). Career: speech/language pathologist Chino Unified Sch. Dist., Chino 1978-86; Rim of the World Sch. Dist. (pre-K.- 8th gr.), Lake Arrowhead 1986–, also San Bernardino Co. Pre-Sch. (S.B. 2666) Home Pgm. Mountain Communities, 1988-89; master tchr. for Speech/Language Pathology Interns, Univ. Redlands, 1990-91; cons. Cedu Middle and High Sch. Running Springs 1991–, cons. Dr. Stanley Kaseno, San Bernardino. 1992–, cons. Assoc. Speech & Hearing Svs. of Chino 1984, trainer Pre-sch. and Parent-child interaction 7 yrs., staff Headstart Chino 3 yrs., Boys Republic High Sch. 1 yr., cons. infant lang. devel./student-parent pgm. Buena Vista Continuation H.S. 3 yrs.; mem: Am. Speech-Lang.-Hearing Assn., Calif. Speech and Hearing Assn., Calif. Tchrs. Assn., Am. Assn. Univ. Women (recording secty.),installed into Delta Kappa Gamma Soc. Internat. Nov. 1992 (charter mem., corr. sec.); civic: anchor Mountain Communities News Falcon Cable TV Ch. 6 (Mondays 6pm), mem. bd. of dirs. Ch. 6 Comm. News and Weather Found., Mtn. Shadow Village HOA (pres.); Republican; Presbyterian (bd. deacons, moderator 1991, 1994-97, English Handbell Choir 1988-92, children's story teller, Pastor nom. com. 1994–); rec: interior design, hiking. Res: PO Box 1745 Crestline 92325 Ofc: Rim of the World Unified School Dist. PO Box 430 Lake Arrowhead 92352

KELLEY, JAMES CHARLES, university dean; b. Oct. 5, 1940, Los Angeles; s. James Charles and Margaret (Fitzgerrell) K.; m. Susan Cotner, June 7, 1963; children: Jason b. 1969, Megan b. 1972; edn: BA, Pomona Coll., Claremont, Calif. 1963; PhD, Univ. of Wyoming, Laramie 1966. Career: prof. of oceanography Univ. of Wash., Seattle 1966-75; dean of science, San Francisco St. Univ., S.F. 1975–; bd. of govs. Moss Landing Marine Lab., Moss Landing, Calif. 1975– (chair 1992-94); mem: Calif. Acad. Sci., S.F. (fellow 1981, bd. trustees 1986, pres. 1989-94), AAAS 1967–, Am. Geophysics Union 1967–, Bohemian Club., S.F.; author: 100+ pub. papers; Independent; Roman Catholic; rec: wooden boats, backpacking. Res: Box 909 Montara 94037 Ofc: College of Science San Francisco State University San Francisco 94132

KELLEY, WIN DAVID, emeritus professor, actor, writer; b. Nov. 6, 1923, Pryor, Okla.; s. William O. Kelley and Audrey (Bruce) Woodard; m. Catherine Elizabeth Hann, June 5, 1948; children: Klinda b. 1950, Kasma b. 1951, Kanda b. 1956, Korwin b. 1959; edn: BA cum laude, Pacific Univ. 1950; MEd, Univ. Oreg., 1954; EdD, USC, 1962; also studied at Penn. St. Univ., CSU Long Beach, and CSU Los Angeles. Career: tchr., Prospect, Oreg. 1950-51; tchr., dir. drama and forensics, Coquille, Oreg. 1951-54; Coos Bay, Oreg. 1954-56; prof., dir. drama Compton Coll. 1956-58; prof. (emeritus), dir. drama and forensics Citrus Coll., Glendora 1958-84; vis. prof. USC and Azusa Pacific Univ.; drama columnist Talent Review Mag., N.Y.C.; Coos Bay newspaper; articles pub. Improving Coll. and Univ. Tchg.; freelance writer t.v. and commls.; awards: Portland Civic Theatre Nat. Play awards 1953, Mark Twain Soc. Lit. award 1953, Freedoms Found. George Washington Hon. Medal 1973, DAR Medal of Hon. 1980, biog. listed Leaders in Edn. 4th ed. 1971, Contemporary Authors 1980, Internat. Authors and Writers Who's Who 9th ed. 1982, others; mem: Songwriters Guild of Am., Am. Forensics Assn. (emeritus), Speech Comm. Assn. (emeritus), Actors Equity Assn., Screen Actors Guild, Dramatist Guild, Inland Forensics Assn. (past pres.), Oreg. Speech League (v.p., past pres.), Active Club Internat. (dir. programs 1951-54), Am. Legion (commdr. 1967-68), VFW; author: (play) Waiilatpu: The Place of Rye Grass 1952, (textbook) The Art of Public Address 1962, coauthor Teaching in Community Jr. College 1969, (play) America the Beautiful 1972, Breaking Barriers in Pub. Speaking 1978, (autobiography) The Fades of Memory 1982, The "Elegant" 18th District, Department of California: The First Sixty-Six Years - 1920-1986 (1987), Gertie's Gall: A Collection of Writings By Gertrude Boatright 1991, poetry pub. in Nat. Poetry Anthology 1988 and other anthologies; mil: cpl. US Army Air Corps 1943-45; Republican; Prot.; rec: acting, writing, singing. Res: Carlsbad 92008

KELLOGG, WILLIAM JACKSON, resort manager; b. Sept. 12, 1951, Pasadena; s. William Crowe and Jane Katherine (Jackson) K.; m. Tricia Tenzer, Sept. 23, 1977; children: Tiffany b. 1978, Wendy b. 1981; edn: BA, Dartmouth Coll. 1973. Career: asst. tennis profl. San Marino Tennis Shop, San Marino 1973-74; head tennis profl., gen. mgr. Westlake Tennis & Swim Club, Westlake Village 1974-79; adminstr., La Jolla Beach & Tennis Club, La Jolla 1979-89, pres. 1989–; mem: La Jolla Shores Assn. (chmn., dir. 1985-86), Mt. Soledad Meml. Assn. (pres. 1980–), San Diego Dist. Tennis Assn. (pres. 1980–), Tennis Club Mgmt. Assn. So. Calif., So. Calif. Tennis Assn. (v.p. 1984–); Republican; Episcopalian; rec: tennis. Ofc: La Jolla Beach & Tennis Club 2000 Sprindrift Dr La Jolla 92037

KELLY, BEN RILEY, retired college professor, audiologist; b. Aug. 14, 1942, Oklahoma City, Okla.; s. Keith Kimble and Delta Fern (Earnheart) K.; m. Corallyn Mary Quirk, June 16, 1966 (div. 1986); m. Darlene Marie Azevedo, March 25, 1988; children: Charles Bryan b. 1969, Jonathan b. 1975; edn: BA, Univ. Fla. 1964; MS, Fla. State Univ. 1968; PhD, Case Western Reserve Univ. 1971; reg. audiologist Bd. Med. Quality Assurance 1980. Career: asst. prof. Southwest Tx. State Univ. San Marcos 1971-75; assoc. prof. E. Tenn. State Univ., Johnson City, Tenn. 1975-79; prof. CSU Fresno 1979-94; awards: CSU Fresno Merit. Performance 1989; mem: Am. Speech Language Hearing Assn., Am. Acad. of Audiology, St. Lukes United Methodist Ch. (trustee 1988); coauthor, book (with D. Davis and M.N. Hegde): Clinical Methods and Practicum in Audiology (San Diego: Singular Pub. Group Inc., 1994); articles pub., 1974-79; Democrat; Methodist; rec: family history. Ofc: PO Box 27876 Fresno 93729

KELLY, RALPH G., consulting company executive; b. Aug. 14, 1919, Chicago, Ill.; s. Walter C. and Virginia A. (Victor) K.; m. Claire E. Moore, 1943 (dec. 1980); m. Patricia H., Feb. 14, 1981; children: Randall Brian b. 1944, Linda Elizabeth b. 1946, Jayme Virginia b. 1951, Scott Harrison b. 1952; edn: BSCE, Purdue Univ., 1938-41, 1946-47; Calif. cert. General Bldg. Contractor; Calif. cert. Real Estate Sales Lic.; cert. priv. pilot. Career: engaged in manufacturing, sales and mgmt. in electrical, garment and construction industries, 1964-85; pres. Shirley & Kelly, Inc., general contractors 1964-85, cons. Shirley & Kelly, Inc. 1985–; lectr. various civic groups; founder Jayme Virginia Kelly Meml. Found. (annual scholarships since 1975); author: book on parenting "Here is One Way - Fun"; Christian. Ofc: Shirley & Kelly 3349 Cahuenga Blvd West #3 Los Angeles 90068

KELLY, RANDOLPH O'ROURKE, biologist; b. March 28, 1947, Fresno; s. Robert Milton and Margie May (Muldoon) K.; m. Darlene Curb, 1967 (div. 1971); m. Edith Anne Perry, April 9, 1978; 1 child, Shawn b. 1979; edn: Moss Landing Marine Lab. 1968; BA, Fresno St. Univ. 1970. Career: lab. tech. UC Berkeley, Fresno 1964-70; fish and wildlife seasonal aid Calif. Dept. Fish & Game, Stockton 1970; aquatic biologist, Monterey 1970-77, assoc. marine biologist, Sacto. 1977-81, assoc. fishery biologist, Fresno 1981-93, sr. fishery biolo-

gist 1993–; co-chair Nat. Rec. Com. Oceans 1983; mem: Am. Fisheries Soc., World Aquaculture Soc., Nat. Shellfisheries Assn., San Francisco Bay & Estuary Soc.; num. articles in fishery bulletin and profl. jours.; Republican; rec: fishing, hiking, scuba diving. Res: 17333 Livermore Ct Soulsbyville 95372 Ofc: Calif. Dept. of Fish and Game 1234 E Shaw Ave Fresno 93710

KELLY, RAYMOND L., physicist; b. Feb. 2, 1921, Rockford, Ill.; s. Walter R. and Margaret S. (King) K.; m. Ruth G. Garlock, Nov. 21, 1943; children: Peter b. 1953, Katherine b. 1955; edn: BA, Univ. Wichita 1947; MS, Univ. Wis. 1949; PhD, 1951. Career: research physicist SRI, Menlo Park 1951-60; prof. physics Naval Postgrad. Sch., Monterey 1960-83; ret.; tchr. NPGS 1960–; mem: Optical Soc. Am. (fellow), Sigma Xi; author: Atomic & Ionic Spectrum Lines; mil: sgt. USAF 1943-45; Democrat; Methodist; rec: photog. Res: 26010 Via Portola Carmel 93923

KELLY, ROBIN HUNTER, veterinarian; b. Jan. 23, 1953, New York; d. Noel Rockmore and Elizabeth (Upham) Hunter; m. Andrew Bruzos Kelly, Oct. 25, 1980 (div. 1986); edn: AS, City Coll. San Francisco 1973; BS, UC Davis 1978; DVM, 1983. Career: assoc. veterinarian Dr. William Nissen, Walnut Creek 1983-85; resident Simpson Bridges Arabians, Alamo 1985-86; pvt. practice equine specialty, Contra Costa 1986–; surgical residency, UC Davis Veterinary Sch. 1995-97; cons. veterinarian Make Believe Farm, Danville 1983-84; Simpson Bridges Arabians, Alamo 1985-86; awards: Calif. Thoroughbred Breeders Assn. award 1982, Dept. Surgery & Medicine R. Jean Andrews 1983, Who's Who of Veterinarians; mem: Calif. Vet. Med. Assn., AVMA, AAEP; 9 articles pub. in profl. jours., 1981-82; Republican; Cath.; rec: sports, photog. Ofc: UC Davis Veterinary School Davis 95616

KELSEY, KATHERINE LOUISE, artist; b. Cleveland, Ohio; d. Adam and Katie (Breckel) McKee; m. Francis Overstreet Kelsey; edn: BS and AM, Columbia Univ., NY; Escuela de Pintura & Escultura, Mexico City; spl. studies Cleveland Sch. of Art, John Huntington Polytechnic.; travelling artist: two Around the World trips, and one Around So. Am. (resulting in num. exhibits of paintings), many trips to Europe and Mexico, month in Alaska; art exhibits in museums and galleries; paintings, sculptures, ceramics, enamels, textile designs, lithographs, and etchings sold in mus. shops and art galleries; recipient 1 Special Award, 2 first prizes, num. Hon. Mentions; business rentals of paintings in Berkeley gallery, Contemporary Arts, now from home/studio; life mem. Cleveland Mus. of Art, mem. YMCA, Humane Soc., Kelsey Kindred; Presbyterian; rec: swimming. Studio: 1753 Lexington Ave El Cerrito 94530

KEMP, MARGARET JEAN, judge; b. Sept. 3, 1944, Chgo.; d. Leonard Dexter, Jr. and Myrtle Alice (Turney) Kemp; edn: BS in edn., Univ. Ill. 1965; MA pol. sci., UC Berkeley 1966; JD, UCB Boalt Hall 1971. Career: tchr. Chgo. Public Schs., 1966-68; dep. dist. atty. San Mateo Co., Redwood City 1972-76; lawyer, ptnr. Thirkell, Pierpoint & Kemp 1976-78; judge San Mateo Co. Municipal Ct., South San Francisco 1978-86, San Mateo 1986-87; judge Superior Ct., Redwood City 1987–; honors: Women on the Bench, var. Women Lawyers Orgns., S.F. (1982); mem: Calif. Judges Assn. (exec. bd. 1981-83, chair muni. cts. com. 1980-81, mem. ethics com. 1983-87), Calif. Women Lawyers, Nat. Assn. of Women Judges, Am. Judges Assn.; civic: Rotary Club, Drug Advy. Bd. San Mateo 1985–, Suicide Prevention, Burlingame (exec. bd. 1979-80); Republican; Prot. Ofc: San Mateo County Seat Marshall St Redwood City 94063

KENNEDY, DONALD PARKER, title insurance company executive; b. Oct. 16, 1918, San Jacinto, Calif.; s. Lewis Rex and Elsie (Parker) K.; m. Dorothy Suppiger, Dec. 20, 1946; children: Parker S. b. 1948, Elizabeth Riney b. 1950, Amy F. b. 1964; edn: BA, Stanford Univ., 1940; LLB, USC Sch. of Law, 1948; admitted bar: Calif. 1949. Career: assoc. counsel Orange Co. Title Co., and successor First American Title Ins. Co., Santa Ana 1948-58, exec. v.p. 1958-63, pres., dir. First American Title Ins. Co., 1963-89, chmn. bd. 1989–, pres., dir. The First American Financial Corp., 1963–; honors: Stanford Univ. Golf Team and NCCA Champion 1939, Nat. Amateur -Pebble Beach, Ca. 1947, inducted Calif. Building Industry Hall of Fame 1989; past pres. and dir. So. Calif. Racing Assn.; mem: Orange Co. Bar Assn., Phi Delta Phi and Zeta Psi frat., Calif. Land Title Assn. (bd. govs., exec. com. 1957–, pres. 1960-61), Am. Land Title Assn. (pres. 1983-84); civic: Chapman Univ. (trustee), USC Presdl. Associates 1990–, UC Riverside Found. (dir. 1990-93), Festival of Learning & Performing O.C. (dir.), South Coast Repertory (trustee, dir.), O.C. Bus. Com. for the Arts, Golden Eagle Club of BSA (chmn. 1984), Goodwill Industries (dir. 1986-93), past: Santa Ana-Tustin Comm. Chest (pres. 1952), US Savings Bond Pgm. Orange (past chair), Santa Ana Board of Edn. 1953; clubs: Santa Ana CC (pres. 1952), La Quinta CC, Eldorado CC, Lake Arrowhead CC, California, Center, Pacific; mil: lt. M.I. USN 1942-46, PTO, ATO; Republican; Episcopalian; rec: golf. Res: 1628 La Loma Dr Santa Ana 92705 Ofc: First American Title Insurance Co. 114 E Fifth St Santa Ana 92701

KENNEDY, HAROLD LEE, colon rectal surgeon; b. Oct. 1, 1948, Amarillo, TX; s. Hugh Leroy and Marilyn Ruth (Kelley) Kennedy; m. Cynthia Louise Garst; children: Rachael, Nikki, Jason, Megan; edn: MD, Louisiana State Univ., New Orleans, La. 1973; lic. physician Calif. Career: internship, Navy Hosp.,

Oakland 1973-74, surgical residency 1974-78; staff surgeon Navy Hosp., Bremerton, WA 1978-81; colo-rectal fellowship Univ. of Minn., Minneapolis 1981-82; surgeon Sacto. Colon Rectal Surgery, Sacto. 1982–; clin. asst. prof. surgery, UC Davis 1984-89; guest lectr. Univ. of Minn. 1983-89, Am. Coll. of Surgery, Chgo. 1991, Northwest Soc. Colo-Rectal Surgeons, Idaho 1993; honors: Alpha Omega Alpha 1973, recipient of FDA approval for investigational work in stimulated gracilus sphincteroplasty (current); mem: Am. Coll. of Surgeons (fellow 1983–), Am. Soc. Colo-Rectal Surgeons (fellow 1983–), Sacto. Surgical Soc. 1983–, Am. Soc. G I Endoscopy 1983–; club: developing "20-30" club for 40-50's, Sacto., 1994; author, book chpts.: Problems in General Surgery, 1992, Surgery of Colon Rectal Anus, 1993; contbr. num. articles to profl. jours.; mil: comdr. USNR 1972-81; rec: hunting, fishing, water sports, snow skiing. Ofc: Sacramento Colon Rectal Surgery 1020 29th St Sacramento 95816

KENNEDY, "SARGE" JAMES WILLIAM, JR., special education administrator, consultant; b. Oct. 6, 1940, Santa Rosa; s. James William and Kay Jean (Eaton) K.; m. Lorene Adele Dunaway, May 12, 1962 (div. 1971); children: Sean b. 1962, Erin b. 1964, Mark b. 1966, stepdau., Joy b. 1971; m. Carolyn Judith Nighsonger, Mar. 30, 1972 (div. 1979); m. Patricia Carter Critchlow, Nov. 5, 1988; edn: AA, Napa Coll., 1961; BA, San Francisco State Univ., 1964, MA, 1970. Career: tchr. Napa County Office of Edn. 1968-74, principal 1974-77, SELPA (spl. edn. local plan area) director 1977-83; special edn. compliance cons. DoD Overseas Dependent Schs., Madrid, Spain 1983-84; dir. special programs and svs. Tehama County Dept. Edn., Red Bluff, Calif. 1985–; appt. Wilson Riles Special Edn. Task Force, Calif. 1981-82, Special Edn. Fiscal Task Force, Calif. 1987-89; mem: Calif. Fedn. Council for Exceptional Children (treas. 1990–, jour. editor 1971-77, 81-83), Coun. Exceptional Children (sgt. at arms 1980-95), Council of Adminstrs. of Spl. Edn., Calif. Assn. of SELPA Adminstrs., Spl. Edn. Adminstrs. in Co. Ofcs., SFSU Alumni Assn., Phi Delta Kappa; Democrat; rec: history of sports, hist. pop music, Spanish and Portuguese cultures. Ofc: Tehama County Dept. Education PO Box 689 Red Bluff 96080 Ph: 916/527-5811

KENNELLY, KAREN MARGARET, college president; b. Aug. 4, 1933, Graceville, Minn.; d. Walter John and Clara Stella (Eastman) Kennelly; mem. religious order Sisters of St. Joseph of Carondelet, 1952–; edn: BA, Coll. of St. Catherine, St. Paul, Minn. 1956; MA, Catholic Univ. of Am., Wash., DC 1958, PhD, UC Berkeley 1962. Career: tchr. European & Am. hist., Coll. of St. Catherine, St. Paul, Minn. 1956-59, 1980-87; tchr. history religious life, Sisters of St. Joseph of Carondelet, St. Paul, Minn. 1979-85, St. Paul Province Inter-Comm. Novitiate, St. Paul, Minn. 1979-85; province dir. Sisters of St. Joseph of Carondelet, St. Province 1982-88; pres. Mount Saint Mary's Coll., Los Angeles 1989–; cons./evaluator No. Central Regional Accred. Assn., Chicago, Ill. 1974-84; cons. Ohio Bd. of Regents, Columbus, Ohio 1980-89; coord. & editor History of Women Religious Network, L.A., 1987–; honors: Phi Beta Kappa 1962–, Fulbright fellowship, Spain, 1964, Am. Council of Learned Societies fellowship, Spain, 1965; mem: Am. Historical Assn. 1962–, Am. Catholic Assn. 1962–, Am. Acad. of Research Historians on Medieval Spain 1972, Am. Council on Edn. 1971-79, 1989–; editor/author (book): American Catholic Women, 1989; author numerous articles. Democrat; Roman Catholic; rec: reading skiing, botany. Ofc: 12001 Chalon Rd Los Angeles 90049

KENNEY, H(ARRY) WESLEY, JR., television producer, director; b. Jan. 3, 1926, Dayton, Ohio; s. Harry Wesley and Minnie Ruth (Keeton) K.; m. Kay Ann Snure (div. 1964); m. Heather North, May 22, 1971; children: Nina, Harry W. III, Kara, Kevin; edn: BFA, Carnegie Inst. Tech., 1950. Career: director Fights at St. Nicks, Rocky King Detective, Night Beat, Dumont Network, N.Y.C. 1950-57; producer, director t.v. shows True Story, Modern Romances, NBC, N.Y.C. 1950-61; freelance director Omnibus, N.Y.C. 1958; director theater prodn. My Three Angels, Totem Pole Playhouse, 1955; The King and I, Melody Fair Summer Theatre, Niagara Falls 1959; Twelfth Night, Antioch, Yellow Springs, Oh. 1962; director t.v. series My Favorite Martian, 1964; The Doctors, NBC, N.Y.C. 1964-66; exec. producer, director t.v. series Days of Our Lives, NBC, Los Angeles 1967-77; All in the Family, CBS, L.A. 1974; director pilots: The Jeffersons, Filthy Rich, Ladies Man, Side By Side, Rosenthal & Jones; producer, director (spl.) Miss Kline, We Love You, ABC, 1974; exec. producer, director t.v. series The Young and the Restless, 1981-86; General Hospital, ABC, L.A. 1987-89; guest lectr. Televisia Corp., Mexico City 1990; dir. Agatha Christie "Ten Little Indians" Advent Theatre Los Angeles 1991; dir. "The Best Christmas Pagent Ever" Advent Theatre L.A. 1993; dir. "Love Letters" W. Virginia Public Theater, Morgantown, W.Va. 1994; dir. Infomercials: Elements of Beauty, The Merle Norman Experience; guest instr. Multiple Camera Direction, UCLA Ext. Sch. 1991, Television Production, UCLA Sch. of Theater, Motion Pictures & Television 1993, assoc. prof. 1994, 95; dir. "Shadowlands", Tracey Roberts Theatre, L.A. 1995; dir. Soap Break (CBS) 1994-95; recipient 7 Emmy awards, 13 Emmy nominations (1972-88); mem: Directors Guild Am., Producers Guild Am., Actors Equity, Omega Delta Kappa; rec: athletics, tennis, travel. Res: 12996 Galewood St Studio City 91604

KENNEY, WILLIAM CLARK, scientist; b. Feb. 25, 1940, Grand Forks, No.Dak.; s. James Clement and Dorothy (Clark) K.; edn: BA w. hons., Carleton Coll. 1962; PhD, UC Berkeley 1967. Career: postgrad. research biochemist

UCSF 1970-71, asst. and assoc. research biochemist 1972-79, assoc. prof. biochemistry (in med.) 1979-84; research chemist Veterans Adminstrn. San Francisco 1979-84; dir., protein chemistry, Amgen, Thousand Oaks 1992–, lab. head, 1989-92, research scientist 1984-89; cons. Veterans Adminstrn. San Francisco 1972-77; honors: Sigma Xi, Alpha Chi Sigma, Am. Cancer Soc. Postdoctoral fellow 1968-69, Veterans Adminstrn. S.F. Alcoholism Research award 1979; mem: Am. Chemical Soc., Am. Soc. Biochemistry & Molecular Biology, AAAS, N.Y. Acad. Scis., Protein Soc., Research Soc. Alcoholism; num. articles pub. in sci. jours., speaker at num. symposia; rec: skiing, philately, model railroads. Res: 2654 Castillo Circle Thousand Oaks 91360 Ofc: AMGEN 1840 DeHavilland Dr Thousand Oaks 91320

KENOFF, JAY STEWART, lawyer; b. Apr. 29, 1946, Los Angeles; s. Charles Kapp and Martha (Minchenberg) K.; m. Pamela Fran Benyas, Sept. 1, 1979 (div. 1981); m. Luz Elena Chavira, June 9, 1991; edn: BA, UCLA, 1967; JD, Harvard Law Sch., 1970; MS, USC, 1974; admitted bar: Calif. 1971, W.D.C. 1970, U.S. Ct. Appeals (9th cir.) 1974, U.S. Dist. Cts. (so., cent. dists. Calif.) 1974, U.S. Ct. Mil. Appeals 1974. Career: atty., assoc. WymanBautzer Rothman & Kuchel, L.A. 1974-76; Epport & Delevie, Beverly Hills 1976-78; Bushkin Gaims Gaines & Jonas, L.A. 1978-83, ptnr. 1983-86; ptnr. Kenoff & Machtinger, L.A. 1986–; law prof. Northrop Univ. Sch. of Law, L.A. 1980-84; judge pro tem L.A. Municipal Ct. 1984–; W. Dist. Voluntary Settlement Panel L.A. Superior Ct. 1986–; awards: Judge Pro Tem Achievement Award L.A. Mun. Ct. 1986, Freedom Found. Medal, Valley Forge 1973, Phi Beta Kappa 1967; mem: U.S. Naval Inst. 1973–, Naval Reserve Assn. (life), USC Inst. of Sci. & Systems Mgmt. (founding mem., bd. dirs. 1984), UCLA Alumni Assn. (life), USC Alumni Assn. (life), Harvard-Radcliffe Club So. Calif. 1971–; author: Entertainment Industry Contracts: Negotiating & Drafting Guide, vol.1 Motion Pictures, periodic supplements (1986–), contbr. ed. "Entertainment Law & Finance", misc. law jour. articles; mil: cmdr. USNR 1968-91; Democrat; Jewish; rec: tennis, skiing, sailing, motion pictures. Ofc: Kenoff & Machtinger 1999 Avenue of the Stars Ste 1250 Los Angeles 90067

KENYON, DOUGLAS ALAN, risk management & loss control executive; b. Jan. 8, 1953, Binghamton, NY; s. Douglas W. and Edith (Noble) K.; m. Marsha Smith, Mar. 17, 1973; 1 son, Jared b. 1981; edn: cert., Ohlone Coll. 1978; AS, Merrit Coll. 1979; BS, Univ. Redlands 1983; JD, Peninsula Univ., 1990. Career: safety coord., Washington Hosp., Fremont 1975-77; safety & health asst. Stanford Med. Ctr. 1977-78; mgr. safety & environmental health Pacific Med. Ctr. S.F. 1978-83, safety mgr. Browning-Ferris Industries, San Jose, 1983-88, reg. claims mgr. 1988–; instr. safety studies Cogswell Coll., S.F. 1980-83; exec. dir. Instnl. Safety Mgmt. Assocs. 1980-83; recipient Tri-Cities Stamp Out Crime Award 1968; mem: Nat. Safety Council (chmn. reg. 9, Healthcare Sect. 1980-83), Profl. Healthcare Safety Assn. (chmn. exec. bd. 1978-83), Am. Soc. Safety Engrs., No. Calif. Indsl. Safety Soc., Nat. Safety Mgmt. Soc., World Safety Orgn.; publs: arts. in var. profl. publs.; mil: E4 USN 1970-74, E5 USAR 1976-82, Presdl. Unit Cit., Good Conduct, Vietnam Svc., Navy Unit Cit., Armed Forces Expeditionary, Vietnam Cross of Gallantry, Vietnam Campaign; Prot.; rec: woodworking, wine tasting. Res: PO Box 225 Moss Landing 95039 Ofc: Browning-Ferris Industries 1601 Dixon Landing Rd Milpitas 95039

KERBER, GEORGE ALEXANDER, urban planning consultant; b. Sept. 4, 1925, Fresno; s. George and Leona (Flohr) K.; m. Esther L. Williams, Feb. 4, 1949; children: George b. 1950, Gary b. 1954; edn: BA, Fresno State Coll., 1950, cert. in public adminstrn., 1957; cert. planner AICP/Am. Inst. Cert. Planners, 1978. Career: city planner City of Fresno 1947-57, asst. planning dir. 1957-72, dir. planning & comm. devel. 1972-82, dir. city development 1982-89; planning consultant 1990–; planning advisor Council of Fresno County Govts. 1965–; plng. cons. Mangore Assocs. 1957-58; honors: Meritorious public service A.I.A. Fresno (1983), Resolution Fresno City Council for 40 years meritorious public service (1987); mem: Am. Inst. Cert. Planners (charter 1950–), Am. Soc. Public Adminstrn., Urban Land Inst., Nat. Assn. Housing & Redevel. Ofcls.; civic: People to People Found. (del. 1982–), Fresno County Hist. Soc., Am. Hist. Soc. of Germans from Russia, San Joaquin River Com. (1991–); contbr. book chpt., Fresno County - The 20th Century (1987); mil: mach. mate 2c USN 1944-47; Republican; Lutheran; rec: photog., sculpture, architecture, history. Res: 9132 N Rittenhouse Ln Fresno 93720-1282

KERCHNER, CHARLES TAYLOR, education professor; b. Feb. 18, 1940, Chgo.; s. Charles Wesley and Dorothy Leticia (Taylor); m. Leanne Rose Bauman, Sept. 2, 1962; children: Paige b. 1966, Charles Arthur b. 1968; edn: BS, Univ. Ill., Urbana 1962, MBA, 1964; PhD, Northwestern Univ., 1976. Career: news editor, asst. to gen. mgr. St. Petersburg Times, Fla. 1964-70; assoc. director Illinois Board of Higher Education, Chgo. 1970-72; dir. of funded programs City Colls. of Chicago, 1972; project dir., prof. Northwestern Univ., Evanston, Ill. 1974, 75; prof. edn. and dir. ednl. leadership project The Claremont Grad. Sch., Claremont, Calif. 1976–; cons. num. school dists. and other orgs., 1965–, Rockefeller Found., N.Y. 1990; awards: res. grantee US Dept. of Labor 1990, Carnegie Corp. 1990, Stuart Foundations 1986-90, Nat. Inst. of Edn. 1980; mem. Am. Ednl. Res. Assn. (com. 1976), Bulletin editor: Politics of Edn. Assn. 1980-85; author: The Changing Idea of a Teachers' Union

(1988), The Politics of Choice and Excellence (1989), A Union of Professionals (1993); Democrat; Presbyterian; rec: photography. Ofc: The Claremont Graduate School 150 E Tenth St Claremont 91711-6160

KERFOOT, BRANCH PRICE, scientist in electronics; b. May 9, 1925, NY, NY; s. Branch Price and Henrietta McBrayer (Bartlett) K.; m. Carol Saindon, Feb. 13, 1965; 1 son B. Price, III b. 1967; edn: BE, Yale Univ., 1945; MSE and PhD, Univ. Mich., Ann Arbor, 1947, 1955; JD, Western State Univ., Fullerton 1987; reg. profl. engr. Calif. Career: ensign USNR, Pacific 1945-46, served to lt. cmdr. US Naval Reserve 1942-66; research engr. Westinghouse Electric, E. Pittsburgh, Pa. 1948; AA engr. Radio Corp. of Am., Moorestown, N.J. 1949-57; prin. engr. Aeronutronic Div. Ford Motor Co., Newport Beach, Calif. 1958-68; prin. scientist McDonnell Douglas, Huntington Beach 1968-90, ret.; tchr. Pasadena City Coll. 1958; advisor Jr. Achievement Calif., 1964, 1979; awards: Sigma Xi 1955, comm. service Ford Motor Co., Newport Beach 1962, 65, prize for patent Inventors Workshop 1990; Life sr. mem. IEEE 1944–, mem. Soc. of the Cincinnati 1950–, Baronial Order of Magna Charta 1992–, Order of the Crown of Charlemagne 1993–, Order of the Founders and Patriots of Am. 1993–, Yale Club of Orange Co. 1970–, Classic Car Club Am. 1980–, USNR Assn. (life 1988–), Inventors Forum, Irvine, Calif. (dir. 1990–), Kappa Sigma frat., Newport Harbor Art Mus. (trustee 1973-76); club: Balboa Bay (N.B.); inventor Fluid-Flow Drag Reducers (pat. 1989); pub. tech. articles, 1956, 65, 70, editor book: Kerfoot & Related Families Ancestors, 1992; Republican; Prot.; rec: classic automobile restoration. Res: 1420 Antigua Way Newport Beach 92660

KERN, WILLIAM HENRY, pathologist; b. Dec. 25, 1927, Nurnberg, Germany, nat. USA 1957; s. Judge Wilhelm and Julie (Maedl) K.; m. Lynn Williams, Aug. 14, 1966; children: Julie Lynn b. 1969, Lisa Catherine b. 1970; edn: Univs. of Erlangen, Vienna and Munich, 1947-52; MD, Univ. of Munich 1952; bd. certified Am. Bd. of Pathology 1958. Career: intern Good Samaritan Hosp. Cincinnati 1952-53, res. in pathology Good Sam Hosp. Cinti and Univ. of Colo., 1953-56; dir. of pathology Hosp. of the Good Samaritan, Los Angeles 1966-91, v.p. bd. of trustees 1975-89, and chmn. medical staff 1972-74, 1987-89; em. clin. prof. of path. USC Sch. of Medicine 1972–; v.p. bd. dirs. Am. Red Cross, L.A. Chapter 1983-86, and chmn. Blood Op. Com. of L.A. and Orange Counties 1984-86; mem: L.A. Acad. of Medicine (pres. 1980-81), L.A. Soc. of Pathologists (pres. 1968), Am. Soc. of Cytology (pres. 1980-81), Fellow Coll. of Am. Pathologist; clubs: Saddle & Sirloin (pres. 1980), Jonathan, Rancheros Visitadores (Charro Camp); publs: 120+ sci. papers & book chapters in field of pathology and cancer; mil: capt. M.C. USAR 1956-58; Republican; Prot.; rec: riding, skiing, history, writing. Res: 1540 Kenmore Rd Pasadena 91106

KERR, GIB, financial planner; b. Apr. 21, 1927; s. Frances and Gladys (Larmondra) K.; m. Shirley Cochrane, June 15, 1952 (div. 1971); children: Brian, Barry, Randy, Judy, Sandy; edn: grad. Ottawa Tech. H.Sch., Ottawa, Ont., Can. 1945; desig: CFP, ChFC, CLU. Career: lab. asst. Eddy Pulp & Paper, Hull, Quebec, Can. 1946-47; special svs. mgr. Bell Tel. Co., Ottawa 1947-57; owner opr. Spotlight Studios 1957-57; corp. pres. G.K.E. Inc. 1957-70; entertainer, Los Angeles, 1970-77; financial planner, life underwriter, 1977–; lectr. in field; civic: W.L.A. LeTip (pres. 1988-90), LAS-ICFP (bd. 1991–, pres. 1994-96), Beverlywood Mental Health Ctr. (bd. 1989-91); publs: (lectures) Budget for a Lazy Person, 1988, Who's The Boss, 1989; coauthor: Talk and the Secrets of Communication, 1990; tchr., author: Sing-A-Long Guitar 1992; rec: music, philosophy, politics, poetry.

KERTZ, MARSHA HELENE, college professor, certified public accountant; b. May 29, 1946, Palo Alto; d. Joe and Ruth (Lazear) Kertz; edn: BS in acctg., San Jose State Univ. 1976, MBA, 1977; Cert. Pub. Acct. Calif. 1977; Cert. Tax Profl., Am. Inst. of Tax Studies 1993. Career: staff acct. Steven Kroff and Co., Palo Alto 1968-71, 1973-74; controller Rand Teleprocessing Corp., San Francisco 1972; staff acct. Ben F. Priest Acctg. Corp., Mountain View 1974-81; acctg. lectr. San Jose State Univ. 1977–; self employed CPA, audits, tax planning, tax preparation, mgmt. advy. svcs. 1977–; honors: Beta Gamma Sigma 1975, Beta Alpha Psi 1974; mem: Calif. Society of CPAs, Am. Inst. CPAs, Nat. Soc. of Tax Profls., Am. Acctg. Assn.; Democrat; Jewish; rec: play piano. Res: 4544 Strawberry Park Dr San Jose 95129 Ofc: San Jose State Univ. Acctg. - Fin. Dept., San Jose 95192

KETTEMBOROUGH, CLIFFORD RUSSELL, computer scientist, manager, professor; b. June 8, 1953, Pitesti, Romania, naturalized U.S. 1989; s. Petre and Constanta (Dascalu) Ionescu; m. Nelia Marie Miller; edn: MS math., Univ. Bucharest, 1976; MS computer sci., West Coast Univ., L.A. 1985, MMIS, 1986; PhD, Pacific Western Univ., 1988; MBA, Univ. of La Verne, 1992; cert. computer programmer, cert. quality analyst, cert. hardware. Career: pgmr. Nat. Dept. of Chemistry, Bucharest, Rom. 1976-80; sr. pgmr. analyst Nat. Dept. Metallurgy, Bucharest, Rom. 1980-82; sr. s/w eng. Xerox Corp., El Segundo, Calif. 1983-88; mem. tech. staff NASA/Jet Propulsion Lab., Pasadena 1988-89; task mgr. Rockwell Internat., Canoga Park 1989-91; cons. software engring. tech. 1991-93; project mgr. Transamerica Corp., L.A. 1993-95, dir. MIS, Maxicare, Inc., L.A. 1995–; adj. prof.: Univ of Redlands, West Coast Univ., National Univ., Chapman Univ., Azusa Pacific Univ.; past pres., sec. Romanian

BB Fedn., Bucharest 1978-82; mem. ACM, AMA, MAA, IEEE, AIAA, DECUS; author: book, 1978, various sci. articles, 1980–; mil: major lt. 1978-79; Republican; First United Methodist; rec: sports, travel.

KETTENHOFEN, ROBERT FRANK, optometrist; b. April 26, 1923, Pomona; s. Frank G. and May Catherine (Hofer) K.; m. Martha Dickey, Nov. 20, 1941; children: Jon b. 1943, Janis b. 1948, Judith b. 1950; edn: Pomona Coll.; Chaffey Coll.; USC; OD, So. Calif. Coll. of Optometry 1946. Career: pvt. practice optometry; awards: Univ. of Laverne Comm. Builder of Year 1970, Optometrist of Year 1956, 78, So. Calif. Coll. Optometry Disting. Alumnus of Year 1988, Dist. Service award JCC 1954; mem: Rotary (pres. 1968-69), So. Calif. Coll. Optometry (chmn. bd. 1974-78, new campus founder 1973), Inland Hospice Assn. (bd. mem. 1986), YMCA (pres. 1976-78), United Way, Red Hill Country Club; Republican; Methodist; rec: golf. Res: 8070 Calle Carabe Ct Rancho Cucamonga 91730

KEWER, RICHARD LEE, educator; b. Dec. 11, 1939, Batavia, N.Y.; s. Joseph John Kewer and Helen (Muschinski) Goffard; m. Linda Decker, Jan. 13, 1963, div. 1969; children: Rod b. 1963, Cindy b. 1965; edn: MA, Long Beach State Univ., 1983. Career: pres. Action Management Systems, Newport Beach, Calif. 1981–; educational consultant Long Beach State 1982–; mem. Southern Counties Training Officers Assn., 1985–; author workbooks: Understanding Leadership, 1986, Performance Appraisal, 1987, Management Principles, 1989; mil: E-5, U.S. Navy, 1958-62; Libertarian; rec: volunteer, Special Olympics. Ofc: Action Management Systems Box 9015 Newport Beach 92660

KEYES, JUDITH DROZ, lawyer; b. Jan. 16, 1946, Pittsburgh, Pa.; d. Blair Guthrie Huddart and Barbara Jane (Tilden) McCoy; m. Donald G. Droz, May 25, 1968 (dec. 1969); m. David P. Keyes, June 6, 1970; 1 dau., Tracy b. 1969; edn: BS, Pa. St. Univ. 1966; MA, Univ. Mo. 1970; JD, UC Berkeley Boalt Hall 1975; admitted St. Bar Calif. 1975. Career: tchr. Schaumburg (Ill.) High Sch., 1966-67; research asst. Center for Research in Social Behavior, Columbia, Mo. 1970-71; field atty. Nat. Labor Rels. Bd., San Francisco 1975-76; vis. assoc. prof. Suffolk Univ. Law Sch., Boston, Mass. 1986-87; atty. Corbett & Kane, San Francisco 1976-81, ptnr. 1981–; dir. Calif.-Nev. Methodist Homes, Oakland 1988-94; neutral evaluator and mediator U.S. Dist. Ct., San Francisco 1988–; honors: Order of Coif, Phi Delta Kappa, Sigma Tau Delta; mem: Am. Bar Assn. (sect. internat. and labor and employment law), State Bar of Calif. (sect. labor and employment law; del. Conf. of Delegates), Alameda Co. Bar Assn. (v.p. 1995), San Francisco Bar Assn. (exec. com., labor and employment law sect.), Boalt Hall Alumni Assn. (dir. 1982-84); author: articles pub. in profl. jours., 1974, 88; Democrat; Unitarian Universalist. Res: 8515 Terrace Dr El Cerrito 94530 Ofc: Corbett & Kane 2000 Powell St Ste 1450 Emeryville 94608

KHANNA, SATISH KUMAR, physicist; b. Dec. 2, 1947, Delhi, India; s. Kishan Chand and Sita Bai (Malhotra) K.; m. Neelam, Dec. 5, 1976; children: Neetu b. 1980, Rohini b. 1983; edn: BS, and MS, Univ. of Delhi, India, 1967, 1969; PhD, Univ. Penn, Phila., 1974. Career: tch. asst., postdoc. Univ. Penn., 1969-76; vis. scientist Univ. de Paris - Sud, Orsay, France 1976; physicist, mem. tech. staff (MTS) Jet Propulsion Lab., Pasadena 1977-84, tech. group supr. 1984-87, asst. section mgr. 1987-89, dep. section mgr. 1989-91, asst. pgm. mgr. 1991–; awards: nat. scholar Univ. Delhi, India 1967-69, fellow Univ. Penn., Phila. 1969-74, Exceptional Service medal NASA 1990; mem. Am. Physical Soc. 1974–, Indian Students Assn. (U.Penn. pres. 1972-74); publs: 50+ tech. papers and 40+ presentations; rec: tennis, travel. Res: 3760 Shadow Grove Rd Pasadena 91107 Ofc: Jet Propulsion Lab 4800 Oak Grove Dr Pasadena 91109

KHORRAMIAN, ABID, bioanalyst, doctor of oriental medicine; b. July 30, 1952, Teheran, Iran, nat. US cit. 1984; s. Nourollah and Anice (Cohansedgh) K.; m. Mojgan Lavi; edn: BS, Cal. Poly. Pomona 1974; MS, CSU Los Angeles 1976; OMD Samra Univ. 1988; clinical laboratory bioanalyst 1994; lic. acupuncturist Calif. 1987; acupuncture cert., Emperor Coll. 1986; med. technologist, Dept. Pub. Health 1977; real estate broker Calif. 1980. Career: tchr. Azusa Pacific Coll. 1978; med. technol. Foothill Presbyterian Hosp. 1978-81; independent real estate broker 1980–; med. technol. Washington Med. Ctr. Culver City 1981–; honors: Dean's List (Cal. Poly. Pomona, Emperor's Coll. Santa Monica); mem: Calif. Assn. Realtors, Calif. Acupuncture Alliance; Beverly Hills Gun Club (Turkey Shoot 2nd pl. champion 1987); rec: chess, backgammon. Res: Woodland Hills 91367 Ofc: Washington Hospital 12101 Washington Blvd Culver City 91230

KHOSLA, ANAND PRAKASH, engineer; b. May 7, 1933, Simla, India; nat. US citizen 1979; s. Mulkh Raj and Sita Wati (Sarin) K.; m. Asha L., Nov. 18, 1957; 1 son, Dr. Rakesh K. b. 1958; edn: BE (Elec.), Univ. of Delhi, India 1955; ME (Elec.), Univ. of Roorkee, India 1962; Reg. Profl. Engr. (Elec.), Mich. 1973, Calif. 1976. Career: project engr. (switchgear), G.E.C., Calcutta, India 1956-70; elect. designer on contract to Union Carbide Corp., Niagara Falls, NY 1970-71; elect. engr. designer Wilson Klaes Brucker & Worden, Buffalo, NY 1971-72; sr. elect. engr. Bechtel Power Corp., Ann Arbor, Mich. 1972-75; supervising elect. engr. Ralph M. Parsons Co., Pasadena 1975-; honors: Martin Marietta Corp. subcontractor employee of yr. (1984) for Ground Support Sys. Pgm. at

Vandenberg AFB, Launch honoree NASA Manned Flight Awareness Pgm. (9/84); mem: IEEE, Indsl. Appl. Socs.; rec: swimming, photography. Res: 3790 Startouch Dr Pasadena 91107 Ofc: Ralph M. Parsons Co. 100 W Walnut St Pasadena 91124

KIBBE, EUGENE VINCENT, photographic artist; b. Mar. 22, 1907, Chgo.; s. Fred and Elsa (Erwig) K.; m. Mary Alice Eger, 1962 (div. 1971); children: Roger b. 1964, Frances b. 1968; high sch. grad. Strafford, Mo. 1924. Career: news photographer Wide World Photos, Chgo. 1931-38; civilian photographer U.S. War Dept., St. Louis, Mo. 1938-40, 1941-42, chief photog. U.S. War Dept., Alaska Hwy. 1943; H.S. tchr. photography, Springfield, Mo. 1940-41; photog. Olin Industries, East Alton, Ill. 1944-45; legal photographer/prin., San Francisco 1946-48; commercial photog./prin., Fairfax 1948-54; photography instr. Coll. of Marin, Kentfield 1954-75, ret.; artist photographer, photos in museum and private collections, exhibited 373 photographs worldwide 1941-46 (24th ranking photo exhibitor internat.), Am. Annual of Photography list of leading exhibiting photographers 1940s; past bd. dirs. Emeritus Coll. Marin County; Hon. life mem. Royal Photographic Soc. U.K. 1943–, Hon. life mem. Photographic Soc. Am. 1942–,(recipient writing award), mem. Marin Soc. of Artists 1985–; contbr. numerous articles re the art of photography, J. Photog. Soc. Am. 1945-86; Democrat; Humanist; rec: travel (54+ countries). Res: 416 4th St San Rafael 94901

KIBEL, HARVEY RONALD, real estate developer, business advisor; b. Jun. 15, 1937, NY, NY; s. Ned and Sylvia (Pearlman) K.; m. Isabel Ruth Rogers, June 7, 1959; children: Ellen b. 1964, Paul b. 1967; edn: BSE, Columbia Univ., 1959; MS, USC, 1960; Calif. lic. C.P.A. 1968, R.E. Broker 1970. Career: ptnr. in chg. gen. consulting Peat, Marwick, Mitchell, Los Angeles 1964-71; pres. Open Road, 1971-77; co-founder/pres. Kibel, Jonas, Inc. 1977-84; co-founder/CEO Kibel, Green, Inc., mgrs. of crossroad, conflict & crisis, Los Angeles 1984–; faculty USC, 1960-67; civic bds: UCLA Johnson Cancer Ctr., L.A. (pres. 1990-92), Amer. Cancer Soc. S.F. (chmn. bd. 1970-84), United Way Bd., Boy Scouts Am. Bd. Govs., Chief Execs. Orgn., World Presidents Council, Young Presidents Orgn. (L.A. chmn., Forum pres. 1975-87); awards: best bus. book/top 10 Library Jour. 1982, nat. award of excellence SBIC, W.D.C. 1983, vol. of yr. Amer. Cancer Soc. 1984; mem: Chief Execs. Orgn., World Bus. Council, T. Mgmt. Assn. (bd. 1989); clubs: Regency (L.A.), Riviera CC (L.A.); author: How To Turn Around a Financially Troubled Co. (McGraw-Hill, 1982); rec: tennis, skiing, biking. Ofc: KGI, 2001 Wilshire Blvd Ste 420 Santa Monica 90403

KIDDE, JOHN EDGAR, food processing company executive; b. May 4, 1946, Kansas City, Mo.; s. Gustave Edgar and Mary Sloan (Orear) K.; m. Donna Carolyn Peterson, Aug. 4, 1973; children: Kari b. 1978, Laurie b. 1981, Kellie b. 1984; edn: BA, Stanford Univ., 1968; MBA, Northwestern Univ., 1971. Career: corp. banking ofcr. First Interstate Bank, Los Angeles 1971-73; v.p. ops. Colony Foods Inc., Newport Beach 1973-78; pres. Western Host Food Services, Newport Beach 1978-81; pres., dir. Giuliano's Delicatessen & Bakery, Carson 1981-90; pres., dir., c.e.o. Sona & Hollen Foods, Los Alamitos 1990–; dir. Restaurant Business Mag., NY, NY 1975-78; alumni admissions com. Phillips Acad. 1985–; trustee Harbor Day Sch. 1989–; mem. Stanford Buck Club 1971–, Stanford Club Orange County (pres. 1987-89); club: Balboa Bay 1992–; mil: 1st lt. US Army Reserves 1969-75; Republican; Episcopalian; rec: skiing, scuba, triathlons. Res: 3907 Inlet Isle Dr Corona Del Mar 92625 Ofc: Sona & Hollen Foods, Inc. 3712 Cerritos Ave Los Alamitos 90720

KIDDOO, ROBERT MICHAEL, assistant professor of clinical accounting; b. Jan. 13, 1960, Santa Monica; s. Robert James and Patricia Anne (Wakefield) K.; edn: BS, CSU Northridge 1983; MBA, CSU Northridge 1987; ABD, UCLA 1995; C.P.A. Calif. 1985. Career: acct. Peat Marwick Mitchell & Co., Los Angeles 1983-85; cons. Kirk-Mayer Inc. 1986-88; lectr. CSU Northridge 1988–, Univ. So. Calif. 1995–; honors: Beta Alpha Psi (pres. 1983), Beta Gamma Sigma, Calif. Soc. C.P.A. doctoral fellow 1986-89; mem: Am. Acctg. Assn., Am. Inst. C.P.A., Calif. Soc. C.P.A., Nat. Assn. Accts., Mensa, Delta Sigma Pi; article pub. in profl. jour., 1988; Republican; Prot.; rec: computers, car restoration, sports. Res: 19348 Crystal Ridge Lane Northridge 91326 Ofc: California State University School of Business Administration and Economics 18111 Nordhoff St Northridge 91330

KIDNEY, ROBERT BRIAN, consultant-governmental affairs, former state legislative chief clerk; b. Dec. 15, 1930, San Mateo; s. Robert Henry and Sarah Alina (MacInnis) K.; edn: BA pol. sci., Univ. Mich., Ann Arbor 1960; MA govt., Univ. San Francisco, 1974. Career: asst. clerk of the Assembly, Calif. Legislature, Sacto. 1963-65, asst. chief clerk 1965-88, chief clerk 1988-91, ret.; cons. The Gualco Group (govt. rels. firm) 1993–; guest lectr. on public affairs UC Davis, Hastings. Coll. Law, State Training Ctr. Sacto., Calif. Jour., others 1974-91; participant symposium on draft rules for the Hungarian Nat. Assembly, Budapest (4/91), seminars- "The Calif. Legislature in Transition" No. Calif. Polit. Sci. Assn., Univ. of Pacific (5/91), "Calif.'s Legislative Process" Assn. of Calif. Ins. Cos., Sacto. (7/91), California Journal, Sacto. (6/92); mem. Sacramento Club, Comstock Club of Sacto., Knights of the Vine, local cultural orgns.; contbg. author: California's Legislature (biennial revised edits. 1964-86); judicial chpt.

editor: California Blue Book (1967, 71, 75); co-editor, editor (booklet) Calif. State Assembly (1969-90); mil: USAF 1951-54; R.Cath.; rec: skiing, bicycling, lively arts, entertaining. Res: 317 Hartnell Pl Sacramento 95825-6613

KIELAROWSKI, HENRY EDWARD, marketing executive; b. Dec. 29, 1946, Pittsburgh, Pa.; s. Henry Andrew K. and Evelyn Marie (Kline) Boileau; m. Lynda Blair Powell, Aug. 1971 (div. 1976); children: Amorette, Blair; edn: BA, Duquesne Univ., 1969, MA, 1974, PhD, 1974. Career: pres. Communicators Inc., Pitts. 1974-76; mktg. specialist McGraw-Hill Inc., N.Y.C. 1976-81; mktg. dir. Fidelity S.A., Allison Park, Pa. 1981-86; exec. v.p. ARC Systems Inc., Pitts. 1986-88; v.p. mktg. Providian Bancorp, San Francisco 1988–; mem: Am. Mktg. Assn. (recipient award for Mktg. Excellence 1988), Direct Mktg. Assn.; author: Microcomputer Consulting in the CPA Environment (1987); contbr. articles to profl. jours.; Democrat; rec: fiction writing, music, dance, travel, filmmaking. Res: 107 Lyon St San Francisco 94117

KIERULFF, STEPHEN, clinical psychologist; b. June 17, 1942, Los Angeles; m. Carol Winter, 1970 (div. 1983); 1 son, Benjamin b. 1976; edn: BA, UC Berkeley 1963; PhD, U.S. Internat. Univ. 1980; lic. clin. psychologist Calif. Career: research assoc. System Devel. Corp., Santa Monica 1980; assoc. prof. psych. Chapman Coll., San Diego 1981; lectr. psych. CSU Long Beach 1982-84; clin. psychologist Orange Co., Anaheim 1985-86; adj. prof. psychology U.S. Internat. Univ., Glendale 1984-91; Calif. Sch. Profl. Psychology, Los Angeles 1987-90; honors: MIT Dean's List 1960, Psi Chi 1978, disting. scholar UCB 1963, USN Journalism award 1959; mem: Am. Psychol. Assn., Assn. Humanistic Psychology, Calif. Psychol. Assn.; articles pub. in profl. jours., 1984, 88, 91, 92. Ofc: 3201 Wilshire Blvd Ste 201 Santa Monica 90403; also 110 South La Brea Ave Ste 220 Inglewood 90301

KILBURN, KAYE HATCH, physician, educator; b. Sept. 20, 1931, Logan, Utah; s. Hyrum Parley and Winona (Hatch) Kilburn; m. Gerrie Griffin, June 7, 1954; children: Ann b. 1958, Scott b. 1961, Jean b. 1963; edn: BS, Univ. Utah, 1951; MD, Univ. Utah Coll. of Med., 1954. Career: capt. Army Med. Corps 1958-60, asst. clin. prof. USA Med. Res. Nat. Lab. Univ. Colorado Sch. Med., Denver 1958-60; asst. prof. medicine Wash. Univ. Med. Sch., St. Louis, Mo. 1960-62; asso. prof. medicine Duke Univ., 1962-69, prof. medicine/dir. environ. medicine 1969-73; prof. medicine and chief, pulmonary div. Univ. Missouri, Columbia 1973-77; prof. medicine, commun. medicine Mt. Sinai Sch. Medicine 1977-80; Ralph Edgington prof. of medicine Univ. of So. Calif., Los Angeles 1980–, dir. Barlow Occup. Health Ctr. 1980-84, dir. pulm. div. USC 1982-84, dir. Workers Disease Detection Service, San Dimas 1985–; awards: Trudeau fellow Am. Lung Assn. 1957-58, NIH fellow in London, G.B. 1960-61, Duke Univ. NIEHS Res. Career Devel. Award 1969-73; asso. editor Am. Jour. Industrial Med. 1970-, editor-in-chief Archives Environmental Health 1986-; mem: AAAS, Am. Thoracic Soc., Am. Fed. Clin. Res., Am. Physiol. Soc., Sigma Xi, Am. Soc. Exptl. Path., Am. Soc. Cellular Biology, W. Assn. Physicians, Collegium Ramazzinas, Am. Heart Assn., Am. Pub. Health Assn., Central Soc. Clin. Research, Soc. Occup. Environ. Health, Internat. Epidemiol. Assn., So. Soc. Clin. Investig., Cosmos Club; publs: 200+ papers re lung disease, physiology and pathology-environmental medicine, byssinosis, asbestosis, neurobehav. toxicology, air pollution, 1958-. Res: 3250 Mesaloa Ln Pasadena 91107 Ofc: USC School of Medicine 2025 Zonal Ave CSC-201 Los Angeles 90033

KILEY, ROBERT RALPH, political consultant; b. Apr. 21, 1948, Honolulu; s. Kenneth John and Dorothy Irene (Ambrozich) K.; m. Barbara Lynn Weber, Mar. 16, 1985; children: Tiryn b. 1977, Kristin b. 1980; edn: BA psychology, USC, 1975. Career: exec. dir. Republican Party, Orange County, Calif. 1976-79; v.p. Nason Lundberg & Kiley, Orange 1978-80; owner, pres. Robert Kiley & Assocs., Yorba Linda 1980–; instr. American Campaign Sch., 1990–; advanceman Pres. Ronald Reagan, W.D.C., 1979-88; bd. mem. Board of Psychology, Sacto. 1989-92; honors: dean's list USC 1974-75, Outstanding Young Man of Am. 1977-78; mem. USC Alumni Assn. 1975–; Republican. Res: 5028 Vista Montana Yorba Linda 92686 Ofc: Robert Kiley & Associates, 5028 Vista Montana Yorba Linda 92686

KILKENNY, JOHN EDWARD, petroleum geologist; b. March 25, 1913, Salinas; s. Lucas Edward and Myrtle (Guidary) K.; m. Dorothy Genevieve Mattingly, Jan. 22, 1939; children: Michael b. 1944, Kathy b. 1948; edn: BA, UC Berkeley 1935. Career: geologist Pure Oil Co., Bakersfield 1940-46; chief geologist Santa Fe Energy Co., Los Angeles 1946-50; sr. geologist Union Oil Co. Calif. 1950-53, chief geologist 1953-64, geological coordinator U.S. 1964-69, coordinator 1969-77; geothermal div. cons. 1977–; cons. U.S. Dept. Energy, Wash. D.C. 1976; program chmn. Circum Pacific Energy & Mineral Conf., Honolulu 1978; honors: Who's Who in U.S., Am. Assn. Petroleum Geologists Best Paper Award (1964) and Sidney Powers Award (1991); mem: Am. Assn. Petroleum Geologists (hon. pres. 1976-77), Native Sons of Golden West; articles pub. in profl. jours. (1952, 71); Republican; Quaker; rec: golf. Res: 1120 S 4th St Alhambra 91801

KILLEA, LUCY L., California state senator; b. July 31, 1922, San Antonio, Tx.; d. Nelson and Zelime (Pettus) Lytle; m. John F. (Jack) Killea, May 11, 1946; children: Jay b. 1946, Paul b. 1956; edn: BA, Incarnate Word Coll., San Antonio, Tx.;

MA, Univ. of S.D.; PhD, UC S.D. Career: analyst M.I. and CIA, 1943-56; mem. S.D. Historical Site Bd., 1969; tchg. and res. asst. UC S.D., 1967-72; lectr. S.D. State Univ., 1976-77; councilwoman S.D. City Council, mem. Metropolitan Transit Devel. Bd. and S.D. County Assn. of Govt., 1978-82; mem., S.D. County Cultural Commn. 1971-78; exec. dir., Fronteras de las Californias 1974-78; commr. S.D. Planning Commn. 1978; deputy mayor City of S.D. 1982; assembly mem. Calif. State Assembly 1982-89; senator Calif. State Senate 1989-; awards: grant, Justice Found., for res. in Spanish lang. manuscripts; Award of Merit, Outstanding Student of Year, Conf. of Calif. Historical Soc., 1966; One of 12 Women of Valor award, Temple Beth Israel, S.D., 1966; res. grant, Mexican and Spanish archival material, UC S.D., 1971; Reg. Planning Award, S.D. Assn. of Planners, 1977; Alumnae of Distinction award, Incarnate Word Coll., 1981; Woman of Year, S.D. Irish Council, 1981; Alice Paul award, Nat. Women's Political Caucus, 1981; Legislative Rookie of Year, Calif. Jour., 1982; Legislator of Year, United Fedn. of Small Bus., 1985; Legislator of Year, Trial Lawyers Assn. and S.D. Bar Assn., 1987; Legislator of Year, Calif. Narcotics Officers Assn., 1988; Media award, Nat. Conf. on Christians and Jews, 1989; Headliner of Year, S.D. Press Club, 1989; Free Speech award, Calif. Common Cause, 1990; Legislator of Year, Vietnam Veterans of S.D. Co. 1991; Special Achievement award, Calif. Resource Recovery Assn., 1991; BPW Hall of Fame, Calif. Fedn. of Bus. and Profl. Women, 1991; Eleventh Person award, Women's Internat. Ctr., Living Legacy Program, 1992; Legislator of Year, Calif. Narcotics Officers Assn., 1992; Legislator of Year, Calif. Women Lawyers Assn., 1993; advy. bd. mem.: UC S.D. Med. Ctr., ElderHelp Comm., Junior League, Girl Scouts; mem: S.D.-Imperial County Council, Bus. and Profl. Women, Calif. Elected Women's Assn. for Edn & Res., Greater S.D. C.of C., Sierra Club, LWV; author: profl. articles pub. in S.D. Jour. of History, 1966, 1976-77; ed., article pub. in Proceedings, 1976; mil: intelligence ofcr., US Army M.I., CIA 1943-56; Independent; Catholic; rec: running, golf, chamber music. Ofc: 2550 5th Ave. San Diego 92103

KILLEBREW, ELLEN JANE, physician, medical educator; b. Oct. 8, 1937, Tiffin, Ohio; d. Joseph Arthur and Stephanie (Beriont) Killebrew; m. Edward S. Graves, Sept. 12, 1970; edn: BS, Bucknell Univ. 1959; MD, N.J. Coll. Medicine 1965. Career: assoc. prof. medicine UCSF 1980-, clin. prof. 1990; dir. coronary care Permanente Med. Group, Oakland 1978-; awards: Pacific Med. Center Robert Kirkwood scholar 1969; mem: Am. Heart Assn. (pres. Oakland Piedmont Branch 1995-); Presbyterian; rec: sailing, writing, skiing, scuba diving. Res: 30 Redding Ct Tiburon 94920-1318 Ofc: Permanente Medical Group 380 W MacArthur Blvd Oakland 94611

KIM, COLUMBA YEUNG-BOON, psychotherapist/religious sister; b. Feb. 1, 1935, Seoul, Korea; d. Casimiro Duk-Hyun and Lucia Myung-Kyu (Kwon) Kim; edn: BA, Ewha Womans Univ., Seoul 1959; theology St. Catherine's Ctr., London 1968-69; soc. scis. Univ. of Leicester, U.K. 1970-71; MSW, Saint Louis Univ., Mo. 1975; fam. therapy Inst. of Psychiat. Northwestern Univ., Chgo. 1983-84; Lic. Clin. Soc. Wkr. Calif. (1986). Career: tchr. soc. studies Sacred Heart Girl's H.S., Seoul 1959-60, 63-66; dir. of boarders' residence Sacred Heart Coll. for Women, Korea 1967, assoc. prof. 1975-82; fam. therapy intern Doyle Ctr. Loyola Univ., Chgo. 1983-84; psychotherapist Catholic Charities, San Francisco, Calif. 1985-91; pvt. practice 1992-; mem: Am. Nat. Assn. Soc. Wkrs., Am. Assn. Marriage and Fam. Therapy, Internat. Assn. of Schs. of Soc. Wk.; author: Welfare for Women, 1977, 4 profl. jour. articles (Korea); Religious of the Sacred Heart Order; rec: painting, gardening. Ofc: 5430 Geary Blvd Ste 204 San Francisco 94121

KIM, JAE-MAN, professor, Chi-Gong master, acupuncturist, Tui-Na doctor (Chinese masso-therapy); b. Nov. 28, 1958, Seoul, Korea; s. In-Ok and Yong-Rhea (Shin) Kim; edn: master of Kung-Fu, Choong-Moo Kung-Fu Sch., Seoul, Korea, 1982; cert., gynecology & pediatrics, Royal Univ. of Am., L.A., Calif., 1989; cert., Tui-Na training prog., Calif. Chinese Tui-Na Medical Coll., L.A., 1992; master of Oriental medicine, Royal Univ. of Am., L.A., 1992; res. Zhejing Coll. of Traditional Chinese Med., Hangzhou, China 1993. Career: Kung-Fu master, Be-Ho & Choong-Moo Kung-Fu Schools, Seoul, Korea, 1982-84; Kung-Fu master, Korean Martial Art Ctr., Yorba Linda, Calif., 1986-87; acupuncturist, C.F Clinic, Monterey Park, Calif., 1989-; prof. of Tui-Na, Royal Univ. of Am., L.A., 1991-; Tui-Na therapist, Royal Univ. of Am. Oriental Med. Ctr., 1993-; prof. of Chi-Gong, Royal Univ. of Am., 1993; prof. acupuncture therapeutics Royal Univ. of Am. 1994- awards: Superior Acad. Achievement award 1989, Active Participant award 1991, Cert. Appreciation 1993, Royal Univ. of Am.; mem: Nat. Commn. for the Certification of Acupuncturists 1989, Calif. Acupuncture Com. 1990, Korean Acupuncture and Oriental Medicine Assn. in Calif. 1991; translator: book (from Chinese to Korean), Tui-Na Therapeutics, 1991. Ofc: Royal University of America Oriental Medical Ctr 1125 W 6th St LA 90017

KIM, JAY, congressman; b. 1939, Korea; m. June, 1961; children: Richard, Kathy, Eugene; edn: BS, Univ. So. Calif., MCE, MPA, Calif. State Univ. Career: mem. city council City of Diamond Bar, Calif. 1990, mayor 1991; mem. 103-104th Congresses from 41st dist. Calif. 1993-; pres., founder Jaykim Engrs. Inc.; awards: Outstanding Achievement in Bus. and Comm. Devel. award, Engr. of Yr. award, Caballero de Distinction award, Engr. Bus. of the Yr. award, others; Republican; Methodist. Ofc. US House of Representatives Office of House Members Washington DC 20515

KIM, KWANG EUN, acupuncturist, chiropractor, herbal/nutritionist; b. Sept. 15, 1938, Seoul, Korea, nat. 1974; s. Ick Chae and Tan (Ock) K.; m. Kyung Sook Yoo, June 17, 1966; children: Sion, b. 1967; Yale, b. 1969; Royle, b. 1975; edn: BA, Union Christian Coll., Seoul 1960; MA, Yonsei Univ., Seoul 1962; DC, Cleveland Chiropractic Coll. 1973; M.Herb., Emerson Coll. of Herbology 1981; PhD, Donsbach Univ. 1987. Career: pvt. practice acupuncturist, chiropractor, herbalist, nutritionist; pres. Dr. Kwang Eun Kim, DC, Inc., Los Angeles; clin. asst. tchr. Cleveland Chiro. Coll., L.A. 1972-73; bd. dirs. New Internat. Mortgage Corp.; apptd. by Calif. State Senate as mem. Council on Technology Edn.; mem: Am. Chiro. Assn., Found. for Chiro. Edn. & Research/USA, Fellow Research Council on Botanic Medicine/Canada, Am. Acupuncture Assn., Am. Nutrition & Herbal Med. Assn., Korean Chiropractic Assn. of US (pres.), Korean-Am. Christian Bus. Mens Com. of So. Calif., Korean Ch. Music Assn.(pres.); Repub.; Presbyterian; rec: pictures, coins, stamps. Res: 645 Hillcrest Ave, Flintridge 91011 Ofc: Dr. Kwang Eun Kim, DC, Inc. 252 S Oxford Ave Los Angeles 90004

KIM, KWANG SIK, physician; b. June 9, 1947, Seoul, Korea; s. Tae Jong and Kyung Ja K.; m. Aeran Y., July 30, 1983; children: Melissa Y. b. 1984, Brian Y. b. 1987; edn: BS, Seoul Nat. Univ. 1967; MD, 1971. Career: asst. prof. pediatrics Harbor-UCLA Med. Center 1980-86; assoc. prof. pediatrics Children's Hosp., Los Angeles 1986-91; currently prof. of pediatrics, USC Sch. of Medicine and head, Div. of Infectious Diseases, Children's Hosp. L.A.; awards: Mead Johnson Lab. Outstanding Pediatric Resident 1977, March of Dimes Basic O'Connor grant 1982, Am. Heart Assn. sr. investigator 1983; mem: Am. Soc. Microbiology, Lancefield Soc., Western Soc. Pediatric Res., Am. Pediatric Soc., Pediatric Infectious Diseases Soc., Am. Fedn. for Clinical Res., Soc. for Pediatric Res., Am. Soc. for Cell Biology, Infectious Diseases Soc. of Am.; author: 91 articles and chpt. pub. in profl. jours.; mil: flight surgeon Korean Air Force 1971-74. Res: 4808 Asteria St Torrance 90503 Ofc: Children's Hospital of Los Angeles Division of Infectious Diseases 4650 Sunset Blvd Los Angeles 90027

KIMMICH, ROBERT ANDRÉ, physician, psychiatrist; b. Nov. 2, 1920, Idpls.; s. Dr. John Martin (M.D.) and Renee Marie (Baron) K.; m. Nancy E. Smith, 1945 (div.); children: Robert, John, Nancy; edn: BS, MD, Indiana Univ., 1943, Rockefeller fellow Inst. of Penna. Hosp., Phila. 1944-45. Career: chief male section Worcester State Hos. 1947-49; dir. Territorial Hosp., Honolulu, 1951-58;clin. dir. Ill. Psychol. Inst. 1958-60; dir. Mental Health Dept. San Francisco, 1960-64; dir. Michigan Dept. Mental Health, Lansing, Mi. 1964-68; chmn. Psychiatric Dept. Childrens' Hosp., San Francisco, 1968-76; asst. prof. Yale Univ. Sch. of Med., 1949-51; assoc. clin. prof. Univ. of Mich. Sch. of Med. 1964-66; assoc. clin. prof. Stanford Univ. Sch. of Med., 1968-82; recipient Distinguished Service Award, No. Calif. Psychiatric Soc., S.F. 1990; Life Fellow Am. Psychiatric Assn. (nat. rep. 1988-), No. Calif. Psychiatric Soc. (pres. elect. 1991-93, pres. 1993-95, newsletter editor 1985-93), Childrens Hosp. Physicians Assocs. (bd. 1985-); mil: capt. Med. Corps AUS 1945-47; rec: sailing, guitar, hiking. Ofc: 341 Spruce San Francisco 94118

KINANE, MICHAEL JOSEPH, lawyer, community advocate; b. Dec. 28, 1956, Inglewood; s. Arthur David and Rosalee Marie (Peralta) K.; m. Patricia M.Y. Wong, Jan. 1, 1994; 1 son, Michael Joseph Kai Ming Kinane b. 1995; edn: BS in bus., acctg. also BA in sociology, UC Berkeley, 1979, MBA internat. trade, UCB, 1982; JD, Hastings Coll. of Law, 1991; admitted bar: Calif., US Dist. Ct., US Ct. Appeals. Career: sales Thom McAn Shoes, Torrance, 1972-76; research cons. Carnegie Council, Berkeley 1978-79; account exec. Comml. Credit Corp., San Francisco 1979-80; pres. CCE Biotech, Oakland 1983-92; Comm. Design 1983-84; Calif. Capital Exports Inc. 1982-92; atty., of counsel Law offices of Kinane & Bonner, Sausalito; adj. prof. Nat. Univ., Oakland 1985-86; columnist, The First Edition; jury chair Nat. Ednl. Film Festival; mem: Calif. Trial Lawyers Assn. (bd. dir.), Am. Trial Lawyers Assn., Calif. Bar Assn., Italian Am. Bar Assn.; Fruitvale Merchants Assn. (pres.), Oakland C.of C., Oakland Comm. Action Agency (bd. dirs.), Spanish Speaking Citizens Found. (bd. dir.), Camara de Comercia Mexicana-Americana, Gael Olde Boys Rugby Club, Fruitvale Comm. Devel. Dist. Council (bd. dir.), Consumer Attorneys of Calif. (bd. dirs.); rec: rugby, skiing, collect childrens' literature. Res: 1844 33rd Ave Oakland 94601 Ofc: Law Offices of Kinane & Bonner 180 Harbor Dr Ste 220 Sausalito 94965

KING, FREDERIC, health services management professional, association executive director; b. May 9, 1937, NYC; s. Benjamin and Jeanne (Fritz) K.; m. Linda Ann Udell, Mar. 17, 1976; children by previous marriage: Coby Allen, Allison Beth, Lisa Robyn, Daniel Seth; edn: BBA cum laude, Bernard M. Baruch Sch. Bus. and Pub. Adminstrn., CUNY, 1958. Career: dir. adminstrn. Albert Einstein Coll. Medicine, Bronx 1970-72; assoc. v.p. health affairs Tulane Med. Ctr., New Orleans 1972-77; dir. fin. Mt. Sinai Med. Ctr., NYC 1977-78; v.p. fin. Cedars-Sinai Med. Ctr., Los Angeles 1978-82; pres. Vascular Diagnostic Services Inc., Woodland Hills 1982-84; exec. dir. South Bay Independent Physicians Med. Group Inc., Torrance 1984-; asso. adj. prof. Tulane Univ. Sch. Pub. Health; asst. prof. Mt. Sinai Med. Ctr.; instr. Pierce Coll., L.A.; listed Who's Who in the West, Who's Who in Soc.; mem: Healthcare Forum, Am. Hosp. Assn., Calif. Assn. Hosps. and Health Systems, The

Presidents Assn., Am. Assn. of Preferred Provider Organizations (dir. Pacific region); civic: pres./chmn. bd. dirs. Torah Learning Ctr.; dir. Ohr Eliyahu Academy; mil: AUS 1959-62; Republican; Jewish. Res: 1116 Rose Ave Venice 90291 Ofc: 3480 Torrance Blvd Ste 220 Torrance 90503

KING, GEORGE (H.S.H. Prince de Santorini, Count de Florina, Lord of Allington), clergyman, writer, broadcaster; b. Jan. 23, 1919, Wellington, Shropshire, Eng.; s. George and Mary King; m. Dr. Monique Noppe, Jan. 30, 1971; ed. Guisborough Public Sch., Eng., Regent St Polytechnic Coll., London; DD, Bodkin Bible Inst.; PhD in theol. Internat. Theol. Sem.; internat. advy. bd. and ordained minister Internat. Evangelism Crusades Inc.; author 30 pub. books, lectr., tchr. religious bdcstr., producer/dir. num. 16mm docu. films and video-tapes, ednl. cassettes; dep. dir. gen. Internat. Biographical Ctr., dep. gov. Am. Biographical Inst. Res. Assn.; founder/pres. The Aetherius Soc., (rel., sci., edn. orgn.), met. archbishop The Aetherius Churches; founder, pres., grand master Mystical Order of St. Peter (reg. charity US, reg. UCCI); founder, pres. Coll. of Spiritual Scis., London, Los Angeles; grand master Internat. Chivalric Order Kts. of Justice (reg. charity); hon. lt. grand master The Grand Sovereign Dynastic Hospitaller Order of St. John, Kts. of Malta (reg. UCCI); grand collier The Imperial Sovereign Mil. Orthodox Dynastic Constantinian Order of St. Georges (reg. UCCI); internat. chaplain Am. Fedn. of Police, nat. chaplain Am. Park Rangers Assn., nat. advy. bd. Nat. Chaplains Assn. USA, patron Internat. Acad. of Criminology, nat. advy. bd. Am. Security Council, advy. bd. Intl. Evangelism Crusades Inc. (peace award 1982), granted Letters Patent of Armorial Bearings by Her Majesty's Coll. of Arms, England; mem: Internat. Acad. for Advance. Arts & Scis. (life), Freeman of the City of London, Guild of Freemen City of London (life), Assn. of Freemen of England, Manorial Soc. G.B., Fellow Royal Soc. of Tropical Medicine and Hygiene G.B., Fellow Royal Commonwealth Soc., The Heraldry Soc. G.B., Royal Nat. Lifeboat Instn. G.B., Hon. Order Ky. Colonels, Nat. Rifle Assn., Calif. Rifle and Pistol Club; mil. awards: Grande Croix, l'Etoile de la Paix (France), hon. gen. Polish Armed Forces (in Exile), gold medal for svc. Imperial House of Byzantium, Order of the White Eagle and Order of Virtuti Militari (former) Rep. of Poland (govt. in exile), WWII Def. Medal (U.K.), Battle for Brit. commemorative medal, Cross of Europe, Medal of the Secret Army of Belgium, Cross of Merit w/Swords (Poland), Gen. Wladyslawe Sikorski Centenary Medal; Republican (U.S. Congl. Advy. Bd., life Presdl. Task Force); Address: 6216 Afton Place Hollywood 90028-8205

KING, JON LANNING, consulting actuary, executive; b. May 8, 1948, Columbus, Nebr.; s. Edward Lanning and Elizabeth Ann (Jaworski) K.; m. Peggy Louise Wright, May 27, 1971 (div. 1988); m. Diana Rae Green, July 29, 1989; edn: BS, Univ. Neb. 1970. Career: systems analyst Transamerica Life, Los Angeles 1972, mgr. direct life product 1973-74; cons. actuary TPF&C 1975-80, prin., cons. actuary 1981-86, v.p., cons. actuary 1986-88; office mgr., cons. actuary Buck Cons. 1986–; mem: Am. Acad. Actuaries, L.A. Actuarial Club (treas. 1982), Western Pension Conf., Pacific States Actuarial Club, Soc. Actuaries, Conf. Actuaries in Pub. Practice; speaker on employee benefits 1979–; rec: golf, bridge, football. Res: 6 Fleet #301 Marina Del Rey 90292 Ofc: Buck Consultants 1801 Century Park E Ste 480 Los Angeles 90067

KING, NANCY GARRETT, educator/communication consultant; b. May 10, 1945, Blytheville, Ark.; d. Willie Lee and Janie (Jones) Garrett; m. Perry, King, June 17, 1967; children: Perry, Jr. b. 1967, Tiffany b. 1970, Christopher b. 1971; edn: BA and MA in speech comm., CSU Los Angeles, 1974, 1981. Career: asst. supr. Pacific Tel. & Tel., 1968-70; computer opr. West Coast Commodity Exchange Fenton & Lavine, Los Angeles 1970-71; So. Calif. Gas Co., 1972-81; communication cons. 1982–, devel. language splst. Charles Drew Headstart Pgm., speechwriter var. regional ofcls.; instr. CSULA, 1979-86; asst. prof. speech dept. Marymount Coll., Rancho Palos Verdes 1986; gub. appt. Calif. State Library Svs. Bd. 1984-94, pres. 1988-89; appt. by State Librarian mem. Calif. Library Networking Task Force 1985; bds: Calif. Libraries LSCA Advy. Bd. 1984, Orange County Friends of the Library Found. 1988, L.A. Southwest Coll. Literacy Council 1988, Calif. State Alliance for Literacy Task Force 1988; mem: Nat. Edn. Assn., Nat. Speech Comm. Assn., Western Speech Comm. Assn., Am. Fedn. Tchrs., AAUW, Orange County Hist. & Cultural Found./Black Council (pgm. dir.), L.A. Southcentral Planning Council (bd.); Republican (Calif. Black Rep. Council, active local, state, nat. campaigns); contbr. articles to profl. jours.; Republican; Cath.; rec: reading, swimming. Ofc: Marymount College 30800 Palos Verdes Dr East Rancho Palos Verdes 90274

KINNANE, DENNIS GEORGE, doctor of Oriental medicine, acupuncturist; b. Sept. 28, 1946, Hammond, Ind.; s. George Vincent and Irene Ethel (Smith) K.; edn: BS in pharmacy, Purdue Univ., Lafayette, Ind. 1969; MS in acupuncture, herbology, SAMRA Univ., L.A., Calif. 1987; OMD, SAMRA Univ. 1988; reg. pharmacist; lic. acupuncturist. Career: pharmacist Hook's Drugs, Indianapolis, Ind. 1970-74; Savon Drugs, L.A., Calif. 1975-78; independent pharmacist, L.A., 1978-88; lic. acupuncturist, private practice, Torrance, Calif. 1988–; faculty mem.: SAMRA Univ., L.A. 1988–, So. Bay Adult Sch., Redondo Beach 1989–, Am. Inst. of Oriental Medicine, San Diego 1990–; mem: Calif. Acupuncture

Assn. 1990–, Purdue Alumni Assn. 1990–; rec: music, travel, metaphysics. Res: 702 Manhattan Beach Blvd Apt #6 Manhattan Beach 90266 Ofc: Dr. Dennis Kinnane 4015 Pacific Coast Hwy, Ste. 101 Torrance 90505

KINSELL, JEFFREY CLIFT, investment banker; b. Sept. 13, 1951, Santa Barbara; s. Dr. Clift Seybert and Shirlee Grace (Burwash) K.; m. Sherry Anne Majerus, July 4, 1980 (div. 1985); m. Sondra Amy Silvey, May 21, 1987; children: Amy Elizabeth b. 1989, Pamela Suzanne b. 1991; edn: BS biology, Coll. Arts & Sci., Tulane Univ., 1973; MBA in fin., John Anderson Grad. Sch. of Mgmt., UCLA, 1976. Career: asst. v.p. First Boston Corp., N.Y.C., 1976-78, v.p. First Boston Corp., San Francisco 1978-88; v.p., western reg. mgr. Paine Webber Capital Markets Inc., S.F. 1988-94; v.p. A.G. Edwards & Sons, Inc. 1994–; honors: Beta Beta Beta, Sigma Alpha Epsilon 1969-73; mem. San Francisco Municipal Bond Club 1978–; Republican; Episcopalian; rec: sailing, travel, photography, scrimshaw. Res: 93 La Espiral Orinda 94563 Ofc: A.G. Edwards & Sons Inc 275 Battery St Ste 2120 San Francisco 94111

KINSELLA, KEVIN JOHN, venture capitalist; b. Dec. 23, 1945, New York; s. Walter Aloysius Kinsella and Jane Andrew (Davis) Southwell; edn: BS mgmt., M.I.T., 1967; MA internat. econ., Johns Hopkins Sch. Advanced Internat. Studies 1969. Career: pres. and chief exec., Sequana Therapeutics; founder, mng. gen. ptnr. Avalon Ventures (pvt. venture capital firm), La Jolla 1983–; dir: Gryphon Software (San Diego), Microcide Pharmaceuticals (Mtn. View), Onyx Pharmaceuticals (Richmond, Calif.); trustee, Boston Univ.; mem. MIT Corp. Devel. Com., Democratic Found. S.D. Co. (chmn.); publs: 24+ columns in the Boston Globe, Boston Herald American, Boston Sunday Globe, 1976-78; Siberian Journey, NY Times 1971; In the Eye of the Storm, MIT Literary Mag. 1971; Computer Graphics, Digital Design 1972; Democrat (S.D. Co. Central Com.); Cath.; rec: tennis, swimming, hiking. Ofc: Avalon Ventures, 1020 Prospect St Ste 405 La Jolla 92037; Sequana Therapeutics 11099 N Torrey Pines Rd #160 La Jolla 92037

KINSEY, THOMAS DU WAYNE, marketing consultant, business directory specialist; b. July 4, 1937, Gerrett, Ind.; s. Elza DuWayne and Teresa Virgilia (Moran) K.; m. Suzanne, June 20, 1959; children: Keith b. 1960, Kerryn b. 1961, Kevin b. 1964; edn: BA, CSU Long Beach 1959. Career: nat. accts. mgr. CompuCorp. Santa Monica 1971-74; owner Thomas D. Kinsey & Assocs. Fillmore 1974-75; shareholder, nat. mktg. mgr. Delphi Info. Sciences Corp. Santa Monica 1975-81; owner Ergo Mktg. & Advtg. Thousand Oaks, Summa Books, Thousand Oaks, and ptnr. Direct Publications, 1981–; evening bus. div. Moorpark Coll.; lectr. UCLA Entrepreneurial Pgm.; mem. Bardsdale Homeowners Assn. (dir. 1984), Rotary (pres. 1988); author: Double Your Income in 2 Years or Less... (Summa Pub.), Pocket Graphic Arts and Desktop Publishing Dictionary; editor: Compound Interest Tables, Complete Compound Interest Tables (Contemporary Books); Republican; Cath.; rec: tennis, biking, rock & mountain climbing. Res: 1401 Pasadena Ave Fillmore 93015 Ofc: Ergo Marketing & Summa Books 560 N Moorpark Rd Ste 134 Thousand Oaks 91360

KINTNER, JANET IDE, judge; b. Feb. 25, 1944, Tucson, Az.; d. Herbert A. and Marian G. (Hetzler) Ide; m. Charles Kintner, Sept. 14, 1968; children: Zachary b. 1976, Darien b. 1978, Cassady b. 1985; edn: BA, Univ. Ariz., 1966, JD, UA Coll. of Law, 1968. Career: staff atty. Legal Aid Soc., S.D. 1969-70; dep. city atty. San Diego 1971-74; pvt. solo law practice 1974-76; apptd. judge San Diego Municipal Ct., 1976, elected 1978, spl. assignment as judge Superior Ct. 1977; spl. assignment to Ct. of Appeals Nov.-Dec. 1985; instr. San Diego Eve. Coll., 1973, 75, SDSU Ext. 1974; lectr. on law for new judges, Calif. Judicial Coll. 1981-93, tchr. and team ldr. adv. civil law for experienced Muni. and Superior Ct. judges, Calif. Judicial Studies Pgm. 1982-89; team ldr. of cause entitled Judicial Factfinding and Decision Making (for judges), 1985-95; taught judges in Canada, Iowa and Minn.; honors: UA Debate Team, Women's Scholastic Honors 1962-66, pres. legal sor. UA 1966-68; lectr. Cont. Edn. of the Bar; mem: Calif. Bar Assn. (1st woman and 1st judge on State Bar Jour. com.) San Diego County Bar Assn. (bd. 1973-76, v.p. 1976, founding chair consumer fraud sect., del. State Bar Conv. 1973, 74, 75, del. chair 1975-78, columnist, staff writer DICTA mag. 1972-75), Lawyers Club (founding mem. 1972, founding ed. L.C. Newsletter 1977), Calif. Women Lawyers Assn. (founding mem.), Calif. Atty. Gen.'s Task Force on Consumer Protection 1972-76, Nat. Assn. of Women Judges (founding mem. and bd. dirs. 1989-91), S.D. Trial Lawyers Assn. 1975, Calif. Judges Assn. (1976, ethics com., govng. com. CJER Jour., assoc. ed. Courts Commentary), S.D. Co. Judges Assn. (pres. 1990), S.D. Psych. and Law Soc. (hon.), Nat. Council on Alcoholism, Bus. & Profl. Women, Big Sisters League (bd. 1984-87), Crime Victims Fund (bd. 1984-88), New Entra Casa (women's half-way house) (bd. 1981-92), Home Start Inc. child abuse prevention pgm. (bd. 1983-88), Judicial Council Civil & Small Claims Advy. Com. 1993– (chair 1995); contbr. articles in law jours.; rec: bridge, music. Ofc: San Diego Municipal Court 220 W Broadway San Diego 92101

KIPROV, DOBRI DOBREV, immunology/apheresis physician; b. May 1, 1949, Sofia, Bulgaria; s. Dobri I. and Zvetana M. (Popov) K.; 1 son, Dobri b. 1973; edn: BS, Sofia H.S., Bulgaria 1968; MD, Med. Acad., Sofia, Bulgaria 1974. resident pathol. Sackler Sch. Med., Tel Aviv, Israel 1974-77, instr. pathol.

1975-77; resident pathol. Mt. Sinai Hosp., Cleveland 1977-79; clin. and res. fellowship Harvard Med. Sch., Mass. Gen. Hosp., Boston 1979-81; fellowship immunol. and plasmapheresis Calif. Pacific Med. Ctr., San Francisco, Calif. 1981-82, chief div. of immunotheraphy and dir. clin. immunology lab.; instr. UCSF 1984–; cons. immunopathol. 1982–; awards: NIH res. award 1979-81; recipient: res. grants Myasthenia Gravis Found., 1982, 83, 84, Cobe Labs Inc., 1982-83; mem: AAAS, AMA, Am. Soc. Clin. Pathols., Am. Soc. Apheresis, SFMS, Coll. Am. Pathols., World Med. Assn., Nat. Inst. Allergy and Infectious Diseases; 100+ articles publ. in profl. jours.; rec: ski, windsurf. Ofc: Centers for Aperesis & Immunology 2351 Clay St #603 San Francisco 94115

KIRBY, ROBERT WILLIAM, real estate broker; b. Nov. 8, 1937, Westwood; s. Oliver William and Nell Vivian (Trickett) K.; edn: BA, Azusa Pac. Univ., 1959; gen. elem. tchg. cred., CSU Stanislaus, 1964; gen. sec. tchg. cred., Univ. of Pacific, 1967; grad. journalism, CSU Fullerton, 1971-74; lic. R.E. broker Calif. 1986. Career: tchr. Lincoln Jr. High Sch., Stockton 1964-68, YMCA Club adv. 1965-68; tchr. Maranatha High Sch., Arcadia 1969-76, baseball coach 1970-76, yearbook /newspaper adv. 1972-76, Key Club adv. 1971-76; real estate agt. Herbert Hawkins Co., Pasadena 1976-82, National Consolidated, Pasadena 1982-86; real estate broker Kirby Properties, Pasadena 1986–; honors: Youth in City Govt., Stockton Unified 1953, pres. Soph. Class, Choir chaplain, editor newspaper Azusa Pacific Univ. (1956-59); mem: Nat. Assn. Realtors, Calif. Assn. Realtors, Pasadena Bd. Realtors, Azusa Pacific Univ. Alumni (bd. dirs. 1972-78, pres. 1976-77, sec. 1974-76), Foothill Apt. Owners Assn.; lodge: Crown City Kiwanis (sec. 1987-88, 91–, bd. 1988-90, v.p. 1988-89); contbr. num. articles to religious, college and club publs., editor: Y.F.C. Jour. "Herald" (1956-57), coll. newspaper "The Interceptor" (1958-59), coll. yearbook "The Sceptor" (1956-57), alumni newsletter "The Collegian" (1974-75); Republican: GOP Nat. Com., Calif. Rep. Party, Citizens Against Govt. Waste, H.A.L.T., Nat. Taxpayer's Union; Congregational; rec: travel, golf, oil painting. Ofc: Kirby Properties 1245 E Walnut Ste 114 Pasadena 91106

KIRCHNER, ERNST KARL, manufacturing company executive; b. June 18, 1937, San Francisco; s. Karl Ewald and Theresa (Muller) K.; m. Ursula Martha Karmann, Sept. 3, 1960; children: Mark Ernst b. 1967, Christl Elaine b. 1968, Steven Thomas b. 1970; edn: BSEE, Stanford Univ., 1959, MSEE, 1960, PhD in E.E., 1963. Career: tchr. Univ. Arizona, Tucson 1963-65; mem. technical staff Teledyne MEC, Palo Alto 1965-72, project engr. 1972-79, staff engr. 1979-81, mgr. 1981-82, operation mgr. 1982-83, sr. mgr. 1983-84; mgr. engring. Teledyne Microwave, Mountain View 1984-87, dir. engring. 1987-88, v.p. bus. devel. 1988-93, v.p. delay device products 1990-93; dir. microwave components Teledyne Electronic Technologies 1993–; honors: Kappa Kappa Psi 1956, Sigma Xi 1959, Tau Beta Pi 1959; mem: Bd. of Hope Unlimited Internat., IEEE, Am. Physical Soc., Am. Mktg. Assn., Assn. of Old Crows; commr. Town of Atherton 1986-87; patentee; contbr. articles in tech. jours. (1963–); mil: 1st lt. US Army 1963-65, Army Commendn. Medal 1965; Republican; Presbyterian (deacon, elder). Res: 41 Ashfield Rd Atherton 94027 Ofc: Teledyne Electronic Technologies 1274 Terra Bella Ave Mountain View 94043

KIRK, CASSIUS LAMB, JR., lawyer, investor; b. June 8, 1929, Bozeman, Mont.; s. Cassius L. and Gertrude V. (McCarthy) K.; edn: AB, pol. sci., Stanford Univ. 1951; JD, UC Berkeley 1954. Career: assoc. law firm of Cooley, Godward, Castro, Huddleson & Tatum, San Francisco 1956-60; staff counsel business affairs, Stanford Univ. 1960-78; chief bus. ofcr., staff counsel, Menlo Sch. and Coll., Menlo Park 1978-81; chmn. bd. Elberli-Kirk Properties, Inc., Menlo Park 1981-94; dir: Just Closets Inc., San Rafael, 1987-91; faculty, UC Santa Barbara Wkshop for Coll. Adminstrs. 1965-73; honors: Order of the Coif, Phi Sigma Alpha, Phi Alpha Delta; mem. Calif. Bar Assn.(inactive), Stanford Faculty Club; civic: Menlo Towers Assn. (pres. 1978-79, 82-83, 87-88), Palo Alto C.of C. (v.p. for community affairs 1969-70), Allied Arts Guild, City of Menlo Park Advy. Bd.); mil: sp3 US Army, Occ. Ger., GCM; Republican; rec: jogging, travel, opera. Res: 1330 University Dr #52 Menlo Park 94025

KITADA, SHINICHI, research biochemist; b. Dec. 9, 1948, Osaka, Japan; came to U.S. 1975; s. Koichi and Asako (Seki) K.; edn: MD, Kyoto Univ., 1973; MS in biol. chem., UCLA, 1977, PhD, 1979. Career: intern Kyoto Univ. Hosp. 1973-74; resident physician Chest Disease Research Inst. 1974-75; res. scholar Lab. Nuclear Medicine and Radiation Biology UCLA 1979-89, asst. res. biochemist Jules Stein Eye Inst. UCLA, 1989-92; research biochemist La Jolla Cancer Research Found., 1992–; awards: Japan Soc. Promotion Sci. fellow 1975-76, Edna Lievre fellow Am. Cancer Soc. 1981-82; mem: Am. Oil Chemists Soc., Sigma Xi, N.Y. Acad. of Scis.; res. papers in field; Presbyterian; rec: swimming, tennis. Res: 920 Kline St #301 La Jolla 92037 Ofc: La Jolla Cancer Research Foundation 10901 N Torrey Pines Rd La Jolla 92037

KITCHEN, JONATHAN SAVILLE, lawyer; b. June 7, 1948, Lincoln, Eng.; s. Walter Lawrence Michael and Helen Margaret (Hastings) K.; m. Nina Hatvany, 1982; children: Natalie b. 1982, Vanessa b. 1984, Paul b. 1985; edn: stu., Strasbourg Univ., France 1966-67; BA (honors) Durham Univ., Eng. 1970; LLM, Univ. Coll., London 1971; MA, Cambridge Univ., Eng. 1974, PhD, 1976; admitted bar: England & Wales, 1977, Calif., 1978. Career: research fellow Churchill

Coll., Cambridge, Eng. 1974-77; teaching fellow, Stanford Law Sch., Palo Alto 1975-76; atty. McCutchen, Doyle, San Francisco 1977-81; ptnr., atty. Baker & McKenzie, San Francisco 1981–; honors: Duke of Edinburgh Scholar, Inner Temple, 1970, Evans Lewis-Thomas Scholar, Sydney Sussex Coll., Cambridge, Eng., 1972-74, Fulbright Scholar in Law to U.S, 1975-76, Bodossaks Fellowship, Churchill Coll., Cambridge, 1974-77; mem: State Bar of Calif., Bar Assn. of San Francisco, Am. Bar Assn., St. Francis Yacht Club; author: 2 books and numerous articles in domestic and foreign law jours.; rec: sailing, skiing. Ofc: Baker & McKenzie, Two Embarcadero Ctr 24th Flr San Francisco 94111-3909

KITCHING, GILBERT EDWARD, obstetrician/gynecologist; b. July 7, 1929, Brooklyn, NY; s. Gilbert James and Kathryn Patricia (Stubbert) K.; m. Joane, Aug. 20, 1955; children: Alfred b. 1951, Gilbert b. 1956, Kenneth b. 1958, Charles b. 1963; edn: BS, Calif. Inst. of Tech. 1952; MD, Univ. of So. Calif. 1956; diplomate Am. Bd. Ob-Gyn. 1967. Career: served to col. US Air Force, 1956-75; med. intern Tripler Army Hosp. Hosp. 1956-58, ob.-gyn. residency, 1959-62; wing flt. surgeon Travis AFB 1958-59; chief Ob-Gyn, Clark AFB, Philippines 1962-64, Home AFB, Ida. 1964-65, Vandenberg AFB, Ca. 1965-70, Wiesbaden (W.Ger.) Hosp. 1970-73, Sheppard AFB, Tx. 1973-75, ret. USAF 1975, AF commendn. medal 1970; cmdr. hosps. Chanute AFB 1976-78, and Homestead AFB, Fla. 1978-81; tchr. med. inspection USAF 1981-83, study dir. evaluation of USAF med. services 1982, dep. dir. profl. services USAF Med. Service, 1983-85; staff ob-gyn. Riverside Med. Clinic, Corona, Calif. 1986-88; staff gyn. St. Bernardine Med. Ctr. 1988–; honors: AF meritorious service medal 1976, 78 81, 83, Legion of Merit 1985; Fellow Am. Coll. Obstets. & Gynecol., mem. AMA, CMA, San Bernardino Co. Med. Assn., Soc. of AF Clin. Surgeons; Boy Scouts Am. scoutmaster 1968-71; num. lectures, workshops, and articles in med. and mil. jours.; Republican; R.Cath.; rec: photog., electronics, carpentry. Ofc: 399 E Highland Ave Ste 502 San Bernardino 92404

KITE, DENNIS S., institutional securities sales executive; b. May 10, 1945, Chgo.; s. Allen M. and June T. (Hillman) K.; m. Aleta Lindbeck, Feb. 14, 1982; children: Debra b. 1968, Suzanne b. 1990; edn: BBA, Univ. Wis. 1967; MBA, Univ. Chgo. 1973; desig: Prin., Mcpl. Securities Rulemaking Bd. 1985, Gen. Investment Securities Rep. 1988. Career: trainee, mail clk., teller Nat. City Bank, now Manufacturers Bank, Chgo. 1967-68; adminstrv. asst. Inv. Div. Am. Nat. Bank, Chgo. 1968-70; asst. v.p./reg. mgr. Montgomery Ward Credit Corp., Chgo. 1970-77; account exec. Bank of Am., Bank Investment Sec. Div., Los Angeles 1977-79, v.p./ Houston reg. sales mgr. 1979-82, v.p./reg. sales mgr./dir. BA Asia Ltd., Tokyo, Japan 1982-84, v.p./mgr. retail securities sales So. Calif., Bank of Am. Capital Markets Group, 1984-86, v.p./sr. account exec. 1986-87; instl. sales account exec. Liberty Capital Markets Inc., 1988–; mem: Calif. Municipal Treasurers Assn., Big Ten Club of So. Calif., Univ. Chgo. Grad. Sch. of Bus. Alumni Club, Univ. Wis. Alumni Assn.; civic: Zool. Soc. San Diego, L.A. Art Mus., Sierra Club, Smithsonian, Save the Children (sponsor); contbr. material to Marcia Stigum's book: The Money Markets, Myth Reality & Practice (1978); mil: s/sgt. USAFR 1968-73; Jewish; rec: music, golf, skiing, racquetball. Res: 4 Mondano Laguna Niguel 92677 Ofc: Liberty Capital Markets, Inc. 4 Park Plaza Ste 2000 Irvine 92714

KITTLESON, HAROLD ALVER, electronic manufacturers' representative; b. Jan. 9, 1912, Malta, Ill.; s. Elon Edwin and Anna Olena (Hobbet) K.; Great Uncle Ole Kittleson invented and patented barbed wire (1875); m. Ella Hartshorn, Apr. 5, 1941; 1 dau. Betty Ann (York) b. 1942; edn: tchr. cred. Iowa State Tchrs. Coll., Cedar Falls 1932; elec. engrg. Iowa State Coll., Ames 1934-38; cert. Micro-wave Engring., Cal. Tech., 1941; cert. USN Radar Sch., Phila. 1943; tech. & bus. courses, Lockheed Co., Sperry Electronic Corp. (NY), MIT, UCLA; bus. mgmt. certs., Stanford Univ., 1961-62. Career: wkr. on family farm, Woden, Iowa, -1932; country sch. tchr., Iowa, 1932-34; resrch. asst., E.E., Iowa State Coll. 1936-39; chief elec. engr. American Pubs. supply, Lynn, Mass. 1939-40; hd. electronic test equip. engring. on design, Lockheed Aircraft, No. Hollywood, Ca. 1940-43; coord. engr. AEW Proj., MIT Radiation Lab., Cambridge, Mass. 1944-45; founder/owner/pres. Kittleson Co. (electronic mfrs. rep), Los Angeles 1946–, Continental Components 1955-60; lectr. Lockheed Aircraft 1943; cons. No. Am. Phillips Co. 1957, Gen. Equip. Corp. 1958, Fairchild Recording Equip. Corp. 1960, Airtron 1965; honors: recipient appreciation awards num. profl. and cult. organizations, banquet honoree, named No. 1 Booth Choice (1000 exhibitors) WESCON Show and Conv. 1969; mem: Internat. Platform Assn., Electronic Reps Assn. (pres. 1950), Mfrs. Agents Nat. Assn. (pres. 1955), Precision Measurement Assn. (charter, internat. pres. 1970-72), Meals for Millions Found. (trustee 1975-80); active in charity fundraising; publs: tech. reports, mkt. studies; book on family recollections, 3 vols.; US patent application, 1983; Republican (Election Bd.); Presbyterian (commnr. Gen. Assem.); rec: painting (exhibition of oil paintings, 1992), cosmology, experimental gardening. Res: 20315 Runnymede St Canoga Park 91306

KITTLESON, MARK DOUGLAS, educator, cardiovascular researcher, veterinary cardiologist; b. Sept. 21, 1950, Sherburn, Minn.; s. Norman Leonard and LaVonne Elaine (Meister) K.; m. Judith Ann, June 11, 1972; children: Ashlie b. 1980, Natalie b. 1984; edn: BS, Univ. of Minn., 1972, DVM, 1974; MS, Kansas State Univ., 1978; PhD, The Ohio State Univ., 1982; Diplomate American Coll.

of Veterinary Internal Medicine, cardiology splty., 1979. Career: staff veterinarian Westfield Vet. Group, Westfield, N.J. 1974-76; resident Kansas State Univ., Manhattan, Kans. 1976-78; graduate tchg. asst. The Ohio State Univ., Columbus 1978-80; asst., assoc. prof. Mich. State Univ., East Lansing 1980-84; asst., assoc., full prof. UC Davis, 1984–; cardiovascular researcher/ cons. Sterling-Winthrop Res. Inst. (1982–); awards: Phi Zeta, Phi Kappa Phi, recipient Ralston Purina Small Animal Research Award (1989); Diplomate Am. Coll. Vet. Internal Medicine- Cardiology (pres. 1984-87); assoc. editor Jour. of Veterinary Internal Medicine (1986-90); mem: Am. Vet. Med. Assn. (1974–), Am. Heart Assn. (1982–), Am. Acad. of Vet. Pharmacology and Therapeutics (1986–); co-discoverer of taurine deficiency as cause of feline dilated cardiomyopathy (Science, 1987), contbr. 40+ sci. articles in refereed jours. (1980–); rec: basketball, tennis. Ofc: Rm 224 VMII, University of California, Davis 95616

KLAFTER, CARY IRA, lawyer; b. Sept. 15, 1948, Chicago, Ill.; s. Herman Nicholas and Bernice Ruth (Maremont) K.; m. Kathleen Ann Kerr, July 21, 1974; children: Anastasia b. 1976, Benjamin b. 1979, Eileen b. 1982; edn: BA, Mich. St. Univ. 1968; MS, 1971; JD, Univ. Chgo. 1972; admitted St. Bar Calif. 1972. Career: assoc. atty. Morrison & Foerster, San Francisco 1972-79, ptnr. 1979–; instr., Stanford Univ. Law Sch.; mem: St. Bar Calif., Great No. Railway. Hist. Soc.; mil: capt. USAR Mil. Police 1972-78. Ofc: Morrison & Foerster 345 California St San Francisco 94104

KLASSEN, ALVIN HENRY, mathematics educator, tennis official; b. July 18, 1949, San Bernardino; s. Herman Arthur and Elsie Frieda (Lille) K.; edn: BA, CSU San Bernardino, 1971; MA, San Diego State Univ. 1990; Calif. sec. tchg. cred., 1987; internat. tennis official (Bronze badge) Internat. Tennis Fedn. (ITF), 1992. Career: Supply Corps US Navy, active duty 1975-84; cdg. ofcr. US Navy Reserve, Santa Ana, 1990-92, Unit: NR Naval Supply Ctr. San Diego Det. A219; physics instr. and dept. chmn. NROTC Preparatory Sch., USN, San Diego summers 1988-91; math. instr. San Diego St. Univ., 1989-92; training ofcr. Defense Contract Mgmt. Dist. West A919, 1992–; tennis ofcl. U.S. Tennis Assn., White Plains, N.Y. 1985–; awards: Phi Kappa Phi 1987–, Univ. scholar award SDSU 1989, Nat. Def. Service, Navy Achiev. 1991, Joint Service Achievement Medal 1993; mem: Naval Reserve Assn. (1984–, San Diego chapt. v.p. 1990-92, named Jr. Ofcr. of Yr. 1989, Diamond in the Rough award 1990), Math. Assn. of Am., San Diego County Tennis Umpires Assn. (1985–, bd. of dir.), U.S. Tennis Assn. 1985–; civic: judge math div. Greater San Diego Science & Engring. Fair 1988–, San Diego County Blood Bank (Gallon Club 1985–); Ind.; Lutheran; rec: tennis, scuba, skiing, reading. Res: 13119 Bonita Vista #232 Poway 92064-5721

KLASSEN, MARGRETA, counselor, educator; b. May 4, 1928, Los Angeles; d. David Charles·and Jessie (Birch-Layng) Klassen; m. Richard C. Calhoun, May 31, 1946 (div. 1962); m. Norman K. Dunn, July 25, 1962 (div. 1969); m. Donald Cole Wargin, Feb. 14, 1970 (dec. 1984); children: Cathleen b. 1947, Melissa b. 1950, Nancy b. 1953, Richard D. b. 1955; edn: AA, Chaffey Coll. 1966; BA, Pitzer Coll. 1968; MA, CSU Los Angeles 1972; PhD, Claremont Grad. Sch. 1982. Career: examiner Biofeedback Cert. Inst. Am., Wheatridge, Colo. 1984-90; oral commr. Dept. Consumer Affairs, Sacto. 1986-89; asst. prof. Univ. LaVerne 1974-76, 1988; asst. prof. Calif. St. Polytech. Univ., Pomona 1986-88; dir. Associates for Wellness, Claremont 1974-88; lic. marriage, family counselor 1974-95; stress mgmt. prog. coord. Claremont Colls., Claremont 1988–; workshop presenter Biofeedback Soc. Calif. 1985-88; alumni council Pitzer Coll. 1985-87; honors: Pi Lambda Theta (nat. edn. honor soc.), Pomona Valley NOW Susan B. Anthony award (1975), Golden Poet, Internat. Cong. of Poets 1992; mem: Biofeedback Soc. Calif. (bd. dirs. 1983-86), Inland Empire Bus. Women's Assn. (pres. 1984), Am. Psychological Assn., Assn. for Applied Psychophysiology & Biofeedback (presenter 1992), Internat. Soc. Stress Mgmt.; publs: articles in profl. jours., 1988, 89, ed. The History of Arabian Horse, 1968; Republican; Prot.; rec: swimming (medalist Reg. Sr. Olympics 1992-94), poetry. Res: 230 Lille Lane #212 Newport Beach 92663

KLEEMAN, MICHAEL JEFFREY, consultant, executive; b. July 13, 1949, Santa Monica; s. Eugene Stanley and Sylvia (Liebman) K.; m. Janet Louise DePree, Jan. 1, 1977 (div. 1980); m. Veronica Lazarus Napoles, May 5, 1985; 1 son, Samuel b. 1987; edn: BA, Syracuse Univ. 1970; MA, Claremont Grad. Sch. 1975. Career: asst. research psychologist UCSF Med. Center, San Francisco 1975-79; dir. govt. systems Teknekron Inc., Berkeley 1979-81, mgr. systems SW SAI Inc., San Rafael 1981-82; mgr. overseas GTE Sprint, Burlingame 1982-84; sr.v.p. San Francisco-Moscow Teleport, San Francisco 1986-89; dir. telcom Arthur D. Little, San Francisco 1985-89; dir. tech. case TMI Class Action, Phila., Pa. 1980-81; bd. mem. Found. Arts of Peace, Berkeley 1982-87; SOVAM Teleport (SFMT, Global Telesystems Group Inc.), Moscow 1989-91; v.p. Boston Consulting Group Inc., San Francisco 1994–; mem: AAAS, IEEE, Assn. Computing Machinery, Am. Psychological Assn., West Point Inn Assn. (dir.); author: PC LAN Primer, 1985, 2 patents for computer keyboard dolphins, 1983, optical disk system, 1986; Democrat; Jewish; rec: photog., writing, rowing. Ofc: Boston Consulting Group Inc 2 Embarcadero Ctr San Francisco 94111

KLEIN, ARNOLD WILLIAM, physician; b. Feb. 27, 1945, Mt. Clemens, Mich.; m. Malvina Kraemer; edn: BA biology (cum laude), Univ. Pa., 1967; MD, Univ. Pa. Sch. of Medicine, 1971; bd. cert. Am. Bd. Dermatology 1977. Career: med. intern Cedars-Sinai Med. Ctr., Los Angeles 1971-72, attdg. physician; dermatology resident Hosp. of Univ. Pa., 1972-73, UCLA Med. Ctr., Los Angeles 1973-75, chief res. dermatology 1975; pvt. practice dermatology, Beverly Hills 1975–; asst. clin. prof. derm. Stanford Univ. 1982-89; assoc. clin. prof. medicine/dermatology UCLA; dir. Am. Found. for AIDS Research; med. advy. bd. Collagen Corp., Lupus Found. of Am., Skin Cancer Found.; editorial bd. Men's Fitness Mag., Shape Mag.; reviewer J. Dermatologic Surgery and Oncology, J. of Sexually Transmitted Diseases, J. of Am. Acad. of Dermatology; Calif. Senate appt. commr. Malpractice Advy. Commn. 1983-88; awards: Phi Beta Kappa, Sigma Tau Sigma, Delphos, Haney scholar Univ. Pa., Measey scholar Univ. Pa., Phila. Found. fellow, Pub. Health Service post-doc. fellow; media appearances on network t.v., radio and mags.; lectr. and presentations num. med. meetings; author med. textbooks, chapters and articles in profl. jours., 3 ednl. video tapes r Collagen Implantation, 1982, 83, 87. Ofc: 435 N Roxbury Dr Ste 204 Beverly Hills 90210

KLEIN, DAVID, diplomat, foreign service officer, educator and university staff executive; b. Sept. 2, 1919, NY, NY; s. Sam N. Klein and Fannie Helen (Falk) Albam; m. Anne Cochran, Mar. 24, 1953; children: Peter b. 1954, Steven b. 1955, John b. 1956, Barbara b. 1956, Richard b. 1958, Suzanne b. 1958; edn: AB, Bklyn. Coll., 1939; MBA (w. high distinction) Harvard Univ., 1948/1988; MA, Columbia Univ., 1952; PhD cand. Univ. of Md., 1964-65; grad. Nat. War Coll., 1966. Career: ofcr. US Fgn. Service, 1947-75: v.consul Mozambique 1947-49, econ. ofcr. US Emb. Rangoon, Burma 1949-51, 2d secty. US Emb. Moscow 1952-54, pol./econ. ofcr. US Mission, Berlin, Ger. 1955-57, 1st secty. US Emb., Bonn 1957-60, Soviet Desk, US State Dept. 1960-62, senior mem. Nat. Security Council The White House 1962-65, econ., then polit. counselor US Emb. Moscow 1966-68, polit. advr. US Mission Berlin 1968-71, US minister & dep. commandant Berlin, Ger. 1971-74, asst. dir. US Arms Control and Disarmament Agy. 1974-75; exec. dir. John J. McCloy Fund 1975-88; exec. dir. and bd. dirs. American Council on Germany 1975-88; instr., govt., Univ. of Md., 1969-71; asst. to the pres., internat. pgms., Fairleigh Dickinson Univ. 1986-90; vis. prof. Univ. San Diego and UC San Diego 1989–; asst. to pres. internat. pgms. Univ. of Tulsa 1990-95; mem: Council on Fgn. Relations (N.Y.), Century Assn. (N.Y.), University Club (N.Y.), Am. Fgn. Service Assn. (W.D.C.); author: The Basmachi, A Study of Soviet Nationalities, 1952, Berlin: From Symbol of Confrontation to Touchstone of Stability (Praeger, 1989); mil: US Army 1941-46, col. USAR (Ret.); Unitarian; rec: tennis, golf, music. Res: 6535 Caminito Kittansett La Jolla 92037

KLEIN, HERBERT GEORGE, newspaper editor; b. Apr. 1, 1918, Los Angeles; s. George and Amy (Cordes) K.; m. Marjorie G. Galbraith, Nov. 1, 1941; children: Joanne L. (Mrs. Robert Mayne), Patricia A. (Mrs. John Root); edn: AB, USC, 1940; Hon. Doctorate, Univ. San Diego, 1989. Career: reporter Alhambra Post-Advocate, 1940-42, news editor, 1946-50; spl. corr. Copley Newspapers, 1946-50, Washington corr., 1950; with San Diego Union, 1950-68: editorial writer 1950-52, editorial page editor 1952-56, associate editor 1956-57, executive editor 1957-58, editor 1959-68; mgr. communications Nixon for President Campaign 1968-69, director communications Executive Branch U.S. Govt., White House, 1969-73; v.p. corp. relations Metromedia, Inc. 1973-77; media cons. 1977-80; editor-in-chief, v.p. Copley Newspapers Inc., San Diego 1980–; mem. Advertising Council, N.Y.; publicity dir. Eisenhower-Nixon campaign in Calif., 1952; asst. press secty. V.P. Nixon campaign, 1956; press secty. Nixon inaugural, 1957, Nixon campaign, 1958; spl. asst., press secty. to Nixon, 1959-61, press secty. Nixon for Gov. campaign, 1962; dir. communications Nixon Presdl. campaign, 1968; awards: Fourth Estate award USC 1947, Alumnus of Yr. USC 1971, Gen. Alumni merit award 1977, spl. service to journalism award 1969, headliner of yr. Greater Los Angeles Press Club 1971, 1st Fourth Estate award of San Diego St. Univ. 1986, Comm. Champion Hall of Champions 1993, Boys and Girls Club Golden Man Award 1993, Chamber of Commerce "Spirit of San Diego" award 1995; civic bds: USC (trustee), Holiday Bowl (chmn.), Clair Burgener Found. of Gr. San Diego Sports Assn. (dir.), Scripps Found. (chair, internat. com.), Super Bowl XXII and XXXII, Olympic Tng. Site Com., San Diego Econ. Devel. Com. (bd.); mem. Am. Soc. Newspaper Editors (past dir.), Calif. Press Assn., Pub. Relations Soc. Am., Gen. Alumni USC (past pres.), Alhambra Jr. C.of C. (past pres.), Greater San Diego C.of C. (exec. com.), Sigma Delta Chi (nat. com. chmn., gen. activities chmn. nat. conv. 1958), Delta Chi, Kiwanis, Rotary (hon.), Commonwealth Club Calif., Bohemian Club, Fairbanks CC; mil: comdr. USNR 1942-46. Res: 5110 Saddlery Sq POB 8935 Rancho Santa Fe 92067

KLEIN, JAMES MIKEL, musician, university professor, orchestra director; b. Aug. 27, 1953, Greenville, S.C.; s. Rubin Harry Klein and Billie Joyce (Mikel) Newton; edn: BMus, Univ. of Texas, Austin 1975, MM, 1977; DMA, Univ. Cincinnati, 1981. Career: tchg. asst. Univ. of Texas, Austin 1975-77, Univ. Cinti. 1977-78; asst. prof. Valparaiso Univ., Ind. 1978-84; prof. CSU Stanislaus, Turlock, Calif. 1984–; music director Modesto Symphony Youth Orch., 1986–; guest conductor/clinician, worldwide 1984–; adjudicator (music) nat., 1978–;

prin. trombone Austin Sym. Orch., Tx. 1973-77, trombone Modesto Sym. Orch., Ca. 1984–; awards: Meritorious Prof. CSU Stanislaus 1988, Outstanding Young Men of Am. 1990, Calif. Orchestra Director of Yr. 1994, listed Who's Who in Edn., in Entertainment, in the West; mem: Calif. Orch. Directors Assn. (pres. 1990-92), Am. Sym. Orch. League 1984–, Calif. Music Educators Assn. (bd. 1990-94), Am. Fedn. Musicians 1973–, Nat. Sch. Orchestra Assn. (public relations chair, 1994–); civic: Turlock Arts Fund for Youth (pres. 1986-88), Internat. Friendship Com. City Modesto (subcom. 1989-91), Big Bros./Bis Sisters Modesto (vol.); contbr. articles in various publs., 1978–; rec: backpacking, reading, sailing, racquet sports.

KLEIN, RAYMOND MARTIN, periodontist; b. Jan. 4, 1947, New York; s. Max Ludwig and Suzette Martina (Perls) K.; edn: BS, City Coll. N.Y. 1968; DMD, Univ. Pa. 1972; lic. periodontist Calif., Ga., N.Y. Career: resident periodontics Ga. Retardation Center, 1975-76; periodontics splst., Fairfield 1976–; San Jose 1976-77; Dixon 1980-83; Vallejo 1981-87; cons. dental research Nutran Inc., Atlanta 1974-86; author weekly newspaper column Daily Republic, Fairfield 1983–; contbr. articles to profl. jours.; awards: NIH grant (1971); mem: Downtown Homeowners Assn. Fairfield (pres. 1977), Fairfield City Center Redevel. Project, Acad. Gen. Dentistry (fellow), Am. Acad. Periodontology, ADA, Bay Area Dentists Study Club, Calif. Dental Assn., Calif. Soc. Periodontists, Napa Solano Dentist Soc. (chmn. pub. rels. com. 1983-84, chmn. contg. end. com. 1985, bd. dirs., pres. elect 1989), Western Soc. Periodontology, Travis Hist. Soc. (chmn. audio-visual dept. Travis Air Force Museum); mil: USAF 1972-74; lt. col. USAFR 1985–. Res: 745 Jackson St Fairfield 94533 Ofc: 1225 Travis Blvd Fairfield 94533

KLEIN, STANLEY R., vascular surgeon; b. Jan. 18, 1950, Los Angeles; s. Harold J. and Helen P. Klein; m. Joan F. Wright, MD, May 28, 1988; edn: BS magna cum laude, UCLA, 1971; MD, UC San Diego, 1976; cert. Am. Bd. Surgery, 1981, spl. cert. in vascular surgery, and in critical care, 1987; qualified Bd. of Emergency Med., 1987. Career: nucleic acid resrch. fellow Molecular Biology Inst. UCLA 1970-71; intern Harbor/UCLA Med. Ctr., Torrance 1976-77, gen. surgery resident (chief res. 1980-81) 1977-81, vascular surgery fellow 1981-82, clin. fellow in emergency med. 1972; instr. human anat. UCSD 1979-80, instr. dept. surg. Harbor/UCLA Med. Ctr. 1981-82; assoc. prof. surg. UCLA Sch. of Medicine, Los Angeles, 1982, and assoc. prof. anat., 1985; vascular surgeon, dir. trauma svs. Harbor/UCLA Med. Ctr., Torrance 1984–; recipient distinguished tchg. award UCSD 1980, golden apple tchg. award UCLA Med. Sch. 1986; mem: Am. Heart Assn., So. Calif. Vascular Surg. Soc., L.A. Surg. Soc., Am. Diabetes Assn., Am. Lung Soc., Long Beach Surg. Soc., Am. Coll. Surgeons (Fellow), Clin. Soc. for Vascular Surgery, Assn. for Acad. Surg., Univ. Assn. of Emergency Med., Critical Care Soc., N.Y. Acad. Scis., Soc. of Surgey for the Alimentary Tract, Am. Assn. of Clin. Anatomists, Internat. Cardiovascular Soc., Am. Assn. for Surgery of Trauma; contbr. numerous research papers, abstracts, med. jour. articles and book chapts.; sci. exhibs. and spkr. nat. symposia; rec: fishing, mt. climbing. Ofc: Harbor-UCLA Medical Center 1000 W Carson St Torrance 90509

KLERER, JOSEPH, gynecologist; b. Dec. 11, 1936, Poland, nat. 1955; s. Sam and Anna (Schwartz) K.; m. Lenore Lewis, div. 1977; 1 son, Andy b. 1965; m. Dahana L., July 30, 1979; edn: BA, N.Y. Univ., 1958; MD, Albert Einstein Coll. of Med., 1962; Diplomate Am. Bd. OB-Gyn. Career: intern King Co. Med. Ctr., Bklyn. 1962-63; ob-gyn resident Bronx Municipal Hosp., NY 1963-67; clin. instr. Albert Einstein Coll. of Med., 1966-67; gynecologist pvt. practice, 1969–; chief of service Dept. Ob-Gyn Whittier Hosp. Med. Ctr., Whittier, Calif. 1988-92; chief of staff Whittier Hospital Med. Ctr. 1993; honors: Phi Beta Kappa, Alpha Omega Alpha; mem: Fellow Am. Coll. Obstets. & Gynecol., L.A. Co. Ob-Gyn Soc., Am. Soc. for Colposcopy & Cervical Pathology, PSRO (v.p.); editl. bd. OB-Gyn Collected Letters Internat. (1976–); mil: capt. USAF 1967-69; rec: computers, tennis. Res: 110 Ramona Dr Fullerton 92633 Ofc: 15141 E Whittier Blvd Ste 300 Whittier 90603

KLIMOSKI, DAVID BRUCE, personnel consultant, consulting chemical engineer; b. June 20, 1946, Denver, Colo.; s. Stephen and Helen W. (Schon) K.; m. Marilyn Simpson, Aug. 29, 1970; edn: BS chem. engrg. Univ. of Colo., Boulder 1968; grad. stu. Chem. Eng., UC Berkeley 1970-71; Reg. Chem. Engr. Calif. 1977; Cert. Employment Splst., Calif. Inst. for Educating Employment Counselors (CIEPC) 1987; Cert. Personnel Cons., Nat. Aassn. of Personnel Consultants (NAPC). Career: design engr. Standard Oil Co. of Calif., S.F. 1968-73; sr. project engr. Procon, Inc. Div. Universal Oil Products, Walnut Creek 1977; sr. project engr. Enserv, Inc., Concord 1978; owner Professional Design Services, Consulting Engineer 1978–; owner Diablo Personnel Services, placement agy. 1985-92; owner Continental Training Center, vocational edn. 1990–; dir. Chief Equipment Corp., Denver, Colo. 1978-95; prof. Chapman Univ., Concord Campus 1995–; recipient Community Service Award (Profl. Design Services), Peralta Comm. Coll. Dist., East Bay Skills Ctr., Oakland; mem: Instrument Soc. of Am., Am. Inst. of Chem. Engrs. (senior), Calif. Assn. of Personnel Consultants (state dir. 1987-88, treas. 1988-89, 2d v.p. 1989-91, 1st v.p. 1991-92; chapt. pres. Mt. Diablo 1987-88), Calif. Assn. of Rehab. Profls. (CARP) 1989–, Concord C.of C.; civic: Indsl. Edn. Council Office Support Task

Force Contra Costa Co., advy. com. Engring. Aide Pgm. ROP, Central Contra Costa Co. Employer Advy. Group, employer advy. com. East Bay Skills Ctr. Oakland; rec: golf, swim. Ofc: Continental Training Center 1333 Willow Pass Rd Ste 212 Concord 94520

KLINE, CARL GEORGE, consulting company president; b. Sept. 5, 1935, La Harpe, Ill.; s. Davis Carl and Helen Harriet (Gillette) K.; m. Nancy Truran, Dec. 28, 1957 (div. 1971); m. Leona Tompkins, Nov. 26, 1988; children: Stephen b. 1961, Douglas b. 1965, Dana b. 1968; edn: BS, Central Mo. St. Univ. 1959; MBA, Ohio Univ. 1983. Career: regional rep. Gillette Co., Boston, Mass. 1960-64; mgr. human resources, Magnavox Co., Ft. Wayne, Ind. 1964-67; dir. personnel Emerson Electric Co., St. Louis, Mo. 1967-70; pres. Kline Co., Dayton, Ohio 1970-77; mgr. manpower NCR, Cambridge, Ohio 1977-82, product mgr. 1982-84; pres. Nat. Cons. Referrals, San Diego 1984–; tchr. Palomar Coll., San Marcos 1987-88; Mira Costa Coll., Oceanside 1987-88; Nat. Univ., S.D. 1986-88; awards: Bd. Health Guernsey Co. plaque 1983, Six Co. Mental Health plaque 1983; mem: Cambridge Democratic Soc. (pres. 1982-83), Cambridge C.of C. (v.p. 1982), Guernsey Co. Bd. Health (pres. 1983), Six Co. Mental Health (trustee 1983); author Coll. Recruiting, 1983, How to Select Computer Hardware & Software, 1983, Practical Tools of Consulting, 1987; mil: pvt. 1c. AUS 1954-56; rec: writing, public speaking, sailing. Address: San Diego 92121

KLINE, PAMELA IRIS, marketing consultant; b. Aug. 23, 1958, Pittsburgh, Pa.; s. Robert Edward and Rae (Marks) Kline; edn: cert. Univ. of Paris, Fr. 1979; BA, Harvard Coll., 1980; MBA, Harvard Bus. Sch., 1984. Career: mgr. AT&T, Phila. 1980-82; VISA, San Francisco 1983; v.p. Prognostics, Menlo Park 1984-91; dir. Diefenbach Elkins, S.F. 1991-93; ptnr. Regis McKenna, Inc. 1992–; mem: Harvard Fundraising Gp. 1980- (chair Harvard Schs. & Scholarship, San Mateo 1984–), BRAVO 1992–; Republican; rec: scuba, aerobics, swimming, travel, reading. Res: 570 Beale St #416 San Francisco 94105

KLINGE, JOHN EDGAR, investment banker; b. Mar. 1, 1956, Vallejo; s. Andy and Christine Nova (Pasley) K.; edn: BS acctg., summa cum laude, Golden Gate Univ. 1978; MBA, UCLA 1985; C.P.A. Calif. 1980. Career: mgr. Peat Marwick Mitchell & Co., San Francisco 1978-83; assoc. Bank of Am. Capital Markets 1983-85; v.p. investment banking, corp. restructures Security Pacific Merchant Bank (now Bank of Am.), Los Angeles 1985–; honors: Beta Gamma Sigma, Golden Gate Acctg. Scholarship; mem: Am. Inst. CPA, UCLA Mgmt. Alumni Assn., Urban Land Inst.; rec: classic cars, golf, water skiing. Res: 1468 N Grand Oaks Ave Pasadena 91104 Ofc: Bank of America 333 S Beaudry Ave Dept 4346 Los Angeles 90017

KLINGENSMITH, ARTHUR PAUL, relocation and redevelopment consultant; b. May 23, 1949, Los Angeles; s. Paul A. and Hermine Elinore (Wacek) K.; edn: AA soc. sci., Indian Valley Jr. Coll. 1976; BA indsl. psych., San Francisco State Univ. 1979; MA indsl. psych., Columbia Pacific Univ. 1980; desig: senior right of way cand., Internat. Right of Way Assn. Career: USAF radio ops. instr., Biloxi, Miss. 1968-72; air traffic controller, Novato, Ca. 1972-74; right of way agent Calif. Dept. Transp., San Francisco 1978-85, sr. right of way agent, Sacto. 1985-87; relocation and redevel. cons., statewide Calif., 1984–, founder, v.p. Associated Right of Way Services Inc., 1989-92; tech. cons. computerization of Right of Way process, CalTrans; mem: Am. Arbitration Assn., Internat. Right of Way Assn. (course instr. 1980–), Marin Co. Bd. of Realtors, Nat. Assn. of Housing and Redevel. Officials (NAHRO), Inst. for Noetic Sciences, Am. Presidents Assn.; civic: Kentfield Med. Found. (bd. 1987-89), P.A.S.T. Found. (bd. 1994–); mil: s/sgt. US Air Force 1968-74, merit service award; Republican; Prot.; rec: auto. restoration, painting, study of Light. Res: POB 1050 Novato 94948

KLONER, MARC OWEN, computer software company president; b. Sept. 23, 1946, Canton, Ohio; s. Simon and Mildred K.; m. Jane, Feb. 15, 1970; child: Megan b. 1983; edn: BE in aero. & astro. engrng., Ohio St. Univ. 1968, MS, 1969. Career: assoc. engr. McDonnell Douglas, St. Louis, Mo. 1968; senior engr. Lockheed, Burbank 1969-72; systems analyst NASA Jet Propulsion Lab., La Canada 1972-79; founder/pres. KComp Systems Inc. (computer software co.), Glendale 1979–; rec: tennis. Res: 290 Kempton Rd Glendale 91203 Ofc: KComp Systems Inc 535 N Brand Blvd Ste 601 Glendale 91203

KLOTZ, RICHARD DAVID, ophthalmologist; b. Sept. 6, 1942, NY, NY; s. Arthur Aaron and Rose (Cohen) K.; m. Barbara Joan Caplin, Feb. 19, 1972; children: Alison b. 1975, Evan b. 1978, Julie b. 1987; edn: exchange student in internal med. Naestved Hosp., Denmark 1967; BA biology, Grinnell Coll., 1964; MD, St. Univ. N.Y., Upstate 1968; cert. Am. Bd. Ophthalmology, 1976. Career: rotating intern, surgeon USPHS Hosp., San Francisco 1968-70; ophthalmology resident North Shore Univ. Hosp., Cornell Univ., Manhasset, N.Y. 1970-73, instr. ophth. 1973-80; pvt. practice Manhasset and Great Neck, N.Y. 1973-80; staff phys. Long Beach (Calif.) Eye Inst., 1980-81; solo practice, Huntington Beach 1981–, med. dir. Pacifica Eye Ctr., H.B.; assoc. med. dir. St. Mary's Eye Surgical Ctr., Santa Monica; bd. dirs. Assn. Ophth. (asst. v.p.), bd. dirs. Cataract Resrch. Inst. Calif., bd. dirs. MD Eye Pac of Calif.; awards: Western Ophthalmic Laser Svs. co-investigator/grantee, AMA phys. recogn. (4); Fellow Am. Acad. Ophthalmology, A.C.S., Interam. Coll. Phys. and Surgeons, Internat.

Coll. Surgeons, Eye Bank Assn. of Am.; Republican; Jewish; rec: oenophile, skiing. Res: 1 Orion Irvine 92715 Ofc: Pacifica Eye Center 18800 Main St Ste 101 Huntington Beach 92648

KLOWDEN, MICHAEL LOUIS, lawyer; b. April 7, 1945, Chicago, Ill.; s. Roy and Esther (Siegal) K.; m. Patricia Doede, June 15, 1968; children: Kevin B. b. 1972, Deborah C. b. 1979; edn: BA, Univ. Chgo. 1967; JD, Harvard Univ. 1970; admitted St. Bar Calif. 1970. Career: atty., assoc., ptnr. Mitchell Silberberg & Knupp, Los Angeles 1970-78; mng. ptnr., mem. Nat. Mgmt. Com., Morgan Lewis & Bockius, L.A. 1978–; dir. Jefferies & Co. 1987; trustee Univ. Chgo. 1988; mem: Am. Bar Assn. Ofc: Morgan Lewis & Bockius 801 S Grand Ave Los Angeles 90017

KMET, JOSEPH PAUL, pharmacist; b. Jan. 11, 1942, Chgo.; s. John Norman and Elizabeth Charlotte (Posh) K.; m. Rebecca Patterson, Mar. 29, 1969; edn: BS pharm., Univ. Ariz. 1971; MS nuclear pharmacy, USC 1973; MS computer sci., Corpus Christi St. Univ. 1984; reg. pharm. Calif., Ariz. Career: enlisted USN 1959-63, USNR 1963-75, staff pharmacist Wadsworth VA Hosp., Los Angeles 1973-75, commd. lt. comdr. Med. Service Corps USN 1975-: nuclear pharmacist Naval Regional Med. Center, San Diego 1975-82; asst. chief pharmacist, radiation safety ofcr. Naval Hosp., Corpus Christi, Tx. 1982-85; chief pharmacist 1985, chmn. Mgmt. Info. Sys. Com. 1983-85; hd. Mgmt. Info. Dept., Naval Medical Command, Mid-Atlantic Region, Norfolk, Va. 1985-89; pharmacist ofcr. Naval Hosp., Portsmouth, Va. 1989-90; pharmacist ofcr. Naval Hosp., N.A.S. Lemoore, Calif. 1990-93; pharmacist, Kaweah Delta Hosp., Visalia, Calif. 1993–; awards: USPHS scholar, 1968-70; mem: Am. Soc. Hosp. Pharmacists 1968–, Soc. of Nuclear Medicine, Calif., So. Calif. Soc. Hosp. Pharmacists 1973-82; contbr. article in J. Nucl. Med., 1979; sci. exhib. Radiol. Soc. N. Am., Chgo. 11/81; mil: lt. cmdr. US Navy 1975-93; Republican; Episcopalian; rec: reading, bicycling, gardening. Ofc: Kaweah Delta Hospital Pharmacy, Visalia

KMET, REBECCA EUGENIA (PATTERSON), pharmacist; b. June 17, 1948, Ellisville, Miss.; d. Eugene Roberts and Ruth Winn (Pettis) Patterson; m. Joseph Kmet, March 29, 1969; edn: BS, Univ. of Ariz. 1970; MBA, National Univ. 1980; reg. pharmacist Calif., Ariz., Tex. Career: pharmacist Defender Star Community Pharmacy, Tucson, Ariz. 1971-72, Santa Monica Bldg. Profl. Pharmacy, Santa Monica 1972-73; US Veteran's Admin., Wadsworth VA Hosp., W. Los Angeles 1974-75; pharmacist Kaiser San Diego Med. Ctr., San Diego 1979-82; participant Current Strategy Forum, Naval War Coll., 1981; profl. continuing edn. instr.; honors: Presdl. achiev. Nat. Congl. Com. 1987, Rho Chi, USPHS Scholar 1968-70; mem: Marine Corps Historical Found., Navy Historical Found., Wilson Assocs., U.S. English PAC, Am. Immigration Control PAC, Kappa Epsilon; mil: Med. Service Corps USNR 1975-78; pub. article "Is U.S. Military Power Weakened by Women in the Services?" Amphibious Warfare Rev., Summer 1988; Independent; Episcopalian; rec: reading, art needlework, gardening, writing. Res: 985 Murphy Dr Lemoore 93245

KNAPP, GLENN, educator, lobbyist; b. Nov. 14, 1939, Salinas; s. Manuel M. and Laura Knapp; m. Jacqueline Barbara Godel, Oct. 25, 1979; edn: AA, Monterey Peninsula Coll., 1961; BS econs., Coll. of Notre Dame, 1974, MBA in fin., 1975; JD, Blackstone Law Ctr., 1975; PhD in fin. & econs., Nova Colleges, 1983; Calif. tchg. creds. in acctg. and mgmt. 1980, comp. sci. 1987. Career: pub. acct. prin., Redwood City 1972-79; co. pres. Western, Redwood City 1977-79; computer analyst 1979–; asst. prof. bus. Embry Riddle Aero. Univ., Moffett Field, and Coll. Notre Dame, Belmont 1976-79; assoc. prof. fin. & computer Armstrong Univ., Berkeley 1982-91; assoc. prof. Nat. Hispanic Univ., San Jose 1991–; City College of San Francisco, S.F. 1991–; reg. lobbyist U.S. House of Representatives, Wash. D.C. 1982–; faculty City Univ., Bellevue, Wash. 1989–; honors: Armstrong Coll. tchr. of yr. (1984, 86); mem: Cert. Internal Auditors, Am. Mensa Soc., Fin. Club Armstrong Univ., San Mateo Co. Investment Club San Carlos (pres.); insp. and precinct judge Precinct 460047 San Mateo Co.; author 4 books: Assembly Language Programming (1988) Basic Computer Programming (1987), Ednl. Research & Evaluation (1987), Cobol Handbook for Microcomputers (1990); mil: lt. Fin. Corps USAR; Republican; R.Cath.; rec: computer, boating, reading. Res: 773 Dartmouth Ave San Carlos 94070

KNAPP, J. BURKE, international consultant; b. Jan. 25, 1913, Portland, Ore.; s. Joseph Burke and Cornelia Ann (Pinkham) K.; m. Hilary Eaves, April 5, 1939; m. Iris Hay Edie, Oct. 19, 1976; children: Louis b. 1942, Rosalind b. 1945, Elise b. 1954, Michael b. 1955; edn: AB in econs., Stanford Univ., 1933; BA in politics, philosophy and econs. (Rhodes Scholar), Oxford Univ., 1935, B.Litt, 1936, MA, 1939. Career: asst. to mng. dir. Brown Harriman & Co. Ltd., internat. inv. banking firm, London, Eng. 1936-40; with the Federal Reserve 1940-48, economist Internat. Sect., dir. Internat. Div. and spl. asst. to the Chmn., on leave with State Dept. as econ. adv. in occupied Ger. 1944-45; with U.S. State Dept. 1948-52, economic adv. to 1st U.S. Delegation to NATO in London, Eng. 1 yr., U.S. co-chmn. of Jt. Brazilian-U.S. Econ. Devel. Commn., Rio de Janeiro, Brazil 1 yr.; with the World Bank 1952-78: dir. ops. in Latin Am. 1952-56, v.p. in chg. worldwide lending ops. and chmn. loan com. 1956-72, senior v.p. for ops. and chmn. bd. dirs. in absence of the pres. 1972-78, ret. 1978; cons. to World Bank on policy matters, 1978-81; internat. cons. 1982-: sr. adv.

Morgan Grenfell & Co., London, Eng. 1983–; honors: Order of Boyaca, 1980, Stanford Univ. disting. service, 1981, Order of Rising Sun, 1978, Rhodes Scholar Oxford Univ., 1933-36; mem: Wash. Drama Soc. (trustee, pres. 1953-65), Mt. Vernon Coll. (trustee, chmn. exec. com. 1966-72), Stanford Univ. Libraries (vis. com.), Metropolitan Club; Democrat; Prot.; rec: swimming, theatre. Res: 8 Arastradero Rd Portola Valley 94028

KNAUFT, MILFORD ROY, JR., chairman Orange County assessment appeals board; b. Aug. 26, 1918, St. Paul, Minn.; s. Milford Roy and Marie Camille (Simonet) K.; m. Doris Louise Bovee, Jan. 18, 1946; children: Robert Lee b. 1946, Nancy Louise b. 1949, Sally Ann b. 1954; edn: UCLA 1936-40. Career: co-owner, gen. mgr. Hollywood Wholesale Paper Corp., Hollywood 1938-61; dist. rep. Congressman Charles Wiggins, Fullerton 1975-79; Cong. Wm. Dannemeyer 1980; exec. dir. World Affairs Council of Orange Co., Santa Ana 1979-88; dir. Yorba Linda Water Dist. 1966-92, Metropolitan Water Dist., L.A. 1979-93; awards: Golden Bear and Silver Beaver BSA 1979, 81; civic: Orange Co. BSA (past pres.), World Affairs Council Orange Co. (bd. dirs.), Rotary Intl. Yorba Linda (Paul Harris Fellow 1983), Richard Nixon Library & Found. (bd. dir.), Orange Co. Council B.S.A. (bd. dir.); mil: lt. US Army Air Corps 1943-46, decorated D.F.C. and Air Medal, 1945; Republican; Presbyterian. Res: 5765 Sunmist Ln Yorba Linda 92686

KNEBEL, JACK GILLEN, lawyer; b. Jan. 28, 1939, Washington, D.C.; s. Fletcher and Amalia Eleanor (Rauppius) K.; m. Linda Karin Ropertz, Feb. 22, 1963; children: Hollis Anne b. 1966 (dec. 1983), Lauren Beth b. 1968; edn: BA, Yale Univ. 1960; LL.B, Harvard Law Sch. 1966; admitted St. Bar Calif. Career: atty., assoc. McCutchen Doyle Brown & Enersen, San Francisco 1966-74; ptnr. 1974-94, of counsel 1994–; advy. council Hastings Coll. Trial Advocacy 1981-91, chair 1990-91; dir. Assoc. mem. S.F. Lawyers Com. for Urban Affairs 1991-93; mem: Am. Coll. Trial Lawyers (fellow), Maritime Law Assn. U.S., Am.Bar Assn., Orinda Assn. (dir., pres. 1972-74), Sea Ranch Assn. (dir., pres. 1978-79), Citizens to Preserve Orinda (co-chair), World Trade Club; article pub. in profl. jour., 1989; mil: lt.j.g. USN 1960-63; Democrat; United Ch. of Christ; rec: rowing, running. Ofc: McCutchen Doyle Brown & Enersen 3 Embarcadero Center San Francisco 94111

KNEISEL, CHRISTOPHER DWIGHT, teacher; b. Jan. 31, 1956, Burbank; s. William George and Joyce Rosemary (Fainot) K.; m. Josephine Bernadette Vasari, June 30, 1984; children: Elizabeth Anna-Maria b. 1991, Gregory John Paul b. 1993; edn: AA cum laude L.A. Valley Coll. 1977; BA, CSU Los Angeles, 1980, music credential, 1982, grad. studies CSU, 1987, 1991–. Career: instrumental music tchr. Hollenbeck Jr. H.S., L.A. 1982-85; Don Benito, Madison & Linda Vista Elem. Schs., Pasadena 1985-87; tchr. Don Benito Fundamental Sch. 1987–; participant Path to Math., UCLA, 1988-90; mem: Music Educators Nat. Conf. L.A. 1986; honors: Sigma Alpha Phi music scholar 1976, Burbank Womens Chorus music scholar 1974, CSU music scholarships, outstanding service award CSULA, CSULA Newman Club (pres. 1981); founding bd. mem. Burbank Chamber Orchestra 1991–; mem: Burbank Chamber Orchestra (cellist), West Los Angeles Symphony (cellist), Phi Alpha Theta history frat., Eta Xi chpt. CSULA 1992–; mem: United Tchrs. of Pasadena (former dir. area 8), Calif. Tchrs. Assn., Nat. Space Soc., former Burbank Symphony (cellist), former Pasadena Community Orch. (cellist); former mem: Burbank Symphony Assn., So. Calif. Sch. Band & Orchestra Assn. (mgr. hon. orch. 1983), L.A. Music Tchrs. Assn.; Republican; R.Cath. (usher), mem. Confraternity of the Most Holy Rosary; rec: cello, history, model railroads, hiking, writing. Res: 1920 N Niagara St Burbank 91505 Ofc: Don Benito Fundamental School 3700 Denair St Pasadena 91107

KNIGHT, JEFFREY RICHARD, senior systems requirements analyst; b. Apr. 22, 1962, Salt Lake City; s. Richard M. and Donna H. (Hallman) K.; m. Carrie Lyn Jackson; edn: BBA, Cal Poly, 1984, MBA, 1986. Career: senior systems requirements analyst Loral, Camarillo 1985–; mem.: Toastmasters Internat. 1995–, Co. Mgmt. Assn., Co. Activities Coord. Com. (pres. 1990-93), Rose Float Alumni Assn. (pres. 1991-93, treas. 1985-86, bd. 1987-88), Rose Float Com. (pub. rel. 1983-84, chmn. 1984-85), Thailand Dart Assn., So. Calif. Darts Assn., Hillcrest Park HOA (treas. 1990-92, pres. 1992-93); Republican. Res: 2143 Saxe Court Thousand Oaks 91360 Ofc: Unisys 5151 Camino Ruiz Camarillo 93011-6004

KNIGHT, JESSIE J., JR., association executive; b. Oct. 27, 1950, Springfield, Mo.; s. Jessie J., Sr. and Doris Marie (Hanks) K.; m. B. Camille Williams M.D., Aug. 19, 1978; child: Jessica b. 1980; edn: BA psych., St. Louis Univ., 1973; S.L.U. fellowship Univ. of Madrid, Spain 1972; MBA in mktg., Univ. Wis., Madison 1975; U.S. mem. British-Am. Project for the Successor Generation (lifetime), Johns Hopkins/ Royal Inst. of Internat. Affairs 1990. Career: mktg. mgr. Cervecuria Hondurena, div. Castle & Cooke Foods, San Pedro Sula, Honduras, Central Am. 1975-77; sales plng. mgr. Bumble Bee Seafoods, Castle & Cooke Foods, San Francisco 1974-77; mktg. plng. mgr., group product mgr. Dole Pineapple, Castle & Cooke Foods, S.F. 1979-81; dir. new bus. devel. Castle & Cooke Foods, 1981-83; dir. U.S. and Canadian mktg. Dole Food Co., Castle & Cooke, S.F. 1983-85; v.p. mktg. and corp. ofcr. San Francisco Chronicle, San

Francisco Examiner, 1985-92; senior v.p. San Francisco Chamber of Commerce, 1992–; instr., cons. American Press Inst., Reston, Va. 1988; awards: CLIO awards for ad excellence 1986, 87, Golden Lion, Cannes Film Fest., Fr. 1986, best of show advt. Internat. Newspaper Mktg. Assn., Toronto 1987, 1991, Eleanor Roosevelt Humanitarian Award of UN Assn. 1991; bd. trustees Golden Gate Univ.; bd. Wis. Bus. Alumni, Univ. Wis. Sch. of Bus.; mem. World Affairs Council S.F. (trustee 1986–, v.chmn. exec. com.), Council on Fgn. Rels. (N.Y.), S.F. Com. on Fgn. Affairs, Internat. Visitors Ctr., St. Francis Found., The Asia Found. Ctr. for Asian & Pacific Affairs; clubs: Olympic, The City; Republican (Nat. Com.'s Pres.'s Club); R.Cath.; rec: classical guitar. Ofc: San Francisco Chamber of Commerce 465 California St San Francisco 94104

KNIGHT, NANCY MORSE, lawyer; b. March 7, 1931, Boston, Mass.; d. Charles William and Lillian Frances (Kerrigan) Morse; m. H. Warren Knight, III, June 12, 1951 (div. 1974); children: Andrew b. 1956, Ellen b. 1957, Elizabeth b. 1962, John b. 1964; edn: BA cum laude, Smith Coll. 1952; JD, UCLA 1974. Career: womens program dir. WCHV radio, Charlottesville, Va. 1952-55; atty., assoc. Sheldon L. Foreman, Tustin 1974-86; Theodore S. Wentworth, Newport Beach 1986–; honors: Phi Beta Kappa; mem: Jr. League, St. James Episcopal Ch., Episcopal Seminary Claremont (bd. 1974-84); Episcopalian. Res: 2517 Vista Baya Newport Beach 92660 Ofc: Law Office of Theodore S. Wentworth 4631 Teller Ave Ste 100 Newport Beach 92660

KNIGHT, VIRGINIA FRANCES, writer, former first lady of California; b. Oct. 12, 1918, Fort Dodge, Iowa; d. Lawrence Frederick and Emma Julia (Miller) Piergue: stepfather: 1923–, E. B. Hershberger, advt. exec. Internat. Harvester Co.; 2 bros: Ralph Gotch Piergue (dec. 1982), Richard B. Hershberger, atty.; mother wrote ofcl. welcome song for 1932 LA Olympic Games; m. C. Lyle Carlson (lt. 15th AF, killed in action WWII 1944), June 28, 1940; m. 2d. Goodwin Jess Knight, Aug. 2, 1954 (Superior Ct. judge 1935-46, lt. gov. Calif. 1946-53, gov. Calif. 1953-59); grad. Los Angeles H.S. 1937. Career: fashion model, Warner Bros. theatres, radio 1937-42, pioneer TV pgms. KHJ, Don Lee Network 1937; Douglas Aircraft 'accomodation sales & emergency procurement/ civic and vets rehabilitation work/ entertainment pgms. for vets. hosps., "Victory House" Pershing Sq./active war bond drives, WWII; assoc. producer, participant TV Tele-Forum and Freedom Forum, 1947-54; First Lady of Calif. 1954-58, ofcl. hostess Nat. Republican Conv., S.F. 1956, planted Virginia Knight Camellia Capitol Park 1958, estab. collection of portraits of Calif. First Ladies for Gov.'s Mansion forseeing it would become a museum; current owner/opr. Elephant-Eagle Gold Mines, Mojave; honors: nat. cit. for sale of war bonds 1941-46, Nat. Viola Queen, Mil. Order of the Purple Heart 1954-55, Dr. in Metaphysics, St. Andrews Ecumen. Coll., London 1955, Hon. Poet Laureate State of Del. 1955, Outstanding Woman of Calif. press award 1956, Ten Best Dressed Women list So. Calif. Fashion Council 1959, fellow (poetry) Am. Inst. of Fine Arts 1969, life mem. Internat. Clover Poetry Assn., Soc. of Literary Designates, Wash DC 1970, Dame Commander, Order of the Crown of Thorns, San Luigi "Disting. Humanitarian" 1977, listed World Who's Who of Women (1989, 90, 91, 92, 93, 94, 95), Ctf. Appreciation, City of Hope Med. Ctr. 1991, Golden State Award 1992, Comdr. Club "Silver Ldr." D.A.V. 1991-93, 94-95; mem: Am. Legion Aux. (past pres.), VFW Aux. (hon), Edwin Markham Poetry Soc., Repuplican Nat. Com. 1993-95; civic: founder The Music Center Building Fund Com., Soc. of Arts & Letters (nat. advy. council 1956-58), Ettie Lee Homes for Youth (nat. advy. com.), Stanford Univ. Libraries, Navy League (life mem.); author: The Golden Heritage of Goodwin Knight 1975, series of oral hist. interviews Bancroft Library, UCB 1977-80, mss. Reflections on Life with Goodwin J. Knight; "Virginia Knight California's First Lady, 1954-58," The Bancroft lib. UCB 1987; World of Poetry Golden Globe Award for "A Tribute to the Unknown Soldier" dedicated to Gen. Douglas MacArthur 1988, "Caressing Rain" 1989, "Words" 1989, Who's Who In Poetry 1989; Republican; rec: writing verse, tennis, swim. Res: 540 S Arden Blvd Los Angeles 90020-4738

KNIGHT, WILLIAM J., state assemblyman; b. Nov. 18, 1929, Noblesville, Ind.; s. William Thomas and Mary Emma (Illyes) K.; m. Gail A. Johnson, Sept. 3, 1983; edn: attended Butler Univ., Ind., Purdue Univ., Ind.; received Commission through Aviation Cadet Program. Career: USAF combat service, 253 missions, So. Vietnam; dir. USAF Fighter Attack Sys. program office, Aeronautical Sys. Div., Wright-Patterson AFB, Ohio; vice comdr. USAF Flight Test Ctr, AF Sys. Command, Edwards AFB; tech. adv. TV show, Call to Glory; councilman City of Palmdale, Calif.; mayor, City of Palmdale; Calif. State Assemblyman, elected 1992; mem. AF Sys. Command Primus Club 1988; chmn. AF Flight Test Hist. Found.; fellow, Soc. of Experimental Test Pilots; assoc. fellow, AM. Inst. of Aeronautics & Astronautics; awards: Allison Jet Trophy Race, Nat. Air Show, Dayton, Oh. 1954; Harmon Internat. Aviator's Trophy, Pres. Lyndon B. Johnson 1968; Octave Chanute Award, Inst. of Aeronautical Sciences; Nat. Aviation Hall of Fame, Dayton, Oh. 1988; Mil. honors: Disting. Flying Cross with two Oak Leaf Clusters; AF Medal with ten Oak Leaf Clusters; Legion of Merit with two Oak Leaf Clusters; mil: col., USAF; Republican; Lutheran. Ofc: State Capitol Sacramento 95814

KNORR, THEODORE HARRY, marketing consultant, editor, publisher; b. March 31, 1935, Toledo, Ohio; s. Harold T. and Eleanor (Worden) K.; m.

Donna Lee Glosup, Nov. 6, 1971; children: Susan b. 1958, Sandra b. 1959, Stephen b. 1961, Stewart b. 1964; edn: BA, Univ. of Toledo 1959; grad. studies USC 1964-65, CSU Fullerton 1978, 89; var. courses Orange Coast Coll. 1972-89. Career: printer Kahl Bros., Toledo 1951-57; sr. copywriter Toledo Scale 1957-59; copy contact J.J. Dugan Agy., Mich. 1959-63; advtg. mgr. Avery Label Co., Monrovia, Calif. 1963-65; acct. exec. Barnes Chase Advtg., Santa Ana 1965-69; owner, CASA Advtg., Orange 1970-82; mktg. dir. Ad Com/West Coast, Shrieveport, La. 1982-84; mktg. dir. J.P. Kapp & Assoc., Tustin 1984-86; owner CORE Organization Costa Mesa, 1986–; editor/pub. Today's Old West Traveler, 1989–; awards: honorary life mem. Orange Co. Ad Club, 1979, Linda Blum Award Costa Mesa Civic Playhouse, 1980, 32 various creative awards for advtg. O.C. Ad Club, 1972-82, Nat. Addy award Nat. Ad Fed., 1978, Creative Awards from Western States Advtg. Assn., 1981; mem: Bus./Devel. Assoc. of Orange Co. (pres. 1986-87), O.C. Ad Federation (pres. 1975-77), Comml. Indsl. Devel. Assn.; mem. Costa Mesa Civic Playhouse 1965–; author: bldg. industry articles, 1984; sporting goods msdg. articles, 1986, western non-fict. articles, 1989-91, mil: priv. 1st class, U.S. Army, 1956-57; Independent; rec: dude ranches, western heritage, racquetball, walking. Res: 2614A Columbine Ave Santa Ana 92704 Ofc: Today's Old West Traveler, 2796 Harbor Blvd Ste 410 Costa Mesa 92626

KNOWLES, RICHARD SETH, teacher; b. April 22, 1935, Lansing, Mich.; s. Albert Walter and Helen May (Green) K.; m. Beverly Ann Willis, Sept. 1, 1956; children: Todd Richard b. 1959, Delcinda Lee b. 1963; edn: BA, Alma Coll. 1957; MA, Mich. St. Univ. 1959; M.Min, Princeton Theology Seminary 1962. Career: asst. minister 1st Presbyterian Ch., Mineola, N.Y. 1962-63; pastor, Decatur, Mich. 1963-65, asst. minister Christian edn. Pleasant Ridge Presbyn. Ch., Cinti. 1965-68, Palm Desert Comm. Presbyn. Ch. 1968-69; tchr. Desert Sands Unified Sch. Dist. 1969–; mem: Desert Sands Tchr. Assn., Shriners, Lions. Masons; Democrat; Presbyterian; rec: coaching basketball, golf, travel. Address: 71540 Halgar Rd Rancho Mirage 92270

KOBAYASHI, TAKASHI, company president; b. Feb. 27, 1941, Tokyo, Japan; s. Mikio and Ishi (Shinozaki) K.; m. Kozue Shimada, June 15, 1969; children: Miki b. 1970, Aki b. 1974; edn: BS, Doshisha Univ. Kyoto Japan. Career: controller Akai Electric, Tokyo, Japan 1968-74; v.p. Akai Am., Compton 1974-88; pres. Exel Microelectronics, San Jose 1988–; rec: golf. Ofc: Exel Microelectronics 2150 Commerce Dr San Jose 95131

KOBLIN, DONALD DARYL, anesthesiologist, educator; b. Sept. 1, 1949, Chgo.; s. Alvin and Vera K.; edn: BS, UCLA, 1971; PhD, UC Santa Cruz, 1975; MD, Univ. Miami, 1983; residency in anesthesia, Penn State Univ., Hershey, Pa. 1983-86; bd. certified 1987. Career: postdoctoral fellow Caltech, Pasadena 1975-76; research chemist UC San Francisco, 1976-81, asst. prof. 1986-88; assoc. prof. 1988-94, prof. 1994–; honors: Phi Beta Kappa 1971; mem. AMA, ASA, IARS. Ofc: Veterans Administration Hospital, Anesthesiology Service (129), 4150 Clement St San Francisco 94121

KOBZA, DENNIS JEROME, architect; b. Sept. 30, 1933, Ullysses, Nebr.; s. Jerry Frank and Agnes Elizabeth (Lavicky) K.; m. Doris Mae Riemann, Dec. 26, 1953; children: Dennis Jerome, Diana Jill, David John; edn: BS, Healds Archtl. Engring. 1959. Career: draftsman, designer B.L. Schroder, Palo Alto 1959-60; senior draftsman, designer Ned Abrams Architect, Sunnyvale 1960-61; Kenneth Elvin Architect, Los Altos 1961-62; ptr. B.L. Schroder Architect, Palo Alto 1962-66; pvt. practice architecture, Mountain View 1966–; recipient, Solar PAL Design Award, 1983; mem: C.of C., Am. Inst. Architects, Constrn. Specifications Inst., Am. Inst. of Plant Engrs., Nat. Fedn. Ind. Bus. Org.; Rotary (pres. 1986-87); mil: USAF 1952-56. Res: 3840 May Ct Palo Alto 94303 Ofc: 2083 Old Middlefield Way Mountain View 94043

KOEHLER, CRAIG CURTIS, chiropractic doctor; b. Sept. 12, 1960 Fresno, Calif.; s. August and Rita Mae (Sherman) Koehler; edn: AA, Fresno Comm. Coll. 1981; DC, L.A. Coll. of Chiropractic 1986, BS 1986; Masters Cert. Permanent Impairment Evaluator 1994. Career: internship, Helzer Chiropractic, Bellflower, Calif. 1984-86; internship, L.A. Coll. of Chiropractic, Wittier, Calif. 1986; doctor on staff, Advanced Chiropractic, Huntington Beach, Calif. 1987-88; doctor on staff, Chiropractic Med. Ctr., Westminster, Calif. 1989-91; owner/clinic dir., Koehler Chiropractic, Huntington Beach, Calif. 1992–; instr./cons. Chiropractic Asst. Assoc., Anaheim 1985, L.A. Coll. of Chiropractic 1986, Family Fitness Ctr., Huntington Beach 1987-90, Sports Chalet, Huntington Beach 1988-89; team doctor, Oakland Ballet Co. 1988, Long Beach Ballet Co. 1989; awards: chmn. annual auction, Westminster Chamber, Westminster, Calif. 1990; humorous toastmaster, Toastmasters Internat., Santa Ana 1991; advanced presentation skills, The Cleve. Inst., San Diego 1991; mem: Orange County Chiropractic Assn. 1987-92; Council on Roentgenology 1987; Back School Adminstrn. 1986-87; Calif. Chiropractic Assn. 1988-91; civic: Westminster C. of C. 1990-92; author: publ. articles in Westminster Business Digest 1991 and Orange Co. Register; host, prod., writer, t.v. program Focus On Health 1988-91; rec: golf, skiing. Ofc: Koehler Chiropractic 5891 Warner Ave. Huntington Beach 92649

KOENIG, JAMES BENNETT, company president, geothermal scientist; b. Nov. 25, 1932, New York; s. Philip Edward and Lorraine Rose (Woldar) K.; children: Laura Bethune b. 1966, Andrea Croft b. 1968, Cassandra Gregory b. 1970; m. 2d. Deborah Grossman, 1992; edn: BS geology, Bklyn. Coll. 1954; MA geology, Ind. Univ. Bloomington 1955; USN Postgrad. Sch. 1957-58; Univ. Nev. Reno 1963-65. Career: geologic aide Howe Sound Mining Co., Snow Lake, Canada 1953; groundwater geologist U.S. Geological Survey, St. Paul, Minn. 1955-56; jr. and asst. mining geologist Calif. Div. Mines & Geology, San Francisco 1956-57, 1960-63, assoc. and sr. geologist 1965-71, supervising geologist 1971-72; pres. GeothermEx Inc., Richmond 1973–; lectr. Coll. William & Mary, Norfolk, Va. 1959-60; UC Berkeley 1968-71; cons. U.N., Ethiopia and El Salvador 1971, Viet Nam and Mozambique, 1981; World Bank, Djibouti 1985-88 and Kenya 1987–; Asian Devel. Bank, Indonesia and Philippines 1983; awards: Geothermal Resources Council J.W. Aidlin 1987; mem: Geothermal Resources Council (pres. 1989-91), Internat. Geothermal Assn. (dir. 1989-95), fin. chmn. World Geothermal Congress, Italy 1995, Geological Soc. Am. (fellow), Am. Geophysical Union, Am. Name Soc.; 80+ articles and papers pub. in profl. jours. and popular mags., 1956-95; mil: lt. USNR 1957-60; Jewish; rec: hiking, onomastics, linguistics. Res: 6332 Barrett Ave El Cerrito 94530 Ofc: GeothermEx Inc. 5221 Central Ave Ste 201 Richmond 94804

KOENIG, MARIE HARRIET KING, public relations and fundraising professional; b. Feb. 19, 1919, New Orleans, La.; d. Harold Paul and Sadie Louise (Bole) King; m. Walter William Koenig, June 24, 1956; children: Margaret Marie b. 1957, Susan Patricia b. 1957; edn: La. State Univ. Sch. of Music 1937-39; pre-law Loyola Univ. of S. New Orleans 1942-43; BS history, Univ. LaVerne, 1985. Career: secty. to the state atty. gen. of La., New Orleans 1940-44; contract writer in legal dept. Metro-Goldwyn-Mayer Studios, Culver City 1944-46; legal asst. in law firms, 1946-50; contbns. dept. mgr. of nonprofit group, also sec. asst. treas. of Found. for Soc. Res. (pub. soc. sci. books), and the Found. for Independence, L.A., 1950-56; res. supr. devel. dept. CalTech, Pasadena 1969-70; adv. fin. planning asst. Incentive Res.Corp., L.A. 1970-78; dir. comms., contbns. and pub. rels., IRC, 1978-79; fundraising cons., prin. Res. Cons. Assocs., Pasa. 1979-82; dir. devel. Republican Party of L.A. Co., 1990-92; awards: Proclamation U.S. Hse. of Reps., certs. from Eisenhower-Nixon Nat. Cpgn., Rep. Nat. Com., Calif. State Assembly; mem: Gr. L.A. Press Club, Women in Comms. Inc.; civic: Freedoms Found. at Valley Forge (charter mem. L.A. chpt., coms., mem. Advy. Coun. 21 yrs.); Nat. Trust for Hist. Preserv., Friends of the Nat. Parks at Gettysburg, Town Hall of Calif., L.A. World Affairs Council, Pacific Clinics for abused children (past devel. com.), Pasa. Opera Guild (publicity chair 2t, life Pasa. Area Opera Trust), Masquers Club, Friends of Huntington Library, L.A. Co. Mus. Art, Gene Autry Mus. We. Heritage (charter), Nat. Mus. of Women in the Arts (charter), Pasa. Arts Council (past bd. dirs.), Colonial Williamsburg (Hon. citizen); Republican (campaigner: Poulson for Mayor L.A., Eisenhower-Nixon, Goldwater for Pres., att. 1964 conv. S.F., mem. Rep. Nat. Com., Nat. Fedn. Rep. Women 1956–, East Pasa. Rep. Women (fmr.), charter Pasa. Rep. Women Fed., founder Altadena Unit #1 United Republicans of Calif., was mem. YR Club L.A., Bel Air Rep. Women); author: While Treason Flourished Over Us (lecture series), Does the Nat. Council Speak for You?; Prot.; rec: res., history, opera. Res: 205 Madeline Dr Pasadena 91105

KOERPER, MARION ALLEN, physician; b. July 8, 1943, Washington, D.C.; d. Robert Allen and Marion Russell Koerper; m. Robert Stephen Blumberg; children: Marc b. 1978, Andrew b. 1981; edn: BA, Stanford Univ. 1965; MD, UCSF 1970. Career: research asst. Carnegie Inst. Wash., Palo Alto 1965-66; intern pediatrics San Francisco Gen. Hosp. 1970-71; resident pediatrics Kaiser Found. Hosp. 1971-72; sr. resident pediatrics UCSF 1972-73, fellow pediatric hematology/oncology 1973-76, asst. clin. prof. pediatrics 1976-84, assoc. clin. prof. 1984–, dir. hemophilia treatment ctr. UCSF, 1976–; med. and sci. advy. council Nat. Hemophilia Found., N.Y.C. 1986–, v.p. for med. affairs 1994–; bd. dirs., med. advisor, past pres. Infant Devel. Center, San Francisco 1979-86; bd. dirs., med. advisor, past pres. No. Calif. Hemophilia Found. 1977–; awards: No. Calif. Hemophilia Found. Outstanding Service 1988, Alaska Hemophilia Assn. Outstanding Svc. 1993; mem: Am. Soc. of Hematology, World Fedn. Hemophilia; articles and book chpts. pub. on AIDS, hemophilia and bleeding disorders, 1976–; Democrat; rec: food, wine, travel. Ofc: University of California Dept. of Pediatrics San Francisco 94143-0106

KOHLER-LOUGIE, CHERYL, registered nurse; b. March 10, 1960, Boston, Mass.; d. Robert J. and Grace D. (DeVito) Kohler; m. Kenneth B. Lougie, June 25, 1983; edn: BS nursing, Northeastern Univ. 1983; MPH, MHSA, Univ. S.F. 1988. Career: staff nse. II Sequoia Hosp., Redwood City 1984-85; Kaiser Hosp., Santa Clara 1985-89; house supr. AMI 1988-89; charge nse. Kaiser Permanente, Santa Clara 1989-92, instr. 1989–; rep. CNA 1989-92; asst. clinical supv. Kaiser Permante, Redwood City 1992-94; cardiac cath. nurse Kaiser Permante, Santa Teresa 1994–; rec: outdoor sports, computer programming, swimming, bicycling. Address: San Jose 95136

KOHNKE, JAMES IRVING, commercial printing company executive; b. May 31, 1966, San Mateo; s. David John and Loraine (Govier) K.; m. Cathy Sue Lingenfelter; edn: BS bus. adminstrn., fin. and mktg., USC 1988. Career: v.p.,

treas. Kohnke Printing Co. Inc., San Francisco 1988–; mem: Nat. Assn. Printers & Lithographers (certified graphic arts exec. 1991), Craftsman Club-Litho. Club San Francisco, Alpha Kappa Psi, Olympic Club S.F., San Mateo Elks; Republican; R.Cath.; rec: scuba diving, automobiles, mountain biking, photography. Ofc: Kohnke Printing 375 Fremont St San Francisco 94105

KOKSHANIAN, ARTINE, physician-otolaryngologist; b. Oct. 29, 1936, Aleppo, Syria, naturalized 1981; s. Hagop and Hripsime (Aghayan) K.; m. Billie Jo Olson; children: Ara Arthur b. Feb. 10, 1989, Rita Hripsime b. Mar. 25, 1990, Alex Artin b. Feb. 5, 1992; edn: dipl. Melkonian Edn. Inst., Cyprus 1956; BS, Am. Univ. of Beirut, 1960, MD, 1965; ENT splty. tng. in Baltimore and Toronto; Fellow Am. Coll. of Otolaryngology 1976. Career: residency and fellowship Univ. of Toronto, Can.; chief of otolaryngology Service VA Hosp., Columbia, S.C. 1974-76; pvt. practice physician, ear, nose and throat splst., head and neck surgeon, Glendale, Calif. 1976–; tchg. staff White Memorial Medical Ctr., Los Angeles 1977–; named Teacher of Yr. White Memorial Otolaryngology Found. 1984; mem: Am. Acad. of Otol., L.A. Soc. of Otol., L.A. Co. Med. Assn., Calif. Med. Assn.; Glendale Masonic Lodge; publs: res. papers related to noise and Ototoxic drugs, their effect on human inner ear and hearing; Armenian Apostolic Ch.; rec: music, painting, tennis, skiing. Res: 832 Moorside Dr Glendale 91207 Ofc: Artine Kokshanian M.D. Inc. 1030 S Glendale Ave Ste 506 Glendale 91205

KOLARCZYK, ROBERT ANTHONY, physician, ophthalmologist; b. April 14, 1957, Buffalo, N.Y.; s. Thomas Tony and Josephine Anne (Wieczorek) K.; m. Karen Deanne Cherness, Sept. 5, 1983; edn: BA, summa cum laude, biochemistry, Canisius Coll. 1978; MD, Johns Hopkins Univ. Sch. Medicine 1982; cert. Am. Bd. Ophthalmology 1988. Career: ophthalmologist FHP, Fountain Valley 1986-87; Kaiser Permanente, Anaheim 1987; pvt. practice ophthalmology, Santa Barbara 1987–; mem: Am. Acad. Ophthalmology, Calif. Assn. of Ophthalmology, S.B. Ophthalmological Soc., AMA, Calif. Med. Assn., S.B. Co. Med. Soc., Johns Hopkins Med. & Surgical Soc.; Democrat; R.Cath.; rec: tennis. Res: 1220 Coast Village Rd #310 Montecito 93108 Ofc: 1801 State St Ste C Santa Barbara 93101

KOLKEY, DANIEL MILES, lawyer; b. April 21, 1952, Chicago, Ill.; s. Eugene Louis and Gilda Penelope (Cowan) K.; m. Donna Christie, May 15, 1982; children: Eugene b. 1984, William b. 1986, Christopher b. 1988, Jonathan b. 1988; edn: BA, Stanford Univ. 1974; JD magna cum laude, Harvard Law Sch. 1977. Career: law clk. to U.S. Dist. Judge Dudley Bonsal, N.Y.C. 1977-78; atty., assoc. Gibson Dunn & Crutcher, L.A. 1978-84, ptnr. 1985-94; legal affairs secty. and counsel to Gov. Pete Wilson, 1995–; dir., v.p. and c.f.o. Los Angeles Ctr. for Internat. Commercial Arbitration, 1986-90, pres. and dir., 1990-94; mem. Panel of Arbitrators, Am. Arb. Assn., 1990–; apptd. arbitrator bi-nat. panel U.S.-Canada Free Trade Agreement 1990-94; commr. Calif. Law Revision Commn. 1992- 94(v.chair 1993-94, chair 1994); honors: Phi Beta Kappa; mem: L.A. Area C.of C. (chair internat. trade legislation com. 1985-91, law and justice com. 1992-94), Chartered Inst. Arbitrators London (assoc. 1986–), Town Hall Calif. (co-chair Internat. Rels. Sect. 1987-90), Friends of Wilton Park So. Calif. (chair 1987-94; mem. exec. com. 1986–), L.A. Co. Bar Assn. (v.chair exec. com. internat. law sect. 1989-91, chair 1991-92), L.A. Com. on Fgn. Relations, Internat. Bar Assn., Am. Bar Assn.; publs: 5+ profl. jour. articles, 1983-92, num. editorials in L.A. Herald Examiner, 1986–, L.A. Times, 1992–; Republican (dep. gen. counsel, Cred. Com., Nat. Conv. 1992); rec: fgn. affairs. Ofc: Governor's Office State Capitol Sacramento 95814

KOLTAI, STEPHEN M., economist, consulting engineer, writer, educator; b. Nov. 5, 1922, Ujpest, Hungary, nat. US cit.; s. Maximilian and Elisabeth (Rado) K.; m. Franciska Gabor, Sept. 14, 1948; children: Eva b. 1951, Susanne b. 1955; edn: M. Engring., Tech. Inst. of Budapest 1948; MBA econs., Univ. of Budapest 1955. Career: engring. cons., var. European countries, 1948-58; economic adviser/secty. Fgn. Diplomatic Service 1958-62; engring. exec. in Switzerland 1963-76; cons. engr./pres. Pan Business Consulting Corp., Palm Springs 1977–; patentee inventions in computer & printing process; charter mem. Republican Presdl. Task Force; rec: tennis, golf.

KOLTUNOV, SAMSON I., orthopedist-traumatologist; b. Mar. 31, 1923, Zaporozye, USSR; s. Isaak Mark Koltunov and Eugenia Sam. (Zuravitskaya) Koltunova; m. Anna A. Mints MD, Aug. 16, 1947; 1 d., Marinas Levitan b. 1954; edn: H.S. Certif., Zaporozye, USSR, 1940; MD, Medical Institute, Moscow & Lvov, 1948; PhD , Medinstitut, Lvov, 1959; Docent/Assoc. Prof., Medinstitute, Lvov, 1969. Career: Dept. Chief, Traumatology & Orthopedics, State Medical Inst. Training Hosp., Lvov 1948-81, Chief Traumatologist & Orthopedist, City of Lvov 1955-80, Assoc. Prof./Docent, Institut Physical Health, Lvov 1968-78, Med. research, Mobile Cardio-Vascular Service, Inc., L.A. 1982-84, Pres., Functional Health Diagnostic, L.A., 1984–; author: 42 pub. sci. works, 4 in Natl. Lib. of Medicine; mil: maj. Soviet Army Med. Svc.. 1941-45; Republican. Res: 642 West Knoll Dr # 204. Los Angeles 90069 Ofc: Function Health Diagnostic, 642 West Knoll Dr., S-204, Los Angeles 90069

KOMAI, DALE S., multimedia developer, consultant; b. Aug. 19, 1952, Santa Monica; s. Hiroshi and Lillie Y. (Yamato) K.; edn: BS in bus. adm., Univ. So. Calif. 1974. Career: field examiner Federal Home Loan Bank Board, San

Francisco 1974-80; owner/photographer Timely Photo, San Diego 1980-84; business cons. Transcontinental Foods, Inc. Escondido 1983-84; field examiner Federal Home Loan Bank Bd., San Francisco 1984-85, tng. instr. new examiners, field mgr., 1985-88, FHLB S.F. sr. program devel. analyst 1988-89; MIS analyst US Treasury Dept. 1989-91; computer consultant, tnr., 1991–; multimedia trade show coordinator, 1991; honors: bowling trophy USC 1971, Dean's List 1973, 74, merit awards FHLBB 1985, FHLB S.F. 1987, profiled in FHLB's Record Copy newsletter 1988, 2d pl. monologue competition Internat. Platform Assn. Conv. 1990; participant & newsletter staff writer 1988-89, Amer. Dance Friendship Tour to Finland, Soviet Union, 1988; ed. and contbg. writer, IICS Chapter Notes, 1991-93; mem: Internat. Interactive Communications Soc., Bay Area Country Dance Soc.; Calif. Hist. Soc., Ctr. for Citizen Initiatives; performed on stage in Speak Up and Dance, 1994, They're Playing Our Song, 1995, The Time of Your Life, 1995; photographer contbr. Jugglers World mag., 1982, 86, San Diego Union newspaper, 1982, Access to Learning newspaper (cover 1982), Daily Trojan newspaper, 1973; Rel. Sci.; rec: dancing, singing, computers, fgn. languages. Address: 39120 Argonaut Way #392 Fremont 94538

KOMAN, DIRK VAN ESS, musician/teacher; b. June 19, 1947, Wash. DC; s. John vanEss and Anne (Singleton) K.; edn: New England Conservatory, Boston 1965-66; USN Sch. of Music, Norfolk 1967; BFA, U.S. Internat. Univ. Sch. of Performing Arts, San Diego 1975. Career: conservatory tchr. USIU Sch. Performing Arts, San Diego 1973-75; third trumpet San Diego Symphony, 1975; principal trumpet Mesa Coll. Orch. 1976-78, Univ. San Diego Orch. 1977-86, La Jolla Symphony 1982-86, San Diego St. Univ. Orch. 1985-86, Gilbert & Sullivan/ Comic Opera Orch. S.D. 1979–; tchr., band dir. Coronado Elem. Schs., 1983-85; leader Young Audiences Inc., S.D. 1980–; assoc. prof. Univ. San Diego, and condr. U.S.D. Trumpet Ensemble, 1987–; dir. Classic Brass, S.D. 1980–; orchestra contractor Pacific Chamber Opera, S.D. 1986; music dir. Ira Harbison Sch. Arts Magnet for Nat. City Dist. 1990-92; dir. Brass Choir, La Jolla Presb. Church 1991–; band dir. Univ. S.D. High Sch. 1993–; awards: full scholarship Aspen Music Festival, Colo. (1986); mem. Internat. Trumpet Guild; author: (Young Audience shows) Let's Get Down to Brass Facts (1982), What Makes Music Tic (1983), (edn'l. video) How to Play the Trumpet (1989), (piano tchg. method) Music Essentials at the Piano (1987); mil: musician E5 US Navy 1967-71; Republican; Prot.; rec: cooking, swimming. Res: 601 I Ave Coronado 92118

KOMATSU, S. RICHARD, architect; b. May 5, 1916, San Francisco; s. Denzo and Tome (Fujimoto) K.; m. Chisato Frances Kuwata, Aug. 6, 1943; children: Richard b. 1946, Kathryn Kay b. 1949; edn: BA, UC Berkeley, 1938; cert. in Interior Design, 1939, cert. in Machine Design, 1944, reg. architect, Calif. 1951, NCARB, 1975. Career: landscape planner Golden Gate Internat. Exposition, San Francisco, 1938-39; designer, architect Charles F. Strothoff, S.F. 1939-42, 1946-52; asst. proj. engr. Federal Public Housing Authority, Detroit, Mich. 1943-44; designer Harley, Ellington & Day 1944; architect assoc. Donald L. Hardison & Assocs., Richmond, Calif. 1952-57; prin., secty. Hardison & Komatsu Assocs., San Francisco 1957-79; pres., prin. Hardison Komatsu Ivelich & Tucker, S.F. 1979-88, cons. 1988–; architect: 47 water treatment plants and related facilities for East Bay Municipal Utility Dist. 1964-84, 24 water treatment plants and related facilities for Contra Costa Water Dist. 1967-88, adv. waste water treatment plant Clark Co. Sanitation Dist., Las Vegas, NV 1979, S. Valley Water Reclamation Facility, Midvale, UT 1987, E. Bank Wastewater Treatment Plant, Metairie, LA 1988, main ofc. complex Turlock Irrigation Dist. 1988, pre-design of 6 water reclamation plants, 3 pumping plants and 1 dechlorination facility for the Clean Water Pgm. for Gr. San Diego 1990-92; design advr.: admin., ops. & lab. bldg. Santa Rosa Wastewater Treatment Plant, admin. bldg. Dublin San Ramon Svs. Dis., plant op. ctr. Delta Diablo Sanitation Dist. 1991-92; vis. archtl. advr. Cogswell Coll., S.F. 1981-82; appt. City of El Cerrito design review bd. 1969-78, chmn. 1973-77, planning commn. 1962-75, chmn. 1966-67, var. municipal coms. El Cerrito, and Richmond; numerous design awards incl. AIA award for East Bay Municipal Util. Dist. 1974 and Gov's. Award 1966, Concord City Award 1972, Eminent Conceptor award Cons. Engrs. Assn. of Calif. for Florin Reservoir and Pumping Station, Sacto. 1974, Southeast Water Pollution Control Plant Gold Nugget Award, S.F. 1984, Fairfield-Suisun Waste Water Mgmt. Plant, Cons. Engrs. Assn. of Calif., Fairfield 1978, AIA award for Student Ctr. Complex UC Berkeley 1978, Fellow AIA 1984, Silver Pin achiev. award Nat. Japanese Am. Citizens League, S.F. 1966; invited speaker nat. confs. Nat. Assn. of Home Builders Nat. Conv., Chgo. 1966, Am. Water Works Assn., Newport Beach 1967, S.F. 1970, 72, San Diego 1971, ASCE, Calif./ Nev. Assn. Water Pollution Control Assn., Lake Tahoe 1972; mem: Am. Inst. of Architects (bd. dirs. 1968-69, chair num. coms.), Am. Water Works Assn., Japanese Am. Citizens League Contra Costa (pres. 1957, dir. 1956-60), Kiwanis Club S.F. (v.p. 1983, dir. 1984-86), Richmond Art Center (dir. 1956-60), Richmond Ballet Co. (dir. 1956-60); publs: 3 articles on arch. design of water and wastewater fac. 1968, 70, 73; mil: master sergeant U.S. Army, 1944-46; Republican; Presbyterian; rec: watercolor artist, architectural delineator, golf. Res: 1323 Devonshire Dr El Cerrito 94530-2572

KONDO, SADAO, trading company executive; b. Sept. 9, 1918, Hirosakishi, Japan; s. Saikichi and Shino (Yannai) K.; m. Setsuko Itoh, May 27, 1943; 1 dau., Michiko; edn: grad. Communication Acad. Japan 1942. Career: staff Ministry Communications Japan 1942-45; Ministry Fgn. Affairs 1945-56; J. Osawa Co., Tokyo 1956-69, mgr. Los Angeles branch 1969; mgr. Nihon Seimitsu Sokki K.K., Los Angeles 1970-74; v.p. JPI, Santa Monica 1974-76, pres. 1976–, dir. Address: 1507 San Vicente Blvd Santa Monica 90402

KONO, NORM N., insurance executive; b. May 13, 1938, New York; s. Heitaro and Nellie N. (Tanabe) K.; m. Carol A., Nov. 25, 1967; children: Keli Kariko b. 1969, Kevin Shaw b. 1971; edn: BS bus. adminstrn., Roosevelt Univ. 1960. Career: underwriter Bankers Life & Casualty, Chgo., Ill. 1958-60; reinsurance underwriter CNA 1960-68; v.p., dir. Am. Pacific Life & Comml. Bankers Life, Irvine 1968-75; pres. Wespac Life, Tustin 1975-78; sr. v.p. S.C.O.R. Life, Dallas, Tx. 1978-81, Hudson R.E. Life, Sarasota, Fla. 1981-82; pres. Hawaii Underwriters Life Assn., Honolulu 1969-70; mem: Greater Irvine Lions (charter), Hawaii Kai Lions; mil: SP-4 AUS 1962-64; Republican. Res: 1052-C Walnut St Tustin 92680 Ofc: Beech Street Inc. 2 Ada St Irvine 92718

KONSTIN, CONSTANTINE, restauranteur; b. May 21, 1931, Agrinion, Greece; nat. 153; s. Christos and Anastasia (Emirzas) Konstantinidis; m. Sydna Pantoja, Feb. 25, 1955; children: Constantine, Jr. b. 1956, Sydna Christina b. 1959, Ann b. 1961, John b. 1963. Career: restaurateur Historic John's Grill Restaurant, San Francisco 1974–; recipient Key of New Orleans (1972, 85), Dashiell Hammett Soc. Award, 1978, Proclamation from Sen. Milton Marks, 1981; mem: San Francisco C.of C. 1980–, Dashiell Hammett Soc. (1976–, researcher), Market Street Devel. Proj., S.F. 1980–, AHEPA 1963–, Godfathers Club; fund raiser for San Francisco and Calif. polit. candidates, Red Cross Fund Raiser; Catholic; rec: swimming, travel, walking, golf, fishing. Res: 1306 Portola Dr San Francisco 94127 Ofc: John's Grill, 63 Ellis St San Francisco 94102

KONTNY, VINCENT L., engineering and construction company president; b. July 19, 1937, Chappell, Nebr.; s. Edward James and Ruth Regina (Schumann) K.; m. Joan Dashwood Fitzgibbon, Feb. 20, 1970; children: Natascha Marie, Michael Christian, Amber Brooke; edn: BS in C.E., Univ. Colo., 1958. Career: hvy. equip. opr./grade foreman Peter Kiewit Son's Co., Denver 1958-59; lt. U.S. Navy Civil Engr. Corps 1959-65; project mgr. Utah Const. & Mining Co., We. Australia 1965-69; project mgr. Fluor Australia, Queensland 1969-72; senior project mgr. Fluor Utah, San Mateo, Calif. 1972-73; senior v.p. Holmes & Narver Inc., Orange 1973-79; mng. dir. Fluor Australia, Melbourne, Aust. 1979-82; group v.p. Fluor Engineers Inc., Irvine 1982-85, pres. and CEO 1985-87, group pres. Fluor Daniel, 1987, pres. and CEO 1988, v.chmn. and pres. Fluor Corp., 1989-94 (ret.); lectr. Stanford Univ. Grad. Pgm. of Civil Engring.-Constrn., 1975-78; mem: Soc. of Mining Engrs. of AIME, Am. Assn. of Cost Engrs., Australian Assn. of Engrs., Am. Petroleum Inst.; clubs: Center (Costa Mesa), Victoria Racing (Melbourne), The Athenaeum (Melbourne); publs: The Cities Service Sx-EW Project Story (AIME, 1977), Business and Edn.: A Crucial Connection, speech before Calif. Bus. Edn. Assn. conf. 1986 (pub. Vital Speeches of the Day, 4/1/86); Republican; R. Cath.; rec: skiing, hunting, fishing. Res: 601 Lido Park Drive, 2AB Newport Beach 92663

KONWIN, THOR W., business executive, real estate developer; b. Aug. 17, 1943, Berwyn, Ill.; s. Frank and Alice S. (Johnson) K.; m. Carol Svitak, Aug. 4, 1967 (div. 1990); 1 son, Christopher b. 1970; edn: AA, Morton Jr. Coll. 1966; BS, Northern Ill. Univ. 1967; MS, Roosevelt Univ. 1971; Career: cost acct. Sunbeam Appliance Co., Chgo. 1968-71, asst. controller 1975-78, controller 1978-81; controller General Molded Products div. Sunbeam Corp., Des Plaines, Ill. 1971-75; c.f.o. Bear Medical Systems Inc., Riverside, Calif. 1981-84 (designed & developed high tech. bldg. for Bear Medical Corp. corp. hq.); structered LBO acquisition from 3M Co., co-founder, cfo, v.p./fin. Bird Products Corp., Palm Springs 1984–; founder, mng. ptnr. TUCKO Rental, Ltd., commercial equip. leasing co., 1985–; co-founder, pres. B&B Ventures Ltd., commercial R.E. devel., 1987–, devel. Fairmont Office Plaza, Riverside; coo BP Holding Inc. 1987-90, acquired W. Stackhouse Assocs. Inc. (laser surgery co.) 1988; exec. v.p. Bird Medical Technologies, 1990–; founder and ceo Equilink Inc. 1990, commercial R.E. devel.; founder and ceo Med One Financial Group 1991, commercial equip. leasing co.; acquired Life Design Systems Inc. (respiratory disposable co.) 1991; designed & devel. high tech. bldg. for Bird Med. Technologies corp. hq., 1991; mil: E-4 US Army 1969-71; rec: buy and sell antiques. Res:45500 Verba Santa Rd Palm Desert 92260 Ofc: This Olde Office 68845 Perez Rd Cathedral City 92254

KOPECKY, YVONNE ANNE, CFA, investment executive; b. Sept. 25, 1959, Santa Barbara; d. Leland Gerhart and Colleen Ann (Weaver) Miller; m. Louis Anthony Kopecky, June 16, 1984; edn: AA, F.I.D.M. 1980; BA mktg., CSU Hayward 1984; Gonzaga Univ. 1977-79; Univ. London England 1978. Career: account coordinator D.J.M.C. Advt., San Francisco 1980-82; asst. account exec. Mandabach & Simms, Emeryville 1984-85; advt. mgr. S&K Toyota, Hayward 1985-87; assoc. investment mgr. Security Pacific FM&TS/Bank of America, San Francisco 1988-94, asst. v.p. 1994–; asst. to chair auction com. Acalanes H.S., Lafayette 1986; awards: Security Pacific Insider 1988, logo competition award Am. Cons. Theatre Assn. 1979; mem: Inst. Chartered Fin. Analysts, Securiteam; works: illustrator, Hackers Hints, 1989, graphic brochures and flyers, 1980; rec: oil paintings, golf. Ofc: Bank of America The Private Bank 50 California St 28th Flr #2653 San Francisco 94111

KOPERSKI, JUDITH ANN, physician, dermatologist; b. Jan. 23, 1955, Chicago, Ill.; d. William S. and Ethel Ann (Friday) Koperski; m. Claude Harold Organ, III, Aug. 18, 1979; children: Cynthia b. 1988, Daniel b. 1990; edn: BA human biology, Stanford Univ. 1977; MD, 1982; cert. Am. Bd. Dermatology (1986). Career: medical intern Mt. Zion Hosp., San Francisco 1982-83; research fellowship, dermatology Stanford Univ., Stanford 1983-84, dermatology resident 1984-86; dermatologist So. Calif. Permanente Med. Group, Garden Grove 1986-87; Scripps Clinic Med. Group, La Jolla 1987–; clin. faculty, cons., tchr. VA Hosp. La Jolla and UCSD Med. Center 1987–; awards: NIH Young Investigator, Danish Inst. Cancer Jr. Investigator, Stanford Univ. Robert G. Walton 1984; mem: Am. Acad. Dermatology (fellow), San Diego Dermatological Soc. (secty./treas. 1994; pres. 1995), Pacific Dermatology Assn., N. Am. Soc. Phlebology, Am. Cancer Soc.; investigative dermatology articles pub. various med. jours., Healthline mag. (1985, 86, 87); Democrat; R.Cath.; rec: tennis, jogging, hiking. Ofc: Scripps Clinic & Research Foundation 10666 N Torrey Pines Rd La Jolla 92037

KOPLEY, MARGOT B., psychologist; b. Boston, Mass.; d. Edwin S. and Irene J. Kopley; edn: BA, Univ. Rochester 1974; MS, Univ. Miami 1976; MS, Pace Univ. 1982, Psy.D., 1983; lic. psychologist N.Y. 1984, Calif. 1985; cert. sch. psychologist, Calif. 1984, N.Y. 1985. Career: grad. fellowship Mailman Center, Miami, Fla. 1975-76; psychol. intern White Plains Public Schs., 1980-81; psychol. extern Childrens Village, Dobbs Ferry, N.Y. 1981-82; psychol. intern Bergen Pines Co. Hosp., Paramus, N.J. 1982-83; psychologist Ladson Coastal Center, S.C. 1977-78; Putnam Assn. for Retarded Citizens, N.Y. 1979-80; psychologist/clin. dir. Greystone House Inc., Poughkeepsie 1981-84; sch. psychol. Bd. of Cooperative Edn., Valhalla 1983-84; pvt. practice, cons., therapist, Westchester 1980-84; pvt. practice psychologist, North San Diego Co., Calif. 1984–; vol. therapist Parents/ Daughter's/ Son's United, North Coastal Chpt. 1985-87; adj. faculty Nat. Univ., San Diego 1987; recipient appreciation awards San Diego Comm. Child Abuse Council 1986-87, S.D. Dept. Social Svcs. (1985, 86, 87, 88) and North County Assn. Retarded Citizens 1984, listed Nat. Register Health Svc. Providers Psychol.; mem: Am. Bd. of Med. Psychotherapists (Diplomate, Fellow), Am. Psychol. Assn., Nat. Assn. Sch. Psychologists, Calif. State Psychol. Assn. (bd. 1990), San Diego Psychol. Assn. (legis. com. 1988-91, 93, chair 1989-90, women's com. 1988-90), Soc. of Mental Health Profls. (pres. 1985-86), San Diego Com. Child Abuse Coordinating Council (bd., co-chair res. com. 1986-88), North Co. Child Abuse Coalition (case rev. com. 1987-90), Volunteers in Probation Inc. (mem., bd. mem. 1986-87); paper: Eval. of Effects of Residential Placement Upon Psychosocial Competence and Self-Esteem, CASP/NASP 1985, Women: Surviving the Unspoken Tragedies (newsletter, Acad. of S.D. Psychologists 1989); rec: sailing. Ofc: 2003 El Camino Real Ste 202 Oceanside 92054 also: PO Box 230336, 220 Second St Encinitas 92023-0336

KOPLIN, DONALD LEROY, consumer advocate, executive; b. Dec. 31, 1932, Greenleaf, Kans.; s. Henry G. Koplin and Edith Mary Stevens; m. Patricia Joynes, June 2, 1962 (div. 1974); children: Marie Claire, Marie Joelle (adopted); edn: Univ. San Diego, 1957-59, 67-68. Career: electronics test insp. Gen. Dynamics, San Diego 1956-59; cryptographer U.S. Dept. of State, W.D.C., 1959-67; communications programs officer Foreign Service in France, Angola, Madagascar, Qatar, India, Oman, Benin, and the Bahamas, 1977-86; tech. writer Ryan Aero. Corp., San Diego, 1967-68; commercial dir., tech. advisor, pub. relations ofcr. Societe AGM, San Francisco, Athens, Gr., Antananarivo and Morondava, Democratic Republic of Madagascar, 1968-72; founder, dir. Societe BECA, Antananarivo, 1972-74; founder, ptnr., assoc. editor, corr., polit. reporter Angola Report, Luanda 1974-76; supr. Texas Instruments, Lubbock 1976-77; exec. Dial A Contact Lens, Inc., La Jolla 1986-90; ARC, San Diego 1991-92, Club Med, Copper Mtn, CO 1992-94; mil: USN 1951-55, Korea; Republican; R.Cath. Res: 436 Rosemont La Jolla 92037

KOPP, QUENTIN L., lawyer, state legislator; b. Syracuse, N.Y.; m. Mara Sikaters; children: Shepard, Bradley, Jennifer; edn: student, Dartmouth Coll.; JD, Harvard Univ. Career: sr. ptnr. Kopp & DiFranco; mem. State Senate, 1986–, mem. various coms.; commentator Sta. KTVU-TV; bd. suprs. rep. San Francisco Bay Conservation and Devel. Commn., 1972-78, Met. Transp. Commn., 1976-86, chmn., 1983-85, Bay Area Air Quality Mgmt. Dist., 1978-79; pres. San Francisco Bd. Suprs., 1976-78, 1982; founding mem. San Francisco/San Mateo Joint County Task Force, 1982-86; originator, chmn. Bay Area Super Bowl Task Force; ex officio mem. Calif. Transp. Commn.; bd. dirs. Bay Area Rapid Transit Dist., 1973-74, Golden Gate Bridge, Hwy. and Transp. Dist., 1977-86, v.p., 1984-86; pres. County Supervisors Assn. of Calif.; mem: State Bar of Calif., Bar Assn. of San Francisco, Am. Bar Assn., S.F. Lawyer's Club, Olympic Club, St. Francis Yacht Club, Marines Meml. Club (hon. life); mil: lt., USAF, 1952-54. Ofc: Office of State Senate 363 El Camino Real #205 South San Francisco CA 94080

KORDIK, MICHAEL WILLIAM, sales and marketing executive; b. March 30, 1946, Chicago, Ill.; s. George Anton and Mary Aileen (Rinkle) K.; m. Nickcol Karen Peters, Sept. 6, 1968; children: Kimberly b. 1972, Matthew b. 1974, Nathan b. 1981; edn: BS bus. adminstrn., Univ. Ariz. 1968; MBA, Nat.

Univ. 1981. Career: ops. mgr. Gen. Electric, Ventura 1969-74; area mgr., San Diego 1975-78, dist. mgr. 1979-80; dir. sales Elgar Corp. 1981-84; cons. Mike Kordik & Assoc., Encinitas 1985-86; controller Agents West Inc., Norwalk 1987-92; pres. Maddox Sales Co., Pico Rivera 1993-94; founder, pres. Target Marketing Group 1994–; awards: Gen. Electric top 3% mgr. 1980; mem: MACS Users Group (pres. 1991), Nat. Electric Mfg. Rep. Assn., Esperanza H.S. Boosters; author of computer program for sales tracking and order entry 1986; Republican; Fundamentalist; rec: remote control aircraft. Res: 19998 Hibiscus Circle Yorba Linda 92686 Ofc: Target Marketing Group 20503 Yorba Linda Blvd Ste 303 Yorba Linda 92686-7129

KORDUS, MARIE RAMONA, sales executive; b. Aug. 9, 1955, Milwaukee, Wis.; d. Benedict Nicholas and Ramona Dolores (Hintz) Kordus; edn: BFA, Cardinal Stritch Coll. 1977. Career: freelance art dir., Los Angeles 1977-79; talent agent Beckman Kordus Agency 1979-82; account exec. WMIL WOKY Radio, Milwaukee, Wis. 1982-84; WISN T.V. 1984-85; KPWR Radio, Los Angeles 1985-87, local sales mgr. 1987-88, gen. sales mgr. 1988–; rec: art, running, tennis. Res: 3448 Oak Glen Dr Los Angeles 90068 Ofc: KPWR RAdio 2600 W Olive Ave Ste 850 Burbank 91505

KORETZ, PAUL (LOUIS), city councilman; b. Apr. 3, 1955, Los Angeles; s. Erich Werner and Doris (Wolinsky) K.; m. Gail Cooper, Oct. 13, 1985; 1 dau., Rachel Elizabeth b. 1991; edn: BA in history, UCLA, 1979. Career: councilman's aide City of Los Angeles, 1975; small bus. owner The Political Scientists (polit. memorabilia), L.A. 1977-81; gen. mgr. sales co. Roadpower, L.A. 1981-83; councilman's aide City of Los Angeles, 1984; dep. councilman City of West Hollywood, 1985-88, elected city councilman 1988–; regional dir. Calif. League of Conservation Voters, 1989; chief of staff Bd. of Equalization, chair Brad Sherman, 1992; Democrat; rec: writing sci-fi., playing softball. Res: 9015 Cynthia St #1 West Hollywood 90069 Ofc: West Hollywood City Hall 8300 Santa Monica Blvd, West Hollywood 90069

KORF, RICHARD EARL, computer science educator; b. Dec. 7, 1956, Geneva, Switzerland; s. Earl Watkin and Suzanne Michelle (Nacouz) K.; edn: BS E.E. and C.S., M.I.T., 1977; MS, and PhD in computer sci., Carnegie-Mellon Univ., 1980, 1983. Career: asst. prof. computer sci. Columbia Univ., N.Y.C. 1983-85; asst. prof., assoc. prof., prof. computer sci. UCLA, Los Angeles 1985–; awards: NSF Presdl. Young Investigator 1986, Faculty devel. award IBM 1985; Fellow, Am. Assn. for Artificial Intelligence 1994 (mem.1983–); author: Learning to Solve Problems by Searching for Macro-Operators (1985), 75+ articles in profl. jours. (1977–); Democrat; Presbyterian; rec: mountain climbing. Res: 10470 Colina Way Los Angeles 90077 Ofc: Computer Science Dept. 4532E Boelter Hall Univ. California, L.A. 90024

KORFF, DONALD BRENT, state government management expert; b. June 3, 1950, Sacramento; s. Don and Roberta (Borden) K.; m. Catherine Marie Mullen, Apr. 24, 1982; children: Jason b. 1986, Shannon b. 1989; edn: BS in bus. adminstrn. CSU Sacto., 1972. Career: staff Calif. St. Dept. of Gen. Svs., Sacto. 1972-: budget analyst 1972-75, asst. budget ofcr. 1975-79, budget ofcr. 1979-83, chief of support svs., 1983-89, deputy local asst. ofcr. 1989-94, asst. to state printer 1995–; awards: appreciation United Way Sacto. 1984, March of Dimes Sacto. 1986, named outstanding mgr. St. Dept. of Gen. Svs. 1986, 87, 88; active United Way (community agencies svs. com. 1985-86); Methodist; rec: golf, fishing, gardening, coaching. Ofc: State Printing, 344 N. &th St., Sacramento 95814

KORN, LESTER BERNARD, business executive; b. Jan. 11, 1936, New York; edn: BS hons., UCLA 1959; MBA, 1960; postgrad. Harvard Bus. Sch. 1961. Career: mgmt. cons. Peat Marwick Mitchell & Co., Los Angeles 1961-66,ptnr. 1966-69; chmn., co-founder Korn Ferry Internat. 1969–; U.S. ambassador, U.S. rep. Econ. & Social Council U.N. 1977-88; alt. rep. 42d. and 43rd U.N. Gen. Assembly; bd. dirs: Continental Am. Properties, Tenet Healthcare Corp., L.A. Music Center Operating Co.; trustee UCLA Found; bd. overseers, bd. visitors, Anderson Grad. Sch. Mgmt. UCLA; mem. advy. council Am. Heart Assn.; spl. advisor, del. UNESCO Inter-gov. Conf. on Edn. for Internat. Understanding Coop., Peace 1983; advy. bd. Women in Film Found. 1983-84; chmn. Commn. on Citizen Participation in Govt., Calif. 1979-82; bd. dirs. John Douglas French Found. for Alzheimers Disease; mem. Republican Nat. Exec. Fin. Com. 1985; Pres. Commn. White House Fellowships; hon. chair 50th Am. Presdl. Inaugural 1985; co-chmn. So. Calif. region NCCJ; trustee Acad. for Advancement Corp. Governance, Fordham Univ. Grad. Sch. Adminstrn; awards: UCLA Alumni Profl. Achievement 1984; mem: Am. Bus. Conf. (founding mem.), Am. Inst. CPA, Calif. Soc. CPA, Council Am. Ambassadors; clubs: City (Bunker Hill), Hillcrest CC, LA Athletic, Regency, Board Room (NYC); author: The Success Profile (Simon & Schuster 1989). Res: 237 Park Ave New York N.Y. 10017 Ofc: Korn Ferry International 1800 Century Park E Ste 900 Los Angeles 90067

KORNIEWICZ, HELEN MARIE, lawyer; b. July 7, 1952, New York; d. John Alexander and Joan Anne (Parslow) Korniewicz; m. Charles Gordon Lambert, March 16, 1987; children: Graham Gordon b. 1988, Marissa Paige b. 1990; edn: St. Marys Coll. 1970-71; Istituto Santa Maria, Rome 1971-72; BA hist., Univ. Notre Dame 1974; JD, St. Johns Univ. 1977. Career: assoc. atty. John S. Zachary,

Staten Island, N.Y. 1977-78; mktg. atty. Chevron USA Inc., Perth Amboy, N.J. 1978-81; trademark atty. Chevron Research Co., S.F. 1981-85, licensing atty. 1985-86, sr. staff counsel Chevron Corp. 1986-88, corp. counsel 1988–; mem: Am. Bar Assn., Calif. Bar Assn., N.Y. Bar, Bar Assn. S.F., Internat. Trademark Assn., World Affairs Council S.F. Res: 6 Flying Cloud Course Corte Madera 94925 Ofc: Chevron Corp. 555 Market St Ste 4023 San Francisco 94105

KORPMAN, RALPH A., physician, executive, pathologist, researcher, educator; b. Aug. 9, 1952, New York City, N.Y.; s. Ralf and Vera Henriette (Terry) K.; edn: BA, Loma Linda Univ., 1971, MD 1974, intern Loma Linda Univ. Sch. of Medicine, Calif. 1974-75, resident 1975-78, fellow 1978; cert. in exec. mgmt., Claremont Grad. Sch. 1979; diplomate: Am. Bd. of Path., Nat. Bd. of Med. Examiners, Am. Coll. of Phys. Execs. Career: lead systems designer Acad. Records, Loma Linda Univ. 1969-74, systems dir., dept. of path. and lab. med. 1974–; cons., dir. Med. Data Corp., San Bernardino 1976-81; dir. of labs., faculty med. lab., Loma Linda 1979–; asst. prof. Loma Linda Univ. Sch. of Med. 1979-84, assoc. prof. 1984-87, prof. 1987–; dir. KM Corp., Los Angeles 1979–; cons., dir. Creative Ventures Capital Group 1980–; cons., dir. BK Med. Research Found. 1980–; chief scientific adv. to the pres. and bd. chmn. HBO & Co. 1981-83; dir. Med. Devices Corp. 1982–; chmn. and CEO, Health Data Sciences Corp. 1983–; dir. Pacific Union Coll. Found. 1984–; trustee Pacific Union Coll. 1985–; dir. Burdick Corp. 1986-88; cons. to num. hosps. and corps. 1977–; lectr. various schools, conferences, orgns.; awards: Healthcare Pioneer Award 1993, Entrepreneur of the Year Award, 1992, Sheard-Sanford Award, Am. Soc. Clin. Pathologists, 1975, Harold Hoxie Award, Loma Linda Univ., 1974, Alumni Award, 1974; Alpha Omega Alpha, Sigma Xi; mem: Am. Acad. Med. Dirs., Am. Coll. of Physician Execs. (Distinguished Fellow, chmn. Forum On Med. Informatics), Am. Mgmt. Assn., Am. Med. Assn., Am. Nat. Standards Inst. (ANSI/Healthcare Informatics Standards Planning Panel.), Am. Soc. Clin. Pathologists (Fellow, dir., exhibits advy. com., chmn. govt. rels. com., nom. com.), Am. Soc. Hematology, Assn. for Computing Machinery, Assn. Clin. Scientists (fellow), Calif. Med. Assn., Coll. Am. Pathologists (fellow), Data Processing Mgmt. Assn., Health Industry Mfrs. Assn., IEEE Computer Section, Internat. Health Econ. and Mgmt. Inst., MUMPS User Group (med. informatics com.), NY Acad. Scis., President's Assn., Rand Inst. for Res. on interactive Systems, San Bernardino Co. Med. Soc., Young Pres. Orgn.; author "Managing Health Care Costs, Quality, and Technology" book publ. 1986; author 50+ articles, 1984–. Res: POB 6406 San Bernardino 92412 Ofc: Health Data Sciences Corp 268 W Hospitality Ln Ste 300 San Bernardino 92408

KORZELIUS, JOHN MICHAEL, plastic and reconstructive surgeon; b. Dec. 21, 1951, Buffalo, N.Y.; s. Edward Gerald and Teresa (Taaffe) K.; edn: BA biol., SUNY at Buffalo, 1973, MS immunology, 1977, PhD pathology, 1980; MD, Medical Coll. of Wis., 1981. Career: resident surgeon dept. surgery UCLA Sch. of Medicine, Los Angeles 1981-88; awards: NSF res. and tchg. fellow 1975, NIH scientist in tng. fellow 1975-77, N.Y. State predoctoral res. fellow 1977-79 Roswell Park Memorial Inst.; mem: Am. Soc. of Tropical Medicine and Hygiene, Am. Soc. Plastic and Reconstrv. Surg. (affil.), Assn. for Academic Surgery, Assn. of Gnotobiotics, Calif. Med. Assn., Internat. Assn. for Gnotobiology, L.A. Co. Med. Assn., Nat. Council on Internat. Health, N.Y. Acad. of Scis.; author 10+ book chapts., sci. articles on immunology, cancer and reconstrv. surgery; rec: frequent travel as volunteer surgeon in Mexico, SE Asia and Africa. Res: 7861 Woodrow Wilson Dr Los Angeles 90046 Ofc: 2601 W Alameda Ave Ste 314 Burbank 91505

KOSTY, MICHAEL PAUL, physician; b. Sept. 17, 1950, South Bend, Ind.; s. Michael Peter and Irene Wanda (Czajkowski) K.; m. Antonette Christine Leone, May 18, 1980; children: Michael b. 1984, Allison b. 1987; edn: BS engring., UC Berkeley 1972; Cornell Univ. 1973; MA biophysics, UC Berkeley 1975; MD, George Washington Univ. 1979. Career: intern Naval Hosp., San Diego 1979-80; med. ofcr. USS Belleau Wood 1980-81; med. resident Naval Hosp., San Diego 1981-83, fellow 1983-86, staff physician, asst. head div. hematology/oncology 1986-89; asst. clin. prof. UCSD 1986–; currently assoc. dir. edn. & training, Ida M. & Cecil H. Green Cancer Ctr., Scripps Clinic and Research Found., La Jolla; honors: Phi Beta Kappa, Tau Beta Pi; mem: A.C.P. (Fellow), Am. Soc. Clin. Oncology, Am. Soc. Hematology Cancer and Leukemia Group B; articles pub. in med. jours. 1987–, research 1989-93; mil: commdr. USN 1979-89, active in USNR (capt. Med. Corps); Democrat; Protestant; rec: amateur radio, woodworking, gardening. Ofc: Ida M. & Cecil H. Green Cancer Center Scripps Clinic and Research Foundation 10666 N. Torrey Pines Rd La Jolla 92037

KOWELL, ARTHUR PRESTON, neurologist, educator; edn: BA (honors), Johns Hopkins Univ., 1968; MD, Univ. Penn. Sch. of Med., 1974, PhD in anatomy 1974; cert. in clin. aspects of the BEAM technique dept. neurology The Children's Hosp., Boston 1984; Diplomate Am. Bd. of Psychiatry & Neurology 1980, Am. Bd. of Clin. Neurophysiology 1983. Career: med. intern UCLA Hosp., Los Angeles 1974-75, 3-yr neurology residency pgm., 1975-78; pvt. practice neurologist, 1978–; clin. neurology UCLA 1978- (clin. prof. neurology 1992–); honors: Phi Beta Kappa 1968, Alpha Epsilon Delta, Sigma Xi, the Augustus S. Rose Award to a neurology resident for excellence in tchg. UCLA

1978; mem: Am. Acad. Neurology (Fellow), Am. Electroencephalographic Soc. (Fellow), Am. Epilepsy Soc., AMA, CMA, L.A. Co. Med. Assn., NY Acad. Scis., Santa Clarita Valley Med. Soc., W. Electroencephalographic Soc.; publs: contbr. articles in med. jours. and presentations nat. confs. Ofc: 16311 Ventura Blvd Ste 680 Encino 91436

KOZITZA, GEORGE ANTHONY, college executive; b. June 5, 1941, Mannato, Minn.; s. Andrew Anthony and Mary (Tabet) K.; m. Mary Grace Cedillos, Sept. 1, 1964 (dec. 1976); m. Linda Lee Pepper, Nov. 4, 1978; children: Mary, Michael, Elizabeth, Rebecca; edn: BA, CSU Los Angeles 1961; MA, 1963; Ed.D, USC 1969. Career: asst. supt. Dixon Unified Sch. Dist. 1969-73; asst. supt. bus. Santa Cruz City Sch. 1973-77; bus. mgr. Merced Comm. Coll., Merced 1977-81; asst. supt. bus. Ventura Co. Comm. Coll. Dist. 1981-83; dep. supt. Santa Barbara Co. Sch. 1983-85; v.p. adminstrn. Marin Comm. Coll. Dist., Kentfield 1985–; guest speaker Nat. Assn. Bus. Officials, Atlanta, Ga. 1982; mem: Calif. Assn. Schs. (st. chair fin. com. 1972-74), Assn. Calif. Sch. Adminstrs., Calif. Assn. Sch. Bus., Phi Delta Kappa, Novato Priorities (bd. dirs.), Friends of Indian Valley (founding mem.); publs: Tng. of Maintenance & Ops. Personnel (1969), article in profl. jour. (1973); Democrat; R.Cath. Ofc: Marin Community College District Indian Valley Campus 1800 Ignacio Blvd Novato 94949

KOZLOFF, THEODORE J., lawyer; b. Dec. 21, 1941, Reading, Pa.; s. Jacob and Fern K.; m. Sharron Black, Aug. 1, 1980; edn: BA econ., Univ. Pa. 1964; MA, 1964; LL.B, 1967; admitted st. Bar Calif. 1967, N.Y. 1968. Career: atty., assoc. Skadden Arps, N.Y. 1968-75, ptnr., N.Y. and Calif. 1976–; mem: The Hill Sch. (trustee); ed. Univ. Pa. Law Review, 1966-67; rec: sailing. Ofc: Skadden Arps Slate Meagher & Flom 4 Embarcadero Ste 3800 San Francisco 94111

KRAFT, ROBERT ARNOLD, physician, ret.; b. Mar. 27, 1924, Seattle, Wash.; s. Vincent Irving and Blanche (Palmer) K.; m. Robby Lee Roberson, June 12, 1949; children: Angela b. 1958, Peter b. 1961, Darius b. 1963; edn: BA, Univ. Wash. 1948, MD, 1954; bd. cert. anatomic & clin. pathology, Am. Bd. Pathology 1962, bd. cert. Am. Bd. Nuclear Medicine 1972. Career: family physician practice, Puyallup, Wash. 1955-58; pathologist/nuclear medicine physician Peninsula Hosp., Burlingame 1962-91, dir. Dept. Nuclear Medicine; asst. clin. prof. Pathol. & Nuclear Medicine, UCSF, 1962–; mem. Calif. Radioactive Mats. Mgmt. Forum (state multidisciplinary orgn. for safe low level radioactive waste mgmt.); honors: spl. service award, W. regl. chpts. Soc. of Nuclear Medicine 1986; elected Am. Board of Nuclear Medicine 1990; mem: Soc. Nuclear Medicine (pres. No. Calif. chpt. 1974-75), Am. Coll. of Nuclear Physicians (nat. bd. trustees 1981-84, pres. Calif. chpt. 1978-79, nat. regent 1987-92), South Bay Pathology Soc. (pres. 1968-69); Rotary 1955-58; author book chpt., Nuclear Medicine; mil: capt. USAAF, WWII, lead navigator (30 missions) 8th Air Force; Methodist; rec: philately, amateur astronomer, orchidist, golf, mining history.

KRAMER, KAREN SUE, community organizational and mind-body psychologist; b. Sept. 6, 1942, Los Angeles; d. Frank Pacheco Kramer and Velma Eileen (Devlin) Moore; m. Stewart A. Sterling, Dec. 30, 1965 (div. 1974); 1 son, Scott b. 1970; edn: BA, UC Berkeley 1966; MA, U.S. Internat. Univ., S.D. 1977; PhD, Profl. Sch. of Psychology, 1980; lic. marriage famiy and child counselor Calif. 1979. Career: psychometrist UC Berkeley Counseling Center 1966-67; social worker Alameda County 1967-69; probation ofcr. San Diego Co. Probation Dept. 1971-76; clin. and outreach supr. Western Inst., San Diego 1976-77; project dir. Womens Resource Center, San Luis Rey 1977-78; advr. USMC Human Resources dept. Camp Pendleton, 1978-80; pvt. practice therapy, Vista 1978-81; prof. human behavior Nat. Univ., San Diego 1979-81; planner San Diego Co. Dept. Health Services 1979-81; social service cons. Calif. Dept. Social Services, 1981-83; affirmative action ofcr. St. Compensation Ins. Fund., San Francisco 1983-87; cons. psychologist Calif. Dept. Mental Health S.F. 1987-89; personnel cons. State Compensation Ins. Fund, 1989-91; reg. property mgr. State Compensation Ins. Fund, 1991–; indep. consulting psychologist for organizational devel., community devel., wellness programing, personal health issues, 1990–; honors: listed Who's Who in Am. Women 1989,90, 91, 92, Who's Who in Behavioral Scis. 1991; mem. bd. dirs: Network Consulting Services Napa (1989–, bd. v.p. 1993-94), Calif. Prevention Network (1989-93, editorial advy. bd. 1992-93), Calif. Peer Counseling Assn., San Francisco Rehab. Ctr., Chinatown Resource Devel. Ctr., Personnel Mgmt. Assn. Aztlan 1984-87, North County Council Social Concerns (pres. 1977-78); rec: interior design, garden design, travel. Address: 1314 Ordway St Berkeley 94702

KRAMER, LAWRENCE STEPHEN, journalist; b. Apr. 24, 1950, Hackensack, N.J.; s. Abraham and Ann Eve (Glasser) K.; m. Myla F. Lerner, Sept. 3, 1978; children: Matthew b. 1982, Erika b. 1987; edn: BS in journ., pol. sci., Syracuse Univ., 1972; MBA, Harvard Univ., 1974. Career: reporter San Francisco Examiner, S.F. 1974-77; Washington Post, W.D.C. 1977-80; exec. editor The Trenton Times, N.J. 1980-82; asst. mng. editor Washington Post, 1982-86; exec. editor San Francisco Examiner, S.F. 1986-92; pres., dir., exec. editor Data Sport, San Mateo, Calif. 1992–; v.p. news and sports ops. Data Broadcasting Corp., San Mateo; guest lectr. Harvard Univ. 1980-89; awards:

Gerald E. Loeb Award, USC 1977, Nat. Press Club Award, W.D.C. 1979; mem. Soc. Profl. Journalists 1975–, Am. Soc. Newspaper Editors 1980-90 (com. chair 1990); civic: commr. Little League, Tiburon 1992–; Jewish. Res: 8 Auburn Ct Tiburon 94920 Ofc: Data Broadcasting Inc. 1900 S Norfolk St San Mateo 94403

KRANZ, KATHLEEN NEE, performing musician/pianist; b. May 31, 1951, Fontana; d. Bruce Lester and Margaret Joanne (Nee) Brown; m. Tomas Patten Kranz, July 4, 1978; child: Michael Alexander b. 1988; edn: BA, Fla. State Univ., Tallahassee, 1973, MM, 1977; PhD in music/ theoretical studies, UC San Diego, 1985. Career: musical dir. Actor's Theatre of Louisville, Ky., 1973-74; musical dir. Asolo State Theatre, Sarasota, Fla., 1974-75; faculty, piano, UC San Diego, La Jolla, 1983-87; pvt. tchr. piano, San Diego, 1977–; performer- Sonos, Chamber Music Seattle, Wash. (ea. summer ongoing), Chamber music, San Diego 1978–; master tchr.- Am. Music Scholarship Assn., Batiquitos Festival Del Mar, Calif. 1988, AM Music Scholarship, Cinti., Oh. 1984-86; 20th century music and theory tchr. Suzuki Assn. of Calif., San Diego 1984-88; pvt. study Aube Tzerko, L.A./Aspen, 1979-88, 91; awards: $500 cash award Fla. Fedn. of Music Clubs 1976, Young Artist in the Schools, Leon County, Fla. 1977, Fulbright Finalist, Fulbright Grant Rotary Club 1977, grad. opportunity fellow UCSD 1981, UCSD Grad. Sch. Alice Hohn fee scholar 1981 and In-candidacy fee grantee (1983, 84); mem: Music Tchrs. Assn. of Calif. (1977–, MTAC high sch. credit chair 1991), Suzuki Assn. of Calif. (sec. 1986-87), College Music Soc. 1985–; publs: (diss.) Structural Functions of Rests in the Piano Works of Franz Schubert (1985); Methodist. Res: San Diego.

KRATOFIL, STEVEN ELLIOTT, dentist; b. Feb. 17, 1959, Inglewood; s. Alexander B. and Lois Roberta (Elliott) K.; m. Elaine Kay Rollos, June 27, 1981; children: Alexander b. 1986, Michael b. 1989; edn: AS, San Bernardino Valley Coll. 1979; BA magna cum laude, USC 1981; DDS, 1985; Praxis Orthodontic Coll., 1987. Career: private practice, Apple Valley 1985–; instr. USC Dental Sch., L.A. 1985-86; team dentist High Desert Mavericks profl. baseball team 1992–; cons. dentist, Apple Valley Care Ctr. 1991–; honors: Phi Beta Kappa, Psi Omega, Omicron Kappa Upsilon, USC hons. at entrance 1979, Calif. Scholarship Fedn. 1977; contbr. Dental Sch. Yearbook 1982-85, co-editor Dental Sch. Yearbook 1985; mem: ADA, Calif. Dental Assn., Tri County Dental Soc., Internat. Assn. for Orthodontics, Rotary Intl.; rec: tennis, golf. Address: Apple Valley 92307

KRAUS, PANSY DAEGLING, gemology consultant, author; b. Sept. 21, 1916, Santa Paula; d. Arthur David and Elsie (Pardee) Daegling; m. Charles Frederick Kraus, Mar. 1, 1941 (div. 1961); edn: AA, San Bernardino Valley Jr. Coll., 1938; edn: Longmeyer's Bus. Coll., 1940; grad. gemologist dipl. Gemmological Assn. Gt. Britain, 1960, Gemological Inst. Am., 1966; career: clk. Convair, San Diego 1943-48; clk. San Diego County Schs. Publs., 1948-57; mgr. Rogers and Boblet Art Craft, San Diego 1958-64; p.t. editorial asst. Lapidary Jour., San Diego 1963-64, assoc. editor 1964-69, ed. 1970–, sr. ed. 1984-85; pvt. practice cons., San Diego 1985–; lectr. local gem and mineral groups, gem & mineral club bulletin editor groups; mem: San Diego Mineral & Gem Soc., Gemol. Soc. San Diego, Gemmol. Assn. Gt. Brit., Epsilon Sigma Alpha; publs: ed., layout dir. Gem Cutting Shop Helps 1964, The Fundamentals of Gemstone Carving 1967, Appalachian Mineral and Gem Trails 1968, Practical Gem Knowledge for the Amateur 1969, Southwest Mineral and Gem Trails 1972, revision ed. Gemcraft (Quick and Leiper, 1977); author Introduction to Lapidary 1987, contbr. articles to Lapidary jour., Keystone Mktg. catalog. Ofc: PO Box 600908 San Diego 92160

KRAUS, RICHARD SHOLOM, librarian; b. Nov. 18, 1956, Bklyn.; s. Leonard Henry and Aviva (Rubby) K.; edn: BA, UC Los Angeles, 1978, MLS, 1980. Career: library intern and archival asst. Acad. of Motion Picture Arts & Scis., Beverly Hills 1979-80; lab asst. Instructional Materials Lab. CSU Northridge 1980-83; catalog librarian Cat. Dept. Los Angeles Pub. Library, L.A. 1983-85, serials librarian Acquisitions Dept. 1985-86, adult reference librarian West L.A. reg. branch library 1986–; honors: Phi Beta Kappa 1978, Beta Phi Mu 1980; mem: Am. Library Assn., Special Libraries Assn., Calif. Library Assn., Nat. Librarians Assn.; newsletter editor UCLA/GSLIS Alumni News 1984-87, pub. article in Am. Libraries Jour. (1983); Democrat; rec: baking. Res: 1515 Purdue Ave Apt 5 Los Angeles 90025 Ofc: Los Angeles Public Library, W.L.A. Reg. Br. 11360 Santa Monica Blvd Los Angeles 90025

KRAUTHAMMER, JUERGEN P., physician-surgeon; b. Dec. 19, 1935, Berlin, Germany; s. Simon and Maria Theresa (Karl) S.; m. E. Elizabeth Otero; m. Maureen Laughnan, July 19, 1980; children: William b. 1962, Elizabeth b. 1965; edn: MD, Univ. Buenos Aires Sch. Medicine 1961. Career: clin. research diabetes Joslin Clin. & Baker Clinic Research Lab., Boston, Mass. 1962-63; intern Delaware Co. Memorial Hosp., Drexel Hill, Pa. 1963-64; resident Grad. Hosp. Univ. Pa., Phila. 1964-66; Bryn Mawr Hosp. 1966-69; Henry Ford Hosp., Detroit, Mich. 1969-70; Shadyside Hosp. 1970-71; pvt. practice, Fresno, currently; pres. med. staff Clovis Comm. Hosp., 1984; bd. dirs. Comm. Hosp./St. Agnes Med. Ctr.. Res: 458 E Feather River Dr Fresno 93720 Ofc: 6177 N Thesta #102 Fresno 93710

KRAVETZ, NATHAN, author, editor, educator; b. Feb. 11, 1921, New York, N.Y.; s. Louis Kravetz and Anna Tau; m. Evelyn Cottan, Dec. 10, 1944; children: Deborah Ruth b. 1948, Daniel b. 1951; edn: BEd, UCLA 1941, MA, 1949, EdD, 1954. Career: teacher, principal Los Angeles Unified Sch. Dist. 1946-64; foreign service ofcr. U.S. Dept. of State, Lima, Peru 1958-60; prof., chmn. Lehman Coll., New York, N.Y. 1964-76, prof. emeritus of edn. 1979; sr. staff ofcr. UNESCO, Paris, France 1969-72; dir. eval. research Ctr. Urban Edn., New York, N.Y. 1965-69; dean, prof. CSU San Bernardino 1976-91, prof. emeritus of edn. 1984; cons.: Ford Foundation, U.S. AID, United Nations Devel. Pgm., UNESCO, Univ. of Lima, Peru.; awards: Sr. Research award, Argentina, Fulbright 1980, fellowship Harvard Univ. 1951-52; mem: Authors Guild, Authors League of Am., PEN, B'nai B'rith, Jewish Historical Soc. of So. Calif.; author: 8 books, 1954–; editor, Legacy, JHS/SC; editor, the Borgo Press: Studies in Judaica and the Holocaust, 1991–; mil: sgt., U.S. Army Air Corps, 1942-46

KRAVITZ, HILARD LEONARD, physician; b. June 26, 1917, Dayton, Ohio; s. Philip and Elizabeth (Charek) K.; m. Marjorie Evelyn Rigler, Dec. 4, 1947 (div. 1969); m. Ellen Frances King, Jan. 9, 1972; children: Kent b. 1949, Kerry b. 1952, Jay b. 1955, Julie b. 1979; edn: BA, Univ. Cincinnati 1939; MD, 1943; postgrad., 1948; USC 1947. Career: pvt. practice internal medicine, Dayton, Ohio 1950-54; Beverly Hills, and Los Angeles 1955–; attdg. physician Cedars-Sinai Med. Center 1955; cons., med. dir. Adolphs Ltd., L.A. 1955-74; mem: Presdl. Pain Commn., Wash. D.C. 1985-86; exec. com. Reiss Davis Clinic, L.A.1966-70; chmn. pharmacy and therapeutic com. Century City Hosp. 1974-79; mem: Friends of Musc CSU (v.p. 1979-81), Los Angeles Co. Med. Assn., CMA, AMA, Am. Soc. Internal Medicine, Calif. Soc. Internal Medicine; patents for sugar substitute, 1959, and mineral based salt, 1978; mil: Capt. AUS 1944-46; Jewish; rec: flying, bicycling, computers. Ofc: 436 N Bedford Dr #211 Beverly Hills 90210

KREBS, STEPHEN JEFFREY, professor of viticulture and wine making; b. July 29, 1950, Belvedere, Ill.; s. Leo Gerard and Jean Catherine (Fiedler) K.; m. Julie Lynn, May 6, 1989; edn: BS, plant sci., UC Davis, 1976; MS, horticulture, UC Davis, 1977; PhD, ecology, UC Davis, 1992. Career: student asst. Loan Dept. Peter J. Shields Main Lib., UC Davis, 1970-72, lib. asst. II, 1972-77; tchg. asst. Pomology, UC Davis, 1977; viticulturist and mgr. San Pasqual Vineyards, Escondido, Calif., 1977-79, Mayacamas Vineyards, Napa, Calif., 1980-83; viticultural researcher in Europe and Calif. for book Vines, Grapes and Wine by Jancis Robinson, 1984; viticulturist and mgr. Matanzas Creek Winery, Santa Rosa, Calif., 1984-85, Sunny Slope Ranch, Glen Ellen, Calif., 1986-89; coord. Viticulture and Winery Technology, Napa Valley Coll., 1986–; grower-cooperator Monsanto, pre-registration round-up trials, 1978; wine judge Del Mar Nat. Wine Competition, 1982; instr. Viticulture Dept., Santa Rosa Jr. Coll., 1986-87; viticultural cons. 1978–; curriculum cons. La Comunidad Drop-out Prevention Program; instr. Internat. Wine Acad., S.F., Calif.; awards: Calif. Comm. Coll. Lifetime Credential in Plant Production, Calif. Dept. of Food & Agric. Pest Control Advisor License; scholarship recipient: Wine Spectator, 1989, 90; ASEV, 1989; ASEV Myron Nightingale Scholarship, 1990; profl. mem Am. Soc. for Enology and Viticulture, 1978; mem: Sonoma County Grapegrowers Assn. 1984-89, Sonoma County Vineyard Tech. Group 1984-89, Napa Valley Coll. Environmental Com., Instructional Excellence Com., Napa County Resource Conservation Dist. (advy. com.), Napa County Farm Bureau, Napa Valley Vineyard Tech. Group, Napa Valley Grape Growers Assn.; rec: guitar, auto restoration. Ofc: Viticulture & Winery Technology Napa Valley College Napa 94558

KREEP, GARY G., lawyer; b. July 1, 1950, San Francisco; s. George H. and Clara Irene (Jones) K.; m. Carol Cole, April 23, 1983; stepchildren: Jason b. 1969, Alissia Michelle b. 1973; edn: UCSD 1972; Univ. San Diego 1975; admitted St. Bar Calif. 1975. Career: political cons., San Diego 1974-76; atty., Escondido 1977–, San Diego 1975-77; exec. dir. U.S. Justice Found., Escondido 1979–; awards: San Diego Co. Bd. Suprs. Cert. Appreciation, Boys & Girls Clubs Escondido Cert. Appreciation 1981, Outstanding Young Americans; mem: Am. Bar Assn., San Diego Trial Lawyers Assn., San Diego Co. Bar Assn., North S.D. Co. Bar Assn.; Republican. Ofc: 2091 E Valley Parkway 1D Escondido 92027

KREGER, MELVIN JOSEPH, tax lawyer; b. Feb. 21, 1937, Buffalo, N.Y.; s. Philip and Bernice (Gerstman) K.; m. Patricia Anderson, July 1, 1955 (div. 1963); children: Beth Barbour, Arlene Roux; m. 2d. Renate Hochleitner, Aug. 15, 1975; edn: JD, Mid-valley Coll. of Law, 1978; LLM in taxation, Univ. San Diego, 1988; admitted bar: Calif. (1978), U.S. Dist. Ct. central dist., Calif. (1979), U.S. Tax Ct. (1979), Calif. State Bar certified specialist- in Tax Law (1990), in Probate Law, Trust Law & Estate Planning Law (1991). Career: life underwriter Met. Life Ins. Co., Buffalo 1958-63; bus. mgr. prin. M. Kreger Bus. Mgmt., Sherman Oaks 1963-78, enrolled agt. 1971-78, sole practice North Hollywood, 1978–; mem: Nat. Assn. Enrolled Agts., Calif. Soc. Enrolled Agts., Calif. State Bar, LA County Bar Assn., San Fernando Valley Bar Assn. (probate and tax. sects.); Jewish; rec: computers, travel. Ofc: 11424 Burbank Blvd North Hollywood 91601

KREITENBERG, ARTHUR, orthopaedic surgeon; b. Apr. 24, 1957, Los Angeles; s. Sam and Irene (Deutsch) K.; m. Melissa C. Carr, JD, Sept. 4, 1988; children: Elliot M. b. 1992, Zoe R. 1994; edn: AB magna cum laude, UCLA, 1978; MD, UC San Diego, 1982; grad. cert. biomed. engring. UC Irvine, 1984;

Dipl. Am. Bd. of Orthopaedic Surgery. Career: summer intern NASA, Johnson Space Center, Houston 1979; gen. surg. resident UCI Med. Center, Orange 1982-84, orthopaedic surg. resident 1984-87; pvt. practice in orthopaedic surgery, Beverly Hills 1989–; asst. clin. prof. UC Irvine; emergency med. disaster relief team following earthquake San Salvador, El Salvador, 10/86, vol. med. work India 1989, diasaster med. assistance team Northridge Earthquake Jan. 1994; mem. bd. trustees Calif. Handicapped Skiers, Southwest Medical Teams; Fellow, Am. Acad. Orthopaedic Surgeons; Fellow Am. Coll. of Surgeons; awards: Samuel Hamburger Award for outstanding thesis, UCSD 1982; club: Zeta Beta Tau frat.; publs. in med. jours., Am. J. of Cardiology, 1982, Paraplegia, 1984; inventions: Neck Venous and Arterial Examination Tchg. Instrument (1983, US Patent #4,380,439), Safety Releasing Ski Boot (1992, US Patent #5,107,608), Self-Powered Human Centrifuge (1995, US Patent #5,378,214); spl. interest in devel. of space for benefit of man. Res: Los Angeles

KREITZBERG, FRED CHARLES, construction management company chief executive; b. June 1, 1934, Paterson, N.J.; s. William and Ella (Bohen) K.; m. Barbara, June 9, 1957; children: Kim b. 1959, Caroline b. 1962, Allison b. 1964, Bruce b. 1968, Catherine b. 1969; edn: BS civil engring., Norwich Univ. 1957; hon. deg.: Doctor Business Mgmt., Norwich Univ. 1994; Reg. Profl. Engr.: Ala., Alaska, Ark., Az., Calif., Colo., D.C., Dela., Fla., Ga., Ia., Ida., Ill., Ind., Kans., Ky., Md., Mass., Miss., Mo., Nebr., Nev., Minnesota, N.H., N.J., N.M., N.Y., Oh., Okla., Oreg., S.C., S.Dak., Tenn., Va., Vt., Wash., Wis., W.V. and Wyo. Career: asst. supt. Turner Constrn. Co., N.Y.C. 1957; project mgr. for Project Mercury before first astronaut launching, RCA, N.J. 1958-62; schedule and cost mgr. Catalytic Constrn. Co., Pa. 1963-65; cons. Meridien Engring., 1965-68; prin. MDC Systems Corp., 1968-72; CEO, O'Brien-Kreitzberg Inc. (OKI), San Francisco 1972–, constrn. mgmt. major pvt. and govt. projects nat., including S.F. Cable Car rehabilitation, S.F. Airport expansion, Silicon Valley Rail System, L.A. Rail System, world's largest wind tunnel for NASA, Libr. of Congress, Bellevue Hosp., Walter Reed Hosp., John F. Kennedy Internat. Airport Redevel. Pgm., Dallas Area Rapid Transit, New York Schools Pgm., provided emergency scheduling following the Oct. 17, 1989 San Francisco Earthquake; leading nat. authority and expert witness in constrn. mgmt. claims; lectr. Stanford Univ. and UC Berkeley engineering students; awards: Community Fields Amphitheater dedicated in honor of Fred Kreitzberg family by the Marin Comm. Fields Assn. 1987, Disting. Alumnus Norwich Univ., Vt. 1987, Norwich Univ. Kreitzberg Library dedicated 1992, ASCE Construction Mgr. of the Year 1982, Boss of Yr. Nat. Assn. of Women in Constrn. 1987, Engineering News Record Man of Year nominee 1984; mem: ASCE (Fellow 1956), Am. Arbitration Assn., Constrn. Mgmt. Assn. of Am. (founding mem. 1982, bd. dirs.), Soc. of Am. Value Engrs.; civic: Alden Partridge Soc., Norwich Univ. (bd. dirs.), Comm. Field Assn. (Marin Co. bd. dirs.), Ross Hist. Soc.; works: designed catenary support system for World's largest radio telescope, patent app. by RCA, 1960; contbg. author to Critical Path Method Scheduling for Contractor's Mgmt. Handbook, 1971; key articles: Repetitive Scheduling (ASCE J. 1984), Cable Car Renovation Project: On Time and On Budget (Proceedings of the Splty. Conf. on Orgn. & Mgmt.), The Constrn. Mgr.-Contractor's Friend or Foe? (Constrn. Consultant, 3 & 4, 87); mil: 1st lt. Corps of Engrs. (Airborne) 1957-58; Cong. Rodef Sholom; rec: running, biking, tropical fish. Res: 19 Spring Rd Box 1200 Ross 94957 Ofc: O'Brien-Kreitzberg Inc. 188 The Embarcadero San Francisco 94105

KREITZER, DAVID MARTIN, artist; b. Oct. 23, 1942, Ord, Nebr.; s. David and Norma (Buls) K.; m. Ana Bueno, June 4, 1973 (div. Feb. 1988); m. Jacalyn Marie Bower, Nov. 25, 1988; children: Anatol b. 1974, Fredricka b. 1989; edn: BS, Concordia Coll., 1965; MA, San Jose State Univ., 1967. Career: faculty San Jose State Univ., 1969-70; Calif. Polytechnic State Univ., San Luis Obispo 1981-91; one-man shows Maxwell Gal., San Francisco 1967-74, Ankrum Gal., Los Angeles 1970-89; represented by Summa Gal., N.Y.C., 1989–, Stary-Sheets Gal., Irvine, Calif. 1991–, Campanile Gallery, Chgo. 1995–; awards: Ciba Geigy Award, Sixth Mobile (Ala.) Annual 1971, Gold medal San Francisco Art Directors Club 1970; publs. include covers (2) Atlantic Monthly 1970, reproduction in book "The Sacred Landscape" 1988, posters (4) Seattle Opera 1981-82; Lutheran. Res: 1442 12th St Los Osos 93402

KREMEN, ALAN FRAZIER, physician-surgeon; b. Dec. 17, 1946, Mpls.; s. Arnold J. and Virginia (Frazier) K.; m. Jodi Catherine Mayo, June 6, 1976; children: Jennifer b. 1981, Elizabeth b. 1985; edn: BA, Stanford Univ., 1968; PhD, Univ. Cologne, Germany 1971; Cambridge Univ., England 1972; MD, Univ. Minn., 1976; diplomate Am. Bd. Surgery 1983. Career: pvt. practice gen. surgery, vascular and thoracic surgery, Healdsburg 1986-88; cons., mem. fellow Hoover Inst., Stanford Univ. 1994-96, res.: health policy and med. ethics; honors: Alpha Omega Alpha; mem: Sonoma Co. Med. Soc., A.C.S., Deaton Cooley Internat. Surgical Soc., Michael Degailey Cardiovascular Surgical Soc., Healdsburg C.of C.; author: The Idea of the Psyche in European Culture, 1976; Beyond Ideology, Philosophy, Public Policy, and Health Care Reform, Stanford: Hoover Inst. Press, 1994. Ofc: 421 March Ave Ste C Healdsburg 95448

KREMPEL, RALF HUGO BERNHARD, artist, inventor, author; b. June 5, 1935, Groitzsch, Saxony, Ger.; s. Curt Bernhard and Liesbeth Anna Margarete (Franz) K.; m. Barbara von Eberhardt, Dec. 21, 1967 (div. 1985); 1 son, Karma b.

1983; edn: Wood and Steel Constrn. Coll., Leipzig, Ger. 1949-55. Career: constrn. specialist var. projects world-wide incl. Germany, Congo (Kinshasa), New Guinea, South Pacific; co-owner w/wife San Francisco Private Mint, commemorative medals and bars in silver and platinum 1973-81; artist/prin. San Francisco Painter Magnate 1982–; prop. Stadtgalerie Wiprechtsburg Groitzsch, Saxony, Germany 1991–; paintings exhib: Galerie Salammbo-Atlante, Paris, Fr., invite d'honneur Expo. Artistes Contemporains, le Salon des Nations a Paris (1985); mem: The Museum Soc., S.F. Mus. of Modern Art; invention: Visual Communication System, world-wide message relay, utilizing colors rather than letters in transmission and depiction; 2 USA patents 4/439/160 (1984), 4/552/534 (1985); European patent 0113720 (1988); 3 reg. trademarks; publs: World Intellectual Property Orgn., PCT Gazette (1984), European Patent Bulletin (1984, 1988); rec: art res., photog., writing. Res: 2400 Pacific Ave San Francisco 94115-1275 Ofc: San Francisco Painter Magnate Rincon Ctr San Francisco 94119-3368

KRIEGBAUM, RICHARD, college president; b. Mar. 26, 1941, Long Beach; s. Arnold Richard and Laura Elizabeth (Miller) K.; m. Elona Alice, Aug. 25, 1962; children: Arnold Richard b. 1963, Sonya Christina Wainscott b. 1965; edn: BA in Spanish, Wheaton Coll., 1963; MA in Spanish, Ball St. Univ., 1966; PhD edn., SUNY at Buffalo, 1976. Career: tchr. Warsaw Christian, Warsaw, Ind. 1964-65; Warsaw Comm. High Sch., 1965-66; instr. Grace Coll., Winona Lake, Ind. 1966-67; assoc. prof. Wheaton Coll., Wheaton, Ill. 1967-76, dir. d.p. & research 1976-79, dir. plan. & research 1979-83, dir. plan. & mktg. 1983-84; v.p. adminstrn. Fresno Pacific Coll., Fresno, Calif. 1984-85, pres. 1985–; trustee Grace Coll. & Sem., Ind. 1971-76; dir. Scripture Press Publs., Wheaton, Ill. 1980-; resource scholar Christianity Today, Carol Stream, Ill. 1985–; mem. Christian Coll. Coalition (dir. 1988-91, com. for nat. mktg. 86-), Indep. Colls. of No. Calif. (exec. bd. 1985-), Rotary Internat. (chair internat. student com. 1988-89); author: A Marketing Approach to Program Development, 1979, Marketing to Advance the Small College, 1981; Mennonite Brethren. Res: 5432 E Montecito Ave Fresno 93727 Ofc: Fresno Pacific College, 1717 S Chestnut Ave Fresno 93702

KRISSOFF, WILLIAM BRUCE, orthopaedic surgeon; b. Oct. 16, 1946, Grand Rapids, Mich.; s. Abraham and Sylvia (Gittlen) K.; m. Christine McGee, Sept. 16, 1978; children: Nathan Michael b. 1981, Austin Price b. 1983; edn: BA cum laude, Oberlin Coll. 1968; MD Univ. Colo., Denver 1972; S.F. Gen. 1972-73; Univ. Colo., Denver 1973-74; Univ. Calif., Davis 1975-79; dipl. Am. Bd. Orthopaedic Surgery 1980. Career: emergency room physician St. Anthony Hosp., Denver, Colo. 1974-75; pvt. practice orthopaedic surgery, Truckee 1979–; clin. asst. prof. orthopaedics, Univ. Calif. Davis, Sacto. 1981-94; clin. asst. prof. Univ. of Nevada, Reno; chief surgery Tahoe Forest Hosp., Truckee (1987-88, 93); vice chief of staff 1985-86; mem: Am. Acad. Orthopaedic Surgeons, Am. Soc. for Sports Medicine, We. Orthopaedic Assn.; author: num. articles pub. in med. jours. rec: white water kayaking, skiing, running. Ofc: Mountain Medical Center 10051 Lake St. Truckee 96161

KROEGER, HELGA ELIZABETH, lawyer; b. Oct. 26, 1954, Winnipeg, Canada; d. Arthur and Elfriede (Hirsack) Kroeger; edn: JD, Freiburg Law Sch. Germany 1978; PhD, 1983; LL.M, UC Berkeley Boalt Hall 1986. Career: atty. Boesebeck Barz et al, Frankfurt, W. Germany 1984-85; Skadden Arps et al, Los Angeles 1987-94; of counsel, Jones, Day, Reavis & Pogue 1994–; asst. prof. Univ. Freiburg Law Sch. 1981-84; awards: Deutscher Akademischer Austauschdienst scholarship 1985, UC Berkeley Boalt Hall Prosser Prize 1986; mem: German Am. Lawyers Assn., Calif. Bar Assn., Vereinigung Ehemaliger und Freunde des Deutschen Akademischen Austausch Dienstes; author: Die Marktshwaechere Partei im Internationalen Vertragsrecht (1984). Ofc: Jones, Day, Reavis & Pogue, Westendstrasse 41, 60325 Frankfurt, Germany

KROGH, PETER SUNDEHL, III, family physician, educator; b. Jan. 29, 1953, Chgo.; s. Peter Sundehl Krogh Jr. and Audrey Rose (Kalal) Morgan; m. Cynthia Marie Umano, Mar. 4, 1978; children: Amy b. 1979, Christen b. 1980, Gina b. 1984, Julie b. 1986; edn: BS, USAF Acad., 1975; MD, Rush Med. Coll., 1979; nat. bd. cert. 1980. Career: served to Lt. Col. US Air Force 1975–; family practice resident David Grant USAF Med. Ctr., Travis AFB, Calif. 1979-82; staff family physician Scott USAF Med. Ctr., Scott AFB, Ill. 1982-84; Irsklion USAF Hosp., Crete, Greece 1984-86; David Grant USAF Med. Ctr., Travis AFB, Calif. 1986–, faculty residency pgm. 1986–, dir. family practice residency pgm. 1992–; awarded Fam. Practice tchr. of year David Grant USAF Med. Ctr. 1987-88; mem. Am. Acad. Fam. Physicians 1982–, Uniformed Services Acad. of Fam. Physicians 1982–; Evangelical Christian; rec: outdoors, biking, music. Res: 140 Alturas Ct Vacaville 95688 Ofc: David Grant USAF Med. Ctr./SGHF Travis Air Force Base CA 94535

KRUEGER, KENNETH JOHN, nutrition and exercise consultant and international lecturer, educator, corporate executive; b. Jan. 29, 1946, Los Angeles; s. Charles Herbert and Adelaide Marie K.; m. Ellen Santucci, June 16, 1979 (div. 1989); children: Kenneth b. 1980, Michael b. 1982, Scott b. 1983, David b. 1985; edn: BS humanities, USC, 1968; MS in edn., psych., Mt. St. Mary's Coll., 1972. Career: English tchr. Corcoran (Calif.) High Sch., 1968, Charter Oak High Sch., Covina 1969-90; nutrition and exercise instr. Mt. San Antonio Coll., Walnut 1974-

79; coach, v.p. Trojan Swim Club, Newport Beach 1978–; dir. Nutrition & Exercise Consultants, Sacramento 1985–; nutrition & exercise dir. Health America 1987-90, pres. The Krueger Group, 1991–, pres. Swiss Nat. Team Nutritionist 1995–; chmn. nutrition & fitness com. of Internat. Eating Disorders Week 1988; recruiter Club Med, Paris, Fr. 1976-78; program coord. Pacific Am. Inst., San Francisco 1983; asst. swim coach Swiss National Team 1968, 1985; chief marshall U.S. Olympic Swim Trials, Irvine 1980, linguistics chmn. protocol, USC Venue, L.A. Olympic Com. 1983-84; mem.-at-lg. long distance com. U.S. Swimming, Colo. Spgs. 1987-91, coach So. Calif. long distance Swimming, 1987-89; Meet dir. 1988 and 1989 U.S. 25K Long Distance Swimming Championships, Long Beach also 1988 FINA Cup Trials, Long Beach, U.S. Nat. team nutritionist for FINA World Cup 1988 Champions; coach and swimmer So. Calif. Swimming for Internat. Crossing of Lake Geneva, Switz. (1st competition sponsored by Internat. Olympic Com. other than the Olympics, 1987); awards: NCAA Nat. Champion, All American, USC 1966, U.S. Masters Swimming Champion (1972, 74, 75, 76, 77, 78, 79, 80, 81), Internat. Senior Olympics Champion, L.A. (1972, 74, 75, 76, 77, 78, 79, 80, 81, 84, 85), recipient commendations U.S. Congress, Calif. Senate 1986, and L.A. Co. Bd. Suprs. 1984, 86; lodge: K.C.; author: Reflections and Refractions, 1973, papers: Nutrition and Exercise for the Olympic Family, Healthful Hints, Nutrition & Exercise: Health Twins, Dozen Simple Rules of Good Nutrition; Republican; Cath.; rec: sports, reading. Ofc: The Krueger Group 3445 Mayhew Rd #79 Sacramento 95827

KRUEGER, KURT A., educator, consultant; b. Jan. 29, 1946, Los Angeles; s. Charles H. and Adlaide M. Krueger; m. Teresa A.; 1 son, Keith; edn: AA, L.A. Valley Coll., 1967; BA, Univ. of Colo. 1969; MS, Mt. St. Mary's Coll. 1972; cert. Siddha Yoga Instr. 1981, USC 1985; Calif. Secondary Teaching Cred. (life) 1972. Career: swim instr., coach Kris Kristenson and Woodland Hills Swim Schools, Van Nuys 1965-70; water polo coach Univ. of Colo. 1968; instr. L.A. Unified Sch. Dist. 1969, 1972-81, 1984-91, 1992– Torrance Unified Sch. Dist. 1969-72; faculty Calif. State Univ. L.A. 1980-86; faculty Glendale Coll. 1978-81; founder, dir. Inst. of Sports Psychology, Bombay and Dept. of Practical Sports Psychology, Tarzana 1982–; instr. sports psychology CSU Long Beach 1979, CSU Dominguez Hills 1980, Nat. Inst. of Sports, India 1982, Stockholm Univ. 1983; taught sports psychol. to nat. athletes and coaches of: Am., Argentina, Austr., Great Britain, Finland, India, Japan, New Zealand, Sweden, Switzerland, 1978–; instr. Stress Mgmt., Peak Performance, Yoga, Mediation, Winning Ways at L.A.: Valley, Pierce and City Colleges, and Mt. San Antonio, Cerrritos, Glendale, Orange Coast, Rio Hondo, Saddleback, Long Beach City, Moorpark and Ventura Colleges, and Calif. State Univ. L.A., U.S. Mil. Acad., St. Xavier's & Somaiya Colleges, Assn. of Sports Medicine (India), IBD Tokyo, GIH-Pedagogic Inst. (Sweden) 1974–; instr. of Stress Mgmt. or Success Systems for: L.A. Unified Sch. Dist. teachers 1978-80, the UN, Calif. State Employees Assn., IBM, Learning Annex, Bozell Advertising Inc, Oxford Univ. Med. Sch., Bajaj Elec. Corp., Young Pres.'s Orgn., Rotary Clubs of Bombay and New Delhi, Delhi Devel. Auth., All India Inst. of Med. Scis.; honors: All-Metropolitan Conf. Water Polo Team 1964, 65, All-American Jr. Coll. Swim Team, Helms Athletic Found. 1966, 4 sch. swimming records Univ. Colo. 1968, sr. Olympic swim championship medals: 4 gold (1979), 3 gold, 3 silver (1980), 2 gold, 1 silver (1981), 2 gold, 1 silver (1984), 2 gold, 1 silver (1985); mem: Internat. Soc. of Sport Psychology, Assn. for Advancement of Applied Sport Psychology (charter), Calif. Parent Teacher Student Assn., Calif. Assn. for Health, Physical Edn., Recreation and Dance; co-cons. on creation of vision-tng. device "AcuVision 2000" for AcuVision Systems Inc, New York, 1986; author 2 books: Japan Hijack, 1978, Winning Ways, 1996; audio tape: Winning Ways, 1988; num. articles in profl. jours. and mags.; rec: skiing, beach volleyball, basketball, hiking, world travel, imitating Christ, writing, bicycling. Address: Kurt A. Krueger, Inst. of Sports Psychology 5175 Mecca Ave Tarzana 91356 Tel: 818/377-4012

KUHN, IRVIN NELSON, physician, educator; b. Aug. 18, 1928, Winnipeg, Canada; nat. 1977; s. Gottfred and Wanda L. K.; m. Doreen M. L., July 3, 1956; children: Jill b. 1968, Erin b. 1968, Jay b. 1970; edn: BA, Loma Linda Univ. 1950; MD, 1955. Career: instr. medicine Loma Linda Univ. 1961, asst. prof. 1965, assoc. prof. 1972, prof. 1978–; honors: Alpha Omega Alpha, Who's Who Cancer Prof.; mem: CMA, AMA, FACP, FRCP (Can.), Nat. Assn. VA Physicians, L.A. Acad. Medicine, Nat. Assn. Advancement of Sci., Am. Coll. Physician Execs.; author num. articles, abstracts and presentations; SDA; rec: travel, carving, wilderness adventure. Res: 36333 Panorama Dr Yucaipa 92399 Ofc: ACOS(E), JLPMVAH, Loma Linda 92357

KUKKONEN, CARL ALLAN, physicist/research director space microelectronics and advanced computing technology; b. Jan. 25, 1945, Duluth, Minn.; s. Carl Allan and Shirley Minette (Miller) K.; m. Noreen Dorothy Cullen, June 22, 1968; children: Carl b. 1973, Daniel b. 1975; edn: AA, Foothill Coll., 1966; BS in physics UC Davis, 1968; MS and PhD in physics, Cornell Univ., 1970, 1975. Career: research assoc. Purdue Univ., 1975-77; sr. res. scientist Ford Motor Co., Dearborn 1977-79, prin. res. scientist assoc. 1979-80, prin. res. engr. 1980-84; dir. advanced microelectronics pgm. Jet Propulsion Laboratory, Pasadena 1984-87, dir. Ctr. for Space Microelectronics, 1987–, also mgr. Supercomputing Project 1988–; mgr. microelectronics technology pgm. 1988-90, mgr. microelectronics and adv. computing tech., 1990–; awarded NASA Exceptional Achiev.

Medal 1992; mem. Am. Physical Soc. 1973–, Nat. Assn. of Watch and Clock Collectors 1970–. Res: 5467 La Forest Dr La Canada 91011 Ofc: JPL M/S 180-604, 4800 Oak Grove Dr Pasadena 91109

KUMLI, RAYMOND PAUL, executive, information consultant; b. June 6, 1938, San Francisco; s. Wilfred Julius and Nancy Henrietta (Outsen) K.; m. Sherryl Anne Spietz, Oct. 2, 1965; 1 son, Paul b. 1968; edn: BA econ., UC Berkeley 1961. Career: portfolio mgr. Bank of Am., San Francisco 1965-68; municipal splst. L.F. Rothschild & Co. 1968-69; municipal bond dept. mgr. Kidder Peabody & Co. 1969-73; municipal bond splst. First Boston Corp., NYC 1973-76; pres. and CEO, McCord Co., San Francisco 1976-89; pres. Goosecross Cellars Inc., a Napa Valley winery, 1991-92; exec. v.p. Resource Biometrics Inc., Emeryville 1994; v.p. Transvivo Inc. 1994–; instr. Coll. of Marin, Kentfield 1989–; club: Olympic; mil: lt. USN 1961-64; Democrat; Episcopalian; rec: golf. Res: POB 846 Ross 94957 Ofc: Resource Biometrics Inc. Emeryville 94608

KUMP, KARY RONALD, lawyer; b. April 27, 1952, Provo, Utah; s. Ronald and Ann (Thomas) K.; m. Terri Renee Farley, Aug. 11, 1978; 5 sons: Kasey Ronald b. 1979, Kyle Thomas b. 1982, Kristopher Lewis b. 1984, Kolby Lawrence b. 1987, and Karson Jack b. 1990; edn: AA, Rio Hondo Coll. 1972; BA, CSU Fullerton 1977; JD, Western St. Coll. of Law 1980. Career: atty., assoc. Kellen & Luchs Atts., Riverside 1980-84; ptnr. Luchs Kump & Mihelich 1984-86; Carter & Kump 1986-87; Kump & Kennedy, Attys. at Law, 1987–; judge pro tem Riverside Municipal Ct.; mediator 4th Dist. Court of Appeals; arbitrator Riverside Superior Ct.; honors: St. Bd. Govs. Calif. Vol. Legal Services 1984; mem: Riverside Bar Assn., Am. Bar Assn., Calif. Trial Lawyers Assn., Am. Trial Lawyers Assn., BSA, Am. Platform Soc.; Republican; Mormon; rec: tennis, golf, scuba. Ofc: 6956 Indiana Ave. Ste 11 Riverside 92506

KUPERS, TERRY ALLEN, psychiatrist; b. Oct. 14, 1943, Phila. Pa.; s. Edward Carlton and Frances Shirley (Praissman) K.; m. Ruth Tavlin, June 23, 1968 (div. 1979); m. 2d. Arlene Marilyn Shmaeff, Jan. 16, 1982; children: Eric b. 1971, Jake b. 1973 (adopted, 1989), Jesse b. 1975; edn: BA, psychology (with distinction), Stanford Univ. 1964; MD, UCLA Sch. Medicine 1968; Masters in Social Psychiatry (M.S.P.), UCLA Neuropsychiatric Inst. 1974; lic. physician, Calif. 1968; cert. Am. Bd. of Psychiatry and Neurology 1974. Career: intern Kings. Co. Hosp./Downstate Med. Ctr., Brooklyn, NY 1968-69; resident in psychiatry UCLA Neuropsychiatric Inst. 1969-72; registrar in psychiatry Tavistock Inst. London, Eng. 1971-72; fellow in social and comm. psychiatry, UCLA Neuropsychiatric Inst. 1972-74; pvt. practice psychiatry, L.A. and Oakland 1972–; staff psychiatrist LA. Co., SouthEast Mental Health Ctr. 1972-74; staff psychiatrist, co-dir. outpatient dept. Martin Luther King, Jr. Hosp., L.A. 1974-77; asst. prof. psychiatry, asst. dir. psychiatry residency edn. Charles Drew Postgrad. Med. Sch., L.A. 1974-77; staff psychiatrist and co-dir. Partial Hosp., Richmond Comm. Mental Health Ctr., Contra Costa Co. 1977-81; prof. Grad. Sch. of Psychology, The Wright Inst., Berkeley 1981–; hosp. staff Alta Bates Med. Ctr., Berkeley (credentials com., chair sub. com. to credential lic. clin. social workers, 1989–); cons./staff trainer: Contra Costa Co. Mental Health Svs., Merrithew Mem. Hosp. Nsg. Svc., Bay Area Comm. Svs., Oakland 1988–, Progress Found., S.F., Operation Concern, S.F., Marin Co. Mental Health Svs., Berkeley Psychotherapy Inst., Berkeley Mental Health Clinic, Ore. Dept. Mental Health, Kaiser Permanente Depts. of Psychiatry, Oakland, San Rafael, Martinez, Walnut Creek; expert witness, forensic psychiatry (num. testimonies on conditions and mental health svs. in Calif. jails and prisons, 1977–); mem. editl. advy. panel, Free Associations (jour.), London, Eng. 1990–; honors: Alpha Omega Alpha, listed Who's Who Among Human Svs. Profls.; mem: Am. Psychiatric Assn. 1972- (fellow, 1984), No. Calif. Psychiatric Soc., East Bay Psychiatric Soc., Am. Orthopsychiatric Assn. (fellow, 1978–), Nat. Orgn. for Men Against Sexism 1990; author (books): Public Therapy: The Practice of Psychotherapy in the Public Mental Health Clinic (Free Press/MacMillan, 1981), Ending Therapy: The Meaning of Termination (NY Univ. Press, 1988; Italian translation pub. in Rome, 1992), Revisioning Men's Lives: Gender, Intimacy and Power (Guilford Publs., 1993), contbr. num. articles to profl. jours., 1970-93; editor (book): Using Psychodynamic Principles in Public Mental Health (Jossey-Bass, 1990); Jewish; rec: playing flute, wilderness. Ofc: 8 Wildwood Ave Oakland 94610

KURAISHI, AKARI LUKE, real estate company executive; b. July 29, 1959, Nagano, Japan; came to U.S., 1984; s. Atsushi and Kuniko (Tomita) K.; m. Hiromi Lydia Hatae, Oct. 10, 1987; children: Katrina Ayumi b. 1988, Kristin Kasumi b. 1991; edn: BA, Nat. Defense Acad., Yokosuka, Japan 1982; MBA, Univ. of Dallas, Tx. 1986; RIM, Internat. R.E. Inst., 1990. Career: mgr. Gateway Travel & Tours, Dallas 1985-87; staff mem. portfolio investments dept. Mitsui Real Estate Sales U.S.A. Co., Ltd., Los Angeles 1987-90, mgr. 1990-91, asst. vice pres. Mitsui Real Estate Sales U.S.A. Co., Ltd., Los Angeles 1991-95, v.p. 1995–; dir: Alkaly Inc., Orange 1991–, v.p. Santa Ana Corp., Santa Ana 1992–; v.p. Santa Ana Management Corp., Santa Ana 1992–; secty. MI Partners (LA) Co., Ltd., Los Angeles 1993–; mem: Internat. R.E. Inst. 1990–, Univ. Dallas Alumni Assn. 1986–, Orange Co. Japanese Am. Assn. (1993–, dir. 1994–), Japanese/Am. Network 1994–, Nat. Rifle Assn. 1993–; rec: shooting, music. Res: 2348 E Trenton Ave Orange 92667 Ofc: Mitsui Real Estate Sales U.S.A. Co. Ltd. 601 S Figueroa St Ste 4600 Los Angeles 90017

KURNICK, NATHANIEL B., cancer research physician; b. Nov. 8, 1917, New York; s. Jacob and Celia (Levine) K.; m. Dorothy Manheimer, Oct. 4, 1940 (dec. 1985); m. Sally Anne Kreeger, June 23, 1989; children: John E. Kurnick b. 1942, Katherine b. 1946 (dec. 1965), James T. Kurnick b. 1947; edn: BA, Harvard Univ. 1936; MD, Harvard Med. Sch. 1940; fellow Harvard Med. Sch. 1940-41; intern Mt. Sinai Hosp. 1942, sr. resident, 1946; fellow Rockefeller Inst. 1947; fellow Nobel Inst. 1948-49. Career: asst. prof. medicine Tulane Med. Sch., New Orleans, La. 1949-54; chief hematology service VA Hosp., Long Beach 1954-59; assoc. clin. prof. medicine UCLA 1954-64; pvt. practice, Long Beach 1959-83; clin. prof. medicine UC Irvine 1964–; dir. Bixby Lab. Long Beach Comm. Hosp., Long Beach 1982–; cons. VA Hosp. Long Beach 1954–; chmn. cancer act. Long Beach Comm. Hosp. 1968-89, chmn. dept. med. oncology hematology 1982-87; honors: Sigma Xi; mem: Long Beach Soc. Internal Medicine (pres. 1971), A.C.P. (fellow), Internat. Soc. Exptl. Hematology, Am. Soc. Hematology, Western Soc. Clin. Research, Central Soc. Clin. Research, Condit Club, Harvard Club, Garden Grove Union H.S. Dist. (trustee 1960-64); research papers pub. in sci. jours., 1942–; mil: capt. AUS MC 1942-46; Democrat; Jewish; rec: sailing, skiing. Ofc: 1760 Termino Ave Ste G-20 Long Beach 90804

KUROKAWA, TORU, financial executive; b. Feb. 27, 1948, Tokyo, Japan; s. Yu and Tomiko (Fukuda) K.; m. Michiko Meguro, Jan. 12, 1974; children: Ayako b. 1976, Chihiro George b. 1980; edn: BA bus. adminstrn., Adyama Univ. Tokyo 1970; Facom Computer Sch. Tokyo 1973; Cornell Univ. 1977. Career: trainee bus. New Otani Hotel, Tokyo, Japan 1969-70, restaurant waiter 1970-73, computer programmer 1973-76, system planner 1976-78, project mgr. New Otani Co. Ltd. 1978-79, asst. v.p., c.f.o., secty. New Otani Am., Los Angeles 1979–; mem: Little Tokyo Lions (pres.), Little Tokyo Bus. Assn. (secty.), Little Tokyo Comm. Devel. Advy. Com. (bd. mem.), Nisei Week Japanese Festival, Concordia Orchestra Soc. (UP); clubs: Adyama Gakuin Alumni, California CC; R.Cath.; rec: skiing, golf, violin. Res: 20804 Covina Hills Rd Covina 91724 Ofc: The New Otani America 120 S Los Angeles St Los Angeles 90012

KURTZ-ABBOTT, PAULA J., accounting manager; b. April 20, 1962, Merced; d. Donald G. and Patsy A. (Bradshaw) Kurtz; m. John K. Abbott, Feb. 21, 1987; edn: BA internat. rels., UC Davis 1984; CSU Bakersfield 1985-87. Career: mgmt. trainee Household Fin., Bakersfield 1985; bookkeeper, acct. Barbich Longcrier Hooper & King 1985-87, retirement plan adminstr. 1987-90; accountant Contel 1990-91; acctg. mgr. Pepsi Cola Bottling Co. 1991–; mem: Inst. of Management Accountants, Soc. Prevention Cruelty to Animals; Democrat; rec: home remodelling, bicycling, gardening. Ofc: Pepsi Cola Bottling Co 215 E 21st St Bakersfield 93305

KUSHNER, JAMES ALAN, law professor, author; b. April 14, 1945, Philadelphia, Pa.; s. Solomon L. and Lois Ethel (Gerson) K.; m. Jacki Fregean, May 15, 1970; children: Gretchen b. 1972, Andrew b. 1976, Ryan b. 1983; edn: BA, Univ. Miami 1967; JD, LL.B. Univ. Md. 1968. Career: legal cons. Urban League, Canton, Ohio 1969; dir. housing Office Econ. Opportunity 1969-70; mng. atty. Legal Aid of Western Mo., Kansas City 1970-73; project atty. Nat. Housing Law Project, Berkeley 1973-75; prof. of law Southwestern Univ., Los Angeles 1975–; vis. lectr. UC Berkeley 1974-75; Univ. Va., Charlottesville 1981; vis. prof. law UCLA, 1983, 93; Rubey M. Hulen vis. prof. law Univ. Mo., Kansas City 1985-86; author Apartheid in Am., 1980, Housing and Comm.Devel., 1981, 2nd edit., 1989, Fair Housing, 2d edit., 1995, Govt. Discrimination, 1988, Subdivision Law and Growth Management, 1991; rec: coach-youth sports. Ofc: Southwestern University 675 S Westmoreland Ave Los Angeles 90005

KUWAHARA, STEVEN SADAO, biochemist; b. July 20, 1940, Lahaina, Maui, Hawaii; s. Toshio and Hideko (Sasaki) K.; m. Rene M. Miyajima, June 24, 1972; children: Daniel T. b. 1974, Sara S. b. 1978; edn: BS, Cornell Univ. 1962; MS, Univ. Wisc. 1965, PhD, 1967. Career: research asst. Univ. Wisc. 1962-66; res. assoc. Univ. Wash. Seattle 1966-67; asst. prof. CSU Long Beach 1967-71; asst. res. biol. UC Irvine 1971-73; unit chief Mich. Dept. of Public Health, Lansing 1973-76, sect. chief 1976-82; mgr. test technol. Hyland Therapeutics, L.A. 1982-90; mgr. validations Baxter Immunotherapy, Duarte 1990–; adj. res. assoc. Coll. of Human Med., Mich. State Univ. 1980-82; honors: Award of Merit (Long Beach Heart Assn. 1969), Spl. Res. Fellowship (NIH 1971-73); mem: AAAS, Am. Assn. Blood Banks, Am. Chem. Soc., Am. Fedn. Clin. Res., Am. Soc. Microbiology, Soc. for Exptl. Biol. & Med., NY Acad. of Scis., BSA (scoutmaster); publ: 28 sci. papers, 20 presentations; Buddhist (treas. W. Covina Buddhist Ch.); rec: stamps, gardening. Res: 975 W Amador St Claremont 91711 Ofc: Baxter Healthcare-Immunotherapy 9 Parker Irvine 92718

KUWAYAMA, GEORGE, art museum senior curator; b. Feb. 25, 1925, N.Y.C.; s. Senzo and Kuma K.; m. Lillian Y. Yamashita, Dec. 11, 1961; children: Holly b. 1964, Mark b. 1966, Jeremy b. 1972; edn: BA, Williams Coll. 1948; Inst. of Fine Arts N.Y. Univ.; MA, Univ. Mich., Ann Arbor 1956. Career: Keeper's asst. Cooper Union Museum, N.Y. summer 1954; curator Los Angeles County Mus. of Art, 1959-69, senior curator, 1969–; lectr. Univ. So. Calif., UCLA, CSU Northridge; awards: Charles Freer Scholar, Louise Hackney Fellow, Inter-University Fellow; mem: College Art Assn., Assn. for Asian Studies, Am. Oriental Soc., Internat. House of Japan, China Colloquium; editor

and author: Imperial Taste (1989); author: Shippo: The Art of Enameling in Japan (1987), The Quest for Eternity (1987), Japanese Ink Printing (1985); ed. New Perspectives on the Art of Ceramics (1992), ed. Ancient Mortuary Traditions of China (1991), ed. Papers on Chinese Funeral Sculptures (1991); mil: pfc Parachute Inf. US Army 1944-46; Indep.; Methodist. Res: 1417 Comstock Ave Los Angeles 90024 Ofc: L.A. County Museum of Art 5905 Wilshire Blvd Los Angeles 90036

KWASKY, ALBERT JOSEPH, naval architecture and marine engineering company president; b. Nov. 2, 1919, Manistee, Mich.; s. Joseph Albert and Antonia Regenia (Krasniewski) K.; m. Virginia Moore, Aug. 26, 1949; edn: BA, Columbia Coll.; postgrad. electronics engring., 1943-44, Stanford Univ.; electrical engring., 1945, Univ. Calif.; Registered Professional Engr., Calif. 1946. Career: elect. engr. Hurley Marine Works, Oakland 1942-45; elec. engr. Pillsbury & Martignoni, Inc., San Francisco 1946-62, marine engr. 1963-71, marine engr. supvr. 1972-78, mgr. 1979-81, pres. 1982- (only the third pres. of firm founded in 1901, as the first pres. Capt. Albert Pillsbury lived to age 94, and 2d pres. Walter L. Martignoni lived to 101 yrs); editor Electronics Systems Tech. Manual for USS Hancock (CVA-19) and USS Oriskany (CVA-34); mem: US Naval Institute, Navy League of the US, Soc. of Naval Archs. and Marine Engrs.; civic: The Nature Conservancy, Nat. Audubon Soc., Sierra Club, New England Anti-Vivisection Soc.; publs: The Old Lady in Dubuque, The Old Lady in Dubuque's Other Son, The Old Lady in Dubuque's Town, The Old Lady in Dubuque's Neighbors; R.Cath.; rec: tennis, chess, mtn. climbing, bird watching. Res: 2418 Ashby Ave Berkeley 94705 Ofc: Pillsbury & Martignoni, Inc. Pier 1 San Francisco 94111

KYLE, ROBERT TOURVILLE, executive engineer; b. Jan. 15, 1910, Deadwood, So.Dak.; s. Robert Doughty and Mellanie Irene (DeTourville) K.; m. Colette Bertha Hart, May 29, 1937; 1 son, Robert b. 1941; edn: BES, Johns Hopkins Univ. 1931; MBA, Northeastern Univ. 1965; reg. profl. mechanical engr. Calif. 1975. Career: research engr. Am. Gas Assn., Cleveland, Ohio 1931-35; gas engr. Iroquois Gas Co., Buffalo, N.Y. 1935-47; branch mgr. Gen. Controls Co., Cleveland, Ohio 1947-48; v.p. Gas Machinery Co. 1948-59; sr. cons. Commonwealth Services, N.Y.C. 1959-61; v.p. Bay State Gas Co., Boston, Mass. 1961-74; pres. Kyle Assoc. Inc., San Diego 1975-86; honors: Hall of Fame 1979, San Diego City Council Commend. 1983, Rancho Bernardo Town Council Disting. Service 1975; mem: Am. Gas Assn., N. England Guild Gas Mgrs., Rotary; inventor: Oil Gas Apparatus, 1952; Christian; avocation: community service. Res: 16925 Hierba Dr Apt 112 San Diego 92128-2659

LABBÉ, ARMAND JOSEPH, museum anthropologist; b. June 13, 1944, Lawrence, Mass.; s. Armand Henri and Gertrude (Martineau) L.; div.; edn: studies in philosophy, Marist Coll., 1962-63, Russian lang., Indiana Univ., 1963-65, Ger. lang., Univ. Md., West Berlin 1965-67; BA anthropology (cum laude) Univ. Mass., 1969, doctoral pgm. in anthropology 1969-71; MA anthropology, CSU Fullerton, 1986; seminars and workshops UCLA, Smithsonian Instn., Bowers Mus., San Diego Mus. Art; Calif. Comm. Colls. (life) instr. credential anthropology, 1983. Career: Russian language and intelligence analysis US Air Force, W.Berlin, 1965-67; curatorial asst. Bowers Mus., Santa Ana 1978-79, curator anthropology 1979–, chief curator 1986–, director for research and collections 1991–; p.t. faculty Santa Ana Coll., 1981-86, UC Irvine, 1983, 87, 91, CSU Fullerton, 1982-84, 88, UC Irvine 1993; trustee Americas Found. (for purpose of understanding cultures and histories of the Americas), Mass. 1985–; trustee Balboa Art Conservation Ctr., San Diego 1989–, adv. bd. Elan Internat., Newport Beach; trustee Mingei Internat. Mus., San Diego; hon. bd. mem. Ethnic Arts Council of L.A.; author: Man and Cosmos in Prehispanic Mesoamerica, 1982, Skywatchers of Ancient California, 1983, Ban Chiang: Art and Prehistory of Northeast Thailand, 1985, Colombia Before Columbus: The People, Culture and Ceramic Art of Prehispanic Colombia (1986, Spanish edit. 1988), Leigh Wiener: Portraits, 1989, Images of Power, 1992, co-author Tribute to the Gods: Treasures of the Museo de Oro, 1992, Guardians of the Life Stream, 1995; numerous scholarly papers, interviews (t.v. and print media) and lectures; contbg. and sole photographer books and art mags., 1980–; awards: honoree of the Colombian govt. and Colombian Inst. of Anthropology at Museo de Oro, Bogotá 1988, Colombian nat. postage stamp inspired by cover of book Colombia Antes de Colon 1989, author-honoree Friends of Library UC Irvine, 1987, 1988, inaugural guest lectr. for Lewis K. Land Memorial Lecture endowed by Friends of Ethnic Art of S.F. at M.H. de Young Mus. 1988, gold 1st pl. award for book entry Ad Club of We. Mass. 1987, recogn. Orange Cty. Bd. Suprs. 1982, Bowers Mus. Found. Bd. Dirs. 1982; mem: AAAS, NY Acad. Scis., Am. Anthropol. Assn. (Fellow), Southwestern Anthropol. Assn., Am. Assn. Museums, We. Museums Conf., Nat. Trust Hist. Preserv., Am. Assn. for State/Local History, Nat. Assn. for Mus. Exh., Am. Mus. Natural History, Smithsonian Instn., San Diego Mus. of Man, Newport Harbor Art Mus., Wilson Ctr. Assocs., Art Asia Mus. (Monterey), Acad. of Polit. Sci., Assn. Corporate Art Curators. Ofc: Bowers Museum 2002 N Main St Santa Ana 92706

LABENSKE, VICTOR KRIS, college professor; b. Dec. 26, 1963, Jonesboro, Ark.; s. George Elbert and Lois (Santo) L.; m. Judith Spaite, June 10, 1989; edn: BA in Music, Point Loma Nazarene Coll., S.D., Calif. 1985; M. of Music, Piano Performance, Univ. of Mo. Conservatory of Music, Kan. City, Mo. 1987; D.M.A.

in Piano Performance, Univ. of So. Calif., L.A. 1993. Career: grad. tchg. asst., Univ. of Mo., Kan. City 1985-87; assoc. prof. of music, Point Loma Nazarene Coll., S.D., Calif. 1987–; pianist, Opening Ceremonies 1984 Olympics, L.A.; awards: Herb Alpert Music Scholarship, L.A. 1981; 1st pl. SAI Composition Competition, Sigma Alpha Iota, Kan. City, Mo. 1986; Acad. All-Am. Scholar, Kan. City 1987; Scholarship, Mu Phi Epsilon, Kan. City 1987; Pi Kappa Lambda Award, L.A. 1993, 1st pl. Mu Phi Epsilon Nat. Composition Competition 1993; mem: Mu Phi Epsilon 1986–, Phi Kappa Phi 1987, Pi Kappa Lambda 1987, ASCAP 1987–; nat. certified mem. Music Teachers Nat. Assn. 1988–, Calif. Assn. of Profl. Music Tchrs. 1988–, Point Loma Nazarene Coll. Music Alumni Assn. (v.p. 1991-94); handbell choir dir., First Ch. of the Nazarene, S.D. 1987–; creative works: arranger of pub. piano hymn arrangements: Take My Life and Let It Be, 1987; It Is Well With My Soul, 1989; Manger Trilogy, 1990; There Is A Savior, 1990; Church of the Nazarene; rec: gardening. Ofc: Point Loma Nazarene College, 3900 Lomaland Dr. San Diego 92106-2899

LABOE, ART, broadcast and music entertainment executive; b. Aug. 7, 1925, Salt Lake City; s. John Egnoian and Hosanna Kezerian; m. Deidre Thompson, June 10, 1961 (div. 1964); children: Arthur b. 1953, Charles b. 1955; edn: Stanford Univ. 1942-44, San Mateo Jr. Coll. 1942, L.A. City Coll. 1946-47; electronic engr. cert., US Army, 1943. Career: radio personality KOLO Radio, Reno, Nev. 1948-49; radio personality freelance various stations Los Angeles 1949-59; mgr. operations KRLA Radio, L.A. 1976-79, senior v.p. 1979-81; pres. Original Sound Ent., Hollywood 1959–; cons. Royal Programs, Hollywood 1976–, cons. KRLA Radio 1985-87; instr. Spear Sch. of Radio, Hollywood 1952-55; awards: music achievement awards ASCAP, N.Y. (1959), and BMI, N.Y. (1960), star Hollywood Blvd. Walk of Fame (1981); mem. Hollywood C.of C.; author: D.J.: Life of A Disc Jockey (1989); mil: capt. USAR 1948-65; Republican (charter Presdl. Task Force 1980–); Republican; Mormon; rec: horses, swimming, tennis. Ofc: Original Sound 7120 Sunset Blvd Los Angeles 90046

LACHMAN, BRANTON GEORGE, lawyer; b. Nov. 7, 1952, Altadena; s. Richard George and Blanche Marie (Bayless) L.; m. Sally Reid Johnson, Jan. 10, 1981; children: Hannah, Rose; edn: BA music edn., chem., CSU Fullerton, 1975; PharmD, USC Sch. Pharmacy, 1979; JD (summa cum laude, Valedictorian), Western State Univ. Coll. of Law, Fullerton 1992. Career: lic. pharmacist pvt. practice, Riverside 1979-81; hosp. pharmacist Western Med. Ctr., Santa Ana 1981-83; tchr. music Yucaipa High Sch. 1983-84; v.p. Pontil, Inc. Corona 1984-89; clin. asst. prof. pharmacy, adj., USC, 1986-92; clin. pharmacist PHI Health Care Mgmt. Inc., Laguna Hills 1989-90; sci. and music tchr. Centennial High Sch., Corona-Norco Unified Sch. Dist., 1990-92; judicial extern Hon. Edward J. Wallin, 4th Dist. Ct. Appeal, Div. III, 1991; patent litigation extern law firm Christie, Parker & Hale, 1992; civil litigation extern law firm Clayson, Mann, Arend & Yaeger, 1991, joined firm, atty., assoc. 1992-93; atty. assoc. Brunick, Alvarez & Batttersby 1993-94; corporate counsel The Guffey Companies, Inc. 1994–; of counsel, Law Ofcs. of T.W. Ronald Danieri, Corona; adj. prof. law West. St. Coll. Law and Calif. St. Law Sch.; chemistry tchr. La Sierra H.S.; awards: preceptor svc. USC Sch. Pharm 1987, fellow Wm. S. Apple Pharmacy Mgmt. Pgm. 1988, Outstanding Young Men of Am. 1989, editor in chief Western State Univ. Law Rev. (Spring 1991), Honors Moot Ct. semi-finalist best team 1990, outstanding scholastic achiev. West Pub. Co. 1991-92, Am. Jurisprudence Awards, Don Program instr. (torts, property, constnl. law), Who's Who Among Students in Am. Univs. and Colls. 1992, Who's Who in the West 1990, mem. Peter M. Elliott Inn of Ct. (Spring 1992); mem: Am. Pharm. Assn. (nat. chair Home Care sect. 1987), Calif. Pharm. Assn. (founding chair Acad. Home Health Care 1987-90); civic: Corona-Norco USD (science fair judge 1986, 89), Hedrick for Sch. Board (treas. 1988, 92), Hedrick for Supervisor, Corona Peace Watch (founding mem. 1987), Inland Counties Hypertension Coord. Coun. (bd. 1985-90), Corona Fine Arts Com. (pres. 1985), Corona Sr. Citizens Ctr. (med. cons. 1979-89); Republican. Ofc: The Guffey Companies, Inc. 2625 Whispering Pines Dr Running Springs 92382

LACKRITZ, JAMES ROBERT, university educator, administrator; b. Dec. 30, 1950, Columbus, Ohio; s. Irving Ross and Dorothy (Krakoff) L.; m. Karen Marie Kearney, March 23, 1974; children: Kristen b. 1980, Robert b. 1982; edn: BS, Bucknell Univ. 1972; M.Stat., Univ. Fla. 1974; PhD, 1977. Career: tchg. asst., dept. statistics Univ. Fla., Gainesville 1972-77; asst. prof. mgmt. dept. San Diego St. Univ. 1977-81, assoc. prof. 1981-84, prof. 1984-85, prof. IDS dept. 1985–, chair 1986-93; founding faculty Inst. Quality & Productivity 1987–; awards: San Diego St. Univ. MPPP 1985, 89, Outstanding Faculty 1987, Am. Statistical Assn. Best Paper 1979; mem: Am. Statistical Assn., Decision Scis. Inst., Balboa Tennis Club (bd. mem. 1980-82, v.p. 1982-84); num. articles pub. in profl. jours., 1977–, author Statistics for Bus., 1990; rec: tennis, skiing. Ofc: San Diego State University IDS Dept. San Diego 92182-0127

LAFFER, ARTHUR BETZ, economist; b. Aug. 14, 1940, Youngstown, Ohio; s. William G. and Molly (Betz) L.; m. Traci Hickman, Nov. 7, 1982; children: Tricia b. 1964, Art Jr. b. 1966, Molly b. 1969, Rachael b. 1972, Justin b. 1983, Allison b. 1984; edn: courses, Univ. of Munich, Germany; BA economics Yale Univ. 1963; MBA, PhD economics, Stanford Univ. 1972. Career: assoc. prof. Bus. Econ., Univ. of Chicago 1970-76; economist, Ofc. of Mgmt. and Budget U.S. Govt.

1970-72; cons. U.S. Secty. Treasury and Secty. Def., 1972-1977; assoc. editorial pages, Wall Street Journal 1972-77; prof. Bus. Econ. USC 1976-84; disting. univ. prof. Pepperdine Univ., bd. dir. Pepperdine Univ., Santa Monica; founder and chmn. A.B. Laffer Assocs., Lomita; founder and ptnr. A.B. Laffer, V.A. Canto & Assocs. (economics Cons.), La Jolla ; co-founder Calport Asset Mgmt. 1993- mem. policy com. and bd. dirs. Am. Council for Capital Formation, WDC; mem. Econ. Policy Adv. Bd. to the President; ed. Marcel Dekker, Inc. series on Econ., Fin. and Bus.; contbg. ed. Conservative Digest; dir. Gillespie, Laffer, Canto, Inc. (res. firm); honors: two Graham and Dodd awards Fin. Analyst Fed. for articles pub. in Fin. Analysts Jour., disting. svc. award Nat. Assoc. of Investment Clubs, Adam Smith Award 1983, Daniel Webster Award Internat. Platform Assoc. 1979; mem: bd. of dirs. Los Angeles Co. Mus. of Natural Hist. (hon. mem.); adv. bd. Taxpayer's Found., bd. mem. Peninsula Chamber Orch.; adv. bds. SIT Investment Assocs., Inc., Bradford & Marzec, Inc.; bd. mem. Boys Club of Am.; publs: The Financial Analysts Guide to Monetary Policy (1986), The Financial Analysts Guide to Fiscal Policy (1986), Conference on International Trade, Foundations of Supply-side Economics, International Economics in an Integrated World (1983), Future American Energy Policy (1982), De Fiscus Order Het Mes (1981), L'ellipse ou la Loi des Rendements Fiscaux Decroissants (1981), The Economics of the Tax Revolt: A Reader (1976), Private Short-term Capital Flows, The Phenomenon of Worldwide Inflation (1975); Republican; rec: exotic birds, animals, plants. Ofc: A.B Laffer, V.A. Canto & Assocs. La Jolla 92037

LAFLER, DARLYNN JOAN, clinical laboratory scientist; medical technologist; b. July 3, 1961, San Diego; d. David Adam and Carole Joyce (Nicewicz) Lasky; m. Kirk Paul Lafler, July 7, 1984; edn: AS, Grossmont Coll. 1982; BS in microbiol., San Diego St. Univ. 1985; Calif. lic. medical technologist, 1987;cert. clin. lab. scientist, 1987. Career: lab. tech. San Diego Co. Vet., S.D. 1982-85; clin. lab. scientist, med. technologist- Technical Supervisor Sharp Memorial Hospital Laboratory, San Diego 1986–; mem: Am. Soc. Clin. Pathologists, Calif. Assn. for Medical Laboratory Technology, So. Calif. Am. Soc. Microbiology, Nat. Certification Agency for Med. Lab. Personnel Inc., Am. Soc. for Clin. Lab. Sci.; articles publs. in profl. journ. 1989–, res. papers related to Fetal Lung Maturity and Lamellar Body Density Counts 1994–; Republican; R.Cath.; rec: inline skating, computers, swimming. Ofc: Sharp Memorial Hospital (Pathology) San Diego 92123

LAFLER, KIRK PAUL, management and computer services executive; b. Feb. 27, 1956, Penn Yan, N.Y.; s. Paul Alton and Eleanor Theresa (Gombar) L.; m. Darlynn Joan, July 7, 1984; edn: BS, Univ. Miami, 1978; MS, 1982; George Washington Univ., 1981. Career: indep. cons., Miami, Fla. 1976-78; jr. programmer analyst Rydacom Inc. 1978-79; systems engr. Electronic Data Systems, W.D.C. 1979-81; programmer analyst Great American Federal, San Diego 1981-82; systems analyst S.D. Gas & Electric 1982-83; sr. systems analyst, engring. prin., 1983-86; pres./CEO Software Intelligence Corp., S.D. 1984–; honors: Electronic Data Systems commendn. 1981, U.S. DOE commendn. 1981, listed in Who's Who in Computer Industry 1989, Who's Who in West 1989-90; mem: Am. Assn. Artificial Intelligence, So. Calif. SAS Users Group (chmn./pres. 1989–), Assn. Computing Machinery, Internat. Platform Assn.; articles pub. in profl. jours. 1981–; Republican; R.Cath.; rec: computers, sailing, scuba diving, marine biology, basketball. Ofc: Software Intelligence Corp. POB 1390 Spring Valley 91979-1390

LAGASSE, LEO DARRELL, physician, medical educator; b. June 13, 1931, Los Angeles; s. Leo Simeon and Mercedes Myrtle (Condley) L.; m. Ann Atkins, Aug. 19, 1961; children: Susan b. 1963, Janet b. 1964, Peter b. 1967; edn: BS, Loyola Univ. 1952; MD, Univ. Va. Charlottesville 1959. Career: dir. gyn. oncology UCLA Sch. Medicine, Los Angeles 1970-85, prof. ob-gyn. 1976–; dir. gyn. oncology Cedars Sinai Med. Center 1986–; bd. trustees Loyola Marymount Univ. 1970-80; mem: Soc. Gynecologic Oncologists (pres. 1980), A.C.S. (fellow); Soc. Pelvic Surgeons, Western Assn. Gyn. Oncologists (pres. 1976); 100+ papers pub. in sci. jours.; mil: capt. USAFR 1952-54; Republican; R.Cath.; rec: tennis, lecturing. Res: 22866 Beckledge Terrace Malibu 90265 Ofc: Cedars Sinai Medical Center 8700 Beverly Blvd Los Angeles 90048

LAGREEN, ALAN LENNART, radio personality and public relations executive; b. May 20, 1951, Burbank, Calif.; s. Lennart F. and Mary (Cassara) LaGreen; m. Wendy D. Gilmaker, June 28, 1975; l child: Cara b. 1980; edn: BA, Univ. of So. Calif., L.A. 1972. Career: public relations asst. Dames & Moore, L.A., 1972-75; asst. pub. Orange County Illustrated, Newport Beach, 1975; membership mgr. Toastmasters Internat., Santa Ana, 1975-79; dist. adminstrn. mgr. Toastmasters Internat., Santa Ana, 1979-86; meetings mgr. Fluor Corp., Irvine, 1986-87; v.p. CCRA, Inc., Santa Ana, 1987–; publicity chmn. Orange County Visual Artists, Garden Grove, Calif., 1990–; afternoon radio personality KSBR Radio, Mission Viejo; mem: Am. Soc. of Assn. Executives (ASAE), 1979–; Reformed Ch. in Am.; rec: photography, model railroads. Res: 120 W. 20th St. Santa Ana 92706

LAI, DAVID D., international investment advisor, developer, real estate syndicator; b. Dec. 30, 1959, Hong Kong; s. Man Yau and Yuek Ling (Lau) L.; m. Joannie; edn: BA, UCLA, 1982; Worcester Coll., Oxford Univ., 1981; London

Sch. Economics, 1983; MBA, USC, 1986. Career: asst. mgr. Yan Seng Securities, Hong Kong 1983-84; mem. Hong Kong Far East Exchange 1983-84; controller/dir. Wing On Realty Co., Monterey Park 1984-89; dir. Tru-Art Prod. 1985-87; investment syndicator, Syndication Plus Inc., Monterey Park 1992–; dir. Man Kee Wollen Garment Mfr., H.K., 1988–; chief investment ofcr. & v.p. Titan Group, South Pasadena, 1990-92; finance dir. Calif. Sec. of State March Fong Eu Campaign Com. 1989, finance chmn. 1990-92; recipient Assn. College Entrepreneurs-Young Entrepreneur award 1987, Nat. Top 100 Entrepreneurs 30 and under 1988, 89, 90; mem: Orgn. of Chinese-Ams.; civic: Lions Club 1987, Friends of March Fong Eu (steering com. 1986-88), March Fong Eu for Senate 1988, Calif. Hon. Goodwill Amb. 1988-89, 89-90, 90-91, Friends of Hong Kong & Macau (economic & political advr.), Guangdong Clan Assn. (vice supr.), Tuen Kong Found. (bd. dirs. and sec.); R.Cath.; rec: golf, horseback riding, swimming. Res: 10535 Wilshire Blvd Los Angeles Ofc: Syndication Plus Inc 1008 E Garvey Ave Monterey Park 91754 Tel: 818/288-6988

LAKOCY, JACQUELINE M., financial consultant; b. May 13, 1961, Athens, Ohio; d. Edward J. and Mollie Scott (Rippeth) Collins; edn: bus., USC 1986. Career: reg. rep. Merrill Lynch, Los Angeles 1980-85; fin. cons. 1986–; branch mgr., reg. principal Titan Capital, San Francisco 1988-1991; branch mgr., reg. principal Aragon Financial, 1991–; mem: IAFP, Am. Paragliding Assn., USHGA, civic: Sierra Club; rec: windsurfing, mtn. biking, parapente, scuba, skiing. Ofc: 2146 Union St San Francisco 94123

LAKOFF, SANFORD ALLAN, political scientist; b. May 12, 1931, Bayonne, N.J.; s. Herman and Gertrude (Robins) L.; m. Evelyn Schleifer, June 4, 1969; edn: BA, Brandeis Univ. 1953; MA, Harvard Univ. 1955; PhD, 1959. Career: asst. prof. govt. Harvard Univ., Cambridge 1958-64; prof. political sci. St. Univ. N.Y., Stony Brook 1964-66; Univ. Toronto, Canada 1966-74; UCSD, La Jolla 1974–; awards: Brandeis Univ. Behr Prize 1949, Fechter Prize 1953, Harvard Univ. Bowdoin Prize 1955, Warren Coll., UCSD Outstanding Teacher of Yr. 1992; mem: Am. Political Sci. Assn., AAAS, World Affairs Council San Diego; author: Equality in Political Philosophy, 1964, coauthor, A Shield in Space, 1989, editor, Knowledge & Power, 1966, co-editor, Strategic Defense & Western Alliance, 1987; Democrat; Jewish. Ofc: Dept. Polit. Sci. Univ. of Calif. San Diego, La Jolla 92093

LALA, TAPAN KANTI, engineering executive; nat. 1986; s. Deendravijay and Swarna Pratima (Chowdhwry) L.; edn: BSEE, Jadaupur Univ. India 1972; MSEE, Queens Univ. Canada 1977; Univ. Toledo 1977-79. Career: tech. staff Mitre Corp., Bedford, Mass. 1980-81; AT&T Bell Labs., Holmdel, N.J. 1981-84; prin. engr. Motorola Four Phase, Cupertino 1984-85; sr. system engr. Fujitsu Am., San Jose 1985-86; mgr., group leader Granger Assoc. 1986; asst. to asst. gen. mgr. NEC Am. 1986–; sr. dir. ATM Systems; lectr. Univ. Toledo 1977-79; instr., tchg. asst. Queens Univ. 1975-77; awards: Govt. of India grad. fellowship 1974-75, undergrad. fellowships 1967-72; represent NEC in ANSI subcoms.; mem: IEEE (computer soc. and comm. soc.), Univ. Toledo Grad. Student Assn. Activities Com. (chmn. 1977-79); papers reviewed in IEEE conf. tech. jours.; mil: sgt. Air Squadron India 1967-72. Res: 15771 Simoni Dr San Jose 95127

LAM, LUI, physicist, educator; b. Nov. 17, 1944, Lianxian, China; s. Lap-Chung and Lai-Jane (Wong) L.; m. Heung-Mee Lee, July 1, 1972; children: Charlene b. 1977; edn: BS, Univ. Hong Kong, 1965; MS, Univ. Brit. Col., Vancouver 1968; MA, Columbia Univ., NY 1969, PhD, 1973. Career: res. assoc. CUNY City Coll., N.Y. 1972-75; res. scientist Univ. Instelling Antwerpen, Antwerp, Belgium 1975-76; Univ. Saarlandes, Saarbrucken, Germany 1976-77; assoc. res. prof. Academia Sinica, Inst. of Physics, Beijing, China 1978-83; assoc. prof. Queensborough Comm. Coll., N.Y. 1984-87, and adj. prof. CUNY City Coll., 1985-87; prof. San Jose State Univ., Calif. 1987–; founder, co-editor: Springer Series on Partially Ordered Systems, 1987–, Woodward Conf. Series, 1988–, Springer-Verlag, N.Y.; planning & steering com. Intl. Liquid Crystal Confs., 1984-90; dir. NATO Advanced Res. Workshop, 1990; assoc. ed. Molecular Crystals & Liquid Crystals Jour., 1981-93, editl. mem. Liquid Crystals Jour., 1986-90; awards: Li Po Kwai scholar Univ. H.K. 1963-65, Eugene Higgin fellow Columbia Univ. 1966-67, Nordita fellow, Denmark 1976, DOE-Assoc. Western Univs. fellow 1989; mem: Am. Physical Soc. 1984–, Intl. Liquid Crystal Soc. (founder, bd. dirs., chair conf. com., 1990-94); co-editor 6 books: Wave Phenomena, 1989, Nonlinear Structures in Physical Systems, 1990, Solitons in Liquid Crystals, 1992, Modeling Complex Phenomena, 1992, Liquid Crystalline and Mesomorphic Polymers, 1994, Novel Laser Sources and Applications, 1994. Ofc: Dept. Physics, San Jose State Univ., San Jose, CA 95192-0106

LAMBERT, THOMAS RICHARD, biologist; b. Dec. 5, 1946, Oakland; s. Harold Wilson and Grace (McHaffie) L.; m. Sally Crenshaw, June 2, 1990; edn: BS, CSU Chico 1969; MS, Humboldt St. Univ. 1973; cert. fishery bilogist (1975). Career: biologist Pacific Gas & Electric, 1971–; mem: Am. Fisheries Soc., Am. Inst. Fishery Research Biologists (dir. 1992–), Conservation Unlimited Alumni Assn. (pres. 1991), Pacific Fishery Biologists, Assn. Power Biologists, Calif. Acad. Sci., Pt. Reyes Bird Observatory, Lindsay Museum, Nat. Audubon Soc.; articles pub. in profl. jours., 1972-94; rec: scuba diving, birdwatching, travel. Ofc: PG&E 3400 Crow Canyon Rd San Ramon 94583

LAMONT, GARY MARTIN, marketing executive; b. Feb. 29, 1956, Newton, Mass.; s. Alton Woodbrey and Joan Carol (Martin) L.; m. Kathryn Margaret Lewis, Oct. 5, 1985; children: Michelle b. 1987, Ryan b. 1989; edn: BA (magna cum laude) bus./economics/math, Colby Coll., Waterville, Me. 1978; MBA, Harvard Grad. Sch. of Bus. Adminstrn. 1982. Career: staff accountant Deloitte, Haskins & Sells, Boston, Mass. 1978-80; product mgr. General Mills, Inc., Minneapolis, Minn. 1982-87; v.p./dir. of mktg. First Interstate Bank of Calif., Los Angeles 1987-91; v.p. mktg. & sales McKesson Water Products Company, Pasadena 1992–; honors: Phi Beta Kappa, Baker Scholar in Business; mem: Internat. Bottled Water Assn. (communications com. 1992–); exec. mem. Am. Mktg. Assn. 1989–. Res: 4351 Oakwood Avenue La Canada 91011 Ofc: McKesson Water Products 3280 East Foothill Blvd Pasadena 91107

LAMPERT, SHIRLEY RUTH, marriage and family therapist, lecturer, educator; b. Jan. 11, Baltimore, Md.; d. Herman and Ida (Tossman) Axelrod; m. Seymour Lampert, March 21; children: Rachel, David, Martin; edn: BA, CSU Fullerton 1970; MA, 1971; USC, 1972-76; lic. marriage and family therapist Calif. (1976); cert. sex therapy supvr. Career: instr. Orange Coast Coll., Costa Mesa 1975-84; Irvine Valley Coll., Irvine 1984-87; Fullerton Coll. 1987-89; Long Beach City Coll. 1986–; pvt. practice psychotherapy, Newport Beach 1976–; lectr. UC Irvine Med. Coll. 1988; City of Irvine Recreation Dept., Community Services 1987; Orange Coast Coll. Community Services 1990–; western reg. conf. chair Am. Assn. Sex Educators Counselors and Therapists 1985-87, 89, 90, pres., So. Calif. sect. 1983-85, 86-89; mem: Am. Assn. Marriage & Family Therapists, Calif. Assn. Marriage & Family Therapists; civic bds: People for Irvine Comm. Health (health, edn. & wellness com.), South Coast Repertory Theatre Bd Govs. (1980-84), Newport Beach Guild (chair 1983-84), Stage Door Guild, Orange Co. Performing Arts Ctr. (v.p. 1987-88); classroom workbook pub., 1980, video ed., 1988; rec: travel, antiques. Ofc: 1151 Dove St Ste 105 Newport Beach 92660

LAMPLEY, EDWARD CHARLES, SR., obstetrician-gynecologist; b. June 21, 1931, Hattiesburg, Miss.; s. Willie Lee Lampley, Sr. and Elma (Wilson) L.; m. Norma Jean Mosley, CNM, Ph.D., Sept. 11, 1959; children: Edward C. Lampley, Jr., MD b. 1961, Marguerite Annette b. 1964, Karl W. b. 1971; edn: AB, biology, Wayne Univ., Detroit, Mich. 1956; liberal arts, Alcorn Coll., Lorman, Miss. 1952-53; MD, Howard Univ., Wash. D.C. 1960; Diplomate Am. Bd. Ob-Gyn 1968, recert. 1978. Career: internship, Det. Receiving Hosp./Wayne Univ. , Detroit, Mich. 1960-61; resident, ob-gyn, Provident Hosp., Chgo., Ill. 1961-63; lectr. Provident Hosp. Sch. of Nsg., Chgo., Ill. 1961-63; resident, ob-gyn Harlem Hosp., NY, NY 1963-66; founder, pres. East Oakland Med. Ctr., Oakland 1979–; chmn. dept. ob-gyn San Leandro Med. Ctr., San Leandro, Calif. 1986-88; mem. ob-gyn quality assurance com. Summit Med. Ctr. 1992–; lectr. San Leandro Mem. Hosp. Nsg. Staff 1971-87; awards: Man of Year, E. Palo Alto Sch. Dist. 1989; mem: Am. Coll. Ob-Gyn (fellow 1968), East Bay Gyn Soc. 1969–, S.F. Gyn Soc. 1972–, Am. Fertility Soc. 1971–, Am. Coll. of Surgeons (diplomate, 1972–), Nat. Med. Assn. (delegate 1990-93), CMA (delegate 1986–), S.F. Surgery Soc., Alameda-Contra Costa Med. Soc. (councilman 1986–), Kappa Alpha Psi 1952 (Berkeley Alumni Chpt. 1971-72), BSA (adult supvy. group, 2 chapters, 1983-88), E. Palo Alto Redevelopment Bd. (chmn. bd. dirs. 1989-91), Downs Mem. Church (chmn. advy. group, v.p. Chapel Ch. and soloist 1969–, lay leader 1988-91, chmn. scholarship com. 1988-92); author: sci. papers presented to Nat. Med. Assn., Chgo. Chpt. 1964, 66; mil: staff sgt. sr. clerk, USAF 1949-52; Democrat; Methodist; rec: swimming, soloist, reading. Ofc: East Oakland Ob-Gyn Medical Group Inc. 9925 E 14th St PO Box 6097 Oakland 94603-0097

LANDERS, VERNETTE, writer, retired school district counselor, civic activist; b. May 3, 1912, Lawton, Okla.; d. Fred and La Verne Trosper; m. Major Paul A. Lum M.D. (dec. 1955); children: William Tappan; m. 2d. Newlin Landers, May 2, 1959 (dec. Apr. 6, 1990); children: Larry, Marlin; edn: AB (honors), UCLA 1933; MA, 1935; EdD, 1953; tchg. life diploma 1940; gen. pupil personnel svcs. life diploma 1970. Career: tchr. Montebello, Ca. schs., 1935-45, 1948-50, 1951-59; prof. Long Beach City Coll. 1946-47, Los Angeles State Coll. 1950; dean of girls 29 Palms H.S., 1960-65; dist. counselor Morongo Unified Sch. Dist., 1965-72; coord. Adult Edn. 1965-67; dir. Guidance Project 1967; chg. clk., vol. Landers Post Office, 1962-83; secty. Landers Volunteer Fire Dept. 1972; v.p. Landers Assn. Inc., 1969-71; dir., secty. Desert Ears, emergency radio svc. 1970-73; freelance writer 1944–; recipient silver medal and Dedication pages in biographical ref. books Intl. Biog. Centre 1985, I.B.C. grand amb. of achiev. and life fellow, dep. dir. gen. of the Americas and Intl. Biog. Assn. Honors List of foremost women 20th century for contbns. to research 1987, life fellow and life dep. gov. Am. Biog. Inst. 1986; honors: Intl. Acad. of Poets, London, 1973, hon. degrees Univ. of Arts, Parma, Italy 1982, Leonardo DaVinci Intl. Acad., Rome 1982, World Univ., Tucson 1985; appreciation US Postal Svc. 1984, Morongo Unified. Sch. Dist. 1984, San Gorgonio Girl Scout Council, Certificates of Appreciation 1984-93, life fellow World Literary Acad., Cambridge, Eng. 1985, citizen of yr. Goat Mt. Grange 1987, guest of honor Landers Elementary Sch. groundbreaking ceremony 1989 and Dedication Ceremony LES 1991, Gold Commemorative Medal of Honor Am. Biog. Inst. 1987, Golden Acad. Oscar Award for lifetime achievement, life mem., World

Inst. of Achievement 1991, Presdl. Order of Merit from Pres. George Bush 1991, Golden State Award Who's Who Hist. Soc. 1991, One in a Million Award- Internat. Biog. Ctr. 1992, Am. Biog. Inst.-Most Admired Woman of the Decade, Woman of the Yr. 1992; mem: Internat. Platform Assn., Am., Calif., Personnel and Guidance Assns., Am. Assn. for Counseling & Devel. (25 Yr. mem. pin 1991), NEA, Nat. Assn. Women Deans and Adminstrs., Calif. Tchrs. Assn., I.P.A., Nat. League of Am. Penwomen, Bus. & Profl. Women's Club (pres. Montebello 1940), Toastmistress (pres., Whittier 1957), Soroptimist (29 Palms mem. of year 1967, life 1983, woman of distinc. 1987), Landers Area C.of C. (secty. 1983, presdl. trophy 1986), Friends of Copper Mt. Coll. (bd. 1990-92), Desert Memorial Hosp. Guild (life), Hi Desert Playhouse Guild (life), Hi Desert Nature Museum (life), Homestead Valley Women's Club (life), Phi Beta Kappa, Pi Lambda Theta, Sigma Delta Pi, Alpha Xi Delta Order of the Rose and Order of the Pearl 1989, Pi Delta Phi, Mortar Board, Prytanean Spurs, Morongo Basin Humane Soc. (life 1990), Who's Who of the Yr. 1993, Internat. Woman of Yr. 1993, Internat. Cultural Diploma of Honor 1993; works: Impy 1974, Talkie 1975, Impy's Children 1975, Nineteen O Four 1976, Little Brown Bat 1976, Slo Go 1977, Who and Who Who 1978, Sandy The Coydog 1979, The Kit Fox and the Walking Stick 1980, Poems in New Voices in Amer. Poetry 1974, 75, An Anthol. on World Brotherhood 1975, 81, Rainbow 1984, contbr. "History of Comanche County, Okla." Vol. I 1985, sketch in "The Pen Woman" 1984; rec: wild animals, flying. Res: 632 N Landers Ln Landers 92285

LANDMAN, MICHAEL DENNIS, physician, head and neck surgeon; b. Dec. 18, 1942, Los Angeles; s. Maurice Seymour and Mary (Silver) L.; m. Erica Mary Ann Berk, Nov. 27, 1971; children: Aaron b. 1973, Shelby b. 1975, Courtney b. 1978, Megan b. 1982; edn: BA w. honors, UCLA 1964; MD w. honors, UCLA Sch. Medicine 1967. Career: intern Harbor Gen. Hosp., Torrance 1967-68; resident gen. surgery UCLA Med. Center, Los Angeles 1968-69, resident head and neck surgery 1969-72; pvt. practice, Los Angeles 1974–; asst. clin. prof. dept. head & neck surgery, UCLA 1974–; staff Valley Presbyterian Hosp., Van Nuys (staff chief 1985); bd. dirs. Research Study Club, L.A. 1988–; honors: Alpha Omega Alpha, fellow Am. Acad. Otolaryngology, fellow Am. Coll. Surgeons, fellow Am. Acad. Facial Plastic & Reconstructive Surgery, fellow Am. Soc. Head & Neck Surgery; mem: L.A. Soc. Otolaryngology (pres. 1962-63), L.A. Co. Med. Assn., CMA, AMA; contbr. articles to med. jours 1970–; mil: major USAF 1972-74. Ofc: 15243 Vanowen St Ste 203 Van Nuys 91405

LANDOLPH, JOSEPH RICHARD, JR., cancer researcher, medical educator; b. Nov. 9, 1948, Upper Darby, Pa.; s. Joseph Richard and Ada Nolia (Welch) L.; m. Alice Lee Kaufman, Jan. 9, 1980; children: Joseph R. b. 1980, Louis Samuel b. 1983; edn: BS chemistry, Drexel Univ. 1971; PhD, UC Berkeley 1976. Career: research asst., UC Berkeley Dept. of Chemistry 1971-76; postdoctoral fellow USC Comprehensive Cancer Center, Los Angeles 1977-80; asst. prof. pathology USC Sch. Medicine 1980-82, asst. prof. microbiol. and pathology 1982-87, assoc. prof. microbiol., pathology and molecular pharmacology and toxicology 1987–; p.t. pvt. toxicology cons., cons. to U.S. Environ. Protection Agy. on Ozone Genotoxicity 1993-95, mem. Carcinogen Identification Bd., Ofc. Environ. Health Hazard Assessment, Calif. EPA, 1994–; awards: Merck Co. award 1971, Am. Cancer Soc. postdoctoral fellow 1977-79, USC Dept. Pathology Excellence in Tchg. 1985, ICI Traveling Lectureship award Thrust Soc. of Toxicologists 1990; mem: Am. Soc. Cell Biology, Am. Assn. Cancer Research, Environ. Mutagen Soc., Soc. Toxicologists, Am. Chemical Soc., Tissue Culture Assn., Am. Soc. for Biochem. and Molecular Biology; editl. bd. Environ. and Molecular Mutgenesis, 1988-93, Cancer Biochemistry & Biophysics, 1988–; articles pub. in research jours.; mil: capt. U.S. Army Medical Svc. Corps 1976-77; Republican; Unitarian; rec: jogging, skiing, karate. Res: 1009 E Mendocino St Altadena 90001

LANEY, MICHAEL L., company executive; b. Sept. 10, 1945, Los Angeles: s. Roy and Wanda L.; m. Marti, Dec. 31, 1964; children: Tynna b. 1962, Kristen b. 1968; edn: BS w. honors, CSU Northridge 1967; MBA, UCLA 1969; C.P.A. Calif. 1969. Career: tax splst. Deloitte Haskins & Sells, L.A. 1967-70; asst. prof. acctg. CSU Northridge 1969-71; tax splst., L.A. 1972-75; owner Michael L. Laney, CPA's, Beverly Hills 1975-80; v.p., controller Ducommun Inc., L.A. 1980-87; sr. v.p., fin. & adminstrn. Monarch Mirror Door Co. Inc., Chatsworth 1987-92; v.p. feature animation div. Walt Disney Co., Glendale 1992-93; sr. v.p. Feature Animation Div., Warner Bros., Sherman Oaks 1994–; p.t. instr. CSU Northridge 1970-80; mem: Am. Inst. CPA, Calif. Soc. CPA, Fin. Execs. Inst., Tax Execs. Inst.; rec: golf. Ofc: Warner Bros. Feature Animation 15303 Ventura Blvd Ste 500 Sherman Oaks 91403

LANG, DUDLEY M., lawyer; b. Dec. 17, 1936, Chandler, Ariz.; s. William F. and Eva Mae (Bowman) L.; m. Gail Simms, Oct. 7, 1979; 1 dau., Kathryn Louise; edn: BA, UCLA 1957; LL.B, UCLA Sch. Law 1962. Career: ptnr. Willis Butler Scheifly Leydorf & Grant, Los Angeles 1963-81; Bryan Cave McPheeters & McRoberts 1981-83; McCutchen Black Verleger & Shea 1984-89; Hufstedler &Kaus, 1989-95, Stephens, Berg & Lasater, 1995–; instr. law USC Law Center 1972-75, lectr. 1967; instr. in law Univ. S.D. 1987; awards: Calif. St. Bar V. Judson Klein 1978, L.A. Co. Bar Assn. Dana Latham Meml. (1985); mem: Am. Bar Assn. (chmn. com. on S corps. 1978-80), Calif. St. Bar

(exec. com. 1986), Calif. Bd. Legal Specialization (tax advy. 1971-76), L.A. Co. Bar Assn. (chmn. 1975-76), USC Tax Inst. Planning Com., L.A. Econ. Round Table (pres. 1992-93), Lions Club L.A. (pres. 1987-88), Lark Ellen Lions Charities (dir., secty. 1983); articles pub. in profl. jours., 1982-83, chpts. pub. 1985-88; Republican; rec: tennis, music. Ofc: Stephens, Berg & Lasater, 1055 W. Seventh St. 29th fl., Los Angeles 90017

LANG, TZU-WANG, professor of medicine; b. Apr. 15, 1929, Hsiang-Shan Hsien, Chekiang Province, China, nat. US cit. 1977; s. Wang-Chieh and Chun-Hsiang (Chang) L.; grandson of Jing-Bang Lang, the Scholar of the Ching Dynasty (1884-1950); m. Winnie Chi, Apr. 15, 1960; children: Daniel b. 1962, Cathy Mae b. 1972; edn: MB, Nat. Defense Medical Center 1955; MD, Nat. Acad. Bd. in Med. 1955. Career: res. fellow Am. Coll. of Cardiology, 1963-65; prin. investigator Cardiovascular Res., VA Gen. Hosp., Taiwan 1966-68; chief of cardiology, Tri-Service Gen. Hosp., Taiwan 1967-69; sr. res. scientist dept. med. Cedars-Sinai Med. Center, Los Angeles 1969-78; adj. assoc. prof. med. UC Los Angeles 1969-76, assoc. clin. prof. med. UC Los Angeles, 1976–; awards: Gold Medal in sci., Taiwan 1962, Young Investigator award finalist, Am. Coll. Cardiology, Boston 1965; mem: Fellow Am. Coll. Cardiology, Am. Heart Assn., AMA, Calif. Med. Assn.; works:one of the pioneers of synchronized retro-perfusion (SRP) for the treatment of coronary artery disease (Am. Jour. Cardiol. 1976, 78); author over 90 sci. papers and contbr. chapters to 4 textbooks on cardiology; Confucianism. Res: 301 N Elm Dr Beverly Hills 90210. Ofc: 8920 Wilshire Blvd Ste 104 Beverly Hills 90211

LANGENHEIM, JEAN H., professor of biology; b. Sept. 5, 1925, Homer, La.; d. Vergil W. and Jeanette (Smith) Harmon; m. Ralph L. Langenheim, Dec. 21, 1946 (div. 1962); edn: BS, Univ. Tulsa 1946; MS, Univ. Minn. 1949; PhD, 1953. Career: research assoc. UC Berkeley 1954-59; asst. prof. San Francisco Coll. for Women 1957-59; res., tchg. assoc. Univ. Ill., Urbana 1959-62; res. fellow Harvard Univ. Cambridge, Mass. 1962-66; fellow Bunting Inst. 1964-65; asst. prof. UC Santa Cruz 1966-68, assoc. prof. 1968-73, prof. 1973–; awards: Calif. Acad. Sci. fellow 1973, Univ. Tulsa disting. alumni 1979, Australian Nat. Univ. fellow 1980, Radcliffe-Harvard Bunting Inst. annual sci. lectr. 1986, Univ. N.M. Sandia Found. annual lectr. 1987; mem: Assn. Tropical Biology (pres. 1985-86), Ecological Soc. Am. (pres. 1986-87), Internat. Soc. Chemical Ecology (pres. 1986-87), Soc. Econ. Botany (pres. 1993-94), Sierra Club, Am. Assn. Univ. Women, Soc. Prevention of Cruelty to Animals; coauthor Botany: Plant Biology & Its Relation to Human Affairs, 1982, 150+ articles in sci. jours., 1955–; Democrat; rec: photog., gardening, travel. Res: 191 Palo Verde Terrace Santa Cruz 95060 Ofc: Dept. Biology University California Santa Cruz 95064

LANGLOIS, CHARLES ALFRED, retired air force senior non-commissioned officer, real estate broker, consultant, world traveler; b. Dec. 18, 1933, Santiago, Chile, S.A., nat. 1954; s. Harold North and Alice Winefred (Armstrong) L.; m. Loretta May Miller, Aug. 28, 1954; children: Susan b. 1955, Charles b. 1956, Jeanne b. 1957, Eileen b. 1959, Alicia b. 1961, David b. 1966; edn: grad. Santa Barbara H.S. 1951; spl. courses Saddleback Coll. 1972-74; lic. R.E. broker Calif. 1974. Military Career: served to M/Sgt. (Ret.) USAF 1952-72: Adak, Aleutian Islands 1952-53; M/Instr. Supply/Logistics Ofcrs. Course, Sch. for Latin Am., USAF, Panama C.Z. 1955-59; logistics advisor to AF of Rep. of Ecuador 1960-63, to AF of Rep. of Peru 1964-69, to Cdr., Aerospace Cartographic and Geodetic Svc. USAF 1969-70, Thailand 1970-71; logistics advisor to Cdr. 60th Mil. Airlift Wing, 22d AF, Mil. Airlift Command 1971-72, ret.; decorated Meritorious Svc. Medal presented by direction of Pres. of U.S., USAF Commendn. Medal, Presdl. Unit Cit., Outstanding Unit Award w. 2 o.l.c., Army Good Conduct Medals w. 3 Bronze Loops, AF Good Conduct Medal w. 3 o.l.c., Nat. Defense Svc. Medal w. Bronze star, Vietnam Svc. Medal w. Bronze star, USAF Longevity Svc. Medal w. 4 o.l.c., US Marksmanship Medal and Rep. of Vietnam Commendn. Medal w. bar. Civilian Career: asst. mgr. Tustin Realty, Tustin, Calif. 1972; mgr. Ranch Realty, Irvine 1973-80; broker/pres. Irvine Associates, Irvine 1974–; awards: Multi Million Dollar Club (1972-85), Ranch Realty salesman of yr. award (8 yrs. consec. 1973-80), Distinguished Leadership Award for extraordinary service to the R.E. Profession; listed Who's Who In Calif. (1981, 82, 90, 91, 92, 93, 94), Am. Biog. Inst. 1990, The Intl. Directory of Disting. Leadership; mem: Non-Commd. Ofcrs. Assn. (life), Disabled Am. Vets. (life), Air Force Sgts. Assn. (life), Navy League (life), V.F.W. (life), Kts. of Col., Am. Legion, Nat. Assn. for Uniformed Services (life), AARP, Retired Enlisted Assn. (life), East Orange Co. Bd. of Realtors 1972-80, Newport Harbor Costa Mesa Bd. Realtors 1974-80, Irvine Assn. Realtors (charter mem.), Calif. Assn. Realtors 1972–, Nat. Assn. Realtors 1972–; club: Shark Island Yacht, Newport Beach (dir. 1981-82, Cruise chmn. 1982, Fleet Capt. 1982, R.Commodore 1983, v.Commodore 1984, Commodore 1985, Staff Commodore 1986–, Internat. Order of Blue Gavel 1986–); rec: boating, travel. Res: 19165 Croyden Terrace Irvine CA 92715

LANHAM, RICHARD H., JR., podiatrist, medical college president; b. Oct. 23, 1935, Shelbyville, Ill.; s. Richard H. and Fern (Litchenwalker) L.; m. Shirley M. Allen, July 31, 1959; children: Rick, Lisa; edn: DPM, Ohio Coll. Podiatric Medicine 1958; M.Ed, Univ. Louisville 1980. Career: pvt. practice podiatric medicine, Clarksville, Ind. 1964-85; v.p., dean acad. affairs CCPM, San

Francisco 1985-86, pres. 1986–; awards: Ind. PMA Podiatrist of Year (1977, 81); mem: Am. Podiatric Med. Assn. (pres. 1985-86), Ind. Podiatric Med. Assn. (pres. 1972-73), Am. Coll. Foot Surgeons (fellow), Council on Podiatric Med. Edn. (chmn. 1977-79), Calif. Podiatric Med. Assn.; article and lectr. pub.; mil: capt. Med. Service Corps 1959-64; Democrat; Presbyterian; rec: photog. Res: 53 Everson San Francisco 94131 Ofc: California College of Podiatric Medicine 1210 Scott St San Francisco 94115

LANSER, HERBERT RAYMOND, financial planner, photographer; b. Dec. 10, 1932, Hollywood; s. Hugo and Anna (Strandlund) L.; m. Evana E. Conway, Apr. 1, 1980 (div.); children: Lynn (dec.), Deborah, Cynthia, Karen, Rick; m. Judy Kay Skousen; children: Zachary, Joshua, Ezekiel; Cert. Fin. Planner (CFP) 1962. Career: prin. Herb Lanser Financial Services, San Mateo 1956-62; Morro Bay 1986-92; fin. planner 1962-92 (ret.), cons. various orgns. 1975–, cons. Lanser Vermiculture Svs., Herb Lanser Fin. Svs., Nurnberg, Fed. Republic Germany 1983-85; accomplished photographer, known best for scenic photo-art, supplies publishers and collectors worldwide, num. published photos incl. telephone directory and book covers, photog. Internat. Freelance Photog. Orgn. Am. Image, Washington, DC 1991–, model cons. Internat. Freelance Models Orgn., Washington, DC 1992- ; awards: nat. sales leader Prudential Ins. Co., Europe (1985, 87); mem. Nat. Assn. Life Underwriters (S.L.O. Co. chapt. bd. dirs., chmn. pub. service 1989-90, v.p. 1991), Morro Bay C.of C. (bd. dirs., chmn. econ. devel. com. 1990, v.p. 1991, pres. 1992); mil: sgt. US Army 1953-55; author: Profit From Earthworms 1976, articles in profl. jours.; Republican. Studio: Photography by Herb Lanser PO Box 834 Morro Bay 93443

LANTOS, THOMAS PETER, congressman; b. Feb. 1, 1928, Budapest, Hungary; m. Annette Tillemann; children: Annette, Katrina; edn: BA, Univ. Washington, 1949, MA, 1950; PhD, UC Berkeley, 1953. Career: mem. faculty Univ. Wash., San Francisco State Univ., 1950-83; TV news analyst, commentator, sr. econ. and fgn. policy adviser to several U.S. senators; mem. Presdl. Task Force on Def. and Fgn. Policy, 97th-104th Congresses from 11th (now 12th) Calif. dist. (Mid. East subcom. of fgn. affairs com., employment and housing subcom. govt. ops. corn.), 1981–; chmn. subcom. internat. security, internat. orgns. and human rights Fgn. Affairs Com.; founder study abroad program Calif. State Univ. and Coll. System; mem. Millbrae Bd. Edn., 1950-66; Democrat. Ofc: US House of Representatives 2182 Rayburn House Office Bldg Washington DC 20515

LANTZ, NORMAN FOSTER, aerospace engineer; b. June 8, 1937, Pekin, Ill.; s. Norman Gough and Lenore Moffett (Elsbury) L.; m. Donnis Ballinger, Sept. 7, 1958 (div. Aug. 1991); children: Katherine b. 1961, Deborah b. 1964, Norman Daniel b. 1967; m. Judith Elaine Peach, Dec. 7, 1991; edn: BSEE, and MSEE, Purdue Univ., 1959, 1961; lic. E.I.T., Ind., 1959. Career: engr. General Electric Co., Phila. 1961-72; senior project engr. The Aerospace Corp., El Segundo 1972–; dir. Internat. Found. for Telemetry, L.A. 1988–; mem. IEEE 1959–, Am. Mgmt. Assn.; sr. mem. AIAA 1991–, mil: 2d lt. US Army 1959-67; Republican; South Bay Christian Ch., Redondo Beach (elder, chmn.). Res: 2801 W Sepulveda Blvd #10 Torrance 90505 Ofc: The Aerospace Corp. PO Box 92957 Los Angeles 90009

LAPLANTE, DONALD EUGENE, teacher; b. Jan. 27, 1955, Los Angeles; s. Victor Donald and Elrose Muriel (Schwartz) LaP.; edn: BA, Univ. So. Calif., 1976; teaching cred., CSU Long Beach, 1992. Career: mgr. USC Copy Centers, Los Angeles 1978-85; Olympic Graphics 1985-90; teacher 1990–; honors: Skull & Dagger (pres. 1985-87), USC Trojan Fourth Estate (pres. 1987-89); mem: Delta Chi (mem. Bd. of Regents 1991-95), Downey Unified Sch. Dist. Bd. of Edn., 1979– (pres. 1982-83, 90, 95, v.p. 1981-82, 1988-89, chmn. audit com.). Res: 11908 Susan St Downey 90242

LARBALESTRIER, DEBORAH ELIZABETH, paralegal, writer, training executive; b. July 17, 1934, Pittsburgh, Pa.; d. Theron Benjamin and Granetha (Crenshaw) Cowherd; edn: BA in hist. and sociol. (cum laude), Storer Coll.; stu. Robert H. Terrell Law Sch., Wash. D.C. 3-1/2 yrs.; paralegal certs., litigation and gen. splst., splst. in worker's compensation, Univ. of West L.A. Sch. of Paralegal Studies; spl. courses Woodbury Coll. and UCLA Ext. Career: owner/tnr. Exec. Tutoring Service for legal sectys., 1963-65; legal asst. in gen. practice 1969-85; paralegal instr. Southland Career Inst., 1985-88; cons. and tng. splst., paralegal mgr. Lynberg & Watkins, Los Angeles; exec. dir. American Paralegal Assn. (charter mem., past pres.); listed Who's Who in the West (21st, 22nd edit.) mem. adv. bd. Sch. of Paralegal Studies, Univ. of West L.A., 1988; keynote speakergrad. class of inmate paralegals (max. security) Mo. State Penitentiary, 1983, founder/nat. chmn. Am. Inmate Paralegal Assn., Mo. State Penitentiary 1984–, radio talk show guest re-edn. for inmate paralegals, Okla. City, Ok. 1984, San Antonio, Tex. 86; panelist "Headlines on Trial" KNBC-TV Ch. 4 (9/85, 12/84, 3/85); career day spkr. Eagle Rock H.S.; author 5 texts in field: Practice and Procedures: A Practical Guide for Legal Assistants (1977, ppb. 1979, 2d edit. 1986, 3rd. edit. 1994-95), Paralegal Training Manual (1981), Handbook of Paralegal Forms... (1982), Self-study Course for Inmate Paralegals (w. cassettes 1985), Prentice-Hall, Inc.; (pamphlet) Legal Secretary: A Specialty (1963-65), statement in US Congl. Record re use, tng. and edn. of legal assts. (7/74), articles in legal newspapers; civic: Wilshire

Comm. Police Council (1984–), LAPD Wilshire Div. (sr. dep. aux. police ofcr. 1984–), Neighborhood Watch Pgm. (block capt. 1984-88); rec: writing, bowling. Res: 1321-1/2 S Sycamore Ave Los Angeles 90019

LAREDO, DAVID CARY, lawyer; b. Feb. 1, 1950, N.Y.C.; s. Joseph A. and Ruth Helen (Mautner) L.; m. Virginia Isabelle Smith, Sept. 23, 1972; children: Christina b. 1980, Josef b. 1984, Michael b. 1987, Matthew b. 1989; edn: BA in English, UCLA, 1972; JD, Southwestern Univ., 1975. Career: served to lt. USNR, 1975-79, staff judge advocate Naval Postgrad. Sch., Monterey; dep. county counsel Monterey County, 1979-81; atty., ptnr. De Lay & Laredo, Pacific Grove 1981–; general counsel Monterey Peninsula Water Mgmt. Dist., 1979–, Pajaro Valley Water Mgmt. Agy., 1986–; instr. Monterey Coll. of Law 1979-82, Monterey Peninsula Coll. 1977-78; dir. Monterey Federal Credit Union (1984–, chmn. bd. 1988–); dir. Children's Services Center (1984-94, chmn. bd. 1988-89); dir. Kinship Center 1984–; mem., v.p. Monterey Penin. Jaycees 1979-84; pub. article: Conducting Effective Meetings, 1992, Taking "Charge" of Board Meetings, 1992; rec: skiing. Ofc: De Lay & Laredo 606 Forest Ave Pacific Grove 93950

LARSEN, DONNA K., media consultant, writer; b. Feb. 14, Anniston, Ala.; d. James M. and Lucy Bible; edn: BA, Univ. Alabama, 1970. Career: intern, reporter Anniston (Ala.) Star, 1967-69; feature writer Los Angeles Times, L.A. 1970-75; owner, pres. Larsen Promotions, L.A. 1977–; mem: Book Publicists So. Calif., L.A. World Affairs Council, Internat. Women's Media Found., Ebell Club; co-author (book): Superior Healing Power; rec: astronomy, astrology, cinema hist., tennis. Ofc: Larsen Promotions 720 S Plymouth Blvd Ste 11 Los Angeles 90005

LARSON, ERIC VICTOR, policy analyst; b. May 29, 1957, Buffalo, N.Y.; s. Ralph William and Marilyn Ruth (Werner) L.; edn: AB polit. sci., Univ. Mich., 1980; policy analysis, RAND Grad. Sch., Santa Monica, PhD cand. Career: statistician Office of Mgmt. & Budget, W.D.C., 1980-82; policy analyst Office of Planning & Evaluation, The White House, 1982-83; policy and systems analyst Nat. Security Council, 1983-88; res. staff mem. Inst. for Defense Analyses, Alexandria, Va. 1988-89; graduate fellow RAND, Santa Monica 1989–, tchg. asst. RAND Grad. Sch., 1990; recipient 2 scholastic distinction honors RAND Grad. Sch. 1991, vis. student to Oxford Univ., St. Antony's Coll., U.K. 1991, Outstanding Young Man of Am. 1986; mem: Operations Research Soc. Am., AAAS, Assn. for Pub. Policy Analysis and Mgmt., Internat. Inst. for the Systems Sciences; mentor Minority Assistance Pgm., RAND (1990, 92); faculty Distinguished Scholars Pgm. Santa Monica High Sch. 1992; First Presbyterian Ch., Santa Monica (trustee); publs: 4+ articles & monographs in field, 1991, 92, 93, 94; Presbyterian; rec: music. Ofc: RAND, 1700 Main St Santa Monica 90407

LARSON, ROGER KEITH, physician; b. Apr. 27, 1924, Cadillac, Mich.; s. William Ernest and Ethel Lydia (Rose) L.; m. Frances Ann Appel, July 1, 1949; children: John b. 1950, Ronald b. 1950, Joan b. 1956, Sharon b. 1960; edn: student, Northwestern Univ. 1942, Wheaton Coll. 1943-44; MD, Univ. of Ill., Chgo. 1947; internship, Cook Co. Hosp., Chgo., Ill. 1947-49; residency, internal medicine, Kern Gen. Hosp., Bakersfield, CA 1949-52; lic. Calif. 1949; cert. Am. Bd. of Internal Medicine 1956; cert. subspecialty of pulmonary disease 1978. Career: dir. of UCLA medicine clerkships Harbor Gen. Hosp., UCLA, Torrance 1954-57; pvt. practice, internal medicine, Fresno 1957-61; chief of medicine Valley Med. Ctr. of Fresno 1961-90 (acting med. dir. 1980-81); med. dir.-AIDS profl. edn. & tng. grant for 4 we. states, HRSA and NIMH, Fresno 1990-94; instr., clin. prof. of medicine UCLA Med. Sch. 1955-76; p.t. med. practice and medico-legal cons. 1965-92; adj. prof. of allied health CSU Fresno 1972-76; clin. prof. of medicine UCSF 1976-92; v. chmn. dept. of medicine, UCSF (in alternate yrs.) 1975-90; acting asst. dean UCSF 1980-81; clin. prof. of medicine UC Davis 1990-92; pres. UCSF Valley Med. Edn. Found. 1991-94; editl. bd. Western Jour. of Medicine 1977-84; v.p. Central Calif. Faculty Med. Group 1979-88, chmn. bd. dirs. 1985-89; awards: Disting. Svc. award Am. Heart Assn. 1969, Henry E. Randel award, Central Valley Lung Assn. 1980, Kaiser award for excellence in tchg., UCSF 1981, establishment of the Roger K. Larson, Disting. Vis. Professorship, UCSF 1989, Fresno-Madera Med. Soc. award for outstanding comm. svc. 1991, Laureate of CA chpt. of Am. Coll. of Physicians award 1992; mem: Am. Coll. of Physicians (fellow 1956–), CMA 1980–, AAAS 1984–, Am. Thoracic Soc. (councilor 1969-72); established (w. Dr. Thomas Eliason) the 1st cardiac catheterization & blood gas lab in San Joaquin Valley & did the 1st catheterizations, 1957; established (w. Dr. Bryon Evans and Dr. Eliason) the 1st open heart surgery prog. in San Joaquin Valley; author, book (biography): Controversial James: An Essay on the Life and Work of George Wharton James, 1991, num. pub. med./scientific articles, 1953-89; editor and chief author, The Bulletin of the We. AIDS Edn. Ctr. 1989-94; exhibits of portions of book and historical collection on Calif. and the West, 1991, 92, 93; mil: capt. US Army Med. Corps 1952-54; rec: music: playing organ, collecting books, writing, photography. Res: 2285 W San Madele Ave Fresno 93711 Ofc: Valley Medical Center of Fresno 445 S Cedar Fresno 93702

LARSON, STEVEN EDWIN, physician, medical group executive; b. Sept. 22, 1950, Baldwin, Wis.; s. Howard George and Doris Henrietta (DeRoy) L.; m. Mary E. Hauch, July 14, 1973 (div. 1981); m. Catherine Ann Price, May 30, 1981; children: Brian b. 1975, Julie b. 1977, Andrew b. 1989; edn: BA chemistry, Augsburg Univ. 1971; MD, Med. Coll. Wis. 1975; MPH, Loma Linda Univ. 1988. Career: ptnr. Riverside Med. Clinic, Riverside 1980–, CEO, chmn. of bd. 1988–; asst. clin. prof. medicine Loma Linda Univ. 1983–; adj. assoc. prof. biomed. scis. UC Riverside 1987–; dir. infectious disease clinic Riverside Gen. Hosp., Univ. Med. Center 1986–; awards: Jr. C.of C. Young Profl. of Year 1984; mem: L.A. Acad. Medicine, AMA, A.C.P. (fellow 1993), Infectious Diseases Soc. Am.; 4 articles pub. in med. jours., 1979-87; Lutheran. Ofc: Riverside Medical Clinic 3660 Arlington Riverside 92506

LASHGARI, BIJAN, engineering and scientific consultant; b. Feb. 12, 1951, Tehran, Iran; nat. 1981; s. Alireza and Batoul (Khajeh-Nasiri) Lashgari-Irvani; m. Shahla Arizi, Jan. 2, 1987; edn: BS, USC, 1975; MS, 1977; PhD, 1981. Career: cons. USC, 1981-83; instr. electrical engring. dept. CSU, Fullerton 1983-85; UC Irvine 1989–; advising scientist Unocal Corp., Brea 1982-94; pres. GeoPars, 1994–; assoc. ed. Am. Geophysical Union; awards: USC Archimedes Circle 1975; mem: IEEE (edn. chmn. Orange Co. 1988, chmn. geosci. & remote sensing 1984), Inst. Advancement of Engrings., Tau Beta Phi, Eta Kapa Nu; 20 articles pub. in sci. jours., 1982-86; rec: tennis, skiing, swimming. Ofc: 25412 Burntwood Laguna Niguel 92677

LASKA, MARK SROL, dentist; b. Apr. 26, 1945, Pittsburgh, Pa.; s. Sol and Lena Irene (Berman) L.; m. Joan Dunlap, 1973; children: Shawn b. 1963, Sheila b. 1964, Shaye b. 1976; edn: UC Los Angeles 1963-66; DDS, USC Sch. of Dentistry 1970. Career: dentist Group Dental Service, 1970-81, head dentist Group Dental Service, A., 1973-81, dental dir. Group Dental Serv., 1980-81; pvt. practice, Los Angeles 1981–; assoc. with S. Jay Welborn, Pasadena 1981-82; official dentist Los Angeles Clippers Basketball Team (NBA) 1989-94; mem. Los Angeles Olympic Citizens Advy. Commn., and L.A. Olympic Medical/ Dental Advy. Commn. 1984; staff dentist Olympic Games, USC Polyclinic 1984; honors: Zeta Beta Tau, Alpha Omega; mem: Acad. of General Dentistry, Am. Acad. of Cosmetic Dentistry, Am. Dental Assn., Calif. Dental Assn., Los Angeles Dental Soc. (Comm. on Dental Care, 1981-84); civic: Hollywood Los Feliz Jewish Comm. Ctr. (bd. 1979-85, chmn. phys. ed. com. 1981-2), YMCA, Laughlin Park HOA (dir. 1980–, pres. 1981, 84, 86, 87, 89, 90, 93, 94 v.p. 1985, 88, 91, 92, treas. 1983), Los Feliz Improvement Assn. (dir. 1986-87), Los Feliz Mobility Action Com. 1990–, Los Feliz Emergency Communications 1993; Democrat; Jewish; rec: politics, racquetball, running. Res: Los Angeles 90027 Ofc: 3460 Wilshire Blvd Ste 104 Los Angeles 90010

LASLETT, LAWRENCE JACKSON, physician; b. Apr. 17, 1942, Boston, Mass.; s. Lawrence Jackson and Barbara Elisabeth (Bridgeford) L.; m. Laurie Winthers, Nov. 3, 1978; children: Jonathan b. 1980, Amy b. 1986; edn: BS, Iowa State Univ. 1964; MD, Univ. of Iowa 1969. Career: asst. prof. of medicine, UC Davis 1978-85; assoc. prof. of medicine UC Davis 1985–; mem: Am. Coll. of Cardiology (fellow 1982–), Am. Coll. of Physicians 1978–, Am. Heart Assn. 1978–; author: 30 book chpts. and jour. articles; mil: USPHS 1970-72. Ofc: University of California Davis, Cardiology Division 4301 X St Sacramento 95817

LASSER, DAVID, writer, editor, labor executive, retired; b. Mar. 20, 1902, Balt.; s. Leon and Lena (Jaffe) L.; m. Florence Glassberg, Aug. 26, 1927 (div. 1937); son, Daniel Joseph; m. Helen Gerber, Oct. 1937 (div. 1947); m. Amelia Tolbert, Dec. 23, 1963; edn: BS engring., M.I.T., 1924. Career: engr. Rossendale-Reddaway Co., Newark, N.J. 1924; prodn. mgr. Halperin Mills, Bklyn. 1925-26; mng. editor Sci., Wonder Stories 1927-34; author: Conquest of Space (1931), Private Monopoly, Enemy at Home (1945); founding pres. Am. Interplanetary Soc. (became Am. Rocket Soc., now renamed AIAA), 1930-33; organized, charter pres. Workers Alliance of Am. (W.A.A.) 1933-40 (resigned 1940); organized American Security Union, 1940-42; asst. dir. plant prodn. div. War Prodn. Bd., Wash. DC 1942, dir. office labor advy. comms. 1944-47, requested by Averill Harriman to consult on handling European work of the Marshall Plan, 1945, special advisor to U.S. Secty. of Commerce, 1947-48, asst. to pres. IUE AFL-CIO, 1950-69; cons. U.S. Dept. State, 1968-72; v.p. instrn. and lectr. Continuing Edn. Ctr. San Diego St. Univ. 1979-82; mem. Am. Inst. Aero. & Astro. (Founding Pres. Award 1981), AAAS, DAV; mil: sgt. US Army 1918-19. Res: 12539 Plaza Centrada San Diego 92128

LAST, JEROLD ALAN, professor of medicine and biological chemistry; b. June 5, 1940, N.Y.C.; s. Herbert and Florence L.; m. Elaine Zimelis, June 1, 1975; children: Andrew b. 1968, Matthew b. 1976, Michael b. 1978; edn: BS chemistry, Univ. Wis., 1959, MS biochemistry, Univ. Wis., 1961; PhD biochemistry, Ohio State Univ., 1965; postdoctoral fellow biochemistry, N.Y. Univ. 1966-67. Career: sr. res. scientist Squibb Inst. for Medical Res., New Brunswick, N.J. 1967-69; ed. Proceedings of the NAS, W.D.C., 1970-73; res. assoc. Harvard Univ., Cambridge, Mass. 1973-76; prof. UC Davis, 1976–, dir. UC Systemwide Toxic Substances Res. & Teaching Pgm. 1985–, unit ldr. Respiratory Diseases Unit, Calif. Regional Primate Res. Ctr., Davis 1985-94; v. chair Dept. of Internal Med. UC Davis 1985–; mem. editorial bds. various sci. journals, review panels various granting agys.; awards: Frank R. Blood Award Soc. of Toxicology 1979, Joan Oettinger Meml. res. award UC Davis (1979, 1983), Fulbright prof. Montevideo, Uruguay 1983, UCD Sch. of Medicine Faculty res. award 1990, ICI travelling lectr. Soc. of Toxicology 1992, prin.

investigator numerous grants in lung biology & toxicology; mem: Am. Soc. Biol. Chemistry and Mol. Biology, Soc. of Toxicology, Am. Thoracic Soc., Calif. Lung Assn.; inventor (3) patents: antimicrobial agents; editor book series: Methods in Molecular Biology, 150+ sci. papers and monographs; rec: referee Am. Youth Soccer Org. Ofc: Univ. California CRPRC, Davis 95616-8542

LATHROP, DONALD BRANUM, physician, pediatrician; b. Nov. 1, 1931, Plainfield, N.J.; s. Frederic William and Dorothy Webster (Smith) L.; m. Flora Smyers, Nov. 15, 1954 (dec. 1968); children: Debbie b. 1955, Suzanne b. 1956, Lydia b. 1958, Steven b. 1970, Michael b. 1972, Christina b. 1977; edn: BA, Cornell Univ. 1953; MD, Cornell Univ. Med. Coll. 1957. Career: pvt. practice pediatrics, Mountain View 1963-89; clin. prof. pediatrics Stanford Med. Sch. 1964-89; chief med. staff El Camino Hosp., Mountain View 1980-81; mem: AMA, CMA, Santa Clara Co. Med. Soc.; mil: capt. AUS MC 1960-62, Commendation Medal 1963; Republican; rec: golf, bridge. Ofc: 2500 Hospital Dr #12 Mountain View 94040

LATHROP, JOYCE KEEN, administrative manager, civic philanthropist; b. Nov. 25, 1939, Los Angeles; d. William Lavern Trewin and Reserl (Wenig) Keen; m. Mitchell Lee Lathrop, 1959 (div. 1977); children: Christin, Alexander, Timothy; edn: BA, USC 1961; USC 1962-63. Career: admin. mgr. The Ralph M. Parsons Co.; civic bds: Assistance League of Glendale (dir. 1964-70), Los Angeles Orphanage Guild Juniors (dir. 1968-78, 1983-89, pres. 1974-75, v.p. 1973-74), Calif. Museum of Sci. & Industry Council (dir. 1979-94, pres. 1981-83, 95-96, chmn. bd. 1983-85), Los Angeles Music Center Opera Assn. (dir. 1973-74), active vol. United Way, Am. Cancer Soc., Good Samaritan Hosp. Aux. 1970-95, Metropolitan Assocs. 1977-95; awards: Calif. Mus. Sci. & Industry awards 1982-93, Huntington Memorial Hosp. vol. service 1968, Order of St. Lazarus of Jerusalem; clubs: The Valley Hunt, Pasadena Athletic; rec: music, travel, cooking. Res: 601 E Del Mar Blvd Pasadena 91101 Ofc: The Ralph M. Parsons Co. 100 W Walnut St Pasadena 91124

LATHROP, MITCHELL LEE, lawyer; b. Dec. 15, 1937, Los Angeles; s. Alfred Lee and Barbara Isabella (Mitchell) L.; m. Denice Annette Davis; children: Christin b. 1964, Alexander b. 1967, Timothy b. 1971; edn: BS, US Naval Acad. 1959; JD, USC Law Sch. 1966; admitted bar: Calif., New York, Dist. Col.; cert. civil trial specialist Nat. Bd. Trial Advocacy. Career: dep. county counsel Los Angeles County, 1966-69; atty., assoc., then ptnr. Brill, Hunt, DeBuys & Burby, L.A. 1969-71; ptnr. Macdonald, Halsted & Laybourne, L.A. and San Diego, 1971-80; senior ptnr. Rogers & Wells, S.D., L.A., N.Y., 1980-86; senior ptnr., exec. com. and firm chmn. Adams, Duque and Hazeltine, S.D., L.A., S.F., N.Y.C., 1986-94; ptnr. Luce, Forward, Hamilton & Scripps, S.D., N.Y.C., L.A., S.F. 1994–; presiding referee Calif. State Bar Court (1985-87); lectr. in law, Am. Bar Assn., Calif. Judges Assn., Calif. State Bar, Univ. of San Diego, Calif. Western Univ., Practising Law Inst.; mem. bds: Metropolitan Opera Assn., N.Y. (dir.), Met. Opera Nat. Council (v.p., exec. com. chmn., and dir.), San Diego Opera Assn. (v.p. 1985-89, dir., pres.-elect 1994), National Actors Theatre, N.Y. (nat. steering com.); mem: Am., Calif., N.Y., D.C. bar assns., San Diego County Bar Assn. (v.p., dir. 1983-85), Am. Bd. of Trial Advocates, San Diego Co. Bar Found. (dir. 1984-86), Internat. Assn. of Defense Counsel; author: State Hazardous Waste Regulation (Butterworth Legal Pubs., 1991), Environmental Insurance Coverage: State Law and Regulation (Butterworth Legal Pubs., 1991), Insurance Coverage for Environmental Claims (Matthew Bender & Co., 1992); mil: capt. JAGC, USNR (Ret.), active duty 1959-63, Vietnam Svc.; Republican; R.Cath.; rec: classical music, scuba. Res: 455 Silvergate Ave San Diego 92106-3327 Ofc: Luce, Forward, Hamilton & Scripps 600 W Broadway 26th Fl San Diego 92101-3391 and 153 E 53rd St 26th Fl New York 10022

LAU, B. PECK, radiation oncologist; b. Nov. 27, 1932, Singapore (nat. 1970); s. T.K. and L.H. (Ding) L.; m. Judith T., June 1, 1962; children: Laura, Benjamin, Estelle; edn: BS, Randolph-Macon Coll., Ashland, Va. 1955; MD, Med. Coll. of Va., Richmond 1959; diplomate, radiology 1965. Career: instr. radiology UCSF Med. Ctr., S.F. 1964-65; assoc. prof. Med. Coll. of Va., Richmond 1967-68; chief, radiation oncologist L.A. County Harbour Gen. Hosp. 1969-71, Valley Med. Ctr., Fresno 1972-94; honors: Phi Beta Kappa 1954; mem: Am. Soc. of Therapeutic Radiology, Am. Coll. of Radiation Oncology, Calif. Coll. of Radiology, CMA; rec: championship squash, tennis, wines. Res: 5331 N Sequoia Dr Fresno 93711 Ofc: Radiation Oncology Groups of California 1201 E Herndon #101 Fresno

LAU, LAWRENCE JUEN-YEE, Kwoh-Ting Li professor of economic development; b. Dec. 12, 1944, China; nat. 1974; s. Shai Tat and Chi-Hing (Yu) Liu; m. Eva C. Ching, 1975 (div. 1978); m. Tamara Katherine Jablonski, June 23, 1984; edn: BS great distinction, Stanford Univ. 1964; MA, UC Berkeley 1966; PhD, 1969. Career: acting prof. of economics Stanford Univ. 1966-67, asst. prof. econ., 1967-73, assoc. prof. econ. 1973-76, prof. econ. 1976–, Kwoh-Ting Li prof. econ. devel., co-dir. Asia/Pacific Res. Ctr. 1992–; cons. World Bank, Wash. D.C. 1975–; Asian Devel. Bank, Manila, Philippines 1988–; mem. Governor's Council of Econ. Policy Advisors, State of Calif.; author: Farmer Edn. & Farm Efficiency, 1982, author, ed. Models of Devel.: A Comparative

Study of Econ. Growth in S. Korea and Taiwan, 1986, revised and expanded ed., 1990; Republican; Episcopalian. Ofc: Stanford Univ. Dept. of Economics Stanford 94305-6072

LAUBSCHER, RODERICK, public relations executive; b. April 26, 1949, San Francisco; s. Fred Harold and Myrtle Louise (Bazzini) L.; edn: BA, UC Santa Cruz 1970; MS, Columbia Univ. 1972. Career: reporter, writer KSFO Radio, San Francisco 1970-74; reporter, anchor KGTV, San Diego 1975-77; reporter KRON T.V., San Francisco 1977-80; pub. rels. exec. Bechtel Group Inc. 1981–; dir. Market St. Railway Co. 1983–; awards: N. Calif. Acad. T.V. Arts & Scis. Emmy 1978, Columbia Univ. Pulitzer fellow 1972; mem: San Francisco Planning & Urban Research, Commonwealth Club Calif., World Affairs Council No. Calif., City Club S.F. (chmn. bd. 1987-89), San Francisco C.of C. (dir. 1987); writer, producer of documentary film Songs of A Distant Jungle, 1985; rec: bicycling. Ofc: Bechtel Group Inc. 50 Beale St San Francisco 94105

LAUER, JEANETTE CAROL, historian, author; b. July 14, 1935, St. Louis, Mo.; d. Clinton Jones and Blanche Aldine (Gideon) Pentecost; m. Robert Harold Lauer, July 14, 1954; children: Jon b. 1955, Julie b. 1957, Jeffrey b. 1961; edn: BS Univ. Mo. St. Louis 1970; MA, Wash. Univ. St. Louis 1972; PhD, 1975. Career: instr., Wash. Univ., St. Louis, Mo. 1972-73; assoc. prof. Comm. Coll. 1974-82; prof., dean of arts & scis.U.S. Internat. Univ., San Diego 1983-94; ed. Am. Historical Assn., WDC 1980-88; awards: Univ. Mo. hon. scholarship 1966-69, Woodrow Wilson fellow 1970, Wash. Univ. fellowship 1971-75; mem: Orgn. Am. Historians, Am. Historical Soc.; author: Fashion Power, 1981, Spirit & The Flesh, 1983, Till Death Do Us Part, 1986, Watersheds, 1988, The Quest for Intimacy, 1991 (2nd edit. 1994), No Secrets, 1993, The Joy Ride, 1994, For Better or Better, 1995, num. articles pub. in jours.; Democrat; Presbyterian; rec: jogging, hiking, art. Res: 18147 Sun Maiden Ct San Diego 92127

LAUGHLIN-MILLER, KATHLEEN ANN, pharmacist; b. Nov. 18, 1961, San Fernando; d. Clarence Edward and Carol Ruth (Anderson) Laughlin; m. Gregory Lee Miller, Mar. 10, 1987; edn: AS, Am. River Coll., 1982; PharmD, Univ. of Pacific, 1985; reg. pharmacist (RPh) Calif., Nev. 1985. Career: pharmacy intern Valley Pharmacy, and Am. River Hosp., Sacto. 1983, San Joaquin Hosp., French Camp 1985; pharmacy tech. Methodist Hosp., Sacto. 1979-82, intern, pharmacist 1983-86; pharmacist Sutter Community Hosps., Sacto. 1985–; assoc. clin. prof. UC San Francisco 1986; recipient Sutter Spirit award Sutter Community Hosps. (1988); dir. of pharmacy, Kangaroo Kids Ctr. for Fragile Children/Home Therapy, Sacto. 1991-93; pharmacist, Kaiser Permanente, Roseville 1993–; mem: Am. Pharm. Assn., Calif. Soc. Hosp. Pharmacists, Am. Soc. Hosp. Pharmacists, Calif. Pharmacists Assn., S.F. Caledonian Soc., Sacto. Youth for Christ/ Campus Life (assoc. staff 1979-82), Precious Moments Collectors Club; Republican; Reformed Ch. of America; rec: counted cross stitch, pharmacy antiques, reading. Ofc: Sutter Memorial Hospital 52nd & F Streets Sacramento 95819

LAUSEN, P. SANDER, optician; b. Oct. 29, 1934, Aarhus, Denmark, nat. 1973; s. Daniel Severin and Ragnhilde (Faurholt) L.; m. Jytte Rasmussen, Jan. 25, 1958 (div. 1984); children: Pia, b. 1960; Rene, b. 1963; edn: BS, Inst. of Tech., Copenhagen, Denmark 1956; M.Ophthalmic Optics 1972; bd. cert. Am. Bd. Opticianry 1967; Fellow Nat. Acad. Opticianry 1967. Career: optician, optometrist Cornelius Knudsen, Aarhus, Denmark 1952-57, C.F. Mc William Ltd., Auckland, NZ 1957-65; dispensing optician/ mgr. Superior Optical Co., Newport Beach 1965-74; mgr. Victor Optical, Laguna Hills 1974-76; prop. Continental Eyewear, Newport Beach 1976–; awards: Man of the Month (2), and Award of Merit Hi-Lite, Superior Optical Co. 1971; mem: Calif. Soc. Ophthalmic Dispensers (bd. dirs. 1971-76), Eastbluff Merchants' Assn. (pres. 1983-84), Newport-Balboa Rotary Club 1977- (sgt. at arms 1983), Newport Beach Tennis Club, Newport Ctr. Toastmasters, Conservative Caucus; research: Aniseikonia and Iseikonic Lenses; Republican; Lutheran; rec: soccer (chief referee Newport-Irvine AYSO 1972-77, bd. dirs. AYSO 1972-77), tennis. Res: 725 Domingo Dr Newport Beach 92660 Ofc: Continental Eyewear "Optique Mobile" 725 Domingo Dr Newport Beach 92660 Tel: 714/640-2020

LAVAL, CLAUDE CONSTANT, III, manufacturing executive; b. May 9, 1935, Fresno; s. Claude Constant Jr. and Marian B. (Kahn) L.; m. Betty Lou Scarbrough, Feb. 1, 1958; children: Melinda, Luann Laval Williams; edn: BA, Stanford Univ. 1957. Career: sales mgr. Suppliers Inc., Fresno 1957-60; pres. A-V Electronics Inc. 1960-71; Claude Laval Corp. 1971–; dir. bus. advy. council CSU 1984-94; chmn. Parking Authority Fresno 1964-68; mem: Irrigation Assn. (pres. 1983-84), Downtown Assn. Fresno (pres. 1966-68), No. Calif. Dist. Export Council, Water Resource Export Council, Young Pres. Orgn. (chmn. 1983-84), World Bus. Forum (secty., treas. 1985–), Rotary, Sunnyside CC, Fig Garden Swim & Racquet Club, Beta Gamma Sigma. Ofc: Claude Laval Corp. 1365 N Clovis Ave Fresno 93727

LAVELLA, CHERYL ANN, management information systems and materials management executive; b. Sept. 24, 1948, Greensburgh, Pa.; d. Louis J. and Grace M. (Fallovallitta) LaVella; edn: CSU Dominguez Hills 1981; AS, Mt. San Antonio 1982. Career: assembler Filtex, LaVerne 1969-75, stockroom 1975-79; planner Natter Mfg., Temple City 1979-83; supr. Fairchild Ind. 1983-85; master

scheduler Tubing Seal Cap, Azusa 1985-87, system analyst 1987-88; MIS mgr. Pacific Precision Metal 1988–; cons., Claremont 1988-89; master scheduler Lynx Golf, City of Industry 1992-93; prodn. and inventory control mgr. HyCAL, El Monte 1994–; pres. Inland ASK User Group, Temple City 1989–; prof. materials program (part-time) UC Riverside 1991-93; awards: Fairchild Ind. achievement 1985, BPW bus. woman runner-up 1988, Milt Cook Award of Distinction 1992, nominated for APICS Outstanding Mem. 1993; mem: APICS (pres. Inland Chpt. 1994-95, v.p. membership 1986-87, v.p. publicity 1981-85), Calif. Literacy (tutor 1987-88), MADD; civic: vol. Riverside Am. Indian Ctr. 1992-93; crisis/suicide counselor Riverside "Helpline" 1992–; rec: classical guitar, antiques, needlecraft. Res: 12399 Blazing Star Ct Rancho Cucamonga 91739 Ofc: HyCAL 9650 Telstar Ave El Monte 91731

LAVENTHOL, DAVID A., media company president; b. July 15, 1933, Phila., Pa.; s. Jesse and Clare (Horwald) L.; m. Esther Coons, Mar. 8, 1958; children: Peter b. 1959, Sarah b. 1960; edn: AB, Yale Univ., 1957; MA, Univ. Minn., 1960. Career: reporter, news editor St. Petersburg (Fla.) Times, 1957-62; asst. editor, city editor N.Y. Herald-Tribune, 1963-66; asst. mng. editor Washington Post, 1966-69; exec. editor Newsday, Long Island, NY, 1969, v.p./ed. Newsday (Times Mirror), 1970-78, publisher/CEO 1978-80; group v.p. Times Mirror Co. eastern newspapers gp. 1981-86, sr. v.p. Times Mirror and chmn. Newsday 1986; pres. Times Mirror Co., 1987–; publisher Los Angeles Times 1990-93; bds: Pulitzer Prize Board 1982–, Internat. Press Inst., London (v. chr. 1985–), Newspaper Advt. Bureau, N.Y. (dir. 1987–), American Press Inst. Reston, Va. (dir. 1988–, chmn. 1988), United Negro Coll. Fund (dir. 1988–), Mus. of Contemporary Art, L.A. (trustee 1989), Calif. Mus. Found. (trustee 1989–), NY City Partnership (dir. 1985-87); awards: (hon.) LittD Dowling Coll., Long Island, NY 1979, (hon.) LLD Hofstra Univ., Long Island, NY 1986; mem. Am. Soc. Newspaper Editors, Am. Newspaper Publishers Assn., Council on Fgn. Rel., Century Club (NY), City Club on Bunker Hill (LA, bd. govs. 1989–); mil: AUS Signal Corps 1953-55. Res: 800 West First St #3202 Los Angeles 90012 Ofc: Times Mirror Co. Times Mirror Sq Los Angeles 90053

LAVERTY, BEN WILLIAM, III, safety consultant; b. Oct. 26, 1945, Taft; s. Ben Wm., Jr. and Marilyn Edith (Kruger) L.; children: Ben IV, Bret, Tim, Terra, Tallie; edn: Bakersfield Jr. Coll. 1964-65; BS, Brigham Young Univ. 1967; reg. environmental assessor, Calif.; cert. farm equipt. appraiser, cert. environmental insp. Career: tree crop supt. Belridge Farms, Bakersfield 1968-73; bd. dirs./owner Willow Creek Farms, Oakley, Ida. 1973-80; pres. and c.e.o. Calif. Safety Training Corp., Bakersfield 1980–; mgr./agt. Cal Farm Invest; irrigation cons. Kester Bros. 1978-80, agri. cons. Mobil Oil Corp. 1982–; pres. bd. dirs. Western Kern Resource Conservation Dist. 1982-86; pres. Calif. Resource Conservation Area IX, 1987-88; mem: Calif. Agricultural Prodn. Consultants Assn., Am. Consultants League, Am. Mgmt. Assn.; civic: Boy Scouts Am. Explorer Post Advisor, Bakersfield Coll. Alumni Assn. and Helmet Club (membership. chmn. 1983–), BYU Cougar Club; publs: agri. economic outlook 1986, Bakersfield Lifestyle mag.; Republican; rec: Masters Track All American 1986, woodworking, geneology. Ofc: California Safety Training Corp. 4909 Stockdale Hwy Ste 132 Bakersfield 93309-2637

LAVINE, STEVEN DAVID, college president; b. June 7, 1947, Sparta, Wis.; s. Israel Harry and Harriet Hauda (Rosen) L.; m. Janet M. Sternburg, May 29, 1988; edn: BA, Stanford Univ., 1969; MA, Harvard Univ., 1970, PhD, 1976. Career: tchg. fellow dept. English & Am. lit. Harvard Univ., Cambridge 1971-74; asst. prof. English & Am. lit. Univ. of Mich., Ann Arbor 1974-81, asst. ed. Mich. Quarterly Rev. 1978-81; vis. res. fellow in humanities Rockefeller Found., NY, NY 1981-82, asst., assoc. dir. for arts & humanities, 1983-88; adj. assoc. prof. Grad Sch. of Bus. N.Y. Univ. 1984-85; pres. Calif. Inst. of the Arts, Valencia 1988–; cons. Wexner Found., Columbus, Ohio 1986-87; cons., panelist Nat. Endowment for the Humanities 1981-85; selection panelist INPUT Television Screening Conf., Montreal Canada and Granada, Spain 1985-86; awards: Ford Graduate Prize Fellow, Harvard 1969-74, Charles B. Dexter Travelling Fellow, Harvard 1972, Horace H. Rackham Res.Fellow (18th-c. poetry) and UM Faculty devel. grantee 1978, UM Class of 1923 Award for outstanding tchg. in lit., arts and scis. 1979, UM Faculty recogn. award for disting. res. & tchg. 1980, Mich. Council for the Humanities grant/ organized nat. creative writing conf. 1980; mem: nat. advy. com. Smithsonian Exptl. Gallery, Task Force of Edn. Am. Assn. of Mus., KCRW-FM NPR (bd.), J.Paul Getty Mus. (vis. com.), L.A. Philharmonic Assn. 1994–, Endowments, Inc., Bonds Portfolio for Endowments, Inc. 1994–; co-editor w. Harry Thomas, The Hopwood Anthology: Five Decades of American Poetry (UM Press, 1981), co-editor w/Ivan Karp, Exhibiting Cultures: The Politics and Poetics of Museum Display (Smithsonian Instn. Press 1991), Museums and Communities (Smithsonian Instn. Press 1992), article, Museum News, 1989, num. articles in literary revs. and jours., ed. spl. jour. issue Prooftexts, 1984. Ofc: Calif. Inst. of the Arts 24700 McBean Pkwy Santa Clarita 91355-2397

LAW, H. DAVID, optoelectric company executive; b. Feb. 12, 1949, Hong Kong; nat. 1978; s. Wan Hei and Yee Hwui (Lin) Lo; m. Ruby Harr Yee, June 16, 1973; children: Jeremy b. 1982, George b. 1985; edn: BSEE, Univ. Wash. 1972; MSEE, Cornell Univ. 1975; PhD, Cornel Univ. 1977. Career: tech. staff

Rockwell Sci. Center, Thousand Oaks 1977-80; lab. mgr. TRW Tech. Research Center, El Segundo 1980-84; v.p. PCO Inc., Chatsworth 1984-91; pres. ArterNet Corp., Woodland Hills 1991–; sr. mem: IEEE, Am. Physical Soc.; 35+ articles pub. in tech. jours.; patentee in field; book chpt. pub.; Prot.; rec: bridge, violin, classical music. Res: 29776 Woodbrook Dr Agoura Hills 91301 Ofc: ArterNet Corp., 22543 Ventura Blvd. Ste 215, Woodland Hills 91364

LAWSON, CAROL WOO, clinical laboratory microbiology section chief; b. Jan. 4, 1948, Artesia; d. Hong Ngoon and Mary (Cho) Woo; m. Robert Wayne Lawson, July 18, 1974; children: Jeffrey Alan b. 1978; edn: BS med. tech., CSU Los Angeles 1971. Career: employee Clinical Lab. Med. Group, 1971-86, as rotating med. tech. St. Francis Med. Center Lab., Lynwood 1971-74, asst. microbiology supr., 1974-78; microbiology supr. St. Francis Med. Ctr. 1978-85, Inter-Community Medical Ctr., 1985–; mem: Am. Soc. Clin. Pathologists, Nat. Cert. Agency Med. Lab. Personnel, Am. Soc. Microbiology, So. Calif.- Am. Soc. of Microbiol., PTA 1983- (San Rafael pres. 1988-89, service award 1989, Pasadena svc. award 1994); Republican; Baptist. Ofc: Inter-Community Medical Center Clinical Laboratory 210 W San Bernardino Rd Covina 91723

LAWSON, JAMES RUSSELL, real estate broker; b. Feb. 23, 1935, Woodland; s. Edwin Leo and Abbie Fern (Fowler) L.; m. Lois Ann Hazeman, Dec. 28, 1957; children: Cynthia b. 1958, Lynda b. 1963, Brenda b. 1965; edn: AA, Yuba Coll. 1979. Career: life ins. sales Equitable, Sacto. 1958-62; sales Sunbeam Bread Co. 1962-68; life ins. and real estate sales Yolo Co. Real Estate, Woodland 1968-70; real estate broker Lawson Real Estate 1970–; instr. Yuba Coll. 1978-80, 1982-84; service broker ERA Real Estate 1976–; awards: Yolo Co. Bd. Realtors Realtor of Year 1976; mem: Yolo Co. Bd. Realtors (pres. 1975), Calif. Assn. Realtors, Nat. Assn. Realtors, Kiwanis (pres. 1974), Comm. Care Center (pres. 1973), AARP, Yolo C.of C., Elderly Transp. (founder, pres. 1973); mil: USN 1952-56; Democrat; Prot.; rec: Golf, tennis, fishing. Res: 742 1st Woodland 95695 Ofc: ERA Lawson Real Estate 413 Court Woodland 95695

LAWSON, KAY, educator; b. Apr. 21, 1933, Salem, Ore.; d. Arlo C. and Ethel L. (Jones) Davis; m. William Lawson, Apr. 30, 1952; children: Kevin b. 1953, Marta b. 1962; edn: BA, UC Berkeley 1959; MA, 1962; PhD, 1971. Career: prof. political sci. San Francisco St. Univ. 1968–; vis. prof. (spring semesters): Rutgers Univ., New Brunswick, N.J. 1982, Columbia Univ., N.Y.C. 1982, Univ. London, England 1987, London Sch. Political Sci. and Economics 1987, Univ. Paris, Nanterre, France 1987, Univ. Paris, Sorbonne 1992, 1994, 1995 and 1996, Fondation Nationale des Sciences Politiques 1992, 1994 and 1996; editorial bds.: P.S., Comparative Political Studies, Party Politics, Modern and Contemporary France; reviewer for Am. Political Sci. Review, Jour. of Politics, Comparative Political Studies, Comparative Politics, Am. Jour. of Political Sci.; mem. of conf. group on French Politics and Society; currently Am. co-editor book series: Perspectives in Comparative Politics (for Longman, England), and co-editor volume of studies tentatively titled: Political Cleavages and Parties in the New Europe; honors: listed World Who's Who of Women, Who's Who in West, Who's Who in Calif., Who's Who in Am. Edn., 2,000 Women of Achievement; mem: Assn. for Study of Modern and Contemporary France, Inter-univ. Consortium for Social Res. on France, Internat. Political Sci. Assn. French Political Sci. Assn., Am. Political Sci. Assn. (section mem.: Political Organizations and Parties, Politics and Society in W. Europe, Comparative Politics), Western Political Sci. Assn., Bay Area Women in Political Sci.; author: Political Parties and Democracy in the United States (Scribners 1968), The Comparative Study of Political Parties (St. Martin's 1976), The Human Polity: An Introduction to Political Science (Houghton Mifflin 1984, 2d. edit., 1989, 3d. edit., 1993, 4th edit., 1996); 25+ book reviews pub. in political sci. jours., 1970-, 30+ pub. articles and chapters, 1971-; editor and contbg. author: How Political Parties Work: Perspectives from Within (Praeger 1994), Political Parties and Linkage: A Comparative Perspective (Yale Univ. Press 1980); co-editor & contbg. author: When Parties Fail: Emerging Alternative Organizations (Princeton Univ. Press 1988); Democrat; rec: travel. Res: 389 Gravatt Dr Berkeley 94705 Ofc: Dept of Political Sci. & Internat. Relations San Francisco State Univ. San Francisco 94132 and Departement de Science Politique, Université de Paris I, Sorbonne, Paris 75005

LAWSON, THOMAS, artist; b. July 16, 1951, Glasgow, Scotland; s. Edward and Margaret L.; m. Susan Morgan; edn: BA (honors), Univ. St. Andrews, Scotland 1973; MA, Univ. Edinburgh, Scotland 1975; MPhil, CUNY, NY 1979. Career: founding editor Real Life Magazine, NY, NY 1979-94; curatorial mem. The Drawing Ctr., NY, NY 1979-81; instr. Sch. of Visual Arts, NY, NY 1981-90; vis. instr. Rhode Isl. Sch. Design, Providence 1988-89; vis faculty Calif. Inst. of the Arts, Valencia 1986, 89; dean art sch. Calif. Inst. of the Arts 1990–; panelist, visual arts, NY St. Council on Arts 1983-90; editl. adv. Alba Magazine, Edinburgh, Scotland 1984-89; artist adv. Rotunda Gallery, Brooklyn, NY 1985-90; honors: artist fellowships: Nat. Endowment for Arts, WDC 1982-83, 85-86, 89-90; mem: Coll. Art Assn. 1986–; artist: paintings on display in various cities worldwide, 1975–, temporary murals Manhattan Municipal Bldg., NY 1989-92, Newcastle, England, 1990; author: num. articles pub. in profl. jours., 1979–. Ofc: Art School California Institute of the Arts 24700 McBean Pkwy Valencia 91355

LAWSON, THOMAS CHENEY, certified fraud examiner, certified international investigator; b. Sept. 21, 1955, Pasadena; s. Wm. McDonald and Joan Bell (Jaffee) L.; children: Christopher, Brittany; edn: CSU Sacto. 1973-77. Career: pres. Tomatron Co., Pasadena 1970–, Tom's Tune Up & Detail, Pasadena 1971–, Tom's Pool Service, Sacto. 1975–, Tom Supply Co., 1975–; mgmt. trainee Permoid Process Co., Los Angeles 1970-75; regional sales cons. Hoover Co., Burlingame 1974-76; mktg. exec. River City Prodns., Sacto. 1977-78; prof. automechanics CSU Sacto. 1973-75; territorial rep. Globe div. Burlington House Furniture Co., 1978; So. Calif. territorial rep. Marge Carson Furniture Inc. 1978-80; pres. Ted L. Gunderson & Assocs., Inc., Westwood 1980-81; pres/c.e.o. Apscreen, Newport Beach 1980–; pres./c.e.o. Creditbase Co., Newport Beach 1982-89; pres. Worldata Corp., Newport Beach 1985-89; shareholder Trademark Enforcement Corp. 1986-93; c.e.o. Carecheck Inc., 1989–; awards: Calif. Rehab. scholar 1974-77; mem. Am. Soc. Indsl. Security (chmn. Orange Co. chpt. 1990), Christian Businessmens' Com., Council of Internat. Investigators, Nat. Pub. Records Research Assn., Personnel & Indsl. Relations Assn., Assn. of Certified Fraud Examiners, Soc. for Human Resourcement. Ofc: 2043 Westcliff Dr Ste 300 Newport Beach 92660

LAYTON, EDWARD NORMAN, construction executive; b. June 29, 1928, Kellogg, Idaho; s. Ernest Alfred and Ruth Eloise (Thwing) L.;m. Mary Katherine Ketchum, June 29, 1948; children: Norman b. 1950, Cheryl b. 1954, Terri b. 1957, Dennis b. 1958; edn: cert. bus. mgmt., UCLA 1957; lic. General Contractor B1, Calif. 1958. Career: cowboy for Davis Ranch, Ariz. 1944; shop foreman Fiat Metal Products 1948; carpenter 1949-52; carpenter supt. Casnor Constrn. 1952-63, v.p./ part owner 1964-77; founder, past pres. (1978-90), chmn. bd. Ed Layton Construction Co., 1978–; pres. Layton Enterprises Inc.; chmn. bd. Tri-Co. Investment Group Inc., 1976–; dir. Building Industry Assn. So. Calif., 1976-84, v.p. labor 1981-83, chmn. Labor Negotiation Com. 1982-83; mem. bd. trustees: Carpenters Pension Trust for So. Cal., C.I.A.F. Trust Fund for So. Cal., F.C.I.A.F Trust Fund for So. Cal., v.-chmn. F.C.I.A. Trustee Bd.; elected bd. Walnut Valley County Water Dist. 1985–, pres. 1991; commr. Puente Basin Water Agy.; awards: Walnut Valley Citizen of Year 1975, A.I.A. Cabrillo Award for excellence of constrn.- La Mirada City Hall 1970, Pacific Coast Builders Conf. 14 Western States Gold Nugget Award of Merit for excellence of commercial remodel 1981; mem: Building Industry Assn. (rewrote BIA Master Labor Agreement 1980), BIA-Pasadena San Gabriel Valley (Commercial Industrial Council), Nat. Assn. Home Builders, NAHB Spike Club (So. Calif. labor policy dir.), So.Calif. Archeol. Survey Assn.; civic: Men's Club Queen of Valley Hosp., Walnut San Dimas Sheriff Station Booster Club (founding dir.), Citizens Advy. Com. Diamond Bar City General Plan, Citizens Advy. Com. Intercomm. Hosp. Diamond Bar Complex, Walnut Valley C.of C. (bd.), Kiwanis Intl. (Cal-Nev-Ha Found.); club: Via Verde Country; works: first fiberglass domed bldg. for projection and display of stellar films of space flts. 1965; constrn. of 300+ million projects; Republican (Presdl. Task Force); Prot.; rec: amateur archeologist, lapidarist, mineorologist. Res: 404 S Lemon Ave Walnut 91789 Ofc: Ed Layton Constrn. Co., Inc., POB 60, Walnut 91789

LA ZARE, HOWARD TED, engineering executive; b. Oct. 10, 1936, Chicago, Ill.; s. Henry and Jeanne (Sodakoff) La Z.; m. Phyllis F., July 15, 1960; children: Adam b. 1961, Kim b. 1965; edn: BSEE cum laude, West Coast Univ. Sch. of Engring. 1969; BSME magna cum laude, 1970; lic. electrical engr. Calif. 1978. Career: v.p. engring Consolidated Film Industries, Hollywood 1964-84; sr. v.p. engring. Deluxe Labs. Inc. 1984-92; pres. FilmTec International, Chatsworth 1992–; gov. Soc. Motion Picture & TV Engrs., White Plains, N.Y. 1984-85 and 1990-96, editorial v.p. 1985-88, dir. engring. 1984, v.p. motion picture affairs 1982-83, chmn./mem. num. committees 1981–; honors: Academy Awards Class II, 1973, 82; listed Who's Who in U.S. Execs., Who's Who in Calif., Who's Who in Entertainment, Who's Who in Fin. & Ind., Who's Who in Sci. & Engring., Who's Who Environmental Registry, Standard & Poor's Register for Corporations, Dirs. & Execs., Personalities in Am., Men of Achievement, Internat. Dir. of Disting. Leadership; mem: Soc. Motion Picture & TV Engrs. (fellow), AMPAS 1985–, Am. Soc. Cinematographers, IEEE (sr. mem.), British Kinematograph Sound & TV Engrs.; author: 2 papers pub. in tech. jours., 1972, 75; inventor: shutterless film projector, Patent #4509836, 1985; Republican; Jewish; rec: chess, tennis, golf. Res: 10825 Fullbright Ave Chatsworth 91311 Ofc: FilmTec International 10825 Fullbright Ave Chatsworth 91311

LAZEROW, HERBERT IRVIN, professor of law; b. April 12, 1939, Baltimore, Md.; s. Julius and Beatrice Lilian (Kimmelman) L.; m. Jane Frances Goding, Aug. 25, 1963; children: Erica b. 1969, Shana Deborah b. 1971; edn: BA, Univ. Pa. 1960; JD, Harvard Law Sch. 1963; LLM, George Washington Univ. 1964; DESS, Univ. Paris I Pantheon-Sorbonne 1981. Career: atty. IRS Chief Counsel, Wash. D.C. 1964-66; asst. prof. Univ. Louisville, Ky. 1966-67; assoc. prof. Univ. San Diego 1967-70, prof. 1970–, dir. Inst. Internat. & Comparative Law 1973–, assoc. dean for academics 1973-79; ed. in chief Internat. Tax Jour., N.Y.C. 1987-91; chair ACLU Legal Panel, San Diego 1968-70; mem. San Diego Co. Employee Rels. Panel 1971-73; chair Mayors Social Sci. Advy. Panel 1970-71; honors: Phi Beta Kappa, Fed. Bar Assn. Essay Winner, 1962; mem: Am. Law Inst., Landmark Arts Projects; author: OECD

Draft Influence on U.S. Income Tax Treaties, 1976, Fiscalite Americaine: l'Impot sur le Revenu, 1987. Ofc: Univ. San Diego Law School, 5998 Alcala Park, San Diego 92110-2492

LEADER, JEFFERY JAMES, educator; b. Oct. 27, 1963, Elmira, N.Y.; s. Dennis Thomas and Jeanne Diane (Smith) L.; m. Margaret Ellen Nieburg, Aug. 26, 1989; children: Derek b. 1990, Corrinne b. 1994; edn: BS, and BSEE, Syracuse Univ., 1985; ScM, Brown Univ., 1987, PhD, 1989. Career: vis. asst. prof. Harvey Mudd Coll., Claremont 1989-90; asst. prof. math. Naval Postgraduate Sch., Monterey 1990-93; asst. prof. Math. Sci., U.S. Military Acad., West Point, N.Y. 1993–; honors: Phi Beta Kappa, Tau Beta Pi, Sigma Xi; mem. Am. Math. Soc., Soc. for Indsl. and Appl. Math.; publs: articles in Applied Math. Letters (3), 1991, Rocky Mountain Math. Jour., 1993; rec: martial arts. Ofc: Dept. of Math. Sci., U.S. Military Academy West Point NY 10996-1786

LEAHY, T. LIAM, management analyst; b. Apr. 15, 1952, Camp Lejeune, N.C.; s. Thomas James and Margaret (Munnelly) L.; m. Shannon Kelly Brooks, Apr. 21, 1990; edn: MA, St. Louis Univ., 1975; spl. tng. Hubbard Coll. of Adminstrn., L.A. 1989. Career: senior mgmt. analyst Leahy and Assocs., Tarzana, Calif. 1982–; pres. Generation Dynamics, N.Y.C. 1985; pres. Journal Graphics, N.Y.C. 1984; assoc, Am. Council of Execs. Assn., Burbank, Calif. 1991–; bd. dirs.: Laser Impact Comproteck Svs., Inc., Austin, Tx. 1995-96, Art Boom Internat. Inc., Canyon Country, Calif. 1994-96, Voiceworks, Irvine, Calif; senior fellow, Effective Mgmt. Centers, Houston & Austin, Tx. 1994–; mem: Turnaround Mgmt Assn. (bd. dirs. 1990-95), Am. Council of Execs. (bd. dirs. 1993-95), Consultants Assn. (bd. 1992), U.S. Chamber of Commerce 1985–; numerous articles in gen. and trade periodicals, 1980–; rec: musician. Ofc: Leahy & Associates 19131 Enadia Way Reseda 91335-3828

LEAKE, DONALD LEWIS, surgeon, medical educator; b. Nov. 6, 1931, Cleveland, Okla.; s. Walter Wilson and Martha Lee (Crow) L.; m. Rosemary Dobson, Aug. 20, 1964; children: John Andrew b. 1965, Elizabeth Victoria b. 1967, Catherine Anne b. 1969; edn: BA, USC 1953; MA, 1957; DMD, Harvard Univ. 1962; MD, Stanford Univ. 1969. Career: assoc. prof. UCLA 1970-74, prof. 1974–; honors: Phi Kappa Phi, Phi Beta Kappa; Royal Conservatory of Music Brussels, Premier Prix 1956; mem: A.C.S. (fellow), British Assn. Oral & Maxillofacial Surgeons, Am. Assn. Oral & Maxillofacial Surgeons (fellow), AAAS, Soc. Biomaterials, ASTM, European Assn. Maxillofacial Surgeons, Internat. Gesellschaft fur Kiefer-Gesichts-Chururgie, Harvard Club Boston, Harvard Club N.Y.C., Beefeater Club; num. papers and articles pub. in med. and sci. jours.; rec: oboe, chamber music. Ofc: Univ. California 1000 W Carson St Torrance 90509

LEAVITT, TODD PAGE, entertainment industry executive; b. March 27, 1951, Detroit, Mich.; s. Gerald Matthew and Ann (Ruttenberg) L.; m. Lauren Iris Luchnick, Jan. 6, 1979; children: Julia b. 1982, Chloe b. 1988, Eliza b. 1988; edn: BA, Kenyon Coll. 1973; JD, N.Y. Univ. Sch. Law 1977. Career: atty. Viacom Internat., N.Y.C. 1975-79; Franklin Weinrib et al 1979-81; v.p. bus. affairs Disney Channel 1981-83; sr. v.p. programming CBS/Fox Video 1983-86; COO D.L. Taffner Ltd. 1986-87; exec. v.p. Reeves Entertainment, Burbank 1987-90; exec. v.p. NBC Productions, Burbank 1990–; lectr. Practicing Law Inst., N.Y.C.; UCLA Ext.; Am. Film Inst., L.A.; honors: Phi Beta Kappa, Nathan Burkan award ASCAP (1977). Address: Santa Monica 90402

LEBEAU, CHARLES PAUL, business, tax and international lawyer; b. Dec. 11, 1944, Detroit; s. Charles Henry, Jr. and Mary Barbara (Moran) L.; m. Victoria Joy (Huchin), May 15, 1970; 2 sons: Jeffrey Kevin, Timothy Paul; edn: AA, Macomb Co. Community Coll., 1967; BA, Wayne St. Univ., 1969; JD, Univ. Detroit Sch. of Law, 1972; postgrad. tax pgm. N.Y.U. Sch. Law 1972-73; admitted bar: Calif., Mich., U.S. Supreme Ct., U.S. Tax Ct., U.S. Ct. Internat. Trade. Career: tax atty. Ford Motor Co., Dearborn, Mich. 1973-75; atty. Hoops & Huff, Detroit 1975-76; tax and internat. atty. Miller, Canfield, Paddock & Stone, Detroit 1976-78; tax mgr. Oceaneering Internat., Santa Barbara 1978-79; tax counsel Signal Cos. Inc., Beverly Hills and La Jolla, 1978-83; tax and internat. atty. Gray, Cary, Ames & Frye, San Diego 1983-84; of counsel James Watts Esq., La Jolla 1985; Murfey, Griggs & Frederick, La Jolla 1986; business, tax and internat. law practice, La Jolla and San Diego, 1987–; lectr. grad. tax pgm. Golden Gate Univ., San Diego 1979-87; adj. prof. law Univ. San Diego 1982-85, 88–; honors: Pi Sigma Alpha, Univ. Detroit Law Sch. law rev. staff (1971) and moot court (1971-72); mem: ABA, Mich. Bar Assn., Calif. Bar Assn., San Diego Co. Bar Assn., Am. Arbitration Assn. S.D. (arb. panelist 1990–); civic: United Way Santa Barbara campaign coord. (1979), Univ. San Diego Charitable Contbns. Com. (1982-83); publs: monthly commentary on tax cases in Taxes Internat., London (1981-85), contbr. articles on internat. tax to profl. jours.; rec: sailing, tennis, walking. Res: 1999 Via Segovia La Jolla 92037 Ofc: 4660 La Jolla Village Dr Ste 1070 San Diego 92122 Ph: 619/456-1100 Fax: 619/455-5024

LEBLANC, GILBERT ARTHUR, physician; b. Sept. 27, 1927, Worcester, Mass.; s. Arthur Eugene and Regina Lea (Pelletier) L.; m. Helene Marie Kennedy, Feb. 27, 1954; children: Stephen b. 1954, Michele b. 1956, Christopher b. 1958, Dominique b. 1967; edn: BA, Assumption Coll.,

Worcester, Mass. 1950; MD, Georgetown Univ., Wash. D.C. 1954. Career: asst. chief urology Navy Hosp., St. Albans, NY 1959-61; chief of urology Navy Hosp., Newport, R.I. 1961-65, Yokosuka, Japan 1965-68; chmn., dept. urology NMC, Oakland 1968-77; chief of urology Holderman Hosp., Yountville, Calif. 1977–; mem: AUA, ACS, SPU; mil: capt. USN, 1954-77; Republican; Catholic; avocation: vineyard owner. Ofc: Holderman Hospital Yountville 94599

LECKIE, BERNARD ARTHUR, lawyer; b. Dec. 10, 1932, Los Angeles; s. Arthur Bernard and Lorene Dorothy (Kiesan) L.; m. Maryanne Hammatt, Dec. 21, 1959; children: Scott, b. 1962, Karin, b. 1964; edn: BS, USC Sch. of Commerce, 1959, LLB, JD, USC Law Sch. 1959. Career: deputy dist. atty. Los Angeles, 1960-61; atty. firms of Betts, Ely, & Loomis, 1961-63, Ely, Kadison & Quinn, 1963-65, Bernard A. Leckie, Atty. at Law, 1964-80, ptnr. law firm Meserve, Mumper & Hughes, 1980–; instr. P.E. law, LA City Adult Edn., 1960-62; instr. R.E. Practice, LA City Coll. 1962-66; judge pro tem Orange County Superior Ct. 1982–; honors: Law Week Award, USC Law Class, 1959; mem: Bar Assn. (Am., Calif., L.A. County, Orange County), Trial Lawyers Assn. (Am., Calif., L.A. Cty., Orange Cty.), Special Master Orange Cty., Legion Lex Orange Co. Inns of Court (bd. mem. 1990–), Orange Co. Legion Lex (bd. dirs. 1992–, pres. 1994-95), Am. Arbitration Assn. (arbitrator), Orange Cty. Superior Court Arb. Panel (arbitrator), Martindale-Hubbell A.V. rating, State Bar of Calif. (mem. investigative com. panel dist. 8, chmn. admin. com. 16, 1972), Phi Delta Theta (social), Phi Delta Phi (legal); mil: cpl. US Army 1951-53; Republican; Prot.; rec: sports, tennis, running, golf. Ofc: 18500 Von Karman Ste 600 Irvine 92715

LE CLERC, MICHAEL WARD, consultant, manufacturing and microcontamination service company president, expert witness; b. May 29, 1948, Detroit, Mich.; s. Ernest Frederick and Mary Ann (Williams) LeC.; edn: resident agent National Life Ins., Pontiac, Mich. 1971-72; techn. Custom Controls, Warren, Mich. 1972-74; foreman Environator Corp., Columbia, S.C. 1974-75; mgr. Calumet Scientific, Elk Grove Village, Ill. 1975-77; automatic equip. specialist IBM, San Jose, Calif. 1977-80; mgr. Trilogy Systems, Cupertino 1981-84; pres./bd. chmn. Class-10 Technologies Inc., San Jose 1984–; ptnr. M & J Associates, 1988-91; sr. mem. Inst. of Environmental Scis. 1986–; publs: 6+ tech. articles in trade mags.; mil: s/sgt. USAF 1967-71; rec: fishing, gardening, gourmet cooking. Ofc: Class-10 Technologies, Inc. 1719-D Little Orchard St San Jose 95125

LEDFORD, GARY ALAN, designer, builder, developer; b. Dec. 30, 1946, San Diego; s. Loren Oscar and Madge Francis (Condon) L.; m. Winifred Eleanor Jess, Nov. 19, 1994; children: Kelly b. 1969, Jeanne b. 1970, Robert b. 1972, Kevin b. 1973; edn: CE, US Army Engrg. Sch. 1967; grad. courses in structures, Univ. of Colo. 1969; sr. housing mktg. specialist, 1990; Calif. lic.: Gen. Engr. Contr., Gen. Bldg. Contr., Hazardous Waste Contr. #328361, Pvt. Patrol Opr. #PPO11098; mem. Spl. Svs. Bur. San Bernardino Co. Sheriff (Badge 5224). Career: platoon ldr., co. comdr., Battalion Civil Engr., US Army Corps of Engrs. (Airborne), Vietnam, 1969; pres. Mastercraft Contractors, Inc., Colorado Springs 1969-73; v.p./ gen. mgr. K.L. Redfern, Inc., Orange, Calif. 1973-75; past pres. Watt Jess Ranch Inc.; pres. Mojave Feed & Fuel Corp., chmn. mgmt. com. Watt-Jess/Ledford Ptnrship; pres. LJ&J Investment Corp.; pres. Jess Ranch Security Corp.; gen. ptnr. Ledford/ Schaffer-Rogers Ltd., past mng. ptnr. Apple Valley Mall; current private practice, G.A. Ledford & Assocs.; projects incl. retirement comm., residential devel., shopping ctr., and office park; instr. (Command & Staff), US Army Eng. Sch., Ft. Belvoir, VA 1966 (Nike Missile Support Sys.); awards: 2nd pl. design, Colo. Springs Parade of Homes 1972; mem: Urban Land Inst., Nat. Assn. Home Builders, Nat. Council Sr. Housing, Nat. Rifle Assn. (life), Nat. Plng. Assn., Bldg. Industry Assn., VFW, Internat. Council of Shopping Ctrs., High Desert Constrn. Inds. Assn., Victor Valley Mus. Assn. (life, past pres.), Victor Valley Cultural Arts Found. (founding, past pres.), Apple Valley Christian Care Ctrs. (trustee, bd., sec.); works: design, engineering, constrn. projects include. 4,700 residential homes, 26 shopping ctrs., 44 restaurants, 3 Edwards Theatres, 3 schools (L.A. Bd. Edn), Malibu Grand Prix (Pomona), over 100 svc. stations, num. indsl. bldgs., med. facilities, and var. mil. projects; design & devel. contractor computer software (copyrighted 1979), Tuffcore Bldg. Sys. (pat pend. 1981); mil. decorations: Bronze Star (2), Army Commdn. (2), Purple Heart; Republican; Prot.; rec: hunting, equestrian, chess. Res: 11401 Apple Valley Rd, Apple Valley 92308 Ofc: Jess Ranch 11401 Apple Valley Rd Apple Valley 92308

LEDIN, JAMES ALAN, aerospace engineer; b. July 29, 1961, Clinton, Iowa; s. John Ronald and Rosemary Theresa (Dunlavey) L.; m. Lynda Schmidt, Oct. 12, 1991; edn: BS aero. eng., Iowa State Univ., Ames 1983; Reg. Profl. Elec. Engr., State of Calif. 1994. Career: aerospace/electronics engr. Naval Air Warfare Ctr., Pt. Mugu, Ca. 1983–; awards: Nat. Merit Scholar, Ankeny, Ia. 1979, Sigma Gamma Tau 1983–, Tau Beta Pi 1983–; mem: Nat. Soc. of Profl. Engrs. 1994–, Calif. Soc. of Profl. Engrs. 1994–, ADI User's Soc. Applied Dynamics Internat., Ann Arbor, Mich. (1984-92, bd. and software librarian 1990–), Mensa 1988–, Simulation Computer Soc., We. Simulation Council Steeering Com. 1993–; Libertarian; rec: computer programming, guitar, photog., reading. Ofc: Naval Air Warfare Ctr Code 4KM400E Pt Mugu 93042-5000

LEE, CHUCK-KWAN KETCHUM, physician, hematologist, oncologist; b. Nov. 29, 1944, China; s. Eu-Dien Eddy and Fei-Ching (Chen) L.; m. Yuk-Ki Yolanda, Nov. 22, 1975; children: Isadora b. 1977, Georgiana b. 1982; edn: MB, BS, Univ. Hong Kong 1967. Career: hematologist-oncologist Bklyn. Jewish Med. Center, Bklyn., N.Y. 1974-77; cons. pvt. practice, Bakersfield 1977–; mem: CMA, Kern Co. Med. Soc., L.A. Pediatric Soc., Am. Acad. Pediatrics, Bakersfield Racquet Club; Republican; rec: music. Res: 1506 Calle Castana Bakersfield 93309 Ofc: 1700 A St Bakersfield 93301

LEE, CHUNG NAM, Oriental medical doctor; b. Feb. 3, 1942, Pusan, Korea (nat. Aug., 1990); s. Kyungtaek and Sobong (Son) L.; m. Jungja Choi, Feb. 16, 1985; children: Diana b. 1975; edn: BA, Yon Sei Univ., Seoul, Korea, 1965; MSA, OMS of SAMRA, L.A., Calif., 1991; ELD, Golden Gate Sem., LA., Calif., 1991; lic. acupuncturist, MBCAC, 1992. Career: dir., Chun Bo Clinic, L.A., Calif., 1991-92, God's Grace Oriental Med. Clinic, Costa Mesa; mem. CAA, 1992, NCCA. Res: 822 1/2 S. Crenshaw Blvd., Los Angeles 90005 Ofc: Traditional Chinese Med. Clinic 1042 E 4th St Ontario 91764 Tel: 909/391-4202, 213/936-9274

LEE, DONNA JEAN, registered nurse; b. Nov. 12, 1931, Huntington Park; d. Louis Frederick and Lena Adelaide (Hinson) Munyon; m. Frank Bernard Lee, July 16, 1949; children: Frank b. 1950, Robert b. 1952, John b. 1954; edn: Bell H.S. grad.; AA in nsg., Fullerton Jr. Coll. 1966; USC Ext. classes Orange Co. Med. Ctr. 1966-71; student 2 wks. abroad Russia Pgm., N.M. Univ., 1982; Calif. lic. RN 1966, AACN/CCRN cert. in intensive care 1972; Career: critical care nursing pos. 1969-85: staff nse. Orange Co. Med. Center, Orange 1966-69, charge nse. relief all intensive care units 1968-69, charge nse. communicable disease unit 1969-71, charge nse. neonatal unit, 5 mos. 1971; staff & charge nse. intensive care units, emergency rm., med.-surgical, maternity, Anaheim Memorial Hosp. 1971-74; agency nse. (staff relief ICU/CCU many hosps. in Orange Co.) Staff Builders, Orange 1974-82; plasma pheresis RN, Med. Lab. of Orange, 5 mos. 1978; asst. dir. nurses Skilled Nursing Facility, 1984; past empl. N.S. International, 1978-89; staff nse. Upjohn HealthCare (now Olsten Healthcare of Orange) 1985-90, also pediatric and geriatric nsg.; employed Visiting Nurses Assoc. Support Services (VNASS) of Orange Co. and Olsten Healthcare of Orange Co.(Home Health-Care, Respite and Nat. Certification in IV Therapy), 1990-93 (ret.); listed Who's Who Among Human Service Profls., Who's Who in Am. Nursing; mem. Am. Assn. Critical Care Nurses, Am. Heart Assn., Am. Cancer Soc., Nat. Assn. M.S., Am. Lung Assn., LM,RPTF 1982–, NRA, CIS, NRCC, NRC, NRSC, CRP, Heritage Found., ARC; Republican (Presdl. Task Force, Presdl. Advy. Com.); Baptist Fundamentalist; rec: travel, aviation, RV-ing, swimming, M.S. res., baking, new friends. Res: 924 S Hampstreet Anaheim 92802

LEE, EDWARD B., financial consultant; b. Sept. 19, 1962, Los Angeles; s. Bok and Suzie L.; edn: BA, and MS, UC San Diego, 1985, 1986. Career: staff research biochemist UC San Diego Cancer Ctr., 1986-88; asst. mgr. The Equitable, San Diego 1988-92; Asian mktg. mgr. Mutual of New York 1992-93; pres. E. Lee & Assoc. 1994–; bd. dirs. Asian Bus. Assn.; bd. dir. Korean Assn. of San Diego; pres. Korean-Am. Profl. Assn.; honors: Who's Who Among Young Am Profls. 1988-92, Who's Who in Am. 1992; mem. San Diego Assn. Life Underwriters 1988–, Le Tip Profl. Bus. Networking Orgn. (1988–, pres. 1992, 93); publs: 6+ sci. research papers and abstracts; rec: karate instr. World Tang Soo Do Karate Assn. Ofc: Lee & Associates 7955-A Dunbrook Road San Diego 92126

LEE, HANFU, dentist; b. May 28, 1960, Indonesia; s. James Djitseng and Louise L.; m. Prisca, Aug. 6, 1982; children: Carolyn b. 1986, Brian b. 1989; edn: Cal Poly Pomona; DDS, UCLA Sch. Dentistry; Univ. Hosp. Career: dentist Univ. Hosp., Jacksonville, Fla. 1985-86; Temple City 1986–; pres. San Gabriel Valley Periodontal Study Group 1987–; mem: ADA, Calif. Dental Assn., San Gabriel Valley Dental Soc., Fellow Acad. Gen. Dentistry; Presbyterian; rec: tennis. Ofc: Lee & Sons 9925 E Las Tunas Dr Temple City 91780

LEE, JERRY C., university president; b. Nov. 21, 1941; m. Joan Marie Leo; 1 child: Zan Carlton b. 1985; edn: BA, W.Va. Wesleyan Coll. 1963, grad. sch. 1963-64; Sch. of Law, Univ. Baltimore 1967-69; MA, Va. Polytechnic Inst. and State Univ. 1975, EdD, 1977. Career: indsl. rels. adminstr. Gen. Motors Corp., Balt. 1964-65; v.p. adminstrn. Commercial Credit Indsl. Corp., Balt.; v.p., adminstrn. and bus. Gallaudet Univ., WDC 1971-84, pres. 1984-88; pres. National University, San Diego 1988–; lectr. Gallaudet Univ.; lectr. nat. and internat.; honors: 1st honorary doctor of laws degree, Gallaudet Univ. 1986, disting. alumni award Va. Polytechnic Inst. and State Univ. 1985, Eileen Tosney award Am. Assn. of Univ. Admins. 1987, Advancement of Human Rights and Fundamental Freedoms award U.N. Assn. of the USA, One-of-a-kind award from People-To-People 1987, honorary pres., and National Service award Council for Better Speech and Hearing Month 1986, Nat. Assn. of Coll. Auxiliary Svcs. Excellence in Journalism award, Man of Yr. award Alpha Sigma Pi 1984, Gallaudet Coll. Alumni Assn. President's award, Gallaudet Comm. Rels. Award, U.S. Steel Foundation Cost Reduction Incentive award, Nat. Assn. of Coll. and Univ. Bus. Ofcrs., Am. Athletic Assn. of the Deaf award 1987; mem: Am. Assn. of Higher Edn., Am. Assn. of Univ. Admins., Am. Assn. of Univ. Prof., Am. Assn. of

School Admins., Am. Mgmt. Assn., Am. Soc. for Personnel Admins., Nat. Assn. of Coll. and Univ. Bus. Ofcrs., Nat. Assn. for Independent Coll. and Univs., Coll. and Univ. Personnel Assn., Soc. for Mgmt. Information Systems; civic: Nat. Collegiate Athletic Assn. Pres.'s Commn., hon. bd. dirs. District of Columbia Spl. Olympics, Sertoma Foundation Nat. Advy. Com. (life mem.), commn. on administration orgn. Rehabilitation International, bd. dirs. People-to-People, bd. dirs. Deafness Res. Foundn., journal advy. bd. Nat. Assn. of College Aux. Services, exec. com. Consortium of Universities of the Wash. Metro. Area, hon. advocacy bd. mem. Nat. Capital Assn. for Coop. Edn., Bureau of Nat. Affairs Personnel Policies Forum; num. articles pub. profl. jours.; rec: tennis. Ofc: National University, 4025 Camino del Rio So, San Diego 92108-4194

LEE, JOHN SUN-CHUNG, certified public accountant; b. Aug. 3, 1955, China; m. Jan-Lih Wang, Apr. 27, 1987; children: Johnson b. 1988, Jennifer b. 1989; edn: BS, CSU Sacramento, 1979; MS, taxation, Golden Gate Univ. 1993; CPA, Calif. (1985); cert. of ednl. achiev. in microcomputer consulting, Calif. Soc. CPAs, 1991. Career: owner John S. Lee, CPA, Monterey Park 1987–; mem: Am. Inst. of CPAs, Calif. Soc. of CPAs; rec: reading. Ofc: John S. Lee, CPA, 2063 S Atlantic Blvd Stes 2J & 2K Monterey Park 91754

LEE, JONG MOON, dentist; b. Aug. 4, 1946, Chung Joo, Choong Book, Korea; s. Young Kie and Choon Young (Song) L.; m. Yee, Oct. 6, 1973; children: Joon Y. b. 1974 (USC Dental Sch.), Sung W. b. 1976 (USC Pre-dental Sch.), Sue Y. b. 1981 (Diamond Bar H.S.); edn: grad. Seoul Nat. Univ. Literature and Sci. Sch. 1968; DDS, Seoul Nat. Univ. Sch. Dentistry 1972; DDS, USC Dental Sch. 1979. Career: dentist, capt. Korean Army 1972-75, O.J.T. tng. US Mil. Dental Detach., Seoul 1973-74, secty. of Surgeon Gen., Korean Army HQ 1974-75; postgrad. dental tng. USC 1976-79; dentist/owner Dr. Lee's Dental Office, first office Diamond Bar, 1982–, second office in Ontario; mem: American Dental Assn., Calif. Dental Assn., Korean Dental Assn. of USA (auditor 1994-95), USC Korean Dental Alumni Assn. (pres.-elect 1995-96), USC Alumni Assn., Seoul National Univ. Alumni Assn., Kyunggi H.S. Alumni Assn., Choong Chung Soc. (v.p. 1994-96), Diamond Bar Chamber of Commerce, Korean Am. Fedn. of Eastern Los Angeles (pres.); R.Cath.; rec: golf, Aikido instr. Res: 2177 Rocky View Rd Diamond Bar 91765 Tel. 909/861-5579 Dr. Lee's Dental Ofcs: 1108 S Diamond Bar Blvd Diamond Bar 91765 Tel: 909/861-4444 also: 2409-D Vineyard Ave Ontario 91761 Tel: 909/923-9557

LEE, MARGARET ANNE, psychotherapist; b. Nov. 23, 1930, Scribner, Nebr.; d. Wm. Christian and Caroline Bertha (Benner) Joens; m. Robert Lee, May 21, 1950, div. 1972; children: Lawrence b. 1951, James b. 1953, Daniel b. 1954; edn: AA, Napa Coll. 1949; journalism major UCB, 1949-50; BA, CSC Sonoma 1975; MSW, CSU Sacto. 1977; Calif. lic: Comm. Coll. Tchr. Credential, MFCC (Marriage Family Child Counselor), LCSW (Lic. Clin. Soc. Wkr.), 1979. Career: columnist local news for Napa Register 1946-50; eligibility wkr./supr. Napa Co. Dept. Social Svcs. 1968-75; psychotherapist, self-empl., Napa Valley Center, 1977–; p.t. instr. Napa Valley Coll. 1978-83; mem. bd. trustees Napa Valley Coll. (1983, pres. 1986, 90, 95), bd. of dir., CCCT (Calif. Comm. College Trustees), 1989–, pres. 1993-94; bd. of dir. CCLC (Comm. College League of Calif.), 1992-95, v.p. 1993-94; recipient Self mag. Fresh Start Award for achiev. as polio quadraplegic confined to wheelchair since 1954 (1984), luncheon guest of honor Congressional Caucus on Womens Issues, Wash DC (2/84); mem. Nat. Assn. of Soc. Wkrs., Napa County Council Econ. Opportunity (bd. 1984-5), Mental Health Assn. of Napa Co. (bd.), Nat. Women's Polit. Caucus, Soroptimist (1985-7), March of Dimes (vol. 1957-71); Democrat (Napa Dem. Caucus); Lutheran. Res: 15 Camilla Dr Napa 94558 Ofc: Margaret A. Lee, 1100 Trancas Ste 300 POB 2099 Napa 94558

LEE, MICHAEL GEORGE WAH, lawyer; b. Nov. 26, 1947, Honolulu, Hawaii; s. Wilson Wai and Hilda (Fong) L.; m. Teresa Gail Tucker, Nov. 15, 1986; edn: BA, UC Berkeley 1969; JD, UC Berkeley Sch. of Law 1972; admitted St. Bar Calif. (1972). Career: Law Ofc. of Michael G.W. Lee, S.F., 1993–; lectr. Golden Gate Univ. Sch. Law, S.F. 1977-78; adj. faculty Hastings Coll. of Law 1978; mem: Bar Assn. S.F. (pres. 1990), Asian Am. Bar Assn. (pres. 1978), Am. Immigration Lawyers Assn. (No. Calif. chpt. chair 1980-81), Legal Aid Soc. of S.F. (v.p. 1995), Am. Bar Assn. (del., House of Dels. 1994-97), Commonwealth Club Calif. (quarterly chair 1984, bd. govs. exec. com. 1987-88, 94-97); contbr. Immigration Law & Defense (Clark Boardman 1979). Ofc: Law Offices of Michael G.W. Lee 388 Market St Ste 1080 San Francisco 94111-5315

LEE, RALPH K., real estate developer; b. Oct. 9, 1951, Salt Lake City; s. Ralph H. and Hattie (Hadlock) L.; m. Jacquelyn Dowdle, Jan. 15, 1974 (div. 1985); children: Ralph Adam b. 1974, Daniel Spencer b. 1976, Linzi b. 1979, Jayme b. 1980, Jordan Duke b. 1982; m. Carol Elaine Redelings, Oct. 24, 1987; st. dau. Annie Rebecca Anderson b. 1978; edn: Cert. urban planning, BS geography, BS polit. sci., Univ. of Utah, 1979; MBA, Univ. of Phoenix, Az. 1987. Career: forward planning dir. PF West Inc., Dallas, Tx., Utah div. 1983-88; forward planning dir. Systems Constrn. Co., Anaheim Hills, 1989-90; proj. mgr. The Orange Coast Group, Seal Beach, Calif. 1990-91; mem. faculty Church Educational Svs., Cypress 1990-93, faculty Univ. of Phoenix, Fountain Valley 1991–; dir. special projects Hill Williams Devel. Corp., Anaheim Hills 1991-93;

computer pgmr. Stewart Title 1993-95; project mgr., Glenwood Devel. Co. 1995–; minister L.D.S. Ch., Perth, Australia 1971-72, Adelaide, Austr. 1972-73; designer, cons. R.K. Lee & Assocs., Anaheim Hills 1990–; awards: Eagle Scout 1970, Duty to God Award Mormon Ch. S.L.C. 1971, ranked in top 2% in nation (GATB) Gen. Aptitude Test Battery 1987, Seminary Ch. Ednl. System Award Mormon Ch. Anaheim Hills, Ca. 1991; mem. Nat. Assn. of Home Builders 1991-93, Bldg. Industry Assn. of So. Calif. Inc. 1991-93; scout master BSA, S.L.C., Ut. 1975-78; composer (new age albums): City Moods (c. 1987), performer, Mac computer synthesizer album: Lucky Dreams (c. 1987); Republican; Ch. of Jesus Christ of Latter-Day Saints; rec: Macintosh & IBM computers, music, basketball, reading, racquetball. Res: 530 S Ranch View Cir #43, Anaheim Hills 92807 Ofc: Glenwood Development Co 100 W Broadway #990 Glendale 91210

LEE, ROBERT ERICH, business consultant; b. Dec. 26, 1955, Spokane, Wash.; s. Robert Edward Lee and Edith Frieda (Klasen) Moore; m. Vicky Ann Rowland, Jan. 31, 1981; children: Erich b. 1985, Christopher b. 1988; edn: Vanderbilt Univ. 1973-77; Corpus Christi St. Univ. 1977; Univ. Tx. El Paso 1980. Career: mgr., instr. Neptune Equipment Co., Nashville, Tenn. 1976-77; customer engr. Hewlett Packard, Los Angeles 1977-82, dist. mgr. 1982-85, regional service adminstrn. mgr., North Hollywood 1985-86; dir. MIS Tova Corp., Beverly Hills 1986-87; dir. information technology PrimeSource Inc., Irvine 1987-92; pres. Results from Technology!, Irvine 1992–; speaker in industry, 1993–; listed Who's Who in Fin. & Ind. 1989–, Personalities in Am. 1990; mem. Assn. for Computing Machinery, IEEE, Interex, Town Hall of Calif.; columnist Interex Press, 1995–, writer Interact, 1995–; Republican; Prot.; rec: skiing, scuba diving, travel. Res: 1 Shenandoah Irvine 92720 Ofc: Results from Technology! 1 Shenandoah Irvine 92720

LEE, SCOTT S., ophthalmologist (retinal surgeon); b. June 30, 1960; edn: MD, Melbourne Univ., Australia 1984. Career: med. intern St. Vincent's Hosp., Melbourne, Australia 1955-86; internal medicine resident Hartford Hosp., Hartford, Conn. 1986-88; ophthalmology res. fellow (retina) Pacific Med. Ctr., San Francisco 1988-89; ophthalmology resident Univ. of Fla. 1989-92; retinal fellow Harvard Med. Sch., Boston, Mass. 1992-93; retinal surgeon East Bay Retina Consultants, Oakland 1993–; clin. retinal faculty UC San Francisco, S.F. Gen. Hosp., Calif. Pacific Med. Ctr., S.F.; awards: First Prize, Royal Australian Coll. of Surgeons 1984, First Prize, Australian Med. Assn. 1984, First Prize, Am. Diabetes Assn. Res. Symposium 1988, Gold Medal, XXVI Internat. Congress of Ophthalmology 1990; mem: Am. Acad. of Ophthalmology (fellow), CMA, Alameda Contra Costa Med. Assn. Mass. Eye & Ear Infirmary Alumni Assn., Barkan Assn.; co-author, med. textbook: Diagnosis and Management of Medical and Surgical Diseases of the Retina (in print), chapters on clin. ophthalmology in multiple med. textbooks, 1993, multiple publications in med. jours. Ofc: East Bay Retina Consultants 3300 Webster St #1110 Oakland 94609 Tel: 510/444-1600

LEE, WILSON, engineering manager; s. Hom Hai and Kam Fung L.; m. Magnolia Shell Ho Wong, Sept. 16, 1989; edn: BS in EECS, UC Berkeley, 1984. Career: project mgmt. assoc. Rolm Systems, Santa Clara 1984-85, design engr. 1985-88, mfg. engr. 1988-91, engring. mgr. 1991–; honors: Eta Kappa Nu 1983; pub. articles in California Engineer, 1984, 86. Ofc: Rolm Systems 4900 Old Ironsides Dr Santa Clara 95052

LEESE, DAVID ALLEN, educator, lawyer; b. Jan. 5, 1944, Detroit, Mich.; s. Sydney and Marcella (Taylor) L.; m. Judith Parker, June 7, 1969; children: Bradley b. 1975, Cindy b. 1978; edn: BA philosophy, Amherst Coll. 1965; JD, Northwestern Law Coll. 1968; PhD eng., Brandeis Univ. 1974; MBA, CSU Northridge 1984. Career: atty. sole practice, Los Angeles 1969–; lectr. Brandeis Univ., Waltham, Mass. 1971-74; asst. prof. Ariz. St. Univ., Tempe, Ariz. 1974-75; prof. Mount St. Marys Coll., L.A. 1975–, chmn. bus. dept. 1975-93, dir. cont. edn. 1986-93; bd. dirs. Am. Financial Assn. 1994–, chmn. 1994 convention; pres. Realcorps Real Estate Investment Firm, Agoura 1978; exchange lectr. L.A.-Guangzhon Assn., China 1987; mem: Calif. St. Bar Assn., Agoura Hills Christian Ch. (elder 1986-89, 1993-95, chair 1993, 94); Republican; rec: photog., hiking. Ofc: Mount St. Marys College 12001 Chalon Rd Los Angeles 90049

LEFF, HARVEY SHERWIN, physicist, educator; b. July 24, 1937, Chicago; s. Jack William and Anne Sharon (Maiman) L.; m. Ellen Janice Wine, Aug. 17, 1958; children: Lisa Michele b. 1962, Robyn Joy b. 1964, Jordan William b. 1969, Jeremy Matthew b. 1969; edn: BS physics, Ill. Inst. of Tech., 1959; MS physics, Northwestern Univ., 1960; PhD physics, Univ. Iowa, 1963. Career: res. assoc. Case Inst. of Technology, 1963-64, asst. to assoc. prof. physics Case Western Reserve Univ., 1964-71; assoc. prof. to prof. physics Chicago State Univ., 1971-79; vis. prof. physics Harvey Mudd Coll. of Sci. & Engring., Claremont, Ca. 1977-78; scientist Oak Ridge Associated Univs., Tenn. 1979-83; prof. physics and dept. chair Calif. State Polytech. Univ., Pomona 1983-95; leader in-service workshops (TI-IN Network, Cal Poly U., So. Calif. Edison, Nat. Sci. Tchrs. Assn.) 1985–; state co-coordinator Calif. State Univ. Inst. for Teaching & Learning, Long Beach 1989-95; assoc. ed. Am. Jour. of Physics, 1992-95; recipient awards for merit. performance Calif. State Polytech. Univ.,

Pomona (1987, 88, 90); mem: Am. Assn. of Physics Tchrs. (So. Calif. pres. 1991-93), Sigma Xi Sci. Research Soc. (Cal Poly past pres. 1991-92), Calif. Sci. Tchrs. Assn., Am. Physical Soc., Assn. Women in Sci.; civic: vol. reader Recording for the Blind, Upland; editor (w/A.F. Rex) Maxwell's Demon: Entropy, Information, Computing (1990), author num. articles in profl. jours. (1964–). Res: 538 E Bishop Pl Claremont 91711 Ofc: Calif. State Polytechnic Univ. 3801 W Temple Physics Dept. Pomona 91768

LEFTWICH, JAMES STEPHEN, retail corporate executive; b. Nov. 30, 1956, Stevenage, England; s. James Wright and Del M. (Thompson) L.; m. Carol Anne Petersen, Nov. 7, 1980 (div. Jan. 1982); edn: AA criminal justice, Butte Coll., 1982; BA criminal justice, Southwest Univ., 1992; lic. Hazardous Material Specialist (HMS) 1989, internat. accredited safety auditor 1990. Career: prodn. mgr. Artistic Dyers Inc., El Monte 1976-80; mgr. loss control & risk mgmt. Mervyn's Dept. Store, Hayward 1982-91; dir. risk mgmt. Save Mart Corp., Modesto 1991-93; v.p. ops. I.C.S. Corp, Irvine 1993; pres. I.C.S. Corp., San Ramon 1993–; dir. Safety Center of Calif., Sacramento 1990–, trustee 1989-90; dir. Bay Area Safety Council, Oakland 1987-88; Reserve Police ofcr., Cotati 1983-85; honors: Class Comdr. 39th Police Acad., Butte County 1982, listed Who's Who in West 1992; mem: Am. Soc. Safety Engrs. 1988–, Nat. Safety Mgmt. Soc., Risk & Ins. Mgmt. Soc., Nat. Fire Protection Assn., Nat. Environmental Tng. Assn. 1989–; co-writer and tech. advisor Safety Tng. videos, 12 1989-91, pub. articles re risk mgmt. 1989–; Republican; R.Cath.; rec: skiing, swimming, biking, hunting.

LEHANE, JOHN FRANCIS, retired educator; b. July 22, 1936, Chicago, Ill.; s. Thomas S. and Alice (Donovan) L.; m. Farelyn Ann Brady, June 25, 1966; children: Anne b. 1967, Cathie b. 1970; edn: BS aeronautical engring., Univ. Ill. 1962; MBA, Univ. Santa Clara 1964; PhD, 1971. Career: assoc. engr. Lockheed Misilles & Space, Sunnyvale 1962-64; ops. analyst Stanford Research Inst., Menlo Park 1965-70; sr. field cost engr. Bechtel Constrn., San Francisco 1970-71; prof. mgmt. Golden Gate Univ. 1971-82; indep. cons. JFL Assocs., 1975–; prof. San Jose St. Univ. 1983-91; prin. cons. DPCS of No. Calif. 1985-94; honors: SJSU Sch. of Bus. acad. achievement award (1984); mem: Calif. Faculty Assn., Assn. Systems Mgmt., Data Processing Mgmt. Assn., Interex, Evergreen Comm. Coll. Info. Planning com.; article pub. in profl. jour., 1987; mil: AUS 1956-58; Republican; Cath.; rec: sports, gardening. Res: 1227 Regency Pl San Jose 95129

LEHMAN, ELLEN J., psychologist; b. Feb. 21, 1944, Pittsburgh, Pa.; d. Alan G. and Jane (Anathan) Lehman; m. Charles Kennel; edn: AB, Vassar Coll. 1966; PhD, Cornell Univ. 1975. Career: staff psychologist Marianne Frostig Center for Ednl. Therapy, L.A. 1974-75; contract instr. Calif. Sch. Profl. Psychology 1975-76; instr. Center for Early Edn. 1979-80; pvt. practice, Santa Monica 1975–; supr. Wright Inst., L.A. 1983–; asst. clin. prof. UCLA 1990–; honors: Phi Kappa Phi; mem: Inst. of Contemporary Psychoanalysis 1991– (supervising & tng. analyst 1993–), Am. Psychological Assn., Soc. Research in Child Devel., Vassar Club So. Calif. (admissions chair 1980-84), Topanga Canyon Docents; papers pub. in profl. jours. 1971, 85–. Ofc: 1132 26th St Santa Monica 90403

LEHMAN, RONALD G., physician, pediatrician; b. Nov. 23, 1942, Dayton, Ohio; s. Cleo D. and Donna (Davis) L.; m. Susan Jean Ross, June 13, 1965; children: Andrea b. 1970, Nathan b. 1975; edn: BA, Miami Univ. Oxford 1964; MD, Ohio St. Univ. Columbus 1968. Career: intern Mercy Hosp., San Diego 1968-69, med. resident 1969; pediatric resident University Hosp., San Diego 1970-72; pvt. practice pediatrics, San Diego 1974–; mem: Am. Acad. of Pediatrics (fellow), CMA, San Diego Co. Med. Soc.; mil: major AUS 1972-74. Ofc: 685 3rd Ave Chula Vista 91910

LEHR, JEFFREY M., allergist; b. April 29, 1942, New York; s. Arthur Elias and Stella (Smellow) L.; m. Suzanne, July 10, 1965; children: Elisa b. 1968, Alexandra b. 1971, Vanessa b. 1977, Ryan b. 1980; edn: BS, Bklyn. Coll. 1963; MD, N.Y. Univ. 1967. Career: pvt. practice Jeffrey M. Lehr, Monterey 1974–; honors: Phi Beta Kappa, Pi Mu Epsilon; mem: CMA, AMA, Acad. Allergists (fellow), Am. Assn. Cert. Allergists (fellow), Am. Lung Assn. (bd. dirs.), Pebble Beach Tennis Club; mil: major USAF 1972-74; Democrat; Jewish; rec: tennis, sailing, jogging. Res: POB 1262 Pebble Beach 93953 Ofc: 798 Cass St Monterey 93940

LEIBENHAUT, MARK HARRIS, radiation oncologist; b. Nov. 7, 1958, Long Beach, NY; m. Susan; 1 son Jeffrey b. 1994; edn: BA, Princeton Univ. 1980; MD, Columbia Univ. 1984; cert. Am. Bd. of Radiology 1988. Career: computer cons. Sage Data, Inc., Princeton, N.J. 1978-84; radiation oncologist Lahey Med. Clinic, Burlington, Mass. 1988-91; radiation oncologist Radiological Assoc., Sacramento, Calif. 1991–; principal investigator, NSABP 1993–; reviewer (jour.), Radiology 1993–; honors: Phi Beta Kappa 1980, NY State Regent's Scholarship 1980-84, Kleinholz Pathology Prize 1985, vis. prof. Inst. of Oncology, Ljubljana, Yugoslavia 1990; mem: Radiological Soc. of N. Am. 1989–, Am. Radium Soc. 1990–, Am. Coll. of Radiology 1989–, Am. Soc. for Therapeutic Radiology & Oncology 1989–, Am. Soc. for Clin. Oncology 1989–; contbg. author: num. articles to sci. jours., 1985-92, textbook chpt., 1993. Ofc: 5271 F Street Sacramento 95819

LEIBERT, RICHARD WILLIAM, producer of public spectacles; b. Nov. 11, 1948, NY, NY; s. Richard Wm. and Rosemarie Martha (Bruns) L.; edn: BS, Boston Univ., 1972. career: prod. WBZ-AM/FM, Boston 1968-70; prodn. dir. WMMR-FM, Phila. 1970; exec. prod. WIND-AM, Chgo. 1970-72; program dir. KGB-AM/FM, San Diego 1972-80; pres. Events Marketing Inc., Los Angeles 1980–, creator/dir. National Fireworks Ensemble (touring co. of fireworks artists), L.A. 1985–; awards: CLIO advt. award, NY 1975, prod. program of year and program dir. of year Billboard Mag. 1976, Emmy award, TV, San Diego 1978; works: creator radio sta. mascot publicity stunt KGB Chicken, 1974, creator/prod. radio fireworks show "Sky Show", 1976, writer/prod. network radio show "New Music News", 1983; rec: sailing, Dodgers fan. Res: 3743 S Bluff Pl San Pedro 90731 Ofc: Events Marketing, Inc. PO Box 65694 Los Angeles 90065

LEIGHTON, DOREEN, physician; b. Nov. 2, 1946, Wash., D.C.; d. Alexander Hamilton and Dorothea (Cross) Leighton; m. George K. Uehara, Sept. 27, 1969 (div. 1976); m. 2d. Simon William Walker, Sept. 24, 1983; children: Catherine Cross Uehara b. 1971, Dorothea Anne Uehara b. 1974, Simon Alexander Walker b. 1987; edn: BA, Stanford Univ. 1968; pre-med., Calif. State Univ.-Hayward 1974-78; MD, UCSF 1982; family practice residency Valley Med. Ctr., Fresno 1982-85. Career: site dir., staff physician Health America-Maxicare, S.F. 1986-87; site dir. Health America-Maxicare, Albany, Calif. 1987-89; pvt. practice, Doreen Leighton, MD, Oakland 1989–; chair, dept. of family practice Summit Med. Ctr., Oakland 1993-95; assoc. clin. prof. UCSF 1993–; Democrat; Unitarian-Universalist. Res: 2600 Piedmont #1 Berkeley 94704 Ofc: D. Leighton, MD 3300 Webster #1105 Oakland 94609

LEISER, ERIC J., engineer, international sales executive; b. Oct. 13, 1960, NY, NY; s. Werner and Laura (Goldschmidt) L.; m. Cynthia Joy Gordon, May 5, 1991; edn: BS, M.I.T., 1982. Career: engr. Motorola, Phoenix, Az. 1982-85; engr. and sales staff Merck, Germany and Taiwan, 1985-89; mgr. Far Eastern sales and applications Allied-Signal, Milpitas, Calif. 1989-94; worldwide technical sales mgr. 1995–. Res: 5466 Drysdale Dr San Jose 95124 Ofc: Allied-Signal 3500 Garrett Drive Santa Clara 95054

LEITMANN, GEORGE, professor of engineering science; b. May 24, 1925, Vienna, Austria, naturalized U.S., 1944; s. Josef and Stella (Fischer) L.; m. Nancy Lloyd, Jan. 28, 1955; children: Josef b. 1957, Elaine b. 1959; edn: BS, Columbia Univ., 1949, MA, 1950; PhD, UC Berkeley, 1956. Career: hd. aeroballistics USN OTS, China Lake, Calif. 1950-57; staff scientist Lockheed Corp., Palo Alto 1957-63; asst., assoc., prof. engring. sci. UC Berkeley, 1957-59, 59-63, 63-91, assoc. dean 1980–, prof. emeritus 1991–; instr. USAF Acad., Colo. Springs 1960-65; cons. Martin Co., Denver 1957-65, Aerojet Gen., Sacto. 1960-63, Guggenheim Lab. Princeton, N.J. 1958-60; awards: Pendray Medal, AIAA 1974, Flight Medal, AIAA 1978, Levy Medal, Franklin Inst., Phila. 1982, V. Humboldt Found. Medal, Bonn, Ger. 1991, Berkeley citation UCB 1991, Hon. doctorates Paris, Vienna, Darmstadt, Rufus Oldenburger Medal, ASME 1995; mem: US Nat. Acad. Engring. 1982–, Internat. Acad. Astron. 1978–, fgn. mem. Argentine Acad. Engring. 1987–, AC. Science, Bologna 1978–, AC. Natural Sciences, Russia 1992–, Georgian AC. Engring. 1994–, corresp. mem. Bavarian AC. Science 1995–; author 11 books in engineering, 1962–, 250+ articles in sci. jours., 1956–; mil: 2d. lt. Mil. Intell.; rec: swimming, art collecting, oenology. Ofc: Chair of Faculty, College of Engineering, Univ. Calif., Berkeley 94720

LEMESH, RUSSELL ALAN, physician, internist; b. Sept. 24, 1958, San Francisco; s. Martin and Stella Mildred (Rosenthal) L. (dec. 1989); m. Shelly Benyohai, Jan. 6, 1980 (dec. 1987); m. 2d. Cynthia Ann Weisman, Nov. 19, 1988; edn: BS magna cum laude, Univ. San Francisco 1980; MS, 1981; MD, Hahnemann Univ. Sch. Medicine 1985. Career: group practice internal medicine, San Francisco 1988–; dir. clin. clerkship program St. Mary's Hosp. and Med. Center 1991-93; asst. prof. UCSF 1988–; pres. Health Professions Soc. UCSF 1992-93; bd. of govs. Univ. of San Francisco 1992-93; awards: Bank of Am. sci. scholarship 1976, Achievement Rewards for Coll. Scientists Found. research grant 1980, Hahneman Univ. Distinction Internal Medicine 1985, Honors in Pharmacology 1985; mem: Am. Coll. of Physicians (fellow 1993), Am. Coll. of Clin. Pharmacology (fellow 1993), Royal Soc. of Medicine (fellow 1992), Am. Geriatrics Soc., Phi Delta Epsilon, Phi Lambda Kappa, Alpha Sigma Nu; author: 6 articles (peer reviewed), 1984-93. Ofc: The Permanente Medical Group 97 San Marin Drive Novato 94945

LENAHAN, SCOTT GREGORY, industrial designer; b. Feb. 19, 1958, North Hollywood; s. Thomas Don Lenahan and Marjorie Ellen Brewer; m. Nancy Jane Freeman, July 18, 1987; edn: airframe and power plant mechanics, No. Valley Occupational Ctr.; AA, L.A. Valley Coll.; BA, CSU Northridge. Career: lic. airframe and powerplant jet engine mechanic, Pacific Airmotive Corp., Burbank 1977-79; airframe mechanic Aircraft Tank Service, Sun Valley 1980-81; photo retouch artist Spectra Color Lab. 1981; graphic designer, Vision Press Inc., Sylmar 1983; designer/sculptor Rafe Afflic Inc., N. Hollywood 1983-84; designer Hydro-Spa Inc., Piru 1984; designer Gruber Systems, Valencia 1984-90; artist Six Elevan Ltd., N. Hollywood 1990-91; designer, Zurhuit Design Assocs., Valencia 1992; security ofcr. Six Flags Magic Mountain, Valencia 1992; designer Melvin Best Design Assocs., Topanga Canyon 1992; aircraft structural sheet metal fabricator Continental Airlines, LAX 1992-95; mem: Indsl. Design Soc. of Am., Am. Red Cross (cert. Advanced First Aid and Mountaineering, Nat. Ski Patrol); patentee: issued 15 design patents for kitchen and bathroom products; conceived and executed award-winning exhibits with related promotional material; designed an entire line of cast polymer bath fixtures and accessories, including Hydrotherapy tub units and spas; Republican; Christian; rec: skiing, mountain bicycling, scuba diving, off-roading, photog., painting, martial arts. Res: 32328 N Greenhill Dr Castaic 91384

LENARD, MICHAEL BARRY, lawyer; b. May 20, 1955, Chicago; s. Henry Madart and Jacqueline Jo Anne (Silver) L.; m. Amy Jeanne Rifenbergh, Oct. 10, 1987; children: Madeline M., Nicholas X; edn: BBA, Univ. Wis., 1977; student, NYU, 1981-82; JD, Univ. So. Calif., 1982. Career: assoc. Whitman & Ransom. N.Y.C., 1982-83, 1984-91; ptnr. Latham & Watkins, L.A., 1992-93, Whitman & Ransom, N.Y.C., 1992-93; assoc. Latham & Watkins, L.A., 1984-91; ptnr. Latham & Watkins, 1991-93; councillor William E. Simon & Sons, L.A., 1993–; with So. Calif. Law Rev. mag., 1980-81; vice-pres. U.S. Olympic Com., 1989–, exec. com. and bd. dirs., 1985–, athletes' adv. coun. (vice-chmn. 1985-89), 1981-89, bd. dirs. L.A. Sports Coun., 1988–, Atlanta Com. for Olympic Games, 1990–; awards: named semi-finalist Outstanding Undergrad. Achievement award, 1977, recipient Harry A. Bunis scholarship, 1977, named LISA Team Handball Athlete of the Yr. 1985, USOC Olympian Mag. Team Handball SportsMan of the Yr., 1985, participated in 6 U.S. Olympic Festivals winning 3 Gold, 2 Silver and 1 Bronze Medals, and 16 U.S. Nat. Championships winning 6 Gold, 4 Silver and 3 Bronze Medals; mem. 1984 Olympic Team, U.S. Nat. Team, 1977-85 (capt. 1985); mem. Order of the Coif, Phi Kappa Phi, Beta Gamma Sigina, Beta Alpha Psi, Phi Eta Sigma. Res: 617 Las Casas Ave Pacific Palisades 90272-3313 Ofc: William E Simon & Sons 10990 Wilshire Blvd Ste 1750 Los Angeles CA 90024

LENZ, PHILIP JOSEPH, county probation deputy chief; b. Sept. 15, 1940, Monterey Park; s. Philip George and Irene (Bowers) L.; m. Mary Lou Antista, July 16, 1966; children: Brian Joseph b. 1972, Jonathan Thomas b. 1975; edn: BA in sociol., CSU Los Angeles, 1966; MS corrections, Pepperdine Univ., 1974. Career: with San Bernardino County Probation Dept., 1966–: dir. Verdemont Boys' Ranch,1974-76; dir. diversion svs. 1976-77; dir. West Valley Div. 1977-79; dir. Juvenile Div. 1979-82; dir. adminstrv. svs. 1982-88; dir. dist. svs. 1988–; dir. dist. svs. 1988-89; dir adult svs. 1989-94; deputy chief 1994–; instr. Loma Linda Univ., 1988, Calif. St. Univ. San Bernardino 1991-94; mem./cons. Cadre of Consultants, Sacto. 1986, Calif. Youth Auth.; awards: Tim Fitzharris award Chief Probation Ofcrs. of Calif., San Diego 1987; mem: Calif. Probation Parole Correctional Assn. (1966, pres. 1988), Assn. of Crim. Justice Research (bd. dirs. 1990-93, 1995–), West. Correctional Assn., Nat. Council on Crime & Delinquency; civic bds: Upland Unified Sch. Dist. (pres. bd. trustees 1987-88, 1993-95), Upland Parks & Rec. Com. (chmn. 1987-90), Highlander Ednl. Found. Upland 1986-93, Upland Comm. Svc. Council 1986; Democrat; Cath.; rec: baseball, bicycle riding.

LENZI, ALBERT JAMES, JR., lawyer; b. Feb. 15, 1955, Chicago, Ill.; s. Albert Joseph and Helen (Katsuleas) L.; m. Erin Jennifer Crowley, Dec. 30, 1955 (div. 1989); m. Darlene Lenzi, Mar. 5, 1994; children: April Lynn b. 1978, Sean Patrick b. 1979; edn: U.S. Naval Acad. 1972-74; BA, Loyola Univ. 1976; JD, Univ. Pacific McGeorge Sch. Law 1979. Career: prof. law Willamette Univ., Salem, Ore. 1979-80; atty., assoc. Thompson Mayhew & Michel, Sacto. 1980-81; Goldstein Barceloux & Goldstein, Chico 1981-82; Brislain & Zink 1982-84, ptnr. Brislain Zink & Lenzi 1984-89, Brislain Zink Lenzi & Artz 1989-90, Brislain Zink & Lenzi 1990-94, Zink & Lenzi 1994–; mem: Calif. Trial Lawyers Assn., Assn. Trial Lawyers of Am., Am. Bar Assn., Calif. Bar Assn., Eagles, Eastside Little League; articles pub. in profl. jours., 1987-95; mil: USN 1972-74; Democrat; rec: sports, little league coaching. Res: 275 Chico Canyon Rd Chico 95928-9128 Ofc: Zink & Lenzi 20 Independence Circle Chico 95926

LENZO, THOMAS JOHN, training and development consultant; b. Nov. 19, 1949, Waterbury, Conn.; s. John Anthony and Mary Louise (Perezella) L.; edn: BA, Fairfield Univ., 1971; MEd., CSU Los Angeles, 1980. Career: media coordinator Valley Vocat. Ctr., Industry, Calif. 1977-78; librarian Washington Sch., Pasadena 1978-79; tng. specialist Data Electronics, 1979-82; engring. instr. Litton Data Sys., Van Nuys 1982-83; cons. B.P.W. Inc., Costa Mesa 1984-85; cons. pvt. practice, Pasadena 1986–; honors: outstanding student 1979, accomplishment in media 1979, 80, CSU Los Angeles; mem. Soc. for Tech. Communication (sr. mem. 1986–), Am. Soc. for Tng. & Devel. 1978–, Nat. Soc. for Performance Inst. 1982–, Pasadena IBM PC Users Gp. (v.p. 1986–); civic: Towards 2000 Mayoral Commn. Pasadena 1984-85; mil: sgt. E/4 USAF 1972-76, Commendn. medal 1976; R.Cath.; rec: hiking, photography, travel. Res: 2473 Oswego St, 10, Pasadena 91107

LEONE, LUCILE PETRY, nurse, educator, retired assistant surgeon general; b. Jan. 23, 1902, Lewisburg, Ohio; d. David A. and Dora (Murray) P.; m. Nicholas Charles, June 1, 1952 (div. 1967); edn: BA, Univ. Del., 1924; Profl. Nse., Johns Hopkins Sch. of Nsg., Balt. 1927; MA, Tchrs. Coll. Columbia Univ., 1927, grad. study 1936-37. Career: instr., asso. prof. Univ. Minn. Sch. of

Nursing, Mpls. 1929-41; cons., then dir. U.S. Cadet Nurse Corps, USPHS, Wash. DC 1941-49; chief nurse ofcr. and asst. surgeon general USPHS 1949-66, ret. 1966; prof. and assoc. dean Sch. of Nursing Texas Womans Univ., Houston, Dallas, Tex. 1967-73; coord. internat. student pgm. Sch. of Nursing UC San Francisco, S.F. 1978-83; pres. Nat. League for Nursing, N.Y.C. 1959-63; chmn. bd. Amer. Journal Co., N.Y.C. 1950-51; mem. govng. council Amer. Pub. Health Assn., N.Y.C. 1955-67 (intermittently); research. study of minority students in nsg. schs. for Rockefeller Brothers Fund 1966; nsg. advy. coms. Kellogg Found. 1952-60, Mental Health Commn. of So. Regl. Edn. Bd. 1949-59, WHO Expert Com. on Nsg. Geneva, Switz.; awarded 10 hon. doctoral degrees- Boston Univ., Syracuse Univ., Adelphi, Univ. Del., Johns Hopkins Univ., others, 1950-95, Nightingale Internat. Award Internat. Red Cross, Geneva, 1954, Lasker award (shared) APHS 1954, Chancellors award for contbn. to community UCSF 1983, Leone Professorship in Internat. Nursing & Health estab. UCSF Sch. of Nursing 1983, Sigma Theta Tau/Intl. Nsg. Hon. Soc. Founder's Award for Leadership 1987, charter mem. Inst. of Medicine Nat. Acad. of Scis. 1970, hon. fellow Am. Acad. of Nsg. 1979. Res: 1400 Geary Blvd San Francisco 94109

LEONG, CAROL JEAN, electrologist, designer; B. Jan. 9, 1942, Sacramento; d. Walter Richard and Edith (Bond) Bloss; m. Oliver Arthur Fisk III, Apr. 12, 1964 (div. 1973); children: Victoria Kay; edn: BA sociology, San Jose State Univ., 1963; degree, Western Bus. Coll., 1964; cert. profl., Bay Area Coll. Electrolysis, 1978; Calif. reg. clin. and profl. electrologist. Career: profl. model, 1951-64; employment counselor Businessmen's Clearinghouse, Cinti. 1966-67; dir. personnel Kroger Food Corp., Cinti. 1967-68; prop. Carol Leong Electrolysis, San Mateo, Calif. 1978–, Designs by Carol, 1987–; recipient appreciation San Francisco Lighthouse for the Blind (1981-82, 83); biographical listings in Who's Who in World, Who's Who in Am. Women, Who's Who in Fin. and Ind., Who's Who in West, others; mem: Internat. Guild Profl. Electrologists (cont. edn. com.), Profl. Women's Forum 1988–, Nat. Assn. Female Execs., Am. Electrologists Assn., Electrologists Assn. Calif., Internat. Platform Assn., Chi Omega; civic: Peninsula Humane Soc., San Francisco Zool. Soc., Friends of Filoli; contbr. articles to profl. publs.; Republican; Presbyterian; rec: photog., golf, tennis, ballet, theater. Res: 1447 Woodberry Ave San Mateo 94403 Ofc: Carol Leong Electrolysis 359 N San Mateo Dr Ste 4 San Mateo 94401

LEPKOWSKY, CHARLES MICHAEL, psychologist; b. Mar. 26, 1956, Inglewood; m. Mary Beth; edn: BS psych., UC Davis, 1977; MA and PhD in counseling psych., Univ. Notre Dame, 1983, 1984; lic. psychologist Calif. 1985–. Career: counselor intern Counseling Ctr., UC Davis, 1981-82, Madison Ctr., South Bend, Ind. 1982-83; intern psychologist UC Santa Barbara, 1983-84; counselor Pinecrest Hosp., Santa Barbara 1984-85; pvt. practice 1985–; clin. dir. KBSAY, Santa Barbara 1988-89, codir. Eating Disorders Council S.B. 1985-88, asst. dir. and clin. coord. Child Abuse Listening and Mediation (CALM) S.B. 1987-88; instr. Univ. Notre Dame, 1979-80, dir. human relations tng. 1980-81; instr. Univ. San Francisco, Santa Barbara 1987, adj. faculty Antioch Univ., S.B. 1986, instr. Brooks Inst. Photography, S.B. 1986, adj. faculty, UC Santa Barbara 1991–; chair, dept. of adolescent & child psychiatry, S.B. Cottage Hosp. 1992-94; mem. Am. Psychol. Assn., Calif. St. Psychol. Assn., Santa Barbara Co. Psychol. Assn., Nat. Register of Health Svc. Providers in Psych., 1987; numerous paper presentations internat., nat. and local confs. and articles in profl. jours. Ofc: 122 S Patterson Ave Ste 200 Santa Barbara 93111

LEPORIERE, RALPH DENNIS, quality engineer; b. Nov. 8, 1932, Elizabeth, NJ; s. Maximo and Christian Leporiere; m. Judith Louise Crowhurst, Nov. 19, 1960; children: Bonnie Ann, b. 1961; David Anthony, b. 1964; edn: BS, Rutgers Univ. 1954; postgrad. Rutgers Statistics Center 1955-6, 1958-9; Coll. of the Holy Names, Oakland 1965-66; Reg. Profl. Quality Engr., Calif. Career: chemist NY Quinine & Chem. Works, Inc., Newark NJ 1954-55; asst. to chief chemist/qual. control C.D. Smith Pharmaceutical Co., New Brunswick, NJ 1955-56; asst. supvr. qual. control White Labs, Inc., Kenilworth, NJ 1958-60; staff cons. qual. eng. Calif. & Hawaiian Sugar Co., Crockett, Calif. 1960–; chmn./ instr. Qual. Control Dept. Laney Coll., Oakland 1967-87; chmn./ asst. prof. JFK Univ., Martinez 1967-72; instr., mem. advy. com. Annual Stat. Short Course, UC Davis 1969-94; mem: Fellow ASQC (S.F. & East Bay Sects.), Soc. of Mfg. Engrs. (senior mem.), Am. Statistical Assn., Am. Chem. Soc., Toastmasters (Vallejo pres. 1965); civic: Am. Canyon Co. Water Dist. (pres. 1973-83, v.p. 1971-73); biog. listings Who's Who in the West, 1970–, Dict. of Internat. Biography, 1984–; mil: Med. Svc. Corps, US Army Environmental Health Labs, Edgewood, MD 1956-58. Res: 618 Kilpatrick St Vallejo 94589 Ofc: Calif. & Hawaiian Sugar Co., 830 Loring Ave Crockett 94525

LERNER, LAWRENCE, interior architect, industrial designer, corporate executive; b. Sept. 21, 1923, New York; s. Abraham and May (Epstein) L.; m. Leslie Karpen, June 1, 1950; 1 son, Erik b. 1951; edn: BA, Bklyn. Coll. 1948. Career: exec. v.p. Michael Saphier Assoc., N.Y. 1948-58; pres. Saphier, Lerner, Schindler, N.Y. 1958-72; div. pres. Environetics Div. Litton Industries, N.Y. 1972-77; chmn. bd./pres. Environetics Internat. 1977-81, N.Y.; pres. Lerner Devel. Corp. (LDC Cal Inc.), Beverly Hills 1981–; chmn. bd./pres. Mega-Erg Inc., B.H. 1986-89; vis. prof. Ohio Univ. Sch. Architecture 1972; contbg. ed.

Contract Mag., N.Y. 1965-70; dir. Pilot Woodworking Inc., Carlstadt, N.J. 1968-74; honors: Hall of Fame, Interior Design Mag. 1982; mem. bd. govs. Cedars-Sinai Med. Center 1986; mem. Chief Execs. Orgn., past mem. Young Pres.'s Orgn. (chair N.Y. 1969), chmn. architectural commn., City of Beverly Hills 1995-96; articles and feasibilty study pub., 1965-72, designer interior of Sears Tower, 1969-73; mil: 2d lt. AUS 1942-46. Res: 516 N Beverly Hills Dr Beverly Hills 90210

LESAVOY, MALCOLM ALAN, plastic surgeon/educator; b. June 27, 1942, Allentown, Pa.; s. Harry Aaron and Rachel L.; children: Brian b. 1969, Jordan b. 1971, Nicole b. 1975; edn: BA, Univ. N.C., 1964; research fellow Chicago Med. Sch., 1964-5, MD, 1969; diplomate Am. Bd. of Plastic Surgery. Career: prof. of surgery Div. Plastic Surgery UCLA Med. Ctr., Los Angeles 1976–, and chief Plastic & Reconstrv. Surg., Harbor/UCLA Med. Ctr., Torrance 1976–; cons. in plastic surg. Wadsworth VA Hosp., L.A., and Sepulveda VA Hosp., Sepulveda, 1977; cons. plastic and reconstrv. surg. City of Hope Nat. Med. Ctr., Duarte 1981; mem. community advy. bd. Ctr. for the Partially Sighted, Santa Monica 1988, comm. advy. bd. Nat. Ctr. for Hyperactive Children, Encino 1985-87; awards: Merk outstanding sr. clerkship 1969, Lange sr. med. student 1969, outstanding clin. tchr. UCLA Sch. of Med. Class of 1978, 90, disting. alumnus 1983 Chgo. Med. Sch., Alpha Omega Alpha 1983; mem: A.C.S., Am. Soc. Plastic & Reconstrv. Surgeons (bd. Ednl. Found. 1984, treas. Plastic Surg. Ednl. Found. 1986, pres. 1992), Am. Assn. of Plastic Surg., Plastic Surg. Resrch. Council, Am. Assn. for Hand Surg., Am. Cleft Palate Assn., Calif. Soc. Plastic & Reconstrv. Surg., Internat. Soc. of Reconstrv. Microsurg., Am. Soc. Reconstrv. Microsurg. (founding mem.), Internat. Coll. Surgeons, Assn. for Academic Surg., Am. Burn Assn., Millard Plastic Surg. Soc. (nat. pres. 1987), UCLA Plastic Surg. Soc., L.A. Area Hand Club (co-founder 1980), L.A. Surg. Soc., Am. Soc. for Laser Med. and Surgery, Pan Pac. Surg. Assn., Assn. of Emergency Physicians, Am. Thoracic Soc., Am. Soc. for Aesthetic Plastic Surg.; publs: editl. bd. Annals of Plastic Surgery, 1982-85, cons. Jour. of AMA, internat. editl. bd. Jour. of Reconstrv. Microsurgery, 1983, guest ed. Plastic and Reconstrv. Surgery; 3 books: Reconstruction of the Head and Neck, 1981, (coauthor w. Roy Meals) Review of Hand Surgery (1981, 2d ed. 1985), contbr. book chapters in 13+ med. texts, numerous med. jour. articles, abstracts, spkr. nat. and internat. confs.; capt. USAR 1969-76; Synagogue for the Performing Arts, L.A. (bd. dirs. 1988-90); rec: all sports. Ofc: Div. of Plastic Surgery, Rm 64-128, UCLA Medical Center, 10833 Le Conte Ave Los Angeles 90024

LESLIE, MICHAEL ROSS, lawyer; b. Sept. 30, 1957, Erie, Pa.; s. Donald Spence and Miriam (Bennett) L.; m. Maria Dante Brown, May 21, 1988; edn: BA, Dartmouth Coll. 1980; JD, Stanford Law Sch. 1985; admitted St. Bar Calif. (1986), U.S. Ct. Appeals 9th Circuit (1986). Career: law clk. Hon. A. Wallace Tashima, Los Angeles 1985-86; atty., assoc. O'Donnell & Gordon 1986-88; ptnr. Hedges Powe & Caldwell 1988–; honors: Phi Beta Kappa, Dartmouth Coll. Rufus Choate scholar 1980; mem: Am. Bar Assn., L.A. Co. Bar Assn.; author, ed. Land Use Regulation, 1984, ed. Wilderness Preservation, 1985; rec: skiing, rock climbing. Ofc: Hedges Powe & Caldwell 606 S Olive St Ste 500 Los Angeles 90014

LESMEZ, ARTHUR GERARD, lawyer; b. July 26, 1959, Nassau County, N.Y.; s. Alvaro Vincent and Betty Jane (Kirchheimer) L.; m. Gwendolyn Ann Billings, June 17, 1989; edn: BA, Syracuse Univ. 1981; JD, Calif. Western Sch. of Law 1984; admitted St. Bar Calif. Career: assoc. outside cousel Forest Lawn Mem. Park, Los Angeles 1985; staff atty. Comml. Union Ins. Co. 1985-87; atty. assoc. O'Flaherty Presholt & Bennington 1987; Liebman Reiner & McNeil 1987–; mem: Am. Bar Assn., Los Angeles Co. Bar Assn., Assn. Trial Lawyers Am., So. Calif. Defense Counsel. Ofc: Liebman Reiner et al 3255 Wilshire Blvd Ste 1200 Los Angeles 92101

LESSARD, ARTHUR GILBERT, meteorologist; b. Apr. 18, 1929, New Bedford, Mass.; s. Arthur P. and Juliette M. (Montminy) L.; m. Maria G. Konrad, Dec. 19, 1960; 1 son, Arthur Jr. b. 1963; m. Crystal A. Ford, Mar. 23, 1985; edn: Eastern N.M. Univ. 1964-66; BS atmospheric sci., Univ. of Hawaii 1971. Career: meteorologist Nat. Weather Service, Wake Island, Pacific 1971-72; Nat. Weather Service Severe Storms Forecast Ctr., Kansas City, Mo. 1972-73; leading forecaster Nat. Weather Service, Topeka, Kans. 1973-74; quality control ofcr. Nat. Weather Service, San Francisco 1974-77; dep. meteorologist in charge Nat. Weather Serv. Los Angeles 1977-79, area mgr./meteorologist in chg. Nat. Weather Serv. Forecast Office, LA 1979-92; dep. dir. National Climate Analysis Ctr., Wash. DC 1992–; govt. liaison to Los Angeles Olympic Organizing Com., 1984 Olympic Games; So. Calif. Nat. Weather Serv. liaison to the Fed. Emergency Mgmt. Agency; mem. Los Angeles Federal Exec. Bd.; Nat. Weather Service Modernization and Associated Restructuring Coordinator for So. Calif.; On US Dept. of Commerce, Nat. Weather Serv. Line Forecasters Honors List 1971, 73; honors: recipient L.A. Co. Bd. Suprs. Award and Scroll for outstanding public service 1989, recogn. by Mayor of Los Angeles for outstanding support to city homeless shelter program (1988, 1992); mem: Am. Meteorol. Soc., Fellow Royal Meteorological Soc., Nat. Weather Assn., Aircraft Owners and Pilots Assn., Nat. Pilots Assn., Nat. Geographic Soc. (contbg. writer NGS publs.), Am. Legion; mil: SMS (E-8) USAF 1951-71, Korean Service, United Nations, Nat. Defense Service medals, USN Merit. Service Commendn. while attached to USN

1966-70; R.Cath.; rec: flying, philately. Res: 11707 Sunset Blvd Los Angeles 90049. Ofcs: NOAA/National Weather Service, Rm 11102 Federal Bldg 11000 Wilshire Blvd Los Angeles 90024; Climate Analysis Center, NOAA Science Center World Weather Bldg 5200 Auth Road Wash DC 20233

LESSER, HENRY, lawyer; b. Feb. 28, 1947, London, England; s. Bernard Martin and Valerie Joan (Leslie) L.; m. Jane, June 29, 1969; edn: BA (honors), Cambridge Univ. England 1968; MA hons, 1972; LL.M, Harvard Law Sch. 1973. Career: law lectr. Lincoln Coll., Oxford, Eng. 1968-69; barrister, London 1969-70; law lectr. Fitzwilliam Coll., Cambridge 1970-71; atty., assoc. Spear & Hill, N.Y. and London 1973-75; Webster & Sheffield 1976-77; assoc., ptnr. Wachtell Lipton Rosen & Katz, N.Y. 1977-83; ptnr. Gibson Dunn & Crutcher, L.A. 1983-87; ptnr. Fried Frank Harris Shriver & Jacobson 1987-91; ptnr. Irell & Manella, 1991–; honors: Lucas Smith Prize Queens Coll. Cambridge 1966, 67, 68, Squire Law scholar Cambridge Univ. 1968, Harkness fellow Commonwealth Fund of N.Y. 1971, Kennedy scholar Lincolns Inn 1968; mem: Am. Law Inst., Calif. State Bar (vice-chair 1993-94, secty. 1992-93, bus. law sect. exec. com. 1991-92, corporations com. chair 1990-91), L.A. County Bar Assn. (exec. com. bus. law sect.), New York State Bar, Am. Bar Assn., Internat. Bar Assn.; num. articles pub. in U.S. and U.K., contbr. 2 legal treatises; rec: long distance running, squash. Res: 1375 Belfast Dr Los Angeles 90069 Ofc: Irell & Manella, 333 S Hope St Ste 3300 L.A. 90071

LESTER, DON KEVIN, orthopaedic surgeon; b. July 21, 1950, Chgo.; s. Donald C. and Bonna E. (Esterson) L.; m. Linda, June 7, 1979; children: Tyler b. 1982, Morgan b. 1986; edn: BA, UC San Diego 1973; MD, UC Irvine Coll. of Med. 1979; bd. certified 1986. Career: orthopaedic intern L.A. Co.-USC Med. Center 1980, grad. orthopaedic residency Penn. State Univ. Hershey Med. Center, Div. Orthopaedic Surgery, 1984; orthopaedic surgeon in pvt. practice, Fresno 1984–; mem. Orthopaedic Res. Soc., Western Med. Assn., Fresno Madera Med. Assn.; contbr. 20 publs. in med. jours., num. presentations nat. profl. meetings, 1979–; current research: hip replacements; mil: sgt. USAF Nat. Guard, hon. disch. 1973. Ofc: D. Kevin Lester, MD, Inc. 6085 N First St Fresno 93710

LEUNG, CHARLES C., manufacturing company president; b. June 27 1946, Hong Kong; nat. 1981; s. Mo-Fan and Lai-Ping (Tam) L.; m. Jessica Lan Lee; children: Jennifer b. 1975, Cheryl b. 1979, Albert b. 1985; edn: BS, Univ. Hong Kong 1969; MS, Univ. Chgo. 1971; PhD, 1976. Career: sr. scientist Corning Glass Works, Corning, N.Y. 1975-79; sr. staff engr. Motorola, Mesa, Ariz. 1979-81; engring. mgr. Avantek Inc., Newark 1981-88; pres., founder Bipolarics Inc., Los Gatos 1988–; awards: Univ. Chgo. Badminton Champion 1969-74, Univ. Hong Kong 3000 meter record 1969, Commonwealth Scholar British Commonwealth 1969; mem: IEEE, Soc. of Photo-Optical Instrumentation Engrs., Am. Physical Soc., Am. Vacuum Soc., Asian Am. Mfrs. Assn., ASM Internat.; articles pub. in tech. jours. 1972-88, patent held for planaization of wafers 1987, speaker 22d Internat. Field Emission Symp. 1974, Am. Vacuum Soc. Symp. 1975, 76, 36th Physical Electronics Conf. 1975, IEEE Symp. 1985; rec: history, poetry, tennis. Res: 45920 Sentinal Pl Fremont 94539-6942 Ofc: 108 Albright Way Los Gatos 95030

LEUNG, LAI-SUNG ERIC, eye surgeon; b. Apr. 30, 1944, Shanghai, China, naturalized Am., 1980; s. Chi-Hsuei and Kwai-Han (Lee) L.; m. Kay-Lee Huang, July 5, 1969; children: Loh-Sze b. 1975, Loh-Shan b. 1977; edn: AB, Columbia Univ. 1966; MD, Johns Hopkins Univ. 1970; surg. intern., UC San Diego 1970-71; resident ophthalmologist Univ. of Penna. 1971-74; Diplomate Am. Bd. of Ophthalmology 1976; FACS, Fellow Am. Coll. of Surgeons 1978. Career: estab. pvt. practice ophthalmol., San Francisco 1975–; asst. prof. UC San Francisco; active staff Calif. Pacific Med. Center and Chinese Hosp., S.F.; Fellow Am. Acad. of Ophthalmology 1977; adv. Am. Nat. Bank, S.F. 1983; mem. Chinese Comm. Health Care Assn. (dir., pres. 1986-89), Assn. of Chinese Comm. Physicians (dir., v.p. 1986-89), Am. Assn. of Ophthal., S.F. Med. Soc.,Calif. Med. Assn.; civic: North Peninsular Mandarin Sch. (dir. 1979-83), Chinese Newcomer Services (dir. 1982-86), Chinese Cultural Found. (dir. 1988, v.p. 1989-91), Chinese Time (treas., dir. 1988); med. journal arts., profl. presentations; rec: sailing, skiing, basketball, travel. Ofc: L. Eric Leung MD 929 Clay St San Francisco 94108

LEVEE, ARNOLD LEONARD, physician; b. Oct. 1, 1932, N.Y.C.; s. Lazar and Irene (Rosen) L.; m. Linda Jean Sherman, June 7, 1959; children: James b. 1959, Lawrence b. 1963, Thomas b. 1964; edn: AA, UCLA, 1955; MD, USC, 1959. Career: trainee Harbor Gen. Hosp., Torrance and Wadsworth VA Hosp., Los Angeles; pvt. practice otolaryngolgy, Santa Monica 1964–; honors: Pi Lambda Phi; mem: Calif. Med. Assn., L.A. Co. Med. Soc., Am. Acad. Otolaryngol./Hd. and Neck Surgery, Phi Delta Epsilon, Los Angeles Geod. Club (pres. 1991-92); club: Santa Monica Lions (pres. 1975-76, dist. zone chmn. 1977-78); mil: airman USNR 1950-52; Democrat; Jewish; rec: hiking, ski, backpacking. Res: 13636 Bayliss Rd Los Angeles 90049 Ofc: 1304 15th St Ste 324 Santa Monica 90404

LEVENTER, TERRI, psychologist; b. Sept. 13, New York; d. David and Stella Akrish; m. Seymour E. Leventer, Aug. 20, 1949 (div. 1962); children: David b. 1954, Jerry b. 1956; edn: BA, Hunter Coll. 1944; MA, N.Y. Univ. 1951; EdD,

UCLA 1969; lic. Bd. Med. Examiners Psychology 1971. Career: secty., N.Y. and Calif. 1944-52; psychology intern San Fernando Valley Child Guidance, Van Nuys 1968-70; psychologist Northridge Hosp. 1970-78; pvt. practice psychology, Sepulveda 1972–; mem: Am. Psychology Assn., Calif. St. Psychological Assn., S.F.V. Psychological Assn. (pres. 1980), Assn. Child & Ednl. Psychology, L.A. Co. Psychological Assn., Group Psychotherapy Assn. So Calif. (bd. mem. 1974–), Women's Referral Service; contbr. profl. jour. article; rec: dancing, music. Address: North Hills 91343

LEVI, DAVID F., United States district judge; b. Aug. 29, 1951, Chicago, Ill.; s. Edward H. and Kate (Sulzberger) L.; m. Nancy Ryerson Ranney, July 14, 1973; children: Joseph b. 1981, William b. 1983; edn: BA, Harvard Univ. 1972; MA, 1973; PhD, 1973–; JD, Stanford Univ. 1980. Career: clk. to judge Duniway 9th Circuit Ct., S.F. 1980-81; clk. to Justice Powell Supreme Ct., Wash. D.C. 1981-82; asst. U.S. atty. Dept. of Justice, Sacto. 1983-86, U.S. atty. 1986–; U.S. District judge, 1990–; chair, Ninth Circuit Task Force on Race, Religious and Ethnic Fairness, 1994–; mem. Civil Rules Com. 1994–; pres. Milton L. Schwartz Inn of Court, 1993–; tchg. fellow Harvard Univ. 1973-77; honors: Phi Beta Kappa, Order of Coif; mem: Am. Law Inst. 1991–, Stanford Law Sch. Vis. Com., Atty. Gens. Advy. Com. of U.S. Attys. (pub. corruption subcom. chmn. 1989); article pub. in profl. jour., 1980; Republican; Jewish. Ofc: U.S. District Court 650 Capitol Mall #2504 Sacramento 95814

LEVIN, BARRY RAYMOND, rare book dealer, author; b. June 11, 1946, Phila.; s. Sidney and Bertha (Zwerman) L.; m. Sally Ann Fudge; edn: Santa Monica Coll. 1964-65. Career: production control dispatcher McDonnell Douglas, Santa Monica 1967-69; shot peener Astro Peen Inc., Hawthorn 1969-72; owner Barry R. Levin Science Fiction and Fantasy Literature, Santa Monica 1973–; cons. sci. fiction fantasy and horror films, Hollywood 1976–; firm sponsors annually the Collectors Award for the most collectable author and book of the year in the fields of science fiction, fantasy and horror 1988–; mem: Antiquarian Booksellers Assn. Am., Internat. League of Antiquarian Booksellers, Am. Booksellers Assn., So. Calif. Booksellers Assn., other profl. organizations; co-author: "Book Collectibles By Stephen King: A Price Guide" for The Stephen King Companion, edited by George Beahm 1989; author rare book catalogues: Titles from the Back Room 1981, Great Works & Rarities of Sci. Fiction & Fantasy 1982, One Small Step 1983, others; writer article "The Controversy Over Presentation Copies" AB Bookman's Weekly (8/28/89); profiled in "Pioneering a Sci-Fi Specialty in So. Calif." AB Bookman's Weekly (10/28/91), "Manuscript Collection - An Endangered Species" Publishers Weekly (6/29/92) reprinted The Roundup Quarterly and Sci. Fiction Writers of Am. Bulletin, editorialized by Stanley Schmidt in Analog (2/93); mil: AUS 1965-67, Nat. Defense Service Medal 1966. Store: 720 Santa Monica Blvd Santa Monica 90401

LEVINE, DAVID STEFAN, lawyer; b. April 18, 1948, New York; s. Harry A. and Terry Roth L.; m. Nora L. Skrukrud, Mar. 26, 1995; edn: BA, UC Berkeley 1970; MPA, Princeton Univ. 1972; JD, UC Berkeley 1978; admitted St. Bar Calif. 1979. Career: atty. Crosby Heaffey Roach & May, Oakland 1979; Waysman & Levine, San Francisco 1980; sole practice, San Francisco 1981–; mem: Am. Bar Assn. (com. on victims and witnesses of section on criminal justice), San Francisco Bar Assn.; author: article pub. in profl. jour., 1979; Jewish. Ofc: 220 Montgomery St Ste 810 San Francisco 94104

LEVINE, EDWARD NORMAN, financial executive; b. Port Glasgow, Scotland; s. Edward Calderwood and Kathleen Jessie (Kirkbride) L.; m. Janet Ann Coates, Aug. 26, 1984; children: Alistair b. 1986, Toby b. 1991; edn: BS commerce, Univ. British Columbia Canada 1978; MBA, Stanford Univ. 1981. Career: dir. fin. planning and corp. devel. Ducommun Inc., Los Angeles 1981-85; dir. fin. planning Collins Foods, Los Angeles 1985-87; c.f.o. Il Fornaio, San Francisco 1987-91; principal Vine Assoc. 1991–; c.e.o. Vine Dining Enterprises, Inc. 1992–; dir. Versatron, Healdsburg 1986–; rec: cooking, wine collecting, mtn. biking. Ofc: Vine Associates PO Box 157 Mill Valley 94941 Tel: 415/389-5441

LEVINE, SAMUEL EDWARD, engineer; b. Apr. 23, 1930, Los Angeles; s. Isadore Sydney and Rachael L.; m. Idele Metz, Dec. 20, 1953 (div. Sept., 1972); m. 2d. Beatrice Alice Bystrom, Mar. 23, 1974; children: Robin b. 1956, Michelle b. 1958, Richard b. 1962, Erik b. 1968; granddaus. Alexandra Meyer b. 1991, Michaela Levine b. 1994; edn: BS engring. UCLA 1954; MS, 1962; reg. profl. engr. Calif. 1959. Career: engr. Radio Corp. of Am., Camden, N.J. and Los Angeles 1954-61; dir. advanced space comms., tech. staff Aerospace Corp., El Segundo 1961-79; assoc. Levine/Seegel Assocs., Santa Monica 1979-94; owner, Samuel E. Levine, P.E. 1994–; radar flight test engr. RCA, Palmdale 1955-58; mil. comms. satellite office, D.O.D., Wash., DC 1975, head attack team, Survivability Analysis Group 1977-78; mem: IEEE, Sierra Club, Aircraft Owners & Pilots Assn., Angel Flight; mil: airman 2c. USAFR 1951-52; rec: woodworking, flying, backpacking. Ofc: Samuel E. Levine, P.E., 10825 Ashby Ave Los Angeles 90064

LEVINE, SY, sales executive; b. May 9, 1943, Brooklyn, N.Y.; James and May (Siegel) L.; m. Marlene Kaufman, May 5, 1964 (div. 1982); m. Carol Ann Lichenstein, Aug. 5, 1982; children: Heidi b. 1965, Shana b. 1970, Yosef b.

1973; Career: mgr. Roberts Dept. Store, Santa Fe Springs 1970-75; owner Sylo, Whittier 1975-80; sales mgr. Hygin Supply, Los Angeles 1980-82; sales Western Kosher 1983-86; v.p. M.S. Enterprise, Long Bach 1986-88; salesman W. Pico Foods, Los Angeles 1988-92; cons. tchr. Whitter Union H.S., Santa Fe Springs 1970-74; awards: Hygin Supply Best Salesman 1982; mem: Young Israel Long Beach (v.p. 1985-95), Long Beach Hebrew Acad., Jewish Fedn. Long Beach; Republican; Jewish; rec: fishing, bowling. Res: 3653 Western Pl Long Beach 90807 Ofc: 12121 Wilshire Blvd West Los Angeles

LEVINGSTON, JOHN C.B., company executive; b. Apr. 10, 1929, Pakistan, nat. U.S. citizen 1967; s. Thomas Clarke and Kathleen P. (Farley) L.; m. Elizabeth Baumer, June 6, 1958 (div. 1968); m. Paula Angela Eriksen, Feb. 29, 1980; children: Thomas b. 1981, Alexandra Jane b. 1989; edn: matriculated Harrow, England 1943-47, rec'd mil. commn. Sandhurst, England 1947-49. Career: lt. British Army 1947-52; sales mgr. British-Am. Tobacco, Nairobi, Kenya 1953-55; sales exec. W.L. Mackenzie, Vancouver, Canada 1957-61; pres. Levingston & Assocs., Los Angeles 1978–, chmn. bd. Straightley Films, L.A. 1972–, chmn. and c.e.o. Interactive Telemedia, L.A. 1986-90; mem. Acad. TV Arts & Scis.; lodges: Masonic 1967–, Scottish Rite 1968–, York Rite 1987–, Masonic Press Club 1968–. Ofc: Levingston & Associates PO Box 1951 Beverly Hills 90213

LEVITT, ALVIN T., lawyer; b. Sept. 19, 1935, Denver, Colo.; s. Nathan and Margaret (Chizewere) L.; m. Rosanne Perlman, Nov. 28, 1957; children: Bradley b. 1960, Douglas b. 1963, Susan b. 1966; edn: BS, Univ. Colo. Boulder 1957; LL.B, UC Berkeley 1960; admitted St. Bar Calif. (1961). Career: atty. Dinkelspiel & Dinkelspiel, San Francisco 1961-69; atty., ptnr. Dinkelspiel Pelavin Steefel & Levitt 1970-80; atty., prin. Steefel Levitt & Weiss 1980–; guest lectr. UC Berkeley Sch. of Law 1970-89; honors: Am. Coll. of Tax Counsel (fellow); mem: Am. Bar Assn., San Francisco Bar Assn., Mt. Zion Hosp. (dir., treas. 1987-89), Jewish Comm. Fedn. (dir., v.p. 1986-89, 90-95); author Attorneys Guide to Calif. Profl. Corps., 1973; rec: photog., bicycling. Ofc: Steefel Levitt & Weiss 1 Embarcadero Center 30th Flr San Francisco 94111

LEVKOFF, GEORGE L., investment banker; b. Oct. 2, 1955, NY, NY; s. Henry L. and Violette (Simon) L.; edn: BS in fin., Lehigh Univ., 1977; MBA in fin., Univ. Chgo. 1979; JD, Univ. of Houston, 1985. Career: instnl. bond salesman various firms, Los Angeles 1985-87; v.p. investments National Bank of Long Beach, 1988-90; investment exec. Paine Webber, 1990; Drake Capital Securities Inc., Institutional Sales/Trading, 1990-. Res: PO Box 5235 Playa Del Rey 90296 Ofc: Drake Capital Securities Inc., 1250 Fourth St 5th Fl Santa Monica 90401 Tel: 310/393-1900 FAX 310/393-3948

LEVY, ALLAN, physician, psychiatrist; b. Oct. 30, 1925, Detroit, Mich.; s. David S. and Ida (Diskin) L. m. Phyllis Kulick, Aug. 6, 1950 (dec. 1973); m. 2d. Maria Coia, Jan. 4, 1975; children: Susan b. 1952, Peter b. 1956; edn: Tufts Coll. 1943-45; MD, Univ. Mich. Ann Arbor 1949. Career: intern Univ. Hosp., Ann Arbor, Mich. 1949-50, resident 1950-53; Agnew St. Hosp., Agnew 1953-54; pvt. practice, San Mateo 1954-70; Peninsula Psychiatric Assn. 1970–; asst. clin. prof. Stanford Univ. 1959-74; councilor N. Calif. Psychiatric Soc., S.F. 1978-79; pres. Peninsula Psychiatric Assn., San Mateo 1970-80; chmn. dept. psychiatry Peninsula Hosp., Burlingame 1970-72; mem: Am. Psychiatric Assn. (life fellow), CMA, San Mateo Co. Med. Assn.; 5 articles pub. in profl. jours. 1954–, book chpt. pub. 1978, paper pub. 1985; mil: lt. USNR 1950-52; Jewish; rec: golf. Res: 50 Mounds Rd #503 San Mateo 94402 Ofc: Peninsula Psychiatric Association 215 N San Mateo Dr Ste 7 San Mateo 94401

LEVY, DAVID STEVEN, college administrator; b. Mar. 9, 1955, Los Angeles; s. Henry and Gloria (Barouh) L.; children: Rachel b. 1986; edn: BA, Occidental Coll., 1977, MA, 1979. Career: student loan ofcr. Bank of Am., Los Angeles 1975-78; financial aid counselor CSU San Bernardino 1978-79, CSU Northridge 1979-80, assoc. dir. fin. aid CSU Dominguez Hills, Carson 1980-82; dir. fin. aid Occidental Coll., L.A. 1982-88; dir. fin. aid Calif. Inst. of Tech., Pasadena 1988–; cons., instr. The College Board, San Jose 1987–; awards: merit. achiev. Nat. Assn. of Student Financial Aid Adminstrs., Denver 1988, disting. service Western Assn. Stu. Fin. Aid Adminstrs., Long Beach 1990, creative leadership, Pres.'s disting. recogn. awards Calif. Assn. Stu. Fin. Aid Adminstrs., Anaheim (1987, 90, 93); mem. Nat. Assn. SFAA (bd. 1980–), Western Assn. SFAA (ofcr. 1978–), Calif. Assn. SFAA (ofcr. 1978–); publs: consumer info. brochures (3). Res: 368 Mt. Carmel Dr Glendale 91206-2970 Ofc: California Institute of Technology MC 12-63 Pasadena 91125

LEVY, JANE, librarian; b. Jan. 31, 1945, Chgo.; d. Robert William and Betty (Amos) Van Brunt; m. Neil Martin Levy, Oct. 19, 1969; children: Ariel, Shoshi, Amos; edn: BA, UC Berkeley, 1967, MLS, 1968. Career: librarian/archivist John Steinbeck Library, Salinas 1970-71, Soc. of California Pioneers, San Francisco 1972-73; librarian Blumenthal Rare Book & Manuscript Library, Magnes Museum, Berkeley 1980–; mem. Soc. of Am. Archivist, Assn. of Jewish Libraries, Latin Am. Jewish Studies Asns., Am. Museum Assn.; coauthor The Jewish Illustrated Book 1986, 2 pub. articles 1986, 91. Res: 953 Shattuck Berkeley 94707 Ofc: Magnes Museum 2911 Russell Berkeley 94705

LEVY, JOSEPH VICTOR, professor of physiology and pharmacology; b. Apr. 7, 1928, Los Angeles; s. Victor Marcus and Rachel Lea (Alhadeff) L.; m. Joanne P., Dec. 18, 1954; children: Virginia Rachel b. 1956, Suzanne Joyce Garrett b. 1959; edn: BA, Stanford Univ., 1950; MS, UCLA, 1956; PhD, Univ. of Wash., 1959. Career: research asst. pharmacology Stanford Univ. 1954-56; Univ. of Wash. res. asst. pharmacol. 1956-57, NIH pre-doc. research fellow 1957-58, res. fellow anesthesiology 1958-59, Am. Heart Assn. advanced res. fellow 1959-60; affil. staff Pacific Med. Ctr. Hosp., San Francisco 1960–; clin. assoc. prof., 1972-84, clin. prof. physiology and pharmacology, Univ. of the Pacific, San Francisco 1985–, prof. and chair, Dept. Physiology/Pharmacology 1991–; featured lectr. 300+ confs., symposia, post-grad. courses, grand rounds; mem. editl. bds: Proceedings Soc. for Exptl. Biol. & Med. 1980-86, Clinical and Exptl. Hypertension 1979-82; mem. NIH Hypertension Task Force 1976-77, res. com. Calif. Heart Assn. 1975-77, Drug Interactions Task Force panelist Am. Pharmaceut. Assn. 1973-85, expert advy. panel on geriatrics U.S. Pharmacopeia 1985-95, comm. hypertension com. S.F. Heart Assn. 1975-77; awards: Stanford Univ. scholar in pharmacol. 1954-55, res. career devel. Nat. Heart Inst./NIH 1965-70, res. travel fellow Internat. Union Physiol. Scis. 1961, 65, 71, 77, Internat. Union of Pharmacol. Scis. 1969, 75, 78, 84; mem: Am. Soc. of Pharmacology & Exptl. Therapeutics, Am. Soc. Clin. Pharmacol. and Therapeutics, Soc. for Exptl. Biology & Medicine, Am. Physiol. Soc., Am. Chem. Soc. Medicinal Chem. Sect., Council on Basic Res., Am. Heart Assn.; coauthor: Vitamins: Their Use and Abuse, 1976; prin. author 120+ sci. articles in sci. jours., books, monographs, proceedings, handbooks, 1957–.

LEVY, MARK ALLEN, physician; b. Apr. 11, 1948, Sacramento, Calif.; s. Robert Bernard and Birdie (Kutzen) L.; m. Stacia Ann Zerebecki, June 28, 1987; edn: BS, UC Davis 1971; BS, pharmacy, Creighton Univ., Omaha, Nebr. 1975, MD, 1980; cert. Am. Bd. of Internal Medicine 1988. Career: internist Foundation Health, Sacramento; asst. clin. prof. family practice, UC Davis Med. Ctr., Sacto. 1993–; mem: AMA 1984–, Sacto. Med. Soc. 1987–. Ofc: Foundation Health 500 University Ave Sacramento 95825

LEWIN, KLAUS JONATHAN, physician, pathologist, medical educator; b. Aug. 10, 1936, Jerusalem, Israel; nat. 1978; s. Bruno and Charlotte (Nawratzki) L.; m. Patricia Coutts Milne, Sept. 26, 1964; children: David b. 1965, Nicky b. 1967, Bruno b. 1971; edn: MBBS, Univ. London England 1959; MRCS, LRCP 1959; MD, 1966. Career: asst. prof. Stanford Univ., Stanford 1968-76; assoc. prof. UC Los Angeles 1976-80, prof. pathology 1980–, prof. medicine 1986–, dir. diagnostic immunopathology 1976–, chief, surgical pathology 1994–; mem: Internat. Acad. Pathology, Am. Gastroenterological Assn., Pathological Soc. Gt. Britain, Arthur Purdy Stout Soc., Gastrointestinal Pathology Soc. (past pres.), L.A. Pathology Soc. (past pres.); 200+ articles, book chpts. and abstracts pub.; rec: travel, internat. affairs, geographic pathology. Res: 333 Las Casas Ave Pacific Palisades 90272 Ofc: Univ. California Center for Health Sciences Los Angeles 90024

LEWIS, BRADLEY HOWARD, physician; b. Mar. 16, 1950, Los Angeles, Calif.; s. Mortimer Kenneth and Doris Jean (Lasky) L.; m. Nancy Ruth Church, M.D., Oct. 22, 1981; children: Jess b. 1982, Rebecca b. 1987; edn: BS, history, Mass. Inst. Technology 1972; MA, history, Brandeis Univ. 1974; MD, UCLA Sch. Medicine 1979; lic. physician St. of Calif.; cert.: Nat. Bd. of Med. Examiners 1979, Am. Bd. of Internal Medicine 1982, Hematology 1984. Career: resident, internal medicine Univ. of Rochester, Strong Mem. Hosp. 1979-82; clin. fellow, hematology, Dept. Medicine, Strong Mem. Hosp. 1982-83, res. fellow 1983-84; pvt. practice, hematology, Berkeley, Calif. 1984–; dir. hematology prog. Alta Bates Med. Ctr., Berkeley 1984-86, dir. Hemophilia and Thalassemia progs. 1984–; co-founder, co-dir. East Bay AIDS Ctr., Berkeley 1986-88, oncology cons. 1988–; clin. instr. medicine/hematology UC San Francisco 1984-89, asst. clin prof. 1989–; lectr. med. hematology UC Berkeley 1990–; advy. bd. Alameda-Contra Costa Co. Blood Bank 1991–; com. mem., Alta Bates Hosp: Transfusion Quality Assurance 1984–, chmn. 1986–; Med. Edn. 1985–, chmn. 1987-90; AIDS Conf. Planning 1987–; County Comm. Consortium 1988–; chmn. AIDS Quality Assurance 1989–; Pharmacy and Therapeutics 1989–; Scientific Advy. Com. 1990–; hosp. comm. membership com. 1990–; awards: Mosby Scholarship 1979, Alpha Omega Alpha 1979, UC Berkeley Med. Sch. Tchr. of Yr. 1991; author/contbg. author: 11 scientific abstracts and jour. articles; rec: fly fishing, skiing, mountain biking. Ofc: Comprehensive Cancer Center 2001 Dwight Way Berkeley 94701

LEWIS, EDWARD B., biology educator, Nobel Prize winner; b. May 20, 1918, Wilkes-Barre, Pa.; s. Edward B. and Laura (Histed) L.; m. Pamela Harrah, Sept. 26,1946; children: Hugh, Glenn (dec.), Keith; edn: BA, Univ. Minn. 1939; PhD, Calif. Inst. Tech. 1942; Phil.D., Univ. Umea, Sweden 1982. Career: instr. biology Calif. Inst. Tech., Pasadena 1946-48, asst. prof. 1949-56, prof. 1956-66, Thomas Hunt Morgan prof. 1966-88, prof. emeritus 1988–; Rockefeller Found. fellow Sch. Botany, Cambridge Univ., Eng. 1948-49; mem. Nat. Adv. Com. Radiation 1958-61; vis prof. Univ. Copenhagen 1975-76, 82; researcher in developmental genetics, somatic effects of radiation; awards: Gairdner Found. Internat. award 1987, Wolf Found. prize in medicine 1989, Rosenstiel award 1990, Nat. Medal of Sci. 1990, Albert Lasker Basic Med. Res. award 1991,

Louisa Gross Horwitz prize 1992, Nobel Prize in Medicine (with Eric F. Wieschaus and Christiane Nuesslein-Volhard) for studies of how genes control embryonic development, 1995; Fellow AAAS; mem: NAS, Genetics Soc. Am. (sec. 1962-64, pres. 1967-69, Thomas Hunt Morgan medal), Am. Acad. Arts & Scis., Royal Soc., London (fgn. mem.), Am. Philos. Soc., Genetical Soc. Great Britain (hon.); editor Genetics and Evolution, 1961; mil: capt. USAAF, 1942-46. Res: 805 Winthrop Rd San Marino 91108-1709 Ofc: Calif Inst Tech Div Biology 1201 E California Blvd Pasadena 91125*

LEWIS, EDWARD NORMAN, marketing executive; b. Aug. 8, 1951, Canandaigua, N.Y. s. Raymond Eugene and Marion Francis (Norman) L.; m. Valerie Lynn Tomlin, Sept. 5, 1970 (div. 1979); son, Christopher b. 1976; m. Nancy Doyle, June 8, 1980; edn: AA, Pasa. City Coll., 1971; BA, CSU Los Angeles, 1973, MS pub. adminstrn. 1988. Career: athletic dir., program splst. Pasadena Boys Club 1968-73; mktg. rep. Merchants & Mfrs. Assn., L.A. 1973-77; mgr. sales & promotions Marineland, Palos Verdes 1977-80; exec. dir. L.A. County Republican Party, 1979-80; area mgr. L.A. Chamber of Commerce 1980-84; v.p. mktg. and sales Hollywood Chamber of Commerce 1984-87, exec. v.p., c.o.o. 1987-90, originator: new Cause-Related mktg. pgms. - Hollywood Walk of Fame, Hollywood Sign, Hollywood community name; dir. of devel. Riverside Comm. Hosp. Found., Riverside 1991-93, exec. dir. 1993-95; dir. of devel. San Antonio Hosp. Found. 1995–; instr. UC Riverside Ext.; instr. in mktg. principles, La Sierra Univ.; honors: Boy of Year Pasadena Boys Club/Calif., Utah & Nev. 1968, Pasa. City Coll. freshman class pres. 1970; listed Who's Who in the West 1991; mem: Nat. Soc. of Fund Raising Executives (found. devel. chair, CA Inland Chpt. 1993/94), La Sierra Univ. Sch. of Bus. & Mgmt. (advy. council), bd. mem. So. Area Fostercare Effort (SAFE); Republican; Presbyterian; rec: tennis, basketball, equestrian, poet. Ofc: San Antonio Hospital Foundation 999 San Bernardino Rd Upland 91786 Tel: 909/920-4965

LEWIS, HILDA PRESENT, educator; b. Mar. 28, 1925, Bridgeport, Ct.; d. Louis David and Yetta (Elstein) Present; children: Daniel b. 1948, David b. 1952, Jonathan b. 1967, Rachel b. 1969; edn: BA, UC Berkeley, 1948, MA, 1956, PhD, 1959. Career: tchr. Richmond Unified Sch. Dist., 1950-52; lectr. Coll. of the Holy Names, Oakland 1957-59; lectr. UC Berkeley, 1958-62; asst. to full prof. and dept. chair San Francisco State Univ., 1962–; vis. prof. Stanford Univ. 1970, 71-72; Leicester Polytechnic, U.K. 1986; researcher in the arts I/D/E/A, L.A. 1973-76; res. assoc. Inst. of Human Devel. UC Berkeley, 1976-78; mem. Nat. Art Edn. Assn. 1964–, editor Art Education 1987-89; mem. U.S. Soc. for Edn. through Art (1978–, v.p. 1983-84), Am. Ednl. Res. Assn. 1962–, Internat. Soc. for Edn. Through Art 1976–; coauthor: Understanding Children's Art For Better Teaching (1973), editor: Art for the Pre-primary Child (1972), Child Art: The Beginnings of Self Affirmation (1966). Res: 17749 Chateau Ct Castro Valley 94552

LEWIS, JASON ALVERT, JR., telecommunications systems technician; b. Aug. 17, 1941, Clarksville, Tex.; s. Jason Allen and Mary (Dinwiddie) L.; edn: Stockton Coll. 1959-60, San Jose Jr. Coll. 1962-63. Career: field engr., telephone technician Pacific Bell, San Francisco, 1983-84; systems technician AT&T, 1984–; patentee in field; biographical listings in Who's Who in West, Who's Who in World, Internat. Who's Who of Intellectuals, Dict. Internat. Biography, Who's Who in Finance and Industry; mem: Internat. Platform Soc., The Planetary Soc., U.S. Naval Inst.; civic: Cousteau Soc., Astron. Soc. Pacific, S.F. Zool. Soc.; mil: US Army 1964-66; Democrat. Res: 139 Pecks Ln South San Francisco 94080 Ofc: Deputy Governor of American Biographical Institute.

LEWIS, JERRY, congressman; b. Oct. 21, 1934; edn: BA, UCLA, 1956. Career: former underwriter life ins. underwriter; field rep. for former U.S. Rep. Jerry Pettis; mem. Calif. State Assembly, 1968-78; vice chmn. rules com., chmn. subcom. on air quality; mem. 96th-104th Congresses from 35th (now 40th) Calif. dist., 1979–; mem. appropriation com., ranking minority mem. Va.-HUD subcom., mem. defense subcom., select com. on intelligence; Republican; Presbyterian. Ofc: House of Representatives Washington DC 20515*

LEWIS, PHILLIP VERNON, business and management educator, dean; b. Mar. 27, 1942, Eastland, Tx.; s. Walter Vernon and Doris (Nelms) L.; m. Marilyn Hermann, Dec. 14, 1963; children: Brook b. 1968, Blair b. 1972; edn: BS, Abilene Christian Univ. 1964; MA, Univ. of Denver 1966; EdD, Univ. of Houston 1970. Career: instr. No. Arizona Univ., Flagstaff 1966-68; prof. Coll. of Bus., Okla. State Univ., Stillwater 1970-82; dean and prof. Coll. of Bus., Abilene Christian Univ., Abilene, Tx. 1982-92; dean Sch. of Bus., Azusa Pacific Univ., Azusa, Calif. 1992–; awards: Ambassador Goodwill, St. of Okla. 1981, Disting. Paper, SW Fed. Adminstrn. Discip., New Orleans, La. 1984; Weeks Award of Merit, Assn. for Bus. Communications, Las Vegas, NV 1989; mem: Assn. for Bus. Communications 1972– (fellow, 1984), Academy of Mgmt. 1972–, SGV Commerce & Cities Consortium, Covina, Calif. (exec. bd. 1994–), Glendora C.of C. (economic devel. com. 1995–); author: Organizational Communication, 1975, 2nd edit. 1980, 3rd edit. 1987; Republican; Ch. of Christ. Ofc: School of Business & Mgmt. Azusa Pacific University 901 E Alosta Azusa 91702-7000

LEWIS, RICHARD BOND, advertising agency president; b. April 14, 1925, Atkinson, Nebr.; s. Monte Claire and Lula Pearl (Bond) L.; m. Carol Ann Bigglestone, Nov. 23, 1948; children: Eric b. 1957, Shannon b. 1958, Carrie b. 1961; edn: BA, Art Center Coll. of Design Pasadena 1953; Univ. Ariz. Career: art dir., account exec. Hal Stebbins Inc. advt. agency, Los Angeles 1953-64; account exec. Buxton Advt., Pasadena 1964-65; account mgr. McCann Erickson, Los Angeles 1965-71; pres. Richard Bond Lewis & Assocs., West Covina 1971–; city councilman West Covina 1989-91; bd. dirs., past pres. Vis. Nurses Assn.; chmn. bd. Comm. Counseling Ctr.; commr. West Covina Personnel Dept.; v.p. West Covina Waste Mgmt. Commn.; presdl. appointee Selective Service Civilian Rev. Bd.; lay leader, del., mem. comms. com. Pacific S.W. Conf., United Methodist Ch. 1979-82; P.R. dir. United Methodist Ch., Calif., Hawaii, Guam; appt. West Covina City Council 1988; awards: Camp Fire Girls spl. svc. 1979, West Covina City Council resolution for svc. 1982, West Covina City Council svc. medal 1988, West Covina Citizen of the Yr. 1991, num. art dir. awards; mem: West Covina C.of C. (com. mem. 1971, 72, 76, pres. 1981-82), West Covina Hist. Soc. (pres.), Kiwanis (disting. pres. 1986-87), Queen of the Valley Hosp. (secty. 2100 Club), Lambda Chi Alpha, Hall of Fame; mil: staff sgt. AUS 1945-46; Republican. Address: 1112 W Cameron Ave West Covina 91790

LEWIS, TED HOWARD, electrical engineer; b. April 4, 1942, Chgo.; s. Howard Estes and Vivian Irene (Lay) L.; m. Susan, May 9, 1971; m. 2d. Judith, June 2, 1984; edn: BS, Ill. Inst. Tech., 1968, MS 1969; reg. profl. engr. (PE) Calif. Career: project engr. Motorola, Chgo. 1970-72, account exec., Los Angeles 1972-74; project engr. County of Los Angeles 1974-78, communications engr. L.A. Co. Sheriff 1978-84; mfrs. rep. Great Am. Rep Co., Encino 1984-87; project engr. L.A. County Metropolitan Transp. Authority, L.A. 1987–; telecomms. cons. L.A. Olympic Org. Com. 1982-84; honors: Tau Beta Pi, Eta Kappa Nu, NASA fellow 1969; mem. IEEE, Intertel, Mensa; Ch. Religious Sci.; rec: guitar, bowling, golf. Res: 4057 Warner Ave Huntington Beach 92649 Ofc: LACMTA (M/S 8520-4) 818 W 7th St Los Angeles 90017

LEX, WILLIAM JOSEPH, college administrator; b. Sept. 3, 1944, Temple, Tx.; s. Henry Joseph and Mary Dorothy (Jeske) L.; m. Diane Chostner, Nov. 25, 1967; children: Carolyn Kimberly b. 1977; edn: AA, San Francisco City Coll. 1965; BA UC Santa Barbara 1967; MS Oregon State Univ. 1973; PhD Univ. of Texas, Austin 1984. Career: head resident Oreg. State Univ., Corvallis 1971-73; ass. dir. housing Univ. of Alaska, Fairbanks 1973-74, dir. residence edn. 1974-76; aviation instr. Tanana Valley Comm. Coll., Fairbanks, Alaska 1976-78, coord. aviation dept. 1978-80, dir. service technology 1980-81, dir. vocat.-tech. programs 1984-86; assoc. dean No. Campus, Pa. Coll. of Technology, Wellsboro, Pa. 1986-91; assoc. v.p., Mendocino Coast Campus, College of the Redwoods, Ft. Bragg, Calif. 1991–; bd. dirs.: Ft. Bragg/Mendocino Coast C.of C. 1991–, Mendocino Co. Arts Council 1991–, Fort Bragg Ctr. for the Arts 1995–, Mendocino Co. Private Industry Council 1992–, Leadership Mendocino 1993–, Mendocino Co. Econ. Devel. & Finance Corp. 1994–; awards: Disting. Graduate USAF Ofcr. Training Sch. 1967, USAF Commendation Medal 1971, Dist. Teaching award, Univ. of Alaska 1977, Phi Kappa Phi 1973, Kappa Delta Pi 1984; mem: Phi Delta Kappa (past pres.) Mansfield, Pa. chpt. 1986–, Nat. Council of Instructional Administrators 1984–; Ft. Bragg Rotary Club (youth leadership chair 1991–), United Way (coastal steering com. 1993–), Ft. Bragg H.S. SSP (advy. com. chair 1993–), Mendocino H.S. Windows Project (advy. com. 1991–); mil: capt. USAF 1967-71; Democrat; Episcopalian; rec: flying, reading, wines, cooking. Res: 45261 Mar Vista Drive Mendocino 95460 Ofc: College of the Redwoods Mendocino Coast Campus 1211 Del Mar Drive Ft Bragg 95437

LEZA, RICHARD L., venture capitalist; b. April 16, 1947, Laredo, Tx.; s. Gustavo G. and Corina C. (Cordova) L.; m. Cindy G. Rocha, Jan. 6, 1967; children: Richard b. 1968; edn: East L.A. City Coll. 1968; BSCE hons., N.M. St. Univ. 1973; MBA, Stanford Grad. Sch. 1978. Career: sr. engr. Stearns Rogers Inc., Denver, Colo. 1973-74; structural and systems engr. Gen. Atomic Co., San Diego 1974-76; fin. analyst Envirotech Corp., Menlo Park 1977-78; internat. dir. Qume Corp., San Jose 1978-80; chmn. RMC Group Inc., Santa Clara 1981-88; AI Research Corp., Palo Alto 1989–; dir. Floormasters Inc., Azusa 1985–; Bytec S.A. de CV, Mexico City 1985–; AI Research Corp., Palo Alto 1989–; EMS Inc., Oakland 1987–; awards: Hispanic Bus. hon. 1985, Oasis Press outstanding bus. author 1987, N.M.St. Univ. outstanding alumni 1988; mem: Phi Kappa Phi, Stanford Bus. Sch. Alumni Assn., Asia Am. Mfg. Assn.; clubs: NMSU Pres.'s Assn., Stanford (Palo Alto), Mission Lakes CC, Catholic (Palo Alto); author: Develop Your Bus. Plan, 1983, 88, Export Now, 1988, newspaper interviews, 1984, 88; Stanford Bus. Sch. Mag. profile 1994, Hispanic Bus. Mag. profile 1994; Republican; R.Cath.; rec: tennis, golf, skiing. Res: 4191 Briarwood Way Palo Alto 94306 Ofc: AI Research Corp. 2003 St Julien Ct Ste 67 Mountain View 94043

LI, PEI-CHING, engineer; b. Nov. 2, 1919, Yencheng, China; nat. 1970; s. Sou-Bing and Wong L.; m. Ai-Juei H., Nov. 20, 1945; children: Robert b. 1946, Lilian b. 1949, Richard b. 1962; edn: BE, Tsing Hwa Univ. China 1945; MS, Univ. Rochester 1955; PhD, 1959. Career: supr. Taiwan Sugar Corp., China 1947-53; research assoc. Univ. Rochester, N.Y. 1954-59; research scientist Raytheon Co., Waltham, Mass. 1959-64; Am. Standard, New Brunswick, N.J. 1964-65; IITRI, Chgo., Ill. 1965-68; advy. engr. IBM Corp., E. Fishkill, N.Y.

1968-95 (ret.); awards: IBM Corp. Outstanding Tech. Achievement 1984; mem: Sigma Xi, Am. Ceramic Soc., Am. Chemical Soc.; num. articles pub. in trade and profl. jours. Ofc: IBM Corp. 2427 W Hillcrest St Newbury Park 91320

LIBANOFF, ARTHUR, podiatrist; b. May 17, 1931, Chgo.; s. Leo and Sylvia (Goodman) L.; m. Erliss Ruff, 1955; edn: BS, Univ. of Ill. 1953; DPM, Ill. Coll. of Podiatry 1959. Career: pvt. practice podiatry, La Habra 1960–; residency pgm. and credential com., Podiatric Surg., Beach Comm. Hosp.; honors: Univ. Ill. Dean's List 1949, pres. German Club 1950, pres. Durlacher Honor Soc., Ill. Coll. Podiat. 1955; mil: cpl. US Army 1955-57; Jewish. Ofc: 740 W La Habra Blvd La Habra 90631

LIBBY, RICHARD ALLAN, mathematician; b. Apr. 9, 1958, Pasadena; s. Harold Dean and Ruth Carol (Geerlings) L.; edn: BA Univ. of Calif., San Diego, 1980; MA, 1982; PhD, Univ. of Calif., Santa Cruz 1990; career: res. asst., Stanford Linear Accelerator Ctr., Stanford 1985; tchg. asst., Univ. of Calif., S.D. 1980-82; mathematics instr. 1986-90; res. analyst, Bankers Trust Co. of Calif., San Francisco 1991-92; financial consultant, Bank of America, S.F. 1993–; tutor, mathematics, 1983–; record broker, Glen Canyon Records 1983-84; classical and theater pianist, Santa Cruz Cty. Symphony 1986; deputy court clerk, State Bar of Calif. 1991; awards: assistantship in mathematics, Univ. of Calif., Santa Cruz 1984-90; Who's Who in the West, 1991; mem: Am. Mathematical Soc., Mathematical Assn. of Am., Soc. for Industrial and Applied Mathematics; author: Asymptotics of Determinants and Eigenvalue Distributions for Toeplitz Matrices Associated with Certain Discontinuous Symbols, 1990; Democrat; rec: classical pianist. Res: 1456 Jones St #25 San Francisco 94109. Ofc:Bank of America, Systems & Procedures Devel #2576, 555 California St 3rd Flr San Francisco 94104

LIBERMAN, ALAN DOUGLAS, clinical psychologist; b. April 30, 1947, Seattle, Wash.; s. Martin and Florence L.; children: Dana, Matthew, Zachary; edn: BA, CSU Northridge 1969; MS, CSU Los Angeles 1971; PhD, Calif. Profl. Sch. Psychology 1976. Career: clin. psychologist Dept. Vocational Rehab., Norwalk 1977-78; Metropolitan St. Hosp. 1978-80; pvt. practice clin. psychology, Tustin 1980–. Address: Tustin 92680

LICHTER-HEATH, LAURIE JEAN, educator, lawyer, writer; b. March 13, 1951, Brooklyn, N.Y.; d. Irving and Beatrice (Gelber) Lichter; m. Donald Wayne Heath, Feb. 28, 1981; children: Michele Samuel b. 1983, Adam Ryan b. 1988, Jason Charles b. 1990; edn: JD, John Marshall Law Sch. 1975; LL.M, Georgetown Univ. Law Center 1979; admitted St. Bars Ill. (1975), Wash. D.C. (1977), N.Y. (1980), Nev. (1981). Career: law clk. Wash. D.C. Ct. Appeals, 1975-77; staff atty. SEC, Wash. D.C. 1977-78; lectr. N.Y. Univ. Sch. Contg. Edn. in Law & Tax., N.Y.C. 1980-81; atty., govt. rels. asst. Metropolitan Life Ins. Co. 1978-81; atty., assoc. Miller & Daar, Reno, Nev. 1981; legal cons., Stockton 1981-84; asst. prof. Univ. of Pacific 1984-92; writer, 1992–; dir. Laurnan B. Mktg. Inc., Boca Raton, Fla. 1981, Heath Fin. Services Corp., Stockton 1986; honors: Univ. of Pacific-SBPA Outstanding Faculty Mem. 1991, Who's Who of Emerging Leaders in Am., Who's Who in West, Who's Who in Am. Law, Who's Who Emerging Young Leaders, Who's Who Am. Women, Univ. Ill. fellowship 1972; mem: Acad. of Legal Studies in Bus. (ALSB), Western Bus. Law Assn., Am. Bar Assn.; co-author Labor Management Relations in a Changing Environment, 1990, 2d edit. 1995, articles pub. in profl. jours., 1986-91; Democrat. Ofc: 18252 Smokesignal Dr San Diego 92127

LIDMAN, DANIEL HARVEY, lawyer; b. June 8, 1945, Albany, N.Y.; s. Milton and Anita (Rosenthal) L.; m. Elizabeth A. Varon, Dec. 28, 1984; children: Andrew b. 1971, Scott b. 1973; edn: BA magna cum laude, Syracuse Univ. 1967; JD, summa cum laude, Boston Coll. Law Sch. 1971; admitted St. Bar N.J. 1971, Calif. 1973. Career: atty., assoc. Lowenstein Sandler Brochin Kohl & Fisher, Newark, N.J. 1971-73; Ervin Cohen & Jessup, Beverly Hills 1973-76, ptnr, 1976-84; Stern & Lidman 1984-89; sole practice Law Ofc. of Daniel H. Lidman, 1990–; lectr. Calif. Cont. Edn. Bar, L.A. 1974-84; Hastings Coll. Law 1984-89; honors: Phi Beta Kappa, Boston Coll. Outstanding Grad. 1971; mem: L.A. Co. Bar Assn. (ofcr. of unfair competition sect. 1980-84), Am. Bar Assn., Beverly Hills Bar Assn., Bus. Trial Lawyers; book chpt. pub., 1983, articles pub. in profl. jours., 1982, 84; mil: s.sgt. U.S. Air Nat. Guard 1968-74; Democrat; Jewish; rec: numismatics, philately. Res: 13010 Maxella Ave #7 Marina del Rey 90292 Ofc: 9777 Wilshire Blvd Ste 512 Beverly Hills 90212

LIEBERMAN, ALVIN, engineer; b. June 14, 1921, Chicago, Ill.; s. Louis and Jennie (Kuznetsky) L.; m. Tillie Bess Lavin, Aug. 24, 1947; children: Gary b. 1952, Harold b. 1954; edn: BA, Central Univ. Chgo. 1942; BSCE, Ill. Inst. Tech. 1948; MSCE, 1949. Career: research assoc. Alfred Univ., N.Y. 1949-51; group mgr. IIT Research Inst., Chgo., Ill. 1951-68; v.p. research & devel. Hiac/Royco Instruments, Menlo Park 1968-83, 1985-87; tech. splst. Particle Measuring Systems, Boulder, Colo. 1983-85, 1987–; ed. powder tech. Elsevier Sequoia, Lausanne, Switzerland 1968; tech. advisor USDDE Filter Test, Oak Ridge, Tenn. 1981; convenor to ISO Tech. Com. Working Group on particle interaction with light, and WG mem. on ISO cleanrooms, 1994; awards: Fine Particle Soc. Hausner 1985, Inst. Environ. Sci. Whitfield 1987; mem: Fine

Particle Soc. (past pres.), Inst. Environ. Sci. (fellow), ASTM, ACS, Am. Inst. Chem. Engrs., AIHA, APCA; 150 articles pub. in tech. jours., 1952, book chpts. pub., 1975; mil: AUS 1942-45; rec: classical music. Ofc: Particle Measuring Systems 46500 Fremont Blvd Fremont 94538

LIEBERMAN, STEPHEN CLARK, lawyer; b. Aug. 15, 1941, Zurich, Switzerland; s. Sali and Jean Ainsley (Clark) L.; m. M. Tamara Marte, Aug. 20, 1966; children: Nicole b. 1967, Eric b. 1969, Joshua b. 1971; edn: BA, Stanford Univ. 1963; JD, UC Berkeley Boalt Hall 1968; admitted St. Bar Calif. 1969, D.C. 1970, U.S. Supreme Ct. 1974. Career: v.p., gen. counsel Vol. Tng. Services, Wash. D.C. 1968-69; atty., assoc. Squire Sanders & Dempsey 1969-75; atty. sole practice, Truckee 1975-87; sr. ptnr. Jones & Lieberman 1987-91; ptnr. Hoffman, Lien, Faccinto, Garnett & Lieberman, 1991-94; ptnr. Porter Simon, P.C., 1994–; mem: Tahoe-Truckee Bar Assn. (pres. 1989), Am. Bar Assn., Nev. Co. Bar Assn., Placer Co. Bar Assn., Calif. Soc. Healthcare Attys., Calif. Rescue & Paramedics Assn., Far West Profl. Ski Patrol Assn., Donner Summit Fire Dept. (chief 1979-87, 1988-93, asst. chief 1993–); mil: U.S. Peace Corps 1964-66; Democrat; rec: firefighting, rescue, skiing. Res: POB 910 Soda Springs 95728 Ofc: 40200 Truckee Airport Rd Truckee 96161

LIEBIG, PHOEBE STONE, educator, gerontologist; b. Dec. 28, 1933, Cambridge, Mass.; d. Marshall Harvey Stone and Emmy Melita (Portmann) Allen; m. Anthony E. Liebig, June 19, 1954 (div. 1961); child, Steuart b. 1956; edn: Radcliffe Coll., 1951-54; BA, MA, UCLA, 1954-56; postgrad., Info. Sci., UCLA, 1961; PhD, USC, 1983. Career: tchr. Los Angeles Unified Sch. Dist., 1961-70; systems documentation splst. Ancom Systems, Los Angeles, 1970-71; grants adminstr. Univ. So. Calif., LA 1971-83; academic planner, res. prof. and geriatric edn. dir. USC, 1984-86; sr. policy analyst Am. Assn. of Retired Persons, WDC 1986-88; dir. res. pgm., 1988-89, asst. prof. USC, LA 1988–; cons. UCLA Div. of Geriatric Medicine, 1988–; cons. Minority Resource Ctr. on Aging, San Diego, 1989-93; Calif. Council of Gerontology & Geriatrics, L.A., (mem. bd. 1989–, pres. 1993-95); subcontract Nat. Inst. for Disability and Rehab. Research, WDC 1994–; mem. editorial bds: Jour. of Aging & Social Policy, Boston 1989–, We. Govtl. Researcher, LA 1990–; awards: Hanson Family Asst. Professor USC 1990-1993, grantee Adminstrn. on Aging, WDC 1988–, AARP Women's Initiative, WDC 1989-90, Haynes Found., LA 1989-90, fellow UCLA/USC Long Term Care Gerontology Ctr., LA 1980, fellow Gerontol. Soc. of Am., WDC 1990; mem: Assn. for Pub. Policy and Mgmt. 1985–, Gerontol. Soc. of Am. (1976–, sect. com. 1979-81), Am. Soc. on Aging (1977–, secty. 1981-83), Am. Soc. for Pub. Adminstrn. 1981–, Am. Political Sci. Assn. 1992–; civic: LA Co. Mus. of Art, Musical Arts Soc., Neo Renaissance Soc. LA (v.p. 1978-83); publs: (monograph) State Teachers' Retirement Systems (1987), num. articles and reports on care and svs. for the elderly, 1977–, author and co-editor (books): Calif. Policy Choices for Long-Term Care, 1990, Housing Frail Elders: International Policies, Perspectives and Prospects, 1995; Democrat; rec: choral singing, bird watching, gardening, travel. Ofc: Andrus Gerontology Center, Univ. of Southern Calif., Los Angeles 90089-0191

LIEBLING, JEROME ROBERT, financial executive; b. Jan. 27, 1944, Chgo.; s. Herman George and Tommy Mildred (Sanders) L.; edn: BSCE, Purdue Univ. 1965; MBA, Stanford Univ. 1967; Indiana Univ. 1973-74; C.P.A. lic. Ind. (1975), Wis. (1978). Career: fin. and systems analysis Texas Instruments 1967-71; v.p. ops. Industrial Materials Inc., Lexington, Ky. 1971-72; controller Central States Operating Co., Youngstown Sheet & Tube, 1972-76; v.p./controller EZ Paintr Corp., Milwaukee 1976-78; div. controller Sun Electric, San Jose, Calif. 1979-81; worldwide sales controller, Signetics Corp., Sunnyvale 1981-83; controller County Sch. Service Fund, acting dir. internal bus. svs. Santa Clara County Office of Edn., 1983–; fin. control, plnng. systems analysis, public sector fin. mgmt., cons. to H.P.3000 Users Gp. (1983); honors: Outstanding Young Man in Am.; mem: Calif. Soc. CPAs, APICS, Stanford Bus. Sch. Alumni Consulting Team (bd. dir., mgmt. com., proj. devel. coord.), Stanford Bachelors; civic: U.S.A. Hockey Referee, Hockey No. Am. (capt., coach, adminstr.), Apres Ski Club, United Way Loaned Execs.; rec: ice hockey, photog., sports. Res: 826 S San Tomas Aquino Rd Campbell 95008 Ofc: Santa Clara COE 100 Skyport Dr Ste 242 San Jose 95110-1374

LIEBMAN, WILLIAM MARTIN, physician; b. June 11, 1940, San Francisco, Calif.; s. Simon Liebman and Sonia Sigel; m. Donna Abel, June 30, 1963; children: Laura b. 1965, Steven b. 1968, Adrienne b. 1971; edn: AB, physiology, UC Berkeley 1961; MD, Chicago Med. Sch./Univ. of Health Sciences 1965; lic. physician St. of Calif.; bd. cert.: Pediatrics 1970, Pediatric Gastroenterology and Nutrition 1990. Career: internship L.A. Co. Gen. Hosp. 1965-66; jr. resident pediatrics UCLA Med. Ctr. and Harbor Gen. Hosp., Torrance 1966-67, sr. resident pediatrics 1967-68; clin. fellowship gastroenterology Harbor Gen. Hosp. 1970-71; trainee to sr. trainee gastroenterology NIH 1971-73; asst. prof. pediatrics Harbor Gen. Hosp. and UCLA Sch. Medicine 1972-73; asst. clin prof. UCLA Sch. Medicine 1973-76; asst. prof. pediatrics III to asst. prof. V, UCSF Sch. Medicine 1976-81; tchg. faculty Calif.-Pacific Med. Ctr., S.F. 1981–; attending faculty Children's Hosp., Oakland and Mt. Zion Hosp., UCSF 1981–; tchg./attending faculty Children's Hosp., S.F. and Oakland 1981–; vis. prof.

pediatrics UC Irvine Sch. Medicine 1978; mem: Am. Acad. of Pediatrics (fellow, comm. health and sch. health coms., No. Calif. Chpt. I), Am. Fedn. for Clin. Res., Am. Physicians Fellowship Inc. for Israel Med. Assn., L.A. Pediatric Soc., Phi Delta Epsilon, Am. Gastroenterological Assn., So. Calif. Soc. of Gastroenterology, So. Calif. Soc. of Gastrointestinal Endoscopy, Am. Soc. of Gastrointestinal Endoscopy, No. Calif. Soc. for Clinical Gastroenterology, We. Soc. for Pediatric Res., N.Am. Soc. for Pediatric Gastroenterology, Am. Soc. for Parenteral and Enteral Nutrition Inc., Soc. for Pediatric Res., Internat. Coll. of Pediatrics; contbg. author 3 book chpts., 1978; author/contbg. author: 60+ articles pub. in profl. jours., 30 pub. abstracts; mil: lt. comdr. Med. Corps USNR 1968-70, capt. 1984-92; Democrat; Jewish; rec: golf. Res: 70 Green Valley Court San Anselmo 94960 Ofc: 2620 Northgate Mall San Rafael 94903

LIEPMANN, HANS WOLFGANG, physicist; b. July 3, 1914, Berlin, nat. 1945; s. Prof. Dr. Wilhelm L. (M.D.) and Emma (Leser) L.; m. Kate Kaschinsky, June 19, 1939 (div. 1954); m. Dietlind Wegener Goldschmidt, Sept. 27, 1954; children: Till W. b. 1955, Dorian b. 1957; edn: exptl. physics, Univ. of Istanbul 1933-35, Univ. Prague, Czech. 1935, PhD, Univ. of Zurich, Switz. 1938. Career: research fellow Univ. of Zurich 1938-39; res. fellow Calif. Inst. of Tech., Pasadena 1939-45, asst. prof. 1945-46, assoc. prof. 1946-49, prof. 1949-76, Charles Lee Powell Prof. of Fluid Mechanics and Thermodynamics 1976-83, Theodore von Karman Prof. of Aeronautics 1983-85, dir. Graduate Aeronautical Labs. 1972-85, exec. ofcr. for aeronautics 1976-85; mem. res. & tech. advy. com. on basic res. NASA, Wash. DC; awards: physics prize Univ. Zurich 1939, Am. Acad. of Arts and Scis. fellow 1960, Nat. Acad. of Engring. 1965, Ludwig Prandtl Ring - Deutsche Gesellschaft fur Luft - und Raumfahrt (Ger. Soc. for Aero.) 1968, Nat. Acad. of Scis. 1971, Monie A. Ferst award Sigma Xi 1978, Michelson-Morley award 1979, fluid dynamics prize Am. Physical Soc. 1980, fluids engring. award ASME 1984, Indian Acad. of Scis. hon. fellow 1985, Hon. Dr. Engring. Technical Univ. Aachen 1985, Otto Laporte award Am.. Physical Soc. 1985, Nat. Medal of Sci. 1986, Guggenheim medal 1986, Max Planck Inst. fgn. fellow 1988, National Medal of Technology 1993; mem: Am. Inst. Aero. & Astro. (hon. fellow), Am. Physical Soc. (fellow), AAAS (fellow), Sigma Xi, Ger. Soc. for Applied Math. and Mechs.; coauthor: Aerodynamics of a Compressible Fluid (w. A.E. Puckett, 1947), Elements of Gasdynamics (w. A.Roshko, 1957); rec: tennis. Res: 555 Haverstock Rd La Canada-Flintridge 91011 Ofc: Caltech MC 105-50 1201 E California Blvd Pasadena 91125

LIGGINS, GEORGE LAWSON, microbiologist, manufacturing company president; b. June 19, 1937, Roanoke, Va.; m. Joyce Preston, Sept. 3, 1966; 1 son, George Lawson b. 1971; edn: BA, Hampton Inst. 1962; MeHarry Med. Coll. 1963; Duke Univ. 1966; MPH, Univ. N.C. 1969; PhD, Univ. Va. 1975; career: med. technologist Vets. Hosp., Hampton, Va. 1964-66; research tech. Univ. N.C. Med. Sch., Chapel Hill 1967-69; postdoctorate Scripps Clinic, La Jolla 1975-76; Salk Inst. 1976-77; research and devel. dir. Baxter Travenol, Round Lake, Ill. 1977-83; pres., COO Internat. Immunology, Murrieta 1983-86; pres., ceo Bacton Assay Systems Inc. 1986–; cons. Beckman Instruments, Brea 1987-88; Baxter Paramax, Irvine 1988-89; awards: NIH HHS fellowship 1975, Am. Cancer Soc. fellowship 1975, Outstanding Alumnus award Hampton Univ. 1994; mem: Am. Assn. Clin. Chemist, Am.Heart Assn., Am. Soc. Microbiology, Am. Chemical Soc., Am. Soc. Pub. Health; tech. papers abstracts and papers pub. in sci. jours. 1974–; Republican; Methodist; rec: music, golf, tennis. Ofc: Bacton Assay Systems, Inc. 772-A North Twin Oaks Valley Rd San Marcos 92069

LIGHTFOOT, WILLIAM HUGH, lawyer; b. Sept. 3, Minneapolis, Minn.; s. William Homer and Elva Asenith (Albright) L.; m. Trudi; edn: BA, JD, Drake Univ.; LLM (taxation), Golden Gate Univ.; admitted bar: Calif., Tenn., U.S. Supreme Ct. Career: Law Office, William H. Lightfoot, 1973–; estate planning, Pruneyard, Campbell; mem: Santa Clara Co. Bar Assn., Commonwealth Club of Calif., Masons, Scottish Rite, Shriner, Am. Legion; mil: 2nd lt., USMC, UN Medal, Korean Service, Presdl. Unit Citation; Republican; rec: exercise, politics, social problems. Res: Cambell.

LIJPHART, AREND, political scientist; b. Aug. 17, 1936, Apeldoorn, Netherlands; s. Anthonius and Mathilde Theodora (d'Angremond) L.; m. Eva Tamm, Aug. 10, 1959; m. Gisela Meyers, June 24, 1988; children: Antony b. 1962, Anna b. 1965; edn: BA, Principia Coll. 1958; MA, Yale Univ. 1959; PhD, 1963. Career: instr. political sci. Elmira Coll., N.Y. 1961-63; asst. prof. political sci. UC Berkeley 1963-68; prof. internat. rels. Univ. Leiden, Netherlands 1968-78; prof. political sci. UCSD, La Jolla 1978–; ed. European Jour. of Political Research, Colchester, U.K. 1971-75; awards: Fulbright grant 1955-56, Am. Political Sci. Assn. Ralph J. Bunche 1979, German Marshall Fund fellowship 1983-84, Guggenheim fellowship 1984-85; mem: Internat. Studies Assn. (v.p. 1976-77), Am. Political Sci. Assn. (secty. 1983-84, v.p. 1987-88, pres. 1995-96), Council for European Studies (exec. com. 1983-85), Royal Netherlands Acad. Scis., Am. Acad. Arts & Scis.; author: Politics of Accomodation, 1968, Democracy in Plural Socs., 1977, Democracies, 1984, Power-Sharing in S.Africa, 1985, Electoral Systems and Party Systems, 1994; rec: classical music, table tennis. Ofc: Univ. of Calif. San Diego La Jolla 92093-0521

LIKENS, ROBERT LEE, computer consultant; b. March 7, 1949, Louisville, Ky.; s. Carl Robert and Thelma Lee (Gambrell) L.; m. In Ja Um, July 12, 1971; children: Michelle Lee b. 1972, Natalie Lynn b. 1976; edn: Ohio St. Univ. 1967-68; BSBA, Franklin Univ. 1978. Career: systems analyst J.C. Penney, Columbus, Ohio 1975-80; v.p. Security Pacific Automation Co., Brea 1980-94; instr. N. Orange Co. Regional Occupational Program, La Palma 1984-89; mem: Seven Tech. Users Forum (pres. 1983-85); mil: sgt. AUS 1969-71; Republican; rec: archaeology. Res: 11532 E 186th St #5 Artesia 90701 Ofc: Sphinx Research Group Inc. 15935 Foothill Blvd Sylmar 91342

LILIEN, DAVID M., economist; b. Feb. 10, 1951, Los Angeles; s. Sam and Cecil (Lewis) L.; m. Carolyn Stone, July 4, 1987; 1 son, Mark b. 1987; edn: BA magna cum laude, UC Berkeley 1973; PhD, MIT 1977. Career: asst. prof. UCSD, La Jolla 1977-82; USC, L.A. 1982-84; prof. UC Irvine 1985–; owner, developer Quantitative Micro Software 1981–; honors: Phi Beta Kappa; mem: Am. Econ. Assn., Econometric Soc.; articles pub. in profl. jours. (1979–), software pub. (1981–). Ofc: Quantitative Micro Software 4521 Campus Dr Ste 336 Irvine 92715

LILLIE, MILDRED L., presiding justice State Court of Appeal; b. Jan. 25, 1915, Ida Grove, Ia.; d. Ottmar A. and Florence E. (Martin) Kluckhohn; m. Cameron L. Lillie, Mar. 18, 1947 (dec. 1959); m. 2d A. V. Falcone, Aug. 27, 1966; edn: AB, UC Berkeley 1935; JD, UC Boalt Hall of Law 1938; hon. degrees: LLD, Western States Univ. Coll. of Law 1966; LLD, Pepperdine Univ. 1979; admitted to practice, State Bar of Calif. 1938, Fed. Ct. 1942, US Supreme Ct. 1961. Career: with the City Atty.'s Ofc., Alameda 1938-39; pvt. law practice Fresno, 1939-42, Los Angeles 1946-47; asst. US Atty., LA 1942-46; judge, Municipal Ct., City of LA 1947-49; judge, Superior Ct., Co. of LA 1949-58; justice Ct.of Appeal, State of Calif. 1958-84, presiding justice, 1984–, assoc. justice pro tem Supreme Ct. of Calif. 1960–; adminstrv. presiding justice 2nd Appellate Dist. Ct. of Appeal, 1988–; mem: Calif. Judicial Council 1961-63, 1987-89; bd. trustees Boalt Hall Fund 1986–; bd. vis. Pepperdine Law Sch. 1985–; awards: Cardinals' award 1994, Cardinal McIntyre award Cath. Press Club LA 1981, LA Times woman of yr. 1952, Muses woman of yr. Mus. of Sci. & Ind. 1980, citation Boalt Hall of Law Alumni Assn. 1985, appellate justice of yr. LA Trial Lawyers Assn. 1986, Humanitarian Award NCCJ 1991; mem: ABA, Fed. Bar Assn., LA Co. Bar Assn., Calif. Judges Assn., Nat. Assn. of Women Judges, Women Lawyers Assn.; civic: LA Area C.of C. (bd. dirs. 1975-82), Town Hall of Calif., Les Dames de Champagne, Pepperdine Univ. Assocs., NCCJ (presiding co-chair 1986-87), Orphanage Guild, Ladies of Charity; clubs: Los Angeles Athletic, Ebell (LA), Soroptimist Internat. LA; rec: reading, writing, painting, cooking. Ofc: 300 S Spring St South Tower Los Angeles 90013

LIM, EUSEBIO GAN, otolaryngologist; b. Aug. 14, Manila, Philippines; s. Bien Liong and Bella (Gan) L.; edn: MD, Univ. Santo Tomas, 1952, AA, 1947 Fellow Internat. Acad. of Cosmetic Surgery. Career: otolaryngologist Union Medical Clinic, Huntington Park, Calif.; honors: mem. Am. Biog. Inst. (res. advy. bd.), Internat. Who's Who Intellectuals, Confederation of Chivalry 1991–, Fellow Intl. Biog. Centre, Cambridge, Eng. (dep. dir. general 1995–); mem: L.A. Co. Med. Assn.; Fellow Am. Acad. Otol., Am. Acad. Plastic and Reconstrv. Surg., Pan Am. Otorhinolaryngology; R.Cath.; rec: photog., car racing. Res: 11730 Sunset Blvd Los Angeles 90049 Ofc: Union Medical Clinic 5421 Pacific Blvd Huntington Park 90255

LIMBAUGH, RONALD HADLEY, historian, educator, administrator; b. Jan. 22, 1938, Emmett, Ida.; s. John Hadley and Evelyn Eloise (Mortimore) L.; m. Marilyn Kay Rice, June 16, 1963; 1 dau. Sally Ann b. 1973; edn: BA, Coll. of Idaho, 1960; MA, Univ. Idaho, 1962, PhD, 1967. Career: history librarian Idaho Historical Soc., Boise 1963-66; instr. Boise Coll., 1964-66; prof. of history Univ. of the Pacific, Stockton, Calif. 1966–, archivist U.O.P. 1968-87, actg. assoc. dean 1975-76, dir. John Muir Center U.O.P., 1989–; dir. Holt-Atherton Ctr., Stockton 1984-87; exec. dir. Conf. of Calif. Hist. Soc., Stockton 1990–; awards: NDEA fellow Univ. Idaho 1960-63, Phi Kappa Phi 1962, Rockwell Hunt Prof. of Calif. Hist. U.O.P. 1989–; mem. Org. Am. Historians 1963–, Western History Assn. 1965–, AAUP 1970–, Phi Kappa Phi (pres. U.O.P. chapt. 1974, 88), Stockton Corral of Westerners (pres. "sheriff" 1978), Jedediah Smith Soc., Stockton (sec. 1989–), Mining Hist. Assn. (1992–, nom. com. 1993–); author: Rocky Mountain Carpetbaggers, 1982, numerous articles in hist. jours., 1969–, editor (microform edit.) John Muir Papers, 1986, contbg. writer John Muir Newsletter, 1991–; mil: pvt. US Army 1955-56; Indep.; Christian Humanist; rec: hiking, golf, birding. Ofc: Univ. of the Pacific 3601 Pacific Ave Stockton 95211

LIN, HARRY CHING-JYI, certified public accountant; b. July 22, 1954, Taichung, Taiwan, R.O.C.; s. Mu-Tze and Yu-Yen L.; m. Mei-Hwa Lin, July 31, 1961; 1 son Michael Yen-Ting b. 1990; edn: Master's degree, Eastern New Mexico Univ., Portales, 1981; cert. public accountant, 1992. Career: accountant James S. Chang, CPA, Orange, Calif., 1981-85; supervisor Price Waterhouse CPA's, Taipei, Taiwan, 1985-87; CEO, Grand Foremost Inc., Commerce, Calif., 1988-92; ptnr. Chang & Lin CPA's, City of Industry, Calif., 1992-94; ptnr. Tang, Chen, Chang & Lin CPA's, City of Industry, 1994–; accounting advisor: Taiwan Innkeeper Assn.

of So. Calif., L.A. 1992-95, SCCAEPA, L.A. 1994-95, Am. Internat. Bank, City of Industry 1995; advisor Greater L.A. Hotel & Motel Assn. 1990-92; mem: Am. Inst. of CPA's 1992–, Calif. Soc. of CPA's 1992–, Sino-Am. CPA Assn. (pres. 1993-94), Rowland Heights Chinese Lions Club (v.p. 1993-95), Taiwanese-Am. C.of C. 1995–, Overseas Chinese Assn. (treas. 1995–), Disting. Citizens Soc. Internat., World Assn. of So. Calif. (treas. 1995–); rec: swimming. Ofc: Tang, Chen, Chang & Lin CPA's 17800 Castleton St #600 City of Industry 91748

LIN, HUA L., physician-gastroenterologist; b. July 2, 1947, Taiwan, nat. 1984; s. Tsu W. and Yuen (Lu) L.; m. Ching L., May 30, 1976; child: James C. b. 1983; edn: MD, Nat. Taiwan Unvi. Sch. of Med., 7 yrs. Career: intern Beekman Downtown Hosp., N.Y.C. 1974-75, med. resident 1975-76; med. res. Catholic Medical Ctr., Jamaica, N.Y. 1976-77; G.I. fellow Good Samaritan Hosp., Phoenix, Az. 1977-79; gastroenterologist pvt. practice, 1979–, mem. med. staff Mercy Hosp. (also med. dir. GI Lab), Gr. Bakersfield Memorial Hosp. and San Joaquin Hosp., Bakersfield, Calif. 1979–; chmn., dept. of medicine, Mercy Hosp., Bakersfield 1993; bd. certified internal medicine ABIM 1978, cert. subsplty. gastroent. 1983; Fellow Am. Coll. Gastroent., mem. Am. Gastroenterol. Assn., Am. Soc. for Gastrointestinal Endoscopy, fellow Am. Coll. Physicians (nat. mem.), Calif. Med. Assn., Kern Co. Med. Soc.; club: Bakersfield Country; Republican; rec: fishing, travel. Ofc: Hua L. Lin MD Inc. 2225 19th St Bakersfield 93301

LIN, JAMES PEICHENG, professor of mathematics; b. Sept. 30, 1949, NY, NY; s. Tung Hua and Susan L.; m. Julie Sano, June 24, 1990; edn: BS, UC Berkeley, PhD, Princeton. Career: asst., asso., prof. math. UC San Diego, 1974-78, 78-81, 81–; vis. prof. Princeton 1978, Hebrew Univ., Jerusalem 1981-82, Neuchatel Univ., Switz. 1984; appt. task force Nat. Res. Council Minority Edn. Bd., 1992–; bd. Asians in Higher Edn., 1987-91; chair, panel on equity and diversity, Mathematical Scis. Edn. Bd.; awards: Sloan Found. fellow 1977-78, Phi Beta Kappa, Chancellor's Tchg. Award UCSD 1981, NSF grantee 1974-90; mem. Am. Math. Soc. 1974–; author: Steenrod Squares and Connectivity in H-Spaces, 1990; rec: tennis, fishing, backpacking. Res: 8239 Paseo del Ocaso La Jolla 92037 Ofc: 7157 APM, Univ. Calif. San Diego, La Jolla 92093

LIN, TAO, applications manager; b. Aug. 6, 1958, Shanghai, P.R.O.C.; came to U.S. 1986; s. Zeng-hui Lin and Wei-jing (Wu) Wu; m. Ping Kuo, Aug. 18, 1989; son, Jason b. 1990, dau. Jessie b. 1992; edn: BS, East China Normal Univ., Shanghai, 1982; MS, Tohoku Univ., Sendai, Japan 1985; PhD, Tohoku Univ., 1990. Career: technician Dongfong Electronics Inc., Shanghai 1977-78; research asst. Electronics Research Lab. UC Berkeley, 1986-87, postgrad. researcher 1987-88; application engr. Integrated Device Technology Inc., Santa Clara 1988-90; sr. applications engr. Sierra Semiconductor Corp., San Jose 1990-91; applications mgr. Sierra Semiconductor Corp., San Jose 1991–; mem. IEEE; pub. articles in tech. jours. Res: 3552 Rockett Dr Fremont 94538 Ofc: Sierra Semiconductor Corp. 2075 N Capitol Ave San Jose 95132

LINAWEAVER, WALTER ELLSWORTH, JR., physician, educator; b. Oct 16, 1928, San Pedro; s. Walter Ellsworth (dec. 1989) and Catherine Breathed (Bridges) L.; m. Anne Whitlock, Oct. 5, 1957; children: Catherine b. 1958, Nancy b. 1959, Walter, III b. 1962; edn: BA cum laude, Pomona Coll. Claremont 1952; MD, Univ. Rochester Sch. Med. 1956. Career: intern pediatrics Univ. Rochester Med.Center 1956-57; asst. resident UCLA 1957-58; resident pediatrics Univ. Rochester Med. Ctr. 1958-59; fellow allergy and immunology Univ. Colo. 1959-61, instr. pediatrics Univ. Colo. Sch. Med. 1961; pvt. practice, Riverside 1962–; bd. dirs. Riverside Med. Clin. 1983-89; asst. clin. prof. pediatrics Loma Linda Univ. Sch. Med. 1963–; staff Riverside Comm. Hosp. 1962–; cons. Head Start, River Co. 1965–; honors: Pomona Coll. Athletic Hall of Fame (1979); mem: Am. Acad. Allergy & Immunology (fellow 1965), Am. Acad. Pediatrics (fellow 1962), L.A. Acad. Med. (fellow 1980), Southwestern Pediatric Soc. (fellow 1970), AMA, CMA, River Co. Med. Assn. (1962–); 2 case reports pub. (1960, 76); mil: s.sgt. AUS 1946-48; Republican; Presbyterian; rec: gardening, Am. and Mil. history. Res: 1296 Tiger Tail Dr. Riverside 92506 Ofc: Riverside Medical Clinic 3660 Arlington Ave. Riverside 92506

LINDE, GERALD (JED) B., psychotherapist; b. Sept. 11, 1938, New York; s. Roland Oskar and Aileen M. (Man) L.; m. 2d. Maria Esther Manni, Feb. 25, 1960; children: Beth b. 1955, Monica b. 1961; edn: AA, Pasadena City Coll. 1958; BA summa cum laude, Univ. Americas Mexico City 1960; MA, Internat. Coll. L.A. 1980; PhD, Sierra Univ. 1987; Lic. Marriage Family and Child Counselor (MFCC) Calif. 1981). Career: fgn. correspondent Copley, Mexico City 1964-67; adminstr. San Francisco Zen Center 1967-76; chief counselor Monterey Youth Project 1976-83; field faculty Sierra Univ. 1983-88; chief counselor RHP Services, King City 1984–; pvt. practice, Carmel Valley and Salinas 1981–; honors: Who's Who Students in Am. Colls. & Univs.; mem: Calif. Assn. Marriage Family Therapists; author: Zen & The Ugly Duckling, 1987, num. articles pub. in profl. jours., 1961-73; R.Cath., Zen Buddhist; rec: hiking, skindiving, travel. Res: 19 Catalina Ave Salinas 93901-1319

LINDQUIST, MICHAEL LEE, financial services executive; b. Aug. 16, 1953, Augsburg, Germany; s. John D. and Lucille (Casto) L.; m. Lana L. Chism, Apr. 19, 1975; edn: BA in acctg., Central Mo. Univ., 1978. Career: bank examiner

Div. Fin., Jefferson City, Mo. 1978-81; job acctg. coord. Farmland Inds., Kansas City, Mo. 1981-83; EDP auditor Broad Inc., Atlanta, Ga. 1983-85, audit mgr. 1985-89, audit director SunAmerica, Inc. (formerly Broad, Inc.), Los Angeles, 1989-93, v.p. 1993–; mil: cpl. USMC 1971-73; rec: hang gliding. Ofc: SunAmerica, Inc. 11601 Wilshire Blvd Los Angeles 90025

LINDQUIST, STANLEY E., professor emeritus, psychologist; b. Nov. 9, 1917, Georgetown, Tx.; s. Elmer H. and Esther Lovina (Nyberg) L.; m. Ingrid Waldren, Aug. 26; children: Douglas b. 1943, Russell b. 1946, Brent b. 1953; edn: BA, Calif. State Univ., Fresno 1940; PhD, Univ. of Chicago 1950; LLD (hon.), Trinity Coll. 1976; career: prof., Trinity Coll. Chgo. 1946-53; res. assoc., Univ. of Chgo. 1949-53; prof., Calif. State Univ., Fresno 1953-89, prof. emeritus 1989–; founder/ pres., Link Care Found., Fresno 1964–, pres. emeritus, 1991–; cons., Liberia, Agape, Monrovia, Liberia 1990–;mem: Am. Psychology Assn. 1950–; pres., ofcr., Am. Sci. Affiliation 1960–; ofcr., pres., Christian Edn. Assn. 1953–; ofcr., pres., Christian Assn. for Psychological Studies 1958–; bd. mem., Pastoral Counseling Inst. 1989–; author: Action Helping Skills, 1975; Reach Out, Become An Encourager, 1983; mil: pfc. US Army Medics, 1943-46; Republican; Evangelical Free Ch.; rec: woodworking, fishing. Res: 5142 N. College Fresno 93704

LINDSEY, MORT, conductor, composer, musical administrator; b. Mar. 21, 1923, Newark, N.J.; s. Irving Otto and Tessie (Henoch) L.; m. Betty Bonney, Oct. 9, 1954; children: Bonney b. 1946, Steven b. 1956, Trevor b. 1963; edn: BA, Columbia Univ., 1944; MA, Teachers Coll. Columbia, 1948, EdD, 1974. Career: staff pianist Nat. Bdcstg. Co., NY, NY 1948-50; staff conductor Columbia Bdcstg. Co., 1950-54; Am. Bdcstg. Co., 1957-59; musical dir. Judy Garland TV Special Series, Hollywood 1960-64; musical dir. Merv Griffin, NY and Hollywood 1964–; musical dir. Barbra Streisand, 2 TV Specials, NY 1969; assoc. conductor Barbra Streisand concert tour 1994; composer, 8 motion pictures, 1963-78; awards: Grammy, album of year- Judy Garland at Carnegie Hall, Am. Acad. Recording Artists 1961, Emmy, outstanding achiev. in music-Barbra Streisand in Central Park, Nat. Acad. TV Arts & Scis.; mem: Sinfonia Frat. 1948, ASCAP 1957, Am. Guild of Authors & Composers 1960, Acad. of TV Artists 1962, Acad. of Recording Artists 1972; composer motion pictures: 40 Pounds of Trouble (Universal, 1963), Stolen Hours (United Artists, 1964), The Best Man (UA, 1964), Gay Purree (U.P.A., 1964), I Could Go On Singing (UA, 1964), Real Life (Paramount, 1978); mil: 2d lt. USAF 1943-46; Christian Sci.; rec: oil painting, raising show horses. Res: 6970 Fernhill Dr Malibu 90265 Ofc: Merv Griffin Productions 9860 Wilshire Blvd Beverly Hills 90210

LINDSLEY, ALAN LAWRENCE, architect; b. April 18, 1955, Dallas, Tx.; s. Robert Porter and Dorothy Gertrude (Johnston) L.; m. Karen Jess, Aug. 5, 1978; children: Ryan b. 1982, Bryce b. 1985, Devon b. 1989; edn: Univ. Colo. Boulder 1977. Career: architect, assoc. Gensler & Assocs., S.F. 1977-90; Brereton Architects, 1990-94; Lindsley Architecture & Lighting, 1994–; event coordinator AIA Learning Through Edn. Arts Program, S.F. 1986-87; design cons. TOPS, Orinda 1986, 88, 89; mem: AIA, Illumination Engring. Soc., Nat. Council Arch. Registration Bds., Bohemian Club, Historic Landmarks Com. Orinda; Episcopalian; rec: wilderness sports, photog., music. Res: 261 La Espiral Orinda 94563 Ofc: Lindsley Architecture & Lighting 261 La Espiral Orinda 94563

LINK, GEORGE H., lawyer; b. March 26, 1939, Sacramento; s. Hoyle and Corrie Elizabeth (Evans) L.; m. Betsy Leland; children: Thomas Hamilton and Christopher Leland b. 1968; edn: BA, UC Berkeley 1961; LL.B, Harvard Univ. Law Sch. 1964. Career: atty. assoc. Brobeck Phleger & Harrison, San Francisco 1964-70, ptnr., Los Angeles 1970–, mng. ptnr. 1976–, mng. ptnr. of the firm 1992-; chmn. Pacific Rim Advisory Council 1992–; mem. Univ. Calif. Bd. Regents 1971-74, pres. Calif. Alumni Assn. (1970-75), trustee Berkeley Found. 1970-74; mem: Am. Bar Found. (fellow), Calif. Bar Assn., Calif. Hist. Soc. (bd. of trustees, reg. v.p.), Yosemite Fund (bd. govs.), Bohemian Club, Calif. Club, Jonathan Club; Republican; Methodist. Res: 315 N Carmelina Ave Los Angeles 90049 Ofc: Brobeck Phleger & Harrison 550 S Hope St Los Angeles 90071

LINKLETTER, ARTHUR GORDON, public speaker, television personality; b. July 17, 1912, Moosejaw, Saskatchewan, Canada; s. Rev. Fulton and Mary (Metzler) L.; m. Lois Foerster, Nov. 28, 1935; children: Jack L. b. 1937, Dawn b. 1939, Sharon b. 1946; edn: BA, San Diego State 1934. Career: announcer KGO, San Diego; TV host House Party Is Funny (29 yrs.) 1947; House Party, CBS TV daytime, 5 days weekly (30 yrs.) 1946; Talent Scouts, CBS night time, once weekly (2 yrs.) 1958; The Linkletter Show, NBC weekly, night time (2 yrs.) 1970; speaker 100 times yearly; trustee Oil and Gas Exploration, Pepperdine Univ.; mem. 12 bds. of dirs. Springfield Coll., Md.; commr. gen. U.S. Exhibit to Expo '88, Brisbane, Australia, rank of Ambassador; entertainer workers in shipyards No. Calif. during WWII; awards: 9 hon. coll./univ. degrees; disting. svc.: Crusade for Freedom and Mt. Sinai Men's Club and Heart of Gold award 1960; citation disting. svc. Comm. Chests Am., citation meritorious svc. Nat. Council Child Safety, Radio-TV Eds. So. Calif. award outstanding contbn. home entertainment, TV-Radio-Mirror award TV/radio excellence 1949-58, LA City Council/Co. awards work w/youth and fostering good citizenship; svc. awards: Newpaper Boys Am.,

Nat. Found. Infantile Paralysis, Nat. Nephrosis Found.; Goodwill Award Goodwill Indus. Am., Brotherhood of Children award Foster Parents Plan for War Orphans, Brotherhood award Nat. Conf. of Christians and Jews, Grandfather of Yr. Nat. Father's Day Com. 1962, d'Officier Commandeur Confrerie des Chevaliers du Tastevin 1961, salesman of yr., Houston 1961, Sports award of Yr., Chgo. 1962, House Party nominated for Emmy, best daytime TV pgm. 1962, Man of Yr. City of Hope 1964; civic: Bohemian Club (30 yrs.), YMCA, Foster Parents Plan, World Vision Inst., Toastmasters Supreme, The Masquers, Pres. Council Physical Fitness; BSA, Nat. Heart Fund, chmn. Easter Seals 1961; author: 17 books incl. Kids Say The Darndest Things, 2 yr. best seller list plus 16 other titles; Republican; Prot.; rec: surfing, ski. Res: 1100 Bel Air Rd Los Angeles 90077 Ofc: 8500 Wilshire Blvd Ste 815 Beverly Hills 90211

LINN, ROGER DAVID, lawyer; b. Nov. 7, 1949, Chicago, Ill.; s. Russell Edwin and Ruth Anita (Mueller) L.; m. Debra, June 27, 1981; children: Rachel Erin b. 1983, Tyler Russell b. 1986, Trevor William b. 1990; edn: Florissant Valley Comm. Coll. 1967-68; BS bus. admin., Drake Univ. 1971; JD, Calif. Western Sch. Law 1978; admitted State Bar Calif. 1978. Career: staff atty. U.S. Securities & Exchange Commn., Wash. DC 1978-80, branch chief, Los Angeles 1980-82; corp. counsel Nat. Investment Devel. Corp. 1982-85; ptnr. Van Camp & Johnson, Sacto. 1985-90; Downey Brand Seymour & Rohwer 1990-91; Bartel Eng Linn & Schroder, Sacto. 1991–; instr. UCLA para-legal program 1981-83; mem: Sacto. Co. Bar, Calif. St. Bar (franchise sect.), Calif. Bar Assn., Roseville Rotary, Alpha Kappa Psi, Rotary Internat.; mil: petty ofcr. USN 1971-75, cmdr. USNR, JAGC 1980–; Lutheran; rec: tennis, camping. Ofc: Bartel Eng Linn & Schroder 300 Capitol Mall Ste 1100 Sacramento 95814

LINSON, DENNIS RICHARD, healthcare executive; b. Nov. 16, 1951, Hollywood; s. Bernard and Rose Carole (Vinokur) L.; m. Sima Levy, March 24, 1974; children: Adam Dean b. 1975, Jeremy Michael b. 1980, Maya Naomi b. 1983; edn: BA, UC Berkeley 1974; MBA, Golden Gate Univ. 1978. Career: v.p. Santa Monica Hosp., UniHealth Inc., Santa Monica 1974-80; sr. cons. Compucare Inc., Reston, Va. 1980-84; v.p. Methodist Hosp., Arcadia 1984–; instr. Chapman Univ., Orange 1983–, chmn. advy. council MHA program 1984-85; honors: BSA Eagle Scout 1966, Encino Jaycees Outstanding Young Man 1969; mem: Am. Coll. Healthcare Execs. (fellow), Healthcare Execs. of So. Calif., College Healthcare Information Mgmt. Execs. (CHIME), Healthcare Info. & Mgmt. Systems Soc., Congregation Bnai Israel; Jewish; rec: reading. Address: Irvine 92720-1952

LIPCHIK, HAROLD, corporate executive; b. Apr. 17, 1928, N.Y.C.; s. Samuel W. and Ida (Gutterman) L. m. Elaine Greenberg, Mar. 23, 1952; children: Alan b. 1953, Debra b. 1956; edn: BSME, Carnegie Mellon Univ., 1948; grad. work in bus. adm. N.Y. Univ., 1948-49. Career: project engr. 1950-54; v.p. AMF Inc., N.Y. 1954-66; v.p. Chromalloy Am. Corp., Clayton, Mo. 1966-71; pres. Water Treatment Corp., City of Industry, Calif. 1968-71; pres., dir. Halco Assocs., Tarzana 1971–; v.p. National Technical Systems, Calabasas 1984–; mem. Assn. for Corporate Growth 1988–; pres. L.A. Hebrew H.S., 1978-84; United Synagogue of Am., L.A. (pres. 1976-78); rec: golf, swimming, fishing. Res: 4429 Trancas Pl Tarzana 91356 Ofc: National Technical Systems 24007 Ventura Blvd Calabasas 91302

LIPPITT, LOUIS, aerospace engineer (retired); b. Mar. 19, 1924, N.Y., N.Y.; s. Louis Lippitt, Sr. and Susan Davie (Anderson) L.; m. Adele Dorothy Wissmann, June 27, 1948; children: Laurie b. 1951, Craig b. 1953, Bonnie b. 1957, Nancie b. 1961; edn: BS in physics, City Coll. NY 1947; MA in geology, Columbia Univ., NY 1953; PhD in geology, Columbia Univ. 1959; reg. geophysicist, reg. geologist, Calif., 1969. Career: physicist Columbia Univ. 1947-51; physicist N.Y. Univ. 1952-53; geologist/geophysicist Standard Oil Co. Calif. (now Chevron), Oildale, Calif. 1954-58; staff engr. Lockheed Missiles & Space Co., Vandenberg AFB, Calif. 1958-87; part-time instr. Hancock Coll., Santa Maria, Calif. 1969–; part-time instr. Chapman Coll., VAFB, Calif. 1985-86; awards: Honorarium, N.Y. State 1952; fellow (sr.) Geological Soc. of Am. 1954–; mem: Sigma Xi 1954–, Am. Geophysical Union 1958–; civic: project leader 4H, Calif. 1960-77; author: profl. article, 1959. Mil: PFC, US Army 1943-46; Lutheran; rec: sailing, masters swimming. Res: 696 Raymond Ave. Santa Maria 93455-2760

LIPSHITZ, HOWARD DAVID, biologist; b. Oct. 30, 1955, Durban, S.A., naturalized U.S., 1991; s. Marcus and Annie Zelda (Cohen) L.; m. Susanna Maxwell Lewis, Sept. 13, 1986; children: Sarah Starr b. 1990; edn: BS, Univ. of Natal, S.A. 1975, BSc. (hons) 1976; M.Phil., Yale Univ., 1980, PhD, 1983. Career: postdoctoral fellow Stanford Univ., 1983-86; asst. prof. Calif. Inst. of Tech., Pasadena 1986-92, assoc. prof. 1992–; awards: Damant Science Prize, Univ. of Natal 1975, S.A. National Scholarship Yale Univ. 1978-80, Helen Hay Whitney Found. Fellow, Stanford Univ. 1983-86, Searle Found. scholar Calif. Inst. of Tech. 1988-91; mem. Genetics Soc. of Am. 1979–, AAAS (Fellow), Nat. Sci. Found. (Eukaryotic Genetics Panel 1993–), Am. Soc. for Cell Biology 1993–, Soc. for Devel. Biology 1993–; assoc. ed. "Zygote" 1993–;author book chapters (4, 1981–), jour. articles (17+, 1975–). Ofc: Calif. Inst. of Technology Div. Biology 156-29 Pasadena 91125

LIPSIG, ETHAN, lawyer; b. Dec. 11, 1948, New York; s. Daniel Allen and Hadassah (Adler) L.; edn: BA, Pomona Coll. 1969; postgrad. studies, St. Edmund Hall 1969-70; JD, UCLA Law Sch. 1974. Career: assoc. atty. Latham & Watkins, Los Angeles 1974-80; assoc. atty., ptnr. Paul Hastings Janofsky & Walker 1980–; honors: Order of Coif; mem: Am. Bar Assn. (employee benefit com., tax. and labor rels. sect. 1975), Calif. C.of C. (healthcare com. 1988), Calif. Club, Los Angeles Men's Garden Club; author: Downsizing: Practice and Law (BNA, 1996), num. articles pub. in profl. jours.; rec: travel, gardening, wine. Ofc: Paul Hastings Janofsky & Walker 555 S Flower St Los Angeles 90071

LITZ, CHARLES JOSEPH, JR., P.E. aerospace engineer; b. Nov. 5, 1928, Phila.; s. Charles J. Sr. and Marie Anna (Muth) L.; m. Ronalda Clara, Apr. 17, 1971; children: Stacey Ann, Mark Charles; edn: AE, Martin Coll., 1948; BSME, Univ. Dela., 1951; postgrad., Texas Western, 1954-56; MS, La Salle Coll., 1959; M.I.T., Cambridge, MA 1958-62; reg. profl. engr.1960–. Career: mech. engr. U.S. Naval Air Devel. Ctr., Johnsville, Pa. 1951-54; mil. service U.S. Army, instr. Army Air Defense Sch., 1954-56; res. assoc., project engr. U.S. Army Advanced Res. Agy., Phila. 1956-60; cons. ballistic missile command for minute man missiles USAF, Phila., 1959-63; elec.-mech. engr. Brown Inst. Minn-Honeywell, Phila. 1956-58; sr. mech. engr. U.S. Army Frankford Arsenal, Phila. 1959-77; sr. design engr. Ford Motor Co., Dearborn, Mich. 1977-81; sr. mfg. engr. Ford Aerospace Co., Newport Beach, Calif. 1981-86; sr. engr. scientist Space Systems Lab., McDonnell-Douglas, Huntington Beach 1986–; recipient award for sci. res. Secty. U.S. Army 1968; mem: ASME; publ. articles: "Simulation Modeling & Testing of a Satellite Despin System" AIAA Flight Simulation Tech. Conf., Boston 1989, "Testing of PAM-S/ULYSSES Despin System" 12th Aerospace Testing Sem., Manhattan Beach 1990, "Unique Utilization of the Design of Experiment Taguchi Methodology and Math Modeling for Cost Effective Pyroshock Testing & Analysis" 14th Aerospace Testing Sem. Manhattan Beach 1993, "Laser Doppler Vibrometer - Unique Use in Pyroshock Response Spectra", 1st Internat. Conf. on Vibration Measurement by Laser Techniques, Advances & Applications, Ancona, Italy 1994, "Design of Experiment Application of Technology in Changing Times to Evaluate Three Different Measurement Systems", Measurement Sci. Conf., Anaheim 1995; contbr. num. articles to profl. jours., 11 patents in field; rec: music, reading, fitness, writing, philosophy. Res: 29221 Tieree Laguna Niguel 92677 Ofc: McDonnell Douglas Aerospace-West 5301 Bolsa Ave Huntington Beach 92647 Tel: 714/896-2172

LIU, JIA-MING, electrical engineering educator; b. July 13, 1953, Taichung, Taiwan, naturalized US 1990; s. Min-chih and Hsin (Lin) L.; m. Vida Hang Chang; children: Janelle b. 1991; edn: BS in electrophysics Nat. Chiao Tung Univ., 1975; SM in applied physics, Harvard Univ., 1979, PhD applied physics, 1982; reg. profl. electrical engr. Taiwan 1977. Career: asst. prof. SUNY at Buffalo, N.Y. 1982-84; sr. mem. tech. staff GTE Labs Inc., Waltham, Mass. 1983-86; assoc. prof. UCLA, Los Angeles 1986-93, prof. UCLA 1993–; cons. JAYCOR, San Diego 1987–, Battelle Inst. 1989-90; awards: Sigma Xi 1984–, Phi Tau Phi 1975–, Patent award GTE Labs Inc. (1986, 87, 88, 89); mem: Optical Soc. of Am. (Fellow 1979–), IEEE Laser and Electro-Optics Soc. (sr. mem. 1982–), Am. Physical Soc. 1980–, Photonics Soc. of Chinese Americans (founding mem. 1988–); author 7 US patents, contbr. articles in profl. jours. Ofc: UCLA 56-147C Eng. IV, E.E. Dept., Los Angeles 90024-1594

LIVINGSTON, ALVIN J., state agency administrator; b. June 12, 1929, New Orleans, La.; s. Bernard and Annette Hanna (Steckler) L.; m. Rita C. Powers, Oct. 29, 1961; edn: BS hons., UCLA 1953. Career: labor law tchg. asst. UCLA Sch. Bus. 1952-54; spl. asst. to pres. So. Calif. Freight Lines 1954-57; v.p., gen. mgr. Torre Safety Devices Co. 1957-59; v.p. fin. and adminstrn., secty., treas., mktg. dir. Mammoth Mountain Inn & 20th Century Engineering and affiliates, 1959-78; pub. rels., fin., political cons. Woodlands Hills, 1959-83; dep. dir. Calif. Dept. Motor Vehicles, 1983–; mem. Electoral Coll., Calif. 1976; mem. Calif. Republican Party 1956-84, 1987–; L.A. Co. Republican Party, L.A. 1956-83; mem; No. Calif. UCLA Alumni Assn.(pres. 1985-89), Vol. Center Sacto. (bd. 1984–, pres. 1994-95), Masons; ed. L.A. Co. Guide to Govt., 1983, chmn. editl. bd., 1970-82; Republican; Jewish; rec: politics, travel. Ofc: Calif. Dept. Motor Vehicles 2415 1st Ave Sacramento 95818

LLEWELLYN, JOHN FREDERICK, cemetery executive; b. Nov. 16, 1947, Los Angeles; s. Frederick Eaton and Jane Elizabeth (Althouse) L.; d. Sharon b. 1978; m. Linda Garrison, 1989; edn: BA, Univ. Redlands 1970; MBA, USC 1972. Career: foreman Pacific T&T, Orange 1970; underwriter Allstate Ins. Co., Santa Ana 1971-72; asst. to controller Forest Lawn Co., Glendale 1972-73, v.p. 1973-75, exec. v.p. Forest Lawn Memorial-Parks and Mortuaries 1976-88, treas./CFO 1978-83, secty. bd. dirs. 1983–, gen. mgr./c.e.o. 1988–; v.p. Forest Lawn Found. 1978–, trustee 1979–, secty. 1980–, treas./c.f.o. 1978-83; dir. Beneficial Standard Life Ins. Co. 1985-91; mem: Nat. Assn. of Cemeteries (dir. 1977-80), Am. Cemetery Assn. (dir. 1983-91, pres. 1988), Calif. Mortuary Alliance (dir. 1985–), Interment Assn. of Calif. (dir. 1984–, v.p. 1985–, state pres. 1988), Western Cemetery Alliance (dir. 1987–, v.p. 1987–); clubs: Economic Round Table (sec.treas. 1983-85), Newcomen Soc. No. Am., California, Lincoln; civic: Braille Inst. Am. (dir. 1983–), Gr. Los Angeles Visitors & Conv. Bur. (dir. 1981–, v.p. 1985-86, pres. and chmn. 1989-90),

Calif. C.of C. (dir. 1991–), Employers Group. (dir. 1991–), Emphysema Found. of Am. (dir. 1981-82), Glendale Devel. Council (dir. 1984-90, sec. 1986-87), Pershing Square Mgmt. Assn. (dir. 1985-86), Glendale Mem. Hosp. (trustee 1985-91), Jr. Achievement of So. Calif. (Bd. Governors 1993–), L.A. Area Council Boy Scouts Am. (dir. 1980–, treas. 1984-85, chmn. Council Advy. Com. on Scouting for Handicapped 1984-86, v. chmn. 1987-93, Commr. 1990-92, chmn. 1992-94), Arcadia Methodist Hosp. (dir. 1995–), Volunteers of Am. (dir.1995–), Claremont Grad. Sch. (Bd. of Visitors 1995–); publs: Fundamentals of Supervision of Cemetery Managers (3/82), Survey of Interment and Crematory-Columbarium Practices (c 1986), articles in trade mags. and jours., 1975–. Res: 1130 Oakwood Pl Sierra Madre 91024 Ofc: Forest Lawn Memorial-Parks and Mortuaries 1712 S Glendale Ave Glendale 91205

LLOYD, CAROL, food technologist; b. Feb. 10, 1952, La Porte, Ind.; d. John Cyrus and Catherine (Rus) Lloyd; m. Roger Allen Lah, Dec. 26, 1977 (div. Dec. 1991); children: Jenny b. 1981, Jessica b. 1984; edn: BS, Purdue Univ., 1974; MS in food sci., Univ. Ill., Champaign, 1979; MBA, Univ. of La Verne, 1985. Career: assoc. food chemist A.E. Staley Co., Decatur, Il. 1979-81; senior food tech. Hunt-Wesson Foods, Fullerton, Calif., 1982-87; project leader Basic American Foods, Blackfoot, Id., 1987; consultant to food industry, owner Austin Food Tech Inc., Newport Beach 1988–; mem. Inst. of Food Technologists (1977–); civic: Peace Corps vol. Brazil (1974-76); rec: astrologer. Ofc: Austin Food Technology, Inc. 3818 E LaPalma Anaheim 92807

LOBODOVSKY, KONSTANTIN K., electrical/mechanical engineer; b. Sept. 7, 1937, Harbin, China; s. Konstantin A. and Alexandra I. (Klariovich) L.; m. Barbara Morgan, Feb. 7, 1975; edn: BS, elec. eng., Heald Coll. 1973; BS, mech. eng., 1978; Calif. Comm. Coll. Tchg. Credential; Cert. Energy Auditor. Career: with Pacific Gas & Electric Co. 1955-93 (ret.); draftsman 1955; land dept. surveyor, computer draftsman, land mgmt. real property admin. 1957; San Francisco liaison, city & co. depts., illuminating engr., indsl. power engr. 1973; energy conservation svs. tech. svs. unit, sr. energy svs. engr./ proj. mgr., staff instr./ lectr. 1979; elec. engr. Electric Distb. PG&E 1989-91; dir. Gas &Electric Distb. stds.; cons./lectr. Motor Mgr. Training 1993; instr. math. & elec. engr. Heald Engring. Coll. Evening Div. 1968-77; dean of engring. & tech. schs. Heald Coll. Even. Div. 1977-79; awards: Energy Engr. of the Yr. (Bay Area chpt.) 1980, (13 Western States) 1981, Assn. of Energy Engrs., Atlanta, Ga.; Spkr. Awd., PG&E 1979; mem: Assn. Energy Engrs. (nat. pres. 1988, chapt. pres. 1979-81, exec. com.); World Energy Engring. Congress Adv. Bd.; Russian Orthodox Ch. West Coast Diocese (tech. advr., bd. mem.); Engrs. Club of San Francisco; S.F. Proj. S.A.F.E.; US patent; tech. publs. in field, 1979-84; mil: sp4 US Army Honor Guard/Drill Team 1961-63, GCM, Expert Rifle, Letters of Commdn., Spl. Assignment to Pentagon; Republican; Russian Orthodox; rec: video filming/editing, boating, woodworking, computers, photog. Res: Penn Valley 95946

LOCATELL, KATHRYN LEE, physician; b. Jan. 21, 1957, Iowa City, Iowa; d. Louis and Marian Lucille (Anderson) Locatell; m. Kenneth E. Payne, Oct. 1, 1982 (div. 1991); m. 2d. Calvin Layman Joseph, July 4, 1991; children: Ian T. Joseph b. 1992, Sophie K. Joseph b. 1994; edn: BA, Clark Univ., Worcester, Mass. 1979; MD, Univ. of Mass. Med. Sch., Worcester, Mass. 1985; diplomate. Am. Bd. of Internal Medicine 1988, cert. geriatric medicine 1994. Career: resident UC Davis Med. Ctr., Sacramento 1985-88; career physician The Permanente Med. Group, Sacto. 1988-90, sr. physician 1991–, chief elder care svs. 1994–; asst. clin. prof. UC Davis Med. Sch. 1988–; co-author: 4 scientific articles pub. in profl. jours., 1980-82; Democrat. Ofc: The Permanente Medical Group 2025 Morse Ave Sacramento 95825

LOCATELLI, PAUL LEO, university administrator, clergyman; b. Sept. 16, 1938, Santa Cruz; s. Vincent D. and Marie J. (Piccone) L.; edn: BSc, Univ. Santa Clara 1961; MDiv, Jesuit Sch. of Theol., Berkeley 1974; BDA, USC 1971; Cert. CPA, Calif. 1965; ordained priest (S.J.) Soc. of Jesus, R.Cath. Ch. Career: profl. acct. Lautze & Lautze (Wolf & Co.) 1960-64, 74; lectr. Jesuit Sch. of Theol., Berkeley 1973-74; with Univ. of Santa Clara 1974–: prof. of acctg. 1974–; assoc. dean Sch. of Bus. 1976-78; academic v.p. 1978–; bd. trustees: Seattle Univ., Seattle, Wash. 1983; Univ. of San Francisco 1979-85; Bellarmine Coll. Prep. 1975–; bd. dirs. and Senior Commn., Western Assn. of Schs. and Colls.; chmn. jury for Calif. Mus. Sci. and Industry 1978-79, and chmn. for selection of Industrialist of the Yr. 1979; honors: Teacher of the Yr. 1977-78, Beta Gamma Sigma 1978; mem: Am. Inst. & Calif. Soc. of CPAs, Am. Acctg. Assn.; Democrat; rec: photog. Address: Univ. Santa Clara, Santa Clara 95053

LOCKARD-DIGRE, SUSAN ANNE, educator, consultant; b. Apr. 5, 1942, Youngstown, Ohio; d. Charles William and Anna Gabriella (Choppa) Lockard; m. Erick Loyd Digre, Oct. 21, 1977; children: Colleen b. 1978, Sean b. 1980, Michael b. 1981, Scott b. 1983; edn: BA biol. scis., Coll. of Notre Dame, Belmont, 1964; Calif. State Elementary tchg. credential - Life 1969. Career: educator Sisters of Notre Dame, Saratoga, 1964-68, Our Lady of Angels Sch., Burlingame, Calif. 1968-78, 88–; ednl. cons. (creative approaches for difficult situations) S.S.S. Consultant Services, San Bruno and Pacifica, 1986–; political activist: Dem. Write-In Candidate for Gov. of Calif. 6/90 and 11/94, rec'd local & nat. media

coverage; mem. bds: S.F. Archdiocese Pastoral Council to Archbishop John Quinn (1986-89, 90–), San Mateo Co. Crisis Pregnancy Ctr. (founding bd., grantwriter 1989–), Concerned Parents and Associates (founder 1989), Burlingame Civic Action Forum 1972-76, Sierra Club Loma Prieta Chpt. (bd. 1972-74); entrepreneur, inventor (math learning game) Math Match-It, several interactive games also practical products for children & adults; author (childrens story) CandyCane&GummyGumDrop, 1975; Democrat (Maverick); R.Cath.; rec: writing, problem solving, horseback riding. Res: 780 Edgemar Ave Pacifica 94044

LOCKWOOD, WILLIAM H., theatrical producer, music director; b. March 16, 1925, Sullivan, Indiana; s. W.H. and Eva C. (Brown) L.; edn: MusM, DePauw Univ., 1949, MusD, 1951. Career: vocal coach, condr. with various clients incl. Dorothy Lamour, Bob Hope, Gordon MacRae, Kaye Ballard, worldwide; music dir. Jonathan Winters TV Show, Hollywood, 1952-54; actor, pianist Days of Our Lives NBC-TV, Hollywood, 1955-60; arranger, condr. Golddiggers Dean Martin TV, Hollywood, 1961-70; pres. Sebastians Dinner Theatre, San Clemente, 1972-75; music dir. Grand Dinner Theatre, Anaheim, 1976–; career cons. San Bernardino Schs., 1975-78; composer, arranger, condr. Sebastian's Hari Prodns., L.A., 1982-85; composer: (tone poem) North of Boston, 1976, (ballet) Tarleton, 1976 (ASCAP award 1977), works for num. films, 1978–; Republican; rec: metaphysics. Address: 3379 N Knoll Dr Hollywood 90068

LOEBL, JAMES DAVID, lawyer; b. July 4, 1927, Chgo. Ill.; s. Jerrold and Ruth Diana (Weil) L; m. Joan Dorothy Hirsch, Apr. 8, 1960; children: Jeffrey William b. 1961, Susan Diana Loebl Grasso b. 1962, Ellen Cynthia b. 1965; edn: AB, Princeton Univ. 1948; Grad. Sch., Dept. of Sociology, Univ. of Chgo. 1948-49; JD, Stanford Univ. Sch. of Law 1952. Career: sec., com. on rules US House of Representatives 1949; deputy atty. gen. Calif. Dept. of Justice 1953-58; travel sec. to Gov. Edmund G. Brown 1959-60; Dept. of Profl. & Vocat. Standards, asst. to dir. 1959-60, deputy dir. 1960, chief deputy dir. 1961, dir. 1961-63; ptnr.: Willard & Loebl 1963-64; Loebl & Bringgold 1964-65; Loebl, Bringgold & Peck 1965-75; Loebl, Bringgold, Peck & Parker 1976-80; Loebl & Parker 1980-81; Loebl, Parker, Murphy & Nelson 1981-87; Loebl, Parker & Nelson 1987-93; of counsel, Muegenburg, Norman & Dowler 1993–; mem. of bars of Ventura County (pres. 1983), L.A. County, Federal, Calif., Ill., and US Supreme Court; mem., State Bar Adminstrv. Law & Tribunals Comm. 1963-68; dir. Employment Aptitude & Placement Assn. 1970-72; Ventura Co. Superior Ct., judge pro tempore 1972, 74, 85-86; fellow, Am. Bar Found. 1989–; civic: asst. city atty., Ojai, Calif. 1964; bd. dirs. Ventura Co. Forum of the Arts 1965, Ojai Music Festivals 1967-68; v.p. & trustee, Monica Ros Sch., Ojai 1967-74; mem., Ojai City Council 1968–, Ventura Co. Sheriff's Prisoner Classification Comm. 1969-72, Comprehensive Health Svc. Comm. 1970, Sheriff's Civil Svc. Examining Bd., Princeton Sch. Admissions Com.; mayor, City of Ojai 1972-75, 1986-87, 1991-92; exec. comm., Ventura County Assn. of Govt. 1972-75, 1986-87; Ojai representative, So. Calif. Assn. of Govt. 1972-75; Ventura County Reg. Sanitation Dist. 1972-75; Calif. Council on Criminal Justice 1972-75; nominee for Congress, 19th Dist. of Calif. 1974. Mil: lt. comdr., US Coast Guard Res., 1964-74. Res: 715 El Toro Rd Ojai 93023. Ofc: Of Counsel, Muegenburg, Norman & Dowler 840 County Square Dr. Ventura 93003

LOEWENSTEIN, WALTER B., consultant on science and technology; b. Dec. 23, 1926, Gensungen, Germany; nat. 1943; s. Louis and Johanna (Katz) L.; m. Lenore C. Pearlman, June 21, 1959; children: Mark b. 1961, Marcia b. 1964; edn: BS cum laude, Univ. Puget Sound 1949; Univ. Wash. Seattle 1949-50; PhD, Ohio St. Univ. 1954; reg. profl. engr. Calif. 1976. Career: physicist Argonne Nat. Lab., Argonne, Ill. 1954-68, project dir. 1968-72, div. dir. 1972-73; dept. dir. Electric Power Research Inst., Palo Alto 1973-86, dep. div. dir. 1981-89; cons., Palo Alto 1989–; tchr. UC Berkeley 1981; mem: Am. Assn. Engring. Soc. (bd. dirs. 1989-90, exec. com. 1989, treas. 1990), Am. Physical Soc. (fellow), Am. Nuclear Soc. (fellow, bd. dirs. 1985-88, v.p. 1988-89, pres. 1989-90), Nat. Acad. Engring. 1991–; 3 patents in field, 1959-88, 50 articles pub. in tech. jours.; mil: USNR 1945-46. Res: 515 Jefferson Palo Alto 94303

LOFGREN, DENNIS CARL, filmmaker; b. May 30, 1947, Duluth, Minn.; s. Carl Oscar and June LaVerne (Johnson) L.; m. Patricia Joyce Tarzian, Feb. 21, 1981 (div. 1984); 1 son, Kristofor b. 1982; m., 2d. Lori Renee Winning, Nov. 16, 1991; edn: BA sci., Gustavus Adolphus Coll. 1970; MS family & child devel., Kansas St. Univ. 1973. Career: pres., owner Auroean Film Co., Mpls., Minn. 1974-76; asst. to pres. Esmeralda Film Co., Los Angeles 1977-78; producer/dir./writer t.v. documentaries and t.v. specials, 1980–; owner/pres. Dennis Lofgren Productions, Santa Monica 1988–; profl. awards include Dupont/Columbia for bdcst. journalism, Christopher for t.v. Specials, ACE award nominations for cable excellence Nat. Acad. of Cable Pgmmg., Best Documentary for t.v. Chgo. Film Fest., Blue rib. American Film Fest., Cine Golden Eagles, Prix Italia (2d) World TV Fest., T.V. Guide year's list `Best We Saw'; mem: Internat. Documentary Assn., Director's Guild Am., Earth Island Inst., Nat. Wildlife Fedn., Environ. Media Assn.; senior thesis "The Lotus and The Robot, A Report on Traditional Medicine in Modern Taiwan" pub. Minn. Student Proj. for Amity Among Nations 1970; mil: cpl. USMCR 1966-72; rec: tennis, painting. Address: Santa Monica 90403

LOHAFER, DOUGLAS ALLEN, health physicist; b. June 7, 1949, Cherokee, Iowa; s. Walter Jessen and Dorothy Ann (Thies) L.; edn: AA in lib. arts (magna cum laude), Waldorf Coll., 1975; Mankato State Univ., 1974-75; Mayo Sch. Health Related Scis., Iowa State Univ., 1976; BA in biology, chemistry, Luther Coll., 1977, St. Olaf Coll., 1977; MS in radiological health physics, San Jose State Univ., 1993. Career: senior satellite ops. engr. Lockheed Missiles & Space Co. Inc., Sunnyvale 1978-87, Lockheed Tech. Ops. Co. Inc., Sunnyvale, 1987-92; chemist, KEL/T, Lawrence Livermore Nat. Lab., Livermore 1995–; honors: Phi Theta Kappa 1975, Eagle Scout 1967; mem: Am. Chem. Soc. (asso. Santa Clara Valley Sect., div. biol. chemistry, div. nuclear chemistry and tech.), Health Physics Soc. (asso. N.Ca. chpt.), Obsessive Compulsive Found., U.S. Parachute Assn., Parachutists Over Phorty Soc., C.S. Lewis Soc. N.Y., Soren Kierkegaard Soc., Fellowship of Confessional Lutherans; Lutheran; Democrat. Res: 403 Los Encinos Ave San Jose 95134

LOKEY, R. EUGENE, governmental affairs executive; b. Sept. 3, 1944, Washington, Ga.; s. Walter EuGene and Zelma May L.; edn: BA, San Jose St. Univ. 1966, 1968; MA, 1974. Career: pub. rels. dir. Alumni Students, San Jose 1966-68; sales mgr. Spartan Engring., Sunnyvale 1968-70; research dir. Council for Action, San Jose 1970-71; v.p. Patrick Andrews Adv. 1972-74; gen. mgr. Photo Lab Express, Berkeley 1974; exec. dir. E. Valley Comm. Clinic, San Jose 1975; dir. tng. Inter Agency Family Council 1975-76; pres. Sunrise Winery, Santa Cruz 1976-79; pres. Calif. Planners & Cons., Sacto. 1979–; awards: Phil Theat Phi La Torre 1966; mem: San Jose Airport Assn. (bd. mem.), Friends of Guadalupe River Park (bd. mem.), Aricraft Owners & Pilots Assn., Democratic Century Club of Santa Clara Co., Nat. Council Against Health Fraud; Democrat; Prot.; rec: beekeeping, winemaking. Address: Sacramento 95814

LOMELI, MARTA, bilingual education teacher; b. Oct. 28, 1952, Tijuana, Mex., naturalized U.S. 1978; d. Jesus Ramirez and Guadalupe (Ascencio) Lomeli; m. Rudolph Benitez Jr., 1978 (div. 1982); children: Pascual b. 1979; m. David Everett Miller, Aug. 16, 1991; edn: BA, San Diego State Univ., 1977; Calif. tchr. credential, 1978. Career: librarian Vista Boy's Club, Vista 1969-70; student recruiter UC San Diego, La Jolla 1970-72; bilingual tchr., 6th grade, National Sch. Dist., 1978–, Nat. Sch. Dist. High Tech. Com. 1993–; advy. coms. prin. and supt., 1986-88; volunteer tutor MECHA, UCSD, 1971-73, St. Vincent de Paul Ctr. for the Homeless, San Diego 1991–; mem. anti-Graffiti Patrol, Bell Jr. H.S. 1991–; awards: Mexican Am. Educators scholar, Vista 1970, Black Belt 1st degree in Shaolin Kempo 1992, listed Who's Who Am. Women, Who's Who in West, Who's Who Am. Educators, Who's Who of Emerging Leaders; mem. Nat. Assn. Bilingual Edn, Calif. Assn. Bilingual Edn. 1982–, World Federalist Orgn. 1992–; past pres., co-founder La Raza Club, Vista H.S. 1970; pub. poems (1969, 70, 92); Democrat; rec: drawing cartoons, Karate. Res: 6920 Alsacia St San Diego 92139-2101

LONDRE, LARRY STEVEN, marketing executive; b. Feb. 18, 1949, Los Angeles; s. E. M. and Thelma D. (Loose) L.; m. Patricia Mathys, May 20, 1978; edn: BS, USC 1971; MBA, 1974. Career: mktg. ofcr. Security Pacific Bank 1971-75; mktg. mgr. Walt Disney Productions, L.A. 1980; v.p. Grey Advtg. 1975-83; sr. v.p. Abert Newhoff & Burr 1983-87; Grey Entertainment Media 1988-89; v.p. mktg. The Music Center of Los Angeles 1988-94; mng. ptnr., CFO, The Londre Co Inc. L.A. 1994–; sr. lectr. USC, 1980–; CSU Northridge 1978-80; awards: Bd. Fire Commrs. Resolution 1987; mem: Advtg. Club of L.A. (bd. dirs. 1975), Studio City Homeowners, HRTS, Sherman Oaks Homeowners, Calif. Spl. Olympics; 3 articles pub. in profl. jour. Ofc: The Londre Co Inc 3393 Barham Blvd Los Angeles 90068

LONEY, TIMOTHY JOHN, change management director; b. June 19, 1942, Middletown, Conn.; edn: BS, So. Conn. St. Univ. New Haven 1965; MSA, George Washington Univ. 1971; MPA, USC L.A. 1981; DPA, 1983. Career: lab. rels. splst. U.S. Dept. Treasury, Wash. D.C. 1971-74; employee rels. advisor U.S. Dept. Labor 1974; regional lab. rels. ofcr. General Service Adminstrn., S.F. 1974-80; tng. mgr. 1980-82, dir. employee rels. 1982–; sr. v.p. Timner Cons. Group, Oakland 1983–; editl. bd. Personnel Jour., Costa Mesa 1985, Pub. Adminstrn. Review, Wash. DC 1988; human resource prof. Univ. S.F. 1981, adj. prof. Golden Gate Univ. 1976, USC 1981; honors: Internat. Businessmen Who's Who 1985, Who's Who in West 1985; mem: Am. Soc. Pub. Adminstrn. (exec. com. personnel adminstrn. section), Soc. Fed. Labor Rels. Profls. (past pres.), Labor Rels. Com. (fed. personnel council No. Calif.); civic: BSA (S.F., v. chmn. Troop 39); contbr. Grievance Arbitration in Fed. Service, 1987, 3 articles pub. in profl. jours., 1981-85; mil: lt. comdr. USNR-Ret. Ofc: Timner Consultant Group 403 Chupcan Place Clayton 94517

LONG, ANTHONY ARTHUR, professor of classics; b. Aug. 17, 1937, Manchester, England; s. Tom Arthur and Phyllis Joan (LeGrice) L.; m. Janice Calloway, Dec. 30, 1960 (div. 1969); m. Mary Kay Flavell, May 25, 1970 (div. 1990); children: Stephen Arthur, Rebecca Jane; edn: BA, University Coll. London, 1960; PhD, Univ. London, 1964. Career: lectr. classics Univ. Otago, Dunedin, N.Z. 1961-64; Univ. Nottingham, Eng. 1964-66; lectr. in Greek and Latin University Coll. London, 1966-71; reader in Greek and Latin Univ. London, 1971-73; Gladstone prof. Greek Univ. Liverpool, Eng. 1973-83; prof.

classics UC Berkeley, 1982–, dept. chmn. 1986-90, Irving Stone Prof. Literature, 1991–; vis. prof.: Univ. Munich, 1973, Ecole Normale Supériere, Paris, 1993; mem. Mellon Fellowships Selection Com. 1984-90; mem. selection com. Stanford Univ. Humanities Council 1985-86; awards: Bye fellow Robinson Coll., Cambridge 1982, Guggenheim fellow 1986-87, Inst. Advanced Study, Princeton 1970, 79, NEH 1991, Wissenschaftskolleg, Berlin 1991-92, fellow Am. Acad. Arts & Scis. 1989–, British Acad. (corresp.) 1992–, ØBK (hon.) 1993; mem: Classical Assn., Aristotelian Soc., Am. Philological Soc.; author: Language and Thought in Sophocles (1968, winner Cromer Greek prize 1968), Problems in Stoicism, 1971, Hellenistic Philosophy (1974, 2d edit. 1986), coauthor w/Sedley, The Hellenistic Philosophers, 1987, w/Dillon, The Question of Eclecticism, 1988; co-editor Images and Ideologies, 1993, editor Classical Quarterly, 1975-81, gen. editor w/Barnes, Clarendon Later Ancient Philosophers, 1987; mil: lt. Royal Arty., Eng. 1955-57; rec: music, walking, travel. Res: 1088 Tevlin St Albany 94706 Ofc: Dept. Classics, Dwinelle Hall, Univ. Calif., Berkeley 94720

LONG, GREGORY ALAN, lawyer; b. Aug. 28, 1948, San Francisco; s. William F. and Ellen L. (Webber) L.; m. Jane Hayes Barrett; children: Matthew, Brian, Michael, Gregory; edn: BA magna cum laude, Claremont Mens Coll. 1970; JD cum laude, Harvard Law Sch. 1973. Career: assoc. atty. Overton Lyman & Prince, L.A. 1973-78, ptnr. 1978-86; Sheppard Mullin Richter & Hampton 1986–; del. St. Bar Conf. Dels. 1976-82, 1987; arbitrator L.A. Superior Ct. 1982-84; mem. Fed. Habeas Corpus Panel U.S. Dist. Ct. 1988; mem: Am. Bar Found. (fellow), Am. Bar Assn. (fellow lit. sect.), L.A. Co. Bar Assn. (Barristers exec. com. 1977-82, pres. 1981-82, bd. trustees and exec. com. 1980-82), Am. Bar Assn. (Young Lawyers Div. exec. council 1979-84, chmn. 1984, lit. sect. exec. council 1982-84, house of dels. 1982-88); Republican; Cath. Ofc: Sheppard Mullin Richter et al 333 S Hope Los Angeles 90071

LONG, STEPHEN INGALLS, professor, electrical and computer engineering; b. Jan. 11, 1946 Alameda, Calif.; s. Stanley M. and Mabel C. (Ingalls) L.; m. Molly S. Hammer, Dec. 17, 1966; children: Christopher b. 1971, Betsy b. 1974; edn.: BS, UC Berkeley 1967; MS, Cornell Univ., Ithaca, NY 1969; PhD, Cornell Univ. 1974. Career: sr. engr., Varian Assoc., Palo Alto, Calif. 1974-77; mem. of tech. staff, Rockwell, Thousand Oaks, Calif. 1978-81; prof., Univ. of Calif. Santa Barbara 1981–; guest prof., Technical Univ. of Denmark 1994; cons., Jet Propulsion Labs., Pasadena 1990-92; Superconductor Technologies, Inc., Santa Barbara 1991–; awards: Microwave Application award IEEE 1978, Fulbright Scholar, Tampere Univ. of Technology, Finland 1994; sr. mem. IEEE 1974–; mem. Am. Scientific Affiliation 1989–; author: Gallium Arsenide Digital Integrated Circuit Design, 1990; over 70 profl. jour. articles and conf. papers, 1974–; mil: staff sgt., USAF, 1969-73; Grace Ch. of Santa Barbara; rec: amateur radio, Christian edn., classical guitar. Res: 895 N. Patterson Ave. Santa Barbara 93111. Ofc: Univ. of Calif. ECE Dept. Santa Barbara 93106

LOOMIS, JOHN RUSSELL, materiels & process engineer; b. Elmhurst, Ill.; edn: AA in physical sci., Santa Barbara Comm. Coll., 1977; BS indsl. tech., CSU Fresno, 1981; certif. mfg. engring., UCLA, 1985; cert. mfg. engr. SME, 1985; Airframe lic. FAA, 1987; cert. Frontline Leadership Pgm., Zenger & Miller. 1991, FAA DER, Airframe & Powerplant, 1993; Hazardous Waste Mgmt. Prog., UCSB (in progress) 1994. Career: mechanic County of Santa Barbara, 1974-79; systems tech. Sloan Technology, 1979-80; liaison engr. Hughes Aircraft Co., El Segundo 1981-85; design engr. Lucas Aviation Inc., Goleta 1985-92; cons. engr. 1992–; instr. vocat. arts, Proteus Adult Training, Inc. Fresno 1981; cons. tchr. Junior Achievement Pgm., Torrance 1982; advisor, student faculty Formula (SAE) Car, UC Santa Barbara, 1991; engring. lectr. Santa Barbara Comm. Coll., 1991; mem: Soc. Mfg. Engrs., Soc. Automotive & Aerospace Engrs. (assoc.), UCLA Alumni; author: Mechanization in the Modern Foundry (1981); 1st Methodist Ch., Santa Barbara (tchr., ofcr./pastor parish com. 1991); rec: walking, bicycling. Res: 3669 Eileen Way Santa Barbara 93105

LOONEY, CLAUDIA A., academic administrator; b. June 13, 1946, Fullerton; d. Donald F. and Mildred B. (Gage) Schneider; m. James K. Looney, Oct. 8, 1967; 1 son, Christopher K.; edn: BA, CSU Fullerton 1969. Career: youth dir. YWCA No. Orange Co., Fullerton 1967-70; dist. director Camp Fire Girls, San Francisco 1971-73; asst. exec. director Camp Fire Girls, Los Angeles 1973-77; asst. dir. community resources Childrens Hosp. of Los Angeles, 1977-80; dir. community devel. Orthopaedic Hosp., L.A. 1980-82; sr. v.p. Saddleback Meml. Found./Saddleback Meml. Med. Ctr., Laguna Hills 1982-92; v.p. planning and advancement Calif. Inst. Arts, Santa Clarita 1992–; instr. UC Irvine, Univ. Irvine; mem. steering com. Univ. Irvine; mem. steering com. United Way, L.A. 1984-86; Fellow Assn. Healthcare Philanthropy (nat. chair-elect, chmn. program Nat. End. Conf. 1986, chair-elect, regional dir. 1985-89, fin. com. 1988–, pres., com. chmn. 1987–, Give to Life com. chmn. 1987-91, Orange Co. Fund Raiser of Yr. 1992); mem. Nat. Soc. Fund Raising Execs. Found. (cert., vice chmn. 1985-90, chair 1994–), So. Calif. Assn. Hosp. Devel. (past pres., bd. dirs.), Profl. Ptnrs. (chmn. 1986, instr. 1988–), Philanthropic Ednl. Orgn. (past pres.); avocations: swimming, sailing, photography. Ofc: California Institute of the Arts 24700 McBean Pkwy Valencia 91355-9999

LOPATA, MARTIN BARRY, service executive; b. Apr. 6, 1939, Bronx, N.Y.; s. Julius A. and Rose (Silverman) L.; m. Sarah G., July 4, 1965 (div. 1978); children: Warren A., Lawrence M.; m. Lynette Wyrick, May 6, 1989 (div. 1990); edn: grad. High Sch. of Art and Design, N.Y.C.; att. N.Y.C. Community Coll., Bklyn. Career: sales mgr. H. Natoway Co., Los Angeles 1961-62; contract mgr. A.S. Aloe Co., L.A. 1962-64; mdse. mgr. S.E. Rykoff Co., L.A. 1964-70; v.p. Kirby Sales, L.A. 1970-71; pres. MBL Industries Inc., Santa Ana 1971-87, Unicorn Seminars Inc., Huntington Beach 1987–, Unicorn Internat., 1988-91; mem. bd. dirs. Internat. Sanitary Supply Assn., 1979-81; chmn. Soviet Am. Internat. Co., 1988-91; bus. chmn. Ctr. for Soviet-Am. Dialogue, W.D.C. 1987-91; chmn. Com. on Business - A New Way of Thinking in a New Age, Moscow 1987; bd. dirs. Three Mountain Found., Lone Pine, Calif. 1987-88, Inside Edge, Irvine, 1987–; patron Am. Mus. Natural Hist., N.Y.C. 1984–; mem. Masons (32d degree), Shriners; Religious Sci. (bd. 1985, 86-87). Res: 16391 Wimbledon Huntington Beach 92649

LOPER, JAMES L., association executive; b. Sept. 4, 1931, Phoenix, Ariz.; s. John D. and Ellen H. (Leaders) L.; m. Mary Louise Brion, Sept. 1, 1955; children: Elizabeth Serhan b. 1964, James, Jr. b. 1966; edn: BA in journ., Ariz. St. Univ., Tempe 1953; MA in radio & t.v., Univ. Denver, 1957; PhD comm., USC, 1966. Career: Weekend News editor and announcer, p.t. KTAR, NBC Radio, Phoenix and 8-sta. Ariz. Bdcst. System, 1955-56; asst., actg. dir. Bur. of Bdcstg. = Ariz. St. Univ., Tempe 1953-59; asst. prof. and dir. ednl. t.v. CSU Los Angeles, 1960-64; exec. Community Television of So. Calif. (KCET- Ch. 28), Los Angeles 1963-82: v.p. and asst. to pres. 1963-64, dir. ednl. svs. 1964-65, asst. gen. mgr. 1965-66, v.p. and gen. mgr. 1967-71, pres. and gen. mgr. 1971-77, pres. and c.e.o. 1977-82; indep. communications cons., 1982-83; blt. KCET into one of largest public t.v. stations nat., pgmmg. won all major nat. awards incl. Peabody, DuPont, Ohio State, Emmy; founding chmn. Public Broadcasting Service (3 yrs.), spokesman for pub. bdcstg., devel. legislation, appt. to CPB Commn. by Gov. Reagan; founding chmn. Pub. TV Playhouse Inc., N.Y., prod. "American Playhouse" 1980-82; exec. prod. internat. t.v. series "Music in Time" 1982; exec. dir. Acad. of Television Arts and Sciences, and ATAS Foundation (the largest acad. for profls. in t.v. industry with 7000+ mbrs., orgn. presents annual Primetime Emmy Awards, seminars and forums, pub. EMMY Mag., and supr. ATAS/UCLA Archives a collection of 25,000+ films and tapes of t.v. pgmmg. dating from 1940s), 1984–; adj. prof. USC Sch. of Cinema-TV 1985–; appt. by Gov. Pete Wilson to Calif. Arts Council 1991–; honors: Sigma Delta Chi, Alpha Delta Sigma, Pi Delta Epsilon, Phi Sigma Kappa (Grand Council 1987-90), Alpha Epsilon Rho, disting. alumnus Ariz. St. Univ. 1972, man of yr. Calif. Mus. Sci. and Indus. 1972, Hon. HDL Columbia Coll. 1973, juror rep. U.S. PBS, the Japan Prize Japan Bdcstg. Co., Tokyo 1975, Alumni award of merit USC 1975, gov's award Hollywood chpt. Nat. ATAS 1975, Hon. LLD Pepperdine Univ. 1978, Alumni Hall of Fame Ariz. St. Univ. 1985 and named Centennial Alumnus 1988; exec. bd. Art Center Coll. of Design, Pasa. 1979–; past pres. Assn. of Calif. Pub. TV Stations and We. Ednl. Network; past dir./treas. Hollywood Radio and TV Soc.; mem. Acad. TV Arts & Scis. (former gov., trustee Internat. Council 1979-83, 88–); mem. Mayor's Com. for the Entertainment Indus., L.A. 1989–; mem. Western Fed. Sav. & Loan Assn., L.A. (dir. 1979-93); civic bds: Performing Tree, L.A. (chmn., dir. 1976-87), Permanent Charities Com. of Entertainment Indus. (dir. 1984–), Polytechnic Sch., Pasa. (trustee 1976-82), Town Hall of Calif. (dir. 1981-82), Calif. Civic Light Opera Co. (dir. 1977–, chmn. Musical Theatre Workshop Com.), Pasa. Chamber Orch. (dir. 1983-84), Assocs. of Otis Art Inst. (past pres.), Acad. of Performing and Visual Arts Found. (bd. 1984-89), Salvation Army (advy. bd. 1981-82); author book chapts., contbr. articles in profl. jours., Performing Arts Mag., Passenger Train Jour.; Republican; Presbyterian; rec: R.R. hist. Ofc: Academy of TV Arts and Sciences, 5220 Lankershim Blvd North Hollywood 91601

LOPEZ, JOHN, JR., infantry officer; b. July 14, 1954, Los Angeles; s. John Soto and Elvira (Jimenez) L.; edn: BA in bus. mgmt., St. Martins Coll., 1983; spl. mil. tng. Army Armor Sch., Fort Knox, 1982, Army Organizational Effectiveness Sch., Fort Ord, 1984, Army Combined Arms Svs. & Staff Sch., Fort Leavenworth, 1986, Defense Language Inst., Presidio of Monterey, 1991; Command & Gen. Staff Coll., Ft. Leavenworth, 1993; Civil Affairs Ofcr. Course, Ft. Bragg, 1994. Career: major US Army 1975–: platoon ldr. 2d Batt. 39th Inf., 9th Inf. Div., Fort Lewis, Wash. 1978-79, company executive ofcr. 1980, 1st Brigade air ops. ofcr. 1980-82; Div. organizational effectiveness cons. Hq., 2d Inf. Div., Camp Casey, South Korea 1984-85, 2d Brigade co. comdr., 1985-86; recruiting ofcr., San Jose 1986-90; inf. advr. U.S. Military Group, El Salvador 1991-92; corps civil affairs ofcr., HQs., I Corps, Ft. Lewis, Wash. 1992–; decorated Parachute Badge, Expert Inf. Badge, Merit. Svc. Medal (2), Army Commendation Medal (5), Army Achiev. Medal (2), Joint Service Achiev. Medal, Joint Merit, Unit Award; mem. Assn. of the US Army; civic: Santa Clara Co. Council Boy Scouts 1989, San Jose City C.of C., Civil Air Patrol/ San Gabriel Valley 1969-76, Nat. Rifle Assn., 82nd Airborne Div. Assn., Wash. State Arms Collectors; Republican; Baptist; rec: hiking, hunting, mil. history, marksmanship. Res: 317 S Aspen Ave Azusa 91702

LOPEZ, TRICIA DEINI, real estate broker; b. Aug. 27, 1943, Tulsa, Okla.; d. Paul James and Beverly Jean (St. John) Jones; m. George H. Deini, Aug. 26, 1971 (dec. 1979); children: Mercy Michelle b. 1974, Wendy Colleen b. 1977; m.

Harold O. Lopez, June 14, 1980; edn: Univ. of Tulsa, Okla. 1960-65; desig: Profl. Legal Secty. 1963; Calif. lic. R.E. agent 1983, R.E. broker 1986. Career: legal secty. Charles E. Kothe, Tulsa 1963-65; John E. Virga, Sacto. 1972-76; Superior Courtroom Clerk to Hon. Rothwell B. Mason, Sacramento Co. 1976-80; real estate agt. Kiernan Realtors, Sacto. 1983-86; real estate broker Elliott Real Estate, Sacto. 1986, GBC Realtors, Sacto. 1986-94, Century 21 Valley Oak Realty 1994–; charter mem. (1990) and current nat. v.p. Select Equestrian Properties, a relocation network of horse property splsts.; awards: Kiernan Realtors Pres.'s Club 1985, 86, GBC 1986-94, Top Prod. 1986, Sacto. Assn. of Realtors Master's Club 1986, 87, 88, 90, GBC Realtors Top Prod. 1988; mem: Nat. Assn. of Profl. Saleswomen, Nat. Assn. Realtors, Calif. Assn. Realtors, Sacto. Assn. Realtors; civic: Job's Daughters Elk Grove (parent 1988, 89), Cosumnes Area Plng. Advy. Council, Wilton (1988, chair 1989); Republican; Prot.; rec: Arabian horses, endurance and competitive trail riding. Res: 9669 La Clair Rd Wilton 95693 Ofc: Century 21 Valley Oak Realty 8694 Elk Grove Blvd Ste 9 Elk Grove 95624

LORD, HAROLD WILBUR, consulting electrical engineer; b. Aug. 20, 1905, Eureka; s. Charles Wilbur and Rossina Camilla (Hansen) L.; m. Doris Shirley Huff, July 25, 1928; children: Joann b. 1929, Alan b. 1932, Nancy b. 1934, Wayne b. 1942; edn: BS in E.E., Calif. Inst. of Tech., 1926; reg. profl. electrical engr., Calif. 1968. Career: electrical engr., res. and devel. electronics engr. Gen. Electric Co., Schenectady, N.Y. 1926-66; consulting elec. engr., 1966–; awards: Coffin Award GE Co. 1933, Inventors Award GE 1966, Centennial Medal IEEE, nat. 1984, Achiev. Award IEEE Magnetics Soc., nat. 1984; mem.: IEEE (Life Fellow, 1967–), AIEE/IEEE (tech. v.p. 1962); inventor, 96 patents (1930-72), tech. publs. J. AIEE/IEEE (8+, 1930-68); mil. 1st lt. Engineer Corps Reserve 1927-31; Republican; Prot.; rec: photography, hi-fi systems. Res: 1565 Golf Course Dr Rohnert Park 94928

LORD, JACK, actor, director, producer, artist, writer; b. Dec. 30, 1930, NYC; s. William Lawrence and Ellen Josephine (O'Brien) Ryan; m. Marie de Narde, Apr. 1, 1952; edn: BFA, N.Y. Univ. 1954. Career: exhibited galleries and museums incl. Corcoran Gallery, Nat. Acad. Design, Whitney Mus., Brooklyn Mus., Lib. of Congress, Biblioteque Nationale, Paris, France; rep. in 37 major mus. permanent collections incl. Met. Mus. of Art, Mus. Modern Art NYC, Fogg Mus., Harvard U., Santa Barbara Mus. Art, Fine Arts Gal. San Diego, Colby Coll. Art Mus., Ga. Mus. Art, Chouinard Art Inst. LA, Calif. Inst. Art, Brit. Mus., others; appearances on Broadway in Traveling Lady (Theatre World award 1959), Cat On A Hot Tin Roof; motion picture performances: Court Martial of Billy Mitchell, Williamsburg - the Story of a Patriot, Tip on a Dead Jockey, God's Little Acre, Man of the West, Hangman, True Story of Lynn Stuart, Walk like a Dragon, Doctor No.; leading roles in TV prodns: Constitution series Omnibus, Playhouse 90, Goodyear Playhouse, Studio One, U.S. Steel; TV film appearances: Have Gun Will Travel (pilot), Untouchables, Naked City Rawhide, Bonanza, Americans, Route 66, Gunsmoke, Stagecoach West, Dr. Kildare, Greatest Show Earth, Combat, Chrysler Theater, 12 O'Clock High, Loner, Laredo, FBI, Invaders, Fugitive, Virginian, Man from Uncle, High Chaparral, Ironside, Twilight Zone, num. others; star series Stoney Burke; prod./star: Hawaii 5-O; creator TV shows: Tramp Ship, Yankee Trader, McAdoo, The Hunter series; writer original screenplay Mellissa 1968; pres. Lord & Lady Ents., Inc. 1968–; honors: St. Gauden's Artist Award 1948, Fame Award 1963, Cowboy Hall of Fame 1963, Am. Legion spl. law enforcement award 1973, City and Co. of Honolulu award for contbn. to tourism 1973, Fed. Exec. Bd. award 1978, Tripler Army Med. Ctr. Citizen of Year 1979, Hawaii Assn. of Bdcstrs. Award 1980, Am. Legion Good Guy award 1981; mem: Screen Actors Guild, Am. Fedn. of T.V. & Radio Actors, Actors Equity Assn., Am. Guild of Variety Artists, Dirs. Guild of Am.; mil: 2nd ofcr., navigator US Merchant Marines; rec: running, swimming. Ofc: Hawaii Five-O Studios, Ft. Ruger Honolulu HI 96816; c/o J. Wm. Hayes, 132 S Rodeo Dr Beverly Hills 90212

LO SCHIAVO, JOHN JOSEPH, university chancellor, clergyman; b. Feb. 25, 1925, San Francisco; s. Joseph and Anna (Re) Lo Schiavo; edn: AB, Gonzaga Univ., Spokane 1948, MA, 1949; STL (Licentiate in Sacred Theol.), Alma Coll., Los Gatos 1962; ordained priest (S.J.) Soc. of Jesus, R.Cath. Ch. (1955). Career: v. principal Brophy Coll. Prep, Phoenix, Ariz. 1958-61; instr. Philos. and Theol., Univ. San Francisco, 1950-52, 1956-57, 61-62, dean of students 1962-66, v.p. Student Affairs 1966-68; pres. Bellarmine Coll. Prep., San Jose 1968-75; rector Jesuit Community Univ. San Francisco 1975-77; pres. Univ. San Francisco 1977-91, chancellor, 1991–, univ. bd. trustees 1964-63, 1969-91, bd. chmn. 1970-73; mem. bd. dirs. St. Mary's Hosp. 1990–; trustee Sacred Heart Schs. 1991–; trustee San Francisco Consortium 1977-91; mem. Assn. of Jesuit Colls. and Univs. (dir. 1977-91), Assn. of Independent Calif. Colls. and Univs. (exec. com. 1978-91); honors: Alpha Sigma Nu (life), Nat. Jesuit Honor Soc., NCCJ Inc. (S.F. dir. 1982–); clubs: Olympic, Bohemian, Il Cenacolo; Republican; rec: golf. Address: Univ. of San Francisco 2130 Fulton St San Francisco 94117

LOTITO, MICHAEL JOSEPH, lawyer; b. July 22, 1948, Carbondale, Pa.; s. Dominic J. and Margaret Mary (Miller) L.; m. Luanne McMaster, Nov. 9, 1985; 1 child, Kelly b. 1977; edn: AB, and JD, Villanova Univ., 1970, 1974. Career: atty., assoc. Barley, Snyder, Cooper & Barber, Lancaster, Pa. 1974-76; assoc. Jackson,

Lewis, Schnitzler & Krupman, N.Y.C. 1976-81, ptnr. 1981, San Francisco mng. ptnr. 1982–; speaker nat. on labor and employment law for: Advanced Mgmt. Reports, Am. Health Care Assn., Soc. for Human Resource Mgmt., PBS Nightly Bus. Report, local radio, newspapers and periodicals incl. Wall Street Journal, S.F. Chronicle, L.A. Times; appt. wage bd. Indsl. Welfare Commn., bd. dirs. No. Calif. Human Resources Council (appt. 1983, elected 1986, chair legis. action com. 1983-87); rated AV Martindale-Hubbell (1986–); former mem: Calif. C.of C. (labor ind. com.), Soc. for Human Resource Mgmt. (bd. dirs. 1990–, chair nat. legislative affairs com. 1988-90, mem. nat. labor & empl. com. 1982-87), Am. Bar Assn. (labor rels. sect. 1974–), Pa. Bar Assn. (labor rels. sect. 1974-93), Calif. Bar Assn.; mem. Calif. Hist. Soc. (bd. 1987-89); coauthor: Making The ADA Work For You (1990), revised (1992); A Comprehensive Guide For Title I of the ADA (1992); What Managers & Supervisors Need to Know About the ADA (1992); Republican; R.Cath. Ofc: Jackson, Lewis, Schnitzler & Krupman 525 Market St Ste 3400 San Francisco 94105

LOTSPEICH, DIANE SUSAN, operations research analyst/systems engineer; b. Jan. 6, 1947, Dayton, Ohio; d. Robert Alexander and Clara Ellen (Stout) Hutton; m. James Edwin Lotspeich, Oct. 5, 1968; children: James Robert b. 1969, Jeffrey Wayne b. 1970; edn: AA, Cerritos Coll. 1974; BA, and MA, CSU Long Beach 1975, 1978; cand. MSSM, USC, 1990. Career: faculty Sawyer Coll, Ventura 1977-81; operations res. analyst/systems engr. Naval Air Warfare Ctr. Weapons Div., Point Mugu 1981–; instr. Ventura Coll. 1978-92; awards: Outstanding Young Women of Am. 1980, Ventura County Fair Bd. 1st Place-clothing & textiles 1987; mem: Apple Corps, Nat. Assn. Female Execs., Order of Eastern Star (Worthy Matron 1995), BSA; rec: counted cross stitch, sewing, hiking. Res: 1316 Crestlake Ave Ventura 93004-2739 Ofc: Naval Air Warfare Ctr Weapons Div Code 4KM200E Test Operations Branch Point Mugu 93042-5001

LOUCA, ALEXANDRE, systems technology manager; b. June 14, 1944, Cairo, Egypt, nat. 1987; s. Sadek Louca and Yvonne (Assaf) Papouchado; m. Georgette El Sokary, Jan. 30, 1972 (div. Dec. 1987); children: Karine b. 1977, Christine b. 1984; edn: BSc aeronautical engring. Faculty of Polytechnique Cairo Univ., 1969; 3-yr. PhD degree in fluid mechanics, Faculty of Polytechnique, Univ. of Paris VI, Fr.; dipl. computer pgmg. Control Data Inst., Paris, Fr., 1972; courses in computer "C" lang., also Spanish lang. (4.0 g.p.a.), El Camino Coll. 1991; Calif. real estate lic., 1992; fluent in English, Arabic, French. Career: pgmr./analyst Jacques Borel Internat., Paris, Fr. 1974-78; pgmr./analyst California Milling Corp., Los Angeles 1979-80; sr. systems cons. American Savings & Loan, Fullerton 1980-82, d.p. cons., 1982; data systems mgr. First Interstate Services, Los Angeles 1982-85; data systems mgr. Toyota Motor Sales USA, HQ, Torrance 1985-90, planned & installed complete data systems dept. supporting Toyota Motor Credit Corp. (TMCC), systems technology mgr. TMCC, 1990–; awards: Sporting Club (Egypt): champion of Egypt in diving 1968, and in table tennis 1964, champion of English schs. in boxing 1962, drummer Cairo Univ. Orch. 1968, technical achiev. First Interstate Svs. of Calif. 1983, feature article Spotlight - Toyota fitness mag. 1990; rec: dancing, working out, drumming, travel, swimming, flying. Ofc: Toyota Motor Credit Corp. 19001 S. Western Ave. Torrance 90509

LOUGHEED, ARTHUR LAWRENCE, financial/pension services firm principal, registered investment advisor, enrolled agent; b. Aug. 11, 1944, Fresno; s. Evan A. and Irene E. (Westby) L.; m. Nancy L. Sanderson; children: Christopher, b. 1967; Jennifer, b. 1969; Evan, b. 1975; edn: Albion Coll. 1963-64; AA, Orange Coast Coll. 1964; USC Grad. Sch. of Law 1964-65; MS finl. svcs., American Coll., Bryn Mawr 1980, MS mgmt., 1985; desig: ChFC, Chartered Fin. Cons. 1987, CLU, Am. Soc. Chartered Life Underwriters 1973, Chartered Property and Casualty Underwriter, Soc. CPCU 1980, Certified Financial Planner (CFP) 1992. Career: Farmers Ins. Gp., Los Angeles, served Santa Ana, Calif. & Pocatello, Idaho; agent./ Div. Agcy. mgr./ Regional life mgr. Aetna Life & Casualty Ins. Co., Hartford Conn., served Los Angeles 1974-77; mgr. of estate, bus. & pension sales CNA Ins. Cos., Chgo., Ill., served Los Angeles & Chgo. 1977-81; reg. dir. life sales ofcs./ nat. dir. mktg. & sales tng. Berkshire Group 1981–; currently pres./dir. of pension svs., The Bershire Life Ins. Co., San Diego; lectr. on ins. Glendale Coll., Univ. of Ill., Chgo, De Paul Univ., Chgo., UC San Diego, UC Irvine; reg. instr./ sem. leader Ins. Ednl. Assn. of San Francisco; honors: Alpha Gamma Sigma 1964, Toppers Club Farmers Ins. Group 1965-69, Regionaire Aetna Life & Casualty 1975–; mem. Nat., Calif., San Diego & Glendale/ Burbank Assns. of Life Underwriters, Am. Soc. CLUs; Soc. Chart. Property & Casualty Underwriters, Internat. Assn. of Financial Plnng., Saddleback Kiwanis (Mission Viejo), San Diego C.of C.; mem. curriculum advy. com. fin. planning UC San Diego, 1988–; editor assoc. CALUnderwriter mag. 1976, contbg. ed. California Broker mag. 1987–, contbr. articles on fin. and photog. in var. newspapers and mags.; Republican; Luthern; rec: fishing, history, literature. Res: 4793 Panorama Dr San Diego 92116 Ofc: Berkshire Group, 3545 Camino del Rio S San Diego 92108

LOVELL, JEFFREY D., investment banker; b. Apr. 21, 1952, N.Y.C.; s. Lewis Frederick and Pauline (Dailey) L.; m. Elaine Worley, Apr. 26, 1980; children: McKenzie b. 1984, Alexander b. 1987; edn: BS in bus. adm., Univ. Colorado, Boulder 1974; grad. studies internat. relations, Regents Coll., London (w/ Univ.

So. Calif.) 1986-87; reg. securities prin. NASD, 1984. Career: financial analyst General Dynamics Corp., San Diego 1974-76; mktg. rep./cons. SEI Corp., Wayne, Pa. 1976-79, regional v.p. SEI Corp., Los Angeles 1980-81, v.p. nat. sales SEI Corp., Wayne, Pa. 1982-83, sr. v.p. SEI Corp., L.A., 1983-85, mng. director SEI Financial Services (U.K.) London, 1985-88; pres., prin., co-founder Putnam, Lovell & Thornton Inc., Manhattan Beach, Calif. 1988–; trustee PIC Investment Trust (a series mutual fund) Pasadena 1992–; ptnr. Crestline Investment Ptnrs. (venture capital L.P.), Manhattan Beach 1992–;.ptnr. Highland Capital Advisors L.P. (venture capital L.P.) 1988–; honors: Sigma Nu 1971, Beta Gamma Sigma 1974; mem: Univ. Colo. Alumni Assn. 1988–, Univ. Colo. Coll. of Bus. Dean's Circle 1995, Empower America 1994–, Heritage Found. 1995–, Manhattan CC 1984–; pub. articles re internat. investing in trade jours. 1984-86; Republican (Rep. Nat. Com. 1980–); St. Andrews Presbyterian Ch., Redondo Beach; rec: skiing, tennis. Res: 99 Village Circle Manhattan Beach 90266 Ofcs: Putnam, Lovell & Thornton Inc. 317 Rosecrans Ave Manhattan Beach 90266, 19 Fulton St NY, NY 10038, and Pier 5, Embarcadero, San Francisco 94111

LOW, HARRY W., police commission president, retired appellate presiding justice; b. Mar. 12, 1931, Oakdale; s. Tong and Ying (Gong) L. m. Mayling Jue, Aug. 24, 1952; children: Lawrence b. 1953, Kathleen b. 1957, Allan b. 1962; edn: AA, Modesto Jr. Coll. 1950, AB, UC Berkeley 1952, LLB, 1955. Career: tchg. assoc. Boalt Hall 1955-56; dep. atty. gen. Calif. Dept. of Justice, 1956-66; commnr. Workers' Compensation Appeals Bd. 1966; municipal ct. judge 1966-74, presiding judge 1972-73; superior ct. judge 1974-82, supvg. judge Juvenile Ct. 1981-82; presiding justice Ct. of Appeal, San Francisco 1982-92; pres. S.F. Police Commn., 1992–; bd. dirs. Union Bank 1993–; speaker, instr. var. judicial seminars and study coms.; faculty Calif. Judges Coll. 1976-83, Nat. Coll. of Judiciary 1977-79, Inst. of Ct. Mgmt. 1976-81; bd. CJER Journal; chmn. ABA Appellate Judges Conf. 1990-91; mem. bd. dirs. Nat. Center for State Cts.; conf. guest lectr. at meetings of Ida., Wash., Ariz., Va., Mich. and Nev. Judiciaries; co-chmn. past confs. on Media and the Law; ed. Courts Commentary 1973-76; chmn. bd. vis. US Mil. Acad., West Point 1981; mem: Calif. Judges Assn. (pres. 1978-79), Calif. Council on Criminal Justice, Edn. Center for Chinese (bd. chmn. 1969–), S.F. City Coll. Found. (pres. 1978-87), Chinese-Am. Citizens Alliance (nat. pres. 1989-93, Grand Bd.), Calif. Jud. Council 1979-81, USF (pres. 1987-88), Inst. of Chinese-Western History; mem. bd. dirs: Salesian Boys Club, St. Vincent's Home for Boys, Friends of Rec. and Parks, S.F. Zoological Soc., Law in the Free Soc., NCCJ, World Affairs Council, Chinatown Youth Task Force, Mayor's China Gateway Com.; Democrat; rec: gardening, S.F. hist. Res: 104 Turquoise 94131 Ofc: Judicial Arbitration and Mediation Services, 2 Embarcadero #1100 San Francisco 94111

LOWE, KAROLYN MARIE, certified public accountant, agricultural company chief financial officer; b. May 4, 1948, Chicago, Ill.; d. Leonard Herald and Juanita Leslie (Register) Lowe; children: Mishaela b. 1983; edn: BS edn., Syracuse Univ. 1970. Career: sr. staff acct. Berry Dunne McNeil CPA, Portland, Me. 1978-81; fin. analyst 7-Up Foods (citrus products div.), Ventura 1981-85; controller Armstrong Roses (div. Moet Hennessey), Somis 1985-88; San Miguel Produce, Oxnard 1988–; awards: Syracuse Univ. centennial scholar 1970; mem: Am. Inst. C.P.A., NAA, ASWCPA, Kimball Road Homeowners Assn. (treas. 1985-93); leader Girl Scout Troop #871, 1982-95. Ofc: San Miguel Produce 4444 Navalair Rd Oxnard 93033

LOWNDES, DAVID ALAN, programmer-analyst; b. Oct. 28, 1947, Schenectady, N.Y.; s. John Henry and Iris Anne (Hepburn) L.; m. Peggy Welco, May 3, 1970; children: Diana b. 1978, Julie b. 1982; edn: AB, UC Berkeley, 1969, grad. study 1972-73. Career: acct., credit mgr. The Daily Californian, Berkeley 1973-75, bus. mgr., 1975-76; acct. Pacific Union Assurance, San Francisco 1976-77; acctg. mgr. 1977-78; senior acct. Univ. Calif., San Francisco 1978-88, pgmr.-analyst, 1988–; mem. Birmingham and Midlands Soc. for Genealogy and Heraldry 1987–, Bay Area Roots Users Group 1990–, Am. Canadian Geneal. Soc. 1991–; rec: genealogy, microcomputing. Ofc: Univ. of California, 250 Executive Park Blvd. Ste 2000 San Francisco 94143

LOWRY, RONALD RALPH, architect; b. Jan. 1, 1937, Oakland; s. Ralph Clair and Desiree A. (Queyrel) L.; m. Roberta Lynn Coffield, Oct. 31, 1964; children: Ronda Lynn b. 1967, Julie Ree b. 1970, Joel Justin b. 1971; edn: AA, Sacramento City Coll.; Calif. State Polytechnic Coll.; BA, CSU Sacramento; reg. architect Calif. 1972, NCARB, 1980. Career: architectural asst. Calif. Dept. of Water Resources 1961-69; archtl. planner Calif. Dept. Gen. Svcs. 1969-71; retirement ofcr. Calif. Tchrs. Retirement System 1971-72; govt. program analyst/architect Calif. Dept. Gen. Services, 1972-76; deptl. constrn. and maint. supvr. Calif. Dept. of Development Services, 1976-80; chief, Facilities Plng. Div.,Calif. Youth Authority 1980–; arch./prin. Ronald R. Lowry Architect; mem. Constrn. Specification Inst.; civic bds: Consumnes Area Community Plng. Advy. Council (1980-86, v.chair 1980, chair 1981), Sloughhouse Fire Protection Dist. (dir. 1981-84), Omochumne-Hartnell Water Dist. (elected dir. 1987–, pres. 1989–), County Service Area 4B (appt. 1990-94), Assn. of Calif. Water Agys.- Jt. Powers Ins. Auth. (appt. 1989-94), Sacramento Met. Water Auth. (1989–), Sheldon Hills HOA (pres. 1974-80, 1993–); mil: USNR 1962; Republican; Agnostic; rec: local govt., hunting, camping. Res: 7515 Lakehill Ct. Elk Grove 95624 Ofc: Calif. Youth Authority, 4343 Williamsborough Dr Sacramento 95823

LOZANO, CARLOS, educator; b. Jan. 12, 1913, Zamora, Mexico; nat. 1942; s. Epifanio and Julia (Tejeda) L.; edn: BA, UC Berkeley 1941; PhD, 1962. Career: asst. prof. George Washington Univ., Wash., D.C. 1959-63; assoc. prof. St. Louis Univ., Mo. 1963-64; prof. Univ. Oreg., Eugene 1964-66; prof. and chair dept. of modern languages, St. Marys Coll., Moraga, CA 1966-70; prof. and founding chair, dept. of fgn. languages, CSU Bakersfield 1970-81, NEH chair Comparative Literature, Scranton Univ., 1982, prof. emeritus, spl. asst. to pres., CSU Bakersfield 1984–; honors: AUS Legion of Merit 1949, Govt. of Chile Medalla Militar del Ejercito 1949, UC Berkeley Therese F. Collin travelling fellowship 1955-56, Calif. Fgn. Language Tchrs. Assn. tchr. of year 1973, Calif. St. Senate commend. 1981; mem: Acad. Spanish Language of Americas, Explicacon de Textos Literarios (ed. CSU Sacto.); Hispanic Press CSU (cofounder); Hispanic Excellence Scholarship Fund, CSU Bakersfield; Liaison Com. Bilingual Cultural Com. Univ. Calif. Articulation Conf., Mex. Am. Educators Assn.; author: Elemental Odes of Pablo Neruda (1961); My Horse Gonzalez, transl. of "Caballo de Copas", novel of F. Alegria (1964); with F. Alegria, Novelistas Contemporaneos Hispano-Americanos (1964); Ruben Dario y El Modernismo en Espana (1968); The Other Fire, transl. of "El Otro Fuego" poetry of David Valjalo, Madrid (1989); La Influencia de Ruben Dario en Espana; The Maypole Warriors, transl. of Manana Los Guerreros, novel of F. Alegria (Latin Am. Literary Rev. Press, Pittsburg, Pa. 1992); Rafe and the Sun Arrow, novel (pending 1992/3); 25+ articles in profl. jours.; mil: major AUS 1942-53; Democrat; R.Cath.; rec: poetry and prose, translating. Res: 2807 Elm Bakersfield 93301 Ofc: California State University Office of the President Bakersfield 93301

LU, NANCY CHAO, professor; b. May 29, Sian, China; d. Lun Yuan Chao and Su-mei (Tsang) Chao; m. Chyi Kang Lu, Mar. 19, 1966; children: Richard Hsiang, 1967; edn: BS, Nat. Taiwan Univ., Taipei, 1963; MS, Univ. Wyoming, Laramie, 1965; PhD, Univ. Calif., Berkeley, 1973; registered dietitian, Am. Dietetic Assn., 1988. Career: tchg. asst. Univ. Wyoming, Laramie, 1963-64, Univ. Calif., Berkeley, 1964, 70; tchg. assoc. UC Berkeley, 1978, 1979-80; lectr. San Jose State Univ., 1980-82; assoc. prof. San Jose State Univ., 1982-87 (tenured 1986), prof., 1987–; proj. coordinator NIH Nematode grant, UC Berkeley, 1978-80; awards: Most Outstanding Nutrition & Food Sci. Prof. (1989, 93); Meritorious Performance and Professional Promise Award, San Jose State Univ., 1986; Who's Who In Calif., 1986; Calif. State Univ. Affirmative Action Faculty Devel. Award, 1984, 1985, 1986; Who's Who of Am. Women, 1977; Ellsworth Dougherty Award, 1976; NIH Postdoctoral Fellowship, 1973-75; UC Berkeley Postdoctoral Fellow, 1976-78; mem: Am. Dietetic Assn., Am. Inst. Nutrition, Inst. Food Technologists, Iota Sigma Pi (pres. 1977), Sigma Xi, Soc. Experimental Biology and Medicine, Soc. Nematology; author and coauthor of numerous publ. articles and res. papers. Ofc: Dept. Nutrition & Food Science, San Jose State Univ. San Jose 95192

LUCAS, GEORGE W., JR., film director, producer, screenwriter; b. May 14, 1944, Modesto, Calif.; edn: Modesto Jr. College; BA, Univ. Southern Calif., 1966. Career: chmn. Lucasfilm Ltd., San Rafael, Calif.; creator short THX-1138 (Grand prize Nat. Student Film Festival, 1967); asst. to Francis Ford Coppola on The Rain People; dir. Filmmaker (documentary on making of The Rain People); dir., co-writer THX-1138, 1970, American Graffiti 1973; dir., author screenplay Star Wars, 1977; exec. producer More American Graffiti, 1979; The Empire Strikes Back, 1980; Raiders of the Lost Ark, 1981; Indiana Jones and the Temple of Doom, 1984; Labyrinth, 1986; Howard the Duck, 1986; Willow, 1988; Tucker, 1988; exec. producer, author screenplay Return of the Jedi, 1983; co-prod. producer Mishima, 1985; co-author, co-exec producer Indiana Jones and the Last Crusade, 1989; exec. producer (TV series) The Young Indiana Jones Chronicles, 1992-93, Radioland Murders, 1994. Ofc: Lucasfilm Ltd PO Box 2009 San Rafael 94912-2009

LUCAS, MALCOLM MILLAR, state supreme court chief justice; b. Apr. 19, 1927, Berkeley, Calif.; s. Robert and Georgina (Campbell) L.; m. Joan Fisher, June 23, 1956; children: Gregory, Lisa Georgina; edn: B.A., Univ. Southern Calif., 1950, LLB, 1953; Calif. Bar 1954. Career: ptnr. firm Lucas, Deukmejian and Lucas, Long Beach, Calif., 1955-67; judge Superior Ct., L.A., 1967-71 U.S. Dist. Ct. (central dist.) Calif., 1971-84; assoc. justice Calif. Supreme Ct. 1984-87, chief justice, 1987–; mem: Calif. State Bar Assn. Ofc: California Supreme Ct 303 2nd St # S023S San Francisco 94107-1366

LUCAS, SUZANNE, statistician, educational consultant; b. Jan. 16, 1939, Baxter Springs, Kans.; d. Ralph Beaver and Marguerite (Sansocie) L.; edn: BA math., Calif. State Univ., Fresno, 1967, MA ednl. theory, 1969; MS stats., Univ. Southern. Calif., 1979; children: Patricia Sue Jennings, Neil Patric Jennings. Career: asst. to dir. NSF Inst., Calif. State Univ., Fresno, 1968; tchr. secondary math. Fresno city schs, 1968-78; statistician corp. indsl. relations Hughes Aircraft Co., Los Angeles, 1979-80; personnel adminstr. Hughes Aircraft Co. Space and Communications Group, Los Angeles, 1981-82, mem. tech. staff in math., 1982-85, staff engr., 1986-87; mem. tech. staff cost analysis The Aerospace Corp., 1987-90; sr. staff engr. Hughes Aircraft Co. Electro Optical Systems, 1990-93, scientist, engr., 1993–; owner, math. cons. Lucas Educational Consultants, Manhattan Beach, Calif., 1989–; lectr. in biostats. Univ. So. Calif.,

1979; awards: Kiwanis scholar, 1958; mem.: Internat. Soc. Parametric Analysts (pres. So. Calif. chpt. 1991-92), Soc. Cost Estimating and Analysis (cert.), Am. Psychol. Assn., Nat. Coun. Tchrs. of Math., Am. Statis. Assn., Univ. So. Calif. Alumni Assn. (life), Kappa Mu Epsilon. Ofc: Hughes Aircraft Co PO Box 902 E0/E1/A118 El Segundo CA 90245-0902 also: Lucas Educational Consultants PO Box 3868 Manhattan Beach 90266

LUCE, R(OBERT) DUNCAN, distinguished research professor of cognitive science and research professor of economics; b. May 16, 1925, Scranton, Pa.; s. Robert Renselaer and Ruth Lillian (Downer) L.; m. Gay Gaer, June 1950 (div. 1967); m. Cynthia Newby, Oct., 1967 (div. 1977); m. Carolyn Ann Scheer, Feb. 27, 1988; children: Aurora b. 1972; edn: BS, MIT 1945; PhD, 1950. Career: staff MIT, Cambridge, Mass. 1950-53; asst. prof. Columbia Univ., NYC 1953-57; lectr. Harvard Univ., Cambridge, Mass. 1957-59; prof. Univ. Pa., Phila. 1959-69; vis. prof. Inst. Advanced Study, Princeton, N.J. 1969-72; prof. UC Irvine 1972-75; prof. Harvard Univ. 1976-88, emeritus 1988–; distinguished prof. UC Irvine 1988–; fellow Center Advanced Study in Behavioral Scis., Stanford 1954-55, 66-67, 87-88; awards: Am. Acad. Arts & Scis. fellow 1966, Am. Psychol. Assn. Disting. Research award 1970, Nat. Acad. Sci. 1972, Am. Philosophical Soc. 1994, UCI Distinguished Faculty Lectureship Award for Res. 1994; mem: Soc. Math. Psychology (past pres.), Psychometric Soc. (past pres.), Am. Psychological Soc. (bd. of scientific affairs, past bd. dirs.), Fedn. of Cognitive, Behavioral and Psychol. Scis. (past pres.); coauthor: Games & Decisions, 1957, Foundations of Measurement, 1971, 89, 90; author: Individual Choice Behavior, 1959, Response Times, 1986, Sound & Hearing, 1993; mil: ensign USNR 1943-46; rec: art and antiques, gardening. Res: 20 Whitman Ct Irvine 92715-4057 Ofc: Univ. of Calif. Social Science Tower Irvine 92717

LUCE, TERRY JEAN, medical-legal consultant; b. Sept. 21, 1954, La Cross, Wis.; d. Charles Harold and Sharon Gail (Schuttenhelm) Luce, Jr.; edn: AA, East L.A. City Coll. 1975; BS, St. Josephs Coll. 1985; reg. nurse Calif. (1975). Career: nursing supr. Covina Valley Comm. Hosp., 1979-80, pediatric cons. 1980-81; coordinator Utilization Rev. and Quality of Care, Calif. Medical Review Inc., San Francisco 1981-85, medicare contracts adminstr., 1985-87; asst. dir. of nursing St. Francis Heights Hosp., 1987; independent health care consultant, 1987-93; utilization review nse. Health Plan of San Mateo, supplemental case mgr. 1989-92, Health Services asst. mgr. 1992–; listed Who's Who in Nursing 1987, Who's Who in Women of Am. 1978; publ: article in J. of Am. Sociol. March, 1974. Res: 1551 Southgate Ave #117 Daly City 94015 Ofc: Health Plan of San Mateo 1500 Fashion Island Blvd Ste 300 San Mateo 94404

LUCEY, JACK, artist, instructor; b. Feb. 11, 1929, San Francisco; s. John and Julia C. (Casey) L.; m. Charlotte M. Wyckoff, July 28, 1956; children: John, Robert, Michael; edn: BA vocat. edn., San Francisco State Univ.; AA, Indian Valley Coll.; postgrad, Univ. of Calif., 1980; BA, Acad. Art Coll., San Francisco, 1979. Career: art dir. Indl. Jour. Newspaper, San Rafael, 1956–; illustrator Lucey Studio & Gallery. San Rafael Calif., 1956–; instr. Coll. of Marin, Kentfield, Calif., 1975–, Acad. of Art San Francisco·1976-77, speaker Internat. Newspaper Internat. Graphics Inst., San Jose 1977; mem: adv. bd. Marin Comm. Colls., Contra Costa Regional Occupational Program, Marin County Substitute Tchr. Assn., Soc. Western Artists, art dir. Club of San Francisco; mil: sgt. USMC, 1950-52. Res/Studio: 84 Crestwood Dr San Rafael 94901

LUCIA, MARILYN REED, physician; b. Boston, Mass.; m. Salvatore P. Lucia, 1959 (dec. 1984); m. C. Robert Russell; children: Elizabeth, Walter, Salvatore, Darryl; edn: MD, UCSF 1956. Career: clin. prof. psychiatry Univ. Calif. at San Francisco 1982–; founder/cons. Marilyn Reed Lucia Child Care Study Ctr. UCSF; cons. Cranio-facial Ctr. UCSF; cons. No. Calif. Diagnostic Sch. for Neurologically Handicapped Children; director Childrens Psychiatric Services, Contra Costa Co. Hosp., Martinez; honors: Phi Beta Kappa; mem: Am. Psychiatric Assn. (fellow), Am. Acad. Child Psychiatry (fellow), Am. Cleft Palate Assn. Ofc: 350 Parnassus Ave Ste 602 San Francisco 94117

LUDDEN, JEROME A., JR., physician, surgeon; b. July 7, 1911, Pomona; s. Jerome A. and Minnie Alta (Newkirk) L.; m. Ruth Adelaide Frary, June 12, 1937; children: James Robert b. 1939, Elizabeth Ann b. 1942; edn: BA, Pomona Coll. 1933; BS medicine, Univ. So. Dakota Vermillion 1935; MD, Tufts Univ. 1937. Career: physician and surgeon; mem: Santa Cruz Co. Med. Soc. (pres. 1952), Lions (pres. 1948); mil: lt. cmdr. USN 1942-51; rec: jewelry making, woodworking, gardening. Res: Dominican Oaks-C202, 3400 Paul Sweet Road Santa Cruz 95065

LUDWICK, JACK RYDEL, physician-surgeon; b. Apr. 7, 1935, Detroit, Mich.; s. Jack Robert and Elna Mary (Loynes) L.; m. Shirley J.E. Hilving, Apr. 5, 1957; children:. Kathleen b. 1960; edn: AB, Wayne State Univ., 1957; MD, Univ. of Mich., 1961; diplomate Am. Bd. Surgery (1968). Career: intern St. Joseph Mercy Hosp. 1961-62; residency tng., Univ. of Mich., 1962-67; surgeon U.S. Army, Ft. Riley, Kans. 1968-70; asst. prof. Univ. Mich., Ann Arbor 1970-72; pvt. practice general and vascular surgeon, Torrance 1972–; asst. clin. prof. UCLA Harbor Gen. Hosp. 1973–; med. staff Little Company of Mary Hosp., Torrance (chief of staff 1993-95, v.chief staff 1991-93, chmn. dept. surg. 1987-

89); awards: USPHS Trainee Surg. (1963-67), Alpha Omega Alpha (1960); mem: Fellow Am. Coll. Surgeons, Collegium Internat. Chiruriae, Soc. Surg. Alimentary Tract; civic: World Wildlife Fund, Sierra Club, Nature Conservancy; contbr. 5 med. jour. articles (1966-70); mil: major AUS 1968-70; rec: wood sculpture, nature photog. Ofc: 4201 Torrance Blvd Ste 550 Torrance 90503

LUDWIG, RONALD LEWIS, lawyer; b. June 25, 1943, Cleveland, Ohio; s. Julius and Helen (Saltzman) L.; m. Carrie B. Glaser, Dec. 28, 1968; edn: AB, Duke Univ. 1965; JD, Univ. Mich. 1968; admitted St. Bar Calif. Career: tax law splst. I.R.S., Wash., D.C. 1968-69; atty. sole practice, Wash. D.C. 1969-73; mem. Kelso Hunt & Ludwig, San Francisco 1973-77; Ludwig Goldberg & Krenzel 1977–; spl. counsel ESOP Assn. 1978-94; adj. prof. Georgetown Univ. Law Center 1971-73; lectr. Golden Gate Univ. Law Sch. 1980-82; awards: ESOP Assn. Spl. Recognition 1986, ESOP Assn. Life Svs. award 1992; mem: Am. Bar Assn., Bar Assn. San Francisco, Western Pension & Benefits Conf. S.F.; mem., bd. of editors, The Journal of Employee Ownership Law and Fin. Res: 640 Davis St Unit 17 San Francisco 94111 Ofc: Ludwig Goldberg & Krenzel 50 California St 36th Floor San Francisco 94111

LUEGGE, WILLARD ARTHUR, chemist; b. Mar. 19, 1931, Oak Park, Ill.; s. Theodore Wilhelm and Irma Minnie (Schoepfer) L.; m. Joanna Carleen Wechter, Sept. 1, 1951; children: Sherylene b. 1952, Lynette b. 1959; edn: BA, Indiana Univ., 1953, grad. work Ind. Univ. Ext., Univ. Louisville, UCLA, 1955-65; Calif. tchg. credential, sec. sci. tchr. 1961. Career: res. chemist Louisville Cement Co., Speed, Ind. 1956-60; quality control chemist Calif. Portland Cement Co., Mojave, Calif. 1960-61; chemistry tchr. Palmdale (Calif.) High Sch., 1961-90, sci. dept. chair 1964-79; res. chemist USAF Rocket Propulsion Lab., Edwards AFB, summers 1966, 67, 68; owner, dir. PM Labs, Lancaster 1968-89; cons. prin. extractive metallurgical chemistry, Lancaster 1989–; bd. dir. Bryman Refining Co., Inc. 1992–, v.p. 1993–; awards: Chem. Tchr. of Year, Am. Chemical Soc., W.D.C. 1967, NSF grantee (1963, 64); mem: Western Mining Council 1989–, Western Public Lands Coalition 1992–; inventor assay kit (1970); Presbyterian; rec: travel, reading, mining archaeology, spectator- baseball, basketball, auto racing. Res: 560 E Avenue J-1 Lancaster 93535 Ph: 805/948-1915

LUENBERGER, DAVID GILBERT, educator; b. Sept. 16, 1937, Los Angeles; s. Frederick Otto and Marion (Crumly) L.; m. Nancy Ann Iversen, Jan. 7, 1962; children: Susan b. 1963, Robert b. 1965, Jill b. 1967, Jenna b. 1975; edn: BSEE, Caltech, 1959; MSEE, Stanford Univ., 1961, PhD, 1963. Career: asst. prof., assoc. prof., prof. Stanford Univ., 1963–; dept. chair EES Dept. 1980; tech. asst. US Office Science and Technology, Wash. DC 1971; vis. prof. M.I.T., 1976; guest prof. Tech. Univ. Denmark, Lyngby 1986; honors: Sigma Xi, Tau Beta Pi; mem: IEEE (fellow), AAUP, Am. Fin. Assn., Soc. for Economic Dynamics and Control (pres. 1987-88), Econometric Soc., Soc. for Promotion of Econ. Theory, Soc. for Promotion of Mgmt. Sci., Mathematical Pgmg. Soc.; club: Palo Alto Camera; author 3 books: Optimization by Vector Space Methods, 1969, Linear and Nonlinear Programming (2d ed. 1973), Intro. to Dynamic Systems, 1979, Microeconomic Theory, 1995; Republican; Lutheran; rec: photog. Res: 813 Tolman Dr Stanford 94305 Ofc: Stanford Univ., EES Dept., Terman Center, Stanford 94305-4025

LUEVANO, FRED, JR., computer systems executive; b. June 21, 1943, Alamogordo, N.M.; s. Fred Macias and Margaret (Baca) L.; m. Lupe Olmos, July 11, 1964; children: Michael b. 1965, James Paul b. 1971; edn: AA, Fullerton Coll. 1975; BA, Univ. Redlands 1979; MAM, 1985. Career: mgr. computer ops. Hoffman Electronics, El Monte 1971-76; mgr. computer ops. and tech. services, City of Anaheim 1976-79; mgr. data processing Wyle Data Services, Huntington Beach 1979-83; mgr. corp. computing Northrop Corp., Hawthorne 1983-85; mgr. computer ops. Northrop Aircraft 1985–, dir. disaster recovery Northrop Corp. 1983-85, dir. disaster recovery & security 1985-91, mgr. systems mgmt. 1991–; cons. info. systems, La Habra Heights 1971–; city council cand. City of La Habra Heights 1982; chmn.. bd. dirs. Disaster Recovery Inst., 1990–; speaker Assn. Computer Ops. Mgrs., Chgo., Ill. 1983, San Diego 1988; mem: Am. Mgmt. Assn., Telecomms. Assn., Assn. Computer Ops. Mgrs., Northrop Mgmt. Club, BSA (cub master 1979-84, com. chmn. 1975-79), La Habra Parents for Swimming Inc. (pres. 1986-89), Red Coach Club (pres. 1979-80); article pub. in profl. jour. (1989); mil: E-5 USN 1961-65; Republican; R.Cath.; rec: fishing, basketball, art collecting. Ofc: Northrop Grumman 8900 E Washington Blvd M/S 770/XC Pico Rivera 90660

LUFT, LORRAINE LEVINSON, psychologist; b. June 23, 1947, Washington, D.C.; d. Irving and Gladys (Dolgin) Levinson; m. Harold Luft, May 24, 1970; children: Shira b. 1977, Jana b. 1983; edn: BA, Brandeis Univ. 1969; MCP, MIT 1971; MS, Pacific Grad. Sch. 1980; PhD, 1983; lic. psychologist Calif. 1986. Career: dir. program planning and evaluation Cambridge-Somerville Mental Health Center, Cambridge, Mass. 1971-73; dir. program evaluation Peninsula Hosp. Mental Health Center, Burlingame 1973-75 dir. program evaluation, inservice edn. 1975-82, dir. program evaluation, inservice edn., comm. service 1982-86, assoc. dir. 1986-89; pvt. practice clin. psychology, San Mateo 1986–; Peninsula Psychiatric Assocs. 1991–; cons. UCSF Langley Porter 1982–; honors: Phi Beta Kappa, Nat. Econs. Hon. Soc., Univ. Pa. Urban Planning fellow-

ship 1970, MIT Nat. Sci. Fedn. fellowship 1971, Peninsula Hosp. Outstanding Major Accomplishments 1989; mem: Am. Psychological Assn., San Mateo Co. Psychological Assn., Calif. St. Psychological Assn., PTA Palo Alto; num. articles pub. in profl. jours.; rec: travel, cooking, hiking. Ofc: 39 North San Mateo Drive Ste 8 San Mateo 94401

LUNDE, DOLORES BENITEZ, retired teacher; b. Apr. 12, 1929, Honolulu, Hawaii; d. Frank Molero and Matilda (Francisco) Benitez; m. Nuell Carlton Lunde, July 6, 1957; 1 dau. Laurelle b. 1959; edn: BA, Univ. Oregon, Eugene 1951, grad. work 1951-52, USC, 1953-54, Colo. State Univ. 1957-58, CSU Fullerton 1967-68; Calif. tchg. credentials: gen. secondary life, 1952, language devel. specialist, 1990; career: tchr. Brawley Union High Sch. Dist., Brawley, Calif. 1952-55; Fullerton Union High Sch. Dist. 1955-73, 1985-94; tchr. aide Placentia Unified Sch. Dist. 1983-85; tchr. Fullerton Sch. Dist. 1988, Fullerton Union HSD Alternative and Cont. Edn., 1985-91, Fullerton Union High Sch. Dist. 1989-94 (ret.); innovator in tests, tchg. tools and audio-visual aids 25+ yrs.; presenter regional and state convs. 1986-87; advisor internat. & Spanish clubs, La Habra 1965-72; awards: named gift honoree AAUW Fullerton 1985, tchr. of year Fullerton Union HSD 1989; mem: Nat. Edn. Assn., Calif. Tchrs. Assn., Fullerton Secondary Tchrs. Assn., Tchrs. of English to Speakers of Other Languages, AAUW (life mem.), ed. 1979-80, corr. sec. 1981-83, pgm. v.p. 1983-84, vol. tchr. 1974-77); Lutheran (Luth. Soc. Svs. vol. 1981-82); rec: singing, folk dancing, guitar, travel. Res: 4872 N Ohio Yorba Linda 92686

LUNDE, GREGORY JAMES, management consultant; b. Feb. 27, 1949, Fargo, ND; s. Palmer James and Freda M. L.; m. Sherryl, Jan. 12, 1986; children: Mark b. 1988, Erik b. 1989; edn: BA, Augsburg Coll., 1971; AM, Univ. S. Dak., 1972; MBA, Claremont Graduate Sch., 1983, MA, 1989; PhD, So. Calif. Inst., 1991; profl. desig: cert. mgmt. cons. (CMC), Inst. of Mgmt. Consultants, NY, 1991. Career: quality control analyst 3M Co., St. Paul, Minn. 1972-76; economic planner ND State Planning Div., Bismarck 1976; planning and mgmt. cons. prin., pres. NOR-CON Devel. Corp., ND, 1976-82; systems coordinator Hughes Aircraft Co., Los Angeles 1984-85; dir. of planning Bank of North Dakota, Bismarck 1986; pres. Poly-Centric Strategies II (exec. & MIS cons.), Los Alamitos 1987-93; pres. COLLIGATED® Solutions and Systems (CEO bus. intelligence, mgmt. cons.), Los Alamitos 1993–; instr., history, Jamestown (N.D.) Coll. 1981; awards: Claremont Grad. Sch. univ. fellow 1981-83, tchg. asst. grant Univ. So. Dak. 1971-72; mem: Inst. of Mgmt. Consultants, Cypress C.of C., Los Alamitos C.of C.; publs: Colligation: Colligation and Covering Law, two theories of historical explanation for decision-making applications (Vantage Press, NY, 1995), Business Intelligence: Strategic Information Management, 1993, Strategic Management and Planning Systems, 1988, Bank of ND Strategic Plan, 1986, land use manual Town & Country Pgm., 1980, ND Econ. Dev. Strategy, 1979-80; Presbyn.; rec: bicycling, running, hunting, fishing. Ofc: COLLIGATED® Solutions and Systems, 12100-131 Montecito Rd Los Alamitos 90720

LUNDELL, BRETTA CHRISTINA, retired banker; b. Aug. 21, 1911, St. Helena; d. Hjalmar Ernest and Anna Caroline (Osterman) Lundell; 1 dau., Carolyn b. 1945; edn: grad. Calistoga H.S. 1928. Career: bookkeeper Bank of Am., Calistoga 1929-37, secty. 1937-43, teller 1945-68, pro. asst. cashier 1968-71; awards: Am. Legion Cert. of Appreciation (1975), Napa Co. Fair Mem. of Year (1971); mem: Native Daughters of Golden West (1st v.p. 1988-89), Am. Legion Aux. (treas. 1975-89), Soroptimist Internat. Calistoga, Am. Legion, Waves Nat., Vets. Rep. Fed. Womans Club, Napa Co. Fair Assn.; mil: USN 1943-45; Democrat; Episcopalian; rec: crafts. Res: 250 Crystal Springs Rd St Helena 94574

LUNDSTROM, MARY FRANCES, contract procurement for the Navy; b. June 23, 1948, Hollywood; d. Archibald DeNorville and Ivy Kate (Whitworth) Meyer; children: Tara Carina b. 1979; edn: BA art, San Diego State Univ., 1971; numerous art workshops and real estate classes; currently working on MBA. Career: draftsman Genge Inds., Ridgecrest 1967-68; draftsman, illustrator Naval Weapons Ctr., China Lake 1969-70; subs. tchr. Albuquerque Pub. Sch., N.M. 1971-72; subs. tchr. Kern County High Sch., China Lake 1972-74; real estate sales Coldwell Banker, Ridgecrest 1974-86; art instr. Cerro Coso Comm. Coll., 1986-91; art curator Maturango Museum, Ridgecrest 1986-95, museum store mgr. 1993-95; free lance artist, 1970–; grants reviewer Inst. of Mus. Svcs. 1993-95; juror for Artfest at Bakersfield Coll. 1995; awards: fellowship name grant award AAUW, China Lake 1987; juror mixed media show Lancaster (Calif.) Art Mus., 1990; mem: AAUW (1972–, past pres.), High Desert Council of the Arts 1979-94, Arts Council of Kern 1986-95, Enamel Guild West 1980–, Enamelist Soc. 1980–, Calif. Assn. of Museums 1986-95; Rotary, Sister City Assn., Am. Assn. of Univ. Women Publications; Democrat; Episcopalian; rec: art, swimming, travel. Res: 731 W Howell Ave Ridgecrest 93555 Ofc: Naval Air Warfare Center China Lake 93555

LUNGREN, DANIEL EDWARD, attorney general; b. Sept. 22, 1946, Long Beach, Calif.; s. John Charles and Lorain Kathleen (Youngberg) L.; m. Barbara Kolls, Aug. 2, 1969; children: Jeffrey Edward, Kelly Christine, Kathleen Marie; edn: AB (cum Laude), Notre Dame Univ., Ind. 1968; post grad., Univ. of So. Calif. Law Sch. 1968-69; JD, Georgetown Univ., Washington, D.C. 1971; admitted Calif. Bar 1972. Career: staff asst. to Senators George Murphy and William Brock 1969-71; spl. asst. to co-chmn., Republican Nat. Comm. & dir., spl. programs 1971-72; assoc., selected as partner, Ball, Hunt, Hart, Brown & Baerwitz, Long Beach 1973-78; mem. 96-97th Cong. from 34th Calif. Dist., and 98-100th Cong. from 42nd Calif. Dist. 1979-89; partner, Diepenbrock, Wulff, Plant & Hannegan, Sacramento 1989-90; elected Atty. Gen., State of Calif. 1990–; Nat. Comm. Representative from Calif. 1988–; awards: Good Samaritan Award, L.A. Council of Mormon Churches 1976; mem: Calif. State Peace Officers Standards & Training Commn. 1991–, Calif. Judicial Council's Commn. on the Future of the Courts 1991–, Conf. of We. Attorneys Gen. 1991–, Nat. Assn. of Attorneys Gen. 1991–, President's Commn. on Model State Drug Laws 1992-93; civic: bd. dir. Long Beach Chpt. Am. Red Cross 1976-88; bd. dir. Long Beach Boys Club 1978-88; author: publ. articles in The Journal of the Inst. for Socioeconomic Studies, 1985 and the San Diego Law Review, 1987; co-author: publ. articles in Loyola Law Review, 1984 and UCLA Law Review, 1992; Republican; Roman Catholic; rec: weight lifting, racquetball, bicycling. Ofc: 1300 I Street Sacramento 95814

LUO, ANNA S., stock analyst; b. Mar. 26, 1963; d. George Y. and Amy J. (Fine) L.; m. George C. Tan, Jan. 16, 1985; edn: BA, UC Berkeley, 1985; att. M.I.T. Sch. of Arch. 1988-90, MS in R.E. Devel. and Investment, M.I.T. Ctr. for Real Estate, 1991. Career: design team Rasmussen Ingle Anderson Architects & Engrs., San Francisco 1986-87; designer, coordinator Community Design Collaborative, S.F. 1987-88; real estate cons. The Beacon Co., Devel. Group, Boston 1989;real estate cons. Pacific Union Co., San Francisco 1992; sr. cons. The Real Estate Consulting Group, Deloitte & Touche, San Francisco 1992-93; stock analyst The Penobscot Group, Inc., Real Estate Stock Research, Boston 1993–; awards: Nat. Honor Soc., S.F. 1977-81, Who's Who Among Am. H.S. Students 1979-81, Blue Chip Co. Award Jr. Achiev. of the Bay Area 1981, Bank of Am. Award 1981, Calif. State Scholar 1981-85, Emerson Award M.I.T. 1988; mem: SFAIA (steering com. Intern Devel. Pgm. 1986-88), MIT Real Estate Assoc. (steering com. 1991-93), NAIOP (educ. com 1994–); seminar chair & moderator "Asian Pacific Investment in U.S. Real Estate", 1992; panel speaker "REITs and Instl. Securitization of Real Estate", 1994; rec: MIT Masters swim team, 1994 NYC marathon, worldwide travel. Res: 2390 39th Ave Ste 1 San Francisco 94116

LUST, PETER, JR., microwave engineer; b. Apr. 21, 1960, Montreal, Que., Can.; came to U.S. 1975, naturalized 1987; s. Peter Clark and Evelyn (Heymanson) L.; Gloria Ruth Bingle, Apr. 5, 1985; children: Peter Alexander III, Elizabeth Ann, Mathew Eric; edn: stu. Lowry Tech. Tng. Ctr., Comm. Coll. A.F., Albuquerque, US Air Force Acad.; BSEE, Pcific Western Univ., 1990. Career: enlisted USAF, 1979, resigned, 1982; computer meterologist Electro Rent, Burbank 1982-84; microwave engr., program mgr. satellite and space shuttle communications systems Transco Products, Camarillo 1984-90, internat. tech. mktg. mgr. 1990–; prin. Electronic Note Company, Oxnard, 1984–; cons. satellite & microwave comms. and spacecraft altitude control, 1984–; currently pres. The Electronic Note Company (spacecraft cons.); awards: Technology award USAF 1980, Discovery award NASA 1987, Internat. Leaders in Achiev. Cambridge; mem: Assn. Old Crows, Channel Islands Health Club; Republican; rec: computer programming, hiking, swimming, model airplanes. Ofc: Electronic Note Co 300 Esplande Dr #900 Oxnard 93030 Tel: 805/981-9178

LUSTMAN, JEFFREY PAUL, private investigator; b. Jan. 27, 1952, Baltimore, Md.; s. Irving and Doris (Hyman) L.; edn: BA, Univ. Md., 1973; Calif. lic. pvt. investigator, claims adjuster. Career: claims processor Farmers Ins. Group, Los Angeles 1974-77, claims rep., Torrance and Culver City offices, 1977-83; pvt. investigator R.J. Frasco Agcy., L.A. 1983-85; owner/prin. L.A. Claims & Investigations, 1985–; prod./host Cable-T.V. public access programs: The Johnny Revolting Show, 1980-85, Taped From L.A., 1985) Century Cable, Santa Monica. Res: PO Box 38653 Hollywood 90038 Ofc: L.A. Claims & Investigations POB 38653 Los Angeles 90038

LYKINS, JAY ARNOLD, religious mission founder, president; b. Feb. 13, 1947, Shattuck, Okla.; s. George Eldridge and Lucy Lee (Croom) L.; m. (Mary) Lynn Turner, Jan. 3, 1970; children: Marilee b. 1974, Amy b. 1974, Jason b. 1977; edn: BA, Covenant Coll., 1973; MBA, Kennedy-Western Univ., 1987, PhD, 1988. Career: owner Environment Control, Nashville, Tenn. 1974-78; bus. adminstr. Youth for Christ, Atlanta, Ga. 1978-81; internat. adminstr. Young Life, Colorado Springs, Colo. 1981-86; founder, pres. Global Reach, Pleasanton, Calif. 1982–; mem: Assn. of MBA Execs., Ctr. for Entrepreneurial Mgmt., Internat. Council for Small Bus., Am. Consultants League; club: Nob Hill CC, Snellville, Ga. (pres. 1980-81); author: Values In the Marketplace (1982), 200+ tng. manuals re bus./Biblical principles (1982–), thesis: Islamic Bus. (1988); mil: E5 USN 1966-68; Republican; Presbyterian; rec: scuba, biking. Res: 7897 Meadowbrook Ct Pleasanton 94588 Ofc: Global Reach PO Box 234 Pleasanton 94566

LYNCH, JOHN WILLIAM, JR., company chairman; b. April 23, 1927, Detroit, Mich.; s. John William and Shirley Olive (Block) L.; m. Dixie June Kirby, Aug. 20, 1949; children: John b. 1950, Daniel b. 1952, Theodore b. 1954, David b. 1962; edn: AA, Coll. of Sequoias, 1949; Stanford Grad. Sch. Bus. 1953-54; BA, San Jose St. Univ., 1951. Career: exec. Westinghouse, Sunnyvale 1951-54; exec. U.S. Steel, Pittsburg Wks. 1954-67; exec. Whittaker Corp., L.A. 1967-72; sr. associate Hergenrather & Co. 1972-73; exec. U.S. Postal Service, Wash. D.C. 1973-76; chmn. bd. J. W. Lynch & Associates, Inc., Newport Beach

1978–; chmn. Lynch & Co., Palm Desert; chmn. Clarity Capital Corp., Orange 1985–; dir. Mederi Med. Systems Inc., Tustin 1988-93; dir. Trans World Express, Costa Mesa 1985-88; awards: Air Force Assn. Nat. Pres.'s Citation 1990, Nat. Exceptional Service Award 1989, Nat. Medal of Merit 1988, listed Who's Who in the West, Who's Who in California; mem: Calif. Air Force Assn. (pres. 1988-90, chmn. 1990-91), Aircraft Owners & Pilots Assn., Stanford Grad. Sch. Bus. Alumni Assn.; civic: Duell Voc. Inst. Ind. Advy. Council 1961-64, nom. Concord Young Man of the Year 1958, Contr Costa Cty. Taxpayers Assn. 1961-64, United Way (loaned exec. 1961-63), BSA (inst. rep. 1962-66), Concord Personnel Board (chmn. 1963-67), Chatsworth C.of C. (dir. 1967-69), Mt. Vernon, VA Youth Athletic League (dir., baseball, basketball coach 1974-76), Newport Beach C.of C. (dir. 1982-83), E. Clampus Vitus, Rotary Internat. (dir. Newport Beach Sunrise Rotary Club 1990- dir. 1991–, pres. 1992-93), Paul Harris Fellow, Gen. Curtis E. LeMay Found. (Orange cty. chmn. 1991-93, chmn. LeMay Golf Scholarship Tour. 1993-94); mem: Columbia Toastmasters (pres. 1958); Holbrook Hgts. Comm. Assn. (dir. 1956-58), Pacific Light Opera Assn. 1956-66, N. Calif. Indsl. Rel. Council (ch. mem. 1963-67), Chatsworth Rotary Club 1967-69, Pers. & Indsl. Rel. Assn. 1967-71, Fresno Rotary Club 1977-78, Fresno Exchange club 1977-78, Dick Richards Breakfast Club 1985-92, Town Hall of Calif. 1967-88, Commonwealth Club of S.F. 1959-75, Nat. Rifle Assn., candidate Calif. State Board of Equalization 1978, nom. Calif. Pub. Utilities Commn. 1978, Air Force Assn., nat. v.p. -Far W. Reg. 1993-94; mil: USAAC 1944-46; Republican (pres. Concord YR 1958-60); Prot.; rec: flying, golf, hunting. Address: 44-259 Portofino Court Palm Desert 92260

LYNCH, MARGARET MARY-MAHONEY, hotel executive, financial executive, civic worker, socialite; b. Sept. 8, 1920, San Francisco; d. Jeremiah John (financier and civic leader) and Suzanne (McKeen) Mahoney; m. Joseph David Lynch, June 10, 1945; children: Timothy J. M. b. 1952, Suzanne Marie; edn: dipl. St. Paul's Sch., S.F., 1940; cert. in realty & hotel mgmt., CSU San Francisco, 1967; CPM, Cert. Property Mgr., Calif. Assn. Realtors, 1988. Career: accounts clk. Mahoney Estates Corp., San Francisco;, 1940-45; property mgr. Mahoney Estates Group, 1945–, mng. ptnr./owner, 1950, gen. ptnr./chief fin. ofcr., 1950-62; owner/ptnr./dir. finance Hotel Pierre, 1962-78; majority owner, ptnr. Lynch Corp. Group, 1978–, chief fin. ofcr. 1985–, gen. ptnr. Lynch Realty & Investments Corp.; honors: exec. of yr. Nat. Assn. Female Execs., S.F. 1990, biog. listings in Who's Who in Am. Women, World's Leading & Most Influential Women, Personalities of U.S. & World, Am.'s 2000 Notable Women, Who's Who World Intellectuals, Register Disting. Intl. Leadership, Intl. Social Register, Am. Biog. Inst. Woman of Year 1991, Intl. Order of Merit award Intl. Biog. Ctr., Cambridge, Eng., Dictionary of Internat. Biogr. (23rd) named 1 of 10 most Prominent Women Leaders; mem: Calif. Hotel & Motel Assn./ S.F. (exec. policy com. 1978), Calif. Assn. Realtors (cons. 1988-92), Calif. Credit / Metro Assn. Sacto. (bd. dirs. 1970-92), NAFE, San Francisco C.of C. (policy coms. 1986–), Bay Area Council (social coms. 1988–), U.S.-China Business Council (fin. com. 1989–); clubs: Palo Alto Womens' (social com. 1973–), San Francisco Womens' (pub. rels. com. 1982–), Villa Taverna (social coms. 1990–); publs: research, essays and jour. articles re hotel & motel mgmt., legal aspects of realty & hotel mgmt., social protocol & entertainment (1986, 90, 91); Republican; R.Cath.; rec: theatre, opera, ballet, gardening. Res: 501 Forest Ave Palo Alto 94301 Ofc: Hotel Pierre Group - Lynch Corp. 540 Jones St Ste 210 San Francisco 94102

LYNCH, MILTON TERRENCE, advertising agency executive; b. Feb. 27, 1931, Denver, Colo.; s. Thomas Lillis and Pauline Regina (Yaeger) L.; m Katherine Marie Stamey, July 19, 1958; children: Carrie b. 1959, Michael b. 1961, Brian b. 1964; edn: BA fine arts, Wash. St. Univ. Pullman 1953. Career: promotion mgr. General Mills Inc., San Francisco and Palo Alto 1956-62; v.p. Robert Ebey Co., Palo Alto 1962-66; exec. v.p. Steedman Cooper & Busse, San Francisco 1966-74; owner Lynch & Assocs., S.F. 1974-78; exec. v.p. Lynch & Rockey Advt., S.F. 1978-84; pres., CEO Evans/ Lynch, Rockey, S.F. 1984-87; chmn. and CEO Evans/San Francisco, S.F. 1987-90; vol. exec. Internat. Exec. Service Corps, 1991–; dir. Evans Communications, Salt Lake City, Ut. 1984; mem. S.F. Advt. Golf Assn. (past pres., 1974); clubs: S.F. Advt., Olympic, S.F. Tennis; mil: capt. US Army Inf. 1953-55; Republican; Cath.; rec: golf, tennis, gardening. Res: 12779 Homes Dr Saratoga 95070

LYNCH, ROBERT BERGER, lawyer; b. June 10, 1931, LaCrosse, Wis.; s. Jan Potter and Eve (Berger) L.; m. Ann Godfrey, May 30, 1980; 2 sons: Jan Fredrick Lynch b. 1956, Jerry Coggins b. 1957; edn: BS in marine engnrg., US Merchant Marine Acad. 1955; JD, McGeorge Sch. of Law, Univ. of Pacific 1967; admitted Calif. State Bar 1969. Career: senior design engr. Aerojet, Sacramento 1955-62, contract adminstr. and pgm. mgr. Liquid Rocket and Nuclear Rocket operations 1962-70; atty. pvt. practice, 1970–; instr. San Joaquin Delta Coll. 1973-76, Solano Coll. 1973-75, cons. CFT 1971, cons. K&B Inc. 1971-73; recipient N.Y. Port Engineers Award (1955); mem: Marines Memorial Assn., Fed. Bar Assn./Sacto. (pres. 1970-72), Sacto. County Bar Council (1970), Mensa, Am. Legion, Calif. Wildlife Fedn., Turtle Club; tech. paper, 16 Years of Rocket Safety- RRI No 2, presented IAF, Paris, Fr. (1967); mil: USCG 1949-51, Lcdr. USNR-R 1951-80, major Calif. Nat. Guard 1989-91 (ret.); Libertarian; Episcopalian; rec: models, hist. research and writing, book revs. for mil. mag. Law Ofc: 10615 Coloma Rd Rancho Cordova 95670

LYNCH, ROBERT MONTGOMERY, newspaper publisher; b. Aug. 9, 1920, San Francisco; s. Ernest Glenn and Alice Ramona (Granice) L.; m. Jean Allen, Nov. 9, 1941; children: William b. 1942, James b. 1948, John b. 1953; edn: AA, Santa Rosa Jr. Coll., 1939; courses Univ. San Francisco, Univ. Penna., Cornell Univ. Career: reporter, ad salesman, photographer, sports editor The Sonoma Index-Tribune, 1946-49, editor and publisher, 1949-88, publisher, 1949–; honors: Hon. Alcalde City of Sonoma 1979; mem: Calif. Newspaper Pubs. Assn. (pres. 1980), Calif. Press Assn./S.F. (pres. 1981-82), Nat. Newspaper Assn., Am. Newspaper Pubs. Assn., Sigma Delta Chi, S.F. Press Club, Internat. Soc. of Weekly Newspaper Editors; civic: Hanna Boys Center, Sonoma (bd. 1995), Kiwanis Club (pres. 1965); mil: enlisted USN 1942-45, Line officer 1945-46; Republican; Catholic; rec: golf, fishing. Ofc: The Sonoma Index-Tribune 117 W Napa St Sonoma 95476

LYNCH, TIMOTHY JEREMIAH MAHONEY, lawyer, real estate holding company executive, civic leader, author; b. June 10, 1952, San Francisco; s. Joseph D. and Margaret Mary (Mahoney) L.; edn: MS, JD, Golden Gate Univ., 1981; MA, PhD, Univ. S.F., 1983; adv. law degrees Inter-Am. Acad. of Internat. Law, 1988, Harvard Ctr. for Internat. Affairs, 1989; cert. atty.-arb. Am. Arbitration Assn., Calif. St. Bar, Internat. Bar, London Ct. of Arbitration; Harvard Bus. Sch. Adv. Mgmt. Pgm., 1991. Career: pres. Lynch Real Estate Co., San Francisco, 1978-82; CEO and chmn. Lynch Realty & Investment Corp. 1985–; chmn., mng. dir. law firm T. Lynch & Assocs., P.C. 1987–; CEO and chmn. Lynch Holdings Group (leverage buy-outs, acquisitions in banking, petroleum, electronics, auto. ind., agric. land, hotels, properties) 1991–; sr. ptnr., corporate counsel L.A. Ctr. for Internat. Commercial Arbitration and Municipal Securities Rule-Making Bd., W.D.C.; arbitrator: Iran-U.S. Claims Tribunal, The Hague 1989–; advy. bd. J.P. Morgan & Co. 1993–; dir. Morgan Stanley Internat. Finance Group; mem: Arb. Panels Pacific Coast Stock Exchange, NASD; Nat. Assn. Corporate Directors (ceo's pub. policy conf. mem. 1992–); corp. mem. U.S.-China Bus. Council, W.D.C. 1987–; bd. councilors Fgn. Svc. Inst., U.S. St. Dept., W.D.C. 1988–; chmn. U.S.-Middle East Relations Com., W.D.C. 1989–; chmn. legis. inv. com. Calif. Council for Internat. Trade, 1988–; chmn. Calif. State Commn. on Internat. Edn. & Culture, 1990-91; mem. Fin. and Industry Employment Policy Advy. Bds., DECD, Paris France 1995; corp. mem. 1991–: Trilateral Commn., Conference Board, Nat. Assn. of Corp. Dirs., Fin. Execs. Inst., World Bus. Acad., Council on Fgn. Relations, Calif. Council on Internat. Trade (PAC); Special Projects on U.S.-Vietnam Trade/Econ. Normalization Council, Ctr. for Internat. Devel. Policy, W.D.C., Stanford Univ. Bus. Sch. Adv. Bd. 1994–, Urban Land Inst., W.D.C., Soc. Indsl. Ofc. Realtors, W.D.C. (Diplomate Indsl. & Ofc. Brokerage, Roundtable on Inv./Fin. Brokerage), Intl. Assn. Entertainment Lawyers, London; awards: Internat. Leader of Achievement, Internat. Who's Who Authors and Writers 1995, 1 of 10 Most Admired Man of 1990's Decade, Am. Biog. Inst. Bd. of Intl. Res., 1994 Intl. Man of the Yr. by IBC Cambridge, England for outstanding leadership and svc. to the intl. comm., 20th Century Leadership Award, IBC 1994, listed ABI's Dictionary of Intl. Leadership 1994, 5000 Personalities of the World 1994, Intl. Biog. Ctr. 1994 Men of Achievement, Dictionary of Intl. Biog. 1994, Who's Who Global Business Leaders 1993-94, Presdl. Order of Merit for outstanding civic leadership and svc. to nation 1991, civic leader of yr. Downtown Assn. S.F. 1986, contbns. to theatre arts S.F. Theatrical Assn. 1989, Am. Law Inst./ABA Special Award for Outstanding Service to Law Profession 1990, Georgetown Univ. Sch. of Fgn. Service ldrship com. and 1 of 5 outstanding bus. ldrs. in Am. 1992, Euro Money Publ. list of Corporate World's Top Lawyers in field of internat. corp. law 1992, listed Intl. Social Register, Who's Who in Am. Law, Who's Who in Am., Who's Who in U.S. Leaders, Who's Who Emerging Leaders of Am., Who's Who in World, Who's Who in West (25th edit.), Who's Who in Fin. and Ind. (29th edit.), Who's Who Internat., London (55th edit., 1991/2), Who's Who Worldwide 1993 (life mem., elected Bus. Leaders Hall of Fame 1995), Who's Who in Am. Bus., Dictionary of Internat. Biog. (named 1 of 20 most prominent leaders 1993), Dir. of Litigation Attorneys, Dir. of Corporate Counsel (ABA/ Prentiss-Hall), Dir. of World Arbitrators (Parker Sch.), Columbia Sch. of Law), Dir. of Trial Lawyers, Dir. of Trial Judges (ATL), Dir. of Alternative Dispute Resolution Specialists (Soc. Profls. in Dispute Resolution, W.D.C.), Dir. of Am. Bank Attys. (Capron Publs.); recipient Golden State Award for outstanding leadership & civic service to Calif., Award of Honor for exceptional achiev.; elected Am. Acad. of Diplomacy (W.D.C.), Nat. Acad. of Conciliators Award for Contbns. to Commercial Dispute Settlement, Nat. Acad. of Arbitrators Univ. Mich. Bus. Sch., British Inst. of Internat. & Comparative Law (U.K.), Practicing Law Inst. (N.Y., S.F.); mem: Internat. Bar Assn., Am. Trial Lawyers Assn., S.F. Trial Lawyers Assn., Internat. Law Assn., S.F. Realtors Assn., Inter-Am. Bar Assn., Am. Fgn. Law Assn., Am. Soc. of Internat. Law (W.D.C.), W.D.C. Fgn. Law Soc., Soc. of Profls. in Dispute Resolution, Al-Shaybani Soc. of Internat. Law, Westchester-Fairfield Corporate Counsel Assn., Am. Assn. for Advancement of Slavic Studies, Nat. Inst. of Soviet & E.European Studies, Middle East Inst. (W.D.C.), Am. Poli. Sci. Assn., Asia Soc. (NY, NY), Univ. S.F. Alumni Assn., Middle East Studies Assn. (Univ. Ariz.), European Comm. Studies Assn., Latin Am. Studies Assn., Japan Soc. of N.Calif. (S.F.), Internat. Platform Assn.; civic bds: Connacher Gal. of Late Modern Euro. and Am. Art, Wash. D.C. Opera Soc. (trustee), Downtown Assn. of S.F. (chmn. Bay Area Economic Forum), Bay Area Council, S.F. C.of C. Downtown Assn. S.F. (bd.), S.F. Planning & Urban Res. Assn. (chmn. city policy groups 1984), Internat. Vis.

Ctr. (advy. bd. 1987–, citizen diplomatic corps), Heritage Found. (elected Pres.'s Club, named Most Influential Conservative Leader in U.S. 1991), Ford Found. - UNESCO Human Rights Edn. Fund (NY, NY), UN Fund for Human Rights & Justice, World Affairs Council of No. Calif., Boys Town of Italy Orgn. (co-ch. Exec. Dinner com.), Jesuit Seminary Assn. (elected Sr. Fellow, Minister of Scapular: Order of Our Lady of Mount Carmel), Christo del Rey Monastery (elected Inst. of Patristic & Byzantine Studies; installed Ancient Clerics of Pope St. Sylvester III of Rome, Vatican, Italy for leadership and service to Cath. Community of U.S. and world), Am. Bus Roundtable 1993, Com. for Economic Devel. (assoc. mem.), Cannes Film Festival (Patron 1994), Intl. Ball 1993 (Dinner Com. 1990-94), S.F. Opera Ball, S.F. Opera Guild (Social Com.) 1993-94; clubs: Commercial, Commonwealth, Calif. Yacht, Pebble Beach Tennis, Villa Taverna, Palm Beach Yacht, Saks Fifth Avenue Fashion; num. publs. in areas of internat. law, trade, and fgn. rels.; Republican (Rep. Senatl. Inner Circle); R.Cath.; rec: music, fine arts, yachting, corp. Learjet. Ofc: Lynch Realty Investment Corp. 540 Jones St Ste 201 San Francisco 94102

LYNN, BERT DANIEL, airline executive, retired; b. Dec. 22, 1916, Cleveland Ohio; s. Abraham and Helen (Bellick) L.; m. June Beckstrand, June 4, 1946; children: Karen b. 1948, Gary b. 1953; edn: BA magna cum laude, Western Reserve Univ. 1938. Career: aviation editor Steel Mag., Cleveland, Oh. 1938-39; exec. asst. to v.p. pub. rels., Douglas Aircraft Co., Santa Monica 1940-47; gen. mgr. Lynn-Western Advt. Agency, Los Angeles 1948-49; dir. advt. and pub. rels. Western Airlines 1950-64, v.p. advt. and sales promotion 1965-82; ret.; p.t. mktg. instr. Brigham Young Univ., Provo, Utah 1982-84, CSU Long Beach 1982-84; mktg. cons., Laguna Niguel 1986–; dir. publicity and promotion Hill Cumorah Pageant, Palmyra, N.Y. 1988-89; honors: Phi Beta Kappa, Western Reserve Univ. Warion Soc. 1938, L.A. Olympic Games Citizens Advy. Commn. 1983-84, Air Force Assn. Airpower award 1951, Adviews Socrates award 1963, 64, 68, 69; mem: Air Force Assn. (western regional v.p. 1950), Calif. Tourism Commn. 1965, Assoc. Latter-Day Media Artists (2d. v.p. 1985), L.A. Better Bus. Bur. (dir. 1955-56), Visitor & Convention Bur. L.A. (chmn. advt. com. 1980-81); mil: major USAF 1944-46, USAFR 1950-58; Republican; Mormon; rec: archaeology. Res: Laguna Niguel 92677

LYON, IRVING, biomedical researcher; b. May 10, 1921, Los Angeles; s. Charles and Bella (Kvitky) L.; m. Harriette Goodman, Oct. 16, 1948; children: David b. 1950, Charles b. 1953, Lawrence b. 1956; edn: AB, UCLA, 1942, MA, 1949; PhD physiol. (mammalian, gen.), UC Berkeley, 1952; grad. studies USC 1947-48. Career: research asst. endocrinol. UCLA, 1941; lab. asst. and tchg. asst., mammal. anat. & gen. embryol., USC, 1947-49; res. lab. asst. physiol. dept. UC Berkeley, 1949-52; res. biochem. The Toni Co. Med. Dept., Chgo. 1954-58; asst. prof. biol. chem. and res. assoc. orthopedic surg., Univ. Ill., Chgo. 1958-62; assoc. prof. biochem. dept. The Chicago Med. Sch., Chgo. 1962-67; prof. biol. Bennington (Vt.) Coll., 1967-72; sr. visitor Inst. Biol. Chem., Univ. Copenhagen, Denmark 1972-74; special cons. Calif. State Energy Resources Conservation & Devel., L.A. 1975; indep. cons. environ. health & nutrition, L.A. 1975-89; asst. res. physiologist UCLA Med. Sch., p.t. 1979-81; res. asst. UCLA Med. Sch. and res. biochemist US Veterans Adminstrn., L.A. 1981-89, ret.; awards: Rockefeller Found. Fellow, Harvard Sch. Pub. Health 1952-54, Soc. Sigma Xi (pres. Chgo. Med. Sch. chapt. 1967-68), NSF res. fellow, Urbana, Ill. 1970, NSF grant participant, Amherst, Mass. (1971, 72), vis. investigator Jackson Lab., Bar Harbor, Me. 1971, invited lectures various univs. and res. insts. (1963, 4 in 1968); Fellow Internat. Coll. Appl. Nutr., L.A. 1976-89, Fellow AAAS 1967, mem. Am. Physiol. Soc., N.Y. Acad. Scis.; civic: W.O. Douglas Outdoor Classroom (docent Santa Monica Mtns. 1989–), Audubon Soc. (docent Ballona Wetlands, Playa del Rey 1991–); co-inventor w/wife Bile Acid Emulsions (pat. 1978); author, contbr. 46+ tech. publs. in field of nutritional biochem. (1952-89), 18 energy resources reports (1975); mil: capt. US Army 1942-46; Indep.; rec: classical music, painting, ceramics, ecol./environ. Res: 708-A Grant St Santa Monica 90405-1221

LYON, RICHARDS PARKER, physician-urologist; b. Nov. 8, 1916, Oakland; s. Harvey Blanchard and Eleanor (Richards) L.; m. Carol Kiessig, Aug. 7, 1946; children: Kathleen, Joan, Laura; edn: AB engring., Stanford Univ., 1939, MD, 1944. Career: intern Boston City Hosp., 1944, surgical resident Mass. Mem. Hosp., 1947-48, urologic resident UCSF, 1948-52; pvt. med. practice, Oakland 1951-52, Berkeley 1953-83; clin. prof. UCSF Sch. of Med., San Francisco 1969-95; staff Alta Bates Hosp.; honors: Tau Beta Pi 1938, Phi Beta Kappa 1939, Zadig Soc. Med. 1942, Bronze Bambino Children's Hosp. & Med. Ctr. Oakland 1978; mem: Am. Assn. of Genitourinary Surgeons 1969–, Soc. for Pediatric Urology (pres. 1976); publs: 68+ med. jour. articles and abstracts; mil: physician/lt. M.C. USNR att. 4th Marine Div., 1944-46; Republican; Episcopalian; rec: photography -2 books on wine pub. "Vine to Wine" 5 vols., 1985, 1995. Address: 600 Stonecrest Napa 94558

MA, FAI, professor mechanical engineering; b. Aug. 6, 1954, Canton, China, came to U.S. 1977, naturalized 1988; s. Rui-Qi and Shao-Fen (Luo) M.; edn: BS, Univ. Hong Kong, 1977; MS, PhD, Calif. Inst. Tech., 1981. Career: senior research engr. Weidlinger Assocs., Menlo Park, Calif. 1981-82; research fellow IBM, Yorktown Hts., N.Y. 1982-83; senior engr. Standard Oil Co., Cleveland,

Ohio 1983-86; assoc. prof. mech. engring. UC Berkeley, 1986–; vis. scholar Oxford Univ., England 1992, Univ. of Stuttgart, Germany 1993; awards: NSF presdl. young investigator grantee 1987, Humboldt Fellowship of Germany 1992, grantee of various agencies 1987–; mem. ASME; publs: Probabilistic Analysis 1983, Computational Mechanics 1989, contbr. articles to profl. jours. Ofc: Mech. Engrg. Dept. Univ. California Berkeley 94720

MA, TINA MARK, stockbroker, associate vice president; b. June 25, 1960, Stockton; d. Bing Wai and Wun Ho (Chinn) Mark; edn: BA, political sci., UC Berkeley, 1982; profl licenses: NYSE, NASD, Nat. Commodities Futures, Interst Rate Options, Calif. St. Life and Variable Ins., Restricted Securities and Stock Options, Retirement Planning Splst. Career: asst. buyer Emporium-Capwell, San Francisco 1982-84; coordinator Town School, S.F. 1984-85; account exec. to assoc. v.p. of investments, Dean Witter Reynolds, 1985–; honors: life mem. Calif. Alumni Assn., Nat. Honor Soc. and Calif. Scholarship Fedn., lifetime honor Nat. Forensic League; mem. Commonwealth Club, UCB Alumni Assn. Res: 10201 Phar Lap Dr Cupertino 95014 Ofc: Dean Witter Reynolds, Inc. 181 E Second Ave San Mateo 94401

MABEE, SANDRA IVONNE, musician, clergy; b. Jan. 13, 1955, Puerto Rico; d. Nelson Custodio Noriega and Norma Ruth Eiseman Lee; m. Carl David Mabee, Aug. 2, 1980; children: Rebecca Lee b. 1985; edn.: MA in music, Calif. State Univ., Hayward 1985; BM in music, S.F. Conservatory of Music 1983; BA in biblical studies, Patten Coll. 1977; cert. with S.A.C.C., 1995. Career: instr., Patten Coll. 1980-88; chairperson, prof. studies div., Patten Coll. 1986-88; minister of music, El Cerrito Christian Ctr. 1988-91; music inst., Hayward Christian Sch. 1989-91; pastor, dir. of music ministries, Evangelical Ch. Alliance 1991; pastor, dir. music ministries, Trinity Church 1992-93; pastor, Unveiled Ch. Ministries, dir. of Music Ministries 1993–; seminar inst., Landmark Sch. of Ministries 1989-91; music inst., Landmark Acad. 1991; adjudicator, Singspiration 1989; principle tympanist, Women's Philharmonic, S.F. 1980–; concerto soloist, Redwood Symphony, Redwood City 1988; awards: scholarship, S. F. Conservatory of Music 1980-83; Internat. Who's Who in Music 1989, Who's Who in the West 1991; Proclamation for Service to Tchg. 1989; 5000 Personalities of the World 1990; compiled seminar Praise and Worship 1990; Women's Philharmonic recording on Koch, 1992; Protestant. Res: 2805 Gomes Ct Tracy 95376

MAC ALISTER, ROBERT STUART, petroleum co. executive; b. May 22, 1924, Los Angeles; s. Robert Stuart and Iris Grace (Doman) MacA.; m. Catherine Willby, Nov. 15, 1947; children: Rodney James b. 1954, Sara Marjorie b. 1956; edn: BSME, Calif. Inst. Tech. 1947; engring. courses Brighton Tech. Coll., Sussex; reg. profl. engr. Tx. (1967). Career: engring., supervisory and mgmt. positions Shell Oil Co. and other affiliates of Royal Dutch Shell 1947-68; v.p., ops mgr. Occidental of Libya, Tripoli 1968-71; mng. dir. subsidiaries, London 1971-76; pres. Occidental Internat. Oil Inc. 1976-78; pres., c.e.o. and chmn. bd. Canadian Occidental Petroleum Ltd., Calgary, Alberta 1978-81; mng. dir. Australian Occidental Petroleum Pty., Sydney 1982-83; mng. dir. Hamilton Brothers Oil & Gas Ltd., London 1983-86; indep. cons., 1986–; dir: Petrogas Processing Ltd. (1978-81), Cansulex Ltd. (1978-81); mem: Soc. Petroleum Engrs., AIME (1954–); civic: BSA (cubmaster 1963-65, scoutmaster 1965-68), Caltech Alumni Assn. (life mem.), Los Posas Country Club (1986–); mil: T-4 US Army Inf. 1944-46, Third Army ETO, expt. combat inf. badge, Euro. campaign rib. w/3 battle stars; Republican; Episcopalian; rec: carpentry, water color painting, golf. Res: 78 Lopaco Ct Camarillo 93010

MACALLISTER, DONALD, marketing company president, city official; b. Nov. 26, 1932, Hollywood, Calif.; s. Donald and Ruth (Waidlich) MacA.; m. Marilyn Jean Simmons, Sept. 25, 1955; children: Denise b. 1956, Gayle b. 1960, Michelle b. 1963; edn: AA, Pasadena City Coll. 1958; CSU Los Angeles, 2-1/2 yrs.; grad. (top 10%), USN Aviation Prep. Sch. and Electronics Sch. 1950. Career: electronics tech. Collins Radio, Burbank 1954-57; engrg. prodn. mgr. C.A. Rypinski Co., Pasadena 1957-59; mgr. planning and sch. Wiancko Engrg. Co., Pasadena 1959-60; sales engr. A-F Sales Engrg. Inc., Pasadena 1960-65; ops. mgr. No. Andros Devel. Co., Bahamas 1965-67; reg. & internat. sales mgr. Duncan Electronics, Costa Mesa 1967-69; v.p., A-F Sales Engrg. Inc., Pasadena 1969-83; founder/pres. Seevid Inc., Huntington Beach 1983–; dir. Huntington Nat. Bank 1982-95; elected City Council Huntington Bch. 1978-86, 87-92, mayor 1979-80, 82; mem: Public Cable-TV Auth. 1978-86, 87-92, chmn. 1981, commr. Harbors, Beaches & Parks Commn. Orange Co. 1983-86, commr. John Wayne Airport, O.C. 1986-91, dir. Huntington Bch. Conf. & Visitor Bur. 1989–; honors: Outstanding Jaycee Costa Mesa 1968, H.B. High Sch. P.T.A. hon. service award and HBHS Citizen of the Year 1974, Outstanding Citizen of Yr., City of Huntington Beach 1994; mem: Electronics Representatives Assn., Soc. for Information Display, Am Soc. for Indsl. Security; civic: H.B. Chamber of Commerce (dir. 1987-88), Elks, Huntington Valley Boys & Girls Club (dir. 1982-86), BSA (area chmn. 1987-88), bd. trustees H.B. Union High Sch. Dist. (1976-79, pres. 1978-79), H. B. 4th of July Parade & Fireworks (pres. 1987-88, dir. 1994-95), trustee H.B. Int. Surfing Mus. 1993–, Surfing Walk of Fame 1994- (chmn. 1994-95); mil: aviation electronics tech. 3/c USN 1951; Republican; Prot.; rec: politics, woodworking, photog., computers. Res: 1121 Park St Huntington Beach 92648 Ofc: Seevid Inc., 15178 Transistor Ln Huntington Beach 92649

MAC ALPIN, REX NERE, physician, professor emeritus; b. Apr. 25, 1932, Glendale. s. Frederic and Christine C. (Wright) MacA.; m. Carol Elizabeth White, June 22, 1957; children: Anne b. 1962, David. b. 1964; edn: Harvard Coll. 1949-51; BA, Pomona Coll. 1953; MD, UCSF 1957; cert. Am. Bd. Internal Medicine 1965. Career: intern, resident UCSF 1957-60; prof. medicine, cardiology UCLA 1963-88, prof. emeritus 1988–; 100+ articles pub. in sci. jours. 1954-93; mil: lt. cmdr. USNR 1961-63; rec: tennis. Ofc: University of California Division of Cardiology 10833 Le Conte Ave Los Angeles 90024-1679

MACBRIDE, DEXTER DU PONT, mediation-arbitration consultant; b. Aug. 18, 1917, Elizabeth, N.J.; s. Charles Munnerlyn and Flora Theolyn (Jerome) MacB.; m. Grace Anderson, Dec. 23, 1963; 1 son. Charles Dexter b. 1964; edn: LL.B, Cumberland Univ. 1938; JD, Samford Univ. 1969; MA, Hofstra Univ. 1970; admitted Va. Bar Assn. 1939; ASA, Am. Soc. of Appraisers 1965, SR/WA, Am. Right of Way Assn. 1968, CAE, Am. Soc. Assn. Execs. 1975, cert. mediator State of Calif. 1989. Career: right of way agent Public Works, Los Angeles 1946-47; negotiator to chief appraiser Pub. Works, Los Angeles and Sacto. 1948-70; exec. v.p. Am. Soc. Appraisers, Wash. D.C. 1970-83; v.p. MacBride Enterprises, San Antonio, Tx. and Diamond Bar 1983–; dir. Diamond Bar Improvement Assn. 1987; project mgr. Diamond Bar Recycling 1988; assoc. Claremont Dispute Resolution Center, Glendora 1989; V.E., Internat. Exec. Svc. Corps; cons. Kaunas Univ. of Tech., Lithuania; trustee, Greater L.A. Co. Vector Control Dist.; awards: Calif. Apprails Council Leadership 1971, Internat. Right of Way Assn. Pub. Service 1983; mem: ASA Coll. of Fellows (fellow 1975), Am. Soc. Appraisers (life), Internat. Right of Way Assn. (life), Lambda Alpha, Va. Bar Assn., Am. Bar Assn., Am. Right of Way Assn., Am. Soc. Assn. Execs.; author Power & Process, 1969, co-author Freedom-USA, 1976, ed. Bibliography of Appraisal Literature, 1974, Opportunities in Appraising Valuation Scis., 1980, news column Value Forum, 1979-83, 60+ articles pub. in profl. jours.; Republican; Quaker; rec: public speaking, travel. Res: 435 Willapa Ln Diamond Bar 91765

MACCAULEY, HUGH BOURNONVILLE, stockbroker, banker; b. March 12, 1922, Mt. Vernon, NY; s. Morris Baker and Alma Orcutt (Gardiner) MacC.; m. Felice Cooper, Dec. 2, 1980; edn: Rutgers Univ. 1939-40; Texas Christian Univ. 1948-50; Omaha Univ. 1957-59. Career: acct. exec. Dean Witter, San Bernardino 1974-79; v.p. Great American Securities, San Bernardino 1980-94; stockbroker, Gorian Thornes, San Bernardino 1994–; chmn. emeritus, dir., Desert Comm. Bank, Victorville 1994–; chmn. bd. Desert Community Bank, Victorville 1980-94;; chmn. bd. KIST Corp., Riverside 1982-87; dir., chmn. fin. com. Air Force Village West Inc. 1986-88; chmn. bd. Gen & Mrs. Curtis E. LeMay Found., 1988–; mem: Daedalian Soc., Riverside Rotary (dir.); club: Victoria CC; mil: mem. Essex Troop, 102nd Cavalry N.J. Nat. Guard 1940-42, capt. US Army 1943-48, col. US Air Force 1949-73, decorated Legion of Merit w/o.l.c. Air Medal w/2 o.l.c., Air Force Commdn. w/3 o.l.c.; Republican; Presbyterian; rec: golf, aviation, equestrian. Res: 1630 Monroe St Riverside 92504 Ofc: Gorian Thornes Inc. 350 W 5th St Ste 103 San Bernardino 92402

MAC DONALD, DONALD KEITH, inventor, electronics company president; b. May 20, 1944, Annapolis, Md.; s. Frank Wadsworth and Henrietta Maria (Scott) MacD.; edn: AA, Foothill Coll.; MD, Harvard, 1975, Psychiatrist, 1980; computer degree, Stanford Univ., 1990. Career: chem. tech. res. US Geol. Survey, Menlo Park 1963-70; inventor/mfr. Puzzlepaper (US patent 1970), 1968–; inventor, owner MacDonald Co., MacDonald Controls and Schematic Control, 1967–; owner High Tech Esoteric HiFi and Video Stores (Century Stereo™), San Jose; recording engr./prod. Neely Plumb™ 1960–, recording studio in Sonora, Calif.; owner MacDonald Play Art Co., Inc., Sonora 1991–; Calendar Prodns., Memphis, Tn. (will print old year and new year calendars w/new or old H.S. or coll. photos by satellites/Lockheed, pat. 1991); sole owner MacDonald Bank (F.R.B.) 1988–; owner MacDonald-Cleworth Publishing, Hollywood 1991–; sales dealer Gray & Martin banjo's & guitars by word pgm. on phone & credit card verbal ESS buying & selling by access codes (AT&T, IBM, APPLE, H.P.), also distbr. (wholesale, retail) Masterpiece Art canvass, signed Fine Art prints; mgr., Isle of Skye Brand Co.; prin., The Good Catalog Co. and Q.V.C.; abstract paintings: "Clown Music" (as Donald Keith Gougan™), 1995, others as Donald Keith Gougain™, 1995; num. inventions include Puzzlepaper-Puzzlemate™, Puzzlebook™, 1960, programmable mirrors & power seat (for Ford), Abstract Painting & Woodwork Desk-Table & Lamp, 1970, Presidential Phone, 1970, Two-Conductor Remote Switching and Transmitting Control System (pat. 1971), Indicator and Shutoff for Cartridge Type Tape Recorders; trademarked inventions include- Playwrite Play FM, PlayToy, Play Art, Play Press, Play Sport, 1986-88, Play Show Mate, 1991, product Play BodyLotion by Vidal Sassoon, 1991; Proton surgery & res. to de-age (pat. 1991); DI Galog™ recording & playback for hi-fi audio close to C.D. quality on reg. Phillips cassette (pat. 1991, lic. to Warner Comm. & Chrysler Flextronics Baby Car Stereo 1992, lic. to Playboy for Neely Plumb™ Art. & FTD Florists to sell, also GEO, dealers); for IBM: Laser Disc Programmable Record Player, Compact Disc Case, design of case Logic Portable Laser Disc Cases: Variable Rate, Digital TV and Stereo FM Computersound, 35mm Color or Black in White Slide,w/ Oscilliscopic Info. circ. print code for music or video multiplexed, playback with no moving parts (IBM, H.P., & Kodak) pat. appls. pending; Right Eye to brain & systems to read as compatible music (sent to

Harvard and IBM, 1970), system of typing- by moving fingers on a surface- to a phone or FM holograph of brainwave to satellites for bdcst. FM Radio system (IBM Brainal Computers 1974), Porkie Pine Navy Stero Project, 1970; recording by feedback to Hi Fi speakers or secret systems (Neely Plumb™, 1960s, RCA); DAT Digital Audio Tape & compatible verbal & written code to produce with aid of main frame computer a video monitor picture of what eyes see as stored human brainal computer memory (lic. to Ford, IBM, H.P., Kodak); Verbal & written digital & analoge fractial stereo & multitrack multiplex code for FM and TV bdcstg. (pat. 1989, lic. McIntosh Labs, RCA, CBS, IBM); publ. original "Play Art"™, "Children's Stickback Puzzlepaper"™, "Puzzlebook"™ "by Neely Plumb"™ DKMD (c. 1989 Puzzart Co.); "Sunset Valley"™; "New Town"™; Republican (non-partisan presdl. cand. 1980, 83, 88, 92, 94, 96); R.Cath.; rec: hi-fi, electronics. Ofc: MacDonald Controls-PlayArt Div 20400 Brook Dr Sonora 95370

MACDONALD, JOHN, county supervisor; b. Oct. 17, 1921, Palisade, Colo.; s. Joseph and Lillian Mae (Shawhan) M.; m. Gloria, Apr. 10, 1949; children: Kirk b. 1955, Erick b. 1957, Michael b. 1960; edn: AA, Oceanside-Carlsbad Jr. Coll., BA and MA, CSU Humboldt, EdD, UCLA. Career: coll. dean of Extended Day Div. Oceanside-Carlsbad Jr. Coll., 1957-61; actg. supt., asst. supt. Oceanside/Carlsbad H.S. Dist., 1961-63; supt./pres. Mira Costa Community Coll. Dist., 1963-82; elected mem., dep. mayor Oceanside City Council, 1982-86; elected supr. 5th dist. San Diego Co. Bd. Suprs., 1987–, mem. CSAC (chmn. growth mgmt. and land use subcom.), LEAD Advy. Com., North S.D. Co. Advy. Council; awards: headliner of yr. S.D. Press Club 1986, man of yr. BECA Found. 1987, Nat. Com. for Employer Support of the Guard and Reserve 1987; civic bds: Mira Costa Theatre Arts Found., Mira Costa Coll. Found. (bd.), Spartan Sports Found., Rotary, BECA Found.; mil: radioman 1/c USN 1942-45; Republican; Episcopal; rec: sports. Res: 1725 Cassidy St Oceanside 92054 Ofc: San Diego County 1600 Pacific Hwy Rm 335 San Diego 92101

MACDONALD, JOHN KENYON, naval officer, business executive, state and county legislator; b. June 15, 1916, Pasadena; s. John Forrest and Lois Helen (Warren) MacD.; m. Helen Louise Sweat, June 14, 1947 (dec. 1958); m. Leslie Bune Hodge, May 30, 1968; children: Stuart b. 1948, Stephen b. 1950, Scott b. 1955; edn: BS bus. USC, 1939. Career: dist. mgr. Witt Ice & Gas Co., 1940-41; fleet sales mgr. James E. Waters Dodge and Plymouth, 1946-51; pres., gen. mgr. Ken MacDonald Chevrolet Inc., Ojai 1955-60; owner "Mr. Transportation" Ventura 1958-62; county supr. Ventura Co. Bd. Supervisors 1961-67, 1977-81, chmn. 1962, 65, 79; state assemblyman Calif. Legislature, Sacto. 1967-76; commr. Area Housing Authority, Ventura Co., Camarillo 1986-89; superior ct. referee Ventura Co. 1964-65, superior ct. receiver 1965; honors: USC Skull & Dagger Soc., L.A. Ephebian Soc.; mem: Ojai Valley Retired Profl. Businessmen (past pres.), Am. Legion (past commdr.), Masons, Scottish Rite, Rotary Internat. (Paul Harris Fellow, Ojai bd. dirs. 1978-79); mil: lt. cmdr. USNR 1941-58, active duty 1941-45, 1951-52; Democrat; Presbyterian; rec: boating, landscaping, geneaology. Address: Ojai 93023

MACE, JOHN WELDON, physician, medical educator; b. July 9, 1938, Buena Vista; s. John Henry and Gladys Elizabeth (Edwards) M.; m. Janice Marie Koerber, Jan. 28, 1962; children: Karin b. 1963, John b. 1965, James b. 1970; edn: BA, Columbia Union Coll. 1960; MD, Loma Linda Univ. 1964. Career: rotating intern Naval Hosp. San Diego 1964-65, resident pediatrics 1965-68; fellow endocrinology Univ. Colo., Denver 1968-70; asst. prof. pediatrics Loma Linda Univ. 1970-75, prof., chair dept. pediatrics 1975–; chief of pediatrics Loma Linda Med. Center 1975–, phys.-in-chief Loma Linda Children's Hosp. 1992–; pres. bd. dirs. Inland Co. Devel. Disabilities Services, San Bernardino 1972-86; pres. Found. for Med. Care 1980-82; Congressional Advy. Bd. 1986–; chmn. St. Calif. Advy. Bd. 1986–, bd. dir. Loma Linda Univ. Health Care 1995; honors: Alpha Omega Alpha, Sigma Xi; mem: N.Y. Acad. Sci., AAAS, Western Soc. Pediatric Research, Lawson Wilkins Pediatric Endocrine Soc., AMA (chmn. pediatric dept.); papers pub. in sci. jours., 1968–; mil: lt.comdr. USN 1963-70; Republican; Prot.; rec: antiques. Ofc: Loma Linda University School of Medicine Loma Linda 92350

MACHADO, MARIO J., television broadcaster, producer; b. Apr. 22, 1935, Shanghai, China; s. Carlos Jacinto M.; edn: British pub. sch., Shanghai (multilingual: Portuguese, 2 Chinese dialects); St. Johns Mil. Acad., L.A.; St. Francis Xavier Coll; Career: with IBM five yrs.; controller nat. company; creator/co-pub. Soccer Corner (1st Amer. soccer mag.); founder/pres. Specials' Ink, Sports Inc., Primo and Trident Publs., MJM Communications, ICVC and EMMI Ink; profl. bdcstr. 1967–; Host, nat. syndicated series MEDIX, KRLA Connection, Good Day LA, and Calif. People (KTTV-Metromedia); news reporter/anchorman KNXT (CBS) Los Angeles; co-host Noontime Daily KNXT (CBS); analyst for sporting events, KHJ-TV, L.A., 1967–; commentator L.A. Olympics '84 (ABC-TV net.); voice of soccer for CBS-TV Network, 1968, 76; World Cup Soccer Championships bdcst. Mex. 1970, Ger. 1974, Argentina 1978, Spain 1982 ABC-TV; host Star Soccer, English PBS netwk.; bdcst. 6 yrs. Football League Cup Final, Wembley, 1977; host, The Best of the World Cup, Spanish Intl. Netwk. Argentinian Soccer/Syn.; host weekly series It Takes All Kinds, KNXT; host for Asian comm., Sunset series; host AMA - Cont. Medical

Education; in-flt. narrator, TWA's Executive Report, American Airlines, Western Airlines, Singapore Airlines; narrator indsl. film/video tapes; movie credits incl: Blue Thunder, Scarface, King Kong, Brian's Song, Oh God, St. Elmo's Fire, Robocop I, II & III; guest appearances episodic TV; voice of Virginia Slims Tennis Championships, L.A.; co-prod. w/Doron Kauper, docu. on Irving Stone, docu. on Fire Safety; prod. Internat. Stars in Concert and Una Serata Italiana (for Internat. Student Center, UCLA); prod. World Song Fest. in America, and Golden Gate to Spruce Goose Chase; prod: Bev. Hills St. Patricks Day Parade, 1985, 86; El Grito Parade, 1986; Offc'l Spanish Language of TV Rose Parade, 1987; Pet Parade 1987; Jimmie Awards, AAPAA 1988-89; creator, producer: La Linea De La Salud (KWKW Radio), A Tu Salud (KMEX-TV34), Hispanic World of Fords, Hispanic Family of the Year -Entenmans; awards: Father of the Year Awards, Interceptor Award for best documentary, S.F. 1975, Asian of the Year, L.A. City Asian-Amer. Assn. (1978), 7 Emmys and Emmy nominations 1971-77; civic: fmr. commr. cultural affairs City of L.A., presdl. appt. Child Safety Partnership, dir. Calif. Special Olympics, dir. Sprint UCLA, Internat. Student Ctr. UCLA, dir. Am. Beach Volleyball League, dir. Asian Am. Games, dir. Genesis Internat., hon. dir. Amer. Youth Soccer Orgn., founder S.F.V. youth soccer league; host many benefit tennis tourn.; R.Cath.; rec: record collection, tennis, soccer. Ofc: 1109 N Vermont Los Angeles 90029

MACK, CHARLES DANIEL, III, labor union official; b. Apr. 16, 1942, Oakland; s. Charles Daniel, Jr. and Berna (Ferguson) M.; m. Marlene Helen Fagundes, 1960; children: Tammy b. 1961, Kelly b. 1967, Kerry b. 1970, Shannon b. 1972; edn: BA, San Francisco St. Univ., 1964; labor studies, Univ. Calif. Career: elected bus. agent Teamsters Local No. 70, 1966-72, legislative rep. Teamsters 1970-71, secty.-treas. Local 70, 1972–; past trustee and recording secty. Teamster Jt. Council No. 7, apptd. pres. 1982, elected pres. 1984; elected 2d v.p. Alameda County Cent. Labor Council, 1988; mem. Calif. Teamsters Pub. Affairs Coun. (exec. bd.), Nat. Freight Negotiating Com., trustee We. Conf. Teamsters Pension Trust; bd. dirs. Calif. Inst. for Federal Policy Research; bd. dirs. East Base Conversion and Reinvestment Commn.; past bd. dirs. State Compensation Ins. Fund; civic: New Oakland Com., Peralta Comm. Coll. Advy. Com., past bd. dirs. Children's Hosp. of East Bay; Democrat; R.Cath.; rec: jogging. Ofc: Teamsters' Joint Council No. 7 150 Executive Park Blvd Ste 2900 San Francisco 94134

MACLEOD, KATHLEEN BROMLEY, physician; b. Mar. 25, 1953, Oakland; d. LeRoy Alton Bromley and Bernice Honora Doyle; m. Glen Earl MacLeod, Dec. 22, 1973; edn: salutatorian Miramonte H.S., Orinda; BA in bacteriology (high honors), UC Berkeley, 1975; MD, UCLA Sch. of Med., 1984; bd. cert. Am. Bd. Internal Medicine (ABIM) 1987, Am. Bd. Infectious Diseases 1990. Career: staff research assoc. dept. genetics, UC Berkeley, 1976-77 (discovery of one of gene loci regulating expression of mating type in Saccharomyces cerevisiae pub. J. Genetics (9/79); microbiologist Bur. of Epidemiology, Bacterial Zoonoses Br., Ctrs. for Disease Control, Atlanta, Ga. 1978-80, PHS award for isolating Legionella pneumophila from the environment; NIH resrch. fellow 1981, 82; resident internal med. Wadsworth VA Med. Ctr., Los Angeles 1984-87 (infectious diseases rotations at Harbor-UCLA Med. Ctr., Hosp. for Tropical Diseases, London, and Princess Margaret Hosp. for Infectious Diseases, Hong Kong); fellow Infectious Diseases UC Irvine Sch. of Med., Orange 1987-89; solo practice Infectious Diseases, Long Beach, Los Alamitos, and Lakewood. Tel: 213/432-4357 (ID2-HELP) Res: 6310 Bayshore Walk Long Beach 90803

MACY, GARY ALLAN, educator; b. March 24, 1950, Milwaukee, Wis.; s. Leland Francis and Joan Marie (La Valle) M.; m. Saralynn Theresa Ferrara, June 20, 1987; edn: HBA, Marquette Univ. 1971; MA, 1973; PhD, Univ. Cambridge England 1978. Career: vis. lectr. Notre Dame Univ., Ind. 1978; prof. Univ. San Diego 1978–; honors: Phi Beta Kappa, Cambridge Univ. Bethune Baker award 1974, Associated Ch. Press Best Humorous Article 1984, College Theology Soc. Book award 1992; mem: Coll. Theology Soc. (bd. dirs.), Medieval Acad. Am., Ecclesiastical Hist. Soc. England, Peace Through Law Inst., Inst. for Advanced Studies (fellow, 1991-92); author: Theologies of Eucharist, 1984, articles pub. in profl. jours., 1984-85, The Banquet's Wisdom, 1992; Cath.; rec: computers. Ofc: Univ. of San Diego Alcala Park San Diego 92110

MACY, JONATHAN ISAAC, physician, medical educator; s. Isaac and Florence M.; m. Jeannette, Nov. 28, 1976; children: Alexandra b. 1980, Adam b. 1983; edn: BA, Boston Univ. 1972; MD, 1976. Career: intern USC Med. Center, Los Angeles 1976-77; research fellow Doheny Eye Fedn. 1977-78; resident physician USC Med. Center 1978-81; assoc. Century City Eye 1981-82; ptnr. Am. Eye Inst. 1982–; bd. dirs. Midway Med. Center 1987–; asst. clin. prof. UCLA 1984–; chief ophthalmology Midway Med. Center 1986-87; cons. St. Dept. Soc. Service 1982–; honors: Phi Beta Kappa 1972, Psi Chi 1987, Los Angeles Eye Soc. Merit research award 1980; mem: A.C.S. (fellow), Am. Acad. Ophthalmology, Calif. Assn. Ophthalmology, Internat. Cornea Soc., World Med. Assn., Los Angeles Co. Med. Assn., CMA; civic: Myasthenia Gravis Fedn. (v.p.), Found. Jr. Blind (bd. mem.); 23 articles pub. in med. jours.; rec: racquetball, reading. Ofc: American Eye Institute 8635 W Third St Ste 390W Los Angeles 90048

MADDALENA, RICHARD KENNETH, risk financing consultant; b. March 23, 1938, Portola; s. Louie Kenneth and Hazel Alexandra (Adams) M.; m. Cheryl Langston, April 27, 1968 (div. 1972); m. 2d. Marilyn Bowlsby Moore, Nov. 5, 1977 (div. 1994); children: Jeff b. 1958, Randy b. 1960, Scott b. 1962, Margot b. 1970; edn: AA, Yuba Coll. 1957; BS, CSU Chico 1962; CPA Calif. (1967). Career: staff accountant Peat Marwick Mitchell, San Francisco 1962-63; ptnr. McDaniel Anderson & Maddalena, Redding 1963-72; owner R.K. Maddalena, CPA, Weaverville 1972-86; adminstr. (founding pres.) Special Dist. Risk Mgmt. Auth. 1986-94; pres. Maddalena & Co. 1994–, pres. Local Agy., Self Insurance Auth., Sacto. 1987-90; pres. Prima Pooling Section 1991-92; awards: num. awards incl. Rotary Internat. Svc. Above Self Award 1993, Trinity Co. Fair Blue Ribbon (1986), Rotary Paul Harris Fellow (1981), Redding Jaycees Outstanding Young Man (1966), CSU Chico Outstanding Grad. (1962); mem: Am. Inst. CPA, Calif. Soc. CPA; civic bds: Weaverville C.of C., dir. PRIMA Pooling Sect., Rotary, Trinity H.S. Advy. Com. (chair 1985), Trinity Players (pres., treas., dir.); Republican; rec: acting, singing, theatre directing. Address: Sacramento 95833

MADDY, DONALD LEE, computer company executive, application programming developer; b. Aug. 27, 1949, Whittier, Calif.; s. Keith Thomas and Colleen Joanne (Barlow) M.; m. Lynne Louise Juhnke, June 29, 1985; children: Crystal Lynne b. 1987, Michael Donald b. 1991; edn: nuclear weapons electronics student, Sandia AFB, N.M. 1970; BS in Computer Sci., Calif. State Univ., Sacto., Calif. 1976; Certificate in Data Processing (CDP) 1982. Career: nuclear weapons electronics splst., US Army, Istanbul, Turkey 1970-71; programmer, Water Resources Control Bd., Div. Water Quality, Sacto. 1974-75; programmer, Calif. State Coll., Bakersfield 1976-78; programmer/analyst, Sierra Pacific Power Co., Reno, Nev. 1979-80; sr. programmer/analyst, State of Idaho Transp. Dept., Boise 1980-81, United Grocers Warehouse, Oakland 1981-84; sr. programming cons., Farmers Savings & Loan, Davis 1984-87; Pacific Gas & Electric, Avila Beach 1987–; mem: Assn. for Computing Machinery 1973-74, Realtor 1977-78, Assn. of Sys. Mgrs. 1979-80, Data Processing Mgmt. Assn. 1980-81, Amer. Nuclear Soc. 1987-89, Cal Poly Swanton Railroad Soc. 1993–; co-author: Computer Software Security System for the Plant Information Management System, 1992; mil: splst. fifth class, US Army, 1969-72; Republican; rec: model railroading, downhill and cross-country skiing. Ofc: The Maddy Corporation 1220 16th St. Los Osos 93402-1422

MADDY, KENNETH LEON, state legislator; b. May 22, 1934, Santa Monica; s. Russell T. and Anna M. (Balzer) M.; m. Beverly Chinello, Feb. 7, 1957 (div.); m. Norma Quesenberry Foster, Nov. 28, 1981; children: Deanna G. b. 1958, Donald P. b. 1960, Marilyn b. 1964, (step): Jayne, Ron, Janet, Suzi, Carrie, Lori; edn: BS, CSU Fresno 1956; JD, UCLA, 1963. Career: atty. ptnr. law firm Chinello, Chinello & Maddy, Fresno 1963-77; assemblyman from 32nd dist. Calif. State Assembly 1970-78; senator from 14th dist. Calif. State Senate 1979–, Senate Republican floor leader 1987, Republican Caucus State Senate chmn. 1979-83; honors: CSUF Alumnus of Yr. 1981, Fabulous Fresnan Fresno C.of C. 1985, UCLA Sch. of Law Alumnus of Yr. 1985, Man of Yr. Whinney Awards, Calif. 1986, Man of Yr. Horsemen & Jockey Guild, Calif. 1987, Lee Atwater Meml. Minority Leader of Yr. 1992; mem: CSUF Bulldog Found. and Pres.'s Club, Rotary, Fresno Philharmonic Assn., Sigma Nu frat., Phi Delta Phi; mil: 1st lt. USAF 1957-60; Republican; rec: golf, tennis, horses. Ofc: State Capitol Rm 305 Sacramento 95814

MADIX, ROBERT JAMES, chemical engineer, educator; b. June 22, 1938, Beach Grove, Ind.; s. James L. and Marjorie A. (Strohl) M.; children: Bradley Alan, David Eric, Michella Lynn, Evan Scott; edn: BS, Univ. Ill., 1961, PhD, Univ. Calif., 1964. Career: NSF post doctoral fellow Max Planck Inst., Göttingen, Fed. Republic of Germany, 1964-65; asst. prof., chem. engr. Stanford Univ., 1965-72, assoc. prof., chem. engr., 1972-77; prof. chem. engring. Stanford Univ., 1977–, chmn., chem. engr., 1983-87, prof. chemistry, 1981–; cons. Monsanto Chem., St. Louis, 1975-84, Shell Oil Co., Houston, 1985-86; Peter Debye lectureship Cornell Univ. 1985; Eyring lectr. chemistry Ariz. State Univ. 1990; disting. prof. lectr. Univ. Texas, Austin 1980; awards: Alpha Chi Sigma award Am. Inst. Chem. Engrs. 1990, Paul Emmett award Catalysis Soc. N.Am. 1984, Irving Langmuir Disting. Lectureship award Am. Chem. Soc. 1981, Humboldt U.S. Sr. Scientist award 1978; Ford Found. fellow 1969-72; chmn. Gordon Res. Conf. on Reactions on Surfaces, 1995; mem. Am. Chem. Soc., Am. Phy. Soc., Am. Vacuum Soc., Am. Inst. Chem. Engineers, Calif. Catalysis Soc. (assoc. editor catalysis revs., 1986–, editl. bd. catalysis letters, 1992–, res. on chem. intermediates, 1994–; editl. bd. Jour. Mol. Catal., 1985–; contbr. 270+ articles to profl. jours. Ofc: Stanford Univ Dept Chemical Engring Stanford 94305

MADORSKY, JULIE G., physician; b. June 17, 1945, Hungary; nat. 1967; d. Imre and Georgina (Fazekas) Geiger; m. Melvin A. Botvin, June 12, 1965 (div. 1977); m. 2d. Arthur G. Madorsky, Sept. 17, 1978; children: Ari b. 1969, Danya b. 1971; edn: Univ. London 1961-65; Univ. Pa. Phila. 1965-66; MD, Med. Coll. Pa. 1969; lic. physician and surgeon Nat. Bd. Med. Examiners 1969. Career: asst. prof. rehab. medicine Temple Univ. Hosp., Phila., Pa. 1973-74; program med. dir. Casa Colina Hosp., Pomona 1974–; clin. assoc. prof. UC Irvine 1974–, UCLA 1979–; clin. prof. Coll. Osteopathic Medicine of Pacific, Pomona 1987–;

awards: Calif. Govs. Com. Calif. Physician of Year 1987, Pres.'s Com. Employment of Disabled Persons U.S. Physician of Year 1988; mem: Calif. Soc. Physical Medicine & Rehab. (pres. 1992–), So. Calif. Soc. Physical Medicine & Rehab. (pres. 1987-90), AMA, CMA, Am. Acad. Physical Medicine & Rehab., Am. Spinal Injury Assn., Am. Med. Women's Assn., Services Center for Indep. Living (bd. mem. 1986–); rec: art, music. Ofc: 255 E Bonita Ave Pomona 91767

MADSEN, GEORGE EVERETTE, civil engineer; b. Mar. 15, 1934, Fresno; s. Edward George and Dorothy L. (Smith) M.; m. Sandra Marie Johannes, July 10, 1960; children: Vivian b. 1961, Cheryl b. 1966; edn: BS civil engring w. honors, Calif. Inst. Tech. Pasadena 1955; MS, 1958; reg. civil (1960) and traffic engr. Calif. Career: jr. asst., asst. sanitary engr./lt. j.g. USPHS, Wash. DC 1955-56, Anchorage, Ak. 1956-57; asst. civil engr. Orange Co. Flood Control Dist., Santa Ana 1958-59; sr. sanitary engr. Co. of San Diego 1959-60; asst. city engr., city engr., pub. works dir. City of Costa Mesa 1960-71; mgr. Costa Mesa Sanitary Dist. 1969-71; sr. v.p. Woodside/Kubota & Assoc., Inc. Santa Ana 1971-88; civil engr. Williamson & Schmid, Irvine 1988–; honors: BSA Eagle Scout 1950, Tau Beta Phi, ASCE Outstanding C.E. student 1955, Engineer of Yr., ASCE Orange Co. Br. 1994, Outstanding Engr. Merit Award, Orange Co. Engring. Council 1995; mem: ASCE (fellow; Orange Co. Br. secty., treas., v.p., pres. 1967-70, History & Heritage Com., del. L.A. section to L.A. Council of Engrs. & Scientists); Am. Pub. Works Assn., Orange Co. Water Assn., Inst. for the Advancement of Engring. (fellow, bd. dirs.; treas. 1994-96), Cons. Engrs. & Land Surveyors of Calif., Newport-Mesa Assn. Realtors, Calif. Assn. Realtors, Nat. Assn. Realtors; Presbyterian (elder); rec: skiing, watching sports. Ofc: Williamson & Schmid/Huitt-Zollars 15101 Redhill Ave Tustin 92680

MAESTRONE, FRANK EUSEBIO, diplomat; b. Dec. 20, 1922, Springfield, Mass.; s. John Battista and Margaret Carlotta (Villanova) M.; m. Jo Colwell; edn: BA, Yale Univ. 1943; cert., U.S. Naval War Coll. 1962-63. Career: 3d. secty. Am. Legation, Vienna, Austria 1948-49; v.consul U.S. Consulate Gen., Hamburg, Germany 1949-53; consul U.S. Consulate, Salzburg, Austria 1954-56; asst. chief, Exec. Secretariat, St. Dept., Wash. D.C. 1956-58; Italian desk ofcr. St. Dept. 1958-60; consul U.S. Consulate, Khorramshahr, Iran 1960-62; political adviser NATO, Paris, France 1963-65; dep. dir. Western Europe, St. Dept., WDC 1965-68; dep. asst. secty. gen. NATO, Brussels, Belgium 1968-71; counselor of embassy U.S. Embassy, Manila, Philippines 1971-73; advisor to pres. U.S. Naval War Coll., Newport, R.I. 1973-74; minister counselor U.S. Embassy, Cairo, Egypt 1974-76; US Ambassador, Kuwait 1976-79; spl. rep. of pres. and dir. Sinai Peacekeeping Mission, WDC 1980-83; exec. dir. World Affairs Council, San Diego 1984-86, mem. bd. 1986–; resident ambassador U.S. Internat. Univ., San Diego 1986-90; mem. Internat. Inst. Strategic Studies, London 1975–; honors: Chevalier du Merite Agricole France 1946; numerous newspaper articles pub. on internat. affairs, 1984–; mil: 1st lt. AUS 1943-46; R.Cath.; rec: golf. Res/Ofc: 2824 Curie Place San Diego 92122

MAGARAM, PHILIP S., lawyer; b. July 29, 1937, New York; s. Bernard and Ida (Weiss) M.; m. Marilyn F. Tepper, Feb. 20, 1966 (dec. 1989); m. Sally Kalish, Aug. 22, 1993; children: Justin b. 1968, Jodi b. 1970; edn: BS, UCLA 1958; LL.B, 1961. Career: atty., ptnr. Magaram Riskin Wayne & Minikes, Los Angeles 1963-83; Irell & Manella 1983-84; Valensi Rose & Magaram 1984–; mem: Joseph Drown Found. (dir., 1982), UCLA Found. (trustee 1984), Arthritis Found. (gov. 1980), Nat. Found. Ileitis & Collitis (dir. 1987), Regency Club; 4 articles pub. in profl. jours., 1975-85; Democrat; Jewish; rec: running, tennis. Ofc: Valensi Rose & Magaram 1800 Ave of Stars Ste 1000 Los Angeles 90067

MAGARIAN, STEVEN DAN, county sheriff; b. Oct. 13, 1942, Fresno; s. Dan Steve and Alice (Ekparian) M.; m. Joanne Louise Massicci, June 15, 1985; 1 dau. Erica b. 1987; edn: BS, and MS, CSU Fresno, 1972, 1974; Calif. Comm. Colls. life tchg. cred. 1974. Career: dep. sheriff Fresno County Sheriff's Dept., 1968-72, sheriff's sgt. 1972-76, sheriff's lt. 1976-81, sheriff's capt. 1981-83, asst. sheriff 1983-87, sheriff Fresno County 1987–, chmn. Fresno Co. Identification RAN Bd.; instr. CSU Fresno, State Center Jr. Colls., 1984–; appt. by Gov. Deukmejian to Calif. Council of Crim. Justice 1989; awards: outstanding law enforcement ofcr. Fresno Jaycees 1980, recogn. Calif. Nat. Guard, Sacto. 1987, Am. Heart Assn. Fresno 1988, Central Calif. Blood Bank, Fresno 1989, appreciation U.S. Secret Svc., Sacto. 1989; mem: Calif. St. Sheriffs Assn., Calif. Peace Ofcrs. Assn., FBI National Academy Graduates 1980–, Fresno County Inter Agy. 1986–; civic: Am. Heart Assn. (dir. 1988–); mil: airman USAF 1961; Republican; Prot. Ofc: Fresno County Sheriff's Dept. 2200 Fresno St Fresno 93721

MAGGI, SERGIO, electronics scientist/design manager; b. May 10, 1949, Rome, Italy; s. Remo and Concetta (Longobardi) M.; m. Rebecca Anne Triggs; children: Mirella b. 1986, Sergio Alexander b. 1989; edn: MSEE (equiv.) Univ. of Rome, 1973. Career: engr. Texas Instruments, Rome, Italy 1973-76; microcomputer designer Texas Instruments, Houston, Tx. 1976-82; system designer Schlumberger, Houston 1982-86; senior scientist Fairchild, Palo Alto, Calif. 1986; design mgr. Micro Power Systems, Santa Clara 1987–, cons. dir. Logitech, Fremont, Calif. 1991–; mem. IEEE; civic: Project G Theatre Club, Houston (pres. 1983-86); co-inventor: TMS 34010, 1st graphic computer in a microchip, 1986; Cath.; rec: theatre, gardening. Res: 925 Laguna Ave Burlingame 94010

MAGNES, HARRY ALAN, physician; b. Dec. 3, 1948, Orange, N.J.; s. Sam and Shirley Sandra (Daniels) M.; m. Patricia Bruce; edn: AB biol. (magna cum laude), Brown Univ., 1970; MD, Yale Univ., 1974. Career: internist and ptnr. Gallatin Medical Corp., Downey, Calif. 1977–, exec. com. 1988-94, pres./ceo 1992-94, med. dir. Gallatin Med. Found. 1993–; clin. specialist/ instr. Rancho Los Amigos Hosp./ USC 1979-81; med. staff Downey Comm. Hosp. 1977–; med. staff Presbyterian Intercommunity Hosp. 1992–; awards: James Manning scholar Brown Univ. 1968, Phi Beta Kappa 1970; mem: Calif. Med. Assn. (faculty Quality Assur. Workshop, Sacto. 1979-83), L.A. Co. Med. Soc. (dist. 10 bd. govs. 1980-81), Am. Coll of Physician Executives 1992–, Unified Med. Group Assn. 1993–, Calif. Assn. Healthcare Provider Foundations 1993–, Med. Group Mgmt. Assn. 1994–, Am. Coll. of Med. Practice Executives (nom.) 1994–; 2 pub. research papers (1965, 74); rec: racquetball, scuba, tennis, magic, fin. advising. Ofc: Gallatin Medical Foundation 10720 Paramount Blvd Downey 90241

MAGNESI, ALEXIS VERONICA, corporate executive; b. June 12, 1955, Bridgeport, Conn.; d. Alex Vincent and Veronica (Pape) Fucci; m. Nathan L. Magnesi, Jr., Dec. 28, 1985; children: Ashley S. b. 1988, Miles A. b. 1989; edn: major eng./jour., So. Conn. State Coll., 2 yrs., bus./personnel mgmt. major UCLA, 1 yr. Career: personnel/acctg. mgr. Postal Instant Press, Los Angeles 1976-80; v.p. personnel Imperial Internat. Inc., Torrance 1980-85; exec. v.p./co-owner USPS Security Inc., Los Angeles 1985–; owner USPS Patrol Inc., 1989–; civic: Youth Employment Summer Pgm., Torrance (chair 1981); recipient appreciation Private Industry Council, Torrance (1981, 82, 83). Ofc: 1264 San Dimas Canyon Rd San Dimas 91773

MAGNUSON, DONALD RICHARD, motion picture and television screenwriter; b. Apr. 23, 1951, Chgo., Ill.; s. Donald O. and Olive J. (O'Keefe) M.; m. Debra Michelle Ruzek, June 9, 1973; children: Jennifer Jean b. 1974, Erick Richard b. 1976; edn: St. Hugh's, Lyons, Ill. 1965; Downers Grove So. H.S. 1969; N. Ill. Univ., journalism, 1969; Coll. of DuPage, Glen Ellyn, Ill., journalism, 1969-71. Career: asst. tchg. tennis pro - Westside Racquet Club 1970-73; Tennaqua Racquet Club 1972; film/t.v. screenwriter/producer Chicagoland Pictures, Ltd., Yorba Linda 1987-92; co-chmn. Chicagoland Pictures, Ltd. 1992–; mem: Ferrari Club of Amer. 1987-91, Porsche Club of Amer. 1986-88; screenwriter: teleplay pilot, Black & White, 1989; eight screenplays: The Taiwan Factor, 1989, Another Autumn, 1989, Reunion, 1990, Harry's Harem (co-written with Fabiola Sarah Volante 1991), An Aspen Affair (co-written with Christina Cardan 1992), Dancer, 1993, Best Medicine, 1993, Midnight Internment, 1993, Love the One You're With (co-written with Deirdre S. Hamilton, 1995); Roman Catholic. Ofc: Chicagoland Pictures Ltd 19866 Ridge Manor Way Yorba Linda 92686

MAGUIRE, EVERETT WILLIAM, lawyer; b. Jan. 2, 1928, San Bernardino; s. Everett Henry and Edith Marie (Droscha) M.; m. Nancy Lee Grant, Oct. 7, 1951; children: Nanette Eileen, William E., Constance Sue; edn: AA in civil eng., San Bdo. Valley Coll., 1948; BSCE, UC Berkeley, 1950; JD, UCLA, 1957; admitted bar: Calif. 1958, US Dist. Ct. (Cent., So., Eastern, No. dists. Calif.), US Ct. Appeals (9th cir.) 1963, US Supreme Ct. 1975; reg. profl. engr. (PE) Calif. 1955. Career: atty. Calif. Dept. Pub. Works, Los Angeles 1958-66; atty., assoc. Grant & Popovich, Beverly Hills 1966-68; ptnr. Shapiro & Maguire, Beverly Hills 1968-88; Maguire & Orbach, Lawyers, L.A. 1989–; mem: ABA, Calif. Bar Assn., L.A. Co. Bar Assn., Santa Monica Bar Assn., ASCE, Soc. Am. Mil. Engrs., Am. Legion, Masons, Shriners, Moose; dir. Palisades-Malibu YMCA 1970–; trustee Pac. Palisades Methodist Ch. & P.P. Meth. Memorial Fund 1981–; mil: sgt. Army Corps Engrs. 1950-52. Res: 927 Lachman Ln Pacific Palisades Ofc: Maguire & Orbach, 10866 Wilshire Blvd Ste 300 Los Angeles 90024-4311

MAGUIRE, JOHN DAVID, university president, educator, writer; b. Aug. 7, 1932, Montgomery, Ala.; s. John Henry and Clyde (Merrill) M.; m. Lillian Louise Parrish, Aug. 29, 1953; children: Catherine Merrill, Mary Elizabeth, Anne King; edn: AB, magna cum laude, Washington and Lee Univ. 1953; Litt.D, hon., 1979; Fulbright scholar, Edinburgh Univ., Scotland 1953-54; BD, summa cum laude, Yale 1956, PhD, 1960; postdoctoral research, Yale Univ. and Univ. Tubingen, Germany 1964-65; UC Berkeley 1968-69, Silliman Univ., Philippines and Chinese Univ., Hong Kong 1976-77; HLD (hon.) Transylvania Univ., 1990. Career: dir. Internat. Student Ctr., New Haven 1956-58; faculty Wesleyan Univ., Middletown, Conn. 1960-70, assoc. provost 1967-68; vis. lectr. Pacific Sch. Religion and Grad. Theol. Union, Berkeley 1968-69; coll. pres. SUNY Coll. at Old Westbury, N.Y. 1970-81; pres. Claremont Univ. Center and Graduate Sch., 1981–; appt. Conn. advy. com. U.S. Commn. Civil Rights 1961-70, participant White House Conf. on Civil Rights 1966; advisor, permanent trustee, dir. M.L.K. Ctr. for Soc. Change, Atlanta 1968–; bd. dirs. Nassau Co. Health and Welfare Council 1971-81, pres. 1974-76; bd. dirs. NAACP Legal Defense and Ednl. Fund Inc., 1991–, West Coast bd. dirs. 1981–; bd. dirs. Salzburg Seminar, 1992–; trustee Inst. Internat. Edn. 1980-86, Tomas Rivera Ctr. Claremont (1984–, v.chmn. 87–), Assn. Indep. Calif. Colls. and Univs. (1985–, v.chmn. 88-89, chmn. 1990-92, exec. com. 1992–), Calif. Achiev. Council (1985-94, chmn. 90-94), Transylvania Univ. Bingham Trust 1987–, Lincoln Found. and Lincoln Inst. of Land Policy Inc. 1987-94, The JL Found.

1988–, Thacher Sch., Ojai, Calif. (1982–, v. chmn. 86–), The Business Enterprise Trust (1989–), Assn. of Am. Colls. and Univs. (1966–, dir. 1981-86, bd. chair 84-85), Ednl. Found. for African Americans 1991–; founder and chair, Calif. Red-Ox Consortium of Higher Edn. 1981–; advy. bd., RAND Ctr. for Research on Immigration Policy 1994–; mem. Am. Com. U.S.-Soviet Relations 1981-92, Blue Ribbon Calif. Commn. on Tchg. Profession 1984-86, Aspen Inst. Wye Faculty Seminar (govng. council 1984-94), Council on Fgn. Rels. 1983–, Pres.'s Advy. Council to Commn. on Calif. Master Plan for Higher Edn. 1986-87, Council of Trustees L.A. Ednl. Alliance for Restructuring Now 1992–, Calif. Bus.- Higher Educ. Forum 1992–; awards: Julia A. Archibald high scholar Yale Div. Sch. 1956; Day fellow 1956-57, Kent fellow Yale Grad. Sch. 1957-60; Howard Found. postdoc. fellow Brown Univ. Grad. Sch. 1964-65; Fenn lectr. 7 Asian countries 1976-77; recipient Conn. Prince Hall Masonic award for contbns. to human rights in Conn. 1965; E. Harris Harbison great tchr. prize Danforth Found. 1968; mem: Soc. Values Higher Edn. (bd. dirs. 1972-88, pres. 1974-81); Phi Beta Kappa; Omicron Delta Kappa; author: The Dance of the Pilgrim: A Christian Style of Life for Today, 1967; num. arts.; Democrat. Ofc: Office of the President, Claremont University Center and Graduate School, 160 E Tenth St Claremont CA 91711

MAHAFFEY, CANDACE MARIE, political organization executive, editor; b. Feb. 11, 1955, Anderson, S.C.; d. Joe Gentry Mahaffey; edn: 4 years in electronics & elec. tech., law studies, Northwestern Calif. Univ. Career: political organizer The Conservative Action Lobby, Los Angeles 1988–, editor political newsletter: The Economic Watch, 1989–; sci. fiction writer; Prot.; rec: karate, weightlifting, music. Ofc: The Conservative Action Lobby PO Box 931602 Los Angeles 90093

MAHANEY, JOHN GAGE, retired surgeon, councilman; b. Mar. 6, 1927, Owosso, Mich.; s. Reynolds Cornelius and Rachel (Preston) M.; m. Billie Kathleen Benzie, RN, Oct. 28, 1956; children: John H, Mark, Michael, Erin; edn: BS, Mich. State Univ., 1949; MD, George Washington Univ., 1954, Diplomate Am. Bd. Orthopedic Surgeons 1964. Career: intern USPHS, San Francisco, 1955, resident, 1957-58, 59-60; resident USPHS Hosp., Staten Island, N.Y., 1956-57; Shriners Hosp. for Crippled Children, Salt Lake City, 1958-59; pvt. practice Santa Cruz (Calif.) Med. Clinic, 1960-92; retired, 1992; councilman City of Santa Cruz, 1973-83, 1988-92; mayor, 1976, 79; pres. Monterey Div. League of Calif. Cities, 1979; Fellow ACS, Am. Acad. Orthopedic Surgeons; mem: Western Orthopedic Assn., Calif. Med. Soc., Am. Orthopedic Soc. for Sports Medicine (emeritus), Santa Cruz Rotary (dir.; pres. elect 1996); mil: USPHS, 1954-60; Republican.

MAHONY, ROGER MICHAEL, archbishop; b. Feb. 27, 1936, Hollywood; s. Victory James and Loretta Marie (Baron) M.; edn: AA, Our Lady of Queen of Angels Sem., 1956; BA, St. John's Sem. Coll., 1958, BST, 1962; MSW, Catholic Univ. Am., 1964; ordained priest Roman Cath. Ch., 1962, ordained bishop, 1975; Career: ast. pastor St. Johyn's Cathedral, Fresno, 1962, 68-73, rector 1973–; residence St. Genevieve's Parish, Fresno 1964–, adminstr., 1964-67, pastor 1967-68; titular bishop of Tamascani, aux. bishop of Fresno 1975-80; chancellor Diocese of Fresno, 1970, vicar gen., 1975-80; bishop Diocese of Stockton, 1980-85; archbishop Diocese of Los Angeles, 1985–; diocesan dir. Cath. Charities and Social Service Fresno, 1964-70, exec. dir. Cath. Welfare Bur., 1964-70; exec. dir. Cath Welfare Bur. Infant of Prague Adoption Svc., 1964-70; chaplain St. Vincent de Paul Soc., Fresno 1964-70; chaplain to Pope Paul VI, 1967; mem. faculty extension div. Fresno State Univ., 1965-67; sec. U.S. Cath. bishops ad hoc com. on farm labor Nat. Conf. Bishops, 1970-75; chmn. com. on pub. welfare and income maintenance Nat. Conf. Cath. Charities, 1969-70; bd. dirs. West Coast Reg. Ofc. Bishops Com. for Spanish-speaking, 1967-70; chmn. Calif. Assn. Cath. Charities Dirs., 1965-69; trustee St. Patrick's Sem., Archdiocese of San Francisco, 1974-75; bd. dirs. Fresno Comm. Workshop, 1965-67; trustee St. Agnes Hosp., Fresno; honors: named Young Man of Yr. Fresno Jr. C.of C. 1967; mem: Urban Coalition of Fresno 1968-72, Fresno Co. Econ. Opportunities Commn. 1964-65, Fresno Co. Alcoholic Rehab. Com. 1966-67, Fresno City Charter Rev. Com. 1968-70, Mexican - Am. Council for Better Housing 1968-72, Fresno Redevel. Agy. 1970-75, Canon Law Soc. Am., Nat. Assn. Social Wkrs. Res: 114 E 2nd St Los Angeles 90012 Ofc: Archdiocese of Los Angeles 1531 N 9th St Los Angeles 90012

MAHRER, PETER RAOUL, physician, educator; b. Oct. 27, 1926, Prague, Czechoslovakia; s. Paul and Betty (Gutman) M.; m. Eva, Jan. 21, 1950 (dec. 1983); m. Gabrielle, June 6, 1989; children: Thomas b. 1953, Susan b. 1955, Kenneth b. 1957; edn: BA, Bklyn. Coll. 1949; MD, Cornell Univ. 1953; cert. Am. Bd. Internal Medicine (1957); cert. Subsp. Cardiovascular Disease (1975). Career: intern Bellevue Hosp., N.Y.C. 1953-54, resident 1954-55; cardiology fellow N.Y. Hosp. 1955-56; Mt. Sinai Hosp. 1956-57; vis. prof. Nat. Heart Hosp., London, England 1968, 72; ptnr. So. Calif. Permanente Med. Group, Los Angeles 1959–; dir. cardiology cath. lab. Kaiser Hosp. 1983–, chief cardiology section 1983–; clin. prof. medicine USC Sch. Medicine 1980–; mem: Am. Coll. Cardiology (fellow, gov., So. Cal. 1995-97), L.A. Cardiology Soc. (pres. 1988); 20+ articles pub. in med. jours., 2 book chpt., 1957; mil: pvt. 1c. USAF 1949; Democrat; rec: skiing, tennis. Res: 3490 Berry Dr Studio City 91604 Ofc: 1526 N Edgemont Los Angeles 90027

MAIBACH, HOWARD, professor; b. July 18, 1929, NY, NY; s. Jack Louis and Sidonia (Fink) M.; m. Siesel W., July 8, 1933; children, Lisa, Ed, Todd; edn: AB, Tulane Univ., New Orleans, La. 1950; MD, Tulane Univ. 1955. Career: prof., dermatology, Univ. of Calif. Med. Sch., S.F. 1961–; mem: SID, AMA, ICDR; author and editior of over forty books since 1965; mil: capt., U. S. Army, 1955-58. Ofc: Univ. of Calif. Medical School, San Francisco 94143

MAIBACH, MICHAEL CHARLES, corporate government affairs executive; b. May 14, 1951, Peoria, Ill.; s. Charles Edward and Annette Claire (Pilon) M.; edn: BA (cum laude), No. Ill. Univ. 1973, MA, 1980; BA (cum laude), CSU Hayward 1983; BS, Am. University, Wash. D.C. 1989; att. AU European Inst., summer 1986, Inst. for Internat. Studies, Tokyo, spring 1985, Universidad Ibero-Americana, Mex. City, summer 1974, Oxford Univ., England, summer 1973, World Affairs Council, S.F.-Central Am. study trip 1987, Ea. European study trip 1990. Career: machine shop foreman Caterpillar, Inc. 1976-77, Ill. issues mgr., govt. affairs 1977-79, west coast rep. 1979-82, domestic issues mgr. 1983; dir. govt. affairs, Intel Corp., Santa Clara, Calif. and Wash., D.C. 1983–; govt: staff asst. Pres. Bush's Nat. Advy. Commn. on Semiconductors 1991, Pres. Reagan's Commn. on Industrial Competitiveness 1983-85, mem. Bd. of Zoning Adjustment, Menlo Park 1985, staff intern, Ill. State Senate, Springfield, 1975-76, Illinois Humanities Council 1973-75, Dekalb County Bd., Ill. 1972-75, Gov's Fellow, Ill. Dept. of Local Govt., summers 1970, 71; author numerous essays; Republican. Res: 1047 Noel Drive Menlo Park 94025 Ofc: Intel Corporation 2200 Mission College Blvd Santa Clara 95052-8119

MAIBAUM, MATTHEW, consulting social scientist, writer; b. Aug. 14, 1946, Chgo.; s. Richard W. and Sylvia M.; edn: AB, UC Berkeley, 1969; MPA, UCLA, 1973; PhD, Calif. Sch. Profl. Psychology, L.A. 1975; PhD, Claremont Grad. Sch., 1980; lic. psychologist Calif. Career: postdoct. intern Pacific State Hosp., Pomona 1976-77, Metropolitan State Hosp., Norwalk 1977-78; pvt. practice psychologist, Los Angeles 1978–; writer, researcher soc. scis., 1972–; instr. Univ. Redlands 1976, 77, UCLA Sch. Pub. Health 1978-79, instr. indus. psy. Cal Poly Pomona 1984; honors: Pi Gamma Mu, Sigma Xi, grant in aid award Soc. Psy Study Soc. Issues, Ann Arbor, Mich. 1972, best paper co-winner Cal State Psychol. Assn. 1975; Diplomate Am. Bd. Med. Psychotherapists; mem.: Authors Guild Am., Dramatists Guild Am. (assoc.), Amity Circle L.A. (pres. 1973), Soc. Advancement Field Theory, Soc. of Authors (Engl.); author fiction, 3 plays: Sly Times, 1986, Wiggling in The Rain, 1988, The Lilac Bush, 1990. Ofc: 253A 26th St. #106, Santa Monica 90402

MAK, JOSEPHINE HUEY JU, physician; b. Aug. 28, 1931, Shanghai, China, nat. 1978; d. Min-Ju and Rong Fen (Liu) Chang; m. Timothy Mak, Aug. 20, 1965; children: Calvin, Grace, Esther, Andrew; edn: MD, Kiangsu (China) Med. Coll., 1956; dipl. child health Royal Coll. Physicians, Dublin, Ireland 1967. Career: intern Kiangsu Med. Coll. Hosp., Kiangsu, China 1955-56; house physician People's Hosp., 1956-57; med. ofcr. Ardkeen Hosp., Waterford, S. Ireland 1962-63; sr. med. ofcr. Infirmary, Cork, S. Ire. 1963-64; sr. med. ofcr. OB-Gyn and pediatrics, St. Finnbarr's Hosp., 1964-65; sr. ofcr. psychiatry Our Lady's Hosp., 1965-66; sr. ofcr. peds. Nat. Children's Hosp., Dublin 1967-70; pub. health (peds) Dublin Health Auth., 1970-71; pediatrics The Jewish Hosp. Med. Ctr., Bklyn. 1979-80; med. staff N.E. Medical Service, San Francisco 1980-81; pvt. med. practice office, family and peds., S.F. 1981–; mem: AMA, Calif. Med. Assn., S.F. Med. Soc., Brit. Med. Assn. (1963-70), Irish Med. Assn. (1963-70); Christian. Ofc: Josephine Mak MD 835 Jackson St Ste 202 San Francisco 94133

MAKSYMOWICZ, JOHN, electrical engineer; b. Feb. 3, 1956, Bklyn.; s. Theodore John and Helen Mary (Kisinski) M.; edn: BEE (highest hon.), Pratt Inst., Bklyn., N.Y., 1983. Career: electrical engr. RF & digital test equip., IBM Corp., Poughkeepsie, N.Y. 1983; AWACS airborne early warning radar, Grumman Aerospace Corp., Bethpage, N.Y. 1983-87; radar & spread spectrum comms., Plessey Electronics, Totowa, N.J. 1987-88; sr. mem. tech. staff, radar designer, The Aerospace Corp., Los Angeles 1989-95, Fairfax, VA 1995–; awards: Fred G. Flickinger scholarship 1980-83, Samuel Brown scholar, Cook-Marsh scholar, Pratt Inst. 1979-83, Tau Beta Pi (coll. chpt. pres. 1981-82), Eta Kappa Nu (coll. chpt. pres. 1981-82), Program Recogn. Award, The Aerospace Corp. 1991, 1992; listed Who's Who in West 1992-3, Who's Who in World 1993-4, Who's Who in Sci. and Engring. 1994-95; mem: IEEE 1980–, Assn. of Old Crows 1982–, US Space Found. 1992–, SPIE 1994–; profl. papers: Pulse Compression Techniques, 1990; Examination of Cross-Polarization ECM, 1991; Detection of Low Earth Orbit Space Debris by a Ground Based Phased Array Radar, 1992; R.Cath.; rec: running, photography, reading, music.

MALACHOWSKI, MICHAEL JON, biophysicist, educator; b. Sept. 4, 1945, Chicago, Ill.; s. Thaddeus Antony and Natalie Constance (Kryczewski) M.; children: Jessica Lynn, Justin Skye; edn: Colo. Coll. 1963-65; AB physics and EE, UC Berkeley 1968; PhD biophysics and health sci. 1978. Career: cert. instr. Calif. Engr. Coherent Radiation Lab., Palo Alto 1966-67; v.p. Centurion Enterprises, Berkeley 1968-72; research assoc. Lawrence Berkeley Labs., 1973-77; NRC fellow Univ. Western Ontario, London, Canada 1977-80; chief exec. CCE-Robotics/Electronic Photography, 1978-; assoc. NASA, Moffett Field 1975-80; Peralta CCD 1980–; CCSF 1981–; PETE (Ptnrs. in Environmental

Tech. Edn.) 1994, 95; instr. biophysics 1981; faculty S.F. State Univ. 1993-; chair No. Calif. Environmental Tech. Consortium 1993-; bd. dirs. Bay Area Multimedia Coll. Consortium 1992-; co-chair edn. & tng. com., No. Calif. Minority Bus. Opportunity Com. 1995; honors: pres. UCB Student Body President's Council 1974-76, chmn. Grad. Assembly 1976. Ofc: CCE Box 9315 Berkeley 94709

MALCOLM, MACKEY H., judge; b. July 20, 1929, Hoboken, N.J.; s. William Gasden and Winifred Walker (Hamilton) M.; m. Sharon Scovill, Sept. 1963 (dec. 1986); children: Michael b. 1969, Kristie b. 1973; edn: AB, New York Univ. 1951; JD, Southwestern Univ. 1958; admitted Calif. State Bar 1959. Career: sales rep. Tidewater Oil Corp. 1951-54, Richfield Oil Corp. 1954-55; claims rep. Allstate Insurance Co. 1955-57; assoc. atty. Dalton, Groff & Dunne 1958-59; trial lawyer pvt. practice 1959-78; elected judge Los Angeles Municipal Ct. 1978-84, 1984-1990; actg. justice Ct. of Appeals, 2nd Dist. div. 7, 1986, presiding judge Los Angeles Municipal Ct. 1985; elected L.A. Superior Court 1988-2001; mem: Calif., L.A. County (trustee 1978-79) bar assns., L.A. Co. Mcpl. Ct. Judges Assn. (secty. 1986-87, v. chmn. 1987-88), Lawyers Club of L.A. (past pres.), Calif. Judges Assn., Masons, Am. Fedn. Radio & TV Artists; author Small Claims Procedural Manual, L.A. Mcpl. Ct.; mil: cpl. USMC 1946-48, Navy GCM and Occup. medals; Democrat; Church Rel. Science. Ofc: Superior Court Dept. 84, N. Hill St. #21, Los Angeles 90012

MALHOSKI, WALTER EDWARD, physician, urologist; b. Aug. 11, 1942, Carbondale, Pa.; s. Edward Walter and Mary Teresa (Leputa) M.; m. Patti Louise West, Oct. 22, 1983; children: Ryan b. 1985, Sonja b. 1989; edn: BS, Univ. Scranton Pa. 1963; MD, Georgetown Univ. 1967. Career: urologist TPMG Inc., Sacto. 1977–; assoc. clin. prof. UC Davis Sch. Medicine, Sacto. 1979–; mem: Am. Urological Assn., CMA, Sacto. Co. Med. Assn.; mil: lt. USN, USMC 1969-71; Republican; R.Cath. Ofc: TPMG Inc. 6600 Bruceville Rd Sacramento 95823

MALI, DHIRU B., structural engineer; b. June 26, 1934, Karachi, Pakistant; nat. 1977; s. Bhagwanji L. and Shantaben B. M.; m. Radha D. B. Rami, Feb. 5, 1953; children: Kashmira b. 1960, Bindu b. 1963; edn: BSCE, Gujarat Univ. 1960; MS, Univ. Ill. 1962. Career: assoc. Booker & Assoc., St. Louis, Mo. 1962-69; sr. engr. Engring. Cons., New Delhi, India 1970-71; project engr. Daverman Assocs., Grand Rapids, Mo. 1973-76; prin. Jack Gillum & Assoc., St. Louis 1976-79; Gillum Polk Assoc., Manchester 1979-83; pres. Mali Engring. Cons., Artesia 1984–; grading examiner St. Bd. Registration 1988; dir. awards: Gujarat Univ. Dr. Shah Prize 1960, YMCA Bailey scholar 1961, India Assn. Chmn.'s award 1983, appreciation ABC Sch. Dist. 1987, 88; mem: India Assn. (bd. trustees 1981-83), ASCE, Nat. Soc. Profl. Engrs., CSPE (Long Beach dir. 1985-87), Structural Engrs. Assn. So. Calif., Am. Inst. Steel Constrn., Internat. Conf. Bldg. Ofcls., Rotary (dir. 1986-89, pres. 1990-91), Artesia C.of C. (dir. 1985-87), Cerritos C.of C., Bellflower C.of C.; pub. engring. article: Str. Systems for Todays Housing, 1985; rec: travel, golf. Ofc: Mali Engineering Consultants 11756 Artesia Blvd Ste A Artesia 90701-3878

MALKIN, JERROLD ALLEN, deputy county counsel; b. Oct. 28, 1959, Norfolk, Va.; s. Leslie and Enid Lenore (Goldberg) M.; edn: BA political sci., Santa Clara Univ. 1980; MCRP, Rutgers Grad. Sch. 1983; JD, Rutgers Univ. 1984; admitted St. Bar Pa. 1985, N.J. 1985, Calif. 1984. Career: atty., assoc. Toff & Paul, San Jose 1984-85; dep. co. counsel Co. of Imperial, El Centro 1985-86; Co. of Monterey, Salinas 1986–; law clk. N.J. Turnpike Authority, New Brunswick 1982-84; tchg. asst. Rutgers Univ. 1981-82; planning intern Santa Clara Planning Dept., San Jose 1980; mem: Co. Counsel Assn.Probate Mental Health Sect., Pub. Attys. for Protection of Children, Co. Counsel (tax. sect.), Monterey Co. Child Abuse Prevention Counsel, Family of Man; Democrat; Jewish; rec: woodworking, construction. Ofc: County Counsel County of Monterey 240 Church St Room 214 Salinas 93901

MALLETT, WILLIAM ROBERT, research chemist, fuels consultant; b. Sept. 12, 1932, Painesville, Ohio; s. Richard Colton and Luella Louise (Dewald) M.; m. Masuko Sano, Mar. 18, 1957; children: Daryl b. 1969, Stacie b. 1971; edn: BA, Miami Univ., Oxford, Oh. 1961, MS, 1963; PhD, Rensselaer Polytech., Troy, NY 1966. Career: res. chem. Union Oil Co., Brea, Calif. 1966-68, sr. res. chem. 1968-73; vis. res. scientist Maruzen Oil Co., Satte, Japan 1973-75; res. assoc. Union Oil Co., Brea 1975-84; supr. fuels res. Unocal Corp., Brea 1984-90, staff consultant 1990-92; fuels consultant Fuels Consulting Services, Placentia 1992–; mem. Soc. of Automotive Engrs. 1970–, Am. Chemical Soc. 1961–, Am. Soc. for Testing & Mats. 1979–; invention: Gasoline additive, 1971; pub. article Gasoline Analysis, 1975; mil: s/sgt USAF 1951-55; rec: personal computers, photography, ham radio, astronomy. Res/Ofc: Fuels Consulting Svs. 1273 Genoa Pl Placentia 92670

MALMSTROM, DOROTHY ELVIRA, private school director; b. April 4, 1945, Guatemala City, Guatemala; d. Carl Olof and Esther (Butler) Malmstrom; edn: AA, Chaffey Coll., 1966; BA sociol. (honors), UC Riverside 1969; MA social sci., Azusa Pacific Univ. 1980; postgrad. work, US Internat. Univ. 1983-86; PhD clin. psychology, The Graduate Sch. of The Union Institute, 1992. Career: research sociologist UC Riverside, 1969-70; adminstrv. coord. Yamaha,

Indio, Calif. 1971-73; mktg. exec. Good Stuff Natural Bakery, Los Angeles 1974-81; founder/pres. Health Network Inst. Santa Monica 1981-82; co-founder Advance Financial Services Inc., Santa Monica 1982-87; psychol. intern Professional Consultation Services Inc., Los Angeles, 1988-92; dir. Progress School, Santa Monica 1993–; mem: Am. Psychol. Assn., Calif. State Psychol. Assn., L.A. Co. Psychol. Assn., So. Calif. Soc. of Clin. Hypnosis, Nat. Psychol. Advy. Assn.; rec: music, art, nature, walking, hiking, community. Ofc: Progress School 1305 Pico Blvd Santa Monica 90405 Tel: 310/450-1116

MALONE, MARVIN HERBERT, pharmacologist-toxicologist, editor, educator, researcher; b. Apr. 2, 1930, Fairbury, Nebr.; s. Herbert August Frederick and Elizabeth Florinda (Torrey) M.; m. Shirley Ruth Cane, Dec. 21, 1952; children: Carla Margaret, Gayla Christa; edn: BS in pharmacy, Univ. Nebr., 1951, MS in physiology and pharmacology, 1953; postgrad. Rutgers Univ., 1954-55; PhD in pharmacology and pharm. scis., Univ. Nebr., 1958. Career: student asst. Univ. Nebr., Lincoln, 1951-53, 1956-58; research asst. Squibb Inst. Med. Research, New Brunswick, N.J. 1953-56; asst. prof. Univ. New Mexico, Albuq. 1958-60; assoc. prof. Univ. Connecticut, Storrs 1960-69; prof. pharmacology and toxicology Univ. of the Pacific, Stockton 1969-84, Distinguished Prof. 1984-90, chair dept. physiology and pharmacology 1969-70, 1987-90, emeritus prof. 1990–; publisher Wormwood Books and Magazines, 1991–; prin., consulting svs., Wormwood Associates, 1990–; cons.: U. Wash. Drug Plant Labs. 1960-64, Research Pathology Assoc. 1967-70, Amazon Natural Drug Co. 1967-70, Atlas Chem. Inds. ICI USA Inc. 1968-78, SISA Inst. Research Northeastern U. 1977-82, Task Force on Plants for Fertility Regulation WHO Spl. Pgm. for R&D & Rsch. Tng. in Human Reprodn. 1982-88, gubnat. appt. Calif. St. Med. Therap. and Drug Advy. Commn. 1985-90, Herb Research Found. 1990–, Emprise Inc. 1990-92; author: Bucolics and Cheromanics 1963, Experiments in the Pharmaceutical Biol. Scis. 1973; editorial bds: J. Natural Products: Lloydia 1971-93, J. Ethnopharmacology 1978-84, 90–, Internat. Jour. Pharmacognosy 1992–; editor: The Wormwood Review, lit. jour. 1960–, Pacific Info. Service on Street-Drugs 1971-78, Am. J. Pharmaceutical Education 1974-79, Pharmat 1984-87, J. Ethnopharmacology 1985-91; contbr. 240+ articles to profl. jours.; awards: special citation UOP Sch. Pharmacy 1991, UOP Order of Pacific 1991, UOP distinction of merit 1980, outstanding svs. plaque Am. Assn. Colls. of Pharmacy 1980, Mead Johnson Labs. award 1964, grantee: USPHS (1960-63, 68-73), US Army 1962-63, Univ. Conn. Research Found. 1964-68, UOP Research 1970-73; Fellow Am. Found. Pharm. Edn. 1956-58; mem. Am. Inst. Chemists (Fellow), AAAS (Fellow), Am. Soc. Pharmacology and Exptl. Therap., Am. Soc. Pharmacognosy, Sigma Xi, Rho Chi, Phi Lambda Upsilon, Phi Kappa Phi; specialties: screening and assay of natural principles from plants and higher fungi, biometrics, pharmacology of inflammation and antiinflamation, pharmacodynamics of psychotropic and autonomic agents, fertility regulation; rec: book, art and little magazine collecting. Res/Ofc: 722 Bedford Rd Stockton 95204-5214 Tel 209/466-8231

MALONEY, DOUGLAS JAMES, lawyer; b. May 26, 1933, San Francisco; s. James Douglas and Loretta Patricia (O'Donnell) M.; m. Elenore Maloney, Dec. 31, 1976 (div. 1986); m. Ellen R. Caulfield, May 14, 1988; children: Lynne b. 1956, Karen b. 1958, Douglas Jr. b. 1961, Susan b. 1962, Pamela b. 1963; edn: BS, Calif. Maritime Acad. 1954; JDS, Univ. San Francisco 1958. Career: dep. county counsel Sonoma County, Santa Rosa 1959-60; asst. county counsel Marin County, San Rafael 1960-62, county counsel 1962–93, ptnr., Nossaman, Guthner, Knox & Elliott; bd. dirs. Buck Center on Aging 1987; Living History Center 1983-86; awards: City of San Rafael Citizen of Year 1986; mem: Irish Am. Bar Assn. (bd. dirs. 1984-86), County Counsels Assn., Nat. Assn. County Civil Attys.; author musical satires Scandals of 1933, Electric Politician, Pigmalian, Blazing Ballots, Marilot; mil: USMM 1955-56; Democrat; Cath.; rec: writing, amateur theatre. Res: 204 Forbes San Rafael 94901 Ofc: Nossaman, Guthner, Knox & Elliott, 50 California St., 34th Flr. San Francisco 94111

MALONEY, JOHN JOSEPH, business manager; b. Aug. 22, 1935, Brooklyn, N.Y.; s. William Francis and Gertrude Elizabeth (Ryder) M.; m. Mary Gail Heller, Dec. 29, 1956; children: John b. 1957, Tamara b. 1958, Sandra b. 1960, Michael b. 1961; edn: BS, N.Y. St. Maritime Coll. 1956; BS, USN Postgrad. Coll. 1964; MS, 1972; MBA, Pepperdine Univ. 1982. Career: v.p. Oceanroutes Inc., Sunnyvale 1980-94; Weather Network Inc., Chico 1985-94; cons. meteorology/oceanography, marine environment, applications, internat., forensic, business, 1994–; mem: Navy League; mil: capt. USN 1956-80; R.Cath.; rec: flying, golf. Address: Saratoga 95070

MALOUF, FREDERICK LEROY, composer, software engineer; b. Oct. 7, 1954, Fort Worth, Tx.; s. LeRoy Gabriel and Antoinette Alice (Antoine) M.; m. Bonnie Elizabeth Johanson, Aug. 21, 1977; children: Eric b. 1986, Vanita b. 1990; edn: MusB, Berklee Coll. of Music, Boston 1979; MusM, Bowling Green State Univ., 1981; ArtsD, Ball State Univ., 1985. Career: tech. support mgr. Quintus Computer Systems, Palo Alto 1985-87; software engr. Sequential Circuits Inc., San Jose 1987; Digideck Inc., Mountain View 1987-88; Apple Computer, Cupertino 1988-92; Kaleida Labs Inc., Mountain View 1992-94; Vicarious Inc., Redwood City 1994–; concert producer Chromatonal Productions, Mountain View 1987–; performer with mus. ensemble "Qwire";

compositions: Piano Sonato No. 1, 1979, Avatar, 1981, Chromatonal, 1985, Sacrifice, 1988, Variations on Goodbye Pork Pie Hat, 1989, Bali Jam, 1991, Imijimi, 1992, Miles, 1992, Patterns, 1994, Between the Lines, 1995; awards: Richard Levy composition award Berklee Coll. of Music 1979, Stanford Univ. composer in residence Rockefeller Found. 1984, Arts Internat. travel grantee to festivals Warsaw, Poland 1990, 91; mem. IEEE 1987–, Computer Music Assn. 1987–, ASCAP 1988–; Indep.; rec: camping, hiking, swimming, movies. Res: 379 Palo Alto Ave Mountain View 94041 Ofc: Vicarious Inc 3 Lagoon Dr Ste 300 Redwood City 94065

MALTZ, ANDREW HAL, computer company executive; b. Feb. 27, 1960, Mineola, N.Y.; s. Joseph A. and Marilyn (Rothchild) M.; m. Leslie Ann Stewart, May 24, 1987; children: Haley b. 1991, Dalton b. 1994; edn: BSEE, SUNY at Buffalo, N.Y. 1982. Career: development engr. Ruxton Ltd., Burbank 1982-85; v.p. engring. Cinedco Inc., Burbank 1985-89; v.p. engring. Ediflex Systems Inc., Glendale 1989-91, v.p. operations & engring., 1991-93; exec. vp. ops. & engring. Ediflex Digital Systems Inc. 1993-94; pres. Digital Media Technologies, Inc. 1994–; awards: Tau Beta Pi 1981, Eta Kappa Nu 1981, Emmy for engring. achiev. Acad. of TV Arts & Scis., Hollywood 1986; mem. Soc. of Motion Picture & TV Engrs. 1982–, Tech. Council Motion Picture & Television Industries; Democrat; rec: wine, skiing, cycling. Res: 15106 Weddington St Sherman Oaks 91411 Ofc: Digital Media Technologies Inc.

MANCINI, ROBERT KARL, computer analyst; b. May 13, 1954, Burbank; s. Alfred Robert and Phyllis Elaine (Pflugel) M.; m. Barbara Diane Bacon, Aug. 4, 1979; children: Benjamin b. 1981, Bonnie b. 1983, Brandon b. 1993; edn: BA econ., UCLA 1976; cert. biblical studies, Multnomah Sch. of Bible 1981; MBA quantatative methods, Santa Clara Univ. 1987. Career: process clk. Am. Funds Service Co., Los Angeles 1976-77; exec. asst. Sierra Thrift & Loan Co., San Mateo 1977-78; scientific programming splst. Lockheed Missiles & Space, Sunnyvale 1978-90; product mgr. Diversified Software Systems Inc., Morgan Hill 1990–; pres. Mancini Computer Services, San Jose 1985–; computer software instr. Heald Coll., San Jose 1990; computer cons. Mary Kay Cosmetics, Cupertino 1985-86, Valor Software, San Jose 1987, Century 21, Campbell 1987-92, Major Freight Systems, Milpitas 1989-91; honors: Phi Kappa Sigma, LMSC commendn. 1979, 81; mem. UCLA Alumni, Heritage House; civic: City of Morgan Hill Blue Rib. Budget Com. 1992; Republican; Christian (Hillside Ch. Fin. Council, S. Valley Christian Ch. Missions Com.); rec: tennis, photography and video photog., gardening. Res: PO Box 1602 Morgan Hill 95038

MANDEL, MAURICE, II, lawyer; b. Hollywood, Calif.; s. Maurice and Wynne M.; edn: Beverly Hills H.S.; BS, USC Sch. of Bus. Adm., 1971, MS, USC Sch. of Edn., 1972; JD, Western State Univ. Coll. of Law, 1979; Calif. life tchg. cred., elem. edn. and adminstrn.; admitted bar: Calif. 1980, U.S. Dist. Cts. (cent. dist. Calif. 1983, we. dist. Tenn. 1987, dist. Az. 1990, so. dist. Calif. 1991), U.S. Ct. Appeals (9th cir. 1983, Fed. cir. 1988, 5th cir. 1995), U.S. Supreme Ct. 1987. Career: elementary sch. tchr. Orange Co. 1972-82; lawyer sole practice, Newport Beach 1982–; Comm. Coll. instr. 1987-95, Comm. Coll. full prof. 1995–; prof. of law Irvine Univ. Coll. of Law 1994–; ski instr., Bear Mountain, Calif. 1994–; FBA/OCC MCLE provider 1994–; O.C.B.A. instr., Coll. of Trial Advocacy 1994–; honors: USC honored senior 1971 and rider of Trojan Horse (sch. mascot), Calif. Bar Assn. pro bono service awards 1983-87, US Dist. Ct. pro bono service award 1986, OCBA Award of Merit 1987, FBA Award of Merit 1990, Thwarted Thwart award Newport Harbor C.of C. 1989, Kirov Ballet Tovarich award 1989 and Marinskii Teatp award 1992, Perestroika award Moscow Classical Ballet 1988-89, 94, Skrasivi Nogi award Bolshoi Ballet 1990, Kirov Negotiator 1995; mem: Am. Bar Assn., Calif. Bar Assn., Orange Co. Bar Assn. (charter mem., O.C. Bar Found. trustee 1984-87, chmn. legal edn. for youth com. 1984-87), Federal Bar Assn. (spl. appointee nat. membership com., reg. v.chair membership; Orange Co. Chpt. founding pres., del. Calif. Bar, del. nat. conv.; O.C. chpt. coms.-programs, courthouse, judicial selection, reception, newsletter, crim. indigent def., constnl. bi-centennial, Bill of Rights; awards for Chpt. activity and FBA membership, 1987) Am. Trial Lawyers Assn., Calif. Trial Lawyers Assn., Plaintiff Employee Lawyers Assn., Bar Leaders Coun. Dist. 8, Amicus Publico, Orange Co. Women Lawyers, Calif. Employment Lawyers Assn., Employees Rights Council, USC Alumni, MENSA, American Inns of Ct., U.S. Olympic Com. Assoc., U.S. Ski Team associate 1975–, Smithsonian Instn., Friends Am. Ballet Theatre, Opera Pacific Guild, Friends Joffrey Ballet, Calypso Soc., World Wildlife Fedn., L.A. County Mus. Art, Newport Beach Art Mus., Laguna Beach Art Mus., Beverly Hills H.S. Alumni and Scholarship Com., Center Dance Alliance, U.S. Supreme Ct. Hist. Soc., 9th Jud. Cir. Hist. Soc.; rec: sailing, skiing. Res: PO Box 411 Balboa Island 92662 Ofc: 160 Newport Center Dr Ste 260 Newport Beach 92660

MANGUM, WILLIAM THOMAS, management consultant, company executive; b. Dec. 7, 1931, Memphis, Tenn.; s. Cary and Jennie (Matthews) M.; m. Maria Elena Smith, April 2, 1984; children: Stacy Ann b. 1959, Christopher Lee b. 1961; edn: AA, Santa Monica Coll. 1952; BS cum laude AV USC 1954. Career: Psychol Research Corp., N.Y. 1952-54; employee rels. splst. Beckman Instruments, Fullerton 1954-55; dir. personnel, asst. gen. mgr. Fairchild Camera & Instruments, Los Angeles 1955-60; ptnr. Deane-Thomas Co. 1960-64; pres.

Thomas Mangum Co. 1965–; cons. dir. TMI Mgmt. Inc. 1965–; prof. indsl. rels. Whittier Coll. 1958-60; listed in The Career Makers - America's Top 100 Recruiters; mem: IEEE, AIAA, USC Personnel & Indsl. Rels. Assn. (pres. 1961-62), Internat. Assn. Corp. Profl. Recruiters, Am. Mgmt. Assn., Merchants & Mfrs. Assn., Old Crows Assn., Calif. Exec. Recruiters Assn., Am. Ordnance Assn., Personnel Indsl. Rels. Assn.; author: (books) 99 Minutes to Your Ideal Job, Job Search Workbook, articles pub. in profl. jours.; civic: Save Our Rural Environ. (pres. 1976-92), La Habra Heights Improvement Assoc. (pres. award 1984), La Habra Heights Planning Com. (pres., bd. dirs.); mil: USNR 1950-58. Ofc: Thomas Mangum Co. 500 E Del Mar Blvd #19 Pasadena 91101

MANINGER, R(ALPH) CARROLL, engineer; b. Dec. 24, 1918, Harper, Kans.; s. Earl Dotterer and Mabel Velma (Haskin) M.; m. Jean Kidder, July 1, 1942; children: Margaret b. 1943, Mary-Carroll b. 1950, Emily b. 1950; edn: BS, Calif. Inst. Tech. 1941. Career: mgr. Gen. Precision Inc., Sunnyvale br. 1957-62; head, elec. engring. res. Lawrence Livermore Nat. Laboratory, 1962-85, consultant 1985–. Res: 146 Roan Dr Danville 94526

MANKOFF, ALBERT WILLIAM, writer, institute president; b. Aug. 24, 1926, Newark, N.J.; s. Albert and Dorothy M.; m. Audrey Emery, Mar. 17, 1972; 1 son, Robert M.; stepfather to Alison, Cynthia, and Robert E. Lee; edn: BLS, Univ. Oklahoma, 1967. Career: mgr. organization devel. American Airlines, Tulsa, Okla. 1947-69; dir. human resources Peat, Marwick, Mitchell, Chgo. 1969-72; personnel mgr.-Europe, Digital Equip. Co., Geneva, Switz. 1972; ptnr. Lexicon Consulting, Raleigh, N.C. 1973-80; founder Monterey Inst. of Mgmt., Monterey, Calif. 1980; total quality mgmt. cons. State of Calif., Sacto. 1980-91; pres. Inst. of Am. Historic Technology, Ojai, Calif. 1987–; bd. dirs., v.p. Meditation Groups, Inc., Ojai 1992; lectr., facilitator Meditation Mount, Ojai 1992–; bd. dirs, v.p., Psychosynthesis Internat., Ojai 1993–; bd. dirs. The Internat. Assn. for Managerial and Organizational Psychosynthesis, Thousand Oaks; past mem. Tulsa Urban League (bd. 1961-69), Oasis The Midwest Ctr. for Human Potential Chgo. (bd. 1970-73), Tulsa Employers Assn. for Merit Employment (founder 1967), Monterey (Calif.) Inst. of Mgmt. (founder 1980); author: The Star Gods, 1973, Trolley Treasures (3 vols., 1985, 88, 92), The Glory Days, 1989, The Edison Paradigm, 1994, pub. articles re mgmt., historic streetcars, light rail systems, reincarnation, meditation; mil: Army Air Corps 1943-46; Indep. Res: 1223 Gregory St. Ojai 93023 Ofc: PO Box 494 Ojai 93024

MANN, MICHAEL MARTIN, corporate development executive; b. Nov. 28, 1939, N.Y.C.; s. Dr. Herbert and Rosalind (Kaplan) M.; m. Mariel Joy Steinberg, Apr. 25, 1965; edn: BS in E.E., Calif. Inst. of Tech., 1960, MS E.E., 1961; PhD E.E., USC, 1969; Exec. MBA, UCLA, 1984; Calif. lic. R.E. broker; bd. cert. in business appraisal, cert. profl. consultant, cert. mgmt. consultant. Career: exec. v.p. Helionetics Inc., Irvine 1984-85, pres. and CEO, 1985-86; ptnr. Mann Kavanaugh Chernove & Associates, Los Angeles 1986-87; sr. cons. Arthur D. Little Inc., L.A. 1987-88; pres. Blue Marble Devel. Group Inc., Palos Verdes Estates 1988–; chmn. and CEO, Blue Marble Partners, L.A. 1991–; dir: Datum Inc., Anaheim 1988–, Safeguard Health Ents. Inc. 1988–, Decade Optical Systems, Albuq. 1990–, chmn. bd. Management Technology Inc., L.A. 1990–; dir. Am. Bus. Consultants, Inc. 1993–, Encompass Technologies, Inc. 1994–; appt. Army-Sci. Bd. subgroup chmn. Ballistic Missile Def., W.D.C. 1984-88; awards: Hicks fellow CalTech 1961, leadership Soc. Calif. Technology Execs. Network, Newport Beach 1986, patriotic civilian svc. commendn. Sec. of Army, W.D.C. 1988; mem: Presidents Assn. 1991–, Consultants Round Table 1991–, IEEE (sr. mem. 1957–), Am. Mgmt. Assn. 1988–; clubs: Palos Verdes Beach & Athletic (P.V.E.), King Harbor Yacht (Redondo Beach); inventor, 12 patents, 1962-86, author two books, 50+ articles, 1961–; Republican; rec: sailing. Ofc: Blue Marble Partners 406 Amapola Ave Ste 200 Torrance 90501

MANNING, MICHAEL M., certified public accountant; b. Nov. 23, 1939, Los Angeles; s. Earl Francis and Isabel Mary (Hanley) M.; father, Capt. Earl F. Manning, US Merch. Marine, WWII (veteran of 2 sinkings, 19 days and 1200 mi. in lifeboat to safety); m. Phyllis M.H. Underwood, 1963; children: Phyllis E. b. 1964, Helen b. 1965, twins, Patrick F. and Michael G. b. 1969; edn: BS, Golden Gate Univ. 1961-64; CPA, 1971; FAA Cert. comml. pilot Instrument Rating (Land & Sea). Career: pub. acct., staff acct. 1960-64; res. auditor in charge States Steamship Co., Maritime Admin., Dept. of Commerce 1965-70; principal, pub. acctg. firm Michael M. Manning, CPA 1971-80; partner, pub. acctg. firm. Manning & Carroll, CPAs 1980-93; director Nat. Real Estate Fund ($20,000,000 R.E.Inv. Trust) 1980-85; mem: Fed. Govt. Acct. Assn., Am. Inst. of CPAS, Soc. of Calif. Accts. (No. Bay pres. 1976-77, pres. elec. 1975-76), Calif. Soc. of CPAs, S.F., Marin Estate Plng. Council (dir. 1987, pres. 1993-94), Rotary, Mill Valley (pres. 1985-86), Elks, San Rafael, Native Sons of the Golden West; mil: SK3 USNR 1957-65; Republican; R.Cath.; rec: music (active in var. Dixieland & big bands), flying, jogging. Address: Manning & Carroll, CPAs, 169 Miller Ave Mill Valley 94941 Tel:415/388-1980

MANNING, PHIL RICHARD, university administrator; b. May 14, 1921, Kansas City, Miss.; s. Phil Richard and Marion M. (Nicholson) M.; m. Mary Richter, June 17, 1949; children: Carol b. 1950, Robert b. 1954; edn: MD, USC 1948; BA cum laude 1945. Career: instr. of med. USC 1954-55; asst. prof. med.

1955-59; dir. postgrad med. 1955-58; assoc. prof. med. 1959-64; prof. of med. 1964–; assoc. dean Postgrad Med. 1958–; assoc. v.p. for health affairs USC 1979–; editor-in-chief Audio-Digest, 1970; named Alumnus of Year USC Med. Alumni Assn. 1974; Fellow Am. Coll. Cardiology, Fellow Am. Coll. Physicians (gov. 1977-81, regent 1981-86, v.p. 1986-87), mem. Soc. of Med. Coll. Dirs. of Cont. Med. Edn., Am. Assn. Med. Systems and Informatics, AMA, CMA, L.A. Co. Med. Assn.; mil: capt. USAF Med. Corps 1952-54. Res: 19 Point Loma Dr., Corona Del Mar 92625 Ofc: Univ. Southern California 1975 Zonal Ave Ste 317 KAM Los Angeles 90033

MANOLIS, PAUL GEORGE, corporate executive, university administrator; b. Feb. 4, 1928, Sacramento; s. George C. and Vasileki (Kalanjopoulos) M.; m. Elene Angelica Zahas, Mar. 7, 1964; children: Alexandra, George, Dimitri, Damian; edn: BA, UC Berkeley, 1952; MA, Harvard Univ., 1954. Career: exec. sec. U.S. Sen. William F. Knowland, Wash. DC 1954-59; with Oakland Tribune, 1959-77, exec. editor 1965-74, asst. gen. mgr. 1968-72, corp. sec. Tribune Pub. Co. 1965-77; pres. BenePlus of Calif., 1979–; v.p. Hellenic Am. Devel. Corp., 1980–; Development Programs, UC Berkeley, 1983-92; dir. Patriarchal Orthodox Inst. 1992–; dir: Franklin Inv. Co., Tribune Bldg. Co.; appt. commr. Calif. Arts Commn., v. chair 1967-71; mem.: jury Pulitzer Prizes 1972, 73; bd. trustees Patriarch Athenagoras Orthodox Inst. at Grad. Theol. Union, Berkeley, (bd. pres. 1986–), Grad. Theol. Union, Anna Head Sch. Oakland, bd. dirs. Holy Cross Coll., Brookline, Mass., Archdiocesan Council Greek Orthodox Ch.; honors: Sigma Delta Chi, Sigma Alpha Epsilon, decorated Gold Cross, Crusader of Holy Sepulchre, Patriarch of Jerusalem; Gold Cross of Mount Athos Ecumenical Patriarch of Constantinople, Archon of Ecumenical Patriarchate; mem. Am. Soc. Newspaper Editors, Calif. Newspaper Pubs. Assn. (dir.); civic bds: Oakland Mus., Oakland Sym., Western Opera Theatre; chmn. bpu. bd. Orthodox Observer; Republican. Res: 100 Guilford Rd Piedmont 94611 Ofc: Orthodox Institute 2309 Hearst Ave Berkeley 94709

MANSON, DAVID JOSEPH, film producer, director; b. Jan. 6, 1952, N.Y.C.; s. Eddy Lawrence and Margery May (Abramson) M.; m. Arla Mae Nudelman (screenwriter/producer, Arla Sorkin), Apr. 4, 1982; stepdau., Lainie Sorkin b. 1971; edn: att. UC Santa Cruz 1970-71; BA (magna cum laude), UC Irvine, 1974. Career: director, actor and stage mgr. for theaters incl. Mark Taper Forum, the Los Angeles Free Shakespeare Fest., Playwrights Horizons and Manhattan Theater Club; senior v.p. creative affairs Stonehenge Prodns., L.A. 1975-80; pres. and CEO Sarabande Prodns., L.A. 1980–, prod. features for Touchstone Pictures, The Walt Disney Co., Tri-Star and Warner Brothers, TV prodns. for cable and network focus on long-forms- miniseries and movies-for-TV; credits: features: Mad Love, The Cemetery Club, Birdy (Cannes Film Fest. special jury award), Bring On the Night (Grammy Award best longform video); miniseries: A Rumor of War (Writer's Guild Award best miniseries), The Word; TV-movies: Those Secrets (directed), Original Sins, Rising Son, Eye On The Sparrow (Christopher Award), The King Of Love, Sessions, Best Kept Secrets, Night Cries, A Love Affair: The Eleanor and Lou Gehrig Story, The Spell, Louis Armstrong: Chicago Style; series: Against The Law (pilot and six episodes), Gang of Four (pilot), Elysian Fields (pilot); mem. Directors Guild Am., Writers Guild Am. Ofc: Sarabande Productions 530 Wilshire Blvd Ste 308 Santa Monica 90401

MAPP, JERRY WALTER, medical foundation president and chief executive; b. Sept. 1, 1945, Columbia, Miss.; s. Jerry M. and Louise E. (Foreman) M.; children: Michael A.; edn: BA in religion, Abilene Christian Univ., 1968; postgrad. in religion, Earlham Coll., 1968-69. Career: minister Texas Ch. of Christ, 1968; US Army Chaplaincy 1969-71, Vietnam, decorated Bronze star; residential treatment social worker Good Samaritan Ctr., adminstrv. asst. in chg. devel. and p.r., 1971-74; devel. assoc. Daniel Freeman Med. Ctr., Inglewood 1974-76; spl. edn. dept. Santa Monica Unified Sch. Dist., 1976-77; assoc. dir. devel. Anaheim Memorial Hosp. Devel. Found., 1977-78; dir. devel. and community relations York Sch., 1978-83; indep. cons. not-for-profit orgns. 1983–; v.p. devel. and exec. director Pacific Presbyterian Med. Ctr. Found., San Francisco 1984-91; pres. and c.e.o. Calif. Pacific Med. Ctr. Found. (merger of PPMC and CH of S.F., 6/91) 1991–; dir. workshops on planned giving, grantsmanship and trusteeship; regional conf. speaker for Calif. Assn. of Independent Schs., Council for Advance. and Support of Edn., Nat. Assn. Hosp. Devel., Nat. Soc. Fund Raising Execs.; cons. numerous orgns. including Festival Theater Calif., Monterey Peninsula Found., Family Service Agy., Ctr. for Attitudinal Healing, Eskaton Monterey Hosp., West Coast Univ., Notre Dame Sch., Merritt Peralta Med. Ctr.; bd. mem. KQED Inc.; past bd. mem. Children's Garden Marin County; former instr., devel. & comm. rels. for non-profits, Hartnell Coll., Monterey Peninsula Coll.; mem: Assn. for Healthcare Philanthropy, Nat. Soc. Fund Raising Execs., Commonwealth Club Calif., Rotary Intl. Ofc: California Pacific Medical Center Foundation PO Box 7999 San Francisco 94120 Tel:415/923-3269

MARC, DAVID, American studies educator, writer; b. Apr. 27, 1951, Brooklyn, NY.; s. Benjamin Cohen and Jeanette (Pistiner) Cohen Nissenbaum; edn: BA in English, SUNY-Binghamton, 1972, MA in English, 1976; PhD in Am. Studies, Univ. Iowa, 1982. Career: jr. research team NBC-TV, NYC, 1976-77; adj. English faculty mem. Wells Coll., Aurora, NY, 1980; adj. mem. writing faculty Cornell Univ., Ithaca. NY, 1981; lectr. Am. civilization Brown Univ., Providence, 1982-

85; asst. prof. Am. studies Brandeis Univ., Waltham, Mass., 1985-89; vis. prof. Annenberg Sch. Communications, Univ. So. Calif., 1988-93; assoc. prof. Film and Television, UCLA., 1993–; mem: Author's Guild, Phi Beta Kappa; author: Demographic Vistas, l984, Comic Visions, 1989, Prime Time, Prime Movers, 1992; TV appearances include: 60 Minutes, Today and CBC Jour.; radio commentator Performance Today; author: Bonfire of the Humanities, 1995; contbr. 100+ articles to profl. jours.including Atlantic Monthly, Village Voice, contbr. to mag. Sight and Sound. Res: 840 Larrabee St # 2-318 Los Angeles 90069 Ofc: UCLA Dept Film & TV 405 Hilgard Ave Los Angeles CA 90024

MARCELLA, MARY ALICE, publisher, writer; b. July 23, 1922, Warren, Ohio; d. Anthony and Angela Marie (DeSanti) Marcella; m. Arley James Bailes Nov. 19, 1941 (div. 1974); children: Roger James b. 1942, Faith Orpha Ann b. 1950; 2 grandchildren; m. 2d Jack H. Bell, May 10, 1986 (dec. 1989); edn: CSU Long Beach 1963; Orange Coast Jr. Coll. 1968; Palomar Jr. Coll. 1971; Cuesta Jr. Coll. 1977; pre-std. cert., other courses, Am. Inst. Banking 1956-68. Career: direct sales Watkins Prods. Warren, Ohio 1940; owner, oper. refreshment concession, Lake Milton, Ohio 1941; real estate sales Gordon Ball, Warren, Ohio 1952-53; sampler Trumbull Co.- Coca Cola Co. Warren, Ohio 1953-54; teller, escrow ofcr. Bank of Am., var. So. Calif. branches 1956-68; automobile sales Sam Priestly Lincoln Mercury Dealership, Oceanside 1968; escrow ofcr. Escondido Nat. Bank, Poway 1969-71, US Nat. Bank, LaVerne 1972-74, br. mgr. Marina Fed. Savings & Loan, Avalon 1974-76, Crocker Nat. Bank, Paso Robles 1976-78, Indian Wells 1978-80 (opened 5 new escrow ofcs. for above banks); owner, publr. Marcella Press, La Quinta 1980–; correspondent writer Daily News, Palm Desert Post, contbr. Carlsbad Journal, 1980–; auto leasing rep. Golden Bear Leasing, Del Mar 1982–; lic. life ins. sales rep.; honors: Eisteddford Contest Winner 1939, Nat. Honor Soc., speech contest winner (Crocker Nat. Bank 1974), listed Internat. Who's Who of Intellectuals 1990; mem: Norwalk Bus. & Profl. Women's Club (treas. 1960), Chiche's, Bank of Am. Women's Speech Club, Desertair Toastmasters (charter mem., pres. 1979-82), No. County Toastmasters 1982–, Desert Beautiful (Palm Desert 1979–), Desert Four Repub. Women Federated (1st v.p. 1981-82), La Quinta Historical Soc. (founding pres. 1984-87, life mem.), Internat. Platform Assn.; past mem: Bd. of Realtors, Calif. Escrow Assn., Avalon C.of C., Quota Club (Paso Robles, corr. secty. 1978), Dateland Toastmistress Club (historian 1979); author (book of poems) Rhyme and Thought, (song) Color Fills the World, (song lyrics) Between You and Me, Forty Days & Forty Nights, A Million Paths Within My Mind; rec: golf, travel, sewing. Address: P.O. Box 1057 La Quinta 92253-1057

MARCHICK, RICHARD, gynecologist; b. Mar. 18, 1934, Cheyenne, Wyoming; s. Ben and Rose (Rabinowitz) M.; m. Gloria Ann Becker, Dec. 18, 1960; children: Patricia Sue b. 1963, David Matthew b. 1966, Sarah Lynn b. 1970; edn: BA (cum laude), Harvard Univ. 1956; MD, Washington Univ., St. Louis, Mo. 1961; Diplomate, Am. Bd. of Ob-Gyn 1968, recert. 1978; med. lic. Calif. 1962. Career: rotating internship Wash. Univ. Med. Ctr., St. Louis, Mo. 1961-62, ob-gyn residency 1962-66; pvt. practice, mng. ptnr. OB-GYN & Fertility Specialists, Berkeley and Lafayette, Calif. 1966-94; staff mem. Alta Bates Med. Ctr., Berkeley 1966–, S.F. Gen. Hosp. 1966-94, UCSF Med. Ctr. 1966-94, Summit Med. Ctr., Oakland 1984-94; clin. instr. UCSF Sch. Medicine 1966-72, asst. clin. prof. 1973-84, assoc. clin. prof. 1984–; bd. dirs.: Alameda-Contra Costa Med. Assn. Retirement Investment Prog. 1988–, Alta Bates Med. Resources 1993, Alta Bates Med. Group IPA 1989-91, 1993-94 (chmn. credentials com. 1988-91, 1993-94, mem. fin. com. 1988-91, 1993-94, ob-gyn capitation com. 1992-94, physician-in-charge ob-gyn capitation com. 1993-94, ob-gyn utilization cons. to med. dir. 1993-94); bd. dirs. No. Calif. Am. Israel Public Affairs Com. 1994–; Fellow Am. Coll. of Obstetrics & Gynecology 1969 (bd. dirs. Calif. Dist. 1985-91, vice chmn. S.F./Bay Area Sect. 1985-88, chmn. 1989-91); med. exec. bd. Alta Bates Comm. Hosp., Berkeley 1981-83 (chmn. dept. ob-gyn & high risk obstetrics 1982-83, vice chmn. quality assurance dept. and chmn. quality assurance com. 1979-81); pres. Eastbay Gynecological Soc. 1977-78 (mem. 1968-90, sec./treas. 1974-77); chmn. ob-gyn com. Heals/QualMed HMO 1988-90; honors: listed Who's Who in West, Who's Who in Calif.; mem: AMA 1967–, CMA 1967–, Alameda-Contra Costa Med. Assn. 1967–, Am. Fertility Soc. 1971-94, S.F. Gynecological Soc. 1972- (sec./treas. 1993), Am. Assn. of Gynecologic Laparoscopists 1974-94, Am. Soc. of Psycho-prophylaxis in Obstetrics (mem. nat. bd. dirs. 1972-73, Bay Area Soc. exec. com. 1970-73, chmn. physicians div. 1971-72, med. advy. bd., jour. 1971-72), Pacific Coast Obstetrical & Gynecological Soc. 1987–, Sierra Club (life), Bay Area Council on Soviet Jewry 1977–, Hebrew Free Laon Soc. (life); med. cons. Jour. of Childbirth Edn. 1970-71; assoc. editor Birth and Family Journal, 1973-80; author 2 articles pub. in profl. jours., 1964, 1988; rec: hiking, bicycling. Ofc: Berkeley 94705

MARCO, DAVID DUANE, biomedical engineer; b. Feb. 3, 1951, Apollo, Pa.; s. Peter M. and Jean Martha (Merlo) M.; m. Nancy Elizabeth Bierman, Nov. 16, 1985; 1 dau. Phoebe Elizabeth b. 1992; edn: BS in biomed. engring., Rensselaer Polytech. Inst., 1973; cert. special competency in cardiac pacing for non-physicians N.Am. Soc. of Pacing & Electrophysiology 1991. Career: clin. engr. Shock & Trauma Unit Albany (N.Y.) Med. Ctr. 1973-75; jr. research engr. Abcor Inc., Wilmington, Mass. 1975-76; biomed. engr. University Hosp., Boston 1976-77;

sales rep. and field clin. engr. ARCO Med. Products, San Francisco 1977-81; field clin. engr. Pacesetter, Oakland 1981–, Western field engring. mgr. 1993-; mem.: N.Am. Soc. Pacing & Electrophysiology (assoc. 1986–), Shiloh Christian Fellowship Oakland (dist. dir. 1990–); contbr. jour. articles in cardiac pacing, trauma (1973–); Republican; Christian; rec: singing, worship music, photography, computing. Res: 140 Hermosa Ave Oakland 94618 Ofc: Pacesetter 3470 Mt Diablo Blvd Ste A150 Lafayette 94549-3939

MARCUS, AARON, graphic artist; b. May 22, 1943, Omaha, Neb.; s. Nathan and Libbie (Burstein) M.; m. Susan Wightman Douglas, Sept. 9, 1968; children: Joshua, Elisheva; m. Leslie Becker, Dec. 15, 1985; edn: BA, Princeton Univ., 1965; BFA, MFA, Yale Univ., 1968. Career: asst. prof. Princeton Univ., 1969-77; research fellow East-West Ctr., Honolulu, 1978; lectr. UC Berkeley, 1979-80; staff scientist Lawrence Berkeley Lab., 1980-82; pres. Aaron Marcus and Assocs., Emeryville, Calif., 1983–; awards: recipient Design awards Soc. of Typographic Arts, Dirs. Club of N.Y., Soc. of Publ. Designers 1974-76; mem: Nat. Computer Graphics Assn., Human Factors Soc., Am. Inst. Graphic Arts, Spl. Interest Group On Computer Graphics and Interactive Techniques of Assn. Computing Machinery, Spl. Interest Group on Computer and Human Interaction of Assn. Computing Machinery, Soc. Tech. Communicators, IEEE; author: (monograph) Soft Where, Inc. (2 vols. 1976, 1981), (w/Ron Baecker) Human Factors and Typography for More Readable Programs, 1990, Graphic Design for Electronic Documents and User Interfaces, 1992, The Cross-GUI Handbook for Multiplatform User Interface Design, with Smilovich and Thompson; Democrat; Ofc: Aaron Marcus and Assocs., Inc., 1144 65th St, Ste F Emeryville 94608-1109

MARCUS, ALON, doctor of Oriental medicine; b. 1957, Tel Aviv, Israel; s. Johseph Marcus, MD and Cilla (Furmanovich) M.; m. Ruth P. Goldenberg, MD, Feb. 4, 1990; children: Sivan b. 1993; edn: gen. study, film, Columbia Coll., Chgo., Ill. 1979; AS Merritt Coll., Oakland, Calif. 1982; L.Ac. Am. Coll. of Chinese Medicine, S.F., Calif. 1983; doctor of Oriental medicine, S.A.M.R.A., L.A., Calif. 1986. Career: preceptor Chinese med. A. Wu, OMD, S.F. 1983; preceptor acupuncture, Dr. M. Lee, 1983-84; resident, Canton Muni Hosp., Canton, China 1985; private practice, Berkeley, Calif., 1984–; doctor, Haight Ashbury Free Clinic, S.F., Calif., 1988; preceptor orthopedic med., R.I. Gracer, MD, Lafayette 1992-93; tchg. asst., Basics of Orthopedics, Golden State Rehabilitation Ctr., San Ramon, Calif., 1993–; preceptor acupuncture and herbology Alcatraz Med. Group, Berkeley 1990–; awards: Award of Honor 1993, listed Who's Who in California 23rd edit.; mem: Calif. Acupuncture Assn. 1985–, Am. Assn. of Acupuncture and Oriental Med. (1985–, bd. dirs.), Am. Assn. of Orthopedic Medicine 1992–; author: Acute Abdominal Syndromes, Combined Chinese-Western (1991); A Modern Approach to Shoulder Pain Using Combined Methods of Acupuncture and Cyriax-Based Orthopedic Medicine, with R. Gracer (1994); The Future of Oriental Mediicine in the US: A Plea for Higher Standards (1994). Ofc: 1650 Alcatraz Ave Berkeley 94703

MARCUS, STEPHEN HOWARD, lawyer; b. June 30, 1945, New York; s. Jacob and Mildred (Cohen) M.; m. Carol Sylvia Beatrice, June 11, 1967; children: Joshua b. 1970, Rebecca b. 1973, Daniel b. 1974; edn: BSME, MIT 1967; JD, Harvard Law Sch. 1970. Career: atty., assoc. Mitchell Silbeberg & Knupp, Los Angeles 1970-72; Greenberg Bernard Weis & Rosin 1972-75, ptnr. 1976-85; atty., assoc. Frandzel & Share 1985-87, ptnr. 1987–; Century City Bar Assn. (bd. govs. 1985-93, contg. edn. chmn. 1984), Town Hall So. Calif., Valley Jewish Bus. Leaders Assoc., MIT Club So. Calif. (pres. 1977-78, treas. 1978-79); article pub. in profl. jour., 1971, book chpt. pub., 1983; mil: capt. USAR 1970-76; Democrat; Jewish; rec: youth sports, senior soccer. Ofc: Frandzel & Share 6500 Wilshire Blvd 17th Floor Los Angeles 90048

MARDIAN, ROBERT CHARLES, JR., restaurant corporation executive; b. Feb. 1, 1947, Orange; s. Robert Charles and Dorothy Driscilla (Denniss) M.; m. Kathleen, Oct. 13, 1984; children: Robert, III b. 1975, Alexandra b. 1986, Ashley b. 1987. Career: BA, Stanford Univ. 1969; MBA, Pepperdine Univ. 1986. Career: founder/pres./bd. chmn. Wind & Sea Restaurants, Inc. (op. restaurants in Calif. and Hawaii), 1970–; dir: Dana Niguel Bank; spl. cons. to 1988 U.S. Olympic Com.; mem: Young Presidents Orgn., Waikiki Rod & Gun Club, Nat. Restaurant Assn., Stanford Alumni Assn., San Onofre Surfing Club; Republican; rec: surfing, skiing, volleyball, Hawaiian Ironman Triathlon 1984. Res: 34342 Cove Lantern Dana Point 92629 Ofc: Wind & Sea Restaurants Inc. 34699 Golden Lantern Dana Point 92629

MARGOLIN, FRANCES, psychologist; b. Mar. 17, 1922, Montgomery Co., Pa.; d. Harry and Dorothy (Blanc) Mongin; m. Elias Margolin, Mar. 12, 1944; children: Janice b. 1959, John b. 1965, Carol b. 1966, Paul b. 1967; edn: BA, Temple Univ. 1948; MA, Ohio Univ. 1955; PhD, U.S. Internat. Univ., S.D. 1972; lic. Clin. Psychologist, Marriage and Family Counselor, Calif. 1960; Diplomate, Am. Bd. of Profl. Psychology 1982. Career: clin. psychologist Dayton St. Hosp., Dayton, Ohio 1948-55; San Diego Superior Ct., 1955-74; pvt. practice, La Jolla 1974–; honors: listed Nat. Register of Health Care Providers. Res: 887 La Jolla Rancho Rd La Jolla 92037 Ofc: PO Box 3056 La Jolla 92038

MARGOLIS, DONALD LEE, mechanical engineering educator, consultant; b. Nov. 13, 1945, Washington; s. Joel and Jeanette (Lowenwirth) M.; children: Scott, David; edn: BSME, Va. Poly. and State Univ., 1967; MSME, MIT, 1969, PhD, 1972. Career: instr. dept. mech. engring. MIT, Cambridge, Mass., 1969-72; prof. dept. mech. engring. Univ. Calif., Davis, 1972–; cons. various industries, nat. labs., U.S., Japan; Fellow ASME (Outstanding Teaching award 1980); mem. Soc. Automotive Engrs. (Ralph R. Teeter Ednl. award 1986); author (textbook) System Dynamics: A Unified Approach, 1990; contbr. 90+ tech. articles to sci. jours.; rec: squash (nationally ranked). Ofc: University of Calif Davis Dept Mech Engring Davis 95616

MARHOEFER, GORDON JOSEPH, chartered life underwriter, lawyer; b. Aug. 25, 1932, Detroit, Mich.; s. Edwin Louis and Lucy Cecilia (Cavanaugh) Marhoefer; m. Patricia Black Nutter, 1978; children: George, b. 1956; Clifford, b. 1956; Thomas, b. 1958; Robert, b. 1960; (step) Darci, b. 1969; edn: BA, Loyola Univ., L.A. 1954; CLU, Am. College 1966; JD, Loyola Law Sch. 1972; ChFC, Am. College 1983. Career: Pacific Mutual Life Ins. Co., L.A.: adminstrv. trainee 1955-57, agent (Sherman Oaks) 1957-59, adminstrv. asst. 1959-61, mgr. of conservation 1961-64, mgr. advanced underwriting, 1964-67, dir. estate & bus. planning, 1967-72; life underwriter/atty., Newport Beach 1972–; instr. CLU, instr. Life Mgmt. Assn.; honors: Million Dollar Round Table 1977-94; mem: Newport Beach-Irvine Estate Plng. Council (founding dir., bd. 1982-87, pres. 1986-87), Orange Coast Estate Plng. Council, Planned Giving Round Table of Orange County, Calif. Bar Assn., Am. Soc. of CLUs, Nat. Assn. Life Underwriters, Mensa; civic: Wellness Community of Orange County (dir. 1992), Newport Theatre Arts Ctr. (dir. 1988-91), Costa Mesa Civic Playhouse, Alano Club of Costa Mesa (v.chmn. 1975-76), Burbank Parochial Baseball League (v.chmn. 1968-71); contbr. articles in profl. jours.; Republican (charter pres. Burbank YR); R.Cath.; rec: drama & musical comedy, camping. Res: 342 Sydney Ln Costa Mesa 92627 Ofc: Massachusetts Mutual Life Ins. Co., 610 Newport Ctr Dr Ste 300 Newport Beach 92660

MARIANO, MISHAEL JORDAN, medical technologist; b. Jan. 11, 1927, Manila, Philippines; nat. 1947; s. Victorino E. and Josefa Visita (Jordan) M.; m. Columbia Trinidad, April 30, 1960; children: Mishael Collier b. 1961, Myron Colin b. 1965, Milbert Clyde b. 1969; edn: BA, Philippine Union Coll. 1954; MA, Theological Seminary of S.D.A. 1959; BD, Potomac Univ. 1961; pre-med., USC 1963-64. Career: med. technologist Bio Sci. Lab., Van Nuys 1967-75; Kaiser Permanente, L.A. 1968-76; Valley Med. Center, Fresno 1976-90; mem: Philippine Union Coll. Alumni Assn. (pres. 1977-87, v.p. 1988-95), Fil-Am. Assn. (pub. rels. 1977-78), Fil-Am. Ch. (elder 1964-95, head elder for 15 yrs.); mil: USN 1945-49; Republican; SDA. Res: 1540 Armstrong Clovis 93612

MARIGOLD, LAWRENCE LEE, management consultant; b. Oct. 14, 1940, Tehachapi; s. George Austin and Pauline Marie (Vukich) M.; m. Mary Ilene O'Connel, Jan. 25, 1964 (div. 1977); m. Julie Ann Chohon, Sept. 9, 1978; children: Eric b. 1967, Michelle b. 1970; edn: AA, Contra Costa Coll. 1961; BS, Univ. San Francisco 1964; MBA, Golden Gate Univ. 1967. Career: exchange analyst Chevron, San Francisco1962-67; v.p., dir. fuel supply Unigas (subsidiary Unocal), Denver, Colo. 1967-70; mgr. residual products Unocal, Chgo., Ill. 1970-74; dir. corp. rep. Anheuser Busch, St. Louis and Sacto. 1974-84; mgmt. cons. Ocelot Chemical, Metallgesellschaft Ag., Calif. Energy Commn., Sacto. 1984–; instr. CSU 1989–; mem. Coal Advy. Com., DOE 1978; mem: Elks; Republican; Cath. Res: 4925 St Thomas Dr Fair Oaks 95628

MARINER, WILLIAM MARTIN, chiropractor; b. Jan. 2, 1949, Baltimore, Md.; s. Wm. Joseph and Ellen (Dexter) M.; m. Judith Mecey, div. 1979; edn: AA, Phoenix Coll., 1976; BSc, and DC (summa cum laude), Los Angeles Coll. of Chiropractic, Whittier 1980. Career: mgr. health food store and restaurant, Nanak Dwara Ents., Phoenix 1974-75; physical therapist A.R.E. Clinic, 1975-76; adminstrv. asst. to the academic dean Los Angeles Coll. Chiropractic, Whittier 1977-80; adminstrv. cons. and faculty mgr. Calif. Acupuncture Coll., Los Angeles 1978-80; founder, dir. Pacific Healing Arts Center, Mt. Shasta 1980–; ednl. cons. John Panama Consulting, San Francisco 1986–; honors: outstanding senior L.A.C.C. 1980, Delta Sigma 1980, Nat. Dean honors 1979-80, Who's Who Young Profls. 1989-94, Who's Who in West 1990-96, Who's Who in the World 1990-96, Dict. of Internat. Biographies 1990, Personalities in Am. 1983-91, Intl. Directory Disting. Leadership 1990; mem: Calif. Chiropractic Assn., Am. Chiropractic Assn., Internat. Coll. Applied Kinesiology, Holistic Dental Assn., British Homeopathic Assn.; Democrat; rec: yoga, meditation, cooking. Ofc: Pacific Healing Arts Center PO Box 192 Mt. Shasta 96067

MARKEN, GIDEON ANDREW, III, advertising and public relations executive; b. June 24, 1940, Hampton, Iowa; s. Gideon Andrew, II and Cleone Marie (Riis) M.; m. Jeannine Gay Hill, Dec. 28, 1963; children: Tracy Lynn b. 1967, Gideon A. b. 1969; edn: BS, Iowa State Univ., 1962; MBA, Hamilton Inst., 1975; APR, accredited Pub. Relations Am. Career: pub. relations mgr. Fairchild Instrumentation, Mountain View 1965-66; dir. pub. relations Barnes-Hind Pharmaceuticals, Sunnyvale 1966-67; v.p and pub. relations dir. Bozell-Jacobs Advt., Palo Alto 1967-77; pres. Marken Communications, Santa Clara 1977–; recipient Bronze Awards PRSA, Peninsula chapt. (1977, 80, 85); mem:

Pub. Relations Soc. Am. (chapt. pres. 1972, 75), Am. Med. Writers Assn. (pres. 1967), BPAA 1982–, Am. Mgmt. Assn. 1982–, PMA 1982–; publs: 100+ articles on mgmt., mktg., advt., and PR (1967–); mil: sgt. USAF 1962-65; Republican; Lutheran; rec: scuba, sailing, aerobics. Ofc: Marken Communications 3375 Scott Blvd #108 Santa Clara 95054

MARKER, MARC LINTHACUM, lawyer, investor; b. July 19, 1941, Los Angeles; s. Clifford Harry and Voris (Linthacum) M.; m. Sandra Yocom, Aug. 28, 1965; children: Victor b. 1970, Gwendolyn b. 1974; edn: Harvard Sch.; AB, UC Riverside 1965; JD, USC 1967. Career: asst. v.p., asst. secty. Security Pacific Nat. Bank, Los Angeles 1970-73; chief counsel Security Pacific Leasing Corp., San Francisco 1973-92; secty. 1980, senior v.p. 1981-92, also pres./secty./counsel Security Pacific Leasing Services Corp. 1977-92; dir: Refiners Petroleum Corp. 1977-81, Voris, Inc. (dir., sec. 1973-86); instr. comml. law Am. Inst. of Banking, 1971-72; lectr. Practicing Law Inst., Am. Assn. of Equip. Lessors, 1976–; mem: Am. Bar Assn., Am. Assn. of Equip. Lessors Lawyers Com. (1977-81); clubs: University (L.A.), Army & Navy; mil: cmdr. USCGR 1966-89; Republican; Lutheran; rec: scuba, mountaineering. Res: 41 Lakeside Dr Corte Madera 94925

MARKEY, MICHAEL LYNN, certified financial planner; b. June 6, 1943, Ft. Wayne, Indiana; s. Arnold Leo and Wanda L. (McGowan) M.; m. Irene Torngren, Mar. 11, 1978; children: Michael Arnold b. 1981, Victoria Ingrid b. 1983; edn: CFP, Coll. for Financial Planning, Denver, Co., 1977; MBA, Santa Clara Univ., 1967; BS, San Jose State Univ., 1966; cert. financial planner; cert. real estate broker (Calif) 1971; ptnr. Markey/Coit Investments 1969–; v.p. First Orinda Corp., Orinda, Calif. 1971-73; pres., founder, CEO Orinda Financial Group, Walnut Creek 1973–; NASD registered prin. w/Finl. Planners Equity Corp. and American Investors Co.; mem: Internat. Assn. for Finl. Planning (past v.p. and past dir. East Bay Chapt.) 1973–, Institute of Cert. Financial Planners; co-chmn. of 1980 Greater Bay Area Finl. Planning Conf. and pgm. chmn. 1984 conf.; chmn. Real Estate Outlook Pgms. 1980, 81; ed. advy. bd. to Digest of Finl. Planning Ideas; mil: USAF Reserves, 1967-73; Independent; rec: golf. Res: 48 Tappan Ln Orinda 94563

MARKHAM, REED B., author, educator; b. Feb. 14, 1957, Alhambra; s. John Frederick and Reeda Margaret (Bjarnson) M.; edn: AA, BA, MA, Brigham Young Univ., Provo 1981, 81, 82; AS, BS, Regents Coll., Albany, N.Y. 1981, 82; MPA, USC, 1983; MA, UCLA, 1989; PhD, CPU, San Rafael 1992; career: prof. Chaffey Coll., 1986-87; prof. communications dept. Calif. State Polytech. Univ., Pomona 1987–, mem. EOP acad. planning com. 1989–; pres. bd. trustees Regents Coll., Albany, N.Y. 1983-86; accreditation commn. NAPNSC, Denver, Co. 1989-92; evaluator Am. Council on Edn., W.D.C. 1991-92; awards: Golden Leaves Cal Poly Pres.'s Office (1988, 89, 90), leadership Bicentennial of U.S. Constn., W.D.C. 1989, C-Span Prof. C-Span Network, W.D.C. 1991, Points of Light award The White House 1991; mem: Pub. Relations Soc. of Am., Nat. Assn. of Scholars (D.C.), Doctorate Assn. of N.Y. Scholars, NSIEE (D.C. devel. com. 1985-86), BYU Alumni Assn. (SDA pres.); civic: Tourn. of Roses Parade Club 1988-90; editorial bds: Education Digest, Speaker and Gavel, Public Relations Rev., Nat. Forensic Jour., Forensic Educator, Clearinghouse for the Contemporary Educator; author: Advances in Public Speaking 1990, Public Opinion: R&R 1990, Power Speaking 1990, Effective Speechwriting 1984; LDS Ch.; rec: athletics. Res: 801 E Alosta Ave T307 Azusa 91702 Ofc: Cal Poly Comm. Dept. 3801 W Temple Ave Pomona 91768

MARKLAND, FRANCIS SWABY, JR., biochemist, educator; b. Jan. 15, 1936, Phila.; s. Francis S. and Willie Lawrence (Averitt) M.; m. Barbara Blake, June 27, 1959; children: Cathy b. 1961, Mark b. 1964; edn: BS, Penn State Univ. 1957; PhD, Johns Hopkins Univ. 1964. Career: postdoc. fellow UCLA Sch. of Medicine, Los Angeles 1964-66, asst. prof. biochem. 1966-73; vis. asst. prof. medicine and biochem., USC Sch. of Medicine 1973-74, assoc. prof. biochem. 1974-83, prof. biochemistry USC Sch. of Med. 1983–, actg. dept. chmn. 1986-88, vice chmn. 1988-92; cons. CLMG Los Angeles 1977-89, Cortech Denver 1983; mem. NIH Study Sect. 1986-90; editl. bd. Toxicon (internat. jour. of toxinology); awards: USPHS NIH Research Career Devel. Award, UCLA 1968-73, USPHS grants from Nat. Cancer Inst. 1979 and Nat. Heart, Lung and Blood Inst. 1984; mem: Am. Chem. Soc., Am. Soc. Biological Chemists, Sigma Xi, Internat. Soc. of Toxicology, Am. Assn. for Cancer Research, Endocrine Soc., Am. Soc. of Hematol., Am. Heart Assn., Internat. Soc. of Thrombosis and Haemostasis (chmn., Registry of Exogenous Hemostatic Factors); civic: Angeles Chorale, SAR, Soc. of the Cincinnati; author 90 papers in sci. books and jours., co-editor 1 book; mil: capt. USNR-R 1957, Active duty 1957-59; Republican; Prot.; rec: ski, jog, tennis, sing. Ofc: USC School of Medicine, Cancer Research Lab. No. 106, 1303 N Mission Rd Los Angeles 90033

MARKOVICH, PATRICIA H., economic & political consultant/artist; b. Oakland, Calif.; d. Patrick Joseph and Helen Emily (Prydz) Markovich; children: Michael Sean Treece b. 1965, Bryan Jeffry Treece b. 1967, Tiffany Helene Treece b. 1970; edn: BA in econ., MS in econ., UC Berkeley; postgrad. (Lilly Found. grantee) Stanford Univ., (NSF grantee) Oreg. Grad. Res. Ctr.; Cert. Emergency Mgmt. Planner, UC Berkeley. Career: with public rels. dept. Pettler

Advt., Inc.; private practice political and econ. cons.; aide to majority whip Oreg. House of Reps.; lectr., instr., various Calif. institutions., Chemeketa Coll., Oreg., Portland State Univ., Oreg.; commr. City of Oakland, Calif., 1970-74; chairperson, bd. dirs. Cable Sta. KCOM, Piedmont; coord. City of Piedmont, Calif. Gen. Planning Commn.; mem: Piedmont Civic Assn., Core Advy. Com. City of Oakland, Oakland Mus. Archives of Calif. Artists; Internat. Soc. Philos. Enquiry, Mensa (ofcr. S.F. reg.), Bay Area Artists Assn. (coord., founding mem.), Berkeley Art Ctr. Assn., S.F. Arts Commn. File, Calif. Index for Contemporary Arts, Pro Arts. No. Calif. Public Edn. and Govt. Access Cable TV Com. (founding), Triple Nine Soc., YLEM (Artists Using Sci. & Tech.), SOLART (Ctr. for Extreme Ultraviolet Astronomy, NASA, Univ. of Calif., Berkeley); Democrat; rec: home improvement. Res/Ofc: 132 Olive Ave. Piedmont 94611-4430

MARKOWITZ, SAMUEL SOLOMON, professor of chemistry; b. Oct. 31, 1931, Bklyn.; s. Max and Florence Ethel (Goldman) M.; children: Michael b. 1960, Daniel b. 1963, Jonah b. 1965; edn: BS, Rensselaer Poly Inst., 1953; MA, Princeton Univ., 1955, PhD, 1957; thesis res. stu. Brookhaven Nat. Lab, Upton, N.Y. 1955-57. Career: NSF postdoctoral fellow Univ. of Birmingham, England 1957-58; U.S. sr. postdoctoral fellow, vis. prof. Faculte Des Scis. de L'Universite de Paris, Orsay, France 1964-65; vis. prof. Weizmann Inst. of Science, Rehovot, Israel 1973-74; prof. of chemistry (freshman, nuclear, ana- lytical chem.) and faculty sr. scientist Univ. Calif. Berkeley and Lawrence Berkeley Lab., Calif. 1958–; elected Berkeley Board of Edn. 1969-73 (pres. 1971-72); awards: Coll. letters in athletics (6) baseball, basketball, soccer, Mary D'Urso Award for Outstanding public servant in pub. edn., Alameda Co. 1973; mem: Am. Chem. Soc. (1953–, chair Calif. sect. 1991, nat. councilor, bd. dirs. 1989–), Am. Physical Soc. 1955–, AAAS (1957–, Fellow); publs: original sci. research in nuclear and environmental chemistry, 1953–; Jewish, Cong. Beth Israel, Berkeley (pres., bd. trustees 1960–); rec: sports, athletics. Res: 317 Tideway Dr #B Alameda 94501 Ofc: Dept Chemistry Univ California Berkeley 94720

MARKS, FREDRIC A., physician; b. Nov. 15, 1952, Albuquerque, N.M.; edn: MD, Hahnemann Med. Coll., Phila., Pa. 1979. mil: maj. US Army 1979-89. Address: Citrus Heights

MARKS, MILTON, state senator; b. July 22, 1920, San Francisco; s. Milton and Olita M. (Meyer) M.; edn: BA, Stanford Univ., 1940; LL.B., San Francisco Law Sch., 1949; m. Carolene Wachenheimer, Aug. 14, 1955; children: Carol, Milton, Edward David. Career: mem. Calif. Assembly from 1959; judge munici- pal ct., San Francisco, 1966-67; mem. Calif. Senate, 1967–, chmn. election coms., select com. on maritime industry, com. on disabled; bd. dirs. Nat. Council on Alcoholism, Calif. League for Handicapped, St. Anthony's Dining Room, Mex. Am. Polit. Assn., Chinese-Am. Citizens Alliance; recipient num. awards including Bronze Key award Nat. Council on Alcoholism; Man of Yr. award Council for Civic Unity of San Francisco Bay Area, 1973, Legislator of Yr. award Calif. Assn. Physically Handicapped, 1973, Consumer Legislator of Yr. award, 1981, Calif. Preservation award, 1982, Legislator of Yr. award Students of Calif. State Univ. System, Legislator of Yr. award Planning and Conservation League Calif., 1984; mem. Am. Legion, VFW, Press Club (San Francisco), Lions; mil: served with U. S. Army, World War II; Democrat; Jewish. Office: 711 Van Ness Ave Ste 310 San Francisco CA 94102*

MARMANN, SIGRID, executive (principal/president); b. Feb. 8, 1938, Voelklingen/Saarland, Germany; d. Leo and Karoline Anna (Weidenhof) Marmann; edn: BS, accounting, Ind. & Handelskammer, Saarbrueckn, Germany 1956; postgraduate study, Norwood College, London, Eng. 1962; postgrad. study, Golden Gate Univ., S.F., Calif. 1970-85; BA, management, St. Mary's Coll., Moraga, Calif. 1984. Career: controller, MOM, Paris, France 1965-69; bookkeeper, Chrissa Imports, Brisbane, Calif. 1970-78; accounting mgr., Highcity Internat., San Anselmo, Calif. 1978-80; accounting mgr. & systems analyst, Kukje Korean Trading Co., E. Rutherford, N.J. 1980-81; asst. treas., Amer. Mercantile Co., Brisbane, Calif. 1981-84; controller, Provident Credit Union, Burlingame 1984; owner, Datatech EDI Systems, San Rafael 1984–; pres./prin., Datatech EDI Systems & Telepay Express, San Rafael 1989–; quali- fied installer, Great Plains Software; installer, developer, Computer Assoc. Internat., Islandia, NY; devel. of application software for EDI/EFT and fin. svs. for businesses; awards: Nominee Membership award, Electronic Data Interchange, Va. 1990; mem: ANSI ASC X12 Electronic Data Interchange 1989–; primary founder, No. Calif. EDI Users Group 1990–; author: publ. article on EDI, 1992; rec: traveling, skiing, swimming, sailing, fishing, baking. Res: 30 Newport Way, San Rafael 94901

MARMEL, ROSALIND SUSAN, publicity agency and management consult- ing president; b. Oct. 21, 1949, Winnipeg, Canada; d. Max and Bernice (Macklin) Marmel; edn: BA, B.Edn, Univ. Manitoba Canada. Career: entertain- ment and cultural ed. Century City News 1990–; gen. mgr. Michelango Restaurant, Beverly Hills 1977-80; east coast ed. Calif. Press Bureau, N.Y.C. 1986-87; fin. mgr. Century City News 1984-86; gen. mgr. and publicist Romeo & Juliet Restaurant, Beverly Hills 1980-86; pres. Marmel Agency 1987–; tchr.

Page Mil. Acad., Los Angeles 1974-76; Hollywood Profl. Sch. 1972-74; Winnipeg Sch. Div. 1968-71; rec: travel, writing. Ofc: Marmel Agency 428 N Palm Dr Ste 101 Beverly Hills 90210

MARQUEZ, ALBERT JOHN, senior bank examiner; b. June 3, 1961, Astoria, Oreg.; s. Domingo Cruz and Socorro Camps (Sungahid) M.; m. Annabelle, May 28, 1988; children: Ashley Marie b. 1989, Anthony John b. 1991, Amanda Nicole b. 1992; edn: BS kinesiology, UCLA; MBA, San Diego State Univ. Career: acct. Dion G. Dyer, APC, San Diego 1984-87; asst. ops. mgr. Reliance Mgmt. Corp., San Diego 1985-86; bank examiner Calif. State Banking Dept.1987–; mem. Soc. of Fin. Examiners, Assn. of MBA Execs.; R.Cath.; rec: tennis, photog., computers. Res: Scripps Ranch San Diego 92131 Ofc: Calif. State Banking Dept. 111 Pine St Ste 1100 San Francisco 94111

MARROQUIN, PATRICIA, journalist; b. Feb. 1, 1957, West Covina; d. Humberto and Josephine (Aragon) Marroquin; edn: BS, Cal Poly Pomona 1980; MA, Stanford Univ. 1981. Career: newsroom typist San Gabriel Valley Tribune, West Covina 1974-79; newsletter ed. East San Gabriel Valley Consortium 1979- 80; nat. copy desk intern Wall Street Jour., NYC 1980; nat. desk copy ed. San Jose Mercury News, San Jose 1981-86; mng. ed. Micro Market World, Menlo Park 1987; copy ed., news ed., makeup ed., slot ed. Los Angeles Times, Costa Mesa 1987-94, suburban asst. copy chief Los Angeles Times, L.A. 1994-95, metro asst. slot editor 1995–; fellow Inst. for Journalism Edn., Mgt. Tng. Ctr., Northwestern Univ., 1990; panel organizer Nat. Assn. of Hispanic Journalists Conf., S.F., 1990 and NYC, 1991; judge Pacific Northwest Soc. Profl. Journalists, Sigma Delta Chi Contest 1989; honors: Press Club So. Calif. "Writes of Spring Award" 1979, Opus Mag. Writer of Year 1978-9, Sigma Delta Chi, Soc. Profl. Journalists Graduate of Year 1980, Dean's List and acad. hons. Cal Poly 1975-80, listed Who's Who Among Am. H.S. Students, Who's Who Among Students in Am. Univs. & Colls., Who's Who Among Hispanic Americans 1990–, Who's Who of Am. Women, Who's Who of Profl. and Bus. Women; mem: Nat. Assn. Hispanic Journalists, Calif. Chicano News Media Assn.; co-founder, ed., writer Perspectiva: The Hispanic Newspaper of Record (1988); rec: writing, photog., jogging. Res: 3312 Van Nostran Dr Lakewood 90712 Ofc: LA Times Editorial Dept., Metro Copy Desk, Times Mirror Square, Los Angeles 90053

MARROW, MARVA JAN, photographer, author; b. Apr. 22, 1948, Denver; d. Sydney and Helen Berniece (Garber) M.; edn: Carnegie-Mellon Univ. 1965-67. Career: singer, songwriter RCA Records, Italy 1972-77, lyricist songs for Italian pop artists incl. Lucio Battisti, Battiato, Premiata Forneria Marconi (PFM), Patty Pravo, 1972–; freelance photographer Italy and U.S., 1976–, corr., photographer Italian TV Guide, Milan 1979–, collaborator, photog. various periodicals in U.S. and Europe, contbr. photos for covers and articles in nat. and internat. mags.; museum exhibits (photo), Tokyo, Palm Springs, Palos Verdes; project dir., Digital Art Museum (CD-ROM) 1994-95; producer: the Kat's Meow (CD- ROM), 1995, The Top Dog (CD-ROM), 1995; author photobook: Inside the L.A. Artist, 1988; dir. acquisitions RAI-TV, Los Angeles, 1990-91, also produc- er RAI-TV and Radio 1990–; represented by Shooting Star Photo Agy., USA, Agenzia Marka, Agenzia Masi, Italy, Uniphoto Press Internat., Japan; mem: Motion Picture Assn. of Am., Fgn. Press Assn.; Democrat; rec: cooking, travel, people, breeding show cats. Studio: Altadena Ofc: Ayzenberg Design Group 39 E Walnut St Pasadena 91103

MARSDEN, SULLIVAN SAMUEL, JR., professor emeritus of petroleum engineering; b. June 3, 1922, St. Louis, Mo.; s. Sullivan S., Sr. and Irene Margaret (Frick) M.; m. Margaret Coolidge, Sept. 4, 1948; children: Sullivan F. b. 1949, Robert S. b. 1951, Mary V. b. 1953, Anastasia E. b. 1955; edn: BA engrg. chem., Stanford Univ., 1944, PhD physical chem., 1948. Career: phys. chemist Tenn. Eastman Co., Oak Ridge, Tenn., 1945; phys. chemist Stanford Res. Inst., Menlo Park, 1947-50; asst. dir. National Chem. Lab., Poona, India, 1950-53; assoc. prof. pet. engrg. Penn. State Univ., Pa. 1953-57; Stanford Univ., 1957-62, prof. pet. engring., 1963-92, prof. emeritus pet. engring. 1993–; awards: Fulbright Awards- Univ. Tokyo, Japan 1963-64, Gubkin Inst., Moscow, USSR 1978, Oil & Gas Inst., Bucharest, Romania 1978; sr. mem. Soc. Petroleum Engrs. 1953–; publs: 100+ tech. papers and presentations, 3 patents issued; Republican; rec: hiking, skiing, photog., gardening. Res: 868 Lathrop Dr Stanford 94305 Ofc: Petroleum Engineering Dept. Stanford 94305-2220

MARSH, THOMAS ARCHIE, sculptor; b. May 7, 1951; s. Archie Glen and Florence Margaret (Weber) M.; m. Marie Jean Sovey, June 14, 1975 (div. Mar., 1981); m. Siobhan Elisabeth Kelly, July 8, 1995; edn: BFA, Layton Sch. of Art, Milwaukee, Wis. 1971-74; anatomy study, Med. Coll. of Wis., Milwaukee 1973- 74; aesthetics study, Univ. of So. Calif., L.A. 1975-76; MFA, Calif. State Univ., Long Beach 1974-77. Career: instr. of sculpture, Calif. State Univ., Long Beach 1978-79; instr. of sculpture, S.F. State Univ., S.F. 1979-80; instr. of anatomy, Acad. of Art Coll., S.F. 1981–; studio asst., Milton Hebald, Sculptor, Rome, Italy 1977-78; public lectures, Univ. of S.F. 1983, 1984, 1986, 1987; solo exhib., Alliance Francaise, S.F. 1982; solo exhib., Univ. of S.F. 1987; co-curated exhib., The Goddess of Democracy, Bedford Gallery, Reg. Ctr. for the Arts, Walnut Creek 1991; awards: Elizabeth Greenshields Found. Award, Montreal, Can.

1977; public installation of drawings (permanent) Univ. of S.F., Lone Mountain Coll., Rossi Lib. 1985; Outstanding Contribution Award, Svc. Ctr. for Chinese Democracy, S.F. 1991; Cert. of Appreciation, Marin Philosophical Soc., Tiburon 1992, Chinese Democratic Edn. Found., S.F. 1992; Outstanding Educator Award, Liberal Arts Dept., Acad. of Art Coll., S.F. 1992; S.C.O.P.E. Award for city beautification (bronze sculpture), Santa Cruz 1992; mem: Found. for Chinese Democracy (bd. dirs. 1990–), Acad. of Art Coll., S.F. (bd. dirs. 1992–) sculptor: (public) bronze figure, Calif. State Univ., Long Beach campus 1977; (public) bronze portrait bust, UC Berkeley Minor Hall 1984; (public) bronze relief, 343 Sansome St., S.F. 1990, (public) bronze portrait bust, Richard M. Lucas Ctr., Stanford Univ. Med. Sch. 1992; sculptor & co-designer: (public) bronze reliefs, 235 Pine St., S.F. 1990, (public) bronze monument with figure, West Cliff Dr., Santa Cruz 1991, Goddess of Democracy (public) bronze figure Portsmouth Sq., S.F. 1994; Libertarian; Lutheran; rec: opera. Ofc: Thomas Marsh, Sculptor 2377 San Jose Ave. San Francisco 94112

MARSHALL, ANN ELLEN, psychologist; b. April 17, 1952, San Diego; d. William Francis and Margaret Claire (Fane) Drummy; m. Anthony Marshall, Sept. 19, 1976; 1 son, Christopher; edn: BA, UCLA 1974; MA, CSU Long Beach 1976; PhD, UCLA 1986; lic. psychologist Calif. Bd. Med. Examiners 1986. Career: psychology instr. CSU, Long Beach 1979-80; instr. UCLA Ext. 1981-83; counselor SW Tx. St. Univ., San Marcos, Tx. 1984-85; psychology instr. San Diego Comm. Colls. 1985-89; pvt. practice psychology, San Diego 1985–; cons. Abraxas H.S., Poway 1988-92; instr. National Univ., San Diego 1982-84; career counselor UCLA 1977-80, appear in weekly television segment on Psychology, KFMB-TV 1993–; awards: Women in Comm. Service Outstanding Vol. (1984); mem: Am. Psychological Assn; 5 publs. in profl. jours., 1979-85. Res: 10641 Bernabe Dr San Diego 92129-3410 Ofc: 16935 W. Bernardo Dr. Ste 110, San Diego 92127

MARSTON, RICHARD WELDEN, lawyer; b. May 8, 1933, Ithaca, NY; s. Winthrop Simon and Sylva Orabelle (Jones) M.; m. Margaret Scholz, Feb. 20, 1960; children: John b. 1962, Ann b. 1964, Robert b. 1965; edn: BS, UC Berkeley 1955; JD, UC Hastings Coll. of Law 1963; admitted U.S. Supreme Ct. 1971. Career: pvt. practice law, San Jose 1964-68; municipal atty. San Jose, Glendale, Beverly Hills & Burbank 1968-88; atty., private practice, 1988–; mem: Calif. Bar Assn., Los Angeles Co. Bar Assn., Glendale Bar Assn., Kiwanis Glendale (dir. 1987-89, v.p. 89-90), SAR (chancellor 1990-94), So. Calif. Genealogical Soc. (dir. 1985-86), F&A Masons Jewel City Lodge No. 368, Royal Canyon Property Owners Assn. (dir. 1991–, secty. 1992-93); mil: capt. USAFR 1971; Republican; R.Cath.; rec: dist. running, backpacking, genealogy. Res: 1224 Imperial Dr Glendale 91207-1526

MARSZALEK, GEORGIA, marketing executive; b. Nov. 14, 1946, Buffalo, N.Y.; d. Edward S. and Helen A. (Rudick) Marszalek; m. Peter J. Loranger, Jan. 15, 1990; edn: BA, St. Univ. N.Y. 1969; MBA, Pepperdine Univ. 1979. Career: mktg. mgr. Atari Inc., 1979-83; Convergent Tech.Inc., Santa Clara 1983-84; mktg. dir. Tektronix Inc. 1984-85; Aida corp. 1985-87; Teradyne 1987-89; mktg. cons., San Mateo 1989–; mem: BPAA. Res: 773 Widgeon St Foster City 94404 Ofc: Georgia Marszalek, Marketing Consultant, POB 4032 Foster City 94404

MART, BRADLEY CURTIS, lawyer, executive; b. Oct. 12, 1957, Los Angeles; s. Donald Sanford and Roberta Mart (Blank) M.; edn: BS pub. affairs/pub. admin. (honors), USC 1979; JD, Univ. Santa Clara 1983; admitted Calif. St. Bar 1983. Career: asst. exec. dir. Bay Planning Coalition, San Francisco 1983-88; atty. pvt. general law practice, 1983–; dir. Bay World Trading, Ltd. (export-import co.), S.F. 1985–; appt. del. White House Conf. on Small Bus. (1986 chmn. state & regional coms.), advy. bd. Senate Select Com. on Small Bus. Ents. (co-ch.), S.F. Leadership Council 1987; awards: outstanding participant Nat. Assn. of Comm. Leadership Orgns. (S.F. class of 1987), publs: articles in Meat Plant Mag. (9/88), Meat & Poultry Mag. (1/88), ArborAge Mag. (8/89), Export Today Mag. (3/94, 1/95, 3/95, 5/95); res. pub. by Bay Planning Coalition: Landowner Liability and Public Access, 1985, The Saved Bay, 1987; contbr. poems var. anthologies; rec: travel, photog., writing, rowing, distance swimming. Ofc: Bay World Trading, Ltd., Pier 9 No.112, The Embarcadero, San Francisco 94111-1419

MARTELLA, VINCENT NICHOLAS, engineer; b. Sept. 12, 1935, New York City; s. Michael and Anna (D'Andrea) Martella; nephew of Dr. Luigi Martella (1911-1971), distinguished Italian architect, professor and painter; m. Jean Susan Scrivani, June 29, 1963; children: Denise, b. 1967, Paul, b. 1970, JoAnne, b. 1978; edn: BSME, Polytech. Inst. of New York, 1966; MSME, Loyola Univ. of Los Angeles, 1972; grad. Cal Tech engring. mgmt. pgm. 1989; Reg. Profl. Mech. Engr., Calif. 1978. Career: stress analyst, F-5 supersonic fighter and 747 comml. jet, Northrop Corp., Hawthorne 1966-68; stress analyst, mil. and comml. helicopters incl. advanced rotorcraft design, Hughes Helicopters Inc., Culver City 1968-71; stress analyst, B-1 Bomber, Rockwell Internat., Los Angeles Div., El Segundo 1971-72; lead engr., San Onofre nuclear power plant, Bechtel Power Corp., Norwalk 1972-77; prin. engr., oil refineries, gas-oil separation units and nuclear power plants, Brown & Root Braun, Alhambra 1977-85; senior engr., F-20 Tigershark aft fuselage structural analysis and loads test; engring. splst. and

lead engr., Adv. Tactical Fighter pgm.; senior lead engr., aircraft structural design and analysis, Northrop Grumman Corp., Aircraft Div., Hawthorne 1985–; mem: The New York Acad. of Sciences, The Mathematical Assn. of Am., U.S. Naval Inst.; civic: tutor in math.; Republican; R.Cath.; rec: historical aircraft, travel, sailing. Res: 5308 Vista Del Mar, Cypress 90630 Ofc: Northrop Grumman Corp., Aircraft Div., One Northrop Ave, Hawthorne 90250-3277

MARTIN, BEVERLY, hospital sleep disorders center polysomnograph technician; b. Nov. 29, 1946, Port Hueneme; d. Raymond Lindsay Bowden and Virginia Lee Jones; m. David M. Montag, Sept. 24, 1967 (div. 1988); m. Gerald Lee Martin, May 5, 1988; children: Daniel b. 1972, Esther b. 1975, Michael b. 1979, Jennifer b. 1990, Rochelle b. 1992; edn: AA, East L.A. Coll. 1968; AA, L.A. City Coll. 1975; BA, CSU Los Angeles 1973; cert. sleep disorders, Stanford Univ. 1989. Career: sleep center Huntington Meml. Hosp., Pasadena 1982–; honors: Mabel Wilson Richards Scholarship, East L.A. Coll.; mem: Calif. Soc. Respiratory Care, Nat. Soc. Cardio Pulmonary Tech., Nat. Soc. Polysomnographic Techs., BSA (asst. leader 1988); rec: quiltmaking.

MARTIN, CLYDE VERNE, psychiatrist; b. Apr. 7, 1933, Coffeyville, Kans.; s. Howard Verne and Elfrieda Louise (Moehn) M.; m. Barbara Jean McNeilly, June 24, 1956; children: Kent b. 1959, Kristin b. 1960, Kerry b. 1962, Kyle b. 1965; edn: BA, Univ. Kans. 1955; MD, Univ. Kans. Sch. of Med., 1958; MA, Webster Univ. (Mo.) 1977; JD, Thomas Jefferson Coll. of Law (L.A.) 1985; diplomate in psychiatry Am. Bd. Psychiat. and Neurol. 1982; career: minister, supply pastor and co-dir. rel. edn., Methodist Ch., 1951-58; pvt. practice psychiatry in Kansas City, Mo. 1958-84; founder Mid-Continent Psychiatric Hosp., Olathe, Kans. 1972, pres. bd. dirs. Martin Psychiatric Res. Found. 1976–; public practice, 1986–, surveyor Jt. Commn. for Accreditation of Hosps.; editor Corrective and Social Psychiatry 1970–, clin. prof. psychiat. UCSF Med. Sch. 1985–; awards: Phi Beta Pi, Phi Theta Kappa, Nat. Honor Soc. 1950-51, Danforth Scholar 1951, Am. Legion Oratory Contest Winner 1951, dist. gov. Key Clubs Internat. 1951, pres. Kans. Conf. United Meth. Youth 1951-53, Dean's List 1952-54, bd. dirs. Meth. Youthville, Newton, Kans. 1964-74, Outstanding Young Men Am. 1970, lay mem. United Meth. Annual Conf. 1972-80, pres. Kansas Area U.M. Com. on Episcopacy 1976-80, AMA phys. recogn. award 1977-92; apptd. FAA Spl. Com. on Major Aircraft Disasters 1978; Fellow: Am. Psychiatric Assn., Royal Soc. of Health (London), Am. Assn. Mental Health Profls. in Corrections, Am. Assn. of Social Psychiatry, World Assn. Social Psychiatry, Masters and Johnson Inst., and Am. Orthopsychiatric Assn.; mem: AMA, Internat. Assn. Group Psychotherapy, Assn. of USAF Psychiatrists, Assn. Mental Health Adminstrs., Am. Assn. Psychiat. Adminstrs., Am. Pub. Health Assn., Am. Acad. Med. Dirs., Am. Correctional Assn., Am. Acad. Psychiat. and the Law, Am. Assn. Sex Educators, Counselors & Therapists, Soc. for Sci. Study of Sex, Pi Kappa Alpha frat.; civic: Native Sons and Daus. Kans., Kans. St. Hist. Soc., Smithsonian Instn., Am. Iris Soc., Am. Horticultural Assn., Univ. Kans. Alumni Assn.; publs: contbr. 4 books, numerous profl. papers and jour. articles, presentations var. nat. and internat. confs. include 10-year study Confrontation gp. therapy with adolescent delinquents using therapists, closed circuit t.v. instant replay and peer confrontation, Proceedings World Cong. Psychiatry, Vienna 1983; mil: col. USAFR-ret. 1964-86, comdr. Med. Svc. USAF 1970-74; United Methodist (local preacher lic. 1951); rec: pvt. pilot, sailor. Res: 4741 Valley End Ln Green Valley/Suisan 94585. Ofc: Box 3365 Fairfield 94533-0587

MARTIN, D. KEVIN, travel company executive; b. Apr. 2, 1954, Santa Monica; s. Robert Ney and Marilyn Joy (Johns) M.; m. Cynthia Jean Andary, Aug. 6, 1977; children: Brian b. 1982, Christine b. 1984, Katie b. 1991; edn: UC Irvine 1972-73; BSBA, CSU Fullerton, 1977; C.P.A. Calif. 1981. Career: fin. analyst McDonnell Douglas, Huntington Beach 1977-78; staff acct. Price Waterhouse, Newport Beach 1979-81; chief fin. analyst Fluor Corp., Irvine 1981-84; reg. v.p. Thomas Cook Travel, Irvine 1984-90, v.p. ops. Associated Travel Internat., Santa Ana 1990–

MARTIN, DONALD WALTER, writer/publisher; b. Apr. 22, 1934, Grants Pass, Ore.; s. George E. and Irma Ann (Dallas) M.; m. Kathleen Elizabeth Murphy July, 1970 (div. May, 1979); m. Betty Woo Mar. 18, 1985; children: Kimberly Ann b. 1959, Daniel Clayton b. 1975. Career: reporter, asst. sports ed., Blade-Tribune, Oceanside, Calif. 1961-65; Sunday ed., Press-Courier, Oxnard, Calif. 1965-69; managing ed., Argus-Courier, Petaluma, Calif. 1969-70; assoc. ed., Motorland Mag., S.F., Calif. 1970-88; founder, CEO, Pine Cone Press, Inc., Columbia, Calif. 1988–; mem: Internat. Assn. of Indep. Publishers 1991–, Soc. of Am. Travel Writers 1992–, Calif. Press Photographers Assn. 1965-70, Kiwanis Club, Petaluma 1969-70; author, travel books: Best of San Francisco, 1986, 90, 94, Best of the Gold Country, 1987, 92, Best of Arizona, 1990, 93, Inside San Francisco, 1991, Best of Nevada, 1992; Best of the Wine Country, 1991, 95, Oregon Discovery Guide, 1993, 95, N. Calif. Discovery Guide, 1993, Ultimate Wine Book, 1993, Washington Discovery Guide, 1994, Utah Discovery Guide, 1995; mil: staff sgt., USMC, 1952-61; Green Party; rec: hiking, whitewater kayaking, bicycling, travel. Res: 11362 Yankee Hill Rd. P.O. Box 1494 Columbia 95310. Ofc: Pine Cone Press Inc11362 Yankee Hill Rd. Columbia 95310

MARTIN, EDWARD HENRY, aerospace program executive; b. July 15, 1933, Lakewood, Ohio; s. Paul Joseph and Susan Rose (Kudravy) M.; m. Janice Joy Morgan, June 1, 1957; children: Kim Luise b. 1958, Michael Edward b. 1960; edn: Fenn Coll. 1951-53, BSEE, Ohio St. Univ., 1957, MSEE, 1964; reg. profl. engr. Calif. Career: GS-13 aerospace splst. USAF Systems Command, Dayton, Ohio 1962-64; sr. research engr. N.Am. Aviation, Anaheim 1964-67, analysis supr. 1967-72; advanced systems mgr. Magnavox Govt. Indsl., Torrance 1972-78; tech. dir. Rockwell Collins, Seal Beach 1978-81, program mgr. Rockwell Internat., Satellite Systems Div. 1981-91, Rockwell Strategic Defense Center staff, 1991-93; principal staff engr. Transportation Systems, Rockwell Autonetics 1993–; postgrad. seminars 1968-72; lectr. Tech. Mktg. Soc. Am. 1978-82; organizer, chmn. Inst. Navigation, Monterey 1980; honors: Jane's Who's Who in Aviation, Who's Who Frontier of Sci., Marquis Who's Who; mem: IEEE, Inst. Navigation, Air Force Assn., Beta Theta Pi, Corona del Mar Track Club, USA Track & Field; 5 papers pub. (1974-82), articles pub. in profl. jours. (1977), patent disclosures (1972, 91, 92, 94); mil: capt. USAF 1959-62; Republican; rec: Master's Track & Field, Pentathlon. Res: 5221 Nantucket Ln Anaheim 92807 Ofc: Rockwell Autonetics Electronic Systems 3370 Miraloma Ave POB 3105 Anaheim 92803-3105

MARTIN, GORDON EUGENE, company president and principal research scientist; b. Aug. 22, 1925, San Diego; s. Carl Amos and Ruth Marie (Fountain) Martin; m. Tricia Jane Totten, June 10, 1949; children: Gloria b. 1950, Theodore b. 1953, Kathryn b. 1956, Susan b. 1957; edn: BS in E.E., UC Berkeley, 1947; MS engring., UCLA, 1951, MA physics, San Diego St. Univ., 1961; PhD in E.E., Univ. Texas, Austin 1966. Career: communications officer US Navy, Pacific Ocean, 1943-45; electrical engr. Convair (Gen. Dyn.), San Diego 1947; res. physicist Navy Electronics Lab., San Diego 1947-52; lt. USNR, asst. ofcr. in chg., USN, Bahamas and Conn., 1952-54; res. physicist Naval Ocean Systems Center, San Diego 1954-80; pres. Martin Analysis, San Diego 1980–; cons. USN, Wash. D.C., 1954-80, mem. Piezoelectric Boards USN, W.D.C., 1960-80; acoustics dept. hd. Systems Exploration, San Diego, 1980-82; awards: Outstanding, Navy Lab. San Diego (1954, 56, 60, 62, others), commendn. letter from Dir. of All Navy Labs, Wash. D.C. 1968, num. commendn. letters USN 1973–; mem: Acoustical Soc. of Am. (1950–, Fellow 1980), Inst. Electronics & Electrical Engrs. (1948–, Senior Mem. 1964), NY Acad. of Scis. 1964–, Sigma Xi 1965–, Sigma Pi Sigma 1960–, Acoustical Soc. (S.D. chpt. pres. 1970); patentee -Sonar, Materials, others (1954-80); author: CAE For Piezoelectric Arrays (originator theory and software, 1954–), Inverse Piezoelectric Parameter Method (theory, paper, software 1964), jour. articles re Piezoelectricity (1954–); Prot. (statistician 1968-82, other offices); rec: old rare books, sci. books, square dancing. Res: 3675 Syracuse Ave San Diego 92122-3322 Ofc: M.A.S.T., Inc. 3675 Syracuse Ave. San Diego 92122-3322

MARTIN, JOSEPH, JR., lawyer; b. May 21, 1915; edn: BA, Yale Univ., 1936, LLB, Yale Law Sch. 1939; mem. State Bars of Calif., NY, and D.C.; career: assoc. Cadwalader, Wickersham & Taft, NY, 1939-41; USN (to Lt. Cdr.) 1941-46; ptnr. Wallace, Garrison, Norton & Ray, San Francisco 1946-55; ptnr. Allan, Miller, Groezinger, Keesling & Martin, 1955-70; Pettit, Evers & Martin 1973-95, (Pettit & Martin); gen. counsel Fed. Trade Commn., Wash DC 1970-71; US Amb., US rep. to Geneva Disarmarment Conf., 1971-76. Fellow Am. Bar Found.; mem. President's Advy. Com. for Arms Control & Disarmament, 1974-78; pres. S.F. Public Utilities Commn. 1956-60; Republican Nat. Committeeman for Calif. 1960-64; dir. Arms Control Assn. 1977-84; dir. Legal Assistance to the Elderly 1981-87; dir.: Arcata Corp. 1982, Astec Industries, Inc. 1987, Allstar Inns, Inc. 1983; treas. Republican Party of Calif. 1956-58; dir. Patrons of Art & Music, Calif. Palace of Legion of Honor, 1958-70, pres. 1963-68; clubs: Pacific-Union (S.F.), Burlingame CC, Yale (of N.Y.); honors: ofcl. commendn. for outstanding service as gen. counsel, FTC 1973, distinguished honoree US Arms Control & Disarmament Agy. 1973, Lifetime achiev., Legal Assistance to the Elderly 1981; Address: Three Embarcadero Ctr #2280 San Francisco 94111

MARTIN, MARY, lawyer; b. June 24, 1941, Buffalo, N.Y.; d. Francis Harold and Eileen May (Carney) Martin; m. Michael F. Grisanti, Jr., April 20, 1963 (div. Oct. 27, 1992); children: Michael b. 1964, Jennifer b. 1966, Maureen b. 1969; edn: reg. nurse, Mercy Hosp. Sch. Nursing 1962, BS, Chapman Coll. 1980, JD, Western St. Sch. law 1983; admitted St. Bar Calif. (1985). Career: staff nurse Mercy Hosp., Buffalo, N.Y. 1962-63; coronary care nurse Milalrd Fillmore Hosp. 1963-64; law clk. Burton Halloren Schwartz, Newport 1984-85; assoc. atty. Beam, Brobeck, DiCaro & D'Antony, Santa Ana 1986-87; Robinson, Robinson & Phillips, Mission Viejo 1986-89; awards: Mercy Hosp. Excellent Bedside Nursing 1962, Moot Court Award 1983, Western St. Law Sch. Hon. Roll 1980-83; mem: Orange Co. Trial Lawyers, Orange Co. Bar Assn., Calif. Trial Lawyers, Orange Co. Bar Assn., Orange Co. Med. Assn., San Diego Co. Bar Assn., Whit PTA (pres. 1976-77), Little League Baseball (scorekeeper 1974-78); article pub. in profl. jour., 1983, num. poems pub.; Cath.; rec: writing. Res & Ofc.: 5383 Chelsea Ave #203 La Jolla 92037

MARTIN, MICHAEL LEE, orthotist; b. May 30, 1947, Long Beach; s. Troy Lee and Ruth Elizabeth (Hummer) M.; m. Sharon Lee Johnson, Aug. 23, 1969; children: Tanya Lee; edn: att. Northwestern Univ. 1973; AA, Cerritos Coll.

1976; att. UCLA 1976; Diplomate Am. Bd. Orthotists and Prosthetists. Career: cable splicer Gen. Telephone, Dairy Valley, 1965-66; orthotic technician Johnson's Orthopedic, Santa Ana, 1969-73, orthotist, 1974–, pres. Johnson's Orthopedic, Orange, 1989–; pres. Johnson's Orthopedic Designs, Corona; dir. Nat. Academy of Orthotists & Prosthetists 1993; res. advy. bd. mem. Rancho Los Amigos Hosp., Rehab Engring.; research orthotist Rancho Los Amigos Hosp., Downey, 1973; mem: Am. Acad. Orthotists and Prosthetists (sec., pres. So. Calif. chpt. 1976-79, sec., pres. Region IX 1979-87), Orthotic and Prosthetic Provider Network (pres. Calif. chpt. 1980–), Internat. Soc. of Prosthetists & Orthotists; mil: US Army 1966-68, Vietnam; Republican. Res: 16 Oakmont Coto De Caza 92679 Ofc: Johnson's Orthopedic 1920 E. Katella Ste G Orange 92667

MARTIN, PORT ROBERT, engineering executive; b. Aug. 27, 1944, Norfolk, Va.; s. Port Corbett and Edith (Chandler) M.; m. Sandra Lee Polasik, Aug. 20, 1968 (div. 1977); m. Barbara Jeanne Green, Sept. 1, 1979 (div. 1985); children: Michael b. 1971, Theresa b. 1973; edn: BS engring., US Naval Acad. 1966; MA bus., Univ. N.Colo. 1976; EdD, Univ. San Diego 1995. Career: real estate sales Mascot Realty, Bonita 1976-77; tng. splst. Cubic Corp., San Diego 1977-78; engr., branch head, dep. div. head Naval Ocean Systems Center 1983-94; assoc. Booz Allen & Hamilton 1994–; adj. prof. Naval War Coll., Newport, R.I. 1985-90; awards: Freedom Found. 1965, Fulbright scholar 1966-67; mem: U.S. Naval Inst., Internat. Assn. Marathoners; author: Jr. Ofcr. Orientation Guide, 1983, Chief Petty Ofcr. Orientation, 1985; poetry writer, 1961–, article pub. 1985; mil: capt. USN 1961-91, Burke scholar 1966, 2 commendation medals 1981, 83; Prot.; rec: running, writing. Res: 1661 Azusa Ct Bonita 91902-4028 Ofc: Booz Allen & Hamilton 1455 Frazee Rd Ste 300 San Diego 92108

MARTIN, PRESTON, financial institution executive; b. Dec. 5, 1923, Los Angeles; s. Oscar H. and Gaynell A. (Horne) M.; m. Genevieve DeVere, Aug. 12, 1983; 1 child, Pier b. 1964; edn: BS fin. USC 1947; MBA, 1948; PhD monetary econ., Ind. Univ. 1954. Career: commr. Calif. S&L 1967-69; chmn. Federal Home Loan Bank Board 1969-72; founder Fed. Home Loan Mortgage Corp. (Freddie Mac); founder Neighborhood Housing Services of Am. (NHSA); founder PMI Mortgage Ins. Co., PMI Ins. Co., PMI Mortgage Corp., 1972-79; bd. chmn./CEO Seraco Enterprises Inc. (Sears Roebuck) 1980-81; vice chmn. Federal Reserve Board Govs. 1982-86; chmn HomeVest Financial Group, Inc.; awards: Nat. Assn. Home Builders Turntable Builders award 1973, Engineering News Record 1971, Top Performer House and Home 1969, USC Alumni award 1972, USC Sch. of Bus. Admin. Alum. Award for Bus. Excellence 1988, 2 White House awards for Govtl. Organization Mgmt. Excellence; author: Principles and Practices of Real Estate (The MacMillan Co. 1969); mil: tech-4 AUS WWII; Republican; Presbyterian; rec: bicycling. Ofc: HomeVest Financial Group Inc. 580 California St Ste 600 San Francisco 94104

MARTIN, ROBERT A., II, healthcare products company owner; b. Dec. 8, 1950, Fesno; s. Robert A. Martin; m. Sandra L. Brown, April 5, 1973 (div. 1980); edn: AA, Fresno City Coll. 1971; var. courses CSU Fresno 1971-79. Career: sales rep. PDM Steel, Fresno 1974-78; chief operating ofcr. Calif. Chrome 1978-81; pres. Ram Dental 1980-82; pres. Del-Rio Calif. 1983-85; owner, pres. Professional Healthcare, Fresno 1980–; chmn. Fresno Citizens Advy. Commn.; pres. emeritus Fresno Bus. & Profl. Assn.; bd. dirs. Fresno CofC. (elected v.p. 1982, 83, Chamber Mem. of Month 1983); chmn. Fresno Co. Crime Prevention Council; bd. dirs. Calif. Bowl 1983, v.p. mktg. 1985; appt. to Calif. State Conf. on Small Bus., legis. implementation ch. Fresno dist., 1984; bd. mem. Fresno Am. Mktg. Assn.; ch. Fresno City Budget Task Force, 1985, 86; appt. mem. Fresno Citizen Advy. Commission, 1986; bd. dirs. Easter Seals, 1987; elected bd. Valley Children's Hosp., chmn. Hearts Desire, 1987; elected bd. Am. Heart Assn., Am. Cancer Soc., 1988; founder, elected charter pres. Fresno Bus. and Profl. Singles, 1987; honors: Jaycee of Month (1975), Jaycee of Quarter, Yr. (1976); Rookie of Yr., PDM Steel (1978), Salesman of the Quarter, PDM Steel (1979); mem. ACS, Fresno; Republican. Ofc: Professional Healthcare POB 26600 Fresno 93729

MARTIN, RONALD GENE, federal government acquisition program manager; b. April 24, 1954, San Bernardino; s. Donald Arthur and Beverly Jean (Willis) M.; m. Mary Alice Acosta, Oct. 14, 1978 (div. March 30, 1990); 2 dau., Natalie b. 1980, Tara b. 1986; m. Desiree A. Pietzsch, Jan. 9, 1991; edn: AA, San Bernardino Valley Coll. 1977; BA history, CSU San Bernardino 1981; MA, nat. security, 1989. Career: VA counselor San Bernardino Valley Coll. Office 1977-78; aircraft maintenance splst. Norton AFB 1978-81, jet engine maintenance splst. 1981-82, quality assurance rep., Air Force plant rep. Boeing, Seattle, Wash. 1982-84; quality assurance rep. space shuttle program H.Q. Western Space & Missile Center, Vandenberg AFB 1984-85; sr. logistics mgr., peacekeeper ICBM program, H.Q. Ballistic Missile Orgn., Norton AFB 1985-91; dep. dir. logistics, HQ Pacific Air Force, Hickam AFB, Hawaii 1991-93; logistics program mgr., Space and Missile Systems Ctr., Los Angeles AFB, Calif. 1993–; awards: Air Force Plant Rep. Spl. Act 1983, Superior Performance H.Q. Ballistic Systems 1987, 89; mil: E-6 USAFR 1972-84; Democrat; Christian; rec: classic automobile restoration, golf. Res: 1418 N. University St. Redlands 92374 Ofc: Space and Missile Systems Center, Dept. of the Air Force, 2420 Vela Way, Ste 1467 A-8, Los Angeles AFB 90245

MARTIN, STANLEY ROLAND, general manager, sales and marketing executive; b. Dec. 25, 1943, Jersey City, N.J.; s. Walter John and Lucille (Guadagno) M.; m. Linda Marie Marson, Oct. 11, 1975; children: Craig b. 1987, David b. 1989; edn: BA, Newark St. Coll. 1969; MA, Univ. Md. 1971. Career: vocational coordinator Anne Arundel Co., Annapolis, Md. 1971-77; regional sales 3M Co., St. Paul, Minn. 1978-87; regional sales mgr. FIGA Group, Itasca, Ill. 1987-92; gen. mgr. Hotsy Equipment Co., Anaheim 1992-93; dir. advance svs. Westminster Mem. Park, Westminster, Calif. 1993–; sr. arbitrator L.A. Autoline Better Bus. Bureau 1986–; awards: Carnation Co. cert. appreciation 1987, A.K.C.A. Koi person of year 1987; mem: Orange Co. Zen Nippon Airinkai (pres. 1987-88, v.p. 1985-87), OCCCO; mil: E-4 N.J. Nat. Guard 1964-70; rec: deep sea fishing, golf, koi. Res: 2421 N Park Blvd Santa Ana 92706 Ofc: Westminster Memorial Park 14801 Beach Blvd Westminster 92683

MARTIN, TIMOTHY PATRICK, executive search/consulting executive; b. Feb. 5, 1944, Santa Barbara; s. Dr. Walter Patrick and Kathrine Georgia (Runions) M.; stepmother, Margaret Ann Martin; m. Maria Maingot, Aug. 10, 1963; children: Timothy P. Jr. b. 1966, Kathie b. 1967, Rob b. 1971, Dave b. 1972; m. 2d. Lois Goldberg, Mar. 12, 1988; edn: BSBA, Univ. Ariz., 1966; P.M.D., Harvard Grad. Sch., 1980. Career: acct. Atkinson, Lee, Fannelli & Co., Willow Glen 1966-69; sr. acct. Boise Cascade Corp., Sunnyvale 1969-70, plant controller Boise Cascade, Wallula, Wash. 1970-72, div. controller, Boise 1972-77, div. fin. mgr. Itasca, Ill. 1977-81, dir. of information, Boise 1981-84; sr. v.p. adminstrn. Lucky Stores, Inc. San Leandro, Ca. 1984-89; exec. search/ cons. and c.e.o. The Martin Group, Walnut Creek 1989–; civic: Right Direction Project (pres. 1987-88), Bishop Kelly H.S. Bd. (pres. 1982-84); Republican; R.Cath.; rec: boating, water sports. Res: 328 Saclan Terrace Clayton 94517 Ofc: The Martin Group, 1981 N Broadway Ste 430 Walnut Creek 94596

MARTINEZ, ANDRES A., corporate executive; b. April 10, 1949, Havana, Cuba; nat. 1979; s. Arturo V. and Dora G. (Diaz) M.; m. Vivian M. Alfonso, May 24, 1969 (div. 1983); m. Susan L. Sanders, July 16, 1983 (div. 1992); children: Lizette b. 1973, Jonathan b. 1985, Samantha b. 1986; edn: BS acctg., CSU Los Angeles 1975. Career: jr. acct. Hilton Rent a Car Corp., Beverly Hills 1969-70; acctg. supr. Empress Pearls Inc., Hollywood 1970-72; cost acct. Larwin Group Inc., Los Angeles 1972-75; vice pres. and corp. controller Environmental Industries Inc., Calabasas 1975-95; CFO, Worldwide Security Assocs., Inc., L.A. 1995–; Republican; R.Cath. Res: 11561 Butter Creek Rd Moorpark 93021 Ofc: Worldwide Security Assocs Inc 10302 Glasgow Place Los Ageles 90045

MARTINEZ, ANTONIO ESPINOZA, county mental health therapist; b. June 5, 1947, Stockton; s. Joe Galvez and Guadalupe (Espinoza) M.; m. Barbara Santos, May 15, 1976; son, Anton b. 1977; edn: AA, San Joaquin Delta Coll., 1970; BA, and MA, CSU Sonoma, 1973, 1974. Career: counselor Skyline Coll., San Bruno 1974-75; dean of students D-Q Univ., Davis 1975-78; dir. ednl. opportunity pgm. Sonoma St. Univ., Rohnert Park 1978-80; counselor Napa County Alcohol Pgm., Napa 1980-84, also coord. Title I pgm. Ridgeview Jr. High Sch., Napa 1981-82; therapist Solano County Mental Health, Fairfield 1983–, devel. & implemented "The Solano Model" (drug prevention pgm.); cons. El Ballet Folklorico De Aztlan, Vacaville 1984–; keynote spkr. Council for the Spanish Speaking, Stockton 1989; awards: inducted Mexican Am. Hall of Fame for City of Stockton (7/90), inducted Edison H.S. Acad. Hall of Fame, Stockton (5/89), achiev. Nat. Assn. of Counties, W.D.C. (7/86), `Well, Well, Well' award Calif. St. Dept. Mental Hlth./ Conf. Local Mental Health Dirs. (5/85), Exemplary Prevention Pgm. award Calif. St. Dept. Alc. and Drug Pgms. (1/90); mem. Calif. Alcohol Pgm. Adminstrn. Assn., Assn. of Latin Am. Svs.; publ: Profile of Calif.'s Award Winning Pgms. (Calif. Dept. Mental Hlth., 1985); Democrat; Christian; rec: sports & fitness. Res: 1740 Lilac Dr Walnut Creek 94596

MARTINEZ, FRANK ROBERT, educator, college administrator; b. Dec. 28, 1921, Los Angeles; s. Frank and Caroline (Bassett) M.; m. Lois Margaret Weber, March 16, 1951; children: Larry b. 1953, Jay b. 1955, Mark b. 1956, Barbara b. 1960; edn: BA, Univ. Redlands, 1947; MA, USC, 1953, EdD, 1963. Career: history prof. Citrus Coll., Glendora 1947-52, dean of students 1952-59, dean of instruction 1959-64; v.p. Cuesta Coll., San Luis Obispo 1964-77, pres. 1977-88; mem. and chmn. Calif. Council for Pvt. Postsec. and Vocat. Edn., Sacto. 1990–; mem: Calif. Postsecondary Edn. Commn. 1991, Chancellor's Advy. Com., Calif. Comm. Colls. 1979-84; We. Assn. Schs. & Colls. (chmn. accreditation com.1978-88), Coll. Opportunity Grants Commn., Calif. 1970-75; awards: Univ. Redlands outstanding alumni 1974, La Fiesta Days San Luis Obispo grand marshall 1980; civic bds: United Way (dir. 1958-94), Civil Service Commn., Rotary (pres. 1960); contbr. articles in field of adult edn., 1963-80; mil: cpl. USMC 1942-46; Presbyterian; rec: bullfighting. Res: 2383 Sunset Dr San Luis Obispo 93401

MARTINEZ, LENORE, licensed clinical social worker; b. June 26, 1930, Santa Rita, N.M.; d. Maria Rivas Martinez; edn: BA, USC 1963; MSW, San Diego St. Univ. 1968; lic. Nat. Bd. Examiners Clin. Social Work 1987; diplomate Am. Bd. Examiners Clin. Social Work. Career: psychiatric social worker Calif. St. Dept. Mental Hygiene, Bakersfield 1968-73; sch. social worker Santa Barbara City Schs. 1973-75; supr., clin. and case worker services Cath.

Charities, Santa Barbara 1975-81, dir. 1981-87, regional dir. 1987-91; pvt. practice psychotherapy, Santa Barbara 1991–; awards: Catholic Charities Recognition of Dedicated Service 1975-91, Cert. of Recognition Santa Barbara City Council 1991 and Santa Barbara Bd. Supervisors, Benemerenti Medal (Medal of Merit) from Pope John Paul II, 1992; mem: Calif. Bd. Behavioral Sci., Soc. Clin. Social Work Fellowship; radio show Sunny Today, 1972; Democrat; Cath. Res: 4210 Croydon Rd San Diego 92130 Ofc: Santa Barbara

MARTINEZ, MATTHEW GILBERT, congressman; b. Feb. 14, 1929, Walsenburg, Colo.; children: Matthew, Diane, Susan, Michael, Carol Ann; edn: Cert. of competence, Los Angeles Trade Sch. 1959. Career: small businessman and bldg. contractor; mem. Monterey Park Planning Commn. 1971-74; mayor City of Monterey Park 1974-75; mem. Monterey Park City Council 1974-80, Calif. State Assembly 1980-82; mem. 97th-104th Congresses from 31st Calif. Dist. 1982–, mem. edn. and labor com., fgn. affairs com.; mem: Congl. Hispanic Caucus, Hispanic Am. Democrats, Nat. Assn. Latino Elected and Apt. Officials, Communications Workers Am., VFW, Am. Legion, Latin Bus. Assn., Monterey Park C. of C., Navy League (dir.), San Gabriel Valley YMCA (bd. dirs.), Rotary; mil: USMC 1947-50; Democrat; Ofc: US House of Reps 2231 Rayburn House Office Bldg Washington DC 20515-0531*

MARTINEZ y FERRER, MARCELINO JUAN CARLOS CODILLA, JR., political/health care consultant and legislative advocate.; b. Sept. 28, 1947, San Francisco; s. Marcelino Cerenio Martinez and Jacinta Parrilla Codilla; edn: BA, CSU Sacto. 1972; BS, Univ. Md. 1980; MPA, CSU Hayward 1990; cert. in hosp. adminstrn. S.D. St. Univ. 1975, instr/educator tng. Naval Post-Grad. Sch. 1987, total quality mgmt. Stanford Univ. Hosp. 1993. Career: adminstrv. asst. Ofc. of Calif. Lt. Gov. 1969-70; adminstrv. analyst Ofc. of Elections, Sacto. Co. 1970-73; dir. Tayo Corp., Manila, Philippines 1970–; dir. Ofc. of Asian/Pacific Affairs, legis. cons. Joint Senate/Assembly Com. on Aging, Calif. St. Legis. 1973-74; hosp. adminstr. DOD, 1974-90; COS and ex. adminstr., pres. PUC, City/Co. of San Francisco 1991-92; dir. med. staff svs. HHMC, San Benito Co.; dir./treas. Westbay Filipino Multi-Svc. Ctr., S.F. 1992-94; cons., mem. The Garamendi Com. 1993-94; ex-dir. Martinez and Assocs. Ltd. 1994–; dep. treas. CDP, 1995–; mem. Sch. to Careers Task Force, Resource Group, Ofc. of Gov., Calif. 1994–; mem. Regional Lab., Resource Group, U.S. Dept. Edn. 1994–; deputy treas., Clinton-Gore '96, 1995–; honors: Phi Kappa Phi, Pi Sigma Alpha, Psi Chi, Phi Alpha Theta, Alpha Sigma Lambda, Golden Key, Order of Merit Pres. Reagan 1981, Medal of Merit Pres. Bush 1989, PAAC, CAA, UC Berkeley Alumni Mentor of Yr. 1993, Republican Senatorial Medal of Freedom 1994; mem: Am. Acad. Political & Social Sci., Am. Acad. Political Sci., Filipino Am. Caucus, Sigma Phi Epsilon Frat., Calif. Democratic Party (St. Central Com., First Dist. 1994–, Nat. Campaign Coord. Com.) Alumni Assns. UC Berkeley, CSU Sacto., Univ. of Md., CSU Hayward, Manila-San Francisco Sister City Commn. 1994–. Res: 3325 South B St Stockton 95206 Ofc: 39412 Sundale Drive Fremont 94538

MARZELL, HAL MARC, lawyer; b. Sept. 14, 1955, Atlantic City, N.J.; s. Norman and Mildred Rose (Heller) M.; m. Cecily Claire French, Feb. 18, 1978, div. Jan., 1991; children: Joshua b. 1978, Adam b. 1986; edn: BS (cum laude) in comm. arts, Calif. St. Polytechic Univ., Pomona 1977; JD, Southwestern Univ. Sch. of Law, 1980; admitted Calif. St. Bar 1981. Career: atty., assoc. Lon B. Isaacson and Assocs., Santa Monica 1982; solo law practice, Los Angeles 1982-84; staff atty. Jacoby & Meyers Law Ofcs., L.A. 1984-87; asst. counsel Home Savings of Am., FA, Pasadena 1987-91, assoc. counsel 1991-94, counsel 1994–; mem: ABA, Calif. St. Bar, L.A. Co. Bar Assn., The L.A. Co. Bankruptcy Forum. Ofc: Home Savings of America, FSB, 4900 Rivergrade Rd. Irwindale 91706

MARZOUK, JOSEPH BAROUKH, physician; b. Nov. 6, 1950, Cairo, Egypt; nat. 1962; s. Baroukh Youseff and Claire (El Gazzar) M.; m. Anna Vedouras, Jan. 27, 1988; children: Tamara b. 1988, Ceseana b. 1989; edn: AB, Princeton Univ. 1972; MD, Boston Univ. Sch. Medicine 1976; lic. physician Ariz. 1980–, Calif. 1980–; cert. Am. Bd. of Internal Medicine 1979, infectious diseases 1982; cert. Bd. of Infection Control 1990. Career: internship and residency, internal medicine, Wayne St. Univ. Affiliated Hosps., Detroit, Mich. 1976-79, chief med. residency 1979-80; fellowship, infectious diseases, UC San Francisco 1980-82; med. staff Providence Hosp., Oakland 1982-92, Merritt-Peralta Med. Ctr., Oakland 1982-92 (adult immunology clinic 1987-92); chief, Div. of Infectious Diseases, Highland Gen. Hosp., Oakland 1990-92; dir. Antimicrobial Utilization Svc. and assoc. chief Infectious Disease Svc., Summit Med. Ctr., Oakland 1992–; active staff: Summit Med. Ctr., Oakland, Alameda Hosp., Alameda, Adult Immunology Clinic, Summit Med. Ctr.; courtesy staff: Alta Bates Med. Ctr., Berkeley, San Leandro Hosp., Eden Hosp., Castro Valley, San Ramon Reg. Med. Ctr., Golden State Rehab. Hosp., San Ramon; bd. dirs. Summit Med. Ctr 1992– (bd. quality com., bd. planning com. 1992–, med. exec. com., officer's/finance com. 1992–, vice-chmn., pharm. and therapeutics com. 1992–, edn. & lib. com. 1992–, infection control com. 1992–, utilization com. 1992–, pres. med. staff, med. exec. com. and officer's/fin. com. 1992-94, exec. com.-bd. dirs. 1993-94 joint quality council 1994–, chmn. credentials com. and president's advy. com. 1994–); v.p. med. staff Providence Hosp. 1991-92 (chmn. quality assurance com., mem. credentials com. 1990-92, sec.-treas. med. staff

1990-91, chmn. budget com. 1990-91, med. exec. com. 1988-92, ICU com. 1987-90, utilization review com. 1984, infection control com. 1982-92); chmn. infection control com. Highland Gen. Hosp. 1990-92; mem. AIDS Task Force, Sisters of Providence Hosps., Seattle, Wash. 1988; mem. num. coms. Merritt-Peralta Med. Ctr. 1982-92; lectr. in field; honors: Am. Coll. of Physician Execs. honored The Antimicrobial Utilization Svc. for innovation and significant advance in med. mgmt., Nat. Speaker's Faculty for "Infectious Disease Challenges in AIDS"; mem: Infectious Disease Soc. of Am., Bay Area Infectious Disease Soc., East Bay Infectious Disease. Soc., Am. Bd. of Forensic Examiners, Am. Coll. of Physicians, Am. Coll. of Physician Execs., Am. Soc. of Microbiology, Alameda-Contra Costa Co. Med. Assn. (mediation com. 1994–, profl. liability com. 1988–), CMA (appeals com. 1994–), Am. Med. Writers Assn., Outpatient Intravenous Infusion Therapy Assn., Med. Speakers Internat.; cons. reviewer: Jour. of Respiratory Diseases, Jour. of Critical Illness; author/contbg. author: 26 pub. profl. articles and abstracts, 1982-93. Ofc: Infectious Disease Medical Group 350 30th St Ste 511 Oakland 94609

MASLIN, HARRY, music record company president; b. Apr. 4, 1948, Phila.; s. Philip and Sarah (Jacobs) M.; m. Ada Allister, Mar. 4, 1985. Career: recording engr. Regent Sound, N.Y.C. 1969-71; chief engr. Hit Factory Studios, N.Y.C. 1971-73, 74-75; recvording engr. Record Plant Studios, N.Y.C. 1973-74; record producer HRM Productions., Hollywood 1975–; co-owner, pres. Image Recording Studios, 1983–; awards: 20 gold and platinum records Rec. Industry Assn. of Am.; mem: Nat. Acad. Recording Arts and Scis., ASCAP, Audio Engring. Soc. Ofc: Image Recording Studios 1020 N Sycamore Ave Hollywood 90038

MASON, DEAN TOWLE, cardiologist; b. Sept. 20, 1932, Berkeley, Calif.; s. Ira Jenckes and Florence Mabel (Towle) M.; m. Maureen O'Brien, June 22, 1957; children: Kathleen, Alison; edn: BA chem., Duke Univ. 1954, MD, 1958; Diplomate Nat. Bd. Med. Examiners, Am. Bd. Internal Med. (cardiovascular diseases). Career: intern, med. resident Johns Hopkins Hosp. 1958-61; clin. assoc. cardiol., sr. asst. surgeon USPHS, Nat. Heart Inst., NIH 1961-63, asst. sect. dir. cardiovasc. diagnosis, attg. phys., sr. investigator cardiol. 1963-68; prof. med., physiol., chief cardiovasc. med. UC Davis Med. Sch.-Sacto. Med. Ctr. 1968-82; chief phys. Western Heart Inst. and chmn. dept. cardiovascular med. St. Mary's Med. Ctr. S.F. 1983–; co-chmn. cardiovasc.-renal drugs US Pharmacopeia Com. Revision 1970-75; mem. life scis. com. NASA; med. res. review bd. VA, NIH; vis. prof. num. univs.; cons. in field; mem. Am. Cardiovasc. Splty. Cert. Bd. 1970-78; awards: Phi Beta Kappa, Alpha Omega Alpha, res. award Am. Therapeutic Soc. 1965, outstanding prof. UC Davis Med. Sch. 1972, Theodore and Susan B. Cummings Humanitarian award US State Dept./Am. Coll. Cardiol. (1972, 73, 75, 78), Skylab achiev. NASA 1974, merit World Cong. Vascular Diseases 1976, UC Faculty research award 1978, Recogn. for service to internat. cardiol. Am. Coll. Cardiol. 1978, Tex. Heart Inst. award 1979, disting. alumnus Duke Univ. Med. Sch. 1979, sci. citation Inst. Sci. Info. 1980, World Congress on Coronary Heart Disease award 1984; Fellow: Am. Coll. Cardiol. (pres. 1977-78), Am. Coll. Phys., Am. Heart Assn., Am. Coll. Chest Phys., Royal Soc. Med.; mem: Am. Soc. Clin. Investigation, Am. Physiol. Soc., Am. Soc. Pharmacol. and Exptl. Therapeutics (exptl. ther. award 1973), Am. Fedn. Clin. Res., NY Acad Scis., Am. Assn. Univ. Cardiols., Am. Soc. Clin. Pharmacol. and Therapeutics, We. Assn. Phys., AAUP, Western Soc. Clin. Res. (past pres.), El Macero CC; author: Cardiovascular Management (1974), Congestive Heart Failure (1976), Advances in Heart Disease (Vol. 1 1977, Vol. 2 1978, Vol. 3 1980), Cardiovascular Emergencies (1978), Clinical Methods in Study of Cholesterol Metabolism (1979), Principles of Noninvasive Cardiac Imaging (1980), Clinical Nuclear Cardiology (1981), Myocardial Revascularization (1981), Love Your Heart (1982), Cardiology (yearly 1981–), numerous articles, assoc. editor Clinical Cardiology; ed.-in-chief Am. Heart Jour., mem. editl. bds. sci. jours.; Republican; Methodist. Res: 44725 Country Club Dr El Macero 95618 Ofc: Western Heart Institute, St. Mary's Medical Center 450 Stanyan St San Francisco 94117

MASON, DOUGLAS ALAN, history professor; b. Sept. 10, 1945, Ventura; s. George Lamay and Barbara (Reed) M.; m. Susanne Beth Willard, Jan. 24, 1976; children: Julie b. 1979, Paul b. 1981; edn: BA, 1967, MA, 1968, UC Santa Barbara 1968; MLIS, UCLA 1974. Career: librarian Orange Coast Coll., Costa Mesa 1974-81, prof. history 1981–; mem: Orgn. Am. Historians, Univ. United Methodist Church; mil: sgt. USAF 1969-72; Democrat, Methodist; rec: camping, hiking, gardening. Ofc: Orange Coast College 2701 Fairview Rd Costa Mesa 92628

MASON, HAROLD FREDERICK, retired research chemist; b. Feb. 15, 1925, Porterville; s. Arthur Charles and Mary (McConchie) M.; m. Marian Elizabeth Caldwell, Jan. 30, 1954; children: Charles b. 1955, Richard b. 1956, Catharine b. 1964; edn: BSChE, Cornell Univ. 1950; PhD, Univ. Wis. 1954. Career: chemical engr. Rohm & Haas, Bristol, Pa. 1950-51; research chemist Chevron Research Co., Richmond 1954-61, res. supr. 1961-67, res. mgr. 1967-86; mem: Am. Chem. Soc., Am. Inst. Chem. Engrs., St. Anselms Episcopal Ch. (sr. warden 1976-77, 1991-92); patents for petroleum processing and catalysis; mil: 2d. lt. USAAF 1943-46; Republican; Episcopalian; rec: photog., astronomy, botany. Res: 553 Monarch Ridge Dr Walnut Creek 94596

MASON, JEFFREY LYNN, lawyer; b. Nov. 1, 1944, Philadelphia, Pa.; s. Herbert Lester and Phyllis Louise (Reader) M.; m. Michele Meyer, Aug. 12, 1967 (div. 1989); m. 2d. Kathryn Eileen Karcher, Aug. 26, 1989; children: Jeffrey b. 1970, Meredith b. 1977, Lauren b. 1991, Kendall b. 1994; edn: BA, Stanford Univ. 1966; JD, Stanford Univ. Sch. Law 1969; admitted State Bar Calif. 1970, U.S. Court Mil. Appeals 1970, U.S. Supreme Court 1973. Career: assoc. staff, legal counsel Stanford Univ. 1969-70; assoc. Seltzer Caplan Wilkins & McMahon, San Diego 1974-77, ptnr. 1977-91, v.p. bd. dirs. 1977-91, of counsel 1992-93; Law Office of Jeffrey L. Mason, San Diego 1993–; adj. prof. Univ. San Diego Sch. Law 1979-81; awards: U.S. Jaycees Outstanding Young Man Am. 1977; mem: Am. Bar Assn., San Diego Co. Bar Assn., Francis W. Parker Sch. (bd. dirs. 1978-87, v.p. 1981-82, pres. 1982-85), Sigma Alpha Epsilon; mil: capt. AUS Judge Advocate Gen. Corps 1970-74, USAR 1974-77. Ofc: Law Office of Jeffrey L. Mason 550 West C St Ste 1350 San Diego 92101

MASSEY, GAIL AUSTIN, professor of electrical engineering; b. Dec. 2, 1936, El Paso, Tx.; s. Albert Harley and Mary Frances (Edmondson) M.; m. Barbara Suzanne Koch, July 2, 1960; edn: BS, Calif. Inst. Tech. 1959; MS, Stanford Univ. 1967; PhD, 1970. Career: engr. Raytheon Co., Santa Barbara 1959-63; sr. engr. GTE Sylvania, Mountain View 1963-72; assoc. prof. Oreg. Grad. Inst., Portland 1972-74, prof. 1974-80; San Diego State Univ. 1981–; cons., San Diego 1981–; mem: IEEE (sr.), Optical Soc. Am. (fellow), Soc. Photo-Optical Instrumentation Engrs.; 60 articles pub. in tech. jours., 1965–. Ofc: San Diego State Univ. Electrical Engineering Dept. San Diego 92182-1309

MASSIE, BARRY MICHAEL, physician; b. May 23, 1944, St. Louis, Mo.; s. Edward and Felice (Ozerovich) M.; m. Ellen Sue Weisberg, May 29, 1970; children: Jennifer b. 1977, Rebecca b. 1981; edn: BA, biochem., Harvard Coll. 1966; MD, Columbia Univ. 1970; lic. physician St. of NY 1971, Calif. 1975; cert. in medicine Nat. Bd. of Med. Examiners 1971, cert. in internal medicine Am. Bd. of Internal Medicine 1974, cardiovascular disease 1978. Career: internship in internal medicine Bellevue Hosp.-NY Univ. Med. Ctr. 1970-71, residency 1971-73, asst. in medicine 1972-74; chief resident 1973-74; fellow in clin. cardiology Univ. of Calif. Med. Ctr., San Francisco 1975-76; res. fellow in cardiology Cardiovascular Res. Ins., UC San Francisco 1976-78, assoc. staff 1982–; dir. cardiology clinics UC Med. Ctr., S.F. 1977-78; dir. hypertension clinic Veterans Adminstrn. Med. Ctr., S.F. 1978–, dir. coronary care clinic 1978–; instr. in medicine in residence UC San Francisco 1977-78, asst. prof. of medicine in residence 1978-83, assoc. prof. of medicine in residence 1983-89; vis. prof. Univ. of Oxford and hon. cons. John Radcliffe Hosp., Oxford, England 1985-86; prof. of medicine in residence UC San Francisco 1989–; editl. bds: Jour. of Am. Coll. of Cardiology, Jour. of Cardiac Failure, Heart Failure (sect. ed.), Index and Reviews in Congestive Heart Failure, Advances in Therapy; jour. referee: New England Jour. of Medicine, Annals of Internal Medicine, Jour. of Clin. Investigation, Circulation Res., Circulation, Jour. of Am. Coll. of Cardiology, Am. Jour. of Cardiology, Am. Heart Jour., Euro. Jour. of Cardiology, Chest, Internat. Jour. of Cardiology, Jour. of Cardiovascular Pharmacology, Cardiovascular Drugs and Therapy, Hypertension, Am. Jour. of Hypertension, Jour. of Hypertension, Jour. of Applied Physiology, Magnetic Resonance in Medicine, Radiology, Archives of Internal Medicine, We. Jour. of Medicine; mem. intensive care unit com. VA Hosp. 1979–, R&D com. VA Med. Ctr. 1990–; num. ad hoc coms. UCSF 1983–; chair, cardiology tng. prog. review com. UCSF 1987–; peer review res. com. Am. Heart Assn. Calif. Affiliate 1982–; abstract reviewer Am. Soc. for Hypertension 1991–; ad hoc study sect. reviewer, NHLBI 1990–; data safety and monitoring bd. PRAISE Trial 1991–; U.S. prin. investigator ATLAS Trial 1992–; cardiorenal advy. panel Food and Drug Adminstrn. 1992–; honors: Nat. Merit Scholarship 1962-66, Harvard Hon. Nat. Scholarship 1963-65, Alpha Omega Alpha 1969, VA Clin. Investigator award 1980-83, We. Soc. for Clin. Investigation 1981, We. Assn. of Physicians 1993; res. grantee: VA Merit Review 1980-82, 84-87, 87-90, 90-95, 93-97, NHLBI 1982-87, 86-91, 89-93, Calif. Heart Assn. 1983-85, 85-87, 88-90, 90-92, VA 1987-88, VA Cooperative Study 1986-90, 89-94; mem: Am. Coll. of Cardiology (fellow, abstract reviewer 1986–), Am. Heart Assn. (fellow, mem. council on clin. cardiology, council for high blood pressure res., abstract reviewer 1986–), Am. Fedn. for Clin. Res., We. Soc. for Clin. Investigation, We. Assn. of Physicians, Soc. of Magnetic Resonance in Medicine; contbg. author: 30 book chpts. 1977-93, num. jour. articles 1973–; author: 200+ pub. manuscripts; rec: travel. Ofc: VA Hospital (111C) 4150 Clement St San Francisco 94121

MASSIE, HENRY NORTON, physician, child and adult psychiatrist; b. June 28, 1941, St. Louis, Mo.; s. Edward and Felice (Ozerovich) M.; m. Bridget Connelly, April 20, 1941; 1 dau., Kathryn b. 1981; edn: BA, Harvard Coll. 1963; MD, Wash. Univ. Sch. Medicine St. Louis 1967. Career: assoc. clin. prof. psychiatry UCSF Sch. Medicine; fmr. dir. child psychiatry residency tng. St. Marys Hosp., San Francisco; awards: Am. Acad. Psychoanalysis Esther Haar award (1988); mem: Am. Acad. Child & Adolescent Psychiatry (fellow), Am. Psychiatric Assn., E. Bay French Am. Sch. (bd. trustees 1988); author Childhood Psychosis in First Four Years of Life, 1984, 20+ articles pub. in sci. jours.; rec: writing, hiking. Address: Berkeley 94705

MASSIER, PAUL FERDINAND, engineer; b. July 22, 1923, Pocatello, Idaho; s. John and Kathryn (Arki) M.; m. Miriam Parks, May 1, 1948 (dec. 1975); children: Marilyn b. 1951, Paulette b. 1953; m. 2d Dorothy Hedlund Wright, Sept. 12, 1978; edn: mech. engrg. cert., Univ. Idaho So. Branch (now Idaho State Univ.) 1943; BSME honors, Univ. Colo. 1948; MSME, M.I.T. 1949. Career: engr. Pan Am. Refining Corp. Texas City, Tex. 1948; design engr. Maytag Co. Newton, Iowa 1949-50; research engr. Boeing Co. Seattle, Wash. 1950-55; sr. res. engr. Jet Propulsion Lab. CalTech Pasadena 1955-58, group supr. 1958-82, exec. asst. 1982-83, task mgr. 1983-86, mem. technical staff 1986-94; honors: Sigma Xi, Tau Beta Pi, Pi Tau Sigma, Sigma Tau, Professional Achiev. Award Idaho State Univ. 1991, Life Mem. Svc. Award PTA of Calif. 1970, NASA-Apollo Achievement Award 1969 and Basic Noise Research Award 1980, AIAA Sustained Svc. Award 1980-81, Arcadia Congregational Ch. Layman of Year 1971; mem: Am. Inst. Aero. and Astro. (Assoc. Fellow, mem. coms.), Planetary Soc., Am. Biog. Res. Assn. (life fellow), Internat. Biog.Assn. (fellow), Family Genealogy and Hist.; publs: num. articles in tech. jours., reviewer 7 tech. jours.; mem. plnng. coms./session chmn. for num. tech. confs.; mil: T/4 US Army 1943-46, Good Conduct, Unit Citn.; Congregational; rec: presentation motion picture travelogs, antiques, collectibles. Res: 1000 N First Ave Arcadia 91006

MASSOLETTI, DEXTER JAMES, scientist; b. Feb. 8, 1941, San Francisco; s. James Michael and Stella; children: Jessica b. 1982, Dexter b. 1986; Career: ops. supr. Magnetic Fusion Energy group Lawrence Berkeley Lab., Berkeley 1975-83, sr. scientific assoc. Lawrence Livermore Nat. Lab., Livermore 1983-89; Scientific/Engring. Assoc. Adv. Light Source Lawrence Berkeley Laboratory, Berkeley 1989–; mem: Am. Physical Soc., AAAS, ISA; AUS 1963-65. Res: 1126 6th Ave Oakland 94606 Ofc: Lawrence Berkeley Laboratory, One Cyclotron Rd. MS 80-101, Berkeley 94720

MASTERS, MARGARET LEE, pediatrician; b. Dec. 3, 1924, Canton, China, naturalized 1950; d. Shau Yan and Wah (Ying) Lee; m. Joseph Henry Masters, Aug. 25, 1947; children: Margo Dianne b. 1952 (dec. 1988), David Joseph b. 1954, Katherine Mildred b. 1958; edn: AA, William & Mary Coll., 1945; MD, Virginia Commonwealth Univ., 1950; MPH, maternal and child hlth., UC Berkeley, 1977; cert. Am. Bd. Pediatrics 1964. Career: staff pediatrician Childrens Hosp., San Francisco 1951-54; chief pediatrics dept. 98th Gen. Hosp., US Army, Germany 1954-57; pvt. practice pediatrics, Sacramento 1959–, and ped. cons. Sacto. City and County pub. health pgms., sch. health pgms., Children's Home and City Sch Dist. spl. edn. pgms., 1960-78; asst. clin. prof. peds. UC Davis, Davis and Sacto. campuses, 1971-75; honors: physician recogn. award AMA, CMA, CME 1969-95; mem. AMA, Calif. Med. Assn. 1963-95, Sacto-Eldorado Med. Soc. 1963-95, Sacto. Co. Med. Soc., No. Calif. Chpt. Acad. of Pediatrics; active civic groups and local health coms. Sacto.; Republican; Baptist. Address: 3937 Orangewood Dr Fair Oaks 95628

MATARE, HERBERT FRANZ, physicist; b. Sept. 22, 1912, Aachen, W. Germany, nat. 1967; s. Joseph Peter and Paula (Broicher) M.; m. Ursula Krenzien, Dec. 2, 1939; children: Felicitas b. 1944, Vitus b. 1955; m. Dr. Elisabeth Walbert, 1980; child, Victor b. 1983; edn: BS (Abitur) Realgymnasium Aachen/Univ. Geneva 1933; MS (Dipl.Ing.) in physics, Univ. Aachen 1939; PhD (Dr.Ing.) electronics, Univ. of Berlin 1942; PhD solid state physics, Univ. Paris 1950. Career: head Microwave Lab., Telefunken, Berlin, W.Ger. 1939-45; dir. Semiconductor Lab., Westinghouse, Paris, Fr. 1946-52; founder/pres. Intermetall Inc., Dusseldorf, W.Ger. 1952-56; head Semiconductor R&D, Gen. Tel. & Electronics Co., NY 1956-59; dir. of res. TEKADE, Semiconductor Dept. Nuernberg, W.Ger. 1959-61; hd. Quantum Electronics Dept. The Bendix Corp.Res. Labs., Southfield, Mich. 1961-63; tech. dir./mgr. Lear-Siegler Res. Labs. Santa Monica, Ca. 1963-64; asst. chief engr. Douglas Aircraft Co., Santa Monica 1964-66; sci. adv. Rockwell Internat. Anaheim 1966-69; pres. ISSEC (Internat. Solid State Electronics Consultants) 1970–; asst. prof. Univ. Aachen, W.Ger. 1936-45; prof. Univ. Buenos Aires, 1953-54; vis. prof. UCLA 1968-69; vis. prof. CSUF 1969-70, dir. Compound Crystal, Ltd., London, England 1985–; mem: Life Fellow IEEE, NY 1976–; Conf. chmn. internat. meetings: Electrochemical Soc., Chgo. 1955; New York (1958, 1969) Internat. Solid State Conf., Brussels 1959; cons. for UNIDO (United Nations Indsl. Devel. Organization) to Indian Semicond. Industry, 1978; mem. emeritus NY Acad. of Sci.; hon. mem. Inst. for the Advancement of Man; mem: Am. Physical Soc. (Solid State Div.), Electrochem. Soc., Thin Film Div. Am. Vacuum Soc., AAAS, Materials Res. Soc., IEEE- Lasers and Electro-Optics Soc., Nuclear and Plasma Scis. Soc., Power Engring. Soc.; author 5 books: Microwave Receiver Technology (Oldenbourg 1951), Defect Electronics in Semiconductors (Wiley - Interscience 1971), Conscientious Evolution (Carlton Press 1982), Energy: Facts and Future (CRC Press 1988); co-author: Renewable Energy (VDI-Verlag with P. Faber 1994); contbr. 100+ papers to sci. journals; approx. 60 patents incl. First transistor patents from 1948 (Westinghouse, Paris), Semicondr. diode mixer theory and tech., 1st vacuum growth of silicon monocrystals and patent on levitation (1952), growth and study of bicrystals (1955-60), first low temp. transistor (1958, GTE), devel. optical heterodyning with bicrystals (1963), 1st crystal-to-crystal optical comm. link (1961), crystal tv- transmission link (1963), unipolar tunnel transistor (1965), first light potentiometer patent (1965), LPE for LED's (1975), 1st batch process for LPE of III-

V-compounds for solar cells (1975); author: review article pub. Jour. Applied Physics, 1984; rec: astronomy, biology. Address: PO Box 2661 Malibu 90265 and PF. Thomas Str. 8, 41836 Hueckelhoven Germany.

MATHES, STEPHEN JOHN, plastic surgeon, medical educator; b. Aug. 17, 1943, New Orleans, La.; s. John Ernest and Norma (Deutsch) M.; m. Jennifer, Nov. 26, 1966; children: David b. 1970, Brian b. 1972, Edward b. 1974; edn: BS, La. State Univ., 1964, MD, 1968. Career: gen. surgery fellow, 1975, plastic surg. fellow, 1977, Emory Univ.; asst. prof. dept. surg., div. plastic surg. Washington Univ., St. Louis, Mo. 1977-78; dir. Hartford Burn Unit, Barns Hosp., St. Louis 1977-78; dir. microvascular serv. Washington Univ. Sch. Med., St. Louis 1977-78; assoc. prof. surg. 1978-83, prof. surg. 1983-84, Div. Plastic Surg., Univ. UC San Francisco; prof. surg. and hd. sect. plastic surg. Univ. Mich., Ann Arbor 1984-85; prof. surg. and hd. div. plastic & reconstrv. surg. Univ. Calif. Sch. of Medicine, S.F. 1985–, prof. growth and devel., Univ. Calif. Sch. of Dentistry, S.F. 1985–; mem. Ethicon Plastic Surgery Advy. Panel; editorial bds. Jour. of Microsurgery 1984–, Contemporary Surgery 1985–, Perspectives in Plastic Surgery 1987, J. of Plastic and Reconstrv. Surg. 1991–; awards: James Barrett Brown Prize for best paper 1982, AMWA best medical book award 1983, 1st prize Plastic Surg. Ednl. Found., Basic Science (1981, 83, 84, 86), Assoc. vis. prof. 1990 for U.S. sponsored by Plastic Surg. Ednl. Found. 1990; mem: Am. Assn. Plastic Surgeons, Am. Soc. Plastic Surgeons, Am. Coll. of Surgeons, Am. Cleft Palate Assn., Am. Trauma Soc., Calif. Soc. Plastic Surgery, Plastic Surgery Research Council (pres. 1987-88), Soc. Univ. Surgeons, Soc. Head and Neck Surgeons, Soc. Surgery of the Hand, Am. Surgical Assn., Pacific Coast Surg. Assn.; author: Clinical Atlas of Muscle & Musculocutaneous Flaps (C.V. Mosby, 1979), Clinical Applications for Muscle and Musculocutaneous Flaps (C.V. Mosby 1982), Plastic Surgery: Principles and Practice (C.V. Mosby 1990); mil: major Ft. Polk Army Hosp. 1970-72; Republican; Episcopal; rec: tennis, gardening. Res: 30 Trophy Ct Hillsborough 94010 Ofc: Div. of Plastic Surgery Univ. of Calif. Ste 509, 350 Parnassus St San Francisco 94143

MATHEWS, BARBARA EDITH, physician-gynecologist; b. Oct. 5, 1946, Santa Barbara; d. Joseph Chesley and Pearl Lula (Cieri) Mathews; m. Michael Joseph Zirolli, July 5, 1980; edn: AB, UC Santa Barbara, 1969; MD, Tufts Univ. Sch. Med., 1972; Diplomate Am. Bd. Obstetrics & Gynecology. Career: intern Cottage Hosp. and County Hosp., Santa Barbara 1972-73; resident Beth Israel Hosp., Boston 1973-77; clin. fellow Harvard Med. Sch., 1973-76, instr. 1976-77; gynecologist Sansum Med. Clinic, Santa Barbara 1977–; mem. contg. edn. advy. council Santa Barbara Comm. Coll.; bd. dirs. Memorial Rehabilitation Found., S.B., Music Acad. of the West, S.B.; honors: Phi Beta Kappa; Fellow A.C.S., Fellow Am. Coll. Obstets. & Gynecols., mem. AMA, Am. Soc. for Colposcopy & Cervical Pathology (bd. 1982-84), Harvard Univ. Med. Sch. Alumni Assn., Tri-Counties Ob-Gyn Soc. (pres. 1981-82); clubs: Birnam Wood Golf, Channel City (bd.); author (w. L.Burke) Colposcopy in Clinical Practice, 1977, contbg. author Manual of Ambulatory Surgery, 1982. Res: 2105 Anacapa St Santa Barbara 93105 Ofc: Sansum Medical Clinic 317 W Pueblo St Santa Barbara 93105

MATIN, ABDUL, microbiology educator, consultant; b. May 8, 1941 Delhi, India, nat. 1983; s. Mohammed and Zohra (Begum) Said; m. Mimi Keyhan, June 21, 1968; edn: BS, Univ. Karachi, Pakistan, 1960, MS, 1962; PhD, UCLA, 1969; career: lectr., St. Joseph's Coll., Karachi 1962-64; res. assoc., UCLA 1964-71; sci. officer Univ. Groningen, Kerklaan, The Netherlands 1971-75; from asst. to full prof. microbiology and immunology Stanford Univ., Calif. 1975–; prof. WE. Hazardous Substances Research Ctr., Stanford Univ.; cons. Engenics 1982-84, Monsanto 1984–; chmn. Stanford Recombinant DNA panel; lectr. ASM Found.; DOE Panel for Yucca Mountain Microbial Activity; convener of microbiological workshop and confs.; mem, editorial bd. Jour. of Bacteriology; Ann. Rev. Microbiology, Rev. of NSF and other Grants; awards: Fellow Fulbright Found. 1964, NSF 1981–, Ctr. for Biotech. Res. 1981-85, EPA 1981-84, NIH Coll. Biotech., UN. Tokten 1987; mem: AAAS, AAUP, Am. Soc. for Microbiology (found. lectr. 1991-92), Soc. Gen. Microbiology, Soc. Indsl. Microbiology, No. Soc. Indsl. Microbiology (bd. dirs.), Biophysics Soc.; author: contbr. numerous publs. to sci. jours.; rec: reading, music, walking. Res: 690 Coronado Ave Palo Alto 94305-1039. Ofc: Stanford Univ./Dept. of Microbiology & Immunology Fairchild Sci. Bldg. D317 Stanford 94305-5402

MATIS, HOWARD S., physicist; b. Sept. 19, 1948, New York; s. Irving and Bea (Lieberman) M.; m. Mary Smith, Jan. 15, 1977; children: Kenneth b.1978, Justin b. 1980; edn: BS, Rensselaer Polytech. Inst., Troy, N.Y. 1970; MS, Univ. Chgo. 1971; PhD, 1976. Career: research asst. Univ. Chgo., Ill. 1976-78; post-doctoral fellow Los Alamos, N.M. 1978-81, staff 1981-83; staff physicist Lawrence Berkeley Lab., Berkeley 1983–; mem: Am. Physical Soc., AAAS; 100+ articles pub. in tech. jours. Ofc: MS 70A-3307 Lawrence Berkeley Laboratory Berkeley 94720

MATLEY, BEN GILBERT, mathematics professor; b. Sept. 8, 1930, Monroe, La.; s. Welcome Gilbert and Lucette Marie (Renaud) M.; m. Patricia Jean McWilliams, June 21, 1959; children: Elizabeth b. 1960, Katherine b. 1962, John b. 1963, Stephen b. 1964, Richard b. 1971, David b. 1973; edn: BA, San Diego St. Coll. 1960; cert. UCLA Ext. 1964; MBA, USC 1964; EdD, Nova

Univ. 1980; cert. data processor Inst. Cert. of Computing Profls. 1965. Career: mathematician Ryan Aero. Co., San Diego 1956-59; computer engr. Autonetics (div. R.I.), Anaheim 1960-62, software quality engr. Collins (div. R.I.), Newport Beach 1962-64; computer systems engr. Nortronis (div. Northrop), Hawthorne 1965-69; prof. data processing and mathematics Ventura Coll. 1970–; lectr. info. systems West Coast Univ., L.A. 1982–; cons., Ventura 1985–; reviewer profl. computer jours. and conf. papers; honors: IEEE Computer Soc. Disting. Visitor 1988; mem: IEEE (Computer Soc., com. on pub. policy 1987), Assn. Computing Machinery, Data Processing Mgmt. Assn., Computer Profls. for Social Responsibilty, BSA Ventura County Council (computer merit badge examiner 1978-82); sr. author: Nat. Computer Policies, 1987, computer conf. papers pub., 1984-89, articles pub. in profl. jours., 1964; mil: lt.j.g. USNR 1953-55; rec: writing, public speaking. Ofc: Ventura College 4667 Telegraph Rd Ventura 93003

MATOSSIAN, JESSE NERSES, scientist; b. Feb. 3, 1952, Los Angeles; s. Hagop Sarkis and Alice Elizabeth (Barsoomian) M.; edn: BS Physics, USC, 1975; MS and PhD Physics, Stevens Inst. of Tech., 1983; career: Hughes Research Labs., Malibu 1983–, mem. tech. staff Plasma Physics Laboratory 1983-91, sr. mem. tech. staff/senior research staff physicist, 1992–; awards: Hughes Res. Labs. "Superior Performance Award" nominee 1985 and recipient 1992, Highes Res. Labs. "Sector Patent Award" recipient 1993, recipient 34 division invention awards Hughes Res. Labs., recipient 6 issued patents, 9 patents pending; listed Amer. Men and Women of Sci. (17th, 18th, 19th ed.); mem: Am. Physical Soc. (life), Am. Inst. Aero. and Astro., IEEE, MRS, ASM, N.Y. Acad. Scis., Sigma Xi, patron mem. L.A. Cty Mus. of Art, sustaining mem/graphic arts council/L.A. Cty Mus. of Art; reviewer Jour. of Propulsion and Power, IEEE Trans. on Electron Devices; rec: art hist., collector 19th and 20th century European paintings, 16th century engravings, classical music, travel. Ofc: Hughes Research Labs. 3011 Malibu Cyn Rd Malibu 90265

MATSUI, ROBERT TAKEO, congressman; b. Sept. 17, 1941, Sacramento; s. Yasuji and Alice (Nagata) M.; m. Doris Kazue Okada, Sept. 17, 1966; 1 son, Brian Robert; edn: AB, poli. sci., UC Berkeley 1963; JD, Hastings Coll. Law, UC San Francisco 1966; admitted to bar Calif. 1967. Career: practices law, Sacramento 1967-78; mem. Sacramento. City Council 1971-78, vice mayor 1977; mem. 96th-104th Congresses from 3rd Calif. dist. 1979–; mem. budget com. 96-102nd Congresses from 3rd. Calif. dist.; mem. ways and means com. 96th-103rd Congresses from 5th Calif. dist. 1979–; chmn. bus. forum Dem. Congl. Campaign Com.; congl. liaison nat. fin. council, Dem. Nat. Com.; mem. advy. council on fiscal policy Am. Enterprise Inst.; awards: named Young Man of Yr. Jr. C.of C. 1973, recipient Disting. Svc. Award 1973; mem: Sacramento Japanese Am. Citizens League (pres. 1969), Sacto. Metropolitan C.of C. (dir. 1976), Sacto. Rotary, 20-30 Club Sacto. (pres. 1972); Democrat. Ofc: US House of Reps 2311 Rayburn House Office Bldg Washington DC 20515-0505*

MATSUNAGA, GEOFFREY DEAN, lawyer; b. Sept. 30, 1949, Los Angeles; s. Hideo Arthur and Yuri (Yamazaki) M.; m. Masako Inoue, Aug. 20, 1981; children: Ayako, Hideko, Lisa; edn: BS, USAF Acad., Colo. 1971; MBA, UCLA, 1972; JD, UC Berkeley, 1982; admitted bar: Calif. 1982, N.Y. 1983. Career: atty. Milbank, Tweed, Hadley, & McCloy, N.Y. 1982-84, Tokyo, Japan 1984-87; atty. Sidley & Austin, Tokyo, Japan 1987-88, Los Angeles 1988-91; atty. Sheppard, Mullin, Richter, & Hampton, Los Angeles 1991-94; atty. Kagei Briggs & Matsunaga, Los Angeles 1994-; mem: L.A. County Bar Assn., Japan Business Assn. of So. Calif., Japan Am. Soc. of So. Calif.; mil: lt. USN 1972-78. Ofc: Kagei Briggs & Matsunaga 879 West 190th St Los Angeles 90248

MATTESON, BYRON ROGER, city official, business executive; b. Jan. 7, 1937, Hartford, Wis.; s. Floyd B. and Martha (Boettcher) M.; children: Tamara b. 1962, Mark b. 1963; edn: AA, San Bernardino Valley Coll., 1957; CSU San Bernardino, 2 yrs. Career: founder/pres. Allstate Business Forms, Inc. 1974-89, Allstate Instant Printing, 1976–, Bear Tanning Salon, 1986–; co-founder Inland Community Bank, 1990–; co-founder Little Sister Truck Wash, 1991–; elected councilman (mayor pro tem) Grand Terrace City Council, 1984-87, mayor 1987–, mem. League of Calif. Cities (pres. Inland Div. 1989); named Outstanding Jaycee of Year 1969; mem. Bus. Forms Distbrs. Assn. of So. Calif. (pres. 1982); civic: Grand Terrace C.of C., Colton C.of C., San Bernardino C.of C., Trade Club of the Inland Empire (hd. trader 1984), Kiwanis, B&B Square Dancers, Grand Terrace Sch. Advy. Bd. (past pres.), 20-30 Club (past pres.), Jaycees (past pres.), Grand Terrace Lions Club 1988–, Indian Y-Guides (chief), Rolling Start, Inc. (bd.); Republican; Methodist; rec: hunting, swimming. Res: 12175 Michigan St Grand Terrace 92313 Ofc: Allstate Printing, 250 N La Cadena Colton 92324

MATTESON, WILLIAM ROBERT, real estate executive; b. July 14, 1922, Kellhier, Minn.; s. Charles James and Maude Jesse (Jones) M.; m. Dolores Elaine; children: Robert b. 1952, Lorraine b. 1962; edn: BS, Bryant & Stratton Coll. 1948; PhD in bus. mgmt., Internat. Coll. 1982; Calif. lic: Road Builder, Gen. Contractor, Real Estate Broker. Career: past pres. Title Realty Co.; past chmn. bd. Portafone Corp.; past chmn. bd. S.U.S. Enterprises., Diversified Financial Corp.; current: chmn. bd. Palm Springs Studios & Theme Park, pres. Palm Springs I Love You Realty; pres. Matteson Constrn. Co.; pres. Palm

Springs Devel. Group; bd. dirs. num. mutual funds, and other corps.; author, lectr. var. colls. statewide; awards: Mexico-US Cultural Exch. Award; mem: Internat. Congress of Shopping Ctr. Developers, Palm Springs Bd. of Realtors, Palm Springs C.of C., Aircraft Owners & Pilots Assn., The Magic Castle; civic: Desert Blind & Handicapped Assn. (bd. chmn.), Angleview Crippled Childrens Hosp. (past bd. dirs.); author, 1st Am. book on Timeshare: The Prepaid Vacation; inventor and devel. of the cordless telephone; mil: US Army 1942-45, ETO, Bronze Star, Purple Heart, Pres. Citation (2); Republican (pres. The Republican Club, So. Calif. co-chmn. the Pres.'s Club, Reagan coord. counsel, 3d Dist. Republican Central Com., pres. Palm Springs Republican Assembly.); Presbyterian; rec: pilot, golf. Ofc: 431 S Palm Canyon Dr Palm Springs 92262

MATTHEWS, JUSTUS, composer, university professor; b. Jan. 13, 1945, Peoria, Ill.; s. Charles Justus and Dorothea (Maurer) M.; m. Barbara Matthews, Aug. 15, 1971; children: David b. 1973, Laura b. 1977; edn: BA, Calif. State Univ., Northridge, 1967; MA, 1968; PhD, SUNY Buffalo, 1971. Career: prof., Calif. State Univ. Long Beach, 1971–; num. awards and honors from Calif. State Univ. Long Beach, various universities and the French Ministry of Culture, Drama - Logue Critics Awards, Robby Awards theater music; creative works: num. compositions for various vocal and instrumental ensembles, one opera, several electronic music compositions; num. sound designs for plays. Res: 245 Harvard Lane Seal Beach 90740 Ofc:CSU Long Beach Univ Music Ctr 1250 Bellflower Blvd Long Beach 90840-7101

MATTHEWS, PHILIP R., lawyer; b. Aug. 27, 1952, San Francisco; s. Richard T. and Marjorie (Dean) M.; m. Dana L. Meier, Aug. 8, 1981; children: Lauren b. 1983, Lyndsey b. 1987; edn: BA, George Washington Univ. 1974; JD, UCSF Hastings Coll. of Law 1977. Career: assoc. atty. Dinkelspiel, Pelavin, et al., San Francisco 1978-80; ptnr. Hancock Rothert et al, San Francisco 1980- (mgmt com. 1989-94, mng. ptnr. S.F. 1992-94); mem: Commonwealth Club, Am. Bar Assn.; Democrat; Episcopalian; rec: sports, genealogy, travel, and outdoors. Ofc: Hancock Rothert et al 4 Embarcadero Center 1000 San Francisco 94111

MATTHEWS, ROBERT LOUIS, community college president (retired); b. June 2, 1930, Tonganoxie, Kans.; s. Mark Hanna, Sr. and Suzie Jane (Brown) M.; m. Ardelle Marie Dunlap, Aug. 26, 1952; children: Mark b. 1953, Brian b. 1957, Scott b. 1962; edn: BS edn., Emporia State Univ., 1952; MA edn., Columbia Univ., 1955; PhD educational leadership/ human behavior, U.S. Internat. Univ., 1971. Career: tchr. San Diego City Sch. Dist. 1955-64, sch. principal 1965-72, dist. dir. of edn. 1972-84; pres. /ECC and Continuing Edn. Centers, San Diego Community Coll. Dist., 1984-94 (ret.); awards: NDEA fellow U.S. Dept. of Edn., WDC 1965, Corant travel award Australian Council of Churches 1971, Rockefeller fellow Rockefeller Found., NYC 1971-72, humanities fellow N.E.H., WDC 1976; mem: Alpha Phi Alpha Frat., S.D. (1951–, past pres., chmn. M.L.King Parade Com. 1984–); civic bds: Southeast Comm. Theatre (1964–, treas.), S.D. Zoological Soc. (edn. com.), Mus. Natural Hist. 1982–, NAACP, S.D. (life), Urban League, S.D. (1965–, pres., Life mem.); author: Black Studies Academic Achievement and the Self Concept of Black Students (1971); mil: cpl. US Army 1952-54; Democrat; Presbyterian; rec: reading, community service, spectator sports. Res: 4931 Dassco Ct San Diego 92102-3717

MATTSON, C. DUDLEY, economist; b. Feb. 11, 1915, Mansfield, Ohio; s. Bernard Gause and Elizabeth Mahala (Dudley) M.; m. Elsie Porter, May 20, 1942; children: Carolbeth b. 1943, Judith b. 1945, Kathleen b. 1946, Christopher b. 1947, Robert b. 1951, Wendy b. 1953, Malcom b. 1953; edn: BS, Hillsdale Coll. 1937; BS forestry, Univ. Mich. 1941; PhD econ., Iowa St. Univ. 1971. Career: forester Mansfield Hardware Lumber, Winnfield, La. 1946-51; regional forester Kirby Lumber Co., Kirbyville, Tx. 1951-60; research forester U.S. Forest Service 1960-61, 1962; asst. prof. Dept. Forestry Wash. St. Univ., Pullman 1965-70; research economist Econ. Research Service U.S. Dept. Agri., Wash. D.C. 1970-74; economist U.S. EPA, Wash. D.C. and Berkeley 1974-81; ret.; mem: Soc. Am. Foresters; 7 articles pub. in profl. jours., 1981; mil: capt. USAAC 1942-45; rec: soaring. Res: 63 Sandy Dr Vallejo 94590

MATUSZAK, ALICE JEAN, educator; b. June 22, 1935, Newark, Ohio; d. James Emery and Elizabeth Hawthorn (Irvine) Boyer; m. Charles A. Matuszak, Aug. 27, 1955; children: Matthew b. 1967, James b. 1969; edn: BS, Ohio St. Univ. 1958; MS, 1959; PhD, Univ. Kans. 1963; reg. pharmacist Ohio 1958, Calif. 1964. Career: apprentice pharmacist Arensberg Pharm., Newark, Ohio 1953-58; research asst. Ohio St. Univ., Columbus 1958, lab. asst. 1958-59; res. asst. Univ. Wis., Madison 1959-60; Univ. Kans., Lawrence 1960-63; asst. prof. Univ. Pacific, Stockton 1963-67, assoc. prof. 1971-78, prof. 1978–; visiting prof. Kobe- Bakuin Univ., Japan 1992; honors: Rho Chi (exec. council 1981-83, 84-85), Sigma Xi, Phi Kappa Phi, tchr. of year UOP Sch. of Pharmacy 1987, Am. Inst. Hist. Pharm. certif. of commendn. 1990, Thomas J. Long Faculty Fellow (1991, 93, 94), Kappa Epsilon Unicorn Award 1993, Ohio St. Univ. Distinguished Pharm. Alumna 1994; mem: Am. Chemical Soc., Am. Assn. Coll. Pharmacists (bd. dirs. 1993-95), Am. Pharmaceutical Assn. (chair com. on women's affairs 1988-90, chair sect. on basic pharm. sci. 1990), Acad. Pharm. Res. and Sci. (pres. 1993-94), Am. Inst. Hist. Pharm. (exec. council 1984-88, 90-95, pres.-elect 1995-97), Calif. Pharmacists Assn., Internat. Fedn. Pharmacists; articles pub. in profl. jours., 1968–; Democrat; Episcopalian; rec: collect historical pharm. artifacts. Res: 1130 W Mariposa Ave Stockton 95204 Ofc: Univ. of the Pacific Stockton 95211

MAUNDER, ELWOOD RONDEAU, historian, forest conservationist; b. Apr. 11, 1917, Bottineau, N.Dak.; s. Henry Langham and Florence (Blackmore) M.; m. Margaret Fornell, Sept. 19, 1941 (div. 1971); children: Jean Michele b. 1951, Martha b. 1952, Elizabeth b. 1956; m. Eleanor Arge, Feb. 14, 1973; edn: BA journ. Univ. Minn. 1945; MA hist. Washington Univ., St. Louis, Mo. 1947; London Sch. of Econ., 1947-48. Career: reporter Minneapolis Times, 1939-40; feature writer Mpls. Star Journal, 1940-41; served with US Coast Guard Reserve 1941-45, combat corresp. European /Mediterranean area 1944-45; mem. staff US delegation at Conf. of Fgn. Ministers, London, Eng. 1947-48; dir. pub. relations fgn. missions Methodist Nat. Mission Bd., NY, NY 1948-50, Ohio Area Methodist Ch., Columbus 1950-52; chmn. world svc. com. Hennepin Ave. Meth. Ch., Mpls. 1958-61; exec. director Forest History Soc. 1952-78, hq. Mpls./St. Paul 1952-64, New Haven, Conn. 1964-69, Santa Cruz, Calif. 1969-78, senior historian FHS 1978-79; curator Forest Hist. Collection Yale Univ. 1964-69; editor-in-chief J. of Forest History, 1956-76 (and preceding publs. FHS newsletter, estab. 1956, and quarterly, Forest History); mem. planning com. 6th Am. Forestry Congress 1974-75; oral history interviewer, 1953-78; author, coauthor 28+ books and numerous articles on hist. of forestry, numerous articles based on 200+ interviews with pub. and pvt. conservation leaders; 4 of these interviews collected in book: Voices from the South: Recollections of Four Foresters 1977; awards: grantee Weyerhaeuser Found. 1960-62, 72-75, Nat. Endowment for Humanities 1973-75, 75-77, Louis and Maud Hill Family Found. 1960-62, 69, Simpson Found. 1974-75, Nat. Resources Council Am. 1974-75, Edwin W. and Catherine M. Davis Found. 1974-75; mem: Oral History Assn. (a founder, mem. first exec. council, first editor OHA quarterly newsletter), Am. Hist. Assn., Soc. Am. Archivists, Orgn. Am. Historians, Am. Forestry Assn., Soc. Am. Foresters, Commonwealth Club of Calif., Midcounty Sr. Citizens Ctr., Capitola (dir. 1989-95); clubs: Tennis (Rio Del Mar), Santa Cruz Lawn Bowling (dir. 1990-95); Democrat; Prot.; rec: gardening, internat. peacemaking. Res: 407 Gay Road Aptos 95003

MAXWELL, RAYMOND ROGER, accountant; b. Jan. 7, 1918, Parmer County, Tx.; s. Frederick W. and Hazel Belle (Rogers) M.; m. Jeanne Hollarn, June 16, 1945 (dec. Dec., 1987); children: Donald R., Bruce E., Sabrina G. Spiering Warren Kleinecke; edn: EdB, Western Ill. State Teachers Coll., 1941, MBA in Acctg., Univ. Fla., 1949; postgrad., UCLA 1965-68. Career: asst. to bus. mgr. Western Ill. State Tchrs. Coll., Macomb 1939-41; apprentice acct. Chas. H. Lindfors, CPA, Ft. Lauderdale, Fla. 1946-48; acct./auditor Frederic Dunn-Rankin & Co., CPA, Miami 1948-49; CPA staff Charles Costar, CPA, Miami 1951; resident auditor/CPA prin., Raymond R. Maxwell CPA, Ft. Lauderdale, Fla. 1951-56; supt. public instrn. Broward Co., Fla., 1956-61; staff asst. in fin., North Am. Aviation, Inc., El Segundo, Calif. 1961-65; acctg. prin. Raymond R. Maxwell, CPA, Whittier, Calif. 1968–; part-time res. asst. UCLA, 1965-68, tchg. asst. 1966, 67; tchr. Calif. Polytechnic, 1967, CSU Fullerton, 1989; active precinct election bds., Whittier, L.A. County, 1989; 1st reader First Ch. of Christ Scientist, Whittier 1990-92, exec. bd. 1989, exec. bd. chmn. 1993, participant Bible Explorations 1991-92; mil: 1st lt. USAAF 1942-46; Republican; rec: dancing, swimming. Ofc: 13217 E Whittier Blvd Unit C Whittier 90602

MAY, JOHN LOUIS, investment counselor; b. Oct. 15, 1936, New York; s. John Valentine and Anne (Striano) M.; m. Margaret Smith, Sept. 23, 1939; children John b. 1961, Jacqueline b. 1971; edn: BA, Baruch Sch. N.Y. 1958; MBA, Baruch City Univ. 1960. Career: investment analyst Reynolds & Co., N.Y.C. 1960-74; portfolio mgr., adminstr. Petrolane, Long Beach; 1974-86; investment counsel Alpha Capital Mgmt. 1986–; mem: L.A. Soc. Fin. Analysts, Inst. Chartered Fin. Analysts, Fin. Analysts Fedn., Boys & Girls Clubs of Long Beach (v.p. fin. 1986); Republican; rec: tennis, sailing. Res: 1529 Craig Pl., San Pedro 90732 Ofc: Alpha Capital Management 200 Pine Ave Ste 620 Long Beach 90802

MAY, LEWIS GLOVER, promotions executive; b. Aug. 29, 1943, NY, NY; s. Arthur Glover and Esther Ruth (Boudo) M.; m. Mary Kathleen McKernan, May 9, 1970; son, Dean Glover b. 1976; edn: BA, St. Lawrence Univ., 1965. Career: research coord., asst. nat. advtg. mgr. House of Seagram, NY, NY 1965-72; we. div. mgr. Schenley Industries, NY, NY 1973-78; v.p./gen. mgr. Robert Landau Assocs., NY, NY 1978-79; pres. May & Associates Inc., Los Angeles 1980-86 (sold firm, became HMG West, to Saatchi and Saatchi Comms. Group), pres. The Howard Marlboro Group West (div. Saatchi, PLC, London), NY, NY 1987-89, bd. dirs. The Howard Marlboro Group, worldwide 1988-89; sr. v.p. Francis, Killingbeck, Bain (FKB, USA) West, 1990; sr. v.p. QLM Associates, 1991-92; sr. v.p. Gage Marketing Group 1993; pres. MBA Group 1994–; honors: `Angel' Peninsula Edn. Found., P.V. Estates 1989–; civic: Town Hall of Calif. (exec. bd. 1988–), Internat. Platform Assn. 1990–, P.V. Estates Breakfast Club 1984–; mil: USN 1965-67; Republican; Episcopalian; rec: golf, boating, fishing. Res: 1705 Via Boronada Palos Verdes Estates 90274 Ofc: The MBA Group 3408 Highland Ave Manhattan Beach 90266

MAY, RONALD VARNELLE, county official, archaeologist; b. Oct. 26, 1946, Salt Lake City, Utah; s. Russell and Dorothy (Jensen) M.; m. Dale Ellen Ballou, May 8, 1983; edn: AA, Mesa Coll., 1967; BA, San Diego State Univ., 1970; postgrad. work 1972-75, 85-88, grad. cert. pub. history SDSU, 1988; DOD workshop tng. cert., hist. & archaeol. preserv., 1992. Career: dist. liaison archaeologist Calif. Div. Hwys., San Diego County, 1970-73; supvy. archaeologist SDSU Found., San Diego Co., 1971, 73; indep. archaeol. consultant, 1971–; sr. archaeologist David D. Smith & Assocs., So. Calif., 1972-74; anthropology instr. Mesa Coll., 1976-77; environmental mgmt. splst. County San Diego, 1974–, staff mem. County Historical Site Bd., 1986-90; archaeology advr. City of Oceanside 1990-94, Certified Local Govt. Pgm., 1991; chmn. bd. dirs. Fort Guijarros Mus. Found., San Diego 1981–, editor quarterly jour.; contbr. res. articles on Spanish fortifications, shore-whaling, Calif. Indian pottery, Asian-Am. hist. archaeology to acad. and hist. jours.; awards: Sigma Xi, merit award Inst. History 1982, conservation grantee San Diego Community Found. 1983, Cabrillo award Inst. of History 1985, comm. service Peninsula C.of C. 1987, Mark Raymond Harrington award for conservation archaeology 1987, Knight's Officer, de la Cruz, Order of Civic Merit by King Juan Carlos for promotion of heritage of Spain in Am. announced by Amb. Pedro Temboury, Consul Gen. of Spain at 186th ann. Fiesta of Battle of San Diego Bay (3/19/89), grantee San Diego Co. comm. enhancement 1987, 88, 89, 90, San Diego Cultural Arts Coun. 1990, Cultural Ministry of Spain 1991, Legacy Program Grant ($95,000) for museum devel. 1993; mem: Soc. Am. Archaeology, Soc. Profl. Archaeologists (cert. rev. com. 1990-91), Assn. Conservation Archaeology (reg. coord.), Soc. Hist. Archaeology (mil., urban archaeology groups), San Diego Co. Archaeol. Soc. (pres. 1980-81), Soc. Calif. Archaeology (v.p., ethics chmn., editor 1977-82, special achiev. award 1983, symp. chair `A Visionary Approach to Curation for the 21st Century' 1991), Archaeol. Resource Mgmt. Soc. (treas. 1980-82), Calif. Council for Promotion of History, Save Our Heritage Orgn. (bd. dirs. 1992-94; dir. collections mgmt. 1993-95), San Diego Repository Corp. (bd. dirs.), San Diego Hist. Soc., Nature Conservancy, Greenpeace, San Diego Maritime Soc., E. Clampus Vitus (Clamper of Yr. 1985), SDSU Anthropol. Soc. (pres. 1969, 72), Coun. on Am. Mil. Past; Republican. Ofc: Planning Dept. County of San Diego 5201 Ruffin Rd Ste 5B San Diego 92123

MAYBAY, DUANE CHARLES, recycling systems equipment dealer executive; b. Oct. 5, 1922, Fort Dodge, Iowa; s. Bert and Flo (Hibbard) Lungren; m. Mary Trible Parrish, Dec. 18, 1947 (div. 1972); children: Tina b. 1949, Karen b. 1955; edn: BA, Univ. Wis. 1948. Career: sales engr. Gates Rubber Co., Denver, Colo. 1948-53; asst. sales and mktg. dir. Minute Maid Corp., N.Y.C. 1953-63; pres. Mountain Foods, Los Angeles 1963-75; pres. Resource Recovery Systems 1975–; dir. Shaw Group, Los Angeles 1980-84; Mapletown USA, Tustin 1984-87; mil: lt. col. USAF 1943-45; Republican; rec: antique collecting. Res: 104 Pergola Irvine 92715 Ofc: Resource Recovery Systems POB 17426 Irvine 92713

MAYER, JAMES HOCK, mediator/lawyer; b. Nov. 1, 1935, Neptune City, N.J.; s. J. Kenneth and Marie Ruth (Hock) M.; m. Carol I. Keating, Sept. 20, 1958 (div. 1981); m. Patrisha Renk, March 28, 1981; children: Craig b. 1960, Jeffrey b. 1964; edn: BA w. distinction, Dartmouth Coll. 1957; JD, Harvard Univ. 1964. Career: atty., assoc. Pillsbury Madison & Sutro, San Francisco 1964-72; ptnr. 1973–, San Diego office since 1988; awards: Dartmouth Coll. Rufus Choate scholar 1956-57; mem: Newcomen Soc., Navy League, Naval Order of U.S., Harvard Club S.D., San Diego C.of C.; mil: Rear Admiral USNR 1957–; Presbyterian; rec: decathalon, masters track meets. Res: 1328 Sun Valley Rd Solana Beach 92075-1647 Ofc: 101 W. Broadway Ste 1800, San Diego 92101-8201

MAYER, PATRICIA JAYNE, C.M.A., chief financial officer; b. Apr. 27, 1950, Chgo.; d. Arthur and Ruth J. (Greenberger) Hersh; m. Wm. A. Mayer, Jr. Apr. 30, 1971; edn: BS in acctg., CSU Hayward 1975; passed CPA test 1978; Cert. Management Accountant (CMA) 1992. Career: auditor Elmer Fox, Westheimer CPAs, 1976; supvsg. auditor Alameda County Auditors Office, 1976-78, devel. and wrote new auditing procedures 1976; asst. mgr. Gen. Acctg. Dept., CBS Retail Stores dba Pacific Stereo, 1978-79; controller Oakland Unified Sch. Dist., 1979-84; v.p. finance YMCA of San Francisco 1984–; instr. in-house acctg. seminars; mem. Inst. of Management Accountants, Financial Executives Inst.; civic: Dep. County Registrar of Voters 1971-76, draft counselor Mt. Diablo Peace Ctr. 1971-73; Democrat; rec: Dalmatian dogs. Res: 2395 Lake Meadow Circle Martinez 94553 Ofc: YMCA of San Francisco 44 Montgomery St Ste 770 San Francisco 94104

MAYNARD, WALTER PRESTON, physician; b. Nov. 20, 1946, Macon, Ga.; s. Eugene Demelvin and Rita (Brown) M.; m. Lillian Brack, Dec. 30, 1971; children: Walter b. 1974, Kimberley b. 1977; edn: AB biol., Talladega Coll., 1966; MD, Meharry Med. Coll., 1970; Diplomate Am. Bd. Radiology (1974), Am. Bd. Nuclear Med. (1974). Career: intern UCLA Affil. Hosp., Los Angeles 1970-71; radiology resident Harbor Gen. Hosp., Torrance 1971-72; rad. resident, nuclear medicine fellow M.L. King, Jr. Gen. Hosp., L.A. 1972-74, 74-75; fellow Johns Hopkins, Baltimore 1974; staff radiologist El Monte Community Hosp., 1975-78; radiologist, pres. North Prairie Med. Grp., Inglewood 1978–; CEO Taxco, L.A. 1988–; trustee Univ. of West L.A. Law Sch.; bd. dirs. The Maple Counseling Ctr. of Beverly Hills; bd. of mgmt. Meharry Med. Coll.; awards: nat.

chemical achiev. Am. Chem. Soc. 1964, merit cert. E.M.I. Med. Corp., Northbook, Ill. 1978, Maripose award Compton Unified Sch. Dist. 1984; mem: Charles Drew Med. Soc., Los Angeles Radiological Soc., Nat. Med. Assn., Omega Psi Phi Frat. 1964–, Meharry Med. Coll. Alumni (L.A. chpt. pres. 1984); civic: Boy Scouts Am. (ldr. 1982–), Beverly Hills Little League (bd.); publs: articles in Am. Jour. Radiology, 1975, Am. Jour. Nuclear Med., 1975; mil: lst lt. USAR 1971-72; Democrat; R.Cath.; rec: tennis, sailing. Res: 913 N Beverly Dr Beverly Hills 90210 Ofc: North Prairie Medical Group 125 N Prairie Ave Inglewood 90301

MAYO, BYRON W., advertising agency executive; b. Jan. 14, 1922, Portland, Oreg.; s. Byron Albert and Della Martell (Dewey) M.; m. Mary G. Bovee, Jan. 28, 1950; children: Cathye M. b. 1946, Byron R. b. 1951; edn: BS, Univ. Oreg. Journalism Sch. 1947. Career: v.p., mgmt. supr. Foote Cone & Belding, San Francisco 1957-65; pres., CEO Sea & Ski Corp. 1966-71; pres. FCB Cablevision, Irvine 1971-72; sr. v.p., mgmt. supr. Foote Cone & Belding, L.A. 1973-75; pres. Jennings & Thompson FCB, Phoenix, Ariz. 1976-80; sr. v.p. Foote Cone & Belding, San Francisco 1980–; v.p., dir. Sonoma Valley Visitors Bureau 1988-90; dir. Arts Guid of Sonoma 1987-88; dir. 4A Sun Country Council 1976-80; pres. Assn. Corp. Growth Phoenix 1980-81; awards: Am. Mktg. Assn. Achievement (1968); mem: Am. Assn. Advt. Agencies (dir. western region 1976-80), Sonoma Valley Grape Growers (hon.), USMCR Assn., Reno C.of C. (dir. 1970), Alpha Tau Omega, Sausalito Citizens Council (pres. 1958-59); travel articles pub. on Alaska, 1986-87; mil: capt. (pilot) USMC 1942-45; rec: writing, photog. Res: 880 Oak Ln Sonoma 95476

MAZZA, JEAN MARIE, sales executive; b. Sept. 17, 1947, St. Louis, Mo.; d. Henry E. and Bernice Marie (Juengling) Johns; m. Frank Alexander Mazza, Feb. 14, 1974 (div. 1985); edn: Omaha Univ. 1966-68. Career: customer service rep. Northwestern Bell, Omaha, Neb. 1966-68; adminstrv. asst. JBR Devel., Beverly Hills 1969-72; v.p., co-owner Maverick Fashion, Sylmar 1972-78; sales mgr., co-owner Beck Mktg., Studio City 1978-82; v.p. promo. div. Arrowhead Jewelry, San Rafael 1982-86; nat. sales mgr. Terragrafics Inc., Brisbane 1986–; sales management training & consulting to small/med. mfgrs. and importers (self-employed) 1991–; rec: skiing, hiking, collecting antiques. Res: 241 El Faisan Ave San Rafael 94903 Ofc: P.O. Box 6246 San Rafael 94903

MAZZOLA, ROBERT A., engineer/project manager; b. Oct. 20, 1948, N.Y., N.Y.; s. Vincent and Mildred (Zollo) M.; m. Christine Anne Petersen, Aug. 1, 1987; children: Elizabeth and Christine (twins by prior m.) b. 1975, Robert Vincent b. 1989; edn: BA, Queens Coll., 1972; BS radiology, Long Island Univ., 1975; MBA, Univ. Ariz., 1984; cert. radiology technologist, ARRT. Career: imaging tech. Nassau County Med. Ctr., East Meadow, N.Y. 1973-76; radiologic tech. SUNY at Stony Brook, N.Y. 1976-77; radiology mgr. FHP, Long Beach, Calif. 1977-78; project engr. Pacific Bell, L.A. 1978-81; project engr. GTE Cal, Westminster 1981–; indep. project mgr., cons., 1988–; awards: Queens Coll. varsity sports 1966-72, Long Island Univ. deans list 1973-74, Guttman Scholar 1975; Republican; Christian; rec: ice hockey, bass guitarist. Res: 7251 Elk Circle Apt 2 Huntington Beach 92647 Ofc: GTE Cal 7292 Slater Ave Huntington Beach 92647

MAZZONI, KERRY, state assembly member; b. Jan. 9, 1949, Springfield, Ohio; d. Stanley and Virginia (Huss) Onderdonk; m. Michael Mazzoni, August 15, 1970; children: Casey, b. 1972, Peter b. 1976; edn: BS, child devel., UC Davis 1971. Career: elected Novato Unified Sch. Dist. Bd. Trustees, 1987-91, 91-94; pres. Bd. of Trustees, 1990, 93; elected to the Calif. State Assembly, 6th Dist. 1994–; awards: Marin County Sch. Trustee of Year 1992, North Marin Council PTA Hon. Svc. Award 1986; mem: Am. Assns. of Univ. Women, Soroptimist Internat., Nat. Women's Political Caucus, League of Women Voters, UC Davis Alumni Assn., Surfrider Found., Nat. Orgn. of Women, Sierra Club, Sonoma Co. Conservation Action; civic: chair, Marin County No on Vouchers, Prop. 174 Campaign, mem. Novato Recycling Campaign Advy. Council, Friends of the Novato Youth Ctr., Young Imaginations Advy. Bd.; participant: Human Needs Ctr. Job Forum, State of Calif. hearing on Multi-cultural Edn., ABAG Com. on Interagency Fiscal Interdependency; rep. Novato Unified Sch. Dist. on Novato Police Chief Recruitment Com.; presenter, Novato Leadership Training; Public Edn. Coalition of Marin (past chair), Novato Human Needs Ctr. (past mem. bd. dirs.), Calif. Sch. Bds. Assn. (former del.), 14th Dist. PTA (past v.p.), Marin Co. Sch. Bds. Assn. (pres. 1990-91), Novato Edn. Found. (past mem. advy. bd.). Ofc: State Capitol PO Box 924849 Sacramento 94249-0001

MCALLISTER, JAMES WILLIAM, college president; b. Oct. 29, 1936, Lebanon, Md.; s. John Wesley and Ruby Eunice (Biggs) McA.; m. Helen Lydia Seibold, June 30, 1956; children: Greg b. 1957, Tambra b. 1958, Jennifer b. 1962, Stacia b. 1966; edn: BS, Toledo Bible Coll. 1980; M.Ministry, Trinity Seminary 1981; DM cand., Luther Rice Sem. 1996. Career: pastor New Hope Free Will Baptist Ch., Kansas City, Kans. 1958-62; Central Free Will Baptist Ch., Kansas City, Mo. 1963-69; First Free Will Baptist Ch., Monett, Mo. 1970-74; Farmington, Mo. 1974-86; pres. Calif. Christian Coll., Fresno 1986–; pastor Harmony Free Will Baptist Ch. 1986–, chmn. Nat. Home Mission Bd., Nashville, Tenn. 1972-84; moderator Missouri State Assoc. of FWB 1972-76;

dir. Farmington Christian Acad., Farmington, Md. 1975-86; v.chmn. bd. dirs. Randal House 1984–; author: Points for Pastors & People (1981), num. articles pub. 1976-94, monthly mag. articles pub. 1986–; mil: G-5, USAR 1957-62; Republican; Free Will Baptist; rec: golf. Res: 370 North Orangewood Fresno 93727 Ofc: California Christian College 4881 E University Fresno 93703

MC BEATH, RONALD JAMES, university professor; b. April 15, 1927, Auckland, N.Z.; s. James and Eliza Marion (McLean) McB.; m. Marjorie Nicholson, July 24, 1954; children: Scot b. 1957, Heather b. 1959, Andrew b. 1961, Kathryn b. 1962; edn: B.Ed., Univ. Alberta Canada 1957; MS, USC 1958; PhD, 1961. Career: tchr. Auckland Schools, New Zealand 1946-51, London Schs., England 1951-54; Calgary Schs., Canada 1954-57; lectr. USC, Los Angeles 1958-61; sr. lectr. Auckland Tchrs. Coll., N.Z. 1961-67; dir. Instructional Res. Center, Univ. of Hawaii 1967-69; San Jose St. Univ. 1969–; internat. cons. Faculty Devel. 1972-89; honors: Phi Kappa Phi Disting. Achievement 1987; mem: Internat. Council for Ednl. Media, Assn. Ednl. Comms. & Tech. (internat. div.), Calif. Library Media Educator (v.p. 1982), Morrin C.of C. (secty. 1955-56); ed. CMLEA Jour. (1982-86), cons. ed. Tech. Trends, Educ. Technology, Ednl. Media Internat. (1985-92), author, editor textbooks (1964, 72, 73, 92); rec: coaching rugby. Res: 888 Helena Dr Sunnyvale 94087 Ofc: San Jose State University Instructional Resources Center, San Jose 95192-0026

MCCAFFREY, STANLEY E(UGENE), retired university president; b. Feb. 26, 1917, Taft, Calif.; s. Joseph Cormack and Dorothy (Bunyard) McC.; m. Beth Connolley, July 6, 1941 (div. Jan. 1991); children: Stephen (Prof., McGeorge Sch. of Law, Sacto.), Nancy (dec. 1984); m. Sue Richardson Heapes; edn: AB, Univ. Calif., Berkeley 1938; LLD (hon.) Golden Gate Univ. 1972, Pepperdine Univ. 1978, Korea Univ. 1981. Career: adminstr. Univ. Calif., Berkeley, 13 years: coord. veterans affairs 1946, exec. mgr. Calif. Alumni Assn. 1948-56, univ. v.p. 1956-60; pres. San Francisco Bay Area Council 1961-71; pres. Univ. of the Pacific, Stockton 1971-87, ret.- during 16 yr. tenure expanded physical campus, budget ($22 mil. to $70+ mil.), enrollment (to 6,000), estab. new Sch. of Bus. and Pub. Adminstrn., and new Sch. of Internat. Studies; internat. pres. Rotary Internat., Evanston, Ill. 1981-82 (emphasis "World Understanding and Peace Through Rotary"); awards: recipient numerous honors and decorations from heads of state of countries visited (75+) as Pres. Rotary Intl. 1981-82, UCB student body pres., varsity football and baseball, Phi Beta Kappa 1938, Order of Golden Bear, The Berkeley Citation for contbns. to the univ. 1969, named to Berkeley Fellows (100 outstanding UC alumni); past pres. Assn. of Indep. Calif. Colls. (2x), Western Coll. Assn.; former bd. trustees Peralta Junior Coll. (pres.), Golden Gate Univ., Coll. of Holy Names; mil: US Navy 1940-45, WWII, decorated Silver Star and Legion of Merit for gal. in action and exceptionally meritorious svc. in the China Theatre; clubs: The Family (S.F.), Bohemian (S.F.), St. Francis Yacht (S.F.), Moraga CC; Congregationalist. Res: 557 Augusta Dr Moraga 94556

MCCAIN GONG, GLORIA MARGARET, pharmacist; b. Oct. 12, 1953, Yreka; d. Kenneth Wayne and Patricia Ann (Farley) McCain; m. Peter-Poon Gong, Apr. 3, 1976; children: George Wayne b. 1977, Cynthia May b. 1978, Miranda Lin b. 1979; edn: AA, Bakersfield Coll., 1972; CSU San Diego, 1972-73; PharmD, Univ. of Pacific, 1976. Career: asst. chief pharmacist West Hills Hosp., Canoga Park 1976-78; pharmacist/owner Gong's Rexall Drugs, Tehachapi 1978–; mem. AAUW (local publ. dir.); R.Cath.; rec: organic gardening, gourmet cooking club. Res: 800 Anita Dr Tehachapi 93561 Ofc: Gong's Rexall Drugs, 201 S Green St Tehachapi 93561

MCCALLA, GARY P., physician; b. July 20, 1962, Edmonton, Alberta, Canada; edn: BA, biology (with honors), Univ. of Calif., Santa Cruz 1984; MS, animal physiology, UC Davis 1986; MD, Univ. of So. Calif. Sch. of Medicine 1990; lic. physician, St. of Calif.; Physician Asst. Supervising Cert.; lic. ACLS Instructor, ACLS Provider, ATLS Provider. Career: internship Highland Gen. Hosp., Oakland 1990-91, residency 1991-94; attending physician Emergency Physicians Med. Group, Emergency Rm. Mt. Zion-UCSF Med. Ctr., S.F. 1994–; honors: Crown College Svc. Award, Commencement speaker, UC Santa Cruz 1984, USC Sch. of Medicine: honors in physiology, family and preventative medicine 1981, psychiatry and blood, musculo-skeletal and cardiovascular sys. 1982, med. clerkship 1983, 84; mem: Am. Coll. of Emergency Physicians, AMA, Wilderness Med. Soc., CMA, Phi Delta Epsilon, Salerni Collegium; civic: vol. flight medic East Bay Regional Parks Helicopter Unit; vol. mem.: Alameda Co. Sheriff's Dept. Search and Rescue Team, Westgate Comm. Assn. Emergency Preparedness Com.; author: res. paper pub. in Annals of Emergency Medicine, 1994; rec: cycling, mountain biking, rock climbing, skiing, running, swimming, scuba diving, piano playing. Res: 2 Admiral Drive #285 Emeryville 94608

MC CANDLESS, DAVID MATTHEW, UP product development; b. Aug. 13, 1959, Fairfield, Calif.; s. Frederick Eugene and Margaret Mary (Walsh) McC.; edn: undergrad. Old Dominion Univ., 1978-79, BSCS, Wash. St. Univ., Pullman 1981; MS in comp. sci., Univ. Wis., Madison 1982. Career: systems analyst Chevron Corp., San Francisco 1980; mem. tech. staff Bell Labs., Piscataway, N.J. 1981-83; systems pgmr. Chevron Corp., San Ramon 1983-86; senior tech. staff Oracle Corp., Belmont 1986-88, devel. mgr. 1988-90, devel. dir. 1990-93; engring. mgr. Open Vision, Pleasanton 1993-94; UP Product Devel. ASNA, Big

Bear Lake, Calif. 1994–; instr. UC Berkeley Ext. 1984-94; honors: appt. USAF Acad. 1978, Phi Beta Kappa 1981, Mensa 1979; rec: sports, flying, golf. Res: 712 Bancroft Rd. #514, Walnut Creek 94598

MC CARTHY, ANTHONY JOSEPH, lawyer; b. Feb. 1, 1951, Butte, Mont.; s. John Joseph and Mercedes (Thomas) McCarthy; edn: BS, Santa Clara Univ. 1973; JD, 1976; LLM, N.Y. Univ. 1977. Career: salesman Eli Thomas of San Jose 1973-77; atty. Anthony J. McCarthy 1977-80, McCarthy & Hager 1980–; assoc. prof. Peninsula Law Sch. 1977-78; mem. Santa Clara Co. Estate Planning Council; mem: Am. Bar Assn., Calif. St. Bar Assn., Santa Clara Co. Bar Assn.; Cath.; rec: skiing, bicycling, racquetball. Ofc: McCarthy & Hager Law Corp. 10 Almaden Blvd Ste 550 San Jose 95113

MCCARTHY, JOHN CHARLES, lawyer; b. Nov. 14, 1923, Chgo., Ill.; s. Thomas James and Margaret Mary (Schollmeyer) McC.; m. Lorraine Donovan, Feb. 5, 1960; children: Michael, b. 1961; Mary, b 1962; Sheila, b. 1964; edn: Miami Univ. 1942-44; BSBA, USC, 1947; JD, UCLA, 1952; admitted bar: Calif. 1953. Career: pvt. law practice, Claremont 1954-63; dir. Peace Corps in Thailand, Bangkok 1963-66; ptnr. law firm Young, Henrie & McCarthy, Pomona 1966-75; pres. law firm John C.McCarthy and Associates, Claremont 1975–; spec. trial counsel City of Beverly Hills 1973-80; lectr./ writer for var. legal groups (incl. Calif. State Bar, Assn. of Am. Trial Lawyers, law schs., Consumer Attorneys of Calif., others); honors: UCLA Law Sch. Alumnus of Year 1973, Trial Lawyer of Yr. Calif. Employment Lawyers Assn. 1989, Bar Register of Pre-eminent Lawyers (civil trial, employment), Best Lawyers in Am. (employment, ins.), Diplomate, Am. Bd. of Trial Advocates; mem: Am. Trial Lawyers Assn. (nat. chmn. Environ. Law Sect. 1972-74), Calif. Trial Lawyers Assn. (pres. Inland chpt. 1969); clubs: University (pres. 1969), Bahia Corinthian Yacht (Newport Beach); author: Sucessful Techniques in Handling Bad Faith Cases (book & cassettes, 1973), Recovery of Damages in Bad Faith Cases (5th edit. 1990), Recovery of Damages in Wrongful Discharge Cases (Lawpress Corp., Tiburon 2d edit. 1990), book chpts: "Successful Ins. Bad Faith Trials" in Masters of Trial Practice (Wiley Law Publs., 1988), and "Punitive Damages" in Calif. Torts (Matthew Bender 1985); mil: lt. j.g. USN 1943-46; Democrat; R.Cath.; rec: skiing, sailing, golf. Res: 1920 Indian Hill Blvd Claremont 91711 Ofc: 401 Harvard Ave Claremont 91711

MCCARTHY, LEO TARCISIUS, state lieutenant governor; b. Auckland, N.Z., Aug. 15, 1930; came to U.S. 1934, nat. 1942; s. Daniel and Nora Teresa (Roche) McC.; m. Jacqueline Lee Burke, Dec. 17, 1955; children: Sharon, Conna, Adam, Niall; edn: BS, Univ. of San Francisco 1955; JD, San Francisco Law Sch. 1961; admitted Calif. St. Bar 1963. Career: supr. Bd. of Supr., San Francisco 1964-68; assemblyman Calif. State Legislature, Sacramento 1969-82, assembly speaker 1974-80; lt. gov. State of Calif., Sacramento 1983–; Democratic nominee U.S. Senate 1988; chmn. Econ. Devel. Commn. of Calif. 1983–; chmn. State Lands Commn. 1989–; regent Univ. Calif. 1983–; trustee State Coll. and Univ. System, Calif. 1983–; chmn. Task Force on Nursing Home Care, Calif. 1982–; mem. Dem. State Cen. Com. 1969–; awards: Outstanding Legislator Planning & Conservation League of Calif. 1971, Outstanding Legislator in U.S. Nat. Council Sr. Citizens 1972, Torch of Liberty award B'nai B'rith 1976; mil: USAF 1951-52. Ofc: Office of Lieutenant Governor State Capitol Rm 1114 Sacramento 95814

MC CARTHY, MARY ELLEN, speech pathologist; b. Aug. 26, 1934, Prescott, Ariz.; d. David J. and Elise Louise (Shupp) Dougherty; m. George E. McCarthy, June 22, 1957; children: George Robert b. 1963, Bryan Patrick b. 1965; edn: BA w. hons., UCSB 1957; post grad., Long Beach St. Univ. 1958-60; San Jose St. Univ. 1967; Santa Clara Univ. 1970–. Career: tchr. Anaheim Unified Sch. Dist., Anaheim 1957-58; speech pathologist Garden Grove Schs., Garden Grove 1958-60; San Luis Obispo Co. 1960-64; Morgan Hill Unified Schs., Morgan Hill 1967–; master clinician student tchrs. Morgan Hill Unified 1975–; awards: Calif. Speech Haring Assn. Outstanding Achievement 1988; mem: Santa Clara Co. Speech & Hearing Assn. (pres. 1979-80), Calif. Speech & Hearing Assn. (advy. bd. 1982), Am. Speech & Hearing Assn., Council Exceptional Children, Calif. Assn. Neurologically Handicapped Children, St. Timothys Lutheran Ch. (bd. mem. 1984-88); Lutheran; rec: travel, camping, sewing. Res: 717 Bolivar Dr San Jose 95123-3910

MCCARTHY, MICHAEL PATRICK, physician, educator; b. June 7, 1939, Pittsburgh, Pa.; s. Wm. Charles and Mary G. (Wallace) McC.; m. Alice Kathleen Hau, June 9, 1965; children: Sean b. 1966, Tara b. 1968, Mallary b. 1969, Michael b. 1970, Brendan b. 1976; edn: BA, St. Vincent Coll., 1961; MD, Univ. Pittsburgh, 1965. Career: served to capt. US Navy, med. intern USN, Phila. 1965-66; submarine med. ofcr. 1966-68, resident surgeon in urology USN, San Diego 1968-72, staff urologist Camp Pendleton 1972-77, chmn. of urology residency USN San Diego 1977-88; chief urology VA Med. Center, La Jolla 1988-94 (ret.); assoc. prof., clinical prof. urology UC San Diego 1988-94 (ret.); awards: outstanding tchr. Family Practice Residents, Camp Pendleton (1974, 75, 76), Kaiser Permanente tchg. award UCSD (1989); mem. Am. Coll. Surgeons, Am. Urol. Assn., Soc. of Govt. Service Urol. (pres. 1979-80); club: El Camino CC; Democrat; R.Cath.; rec: sports. Res: 4073 Skyline Rd Carlsbad 92008

MCCARTHY, ROGER LEE, mechanical engineer; edn: BA high distinction, philosophy, Univ. Mich. 1972; BSME summa cum laude, 1972; MSME, MIT 1973; MechE, 1975; PhD, mech. engring., 1977; reg. profl. engr. Calif., Ariz. Career: project engr. machine design and devel. engring. div. Proctor & Gamble Inc., Cincinati 1973-74; program mgr. Spl. Machinery Group Foster Miller Assoc. Inc., Waltham, Mass. 1976-78; prin. design engr. Failure Analysis Assocs., Palo Alto 1978–, pres. 1982-93, CEO 1982–, chmn. bd. 1988-93; awards NSF fellow 1972-75, James B. Angell scholar; mem: Am. Soc. Metals, ASME, Soc. Automotive Engrs., Am. Welding Soc., Am. Soc. Testing & Materials, Human Factors Soc., ASHRAE, Nat. Fire Protection Assn., Phi Beta Kappa, Sigma Xi, President's Com. on the Nat. Medal of Science 1992-94, Army Sci. Bd. (cons. 1994-95); contbr. num. articles to profl. jours. Ofc: Failure Analysis Associates 149 Commonwealth Dr POB 3015 Menlo Park 94025

MC CLAIN, CHARLES JOSEPH, JR., law school administrator, lecturer; b. Oct. 24, 1943, New Orleans, La.; s. Charles Joseph and Loretta (Cahill) McClain; m. Laurene Wu, June 25, 1966; 1 son, Christopher b. 1967; edn: HAB, Xavier Univ. 1964; PhD, Stanford Univ. 1972; JD, UC Hastings Coll. Law 1974; admitted St. Bar Calif. (1974). Career: atty. Am. Assn. Univ. Profs., San Francisco 1974-77; v.chmn., lectr. UC Berkeley Sch. Law 1977–; awards: Hist. Soc. No. Dist. Calif. Ct. Writing award 1984; mem: Am. Arbitration Assn., Am. Hist. Assn., Calif. St. Bar Assn., World Affairs Council No. Calif.; num. articles pub. in profl. jours, author: In Search of Equality: The Chinese Struggle Against Discrimination in 19th Century Am., Asian Am. and the Law. Ofc: Univ. California School of Law Berkeley 94720

MCCLAIN, GEORGETTE, manufacturing company executive, general engineering contractor; b. May 18, 1927, Ventura; d. George W. and Harriet Josephine (Hanawalt) Floyd; m. James Weston McClain, Sept. 3, 1950; children: David b. 1952, Paul b. 1954, Mark b. 1961; edn: BA, Mills Coll. 1949; grad. Sawyer Bus. Coll. 1975; lic. Gen. Engring. Contr., Calif., Nev. (1985). Career: self-empl. piano tchr., Grass Valley 1950-74; office mgr. Gabe Mendez Inc., Newcastle 1976-79, Livingstons Grading & Paving Co., Newcastle 1979-81; pres. A.C. Dike Co., gen. engring. contrs., 1981–; owner Specialty Paving Equipment Co. (mfr. automatic paving equipment) 1981–; mem. Assn. Engring. Constrn. Employers; Republican; Episcopalian. Ofc: A.C. Dike Co., 2788 Venture Dr Lincoln 95648

MC CLANAHAN, CLARENCE, educator; edn: BA, William Paterson Coll. 1973; MA, N.Y. Univ. 1977; MPhil, N.Y. Univ. 1979; PhD, N.Y. Univ. 1981. Career: adj. prof., Calif. colleges, 1980-90; adminstr., Stanford Univ., 1991–; awards: World of Poetry 1986; mem: Modern Language Assn. Am.; author: European Romanticism: Literary Socs. Poets and Poetry, 1990, collection of papers on gay studies, 1995; Democrat. Res: 360 Hyde St #202 San Francisco 94109

MCCLELLAN, CRAIG RENE, lawyer; b. June 28, 1947, Portland, Oreg.; s. Charles Russell and Annette Irene (Benedict) McC.; m. Susan Armistead Nash, June 7, 1975; children: Ryan Alexander, Shannon Lea; edn: BS in econs., Univ. Oregon, 1969; JD (magna cum laude), Calif. Western Sch. of Law, 1976; admitted bar: Calif. 1976, U.S. District Courts CA, So. 1976, Ea. 1991, No. 1991, Cent. 1992, U.S. Supreme Ct. 1991. Career: compliance specialist Cost of Living Council W.D.C., Price Commn., W.D.C., 1972-73; dir. Oil Policy Subcom., 1973; ptnr. law firm Luce, Forward, Hamilton & Scripps, San Diego 1976-87; prin. McClellan & Assocs., San Diego 1987–; honors: Master, American Inns of Court (1991–), Outstanding trial lawyer award San Diego Trial Lawyers Assn. (1981, 83); mem: Am. Bd. of Trial Advocates, Calif. Bar Assn., San Diego County Bar Assn., Assn. Trial Lawyers Am., Calif. Trial Lawyers Assn. (bd. govs. 1985-87), San Diego Trial Lawyers Assn. (bd. 1983-90), Nat. Forensics League; civic: Calif. Western Law Sch. (bd. trustees 1985-89), Sta. KPBS (chair Annual Fundraising Auction 1984); mil: capt. USMC 1969-72. Ofc: McClellan & Associates, 1144 State St San Diego 92101

MCCLURE, HOWE ELLIOTT, wildlife biologist, author; b. Apr. 29, 1910, Chgo.; s. Howe Alexander and Clara (Phillips) McC.; m. Lucy Esther Lou Fairchild, Oct. 1, 1933 (dec.); children: Lucy Jeannette b. 1941, Clara Ann b. 1942; m. Nobuko K. Bowden, Oct. 14, 1994; edn: BS, Univ. of Illinois, Urbana 1933, MS, 1936; PhD, Iowa State Univ., 1941. Career: asst. entomologist Univ. Ill., Urbana 1930-33; tree expert Ill. Tree Service Co., Peru, Ill. 1934-37; grad. asst. Iowa State Univ., Ames 1937-41; biologist Nebra. Game Forestation & Parks, Ord, Nebr. 1941-44; biologist USPHS, Bakersfield, Calif. 1946-50; ornithologist Walter Reed Army Inst. of Research, Tokyo, Kuala Lumpur, honors: Silver Beaver BSA, Tokyo 1958, Sigma Xi 1933–; mem: Nat. Audubon Soc. (conserv. chmn. Conejo Soc. 1976–), N.E., E., Inland and Western Birdbanding Socs. 1940–, Malayan Nature Soc. (pres. 1962-63), Defenders of Wildlife (1976–, bd. 1978-89); scoutmaster BSA 1933-58; author: Migration and Survival of the Birds of Asia 1974, Haematozoa in the Birds of Eastern and Southern Asia 1978, Bird Banding 1984, Whistling Wings - The Dove Chronicles, 1991, Inago - Children of Rice, 1993, Stories I Like to Tell - An Autobiography, 1995; mil: lt (jg) USN 1944-46; rec: bird watching, bird banding, stamps. Res: 69 E Loop Camarillo 93010

MCCONNEL, RICHARD APPLETON, aerospace engineer; b. May 29, 1933, Rochester, Pa.; s. Richard A., Sr. and Dorothy (Merriman) McC.; m. Mary Francis McInnis, Apr. 11, 1966 (div. 1984); children: Amy Ellen b. 1967, Sarah Cathrine b. 1971; m.2d. Penny Kendzie, Jun. 5, 1993; edn: Washington and Jefferson Coll., Pa. 1951-53; BS engring. US Naval Acad., Annapolis 1957; naval aviator USN 1959; MS aero. engring.; US Naval Postgrad. Sch., Monterey 1966; prog. mgr. NAVAIRDEVCEN, Warminster, Pa. P3C prgms 1971-75; prog. mgr. PACMISTESTCEN, Pt. Mugu, CA, Range Systems 1979-82. Career: advanced through ranks of ensign to cdr. US Navy 1957-82; engr. Raytheon Electro-Magnetic Systems, Goleta, Calif. 1982-87; sr. engr. SRS Technologies, Camarillo 1987-92; sr. engr. High Technology Solutions, Camarillo 1992–; mem. Assn. Old Crows 1982–; rec: skiing, hiking, camping. Res: Camarillo 93010 Ofc: 1000 Paseo Camarillo 93010

MCCONNELL, JOHN DOUGLAS, executive; b. May 13, 1932, Dimboola, Australia; s. William Thomas and Ada Maud (Gardner) McC.; m. Patricia Rosemary Noakes, 1958 (div. 1967); m. Gloria Ann Kubis Revak, Oct. 12, 1968; children: Joanne Patricia b. 1961, Meredith Lorraine b. 1963; edn: BA, Univ. Melbourne Australia 1955; PhD, Stanford Univ. 1967. Career: dir. mgmt. systems SRI Internat., Wash. D.C., dir., London, dir. food and forest products, dir. we. region, Menlo Park 1975-83; chmn. exec. com., v.p. Sungene Tech., Palo Alto 1983-85, dir. fin. services SRI, Menlo Park 1986-87, prin. 1987-91, sr. economist 1967-74; mgr. Eagle Market, S. Melbourne, Australia 1959-64; asst. to mng. dir. Automotive & Gen. Industries 1957-59, personnel mgr. 1954-57; asst. personnel ofcr. Dept. Social Services 1950-54; owner and pres. Remnant World, Inc., San Jose, Calif 1991–; awards: Stanford Univ. Alfred P. Sloan fellow 1964-65, 1965-66, G.E. fellow 1966, BSA Silver Beaver; mem: Australian Inst. of Mgmt. (fellow), Advtg.Inst. Australia (fellow), Royal Victorian Inst. for the Blind (life gov.), invested ofcr., Most Venerable Order of St. John of Jerusalem 1992, Masons, Army & Navy Club, St. Andrews Soc., Royal Scottish Country Dance Soc., Queens Club; mil: Flt Lt. Royal Australian Air Force 1951-64; Presbyterian; rec: tennis, Scottish country dancing, skiing. Res: 4174 Oak Hill Ave Palo Alto 94306 Ofc: Remnant World, Inc., 5158 Stevens Creek Blvd San Jose 95129

MCCORMICK, JOSEPH PAUL, certified public accountant; b. March 29, 1926, Grand Rapids, Mich.; s. William Albert and Irma Evelyn (Doran) McC.; m. Mary Geraldine Erhardt, July 8, 1950 (dec. 1993); children: Eileen b. 1951, Geri b. 1952, Peggy b. 1954, Joe b. 1955, Teri b. 1956, Tim b. 1959, Rick b. 1961, Pat b. 1962, Katie b. 1965, Mike b. 1966; edn: BA, Mich. St. Univ. 1951; C.P.A. (1956). Career: acct. Ernst & Ernst, Grand Rapids, Mich. 1951-60, mgr., Los Angeles 1960-65, ptrn., Santa Ana 1965-80; Ernst & Whinney, Newport Beach 1980-81; owner Joseph P. McCormick 1981–; mem: Big Canyon CC, Big Ten Club (pres. 1973), Calif. Soc. C.P.A. (pres. 1973), Orange Co. C.of C. (chmn. bd. 1979), St. Joseph Hosp. (chmn. bd. 1979-80); mil: lt. comdr. USNR 1944-49; Republican; R.Cath.; rec: golf, water skiing. Res: 2322 Aralia St Newport Beach 92660 Ofc: 2322 Aralia St Newport Beach 92660

MCCORQUODALE, DANIEL ALFRED, senator, educator; b. Dec. 17,1934, Longville, LA; s. Daniel Alfred and Lalla May (Thornton) M.; m. Jean Adrian Botsford; children: Michael; Sharon; Daniel; edn: BS, San Diego State Univ., 1960; tchg. cred., San Diego State Univ., 1960; career: elem. educator National City, Pasadena, and San Jose sch. systems, 1960-72; city council/mayor, Chula Vista, 1964-68; county supervisor, Santa Clara Co., 1972-82; state senator, 12th senate dist., 1982–; chair Select Com. on Citizen Participation in Gov.; mem: Senate Natural Resources and Wildlife Com.; chair Agric. and Water Resources Com.; Budget and Fiscal Review Com.; chmn., Subcom. on Justice, Corrections, Resources; and Agric.; Bus. and Professions, Ins., Claims, and Corporations; Transportation; Constitutional Amendments; Public Employment and Retirement; chmn., Special Com. on Developmental Disabilities and Mental Health; mem: Napa State Hosp. Advy. Bd.; Multiple Sclerosis Soc.; chmn, Area VII Developmental Disabilities Bd.; mem: Marine Corps Lge., Modesto; awards: Legislator of Year: Calif. Planning & Conservation League, Peace Officers Res. Assn., Nat. Org. for Women, Sacto.; Advocate of Year, Calif. Assn. Svs. for Children; Outstanding Legislator, Calif. Council Developmental Disabilities; Calif. Governor's Com. for Employment of Disabled Persons; N. Calif. Psychiatric Soc.; United Cerebral Palsy Assn. of Calif.; Calif. Coalition for Mental Health; Calif. Assn. of Retarded Citizens; Parents Helping Parents; Calif. Assn. of Reg. Ctr. Agencies; civic: Haven Women's Ctr., Calif. Women for Agric., Farm Bureau Fedn., Sr. Opportunity Svc. Prog.; author: pamphlet, The Legislative Process, 1990; report, The Lanterman Developmental Disabilities Services Act, 1992; author, SB 124, creates eight cty. reg. air pollution control dist.; SB 238, equalize sch. dist. funding; SB 1383, developmental disabilities reform; SB 1665, increase penalties for infractions to irrigation facilities; SB 387, park bond; SB 1296 create Mentally Disordered Offender Prog.; SB 1541, protections for victims of domestic violence; SB 1862, stalker legislation; SB 354, programs to keep pregnant and parenting teens in sch.; SB 463, wetlands; SB 1563, retirement sys. for judges, SB 1470, money laundering; SB 1112, est. standards for developmental svs.; SB 960, exempt Special Olympics; SB 2210, training law enforcement; SB 1115, treatment of mentally retarded defendants; SB 1045, reg. ctr. budget reduction; mil: sgt., USMC, 1953-56; Democrat; Protestant. Res: Modesto Ofc: State Senate, State of Calif., State Capitol Rm. 4032 Sacramento 95814

MCCRACKEN, SHIRLEY ANN, educational consultant; b. Aug. 15, 1937, Rochester, N.Y.; d. Bernard Anthony Ross and Marian Elizabeth (Taliento) Heimann; m. Paul Arthur McCracken, June 25, 1971; children: Donna b. 1967, Glenn b. 1971; edn: BA in math., Nazareth Coll., Rochester, N.Y. 1959; MS math., Marquette Univ., Milw. 1968; PhD human behavior, La Jolla Univ., 1980. Career: tchr., dept. chair Mt. Carmel High Sch., Auburn, N.Y. 1959-68; training asst. Jewish Vocational Svc., Milw. 1969; rehabilitation counselor Curative Workshop, Milw. 1968-69; tchr. Anaheim Union High Sch., Calif. 1969-72; program dir. San Antonio Church, Anaheim 1987-90; trainer, cons., Anaheim 1990–; tchr. Orange Catechetical Inst., Orange 1989–; awards: scholarship Nazareth Coll. 1954-59, NSF inst. grantee- Marquette Univ. 1963, 64, 66, 67 and Anaheim, Ca. 1990, Annie Accolade women's div. Anaheim C.of C. 1978, Named Gift, EF AAUW- Anaheim 1978, Anaheim Hills 1984, and Calif. State AAUW, Sacto. 1991; civic: Ebell Club Anaheim 1975–, Anaheim Hills AAUW 1982–, Anaheim AAUW 1972–, Anaheim Mus., Anaheim Sister Cities Assn., Anaheim Arts Council (pgm. v.p. 1993-95, pres. 1995-96), Anaheim Budget Comm. (1991-95, chair 1992-95); author: Creative Leadership, 1980; book editor: Planning Model for Leadership, Decision Making, Mgmt. Training, 1982; Republican; R.Cath. Res: 6553 Calle Del Norte Anaheim 92807

MCCRARY, BARBARA JO, antique auto dealer, insurance agent; b. Jan. 6, 1934, Quinton, Okla.; d. Ben H. and Nan V. (Murrell) Brackett; m. Bill Johnston (div.); m. 2d. Jerry Lee McCrary, Oct. 19, 1973; children: Julie Johnston Hermosillo b. 1952, Terry Ellen Hauff b. 1954, Vickie Lynn Johnston-DiPaolo b. 1956; 6 grandchildren: (nee Hermosillo) Harley and Jay, (nee Hauff) Barbara Jo, Belinda Jean and Christian, (nee DiPaolo) Julian Paolo b. 1994; gt. grandchildren: Alexie A. Hauff, David Lee Hauff, III (children of David Lee, Jr.) and Jason A. Grissom, Jr., Samantha Grissom (children of Belinda Jean); Calif. lic.: Life & Disability, Fire & Casualty (life), Variable Contract agent; lic. Contractor, P.U.C. lic. (freight of mobile homes), lic. Auto dealer. Career: retail sales clerk, Merced 1968-69; auto sales Town & Country Chrysler, Merced 1969; sales Travelon Trailer Co., Modesto 1973; ptnr. Bill's Trailer Sales, Merced 1974-77; prop. McCrary's Mobile Homes, Merced 1977-93, Antique Auto dealership, 1987–, My Body Shop (antique auto restoration), 1988–, investor rental property, almond ranch; full time ins. broker, 1991–; mem. Am. Biographical Inst., Inc.; Republican; Prot.; rec: dancing, fishing, gardening. Res/Ofc: 1950 Ashby Rd Merced 95340

MC CRAVEN, EVA STEWART MAPES, mental health center administrator; b. Sept. 26, 1936, Los Angeles; d. Paul Melvin and Wilma Zech (Ziegler) Stewart; m. Carl Clarke McCraven, Mar. 18, 1978; children: David Anthony, Lawrence James, Maria Lynn Mapes; edn: BS (magna cum laude) CSU Northridge, 1974; MS, Cambridge Grad. Sch. Psychology, 1987, PhD 1991. Career: dir. special projects Pacoima Memorial Hosp. 1969-71, dir. health edn. 1971-74; asst. exec. dir. Hillview Community Mental Health Ctr., Lakeview Terrace, 1974–, developer, mgr. Long-term Residential Program 1983-90, past prog. mgr. Crisis Residential Program, prog. mgr. Mentally Ill Offender Residential Treatment Prog.; current dir. of Hillview Integrated Services Agency; past dir. dept. consultation and edn.; dir: N.E. Valley Health Corp. 1990-93; developer and prog. dir. Hillview Integrated Svs. Agency 1993–; bd. dir. Golden State Comm. Mental Health Ctr. 1970-73; awards: nominee Hourglass award Hiltoppers Aux. of Assistance League of So. Calif. 1985, resolution Calif. St. Senate 1988, commendn. and spl. mayor's plaque L.A. Mayor Tom Bradley 1988, recipient commendations for comm. service City & Co. of L.A., Calif. St. Assembly and Senate, Sunland Tujunga Police Support Council & C.of C. 1989; woman of achiev. Sunland Tujunga BPW 1990; mem: Assn. Mental Health Adminstrs., Am. Pub. Health Assn., Women in Health Adminstrn., Health Svs. Adminstrn. Alumni Assn. (former v.p.), Bus. and Profl. Women (v.p.), L.W.V.; civic: S.F.V. Coordinating Council Area Assn. (past pres.), Sunland-Tujunga Coordinating Council (past pres.). Ofc: Hillview Center 11500 Eldridge Ave Lake View Terrace 91342

MCCRONE, ALISTAIR WILLIAM, university president; b. Oct. 7, 1931, Regina, Saskatchewan, Can., nat. U.S. 1961; s. Hugh MacMillan and Kathleen Maude Tallent (Forth) McC.; m. Judith Saari, May 8, 1958; children: Bruce b. 1960, Craig b. 1962, Mary b. 1963; edn: B.A. Univ. Saskatchewan 1953; M.Sc. (Shell fellow) Univ. Nebr., 1955; PhD geol., Univ. Kans., 1961. Career: wellsite geologist Brit. Am. Oil Co. 1953; field geologist Shell Oil Co. 1954-55, field party chief exploration and mapping 1956-58; instr. New York Univ., 1959-61, asst. prof. 1961-64, assoc. prof. 1964-69, assoc. dean Grad. Sch. Arts and Scis./ prof. of geology 1969-70; academic v.p./prof. geol. Univ. of the Pacific, 1970-74, acting pres. 1971; univ. pres./prof. geol., Humboldt State Univ., 1974–; lectr. CBS-TV Sunrise Semester 1969-70; mem. CSU Commn. on Ednl. Telecomm. 1983-85, advy. group Exec. Council CSU System 1980-81; awards: Golden Dozen HSU 1982, Sigma Xi (NYU chpt. pres. 1967-69, v.p. 1965-67, sec. 1965-66, full mem 1962), Phi Kappa Phi (life 1986), Erasmus Haworth Honors Univ. Kans. 1957, Danforth Assoc. Convenor NYU 1964-68, listed Who's Who in Am. 1976, Am. Men and Women of Sci. 1976, Outstanding Educators of Am. 1975, Leaders in Am Educ. 1974, Who's Who in the West 1973, Am. Men of Sci. 1972 Who's Who in the East 1969; mem: Am. Assn. Univ. Adminstrs. (bd. 1986-89), Assn. of Am. Colls. (bd. 1989-93, v.chair 1990, chair 1991), Am. Assn. State Colls. and Univs.

(state del. 1977-80), Calif. State Auto Assn. (bd. 1988–), Am. Auto. Assn. (bd. 1990-93), Calif. St. Parks Found. Bd. 1994–, Geol. Soc. Am. (fellow), AAAS (fellow), Calif. Acad. Scis. (fellow), , Soc. of Econ. Paleontologists and Mineralogists (nat. del. 1967, 68, 69), Humboldt Conv. and Visitors Bur. (bd. 1980-87), Redwood Empire Assn. (bd. 1983-89), Calif. Council for the Humanities (1977-82, prog. com. chair 1981-82), BSA Redwood Empire Council 1975-80, Western Assn. of Schools and Coll. chair and mem. of accreditation teams; clubs: Rotary, Saint Andrews Soc. N.Y. (life); frequent speaker, panelist; num. articles pub. in profl. jour.; Presbyn. Hosp. Pacific Med. Ctr. S.F. (trustee 1971-74); rec: golf, reading. Ofc: Humboldt State University Arcata 95521

MCCURDY, STEPHEN RANKIN, interior landscaping company president; b. April 19, 1960, Belfast, No. Ireland; s. Samuel and Daphne (Rushbrook) McCurdy; m. Janet Faith McFarland, July 3, 1982; children: Timothy b. 1989, James b. 1991, Jonathan b. 1994; edn: cert. craftsman Oakland College of Horticulture, Hertfordshire, Eng. 1979. Career: grower Buena Park Greenhouses, Encinitas 1979-80; sales rep. Thomas Rochford & Sons, Hertfordshire, Eng. 1980-82; grower, mgr. Calif. Exotique, Los Angeles 1983, general mgr. Carson 1984; owner, prin. British Indoor Gardens dba Landscape Images, L.A. 1984–; pres. British Indoor Gardens, Inc., Lake Forest 1987–; instr. seminar San Diego Plantscape, San Diego 1989; judge Norcal Awards, San Francisco 1989; instr., speaker Assoc. Landscape Contractors of Am. (1993, 94); awards: recipient Best Project award from Interiorscape mag. (1986, 90), PIPA awards: service (1987, 88, 92, 94), installation 1986-95, design (1989, 91, 92), judges award (1989, 91); Distinction Awards Assoc. Landscape Contractors of Am. (1992, 94); mem: Profl. Interior Plantscape Assn. (dir. fin. com.1986-88, dir. ways & means com. 1988-91), Associated Landscape Contractors of Am., Bldg. Industry Assn., Sales & Mktg. Council, Foilage for Clean Air Council, Calif. Interior Plantscape Assn. (4 awards 1993, 6 awards 1994, v. chair 1994-95); rec: stamp collecting. Ofc: Landscape Images 20611 Cañada Rd Lake Forest 92630

MC CURRY, MARGUERITE FAYE, academic administrator; b. Feb. 23, 1935, Roswell, N.M.; d. John Robert and Alice Marguerite (Gordon) Wilhite; m. O.L. Ted Taylor, Feb. 18, 1954 (dec. 1969); m. Liam R.A. McCurry III, Dec. 18, 1971; children: Lois b. 1959, M. Lee b. 1962, Michael b. 1963; edn: BA, Univ. N.M. 1974; MAPA, 1976; PhD, 1980; cert. fund raising exec. 1988. Career: pub. info. staff Univ. New Mexico, Albuquerque 1967-76, dir. med. center pub. info. 1976-80, dir. devel. pub. affairs 1981-85; res. splst. NIH, Bethesda, Md. 1980-81; exec. dir. coll. advancement Stephens Coll., Columbia, Mo. 1985-86; exec. dir. univ. advancement CSU, Sacto. 1986-92, asst. v.p. univ. affairs, CSU, Sacto. 1992–; mem. bd. dirs. Sacto. Opera Assn., Med. Alert Fedn. N.M. (chmn. 1982-85), Lovelace Med. Ctr., Albuquerque (dir. 1982-85), Nat. Health Agys. N.M. (pres. 1985); awards: John McGovern scholarship 1979; mem: Planned Giving Forum of Sacto. (pres. 1989-90); 50+ articles pub. in profl. jours. and newspapers 1985; Episcopalian. Res: 8366 Mediterranean Way Sacramento 95826 Ofc: California State University Sacramento 95819-6026

MC DONALD, JOHN GREGORY, educator; b. May 21, 1937, Stockton; s. Earl and Dora (Mitchell) McD.; m. Melody June 19, 1973; edn: BS, Stanford Univ. 1960, MBA, 1962, PhD, 1967. Career: faculty Stanford Univ. Grad. Sch. of Bus.: asst. prof. 1968-71, assoc. prof. 1971-75, prof. of fin. 1975-78, The Joseph McDonald prof. of fin. 1979-87, The IBJ Prof. of Finance, 1987–; dir: Investment Co. of Am., Growth Fund of Am., New Perspective Fund, EuroPacific Growth Fund, Scholastic Inc.; mem. advy. bd. InterWest Venture Capital; awards: Fulbright fellow in Paris 1967-68, vis. prof. Univ. of Paris 1972, Columbia Univ. 1975, Harvard Univ. 1986; mil: 1s lt. US Army 1962-64. Ofc: Graduate School of Business Stanford University Stanford 94305

MCDONALD, MARIANNE, classicist; b. Jan. 2, 1937, Chgo.; d. Eugene Francis and Inez (Riddle) McDonald; children: Eugene, Conrad, Bryan, Bridget, Kirstie (dec.), Hiroshi; edn: BA (magna cum laude), Bryn Mawr Coll., 1958; MA, Univ. Chgo., 1960; PhD, UC Irvine, 1975. Career: tchg. asst. classics UC Irvine, 1972-74, instr. Greek, Latin and English, mythology, modern cinema, 1975-79, research Thesaurus Linguae Graecae Project, 1979–; prof. Dept. Theatre, UC San Diego, 1990–; vis. research fellow Sch. of Classics, Univ. of Dublin, Trinity Coll., Eire. 1990; bd. dirs. Centrum, Am. Coll. of Greece 1981-94, Scripps Hosp. 1981, Am. Sch. Classical Studies 1986–; bd. overseers UC San Diego 1985–; honors: Ellen Browning Scripps Humanitarian 1975, disting. service UC Irvine 1982, Irvine Medal 1987, 3rd Prize Midwest Poetry Ctr. Contest 1987, philanthropist of yr. NCCJ 1986, woman of yr. AHEPA 1988, Hon. Doctorate Am. Coll. of Greece 1988, Woman of Distinction San Diego Regl. Conf. for Women 1990, Gold medal Soc. for the Internationalization of the Greek Language 1991, Gold medal from Mayor of Athens 1991, Gold medal from Mayor of Piraeus 1991, Hon. Dipl. the Archeol. Assn. of Athens 1991, Axios Woman of Year 1991, Hellenic Univ. Women's Assn. of Greece Hypatia Award 1992, AHEPA Acad. of Achievement Award 1992, UC San Diego Civis Universitatis Award 1993, Doctor of Letters honoris causa Univ. of Athens 1994, Am.- Heritage Award 1994, Aristotle Univ. of Thessaloniki award for contr. to Greek letters 1994, Order of the Phoenix (Greece) 1994, Am. Ireland Fund Award 1994, Women's Internat. Ctr. Volunteer of the Decade 1994, Doctor of Letters honoris causa Univ. of Dublin 1994; mem: Am. Philol. Assn., Philol.

Assn. Pacific Coast, Am. Classical League, MLA, Am. Comparative Lit. Assn., Modern and Classical Language Assn., AAUP So. Calif., Hellenic Soc., Calif. Fgn. Language Tchrs. Assn., Royal Irish Academy, Internat. Platform Assn., Am. Biog. Inst. Nat. Bd. Advisors 1982–, KPBS Producers Club, Hellenic Univ. Club (dir.); author: Terms for Happiness in Euripides, 1978, Semilemmatized Concordances to Euripides' Alcestis, 1977, Cyclops, Andromache, Medea, 1978, Heraclidae, Hippolytus, 1979, Hecuba, 1982, Hercules Furens, 1984, Electra, 1985, Ion, 1985, Trojan Women, 1988, Iphigenia in Taurus, 1988, Euripides in Cinema: The Heart Made Visible, 1983; translator: The Cost of Kindness and Other Fabulous Tales by Shinichi Hoshi, 1986; book chapters in Views of Clytemnestra, Ancient and Modern, 1990; Tony Harrison: A Critical Anthology, 1991; Modern Critical Theory and Classical Lit., 1994; A Challenge to Democracy, 1994; Ancient Sun, Modern Light: Greek Drama on the Modern Stage, 1991; num. articles in scholarly jours. Res: Box 929 Rancho Santa Fe 92067 Ofc: Dept. of Theatre B-044 Univ. California San Diego La Jolla 92093

MCDOWELL, JENNIFER, publisher, composer; b. May 19, 1936, Albuquerque, NM; d. Willard A. and Margaret (Garrison) McDowell; mother is the author, Margaret F. Garrison; grandfather, Lemuel Addison Garrison, former pres. Central College Pella, Iowa; uncle, Lon Garrison, supt. of Yellowstone Nat. Park 1955-63; m. Milton Loventhal (author, playwright and lyricist), July 2, 1973; edn: BA, UC Berkeley, 1957; MA, CSU San Diego, 1958; MLS, UCB, 1963; PhD, Univ. Oregon, Eugene 1973. Career: high sch. tchr. Abraham Lincoln H.S., San Jose 1960-61; freelance ed., Soviet field, 1961-63; res. asst., sociol., Univ. Oreg. 1964-66; ed./pub. Merlin Papers, San Jose 1969–; ed./pub. Merlin Press, 1973–; res. cons. sociol., San Jose 1973–; music publ. Lipstick and Toy Balloons Pub. Co., San Jose 1978–; res., writer Merlin Res. and Writing Center, 1980–; co-creator musical comedy: Russia's Secret Plot To Take Back Alaska, 1983; co-author 4 plays performed off-off Broadway in 1986: Betsy and Phyllis, The Estrogen Party To End War, Mack The Knife Your Friendly Dentist, The Oatmeal Party Comes to Order; coauthor play "Betsy Meets the Wackey Iraqi" performed Burgess Theatre, 1991; tchr. writing workshops 1969-73; manuscript reader for Journ. of the Sci. Study of Religion, 1974–; composer 160+ songs, on list of composers for Paramount Pictures, 1981-88; co-prod. radio shows, Sta. KALX, Berkeley 1971-72; awards: AAUW doctoral fellow 1971-73, Calif. Arts Council grantee 1976-77, 3 songs incl. in Survey of Am. Music for Bicentennial Yr. 1976, 8 awards at Am. Song Festival 1976-79, Poetry Orgn. for Women 1979, Bill Casey Mem. Award 1980, listed Directory of Am. Poets and Fiction Writers 1980, composer for Harold C. Crain Award (1980) winning play, Simple Gifts by Nancy Gilsenan; honors: Sigma Alpha Iota, Phi Beta Kappa, Beta Phi Mu; mem: Soc. for the Sci. Study of Religion, Am. Sociological Assn., Poetry Orgn. for Women, Feminist Writers Guild, Internat. Womens Writing Guild, Kappa Kappa Gamma; author: Black Politics (1971, featured at Smithsonian Institute in 1992),Contemporary Women Poets an Anthology 1977, Ronnie Goose Rhymes for Grown-ups 1984; contbr. num. articles in Bulletin of Bibliography, Jour.for the Sci. Study of Religion, San Jose Studies; poems, essays, plays in num. books and mags. incl. Women's World, Women Talking, Women Listening, X a Journal of the Arts, others; Democrat; Prot.; rec: tennis, Calif. native plants, hiking. Ofc: Merlin Press, POB 5602 San Jose 95150

MCELROY, LEO FRANCIS, public relations consultant; b. Oct. 12, 1932, Los Angeles; s. Leo Francis Sr. and Helen Evelyn (Silliman) McE.; m. Dorothy Montgomery, Nov. 3, 1956 (div. 1981); children: James b. 1961, Maureen b. 1964, Michael b. 1967, Kathleen b. 1969; m. Judy Lewis, May 30, 1992; edn: BS in English, Loyola Univ., 1953. Career: broadcast newsman in Ill., Calif., 1954-63; news director KFI, KRLA, KABC Radio, Los Angeles, 1963-72; reporter/host KCET-TV, L.A. 1965-74; political editor KABC-TV, L.A. 1974-81; pres. McElroy Communications, Sacramento/Los Angeles, 1981–; special asst. Lt. Gov. of Calif. 1983-84; lectr. (politics) UC Davis 1983–, lectr. (journalism) Sacto. St. Univ. 1985–, lectr. (media) Chamber of Commerce, Sacto. 1985–; honors: Emmy nominations Acad. TV Arts & Scis. (1967, 68, 70, 74, 79), Golden Mike award Radio-TV News Assn., L.A. 1973, Gabriel award Catholic Archdiocese, L.A. 1972, announcer of year Calif. State Fair, Sacto. 1960, Hon. Resolution Calif. State Assembly, Sacto. 1981, writing award Gr. L.A. Press Club 1981; mem: Am. Assn. Political Consultants, Am. Soc. Composers Authors Publishers, AFTRA, SAG; civic: Mental Health Assn. Sacto. (dir. 1985–), Rescue Alliance Sacto. (dir. 1987–), Volunteers in Victim Asst. Sacto. (dir. 1984), Leukemia Soc. (bd. 1993–), Americans for Non Smokers Rights (bd. 1995–); author: (book) Uneasy Partners, 1984, (play) To Bury Caesar, 1952, author/lyricist: (musicals) Mermaid Tavern, 1956, Rocket To Olympus, 1960, The Code of Whiskey King, 1994, numerous songs incl. Melanie Goodby, 1963, Wanderin' Song, 1964; mil: 1st lt. USAF 1954-56; Republican; R.Cath.; rec: tennis, songwriting. Res: 8217 Oakenshaw Way Orangevale 95662 Ofc: McElroy Communications 2410 K St Ste C Sacramento 95816 also: 6363 Wilshire Blvd Ste 129 Los Angeles 90048

MC ELWEE, DORIS RYAN, psychotherapist; b. Feb. 15, 1931, Calif.; d. Dennis M. and Emma A. (Klockau) Ryan; m. Dr. Charles McElwee, Feb. 6, 1959; m. 2d. Craig Thomson, May 6, 1988; children: Brent b. 1960, Gregg b. 1963, Cynthia b. 1965; edn: BA, Millikin Univ. Decatur, Ill.; MA, PhD, Univ. Ariz.; Temple Univ. Phila.; USC; UCLA. Career: pvt. practice psychotherapy,

Arcadia; senior therapist American Inst. of Family Relations, Burbank 1969–; Calif. Family Study Center, Burbank 1983-90; grad. faculty Am. Inst. Family Relations, L.A. 1972-85, Pepperdine Univ. 1972-74, Chapman Coll. 1971-72; guest expert Phil Donahue Show; awards: Millikin Univ. Annual Merit 1983, Psi Chi Nat. Hon. Soc. in Psychology; mem: Group Psychotherapy Assn. So. Calif. (ofcr. and exec. bd. 1986–, chair Ethics Com.), Am. Assn. Marriage & Family Therapy, Calif. Assn. Marriage & Family Therapists, So. Calif. Assn. Marriage & Family Therapy, Self Esteem Task Force, AASECT, Soc. Sci. Study of Sex, AACD; civic: NOW (bd. Pasadena), Arcadia Assistance League, Las Alas Orgn., Panhellenic Assn., Pi Beta Phi; author: Techniques of Marriage and Family Counseling; Suicide Prevention for College Students; contbg. author: Woman To Woman; A Place To Rest Your Heart; contbg. writer, Ladies Home Jour. (10 yrs.); Republican; Lutheran; rec: travel, gardening, dancing. Address: Arcadia 91006

MC EWEN, WILLARD WINFIELD, JR., lawyer, federal magistrate, judge; b. Dec. 26, 1934, Ivanston, Ill.; s. Willard Winfield and Esther (Sprenger) McE.; m. Susanne House, Aug., 22, 1959; children: Michael b. 1961, Elizabeth b. 1962, Allison b. 1966; edn: BA, Claremont Men's Coll.; LL.B., UCSF Hastings Coll. Law. Career: dep. legislative counsel Legislative Counsels Office, Sacto. 1959-61; asst. city atty. City Attys. Office, Santa Barbara. 1961-62; atty. Harris Parke Barnes & McEwen 1962-72; magistrate U.S. Dist. Ct. Central Dist. 1972–; atty. sole practice, Santa Barbara. 1972–; atty. Goleta Water Dist. 1986-87; lectr. Santa Barbara Adult Edn. Prog.; awards: Jr. C.of C. Young Man of Year 1965, Santa Barbara C.of C. Testimonial Dinner 1985; mem: Santa Barbara Co. Bar Assn., Am. Bar Assn., Santa Barbara. C.of C.(com. on local govt., state legis. com., pres. 1979, bd. dirs., pres. bd. dirs. 1981-82, chmn. several coms.), Santa Barbara Kiwanis (pres. 1963), Santa Barbara Downtown Kiwanis (pres. 1967), Am. Heart Assn. (pres. Santa Barbara Co. Chpt. 1981-82), Santa Barbara Heart Assn. (bd. dirs., pres. bd. dirs.1981-82, chmn. Heart Sunday 1973, 75); mil: capt. US Army. 1957-64; Republican; Catholic; rec: skiing, golf. Res: 1620 Larsen Rd Santa Barbara 93103 Ofc: US Courthouse 8 E Figueroa St Ste 210 Santa Barbara 93101

MCFARLAND, GARY LYNN, civil engineer; b. May 28, 1947, Wichita, Kans.; s. Duard Edward and Leah Jean (Shiner) McF.; m. Carol, June 22, 1974; children: Joseph b. 1979, Patrick b. 1983, Kevin b. 1984; edn: BE in C.E., Ga. Inst. of Tech. 1970; reg. civil engr. Calif. 1976. Career: field engr. R.S. Delamater & Assocs., Wichita, Kans. 1970-71; jr. engr. Goleta Water Dist., 1974-77; consulting engr. McFarland Engring. Inc., 1977-83; pres. Lawrance, Fisk & McFarland Inc., cons. engrs., 1983-95; sr. project mgr. Martin Northart & Spencer, Civil Engrs., 1995–; elected bd. dirs. Goleta Water Dist. 1979, 1983, mem. Cachuma Ops. & Maint. Bd., Santa Barbara Co. 1985-87; mem: ASCE, Am. Public Works Assn.; mil: 1st lt. AUS 1971-73; Orthodox Christian Ch.; rec: pvt. pilot. Res: 213 Hillview Goleta 93117 Ofc: Lawrance, Fisk & McFarland, Inc. 928 Garden St Santa Barbara 93101

MCGEE, JAMES FRANCIS, lawyer; b. Sept. 19, 1950, New York; s. James Francis and Elizabeth Jane (Mooney) McG.; m. Annamarie Saunders, Feb. 13, 1988; edn: BS, Univ. Pa. 1972; LL.B, JD, Western Univ. 1979; admitted St. Bar Calif. 1980. Career: founder Law Offices James F. McGee, Newport Beach and Irvine 1980–; awards: 20-30 Internat. So. Calif. Man of Year 1985; mem: Newport Beach 20-30 Club (founder 1985), Orange Co. Bar Assn., Orange Co. Trial Lawyers Assn., Calif. Bar Assn., Calif. Trial Lawyers Assn., Am. Bar Assn., Am. Trial Lawyers Assn., Roosters of Chanticleer (membership chmn. 1988), Laguna Beach Bd. of Adjustment (chmn. 1985-87), Laguna Beach Arch. Review Bd. (chmn. 1985-87); rec: sports, flying, public speaking. Ofc: 23 Corporate Plaza Ste 230 Newport Beach 92660

MCGETTIGAN, CHARLES CARROLL, JR., investment banker; b. March 28, 1945, San Francisco; s. Charles Carroll McGettigan and Molly (Fay) Pedley; m. Katharine Havard King, Nov. 1, 1975 (div. 1981); m. Meriwether Lewis Stovall, Aug. 6, 1983; 1 child, Meriwether Lewis Fay; edn: BA govt., Georgetown Univ. 1966; MBA fin., Wharton Sch., Univ. Pa., 1969. Career: assoc., asst. v.p., v.p. Blyth Eastman Dillon, NYC 1970-75, 1st v.p. 1975-78, sr. v.p., San Francisco 1978-80; sr. v.p. Dillon Read & Co., S.F. 1980-83; gen. ptnr. Woodman Kirkpatrick & Gilbreath, S.F. 1983-84; prin., corp. fin. Hambrecht & Quist, Inc., S.F. 1984-88; mng. dir., founder McGettigan, Wick & Co., Inc. S.F. 1988–; gen ptnr., founder Proactive Partners, L.P., S.F. and Fremont Proactive Partners, L.P., S.F. 1991–; dir: Circadian Inc., San Jose 1980-84, Skouras Pictures Inc., Hollywood 1987-94, Sungene Techs. Inc., San Jose 1987-88, Raytel Systems Inc., San Jose 1988-89, Shared Techs. Inc., Hartford, Conn. 1988-90; Phoenix Network, Inc., San Francisco 1990-92, Coded Comm., Carlsbad 1991-95; PMR Corp., San Diego 1992–; I-Flow Corp., Irvine 1992–; Sonex Res., Inc., Annapolis, MD 1992–; Onsite Energy, Carlsbad 1993–, Modtech, Inc., Perris 1994–; Digital Dictation, Inc., Vienna, VA 1995–; NDE Environmental Corp., Austin, Tx. 1995–; Wray-Tech Instruments, Inc., Stratford, Ct. 1995–; advy. dir. Chesapeake Ventures, Baltimore 1984-94; trustee St. Francis Meml. Hosp., S.F. 1980-86; advy. bd. dirs. Leavey Sch. Bus. Adminstrn., Santa Clara Univ. 1984-90; clubs: Brook, Racquet & Tennis (N.Y.), Pacific Union, Bohemian, S.F. Golf (S.F.), Burlingame CC (Hillsborough), California

(L.A.), Boston (New Orleans), Piping Rock (Locust Valley, N.Y.), Conferie des Chevaliers du Tastevin 1991–; mil: USN 1966; Republican (United S.F. Rep. fin. com. 1983–, steering com. 1986–); R.Cath. Res: 3375 Clay St San Francisco 94118 Ofc: McGettigan Wick & Co., Inc. 50 Osgood Pl San Francisco 94133

MCGIFFEN, THOMAS GLENN, electrical engineer; b. Apr. 19, 1964, Clarion, Pa.; s. Milton Earl, Sr. and Rose Mary (Scarnato) McG.; edn: BS in E.E. (honors and high distinction), Pa. State Univ., 1987; MS in elect. and computer engring., Univ. Ill., Urbana 1989. Career: co-op. engr. Packard Electric, Warren, Ohio 1985; systems engr. Hughes Aircraft Co., El Segundo, Calif. 1987-94, DIRECTV 1994–; awards: G.E. Foundation fellow 1987-88; honors: Who's Who in the West 1993; pub. res. articles in E.E., 1989; Christian; rec: guitarist. Res: 1031 W 132nd St Gardena 90247 Ofc: DIRECTV 2230 East Imperial Highway El Segundo 90245

MCGLYNN, BETTY HOAG, art historian; b. Apr. 28, 1914, Deer Lodge, Mont.; d. Arthur James and Elizabeth Tangye (Davey) Lochrie; m. Paul Sterling Hoag, Dec. 28, 1936 (div. 1967); children: Peter Lochrie Hoag, Jane Hoag Brown, Robert Doane Hoag; m. Thomas Arnold McGlynn, July 28, 1973; edn: BA, Stanford Univ., 1936; MA, USC, 1967; Calif. std. tchg. cred., secondary. Career: research dir. So. Calif. Archives of American Art, Los Angeles, 1964-67; Carmel Museum of Art, 1967-69; dir. Triton Museum of Art, Santa Clara, 1970; archivist, librarian San Mateo County Historical Soc. Museum, 1972-74; art instr. Monterey Peninsula Coll., 1970, San Jose City Coll., 1971; art appraiser, City of Carmel, 1967, Monterey, 1981; cons., writer, lectr. in field, 1964–; mem. Pacific Grove (Calif.) Art Ctr., Montana Histrical Soc., Gallantin County (Mont.) Historical Soc., Butte (Mont.) Arts Chateau, Carmel Art Assn. (hon.), Carmel Heritage Soc., Chinese Hist. Soc., Friends of the Bancroft Library, Monterey County Cultural Council, Monterey History and Art Assn. (art cons.), Monterey Peninsula Museum of Art (acquisitions bd.), Robinson Jeffers Tor House Found. (art cons.), Hawaiian Hist. Soc., Nat. Museum of Women in the Arts, The Westerners, P.E.O.; author: The World of Mary DeNeale Morgan 1970; Carmel Art Association: A History 1987; various booklets and museum catalogs; contbg. author: Orchid Art of the Orchid Isle (Malama Arts, Honolulu, 1982); Plein Air Painters of California The North 1986; Hawaiian Island Artists and Friends of the Arts (Malama Arts, Kailua-Kona, 1989); jour. editor, contbr.: La Peninsula 1971-75, Noticias 1983-88; Republican. Address: PO Box 7189 Carmel-by-the-Sea CA 93921

MCGOUGH, RUTH LOIS DICKERSON, lawyer and mediator; b. June 18, 1927, Selma; d. Clovia Floyd and Gertrude May (Groat) Patterson; children: Kevin b. 1957, Dereney b. 1959, Kari b. 1964; m. David L. McGough, Mar., 1993; edn: San Jose St. Univ. 1945-47; admitted St. Bar Calif, U.S. District Court. Career: atty., Walnut Creek 1978–, mediator 1983–; mem: Contra Costa Co. Bar Assn., Calif. Women Lawyers; practicioner mem. Acad. of Family Mediators; rec: music, gardening, hiking. Ofc: 1281 Boulevard Way Ste A Walnut Creek 94595

MC GUIGAN, WILLIAM MARION, lawyer; b. Sept. 11, 1939, San Diego; s. William J. and Irene H. (Coates) McG.; m. Eleanor S., Aug. 6, 1968; children: Shannon D. b. 1968, Tara M. b. 1971; edn: BS aerospace engring., Univ. Colo. Boulder 1961; MS, S.D. St. Univ. 1972; JD, Univ. S.D. 1976. Career: sr. aerodynamacist, analyst Rohr Industries Inc., S.D. 1969-78; atty., assoc. Rose Rockwell & Jennings 1977-78; ptnr. McGuane & McGuigan 1981-85; atty. sole practice 1985–; awards: Am. Jurisprudence award; mem: Am. Bar Assn., S.D. Bar Assn. (bd. dirs. 1977), Criminal Defense Bar Assn., S.D. Trial Lawyers Assn. (bd. dirs. 1991-94), S. Bay Bar Assn. (treas. 1980, pres. 1983, 89), Juvenile Ct. (list panel); co-author USN Tactical Manual, 1970, tech. paper pub.; lectr. child abuse and neglect; mil: lt. USN; Republican; Cath.; rec: golf, sport literature, fishing. Res: 5074 Debby Dr San Diego 92115 Ofc: 315 Third Ave Chula Vista 91911

MC GUINN, JOHN FRANCIS, lawyer; b. Oct. 29, 1940, Chicago, Ill.; s. Martin F. and Margaret (O'Grady) McG.; m. Karen Nuzum, Sept. 27, 1969; edn: BA, Ill. Benedictine Coll. 1962; JD, Univ. Ill. 1965. Career: ptnr. Juergensmeyer McGuinn Chase & Wotan, Elgin, Ill. 1965-67; atty. Bechtel, San Francisco 1967-70; asst. to gen. mgr. Acres Canadian Bechtel, Montreal, Canada 1970-71; asst. mng. atty. Bechtel, San Francisco 1971-74, dep. mng. atty., Paris, France 1974-76, counsel, Kuwait City 1976-78, mgr. internal audit, S.F. 1978-80, chief counsel 1980–, also mgr. dept. ops. 1986–; mem. Am. Bar Assn., Forum on Constrn. Industry (chmn. 1988-89), charter mem. Am. Coll. of Constrn. Lawyers 1989; clubs: World Trade (S.F.), Commonwealth of Calif.; articles pub. in profl. jours.,1964-86. Ofc: Bechtel Power Corp. POB 3965 San Francisco 94119

MCGUIRE, MICHAEL JOHN, consulting, environmental engineer; b. June 29, 1947, San Antonio, Texas; s. James Brendan and Opal Mary (Brady) McG.; m. Deborah Marrow, June 19, 1971; children: David, Anna; edn: BS Civil Engring., Univ. Pa., 1969; MS, and PhD Environmental Engring., Drexel Univ., 1972, 1977; diplomat Am. Acad. Environmental Engring.; reg. profl. engr. Pa., N.J., Calif. Career: sanitary engr. Philadelphia. Water Dept., 1969-73; research assoc. Drexel Univ., Philadelphia. 1976-77; prin. engr. Brown & Caldwell Consulting Engrs., Pasadena 1977-79; water quality engr. Met. Water Dist. of

So. Calif., Los Angeles 1979-84, water quality mgr. 1984-86, dir. water quality 1986-90, asst. general mgr. 1990-92, pres., McGuire Environ. Cons., Inc.; cons. to subcom. on adsorbents, safe drinking water com. Nat. Acad. Scis. 1978-79, cons. mem., Technologies Workgroup, USEPA DBP Reg. Neg. 1992-93; honors: Sigma Xi, Sigma Nu, Sigma Tau, Academic Achiev. Award Am. Water Works Assn. 1978, AWWA Fuller Award 1995, listed Who's Who in West 1981–; mem: Am. Water Works Assn. (edn. div. chmn. 1982-83, Calif.-Nev. sect., governing bd. 1984-87, exec. com. 1989–, chmn. 1991-92, Nat. Dir. 1993–, nat. v.p. 1994–, trustee Research Found. 1983-86), Am. Chem. Soc., ASCE, Internat. Water Supply Assn., Internat. Assn. on Water Quality (1972–, specialist group on taste and odor control 1982–, chmn. organizing 1991 Off-Flavor Symp. 1987-91), Internat. Ozone Assn. (internat. bd. dirs. 1992–); editor: (w/ I.H. Suffet) Activated Carbon Adsorption of Organics from the Aqueous Phase, 2 vols. 1980; Treatment of Water by Granular Activated Carbon 1983; 86 tech. jour. articles on trace contaminant control in the water treatment process; rec: swimming, reading, bicycling, scuba diving. Ofc: McGuire Environ. Cons., Inc., 469 25th St. Santa Monica CA 90402-3103

MC HENRY, MALCOLM MICHAEL, physician, cardiologist; b. Feb. 5, 1934, San Francisco; s. Merl and Marcella (Bricca) McH.; m. Anne Budny, July 3, 1963; edn: BA, Stanford Univ. 1955; MD, USC Med. Sch. 1958. Career: intern, med. resident Univ. Mich., Ann Arbor 1958-61; cardiovascular disease fellowship UCSF 1961-63; staff cardiologist Lackland AFB, San Antonio, Tx. 1963-65; adult cardiologist Sutter Comm. Hosp., Sacto. 1965–; assoc. prof. medicine UC Davis 1969–; awards: Am. Heart Assn. Outstanding Achievement 1974; mem: Am. Coll. Cardiology, A.C.P., Royal Soc. Medicine London; 50 articles pub. in med. jours., 6 textbooks pub.; mil: capt. USAF 1961-63; rec: travel, art collecting. Ofc: 5301 F St Ste 117 Sacramento 95819

MC HUGH, JAMES JOSEPH, lawyer; b. Aug. 12, 1930, Philadelphia, Pa.; s. James Joseph and Patience Mary (McGowan) McH.; m. Rita Marie Huber, May 21, 1960; children: Margaret b. 1961, James b. 1964; edn: BA, Univ. Pa. Phila. 1951; LL.B, Univ. Pa. Law Sch. 1954; MA, George Washington Univ. 1972; admitted Supreme Ct. Pa. 1955. Career: ensign USN, Newport, R.I. 1955; legal ofcr. U.S. Naval Air Station, Pt. Mugu 1955-58, Treasure Island 1958-59, Office of Judge Advocate Gen., Wash. D.C. 1959-63, instr. Naval Justice Sch., Newport, R.I. 1963-65, judge advocate USN Bureau of Naval Personnel, Wash. D.C. 1965-68, staff judge advocate Comdr. in Chief Pacific Fleet, Pearl Harbor 1968-71; student sr. course U.S. Naval War Coll., Newport, R.I. 1971-72; spl. counsel Chief of Navy Ops., Wash. D.C. 1972-76; ofcr. in charge Naval Legal Service Office, San Francisco 1976-78; asst. judge advocate gen. USN, Wash. D.C. 1978-80; dep., judge advocate gen. USN 1980-84; asst. dean McGeorge Sch. Law, Sacto. 1984-86, assoc. dean 1986–; honors: Phi Beta Kappa, Navy Commend. Medal, Merit. Service Medal, Legion of Merit, Disting. Service Medal; mem: Am. Bar Assn., Fed. Bar Assn., Am. Legion, Navy League; Republican; R.Cath.; rec: golf. Res: 4704 Olive Oak Way Carmichael 95608

MCINTOSH, ABRAHAM STEVEN, III, physician; b. July 19, 1963, Carmichael, Calif.; s. Abraham McIntosh, Jr. and Alberta (Campbell) M.; m. Myrna Danette Woods, June 9, 1991; edn: BA, chem., Dartmouth Coll. 1985; postgrad. (MPH cand.), San Diego State Sch. of Public Health 1986-87; MD, Univ. of Ill. Coll. of Medicine 1991; lic. physician, St. of Calif.; cert. Am. Bd. of Internal Medicine 1994. Career: res. asst., hematology, Brigham & Women's Hosp./Harvard Med. Sch. 1985-86; adminstrv. asst. San Diego Co. Dept. Health 1987; internship, primary internal medicine, Highland Gen. Hosp. 1991-92, residency 1992-94, chief residency, internal medicine 1994-95; staff physician, emergency medicine, Kaiser Found. Hosp., Hayward 1993-95; staff physician, acute care, C-3 medicine and adult immunology clinics, Highland Gen. Hosp. 1994-95; fellowship, gastroenterology, Phoenix/VA Good Samaritan Hosp./Univ. of Ariz. Coll. of Medicine Combined Tng. Prog. (7/95-6/97); honors: Casque and Gauntlet Sr. Honor Soc., Alpha Phi Alpha Frat., Outstanding Young Men of Am. 1992; mem: AMA 1991–, Nat. Med. Assn. 1991–, Am. Coll. of Physicians 1991–, Highland Assocs. of Interns and Residents 1991–; rec: golf, weight lifting, sailing, skiing, scuba diving. Res: 6971 Hogan Drive Sacramento 95822

MCINTYRE, ROBERT MALCOLM, utility company executive; b. Dec. 18, 1923, Portland, Oreg.; s. Daniel A. and Bessie W. (Earsley) McI.; m. Marilyn Westcott, Aug. 27, 1949; 1 dau. Julie b. 1951; edn: BA, UCLA, 1950; graduate study UCLA, USC, Columbia Univ. Career: mgmt. positions So. Calif. Gas Co., 1952-68: v.p. 1970, senior v.p. 1974, dir. 1975–, pres. 1980-85, bd. chmn./CEO 1985-88; dir. Pacific Lighting Service Co. 1975-81; mem. Pacific Coast Gas Assn. (past dir.), Am. Gas Assn., trustee Inst. of Gas Technology; Regent's Professor UC Irvine Grad. Sch. of Mgmt.; honors: 49er Club award Pac. Coast Gas Assn. (1979), Nat. Hispanic Scholarship Award 1980, Mex. Amer. Legal Def. and Ednl. Fund (MALDEF) Award for outstanding service, corporate responsibility 1981, Pacific Pioneer Award, Jr. Chamber of Commerce Award of Merit, NCCJ Humanitarian Award, L.A. Area C.of C. Medici Award, L.A. chpt. NAACP Roy Wilkins Award, decorated Order of the Rising Sun With Gold Rays and Ribbon from His Imperial Majesty Emperor Hirohito of Japan 1988; civic bds: L.A. Area C.of C. (past chmn.), NCCJ (dir.), US-Mex. C.of C. (dir.), L.A. Co. Academic Decathlon, MALDEF (dir.), Korean Am. Centennial Commn.,

Calif. Council for Environ. and Econ. Balance (dir.), Calif. Found. on Environ. and Economy (dir.), UCLA Found. (trustee), Town Hall of Calif. (bd. govs., life mem.), Plaza de la Raza Bus. Indus. Advy. Bd. (chmn. 1982), Huntington Library Soc. of Fellows, L.A. Music Ctr. Founders, Newport Harbor Art Mus. Bus. Council, Orange Co. Bus. Com. for the Art (steering com.), L.A. Olympic Citizens Advy. Commn., UCLA GSM Dean's Council, Pepperdine Univ. Assocs., USC Assocs., L.A. United Way (bd.), United Way O.C. (exec. com.), Commn. of the California, Mayor Bradley's Ad Hoc Com. on City Fin., L.A. Orthopaedic Hosp. (trustee, exec. com., Lowman Club), Hoag Memorial Hosp. Found. (pres.); clubs: California, Big Canyon Country, Center, Pacific, 100; Phi Kappa Psi; mil: lt.sg USN 1942-46; Republican; Presbyterian; rec: swimming, fishing, golf. Ofc: So. Calif. Gas Co. 555 W Fifth St Los Angeles 90013-1011

MCINTYRE, ROBERT WHEELER, conservation organization executive; b. Aug. 26, 1936, Chicago, Ill.; s. Henry L. and Winifred (Wheeler) McI.; m. Emily Beardsly Taylor, Oct. 12, 1961 (div. 1985); children: Burley b. 1964, Nancy b. 1965, Oliver b. 1967, Shanna b. 1968, Amanda b. 1971; m. Miriam de Jesus Zarate, June 23, 1990; edn: AB in sociology, Stanford Univ. 1959; MBA, Harvard Univ. 1964. Career: loan analyst Wells Fargo Bank, San Francisco 1964-65; supr. budget analysis Ford Aerospace, Palo Alto 1965-69; controller Allied Life Sciences, San Leandro 1969-70; ptnr. Diplomat Mfg. Co., Palo Alto 1970-71; staff cons. Opportunity Through Ownership, San Francisco 1971-72; gen. mgr. Quality Metal Finishers 1972-73; sr. v.p., c.f.o. The Trust for Public Land 1973–; dir. Environ. Vols., Palo Alto 1980–; advy. bds.: Dorothy Erskine Open Space Fund, San Francisco 1978–; Resource Renewal Inst., Sausalito 1988–; Water Heritage Trust, Sausalito 1988–; Peninsula Open Space Trust, Menlo Park 1978–; Marin Headlands Advy. Com., Sausalito 1978-81; awards: Trust for Pub. Lands Presdl. Citation 1988, Environ. Vols. spl. service 1989; mem: Robert C. Wheeler Found. (dir., treas.), Families Adopting Inter-racially (dir. 1971-74), Palo Alto Jr. Achievement (advisor 1966-67); clubs: Harvard (NY), Harvard (Boston), Sundown Tennis (San Mateo); mil: lt. (jg) USN 1959-62; USNR 1962-64; rec: hiking, backpacking, tennis. Ofc: The Trust for Public Land 116 New Montgomery 4th Floor San Francisco 94105

MCKEAN, KEITH EDWARD, transportation engineer, retired state transportation executive; b. June 1, 1925, Pierre, S. Dak.; s. Harold Ambrose and Essie Irene (Whisler) McK.; m. Emily, Nov. 6, 1954; children: David b. 1955, Patricia b. 1957, Jill b. 1959, Jacquelyn b. 1964; edn: BCE, USC, 1950; Reg. Civil Engr., Calif. (C10691, 1957). Career: project engr. Calif. Div. of Hwys., Los Angeles 1952-61; senior engr. 1961-67; engring. mgr. Calif. Dept. of Transp., Los Angeles 1967-79; Dist. 7 p ogram mgr. for $2 Billion Dollar I-105 Transitway Program, L.A., 1979-83, dir. Dist. 9, Bishop, 1983-87; organizing dir. new state transp. dist., dir. Dist. 12, Santa Ana, 1987-90; v.p. transportation engring. Robert Bein, William Frost & Associates, 1991-94; coauthor, faculty Caltrans Mid-Level Mgmt. Tng., 1986-87; chmn. Caltrans Statewide Mgmt. & Devel. Com., Sacto. 1987; mem. UC Irvine civil engr. advy. com. 1988-90, and chmn. curriculum com. Friends of Civil Engring., UCI, 1991-93; mem: Am. Road and Trans. Builders Assn. 1983-90, Am. Public Works Assn. (exec. com. L.A. sect. 1978-80), Am. Soc. of Civil Engrs. (pres. Desert Area br. 1984-85, chmn. L.A. sect. life mem. com. 1991-93), Soc. for Advancement of Mgmt. (pres. L.A. sect. 1981-83), Santa Ana Rotary Club (dir. 1989-91), Civic Center Optimist Club, L.A. (pres. 1977-78); awards: Outstanding Pres., Gov.'s award, Outstanding Club, Honor Club, 1978); mil: 1st lt. US Amy 1943-46, 1950-52; Republican; R.Cath.; rec: philately, fishing. Res/Ofc: 14503 Biola Ave La Mirada 90638

MC KEE, CHRISTOPHER FULTON, astrophysicist; b. Sept. 6, 1942, Washington, D.C.; s. William Fulton and Gertrude Anna (Scheele) McK.; m. Suzanne Marie Peshette, June 20, 1965; children: William b. 1968, Christopher b. 1973, Maria b. 1979; edn: BA, Harvard Univ. 1963; PhD, UC Berkeley 1970. Career: research physicist Lawrence Livermore Lab., Livermore 1969-70; research assoc. CalTech, Pasadena 1970-71; asst. prof. Harvard Univ., Cambridge, Mass. 1971-74; asst. prof., prof. UC Berkeley 1974–, dir. space scis. lab. 1985–; cons. Lawrence Livermore Labs. 1970–; honors: Phi Beta Kappa, CalTech Sherman Fairchild disting. scholar 1982; mem: Nat. Acad. of Sciences 1992; 100+ research articles pub. in sci. jours. Ofc: Univ. of Calif. Physics Dept. Berkeley 94720

MCKEE, ROGER CURTIS, (presiding) federal magistrate judge; b. Feb. 11, 1931, Waterloo, Ia.; s. James A. and Leonace (Burrell) McK.; m. Roberta Jeanne Orvis, Sept. 4, 1954; children: Andrea b. 1959, Brian b. 1961, Paul b. 1969; edn: BA, Univ. of N.Iowa, 1955; MA, Univ. Ill., Urbana, 1960; JD, Univ. San Diego, 1968; admitted bar Calif., 1970. Career: telegrapher Ill. Cent. R.R., Iowa Div., 1950-55; tng. asst. No. Ill. Gas, Aurora, Ill., 1958-60; industrial rels. General Dynamics Corp., San Diego, 1960-70; law ptnr. Powell & McKee, San Diego, 1970-83; U.S. magistrate judge U.S. Courts, San Diego, 1983–; instr. in law and bus. National Univ., San Diego, 1972-87; mem: Calif. State Bar 1970–, Navy League of the U.S. 1963–, Naval Reserve Assn. 1968–, Submarine League 1978–; civic: Amateur Radio Club of S.D. 1987–, S.D. Dixieland Jazz Soc. (bd. 1984–), Dolphin Mariners (skipper 1986-88); pub. article in Naval Inst. Proceedings, 1958; mil: capt. (ret.) US Naval Reserve 1948-85, Active duty Pacific- Mideast 1955-58; Republican; Presbyterian; rec: amateur radio (KK6XY), hiking, travel, reading. Ofc: U.S. Court House, 940 Front St San Diego 92101

MC KELVEY, GEORGE IRWIN, III, consultant; b. May 5, 1925, Glen Ridge, NJ; s. George and Florence McK.; m. Velma Vergara, 1959; 1 son, George Stuart b. 1965; edn: AB, Univ. Rochester 1950, MA, 1957. Career: exec. secty. Alumni Assn., Univ. Rochester, 1950-54, dir. Alumni relations 1954-56; assoc. dir. American Alumni Council 1956-57; dir. devel. Harvey Mudd Coll. 1957-68, v.p. devel. and planning, 1968-90; asst. dir. Rancho Santa Ana Botanic Garden 1990-92; dir. Raymond M. Alf Museum; mem: Mens Garden Club (L.A.), Psi Upsilon; mil: aviation cadet USNR 1943-44, ensign USMS 1945-46; Presbyterian. Ofc: 1175 Baughman Drive Claremont 91711

MC KENNA, WILLIAM EDWARD, investment company executive; b. Aug. 9, 1919, Boston, Mass.; s. Alfred W. and Mary E.C. (Quigley) McK.; m. M. Eileen Sullivan (div. 1968); m. Mary N. Smith, Oct. 3 1968; children: William P., Kathleen M., Daniel J., Eileen F., Paul V., Mary Ellen; edn: BA, Holy Cross Coll. 1947; MBA, Harvard Univ. 1949; diplomate, C.P.A. N.Y., Calif. Career: staff acct. Touche Niven Bailey & Smart, N.Y.C. 1949-52; v.p., controller Monroe Calculating Machine Co., Orange, N.J. 1952-60; dir., v.p., treas., controller Litton Industries, Beverly Hills 1964-67; dir., chmn. CEO, dir. Hunt Foods & Industries Inc., Fullerton 1967-68; chmn. CEO, dir. Norton Simon Inc.,= 1968-69; bus. cons. 1969-70; chmn., dir. Technicolor Inc., Hollywood 1970-76; chmn. bd. Sambos Restaurants Inc., Santa Barbara 1979-81; Vencap Inc., Irvine 1977-79; dir. Calif. Amplifier Inc.; Safeguard Health Enterprises Inc.; Calprop Corp.; WMS Industries Inc.; Drexler Tech. Inc.; mem. pres. council, regent, assoc. trustee Coll. Holy Cross; trustee St. Johns Hosp. Found.; regent St. Mary's Coll., Moraga; mem: Am. Inst. C.P.A., Nat. Assn. Accts., Fin. Execs. Inst., Calif. Soc. C.P.A., N.Y. Soc. C.P.A., N.J. Soc. C.P.A., Tailhook Assn., Delta Epsilon, Alpha Sigma Nu Soc. Address: 912 Oxford Way Beverly Hills 90210

MCKEON, HOWARD P. (BUCK), congressman; b. Los Angeles; m. Patricia; 6 children; edn: BS, Brigham Young Univ. Career: mem. Council City of Santa Clarita, Calif. 1987-92, mayor 1987-88; mem. 103rd-104th Congresses from 25th Calif. dist. 1993–; founding dir., chmn. Valencia Nat. Bank; co-owner Howard & Phil's Western Wear, Inc.; hon. chmn. Leukemia Soc. Celebrity prog. 1990, Red Cross Com. Support Campaign 1992; active Dist. Com Boy Scouts Am.; chmn., trustee William S. Hart Sch. Dist. 1979-87; chmn., dir. Henry Mayo Newhall Meml. Hosp. 1983-87; mem Calif. Rep. State Central Com. 1988-92; bd. dirs. Santa Clarita Valley Small Bus. Devel. Ctr. 1990-92, Canyon Country C.of C. 1988-92. Ofc: US House of Reps 307 Cannon House Office Bldg Washington DC 20515

MCKEVITT, GERALD L., Jesuit priest and historian; b. July 3, 1939, Longview, Wash.; s. Edward Henry and Evelyn Almeda (Acock) McK.; edn: BA, Univ. San Francisco, 1961; MA, USC, 1964; PhD, UCLA, 1972; BST, Gregorian Univ., Rome 1975, ordained priest S.J., Roman Catholic Ch., 1975. Career: dir. univ. archives Santa Clara Univ., Santa Clara, Calif. 1975-85, chair history dept. 1984-88, univ. historian 1985–, assoc. prof. 1981-93, prof. 1993-rector Jesuit Comm. 1993–; honors: Oscar O. Winther Award, Western Hist. Assn. 1991; mem. bd. trustees Gonzaga Univ., Spokane 1988–, Santa Clara Univ. 1993–, Nat. Seminar on Jesuit Higher Edn. 1990-94; author: The University of Santa Clara, A History, 1851-1979 (1979), and numerous scholarly articles on Calif. and Western U.S. history. Ofc: History Dept. Santa Clara Univ., Santa Clara 95053

MCKINNON, MICHAEL D., broadcast executive; b. June 12, 1939, Los Angeles; s. Clinton D. and Lucille (McVey) M.; m. Sandra E., May 22, 1973; children: Gaylynn b. 1961, Donnie b. 1962, Michael Dean b. 1964, Mark b. 1968; edn: Univ. of Redlands, Calif. 1958-60; worked various dept.'s San Diego Sentinel newspaper 1960-63; publisher The La Jolla Light/ Journal 1963–; owner KUSI-TV Ch. 51, San Diego; bd. chmn., pres., owner KIII-TV Ch. 3, Corpus Christi, Tx.; pres., owner KBMT-TV Ch. 12, Beaumont, Port Arthur; elected Texas State Senate 1972-76; dir. Calif. Bdcstrs. Assn. 1986–; pres. Texas Assn. of Bdcstrs. 1971, dir. 1965-72, mem. Small Market Com. 1972-73; ABC News advy. com. 1979-80; bd. mem., exec. com. Television and Radio Polit. Action Com. 1980-83; honors: Boss of Yr. from Nat. Secty.'s Internat. Assn. 1970, Outstanding Young Man of Yr. from Jr. CofC. 1971, Presidential Citation Holder from Pres. Nixon, recip. Special Citation from Nat. LULAC Council for svc. to Mexican-Americans; statewide and local awards for anti-drug program "Drugs A to Z"; mem: Nat. Assn. Bdcstrs., Bdcsting. Promotion Assn.; Assn. Bdcst. Execs. of Texas; Television Bureau of Advting.; civic: advy. bd. dirs. First City Bank, Corpus Christi, Tx., chmn./bd. govs. Art Mus. of So. Texas, mem. exec. com. Bd. of Trustees of Redlands Univ., Calif., mem. San Diego Historical Soc., San Diego Mus. of Art (President's Cir.), Rest and Aspiration Soc., San Diego. Ofc: KUSI-TV, Channel 51 4575 Viewridge Ave San Diego 92123

MCKOY, B. VINCENT, educator; b. March 25, 1938, Trinidad, British West Indies; s. Allan C. and Doris McK.; m. Anne E. Shannon, March 18, 1967; 1 son, Christopher Allan b. 1973; edn: BSCE, Tech. Univ. Nova Scotia 1960; PhD, Yale Univ. 1964. Career: instr. Calif. Inst. Tech., Pasadena 1964-66, asst. prof. 1966-69, assoc. prof. 1969-75, prof. 1975–; chmn. of the faculty 1985-87; awards: Guggenheim fellow 1973, Gov. Gen. of Canada Medal 1960; Fellow of:

Am. Physical Soc.; 300 papers pub. in sci. jours., ed. conf. proceedings, 1979, 83, 87. Res: 3855 Keswick Rd Flintridge 91011 Ofc: California Institute of Technology Pasadena 91125

MCLURKIN, THOMAS CORNELIUS, JR., government lawyer; b. July 28, 1954, Los Angeles; s. Thomas Cornelius and Willie Mae (O'Connor) McL.; m. Charmaine Bobo, M.D. edn: AB, USC, 1976, MPA, 1980; JD, Univ. LaVerne, S.F.V., 1982; PhD pub. admin., USC, 1995; admitted Calif. Bar 1984. Career: law clk. City of Los Angeles Dept. Water & Power, 1979-82; judicial extern Fed. Magistrate Hon. Ralph J. Geffen (Ret.), L.A. 1982, Fed. Dist. Ct. Judge Hon. Terry J. Hatter, Jr., L.A. 1983; sr. law clk. L.A. County Dist. Atty., 1983; sr. law clk. City of Los Angeles, 1984, dep. city atty., prosecutor criminal br. 1984-89, dep. city atty., tort liability litigator Dept. Water & Power Div. 1989–; honors: Eagle Scout 1970, Honor Medal for Heroism BSA 1984, Outstanding Young Man in Am. Nat. Jaycees 1984; mem: Am. Bar Assn., Assn. of Am. Trial Attys., L.A. Co. Bar Assn., Am. Soc. for Pub. Adminstrn., Langston Law Assn. L.A., USC Gen. Alumni Assn. (bd. govs., exec. com. 1986-90), USC Black Alumni Assn.- Ebonics (bd. dirs., pres. 1988-89), USC Pres.'s Circle (bd. dirs.), Scapa Praetors/USC Sch. Pub. Admin.; civic: L.A. World Affairs Council, BSA L.A. Area Council (bd. dirs., sustaining mem. 1976–), BSA Verdugo Area Council (bd. dirs.), Hillsides Home for Children Pasadena (bd. dirs. 1990-92), Smithsonian Assocs., Optimist Internat. Hollywood (charter mem.), Pasadena Hist. Soc., Pasadena Lodge BPOElks, Am. Legion, Reserve Officers Assn.; coauthor w/Donald R. O'Connor (hist. ref. book) Facts in American History (1968, 2d edition 1989); mil: Major USAR JAGC 1987–, currently chief, criminal law 311th Corps Support Command at Los Angeles (COSCOM); Republican; Holman United Methodist Ch.; rec: sailing, tennis, world history. Res: Glendale. Ofc: Office of the City Attorney Water & Power Div. 111 No. Hope St. Ste. 340 Los Angeles 90051

MCMANUS, RICHARD PHILIP, financial institution executive, lawyer; b. Oct. 20, 1929, Keokuk, Iowa; s. Edward William and Kathleen (O'Connor) McM.; m. Marjorie Theresa Mullaney, Nov. 5, 1955; children: Michael b. 1957, Mark b. 1962, Matthew b. 1967; edn: BA, St. Ambrose Univ. 1949; JD, Univ. Mich. Ann Arbor 1952; MBA, Roosevelt Univ. 1965; admitted St. Bar Iowa 1952, Ill. 1957, Calif. 1982. Career: ptnr. McManus & McManus, Keokuk, Iowa 1952-63; div. counsel Navy Facility Engr. Command, Great Lakes, Ill. 1963-66; v.p., dir. of law Household Fin., Prospect Heights, Ill. 1966-81; trustee Village of Lake Bluff, Ill. 1974-78; exec. v.p., secty., gen. counsel Security Pacific Fin. Services Inc., San Diego 1981-92; lectr. Loyola Univ., Chgo. 1970-71; dir. Security Pacific Fin. Systems Inc., San Diego 1981-92; pres., dir. Mosamac Co. 1980–; honors: Beta Gamma Sigma; mem: Am. Bar Assn., Calif. Bar Assn., Am. Fin. Services Assn. (chmn. law com. 1981-82), Calif. Fin. Services Assn. (chmn. law com. 1981), Conf. Consumer Fin. Law (dir. 1976), Elks, Am. Legion (v.comdr. 1961-63), Tijuana/San Diego Habitat for Humanity (dir. 1992-94); clubs: University (S.D.); num. articles pub. in profl. jours., 1964; mil: lt. col. USAF 1952-53; Democrat; Cath.; rec: golf, cabinet making, flying. Ofc:17305 Campillo Dr San Diego 92128

MCMASTER, LOREN E., lawyer; b. Aug. 13, 1944, Glendale; s. Vernon C. and Doris A. (Pool) McM.; m. Anne Wenneis, Nov. 4, 1966; children: Mary Camille b. 1967, Suzanne b. 1968; edn: BA, UC Davis 1966; JD, 1969; admitted St. Bar Calif., U.S. Supreme Ct., U.S. Ct. Appeals 9th Circuit, U.S. Dist. Ct. Eastern Dist., No. Dist., Central Dist. Career: dep. atty. gen. St. Calif., Sacto. 1969-72; atty. Calif. St. Employees Assn. 1972-73, chief counsel 1973-80; sole practice, Sacto. 1980–; instr. real estate law Sacto. City Coll. 1970-72; arbitrator Sacto. Superior Ct. 1980-88; Superior Ct. judge pro tempore 1988–; awards: Am. Jurisprudence 1967-69, Calif. St. Employees Assn. Outstanding Service 1980, Asian Pacific Am. Coalition Recognition 1987; mem: Am. Bar Assn. (labor law sect.), Sacto. Co. Bar Assn., Calif. St. Bar Assn.; articles pub. in profl. jours., 1969, 77; rec: hiking, camping, travel. Ofc: 2400 22nd St Ste 110 Sacramento 95818

MCMILLAN, HORACE JIM, executive, physician, retired; b. Oct. 30, 1919, Mineola, Tx.; s. Lemon Columbus and Joann Aletha (Zollars) McM.; m. Jessie, Oct. 21, 1942, (div.); children: Yvonne Camille (Sawyer) b. 1943, Michelle Louise b. 1972; edn: BS, Prairie View A&M Coll. 1942; MD, Meharry Medical Coll. 1950; grad. wk. St. Louis Univ. 1945-46; H.M.O. Cert., UC Los Angeles 1975. Career: prin. Family Medical Center, pres. Physicians Inv. Corp., 1988-92; family practice physician, Santa Barbara, 1952-88, ret. 1988; staff Mt. Francis Hosp., Santa Barbara Cottage Hosp., and Goleta Valley Comm. Hosp. (founder GVCH 9/17/71, one of 10, mem. bd. dirs. 1967-77; appt. 1st chmn. Santa Barbara Mayor's Advy. Com. on Human Relations 1968, chmn. Community Health Task Force 1973-81; innovator of Urban Renewal & Devel., Community Rels. Commn., and fed. Low-Cost Housing for Santa Barbara, 1960s; founder Franklin Neighborhood Center, 1975; mem: Am., Calif., Santa Barbara County Acad. Family Practice 1982–, Am. Assn. for Clin. Immunology and Allergy 1982-88, NAACP (life); awards: resolutions for comm. service Calif. Legislature Assem., County of Santa Barbara Bd. of Suprs. 1988, Franklin Neighborhood Ctr. 10th anniversary award of appreciation for making the center a reality (9/28/85), Afro-Am. Community Ctr. award "for helping us to realize the dream of Martin Luther King, Jr." (1/25/86), 35 yrs. of outstanding comm. svc. NAACP, Maharry Med. Coll. pres.'s award for 25 yrs. svc. to mankind 1950-75, Goleta Valley C.of C. award for helping provide outstanding health resource- Goleta V. Comm. Hosp., Com. for Black Culture appreciation for outstanding svc. to comm., appreciation Community Health Task Force, 1990 Endowment for Youth Com. Community Service Award in spl. recogn. for sustaining svs. as a primary mover in improving the quality of life in health svs., housing, employment & edn. in the Santa Barbara Comm. 1990; recipient Santa Barbara Newspress "Lifetime Achiev. Award" with congratulations from House of Representatives and State Senator from S.B. congl. dist.; personal papers deposited in Calif. Ethnic & Multicultural Archives, Davidson Lib., UC Santa Barbara, 4/4/94; mil: chief p.o., chief pharmacist mate USN 1942-46, 1st black pharmacists mate in hist. of US Coast Guard; Democrat; Methodist; rec: travel, sports, reading. Res: 3340 McCaw Ave #103 Santa Barbara 93105

MCMORRIS, CLINT, commercial real estate broker; b. July 5, 1939, Memphis, Tenn.; s. Rudolph J. and Carolyn (Bell) McM.; m. Anita, Sept. 20, 1975; children: Clint b. 1976, Scot b. 1978; edn: BS, Memphis State Univ. 1963. Career: sales/leasing office/indsl. property, senior v.p. Heger Realty Corp., 1972–; mem: Am. Indsl. Real Estate Assn. (bd. dirs., secty., treas., sr. advy. com.), Soc. of Indsl. and Office Realtors (pres. L.A. chpt. 1994), Nat. Assn. Realtors; club: Palos Verdes Tennis Club; Republican; R.Cath.; rec: tennis. Res: 3909 Via Campesina Palos Verdes Estates 90274 Ofc: Heger Realty Corp 5657 E Washington Blvd Los Angeles 90040

MCMULLEN, BRYAN T., chiropractor; b. June 6, 1946, Jacksonville, Fla.; s. Thomas K. and Marie V. (McGraph) McM.; edn: BA, UC Berkeley 1974; DC, Los Angeles Co. Chiropractic 1978. Career: chiropractor, Beverly Hills; awards: Toastmasters Best Speaker 1988; mem: Toastmaster (asst. v.p. 1989-90); rec: marathon running. Address: McMullen Chiropractic 8530 Wilshire Blvd Ste 403 Beverly Hills 90211

MC MULLINS, TOMMY, bank executive; b. Sept. 15, 1942, Macon, Ga.; s. Alummer McMullins and Fannie (Thomas) Anderson; m. Gwendolyn Williams, Dec. 18, 1966; children: Tommy b. 1970, Tyrone b. 1974, Timothy b. 1979. Career: v.p. First Interstate Bank, Los Angeles 1965-81; Wells Fargo, L.A. 1981-94, Citibank FSB 1994–; recipient pres.'s award NAACP Pasadena 1988; mem. Kiwanis, Monrovia (bd. 1973-77), Rotary Intl., Pasa. (Bell Garden bd. 1979-81), Internat. Visitor Council of L.A. (pres. 1994, 95); coauthor (study) The Emerging Hispanic Majority, 1981; mil: cpl. USMC 1966-68; Baptist; rec: fishing, camping. Res: 1245 Rubio Vista Rd Altadena 91001

MCNEES, CARYL, professor; b. Nov. 5, 1938, Sewickley, Pa.; d. Floyd Raymond and Ione (Earl) McNees; edn: BA, English, Grove City Coll., Pa., 1960; M. Edn., English, Univ. of Pitts., 1968; EdD, English, Univ. of Va., Charlottesville, 1972; MS in Marriage, Family, Child Therapy, Univ. of La Verne, Calif., 1992. Career: H.S. English tchr., Pa.; prof. of English, Cal Poly, Pomona 1972–; cons., Claremont, Calif. Unified Sch. Dist. 1977-78; awards: Kappa Delta, Univ. of Va. 1971; Lychenos Soc., Univ. of Va. 1972; Golden Key Award, Calif. State Univ., Pomona 1990; Psi Chi Honorary, Univ. of La Verne, Calif. 1991; mem: Nat. Council Tchrs. of English 1970–, Modern Lang. Assn. 1972, Calif. Assn. of Marriage, Family, Child Therapists 1989–; Kappa Delta Edn. Honorary; Am. Assn. of Univ. Women, Pomona; author: various articles pub. in edn. and English jours.; Presbyterian; rec: keyboard, piano, tennis, bridge. Ofc: Calif. State Univ., Temple Ave. Pomona 91768

MCNEIL, MALCOLM STEPHEN, lawyer; b. Jan. 7, 1956, San Francisco; s. Henry Stephen and Adeline Elizabeth (LaVoie) McN.; m. Shahrezad Mabourakh; children: Jennifer b. 1975, Geoffrey b. 1977, Vanessa b. 1984; edn: AA, L.A. City Coll. 1976; BA, Antioch Univ. 1980; JD, Loyola Law Sch. 1983; admitted bar: Calif. 1983, U.S. Fed. Ct. no. dist. 1984, cent. dist. 1991, Ct. of Appeals 9th cir. 1989. Career: sales mgr. Metropolitan Life Ins. Co. 1977-82; law clerk Gilbert, Kelly, Crowley & Jennett 1982-83; atty. law firm Briedenbach, Swainston, Yokaitis & Crispo 1983-84, Law Offices Brian F. Zimmerman 1984; Law Offices Malcolm S. McNeil, Los Angeles 1984–; corporate counsel: Euram Flight Centres Inc., Security Systems Inc., Pak Trading Co. Inc., Citic Trading USA Inc.; instr. Northrop Univ. 1987–; honors: Sigma Tau Sigma 1975, Dean's List 1982, pres. Rep Law Forum 1981-83, Phi Alpha Delta; mem. Westchester C.of C., Marina del Rey C.of C., Assn. Internationale Des Jeunes Avocats (exec. com.); publs: legal article on pre-judgment interest, 1982; Republican; R.Cath.; rec: Judo, skiing, book collecting. Law Offices of Malcolm S. McNeil, 5777 W Century Blvd Ste 1475 Los Angeles 90045-5631 Tel: 310/216-0747 FAX 310/216-5736

MC NEILL, DANIEL RICHARD, author; b. June 1, 1947, San Francisco; s. Harry Daniel and Maureen Evangeline (Sherriff) McN.; m. Rosalind Deborah Gold, Dec. 21, 1984; edn: BA, UC Berkeley 1975; JD, Harvard Law Sch. 1982. Career: pres. Carnelian Software, Culver City 1988-89; honors: Phi Beta Kappa; author: Fuzzy Logic, 1993 (winner of 1992-93 L.A. Times Book Prize in Sci. & Tech.); rec: mountain climbing. Res: 9905 Farragut Dr #2 Culver City 90232

MCNELLEY, DONALD BENAGH, lawyer; b. Jan. 25, 1934, Birmingham, Ala.; s. William Wert and Dorothy (Benagh) McN.; m. Ann Lovelace Stewart, June 18, 1955; children: Carolyn b. 1956, Anne b. 1958, Donald B. b. 1962; edn: BA, Univ. Ala. 1955; JD, USC, 1969; admitted St. Bar Calif. 1970. Career: human factors splst. System Devel. Corp., Santa Monica 1959-69; atty. Equity Funding Corp., Los Angeles 1969-72; atty., exec., gen. counsel Bateman Eichler Hill Richards Inc 1972-87; ptnr. Kindel & Anderson, Los Angeles 1987-91; of counsel Schlecht, Shevlin and Shoenberger, Palm Springs, 1991–; instr. Univ. W.L.A. Sch. Law, Culver City 1970-72; mem: Am. Bar Assn. (fed. reg. of securities com.), LA Co. Bar Assn., Securities Industry Assn. (legal and compliance div.); mil: 1st lt. USAF 1955-58; Republican; Episcopalian. Ofc: Schlecht Shevlin & Shoenberger, 801 E Tahquitz Cyn Way Ste 100 Palm Springs 92262

MCNERNEY, ROBERT JAMES, educator, retired; b. May 2, 1916, Fairbury, Neb.; s. Harry A. and Blanche (Pantier) McN.; m. Jennie, June 9, 1937; children: R. James b. 1938, Sharon b. 1940, George b. 1941; edn: AB, Univ. Neb. 1938, MA, 1960-61; counseling cert., UC Riverside 1974; pupil personnel svcs. cred. Calif.; comm. coll. supr. cred. Career: inspector US Maritime Commn. Oakland 1941-44; cost analyst 12th Naval Dist. Ind. Mgr. Mare Island 1945-46; real estate developer, planner Lincoln, Neb. 1947-51; asst. dir. Neb. State Real Estate Commn. 1952-57; instr. Neb. Public Schs. 1957-59; admissions counselor Iowa Wesleyan, Univ. Dubuque 1960-64; asst. dir. admissions Park Coll. 1965; registrar, dir. admissions/registrar Calif. Coll. of Med. 1966-68; exec. mgr. Solano County Taxpayers Assn. Fairfield 1969-70; counselor, attendance ofcr. Perris Union H.S. Dist. Sun City 1971-81; real estate broker 1982–; elected bd. dirs. Hemet Dist. Hosp. and chmn. bd. trustees Mt. San Jacinto Coll.; gov. apptd. mem. Calif. State Sunset Review Com. on Edn. 1983-85, Calif. State Advy. Commn. on Aging 1986-92; mem: Calif. Retired Tchrs. Assn. (pres. San Jacinto Mountain Div. 1988), Nat. Assn. of Real Estate Appraisers, SAR (chpt. pres. 1984), Calif. Comm. Coll. Trustees, Am. Comm. Coll. Trustees, Lions, Masons, Scottish Rite, Shriners; Republican (Calif. Central Com.); Christian. Res: 791 Oleander Hemet 92543

MCNICHOLS, STEPHEN LUCID ROBERT, JR., lawyer; b. June 5, 1943, Denver; s. Stephen Lucid Robert and Marjorie Roberta (Hart) McN.; children: Justin, Chelsea; edn: Monterey Inst. Fgn. Studies, 1964-65; BA, Pomona Coll., 1965; JD, UC Berkeley, 1968; admitted bar: Colo. 1968, Calif. 1969. Career: dep. dist. atty. San Luis Obispo Couty, 1970-73; assoc. Varni, Fraser, Hartwell & Van Blois, Hayward 1973-76; ptnr. Varni, Fraser, Hartwell, McNichols & Rodgers, Hayward 1976-86; Hallgrimson, McNichols, McCann & Inderbitzen (& predecessor firm, San Ramon), Pleasanton 1987–; mem: ABA (litigation sect.), Calif. Bar Assn. (adminstrn. justice com.), Alameda County Bar Assn. (bd. 1986-88), So. Alameda County Bar Assn. (bd. 1978-80), Assn. Trial Lawyers Am., Calif. Trial Lawyers Assn., Alameda-Contra Costa County Trial Lawyers Assn. (bd. 1977-78), Barristers (bd. 1974-77); civic: Morro Bay Planning Commn. (1970-72, chmn. 1972), Children's Hosp. Found. (bd. 1980-83); Democrat; rec: skiing, running, golf. Res: 947 Redwood Dr Danville 94526 Ofc: Hallgrimson, McNichols, McCann & Inderbitzen, 5000 Hopyard Rd Ste 400 Pleasanton 94588

MC NICOLL, MICHAEL PATRICK, physician-surgeon; b. 1957; s. Joseph and Joanne McN.; m. Krystyna; edn: BS cum laude, biochemistry, UCLA 1979; MD, St. Univ. N.Y. 1983; dipl. Am. Bd. Otolaryngology (1988). Career: surgical L.A. Co.-USC Med. Center, Los Angeles 1983-84, head and neck surgery resident 1984-88; pvt. practice, Burbank 1988-89; surgeon with So. Calif. Permanente Medical Group, Los Angeles 1989–; clin. instr. otolaryngology L.A.Co.-USC 1988–; Fellow Am. Coll. Surgeons; mem: Am. Acad. Otolaryngology, Head & Neck Surgery; pub. med. jour. article, 1988.

MCNULTY, JOHN KENT, law educator; b. Oct. 13, 1934, Buffalo, N.Y.; s. Robert W. and Margaret D. McN.; m. Linda Conner, Aug. 20, 1955 (div. 1977); children: Martha b. 1956, Jennifer b. 1959, John b. 1961; m. Babette B. Barton, March 23, 1978 (div. 1988); edn: AB, Swarthmore Coll. 1956; LLB, Yale Law Sch. 1959. Career: clk. Justice Hugo L. Black, U.S. Supreme Ct., Wash. D.C. 1959-60; atty., assoc. Jones Day Cockley Reavis, Cleveland, Ohio 1960-64; prof. law UC Berkeley 1964–, Roger J. Traynor Prof. of Law 1991–; cons. on fed. taxation to lawyers, govt. and corps.; honors: Phi Beta Kappa, Order of Coif, Guggenheim Fellow for fiscal studies on "Simplification of US Fed. Income Tax Sys. by Structural Reform", 1977; mem: Am. Bar Assn., Am. Law Inst., Internat. Fiscal Assn. (U.S. bd.), Internat. Tax & Bus. Lawyer (bd.), Berkeley Tennis Club, Women's Faculty Club UC Berkeley; author: Fed. Income Tax. of Individuals (5th ed. 1995), Fed. Estate and Gift and Generation-Skipping Taxation (5th ed. 1994), Federal Income Taxation of S Corporations, 1992, coauthor w/Kragen: Cases & Materials on Fed. Income Taxation (4th ed. 1985); rec: tennis, opera, travel. Ofc: Univ. California 389 Boalt Hall Berkeley 94720 Tel: 510/642-1928

MC PHERSON, ROLF KENNEDY, clergyman, church official; b. March 23, 1913, Providence, R.I.; s. Harold S. and Aimee Elizabeth (Kennedy) McP.; m. Lorna De Smith, July 21, 1931 (dec.); children: Kay b. 1932, Marleen b. 1937 (dec.); edn: grad. So. Calif. Radio Inst., L.A. 1933; Hon. DD, 1944, Hon. LLD, 1988, L.I.F.E. Bible Coll.; ordained Internat. Ch. of Foursquare Gospel 1940.

Career: pres. Internat. Ch. of Foursquare Gospel, Los Angeles 1944-88, pres. emeritus 1988–; pres. LIFE Bible Coll. Inc. 1944-88; Echo Park Evangelistic Assn. (pres. 1944–), Pentecostal Fellowship N. Am. (bd. 1948-88), Nat. Assn. Evangelicals (bd. 1946-88); awards: 1st pl. Missionary Digest Film Festival 1956; editor Foursquare Mag., 1940-43. Ofc: Intl. Church of the Foursquare Gospel 1910 W Sunset Blvd Ste 200 Los Angeles 90026-0176

MCQUEEN, MARJORIE MARIE WYNKOOP, government archivist; b. Mar. 31,1927, Mexico City, Mex.; d. George M. and Marie (Chabert) Wynkoop; m. Halton Stephen McQueen, Mar. 8, 1952 (dec. 1982); children: Kathleen b. 1952, Stephen b. 1958, Patricia b. 1962, Michael b. 1955 (dec. 1955), grandson, James Robert Strong b. 1972; edn: BA, liberal arts, San Antonio (Tx.) Coll., 1952; AA, liberal studies, Coll. of the Desert, 1980; BA poli. sci., UC Riverside, 1983. Career: editor/writer USAF Electronic Security Command, San Antonio, Tx., 1946-52; free lance writer/photographer, 1952–; Librarian, USDA Salinity Lab., Riverside, CA, 1981-83; project officer and archivist USAF 1352 Audiovisual Squadron, Norton AFB, CA, 1984-93; archivist, Defense Visual Information Service, March AFB, CA, 1994–; instr., lectr. Nat. League of Am. Pen Women Inc., 1974-80 (pres. Palm Springs br. 1976-78, state historian 1978-80, mem.-at-large 1989–); indep. cons., Riverside area 1981–; owner/dir. Diversified Services, 1983–; awards: contest winner Writer's Digest Mag 1973; Historian annual award, photog. awards Nat. League of Am. pen Women Inc. 1976-80; Univ. Calif. scholar and grantee 1981-83; suggestor of year Norton AFB 1989; numerous photog. awards include County Fairs, PSA, others; mem: Nat. League of Am. Pen Women; Photographic Soc. of Am., World Affairs Council (Riv.); UCR Alumni Assn. (life); Older Women's League; Rancho Mirage C. of C. (v.p. publicity 1978-81); Fed. Women's Prog. (rep. Norton AFB 1985); Rancho Mirage Comm. Assn. (bd. dirs. 1978-81); The Soc. of Am. Archivists, 1993–; So. Calif. Archivists, 1993–; author/editor med. Doctor's Book on the Brain; writer continuity for radio and TV; contbr. articles to newspapers, jours., mags.; rec: photog., writing, travel. Ofc: DVIC/OM-AM, Bldg 2730,1363Z St., March AFB, CA 92518-2717

MCQUILLIN, RICHARD ROSS, management consultant; b. Oct. 15, 1956, Elyria, Ohio; s. Wayne Rupp and Frana Rose (Romp) McQ.; m. Riko Koga, Apr. 7, 1991; 1 son Richard K., Jr. b. 1995; edn: BSEE, Ohio State Univ., Columbus 1979; MSEE, USC, 1983; MBA, UC Los Angeles, 1990. Career: senior staff TRW, Inc. Redondo Beach 1979-88; senior cons. Deloitte & Touche, Los Angeles 1990-91; consulting mgr. NetBase Computing Inc., Torrance 1993–; awards: TRW fellow 1980-86, UCLA fellow 1989-90; mem: IEEE 1980–, Beta Gamma Sigma (life), USC Alumni Assn. (life), UCLA Alumni Assn. (life), TRW Investment Club Redondo Beach (pres. 1984-87), Patio Creek HOA (treas. 1986-90, pres. 1990–). Res: 19028 Entradero Ave Torrance 90503-1360 Ofc: NetBase Computing Inc 3625 Del Amo Blvd Ste 200 Torrance 90503

MCQUITTY, JOHN C., physician; b. Feb. 12, 1944, Wash. DC; s. Louis L. and Myra (Crocker) M.; m. Suzan J. Powell, Aug. 6, 1966; children: Alissa Ann b. 1972, Angela Lynn b. 1974; edn: MD, Univ. of Michigan, Ann Arbor 1970. Career: dir. pulmonary medicine Children's Hosp. Oakland 1977–; assoc. prof. of pediatrics UC San Francisco 1989–; mem: Am. Thoracic Soc., Am. Acad. of Pediatrics, Calif. Thoracic Soc.; mil: lt. col. US Army (Reserve) 1971–. Res: 160 Estates Dr Piedmont 94611 Ofc: Children's Hospital Oakland 747 52nd St Oakland 94609

MC WALTERS, JAMES G., institutional real estate investment advisory executive; b. Oct. 7, 1940, NYC; s. John and Mary McWalters; edn: midshipman, BS in aeronautical engring. and nuclear sci. (top 2% in grad. class), US Naval Acad., Annapolis, 1964. Career: precision machinist, Arizona Gear, Tucson 1958-60; prodn. supr. No. Am. Aviation, Downey, Calif. 1960; founder/pres. Advanced Protective Systems, Inc., San Diego 1969-71, merged with Sterling Security Svc., 1971; with Grubb and Ellis Comml. Brokerage Co. 1972-78: investment mktg. 1972-73, mgr. new tract sales, San Diego 1973-74, Los Angeles sales mgr. 1974-75, mgr. Investment Bus. Devel. 1975-76, Investment Div. coordinator 1974-78, mgr. L.A. Comml. Brokerage Co. 1975-78, vice pres. 1974-78, bd. dirs. 1976-78; pres. Vistar Comml. Brokerage Co., 1978-80; exec. vice pres./regional dir. Merrill Lynch Commercial Real Estate (developed commercial real estate brokerage network in western states), 1981-85, v.p. Merrill Lynch investment banking 1985-86, responsible for all transactional real estate activities West of Miss., mng. dir. PM Realty Advisors (reg. fin. advy. firm), Newport Beach 1986–; mil: served in USN 1960-69, led 1st bd. & search opns. on minesweeper Excel, Vietnam 1964-65, served 3 yrs. abd. nuclear submarine Snook, Vietnam Svc. Star; rec: flying, golf, tennis, ski. Ofc: PM Realty Advisors, 800 Newport Center Dr Ste 300 Newport Beach CA 92660

MCWATTERS, EDD DAVID, filmmaker and novelist; b. Oct. 27, 1930, Ottawa, Ont., nat. US cit. 1980; s. Vernon Wm. and Irene Elizabeth (Langdon) McW.; m. Betty Josephine Hollingshead, Oct. 14, 1976; children: Jon, Lynn, Cindy, Marc, Celene, Bradley, Janet and Timothy; 10 grandchildren; edn: spl. courses Western Univ., cert. Brooks Inst. of Photog. 1962. Career: formed a comedy tumbling act that toured the province with his scout troop, Hamilton,

Ont., worked as a young volunteer in servicemens canteen during WWII, as swim instr. for blind and disabled children; became an exhibition ballroom dancer in his twenties and won audition to appear on the Hit Parade Show on TV; moved to Santa Barbara, Calif. to study motion picture production, 1960, during student yrs. put on film shows for Hillcrest Home for cerebral palsy residents and for children in hospitals, during his sr. yr. at Brooks Inst. of Photography directed TV pilot aired on ABC satellite Sta. KEYT Channel 3; hd. of movie dept. Brooks Inst. of Photography, 1964-65; cameraman, editor in Hollywood 1965-70, director and writer, completed 108 TV shows, 30 documentaries; wrote and produced 15 of his own productions, won 80+ awards: The Highwayman (comedy), Egghead Meets Vampire (spl. effects), Bikini Capers (comedy), MagicBottle (fantasy), Wildest Surfer (humor), The Hungry Kook Goes Bazook (comedy), photography instr. Santa Barbara County Probation program for young court wards (ages 13-17) 1972-77, innovative rehabilitative pgm. later expanded to Lompoc and Santa Maria; founder, dir. The Santa Barbara Motion Picture Inst. 1972-73; 1980-82: produced TV pilots, TV commercials, videotaped for Japanese network; writer, songwriter and author, 1982–: 12 novels, his 1st Western novel in press (1991); book of verse (pub. 1991), contbr. 100+ poems in 78 anthologies; 28+ articles pub. based on his experience in filmmaking ind.; pub. in SAC TV News and Film; 6+ songs sold 1990–; winner 26 internat. film festival awards incl. A silver cup at Cannes with his first comedy and bronze medallion for his last comedy, 78+ literary awards, golden poet award, hon. dep. gov. Am. Biographical Inst. 1988; personal letters from both Pres. and Mrs. Bush in appreciation of article written, county Best of Fair award and 2 others for still photography 1995; mem: Photog. Soc. of Am., Soc. of Amateur Cinematographers (Fellow), Sierra Club, Audubon, San Diego Zoo, Smithsonian, AARP, P.S.A. Soc.; Jehovahs Witness; rec: photography, writing. Ofc: PO Box 2621 Big River, Earp 92242

MEADE, STEPHEN ALAN, executive director; b. Nov. 22, 1949, Boston, Mass.; s. Richard Alan and Rosemary M.; m. Donna Maria Diauto, Sept. 12, 1971 (div. 1981); m. Mary Lou Fountain, April 23, 1983; children: Christine b. 1973, Michelle b. 1975; edn: BS, Boston St. Coll. 1971. Career: underwriting mgr. Firemans Fund Ins. Co., San Francisco 1972-81; asst. v.p. San Francisco Reinsurance Co. 1981-84; sr. v.p. Balboa Life & Casualty, Irvine 1984-88; pres. Prodigy Group, Santa Ana 1988–; awards: Ins. Inst. of Am. Academic Excellence 1981; mem: Internat. Assn. Fin. Planners; mil: Mass. Army Nat. Guard 1970-76; Episcopalian; rec: photog., tennis, piano. Res: 2329 N Linwood Ave Santa Ana 92705 Ofc: Prodigy Group International 2639 N Grand Ave Ste 270 Santa Ana 92705

MEADOR, ROSS DESHONG, lawyer; b. Aug. 23, 1954, Mexico; s. Bruce Staffle and Betty Lee (DeShong) M.; edn: BA, UC San Diego, 1980; JD, Boalt Hall Sch. of Law UC Berkeley, 1986; admitted Calif. bar, 1987. Career: res. asst. Michael Ashburne, J.D., Oakland 1983-85; lectr. in law Street Law Proj. community legal edn. pgm., Berkeley 1984; summer assoc. law firm Turner & Franzoia, Oakland 1984; Akin, Gump, Strauss, Hauer & Feld, W.D.C., 1985; bus. atty., assoc. Morrison & Foerster, San Francisco 1986–; fgn. legal cons. Kim & Chang, Seoul, Korea 1990–; honors: UCSD Provost's Honor List (1977, 78, 79, 80), Student Council rep. 1978, writer campus newspaper The Guardian (1978, 79), UC Berkeley S.K. Yee Scholarship Award, Outstanding Brief and Oral Argument Awards; mem: Internat. Law Soc. (v.p.), ABA (bus. law, internat. law sects.), Calif. Bar Assn., S.F. Bar Assn., The Japan Soc. of No. Calif., Soc. for Internat. Devel., S.F. Lawyers Com. for Urban Affairs, Am. C.of C. in Korea (chair legal svs. com.); civic: Theatre Bay Area (bd. 1988-89), Friends of Children of Viet Nam (co-dir. overseas ops. 1974, fieldwork South Viet Nam, processed 800 internat. adoptions, prin. orgzr. Operation Babylift, evacuated from roof of US Emb. 4/75), Friends of Children Seoul, Korea (estab. Seoul office, 1976, initiated Korean-Am. adoption pgm.), Internat. Mission of Hope, Calcutta, India (field staff 1982, negotiated release of orphans from prisons in W.Bengal); photographer, featured in sev. galleries and art exhibits. Res: 1410 Hawthorne Terrace Berkeley 94708 Ofc: Morrison & Foerster 345 California St San Francisco 94104-2675 and Kim & Chang 223 Naeja-dong Chong ro-Ku, Seoul, Korea

MEANS, JAMES ANDREW, engineering technical advisor; b. Oct. 11, 1937, Heavener, Okla.; s. Edward Andrew and Altha Lorena (Nobles) M.; m. Therese Louise Zimmermann, Feb. 21, 1959; children: James A., Jr. b. 1959, William R. b. 1961, Charles E. b. 1962, Vicky M. b. 1966; edn: BSEE, Univ. Ariz., 1962, MSEE, 1966; PhD in E.E., UC Santa Barbara, 1972; MSCS, Chapman Univ., 1989. Career: electronic engr. Pacific Missile Test Ctr., Pt. Mugu 1962-78; tech. dir. Targets & Ranges Div., NAVAIR, Camarillo 1978-79; tech. dir. Space & Missile Test Org., Vandenberg AFB, 1979-89; senior technical advisor SRI Internat., Menlo Park 1990–; adj. full prof. Chapman Univ., 1983-89; awards: Tau Beta Pi 1962, Sigma Xi 1966, Eta Kappa Nu 1972, outstanding profl. of year Pacific Missile Test Ctr., Pt. Mugu 1972, meritorious svc. Navy, Pt. Mugu 1979, outstanding career Air Force, Vandenberg AFB 1989, Allen R. Matthews, ITEA, Fairfax, Va. 1991; mem.: Internat. Test & Eval. Org. 1980–, Internat. Found. for Telemetering (pres. 1989–); inventor: Solid State Circuit Breaker (pat. 1966), Semiconductor Test Set (pat. 1966); mil: p.o. 1c USN 1955-58; Democrat; Baptist; rec: old cars, model planes, computer. Res: 284 St. Andrews Way Lompoc 93436

MEANS, RICHARD DENNIS, financial/employee benefit consultant; b. July 10, 1947, Riverside; s. Robert C. Means and Laura Antonia (Flack) White; m. Katharina Magdalena Bruesselbach, Apr. 3, 1970; children: Monica b. 1976, Matthew b. 1978; edn: AA, Santa Monica Coll., 1968; BA, and MA, CSU Northridge, 1973, 75; Cert. Fin. Planner (CFP) 1988; Reg. Health Underwriter (RHU) 1984, Chartered Life Underwriter (CLU) 1992. Career: asst. mgr. Market Basket/Kroger, Los Angeles 1965-75; owner Means Insurance Services, Woodland Hills 1976-83, mgr. brokerage Postil & Assocs., 1978-83; v.p. Resource Fin. Services, Anaheim 1983-86; fin./employee benefit cons. prin. Richard D. Means & Assocs., Orange1987–; cons. benefits & ins. B. Temkin Inc., No. Hollywood 1978–, Mutual Assoc. Profl. Service, San Diego 1977–; honors: Eagles Club-LPRT, Nat. Assn. Health Underwriters 1986, 87, 88, 89, 91, Royal Blue, Penn Mutual Life 1984, pres.'s club Mutual Omaha 1983, 84, 85, painting- purchase award Arco Collection L.A. 1978, hon. mention Laguna Beach Mus. Modern Art 1979; mem: Internat. Assn. Fin. Planners, Nat. Assn. Life Underws., Nat. Assn. Health Underws., Orange Co. Employee Benefits Coun., Orange County C.of C. (small bus. task force), Thousand Oaks Art Assn. (v.p. exhibitions 1975-80), Newport Mus. Modern Art, L.A. Mus. Contemporary Art, Orange Co. Philharmonic Assn.; research article: Complete Analysis, Universal Life (1982); mil: YN3 USN 1969-72; Republican (Rep. Presdl. Task Force charter mem.); Lutheran; avocation: artist, watercolorist, works in pub. and pvt. collections nat. (1970–). Res: 4397 Mahogany Cir Yorba Linda 92686 Ofc: Richard Means and Associates, 2100 Orangewood Ave #115 Orange 92668

MEECHAM, WILLIAM CORYELL, engineering educator; b. Detroit; s. William Edward and Mabel Catherine (Wilcox) M.; m. Barbara Jane Brown, (dec.); children: Janice Lynn, William James; m. Della Fern Carson; edn: MS, PhD, Univ. Mich., Ann Arbor, 1958-60. Career: prof. Univ. Minn., Mpls. 1960-67; prof. fluid mechanics and acoustics, UCLA, 1967–; cons. Aerospace Corp., El Segundo 1975-80, Rand Corp., Santa Monica 1964-74, Bolt, Beranek and Newman, Cambridge, Mass. 1968-73, Arete Assocs., Encino 1976–;advisor U.S. Congress com. on pub. works, Congl. Record Report N.J. 1972; mem. Calif. Space and Def. Council, U.S. Congress, 1982–; awards: Sigma Xi, Tau Beta Pi, Mich. Alumni scholar 1942-44, Donovan scholar Univ. Mich. 1944-45, UCLA Senate res. grantee 1968-78, NASA res. grantee 1971–; mem: Acoustical Soc. Am. (fellow, gen. meeting chmn. 1973), AIAA (asso. fellow, aeroacoustics com. 1972-75), Am. Phys. Soc. (fluid dynamics div.), Inst. Noise Control Engring.; coauthor (w. R. Lutomirski): Lasar Systems, 1973; mil: US Army 1944-46. Res: 927 Glenhaven Dr Pacific Palisades 90272 Ofc: School of Engineering and Applied Sciences Univ. California, Los Angeles 90024

MEEHAN, JOHN JOSEPH, district attorney emeritus; b. Apr. 19, 1932, San Francisco; s. John Patrick and Helen Gertrude (Smith) M.; m. Janet Mangan, June 28, 1958; children: Anne b. 1959, J. Matthew b. 1960, James b. 1961, Mark b. 1965; edn: BS, Univ. S.F., 1954; LLB, JD, USF Sch. of Law, 1959. Career: dep. dist. atty. Alameda County, Oakland 1960-68, senior trial deputy D.A. 1968-70, asst. D.A. 1970-81, chief asst. D.A. 1981, dist. atty. Alameda County, 1981-95; named Calif. Prosecutor of Yr., Calif. D.A. Assn. 1980, Alumnus of Yr. Univ. of S.F. Sch. of Law 1995, Edwin Miller Lifetime Leadership award, Calif. Dist. Attys. Assn. 1995, President's award, Nat. Dist. Attys. Assn. 1995; mem. Calif. D.A. Assn. (bd. 1981-86, pres. 1985-86); host weekly video pgm. Points & Authorities, 1974-81; editor law jour. Point of View, 1970-81, exec. ed. 1981-95; mil: 1st lt. AUS 1954-56; Democrat; Cath.; rec: athletics, music. Ofc: 4 Coast Way San Rafael 94903

MEHAN, ROSS JAMES, photographer; b. Nov. 22, 1955, Columbus, Ga.; s. Chester Jack and Betsy M. (Ross) M.; edn: AA, Foothill Jr. Coll. 1975; BA advt., San Jose St.Univ. 1978. Career: photographer Murry Kalish Photo, Los Altos 1981–; litho tech. Image Tech, Palo Alto 1979-80; proofer Colorscan Inc. 1980-82; scanner tech. Kedie Image Systems, Sunnyvale 1982–; mem: Profl. Photographers of Am.; Republican; Christian; rec: hiking, fishing. Address: Sunnyvale 94086

MEHDIZADEH, PARVIZ, insurance executive; b. Sept. 15, 1934, Tehran, Iran; s. Alexander and Sedigheh (Siavooshy) M.; m. Manijeh Sadri, Sept. 12, 1961; children: Sheida, Peyman, Pejman; edn: BS, Forestry Sch., Tehran 1958; MS, N.C. State Univ., Raleigh, 1963, PhD, 1966. Career: pres. Research Inst. Natural Resources, Tehran 1968-73; assoc. prof. Univ. Tehran, 1973-74; prof. environmental scis. Univ. Tabriz, 1974-76; chmn. resolution com. FAO, Rome 1976-77; chmn. natural resources Central Treaty Orgn., Ankars, Turkey 1977-78; special advisor to sec. Ministry of Agriculture, Tehran 1978-79; cons. Minstry of Sci., Tehran 1972-75, UN Univ., Tokyo 1975-76; dist. mgr. American Family Life Assurance Co., Beverly Hills, Calif. 1981–; v.p. Point Internat. Corp., Inc., L.A. 1986–; author: Flowering Plants of Semi-Arid Regions (1976), Economizing of Water Use in Agriculture (1977); editor Khandamhaych Hafteh, London, Eng. (1979); mem. Life Underwriters Assn. (L.A. chpt. Health Ins. Quality Award 1985, 88); clubs: Beverly Hills CC, Friars (L.A.), Rotary Internat. (pres., founder Rancho Park chpt. 1985-86, chmn Found. Com. dist. 5280, 1992); Republican (U.S. Senatorial Club Wash. D.C., charter mem. Rep. Presdl. Task Force 1984). Ofc: American Family Life Assurance Co. 9301 Wilshire Blvd Ste 508 Beverly Hills 90210

MEHLIG, DONALD HOMER, insurance brokerage company president; b. Feb. 3, 1935, Torrance; s. John Homer Mehlig and Evelyn Wolford; m. Patricia A. Nield, March 19, 1953; children: Steven b. 1954, Sharon b. 1956, Susan b. 1962; edn: BA, UCLA 1957; Am. Coll. 1960, 1983; chartered life underwriter (1960). Career: ins. agent Provident Mutual, Los Angeles 1957-62; pres. Cal-Surance Benefit Plans, Torrance 1962–; dir. Little Co. Mary Hosp. 1987–, bd. trustees 1988-89; bd. trustees Am. Coll. Bryn Mawr, Pa. 1989–; awards: LALUA William G. Farrell (1985), Leaders Mag. outstanding life ins. man (1978, 88), CLU Inst. nat. speaker (1977–); mem: AALU (pres. 1976), Am. soc. CLU & ChFC (pres. 1990-91, v.p. 1989-90, nat. treas. 1988-89, secty. 1987-88, dir. 1987–), Million Dollar Round Table (life), Life Ins. & Trust Council L.A., South Bay Estate Planning Council (pres. 1970), Nat. Assn. Estate Planning (dir. 1976-80), Christian Businessmens Com. (dir. 1987–); author instructional tapes, 1980-85; Republican; Prot.; rec: horseback riding, fishing. Ofc: Cal Surance Benefit Plans Inc. POB 3459 Torrance 90510

MEHLMAN, GERALD JAY, lawyer; b. Jan. 29, 1930, New York; s. Jacob and Leah (Baker) M.; m. Josephine, Dec. 30, 1960 (dec. 1986); m. Barbara McDonald, Nov. 21, 1987; children: BA, Univ. Mich. 1951; LL.B, Yale Law Sch. 1954; admitted St. Bar Calif. Career: mil. judge advocate gen. Dept. of Navy, Wash. D.C. 1955-57; atty. advisor U.S. Tax Ct. 1957-59; ptnr. Kaplan Livingston et al, Beverly Hills 1960-80; Albert Mehlman et al, Los Angeles 1980-81; Finley Kumble et al, Beverly Hills 1981-87; Stroock & Stroock & Lavan, Los Angeles 1987–; moderator, panelist Cont. Edn. Bar 1975; mem: Am. Bar Assn., L.A. Co. Bar Assn., Beverly Hills Bar Assn., Am. Coll. Tax Counsel, Motion Picture & Tax Inst. (chmn. bd. 1962), Citizens for Tax Reform; 3 articles pub. in profl. jours., 1979-88; mil: lt.j.g. USN 1954-57; rec: tennis. Ofc: Stroock & Stroock & Lavan 2029 Century Park E Ste 1800 Los Angeles 90067

MEHTA, ARVIND CHANDULAL, physician; b. Mar. 11, 1934, Bombay, India, nat. 1979; s. Chandulal Hiralal and Chandravidya Chandulal (Gandhi) M.; m. Manjari A. Vadakkan, May 21, 1959; children: Piyush A. b. 1962, Manoj A. b. 1964; edn: MB, BS, Univ. of Bombay, India 1957; MRCP, Royal Coll. of Surgeons of Edinburgh 1964; reg. med. practitioner Maharastra and Gujarat States, India; fully reg. med. practitioner Gen. Med. Council of England and Wales; cert., ECFMG 1961; lic. physician and surgeon Calif. 1974; cert. in neurology, Am. Bd. of Psychiatry and Neurology 1976; diplomate Am. Acad. of Pain Mgmt. 1990; diplomate Am. Bd. of Profl. Disability Consultants 1991. Career: residency, Bombay, India 1957-61; grad. medicine tng., England 1962-65; sr. resident and chief resident internal medicine, Brooklyn, NY 1965-67; sr. resident and chief resident neurology, VA Ctr. & UCLA Sch. of Medicine, L.A. 1967-70; asst. prof. neurology Topiwalla Nat. Med. Coll., Bombay, India 1971-73; assoc. prof. neurology Creighton Univ. and Univ. of Nebr., Omaha 1973-74; attending physician Douglas Co. Hosp., Omaha, Nebr. 1973-74; pvt. practice neurology, Fresno, Calif. 1974–; assoc. clin. prof. neurology UC San Francisco 1974–, UCSF-Fresno Med. Prog. 1974–; staff appointments: Fresno Comm. Hosp. 1974–, St. Agnes Hosp., Fresno 1974–, Valley Children's Hosp., Fresno 1974–, Sierra Hosp., Fresno 1974–, Clovis Comm. Hosp. 1980–, HCA Cedar Vista Hosp., Fresno 1987–, San Joaquin Valley Rehab. Hosp. 1991–; lectr./resource person for seminars on neurological diseases and conditions; honors: Univ. of Bombay Traveling Fellowship for post-grad. med. study in United Kingdom 1961-64; mem: Fresno-Madera Med. Soc. 1974–, CMA 1974–, Am. Acad. of Neurology 1976– (fellow 1986–), Am. Electroencephalographic Soc. 1982–, Am. Assn. of Electrodiagnostic Medicine 1984–, Am. Acad. of Disability Evaluating Physicians (fellow 1989–); civic: leading part in ethnic groups and festivals, Fresno; contbg. author: 15 articles pub. in med. jours., 1958-73; author: 25 articles on Hinduism pub. in ethnic weekly, 1994-95; Hindu; rec: music, painting, travel, writing. Res: 2602 West Bluff Fresno 93711 Ofc: Arvind C. Mehta, M.D., Inc. 110 N Valeria, Ste 405 Fresno 93701

MELLINI, PETER J. D., historian/educator; b. Aug. 16, 1935, Hermosa Beach; s. Oscarre Hummling Mellini and Helen Mildred (Scheck) Baskette; m. Verna Adams, Dec. 4, 1970 (div. 1975); m. Gisela Maria Doppelgatz, Oct. 7, 1977; edn: BA hist., Stanford Univ. 1962; MA, 1965; PhD, 1971. Career: instr. history Stanford Univ. 1966, 1968-70; prof. Sonoma St. Univ., Rohnert Park 1970–; lectr. hist. of journalism San Francisco St. Univ. 1985-90; dir. Inst. Hist. Studies, San Francisco 1980-83; vis. fellow Cartoon Centre, Univ. of Kent, U.K. 1983; advisor Mission San Antonio de Padua, Jolon 1979-82; reviewer, reporter The Economist, London, England 1984–; bd. editors Am. Journalism, 1986; awards: Nat. Endowment for Humanities fellow 1971, 83, 88, Calif. Hist. Soc. Local Preservation award 1980, Leverhulme Found. fellow 1966-67; mem: Larkspur Heritage Commn., No. Am. Conf. on British Studies, Nat. Trust for Historic Preservation, Victorian Soc., Western Assn. Journalism Historians, Inst. for Hist. Study, Big Brothers Marin; author: In Vanity Fair, 1982, Sir Eldon Gorst: The Overshadowed Proconsul, 1977, articles and reviews pub. in profl. jours.; mil: AUS 1956-58; Democrat; Agnostic; rec: collecting political cartoons. Res: 141 Ward St Larkspur 94939 Ofc: Sonoma State Univ. History Dept. Rohnert Park 94928

MELLON, WILLIAM DANIEL, multi-industry communications executive; b. June 2, 1951, Darby, Pa.; s. William D. and Eleanor Lucy M.; m. Nikki Dersin, July 15, 1978; children: William D., Logan, Megan; edn: BA, St. Louis Univ.

1972; MA, 1974. Career: pub. rels. mgr. Boeing Comml. Airplane, Renton, Wash. 1978-80, regional pub. rels. dir. 1980-85; dir. corp. comms. Beech Aircraft Corp., Wichita, Kans. 1985-87; dir. news and info. Rockwell Internat. Corp., El Segundo 1987-92, dir. public rels., Seal Beach 1992-94, dir. internat. comms. and public affairs 1994–; mem: Pub. Rels. Soc. Am., Aviation & Space Writers Assn., Am. Mktg. Assn., Internat. Assn. Bus. Communicators, Council Communication Mgmt., Nat. Investor Rels. Inst., Am. Inst. Aero. & Astronautics, L.A. Press Club; mil: capt. USAF 1973-78. Ofc: Rockwell International Corp. 2201 Seal Beach Blvd Seal Beach 90740

MELMON, KENNETH L., academic physician; b. July 20, 1934, San Francisco; s. Abe Irv and Jean M.; m. Elyce Esther Edelman; children: Brad b. 1960, Debra b. 1963; edn: BA biology, Stanford Univ. 1956; MD, UCSF 1959. Career: chief div. clin. pharmacology, assoc. prof. UCSF Med. Center 1968-73, prof. 1973-78; chmn. dept. medicine Stanford Univ. 1978-84, Arthur L. Bloomfield prof. of medicine 1978-88, prof. medicine and clin. pharmacology 1978–, assoc. chmn. medicine 1989-94, assoc. dean, post-grad. med. edn. 1994–; awards: Burroughs Wellcome Clin. Pharmacology scholar 1966-71, NIH special fellow 1971-72; mem: Am. Fedn. for Clin. Research (pres. 1973-74), Western Assn. Physicians (pres. 1984-85);, Inst. Medicine of Nat. Acad. Sci. (membership com.), Center for Internat. Security & Arms Control (fellow), Physicians for Social Responsibility, Assn. Am. Physicians, Calif. Acad. Sci.; 300+ articles pub. in med. jours., num. med. jour. reviews, books pub. on clin. pharmacoloigy; mil: USPHS 1961-64; Democrat; Jewish; rec: woodworking, hiking, swimming. Res: 51 Cragmont Way Woodside 94062 Ofc: Stanford University Medical Center Clinical Pharmacology Stanford 94305-5423

MELNIKOW, DAVID GREGORY, developer; b. Apr. 19, 1927, San Francisco; s. Henry Peter and Caroline (French) M.; m. Theresa Molinaro, Sept. 13, 1958; children: Susan, b. 1950; David Jr., b. 1953; Christopher, b. 1955; Matthew, b. 1956; edn: BA, UC Berkeley 1951; R.E. Broker, Calif. 1980. Career: police sgt. Berkeley Police Dept. 1956-70; gen. mgr. Wholesale Produce Co., Santa Rosa 1970-79; broker/ owner real estate agency Cameron Park 1980-83; pres./ gen. mgr. Gatrean Homes, Cameron Park 1980-83; Wise Mortgage, 1983-88; pres. Green Valley Equity Fund 1982-83; v.p. Wicket Inc. 1982-83; mem: Contra Costa Bd. Realtos, El Dorado Co. Bd. Realtors, Navy League; lodge: Elks; mil: firecontrolman 3/c USN 1945-46; Republican; R.Cath.; rec: boating, fishing. Ofc: Silver Real Estate, 2960 Camino Diablo Ste 105 Walnut Creek 94596

MENDAL, GEOFFREY OWEN, software company executive; b. May 25, 1961 Chgo., Ill.; s. William Louis and Sandra Ruth (Sol) M.; edn: BS, Univ. of Mich., Ann Arbor, 1983. Career: software engr., Lockheed Corp., Sunnyvale, Calif. 1984-85; res. assoc., Stanford Univ. 1985-90; exec. v.p., SERC, Mountain View, Calif. 1990-94; v.p. Tri-Pacific Corp., Alameda 1994–; cons., Stanford Univ. 1985-90; conf. chair, ACM SIG Ada 1991-92; awards: best paper, IEEE Computer Soc., Hollywood, Fla. 1986; mem: ACM 1984–, IEEE 1991–; author, Exploring Ada, Vol. 1 & 2, 1984-91; Republican; Jewish; rec: wine tasting, photography. Res: 20580 Shady Oak Lane Cupertino 95014. Ofc: Tri-Pacific Corp. 1070 Marina Village Parkway Ste 202 Alameda 94501

MENDE, HOWARD SHIGEHARU, mechanical engineer; b. Nov. 19, 1947, Hilo, Ha.; s. Tsutomu and Harue (Kubomitsu) M.; edn: BSME, Univ. of Hawaii, 1969; MSME, USC, 1975; reg. profl. mech. engr. Calif. 1981. Career: tech. staff I Autonetics Div., Rockwell Internat., Anaheim 1970-71, tech. staff II B-1 Div., Los Angeles 1971-77; devel. engr. AiResearch Mfg. Co. of Calif., Torrance 1977-83; tech. staff IV, North Am. Aircraft Ops., Rockwell Internat., Los Angeles 1984-86; GS-0855-012 DCMAO Santa Ana, Def. Logistics Agency 1987–; lectr. Pacific State Univ. 1974- 75; honors: book acknowledgement in Philosophy and Unified Science by Dr. George R. Talbott 1977, Who's Who Worldwide Registry 1993-94, Who's Who in Sci. and Engring. 1996-97; mem: Pi Tau Sigma, Am. Soc. Mech. Engrs., Internat. Platform Assn.; Democrat; Buddhist; rec: gardening. Res: 1946 West 180th Pl Torrance 90504 Ofc: Defense Logistics Agy. DCMAO Santa Ana, PO Box C-12700 Santa Ana 92712

MENDOZA, FELISE BOBOT ILAHY, financial consultant, real estate broker, b. Oct. 30, 1943, Manila, Phil., naturalized 1976; d. Eufemio Benavedes and Maria Paustino (Ubnimo) Mendoza; children: Vi Leah b. 1963, Ted Paul b. 1964 edn: BSCE, Mapua Inst. Tech., Manila 1961; BSCE, USC, 1974; MPA, CSU Long Beach, 1978; BS in valuation sci., Western State Univ., Doniphan, Mo., MBA, PhD in bus. adminstrn. 1993; Calif. lic. real estate broker 1982; residential constm. cert., 1989, cert. R.E. appraiser (CREA), 1989, Nat. Assn. RE. Appraisers; grad. tng. course mortgage lending, National Schs., and home inspector cert. American Schs., 1989; reg. property mgr. (RPM), Nat. Soc. RPM, 1989. Career jr. civil engr. City of Seal Beach, 1969-72; tech. writer L A. Water Treatment Div., City of Industry 1973-74; pvt. contr. City of Corona, 1975-76; civil engr. Santa Fe R.R., Fullerton 1977-78; pres. Villafd Ents., 1979-81; fin. cons., real estate broker PM Royal Home Co., West Covina 1982-88; fin. planning cons. Sadora Corp., La Puente 1983-86; exec. Marathon Home Loan, Long Beach 1987-88; awards: for thermal analyzing focus on missile design URS Corp., Burlingame 1968, cert. Def. Civil Preparedness Agency,

L.A. 1975, recogn. for outstanding contbns. Los Angeles Mayor 1985; commr. L.A. County Manpower Advy. Bd. 1981-85; biography listed in publs. of Am. Biog. Inst. (N.C.), RLO Publ. Co. Inc. (Irvine, Ca.) and Internat. Biog. Centre (Cambridge, Eng.); mem: Nat. Assn. R.E. Appraisers (sr.), Nat. Soc. Reg. Prop. Mgrs., Philippines Engrs. and Scientists Soc. of So. Calif. (pres. 1978-85), Nat. Assn. Fin. Cons. 1981-, ASCE (Pasadena sec. 1979-80), Soc. of Women Engrs., Internat. Platform Assn., Flipino Am. Political Orgn L.A. (sec.); Republican (sustaining mem.); R.Cath.; rec: education. Ofc: Ilahy Realty PO Box 2570 La Puente 91746

MENKES, DAVID, certified public accountant; b. Aug. 5, 1922, Phila.; s. Morris and Pauline (Friedman) M.; m. Rosalie Saperstone, June 17, 1953; children: Elizabeth b. 1954, Pamela b. 1956, Barbara b. 1957, Robin b. 1959; edn: BS, UCLA 1948; Cert. Pub. Acct. Calif. Career: auditor State of Calif., Los Angeles 1948-53; ptnr. Beaver, Menkes & Co., Bellflower 1953-80, dir./prin. Beaver, Menkes Acctg. Corp. 1980-86, pres. Beaver, Menkes & Hass, 1986-90; secty./dir. Bellflower Nat. Bank 1962-67, dir./v. chmn. Mid Cities Nat. Bank 1983-89, dir. Huntington Nat. Bank 1990–; mem: Am. Inst. CPAs, Calif. Soc. CPAs., Bellflower Kiwanis (Kiwanian of Yr. 1979); mil: T/5 AUS 1942-45; rec: bridge, golf. Ofc: Beaver, Menkes & Hass Accounting Corp. 16739 Bellflower Blvd Bellflower 90706

MENNIE, GARY ROY, medical doctor; b. May 17, 1961, Santa Monica; s. William and Jeannie (Sword) M.; edn: BA, biol., CSU Northridge, 1990; MD, Ross Univ. Sch. of Medicine, 1995, tchg. asst. Gross Anatomy Lab 1991-92; family medicine, Univ. Texas Med. Branch 1995. Career: phlebotomist CSU Health Center, Northridge 1987-88; emergency room EDS Valley Presbyterian Hosp., Van Nuys 1979-91; instr. Helpline Crisis Intervention 1986-91, listener supr. 1987-91; dir. Suicide Prevention Speakers Bur. 1989-90; lab. asst. Los Angeles Community Coll., Woodland Hills 1983-84; honors: Sigma Xi, CSU Found. grant 1988, freshman class pres. Ross Univ. Sch. of Medicine 1991, mem. student affairs com. 1991, honor roll/dean's list 1991, 92, recipient Disting. Scholar Award 1992; mem. Scripps Inst. Research Soc.; Republican (life mem. Rep. Presdl. Task Force, Nat. Rep. Congl. Com.); pub. sci. research in profl. jour., 1988; Res: 8800 Gothic Ave North Hills 91343

MENNING, PATRICIA MAXINE, hospital administrator; b. July 6, 1934, Willows; d. Francis Alexander and Mildred Elizabeth (Howard) Landon; m. Richard Blaine, July 30, 1952; children: Norman b. 1953, Angelo b. 1955, Cari b. 1956, Kim b. 1960; edn: P.H.T., Cal Poly, San Luis Obispo 1953. Career: administrator Trinity Hosp., Weaverville; owner/opr. Granny's House (bed & breakfast inn), 1987–; past pharmacist asst. Fall River Mills, dental office mgr. Burney, bus. office mgr., personnel dir. and asst. adminstr. Modoc Med. Ctr., Alturas; bd. mem. Rural Hosp. Ctr. 1994; honors: employee appreciation Trinity Hosp. 1986, Trinity Co. C.of C. nominee for citizen of yr. 1987, Soroptimists Internat. Women of Distinction Award, Trinity Co. Dept. Hd. of Yr. Award 1988, 2000 Notable Am. Women Award 1991; mem: Calif. Assn. of Hospitals & Health Systems (advy. bd. 1994, delegate to Wash. D.C. legis. advocate for health care reform 1994), Hosp. Council Found. (bd. 1994), Hosp. Council Health Svs. Res. Found. (bd. 1994), Hosp. Council of No. & Central Calif. (bd. 1994), Soroptimists, LDS Young Women's Orgn. (pres. 1984-88); painter primitive oils on misc. media, 1982–; Republican; Latter Day Saints. Res: 313 Taylor St Weaverville 96093 Ofc: Trinity Hospital 410 N Taylor St Weaverville 96093

MENSH, IVAN NORMAN, professor emeritus of medical psychology; b. Washington, D.C.; s. Shea Jacob and Rose (Clayman) M.; m. Frances Levitas; edn: AB, Geo. Washington Univ., 1940, AM, 1942; PhD, Northwestern Univ., 1948; dipl. in clin. psych. Am. Bd. Profl. Psychology 1952, lic. psychologist, Calif. 1958. Career: social sci. analyst NIH, USPHS, Health Edn. Research, Bethesda, Md. 1941-43; res. assist. Navy Res.Unit Northwestern Univ. 1946-47, USPHS senior clin. fellow, 1947-48; prof. and head div. med. psych., dept. psychiatry Sch. of Medicine Washington Univ., St. Louis, Mo. 1948-58; prof. and head div. medical psychology, dept. psychiatry and biobehavioral scis. UCLA Sch. of Medicine, Los Angeles 1958–; Acad. Senate 1958-90, UC Research Com., Calif. Youth Auth. 1990–; cons. Veterans Adminstrn., Mo. and Calif., 1953–; USPHS Special Resrch. Fellow, Inst. Psychiatry, Univ. of London, 1961-62; liaison scientist Office of Naval Resrch, London 1969-70; Fellow: Am. Psychol. Assn., Am. Psychol. Soc., Western Psychol. Assn., Calif. Psychol. Assn., N.Y. Acad. Scis., Am. Board of Profl. Psychology, Nat. Register of Health Service Providers in Psychology 1974–; author 3 books, 200+ chapters, jour. articles, and reviews; mil: capt. USNR 1943–. Ofc: Dept. Psychiatry and Biobehavioral Scis. UCLA School of Medicine, L.A. 90024-1759

MERCANT, JON JEFFRY, lawyer; b. Dec. 17, 1950, San Jose; s. Anthony J. and Margie Vivian (Diaz) M.; edn: BA, UC Berkeley 1972; JD, UCLA 1975; admitted St. Bar Calif. (1975). Career: practicing atty., Redondo Beach; adj. prof. El Camino Coll.; exec. bd. Calif. Democrat Party 1986–, Dem. nominee State Assembly 1986, mem. L.A. Co. Central Com. 1986-90; honors: Phi Beta Kappa 1972), UCB Alumni scholar 1968, Nat. Merit scholar, Outstanding Young Men of Am. 1984; mem. AFM, Local 47; COPE chair Calif. Fedn. of Teachers, Local 1388; civic: Peninsula Symphony Assn. (dir.), South Bay

Concern (dir., founder), Coastal Environ. Coalition (dir., founder), Retired Senior Volunteer Program (v.chmn. and legal counsel), Consumer Coalition Calif. (dir., legal counsel), Redondo Beach C.of C. (pres.), Torrance C.of C., Palos Verdes C.of C., N. Redondo Rotary (pres.-elect), Redondo Beach Library Found. (dir.); Democrat; rec: music performance. Res: 210 The Village Redondo Beach 90277 Ofc: 707 Torrance Blvd Ste 220 Redondo Beach 90277

MERCER, RICHARD HAMPTON, JR., data processing executive; b. Aug. 12, 1952, Abingdon, Va.; s. Richard Hampton Mercer (dec.) and Helen Olivia (Hull) Spencer; m. Carole Ann Stevens, Feb. 14, 1976; children: Sarah b. 1976, Glen b. 1978; edn: AA, Coll. of Siskiyous (COS), 1972; BA in speech path., CSU Sacramento, 1977, BA in drama, 1977; MPA, National Univ. 1985. Career: legislative clerk 1973-76, computer opr. Legislative Counsel, Sacramento 1977-79, senior computer opr. 1979-80, computer operations supr. I, II, 1980-84, data proc. mgr., I, II, III, 1984–; honors: Bank of Am. Scholarship Award -humanities COS 1971, outstanding acad. achievement Drama, student leadership award, COS 1972, v.p. and pres. COS Student Body 1971, 72, Boy Scouts Am. awards: Eagle Scout 1964, God and Country award, Lutheran, BSA 1965, Vigil Honor, Order of the Arrow 1969; mem. Calif. State Univ. Alumni Assn., Nat. Univ. Alumni Assn.; civic: Calif. Youth Soccer Assn. (coach, referee 1983-90); Democrat; Lutheran; rec: backpacking, acting. Res: 9043 Camden Lake Way Elk Grove 95624

MERCHANT, ROLAND SAMUEL, SR., hospital administrator; b. Apr. 18, 1929, NY, NY; s. Samuel and Eleta (McLymont) M.; m. Audrey Bartley, June 6, 1970; children: Orelia b. 1971, Roland, Jr. b. 1972, Huey b. 1973; edn: BA, NY Univ. 1957, MA, 1960; MS, Columbia Univ. 1963, MS hosp. adminstrn., 1974. Career: asst. statistician NYC Dept. of Health 1957-60, statistician 1960-63, NY TB & Health Assn. 1963-65; biostatistician, adminstrv. coord. Inst. for Surgical Studies Montefiore Hosp., Bronx, NY 1965-72; resident hosp. adminstrn. Roosevelt Hosp. NY 1973-74; dir. health & hosp. mgmt. NYC Dept. of Health 1974-76; asst. adminstr. West Adams Comm. Hosp. Los Angeles 1976, adminstr. 1976; spl. asst. to assoc v.p. for med. affairs Stanford Univ. Med. Ctr. 1977-82, dir. ofc. of mgmt. and strategic planning Stanford Univ. Hosp. 1982-85, dir. mgmt. planning 1986-90; v.p. for strategic planning Cedars-Sinai Med. Ctr., 1990–; lectr. div. of health adminstrn. Columbia Univ. Sch. of Pub. Health 1975-76; lectr., clin. asst. prof., clin. assoc. prof. Stanford Univ. Med. Sch. dept. of family, community and preventive medicine 1977-88, dept. health research & policy, 1988-90; honors: USPHS Fellow (Columbia Univ. 1962-63); fellow: Am. Pub. Health Assn. 1965, Am. Coll. Healthcare Execs. 1985; mem: Am. Hosp. Assn., Nat. Assn. Health Svcs. Execs., NY Acad. Scis.; author: Tuberculosis in New York City 1964, Tuberculosis Morbidity Resumes Decreasing Trend 1965, articles in med. and adminstrv. jours.; mil: US Army 1951-53; Democrat; Baptist (deacon); rec: bowling, fishing; Res: 27335 Park Vista Rd Agoura Hills 91301; Ofc: Cedars-Sinai Medical Center 8700 Beverly Blvd Los Angeles 90048-1869

MEREDITH, ROGER L., lawyer; b. May 9, 1942, St. Paul, Minn.; s. Earl Lawrence and Geraldine Elaine (Veilleux) M.; edn: BA, Univ. Chgo. 1964; Rice Univ. 1967-68; JD, New Coll. Law Sch. 1978. Career: atty. sole practice, San Francisco 1978–; bd. dirs. Lawyers Referral Service, San Francisco 1985–, chair 1991; awards: St. Bar Calif. Pres.'s ProBono Service 1988, Award of Merit 1987, S.F. Bar Preivikis Award 1991; mem: San Francisco Bar Assn., Am. Bar Assn., Calif. Lawyers for Arts, Plaintiff Employment Lawyers Assn., Committee of Bar Examiners 1990-94 (chair 1994), Headlands Homeowners Assn. (pres. 1987-94), Belvoran Assn. (pres. 1980-84). Ofc: 220 Montgomery St Ste 996 San Francisco 94104

MERIAM, JAMES LATHROP, retired professor, textbook author; b. Mar. 25, 1917, Columbia, Mo.; s. Junius Lathrop and Mary (Bone) M.; m. Julia Ellen Powers, Dec. 25, 1940; children: Mary Ellen b. 1943, Melissa b. 1946; edn: B.E., Yale Univ., 1939, M.Eng., 1941, Ph.D., 1942; reg. Mech. Engr., Calif., reg. Profl. Engr., N.C. Career: test engr. Pratt & Whitney Aircraft, E.Hartford, Conn., 1940; engr. General Electric Co., W.Lynn, Mass., 1942; instr. to full prof. Univ. Calif. Berkeley, 1942-63; dean and prof. Sch. of Engring. Duke Univ., Durham, N.C., 1963-72; prof. Calif. Polytechnic State Univ., San Luis Obispo, 1972-80; vis. prof. UC Santa Barbara, 1980-90; awards: Yale Engring. Assn. Award for Advancement of Basic & Applied Sci., NYC 1952, Tau Beta Pi Outstanding Faculty award, UCB 1963, Am. Soc. for Engring. Edn., WDC outstanding service award SE Sect. 1975, ASEE Mechanics Div.`Distinguished Educator' and Service award (1978, 1989); mem: Am. Soc. for Engring. Edn. (1952–, Hon. Life mem. 1982), Am. Soc. Mech. Engrs. (1952–, Fellow 1976, Hon. Life mem. 1980), Am. Soc. for Testing & Mats. (affil. 1985-91); author textbooks: Mechanics, Part I Statics, Part II Dynamics (1952, 2d edit. 1959), Statics; Dynamics (1966, 2d edit. 1971), Engr. Mechanics, Vol. 1 Statics, Vol. 2 Dynamics (1978, 2d edit. 1986, 3d edit. 1992); mil: lt.jg. USCG Reserve 1944-45; Independent; Prot.; rec: boat building. Res: 4312 Marina Dr Santa Barbara 93110

MERIN, ROBERT LYNN, dentist-periodontist; b. Jan. 25, 1946, Los Angeles; s. Marcus and Belle Merin; m. Barbara Ann Rosen, June 27, 1971; children: Lori Melissa b. 1974, Kimberly Tracy b. 1978; edn: DDS, UCLA, 1970; MS, Loma Linda Univ., 1972; Diplomate Am. Bd. of Periodontology. Career: lectr.

UCLA Sch. of Dentistry, 1970; major US Air Force, chief periodontal service Mather Air Force Hosp., Sacto. 1972-74; chmn. dental staff Humana-West Hills Hosp., West Hills 1982-84; lectr. in periodontics UCLA Sch. Dent., 1974–; pvt. periodontal practice, Woodland Hills 1974–; cons. LA Olympic Com., 1984; mem. UCLA Dent. Scholarship and Loan Com. 1984–; I.V. Sedation Examiner, Calif. Dent. Bd., Sacto. 1994–; awards: Lactona Award - periodontics UCLA (1970), profl. achiev. USAF (1974), special leadership, service awards UCLA Sch. Dent. (1980, 86), service Human West Hills Hosp. (1984); mem: ADA, Am. Acad. Periodontics, Calif. Soc. Periodontists, S.F.V. Dental Soc. (PAC 1988), UCLA Dent. Alumni Assn. (pres. 1979-80), UCLA Apollonians (pres. 1983-86); contbg. author (textbook) Glickman's Clinical Periodontics (1978, 84, 88), contbr. sci. articles in various dental jours. (1972-76); rec: windsurfing, sailing, magic. Ofc: Robert L. Merin, DDS, MS, Inc. 6342 Fallbrook Ave Ste 101 Woodland Hills 91367

MERRIAM, JOHN LAFAYETTE, irrigation consultant, professor emeritus; b. Nov. 27, 1911, Corona; s. George Henry and Bessie Emily (Baird) M.; m. Sarah Elizabeth Gridley, Oct. 2, 1938; children: Andrew b. 1941, Elisabeth b. 1944; edn: AA, San Bernardino Valley Jr. Coll. 1932; BSCE,Caltech, Pasadena 1938; reg. profl. engr. Calif. 1947. Career: area engr. USDA Soil Cons. Service 1939-56; irrigation engr. Ralph M. Parsons Co., Saudi Arabia 1956-58; prof. Calif. Polytechnic St. Univ., San Luis Obispo 1958-78; cons. engr., Egypt, Tunisia, Saudi Arabia, Thailand, Sri Lanki, India, Pakistan, Nicaragua, Mexico 1962–; mem. water advy. com. Calif. Dept. Water Resources; mem. water advy. com. San Luis Obispo Co.; Co. Flood Control Com. San Luis Obispo Co.; awards: Calif. Polytechnic St. Univ. outstanding prof. 1964, Calif. Polytechnic St. Univ. nominee for Calif. St. Univ. Sys. Outstanding Prof. 1975, Soil Cons. Soc. of Am. Calif. Ch.-Conservationist of Yr. 1978, ASCE Royce J. Tipton 1979, Calif. Irrigation Inst. irrigation man of year 1980, Am. Soc. Agri. Engr. Pacific Coast Section-Engineer of Yr. 1981, Am. Soc. of Civil Engring. Outstanding Service 1994; mem: ASCE (fellow), Am. Soc. Agri. Engrs. (sr.), U.S.Com. Irrigation & Drain., Calif. Irrigation Inst.; established Merriam Endowment for Irrigation & Water Mgmt.; established Fund for Furthering Flexible Irrigation; 2 patents held in field, author 2 books and num. papers on irrigation and water supply; rec: travel, photog. Address: 235 Chaplin Ln San Luis Obispo 93405

MERRIFIELD, DONALD PAUL, priest, university chancellor; b. Nov. 14, 1928, Los Angeles; s. Arthur S. and Elizabeth Marian (Baker) M.; edn: BS (physics) Calif. Inst. of Tech. 1950; MS (physics) Univ. of Notre Dame 1951; Ph.L. (philosophy), St. Louis Univ. 1957; PhD (physics), Mass. Inst. of Tech. 1962; STM (theol.), Univ. of Santa Clara 1966; ordained priest, Soc. of Jesus. Career: instr. physics Loyola Univ. of L.A. 1961-62; lectr. Univ. of Santa Clara Eng. Sch. 1965; cons. theoretical chem. Jet Propulsion Lab, CalTech, 1962-69; pres. Loyola Univ. of Los Angeles, now, Loyola Marymount Univ., 1969-84, chancellor 1984–; awards: S.T.D., USC 1969, service award CalTech 1971; Soc. of Sigma Xi (sci. hon.); mem. bd. dirs. Santa Marta Hosp. Found., bd. of visitors UCLA; rec: sailing, travel. Ofc: Loyola Marymount Univ. Loyola Blvd at W 80th St Los Angeles 90045

MERRILL, STEVEN WILLIAM, pyrotechnic consultant; b. Aug. 6, 1944, Oakland; s. David Howard and Etha Nadine (Wright) M.; edn: B.Chem., CSU Hayward, 1986; MBA cand., CSU San Bernardino, 1989-93; lic. pyrotechnic opr. Calif. 1962–. Career: firework assembler Calif. Display Fireworks, Rialto 1970-71; testing technician Hand Chemical Industries, Ontario, Can. 1972-74; chemist Baron Blakesly/Allied Signal, Newark, Calif. 1988-89; dir. R&D, Astro Pyrotechnics, Rialto 1989-91; pyrotechnic cons. Pyro Spectaculars, Rialto 1991–; dir. Merrill Productions Ordnance, Crestline 1975–; expert witness Superior Ct., San Francisco, 1971, Victorville, 1990-91; awards: Bay Area Sci. Fair 1st prize physics 1960, 2d prize physics 1961, finalist Fannie & John Hearst Engring. Scholarship 1961; mem. Pyrotechnic Guild Internat.(charter) 1960–, Western Pyrotechnics Assn. 1989–, Am. Chem. Soc. (anal. div.) 1987–; Oakland Magic Cir. (sec. 1965-70), Am. Bd. of Forensic Examiners 1994–; Christian; rec: sculpture, writing. Res: PO Box 676-23379 Crestline Rd Crestline 92325 Ofc: Pyro Spectaculars 3196 N Locust Rialto 92377

MERRITT, BRUCE GORDON, lawyer; b. Oct. 4, 1946, Iowa City, Iowa; s. William Olney and Gretchen (Kuever) M.; m. Valerie Sue Jorgensen, Dec. 28, 1969; children: Benjamin b. 1976, Alicia b. 1980; edn: AB, Occidental Coll., 1968; JD, Harvard Law Sch., 1972; admitted bar: Calif. 1973. Career: assoc. Markbys (solicitors), London, Eng. 1972-73; atty. assoc., ptnr. Nossaman, Krueger & Marsh, L.A. 1973-79, 79-81; asst. U.S. Attorney, Cent. Dist., Calif., L.A. 1981-85; ptnr. Hennigan & Mercer, L.A. 1986-88; ptnr. Debevoise & Plimpton, L.A. 1989–; bd. dirs. Inner City Law Ctr., L.A. 1991–; Am. Coll. of Trial Lawyers (fellow 1992); mem: Calif. State Bar Assn. (1973–, exec. com. litigation sect. 1992–), L.A. County Bar Assn. (del. state bar conf. 1984-86). Ofc: Debevoise & Plimpton 601 S Figueroa St Ste 3700 Los Angeles 90017

MERTA, PAUL JAMES, political cartoonist, film producer; b. July 16, 1939, Bakersfield; s. Stanley Franklin and Mary Ana (Herman) M.; edn: AA, Bakersfield Jr. Coll. 1962; BS engring., CSU San Jose 1962. Career: cartoonist for coll. and nat. mags. 1959–; civilian elec. engr. USAF missiles, San

Bernardino Air Material Area 1962-65, elec. countermeasures engr. 1965-72, program mgr., logistics acquisition, Sacto. Air logistics area 1972-90, ret.; t.v./film prod., owner Merge Films 1965; photog./owner The Photo Poster Factory, Salinas 1971–; owner La Rosa Blanca Mexican Restaurant, Sacto. 1979-91; ptnr. Kolinski and Merta Hawaiian Estates (housing devel.), Hilo 1981-92; political cartoonist California Journal 1958-59, Sacramento Union 1979-91, Sacramento Legal Journal 1979; cartoons pub. in nat. mags. and regional periodicals; producer TV show, numerous TV commercials and entertainment shorts; rec: flying, skiing, bridge; Res: 4831 Myrtle Ave #8 Sacramento 95841 Ofc: The Photo Poster Factory 1005 12th St Sacramento 95814

METZER, JOHN EDGAR, hatchery owner; b. March 23, 1956, Corvallis, Ore.; s. Olin Oscar and Lois Jean (Fraser) M.; m. Sharon Kay Green, July 10, 1982; children: Janelle b. 1983, Marc b. 1986, Erin b. 1990; edn: AA (Valedictorian), Hartnell Comm. Coll., 1976; BS animal sci., UC Davis, 1978. Career: owner, mgr. Metzer Farms, Gonzalez 1978–; co. dir. Monterey Co. Farm Bureau, Salinas 1981-92; honors: Phi Kappa Phi, Outstanding Grad. in Animal Sci. UC Davis 1978, valedictorian Gonzales H.S. 1974; mem. Hartnell Coll. Found., Hartnell Comm. Coll. Bd. Govs. 1979-93; Democrat; R.Cath. Res: 26000 Old Stage Rd Gonzales 93926 Ofc: Metzer Farms 26000 Old Stage Rd Gonzales 93926

METZGER, VERNON ARTHUR, management consultant, professor emeritus; b. Aug. 13, 1918, Baldwin Park; s. Vernon and Nellie Catherine (Ross) M.; m. Beth Wilson, Feb. 19, 1955; children: Susan b. 1948, Linda b. 1957; edn: BS, UC Berkeley 1947; MBA, 1948. Career: prof. mgmt. CSU Long Beach 1974-90, founding faculty member and prof. emeritus CSULB Sch. of Bus. Adminstrn.; mgmt. cons.; mem. Calif. Fair Polit. Practices Com. 1978-84, Orange Co. Transit Com., Fountain Valley Fire Commn. 1959-60, Yugoslavia Mgmt. Team 1977; awards: Outstanding Citizens (Orange Co. Bd. of Suprs.), Beta Gamma Sigma; mem: Soc. for Advancement Mgmt. (fellow, pres. & founder Orange Coast Chpt. 1956, 61, 63, regional dir. 1962-63); civic: Orange Co. Democratic League, Orange Co. Indsl. Relations Research Assn.; original founding faculty mem. CSU Long Beach Sch. Bus. Adminstrn. 1949; mil: lt. USNR 1942-45; Democrat; Methodist; rec: backpacking, fishing, hunting. Address: 1938 Balearic Drive Costa Mesa

METZLER, YVONNE LEETE, J.D., realtor; b. Jan. 25, 1930, Bishop; d. Ben Ford and Gladys Edna (Johnson) Leete; m. Richard Metzler, June 2, 1950; children: David b. 1951, Regan b. 1953, Erin b. 1957; edn: UC Berkeley, Empire Coll. Sch. of Law, Santa Rosa; Calif. R.E. lic. 1989, Calif. cert. law clerk 1990; JD, Empire Coll. Sch. of Law, 1992. Career: vocational instr. Ukiah Jr. Acad., Ukiah, 1962-63; bookkeeper Sid Beamer Volkswagen, Ukiah, 1963-64; acct. Ukiah Convalescent Hosp., 1964; Walter Woodard, P.A., 1964-66; assoc. dir. Fashion Two Twenty, Ukiah, 1966-67, dir. Santa Rosa, 1967-71; acct. P.K. Marsh MD, Ukiah, 1971-72; acct. W.W. Woodward, P.A./Clarence White CPA, Ukiah 1973-74; ptnr., owner Redwood Travel Agy., Ukiah 1973-76; travel agent/owner A-1 Travel Planners, Ukiah 1976-90, also A-1 Travel Planners, Willits 1979-88; realtor assoc. Mendo Realty, Ukiah 1989-92; cert. law clerk Sonoma Co. Dist. Attys., 1990-91; freelance legal asst. 1991–; loan ofcr. Allied Bank, Ukiah 1994; realtor Century 21, Ukiah 1995–; mem. Am. Soc. of Travel Agents 1973-90, Sonoma County Bar Assn. 1989-91, Sonoma County Young Lawyers Assn. 1991-92; civic: Ukiah Planning Commn. (commr. 1979-84, chair 1981-83), Ukiah C.of C. (pres. 1981, 1982), Mendocino County C.of C. (dir. 1981), Private Industry Council 1988-90, Mendocino County Visitors & Conv. Bur. (bd. dirs., rep. 1988), Soroptimists (Ukiah pres. 1977-78, 1994-95), Ukiah Bus. & Profl. Womens Club (1964-79, treas. 1977-78, named Woman of the 80s), Am. Soc. BPW Clubs 1968-69; Republican Central Com. 1979-80; Prot.; rec: reading. Res: 1112 W Standley St Ukiah 95482

MEYE, ROBERT PAUL, retired professor, administrator, writer; b. Apr. 1, 1929, Hubbard, OR; s. Robert Carl and Eva Julia (Pfau) M.; m. Mary Alice Cover, June 18, 1951; children: Douglas 1953; Marianne 1954; John 1957; edn: ThM, Fuller Theol. Sem., Pasadena, 1959; BD, Fuller Theol. Sem., Pasadena, 1957; BA, Stanford, 1951; career: prof., N. Baptist Theol. Sem., Lombard, Ill. 1962-77; dean, 1971-77; prof., Fuller Theol. Sem., Pasadena 1977–; dean, Sch. of Theol., Fuller Theol. Sem. 1977-90; assoc. provost, Fuller Theol. Sem. 1990-92; dean emeritus and prof. emeritus, Fuller Theol. Sem. 1992–; awards: Doctor of Divinity, Eastern Baptist Theol. Sem., Phila. 1990; Fellowship, Assoc. Theol. Schs., Pittsburg 1970-71 and 1975-76; mem: Inst. of Biblical Res., Soc. of Biblical Lit., Studiorum Novi Testamentum Societas, Soc. of Biblical Res.; author: Jesus and the Twelve; num. publ. jour. and dictionary articles; mil: lt. (jg), Navy, 1946-54; Republican; Protestant, Am. Baptist Churches; rec: photography; gardening; travel; music; reading. Res: 1170 E. Rubio St. Altadena 91001 Ofc: Fuller Theol. Sem. 135 N. Oakland Ave. Pasadena 91182

MEYER, DEANNA MARIE ARRAS, realtor, entertainment and events executive; b. July 9, 1937, New Britain, Conn.; d. Damiano Francis and Angelina Catherine (Reina) Arras; m. 2d, Richard A. Meyer, July 19, 1986; 2 children by previous marriage (nee Yuhas): John b. 1960, Maryann b. 1962; edn: Syracuse Univ. 1957; Ryder Coll. 1959; Calif. R.E. lic. 1980. Career: ptnr. Fashion

Artistry By-Ka-Dee; librarian, media center dir. Chino Unified Sch. Dist. 1973-80; realtor/ptnr. ERA Diversified Realty, Chino 1980-84; adminstrv. asst. San Bernardino County Supr., 4th dist., 1983-86, chair San Bernardino Co. Day Creek Project 1984-85, chair Gov.'s com. Neighborhood Watch, San Bernardino. Co. 1985; exec. dir. Prado Tiro Grand Prix Corp., 1986-88, sec.-treas. Prado Tiro Found.; exec. director Decathlon Championship, American Outdoor Sports Associates Inc., 1989, mem. corp. com. and co-chair opening & closing ceremonies Chino Corporate Challenge, 1990, 91, 92; realtor The Western Group, 1991–; honors: Inland Business "Women of the Yr." finalist 1990, Paul Harris Fellow Rotary 1987, hon. service PTA, listed World Who's Who of Women, 5000 Personalities of World, Am. Biog. Inst.; mem. Inland Empire West Assn. of Realtors (bd. 1991-92, sec. 1992-93, v. pres. 1993-94, pres. 1994-95, Legis. com. 1980–, chair 1989, v. chair 1992, co-chair comm. relations 1980–, chair BORPAC 1991–,bd. mem. SALE, bd. dir. Jt. Venture), Calif. Assn. of Realtors (dir. 1993-95), Nat. Assn. of Realtors delegate; civic: Chino C.of C. (bd. 1983–), Soroptimist Internat. of Chino, Chino Comm. Hosp. Bd. Trustees (chair citizens bd. 1992-93), Chino Family YMCA (pres. bd. mgrs., bd. pres. Capital Camp, chair P.R. com.), Chaffey Coll. Found. (bd. dirs., chair Chino Friends of Chaffey Coll., co-chair Planetarium Com.), OPARC, Chino Hist. Soc., L.A. Co. Mus. of Art (patron); Republican; R.Cath.; rec: golf, travel. Res: 778 Via Montevideo Claremont 91711

MEYER, JANET JONES, emergency physician; b. Apr. 2, 1944, Midland, Tx.; d. Kyle Everett and Ruth Lorraine (Pickett) Jones; m. John Joseph Weger, May 5, 1962 (dec. 1972); children: Erica Ruth b. 1963, Mark Christopher b. 1964; m. Anthony Francis Meyer, Aug. 4, 1973 (div. 1981); edn: BA, Ind. Univ. 1973; MD, Loyola Stritch Sch. of Med. 1976. Career: res. physician Highland Hosp.-Duke Univ., Asheville, N.C. 1976-77; emergency physician Reid Meml. Hosp., Richmond, Ind. 1977-79, Silver Cross Hosp., Joliet, Ill. 1979-80, Chapman Gen. Hosp., Orange, Calif. 1980-87, FHP, Fountain Valley 1987-88, La Habra Comm. Hosp. 1983-88, Friendly Hills Med. Group 1988–; fellow and diplomate of Am. Coll. EM Physicians; mem: Soc. of Orange Co. EM Physicians, DAR; Democrat; Jewish; rec: boating. Ofc: Friendly Hills Medical Group 1251 W Lambert Rd La Habra 90631

MEYER, KENNETH NORMAN, computer consultant, engineering executive; b. Feb. 7, 1950, Houston, Tx.; s. Benjamin and Enid D. Meyer; edn: BA, Univ. Tx., Austin 1974. Career: dir. KTVV TV, Austin, Tx. 1972-76; assoc. producer Englander Films, Dallas, Tx. 1976-77, freelance prodn. mgr. (TV & film), Los Angeles 1978-82; writer 1982-87; computer cons. 1987–; v.p. devel. Quick Tally Systems 1988-91; ptnr. Piltdown Inc. 1991-93; mem. ACM; Democrat; rec: creative writing, astronomy. Res: 401 E Los Flores Dr Altadena 91001

MEYEROWITZ, BASIL RALPH, physician, surgeon; b. Sept. 14, 1929, Johannesburg, South Africa; nat. 1965; s. Louis and Ray (Nach) M.; m. Miriam Lewinsky, Nov. 3, 1963; children: Robin b. 1965, Eric b. 1967, Lisa b. 1969, Jennifer b. 1972; edn: B.Ch., MB, Univ. Witwatersrand Johanesburg 1952. Career: intern Johanesburg Gen. Hosp. 1952-54; surgical resident Hammersmith Hosp., London, England 1955-60; asst. prof. surgery Einstin Coll. Med. N.Y.C. 1960-67; clin. assoc. prof. surgery Stanford Med. Sch. 1967–; chief med. staff Mills Hosp., San Mateo 1982-88; mem: S.F. Surgical Soc., CMA, Am. Soc. Bariatric Surgery; mil: major USAR 1961-65. Ofc: 101 S San Mateo Dr San Mateo 94401

MEYERS, ELEANOR SCOTT, academic administrator; b. Jan. 3, 1940, Kansas City, Mo.; d. Walter A. and Dorothy Ann (Davis) Meyers; m. Brower R. Burchill, July 2, 1960; (div. 1979); m. 2d, William Duke, Apr. 16, 1992; children: Gaile Burchill b. 1962, Scott Burchill b. 1963; edn: BA, Florida State Univ. 1961, MA, Yale Univ., New Haven, Conn. 1977, MS, Univ. of Wis., Madison 1982, PhD, 1985. Career: campus minister, Univ. of Kansas 1973-78; nat. prog. adminstr. World Student Christian Fedn. 1978-81; assoc. minister First Congregational Ch. Christ, Madison, Wis. 1981-84; asst. prof. of ch. & society Union Theol. Sem., NY, NY 1985-88; academic dean and prof. of ch. & society Saint Paul Sch. of Theology, Kans. City, Mo. 1988-92; pres. Pacific Sch. of Religion, Berkeley, Calif. 1992–; honors: Danforth Fellow 1976-77, Women's Hall of Fame Univ. of Kansas 1978; mem: Society for the Scientific Study of Religion, Am. Acad. of Religion, Religious Res. Assn., Assn. for the Sociology of Religion; Am. Sociological Assn.; editor (book): Envisioning a New City, 1992; United Ch. of Christ Christian Ch. (Disciples of Christ). Ofc: Pacific School of Religion 1798 Scenic Ave Berkeley 94709

MEYERS, ROGER J., telegram company executive; b. Feb. 15, 1955, Kansas City, Mo.; s. Henry Julius and Gloria Ann (Tartaglia) M.; m. Marian Berger, Jan. 2, 1983; 2 children; edn: BFA, New York Univ., 1977. Career: founder and CEO, American Telegram Corp., Beverly Hills 1986–; honors: nom. Entrepreneur of Yr. Ernst & Young, L.A. (1991, 92, 93, 94). Res: 270 N Canon Dr, 1167, Beverly Hills 90212 Ofc: American Telegram Corp. 9230 Olympic Blvd Beverly Hills 90212

MEYSENBURG, JOHN HAROLD, electronic engineer; b. Dec. 2, 1934, Primrose, Nebr.; s. Harold Peter and Agnes Gertrude (Puetz) M.; m. Mary Ann Augustine, June 17, 1967; children: Peter b. 1971, Amy b. 1976; edn: Radio

Engring. Inst. 1954-55, Ricker Coll. 1958, Pasadena City Coll. 1967-71. Career: tech. rep. field engr. Philco Corp. 1959-61; senior tech. TRW Semiconductors 1961-64; sr. electronic tech. in R & D, Quality Control (Project Apollo Spacecraft), Allen Jones Electronics, 1964-65; sr. electronic tech. TRW System, 1965-67; electronic engr. (test asst.) Jet Propulsion Lab., 1967-: helped develop: High Power Solid State Microwave Switch 1968, Micromin and NASA Std. Transponder 1969-75, RF Test System 1975, Transmitter for Total Hip Joint Biotelemetry System 1980, Solid State X Band Transmitter 1981, ISPM Down Converter 1980-81, mem. of team to devel. and deliver the NASA Microwave Limb Sounder 1985, co-developer of Cassai Deep Space Transponder 1983-92; honors: mem. of the JPL Flight Team to deliver an X-band Down Converter to the Galileo and Magellan Spacecrafts; co-developer of the Cassini Ka Band Downlink Transmitter and mem. of the flight team; co-developer MSTI Satellite System 1993; Bausch & Lomb Hon. Science Award 1953; co-inventor on a patent for Beam Lead Integrated Circuit Test Fixture 1974; NASA awards for Cassini Spacecraft Transponder and advanced error-correcting code res. & devel.; 3d. place (color slides - subject Lightning), L.A. Photog. Center 1956; Boy Scouts Am. San Gabriel Valley (mem. Eagle Board and asst. Merit Badge Counselor 1988); mil: Airman 2/c 1954-59, GCM; Democrat; R.Cath.; rec: photog., radio expt. Res: 6725 Brentmead Ave Arcadia 91007 Ofc: Jet Propulsion Laboratory 4800 Oak Grove Dr Pasadena 91009

MEYSENBURG, MARY ANN, private school administrator; b. Sept. 16, 1939, Los Angeles; d. Clarence H. and Mildred (McGee) Augustine; m. John Harold Meysenburg, June 17, 1967; children: Peter b. 1971, Amy b. 1976; edn: BA (magna cum laude), USC, 1960; life tchg. cred., UCLA, 1971; MA, adminstrn., Univ. of San Francisco 1995. Career: escrow ofcr. Union Bank, Los Angeles 1962-64; escrow mgr., v.p. Bank of Downey 1964-66; elem. tchr. St. Bruno's Sch., Whittier 1966-70; elem. tchr. Pasadena Unified 1971-84; elem. tchr. Holy Angels Sch., Arcadia 1985-89; v.principal, tchr. Our Mother of Good Counsel, L.A. 1989-91; consulting tchr. Santa Ana Coll. of Bus. 1964-66; catechist Los Angeles Catholic Archdiocese 1978–, master catechist 1988–; eucharistic minister Our Mother of Good Counsel 1989–; historian Phi Delta Kappa (USC) 1991-92; Foundations rep. Phi Delta Kappa, 1992-93, treas. 1993-94, 1st V.P. 1994-95, pres. 1995-96; Writing to Read coordinator 1991-93; principal St. Stephen's Sch., Monterey Park 1993–; honors: Phi Beta Kappa 1960, Phi Kappa Phi 1960, Phi Alpha Theta nat. hon. hist. soc. 1960, Pius X award L.A. Archdiocese 1979, St. Elizabeth Ann Seton award/St. Anne medal, Cath. Com. for Girl Scouting 1988, 89, Bronze Pelican award Cath. Com. for Boy Scouting 1989, Outstanding New Mem.Phi Delta Kappa 1988, Teacher Incentive grantee Milken Family Found. 1989, 92, Writing to Read Lab. grantee Riordan Found. 1995; civic: Boy Scouts of Am. (counsellor 1985–), Legion of Mary (sec. Senatus 1980-85), Cath. Com. for Girl Scouts and Campfire (v.chmn. acad. affairs 1985–); publs: ms. History of the Arms Control Disarmament Orgn. 1976, editor The Message newspaper 1986-88; Democrat; R. Cath.; rec: history, tennis, scouting. Res: 6725 Brentmead Ave Arcadia 91007

MICHAUD, FREDERICK CHARLES, lawyer; b. November 22, 1940, Winterset, Iowa; s. Elmer Hubert and Harriet Francis (Coffin) M.; m. Bette Camille Berliner, June 27, 1964; children: Camille b. 1967, Katherine b. 1972, Marguerite b. 1976; edn: BA, Stanford Univ. 1962; JD, UC Berkeley 1965; admitted St. Bar Calif. 1966, U.S. Supreme Ct. 1971. Career: dep. dist. atty. Santa Clara Co., San Jose 1966-67; ptnr. Griswold Michaud & Halliday 1968-77; Michaud & Weber, Cupertino 1978-94; judge pro tem and arbitrator Santa Clara Superior Ct.; faculty lit. advocacy programs Stanford Univ. Law Sch., Univ. of Santa Clara Law Sch., Univ. of San Francisco Law Sch., Hastings Coll. of Law, S.F. 1985–; mem: Calif. Trial Lawyers (chmn., council chpt. pres. 1976), Am. Trial Lawyers Assn., Am. Coll. Legal Medicine, Am. Bd. Forensic Examiners, Calif. Dispute Resolution Council, Santa Clara County Bar; Republican; Presbyterian; rec: gardening. Ofc: 27709 Via Cerro Gordo Los Altos Hills 94022-3223

MICHEL, KARON RAE, training company president/owner; b. Dec. 30, 1946, Macomb, Ill.; d. Harry Dale and Jeanette Elvina (Stoke) Shannon; m. Thomas Edward Michel, Apr. 15, 1967, div. 1978; edn: Patricia Stevens Modeling Sch., Milw. 1965-66, Univ. Wisc., Milw. 1966-69. Career: sales promotion mgr. Computer Book Service, Schamburg, Ill. 1969-72; v.p. mktg. Midwestern Mktg. Assn., Charleston, Ill. 1972-75; nat. trainer/mgr. Management Recruiters Intl., Cleveland, Oh. 1977-86; v.p. ops. R.M.E., Inc. Los Angeles 1986-88; internat. tnr. Jenny Craig Centres, Brisbane and Sydney, Austr., Los Angeles 1988-89; dir. tng. Search West, Inc. Los Angeles 1989-93; pres., prin. High Performance Training, Pacific Palisades 1993–; cons. prin. Power Play, Beverly Hills 1986-88; awards: named Hon. Texas Citizen by Texas Gov. 1979, San Francisco mag. list of 100 Most Outstanding Women S.F. 1982, Alan Newman Memorial Award 1992, listed Who's Who of Am. Women (1985-86), World Who's Who of Women (11th), Two Thousand Notable Am. Women (4th), Intl. Dir. of Disting. Leadership 1991; mem: Nat. Assn. for Female Execs., Century City C.of C. (v.p. spkrs. bur. 1986-87), Calif. Personnel Consultants (dir. 1981-83), Am. Mgmt. Assn. 1980-84, Toastmasters (founder/sec. Jefferson, IA 1975-77); civic: Calif. Special Olympics (1972–, past vol. Charleston and Chgo., Ill.), Girl Scouts Am. (Ill., Wis., Ia., 1959-78); author 3 books: How To Be an

Effective Recruiter, 1987, How to Manage Recruiters, 1987, 30 Effective Meetings for Recruiters, 1986; Republican; Prot.; rec: art, games, travel, photography, whitewater rafting, skydiving, theatre, symphony, sports. Ofc: High Performance Training 15415 Sunset Blvd #215 Pacific Palisades 90272

MICHELL-LANGSAM, GEORGIA ANN, lawyer; b. April 15, 1953, Oakland; d. George Louis and Jean Ellen (Starks) Michell; m. Jon Dexter Langsam, Feb. 17, 1985; 1 son, Stephen Edward b. 1987; edn: BA, UC Berkeley 1975; JD, UCSF Hastings Coll. Law 1979; admitted Calif. Supreme Ct. 1980. Career: atty. Pillsbury Madison & Sutro, San Francisco 1979; Western Energy, Fairfield 1979-81; ptnr. Ganong & Michell, Walnut Creek 1981–; awards: Bd. Govs. St. Bar Calif. Pro Bono (1982, 84, 88, 89, 90, 91); mem: Calif. St. Bar Assn. (family law splst.), Am. Bar Assn., Am. Trial Lawyers Assn., Calif. Trial Lawyers Assn., ACCTLA, Jr. League of E. Bay, Sisterhood Bnai Shalom (v.p. 1982-84); Democrat; Jewish; rec: horseback riding, gardening, cooking. Res: 177 Oak Rd Danville 94526-1521 Ofc: Ganong & Michell 500 Ygnacio Valley Rd Ste 360 Walnut Creek 94596

MIECKE, GARY G., engineer/manager; b. March 22, 1946, Buffalo, N.Y.; s. Erwin A. and Ella (Duell) M.; edn: AA, Los Angeles City Coll. 1972; BA, Cal Poly Pomona 1976; Reg. Profl. Engr., Calif. Career: engr./mgr. Selective Services Corp. 1972–; cons. engr., pres. Omni Corp. 1975–; mem. Inst. of Indsl. Engring.; civic: Easter Seal Found./Orange (research, cons.), Kiwanis Club, Republican Inner Circle; mil: sgt. US Army 1967-69; rec: sailing, swimming. Address: Omni Corp. 3010 Wilshire Blvd Ste 614 Los Angeles 90010

MIHALICK, CHARLES RAUTZE, financial executive; b. June 6, 1945, Ashtabula, Ohio; s. Charles and Mary Jane Nina (Williams) M.; m. Lorelei Ann Lindenmayer, Oct. 31, 1964 (div. 1988); m. Nadine Joan Marcon, Sept. 16, 1989; children: Stephanie b. 1972, Chad b. 1974, Christopher b. 1990; edn: BS, Ohio St. Univ. 1971; MBA, USC 1978; C.P.A. Calif. 1973. Career: auditor Coopers & Lybrand, San Francisco 1971-73; corp. acct. Hughes Aircraft, Los Angeles 1973-78; CFO, dir. Pioneer Aluminum Inc. 1978-85; treas. Bell & Howell / Columbia /Paramount Video, Torrance 1985-88; CFO Contain-a-Way Inc., Irvine 1988-89; CFO Enertech, Brea 1989–; honors: Beta Gamma Sigma, Beta Alpha Psi; mem: Am. Inst. C.P.A., Calif. Soc. C.P.A.; mil: E-5 AUS 1966-69; Republican; Episcopalian; rec: skiing, tennis, wt.lifting. Res: 27441 Betanzos Mission Viejo 92692 Ofc: Enertech 2950 Birch St Brea 92621

MIKALOW, ALFRED ALEXANDER, captain/marine diving consultant; b. Jan. 19, 1921, N.Y.C.; m. Janice Brenner, Aug. 1, 1960; children: Alfred Alexander III, Jon Alfred; edn: Rutgers Univ., 1940; Columbia Univ., 1948; MBA, Rochdale Univ., Toronto, Can. 1950; lic. Merchant Marine capt., Cert. Marine Insp. Career: Lt. Cdr. served with USN, 1941-47, 49-50, decorated Purple Heart, Silver Star; capt. and master res. vessel Coastal Researcher I, owner/dir. Coastal Diving Co., Coastal Sch. Deep Sea Diving, Oakland 1950–, Divers Supply, 1952–; pres. Treasury Recovery Inc., 1972-75; comml. diving 44 years, has trained 8,500+ comml. divers including mil. Green Berets, Navy Units, Coast Guard Strike teams, and fgn. students; designer of diving equipment and recompression chambers incl. One-Atmosphere Dive Suit and Remote Observation Vehicle and Semi-Dry Wet Submarine; cons. var. hosps. in treatment of diving disease; marine diving contractor, consultant; active cert. marine insp.; mem. advy. bd. Medic Alert Found., Turlock 1960–; mem: Diver's Assn. of Am. (pres. 1970-74), Calif. Assn. of Marine Surveyors (pres. 1987), Internat. Assn. Profl. Divers, Calif. Assn. of Diving Contrs. (charter), Marine Tech. Soc., Calif. Assn. Pvt. Eductors (N. Calif. v.p. 1971-72), Internat. Authors Guild, Internat. Game Fish Assn., Navy League, US Submarine Veterans of WWII (Vallejo chapter), Reserve Ofcrs. Assn., Navy Tailhook Assn., Explorers Club (S.F.), Masons (Master Sequoia Lodge, Oakland), Lions Club, Medic Alert Found. (fmr. dir., adv. bd. mem.); author: Fell's Guide to Sunken Treasure Ships of the World 1972, (w/ H. Rieseberg), The Knight from Maine 1974, The Sea and I, Salvage; rec: treasure hunting. Res: 52 Mira Loma Orinda 94563 Ofc: 320 29th Ave Oakland 94601

MIKALSON, ROY GALE, college president; b. July 21, 1921, Eureka, Mont.; s. Lawrence Merton and Barbara M. (Patterson) M.; m. Eva Johnson, July 30, 1949; children: Steve b. 1950, Barbara b. 1952, Jeffrey b. 1958, Thomas b. 1960; edn: BA eng., Univ. Wash. Seattle 1947; MA, 1948; PhD, UC Berkeley 1964. Career: instr. Mont. Univ., Missoula 1949-50; dept. chair, instr. Lower Columbia Coll., Longview, Wash. 1950-62; dean, evening coll. Coll. of Marin, Kentfield 1964-66; founding pres. Clackamas Comm. Coll., Oregon City, Oreg. 1966-68; pres. Modesto Jr. Coll. 1968-71; supt., pres. Santa Rosa Jr. Coll. 1971–; honors: Phi Eta Sigma, Phi Beta Kappa, Kellog Found scholar 1962-64, Woodrow Wilson fellow 1963-64, Hall of Fame Lower Columbia Coll., Longview, Wash. 1988; mem: Calif. Assn. Comm. Coll. Adminstrs. 1974, Calif. Comm. Coll. Presidents (dir. 1982), Chancellor's Consulting Board 1986, Pres.'s Assoc. Am. Assn. Comm. Colls. 1968; civic: Rotary Club Santa Rose (pres. 1984-85), YMCA (bd, dirs.), Salvation Army (bd. dirs.), United Way No. Bay (bd. dirs.), bd. dirs. Doctors Hosp., Modesto; mil: 1st lt. Infantry AUS 1940-45, Silver Star; Democrat; Lutheran; rec: writing sports, camping, jogging, travel. Res: 4050 Alta Vista Santa Rosa 95404 Ofc: Santa Rosa Jr. Coll. 1501 Mendocino Santa Rosa

MIKESELL, MARY JANE, psychotherapist; b. Oct. 29, 1943, Rockledge, Fla.; d. John and Mary Christine (Leighty) Wagner; edn: BA, CSU Northridge 1967; MA, Pacific Oaks Coll. 1980; PhD in psych., California Graduate Inst., 1989; lic. Marriage, Family, Child Counselor (MFCC), Calif. Career: tchr. Los Angeles Unified Sch. Dist., 1966-69; photo lab. dir. Oceanograficos de Honduras, Roatan, Honduras, C.A., 1969-70; supr. Los Angeles Life Insurance Co., 1970-72; customer service rep. Beverly Hills Fed. S&L, Beverly Hills 1972-73; consultant, lectr. 1973–; staff CSUN Counseling Center, Northridge 1974-78; hd. office services Pacific Oaks Coll., Pasadena 1978-79; prodn. supr. Frito-Lay Inc., LA 1979-81; circulation supr. Daily News, Van Nuys 1981-82; educational therapist, MFCC intern Ctr. for Human Development, 1982-89, psychol. intern CGI Counseling Ctr., 1987-88; psychol. asst., Calabasas 1989-90; proj. coord. Carlson, Rockey & Assocs., Brentwood 1983-84; mem. press staff Southland Olympic News Bur. 1983-84; press staff ATAS Emmy Awards ceremonies 1983, staff 7-11 Stores/Bicycling mag. Internat. Grand Prix Cycling Race 1983, Sub-Center steward, press ops. 1984 Water Polo Venue, Pepperdine Univ.; proj. coord. and sys. splst. student ins. div. William F. Hooper Inc. 1985-87; cons. psychol. benefits pgm. Brentwood Ins. Claims Adminstrs. 1985-87; problems analyst Com Systems 1987-89; sch. counselor, therapist Poinsettia Found. 1990-91, Calabasas Acad. 1992-, Brighton Acad. 1992-93; currently prin. of Calabasas Acad.; cons. Designer Collection by Pingy, L.A. 1985; mem: Am. Assn. of Counseling & Devel., Internat. Assn. Marriage & Fam. Counselors, Am. Psychol. Assn. (asso.), Nat. Assn. Female Execs., Planetary Soc., Calif. Scholarship Fedn.; works: photog. exhib. Canoga Park Mission Gal. 1966, all photos for the Soo Yin Trade Co. catalog 1977, brochure photos for Miss China Town 1977, Archeology Today (multi-media presentation); Republican; Judeo-Christian; rec: photography, writing, research w. mentally gifted children. Res: 1754 Blackwell Dr Simi Valley 93063-3210 Ofc: Calabasas Academy 25000 W Mureau Rd Calabasas 91302

MIKLOWITZ, DAVID JAY, clinical psychologist, educator; b. July 18, 1957, Pasadena; s. Julius and Gloria (Dubov) M.; m. Lisa E. Goehler, Aug. 24, 1985; edn: BA, Brandeis Univ., 1979; PhD, UCLA, 1985, postdoctoral fellow, 1988; lic. clin. psychologist Calif. 1987. Career: asst. prof. Univ. Colo., Boulder 1989–; awards: dissertation award UCLA 1986, young investigator awards Internat. Congress on Schizophrenia Research, and Nat. Alliance for Research on Schizophrenia & Depression 1987; mem: Am. Psychological Assn., Soc. for Research in Psychopathology, Internat. Congression on Schizophrenia Research; article pub. in profl. jour., 1988; Democrat; Jewish. Ofc: Univ. of Calif. Los Angeles Dept. of Psychology and Univ. of Colorado Campus Box 345 Boulder CO 80309-0345

MILGROM, PAUL ROBERT, economics educator; b. April 20, 1948, Detroit, Mich.; s. Abraham Isaac and Anne (Finkelstein) M.; m. Jan Elise Thurston, Dec. 10, 1977; children: Joshua b. 1978, Elana b. 1982; edn: BA, Univ. Mich. 1970; MS, Stanford Univ. 1978; PhD, 1979. Career: asst. prof. Northwestern Univ. 1979-82; prof. Yale Univ., New Haven, Conn. 1982-87; Stanford Univ., Palo Alto 1987–; co-editor Am. Econ. Review 1990-93; assoc. ed. Jour. Econ. Theory, Ithica, N.Y. 1983-87; Rand Jour. Econ., Wash. D.C. 1985-89; Econometrica, Cambridge, Mass. 1987; Jour. Fin. Intermediation, Evanston, Ill. 1989-92; Jour. Econ. & Mgmt. Strategies 1993; awards: NBER Leonard Savage Prize 1980, Princeton Univ. Olin Disting. Lectr. 1988, J.S. Guggenheim Found. fellow 1986, Inst. Advanced Studies fellow 1985, Soc. Actuaries Annual Papers 1987; mem: Am. Acad. of Arts and Scis. 1992 (fellow), Econometric Soc. (fellow), Am. Econ. Assn., Stanford Inst. Theoretical Econ. (dir. 1989); 50 articles pub. in profl. jours., 1989–. Ofc: Stanford University Dept. of Economics Stanford 94305

MILKS-MARTIN, MARTE ELIZABETH, painting contractor; b. July 4, 1951, Lansing, Mich.; d. Malcolm Leonard and June Elizabeth (McIntosh) Milks; children: Jesse Cheyenne, Taylor Lansing; edn: BFA, Mich. State Univ., 1975; postgrad., Lansing Community Coll., 1975-80, Coll. of Marin, 1985–, Golden Gate Sch. of Law, 1993–. Career: community planner Mich. State Dept. Labor, Lansing 1976-77; exec. dir. Lansing Art Gallery 1977-80; owner Milks Painters & Decorators, San Anselmo, Calif. 1980–; cons. William A. Martin, Gen. Contr., Ross, Calif. 1986–, Lansing Art Gal. & Art Ctr. 1980-81; awards: grantee City of Lansing, Mich. 1977-80, Nat. Endowment for Arts 1979, Oldsmobile 1979, Mich. Mus. Assn. 1979; mem: Am. Trade Assn., Humane Farming Assn., L.W.V., San Anselmo C.of C. Res: 73 Magnolia Ave San Anselmo 94960 Ofc: Milks Painters & Decorators PO Box 2669 San Anselmo 94979

MILLAR, RICHARD W., JR., lawyer; b. May 11, 1938; s. Richard W. and Catherine (Arms) M.; m. Nancy; children: Richard W. III, Kelly Ann, Adam Edward; edn: student Occidental Coll. 1956-59; JD, Univ. San Francisco 1966; admitted bar Calif. 1967, Supreme Ct. 1971. Career: dep. dist. atty., Los Angeles 1967; atty. Iverson & Hogoboom 1967-72; Eilers, Stewart, Pangman & Millar 1973-75; Millar & Heckman 1975-77; ptnr. Millar, Hodges, & Bemis (and predecessor firm), Newport Beach 1979–; lectr. Calif. Contg. Edn. Bar.; judge pro tem Orange Co. Superior Ct.; mem: Am. Bar Assn. (litigation sect., trial practice com., ho. of dels. 1990–), Am. Bar Foundation (fellow), Orange Co. Bar Assn. (real estate sect., chmn. bus. litigation sect. 1981, chmn. judiciary com. 1988-90); civic: Bluffs Homeowners Assn. (pres. 1977-78), Newport Hills. Comm. Assn. (pres. 1972), Los Angeles YMCA Camp Branch (bd. 1970-75); club: Balboa Bay, Bohemian; Republican; Episcopalian. Res: 2546 Crestview Dr Newport Beach 92663 Ofc: Millar, Hodges, & Bemis, One Newport Pl Ste 900 Newport Beach 92660

MILLARD, NEAL STEVEN, lawyer; b. June 6, 1947, Dallas; s. Bernard and Adele (Marks) M.; m. Janet Keast, Mar. 12, 1994; children: Kendall Layne b. 1994; edn: BA (cum laude), Univ. Chgo., 1969; JD, Univ. Chgo., 1972; admitted bar: Calif. 1972, N.Y. 1990, US Dist. Ct. cent. dist. Calif. 1973, US Tax Ct. 1973, US Ct. Appeals 9th cir. 1987. Career: atty., assoc. Willis, Butler & Schiefly, Los Angeles 1972-75; ptnr. Morrison & Foerster, Los Angeles 1975-84; ptnr. Jones, Day, Reavis & Pogue, Los Angeles 1984-93; ptnr. White & Case, Los Angeles 1993–; instr. CSC San Bernardino 1975-76; lectr. Practising Law Inst., N.Y.C. 1983-90, Calif. Cont. Edn. of Bar 1987-89, adj. prof. USC Law Ctr. 1994–; honors: Phi Beta Kappa, Pi Gamma Mu, Phi Delta Phi; mem: ABA, NY State Bar Assn., Calif. Bar Assn., L.A. County Bar Assn. (trustee 1985-87), L.A. County Bar Found. (bd. 1991–), Pub. Counsel (bd. 1984-87, 1990-93), Univ. Chgo. Law Alumni Assn./ So. Calif. Chpt. (bd. 1981–); civic bds: L.A. Olympics Citizens Advy. Com. 1982-84, Woodcraft Rangers/ L.A. (bd. 1982-91, pres. 1986-88), Altadena Library Dist. Bd. Trustees 1985-86, mem. Energy Commn. of Co. and City of L.A.; club: The Calif. Club; mil: capt. AUS 1970-72. Ofc: White & Case 633 W. Fifth St Ste 1900 Los Angeles 90071

MILLARD, RAYMOND KEITH, city official; b. July 29, 1931, Dinuba; s. Maxwell Bankcroft and Olga W. (Reiman) M.; m. Mary, Aug. 8, 1953; children: Karen b. 1959, Susan b. 1963; edn: Coll. of Sequoias 1962-64. Career: staff Tulare County Probation Dept., 1961-81, ret.; Reserve Police Ofcr., City of Dinuba, 1965-75; elected councilman Dinuba City Council 1981–, mayor 1982-84 and 1993-94, v. mayor 1986-88 and 1990-93, Dinuba Redevel. Agy. (first chmn. 1984, v. chmn. 1987-93, chmn. 1993-94), Tulare County Bd. of Govts. (1981–, v.chmn. 1988-94), Community Svs. and Employment Tng. Inc., Visalia (dir., secty. 1988, v.p. 1990, pres. 1992-94), L.A.-Fresno-Bay Area/Sacto. High speed Rail Corridor Study Group Amtrack Rail Service (city mem. from Tulare County), 200th Year of US Census Com. of Tulare Co. 1990, 1st mayor in Dinuba City Charter form of govt. (Jul. 8, 1994); mem: Rotary Club, Am. Legion 1972–, Dinuba C.of C., Dinuba Hist. Soc. (life); Dinuba Union H.S. Advy. Council (1972-76, chmn. 1973-75), Calif. League of Cities (past pres. S. San Joaquin Valley Div. 1990); with wife state lic. foster parents, 1957– Alta Hosp. Found. 1990, Hispanic Council 1992, Social Svc. Transportation Adv. Council 1994, Jt. Powers Agreement Tulare Co. Solid Waste Disposal Mgt. Com. 1994; Democrat; Prot. Res: 1022 Elizabeth Way Dinuba 93618 Ofc: City of Dinuba 405 E El Monte Way Dinuba 93618

MILLER, ARNOLD LAWRENCE, educator; b. Nov. 7, 1942, NY, NY s. Julius and Anne (Blumenfield) M.; m. Barbara Jean Freeman, Nov. 12, 1966 children: Matthew b. 1972, Jeremy b. 1975; edn: BA, Alfred Univ., NY 1961; MS, Syracuse Univ. 1964, PhD, 1968. Career: postgrad. res. neuroscientist UC San Diego 1971-73, asst. res. neurosci. 1973-74, asst. prof. 1974-80, assoc. prof. 1980-85, prof. neurosci. 1985–; dir. grad. studies UC San Diego, 1980–, com. on acad. personnel 1986-88, chemical usage com. 1988–, founder & coord. neurosci. information exchange 1980–; guest lectr. Am. Assn. for the Study of Liver Diseases, Chgo. 1984; awards: res.career develop. award NINDS 1975-80, travel award Monash Univ., Clayton, Victoria, Austr. 1982; mem: Soc. of Neurosci., Am. Soc. for Biological Chemists, Soc. of Complex Carbohydrates, Biochem. Soc., Am. Soc. for Cell Biology, Screen Actors Guild, Am. Federation of Radio & Television Artists, San Dieguito Surf Soccer Club (exec. bd. 1982-86); trustee Temple Solel, Encinitas 1980-83, 1985-88, chmn. Rel. Sch. 1982-84; author: num. scientific articles pub. in profl. jours.; rec: acting, sports. Res: 1364 Ahlrich Ave Encinitas 92024 Ofc: Dept Neurosciences, Univ. Calif. Sch of Medicine M-0624, La Jolla 92093

MILLER, CLIFFORD ALBERT, business consultant; b. Aug. 6, 1928, Salt Lake City, Ut.; s. Clifford Elmer and LaVeryl (Jensen) M.; m. Barbara, June 22, 1951; m. 2d. Judith Auten, Sept. 20, 1976; children: Clifford b. 1959, Christin b. 1959, Stephanie b. 1962, Courtney b. 1978; edn: Univ. Utah, S.L.C. 1945-49, UCLA, 1956. Career: pres. Braun & Company, L.A. 1955-82, chmn. 1982-86; exec. v.p..Great Western Fin. Corp., Beverly Hills 1986-91; chmn. The Clifford Group, Inc. 1992–; dir. First Am. Corp. & Firat Am. Bankshares, Inc. W.D.C. 1994–; dir. L.A. Gear, Santa Monica 1993–; dir. Shamrock Broadcasting, Inc., Burbank 1979–; trustee Harvey Mudd Coll., Claremont 1974–, chmn. bd. 1991–; Los Angeles Master Chorale (1989–, chmn 1989-93, chmn. emeritus 1993–); mem. chmn.'s coun. Music Ctr. Unified Fund Campaign, past ofcr., dir. L.A. Jr. Chamber of Commerce; mem. Pi Kappa Alpha, Skull & Bones, Sigma Delta Chi; clubs: California, L.A. Tennis, Lakes CC (Palm Desert), Wilshire CC, Jeremy Golf & CC (Park City, Utah). Ofc: The Clifford Group Inc. 4444 Lakeside Dr Ste 120 Burbank 91505

MILLER, EDWARD FRANCIS, manufacturing company owner; b. June 25, 1925, Boston, Mass.; s. Andrew George Miller and Anna Frances (Dugan) Armstrong; m. Virginia Marie Lynch, Feb. 13, 1944; children: Judith Marie b. 1945, Edward Francis b. 1949; edn: Univ. Ala. 1944; Lowell Inst. 1948; BS magna cum laude, econ., Babson Coll. 1952. Career: gen. mgr. mfg. Vypak

Corp., Rockaway, N.J. 1965-66; owner Miller Assoc., Wayne, N.J. 1966; product sales mgr. Waldron Hartig, New Brunswick, N.J. 1966-69; gen. mgr. Plastaloy Inc., Prescott, Ariz. 1969-74; v.p., gen. mgr. Pacific Molded Plastics, Carlsbad 1974-82; owner Hi Tech Molded Polymers, Escondido 1982–; plastics advy. com. San Diego Comm. Coll. 1974–; honors: Blue Key 1952; mem: Am. Mgmt. Assn. (speaker 1968), Delta Sigma Pi, Soc. Plastics Engrs. (sr.), St. Patricks Ch. (chmn. lectors and eucharistic min.), Rotary (pres. Prescott 1972-74), Wildwood Estates Mgmt. Assn. (pres. 1969-74), Altamira Mgmt. Assn. (secty., v.p., pres. 1974–); inventor bottle handling, 1962, paper pub. in tech. paper, 1964; mil: air cadet USAAF 1943-46; Republican; R.Cath.; rec: photog. Res: 900-B Caminito Madrigal Carlsbad 92009-2435 Ofc: 115-B S Market Place Escondido 92029-1353

MILLER, GEORGE, congressman; b. May 17, 1945, Richmond, Calif.; s. George and Dorothy (Rumsey) M.; m. Cynthia Caccavo, 1964; children: George, Stephen; edn: BA, San Francisco State Coll. 1968; JD, Univ. Calif., Davis 1972. Career: legis. counsel Calif. Senate majority leader, 1969-73; mem. 94th-104th Congresses from 7th Calif. dist., 1975–; chmn. subcom. on oversight and investigations, 1985–, mem. subcom., 1993–; chmn. subcom. on labor standards, 1981-84; chmn. select com. on children, youth and families, 1983-91, chmn. com. on natural resources, 1992–; mem. com. on edn. and lab., dep. majority whip, 1989–; mem: Calif. Bar Assn. Ofc: US House of Reps House Office Bldg 2205 Rayburn Washington DC 20515*

MILLER, HARRIET EVELYN, management consultant; b. July 4, 1919, Council, Idaho; d. Colwell and Vera (Crome) Miller; edn: BA in chemistry (magna cum laude) Whitman Coll., 1941; MA polit. sci., Univ. Pa., 1949; DHL (Hon.), Whitman Coll., 1979. Career: res. chemist Atlantic-Richfield, Phila. 1944-50; student personnel adminstr., assoc. prof. and assoc. dean of students Univ. Montana, Missoula, 1950-56; elected Supt. of Pub. Instrn., State of Montana, 1956-69; mgmt. cons., pres. Harriet Miller Assocs., Helena, Mont. 1969-75; assoc. director Am. Assn. Retired Persons/Nat. Retired Tchrs. Assn., Wash. DC, 1975-76; exec. director 1976-77, mgmt. cons. 1977–; exec. dir. US Occupational Safety and Health Rev. Commn., Wash. DC, 1979-81; pres. HMA, Inc., mgmt. consulting firm, 1984-88; commr. Santa Barbara County Parole Commn. 1981-84; commr. Housing Auth. City of Santa Barbara 1982-87, chair 1984-86; elected Santa Barbara City Council 1987–; mayor, City of Santa Barbara 1995–; awards: disting. libr. svc. Mont. Library Assn., spl. award for leadership and svc. in tng. of firemen Mont. State Fire Chiefs Assn., outstanding svc. to Job Corps Office of Economic Opp., "Morning Star Woman" Hon. mem.: Blackfeet Indian Tribe; mem. bd. overseers Whitman Coll., 1983–; lectr. and author numerous articles, speaker nat. and internat. confs. incl. White House Confs. on Edn., Ednl. Demo. Tour Germany, Internat. Symp. on Housing and Environmental Design, W.D.C., UN Sem. on Financing Housing, Geneva, Internat. Council of Homehelp Svs., Frankfurt, Internat. Conf. on Volunteerism, Vienna, Internat. Fedn. on Aging Conf., Madid; mem: Homes for People, Channel City Club, Shelter Svs. for Women, Get Oil Out, Humane Soc. U.S., AAUW, Delta Kappa Gamma, Phi Kappa Phi, Psi Chi, Phi Beta Kappa, Gray Panthers; local bds.: United Against Crime 1989-94, Heath House for people with AIDS 1989–, Westside Neighborhood Med. Clinic 1981–; Unitarian (past trustee). Address: PO Box 1346 Santa Barbara 93102 Tel: 805/564-5319

MILLER, JERRY, university president emeritus; b. June 15, 1931, Salem, Oh.; s. Duber Daniel and Ida Claire (Holdereith) M.; m. Margaret Annette Setter, May 30, 1958; children: Gregory b. 1959, Joy b. 1961, Carol b. 1962, Beth b. 1967, David b. 1971; edn: BA, Harvard Univ., 1953; MDiv, Hamma Sch. of Theol., 1957; DD, Trinity Lutheran Sem., 1981; ordained minister Evangelical Lutheran Ch. in America (ELCA) 1957. Career: instr. Wittenberg Univ., Springfield, Oh. 1955-56; res. assoc., intern Cornell Univ., 1956-57; parish pastor Good Shepherd Ch., Cinti. 1957-62; asst. to pres. Ohio Synod (LCA) Columbus, Oh. 1962-66; senior campus pastor and dir. campus ministry Univ. Wis., Madison 1966-69; reg. dir. Nat. Lutheran Campus Ministry, Madison, Wis. 1969-76, and nat. dir., Chgo., Ill. 1977-81; pres. Calif. Lutheran Univ., Thousand Oaks, Calif. 1981–; bd. dirs. Wittenberg Univ., Augustana Coll.; mem: Council of Indep. Colls. & Univs. (exec. com. 1984-94), Lutheran Coll. Presidents Council, Luth. Ednl. Conf. of No. Am. 1977-94, Am. Assn. of Higher Edn., Council for Advance. & Support of Edn., Harvard Alumni Assn.; honors: man of yr. Salem, Ohio 1974, Siebert Found. fellow for study and travel 1975, listed Who's Who in Midwest, Who's Who in Religion 1975, Who's Who in Am. 1987–, Who's Who in West 1985–; mem. civic bds.: T.O. Rotary Club, YMCA, Los Robles Hosp., C.of C., United Way, Am. Red Cross Ventura Co.; rec: skiing, golf, hiking, travel. Ofc: 3148 Thistlewood St Thousand Oaks 91360

MILLER, KELLY RENÉE, physician; b. Aug. 27, 1960, San Jose, Calif.; d. Ernest Lee and Theresa Mary (Giluso) M.; edn: BA (with honors), UC Davis 1981; master's level work in biomed. engring. CSU Sacramento 1981-83; MD, Univ. of Vermont 1988; diplomate Nat. Bd. of Med. Examiners 1989; Management of Multiple Trauma Cert. 1990; med. lic., State of Calif. 1991; diplomate Am. Bd. of Family Practice 1992; Neonatal Resuscitation Program Provider 1992; recertified, Advanced Cardiac Life Support 1995. Career: family

practice internship and residency St. Joseph's Hosp. and Med. Ctr., Phoenix, Ariz. 1988-91; family practice physician Palo Alto Med. Ctr., Fremont, Calif. 1991-94; San Jose Med. Group, San Jose 1994–; active med. staff Washington Hosp., Fremont 1991-94; quality assurance com. mem. Cigna of No. Calif., Oakland 1993–; awards: Silver Pen Award, San Jose Mercury News 1993; mem.: AMA 1983-94, Am. Acad. of Family Practice 1988–, Physicians for a Nat. Health Program 1990–, Fremont Freewheelers; lectures and presentation in field, 1988-91; Democrat; Christian; rec: bicycling, computers, travel, writing. Ofc: San Jose Medical Group 500 E Calaveras Blvd Milpitas 95035

MILLER, MICHAEL DAVID, physician; b. Feb. 12, 1935, Nyack, NY; s. Joseph Samuel Arluck Miller, M.D. and Sarah Elizabeth (Cardin) M.; m. Merle Judith Jablin, Aug. 16, 1959; children: Nicole b. 1962, Steven b. 1967; edn: BSc, Union Coll., Schenectady, NY 1957; MD, Albert Einstein Coll. of Medicine, NY, NY 1962. Career: intern, resident in ob/gyn Downstate Med. Ctr., NY, NY 1962-67; obstetrician/gynecologist U.S. Army, Monterey, Calif. 1967-69; staff obstetrician/gynecologist The Permanente Med. Group, Inc., San Francisco 1969-; perinatologist TPMG, Inc., San Francisco 1979-; mem., past chair Perinatal Review Com., Kaiser Found. Hosp., S.F. 1969-; mem., past chair Med. Advy. Com. to City and County of San Francisco Perinatal Forum 1979-84; mem: CMA, San Francisco Med. Soc., Am. Coll. of Obstetricians & Gynecologists (fellow 1969-), Soc. of Perinatal Obstetricians (assoc. fellow 1979-); author: num. articles and scientific papers in field, 1967-; mil: maj. U.S. Army 1967-69; rec: harpsichord, photography, tennis, skiing, hiking. Res: 26 Mt. Wittenburg Ct San Rafael 94903 Ofc: TPMG, Inc. 2200 O'Farrell St San Francisco 94115

MILLER, PAMELA JOYCE LARAYNE, optometrist; b. Nov. 11, 1948, San Bernardino; d. Robert Warburton and Joyce Larayne (Maxey) Miller; edn: BS, Univ. Redlands 1969; BS, So. Calif. Coll. Optometry 1971; OD, 1973; JD, Loma Linda Coll. Law 1983. Career: optometrist, Highland 1973–; con. 1975–; lectr. 1973–; awards: Calif. Optometric Assn. Young Optometrist 1978, LWV Woman of Achievement 1980; mem: Am. Optometric Assn., Calif. Optometric Assn., Am. Acad. Optometry, Calif. St. Bd. Examiners in Optometry 1986-94; 75+ articles pub. in profl. jours., 1973; author: Introductory Handbook for Vision Care Asst., 1989, 92, Introductory Handbook for the Contact Lens Care Assistant, 1995; rec: writing, investments, travel. Address: 6836 Palm Ave Highland 92346

MILLER, PAUL JAMES, coffee company executive; b. Aug. 23, 1939, San Mateo; s. Paul and Rita M.; m. Patricia Ann Deruette, Aug. 22, 1964; children: Mike, Britt, Brian; edn: BSBA (hons.), San Jose State Univ., 1962; MBA mktg., Santa Clara Univ., 1964. Career: with Hill Bros. Coffee Inc. (acquired by Nestle 1989), San Francisco 1964-: advt. mgr., then dir. mktg. 1971-75, pres. 1975-83, chmn. bd. and c.e.o. 1983-89, pres. and c.e.o. 1989-91, pres. and c.e.o. Nestle Beverage Co. 1991–; mem: Am. Mgmt. Assn., Grocery Mfrs. Assn., Am. Better Bus. Bur. San Francisco, Conf. Board, U.S. C.of C., Calif. C.of C.; clubs: World Trade, Olympic. Res: 681 Brewer Dr Hillsborough 94010 Ofc: Nestle-Hills, Inc. 345 Spear St San Francisco 94105

MILLER, PHOEBE AMELIA, computer software marketing consultant; b. Jan. 13, 1948, Evanston, Ill.; d. William Prescott and Elizabeth Helen (Lucker) Miller; edn: BA, honors, Univ. of Wis. 1970; grad. work, Stanford Univ. 1973; MBA work, Golden Gate Univ. 1978; ICP Sales Tng. 1979. Career: optics analyst Coherent Radiation, Palo Alto 1970-72; engr. Bechtel Inc. 1972-77; asst. div. mgr. Rand Info. Systems, San Francisco 1977-79; sr. mktg. rep. Computer Scis. Corp., S.F. 1979-81; sr. mktg. cons., mgr. VAR/ distbr. Cognos Corp., Walnut Creek 1981-86; pres. P.A. Miller & Assocs. Inc., S.F. 1986–; awards: ICP Million Dollar Super Seller 1983, Cognos Sales Honor Roll 1982, 83, 84 and Pres.'s Award 1982, 83, V.P. Achiev. Club, Computer Scis. Corp. 1981, Bechtel Corp. Award of Merit for tech. contbn., listed in Who's Who of Am. Bus. Leaders 1991, Who's Who of Women 1994-95, 5,000 Personalities of World, Who's Who Registry (1992-93, 1994-95), Oxford Who's Who 1992-93, Who's Who Among Outstanding Americans 1994-95, Who's Who of Am. Women (1993-94, 1995-96); publs: contbr. Nat. Structural Engring. Conf. 1976. Res: PO Box 894 Belmont 94002 Ofc: P.A. Miller & Assocs. Inc., 1750 Montgomery St San Francisco 94111

MILLER, RALPH HENRY, educator; b. Nov. 4, 1944, Berkeley; s. Russell Sparks and Ruth Elizabeth (Bailey) M.; m. Linnea Ann Pregler, Jan. 27, 1968 (div. 1972); m. Nancy Sabin Root, Sept. 29, 1976; edn: BA psychology, UC Berkeley 1967; MA, San Jose St. Univ. 1969; PhD, Claremont Grad. Sch. 1979. Career: NDEA fellow Claremont Grad. Sch., Claremont 1970-73, asst. dir. computer services 1973-76; lectr. ops. mgmt. Calif. St. Polytech., Pomona 1976-79, asst. prof. 1979-83, assoc. prof. 1983-88, prof. and dept. chair 1988–; adj. prof. pub. policy Claremont Grad. Sch. 1984–; v.p. Homestead Farms Inc., Gustine 1980; honors: Blue Key, Psi Chi, Delta Mu Delta, Phi Kappa Phi, Golden Key, U.S. Jaycees Outstanding Young Men Am. 1981, Who's Who in W., Delta Sigma Pi; mem: Am. Psychological Assn., Western Psychological Assn., AAAS, Decision Scis. Inst., INFORMS, Common Cause, Psychologists for Social Responsibility; article pub. in sci. jour., 1973; Democrat; rec: skiing, surfing, sports cars. Ofc: California State Polytechnic University Operations Management Dept. 3801 W Temple Ave Pomona 91768-4083

MILLER, ROBERT RUSSELL, plant engineer/manager; b. Aug. 13, 1928, Ventura; s. Roy Russell and Mary Helen (Britten) M.; m. Wilma Clara Withrow, Aug. 21, 1955; children: Susan b. 1957, Debra b. 1959, Bob b. 1961; edn: ME, ACHV tech., Calif. St. Polytech. Univ., 1946-50; reg. profl. engr., control engring., Calif. (1982). Career: senior engr. Rohr Industries, Chula Vista 1967-68, plant engr. specialist 1968-70, plant engr. supr. 1972-73, plant engr. gen. supr. 1973-80, plant engr. mgr. 1980-92 (ret.); design engr. Calif. Instate Telephone, Bishop 1953-54; project engr. Baker Engring. Cons., Los Angeles 1954-56; cons. engr./v.p. T.H. Parry & Assocs., Pasadena 1956-67; awards: named San Diego engr. of year S.D. Assn. of Engrg. Socs. 1983, energy mgr. regional award Assn. Energy Engrs. S.D. 1985; mem: Assn. Energy Engrs. (pres. 1988-89), Am. Soc. Htg. Refrig. & Air Condtg. Engrs. (pres. 1973-74), Am. Inst. Plant Engrs. (pres. 1983-84), Am. Soc. Plg. Engrs.; publs: tech. jour. articles re energy conserv. and co-generation, 1982-87; mil: cpl. C.I.C. US Army 1952-53; Republican; Baptist; rec: fishing, gardening. Res: 9240 Shirley Dr La Mesa 92041

MILLER, ROBERT STEVEN, educator; b. Aug. 9, 1963, Van Nuys; s. Frederick Earl and Mary Theresa (Brash) M.; edn: AA, L.A. Valley Coll., 1984; BS bus. adm., CSU Los Angeles, 1987, MA hist., 1990. Career: adj. faculty history dept. CSU Los Angeles, 1990-92, study group leader Educational Opportunity Program; v.p. Agate Amethyst Imports 1991–; substitute instr. L.A. Unified Sch. Dist. 1993–; reading instr., summer bridge prog. CSU Los Angeles 1994; awards: Ledeboer scholar Phi Alpha Theta CSULA 1989, Jake Gimbel scholar CSULA 1990, Mu Kappa Tau mktg. hon. soc. 1987, Phi Alpha Theta hist. hon. soc. 1988; mem. Soc. for Historia of Am. Fgn. Relations 1990–, Pi Sigma Epsilon nat. mktg. frat. 1985–; editor hist. jour.: Perspectives, CSULA Hist. Dept. 1991, contbr. articles, 1990, 92, contbr. Glendale Law Rev., 1991; Democrat; R.Cath. Res: 13750 Runnymede St Van Nuys 91405 Ofc: 7712 Gloria Ave #8 Van Nuys 91406

MILLER, ROSS SHELDON, consulting entomologist; b. June 2, 1919; s. Roy Oscar and Lenore (Glen) M.; m. Ruth Carter, May 6, 1944; children: Ross T. b. 1946, Paula S. b. 1945; edn: BS, UC Berkeley 1941; MS, UC Davis 1946; cert. pest control advisor Calif. Career: tech. service mgr. Cal Spray Chem. Corp., Richmond 1946-47; Turlock 1946-48; dist. mgr. United Chem. Corp., 1948-50; gen. mgr. S.A. Camp Fertilizer & Insecticide Co., Shafter 1950-52; mgr. Sunland Industries, Fresno 1952-57; FMC Corp. A.G. Chem. Group 1957-85; cons. 1985–; honors: Alpha Zeta Honor Soc., Who's Who in West 1972; mem: Am. Entomol. Soc., Registry Profl. Entomol., Calif. Crop Prod. Assn., San Joaquin Entomol. Assn., Stockdale Exchange Club, Toastmasters Internat. (past pres.), Reserve Ofcrs. Assn., Navy League of U.S. (life), Retired Ofcrs. Assn. (past pres., life), Naval Aviation Mus. Found. (life), Exchange Club, UC Alumni Assn. (life), Calif. Aggie Alumni Assn. (life), Elks, Am. Legion; contbr. articles Sugar Beet Bull. 1947-48, Implement Record 1948, Agricultural Chemicals 1965, Ariz.-Calif. Farm Press 1980-82; mil: comdr. USNR 1941-61; Republican; Presbyterian; rec: skin diving, gardening, woodwork. Address: 2830 21st St Bakersfield 93301

MILLER, SAMUEL RAY, lawyer; b. Nov. 5, 1948, Miami, Fla.; s. David and Phyllis (Morstein) M.; m. Maude Pervere, July 29, 1979; children: Eli b. 1980, Nathaniel b. 1982; edn: BA, Yale Univ., 1971; JD, UC Berkeley, 1975. Career: lawyer Morrison & Foerster, San Francisco 1976-93; special trial counsel U.S. Dept. of Justice, Antitrust Div. 1994-95; ptnr. Folger & Levin, San Francisco 1995–; faculty Nat. Inst. for Trial Advocacy, Hastings Coll. of Advocacy, and Trial Practice Pgm. of US Dist. Ct. for no. dist. Calif.; mem. Am. Bar Assn. (com. chair consumer & personal rights, sect. lit., 1986-89); coauthor law jour. articles in Santa Clara Law Rev. 41 (1984), Business Lawyer 631 and 1053 (1985, 87). Ofc: Folger & Levin 275 Battery St 23rd Flr San Francisco 94111

MILLER, STEVEN JEFFREY, lawyer; b. Feb. 13, 1954, Chicago, Ill.; s. Hadley Allen and Carol Joan (Prince) M.; m. Mona Joy Deutsch, Aug. 21, 1977; 1 child, Thais b. 1988; edn: BA magna cum laude, Univ. Pa. Phila. 1974; JD, Stanford Sch. Law 1977; admitted St. Bar Calif., U.S. Dist. Courts for the Central, Southern, Northern and Eastern Dists. of Calif., and Dist. of Ariz.; U.S. Courts of Appeals for the Ninth and Tenth Circuits; U.S. Supreme Court. Career: assoc. atty. Lawler Felix & Hall, Los Angeles 1977-84; Wyman Bautzer Kuchel & Silbert 1984-86; sole practice and of counsel Law Offices of Peter J. McNulty, Bel Air 1987-89; assoc. general counsel, Ernst & Young, 1989-94; judge pro tem Los Angeles Municipal Ct. Small Claims 1986-90; honors: Phi Beta Kappa, Univ. Pa. Dean's List w. distinction 1971-74; mem: Am. Bar Assn., Calif. State Bar (mem. corp. counsel com. of Bus. Law Section, 1993-94), Los Angeles Co. Bar Assn., Am. Judicature Soc., Internat. Assn. of Jewish Lawyers & Jurists, Assn. Bus. Trial Lawyers, Am. Corporate Counsel Assn., Univ. Synagogue (bd. trustees 1984–, secty. 1985-89, exec. com. 1985-94, pres. 1989-91); Univ. Pennsylvania Alumni Assn. (bd. dirs. 1986–, treas. 1988-93); Democrat; Jewish; rec: softball, racquetball, bowling, rotisserie league baseball.

MILLER, VICTORIA LOREN, designer, art director; b. May 25, 1957, San Francisco; d. Leon and Malvina (Hoffman) M.; edn: BFA, UCLA, 1979; postgrad. studies Art Center Coll. of Design, Pasadena 1979, 80, UCLA Ext. 1980-82, Otis/Parsons, L.A. 1981. Career: designer Bright and Assocs., L.A. 1979-80;

designer Richard Runyon Design, L.A. 1980-83; art dir. Grey Entertainment Media, Santa Monica 1984; prin. Victoria Miller Design, Santa Monica 1984–; freelance art dir. Backer Spielvogel Bates, L.A. 1987-88; designer Sussman/Prejza & Co., Santa Monica 1984, The Mednick Group, L.A. 1988-89; awards: designer label Grand Cru Vineyards (Clio award 1985), designs selected for inclusion in permanent collection of Library of Cong., Wash. D.C., 1989; pub. in Print Regional Annual, Am. Corp. Identity, Letterheads 5, Vision Mag. (Japan), others; mem: Art Dirs. Club (L.A.), UCLA Alumni Assn., MOCA Photography Council, Am. Inst. of Graphic Arts; Jewish; rec: contemporary art, photography, dance, tennis, cycling. Address: 10650 Kinnard #311 Los Angeles 90024

MILLER, WALTER L., medical scientist, educator; b. Feb. 21, 1944, Alexandria, Va.; s. Luther S. and Beryl R. M.; m. Synthia H. Mellon; edn: SB, MIT 1965; MD, Duke Univ. 1970; lic. Calif. Bd. Med. Quality Assurance, 1974; cert. Am. Bd. of Pediatrics, 1975. Career: intern, resident Mass. Gen. Hosp., Boston 1970-72; sr. resident UCSF, 1974-75, fellow 1975-78, asst. prof. pediatrics 1978-83, assoc. prof. 1983-87, prof. 1987–, faculty grad. program in endocrinology 1982–, dir. Child Health Res. Ctr. 1992–; awards: Western Soc. Pediatric Research Ross Research award 1982, Endocrine Soc. Edwin B. Astwood award 1988, N.Y. St. Med. Soc. Albion O. Bernstein award 1993, British Endocrine Soc. Clin. Endocrinology Trust Medal 1993, European Soc. for Paediatric Endocrinology Henning Andersen Prize 1993; Fellow AAAS 1994; mem: Assn. of Am. Physicians, Am. Pediatric Soc., Am. Soc. Clin. Investigation, Soc. Pediatric Research, Western Soc. Pediatric Research (councillor 1986-89), Endocrine Soc., Am. Soc. Human Genetics, Am. Soc. Microbiology, Lawson Wilkins Pediatric Endocrine Soc. (edn. com. 1992-96, dir. 1995-98), Japanese Pediatric Endocrine Soc. (hon.), Democratic Party (del. Nat. Convention 1976); ed.-in-chief DNA jour., 1983, 160+ articles and book chpts. pub., 1967, patentee in field of biotech.; mil: lt. comdr. USPHS 1972-74; Democrat; rec: science, politics, enology. Ofc: Bldg MR-IV, Rm 209, Pediatrics, Univ. California San Francisco 94143-0978

MILLER-BLAIR, DANA JEANNE, physician; b. Nov. 4, 1957, Berkeley, Calif.; d. Daniel Holmes and Dorothy Natalie (Cake) Miller; m. Gregory Robb Blair, June 30, 1979; children: Jeffrey Alden Blair b. 1986, Katherine Jeanne Blair b. 1988; edn: BS, biol. scis. (highest honors), UC Davis 1979; MD (cum laude), St. Louis Univ. Sch. Medicine 1983; lic. physician Utah, Calif.; cert. in adv. cardiac life support 1983–; diplomate, Nat. Bd. Med. Examiners 1984; diplomate in internal medicine, Am. Bd. Internal Medicine 1986, diplomate in rheumatology 1992. Career: intern, resident in internal medicine, Univ. of Utah Med. Ctr. 1983-86; physician FHP Acute Care Clinic, Salt Lake City, Utah 1985-86; med. ofcr./internist, USPHS, Choctaw Nation Indian Hosp., Talihina, Okla. 1986-88, W.W. Hastings Indian Health Svc. Hosp., Tahlequah, Okla. 1988-90; fellowship, rheumatology, UC Davis 1990-92; rheumatologist, career physician Kaiser Permanente Med. Ctr., S. Sacto. 1991–; asst. clin prof. rheumatology (tchg. and res.) UC Davis 1992–, honors: Phi Kappa Phi (life mem.), Am. Med. Women's Assn. Achievement Citation, Merck Scholarship Book award, recipient Ruth G. White and Phi Mu Scholarship awards, St. Louis Univ. Sch. Medicine, USPHS Isolated Hardship award 1987, Young Career Woman award Talihina Bus. & Profl. Woman's Club 1987, AMA Physician's Recognition award 1987, USPHS Achievement Medal 1989, KFRI research award, Oakland 1993–; mem: Am. Coll. of Physicians 1981- (health care reform com.), Alpha Omega Alpha 1982–, Am. Coll. of Rheumatology (fellow 1990–), CMA 1990–, Sacramento El Dorado Med. Soc. 1992–, PEO, Sacto. 1993–; contbr. 3 articles to sci. jours., 1983–; mil: lt. comdr., USPHS 1986-90; Presbyterian; rec: skiing, sailing, piano. Ofc: 6600 Bruceville Rd Sacramento 95823

MILLS, BASIL EUGENE, agri-business executive; b. Jan. 18, 1930, Montevideo, Minn.; s. Charles E. and Mary Clare (Brainard) M.; m. Evangeline C., July 2, 1955; children: David G., James L., Susan Elizabeth, Katherine Anne; edn: S.E. Mo. St. Univ., Cape Girardeau 1948, Univ. Colo., Boulder 1948-51. Career: produce buyer Walter S. Markham, Salinas 1953-55; lettuce salesman Royal Packing Co., Salinas 1955-58; pres. Mills Dist. Co., Salinas 1958–; appt. Calif. Iceberg Lettuce Commn. (commr. 1978-92, chmn. 1986-88); mem. bds.: Western Growers Assn. (dir. 1985–, vice pres. 1995), Grower-Shipper Vegetable Assn. of Central Calif. (dir. 1988-93, chmn. 1991-92); honors: Salinas citizen of year 1989, Salinas bus. excellence award Agribus. Div. 1988, Monterey Co. Agricultural Leadership award 1993; civic: Salinas Rotary Club (pres. 1988-89), Salvation Army (dir.), Community Found. for Monterey County (pres.), Legal Services for Seniors (Coun. of Advisors), Meals on Wheels of Salinas (advy. bd.), Center for Community Advocacy (bd. dirs.), Found. for Monterey Co. Free Libraries (advy. bd.), F.O.O.D. Crops (bd. dirs.); mil: sgt. AUS 7th Army Hq. Stuttgart, W.Ger. 1951-53; Republican; Episcopalian; rec: golf, reading. Res: 25951 Red Pony Lane Salinas 93908 Ofc: Mills Distributing Co. PO Box 3070 Salinas 93912

MILLS, EUGENE SUMNER, college president emeritus; b. Sept. 13, 1924, West Newton, Ind.; s. Sumner Amos and Lela (Weatherly) M.; m. Dorothy Frances Wildman, Oct. 22, 1945; children: David Walden, Sara Anne; edn: AB, Earlham Coll. 1948; MA, Claremont Grad. Sch. 1949, PhD, 1952; postgrad. Harvard Univ. 1958-59; LLD, New Hampshire Coll., 1979; LHD, Earlham

Coll., 1987; LLD, Univ. New Hampshire, 1988. Career: instr. psychology Whittier Coll. 1950-52, asst. prof. 1952-55, assoc. prof. 1955-60, prof. psychol. 1960-62, dept. chmn. 1952-62; prof. psychol. Univ. New Hampshire, Durham, 1962-79, chmn. dept. 1962-65, dean Grad. Sch. and coordinator research, 1963-67, dean Coll. Liberal Arts, 1967-70, acad. vice pres., 1970-71, provost, 1971-74, provost, actg. pres. 1974, pres. 1974-79; pres./prof. psych. Whittier Coll. and Whittier Coll. Sch. of Law, 1979-89, 1989: pres. emeritus and emeritus prof. psychology, Whittier Coll.; vis. prof. Univ. Victoria, B.C. 1958, 60; bd. dirs. Elderhostel, Inc. 1977–, bd. chmn. 1984-90; bd. dirs. Fedco, Inc. 1988–; awards: Danforth Found. grantee 1956-57, NSF grantee, 1963-66, Sigma Xi, Phi Kappa Phi, Omicron Delta Kappa; mem: Independent Colls. of So. Calif. (bd. 1979-89), Assn. of Indep. Calif. Colls. and Univs. (exec. com. 1987-89), Am. Psychol. Assn. (fellow), Western Psychol. Assn., Eastern Psychol. Assn., N.H. Psychol. Assn. (pres. 1969-70, dir. 1967-70), LA Area Council BSA (exec. bd. 1981-89), N.H. Council on World Affairs (bd. 1976-79); author: George Trumbull Ladd: Pioneer American Psychologist, 1969, The Story of Elderhostel, 1993, articles in profl. jours.; Quaker. Res: 331 Prospect Park South, Tustin 92680-3208

MINETA, NORMAN YOSHIO, congressman; b. Nov. 12, 1931, San Jose, Calif.; s. Kay Kunisaku and Kane (Watanabe) M.; m. Danealia; children: David K., Stuart S.; edn: BS, UC Berkeley, 1953; D of Public Svc., Santa Clara Univ., 1989. Career: agent/broker Mineta Ins. Agy., San Jose 1956-89; mem. advy. bd. Bank of Tokyo in Calif., 1969-71; mem. San Jose City Council, 1967-71; vice mayor San Jose, 1969-71, mayor, 1971-75; mem. 94th-104th Congresses from 13th (now 15th) Calif. dist., 1975–. chmn. house com. on public works and trans., subcom. surface trans.; mem. sci., space and tech., select com. on intelligence; mem. budget com. 95th-97th Congresses; dep. Dem. whip 94th Congress; chmn. fin. com. Santa Clara County Council Chs., 1960-62; commr. San Jose Human Relations Commn. 1962-64, San Jose Housing Authority, 1966–; precinct chmn. Comm. Theater Bond Issue, 1964; mem. spl. gifts com. Santa Clara Co. council BSA, 1967; sec. Santa Clara Co. Grand Jury, 1964; bd. dirs. Wesley Found., San Jose State Coll., 1956-58, Pacific Neighbors, Comm. Council Central Santa Clara Co., Japan Soc., San Francisco, Santa Clara Co. chpt. NCCJ, Mexican-Am. Comm. Svs. Agy.; mem. exec. bd. No. Calif.-We. Nevada dist council Japanese Am. Citizens League, 1960-62, pres. San Jose chpt., 1957-59; bd. regents Smithsonian Inst., 1979–; chmn. Smithsonian vis. com. for Freer Gallery, 1981–; bd. regents Santa Clara Univ.; mem: Greater San Jose C.of C., Nat. Assn. Indsl. Ins. Agents, Calif. Assn. Indsl. Ins. Agents, San Jose Assn. Indsl. Ins. Agents (dir. 1960-62), No. San Jose Optimists Club (pres. 1956-58), Jackson-Taylor Bus. and Profl. Assn. (dir. 1963); mil: lt. AUS, 1954-56; Methodist. Ofc: US House of Reps 2221 Rayburn House Office Bldg Washington DC 20515-0515*

MINTZ, LEIGH WAYNE, university administrator; b. June 12, 1939, Cleveland, Ohio; s. William Michael and Laverne (Bulicek) M.; m. Carol Jackson, Aug. 4, 1962; children: Kevin b. 1969, Susan b. 1972; edn: stu. Univ. of Pacific, Pacific Marine Station 1963; BS geol., Univ. of Michigan 1961, MS 1962; PhD paleontology, UC Berkeley 1966. Career: asst., assoc. prof. of earth scis. CSU Hayward, 1965-75, prof. geological scis., 1975–; also assoc. dean instrn. 1969-70, assoc. dean of sci. 1971-72, acting dean of instrn. 1972-73, dean of undergrad. studies 1973-79, assoc. vice pres. academic programs 1979-93, assoc. v.p. admissions and enrollment svs. 1992-93, assoc. v.p. academic svs. and programs 1993-94, assoc. v.p. curriculum and acad. programs 1994–; judge of geol. exhibits Alameda County Fair 1968-91; Jt. Hill Area Planning Prog. with City of Hayward 1969; awards: Morris Miller Wells Scholar 1965-66, NSF grad. fellow 1961-64, Alfred E. Sloan Found. scholar 1959-61, Phi Sigma Soc. undergrad. award 1961, Palmer Prize, UC Dept. Paleontology 1966; mem: Fellow Geol. Soc. of Am., Paleontol. Soc., Sigma Xi, Wilderness Soc., Nat. Parks & Conservation Assn., Sierra Club, Nature Conservancy; author textbooks: Historical Geology, 1972, 77, 81, Physical Geology (6 coauthors, 1982), both for C.E. Merrill Pub. Co.; articles on paleontol. and geol., Academic American Ency.; sci. articles and papers; rec: travel, photog. Res: 5940 Highwood Rd. Castro Valley 94552; Ofc: Calif. State Univ. Hayward 94542

MIR, CARL J., accountant; b. May 14, 1956, New York; s. Jorge E. and Carmen (Diaz) M.; m. Norma Hallado, Aug. 29, 1981; d. Carissa b. 1982, s. Christopher Andrew b. 1993; edn: BA, USC, 1979. Career: Ralphs Grocery Co., Compton, staff accountant 1984-85, supr. 1985-89, asst. mgr. 1989–; honors: Alpha Mu Gamma, Delta Phi Epsilon, Delta Alpha Psi, listed Who's Who Among Hispanic Americans 1991, 93, 2000 Notable Am. Men 1991, Who's Who In Poetry 1992; mem: USC Alumni Assn. (life), Nat. Assn. Accountants, Cuban Am. Nat. Found., Mission Marti; publs: contbr. World of Poetry, 1979, 80, 88, Magill's Survey of Cinema, 1980; R.Cath.; rec: photog. Address: Downey 90242

MIRASSOU, MARLENE MARIE, psychiatrist; b. Dec. 12, 1948, San Jose, Calif.; d. Donald Charles and Joyce Jacqueline M.; m. Mervyn Stouffer, Jan. 28, 1984 (div. 1988); edn: BA, San Jose State Univ. 1971, pre-med. studies 1971-72; MD, Med. Coll. of Wisconsin 1976; med. lic. Calif., Wisconsin; Diplomate, Nat. Bd. of Examiners 1977; cert. Am. Bd. of Psychiatry and Neurology 1982. Career: medicine residency Med. Coll. of Wis. Affiliated Hosp. 1976-77, psychi-

atry residency 1977-80, chief resident 1979-80; fellowship Yale Univ. 1981-82; asst. prof. psychiatry, dir. crisis intervention svc. Med. Coll. of Wis. 1980-81; instr. dept. of psychiatry Yale Univ. 1981-82; asst. clin. prof. psychiatry Sch. of Medicine, UC Davis 1982-88, asst. dean for student affairs 1983-86, assoc. clin. prof. 1988–; dir. inpatient psychiatric svs. Jail Psychiatry Svc., UC Davis at Sacto Co. Main Jail 1986-90; med. dir. inpatient psychiatric unit, UC Davis Med. Ctr. 1990-91; attending psychiatrist, site coord. residency tng. Sacto. Co. Mental Health Treatment Ctr., UC Davis 1991; attending psychiatrist, psychiatric consultation liaison svc. UC Davis Med. Ctr. 1991–; examiner Am. Bd. of Psychiatry and Neurology 1988–; mem. UC Davis Med. Ctr. severe agitation com., surgical intensive care unit 1994–, stress com. 1992–, com. on physician health 1992–, patient edn advy. com. 1992-93; mem. UC Davis Sch. of Medicine Admissions selection subcom. 1993–; tchr., seminar leader, lectr. and course dir. 1978–; honors: Phi Kappa Phi 1970; mem: Am. Psychiatric Assn. (fellow 1991–); Am. Med. Women's Assn. (pres. Mother Lode Br. 1994, newsletter ed. 1991–, sec. 1992-93, prog. com. annual spring women's health conf. 1990-94, bd. dirs. 1988–), Central Calif. Psychiatric Soc. (edn. com. 1993–), Assn. for Academic Psychiatry, CMA, Sacramento El-Dorado Med. Soc., Acad. of Psychosomatic Medicine, Sacto. Co. Placement Coalition 1991-92, Sacto Co. Sr. Sys. Redesign Subcom. 1992-93, Sierra Club, Sacto. Bike Hikers; contbr. 3 articles, 1 abstract to profl. jours., 1980-83, num. presentations, 1978–; rec: hiking, cross-country skiing, photography, music. Ofc: UCDMC Dept. of Psychiatry 2315 Stockton Blvd Sacramento 95819

MIRDA, DANIEL P., clinical oncologist/hematologist; b. Feb. 7, 1957, Elizabeth, N.J.; m. Marcela, June 21, 1989; edn: BA (cum laude), Cornell Univ., Ithaca, NY 1979; MD, Stanford Univ. 1984. Career: med. intern UCSF 1984-85, med. resident 1985-87, oncology/hematology fellow 1987-90, research fellow 1989-92, asst. prof. 1992–; pvt. practice, Hematology Oncology Group, Napa 1993–; tchr. Cornell Univ. 1977-79, Stanford Univ. 1981-84; honors: Nat. Honor Soc. Scholar, Cornell Univ. 1979, Medical Scholar, Stanford Univ. 1982-83, res. fellowship, Am. Heart Assn., UCSF 1989-91, career devel. res. grant, NIH, UCSF 1992–, res. grant, Elsa Pardee Found., Mich. 1993-94; mem: CMA 1993–, Assn. of No. Calif. Oncologists 1994–, Southwestern Oncology Group 1993–, Am. Coll. of Physicians 1987-89, AMA 1991-93; author: research articles, 1979, 92, 93; Catholic; rec: sailing, bicycling, hiking. Ofc: Hematology Oncology Group 1100 Trancas St Ste 256 Napa 94558

MIRKIN, MARCIA ELICIE, savings and loan association executive; b. July 15, 1934, Morristown, N.J.; d. Irving and Jennie Jean (Lerner) Hirschborn; m. I. Mirk Mirkin, June 20, 1954; children: Karen b. 1954, Stephen b. 1956, Philip b. 1961, Judith b. 1962; edn: Drew Univ. 1951-52; L.A. Valley Coll. 1971-72; AA, Saddleback Coll. 1975. Career: gen. mgr. Fred Wilson Studios, Studio City 1971-72; gen. mgr., sales mgr. Am. Home Realtors, San Fernando Valley 1973-87; loan ofcr. Fidelity Fed. Savings & Loan Assn., Glendale and Sherman Oaks 1987–; dir., v.p. Mirimar Enterprises, Sherman Oaks 1976-89; Mirkin & Assoc., North Hollywood 1980-89; awards: Synagogue of Creative Arts Citizen of Year (1977), Hi Desert Mensa Top Contbn. to Youth (1985); mem: Synagogue of Performing Arts, Synagogue of Creative Arts (bd. mem. 1981-84); Democrat; rec: bridge. Res: 13416 Magnolia Blvd Sherman Oaks 91423

MISA, KENNETH FRANKLIN, management consultant; b. Sept. 24, 1939, Jamaica, N.Y.; s. Frank J. and Mary M. (Soszka) M.; edn: BS psychology, Fairfield Univ. 1961; MS, Purdue Univ. W. Lafayette 1963; PhD, St. Johns Univ. N.Y. 1966. lic. psychologist Calif.; cert. mgmt. cons. Inst. of Mgmt. Consultants. Career: mgmt. psychologist Rohrer Hibler & Replogle, L.A. 1966-67; assoc., sr. assoc. A.T. Kearney Inc. 1968-74, prin. 1975-78, v.p. 1979-86; pres. H.R. Cons. Group Inc., Glendale 1987–; mem: Calif. St. Psychological Assn., Am. Psychological Assn., Am. Psychol. Soc., Am. Soc. Tng. & Devel., Human Resources Planning Soc., Soc. for Human Resource Mgmt.; civic: L.A. World Affairs Council, Town Hall So. Calif., Glendale C.of C.; club: Jonathan; Republican; R.Cath.; rec: tennis, reading, travel. Res: 924C S Orange Grove Blvd Pasadena Ofc: H. R. Consulting Group, 100 N Brand Blvd Ste 200 Glendale 91203

MISKUS, MICHAEL ANTHONY, electrical engineer, b. Dec. 10, 1950, East Chicago, Ind.; s. Paul J. and Josephine (Forstka) M.; edn: BSEE, Purdue Univ. 1972; CM (Cert. Mgmt.), Indiana Central Coll., 1974, CM, Indiana Univ., Purdue Univ., 1975; Cert. Plant Engr. (CPE), AIPE. Career: maint. mgr. supr. Diamond Chain Co., Indpls. 1972-76; plant and primary elec. engr. Johnson Baby Products Co., Park Forest South, Ill. 1976-81; plant engr. Sherwin-Williams, Emulsion Plant, Chgo., Ill. 1981-82; prin. Miskus Consultants, Industrial and Commercial Electrical Consultants, Olympia Fields, Ill.; staff facilities engr., actg. dir. plant engring. Bourns Inc., Riverside 1982-90; plant engring. mgr. 3M/CDI, Inc., Irvine 1990; mgr 3M Corporate Metrology Lab., St. Paul, Minn.; chmn. Nat. Council on Standards Labs., St. Paul/Minneapolis Sect.; 3M Global Plant Engring. Steering Com. 1993–; instr., elec. tech. pgms., Moraine Valley Comm. Coll., Prairie State Coll., 1978; adj. instr. Orange Coast Coll., Costa Mesa, bldg. automation systems and energy mgmt., faculty advy. com.; instr. Plant Engring. Certificate Pgm., lectr. UC Riverside; appt. City of Riverside Energy Commn. 1988-92, chair 1989-90; recipient P & Q Cost

Reduction Award l983, Bourns Inc., "Utility Rate Analysis"; mem: IEEE, Indsl. Applications Soc., Indsl. Electronics & Control Soc. (sr.), Assn. of Energy Engrs. (sr.), Illumination Engrs. Soc. of North Am., Am. Inst. of Plant Engrs. (chpt. pres. Inland Empire #111, we. region dir. of membership AIPE), Internat. Platform Soc.; res.: electrostatic precipitator, Purdue, 1971-72; author: Building Automation and Energy Mgmt. Systems, 1987; Republican; Lutheran; rec: skiing, sailing. Res: 4035 Salem Dr W, Woodbury MN 55125 Ofc: Miscon Assocs., POB 25252 Woodbury MN 55125

MITCHELL, BRUCE TYSON, lawyer; b. Nov. 6, 1928, San Francisco; s. John Robert and Lorraine Christine (Tyson) M.; m. Adrienne Hiscox, Oct. 14, 1951; 1 son, Mark Means b. 1955; edn: BA econ., JD, Stanford Univ.; admitted St. Bar Calif. (1952). Career: estate adminstr. Crocker Nat. Bank, San Francisco 1955-57; sr. counsel, secty. Utah Internat. Inc. 1957-87; atty., San Francisco 1987–; mem: Am. Soc. Corp. Sectys. (dir. 1976-79), Bar Assn. San Francisco, Am. Bar Assn., San Mateo Co. Republican Central Com. (chmn. 1964-71), Commonwealth Club Calif. (pres. 1973), Pacific Union Club, Olympic Club S.F., Capitol Hill Club; mil: lt.j.g. USNR 1952-55; Republican; Congregational. Res: 165 Redwood Dr Hillsborough 94010 Ofc: 400 Montgomery St Ste 1002 San Francisco 94104

MITCHELL, CHERYL RUTH, chemist; b. Dec. 4, 1954, Pomptain Plains, N.J.; d. Wm. Alexander and Ruth (Cobbey) Mitchell; m. Pat Richard Mitchell, Dec. 31, 1980; children: Sarah b. 1982, Catherine Anne b. 1986; edn: BS chem., Bethany Coll. 1976; PhD, Tx. A&M Univ. 1980. Career: lab. technician Gen. Foods Corp., Tarrytown, N.Y. 1974-76; tchg. assoc. Tx. A&M Univ., College Station 1976-78; asst. prof. CSU Sacramento, 1980-82; R&D dir. Calif. Natural Products, Lathrop 1982–; mem: Inst. Food Technologists; inventor, 10 patents; rec: violin, music. Ofc: California Natural Products PO Box 1219 Lathrop 95330

MITCHELL, EARL LAMONT, corporate president; b. Feb. 12, 1912, Sacramento; s. John Wesley and Hilda Maude (Schvalle) M.; m. Doris Aagaard Becker, Sept. 14, 1934; children: Earl, b. 1937; Mary, b. 1940; Jean, b. 1944; att. Jr. Coll. 2 years. Career: Pacific Coast sales rep. Scovill Mfg. Co., San Francisco 1932-45; pres./ treas. Mitchell Ent. Inc., owner State Plumbing & Heating Supplies, San Carlos 1942–; mem: Assn. of US Army (civilian status); Elks; Spy Glass Hill Golf Club; Palo Alto Hill Golf & Country Club; No. Calif. Seniors Golf Club; Senior Assn. NCGA; Seniors Assn. of Am.; Republican; Christian Science; rec: golf, work. Res: 3950 Sand Hill Rd Woodside 94062 Ofc: State Plumbing & Heating Supplies, 1000 American San Carlos 94070

MITCHELL, GWENDOLYN VAN DERBUR, lawyer, financial planner; b. Aug. 29, 1931, Denver, Colo.; d. Francis Stacy and Gwendolyn (Olinger) Van Derbur; m. Robert L. Falkenberg Jr., Feb. 6, 1954 (div. 1971); m. Ernest Albert Mitchell, May 14, 1972; children: Robert L. b. 1955, Nancy b. 1960; edn: BA, Univ. Colo. Boulder 1953; JD, Univ. Mo. 1957; cert. fin. planner 1984. Career: atty., assoc. Henry & Anderson, Overland Park, Kans. 1957-62; atty. Henry Shankel Gilman Falkenberg & Rainey 1962-72; asst. exec. dir. San Francisco Neighborhood Legal Assistance Fedn., San Francisco 1972-75; atty., assoc. Lawrence H. Stotter Law Office 1975-82; Carr McClellan Ingersoll Thompson & Horn, Burlingame 1982-85; sole practice, San Mateo 1986–; mem. Mills-Peninsula Hosp. (bd. dirs.); Republican; Presbyterian. Res: 3220 Ralston Ave Hillsborough 94010 Ofc: 2000 Alameda de las Pulgas Ste 160 San Mateo 94403

MITCHELL, JAMES ELDON, lawyer, investor; b. July 23, 1940, Orange; s. John William and Marguerite Mildred (Reafsnyder) M.; m. Michael Ann Mitchell, July 5, 1963; children: William b. 1966, Andrew b. 1967, Emily b. 1973; edn: BA, Whittier Coll. 1962; JD, Stanford Law Sch. 1965; admitted St. Bar Calif. Career: assoc. counsel 1st Am. Title Ins., Santa Ana 1965-67; ptnr. Mitchell Hart & Brisco 1967-74; sr.v.p., gen. counsel Century 21 Real Estate Corp., Irvine 1974-80; of counsel Millar Hodges & Bemis, Newport Beach 1980-89; gen. ptnr. Capital Investors Ltd. 1979-89, Mitchell Partners, L.P. 1989–; pres. 1st Balboa Securities Corp. 1987–; awards: Am. Lung Assn. Pottinger 1989; mem: Whittier Coll. (trustee, chmn. investment com.), Magic Castle; rec: magic, ballroom dancing. Ofc: Mitchell Partners, L.P., 611 Anton Blvd Ste 1110 Costa Mesa 92626

MITCHELL, MICHAEL EUGENE, financial consultant, venture capitalist; b. June 29, 1930, Kalamazoo, Mich.; s. Otto E. and Helen E. M.; m. Joan H. Beard, 1953 (dec.); children: Michael Thomas, Donald Gregory, Nicole Margaret; edn: BS in E.E./BS in engring. math., Univ. Mich. 1953; grad. courses in electronics and math., Univ. Okla., Syracuse Univ., CSU Fullerton. Career: engr. Bell Tel. Labs, grad. 3-yr. communications devel. tng. pgm., designed hybrid analog/digital computer systems and circuits; consulting engr. adv. systems and tech. Gen. Electric Co., responsible for R&D of adv. modulation, coding and comms. systems, mem. GE Adv. Devel. Council on Comms. and project engr./prin. investigator for 18-year series of DOD contracts and GE res. & devel. projects in military comms.: developed coding and decoding techniques for self-synchronized error control for comm. links, i.e. satellite, EHF, microwave, troposcatter, HF, telephone, and undersea acoustic channels, also developed high-speed memory fault detection techniques; retired senior staff engr., mil. communications resrch.

& devel., Hughes Aircraft Co.; currently pres. Opportunityland, Inc., also Success Funding Group, Inc.; honors: Kalamazoo Jr. C.of C. scholar 1948, Kalamazoo Citizens' grantee 1949, W. Mich. Univ. high scholarship list 1951, Kappa Rho Sigma 1951, Univ. Mich. honor's convocation 1952, 53, Joseph Boyer scholar 1952, Eta Kappa Nu, Tau Beta Pi 1952, Phi Kappa Phi, Sigma Xi 1953, RESA 1960, 70, Univ. Mich. AIEE-IRE annual award 1953; mem: IEEE Profl. Group on Information Theory, IEEE Comuter Soc., IEEE Communications Soc., Math Soc. of Am. 1963-73, AAAS 1972-79; publs: 12+ res. papers in tech. jours., 6 nat. conf. presentations, 8 U.S. patents. Ofc: P.O. Box 5407 Fullerton 92635

MITCHELL, THOMAS EDWARD, JR., president/chief operating officer, retired military officer; b. Apr. 12, 1946, Sacramento; s. Thomas Edward, Sr. and Violet Mae (Southall) M.; m. Terri K. Vance, Apr. 20, 1968; children: Anthony b. 1969, Brian b. 1972; edn: BBA, 1987, MBA, 1988. Career: enlisted ofcr., served to Maj. U.S. Marine Corps (Ret.) 1966-89, assignments all levels of govt. up to Jt. Chiefs of Staff, UN Command, and the Foreign Service; chief tactics instr. USMC, OCS, Quantico, Va. 1973-74; decorated Battlefield Commn. Viet Nam S.E. Asia 1968, Silver Star Viet Nam 1968, DOD Merit. Service Seoul, Korea 1985, JCS Commendation. Medal UN Cmd. 1984, Navy Commendation. Medal Camp Pendleton 1983; exec. Equifax Marketing Decision Systems, mktg. info. co., Encinitas 1989-93; pres./COO and pres., bd. of dirs., Holocomm Systems Inc., San Diego 1993–; dir: Cal-Pacific Steel Structures, Inc., Hawaii and Calif.; honors: Calif. Jr. Coll. Student Govt. Assn./Sacramento v. p. 1965-66, Who's Who Global Bus. Leaders 1994-99; civic: Toys for Tots, Orange Co. (dir. 1974-77), support youth activities, comm. charities; profl. publs.; Republican; Prot.; avocation: internat. affairs. Res: 3264 Chase Ct Oceanside 92056 Ofc: Holocomm Systems Inc 6440 Lusk Blvd Ste D-211 San Diego 92121

MITROFF, NORMAN S., psychologist; b. Aug. 28, 1942, S.F., Calif.; s. Joseph and Mabel M.; children: David b. 1973, Stephen b. 1975; edn: BA, S.F. State Univ., S.F., Calif. 1966, MS, 1968; PhD., Univ. of Portland, Portland, Ore. 1971. Career: psychologist, private practice, Novato, Calif. 1973–; vocat. psychologist, Dept. of Vocat. Rehab., S.F. 1973-78; police psychologist, Fairfax Police Dept., Fairfax, Calif. 1976-86; instr., S.F. State Univ. 1974-75; awards: Diplomate, Am. Bd. of Profl. Psychologists 1976; Certified Sex Therapist, AASECT 1978; Silver Psi, Calif. State Psychol. Assn., 1980; Qualified Med. Evaluator, DIR, Calif. 1991; mem: (past sec.) Calif. State Psychol. Assn.,1971–; (past Pres.) Marin County Psychol. Assn. 1975–; chair, Calif./We., ABPP 1977-81; pres., CPHP 1984-87; author: profl. jour. article 1973, profl. papers on Workers Comp. 1988, 89, 93; rec: racquetball. Ofc: 1025 Fifth St. Novato 94945

MITTMAN, BRIAN S., social scientist; b. Feb. 16, 1960, Chicago, Ill.; s. Charles and Ilene Lois (Pavlow) M.; m. Deborah C. Michlin, May 8, 1993; edn: BS, Princeton Univ. 1981; MA, Stanford Univ. 1984; PhD, Grad. Sch. Bus. Stanford Univ. 1987. Career: assoc. social scientist RAND, Santa Monica 1986–; vis. assoc. prof. UCLA 1986–; faculty RAND Grad. Sch. Policy Studies, Santa Monica 1986–; assoc. dir. Ctr. for Study of Healthcare Provider Behavior, Sepulveda V.A. Med. Ctr. 1992–; honors: Sigma Xi, Tau Beta Pi, Rotary Found. Internat. fellowship 1981-82; mem: Inst. Mgmt. Scis., Am. Sociological Assn., Acad. Mgmt., Am. Public Health Assn., Assn. for Health Svs. Res.; num. reports, book chpts. and jour. articles pub., 1984. Ofc: RAND POB 2138 Santa Monica 90407

MIXON, DAVID G., corporate finance executive; b. Sept. 18, 1952, Tampa, Fla.; s. David S. Waters and Eve Shaw (remarried G. Mixon); m. Deborah, Sept. 10, 1982; children: Shelley, Kristen; edn: BS, Univ. Santa Clara, 1974; MBA, National Univ., 1988; Certified Cash Mgr. (CCM) 1994. Career: branch asst., asst. mgr. Fireside Thrift Co., Newark 1974-76, auditor 1976-79, asst. controller 1979-82, controller 1982-84, asst. treas. 1984-85; v.p./controller First Interstate Financial Services Inc., San Diego 1985-90; exec.v.p. finance & data processing Santel Federal Credit Union, San Diego, 1991–; treas. Executive House Assn., Santa Clara 1981-83; mem: Am. Mgmt. Assn., Treasury Mgmt. Assn.; Republican; rec: skiing, swimming, tennis, golf. Res: 11052 Pinzon Way Rancho Bernardo 92127 Ofc: 5890 Pacific Center Blvd San Diego 92121

MIZE, ROBERT HERBERT, JR., clergyman (ret.); b. Feb. 4, 1907, Emporia, Kans.; s. Robert Herbert and Margaret Talman (Moore) M.; edn: BA, Univ. of Kans., Lawrence, Kans., 1928; General Theol. Sem., NY, NY, 1929-32; STD, General Theol. Sem., 1960. Career: dir., Gen. Sem. Assoc. Mission, Episcopal Ch., Hays, Kans. 1933-41; vicar, St. Stephen's Episcopal Ch., Wakeeney, Kans. 1941-45; founder, dir., St. Francis Boys Homes, Ellsworth & Salina, Kans. 1945-60; bishop of Namibia, Anglican Ch., Windhock, Namibia 1960-68; asst. bishop in Botswana, Anglican Ch., Gaberone, Botswana 1968-70, 73-76; asst. bishop, Diocese of San Joaquin, Episcopal Ch., Fresno, Calif. 1977-89; pres., Boys Homes Assn. of Am. 1958-59; awards: Phi Beta Kappa, Univ. of Kans. 1928; Disting. Svc. Citation, Univ. of Kans. 1954; subject of book, Father Bob and His Boys, by Emily Gardiner Neal, 1960. Res: 530 W. Floradora Apt. 318 Fresno 93728. Ofc: Diocese of San Joaquin 4159 E. Dakota Fresno 93726

MIZER, RICHARD ANTHONY, technology staff; b. San Francisco, Jan. 7, 1952; s. Conrad Xavier and Sally Jo (Hagan) M.; edn: BA bioengring. and economics Univ. Calif., San Diego, 1977. Career: founding ptnr. Microdoctors, Palo Alto, Calif. 1974–; mgr., ptnr. K-Family Corp., dba Harlow's Night Club, Fremont, Calif., 1977-79, Restaurants Unique Inc., dba Bourbon Street, Mountain View, Calif., 1980-83; engring. mgr. Pacific Bell, San Ramon, Calif., 1983-89; tech. mgr. adv. video svs. Pacific Bell, 1989–; product engr. Advanced Broadcast Video Svc., Advanced Digital Network, Switched Multimegabit Data Svc.; exec. producer Cinema of the Future, 1992; assoc. producer Soccer Fest: World Cup Soccer Final in HDTV to Europe and U.S. theaters from Pasadena Rose Bowl, 1994; exec. producer HDTV production of 50th Anniversary of the Signing of the United Nations Charter, 1995; security staff Republican Task Force, San Francisco 1984; tech. staff U.S. Olympic Com., Los Angeles 1984; tech. staff World Cup 94 (Soccer Fest); mem: IEEE, Soc. Motion Picture and TV Engrs., Nat. Assn. Broadcasters; Roman Catholic. Ofc: Pacific Bell 2600 Camino Ramon 1S300 San Ramon 94583

MIZUNO, NOBUKO SHIMOTORI, biochemist; b. Apr. 20, 1916, Oakland; d. Shinichiro and Kii (Niyomura) Shimotori; m. Walter Masami, Mar. 20, 1942 (dec. Aug. 10, 1946); edn: BA, UC Berkeley, 1937, MA, 1939; PhD in biochem., Univ. Minn., 1956. Career: research asst. UC Berkeley, 1939-41; instr. Macalester Coll., St. Paul, Minn. 1943-51; research assoc. Univ. Minn., St. Paul 1956-62, Mpls. 1964-79; research biochemist Veterans Adminstrn. Med. Ctr., Mpls. 1962-79, ret.; awards: NSF fellow 1955-56; mem.: Am. Inst. Nutrition 1963–, Am. Soc. Biochem. Mol. Biology 1974–, Am. Assn. Cancer Res. 1963-79, Soc. Experimental Biology Medicine 1971-79, Iota Sigma Pi (nat. sec., historian 1963-72); author, contbr. 50+ revs. and jour. articles in J. Biol. Chem., Science, Biochem., Biochem. Pharmacol., Cancer Res., Chem.-Biol. Interactions, Cancer Chemo. Reports, Proc. Soc. Exptl. Biol. Med., J. Nutrition, Blood, Nature, others. Res: 3628 Loma Way San Diego 92106

MOACANIN, RADMILA, psychotherapist; b. Belgrade, Yugoslavia; nat. 1956; d. Svetozar and Olga (Pavlovic) Moacanin; edn: dipl. Univ. of Geneva, Switz. 1946; MA, and MSS, N.Y. Univ. 1954, 1960; PhD, Internat. Coll., L.A. 1983. Career: chancellor Mission of Burma to U.N., N.Y.C. 1953-57; psychiatric social worker N.Y. St. Dept. Mental Hygiene, N.Y.C. 1958-59; med. social worker N.Y. Univ. Med. Center, N.Y.C. 1960-62; psychotherapist L.A. Co.-USC Med. Center, Los Angeles 1963-85; pvt. practice psychotherapy, Los Angeles 1986–; cons. Nat. Intensive Jour. Program 1980-94; adj. faculty Pacific Oaks Coll., Pasadena 1991–; adj. faculty Univ. for Humanistic Studies, Del Mar 1994–; vis. lectr. School of Psychology, Moscow 1992; honors: Pi Sigma Alpha, Fulbright fellow Italy 1962-63; author: Jung's Psychology and Tibetan Buddhism; Western and Eastern Paths To the Heart, 1987) 2 articles pub. in profl. jours., 1966, 77. Res: 4228 Los Nietos Dr Los Angeles 90027

MOBLEY, DOROTHY FRANCES, hospital supply company owner; b. June 17, 1925, Louisville, Ky.; d. John Merritt and Edna Pearl (Waldridge) Mobley; edn: BS, UC Berkeley 1959; cert. physical therapy, UC San Francisco Med. Ctr. 1959; reg. physical therapist Bd. Med. Quality Assurance 1959. Career: physical therapist II Camarillo St. Hosp., Camarillo 1959-79; physical therapist Kern Valley Hosp. Home Health Agency, Mt. Mesa 1980-87; owner Lakeview Physical Therapy, Wofford Heights 1981-83; adminstr. owner Lakeview Guest Home 1978–; Lakeview Rehab. Ctr. 1983–; Lakeview Hosp. Supply 1988–; psychiatric technician tng. Camarillo St. Hosp. 1959-79; vol. Lakeview Convalescent Hosp.; honors: Life Scis. Hon. Soc. 1948; mem: Calif. Physical Therapy Assn., Am. Physical Therapy Assn., Assn. Research & Enlightenment, Metaphysical Group of Wofford Heights, Save the Redwoods League, Statue of Liberty Found., Concept Therapy Inst. (chmn. 1987–), Forest Inst.; rec: gardening, hiking, astrology. Ofc: Lakeview Rehabilitation Ctr. 13 Sycamore Dr POB K Wofford Heights 93285

MOBLEY, JONNIEPAT MOORE, theatre instructor; b. Aug. 1, 1932, Detroit, Mich.; d. John Patrick and Charlotte P. (Tillman) Moore; m. Dwight Mobley; 1 dau., Eve; edn: BA, Mount St. Mary's Coll., 1962; MA, CSU Los Angeles, 1964; PhD, USC, 1974. Career: instr. Mount St. Mary's Coll., L.A. 1963-67; prof. West L.A. Coll., 1969-78; prof. theatre arts Cuesta Coll., San Luis Obispo 1985–; dir. St. Peter's Players, Morro Bay dir. of plays: Parish Players, S.L.O., 1982, Mission Prep, S.L.O., 1983, 1985; honors: Outstanding Young Women of Am. 1965; mem.: ALPHA 1985–, PETA 1990–; author: NTC's Dictionary of Theatre and Drama Terms, 1992, NTC's Play Production Today!, Access to Shakespeare Vol. I-IV. Ofc: Cuesta College San Luis Obispo 93403

MOBLEY, ROBERT WESLEY, marketing executive, naval aviation electronics trainer, administrator; b. Dec. 5, 1925, Jerome, Idaho; s. Frank Kenneth and Blanche Alice (Wasson) M.; m. Rosalie Naglik, June 3, 1950; children: Mark b. 1951, Diane b. 1952; edn: McDonnell Aircraft Co. schs. on aircraft sys. maintenance. 1964-65; Litton Ind. solid state computer sch. 1979; grad. mil. tng. schs. Navy/Marine Corps F/A-18, Electric/Instrument and Flight. Control Systems, Jan. 1990. Career: field svc. engr., assoc. McDonnell Aircraft Co., St. Louis, Mo. 1964-66; field svc. assoc. engr. AiResearch Mfg. Co., Torrance 1966-71; electronics tech. supr. Dept. of Navy Naval Aviation Engring. Svc. Unit, Phila.

1971–, train mil. technicians in electronic computer & sys. installed in aircraft; lectr. pilots on sys. fundamentals and ops.; founder, prin. RMR Enterprises, independent mktg. exec., 1991–; honors: num. letters of accomplishment from military commands; mem: South Orange County C.of C., USN Fleet Reserve Assn., Internat. Order of Foresters, Internat. Platform Assn.; works: designed new test bench and wrote test procedures to improve ops. of aircraft computers; mil: E-7 Chief USN 1943-64, gen. medals; Democrat; Lutheran; rec: model trains. Res: 27271 Nubles Mission Viejo 92692 Ofc: Naval Aviation Engineering Service Unit, MCAS El Toro, Santa Ana 92709

MODE, V. ALAN, research executive, inorganic chemist, computer scientist; b. May 25, 1940, Gilroy; s. Vincent Alan and Jewel (Clary) M.; m. Sue A. Oleson, Feb. 14, 1964 (div. 1975); m. Jackie Sue Hill, Dec. 23, 1976; 1 dau., Nicolle A. b. 1969; edn: BA magna cum iaude, Whitman Coll. 1962; PhD inorganic chemistry, Univ. Ill. 1965; MBA, Golden Gate Univ. 1980. Career: chemist Lawrence Livermore Nat. Lab., Livermore 1965-69, group leader 1969-72, section leader 1972-80, facility mgr. 1984-85, dep. assoc. dir. 1985–; exec. dir. BC Research Council, Vancouver, Canada 1980-84; BC Sci. Council 1982-84; honors: Outstanding Young Men Am., Alfred P. Sloan nat. scholar 1958-62, Ford tchg. fellow 1960-62, Sigma Xi; 50+ articles pub. in profl. jours.; rec: gardening, square dancing, ham radio (KK6ZL). Ofc: LLNL, Box 808/L-270 Livermore 94551

MOERBEEK, STANLEY LEONARD, lawyer; b. Nov. 12, 1951, Toronto, Canada; nat. 1963; s. John Jacob and Mary Emily (Giroux) M.; m. Carol Annette Mordaunt, April 17, 1982; children: Sarah b. 1985, Noah b. 1987; edn: BA, CSU Fullerton 1974; JD, Loyola Law Sch. 1979; admitted St. Bar Calif. 1980. Career: law clk., atty., assoc. McAlpin Doonan & Seese, Covina 1977-81; atty., assoc. Robert L. Baker, Pasadena 1981-82; Miller Bush & Minnott, Fullerton 1982-83; sole practice, Fullerton 1984–; honors: Governor's Scholar (1970), Phi Kappa Phi, lt. gov. ABA Law Student Div., 9th cir. 1979, Kiwanis Plaque of Appreciation 1983, Orange Co. Superior Ct. Cert. Appreciation 1984-88; mem. Calif. Assn. of Realtors Atty. Referral Panel; mem: Heritage Found., Orange Co. Bar Assn., Orange Co. Superior Ct. Pro Tem Panel; Republican; R.Cath.; rec: gardening, sports. Ofc: 1370 N Brea Blvd Ste 210 Fullerton 92635

MOFFITT, CHARLES TUTHILL, corporate chief executive; b. Oct. 21, 1942, Orange, Calif.; s. Robert Lovering and Martha Eleanor (Tuthill) M.; m. Gina Gilbert, May 12, 1979; children: (twins) Emily and Julia, b. 1982, Evan b. 1992; edn: BA, UC Los Angeles 1964; MA, Univ. of Wash., Seattle 1966. Career: fgn. svc. ofcr. US Dept. of State 1967-70; spl. asst. to majority leadership US House of Reps. 1970-73; exec. asst. to Mayor of Los Angeles 1973-75; ofcr. United Calif. Bank 1975-79; exec. v.p. Central L.A. Trading Inc. 1979-81; pvt. cons. 1981-82; pres. ST Internat. Inc. 1983-86, Digital Hydraulics Corp. 1984, pres. Lester/Moffitt Inc. 1986-88; CFO, Olympia Industrial, Azusa 1988-90; pres. C.T. Moffitt & Co. 1991–; mem: L.A. Com. on Fgn. Relations., Turnaround Mgt. Assn.

MOGULL, ROBERT GABRIEL, educator; b. Aug. 16, 1939, New York; s. Alexander Aaron and Shirley (Simon) M.; m. Susan Lyn Stalnaker, June 7, 1970; children: Robin b. 1973, Scott b. 1974, Michael b. 1982; edn: BA, Univ. Conn. 1961; MS, L.I. Univ. 1965; MA, St.Univ. N.Y. 1967; PhD, W. Va. Univ. 1969. Career: tchr. Roslyn H.S., N.Y. 1963-65; tchg. fellow St. Univ. N.Y., Buffalo 1965-67; tchg. fellow W. Va. Univ., Morgantown 1967-69; prof. Purdue Univ., Hammond, Ind. 1969-70; prof. CSU Sacto. 1970–; awards: Regional Research Inst. grant 1969, St. Univ. N.Y. tchg. fellow 1965-67, W. Va. Univ. tchg. fellow 1967-69, CSU Sacto. Research award 1972-73, CSUS Merit. Performance 1984-85, 88-89, CSUS Scholarly Activity Grant 1992-93, CSUS Summer Res. Fellowship 1992, Finalist in CSUS Scholarly Achievement Award 1992; mem: Am. Econ. Assn., Atlantic Econ. Soc., Midwest Econ. Assn.; 50 articles pub. in profl. jours.; rec: tennis, philately, gardening. Ofc: California State University School of Business Administration 6000 J St Sacramento 95819

MOHOLY, NOEL FRANCIS, clergyman; b. May 26, 1916, San Francisco; s. John Joseph and Eva Gertrude (Cippa) M.; edn: grad. St. Anthony's Seminary, Santa Barbara; S.T.D., Faculte de Theologie, Universite Laval, Quebec, Can. 1948; joined Franciscan Friars, 1935, ordained priest Roman Catholic Ch., 1941. Career: tchr. fundamental theology Old Mission Santa Barbara, 1942-43, sacred theology 1947-58; tchr. languages St. Anthony's Sem. 1943-44; nat. and internat. authority on Saint Irenaeus, Mariology, Calif. history (esp. Fr. Junipero Serra), occupied num. pulpits, asst. in several Franciscan Retreat Houses, retreat master San Damiano Retreat, Danville 1964-67; adminstr. (in U.S.) Cause of Padre Junipero Serra, 1950-55, vice postulator, 1958–, pres. Fr. Junipero Serra 250th Anniversary Assn. Inc. 1964–; condr. series illustrated lectures on cause of canonization of Padre Junipero Serra in all Franciscan study houses in U.S., summer 1952, also lectr. various clubs of Serra Internat. in U.S., Europe and Far East, on NBC-TV in documentary with Edwin Newman "Padre Serra, Founding Father" (1985), PBS-TV on Firing Line with Wm. F. Buckley "Junipero Serra- Saint or Sinner" (1989), CBS, ABC bdcsts., also conducted own local TV series; dir. Old Spanish Days Ins Santa Barbara Inc., 1948-58; mem. building com. for restoration of the hist. facade and towers of Old Mission Santa Barbara, 1950-54, exec. dir./treas. Old Mission Restoration Project, 1954-58; apptd: Calif. Hist.

Landmarks Advy. Com. 1962-71, U.S. Mint Annual Assay Commn. 1964, Calif. Bicentennial Celebration Commn. 1967-70, Calif. Hist. Resources Commn. 1971-76, Serra Bicentennial Commn. (pres. 1983-86); decorated Knight Comdr. Order of Isabella la Catolica (Spain, 1965), hon. citizen Petra de Mallorca 1969, Palma de Mallorca 1976, Cross of Merit Sovereign Mil. Order of Knights of Malta 1989; mem: Mariology Soc. Am., Native Sons Golden West, Associacion de los Amigos de Padre Serra, Kts. Col., Calif. Missions Study Assn.; author: Our Last Chance (1931), Saint Irenaeus the Father of Mariology (1952), The California Mission Story (1975), The First Californian (1976), (w. Don DeNevi) Junipero Serra (1985); producer phonograph records: Songs of the Calif. Missions (1951), Christmas at Mission Santa Barbara (1953), St. Francis Peace Record (1957); producer film: The Founding Father of the West (1976). Res./Ofc: Rev. Noel Francis Moholy, O.F.M., Serra Cause Old Mission Santa Barbara 93105-3611

MOHUN, GERALD FITZGIBBON, JR., lawyer; b. April 14, 1956, San Francisco; s. Gerald Fitzgibbon and Caroline (Sutro) M.; m. Marcia McGovern, Aug. 16, 1978; 2 sons, Matthew Conor b. 1984, Brendan Riley b. 1989; edn: BA political sci., UCSB 1979; JD, UCSF Hastings Coll. Law 1983; admitted St. Bar Calif. 1983, Nevada 1993. Career: atty. O'Connor Cohn Dillon & Barr, S.F. 1983-85; Forstenzer & Rudder, Bishop 1985-86; Law Offices Paul Rudder, Mammoth Lakes 1986-90; Rudder, Liebersbach, Mohun & Carney 1990–; mem: . Am. Bar Assn. (litigation sect. 1986), Mammoth Lakes C.of C. (bd. dirs.), Park & Recreation Dept. Mammoth Lakes (commr. 1989–); Republican; Cath. Ofc: POB 2127 Mammoth Lakes 93546

MOLDO, BYRON Z., lawyer; b. Sept. 26, 1956, Los Angeles; s. L. Moldo; edn: BS, UCLA 1979; JD, Southwestern Univ. 1982; admitted St. Bar Calif. 1983. Career: atty., partner Saltzburg Ray & Bergman, Los Angeles 1976–; instr. Calif. Coll. Paralegals, Van Nuys 1984; mem: L.A. Co. Bar Assn., Am. Bar Assn., Nat. Lawyers Conf., L.A. Bankruptcy Forum. Ofc: Saltzburg Ray & Bergman 10960 Wilshire Blvd 10th Floor Los Angeles 90024

MOLENKAMP, CHARLES R., atmospheric physicist; b. Aug. 26, 1941, San Francisco; s. Charles and Sophia H. (Lappinga) M.; m. Margaret J. Wattron, Aug. 26, 1967; children: Robin b. 1970, William b. 1974; edn: BS, Calvin Coll., 1963; MS, Univ. Ariz., Tucson 1967, PhD, 1972. Career: physicist Lawrence Livermore Nat. Lab., 1972–; honors: Phi Beta Kappa 1972; mem.: Am. Meteorol. Soc. 1969–, Am. Scientific Affiliation 1980–, Am. Assn. for Aerosol Research 1989–; publs: 17+ jour. articles. Ofc: Lawrence Livermore National Lab. L-262 PO Box 808 Livermore 94550

MOLLOY, JOHN JOSEPH, III, lawyer; b. Aug. 8, 1946, San Antonio, Tx.; s. John Joseph and Nadine Gloria (Pape) M.; m. Joan Susan Cottier, June 8, 1968; children: Kelly b. 1970, Susan b. 1976, Sean b. 1977, Michael b. 1978, Ryan b. 1983; edn: BS, USC, 1968, JD, 1972; admitted Calif. St. Bar 1972. Career: atty., ptnr. Sheppard Mullin Richter & Hampton, Los Angeles 1972-87; Sandler Rolnick & Morse 1987-93; mem: Am. Bar Assn., Los AngelesCo. Bar Assn., Jonathan Club; mil: sgt. Calif. Nat. Guard 1969-75; Republican; Cath.; rec: golf. Res: 244 Tilden Ave Los Angeles 90049 Ofc: Walker Wright Tyler & Ward 626 Wilshire Blvd Los Angeles 90017

MOLTZ, DENNIS MICHAEL, nuclear chemist-physicist; b. Oct. 2, 1952, San Antonio, Tx.; s. Ellis Edward and Alice Rose (Wagner) M.; m. Rosette Margaret Ajemian, Oct. 16, 1983; children: Andrew b. 1985, Christopher b. 1986; edn: BS chemistry, Tx. A&M Univ. 1974; BS math. 1974; PhD, UC Berkeley 1979. Career: postdoctoral fellow Oak Ridge Nat. Lab., Tenn. 1979-82; Univ. S.C., Columbia 1982-84; staff scientist Lawrence Berkeley Lab., Berkeley 1984–; mem: Am. Chemical Soc., Am. Physical Soc., AAAS; Republican; Lutheran; rec: sports, gardening. Ofc: Lawrence Berkeley Laboratory 1 Cyclotron Rd Berkeley 94720

MONDAVI, ROBERT GERALD, executive, vintner; b. Virginia, Minn. June 18, 1913; s. Cesare and Rosa (Grassi) M.; m. Marjorie Declusin 1940 (div.); children: Michael, Timothy, Marcia; m. 2d. Margrit Biever 1980; edn: BA Stanford Univ. 1936. Career: dir. Sunny St. Helena Wine Co., St. Helena 1937-45; v.p. gen. mgr. Chas. Krug Winery, St. Helena 1945-66; pres. Robert Mondavi Winery, Oakville 1966-88, chmn. 1988–. Ofc: Robert Mondavi Winery PO Box 106 Oakville 94562-0106

MONROE, RAY, social scientist, author, archaeologist; b. Dec. 21, 1937, Columbus, Ohio; s. Paul Thompson and Miriam Esther (Young) M.; widower; 1 child, Psyche b. 1963; edn: Texas Tech. 1956-57, Stephen F. Austin St. Coll. 1960-63, BFA San Francisco Art Inst. 1964, Peace Corps Tng. Cornell Univ. 1965 Latin Am. Rural Comm. Dev., MBA La Jolla Univ. 1982, PhD Latin Am. studies 1983; archeol. res. Ashmolean Mus., Oxford Univ. post-doctoral res. 1990; ethics and morality Worchester Coll., Oxford Univ. 1990. Career: res. devel. specialist, antibodies, Chas Pfizer Co. 1957-58, travel to 38 countries for cancer res.; seaman U.S. Merchant Marine 1957–; staff res. and sci. illust. for Jour. of the Arnold Arboretum, Harvard Univ. 1963; freelance writer, num. sci. publs., 1963–; cons. to U.S. Congl. Commn. for study of internat. migration and

coop. econ. devel., also on call for spl. placement Latin Am. affairs Office of Pub. Liaison, The White House, 1989-90; archeol. res. Ramat Hanidiv, Masada, Caesarea, Israel 1991, Rafa, Beersheba, Qumran 1992, memphis, Egypt 1992, Apache Co. Ariz. Anasazi ruins 1990-94; lectr. Biblical archeol. vol. Israel Ministry of Culture and Educ., Dept. of Antiquities 1990-92; awards: Lacy Hunt art scholar Stephen F. Austin St. Univ. 1963, Kappa Phi 1962, NSF travel grantee to Central & So. Am. 1961, L.B. Johnson Found./Univ. Tex. res. grantee 1987-88, Internat. Platform Assn. P.R.O.F. Mex., Am. Biog. Inst. disting. ldrship award US-Mex. rels., SouthWestern Coll. Bd. Govs. grantee, U.S. Pell grantee 1988-89, IBC Gold Medal, Cambridge England, Internat. Biog. Ctr. 1st 500 edit. 1991; publs: Customs of Mexican Comml. Practice (La Jolla Univ. 1983); author 16 books, num. articles and res. publs. re the economy and hist. of Mexico including: Hidden Forces in Europe that Fueled Spanish Expansionism in the New World (Imprinta Salinas, T.J. Mex., 1989); The Impact of Aztec Nahuatl on the Present Usage of the Sp. Lang. in Mexico (ibid); A 20th Century Hist. Perspective for Policy Makers on Issue of Minority Rights (ibid); Epicurs, An Ancient Prescription to Cure Ailing Govts. (ibid); Coyote (Archives Palacio Nac., Mex.); Confessions of an Illegal Alien Smuggler (Carlton Press, N.Y. 1987); The Creation of Employment in Mexico (Ram's Head Press, T.J., Mex. 1988); Violence Related to the Illegal Alien Crossings at the Calif.-Mex. Border, 1988; Ingenious Mexican Migrators Perpetuate the Cycle of Illegal Immigration (ibid); The Impact on the U.S. & Mex. Economy of the Tax and Wages of the Illegal Aliens; L.B.J. and the Illegal Alien as a Precursor to Amnesty; Herodian Pottery, Ibex Press, 1991; Ancient Israel- Lamps, 1993; Canaan Pottery and Style, 1993; Philistine Pottery, Markings and Style, 1993; Papyrus and Scrolls - Methods at Qumran Scriptorium, 1994; Seal Stones and Scarabs for Contact Documents, 1994; Tijuana Quartet, article in S.D. Reader mag., 1988; t.v. news feature- In Search of the Alien Smuggler (CBS-TV Ch. 8, 2/15/88) mil: E5 USNR, 3rd merit. svc. medal, Nat. Defense Medal, Naval Reserve Medal; Republican, mayoral cand. San Diego 1988; Jewish; rec: art, photog. Res: 75 Calle Fuego Tijuana Mexico, Playas 22700 Ofc: 39900 Ranchwood Dr Murrieta 92563

MONTANUCCI, ROBERT, artist; b. June 1, 1953, San Jose; s. Aldo Marcello and Carol (Wawel-Habdank de Dunikowski) M.; edn: AA, Merced Coll. 1974. Career: artist; one-man show: Merced Coll. 1974; Lake Gallery, Tahoe City (1979, 80); SFB Morse Gallery, Pebble Beach 1981; Merced Coll. 1982; Merced Coll. 1988; Zantman Art Galleries, Ltd. Palm Desert 1989; Merced Coll. 1993; lecture and exhib. Dos Palos H.S. (1989, 91, 95); two-man show: Round House Gal., Fallon Indian Reserv., Nev. 1981; Fambrough Gal., Reno 1982; featured artist: Fresno Art Ctr. 1974; Pebble Beach Gal. 1975; Gal. Americana, Carmel 1977; Lindsey Gal., Carmel 1981; group exhib: Mfgs. Hanover Trust Co. Art Gal. 1976; San Bernardino Co. Mus. 1985; Yosemite Renaissance III, Yosemite Nat. Park 1988; Visions of Excellence V, Albuquerque, NM 1991; Panache Gal., Mendocino 1994; nat. finalist Benedictine Art Awards, N.Y. 1976; 2 paintings in permanent collection Favell Museum of Western Art, Klamath Falls, OR 1977; art pub: "The First Collection of Tahoe Artists" 1978; "Duck Stamps and Prints: The Complete Federal and State Editions" 1988; feature articles: Game & Gossip mag., Monterey 1975; Southwest Art mag. 1979; Outdoor Calif. mag. 1984; Horizon mag. 1987; designer of Calif. Dept. of Fish and Game Waterfowl Conservation Stamp, winner 7th annual Calif. Duck Stamp Competition, Sacto. 1984; named Artist of the Year, Ducks Unlimited, S.F. 1986; lectr., slide shows, demonstrations Merced Coll. (1982, 85, 87, 91), Calif. Waterfowl Assn., Monterey 1985, Merced Art League (1985, 87). Ofc: Montanucci Art, PO Box 19155 South Lake Tahoe 96151

MONTEMAYOR, JOANNE MARIE, registered nurse; b. Sept. 10, 1941, Jerome, Ariz.; d. Karl Nickolas and Anna Linda (Worgt) Wilke; m. Casimiro Lopez Montemayor, Oct. 8, 1978; edn: BS nursing, Univ. Colo. Boulder 1965; MN, Univ. Wash. Seattle 1974; reg. nurse, 1989. Career: nursing coord. Redwood Convalescent Center, Castro Valley 1982-83; service dir. Upjohn Health Care Services, Hayward 1983-84; dir. of nursing Wash. Manor Convalescent, San Leandro 1984-86; case mgr. Vesper Hospice 1988, north team leader 1988-89, patient care coord. 1989–; honors: Who's Who Am. Women, Who's Who Am. Nursing Profls., Who's Who Exec. Women; mem: Nat. Hospice Orgn.; author Western Anthology of Poetry, 1989; mil: lt commdr. USN 1959-79; Democrat; Prot.; rec: music, gardening. Res: 2722 Stanton Heights Ct Castro Valley 94546

MONTGOMERY, HOWARD GROMEL, employee benefits company executive, naval reserve officer; b. Jan. 21, 1946, Norfolk, Va.; s. John Archibald and Edna (Gromel) M.; m. Audrey Mae Hibl, Oct. 6, 1973; children: Krista Marie b. 1978, Ashli Lynn b. 1984; edn: BA in polit. sci./internat. rels., UC Berkeley, 1968; reg. health & disability underwriter (RHU) Nat. Assn. Health Underws., 1980; fluent in Fr. and Spanish. Career: pres. and ceo Howard Montgomery Assocs., employee benefit plan sales & consulting, 1971–; dir: World Graphics Inc., Pompano Properties Inc.; columnist "GroupAdvisor" distb. local newspapers and bus. newsletters in Calif.; mem. Nat. Assn. Life Underws., Nat. Assn. Health Underws., Leading Producers Roundtable (life 1978–), Calif. Assn. Life Underws., Peninsula Life Underwrs. Assn. (dir., ofcr. 1978-84, hlth. ins. advr. 1982-84); appt. by Calif. State Assembly to Small Bus. Task Force (chmn.), Small Bus. Reps. Roundtable, Calif. State Conf. on Small Bus. (small bus. advy.

com.), 1987–; appt. regional area advy. com. U.S. SBA, 1987–; White House Council on Small Bus., 1978-80; mem: Better Business Bur./ San Mateo County (dir. 1983–, chmn. bd. 1987-89, Lois J. Bell achiev. awards 1987-88, rec'd Calif. St. Legislature Proclamation 1989), Burlingame Kiwanis Club (pres. 1975-76, Disting. Pres. Award 1976), Foster City Bus. Devel. Club (pres. 1979-84), Burlingame Ambassadors Club (pres. 1978, Top Dog Award 1978), Calif. C.of C. (1985–, v.ch. Small Bus. Advy. Com. 1987–), Foster City C.of C. (bd. 1978-81, 83-86, treas. 84-86), UC Alumni Assn. (life), World Affairs Council S.F., Commonwealth Club of Calif., San Mateo County Council Boy Scouts Am. (bd. 1972-76, county chmn. mem. 1974), Burlingame C.of C. (bd. 1973-77), Burl. Bicentenial Com. (co-chair 1975-76), Miss Burlingame Pageant (co-chair 1974), Airport Land Use Commn. San Mateo Co. 1975-77, Regional Plng. Com. S.M. Co. 1975-77, Am. Cancer Soc. (Burl. chmn. 1974), Heart Fund (Burl. chmn. 1973); mil: Capt. USNR 1968–, decorated Defense Meritorious Service Medal 1994, Meritorious Svc. Medal 1987, , Navy Commendn. Medal (1982, 85, 87, 90), Merit. Unit Commendn., Battle Efficiency "E" USS Wiltsie (DD-716), Nat. Def. Medal w/star, Vietnam Svc. Medal w/star, Naval Reserve Sea Svc. Ribbon w/star, Navy and Marine Corps Overseas Ribbon, Armed Forces Reserve Medal w/hourglass, Repub. Vietnam Campaign Medal, Navy Expert Rifleman, Navy Expert Pistol Shot; mem. Naval Reserve Assn.: 12th Dist. (pres. 1988–), Polaris Chpt. (pres. 1985-87, awarded Navy Recruiting Command's #1 NRA Chapt. in Nation 1987 and #2 Chapt. 1986, Twice A Citizen Award 1987), dir., coord. Chief of Naval Ops. Presentation & Speakers Pgm. (awarded 4 certs. of merit and 3 top nat. ranking awards) 1985–, coord. Command Excellence Sem. Pgm./TQL Pgm. for NAVRESREDCOM reg. 20, 1991–; mem. Navy League of U.S. (life, dir. S.F. Council 1987–), Surface Navy Assn., Reserve Ofcrs. Assn., US Naval Inst., Naval Order of U.S., Naval Enlisted Reserve Assn., Naval War Coll. Found. (alumni mem. 1982–), Nat. Def. Univ. Found. (grad. mem. 1983–), Navy Memorial Found. (charter 1987–); Republican; Presbyterian. Ofc: 1181 Chess Dr Ste B Foster City 94404

MONTGOMERY, JOHN ALAN, surgeon; b. Jan. 24, 1944, Los Angeles; s. Milford Jefferson and Ilah Claudine (Whitely) M.; m. Jean Nishita, March 28, 1970; children: Maggie Mae b. 1977, Max Alan b. 1979; edn: BA, UCLA 1965; MD, USC Med. Sch. 1969; cert. Am. Bd. Surgeons (1978, 88). Career: intern L.A.Co.-USC Med. Center, L.A. 1969-70, surgical resident 1970-74; pvt. practice gen. vascular thoracic surgery, Fortuna 1976–; clin. prof. L.A. Co.-USC Med. Center 1982–; honors: Exchange Club Man of Year 1961, USC Med. Sch. Assoc. Students Pres. 1968-69, Skull & Dagger USC 1969; Fellow A.C.S., mem. Calif. Med. Assn., Internat. Soc. Philosophical Enquiry, Triple 9 Soc.; paper pub., 1974, one man show of recent drawings, 1987; mil: major USAF 1974-76; rec: art, music. Res: 4175 Mill St Fortuna 95540 Ofc: 3301 Renner Dr Fortuna 95540

MOORE, C. BRADLEY, chemistry professor; b. Dec. 7, 1939, Boston; s. Charles Walden and Dorothy (Lutz) M.; m. Penelope Williamson Percival, Aug. 27, 1960; children: Megan Bradley, Scott Woodward; edn: BA, Harvard Univ., 1960; PhD, UC Berkeley, 1963. Career: asst. prof. chemistry UC Berkeley, 1963-68, assoc. prof. 1968-72, prof. 1972–, chemistry dept. v.chair 1971-75, dept. chmn. 1982-86, dean Coll. of Chemistry, 1988-94; vis. prof. Faculté des Scis., Paris 1970, 75, Inst. for Molecular Sci., Okazaki, Japan 1979, Fudan Univ., Shanghai 1979, adv. prof. 1988–, vis. prof. Joint Inst. for Lab. Astrophysics, Univ. Colo., Boulder 1981-82; awards: Alfred P. Sloan Found. fellow 1968, Guggenheim Found. fellow 1969, Coblentz award 1973, E.O. Lawrence award 1986, Lippincott award 1987, 1st Inter-Am. Photochem. Soc. award 1988, Earle K. Plyler Prize, Am. Physical Soc. 1994, Humboldt Research Award for Sr. U.S. Scientists 1994; mem: Am. Phys. Soc. (Fellow), AAAS (Fellow), Am. Chem. Soc. (past chmn. div. phys. chemistry, Calif. sect. award 1977), Nat. Acad. Scis. (chmn. Com. Undergrad. Sci. Educ.); contbr. articles to profl. jours.; editor: Chemical and Biochemical Applications of Lasers; rec: cycling. Res: 936 Oxford St Berkeley 94707-2435 Ofc: Dept. Chemistry Univ. Calif. 211 Lewis Hall Berkeley 94720-1460 Tel: 415/642-3453

MOORE, DONALD ARTHUR, economics and statistics professor emeritus; b. Aug. 20, 1916, Vegreville, Canada; nat. 1937; s. James Darien and Edith Carolyn (Hatch) M.; m. Kathleen Mae Ross, May 23, 1942; children: Margaret b. 1946, David b. 1950, Kathleen b. 1959; edn: BA bus., Linfield Coll. 1942; MA internat. rels., Tufts Univ. 1942; PhD econ., Mich. St. Univ. 1956. Career: instr. econ. Brown Univ. Providence, R.I. 1948-50; Bowdoin Coll., Brunswick, Me. 1947-48; Mich. St. Univ., E. Lansing, Mich. 1950-56; asst. prof., assoc. prof., prof. econ. CSU Los Angeles 1956-82, prof. emeritus 1983–, chair Academic Senate 1979-81; cons. Assn. Calif. St. Univ. Profs. 1980-89; mem: So. Calif. Econ. Assn. (pres. 1967-68), Assn. Calif. St. Univ. Profs. (pres. 1979-80), Am. Econ. Assn., Western Econ. Assn., Episcopal Diocese of L.A. Housing Commn. 1990-95, Foothill Family Shelter, Univ. Club of Claremont (pres. 1994-95), United Way (vol.); ed. 2 proceedings, 1987, 89, articles pub. in profl. jour.; mil: major AUS 1937-61; Democrat; Episcopalian; rec: flying. Res: 1121 W 23d St Upland 91784-1213 Ofc: Dept. Econ. California State University Los Angeles 90032

MOORE, JACQUELINE URSULA, lawyer; b. Oct. 23, 1952, Palo Alto; edn: BA, Stanford Univ. 1974; JD, 1977; admitted St. Bar Calif. Career: atty., assoc. Morrison & Foerster, San Francisco 1977-84; v.p., real estate counsel Triton Nat.,

Danville 1984-87; spl. counsel Farella Braun & Martel, San Francisco 1988–; honors: Stanford Law Sch. Hilmer Olemer 1975, Phi Beta Kappa; mem: Am. Bar Assn. Ofc: Farella Braun & Martel 235 Montgomery St San Francisco 94104

MOORE, JOHN WILLIAM, university president; b. Aug. 1, 1939, Bayonne, N.J.; s. Frederick A. and Marian R. (Faser) M.; m. Nancy Baumann, Aug. 10, 1968; children: Matthew b. 1972, Sarah b. 1974, David b. 1979; edn: BS soc. sci./edn., Rutgers Univ., 1961; MS, counseling & student personnel svs., Indiana Univ., 1963; EdD, Penn. State Univ., 1970. Career: asst. v.p. acad. affairs Univ. of Vermont, Burlington 1973-76, assoc. v.p. acad. affairs, 1976-77; v.p. policy & planning Old Dominion Univ., Norfolk, Va. 1977-78, v.p. ednl. svs. 1978-82, exec. v.p. and prof. edn. 1982-85; pres. CSU Stanislaus, Turlock, Calif. 1985–; trustee Gould Med. Found., Modesto 1988–; awards: Disting. service Old Dominion Univ. Alumni Assn. 1985, community svc. Norfolk Commn. for Edn. 1985, leadership United Way Modesto 1986, service Private Industry Council Modesto 1989, Alumni Fellow Penn State Univ. 1990; mem: Soc. for Coll. and Univ. Planning (nat. pres. 1985-86), Am. Assn. of State Colls. & Univs. (Calif. state rep. 1988–), United Way Stanislaus Co. (pres. 1988-89), Turlock C.of C. (bd. 1988–), Pvt. Industry Council Modesto 1987–, Union Safe Bank Advy. Com. 1988–, Rotary Turlock, Sportsmen of Stanislaus 1985–; Methodist; rec: youth soccer coach. Ofc: CSU Stanislaus 801 W Monte Vista Turlock 95380

MOORE, THOMAS PRESTON, educator; b. Mar. 22, 1951, New Britain, Conn.; s. James Mendon and Lenna Mary (Maguire) M.; m. Monique Pierrette Fargues, July 2, 1989; edn: att. Univ. of Helsinki, Finland 1968-69; BA, Northeastern Univ., Boston 1974; MS, Stanford Univ., 1975; PhD., Virginia Tech, 1986; Cert. Profl. Logistician, Soc. of Log. Engrs. 1988. Career: lab. tech. Cabot Corp. Res. Lab., Billerica, Mass., 1970; res. asst. Avco-Everett Res. Lab., Everett, Mass., 1971; marine engr. trainee Nat. Data Buoy Ctr., Bay St. Louis, Ms., 1972-73; served to Lt.Col. US Army (active duty 1976-80 , res. 1980–); instr. Army Logistics Mgmt. College, Fort Lee, Va. 1977-80; tchg. asst. IEOR Dept. Virginia Tech, Blacksburg, Va. 1980-81; res. assoc. VA Ctr. for Coal & Energy Res., 1981-82; res. asst. Mgmt. Systems Lab, Virginia Tech, 1982-83, res. assoc. IEOR Dept. 1983-85; asst. prof. of mgmt. sci. Naval Postgraduate Sch., Monterey, Calif. 1986-93; Moore Productivity Associates, 1993–; honors: Phi Kappa Phi 1974, Alpha Pi Mu IE Honor Soc. 1981, fellowship Soc. of Log. Engrs. 1984, Sigma Xi 1993; mem: Decision Scis. Inst. 1988–, Inst. of Indsl. Engrs. (1980–, sr. mem. 1995–), Ops. Res. Soc. of Am. 1974–, Soc. of Logistics Engrs. (1985–, sr. mem. 1993–), Mil. Ops. Res. Soc. 1987–, Am. Soc. of Engring. Educ. 1992, Fellow Inter-Univ. Seminar on Armed Forces and Society 1992–, Bikecentennial (life 1980–), Sierra Club 1977–; civic bds: Marina Coast Water Dist. (dir. 1993–, pres. 1994–), Marina City Planning Commn. 1989-93, Marina Water Conservation Com. (chair 1990–), Monterey Penn. Soccer League (pres. 1987–), SW Va. Soccer Assn., Blacksburg, Va. (founder & pres. 1981-84), Metro DC-Va. Soccer Assn. (v.p. 1982-83, newsletter ed. 1982-84), Monterey Penn. Choral Soc. (bd. 1993–), Am. Heart Assn. (CPR instr. 1978-80); publs: (diss.) Optimal Design, Procurement and Support of Multiple Repairable Equipt. and Log. Systems, 1986, contbr. jour. articles to: Transportation Res., Proceedings of the 1985 Fed. Acquisition Res. Symposium, Proceedings of 20th Annual Internat. Logistics Symposium, 1985, Supply J. Royal Australian Navy, 1990. Ofc: Dept. Systems Mgmt., Code SM/Mr, Naval Postgraduate School, Monterey CA 93943-5103

MOORE, TILLMAN M., vice president and medical director of tissue bank, emeritus professor of clinical orthopaedics; b. July 18, 1927, Amarillo, Tx.; s. Tillman Marion and Velma (Truett) M.; m. Shirley Mayer, Dec. 22, 1950; children: Paul b. 1954, Shannon b. 1956, Anne b. 1959, Elizabeth b. 1961; edn: BS, Iowa St. Univ. 1949; MD, Wash. Univ. Sch. Medicine St. Louis 1953; diplomate Am. Bd. Surgery 1959, Am. Bd. Orthopaedic Surgery 1972; ordained priest Episcopal Ch. 1968. Career: surgery resident Barnes Hosp., St. Louis, Mo. 1953-58; pvt. practice surgery, Sitka, Alaska 1958-67; orthopaedic surgeon L.A. Co.-USC Med. Center, L.A. 1967-70; asst. clin. prof. orthopaedic surgery, 1970-87, emeritus prof. clin. orthopaedics Univ. So. Calif., 1987–; med. dir. Pacific Coast Tissue Bank 1987–; chief oncology Orthopaedic Hosp. 1980-88; chief orthopaedics Norris Cancer Hosp. 1984-88; cons. kinesiology Los Amigos Hosp., Downey 1970-72, cons. orthopaedic reconstrn. 1972-80; bd. dirs. Hosp. of Good Samaritan, L.A. 1986; chmn. bd. dirs. KSEW-Radio, Sitka 1962-67; honors: Orthopaedic Research & Edn. Found. Order of Merit 1983-85, Assn. Bone & Joint Surgery Nicolas Audrey award 1980, Am. Acad. Orthopaedic Surgery Carl Berg fellow 1971, Am. Cancer Soc. grantee 1973; mem: A.C.S. (Fellow), Am. Acad. Orthopaedic Surgeons (Fellow), Soc. Surgical Oncology, Am. Orthopaedic Assn.; past mem. Sitka Jr. C.of C., Wilson-Bost Interurban Club Calif., Sigma Alpha Epsilon, Phi Beta Pi; ed. Injuries to Leg and Sequellae, 1981, Symp. on Tumors of Musculo-skel. System, 1977, 6 book chpts. pub., 50 articles pub. in med. jours., 1969-88; mil: lt.j.g. USN 1956; Republican; Episcopal; rec: music, numismatics, tennis. Res: 5535 Peregrine Way Blaine WA 98230 Ofc: Pacific Coast Tissue Bank 2500-19 S Flower St Los Angeles 90007

MOORE, WILLIAM JAMES, journalist; b. Oct. 7, 1943, Corpus Christi, Tx.; s. Edwin Ruthven and Mary Wilson (Clokey) M.; son, Matthew b. 1982; edn: BA comm. & polit. sci., Stanford Univ., 1965, MA comm., 1966. Career:

reporter Arizona Daily Star, Tucson 1962; editor-in-chief Stanford Daily, Stanford, Ca. 1964; reporter San Francisco Chronicle, 1967-79; news editor Oakland Tribune /East Bay Today, 1979-81; metropolitan editor Sacramento Bee, 1982, Forum editor, McClatchy Newspapers (Sacramento Bee), Sacto. 1982–; press aide/volunteer Robert F. Kennedy Presdl. Campaign, S.F. 1968; awards: Silver Award for editing best overall newspaper sect. in U.S., The Assn. of Opinion Page Editors 1993, Best feature writing in No. Calif., S.F. Press Club 1973, 78, Copley Found. fellow at Stanford Univ. 1965-66, two gold medals for newswriting Hearst Found., NYC 1963; contbg. writer Stanford Review 1965, Rolling Stone Mag. 1975; mil: USCG Reserve 1967-73; rec: skiing, pub. speaking (western storyteller). Ofc: McClatchy Newspapers PO Box 15779 Sacramento 95852

MOORHEAD, CARLOS J., congressman; b. May 6, 1922, Long Beach, Calif.; s. Carlos Arthur and Florence (Gravers) M.; m. Valery Joan Tyler, July 19, 1969; children: Theresa, Catharine, Steven, Teri, Paul; edn: BA, UCLA, 1943; JD, Univ. So. Calif., 1949; admitted Bar: Calif. 1949, U.S. Supreme Court 1973. Career: pvt. practice law, Glendale, Calif. 1949-72; dir. Lawyers Reference Svc., Glendale, 1950-66; mem. Calif. Assembly 1967-72; mem. Calif. Law Revision Commn., 1971-72; pres. 43rd Dist. Republican Assembly, Glendale Young Republicans; mem. 93rd-104th Congresses from 22nd (now 27th) Calif. dist. 1973–, judiciary com.; ranking Rep. energy and commerce com.; dean Calif. Congl. Rep. Delegation; appt. to Fed. Cts. Study Com.; mem. L.A. Co. Republican Central Com., Calif. Rep. Central Com.; pres. Glendale Hi-Twelve Club; awards: Man of Yr. award USO, 1979; mem: Calif. Bar Assn., L.A. County Bar Assn., Glendale Bar Assn. (past pres.), Glendale C.of C., Verdugo Hills council BSA, Glendale La Crescenta Camp Fire Girls Inc. (pres.), Masons, Shriners, Lions, Moose, VFW; Presbyterian. Ofc: US House of Reps 2346 Rayburn House Office Bldg Washington DC 20515

MOOSSA, A. R., academic surgeon; b. Oct. 10, 1939, Port-Louis, Mauritius; s. Yacoob and Maude (Rochecoute) M.; m. Denise Willoughby, Dec. 28, 1973; children: Pierre b. 1977, Noel b. 1981, Claude b. 1984, Valentine b. 1987; edn: BS, Univ. of Liverpool 1962, MD, 1965; postgrad. tng. Johns Hopkins Univ. 1972-73, The Univ. of Chgo. 1973-74; FRCS, Royal Coll. of Surgeons of England 1970; FRCS Royal Coll. of Surgeons of Edinburgh 1970; FACS, Fellow Am. Coll. of Surgeons. Career: asst. prof. of surgery Univ. of Chgo. 1974, assoc. prof. of surgery 1975, prof. of surg., dir. Surgical Research, and chief Gen. Surgery Service, vice chmn. Dept. of Surgery, Univ. of Chgo. 1977-83; prof. and chmn. Dept. of Surgery, UC San Diego and surgeon-in-chief UCSD Medical Center, 1983–; awards: Hunterian Prof., Royal Coll. of Surgeons 1977, Litchfield lectr. Univ. of Oxford, Eng. 1978, Praelector in Surgery, Univ. of Dundee, Scotland 1979, Hon. Fellow Brazilian Coll. & Surgeons 1988, Hon. Doctor of Medicine, Univ. of Liverpool 1990, G.B. Ong vis. prof. Univ. of Hong Kong 1992, Hampson Trust vis. prof. Univ. of Liverpool 1992, hon. mem. Assn. de Chirurgie Francaise 1992, hon. mem. Paraguan Surgical Soc. 1992; mem: Am. Coll. of Surgeons, Am. Surgical Assn., Soc. of Univ. Surgeons, Soc. of Surgical Oncology, Am. Soc. of Clin. Oncology, Soc. for Surgery of the Alimentary Tract, Internat. Hepato-Biliary-Pancreatic Assn. (pres. 1989); club: La Jolla Beach and Tennis, Fairbanks Ranch Country; R.Cath.; rec: travel, soccer. Ofc: Dept. of Surgery, UCSD Medical Center 225 Dickinson St San Diego 92103

MOOZ, WILLIAM ERNST, chemical company president; b. Feb. 28, 1929, Staten Island, NY; s. Harold Adolph and Kathryn Jameison (Neuschwander) M.; m. Melodie Ione Linn, Sept. 11, 1982; edn: BS, MIT 1950; reg. profl. engr. Calif. Career: asst. to plant mgr. Titanium Metals Corp., Henderson, Nev. 1950-60; econ. engr. U.S. Borax & Chem., Los Angeles 1960-62; exec. v.p. G.B. Smith Chem. Works, Maple Park, Ill. 1962-63; sr. research staff Rand Corp., Santa Monica 1963-88; pres. Met-L-Chek Co. 1963–, dir. 1963–; NDT Europa BV, Amsterdam, Netherlands 1963–; awards: Earl P.L. Apfelbaum Meml. 1985; mem: Am. Inst. Mining & Metallurgical Engrs., Am. Soc. Nondestructive Testing; 2 patents 1952, 100 reports pub. 1963–, author of 7 books; mil: cpl. AUS 1953-55; rec: whitewater river rafting, hiking. Res: Box 1714 Santa Monica 90406 Ofc: Met-L-Chek Co 1639 Euclid St Santa Monica 90404

MORALES, JUSTO JAVIER, business owner; b. March 14, 1962, El Gurllo Jalisco, Mex.; nat. 1962; s. Salvador D. and Dolores H. (Garcia) M.; edn: BS mktg. and mgmt., Chapman Coll. 1985; MBA, Humboldt St. Univ. 1988. Career: asst. mgr. Dolphin Fin., Anaheim 1988-89; claim specialist State Farm Ins., Irvine 1989–; owner, entrepreneur Astro Services, La Habra 1989–; cons. Taipaku, Arcata 1988–; mentor Neighborhood Housing Svc., Santa Ana 1994-95; mentor Career Beginnings, Rancho Santiago Coll., 1989-92; mem: PIRA (pres. 1985-86), Internat. Club Chapman Coll., Bus. & Econ. Humboldt St. Univ.; pub. thesis on hispanic mktg.; R.Cath.; rec: swimming, racquetball. Res: 518 N Eastside Ave Santa Ana 92701

MORENA, GITA DOROTHY, psychotherapist; b. Aug. 1, 1947, Los Angeles; d. Kenneth Austin and Ozma (Baum) Mantele; m. David Morena, July 5, 1969 (div. 1981); children: Brian b. 1973, Gregory b. 1977; edn: BS biol., Santa Clara Univ.; MS clin. psychol., San Diego St. Univ.; lic. marriage family and child therapist 1973. Career: program dir. Western Inst., San Diego 1974-76; treat-

ment dir. Windmill House 1976-78; cons. Learning Devel. 1975-78; faculty Nat. Univ. 1978-91; pvt. practice, San Diego 1976–; graphic artist Gita's Graphics 1985–; honors: Psi Chi; mem: Calif. Assn. Marriage & Family Therapists, Sandplay Therapists of Am., Internat. Soc. of Sandplay Therapists; contbr. interpretation of projective drawings 1984, article pub. in profl. jour. 1974; rec: music, meditation, yoga, metaphysics. Address: 3855 Camino Litoral Ste 222 San Diego 92107

MORETTI, AUGUST JOSEPH, lawyer; b. Aug. 18, 1950, Elmira, N.Y.; s. John Anthony and Dorothy M. (DeBlasio) M.; m. Audrey B. Kavka, M.D., Nov. 8, 1981; children: David Anthony b. 1983, Matthew Alexander b. 1987; edn: BA econ., Princeton Univ. 1972; JD, Harvard Sch. Law 1975. Career: atty., assoc. Heller Ehrman White & McAuliffe, San Francisco 1976-82, ptnr. 1982–; lectr. fin. UC Berkeley Sch. Bus. Adminstrn. 1976-79; mem. advy. bd. UC Berkeley Lester Ctr. for Entrepreneurship; dir. Ann Martin Childrens Ctr. Ofc: Heller Ehrman White & McAuliffe 525 University Ave Palo Alto 94301

MORGAN, HENRY MILES, sales executive, city official; b. March 25, 1927, La Jolla; s. Henry M. and Beatrice F. (Lacy) M.; m. Joy Carmichael, June 14, 1952; children: Melinda b. 1953, Steven b. 1955, Laura b. 1956, William b. 1960, Jennifer b. 1962, Mary b. 1964; edn: BA physics, Pomona Coll. 1951. Career: sr. mktg. rep. IBM Corp., Los Angeles 1951-87; mayor City of Covina 1982-84, 1992-93, councilman 1978-93; pres. Calif. League of Cities, L.A. 1988-89; awards: So. Calif. Council Vol. Action Outstanding Vol. 1980; mem: Pomona Coll. Alumni Council, Intercomm. Med. Center (foundation dir., Men's Club 1984, pres. Men's Club 1993), E. San Gabriel Valley Manpower Tng. Consortium 1978-93 (chair 1984-93), San Gabriel Valley Assn. Cities (pres. 1980-83), Rotary Club (pres. 1988-89); mil: USN 1945-47; Republican; Episcopalian; rec: sailing, gardening, travel. Res: 768 Casad St Covina 91723

MORGAN, KERMIT JOHNSON, lawyer; b. Feb. 13, 1914, Henderson, Iowa; s. Samuel and Jennie Amelia M.; m. Ortrud Impol, Dec. 9, 1960; children: Georgina b. 1942, Wilson b. 1945; edn: BA, Univ. Iowa 1935; JD, USC 1937; admitted Calif. St. Bar (1937). Career: atty./of counsel to Morgan & Armbrister, Los Angeles 1937–; honors: Alpha Tau Omega, Phi Delta Phi; mem: Am. Board of Trial Advocates (nat. pres. 1973, pres. L.A. Chpt. 1971), Internat. Assn. of Defense Council, Assn. of Defense Trial Attys. (bd. dirs. 1963-66), Am. Bar Assn., Calif. Bar Assn., L.A. County Bar Assn., Wilshire Bar Assn.; Republican; Congregational; rec: golf, fishing. Res: 2108 Stradella Rd Los Angeles 90077 Ofc: Kermit J. Morgan 2850 28th St Santa Monica 90405

MORGAN, KILE, city mayor; b. Mar. 22, 1920, Hancock County, Tenn.; s. George Preston and Geneva Mary (Barnard) M.; m. Donna Wilcox, July 28, 1944; children: Janice b. 1945, Kile, Jr. b. 1946, Robert b. 1950; H.S. grad. Ava, Mo. 1938; Calif. lic. real estate broker 1946. Career: prop. car dealer, 1944-46; real estate builder/devel., 1946-66; elected National City City Council, 1960-66, city mayor 1966-86; Kiwanian; Democrat; Baptist; rec: golf. Res: 1223 J Ave National City 91950

MORGAN, KILE, JR., home builder; b. Aug. 6, 1946, National City; s. Kile and Donna Kay (Wilcox) M.; m. Marron Spencer, Aug. 22, 1969; m. Judy Morgan, Feb. 28, 1981; children: Donna Michelle b. 1968; edn: BSCE, and BS bus., Univ. Colo., 1969; MBA, Univ. Santa Clara, 1973. Career: gen. mgr. Kaiser Aetna, Oakland 1973-76; sr. v.p. Broadmoor Homes, Dublin 1977-80; v.p./gen. mgr. Ponderosa Homes, San Ramon 1983-85, exec. v.p. Ponderosa Homes, Pleasanton 1983-85, owner/pres./CEO, 1985–; mem: Building Industry Assn. (state dir. 1987-88, dir., v.p. BIA/No. Calif. 1986-88, pres. BIA/Walnut Creek 1988), Young Pres. Orgn. 1987–; bd. dirs. YMCA/ Hayward 1988; club: Diablo CC; Democrat; Baptist; rec: golf, skiing. Res: 59 Starmont Ln Danville 94526 Ofc: Ponderosa Industries 6671 Owens Dr Pleasanton 94566

MORGAN, ROBERT, management consulting firm president; b. Jan. 27, 1937, Philadelphia, Pa.; s. Maxwell and Hannah (Cohen) M.; m. Delores Vohs, June 2, 1962; children: Phillip b. 1964, Daniel b. 1966, Reisa b. 1971; edn: BA econ., Whittier Coll. 1958; MBA mgmt., Ind. Univ. Bloomington 1959. Career: mktg. research Union Oil Co. Calif., L/A. 1960-63; sales service mgr. R.H. Donnelley (D&B) 1964-65, account exec. 1966-68, regional mgr., Houston, Tx. 1969-71; dir. political direct mail & computer systems for Reelection of President, Wash. D.C. 1972; dir. acquisitions and new bus. devel. D&B (3 divs.), Oakbrook, Ill. 1973-74; v.p. Rocliff Assocs. Inc., Chgo. 1975-76; pres. Morgan & Assoc. Inc., Chgo. 1976-78, Los Angeles 1979–; awards: Whittier Coll. Tennis scholarship 1956-58, Ind. Univ. Acad. scholarship 1958-59; mem. Nat. Assn. Real Estate Appraisers; civic: Big Brothers Houston, Houston Tennis Assn. (v.p. 1971), Oakbrook Little League (pres. 1978); mil: sgt. pc Army Nat. Guard 1959-65; Republican; Jewish; rec: tennis, hunting, fishing. Ofc: 2127 Power St Hermosa Beach 90254

MORI, ALLEN ANTHONY, university dean; b. Nov. 1, 1947, Hazleton, Pa.; s. Primo Philip and Carmella (DeNoia) M.; m. Barbara Epoca, June 26, 1971; children: Kirsten Lynn; edn: BA, Franklin and Marshall Coll., 1969; MEd, Bloomsburg Univ., 1971; PhD, Univ. Pittsburgh, 1975. Career: Special edn. tchr. White Haven State Sch. and Hosp., White Haven, Pa. 1969-70, Hazleton

Area Sch. Dist. 1970-71, Pittsburgh Pub. Schs., 1971-74; supr. student tchrs. Univ. Pittsburgh, 1974-75; prof. special edn. Univ. Nevada, Las Vegas 1975-84; dean Coll. Edn., Marshall Univ., Huntington W.Va. 1984-87; dean Sch. Edn., CSU Los Angeles 1987–; hearing officer pub. law 94-142 Nev. Dept. Edn., Carson City 1978–; appt. Nev. gubnat. com. on mental health and mental retardation 1983-84; cons. Ministry of Edn., Manitoba, Can. 1980-82; honors: Phi Beta Delta, Phi Delta Kappa, Pi Lambda Theta, grantee US Dept. Edn. 1976-91, Nev. Dept. Edn., W.Va. Dept. Edn., Calif. State Univ. Chancellor's Office; mem: Assn. Tchr. Educators, Coun. for Exceptional Children (career devel. exec. com. 1981-83), Nat. Soc. for Study of Edn.; Kiwanis Club; author: Families of Children with Special Needs (1983); coauthor: Teaching the Severely Retarded (1980), Handbook of Preschool, Special Education (1980), Adapted Physical Education (1983), A Vocat. Tng. Continuum for the Mentally and Physically Disabled (1985), Teaching Sec. Students with Mild Learning and Beh. Problems (2nd. ed. 1993); contbr. numerous articles, book revs. and monographs to scholarly jours. Ofc: Calif. State Univ. 5151 State University Dr Los Angeles 90032

MORIARTY, DONALD PETER, II, engineering executive; b. Jan. 26, 1935, Alexandria, La.; s. Donald Peter and Catherine Graham (Stafford) M.; m. Diana Mary Blackburn, Feb. 4, 1984; children by previous marriage: Erin b. 1957, Donald, III b. 1960; edn: BS, La. State Univ., 1957; MA, Fla. Atlantic Univ., 1973; grad. US Army Command & Gen. Staff Coll., Fort Leavenworth, Ks. 1977. Career: served to lt. col. US Army (Artillery) 1957-80: commd. arty. ofcr. 1957-74, ops. ofcr. and dir. of instrn. US Army Advisor Sch., Di An, Viet Nam 1970-71; strategic plans ofcr. 32d Air Defense Command, Darmstadt, Ger. 1975-77; C3I Dept. dir. Army Air Defense Ctr., Fort Bliss, Tx. 1977-80; mem. NATO HQ, Brussels Tactical Airpower Com. 1977-79, Tri-Svc Group on Air Def. 1978-80, Air Def. Elect. Equip. Com. 1978-80; decorated Air Medal w/clusters 1967, Cross of Gal. w/Palm 1967, Bronze Star w/cluster 1971, Merit. Svc. Medal w/cluster 1977, Legion of Merit 1980; sr. systems engr. Hughes Aircraft Co., Fullerton 1980-82, mgr. eng. design dept. 1982-84, program mgr. 1984–; mem: Gen. Soc. of Mayflower Descendants, Sons of Am. Rev., Phi Alpha Theta, Armed Forces Comms.-Electronics Assn., Acacia Frat. (chapt. sec. 1956-57), Kiwanis West Palm Beach, Fla. (dir. 1972-73), Episcopal Service Alliance (O.C. dir. 1988-89), Am. Coll. of Genealogists (Fellow 1992), pres. Episcopal Synod of Am. 1993–; author: The US Army Officer As Military Statesman, 1930-1965 (1973), Louisiana Ante Bellum (1992); Republican; Episcopalian; rec: cosmology, genealogy. Res: 626 E Riverview Ave Orange 92665 Ofc: Hughes Aircraft Co., 1901 W Malvern St Fullerton 92634

MORLER, EDWARD EDWIN, international negotiator and management consultant; b. May 7, 1940, Oak Park, Ill.; s. Edwin Edward and Malva Ida (Pospicil) M.; edn: BS, Ill. Inst. Tech. 1962; MBA, Univ. Chgo. 1968; PhD, Univ. Md. 1973. Career: cons. Fry Cons. Inc., Chgo., Ill. 1968-69; dir. adminstrv. services Airline Pilots Assn., Wash. D.C. 1969-71; spl. cons. Dept. of Labor 1972; indep. cons. 1973-76; cons. Effective Comm. Skills Inc., N.Y.C. 1976-78; founder, chmn. Morler Internat. Inc., Sonoma, Ca. 1978–; honors: BSA Eagle Scout 1957, Book of Honor, Comm. Leaders of Am., Disting. Am., Internat. Who's Who of Intellectuals; mem: Bel Aire Navy League; mil: lt. USN 1962-66; rec: artist in oils & watercolors, golf, sailing, tennis, writing. Ofc: 1140 Brockman Dr Sonoma 95476

MORRIS, EFFIE LEE, library consultant/lecturer; b. Apr. 20, Richmond, Va.; d. William H. and Erma (Caskie) M; m. Leonard Jones, Aug. 25, 1971; edn: BA, Case Western Res. Univ., 1945; BLS, 1946; MSLS, 1956; EdD, in progress, Univ. of San Francisco 1978–. Career: childs splst. Library for the Blind 1958-63; N.Y. Pub. Library; coord. Childrens Svcs., San Francisco Pub. Lib. 1963-78; senior ed. Harcourt Brace Jovanovich 1978-79; lectr. Childrens Literature, Mills Coll. 1981–; contbg. writer var. profl. publs. honors: The San Francisco Pub. Lib. designated The Effie Lee Morris Hist. & Research Collections of Childrens Literature, Nov. 1981; recipient 1984 Women's National Book Assn. Award; mem. advy. council Mayor's Office of Child Care 1979; apptd. Calif. Library Svcs. Board 1982-84, 1984, v.p. 1987; advy. bd. The Center for The Book-Library of Congress 1979; mem: Childrens Svcs. Lib., Calif. Lib. Assn. (pres. 1969-71), Am. Lib. Assn. (mem. Council 1984-88, pres. Pub. Library Assn. 1971-72, Caldecott Award Com. 1987), Women's Nat. Book Assn. (S.F. chpt. pres. 1968-70, nat. secty. 1974-76), Alpha Kappa Alpha Sor., Commonwealth Club of Calif., S.F.-Abijan Sister City Com. 1986, English-Speaking Union S.F. (bd.). rec: reading. Res: 66 Cleary Ct #1009 San Francisco 94109

MORRIS, GRANT HAROLD, professor of law; b. Dec. 10, 1940, Syracuse, N.Y.; s. Benjamin and Caroline Grace (Judelson) M.; m. Phyllis A. Silberstein, July 4, 1967; children: Joshua b. 1970, Sara b. 1972; edn: BA, Syracuse Univ. 1962; JD, 1964; LLM, Harvard Univ. 1971. Career: atty., Mental Hygiene Law Recodification Project, Inst. Pub. Adminstrn., N.Y.C. 1964-66; prof. law Wayne St. Univ. Law Sch., Detroit, Mich. 1967-73, also prof. law-psychiatry Wayne St. Univ. Sch. Medicine, 1970-73; law prof. Univ. San Diego Law Sch. 1973–, actg. dean 1977-78, 1988-89; adj. prof. UCSD Sch. Medicine 1974-84, clin. prof. 1984–; legal reporter Am. Bar Assn. 1981-84; cert. review hearing ofcr. San Diego Co. Superior Ct. 1984-90, ct. commnr./judge pro tem, 1990-92, mental health hearing ofcr., 1992–; hearing ofcr. San Diego Co. Housing Com. 1988-

92; honors: Phi Kappa Phi, Wayne St. Univ. Research Recognition 1968, Phi Alpha Delta; mem: Assn. Am. Law Schs. law and mental disability sect. (organizer and chair, 1973-74; exec. com. 1990–), San Diego Vol. Lawyer Program (bd. dirs., exec. com. 1988-89), San Diego Law Center (advy. bd. 1988-89); author: Insanity Defense: A Blueprint for Legislative Reform, 1975; co-author: Mental Disorder in the Criminal Process: Stan Stress and the Vietnam/Sports Conspiracy, 1993; contbg. ed. Mentally Ill & Right to Treatment, 1970; contbr. 30+ articles to profl. jours., 1970-95; rec: jogging, biking, hiking. Ofc: Univ. of San Diego Law School 5998 Alcala Park San Diego 92110-2492

MORRISH, WILLIAM BRADFORD, title insurance executive; b. June 6, 1931, Berkeley; s. Kendric Bradford and Marian Lathrop (Thomas) M.; m. Eva-Marie von Arnim, Mar. 31, 1962; children: Bettina b. 1964, Kendric b. 1966; edn: AB letters & sci., UC Berkeley, 1954; MBA, Stanford Univ., 1959. Career: various pos. in market res., product devel. and sales Hexcel Products, Berkeley 1956-63; asst. division mgr. Transamerica Title Ins. Co., San Francisco, then Berkeley branch mgr., 1963-67; founder, pres., dir. First American Title of Alameda County, Oakland 1967-70, corporate merger 1970, dir. and pres. First American Title Guaranty Co., Oakland, with br. offices S.F. Bay Area, 1970–, chmn. bd. and c.e.o. 1987–; pres., dir. and c.e.o. First Am. Title Guaranty Holding Co., 1983–; regional v.p. First Am. Title Ins. Co., Santa Ana 1984–; chmn. bd. First Security Thrift (indsl. bank), Orange 1988–; honors: Lambda Alpha, R.E. Soc. hon. 1988–, Trustee's citation UC Berkeley Found. 1990, William F. Knowland Award 1992; mem: Associated Building Industry (dir. 1977-78), Calif. Land Title Assn. (bd. govs. 1979–, chmn. pub. affairs com. 1981–, pres. 1988-89), Mortgage Bankers Assn. of No. Calif. (dir. 1972-74), No. Calif. R.E. Research Inst. (dir. 1985-86), The Urban Land Inst. (assoc. 1980–); civic: Bishop O'Dowd H.Sch. Bd. Regents 1983-86, The Coll. Preparatory Sch. (trustee 1970-86, v.p. 80-82), Samuel Merrit Hosp. (dir. 1976-79), The Nat. Outdoor Leadership Sch. (trustee 1982-88, v.chmn. 83-85, chmn. 86-88), New Oakland Com. (dir. 1970–, pres. 76), Oakland-Alameda County Coliseum (dir. 1978-87, v.chmn. 82-84), Oakland Boys Club (dir. 1967–), Oakland C.of C. (dir. 1978-82, 86–, treas. 80-81, v.chmn. 84-86), Oakland Citizen's Com. for Urban Renewal (pres. 1968-71), Oakland Mus. Assn. (dir. 1976-77), Oakland Symphony Orch. Assn. (dir. 1975-76), The 100 Club Oakland (past pres.), UCB Found. (trustee 1976-78, 1990–), East Bay Comm. Found. (trustee 1993–), UCB Order of the Golden Bear; clubs: Bohemian (SF), The Lakeview (dir., Oakland); mil: 1st lt. US Army 1954-55; Republican; Congregationalist; rec: canoeing, kayaking, hiking, flyfishing, photography, travel. Res: 5950 McAndrew Dr Oakland 94611 Ofc: First American Title Guaranty Co. 1939 Harrison St Oakland 94612

MORRISON, JAMES IAN, research institute president; b. Dec. 22, 1952, Irvine, Scotland; s. James Morrison and Janet Miller (McConachy) Munro; m. Nora Cadham, Dec. 6, 1980; children: David b. 1984, Caitlin b. 1986; edn: B.Phil., Univ. of Newcastle-upon-Tyne, England 1976; MA, Univ. Edinburgh, 1974; PhD, Univ. Brit. Columbia, Vancouver 1985. Career: instr. British Columbia Inst. of Tech., Vancouver, BC, Can. 1980-85, research assoc. 1980-85; research fellow Inst. for the Future, Menlo Park, Calif. 1985-86, dir. health care research pgm. 1986–, pres. 1990–; bd. dirs. Interim Services, Ft. Lauderdale, Fla. mem.: nat. advy. bd. Interim Healthcare, Ft. Lauderdale, Fla. 1992–, mem. corp. advy. bd. Bristol-Myers Squibb, Princeton, N.J. 1992–, Environmental Scanning Com. of United Way of Am. 1990–, UNIS Press Advy. Bd. 1990–; awards: Lind Prize for geography Edinburgh Univ. 1973, SSRC scholar Social Sci. Rsch. Council, Univ. of Newcastle-upon-Tyne 1974-76; coauthor 4 books incl.: Future Tense: The Business Realities of the Next Ten Years (1994), System in Crisis: The Case for Health Care Reform (1991), article "Satisfaction with Health Systems in Ten Nations" (1990); rec: golf. Ofc: Institute for the Future 2744 Sand Hill Rd Menlo Park 94025-7020

MORRISSEY, THOMAS FRANCIS, hospital financial executive; b. Dec. 2, 1949, Vincennes, Ind.; s. Thomas Francis and Martha (Dunn) M.; m. Elizabeth Bruce, Dec. 9, 1992; children: Jonathan b. 1978, Kristen b. 1983, Danielle b. 1990; edn: BBA acct., fin., Univ. Notre Dame 1972; MBA, Golden Gate Univ. 1984. Career: acctg. Bank of Am., San Francisco 1972-75; fin. aid office bus. mgr. UC Davis 1975-78, sr. budget analyst UC Davis Med. Center, Sacto. 1978-80, spl. service group mgr. 1980-82; budget and reimbursement dir. St.Josephs Hosp., Stockton 1982-87; v.p. fin. Sierra Nevada Meml. Hosp., Grass Valley 1987–; treas. Fazio for Congress Com., Sacto.; Howe for City Council; Fazio for Assembly Com.; mem: Hosp. Council No. Calif. (fin. com.), Health Care Fin. Mgmt. Assn., Health Care Execs. Greater Sacto. Valley, Notre Dame Alumni Assn., Golden Gate Alumni Assn., Gold County Kiwanis, Friends of Hospice; Democrat; R.Cath.; rec: hunting, fishing, boating. Res: 12568 Lakeshore N Auburn 95602 Ofc: Sierra Nevada Memorial Hospital 155 Glasson Way Grass Valley 95945

MORROW, W. AUBREY, financial planner; b. July 31, 1945, Oxnard; s. Claude Aubrey and Willie Hazel (Cumberland) M.; m. Debbie Foster, Sept. 10, 1977; 1 dau., Devin b. 1983; edn: BS bus., Univ. So. Mo. 1968; Mo. Coll. 1968-70; cert. fin. planner. Career: mktg. rep. IBM, Detroit, Mich. 1973-76; estate planner Cigna, San Diego 1976-79; fin. advisor/pres. Financial Designs Ltd., 1979–; assoc. prof. fin. plng. UC San Diego, and San Diego St. Univ.; pub.

speaker on fin. matters; host Nat. P.B.S.-TV and local radio series: The Financial Advisors; mem: San Diego Soc. Inst. Cert. Fin. Planners (dir. 1986-87), Internat. Assn. Fin. Planners (pres. 1987-88, nat. dir. 1989-90, chmn. Fin. Independence Week 1988), San Diego Estate Planning Council, Kiwanis Torrey Pines (pres. 1984-85, outstanding pres. award 1985); numerous articles in field; listed Who's Who in Am. Industry and Fin.; mil: capt. USMC 1969-73; Republican; rec: sports. Ofc: Financial Designs Ltd. 5075 Shoreham Place Ste 230 San Diego 92122-5986

MORTENSEN, STEWART SOREN, credit data company president; b. Apr. 14, 1940, Santa Monica; s. Elmer Soren and Elizabeth Margaret (Stewart) M.; m. Diane, 1962, div.; children: Michael b. 1962, Jonathan b. 1967; m. 2d. Lois, Aug. 17, 1986; edn: BS in bus., Loma Linda Univ. Career: asst. mgr. Fireside Thrift, Pomona 1965-67; mgr. Credit Bur. of Pomona, 1967-69; owner/opr. Credit Bureau Services, Capistrano Beach 1969–; pres. Calif. Credit Data, Capistrano Beach 1986–; bd. chmn. Mission Valley Bank, San Clemente 1982-91; recipient recogn. award City of San Clemente (1973); mem: San Clemente C.of C., Associated Credit Bureaus of Calif. (mem. 1970–, bd.dirs. 1985–, pres. 1991-92, instr. cert. 1975), Saddleback C.of C., Medical-Dental Hosp. Bureaus of Am., Am. Bankers Assn.; contbr. newspaper articles to Daily Sun Post, San Clemente, "Bank Notes" (1984, 85, 86); Democrat; Seventh Day Adventist; rec: boating, tennis. Ofc: Credit Bureau Services 34175 Camino Capistrano #201 Capistrano Beach 92624

MORTON, HUGH WESLEY, IV, performing arts producer; b. Dec. 8, 1931, Pasadena; s. Hugh Wesley and Timey De Lacey (Hopper) M.; m. Paula Dozois, Nov. 30, 1951 (dec.); son, Wil Guido b. Aug. 11, 1964; edn: BS, Univ. Mont. Billings 1958; Northwestern Univ. Evanston; Univ. Oreg. 1960. Career: mail boy, prod. office clk. Paramount Pictures 1962-64; tchr. and dir. profl. workshop Desilu Studios 1964-66; asst. to controller, asst. to exec. v.p. t.v. production Columbia Pictures T.V. 1966-75; asst. to pres. Burbank Studios 1975-78; dir. Hollywood Central 1978-82; special events producer, director, studio fac coord. Twentieth Century Fox, 1982-90; owner IV Productions; has worked on 300+ episodes of TV pgms., 60+ feature films, music videos and special events including work with Canadian TV and a Russian Documentary in 1987; vol. tchr., dir. Notre Dame Girls Acad. 1965-82; actor Hollywood First Presbyterian Ch., concerts, light opera and soaps; awards: Warn Fed. C.U. Outstanding Contbn. (1977-81), Dirs. Guild Am. Guest Faculty Contbn., Am. Cancer Soc. cert. merit, Glendale C. of C. cert. appreciation, Drama Tchrs. Assn. So. Calif. Blue Ribbon judge, Delta Psi, Omega, Alpha Psi Omega; mem: IATSE, AFTRA, SAG, Acad. of TV Arts and Scis., Internat. Platform Assn., Glendale C.of C., St. Charles Comm. Fair, St. Charles Choir, Hollywood Presbyterian Ch. (drama guild, cathedral choir), L.A. Music Center, Festival of Arts Laguna Beach, Colony Players; actor in Eagles Mere Playhouse Pa., Ashland Oreg. Shakespeare Festival, poetry pub., concert tour of Europe; Presbyterian; rec: singing, teaching theatre. Address: POB 2517 Toluca Lake 91610-0517

MOSBY, DOROTHEA SUSAN, parks and recreation director; b. May 13, 1948, Sacramento; d. William Laurence and Esther Ida (Lux) M.; edn: AA sociol., Bakersfield Coll., 1969; BS recreation, San Jose State Univ., 1972; MPA pub. adm., CSU Dominguez Hills, 1982; cert. Calif. Bd. Rec./Pks., Sacto. 1972. Career: personnel dept. asst. San Jose Parks & Rec. Dept., San Jose 1972-73; neighborhood ctr. dir. 1973-74; sr. rec. leader Santa Monica Rec. & Parks Dept., Santa Monica 1974-76, rec. supr. 1976-83, business div. hd. 1983-88, bus. adminstr. Santa Monica Cultural & Rec. Services, 1988-91; dir. South Gate Parks & Rec. Dept., South Gate 1991–; appt. bd. Calif. Bd. Rec. & Park Cert., 1990–, CPRS State Scholarship Found., 1992–; v.p. CPRS District Ten 1994–; mem. pub. sector advy. bd. Loyola Marymount Univ. Cont. Edn., 1991–; honors: Pi Alpha Alpha (life mem. 1982); mem.: Los Angeles Philharmonic Bus. & Profl. Com. 1993–, L.A. World Affairs Council 1993–, Calif. Park & Rec. Soc. 1976–, Nat. Rec. & Park Assn. 1983–, South Gate Kiwanis (bd. 1992-94), Windsor Sq. Hancock Park Hist. Soc. (chair 1988-90); Democrat; Lutheran (ch. treas. 1984-86); rec: flute, piano, reading, biking, tennis. Res: 9329 Elm Vista Dr #103 Downey 90242 Ofc: Parks & Recreation Dept. 4900 Southern Ave South Gate 90280

MOSER, LEO JOHN, diplomat, educator; b. Jan. 19, 1929, Los Angeles; s. Carl and Rosa Elizabeth (Wininger) M.; m. Helen Ann, Aug. 17, 1952; children: Mark William, Ann Elizabeth, Carol Marie, Robert Dodd; edn: BA, MA, and PhD, Univ. So. Calif., 1951, 52, 57; MPA, Harvard Univ., 1960; Fgn. Service Inst. 1958-60, 1965-67, Canadian Nat. Defense Coll. 1970. Career: tchr. Los Angeles City Schs. 1952-53; tchg. asst. USC 1953-54; v. consul Am. Consulate Gen., Hong Kong 1954-56; cultural affairs Am. Embassy, Moscow, USSR 1960-62; political affairs Am. Embassy, Caracas, Venezuela 1963-65, Taipei, Taiwan 1967-70; dir. Dept. of State, Wash. D.C. 1970-74; chief. of mission Am. Embassy, Vientaine, Laos 1979-81; prof. CSU, Sacto. 19974-75; dir. Center for Study of Fgn. Affairs, Wash. D.C. 1982-85; dep. asst. secty. of state Wash. D.C. 1985-86; prof. Mansfield Center 1986-88; instr. Gavilan Coll., 1993–; Foreign Affairs Reserve Corps, Dept. of State, 1993–; awards: Dept. of State Merit. Service 1977, St. of Calif. Commend. for Outstanding Service, Secty. of States Open Forum 1985; mem: Assn. for Asian Studies, Harvard Club of China, Assn.

Computational Linguistics, Internat. Inst. Strategic Studies, Am. Assn. Artificial Intelligence, World Future Soc.; author Tech. Trap, 1979, Chinese Mosaic, 1985, ed. Toward a Better Relationship: U.S.-Japan Rels., 1986, The Political Culture of the United States, 1995; rec: linguistics. Ofc: 7620 Westwood Dr Gilroy 95020

MOSER, VIRGINIA STROTHER, art enthusiast, homemaker; b. Aug. 5, 1917, Memphis, Tenn.; d. William Carey and Marion (McConnel) Strother; m. Gordon Moser, Dec. 5, 1936; children: Marilyn b. 1938, Julie b. 1949, Deborah b. 1950; edn: grad. Beverly Hills H.S.; att. Sawyers Bus. Sch., Los Angeles. Career: chmn. La Jolla Rotary Club 1977-78; ball chmn. Children's Home Soc., La Jolla; chmn. La Jolla Opera Guild; mem: St. Germain, San Diego Museum of Art, La Jolla Country Club; creative works: flower arrangements for receptions and hangings for shows, La Jolla Mus. of Contemporary Art. Res: 2879 Caminito Merion La Jolla 92037

MOSES, LIONEL ELLIOTT, rabbi; b. Sept. 4, 1949, Toronto, Canada; s. Joseph Phillip and Molly (Stone) M.; m. Joyce Rappaport, Dec. 20, 1981; children: Zev Gershon b. 1983, Jeremy Samuel b. 1986, Ezra Melekh b. 1990; edn: BS, Univ. Toronto 1970; MA, Univ. of Toronto, 1973; MA, Jewish Theological Seminary of Am. 1976; ordained rabbi Jewish Theological Seminary of Am. 1977. Career: asst. rabbi Westchester Jewish Center, Mamaroneck, N.Y. 1977-81; rabbi Jewish Center of Jackson Heights, N.Y. 1981-87; Mosaic Law Congregation, Sacto. 1987–; mem: Westchester Assn. Hebrew Educators (pres. 1979-81), Commn. on Synagogue Rels. (v.p. 1985-87), Com. on Jewish Law & Standards, Joint Bet Din of Conservative Movement, Sacto. Jewish Profl. Orgn. (founding chair 1987-89), Sacto. Jewish Fedn. (bd. dirs. 1987–), Clergy Concens. Council, Interfaith Svc. Bureau 1989–, med. ethics com. Mercy Hosps. 1990–, Rabbinical Assembly, N.Y. Bd. of Rabbis, No. Calif. Bd. Rabbis, Soc. Biblical Literature, Center for Learning & Leadership, Multicultural Living Assn. (v.p., founder 1986-87), Jackson Heights Elmhurst Kehillah (bd. mem. 1981-87); Jewish; rec: scholarly writing, travel, reading. Res: 181 Middleton Way Sacramento 95864 Ofc: Mosaic Law Congregation 2300 Sierra Blvd Sacramento 95825

MOSES, ORRIN DOUGLAS, educator; b. Feb. 4, 1948, Salem, Mass.; s. Orrin Judd and Ruth Majorie (Staples) M.; m. Jennifer Europa Benitez, June 18, 1988; edn: BA, Cornell Univ., 1969; MBA, CSU San Diego, 1976; PhD, UC Los Angeles, 1983. Career: tchg. assoc. UCLA, 1976-78; assoc. prof. CSU Los Angeles 1978-84; assoc. prof. Naval Postgrad. Sch., Monterey 1985–; vis. assoc. prof. UC Berkeley 1984-85; lectr. CSU Hayward 1985; vis. asst. prof. Stanford Univ. 1988-89; lectr. CSU San Jose, 1992-94; reseach intern Price Waterhouse, L.A. 1977; awards: Beta Gamma Sigma 1976, disting. tchg. UCLA 1979, Schieffelin Tchg. award, Naval Postgrad. Sch. 1993, Griffin Tchg. Excellence award, Monterey Co. 1994; mem. Am. Acctg. Assn., Decision Scis. Inst., Soc. of Cost Estimating and Analysis; publs: 30+ jour. articles, tech. reports incl. articles in Jour. of Commercial Bank Lending, 1987, Accounting Rev., 1987, Business Forum, 1984; mil: lt. USN 1969-73. Ofc: Naval Postgraduate School Code SM/MO Monterey 93943

MOSK, STANLEY, state supreme court justice; b. Sept. 4, 1912, San Antonio, Tex.; s. Paul and Minna (Perl) M.; m. Edna Mitchell, Sept. 27, 1936 (dec); children: Richard Mitchell; m. 2d. Susan Jane Hines, Aug. 27, 1982 (div.); m. Kaygey Kash, Jan. 15, 1995; edn: student, Univ. of Tex. 1931; PhB, Univ. of Chicago 1933, student, Law Sch. 1935, Hague Acad. Internat. Law 1970; LLD, Univ. of the Pacific 1970, Univ. of San Diego 1971, Univ. of Santa Clara 1976; Cal Western Univ. 1984; Southwestern Univ. 1986, Whittier Coll. 1993; admitted State Bar of Calif. 1935. Career: practicing atty., Los Angeles 1935-39; exec. secty. to gov. Calif., 1939-42; judge superior ct. Los Angeles County, 1943-58; pro tem justice Dist. Ct. Appeal, Calif., 1954; state atty. gen., also head state dept. justice, 1959-64; justice Calif. Supreme Ct., 1964–; vis. prof. Santa Clara Univ. 1981-82; mem. Calif. Commn. Jud. Qualifications, Calif. Disaster Council, Colo. River Boundary Commn., Calif. Commn.; Peace Ofcr. Stds., Dist. Securities Commn., Calif. Commn. Ofcl. Reports of Cts., Calif. Reapportionment Commn.; state chmn. Thanks to Scandinavia Fund, 1967-8; chmn. S.F. Internat. Film Festival, 1967; bd. regents Univ. Calif., 1940; pres. Vista Del Mar Child Care Svc., 1954-8; recipient disting. alumnus award Univ. Chgo., 1958; mem: Nat. Assn. Attys. Gen. (exec. bd.), Western Assn. Attys. Gen., (pres. 1963), ALA, L.A., Santa Monica, S.F., Korean bar assns., Am. Judicature Soc., Am. Legion, Manuscript Soc., Univ. Chgo. Alumni Assn. (pres. No. Calif. 1966-8), Phi Alpha Delta, Bnai Brith; clubs: Commonwealth (S.F.), Beverly Hills Tennis, Hillcrest Co. (L.A.); mil: served in US Army WWII; mem. Democratic Nat. Com. 1960-64. Res: 1200 California St San Francisco 94109 Ofc: 303 Second St San Francisco 94107

MOSKOWITZ, JOEL, lawyer; b. Jan. 14, 1947, New York; s. Jack I. and Myra (Shor) M.; children: David b. 1973, Michael b. 1975, Ellen b. 1979; edn: BA, UCLA 1967; JD, UCLA Law Sch. 1971. Career: dep. atty. gen. Calif. Dept. Justice, Sacto. 1970-83; dep. dir. Calif. Dept. Health Services 1983-85; ptnr. Gibson Dunn & Crutcher, Los Angeles 1985–; honors: Phi Beta Kappa; author: Environ. Liability in Real Property Transactions, 1989. Ofc: Gibson Dun & Crutcher 333 S Grand Ave Ste 4763 Los Angeles 90071

MOSS, CHARLES NORMAN, physician; b. June 13, 1914, Los Angeles; m. Margaret Louise; children: C. Eric b. 1953, Gail L. b. 1956, Lori Anne b. 1967; edn: AB, Stanford Univ. 1940; MD, Harvard Med. Sch. 1944; MPH, UC Berkeley 1955; Senior Flight Surgeon, USAF 1956; Dr.PH, UC Los Angeles 1970; Aviation Med. Examiner, FAA (1970). Career: surg. intern Peter Bent Brigham Hosp., Boston 1944-45; med. ofcr. US Army 1945-49: female ward, Birmingham Gen. Hosp., Van Nuys, 1945; Battalion surg., Shanghai and Peiping, China 1945 47 (responsible med. care for 2500, supr. 18 personnel);med. ofcr. US Air Force 1949-65: Wing Base surg., Wing Flight urg. and Med. Group comdr. 86th Fighter-Bomber Wing, Germany 1949-52, ed. care 6000, supr. 48 personnel; surg., flight surg., and med. group omdr. San Antonio Air Material Area, Kelly AFB, Tx. 1952-54, med. care or 45,000, supr. 65 personnel; Preventive Med. Div., Communicable Disease fcr., Office of AF Surg. Gen., Wash DC 1955-59, supr. preparation & publ. of num. AF regulations and pamphlets, served on var. boards and coms. incl. Nat. Acad. of Sci., Nat. Research Council, Army-AF Master Menu Bd., US Civil Service Examiners; hosp. comdr. and flight surg. NATO Hdqtrs., AF & Army, Izmir, Turkey 1959, med. care for 10,000, supr. 45 med. personnel; chief Missile Test and Range Support Div., Staff Surgeon's Ofc., Atlantic Missile Range and Cape Canaveral 1959-61, med. care for 18,000, supr. up to 80; safety ofcr. and occupational med., Orlando AFB, Fla. and Lookout Mtn. AF Station, Los Angeles, 1961-64, ret. lt. col. 1965; med. dir. No. Am. Rockwell Corp., L.A. div. 1969-70; physician, Los Angeles Co. 1970-: Occupational Health Svc., Dept. of Personnel 1970-73, chief Med. Adv. Unit L.A. Co. Bd. of Retirement, Community Health Servs. 1973-79, med. cons. Health Facilities div. Dept. Health Servs. 1979-81; recipient Physician's Recogn. Awards, AMA, 1969, 72, 76, 79, 82; team physician Am. Weightlifting Team winner World Championships in Paris (1950), and Milan (1951); mem: Assn. Oldetime Barbell and Strongmen (1984–); Presbyterian; rec: nutrition, wt.lifting, photog. Res: 7714 Cowan Ave Los Angeles 90045

MOSTELLER, JAMES WILBUR, III, computer scientist; b. June 21, 1940, Ft. Riley, Kans.; s. James Wilbur and Ruth Rentfro (Thompson) M.; m. Sandra Stevenson, Oct. 13, 1962; children: Margaret b. 1965, Steven b. 1967, Michael b. 1971; edn: BS econ., Rensselaer Polytech. Inst. 1962; MBA indsl. mgmt., Temple Univ. 1971; UCSD 1965-66; cert. data processing DPMA (1972). Career: systems assoc. Philco-Ford Corp. 1966-69; systems project supr. Merck & Co. 1969-75, mgr. of systems and programming 1975-81, dir., mgmt. info. systems (Kelco Div.) 1981-87 (co. rep. to S.D. Coalition 1977-78, S.D. Res. Park Com. 1979-87); dir., info. resource mgmt. Advanced Sys. Div. of United Technologies, 1987-88; computer scientist Navy Personnel R & D Center, 1988–; honors: Beta Gamma Sigma 1971, Nat. Merit scholar 1958; mem: Data Processing Mgmt. Assn., Naval Reserve Assn. (life), Naval Inst. (life); civic: San Diego Space & Sci. Found. (1st v.p. and exec. com.), New Horizons Montessori Sch. (bd. 1971-73); mil: capt. USNR Security Group 1962-93. Res: 801 Santa Regina Solana Beach 92075 Ofc: Navy Personnel R & D Center San Diego 92152

MOYA, R. ANTHONY, lawyer; b. June 20, 1958, El Paso, Tx.; s. M. Nicolas and Alicia (Villalva) M.; m. Lucinda Kate McCarthy, June 19, 1982; children: Nicolas b. 1982, Rachel b. 1986; edn: BA, Univ. Tex., Austin 1983, JD, 1987; admitted bar: Tex. 1987, Calif. 1988. Career: atty., assoc. Lewis, D'Amato, Brisbois & Bisgaard, San Diego 1987–; mem: Am. Bar Assn. (mem. Litigation and Arbitration Com., Real Estate, Probate & Trust Sect.), Tex. Bar Assn., Calif. Bar Assn., San Diego Co. Bar Assn., L.A. Co. Bar Assn., Barristers Club; civic: S.D. Zool. Soc., S.D. Mus. Art, L.A. Co. Mus. Art; rec: long dist. running, antique furniture restoration, ancient Greek hist. Res: 3145 Ivy St San Diego 92104 Ofc: Lewis, D'Amato, Brisbois & Bisgaard 550 West "C" St Ste 800 San Diego 92101

MOYER, CRAIG ALAN, lawyer, educator; b. Oct. 17, 1955, Bethlehem, Pa.; s. Charles Alvin and Doris Mae (Schantz) M.; m. Candace, May 3, 1986; children: Jason b. 1976 (step), Chelsea A. b. 1988; edn: BA, USC, 1977; JD, UCLA, 1980. Career: atty., assoc. Nossaman, Krueger, et al, Los Angeles 1980-83; Finley, Kumble, et al, Beverly Hills 1983-85; ptnr. Demetriou, Del Guercio, Springer & Moyer, L.A. 1985–; gen. counsel American Independent Refiners Assn., 1985–, exec. dir. 1991–; instr. regulatory framework UC Los Angeles, Environmental Law, Hazardous Materials Certificate Pgm.; instr. regulatory framework environmental law, UC Santa Barbara; lectr. environmental edn. for Pac. Auto Show; spkr. Hazmat Confs. Long Beach 1986–, instr. Air Researchers Bd. Symposium Sacto. 1985–; honors: Tau Kappa Epsilon pres. 1975-76 and Outstanding Alumnus 1983; mem: Calif. Public Interest Research Group (pres. 1978-80), Am. Bar Assn., Calif. St. Bar, L.A. County Bar Assn. (Environmental Law Sect., chair Legislative Rev. Com., Exec. Com.); author: The Hazard Communication Handbook, A Right to Know Compliance Guide, 1990, The Clean Air Act Handbook, (1991, Clark-Boardman Pub.), contbr. articles in law jours.; Republican; Prot.; rec: bicycling. Ofc: Demetriou, Del Guercio, Springer & Moyer 801 S Grand Ave Ste 1000 Los Angeles 90017

MUELLER, ROBERT WILLIAM, JR., manufacturing company executive; b. June 16, 1936, Rahway, N.J.; s. Robert William and Sara Elizabeth (Smoak) M.; m. Johanne Bleakley Wright, Feb. 26, 1936; children: Kim b. 1959, Katherine b. 1960, Johnna b. 1962, Robert b. 1965; edn: BA, Dartmouth Coll. 1958; MBA, Amos Tuck Sch. of Bus. Adminstrn. 1959. Career: contract adminstrn. and

mktg. mgmt. Honeywell, Mpls., Minn. 1962-81; v.p. bus. devel. Northrop (electronics div.), Hawthorne 1981-88; Loral Electro-Optical Systems, Pasadena 1988-89, pres. 1989–; mil: 1st lt. USAF 1959-62; Republican; rec: skiing, motorcycling, riding. Ofc: Loral Electro Optical Systems 300 N Halstead Pasadena 91109

MUELLER, VIRGINIA SCHWARTZ, lawyer; b. April 27, 1924, Palo Alto; d. William Leonard and Anstrice (Bryant) Schwartz; m. Paul F. C. Mueller, Sept. 24, 1945; children: Christian b. 1949, Lisa b. 1956; edn: BA, Stanford Univ. 1944; LL.D, Cornell Univ. 1946; Doctor of Univ. Paris France 1950; admitted Supreme Ct. Calif. 1946, Wash. 1952, U.S.A. 1966. Career: research atty. Calif. Dist. of Appeal, San Francisco 1946-49; dept. prosecuting atty. King Co. Dist. Atty., Seattle, Wash. 1953-56; asst. counsel Calif. Bd. Equalization, Sacto. 1959; dep. dist. atty. Sacto. Co. Dist. Atty. 1959-60; legal counsel Legal Aid Soc. Sacto. 1966-71; sole practice, Sacto. 1971–; chmn. Port of Sacto. 1988, commr. 1983; awards: YMCA Outstanding Woman 1985, Am. Assn.Univ. Women Centennial 1981, Sacto. Metro. C.of C. Disting. Bus. Woman 1980; mem: Sister Cities Internat. (No. Calif. St. coord. 1994–), Am. Bar Assn. House of Delegates 1991-95, Alternative Sentencing Pgm. (advy. bd. 1976–), Soc. Mayflower Descendents Calif. (counselor 1981–), Matsuyama-Sacto. Sister City Corp. (past pres.), Jinan-Sacto. Sister Cities (bd.), Soroptimist Internat. (pres. 1975-76), Am. Assn. Univ. Women (pres. 1978-79), Nat. Assn. Women Lawyers (pres. 1985-86), Women Lawyers Sacto. (pres. 1964-65); 3 articles pub. in profl. jours., 1946-74; Democrat; rec: travel, gardening, swimming. Res: 4310 Moss Dr Sacramento 95822 Ofc: 106 L St Sacramento 95814

MUHAMMAD, RAQUEL ANNISSA, teacher; b. Sept. 3, 1932, Beggs, Okla.; d. John Lovings and Elnora DuBose Crenshaw; m. Amos Muhammad Sr., Nov. 25, 1951; children: Duane Bradford b. 1952, Sharon Hammons b. 1955, Valerie b. 1969, Shana b. 1972, Sita b. 1973, Amos Jr. b. 1974; edn: BA, BS, San Diego State Univ., 1961; MA, U.S. Internat. Univ. San Diego 1975, PhD, 1980; degree Alliance Francaise, Paris, Fr. 1966; Calif. tchg. credentials, adj. prof. and sec. English instr. 1961-95. Career: edn: analyst IDEP/UNESCO, Dakar, Senegal, W.Africa 1964; site administr. Univ. of Islam #8, San Diego, Calif. 1965-75; coord. Clark County Comm. Coll., Las Vegas, Nev. 1978; edn. cons. Operation Independence, 1979; tng. analyst Northrop Corp., San Diego 1979; sec. English tchr. San Diego Unified Sch. Dist., 1980–; adj. prof. Eng. San Diego Comm. Coll., 1989-91; adj. prof. Tulsa Jr. Coll. & UCT, Langston Univ. 1994-95; cons. prin. R. Muhammad Educational Services, San Diego 1980–; reader ETS, Berkeley, San Diego, 1987, 88, 90; chair Univ. Islam #2, Chgo. 1987-88; awards: fellow SDAWP, UCSD 1982, listed Who's Who Am. Women, Who's Who Am., Who's Who in West; mem. Nat. Assn. Female Execs., Nat. Edn. Assn. 1978–, Calif. Tchrs. Assn. 1978–, SDTA (1978–, minority affairs coun. 1980-90), CATE 1978–, CATESOL 1978-88, Assn. Black Educators S.D., Nat. Assn. Female Exec., Nat. Coun. Tchrs. of English, Nat. Assn. Univ. Women; publs: newspapers series "Social Change Through Education", 1979, curric. and tchg. guides (4), translator "Histoire d'/Afrique Occidentale", 1982-92; Democrat; Islam; rec: travel. Res: 898 Valencia Pky San Diego 92114

MUIR, WILLIAM KER, JR., political scientist; b. Oct. 30, 1931, Detroit, Mich.; s. William Ker and Florence Taylor (Bodman) M.; m. Paulette Irene Wauters, Jan. 16, 1960; children: Kerry b. 1962, Harriet b. 1967; edn: BA, Yale Univ., 1954; JD, Univ. Mich., 1958; PhD, Yale Univ., 1965. Career: instr. law Univ. Mich., Ann Arbor 1958-59; assoc., law, Davis Polk, N.Y.C. 1959-60; instr. polit. sci. Yale Univ., 1960-67; law ptnr. Tyler Cooper, New Haven, Ct. 1964-68; prof. political sci. UC Berkeley 1968–, dept. chmn. 1980-83; cons. Oakland Police Dept. 1969-74, Calif. State Legislature, Sacto. 1975-76; commr. Police Review Commn. Berkeley 1980-83; speechwriter Office of US Vice Pres., W.D.C., 1983-85; weekly columnist Oakland Tribune 1992-93; speechwriter Gov. Pete Wilson of Calif., Sacto. 1994; awards: Edward S. Corwin Prize, Am. Polit. Sci. Assn., W.D.C. 1967, Distinguished tchg. UCB 1974, Hadley B. Cantril Prize Cantril Found., N.Y.C. 1979, Excellence in Tchg. Award Phi Kappa No. Calif. Assn. 1994; author: Law and Attitude Change, 1967, 74, Police: Streetcorner Politicians, 1976, Legislature: California's School for Politics, 1983, The Bully Pulpit, 1992; mil: 2d lt. US Army 1954; Republican; Presbyterian. Res: 59 Parkside Dr Berkeley 94705 Ofc: Dept. Political Science Univ. Calif Berkeley 94720

MULFORD, RAND PERRY, biomedical company executive; b. Sept. 30, 1943 Denver, Colo.; s. Roger Wayne and Ann Louise (Perry) M.; m. Paula Marie Skelley, Aug. 24, 1987; children: Conrad P. Mulford b. 1982, Jeffrey G. Da Vanon b. 1973, Kelley J. Da Vanon b. 1970; edn: BSE in basic engring. (cum laude, NROTC), Princeton, 1965; MBA (high distinction, Baker Scholar), Harvard Bus. Sch., 1972; USN adv. tng. Nuclear Power Sch., Nuclear Reactor Prototype, Submarine Sch., Inertial Navigation, 1965-67; Career: served to Lt. US Navy 1965-70, abd. nuclear-powered Polaris missile submarine, Flotilla commendn. for communications work, meritorious unit citation; mgmt. cons. McKinsey & Co., Inc., Chgo. 1972-80; v.p. planning & control Occidental Chem. Co., Houston, Tx. 1980-82; founder, pres. Technivest Inc., Houston 1982-84; exec. dir. corp. planning Merck & Co., Inc. Rahway, N.J. 1985-89; v.p. fin. and adminstrn. Advanced Tissue Sciences, La Jolla, Calif. 1989-90; CEO, Chiron

Mimotopes Peptide Systems 1990-94; COO, XYTRONYX, Inc., San Diego 1994-95; chmn. of the bd. Medication Delivery Devices, Inc., San Diego 1994–; dir: L.Karp & Sons Inc., Chgo. Res: 2178 Caminito Del Barco Del Mar 92014 Ofc: Medication Delivery Devices Inc 10125 Mesa Rim Rd San Diego 92121

MULLEN, JOHN, lawyer; b. June 14, 1929, Green, Kans.; s. Henry James and Susan Jane (McQuillan) M.; m. Beth Daley, Nov. 22, 1975; children: Susan b. 1956, Lavra b. 1958, Stephen b. 1959; edn: BS, Sacto. St. Univ. 1960; JD, Univ. Pacific McGeorge Coll. Law 1965. Career: state traffic ofcr. Calif. Hwy. Patrol, Indio 1955-65; criminal defense lawyer, Sacto. 1965–; mem: Calif. Atty. Criminal Justice, Calif. Trial Lawyers, Am. Bar Assn. (criminal law sect.); author I Object, 1984; mil: AUS 1951-53; Democrat; Cath.; rec: music. Res: 5263 Rimwood St Fairoaks 95628 Ofc: 2631 K St Sacramento 95816

MULLEN, RONALD ELWYN, executive; b. Jan. 3, 1939, Albany, Oreg.; s. Harold Kermit and Mable Tora (Jensen) M.; m. Donna Jean Porter, Sept. 23, 1959; children: Kevin b. 1961, Diana b. 1963; edn: BSME, Oreg. State Univ. 1961; MBA, CSU Fullerton 1973. Career: systems engr. Rockwell, Anaheim 1967-69; chief engr. Resource Scis., Santa Ana 1969-71; mktg. mgr. Aerojet, Fullerton 1971-80; mgr. contracts and programs Lucas Western, City of Industry 1980-92; dist. mgr. Southern Calif. Water Co., Santa Fe Springs 1992–; honors: Pi Tau Sigma; mem: Am. Nuclear Soc., Machinery & Allied Products Inst., Linhurst Recreation Club (pres. 1980-85), Nutwood St. Ch.; author: articles pub. in profl. jours., 1966-77; inventor: solid waste selection rejection, 1971; mil: capt. USAF 1961-67, Vietnam Service Medal 1966, Air Medal 1967; Republican; Prot.; rec: woodworking, antique car restoration. Res: 312 N Monterey St Anaheim 92801 Ofc: Southern California Water Company 12035 Burke St Ste 1 Santa Fe Springs 90670

MULLER, JEROME KENNETH, photographer, editor, painter, psychologist; b. July 18, 1934, Amityville, N.Y.; s. Alphons and Helen (Haberl) M.; m. Nora Marie Nestor, Dec. 21, 1974; edn: BS, Marquette Univ., 1961; postgrad. CSU Fullerton, 1985-86; MA, National Univ., San Diego, 1988, Newport Psychoanalytic Inst., 1988-90. Career: commercial and editorial photographer, N.Y.C., 1952-55; mng. editor Country Beautiful mag., Milwaukee 1961-62, Reproductions Review mag., N.Y.C. 1967-68; editor, art dir. Orange County Illustrated, Newport Beach 1962-67, art editor, 1970-79, exec. editor/art dir. 1968-69; owner/CEO Creative Services Advt. Agcy., Newport Beach 1969-79; founder/CEO Museum Graphics, Costa Mesa 1978–; tchr. photography Lindenhurst (NY) High Sch., 1952-54; tchr. comic art UC Irvine, 1979; guest curator 50th Anniversary Exhib. Mickey Mouse 1928-78 at The Bowers Museum, Santa Ana 1978; organized Moving Image Exhbn. Museum of Sci. and Indus., Chgo., Cooper-Hewitt Museum., NYC, William Rockhill Nelson Gal., Kansas City, 1981; collect original works of outstanding Am. cartoonists, exhibited in major museums nat.; One-man shows include Souk Gallery, Newport Beach 1970, Gallery 2, Santa Ana 1972, Cannery Gallery Newport Bch. 1974; author: Rex Brandt 1972; contbr. photographs and articles to mags.; awards include two silver medals 20th Ann. Exhbn. Advt. and Editorial Art in West 1965; mem: Am. Assn. Profl. Hypnotherapists, Am. Psychol. Assn., Newport Harbor Art Mus., Mus. Modern Art (NYC), Met. Mus. Art, Am. Fedn. of Arts, Laguna Beach Mus. Art, Alpha Sigma Nu; clubs: Newport Beach Tennis, Gr. Los Angeles Press; mil: USAF 1956-57. Res: 2438 Bowdoin Pl Costa Mesa 92626 Ofc: PO Box 10743 Costa Mesa 92627

MULLER, THOMAS FRANCIS, restauranteur, musician, broadcaster; b. Nov. 17, 1946, San Jose; s. Francis Paul and Gloria Marie (Santoro) M.; m. Sally Ericksen, July 6, 1968; children: Thor Emil b. 1971, Kacy Lauren b. 1973; m. 2d. Janice Tilford, May 8, 1977; dau. Alexandra Kahili b. 1989; edn: BA in bdcst. comms., San Jose St. Univ., 1968. Career: profl. musician and composer, 1963-68, 1971-76; owner Lou's Village, San Jose's oldest restaurant, 1976–; estab. new AM radio stations, Clear Channel Assocs., 1981–, dir. "Alive After Five" 1986–, chmn. bd. 1988–; estab. "Classics of Rock and Roll" Concert Series, 1987 (voted concert of the yr. with Chuck Berry and New Arrivals); mem. Santa Clara Valley Hotel & Rest. Assn., San Jose C.of C., San Jose Conv. & Vis. Bur. (dir. 1989–, treas. 1992), San Jose Downtown Assn. (exec. com. bd. dirs.); honors: winner Cross Puget Sound Row doubles 1987, co-winner Monterey Crossing, co-share course record (Quad Alexandra, 1990); mem. New England and S.F. Peninsula MG"T" Register; clubs: Santa Cruz Yacht, Santa Cruz Rowing (pres. 1984-89); organizer successful annual SCRC Lobster Row 1984–, instrumental in estab. of Lee Faraola Rowing Facility in S.C.Harbor 1989; songwriter: Take Me Back to Lahaina (released 1988); mil: lt. jg USN 1969-71, Vietnam Service medal; Democrat; Christian; rec: ocean rowing, sailing, mountain biking. Ofc: Lou's Village 1465 W San Carlos St San Jose 95126

MUNITZ, BARRY ALLEN, state university system chief executive; b. July 26, 1941, Bklyn.; s. Raymond J. and Vivian (LeVoff) M.; m. Anne Tomfohrde (former assoc. director Houston Grand Opera), Dec. 15, 1987; edn: BA (magna cum laude), Brooklyn Coll. CUNY, 1963; MA, Princeton Univ., 1965, PhD, 1968; cert. Univ. Leiden, Netherlands 1962. Career: asst. prof. lit. and drama UC Berkeley, 1966-68; staff assoc. Carnegie Commn. on Higher Edn. 1968-70; mem. pres.'s staff, then assoc. provost Univ. Illinois System, 1970-72, acad. v.p.

1972-76; v.p., dean faculties Univ. of Houston, Tx., Central Campus, 1976-77, chancellor 1977-82, chmn. Texas Long Range Planning 1980-82; pres. and c.o.o. Federated Devel. Co., N.Y. 1982-91; v.chmn. MAXXAM Inc., L.A. 1982-91; chmn. and c.e.o. United Financial Group; chancellor and CEO, Calif. State Univ. System (22 campuses and 8 off-campus ctrs., 34,000 faculty & staff, 320,000 students, offers approx. 1,500 bachelor's degree pgms., 600 master's pgms., 8 jt. doctoral pgms. in 240 areas), 1991–; prof. English literature, CSU Los Angeles 1991–; cons. in univ. governance; mem. Nat. Acad. of Scis. (task force), Nat. Acad. Engring.; chair Calif. Edn. Roundtable; dir.: Calif. Econ. Devel. Corp., Sun America; KCET Public TV; dir., chair-elect Am. Council on Educ.; awards: Distinguished Alumnus Bklyn. Coll. 1979, Univ. Houston Alumni Pres.'s medal 1981, Woodrow Wilson fellow 1963; mem: Phi Beta Kappa (S.W. Region Bd.); author: Leadership in Colleges & Universities: Assessment & Search, 1977, monographs, articles. Office of the Chancellor Calif. State University, 400 Golden Shore Long Beach 90802-4275

MUNOZ, ADOLFO HOMERO, III, organizational psychologist; b. March 1, 1945, Laredo, Tx.; s. Adolfo H. and Elvira (Alvarado) M.; m. Angeline Carmen Castillo, Sept. 20, 1969; children: Adolfo IV b. 1971, Jose, Miguel and Mercedes b. 1973; edn: BA, St. Marys Univ. 1968; MA, Antioch Univ. 1974; PhD, Columbia Pacific Univ. 1991. Career: planning coordinator Model Cities Program, San Antonio, Tx. 1968-71; sr. tng. ofcr. Leadership Inst., Wash. D.C. 1971-72; research coordinator Development Assocs. Inc., San Antonio, Tx. 1972-74, project dir., Los Angeles 1974-76, v.p., San Francisco office 1976–, v.p. West Coast operations 1983–; senior cons. AID, U.S. State Dept., 1980; mem: San Ramon Edn. Found. (bd. mem. 1988), Leadership San Ramon (bd. 1994), San Ramon Comm. Svs. Group (bd. 1992-95); rec: tennis. Ofc: Development Associates, Inc. 1475 N Broadway Ste 200 Walnut Creek 94596

MUNOZ, JULIAN D., architect, developer and software company executive; b. July 11, 1946, San Francisco; s. Clodovaldo Julian and Carmen Mercedes (Zuniga) M.; edn: AA, San Francisco City Coll. 1967; BA, UC Berkeley 1970, B.Arch, 1972; reg. architect Calif. Career: cons. arch. Ueli Roth Inc., Zurich, Switz. 1972-73; pres., prin. Group 4 Architects., South S.F. 1973-88; CEO, pres. InterAm. Consortium 1989–; instr. arch. City Coll. San Francisco 1974-82; Calif. Energy Commn. 1980-82; advisor, ex-Pres. Oscar Arias of Costa Rica; adv. UN 50 Committee, Nobel Laureates Prog., S.F.; honors: Consulate of Costa Rica Diplomatic Attache 1983-86; mem: Costa Rica Olympic Ski Team and Nat. Olympic Com., Fgn. Affairs Council, Pan Am. Soc. of Calif. (pres. 1995-96), Peninsula Humane Soc. (bd. dirs. 1986–); Democrat; R.Cath.; rec: music, art, skiing, sailing. Address: San Francisco 94110

MUNZ, LARRY MARTIN, educator; b. May 23, 1940, Prescott, Ariz.; s. Martin Henry and Dorothy (Draper) M.; m. Carol Blackburn, Jan. 7, 1962 (div. 1984); m. Cynthia Hardy, Mar. 17, 1984; children: Laurence b. 1962, Megan b. 1987; edn: BA, Oreg. St. Univ., 1962; MA, Univ. Redlands, 1971; Calif. St. tchg. and adminstrn. credentials. Career: tchr. San Bernardino City Schs., 1963-64; Redlands Unified Schs., 1964-71; cons. San Bdo. County Schs., 1971, dir. San Jacinto-Moreno Valleys Regional Occupational Pgm., Hemet 1971-72; coordinator Riverside County Schs., 1972-73, San Bdo. County Schs. 1973-87; supt. Colton-Redlands-Yucaipa Regional Occupational Pgm., Redlands 1987-90; pres. A-1 Construction Services 1990–; asst. prof. CSU San Bdo. 1975-86; chmn. Statutory Plng. Commn. for Vocat. Edn. 1980-82; honors: Phi Delta Kappa (Young Edn. Leader of Am. 1981, chpt. v.p. 1987-88); mem: Calif. Assn. of ROP Ctrs. & Pgms. (So. Calif. rep.), Calif. Assn. of Vocat. Edn. (bd. govs., pres. 1987-88), So. Calif. Council of Vocat. Edn. Adminstrn. (pres. 1977-78), Assn. Calif. Sch. Adminstrs. (vocat. edn. com. chmn. 1979-82, Outstanding vocat. ed. adminstr. award 1983), Am. Vocat. Assn.; civic: Historic & Scenic Preserv. Commn. Redlands (chair 1986), Redlands Bicycle Classic (bd. dirs. 1986-88, sponsor events chair 1986), Redlands Historical Soc. (bd. dirs. 1991-95), Redlands Conservancy (bd. dirs. 1994–), Run Thru Redland B Com. 1991–, Kiwanis (pres. elect 1995-96); publisher Calif. Jour. of Vocational Education, 1987-88; contbr. articles in ednl. jours.; Republican; rec: woodworking, stained glass, running. Ofc: 1125 Olive Ave Redlands 92373

MURAKAMI, RICHARD MICHIO, state official; b. Jan. 29, 1932, Florin; s. Kazuo Harvey and Yomiko (Inouye) M.; edn: BS actg., USC 1959. Career: accountant City of L.A. 1958-59; corporation examiner I and II, Calif. State Dept. Corporations, 1959-65, corp. examiner III, 1965-68, supr. corporation examiner 1968-79, chief examiner 1979-86; asst. commr. Div. Fin. Services, asst. commr. Div. Health Care Svc. Plans 1986–, chmn. bd. dirs. Regulatory Devel. Com.; mem. Nat. Assn. Credit Union Suprs. (chmn. Program Com.); awards: Optimist of Year (Optimist Club Uptown L.A. 1971-72), Optimist of Year (Zone 2 Pacific S.W. Dist. Optimist Internat. 1973-74); mem: Nat. Assn. Credit Union Suprs., Nat. Assn. Consumer Credit Admnstrn.; civic: Optimist Club Uptown L.A. (pres.), Montebello-Bella Vista Optimist Club, L.A.-Nagoya Sister City Affliation, Nisei Week Japanese Festival, Pacific S.W. Dist. Optimist Internat. (past lt. gov.); mil: cpl. AUS 1953-55; Republican; Episcopal; rec: photog., bowling. Ofc: Dept Corporations 3700 Wilshire Blvd Los Angeles 90010

MURANAKA, HIDEO, artist; b. Feb. 4, 1946, Mitaka-shi, Tokyo, Japan; came to U.S.A. 1974; s. Nobukichi and Hisae Muranaka; edn: BFA, Tokyo Nat. Univ. of Fine Arts & Music, 1970, MFA, 1972; research stu., traditional Japanese painting 1972-73; mural painting, Fresco 1973-74; faculty of Fine Arts; "INYU" desig., assn. Art Exhibition of INTEN (assn. of traditional Japanese style painting) 1972. Career: artist, painting, printmaking, traditional calligraphy; art tchr. traditional Japanese style painting; exhibits: Eberhard Faber Art Contest 1974, S.F. Art Fest. (1974-77, 82, 85), Internat. Exh. of Botanical Drawings Hunterdon Art Ctr., N.J. 1977, 100 New Acquisitions Brooklyn (NY) Mus. 1978, Calif. State Fair 1978, Pacific Coast States Collection at Vice President's House W.D.C. (1980, 81), Calif. Palace of Legion of Honor, S.F. (purchase 1980), 3d Alaskan Wildlife Art Exh. Anchorage Hist. and Fine Art Mus. 1982, Coos Art Mus. 17th Nov. Annual 1982, Alabama Works on Paper (touring 1983), IEEE Centennial Art Contest, N.Y. (purchase award 1983), El Paso (Tx.) Mus. of Art "24th nat. Sun Carnival" 1986, 30th Nat. Print Exh. Hunterdon Art Ctr., Clinton, NJ 1986, San Diego Art Inst. 33rd Exh. 1987, "Stockton National '88" Haggin Mus., Stockton, Calif., "Am. Drawing Biennial" Muscarelle Mus. of Art Coll. of William and Mary 1988, "The Electrum XVIII" Holter Mus. of Art, Helena, MT 1989, "Fine Arts Inst. 24th Annual" San Bdo. Co. Mus., Redlands, Calif. 1989, The Expo. Internat. d'Arts Plastiques" Chapelle de la Sorbone, Paris and the Mus. de la Commanderie, Bordeaux, Fr. 1990, num. others; awards include 1st prize Internat. Art Exh. for Museo Hosio in Palazzo Castel Sant'Elia, Viterbo, Italy 1988, 2d prize Internat. Art Exh. for Museo Hosio, Capranica-Viterbo, Italy 1984, Kasaku Prize Shell Oil Co. (1971), Wesleyan Coll. Intl. Exh. of Prints and Drawings (purchase award 1980), Owensboro Mus. of Fine Art, Ky. Mid-Am. Biennial (purchase award 1982), 20th Dulin Nat. Works on Paper Exh. Knoxville (Tenn.) Mus. of Art (purchase award 1988), YERGEAU-Musee Internat. d'Art (Collection Permanente 1991) Canada; listed Who's Who in Am. Art 1986, Who's Who in Soc. 1986, Printworld Dir. 1988, Men of Achiev. 1988, The N.Y. Art Rev. 1988, The Calif. Art Rev. 1989, World Biog. Hall of Fame 1990, American Artists 1990; mem. Lepidopterists Soc.; publs: City Mag. (5/75), S.F. Chronicle (5/75); Christian; rec: music, butterfly collector. Res: 179 Oak St #W San Francisco 94102

MURDOCH, BROCK GORDON, educator; b. Apr. 25, 1948, Vancouver, B.C., Canada, nat. U.S. 1977; s. Groffe Watson and Joyce Isabelle (Armstrong) M.; m. Judith Ann James, June 22, 1971; children: Shandi b. 1975; edn: BA, CSU Fullerton, 1970; MBA, CSU Long Beach, 1977; PhD, UC Irvine, 1984; C.P.A., Calif. 1974. Career: asst. controller W.R. Grace Properties Inc., Newport Beach 1973-76; acctg. instr. Georgia Southern Coll., Statesboro, Ga. 1977-78; assoc. prof. acctg. Chapman Coll., Orange 1978-85; prof. acctg. CSU Chico, 1985–; awards: CSU Profl. Promise (1985-86, 88-89), CSU Chico Coll. of Bus. outstanding researcher and outstanding faculty member, also Inter-Bus. Student Council outstanding tchr. 1988-89; mem. Am. Acctg. Assn. (1977–); contbr. num. articles in refereed jours.; rec: rugby, waterskiing, softball. Ofc: Dept. Acctg. & MIS. Calif. State Univ. Chico 95929-0011

MURPHY, MICHAEL JAMES, architect; b. May 8, 1927, Los Angeles; s. Michael J. and Alta T. (Wedemeyer) M.; m. Patricia Jean Warren, May 25, 1958; children: Marc b. 1959, Michele b. 1960; edn: AA, Art Center Pasadena 1953; BA, Univ. Oreg. 1951. Career: chief designer Fetridge & De Vieloa Arch. and Design, San Bernardino 1951-53; arch./prin. M.J. Murphy Assoc. 1953-86; Parsons & Murphy Architects Assoc. 1978-82; Hiller & Murphy 1968-78; M.J. Murphy 1986–; p.t. tchr. Univ. Calif. Real Estate Sch. 1958-64; pres., co-owner Tee & Murphy Enterprise 1980-83; Doer Inc. Constrn. 1980-83; pres. Butterfield Constrn. 1975-77; Dramus Constrn. 1976-77; awards: LWV Citizen of Year (1982); mem: Assn. Bldg. Professions (pres. 1981-84), Arch. Computer (v.p. 1980-86), Emergency Med. Services (pres. 1978-85), Calif. Council AIA, San Bernardino City Rose Parade Com. (bd. dirs. 1980-83), City of San Bernardino Advy. Com., Light House for Blind (bd. dirs. 1973-77), Sister City Program (v.p., bd. dirs. 1973-88), Mayors Council for Internat. Friendship (1975-93), Am. Heart Assn. (pres. 1974), San Bernardino Expo 81 (com. 1977); mil: U.S. Navy 1943-45. Res: POB 1442 Running Springs 92382 Ofc: Michael J. Murphy, A.I.A., 2601 N Del Rosa Ste 220 San Bernardino 92404

MURRAY, FRANK EARL, medical director, educator; b. Oct. 30, 1930, Hazelgreen, Wis.; s. Earl Laverne and Elizabeth Lois (Cottingham) M.; m. Ione Leah Klimke, Nov. 26, 1955; children: David b. 1956, Timothy b. 1958, John b. 1961, Amy b. 1963, Polly Ann b. 1965, Frank b. 1972; edn: BS, Univ. Wis. Madison 1952; MD, 1960; advanced mgmt. program, Harvard Univ. Grad. Sch. Bus. 1979. Career: physician Harwood Med. Assoc., Wauwatosa, Wis. 1964-71; staff physician So. Calif. Permanente, Harbor City 1971-76; area assoc. med. dir. Med. Group SCPMG 1976-80, med. dir. elect SCPMG, Los Angeles 1980-81, med. dir. 1982-93; sr. physician consultant Kaiser Permanente of Ga. 1994-95; asst. clin. prof. medicine UCLA 1972-93; pres. bd. dirs. Sch. of Health & Human Services, CSU Los Angeles 1986-90; bd. dirs. Kaiser Found. Health Plan & Hosps., Kans. 1985-95; Dallas Tx. 1985-93; Permanente Med. Assn. Tx. 1987-90; Group Health Assn. Am., Wash. D.C. 1986-93; Wis. Med. Alumni Assn., Madison 1985–; honors: Sigma Sigma, Alpha Omega Alpha; mem: L.A. Co. Med. Assn., CMA, A.C.P., Am. Coll. Physician Execs., Group Health Assn.

Am., Am. Group Practice Assn.; mil: cpl. AUS 1952-54; Presbyterian; rec: astrophysics, astronomy, orchid growing. Ofc: Kaiser Permanente Piedmont Center 3495 Piedmont Rd NE, Atlanta GA 30305-1736

MURRAY, WILLIAM EDWARD, electrical engineer; b. March 14, 1924, Chickasha, Okla.; s. William Clifford and Blanche Winifred (McIntyre) M.; m. Jeannie Morris, April 27, 1946; children: Robert b. 1947, Richard b. 1948, Daniel b. 1953, John b. 1955, Alan b. 1962; edn: BS, UC Berkeley 1947; MSEE, USC 1954; postgrad. stu., UC Irvine 1978-80. reg. prof.elec. engr (CA E2830), Life Cert. in Voc. Engr Educ (CA 3536 VPL). Career: br. chief McDonnell Douglas Astronautics Co., Huntington Beach 1969-74; senior engr., scientist Douglas Aircraft Co., Long Beach 1974-78, prin. engr., scientist 1978-84, senior staff engr.1984-85, prin. staff engr. 1985-90, prin. specialist -design 1990–; instr. engring. UC Irvine 1978-84, UCLA 1960-66, 1985–, Golden West Coll. 1972-76, CSU Northridge 1974, Los Angeles Dept. of Edn. 1960-84; honors: IEEE Centennial Medal 1984, elected eminent member, Eta Kappa Nu, 1987, elected WESCON dir. 1987-92, chmn. exec. com. 1990, chmn. bd. dirs. 1992, 6 NASA citations, 6 McDonnell Doug. cits. elected fellow, Inst. for the Adv. of Engring. 1982; IEEE-AES Internat. Tech. Paper Award, Wash. DC 1963; mem: Eta Kappa Nu (nat. pres. 1973-74, Western Rep. Award Orgn. Comm. 1983–, Vladymer Karapetoff Eminent Member Award 1990–, nat. v.p. 1972-73, nat. dir. 1970-72, pres. L.A. Alumni chpt. 1965-66), IEEE (Region 6 dir.-elect 1993-94,Los Angeles Council, chmn. 1985-86, v.chmn., secty. 1984-85, treas. 1983-84, chmn. Sects. Com. 1982-83; Orange Co. sect., chmn. 1981-82, v.chmn. 1979-81, secty. 1978-79; gen. chmn. 1982 Reg. 6 Conf., awards chmn. Power Electronics Splsts. Conf. 1977-85, secty. Elec. Power/ Energy Sys. Panel 1977–, mem. 1948-60, sr. mem. 1960-90, Life sr. mem. 1990–), Tau Beta Pi, Pi Tau Pi Sigma, Pi Kappa Alpha, Aerospace Electrical Soc., Am. Inst. Aero. & Astro.; author, 8 engring. papers presented and publ. at confs.; mil: 1st lt. US Army Signal Corps 1943-45, 1950-52; Republican; Methodist; rec: literature, technology, travel. Res: 1531 Wyndham Court Rd Santa Ana 92705 Ofc: Douglas Aircraft Co., 3855 Lakewood Blvd Long Beach 90846

MUSKET, RONALD GEORGE, scientist; b. Feb. 4, 1940, St. Louis, Mo.; s. George Henry and Geraldine (Morris) M.; m. Yvona Marie Hoehne, Aug. 19, 1961; children: Kevin b. 1966, Brian b. 1968, Daren b. 1970; edn: BS engring. physics, Univ. Colorado, Boulder 1962; PhD engring. sci., UC Berkeley, 1967. Career: physicist NASA Lewis Research Ctr., Cleveland, Oh. 1967-69; lectr. Cleveland State Univ., p.t. 1968-69; physicist Sandia Lab., Livermore, Calif. 1969-77; mgr. surface instrumentation Kevex Corp., Foster City 1977-80; physicist Lawrence Livermore Nat. Lab., Livermore 1980–; awards: AEC nuclear sci. & engring. fellow UCB 1962-65, NASA predoctoral fellow UCB 1965-67; mem. Am. Physical Soc., Am. Vacuum Soc., Materials Research Soc.; publs: 70+ sci. papers; mil: capt. US Army 1967-69; rec: reading, tennis, travel, jogging. Res: 4466 Fleetwood Rd Danville 94506-1288 Ofc: LLNL, Livermore 94550

MUTSCHLER, LAWRENCE HOWARD, real estate investment; b. Oct. 9, 1934, St. Cloud, Minn.; s. Lawrence V. and Leah Mildred (Luther); edn: Claremont McKenna Coll. 1953-54, USC 1959, BS; Art Center Coll. 1960; UCLA 1980-84.; mem. Bel Air Navy League, Presidents Councils CMC; clubs: Palm Valley CC (Palm Desert), Riviera CC, L.A. Athletic, Calif. Yacht, Fredricksburg CC.,Virginia; R.Cath.; rec: collecting antiques & art, travel. Res: 7172 Hawthorn Ave Los Angeles 90046, 38769 Palm Valley Dr Palm Desert and 306 Caroline St Fredricksburg, VA

MYERS, JOHN L., mineral fibers manufacturing company president (retired); b. Aug. 8, 1928, Columbus, Ind.; s. J. Lester and Elna Clara (Schoessel) M.; m. Donna, Sept. 4, 1976; dau. Kimberly b. 1969; edn: BSChE, Purdue Univ., 1951. Career: tech. supr. Union Carbide Corp., Oak Ridge Tenn., Paducah, Ky., 1951-66, res. engr. in Niagara Falls, N.Y. plant, 1966-67, tech. supt. King City, Calif. plant 1967-70, mktg. mgr., Niagara Falls, N.Y. 1970-81, ops. mgr. King City, Calif. 1981-85; pres./dir. KCAC, Inc. (mining, milling & mktg. of mineral fibers), King City 1985-93; bd. chmn. Asbestos Info. Assn. of No. Am., 1981-95; mem: Am. Chem. Soc., Am. Inst. of Chem. Engrs.; appt. King City Planning Commn. 1984-86, elected King City City Council 1986, 90, 94; mayor King City 1993–; civic bds: Somoco Community Concerts Assn. (pres. 1987), Mee Mem. Hosp. (trustee 1982, chmn. 1987-88); patentee in field (US Pats. 3838085, 3947286); Republican; Lutheran; rec: golf, furniture restoration. Ofc: KCAC, Inc. Box K King City 93930

MYERS, VERNE STEELE, consultant; b. Apr. 11, 1907, Hillsdale, Mich.; s. Harry Silas and Ellen Mae (Steele) M.; m. Edna Cottle, Nov. 12, 1932; children: Monica b. 1936, Virginia b. 1942; edn: undergrad. Univ. Mich. 1928; BS, Hillsdale Coll. 1930; BS, Columbia Univ. 1932, MS, 1935; Reg. Profl. Engr., Calif. 1945. Career: indsl. engr. R.A. Lasley and R.W. Kelsey Consults., NYC 1934-35; econometric asst. to the pres. Tide Water Ass'd Oil Co., NYC 1935-41; supvrsg. statistical engr. Lockheed-Cal. Co., Burbank 1941-71; prof. (Statistical Decision-Making for Graduate Engrs.) USC, 1958-68; statistical scientist C.W. Whitston Assoc., Pasadena 1969-70; cons. mgmt. engr. prin., La Canada Flintridge 1950–; honors: Bridgham Fellow, Columbia Univ. (1939), Alumni Achievement Award, Hillsdale Coll. (1973), humanitarian award, Advocates for the Quiet Minority (1969); mem: Greater L.A. Mgmt. Club (pres. 1944-49), Econometric Soc. 1935-65, Ops. Rsch Soc., Am. Indsl. Engring. Soc., Nat. Soc. Profl. Engrs. (chmn. edn. com.), Am. Soc. Engring. Educators, Delta Sigma Phi; Assocs. of Villa Esperanza (pres. 1985-86), SAR (pres. 1950-52), Mayflower Soc., Pasadena League for Spastic Children (chmn. Parents Aux. 1949-51), Cancer Control Soc. (bd. 1984–); publs: Statistical Decision-Making Reversible Relationship between GNP and R&D, J. IE Soc. (1964), articles on wellness and objective enumerative interpretation in Townsend Letter for Doctors, and Nutritional Consultant; America's Elliptical and Square Wheel Economy, L.A. Times; vol. worker for handicapped; rec: wellness (complete nutritional recovery from cancer 1973–), Senior Olympics swimming. Address: Verne S. Myers, P.E., 4610 Commonwealth, La Canada Flintridge 91011

NADARAJA, RAVEENDRA, cardiovascular surgeon; b. Jan. 14, 1944, Colombo, Sri Lanka; s. Nallathamby and Nithiya (Ratnam) N.; m. Iswara Gowri, Feb. 1977; children: Garani Shiranthana b. 1981, Divani Raveena b. 1982; edn: attended Royal Coll., Colombo, Sri Lanka 1961; med. edn., MBBS, Univ. of Ceylon, Colombo, Sri Lanka 1967. Career: rotating intern Colombo Group Tchg. Hosp., Sri Lanka 1967-68; med. ofcr. outpatient surgery Colombo Gen. Hosp., Sri Lanka 1969-70; sr. house ofcr. Accident Svc. Hosp., Colombo, Sri Lanka 1970-71; sr. house ofcr. surgery, Badulla Skandy Gen. Hosp., Sri Lanka 1971-72; sr. registrar St. Anthony's Hosp.. U.K. 1972-75; locum sr. registrar St. Mary's Hosp., Portsmouth, U.K. 1975; residency in surgery Univ. of Rochester, N.Y. 1975-78; chief resident 1978-79; fellow, cardiovascular thoracic surgery Texas Heart Inst., Houston 1979-80; pvt. practice, Castro Valley, Calif. 1980–; chief of surgery St. Rose Hosp., Hayward 1990-92, v.p. of staff 1994; chief of vascular surgery Eden Hosp., Castro Valley 1988-94; awards: E.W. Perera scholarship, Royal Coll., Colombo, Sri Lanka 1960, H.W. Wijesinghe Prize for Chemistry, Royal Coll. 1959, class prizes, Royal Coll. 1960, 61, GCE Ordinary Level, 1st Div. 1959; mem: Royal Coll. of Surgeons, Edinburgh, U.K. (fellow 1973), Royal Coll. of Surgeons, England (fellow 1975), Am. Coll. of Surgeons (fellow 1980), Internat. Coll. of Surgeons (fellow 1980), Cooley Cardiovascular Soc. 1980–, CMA 1980–, ACCMA 1980–; rec: photography, music. Res: 4120 Picea Court Hayward 94546 Ofc: 20440 Lake Chabot Rd Ste 7 Castro Valley 94546

NADLER, GERALD, management consultant, educator; b. Mar. 12, 1924, Cincinnati, Ohio; s. Samuel and Minnie (Krumbein) N.; m. Elaine M. Dubin, June 22, 1947; children: Burton Alan b. 1949, Janice Susan b. 1952, Robert Daniel b. 1955; edn: attended Univ. of Cincinnati 1942-43; BSME, Purdue Univ. 1945, MSIE, 1946, PhD, 1949; reg. Profl. Engr. (IE), Mo. and Wis. (until 1994). Career: plant industrial engr. Central Wisconsin Canneries, Beaver Dam, Wis. (summer) 1948; instr. indsl. engring Purdue Univ. 1948-49; asst. prof. , assoc. prof. to prof. indsl. engring., Washington Univ., St. Louis 1949-64, dept. head 1955-64; v.p. gen. ops. Artcraft Venetian Blind Mfg. Co., St. Louis, Mo. 1956-57; prof. indsl. engring Univ. of Wisconsin, Madison 1964-83; prof. & chmn. Univ. of So. Calif. Industrial & Systems Engring 1983-93; IBM chair in Engring. Mgmt., USC 1986-93; dir. Ctr. on the Mgmt. of Engring., Res, and Innovation in Technology (MERIT), USC 1986-93; IBM chair emeritus in Engring. Mgmt. and prof. emeritus of Indsl. and Sys. Engring, USC 1993–; dir. Breakthrough Thinking Group of the MERIT Ctr., USC 1990–; pres. The Ctr. for Breakthrough Thinking Inc., L.A. 1990–; mem. USC Engring. Committee. 1989–, Mgmt. of Technology Master's Prog. Com. 1992–; bd. dirs. USC Federal Credit Union 1993–; mem. 4 PhD committees; reviewer, various univ. programs, books and papers for jours, res. proposals; cons. to over 60 Am. and internat. companies and orgns.; internat. invited speaker and lectr. in field (750+), 1959-94; editl. bd. Design Studies 1979–; chair Internat. Congress on Planning and Design Theory; editl. adv. Design Mgmt. Jour. 1990–; advy. com. 13th Internat. Conf. on Prodn. Res., Jerusalem 1995 (1992-95); bd. dirs. Intertherm Inc. 1969-85; arbitrator for company-union disputes 1952-73; Lucas vis. prof. of engring. prodn. Univ. of Birmingham, England 1959; vis. prof. indsl. engring. Waseda Univ., Tokyo, Japan 1963-64; vis. prof. prodn. mgmt. Indiana Univ. 1964; vis. prof. of orgn. and adminstrn. Univ. of Louvain, Belgium 1975; Lady Davis vis. prof., indsl. engring. and mgmt., Technion, Israel Inst. of Technology, Haifa 1975-76; honors: Alpha Pi Mu (nat. v.p. 1950-52), Pi Tau Sigma, Omega Rho, Sigma Xi, Tau Beta Pi, awarded Gilbreth Medal by Soc. for Advancement of Mgmt. 1961, editl. award Hosp. Mgmt. Mag. 1966, Disting. Engring. Alumnus award Purdue Univ. 1975, Book of Yr. award Inst. of Indsl. Engrs. 1983, Phi Kappa Phi Faculty Recognition Prize 1990, Frank and Lillian Gilbreth award Inst. of Indsl. Engr. 1992, listed Who's Who in World, Who's Who in Am., and 6 others, recipient num. res. grants/contracts from NSF, NIE, HEW, USDA, Sloan, many other agys., founds., and cos. 1949–; mem: Inst. of Indsl. Engrs. 1952– (fellow 1969, life mem., internat. pres. 1989-90, track co-chair Quality and Beyond, internat. conf. 1995, past mem./dir./chair/co-chair num. coms.), Am. Soc. for Engring. Edn. 1956– (fellow 1991, chmn. IE Div. 1958-59, exec. com IE Div. 1959-62), AAAS (fellow 1984), Inst. for Advancement of Engring. (fellow 1990), Acad. of Mgmt., The Planning Forum, Engring. Mgmt. Soc. of IEEE, Inst. of Mgmt. Sciences (exec. com. 1982-85, chair sum. sessions 1980-88), Nat. Acad. of Engring. (elected mem. 1986–), Inst. for High Performance Planners; patentee, developer (with J. Goldman), Universal Operator Performance Analyzer and Recorder (UNOPAR); author (13 books): Motion and Time Study (and Teacher's Manual; McGraw-Hill, 1955), Workbook for Motion and Time Study (McGraw-Hill, 1955), Work Simplification (McGraw-Hill, 1957), Work Design (and Teacher's Manual; Richard D. Irwin, Inc., 1963), Work Systems Design: The IDEALS Concept (Richard D. Irwin, Inc., 1967; transl. into 6 langs.), Work Design: A Systems Concept (and Solutions Manual; Richard D. Irwin, Inc., 1970), Design Concepts for Information Systems (with J.T. Johnston and J.E. Bailey, 1975), SPARK: Student Planned Acquisition of Required Knowledge (with M. Norton and W.C. Bozeman; Ednl. Tech. Pubs., 1980), The Planning and Design Approach (John Wiley & Sons, 1981), Breakthrough Thinking: Why We Must Change the Way We Solve Problems, and the Seven Principles to Achieve This (with Shozo Hibino; Prima Pub./St. Martins Press, 1990; transl. into 3 langs.), Breakthrough Thinking in Total Quality Management (with G. Hoffherr and J. Moran; Prentice-Hall, 1994), Breakthrough Thinking: The Seven Principles of Creative Problem Solving (with S. Hibino; 2nd Edit., Prima Pub., 1994), Creative Solution Finding: The Triumph of Full Spectrum Creativity Over Conventional Thinking (with S. Hibino; Prima Pub., 1995); contbr. 200+ articles to profl. jours. and trade mags.; mil: USN 1943-45; rec: tennis, piano, bridge, grandchildren. Ofc: The Center for Breakthrough Thinking Inc PO Box 18A12 Los Angeles 90018

NADLER, RICHARD LEE, certified public accountant; b. Nov. 27, 1932, San Francisco; s. Max and Leona G. (Urbanus) N.; m. Joan Chrisman, June 24, 1950 (div. 1958); m. Barbara Beaver, June 17, 1960; children: Deborah b. 1951, Rhonda b. 1954, Jeffrey b. 1955, Daniel b. 1963, David b. 1965; edn: C.P.A. Calif. (1961). Career: pub. acct. trainee Arthur M. Haddock, Redwood City 1950-54; govt. contract splst. Hiller Helicopters, Palo Alto 1955-57; chief acct. Pulse Engring. Inc. 1957-58; govt. contract splst. Aerojet Gen. Corp., Sacto. 1958-62; owner Nadler Accountancy Corp., Orangevale 1962–; bd. dir. Christian Estate Planners 1973–; adult edn. tchr. Folsom Cordova Unified Sch. Dist., Rancho Cordova 1965-73; mem: Am. Inst. C.P.A., Calif. Soc. C.P.A., Soc. Calif. Accts., Nat. Soc. Accts., Sacto. Estate Planning Council, Linc Soc. of C.P.A. Fin. Planners, Orangevale Rotary (pres. 1977-78), Orangevale C.of C. (bd. dirs. 1962-64); article pub. in profl. jour. 1981, contbr. Simplified Bookkeeping for Churches 1990; Republican; Conservative Baptist; rec: sports, music. Res: 9400 Shumway Dr Orangevale 95662 Ofc: Nadler Accountancy Corp. 8836 Greenback Lane Ste E Orangevale 95662

NAGLE, ROBERT E., corporate attorney; b. Nov. 2, 1948, Chicago, Ill.; s. Milton and Lillian N.; m. Lynne S., April 5, 1975; children: David b. 1987, Katherine b. 1990; edn: Wabash Coll. 1967-71; BS, Pepperdine Univ. 1979; JD, Southwestern Univ. 1983. Career: v.p. Mid-West Veal Dist., l.A. 1973-80; contract adminstr. Northrop Corp., Hawthorne 1980-84; atty. Bakst & Garber, L.A. 1984-86; senior corp. counsel Farmers Group Inc. 1986–; adj. prof. Whittier Coll. Sch. of Law, L.A. 1987-90; mem: L.A. Co. Bar Assn., Glendale Bar Assn., Am. Bar Assn. Ofc: Farmers Group Inc. 4680 Wilshire Blvd 2d Floor Los Angeles 90010

NAGY, KENNETH ALEX, university professor; b. July 1, 1943, Santa Monica, Calif.; m. Patricia, Aug. 12, 1967; children: Mark, Erik; edn: AB, zoology, UC Riverside 1967, PhD, biology, 1971. Career: asst. prof. of biology, UCLA 1971-77, assoc. prof. 1977-83, prof. of biology 1983–; honors: Fulbright Fellow, Africa 1986-87, Paul Levy Meml. Lecture, Univ. of Witwatersrand Med. Sch., Johannesburg, S. Africa 1989, Vis. Disting. Prof., Chengdu, China 1990, Fulbright Disting. Lectureship, Morocco 1994; mem. editl. bds.: Ecological Soc. of Am. 1987-91, Am. Soc. of Zoologists 1989–, Am. Physiological Soc. 1990–; mem. Boy Scouts of Am. (treas. and merit badge counselor 1982–); author: 110+ res. articles, chapters, and books on animal physiological ecology and desert biology; mil: 3rd class petty ofcr., U.S. Navy 1962-64; rec: photography. Res: 11833 Allaseba Dr Los Angeles 90066-1112 Ofc: Warren Hall, UCLA 900 Veteran Ave Los Angeles 90024-1786

NAHMIAS, STEVEN, educator; b. June 19, 1945, New York; s. Morris and Elizabeth (Saffan) N.; m. Susan Lynn Esses, Aug. 13, 1972 (div. 1979); m. Vivian Sau Kwan Loh, Aug. 21, 1988; edn: BA, Queens Coll. 1966; BS, Columbia Univ. 1968; MS, Northwestern Univ. 1971; PhD, 1972. Career: asst. prof. Univ. Pittsburgh, Pa. 1972-76, assoc. prof. 1976-78; vis. assoc. prof. Stanford Univ. 1978-79; assoc. prof. Santa Clara Univ. 1979-81, prof. 1981–; chmn. DIS dept. 1987-92; dir. Competitive Manufacturing Inst. 1992–; cons. Santa Clara Co. Dept. Transp. 1986; Lotus Cons., Los Altos 1985; Shaklee Corp., San Francisco 1982; Lex Automative 1981; honors: Alpha Pi Mu, Beta Gamma Sigma, Omega Rho, Sigma Xi; mem: Ops. Research Soc. Am., Inst. Mgmt. Scis.; 50 articles pub. in profl. jours.; author Production & Ops. Analysis, 1989 and 1993; rec: jazz musician, golf. Ofc: Santa Clara University Decision and Information Science Dept. Santa Clara 95053

NAKAGAWA, ALLEN DONALD, radiologic technologist; b. Mar. 14, 1955, N.Y.C.; s. Walter Tsunehiko and Alyce Tsuneko (Kinoshita) N.; edn: BS in environmental studies, St. John's Univ., Jamaica, N.Y. 1977; MS in marine biol., C.W. Post Coll., 1980; Cert. radiologic technologist, 1986, Cert. in fluoroscopy, 1987. Career: research asst. environ. studies St. John's Univ., 1976-78; lab. asst. Bur. of Water Surveillance, Nassau County Health Dept., Wantaugh, N.Y. 1978; clin.

endocrinology asst. Univ. Calif. VA Hosp., San Francisco 1981-83; student technologist St. Mary's Hosp., S.F. 1985-86; radiologic technologist Mt. Zion Hosp., S.F. 1986-88; Univ. Calif. San Francisco 1988–, senior rad. technologist UCSF 1989–; awards: UCSF Medical Ctr. Director's Commendn. letter for 1989 earthquake preparedness, biog. listings in Who's Who in West, Who's Who in Am. 49th & 50th Edit., Internat. Directory of Disting. Leadership (2d edit.), Who's Who in the World 12th edit.; mem: Sigma Xi, Calif. Soc. Radiologic Technologists, AAAS, Am. Registry RTs (Cert.), Calif. Acad. Scis., ACLU, Japanese-Am. Nat. Mus. (charter mem. 1991), Marine Mammal Ctr. (formerly Calif. MMC), World Affairs Council 1993–; recruiting chmn. hunger project C.W. Post Coll. 1979; att. radiology, biotech. and computer related confs.; Democrat; Methodist; rec: computer illustration, reading, bowling, vol. activities, studying advanced technologies, photog. Ofc: Univ. Calif. Dept. Radiology Box 06

NAKAMURA, ROBERT M., medical group president emeritus, department of pathology chairman emeritus; b. June 10, 1927, Montebello; m. Shigeyo Jane Hayashi; edn: UC Berkeley 1949-50; Temple Univ. Sch. Medicine 195-54; MD, 1959. Career: gen. rotating intern Los Angeles Co. Gen. Hosp. 1954-55; pathology resident Long Beach VA Hosp. 1955-59; clin. mem. dept. of molecular immunology Scripps Clinic and Research Found., La Jolla 1974-80, chmn. dept. pathology 1974-92; adj. prof. pathology UCSD 1975-93; cons. pathologist dept. pathology UCSD Med. Center 1976-93; dept. molecular immunology Scripps Clinic & Research Found. 1980–, pres. Scripps Clinic Med. Group 1981-91; mem: Coll. Am. Pathologist (fellow), Am. Soc. Clin. Pathologists (fellow), Am. Soc. Blood Banks, Am. Soc. Exptl. Pathology, Am. Soc. Microbiology, Am. Coll. Nutrition; co-ed. Jour. Clin. Lab. Analysis, 1987, author 100+ articles pub. in med. jours., 40 books pub.; Republican; rec: films. Res: 8841 Nottingham Pl La Jolla 92037 Ofc: Scripps Clinic & Research Foundation 10666 N Torrey Pines Rd La Jolla 92037

NAKANO, FRANK HIROSHI, physician/professor; b. Dec. 21, 1935, Modesto; s. George Gonkichi and Haruko (Harano) N.; m. Josephine van Nieuwpoort, July 25, 1979; children: Genji C., b. 1980; Bastiaan G., b. 1982; edn: BS, honors, UC Sch. of Pharmacy 1958; MD, UCLA Sch. of Med. 1962. Career: asst. clin. instr. medicine, UCLA 1965-67, clin. instr. in med. 1970-74, attdg. general med.1970-71, cardiac catheterization lab 1971-74; attdg. cardiology svcs., VA Hosp. Los Angeles, 1972-74, 77–, asst. clin. prof. UCLA 1974–; chief med. svc. Washington Hosp., 1971-73, assoc. chief med. svc. 1973-74, dir. coronary intensive care unit 1972-82; ECG reader 1970–, dir. cardiology svcs. 1972–, chief of staff 1982-84, dir. TAU 1984–; chmn. cardiology com. Brotman Med. Ctr. 1976-82; currently, cardiologist, pvt. practice; honors: Rho Chi hon soc., Sch. of Pharmacy; Bear Photo Awd. for Scholarship, Sch. of Pharmacy; mem: Fellow Council on Clin. Cardiology, Am. Heart Assn.; Fellow Am.Coll. of Cardiology; Japanes-American Citizens League; publs: Fatal Lung Scan in a Case of Pulmonary Hypertension due to Obliterative Pulmonary Vascular Disease, in Chest; Computer Enhanced Digital Angiography, in Clin. Cardiology; Computer Enhanced Digital Angiography: Correlation of Clinical Assessment of Left Ventricular Ejection Fraction and Regional Wall Motion, in Am. Heart Journ.; mil: major, chief Cardiology Svc., US Army Japan 1967-69; Republican; Buddhist; rec: koi, skiing. Res: 10853 Marietta Ave Culver City 90232 Ofc: 3831 Hughes Ave Ste 604 Culver City 90232

NAKANO, HIROYUKI, company executive; b. Sept. 20, 1935, Matsumoto, Japan; s. Homare and Kogane N.; m. Yuki, Apr. 14, 1964; children: Tomoyo b. 1965, Takayo b. 1967; edn: BA, Tokyo Univ. 1959. Career: engr. Hitachi Ltd., Tokyo, Japan 1967–, devel. of Tel. Exchange System 1967-68, chief design engr. Real Time Computer Sys. 1978-82, dept. mgr. Microprocessor devel. 1983-85, dept. mgr. product plnng. of small computer sys. 1986-90, gen. mgr. 1991-94, current sr. v.p. & gen. mgr. Hitachi Computer Products, Santa Clara, Calif.; mem. IEEE (sr. v.p.); Buddhist; rec: classical music, golf. Res: 288 Casitas Bulevar Los Gatos 95030 Ofc: Hitachi Computer Products 3101 Tasman Dr Santa Clara 95054

NAKANO-MATSUMOTO, NAOMI NAMIKO, social worker; b. May 3, 1960, Salt Lake City, Utah; d. Rokuro "George" and Miyuki (Tashima) Nakano; m. Robert Hideo Matsumoto, Aug. 10, 1991; edn: BS sociology, soc. work, Weber State Coll., Ogden, UT 1982; MSW, Univ. Denver, 1986; Lic. clin. soc. wkr. Colo. 1991, Calif. 1992–. Career: caseworker Children's Aid Soc. of Utah, Ogden 1982-85; social worker Asian/Pacific Ctr. for Human Devel., Denver 1985-87; soc. worker II, Santa Clara County Dept. Soc. Svs., San Jose 1988; school soc. worker Denver Public Schs., Denver 1986-91, mem. Asian Edn. Advy. Coun. Denver Pub. Schs. 1988-91; soc. worker/supr. Asian Americans for Comm. Involvement, San Jose, Calif. 1991-94; co-dir. Asians & Pacific Islanders for Reproductive Health, Oakland 1994–; awards: Outstanding Young Women of Am. 1988, Outstanding Volunteer Denver Girls Inc. 1990, listed Who's Who in West 1992; mem: Nat. Assn. Soc. Workers 1987–, Coalition for Asian/Pacific Islander Youth 1992–, Nat. Assn. Asian & Pacific Am. Educators 1986–, Asian Am. Psychol. Assn. 1986–, Am. Inst. for Asian Am. Families 1993–, Asian Human Svs. Assn. 1985-91, Coalition for Multi-Ethnic Svc. Providers 1988-91, Japanese Am. Citizens League San Jose, Asian Women Advocating for Rights & Empowerment 1992–, Asian Pacific Islanders for

Reproductive Health 1993–, Yu Ai Kai-Japanese Am. Sr. Svc. Ctr. 1993–; Democrat; Jodo Shinshu Buddhist; rec: jogging, biking. Ofc: Asians & Pacific Islanders for Reproductive Health 310 8th St Ste 305A Oakland 94607

NANUS, BURTON BENJAMIN, emeritus professor of management; b. March 21, 1936, New York; s. Max and Mollie (Rothstein) N.; m. Marlene Guttman, June 29, 1969; 1 dau., Leora b. 1973; edn: mech. engring., Stevens Inst. 1957; MSIM, MIT 1959; DBA, USC 1967. Career: mgr. advance edn. tech. Sperry Rand Univac, N.Y.C. 1959-62; sr. tech. advisor to mgmt. System Devel. Corp., Santa Monica 1962-67; pres. Planning Tech. Inc., Los Angeles 1967-69; prof. mgmt. USC, 1969-94; dir. Center for Futures Research 1971-87; Pvt. Industry Council 1986-87; mem: Futures Research Quarterly (editl. bd. 1985), Tech. Forecasting & Social Change (editl. bd. 1986); author: Visionary Leadership, 1992, The Leaders Edge, 1989; co-author: Leaders, 1985, Emerging Network Marketplace, 1981, Mgmt. Games, 1961; rec: tennis. Ofc: Univ. of Southern California University Park Los Angeles 90089

NAPLES, CAESAR J., attorney, consultant, professor, university administrator (retired); b. Sept. 4, 1938, Buffalo, N.Y.; s. Caesar M. and Fannie (Occhipinti) N.; children: Jennifer b. 1965, Caesar b. 1967; m. Sandra L. Harrison, 1983; edn: AB, Yale Univ., 1960; JD, SUNY at Buffalo, 1963; admitted bar: N.Y. 1963, Fla. 1977, Calif. 1987, U.S. Supreme Ct. 1969. Career: atty. Moot & Sprague, Buffalo, NY 1965-70; counsel and staff dir. Select Jt. Legislative Com. on employee rels. New York Legislature, Albany 1969; asst. dir. Gov.'s Office on Employee Rels., N.Y. 1969-70; assoc. v.chancellor State Univ. New York, 1970-74; gen. counsel State Univ. Sys. of Florida, 1974-83; prof. CSU Long Beach, 1983–; v.chancellor The Calif. State Univ., 1983-92, vice chancellor emeritus and Trustee Professor, 1992–; gen. counsel Walden Univ. 1991–; cons. Univ. System of Nev. 1992–, Curtin Univ., Perth, Austr. 1992, CUNY, N.Y.C. 1992, Minn. State Univ. System, Mpls. 1987–, Canadian Public Univs., Can. 1971–; bd. chair Metlife Higher Edn. Bd., N.Y.C. 1987–; mem: Acad. for Academic Personnel Adminstrn. (co-founder 1972–), Ctr. for the Study of Collective Bargaining in Higher Adminstrn. (dir. 1973–); coauthor w/Victor Baldrige (novel) Romanoff Succession 1988; mil: capt. US Army, Armor, 1963-72; rec: writing, tennis, opera. Ofc: 816-B N Juanita Ave Redondo Beach 90277

NAPPA, JOSEPH AUGUST, lawyer; b. Oct. 16, 1954, Phoenix, Ariz.; s. Emanuelle G. and Evelyn Ann (Cortese) N.; edn: BS, Western St. Univ.1979; JD, 1982. Career: freelance musician, conductor 1973–; atty. Gardiner & Nappa, Newport Beach 1982-83; sole practice, Huntington Beach 1983–; awards: Am. Jurisprudence 1979; mem: W. Orange Co. Bar Assn. (pres. 1988, 89, 90, 92, 94, 95, sec. 1987, 88, dir. 1983, trustee 1983), L.A. Co. Bar Assn., Orange Co. Bar Assn., Assn. Trial Lawyers of Am., Am. Fedn. Musicians; Cath.; rec: music, theatrical performance, baseball, basketball. Ofc: 315 3rd St Suite G Huntington Beach 92648

NAUGHTEN, ROBERT NORMAN, pediatrician, educator, consultant; b. Oct. 13, 1928, Stockton; s. Norman Stafford and Junetta Marie (Doherty) N.; m. Ann Louise Charkins, June 26, 1954; children: Robert James b. 1955, Annette Marie b. 1958, Patricia Louise b. 1961; edn: AA, San Jose City Coll. 1948; BA, UC Berkeley 1950; MA, Stanford Univ. 1955; MD, Hahnemann Univ. 1959; lic. physician and surgeon Calif. Career: intern Highland-Alameda Co. Hosp., Oakland 1959-60; research fellow Nat. Cancer Inst., Stanford 1960-61; resident pediatrics Stanford Med. Center 1961-63; pvt. practice pediatrics, Los Gatos 1963–; instr. Santa Clara Valley Med. Center, San Jose 1963–, dept. pediatrics Stanford Univ. 1963-73; drug abuse cons. San Jose Police Dept. 1963-68, child abuse cons. Santa Clara Co. Dist. Attorney, 1984–, cons. Calif. St. Dept. Social Services 1990–; awards: Soc. of the Sigma Xi (Stanford), San Jose City Coll. Alumnus of Year (1967), Chef of the West, Sunset Mag. (1989); mem: Phila Coll. of Physicians (fellow), AMA, CMA, Santa Clara Co. Med. Assn., Am. Acad. Pediatrics, Am. Acad. Allergy & Clin. Immunology, Commonwealth Club Calif., Sierra Club, Calif. Alumni Assn., Stanford Alumni Assn., Out Reach & Escort (dir., v.p. 1985-88); 2 articles pub. in med. jours. (1957-86); mil: USN 1951-53; Democrat; R.Cath.; rec: cooking, philately, sailing. Ofc: 777 Knowles Dr Ste 14 Los Gatos 95030

NAUSS, ALLEN HENRY, college professor, ret.; b. Nov. 5, 1923, Fargo, N.D.; s. John Carl and Amanda Margaret (Krato) N.; m. Victoria Louise Hinck, June 10, 1937; children: Ellen b. 1959, Ruth b. 1960, John b. 1962, Victoria b. 1965; edn: Concordia Coll. 1942-44; BA, Concordia Seminary 1944; M.Div. 1948; M.Ed, Univ. Oreg. 1950; Univ. Denver 1951-52; PhD, Univ. Mo. 1960. Career: tchr. Concordia Acad., Portland, Oreg. 1945-46; prof., registrar, dean of students St. Pauls Coll., Concordia, Mo. 1948-60; asst. pastor Trinity Lutheran Ch., Alma, Mo. 1948-59; counselor Univ. Mo., Columbia 1959-60; prof., registrar, dir. student personnel Concordia Theological Seminary, Springfield, Ill. 1960-77; prof., dean of students Christ Coll. Irvine 1978-88; awards: Lutheran Ch. Synod J.W. Behnken fellow 1970-71; mem: Synodical Service Com., Ill. Council of Chs. (personnel com. 1964-70), Lutheran Ch. Mo. Synod, Am. Psychological Assn., Internat. Soc. Gen. Semantics, Lions, Advy. Com. on Pub. Aid Sangamon Co. Ill.; articles pub. in profl. jours., 1962; Republican; Lutheran; rec: golf. Res: 261 N Malena Orange 92669

NAVARRE, GERALD LEO, obstetrician-gynecologist, educator; b. April 10, 1931, Ecorse, Mich.; s. Leo Curtis and Harriet Celina (Raupp) N.; m. Rita, June 11, 1960; children: Mark b. 1961, Mary b. 1963, Matt b. 1965, Michael b. 1966, Martin b. 1970; edn: BS chem., Mich. St. Univ. E. Lansing 1953; MD, Univ. Mich. Ann Arbor 1957; cert. Am. Coll. Ob-Gyn. 1968. Career: intern San Bernardino Co. Hosp. 1957-58; resident ob-gyn. Fresno Co. Hosp. 1962-65; physician Kaiser Found. Hosps. in Bellflower 1965-83, in Anaheim 1983–; asst. clin. prof. Harbor UCLA Med. Center, Torrance 1970-84; clinical prof. UC Irvine 1981–; mem: Am. Soc. Colposcopy & Cervical Pathology 1972–, Internat. Fedn. Colposcopy, Am. Assn. Pro-Life Obstetricians & Gynecologists (Fla.), Pro-Life Med. Assn.; 4+ pub. articles in med. jours. (1975-84); mil: capt. USAF 1956-62; Republican; R.Cath.; rec: golf, scuba diving. Res: 4965 Westfield Ct Anaheim Hills 92807 Ofc: So. California Permanente Medical Group 441 Lakeview Anaheim 92807-3089

NAVE, ROBERT HARRY, federal agency manager; b. March 14, 1933, Rexburg, Ida.; s. Martin Louis and Ethel Ann (Reese) N.; m. Darlene Ellen Hunter, June 28, 1957; children: Lori Jo b. 1960, Nancy Ann b. 1964, Linda Lee b. 1968; edn: BS, Univ Utah 1959; MS, 1960. Career: inspector U.S. Dept. Agriculture, N.Y.C. 1960, agricultural inspector, Honolulu, Hawaii 1960-64, Travis AFB 1964-66, supr. protection and quarantine, Norton AFB 1966-67, asst. to regional dir., Berkeley 1967-71, project mgr., instr., Battle Creek 1971-75, dist. dir., San Francisco 1975-81, area dir., Oakland 1981-87, asst. regional dir., Sacto. 1987–; awards: U.S. Dept. Agriculture Quality award 1974, 78, 87, and Honor award 1990-91, Animal & Plant Health Insp. Svc. Honor award, Hon. Svc. to USDA in Saudia Arabia during Gulf War, recognized for svc. in Somalia by US Army, USAF and Marines 1993, Spl Svc. Assignment in Germany for US Armed Forces 1994; mem: Calif. Dept. Real Estate; mil: capt. USAR 1981; Republican; Mormon; rec: skiing, water skiing, fishing, traveling, gardening. Res: 58 Dobbs Dr Pleasant Hill 94523

NAY, SAMUEL W., JR., retired consulting engineer; b. May 29, 1914, Steamboat Springs, Colo.; s. Samuel W. and Josephine L. (Bartz) N.; m. Edythe L. Winberg, May 31, 1942; 1 son, Samuel W. III b. 1943 (decd.); edn: BS engrg., CSU Los Angeles; Reg. Mech. Engr. Calif., Fire Protection Engr. Calif. Career: tooling Lockheed Aircraft Burbank 1940-47; mech. engr. assoc. Dept. of Water & Power L.A. 1947-78; tchr. UCLA Extn. 1978-81; cons. engr. S.W. Nay Assoc., owner/ ptnr. in cons. engr. & parliamentary law firm 1978–; mem: Soc. Fire Protection Engrs. (life mem., past chpt. pres.), L.A. Council of Engineers & Scientists (pres. 1990-91), Am. Soc. Mech. Engrs. (life mem.), Inst. for Advancement of Engrs. (past treas.), Toastmasters Internat. (past area gov., ATM), Brookside Men's Golf Club; editor: The Flame (tech. soc. publ. 1978-81); mil: sgt. USAAF 1942-45, Meritorious Svc.; Republican; Prot.; rec: golf, photog. Ofc: POB 4663 Glendale 91202

NAZZARO, DAVID ALFRED, sales executive; b. Sept. 15, 1940, Malden, Mass.; s. Alfred Anthony and Louise (Cunningham) N.; m. Jane Valentine, June 26, 1971; children: David Thomas; edn: BME, US Merchant Marine Acad., 1962; MS, Columbia Univ., 1965; MBA, Pepperdine Univ., 1975. Career: regional mgr. Turbo Power and Marine Systems div. United Technologies, Hartford, Conn. 1965-74; mgr. bus. devel. S & Q Corp., San Francisco 1974-78; v.p. and gen. mgr. Con-Val, Oakland 1978-85; pres. and c.e.o. Dasa Controls, Belmont 1985-87; mgr. bus. devel. Johnson Yokogawa Corp., San Francisco 1987–; mem: Instrument Soc. Am. (Sr. Mem., pres. No. Calif. sect. 1987-88), ASME, Am. Water Works Assn., Elks, Jaycees, Clearview HOA (bd. 1976); mil: lt. USNR 1963-69; St. Bartholomew's Ch. San Mateo (Parish Council pres. 1986, Mens Club pres. 1977); rec: skiing, tennis, racquetball, handball, bridge. Res: 30 Tollridge Ct San Mateo 94402 Ofc: Johnson Controls, Inc. 50 Park Lane Brisbane 94005

NEBEKER, NEIL R., optometrist; b. April 28, 1952, Ogden, Utah; s. E. Ross and Lucille (Chugg) N.; m. Leslie Adamson, Aug. 4, 1976; children: Heidi b. 1977, Mark b. 1979, Robert b. 1981, Lindsey b. 1983, Todd b. 1984, Alan b. 1989; edn: BA, Weber St. Coll. 1977; BS, and OD, So. Calif. Coll. Optometry, 1979, 1981; therapeutics for optometric practioner, Penn. Coll. of Optometry 1984. Career: optometrist, mgr. Bischoff Optical, Salt Lake City, Utah 1981-83; optometrist Royal Optical 1983-85; pvt. practice optometry, Merced 1985–; assoc. Vision Care Center, Fresno 1986-93; recipient Optometric Recognition award. Am. Optometric Assn. 1985; mem. N. Merced Rotary Club; Republican; Ch. of Jesus Christ of Latter-day Saints; rec: woodworking, water & snow skiing. Ofc: Family Optometric Center 2908 North G St Merced 95340

NEBELKOPF, ETHAN, psychologist; b. June 14, 1946, NY, NY; s. Jacob Aloysius and Fega (Carver) N.; m. Ellen Rozek, Nov. 15, 1966 (div. 1971); m. Karen Horrocks, July 25, 1974; children: Demian b. 1967, Sarah b. 1974; edn: BA, City Coll. N.Y., 1966; MA, Univ. Mich., 1969; PhD, Summit Univ., 1989; lic. Marriage Family and Child Counselor, Calif. 1979. Career: social worker Proj. Headstart, N.Y.C. 1965; coord. Proj. Outreach, Ann Arbor, Mich. 1968-69; dir. White Bird Clinic, Eugene, Oreg. 1970-75; tng. dir. Walden House Inc., San Francisco 1979-93; cons. Berkeley Holistic Health Ctr., 1979-84; herbalist Medcine Wheel, San Diego 1977-80; adj. prof. S.F. State Univ. 1982-87; lectr.

Univ. of Calif. Berkeley Ext. 1993-94; awards: Silver Key, House Plan Assn. 1966, Phi Beta Kappa 1966; mem: Calif. Assn. of Drug Pgms. (pres. 1988-92), Calif. Assn. of Family Therapists, Calif. Assn. of Drug Educators 1990–; appt. S.F. Mayor's Task Force on Drugs 1988-92, Gov's. Policy Council on Drugs, Treatment Com., Sacto. 1989-92; author: White Bird Flies to Phoenix (1973), The Herbal Connection (1981); rec: baseball cards, rocks, yoga, herbs. Res/Ofc: 6641 Simson St Oakland 94605

NEEDLER, MARTIN CYRIL, university administrator; b. Mar. 23, 1933, Manchester, England, naturalized U.S., 1954; s. Thomas Anthony and Beatrice (Rosenberg) N.; m. E. Lore Heyman, Mar. 16, 1955 (div. Mar. 1976); children: Stephen b. 1956, Daniel b. 1970; m. Jan Knippers Black, July 23, 1976; edn: AB, magna cum laude, Harvard Univ., 1954, PhD, 1960. Career: tchg. fellow Harvard 1957-59; instr. Dartmouth, 1959-60; instr., asst. prof. Univ. Mich., Ann Arbor 1960-65; research assoc. Harvard 1965-66; assoc. prof., prof., dir. Univ. of New Mexico, Albuquerque 1966-90; dean Sch. of Internat. Studies, Univ. of the Pacific, Stockton 1990–; lectr. Foreign Service Inst., Rosslyn, Va. 1967, 80, 81; cons. NSF, NEH, Smithsonian, W.D.C., 1970–, Dept. of State, W.D.C., 1976-77, various members U.S. Congress, 1962-86; vis. prof. Univ. Pitts., Inst. for Shipboard Edn., 1988; awards: postdoctoral fellow UCLA 1962, sr. assoc. mem. St. Antony's Coll., Oxford 1971, sr. res. fellow Univ. Southampton, Eng. 1974, Bishop Miller Lectr. Covell Coll. U.O.P. 1977, Phi Beta Kappa (Alpha of N.Mex. pres. 1987-88); mem. Consortium of Latin Am. Studies Pgms. (chmn. steering com. 1970), Latin Am. Studies Assn. (pgm. chmn. 1972-73), "Armed Forces & Society" (assoc. editor 1983–); author: Political Devel. in Latin Am. 1968, Politics & Society in Mexico 1971, The Problem of Democracy in L.A. 1987, The Concepts of Comparative Politics 1991 and 10 other books; mil: pfc US Army 1954-56; Democrat; Jewish; rec: cooking, acting, singing, swimming, languages. Res: 4 La Playa Monterey 93940 Ofc: Sch. of Internat. Studies, Univ. of the Pacific, Stockton 95211

NEEL, PAUL R., architecture educator, dean; edn: BS, arch. engring., Calif. Polytechnic St. Univ.; Bachelor of Architecture, Univ. of So. Calif.; Master of Architecture, Univ. of Sheffield, England. Career: architectural practice, Monterey, L.A. and San Luis Obispo 1958-62; prof. of arch. Sch. of Arch. & Environ. Design, Calif. Polytechnic St. Univ. 1962-89, dir., Sch. of Arch. & Environ. Design 1968-78, dean Coll. of Arch. & Environ. Design 1991–; state architect, appt. by Gov. George Deukmejian 1989-91; arch. cons. to U.S. Dept. of State; pres. Calif. Council, Am. Inst. of Architects 1983; regional dir., bd. dirs. Am. Inst. of Architects 1984-86; mem: Calif. Bd. of Arch. Examiners (appt. by Gov. George Deukmejian) 1985-93; pres. Calif. Bd. of Arch. Examiners 1986-91; chair, fellowship jury, Coll. of Fellows, Am. Inst. of Architects 1991; awards: Commendation from Gov. George Deukmejian and Presdl. Commendation from Pres. Ronald Reagan for assisting City of Coalinga after the earthquake, 1983, Man of Yr. award Nat. Engring News Record 1988, recipient 6 awards from Calif. Council, Am. Inst. Architects: Honor Award Residential Design 1982, 85, Disting. Svc. Citation 1986, Presdl. Citations 1988, 90, Educator of Yr. 1991-92, Kemper award 1995; civic: mem: CCAIA Earthquake Response Team 1983–, CCAIA Earthquake Design Assistance Team, Coalinga; chair Earthquake Design Assistance Teams in Whittier, Mexico City, Santa Cruz, Hollister. Ofc: College of Architecture & Environ. Design California Polytechnic State University San Luis Obispo 93407

NEES, OLIVER ROSCOE, JR., physician, ophthalmologist; b. Jan. 15, 1927, Long Beach; s. Oliver R. and Clara (McCullough) N.; m. Margaret Huefner b. Oct. 31, 1928; children: Daryl Lynn b. 1953, Robert Oliver b. 1956, Kelly Jean b. 1958, Paige Ann b. 1961; edn: AB, UCLA 1948; MD, UCSF 1952. Career: physician, Long Beach 1956–; clin. prof. UC Irvine 1986–; cons. Long Beach VA Hosp. 1957–; mem: AMA, CMA, L.A. Co. Med. Assn.; mil: USNR 1944-46; Republican; rec: flying. Res: 6481 Mantova St Long Beach 90815

NEFF, LESTER LEROY, clergyman, church executive; b. Nov. 20, 1923, Medford, Ore.; s. James Asher and Ruth (Turnbow) N.; m. Avon Maxine Bostwick, Aug. 15, 1942; children: Lawrence b. 1944, Carol b. 1948, Donald b. 1950; edn: BA, Ambassador Coll., 1959; MA theol., 1962. Career: dept. mgr. Ambassador Coll., Worldwide Ch. of God, Pasadena 1955-81, ch. pastor, faculty, treas., chief fin. ofcr. 1981-90, corp. secr. 1981–; pub. articles in religious jours., 1957, 1990; mil: sgt. USAAF 1943-46. Ofc: Worldwide Church of God Pasadena 91129

NEHAMEN, CLIFFORD ALVIN, corporate credit director; b. Sept. 10, 1948, Los Angeles; s. Norman and Edith (Gootman) N.; m. Gail Ann Olken, July 15, 1973; children: Marc, Megan; edn: AA in indsl. arts, Santa Monica City Coll., 1968, BSBA, Woodbury Coll., 1970; student UCLA 1978.; Cert. credit mgmt. Career: senior asst. mgr. Household Fin. Corp., various, 1971-74; collection mgr. Fireside Thrift and Loan, various, 1974-76; credit mgr. Forecast Lighting Co., Inglewood, Calif. 1976-80; dir. corp. credit Hoffinger Industries Inc., Rancho Cucamonga 1980–; mem: New York Credit Assn. (chmn. 1983-88, legis. com. 1984-87, Distinguished Chmn. award, named Fin. Mgr. of Yr. 1987, 88, 94); civic: City of Hope, Rancho Cucamonga (pres. 1986), Citrus Little League (coach 1983). Ofc: Hoffinger Industries, Inc. 10959 Jersey Blvd Rancho Cucamonga 91730

NEIL-WILSON, JOYCE, caterer; b. Dec. 3, 1926, Chgo.; d. Floyd Barkley and Irene Emma (Serville) Parker; m. Douglas Stoddard Neil, Oct. 2, 1982; children Leslie Floyd Wilson b. 1946, James Harrison Wilson b. 1947, Deborah L. Wilson b. 1949. Career: U.S. Post Office, Richmond, Calif. 1942-44; Veteran's Admin., San Francisco 1944-46; Party Time Caterer, San Pablo 1956–; bd. dirs. Scholarship Found., Contra Costa Coll., 1991–; honors: recipient personal letter of commendn. from US President, woman of Year City of San Pablo (1974), feature subject in natl. mag. Entrepreneur (11/87), honoree Exchangite of Year and Exchangite of Sierra Pacific Dist. (1990), Goodwill Amb. to Japan (1975), Indonesia (1977), to Mexico, Proclaimed One of the Best Caterers in Bay Area by Restaurant Assn, 1993, Worldwide Business Women 1993, C. of C. 1st Business Person of the Yr. Award 1994; civic: Richmond Soroptimist (v.p.), Exchange Club (dir. 1987-89), Bus. & Profl. Women (3-time pres.), Salesian Boys Club (2-time pres., dir. 1965–), Soroptimist (1965–, Woman of Achiev. 1987), Beautification Commn. (2-time pres.), Museum and Historical Soc. (2-time pres.), Portuguese-LUSO (2-time pres.), San Pablo-Manzanilla, Mexico Sister City Bd. (pres.), S.F. Opera, Mill Valley Film Festival; lodges: Richmond Moose, San Pablo Eagles, Rod & Gun Club; author cookbook: From Katerer's Kitchen To You (1978); restored (15 yr. project) the garden estate that once belonged to John Rockefeller for partytime catering; catered Robin Williams' movie premiere "Awakening."

NEIMANN, ALBERT ALEXANDER, mathematician; b. Nov. 29, 1939, Torrington, Wyo.; s. Alexander and Lydia (Temple) N.; m. Barbara, May 6, 1962; children: Debbie b. 1964, Todd b. 1969, Amy b. 1971, Kelly b. 1974; edn: BA, Willamette Univ. 1967. Career: mathematician Quality Evaluation & Engring. Lab., Naval Torpedo Station, Keyport, Wash. 1968-70; mathematical statistician Weapons Quality Engring. Center, Concord (Calif.) Naval Weapons Station, 1970-85, engring. statistician 1985-90, mathematician 1990–; recipient outstanding performance award Concord Naval Weapons Sta. (1979, 88, 89, 90, 91, 92, 93), employee of the yr. award (1992, 93); mem: Am. Soc. Quality Control, Am. Stat. Assn., Nat. Council of Teachers of Math.; civic: mgr. Little League softball and baseball teams; mil: E4 USAF 1961-65; Democrat; Grace Baptist Ch. (Sun. Sch. tchr. 1980-90); rec: jogging, electronics, gardening, basketball. Address: Antioch 94509

NELSON, CHARLES ROBERT, financial planner; b. Jan. 14, 1930, Philippines; m. Beverly Ann Nelson, May 17, 1980. Career: v.p., mgr. Paine Webber Jackson and Curtis, Newport Beach, Calif. 1972-73; Bache Halsey Stuart, Tucson, Az., 1973-77; owner, mgr. King of the North, Irvine, Calif. 1978-84; owner, mgr. Nelson Fin., Laguna Hills, 1983-84; gen. mgr. First Liberty Securities, Carlsbad 1984-86; sr. ptnr. Nelson Financial Assocs., Dana Point 1986–; advy. bd. Monarch Bank, Laguna Niguel; mem. Internat. Assn. Fin. Planners, Alpha Delta Phi, Rotary Internat. (past pres.); civic bds: Orange County Hosp. Planning Advy. Com. 1979, Palm Desert Resort Country HOA (bd., v.p. 1982-83), South Coast YMCA (bd. mgrs. 1988–), C.of C. (Dana Point bd. dir. 1990-91), vol. bus. editor Dana Point News; club: Marbella CC (San Juan Capistrano). Res: 33945 Primavera Dana Point 92629 Ofc: Nelson Financial Associates 24681 La Plaza #260 Dana Point 92629

NELSON, DAVID EDWARD, lawyer; b. Oct. 26, 1930, Passaic, N.J.; s. David Charles and Ann Ellen (Pardoe) N.; m. Stuart McKenna, May 28, 1953; m2d. Elizabeth A. Carlston, Dec. 28, 1974; children: Douglas b. 1961, Kathryn b. 1963, Ann b. 1967, Lynn b. 1964, Kathleen b. 1966; Dec. 28, 1974 edn: BA, UCLA 1952; LL.B, UC Berkeley 1959; Cambridge Univ. England 1960; admitted St. Bar Calif. 1960. Career: assoc. atty. Morrison & Foerster, San Francisco 1960-65, ptnr. 1966–; honors: ed. Order of Coif Law Review (1958-59), v.chair, ed. Bus. Lawyer 1986-87; mem: San Francisco Bar Assn., Barristers Club, Am. Bar Assn. (chmn. bus. law sect. 1988-89), Am. Coll. Investment Counsel, Am. Law Inst., N.Y. Stock Exchange (legal advy. bd.), Oakland Museum Assn. (bd. 1985-89), Internat. Bar Assn., Southwestern Legal Assn., Bankers Club S.F., Berkeley Tennis Club, Berkeley Bd. Edn. (bd. 1967-69), Head-Royce Sch. (chmn. bd. dirs. 1974-79); mil: lt.j.g. USN 1952-56; Democrat. Res: 399 Camino Sobrante Orinda 94563 Ofc: Morrison & Foerster 345 California St San Francisco 94104

NELSON, JAMES AUGUSTUS, II, real estate executive, architect, banker; b. July 26, 1947, Damrascotta, Maine; s. Robert Maynard and Margret Rebecca (Harmision) N.; m. Linda Ray, Aug. 15, 1975 (div. 1985); m. Tina Nides, Oct. 22, 1986 (div. 1992); 1 dau., Jennifer Alexandria; edn: BArch, Columbia Univ., 1973, MBA, 1974. Career: resident v.p. Citibank, N.Y.C., 1974-77; group v.p. Bank of Am., San Francisco, 1977-82; assoc. John Portman and Assocs., Atlanta 1983-85; pres. J.A. Nelson and Assocs., Los Angeles 1986-88; dir. real estate planning and devel. MCA Development Co., L.A. 1988–; author: Banker's Guide to Construction (1978), Doing Business in Saudi Arabia (1979); civic: Laurel Canyon Coalition, L.A. (chmn.), Laurel Canyon Area Assn. (pres.), Hillside Fedn., L.A. (representative), Lookout Mountain Assocs., L.A. (v.p.), Hollywood Heritage (v.p.); club: Los Angeles Athletic. Res: 8306 Grandview Dr Hollywood 90046 Ofc: MCA Development Co. 100 Universal City Plaza Universal City 91608

NELSON, JOHN RONALD, physician, cardiologist; b. May 26, 1956, Anchorage, Alaska; s. Ronald Stuart and Janice Rae (Williams) N.; m. Zarrin Izadkhah, Dec. 20. 1981; children: Ashley R. b. 1984, Kristen M. b. 1986, Liane W. b. 1991; edn: BS (with distinction), Univ. of New Mexico 1978; MD, Univ. of Louisville 1982; internship VA Med. Ctr./UC San Francisco Sch. of Medicine, Fresno-Central San Joaquin Valley Med. Edn. Prog. 1982-83, resident in internal medicine 1983-85, fellow in adult cardiovascular diseases 1985-87, sr. cardiology fellow 1987-88; sr. cardiology fellow Mount Carmel Med. Ctr., Columbus, Ohio 1988-89; lic. physician Calif.; cert. Am. Bd. Internal Medicine 1987, cert. subspecialty cardiovascular disease 1989. Career: pvt. practice cardiology, Clovis 1989–; dir. Calif. Cardiovascular Inst., Clovis 1989–; dir. of res. California Vascular Inst., Fresno 1990–; active staff: Clovis Comm. Hosp. 1989-, Fresno Comm. Hosp. 1989-, Sierra Hosp. 1989-; dir. res. Central Calif. Laser Vascular Inst. 1991; currently prin. investigator laser res. study and co-investigator MRI res. study; past co-investigator 10 res. studies in field; awards: Eagle Scout 1972, Dean's List UC Davis 1974; 1st Annual House Staff Res. award UCSF, Fresno-Central San Joaquin Valley 1986, Am. Coll. of Cardiology Tng. Director's Com. Travel Award 1988; mem. AMA, CMA, Am. Coll. of Cardiology (fellow 1991), Am. Soc. of Cardiovascular Interventionists (fellow 1991), Am. Coll. of Physicians, Internat. Soc. of Endovascular Surgery, Am. Soc. of Internal Medicine, Calif. Soc. of Internal Medicine, Am. Soc. of Hypertension (charter), Fresno-Madera Med. Soc., Am. Heart Assn., Am. Assn. of Cardiovascular and Pulmonary Rehab., BSA, Biological Soc. of N.M., Sierra Hosp. Found., Good Shepherd Lutheran Ch.; author/co-author 25 abstracts, 1980-; author case report 1989; co-author: 3 pub. manuscripts, 1989, 90, 91, book chpt., Measuring Arterial Blood Flow by Nuclear Magnetic Resonance, 1994; Republican; Lutheran; rec: hunting, fishing. Ofc: John R. Nelson, MD, Inc. 684 Medical Center Drive East Ste 106 Clovis 93612

NELSON, LUELLA ELINE, arbitrator; b. April 11, 1952, Portland, Oreg.; d. Alben Wayne and Geneva Esther (Larsen) Nelson; edn: BS econ. and pol. scis., Macalester Coll. 1973; JD, Harvard Law Sch. 1976; admitted St. Bar Calif. 1984, St. Bar Oreg. 1976. Career: N.Y.C. urban fellow Office of Mayor 1972-73; hearing ofcr. UMWA Retirement Fund, Wash. D.C. 1975; counsel, sr. counsel NLRB Region 32, Wash., D.C. 1976-81; field atty., Oakland, Calif. 1981-86; arbitrator, mediator and factfinder, Oakland. Calif. and Portland, Ore. 1986–; instr. Golden Gate Univ., S.F. 1987-88; awards; City of N.Y. Urban Fellow 1972-73; mem: Soc. Profls. in Dispute Resolution (v.p. No. Calif. 1988-89, bd. dirs. 1987-88), Am. Arbitration Assn., Indsl. Rels. Research Assn., Am. Bar Assn., Calif. Bar (chair, exec. com. and pgm. chair, labor sect.), Oregon Bar (exec. com., labor sect.), Industrial Relations Research Assn. (steering com., program chair, Ore. chpt.), San Francisco Civic Chorale (Chorale Council 1988-90), Thomas Circle Singers; 4 articles pub. in profl. jours., 1988, 94; Independent; Methodist; rec: singing, hiking, cross country skiing. Ofcs: 4306 NE Mason St Portland OR 97218-1737 and POB 21268 Oakland 94620-1268

NELSON, WILLIAM ROBERT, business owner; b. April 15, 1945, Miami, Fla.; s. Thomas Robert and Eunice (Davis) N.; m. Darrell Shone, Aug. 12, 1967; children: William, Pamela, Jed; edn: BA, Univ. Nev., Reno 1967; MBA, UC Berkeley, 1969. Career: reg. mgr. Frito Lay Corp., Dallas, Tx. 1969-72; mgr. Central Soya, Ft. Wayne, Ind. 1972-74; account mgr. Foote, Cone & Belding/Honig, San Francisco 1974-75; dept. mgr., sugar, C&H Sugar, San Francisco 1975-78, SFSP mgr., 1978-87; gen. ptnr. Quick Lube of San Rafael and Santa Rosa, currently; Republican; rec: fishing. Res: POB 1165 Ross 94957

NEMIR, DONALD PHILIP, lawyer; b. Oct. 31, 1931, Oakland; s. Frank and Mary Madelyn (Shavor) N.; edn: BA, UC Berkeley, 1957, JD, Boalt Hall, Sch. of Law, 1960; admitted bar: Calif. 1961. Career: pvt. law practice, San Francisco 1961–; mdm. Am. Bar Assn., Calif. State Bar, S.F. Bar Assn., Phi Delta Phi; rec: chess, hiking. Res: PO Box 1089 Mill Valley 94942 Law Offices of Donald Nemir, APC, One Sansome St. Ste 2000 San Francisco 94104

NEMIROW, LAWRENCE HARVEY, risk manager/consulting services company president; b. Dec. 4, 1948, Bklyn.; s. Hyman Wolf and Irma Carver (Schnitzer) N.; m. Rochelle, Oct. 12, 1969 (div.); m. Shari, June 5, 1983; children: Jennifer b. 1971, Adam b. 1976, Aaron b. 1977, Jaime b. 1980; edn: BBA, Univ. Detroit, 1978, MBA, 1980; JD, Western State Univ. Coll. of Law 1995; desig: ARM (Risk Mgmt.) 1991. Career: subrogations supr. Royal Globe Ins. Co., NY, NY 1971-73; insurance splst. Ford Motor Co., Dearborn, Mich. 1973-80; dir. insurance and benefits John Morrell & Co., Chgo. 1980-84; risk mgr. Honda North America, Torrance 1985-88; prin. risk mgmt. consulting div. Windes & McClaughry Acctncy. Corp., Long Beach 1988-89; pres. The Nemirow Group, 1989–; mem: Soc. of Risk Mgmt. Consultants, Risk & Ins. Mgmt. Soc., Nat. Risk Mgmt. Panel (1986–); Democrat; Jewish; rec: golf. Ofc: 3662 Katella Ave Ste 211 Los Alamitos 90720

NENNEY, MILTON JAMES, lawyer, certified public accountant; b. Aug. 17, 1915, East St. Louis, Ill.; s. Claude G. and Amelia Marie (Rubel) N.; m. Janet Allen Vawter Gammon, July 21, 1937 (div. 1952); m. Velma Helen Hunt, April 24, 1953; children: Barbara b. 1938, Carol b. 1941, David b. 1944, James b. 1946; edn: BS commerce, Northwestern Univ. 1937; MBA, 1939; JD, UCLA

1967; UCLA Ext. 1979, 1985. Career: acct. Arthur Andersen & Co., Los Angeles 1943-47; ptnr. Nenney Miller & Hunter 1952-57; prin. MJN Acctg. Offices 1957-68; atty., ptnr. Collins & Woolway 1968-69; prin. MJN Law Offices 1969-86; of counsel Williams & Nenney 1986; awards: UCLA Ext. Profl. in Tax. 1979, Designation Personal Fin. Planning 1985, Brentwood C.of C. Citizen of Year 1981; mem: W. Hollywood Rotary 1978-93 (pres. 1981), W. L.A. Brentwood Rotary 1995-, Al Malaikah Shrine, ARC, Brentwood C.of C., S.O.S. (dir. 1985), Masons; Republican; Methodist; rec: square dancing. Ofc: Williams & Nenney 11520 San Vincente Blvd Ste 206 Los Angeles 90049

NESBITT, PATRICK MICHAEL, lawyer; b. Feb. 7, 1944, Detroit, Mich.; s. Frederick Henry and Marie (Labadie) N.; m. Marji B. Bailey; children: Elizabeth Paige b. 1977, Patrick Michael Jr. b. 1978; Stepchild: Whitney Williams b. 1976; edn: BS, USAF Acad. 1967; MS, Univ. of Mich. 1968; JD, Whittier Coll. 1981. Career: research engr. USAF 1967-71; pres./chmn. bd. Patrick M. Nesbitt Assocs. 1971–; mng. ptr. Nesbitt/Freshman Devel. Co. 1977–; pres. Nesbitt Hospitality Group Inc., 1983–; chmn. bd. Patrick M. Nesbitt Associates of Colorado Inc., 1983–; honors: Congl. appt. to USAF Acad., grad. scholarship Univ. Mich., Exellence in design award, A.I.A. (1981); clubs: Eldorado Polo, Santa Barbara Polo, Empire Polo, Jonathan, Rancho Santa Fe Polo; mil: capt. USAF 1963-81; Republican; R.Cath.; rec: skiing, flying, polo. Res: 273 S Glenroy Ave Los Angeles 90049 Ofc: 11150 W Olympic Blvd Ste 690 Los Angeles 90064 Tel: 310/914-8777

NETZEL, PAUL ARTHUR, management and fund raising consultant; b. Sept. 11, 1941, Tacoma; s. Marden Arthur and Audrey Rose (Jones) N.; m. Diane Viscount, Mar. 21, 1963; children: Paul M., Shari Ann; edn: BS in group work edn., Geo. Williams Coll., 1963. Career: program dir. YMCA South Pasadena-San Marino, 1963-66; exec. dir. Culver-Palms Family YMCA, 1967-73; v.p., metropolitan fin. devel. YMCA Met. Los Angeles, 1973-78, exec. v.p devel. 1979-85; pres. bd. dirs. YMCA Employees Credit Union, 1977-80; chmn. N.Am. Fellowship of YMCA Devel. Officers, 1980-83; adj. faculty USC Coll. Continuing Edn., 1983-86, Loyola Marymount Univ., CSU Los Angeles, 1986–; chmn. bd./c.e.o. Netzel Associates Inc., 1985–; indep. cons., fund raiser; mem. Nat. Soc. Fund Raising Execs. (chpt. pres. Greater L.A. chpt. 1989-90, mem. and vice chair nat. bd. 1989-92, 94, award Profl. of Year 1983); civic: elected Culver City Bd. of Edn. 1975-79, pres. 1977-78; elected Culver City City Council 1980-88 (mayor 1982-83, 86-87, v.mayor 1980-82, 85-86), bd. L.A. Co. Sanitation Dists. (1982-83, 85-87), bd. Culver City Redevel. Agy. (1980-88, chmn. 83-84, 87-88); mem. civic bds: Calif. Youth Model Legislature Bd. Dirs. (chmn. 1987-92), Culver-Palms Family YMCA (bd. of mgrs. 1985–, chmn. bd. 1991-93, 94-95), Culver City Guidance Clinic (pres. 1971-74), Culver City Edn. Found. 1982–, Los Angeles Psychiat. Service, United Way/W. Reg. (1986-93, v.chmn. bd. 1991-92), World Affairs Council L.A. 1989–, Rotary Intl. L.A.#5 (bd. 1989–, pres. 1992-93), Goodwill Industries of So. Calif. (bd. dirs. 1993–); clubs: California Club, Mountaingate CC; R.Cath. Res: 12336 Ridge Circle Los Angeles 90049 Ofc: 9696 Culver Blvd Ste 204 Culver City 90232

NEUDECKER, STEPHEN KRAMER, scientist, marine ecologist; b. Sept. 25, 1953, St. Louis, Mo.; s. Thomas Earl and JoAnn (Kramer) N.; m. Karen D. Worley, CPA, Aug. 31, 1973; children: Austin b. 1983, Stephanie b. 1985; edn: BS zoology, Univ. Ky. 1974; MS biology, Univ. Guam 1979; PhD ecology, UC Davis 1982; cert. Ecological Soc. Am. Career: marine environ. cons. Yamada Engring., Tokyo, Japan 1977-78; sr. scientist Ecological Analysts, Lafayette 1979-84; Lockheed Engring., Las Vegas 1984; prin. Environ. Cons. Services, Davis 1984-87; exec. dir. Bayfront Conservancy Trust, Chula Vista 1987–; mem: AAAS, Ecological Soc. Am., Sigma Xi, Am. Soc. Icthyologists & Hespotologists, Bonita Sunrise Rotary; 45+ articles pub. in sci. and tech. jours., 1976, book chpts. pub., 1987, 89, 93, 95, symposium proceedings; rec: skiing, water skiing. Res: 313 Glen Creek Dr Bonita 91902-4279 Ofc: Bayfront Conservancy Trust 1000 Gunpowder Pt Dr Chula Vista 92010

NEVAREZ, CARMEN RITA, physician; b. Sept. 21, 1951, Riverside; d. Frank Rivas and Bertha (Flores) N.; edn: BA, UCSD 1974; MD, Univ. Minn. 1978; MPH, UC Berkeley 1988. Career: staff physician Planned Parenthood, Portland, Oreg. 1979-80; staff physician student health San Diego St. Univ. 1980-82; med. dir. Beach Area Comm. Clinic 1980-83; cons. San Diego Co. Health Services Agency 1983; med. dir. La Clinica de la Raza, Oakland 1986-88; health ofcr. Dept. Health & Human Services, City of Berkeley 1988-94, dir., 1992-94; cons. Western Consortium for Public Health 1994; community based public health practice adminstr., UC Berkeley 1994-; lectr. Stanford Univ., Palo Alto 1986-88, San Diego St. Univ. 1980-82; Health Career Devel. Program, Sacto. 1985; awards: Joint Houses Calif. Legislature Proclamation 1988, CIBA Pharmaceutical Comm. Service 1975, Merck Pharm. Med. Student Outstanding Achievement 1978, Calif. Lt. Gov. Letter Recognition 1988; mem: Am. Pub. Health Assn., Calif. Pub. Health Assn. (governing council), Pacific Med. Assn. (secty.), Latino Health Policy Advy. Bd., Peri-Natal Network (bd. dirs.), Multi-Cultural Health Task Force (exec. com.). Ofc: Room 19 Warren Hall Univeristy of California Berkeley 94720

NEVIL, DANA CHRISTOPHER, radio station executive; b. Dec. 24, 1956, Los Angeles; s. Charles H. and Irene (Fialkoff) N.; m. Gloria Patricia Gallego, Nov. 16, 1986; 1 dau. Andrea Pilar b. 1991; edn: BA, UCLA 1979. Career: west coast mgr. Caballero Spanish Media Inc., Los Angeles 1980-83; dir. Hispanic mktg. Westwood One, Culver City 1984; v.p., gen. mgr. KALY Radio, El Paso, Tx. 1985; nat. sales mgr. KAMA/KAMZ 1986-87; v.p., gen. sales mgr., we. region Caballero Spanish Media Inc., Los Angeles 1987-93; v.p., gen. mgr. KMQA-FM Radio, L.A. 1993–. Ofc: KMQA-FM Radio 6430 Sunset Blvd 6th Flr Los Angeles 90028

NEWACHECK, DAVID JOHN, lawyer; b. Dec. 8, 1953, San Francisco; s. John Elmer and Estere Ruth Sybil (Nelson) N.; m. Dorothea Quandt, June 2, 1990; edn: AB in English, UC Berkeley, 1976; JD, Pepperdine Univ. Sch of Law, 1979; MBA, CSU Hayward, 1982; LLM (tax) Golden Gate Univ., 1987; admitted bar: Calif. 1979, US Supreme Ct. 1984, Dist. of Col. 1985. Career: tax consultant Pannell Kerr Forster, San Francisco 1982-83; atty. at law, legal writer, Matthew Bender & Co., Oakland 1983–; lectr. in law, Oakland Coll. of Law 1993–; dir. Aztec Custom Cos. 1982–; mem. ABA, Calif. Bar, Alameda County Bar Assn., Mensa, Calif. Alumni Assn., Pepperdine Law Alumni; staff author & consultant: California Taxation, California Closely-Held Corporations, Illinois Tax Service, New Jersey Tax Service, Pennsylvania Tax Service, Bender's Federal Tax Service (pub. Matthew Bender) 1983–; Republican (life mem. Repub. Nat. Com.); Lutheran (deacon); rec: music, competitive running, youth work. Res: 5141 Vannoy Ave Castro Valley 94546-2558 Ofc: Matthew Bender & Co. (POB 2077 Oakland 94604-2077) 2101 Webster St Oakland 94612

NEWBERRY, CONRAD FLOYDE, professor of aeronautics and astronautics; b. Nov. 10, 1931, Neodesha, Kans.; s. Ragan McGregor and Audra Anitia (Newmaster) N.; m. Sarah Louise Thonn, Jan. 26, 1958; children: Conrad, Jr., b. 1958, Thomas b. 1962, Susan b. 1965; edn: AA, Independence Jr. Coll. 1951; BEME (Aeronautical Sequence), USC 1957; MSME, Calif. St. Univ. L.A. 1971; M.Ed., 1974; D.Env., UCLA 1985; profl. engr. Calif. 1970, Kans. 1978, Tx. 1979, N.C. 1978; cert. air pollution control engr. Am. Acad. Environmental Engrs. 1988. Career: mathematician L.A. div. N. Am. Aviation 1951-53; jr. engr. 1953-54, engr. 1954-57, sr. engr. 1957-64; asst. prof. aerospace engring. dept., Calif. St. Polytech. Univ., Pomona 1964-70, assoc. prof. 1970-75, prof. 1975-90, professor emeritus 1990–; staff engr. EPA, Res. Triangle Park, N.C. 1980-82; engring. specialist Rockwell Internat. Space Div., 1984-90; prof. aeronautics and astronautics (academic assoc. for space systems engring. 1992-94) Naval Postgraduate Sch., Monterey 1990–; awards: John Leland Atwood Outstanding Aerospace Engring. Educator award 1986-87, Tau Beta Pi, Sigma Gamma Tau, Kappa Delta Pi; mem: Fellow AIAA (dir. tech.-aircraft systems 1990-93), Fellow Inst. Advancement Engring., Fellow British Interplanetary Soc., ASEE (chmn. PIC II, 1995-97; chmn. Aerospace Div. 1979-80; chmn. Ocean and Marine Engring. Div. 1993-95, pgm. chmn. 1991-93), AHS, EAA, ASME, SNAME, AWMA, AMS, SAE, CSPE, CWPCA, AAEE, NAEP, AAAS, IEEE, NSPE, IES, ASPA, Planetary Soc., Am. Soc. of Naval Engrs., U.S. Naval Inst., Soc. of Allied Weights Engrs., Assn. for Unmanned Vehicle Systems, Royal Aeronautical Soc.; Democrat; Disciples of Christ. Res: 9463 Willow Oak Rd Salinas 93907-1037 Ofc: Naval Postgraduate Sch., Monterey 93943-5000

NEWBRUN, ERNEST, oral biology and periodontology educator, b. Vienna, Austria, Dec. 1, 1932; came to U.S. 1955; s. Victor and Elizabeth (Reichl) N.; m. Eva Miriam, June 17, 1956; children: Deborah Anne, Daniel Eric, Karen Ruth; edn: BDS Univ. Sydney, New South Wales 1954; MS Univ. Rochester 1957; DMD Univ. Ala. 1959; PhD Univ. Calif., San Francisco 1965; Odont. Dr. (hon.) Univ. Lund, Sweden 1988; cert. periodontology. Career: Res. assoc. Eastern Dental Ctr., Rochester, N.Y. 1955-57, Univ. Ala. Med. Ctr., Birmingham 1957-59; res. fellow Inst. Dental Res. Sydney, Australia, 1960-61; res. tchr. trainee Univ. Calif., San Francisco 1961-63, postdoctoral fellow 1963-65, assoc. prof. 1965-70, prof. oral biology 1970-83, prof. oral biology and periodontology 1983-94, prof. emeritus 1994–; cons. FDA 1983–; author: Cariology 1989, Pharmacology and Therapeutic Dentistry 1989, contbr., Pediatrics 1991; editor: Fluorides and Dental Caries 1986; mem. editorial bd. Jour. Periodontal Res. 1985-90, Jour. Peridontology 1990; bd. dirs. Raoul Wallenberg Dem Club, San Francisco, 1987-92. Mem. AAAS (chmn dental section, 1988-89), Internat. Assn. Dental Res. (pres. 1989-90), Dental Health Found. (chmn bd. dirs. 1985-92). Jewish. Ofc: Univ. Calif. San Francisco Div. Oral Biology San Francisco 94143-0512

NEWBURN, REX D., police polygraphist; b. Dec. 2, 1934, Malta, Ohio; s. Clancy E. and Ida Christine (Dougan) N.; edn: BS, State Coll. of Wash. 1958; MA, Wash. St. Univ. 1961; designated Expert Polygraphist, Nat. Tng. Ctr. of Lie Detection, NY 1968; lic. Calif. Polygraph Examiner 1985-90. Career: police ofcr. San Jose Police Dept., 1964-70, police sgt. Bur. of Field Ops., 1970–; bd. dirs. San Jose Police Union, Local 170, 1983-87; mem: Am. Polygraph Assn., Calif. Assn. of Polygraph Examiners, Am. Assn. of Police Polygraphists, Acad. of Certified Polygraphists Inc., Calif. Peace Officers Assn., San Jose Police Benevolent Assn., Monterey Bay Aquarium, American Air Museum (founding mem.), U.S. Senatorial Club 1981–, U.S. Com. for The Battle of Normandy Mus.; Republican (Presdl. Task Force); Christian Ch.; rec: reading. Ofc: San Jose Police Dept POB 270 San Jose 95103-0270

NEWCOMER, OWEN EUGENE, political science educator; b. Dixon, Ill., Feb. 13, 1948; s. M. Burns and Etholine C. (Clingenpeel) N.; m. Kristina Jean Weis, Apr. 3, 1971; edn: AA L.A. Valley C.C. 1970; BA Calif. State Univ. Northridge 1971, MA 1972; PhD Univ. So. Calif. 1980. Career: lectr. polit. sci Coll. of Canyons, Santa Clarita, Calif., 1973-75; prof. polit. sci. Rio Hondo Coll., Whittier, Calif. 1975–; lectr polit. sci. L.A. Pierce Coll., Woodland 1973-75, Moorpark (Calif.) Coll. 1974-75, L.A. City Coll., Hollywood 1974- 75; author: Governing Los Angeles, 1992. Commr. Whittier City Parks & Recreation Commn. 1987-89; pres. Rio Hondo Coll. Faculty Assn.. Whittier 1989-90; bd. dirs. Whittier City Sch. Dist. 1989–, pres. 1991-92; mem: Am. Polit. Sci. Assn., Soc. Calif. Hist. Soc., We. Polit. Sci. Assn., Whittier Hist Soc. Pico Rivera Heritage and Hist. Soc., El Monte Hist. Soc., Model UN of Far West; Democrat. Ofc: Rio Hondo College 3600 Workman Mill Rd Whittier 90608

NEWELL ALMA (LISA NEWELL), company executive, consultant; b. Beaver Falls, Pa., Oct. 21, 1936; d. Charles Edward and Mary Alma (Novak) Kralic; m. Everett William Newell, June 9, 1956 (div. Mar. 1971); children: Lawrenee Dean, Debora Lynn, Everett William II; edn: grad. high sch., Beaver Falls; lic. real estate agt., Calif. Career: adminstr. asst. to dir. sales U.S. Stoneware, Tallmade, Ohio, 1969-71; exec. sec. B.F. Goodrich Co., Akron, Ohio, 1971-76; real estate agt., L.A., 1977-78, Four Seasons Real Estate, 1978, Am. Calif. Devel., 1978; v.p. E.A.C. Constrn. Corp., L.A., 1978-80, com. sec., v.p. Bedford Group, Culver City, Calif., 1980; cons. Pacific Architronics, Pacific Palisades, Calif. Hosp. vol., Ohio, 1972-76; vol. fund raiser for afflicted children, L.A. Co. 1977–; mem: Nat. Notary Assn.; Democrat; R. Cath. Ofc: The Bedford Group 690 Corporate Point Ste 1100 Culver City 90230-7606

NEWELL CASTLE SKIP, III, marketing executive, foundation administrator; b. Detroit, Aug. 10, 1940; s. Castle and Leona (Herrick) N.; m. Nancy Elizabeth Taylor, Aug. 7, 1964; children: Andrew Scott, Samantha Suzanne; edn: AA Orange Coast Coll., Costa Mesa, Calif. 1962. Career: sports announcer Sta. ABC-TV Wide World of Sports, N.Y.C. 1965-70; dir. pub. rels. Kawasaki Inc., Santa Ana, Calif. 1970-73; shovelman Mendocino County Dept. Pub. Works, Laytonnlle, Calif. 1973-74; dir. pub. rels. Harwood Products, Branscomb, Calif. 1974-80; v.p. mktg. pub. rels. Bailey's, Inc., Laytonville, Calif. 1980–; pres. Castle Newell & Assocs.; mem: ANSI B 175 com. Comsumer Products Safety Commn., Washington 1985–; Fireman Laytonville Vol. Fire Dept. 1974, reserve dep. Mendocino County Sheriff's Dept. 1983–; pres., founder Rural Visions Found., Laytonville, 1986–; mem. bd. govs. Mendocino-Lake Community Coll. Found.; Recipient recognition as 237th Daily Point of Light, U.S. Pres. George Bush 1990, Community Svc. tribute U.S. Senate 1990, Commenda- tion award Calif. State Assembly 1987, Congl. salute U.S. Congress 1987 nominee Pres.'s Vol. Action award 1987. Res: PO Box 717 Laytonville 95454-0717 Ofc: Rural Visions Found PO Box 1371 Laytonville 95454-1371

NEWHART, BOB, entertainer; b. Oak Park, Ill., Sept. 29, 1929; m. Virginia Quinn, Jan. 12, 1963; 4 children; edn: BS Loyola Univ., Chgo., 1952. Career: Law clk. U.S. Gypsum Co.; copywriter Fred Niles Film Co.; performer Dan Serkin tv show 1957; appeared on Jack Paar Show, 1960; tv performer num. guest appearances, 1961–; star TV series Newhart, 1982-90; rec. artist (album) Button Down Mind on TV; royal command performance, London 1964; appeared in films Hot Millions 1968, Catch 22 1970, Cold Turkey 1971, First Family 1980, Little Miss Marker 1982; tv films incl. Thursday's Game 1978, Marathon 1980; Grand Marshall Tournament Roses Parade 1991; awards: Emmy award 1961, Peabody award 1961, Sword of Loyola award 1976; named to Acad. Hall of Fame 1993; mil: U.S. Army 1952-54. Ofc: c/o David Capell 2121 Avenue Of The Stars #1240 Los Angeles 90067-5009

NEWHOFF, JAMES ROBERT, airline executive, marketing company owner; b. April 11, 1941, New York; s. Stanley E. and Shirley Alice (Gants) N.; m. Patricia H. Staab, Jan. 23, 1963 (div. 1976); m. Nancy Karen Hollon, May 19, 1983; children: Annemarie (Mrs. Paul Pierre Rousse) b. 1967, Carol b. 1969, Joshua b. 1985, Daniel b. 1986; grandchildren:, Nicholas S. Rousse b. 1990; edn: grad. E. Meadow H.S. 1958. Career: agent Eastern Airlines 1962-78, sales rep., San Francisco 1978-80; sales agent Sato Travel, Charleston, S.C. 1980-82; mgr. Eastern Airlines and Sato Travel, Castle AFB 1982-91; supr./lead agt. Sato, Inc., Castle AFB 1991-92; owner DNJ Mktg. & Sales Group, Merced 1989-1994; owner DNJ Travel Service 1993-95 (ret.); counsellor Non-Commissioned Officers Assn. (NCOA), 1992-94; elected chmn. City of Merced Airport Authority 1994–; mem: N.D.T.A., Full Gospel Bus. Mens Fellowship (pres. 1984, pres. 1990), C5 Computer Club (v.p. 1988-89), Merced C.of C. (com. mem. 1989), Economic Devel. Com. of Merced, Kiwanis 1993–; Republican; Full Gospel Ch.; rec: photog. Res: 3281 Cheyenne Dr Merced 95348-1109

NEWKIRK, RAYMOND LESLIE, management consultant; b. Shreveport, La., July 13, 1944; s. Raymond Clay and Dorothy Emily (Parker) N.; m. Felicisima Guese Calma, Jan. 19, 1985; edn: AA Dayton Comm. Coll. 1973; BS behavioral sci. N.Y. Inst. Tech. 1976; MS philosophy Columbia Pacific Univ. 1980; PhD behavioral sci. 1982; PhD human sci. Saybrook Inst. 1992. Career: c.e.o. Newkirk & Assocs., Ft. Lauderdale, Fla. 1980-84; head dept. ADP Royal Saudi Naval Forces, Jeddah 1984-86; pres., cons. Internat. Assn. Info. Mgmt.,

Santa Clara 1984; cert. quality analyst Quality Assurance Inst., Orlando, Fla., 1986–; prin. cons. Info Impact Internat., Nashville 1988–; exec. dir. Systems Mgmt. Inst., Pleasant Hill 1987; pres., c.o.o. P.Q. Info. Group, The Netherlands 1992–; mem: Union for Concerned Scientists, San Francisco 1988, Fellow Brit. Inst. Mgmt., Internat. Biog. Assn.; Assn. Systems Mgmt., Assn. Profl. Cons., Planetary Soc., Columbia Pacific Alumni Assn. (pres. Mid-east chpt. 1985), Assn. Computing Machinery, IEEE Computer Soc., Phi Theta Kappa (outstanding scholar award 1973); author: Chronicles of the Making of A Philosopher 1983; contbr. articles to profl. jours.; speaker; . R. Cath. Res: 4395 Snowcloud Ct Concord 94518-1938

NEWMAN, ANNETTE GOERLICH, shopping center manager; b. Jan. 19, 1940, Fresno; d. David August and Mary Eloise (Simpson) Goerlich; children: Anne Kristen b. 1963, Mark David b. 1965, Gregory Hartley b. 1966; edn: PharmD, UC San Francisco Sch. of Pharmacy 1963, lic. pharm. Calif. 1963; cert. shopping center mgr., CSM 1977. Career: pharmacist Village Drug, 1963-69; pharmaceutical cons. 1962-72; store mgr. The Drug Store of Fig Garden Village, 1972-77, gen. mgr. Fig Garden Village Shopping Center, Fresno 1977–; corp. secty. Fig Garden Village Inc.; bd. dirs. Fig Garden Village Mchts. Assn.; mem. Calif. Club Hon. Soc. UCSF, Blue Gold Club UC Sch. of Pharm., UC Pharmacy Alumni Assn., Nat. Assn. of Female Execs.; civic: Fresno Arts Center (exec. bd. dirs.), Fresno Arts Center and Museum Council of 100, Junior League of Frresno, CSUF Arts & Humanities Advy. Bd., Sen. Ken Maddy's Central Calif. Conf. on Women Advy. Com., St. Agnes Med. Center Found. (bd. dirs.), Childhelp USA, Fig Garden Village Inc. (sec. treas.); rec: ski, equestrian, metaphysics, phys. fitness. Res: 3909 W Fir Fresno 93711 Ofc: Fig Garden Village Shop Ctr. 5082 N Palm Ste A Fresno 93704

NEWMAN, JEFFREY RICHARD, economic development; b. Nov. 6, 1955, New York, N.Y.; s. Leo and Ellen Ruth (Groer) N.; m. Marushka Ann Wohl, May 29, 1988; edn: BA physics, CSU Fullerton 1978; MS physics, CSU Fresno 1982. Career: teaching asst. CSU Fresno, physics dept., 1978-82; research asst. Univ. Colo., Boulder, Colo. 1983-85; technical staff TRW, Redondo Beach 1985-92; principal Donaldson/Newman Assoc. 1993–; assoc. devel. spec. Calif. Trade & Commerce Agency 1994–; mgr. Gold Strike Partnership; cons. Los Angeles Educational Ptnrship., L.A. 1987-88; cons. Los Angeles Aerospace Task Force 1992; listed Who's Who in Am. Universities, Who's Who Young Am. Profls., Who's Who in the West 24th edit.; mem: L.A. Organizational Devel. Network 1990–, CPSR 1992–, ASTD 1992–, ASM 1992–, Beyond War, Sigma Pi Sigma, Beach Cities Democratic Club, Redondo Bch. (v.ch. 1989–), IEEE-MTT, So. Bay chapt. (v.ch. 1986); author: articles pub. profl. jours., 1987, 92; Democrat (elected L.A. Co. Dem. Cent. Com. 1991–); rec: organizing, reading. Res/Ofc: 2000 Mathews Ave #5 Redondo Beach 90278

NEWMAN, JOHN JOSEPH, electrical engineer; b. Jan. 15, 1936, Wolf Point, Mont.; s. Leon Vincent and Anna Agusta (Muller) N.; m. Linda Carol Hawthorne, July 11, 1964; children: Vincent b. 1965, Penelope b. 1966, Michael b. 1970, Jennifer b. 1975; edn: BSEE, Mont. St. Univ. 1958; MSEE, Univ. N.M. 1961; PhD, Univ. Santa Clara 1968. Career: staff Sandia Corp., Albuquerque, N.M. 1958-61; sr. engr. Lockheed Missiles & Space, Sunnyvale 1961-66; engr. Fairchild Semiconductor, Palo Alto 1967; prin. scientist Memorex Corp., Santa Clara 1967-82; Burroughs Corp. 1982-87; prin. engr. Unisys Corp. 1987-89; cons. in Magnetics and Magnetic Recording, 1989–; tchg. asst. Univ. Santa Clara 1965-67; honors: BSA dist. award of merit 1981, Silver Beaver 1983; mem: IEEE, Santa Clara Valley Magnetics Soc. (secty. 1969, treas. 1970, v.p. 1971, pres. 1972), BSA (scoutmaster 1976-80, dist. membership chair 1980-84, dist. commr. 1984-86, SME chmn. 1987); 14 articles pub. in tech. jours. (1962–), patent held for thermomagnetic copying of mag. rec. (1968); Republican; R.Cath.; rec: photog., auto mechanics, woodworking. Res: POB 24624 San Jose 95154

NEWMAN, NANCY MARILYN, ophthalmologist, educator, consultant, inventor, entrepreneur; b. Mar. 16, 1941, San Francisco; edn: BA psychology (magna cum laude), Stanford Univ., 1962, MD, Stanford Univ. Sch. Medicine, 1967; diplomate Am. Bd. Ophthalmology. Career: NIH trainee neurophysiology, Inst. of Visual Scis., S.F. 1964-65; clin. clk. Nat. Hosp. for Nervous and Mental Disease, Queen Sq., London, Eng. 1966-67; internship Mount Auburn Hosp., Cambridge, Mass. 1967-68; NIH trainee in neuro-ophthalmology, jr., sr. asst. resident, assoc. resident dept. ophthal. Washington Univ. Sch. of Med., St. Louis, 1968-71; Internat. Eye Found. fellow with Dr. Humberto Escapini, San Salvador, El Salvador, 1971; NIH spl. fellow neuro-ophthal. with William F. Hoyt, M.D., Univ. Calif. Sch. of Medicine, S.F. 1971-72; fellow Smith-Kettlewell Inst. of Visual Scis., 1971-72; clin. asst. prof. ophthal. UCSF Sch. Med., 1972, cons. neuro-ophthal. VA Hosp. S.F. 1972-74, cons. nerve fiber contract, Nat. Eye Inst., NIH, DHEW, at UC Sch. Med. S.F. 1973-75; physician/cons. dept. neurology UC Sch. Med./VA Med. Ctr. Martinez, 1978–; asst., assoc. prof. and chief div. neuro-ophthal. Pacific Med. Ctr., S.F. 1972-88; prof. dept. spl. edn. CSU San Francisco 1974-79; vis. prof. Centre Nat. D'Ophtalmologie des Quinze-Vingts, Paris, France 2-5/80; clin. assoc. prof. Sch. Optometry UC Berkeley, 1990–, cons. VDT and Occupational Health Clinic, Sch. Opt. UCB, 1990–; pres. and c.e.o. Minerva Medica, Inc.; cons. num. med.

device and biomed. cos.; recipient merit awards: Internat. Eye Found., NSPI Award for outstanding instrnl. materials in ophthal. SIMO; dir., advy. bds: Fifer Street Fitness, Larkspur 1990-92, Rose Resnick Ctr. for the Blind and Handicapped 1988-92, N.African Ctr. for Sight Tunis, Tunisia (internat. advy. com. 1988–), Internat. Soc. for Orbital Disorders 1983–, Frank B. Walsh Soc. 1974-91, No. Calif. Soc. for Prevention of Blindness 1978-88; mem: AMA (ldr. Calif. delegation cont. med. edn. 1982, 83), S.F. Med. Soc., Calif. Med. Assn. (subcom med. policy coms. 1984–, chair com. on accred. cont. med. edn. 1981-88, chair quality care rev. commn. 1984), Assn. for Res. in Vision and Ophthal., Pan Am. Assn. Ophthal., Soc. of Heed Fellows, Pacific Coast Oto-Ophthal. Soc., Lane Med. Soc. (v.p. 1975-76), Internat. Soc. Neuro-Ophthal. (founding), Cordes Soc., Am. Soc. Ophthalmic Ultrasound (charter), Orbital Soc. (founding), West Bay Health Systems Agy., Oxford Ophthalmol. Soc., Pacific Physicians Assocs., Soc. Fr. d'Ophtalmologie; author: Eye Movement Disorders; Neuro-ophthalmology: A Practical Text (1992); mem. Opthalmology Practice 1993–; editorial bd. J. Clin. Neuro-ophthalmology, Am. J. Ophthalmology 1980-92; contbr. num. articles in profl. jours. Res: 819 Spring Dr Mill Valley 94941

NEWSOM, BERNARD DEAN, physiologist; b. Feb. 8, 1924, Oakland; s. Charles Clarance and Grace Edna (Coughlin) N.; m. Eva Marie Snyder, Dec. 31, 1945 (dec. 1988); m. Marie Alicia Gorman, Apr. 4, 1992; children: Bernard B. b. 1947, Ronald L. b. 1957; edn: BS, UC Berkeley 1949; MS, Univ. San Francisco 1954; PhD, UC Berkeley 1960. Career: staff scientist Naval Radiological Defense Lab., San Francisco 1949-60; chief biomed. research Gen. Dynamics, San Diego 1960-68; asst. to dir. med. research NASA Manned Space Craft Center, Houston, Tx. 1968-72; sr. staff scientist NASA Ames Research Center, Sunnyvale 1972-76; awards: NASA Achievement 1969, Manned Spacecraft Achievement 1969; mem: Radiological Research Soc. (emeritus), Am. Physiological Soc., Aerospace Med. Assn.; research planning study pub., 1978, research reports pub. in sci. jours.; Republican; Cath. Res: 26645 Altamont Rd Los Altos Hills 94022

NEWTON, LYMAN WILLIS, sales and marketing executive; b. Dec. 9, 1936, Seattle, Wash.; s. Ellery Willis and Helen Greta (Morehouse) N.; m. Gloria Trunkey, July 25, 1959; children: Mari b. 1961, Mark b. 1963, Lori b. 1966; edn: BA bus. adminstrn., Univ. Wash. Seattle 1959. Career: market analyst Scott Paper Co., Los Angeles 1960-68; dist. mgr. Sylvania Corp. 1968-70; Berkeley Inst. 1970-72; regional mgr. Baird Atomic, Paramount 1972-74; v.p. sales and mktg. Riverside Bio Engring., Riverside 1974-76; dir. sales and mktg. Medi Nuclear, Baldwin Park 1976–; honors: BSA Eagle Scout; mem. Pasadena Sch. Bd.; founder Pasadena Fundamental Sch. (1973); Club: City (San Marino), Valley Hunt Club; mil: E-7 AUS 1955-63; Republican; Congregational; rec: gardening. Res: 1550 Wilson Ave San Marino 91108

NEWTON, RICHARD HOWARD, engineering executive/program manager; b. Oct. 12, 1932, Milw.; s. Howard Leslie and Evelyn Jennie (Shove) N.; m. Martha Jane Dinsmore, Sept. 11, 1954 (dec.); children: Scott b. 1955, Gayle b. 1957, Jeffrey b. 1958, Mark b. 1962; m. Dorothea Elaine Gregloit, Feb. 19, 1966; edn: BSME, Purdue Univ., 1954; MBA, Claremont Grad. Sch., 1984. Career: engr. Robbius & Myers, Springfield, Oh. 1954; project engr. Aerojet Avionics, Azusa, Calif. 1956-63, dept. mgr. Aerojet Meas. Dept. 1963-67, asst. to div. mgr. Aerojet Microelectronics 1967-68, special projects mgr. Aerojet Astrionics 1968-82, mgr. central program Aerojet Electro Systems 1982–; bd. dirs. Citrus College Found., Glendora 1988–, Recording for the Blind, Pomona 1987-91, L.A. Sanitation Dist. 1978-89, L.A. County Private Ind. Council 1980-84; recipient Awards of Honor: L.A. County Board Suprs. 1980, L.A. County 1st Dist. 1990; mem. ASME 1954–, Air Force Assn. 1988–, Nat. Space Club 1991–, Masonic Lodge (W.Lafayette, Ind.); mil: capt. USAF 1954-56; Republican; Presbyterian; rec: bicycling, golf, skiing. Res: 2270 Tulsa Ave Claremont 91711 Ofc: Aerojet Electronic Systems Div. PO Box 296 Azusa 91702

NEY, MICHAEL JAMES, lawyer; b. Nov. 20, 1943, Oakland; s. George William and Monica Patricia (Ford) N.; m. Jamie Sue Deren, July 13, 1968; children: Molly, Deren; edn: Bach. Sci. and Commerce, Santa Clara Univ. 1965; JD, John F. Kennedy Univ. 1971; admitted Calif. St. Bar 1972, U.S. Dist. Ct. (no. dist.) Calif. 1972. Career: dep. district atty. County of Alameda, Oakland 1972-73; assoc. Helzel, Leighton, Brunn & Deal, Oakland 1973-75; ptnr. McNamara, Houston, Dodge, McClure & Ney, Walnut Creek 1975–; mem: Am. Bar Assn., Calif. Bar Assn., Contra Costa Bar Assn., No. Calif. Assn. of Defense Counsel (bd. 1989-91), Am. Bd. of Trial Advocates (ABOTA), Calif. Trial Lawyers Assn. (guest panelist); civic: Leukemia Found. of No. Calif. (com.); R.Cath. Res: 1031 Via Nueva Lafayette 94549 Ofc: McNamara Houston Dodge McClure & Ney 1211 Newell Ave Walnut Creek 94596

NG, MICHAEL GUAN-YUH, cosmetic chemist; b. Jan. 7, 1942, Singapore; nat. 1972; s. Hee Yin and Fung May (Wong) Ng; m. Pauline Yuen-Ling, Aug. 29, 1970; children: Eric Wai-Choi, Bryant Wai-Wah; edn: BA chem., UC Riverside 1965. Career: quality control chemist Nestle Co., Salinas 1965-66; chemist Max Factor Co., Hollywood 1966-70, research chemist 1970-75, sr. research chemist 1975-80, mgr. 1980-85; project mgr. Redken Lab. Inc., Canoga Park 1985-94; dir. Res. & Devel. Lab, Randall Internat., Carlsbad 1994-95; dir.

R&D Lab., Thibiant Internat., Chatsworth 1995–; mem: Soc. Cosmetic Chemist, Am. Chem. Soc., Chinese Am. Chem. Soc., San Fernando Valley Chinese Assn. (asst. dir. 1982-83); patentee in field (1988); Republican; Christian. Res: 11719 Monte Leon Way Northridge 91326 Ofc: Thibiant International, Chatsworth 91311 Tel: 818/709-1345

NGUYEN, HUGH DAN, juris doctor, business executive; b. Jan. 8, 1944, Saigon, Vietnam; s. Austin Nguyen and Thong Thi (Le) N.; m. Kimberly Chau, Jan. 1, 1974; children: Esther b. 1976, David Dan b. 1980; edn: BA, Saigon Law Sch., 1970. Career: high sch. tchr. Dong-Tien H.S., Vietnam, 1965-70, Nhan-Chu H.S., also An-Lac H.S., Saigon, 1967-70; lawyer, mem. Vietnamese Lawyer Assn., Saigon; job developer Gov.'s Task Force for Indochinese Resettlement, Des Moines, Ia., 1976-77; eligibility worker Dept. Social Svs., Santa Clara County, Calif., 1978-81; real estate agt. West Realty, San Jose, 1980-85; real estate broker West Realty Investments, San Jose, 1985–; owner opr. Monterey AM/PM Mini Mart, San Jose; club: Nautilus; Republican; R.Cath.; rec: tennis, weight lifting. Ofc: 5498 Monterey Rd San Jose 95111

NGUYEN, QUAN HONG, physician; b. Jan. 16, 1963, Saigon, Vietnam (nat. 1984); s. Van Van and My N.; m. Monique Ann B., June 8, 1991; edn: student De Anza Coll., Cupertino 1980-82; BS (cum laude) biology, USF 1985; MS (summa cum laude) molecular biology, USF 1987; MD, Georgetown Univ. Sch. of Medicine, W.D.C. 1991. Career: internship UC Davis Med. Ctr., Sacto. 1991-92; biomed. res. USF Inst. of Chemical Biology, S.F. 1992-93; residency USF/Mt. Zion, S.F. 1993-94; fellowship UCSF Sch. of Medicine Psoriasis Treatment Ctr., S.F. 1994-95; dermatology residency Ohio State Univ. Med. Ctr., Columbus 1995–; honors: Honor Thesis, UCSF 1985, Nat. Tri-Beta Biol. Honor Soc. 1983-87, Frank G. Brooks award for Excellence in Res., Tri-Beta, S.F. 1985, Nat. Dean's List UCSF 1985; mem: AMA 1987–, Vietnamese Physician Assn. of No. Calif. 1991–; author: num. articles pub. in profl. jours, 1987–; research: 4 papers presented to profl. assns., U.S., England & Italy, 1984-89; rec: music: guitar; swimming, ballroom dancing. Ofc: Ohio State University Medical Center Columbus OH

NGUYEN, THINH VAN, physician; b. April 16, 1948, Vietnam; nat. 1983; s. Thao Van and Phuong Thi (Tran) N.; m. Phi Thi Ho, Jan. 2, 1973; children: Anh-Quan b. 1974, Andrew Anh-Tuan b. 1982; edn: BS, Univ. Saigon Vietnam 1970; MS, Univ. Mo. 1974; MD, Univ. Tx. Houston 1982; diplomate Am. Bd. Internal Medicine 1988, Am. Acad. of Pain Mgmt. 1989. Career: research asst. Univ. Tx. SW Med. Sch., Dallas 1974-78; resident physician rep., Texas Med. Assn. Com. on Cardiovascular Diseases 1982-84, Council of Scientific Affairs 1984-85; internist, area chief FHP Inc., Long Beach, Calif. 1985-89; pvt. practice in San Jose, 1989–; chmn. interdisciplinary practice com. Charter Comm. Hosp., Hawaiian Gardens 1989–; chmn. interdisciplinary practice com. San Jose Med. Ctr. 1993–; listed Who's Who in Texas 1985, Who's Who in the West 1994-95, Who's Who in the World 1995; mem: A.C.P., Calif. Assn. Med. Dirs. (bd. dirs.), AMA, Am. Acad. of Otolaryngeal Allergy; articles pub. in med. jours. 1975, 77; rec: photog., tennis, dancing. Address: 2470 Alvin Ave Ste 5 San Jose 95121

NICE, CARTER, symphony conductor; b. Apr. 5, 1940, Jacksonville, Fla.; s. Clarence Carter, Jr. and Elizabeth Jane (Hintermister) N.; m. Jennifer Smith, Apr. 4, 1983; children: Danielle b. 1968, Christian b. 1972, Olivia b. 1993; edn: BMus., Eastman Sch. of Music, 1962; MMus., Manhattan Sch. of Music, 1964. Career: asst. conductor, concertmaster Florida Symphony, Orlando 1965-66; asst. prof. Univ. of Oklahoma, Norman 1966-67; asst. conductor, concertmaster New Orleans Philharmonic, La. 1967-79; music director Sacramento Symphony, Calif. 1979-92; music director Bear Valley Music Festival, Bear Valley, Calif. 1985–. Res: 200 P St #B-36 Sacramento 95814

NICHOLAS, P.K., public accountant; b. May 31, 1917, Orange, N.J.; s. Fred Q. and Edith (Stevens) N.; m. Betty Jane McClure, Pittsburgh, Pa., Dec. 31, 1941; children: Barbara Ann b. 1947, David King b. 1949, Becky Jane b. 1951; edn: BS in bus. adm., Lehigh Univ., 1939. Career: staff acct. U.S. Steel Corp., Pittsburgh, Pa. 1939-41; Beckwith Mach. Co., Pittsburgh 1946-47; pub. acct. practice, Bakersfield, Calif. 1948-89; mem. Soc. of Calif. Accts. (state pres. 1962-63); civic: Little League Baseball Bakersfield (coach 1951-65), Kiwanis Club Kern of Kern (Bakersfield pres. 1958); mil: capt. US Army 1942-45; Presbyterian; rec: golf. Res: 6001 Auburn Street #117 Bakersfield 93306 Tel: 805/873-8412

NICHOLS, DAVID NORTON, elementary school principal; b. Mar. 26, 1954, Lancaster, Calif.; s. Norton, Jr. and Sarah Jane (Jones) N.; edn: AA, Antelope Valley Coll., 1974; BA, UCLA, 1977; MA, San Diego St. Univ., 1986; CSU Long Beach, 1977-79. Career: tchr., 5, 6, 7, 8 gr., Carlsbad Unified Sch. Dist., Carlsbad 1979-90, summer sch. prin. 1987, 88, adminstrv. intern 1985-87; principal Lakeside Union Sch., Lakeside 1990–; sci. staff devel. Calif. Sci. Implementation Network; honors: Mentor tchr. Carlsbad USD 1988-89, Internat. Man of Achiev. 1989, Outstanding Young Man of Yr. 1986, outstanding ranking NASSP Assessment Ctr. #60 (1986), Who's Who in Am. Edn. 1987-88; mem. NEA 1979–, ASCD 1984–, CASCD 1989–, ACSA 1990–, NAESP 1990–, Heartland Sch. Adminstr. Assn.; Democrat; Christian; rec: gourmet cooking, gardening, travel, theatre. Res: 6860-B Caminito Montanoso, 8, San Diego 92119

NIDEVER, JACK EDWARD, psychologist; b. Mar. 6, 1925, Fresno; s. Elza Edward Nidever and Vella Virginia (Foley) Lehrke; m. Alberta Viola Kiehl, Feb. 5, 1948, div. 1976; children: Linda b. 1951, Clare-Mrie b. 1954, Melissa b. 1958; m. Eva Rosenbaum, Jan. 8, 1984 (dec. 1992); m. Franzi Elizabeth Bauer, Mar. 6, 1993; edn: BA, Pomona Coll., Claremont 1950; MA, Univ. Pa., 1952; PhD, UCLA, 1958; diplomate C.G. Jung Inst., Zurich 1965. Career: research staff Rand Corp., Santa Monica 1954-56; research asst. UC Los Angeles 1956-58; research staff Gen. Elec. Computer Dept., Arlington, Va. 1959; human factors IBM Research, San Jose 1959-62; Hinkle Fellow C.G. Jung Inst., Zurich 1962-65; clin. psychologist state and county hosps. Mendocino, Agnews, Porterville, Valley Med. Ctr., San Jose, Calif. 1965-70; pvt. practice Associated Psychologists, San Jose and Arnold 1968-91, ret.; returned to practice 1993–; instr. Calif. Sch. of Profl. Psychology, S.F. 1968-70, Psychol. Studies Inst., Palo Alto 1978-85; mem: Am. Psychol. Assn., Internat. Assn. of Analytical Psychol.; newspaper columnist "Country Shrink" for Sierra Sentinel (1986), Calaveras Californian (1987); mil: T5 AUS 1943-46; Democrat; Prot.; rec: flying, skiing, writing prose and poetry. Res: 3811 Fairway Dr POB 526 Arnold CA 95223 and 30243 SW Heater Rd Sherwood, OR 97140

NIEMAND, SHIRLEY M., stock broker; b. Nov. 20, 1924, Kansas City, Mo.; d. Karl Frederick and Marion (McCutcheon) Maier; m. Donald Wayne Niemand, Sept. 6, 1947; children: Linda b. 1950, Steven b. 1954, Jeffrey b. 1956, William b. 1958, Gary b. 1961; edn: AA, Kans. City, Mo. Jr. Coll. 1945; BS, Iowa St. Univ. 1947; N.Y. Inst. Fin. 1977-78. Career: engr. Iowa Hwy. Commn., Ames 1947-49; clk. AEC, Los Alamos, N.M. 1950; stockbroker Dean Witter, Whittier 1977–, coordinator tax advantaged investments 1982–; awards: Dean Witter Broker of Month 1984, Pres. Merit 1979, Franklin Funds Pres. Club 1985, Pub. Storage Pres. Round Table 1986, 87, A.E. of Month, D.W. Ins. Svs. 1990, Summit Club AIM Funds 1992, 1st Place Branch Winner-D.W. Equity Porfolio Challenge 1993; mem: Soroptimist Internat. (pres., program chmn. 1980-85), Downey Symphonic Soc., First Ch. Christ Scientist (past chmn. bd., Sunday sch. supt., clk.), Am. Assn. Univ. Women (pres. 1966-68), Sister City Com. Downey (v.p. 1976-78), Women's Com. Downey Symphony (program chmn. 1975-78), E. Jr. H.S. PTA (pres.), Downey City Sanitation Com. (v.p. 1974-78); Republican; Christian Scientist; rec: gardening, bridge, travel. Res: 9340 Gallatin Rd Downey 90240 Ofc: Dean Witter 15111 E Whittier Blvd Whittier 90603

NITZ, FREDERIC WILLIAM, electronics company executive; b. June 22, 1943, St. Louis; s. Arthur Carl Paul and Dorothy Louise (Kahm) N. m. Kathleen Sue Rapp, June 8, 1968; children: Frederic Theodore, Anna Louise; edn: AS, Coll. of Marin, 1970; BS in electronics, Calif. Poly. State Univ., S.L.O., 1972. Career: electronic engr. Sierra Electronics, Menlo Park 1973-77; RCA, Somerville, N.J. 1977-79; engring. mgr. EGG-Geometrics, Sunnyvale 1979-83 v.p. engring. Basic Measuring Insts., Foster City 1983-91; exec. v.p. Reliable Power Meters, Los Gatos 1991–; cons. in field, Boulder Creek 1978–; patentee in field; civic bds: San Lorenzo Valley Water Dist., Boulder Creek (dir. 1983–), Water Policy Task Force, Santa Cruz County (1983-84); mil: AUS 1965-67; Democrat. Res: 12711 East St Boulder Creek 95006 Ofc: RPM 400 Blossom Hill Rd Los Gatos 95032-4511

NIXON, GEORGE, tax accountant; b. July 3, 1942, North Belfast, No. Ireland, came to U.S.A. 1971; s. George and Ethel Florence (Cunningham) N.; edn: grad. Instn. of Electronic & Radio Engrs., London 1966; chartered engr., U.K.; tchg. cert. Victoria Univ. of Manchester, Eng. 1969; BS in acctg., Univ. San Francisco 1976. Career: product devel. engr., England 1965-70; instr. Bolton Tech. Coll., England, 1969; acct., owner tax acctg. and bookkeeping bus., San Francisco 1972–, pres. Shamrock Tax & Bookkeeping Corp., 1975–; mem: Nat. Soc. Pub. Accts., Instn. of Elec. Engrs., London; rec: ham radio, writing, civil rights/pol. causes, fitness, programming. Ofc: Shamrock Tax & Bookkeeping Corp. 6033 Geary Blvd San Francisco 94121-1907

NOBLE, JOHN ROBERT, retired mutual fund president, investment adviser; b. June 4, 1921, Manila, Philippines; s. Frederick Handy and Suzanne Maude (Ely) N.; m. Georgia Eleanor Faith, Nov. 21, 1942; children: David b. 1944, Bonnie b. 1947, Cynthia b. 1953; edn: BA, Colgate Univ. 1942. Career: chemist Monsanto Chem. Co., St. Louis, Mo. 1942-43, research chemist, Springfield, Mass. 1943-44; chemist Manhattan Dist., Oak Ridge, Tenn. 1944-46; mktg. asst. Standard Vacuum & Oil, Iloilo and Manila, Philippines 1946-51, area mgr., N.Y.C. 1951, mktg. asst., Bombay, India 1951-54; gen. mgr. Investors Research Co., Santa Barbara 1955-92; pres. Investors Research Fund Inc. 1959-92; honors: Phi Beta Kappa, Alpha Chi Sigma, Mu Pi Delta; U.S. Treasury Silver Life Saving Medal, Boy Scout Life Saving Medal (1938); mem: Fifty Families, Santa Barbara Museum of Art, Pres. Club Colgate Univ., Santa Barbara Symphony (pres., dir. 1962-82); author: How to Start a Mutual Fund (1966), Mgmt. of Money (1962); mil: T-4 Spl. Det. Engrs. 1944-46; Episcopalian; rec: yacht racing, model building.

NOCAS, ANDREW JAMES, lawyer; b. Feb. 4, 1941, Los Angeles; s. John R. and Muriel P. (Harvey) N.; 1 son, Scott b. 1972; edn: BS physics, Stanford Univ. 1962; JD, 1964. Career: ptnr. Thelen Marrin Johnson & Bridges, Los Angeles 1964-91; Law Offices of David M. Harney 1992–; arbitrator Am. Arbitration Assn., L.A. 1979–; speaker legal programs 1970–; mem: Am. Bar Assn. (tort & ins. practice sect., litigation sect., Fellow Am. Bar Found.), Calif. State Bar Conf. (del.), Los Angeles Bar Assn. (trustee 1990-92, chair litigation sect. 1989-90), San Marino City Club; articles pub. in profl. jours.; mil: capt. USAR 1966-72; Republican; Episcopalian. Law Ofcs. of David M. Harney, 201 N Figueroa St Ste 1300 Los Angeles 90012

NOCHIMSON, DAVID, lawyer; b. June 19, 1943, Patterson, N.J.; s. Samuel S. and Mildred (Singer) N.; m. Roberta Maizel, June 5, 1966 (div. 1972); m. Gail Burgess, May 26, 1978; edn: BA, Yale Univ. 1965; LL.B, Columbia Law Sch. 1968; LL.M, Australian Nat. Univ. 1970; admitted St. Bar N.Y. 1970, Calif. 1977. Career: atty., assoc. Paul Weiss Rifkind Wharton & Garrison, N.Y.C. 1970-72; sr. v.p. Comprop Equities Corp. 19872-75; ptnr. Mitchell Silberberg & Knupp, Los Angeles 1977-83; Ziffren Brittenham Branca & Fischer 1983–; awards: Fulbright scholar 1968-69; mem: UCLA Entertainment Symposium Com., Am. Bar Assn. (chmn. Forum Com. on the Entertainment and Sports Industries), Internat. Bar Assn. (com. on copyright and intellectual property), Beverly Hills Bar Assn.; Democrat; Jewish. Ofc: Ziffren Brittenham Branca & Fischer 2121 Ave of Stars 32nd Floor Los Angeles 90067

NOGUCHI, THOMAS TSUNETOMI, professor of forensic pathology; b. Jan. 4, 1927, Fukuoka, Japan, naturalized U.S. citizen 1960; s. Dr. Wataru and Tomika (Narahashi) N.; m. Dr. Hisako Nishihara, Dec. 31, 1960 (div. 1982); edn: pre-med. Nippon Medical Sch., Tokyo 1944-47, MD, 1951; MD (nat. lic.) Japan 1951, Calif. 1955; cert. Am. Bd. of Pathology: Pathologic Anatomy 1960, Clin. Path. 1962, Forensic Path. 1963. Career: asst. prof. path. Loma Linda Univ., L.A. 1960-61; dep. med. examiner, 1961-67, chief med. examiner - coroner County of Los Angeles, 1967-82; prof. forensic pathology USC Sch. of Medicine, also chief of autopsy and forensic pathologist L.A. Co.-USC Med. Ctr. and dep. med. examiner & dep. coroner County of L.A. in LAC-USC Med. Ctr., 1987–; awards: JD (hon.) Univ. of Braz Cubas, Sao Paulo, Brazil 1980, D.Sc. (hon.) Worcester State Coll. 1985, Dutton Prof. of Legal Medicine USC Sch. of Med. 1987, numerous honors from various orgs. incl. Outstanding Svc. Nat. Assn. of Med. Examiners 1991; mem: Nat. Assn. of Med. Examiners (pres. 1982-83, chmn. past pres.'s com. 1985-91), World Assn. of Med. Law (v.p. 1980–), L.A. County Med. & Bar Assns. Jt. Com. on Bio-Med. Ethics Com. 1980-91, Calif. State Coroners Assn. (pres. 1974-75), Am. Acad. Forensic Scis. (Council, sect. chair 1968-69); author (fiction, mystery): Physical Evidence 1990, Unnatural Causes 1988, (non-fiction): Coroner 1983, Coroner At Large 1985, 80+ sci. articles in forensic field; Republican; Christian; rec: fine arts, painting, still & landscape, photography, travel. Ofc: LAC-USC Medical Ctr. 1200 N State St Rm 2520 Los Angeles 90033-1084 Tel:213/226-7126

NOLAN, DENNIS PAUL VINCENT, senior project engineer; b. Dec. 8, 1954, Detroit; s. James Vincent and Anastasia Theresa (Kulick) N.; m. Kushal (Bains); children: Allam Nicholas, Zebulon Vincent; edn: BS in fire protection engrg., Univ. Md. 1977; MS syst. mgmt., Fla. Inst. of Tech. 1979; grad. Sch. of Offshore Ops., Univ. Tex. at Austin, 1981; RGIT, Aberdeen Offshore Survival Sch., 1990; Reg. Profl. Engr. Calif. 1984. Career: fire protection engr. 1977-80 Boeing Aerospace Kennedy Space Ctr. (designed shuttle facilities fire protection systems) 1977-80; risk engr. Marathon Oil Co. Findlay, Ohio 1980-84; senior engr. Lockheed Vandenberg AFB (ops. of shuttle launching) 1984-87; senior project engr. Occidental Petroleum Corp., Los Angeles, Calif., Aberdeen, Scotland (design of offshore oil platforms), Bakersfield, Calif. 1987-94; fire prevention engr. Aramco, Saudi Arabia 1994–; honors: Aerospace Awareness Award, NASA 1979; mem: Soc. of Petroleum Engrs., Am. Soc. of Safety Engrs., Soc. of Fire Protection Engrs., Nat. Fire Protection Assn., Mil. Vehicle Preservation Assn.; research: Mathematical Comparison of Friction Losses in Plastic, Copper, Steel Pipes 1977, Fired Heater Losses and Prevention 1980, LC-39A Fire Protection Assessment 1979, Ground Safety Plan VLS STS 1985; author: (book) Applications of Hazop and What If Safety Reviews to the Petroleum, Petrochemical Industries, Noyes Publ. 1994, (book) Handbook of Fire and Explosion Protection Engineering Principles for Oil, Gas and Related Facilities, Noyes Publ. 1995, num. tech. papers and profl. articles; Republican; rec: restore antique mil. vehicles, ski, white water rafting, theater/cinema, travel. Res: 12700 Overton St Bakersfield 93312-4630 Ofc: Saudi Arabian Oil Co, Abqaiq, Saudi Arabia

NOPAR, ALAN SCOTT, lawyer; b. Nov. 14, 1951, Chicago, Ill.; s. Myron E. and Evelyn R. (Millman) N.; edn: BS, Univ. Ill. 1976; JD, Stanford Univ. 1979; CPA, Ill. 1976; admitted bar: Calif., Ariz. Career: atty., assoc. O'Connor Cavanagh Anderson Westover Killingsworth & Beshears, Phoenix, Ariz. 1979-85; ptnr. 1985-87; of counsel Tower Byrne & Beaugureau 1987-88; ptnr. Minutillo & Gorman, San Jose 1989-91; ptnr. Bosco, Blau, Ward & Nopar, San Jose 1991–; mem: Am. Bar Assn. (bus. law sect., internat. law sect., forum com. on franchising), Calif. St. Bar (bus. law sect.), Ariz. St. Bar (bus. law sect.), Am. Inst. CPAs; article pub. in profl. jour. (1980); Republican; rec: golf, skiing. Ofc: Bosco, Blau, Ward & Nopar 2166 The Alameda San Jose 95126-1187

NORBY, STEVEN JEROME, dentist; b. Sept. 27, 1957, Crescent City; s. Donald Jerome Norby and Mary Ann (Shires) Montgomery; m. Valerie Stacy Axan; children: Kyle b. 1984; edn: BS, UC Davis 1981; DDS, Georgetown Univ. 1985. Career: dentist, owner Baywood Dental, Baywood Park 1985–;

cons. Den Mat Corp., Santa Maria 1987; awards: Georgetown Univ. Research Contbns. (1984), Excellence in Fixed Prosthodontics (1985); mem: ADA, Calif. Dental Assn., Central Coast Dental Soc., Acad. Gen. Dentistry, U.S. Dental Inst., Baywood Park C.of C.; Taoist; rec: paragliding, scuba, backpacking, bicycling, sailing. Res: 433 Woodland Dr Los Osos 93402 Ofc: Baywood Dental 1205 4th Ste B Los Osos 93402

NORDEN, ROBERT AUGUST, insurance claim litigation consultant; b. Aug. 28, 1935, San Jose; s. August Friedrich and Marie Katherine (Mauer) N.; m. Theresa McGuire, July 30, 1960; children: John b. 1961, Maryanne b. 1963, Stephen b. 1964; edn: BS, Santa Clara Univ., 1957; Santa Clara Law Sch. 1958-59, Penn State Univ. 1970-71, Allen Mgmt. Pgm. 1973. Career: trainee INA 1959-60, claim rep., San Jose and Santa Rosa 1960-62, resident rep., Santa Rosa 1962-66, claim supr. 1966-70, San Francisco, home office supr., Phila., Pa. 1970-72, asst. claim mgr., N.Y.C. 1972-74, claim mgr. 1972-76, Chgo. 1976; claim mgr., v.p., asst. secty. Sequoia Ins. Co., Menlo Park, Calif. 1976-90; indep. cons. ins. claim litigation, 1990–; mem. Fedn. of Ins. and Corp. Counsel 1988–, Internat. Assn. of Defense Counsel 1989–, Def. Research Inst. 1988–, past mem. Pacific Claim Exec. Assn. (Calif. Arson Prevention Com. 1978-90); mil: sgt. USMCR 1954-60; Democrat; R.Cath.; rec: sports, travel. Address: 504 Charles Cali Dr San Jose 95117

NORDSTROM, RICHARD DEAN, educator; b. Feb. 7, 1933, Topeka, Kans.; s. Albert Edwin and Wanda Lyle (Officer) N.; m. Margaret Anne Throm, Oct. 25, 1958; children: Neal b. 1960, Pam b. 1962; edn: BS, Univ. Kans. 1954; MBA, Wichita St. Univ. 1969; PhD, Univ. Ark. 1974. Career: dealer Nordstrom Ford, Newton, Kans. 1958-70; asst. prof. Wichita St. Univ., Kans. 1970-71; Univ. Ark., Fayetteville 1971-74; prof. Western Ill. Univ., Macomb, Ill. 1974-81; prof. CSU Fresno, 1981–; awards: Arkansas Purchasing Assn. fellow 1972, Fresno Sch. of Bus. Duncan award 1983; mem: Am. Mktg. Assn., Assn. Forensic Economists, Western Mktg. Educators; lodge: Masonic; author: Introduction to Selling (1981), 41+ articles pub. in profl. jours.; mil: lt.j.g. USN 1954-56; Republican; Lutheran; rec: golf. Address: 93711.

NORMAN, DONALD ARTHUR, cognitive scientist, educator; b. Dec. 25, 1935, N.Y.C.; s. Noah N. and Miriam F. N.; m. Martha Karpati (div.); children: Cynthia, Michael; m. Julie Jacobsen; children: Eric; edn: BSEE, M.I.T., 1957; MSEE, Univ. Pa., 1959, PhD in psychology, 1962. Career: prof. dept. psychology UC San Diego, La Jolla 1966-92, dept. chair 1974-78, dir. cognitive sci. pgm. 1977-88, dir. Inst. for Cognitive Sci. 1981-89, prof. and chair dept. cognitive sci. UCSD, 1988-93 (retired); fellow Apple Computer, Inc., Cupertino 1993; lectr. Harvard Univ. 1982-86; mem. Sci. Advy. Bd., Naval Personnel Res. Ctr., San Diego 1982-86; cons. to industry on human computer interaction and user-centered design; awards: Excellence in Res., UCSD; mem: AAAS (Fellow), Am. Psychol. Soc. (Fellow), Assn. for Computational Machinery, Cognitive Sci. Soc. (chmn. and founding mem.), Am. Assn. for Artificial Intelligence; author: Learning and Memory, 1982, Human Information Processing, 2d edit., 1977, User Centered System Design, 1986, The Psychology of Everyday Things, 1988, Turn Signals Are the Facial Expressions of Automobiles, 1992, Things That Make Us Smart, 1993; ed: Perspectives on Cognitive Science, 1981, series editor: Explorations in Cognition, 1975, Cognitive Science Series Lawrence Earlbaum Assocs., 1979–, Cognitive Science Jour., 1981-85. Ofc: APPLE Computer Inc 1 Infinite Loop Cupertino 95014

NORRIS, ERIC ALEXANDER, urban planner; b. July 5, 1959, Frankfurt, Germany; s. Arthur F. and Jutta M. (Kropf) N.; m. Cynthia Pauleen Abell, Aug. 2, 1986; children: Gregory b. 1991; edn: BA communication, Cal Poly. St. Univ., Pomona 1982, M. Urban & Reg. Planning, 1992; A.I.C.P., Am. Planning Assn., 1989. Career: planner Planning Network, Ontario, Calif. 1985-88; planner EDAW, San Bernardino 1988; dir. plng. RHA Inc., Riverside 1988-92; senior planner City of Chino Hills 1992–; mem: Regional Trails Com. 1991–, Am. Planning Assn. (1985–, awards for disting. svc. Inland Empire chpt. 1988, 89), State Outstanding Planning Award 1992, Am. Inst. Cert. Planners 1989–; civic: Water Bottle Transit Co., Redlands; publs: num. articles on bicycling & planning, 1983–; rec: ultramarathon cycling. Ofc: City of Chino Hills 2001 Grand Ave Chino Hills 91709

NORSELL, PAUL ERNEST, executive recruiter; b. Jan. 28, 1933, Salt Lake City, Utah; s. Alf Raae and Florence Emily (Freer) N.; m. M. Rynda, Sept. 2, 1958; children: Stuart b. 1961, Daryl b. 1964, Paula b. 1967; edn: BSEE, Purdue Univ. 1954; MS engring., UCLA 1956. Career: program mgr. applcn. tech. satellite Hughes Space Systems, El Segundo 1954-64; dir. advanced programs devel. Litton Industries (data systems div.) 1964-67, v.p. engring. and ops. 1967-69, pres. LITCOM div., Melville, N.Y. 1969-73, v.p. Profl. Services & Equipment Group, Beverly Hills 1973; pres. Paul Norsell & Assoc., Inc., Woodland Hills 1974-92, Auburn 1993–; awards: St. Johns Univ. businessman of year 1969, GM-Hughes Electronics masters fellow 1954-56, Purdue Alumni Assn. engring. scholar 1952-54; mem: IEEE, Eta Kappa Nu, Valley Industry & Commerce Assn. (bd. dir., govt. rels. com., exec. com.), Woodland Hills C.of C. (devel. pgms. com.), Calif. Exec. Recruiters Assn., Entrepreneurs of Am., U.S. C.of C., Los Angeles Area C.of C. (econ. devel. council), L.I. Assn. Commerce

& Industry (dir., exec. com. 1970-73); clubs: Transpacific Yacht, Long Beach Yacht, Braemar CC; publs: trade jour. articles re sales and comms. (1963–); rec: transoceanic & local yacht racing. Ofc: POB 6686 Auburn 95604-6686

NORVIEL, VERNON ALAN, lawyer; b. Dec. 23, 1958, Denver, Colo.; s. Vernon Alvin and Pearl (Clark) N.; m. Carmencita Jocson, June 29, 1983; edn: BS chem. eng., Univ. Colo., 1981; JD, Univ. S.F., 1985; MS, elec. engring., Univ. Santa Clara 1991; admitted Calif. St. Bar. Career: process engr. Chevron U.S.A., San Ramon 1981-85; atty. Chevron Corp., San Francisco 1985-88; atty. Townsend & Townsend, Palo Alto 1988–; mem. Am. Intellectual Property Law Assn., Peninsula Patent Law Assn.; Republican; rec: pvt. pilot. Ofc: Townsend & Townsend 379 Lytton Ave Palo Alto 94301-1431

NUGENT, JOHN WILLIAM, company president; b. July 21, 1945; Sharon, Pa.; s. John William and Lillian Elizabeth (Rigby) N.; m. Nancy, Dec. 25, 1967; children: Derric James b. 1968, Shane Elden b. 1972; edn: Univ. Cincinnati 1963-64; BS, Youngstown State 1968. Career: corp. sales N/S Corp. Sharon, Pa. 1968-70, nat. acct. sales mgr. 1970-73, mktg. mgr. 1973-75, v.p. mktg. Inglewood 1975-82, exec. v.p. 1982-90; pres. Nugent International Corp., 1990–; dir.: N/S Corp. 1975-90, Nugent Convalescent Home Inc. 1979–, Nat. Car Wash Council 1981-82; honors: disting. service, NCC 1982, Paul Harris Fellow, Rotary 1985; mem: Advt. Frat. 1967-68, Am. Pub. Works Assn. 1983-85, Assn. School Business Ofcls. 1981-83, Internat. Car Wash Assn. 1970–; civic bds.: Westchester C.of C. (bd. 1990), Rotary Internat. (Westchester Club pres. 1988-89, dir. 1986-90, Dist. #5280 long range planning com. 1990-93, Dist. gov. 1993-94), Westchester YMCA (bd. 1988–, bd. chmn. 1991-92, chmn. major gifts com. 1990); patentee: vehicle washing machine; Republican; Lutheran; rec: horticulture, art, skiing. Res: 7335 Vista Del Mar Playa Del Rey 90293

NUNN, ROBERT HARRY, engineer, educator; b. Nov. 9, 1933, Tacoma, Wash.; s. Harry and Muriel Day (Paul) N.; m. Caroline Lee Stahl, Sept. 13, 1955; children: Michael b. 1957, Theodore b. 1958, William b. 1961; edn: BS engring., UCLA 1955; MSME, 1964; PhD, UC Davis 1967; lic. profl. engr. Career: research aerospace engr. Naval Weapons Center, China Lake 1960-68; prof. mech. engring. Naval Postgrad. Sch., Monterey 1968-89, emeritus prof., 1989–, dept. chmn. 1971-75; dept. sci. dir. Office of Naval Research, London 1975-77; Pacific Grove City Council 1986-92; dir. Assn. Monterey Bay Area Govts. 1986-92; awards: NWC fellow 1964-67, Royal Naval Engring. Coll. vis. research fellow 1982-83; mem: Am. Inst. Aeronautics & Astronautics (assoc. fellow), ASME, Sierra Club; patentee in field, 100+ articles pub. in tech. jours., author Intermediate Fluid Mechanics 1989, ed. Power Condenser Heat Transfer Tech. 1981; mil: lt. USN 1955-60; rec: leaded glass, bicycling, tennis.

NUSBAUM, DANIEL MICHAEL, educator; b. Aug. 27, 1946, Los Angeles; s. Robert A. and Ruth L. (Sperling) N.; 3 sons, Micah b. 1973, Luke b. 1992, Sam b. 1993; edn: BA, St. Univ. N.Y. 1968; MS, St. Univ. Coll. Buffalo 1970. Career: musician 1960-87; substitute tchr., Los Angeles Co. 1973-87; English instr. Los Angeles City Coll. 1987–; mem: AFT Coll. Guild; candidate for Calif. supt. of public instrn., 1982, 86; cand. for L.A. Bd. of Edn., 1983; works: 2 stories, 7 essays, 2 sch. reform plans, 1 poem, 1 book. Res: 1918 N Taft Ave Los Angeles 90068

NUTT, NAN, retired church administrator; b. Dec. 15, 1925, Pasadena; d. Paul Geltmacher and Estelle Boggs (Love) White; m. David Ballard Norris, Jan. 8, 1944 (div. 1966); children: Teresa b. 1945, Anita b. 1947, Carol b. 1947, Steven b. 1951; m. Evan Burchell Nutt, July 12, 1969; edn: AA, Chaffey Coll., 1967; BA, Pomona Coll., 1969; grad. work UC Riverside 1969-70. Career: administrv. asst. to dept. hd. E.E., Univ. of Tenn., Knoxville 1951-53; organizer, administr. troop camping San Gabriel Valley (Calif.) Girl Scouts Am., summers 1953-57; administrv. asst. Church Sch. Claremont UCC, Claremont 1957-64; asst. to personnel dir. Pomona Coll., Claremont 1964, 1964; bus. mgr. First Congregational Ch. of Long Beach, UCC, Long Bech 1982-86, adminstr. 1986-90, ret. 1990, bd. pres. 1993; mem: Plymouth West, Long Beach 1988-89; listed Who's Who of Am. Women 1989-90; civic bds: Nat. Womens Polit. Caucus of Calif. (state advy. bd. 1988–, mem. NWPC nat. bd. 1981-89, nat. bd. steering com. 1972-79, 82–), OASIS/Older Adult Service & Info. Svc. L.B. (advy. com. 1986–), Cultural Heritage Commn. L.B. (mem. 1984–, chair 1987-89), Toastmistress Internat. Knoxville, Tenn. (founding pres. 1951-52), bd.dir. Public Corp. for the Arts, Long Beach; Democrat; Congregational, UCC; rec: politics. Res: 2867 Lomina Ave Long Beach 90815

NUTTER, BEN EARL, port development management and planning consultant; b. May 17, 1911, Baldwin, Kans.; s. John Alva and Lillian Capitola (Boggs) N.; m. Leone Rockhold, Nov. 26, 1936; edn: Glendale City Coll. 1929-31; BSCE Oregon State Univ. 1936; reg. civil engr. Calif. 1938, Hawaii 1946. Career: asst. engr. materials to Chief of Engring. Div. Honolulu Dist. US Army Corps of Engrs., mil. constrn. to harbor and flood control 1941-52; asst. mgr., asst. chief engr. Hawaii Harbor Bd. 1952-53; chmn. Hawaii Irrigation Authority and planning and constrn. for Hawaii Aeronautics Commn. 1953-57; supt. of public works Territory of Hawaii, chmn. Hawaii Harbor Bd., hwy. engr., mem. Honolulu Bd. of Water Supply 1953-57; chief engr., asst. exec. dir. Port of

Oakland 1957-62, exec. director 1962-77; cons. port devel. & mgmt. to ports and steamship cos. 1977–; honors: ASCE Civil Govt. Award 1971, Internat. Ports & Harbors (hon. mem. 1981), Public Works Man of Yr. Kiwanis Internat./Am. Public Works Assn. 1967, Meritorious Civilian Service Overseas US War Dept. 1943, Sigma Xi Sigma, Tau Beta Pi; mem: Am. Soc. Civil Engrs. (past sect. pres.), Am. Assn. Port Authorities (pres. 1974-75), Regional Export Expansion Council, Nat. Defense Exec. Reserve, Internat. Assn. Ports & Harbors (chmn. containers com.), Internat. Cargo Handling Coord. Assn. (hon. mem.), Nat. Defense Trans. Assn., Rotary Internat., Masons, Scottish Rite, KCCH, Beta Theta Pi, Propeller Club; Republican; Christian. Address: Santa Rosa.

NYBERG, LINDLEY VINCENT, SMT process engineer; b. Oct. 19, 1931, Madison, Wis.; s. Alvar F. and Ellen A. (Lund) N.; m. MaryLou Benedict, Apr. 5, 1952; edn: electronics, RCA Inst. Inc., N.Y. 1953-55. Career: display system specialist in research and devel. 1955-70; sales and mktg. 1970-74; mfg. engr. specializing in printed board assembly 1974-92; Surface Mount Technology (SMT) consultant 1992-95; SMT process engr. 1995–; awards: Archery State Champion, N.H. 1968; mem. SMTA (No. Cal. chapt. pres. 1986-89), past mem. Soc. Info. Display, Inst. of Radio Engrs., IEEE, Internat. Soc. of Hybrid Mfrs.; clubs: Masonic, Driftwood Yacht; 2 patent disclosures re cathode ray tube displays, classified, 1965-67; patent pending: direction indicator circuit, 1995; mil: US Coast Guard 1949-51; rec: yachting, photog. Res: 4368 Strawberry Park Dr San Jose 95129-2338

NYBO, L. BRUCE, consulting civil engineer; b. Mar. 6, 1944, Glendale; s. Luverne Bernard and Elise; m. Jean W., May 29, 1965; children: Elisabeth b. 1967, David b. 1969, John b. 1970, Joy b. 1972; edn: Bakersfield Coll. 1961-63; Christian lib. arts Highland Coll. 1965; BSCE UC Los Angeles 1966; Reg. Profl. Engr. Miss. 1977, Reg. Civil Engr. Calif. 1978. Career: transp. ofcr. US Naval Base Adak, Alaska 1966-67; asst. resident ofcr. in charge of constrn. USMCAS Cherry Point, N.C. 1967-69; constrn. engr. The Kroger Co. Houston, Tex. 1969-71; dir. of engrg. Jitney Jungle Stores of Am. Jackson, Miss. 1971-75; corp. dir. engrg. Peter J. Schmidt Co. Buffalo, NY, Erie, Pa. 1975-78; gen. mgr., dir. engrg. and surveying services Smith & Assoc. Bakersfield 1978-79; pres. L. Bruce Nybo Inc., Civil Engineering, Planning & Land Surveying, Bakersfield 1979–; mem: Calif. Council Civil Engrs. and Land Surveyors (past chpt. pres.), Am. Soc. Civil Engrs., Nat., Soc. Profl. Engrs., Profl. Engrg. Assn. of Antelope Valley, Am. Planning Assn., Bakersfield C.of C.; mil: lt. USNR Civil Engineer Corps, active duty 1966-69; Republican. Ofc: L. Bruce Nybo Inc. 4200 Easton Dr Ste 10 Bakersfield 93309 also: 2635 Diamond St Rosamond 93560 and 32255 McLeod Dr Ste A201 Las Vegas NV 89121

NYDAM, WILLIAM JOSEPH, healthcare executive; b. Apr. 11, 1950, Lynwood; s. Bernard John and Marian (Polich) N.; m. Dorothy I. Kowalczewski, Jan. 21, 1984; son, Barron b. 1989, dau. Alexandra b. 1992; edn: BS acctg. (honors), UC Berkeley, 1972, MBA, 1973; C.P.A., Calif., 1975. Career: staff acct., sr. acct., mgr. Audit Staff, Deloitte, Haskins and Sells, 1973-79; treas./c.f.o. and bd. dirs. Centinela Hosp. Medical Ctr., 1979-84; exec. v.p./c.o.o. Memorial Health Technologies (for-profit subs. co.), also v.p. corp. devel. for parent co. (of regional healthcare network with 3 hosps. incl. Memorial Med. Ctr. of Long Beach) 1984-86; sr. v.p./c.f.o./treas. American Healthcare Sys. (AmHS), San Diego, 1986–; tchg. asst. UCB Sch. of Bus. 1972-73; lectr. in fin. Ambassador Coll. Sch. of Bus., Pasadena 1975-78; lectr. fin. acctg. and auditing USC Sch. of Bus. 1978-80; mem. bd. dirs. Vista Hill Found., 1988-95; bd. dirs.: Vision Sciences, Inc. 1993–, Cable Healthcare 1995–, Sensor Medics 1994–; awards: "An Emerging Leader in Healthcare" The Healthcare Forum and Korn/Ferry Internat. 1988, "Up and Comer in Healthcare" Modern Healthcare/Am. Coll. of Healthcare Execs. 1989; mem: Am. Inst. CPAs, Calif. Soc. Public Accts., Hosp. Financial Mgmt. Assn., Financial Execs. Inst., Am. Coll. of Healthcare Execs.; nat. speaker and panelist on topics incl. Medical Liability, Future of Healthcare, Working Capital Loans, Proactive Strategies for Reduction in Malpractice Liability Costs, The Value of a Healthcare Alliance; Republican; R.Cath.; rec: skiing, jogging. Ofc: American Healthcare Systems 12730 High Bluff Dr 3d Flr San Diego 92130-2099

NYERGES, CHRISTOPHER J., writer, educator; b. Jan. 11, 1955, Pasadena; s. Frank and Marie N.; m. Dolores (organic gardener, owner Rainbow Garden Service, Los Angeles 1988–). Career: writer Wild Food Field Guide, L.A. Co. 1974; hiking instr. Pasadena City Coll. 1980, instr. Am. Indian religions City of Pasadena 1975, frequent lectr. on economic, ecological, Am. Indian, & political topics 1978; outdoor columnist Pasadena Star News, 1976-88, Glendale News Press, 1994-; feature columnist "Perspective" for Foothill Papers, L.A. Co. 1985-89; editor "Lament" Mensa, L.A. 1988-91; mem: NRA, WTI Inc.; author: Guide to Wild Foods, 1978, Wild Greens & Salads, 1979, Urban Wilderness, 1980, books in progress: Rotten Apple Report (re fraud factor in our economy), Shining Bear Chronicles (tchgs. of a modern day Shaman). Address: PO Box 41834 Los Angeles 90041

NYERGES, GILBERT, brokerage executive/commodity futures specialist; b. Feb. 27, 1944, Los Angeles; s. Frank Napolean and Marie T. (Jonke) N.; children: Joseph b. 1979, Chavon b. 1981, John b. 1983, James b. 1984, Charlean b.

1985, Justin b. 1987, Jason b. 1990; edn: BS fin., CSU Long Beach 1969. Career: commodity splst. Shearson Loeb Rhodes Hornblower, Beverly Hills 1974-80, Smith Barney, Beverly Hills 1980-82, Prudential Bache, Beverly Hills 1982-84, Paine Webber, Beverly Hills. 1984-88; v.p./commodities splst. Thomson McKinnon Securities Inc., L.A. 1988-91, Dean Witter, Valencia 1991–; guest lectr. UCLA 1985; awards: Pres.'s Council Shearson Loeb 1978, 79, 80, Pres.'s Club Prudential Bache 1982, 83, 84, Pacesetter Club Paine Webber 1984, 85, 86, 87; civic: Amer.-Philippine Assn. Newhall, Right to Life League, L.A. (bd. 1987); clubs: Ray Bradbury Appreciation Soc. (pres. 1970–), Rolling Stones West Coast Fan Club (dir. 1972–), L.A. Blues Club (v.p. 1974–); writer weekly column "Commodity Financial Recap", San Diego Union, 1980-84; baseball coach Valencia Parks & Recreation; Catholic; rec: baseball, sports, music. Ofc: Dean Witter 23827 Valencia Blvd Valencia 91355 Tel: 800/699-2455

OAKS, M. MARLENE, ordained minister; b. Mar. 30, 1940, Grove City, Pa.; d. Allen Roy and Alberta Bell (Pinner) Eakin; m. Lowell B. Chaney, July 30, 1963 (dec. 1977); children: Christopher Allen, Linda Michelle; grandchildren: Scott Nicholas Younger, Alexandra Nicole Younger, Naomi Grace Sanders, Nichole Cherrie Chaney; m. Harold G. Younger, Aug. 1978 (div. 1986); m. Gilbert E. Oaks, Aug. 3, 1987; edn: BA, CSU Los Angeles, 1972; ordained to ministry Ch. Religious Sci., 1986. Career: sch. tchr. Whittier Sch. Dist. 1972-74, Garden Grove Sch. Dist. 1974-78, instr. Fullerton Coll. 1974-75; founding minister Community Ch. of the Islands (now Ch. of Religious Sci.), Honolulu 1978-80; minister Ch. of Divine Sci., Pueblo, Colo. 1980-83; founding minister Ch. of Religious Sci., Palo Alto, Calif. 1983-86; minister Ch. of Religious Sci., Fullerton 1986-94, minister emeritus 1994–; founder, bd. of dirs. Awakening Oaks Found. 1990;second v.chmn./corp. sec. VCC International, Anaheim 1994–; founder, pres. La Vida Inst. 1994; workshop leader Religious Sci. Dist. Conv., San Jose, 1985, Internat. New Thought Alliance Conf., Las Vegas 1984, Calgary, Alb., Canada 1985, Wash. DC, 1988, Denver 1989 and Anaheim 1990, Golden Valley Unity Women's Advance, Mpls. 1986, 87, Qume Corp., San Jose 1985; del. Soviet and Am. Citizens Summit Conf. 1988, 89; pres. Soviet-Am. New Thought Initiatives 1991, chairperson conf. St. Petersburg 1992, Moscow 1992, weekly radio prog. Radio Moscow, The Philippines 1992–; founder Operation K.I.D.S. 1989, pres. SANTI 1991-94; presenter in SANTI Conf. 1992, 93, 94; guest workshop ldr. Ctr. for Life Enrichment 1990-92; speaker Comm. of Tartarstan 1993; mem: Fullerton Interfaith Ministerial Assn. (sec. treas. 1987-88), United Clergy of Religious Sci., Internat. New Thought Alliance (O.C. chpt. pres.), Soroptimists (chair com. internat. coop. and goodwill 1987-88), Kappa Delta Pi; author: 21 Seeds, Values Remembered, Old Time Religion is a Cult, 1985, Forgiveness and Beyond, 1985 revised edit. 1992), Stretch Marks on My Aura, 1987 (revised edit. 1995), Ten Core Concepts of Science of Mind, 1991, Beyond Addiction, 1989, Service, The Sure Path to Enlightenment, 1985, The Christmas in You, 1983 (revised edit. 1994), Ki Aikido, The Inner Martial Art, 1984, num. articles; Republican. Ofc: VCC International 1775 E Lincoln Ste 101 Anaheim 92805

O'BOYLE, SHEILA MARY, lawyer; b. Aug. 28, 1956, San Francisco; d. Frank Vincent and Eleanor (Rodenhausen) O'B.; m. Moshe Litman, Sept. 9, 1978; dau., Marissa Michelle; edn: BSBA in acctg., CSU Northridge, 1978; JD, Univ. of W. L.A., 1982; admitted Calif. Bar 1982. Career: auditor State of Calif. Dept. Corporations, Los Angeles 1979; acct. Transamerica Corp., L.A. 1978-79; sole practice atty., Simi Valley 1982–; awards: John Garfinkel award Univ. W.L.A. 1980, Am. Jurisprudence 1981; mem: ABA, Calif. Bar Assn., Univ. W.L.A. Alumni, AAUW/Simi Valley (dir. 1984-85, treas. 86-87), Simi Valley Rep. Women (v.p. ways & means 1987); Republican. Ofc: 2333 E Birchfield St Simi Valley 93065

O'BRIEN, DANIEL JOSEPH, probation executive; b. Sept. 20, 1927, Boston, Mass.; s. Michael J. and Johanna Anna (Moriarty) O'B.; m. Gloria C. Bryant, Apr. 23, 1949 (div.); children: Pamela F. b. 1950, Daniel F. b. 1953, Thomas J. 1954; edn: BS edn., Boston Univ. 1951. Career: supervising dep. probation ofcr. L.A. Co., Los Angeles 1951-95 (ret.); mem: Am. Legion, Irish-Am. Club; mil: sgt. AUS 1946-47; R.Cath.; rec: sports. Res: 5820 Woodman Ave Van Nuys 91401

O'BRIEN, JOHN ROGER, lawyer; b. Oct. 10, 1943, Omaha, Nebr.; s. James Patrick and Marie T. (Chleborad) O'B.; m. Cheryl Anne Alvey, June 24, 1967; children: Kerri b. 1968, Laurie b. 1971, Shauna b. 1978; edn: BA econ., Creighton Univ. 1965; JD, UCSF Hastings Coll. 1968. Career: capt. U.S. Army Judge Advocate General's Corps, 1969-73; atty., assoc. Bancroft Avery & McAlister, San Francisco 1973-75; assoc. atty., ptnr. Spridgen Barrett Achor Luckhardt Anderson James & Zeigler, Santa Rosa 1975-81; ptnr. O'Brien Watters Davis & McCullough 1981–; legal advy. com. Am. Cancer Soc. 1986; honors: Thurston Hon. Soc., Order of Coif; mem: Sonoma Co. Bar Assn., Calif. St. Bar Assn., Am. Bar Assn., Sonoma Co. Comm. Found. (pres. 1993-95), Am. Cancer Soc. (dir. Sonoma Co. 1981–), Holy Spirit Mens Club (pres. 1988-89), Redwood Empire Cursillos, Redwood Empire Estate Planning Council, Sunrise Club; article pub. in profl. jour., 1968; Democrat; Cath.; rec: tennis, skiing, running. Ofc: O'Brien Watters Davis & McCullough POB 3759 Santa Rosa 95402

O'BRIEN, PHILIP MICHAEL, college librarian; b. Jan. 5, 1940, Albion, Nebr.; s. Lawrence Joseph and Mary Helen (Ruplinger) O'B.; children: Tara Jennine b. 1973, Kirsten Ann b. 1977; m.2d. Ann Johnson Topjon, Mar. 10, 1990; edn: BA, Whittier Coll., 1961; MSLS, USC, 1962; PhD, USC, 1974. Career: asst. librarian Whittier Coll., 1962-66, Special Collections librarian 1970-74, coll. librarian, 1974–; librarian soc. sci. dept. Chico State Coll. 1966-67; librarian US Army Europe, Germany 1967-70; awards: Whittier Coll. Athletic Hall of Fame 1988, Besterman Medal, Library Assn. (GB) London 1989; mem: Am. Library Assn. 1974–, Ronce & Coffin Club 1977–, Los Compadres con Libros 1975–, Am. Coll. & Res. Libraries 1974–, 1195 Club (bd. dirs. 1992); author: T.E. Lawrence & Fine Printing, 1980, T.E. Lawrence: a Bibliography, 1988, contbr. articles in The T.E. Lawrence Puzzle, 1984, Explorations in Doughty's Arabia Deserta, 1987, Sweetbriar Gazette (Spring 88); rec: book collecting, bicycling. Ofc: Wardman Library Whittier College, Whittier 90608

OCHOA, EDUARDO M., university professor, economist; b. Nov. 18, 1950, Buenos Aires, Argentina; s. Ernesto A. and Violeta (Kimelman) O.; m. Holly D. Byers, Dec. 20, 1970; children: Michael b. 1982, Eric b. 1985; edn: BA, Reed Coll. 1973; MS, Columbia Univ. 1976; MA, New Sch. for Social Research N.Y. 1981; PhD, 1984. Career: asst. engr. Gibbs & Hill Inc., N.Y.C. 1976-77; assoc. engr. Ebasco Services Inc. 1977-80; instr. St. Univ. N.Y., Old Westbury 1980-81; lectr. CSU Fresno 1981-84; prof. CSU Los Angeles 1984–, chair, dept. of econ. and statistics 1990-94, assoc. dean, Sch. of Bus. & Econ. 1994–; cons. economist Lorente & Asociados (Barcelona) 1990-94, Cordoba Corp., L.A. 1992-94, Spray Gould & Bowers, L.A. 1987–; Orange Co., Santa Ana 1987; awards: New Sch. Bus. Res. Edith Hansen Outstanding Dissertation 1984, Econ. Found. Rasmussen Prize Essay 1980, NSF Project Dir. 1987; mem: Am. Econ. Assn.; articles pub. in profl. jours.; Democrat. Ofc: California State University 5151 State University Dr Los Angeles 90032

O'CONNOR, GREGORY MICHAEL, optometrist; b. April 8, 1952, South Bend, Ind.; s. Joseph Bernard and Irene Ellen (Kearney) O'C.; m. Patricia Ranville, Dec. 30, 1977, div. Dec. 1991; edn: BS, Univ. of Mich. 1973; BS, Ill. Coll. of Optometry 1975, OD, 1978; Reg. Optometrist, Calif. 1979. Career: staff optometrist Chicago Eye, Ear, Nose & Throat Hosp., Chicago, Ill. 1977-78; chief of optometry svc., Naval Reg. Med. Ctr., Barstow 1978-81; pvt. practice, Malibu 1981–; tchg. asst. Ill. Coll. of Optometry 1977-78; awards: State of Mich. Undergrad. Scholarship, Univ. of Mich. Honors Convocation, Armed Forces Health Professions Scholarship, Tomb & Key, Beta Sigma Kappa; mem: Am. and Calif. Optometric Assns., Mojave Desert and L.A. Co. Optometric Socs., Malibu C.of C. (bd. 1988–, pres. 1992); clubs: Optimist (Malibu dir. 1982, pres.), Rotary Intl. (Barstow dir. 1979-80), Big Ten Club; works: Cataractogenesis and Exposure to Non-ionizing Radiation Sources, Dept. of Defense Study 1979; mil: lt. USN 1976-81, Letter of Commendation.; Republican; Roman Cath.; rec: running (finished Los Angeles Marathon 1988, 89, 90, 91, 92, 93, 95), writing, hiking, woodworking. Res: 5785 Oak Bank Trail, # 101 Agoura Hills 91301 Ofc: 3840 Cross Creek Rd. Malibu 90265

O'DER, JOHN T., real estate broker, retired naval aviator; b. Oct. 31, 1929, Louisville, Ky.; s. John Thomas and Thelma Francis (Jarvis) O.; m. Carol Ann Holton, June 2, 1956; children: Michael b. 1957, Kathleen b. 1960; edn: BA, UC Los Angeles, 1953; USN Postgrad. Sch., Monterey 1969-70; lic. R.E. broker Calif., 1977. Career: naval aviator, served to Cdr. US Navy 1953-74, decorated Bronze Star Medal with Combat "V" Vietnam 1968-69, (2) Air Medals Vietnam 1968-69, Meritorious Service Medal CINCPAC Staff Hawaii 1974; sales agt. Art Leitch Realtors, San Diego 1974-75; broker/mgr. Red Carpet Realtors, S.D. 1975-76; broker/owner John O'Der Realty, 1977–; bus. owner Encinitas Car Wash, Encinitas 1977-85; mem: Nat. Assn. Realtors, Calif. Assn. Realtors, San Diego Assn. Realtors, Retired Ofcrs. Assn., Navy League S.D., Theta Xi Frat. (1947–); civic: Green Valley Highlands Assn. (pres. 1988), Poway Planning & Devel. Pgm. 1976-77; installed first 98% water reclamation system in an automatic car wash in So. Calif., 1977; Republican; Presbyterian; rec: golf, travel. Res: 10918 Rim Road Escondido 92026

O'DOWD, DONALD DAVY, higher education consultant; b. Jan. 23, 1927, Manchester, N.H.; s. Hugh Davy and Laura (Morin) O'D.; m. Janet Louise Fithian, Aug. 23, 1953; children: Daniel b. 1955, Diane b. 1957, James b. 1959, John b. 1962; edn: BA, Dartmouth Coll., 1951; MA, Harvard Univ., 1955, PhD, 1957. Career: asst. prof. Wesleyan Univ., Middletown, Ct. 1955-60; provost and prof. Oakland Univ., Rochester, Mich. 1960-70, pres. 1970-79; exec. v.chancellor State Univ. of N.Y., Albany 1980-84; pres. Univ. of Alaska, Fairbanks 1984-90; chmn. U.S. Arctic Research Commn., W.D.C. 1991–; sr. cons. Assn. of Governing Bds. Univs. and Colls., W.D.C., 1991; cons. Greenhills Software Inc., Santa Barbara 1991–; honors: D.Litt. (Hon.) Oakland Univ. 1980, Presdl. medal Dartmouth Coll. 1991; mem. AAAS 1955–, Am. Psychol. Assn. 1955–, Phi Beta Kappa 1950–, Sigma Xi 1957–; mil: t5 US Army 1945-47. Res: 1550 La Vista Del Oceano Santa Barbara 93109

O'DWYER, MYLES MICHAEL, financial executive; b. Feb. 16, 1952, San Rafael; s. John Stephan and Nora Marie (Costello) O'D.; m. Laurie Lou Larson, March 20, 1982; children: Erin Larson b. 1984, Emily Lou b. 1986, Victoria May (Tory) and Teresa Nora (Tess) b. 1993; edn: BS, UC Berkeley 1974; MBA, USC 1975. Career: asst. trust investment ofcr. Crocker Nat. Bank, San Francisco 1975-78; dir. strategic planning Dart & Kraft Inc., Northbrook, Ill. 1978-84; v.p. fin. American Tng. Internat., Los Angeles 1984-86; v.p., mgr. First Interstate Bank, Ltd. 1986-87; dir. fin. planning Ashton-Tate Corp., Torrance 1987-88; CFO Thrislington Cubicles, Inc., Sun Valley 1989-90; dir. TQM and adminstrn. Hamilton Hallmark, Culver City 1990-94; sr. v.p. Bus. Planning, McKesson Drug Co., San Francisco 1994–; vis. lectr. Loyola Marymount Univ., L.A. 1988-94; dir. Thrislington Cubicles Inc. 1989-90; mem: So. Calif. Planners Assn., Univ. Calif. Alumni Assn., Univ. Calif. Bus.Sch. Alumni Assn.; Republican; R.Cath. (Am. Martyrs' Fair spl. events chmn. 1988-93); rec: skiing, water skiing, automobile restoration. Res: 55 Meadowood Dr Larkspur 94939 Ofc: McKesson Drug Co One Post St San Francisco 94104

OFFENHAUSER, BOB RAY, architect; b. Feb. 8, 1927, Los Angeles; s. O.D. and Laura (Putney) O.; m. Katherine, Apr. 17, 1958; 1 son, Madison b. 1960; edn: B.Arch., USC, 1952; Calif. reg. architect, AIA, Am. Inst. Arch. Career: architect prin. Bob Ray Offenhauser & Assocs., archtl. and interior design co., 1982–, incorporated, now pres. Offenhauser Associates Inc., also Offenhauser Decorating Corp.; mem. Architl. Guild USC, mem./founder L.A. Music Center, New Mus. of Contemporary Art, L.A. County Art Museum, Fellows of Contemporary Art, Frat. of Friends L.A. Music Center; clubs: Valley Hunt (Pasadena), Men's Garden (L.A.); mil: USCG; Republican; rec: gardening. Res: 445 Columbia St South Pasadena 91030 Ofc: Offenhauser Associates Inc., 3800 W Alameda Ave Ste 1190 Burbank 91505

OGAWA, AKINORI, network cabling company executive; b. Sept. 11, 1958, Taiwan; s. Joji and Ryo-Ing (Chou) O.; m. Sheng-Mei Hsiung, Feb. 19, 1989; edn: BS civil engring., Hosei Univ. Japan; lic. R.E. broker, Calif.. Career: supr. Sumitomo Constrn., Tokyo, Japan 1981-86; sales mgr. Kansai Internat., Torrance 1986-88; dir. Project Seven 1988–; dist. mgr. Golden Calif. Fin., Monterey Park 1987–; asst. mgr. R.E. devel., Yaohan U.S.A. Corp. 1993-94; v.p. internat. sales, Tri-Net Technology Inc., Walnut 1994-; mem: Long Beach Bd. Realtors. Res: 422 N Nicholson Ave #C Monterey Park 91754

OGAWA, GARY SHIGEMI, pharmacist, clinical pharmacy educator; b. July 15, 1951, Honolulu, Hawaii; s. Shigeo and Jane Misumi (Kitaoka) O.; m. Elaine, Aug. 16, 1975; children: Rachel b. 1981, Michelle b. 1983; edn: BS biology, Univ. Hawaii Honolulu 1973; grad., USC, 1974; PharmD, 1979. Career: pharm. resident UCSF Sch. Pharm., San Francisco 1979-80; clin. pharmacist Cedars-Sinai Med. Center, Los Angeles 1980-83; Norris Cancer Hosp. 1983-86, asst. dir. pharm. 1986–; asst. prof. USC Sch. Pharm. 1983–; honors: Am. Cancer Soc. Hon. Citation 1987, Rho Chi, Nat. Hon. Soc.; mem: Am. Cancer Soc. (pharma-.cists edn. com. 1985), Am. Soc. Hosp. Pharmacists, Calif. Soc. Hosp. Pharmacists, So. Calif. A.S.P.E.N. (bd. dirs.); num. articles pub. in profl. jours., 1979-88. Ofc: Univ. So. California Norris Cancer Hospital 1441 Eastlake Ave Los Angeles 90033-0804

OGDEN, CHARLES WILLIAM, college administrator, minister; b. Dec. 30, 1927, Brush, Colo.; s. Lloyd Alfred and Doris Irene (Ream) O.; m. Mary Elizabeth Burks, March 3, 1950; children: Karla b. 1953, Kevin b. 1956; edn: BA, Pasadena Coll. 1949. Career: assoc. pastor Ch. of Nazarene, Lincoln, Neb. 1949-51, pastor, Dodson, Tx. 1951-52, San Angelo, Tx. 1952-58, Portland, Oreg. 1958-66, Whittier 1966-85; adminstrv. asst. Nazarene Regional Office, Orange 1986-87; alumni dir., dir. of annual fund Point Loma Nazarene Coll., San Diego 1988-94 (ret.); honors: Who's Who in Am. Colls. & Univs. 1948, 49; mem: Rotary Club, Exchange Club (chaplain 1981-85); writer Young Peoples Jour, 1955; Republican; Ch. of Nazarene; rec: antiques. Res: 1195 Lamoree Rd San Marcos 92069 Ofc: Point Lomma Nazarene College 3900 Lomaland Dr San Diego 92106

OGDEN, JEAN LUCILLE, medical marketing professional; b. Jan. 20, 1950, Chgo.; d. George William and Mary Elizabeth (MacKenzie) Anderson; m. Michael Jude Ogden, Aug. 27, 1977 (div. 1983); edn: BA (hons.) UC Santa Barbara, 1971. Career: sales rep. Am. Hosp. Supply Co., Irvine 1975-77, Abbott Labs, HPD, Los Angeles 1977-78; Gillette Co., Albuquerque 1978-79, Unitek Corp., Monrovia 1979-86, Nat. Patent Dental Products, San Diego 1986-87; area mgr. Branson Ultrasonics Corp., Los Angeles 1987–; honors: Outstanding Young Women Am. (1984); mem: Med. Mktg. Assn., Salesmasters Albuquerque, Soroptimists Internat. (chpt. ofcr. 1983-86), Alpha Phi Sor. (House corp. bd. Long Beach chpt. 1974-75, chpt. advisor 1975-76); civic: Nat. Multiple Sclerosis Soc. (San Diego co-chair 1983–), Am. Cancer Soc. (1985–), Zool. Soc. San Diego (1984-85); Republican. Res: 2634 Levante St Rancho La Costa 92009 Ofc: Branson Ultrasonics Corp. 12955 E Perez Pl City of Industry 91746

OGG, WILSON REID, poet and lyricist, graphic artist, publisher, curator, lawyer, retired administrv. law judge, educator; b. Feb. 26, 1928, Alhambra; s. James Brooks and Mary Newton (Wilson) O.; edn: BA, UC Berkeley 1949; JD, UCB Boalt Hall Sch. of Law 1952; admitted Calif. State Bar 1955, lic. R.E. Broker 1974, Calif. Comm. Colls. tchg. creds., law, real estate and social scis. 1976. Career: psychology instr. 25th Station Hosp., Taegu, Korea, also English instr. Taegu English Language Inst. 1953; pvt. practice of law 1955-78; arbitrator

Am. Arb. Assn. 1963–; sr. ed. Continuing Edn. of the Bar, Univ. of Calif. 1958-63; secty., bd. trustees First Unitarian Ch. of Berkeley 1957-58; pres. Calif. Soc. of Psychical Study 1963-65; treas. The World Univ. 1977-79; dir. admissions The Internat. Soc. for Philosophical Enquiry 1981-84; pub. Pinebrook Press, 1988–; poet, curator-in-residence Pinebrook, 1964–; honors: Cultural Doctorate in Philosophy of Law, The World Univ. Roundtable 1984; Life patron Internat. Biographical Assn. and dep. dir. Internat. Biographical Centre, dep. gov. Am. Biographical Inst. Research Assn.-awarded Grand Amb. of Achievement. (ABIRA), Golden Acad. for lifetime achievement. (ABI 1991), Most Admired Man of Decade (ABI 1992), The Internat. Honors Cup (ABI 1992), 20th Century Award for Achievement (IBC 1992), Internat. Man of Yr. 1991-92 (IBC), Men's Inner Circle of Achievement Am. Bio. Inst. 1993; mem: State Bar of Calif., Am. Arb. Assn., World Future Soc. (proff. mem.), Bar Assn. of S.F., City Commons Club of Berkeley, Am. Soc. for Psychical Research, Inst. of Noetic Scis., The Wisdom Soc., AAAS, Parapsychol. Assn., Berkeley Archtl. Heritage Assn., Internat. Soc. of Poets (life), Artists Embassy Internat., World Acad. of Arts And Culture, The World Literary Acad., Commonwealth Club, Town Hall of Calif., Faculty Club (UCB), Elks, Masonic Orders, Am. Legion, VFW, Amvets, Mensa, Triple Nine Soc.; sr. ed. var. law handbooks (UC Regents, 1958-63), articles in Internat. Soc. of Philosophical Enquiry Jour. 1981-84, poems pub. in The Best Poems of the '90's (Nat. Lib. of Poetry, 1992), Disting. Poets of Am. (The Nat. Lib. of Poets 1993), Windows of the Soul (Nat. Lib. Poetry 1996), Best Poems of 1996 (Nat. Lib. Poetry), other poetry anthologies, Am. Poetry Assn. 1987; mil: cpl. AUS 1952-54, commendation.; Libertarian; Unitarian; rec: theater, horticulture, archtl. design. Address: Pinebrook at Bret Harte Way, 1104 Keith Ave Berkeley 94708-1607 E-Mail: Pinebrook @ incl.com,

OGROD, EUGENE STANLEY, physician; b. July 7, 1944; m. Jean L. Harrison, Sept. 7, 1969; edn: AB, chem. and psychol., TCU 1965; MD, Stanford Univ. Med. Sch. 1970; MA, poli. sci., Stanford Univ. 1970; JD, UC Davis, King Hall Law Sch. 1978. Career: internship Presbyn. Univ. of Pa. Med. Ctr. 1970-71; residency UC Davis Med. Ctr. 1972-74; pvt. practice, Sacramento 1974-78; solo practice in assn. with R.J. Forster, M.D., 1978-82; Sutter Med. Group 1983– (founder 1983, bd. dirs. and v.p. 1983-88, chair, prog. devel. com. 1988-90, planning & fin. com. Sutter Med. Found. 1992-93); clin instr. internal medicine UC Davis Med. Sch. 1987–, clin. instr. family practice 1975-79; Patient Care bd. of editors 1987–; indep. med. examiner and corp. mem. Workers' Compensation Appeals Bd., St. of Calif. 1986–, qualified med. examiner 1991–; staff mem: Sutter Gen., Sutter Mem., and Mercy Gen. Hosps., Sacto.; cons. med. dir. Am. Gen. Group Inc., Am. Health Network, We. Region 1985-86; tech. adv. internal medicine, Harvard/HCFA/AMA, RVS Study 1986-90; physician adv. Blue Shield of Calif. 1988-89, corp. mem. 1988-90; physician cons. Occupational Urgent Care Health, Inc. 1989-91; Physician Payment Review Commn. CPT Advy. Panel 1989-90; awards: 1st Annual Ben H. Read award Public Health League of Calif. 1974, Young Internist of Yr., Am. Soc. of Internal Medicine 1982, Disting. Practitioner, Nat. Academies of Practice 1994; mem: AMA 1972– (mem The Study of the Fedn. 1994–, Res. Subcom. of RUC 1992–, rep. to RUC 1991–, rep. to Practice Parameters Partnership 1991-92, House of Delegates 1982–, other coms.), Am. Soc. of Internal Medicine (pres. 1991-92, bd. trustees 1985-93, fin. com. 1989-90, other coms. and task forces 1976-88), IMCARE (bd. trustees), Federated Council of Internal Medicine 1990-93 (steering com. 1993), CMA 1972– (pres. 1995-96, pres. elect 1994-95, bd. trustees: chair 1992-94, vice chair 1990-92, exec. com. 1990–, trustee Dist. XI 1988–, Commn. of State Legis. 1981-85, 90–, fin. com. and nominations com. 1989, num. other coms.), Audio Digest Found. (bd. dirs. 1991–), Calif. Poli. Action Com. (bd. dirs. 1991–, exec. com. 1992–), Calif. Med. Edn. and Res. Found. (bd. dirs. 1991–), Sacto.-El Dorado Co. Med. Soc. 1972– (pres. 1986, bd. dirs. 1982-87), Sacto. Soc. of Internal Medicine (pres. 1984), Calif. Soc. of Internal Medicine (pres. 1986-87, legis. com. 1978-85, chair 1981-85), Am. Coll. of Legal Medicine 1979– (fellow), Am. Coll. of Physician Execs., Am. Coll. of Physicians (fellow, N. Calif. Govs. advy. com. 1992-93), Am. Cancer Soc. Sacto. Unit, Golden Empire Health Sys. Agy., Nat. Health Svc. Corps, Bd. of Med. Quality Assurance-St. of Calif. Jurisprudence Sect., Calif. Assn. of Hosps. and Health Sys., Calif. Coalition for Childhood Immunization 1995, Jackson Hole Group 1995, Knights of the Vine 1973–, Monterey Bay Aquarium (charter), Friends of Mus. of Modern Latin Am. Art, WDC, Mus. of No. Ariz. Assocs. 1974–, Am. Inst. of Am. Indian Arts, Santa Fe, NM; author: contbr 15+ articles to profl. jours./assns., 1973-90. Res: PO Box 19275 Sacramento 95819 Ofc: 1020 29th St Ste 680 Sacramento 95816

OH, JANG OK, microbiologist-virologist; b. Jan. 15, 1927, Seoul, South Korea; s. Ki Yang and Moo-Duk (Lee) Oh; m. Won Yung Hyun, PhD, June 18, 1955; children: Dennis, MD, PhD b. 1963; edn: MD, Yonsei Univ. Med. Sch., Seoul 1948; PhD, Univ. Washington, Seattle 1960. Career: pathologist Carle Clinic Hosp., Urbana, Ill. 1956-57; res. instr. Univ. Wash., Seattle 1957-61; asst. prof. Univ. Brit. Col. Med. Sch., B.C., Can. 1961-66; res. microbiologist Univ. Calif., San Francisco 1966–, assoc. dir. Proctor Found., UCSF, 1985–; cons. NIH, USPHS, Bethesda, Md. 1979-83, 90-92; awards: NIH res. grantee 1970–, grantee Nat. Soc. Prevention of Blindness, USA 1974, medical exhibit award Am. Med. Assn. 1977, Lederle Med. Faculty Award, Lederle Pharmaceuticals USA 1963; mem: Am. Assn. of Pathologists 1965–, Am. Soc. of Microbiology 1958–, Assn. for Rsrch. in Vision & Ophthalmology (1970–, com. chair 82-85);

author articles in med. books and jours., editor monographs: Herpetic Eye Infections (1976), Intl. Conf. on Herpetic Eye Diseases (1987); Christian; rec: reading, gardening, carpentry. Ofc: Univ. Calif., San Francisco 94143-0412

O'HANLON, GEORGE ALAN, advertising agency executive, author; b. Mar. 29, 1955, San Jose, Calif.; s. Charles Adelbert and Dolores (Palacios) O'H.; m. Laura Colin, Aug. 9, 1974; children: Michele b. 1974, Bianca b. 1977, Sahara b. 1979, Vanesa b. 1981, Shante b. 1984; edn: BS internat. mktg., Univ. Mexico, 1976; BA advt., San Jose St. Univ., 1980. Career: mktg. mgr. Backgammon, S.A., Mexico, D.F. 1976-79; v.p. Advt/Mktg Systems, Santa Clara, Calif. 1980-87; pres., dir. and chief ops. ofcr. AD&MS (subs. of Shin-Etsu, Tokyo, Japan), Union City, Calif. 1987-92; cons. dir. On Target, San Jose 1992–; mem: Business/Profl. Advtg. Assn. (award for excellence B/PAA, L.A. 1988), Western Art Directors Club (show award, S.F. 1988), San Jose Met. C.of C.; author 4 books: How to Get Full Value from Advertising Sales Leads, 1988, Effective Sales Literature for Business Marketers, 1989, How to Increase Profits with Business Direct Mail, 1990, Visual Communication, 1991; Jehovah's Witness. Ofc: 1276 Lincoln Ave San Jose 95125

O'HARE, SANDRA FERNANDEZ, educator; b. Mar. 19, 1941, N.Y.C.; d. Ricardo Enrique and Rosario de Los Angeles (Arenas) Fernandez; m. S. James O'Hare, Oct. 12, 1963; children: James, Richard, Michael, Christopher; edn: BA, Marymount Coll., 1962; MA, Univ. San Francisco, 1980. Career: instr. adult edn., Guam, 1964-66, Spanish Speaking Ctr., Harrisburg, Pa. 1977-79; tchr. Colegio Salesiano, Rota, Spain 1973, 84, Alisal Sch. Dist., Salinas, Calif. 1979-81, Liberty Sch., Petaluma, Calif. 1981-85, Cinnabar Sch., Petaluma 1985–; S.D.B. Fellow Johns Hopkins Univ.; instr. Santa Rosa Jr. Coll., 1982-83; instr. Chapman Univ. 1994–; mem. math. curriculum com. Sonoma County Office of Edn., Santa Rosa 1988; 1990; participant Summer Sci. Connections Inst., Sonoma State Univ. 1994; mem: Calif. Assn. Bilingual Educators, NEA, AAUW (chair ednl. foundations pgm. 1985-86), Hispano-Americano Club Petaluma (pres. 1987-89); civic vol. Am. Red Cross 1975, Boy Scouts Am. 1971, 74, 83; translator: Isabel la Catolica, 1962; R.Cath. Res: 1289 Glenwood Dr Petaluma 94954

O'KEEFE, MICHAEL ADRIAN, physicist; b. Sept. 8, 1942, Melbourne, Australia; s. Peter Francis and Nadezhda O'K.; m. Dianne Patricia Fletcher, June 15, 1976; children: Eleanor b. 1988, Carlene b. 1990; edn: dipl. in physics, RMIT, Melbourne, Aust. 1965; BS physics (First Class hons.), Univ. Melbourne, 1970, PhD physics, 1975. Career: tech. asst. CSIRO, Melbourne 1961-69, exptl. ofcr. 1969-75; res. assoc. Ariz. State Univ., Tempe 1976-79; sr. res. assoc. Cambridge Univ., U.K. 1979-83; staff scientist Univ. Calif./Lawrence Berkeley Lab., 1983-94; acting head, Nat. Ctr. for Electron Microscopy/LBL 1994–; cons. Xerox, Palo Alto 1984–, Shell, Houston 1985-87; recipient cert. of merit Univ. Calif./LBL, Berkeley 1991; Fellow Royal Microscopical Soc. 1983–, mem. Australian Inst. of Physics 1970–, Microscopy Soc. of Am. 1976–; inventor: EREM (pat. 1992); publs: 100+ sci. papers, 1972–, editor conf. proceedings: TMS, 1990, 10th Pfefferkorn, 1991; co-editor Jour. of the Microscopy Soc. of Am. Ofc: Univ. Calif. LBL 1 Cyclotron Rd Berkeley 94720

OKERLUND, ARLENE NAYLOR, university professor and administrator; b. Oct. 13, 1938, Emmitsburg, Md.; d. George Wilbur and Ruth Opal (Sensenbaugh) Naylor; m. Michael Dennis Okerlund, June 6, 1959 (div. 1983); 1 dau., Linda Susan b. 1963; edn: BA, Univ. Md. 1960; PhD, UCSD 1969. Career: sci. instr. Mercy Hosp., Baltimore, Md. 1959-63; tchg. asst. UCSD 1963-69; prof. English, San Jose St. Univ. 1969-, dean of humanities and arts 1980-86, acad. v.p. 1986-93; cons. Ednl. Testing Service, Berkeley 1975-80; splst. reader Modern Language Assn., N.Y. 1970-80; co-chair Instr. Tchg. & Learning, CSU 1987–; awards: YWCA Tribute to Women & Industry 1986; mem: Philological Assn. Pacific Coast (secty., treas. 1975-78), World Forum of Silicon Valley (bd. dirs. 1988-), Am. Beethoven Soc. (bd. dirs. 1984–); founding ed. San Jose Studies jour., 1975-80, num. articles pub. in profl. jours., 1970; rec: hiking, working out, gardening. Ofc: San Jose State University San Jose 95192

OKIMOTO, DANIEL IWAO, college professor; b. Aug. 14, 1942, Santa Anita; s. Tameichi and Kirie (Kumagai) O.; m. Nancy Elizabeth Miller, Jan. 27, 1970; children: Saya b. 1971, Kevin b. 1977; edn: BA, Princeton Univ. 1965; MA, Harvard Univ. 1967; PhD, Mich. Univ. 1977. Career: asst. prof. Stanford Univ. 1977-84, assoc. prof. 1984-92, prof. 1992–; advy. council Dept. Politics, Princeton Univ. 1988–; overseas bd. Research Inst. Ministry of Internat. Trade & Industry, Tokyo, Japan 1988–; cons. Aspen Inst., Colo. 1978-82; awards: Harvard Univ. Nat. Language fellow 1965-67, Aspen Inst. Mellon fellow 1976-77, Hoover Inst. nat. fellow 1979-80; mem: Asia Pacific Res. Ctr. (co-dir. 1980–), Council on Fgn. Rels., Palo Alto Little League (coach, mgr. 1988-89); author: Between MITI & Market, 1989; co-ed.: The Political Econ. of Japan, 1988, Inside Japanese System, 1988, Semiconductor Competition & Nat. Security, 1988; Democrat; Prot.; rec: bicycling, sports. Ofc: Asia Pacific Research Center Stanford University Stanford 94305-6055

OLAH, GEORGE ANDREW, chemist, educator, Nobel Prize winner; b. May 22, 1927, Budapest, Hungary; came to U.S. 1964, naturalized 1970; s. Julius and Magda (Rasznai) O; m. Judith Agnes Lengyel, July 9, 1949; children: George

John, Ronald Peter; edn: PhD, Tech. Univ. Budapest 1949, hon. degree 1989; DSc honoris causa, Univ. Durham 1988, Univ. Munich 1990. Career: mem. faculty Tech. Univ. Budapest 1949-54; assoc. dir. Cen. Chem. Res. Inst., Hungarian Acad. Scis.1954-56; res. scientist Dow Chem. Can. Ltd. 1957-64, Dow Chem. Co., Framingham, Mass. 1964-65; prof. chemistry Case Western Reserve Univ., Cleveland, Ohio 1965-69, C.F. Mabery prof. res. 1969-77; Donald P. and Katherine B. Loker disting. prof. chemistry, dir. Hydrocarbon Res. Inst., Univ. So. Calif., L.A. 1977–; vis. prof. chemistry Ohio State Univ. 1963, Univ. Heidelberg, Germany 1965, Univ. Colo. 1969, Swiss Fed. Inst. Tech. 1972, Univ. Munich 1973, Univ. London 1973-79, L. Pasteur Univ., Strasbourg 1974, Univ. Paris 1981; hon. vis. lectr. Univ. London 1981; cons. to industry; awards: Leo Hendrik Baekeland award N.J. sect. Am. Chem. Soc. 1966, Morley medal Cleveland sect. 1970, Alexander von Humboldt Sr. U.S. Scientist award 1979, Pioneer of Chemistry award Am. Inst. Chemists 1993, Nobel Prize in Chemistry (sole winner), Royal Swedish Acad. of Scis., Stockholm 1994; Fellow AAAS, Chem. Inst. Can.; mem: NAS, Italian NAS, European Acad. Arts, Scis. and Humanities, Italy Chem. Soc. (hon.), Hungarian Acad. Sci. (hon.), Am. Chem. Soc. (award petroleum chemistry 1964, award Synthetic organic chemistry 1979, Roger Adams award in organic chemistry 1989), German Chem. Soc., British Chem. Soc. (Centenary lectr. 1978), Swiss Chem. Soc., Sigma Xi; author: Friedel-Crafts Reactions, Vols. I-IV, 1963-64, (with P. Schleyer) Carbonium Ions, Vols. I-V, 1969-76, Friedel-Crafts Chemistry, 1973, Carbocations and Electrophilic Reactions, 1973, Halonium Ions, 1975, (with G.K.S. Prakash and J. Somer) Superacids, 1984, (with Prakash, R.E. Williams, L.D. Field and K. Wade) Hypercarbon Chemistry, 1987, (with R. Malthotra and S.C. Narang) Nitration, 1989, Cage Hydrocarbons, 1990, (with Wade and Williams) Electron Deficient Boron and Carbon Clusters, 1991, (with Chambers and Prakash) Synthetic Fluorine Chemistry, 1992, also chpts. in books, numerous papers in field; patentee in field (85 patents from 7 countries, including 4 for the transformation of natural gas into the type of hydrocarbons used in gasoline). Res: 2252 Gloaming Way Beverly Hills 90210-1717 Ofc: University of Southern California Dept. Chemistry Los Angeles 90007

OLDFIELD, A. BARNEY, writer, radio commentator, specialist in international relations; b. Dec. 18, 1909, Tecumseh, Nebr.; s. Adam William and Anna Ota (Fink) O.; m. Vada Margaret Kinman, May 6, 1935; edn: AB, Univ. Nebraska, Lincoln 1933. Career: columnist, feature writer Journal, Lincoln, Nebr. 1932-40; publicist Warner Bros. Studio, Burbank, Calif. 1946-47; corporate dir. internat. relations (77 countries) Litton Inds., Beverly Hills 1963-89; adj. prof. Pepperdine Univ., Malibu 1975-81; mil: ROTC commission, June 6, 1932, Univ. of Nebr.; served thru ranks to lt. col. US Army WW II, ETO 1940-45, Col. Reg., USAF, US Air Force 1947-62: worldwide, Korea, first newspaperman to become a paratrooper in early Class 23; decorated Legion of Merit USAF No. Am. Aerospace Def. Command 1962; founder/treas. Radio & TV News Dirs. Found. 1967–; founder/sec.treas. Found. of the Americas for the Handicapped, WDC; founder Aviation/Space Writers Found., WDC 1977-84; bd. mem., trustee Triple L Youth Ranch, Center, Colo. 1978-88; trustee USAF Museum and mem. bd. of nom. Aviation Hall of Fame, Dayton, Oh.; honors: humanitarian award Am. Res. & Med. Svs. Anaheim 1978, disting. svc. Radio & TV News Dirs. Assn. 1978, disting. svc. Aviation/Space Writers Assn., inducted Hall of Champions, Invent America (US Patent Model Found.) Alexandria, Va. 1989, disting. Nebraskalander of year, Lincoln, Nebr. 1983, HDL (Hon.) Univ. Nebr. (5/9/92), Veterans of Fgn. Wars "VFW Distinguished Citizen" 1992, RTNDA established Col. Barney Oldfield Disting. Service Award in his honor 1994; mem: Overseas Press Club of Am. 1962–, Gr. LA Press Club 1963–, Radio & TV News Dirs. Assn. 1949–, Radio & TV News Assn. So. Calif. 1964–, Writers Guild Am./West 1964–, Armed Forces Bdcstrs. Assn. 1970–, AF Assn. (life), Navy League (life); author: Never a Shot in Anger (now in 3d printing); (novel) Operation Narcissus (repub. 1991); Those Wonderful Men in the Cactus Starfighter Squadron (2-vol. set); contbr. to collections: Yanks Meet Reds; Sale I Made Which Did Most For Me; (script) Road to Berlin, for Walter Cronkite's 20th Century. Republican; Prot.; avocation: philanthropy, has estab. 250+ scholarships, awards the George Foreman scholarship annually. Ofc: PO Box 1855 Beverly Hills 90213

OLDHAM, MAXINE JERNIGAN, realtor; b. Oct. 13, 1923, Whittier; d. John K. and Lela H. (Mears) Jernigan; m. Laurance Oldham, Oct. 28, 1941; children: John Laurence, b. 1942; edn: UC San Diego 1951-80; Western State Univ. 1976-77; LaSalle Ext. 1977-78; AA, San Diego City Coll. 1974. Desig: GRI, Grad. Realtors Inst., CAR 1978. Career: Pacific Telephone, S.D. 1952-57; US Civil Svc. Commn., US Naval Aux., Air Sta., Brown Field, Chula Vista 1957-58; San Diego Bd. of Edn., 1958-59; real estate sales 1966–; realtor Shelter Island Realty, S.D. 1977–; awards: Outstanding achiev. public speaking Dale Carnegie 1988; mem: Nat., Calif. Assns. Realtors, San Diego Bd. Realtors, Calif. Assn. GRI, Apartment Owners Assn., FIABCI Internat. Real Estate Fedn., Internat. Platform Assn. (Speakers), S.D. Geneal. Soc., Internat. Fedn. Univ. Women, Native Daus. of Am. Rev., Native Daus. of Golden West, Colonial Dames 17th Century; author: Jernigan Hist. 1982, Mears Genealogy 1985; Republican; R.Cath.; rec: painting, music, theater. Res: 3348 Lowell St San Diego 9106 Ofc: Shelter Island Realty, 2810 Lytton St San Diego 92106

O'LEAR, HAROLD DWIGHT, retired aerospace company engineer; b. July 8, 1926, Warren, Ohio; s. Micheal Jame and Eva May (Shilling) O'L.; m. Carol Langmaid, Feb. 6, 1956 (div.); son, Dennis Harold b. 1957; edn: Univ. Mich., 2 yrs.; engring. and metallurgy courses; desig: Quality Assurance Engr. 1986. Career: insp. Chrysler Corp., Trenton, Mich. 1952-55; chief insp. Bathey's Mfg. Co., Plymouth, Mich. 1955-61; inventory control Ford Motor Co., Rawsonville,Mich. 1961-62; lab tech. Cyclop's Corp., Sharon, Pa. 1962-63; pub. rels. U.S. Steel Corp., Pittsburgh, Pa. 1963-68; carpenter, self employed, Los Angeles 1968-70; quality control mgr. Advantec, Inglewood 1970-72; sr. asst. quality control mgr. Sun Weld Fitting Co., Los Angeles 1972-77; calibrated tool inspector Gultons Inc., Costa Mesa 1977-79; quality control Advanced Control, Irvine 1979-86; quality assurance engr. McDonnell Douglas, Long Beach 1986-92 (ret.); mem. Am. Soc. of Quality Control; club: Holiday Spa (Anaheim); publs: tech. articles on Q.C. (1964, 68, 70); mil: seaman 1/c USN 1944-46; Democrat; Prot.; rec: build model airplanes. Res: 3333 Pacific Pl. Apt. 405 Long Beach 90806

OLIN, JOHN GEORGE, manufacturing company president; b. Aug. 27, 1939, Chgo.; s. George G. and May (Hallberg) O.; m. Jane Eleanor DeLorenzi, June 13, 1964; children: Erica b. 1969, Matthew b. 1971; edn: BSME, Ill. Inst. Tech., 1961; MS in M.E., Stanford Univ., 1962, PhD in M.E., 1966. Career: mem. tech. staff Hughes Aircraft Co., El Segundo, summers 1961-63; principal research engr. AVCO-Everett Res., Everett, Mass. 1966-68; dir. research & engring. Thermo Systems Inc., St. Paul, Minn. 1968-71; dep. exec. director Minn. Pollution Control Agy., 1971-74; founder, owner, pres. Sierra Instruments Inc., Monterey, Calif. 1977–; awards: alumni profl. achiev. Ill. Inst. of Tech., Chgo. 1981, 87, profl. achiev. Delta Tau Delta, Idpls. 1988; mem. Air and Waste Mgmt. Assn. (1972–, pres. 1983-84), SEMI (1980–), ASME (1961–), ISA (1983–); clubs: Pacheco (Monterey), Chamisal Tennis Club; inventor, 7 patents, 1970–; publs: 30+ tech. papers, 1966–; Christian; rec: tennis, skiing, golf. Res: 46 La Rancheria Carmel Valley 93924

OLIPHANT, CHARLES ROMIG, physician; b. Sept. 10, 1917, Waukegan, Ill.; s. Charles L. and Mary (Goss) R.; m. Claire E. Canavan, Nov. 7, 1942; children: James R., Cathy Rose, Mary G., William D.; edn: student St. Louis Univ., 1936-40, MD, 1943; postgrad. Naval Med. Sch., 1946. Career: physician Med Corps US Navy 1943-47; pvt. practice medicine and surgery, San Diego 1947–; pres., chief exec. ofcr. Midway Med. Enterprises; former chief staff Balboa Hosp., Doctors Hosp., Cabrillo Med. Ctr.; chief staff emeritus Sharp Cabrillo Hosp.; awarded Golden Staff Award Sharp Cabrillo Hosp. 1990; mem. staff Mercy Hosp., Children's Hosp., Paradise Valley Hosp., Sharp Memorial Hosp., secty. Sharp Senior Health Care, San Diego; charter mem. Am. Bd. Family Practice; Fellow Emeritus Am. Geriatrics Soc., Fellow Am. Acad. Family Practice, Fellow Am. Assn. Abdominal Surgeons, mem. AMA, Calif. Med. Assn., Am. Acad. Family Physicians (past pres. San Diego chpt., del. Calif. chpt.), San Diego Med. Soc., Pub. Health League, Navy League, San Diego Power Squadron (past comdr), SAR; clubs: San Diego Yacht, Cameron Highlanders. Res: 4310 Trias St San Diego 92103

OLIVER, JOYCE ANNE, international columnist, high technology editorial consultant; b. Sept. 19, 1958, Coral Gables, Fla.; d. John Joseph and Rosalie Cecile (Mack) Oliver; edn: Mathematics scholarship, Miami-Dade Coll. (Fla.) 1972-73; BA, CSU Fullerton 1980, MBA, 1990. Career: corporate editor Norris Industries Inc., Huntington Beach 1979-82; pres. J.A. Oliver Assocs., La Habra Hts. 1982–, editorial clients include Norris Inds., Hunt. Bch. 1982, Better Methods Consultants, Hunt. Harbour 1982-83, The Summit Group, Orange 1982-83, UDS, Encinitas 1983-84, ALS Corp., Anaheim 1984-85, General Power Systems, Anaheim 1984-85, MacroMarketing Corp., Costa Mesa 1985-86, PM Software, Huntington Beach 1985-86, Compu-Quote, Canoga Park 1985-86, Nat. Semiconductor Canada Ltd., Mississauga, Ont. 1986, Maclean Hunter Ltd., Toronto, Ont. 1986-90, Frame Inc., Fullerton 1987, The Johnson-Layton Co., L.A. 1988-89, Corporate Research Inc., Chgo. 1988, Axon Group 1990-91, American Mktg. Assn., Chgo. 1990-92, Kenzaikai Co., Ltd., Tokyo 1991, Bus. Computer Pub., Inc. Peterborough, NH 1991-92, Helmers Pub., Inc., Peterborough, NH 1992, Schnell Pub. Co., Inc. NYC 1992-93, Diversified Pub. Group, Carol Stream, Ill. 1993; contbg. ed. Chemical Bus. 1992; bus. columnist, Marketing News 1990-92; contbg. editor Canadian Electronics Engineering mag., 1986-89; West Coast editor CEE, 1990; special feature editor The Electron (Cleveland Inst. of Electronics), 1986-89; contbg. editor Reseller Mgmt. Mag., 1987-89, Computer Mdsg. Mag., 1982-85; contbg. writer to Business, NOMDA Spokesman, PC Week, Administrative Mgmt., Leadership and Organization Development Journal, Service Mgmt., Entrepreneur, High-Tech Selling, Video Systems, Technical Photography, Computing Canada, Research & Development, Portable Office, American Demogaphics, ID Systems, Materials Engineering, Visual Merchandising and Store Design, H.R. Executive, H.R. Mag. and Stores Mag.; bd. dirs. Action Commtns. 1993–; mem: Soc. of Profl. Journalists, Nat. Writers Club, Internat. Platform Assn., IEEE, L.A. World Affairs Council, Internat. Mktg. Assn., Soc. for Photo-Optical Instrumentation Engrs., Inst. Mgmt. Scis., Assn. Computing Machinery, Research Council of Scripps Clinic and Research Found. (biomed. res.), Internat. Assn. of Bus. Communicators (IABC award for outstanding dedication

1979, pres. Fullerton chpt. 1979-80, treas. Orange Co. chpt. 1982), Communications Advy. Council (pres. Fullerton chpt. 1979-80); Republican; R.Cath.; rec: sailing, water ski. Ofc: J.A. Oliver Associates 2045 Fullerton Rd La Habra Heights 90631-8213

OLIVER, ROBERT HAROLD, municipal court judge; b. June 21, 1943, San Jose; s. Arthur S. and Elsa Mae (Sawyer) O.; m. Stephanie Yates, July 24, 1971; children: Charles A., Bradley R.; edn: BSBA, CSU Fresno, 1966; JD, Golden Gate Univ. Sch. of Law, 1973; CLU, Am. Coll. of Life Underwriters 1974; cert. specialist-estate planning trust and probate law. Career: atty., shareholder Wild, Carter, Tipton & Oliver, APC, Fresno 1973-75; instr. San Joaquin Coll. of Law 1982-87, Humphreys Coll. of Law 1974-75; speaker profl. and comm. groups re bus., estate planning and taxation, 1973-; currently judge, Fresno Municipal Court; pres. Nat. Conference of Bar Foundations 1995-; bd. of govs. CSUF Found. (chmn. 1992-, bd. mem. 1990-), CSUF Bus. Assocs. Exec. Bd. (1989-, chair 1991-), CSUF Planned Gifts Advy. Council 1987-, CSUF Bus. Advy. Council & Univ. Bus. Ldr. Advy. Bd. 1989-; bd. of govs. Fresno Reg. Found. 1992-; bd. of trustees St. Agnes Med. Ctr. 1992-; past pres. Found. of the State Bar of Calif. 1992-94; appt. Commn. on Judicial Nominees Evaluation, 1987-88; mem: State Bar of Calif. (elected bd. govs. 1988-91, v.p. 1990-91; mem. Conf. of Dels. 1983-86 and vi.chmn. exec. com. 1985-86), Fresno County Bar Assn. (dir. 1977-83, pres. 82), Fresno County Young Lawyers (dir. 1974-77, pres. 77), Fresno St. Coll. Alumni Assn. (bd. 1968-70), SAE Alumni Assn. (pres., alumni advr. 1968-70); civic: Sequoia Council BSA (exec. bd. 1988-), Fresno County Emergency Housing and Pgm. Devel. Corp. (sec., dir. 1974), Ad Hoc Com. on Citizens Participation Fresno 1974, Fresno Co. Air Pollution Control Dist. Hearing Bd. 1975-76, Salvation Army Advy. Bd. (1974-92, chmn. 1979-80), YWCA Advy. Bd. 1983, Leadership Fresno Steering Com. 1984-89, Valley Bus. Conf. Exec. Com. 1986-90, Moderator 1989-90, St. Agnes Med. Ctr. Found. 1989- (chair 1989-91, co-chair capital campaign 1987), Fresno Rotary Club (pres. 1986-87), KVPT Ch.18 PBS-TV (bd. trustees 1993-, chair The Great TV Auction 1988-91); mil: lt. col. (ret. 1985) USAF, Calif. Air Nat. Guard; Republican; rec: dixieland jazz. Ofc: Fresno Municipal Court Rm 200, 1100 Van Ness Fresno 93704

OLIVER, ROBERT M., professor emeritus of engineering science and operations research; b. May 5, 1931, Seattle; s. Henry H. and Alice (Velten) O.; m. Donna Bush, Nov. 28, 1959; children: John S., Marquam R., Bryan V.; edn: Phillips Exeter Acad. 1944-48; BSc Physics, M.I.T., 1952; math., Univ. of London, 1952-53; PhD Physics and Ops. Res., M.I.T., 1957. Career: dir. mgmt. scis. Broadview Research Corp., Burlingame, Calif. 1957-61; lectr. and res. engr. UC Berkeley, 1960-62, assoc. prof. engring. sci., 1962-66, full prof. dept. indsl. engring. and ops. res., 1966-: dept. chmn. 1964-68, dir. Ops. Res. Ctr. 1972-80, assoc. dean for res. and devel. 1982-85, dean for budget and adminstrn. 1986-89, editor Jour. of Forecasting and Ops. Res. Letters 1983-; tech. advisor and cons. to U.S. govt. agys.; chmn. bd. trustees Analytic Svs. Corp. (ANSER), Arlington, Va.; bd. dirs. Fair Isaac Companies Inc., San Rafael; mem. bd. dirs. (pres. 1984-85) Berkeley Repertory Theatre Corp.; awards: Fulbright Scholar to Univ. of London (1952-53), jt. recipient (w. Aryeh Samuel) Lanchester Prize of Ops. Res. Soc. of Am., for res. in the scheduling of USPS mail sorting and flow ops. (1963); mem: Ops. Res. Soc. of Am. (pres. 1973-74), Inst. of Mgmt. Scis., Operational Res. Soc. of England, Sigma Xi; works: Zip Code design (USPS), author 100+ papers, journal articles and books in forecasting, prediction and decision-making models of ops. res.; mil: 2d lt. AUS; Democrat; rec: tennis, fly fishing, flying. Ofc: College of Engineering Univ. of California at Berkeley 94720

OLIVER, ROBERT WARNER, professor of economics; b. Oct. 26, 1922, Los Angeles; s. Ernest Warner and Elnore Mae (McConnell) O.; m. Darlene Hubbard, July 1, 1946 (dec. 1987); m. Jean Tupman, July 8, 1989; children: Lesley b. 1949, Stewart b. 1951; edn: BA, USC, 1943; MA, 1948; PhD, Princeton Univ. 1957. Career: instr. USC 1946-47; Princeton Univ. 1948-50; Pomona Coll., Claremont 1950-52; asst. prof. USC, 1952-57; economist Stanford Research Inst., 1957-59; prof. Calif. Inst. of Technology, Pasadena 1959-; cons. economist Soc. Sci. Research, London, Eng. 1954-55, urban econ. World Bank, Wash. D.C. 1970-71, OECD, Paris 1978-79; vis. scholar Cambridge Univ., U.K. 1989; honors: Phi Beta Kappa, outstanding teacher, Hon. Alumnus 1988; civic bds: Pasadena Beautiful Found. (pres. 1973-75), Pasadena Human Rels. Com., Pasadena City Council, 1965-69, Pasadena Planning Commn., Pasadena Utilities Commn.; author: Internat. Economic Cooperation & World Bank, 1973, George Woods and the World Bank, 1995, pub. monographs, 1959, 85; mil: lt.j.g. USNR 1943-46; Democrat; Presbyterian; rec: music, golf, tennis. Ofc: CalTech 1201 California Blvd Pasadena 91125

OLIVER, RON S., city association executive; b. Feb. 5, 1947, San Diego; s. George S. and Anna Mae (Young) O.; m. Stephanie N. Donovan, Dec. 28, 1986; children: Jason b. 1971, Clark b. 1987; edn: AA, Grossmont Coll. 1969; San Diego St. Univ. 1968-71; AA, Mesa Coll. 1973. Career: supt. R.G. Fisher Constrn., San Diego 1978-83; council rep. Councilman Martinez 1983-84; gen. mgr. Fairbanks Ranch Assn., Rancho Santa Fe 1984-86; exec. v.p. Downtown San Diego Partnership, San Diego 1986-; mem. Centre City Advy. Com. 1986-; council mem. City Coll. Advy. Council 1988-; bd. dirs. Downtown

Mktg. Consortium 1988-; instr. Mesa Coll., San Diego 1981-83; awards: Who's Who Am. Jr. Colls., Outstanding Young Man of Am.; mem: Downtown Transp. Mgmt. Assn. (bd. dirs. 1989-), Balboa Park Com., Univ. Heights Comm. Devel. Corp. (pres., bd. dirs.), Lead San Diego (bd. dirs.), Balboa Theatre Found. (bd. dirs.), Rotary, Mission Bay Yacht Club, San Diego Athletic Club (advy. bd.); host, producer KSDS Interview Radio Show (1988-); mil: E-3 USNR 1968-71; Republican; Catholic; rec: sailing. Res: 11404 Via Playa de Cortes San Diego 92124 Ofc: Downtown San Diego Partnership 110 West A Street Ste 101 San Diego 92101

OLOFF, JOAN, podiatrist; b. Nov. 18, 1954, NY, NY; d. Joseph and Gisela (Fleischman) O.; m. Murray Arthur Solomon, Oct. 16, 1982; children: Daniel b. 1985, Matthew b. 1988; edn: BS, N.Y. Univ. 1976, DPM, Pa. Coll. Podiatric Medicine, Phila. 1981, MS, Calif. Coll. Pod. Med., S.F. 1986. Career: asst. prof. Calif. Coll. Podiatric Medicine, San Francisco 1983-; med. dir. Los Gatos Foot & Ankle Center, 1985-; mem. Board of Podiatric Surgery (credentials com. 1988), Am. Coll. of Foot Surg. (fellow), Diabetes Soc.; author/ed. Radiology of the Foot & Ankle, 1988, book chapt. in Metabolic Bone Disease, 1989, sev. articles re arthritis in the foot; rec: skiing, tennis, running. Ofc: Los Gatos Foot & Ankle Center 14601 S Bascom Ave Ste 240 Los Gatos 95032

OLSEN, CLIFFORD WAYNE, physical chemist; b. Jan. 15. 1936, Placerville; s. Christian William and Elsie May (Bishop) O.; m. Margaret Clara Gobel, June 16, 1962 (div. Dec. 1985); children: Anne Olsen Cordes, PhD b. 1964, Charlotte Olsen b. 1966; m. Nancy Mayhew Kruger, July 21, 1990 (div. 1994); edn: AA, Grant Technical Coll., Sacto. 1955; BA, UC Davis, 1957, PhD, 1962. Career: physicist, project leader, task leader, actg. program ldr. Univ. Calif., Lawrence Livermore Nat. Lab., Livermore 1962-93 (ret.), lab. assoc. 1993-95; cons. Aerojet Gen. Nucleonics, San Ramon 1969; organizer 2d Symposium on the Containment of Underground Nuclear Explosions, 1983, also 3rd, 4th, 5th, 6th, 7th (1985, 87, 89, 91, 93), editor symposium proceedings (2d-7th); appt. US Dept. Energy Containment Evaluation Panel, Las Vegas, Nev. 1984-; mem. Cadre for Jt. Verification of Underground Nuclear Testing 1988-; awards: Eagle Scout 1952, Life mem. Alpha Gamma Sigma, Calif. 1955, Chevalier Order of DeMolay 1953; mem.: Sigma Xi 1962-, Seismological Soc. Am. 1969-, AAAS 1970-, Am. Radio Relay League 1988-, Livermore Amateur Radio Club (pres. 1994-96); civic bds: Foothill H.S. Band Boosters, Pleasanton (sec. 1991, parade chmn. 1991-92), Calif. Lutheran Univ. (bd. convocators 1976-78); contbr. profl. papers J. Geophysical Res., Bull. of Seismol. Soc. of Am., J. Am. Chem. Soc., Physics of Fluids, 1960-; Democrat; Lutheran; rec: amateur radio, cooking, gardening. Res: 3550 Pacific Ave #201 Livermore 94550 Ofc: Lawrence Livermore National Lab. PO Box 808 Livermore 94551

OLSEN, ROGER MILTON, lawyer; b. March 27, 1942, San Jose; s. Chester Milton and Alice Louise (Leland) O.; m. Joanne Lee Gordon, Sept. 7, 1974; 1 son, Nicholas b. 1979; edn: BA, UC Berkeley 1964; JD, 1968; LL.M, George Washington Univ. 1977. Career: dep. dist. atty. Alameda Co. Dist. Attys. Office, Oakland 1969-72; trial atty. tax div. U.S. Justice Dept., Wash. D.C. 1972-76; private practice, S.F., Calif, and Wash. D.C. 1977-81; dep. dist. atty. gen. criminal div. U.S. Justice Dept. 1981-83, tax. div. 1983-85, asst. atty. gen. 1985-87; Roger M. Olsen, P.C., Los Angeles 1989-; mem: Am. Bar Assn., Calif. Bar Assn.; 2 articles pub. in profl. jours., 1984-88; Republican. Ofc: Los Angeles 90071

OLSEN, STEVEN KENT, dentist; b. Nov. 20, 1944, Spanish Fork, Utah; s. Earl Clarence and Adela (Faux) O.; m. Karin Hurst, Oct. 5, 1984; children: Christopher Steven b. 1984, Sara Kate b. 1988, Vanessa Leigh b. 1992; edn: L.A. Valley Coll. 1969-70, Univ. of Utah 1967-68; BS, Brigham Young Univ. 1969; DDS, Univ. of Pacific 1974. Career: ptnr., practice dentistry spec. in surg. and endodontic procedures Brooks & Olsen, Salt Lake City, 1974; gen. practice dentistry, San Francisco 1974-, solo 1974-76, Steven K. Olsen, D.D.S., Profl. Corp., 1977-83, ptnr. Olsen & Bergloff, 1984-; med. staff Latter-day Saints Hosp.; chmn. bd. Am. Dentists Ins. Corp., Grand Cayman, W.I., 1978-81; dir. Wilks & Topper, Inc., S.F.; instr. Univ. of Pacific, 1978-, instr. Stanford Inst., Palo Alto 1979-82; cons., dir., editor corr. course, Calif. Inst. for Continuing Edn., S.F., 1981-; cons. Pacific Coast Soc. of Marine Explorers, 1990-; exec. cons. Sea of Cortez Aquarium Found. 1993-; full-time missionary 1964-66 (asst. to the pres.); seminary instr. 1974-80; Bishoprice Stanford Ward 1985-90; High Priest, Ch. of Jesus Christ 1988-; honors: Alpha Epsilon Delta (life), Good Citizenship medal SAR 1963, Hinkley-Roberry Scholar 1963-64; biog. listings in Who's Who in West, Who's Who in World, Who's Who Emerging Leaders Am., Men of Achievement Vol. 1, Internat. Register of Profiles; polio pioneer 1954 initial group; mem: Assn. Coll. of Physicians and Surgeons, Am. Dental Assn., Calif. Dental Assn., Utah Dental Assn., Inst. For Aesthetic Dentistry 1994-; club: Physicians and Surgeons (SF). Res: 385 Old La Honda Rd Woodside 94062 Ofc: Two Embarcadero Ctr Podium Level San Francisco 94111

OLSHEN, ABRAHAM CHARLES, actuarial consultant; b. Apr. 20, 1913, Portland, Oreg.; m. Dorothy Olds, June 21, 1934; children: Richard Allen (PhD), Beverly Ann (Jacobs) (PhD); edn: AB, Reed Coll., 1933; MS, Univ. Iowa, 1935, PhD, 1937. Career: chief statistician City Plnng. Commn., Portland, Oreg. 1933-34; res. asst. math. dept. Univ. Iowa 1934-37, biometrics asst. Med. Ctr., 1936-

37; actuary and chief examiner Oreg. Ins. Dept. 1937-42, 1945-46; actuary West Coast Life Ins. Co., San Francisco 1946–, chief actuary 1953-63, v.p. 1947–, 1st v.p. 1963-67, senior v.p. 1967-68, bd. dirs. 1955-68, ret.; cons. actuarial & ins. mgmt./pres. Olshen & Assocs., San Francisco 1979–; dir. Home Federal Sav. & Loan Assn., S.F. 1972-85, v. chmn. bd. 1979-85, bd. chmn. 1985-86, ret.; guest lectr. var. univs.; mem. Calif. com. Health Insurance Council, Univ. Calif. Med. Care Adminstrn. com., San Mateo County Retirement Bd. 1975-77; awards: Sigma Xi (Fellow), AAAS (Fellow), USN Ordnance Devel. Award 1945, disting. service US Office of Sci. Res. & Devel. 1945, Presdl. Cert. Merit 1947; mem: Health Ins. Assn. Am. (mem., past chmn. Blanks Com., actuarial & stat. com.), Actuarial Club of Pacific States (past pres.), Actuarial Club of S.F. (past pres.), Am. Acad. of Actuaries (charter), Am. Math. Soc., Am. Risk and Ins. Assn., Calif. Math. Council, Commonwealth Club (life), Fellow Conf. of Actuaries in Public Practice, Inst. Mgmt. Scis., Inst. Math. Stats., Internat. Actuarial Assn., Internat. Assn. Consulting Actuaries, Internat. Cong. Actuaries, Ops. Res. Soc., Press Club S.F. (life), San Francisco C.of C. (edn. com.); contbg. writer Ency. Britannica, Underwriters' Report, The Nat. Underwriter, Life Underws. Mag., Annals of Math. Stats., other publs.; mil: resrch. assoc. Div. of War Resrch. 1942-44, Ops. Resrch. Gp., H/Q Comdr.-in-Chief, US Fleet 1944-45. Res: 2800 Hillside Dr Burlingame 94010 Ofc: 760 Market St Ste 739 San Francisco 94102

OLSON, KIM L., insurance executive; b. June 27, 1956, Gary, Ind.; s. Melvin L. and Sylvia A. (Parker) O.; m. Robin Lynn Zabrek, Jan. 18, 1981; children: David Michael b. 1983, Stephanie Lynn b. 1985, Sean Thomas b. 1992; edn: AA, Santa Barbara Comm. Coll., 1976; BA, UC Santa Barbara, 1980. Career: t.v. reporter, talk show host, teleprompter Cable TV, 1972; profl. tennis instr., 1975-81; ins. broker MONY Inc., 1982-83; chmn. bd., pres., c.e.o. Alamar Financial Services Inc. (ins., fin. products), Santa Barbara 1984-88; founder/owner The Olson Group (ins. & fin. products), 1988–; awards: Agent of the Yr. (nat. top prod.) General American Ins. 1992, Million Dollar Round Table Top of the Table 1992, Intv. Gen. Am. magazine 1992, MDRT Court of the Table 1990, Leading Producers' Round Table `Eagles Club' award Nat. Assn. Health Underws. (top award of health ins. ind.), disting. sales awards from Aetna Life, Combined Insurance, Congress Life, Kentucky Central, UNUM, Transamerica-Occidental, Am. Bankers Life, Blue Cross of Calif., Blue Cross/Blue Shield of Ohio, Old Line Life; listed Who's Who in Fin. & Ind. 1992-93; mem: Nat. Assn. Health Underws. (Santa Barbara Co. chpt. bd., past pres. 1987-8), Nat. Assn. Life Underws., Internat. Platform Assn., Nat. Fedn. of Indep. Business (charter mem. nat. Council of 100, moderator Nat. Pub. Policy Forum, Hot Springs, Va. conf. on health ins. crisis in Am., 1990), Santa Barbara C.of C., Easter Seal Soc. (S.B. Co. bd. 1982-83), Young Life Internat. (bd. 1984-86); publs: Life Ins. Selling (11/90), interviewee Transamerica Mag. 1987, Blue Cross Mag. 1989; rec: tennis, basketball. Ofc: The Olson Group, 4141 State St Ste C-4 Santa Barbara 93100

OLSON, THOMAS PETER, building contractor; b. June 6, 1947, Elmhurst, Ill.; s. George Wm. and Ima-Jean Louise (Stenberg) O.; m. Terry Fahrenbacher, July 30, 1983; children: Thomas Michael, Katherine Louise, Terissa Lynn, William Benjamin; edn: BS aerospace engring., Texas A&M, 1969; Calif. lic. contr. 1976, lic. real estate broker. Career: engr. Douglas Aircraft, 1969-70; real estate sales agt. Forest E. Olson 1970-72; contr./prin. Olson Constrn. Co., home remodel projects (250+), build apt. and condominium projects, custom homes, real estate devel. projects, 1972-; mem: Calif. Taxpayers Union, Nat. Tax Reduction Movement, Nat. Rifle Assn. (life), Aircraft Owners & Pilots Assn., Heritage Found., B.P.O.E., Century Club, Smithsonian Instn., Nat. Geog. Soc., Loyal Order of Moose, L.A. Dep. Sheriffs Assn. (sponsor); Republican (Senatorial Club, Nat. Rep. Congl. Com.); Lutheran; rec: pvt. pilot, fishing. Res: 18486 Barroso Rowland Hts 91748

OLVERA, CARLOS NELSON, engineering executive, research consultant; b. Aug. 16, 1942, Antioch, Calif.; s. Manuel Carlos and Faye Sibyl (Ames) O.; m. Pamela Lords, Oct. 20, 1966 (div. 1979); children: Jason b. 1969, Jared b. 1970, Jamie b. 1973, Janel b. 1974; m. Georgelean Nielsen, Mar. 19, 1983; edn: BSME, Brigham Young Univ., 1972; reg. profl. engr. Ida., Calif. Career: engring. mgr. Westinghouse Elec. Corp., Idaho Falls, Ida. 1972-82; maintenance cons. Philippine Nuclear Plant, Manila, Philippines 1982-83; senior engr. So. Calif. Edison, San Clemente, Calif. 1983–; owner, prin. Olvera Research, 1991–; honors: BYU Dean's Honors list 6 of 7 semesters, listed Who's Who in West 1978, 79, Who's Who in Technology Today 1981, Who's Who Calif. 1992, 93, 94; mem. Am. Nuclear Soc., Am. Soc. Mech. Engrs., Naval Reserve Assn., Am. Legion, Mercer County, Pa. Hist. Soc., Polk County, Mo. Hist. Soc., Calif. Preservation Soc., Calif. Hist. Soc.; civic bds.: Dana Point Planning Commn. (chmn. 1990-91, v. chmn. 1993-94, commr. 1989-95), Dana Point Underground Utilities Com. (chmn. 1990-95), Dana Point Hist. Soc. (bd. 1990-95, pres. 1993-95, chmn. Museum Proj. 1991-93, newsletter editor 1991-95, membership chmn. 1991-92), Danawoods HOA (bd. 1989-90), Dana Point C.of C. (10K run com. 1990-92, historian 1992), Capistrano Valley Symphony's Treble Clef Guild (charter mem., bd. 1990-93, parliamentarian 1990-92); author: "Los Olveras, Journey to America" a family history, 400 pp., 1991, profl. article, 1988; mil: nuclear opr. MM1 (SS) US Navy 1963-69, comdr. USNR (Ret.) 1974-91, decorated Merit. unit Commendation, Good Conduct, Nat. Def., Vietnam Service

w/star, Armed Forces Res., Navy Expert Pistol, Navy Expert Rifle medal, Navy and Marine Corps Overseas Svc. rib., Naval Reserve Assn. rib., Qualified in Submarines; Republican; Ch. of Jesus Christ of Latter Day Saints; rec: antique auto restoration, geneal. research. Res: 24901 Danafir Dana Point 92629 Ofc: So. Calif. Edison POB 128 San Clemente 92672

ONIK, FRANK JOSEPH, JR., engineering executive; b. June 12, 1949, Omaha, Nebr.; s. Frank Joseph, Sr. and Irene Rose (Mruk) O.; m. Diane Grace, July 14, 1984; children: Stephanie b. 1985; edn: BS in E.E.T., Univ. Nebr. 1976. Career: project engr. Reach Electronics, Lexington, Nebr. 1977-84; product engr., TCXO Crystal Filter, Dale Electronics, Tempe, Az. 1985-86; engring. mgr. Standard Crystal Corp., El Monte 1986–; mem: American Legion (post cmdr. 1982-83, Lexington, Nebr.), VFW (All State post comdr. 1983-84), K.C. (grand kt. Temple City, Ca. 1987-89), Order of the Alhambra (vice G.C. 1993-94), 4th Degree K.C. (navigator 1992-93); mil: sgt. U.S. Army 1969-72; Democrat; R.Cath.; rec: philately. Ofc: Standard Crystal Corp., 9940 E Baldwin Pl El Monte 91731

OPPENHEIM, BOHDAN W., ocean-aerospace engineer, educator, consultant; b. Dec. 9, 1948, Warsaw, Poland, nat. 1976; s. Roman Wyrzykowski and Danuta (Urbanowicz) Oppenheim; m. Grazyna W. Sochacka, April 15, 1981; children: Peter b. 1983, Tom b. 1985; edn: BSME, Warsaw Polytech. Poland 1970; MS in ocean engring., Stevens Inst. Tech. 1972; ocean engr., M.I.T., 1974; PhD, Southampton Univ., England 1980. Career: mem. tech. staff Global Marine Devel., Newport Beach 1974-80; research assoc. Univ. Southampton, England 1977-80; engring. cons. TRW, DOE, NOAA, offshore industry 1980–; prof. mech. & ocean engring. Loyola Marymount Univ., Los Angeles 1981–; research engr., p.t., Northrop Corp., Hawthorne 1985-88; mem. tech. staff The Aerospace Corp., El Segundo 1989–; author sev. major software suits for offshore industry, 1980; mem: Soc. Naval Architects & Marine Engrs., ASME, Am. Soc. Engring. Educators; lodge: FIUTS (hon. amb.); contbr. 30+ articles to profl. jours., 1980; Cath.; rec: sailing, skiing, travel, modern art. Res: 1733 Ashland Ave Santa Monica 90405

OPPENHEIM, SAMUEL AARON, history educator; b. Nov. 11, 1940, N.Y.C.; s. Harold and Dorothy (Sobel) O.; m. Alyne Faye Bernstein, Aug. 15, 1965; children: Michael b. 1968, Andrew b. 1969, Dorothy b. 1973, Sarah b. 1982; edn: BA, Univ. Ariz., Tucson 1962; AM, Harvard Univ., 1964; PhD, Indiana Univ., 1972. Career: instr. in Russian lang. & hist. Bishop Coll., Dallas, Tx. 1964-67; Austin Coll., Sherman, Tx. p.t. 1965-67; asst., assoc., full prof. history CSU Stanislaus, Turlock, Calif. 1972-74, 1974-79, 1979–, also coord. of Regional Distance Learning (half-time) 1995–; honors: Phi Beta Kappa 1962, Phi Kappa Phi 1962, Phi Alpha Theta 1959, Phi Eta Sigma 1961, w/wife jt. community service award Univ. of Judaism, L.A. 1976; mem: Am. Asssn. for Adv. of Slavic Studies 1965–, Am. Historical Assn. 1970–, Calif. Faculty Assn.; author: The Practical Bolshevik: A.I. Rykov, 1881-1938, 1979, textbook, Russia and the Soviet Union in the Twentieth Century, 1995, 70+ articles in Slavic Rev., Soviet Studies, The History Teacher, Australian Slavonic & E. European Studies, Modern Ency. of Russian & Soviet History; mil: A2c Ariz. Air Nat. Guard, USAF Reserve 1958-65; Democrat; Jewish (pres. Cong. Beth Shalom, Modesto 1973-75); rec: exercising, classical music, reading.

ORENSTEIN, MICHAEL, philatelic dealer, columnist; b. Jan. 6, 1939, Bklyn.; s. Harry and Myra (Klein) O.; m. Linda Turer, June 28, 1964; son, Paul David b. 1970; edn: BS, Clemson Univ. 1960; grad. studies UC Berkeley 1960-61. Career: regional mgr., So. Calif., Minkus Stamp & Pub. Co., 1964-70; mgr. stamp div. Superior Stamp & Coin Co. Inc., Beverly Hills 1970-91;Superior Galleries, director stamp div. 1991-94, dir. space memorabilia 1992-94; Superior Stamp & Coin An A-MARK Company, dir. stamp div. 1994- dir. space memorabilia 1994–; stamp columnist Los Angeles Times 1965-93; tech. advisor "The Video Guide to Stamp Collecting" narrated by Gary Burghoff (of M.A.S.H. fame) 1988; author: The Fun of Stamp Collecting (award winning lighthearted basic guide); bd. govs. Adelphi Univ. N.Y. Inst. of Philatelic & Numismatic Studies 1978-81; mem: Am. Stamp Dealers Assn., C.Z. study group, German Philatelic Soc., Confederate Stamp Alliance, Am. Philatelic Soc. (Writers Unit 1975-80), Internat. Fedn. of Stamp Dealers; listed in 1977 World Book Ency. yearbook as purchaser (agt. Superior Stamp & Coin Co.) of most valuable US stamp (Sc#85A) for $90,000, subsequently handled the resale (Dr. Jerry Buss Auction 1987) for $418,000, highest price ever paid for a single US stamp and 2d highest for any stamp in world (at the time); mil: pfc AUS 1962-64; Republican; rec: fishing. Ofc: Superior Stamp & Coin An A-MARK Company of Beverly Hills9478 W Olympic Blvd Beverly Hills 90212

ORLANDO, ROBERT ANTHONY, pathologist, educator, musician; b. Mar. 5, 1938, NYC, NY; s. Lawrence E. and Ida Ernst (Karnikofsky) O.; m. Joan Crofut Weibel, Nov. 29, 1981; children: William, b. 1959; Robert, b. 1969; Vivian, b. 1971; edn: BA, NY Univ. 1960; MD, NJ Coll. of Med., 1965; PhD, Univ. of Chgo. 1971. Career: faculty, Univ. of Chicago 1966-71; UC Irvine 1971-81; So. Calif. Coll. of Optometry 1972–; chief of pathology Mercy Gen. Hosp. 1972-74; Canyon Gen. Hosp., 1974-1981; Whittier Hosp. Med. Ctr., 1981-91, also chief of staff 1989-90; chief pathology and dir. of labs. Beverly

Hills Hosp., Montebello 1991–;pres. Pathology and Laboratory Med. Group, Inc.; dir. sci. affairs Biomerica, Inc.; med. dir., Salick Health Ctr. Lab, West Anaheim Med. Ctr., Coast Plaza Med. Ctr., Whittier Hosp. Med. Ctr.; bd. dirs: Lancer Corp., Biomerica, Allergy Immunotechnologies, Whittier Hosp. Med. Ctr.; prof. path. So. Calif. Coll. Optometry, 1972–, Univ. Calif. Sch. of Medicine, 1971-73; Fellow Coll. of Am. Pathologists, Am. Soc. Clin. Pathologists, Internat. Acad. Pathologists, Royal Soc. Medicine (London); mem. Orange County Soc. of Pathologists (sec. 1973–), AMA, Calif. Med. Assn., Orange Co. Med. Assn., Am. Fertility Soc., Am. Assn. for Study of Liver Disease, Reticuloendothelial Soc., Am. Assn. for Cancer Res., Internat. Acad. of Pathologists; mem. Trumpet Guild of Am., L.A. Doctors Symphony Orch. co-prin. trumpet (pres. 1990-92). Mail: PO Box 9949 Newport Beach 92658-1949

ORLEBEKE, WILLIAM RONALD, lawyer; b. Jan. 5, 1934, El Paso, Tx.; s. William Ronald Orlebeke and Frances Claire (Cook) Hammon; m. Barbara Pike, Aug. 29, 1954 (div. June 1988); children: Michelle b. 1955, Julene b. 1957, David b. 1959; m. Kathie Menlove Waterson, June 19, 1989; edn: BA, Willamette Univ., 1956; MA, Univ. Kansas, 1957; MA, Oxford Univ., U.K. 1958; JD, Willamette Univ., 1966. Career: senior scholar history Willamette Univ. 1955-56; instr. Univ. Kansas, Lawrence 1956-57; claim supr. Travelers Ins., Sacramento 1958-61; claim mgr. New York Life, San Francisco 1961-62; claim mgr. Transam., S.F. 1962-63; law clk. Oregon Supreme Ct., Salem 1964-65, investigator Ore. State Police, Salem, Ore. 1964-66; atty. law firm Coll, Levy & Orlebeke, Concord, Calif. 1967-77; W. Ronald Orlebeke Law Office, 1977–; judge pro tem Mt. Diablo Jud. Dist., Concord 1973-77; awards: Phi Beta Kappa 1956, Pi Gamma Mu 1956, Woodrow Wilson Fellow 1956-57, Rhodes Scholar, Oxford, Eng. 1957-58, Rotarian of Yr. Dist. 5160 Rotary Intl. 1989-90; clubs: Rotary Club of Clayton Valley-Concord (pres. 1987-88, dist. mem. 1989-90, chair, dist. conf. chmn. 91-92, gov. liaison 90-92), S.A.R. 1980–, Sons of Union Veterans of Civil War 1984–, Sons of Confederate Veterans 1984–, Masonic 1956–, Shrine 1977–, Elks 1972–; coauthor: Orlebeke Family in Europe & America, 1987; mil: 1st lt. USMCR 1952-59; Republican; Prot.; rec: mil. and legal hist. of England. Ofc: 3330-B Clayton Rd Concord 94519

ORNELLAS, DONALD LOUIS, explosives chemist; b. July 7, 1932, San Leandro; s. Louis Donald and Anna (Gerro) O.; m. Linda Vee, Mar. 24, 1972 (div. 1982); children: Timothy b. 1961, Kathy b. 1964, Melinda b. 1975; edn: BS chem., Santa Clara Univ., 1954. Career: chemist Kaiser Gypsum Co., Redwood City 1954-55; Kaiser Aluminum & Chem., Permanente, Calif. 1957-58; Lawrence Livermore Nat. Lab., Livermore 1958–; recipient Annual Medal Award, Am. Inst. of Chemists, Santa Clara 1954; civic: Parents Without Partners (Hayward pres. 1970-72, Livermore bd. 1983-92); inventor, 2 patents on explosives (1973, 76); publs: 18+ jour. articles on detonation chem., 1962–; mil: capt. US Army 1955-57; Democrat; R.Cath.; rec: hunting, fishing, boating, gardening. Res: 559 South N St Livermore 94550 Ofc: LLNL PO Box 808, L-282, Livermore 94550

O'ROURKE, KENNETH RYAN, lawyer; b. June 26, 1959, Los Angeles; s. E. L. and Marilyn J. O'R.; edn: BA, UCLA 1982; JD, Loyola Law Sch. 1985; admitted St. Bar Calif. (1985), U.S. Ct. Appeals 9th Cir., Fed. Cir. (1986, 1991), U.S. Dist. Cts. of Calif. (cent. 1985, no. 1986, so. 1986, east. 1988). Career: atty. O'Melveny & Myers, Los Angeles 1985–; extern U.S. Securities & Exchange Commn., L.A. 1985; L.A. Co. Superior Ct. 1983; honors: St. Thomas More Hon. Soc. (1983-85), Am. Jurisprudence award (1983), UCLA Most Valuable Frosh Oarsman (1978); mem: L.A. Co. Bar Assn; ed. in chief Loyola L.A. Internat. & Comparative Law Jour. (1984-85), staff (1983-84), 1 article pub. in profl. jour. (1984); rec: numismatics. Ofc: O'Melveny & Myers 400 S Hope St Ste 1050 Los Angeles 90071-2899

ORR, LEONARD, rebirthing movement founder, author, resort owner; b. Nov. 15, 1937, Walton, N.Y.; s. William and Eva O.; m. Magdalena Katarzyna, April 3, 1984; 1 child, Spirit b. 1985; edn: BA, L.A. Pacific Coll. 1962. Career: founder Rebirthing, San Francisco 1974–; Money Seminar 1974–; author: Money (book, video, audio tape 1978), Prosperity Consciousness, 1979, How to be a Successful Profl. in the Self-Improvement Bus., 1988, Physical Immortality, 1980, Physical Immortality for Christians, 1986, Bhartriji - Immortal Yogi 2000 Years in the Same Body, 1986, Common Sense of Physical Immortality, 1985, How to Make Democracy Work, 1987, Breath Awareness, 1985, Rebirthing in the New Age, 1977, Turning Senility Misery into Victory, 1991, About Your Femininity, 1991, Fire, Babaji - Angel of the Lord, 1992, Government Without Taxes, 1992, The Secrets of Youthing, 1994, and numerous audio tapes; clubs: 1000 Friends, Sierra; mil: Nat. Guard 1955-56; rec: farming. Res: PO Box 1026 Staunton VA 24402

ORTIZ, LEOPOLD, construction executive, b. May 1, 1926, El Paso, Tx. m. Josephine Lomeli, July 5, 1952, children: Louise b. 1955, Leo b. 1959, Thomas b. 1962, Joann b. 1965; edn: BA w/ distinction and dept. honors, indsl. arts, San Jose State Univ. 1951; MS engring. mgt., Columbia Pacific Univ. 1979, PhD resources mgt./pub. admin., 1980; spl. courses AF Inst. of Tech. (Civil Engring. Sch.) 1968, Indsl. Coll. of Armed Forces, Wash DC 1975-77, US Army Engr.

Sch. 1978, 85; Calif. Life std. designated subjects tchg. credential, Calif. Life community coll. instr. and supr. credentials; cert. plant engr. (CPE) AIPE; Calif. lic. gen. contr. Career: served in US Navy, WWII; col. US Air Force (ret.), Berlin Crisis, Pueblo Crisis, Vietnam Era; base civil engr./squadron comdr., 96th Civil Engring. Sq., Dyess AFB, Tx. 1968-69, chief Pgms. Br., 1969-70; spl. asst. for Reserve Affairs to the Dir. of Civil Engring, HQ USAF, Pentagon, 1971-75; chief Engring. Resources Mgmt., HQ MTMCWA,Oakland (Calif.) Army Base 1976-80, 1981-89, chief engring. plans and svs. 1980-81; pres. Delta West Co., Martinez 1988-94, v.p. 1994–; p.t. faculty mentor Columbia Pacific Univ., 1982-89; decorated Merit Svc. 1975, AF Commendn. 1970, AF Outstanding Unit w/3 o.l.c., Navy GCM, Asia-PacCampaign, WWII Victory, Nat. Def., AF Longevity Svc. w/o.l.c., Armed Forces Reserve w/hour glass device, Small Arms Expert Marksman; honors: Air Force ROTC distinguished military grad. 1951, Epsilon Pi Tau 1950, Air Force scroll of appreciation, Dept. Army commendn.; mem: Am. Inst. of Plant Engrs. (past chpt. secty.), Fellow Soc. of Am. Mil. Engrs. (life, past nat. v.p.), Nat. Assn. of Industrial Tech. (mem. on-site coll./univ. accreditation teams), Reserve Ofcrs. Assn., Phi Sigma Kappa (life), SJSU Alumni Assn. (past chpt. pres., life), Disabled AmVets (life), Martinez Music Forum, Internat. Platform Assn. 1988-91, Assn. of Iron and Steel Engrs. 1954-56, Martinez Jaycees 1955-60 (past chpt. pres.), Jt. Commn. on CATV 1978-80; Democrat; R.Cath. Res: 725 Ulfinian Way Martinez 94553

ORTIZ-FRANCO, LUIS, mathematics educator; b. June 11, 1946, Teocaltiche, Jalisco, Mexico; nat. 1973; s. Luis O. and Antonia F.; m. Judy Weissberg, Nov. 26, 1983; children: Rebeca Xochitl b. 1986, David Tizoc b. 1989; edn: BA, UCLA 1969, MAT, Reed Coll. 1970; PhD, Stanford Univ. 1977. Career: lectr. UCLA Ext., 1971; math. instr. UCLA Spl. Edn. pgm. 1970-72; dir. San Diego St. Univ. Student Support Pgm. 1972-73; math. instr. De Anza Coll., Cupertino 1976-77; Foothill Coll., Los Altos 1974-77; assoc. dir. NSF grant Univ. N.M., Albuquerque 1977-78; ednl. researcher SW Reg. Lab., Los Alamitos 1978-79; res. assoc. NIE U.S. Dept. Edn., WDC 1979-82; res. coord. UCLA Chicano Res. Ctr., L.A. 1983-86; math. instr. East Los Angeles Coll. 1984-87; assoc. prof. math. dept. Chapman Univ., Orange 1986–; awards: Chapman Univ. Summer Res. fellowship 1987, 90, 93, 94, Ford Found. dissertation fellowship 1975-77, U.S. Dept. Edn. fellowship 1973-75, UCLA scholarship 1965-66; mem: Internat. Study Group on Ethnomath. (3d.v.p. 1988–), Nat. Council Tchrs. of Math., Math. Assn. Am., Soc. Advancement Chincanos & Native Am. in Sci., Am. for Democratic Action (bd. dirs. 1981); co-author: Ethnic Groups in Los Angeles, 1987, Bibliography on Civil Rights Lit., Math Power in the School, articles pub. in profl. jours., 1982, 89, 93, 94; Democrat; rec: soccer. Ofc: Chapman University Math. Dept. Orange 92666

ORTON, EVA DOROTHY, dietitian, community volunteer; b. Aug. 21, 1921, San Jose; d. George A. and Marguerite C. (Del Ponte) Prudhomme; edn: AB dietetics, San Jose State Coll. 1943, post grad. 1959; cert. dietitian Calif. (1945). Career: intern Highland-Alameda 1944; dietitian Providence Hosp., Oakland 1944-46; dietitian relief Santa Clara Valley Med. Center, San Jose 1949-51, dietitian 1952-63, dir. of nutrition and food svcs. 1963-86, ret.; hosp. vol. adminstrv. cons.; appt. mem. advy. council to the Council on Aging, Legis. com. 1988; awards: achiev. Interne Class Santa Clara Valley Med. Center 1964, resolution Santa Clara County Bd. Suprs. 1986, recognition award San Jose Peninsula Dist. Calif. Dietetic Assn. 1985, recipient 1st disting. alumnae award San Jose St. Univ. 1982; mem: Interagy. Nutrition Council, San Jose Peninsula Dist. Calif. Dietetic Assn. (var. com. chmn.,dist. council 6 yrs.), Am. Dietetic Assn. (life, 1946), svc. on workshops and panels programs for pub.; civic: League Women Voters (bd. 1988, San Jose/Santa Clara pres. 1993-95), Kids for Camp (advy. bd. 1993-), Council on Aging (advy. bd. 1989-), nat. coord. Dist. #15-AARP Vote; Democrat; Cath.; rec: jogging, bowling, gardening. Res: 4925 Bel Escou Dr San Jose 95124-5441

OSBURN, MELVIN LANE, psychotherapist; b. Nov. 6, 1938, Slaton, Tx.; s. James LeRoy and Donnie Ovetra (Sanders) O.; m. Joyce, June 23, 1961; children: Julia b. 1962 (dec.), Blaine b. 1963, Brenda b. 1967; edn: AA (honors) San Bernardino Valley Coll. 1975; BA (high honors) CSC San Bernardino 1977; MA Chapman Coll. 1981; Calif. lic. Marriage, Family and Child Counselor 1983; Nev. lic. Marriage, Family Therapist 1994. Career: unit supr. Vista Pacifica Psychiat. Hosp., Riverside 1981-82; caseworker Concept Seven Boy's Ranch, Apple Valley 1983-84; vol. therapist Parents United, San Bdo. 1984–; exec. dir. Merrill Community Svcs., Fontana 1984-85; psychotherapist pvt. practice, 1983-87; psychotherapist Mel Osburn & Assocs., San Bdo. 1987–; honors: life mem. Nat. Honor Soc. in Psych. CSCSB 1976, listed Who's Who Among Human Service Profls. (1988), 5,000 Personalities of The World, Personalities of Am., Community Leaders of Am.; mem: Inland Empire Study Group for Multiple Personality and Dissociation (founder), Am. Mental Health Counselors Assn., Am. Assn. of Counseling and Devel., Internat. Soc. for the Study of Multiple Personality and Dissociation/ Orange County, Calif. Assn. of Marriage & Fam. Therapists, People Against Childhood Trauma /San Bdo. (founder 1988, chair 1989, pres. 1990); mil: E3 AUS 1956-59; Democrat; rec: long dist. runner. Res: 27015 Stratford Highland 92346 Ofc: Mel Osburn 971 W Main St Sp. #43 Barstow 92311

O'SHAUGHNESSY, MICHAEL JOHN, physician-obstetrician/gynecologist; b. June 20, 1962, Springfield, Mass.; s. Gerald Michael and Dorothy Anne (Guenerra) O.; m. Evelyne Keiko Gibo-O'Shaughnessy, Sept. 22, 1990; children: Evan Tadashi b. 1992; edn: BA, psychol., Coll. of the Holy Cross, Worcester, Mass. 1984; MD, Dartmouth Coll. Med. Sch. 1988. Career: resident physician Valley Med. Ctr. of Fresno 1988-92, attending physician 1992–, asst. chief of ob-gyn 1992–; clin instr. ob-gyn UC San Francisco 1992-94, asst. prof. ob-gyn 1994–; asst. prof. ob-gyn UCSF-Fresno 1994–; awards: Resident Physician of Yr. and Laproendoscopic Surgery Awards, Valley Med. Ctr. Dept. of Ob-Gyn, Fresno 1992, Physician of Yr. Valley Med. Ctr. Dept. of Nursing 1993; mem. Am. Coll. of Obstetrics and Gynecology 1990–, Fresno-Madera Med. Soc. 1992–, Soc. of Laproendoscopic Surgeons 1992–; author: jour. article pub. 1992; rec: sports, music, medical history. Res: 528 E Clinton Ave Fresno Ofc: Valley Medical Center 445 S Cedar Ave Fresno 93702

OSOFSKY, GENE LOUIS, lawyer; b. Nov. 27, 1944, Berkeley; m. Hilary Merle Stein; edn: BA, UC Berkeley 1966; JD, UCLA 1969; admitted St. Bar Calif. 1970. Career: atty., assoc. Sidney Pilot Inc., Los Angeles 1974-75; vol. atty. Vista 1969-70; staff atty. Los Angeles Neighborhood Legal Services 1970-71; Legal Aid Found. 1971-72; Model Cities 1972-74; sole practice, Hayward 1975-89; ptnr. Osofsky & Osofsky 1989–; dir., co-founder Am. Coll. Law, Anaheim 1972-77, instr. law 1972-73; mem: Calif. St. Bar (cert. splst. family law), So. Alameda Co. Bar assn., Alameda Co. Bar Assn., Calif. St. Bar Assn., Am. Bar Assn., No. Calif. Soc. Cert. Family Law Splsts.; articles pub. in profl. jours.; rec: swimming, jogging. Ofc: Osofsky & Osofsky 24301 Southland Dr Ste 307 Hayward 94545

OSSANLO, DEBORAH ANNE, advertising and design company president; b. July 19, 1958, South Pasadena; d. George John and Loreene Mary (Kunz) Lundie; m. Majid K. Ossanlo, Sept. 21, 1980; edn: BS in acctg., USC, 1980. Career: asst. controller Woodbury Univ., Los Angeles 1978-82; controller Naylor Brothers Restaurants Inc., Westwood 1982-87; owner/pres. Production Art & Graphic Ent. Inc., Los Angeles 1987–; bd. dirs. Product Art Service Inc., L.A. 1976-87; mem: Typographers Internat. Assn. (1987–), Art Directors Club L.A. (1987–), The Industrial Council Commerce (1987–), Commerce C.of C.; awards: acad. scholar USC (1976); Democrat; R.Cath.; avocation: working with H.S. students in field of commercial advtsg. and design. Ofc: 5900 S Eastern Ave Ste 170 Los Angeles 90040

OTTO, JAMES DANIEL, lawyer; b. June 9, 1949, Long Beach; s. Paul Daniel and Bertine (Hudspeth) O.; m. Nancy E. Paulsen, Nov. 24, 1984; children: Christopher Graham b. 1988, Brian James b. 1990; edn: BA, San Diego St. Univ., 1971; JD, Northwestern Univ., 1974. Career: atty., assoc. Cummins, White & Briendenbach, Los Angeles 1974-78, Cummins & White ptnr. 1978–, senior ptnr. 1983–, mng. ptnr. 1981-85, 89-94; faculty Practicing Law Inst., S.F. 1987; spkr. St. Paul Fire & Marine Ins., L.A. 1982, ABA Nat. Inst., Beverly Hills 1986, L.A. Co. Bar Assn. 1989, L.B. Women Lawyers Assn. 1990, Nat. Practice Inst. Environ. Law, Laguna Nigel 1993; mem: State Bar Calif., L.A. Co. Bar Assn. (trustee 1991-93, chair E.& O. Prevention Com. 1990-92, speaker and moderator two pgms. 1992 MCLE Conv., chair CLE planning com. 1992-94, govt. spec. com., ct. unification com.), Defense Research Inst., Internat. Assn. Defense Counsel; civic: East Penin. Edn. Council Rancho Palos Verdes (legal advy. com. 1988–); author: pub. article re ins. coverage, 1987, Trying the Complex Environmental Insurance Case, 1994; co-author: 4 articles pub. 1995; rec: wine tasting, paddle tennis, biking, racquetball. Ofc: Cummins & White, 865 S Figueroa St 24th Flr Los Angeles 90017-2566

OTTO, JOSEPH CLAIR, university educator; b. Nov. 4, 1955, Carroll, Iowa; s. Clair Joseph and Lou Ann Theresa (Wolterman) O.; m. Florita, 1995; children: Tyler b. 1984, Abigail b. 1986, Hayley b. 1993; edn: BS, Iowa St. Univ. 1978; MS, Eastern Ill. Univ. 1982; Ed.D, Memphis St. Univ. 1987. Career: instr. Sparks Coll., Shelbyville, Ill. 1980-84; grad. asst. Eastern Ill. Univ., Charleston 1980-82; instr. Memphis St. Univ., Tenn. 1984-86; prof. CSU Los Angeles 1986–; instr. Shelby St. Comm. Coll., Memphis, Tenn. 1986; cons. J. Cherry & Assoc. 1985-86; honors: Delta Pi Epsilon, Calif. Bus. & Edn. Assn. Cert. Appreciation (1988, 89, 90, 91, 92, 93, 94), Cert. Commend; mem: Nat. Bus. Edn. Assn., Calif. Bus. Edn. Assn. (pres); author: 23 articles pub. in profl. jours., 1986-95, 5 textbooks pub. (Paradigm Pub., Inc.); Cath. Res: 12916 Saratoga Place Chino Hills 91709 Ofc: California State University 5151 State University Dr Los Angeles 90032

OVERTON, LEWIS MARVIN, JR., management/turnaround consultant; b. July 2, 1937, Des Moines, Iowa; s. Lewis Marvin and Helen Jane (Thomas) O.; m. Helen Virginia Hawthorne, Sept. 9, 1961 (div. Feb. 1984); children: Thomas William b. 1966, Anne Hawthorne b. 1971; m. Priscilla Craig Franklin, Dec. 28, 1985; edn: BS chemistry, Stanford Univ., 1961; MBA (honors) Pace Univ., 1967. Career: assoc. A.T. Kearny Consult., N.Y.C., 1967-72; Alan Patricof Assocs., 1972-75; v.p. finance Jon-T Chemicals Inc., Houston, Tx. 1975-79, CEO, 1981-85; pres. Lewis Overton Jr. Consultants 1979–; pres. D-CEMCO Inc., Burbank 1984-87; sr. v.p. The Belet Group Inc., Newport Beach 1987-89; ptnr. Belet Partners, N.B. 1989-92; pres. and c.e.o. Microwave Products of Am., Memphis,

Tenn. 1989-91; mng. dir. Menumaster Inc., Sioux Falls, S.D. 1991-93; receiver District Ct. State of Texas 1981-94; acting exec. dir. Am. Lung Assn. of Los Angeles Co. 1993; mem. Nat. Assn. Bankruptcy Trustees, Am. Bankruptcy Inst., Turnaround Mgmt. Assn.; club: California Yacht; pub. jour. article (1968); Episcopalian; rec: sailing. Res/Ofc: 1021 W Mountain St Glendale 91202

OWADES, JOSEPH L., brewing consultant; b. July 9, 1929, New York, N.Y.; s. Samuel a. and Gussi (Horn) O.; m. Ruth Markowitz, Sept. 2, 1969; edn: BS, Polytechnic Inst. 1947, PhD, 1950. Career: dir. brewing Rheingold Brewing, Brooklyn, N.Y. 1961-69; coord. brewing Anheuser-Busch, Inc., St. Louis, Mo. 1969-72; v.p. brewing Carling Brewing Co., Waltham, Mass. 1972-74; dir. Center for Brewing, San Francisco 1975–; dir. Calyx & Corolla, Inc., San Francisco 1988–; pres. J.L. Owades & Co., Sonoma 1974–; mem: Master Brewers Assn. of Am., Institute of Food Technologists, Am. Soc. Brewing Chemists, Institute of Brewing (London), Am. Assn. Advancement of Sci.; inventor, 4 patents: no-salt pickles (1989), non-alchohol beer (1987), light malta (1987), ginseng beer (1989). Res: 2164 Hyde St San Francisco 94109 Ofc: 3097 Wood Valley Rd Sonoma 95476

OWEN, ROBERT H., information services executive; b. Feb. 25, 1951, Sedalia, Mo.; s. Aubrey W. and Julia Helen (Todd) O.; edn: BA in bus., Loretto Hts., Denver 1983; MA bus., Columbia Pacific Univ., 1988. Career: D.P. mgr. Reyco Mfg., Springfield, Mo. 1973-76; D.P. mgr. Syntex, Springfield, Mo. 1976-78, MIS mgr. Syntex, Des Moines, Iowa 1978-81, Boulder Colo. 1981-84, consulting mgr. Syntex, Palo Alto, Ca. 1984-86; dir. MIS, PMI, Santa Clara, Ca. 1986-__; dir. of IS&T, Burr-Brown Corp., Tuscon, Ariz. 19__–; tchr. adult edn., Pub. Schs., Des Moines, Ia. 1979-81; indep. cons., seminar ldr.; mem. Masonic Lodge, Optimist Club Palo Alto (treas. 1986); author: Guide to Consulting, 1984, jour. articles: User's Guide to Systems Dev., 1982, Intro. to Project Mgmt., 1982; rec: running, scuba, pers. computing. Ofc:Burr-Brown Corp PO Box 11400 Tuscon AZ 85734

OWENS, JACK BYRON, lawyer; b. Oct. 14, 1944, Orange; s. Jack Byron Owens and Lenna Mildred Owens; m. Barbara Kaye Rasbury, Aug. 15, 1981; children: John b. 1971, David b. 1975, James b. 1982, Alexandra b. 1984; edn: BA, Stanford Univ. 1966; JD, 1969; admitted St. Bar Calif. 1970, Wash. D.C. 1970. Career: clk. U.S. Ct. Appeals 9th Dist., 1969-70; atty., assoc. Wilmer Cutler & Pickering, Wash. D.C. 1970-71, 1974-75; law clk. U.S. Supreme Ct., Wash. D.C. 1973-74; law prof. UC Berkeley Boalt Hall 1975-79; ptnr. Orrick Herrington & Sutcliffe, San Francisco 1978-81; exec. v.p., gen. counsel E. & J. Gallo Winery, Modesto 1981–; adj. prof. Georgetown Univ. Law Sch.; honors: Phi Beta Kappa, Order of Coif; mem: Am. Law Inst., Am. Bar Assn.; mil: USAF 1971-73. Address: Modesto 95357

PACE, DENNY, writer, retired law enforcement official, educator; b. Aug. 27, 1926, Clemenceau, Ariz.; s. Leroy and Mauretta (Eager) P.; m. Eleanore Ruth, June 19, 1946; children: Cynthia Ann b. 1947, Susan Carole b. 1948, Taina Marie b. 1949; edn: BS pub. adminstrn., USC, 1955, MSPA, 1964; EdD, Texas A & M, 1975. Career: sgt. Los Angeles Police Dept., 1946-64, decorated Purple Heart LAPD 1948; state crim. justice planner Gov. Office, Austin, Tx. 1970-72; dep. regional adminstr. U.S. Justice Dept., Dallas, Tx. 1972-73; faculty CSU Long Beach, Calif. 1965-67, Kent State Univ., Oh. 1968-70, Tarrant Co. Comm. Coll., Fort Worth, Tx. 1967-68, Univ. Texas, Arlington, 1973-74; dept. head Long Beach City Coll., Calif. 1975-88; researcher, writer in pub. adminstrn., edn. and human relations; author, coauthor 4 textbooks incl. Concept of Vice, Narc. & Org. Crime (1975-92), chpts. in 8 books; mem. Calif. Assn. Crim. Justice Educators (1970s–), V.F.W. (life), Marine Corps Raiders Assn. (life). Res: 3842 Montego Huntington Beach 92649

PACELLI, JOSEPH GERARD, JR., designer, author; b. May 10, 1934, Bklyn.; s. Joseph Gerard and Ann Dorothea (Rescigno) P.; m. Lydia Colon, Aug. 4, 1956; m. 2d. Alesta Ericsson, Sept. 9, 1967; children: Mia Lynn b. 1962, Blayne Joseph b. 1965; edn: BFA, Univ. Conn., 1955, grad. pgm. MFA, 1955-56. Career: archtl. designer, assoc. major architects, Los Angeles 1956-65; commercial interior designer- hotels, restaurants and amusement parks, nat., 1965-78; motion picture set designer, feature film and t.v., 1978–; production designer/art director, feature film, 1983–; mem. Internat. Alliance of Theatrical and Stage Employees 1965–, Am. Football Coaches Assn. 1990–, Big Bear Lake Film Comm. 1988–, mem. Nat. Trust for Hist. Preservation 1992–, Smithsonian Assoc. 1993–; civic: H.S. and jr. college football coach; author: Building Your High School Football Program: In Pursuit of Excellence 1987; coauthor: George Allen's Guide to Special Teams 1989; Republican; R.Cath. Res: 42689 Constellation Dr Big Bear Lake 92315 Ofc: Inter/Plan Limited PO Box 3752 Big Bear Lake 92315

PACHON, HARRY P., educator, researcher; b. June 4, 1945, Miami, Fla.; s. Juan and Rebeca (Perez) P.; m. Barbara Schuld; children: Marc b. 1974, Melissa b. 1990, Nicholas b. 1992; edn: BA, CSU Los Angeles 1967; MA, 1968; PhD, Claremont Grad. Sch. 1973. Career: policy analyst U.S. HEW, Wash. D.C. 1976–; adminstrv. asst. U.S. Congress 1977-81; assoc. prof. City Univ. N.Y. 1981-87; Kenan prof. Pitzer Coll., Claremont 1987–; expert cosn. U.S. Agency for Internat. Devel., Dominican Republic 1982-86; awards: Fulbright scholar

1989, Nat. Assn. Schs. Pub. Affairs postdoctoral fellow 1976, Nat. Endowment for Humanities (postdoctoral fellow 1973); mem: Nat. Assn. Latino Elected & Appointed Officials (nat. dir. 1981-93, edn. fund bd. mem. 1981); pres. Tomas Rivera Center; author: Hispanics in U.S. (Prentice Hall 1985), Americans by Choice (Westview Press, 1994); Democrat; Cath. Res: 2354 N Indian Hill Claremont 91711 Ofc: Tomas Rivera Ctr 241 E 11th St Claremont 91711

PACKARD, BETTY J., marketing consultant, writer; b. Oct. 1, 1937, Idpls.; d. Raymond Roy and Juanita Doris (Copeland) Reed; m. James R. Packard Jr., Nov. 28, 1958 (dec. Oct. 1, 1960); children: Lisa Lynn Packard Beaudry b. 1959, James R. Packard III b. 1961; m. Stephen Milton Voris, Sept. 26, 1975; edn: BA, Franklin Coll., 1967. Career: English tchr. and hd. dept. journalism Ben Davis High Sch., Indianapolis 1967-69; tchr. In H.S. Journalism Assn., Ball State Univ., 1968; ed. Res. & Review Svc. of Am., 1969-75; owner, pres. Packard Consulting, 1975–; co-owner Hoosier Hospitality, 1985-89; dir. Indiana Mutual Fire Ins. Co., 1974-93; seminar instr. financial svs. ind. world-wide, 1973–; ed. WLUC News, Women Life Underwriters, Clinton, Md. 1988-90; awards: 19 nat. writing awards Nat. Fedn. of Press Women, Mo. 1971-94, 91 state writing awards Ind. and Calif. Press Women 1971-94, Woman Writer of Yr. Indiana Women's Press Club 1975, 1989 Sweepstakes Winner annual writing contest Calif. Press Women 1989; mem: Calif. Press Women (exec. bd. 1985–, pres. 1993-95), Nat. Fedn. of Press Women (1967–, nat. bd. 1971-79, 1993-95), Am. Auto Racing Writers & Bdcstrs. Assn. (annual dinner com. 1990–, chair 1991), Championship Auto Race Aux. 1987–, Calif. Abortion Rights Action League (bd. 1985-89); S.F. Symphony Store (vol. 1985–); clubs: Pi Beta Phi Alumnae S.F. (ways & means com. 1984–), Presidio of S.F. Officers' Wives (Xmas Project chair 1982-92), Republican Fed. Womens; author: (book) When Someone Is Crying (1976), (brochure) I Love You (1976); Republican; Disciples of Christ; rec: family, classical music. Res: 1419 DeHaro St San Francisco 94107 Ofcs: Packard Consulting 9571 Edgewater Ct Brownsburg IN 46112 and 1419 DeHaro St San Francisco 94107

PACKARD, RONALD C., congressman; b. Jan. 19, 1931, Meridian, Idaho; s. Forrest LeRoy and Esther (Carter) P.; m. Roma Jean Sorenson, July 18, 1952; children: Chris, Debra, Jeff, Vicki, Scott, Lisa, Theresa; edn: student Brigham Young Univ. 1948-50, Portland State Univ. 1952-53; DMD, Univ. of Ore. 1957; lic. dentist Calif. 1959. Career: gen. practice dentistry, Carlsbad 1959-82; ofcr. Packard Devel. Corp., Carlsbad 1965–; mem. 98th-104th Congresses from 43rd (now 48th) Calif. Dist. 1983–; mem. appropriations com. 103rd Congress from 43rd Dist. Calif., mem. public works and transp. com., sci., space and tech. com.; v.chmn., dir. Bank of North County 1981-83; trustee Carlsbad Unif. Sch. Dist. 1962-74 (chmn. 1968-69, 1972-74), bd. dirs. Carlsbad C.of C. 1972-76; Carlsbad City Council 1976-78; mayor City of Carlsbad 1978-82; ; mem: No. County Armed Svcs YMCA, No. County Transit Dist. (dir. 1978-82), San Diego Assn. of Govts., Coastal Policy Com., Transp. Policy Com.; pres. San Diego div. Calif. League of Cities; mil: lt. USN 1957-59; Republican; Mormon; rec: sports, golf, tennis. Ofc: House Office Bldg 2162 Rayburn Washington DC 20515

PADILLA, JOHN M., lawyer; b. Jan. 1, 1954, San Jose; s. John P. and Stephanie (Martinez) P.; m. Adoralida Lopez, July 13, 1985; 1 son, Jonathan b. 1989; edn: BA history, Santa Clara Univ. 1977; JD, 1980; admitted Supreme Ct. Calif. 1980. Career: atty. sole practice, San Jose 1980–; mediator Small Claims Ct. San Jose 1984–; judge pro tem Municipal Ct. San Jose 1986–; awards: Gretchen Bufford service award 1993; mem: Calif. Trial Lawyers Assn., Am. Trial Lawyers Assn., Calif. Attys. for Criminal Justice, Santa Clara Co. Bar (juvenile dependency exec. com.), La Raza Lawyers Assn., Chicano Alumni Assn., E. Side Union H.S. Dist. (desegregation plan advy. com. 1987); Cath.; rec: computer programming. Ofc: Judge Pro Tem, Superior-Family Division 31 N 2nd St Ste 210 San Jose 95113

PAGE, LESLIE ANDREW, microbiologist, manufacturing company executive; b. June 5, 1924, Minneapolis, Minn.; s. Henry R. and Amelia (Steinmetz) P.; m. DeEtte Griswold, July 6, 1952 (div. 1975); m. Mary Ellen Decker, Nov. 26, 1976; children: Randolph, Michael, Katherine, Caroline; edn: BA, Univ. Minn. 1949; MA bacteriology, UC Berkeley 1953; PhD, 1956. Career: research microbiologist, lectr. UC Davis Vet. Sch. 1956-61; cons. San Diego Zoological Soc. Zoo Hosp. 1957-60; microbiologist, research leader U.S. Dept. of Agri. Nat. Animal Disease Ctr., Ames, Iowa 1961-79; writer and med. text cons. prin. Bay St. Louis, Miss. 1979-87; founder, pres., bd. chmn. SteriDerm Corp., Escondido 1987–; cons. McCormick Distilling Co. 1994–; ed. J. of Wildlife Diseases, 1965-72; awards: Wildlife Disease Assn. disting. service and Emeritus awards 1980, 84, Sigma Xi, Phi Zeta, E. Hancock Fire Dist. disting. service 1983; mem: Am. Acad. Microbiology (fellow), Wildlife Disease Assn. (pres. 1972-73), Am. Soc. Microbiology (emeritus 1979); civic: Garden Island Comm. Assn. (pres. 1980-81), E. Hancock Fire Dist. chief commr. 1982-83, Woodridge Escondido Property Owners Assn. (treas. 1986-88); invention: liquid antiseptic composition (Pat. 1989), author: 12 med. texts and manuals (1965-84), 70+ research papers pub. in sci. jours. (1959-84); mil: cpl. AUS 1943-46; Episcopalian; rec: community service. Ofc: SteriDerm Corp. (Ph: 619-746-5017) 1784 Deavers Drive San Marcos 92069

PAHL, STEPHEN DONALD, lawyer; b. July 23, 1956, Los Angeles; s. Donald Alfred and Verlene Virginia (Dunaway) P.; m. Louise A. Dodd, Feb. 18, 1978; edn: BA, UC Santa Barbara 1977; JD, Univ. Santa Clara 1980. Career: research atty. Santa Clara County Superior Ct., San Jose 1980-81; atty., assoc. Littler Mendelson 1981-82; ptnr. Tarkington et al 1983-89; mng. ptnr. Pahl & Gosselin, San Jose and San Francisco 1989–; dir. St. Johns Restaurant, Sunnyvale 1984–; Nat. Intercity Bank, Santa Clara 1983-86; Texas Turkeys, Inc. Los Altos 1984–; awards: UC regent scholar 1977, St. of Calif. fellow 1977-80; mem: ABA, FBA, Calif. Bankers Assn., Calif. St. Bar Assn. (com. on fed. cts., resolutions com.), Los Altos Hills Planning Commn. (commr. 1989-93); author A Ct. Divided: An Analysis of Polarization on U.S. Supreme Ct.; Republican; Baptist; rec: racquetball, golf, flying. Res: 27431 Black Mountain Rd Los Altos Hills 94022 Ofc: 160 W Santa Clara St 14th Fl San Jose 95113 Ph: 408/286-5100

PAINTER, AMELIA ANN, marketing professional, writer; b. Oct. 26, 1946, Hot Springs, Ark.; d. Jack H. and Emily C. (Hosmer) Chapman; m. Douglas M. Painter, June 12, 1988; children: Katrina b. 1967, Bruce b. 1969, Emily Grace b. 1973; lic. R.E. sales agt. Calif. 1978, Texas 1985. Career: salesmgr. Commercial Systems, Houston 1984-85; mktg. dir. Southmark Mgmt., Dallas 1985-86; sales dir. Noble Design & Set Construction, San Diego 1986-89; mktg. dir. Scenic Drive Set Design & Constrn., Los Angeles 1990-91; freelance writer 1992–; editorial asst. and mem. Houston Motion Picture Council, Tx. ("Newsreel Publication"), Nat. Assn. of Women in Commercial Real Estate, Houston ("Shoptalk Newsletter"), 1984-85; contbg. author: Consumers Form Letter Collection (1991), Cleaning-Up Your Credit (1991); author: Chapman Forum (1993), Surviving College (1995); rec: writing, gardening. Ofc: PO Box 154 San Luis Rey 92068-0154

PAINTER, JOEL HAROLD, clinical psychologist; b. July 3, 1936, Ashland, Ohio; s. Harold Dennis and Margaret Ruth (Stone) P.; children: Daniel b. 1968, Jeremy b. 1973; edn: Westmont Coll. 1954-57; BS hons., Old Dominion Univ. 1967; PhD, Ariz. St. Univ. 1972; lic. clin. psychologist Calif. Career: psychologist VA Hosp. Atlanta 1971-74; coord. DDTP VA Med. Ctr., Long Beach 1974-80; chief psychologist Dept. Vet. Affairs 1980–; pvt. practice, Santa Barbara 1981–; honors: Who's Who West; mem: S.B. Psychol. Assn., Calif. St. Psychol. Assn., Am. Psychol. Assn., Christian Bus. Mens. Com., Am. Legion, Am. Cancer Soc.; author: Modification of Smoking Behavior Controlled Pub. Clinic (1972), 3 articles pub. in profl. jours. (1974-83); mil: sgt. E-5 AUS 1961-64, Army Commend. Medal 1964; Republican; United Methodist; rec: bicycling, music. Ofc: 27 West Micheltorena Santa Barbara 93101

PALFREYMAN, RICHARD WARWICK, financial executive; b. Aug. 14, 1942, Springville, Utah; s. Warwick Charles and Ione (Averett) P.; m. Lindy Olson, June 9, 1966; children: Mandi b. 1968, Scott b. 1968, Michael b. 1972, Matthew b. 1975, Timothy b. 1980; edn: BS, Univ. Utah 1966; MBA, 1967. Career: treasury analyst Kaiser Aluminum & Chemical Corp., Oakland 1967-72; asst. treas. Natomas Co., San Francisco 1972-80; CFO Simmons Oil Corp., Phoenix, Ariz. 1980-83; sr.v.p. fin. Computerland Corp., Hayward 1983-88; CFO Photo & Sound Co., San Francisco 1989–, pres. and c.e.o. 1992–; mem: BSA (exec. bd. 1984–), Cerebral Palsy Center (bd. mem.); mil: SP-4 Army Nat. Guard 1959-66; Republican; Mormon; rec: racquetball. Res: 320 LasSalle Ave Piedmont 94610 Ofc: Photo & Sound Co. 140 Hubbell St San Francisco 94107

PALMER, BEVERLY B., clinical psychologist; b. Nov. 22, 1945, Cleveland, Oh.; d. Lawrence Edwin and Mildred Blazey; m. Richard C. Palmer, M.D., May 5, 1944; son, Ryan b. 1975; edn: BA, Univ. Mich., Ann Arbor 1966; MA, Ohio St. Univ., 1969, PhD, 1972; lic. clin. psychologist Calif. Career: research asst. dept. psychiat. Ohio State Univ., Columbus 1966-68, adminstrv. assoc. 1969-70; tchr. S.W. City Sch., Grove City, Oh. 1967-69; research psychologist UC Los Angeles, 1971-77, counseling adminstr. Harbor Free Clinic, San Pedro 1971-73, clin. supr. CSU Long Beach 1972-73; prof. dept. psychol. CSU Dominguez Hills, Carson 1973–; commr. of public health L.A. Co., 1978-81; ms. reviewer coll. textbook publishers, 1978; bd. dirs. South Bay Ctr. for Counseling, Manhattan Beach 1979-83; honors: L.A. Co. Bd. Suprs. proclamation for comm. svc., for public health svc. 1972, 81, Calif. State Univ. Outstanding Prof. Award 1995; mem: Am. Psychol. Assn., Assn. for Women in Science, Assn. Humanistic Psychol.; contbr. num. articles in profl. jours.; rec: tennis, skiing, travel. Ofc: Dept. Psychol. Calif. State Univ. Dominguez Hills, Carson 90747

PALMER, CHARLES SUMNER, retired business owner; b. Aug. 28, 1918, LeRoy, Minn.; s. Charles Sumner and Nannie George (Griswold) P.; m. Lois Clare Hartmann, Sept. 4, 1948; children: Wendy b. 1949, Charles S., III b. 1951 (dec. 1974), Davis b. 1954, Elizabeth b. 1964; edn: BS, Cal Tech 1940; MBA, Stanford Univ. 1949. Career: engr. Army Corps of Engrs., Los Angeles 1941-42; Arcadia Metal Prod., Arcadia 1949-50; Don Baxter Inc., Glendale 1950-51; Beckman Instruments, South Pasadena 1951-54; v.p. ops. Datex Corp., Monrovia 1954-61; pres. Gambit Corp., Pasadena 1962-93; chmn. of bd. Gambit Corp., Rialto, Calif. 1993–; dir., trustee Foothill Workshop for Handicapped, Pasadena 1985-95; mil: capt. USAF 1942-46; Republican; rec: do-it-yourself, computers. Res: 8545 Carmel Valley Rd Carmel 93923

PALMER, JOHN MATTERN, academic physician/urologist; b. Aug. 1, 1933, Oakland; s. Bean Mark and Laurinne Easter (Mattern) P.; m. Susan Sutton, Feb. 6, 1982; children: John D. b. 1961, Duncan Thomas b. 1963, Amy Jane b. 1967; edn: BA, Dartmouth Coll. 1955; MD, Stanford Univ. Sch. Medicine 1960; cert. Am. Bd. of Med. Examiners 1961; cert. Am. Bd. of Urology 1968. Career: resident Stanford Univ. Sch. Medicine, chief resident dept. urology 1965, instr. in surgery, div. urology Stanford Univ. Hosp. 1965-66, asst. prof. surg. urol. 1967-70; assoc. prof., prof. urology, UC Davis Sch. of Medicine 1970–, dept. chmn. 1970-84, chief pediatric urology UC Davis Sch. of Med. and UCD Med. Center (Sacto.) 1984; mem. staff Sutter Hosps., Sacto.; cons. Martinez VA Hosp.; urol. cons. Kaiser-Permanente orgn.; cons. AMA Journal; honors: Alpha Omega Alpha 1960, Sigma Xi 1976; Fellow: Am. Bd. of Urology 1968, Am. Coll. of Surgeons 1969, Am. Acad. of Pediatrics, Urol. Sect. 1988; mem. Am. Urologic Assn./W. Sect., Soc. for Pediatric Urol., Am. Soc. Transplant Surgeons, Soc. of Univ. Urologists, Sutter Club (Sacto.); contbr. 100+ articles to med. jours. Ofc: Dept. Urology UC Davis School of Medicine 4301 X St Ste 2210 Sacramento 95817

PALMER, PATRICIA TEXTER, educator, administrator; b. June 10, 1932, Detroit, Mich.; d. Elmer Clinton and Helen (Rotchford) Texter; m. David Jean Palmer, June 4, 1955; edn: BA, Univ. Mich. 1953; MEd, Nat. Coll. of Edn. (now National-Louis Univ.) 1958; MA, CSU San Francisco 1966; postgrad. work Stanford Univ. 1968, CSU Hayward 1968-69; Calif. Life Tchg. Creds. (gen. elem., gen. secondary, spl. Speech Arts). Career: chair Speech Dept. Grosse Pointe Univ. Sch., Mich. 1953-55; tchr. South Margerita Sch., Panama 1955-56; tchr. Kipling Sch. Deerfield, Ill. 1955-56; Rio San Gabriel Sch., Downey, Calif. 1957-59; Roosevelt High Sch., Honolulu 1959-62; El Camino High Sch., South San Francisco 1962-68, chair ESL Dept. South S.F. Unified Dist. 1968-81; dir. English as Second Lang. Inst., Millbrae 1978–, Calif. master tchr. ESL, Calif. Council Adult Edn. 1979-82; adj. faculty New Coll. of Calif., 1982–, Skyline Community Coll., San Bruno 1990–; mem. Calif. State Adult Basic Edn. Advy. Com. on vocational ESL; awards: Concours de Francais Prix 1947, Jeanette M. Liggett Meml. award for excellence in hist. 1949, Cum Laude Soc. 1949, Zeta Phi Eta Speech Hon. 1953, Scroll Hon. Soc. 1953, outstanding alumna Univ. of Mich. Sesquicentennial Awards 1968, commendation. for achieve. in journalism Hawaii State Legislature 1962, Women Helping Women award Soroptimist Internat. of Millbrae-San Bruno 1993; mem: Tchrs. of English to Speakers of Other Languages, Calif. affiliation, Faculty Assn. of Calif. Comm. Colls., Assn. for Supvn. and Curriculum Devel., Speech Communication Assn., AAUW, Internat. Platform Assn., Univ. Mich. Alumnae Assn., National-Louis Univ. Assn., Ninety Nines, Chi Omega, Nat. Assn. of Female Execs., Computer Using Educators (CUE), Faculty Assn. of Calif. Comm. Colls., Nat. Assn. for Foreign Student Affairs (NAFSA), Peninsula Lioness Club, Soroptimist Intl., Rotary Club of Millbrae; Republican; R.Cath.; rec: flying. Res: 2917 Franciscan Court San Carlos 94070 Ofc: New College of California 450 Chadbourne Ave Millbrae 94030

PALMQUIST, RICHARD HERMAN, broadcaster, publisher; b. July 11, 1931, Davenport, Iowa; s. Herman Phillip and Margaret (Burchell) P.; m. Dolores Mae Lund, June 28, 1953; children: Philip b. 1955, Stephen b. 1957, Mary b. 1958, Timothy b. 1960, Carol b. 1962; edn: BA, Carthage Coll. 1953; Dallas Theological Seminary 1953-54, 55-56; Northwestern Sch. Seminary 1954-55. Career: pres. Denali Broadcasters Inc., Nome, Alaska 1957; Family Stations Inc., Oakland 1958-64; Tape Networks Inc., Delano 1966–; AIM Inc., Los Angeles 1967–; former owner Enterpise News, Pixley and Delano 1974-92, and Terra Bella News, Terra Bella and Delano 1975-92; Handi Directory Co., Delano 1975-92; mem: Calif. Govs. Advy. Council on Small Bus.; Libertarian; Baptist; rec: econ. Ofc: 1305 Glenwood Delano 93215

PALUMBO, ANTHONY LOUIS, lieutenant general (retired), financial executive (private placements); b. Oct. 25, 1929, Reading, Ohio; s. Gennaro Marian and Esther Rose P.; m. Jean Kathryn LeFeber, Sept. 15, 1951; children: Kathy b. 1953, Jeffrey b. 1955, Maj. Anthony, II (AUS) b. 1958, Maj. Steven (AUS) b. 1960; edn: nuclear weapons employment specialist, grad. Army Armor Sch., Ft. Knox 1959, Command & Gen. Staff Coll., 1962; BA in pub. adm. Univ. Beverly Hills, 1977, MPA, 1978. Career: maj. gen. USA Ret. 1948-86: decorated Combat Inf. Badge, 7th Inf. Div., Korea (1952), merit service medals (3), Legion of Merit (1970), Dist. Service medal (1986); v. chmn. Gov.'s Select Com. Crime & Crim. Justice, 1972-73, special asst. to Gov., exec. dir. Gov.'s Public Safety Planning Com., Sacto. 1973-75, also exec. dir. Office Criminal Justice, 1974-75; dir. region IX, Fed. Emergency Mgmt. Agy., San Francisco 1981; div. comdr. 40th Mech. Inf. Div., US Army, Los Angeles 1981-84; cmdr. Olympic Task Force Grizzly, DOD Olympic Security Force, Los Angeles 1984-85; dir. Task Force CARE, Calif. State Military Dept. , Sacto. 1986–; bd. dirs., foundation pres. Developmentally Disabled Service Orgn., Sacto. 1986–; pres./administr. Ranch House, Inc. 1986–; pres., chmn. bd. ALP & Sons Enterprises, Inc. 1982–; awards: Community service and Res. and Living Award, Assn. for Retarded, Sacto. (1987); mem: Nat. Guard Assn. Calif. (pres. 1974), Calif. State Sheriffs' Assn., Citizens for Law Enforce. Needs, L.A. (advy. bd. 1973-78), Calif. Police Ofcrs. Assn. (1968–), Mil. Order of World War, Calif. Crime Technology Research Found. (exec. bd. 1973-75), Svens Lokrantz Devel. Disabled Parents Gp. (v.p. 1963-65), Commonwealth Club (1976-81), Comstock Club (1985–); sev. publs. in field of crim. justice including crim. justice opnl.

exercises (Cable Splicer Series 1966-70); Republican; R.Cath.; rec: golf, bldg. construction, mosaic murals. Res: 1840 Rockwood Dr Sacramento 95864

PAN, WILLIAM JIAWEI, trading company president; b. July 24, 1935, Shanghai, China; s. You-Yuan Pan and Ruth (Li) Tien; m. Lena Fengqiu Liu, Dec. 26, 1965; 1 child, Song b. 1967; edn: BS, Peking Univ., Beijing 1958; Ching Hwa Univ., Beijing 1961-63. Career: engr. Beijing Radio Factory, Beijing 1958-78; Dong Feng TV Factory, 1978-80; asst. gen. mgr. China National Electronics Imp./Exp. Corp., Beijing br. 1980-91; mgr. electronics dept. China Resource Products, NY, NY 1985-91; pres. and c.e.o. King Trading Inc., San Francisco 1987-91; pres. and CEO Kings International, Inc., San Jose 1991–; rec: photog., tennis, swimming, badminton. Res: 175 Calvert Dr Cupertino 95014

PANCER, STEFAN ROBERT, lawyer; b. Sept. 21, 1945, New York; s. David and Ernestine (Silver) P.; m. Niki Jean Semenick, May 2, 1981; children: Joshua b. 1983, Brennen b. 1986; edn: L.A. Valley Coll.; E. N.M. Univ.; JD, Univ. West L.A., 1976; admitted St. Bar Calif. Career: atty. sole practice, personal injury, San Bernardino and Riverside 1977-87; mng. ptnr. Pancer & Nachlis (a personal injury firm), 1987–; mem: Calif. Trial Lawyers Assn., San Bernardino Co. Bar Assn., Riverside Co. Bar Assn. Ofc: 1201 Brookside Ave Redlands 92373-4402

PANETTA, LEON EDWARD, government official; b. June 28, 1938, Monterey; m. Sylvia Marie Varni, 1962; 3 sons: Christopher, Carmelo, James; edn: BA, magna cum laude, Univ. of Santa Clara 1960, JD, 1963; admitted to Calif. Bar 1965. Career: individual law practice, Monterey; legis. asst. to U.S. Senator Thomas H. Kuchel of Calif. 1966-69; spl. asst. to secty. HEW, WDC. 1969; dir. U.S. Ofc. for Civil Rights, Wash. 1969-70; exec. asst. to mayor, NYC 1970-71; ptr. firm Panetta, Thompson & Panetta, Monterey 1971-76; elected to U.S. House of Reps. from 16th Congl. Dist., Calif. 1976, reelected 1978, 80, 82, 84, 86, 88, 90, 92; chmn. 95th Congress New Members Caucus 1977-78; No. Calif. Majority Regional Whip 1981-84; Dep. Majority Whip for budget issues 1985-93; House Budget Com. mem. 1979-85, 89-93, chmn. 1989-93, appt. Director Office of Mangement and Budget by Pres. Clinton 1993-94, appt. chief of staff by Pres. Clinton 1994–; mem. House Agric. Com., House Adminstrn. Com., House Select Com. on Hunger; founder Monterey Coll. of Law; trustee, Univ. Santa Clara Law Sch.; awards: NEA Lincoln Award 1969, Lawyer of the Year 1970, Bread for the World Award (1978, 80, 82), Nat. Hospice Orgn. Award 1984, Am. Farm Bur. Fedn. Golden Plow Award 1988; mem: Carmel Valley Little League; Parish Council of Our Lady of Mt. Carmel Ch.; mil: 1st lt. US Army 1963-65, Army Commdn.; author: Bring Us Together, 1971; Democrat (Monterey Co. Dem. Central Com. 1972-75); Cath. Ofc: The White House Washington DC 20500

PAPADAKIS, ANGIE, writer, lecturer, advertising executive; b. Dec. 25, 1925, Enid, Okla.; d. John and Alexandra (Papandrian) Lampas; m. Ernest Nickolas Papadakis, Sept. 7, 1946; children: Nickolas b. 1947, John b. 1949, Tom b. 1954; edn: attended USC, UCLA, L.B. State, Harbor Coll. Career: writer Readers Digest 1958; speaker Nat. Artistis & Lecture Service, Beverly Hills 1962-72, Assoc. Profl. Talent, Los Angeles 1972-90, SPEAK, INC., San Diego 1990–; advtg. exec. Papadakis, San Pedro 1975–; numerous awards include 'Arkansas Traveler' Gov. Dale Bumpers 1974, appreciation San Pedro Boys Club 1975, Wm. H. Spurgeon award and citizen of yr. Boy Scouts Am. 1979, 80, amicus colleqii Harbor Coll. 1980, Woman of Yr. award 51st Assembly Dist. 1992, Lions Citizen of Yr. 1995; gubnat. appt. Calif. Nevada-Super Speed Train Commn. 1988; gubnat. appt. Little Hoover Commn. 1990–; vice chmn. U.S. English 1990-92; mem. Calif. State Board of Edn. 1983-88, L.A. Co. Board of Edn. 1978-81, L.A. Ednl. Partnership (dir. 1983), L.A. Harbor Improvement Corp. (dir. 1984), Harbor Round Table (chmn. 1984), Maritime Industries Bd. (v.chmn. 1974-78), L.A. Co. Dept. Pub. Services (commr. 1974-77), L.A. United Way (corp. bd. 1986), L.A. Area Council Boy Scouts Am. (dir. 1978), mem. L.A. Area C.of C., Propeller Club U.S.; co-author: The Howls of Justice, 1988, num. articles pub. in nat. publs., 1958; Republican; Greek Orthodox. Ofc: Papadakis Advertising 267 W 7th St San Pedro 90731

PAPPAS, NICHOLAS, psychiatrist, physician; b. June 30, 1937, Brooklyn, N.Y.; s. Michael George and Chrisanthy Ann (Nicholakakis) P.; m. Margaret Carol Murphy, Nov. 24, 1963; children: Katina b. 1964, Christy b. 1966; edn: BA, Indiana Univ. 1959, MD 1962; lic. psychiatrist, 1970. Career: rotating internship Detroit Receiving Hosp. 1962-63; psychiatric resident Indiana Univ. Med. Ctr. 1963-65; psychiatrist, staff Central State Hosp, Indpls. 1965-66; psychiatric resident Napa St. Hosp., Imola 1968-70, staff psychiatrist 1970-73; priv. psychiatric practice, Novato 1971–; med. dir. Canyon Manor Drug Rehab. Hosp., Novato 1972-73; preceptor, supvr.: Napa St. Hosp. (psych. resident) 1970-73, Sonoma Univ. (nursing stu.) 1974–, Calif. Sch. of Profl. Psychol. 1975–; mil: capt. U.S. Army, chief Mental Hygiene Consultation Service, Ft. McClellan, Ala. 1966-68; Republican; Greek Orthodox; rec: golf, racquetball, woodworking, carpentry, computers. Ofc: Dr. Nicholas Pappas 1025 5th St Novato 94945

PAPPAS, THETIS HERO, real estate broker; b. Sept. 9, 1920, Astoria, N.Y.; d. Thomas John and Andromahe (Krahtis) Hero; m. Costas Ernest Pappas, June 9, 1940; children: Alceste T., Conrad T. E.; edn: BA chemistry, Hofstra Univ.

1943; N.Y. Sch. Interior Design 1954; MS counseling, Long Island Univ. 1967; cert. real estate Coll. San Mateo 1982. Career: investor, developer pvt. practice, Huntington, N.Y. 1950-63; sci. tchr. Hills H.S. 1963-68; cons. engr. Pappas Assoc., Palo Alto and Emeryville 1968-79; real estate broker Pappas Brokers, San Mateo 1979–; real estate advy. bd. Coll. San Mateo 1985–; awards: Hofstra Univ. scholarship (1941-42), George A Thuss award; mem: San Mateo-Burlingam Bd. Realtors (bd. dirs. 1985-88, chmn. membership com. 1984-88, chmn. edn. com. 1982-84), Am. Chemical Soc., Am. Assn. Univ. Women, Commonwealth Club of Calif., Lawrenceville Sch. Women's Aux., Whittier Coll. Aux., Hofstra Univ. Alumni, Redwood City Pub. Library (archive com. 1986–), Calif. Real Estate Edn. Assn., P-47 Thunderbolt Advocates; co-author (with Costas E. Pappas): To The Rainbow and Beyond (memoirs, pub. 1992). Address: San Mateo 94402

PARADY, JOHN EDWARD, information systems executive; b. Sept. 26, 1939, Inglewood; s. Raymond Oliver and Ella Louise (Timm) P.; m. Barbara Louise Pettit, Aug. 13, 1966; children: John b. 1968, Renee b. 1970, Stacy b. 1975; edn: BS, CSU 1966; MS, USC 1969. Career: computer operator Systems Devel. Corp., Santa Monica 1962-64; systems ofcr. Security Pacific Bank, Los Angeles 1964-66; industry analyst IBM Corp. 1966-69; mgmt. cons. Norris & Gottfried Inc. 1969-71; Arthur Young, Santa Ana 1971; Mordy & Co., Los Angeles 1972-75; dir. info. systems Weyerhaeuser Corp., Tacoma, Wash. 1975-82; exec. dir. McKenna Conner & Cuneo, Los Angeles 1983; sr.v.p. techn. Bank of Am., S.F. 1984-85; mgmt. cons., Los Angeles 1986; exec. v.p. tech., Pacific Stock Exchange 1987–; mil: 2d. lt. AUS 1959-63; Republican; Mormon; rec: fishing, hiking, horseriding. Res: 1004 Vista del Valle La Canada 91011 Ofc: The Pacific Stock Exchange 233 S Beavory Ave Los Angeles 90012

PARAYNO, MAXIMO ALANO, JR., physician executive; b. Jan. 25, 1932, Calasiao Pangasinan, Philippines (nat. 1978); s. Maximo Zulueta and Rosa (Alano) P.; m. Teresita Donato, Sept. 10, 1961; children: Max III b. 1962, Michael b. 1964, Marlon b. 1965, May b. 1972; edn: BS, Univ. of Philippines, Manila 1954, MD, 1959, MPH, 1967; psychiatry study, Mich. St. Univ., Lansing 1975-78. Career: health ofcr. Municipal Health Ofc., Mapandan, Pangasinan, Philippines 1963-72; regional med. cons. Dept. of Health, Philippines 1970-72; staff psychiatrist VA Med. Ctr., Battle Creek, Mich. 1978-83, Fresno Co. Mental Health, Fresno. Calif. 1984-86; med. dir. Madera Co. Mental Health, Madera, Calif. 1986-92, Fresno Co. Mental Health 1993–; awards: Phi Kappa Phi 1967, Outstanding Filipino in Midwest, Cavite Assn. of U.S. 1982, Public Svc. Cert. of Appreciation, Mayor Tom Bradley, L.A. 1992; mem: Am. Psychiatric Assn. 1978–, Assn. of Military Surgeons of U.S. 1980–, Am. Acad. of Clin. Psychiatrists 1984–, Am. Coll. of Physician Execs. 1990-92, Filipino-Am. Assn. of Fresno (v.p. 1986-88), Univ. of Philippines Alumni Assn. of Central Calif. (pres. 1990-94); author: jour. article, Philippine Demography/Public Health in Philippines, 1971; editor: Pangasinan Med. Soc. Jour., 1972; mil: lt. col. Med. Corps, 1981–; Republican; Roman Catholic; rec: chess. Res: 529 W. Robinwood Lane Fresno 93704 Ofc: Fresno County Mental Health 4441 E Kings Canyon Rd Fresno 93702

PARER, JULIAN THOMAS, physician, maternal-fetal medicine educator, administrator; b. Sept. 2, 1934, Melbourne, Australia; m. Robin M.W. Fletcher, Apr. 23, 1962; children: William John; edn: B.Agr.Sc., Univ. Melbourne, 1959; M.Rur.Sc., bioclimatology, Univ. of New England, Aus. 1962; PhD, Oregon State Univ., Corvallis 1965; MD, Univ. Washington, Seattle 1971; dipl. Am. Bd. Ob-Gyn, 1976, splty. dipl. maternal-fetal medicine, 1977. Career: res. asst. rural sci. Univ. New England, Aus. 1958-61; grad. fellow dept. animal sci. Oregon State Univ. 1961-63; grad. asst., summer fellow, res. fellow Heart Res. Lab. Univ. Oregon Med. Sch., 1961-66; vis. scientist Oregon Reg. Primate Res. Ctr. 1964-66; instr. dept. ob.-gyn. Univ. Wash., 1966-68, sr. fellow 1969-71, also mem. med. res. unit Child Devel. and Med. Retardation Ctr., mem. Anesthesia Res. Ctr.; res. affiliate Reg. Primate Ctr., Seattle 1969-71; resident ob-gyn. L.A. Co.-USC Sch. of Med., 1971-74; asst. prof., assoc. prof., prof. dept. obstets., gyn. and reproductive scis. UC San Francisco, 1974–, dept. assoc. v.chmn. 1987–, assoc. staff Cardiovascular Res. Inst. 1976–, dir. obstets. 1980-87, dir. maternal-fetal medicine fellowship tng. pgm. 1983–, codir. North Coast Perinatal Access System, UCSF, 1984-89; vis. scientist Nuffield Inst. for Med. Res., Univ. Oxford, Eng. 1981-82, Univ. de Chile, Santiago, Chile 1985, 86, 87, 88, 89, 91, Univ. of Auckland, N.Z. 1988, 89, 90; mem: Am. Coll. OB-Gyn (Fellow), Am. Physiol. Soc., Aus. Perinatal Soc., La Sociedad Chilena de Obstetricia y Ginecologia (hon.), Pac. Coast Obstet. Gynecol. Soc. (pgm. com. 1992), Perinatal Rsch. Soc., S.F. Gynecol. Soc. (pgm. chmn. 1989-90), Soc. for Gynecol. Investigation, Soc. Perinatal Obstets. (bd. 1988-91, pgm. chmn. 1991), Soc. for the Study of Fetal Physiology (org. com. 1990); spl. interests: Fetal responses to asphyxia; the circulation and oxygen transport in pregnancy; clin. fetal monitoring; Rh disease; High risk pregnancy; author: Handbook of Fetal Heart Rate Monitoring 1983; editor: Res. in Perinatal Medicine (w. P.W. Nathanielsz, 1984), Antepartum and Intrapartum Mgmt. 1989, contbr. numerous med. jour. articles and abstracts. Ofc: Univ. Calif. 505 Parnassus Ave San Francisco 94143-0550

PARKER, ROBERT GEORGE, professor of radiation oncology; b. Jan. 29, 1995, Detroit, Mich.; s. Clifford R. and Velma (Ashman) P.; m. Diana Davis, June 30, 1977; children: Thomas, James; edn: attended Univ. Mich. 1942-43; BS,

Univ. of Wis. 1946, MD, 1948. Career: instr. Univ. of Mich., Ann Arbor 1955; prof. Univ. of Wash., Seattle 1956-77; prof. and chair radiation oncology, UCLA Sch. of Medicine 1978–; awards: Gold Medal, Am. Soc. Therapeutic Radiology & Oncology, Alumnus of Yr. Univ. of Wis.; mem: AMA, Am. Soc. Therapeutic Radiology & Oncology (pres.), Am. Radium Soc. (pres.), Am. Bd. Radiology (pres.), Radiological Soc. of N. Am. (pres.); author: textbook, 150+ scientific articles; mil: lt. comdr. USNR 1952; rec: jazz piano, swimming, gardening, cooking. Res: 16840 Adlon Rd Encino 91436 Ofc: Dept Radiation Oncology UCLA Sch of Medicine 200 UCLA Medical Plaza Ste B265 Los Angeles 90024-6951

PARKER, THEODORE CLIFFORD, manufacturing company president; b. Sept. 25, 1929, Dallas, Ore.; s. Theodore C. and Virginia Bernice (Rumsey) P.; m. Jannet Barnes, Nov. 28, 1970; 2 daus: Sally, Peggy; edn: BSEE, magna cum laude, USC 1960. Career: v.p. engring. Telemetrics Inc. 1963-65; chief engr. Information Systems, Northrop-Nortronics 1966-70; pres. Avtel Corp. 1971-74; pres. Aragon Inc. 1975-77; v.p. engring. Teledyne McCormick Selph 1978-82; mgr. electronic systems FMC Corp., Ordnance Div. 1983-85; pres. Power One Switching Products (engring. & mfg.) 1985-86; pres. Condor Inc., D.C. Power Supplies, 1987; pres. Intelligence Power Inc., Camarillo 1988–; chmn. Autotestcon 87; honors: Tau Beta Pi, Eta Kappa Nu; mem: IEEE, Am. Prodn. & Inventory Control Soc., Electronics Assn. of Calif. (founding dir.), Am. Def. Preparedness Assn. Res: 1290 Saturn Ave Camarillo 93010 Ofc: Intelligence Power, Inc. 829 Flynn Rd Camarillo 93010

PARKS, JOHN LAWRENCE, real estate broker; b. June 22, 1951, Berwyn, Ill.; s. Victor Lawrence and Mary Phylis; edn: BS, Univ. Ill. Champaign 1973. Career: charts analyst Billboard Mag., Los Angeles 1973-74; sales rep. Fawcett Pubs. 1974-76; sales assoc. Harleigh Sandler Co., Beverly Hills 1976-78; v.p. Merrill Lynch Realty 1978-88; owner Unicorn Bookstore, W. Hollywood 1986-93; pres. John L. Parks Inc., Los Angeles 1981-894; awards: Million Dollar Club 1978-95, Blue Diamond Club 1979-95, Pres. Club 1983-95, Leading Edge Soc. 1984-95, Rookie of Year 1977; mem: B.H. Board of Realtors, Mt. Olympus Property Owners Assn. (treas. 1979-83, pres. 1984-86), W. Hollywood Chamber of Commerce, W. Hollywood Concerned Citizens (treas. 1984-95), W. Hollywood Community Alliance, Apt. Assn. Greater L.A. (dir. 1984-88); Democrat; Cath.; rec: skiing, bridge, travel. Res: 2500 Jupiter Dr Los Angeles 90046 Ofc: John Aaroe & Assocs 8687 Melrose Ave #B110 Los Angeles 90069

PARKS, RICHARD DEE, theater director; b. Aug. 29, 1938, Omaha; s. Charles and Josephine Marie-Rose P.; edn: BA, San Jose St. Univ., 1961; MA, Univ. Wash., 1963; postgrad. Stanford Univ. Career: faculty San Jose St. Univ., 1964-65, 1966-71, dir. theater SJSU, 1972-79, coordinator performance area, 1979-92, coord. auditions, 1975-92, chmn. performance area, coordinator M.F.A. performance degree program, 1983-92; instr. oral interpretation Stanford Univ., 1965-66, B.F.A. program Univ. Wash., 1971-72; exchange prof. Ventura Coll., spring 1982; actor, dir., prod.; exec. dir. Actors Symposium of Hollywood; sr. prod. Star Weekend projects NBC, 1978-91; cons. profl. and community theater orgns.; interim coordinator theater arts grad. program, 1977-78; dialects coach, voice and diction tutor; research cons. Ednl. Films of Hollywood; cons. Fourth Street Playhouse, Monterey Peninsula; cons. dir. Gen. Electric Sales Conf., Pajaro Dunes, 1983; awards: for new play directing Am. Coll. Theater Festival Reg. I 1975; mem: Calif. Ednl. Theater Assn. (exec. sec. treas. 1978-80), Am. Theater Assn., AAUP, Calif. Assn. Am. Conservatory Theater, Am. Coll. Theater Fest., Am. Film Inst., Dramatists Guild, Authors League Am.; clubs: Brit. Am., San Jose Players; author: plays: Charley Parkhurst Rides Again!, 1978, Wild West Women, 1980, Ken Kesey's Further Inquiry, 1980, stage adaptation of Tamden Prodns. Facts of Life, 1982,This Scepter'd Isle, 1995; books: How to Overcome Stage Fright, 1978, American Drama Anthology, 1979, The Role of Myth in Understanding Amber in the Ancient World, 1983, textbooks: Oral Expression, 1985 (2d rev. edit. 1986, 3d rev. edit. 1988-89, 4th rev. ed. 1994), Voice and Diction, 1990, tchg. supplement: Calendar of Am. Theater Hist., 1982, Principles of Rhetoric, 1993. Ofc: 37428 Centralmont Place Fremont 94536

PARROTT, JAMES EDWARD, chiropractor, acupuncturist, hypnotherapist; b. Aug. 7, 1924, El Paso, Tex.; s. John N. and Marie (Boudreaux) P.; m. Marilyn Fowler, Mar. 5, 1985; children: Joseph, Brynda Monique, Heidi Jacqueline; edn: DC, L.A. Coll. of Chiro. 1957; CBS Cert., basic sci., Ariz. State Univ., 1958; MA, Baptist Comm. Coll.: Oriental preceptorship in acupuncture, herbal med., Hong Kong Intl. 1960; grad. Hypnotism Tng. Inst., 1979; bd. cert. Acad. of Am. Pain Mgmt., 1990; Calif. lic. radiographer 1979, cert. instr. Hunter Safety. Career: lectr. and tchr. basic scis., Oriental Med.; chiropractor, acupuncturist, hypnotherapist, Acutherapy pioneer in U.S. 1960–; bd. chmn. Karmel Kookies Inc.; founder/ pres. San Pedro Prebuilt Homes; honors: Delta Sigma Hon. Scholastic Soc. of the Healing Arts (elected 1957); mem: NY Acad. of Sci., AAAS, Elks, Nat. Rifle Assn. (life), Calif. Rifle & Pistol Club (life), Sigma Chi Omega; mil: pharmacist 2c USN, USMC, WWII, Korean War, decorated Presdl. Unit Citations Korea & USA, Philippine Presdl. Medal, Am. Campaign medal w/ 1 Star, Asia-Pac. w/ 4 Stars, Nat. Def., Victory, United Nations Medal, Korean Svc. w/ 2 Stars; Democrat (State Central Com.); Cath. (Brother); rec: music, art, sculpture. Address: 812 W 5th St Oxnard 93030

PARRY, ROBERT T., economist; b. May 16, 1939, Harrisburg, Pa.; s. Anthony Charles and Margaret Ruth (Troutt) P.; m. Brenda Louise Grumbine, Dec. 27, 1956; children: Robert Richard, Lisa Louise; edn: BA, magna cum laude, Gettysburg Coll., 1960, MA, Univ. Penn., 1961, PhD, 1967. Career: asst. prof. econs. Phila., Coll. of Textiles & Sci. 1963-65; economist Fed. Reserve Bd., Wash. DC 1965-70; v.p., chief economist Security Pacific Nat. Bank 1970-76, senior v.p./chief economist 1976-81, exec. v.p./chief economist Security Pacific Corp. and Security Pacific Nat. Bank, 1981-86; CEO and pres. Fed. Reserve Bank of San Francisco, 1986–; mem. advy. bd. Pacific Rim Bankers Program; dir. Nat. Bur. of Econ. Research; exec. com. and dir. S.F. Bay Area Council; mem. S.F. Bay Area Economic Forum; mem. policy advy. bd. Ctr. for Real Estate & Urban Econs., UC Berkeley; advy. com. Inst. of Bus. & Econ. Res., UC Berkeley; honors: Phi Beta Kappa 1960, Nat. Defense Edn. Act grad. study fellow 1963; mem: SRI Internat. advy. council, Univ. of Pa. Econ. vis. com., Gettysburg Coll. Bd. of Fellows, Nat. Assn. Bus. Economists (pres. 1979-80), Am. Economic Assn., Boy Scouts Am. (exec. bd.), United Way (bd dirs.); contbr. num. articles to business and profl. jours. Res: 90 Overhill Rd Orinda 94563 Ofc: Federal Reserve Bank of San Francisco 101 Market St San Francisco 94105

PARSONS, ROBERT EUGENE, transportation research engineer; b. April 19, 1931, Cincinnati, Ohio; s. Charles Eugene and Samantha Ellen (Snider) P.; m. Beverly Greenhalgh, Dec. 30, 1949; children: Brian b. 1955, Barry b. 1957, Robert b. 1958, Kimberly b. 1960; edn: ME, Univ. Cincinnati 1954; MSME, Drexel Inst. Tech. 1959; reg. profl. engr. Ohio 1959, Md. 1959, Calif. 1982, Nev. 1985. Career: design/devel. engr. Cincinnati Milling Machinery, Cinti. 1950-54; engring. secton chief Martin Co., Baltimore, Md. 1956-62, asst. tech. dir. 1962-64; dept. dir. Super Speed Transp. FAA, Wash. D.C. 1964-71; dir. research and devel. plans/resources Office of Secty. of Transp. 1971-75; assoc. adminstr. research and devel. Fed. RR Adminstrn., Dept. Transp. 1975-80; research mgr. Nat. Bureau of Standards 1980-81; research splst. UC Berkeley 1981-84, dir. prog. of advanced tech. for highway (PATH), 1986-90; pres., cons. Parsons Trans. Assoc., ITS, 1990–; honors: Univ. Cincinnati disting. engring. alumni 1973, Fed. RR Adminstrn. superior achiev. 1976, 77, Dept. Transp. meritorious achiev. 1971, biog. listed Who's Who Aviation, Who's Who in Govt., Who's Who in Fin. and Indus., Who's Who in Calif., Who's Who in Am.; publs: numerous articles in tech. jours., 1964, patent; mil: 1st lt. AUS 1954-56; Methodist; rec: computers, home remodelling, grandchildren.

PARSONS, ROBERT Q., executive; b. May 1, 1915, Roswell, N.M.; s. Wyly and Mary (Quarterman) P.; m. Nancy Nickerson, April 13, 1940; children: Linda b. 1940, Robert b. 1944, William b. 1948; edn: BSME, Univ. Ariz. 1938; reg. profl. mech. engr. Career: sales engr. Firestone Tire & Rubber Co., Los Angeles 1938-50; pres. Century Engrs., Burbank 1950-57; engring. cons., L.A. 1957-64; pres. Frank Kimball Parsons & Daum 1964-74; Robert Q. Parsons & Co., San Marino 1974–; dir: Perrin Mfg. Co., City of Industry 1981–, Zero Corp., L.A. 1950-64; honors: Tau Beta Pi, Young Pres. Orgn. L.A., Univ. Ariz. hon. degree 1955; mem. Young Pres. Orgn. Graduates, Rotary Internat.; author: Anatomy of a Merger (1970); Republican; R.Cath.; rec: travel. Address: San Gabriel 91775

PARSONS, STUART OVERTON, JR., industrial psychologist, human factors consultant, ergonomist educator; b. Aug. 11, 1926, Denver; s. Stuart O. Sr. and Gladys (East) P.; m. Harriet Jaggard, July 11, 1955; children: Carol, Cynthia, Pamela; edn: BA psych., Colorado Univ., 1948; MA psych., USC, 1950, PhD indsl. psychology, 1958; lic. psychologist, reg. profl. engr., Calif., cert. profl. ergonomist. Career: aviation electronics technician USN 1944-46, WWII, served to col. (ret. 1983) Navy and Air Force reserve, assignments in human factors in AF Systems Command, was mobilization asst. to dir. maint. Sacto. Air Logistics Ctr., decorated USAF Total Force Award and Meritorious Service Medal 1983; psychometrician Colo. Merit System, Denver 1947-48; personnel technician City of Denver 1950-51; res. assoc. Psychological Svs. Inc., Los Angeles 1951-53; industrial relations splst. Lockheed Corp. Offices, Burbank 1954-57, engring. mgr. Lockheed Missile & Space Co., Sunnyvale 1958-87; pres. Parsons and Assocs., Saratoga 1987–, cons./splst. human factors/ergonomics, mgmt., organizational and forensic psychology, energy systems, maint., safety, and tng.; condr. mgmt. seminars for execs. of Commonwealth of Independent States (CIS) 1990-91; lectr. Coll. of Notre Dame 1993–; lectr. San Jose State Univ. 1964-92, adj. assoc. prof. USC 1969-91, adj. prof. Univ. Denver 1987-93, res. faculty Waseda Univ., Tokyo 1988-89; past instr. mgmt. courses Lockheed and McClellan AFB; mem. Human Factors and Ergonomics Soc. (fellow), AIAA (assoc. fellow), Bay Area Human Factors Soc. (charter, dir.), Internat. Ergonomics Soc. (U.S. del. 1991–), Reserve Ofcrs. Assn.; author 40+ books and jour. articles, 1960-94; Episcopalian; rec: skiing, golf, tennis, travel. Address: 19740 Via Escuela Dr Saratoga 95070 Ph./Fax: 408/867-0987

PARVIS, RENEE PAPERNER, business communications consultant, writer; b. Sept. 16, 1952, St. Louis, Mo.; d. Boris and Dorothy (Katz) Paperner; m. John G. Parvis, April 8, 1979; edn: BJ journalism, Univ. Mo. 1973. Career: pub. affairs dir., talk show host KSLQ FM, St. Louis, Mo. 1974-79; pub. rels. cons. social service agencies, Akron and Kent, Ohio 1980-81; writer, producer Goodyear Tire & Rubber Co., Akron, Ohio 1981-84; v.p., copy dir. Citicorp Comms. Design, Sacto. 1985-90; prin. Renee Parvis Communications 1990–; comms. cons. Calif.

Arts Council Bus. Vols. for Arts, Sacto. 1988–; guest lectr. UC Davis 1987; awards: Society for Mktng. Profl. Svcs. 1989, Credit Union Mktg. Assn. Golden Mirror 1989, Mo. Broadcasters Assn. Pub. Service Campaign 1977, Sacto. Ad Club: Identity Devel. 1989, 2 Delta awards 1989, 92, 4 Silver awards 1993, 94, Fin. Inst. Mktg. Assn. awards (3), 1990, Internat. Assn. Bus. Communicators Crystal award 1991, Calif. Mktg. Assn. Gold awards 1992, listed Who's Who in Calif., 2000 Notable Am. Women; mem: Calif. Literacy Campaign (tutor 1988). Res/Ofc: 1500 Bolivar Ct El Dorado Hills 95762

PASTEN, LAURA JEAN, veterinarian; b. May 25, 1952, Tacoma, Wash.; edn: Stanford Univ. 1970; BA physiol., UC Davis 1970, DVM, 1974; postgrad., Cornell Univ. 1975; Career: vet. Nevada Co. Vet. Hosp. Grass Valley 1975-80; pvt. practice vet., owner Mother Lode Vet. Hosp. Grass Valley (certified wildlife rehab. ctr.) 1980–; veterinarian for Morris, the 9-Lives cat (of t.v. comml. fame) 1985–; lectr. in field, spokesperson for Nat. Cat Health Month; affil. staff Sierra Nevada Meml. Hosp.; bd. dirs. Sierra Svcs. for the Blind; syndicated TV show on vet. medicine, guest on Today Show re wildlife; honors: Regent's Scholar, Woman of Yr. Am. Biog. Inst. 1991, Woman of Decade Who's Who Soc., Lifetime Achievement Award; mem: Am. Vet. Med. Assn. (ethics com.), Sacto. Valley Vet. Med. Assn. (exec. com., CVMA del.), Mother Lode Vet. Assn., Am. Animal Hosp. Assn., Nat. Ophthalmic Soc., Nat. Pygmy Goat Assn., Nat. Llama Assn., Internat. Assn. of Arabians, Denver Area Med. Soc., Internat. Vet. Assn., Mensa, Nat. Soc. Underwater Instrs., Am. Endurance Riding Soc.; civic: Nevada Co. CofC (bd. dirs.), Grass Valley Bus. Women, affiliate staff mem. Sierra Nevada Meml. Hosp., bd. dirs. Sierra Services for the Blind, adv. bd. Veterinary Forum; publ: Canine Dermatology (w. Dr. Muller 1970), contbr. articles to profl. jours.; Republican; Lutheran. Address: 11509 La Barr Meadows Rd Grass Valley 95949

PATE, CHRISTINE VETTER, superior court judge; b. Sept. 27, 1943, San Diego; d. William Paul and Ethel Marguerite (Waters) Vetter; m. William Craig Pate, Oct. 30, 1966; children: William C., Bryan L., David G., Douglas F.; edn: BA, Univ. Calif., 1965, JD, Univ. San Diego, 1969; admitted bar: Calif., U.S. Dist. Ct. so. dist. Calif. 1970. Career: atty., shareholder law firm Jennings, Engstrand & Henrikson, San Diego, 1970-88; judge Superior Ct., San Diego 1988–; bd. dirs. San Diego Law Center; mem: Calif. Bar Assn. (dist. rep. 1983-86), Calif. Judges Assn., San Diego Co. Bar Assn. (past dir., v.p., sec.), Lawyers Club of San Diego (past pres.), San Diego Vol. Lawyers (bd. 1984-87), Rotary Internat.; Republican; R.Cath. Ofc: Superior Court 220 W Broadway San Diego 92101

PATERSON, THOMAS GLYNN, management consultant, inventor, author and speaker; b. Mar. 12, 1925, Kearny, N.J.; s. Robert Burns and Marion (Glynn) P.; m. Virginia Katherine White, Sept. 30, 1944; children: Thomas b. 1945 (dec.), James b. 1948, Jay b. 1951, Deborah b. 1954 (dec.), Kathleen b. 1959, Carol b. 1961, William b. 1963; edn: BS, Boston Univ., 1947; MBA, Pepperdine Univ., 1978. Career: staff mem. Air Transport Plng. Team, McDonnell Douglas Corp., Santa Monica 1952-55; dir. market plng. Northrop Corp. Electronics Div., Hawthorne 1955-60; dir. bus. plng. IBM Corp. Fed. Systems Div., Wash. DC 1960-62; dir. corporate plng. pgms. RCA Corp., Camden, N.J. 1963-70; pres. Paterson and Company, Acton, Ca. 1970–, recognized internat. for devel. of the "Tom Paterson Process" a form of participation mgmt. enabling instns. to achieve higher levels of performance through enterprise system mgmt. and cross-functional teamwork; founded Thomas G. Paterson Ctr. for cross-functional tng. 1993; dir: Process Equipment Co., Anaheim 1987-90; mem: bd. govs. City of Hope Nat. Med. Ctr., Duarte 1975–, Research Advy. Council, The Planning Forum; honors: Nat. Mktg. Assn. marketing man of yr., NYC 1968, hon. overseas cons. to The Peoples Rep. of China and the Chinese Acad. of Scis., Beijing 1987; listed and 10th Ed. dedication in Who's Who of Intellectuals, Cambridge, Eng. 1992, 5000 Personalities of World for outstanding contbn. to mgmt. scis. (3d. ed.), Human Resources Hall of Fame Ingersoll-Rand Co. 1993; Order of Merit, Internat. Biographical Ctr., Cambridge, England 1993; invention: Automatic Cash Dispensing System (pat. 1969); publs: 200+ articles and essays 1950–; mil: pfc USMC 1943-44; Republican (Pres.'s Club of Rep. Nat. Com., Senatorial Commn. award Rep. Senatl. Inner Circle); Prot.; rec: organist, swimming, garden. Address: Paterson and Company, PO Box 6676 Big Bear Lake 92315

PATRICK, CAROL SUE, real estate executive; b. June 6, 1944, Bakersfield; d. Lester Lewis and Freda Evelyn (Headlee) Williams; m. Charles Patrick, Jan. 13, 1961; children: Kelley b. 1962, LeAnne b. 1966; edn: Bakersfield Coll. 1977; USC 1980; limited svc. cred. Calif. Bd. Edn. 1978. Career: realtor 1971–; gen. bldg. contractor 1979-1983; owner Mid-Valley Real Estate 1976–; secty CMC Corp. 1986–; mem: Bakersfield Bd. of Realtors Calif. Nat. Assn.; civic: First Baptist Ch.; Bakersfield Coll. Alumni Assn.; Republican; Baptist; rec: crafts, sewing, cooking. Res: 12632 Kern Canyon Rd Bakersfield 93306 Ofc: Mid-Valley Real Estate 4664 American Ave Bakersfield 93309

PATRICK, CHARLES LEON, real estate broker/ building contractor; b. Feb. 3, 1938; s. Elby Leon and Dorothy Aline (Hicks) P.; m. Carol Sue, Jan. 13, 1961; children; Kelley, b. 1962; LeAnne, b.1966; edn: Bakersfield Coll. 1968-69; Lumbleau Real Estate Sch. 172, 73, 75; UC Santa Barbara 1977; USC 1982;

Limited Svc. Cred., Calif. State Dept. of Edn. 1977; Cert. Real Estate Appraiser 1986. Career: draftsman, surveyor, instrument-man, engr. Southern Pacific Transp. Co., Bakersfield 1961-75; gen. building contr., real estate broker, Bakersfield 1976–; owner Mid-Valley Real Estate, and C.L. Patrick Construction; mem: Bakersfield Board of Realtors, Calif., Nat. Assns. of Realtors, Independent Contractors Assn. 1971–; clubs: Bakersfield Trade, Meudell Lodge Freemasons, Bakersfield Christian Life Schools Booster, Bakersfield College Alumni Assn., UCSB Alumni Assn., Bakersfield Racquet; Republican; Baptist; rec: antique cars. Res: 12632 Hwy 178 Bakersfield 93306 Ofc: Mid-Valley Real Estate/C.L. Patrick Construction, 4664 American Ave Bakersfield 93309

PATRICK, LEANNE KAY, teacher; b. Aug. 16, 1966, Bakersfield, Calif.; d. Charles Leon and Carol Sue (Williams) Patrick; edn: AA, Bakersfield Coll., 1986; BA, CSU Bakersfield, 1990; Cert. Attorney Asst. Tng. Pgm. (hons.), UC Los Angeles, 1988-89; Calif. tchg. credential (sec., social studies), Calif. Lutheran Univ., 1992. Mem. Nat. Assn. of Legal Assts., CSU Bakersfield Alumni; Republican; Prot.; rec: golf, crafts, roller blading, youth work. Res: 3333 El Encanto Ct #32 Bakersfield 93301

PATSEY, RICHARD LEE, judge; b. April 23, 1935, St. Joseph, Mo.; s. Gerald Julien and Sigrid Sofia (Parson) P.; m. Lois Kathryn Berg, Sept. 13, 1958; children: Shannon b. 1961, Geoffrey b. 1965; edn: BA, Carleton Coll., 1957; LLB, UC Boalt Hall, 1960. Career: counsel Calif. St. Assembly Judiciary Com., Sacto. 1960-61; instr. McGeorge Coll. of Law 1960-61; asst. dist. atty. Contra Costa County, Martinez 1961; asst. pub. defender Alameda County, Oakland 1961; exec. dir. Calif. Constitution Revision Commn., Sacto. 1963-64; ptnr. law firm Leonards & Patsey, San Francisco 1964-80; judge Superior Ct., Martinez 1980–, presiding judge Civil Div. Contra Costa Superior Ct. 1989–; prof. of law J.F. Kennedy Law Sch., Walnut Creek 1985-87; statewide lectr. various law assns. 1980; awards: Ford Found. grant 1960-61, Nat. Endowment for Humanities grantee 1981, Alameda-Contra Costa Trial Lawyers trial judge of yr. 1982; mem: Am. Bar Assn., Calif. Judges Assn., Am. Judicial Soc., Contra Costa Bar Assn.; civic: Right Direction Project Advy. Bd. 1985, Edn. for Foster Parents Pgm. Contra Costa Co. (founder, dir. 1986), Senior Tutors for Youth Inc. Contra Costa Co. (dir. 1988); publs: numerous articles re law and legal procedure, 1960; Democrat; Prot.; rec: music, tennis, skiing. Ofc: Contra Costa Superior Court 1020 Ward St 2d Floor Martinez 94553

PATTEN, BEBE HARRISON, clergywoman, educator; b. Sept. 3, 1913, Waverly, Tenn.; d. Newton Felix and Mattie Priscilla (Whitson) Harrison; m. Carl Thomas Patten, Oct. 23, 1935; children: (twins) Priscilla Carla and Bebe Rebecca, Carl Thomas; edn: DD, McKinley- Roosevelt Coll. 1941; D.Litt., Temple Hall Coll. & Sem. 1943. Career: ordained to ministry, Ministerial Assn. of Evangelism 1935; evangelist in various cities of US 1933-50; founder/pres. Christian Evangelical Churches of Am. Inc. 1944–; founder/pres. Patten Acad. Christian Edn., Oakland 1944–; Patten Bible Coll., Oakland 1944-83; pres.-emeritus/chancellor, Patten Coll. 1983–; founder/pastor Christian Cathedral of Oakland 1950–; condr. pgm., The Shepherd Hour, 1934–, weekly telecast 1976–, nat. telecast 1979–, KUSW world-wide radio ministry heard in 70 countries, 1989-90; WHRI (2 million watts), WWCR (3.5 million watts) world coverage short wave, 1990–; mem. Global bd. trustees 1991, exec. bd. and Hon. Fellow, Bar-Ilan Univ., Israel; Dr. Bebe Patten Chair in Social Action established, Bar-Ilan Univ. 1982; Dr. Bebe Patten Day proclaimed by City of Oakland, 11/4/94; ldr. 20 pilgrimages to Israel in interest of Christian-Judaic relationship since 1962; private interview w/Israeli Prime Ministers: David Ben-Gurion 1972, Menachim Begin 1977, Yitzhak Shamir 1991; awards: medallion, Ministry of Religious Affairs, Israel 1969; medal, Govt. Press Ofc., Jerusalem 1971; Christian honoree of Year, Jewish Nat. Fund of No. Calif. 1975; Hidden Heroine award, S.F. Bay Council, Girl Scouts USA 1976; Ben-Gurion medallion, Ben-Gurion Research Inst. 1977, Resolutions of commendation, Calif. Senate Rules Com. 1978, 94; mem: Am. Assn. for Higher Edn.; Religious Edn. Assn.; Am. Acad. Religion & Soc. Bibl. Lit.; Zionist Orgn. of Am.; Am. Jewish Hist. Soc.; Am. Israel Pub. Affairs Comm. 1983; works: author, Give Me Back My Soul, 1973; editor, Trumpet Call, 1953–; composer 20 gospel & religious songs 1948–; listed in num. biographical publs.; rec: swimming, tennis. Ofc: 2433 Coolidge Ave Oakland 94601

PATTEN, BEBE REBECCA, academic dean, Patten College; b. Jan. 30, 1950, Berkeley, Calif.; d. Carl Thomas and Bebe (Harrison) Patten; edn: BS (summa cum laude), Bible, Patten Bible Coll., Oakland, Calif., 1969; BA, Philosophy, Coll. of the Holy Names, Oakland, Calif., 1971; MA (with honors), New Testament, Wheaton Coll., Chgo., Ill., 1972; PhD (with honors), New Testament, Drew Univ., Madison, N.J., 1976; MA, Philosophy, Dominican Coll., Berkeley, Calif., 1990; 9 units, Higher Edn. Adminstrn., UC Berkeley, 1991-94. Career: co-pastor, Christian Cathedral of the Christian Evangelical Churches of Am., Inc., Oakland 1964–; tchg. fellow prof., Drew Univ. 1974-75; assoc. prof., Patten Bible Coll., Oakland 1975-82; prof. of New Testament, Patten Coll., 1982–; academic dean, Patten Coll. 1977–; mem., bd. of dir., Christian Evangelical Churches of Am., Inc. 1964–; fellowship, Kierkegaard Lib., St. Olaf's Coll. 1990, 91; awards: Patten Bible Coll.: Honor Student 1966, Gold "P" 1969, Most Beloved Student award 1968, Heart award 1971; listed in:

Outstanding Young Women of Am. 1976, 77, 80-81, 82, Notable Americans 1976-77, 78-79, The World Who's Who of Women 1977, 79, 81-82, Personalities of the West and Midwest 1977-78, 80, Book of Honor (A.B.I.) 1979, Dictionary of Internat. Biography 1979-80, Men and Women of Distinction 1979-80, Personalities of Am. 1979, Who's Who in Calif. 1979-80, 81-82, Comm. Leaders and Noteworthy Americans 1980, Who's Who of American Women 1981-82, 83-84, 85-86, 93-94, Who's Who in the West 1985, 92, 93-94, Who's Who in Religion 1985, 92-93, Who's Who in the Humanities 1992, Who's Who in Am. Edn. 1991, 92-93, Who's Who of Emerging Leaders in Am. 1991; mem: Am. Acad. of Religion 1975–, Soc. of Biblical Lit. 1975–, Am. Assn. of Univ. Professors 1975–, Christian Assn. for Student Affairs 1980, Phi Delta Kappa 1980, Inst. for Biblical Res. 1981, Assn. for Christians in Student Devel. 1981; civic: founder, 45-mem. youth orchestra, Christian Cathedral 1969-71; founder/conductor, 45-mem. intermediate orch., Patten Christian Schools 1975-82; violinist, harpist, Christian Cathedral; symphony mem.: Holy Names Coll. 1966-71, Berkeley Symphony Youth Orch. 1968, Wheaton Coll. Symphony 1971-72, Young Artists Symphony (N.J.) 1972-75, Somerset Hill Symphony (N.J.) 1973-74, Peninsula Symphony (Calif.) 1977-81, Madison Chamber Trio (N.J.) 1973-75, Redwood Symphony (Calif.) 1990–; author: Before the Times, 1980; The World of the Early Church, 1990; The Role of Reason in Faith in Kierkegaard and St. Thomas (in process); 7 publ. articles in Internat. Standard Biblical Encyclopedia, Rev. Edit., 1983–; 2 book reviews publ in the Nacada Jour. 1990, 93. Res: 190 Alderwood Lane Walnut Creek 94598. Ofc. 2433 Coolidge Ave Oakland 94601

PATTERSON, J. MICHAEL, certified public accountant; b. Mar. 6, 1946, Washington, Ia.; s. J. Kenneth and Jo Ann P.; m. Marci Feiock, Aug. 28, 1979; children: Lori b. 1964, Lisa b. 1966, Todd b. 1970, Staci b. 1972; edn: BBA, Univ. of Iowa 1968; JD, Univ. of Chgo. 1973; CPA, Iowa 1970, Ill. 1971, Calif. 1973; Realtor, Calif. 1978. Career: acct. Price Waterhouse, Chgo., then San Jose, Calif., ptnr. in charge, San Jose br.; frequent pub. spkr.; honors: Beta Alpha Psi (v.p. 1968), Phi Delta Phi; mem. Am. Inst. CPA, Calif. Inst. CPA, ABA, Calif. St. Bar Assn., Santa Clara Bar Assn. (Tax Sect. exec. com.), Estate Planning Council, Am. Electronics Assn. (tax subcom., No. Calif. exec. com.); civic bds: Kiwanis San Jose (dir.), Southwest YMCA (dir.), Santa Clara Co. Trunk & Tusk Club, Childrens Discovery Mus. (dir.), Villa Montalvo Assn. (pres.), Silicon Valley Capital Club (chmn. 1992-94); mil: spec. E5 US Army 1968-70; Republican (Fin. Com. for Morgan for Senate 1983-93); Methodist; rec: sports. Res: 17286 Clearview Dr Los Gatos 95030 Ofc: Price Waterhouse 150 Almaden Ave San Jose 95113

PATTERSON, MARION L., photographer, college photography instructor; b. Apr. 24, 1933, San Francisco; d. Morrie Leslie and Esther Elizabeth (Parker) P.; edn: BA (cum laude) philosophy w. art minor, Stanford Univ., 1955; MA, San Francisco St. Univ., 1970; adv. studies Calif. Sch. of Fine Arts 1956-58, Univ. Fla. 1969, studies in photography under Ansel Adams, Dorothea Lange, Minor White, Jerry Uelsmann, Don Worth, Beaumont and Nancy Newhall. Career: clk. Best's Studio, Yosemite (Ansel & Virginia Adams owners) 1958-61; asst. to photog. editor Sunset Mag., Menlo Park 1961-64; freelance photog., Oaxaca, Mexico 1964-66; comms. cons. Projects to Advance Creativity in Edn., San Mateo 1966-68; instr. photography Foothill Coll., Los Altos Hills 1968–, photog. dept. chair 86–; instr. DeAnza Coll., Coll. of Marin, Coll. of San Mateo, West Valley Coll., Merced Coll., UC Santa Cruz, S.F. St. Univ.; workshops: Calif. Acad. of Scis., Oakland Mus., The Ansel Adams Workshop, The Friends of Photography Workshop, Nature Expeditions Internat. (NEI), and pvt. workshops; mem. Am. Soc. of Magazine Photographers; rep. by Photo Researchers, NY, NY; rep. in permanent collections: M.I.T., George Eastman House, Univ. Ariz., Oakland Mus., Ansel Adams, Dorothea Lange, Minor White, others; photographic exhibits: one-woman: S.F. Mus. of Modern Art, Focus Gal. Oakland Mus., Gallery 115, Monterey County Mus. of Art, Oaxaca Mus., Stanford Univ., Kasteel Hoensbroeck Holland, Ansel Adams Gal. Yosemite, Univ. of Bayreuth W.Ger. Photographer's Gal.; group: M.I.T., George Eastman House, Polaroid Corp., Art Embassies, Indiana Univ., Univ. Fla., Critics Choice Traveling Exh., CSU Humboldt Arcata, New Light L.A., New Directions Palo Alto; photographic expeditions in East Africa, Cent. Am., Mexico, Nepal, Pakistan, P.R.O.China, India, Sikkim, Bhutan, Tibet, Japan, Thailand, we. U.S.; TV interviews on KQED, KRON, local cable stations, subject 1/2 hr. documentary by First Generation (NEA grant), recipient Point Found. "Most Creative and Extraordinary" award, biog. listed Who's Who of Am. Women, Who's Who in West, Internat. Biography of Women. Res: Box 842 Menlo Park 94026 Ofc: Foothill College 12345 El Monte Rd Los Altos Hills 94022

PAUL, JOASH EPHRAIM, real estate broker, former elected official; b. Sept. 23, 1919, Turlock; s. Philip and Sarah (David) P.; m. Julia David, Feb. 15, 1947; children: Joyce b. 1948, Joan b. 1949, Dean b. 1951, Timothy b. 1956, Therese b. 1958, Bernadette b. 1962, David b. 1965; edn: AA, Modesto Jr. Coll. 1940, att. UC Berkeley, law courses LaSalle Ext. Univ.; lic. R.E. broker Calif. 1949–. Career: active duty US Army 1941-46; grower/owner grape and almond ranch 1946-76; co-owner food and lodging bus. 1952-77; dir.: Town & Country Thrift, Turlock; apptd. Growers' Harvesting Com., 1960, Stanislaus County Grand Jury, 1961, Grape Crush Adminstrn. Com., 1962, College Area Plng. Com., 1963,

Stanislaus County Planning Commn., 1964-68; elected supr. Stanislaus County Board of Supervisors, 3-terms, 1968-80: bd. chmn. 3 yrs., mem. health & welfare com., labor relations com., chmn. bd. Stanislaus County Retirement Bd.; past mem. County Suprs. Assn. of Calif. (chmn. labor relations 2 yrs.), Nat. Assn. of Counties (employee relations steering com. until 1981); mem. Commonwealth Club of Calif., Am. Legion, past dir. Am. Red Cross, K.C. (3d, 4th deg., past Grand Kt., past Navigator), past pres. Parents/Tchrs. cent. Cath. H.S., past pres. Assyrian Am. Civic Club, mem. S.E.S., I.D.E.S., UC Alumni Assn., Modesto J.C. Alumni Assn., Turlock C.of C., Scenic Gen. Hosp. Found. (founding pres.), Cath. Charities Diocese of Stockton corp. bd., Sacred Heart Ch. Turlock. Ofc: JDT Realty PO Box 1821 Turlock 95381

PAUL, ROBERT QUINN, manufacturing company executive (retired); b. Feb. 7, 1929, Chicago, Ill.; s. Peter and Edna (Quinn) P.; m. Judith Mary Smallegan, July 15, 1951; children: Gary Scott b. 1952, Jane Ellen; edn: Hope Coll. 1947-48; Western Mich. Univ. 1948; John Marshall Law Sch. 1948-49; Am. Acad. Art Chgo. 1952. Career: customer service Monsen Typographers, Chgo., Ill. 1948-57, co. pres., L.A. 1957-92; Supertype 1978-92; v.p., treas. The Classic Typographer, Santa Ana 1987-92; chmn. L.A. Internat. Typographical Joint Apprentice Com. 1968-72; mem: Printing Industries of L.A. (exec. com., bd. dirs. 1970), Printing Industries of Am. (union employers sect. 1969-70), Printing Industries of L.A., Westlake Lions (pres. 1963-64); rec: tennis, bowling. Res: 48-571 Valley View Dr Palm Dessert 90028

PAULSEN, PATRICK LAYTON, entertainer/comedian; b. July 6, 1927, South Bend, Wa.; s. Norman Inge and Beulah Inez (Fadden) P.; m. Noma Henriques; children: Terri b. 1959, Monty b. 1962, Justin b. 1964; edn: att. San Francisco City Coll. Career: comedian, entertainer "Smothers Brothers Comedy Hour" 1967-69, 1975, 1987-88, 1989, "Pat Paulsen's Half a Comedy Hour" 1970; film appearances: "Harper Valley PTA", "Elly", "Night Patrol", "They Still Call Me Bruce"; owner Cherry Co. Playhouse, Muskegon, Mich. 1975–; awards: Emmy Award 1968, Smile Award Calif. Travel Industry 1990; mem: Actor's Equity Assn., Comedy Hall of Fame (bd. dirs.), Screen Actors Guild, Am. Federation of Television & Radio Artists; presdl. candidate 1968, 72, 76, 84, 88, 92, 96; mil: USMC 1945-46; rec: tennis, golf, reading. Ofc: Entertainment Alliance PO Box 5734 Santa Rosa 95402-5734

PAULSON, JOHN ERIC, photographer; b. Oct. 14, 1957, Syracuse, N.Y.; s. Roy Wilson and Wanda (Lewandowski) P.; m. Diane Josephine Pifferetti, March 27, 1981; children: Kirsten, A.J.; edn: BA, San Jose St. Univ. 1988. Career: self-employed John Paulson Photog., San Jose 1978–; mem: Profl. Photographers of Am. (master photographer, photographic craftsman), Profl. Photographers of Greater Bay Area (pres. 1989); Republican; Christian. Ofc: John Paulson Photography 2995 Leigh Ave San Jose 95124

PAULSON, RAYMOND ARNOLD, engineering executive, law college founder; b. Dec. 29, 1921, Eagle Rock, Calif.; s. Arnold Edwin and Clara (Martin) P.; m. Beverly Doris, Sept. 21, 1941; children: Larry b. 1949, Jerry b. 1952, Celeste b. 1953; edn: JD, Calif. Coll. of Law; grad. studies Citrus Coll., Nat. Inst., USC. Career: radar navigator USAAF, WWII, crewman on a diversionary aircraft during A-bombing of Heroshiima and Nagasaki, Aug. 1946; law instr. U.S. Armed Forces Inst.; dir., mgr. for nat. major mfr., prod. 1st tactical Army Missile, The Corporal, 1959; sales mgr., asst. dir. So. Calif. Credit Bureau; engr., designer radiation and chem. eval. test laboratories for USAF; dir., mgr. electro-mechanical bus.; founder Calif. Coll. of Law; pres., chmn. bd. Paulson Internat. Corp., 1971-90, ret., hon. chmn. 1990–; pres. World Trust Agency (an agy. of fin. engring. of country and bank fin. re-structuring by the Paulson Private Trust, a Denmark Heritage since 1900), div. Paulson Devel. Corp.; founder Paulson Products Co.; sole prop. Paulson Co.; devel. and taught exec. leadership tng. pgm. Baldwin Park Schs. Adult Edn. Dept.; talent locator for "I Love Lucy Show" (Lucille Ball & Desi Arnaz); w/ Harry Lubke started TV Acad. of Arts and Science (originator, Life Assoc. Member); estab. Paulson Trust (a pvt. trust), Guatemala Private Sector Country Trust Fund (1st country trust fund for mng. and mktg., A country bridge to free trade of S.Am. and the world); designer; assoc. dir. World Internat. Air & Space Show 1993, Las Vegas, Nev., Sky Harbor and McCarron Airports, Hqs. for World Air & Space Tours; assoc. designer of thermal battery and developer of 1st semi-perpetual electric vehicle (1980); pioneered color telecasting as assoc. dir. w/Carlton Winckler of CBS Color TV "Union Pacific - Ed Wynn" (1st full color 2-hr. TV show) Hollywood (1940); recipient merit award L.A. Co. Supt. of Schools div. Research & Sci. Guidance; leadership tng. dir. Boy Scouts Am. Monte Vista dist.; jt. originator of the Toys for Tots (US Marine Corps Christmas Pgm. for underprivileged kids); works: surveyed and designed the U.S. Canal, 1400 hundred mile waterway National City-Brownsville, Tx., feasibility approved by US Congress 1982; designed the Fly by Wire Flight Control System 1983 and mfr. first all composite single eng. two place jet spacecraft in world; Paulson Trust developed the 1st all composite semi perpetual electric jet small passenger train; designed and devel. "VAC-PAC All Purpose Shipping Container" ship, rail & truck (12/91), designed and produced semi-perpetual self-contained charging system for elect. vehicle battery sources. Ofc: World Trust Agency POB 4369 Covina 91723

PAULSON, TERRY LEE, lecturer, author, psychologist; b. Oct. 23, 1945, Panama City, Fla.; s. Homer Frederick and Ann Marie (Carlson) P.; m. Kathleen Wynn Hiebert, Mar. 16, 1968 (div. 1976); m. 2d. Valorie Ann Leland, June 19, 1976; 1 son, Sean Douglas b. 1971; edn: BA psychology, UCLA 1968; MA theology, Fuller Theological Seminary 1975; PhD psychology, Fuller Grad. Sch. Psychology 1974. Career: staff psychologist Orange Co. Mental Health, Anaheim 1974-76; pres., trainer, speaker, author Paulson & Assoc. Inc., Agoura Hills 1974–; ext. lectr. UCLA 1976-91; UC Berkeley 1982-90; awards: Nat. Speakers Assn. CSP Cert. Spkg. Profl. 1988, CPAE Council of Peers Award of Excellence 1991, Am. Soc. Tng. & Devel. Top Presenter 1981; mem: Nat. Speakers Assn. (Nat. Bd.), Am. Soc. Tng. & Devel., Westlake Lutheran Ch., Wellness Comm. (advy. bd.); author: Teacher Training on Discipline, 1975, Making Human Work, 1989, They Shoot Managers Don't They?, 1989, Secrets of Life Every Teen Needs to Know, 1990, Paulson on Change, 1995; author, ed. Management Dialogue, 1980–; Republican; Lutheran; rec: backpacking, running, travel. Ofc: Paulson & Associates Inc 28717 Colina Vista Agoura Hills 91301

PAYNE, MAX BIEHL, petroleum geologist, retired; b. Jan. 23, 1910, Glenns Ferry, Idaho; s. Fred C. and Alice Amanda (Biehl) P.; m. Karen Amundson (div.); m. Charlotte Louise Annin, Dec. 8, 1946; children: Anne b. 1947, Fred b. 1949, Martha b. 1955, Robert b. 1963; edn: undergrad. Univ. Puget Sound, Tacoma, Wa. 1932-34; BS geology, Univ. Wash., Seattle 1936. Career: paleontol. lab. and field geologist Union Oil Co. of Calif., Bakersfield 1936-37; oil field mapping and resrch. Richfield Oil Corp. in Rio Bravo and Coles Levee Oil Fields, Cuyama Valley, and Wheeler Ridge, western U.S. 1937-42; served to lt. cmdr. US Navy 1942-46, So. Pacific during WWII with PB4Y Bomber Sq. VB109, later in chg. field party geologic field mapping for USN Petroleum Reserve #4 Umiat, Alaska on the north slope, decorated 5 campaigns, Bronze Star, Am. Theatre, Presdl. Unit cit. w. bronze star; engring. dept. Union Oil Co., Bakersfield, 1946-47; dist. geologist Signal Oil & Gas Corp., Bkfld. 1947-52; v.p./gen. mgr. Natural Gas Corp. of Calif. (sold to PG&E) 1952-53; oil & mineral cons. Stansbury-Del Webb, 1953-54; res. Eocene/ Cretaceous on west side of San Joaquin Valley, 1936-76; chief geologist Norris Oil Co., Bkfld. 1955-65;Chairman, Am. Assn. of Petroleum Geologists Cross-section Com. for the San Andreas Fault; Texfel Pet. Corp., Westwood 1965-68; indep. exploration cons. 1968-69; mgr. oil concessions for Weaver Pet. of Pa., P.R. and Jamaica, 1969; exploration cons. for oil and gas, hard minerals, geothermal in western U.S., 1970-87; honors: Sigma Alpha Epsilon 1934, guest of Chinese Govt. geol. dept. via People-to-People 1983; mem: Am. Assn. Pet. Geologists (cert. 1938), Soc. Econ. Paleontology and Mineralogy 1960–, Am. Inst. Profl. Geologists (cert. 1962), Am. Assn. for the Advancement of Sci. (elected Fellow 1962), Paleontol. Research Inst., Fellow Geol. Soc. Am., Retired Oilmen Long Beach; publs: guidebooks on geology of Calif. for geol. assns., tech. reports for Calif. Div. Mines; speaker AAPG annual nat. meeting, S.F. on K/T Cretaceous/Late Paleocene Boundary We. San Joaquin Valley, Ca. (1990); Republican; Presbyterian; rec: photog., geology, music, art. Res: 300 Deer Valley Rd #2S San Rafael 94903-5514

PAYTON, PHILLIP W., college and university administrator, educator; b. Dec. 26, 1929, Santa Barbara; s. Curtis Charles and Dorothy (Godfrey) P.; m. Gertrude Payton, Mar. 4, 1961 (div. 1976); m. 2d. Marie Rowe-Payton, 1990; children: Paul b. 1961; edn: BA, Reed Coll. 1951; MA, Stanford Univ. 1954; Ed.D, 1960; postdoctoral, UC Berkeley 1969-70; CSU Hayward 1970-71. Career: assoc. prof., dept. chmn. Golden Gate Univ., San Francisco 1966-70; sr. adminstrv. analyst City of Oakland 1969-73; asst. div. dir. Univ. San Francisco 1980-82; mgr. mgmt. devel. MCI Telecomms. 1985; bus. program coord. Nat. Univ., North Las Vegas, Nev. 1987; coord., dir. bus. and econ. Lincoln Univ., San Francisco 1987–; p.t. data analyst Cushman & Wakefield, Foster City 1994–; p.t. acct. Heath Zenith Electronics, Redwood City 1989-91; BSA, Palo Alto 1987-88; personnel and fin. adminstr. GTE Govt. Systems, Mountain View 1982-85; corp. manuals coordinator McKesson Corp., San Francisco 1973-78; personnel cons. R.J. Carroll Assoc., San Mateo and Phila., Pa. 1969; awards: Reed Coll. scholarships 1947-49, Portland Ore. Jour. All A award 1947; mem: Assn. for Continuing Higher Edn., Western Mktg. Educators Assn., Western Econ. Assn., Am. Econ. Assn., Nat. Univ. Research Inst., City of Oakland (sr. adminstr. 1970-73), City of Mountain View (acct.); author: 2 monographs and 2 articles pub. in profl. jours., 1961-86, 5 profl. papers on adult edn., 1992-95; mil: staff sgt. USAF, U.S. Air Nat. Guard 1948-55; Democrat; Prot.; rec: hist. newspaper collecting, old time music record collecting. Ofc: Lincoln University 281 Masonic Ave San Francisco 94118

PEARSON, SCOTT ROBERTS, economics educator; b. March 13, 1938, Madison, Wis.; s. Carlyle Roberts and Edith (Hope) Smith P.; m. Sandra Carol Anderson, Sept. 12, 1962; children: Sarah Roberts, Elizabeth Hovden; edn: BS, Univ. Wis. 1961; MA, Johns Hopkins Univ. 1965; PhD, Harvard Univ. 1969. Career: asst. prof. Food Research Inst., Stanford Univ. 1968-74, assoc. prof. 1974-80, prof. 1980–, dir., 1992–; cons. U.S.AID, Wash. D.C.; World Bank; awards: Stanford Univ. Dean's Award Tchg. 1978, Am. Agri. Econ. Assn. Profl. Excellence 1984; author, coauthor 10 books incl. Petroleum & Nigerian Econ., 1970, Food Policy Analysis, 1983, The Policy Analysis Matrix for Agri. Devel., 1989, Rice Policy in Indonesia, 1991; mil: USAR 1956-64. Res: 691 Mirada Ave Stanford 94305 Ofc: Food Research Institute Stanford University Stanford 94305

PEASLAND, BRUCE RANDALL, financial executive; b. Mar. 24, 1945, Buffalo, N.Y.; s. Kenneth Arthur and Edith Grace (Bristow) P.; m. Debra Myers, June 13, 1981; children: Michael John, Timothy Scott, Amanda Jean; edn: BS, USC, 1971, MBA in fin. 1978; JD, Western State Univ., 1983. Career: price and cost analyst McDonnell Douglas, Long Beach 1966-70; mgr. cost acctg. The Gillette Co., Santa Monica 1971-78; controller Lear Siegler Inc., Santa Ana 1978-85; British Petro. - Hitco, Newport Beach 1986-87; v.p. fin. & adminstrn. Control Components Inc., Rancho Santa Margarita 1987-90; chief fin. ofcr. MacGillivray Freeman Films Inc., Laguna Beach 1990-91; exec. v.p./cfo Intervest Industries, Inc. 1992–; mem: Nat. Mgmt. Assn. (mgr. of yr. Santa Ana chapt. 1984), USC MBA Assn., USC Trojan Club, USC Alumni Assn.; mil: USMC 1963-69; Republican; Episcopalian; rec: sailing, skiing. Res: 25211 Yacht Dr Dana Point 92629 Ofc: Intervest Industries Inc 7720B El Camino Real Ste 201 Carlsbad 92009

PEDERSON, SAM MARSHALL, aerospace software company executive; b. July 26, 1943, Veblen, S.Dak.; s. E. LeRoy and Ellen (Hestenes) P.; m. Mary Louise Anderson, June 18, 1966; 1 son, Troy, b. 1969; edn: BA, St. Olaf Coll. 1965; MS, Univ. Ill. 1967. Career: research asst. Univ. Ill. 1967; mem. tech. staff TRW Systems, Redondo Beach 1967-70; with Space Applications Corp., currently in Santa Ana, 1970-95: mem. Tech. Staff 1970-71, Seattle Operation mgr. 1972-76, dir./v.p. 1974-77, Irvine Op. mgr. 1977-82, v.p./dir. and gen. mgr. 1982-89, pres./dir. 1989-95; pres. SMP Consulting 1995–; dir. Southland Lutheran Home 1983-89; dir. Lutheran Conferences (camping and retreats 1994–); author: The Software Development Project: Planning and Management (Wiley InterScience 1982); Ind.; Lutheran; rec: photog. Res/Ofc: 657 Virginia Park Dr Laguna Beach 92651

PEDRIN, ROBERT ALAN, family physician; b. Dec. 14, 1937, San Francisco, Calif.; s. Rupert Avrum and Pauline (Feldman) P.; m. Susan Rosenberg, Sept. 11, 1963 (div. 1980); children: Jeffrey b. 1965, Sheri b. 1968, Stephen b. 1970, Sherry b. 1972; m. 2d. Audrey Schwartz, June 1, 1980; edn: AA, UC Berkeley 1958; MD, Univ. of So. Calif. 1962; lic. physician and surgeon, Calif. 1963; charter diplomate Am. Bd. Family Practice 1972, recert. 1978, 84, 91. Career: rotating internship Fresno Co. Hosp. 1962-63; gen. practice residency Ventura Co. Hosp.; pvt. solo practice family physician, Marin County 1967–; assoc. clin. prof. UC San Francisco 1970–; preceptor, 1st & 2nd yr. med. students, UCSF; active staff Marin Gen. Hosp., oncology com. mem. and family practice liaison 1985–; courtesy staff: Ross Psychiatric Hosp., Kentfield Rehab. Hosp., S.F. Gen. Hosp.; pres. Calif. Acad. of Family Physicians 1990-91; chief, family practice dept., Marin Gen. Hosp. 1984-86 vice chief of staff Ross Gen. Hosp. 1978-80; awards: Phi Chi Frat. Service Award (ofcr. 1960-62); mem: AMA, CMA, Marin Acad. Family Physicians 1969– (exec. com. and alternate delegate 1988–, pres. Marin Chpt. 1981-86), Calif. Acad. Family Physicians 1969– (bd. dirs. 1982-92, 93-95, treas. 1986-89, pres. 1990-91, liaison Calif. Primary Care Network 1993–, membership com. 1995–), Calif. Acad. Family Physicians Found. (trustee 1992–, corp. devel. task force 1992-95), Am. Acad. Family Physicians (charter fellow, mem. com. on women 1995–), Marin Med. Soc. (mem. consortium for cont. med. edn. accreditation, family practice 1994–), Marin Independent Practice Assn. (med. policy com. 1993–); mil: lt. comdr. USNR, 1965-67; Democrat; Jewish; rec: tennis, astronomy, stereophile; Ofc: Robert A. Pedrin, M.D. 1300 So Eliseo #204 Greenbrae 94904

PEHL, RICHARD HENRY, physicist; b. Nov. 27, 1936, Raymond, Wash.; s. Henry Leopold and Annabelle (Moyer) P.; m. Paula Bhatia, July 1, 1980; edn: BS chem. eng., Wash. State Univ., Pullman 1958, MS nuclear eng., 1959; PhD nuclear chemistry, UC Berkeley, 1963. Career: grad. asst. Lawrence Berkeley Lab., Berkeley 1960-63, res. assoc. 1963-65, staff mem. 1965-78, senior scientist 1978–; res. physicist UC Berkeley Space Sci. Lab. 1994–; mem. Instrument devel. sci. team NASA, 1984–; adj. staff physicist Indiana Univ. Cyclotron Facility, Bloomington, Ind. 1987–; mem. Am. Physical Soc., IEEE; author chapt. in book Nuclear Spectroscopy and Reactions 1974, 160+ tech. articles, 1960-94; rec: sports. Res: 2550 Dana St, 6D, Berkeley 94704 Ofc: LBL Bldg 29 Berkeley 94720

PEISER, RICHARD B., educator; b. Aug. 12, 1948, Houston, Tx.; s. Maurice Bondy and Patricia (Levy) P.; m. Beverly Gail Siegal M.D., May 23, 1976; children: Allison b. 1981, Michael b. 1985; edn: BA, Yale Univ., 1970; MBA, Harvard Univ., 1973; PhD, Cambridge Univ., Eng. 1980. Career: builder, real estate developer, owner Peiser Corp., Dallas and Los Angeles, 1978–; asst. prof. So. Methodist Univ., Dallas 1978-85; vis. assoc. prof. Stanford Univ., 1981; dir. Lusk Center for Real Estate Devel., Univ. So. Calif., L.A. 1986–; Fellow, Urban Land Inst.; civic: South Coast Botanical Garden (trustee), YMCA Camp Grady Spruce, Dallas (trustee); author: Professional Real Estate Development: The ULI Guide to the Business, 1992. Ofc: 351 VKC, USC, Los Angeles 90089-0042

PELLICORI, SAMUEL FRANK, optical engineer, consultant; b. April 14, 1940, Kenosha, Wis.; s. Sam and Anna (Palese) P.; children: Ariana b. 1976, Thalia b. 1977, Damon b. 1979; edn: BS physics, Univ. Ariz. 1965; MS optical sci. 1969. Career: research asst. Univ. Ariz., Tucson 1961-69; physics staff Hughes Research Center, Santa Barbara 1969-86; cons. Pellicori Optical

1986–; bd. mem., founder Santa Barbara Sci. Discovery Center 1984; awards: NASA Pub. Service 1974, Optical Soc. Am. George Eastman Travel Lectr. 1986; mem: Optical Soc. Am., Sigma Xi, Scientific Research Soc., Shroud of Turin Research Project; 35 papers pub. in tech. jours., 1965, patentee in field of optics, 1975. Ofc: Pellicori Optical Technology Consulting Services POB 60723 Santa Barbara 93160

PELLONE, DAVID THOMAS, financial executive; b. March 15, 1944, Ashtabula, Ohio; s. Frank Joseph and Shirley Edna (Foster) P.; m. Sunny Jewel Unfug, May 28, 1977; children: Todd b. 1970, Michelle b. 1980; edn: BBA in indsl. mgmt., Kent St. Univ. 1967; MBA acctg. and fin., Univ. Santa Clara 1973. Career: product supr., indsl. engr. Owens Corning Fiberglas, Santa Clara 1970-72; line controller Fairchild Semiconductor, Mountain View 1972-74; corp. controller Cermetek Inc., Mountain View 1974-76; mgmt. positions 3M, Ventura 1976-83; area fin. mgr. Genrad Inc., Milpitas 1984-86; v.p., controller Genus Inc., Mountain View 1986-90; v.p. finance AG Processing Technologies, Inc., Sunnyvale 1990-93; c.f.o., sec. Pellone Enterprises, Inc. 1994–; bd. dirs. Santa Clara Univ. MBA Alumni Assn. 1989-92; cons. J&P Associates, Menlo Park 1983-84; instr. Univ. San Francisco 1989-1990, Golden Gate Univ. 1994–; instr. DeAnza Coll. 1991–; mem: Inst. of Indsl. Engrs. (sr.), Inst. Internal Auditors, Am. Acctg. Assn., Am. Mgmt. Assn., Commonwealth Club, Churchill Club; mil: E-5 AUS 1967-69; Republican; Episcopalian; rec: canoeing, hiking, camping. Address: Menlo Park

PELOSI, NANCY, congresswoman; b. Baltimore, Md., Mar. 26, 1941; d. Thomas J. D'Alesandro Jr.; m. Paul Pelosi; children: Nancy Corinne, Christine, Jacqueline, Paul, Alexandra; edn: grad. Trinity College. Career: former chair Calif. State Democratic Com. 1981; committeewoman Dem. Nat. Com. (1976, 80, 84); fin. chmn. Dem. Senatorial Campaign Com. 1987; mem. 99th-102d Congresses from 5th Calif. dist. 1987-1992; 103rd Congress from 8th Calif. dist., 1993–; mem: appropriations com., subcoms. Labor, HHD, Edn., Fgn. Ops., intelligence (select) com., standard official conduct com. Ofc: US House of Representatives 240 Cannon Bldg. Washington DC 20515-0508

PELTON, HAROLD MARCEL, mortgage broker; b. Jan. 24, 1922, Montreal, Quebec, Can.; s. Grover Cleveland and Denise (Pigeon) P.; m. Frances Farley, June 1947 (div. 1968); children: Mary Virginia Joyner, Diane Jean Slagowski; m. Virginia L. King, July 11, 1970; edn: student, L.A. City Coll. 1948-49, Anthony Schs., Van Nuys 1966; lic. R.E. Broker, Calif. Career: stockbroker, agt. Mitchum, Jones, Templeton Assu~nce Co., L.A. 1957-60; owner Assurance Investment Co., Van Nuys 1960-65; sales syndicator TSI Investment Co., L.A. 1965-69; pres., owner Univest Co., Beverly Hills 1970-72, Am. Oil Recovery, L.A. 1973-79; v.p. Newport Pacific Funding Co., Newport Beach 1979-81; chmn. bd. dirs. TD Publs., El Toro 1981-83; pres., broker HP Fin. Inc., Laguna Hills 1983–; mem: L.A. Museum of Art, Laguna Hills CofC., Kiwanis, Toastmasters; contbg. editor Am. Oil Recovery newspaper, 1973-79; editor Trust Deed Jour., 1981-83; mil: served with U.S. Army, 1942-46, PTO; Republican. Res: 24942 Georgia Sue Dr Laguna Hills 92653 Ofc: HP Finance Inc 23276 S Pointe Dr Ste 114 Laguna Hills 92653

PELTZER, DOUGLAS LEA, semiconductor device manufacturing company executive; b. Clinton, Iowa., July 2, 1938; s. Albert and Mary Ardelle (Messer) P.; m. Nancy Jane Strickler, Dec. 22, 1959; children: Katharine, Eric, Kimberly; edn: BA Knox Coll. 1960; MS New Mexico State Univ. 1964; MBA, Univ. Phoenix 1990. Career: res. engr. Gen. Electric Co., Advanced Computer Lab., Sunnyvale 1964-67; large scale integrated circuit engr. Fairchild Camera & Instrument, Res. & Devel. Lab., Palo Alto 1967-70, bipolar memory division, Mountain View 1970-83, tech. dir., 1977-83; v.p. tech. ops. Trilogy Systems Corp., Cupertino 1983-85; pres. Tactical Fabs. Inc., 1985-89; v.p. process devel. Chips and Techs. Inc., 1989- 92; pres, CEO, CAMLAN, Inc., San Jose 1992-94; staff Chip Express, Santa Clara 1994–; prin. Corporate Technology Devel. (consultants) 1994–; awards: NSF fellow 1962- 63; Sherman Fairchild award for tech. excellence 1980, Semiconductor Equipment and Materials Inst. award 1988; Inventor of Yr. award Peninsula Patent Law Assn. 1982; mem: AAAS, IEEE, Sigma Pi Sigma; inventor in field; patentee in field. Res: 10358 Bonny Dr Cupertino 95014-2908

PENG, SHENG YENG, electrical engineering executive; b. May 8, 1937, Kiangsi, China; nat. 1972; s. Jen Huai and Si Mei (Lo) P.; m. Mei-Ho Tu, June 13, 1967; children: Peter b. 1970, John b. 1972, David b. 1976; edn: BSEE, Nat. Cheng Kung Univ. 1961; MSEE, Wash. St. Univ. 1966; PhD, St. Univ. N.Y. 1975. Career: assoc. engr. Boeing Co., Seattle, Wash. 1965-70; sr. engr. Raytheon Co., Goleta 1972-74; staff engr. Interstate Electronics Corp., Anaheim 1974-76; staff splst. Aerojet Electrosystems Co., Azusa 1976-78; supr. tech. Hughes Aircraft Co. Ground Systems Group, Fullerton 1978-83; dir. Teledyne Ryan Electronics, San Diego 1983-90; pres. APC Leading Technology, San Diego 1990-91; pres. Allied Holowave, Inc., Escondido 1992-93; pres. Advanced Antenna Tech., Inc., San Diego 1993–; tchg. fellow St. Univ. N.Y., Albany 1970-72; tchg. asst. Chinese Naval Acad., Tsoying, Taiwan 1962-63; awards: Taiwan Sugar Co. scholar (1958-61), Cheng Kung Univ. Free China Sci. Talent scholar (1957-58); mem: IEEE (Senior), Geophysical Union, Nat.

Mgmt. Assn., Hua-Sheng Singing Club (advisor 1987–, pres. 1985-90), So. Calif. Chinese Culture Assn. (v.p. 1981-82); inventor, 3 patents in field (1974, 87, 90); 20+ papers pub. in tech. jours. (1984-89); rec: music, table tennis, bridge. Res: 731 Inspiration Ln Escondido 92025 Ofc: Advanced Antenna Technology, Inc., San Diego 92128

PENHUNE, JOHN PAUL, science company executive, electrical engineer; b. Flushing, N.Y., Feb. 13, 1936; s. Paul and Helene Marguerite (Beux) P.; m. Nancy Leigh Peabody, Sept. 6, 1958 (div. Apr. 1982); children: Virginia Burdet, James Peabody, Sarah Slipp; m. Marcellite Helen Porath, Feb. 15, 1986; children: Marcellite Helen Broadhurst; edn: BSEE MIT 1957; PhD 1961; postgrad., Univ. Grenoble, France 1959, Harvard Bus. Sch. 1973. Career: asst. prof. elec. engring. MIT, Cambridge, Mass. 1962-64; mem. tech. staff Lincoln Lab. MIT, Lexington, Mass. 1964-66; supr. radar group Bell Telephone Labs., Whippany, N.J. 1966-68; asst. dir. Advanced Ballistic Missile Def. Agy., Washington 1968-69; pres. Concord Res. Corp., Burlington, Mass. 1969-73; pvt. practice sci. cons. Carlisle, Mass. 1973-79; bd. dirs. Phys. Dynamics, Inc., La Jolla 1979-81; sr. v.p. for res. Sci. Applications Internat. Corp., San Diego 1981–; indsl. adv. bd. Inst. for Biomed. Engring., Univ. Calif., San Diego 1992–, CONNECT steering com., Univ. Calif. San Diego 1993–; mem. bd. of visitors UC Davis 1993–; honors: Meritorious Civilian Svc. award Dept. Army 1968; mem: Cosmos Club (Washington), San Diego Yacht Club., Eta Kappa Nu Tau Beta Pi, Sigma Xi, Phi Kappa Sigma, bd. dirs. La Jolla Chamber Music Soc. 1985-87; author: Case Studies in Electromagnetism 1960; patentee in field; mil: 1st It. U.S. Army 1961-62. Res: 6730 Muirlands Dr La Jolla 92037-6315 Office: Science Applications International Corp 1241 Cave St La Jolla 92037

PENN, CHARLES JAMES, writer, editor, publisher; b. May 30, 1914, Perth, W. Australia; s. James Albert and Kate Sarah (Leckie) P.; m. Verle Rowles, 1940, div. 1960; children: Russell b. 1945, Wayne b. 1948, Gary b. 1954; m. 2d Mary Faith Taylor, June 1, 1970; edn: lib. arts, Univ. of W. Australia, Perth Tech. Coll. 1929-36; Santa Monica Coll., UCLA, 1963-64; stu. of Bhagavan Sri Sathya Sai Baba, India 1966–. Career: copy boy, cub reporter Daily News newspaper, Perth 1929-36; ed. West Australian Mining Review and West Australian Mining Annual 1936-39; ed./pub. Canadian Oil & Gas Jour., Toronto 1940-42; dir. Australian War Supplies Mission, W.D.C. 1942-43; ed. Internat. Petroleum Register, Los Angeles 1946-49; mng. dir. Russell Publs. Ltd., London 1950-52; ed./pub. Nat. Indsl. Publs., Los Angeles 1953-60, Western Oil & Gas Jour., L.A. 1961-63; exec. Trade Service Corp., San Diego 1966-92; chmn., ceo The Found. of Higher Learning 1987-89; dir. London Court Ltd., Piccadilly Arcade Ltd., Perth W.A. 1936-39; charter pres., gov. Sertoma Internat. L.A. 1955-59; lectr. in US, Canada, S.Am., guest speaker 4, World Confs., delegate 5th World Conf. Sri Sathya Sai Service Orgn., Bombay and Prasanthi Nilayam, India; author: "My Beloved" The Love and Tchgs. of Bhagavan Sri Sathya Sai Baba (1981, pub. in Hindi, Spanish, Italian, and Chinese edits.), "Finding God" My Journey to Bhagavan Sri Sathya Sai Baba (1990), "Lord Sai and I in Vaikunta," coauthor (w/ Mary Faith Penn) Am. edit. Part I "Sathyam - Sivam - Sundaram" - "Sai Baba" (1969), "Sai Ram" Experiencing the Love and Teachings of Bhagavan Sri Sathya Sai Baba (1985), contbr. "Sanatha Sarathi," "The Divine Master," "Golden Age," "Sai Chandana" (1965), "The Sri Sathya Sai Inst. of Higher Learning (Deemed Univ.) Homage Volume," "Sai Vandana," (1990), "The Sri Prasanthi Soc. Homage Volume," "Sathya Sai -The Eternal Charioteer" (1990), India; Sri Sathya Sai Seva Orgns. Golden Jubilee Homage Volume (1990), "Soham," Canadian Jours. (1986), prin. speaker 1st Annual Symp. Sri Sathya Sai Service orgns. of W. Canada (1984); mem: Boy Scouts of Australia, King Scout, Rover (1921-30); Scarborough Surf Life Saving Assn. West Australia 1931-35, Masonic Grand Lodge of Western Australia 1937-39, Sathya Sai Soc. of Am. (charter v.p. 1968-75); inventor: Letters ejectable help summoning device (pat. 1966); mil: capt. Brit. Army staff, W.D.C. 1944-45, Def., War medals; capt. USAF Civil Air Patrol 1963-66; Republican; rec: lectr. on humanities, travel, biking. Address: San Diego 92054

PENN, MARY FAITH, lecturer, writer, editor; b. Oct. 22, Vancouver, B.C., Canada; d. Henry Boardman and Althea (Marston) Taylor; m. Charles Penn, June 1, 1970; edn: liberal arts major Tower Coll., San Antonio, Tx. 1944-46, Long Beach Coll. 1951-52; Yoga student of Paramahansa Yogananda (Yogas Raja, Bhakti, Karma, Hatha, Selfless Service), Self-Realization Fellowship Internat. Hqtrs., L.A. 1949-52; adv. Yoga studies in India: Sri Aurobindo Inst. 1968, Sri Sathya Sai Inst. of Higher Learning 1968, 72, 75, 80, student of Bhagavan Sri Sathya Sai Baba 1966–. Career: meditation counselor, Yoga instr., West and Southwest U.S. 1953–; pvt. estate mgr. 1954–; exec. secty. Charles Luckman Assocs., Los Angeles 1962-68; pres./cfo The Found. of Higher Learning, 1987-89; lectr. on humanities, E. and W. philosophy and meditation, retreats/confs. and seminars in U.S., Canada, S.Am., Hong Kong, 1961–; author, writer, editor, 1969–; coauthor (w/C.J. Penn) Am. edition Part I "Sathyam - Sivam - Sundaram" "Sai Baba" (1969), "Sai Ram" Experiencing the Love and Teachings of Bhagavan Sri Sathya Sai Baba (1985), contbr. "Soham," Canadian Jours. (1986); prin. speaker 1st Annual Symp. Sri Sathya Sai Service Orgns. of W. Canada 1984, Sri Sathya Sai E. Canada Conf. (1990, 93), Annual Conf. Ariz. 1994, Calif. & Mich. Retreats 1994; guest speaker 4th World Conf. Sri Sathya Sai Service Orgns., Prasanthi Nilayam, India 1985, delegate 5th World Conf.

1990; guest speaker Sri Sathya Sai Foreign Devotees Programs, Prasanthi Nilayam, India 1990; pres. bd. trustees San Antonio Gospel Tabernacle 1985–; First woman recipient Award of Forensic Excellence, S.W. Texas Univ. 1943; Republican; rec: travel, cymbidiums and bromeliads, music, biking. Address: San Diego 92054

PENNELL, LARITA JEANNE, educator; b. Dec. 3, 1927, Portland, Ore.; d. LeRoy Carl and Leona Emma (Flier) Eisele; m. James Kell Pennell, Sept. 2, 1949; edn: BA, Univ. of Ore. 1949; MA, John F. Kennedy Univ. 1979; grad. study: CSU Humboldt, Hayward, Sonoma & San Jose; UC Berkeley 1950–; Univ. de Salamanca, Spain 1967, 68, 80; Univ. de Michoacan, Mex. 1964; Univ. of London, Eng. 1971; Cité Univ., Paris, France 1982; Loyola Univ., Rome, Italy 1985; Univ. Saltzburg, Germany 1986; Tchr. Credentials: Secondary Edn. 1950, Bilingual Edn. 1979, Designated Svc.-Pupil Personnel 1980, Adminstrv. 1981, Calif. Career: computer science, mathematics educator/faculty Wright School Dist., Santa Rosa 1950-51; Lafayette Sch. Dist., Lafayette 1952–; John F. Kennedy Univ., 1981–; computer cons. Microtime 1983; awards: academic NDEA Grants, US Govt. 1964, 65, 66; WHO (We Honor Ours) Award, CTA-NEA Alcosta Council, NEA-Women's Leadership Tng. Cadre; mem: Am. Assn. of Tchrs. of Spanish and Portuguese (secty. Bay Area chpt. 1975), Assn. of Mathematics Educators, Lafayette Edn. Assn. (pres. 1983-85), Orinda-Moraga Rep. Women Fed. (first v.p. 1993-94, pres. 1995-97); Republican; Cath.; rec: swimming, yoga, computer games. Res: 3085 Stonegate Dr Alamo 94507-1761 Ofc: Lafayette School District 3477 School St Lafayette 94549; Mason McDuffie 2051 Mt Diablo Blvd Walnut Creek 94596

PENNER, STANFORD SOLOMON, educator; b. July 5, 1921, Unna, Ger.; nat. 1943; s. Heinrich and Regina (Saal) P.; m. Beverly Preston, Dec. 28, 1942; children: Merilynn Jean, Robert Clark; edn: BS, Union Coll. 1942; MS, Univ. Wis. 1943; PhD, 1946; Dr. rer. nat. (hon.), Technische Hochschule Aachen W. Germany 1981. Career: res. assoc. Allegany Ballistics Lab., Cumberland, Md. 1944-45; res. scientist Standard Oil Devel. Co., Esso Labs., Linden, N.J. 1946; sr. res. engr. Jet Propulsion Lab., Pasadena 1947-50; mem. faculty Calif. Inst. Tech. 1950-63, prof. div. engring., jet propulsion 1957-63; dir. research engring. div. Inst. Def. Analyses, Wash. 1962-64; prof. engring. physics and chmn. dept. aerospace and mech. engring. UC San Diego, 1964-68, vice chancellor acad. affairs 1968-69, dir. Inst. Pure & Applied Physical Scis. 1968-71, dir. Energy Center, 1973-92; chmn. Dept. of Energy, Adv. Fuel-Cell Commercialization Working Group 1993–; dir. Ogden Corp., Optodyne Corp.; U.S. mem. advy. group aero. res. and devel. NATO 1952-68, chmn. combustion and propulsion panel 1958-60; mem. advy. com. engring. scis. USAF Office Sci. Research 1961-65; mem. subcom. combustion NACA 1954-58; res. advy. com. air-breathing engines NASA 1962-64; mem. coms. on gas dynamic and edn. Internat. Acad. Astronautics 1969-80; mem. coms. NRC; cons. to govt. univs. and industry 1953–; chmn. NRC/U.S. com. Internat. Inst. Applied Systems Analysis 1978-81; nat. Sigma Xi lectr. 1977-79; spl. guest Internat. Coal Sci. Confs. 1983, 85, 87, 89; Baetjer speaker Princeton Univ. 1985; awards: spl. awards People to People Program, spl. awards NATO, pub. service award UCSD, N. Manson medal Internat. Colloquia on Gasdynamics of Explosions & Reactive Systems, Internat. Columbus award Internat. Inst. Comms., Genoa Italy, Disting. Assoc. Award of U.S. Dept. of Energy, Guggenheim fellow 1971-72; Fellow: Am. Phys. Soc., Optical Soc. Am, AAAS, N.Y. Acad. Scis., AIAA (dir. 1964-66, past chmn. com., G. Edward Pendray award 1975, Thermophysics award 1983, Energy Systems award 1983), Am. Acad. Arts & Scis.; mem: Internat. Acad. Astronautics, Nat. Acad. Engring., Am. Chem. Soc., Sigma Xi; author: Chemical Reactions in Flow Systems, 1955, Chemistry Problems in Jet Propulsion, 1957, Quantitative Molecular Spectroscopy & Gas Emissivites, 1959, Chemical Rocket Propulsion & Combustion Research, 1962, Thermodynamics, 1968, Radiation & Reentry, 1968; sr. author: Energy, Vol I (Demands, Resources, Impact, Tech. and Policy), 1974, 81; Energy Vol. II (Non-nuclear Energy Technologies), 1975, 77, 84; Energy, Vol. III (Nuclear Energy and Energy Policies), 1976; editor: Chemistry of Propellants, 1960, Advanced Propulsion Techniques, 1961; Detonations & Two-Phase Flow, 1962, Combustion & Propulsion, 1963, Advances in Tactical Rocket Propulsion, 1968, In Situ Shale Oil Recovery, 1975, New Sources of Oil & Gas, 1982, Coal Combustion & Application, 1984, Advanced Fuel Cells, 1986, Coal Gasification: Direct Applications & Syntheses of Chemicals & Fuels, 1987, Commercialization of Fuel Cells, 1995; assoc. ed. Jour. Chem. Physics, 1953-56; ed. Jour. Quantitative Spectroscopy & Radiative Transfer, 1960-92; Jour. Def. Research, 1963-67, Energy-The Internat. Jour., 1975–. Res: 5912 Ave Chamnez La Jolla 92037 Ofc: Univ. of Calif. San Diego 92093-0411

PENROSE, JOHN MORGAN, educator; b. June 16, 1942, Tulsa, Okla.; s. John Morgan and Garnet (Haston) P.; m. Margaret Iwanaga, June 15, 1983; edn: BSJ, and MS, Ohio Univ. 1964, 1966; PhD, Univ. Texas, Austin 1978. Career: dir. of annual giving Ohio Univ., Athens 1966-69; lectr., asst. to dean So. Ill. Univ., Edwardsville 1969-72; lectr., sr. lectr. Univ. Texas, Austin 1972-88; prof. San Diego St. Univ. 1988–; chmn. Info. & Decision Systems Dept. 1993–; cons. Sohio/Standard Oil, British Petroleum, 1980–; honors: recipient F.W. Weeks award, fellow, disting. member and best paper awards Assn. for Bus. Comm. 1985; mem. editl. rev. bd. Mgmt. Comm. Qtr. USC 1985-90, J. of Bus. Comms.,

Abilene Christian Univ. 1984-90, Iowa State J. of BTC 1985–; mem: Assn. for Bus. Comm. (1968–, pres. 1988-89), Internat. Comm. Assn. 1969–, Acad. of Mgmt. 1985–, Nat. Bus. Edn. Assn. 1989–, S.W. Fedn. of Adminstrv. Disciplines 1980–, Delta Sigma Pi (chpt. adv. 1970-88), Phi Kappa Phi 1974–, Sigma Delta Chi 1965–; sr. author (text) Advanced Bus. Comm., 1989, 93; coauthor Bus. Comm. Strategies & Skills (1991 4th edit.), Readings & Applications in Bus. Comm., 1985; contbr. articles in numerous scholarly jours., 1975–; rec: sailing. Res: 1522 Berenda Pl El Cajon 92020 Ofc: San Diego State University IDS Dept. San Diego 92182

PENSO, HORACE ALTON, physician, diplomat; b. June 3, 1932, Jamaica, W.I., naturalized U.S. 1973; s. Harold A. and Hilda L. (Greenwood) P.; m. Faye Yvonne Warner, Aug. 29, 1959; children: Peter John b. 1966, Andrea Faye b. 1970; edn: BS, Howard Univ., 1955, MD, 1960; lic. Med. Coll. of Canada, 1961; cert. Am. Bd. Ob/Gyn 1977, Fellow Am. Coll. Ob/Gyn 1980; med. lic. Canada, U.K.; Fellow Internat. Coll. of Surgeons. Career: rotating intern St. Luke Meth. Hosp., Cedar Rapids, Ia. 1960-61; asst. med. ofcr. Ministry of Health, Black River and Kingston Pub. Hosp., Jamaica 1961-63; pvt. family practice, Kingston 1963-70; resident dept. ob/gyn Highland Gen. Hosp., Oakland 1970-71, Kaiser Found. Hosp., 1971-73, chief resident 1973; pvt. practice ob./gyn., pres. Horace A. Penso, M.D., Inc., Hayward 1973–; cons. Tiburcio Vasquez Health Ctr., Union City, Calif. Perinatal Svs. Prog.; dir. Chabot Med. Group, Jamaica Maritime Corp. Ltd.; chief of staff Hayward Vesper Hosp. 1978, chmn. dept. Ob/Gyn 1982-84; hon. consul for Jamaica, No. Calif., S.F. 1983–; mem: Calif. Med. Assn., Nat. Med. Assn., Alameda-Contra Costa Co. Med. Assn. (mediation com. 1979–), Am. Assn. Gynecologic Laparoscopists, Am. Assn. Planned Parenthood Physicians, Am. Fertility Soc., Am. Soc. for Laser Medicine & Surgery, Royal Med. Soc. (U.K.); mil: capt. Jamaica Defence Force 1966-70; rec: travel, stamps, sailing. Ofc: 22455 Maple Ct Ste 404 Hayward 94541

PERELSON, GLENN H., healthcare executive; b. Oct. 10, 1954, N.Y.C.; s. Bruce I. and Shirley M. P.; m. Sofia, Feb. 21, 1992; children: Adriana b. 1985, Alexander b. 1990, Brandon b. 1992; edn: AB, Hamilton Coll., 1975; MD, Boston Univ.,1979; MBA, Univ. of Phoenix, Fountain Valley 1991; bd. cert. Internist and Cardiologist 1983, bd. cert. Medical Mgmt. 1992. Career: founder, pres. Zero-G Industries, Boston 1985–; med. dir. Physician Med. Ctr., Boston 1985-88; medical director FHP Inc., Fountain Valley, Calif. 1988–; dir: Buckingham Properties, Buckingham, Pa. 1986–; mem. corporate speakers bur. Am. Heart Assn., San Diego 1992–; bd. dir. Am. Heart Assn., Chula Vista; awards: Golden Heart, Cardiovascular Res. in Space Soc., Houston 1990, Winning Idea award FHP Inc. 1991; mem: Am. Coll. of Physician Execs. 1989–, Am. Heart Assn. 1983–, Cardiovascular Res. in Space Soc. (1985–, past pres.), Zero-G Found. (chmn. bd. dirs. 1987–); author (text): Zero-G Medicine, 1989, articles in sci. publs., 1981–; rec: underwater photog., composing music. Ofc: FHP, Inc. 4365 Executive Dr Ste 500 San Diego 92121-2125

PEREYRA-SUAREZ, CHARLES ALBERT, lawyer; b. Sept. 7, 1947, Paysandu, Uruguay; came to U.S. 1954, naturalized 1962; s. Hector and Esther (Enriquez-Sarano) P.-S.; m. Susan H. Cross, Dec. 30, 1983; edn: BA (magna cum laude), Pacific Union Coll. 1970; postgrad. UCLA 1970-71; JD, UC Berkeley 1975; admitted Calif. St. Bar 1975, D.C. 1980. Career: staff atty. Western Ctr. Law and Poverty, Inc., Los Angeles 1976; trial atty. civil rights div. U.S. Dept. Justice, Wash. 1976-79; asst. U.S. atty., criminal div. U.S. Dept. Justice, L.A. 1979-82; sr. litigation assoc. Gibson Dunn & Crutcher, L.A. 1982-84; sole practice L.A. 1984-86; ptnr. McKenna & Cuneo, L.A. 1986–; Democrat. Ofc: McKenna & Cuneo 444 S Flower Los Angeles 90071

PEREZ, DAVID DOUGLAS, judge; b. Sept. 14, 1937, Los Angeles; s. Ygnacio and Cruz (Rivera) P.; m. Penny J., June 1, 1968; children: Jason David b. 1973, Heather Anne b. 1975; edn: BBA, Loyola Univ. L.A. 1959; JD, Southwestern Univ. 1965. Career: chief asst. city atty., Los Angeles 1965-75; appt. judge Municipal Ct., Los Angeles and East L.A., 1975-85; judge Superior Ct., County of Los Angeles, 1985–; mem. Calif. Council on Crim. Justice; honors: Hispanic Mag. list of One Hundred most influential Hispanics in U.S. 1986; mem. Am., Calif. Judges Assn. (exec. com. 1989-91); civic: Corpus Christi Parish Sch. Assn. (pres. 1983-87), Optimists, Rotary, YMCA (bd. mgrs.), Salvation Army (bd. Westmont Br.); Republican; Cath.; rec: running, travel, gardening, reading. Ofc: L.A. Superior Court, 1725 Main St Ste B Santa Monica 90401

PEREZ, KATHERINE DIANA, educator; b. Nov. 15, 1949, Elyria, Ohio; d. Timothy James and Donna Dale (Dickason) Donovan; m. Robert Henry Perez, Aug. 24, 1974; children: Hart b. 1985, Devon b. 1987; edn: BA hons., english, Holy Names Coll. 1971; MS ednl. psychology, CSU Hayward 1977; Ed.D, Brigham Young Univ. 1983. Career: asst. dean and dir. spl. edn. and reading leadership Saint Marys Coll., Moraga 1984–; tchr. Richmond Unified Sch. Dist., Richmond 1973-77, reading splst. 1976-77, spl. edn. tchr. 1977-78, coord. project STEP 1978-81, curriculum and staff devel. splst. 1981-84; lectr. CSU Hayward, UC Berkeley Ext., Contra Costa Coll., 1981-84; cons. Project HATCH, Oakland 1979-84; spl. activities dir. Santa Barbara Recreation Dept. 1971-75; awards: Rotary Internat. Fellow 1979-80; mem: Learning Disabilities Assn. Intl. (ednl. chair, conf. spkr. 1990), Council for Exceptional Children

(com. chair), Calif. Council Edn. of Tchrs. (program com.), Internat. Reading Assn., Calif. Reading Assn., Calif. Assn. Prof. of Spl. Edn., Assn. Supervision & Curriculum Devel. (nat. staff Devel. Coun.), Glide Found. (chair), Delta Kappa Gamma (past pres.), Center for Adaptive Learning (advy. bd.), Clausen House (advy. bd.); author: Teachers Guide (Janus Pub. Co. 1985), Resource Specialist Handbook 1983, 5+ articles pub. in profl. jours. 1983–; Democrat; R.Cath.; rec: swimming, aerobics. Res: 286 Vernon St Oakland 94610 Ofc: Saint Marys College School of Education PO Box 4350 Moraga 94575

PEREZ, RICHARD LEE, lawyer; b. Nov. 17, 1946, Los Angeles; s. Salvador Navarro and Shirley Mae (Selbrede) P.; children: Kristina, Kevin, Ryan; edn: BA, UCLA 1968; JD, UC Berkeley 1971; admitted Calif. U.S. Dist. Ct. (no. dist.) 1974, U.S. Ct. Appeals (9th Cir.) 1974, U.S. Dist. Ct. (ea. dist.) 1982, Tex. U.S. Dist. Ct. (no. dist.) 1984. Career: associate McCutchen, Doyle, Brown & Enersen, San Francisco 1972-74, John R. Hetland, Orinda 1974-75; ptnr. Lempres & Wulsberg, Oakland 1975-82, Perez & McNabb, Orinda 1982–; spkr. real estate brokerage and computer groups and seminars; mem. adv. bd. Computer Litigation Reporter, Wash. 1982-85, Boalt Hall High Tech. Law Jour. 1984-90; mem: ABA, Alameda Co. Bar Assn., Contra Costa Co. Bar Assn.; assoc. ed. Univ. Calif. Law Review 1970-71; mil: capt. U.S. Army, 1968-79. Ofc: Perez & McNabb 140 Brookwood Orinda 94563

PERILLOUX, BRUCE EDGAR, optics manufacturing staff thin film engineer; b. Mar. 24, 1961, New Orleans, La.; s. Louis Francis, Jr. and Edna Eloise P.; m. Anne Mary Jeansonne, Jan. 19, 1985; edn: BS in E.E., Univ. New Orleans, 1983, MSE, 1984. Career: grad. tchg. asst. Univ. New Orleans, 1983-84, grad. res. asst. 1984-85; Thin Film res. & devel. engr. Coherent Inc., Auburn, Calif. 1985-87, sr. Thin Film engr. 1988-89, product line mgr. 1989-93, staff Thin Film engr. 1994–; awards: Sigma Xi 1984, outstanding res. award 1985, employee of yr. nom. Coherent Inc. 1985; mem. Phi Kappa Phi 1984–, Optical Soc. of Am. 1983–, Soc. of Photo Optical and Instrumentation Engrs. 1983-92; inventor in optical engring. (5 Patents 1988, 88, 90, 91, 92); publs: 11+ tech. articles, 1984-95; rec: reading, physics, philosophy, music. Ofc: Coherent, Inc. 2301 Lindbergh St Auburn 95602-9595

PERINO, CARMEN, business owner, former state legislator; b. Dec. 6, 1922, Chatsworth, N.J.; s. Dominic and Rose (Pizzo) P.; m. Della M. Castaldo, July 18, 1943 (div. 1976); children: Angela M. b. 1946, Janet L. b. 1949, Barbara A. b. 1953; edn: grad. Stockton H.S. 1941. Career: Planning Commn. City of Stockton 1950-60; mem. Bd. Suprs., San Joaquin Co. 1961-74; assemblyman Calif. Legislature 1974-80; appt. Parole Bd. Narcotic Addict Auth. 1982-85; awards: House Resolution Calif. St. Assembly (1980), commendn. La Scuola Italiana (1976), hon. mem. Latin Am. Club (1977), AFGE Hon. (1968), Lathrop C.of C. commendn. (1972); mem: VFW, Sierra Club, Amvets (life), Sons Italy, Elks; pub. booklet, paper on planning (1964); mil: sgt. US Army Air Corps 1942-45; Democrat; R.Cath.; rec: woodworking, renovating. Ofc: 421 E Miner Ave Stockton 95202

PERKINS, JAMES HAROLD, lawyer; b. April 30, 1928, Sacramento; s. Harold Bushnell and Opal Lee (Humble) P.; m. Mary Ann Robbins, March 8, 1949 (div. 1952); m. Harriet Joann Storey, March 24, 1956; children: Janis b. 1950, Mitchell b. 1960, Margaret b. 1962; edn: BA, Stanford Univ. 1950; JD, 1953; admitted St. Bar Calif. 1954;. Career: atty., ptnr. Docker Docker Perkins & Shelton, Fresno 1954-69; McCormick Barstow et al, 1969–; lectr. Calif. Cont. Edn. of Bar; mem: Am. Bar Assn., Bar of Calif., Fresno County Bar Assn., Fellow Am. Coll. Trust and Estate Counsel 1980; cert. specialist, probate estate planning and trust law, State Bar Bd. of Legal Specialization; civic: Fresno 20-30 Club (pres. 1960-61), YMCA (pres. 1977); pub. articles re estate planning, 1983; mil: sgt. US Army 1946-47; Republican; Prot. Res: 6687 N Woodson Ave Fresno 93711 Ofc: McCormick Barstow et al Box 28912 Fresno 93727-8912

PERL, MARTIN L., physicist, educator, Nobel Prize winner; b. 1927; edn: PhD, Columbia Univ., 1955 (studied under Prof. I.I. Rabi, winner of 1944 Nobel Prize in physics). Career: mem. faculty Stanford Linear Accelerator Ctr, Stanford Univ., 1963–; Fellow Am. Physical Soc.; awards: Wolf Prize for discovery of the tau lepton, 1982, awarded the Nobel Prize in physics (with Frederick Reines) for discovering subatomic particles, 1995; mem. Nat. Acad. Scis. Ofc: Stanford Linear Accelerator Ctr Stanford 94305*

PERLOFF, JEFFREY MARK, professor of agricultural economics; b. Jan. 28, 1950, Chgo.; s. Harvey S. and Miriam (Seligman) P.; m. Jacqueline B. Persons, Aug. 15, 1976; children: Lisa b. 1986; edn: BA, Univ. Chgo., 1972; PhD, M.I.T., 1976. Career: asst. prof. econ. Univ. of Pa., Phila. 1976-80; asst. prof., assoc. prof., prof. agric. econ. Univ. Calif., Berkeley 1980-82, 82-89, 89–; coauthor: Modern Industrial Organization, 1990, 2nd edit. 1994; numerous articles in profl. jours. Ofc: Dept. Agricultural & Resource Economics 207 Giannini Hall Univ. Calif. Berkeley 94720

PERRINE, RICHARD LEROY, professor of engineering and applied science; b. May 15, 1924, Mountain View; s. George Alexander and Marie Carrie (Axelson) P.; m. Barbara Jean Gale, April 7, 1945; children: Cynthia b. 1954,

Jeffrey b. 1957; edn: BA chemistry, San Jose St. Univ. 1949; MS, Stanford Univ. 1950; PhD, 1953; cert. Nat. Assn. Environ. Profls. 1987). Career: research chemist Calif. Research Corp., La Habra 1953-59; assoc. prof. engring. UCLA 1959-63, prof. engring. and applied sci. 1963-92, prof. emeritus 1992–; exec. v.p. Sage Resources 1987-91; ed. in chief Environ. Profl. mag., Alexandria, Va. 1985-90; advy. com. mem., cons. Nat. Lab., Oak Ridge, Tenn. 1987-90; mem. policy bd., Inst. for Environment and Natural Resource Res. and Policy, Univ. Wyoming, 1994–; awards: Inst. Advancement of Engring. Outstanding Engr. 1975, NAACP Service & Leadership 1984; mem: AAAS (fellow), Air & Waste Mgmt. Assn., Am. Chemical Soc., Am. Inst. Chemical Engrs., Nat. Assn. Environ. Profls., Soc. Petroleum Engrs. of AIME; author, ed. of num. books incl. Paradoxes of Western Energy Devel., 1984, ed. Energy: For Ourselves & Our Posterity, 1985; mil: AUS 1943-46; rec: trout fishing, hiking. Res: 22611 Kittridge St West Hills 91307 Ofc: Univ. California Civil Engineering Dept. Los Angeles 90024

PERRY, DALE LYNN, research chemist; b. May 12, 1947, Greenville, Tex.; s. Francis Leon and Violet (Inabinette) P.; edn: BS, Midwestern Univ., 1969; MS, Lamar Univ., 1972; PhD, Univ. Houston, 1974. Career: NSF fellow dept. chemistry Rice Univ., Houston 1976-77; Miller Research fellow dept. chemistry Univ. Calif. Berkeley 1977-79, prin. investigator solid state chemistry and spectroscopy Lawrence Berkeley Lab. 1979–, sr. scientist 1987–; honors: Sigma Xi nat. research award Univ. Houston 1974, NSF postdoc. fellow (1976-77), Miller research fellow 1977-79; mem: Royal Soc. of Chemistry, London (fellow), Am. Chem. Soc. (chmn. Indsl. Engring. and Chem. Div. 1995–, subdiv. chmn. mats. chemistry and engring. Indsl. and Engring. Div. 1992–), Applied Spectroscopy, Coblentz Soc., Materials Research Soc. (corporate participation com. 1991–); author: (books) Instrumental Surface Analysis of Geologic Materials, 1990, Applications of Analytical Techniques to the Characterization of Materials, 1991, Applications of Synchrotron Radiation Techniques to Materials Science, 1993, Applications of Synchrotron Radiation Techniques to Materials Science II, 1995; contbr. articles to profl. jours. Ofc: Lawrence Berkeley Lab Univ. Calif. MS 70A-1150 Berkeley 94720

PERRY, JACQUELIN, orthopedic surgeon; b. May 31, 1918, Denver, Colo.; edn: B.Edn., UCLA 1940; Walter Reed Army 1940-41; MD, UCSF 1950; orthosurgery, 1958. Career: physical therapist Walter Reed Army Hosp., Wash. D.C. 1953-40; med. physician UCSF 1946-50, intern 1950-51, gen. surgery 1952-55, orthopedic surgery 1952-55; prof. orthopedics USC, 1965–; prof. physical therapy USC 1977–; chief pathokinesiology Rancho Los Amigos Med. Center, Downey 1955, dir. quality assurance 1977, chief polio and gait clinic 1972; awards: L.A. Times Woman of Year Medicine 1969, Jour. Am. Physical Therapy Golden Pen 1965, Univ. Colo. Packard Meml. Lectr. 1970, Ortho. Research Soc. Kappa Delta 1976, Sommer Meml. Lectr. 1978, Goldenson Award in Tech., United Cerebral Palsy Assn. 1981, Joseph F. Dowling Dist. Svc. Award, Rancho Los Amigos Med. Ctr. 1985, Am. Acad. Orthopedic Surgery Shands Lectr. 1988, UCLA Professional Achievement Award 1988, Shands lectr. Am. Orthopedic Assn. 1988, Milton Cohen Disting. Svc. award Nat. Assn. of Rehab. Facilities 1993, Physician of Yr. Calif. Governor's Com., Employment Devel. Dept. St. of Calif. 1994; mem: Am. Acad. Orthopedic Surgeons, Am. Orthopaedic Assn., Western Orthopaedic Assn., CMA, Le Roy Abbott Soc., Am. Physical Therapy Assn., Am. Acad. Cerebral Palsy & Devel. Medicine, Scoliosis Research Soc., Ruth Jackson Soc., Am. Acad. Orthotists/Prosthetist, L.A. Co. Med. Assn., Physical Medicine & Rehab. (editl. bd. of archives 1974-78); inventor dynamic electromyograph, foot switch measurement system, 190 med. references; mil: AUS 1940-41; rec: carpentry, hiking. Ofc: Rancho Los Amigos Medical Center 7601 E Imperial Hwy Downey 90242

PERSCHBACHER, DEBRA LYN BASSETT, lawyer; b. Oct. 28, 1956, Pleasanton; d. James Arthur and Shirley Ann (Russell) Bassett; m. Rex Robert Perschbacher; edn: BA, Univ. Vermont, 1977; MS, CSU San Diego, 1982; JD, UC Davis, 1987. Career: guidance counselor Addison Central, Middlebury, Vt. 1982-83, Milton (Vt.) Elem. Sch., 1983-84; instr. Comm. Coll. of Vt., Winooski 1983-84; law clk. to Hon. Mary Schroeder, Ninth Cir. Ct. Appeals, 1987-88; atty., assoc. Morrison & Foerster, San Francisco 1988-92; senior atty. Ct. of Appeal, 3d Appellate Dist., Sacramento 1992–; instr. Univ. of Calif. Extension 1995–; honors: disting. scholar fellowship UCD 1984-85, Am. Jurisprudence Awards-contracts, civil procedure, and commercial paper 1984-86, Senior articles ed. UCD Law Rev., 1986-87, Civil Procedure tutor UCD, 1985-87; mem: ABA, Calif. St. Bar, Dist. of Col. Bar, Sacramento Co. Bar Assn., Alpha Delta Pi Sor.; contbr. Law Rev. article, 1987, 90; Democrat; rec: travel, photog., hiking. Res: 1438 41st St Sacramento 95819 Ofc: Court of Appeal, Third Appellate Dist. 914 Capitol Mall Sacramento 95814

PERSCHBACHER, REX ROBERT, law professor; b. Aug. 31, 1946, Chgo., Ill.; s. Robert Ray and Nancy Ellen (Beach) P.; m. Debbie Bassett Hamilton; children: Julie b. 1977, Nancy b. 1981; edn: BA, Stanford Univ. 1968; Oxford Univ. 1969; JD, UC Berkeley 1972; admitted St. Bar Calif. 1972. Career: legal writing instr. UC Berkeley 1972-73; law clerk to federal district court judge Alfonso J. Zirpoli 1973-74; asst. prof. Univ. Tx., Austin 1974-75; atty., assoc. Heller Ehrman White & McAuliffe, San Francisco 1975-78; assoc. prof. Univ. San Diego 1978-81; prof. law, assoc. dean UC Davis 1981–; instr. Inst. Internat.

& Comparative Law, Kings Coll., London, England 1984, 88; instr. Nat. Inst. Trial Advocacy 1988; honors: Phi Beta Kappa, Order of Coif, Distinguished tchg. award 1992; mem: Am. Bar Assn., Am. Assn. Law Schs., Inn of Court, Legal Svs. of No. Calif. (bd. dirs.); co-author: Civil Procedure (1987, 2d edit. 1992), California Legal Ethics, 1992, California Trial Practice, 1991, 5 revs. in law jours., 1982–; Democrat; rec: travel, hiking. Res: 1438 41st St Sacramento 95819 Ofc: Univ. California Davis 95616

PESCAN, TODD LINE, stockbroker; b. Feb. 13, 1959, Columbus, Ohio; s. Alexander and Faith Lee (Line) P.; m. Lisa Hix, May 3, 1986; edn: BA in econs./psychol., UCLA 1981; MBA in corp./internat. fin., USC 1983. Career: stockbroker, fin. cons., v.p. Smith Barney Shearson, Beverly Hills; mem: Am. Mktg. Assn., Am. Fin. Assn., Phi Kappa Sigma, Alpha Phi, Sonance; Republican; Presbyterian; rec: coin collecting, tennis. Res: 9802 Ludwig St Villa Park 92667 Ofc: Smith Barney Shearson 9665 Wilshire Blvd Ste 700 Beverly Hills 90212

PETER, CHRISTOPHER RAYMOND, microbiologist; b. Nov. 27, 1948, Sacramento; s. Raymond Vincent and Cynthia Grace (Roberts) P.; m. Dolores Mary Rupprecht, June 23, 1989; children: Brendan b. 1979, Rachel b. 1982; edn: BS, Sacto. St. Coll. 1970; MA, UC Davis 1975; PhD, 1975. Career: clin. lab. tech. trainee UC Davis Med. Center 1970-71; clin. lab. tech. Am. River Hosp., Carmichael 1971-75; postgrad res. microbiologist UC Davis 1972-75; postdoctoral res. fellow Oreg. Regional Primate Res. Ctr., Beaverton, Oreg. 1975-76; adj. faculty biology dept. San Diego St. Univ., 1982–; asst. chief, San Diego Co. Pub. Health Lab. 1976-89, chief 1989–; awards: Landgraf Found. Christine Landgraf Meml. 1974; mem: AAAS, Calif. Assn. Pub. Health Lab. Dirs., Am. Soc. Microbiology, So. Calif. Assn. Pub. Health Microbiologists, Boy Scout leader 1988–; Democrat; R.Cath.; rec: gardening, hiking, bicycling, skiing. Res: 2450 Grafton St El Cajon 92020 Ofc: San Diego County Public Health Laboratory POB 85222 San Diego 92186-5222

PETERS, BARBARA STRATTON, career counselor; b. Apr. 18, 1949, Pocatello, Idaho; d. Richard Wendell and Margaret (Harris) S.; m. Thomas H. Peters, Aug. 7, 1984; edn: BA in govt. Idaho State Univ., 1971, MA edn. student personnel, 1976. Career: asst. dir. Career Planning & Placement, Idaho State Univ., Pocatello 1974-77; assoc. dir. Career Devel. Ctr., Humboldt State Univ., Arcata, Calif. 1977-90, career counselor 1990–, asst. to v.p. for student affairs 1988; honors: Phi Kappa Phi 1970; appt. Coll. of the Redwoods counseling svs. advy. com., Eureka 1987–, Redwoods Occup. Educ. Council, Eureka (pres. 1985-86); Democrat; R.Cath.; rec: singing, baseball, camping. Res: 221 Dollison Eureka 95501 Ofc: Career Development Center, Humboldt State Univ., Arcata 95521

PETERS, DONALD LOUIS, lawyer; b. Sept. 28, 1932, Jacksonville, FL; edn: BSC, Univ. Notre Dame, 1955, JD, Southwestern Univ., 1964; admitted to bar, Calif. and U.S. District Court, So. Dist. of Calif., 1965. Career: asst. trust ofcr., Bank of America 1957-60, exec. asst. to the exec. ofcr. 1962-65 and judge pro tem, 1976-77, probate atty. 1965-66; judge pro tem, Los Angeles Co. Superior Ct., 1994–, Orange Co. Superior Ct.; bd. of dirs., Beverly Hosp., Montebello 1966–, treas. 1967-74, second vice pres. 1991-94; listed: Who's Who in Am. Law, Who's Who in Calif., Martindale-Hubbell's Bar Register of Preeminent Lawyers, Markhams Negligence Counsel; mem: Orange Cty. Bar Assn., State Bar of Calif.; instrument rated private pilot; mil: lt.jg. USNR 1955-57; Democrat; R. Cath.; rec: aviation, tennis. Ofc: Donald Peters, 1300 Dove St. #200, Newport Beach 92660

PETERSEN, DONALD LOREN, realtor; b. Sept. 29, 1936, Tama, Ia.; s. Arthur Paul and Mildred Vera (Lacina) P.; m. Marilyn Zeigler, Sept. 2, 1961; children: Mark b. 1962, Corinn b. 1963, Michael b. 1964, Ronald b. 1967; m. 2d. Adrianne Perelskin, May 9, 1981; edn: BSME, Iowa State Univ., 1962. Career: test engr. U.S. Forest Service, Arcadia 1962-65; prodn. supr. Monsanto Co., Soda Springs, Id. 1965-71, wildfire div. mgr., Ontario, Calif. 1971-91; real estate agent, Upland, Calif. 1991–; mem. Monsanto Bus. Climate Com. 1979; mem: Nat. Fire Protection Assn., Western Forestry & Conservation Assn., mem. 5 Regional Fire Councils 1970; civic: Lions, Soda Springs, Id. (ofcr. 1966-71), City of Hope, Alta Loma chapt. (pres. 1982), BSA, Alta Loma Troop (com. 1972-73, scoutmaster 73-75); mil: sp4 AUS 1957-58; Republican; rec: shooting, RV'ing. Res: 1067 St Andrews Dr Upland 91784 Ofc:450 N Mountain Ste A Upland 91786

PETERSON, MARTHA ANGELL, financial executive, certified public accountant; b. March 28, 1945, Nebr.; d. Robert Geyer and Barbara (Bartlett) Angell; m. Carroll Floyd Peterson, Feb. 5, 1972; children: Andrew b. 1978, Wyatt b. 1983; edn: BS magna cum laude, USC, 1967; C.P.A. Calif. (1970). Career: sr. mgr. Ernst & Young, San Francisco 1967-84; v.p. Crocker Nat. Bank 1985, 1st v.p. 1985-86; CFO Midland Am. Corp. 1986-88; sr. v.p., CFO Bracton Corp. 1986-89; pres. ICON Assoc. Inc. 1989–; guest lectr. UC Berkeley 1986-95; awards: Bus. & Profl. Womens Club Outstanding Young Career Woman 1974, USC Price Waterhouse 1967, Beta Alpha Psi Outstanding Grad. 1968, Panehellenic Assn. Outstanding Sr. Women 1967; mem: Fin. Womens Assn. S.F. (treas.), Calif. Soc. C.P.A., Fin. Execs. Inst., Am. Inst. C.P.A. (Task Force 1982-83), Junior League

S.F. (bd. mem. 1985-86), St. Vincent de Paul Soc. S.F. (treas. 1983), Graphic Arts Council S.F. (chmn. 1984), Commonwealth Club (sect. secty. 1974-76). Ofc: ICON Associates Inc 100 Pine St 6th Fl San Francisco 94111

PETILLON, LEE RITCHEY, lawyer; b. May 6, 1929, Gary, Ind.; s. Charles Ernest and Blanche Lurene (MacKay) P.; m. Mary Anne Keeton, Feb. 20, 1960; children: Andrew G. b. 1960, Joseph R. b. 1968; edn: BBA, Univ. Minn. 1952; LL.B, UC Berkeley 1959. Career: v.p. Creative Investment Capital Inc., Los Angeles 1969-70; corp. counsel Harvest Industries 1970-71; pres. Spring Fin. Services 1970-71; v.p., gen. counsel, dir. Tech. Service Corp., Santa Monica 1971-78; ptnr. Petillon & Davidoff, Los Angeles 1978-92; ptnr. Gipson, Hoffman & Pancione 1992-93; ptnr. Petillon & Hansen 1993–; guest lectr. CSU, Northridge 1980-81; dir., pub. counsel Westside Vol. Bureau 1981-84; chmn. Dispute Resolution Advy. Council 1988-89; dir. Saztec Internat. Inc., Kansas City, Mo. 1988; awards: Moot Ct. Boalt Hall Sch. Law Best Brief 1957, L.A. City Demonstration Agy. Cert. Appreciation 1975, United Inidan Devel. Assn. Cert. Appreciation 1981, St. Bar Calif. Pres. Pro Bono Service 1983, City L.A. Cert. Merit Vol. Service 1984, Griffin Bell Vol. Svc. Award 1993; mem: L.A. Co. Bar Found. (dir. 1986-89), Am. Bar Assn. (small bus. com., securities and regulation and partnerships subcoms. 1986), L.A. Co. Bar Assn. (trustee 1984-85, bus. and corp. law sect., fed. regulation of securities subcom., chair law and tech. sect. 1987), Neighborhood Justice Center Com. (chair 1983-85), St. Bar Calif. Task Force Alternative Dispute Resolution, Middle Income Com. (chair 1983-85), Alternate Dispute Resolution Sect. (chair 1992-94); co-author of handbook Research & Devel. Partnerships (Clark Boardman Co. 1984, 85); co-author, book, Representing Start-Up Companies (Clark Boardman Callaghan, 1995, 3rd edit.); article pub. in profl. jour., 1987; mil: 1st lt. USAF 1952-54; rec: backpacking, music, painting. Res: 1636 Via Machado Palos Verdes Estates 90274 Ofc: Petillon & Hansen 21515 Hawthorne Blvd Ste 1260 Torrance 90503

PETRONE, JOSEPH ANTHONY, professional speaker, author; b. July 6, 1956, Manhattan, NY; s. Louis Richard and Catherine (Devito) P.; m. Deborah Bernice Steele, Sept. 24, 1983; edn: BS in chem., Muhlenberg Coll., 1978. Career: sales rep. Calgon Corp., San Francisco 1979-82, market mgr. Calgon Corp., Pittsburgh, Pa. 1982-85; sales engr. Nicolet Corp., Pitts. 1985-88, regional mgr. San Francisco, 1988–; group ldr. Dale Carnegie 1983-84, instr. Learning Unltd. 1984-85; profl. awards: top sales Calgon, S.F. 1980, Nicolet, Pitts. 1985, biog. listing Internat. Directory of Disting. Leadership 3d edit.; mem.: Sales and Mktg. Execs. (ofcr., pgm. chair 1988, mktg. com. 1988, bd.), Toastmasters (bd. 1993-), Nat. Speakers Assn. (mktg. com. 1993-); civic bds: Economic Devel. and Govt. Affairs Coms. City of Pleasanton 1990, Hospice volunteer, Pitts. 1987-88; author: Building the High Performance Sales Force (AMACOM 1994); rec: tennis, wt. lifting, travel, duathlete. Res/Ofc: 3649 Dunsmuir Cir Pleasanton 94588

PETTERSEN, THOMAS M., financial executive; b. Nov. 9, 1950, Poughkeepsie, N.Y.; s. Olsen T. and Reva (Palmer) P.; edn: BS, SUNY, Albany 1973; lic. CPA, N.Y. 1976. Career: senior acct. Arthur Andersen & Co., N.Y., N.Y. 1973-77; financial analyst Paramount Communications, N.Y., N.Y. 1977-78; dir. acctg. systems, dir. auditing Nat. Broadcasting Co. Inc., Burbank 1979-90; v.p. fin. & adminstrn. Data Dimensions Inc., Culver City 1991-92; cons. Westwood One, Inc., Culver City 1992-93; CFO, Computer Image Systems, Inc., Torrance 1993–; mem. Am. Inst. CPAs 1976–, Financial Execs. Inst. 1992–; Republican; rec: sports, travel. Res: 217 First Place Manhattan Beach 90266 Ofc: Computer Image Systems Inc 20030 Normandie Ave Torrance 90502

PETTIGREW, THOMAS FRASER, social psychologist, educator; b. March 14, 1931, Richmond, Va.; s. Joseph Crane and Janette (Gibb) P.; mm. Ann Hallman, Feb. 25, 1956; 1 son, Mark b. 1966; edn: BA psych., Univ. Va., 1952; MA and PhD in social psychology, Harvard Univ., 1955, 56. Career: asst. prof. Univ. North Carolina, Chapel Hill, 1956-57; Harvard Univ., Cambridge, Mass. 1957-62, lectr., assoc. prof. 1962-68, prof. 1968-80; prof. UC Santa Cruz 1980-94, research prof. 1994–; Univ. Amsterdam, Netherlands 1986-91; mem. White House Task Force on Edn., WDC 1967; Phi Beta Kappa Emerson Book Award Com. 1971-73; trustee Ella Lyman Cabot Trust, Boston, Mass. 1978-80; adj. fellow Joint Center for Political Studies, WDC 1982–; cons. U.S. Office of Edn. 1966-68; U.S. Commn. on Civil Rights 1966-71; awards: Guggenheim Found. Fellow 1967-68, (hon.) HDL, Gov. St. Univ. 1979, Am. Sociol. Assn. Spivack Award 1978, UC Santa Cruz Faculty Res. Award 1988, Soc. Psychol. Study of Social Issues Kurt Lewin Memorial 1987, Gordon Allport Intergroup Relations Res. Award 1988, Bellagio Center Fellow 1991; mem: Am. Psychol. Assn. (fellow), Am. Sociol. Assn., Soc. Psychol. Study of Social Issues (past pres.), European Assn. Exptl. Social Psychology, Soc. Exptl. Social Psychology; author: A Profile of Negro Am. 1964, Racially Separate or Together 1971, Sociology of Race Rels. 1980, How To Think Like A Social Scientist 1995; coauthor: Christians in Racial Crisis, 1959, Prejudice, 1982, Tom Bradley's Campaigns for Governor, 1988, The Future of Social Psychology, 1991; 250+ articles pub. in profl. jours.; mil: 2d. lt. AUS 1952; Democrat; Episcopalian; rec: chess. Ofc: Psychology Dept Univ. Calif., Santa Cruz 95064

PETTUS, JOSEPH HODSON, energy company executive; b. Aug. 1, 1947, Louisville, Ky.; s. Thomas N. and Nancye B. (Trimble) P.; m. Judith C. Nenno,

Aug. 26, 1969; children: Jeffrey W. b. 1976, Jeremy H. b. 1979, Jenna C. b. 1989. edn: BS civil engrg., bus. adminstrn., Univ. Colo. 1970. Career: engr. Exxon Co. USA Houston 1970-75; proj. mgr. Fluor E&C Houston 1976-77; v.p. ops. United Energy Resources Houston 1978-81; senior v.p. supply & transp. Cal Gas Corp., Sacto. 1981-86; dir. Propane Transport Inc. Milford, Ohio, Minden Pipeline Co. Minden, La., Norco Transp. Co. L.A., Beacon Petroleum Co. Shreveport. La.; sr. v.p. Amerigas, Inc., Valley Forge, Pa. 1986-88; pres. Sun Valley Energy Inc., Sacto. 1988–; honors: Chi Epsilon, listed Who's Who in Am.; Gov.'s Internat. Host Com. of Calif.; mem. bd. dirs. KVIE-TV Ch. 6 (PBS); Republican; Protestant. Res: 8800 Triple Crown Ct Fair Oaks 95628

PEZZUTI, THOMAS ALEXANDER, architect; b. Dec. 29, Harrisburg, Pa.; s. Hamil Ralph and Dorothea Marie (Graham) P.; m. Diane Marie Paplham; 2 sons: Graham Alexander and Rhett Alexander; edn: BArch, Univ. of Notre Dame; reg. arch. Pa. 1964, Calif. 1968. Career: div. dir. Maxwell Starkman AIA & Assocs., Beverly Hills 1977-83; mgr. of design and constrn. (acting) US Postal Svc., Santa Monica 1983-87; project mgr. Daniel, Mann, Johnson and Mendenhall, 1986–; instr. design workshop Univ. of Notre Dame, 1963; candidate U.S. Congress, 27th C.D. Calif. 1976; honors: 2d prize Beaux Arts, Paris, France 1963, listed Who's Who in the West 1975, Contemporary Authors 1976; mem. Am. Inst. Architects 1973–, Internat. Mensa Soc. 1962–, Command Performance Telecable (pres. 1982-84); author: You Can Fight City Hall and Win 1974, EZ Golf 1985, invention: Hammerhead Putter (pat. 1989); mil: USAR Corps of Engrs.; Indep.; Cath.; rec: writing, computers, simulation gaming. res: PO Box 2901 Beverly Hills 90213-2901 Ofc: Daniel, Mann, Johnson & Mendenhall, 3250 Wilshire Blvd Los Angeles 90010

PFUHL, JOHN WESLEY, accountant; b. June 26, 1938, Lansing, Mich.; s. Edward Carl, Sr. and Gladys Dorothy (Williams) P.; m. Maren C. Thoresen, June 22, 1965; children: Scott, Shari; edn: BA acctg., Mich. State Univ. 1960; Certified Public Acct., Calif. 1969. Career: staff acct. Arthur Young & Co., Santa Ana office; staff acct. Jones, Elliott & Assocs., Fullerton; ptnr. Sherlock, Soule & Pfuhl, La Jolla; pres. John W. Pfuhl Acctncy. Corp.; pres. Pfuhl & Knight Acctncy. Corp., El Cajon currently; mem: Am. Inst. CPAs, Calif. Soc. CPAs; civic: past pres. Torrey Pines Kiwanis Club (Kiwanian of Year 1975), mem. El Cajon Valley Lions Club, past treas. La Jolla Town Council; mil: Lt. US Navy; Republican; Lutheran; rec: softball, skiing, woodworking. Ofc: 237 Avocado Ave Ste 210 El Cajon 92020

PFUND, EDWARD T., JR., aerospace company engineer, executive; b. Dec. 10, 1923, Methuen, Mass.; s. Edward Theodore Sr. and Mary Elizabeth (Banning) P.; m. Marga Andre, Nov. 10, 1954 (div. 1978); children: Angela b. 1954, Gloria b. 1956, Edward III b. 1961; m. 2d. Ann Lauren Dillie, Jan. 10, 1988 (div. 1990); edn: BS, magna cum laude, Tufts Coll. 1950; grad. studies, USC 1950, Boston Univ. 1950, Columbia Univ. 1953, UCLA 1956, 58. Career: radio engr. WLAW, Lawrence-Boston 1942-50; foreign svc. staff ofcr. US Dept. of State Voice of Am., Tangier, Munich, 1950-54; proj. engr. Crusade for Freedom, Radio Free Europe, Munich, Ger. 1955; proj. mgr./ material splst. United Electrodynamics Inc., Pasadena 1956-59; dir. eng./ chief engr. Electronics Specialty Co., Los Angeles & Thomaston, Conn. 1959-61; with Hughes Aircraft, var. locations 1955, 1961-89: chmn. subcom. on communications Space Flt. Ops. Gp. 1963, chief Johannesburg Ops. 1961-63, dir. Spacecraft Performance Analysis and Command 1964-68 (directed the command control & perf. of all USA unmanned soft lunar landings and the world's first lunar liftoff and translation 1966-68), pgm. mgr. Lunar Rover Ground Data Sys. Design 1969-70, mgr. new bus. devel. Middle & Far East Africa and So. America 1971-84, tech. chmn. Internat. Consortium 1974-78, dir. internat. pgms. devel. Hughes Communications Internat., Inc. 1984-89; dir. pgms. development Asia-Pacific, TRW Space & Technology Group, Redondo Beach, Calif. 1990-93; cons., mng. dir. E.T. Satellite Assocs. Internat. 1989–; cons. H.I. Thompson Co., L.A. 1958-60, Andrew Corp., Chgo. 1959, Satellite Bdcst. Assocs., L.A. 1982; faculty, Pasadena City Coll. 1958-60; honors: Phi Beta Kappa, Sigma Pi Sigma, award of merit Materials in Design Engring. for design devel. 2 unique kinds of coaxial cable having low losses at over 1000 degrees F. for Mach 3 vehicles 1958-59, Surveyor Test Pilot, Surveyor's Hon. Roll, Aviation Week & Space Technology 1966; mem: Am. Inst. of Aero. & Astro. 1973-(tech. com. Commun. Sys. 1973-76), Pacific Telecommunications Council, Honolulu 1993–; publs: num. articles. in fields of communications satellites, real-time control and data processing, distributed amplifiers, transmission lines, transistorized telemetering devel. and elect. insulation; mil: 2nd lt. US Army Air Corps 1942-46; rec: amateur radio K6OUW (1939–). Res: 25 Silver Saddle Ln Rolling Hills Estates 90274

PHAM, PHO VAN, lawyer; b. Feb. 23, 1939, Ninh Binh, Vietnam; s. Tan Van and Che Thi P.; edn: Saigon Univ. Faculty of Law 1974; JD w. honors, Western St. Univ. 1986. Career: journalist, ed. Tu Do Daily News, Saigon, Vietnam 1959-71; press attaché Vietnamese Conf. of Labor 1971-73; tchg. asst. Univ. Hue 1973-75; health plan rep. Calif. Health Plan, Los Angeles 1978-81; ins. agent and broker Pho Van Pham Ins. Agency, Westminster 1981–; real estate broker First Home 1986–; atty. 1987–; mem: Vietnamese Am. Bar Assn. (v.p.), Vietnamese Inter-Faith Council in U.S.A. (hd. Com. for the Struggle of Rel. Freedom in Vietnam) Vietnamese Cath. Comm. in Orange Diocese (v.p. 1992-

94, pres. 1994-), Vietnam Human Rights Watch Inc. (v.p. 1991–), Vietnamese Cath. Overseas Movement (v.p. 1991–), Saigon Students Assn., L.A. Vietnamese Catholics Assn. (gen. secty. 1978-79), Little Saigon Comm. Devel. Orgn.; ed., writer articles and editorials, 1964-75; ed. Hiep Nhat (Solidarity) Mag., 1992–; Catholic; rec: tennis, fishing, travel. Ofc: Pho Van Pham 9361 Bolsa Ave Ste 202 Westminster 92683

PHILLIPS, GENEVA FICKER, academic editor; b. Aug. 1, 1920, Staunton, Ill.; d. Arthur Edwin and Lillian Agnes (Woods) Ficker; m. James Emerson Phillips, Jr., June 6, 1955 (dec. 1979); edn: BS in journalism, Univ. Ill., 1942; MA in English lit., UCLA, 1953. Career: copy desk Chicago Journal of Commerce, 1942-43; editorial asst. patents Radio Research Lab., Harvard Univ., 1943-45; asst. editor adminstrv. publs. Univ. Ill., Urbana, 1946-47; teaching fellow UCLA, 1950-53, grad. fellow 1954-55, editorial asst. Quarterly of Film, Radio and TV, UCLA, 1952-53; mng. editor The Works of John Dryden, Dept. English, UCLA, 1964–; bd. dirs. Univ. Religious Conf., Los Angeles 1979–; mem: Assn. Acad. Women UCLA, Friends of Huntington Library, Friends of UCLA Library, Renaissance Soc. So. Calif., Samuel Johnson Soc. of So. Calif., Associates of Univ. Calif. Press, Conf. Christianity and Literature, Soc. Mayflower Descs.; Lutheran. Res: 213 First Anita Dr Los Angeles 90049 Ofc: UCLA Dept. English 2225 Rolfe Hall Los Angeles 90024

PHILLIPS, GEORGE SCOTT, land developer, home builder, real estate consultant; b. Feb. 28, 1939, Charleroi, Penn.; s. George Francis and Gaynell Pauline (Milliken) P.; m. Rena Louise, Apr. 20, 1985; 1 child Kim b. 1961; edn: BA in geol., UC Berkeley 1961; Cert. in Land Devel. Adminstrn., Golden Gate Univ. 1973; MA bus. adminstrn., Kensington Univ., Glendale 1979, PhD bus. adminstrn., 1980; Calif. State lic. Gen. Building Contractor 1978, Real Estate Broker 1968; SR/WA (Reg. Senior Mem.), Internat. Right of Way Assn. 1970. Career: asst. mgr. Donald D. Davis Constrn. Co., Greenbrae 1960-63; right-of-way agent Calif. Div. Hwys., San Francisco 1963-66; Acquisition and Appraisal Assocs., S.F. 1966-67; dir. R.E. mktg. and bus. devel. San Francisco Redevelopment Agy., 1967-73; v.p., forward planning mgr. Kaufman & Broad, No. Calif., Burlingame 1973-76; dir. planning and devel. Ponderosa Homes, Santa Clara 1976-77; v.p./div. mgr. M.J. Brock & Sons Inc., Dublin 1977-82; pres. Barratt Northern California, Inc., Sacramento 1982-84; pres. Warmington Homes-No. Calif., San Ramon 1985-86; mgr. land acquisition and devel., Davidon Homes, Walnut Creek 1987-94; frequent spkr. var. service and profl. groups, 1969–; qualified expert witness on valuation, mktg. and disposition of real estate, Superior Ct. City and County of San Francisco 1970; appt. mem. qualification appraisal panel for selection of Deputy Real Estate Commr. trainees; awards: Housing design award City of Novato 1974, Special appreciation Capitol Area Devel. Auth. 1983; mem. Internat. Right of Way Assn. (exec. com. 1968-71), Theta Tau (Epsilon Chap. Regent 1960) Land Execs. Assn. (pres. No. Calif. 1971); contbr. articles and interviews in New Homes Mag. 1980, Homes for Sale 1981, 82, Homebuyers Guide 1978; mil: seaman USCGR 1961-69, Calif. Wrestling & Track Teams 1961; Republican; Prot.; rec: fitness, collect Egyptian, Asian and Pre-Columbian artifacts, weapons and coins. Res: 3343 Marsh Hawk Ct Pleasanton 94588 Ofc: San Francisco Redevelopment Agency 770 Golden Gate Ave San Francisco 94102

PHILLIPS, JEFFREY RICHARD, writer/editor; b. Mar. 9, 1947, San Francisco; s. Robert Maxim and Dorothy Marie P.; edn: AA, Coll. of San Mateo; stu. CSU San Francisco, Stanford Univ. Career: editor Sunset Mag., Menlo Park 1969–; congressional appointee to White House Conf. on Travel and Tourism, 1995; cons. PBS documentary; speaker at writers conferences; writer for periodicals; awards: Lowell Thomas journalism award Soc. of Am. Travel Writers, Wash. DC (1986, 89, 92), Western Publications Assn. Maggie awards (1992, 93). Ofc: Sunset Magazine 80 Willow Road Menlo Park 94025

PHILLIPS, JOHN RICHARD, engineering professor; b. Jan. 30, 1934, Albany, Calif.; s. Eric Lester and Adele Catherine (Rengel) P.; m. Joan Elizabeth Soyster Mar. 23, 1957; children: Elizabeth b. 1962, Sarah b. 1963, Kate b. 1966; edn: BS, UC Berkeley, 1956; M.Eng., Yale Univ., 1958, D.Eng., 1960; reg. profl. engr. Calif. Career: chemical engr. SRI, Menlo Park 1960; res. engr. Chevron Research Co., Richmond 1962-66; asst., assoc., prof. engring. Harvey Mudd Coll., Claremont 1966–, dir. Engring. Clinic 1977-93, James Howard Kindleberger Prof. of Engring. 1991–, chair Engring. Dept. 1993–; founder Claremont Engring. Co., Claremont 1973–; vis. prof. Univ. Edinburgh, Scotland 1975, Cambridge Univ., Eng. 1981, ESIEE, Paris 1981, Naval Postgrad. Sch., Monterey, Calif. 1984-85; Calif. Polytechnic Univ., San Luis Obispo 1992; cons. various cos. and govt. 1966–; mem. Am. Inst. Chem. Engrs.; author 3 US patents, 25+ profl. publs.; mil: 1st lt. US Army 1960-62. Ofc: Harvey Mudd College Dept. Engineering, Claremont 91711

PHILLIPS, LACY DARRYL, creative and performing artist; b. Feb. 24, 1963 Brooklyn, NY; s. William Lacy and Sandra Ann (Reaves) P.; edn: diploma (Regents), Springfield Gardens H.S., Queens, NY, 1980; Herbert H. Lehman Coll., Bronx, NY, 1980-81; Sound Master Audio Video Sch., 1994; cert. recording engr 1994. Career: tchr./choreographer Queens Coll., Queens, NY, 1980; choreographer Broadway Dance Ctr., Tokyo, Japan, 1985-90; asst. to dir Red

Bird Productions, L.A., 1988-92; choreographer, Ruthless Records, L.A., 1991; co-dir. Painted Black Productions, L.A., 1991-92; mem: Actors Equity Assn. 1973–, Screen Actors Guild 1978–, AFTRA 1980–, Dancers Alliance 1990–, Soc. of Stage Directors & Choreographers 1991–; song writer/lyricist, Compilation, 1989–; Democrat; Christian; rec: music, writing, singing.

PHILLIPS, PAUL E., university administrator; b. Jan. 31, 1942, Saratoga Springs, N.Y.; s. John Francis and Hazel Jane (Graves) Litke P.; m. Jean C. Craven, Sept. 12, 1964; children: Laura b. 1966, Beth b. 1968; edn: BA, Duke Univ. 1963; MA, Univ. of Pacific 1974. Career: regional personnel mgr. Air Products & Chemicals, Allentown, Pa. 1967-69; asst. dir. admissions, Univ. of Pacific, Stockton 1969-74; dir. of admissions Pacific Univ., Forest Grove, Ore. 1974-78; dir. fin. aid Univ. of Pacific, Stockton 1978-89; CSU San Marcos 1989–; cons. Calif. Student Aid Commn., Sacto. 1980–; profl. presentations Calif., Western and Nat. Assn. Student Fin. Aid Adminstrn., Calif. and Wash. D.C. 1979–; Coll. Bd. San Jose, Calif. and N.Y.C. 1980–; exec. com. Nat. Council Coll. Scholarship Service, N.Y.C. 1987-88; honors: Phi Kappa Phi, Calif. Assn. Student Aid Adminstrn. Disting. Service 1988, Nat. Assn. Student Aid Adminstrn. Outstanding Service 1983, Leadership Award 1992; mem: Calif. Assn. Student Fin. Aid Adminstrs. (past pres.), Western Assn. Student Fin. Aid Adminstrs. (pres. 1990), Nat. Assn. Student Fin. Aid Adminstrs., Pacific Northwest Indep. Colls. (pres. 1977), Nat. Assn. Coll. Admissions Counselors, Planned Parenthood (bd. dirs. 1985-89), Sister City Assn. (bd. dirs. 198889), Lifeline Inc. (bd. dirs. 1971-74); article pub. in profl. jour. (1980); mil: lt. USN 1963-67; Democrat; United Methodist; rec: gardening, soccer, boating. Res: 901 Carriage Dr San Marcos 92069 Ofc: California State University San Marcos 92096

PHILLIPS, ROBERT BROOKS, advertising executive; b. Nov. 28, 1932, St. Louis, Mo.; s. Herbert Curlee and Maud Evelyn (Brooks) P.; m. Georgia Lee Berkley (div. 1988); children: Robert b. 1960, Brook b. 1962, Berkley b. 1964; edn: BS commerce, Univ. Va. 1954. Career: account exec. Ridgway Adv., St. Louis, Mo. 1956-57; production mgr., exec. v.p. Lynch Adv. 1957-68; pres. Phillips Orgn. 1968-72; exec. v.p. Franklin & Assoc., San Diego 1973-74; pres. Phillips Orgn. 1974-86; exec. v.p. Franklin & Assoc. 1987-89; pres. Phillips Mktg. 1989–; awards: Best in West, Clios, Marsys, Nat. Creative Mktg.; mem: San Diego Historical Soc. (bd. dirs. 1983-91), USA Volleyball Inc. (bd. dirs. 1984-90); mil: lt.j.g. USN 1954-56; Republican; Episcopalian; rec: racquetball, golf, country inns. Res: 2945 Kellogg St #B San Diego 92106 Ofc: Phillips Marketing 4011 Ibis St San Diego 92103

PHILLIPS, SAMUEL LAWRENCE, lawyer; b. Feb. 2, 1960, Modesto; s. Neil Harold and L. Carolyn (Goodhue) P.; m. Anita Joan Gildea, June 12, 1982; children: Patrick b. 1984, Sean b. 1991; edn: BA, Univ. San Francisco 1982; JD, 1985. Career: law clk. Conklin Davids & Friedman, San Francisco 1982-85; Newton & Kastner, Mountain View 1985-86; sr. adjuster Home Ins., San Francisco 1986-87; sr. litigation adjuster Underwriters Adjusting Co., San Mateo & Pleasanton 1987; atty., assoc. Glaspy & Glaspy, San Jose 1987-90; assoc. Borton, Petrini & Conron, Modesto 1990-93, ptnr. 1993–; listed Who's Who in Am. Law; mem: Am. Bar Assn., Calif. Bar Assn., Stanislaus Bar Assn.; R.Cath.; rec: Calif. history, fishing, basketball. Ofc: Borton, Petrini & Conron 9th St Modesto 95350

PHILLIPS, TEDDY STEVE, orchestra director; b. June 15, 1916, Chgo., Ill.; s. Steve S. and Kaliope S. (Phillips) Simms; m. Colleen Lovett, Apr. 18, 1957; children: Joe, b. 1961; Teddy, b. 1963; edn: Univ. of Ill. 1935-39. Career: saxophone player with big bands across US 1940-45; staff musician Radio Sta. CBS, Chgo. 1944-45; conductor Teddy Phillips Orch. across country, 1944-55, 1957-62; prin. Teddy Phillips Show, WBKB-TV- ABC, Chgo. 1956-57; conductor Tedd Phillips & Orch.: Ambassador Hotel (L.A.), Flamingo Hotel (Las Vegas), Statler Hotels, Aragon Ballroom, Hilton Hotels (Chgo.) 1962–; recording artist and record producer, pres. P&M Prodns., 1976–; director The Guy Lombardo Orch. 1980–; producer t.v. show: Great Concert in the Sky; hit recording: Bartender Pour Me Another Heartache; songwriter: Do the Camel Hump; honors: Heart Fund medal of distinction, citation Rotary Clubs of Am.; mem. Musicians Union, Masons; mil: US Army 1940-41; Greek Orthodox. Res: 4650 Park Mirasol Calabasas 91302

PHILPOTT, DELBERT EUGENE, biologist; b. Sept. 24, 1923, Loyal, Wis.; s. Lacey D. and Nettie A. (Goering) P.; m. Donna A. Naylor, Dec., 1985; edn: BA, Ind. Univ., 1948, MS, 1949; PhD, Boston Univ., 1963. Career: res. assoc. Univ. Ill. Med. Sch., Chgo. 1949-52; hd.electron microscope lab. Inst. Muscle Research, Woods Hole, Mass. 1952-63; asst. prof. biochem. Univ. Colo. Med. Sch., Denver 1963-66; hd., co-dir. Inst. Biomed. Research, Mercy Hosp. 1966; hd. Electron Microscope Lab., NASA Ames Research Center, Moffett Field 1966-90, sci. coord. Student Space Biology 1974–, Radiation Safety 1987–; sci. coord. Historically Black Colls. 1989; faculty advisor Delta Coll., Stockton 1982–; awards: PhT (hon.) Coll. Optometry 1976, NASA Apollo Biocore Achievement 1974, Joint U.S./USSR Mission 1976, Cosmos 936 Group Achievement 1978; mem: Nat. Bd. Cert. Electron Microscopists, No. Soc. Electron Microscopists (past. pres., v.p.), Electron Microscope Soc. Am., N.Y. Acad. Scis., Sigma Xi, Exptl. Aircraft Assn. (v.p. 1978); 200+ papers pub. in sci.

jours. (1949–), sci. pictures pub. on cover of Jour. Applied Physics, Sci., A.I.B.S. (1951-62); mil: pvt. 1c AUS 1942-45, Bronze Star, Purple Heart; rec: flying, photog. Ofc: NASA Ames Research Center Moffett Field 94035

PIASECKI, JACK O., physician-orthopedic surgeon; b. June 7, 1950, Ontario, Canada, naturalized U.S. cit. 1956; s. Andrew Leon and Christine Anna (Pozniak) P.; m. Tracy Holtzman, May 31, 1980 (div. 1988); m. 2d. Cassie Weiner, Dec. 31, 1993; edn: BS in biology (magna cum laude), Univ. of Pittsburgh, 1972, MD, 1976; MBA, UC Irvine, 1989; qualified medical evaluator, St. of Calif. Indsl. Med. Council; Bd. cert. independent med. examiner. Career: orthopedic surgeon Fronk Clinic, Honolulu 1982-84; chmn. dept. orthopedic surg. Family Health Program, Fountain Valley 1984-88; orthopedic surgeon pvt. practice Griffon Med. Group, Costa Mesa, Calif. 1992–; orthopaedic cons. Internat. Rehab. Assocs., Anaheim 1992–; staff cons. Charter Hosp. 1986–; supr. of P.A. St. of Calif., Sacto. 1988–; tchg. cons. UC Irvine Grad. Sch. of Mgmt. 1988–; honors: Phi Beta Kappa 1972; mem: New York Co. Med. Soc., Orange Co. Med. Assn., Calif. Med. Soc., Calif. Orthopedic Assn., Calif. Soc. of Indsl. Medicine & Surgery; clubs: Laguna Niguel Racquet, Caribou (Aspen); publs: 3 sci. papers re scoliosis, spinal fusion, 1982, 83, 86; Republican; R.Cath.; rec: oil painting, skiing, tennis. Res: 315 Promontory Dr East, Newport Beach 92660 Ofc: South Coast Rehab Inst 1520 Nutmeg Ste 190 Costa Mesa 92626

PICK, ARTHUR JOSEPH, JR., chamber of commerce executive; b. March 22, 1931, Louisville, Ky.; s. Arthur Joseph and Helen Elizabeth (Henzel) P.; edn: BS, UC Riverside 1959; grad., Coro Found., L.A. 1960; MA, urban studies, Occidental Coll. 1969. Career: pres. Greater Riverside Chamber of Commerce 1972–; mem. Calif.-Nevada High Speed Ground Transportation Commn. 1992–; pres. Riverside Monday Morning Group 1992-94; pres. Young Life Riverside 1966-68; pres. Riverside Symphony Orch. Soc. 1966-69; founding pres. Riverside Cultural Arts Council 1969-71; elected Riverside City Council 1967, re-elected 1971; founder Friends of Calif. Bapt. Coll. 1978, Friends of La Sierra Univ., Riverside 1978, Friends of Sherman Indian H.S. 1986, Friends of Calif. Sch. for the Deaf, Riverside 1988; founding pres., Mayors and Council Assn. of Riverside Co. 1968-69; trustee La Sierra Univ., Riverside 1990–; awards: Disting. Svc. award, Riverside Jaycees 1966, Patron of Arts award, Cultural Arts Council 1977, Vernon Jordan Humanitarian award, Riverside Area Urban League 1989, Citizen of Yr. award, Riverside Police Ofcrs. Assn. 1990, Atlas award, Riverside YWCA 1990, Comm. Svc. award 1990, UC Riverside Disting. Alumni award 1990, Riverside Internat. Relations Council Citizen of Yr. 1992; life mem. Riverside Jaycees; v.p. Orange Blossom Festival; treas. Calif. St. Citrus Heritage Park; co-chair Mayor's Vision Com.; chair City/Univ. Task Force Com.; founding chair UCR Ext. Advy. Bd.; mil: cpl. AUS 1953-55; Republican; Presbyterian. Ofc: Greater Riverside Chamber of Commerce 3685 Main St Ste 350 Riverside 92501

PICKFORD, ROLLO SEARS, JR., computer software company executive; b. Aug. 9, 1927, Cedar Rapids, Iowa; s. Rollo Sears and Alta (Fessenden) P.; m. Nadene Katheryn Weltz, Jan. 13, 1928; children: Michael b. 1954, Laura b. 1957, Scott b. 1959; edn: BS, Iowa St. Univ. 1951; reg. profl. engr. Calif. 1957. Career: research engr. Calif. Inst. Tech. Jet Propulsion Lab., Pasadena 1951-55; dept. head combustion research and space environ. lab. Aerojet Gen. Corp., Azusa 1955-60; mgr. mech. and ordnance engring. and research Astropower Inc., Newport Beach 1960-67; sr. group leader McDonnel Douglas Corp., Huntington Beach 1967-69; pres. Thermeon Corp., Santa Ana 1969–; papers and articles pub. in profl. jours., 1955-67, inventor rocket engine testing devices, 1958; Republican; Lutheran; rec: camping, music, teaching. Res: 1111 St Vincent Pl Santa Ana 92705 Ofc: Thermeon Corp. 12241 Newport Ave Santa Ana 92705

PIERCE, RONALD LEE, accounting educator; b. Jan. 8, 1939, El Paso, Tx.; m. Lorraine Schwendiman, June 15, 1964; children: Ronald Merlin b. 1966, Julene b. 1967, Kristin b. 1969, Lee Alvin b. 1974, Larry Thomas b. 1978; edn: BA, Brigham Young Univ., 1963, MA acctg., 1965; postgrad. studies, USC, 1972-75; C.P.A., Utah 1965, Calif. 1976. Career: staff acct. Peat, Marwick, Mitchell & Co., Salt Lake City, Utah 1964-66; asst. to corporate div. controller of Boise Cascade Corp., Boise, Ida. 1966-67; pvt. practice acct. Logan, Utah 1967-72; Claremont, Calif. 1972–; asst. prof. acctg. Utah State Univ., Logan 1967-72, assoc. prof. acctg. CSU Los Angeles, 1972–; missionary for LDS Ch., Argentina, 1959-61; honors: Eagle Scout 1972, H.S. varsity tennis and sch. newspaper editor, BYU 2d counselor 15th Ward bishopric, voted Outstanding Acctg. Prof. by students CSULA 1976; Res: 1644 Paine Ct Claremont 91711

PIEROSE, PERRY NICHOLAS, physician; b. Aug. 15, 1910, Butte, Mont.; s. Nicholas Peter and Mary (Brant) P.; m. Elizabeth Bissel Van Wormer, 1938 (dec. Feb. 1990); m. Dorothy Jane Stout, July 14, 1990; children: Anne, b. 1943; Susan, b. 1945; Gale, b. 1954; edn: AB, Stanford Univ. 1933; Asstship., biochem. research, USC Sch. of Med. 1934, faculty mem., M.D., USC Sch. of Med. 1939. Career: pvt. practice internal medicine; senior staff St. Vincent Medical Centre, Los Angeles, Pasadena; med. dir. Calif. Portland Cement Co.; J.G. Boswell Co.; Doctor of Year honoree St. Vincent Medical Centre, L.A. (10/86); honors: Nu Sigma Nu, Delta Tau Delta Hall of Fame Stanford Univ.; clubs: Stanford, Valley Hunt, (past) Bohemian, S.F. (courtesy mem. WWII),

Balboa Bay Club, Newport Beach, Big Canyon Country Club, Newport Beach; mil: capt. USMC WWII 5th armored div. chief surgery, Ft. McDowell Sta. Hosp., S.F. WWII, four med. commendns.; Republican; Prot.; rec: hunting, fly-fishing, gardening, art. Res: 698 La Loma Rd Pasadena 91105 also: 3622 Blue Key Corona del Mar 92625 Ofc: 201 S Alvarado St Los Angeles 90057

PILLING, STEVE PAUL, telecommunications consultant; b. July 23, 1958, Decatur, Ill.; s. Frank Edward and Lauri Lee (Riesland) P.; m. Marta E. Rogers, Apr. 16, 1994; edn: BS mktg., Millikin Univ. 1980; Nat. Univ. 1984; MBA telecommunications, 1985. Career: sales rep. Burroughs Corp., Decatur, Ill. 1981; Starnet Corp., San Diego 1982-86; regional sales mgr. Com Systems, Newport Beach 1986; cons., pres. Telecom Cons., San Diego 1986–; honors: Kappa Sigma, Who's Who Among Students in Am. Coll.s & Univs., Starnet Corp. Leadership award; mem: Le Tip (pres. 1991, v.p. 1988, inspector 1986-88), Soc. Telecomms. Cons., San Diego C.of C.; Republican; Presbyterian; rec: golf, swimming, sailing. Ofc: Telecom Consultants 23212 Shooting Star Dr Murrieta 92562-3260

PINES, BURT, lawyer, former city attorney; b. May 16, 1939, Burbank; s. Charles and Ruth (Pines) Landeau; m. Karen, Apr. 9, 1966; children: Adam b. 1969, Ethan b. 1970, Alissa b. 1974; edn: BA, USC, 1960; JD, N.Y. Univ., 1963. Career: asst. U.S. atty. U.S. Dept. of Justice, Los Angeles, 1964-66; atty., assoc. law firm Kadison & Quinn, 1966-67; Schwartzman, Greenberg & Fimberg, 1968-69; ptnr. Pines & Dunn, Beverly Hills, 1970-73; city atty. City of Los Angeles, 1973-81; sr. ptnr. Alschuler, Grossman & Pines, Los Angeles, 1981–; mem. bd. trustees NIMLO, Wash. D.C., 1973-81; appt. Calif. Commn. on Personal Privacy (chmn. 1981-82), L.A. Dept. of Airports Citizens Advy. Com. (chmn. 1985-87), Calif. Coun. on Criminal Justice, L.A. (mem. 1974-81); honors: Phi Beta Kappa 1960, Root-Tilden Scholar, N.Y.U. 1960-63, Order of the Coif 1963, recipient num. civic awards; mem: State Bar of Calif. 1964, Am., L.A. County, Fed. bar assns., Public Counsel/L.A. (dir. 1985-86), Constnl. Rights Found./L.A. (dir. 1975-82); civic: Town Hall, World Affairs Council, L.A. C.of C. Ofc: Alschuler, Grossman & Pines, 2049 Century Park East 39th Flr Los Angeles 90067

PINKHAM, CLARKSON WILFRED, structural engineer; b. Nov. 25, 1919, Los Angeles; s. Walter Hampden and Dorothy Rebecca (Burdorf) P.; m. EmmaLu Hull, May 8, 1942; children: Nancy b. 1947, Timothy b. 1949, Anthony b. 1955; edn: BAS in C.E., UC Berkeley, 1943, BS, 1947; reg. civil and structural engr., Calif., Wash.; reg. struc. engr. Ill., Ariz.; reg. profl. engr. Fla., Ga., Ind., Iowa, Ks., Md., Okla., Ore., Tx., Wis. Career: active duty USN 1941-46, retired lt. cmdr. USNR 1954; engr., exec. pres. S.B. Barnes Associates (structural engring. consulting firm), Los Angeles 1947–; mem.: Struc. Engrs. Assn. of So. Calif. (pres. 1971, 75, hon. mem. 1984, Stephenson B. Barnes Award for Research 1985, 90), Am. Soc. Civil Engrs. (life, Fellow), Internat. Assn. Bridge and Struc. Engring., Earthquake Engring. Res. Inst. (bd. dirs. 1994-96), Building Seismic Safety Commn., Am. Concrete Inst. (Fellow, bd. dirs. 1975-78, bldg. code subcom. chmn. on seismic provisions 1983-95, Henry L. Kennedy Award 1986), Am. Soc. Testing and Materials, Am. Welding Soc., The Masonry Soc. (charter, bd. 1986-87), Struc. Stability Research Council, Am. Arbitration Assn., Seismol. Soc. Am., Internat. Conf. Building Ofcls., Am. Inst. Steel Constrn. (specs. com.), Inst. for Adv. Engring., Nat. Inst. of Bldg. Scis. (charter mem. con-sultative council), L.A. Tall Bldg. Struc. Design Council (Pres.'s Award 1989), Am. Iron and Steel Inst. (spec. com. design of cold formed steel struc. members); civic: L.A. Co. Earthquake Commn. 1971-74, Town Hall of Calif., L.A. C.of C. 1957-85; author tech. reports and articles, book chapter "Design Philosophies" in Building Structural Design Handbook, 1987; rec: philately, family genealogy. Ofc: S.B. Barnes Associates 2236 Beverly Blvd Los Angeles 90057

PINOLI, BURT ARTHUR, international airlines management executive; b. Nov. 23, 1954, Santa Rosa, Calif.; s. Norris L. and Grace (Williams) P.; m. So Yen, May 9, 1987; 1 son, Lucas b. 1991; edn: BS agri-bus., CSU Fresno; MIM, Am. Grad. Sch. of Internat. Mgmt., Thunderbird, Glendale, Az.; proficient in Mandarin Chinese. Career: loan ofcr., mgmt. trainee Lloyds Bank Calif., Sanger 1979-81; mgr. sales and bus. devel. Transamerica Airlines, Oakland 1981-86; credit analyst, comml. loan ofcr. Farm Credit Bank System, Ukiah 1986-87; city mgr. Northwest Airlines, Beijing, Peoples Republic of China 1988-90; city mgr. Northwest Airlines, Shanghai, China 1990-94, gen. mgr. sales & mktg., P.R. of China 1995–; honors: Nat. 4-H Council, nat. winner health proj. 1974, BSA Life award 1973, Blue Key 1978, Alpha Gamma Rho (pres. 1978-79), Alpha Zeta, Internat. Farm Youth Exchange del. to India, AGSIM Asia and China Clubs; Ch. of Jesus Christ of Latter Day Saints. Res: 1551 Boonville Rd Ukiah 95482

PINSON, HARLEY FREDERICK, lawyer; b. July 8, 1950, Oakland; s. Robert Franklin and Borghilde (Jorgensen) P.; m. Cynthia Ann West, Aug. 25, 1973; children: Adam b. 1982, Lisa b. 1985; edn: BA political sci., UCSB 1973; JD, Univ. of Pacific McGeorge Sch. Law 1977; admitted St. Bar Calif. 1977. Career: staff counsel Calif. St. Lands Commn., Sacto. 1977-81; atty. Getty Oil Co., Bakersfield 1981-84; counsel Occidental Internat. Exploration & Production Co. 1984-90; legal mgr. Occidental of Pakistan 1990-93; legal and contracts mgr. Occidental of Malaysia 1993–; mem: Am. Bar Assn., Internat. Bar Assn., Internat. Assn. Petroleum Negotiators, Republican; Methodist; rec: running. Ofc: Occidental Petroleum (Malaysia) Ltd PO Box 11174 Bakersfield 93389-1174

PIRNAZAR, SAM (SAEED), entertainment executive; s. Assadollah and Pari Dokht (Ahadpour) P.; edn: MA, Univ. Kans. 1977; PhD, 1982. Career: instr. Univ. Kans., Lawrence 1976-81; mktg. exec. Compu-Psych Inc., Kans. City, Mo. 1981-83; dir. Test Corp. Am. 1982-84; regional mktg. dir. Nat. Computer Systems, Minneapolis, Minn. 1983-87; exec. v.p. Trimark Pictures 1987-94; pres., CEO, founder Tech. Dynamics Inc., Santa Monica 1987–; sr. cons. Tests (directory). Ofc: POB 219 Manhattan Beach 90266

PITCHESS, JOHN PAUL, insurance broker; b. March 21, 1942, Kansas City, Mo.; s. Peter J. and Athena (Takis) P.; m. Wendy M. Marquand, Aug. 28, 1965; children: Peter b. 1967, Julie b. 1969, Kathleen b. 1975; edn: BS, USC 1965; MBA, USC 1967. Career: pres. Pitchess & Perricone Ins., Newport Beach 1973-83; pres. Pitchess Ins. Assoc. 1983–; mem.: Western Assn. Ins. Brokers, S.F. and L.A. 1980-93, Profl. Ins. Agents of Calif. 1983-95; civic: Newport Harbor C.of C. (dir. 1976-83), Vikings of Orange Co.; club: Balboa Bay; Republican; rec: golf, tennis, soccer coaching. Res: 4 Corona Irvine 92715 Ofc: Pitchess Insurance Associates 18400 Von Karman #100 Irvine 92715

PITKIN, ROY MACBETH, physician; b. May 24, 1934, Anthon, Iowa; s. Roy and Pauline (McBeath) P.; m. Marcia Jenkins, Aug. 17, 1957; children: Barbara b. 1959, Robert Macbeth b. 1961, Kathryn b. 1963, William Charles b. 1968; edn: BA (highest distinction), Univ. of Iowa 1955, MD, 1959. Career: intern King Co. Hosp., Seattle, Wash. 1959-60; resident ob-gyn, Univ. of Iowa 1960-63; chief, ob-gyn USMC Air Station Hosp., Cherry Point, NC 1963-65; asst. prof. Univ. of Ill., Chg. 1965-68; assoc. prof. and prof. Univ. of Iowa 1968-87; prof. and chair ob-gyn, UCLA, Los Angeles 1987–; dir. Am. Bd. Obstetrics & Gynecology 1980-88; dir. Am. Bd. of Emergency Medicine 1990–; honors: Career Devel. award, NIH 1972-77, Joseph Goldberger award, AMA 1982, fellowship ad eundem, Royal Coll. of Obstetricians & Gynecologists, United Kingdom 1986, honorary fellowship German Soc. of Gynecology & Obstetrics, Germany 1992; mem: Soc. of Perinatal Obstetricians (pres. 1978-79), Soc. for Gynecologic Investigation (pres. 1986), Am. Gynecological & Obstetrical Soc. (pres. 1994-95); editor, med. periodicals: Clinical Obstetrics and Gynecology, 1978–, Obstetrics and Gynecology, 1986–; author: 150+ scientific publications; mil: lt. comdr. Med. Corps, USNR 1963-65; Independent; Presbyterian. Res: 15500 Sunset Blvd Pacific Palisades 90272 Ofc: UCLA 10833 Le Conte Ave 24-126 CHS Los Angeles 90024-1740

PLANE, FREDRICK ALAN, deputy county administrative officer; b. Dec. 25, 1955, Eugene, Ore.; s. Richard Alan and Dorothy Elizabeth (Morris) Touchstone P.; m. Karen Maureen Dirksen, Aug. 1, 1976 (div. 1987); children: Alison b. 1982, Breanna b. 1985; m. Sheila Kay Brown, Oct. 18, 1992; edn: BS bus. adminstrn., CSU Bakersfield 1978, MPA, 1994. Career: p.t. bus. mgr. Niles Surgical & Med. Group, Bakersfield 1971-78, bus. mgr. 1978-80; sr. buyer Co. of Kern Purchasing Dept. 1980-88; dep. co. adminstv. ofcr. Co. of Kern Adminstrv. Office 1988–; bd. dirs. Kern Co. Econ. Opportunity Corp., Bakersfield 1992–; honors: Outstanding MPA Grad., CSU Bakersfield 1994; mem: Am. Soc. Pub. Adminstrs. (sec. 1991, pres. 1991, 92), Kern Co. Mgmt. Council, Kern Co. Speakers Bureau, Toastmasters Internat., Roadrunner Club CSU Bakersfield, So. Valley Toastmasters (secty., treas. 1988-89, pres. 1989); Democrat; Prot.; rec: golf, basketball. Res: 11901 April Ann Ave Bakersfield 93312 Ofc: County of Kern Administrative Office 1115 Truxtun Ave 5th Fl Bakersfield 93301

PLANT, FRANCIS BENJAMIN, comic book direct mail sales company president; b. May 4, 1952, San Jose; s. Henry Benjamin and Janet Elizabeth (Lynch) P.; m. LeAnn Marie Tauer, Sept. 18, 1974 (div. Mar. 1978); m. Ann Black, Dec. 30, 1983; children: Meadow b. 1974, Ena b. 1978, Alison b. 1984, Philip b. 1986; edn: BS in bus. mktg., San Jose St. Univ., 1975. Career: retail comic book store ptnr. Seven Sons Comic Shop, San Jose 1968; ptnr. Comic World, 1969-70; ptnr. Comics & Comix, chain of 7 stores: Sacto., S.F., Palo Alto, Berkeley, Solano, 1972-88, sole owner 1988; owner/mgr. Bud Plant (mail order/whsle) San Jose/Grass Valley, 1970-78; owner/mgr. Bud Plant, Inc. (7 warehouses) Hayward, L.A., San Diego, Grass Valley, Phoenix, Denver, St. Louis, 1978-88; current owner Bud Plant Comic Art (mail order, retail only) 1988–, and Bud Plant Illustrated Books (Antiquarian books) 1986–; publisher/co-editor (art mag.) Promethean Enterprises #1-5 (1969-75), author and publisher Bud Plant's Incredible Catalog (6x yearly 1970–), publisher (comic book) The First Kingdom #1-24 (1974-87), editor (pamphlet) Help for New Retailers, 1987; awards: Friend of Fandom, San Diego Comic-Con 1975, 50 Who Made DC Comics Great, DC Comics div. Warner Comm., NYC 1983, Inkpot Award, San Diego Comic-Con 1994; mem. Internat. Assn. for Direct Distbn. (pres. 1984, 1987), Am. Booksellers Assn.; organizer comic book conv. Baycon, in conjunction with UC Berkeley, 1973; Indep.; rec: collect old comic books, original artwork, antiquarian illustrated books. Ofc: PO Box 1689, 13393 Grass Valley Dr Ste 7 Grass Valley 95945

PLATZKER, ARNOLD C.G., physician, professor of pediatrics; b. Aug. 26, 1936, N.Y.C.; s. Irving Golembe and Faye (Cassin) P.; m. Marjorie A. Sanek, June 9, 1963; children: David I. b. 1965, Elizabeth F. b. 1967; edn: AB (honors in biology), Brown Univ., 1958; MD, Tufts Univ., 1962; med. lic. Mass. 1963, Calif. 1964. Career: asst. prof. pediatrics Univ. Calif. San Francisco 1971-73; asst. prof. pediatrics USC Sch. of Medicine, L.A. 1973-78, assoc. prof. 1979-85,

prof. 1986–; head div. neonatology/ pulmonology Childrens, L.A. 1973–; bd. dir. University Childrens Med. Group, 1982–, exec. com. 1982-93, pres. 1982-86; steering com. and exec. com. NHLBI Study of Pediatric Pulmonary and Cardiac Complications of Vertically Transmitted HIV Infection (chair Pulmonary Subcom. 1989–); cons. state agys. and hosps.; awards: life mem. Clare Hall, Cambridge Univ., U.K. 1986; mem: We. Soc. for Pediatric Res. 1973–, Calif. Thoracic Soc. 1972–, L.A. Pediatric Soc., Calif. Perinatal Assn. (1977–, pres. 1978-79), Am. Lung Assn. of L.A. Co. (bd. 1988-93, exec. com. 1992-93), Am. Lung Assn. of Calif. (bd. 1990-93), Am. Acad. of Pediatrics (Fellow 1973–, fetus and newborn com. 1973–, chmn. 75-78), Am. Coll. Chest Physicians (Fellow 1974–), Am. Thoracic Soc. (1971–, chmn. Pediatric Assembly 1979, com. health care policy and tech.1987-92, long range plng. com. 85-89, com. ped. pulmonology manpower 85-89), AAAS, NY Acad. Scis., Soc. for Critical Care Medicine, AAUP, Royal Soc. of Medicine, UK (fellow 1986–), European Respiratory Soc. 1991–; author 70+ peer reviewed articles, book chapters; mil: lcdr USNR 1966-68; Democrat; Jewish; rec: swimming, photography. Ofc: Childrens Hospital 4650 Sunset Blvd Box 83 Los Angeles 90027

PLAYER, THERESA JOAN, law professor; b. Nov. 17, 1947, Great Lakes, Ill.; d. Heber and Rita Jane (Mulholland) Player; edn: BA, Univ. San Diego St. Univ. 1970; JD, UCLA 1973; admitted St. Bar Calif. 1973. Career: staff atty. Legal Aid Soc. San Diego 1974-78; Meaney & Player 1979-80; asst. law prof. Univ. San Diego 1980-83, clinic dir. 1983–; vis. prof. Santa Clara Univ. 1986-87; exec. com. Assn. Am. Law Schs. (sect. on clinical edn.), Wash. D.C. 1988; awards: San Diego Vol. Lawyers Appreciation (1985), WOmens Criminal Defense Service (1984); mem: Am. Bar Assn., Calif. Attys. for Criminal Justice, Lawyers Club S.D., Calif. Women Lawyers; contbr. Everywomens Legal Guide, 1982; co-author, California Trial Techniques, 1991; Democrat; rec: running, bicycling, swimming. Ofc: Univ. San Diego Alcala Park San Diego 92110

PLOTT, ELIZABETH ROGINSON, health care executive; b. Jan. 14, 1928, Ontario, Canada; d. Frederick Raymond and Elizabeth Margaret (Collins) Roginson; m. Thomas Plott, Sept. 8, 1958; children: Elizabeth b. 1962, Sarah b. 1965, Jennifer b. 1967; edn: BA, Oberlin Coll., 1949; MSW, UC Los Angeles, 1953; R.N., Chaffey Coll., 1964; reg. nursing home adminstr. Calif. (1988). Career: dep. counselor of mental health Los Angeles Co. Dept. of Mental Health, L.A. 1953-56; adminstr. Los Angeles Sanitarium 1956-58; social work cons. Plott Nursing Home, Ontario 1958-64; co-owner Waterman Convalescent Hosp., Inc. San Bernardino 1964–, social work cons., corp. secty. 1967–; adminstr. Orangetree Conv. Hosp., Arlington; co-owner Mt. Rubidoux Conv. Hosp., Riverside; Del Rosa Villa Conv. Hosp., San Bdo.; Plott Nursing Home, Ontario; corp. secty. Del Rosa Villa Inc. 1981–, Orangetree Conv. Hosp. 1983–; mem: L.A. Co. Mus. of Art President's Circle (1984–), Nat. Hist. Museum of L.A. (Fellow), Sch. Pub. Health UCLA (Dean's Council 1984–), Gr. L.A. Zoo Assn., Am. Coll. Health Care Adminstrs., Nat. Assn. Social Workers; Republican; Presbyterian; rec: travel. Res: 713 N Beverly Dr Beverly Hills 90210

PLOURD, DAVID MEDRICK, obstetrician-gynecologist; b. Oct. 18, 1956, New Haven, Conn.; s. Medrick C. and Letty (Arpaia) P.; m. Fran Sentesy, May 3, 1986; edn: BA, natural sci., Pepperdine Univ. 1978; MD, UCLA Sch. Medicine 1982; ob-gyn specialty, UC Irvine 1982-86. Career: faculty ob-gyn physician S.C.V. Med. Ctr., San Jose 1987–; staff ob-gyn physician U.S. Naval Hosp., Oakland 1993–; ob-gyn lectr. (nationwide), Nat. Bd. Reviews 1988–; honors: Alpha Omega Alpha 1982; mem. CMA 1982–; author: Research on Treating Serious Infections in Women, 1993; peer reviewer, article on contraception, 1995; researcher/author: New Treatments for Sexually Transmitted Diseases, 1995; Catholic; rec: motor yachting. Res: 450 Lowell Place Fremont 94536

PLUMB, DAVID W., certified public accountant; b. Nov. 29, 1962, Santa Monica; s. Walter D. and Edelgard (Wesner) P.; edn: CSU San Bernardino 1981-83; BA acctg., info. systems, Azusa Pacific Univ. 1986. Career: staff auditor Conrad Assoc. CPA, Irvine 1986-87; staff auditor Peat Marwick Main CPA, Los Angeles 1987-88; sr. acct. Managed Health Network 1988-92; controller Krout & Schneider, Inc. 1992–; Republican; Baptist; rec: skiing, acting. Res: 1246 E Carroll Ave Glendora 91741 Ofc: Krout & Schneider, Inc 2250 Lindsay Way Glendora 91740

PLUSKAT, THOMAS J., real estate property manager; b. Aug. 17, 1951, Sheboygan, Wis.; s. Edwin C. and Virginia P.; m. Rosemary T., Apr. 8, 1978; children: David b. 1981, Suzanne b. 1984; edn: BS nuclear engring., Univ. Wis. Madison 1973; DBA, Pacific Western Univ. 1987; real estate cert. Fullerton Coll.; reg. profl. engr. Calif., lic. gen. contractor Calif., lic. real estate salesman Calif. Career: cons. Bechtel Corp., Norwalk 1973-79; prin., CEO Innovative Dynamics, Lakewood 1975–; mem: Tau Beta Pi, Phi Eta Sigma; author: Real Estate To a Better Future & Fin. Independence, 1986; Republican; rec: woodworking, hiking, bicycling. Ofc: Innovative Dynamics Co PO Box 4474 Lakewood 90711

PLUTCHAK, NOEL BERNARD, consulting company executive/scientist; b. Dec. 14, 1932, Green Bay, Wisc.; s. Bernard Edward and Violet Marie (Sherman) P.; m. Sandra Kolvig (div.); 1 child, Channin P. b. 1969; edn: BS geology, Univ. Wisc., 1960; MS meteorology, Fla. State Univ., 1964. Career: research asst.

Columbia Univ., Lamont Inst., 1963-65; hd. theortical studies Bendix - Marine Advisers, La Jolla 1965-69; research assoc. Univ. So. Calif., 1972-75; chief scientist Interstate Electronics Ocean Eng. Div., Anaheim 1975-83; chief scientist Raytheon Services Corp. Ocean Engring. Div., Ventura 1984-87; pres./c.e.o./chief scientist Active Leak Testing, Inc. San Pedro 1985–; mem: Am. Geophysical Union 1960–, Marine Technology Soc. 1968–, Am. Chem. Soc. 1990–, Am. Mgmt. Assn. 1972–, Exptl. Aircraft Assn. 1985–; patentee (2, 1960s); contbr. 40+ jour. articles, reports and papers; mil: sgt. USAF 1952-56; Republican; Prot.; rec: soaring, wind surfing. Res: 1120 W 27th St Los Angeles 90007

PLUTSCHOW, HERBERT EUGEN, cultural historian, educator, author; b. Sept. 8, 1939, Zurich, Switzerland; s. Eugen Franz and Martha (Geiger) P.; m. Yoshiko Kogure, Apr. 5, 1966; children: Patrick b. 1968, Nickolas b. 1971; edn: dipl. Univ. of Paris, Fr. 1962; MA, Waseda Univ., Tokyo 1966; PhD, Columbia Univ., 1973. Career: asst. prof. Univ. of Ill., Urbana, Ill. 1971-73; asst., assoc., prof. of Japanese literature and cultural history, UCLA, Los Angeles 1973-78, 78-86, 86–, dept. chair East Asian Studies, 1983–; mem. Internat. House of Japan 1988–; author: Historical Kyoto, 1986, Historical Nagasaki, 1988, Four Japanese Travel Diaries of the Middle Ages, 1986, Chaos and Cosmos, 1990, others. Ofc: UCLA, 405 Hilgard Ave Los Angeles 90024

POESCHL, THOMAS FRANCIS, JR., lawyer; b. Feb. 6, 1957, San Francisco; s. Thomas Francis and Maureen Genevieve (Flynn) P.; m. Laura Marion Willin, Dec. 22, 1985; children: Elizabeth b. 1987, Thomas III b. 1989, Kathryn b. 1991; edn: BA govt., St. Mary's Coll. 1978; JD, Univ. San Francisco 1983; admitted St. Bar Calif. 1986. Career: Calif. projects dir. U.S. Senator Alan Cranston, Wash. D.C. 1978-80; law clk. Anti-Defamation League of B'Nai B'Rith, San Francisco 1981-82; atty. Crosby Heafey Roach & May, Oakland 1983-85; partner/atty. Bjork, Lawrence, Poeschl & Kohn 1986–; ed. Univ. San Francisco Law Review 1982-83, secty. Student Bar Assn. 1981-82, rep. to Am. Bar Assn. 1981-82; extern U.S. Dist. Ct. Judge Robert P. Aguilar 1982; mem: Death Penalty Focus of Calif. (bd. mem. 1988), Adult Literacy (instr.1987); Democrat; Cath. Ofc: Bjork Lawrence Poeschl & Kohn 483 9th St Oakland 94607

POHL, JOHN HENNING, engineering consultant; b. May 29, 1944, Fort Riley, Kans.; s. Herbert Otto and Ellen Irene (Henning) P.; m. Judith Lynn Sykes, Aug. 10, 1968; children: J. Otto b. 1970, Clint b. 1975; edn: AA, Sacto. City Coll., 1964; BS, UC Berkeley, 1966; SM, M.I.T., 1973, ScD, 1976. Career: inspr. dam constrn. C.O. Henning Const. Engrs., Sacramento 1965; engr. E.I. du Pont Nemours, Wilmington, Dela. 1966-71; res. asst. M.I.T., Cambridge 1971-75, lectr. 1975-76; mem. tech. staff Sandia Nat. Labs., Livermore, Calif. 1976-81; dir. fossil fuels Energy & Environmental Res., Irvine 1981-86; dir. res. & devel. Energy Systems Assocs., Tustin 1986-89; sr. scientist energy W.T. Schafer Assocs., Irvine 1989-91; v.p. Advanced Combustion Technology, Ltd., Hsinchu, Taiwan 1993-94; prin. Energy Internat., Laguna Hills 1988–; v.p. technology Energeo, Inc., San Mateo 1994–; awards: technology achievement US EPA, Raleigh, N.C. 1987, best energy project Energy Com. Taiwan, R.O.C. 1989, 92; mem: Combustion Inst. (pgm. subcom. 1978–, exec. com. Western States sect. 1986-95), ASME (advisor corrosion and deposits combust. gasses 1989–), Am. Inst. Chem. Engrs. (combustion advisor 1988-91), Engring. Found. (steering com. ash deposition 1989–, research project subcom. 1994–); civic: Headstart, Cambridge, Mass. (treas. 1975-76); author 85+ tech. publs., 1972–, inventor (num. pats. 1987–). Res: 26632 Cortina Mission Viejo 92691 Ofc: Energy International 27075 Cabot Rd Ste 114 Laguna Hills 92653

POHLMAN, BARBARA LORI, physician; b. Feb. 10, 1955, Heron Lake, Minn.; d. Leo Roy and Rosella (Sievert) Pohlman; edn: BA, Gustavus Adolphus Coll. 1977; MD, Univ. Minn. 1981; MPH, 1986. Career: locum tenens Cigna Health Plans, Glendale 1986; cons., Orange Co. 1987; med. dir. Pacific Bell, Pasadena 1987-88; cons., Orange Co. 1988; med. review ofcr. and dir. occupational medicine So. Calif. Edison, Rosemead 1988-94; asst. clin. prof. of medicine UC Irvine 1994–; instr. UC Irvine Ext. 1988–; honors: Phi Kappa Phi, Gustavus Adolphus Coll. fellow 1977; mem: A.C.P., Am. Coll. Occupational & Environmental Medicine, Western Occupational & Environmental Med. Assn.; 1 article pub. in med. jour., 1986, 2 papers pub. on cadmium toxicity, 1985, and health effects of video display terminals, 1985; Democrat; Lutheran; rec: scuba diving, tennis, bicycling, golf. Res/Ofc: 23 Hancock St Laguna Niguel 92677

POINDEXTER, WILLIAM MERSEREAU, lawyer; b. June 16, 1925, Los Angeles; s. Robert Wade and Irene (Mersereau) P.; m. Cynthia Converse Pastushin, Nov. 10, 1979; children: James Wade b. 1952, David Graham b. 1954; edn: BA, Yale Univ., 1946; postgrad. Univ. Chicago, 1946-47; LLB, Boalt Hall UC Berkeley, 1949; admitted bar: Calif. 1952. Career: pres. Consolidated Brazing, Riverside 1949-52; atty. Bledsoe, Smith, et al, San Francisco 1952-54; Robertson & Poindexter, L.A. 1954; atty., ptnr. Poindexter & Doutre', Inc., Los Angeles 1964–; dir. Trio Metal Stampings, 1965-80; secty. Production Aids, Inc. 1969-78; secty. MOB, EPD Industries, 1969-72; mem: American Coll. Trust & Estate Counsel (Fellow), Calif. Bar Assn., L.A. Co. Bar Assn., Conf. of Insurance Counsel (pres. 1975); civic: San Marino School Board (1965-69, pres. 67), S.Pasadena-San Marino YMCA (1960-65, pres. 63); publs: Tax Notes, L.A. Bar Jour.; Calif. Cont. Edn. Practice Book Calif.: Non-Profit

Corporations; mil: USMCR 1943; Republican; Presbyterian; rec: fishing. Res: 1825 Braemar Rd Pasadena 91103 Ofc: Poindexter & Doutre', Inc. 624 S Grand Ave Ste 2420 Los Angeles 90017

POKRAS, SHEILA FRANCES GRABELLE, judge; b. Aug. 5, 1935, Newark, N.J.; m. Norman M. Pokras, oral surgeon, 1954; children: Allison b. 1959, Andrea b. 1961, Larry b. 1964; edn: BS in edn., Temple Univ., 1957; JD cum laude, Pepperdine Sch. of Law, 1969; admitted bar: Calif. 1970, US Dist. Cts. 1970, US Supreme Ct. 1975. Career: pub. sch. tchr. jr. and sr. high schs. Phila., Pa. and Newark, N.J. 1957-59; pvt. law practice, Long Beach 1970-80; first woman elected to Lakewood City Council, 1972; apptd. judge Long Beach Municipal Ct., 1978, elected presiding judge 1979, apptd. judge Los Angeles Superior Ct., 1980–, elected exec. bd. 1984, 85, supvg. judge Long Beach 1986; mem: ABA, Nat. Assn. Women Judges (dist. supr. 1986), Calif Bar Assn. Judges Div., Calif. Judges Assn. (sem. com. 1981-2), L.A. Bar Assn. Judges Div. (arbitration com.), Women Lawyers Assn. L.A. Judges Sect., Women Lawyers Assn. Long Beach (founding mem.), Long Beach Bar Assn. (bd. govs. 1957-70, CEB chair, state bar conv. del., fam. law sect. chair 1977-8, Judge of Year 1987); civic: Long Beach Legal Aid Found. (v.p. 1976-78), Soroptimist Internat. L.B. (comm. devel. chair 1979-86, woman of achiev. and Hall of Fame 1984), L.B. C.of C. (dir.), Junior League Advisor 1980, L.B. Alcoholism Council Bd. 1979-80, AAUW, League Women Voters L.B. (woman of yr. 1984 nom.), KLON Advisor, Boys Club (bd. 1981), L.B. Symphony Bd. 1985, Jewish Comm. Fedn. (bd. 1982), Beyond War (bd. advisors); honors: Pepperdine Alumnus of Yr. nom. 1974, B'nai B'rith ADL Torch of Liberty 1974, NOW L.B. woman of yr. 1984, NCCJ honoree 1986; rec: classical music, theater, jogging. Ofc: South Dist. Superior Court 415 W Ocean Blvd Long Beach 90802

POLK, MEREDITH JAY, JR., certified public accountant; b. June 5, 1938, Marked Tree, Alaska; s. Meredith Polk and Myra (Owens) Barnes; children: Kim Isaac b. 1960, Brigitte Isaac b. 1961, Michael J. Polk b. 1962, Corry Polk b. 1978; edn: AA, L.A. City Coll., 1971; BS, Woodbury Univ., 1975; MBA, tax, Golden Gate Univ., 1983; C.P.A. Calif. Career: various pos. IBM Corp. 1963-76, fin. analyst 1976-78, acct. 1978-81; CPA/prin. owner The Sir Meredith Agency, 1969--, cons. to small bus.; honors: Western Ins. Service speaker awards (5), recipient IBM awards for extraordinary effort, service, suggestions (3), listed Who's Who In Am. Univs. and Colls.; mem: Nat. Soc. Pub. Accts., We. Ins. Speakers Bur., Am. Inst. CPAs, Town Hall of Calif.; mil: cpl. USMC 1956-59; R.Cath.; rec: photog., bowling, sports. Res: 724 S Flower St Inglewood 90301 Ofc: The Sir Meredith Agency 5757 W Century Blvd Ste 430 Los Angeles 90045

POLLACK, ALAN MYRON, physician; b. Feb. 16, 1958, N.Y.C.; s. Samuel and Jean Anna (Friedman) P.; edn: BS in biochemistry, UCLA, 1979; MD, Univ. Texas, Southwestern Med. Ctr., Dallas 1983. Career: resident physician Cedars-Sinai Med. Ctr., L.A. 1983-86; staff physician Kaiser Permanente, Panorama City 1986–; honors: Phi Beta Kappa 1979, Alpha Omega Alpha 1982; civic: Lincoln County (N.M.) Heritage Trust; Jewish; rec: collect rare books & documents from Old West, guitar. Ofc: Kaiser Permanente 13652 Cantara St, NS3, Module 4, Panorama City 91402

POLLAK, MARTHA, dentist, educator; b. April 4, 1939, Mercedes, Uruguay; m. Erich W. Pollak, May 5, 1960; children: Adriana E., Elizabeth S.; edn: BA, UC Davvis 1976; DDS, Univ. Mo. 1982. Career: asst. prof. Univ. Mo.Sch. Dentistry, Kansas City, Mo. 1982-83; lectr. oral radiology UCLA Sch. Dentistry 1983; bd. dirs. Truman Med. Center, Kansas City, Mo. 1981; honors: Alpha Omega; rec: tchg. piano. Ofc: 1038 S Glendora Ave Ste 2 West Covina 91790

POLLAK, NORMAN L., certified public accountant; b. Aug. 16, 1931, Chgo.; s. Emery and Helen (Solomon) P.; m. Barbara Zeff, Aug. 21, 1955 (div. 1980); m. Jean Lambert, Sept. 21, 1986 (div. 1991); children: Martin Joel, Elise Susan McNeal, Rhonda Louise; edn: Valedictorian, Hyde Park H.S., Chgo., 1949; BS (Delta Mu Delta), Sch. of Commerce, Northwestern Univ., 1955; C.P.A., R.E. lic., Calif. Career: sr. acct. two C.P.A. firms, 1951-58; public acctg. practice 1958-86, semi-ret.; C.P.A./ fin. and mgmt. cons., pres. Norman L. Pollak Acctncy. Corp., Westlake Village; expert witness on dissolution matters; frequent lectr. profl. orgns.; dir. AmeriVox (div. World Telecom Group); mem: Am. Inst. CPAs, Calif. Soc. CPAs (S.F.V. Tech. Discussions Group chmn. 1960-61), Nat. Assn. Accts., Am. Acctg. Assn., Valley Estate Planning Council (charter, pres. 1964-65), Northwestern Univ. Alumni Club, Westlake Village C.of C., Optimist Club (chmn. Comm. Contest for Hearing Impaired), Conejo Future Found., Oak Forest HOA; past mem. Ventura Co. Estate Planning Council (pres. 1975-78, 78-79), Conejo C.of C., Internat. Assn. Fin. Planners, coach Braille Olympics for Blind, chmn. Emergency Com. for Disaster Preparedness Oak Forest Mobile Estates Assn., dir. Honokowai Palms Homeowners Assn., Kailua -Kona, HI; Guardians of L.A., Westlake Cultural Found. (trustee), Sponsor Code 3 for Homeless Children 1993; publs: article in Conejo Mag. (Nov-Dec 82), biog. listings Who's Who in West, Who's Who in World, Who's Who in Fin. & Ind., Community Leaders of Am., Men of Achiev., Two Thousand Men of Achiev., Dict. of Internat. Biography; Address: 143 Sherwood Dr Westlake Village 91361

POLLARD, HENRY, lawyer; b. Jan. 10, 1931, New York; s. Charles and Sarah P.; m. Adele Ruth Brodie, June 16, 1954; children: Paul Adam b. 1959, Lydia Sara b. 1964; edn: BA, N.Y. City Coll. 1953; JD, Columbia Law Sch. 1954. Career: assoc. atty. Sullivan & Cromwell, N.Y.C. 1956-61; Kaplan Livingston Goodwin & Berkowitz, Beverly Hills 1961-63, ptnr. 1963-81; Pollard Bauman Slome & McIntosh 1981-87; Seyfarth Shaw Fairweather & Geraldson, Los Angeles 1987-95; of counsel Oberstein, Doniger, Fetter, Kibre & Horwitz 1995–; faculty UCLA Ext. Paralegal Program 1980–; judge pro tem Los Angeles Co. Municipal Ct. 1989–; arbitrator/mediator, Am. Arbitration Assn. (Large Complex Case Prog.); honors: ed. Columbia Law Review 1953-54; mem: Am. Bar Assn., L.A. Co. Bar Assn., Calif. Bar Assn., Beverly Hills Bar Assn.; mil: AUS 1954-56. Res: 29704 Zuma Bay Way Malibu 90265 Ofc: 1999 Avenue of the Stars Los Angeles 90067

POLLOCK, RICHARD EDWIN, real estate investor, retired county official; b. Aug. 27, 1928, Phila.; s. Ernest Edwin and Evelyn Marie (Scarlett) P.; m. Yvonne May Graves, Oct. 11, 1952 (div. Aug. 1989); children: Colleen May, Karen Marie, Richard Irvin, Annette Yvonne, Mary Ann; edn: Armstrong Coll., 1947; UC Berkeley, 1949-51, 55; BA (Recreation), San Jose State Univ., 1961; postgrad. San Fernando Valley State Univ., 1969-70, UC Davis, 1963-77, UCLA, 1964, UC Santa Barbara, 1970, Univ. Redlands, 1979; Calif. Comm. Colls. instr. cred., Calif. Std. tchg. creds. elem., sec.; reg. recreator and park mgr.; lic. comml. aircraft pilot 1974–. Career: swim pool mgr./instr. Berkeley Tennis Club, 1955-56; police ofcr. City of Berkeley, 1956; recreation and aquatic supr. Pleasant Hills Rec. & Park Dist., 1956-62; gen. mgr. Pleasant Valley Rec. & Park Dist., Camarillo 1962-68; bldg. insp. Ventura Co. 1969-71; adminstr. Sacramento Co.-Carmichael Rec. & Park Dist., 1971-73; dir. parks and recreation Imperial Co. 1973-81, ret.; faculty Imperial Valley Jr. Coll. 1974–; aquatic cons., 1957–; real estate investor, 1984–; magician, 1944–; hypnotherapist, 1988–; chmn. S.F. Bay Area Conf. for Cooperation in Aquatics, 1958-59; honors: Am. Red Cross recognition for 50 years volunteer svs. (1989); civic: Boy Scouts Am. Desert Trails Council (advr., scoutmaster), Am. Red Cross (bd., instr.), work with devel. disabled and handicapped children and adults; mem: Calif. Nat. Rec. and Park Assn., AAHPER, Calif. Park and Rec. Soc., Calif. Co. Dirs. Parks and Rec. Assn., Calif. Boating Safety Officers Assn., Aircraft Owners and Pilots Assn., Nat. Assn. Emergency Med. Technicians; publs: Bibliography: A Pool of Aquatic Sources, 1960; mil: lt. US Army, Korea 1951-55; Democrat. Address: PO Box 3011 El Centro 92244

POLON, LINDA BETH, educator, writer, illustrator; b. Oct. 7, 1943, Baltimore; d. Harold Bernard and Edith Judith Wolff; m. Marty I. Polon, Dec. 18, 1966 (div. 1983); edn: BA in hist., UCLA, 1966. Career: elem. tchr. Los Angeles Unified Sch. Dist., 1967–; writer-illustrator Scott Foresman Pub. Co., Glenview, Ill. 1979, Frank Schaffer Pub. Co., Torrance 1981-82, Learning Works, Santa Barbara 1981-82; editorial reviewer Prentice Hall Pub. Co., Santa Moncia 1982-83; mem. Soc. of Childrens Book Writers; author juvenile books: Creative Teaching Games, 1974, Teaching Games for Fun, 1976, Making Kids Click, 1979, Write up a Storm, 1979, Stir Up a Story, 1981, Paragraph Production, 1981, Using Words Correctly (3rd-4th grades, 1981, and 5th-6th grades, 1981), Whole Earth Holiday Book, 1983, Writing Whirlwind, 1986, Magic Story Starters, 1987, Kid's Choice Libraries Grades 3-4, 1991, Kid's Choice Libraries K-2, 1991; Democrat; Res: 11640 Kiowa Ave #205 Los Angeles 90049-6244 Ofc: Los Angeles Board of Education 980 S Hobart Blvd Los Angeles 90006

POMBO, RICHARD W., congressman, farmer, rancher; b. 1961, Tracy, Calif.; m. Annette, 1983; children: Richard Jr., Rena; edn: student, Univ. Calif., Pomona 1981-83. Career: councilman City of Tracy, 1991-92; mayor pro-tem Tracy City Council, 1992; mem. 103rd-104th Congresses from 11th Calif. dist., 1993–; co-founder, v.p. San Joaquin County Citizen's Land Alliance, Calif. 1986–; active San Joaquin County Econ. Devel. Assn., Tracy Bus. Improvement Dist., City Council (vice chmn. Community Devel. Agy., Community Parks Com. and Waste Mgmt. Com.), San Joaquin County Rep. Central Com.; mem. Rotary Club; Roman Catholic. Ofc: US House of Reps Washington DC 20515*

POONAWALA, ISMAIL KURBANHUSEIN, educator, author; b. Jan. 7, 1937, Godhra, Gujarat, India, naturalized U.S. 1981; s. Kurbanhusein Fidahusein and Sakina (Sakina) P.; m. Oumayma H. Ali-Ahmad, Jan. 6, 1981; children: Qays b. 1989. edn: MA, Bombay Univ., 1959; MA, Cairo Univ., 1964; PhD, UCLA, 1968. Career: asst. prof. McGill Univ., Montreal, Can. 1968-71; research assoc. Harvard Univ., 1971-74; prof. of Arabic, UCLA, 1974–; author: Al-Sultan al-Khattab, 1967, Al-Urjuza al-Mukhtara, 1971, Bibliography of Ismaili Literature, 1977, History of al-Tabari, vol. ix, 1990; Muslim. Res: 28749 Covecrest Dr Rancho Palos Verdes 90275 Ofc: Dept. Near Eastern Languages and Cultures UCLA, 405 Hilgard Ave Los Angeles 90024

POPKOFF, BURTON R., lawyer; b. Nov. 14, 1942, Chicago, Ill.; s. Paul and Lillian P.; m. Janet S. Sires, Oct. 28, 1962; children: Lisa b. 1963, Hillary b. 1966; edn: BS, UCLA 1963; JD cum laude, Southwestern Univ. 1970; C.P.A. Calif. 1965; admitted Bar: Calif. 1971, U.S. Supreme Ct. 1988. Career: C.P.A. Miller & Co., Los Angeles 1963-65; controller Markab Mgmt. Assn., Beverly

Hills 1965-69; ptnr. Miller Handzel & Co., Encino 1969-71; atty. sole practice, Los Angeles 1971-86; sr. ptnr., atty. Popkoff & Stern 1986–; prof. of law Golden West Univ., Los Angeles 1979-81; referee hearing dept. St. Bar Ct. 1981-89; dir. Miller Fluid Heads USA 1986–, Urethane Service Inc., Torrance 1974–, Tele-Talent Inc., Hollywood 1981–; awards: Southwestern Univ. Am. Jurisprudence 1966-69; mem: Childrens World (life), Am. Assn. Atty-C.P.A., Calif. Soc. Atty.-C.P.A., L.A. Co. Bar Assn., Am. Bar Assn., So. Calif. Council of Elder Attys. (charter mem., dir. 1992–), Wilshire Bar Assn., Desert Bar Assn., No. Hills Jaycees (secty. 1976-78), Police Aux. League (dir. 1981-82), Buhai Ctr. for Family Law (dir. 1992–). Ofc: Popkoff & Stern 501 Shatto Place Ste 100 Los Angeles 90020 and 225 So. Civic Dr. Ste 212 Palm Springs 92262

POPOFSKY, MELVIN LAURENCE, lawyer; b. Feb. 16, 1936, Oskaloosa, Iowa; s. Samuel and Fannye Charlotte (Rosenthal) P.; m. Linda Jane Seltzer, Nov. 25, 1962; children: Mark b. 1967, Kaye b. 1970; edn: BA hist., Univ. Iowa 1958; BA jurispurdence, Oxford Univ. England 1960; LL.B, Harvard Law Sch. 1962. Career: assoc. atty. Heller Ehrman White & McAuliffe, S.F. 1962-69, ptnr. 1969–, exec. com. 1980–, pres. 1984-87, co-chair 1988–; honors: Phi Beta Kappa, Rhodes scholar 1958; mem: S.F. Bar Assn., Calif. St. Bar Assn., Bureau of Nat. Affairs, Am. Bar Assn., Am. Coll. Trial Lawyers (fellow), Am. Bar Found. (fellow), Mt. Zion Hosp. (dir. 1982-88); Democrat; Jewish. Ofc: Heller Ehrman White & McAuliffe 333 Bush St San Francisco 94104

PORTER, EDWIN CLOYD, retired military officer; b. Oct. 8, 1917, Logansport, Ind.; s. Cloyd and Lena Mae (Hinkle) P.; m. Dorothy Ross, Dec. 28, 1940; children: Frederick b. 1941, Timothy b. 1943, Edwin, Jr. b. 1953, Susan b. 1954, Kathleen b. 1959, Deborah b. 1960; edn: diploma, Loganport H.S., 1935; BS, Univ. Minn., 1941; MS, DePaul Univ., 1960; USAF Command Staff Coll., 1967, USAF Air Univ., Montgomery, Ala. 1968, Air War Coll., 1969. Career: served to Col. (Ret.) US Air Force 1942-78; organized and activated 1st Nat. Guard Unit in Logansport, Ind., 38th Inf. Div., Hq. Bn. 293rd Inf. Regt. 1948; dir. USAF Reserve, State of Ill., 1970-79; field rep. Social Security Adminstrn., Kokomo, Ind. 1945-56, dist. mgr., Muncie, Ind. 1952-66, East St. Louis, Ill. 1966-67, Chgo., Ill. 1967-79; substitute coach, Muncie, 1956-66, Downers Grove, 1964-78; honors: mem. Logansport, Ind. High Sch. State Basketball Champions 1934, Univ. Minnesota Nat. Champion Football Team 1940, 1941; mem: Nat. Assn. Ret. Fed. (chapter pres. 1982-86), Reserve Ofcrs. Assn. (life mem.), The Retired Ofcrs. Assn. (chpt. pres. 1991-92, life mem.), Nat. Assn. for Uniformed Services (life mem., chapter pres. 1993, 94, 95); civic: Masons, Rotary, Scottish Rite, Shrine, Elks, Kiwanis, 40/8, Am. Legion; mil. decorations: Unit Citation, Explosive Ordnance Disposal Comdr. Combat Inf. badge, commendation E.O.D. Unit, Army commendation AF commendation US Def. medal, Asiatic Theater, ETO, Am. Theater, Victory medal, Reserve medal Army and AF, Good Conduct w/3 clusters, AF Good Conduct w/2 clusters; Presbyterian; rec: swimming, sports. Res: 20397 Eyota Ln Apple Valley 92308

POSS-HATCHL, NANCY LUCILE VAN DYKE, private investigator; b. Nov. 20, 1934, Los Angeles; d. Douglas and Bernadette Ann (Le Sage) Van Dyke; m. Sidney Hatchl, Aug. 15, 1988; children (nee Poss): Charles b. 1956, Wendy (Milette) b. 1958, Douglas b. 1959; edn: BA, Mt. St. Mary's Coll., L.A. 1956; MA, CSU Long Beach 1971; Lic. Investigator, Calif. 1979. Career: founder/CEO Helios Investigations, Inc. Santa Ana 1979–; pres. Council of Internat. Investigators; mem: Calif. Assn. of Licensed Investigators, Inst. of Profl. Investigators (British), recipient International Investigator of 1993 award, New Delhi, India; Democrat; rec: sailing, tennis, travel. Res: Santa Ana Ofc: Helios Investigations, Inc. PO Box 11783 Santa Ana 92711

POSSNACK, JUDITH ANNE, psychotherapist; b. Aug. 26, 1939, Albion, Nebr.; d. Bruce Arnold and Helen Lavonne Kunkel; m. David Possnack, Aug. 16, 1987; children by prev. marriage (nee Vanderpool): Jeffrey Scott b. 1958, Douglas Brent b. 1960, Kimberly Joy Adair b. 1961; 9 grandchildren; edn: AA, Cypress Comm. Coll., 1979; BA in bus. mgmt., Univ. Redlands, 1986; MA marriage, family therapy, Azusa Pacific Univ., 1988; Calif. lic. Marriage Family Therapist 1988. Career: dep., sgt. L.A. County Sheriff's Dept., 1963-80; internal investigator Safeway Markets, 1981-84; ins. fraud investigator Insurance Crime Prevention Inst., 1984-86; instr. Long Beach City Coll., 1986-88; marriage, family, individual therapist in pvt. pract. 1988–; instr. Leadership Training Inst., Crystal Cathedral; profl. speaker var. coll., community and church groups on: Communicating & Relating, Self-Esteem, Healing of Memories, Self Defense for Women, others; awards: numerous media appearances radio, TV, and print, honors relating to law enforcement 1967-79, Speakers awards various civic and comm. groups, L.A. Co. Bar Assn., Youth Forum 1971; mem: Am. Assn. for Counseling & Devel., Assn. for Psychological Type (bd. 1986–), Assistance League for Bus. & Profl. Women, Executive Women's Club, Alumni Assn. Univ. Redlands, Rep. Women's Club; Republican; Crystal Cathedral Garden Grove; rec: travel, camping, weekends in Baja, Calif., volunteer work. Res: 6022 Marilyn Dr Cypress 90630 Ofc: 3532 Katella Ste 210 Los Alamitos 90720 Tel 714/ 952-7883

POTTER, ROBERT L. ANDREW, education administration; b. May 24, 1932, San Jose; s. Andrew Willis and May Verser P.; m. Peggy Ann Joseph, July 29, 1977; children: Kevin David, Brian Lawrence, Kathryn May-Marie,

Kirk Robert; edn: AA in bus. admin., Hartnell Coll., 1958; BS in organizational behavior, Univ. San Francisco, 1961, MBA, Stanislaus State Coll. 1990, PhD Edn., 1993. Career: served to capt. US Marine Corps 1950-55, Korea, Bronze Star, Purple Heart; asst. controller Honolulu Oil Corp., San Francisco 1959-60; pres. R. Potter Consulting, Merced; mgmt. cons. Allstate Ins., cons. Mercy Hosp., Merced; cons., campaign mgr. Am. Cancer Soc., Merced, Mariposa County; campaign mgr. Calif. State Assembly Seat, Merced, Stanislaus County; Allocations, Merced United Way; American Heart Assn.; mem. Merced C.of C. (amb.), Yosemite Corvett Club (treas.), Elks, Merced Sunrise Rotary (dir.), Graduate Leadership Merced; Republican; R.Cath. Res: 2862 St Thomas Ct Merced 95348

POUTEAU, JEAN L.M., psychiatrist; b. Mar. 26, 1922, Calgary, Alberta, Canada (nat. 1949); s. Constant Lucien and Corinne Josephine (Nadeau) P.; m. Lisa Lynn Larsen, Dec. 24, 1950 (div. 1974); children: Renée b. 1952, Anne-Marie b. 1954, Guy b. 1956, Jean-Christopher b. 1958; m. Vivianne Froschel, Apr. 14, 1990; edn: BA, chem., Reed Coll., Portland, Ore. 1947; MD, Univ. of Oregon Med. Sch. 1949; lic. physician and surgeon, St. of Calif. 1950; bd. cert. in psychiatry/neurology 1958; cert. in addiction medicine 1987. Career: internship So. Pacific RR Hosp. 1949-50, residency in medicine 1950-51; residency in psychiatry Langley-Porter Inst. 1953-58; psychiatrist, acting asst. supt. Sonoma St. Hosp. 1958-60; pvt. practice, Marin Co., Calif. 1960–; staff psychiatrist Alameda Co. Health Dept., Oakland 1960-63; acting prog. chief Alameda Co. Mental Health Svs., Oakland 1963-64; clin. instr. psychiatry Univ. of Calif. San Francisco 1961-63; on-call psychiatrist CMHS Marin Co. 1968-70; cons. Marin Co. Criminal Justice Sys. 1974-77; psychiatric cons. Canyon Manor 1978-79; mem: Am. Psychiatric Assn. (life) 1953–, Calif. Psychiatric Assn. 1965–, Am. Soc. of Addiction Medicine 1986–, Marin Psychiatric Soc. (sec., treas., founding mem., v.p., pres. 1963-65); mil: capt. AUS 1951-53; Democrat; rec: languages (French, Italian), woodworking. Res: 84 Bahama Reef Novato 94949 Ofc: 711 D Street Annex San Rafael 94901

POWELL, HENRY C., pathologist, educator; b. Sept. 1, 1946, Dublin, Ireland; nat. 1986; s. Anthony Gerard and Mary Celine (Delany) P.; m. Geraldine Tierney, July 29, 1970; m.2d. Mary Johnson, Sept. 24, 1981; edn: MB, B.Ch., BAO, MD, Nat. Univ. Ireland 1970; Dsc, Nat. Univ. Ireland 1994. Career: intern Phila. Gen., Pa. 1970-71; resident UCSD 1971-75; fellow Mass. Gen. Hosp., Boston 1975-76; asst. prof. UCSD 1976-81, assoc. prof. 1981-88, prof., head div. of neuropathology 1986–, head div. of anatomical and neuropathology 1993–; Fellow Royal Coll. of Pathologists 1995; mem: Royal Coll. Pathologists U.K., Am. Assn. Neuropathologists, Am. Assn. Pathologists; Democrat; rec: music. Res: 940 Runnymead Ln San Diego 92106 Ofc: Univ. of Calif. San Diego Dept. of Pathology M-012 La Jolla 92093

POWELL, PATRICK EDWARD, anesthesiologist; b. Sept. 10, 1944, New Orleans, La.; s. Edward Walter and Estelle Rita (Grady) P.; edn: BS, Louisiana State Univ., Baton Rouge 1967; MD, Louisiana State Univ. Sch. of Medicine, New Orleans 1970. Career: general medicine U.S. Navy, Phila., Pa. 1970-71; anesthesiologist U.S. Navy, Rota, Spain 1971-74; anesthesiologist, pvt. practice, Hayward, Calif. 1974-89; anesthesiologist Kaiser Permanente, Oakland 1989–; mil: comdr. U.S. Navy 1970-78. Res/Ofc: 1117 Morton St Alameda 94501

POWELL, RODNEY LEROY, scientist; b. Oct. 20, 1927, Moline, Ill.; s. LeRoy and Ella Katherine (Rasmussen) P.; m. Donna, Feb. 2, 1951; m. 2d. Katherine, Nov. 5, 1985; children: Glenn b. 1955, Sherrie b. 1957, Karrie b. 1959, Kathleen b. 1962, Eric b. 1969; edn: AA, Univ. Ill., Urbana 1949; BSME, Ill. Inst. Tech., 1951; MSME, USC, 1955; PhD, 1962; reg. profl. engr. Calif. Career: staff engr. Rockwell Internat., Downey 1951-60; section head Hughes Aircraft, Fullerton 1960-65; sr. staff engr. Rockwell Internat., Seal Beach 1965-87; cons., senior staff scientist Infotec Development Inc., Costa Mesa 1987–; instr. USC, 1955-62; cons. Infotec Devel. Inc., Costa Mesa; honors: Pi Tau Sigma (1951); mem. Am. Inst. Aero. and Astro., Air Force Assn., FAA; 2 patents (1943, 56); mil: pfc AUS 1946-47; Republican; rec: computer, home workshop, flying. Res: 9861 Foxrun Rd Santa Ana 92705 Ofc: Infotec Development, Inc. 3505-M Cadillac Costa Mesa 92626

POWERS, DIANE ELIZABETH, artist, designer, owner international shops and restaurants complex; b. Los Angeles; d. Jack and Virginia Gruss; edn: BA fine arts (honors), San Diego State Univ., 1964. Career: interior designer, owner/opr. Design Center Inc. (int. design bus. and showroom), San Diego 1968–; owner/opr. Bazaar del Mundo (16 retail internat. shops, 4 restaurants), S.D. 1971–; instr. craft and clothing classes at Bazaar del Mundo; guest lectr. on int. design and color San Diego St. Univ., UCSD, Cal Western Univ., Grossmont Union H.S., other schs. and ladies clubs; collect and exhibit crafts of China, India, Morocco, Mexico, Guatamala, and Peru; exhibits of personal art works as well as internat. collection: Fine Arts Gal. S.D., Southwestern Coll., Cal Western Internat. Univ., SDSU Gal., Spanish Village Gal., Mingei Internat. Mus. World Folk Art; awards: Disting. Alumna Coll. of Profl. Studies & Fine Arts SDSU 1982, orchid award A.I.A. for creation of one of most beautiful San Diego environments - Bazaar del Mundo 1979, outstanding San Diegan Pacific Tel. Co. 1983, San Diego Woman of Achiev. L.W.V. 1988, Entrepreneur of Yr.

Calif. Tourism Council 1994; civic: Festival of the Arts (past pres.), S.D. Conv. & Vis. Bur., S.D./ Calif./ Nat. Restaurant Assn., San Diego C.of C., S.D. Old Town C.of C., SDSU Art Council Advy. Bd., S.D. Parking & Plng. Commn., Design Counsel SDSU, Nat. Wildlife Fedn., Mingei Internat. Mus. of World Folk Art, Crafts & Folk Art Mus., S.D. Mus. of Art, Am. Crafts Council, SDSU Alumni & Assoc. Univ. Club, S.D. Hist. Soc., Old Town Task Force, Pub. Arts Advy. Council; rec: fashion and craft design, collect folk art and fine crafts, travel, landscaping, equestrian. Ofc: 2754 Calhoun St 92110

POYNTER, DANIEL FRANK, parachuting expert, author-publisher; b. Sept. 17, 1938, NY, NY; s. William Frank and Josephine (Thompson) P.; edn: BA in soc. sci., CSU Chico, 1960, 4th-yr. study tour 15 European countries; postgrad. S.F. Law Sch., 2 yrs.; numerous spl. courses incl. disaster and rescue, survival, aviation litigation; Fed. lic. master parachute rigger with all ratings: back, seat and chest; lic. pilot: single engine land and gliders; expt. parachutist (D-454), parachuting Instr./Examiner; hang gliding Flt. Examiner; FCC radiotel. opr.; listed as expert witness Nat. Forensic Ctr., Tech. Advy. Svc. for Attys., Defense Research Inst., Expert Resources Inc., others. Author numerous books incl: The Parachute Manual; Parachuting, The Skydivers' Handbook; Parachute Rigging Course; Parachuting Instructor/Examiner Course; Parachuting Manual with Log; Hang Gliding; Manned Kiting; The Self-Publishing Manual, How To Write, Print & Sell Your Own Book; various books pub. in Spanish, German, Russian, Japanese languages; numerous monographs, 400+ tech. and popular articles and num. photographs pub. in Parachutist (mo. column 1963), Skydiver, Skydiving, Soaring, Can Para, Frisbee World, Free Fall Kiwi (N.Z.), Hang Glider Weekly, Publishers Weekly, others; author chapters in books: The Ency. Americana, The Whole Earth Cat., The Next Whole Earth Cat., United We Fall, Skiers Digest, Sportsource, Explorers Unlimited Source Book, Hang Gliding, others; mem: U.S. Parachute Assn. (1962, exec. com. mem., chmn., sec. 12 yrs.; Nat. Para. Championships equip. insp. 10 yrs., participant, competition jury mem., jury pres., tng. judge; team observer, del. chief in Bulgaria 1966, Ger. 1975, Australia 1977; sport parachuting witness state and fed. hearings; del. to Nat. Sport Aviation Council), Parachute Indus. Assn. (pres. 1985, 86, founder/past ed. Para-News briefs), Am. Inst. Aero. & Astro. (sr., tech. coms., session chmn. Houston 1979), Soc. Automotive Engrs. (past com. chmn.), Nat. Aero. Assn., Aviation/Space Writers Assn., Calistoga Skydivers, No. Calif. Parachute Council, NE Sport Parachute Council (past pres., past ed. Spotter Newsmag. 10 yrs.), Exptl. Aircraft Assn., Survival and Flt. Equip. Assn., Brit. Assn. Parascending Clubs, Soaring Soc. Am., U.S. Hang Gliding Assn. (life, chief del. to World Hang Gliding Championships in Austria 1976), Commn. Internat. de Vol Libre of Fedn. Aero. Internat. in Paris (U.S. del., past pres., life hon. pres.), Internat. Frisbee Assn., U.S. Flying Tube Assn. (charter), Internat. Assn. of Indep. Publishers (chapt. pres. 1979, 82), Assn. of Am. Publishers, Publishers Mktg. Assn. (dir., v.p.), Mus. of Parachuting and Air Safety (past dir.), Computer Writers' Assn., Book Publicists So. Calif., Am. Booksellers Assn.; invention: parachute pack, Pop Top Container (U.S. pat., 1975). Res: Rt #1 Goleta 93117-9701 OFc: Para Publishing PO Box 8206 Santa Barbara 93118-8206

PRADA, ALFREDO, computer systems consultant; b. July 20, 1933, Bogota, Colombia, nat. 1985; s. Alfredo and Mercedes (Pulido) P.; m. Maria Elena Pulido, June 30, 1973; children: Constanza, b. 1961, Claudia, b. 1961, Alfredo M., b. 1963, Estella, b. 1966; edn: BSEE, Univ. of Tex. 1958; BSIE, Univ. of Mich. 1961; lic. Indsl. Engr. 1964, Elec. Engr. 1964, Colombia. Career: systems analyst and pgmr. Exxon, Colombia 1959-62; univ. program coordinator, IBM, Colombia 1962-64; systems and pgmg. mgr. Ecopetrol, Colombia 1962-68; systems gen. mgr. Colgate Palmolive, Central Am. 1968-71; ops. res. dept. head Ecopetrol, Colombia 1971-75; ops. res. staff splst. A.G. McKee, Cleveland, Oh. 1975-78; systems cons. Computer Scis. Corp., El Segundo 1978-82; prin./pres. Omni Systems Consultants, Lomita 1982–; coll. lectr. sev. univs. in Bogota, Col. 1961-74; awards: Good Neighbour Scholar, Univ. of Tex. 1956-58, Orgn. of Am. States (OAS) Scholar, Univ. of Mich. 1960-1; past mem. AIEE, ACM; publs: profl. conf. proceedings 1967, 69, 72; series of articles in Software News, 5/11/83; rec: x-country, swimming. Address: Omni Systems Consultants, 1981 Mt. Shasta Dr. San Pedro 90732

PRAG, ARTHUR BARRY, physicist; b. Apr. 14, 1938, Portland, Oregon; s. Arthur Edwin and Margaret (Twombly) P.; m. Mary Ann Tomaschko, Aug. 14, 1986; 1 son, Patrick b. 1961; edn: BS physics (maxima cum laude), Univ. Portland, 1959; MS physics, Univ. Wash., Seattle 1962, PhD, 1964. Career: mem. tech. staff The Aerospace Corp., L.A. 1964-69, staff scientist 1969-75, res. scientist 1975–; awards: Sigma Xi 1960–, NSF co-op fellowshop 1960-61; mem: Am. Physical Soc. 1961–, Am. Geophysical Union 1965–, AAAS 1965–, NY Acad. Scis. 1978–; publs: sci. res. papers in profl. jours. 1961–; R.Cath.; rec: computer pgmg. Res: 17357 Hartland St Van Nuys 91406-4416 Ofc: The Aerospace Corp. PO Box 92957 MS M2/260 Los Angeles 90009-2957

PRAY, RALPH MARBLE, III, lawyer; b. June 7, 1938, San Diego; s. Ralph Marble and Doris (Thomson) P.; m. Karen L., June 13, 1964; m. Sandra Anne Shaw, June 7, 1988; children: Matthew Thomson b. 1969, Kristen Leigh b. 1970; edn: BS, Univ. Redlands 1960; JD, UC Hastings Coll. of Law 1967; admitted St. Bar Calif. 1967. Career: atty., assoc. Gray Cary Ames & Frye, San Diego 1967-

73, ptnr. 1973–, mbr., firm mgmt. com. 1975-80, chmn. commercial law dept. 1985-89; arbiter Am. Arbitration Assn. S.D. 1980, Superior Ct. San Diego 1984; honors: Thurston Soc., Order of Coif; mem: Am. Bar Assn., San Diego Co. Bar Assn., Sons of Am. Revolution, S.D. Zoological Soc., sponsor Ducks Unlimited 1974, NRA, Coronado Rotary Club; mil: lt. USNR 1960-64; Republican; Episcopalian; rec: hunting, fishing, photog. Res: 535 C Ave Coronado 92118 Ofc: Gray Cary Ware & Friedenrich 401 B St Ste 1700 San Diego 92101-4297

PREMO, EUGENE MILTON, appellate court justice; b. Aug. 28, 1936, San Jose; s. Milton A. and Mary Teresa (Fatjo) P.; m. Georgine Drees, Jan. 24, 1959; children: Nicole, b. 1961, Michelle, b. 1965, Patrick, b. 1967, Richard, b. 1968; edn: BS, Santa Clara Univ. 1957, JD, 1962. Career: research atty. Court of Appeal, San Francisco 1962; practicing atty. Santa Clara Co. 1963-69; apptd. judge Municipal Ct, Santa Clara Judicial Dist. 1969-75, judge Superior Ct. 1975-88; associate justice Ct. of Appeal, Sixth Dist., 1988–; lectr. Santa Clara Univ. Sch. of Law; lectr. Rutter Group mem: Alpha Sigma Nu, Calif. Judges Assn. (v.p. 1984-85); civic: West Valley Kiwanis, Bronco Bench, Santa Clara Univ. Athletic Bd., Salvation Army Advy. Bd., Sisters of Notre Dame De Namur Advy. Bd.; mil: 1st lt US Army C.I.C.; Republican; R.Cath.; rec: golf, travel, photography. Res: 19161 Portos Dr Saratoga 95070

PREONAS, GEORGE ELIAS, lawyer; b. Oct. 5, 1943, Dayton, Ohio; s. Louis D. and Mary (Drakos) P.; m. Aileen Strike, May 27, 1968; children: Annemarie b. 1972, Michael b. 1974, Stephen b. 1976; edn: BA, Stanford Univ. 1965; JD, Univ. Mich. 1968. Career: ptnr. Seyfarth Shaw Fairweather & Geraldson, L.A. 1968–; mem: L.A. Co. Bar Assn., Am. Bar Assn., Calif. Bar Assn. Address: 2029 Century Park E Ste 3300 Los Angeles 90067

PRESCOTT, LAWRENCE MALCOLM, writer, health consultant; b. July 31, 1934, Boston, Mass.; s. Benjamin and Lilyan (Stein) P.; m. Ellen Kober, Feb. 19 (dec. 9/15/81); m. 2d Sharon Kirshen, May 16, 1982; children: Jennifer b. 1967, Gary Kirshen b. 1969, Adam b. 1970, Marc Kirshen b. 1973; edn: BA, Harvard Coll. 1957; MS, Geo. Wash. Univ. 1959, PhD, 1966; postdoctoral fellow Nat. Acad. of Scis. 1965-66. Career: microbiol./sci. World Health Orgn., Calcutta, India 1967-70, team leader health lab. svcs., Djarkarta, Indonesia 1970-72, project mgr., Bangkok, Thailand 1973-78, pub. health cons. 1978-81; publisher/ed. Teenage Scene, San Diego 1982-83; freelance med. writer, prin. Prescott Assocs.; awards: medal of merit 1st class Ministry of Pub. Health Govt. of Thailand 1978; mem: Am. Soc. for Microbiol., Soc. of Sigma XI, AAAS, Am. Med. Writers Assn., Nat. Assn. of Sci. Writers; author 40 profl. papers, manuals, pamphlets, and books in fields of microbiology and public health; 3000+ articles on med. and health in profl. jours., 1982–; numerous non-sci. publs. incl. stories, poems, articles, 1977-81; Curry Every Sunday, an Asian Cookbook, 1984; rec: travel, numismatics, philately. Ofc: Prescott Associates 18264 Verano Dr San Diego 92128

PRESS, BARRY HARRIS JAY, plastic surgeon, educator; b. Apr. 10, 1951, Marshalltown, Iowa; s. Robert Alfred and Phyllis Elaine (Rovner) P.; m. Cynthia Jane Witz, Aug. 11, 1973; children: Sarah Jane, Rachel Ann; edn: BS (hons. microbiology), Univ. Iowa, 1973, MD, 1977; Diplomate Am. Bd. Med. Examiners 1979, Am. Bd. Surgery 1989, Am. Bd. Plastic Surgery 1989, cert. surgery of hand 1990. Career: intern, resident gen. surgery Univ. of Minnesota Hosps., Mpls. 1977-78, 78-79, 80-85, chief res. 1984-85, resident otol. 1979-80; resident plastic surgery NY Univ. Med. Ctr., 1985-87, chief res. 1986-87; asst. prof. plastic surgery Stanford Univ. Coll. Med., 1987-94, assoc. prof. 1994–; dir. Burn Ctr. and assoc. chief div. plastic surg. Santa Clara Valley Med. Ctr., San Jose 1987–; awards: Old Gold Scholar Univ. Iowa 1969, summer res. fellow Univ. Iowa Coll. Med. 1974, 1st pl. Resident Trauma Essay competition ACS, Minn. 1981, 1st pl. Resident Res. competition Minn. Surgical Soc. 1983, PSEF res. grantee 1986, NIH biomed. res. grantee 1988; Fellow ACS, mem. Am. Soc. Plastic and Reconstrv. Surgeons, Am. Soc. Surgery of the Hand, Calif. Soc. of Plastic Surgeons, Am. Burn Assn., Santa Clara County Med. Soc., Calif. Med. Assn., AMA; author 25+ med. jour. articles and book chapters, 8+ sci. presentations. Ofc: Santa Clara Valley Medical Ctr. 751 S Bascom Ave San Jose 95128 Tel: 408/885-5315

PRESS, SKIP (LLOYD DOUGLAS JR.), writer; b. July 26, 1950, Commerce, Texas; s. Lloyd Douglas Press, Sr. and Bettie Eleanor (Jacobs) Davidson; m. Debra Ann Hartsog, July 30, 1989; children: Haley Alexander b. 1990, Holly Olivia b. 1992. Career: mng. editor Today's Professionals mag., L.A. 1979-80; editor Entertainment Monthly, L.A. 1984; writer radio show Alien Worlds 1978; freelance writer 1978–; playwright, prod., dir. several stage plays; writer, cons. First Interstate Bank, L.A.; writer TV Zoobilee Zoo 1986;writer, producer how-to-videos, 1986-90; writer, packager video Jan Stephenson's How To Golf 1986; writer, co-prod. video A Woman's Guide to Firearms 1987 (awarded Silver Medal, N.Y. Internat. Film Festival 1987); writer, cons. video Wedding Helper, 1989; instr. UCLA Ext. Writer's Program, 1992–; author: young adult novels: Cliffhanger, 1992, Knucklehead, 1993, The Big Picture, 1993, A Rave of Snakes, 1994, A Web of Ya-Yas, 1994, A Shift of Coyotes, 1994, Zack Zeroes In, 1994; non-fiction: The Kuwaiti Oil Fires, 1993, The Importance of Mark Twain, 1993, Awesome Almanac: California, 1994, Star Families, 1995, How To Write What You Want and Sell What You Write, 1995; writer Allure feature

Chessler Prodn., 1991; co-writer South of Paradise feature Pacific Rim Productions 1994; mem: Dramatists Guild 1984–, Poets and Writers 1986–, Nat. Writer's Union 1993–, Soc. of Children's Book Writers 1993–; rec: golf, music. Address: 710 E Palm Ave Burbank 91501 Tel: 818/954-8900

PRESTON, ROBERT ARTHUR, astronomer; b. June 29, 1944, N.Y.C.; s. Arthur Lloyd and Dorothy Elizabeth (Smith) P.; m. Ann Lee Archer, July 18, 1970; children: Karen b. 1973; edn: BS, Cornell Univ., 1966, M.Aerospace Eng., 1967; PhD, M.I.T., 1972. Career: project scientist Lockheed Research Lab., Palo Alto 1972-73; Jet Propulsion Lab., Pasadena, 1973–, group supr. 1975–, mgr. astrophysics res. pgm. 1979-92, project scientist, 1991–; vis. prof. Calif. Inst. of Tech., 1989-90; prin. investigator Vega Venus Balloon Experiment, Phobos Lander Mission, Hipparcos Mission, Extragalactic Radio Astronomy Grant (NASA); awarded NASA Special Svc. Medal 1986; discoverer of 28 archeoastronomy sites in American Southwest; author 150+ pub. sci. papers; mem. Am. Astronomical Soc. 1973–, Internat. Astronomical Union 1976–; rec: piano, running. Res: 24618 Golf View Dr Valencia 91355 Ofc: Jet Propulsion Lab. 238-600, 4800 Oak Grove Dr Pasadena 91109

PRICE, CLIFFORD WARREN, metallurgist; b. April 22, 1935, Denver, Colo.; s. Warren Wilson and Vivian Fredricka (Cady) P.; m. Carole Joyce Watermon, June 14, 1969; children: Carla b. 1971, Krista b. 1973; edn: Metall. Engr., Colo. Sch. of Mines 1957; MS Metall. Engring., Ohio State Univ. 1970, PhD, 1975. Career: design engr. Sundstrand Aviation, Denver, Colo. 1957-60; materials splst. Denver Research Inst. 1960-63; senior metallurgist Dow Chemical Co. (Rocky Flats div.), Golden, Colo. 1963-66; staff metallurgist Battelle Columbus Labs., Ohio 1966-75; sr. scientist Owens Corning Fiberglass, Granville, Ohio 1975-80; metallurgist Lawrence Livermore Nat. Lab., Livermore 1980-93 (ret.); awards: Battelle Columbus Labs. Staff Fellowship 1972, Am. Soc. Metals Metallographic Best in Class 1960, 65; mem: AIME, ASM Internat., Electron Microscopy Soc. Am.; article pub. and presented in tech. jours.; Republican; Prot.; rec: woodworking, metalworking, sports. Res: 1569 Vancouver Way Livermore 94550

PRICE, DAVID MAC GREGOR, lawyer; b. Nov. 10, 1958, Long Beach; s. William Cecil and Helen (Frederickson) P.; m. Kelli Ruth O'Neill, May 8, 1982; children: BA, Brigham Young Univ. 1982; JD, UC Davis 1985; admitted St. Bar Calif. (1985). Career: atty., partner. Pray Price Williams & Russell, Long Beach 1985–; awards: Brigham Young Univ. Edwin S. Hinckley scholar (1981), UC Davis Law Review 1984, UC Davis Hons. Bd. 1985; mem: Garden Grove Republican Assembly (pres. 1989), Garden Grove Symphony (v.p. bd. dirs. 1988), Ch. of Jesus Christ of Latter-Day Saints (bishop 1988); Republican; Mormon; rec: woodworking. Res: 9316 Marchand Avet Garden Grove 92641 Ofc: Pray Price Williams & Russell 555 E Ocean Blvd Ste 810 Long Beach 90802

PRICE, FRANK, motion picture/television entertainment company executive; b. May 17, 1930, Decatur, Ill.; s. Wm. F., Sr. and Winifred A. (Moran) P.; m. Katherine Huggins, May 15, 1965; children: Stephen, David, Roy, Frank; edn: Mich. State Univ., 1949-51. Career: pres. Universal TV, Universal City 1974-78; v.p./dir. MCA, Inc., 1976-78; chmn. bd./CEO Columbia Pictures, Burbank 1979-84; chmn. bd. MCA Motion Picture Group, Universal City 1984-86; bd. chmn. and c.e.o. Price Entertainment Inc., Burbank 1987-90; chmn. Columbia Pictures, 1990-91; CEO Price Entertainment 1991–; bd. dirs.: Sony Pictures Entertainment, Savoy Pictures, Academy of Motion Pictures, Beverly Hills; bd. trustees Sundance Inst., Park City, Ut. 1983–; honors: motion picture exec. of yr. Nat. Assn. of Theatre Owners 1980, distinguished community service Brandeis Univ. 1982, pioneer of yr. Motion Picture Pioneers 1982; mil: USN 1948-49. Ofc: Price Entertainment 2425 Olympic Blvd Santa Monica 90404

PRICE, FREDERICK KENNETH CERCIE, clergyman; b. Jan. 3, 1932, Santa Monica; s. Fred Cercie and Winnifred Bernice (Ammons) P.; m. Betty Ruth Scott, Mar. 29, 1953; children: Angela Marie P. Evans, Cheryl Ann P. Crabbe, Stephanie Pauline P. Buchanan, Frederick Kenneth; edn: Dipl. (hon.) Rhema Bible Tng. Ctr., Tulsa 1976; DD (hon.), Oral Roberts Univ., 1982; Hon. student Pepperdine Univ., Malibu, Ca., 1/21/90; Ordained to ministry Baptist Ch., 1955, African Methodist Episcopal Ch., 1957, Kenneth Hagin Ministries, 1975; Friends Internat. Christian Univ., Fresno, B. Biblical Stu. 1978, M. Div. 1982, D. Ministry 1988, D. Humane Letters 1991, PhD religious studies 1992, Career: asst. pastor Mount Sinai Baptist Ch., Los Angeles 1955-57; pastor AME Ch., Val Verde, Calif. 1957-59; Christiam Missionary Alliance West Washington Community Ch., Los Angeles 1965-73; Crenshaw Christian Ctr., L.A. 1973–; founding mem. bd. trustees Internat. Convention Faith Ministers Inc., Tulsa 1979–; founder, chmn. bd., pres. Fellowship of Inner City Word of Faith Ministries (FICWFM), L.A., 1990; author: How Faith Works 1976, Explanation to Receiving Your Healing by the Laying On of Hands 1980, High Finance, God's Financial Plan, Tithes and Offerings 1984, How to Believe God for a Mate 1987, Marriage and the Family, Practical Insight for Family Living 1988, The Origin of Satan 1988, Living in the Spiritual Realm 1989, Concerning Them Which are Asleep 1989, Homosexuality, State of Birth or State of Mind 1989, Prosperity on God's Terms 1990, other books; Democrat; Ofc: Crenshaw Christian Center 7901 S Vermont Ave POB 90000 Los Angeles 90009

PRICE, JOE (A.), artist, educator; b. Feb. 6, 1935, Ferriday, La.; s. Edward Neill and Margaret (Hester) P.; edn: BS, Northwestern Univ., 1957; postgrad. Art Center Coll., L.A. 1967-68; MA, Stanford Univ., 1970. Career: actor and freelance artist, illustrator in N.Y.C. 1957-60, in L.A. 1960-68, commercial artist, San Carlos 1968-69; package designer Container Corp. Am., Santa Clara 1969; prof. studio art and filmmaking and chair dept. art Coll. of San Mateo, 1970-94 (ret.); One-man shows incl. Richard Sumner Gal., Palo Alto 1975, San Mateo County Cultural Ctr. 1976, 82, Tahir Gals., New Orleans 1977, 82, Kerwin Gals., Burlingame 1977, Editions Gal., Melbourne, Australia 1977, Ankrum Gal., L.A. 1978, 84, Editions Ltd. West Gal., S.F. 1981, Miriam Perlman Gal., Chgo. 1982, San Mateo County Arts Council Gal. 1982, Candy Stick Gal., Ferndale 1984, Assoc. Am. Artists, N.Y.C. and Phila. 1984, Gallery 30, Burlingame 1991, San Mateo 1984, Triton Mus. Art, Santa Clara 1986, Huntsville Mus. Art, Ala. 1987, Gallery 30, San Mateo 1988-91, Concept Art Gal., Pitts. 1991, Eleonore Austeder Gallery, S.F. 1995; num. group shows nat. incl. 15th Ann. Nat. Invitational Drawing Exhbn. Emporia State Univ., Kansas 1991, internat. group shows incl. Nat. Gal. Australia 1978, Editions Galleries, Melbourne 1988, 6th Internat. Exhbn. Carnegie-Mellon Univ., Pa. 1988, 5th Internat. Biennale Petite Format de Papier, Belgium 1989, 4th Internat. Biennial Print Exh., Taipei Fine Arts Mus. P.R.China 1990, Interprint, Lviv '90, USSR 1990, Internat. Print Triennale, Cracow, Poland 1991, "Directions in Bay Area Printmaking: Three Decades" Palo Alto Cultural Ctr. 1992-93, Am. Printmaking, Haslem Gallery W.D.C. 1993, "Diversity and Visions of the Printed Image", Triton Mus. of Art, Santa Clara 1994, "Alabama Impact: Contemporary Artists with Alabama Ties" Mobile Mus. of Art and Huntsville Mus. of Art 1995; represented in perm. collections San Francisco Mus. Modern Art, Achenbach Found. Graphic Arts, S.F., Phila. Mus. Art, New Orleans Mus. Art, Portland Mus. Art, Me., The Library of Congress, W.D.C., Huntsville Mus. Art, Midwest Mus. Am. Art, Ind., Cracow Nat. Mus., Poland, Cabo Frio Mus., Brazil, Nat. Mus. Am. Art, Smithsonian Instn., W.D.C.; awards: Kempshall Clark award Peoria Art Guild 1981, Paul Lindsay Sample Meml. award 25th Chautauqua Nat. Exhbn. of Am. Art 1982, 1st Ann. Creative Achiev. award Calif. State Legislature /Arts Coun. San Mateo Co. 1989; mem: Am. Color Print Soc., Audubon Artists (Louis Lozowick Meml. award 1978, Silver medal of honor 1991), Boston Printmakers (Ture Bengtz Meml. award 1987), Calif. Soc. Printmakers council 1979-81), L.A. Printmaking Soc., Phila. Print Club (Lessing J. Rosenwald prize 1979), Arts Council of San Mateo Co., Theta Chi; Democrat; Rel. Sci. Res/Studio: PO Box 3305 Sonora 95370-3305

PRICE, LARRY R., government executive; b. Jan. 24, 1947, Portsmouth, Ohio; s. Irby C. and Anna R. (McCoy) P.; m. Linda S. Hosford, June 8, 1968; children: Kevin b. 1971, Kimberly b. 1974; edn: AA, Fullerton Jr. Coll. 1967; BS criminology, CSU Long Beach 1970; MPA, CSU Bakersfield 1982. Career: police ofcr. City of Fullerton 1968-69; dep. probation ofcr. Los Angeles Co. 1969-70; Kern Co. Probation, Bakersfield 1970-73, mgr., adminstr. 1973-88; chief probation ofcr. Tulare Co., Visalia 1988–; instr. Bakersfield Coll. 1973-86; guest prof. CSU Bakersfield 1982-88; guest lectr. McPherson Coll., Kans. 1984-87; cons. Price Talbot & Assoc., Carpenteria 1986–; Calif. Youth Authority Cadre, Sacto. 1984-87; awards: Campfire Luther Halsey Gulick 1983, Calif. Youth Authority Disting. Service 1984, Calif. Probation Parole & Correctional Assn. Lester J. Haye 1986, Calif. St. Juvenile Ofcrs. Model Juvenile Bureau 1987, USAF Model Prevention Program 1987; mem: Am. Probation & Parole Assn., Am. Correctional Assn., Rotary, Chief Probation Ofcrs. of Calif., Am. Soc. Pub. Adminstrs., Western Correctional Assn., Calif. Probation, Parole & Correctional Assn. (pres. 1988-89), Calif. Found. Cont. Edn. in Corrections (pres. 1988-89), Kern Council of Campfire (pres. 1980-83), Kern Co. Advy. Com. on Drug Abuse (v. chmn. 1977-79); num. articles pub. in profl. jours., 1973; Republican; Prot.; rec: camping, hiking, gardening. Ofc: Tulare County Probation Dept. Room 206 Courthouse Visalia 93291

PRIMACK, MARVIN HERBERT, physician, anesthesiologist; b. Mar. 20, 1931, Detroit, Mich.; s. Abraham and Florence (Zeman) P.; m. Bune Rothbart, Dec. 26, 1934; children: Todd b. 1957, Teri b. 1959, Daren b. 1962, Heidi b. 1964; edn: BS, Wayne St. Univ. 1953; MD, Univ. Mich. Ann Arbor 1957. Career: staff Harper & Hutzel Hosp., Detroit, Mich. 1960-66; St. Josephs Med. Center, Stockton 1966–; bd. chmn., pres. Found. Med. Care 1981-83; M.H. Primack MD Inc. 1979-88; v.p. Stockton Anesthesia 1969-79, 1989–; med. dir. Lodi Outpatient Surgery Ctr., Lodi, Calif. 1994–; asst. prof. Wayne Univ. Med. Sch., Detroit, Mich. 1963-66; mem: Calif. Soc. Anesthesiologists, Am. Soc. Anesthesiologists, AMA, CMA, San Joaquin Med. Soc.; rec: computers, photography. Ofc: Stockton Anesthesia Medical Group Inc. 2626 N California Suite G Stockton 95204

PROFFITT, RICHARD THOMAS, research and development biochemist; b. May 13, 1944, Toledo, Ohio; s. Raymond Thomas and Dorothy Louise (Reingruber) P.; m. Barbara Ruth Siechert, June 27, 1969; children: Pamela Ruth b. 1974, Sarah Louise b. 1977, Roger Thomas b. 1983; edn: BA, Occidental Coll. 1966; MS, San Diego St. Univ. 1970; PhD, UC Davis 1973. Career: research fellow U.S. Dept. Agri., Albany 1973; lectr. Calif. Polytech. St. Univ., San Luis Obispo 1974; research fellow St. Louis Univ. Sch. Medicine, Mo. 1974-76; research assoc. Wash. Univ. Sch. Medicine 1977-79; asst. research scientist City of Hope, Duarte 1979-82; dir. pharmacology Vestar Inc.,

San Dimas 1982–; awards: USDA Nat. Research 1973, NIH postdoctoral fellow 1976-77, City of Hope Fred Marik research fellow 1981-82; mem: Am. Chemical Soc., Am. Soc. Microbiology, Am. Assn. for Cancer Res.; 25 research articles pub. in sci. jour., 1972–, 4 book chpts. pub., 5 patents issued, 2 pending, 1982–; Republican; Prot. Res: 11 N Altura Rd Arcadia 91007 Ofc: Nexstar Pharmaceuticals Inc. 650 Cliffside Dr San Dimas 91773

PUCKETT, RICHARD EDWARD, artist, consultant, recreation executive, retired; b. Sept. 9, 1932, Klamath Falls, Ore.; s. Vernon Elijah and Leona Bell (Clevenger) P.; m. Velma Faye Hamrick, Apr. 14, 1957 (dec. 1985); children: Katherine Michelle b. 1958, Deborah Alison b. 1960, Susan Lin b. 1961, Gregory Richard b. 1962; edn: stu. Monterey Peninsula Jr. Coll., Hartnell Jr. Coll., CSUSJ, Lake Forest Coll., Ill., So. Ore. Coll. of Edn.; BA in public service, Univ. San Francisco 1978; desig: profl. recreator Am. Recreation Soc. 1964, Armed Forces Rec. Soc. 1970, Nat. Park & Rec. Soc. 1976. Career: asst. arts and crafts dir. Ft. Leonard Wood, Mo. 1956-57; arts & crafts dir./ asst. spl. services ofcr./museum dir. Fort Sheridan, Ill. 1957-59, designed and opened 1st Fort Sheridan Army Museum; arts & crafts dir. Fort Irwin, Calif. 1959-60; arts & crafts br. dir. Fort Ord, 1960-86, opened first Presidio of Monterey Army Museum 1961; ret. 1986; artist in oils, watercolor, blownglass sculpture, graphics; one-man shows: Seaside, City Hall (1975), Fort Ord Arts & Crafts Center Gal. (1967-85), Presidio of Monterey Art Gal. (1979), exhibits in Mo., Ill., Calif., work in pvt. collections in U.S., Canada and Europe; contrib. author for book to be pub. on Army arts & crafts and Army combat artist prgm; awards: 1st pl. programming Dept. of army (6 awards 1975-85), 1st pl. programming and publicity Armed Forces Command (5 consec. awards 1979-84), Commanders' Award for Civilian Service 1986, 1st & 3d pl. modern sculpture Monterey Fair Fine Arts Exh. 1978, 19 awards for outstanding performance, 2 sustained superior performance awards (1978, 84), numerous ribbons for arts and crafts; Life mem. Am. Biographical Soc., FABA and Golden Acad. Award for lifetime achiev. (1991), Life mem. Internat. Biog. Soc. "FIBA Internat. Man of Yr." (1991-92); past mem. Am. Park & Rec. Soc., Am. Craftsman Assn., Glass Arts Soc., Monterey Mus. Assn., Rogue Valley Art Assn.; current mem. Salinas Valley Fine Arts Assn.; Democrat; Prot.; rec: walking, antiques. Res: 1152 Jean Ave Salinas 93905 also 110 Ashland Ave Medford OR 97504

PUGNO, PERRY ALAN, physician; b. April 28, 1948, San Bernardino; s. Perry and Vanda Diane (Boggio) P.; m. Terry Gail Ren, June 20, 1970; children: Andrew b. 1973, Joseph b. 1976, Benjamin b. 1977; edn: BA, UC Riverside 1970; MD, UC Davis 1974; MPH, Loma Linda Univ. 1983; cert. Am. Bd. Family Practice 1977, Am. Bd. Emergency Medicine 1983. Career: resident physician Ventura Gen. Hosp. 1974-77; residency dir. Riverside Gen. Hosp. 1978-80; emergency dir. Riverside Comm. Hosp. 1980-82; edn. dir. Univ. Conn., Farmington 1982-84; residency dir. Shasta-Cascade Family Practice, Redding 1984–; assoc. clin. prof. Loma Linda Univ. 1978-82; asst. prof. Univ. Conn., Farmington 1982-84; assoc. clin. prof. UC Davis 1984–; awards: Meade-Johnson Grad. Edn. 1977, Lange Med. Publs. 1974; mem: Am. Acad. Family Physicians, Soc. Tchrs. Family Medicine, BSA; articles pub. and reviewed in sci. jours.; mil: sr. surgeon, lt. comdr. USPHS 1977-78; Republican; R.Cath.; rec: backpacking, music. Ofc: 7500 Hospital Dr Sacramento 95823

PUJOL, JOHN JEROME, customs broker; b. July 18, 1954, Landstuhl, Germany; s. Jerome Paul and Gertrud Vera (Lindhorst) P.; m. Karen Jean, Sept. 5, 1976; children: Tyler b. 1989, Griffin b. 1991. Career: plant mgr. Process Control Corp., Atlanta, Ga. 1978-79; account rep. EFI, N.Y.C. 1979-83, v.p. 1983-87, pres. and c.e.o. Valley Stream, N.Y. 1987–; dir: Pier Container Corp., EF Warehousing Inc., E.O.L. Inc., AP Holding Corp.; mem: Young Pres. Orgn., Am. Motorcyclists Assn., Nursery Nature Walks (bd. of dir.); rec: outdoor sports. Ofc: EFI 6033 W Century Blvd Ste 720 Los Angeles 90045

PULGRAM, LAURENCE FAIRLIE, lawyer; b. April 4, 1958, Atlanta, Ga.; s. William Leopold and Lucia Walker (Fairlie) P.; edn: BA summa cum laude, Duke Univ. 1979; JD magna cum laude, Harvard Law Sch. 1983; admitted St. Bar Calif. (1984). Career: legislative asst. Congressman Wyche Fowler Jr., Wash. D.C. 1979-80; law clk. Chief Judge Sam C. Pointer, U.S. Dist. Ct., Birmingham, Ala. 1983-84; atty., assoc. Howard Rice Nemerovski Canady Robertson & Falk, San Francisco 1984–; dir. Feedback Production Inc., San Francisco 1986, pres. 1988; honors: Phi Beta Kappa, Phi Eta Sigma; mem: Am. Bar Assn., San Francisco Bar Assn. (mediator), S.F. Barristers Club; Democrat; Unitarian; rec: yacht racing, cello, soccer. Res: 530 Filbert St. San Francisco 94133 Ofc: Howard Rice Nemerovski Canady Robertson & Falk 3 Embarcadero Center 7th Floor San Francisco 94111

PULLEY, DOUGLAS BOYD, physician, ophthalmologist; b. Apr. 1, 1942, San Francisco; s. Boyd H. and Beth (Paxman) P.; m. Katherine Anne Bennion, June 25, 1966; children: Anne b. 1970, Matthew b. 1972, David b. 1975, Susan b. 1977, Stephen b. 1981; edn: BS zoology, Brigham Young Univ. 1966; MD, UCLA 1970. Career: pres. Douglas B. Pulley MD Inc., San Jose 1976–; mem: Am. Acad. Ophthalmology (fellow), AMA, CMA, SCCMS, Santa Clara Valley Orchid Soc.; mil: capt. AUS 1971-73; Republican; Mormon; rec: orchids, woodturning. Ofc: 393 Blossom Hill Rd Ste 265 San Jose 95123-1602

PUNNETT, AUDREY FRANCES, clinical psychologist; b. Oct. 25, 1947, Bremerton, Wash.; d. Louis and Marjorie Velma (Gibson) Punnett; m. Harlan E. Ratmeyer, July 30, 1988; edn: AA, Victor Valley Coll. 1967; BS, Univ. Utah 1971; MS, 1975; PhD, Calif. Sch. Profl. Psychology 1981. Career: crisis worker Valley Med. Center, Fresno 1980-81; coordinator pediatric psychology Fresno Comm. Hosp. 1981-85; clin. psychology II UCSF Med. Edn. Program 1983-84; instr. W. Hills Coll., Lemoore 1983-84; pvt. practice, Fresno 1981–; pediatric psychologist Valley Childrens Hosp. 1985–; asst. clin. prof. UCSF Med. Edn. Program 1986–; cons. CSU Fresno 1988–; awards: CSPP Outstanding Alumni for Decade nominee 1973-83; mem: Am. Psychology Assn., Soc. Pediatric Psychology, Clin. Child Psychology, Calif. Psychological Assn., Jr. League of Fresno; articles pub. in profl. jours., 1984, 93, 94; Episcopalian; rec: gardening. Ofc: 5151 N Palm Ave Ste 605 Fresno 93704

PURCELL, PATRICK B., motion picture executive; b. March 16, 1943, Dublin, Ireland; nat. 1984; s. James P. and Margaret M. (Donohoe) P.; m. Simone Gros-Long, Feb. 1, 1968; children: Alexander b. 1972, Christopher b. 1973, Benjamin b. 1976; edn: MBA, Fordham Univ. 1973; CPA, U.K. cert. acct. Career: exec. Paramount Pictures Corp. 1970–, exec. v.p., chief fin. & admin. ofcr. 1983–. Ofc: Paramount Pictures Corp. 5555 Melrose Ave Los Angeles 90038

PURCELL, STUART MCLEOD, III, financial planner; b. Feb. 16, 1944, Santa Monica; s. Stuart M., Jr. and Carol (Howe) P.; edn: AA, Santa Monica City Coll., 1964; BS, CSU Northridge, 1967; grad. CPA Adv. Personal Fin. Plnng., 1985; CPA 1976, reg. prin. NASD 1984, Registry of Fin. Plnng. Practitioners 1987; Cert. Financial Planner (CFP) 1995. Career: sr. acct. Pannell, Kerr, Forster CPA, San Francisco 1970-73; fin. cons./prin. Purcell Fin. Services, 1973-74; controller Decimus Corp., S.F. 1974-76; Grubb & Ellis Co., Oakland 1976-78; Marwais Steel Co., Richmond 1979-80; fin. cons./prin. San Rafael 1980–, fin. counselor/owner Purcell Wealth Mgmt., 1981–; guest lectr. Master's Pgm. in fin. plnng. Golden Gate Univ. 1985–, lectr. comm. workshops, Larkspur 1984; awards: Eagle Scout BSA 1959, dean's list CSUN 1967, best fin. advisor and fin. newsletter Marin Indep. Jour., Novato 1987, top prod. Unimarc 1986, achiev. United Way Marin Co. 1984; mem: Am. Inst. CPAs, Calif. Soc. CPAs, Marin Estate Planning Council, Nat. Speakers Assn., Internat. Assn. for Fin. Plnng. North Bay Chpt. (exec.dir. 1984), Soc. of CPA Financial Planners (S.F. dist. mem. chair 1986), Internat. Soc. of PreRetired Planners, Sigma Alpha Epsilon; civic: United Way Marin Co. (div. chair 1984), San Rafael C.of C. 1983–, Salvation Army San Rafael, San Anselmo, Fairfax Chpt. (treas. 1987–), March of Dimes Marin Co. (funding com. 1987–), Arthritis Found. (funding com. 1988–); publs: contbr. articles in newspapers and bus., fin. profl. jours.; mil: lt. j.g. USNR 1968-76; Presbyterian; rec: travel, auto racing, skiing, gardening. Res: 45 Vineyard Dr San Rafael 94901

PURDY, CAROL ANN, licensed clinical social worker, children's book author; b. Jan. 5, 1943, Long Beach; d. Melvin Boyce and Kathryn Delia (Wilbur) Slaughter; m. John Allen Purdy, June 8, 1963; children: Laura b. 1967, Mark b. 1971, Sarah b. 1977; edn: BA, CSU Long Beach, 1964; MSW, CSU Sacto., 1990; Calif. life tchg. credential 1985, pupil personnel svs. cred. 1991. Career: tchr. Orange Unified Sch. Dist., Orange 1964-67; children's book author, 1977–, lectr. in pub. schs. 1986–; high risk youth consultant, Community Mental Health, Red Bluff 1989-93; psychotherapist. pvt. practice 1993–; founder and tnr. The Kid Power Program, Groups for High Risk Children, 1990–; school social worker, 1990-95; mem: Soc. Childrens Book Writers, Nat. Assn. Soc. Workers, Calif. Tchrs. Assn. 1964-67; listed Who's Who Authors and Writers, Two Thousand Notable Am. Women, Intl. Dir. of Distinguished Leadership, Who's Who Among Human Service Profls., 5,000 Personalities of World, Women of Today, Something About the Author, Who's Who of Am. Women; author children's books: Iva Dunnit & The Big Wind (1985, pub. USA, Can., Fr., Gt. Brit.), Least of All, 1987, The Kid Power Program, 1989, Mrs. Merriwether's Musical Cat, 1994, Nesuya's Basket (in press); Ch. of Christ. Res: 25310 68th Ave Los Molinos 96055 Ofc: Kid Power 645 Antelope Blvd #22 Red Bluff 96080

PURDY, RUTH MELISSA SANDERS, family therapist, professor; b. Nov. 5, 1910, Rocky, Okla.; d. Henry Allen and Ada Selena (Payton) Sanders; m. Allen B. Purdy, Sept. 14, 1935; children: Joseph D. b. 1937, John b. 1941; edn: BA, CSU Long Beach, 1951, MA, 1952; PhD, Univ. of Okla., 1966; extensive post doctoral studies. Career: faculty Long Beach City Coll., estab. & devel. 1st college reading lab, 1952-68; Cypress Coll., estab. & devel. 1st individualized instrn. adult edn. lab, 1968-76; marriage, family & child therapist Pacific Counseling Ctr., Fullerton 1976-81; dir. Christian Counseling Ctr., Huntington Beach 1981–; former adj. prof. Sch. of Psych., Azusa Pacific Univ., former faculty Pepperdine Univ.; awards: Lifetime Achievement Award from the White House and State of Calif. 1993, named Californian of Comm. for outstanding volunteer contbns. 1988, Diplomate Am. Bd. of Sexology 1992–; mem: Internat. Reading Assn. (past pres. Long Beach chpt.), Western Coll. Reading Assn. (treas. 1974-75, archivist 1979-86), Am., Calif. Assn. Marriage & Family Therapists (Orange Co. chpt. pres. 1991-92, sec. 1979-80, legis. & ethics chair 1994, CFO 1994–), Calif. Soc. for Hypnosis in Family Therapy (sec. 1982-84, treas. 1985-90), Council for Exceptional Children, Nat. Alliance for Family Life

Inc. (founding clin. mem.), Mothers and others Against Child Abuse (co-founder/co-dir.); author textbook: English Basics for Clerical Workers (1981); Republican; Christian; rec: book and stamp collections, travel. Res: 438 Princeton Dr Costa Mesa 92626 Ofc: Christian Counseling Center of Huntington Beach, 1207 Main St Huntington Beach 92648

PURSELL, PAUL DENNIS, hospital rehabilitation director; b. Jan. 26, 1950, Altadena; s. Robert Ralph and Thelma Winifred P.; edn: BS, CSU Long Beach 1972; reg. physical therapist Calif. Career: asst. athletic trainer CSU Long Beach 1968-71; chief physical therapist Tustin Comm. Hosp., Tustin 1972-78; disaster planning coordinator St. Josephs Hosp., Orange 1984-90, dir. human devel. 1987-91, dir. rehab. 1978–; instr. CSU Long Beach 1989–; chmn. bd. Health Assn. Fed. Credit Union, Orange 1985-86; Orange/Long Beach Area Health Edn. Center 1984-85; chmn. Pres.'s Advy. Council on Phys. Therapy, CSU Long Beach, 1987–; awards: St. Joseph Hosp. spirit of St. Joseph 1987, Carnation Found. commend. for vol. 1984; mem: Orange C.of C. (pres. 1990-91), Am. Physical Therapy Assn. (pres. Calif. chpt. 1983-84), Am. Coll. Sports Medicine, Inst. Profl. Health Services Adminstrn., Nat. Fire Protection Assn. 1990–; civic bds: Orange Citizen of Yr. Selection Com. 1988-89, Mgmt. Audit Com. City of Orange 1991–, Leadership Orange (exec. com. 1991-94, chmn. 1992-94), Finance Com. City of Orange 1993; Providence Bldg. Condominium Assn. (bd. dirs. 1988–, pres. 1991-92); Democrat; R.Cath.; rec: fishing, movies. Ofc: St. Josephs Hospital 1100 W Stewart Orange 92668

PUTNAM, PHILIP CONRAD, lawyer; b. Dec. 7, 1954, Charlottesville, Va.; s. Gerrie Price and Liane Marie (Seim) P.; m. Lori Younger, July 21, 1979; 2 sons, Christian b. 1985, Sean b. 1989; edn: BS bus., USC, 1977; JD, 1980; admitted St. Bar Calif. 1980, C.P.A. Ill. 1978. Career: auditor Times Mirror Co., Los Angeles 1976-79; atty., assoc. Monteleone & McCrory 1980-84, ptnr. 1985–; secty. Rekortan Corp., Los Angeles 1982; dir. Eby Mine Services Inc. 1982; Flocrete Mfg. Co. 1983; Kemper Constrn. Co. 1982; judge pro tem L.A. Co. Municipal Ct. 1987–, L.A. Superior Court 1991–; awards: Outstanding Young Men Am. 1983, USC Top 25 Acctg. Students 1979, Hale Moot Ct. Best Brief 1979; mem: Am. Bar Assn., Wilshire Bar Assn. (v.p., gov. 1984), L.A. Co. Bar Assn., Ill. C.P.A. Soc., Am. Inst. C.P.A., Faith Lutheran Ch., L.A. World Affairs Council, Pasadena Tournament of Roses Assn.; asst. ed. Labyrinth, 1979; Republican; Lutheran; rec: sailing, skiing. Ofc: Monteleone & McCrory 10 Universal City Plaza Ste 2500 Universal City

PYROS, GREGORY GEORGE, architect, computer software author, consultant; b. Jan. 10, 1957, Kingston, Pa.; s. Nicholas Jonathan and Artemis (Veras) P.; m. Susan Stachowiak Gubala; edn: BS Bldg. Sci., Rensselaer Polytech. Inst. 1978, MBA 1979, BArch 1980; Reg. Arch. Calif. 1983, Pa. 1987; cert. Nat. Council of Archit. Registration Bds. (NCARB). Career: owner The Pyros Partnership, Newport Beach 1982–; pres. and chief exec. ofcr. Sno-Tek Inc., Newport Beach 1988-; instr. archtl. design course Orange Coast Coll., 1988; pvt. consulting and seminars on computer applications to bldg. industry; honors: Who's Who Am. Colls. and Univs. 1978; corp. mem. Am. Inst. of Architects (CAD computers in arch. com.), Archtl. Telecommunications Network/So. Calif. (chmn. 1986), So. Orange Co. AutoCAD User's Gp. (charter); coauthor computer pgm: Architect's Office Mgr. (nat. distbn.), author digitizer menu for AutoCAD for Architecture/ Facilities Mgmt.; 3D Multimedia and Film Animations; Republican; Greek Orthodox; rec: sailing, skiing, tennis. Res: 2639 Buckeye Street Newport Beach 92660 Ofc: The Pyros Partnership, 1201 Dove St Ste 550 Newport Beach 92660

QAQUNDAH, PAUL YOUSEF, pediatrician, allergist, educator; b. Feb. 26, 1933, Ramleh; s. Yousef Ibrahim and Soraya Salim (Qare) Q.; m. Susan Salib, Oct. 20, 1966; children: John b. 1967, Joyce b. 1968, Jennifer b. 1970, Michelle b. 1974, James b. 1979; edn: MD, Ein Shams Univ., Cairo 1960; DCH, dipl. child health, Univ. of London 1964; diplomate Am. Bd. of Pediatrics 1969, cert. subsplty. Allergy & Immunology 1975. Career: physician, pres. Pediatric Care Medical Group Inc., Huntington Beach 1971–; asst., assoc. prof. ped. UC Irvine 1971–, clinical prof. ped. UC Irvine, 1987–; vol. tchg. UCI- Childrens Hosp. Orange County; mem: Am. Acad. Pediatrics (charter pres. Orange Co. chpt. 1986), Orange Co. Ped. Soc. (pres. 1982–), Orange Co. Med. Soc. (pres.), Am. Lung Assn. O.C. (ped. com. 1975–, bd. dirs. 1974-85); contbr. num. articles and abstracts in med. jours.; Repub.; Greek Orthodox; rec: deep sea fishing, hunting, tennis. Ofc: Pediatric Care Medical Group 17822 Beach Blvd. Huntington Beach 92647

QUACKENBUSH, CHARLES W., legislator, business executive; b. Apr. 20, 1954, McChord Air Force Base; m. Rita "Chris" Christiansen, Dec. 14, 1978; children: Carrey b. 1979, Joseph b. 1985, Charles b. 1989; edn: BA, Notre Dame Univ., 1976; career: Captain, US Army 1976-82; v.p., Q-Tech 1982-86; state assemblyman, Twenty-Fourth Dist. 1986–; state insurance commissioner 1994–; mem: vice chmn., Com. on Revenue and Taxation; Governmental Orgn.; Ways & Means; former vice chmn: Banking, Finance and Bonded Indebtness, Econ. Devel. and New Technologies, Select Com. on the Census; delegate, Nat. Conf. of State Legislatures; former mem. appointed by Pres. Bush, U. S. Dept. of Defense Environmental CFC Advy. Com.; vice chmn., Assembly Com. on

Revenue and Taxation 1993–; Assembly Com. on Governmental Orgn. 1993–; Assembly Com. on Ways & Means 1993–; awards: Almaden Valley Homeowner's Assn. Appreciation Award 1989, Am. Electronics Assn. High-Tech Legislator of the Year 1991-92, CA Abortion Rights Action League Legislator of the Year 1990, CA Bus. Properties Assn. Appreciation Award 1990, CA Instr. Video Consortium Appreciation Award, CA Sch. Bd. Assn. Hispanic Caucus Award 1989, Cert. Appreciation Jr. League of Palo Alto 1989, Cert. Appreciation San Jose Lions Club, City of Cupertino Proclamation for Resolving Trial Court Funding 1988, City of Saratoga Resolution for Resolving Trial Court Funding 1988, Comm. Svc. Award for Caltrain Track Attack Steering Com. 1991, Computer Using Educators Golden Disk Award 1991, Gann Spending Limit Watchdog Coalition's Taxpayer's Hang Tough Award 1987, L. A. Jr. C. of C. Award, Reg. Educational TV Advy. Council Award, Sr. Citizens Escort & Outreach Paratransit Assn. Cutting Gov. Red Tape Award, U. S. Army Commendation Medal; mem: Calif. Republican Assn., Calif. Cong. of Republicans, Santa Clara Chpt.; delegate, Republican Nat. Conv. 1988; Calif. Republican League; Peninsula Republican Assn.; Republicans for Choice; Santa Clara Cty. Republican Central Com.; mil: capt., US Army, 1976-82. Res: Cupertino Ofc: State Capitol, Rm. 4130 Sacramento 95814

QUE HEE, SHANE STEPHEN, environmental health scientist, educator; b. Oct. 11, 1946, Sydney, New South Wales, Australia; s. Robert and Jean (Byers) Q.H.; edn: BSc (hons.) Univ. Queensland, Brisbane, Aus. 1968, MSc, 1971; PhD, Univ. Saskatchewan, Can. 1976; postdoctoral McMaster Univ., Hamilton, Ont., Can. 1975-78; Fellow Am. Inst. of Chemists 1986. Career: asst., assoc. prof. Univ. Cincinnati, Oh. 1978-84, 1984-89; assoc. prof. dept. environmental health scis. UCLA, Los Angeles 1989-94, prof., 1994–, dept. vice chair 1992-94; reviewer US EPA, ATSDR, Nat. Sci. Found., Wash. DC 1978–; mem. TOXNET, Nat. Library Medicine, Bethesda, Md. 1985-89; mem. editorial bd. CRC Press, Boca Raton, Fl. 1988–, advy. bd. lab. methodology 1987–; awards: noteworthy contbn. US EPA 1981; mem: AAAS 1971–, Am. Chem. Soc. 1971–, Am. Coll. Toxicology 1981–, Am. Conf. Govt. Industrial Hygienists 1987–, Am. Ind. Hygiene Assn. 1978–; civic: Univ. Saskatchewan Squash Club (founder, pres. 1971-72), Saskatoon Cricket Assn. (sec. treas. 1974-75), Saskatchewan Cricket Assn. (sec. treas. 1974), Cincinnati Coal. Against Apartheid (facilitator 1985), Cinti. Gay/Lesbian March Activists (facilitator 1987-89), Lesbian/Gay Health and Health Policy Found. (pres. 1993–); author: The Phenoxyalkanoic Herbicides 1981, contbg. editor: Biological Monitoring: An Introduction, 1993; rec: writing, civil rights, music. Res: 923 Levering Ave, Unit 102, Los Angeles 90024 Ofc: Dept. Env. Hlth. Sciences, and UCLA Ctr for Occupational and Environmental Health, UCLA School Public Health, 10833 Le Conte Ave Los Angeles 90095-1772

QUIEL, CYNTHIA ANN, workers' compensation judge; b. Nov. 5, 1957, Long Beach; d. Charles Hamilton and Mary Louise (Leslie) Ishmael; m. Fred G. Quiel, Jan., 1991; edn: AA, Goldenwest Coll. 1978; BS, Western St. Univ. 1981; JD, 1982; admitted St. Bar Calif. 1983, U.S. Dist. Ct. 1983, U.S. Ct. Appeals 1984, U.S. Supreme Ct. 1988. Career: atty., assoc. Ruston & Nance, Tustin 1983-84; Farano & Kieviet, Anaheim 1984-86; house counsel Aetna Ins., Orange 1986-88; dep. city atty. City of Long Beach 1988-90; workers' compensation judge, WCAB Long Beach 1990–; vol. atty. Amicus Publico, Santa Ana 1986; honors: Delta Theta Phi, St. Bar Calif. Bd. Govs. Commend. 1987, Who's Who Students in Am. Univs. & Colls.; mem: Calif. St. Bar Assn.; Democrat; rec: bicycling. Ofc: Workers' Compensation Appeals Board 245 W Broadway Rm 230 Long Beach 90802

QUINN, JOHN R., archbishop; b. March 28, 1929, Riverside, Calif.; s. Ralph J. and Elizabeth (Carroll) Quinn; 3 siblings: Anthony G., Mrs. William Bash, Mrs. Noel deJarnette (dec.); edn: priesthood studies, St. Francis Sem. and Immaculate Heart Sem., San Diego, 1947-48, philosophy and theology, North American Coll., and Gregorian Univ., Rome, Licentiate in Sacred Theology, 1954; ordained priest in Rome at Ch. of San Marcello, by Archbishop Hector Cunial for the Diocese of San Diego, 1953; Hon. degrees Jesuit Sch. of Theology, Berkeley, Univ. of San Francisco, Santa Clara Univ., Univ. of Notre Dame. Career: apptd. assoc. pastor St. George`s Parish, Ontario, Calif. 1954; mem. theology faculty Immaculate Heart Seminary, San Diego 1955–, apptd. pres. St. Francis Coll. Seminary, 1962, rector Immaculate Heart Sem. Sch. of Theology, 1964; ordained Bishop, San Diego, 1967; apptd. first provost of the Univ. of San Diego, 1968, also mem. bd. trustees; apptd. pastor St. Therese Parish, San Diego, 1969; apptd. by Pope Paul VI as a consultor to the Congregation for the Clergy, Rome, 1971; installed Bishop, Oklahoma City and Tulsa, Okla., 1972, by the Apostolic Del. to the U.S., The Most Rev. Luigi Raimondi; installed as first Archbishop of Oklahoma City, Cathedral of Our Lady of Perpetual Help, 1973; appt. by Pope Paul VI as rep. Fourth Synod of Bishops, Vatican City, 1974; elected pres. Okla Conf. of Churches, 1976-78; Archbishop of San Francisco, 1977–; apptd. by Pope John Paul II Pontifical Del. for Religious in the U.S., 1983; mem: Nat. Conf. of Catholic Bishops (pres. 1977-80, past chmn. com. of the liturgy, elected to att. Synod on the Family in Rome, 10/80, past chmn. com. on doctrine, mem. com. for pro-life activities 1989–), Canon Law Soc. of Am., Cath. Theol. Soc. Am., U.S. Cath. Conf. (past chmn. com. on family life), Calif. Cath. Conf. (pres. 1985-88), Inst. of Living, Hartford, Ct. (bd.

govs.); contbr. articles in L'Osservatore Romano, America, The Priest, The Catholic Ency., Catholic Hospital, and in various newspapers. Address: Office of the Archbishop, 445 Church St San Francisco 94114

QUINN, ROBERT EMMET, JR., public works civil engineer; b. May 11, 1934, Chgo.; s. Robert Emmet and Hazel Theresa (Butt) Q.; m. Judith May Bohlman, June 2, 1956; children: Robert b. 1959, Diane b. 1961, John b. 1962; edn: BS, US Naval Acad., 1956; BCE, Rensselaer Polytech. Inst., 1958; MCE, Stanford Univ., 1965; reg. profl. civil engr. Mass. 1970, Calif. 1978. Career: capt. Civil Engineer Corps, USN 1952-86: pub. works ofcr. naval ammo. depot Fallbrook, Calif. 1958-60, ops. ofcr. Mobile Constrn. Batt. Eleven, Pacific 1960-62, NAS Alameda 1965-67, ops. ofcr. 32nd constrn. regt. Vietnam 1967-68, naval facilities engr. Supreme Hqtrs. Allied Powers Europe, Shape, Belgium 1968-71, NATO infrastructure engr. Joint Chiefs of Staff, Wash. DC 1971-74, c.o. Mobile Constrn. Batt. Forty, Pacific 1974-76, exec. ofcr. Navy Constrn. Batt. Ctr. Port Hueneme, Calif. 1976-78, c.o. Navy Pub. Works Ctr., Yokosuka, Japan 1978-81, c.o. W. Div. Naval Facilities Engring. Command, San Bruno, Calif. 1981-83, dep. cdr. Naval Facilities Engring. Command, Wash. DC 1983-86, decorated (25+) Legion of Merit (3), Bronze Star, Purple Heart, Merit. Svc. (2), Rep. Vietnam Gal. Cross w/palm and w/silver star (2); v.p. ops. Engineering Management Concepts, Camarillo 1986-89; pub. works civil engr. City of Santa Barbara, 1989-90; pub. works dep. dir. engring. County of Ventura, 1990–; honors: Chi Epsilon 1958) mem: Soc. Am. Mil. Engrs. (chpt. dir. 1976–, pres. Tokyo 80-1, S.F. 81-2, Oxnard/Ventura 87-8), CBC Fed. Credit Union (dir. 1987-93), CBC/Seabee Museum (dir. 1988–), Navy League U.S. (Ventura dir. 1986–, v.p. 1988-90, pres. 1991), Am. Pub. Works Assn. 1978–, ASCE (dir.1986–), Nat., Calif. Soc. Profl. Engrs., Naval Inst., Naval Acad. Alumni Assn. (dir. 1982-85), Stanford Univ. Alumni Assn.; civic: Pt. Hueneme C.of C. (dir. Men's Follies 1987–), Tuesday Afternoon Rest & Aspiration, 1977–; pub. article, 1986; Republican; Prot.; rec: house remodeling, electronics, photog. Res: 661 Ivywood Dr Oxnard 93030 Ofc: Public Works Agy. County of Ventura, 800 S Victoria Ave Ventura 93009

QUINN, TERESA MOSS, lawyer; b. Apr. 27, 1952, Logan, Ut.; d. Harold J. and Shirley D. (Farrer) Moss; m. John B. Quinn, Aug. 28, 1976 (div. 1983); children: Meredith b. 1976, Megan b. 1982; edn: BA (magna cum laude), Pomona Coll., 1973; JD, Boston Univ. Sch. of Law, 1977. Career: atty., assoc. Milbank, Tweed, Hadley & McCloy, NY, NY 1977-79; ptnr. Pillsbury Madison & Sutro, Los Angeles 1979–, splst. in internat. banking and finance incl. tax-exempt, LBO, and bankers acceptance financings; co-counsel to Calif. Bankers Clearing House Assn. 1983-84; honors: ed. law rev. Boston Univ. Sch. of Law 1975-76, Norman Neal Pike scholar 1975-76, Book awards, highest grades: contracts, property, best brief, best overall First Year Moot Ct. 1974-75; mem: ABA (corp., banking and bus. law, internat. law sects.), Calif. St. Bar Assn. (exec. com., past chr. bus. law sect., internat. law sects.), L.A. Co. Bar Assn. (state bar del. 1984-5, 85-6, fin. instns., internat. coms.), Financial Lawyers Conf., Barristers Law Assn. (large firm mgmt. com.), The Law Assn. for Asia and the Pacific, Women Lawyers' Assn. of L.A., Inst. for Corporate Counsel (advy. bd. 1985); Democrat; Latter Day Saint; rec: travel. Res: 344 S Hill Ave Pasadena 91106 Ofc: Pillsbury Madison & Sutro 725 S Figueroa St Ste 1200 Los Angeles 90017

QUINN, TOM, communications media executive; b. Mar. 14, 1944, Los Angeles; s. Joseph M. and Grace (Cooper) Q.; m. Amy Lynn, Nov. 25, 1982; children: Douglas b. 1967, Lori b. 1969, Shelby b. 1991; edn: BS, Northwestern Univ. 1965. Career: reporter City News Bureau of Chicago, 1964; reporter WLS Radio, Chgo. 1965; reporter, newswriter ABC Radio, Los Angeles 1965; reporter KXTV Ch. 10, Sacramento 1966; city editor City News Service of Los Angeles, 1966-68; pres. Radio News West, L.A. 1968-70; campaign mgr. Jerry Brown for Secty. of State, L.A. 1970; dep. Secty. of State Calif., Sacto. 1971-74; campaign mgr. Jerry Brown for Gov., 1974; chmn. Calif. Air Resources Board and Secty. of Environmental Quality, State of Calif., Sacto. 1974-79; mem. Calif. Governor's Cabinet, 1975-79; chmn./pres. City News Service, L.A. 1980-85; pres. Americom, L.A. 1985–; pres. KODS-FM, Reno, Nev. 1982–, pres. sta. KFBI, Las Vegas 1989–, pres. KFSO Radio, Fresno 1985–, pres. December Group, L.A. 1981–; Democrat (chmn. Mayor Tom Bradley Reelection Campaign 1985); rec: skiing. Ofc: Americom, 6255 Sunset Blvd Ste 1901 Los Angeles 90028

RABINOWITZ, MARIO, physicist; b. Oct. 24, 1936, Mexico City, Mex.; U.S. citizen by parentage; s. Laib and Rachel (Loschak) R.; m. Laverne Marcotte; children: Daniel, Benjamin, Lisa; edn: BS in physics, Univ. Wash., Seattle, 1959, MS physics, 1960; PhD physics, Wash. St. Univ., Pullman 1963. Career: res. engr. Boeing Co., Seattle 1958-61; res. asst. Wash. St. Univ., Pullman 1961-63; sr. physicist Westinghouse Res. Ctr., Pittsburg, Pa. 1963-66; mgr. gas discharges and vacuum physics Varian Assocs., Palo Alto, Calif. 1966-67; res. physicist Stanford Linear Accel. Ctr., 1967-74; sr. scientist and mgr. Electric Power Res. Inst., Palo Alto 1974–; adj. prof. Case Western Reserve Univ. 1975-77, Boston Univ. 1975-77, Ga. Inst. Tech., Atlanta 1987–, Virginia Commonwealth Univ., Richmond 1990–, Univ. Houston, Tx. 1990–; mem. editl. bd. IEEE Transactions on Applied Superconductivity; awards: del. and counselor Boys State, Am. Legion 1953-55, Vancouver (Wa.) High Sch. Boy of the Yr. 1954, George F. Baker Scholar, Baker Found. 1955-58, Boeing Co. Grad.

Study Pgm. 1958-60, Wash. St. Univ. Alumni Achiev. Award, Pullman, Wa. 1992, EPRI Discovery Award, Palo Alto 1993; inventor 33 U.S. patents, plus many fgn., 1968–, author 131 sci. papers, 1962–, 6 ency. articles incl. 3 feature articles, 1981, 82, 86, 87, 89, 92; rec: philosophy, mathematics. Res: 715 Lakemead Way Redwood City 94062

RABOVSKY, JEAN, staff toxicologist; b. Aug. 18, 1937, Baltimore, Md.; edn: BS, Univ. of Maryland, College Park, Md., 1959; PhD, Brandeis Univ., 1964. Career: research chemist, NIOSH, Morgantown, W. Va., 1978-89; staff toxicologist, State of Calif., Sacto.. Calif., 1989–; mem. Sigma Xi, N.Y. Academy of Sciences, Amer. Chemical Society, Amer. Assn. for the Advancement of Science, Am. Public Health Assn.; author of peer-reviewed journal articles on xenobiotic metabolism and occupational and environmental health issues. Ofc: 2151 Berkeley Way, Annex 11, Berkeley 94704

RABOW, JEROME ALAN, lawyer; b. April 2, 1937, Buffalo, N.Y.; s. Milton and Belle (Weintraub) R.; m. Lola Stricker, Aug. 17, 1958; children: Victoria b. 1962, Michael b. 1965, Amy b. 1968; edn: BA, Harvard Coll. 1958; JD, Harvard Law Sch. 1961; admitted St. Bars. N.Y. (1961), Calif. (1963). Career: atty. U.S. Dept. Justice, Wash. D.C. 1961-63; Irell & Manella, Los Angeles 1963-68; DeCastro West & Chodorow Inc. 1968–; legal edn. lectr. USC Tax Inst., Calif. Cont. Edn. Bar, PLI, and other profl. orgns. 1963–, chmn. planning com. USC Probate & Trust Law Inst. 1981-93, instr. paralegal course UCLA 1974-75; mem: Valley Beth Shalom Synagogue (chmn. bd. dirs. 1989-90); author: A Guide to Jewish Mourning & Condolence (1983). Res: 16303 Meadow Ridge Rd Encino 91436 Ofc: DeCastro West & Chodorow Inc. 10960 Wilshire Blvd Ste 1800 Los Angeles 90024

RACHMELER, MARTIN, university research administrator, technology transfer director; b. Nov. 21, 1928, Bklyn.; s. Jack and Sophie (Rosenbloom) R.; m. Betty Karkalis, June 9, 1956; children: Susan b. 1966, Ann b. 1970, Helen b. 1970; edn: AB, Indiana Univ., 1950, PhD, Case Western Reserve, 1960. Career: asst. res. geneticist UC Berkeley, 1961-62; asst. prof., assoc. prof. microbiology Northwestern Univ., Evanston, Ill. 1962-67, 67-89, dir. Res. Svs. Adminstrn. 1977-89; dir. technology transfer UC San Diego, La Jolla, Calif. 1989–; awards: USPHS postdoctoral fellow 1959-61, USPHS career dev. award 1967-72; mem: Nat. Council of Univ. Res. Adminstrs. 1978–, (reg. chair 1988), Sigma Xi 1960–, Am. Soc. for Microbiology 1957–, AAAS 1962–, Licensing Exec. Soc. 1979–, Assn. of Univ. Technology Mgrs. (pres. 1991); author: med. book chapt. 1966, 22+ articles in microbial genetics 1959-77; mil: cpl. US Army Chem. Corps 1952-54; rec: tennis, plays, movies, jogging. Ofc: UCSD, Technology Transfer Office, 0093, La Jolla 92093

RADADIA, VRAJLAL MANJI, chiropractor; b. June 2, 1944, Devkigalol, Gujarat, India; s. Manji Gangdas and Raliat Manji (Ratanpura) R.; m. Bhanuben, Aug. 17, 1980; children: Nilkanth b. 1984; Anil b. 1985; edn: BSc, Saurashtra Univ., India 1968; BS, Los Angeles Coll. of Chiropractic 1979, DC 1979. Career: draftsman Curt G. Joa Inc., Ft. Worth, Fla. 1973-74, Sensor Techonology Inc., Chatsworth 1974-75; draftsman, machinist, Back Industries, Chatsworth 1975-76; machinist Stainless Steel Prods., Burbank 1976-80; chiropractor Wilshire Center Chiropractic Group, Los Angeles 1981–, also Family Chiropractic Healing Ctr., San Gabriel 1983–; Who's Who Worldwide, Oxford's Who's Who, Doctor of the Year 1987; mem: Am., Calif. Chiropractic Assn., San Gabriel Chiro. Soc., San Gabriel C.of C., Lions Club Internat.; rec: painting, photography, reading. Ofc: Family Chiropractic Healing Center, 915-1/2 E Las Tunas Dr San Gabriel 91776

RADCLIFFE, MARK FLOHN, lawyer; b. March 11, 1952, Dayton, Ohio; s. David Laurance and Kathryn Elizabeth (Stoutenbugh) R.; m. Judy Dianne Brinson, April 29, 1989; edn; BS magna cum laude, chemistry, Univ. Mich. 1974; Univ. Sorbonne Paris 1972; JD, Harvard Law Sch. 1981. Career: judicial law clk., San Diego 1981-82; atty., assoc. Brobeck Phleger & Harrison, San Francisco 1982-87; atty. Gray, Cary, Ware & Freidenrich, Palo Alto 1987–; editl. bd. Computer Lawyer, Los Angeles 1988–; bd. dirs. Computer Law Assn.; mem: Bar Assn. S.F. (chmn. computer law sect. 1986-87), Harvard Club S.F.; num. articles pub. in profl. jours., 1987-95; mil: lt. USNR 1974-78; Episcopalian; rec: skiing, rowing, history. Ofc: Gray Cary Ware & Freidenrich 400 Hamilton Ave Palo Alto 94301

RAE, MATTHEW SANDERSON, JR., lawyer; b. Sept. 12, 1922, Pittsburgh, Pa.; s. Matthew S. and Olive (Waite) R.; m. Janet Hettman, May 2, 1953; children: Mary-Anna b. 1959, Margaret Rae Mallory b. 1961, Janet Rae Dupree b. 1962; edn: AB, Duke Univ. 1946, LLB, 1947; postgrad. Stanford Univ. 1951. Career: asst. to dean, Duke Law Sch. 1947-48; admitted to Md. bar 1948, Calif. bar, 1951, Supreme Ct. of US 1967; assoc. Karl F. Steinmann law firm, Baltimore, Md. 1948-49; nat. field rep. Phi Alpha Delta Law Frat. 1949-51; research atty. Calif. Supreme Ct. 1951-52; partner Darling, Hall & Rae and predecessor firms, 1953–; mem. Calif. Commn. on Uniform State Laws 1985–, chmn. drafting com. for rev. Uniform Principal and Income Act of Nat. Conf. of Commrs. on Uniform State laws, 1991–, mem. Probate Law Consulting Group, Calif. Bd. of Legal Specialization 1977-88; active Republican Party: mem. L.A.

Co. Repub. Assembly (v.p. 1959-64), L.A. County Repub. Central Com. (1960-64, 1977-90, exec. com. 1977-90), 29th Senatorial Dist. (chmn. 1977-90), 17th Congl. Dist. (v. chmn. 1960-62), 28th Congl. Dist. (v. chmn. 1962-64), 46th Assem. Dist. (chmn. 1962-64), Repub. State Central Com. of Calif. (1966–, exec. com. 1966-67), Calif. Repub. League (pres. 1966-67), Repub. Associates (pres. 1983-85); mem. Air Force Assn., Aircraft Owners and Pilots Assn., Allied Post Am. Legion (comdr. 1969-70), South Bay Bar Assn., Fellow Am. Coll. of Trust and Estate Counsel, Internat. Acad. Estate and Trust Law (exec. council 1974-78), L.A. Co. Bar Assn. (chmn. probate and trust law com. 1964-66, chmn. Legislation Com. 1980-86, chmn. Program com. 1981-82, bd. trustees 1983-85), L.A. Co. Bar Found. (bd. dirs. 1987-93), recipient Shattuck-Price Award 1990, Am. Bar Assn. (sect. probate, trust, and real prop. law and taxation), Calif. State Bar (bulletin chmn. 1970-72, chmn. Probate Com. 1974-5, exec. com. 1977-83, Legis. chmn. 1978-89, Legis. co-chmn. 1991-92, Estate Planning. Trust and Probate Law Sect.; Conf. of Dels. exec. com. 1987-90), Breakfast Club (pres. 1989-91), Lawyers Club of L.A. (first v.p. 1983), Phi Alpha Delta (supreme justice 1972-74, elected. to Distinguished Service Chpt. 1978), Legion Lex (pres. 1969-71), Chancery Club (treas. 1994–), World Affairs Council, IPA, Rotary Intl., Commonwealth Club, St. Andrews Soc., Town Hall (pres. 1975), L.A. Com. on Fgn. Relations, Lincoln Club, Phi Beta Kappa (v.p. Alpha Assn. So. Calif. 1984-86, 1994–), Omicron Delta Kappa; mil: 2d lt. USAAF, WWII; United Presbyterian; rec: theater, volleyball, swimming. Res: 600 John St Manhattan Beach 90266 Ofc: 777 S Figueroa St 37th Flr Los Angeles 90017

RAE-VENTER, BARBARA, patent lawyer; b. July 17, 1948, Auckland, New Zealand; nat. 1973; d. John Donald and Veronique (Grant) Rae; m. J. Craig Venter, Nov. 7, 1974 (div. 1980); 1 son, Christopher; m. Joseph Elmer Huff, III, Sept. 21, 1981 (div. 1983); m. Edward J. Morton, Aug. 24, 1990; edn: Coll. San Mateo 1969-70; BA, UCSD 1972; PhD, 1976; JD, Univ. Tx. Austin 1985; admitted St. Bars Tx. 1986, Calif. 1987, Patent and Trademark Ofc. 1987. Career: postdoctoral fellow Roswell Park Meml. Inst., Buffalo, N.Y. 1976-77, cancer research scientist II 1977-79; asst. prof. Univ. Tx. Med. Branch, Galveston 1979-83; research asst. Univ. Tx. Law Sch., Austin 1984; law clk. Davis & Davis, Austin 1984-85; assoc. atty. Richards Harris Medlock & Andrews, Dallas 1985-86; Leydig Voit & Mayer, Palo Alto 1986-87; ptnr. Cooley Godward Castro Huddleson & Tatum, Palo Alto 1990-93; ptnr. Fish & Richardson, Menlo Park 1993-94; ptnr. Weil Gotshal & Manges, Menlo Park 1994–; vis. asst. prof. Stanford Univ. 1988-89; vis. lectr. Santa Clara Univ. Sch. of Law 1995–; awards: Am. Cancer Soc. NIH grantee (1978-81, 1983); mem: Am. Bar Assn., Peninsula Intellectual Property Law Assn.; vol. Bar Assn. San Francisco, 1988; author: articles pub. in profl. jours., 1979-83; rec: travel, skiing, hiking. Res: 903 Loma Verde Ave Palo Alto 94303 Ofc: Weil Gotshal & Manges 2882 Sand Hill Rd Menlo Park 94025

RAFEEDIE, EDWARD, federal judge; b. Jan. 6, 1929, Orange, N.J.; s. Fred and Nabeeha (Hishmeh) R.; m. Ruth Ann Horton, Oct. 8, 1961; children: Frederick Alexander b. 1962, Jennifer Ann b. 1964; edn: BS in Law, USC 1957, JD, 1959; admitted Calif. State Bar 1960. Career: private practice law, Santa Monica 1969-69; judge Municipal Ct. Santa Monica 1969-71; judge Superior Ct., Los Angeles 1971-82; judge U.S. District Ct., Los Angeles 1982–; honors: Dr. of Laws, Pepperdine Univ. (1978); past pres. Santa Monica Bay Dist. Bar Assn. (1968). Ofc: U.S. District Court, 312 N Spring St Los Angeles 90012

RAFFETY, MICHAEL EDWARD, newspaper editor; b. Oct. 23, 1946, Berlin, Germany; nat. 1955; s. Charles Alva and Lois Fae (Nordean) R.; m. Cherie Lynn Albusche, Oct. 18, 1980; children: Natasha Jane b. 1981, Michael Wolfgang b. 1985; edn: AA, City Coll. of San Francisco 1972; BA, San Francisco St. Univ. 1977; BA, Calif. State Univ., Sacramento 1990, MA, 1992. Career: photographer Olan Mills Inc., Atlanta, Ga. 1969-70; Daily Democrat, Woodland 1977; news ed. Amador Progress News, Amador Ledger, Jackson 1977-78; city ed. Mountain Democrat, Placerville 1978-86, chief editor 1986–; photog. instr. Cosumnes River Coll. 1980-93, art history instr. 1993–; awards: Nat. Newspaper Assn. 1 first place and 1 second place, 1992-93, Calif. Newspaper Publishers Assn. 9 first place and 7 second place, 1979-94, Soc. Profl. Journalists 2 first place and 1 second place, 1981-83, Calif. St. Fair 1st place, 1985, Western Fairs Assn. 1st place, 1985; mem: Nat. Press Photographer Assn., Am. Soc. Newspaper Eds., Mother Lode Lions Club (v.p. 1987-90, pres. 1990-91); mil: USN 1965-69; Episcopalian; Ofc: Mountain Democrat POB 1088 Placerville 95667

RAINEY, RICHARD K., state assemblyman; b. Dec. 5, 1938, Medford, Ore.; m. Sue McNulty; 7 children; edn: BA, adminstrn. of justice, Calif. St. Univ., Sacramento 1973; MA, public adminstrn., Golden Gate Univ. 1976. Career: police ofcr. City of Compton, Calif. 1962-64; dep. sheriff to sgt., lt. and capt. Contra Costa Co. Sheriff-Coroner's Dept. 1964-78, elected sheriff-coroner 1978, 82, 86, 90; elected to Calif. State Assembly, Nov. 1992; serves on Assembly committees for Local Govt. (chmn.), Public Safety, Utilities and Commerce, Environmental Safety & Toxic Materials; appt. by Gov. George Deukmejian to St. Bd. of Corrections and Bd. of Trustees of the Robert Presley Inst. of Corrections. Res: Walnut Creek Ofc: 1948 Mt. Diablo Blvd Walnut Creek 94596

RAMCHANDANI, RAJ S., engineering educator/consultant; b. June 6, 1941, Hydrabad, Pakistan, naturalized 1974; s. Shamdas B. and Kishni U. (Bharwani) R.; m. Sheila Nagrani, June 3, 1971 (dec.); children: Suneil b. 1976, Nina b. 1978 edn: BS engring., Birla Inst. of Tech., Ranchi, India 1964; MS, Penn. St. Univ., 1966; PhD, Ohio State Univ., 1975; reg. profl. engr. St. of Ohio (1969–). Career: staff engr. N.C.R. Co., Dayton, Ohio 1966-69; research assoc. Ohio State Univ., Columbus 1969-71; asst. prof. electronic engring., Ohio Inst. of Tech., 1971-74; vis. asst. prof. E.E., Univ. of Toledo, Ohio 1974-75; asst. prof. E.E., Owens Tech. Coll., Perrysburg, Ohio 1975-76; prof. E.E., CSU Los Angeles 1976–, dir. CSULA Adopt-A-School pgm. (1986–), chmn. student activities L.A. Metro sect. (1981-82); prin. investigator for elect. power studies for L.A. Dept. Water & Power, and Pacific Gas & Elec., cons. Los Angeles DWP 1981-85, Gen. Dynamics, Pomona 1979-80, Jet Propulsion Lab 1976-78; honors: Tau Beta Pi, Eta Kappa Nu, appreciation cert. Ind. Council of San Gabriel (1986), MPPA Award for 1989 CSULA (1989); mem: IEEE (1966–), Am. Soc. Engineering Educators (1971–), Power Engring. Soc., Antennas and Propagation Soc.; civic: Mid Valley Industry Edn. Council, El Monte (charter 1988), Ind. Edn. Council San Gabriel, Vedanta Soc., Ch. of Self Realization Fellowship Fullerton; publs: tech. papers on transients in elec. power systems and microwave power transmission thru atmosphere (1976–); Republican; Hindu; rec: model R.R., travel, camping, classical music. Ofc: Dept. E.E. Calif. State Univ. L.A., 5151 University Dr Los Angeles 90032

RAMER, BRUCE M., lawyer; b. Aug. 2, 1933, Teaneck, NJ; s. Sidney and Anne (Strassman) R.; m. Ann Greenberg, Feb. 15, 1965; children: Gregg B. b. 1967, Marc K. b. 1969, Neal I. b. 1972; edn: AB, Princeton Univ. 1955; JD, Harvard Law Sch. 1958. Career: assoc. law firm of Morrison, Lloyd and Griggs, Hackensack, NJ 1959-60; partner law firm Gang, Tyre, Ramer & Brown, Inc., Los Angeles, Ca. 1963–; exec. dir. Entertainment Law Inst., bd. of councilors USC Law Center, 1973–; awards: community service Am. Jewish Com. 1987, Bev. Hills Bar Assn. Exec. Dir.'s Award 1988, NCCJ annual brotherhood award 1990; mem. Am. Bar Assn., Calif. Bar Assn., L.A. County Bar Assn., Beverly Hills Bar Assn., Calif. Copyright Conf. (pres. 1973-74), L.A. Copyright Soc. (pres. 1974-75), The Fellows of the Am. Bar Found., Princeton Club (So. Calif. pres. 1975-78); civic bds: United Way (v.chair 1991–, corporate bd. dirs. 1981–, exec. com., chair Coun. of Presidents 1989–, mem. Comm. Issues Coun.), Loyola Marymount Univ. L.A. (trustee 1987–), Am. Jewish Com. (chair nat. bd. trustees, chair Nat. Exec. Council, chair Pacific Rim Inst., mem. nat. bd. govs., nat. v.p AJC 1982-88, pres. L.A. chapt. AJC 1980-83, chair AJC We. Region 1984-86), Jewish Fedn. Council of Gr. L.A. (bd., mem. comm. relations com.), Jewish TV Network (bd.), L.A. Urban League (bd.), Frat. of Friends of L.A. Music Ctr. (v.p.), Calif. Community Found. (v.chmn. bd. govs.); mil: pvt. U.S. Army 1958-59, 2d lt. 1961-62. Res: 10445 Wilshire Blvd, #1004 Los Angeles 90024 Ofc: Gang, Tyre, Ramer & Brown, Inc., 6400 Sunset Blvd Los Angeles 90028

RANDALL, GERALDINE MARGARET, arbitrator, mediator; b. Oct. 27, 1943, Wayne, Mich.; d. Anthony and Nellie Olga (Navickas) Gronos; 1 dau., Laurelyn G. b. 1964; edn: BA math., UC Berkeley 1970; JD, UC Davis 1973; admitted St. Bar Calif. (1973). Career: tech. writer Kaiser Engrs., Oakland 1967-71; atty. Pacific Gas & Electric, San Francisco 1973-74; counsel Kaiser Industries, Oakland 1974-76; assoc. counsel Bank of Am., San Francisco 1976-77; arbitrator, factfinder, atty. pvt. practice, San Anselmo 1977–; commr. Los Angeles City Employee Rels. Bd. 1985-90; honors: Phi Beta Kappa, Univ. Mich. Regents scholar 1961-62, Calif. St. Moot Ct. 1st (1971), Jessup Internat. Moot Ct. 1st (1972), Disting. Service award Labor Mgmt. Disputes, Am. Arbitration Assn. 1991; mem: Nat. Acad. Arbitrators, Calif. St. Bar Assn., Indsl. Rels. Research Assn., Am. Bar Assn.; 2 articles pub. in profl. jours., 1972; rec: writing, skiing, hiking. Ofc: POB 1540 San Anselmo 94979

RANDALL, JAMES GRAFTON, trial lawyer; b. Dec. 2, 1951, Great Lakes, Ill.; s. Cmdr. John A. (USN, ret.) and Barbara Blanche (Coen) R.; m. Valerie Sue, Oct. 18, 1980; children: Wm. Douglas, Michael Coen (twins) b. 1981; edn: AA, Chaffey Jr. Coll. 1972, BS, Univ. N.Y. 1978, J.D., Western St. Coll. of Law 1981; admitted bar: Mont. 1985, Mont. Fed. Dist. Ct. 1986, Calif. 1986, Ct. of Appeals 9th dist. 1987, U.S. Dist. Ct. Cent. dist. Calif. 1987. Career: personal injury trial lawyer, instr. (evidence/labor law) Am. Coll. of Law 1985; author: California Personal Injury Form Book (Bancroft-Whitney, 1987), num. law jour. articles; contbg. editor L.A. Trial Lawyers Assn. "Advocate" mag., 1990; awards: Speaker of year Chaffey Jr. Coll. 1972, So. Calif. Coll. Debate Champion 1973, Am. Jurisprudence Awards in crim. law 1978 and constnl. law 1979; mem: ABA, Calif. Bar Assn., Los Angeles Trial Lawyers Assn., Calif. Trial Lawyers Assn., Am. Trial Lawyers Assn. (speaker Melvin Belli Seminar, ATLA Conv. 1991, 1992), San Diego Trial Lawyers Assn. (Tort editor S.D. Trial Bar News); mil: sp4c AUS (1969-71, 1973-76, Vietnam Svc., Vietnam Campaign, Vietnam Cross of Gal. w/palm); rec: writing, local politics Res: Anaheim Hills.

RANDHAWA, AJIT SINGH, veterinarian; b. Apr. 8, 1942, Dhunda, Punjab, India, nat. 1980; s. Bhagwan Singh and Ishar Kaur (Sidhu) R.; m. Surinder, Feb. 13, 1967; children: Neena b. 1967, Ruvdeep b. 1974, Inderpal b. 1976; edn: F.Sc., D.A.V. Coll., Jullundur City, Punjab 1962; DVM, Coll. Vet. Med. & Sci., Hissar, Punjab 1966; MSc, 1969, and MPH, 1971, Loma Linda Univ. Sch.

Health. Career: postdoctoral fellow Johns Hopkins Univ., Sch. of Public Health, 1973-75; virologist Univ. Texas Sch. of Med., Galveston 1975-77; virologist Ohio Dept. Agric. Div. Animal, Columbus, O. 1977-78; small animal practitioner Banning Vet. Hosp., and AAA Vet. Hosp., Van Nuys, 1978-79; owner/dir. Abbey Animal Hosp. Inc., Beaumont 1979–, and Abbott Animal Hosp., Hemet 1987–, both certified AAHA hosps.; adj. faculty Coll. Vet. Med. & Sci. PAU, Hissar, 1966-69; res. assoc. LLU Sch. of Med., Loma Linda 1970-73; awards: merit scholar, silver medal Coll. Vet. Med. & Sci. PAU 1965-66, McLaughlin Found. Postdoc. Fellow 1975-77, listed Who's Who in World Vet. Sci. & Med., 1st ed. 1987-88; mem: Am. Animal Hosp. Assn. (dir., mem. 1982–), Am. Vet. Med. Assn. 1977–, Calif. Acad. of Vet. Med. 1976–; publs: 12 research articles, 1969-75; Democrat; Sikh; rec: reading, gardening. Res: 754 E 3d St Beaumont 92223 Ofc: Abbey Animal Hospital 764 E 3rd St Beaumont 92223-2712

RANKIN, HELEN CROSS, cattle ranch/guest ranch owner; b. Kern County, d. John Whisman and Cleo Rebecca (Tilley) Cross; m. Leroy Rankin (dec. 1954), Jan. 4, 1936; children: Julia (Sharr) b. 1939, Patricia (Denvir) b. 1940, William John b. 1945; edn: AB, CSU Fresno 1935. Career: owner/opr. Leroy Rankin Cattle Ranch (founded 1863 by Walker Rankin Sr.) with husband 1936-1954, 1954–, founder, pres. and gen. mgr. Rankin Ranch, Inc., guest ranch with internat. clientele, 1965–; frequent lectr. various groups on Calif. and Rankin family history; mem. US Bur. of Land Mgmt., Sect. 15; honors: mem. US Food and Agri. Leaders Tour China 1983, Tour Australia and N.Z. 1985, Calif. Hist. Soc. award 1983, Kern River Valley Hist. Soc. award 1983, named Kern County Cattlewoman of the Year 1987; mem: Nat. Cattlemens Assn./Kern Co. chpt., Am. Nat. Cowbelles Assn. (pres. Kern Co. Cowbelles 1949); civic: Camp Ronald McDonald for Children (advy. bd.), Childrens Home Soc. of Calif. (pres. Central Sect. 1945), Lori Brock Jr. Mus. (patron), Calif. Hist. Assn., Kern River Valley Hist. Assn.; publs: advt. for Rankin Ranch Inc., hist. research on Calif. and Rankin Family hist.; Republican; Baptist; rec: painting, gardening. Address: Rankin Ranch Box 36 Caliente 93518

RANKINE, BAXTER JAMES, aerospace manufacturing company executive; b. June 30, 1936, Moncks Corner, So. Caro.; s. Baxter Grey and Mary DeLellis (Bradley) R.; m. Joyce Marie Lemery, July 24, 1965; children: David b. 1966, Julie b, 1969; edn: BS engring., UCLA 1959; reg. profl. indsl. engr. Calif. Career: v.p. mktg. Paco Pumps, Oakland 1969-75; dir. of corp. devel. Mark Controls Corp., Skokie, Ill. 1975-77; pres. Center Line, Tulsa, Okla. 1977-78; Pacific Valves, Long Beach 1978-87; Kool Mist Co., Santa Fe Springs 1987–; pres., CEO All Power Mfg. Co. 1987–; material control mgr. Collins Radio Co., Newport Beach 1965-67; indsl. engr. Gen. Electric Co., Schenectady, N.Y. 1960-65; dir. All Power Mfg. Co., Santa Fe Springs 1987–; mem: The Business Network (dir.); mil: lt. comdr. USCGR 1959-67; Republican; R.Cath. Res: 30330 Cartier Dr Rancho Palos Verdes 90274 Ofc: All Power Manufacturing Co. 13141 Molette St Santa Fe Springs 90670

RANNEY, HELEN MARGARET, physician/educator; b. Apr. 12, 1920, Summer Hill, N.Y.; d. Arthur Clark and Alesia Cecilia (Toolan) Ranney; edn: AB (Cum Laude), Barnard Coll., Columbia Univ., 1941; MD, Coll. of Physicians and Surgeons, Columbia Univ., 1947. Career: technician Babies Hosp., New York, 1941-43; med. intern Presbyterian Hosp., 1947-48, asst. med. resident, 1948-50; clin. fellow in medicine Am. Cancer Soc., Dept. Med., Coll. Physicians and Surgeons, Columbia Univ., 1951-53; instr. in medicine 1954-45, assoc. 1956-58, asst. prof. clin. med. 1958-60, Columbia Univ.; assoc. prof. 1960-65, prof. med. Albert Einstein Coll. of Med., New York, 1965-70; prof. med. S.U.N.Y. at Buffalo, 1970-73; prof. med. Dept. Med., UC San Diego, 1973-90, dept. chair 1973-86, prof. emeritus of med. 1990–; distinguished physician Dept. Veterans Affairs, VAMC San Diego, 1986-91; dir: Squibb Corp. 1978-89, Alliance Pharmaceutical Corp., San Diego 1991–; trustee Population Council 1976-88; bd. sci. cons. Memorial Sloan-Kettering Cancer Ctr. 1986-88; awards: Phi Beta Kappa, Alpha Omega Alpha, Sigma Xi (Faculty), Joseph Mather Smith Prize, Columbia Univ. 1955, Dr. M.L.King, Jr. Med. Achiev. Award for outstanding contbn. in field of sickle cell anemia 1972, Gold Medal, Coll. Physicians and Surgeons Alumni Assn. Columbia Univ. 1978, Disting. Alumni Award Barnard Coll. 1980, Mayo H. Soley Award for excellence in res. We. Soc. for Clin. Investigation 1987; mem: Nat. Acad. of Sci. (1973–,council 1977-80, chair Sect. 41 1986-89, class IV sec. 1989-92), Inst. of Med. NAS (1973–, council 1980-83), Assn. of Am. Physicians (1968–, council 1978-85, pres. 1984-85), Am. Coll. Physicians (1968–, Master 1980), Am. Acad. of Arts and Scis. (1975–, Fellow), AAAS (Fellow 1979), We. Assn. of Physicians (1974–, pres. 1976-77), Am. Physiol. Soc. 1973–, Am. Soc. Biol. Chemists, Am. Soc. for Clin. Investigation, Am. Soc. Hematology (pres. 1973-74), Am. Soc. Biochemistry and Molecular Biology 1972–, Central Soc. for Clin. Res.; author: 2 books, 100+ scientific articles. Res: 6229 La Jolla Mesa Dr La Jolla 92037 Ofc: Alliance Pharmaceutical Corp 3040 Science Park Rd San Diego 92121

RASMUSSEN, MIKE JOSEPH, community college financial aid officer; b. Aug. 1, 1947, Avalon, Calif.; s. Herman Joseph and Nina (Walker) R.; m. Phyllis Ann Freedman, Aug. 4, 1968 (div.); children: Dawn Michelle b. 1970, Stephen Michael b. 1973; edn: AA in liberal arts, 1967, bilingual studies, 1980, bus. edn., 1983, BA soc. sci., 1969, MA edn., 1976; stu. West Valley Coll. 1965-67, San Jose State Coll. 1967-69, CSU San Jose 1974-77, Butte Coll. 1977-83; Calif. Comm. Coll. life credentials: counseling 1976, basic pupil personnel svs. 1977, supr. 1980, instr. psych., personnel wkr., and chief adminstrv. ofcr., 1982. Career: Veterans Pgms. coord./counselor Butte Community Coll. Dist., 1977-80, interim dir. fin. aid 1980-81, dir. financial aid and veterans affairs, 1981-92, dir. special pgms. & svs. 1992–; appt. Butte Coll. EOP/S Advy. Com. 1983–, Chancellor's Fin. Aid advy. group 1985-87, 88-91, VA reg. office advy. bd. 1978-79; bd. dirs. Chico Comm. Hosp. Found. 1985–; awards: appreciation Community Companions Inc. (1976, 77), Butte-Glenn Co. Vet. Employment Com. 1979, BSA Troop 770 (1985), Paradise Pride Lioness Club 1986, Butte Coll. EOP/S (1986, 87), pub. service award Calif. Health & Welfare Agy. 1980; mem: Calif. Comm. Coll. Student Fin. Aid Adminstrs. Assn. (1980–, pres. 1989-90, chair Fed. Issues com. 1991-92, state awards: 3 for outstanding service, 7+ appreciation), Calif. Assn. SFAA, Western Assn. SFAA, Nat. Assn. SFAA, Vet. Pgm. Adminstrs. of Calif.; mil: p.o. 2c USN 1970-74, Merit. Unit Cit., Vietnam Svc. Medal, Vietnam Cpgn. Medal, Combat Action Rib.; rec: motorcycling, sports cars, golf, fishing, bicycling. Ofc: Butte College Financial Aid Office, 3536 Butte Campus Dr Oroville 95965

RATALAHTI, HEIKKI, graphics designer; b. June 28, 1937, Kauhajoki, Finland; nat. 1974; s. Eino and Sanni R.; edn: Univ. of Helsinki, Finland, 1962-63; Acad. of Art Coll., S.F., Calif., 1969-70. Career: exec. trainee, Doubleday & Co., NY (US State Dept. student exchange program) 1960-62; operated family-owned book bus. in Finland 1963-67; design staff, Am. Conservatory Theater, S.F. 1967-69; graphics designer, Nagase Advt., S.F. 1970-71; co-founder, v.p., design dir., Jayme, Ratalahti, Inc., Sonoma, Calif. 1971–; mem. guest faculty, Stanford Univ. and Radcliffe Coll. pub. courses; designed graphics for Japan Ctr. complex, S.F. 1970-71; designed promotion materials that launched Smithsonian, Bon Appetit, Air & Space, Food & Wine, Mother Jones, Cooking Light, Worth, Paris Hebdo (France), and other publs. 1971–; awards: numerous profl. awards from art directors' clubs, Folio Magazine, Direct Mktg. Assn.; profiled, NY Times Sunday Magazine, Aug., 1990; mil: 2nd lt., Signal Corps, Finnish Army, 1958-59. Ofc: Jayme, Ratalahti, Inc. 1033 Bart Road Sonoma 95476

RATEAVER, BARGYLA, organic/conservation gardening and farming educator, publisher, writer, international consultant; b. Aug. 13, 1916, Ft. Dauphin, Madagascar; came to U.S. 1935; d. Eugene Alaric and Margaret (Schaffnit) Rateaver; children: Gylver; edn: grad. (Valedictorian) American Sch., Ft. Dauphin, 1934; San Francisco Jr. Coll. 1936-37; AB, botany, UC Berkeley 1943; PhD., botany, Univ. of Mich. 1951; MSLS, lib. sci., UC Berkeley, 1959; Calif. std. jr. coll. Adult Edn. credential, 1966, Eminence cred. for elem. and sec. schs., 1969; Calif. R.E. lic., 1968. Career: plant collecting in Madagascar, 1930-34; plant intro. for USDA, UCB Genetics Dept., 1935; plant collection in U.S. for European collections, 1936; herbarium and bot. dept. res. asst. UC Berkeley, 1938-43; organized herbarium Palm Springs Desert Mus., 1944; res. asst. bot. dept. Univ. Mich. 1945-51; bot. res. UCD, 1951-52, UCLA Hort. Dept. 1953-54, San Diego County, 1954-55; organized biology library, Kaiser Labs., 1958-59; org. sci. libraries in Calif., histology lab. Univ. Alberta, Calgary, 1959-64; lectr. on organic gardening, radio and TV, 1965-67; re-org. sci. collection Santa Rosa City-Co. Library, 1968-69; lectr. on organic gardening radio, TV, univs., demonstrations and expo. booths, pvt. classes, author/pub. books in field, columnist nat. mags., 1968–, promote internat. liaison and maintain internat. corr. service in field, 1972–; initiated and intro. into U.S. ednl. system the first course in organic gardening and farming, intro. first coll. and univ. level course (TM) "Conservation Gardening and Farming" at: San Jose Sch. Sys., 1965, Coll. of Marin, 1966, UC San Diego Ext., Marin County Adult Edn., and private classes San Francisco, 1968; instr. courses Univ. Calif. Extension, Calif. State Univ., jr. colls., campuses statewide, 1970-77, garden plots UC Berkeley, UC Irvine, Santa Rosa Jr. Coll., and Palomar Jr. Coll., 1970, CSU Sacto. (asst. prof.), 1972; lectr., cons. in field; awards: pres.'s scholar DePauw Univ. 1935, award for plant introduction of 1935 for USDA and Joel Spingarn Clematis Collection 1935, honors stu. UCB 1938, 1st prize Della Sizler Graphic Arts Collection, UCB, for collection "Preparation for bot. res. in Madagascar" 1959; grantee Longwood Gardens 1955, award Chgo. Mus. Natural Hist. 1955, Am. Acad. Arts and Scis. 1955, 1st Steward of Sustainable Agri. award CSA 1988, cited Honor Roll, Giraffe Project Gazette 1991; mem. Internat. Fedn. of Organic Agriculture Movements (IFOAM) 1978-: editl. bd. 1988, coord. com. 1978-82, and mem. working Groups: Information, Edn.; exh. of Organic Method Primer in IARC Book Exh., Beijing 1982, multiple exhibits Del Mar Fair, Del Mar, Ca. 1984, 91, lectr. World Food Expo, L.A. 1986, exhibits: IFOAM Internat. Conf., Santa Cruz 1988, Burkina Faso 1989, Eco Farm Conf., Asilomar, Monterey 1989-94 (lectr. 1988, 1990-94); author: Organic Method Primer, 1973, condensation of: Bio Dynamic Farming and Gardening by E.E. Pfeiffer, M.D., 1973, Organic Method Primer UPDATE, 1993; author/cons.: Earthworms 1993, Lawn Care, 1993; author/pub. Organic Method Primer: The Basics, 1994; video for Bali, 1991; book reviews, Ecology & Farming, IFOAM, 1992-93; monthly columns in Clear Creek, 1972, Let's Live, 1972–, Mother Earth News, 1972, Acres USA, 1973–, bimonthly column: Natural Life Styles, 1972-73, Health Quarterly, 1977, Calif. Organic Jour., 1977–, articles: Natural Life, Harrowsmith, Natural Gardening, Health Food Age, Answer mag., Soil & Health (New Zealand), Acres USA, Calif. Grower, others;

weekly bdcast. TV, Ch. 6, Healdsburg, 1969, guest num. talk shows and interviews San Francisco, Los Angeles, San Diego, 1970–, talk show by teleconf. 1991; Bible student. Res/Ofc: 9049 Covina St San Diego 92126

RATLIFF, WILLIAM ELMORE, historian, academic senior research fellow and curator, journalist, arts critic; b. Feb. 11, 1937, Evanston, Ill.; s. Harold Shugart and Marjorie (Elmore) R.; m. Lynn Robbins, June 9, 1959; children: Sharon, Paul, Susan, David, John; edn: BA in English, Oberlin Coll., 1959; MA Chinese history, Univ. Washington, Seattle 1968, PhD Latin Am./Chinese history, 1974. Career: res. fellow Hoover Instn., Stanford Univ., 1968-79, sr. res. fellow, 1986–; chief editorial writer, arts critic Times Tribune, Palo Alto 1979-86; cons. risk analysis Res. Internat., San Francisco 1972-79, indep. cons., 1979–; writer on classical music, music stringer Opera News, 1975-93, Los Angeles Times, 1975–; instr. courses, seminars Stanford Univ., UC Berkeley, 1983-86, San Francisco St. Univ., Univ. of S.F., Univ. Wash., Monterey Naval Postgrad. Sch., Austrian Defense Acad. (Vienna), and Inst. of Internat. Relations (E.Berlin); lectr. for Am. Bar Assn., Amnesty Internat., Wash. Ctr. Strategic and Internat. Studies, US Nat. Def. Univ., U.S. DoD, U.S. Mil. Acad. (West Point), U.S. Air War Coll., other agys.; US Govt. cons. and journalist (50 trips to 45 Asian, Latin Am. & European countries), USIA lecture tours in We. and Ea. Europe and Canada; splst. in politics of Latin Am. and Caribbean and US reg. policy, monitored elections El Salvador, Costa Rica and Chile, talked with Latin Am. presidents incl. Fidel Castro; awards: Oberlin Shansi Memorial 1959-62, Nat. Def. Edn. Act 1963-68, Hoover Instn. Nat. fellow 1971-72; author: Castroism and Communism in Latin America, 1976, author/editor: The Selling of Fidel Castro: The Media and the Cuban Revolution, 1987; editor: Inside the Cuban Interior Ministry, 1994; co-editor (w. S. Amaral) Juan Peron: Cartas del exilio, 1991, coauthor (w. R. Fontaine) Changing Course: The Capitalist Revolution in Argentina, 1990, (w. Roger Miranda) Civil War in Nicaragua: Inside the Sandinistas, 1993, (w. R. Fontaine) Argentina's Capitalist Revolution Revisited, 1993; Latin Am. area ed. of Hoover Instn.'s Yearbook on Internat. Communist Affairs, 24 yrs.; num. articles and revs. in scholarly jours., book anthologies, mags.; rec: classical music, hiking. Ofc: Hoover Institution, Stanford CA 94305

RATNESAR, RAJENDRA MANOHARAN, physician; b. Mar. 7, 1937, Mannar, Sri Lanka; nat. 1985; s. William Charles and Grace (Anketell) R.; m. Queelan, Apr. 17, 1971; children: Neethi b. 1973, Romesh b. 1975, Meera b. 1979; edn: MD, Univ. of Ceylon, Sri Lanka 1967. Career: resident City of London Hosp., London, England 1969-71; intern General Hosp., Perthamboy, NY 1971-72; resident Univ. of Rochester, NY 1972-74; ob-gyn Wilson Health Ctr., Rochester, NY 1974-79; ob-gyn Kaiser Med. Group, Hayward, Calif. 1980-81; pvt. practice ob-gyn, Castro Valley 1981–; clin. asst. prof. of ob-gyn Univ. of Rochester 1974-79, Stanford Univ. 1981–, UC San Francisco 1981–; bd. dirs. Hill Physicians, San Ramon 1991-94; mem: Am. Coll. of Ob-Gyn (fellow 1976–), Am. Fertility Soc. (fellow 1980–), AMA 1981–; organizer and vol. physician, free Prenatal Clinic 1989–; Republican; Methodist. Res: 26851 Greenhaven Rd Hayward 94542 Ofc: 19845 Lake Chabot Rd Castro Valley 94546

RAUCHWERGER, GEORGE PAUL, electronics research & development engineer, instruments company president; b. July 27, 1938, Zilina, Czechoslovakia; nat. 1959; s. Ernest and Augusta (Futterweit) R.; m. Diane Levin, July 30, 1961; children: Lisa Renee, Michael Allan; edn: BS/BA electronics engring. Career: project engr. Edex Corp., Mountain View 1966-67; elec. engr. Fairchild Instrument, Sunnyvale 1967-68; quality engr. Fairchild Semiconductor, Mountain View 1968; project engr. Nytron Inc., Palo Alto 1968-69; Internat. Contronics, Sunnyvale 1969-70; pres. Expo Instruments Inc. 1970–; recipient C.E. Knott award IEEE, San Luis Obispo 1964; inventor, 11 patents: automatic sprinkler control, 1965, capacitive moisture control system having a peak detector, 1971, 73, capacitance probe & system for precision measurement of liquid level, 1973, 75, 76, suction type de-soldering tool, 1982, high speed desoldering tool, 1980, 86, hydrocarbon detector system, 1987, liquid beverage dispenser, 1986; mil: pfc AUS 1956-64; rec: photog. Ofc: 989 E California St Ste 4 Sunnyvale 94086

RAVELO, HUMBERTO ROGELIO, cardiovascular-thoracic surgeon; b. Sept. 16, 1947, Santiago, Cuba, nat. 1971; s. Humberto C., M.D., and Gloria E. (Sanchez) R.; m. Kathryn Walsh, Aug. 4, 1973; edn: BS, Marquette Univ., 1968; MD, Med. Coll. of Wisc. (fmr. Marquette Univ. Sch. of Med.) 1972. Career: intern Univ. of Alabama Hosps. and Clinics, Birmingham 1972-73, gen. surgery resident 1973-78; cardiothoracic fellow Hosp. of Univ. of Penn., Phila. 1978-80; pvt. practice Memorial Medical Ctr. of Long Beach, Calif. 1980–, chmn. dept. surg.1994–, chief cardiovascular and thoracic surg. div. 1989-90; asst. clin. prof. surg. UC Irvine 1984–; vice chief cardiovascular and thoracic surg. div. St. Francis Med. Ctr., Lynwood 1986-87, 87-88, chief 1989-90; honors: Who's Who Students in Am. Univs. and Colls., Phi Sigma nat. biological hon. soc. (pres. 1967), Alpha Sigma Nu nat. scholastic Jesuit hon. soc. 1967; mem: John Webster Kirklin Soc., A.C.S. (fellow), Am. Coll. Chest Phys. (fellow), Am. Coll. Cardiology (fellow), Soc. of Thoracic Surgeons, Phi Delta Epsilon Soc., Long Beach Surgical Soc.; numerous lectures, pub. med. jour. articles and abstracts; Republican; Cath.; rec: tennis, music, travel. Ofc: 2880 Atlantic Ave Ste 160 Long Beach 90806

RAVEN, BERTRAM H(ERBERT), psychology educator; b. Sept. 26, 1926, Youngstown, Ohio; s. Morris and Lillian (Greenfeld) R.; m. Celia Cutler, Jan. 21, 1961; children: Michelle G., Jonathan H.; edn: BA, Ohio State Univ., 1948, MA, 1949; PhD, Univ. Mich., 1953. Career: res. assoc. Res. Ctr. for Group Dynamics, Ann Arbor, Mich. 1952-54; lectr. psychology Univ. Mich., 1953-54; vis. prof. Univ. Nijmegen, Univ. Utrecht, Netherlands, 1954-55; psychologist RAND Corp., Santa Monica, Calif. 1955-56; prof. and chmn. dept. psychology UCLA 1956–, co-dir. Tng. Pgm. in Health Psychology, UCLA, 1979-88; vis. prof. Hebrew Univ., Jerusalem 1962-63, Univ. Wash., Seattle, Univ. Hawaii, Honolulu, 1968, London Sch. of Economics and Polit. Sci., England, 1969-70; external examiner Univ. of the West Indies, Trinidad and Jamaica, 1980–; participant Internat. Expert Conf. on Health Psychology, Tilburg, Netherlands, 1986; cons. in field, expert witness Calif. cts., 1978–, cons. World Health Orgn., Manila 1985-86; author: (with others) People in Groups, 1976, Discovering Psychology, 1977, Social Psychology, 1983, Social Psychology in Chinese, 1994; editor: (with others) Contemporary Health Services, 1982, Policy Studies Rev. Annual, 1980; contbr. articles to profl. jours., editor J. of Social Issues, 1969-74; awards: Guggenheim fellow, Israel 1962-63, Fulbright scholar, Britain 1969-70, Netherlands 1954-55, Israel 1962-63, citation L.A. City Council 1966, NATO sr. fellow, Italy 1989, citation for res. on social power Calif. Sch. Profl. Psychology, L.A. 1991; mem: Am. Psychol. Assn. (Fellow, chair bd. social and ethical responsibility 1978-82), Soc. for Psychol. Study of Social Issues (Fellow, pres. 1973-74), B.H.R. Council 1994-97), AAAS, Am. Sociol. Assn., Internat. Assn. Applied Psychology, Soc. Experimental Social Psychology, Assn. Advance. of Psychology (founding, bd. 1974-81), Am. Psychol. Soc. (fellow), Internat. Soc. Polit. Psychology, Interam. Psychol. Soc., Am. Psychology/Law Soc.; rec: guitar, travel, internat. studies. Res: 2212 Camden Ave Los Angeles 90064-1906 Ofc: UCLA Dept. Psychology Los Angeles 90095-1563 Ph: 310/825-2296

RAYNER, ARNO ALFRED, investment executive; b. Sept. 23, 1928, San Francisco; s. Kurt Hugo and Angela (Flasch) R.; m. Carol Jean Kaufman Aug. 27, 1994; children (prev. m.): Eric b. 1957, Jill b. 1959, Neal b. 1967; edn: BS, UC Berkeley, 1950, MBA, 1954; Chartered Fin. Analyst (C.F.A.) 1967. Career: investment analyst Bank of California, San Francisco 1950-54; sr. v.p. Industrial Indemnity, 1954-74; v.p. Bechtel Corp., 1975-76; pres. Rayner Associates, Mill Valley 1977–; vis. lectr. UC Berkeley, Santa Clara Univ.; mem. bd. dirs. num. corps., and non-profit orgs.; clubs: Bohemian 1979–, World Trade 1962–, San Francisco Bond (1957–, dir.), Tiburon Peninsula (1954–, past pres.), Harbor Pt. Tennis 1991–, S.F.Kiwanis (v.p., dir.), Am. Philatelic Soc. 1988; mil: chief cashier Army. Res: 7 Venado Dr Tiburon 94920 Ofc: Rayner Associates, Inc. 655 Redwood Hwy Ste 370 Mill Valley 94941

REAGAN, JOSEPH BERNARD, aerospace executive; b. Nov. 26, 1934, Somerville, Mass.; s. Joseph Bernard, Sr. and Helen (Lowry) R.; m. Dorothy Marie Hughes, March 2, 1957; children: Patrick b. 1958, Michael b. 1959, Kevin b. 1961, Kathleen b. 1962, Brian b. 1964, John b. 1968, Maureen b. 1975; edn: BS, Boston Coll. 1956. MS, 1959; PhD space scis., Stanford Univ. 1975. Career: tchr. and res. asst. Boston Coll. 1956-58; scientist Lockheed Missile & Space Co. 1959–: sr. scientist 1961-63, res. scientist 1963-68, staff scientist 1968-74, program mgr. space payloads 1974, mgr. Space Scis. Lab. 1975-84, dir. Electronic Scis. Lab. 1984, dir. Physical & Electronic Sci. Lab. 1985-86, Lockheed Res. & Devel. Div. dep. gen. mgr. 1986-88, v.p./asst. gen. mgr. 1988-91, v.p./gen. mgr. 1991–; dir: Southwall Tech. Inc. 1987-92, 1993–, Planning Systems Inc. 1989-91; dir. Technology Ctr. of San Jose 1993–; adv. council Schs. of Engring. at Stanford Univ. and UC Berkeley; awards: Disting. service Pioneer Venus Pgm. NASA, AIAA/ S.F. Chpt. Outstanding Engr. 1988; Fellow AIAA 1990, mem. Am. Geophysical Union, Sigma Pi Sigma, IEEE; patent: Transistorized Amplifier, 1963; publs: 130+ papers in tech. jours.; invited lectr. 12 nat. & internat. tech. soc. meetings; mil: capt. AUS 1956-63; Republican; R.Cath.; rec: computers, woodworking. Res: 13554 Mandarin Way Saratoga 95070 Ofc: Lockheed Martin R&DD (0/90-01 B/201) 3251 Hanover St Palo Alto 94304

REAGAN, NANCY, First Lady during 40th U.S. Presidency; b. July 9, 1923, NYC, raised in Chgo.; d. Dr. Loyal and Edith (Luckett) Davis; father, prof. surgery emeritus, Northwestern Univ. (dec. 1981); bro. Dr. Richard Davis, neurosurgeon, Phila.; m. Ronald Reagan, March 4, 1952; children: Patricia Ann, b. 1952, Ronald Prescott, b. 1958; Pres. Reagan's children by 1st marriage: Maureen, b. 1941, Michael, b. 1946; two grandchildren; edn: grad. Girls' Latin Sch., Chgo.; drama major Smith Coll., 1943. Career: actress, stage (road tours to Broadway and Radio City Music Hall), film (11 films include: The Next Voice You Hear; East Side, West Side; Hellcats of the Navy), TV prodns., 1949-56; First Lady of Calif., 1966-74; First Lady of U.S., 1980-88; ldr. Foster Grandparent Program, 1967–, coauthor (w/Jane Wilkie) To Love A Child, with song by same title written and dedicated to her by Hal David and Joe Raposo, recorded by Frank Sinatra (all book and record sales benefit pgm.); activist for POWs and MIAs, hon. sponsor Vietnam Vets Mem. Fund; spl. project fighting substance abuse among youth, 1980–, traveled 170,000+ miles vis. rehab. centers and schs., held briefing for 30 First Ladies and internat. drug conf. 1985; hon. chair Nat. Fedn. of Parents for Drug-Free Youth, "Just Say No" Found., Nat. Child Watch Campaign, Pres.'s Com. on the Arts and Humanities, Wolf Trap Found. Bd. Trustees, Nat. Trust for Historic Preservation, Cystic Fibrosis Found., Nat. Republican Women's Club, hon. pres. Girl Scouts of Am.; awards: Hon. DHL, Georgetown Univ. 1987, Hon. LLD, Pepperdine Univ. 1983, num. humanitarian awards U.S. C. of C., USO, Salvation Army, Entertainment Inds. Council, Rotary Clubs Intl., Lions Club Intl., var. drug treatment programs, Am. Camping Assn., Nat. Council on Alcoholism, United Cerebral Palsy, Intl. Ctr. for the Disabled, Boys Town Father Flanagan Award, Kiwanis Intl. World Service Medal 1986, Variety Clubs Intl. lifeline award, Gallup Poll list of 10 most admired women in world (1981–, most admired 81, 85, 87), Good Housekeeping mag. survey of 10 most admired women in world (1981–, ranked number one 1984, 85, 86), LA Times Woman of the Year 1968, Permanent Hall of Fame of Ten Best Dressed Women in Am. Res: Bel Air

REAGAN, RONALD WILSON, 40th President of the United States; b. Feb. 6, 1911, Tampico, Ill.; s. John and Nellie (Wilson) R.; m. Jane Wyman, 1940, div. 1948; children: Maureen, Michael; m. 2d. Nancy Davis, Mar. 4, 1952; children: Patricia, Ronald; edn: BA in econ. and sociol., Eureka Coll. 1932. Career: radio sports broadcaster and editor, 1932-37; film actor, over 50 feature-length motion pictures, 1937-50s; prodn. supr./host General Electric Theatre TV series 1950s, host, Death Valley Days TV series 1964-65; elected Gov. of Calif. 1966-70, re-elected 1970-74; syndicated radio commentary pgm., newspaper column, extensive speaking schedule to civic, bus., polit. groups nat., 1974–; mem. Presidential Commn. investigate the CIA, 1974-75; candidate for Repub. presidential nom. 1976, campaigner for 86 candidates in 1978 elections; elected US President (by electoral vote 489-40), Nov. 4, 1980, sworn in as 40th US President Jan. 20, 1981, elected 2d term 1984-88; founder Citizens for the Republic; past bd. dirs. Com. on the Present Danger; past pres. Screen Actors Guild 6 terms; past pres. Motion Picture Indus. Council 2 terms; awards include Nat. Humanitarian, NCCJ; Torch of Life, City of Hope; Horatio Alger; Am. Newspaper Guild; Freedoms Found. awards; Distinguished Am., Nat. Football Found. Hall of Fame; Am. Patriots Hall of Fame; Medal of Valor, State of Israel; mil: capt. USAAF 1942-45, WWII; Tau Kappa Epsilon. Address: Bel Air

REECE, MONTE MEREDITH, lawyer; b. May 29, 1945, Jackson, Tenn.; s. Jerrel Rexford and Marjorie (Ricks) R.; m. Melanie; children: Hugh b. 1970, Bryan b. 1973, Andrew b. 1974, Jerrel b. 1985, Rebecca b. 1986; edn: Louisiana State Univ. 1963-64, 66; Louisiana Coll. 1964-65; LLB, Western State Univ. Coll. of Law 1974; admitted Calif. State Bar 1974. Career: assoc. atty. English & Marotta APC 1974-78; atty. pvt. practice 1978–; US magistrate US Dist. Ct. Eastern Dist of Calif. 1983–; judge pro tem Lake Valley Jud. Dist. El Dorado Co. 1983-85; comm. coll. instr. 1983-85; mem. Lions Club (bd. 1986–); civic: Sudden Infant Death Syndrome S.Lake Tahoe (bd. 1988–, pres. 89-90), Tahoe Human Svs. (legal advisor 1986–), Eldorado County Sheriff Search and Rescue (legal advisor 1988–), AYSO Reg. 82 (bd. 1982–, commr. 1985); mil: SK2 USNR 1967-72, Navy Achievement medal w. combat V, Navy Unit comendn., Vietnam Svc., Viet. Campaign (3), Nat. Def. medals, Viet. Cross of Gallantry w/palm; Republican; Prot.; rec: antique furniture restoration, photography. Address: 3330 Lake Tahoe Blvd Ste 10 S Lake Tahoe 96150

REED, DALE D., executive; b. July 22, 1931, Veedersburg, Ind.; s. Clyde and Aline (Jones) R.; m. Donna Ellen Bartley, April 16, 1955; children: Katherine b. 1956, Richard b. 1957, Ann b. 1960; edn: BS engring., Purdue Univ. 1953. Career: pres. Blakemore Equipment, Oakland 1962-66; Bay Area Kenworth, San Leandro 1966-84; chmn. and CEO Buran & Reed Inc. 1984–; dir: Civic Bank of Commerce 1984–; pres. Nat. Scale Dealers Assn. 1993–; civic bds.: San Leandro Hosp. (trustee 1993–), Alameda Co. Transp. Authority (mem. Citizen's Advy. Com. 1983–), San Leandro Planning Commn. (chmn. 1990), San Leandro Scholarship Found. (trustee 1986–), Goodwill Industries of E. Bay (dir. 1988–), San Leandro C.of C. (pres. 1985-86); mil: 1st. lt. AUS 1954-56; Republican; Prot. Res: 1560 Daily Ct San Leandro 94577 Ofc: Buran & Reed, Inc. 1801 Adams Ave San Leandro 94577

REED, GERARD ALEXANDER, educator; b. Jan. 19, 1941, Colorado Springs, Colo.; s. Paul Alexander and Lula (Taylor) R.; m. Roberta Kay Steininger, May 26, 1963; edn: BA, So. Nazarene Univ., 1963; MA, Univ. Oklahoma, 1964, PhD, 1967. Career: asst. prof. So. Nazarene Univ., Bethany, Okla. 1966-68; assoc. full prof. MidAmerica Nazarene Coll., Olathe, Kans. 1968-82; prof. Point Loma Nazarene Coll., San Diego 1982–; awards: Parriot Found. fellow, Norman, Okla. 1966, "B" Award So. Nazarene, Bethany, Okla. 1980, merit cit. Gen. Assembly Ch. of Nazarene, K.C., Mo. 1980; mem: Am. Maritain Soc., Conf. Faith and History, Wesleyan Theol. Soc., Western History Assn., Nature Conservancy; publs: 12+ articles; Ch. of the Nazarene; rec: running. Res: 4217 Loma Riviera Ln San Diego 92110 Ofc: Point Loma Nazarene College, 3900 Lomaland San Diego 92106

REED, ROBERT DANIEL, publisher, entrepreneur; b. May 24, 1941, Pottsville, Pa.; s. Robert Daniel and Thelma June (Weiss) R.; children: Robert b. 1966, Alan b. 1968, Tanya b. 1969. Career: buyer Viking Labs, Sunnyvale 1962-69; mktg. mgr. Plaza Press 1969-70; pres. R&E Research Assoc., Palo Alto 1971-85, pres., pub. 1986–; pres., CEO Edgecombe Corp., Saratoga 1986-; pres. The Other Money Inc, Saratoga 1986–; awards: incentive award U.S.

Armyu Intelligence Group 1960, 61, 62; mem: Amnesty Internat., Nat. Geographic Soc., Cent. for Democratic Institutions, Friends of the San Jose Library; author and co-author of 60 books 1976–, pub. 1100+ books in edn., sociology, self-help 1966–, 10 copyrights var. products 1980–, var. electro-mech. inventions in works 1970–; mil: U.S. Army, 1959-62; Republican; rec: idea creation, generalist, oil painter, inventions, gardner. Ofc: Robert D. Reed 750 La Playa Ste 647 San Francisco 94121

REEVE, THOMAS VARNEY, II, college administrator; b. Oct. 28, 1934, Los Angeles, Calif.; s. Thomas Varney and Nellie Maurine (Gruwell) R.; m. Christina Ann Schade, June 5, 1965; children: Thomas, III b. 1966, Jessica b. 1969; edn: BS, social sci./edn., Brigham Young Univ. 1956; MA, history, Calif. St. Univ., Long Beach 1961; attended. Duke Univ. 1965, Univ. of Paris, Sorbonne 1964, Brigham Young Univ. 1967(passed doctoral exams in history/poli. sci.), San Diego St. Univ., CSU Fullerton; Life Gen. Secondary Tchg. Cred., Utah 1956, Calif. 1961. Career: tchr. and dept. chair Ch. Coll. of We. Samoa, Apia, We. Samoa 1956-59; tchr. Santa Ana H.S. 1961-64; adj. instr. Brigham Young Univ. 1964-67; prof. of history Cypress Coll., Cypress, Calif. 1967–, dean of social sci. 1975–; adj. instr. UC Irvine and UCLA 1978-84; dept. chair, history/poli. sci , Cypress Coll. 1969-72, chair Social Sci. Div. 1972–, exec. sec. Local History Soc. 1973-91, lectr. and tour guide 1974–, dir. hist. preservation prog. 1975-85; coord. Hist. Survey of Anaheim Township, Anaheim, Calif. 1978-79; awards: Conf. of Calif. Hist. Socs. Award of Excellence 1969, 71, listed Who's Who in Orange Co. 1980; mem: Am. Hist. Assn. (life), Orgn. of Am. Historians (life), Phi Alpha Theta (pres. 1965-66), Orange Co. Hist. Soc. 1967-83 (bd. dirs. 1970-72, v.p. 1971, pres. 1972), Conf. of Calif. Hist, Societies 1968– (bd. dirs. 1968-77, chmn. young historian prog. 1968-71, regional v.p. 1971-77, state exec. com. 1973), Calif. Hist. Soc. 1972– (trustee 1972-84), San Juan Capistrano Hist. Soc. 1972-82, Buena Park Hist. Soc. 1973-76, Orange Co. Antique Soc. (hon. life mem. 1974), Garden Grove Hist. Soc. 1974-77, Orange Comm. Hist. Soc. (charter mem. 1975-79), San Clemente Hist. Soc. (charter mem. 1975), Villa Park Hist. Soc. (charter mem. 1975-84), Anaheim Genealogical Lib. 1976-79 (bd. chair 1976-79), U.S. Bicentennial Com. 1976, Garden Grove Shakespeare Festival Guild (organizer and pres. 1984–), Orange Co. Centennial Com. 1989, Los Amigos of Orange Co. 1989–; author: book chpt. on Cypress in Orange Co. Centennial, 1989; Republican; Ch. of Jesus Christ of LDS (regional exec. sec. 1981-87, So. Calif. area sec. 1984–); rec: gardening. Ofc: Cypress College 9200 Valley View Cypress 90630

REICH, JULIUS MEL, lawyer; b. May 22, 1933, Bronx, N.Y.; s. Arthur Reich and Margaret Molnar; m. Cynthia Haikin, Aug. 30, 1959; children: Shayne b. 1963, Julie b. 1966, Francine b. 1969; edn: BA, UCLA 1959; JD, 1962. Career: atty. Brundage & Hackler, Los Angeles 1962-75; ptnr. Reich Adell & Crost 1975–; adj. prof. Loyola Sch. Law; San Fernando Valley Coll. Law, Van Nuys; lectr. Calif. Cont. Edn. of Bar, L.A.; mem: L.A. Co. Bar Assn. (labor law sect. chair), Am. Bar Assn.; articles pub. in profl. jours., 1962; mil: USCG 1952-56; Democrat; Jewish. Ofc: Reich Adell & Crost 501 Shatto Place Ste 100 Los Angeles 90020

REICHMAN, RONALD PETER, physician, film and television technical advisor; b. Jan. 18, 1951, Chgo.; s. Heinz Charles and Margot (Rovell) R.; m. Carolyn Elizabeth Kean, May 27, 1984; edn: BA psych. (magna cum laude), UCLA, 1973, MD, 1977; cert. Am. Bd. Int. Medicine 1980, cert. subsplty. Rheumatology 1986. Career: intern internal med. Valley Med. Ctr. of Fresno, 1977-78; jr., sr. resident int. med. Cedars Sinai Med. Ctr., L.A. 1978-80, fellow, sr. fellow rheumatology Cedars Sinai Med. Ctr. and UC Los Angeles Hosps. and Clinics, 1981-83, asst. clin. prof. med. 1983–; pvt. consultant, med. tech. advisor T.V. & Motion Pictures, 1980–; pres. San Vicente Rehabilitation Inc., 1985–; cons. Calif. St. Office of Emergency Svs., 1980–; mem. AMA Physician Advy. Panel to TV, Motion Pictures & Radio, 1980–; guest spkr. Am. Medicine Writers Assn. Conv., 1982; honors: Phi Beta Kappa, Pi Gamma Mu, Phi Eta Signa, Pi Lambda Phi Svc. Soc., Medicus Assn., Phi Delta Epsilon Svc. Soc.; mem: Am. Rheumatism Assn. (founding fellow), A.C.P., So. Calif. Rheumatism Assn., AMA, CMA, L.A. Co. Med. Assn.; contbr. articles in med. jours. Ofc: 8631 West Third St Ste 1001E Los Angeles 90048

REID, JOSEPH LEE, physical oceanographer, professor of physical oceanogra-phy; b. Feb. 7, 1923, Franklin, Tx.; s. Joseph Lee and Ruby (Cranford) R.; m. Freda Mary Hunt, April 7, 1953; children: Ian b. 1954, Julian b. 1956; edn: BA math., Univ. Tx. 1942; MS physical oceanography, Scripps Inst. La Jolla 1950. Career: research staff Scripps Inst. Oceanography, La Jolla 1957-64; assoc. dir. Inst. Marine Resources Univ. Calif. 1975-82; dir. marine life research group Scripps Inst. Oceanography 1974-87, prof. oceanography 1974–; cons. Sandia Nat. Labs., Albuquerque, N.M. 1980-86; editl. advy. bd. Ciencias Marinas, Ensenada 1982–; Deep Sea Research Oxford, England 1980-84; awards: Am. Misc. Soc. Albatross 1988, Nat. Oceanographic Data Center Service 1984; mem: AAAS (fellow), Am. Geophysical Union (fellow, pres. ocean scis. sect. 1972-74, 84-86), Am. Soc. Limnology & Oceanography, Am. Meteorological Soc., Oceanography Soc.; articles pub. in oceonography jours., 1965–; mil: lt. USNR 1942-46. Ofc: Scripps Institution of Oceanography MLR Group La Jolla 92093

REINES, FREDERICK. physicist, educator, Nobel Prize winner; b. Mar. 16, 1918, Paterson. N.J.; s. Israel and Gussie (Cohen) R.; m. Sylvia Samuels. Aug. 30, 1940, children: Robert G., Alisa K.; edn: ME, Stevens lnst. Tech., 1939, MS, 1941; PhD, NYU, 1944; D.Sc. (hon.), Univ. Witwatersrand 1966; D. Engring. (hon.), Stevens Inst. Tech. 1994. Career: mem. staff Los Alamos Sci. Lab., 1944-59; group leader Los Alamos Sci. Lab. (Theoretical div.) 1945-59, dir. (AEC expts. on Eniwetok Atoll), 1951; prof. physics, head dept. Case lnst. Tech. 1959-66; prof. physics Univ. Calif., Irvine, 1966-89, dean phys. scis., 1966-74, Disting. prof. physics, 1987-88, prof. emeritus. 1998–; Centennial lectr. Univ. Md., 1956; Disting. Faculty lectr. Univ. Calif., Irvine, 1979; L.I. Schiff Meml. lectr. Stanford Univ., 1988; Albert Einstein Meml. lectr. Israel Acad. Scis. and Humanities, Jerusalem. 1989; Goudschmidt Meml. lectr., 1990; honors: Guggenheim fellow, 1958-59, Sloan fellow 1959-63, recipient J. Robert Oppenheimer Meml. prize 1981, Nat. Medal Sci. 1983, medal Univ. Calif., Irvine 1987, Michelson Morley award 1990, co-recipient Rossi prize Am. Astron. Soc. 1990, Franklin medal Franklin lnst. 1992, awarded the Nobel Prize in Physics (with Martin L. Perl) for discovering subatomic particles, 1995; Fellow Am. Phys. Soc. (W.K.H. Panofsky prize 1992), AAAS; mem: NAS, Am. Assn. Physics Tchrs., Argonne Univ. Assn. (trustee 1965-66), Am. Acad. Arts and Scis., Phi Beta Kappa, Sigma Xi, Tau Beta Pi, mem. Cleve. Symphony Chorus, 1959-62; co-discoverer elementary nuclear particles, free antineutrino, 1956; contbr. numerous articles to profl. jours.; contbg. author: Effects of Atomic Weapons, 1950. Ofc: University of California at Irvine Dept Physics Campus Drive Irvine 92717*

REINICKE, MELINDA JUNE, psychologist, marriage & family therapist; b. May 14, 1956, San Diego; d. Gail Dalmer and Pearl Floye (Foster) Peacock; m. Aaron Reinicke, June 19, 1981; edn: BA in psych. (honors), San Diego St. Univ., 1977; MA in clin. psych., and PsyD, Biola Univ. Rosemead Sch. Psych., 1981, 1986; lic. MFCC, 1986, psychologist, 1988. Career: intern counselor Coll. Ave. Counseling, San Diego 1981-82; intern therapist Alpha Counseling, El Toro 1982-84; intern psychologist U.S. Internat. Univ. Psychology Clin., San Diego 1984-85; therapist Life Dimensions Counseling 1984-89, dir. 1985-89; co-dir. Reinicke Counseling Assocs. 1989–; honors: Phi Beta Kappa, Who's Who Human Service Profls., Calif. St. Grad. fellowship (1980-81, 1981-82); mem: Am. Psychol. Assn., Acad. San Diego Psychologists, N. Am. Soc. Adlerian Psychologists, Christian Assn. Psychol. Studies, First Assembly of God; author: Parables for Personal Growth, 1993; Republican; Christian. Ofc: 3420 Camino del Rio No. #200 San Diego 92108

REINING, DONALD JAMES, association past president, lobbyist; b. Nov. 11, 1923, Bridgeport, Ill.; s. Henry James and Cora A. (Ramsey) R.; m. Jane Ann Linkogle, Aug. 23, 1948; edn: Shurtleff Coll. 1946-48; BS edn., Ind. Univ., 1950; reg. lobbyist State of Calif. 1963-92, City of Los Angeles 1970-92. Career: mgr. Jeffersonville C.of C., Ind. 1950-53; exec. dir. Lafayette C.of C., Ind. 1953-61; mgr. Torrance C.of C., Calif. 1961-62; pres. So. Calif. Rock Products Assn., So. Calif. Ready Mixed Concrete Assn., South Pasadena 1963-92; pres. Rock Castle Consulting 1992–; mem. Western Miners Advy. Council 1967–; att. State Mining and Geology Board meetings from March, 1963-92, active in writing and enforcement of Calif. Surface Mining and Reclamation Act; mem: So. Calif. Soc. Assn. Execs. (pres. 1980-81, Man of Year award 1983-84), Internat. Council Aggregates Assn. (pres. 1970), Am. Soc. Assn. Execs. (Merit Award for mgmt. achiev.), Calif. Transp. Found. (sec., treas.), Californians for Better Transp. (bd.); civic bds: Gen. Planning Adv. Com. City of LaCanada Flintridge, Pub. Works Commission La Canada Flintridge (1987-90, 1990-94, commissioner 1985-93), Little Company of Mary Hosp., Torrance (bd. 1962-64), Clark Co. (Ind.) Planning Commn. 1950-51, Traffic Commn. West Lafayette, Ind. 1957-61; clubs: Elks, Masons, Press Club, University Club (Pasadena); publs: articles in profl. jours.; mil: USN 1943-46; rec: philately, cac-tus growing, English Setter showing. Ofc: Rockcastle Consulting 5535 Rock Castle Dr La Cañada Flintridge 91011

REINJOHN, RICHARD G., lawyer; b. Mar. 24, 1939, Los Angeles; s. George R. and Lorine Reinjohn; m. Ann Thomas (div. Jan. 1988); children: Laura b. 1963, Andrew b. 1966; edn: att. UC Berkeley; BA, UCLA, 1960; JD, USC Law School, 1964; admitted Calif. St. Bar 1965; nat. import-export mgr. Watson Bros. Transportation Co. 1960-61; assoc. Von Herzen & Hutton 1966-67; mng. ptnr. Von Herzen, Catlin, Reinjohn, & Clements 1967-77; mng. ptnr. Reinjohn, Catlin, Clements & Burgess, 1977-80; ptnr. Reinjohn, Clements, Burgess & Holston 1986-87; managing ptnr. law offices of Richard G. Reinjohn 1988–; lectr. num. organizations; advisor pgms. for paraprofessionals and legal assts. at num. univ. and colleges; instr. USC Law Sch. 1971-72, Pasadena Comm. Coll. 1972-74; mem: Am. Bar Assn., LA Co. Bar Assn. (past chmn., exec. bd. Law Ofc. Mgmt. Sect., del. to St. Bar), Lawyers Assistance Com. (exec. bd. mem.), Orange Co. Trial Lawyers Assn., Assn. of So. Calif. Defense Counsel, Am. Trial Lawyers' Assn., special com. on Paraprofessionals and Legal Assts. 1971–, Trial Lawyers Club (bd. govs. 1968–, treas. 1969-70, pres.-elect 1973, pres. 1973-74), Calif. Trial Lawyers Assn., Assn. of Bus. Trial Lawyers, Spkrs. Bureau 1969–; weekly radio host: "Let's Talk About The Law" KBRT Radio, 1984-85. Ofc: Law Office of Richard G. Reinjohn 606 S Olive St Ste 1700 Los Angeles 90014

REISS, JERRY MILBOURNE, municipal official, construction consultant; b. Sept. 15, 1937, Torrance; b. James Milbourne and Emma Helen R.; m. Collette Martin, Aug. 17, 1973; children: Jonathan b. 1968, Devin L. b. 1975; edn: AA, El Camino Coll. 1957; psychol., Univ. Ariz. 1958-61; arch., Calif. Polytech. St. Univ. 1962-64. Career: owner Wildbird Properties 1964-69; pres. and c.e.o. Bunnell Construction Inc. 1968-91; prin., constrn. cons. in area of constrn. defect and contract litigation J.M. Reiss & Assocs., 1991–; honors: Calif. Scholarship Soc. (life); mem. San Luis Obispo Contractors Assn. (bd. dirs., past pres. 1979-82); civic bds: Calif. Consortium for the Prevention of Child Abuse (bd. 1990-92), Mission Coll. Prep. Sch. (regent 1985-87), San Luis Obispo Architectural Review Commn. 1976-81, City Planning Commnr. 1981-87, Economic Opportunity Commn. (bd. 1988-90) City Council San Luis Obispo (elected 1987-92, v. mayor 1989–; introduced the first ordinance in U.S. to ban smoking in all public places, 1990); Republican (congl. nominee 16th C.D. Calif. 6/90); mil: Calif. Air Nat. Guard; Christian. Res: 1364 San Marcos San Luis Obispo 93401

RELYEA, STEVEN WAYNE, university administrator; b. July 11, 1952, Santa Monica; s. Robert Emile Relyea and Carol Lula (Phillips) Siler; m. Ginger Sue Bradley, June 25, 1988; edn: BA, UC Irvine 1974-75, planner 1975-76, asst. to exec. dean 1976-78, dir. budget and planning 1978-79, assoc. dean adminstrn. 1979-83, asst. v.chancellor bus. 1983-85, acting v. chancellor bus. 1985-86; v.chancellor bus. UCSD 1986–; awards: UC Irvine Service 1985, Community Service 1984, UCSD Affirmative Action 1988; mem: Nat. Assn. St. Univ. & Land Grant Colls., Nat. Assn. Coll. & Univ. Bus. Ofcrs., Faculty Club (bd. dirs. 1988–), UCSD Found. (treas. 1986–), Old Mission Beach Athletic Club; Democrat; Presbyterian. Ofc: Univ. of Calif. San Diego La Jolla 92093-0007

REMINGTON, DAVID ASTAIRE, computer and electrical engineer, mathematician; b. Feb. 16, 1948, Colorado Springs, Colo.; s. Vernon Ivor and Mary Jane (Miller) R.; m. Susanna, Nov. 3, 1972; children: David b. 1976, Robert b. 1978, Melanie b. 1981, Timothy b. 1990; edn: BSEE (honors), Univ. Colo. 1971, MSEE, 1974, MA in Math., 1976. Career: staff mem. Los Alamos Sci. Lab., 1976-80: electrical engr. Electronics Div. LASL, control systems programmer for Eight Beam HELIOS Laser Fusion Res. Facility (3 yrs), in chg. E div. Computer Aided Design (1 yr); senior engring. cons. (systems analysis, modeling and simulation) Los Alamos Tech. Assocs. 1980-81, did control systems models for a liquid metal fast breeder reactor, and a complete plant transient model for Tritium Systems Test Assembly of LASL; guest scientist, cons. for Los Alamos Sci. Lab, 1980-81; power prodn. engr. Pacific Gas and Electric, Diablo Canyon Plant 1981–, in chg. plant security computer system, 2 plant turbine control computer sys., turbine network data servers, all real time network data servers and client pgms.; awards: 2 NSF scholarships, Tau Beta Pi 1970, Eta Kappa Nu 1970, Sigma Tau 1970, 5 performance recognition awards PG&E 1984-90; mem. IEEE 1969–, Computer Sci. Book Club, Electronic Engring. Book Club; 6 tech. publs. in field; Republican; bicycle road racing, running. Res: 1821 Royal Way San Luis Obispo 93405 Ofc: PG&E Diablo Canyon PO Box 56 Avila Beach 93424

REMY, RAY, chamber of commerce executive; b. San Francisco; edn: B. in political sci., Claremont Men's Coll. (now Claremont McKenna Coll.); M. in Public Adminstrn., UC Berkeley. Career: adminstrv. intern City of Berkeley 1962-63; with So. Office League of Calif. Cities 1963, then asst. to exec. dir. and mgr. to 1969; exec. dir. So. Calif. Assn. Govt. 1969-76; appt. dep. mayor City of L.A. 1976-84; pres. L.A. Chamber of Commerce 1984–; prin. spokesman Los Angeles Area C. of C.; bd. Mus. Sci. and Industry; past chmn. bd. councilors Sch. Public Adminstrn. Univ. So. Calif., L.A.; vice chmn. bd. dirs. Rose Inst. for State and Local Govt.; vice chmn. bd. trustees, Claremont McKenna Coll., Calif. Trust for the Environment, Bay Delta Advy. Council; pres. Inst. for Local Self Govt.; bd. dirs. RLA, bd. dirs. Achievement Council; chmn. Calif. Trade and Goods Movement Com.; mem. bus. advy. council U.S. Dept. Transp.; awards: num. awards including Fletcher Bowron award, Donald Stone award, Mus. of Sci. and Industry Fellowship award, others; mem: Nat. Acad. Public Administrn., Jr. Statesmen Found. Am. Soc. Public Adminstrn. (past pres.). Ofc: Los Angeles Area Chamber of Commerce PO Box 3696 350 S Bixel St Los Angeles 90017

RENNICK, SYDELLE, speech pathologist; b. Mar. 6, 1941, Bklyn.; d. Alexander Simon and Ethel (Yarvis) Shatkin; m. Harley Rennick, Aug. 6, 1970; dau. Gwen b. 1962; edn: BA, and MA communicative disorders, CSU Long Beach, 1983, 86; lic. speech/lang. pathologist 1987. Career: pathologist Acute Care, La Habra Rehab. Assn. Inc. 1986-89, also Rehabilitation Unit 1987–, covering affil. hosps. Memorial Hosp. of Gardena 1986–, Midway Med. Ctr., L.A. 1986-90; So. Calif. area mgr. Alta Therapies, L.A. 1991-95; advy. bd. Communicative Disorders Dept., CSU Long Beach 1993–; stroke support group United Stroke Found., Hawthorne 1987–; pvt. practice Speech and Hearing Services, Torrance 1987–; honors: Golden Key, Kappa Delta Pi; mem: Acad. Neurologic Communication Disorders and Scis. 1990–, Am. Speech Language Hearing Assn. (PAC), Calif. Speech Language Hearing Assn., So. Calif. Sp.-Lang. Pathology & Audiology Dirs. Council, Soroptimist Internat., Redondo Bch.-P.V. Chpt. (1974–, v.p. 1975-77); rec: breed thoroughbred horses and Shar-Pei dogs, travel. Res: 32706 Via Palacio Rancho Palos Verdes 90274

RENOLLET, HAROLD L., emergency physician; b. Feb. 13, 1928, Frazee, Minn.; s. Louie Wm. and Hilda (Tester) R.; m. Donna Eleanor Reinmuth, Aug. 20, 1955; children: Robyn b. 1958, Mark b. 1960; edn: BA, BS, and MD, Univ. Minn. 1952, 1956, 1956; med. lic. Minn. 1956, Calif. 1957, Wash. 1957. Career: physician pvt. family practice Kilbourne & Renollet, Saratoga, Calif. 1959-69; dir. emergency dept. Los Gatos Community Hosp. 1969-73; asst. dir. emerg. services UC Davis Med. Ctr., Sacto. 1973-75; emerg. physician Sutter Davis Hosp., Davis 1975–, dir. emerg. services 1980-92; med. dir. Nor Cal EMS, Inc. 1980–; asst. clin. prof. UC Davis, Sacto., tch. family practice, 1973–; cons. UCD Poison Ctr., 1975–; honors: Phi Beta Kappa 1952; mem. AMA, Calif. Med. Assn., Am. Acad. Family Physicians, Am. Coll. Emerg. Physicians, EMS Med. Dirs. of Calif., Flying Physician Assn.; mil: sgt. USAF 1945-50; Republican; Lutheran. Res: 8639 Olivewood Ct Fair Oaks 95628 Ofc: Nor Cal EM, Inc. 970 Executive Way PO Box 491989 Redding 96049-1989

REPIC, EDWARD MICHAEL, aerospace executive, consultant; b. June 7, 1935, Cleveland, Ohio; s. Michael and Ann Mary (Purkeli) R.; m. Patricia Rae Deblass, June 30, 1956; children: Terri Lynn, Raymond Anthony, Toni D'Ann, Edward Michael; edn: BS in aero. engring., Ohio State Univ., 1962; MS in aero. engring., USC, 1964; MBA, Pepperdine Univ., 1975; cert. profl. mgr. Career: engr. Rockwell Internat., Anaheim 1962-68, mgr. 1968-81, dir. shuttle processing 1981-82; pres. Effective Mgmt. Resources Corp., 1979–; prof. West Coast Univ.; dir. Key to Travel Inc.; mem: ASME, AIAA, Am. Soc. for Engring. Mgmt., Am. Inst. Indsl. Engrs., Internat. Soc. Philos. Inquiry, Mensa; club: Diogenes (Anaheim); author: Managing Engineers, 1981, Project Management for Engineers, 1981, Improving Engineering Productivity, 1982, Business Development, Planning and Capture, 1983. Ofc: 2229 Nyon Ave Anaheim 92806

RESSA, AMES DANIEL, physician, surgeon; b. Jan. 18, 1954, Rockville Centre, N.Y.; s. Ames Daniel and Roselyn (Maguire) R.; m. Mona Lisa Ascoli, Aug. 12, 1979; children: Ames Edward b. 1985, Thomas Michael b. 1988, Francesca Elyse b. 1991; edn: BA, Brown Univ., R.I. 1976; MD, Columbia Coll. Physicians & Surgeons, N.Y. 1980; cert. Am. Bd. Surgeons 1988. Career: gen. surgical resident St. Vincent's Hosp. & Med. Center, N.Y.C. 1980-85; attdg. surgeon So. Calif. Permanente Med. Group, San Diego 1985–; mem: A.C.S., S.D. Soc. Surgeons. Res: 6898 Bluefield Ct San Diego 92120 Ofc: 4647 Zion Ave San Diego 92120

RESTER, GEORGE G., artist, painter, architect, designer, showman, sculptor; b. Oct. 5, 1923, Panchatoula, La.; s. Kelly C. and Myra V. (Adams) R.; m. Virginia Nacario, June 25, 1955; children: Gina b. 1956, Taira b. 1959, Licia b. 1963; edn: spl. engring. tng., US Combat Engrs. WWII; law, bus. actg. Soule Coll. 1945-48; art, arch. and engring. Delgado Tech. Inst. 1949-50; Art Center Coll. of Design 1961-62; reg. arch. La. 1960, Calif. 1963, Fla. 1984, Ariz., Colo., N.J., Mich., Minn., N.Y., Tx. 1985, Wash. 1986, N.M. 1988; cert. NCARB 1985. Career: artist, painter, builder, theater set designer- painter 1945-53; gen. architectural practice in pvt. practice and with var. firms incl. project arch./designer Welton Becket 1961-64; sr. prin. engr. Ralph M. Parson Co. 1973-76; designer artist, dir. archtl. design- prodn. (chief arch.) Walt Disney Imagineers, Glendale 1965-71, 1976-87, retired; recipient profl. accolades internat. for work incl. Disneyland, Calif., Disneyworld and Epcot, Orlando, Fla., and Tokyo Disneyland; founding pres. and c.e.o. New Visions Resorts Inc., retired; cur. artist, painter pvt. practice George G. Rester Architect A.I.A.E., internat. projects: master plan, design, entertainment ctrs., destination resorts, theme parks and new communities; mem: AIA 1973, New Orleans Amateur Artists Assn. (co-founder), co-host of weekly radio pgm. 1940-42; mil: pfc AUS Combat Engrs. Corps WWII, European, African, Middle Eastern, Purple Heart; Republican; R.Cath.; rec: artist, painting, crafts. Address: 26337 Dunwood Rolling Hills Estates CA 90274

RESTIFO, RONALD ANTHONY, physician; b. Mar. 11, 1933, Erie, Pa.; s. Anthony and Mary (Palmisano) R.; m. Monika Martini, Oct. 21, 1967; children: Stefanie b. 1968, Andreas b. 1970; edn: grad. (1st in class) Cathedral Prep. Sch. 1946-50; Villanova Univ., 1950-52, AB in anat. and physiol., cum laude, Indiana Univ., 1954, MD, cum laude, 1957; diplomate Am. Bd. Internal Med., 1964, subsplty. rheumatology 1972. Career: intern Philadelphia Gen. Hosp., 1957-58; resident internal med. Johns Hopkins Hosp., 1958-59, Phila. VA Hosp., 1959-60; fellow in arthritis and rheumatic disease Univ. Penn. Hosp., 1960-61; capt. US Army, internist and instr. internal med. and rheumatology Walson Army Hosp., Fort Dix, N.J. 1961-63; assoc. in med. Univ. Penn. Sch. of Med., 1963-66: clin. dir. Arthritic Clinic, resrch. assoc. arthritis sect., instr. in med. Grad. Sch. Univ. Penn.; cons. in rheumatology to Surgeon General's Ofc., Walson Army Hosp., 1964-68, also faculty, attdg. physician and rheumatologist Jefferson Med. Coll. Hosp., Phila.; mem: AMA, CMA, Santa Clara Co. Med. Soc., Am. Rheumatism Assn., No. Calif. Rheumatism Assn. (past pres.), Arthritis Found. (past chmn. exec. com. No. Calif. chpt.); author book chapt. in Textbook of Cardiology, research studies, jour. articles and abstracts; Cath.; rec: tennis, flying, art, travel. Res: 22316 Rancho Deep Cliff Drive Cupertino 95014-3928 Ofc: 2512 Samaritan Ct Ste P San Jose 95126

RETTIE, JOHN GARNER, writer, editor; b. July 1, 1949, London, England; s. John Kerr and Dorothea Garner (Barker) R.; m. Lisa Winn, Feb. 25, 1984; 2 sons: Matthew b. 1986, Nicholas b. 1989; edn: BS, Leeds Univ. 1970. Career: assoc. ed. VW Motoring, England 1970-73; tech. ed. Hot VWs, Costa Mesa 1977-79; ed. Import Auto & Parts, N. Hollywood 1981-85; west coast ed. Wards Auto World, Detroit, Mich. 1985-88; ed. J.D. Power & Assoc., Agoura 1988–; mem: Motor Press Guild (pres 1990); author: Kaypro Power, 1986; Prot.; rec: photog. Res: 655 Catania Way Santa Barbara 93105 Ofc: J.D. Power & Associates 30401 Agoura Rd Agoura Hills 91301

REUBEN, LEEDELL, neonatologist-pediatrician; b. Camden, Ala.; s. Willie Frank and Mary (Freeman) R.; m. Sylvia Staton, Dec. 23, 1972; children: Adrienne b. 1976, Annita b. 1980; edn: M.T., Coll. of Med. Technology, Mpls. 1962; undergrad. work, 1967-70, MD, 1974, Univ. Wash., Seattle. Career: rotating intern Letterman Army Med. Ctr., San Francisco 1974-75; pediatric resident Letterman Army Med. Ctr., 1975-77; gen. pediatric practice, chief dept. ped. Darnell Army Hosp., Ft. Hood, Tx. 1977-79; neonatology fellow Tripler Army Med. Ctr., Honolulu 1979-81; staff neonatologist Frankfurt Army Regional Med. Ctr., Frankfurt, W.Ger.; staff neonatologist Kadlec Med. Ctr., Richland, Wash. 1983-84, med. adv. Benton-Franklin Headstart, Tri-Cities March of Dimes, 1984; sr. neonatologist, San Joaquin Gen. Hosp., Stockton, Calif. 1984–, dir. neonatal intensive care unit 1984-88, asst. dir. 1986-91, dir. pediatrics 1991– ; San Joaquin Cty. Fetal-Infant Death Review Team 1992–, San Joaquin Cty. Child Death Review Team 1992; mem. bd. Black Women Initiative Perinatal Bd., med. adv. Black Women Initiative Pgm., 1990–; mem. Maternal, Child and Adolescent Health Bd.; mem. San Joaquin County Drug Abuse and Prevention Advy. Council 1994; mem. Calif. Med. Assn., Calif. Perinatal Assn., San Joaquin Co. Med. Soc. Triplet Connection (bd. dirs. and sci. advy. bd. 1985–); clin. research articles in med. jours.; mil: maj. AUS 1978-83, GCM, Nat. Defense, Commendn. medals, Overseas, Am. Svc. rib.; AME; rec: fitness, family activities.

REVAK, RUDY, company executive; b. Jan. 1, 1947, Altusried, Ger.; s. Steve and Maria (Ditzig) R.; edn: AA, Mercer Coll. 1972. Career: store mgr. Newport Auto Ind., N.J. 1965-67; area coord. R.R. Associates, N.J. 1970-71; v.p. BL Products GMBH, Germany 1972-74; pres. BL Products of Canada, Toronto 1974-78; pres. BL Products Italia, Rome 1978-80; pres. Diamite Corp., Los Gatos, Ca. 1980-95; pres. Symmetry Corp. 1995–; cons. Flemington Mini Storage, Traveline Inc., ReLine Ent. Toronto; recipient chmn's awards, Internat. Mktg. Mgmt.; frequent writer and lectr. internat. on sales, motivation and personal growth; mil: sgt. US Army Quartermaster Corps 1967-70, Vietnam; Republican (Congl. Club, Senatl. Club, Republican Nat. Com., Presdl. Task Force); Christian; rec: pvt. pilot, race car driver. Res: 121 Callecita Los Gatos 95030 Ofc: 1625 McCandless Dr Milpitas 95035

REVEAL, ARLENE HADFIELD, county librarian; b. May 21, 1916, Riverside, Boxelder Co., Utah; d. Job Oliver and Mabel Olive (Smith) Hadfield; children: James L. b. 1941, Jon A. b. 1944; edn: BS (valedictorian), Utah State Univ. 1938; tchg. cred., CSU San Diego 1970; MLIS (Masters of Lib. & Info. Sci.), Brigham Young Univ. 1976. Career: tchr. Logan High Sch., Logan, Utah 1937-38; social case worker Boxelder Co., Utah 1938-39; branch librarian Tuolumne Co. Library, Calif. 1948-54; acct. Strawberry (Calif.) Inn 1954-66, asst. mgr. Dodge Ridge Ski Area, Long Barn 1949-66, office mgr. Pinecrest (Calif.) Permittees Assn. 1955-66; Library Asst., Mono Co. Office of Edn. 1961-64; asst. to co. supt. of Mono Co. Office of Edn. 1964-67; librarian LaMesa-Spring Valley Sch. Dist., LaMesa 1968-71; county librarian Mono Co. Library, Bridgeport 1971–; honors: John Cotton Dana Award 1974, Woman of Year, Beta Sigma Phi 1980, Bridgeport Citizen of the Yr. 1993; mem: Am. Library Assn., Calif. Library Assn., Calif. Media and Library Educators Assn. (historian 1970), Mountain Valley Library System (chair 1988-90), Delta Kappa Gamma (chpt. pres. 1984-88), Beta Sigma Phi, Xi Omicron Upsilon (treas. 1981, 83, 1990–, chpt. pres. 1982, 85); civic: Aurelia Rebekah Assembly (treas. 1973-90), Pinecrest Vol. Fire Dept. (pres. 1953-54), Mono County Friends of the Library 1976–, Mono Co. Hist. Soc. (secty. 1982–), Developmentally Disabled Area Bd. #12 (chair 1990-92); jt. author: Mono County Courthouse; Pinecrest School History; (ERIC document) Team Teaching in the Library; Ch. of Jesus Christ of Latter Day Saints; rec: archaeol., knitting, Native Am. basketry. Res: Kingsley St Bridgeport 93517 Ofc: Mono County Free Library POB 398 Bridgeport 93517

REYBURN, STANLEY SHORTRIDGE, real estate consultant, expert witness, writer, educator; b. May 28, 1930, Los Angeles; s. Wilbur Wm. and Margaret (Leslie) R.; m. Jeanette Smith, May 29, 1982; children: Valerie, b. 1953; Stephen, b. 1955; Stuart, b. 1959; Paul, b. 1971; edn: AA, El Camino Coll. 1956; BS, CSU Los Angeles, 1959; MBA, USC, 1961; grad. Sch. of Mortgage Banking, Northwestern Univ., 1964; postgrad. work, USC 1965-66; DBA, Kensington Univ., 1988; A.I.B. std. certs. 1967; life jr. coll. tchr. cred. (bus. ad., econ.) 1968;licensed R.E. Broker, cert. General Appraiser; cert. Sr. Loan Escrow Ofcr., Calif. Escrow Assn. 1970; desig: CRA, RMU, Nat. Assn. R.E. Appraisers, CREA. Career: asst. secty./asst. treas. Western Mortgage Corp. 1961-66; v.p./mgr. Security Pacific Nat. Bank 1967-77; pres. Commonwealth Escrow Co. and Commonwealth Svc. Co., 1977-79; 1st v.p.; sr. v.p.-admin. Century Bank, L.A. 1979-82; exec. vice pres., corp. secty., loan adminstr. and

dir. Wilshire State Bank, 1982-86; sr. v.p., mgr. real estate industries div. Sterling Bank, 1986-90; real estate consultant, expert witness and writer, 1990–; instr. Calif. Cont. Edn. of the Bar; faculty Pacific States Univ. 1991–, College of the Desert 1990–, UCLA Ext. 1964-68, L.A. Valley Coll. 1968–, CSU Long Beach. 1966-67; mem. Calif. Escrow Assn. (dir. 1970-82, 89, contbr. monthly column in CEA News), L.A. Escrow Assn. (pres. 1968), Am. Escrow Assn., Calif. R.E. Educators Assn. (awarded 1992 Norman Woest Award as Most outstanding real estate teacher), Nat. Assn. Mtg. Underwriters & Appraisers, Toastmasters Intl. (pres. 1990, ATM Silver), Palm Springs Writers Guild (pres. 1991-92), Desert Press Women (sec./treas. 1995); author: R.E. Finance- Calif. Style (Coll. text, Tom Felde 1993), Careers in Escrow (Calif. Escrow Assn. 1976); Calif. Escrow Procedures: A Blueprint for the Nation (c. 1986, Stanley S. Reyburn); co-author Calif. R. E. Finance (coll. text, Scott, Foresman & Co., 1988); Escrow Procedures and Title Ins. (2 separate 8 hr. and 45 hr. courses, Anthony Schools, 1988); How To Get Better Performance and Profitability from Your Escrow Operation (Fulkerson & Assocs., 1988); What A Wonderful World This Could Be (World of Poetry Press, 1990); Appraisal Performance and Standards (Anthony Schools, 1991); Environmental Hazards Disclosure Requirements (3 hr. course, Calif. Comm. Colls. Real Estate Depository, 1991); technical ed. Calif. R.E. Practice (3d. ed. Scott, Foresman & Co., 1988), tech. ed. Basic R.E. Appraisal (3rd ed. Prentice- Hall 1994); co-author: Environmental Issues & Obligations (continuing educ. Anthony Sch. 1993), Trickle Up Economics (Am. Capital Found., 1993), What They Didn't Teach About R.E. Finance in Business School, Winning With Bankers, R.E. Wheel of Fortune, Ignite Your Inner Genius; author: Writing a Business Plan for Starting or Expanding your BBS (Infolink, 1994), California Loan Brokering and Lending Strategies (Coll. Text, Tom Felde, 1995); pub. poetry, radio plays prod. KCSN, 88.5 FM, numerous mag. & newsletter articles; Republican; Presbyterian; rec: numismatics, preservation of radio hist., writing. Res/Ofc: 73-702 Desert Greens Dr N, Palm Desert 92260-1206

REYNOLDS, ALBERT GORDON, retired medical director, spa director; b. Jan. 25, 1926, Vashon Isl., Wash.; s. Albert Hargrave and Claire Louise (Stowell) R.; m. Polly Staples, Aug. 29, 1948 (div. Jan. 1989); children: Scott b. 1949, Debra b. 1952, Lori b. 1956; edn: MD, Univ. of Michigan 1949; Diplomate Am. Bd. of OB-Gyn. 1958. Career: intern, res. OB-Gyn. Univ. of Mich. Ann Arbor; pvt. practice OB-Gyn. Redlands, Calif. 1955-82; asst. clin. prof. UC Los Angeles and Loma Linda Med. Ctr.; past chief of OB-Gyn. dept., chief of staff Redlands Comm. Hosp.; med. and spa dir. La Costa Spa preventive med. and fitness (ret.); Fellow Am. Coll. of Surgeons 1960–, Am. Coll. of Preventive Med. 1984–, Am. Coll. Sports Med., Am. Geriatric Soc.; coauthor: The La Costa Book of Nutrition (Pharos Publ); mil: corpsman Navy Hosp. WWII 1943-45; capt. MC US Army Korean War 1950-51, Med. Combat Medal, Purple Heart, Meritorious Award from Crown Prince Thailand; Republican; Prot. Res: 3190 Piragua St Carlsbad 92009

REZA, JACQUELYN VALERIE, college counselor, educator, therapist; b. Sept. 12, 1953, San Francisco; d. Armando Rosalio and Jacquelyn Joan (Jordan) Reza; edn: BA, La Raza studies, San Francisco State Univ., 1979; BS in Zoology (honors), Ahmadu Bello Univ., Zaria, Nigeria, W. Africa 1978; MS in Rehab. Counseling, San Francisco State Univ., 1981; lic. Marriage Family Child Counselor (MFCC) 1982; Nat. Cert. Counselor 1981–, Cert. Hypnotherapist 1988–, EdD in Internat. and Multicultural Edn., Univ. of San Francisco 1995. Career: counselor SF State Univ. 1980-82, CSU Stanislaus, Turlock 1982-84, Gavilan Community Coll., Gilroy 1984-85, De Anza Community Coll., Cupertino 1985–, exec. bd. De Anza Faculty Assn. 1987-89, pres. De Anza Faculty Senate 1989-91; v.p. Latina Leadership Network of the Calif. Comm. Colls. 1991-93, pres. 1993-94; exec. bd. mem. Academic Senate Calif. Comm. Colls., 1990-92; MFCC therapist and workshop cons., pvt. practice therapist, San Francisco, Sacramento, San Jose, 1982–; cons. examiner Bd. of Beh. Scis., Sacto. 1986-92; cons. Driver Performance Inst., S.F. 1984-91; cons. EOPS Student Leadership 1987–; awards: honored graduate SFSU 1979, Outstanding Young Woman Am. 1987, special recogn. as Faculty Senate pres. DeAnza Coll. 1991, Women Leaders in Education Award 1990, SFSU Alumni Golden Torch Award 1993, Honoree of the Chicana Found. of No. Calif. 1994; mem: Latina Leadership Network of the Calif. Comm. Colleges, Minority Staff Assn., Third World Counselors Assn., La Raza Faculty Assn., Am. Assn. of Women in Comm. & Jr. Colls., Calif. Assn. for Counseling & Devel.; publs: (booklet) A Guide for I.D. and Referral of Students in Stress 1985, (articles) "Faculty Hiring Excellence Affirmatively", 1991 in Rostrum Newsletter, "17 Points of Latina Leadership", 1992, "What is Latina Leadership?", "On Being Latina" in Esperanza Newsletter, 1993; rec: equestrienne, travel. Res: 6262 Thomas Ave Newark 94560 Ofc: De Anza College 21250 Stevens Creek Blvd Cupertino 95014

RHEA, WILLIAM EDWARD, III, physician, pediatrician; b. July 30, 1933, St. Louis, Mo.; s. William Edward and Helen Dorothy (Kelly) R.; m. Rhoda Mary Myers, Dec. 20, 1958; children: William b. 1960, Vincent b. 1960, Siobhan b. 1961, Regan b. 1963, Fiona b. 1965; edn: BS, Georgetown Univ. 1955; MD, Univ. Md. Sch. Medicine 1959; dipl. Am. Bd. Pediatrics 1966. Career: intern Providence Hosp., Wash. D.C. 1959-60; resident Children's Hosp., Oakland 1962-63, chief resident 1963-64; pvt. practice, Berkeley 1964–; tchr. Children's

Hosp., Oakland 1965–, chief medicine 1974-80, pres. med. staff 1985-86; awards: Children's Hosp. Bronze Bambino 1980, Am. Acad. Pediatrics Spl.Cert. Appreciation 1973; mem: E. Bay Pediatric Soc. (pres. 1969-71), Am. Acad. Pediatrics (fellow), CMA, Alameda-Contra Costa Med. Assn., Cath. Physicians Guild (pres. 1976-80); mil: capt. USAF 1960-62; Democrat; R.Cath. Res: 1190 Shattuck Ave Berkeley 94707 Ofc: 2999 Regent St Ste 325 Berkeley 94705-2146

RHEINSCHILD, GARY WAYNE, surgeon; b. Aug. 30, 1934, Los Angeles; s. Rudolph Waldo and Hazel (Allard) R.; m. M. Sue Haukenberry, Aug. 7, 1955; children: Linda Diane b. 1968, Gary Steven b. 1971; edn: BA, Occidental Coll., 1956; MD, Loma Linda Univ., 1966; Dipl. Am. Bd. Urology; Fellow Am. Coll. Surgeons (FACS) 1990. Career: urology intern L.A. Co.-USC Med Ctr. 1966-67, urology resident UC Irvine 1967-71; surgeon, urologist pvt. practice; chief of surgery Anaheim Memorial Hosp., Anaheim 1987-89; bd. dirs. Anaheim Mem. Hosp. Found., 1987–; mem: Am. Urol. Assn., Western Sect. AUA, Orange Co. Urol. Soc., Los Angeles Urol. Assn., Internat. Coll. Surgeons, Am. College of Surgeons (fellow); mil: sp4 US Army Reserve 1957-63; Republican; Presbyterian; rec: golf. Ofc: Gary W. Rheinschild, M.D., Inc. 1211 W La Palma Ave Ste 303 Anaheim 92801

RHETT, WILLIAM MEANS SMITH, marketing executive; b. Jan. 25, 1930, Miami Beach, Fla.; s. Haskell Smith and Eunice Campbell (Emery) R.; m. Ethelyn Eddy, May 29, 1964 (div. 1971); m. Mary Frances Amill, Jan. 1, 1980 (dec. 1988); children: Ian Christopher b. 1967, Allison Wingate b. 1969; edn: BA, Hamilton Coll. 1952; MBA, Harvard Bus. Sch. 1957. Career: account group exec. McCann Erickson Internat., N.Y.C. 1957-60; dir., chief client service Colón S.A., Madrid, Spain 1960-61; mgr. mktg. devel. and advt. Motorola Overseas Corp., Chgo., Ill. 1962-66; account mgr. Marsteller Internat., N.Y.C. 1966-67; area dir. Latin Am. Wells Rich Greene Internat., Lima, Peru 1968-69, account supr., N.Y.C. 1969-70; v.p. Mktg. Control Inc. 1971-73, N.Y.C.; internat. mktg. mgr. Nat. Semiconductor, Santa Clara, Calif. 1974-75; mng. dir. Intermarkets Ltd., Moraga, Calif. 1975–; mem: Internat. Advt. Assn. (dir. at large 1964-66), Hamilton Alumni (pres. Midwest 1964-66, pres. N. Calif. 1982-86, bd. govs. 1986–), S.F. Advt. Club, Naval Order of U.S., Naval Reserve Assn., Stamford Conn. Yacht Club, Am. Club of Madrid, Orinda Crime Com.; articles pub. in profl. jours., 1962–; mil: commdr. USNR 1953–; Republican; Episcopalian; rec: travel, tennis, classic cars. Ofc: Intermarkets Ltd. POB 821 Lafayette 94549

RHODE, DEBORAH L., law professor; b. Jan. 29, 1952, Evanston, Ill.; s. Frederick R. and Hertha Rhode; edn: BA, Yale Univ. 1974; JD, 1977. Career: law clk. U.S. Ct. Appeals 2d Circuit, N.Y.C. 1977-78; U.S. Supreme Ct., Justice Thurgood Marshall, Wash. D.C. 1978-79; prof. Stanford Law Sch. 1979-89; dir. Inst. for Research on Women & Gender, Stanford 1986–; trustee Yale Univ., New Haven, Conn. 1983-89; dir. Nat. Council Research on Women, N.Y.C. 1986-89; author Justice & Gender (1989), co-ed. w. G. Hazard, The Legal Profession: Responsibility & Regulation (1987); articles pub. in profl. jours. (1980-89). Ofc: Stanford University Law School Stanford 94305

RIACH, DOUGLAS ALEXANDER, sales and marketing executive, retired military officer; b. Oct. 8, 1919, Victoria, B.C., Can.; s. Alex and Gladys (Provis) R.; came to U.S., 1925, naturalized, 1942; m. Eleanor Montague, Mar. 28, 1942; dau., Sandra Jean; edn: BA, UCLA, 1948; Fenn Coll. 1959, Grad. Sch. Sales Mgmt. and Mktg. 1960, US Army Command and Gen. Staff Coll. 1966, Armed Forces Staff Coll. 1968, Ind. Coll. Armed Forces 1970-71. Career: field rep. GM Acceptance Corp. 1940-41, 46-47; with Ridings Motors 1947-48; Gen. Foods Corp. 1948-80, territory. sales mgr. San Francisco 1962-80; with Mel-Williams Co., Elgaaen-Booth Co., 1980-86, Summit mktg. 1986-87; exec. v.p. Visual Market Plans Inc., Novato, Calif. 1984-87; account exec. Thunderbird Mktg. 1987-89; territory. mgr. RBT Assoc., 1989-90; territory mgr. Ibbotson, Berri & De Nola & Assoc., 1990–; served to Capt. Mil USAR 1941-46, to Col. Inf. USAR 1968, ret. 1979, decorated Bronze Star w. "v" and o.l.c., Legion of Merit, Purple Heart, Combat Inf. Badge, inducted US Army Infantry Hall of Fame 1982; served as Col. to BGen. 1990, Calif. State Mil. Reserve, dep. comdr. 1980-84, commdr. 1984-87, 2d Inf. BDE, decorated Calif. Medal of Merit (2), and Commendation. Medal w. pendant; 13 fgn. WWII awards- Croix de Guerre Avec Palme (France), Croix de Guerre avec Palme (Belgium), Fouragerre (Belgium), Combattant Cross-Voluntaire (France), Combattant Cross-Soldier (France), Medaille-Commemorative de la Liberee (France), Medaille-Commemorative Francais (France), Medaille-War Wounded (France), Medaille-Commemorative Belgique (Belgium), Medaille-de la Reconnaissance (Belgium), Medaille du Voluntaire (Belgium), Cross of Freedom (Poland), Royal Commemorative War Cross (Yugoslavia), Knight Royal Order of Compassionate Heart (Intl.), Knight Sovereign Mil. Order of the Temple of Jerusalem (Knights Templar) (to Comdr 1989) Comdr., Commandery of Calif. (MOJ) 1992-94, Knight Comdr, Sovereign Order of St. John of Jerusalem (Knights Hospitaller), Comdr, Commandery of St. Francis (OSJ) 1990–, Knight Comdr, Order of Polonia Restituta (Polish State Order), Master Mason, F & AM (Lodge 400), Scottish Rite 32nd Decree, Shriner (Islam Temple), Sojourner chpt. 277; mem: Long Beach Food Sales Assn. (pres. 1950), Assoc. Grocers Mfrs. Reps. (dir. 1955), Am. Security Council (nat. advy. bd. 1975–), Reserve Officers Assn. (S.F. Presidio pres. 1974-6, v.p. 1977-82, v.p. dept. Calif. 1979, exec. v.p. 1980, pres. 1981, nat. councilman 1981-2), Assn.

U.S. Army (gov. East Bay chpt. 1974-82, S.F. chpt. 1982–); civic: Boy Scouts Am. L.A.: asst. scoutmaster 1936-9, asst. dist. commr. 1940-1, Eagle Scout w/ 2 silver palms award; Pasadena Tournament Roses (co-chmn. Long Beach entry 1947, tournament sweepstakes winner); clubs: Exchange (v.p. Long Beach 1955), Mdsg. Execs. S.F. (dir. 1970-5, 1981-6, sec. 1976-7, v.p. 1978-9, pres. 1980), Commonwealth Club of Calif. (nat. def. sect. v. chmn. 1964-6, chmn. 1967-72), Elks. Res: 2609 Trousdale Dr Burlingame CA 94010-5706 Ofc: 5677 Landregan St Emeryville CA 94608

RICARDO-CAMPBELL, RITA, economist; b. Mar. 16, 1920, Boston, Mass.; d. David A. and Elizabeth (Jones) Ricardo; m. W. Glenn Campbell, Sept. 15, 1946; children: Barbara b. 1954, Diane b. 1956, Nancy b. 1960; edn: BS, Simmons Coll. 1941; MA, Harvard Univ. 1945, PhD, 1946. Career: tchg. fellow, tutor, instr. Harvard Univ. 1946-48; asst. prof. Tufts Coll. 1948-51; economist, Nat. Wage Stab. Bd., 1951-53, Ways & Means Com., US House of Reps., 1953; cons. econ., 1957-61; archivist and research assoc., Hoover Instn. 1961-68, senior fellow, 1968–; mem. bd. dirs., chmn. finance com. The Gillete Co., Boston; bd. Watkins-Johnson, Inc., Palo Alto 1974–; mgmt. bd. Samaritan Med. Ctr., San Jose; Pres. appt. Health Services Industry Com., 1971-74; Pres. appt. Nat. Council on Humanities, NEH, 1982-88, Pres.'s Nat. Economic Policy Advy. Bd. 1981-89; mem. advy. council SRI Internat., mem. Pres.'s Medal of Science Com. 1988-94; dir. Mont Pelerin Soc. 1988–, V.P. 1992-94; awards: senior fellow Nat. Endowment for the Humanities 1975, Alumnae achiev. Simmons Coll., Boston 1972, Phi Beta Kappa, Radcliffe Coll., Harvard Univ., Cambridge 1946; recognized authority on the health care sector, Soc. Sec. policy, and drug ind. regulations; lectr. internat. on med. care in U.S.; author: The Economics and Politics of Health (1982, paperback ed. 1985); Social Security: Promise and Reality; Drug Lag: Federal Government Decision Making; Food Safety Regulations; The Economics of Health and Public Policy; coauthor (w/Glenn Campbell) Economics of Mobilization and War (1952); coeditor (w/Edward Lazear) Issues in Contemporary Retirement (1988), coeditor (w/ Kingsley Davis, Mikail S. Bernstam) Below-Replacement Fertility in Industrial Societies (1987). Ofc: The Hoover Instn., HHMB Stanford 94305-6010

RICE, DENNIS KEITH, aerospace executive; b. Dec. 12, 1939, Newell, W. Va.; s. Lyman Glenn and Thelma Mae (Newbrough) R.; m. Rebecca Ann, Dec. 12, 1970; children: Robyn Danielle b. 1961, Erin Coleen b. 1965, Andrew Jason b. 1973; edn: BEE, Cleveland St. Univ., 1964; MSEE, USC, 1966; PhD in E.E., 1969. Career: engr., asst. to sales mgr. (in assn. w. Cleveland St. Univ.) Halstead & Mitchell Co., 1959-64; staff physicist Korad Dept. Union Carbide, Santa Monica 1969-70; engring. mgmt. Northrop Corp., 1971–: prin. engr., dir. engring. Laser Technology Labs, 1971-74, mgr. Laser Lab. 1974-76; high power laser program mgr. 1976-78; mgr. Laser-Optical Engring., 1978-80; asst. to gen. mgr. Electro-Mech. Div., 1980-82, mgr. Adv. Systems Dept. 1982-85, v.p. 1985-86, v.p./chief scientist for Strategic Technology Planning 1986-89, v.p./mgr. Division Consolidation 1989–, v.p. systems engring. and planning 1990-91, v.p. planning 1991-95; mem. Harvey Mudd Coll. President's Advy. Council 1992-95, Independent Colls. of So. Calif. Advy. Bd. 1994-95; chair Northrop Grumman Ednl. Relations Advy. Bd.: engring. steering com. UC Irvine (1983-92, chmn. 1985-86), CSU Fullerton sponsor's council Orange Co. Sci. & Engring. Fair 1981-95, and Fullerton Arboretum Select Com. for Devel. 1986-89, USC Ctr. for Cont. Edn. advy. bd. 1983-89; mem: Am. Mgmt. Assn., Am. Defense Preparedness Assn., Nat. Security Indsl. Assn. (trustee); mil: A2c USAF 1958-64; Presbyterian (elder); rec: guitar/singing, golf, running. Res: 650 S Scout Trail Anaheim 92807 Ofc: Northrop Grumman Corp. 1840 Century Park East, Los Angeles 90067-2199

RICE, SHARON MARGARET, clinical psychologist; b. Sept. 4, 1943, Detroit, Mich.; d. William Christopher and Sylvia Lucille (Lawecki) Rice; m. Robert Rubin Bruner, Aug. 10, 1969 (div. 1973); m. John Robert Speer, Aug. 14, 1977 (dec. 3/17/94); edn: AB, Oberlin Coll. 1965; MA, Boston Univ. 1968; PhD, 1976. Career: psychologist L.A. Co. 1969-75; Las Vegas Mental Health Center, Nev. 1976-81; psychologist, ptnr. Foothills Psychological Associates, Upland 1981–; tchg. fellow Boston Univ., Mass. 1965-67; cons., Claremont 1986–; extern L.A. Psychiatric Service 1968-69; awards: Highest Honors in Psychol. Oberlin Coll., Las Vegas City Schs. Good Apple 1980, Sigma Xi, listed Who's Who in Mental Health, Who's Who in Am. Women; mem: Am. Psychol. Assn., Calif. Psychol. Assn., Internat. Soc. Study of MPD & Dissociation; rec: boating, dog breeding. Ofc: Foothills Psychological Associates 715 N Mountain Ave Ste G Upland 91786

RICH, MICHAEL DAVID, research corporation executive; b. Jan. 23, 1953, Los Angeles; s. Ben R. and Faye (Mayer) R.; m. Debra Paige Granfield, Jan. 12, 1980; children: Matthew b. 1980, William b. 1985; edn: AB, UC Berkeley, 1973; JD, UCLA, 1976; admitted bar Calif., 1976. Career: dir. Resource Mgmt. Pgm., RAND, Santa Monica 1980-86, v.p. Nat. Security Res. and dir. Nat. Defense Res. Inst. 1986-93, sr. v.p. 1993–; immediate past pres., bd. dirs. WISE Senior Services, Santa Monica; awards: Wilson Scholar UCLA Law Sch. 1973-74; mem. Council on Fgn. Rels., Internat. Inst. of Strategic Studies; publs: num. unclassified and classified articles, reports. Ofc: RAND 1700 Main St Santa Monica 90406-2138

RICHARDS, MORRIS DICK, psychotherapist, county agency administrative/staff analyst, educator; b. Aug. 20, 1939, Los Angeles; parents: Morris Dick Richards, Lynn Rich Briggs, Annette (Fox) Briggs; m. Leslie Sondra Lefkowitz, Mar. 22, 1975; edn: BA (cum laude) Claremont Men's Coll., 1962; MA, Univ. Chgo., 1964; MBA, Chapman Coll., 1985; LLB, La Salle Ext. Univ., Chgo. 1971; MS Hygiene, Univ. of Pittsburgh, 1973, PhD, 1973; MPA, USC, 1965; Calif. lic. Marriage Family Child Counselor (MFCC), Clinical Social Worker (LCSW), Psychotherapist, Adminstr.; diplomate, Acad. Cert. Soc. Workers, NASW, 1962. Career: settlement house worker Benton House, Chgo. 1963-64; psychiatric soc. worker Jewish Big Brothers of Gr. L.A., 1964-67; L.A. Co.: Dept. Soc. Svs. supvy. child welfare worker 1967-68, pgm. analyst 1968-69, hd. child welfare wkr. 1970-71, exec. asst. 1971-72; group therapist Spl. Svs. for Groups, Watts, 1967-68; psychiatric soc. worker Calif. State Dept. Soc. Welfare, L.A. 1969-71 p.t.; asst. dep. dir. Mental Health Dept., Santa Ana 1973-77; soc. wkr. Jewish Fam. Svs., Garden Grove 1973-75 p.t.; pvt. practice, Santa Ana 1975-77; gen. mgr. and industrial therapist Paragon West, Anaheim 1977-83; sr. psychiatric counselor and actg. pgm. dir. Horizon Health, Newport Beach 1983-84; Co. of Orange: sr. social worker O.C. Social Svs., Santa Ana 1983-85, adminstrv. analyst O.C Environmental Mgmt. Agy. 1985-88, staff analyst 1988-90, exec. asst. to Env. Mgmt. Dir. of Planning, 1990-92, staff analyst O.C. Services Agency 1992-95 (ret.); ed. dept. newsletter 1991-92; instr. Calif. Graduate Inst., Orange 1988-92; instr. Univ. of Phoenix 1992-95; mem. O.C. Mental Health Advy. Bd. 1981-87, Alliance for the Mentally Ill O.C., Anaheim Affirmative Action ad hoc com., cons. Head Start Agy., Child Abuse Policy Com., Sch. Attendance Rev. Bd., Foster Home Coord. Task Force, Inter-Dept. Cont. Care Task Force, Juv. Delinquence Com., Diversion Comm. Based Alternatives Task Force, Calif. Curriculum Framework Com., coord. United Way; awards: Haynes scholar Claremont Men's Coll. 1959-60, Univ. Chgo. fellow 1962-64, NIMH fellow 1963-64, USC Alumni fellow 1964-65, adj. prof. teaching excellence award Chapman Coll. 1982; mem. Nat. Assn. Soc. Workers (NASW Social Worker of Yr., O.C., 1987), O.C. Mental Health Assn. (1988-91, past sec.), Am. Jewish Com. (1964–, past dir.), Broadmore Northridge Assn. (past sec., newsletter ed. 1991-94), ACLU; mil: sp4 Army, active 1957, Reserve 1958-64; Indep.; Jewish; rec: tennis, wt.lifting, karate, reading.

RICHARDSON, JOHN FRANCIS, business executive, educator; b. Nov. 22, 1938, Newark, NJ; s. John Stanley and Helen Ana (Rathburn) R.; m. Monika Gatzweiler, Mar. 14, 1966; son, Christopher J. b. Dec. 15, 1966; edn: BA, Montclair St. Coll., 1960; IBM computer sys. schs., 1962-67; MS, Polytech. Univ. of New York, 1968; BSL, Calif. Coll. of Law, 1978, JD, 1980; MBA, summa cum laude, Pepperdine Univ., 1982; doctoral pgm. strategic mgmt. and internat. finance, U.S. Internat. Univ., 1991–; grad. studies Purdue Univ., Rutgers Univ., Seton Hall Univ., Fairleigh Dickinson Univ. Career: high sch. math tchr., NJ 1960-62; mktg. rep. IBM Corp., NYC 1962-68; pres Universal Learning Corp., NYC 1968-70; acct. mgr. Realtronics, Inc., NYC 1970; acct. exec. Merrill Lynch, NYC 1970-71; Bache rep. Bache & Co., NYC 1971; v.p. John S. Studwell Assoc., NYC 1972-73; sales rep. Control Data Corp., NYC 1973; asst. prof. Purdue Univ., Fort Wayne, Indiana 1973-74; physics tchr., Kearney (NJ) High Sch. 1975; biochem. tchr. Sparta (NJ) H.S. 1975-76; acct. exec. Dean Witter, Santa Monica 1976; lectr. USC, Los Angeles 1977-78; mktg. rep. National CSS, Inc., Newport Bch. 1977-80; realtor assoc. Coldwell Banker, Santa Ana 1980-81; mktg. rep. Informatics, Inc., L.A. 1981-82; exec. v.p. Computique, Santa Ana 1982-83; pres. ILAR Systems, Inc., Newport Bch. 1983–; past mem. New York C.of C., NYAC, Pepperdine Univ. Assocs.; computer systems cons. numerous cos. internat.; author numerous computer applications pgms. incl. Bottomline-V Plus (tm) and CEO's Strategic Planner (trademark corporate fin. planning system w/ 16,000+ installations worldwide), 12 academic study courses w/ tapes, numerous tape lectures, 6 travel books w/ tapes; honors: Kappa Delta Pi 1958, Am. Jurisprudence award 1978; mem: Internat. Platform Assn., Pepperdine Univ. Mgmt. Partners, U.S. Tennis Assn., U.S. Chess Fedn., staff ofcr. U.S. Coast Guard Auxillary (vol boating safety and public edn.) 1995–; club: John Wayne Tennis (team capt. 1989-91 OCTA Champions); Republican; Presbyterian; rec: travel, writing, tennis, computers, math & sci., chess, fgn. languages. Address: 334 Baywood Dr Newport Beach 92660

RICHARDSON, JOHN VINSON, JR., educator; b. Dec. 27, 1949, Columbus, Ohio; s. John Vinson and Hope Irene (Smith) R.; m. Nancy Lee Brown, Aug. 22, 1971; edn: BA, Ohio State, 1971; MLS, Vanderbilt, Peabody Coll., 1972; PhD, Indiana Univ., 1978. Career: asst. prof. UCLA, Los Angeles 1978-83, assoc. prof. 1983–; chair Grad. Council, UCLA 1995-96; pres. Information Transfer Associates (consulting bus.); pres. Wesley Found., L.A.; vis. scholar ALISE/Russia Project, St. Petersburg and Moscow, 1996; awards: Newberry Fellow, Newberry Library, Chgo. 1982, NEH grantee, W.D.C. 1984, Lancour Scholar, ALISE, Research Tri, N.C. 1986, Justin Winsor Prize, Am. Library Assn., Chgo. 1990, Indiana Univ. Alumni Assn. Louise Maxwell Award 1995; mem: Am. Library Assn. 1972–, Assn. of Lib. and Info. Sci. Edn. 1975–, Beta Phi Mu 1972–, Sigma Xi 1987–, ACM, SIGAI 1990–, Grad. Council UCLA 1992–, Grad. Council UC Statewide 1993–; author: Calligraphy, 1982, Spirit of Inquiry, 1982, Knowledge-Based Systems, 1995, Gospel of Scholarship, 1992; editor-elect The Library Quarterly (7/94-3/95), editor, (4/95–); mil: conscien-

tious objector, alt. svc. 1972-75; Green; United Methodist; rec: travel internat., reading, oenology. Ofc: UCLA GSLIS, GSLIS Bldg Ste 204 Los Angeles 90024-1520 Ph: 310/206-9369

RICHARDSON, MARY ELIZABETH, motion picture film librarian; b. Nov. 27, 1916, Los Angeles; d. Ford Ingalsbe and Frances Caroline (Willey) Beebe; m. Lloyd Leland Richardson, June 6, 1936 (div. 1948); children: Lloyd L. III b. 1939, Mary Elizabeth b. 1943; edn: grad. Benjamin Franklin H.S., L.A. 1932; AA, L.A. Jr. Coll., 1935; undergrad. UC Berkeley, 1935, BA, UCLA, 1937. Career: continuity clk. Republic Studios, Studio City 1945-55, film librarian 1955-57; film librarian Warner Brothers, Burbank 1957-63, Universal Studios, Universal City 1972; head film librarian Banner Prodns., Studio City 1964-65, Columbia Bdcstg., Studio City 1965-67, Desilu (later Paramount/ Gulf Western), Hollywood 1967-71, Columbia Pictures TV, Burbank 1973-82, ret.; also owner/prin. dba The Winged Cap, 1946–: continuity clk. Walter Lantz Prodns. 1946-83, free lance continuity Alperson Prodns. and others 1946-83, office svs. Zahler Prodns. 1971-73; bd. dirs. Valley Water Assn. 29 Palms 1985-87; honors: Calif. Scholarship Soc. (life); mem: Motion Picture Film Eds. Guild (1955–, Gold Card Life), Office & Profl. Employees Internat. Union (founding 1946–), Desert Writers' Guild of 29 Palms (past chmn., treas. 1989–, editor/printer Annual 1991–); civic: Morongo Basin Coalition for Adult Literacy (1987–, bd. 1989–); contbr. poetry, fiction Desert Writers' Guild Annual, 1991–; Republican; Rosicrucian faith; rec: writing, music, sci., rel., health & nutrition. Res: HC02, Box 324L, 29 Palms 92277 Ofc: The Winged Cap PO Box 1896, 29 Palms 92277-1260

RICHENS, MURIEL WHITTAKER, counselor, educator; b. Prineville, Oreg.; d. John Reginald and Victoria Cecilia (Pascale) Whittaker; children: Karen, John, Candice, Stephanie, Rebecca; edn: BS, Oregon State Univ.; MA, San Francisco State Univ., 1962; postgrad. UC Berkeley 1967-69, Univ. Birmingham, Eng. 1973, Univ. Soria, Spain, 1981; spl. postgrad. studies Ctr. for Human Comms., Los Gatos 1974, Univ. P.R. 1977, Univ. Guadalajara, Mex. 1978, Univ. Durango, Mex. 1980, Univ. Guanajuato, Mex. 1982; Lic. marriage, child and family counselor (MFCC), Calif.; Calif. tchg. and sch. administrn. credentials, 7-12, pupil personnel specialist. Career: instr. Springfield H.S., Springfield, Oreg.; San Francisco St. Univ.; instr., counselor Coll. of San Mateo, San Mateo H.S. Dist., 1963-86; therapist AIDS Health Project, Univ. Calif., San Francisco 1988–; pvt. practice MFCC, San Mateo; mem: UC Berkeley Alumni Assn., Am. Contract Bridge League (Diamond Life Master, cert. instr., tournament dir.), Women in Comms., Computer-Using Educators, Pi Lambda Theta, Delta Pi Epsilon, Commonwealth Club; civic: Am. Red Cross (lifeguard); R.Cath. Res/Ofc: 847 N Humboldt St #309 San Mateo 94401-1451

RICHEY, EVERETT ELDON, religious educator; b. Nov. 1, 1923, Claremont, Ill.; s. Hugh Arthur and Elosia Emma (Longnecker) R.; m. Mary Elizabeth Reynolds, Apr. 9, 1944; children: Eldon b. 1947, Clive b. 1950, Loretta b. 1953, Charles b. 1956; edn: ThB, Anderson Univ., 1946; MDiv, Sch. of Theology, Anderson, Ind. 1956; ThD, Iliff Sch. Theology, Denver 1960; ordained minister Ch. of God, 1948. Career: pastor Church of God, Bremen, Ind. 1946-47, Laurel, Miss. 1947-48, First Ch. of God, Fordyce, Ark. 1948-52, Cherry Ave. Ch. of God, Long Beach, Calif. 1964-68; prof. Arlington Coll., Long Beach 1961-68; Azusa Pacific Univ., 1968-93, prof. emeritus 1993–; mem. Commn. on Christian Higher Edn. of Ch. of God, Fullerton, Calif. 1982–; pres. Church Growth Investors, Glendora 1981–; mem: Christian Ministries Training Assn. 1968–, Assn. of Profs. and Researchers of Rel. Edn. 1976–, Rel. Edn. Assn. 1956–, General Assembly Ministers of Ch. of God 1946–; publs: curriculum, ednl. manuals, contbr. ch. periodical 1971-83; Republican; rec: gardening. Res/Ofc: 413 N Valencia Glendora 91741

RICHTAREK, JOHN GREGORY, sales executive; b. May 31, 1952, Hartford, Conn.; s. Wm. John and Patricia Blake (O'Meara) R.; m. Laura Ness, Mar. 7, 1987; edn: BA, Randolph Macon Coll., 1974; MA, Northeastern Univ., 1977. Career: project coordinator C.S.I., Elmsford, NY 1977-79; sales engr. Mergenthaler-Linotype, Hayward, Calif. 1979-80; dir. edn. Shast General Sys., Sunnyvale 1980-82; mgr. systems engring. Fortune Systems, Belmont 1982-84; sales services mgr. Micro Focus Inc., Palo Alto 1984-86; internat. sales mgr., dir. of sales, pres. Presentation Technologies, Sunnyvale 1986-91; v.p. sales Mirus Industries, Milpitas 1991–; honors: outstanding youth leader C.of C. Westfield, N.J. 1972, key employee Fortune Systems, Belmont, Calif. 1983; mem. Am. Motorcyclist Assn., Motorcycle Safety Found. (cert. instr. 1984–), Cousteau Soc.; Episcopalian; rec: motorcycling, sailing, hiking, running. Ofc: Milpitas.

RICHTER, BURTON, physicist/linear accelerator center director; b. Mar. 22, 1931, Bklyn.; s. Abraham and Fannie (Pollack) R.; m. Laurose Becker, July 1, 1960; children: Elizabeth b. 1961, Matthew b. 1963; edn: grad. The Mercersberg Acad., 1948; BS, PhD, M.I.T., 1952, 1956. Career: research assoc. Brookhaven Nat. Lab., Upton, N.Y. 1954; res. assoc. high energy physics, Stanford Univ., 1956-59, asst. prof. dept. physics 1960-63; assoc. prof. Stanford Linear Accelerator Center, 1963-67, prof. 1967–, tech. dir. 1982-84, dir. 1984–; Paul Pigott Prof. in the Physical Scis., Stanford Univ.; mem. bd. dirs.: Varian Corp., Palo Alto, Litel Instruments, San Diego; awards: Loeb lectr. Harvard Univ.

1974, DeShalit lectr. Weizmann Inst. 1975, E.O. Lawrence Medal 1976, Nat. Acad. of Sci. 1976, Nobel Prize in Physics 1976; Fellow Am. Acad. of Arts & Scis., Am. Physical Soc. (pres. 1994), AAAS; mem. European Physical Soc.; rec: skiing, squash, music. Ofc: Stanford Linear Accelerator Center POB 4349 Stanford 94309

RICKARD-RIEGLE, BARBARA KATHERINE, journalist, news broadcaster; b. May 1, 1921, Los Angeles; d. Thomas and Katherine Elizabeth (Blackburn) Rickard; children: Katherine, Karen, Christopher, Melissa, Richard; edn: student pvt. schs.; BA, journalism, Calif. State Univ., Fullerton; grad. studies Paris, Fr.; law studies Western St. Univ. of Law, 1987-94. Career: editor Phenix City (Ala.) Herald, 1957-58; news bdcstr./ed. WRBL Radio T.V., Columbus, Ga. 1958-62; political reporter Esquire Bdcstg. Co., WQXI, Atlanta 1962-63; news commentator WAII-T.V. 1962-63; political writer, columnist L.A. Herald Examiner, 1963-66; Congl. news secty., Wash. DC 1966-67; news writer, guest bdcstr. KNXT, KABC-TV, Hollywood 1964-67; bdcstr., women's news ed. KNX-CBS 1967-71; news bdcstr., prod., reporter, bureau chief Westinghouse Bdcstg. Corp., KFWB 1971-87; guest bdcstr. Pub. Bdcstg. System KCET 1975–; owner/pres. Calico Feature Prodns., Anaheim 1969–; instr. journalism CSU Fullerton 1972-73; Republican candidate for Calif. St. Assembly 1976; recipient recogn. awards NCCJ, Georgia St. Rep. and Dem. Parties (for fairness in campaign reporting), US Army 7th Div. Euro. Command (for editorials), Comdg. Gen. Fort Benning (for volunteerism); named Journalist of Year Cypress Coll. 1980, Angel of Distinction, City of Los Angeles 1973, John Swett Journalist of Year, Calif. Tchrs. Assn. 1974, 79, resolution Orange Co. Bd. Suprs. 1987, commendns.O.C. Status of Women Commn. and Womens Network Alert 1987, YWCA silver medalion 1987, hon. A.A. degree Irvine Valley Coll. 1987; mem: Am. Women in Radio and T.V. (chpt. pres. 1982-83, chair Bus. and Industry forum Ednl. Found. 1979), Nat. Womens's Polit. Caucus, Investigative Reporters and Editors, Orange Co. Press Club (dir. 1979–, pres. 1984-85), Women in Communications (award 1979), Pioneer Bdcstrs. West, Sigma Delta Chi; author: The Long Hot Summer of 1962; Something is Missing, The Majority Sex, 1971; Dinner for One, Soupcon for Singles, 1977; Addresses: 2512 W Chain Ave Anaheim 92804; 2639 SW 347th Place Federal Way WA 98023

RIDDELL, ROBERT JAMES (JR.), physicist, retired; b. June 25, 1923, Peoria, Ill.; s. Robert James and Hazel Marion (Gwathmey) R.; m. Kathryn Jane Gamble, Aug. 12, 1950; children: Cynthia b. 1953, Stephen b. 1955, James b. 1957; edn: BS, Carnegie Inst. of Tech., 1944; MS, Univ. Mich., 1947, PhD, 1951. Career: asst. prof. physics Univ. Calif., Berkeley 1951-55; sr. physicist Lawrence Berkeley Lab., Berkeley 1951-81; physicist AEC, Germantown, Md. 1958-60; Pacific Sch. of Religion 1971- (trustee 1971–, bd. chair 1979-84), Graduate Theological Union 1983- (trustee 1983–, bd. chair 1990–); advy. bd. Coll. Natural Resources, Univ. Calif. 1990-95; mem: Friends of Univ. Calif. Botanical Garden (pres. 1985-95), Calif. Horticultural Soc. (council 1988-94); mil: lt.jg USN 1944-46; United Ch. of Christ, First Congl. Ch., Berkeley (moderator 1973-74, treas. 1989-92); rec: gardening, model making, photography. Res: 1095 Arlington Blvd El Cerrito 94530

RIDGWAY, DAVID WENZEL, academic film producer; b. Dec. 12, 1904, Los Angeles; s. David Nelson and Marie (Wenzel) R.; m. Rochelle Mary Devine, June 22, 1955; edn: AB, UCLA, 1926; MBA, Harvard Univ., 1928. Career: sound engr. RKO Studios, Hollywood 1928-42; producer Ency. Britannica, Wilmette, Ill. 1946-60; film producer/ exec. dir./ dir. Chemical Edn. Material (CHEM) Study, Lawrence Hall of Sci., UC Berkeley, 1960-89, dir. 1989–; advisor CalTech, Pasadena 1982-85; awards: Chris award Film Council Greater Columbus, Ohio 1962, Best film, Brussels 1965, Gold Camera, Chgo. 1971, Golden Eagle (5 awards) CINE, W.D.C. 1973, Diploma of Honor ISFA, Cairo 1978; mem: Soc. Motion Picture & TV Engrs. 1929–, Alpha Kappa Psi 1928–, Delta Upsilon 1928–; clubs: UC Faculty 1963–, Bohemian 1967–, Berkeley City; author: w. R.J.Merrill, The CHEM Study Story (1969), articles in SMPTE J., J. Chem. Edn., Canadian Chem. Edn., Sci. Activities, Ednl. Screen and Audio Visual Guide; mil: lt. cdr. USN 1943-46; Republican; rec: dancing, bridge, travel. Res: 1735 Highland Pl Berkeley 94709 Ofc: University of California, Lawrence Hall of Science, Berkeley 94720

RIEDER, RONALD FREDERICK, public relations/advertising consultant; b. Nov. 10, 1932, Oshawa, Ontario, Can., naturalized 1962; s. Joseph Samuel and Minnie (Collis) R.; m. Pauline Feldman, Sept. 22, 1957; children: Mitchell b. 1961, Stephen b. 1962, Robert b. 1964; edn: BA, Sir Geo. Williams Univ. (now Concordia U.), Montreal, 1955; B.Journalism, Carleton Univ., Ottawa, 1956. Career: reporter Montreal Star, Montreal, Canada 1956-58; night city editor Valley News, Van Nuys, Calif. 1958-66; v.p. Hal Phillips & Assocs., Beverly Hills 1966-72; dir. communications Daylin, Inc., Beverly Hills 1972-80; ptnr. The Phillips Group, Beverly Hills 1980-89; dir. pub. affairs Jewish Fedn. Council of Greater L.A., 1989-92; pres. Ron Rieder & Assocs., Sherman Oaks 1992–; mem: Valley Press Club (1960–, past pres.), Soc. of Profl. Journalists 1962–, Pub. Relations Soc. Am. 1972–. Res: 5420 Sylmar Ave #322 Sherman Oaks 91401 Ofc: Ron Rieder & Associates 5420 Sylmar Ave #322 Sherman Oaks 91401

RIGGS, HENRY E., college president; b. Feb. 25, 1935, Chgo.; s. Joseph Agnew and Gretchen (Walser) R.; m. Gayle Carson, May 17, 1958; children: Elizabeth, Peter, Catharine; edn: BS indsl. engring. (with distinction), Stanford Univ., 1957, MBA (high distinction) Grad. Sch. Bus. Adminstrn., Harvard Univ., 1960. Career: process engr. Ampex Corp., Redwood City 1957-58; industrial economist, techno-economic res. and cons., Stanford Res.Inst., 1960-63; Icore Industries, Sunnyvale 1963-70: treas. controller 1963-64, v.p. ops. 1964-65, exec. v.p. 1965-67, pres. and c.e.o. 1967-70; v.p. fin. Measurex Corp., Cupertino 1970-74; academic splst. in fields of technology mgmt., technical strategy, new venture mgmt., fin. analysis and control; instr. Foothill Coll., Los Altos 1961-66; faculty Stanford Univ. 1967-88: instr. 1967-70, cons. prof. 1970-76, adj. prof. 1976-80, prof. engring. 1980-88, Thomas W. and Joan B. Ford Professor of Engring. 1986-88, Ford Professor of Engring., Emeritus 1990–, chmn. dept. indsl. engring. and engring. mgmt. 1978-82, v.p. devel. Stanford Univ. 1983-88, founder, dir. Stanford-AEA Exec. Inst. for Mgmt. of High Technology Cos. 1975-83, dir. Industrial Affiliates Pgm. 1979-82; pres. and prof. of engring. Harvey Mudd Coll., Claremont 1988–; dir: Income Fund of Am., Growth Fund of Am., Am. Balanced Fund, Fundamental Investors Inc., AMCAP; mem: AIIE (editorial rev. com. Transactions J.); civic bds: Bay Area Com. advy. to SEC, Phillips Acad. (trustee), Stanford Alumni Assn. (dir., chmn, 1993), United Way Campaign Mt. Baldy Region (chmn. univ. and coll. div.), YMCA Palo Alto (dir.), BSA Stanford Area Council (ofcr., dir.), BSA Mt. Baldy Council (dir. 1993–); author: Accounting: A Survey (McGraw-Hill, 1981), Managing High-Technology Companies (Van Norstrand Reinhold, 1983), Financial and Cost Analysis (Wiley Interscience, 1994), 11+ profl. jour. articles and tech. reports (1962–). Res: 495 E 12th St Claremont 91711 Ofc: Harvey Mudd College Kingston Hall 301 E 12th St Claremont 91711

RIGHTER, RHONDA LEE, associate professor; b. Nov. 9, 1959, Washington, D.C.; d. Richard William and Elizabeth (Abernathy) Righter; edn: BS, Carnegie Mellon Univ. 1980; MS, UC Berkeley 1982; PhD, 1986. Career: programmer IBM, Manassas, Va. 1979; research asst. Carnegie Mellon Univ., Pittsburgh, Pa. 1980; engr. Bell Labs., West Long Branch, N.J. 1980-81; mathematician Naval Research Lab., Wash. D.C. 1982; lectr. UC Berkeley 1986-87; prof. Santa Clara Univ. 1987–; awards: Carnegie Mellon Univ. Outstanding Woman 1978, 79, Bell Labs. fellowship 1981, Gen. Electric Found. forgivable loan 1984, 85, Leavey Grant for Research 1989; mem: INFORMS; articles pub. in tech. jours.; rec: hiking, backpacking, cooking. Ofc: Santa Clara University Dept. of Decision & Information Sciences Santa Clara 95053

RILES, WILSON CAMANZA, educational consultant; b. June 27, 1917, Alexandria, La.; s. Wilson Roy and Susie Anna (Jefferson) R.; m. Mary Louise Phillips, Nov. 13, 1941; children: Michael b. 1943, Narvia b. 1945, Wilson Jr. b. 1946 Phillip b. 1947; edn: BA, No. Ariz. Univ., 1940, MA, 1947; awarded Hon. Dr. of Laws degree, Pepperdine Coll., 1965, Claremont Grad. Sch., 1972, USC, 1975, No. Ariz. Univ., 1976, Univ. of Akron, 1976, Golden Gate Univ., 1981, Hon. Dr. Humane Letters degree, St. Mary's Coll., Moraga 1971, Univ. of Pacific, Stockton 1971, Univ. of Judaism, L.A. 1972. Career: elementary sch. tchr., adminstr. Arizona Public Schs., 1940-54; exec. secty. Pacific Coast reg. Fellowship of Reconciliation, L.A. 1954-58; cons., dir. compensatory edn. Calif. Dept. Edn., Sacto. 1958-70; supt. of pub. instrn. Calif. Dept. of Edn., Sacto. 1971-83; pres. Wilson Riles & Associates Inc., Sacto. 1983–; dir. (emeritus) Wells Fargo Bank; awards: Berkeley Citation UCB 1973, Spingarn Medal NAACP 1973, Disting. service Harvard Club S.F. 1978, Robert Maynard Hutchins award Ency. Britannica 1978, Medal for disting. service Teachers Coll. Columbia Univ. 1979, Disting. Alumnus Am. Assn. of State Colls. and Univs. 1979; mem: The Cleveland Conf., NAACP, Phi Beta Kappa, Nat. Advy. Coun. Nat. Schs. Volunteer Pgm., Assn. of Calif. Sch. Adminstrs., Am. Assn. Sch. Adminstrs., Save the Redwoods League Council; editl. advy. bd. Early Years Mag.; mem. nat. com. on U.S.-China Relations Inc.; mil: vet. WWII, US Army Air Corps. Ofc: 400 Capitol Mall Ste 1540 Sacramento 95814

RILEY, BENJAMIN KNEELAND, lawyer; b. June 3, 1957, Pompton Plains, N.J.; s. Christopher Sibley and Katharine Louise (Piper) R.; m. Janet McCormick, Sept. 15, 1984; children: Keith McCormick b. 1989, Jamin McCormick b. 1993; edn: BA, cum laude with distinction in history, Dartmouth Coll. 1979, JD, UC Berkeley Boalt Hall 1983. Career: atty. McCutchen Doyle Brown & Enersen, San Francisco 1983-84; ptnr. Cooley Godward Castro Huddleson & Tatum 1984–; special asst. Dist. Atty., San Francisco 1988; lectr. UC Berkeley Boalt Hall 1989; honors: UC Berkeley Calif. Law Review assoc. ed. 1981-83, Am. Jurisprudence award 1981; mem: Am. Bar Assn., San Francisco Bar Assn. S.F. Barristers Club, Childrens Garden San Rafael (bd. dirs. 1987-92), Dartmouth Club No. Calif., Orinda Parks and Recreation Commn. (chair and commnr. 1991–), Orinda Country Club, Orinda Assn. (v.p. and sub-com. chair 1989-90); 1 article pub. in profl. jour., 1983; Democrat; Prot. Ofc: Cooley Godward 1 Maritime Plaza 20th Floor San Francisco 94111

RILEY, JAMES D(ANIEL), mathematician; b. June 25, 1920, Tuscola, Ill.; s. Fred Thomas and Ruth Elizabeth (Deardurff) R.; m. Elaine Kutschinski, June 2, 1952; children: Dane b. 1953, Gregory b. 1957; edn: AB, Park Coll., 1942; MA, Univ. Kans. 1948, PhD, 1952. Career: mathematician Naval Ordnance Lab.

1952-54; asst. prof. Univ. Ky., 1954-55, Iowa State Univ., 1955-58; staff mem. Space Technology Labs, 1958-61, Aerospace Corp., 1961-66, sr. staff MDAC, 1967-74; lectr. National Univ. of Malaysia, 1975-77; staff mem. Honeywell, 1977-85; sr. staff Lockheed Calif., Burbank 1985-90; instr. Moorpark Coll., 1990–; lectr. USC, UCLA, 1958-68; honors: Phi Beta Kappa 1948, Sigma Xi 1948, Pi Mu Epsilon 1948; mem. var. math. socs., U.S. Power Squadron; contbr. tech. articles in sci. jours.; mil: sgt. AUS 1941-46; Lutheran; rec: nature study, ornithology. Res: 6195 Sylvan Dr Simi Valley 93063

RILEY, REX (CHARLES LOGAN), health administrator; b. Jan. 20, 1946, Toledo, Ohio; s. Charles Allen and Phyllis Mary (Logan) R.; m. Rosemarie Jeanette Webster, Apr. 10, 1971; children: Paul b. 1977, Ross b. 1980; edn: BA, Univ. Mich., 1968; MHA, Univ. of New South Wales, Sydney, Australia 1976; health exec. devel. pgm. Cornell Univ., 1988. Career: prodn. planner Internat. Harvester, Melbourne, Australia 1972-74; adminstrv. staff Royal Women's Community Hosp., 1974-79; chief ops. Preston Northcote, 1979-84; CEO Geelong, Victoria, Australia 1984-89; chief ops. Valley Children's Hosp., Fresno, Calif. 1989–; Fellow Australian Coll. of Healthcare Executives (1976, ofcr. 1982-88, pres. 1987-88); Fellow Am. Coll. of Healthcare Execs. 1989–; civic: Rotary Fresno, Leadership Fresno, Ronald McDonald House, Combined Health Appeal Fresno, Hope Now for Youth; pub. article "Two Avenues to Improve Comm. in an Org.", 1988; mil: capt. USMC 1968-72, Vietnam 70-71, Navy commendn. 1971; Lincoln Republican; Lincoln Presbyterian; rec: family, A. Lincoln, Sir Donald Bradman, Civil War, gardening, walking. Res: 2287 W Pinedale Ave Fresno 93711 Ofc: Valley Children's Hospital 3151 N Millbrook Fresno 93703

RIMOIN, DAVID LAWRENCE, physician, medical investigator, administrator; b. Nov. 9, 1936, Montreal, Quebec, Canada; s. Michael and Fay (Lecker) R.; m. Ann Piilani Garber, July 27, 1980; children: Anne Walsh, Michael Keone Garber, Lauren Piilani; edn: BS, MD, CM, MSc genetics, McGill Univ., Montreal 1957, 61, 61; PhD genetics, Johns Hopkins Univ., 1967. Career: asst. physician Barnes/Allied Hosp., St. Louis, Mo. also asst. prof. med. & pediatrics Washington Univ., 1967-70; chief div. med. genetics Harbor/UCLA Med. Ctr., Torrance, Calif. 1970-86, prof. peds./medicine UCLA Sch. of Med., Los Angeles 1973–, dir. Med. Genetics Ctr. 1986–, dir. dept. peds., Steven Spielberg Chair of Pediatrics, Cedars-Sinai Med. Ctr., L.A. 1986–; cons. Orthopedic Hosp., L.A. 1970–, Shriners Hosp., L.A. 1976–; awards: Forsyth Prize in Surgery 1961, Chipman Gold Medal in Ob/Gyn 1961, Holmes Gold Medal, E. Mead Johnson Award for Res. in Pediatrics 1976, Ross Outstanding Young Investigator award 1976, Johns Hopkins Soc. of Scholars 1990, Inst. of Medicine 1992, Alpha Omega Alpha (fellow); Am. Coll. of Physicians (fellow), Endocrine, Am. Diabetes Assn., Am. Bd. Med. Genetics (pres. 1979-83), Am. Coll. Med. Genetics (founding fellow, pres. 1989–), Western Soc. Clin. Res. (pres. 1978-79), Am. Soc. Human Genetics (pres. 1984), We. Soc. Pediatrics Research (pres. 1995); author, coauthor 10 med. books incl. Atlas of Fetal Skeletal Radiology (Year Book Med. Pubs., Chgo., 1988), Principles and Practice of Medical Genetics, 1983, 1990, contbr. chapters in 20+ med. books. Ofc: Cedars-Sinai Medical Center 8700 Beverly Blvd Ste 4310 Los Angeles 90048

RINEHART, CHARLES ROBERT, financial services company chairman and CEO; b. Jan. 31, 1947, San Francisco; s. Robert E. and Rita Mary (Gianni) R.; m. Maria Theresa Jordan, Dec. 30, 1968 (div. 1986); m. Cynthia L. Abts, Sept. 13, 1987; children: Jeseph b. 1975, Kimberly b. 1978, Michael b. 1981, Scott b. 1980; edn: BS, Univ. San Francisco 1968. Career: exec. v.p. Firemans Fund Ins. Co., Novato 1969-83; pres., CEO, Avco Fin. Services, Irvine 1983-89; chmn., dir. and CEO, H.F. Ahmanson & Co. 1989–; chmn. and CEO, Home Savings of Am. 1989–; mem: Casualty Actuarial Soc. (fellow), Am. Acad. Actuaries, Drug Use is Life Abuse (advy. com.), Tustin Public Sch. Found.; mil: 2d. lt. AUS 1968-69; Republican; R.Cath.; rec: athletics, cooking, model trains. Ofc: Home Savings of America 4900 Rivergrade Rd Irwindale 91706

RINGROSE, JOSEPH STEPHEN, personnel executive; b. Feb. 29, 1936, Boston, Mass.; s. Alan James and Esther Victoria (Gronberg) R.; m. Barbara Ann Ellis, Aug. 29, 1959; children: Katrina b. 1960, Kristina b. 1964; edn: BS hons., San Jose St. Univ. 1962; MBA, 1968. Career: claims rep. Aetna Casualty Co., San Francisco 1962-64; budget analyst City of San Jose 1964-67; asst. city mgr. City of Santa Cruz 1967-70; personnel dir., bus. mgr. City of San Jose 1970-77, bus. mgr., exec. dir. Sunnyvale Med. Center 1977-87; human resource mgr. Natividad Med. Center, Monterey 1987-90, Santa Clara Office of Edn. 1990-94; dir. of classified personnel and benefit programs, pvt. consultant 1995–; mem: Med. Group Mgrs. Assn.; mil: sgt. USAF 1953-57; Republican; rec: golf, tennis. Ofc: 749 Dubanski Dr San Jose 95123

RINN, FAUNEIL JOYCE, retired political science educator; b. Feb. 10, 1926, Boulder, Colo.; d. Michael McDonald and Fauneil Constance (Hall) Rinn; edn: BA eng., Univ. Cincinnati 1946; MS journalism, Columbia Univ. 1947; MA political sci., Univ. Chgo. 1954; PhD, 1960. Career: reporter, copy ed. Watertown Daily Times, Watertown, N.Y. 1948-52; asst. dir. Pub. Adminstrn. Clearing House, Chgo., Ill. 1953-56; head resident Univ. Chgo., Ill. 1956-58; fellow Brookings Inst., Wash. D.C. 1958-59; instr. Univ. Chgo., Ill. 1959-60;

guest scholar Brookings Inst., Wash. D.C. 1965-66; asst. prof., prof. San Jose St. Univ. 1960–; honors: Phi Kappa Phi achievement award 1988, Pacific Sch. of Religion Shedd fellow 1970-71; mem: Am. Political Sci. Assn., Nat. Womens Political Caucus, Am. Assn. Univ. Women, Calif. Women in Higher Edn. (pres. 1976), Charter Review Com.; ed. San Jose Studies, 1985–, ed. monograph Feminist Literary Criticism, 1974, entries pub. in Encyclopedia Americana, 1980-83; Democrat; Prot. Res: 1447 McDaniel Ave San Jose 95126

RIORDAN, CAROL CAMPBELL, university television producer, entertainment and media consultant; b. May 15, 1946, Fresno; d. Alexander Boyle and Jeanne Carol (Yarnell) Campbell; m. Samuel Gresham Riordan, May 27, 1966; children: Loren Jeremy, Rachel Elisabeth; edn: AA, San Diego City Coll., 1976; BA, The Union Inst., 1976; MFA, Drama, San Diego State Univ. 1992. Career: instr., dir. San Diego Jr. Theatre, 1963-66, Actor's Lab., San Francisco, 1966-68; costume designer Playhouse/Interplayers Theatres, San Francisco 1966-68; Stage 7 Dance Theater, San Diego 1981-83; producer TV edn. San Diego Co. Edn. Office, 1974-76; producer, dir. Comm. Video Ctr., San Diego 1976-78, program mgr. 1978-79; designer-in-residence Three's Co. and Dancers, San Diego 1976-89, bd. dirs., 1981; media producer TV San Diego State Univ., 1982–; consultant in field; awards: North County Comm. TV Found. grantee 1985, Calif. Council Humanities grantee 1988; producer, director TV: Poems of Wonder and Magic, 1986 (Emmy award 1987, Best of Western Ednl. Soc. Telecommunications 1986, ITVA Excellence award 1986, CINDY award 1991), The Fearless Vampire Dressers, 1984 (Best of Western Ednl. Soc. Telecommunications 1985); coauthor w/others: Framework & Instructional Units for Teaching CCTV, 1980; mem: Women in Film, Nat. Acad. TV Arts and Scis. (bd. govs. San Diego chpt. 1989-93, secty. 1990-93), Internat. TV Assn. (S.D. chpt. merit award 1986); civic: Sierra Club (com. 1982), Environmental Defense Fund, Greenpeace Internat.; Zen Buddhist. Ofc: San Diego State Univ. Media Tech Svcs San Diego 92182-0524

RIORDAN, RICHARD J., mayor of Los Angeles; b. 1930, Flushing, NY; m. Eugenia (div.); 5 children; m. 2d., Jill; edn: attended UC Santa Clara; grad. of Princeton Univ. 1952; JD, Univ. of Mich. 1956. Career: joined law firm of O'Melveny & Myers, Los Angeles; investor, num. high-tech entrepreneurial firms, 1960's; bd. dirs. Mattel Toys; owner/operator Original Pantry Cafe; co-founder Total Pharmaceutical Care; co-founder LEARN (blueprint to improve local schools) 1991; sponsor (through the non-profit Riordan Found.),"Writing to Read" computer labs for school children, Eastside Boys & Girls Club, PUENTE Learning Ctr.; mayor, City of Los Angeles 1993–. Ofc: Office of the Mayor City Hall Los Angeles 90012

RISKAS, MIKE, coach, physical education instructor; b. June 22, 1934, Ely, Nev.; s. Nicholas Vasiliou and Helen (Massouris) Riskas; m. Barbara Lou Watson, July 16, 1960; children: Michelle b. 1962, Steven b. 1966; edn: BS, UCLA, 1958, MS, 1967. Career: coach, baseball and football, UCLA, 1958-59; journeyman plumber Reese Plumbing Co., Alhambra 1960-61; coach, football, Alhambra High Sch., 1961; actor, extra/Actor Guilds, Hollywood 1958–; physical edn. instr./coach Pomona Coll., Claremont 1961–; baseball clinician US Baseball Fedn./Olympics, Columbia, S.A. 1984, Gt. Brit. 1987, Am. Baseball Coaches Assn., Europe 1970; editor P.E. courses, Azusa Pacific Coll., 1970-73, P.E. curric. advisor Univ. of Laverne, 1973-76; awards: Coach of Year NCAA Div. III Bsb., San Diego 1986, Coach of Quarter Century Am. Bsb. Coaches Assn., San Diego 1986, French Nat. Coach, French Bsb. Fedn., Paris 1988; mem: Am. Football Coaches Assn. 1961–, Am. Baseball Coaches Assn. 1963–, U.S. Baseball Fedn. 1980–, NCAA Baseball Com. (chmn. div. III 1985-86), Internat. Baseball Assn. 1986–, Screen Extras Guild/SAG 1958-86; civic: Inland Hospice Assn. (life), UCLA 10th Player; author: Baseball Course 1972; mil: seaman USNR 1951-55, sp3c US Army 1955-57; Democrat; Greek Orthodox; rec: sports, gardening. Res: 1655 Clemson Claremont 91711 Ofc: Pomona College 220 E Sixth St Claremont 91711

RISLING, DAVID, university president, professor; b. Apr. 10, 1921, Hoopa-Extension, Calif.; s. David W. and Mary Geneva (Orcutt) R.; m. Barbara Phelps, Apr. 28, 1944; children: Katherine b. 1947, Peg b. 1949, Lyn b. 1950, Kenneth b. 1954; edn: BS, Calif. Polytechnic State Univ. 1947, MA, 1953. Career: lt. comdr. USNR, 1942-46; tchr./dir. Caruthers H.S., Calif. 1948-51; tchr./adminstr. Modesto Jr. Coll., Calif. 1951-70; sr. lectr./adminstr. Univ. of Calif., Davis 1970-92; pres. D-Q Univ., Davis, Calif. 1994–; chmn. bd. of trustees D-Q Univ. 1970-94; bd. dirs.: Calif. Indian Legal Svs. Inc. (chmn. 1968-71), Native Am. Rights Fund 1980- (chmn. 1970-80), Nat. Indian Training and Res. Ctr., Nat. Indian Edn. Assn., Calif. League for Am. Indians, Calif. Indian Edn. Assn. 1967- (pres. 1967-72); v.p., bd. dirs. Assn. on Am. Indian Affairs 1970–; cons., lectr. num. Indian Edn. Conferences; speaker at colls. and univs.; awards: Outstanding Agric. Tchr., CATA 1963, Risling Intertribal award CAL Aggie, UC Davis 1991, Native Am. Elder award Calif. Indian Edn Assn. 1990, Outstanding Indian Educator Calif. Dept. of Edn. 1990, Disting. Publ Svc. award UC Davis 1992, Youth-on-the-Move African Am. Educators Hall of Fame 1994; mem.: Calif. Advy. Council on Vocational & Tech. Edn., Am. Indian Edn. Council (St. of Calif.), Calif. St. Dept. of Edn. Equal Opportunities Commn., Am. Indian Higher Edn. Consortium 1973–, No. Calif. Cultural Comms. 1993–,

Lions Club (Caruthers, Calif. 1948-51, Empire, Calif. 1951-76); author: Parliamentary Procedure (booklet), 1954; co-editor (books): Calif. Indian Found., 1969, Handbook of NAS, 1971; co-author (book): Establishment of DQU, 1972; ed. (documentary collection) Comm. Devel. at DQU, 1983; mil: LCDR, US Navy 1942-46; Native Am. Spirituality; rec: fishing, hunting, Am. Indian affairs (legal, civil rights, spirituality, edn.). Res: 2403 Catalina Drive Davis 95616

RITCHIE, ROBERT OLIVER, engineering educator, researcher, administrator; b. Jan. 2, 1948, Plymouth, U.K., nat. U.S., 1989; s. Kenneth Ian and Kathleen Joyce (Sims) R.; m. Connie Olesen, 1969 (div. 1978); children: James b. 1972; m. Hai Ying Song, 1991; edn: BA, Cambridge Univ., 1969, MA, 1973, PhD, 1973, ScD, 1990; C.Eng. (cert. engr.) U.K. Career: Goldsmith's Res. Fellow, Churchill Coll., Cambridge Univ., U.K. 1972-74; Miller Res. Fellow, lectr. UC Berkeley, Calif. 1974-76; assoc. prof. mech. engring. M.I.T., 1977-81; prof. materials sci. UC Berkeley, 1981–; dir. Ctr. for Advanced Mats., Lawrence Berkeley Lab. 1987-94; dep. dir. Mats. Scis. Div. Lawrence Berkeley Lab. 1990-94; head, structural materials dept. Material Scis. Div., Lawrence Berkeley Nat. Lab. 1994–; cons. on topics of engring. and bio-prosthetic implant (medical) devices: Westinghouse, Rockwell, GE, Garrett Turbine, Exxon, Alcan, Allison, Northrop, Chevron, Grumman, St. Jude Med., Shiley Inc., Carbomedics Inc., Baxter Healthcare, USCI/BARD, other cos.; awards: Marcus A. Grossmann award Am. Soc. for Metals 1980, Champion H. Mathewson gold medal, Minerals Metals Mats. Soc. 1985, George R. Irwin medal ASTM 1985, Curtis W. McGraw research award Am. Soc. Engring. Educators 1987, Rosenhain medal Inst. of Materials, London 1992, Science Digest mag. list of Am. Top 100 Young Scientists (12/84); Fellow Am. Soc. for Metals 1980–, Inst. of Materials, U.K. 1972–, Internat. Congress on Fracture (hon. fellow 1989, v.p. 1993), mem. Minerals Metals & Materials Soc. 1975–; publs: 250+ tech. papers and editor 8 books on fatigue, fracture mechanics and materials sci. of structural mats.- metals, intermetallics, ceramics & composites, 1971–; Republican; rec: orchidist, gardening, x-c skiing. Ofc: Dept. Mats. Sci. & Mineral Engring. Univ. Calif., Berkeley 94720

RIVAS, DANIEL E., college administrator; b. Dec. 11, 1945, Camaguey, Cuba (nat. 1970); s. Daniel J. and Hilda (Gonzalez) R.; edn: BA (honors), Marist Coll., Poughkeepsie, NY 1969; AM, Univ. of Ill., Urbana 1972, PhD, 1977. Career: asst. prof. Auburn Univ., Auburn, Ala. 1977-82, assoc. prof. 1982-85; dean, liberal arts, Saddleback Coll., Mission Viejo, Calif. 1985–; cons. Nat. Endowment for the Humanities, W.D.C. 1992–, Am. Assn. of Comm. Colleges, W.D.C. 1993–; bd. dirs. Laguna Beach Comm. Clinic 1994–; awards: undergrad. award in French, Marist Coll. 1967, Univ. Fellow in French, Univ. of Ill. 1971-73; author: pub. articles. Ofc: Liberal Arts Saddleback College 28000 Marguerite Pkwy Mission Viejo 92692

RIVERS, ERNEST LAWRENCE, business executive, motivational speaker; b. Dec. 18, 1927, Eureka, Calif.; s. Jefferson Davis and Pearl (Hammock) R.; m. Patricia Vaneman, Nov. 11, 1962 (dec. 1989); edn: grad. Boulder Creek (Calif.) H.S. 1945; private tutoring in semantics by Dr. S.I. Hiyakawa; cert. massage therapist, So. Calif. Sch. of Massage (annex to Mueller Coll. of Holistic Tng.), San Diego. Career: owner/operator Laguna Plaza Service (auto repair) San Francisco 1956-59; steward/exec. com. Internat. Assn. of Machinists and Aerospace Workers (IAM/AW) Local 1305, 1963-81; business mgr./advisor Beverly Styles Music, Yucca Valley, Calif. 1981–; owner/operator Quiet Place Studio (haven for disadvantaged or physically impaired men and women, including alcoholics and drug addicts), Yucca Valley 1982–; founder, exec. dir. The Lawrence Program of Calif. (recovery prog. for alcohol and drug addiction), Yucca Valley 1990–; founder (with Beverly Styles), dir. Quiet Place Recording Studio (music recording and pub. co.), Yucca Valley 1995–; owner/dir. Grant Fund Research Service (support svc. in applying for grants and scholarships), Yucca Valley 1995–; national motivational speaker on improved lifestyle through structured programs of recovery; awards: 25 Year Pin, IAM/AW Local 1305, 1988; mem: Anti-Drug Prog., San Mateo 1978-81, Am. Council on Alcoholism 1992–, Nat. Council on Alcoholism 1993–, Small Bus. Assn. 1994–; contbg. mem. Calif. Arts Commn.; author: (books) Only the Good Times, 1985, The Hunter Who Spoke, 1993, The Gentle Curmudgeon, 1994, (journal) Alcoholism in the Work Place, 1973, num. articles, manuscripts, tech. pamphlets and tracts; mil: F1/c, USCG/Navy, 1946-47; Republican; Catholic; rec: golf, music, travel, working with the disadvantaged. Ofc: Quiet Place Studio 7839 Aster Ave Ste 2 Yucca Valley 92284-4130 FAX: 619/369-1825

RIZZA, JOSEPH PADULA, U.S. naval officer/president emeritus California State Maritime Academy; b. Jan. 30, 1915, Johnstown, Pa.; s. Paul and Concetta Rizza; m. Marie Follin, Aug. 30, 1947 (widowed Mar. 1, 1992); edn: Dip., Penna. Maritime Acad. 1936; BA, Univ. of Wash. 1950; MA, Boston Univ. 1958; Dip., Naval War Coll., Newport R.I. 1959, Nat. War Coll., Wash DC 1970; Master Mariner, USCG 1942–. Career: Merchant Marine Ofcr. U.S. Lines Co., 1936-1942; during naval career advanced thru Capt. USN, 1942-72. Pacific Fleet WWII 1942-45; Cmdr. Destroyer Escort Squadron Three, U.S. Pacific Fleet 1958-1960; held major command positions ashore and at sea: cmdg. ofcr. USS Spangler, Pacific Fleet 1946-47, USS Gregory (destroyer), Pacific Fleet

1954-56, USS Mountrail (APA 213), Atlantic Fleet 1962-64; cmdg. ofcr. US Naval Adv. Repub. of Korea, 1960-62; mil. policy planner Jt. Chiefs of Staff Wash DC 1964-66; cmdr. Destroyer Squadron 24, U.S. Atlantic Fleet, 1966-68; Chief of Staff US Naval Forces Vietnam 1968-69; dir. of instrn. and curriculum devel. National War Coll. Wash DC 1969-72; pres. California Maritime Academy 1972-84; Rear Admiral US Maritime Service 1972–, decorated Legion of Merit (2), Meritorious Service medal, Jt. Service Commendn. medal, Navy Unit Commendn. medal, 4 USN Battle Efficiency Awards, Calif. Medal of Merit; honors: Phi Beta Kappa 1950, Brass Hat Award for Maritime Man of the Year, Propeller Club of the Golden Gate 1981, Person of Year, Johnstown, Pa. 1983, US Dept. of Transp. highest award for exceptional public service 1983, distinguished alumni, Penna. Maritime Acad. 1980, Commendations, Calif. Senate and Assembly 1983, Maritime Man of Yr. San Diego Propellor Club 1987, Coronado Rotarian of Yr. 1993; mem: Am. Soc. of Internat. Law, Nat. Assn. for Indsl. Technology, Council of Am. Master Mariners, (Lic. Master Mariner unlmtd. tonnage any ocean), Maritime Tng. Advy. Bd., Rotary Intl. (pres. Vallejo Club 1981-82), Coronado Rotary Club 1984–, Vallejo C.of C. (dir. 1980-83), Propeller Club of the U.S. (Golden Gate, pres. San Diego), dir. Navy League (S.D. Council 1984–), Civil Service Commn. San Diego County (pres. 1988, commr. 1986-93); civic: Silverado Council Boy Scouts (v.p. 1979-82), Coronado Roundtable (steering com. 1984–), World Affairs Council San Diego 1980– (bd. dirs. 1994–96), Coronado Hosp. (bd. dirs. 1995–); rec: sailing, golf. Res: 1830 Avenida Del Mundo, 1605, Coronado Shores 92118

ROBBINS, JACK HOWARD, lawyer; b. May 16, 1957, Los Angeles; s. Albert M. and Helen (Karabenick) R.; m. Cindy L. Cannon, Jan. 7, 1990; edn: BA polit. sci. (cum laude) CSU Northridge, 1979; JD, Loyola Law Sch., 1982; admitted bar: Calif. 1982, U.S. Dist. Ct. (Central, So. and Eastern Dists.) 1982, Ct. of Appeals (9th Cir.) 1982. Career: atty., assoc. Wilson, Kenna & Borys, L.A. 1985-88; Bottum & Feliton, L.A. 1988-90; sole law practice, Sacramento 1991–; judge pro tempore Sacramento Co. Superior Court 1994–; mem: Arbitration Panel Sacto. Co. Superior Ct. 1992–, Am. Bar Assn. (mem. Dispute Resolution Sect.), The State Bar of Calif. (mem. Comm. on Admin. of Justice 1993-94), Sacto. Co. Bar Assn. (mem. Atty./Client Relations Com.), Calif. Dispute Resolution Council, 1995–; civic: Citrus Hts. C.of C. 1991–, Fair Oaks Comm. Planning Advy. Council (1991–, chmn.); Democrat (Sacto. Co. Dem. cent. com. 1991–), Culver City Dem. Club (1987-89, past pres.); Jewish; rec: skiing, tennis. Res: 8605 Jaytee Way Fair Oaks 95628-2976 Ofc: Law Office of Jack Robbins 2625 Fair Oaks Blvd Ste 1 Sacramento 95864-4936 Ph 916/486-4444

ROBBINS, WILLIAM CURTIS, JR., film and television producer, director, writer, news reporter, cameraman; b. Dec. 24, 1948, Chgo.; s. William Curtis, Sr. and Jean Vallee (Guyot) R.; edn: grad. San Marcos H.S., Santa Barbara, Calif. 1968; grad. Airline Sch. Pacific, Santa Monica 1969, Danny Rouzer Sch. Motion Picture Photography, Hollywood 1971. Career: producer Marine Movies, Santa Barbara 1966-68, Looking Glass Films, Santa Barbara 1972; producer, director, writer, news reporter and cameraman Cinema Tech Films, Hollywood 1972-76, Jimmy Oz Prodns., Temple City 1976–; founder, exec. dir. Corp. for Children's TV, 1987; cons. various cable and t.v. stations, 1973–; producer t.v. film: Flying Kids 1988; producer, dir., writer (short subjects) The Geni (1988), The Watchdog (1988), The Circus (1988), The Landing (1989); producer Children's Storybook Hour, KIEV 870-AM, Glendale (1990), (children's t.v. show) Beverly's Farm (1991); author: Sunshine the Sea Otter (1976), Her Father's Daughter (1981), How To Land & Takeoff Safely At Santa Catalina's Airport-in-the-Sky (1989), Helicopter Pilot Handbook (1990); accident prevention counselor FAA, 1982–; mem: Soc. Motion Picture and TV Engrs., Order Iron Test Pattern (ofcr. 1986–), Mad Scientists' Group, Temple City (exec. dir., founder 1989); rec: flying, underwater diving and photography. Ofc: Jimmy Oz Productions, PO Box 128 Temple City 91780-0128 Tel:818/285-0144

ROBBOY, MERLE S., physician; b. Feb. 9, 1941, Cleveland, Ohio; s. George M. and Mary Rose (Frankel) R.; m. Christine E. Stevens; children: Susan b. 1961, Meade b. 1964; edn: BA, Western Reserve Univ. 1961; MD, Ohio St. Univ. 1965. Career: rotating intern USPHS, Seattle, Wash. 1965-66, surgeon, San Francisco 1966-68; resident UCLA Med. Center, Los Angeles 1968-71; gen. and surgery oncology City of Hope Med. Center, Duarte 1972–; pvt. practice ob-gyn., Newport Beach 1972-94; assoc. clin. prof. UC Irvine Med. Center 1974-94; chmn. dept. ob-gyn. Hoag Meml. Hosp., Newport Beach 1982-84; awards: Roessleer Research scholarship 1964; mem: Orange Co. Ob-Gyn. Soc. (pres. 1983-84), Pacific Coast Fertility Soc., Am. Fertility Soc., Am. Coll. Ob-Gyn. (fellow), Pacific Coast Ob-Gyn. Soc., Southwest Ob-Gyn. Soc., Am. Assn. Gynecology Laparoscopists, Newport Harbor Orchid Soc., Am. Dahlia Soc.; 3 articles pub. in med. jours. 1971-87; mil: surgeon major USPHS 1966-68; Republican; Jewish; rec: orchids, dahlias, gardening. Ofc: 1401 Avocado Ave Ste 801 Newport Beach 92660

ROBECK, CECIL MELVIN, JR., clergyman, church history educator; b. Mar. 16, 1945, San Jose, Calif.; s. Cecil Melvin and Berdetta Mae (Manley) R.; m. Patsy Jolene Gibbs, June 14, 1969; children: Jason Lloyd b. 1972, John Mark b. 1974, Peter Scott b. 1977, Nathan Eric b. 1979; edn: AA, San Jose City Coll., 1967; BS, Bethany Bible Coll., Santa Cruz 1970; MDiv, Fuller Theol. Sem.,

1973, PhD, 1985; ordained minister Assemblies of God, 1973. Career: grad. tchg. asst. Fuller Theol. Sem., Pasadena 1973-78, adj. instr. 1981-85, asst. prof., assoc. prof. church history 1985-88, 88-92, assoc. prof. church history and ecumenics, 1992–, adminstrv. staff 1974–, dir. admissions 1977-79, dir. student svs. 1979-83, dir. acad. svs. 1983-85, asst. dean, assoc. dean acad. pgms. Sch. of Theology 1985-92; awards: Joseph L. Gerhart scholar 1969, staff devel. grantee Assn. Theol. Schs. in U.S. and Canada 1977; mem. World Council of Churches Plenary Commn. on Faith and Order 1991–; mem. Nat. Council of Churches Commn. on Faith and Order 1985–, NCC Pentecostal Dialogue (co-chair 1988-91, 1995–), Internat. R.Cath./Pentecostal Dialogue, Vatican City (internat. steering com., treas. 1985–, co-chair 1992–), Local Evangelical/R.Cath. Dialogue, L.A. (1987-92, co-chair 1992–), N.Am. Acad. of Ecumenists (bd. 1989–), Secretaries of Christian World Communions 1993–; trustee Bethany Bible Coll. (1985-88, exec. com. 1986-88); fellow Wesleyan/Holiness Studies Ctr. Asbury Theol. Sem. 1987-90; mem. Soc. for Pentecostal Studies (1977–, pres. 1982-83), Am. Acad. of Religion 1984–, Pacific and Am. Assns. of Collegiate Registrars and Admissions Ofcrs. 1975-85, Nat. Assn. Student Personnel Adminstrs. 1980-85, N. Am. Patristics Soc. 1993–; author: Prophecy At Carthage, 1992, editor (books) Charismatic Experiences in History, 1985, Witness To Pentecost, 1985, (journal) Pneuma: The J. of the Society for Pentecostal Studies, 1984-92, num. jour., book and dict. articles, 1974–; Republican; rec: writing, camping, travel. Ofc: Fuller Theological Seminary Pasadena 91182

ROBERTS, CHARLES MORGAN, optometrist; b. June 13, 1932, Roswell, N.M.; s. Clarence A. and Annie Lorene (Perkins) R.; m. Gloria Vivian Lasagna, Feb. 24, 1962; children: Michael b. 1963, Janis b. 1965; edn: AA engring., Mt. San Antonio Coll., 1958; BS organic chem., Univ. La Verne, 1961, MA organic chem., 1970; BS physiol. optics, So. Calif. Coll. Optometry, Fullerton 1972, OD, 1974; Diplomate of Cornea & Contact Lenses Am. Acad. of Opt. 1977, bd. cert. contact lenses N.E.R.F. 1981. Career: electronic engr. Aerojet General, Covina 1955-65; research chemist Sunkist Orange Prod. Div., Ontario 1965-70; cons. physician U.S. Pub. Health Service, San Pedro 1974-77; asst. prof. So. Calif. Coll. Optometry, Fullerton 1974–; Dr. of optometry pvt. practice, San Juan Capistrano, 1975–; awards: res. fellow, outstanding achieve. award Bausch & Lomb 1974, instr. of yr. SCCO 1975, Rotarian of Yr. 1978; mem: Am. Acad. Opt. (fellow 1976–), Am. Opt. Assn. 1970–, Calif. Opt. Assn. 1970–, Orange Co. Opt. Soc. (bd. dirs. 1981-83); clubs: Rotary Intl. (San Juan Cap. pres., bd. dirs. 1975-82), Elks (San Clemente); author: Contact Lens Modification 1980, Math of Contact Lens 1985, editor: Dict. of Visual Science 1990; mil: RM2 USN 1951-55; Republican; Lutheran; rec: computers, aviation. Ofc: Charles M. Roberts, O.D., Inc. 32282 Camino Capistrano "B" San Juan Capistrano 92675

ROBERTS, ERIC STENIUS, computer science educator; b. June 8, 1952, Durham, N.C.; s. James Stenius and Anne Hall (Estep) R.; edn: AB (cum laude), Harvard Coll. 1973; SM, Harvard Univ., 1974, PhD, 1980. Career: asst. prof. Wellesley Coll., 1980-85; research scientist DEC Systems Res. Ctr., Palo Alto 1985-90; assoc. prof. Stanford Univ., 1990–; vis. prof. Harvard Univ., 1984-85; awards: NSF grad. fellow, Harvard 1973-76; pres. Computer Profls. for Social Responsibility 1990–; mem: Assn. for Computing Machinery, IEEE, Democratic Socialists of Am.; author: Thinking Recursively (1986), The Art and Science of C (1995); Democrat; Soc. of Friends. Res: 2256 Bowdoin St Palo Alto 94306 Ofc: Dept. Computer Sci. Stanford University, Stanford 94305

ROBERTS, INES ELEONORE (Lady Roberts), photographer, artist, educator; b. July 15, 1929, Danzig; d. Alfons and Margarete (Labunski) m. Sir Gilbert Howland Rookehurst Roberts; children: Solveig b. 1959, Howland b. 1961; edn: SRN (highest aggregate), Essex Sch. of Nursing, England 1954; BSc, 1955; self-taught in photography. Career: instr. in photography Laguna Blanca High Sch., Santa Barbara, Calif. 1972-86; instr. photog. UC Santa Barbara Extension, 1978–; conv. workshop instr. Calif. Art Educators Conv., Santa Barbara and San Francisco, 1975; co-dir., founder Santa Barbara Photographic Gallery, 1975-80; photographic assignments for Direct Relief Found. in Guatemala 1968, 72; awards: Silver Medal R.P.S. Internat. Print Exhib. 1992, London Salon of Photog. Medal 1988-89, Nikon Internat. Photo. Contest Bronze Medal 1988-89, Sierra Annual Photo Contest 1st Prize 1987, 94, Ventura Art Forum 1st Prize 1970, Johnson of Hendon Chem. All British Competition 1st Prize 1966, Advocate for the Arts nominee Santa Barbara County 1988; Fellow, Royal Photographic Soc. 1992; mem: Photographic Soc. Am., S.B. Museum of Art, Sierra Club, Channel City Camera Club (pres. 1980, 90), U.S. Hang Gliding Assn., Photographers Gallery London, London Salon Photography; public presentations: Ines E. Roberts Harmonic & Visual Synthesis (36+ different programs 1972-89); publs: various articles in "Letter from America" Photo News Weekly, London, 1967-77, Color Foto "Lichwelten" in Munich Portfolio, 1986, Foto Creativ - München, 1991, Photo Digest Canada, 1992, Photographic Yearbook of Great Britain, 1991, 92, Photography "Draussen", 1994, R.P.S. Journal, 1994, Foto Creativ - Munich, 1995; rec: hang gliding.

ROBERTS, LEE MACK, JR., president private investigation, security and alarm company; b. Sept 14, 1948, Gastonia, NC; s. Lee Mack Sr. and Bonnie Estelle (Smallwood) R.; m. Vernon Wooten, Nov 11, 1972; children: Paula b. 1963, Paul b. 1965; edn: AA, Golden West Coll. 1974; BA, Univ. of Redlands

1977; Licenses: pvt. investigator/ pvt. patrol/alarm co.; cert. fraud examiner. Career: detective Newport Beach Police Dept. 1970-81 (med. ret.); pres. Roberts Protection & Investigations, 1982–; instr. Golden West Coll., Criminal Justice Tng. Ctr.; awards: named Outstanding Police Ofcr. of the Yr. 1973, 3 time recipient Police Award of Merit (1976, 77, 79) Newport Beach Police Dept., Am. Law Enforc. Ofcrs. Assn. Legion of Honor, Honored citizen Orange Co. Bd. Supvrs. 1979, listed Who's Who in Am. Law Enforcement; mem: Calif. Conf. & Internat. Assn. of Arson Investigators, Internat. Assn. for Identification, Am. Soc. Industrial Security (A.S.I.S.), Calif. Assn. Licensed Investigators (C.A.L.I.); works: Procedural Crime Scene Investigators Handbook, Newport Bch. PD; proposal for creation of multi-jurisdictional burglary impact team; plan to create Orange Co. Police Mus.; contracted, placed first pvt. security team into Kuwait, 20 days after cease-fire with Iraq to protect Am. owned businesses; solved Tay homicide, dubbed by media "Honor Roll Murder"; mil: cpl. USMC 1965-68; Republican; Baptist; rec: police memorabilia collector. Ofc: Roberts Protection & Investigations, 838 N Van Ness Ave Santa Ana 92701

ROBERTS, MARK SCOTT, lawyer; b. Dec. 31, 1951, Fullerton; s. Emil Siedel and Theda (Wymer) R.; m. Sheri Lyn Smith, Sept. 23, 1977; 3 children; edn: grad. Hampden DuBose Acad., Fla. 1970; BA in theater, Pepperdine Univ., 1975, JD, Western St. Univ., 1978; cert. civil trial advocacy Hastings Coll., 1985; cert. program of instrn. for lawyers Harvard Law Sch., 1990; admitted bar: Calif. 1980, US Supreme Ct. 1989, US Ct. Mil. Appeals 1989, US Tax Ct. 1990. Career: concert mgr. Universal Studios, Hollywood 1973-74; legal intern Dist. Atty. Fullerton, 1978-79; tchr. Anaheim Unif. Sch. Dist. 1979-80; faculty Biola Univ., La Mirada 1980-82; atty. sole practice, Fullerton 1980-85; pres. Mark Scott Roberts and Assocs., PLC, 1985–; judge pro tem Orange County Superior Ct; mem. Orange County Bar Assn.; rec: baseball, skiing. Ofc: 285 E Imperial Hwy Ste 107 Fullerton 92635

ROBERTS, WALTER HERBERT BEATTY, physician, medical educator; b. Jan. 24, 1915, Field, Canada; nat. 1965; s. Walter McWilliam and Sarah Caroline (Orr) R.; m. Olive Louise O'Neal, Sept. 1, 1937; children: Gayle b. 1939, Sharon b. 1942, David b. 1949; edn: MD, Coll. Med. Evangelists Loma Linda Univ. 1939. Career: med. dir. Rest Haven Hosp. & Sanitarium, Sidney, B.C. 1940-53; instr., prof. anatomy, Loma Linda Univ. 1955–; chmn. anatomy dept. 1974-81; honors: Alpha Omega Alpha, Sigma Xi; mem: San Bernardino Co. Med. Assn., CMA Am. Assn. Anatomy; articles pub. in med. jours., 1959-84; Republican: SDA; rec: nature. Res: 11366 Campus Loma Linda 92354 Ofc: Department of Anatomy Loma Linda University Stewart St Loma Linda 92350

ROBERTSON, J. MARTIN, lawyer; b. April 30, 1952, Danville, Ill.; s. Calloway M. and Barbara (Holland) R.; edn: AB, Miami Univ. 1974; JD, Univ. Cincinnati 1978; Ohio St. Univ. 1978-79. Career: atty. Southeastern Ohio Legal Services, Steubenville and Chillicothe, Ohio 1979-80; asst. district counsel, Dept. of Army, Corps of Engrs. Office of Counsel, Huntington, W.Va., and Jacksonville, Fla. 1980-83; asst. atty. gen. Ohio Atty. Gen., Columbus, Ohio 1983-84; trial atty. Dept. of Navy Office of Gen. Counsel, San Francisco and Wash. D.C. 1984-92; mem. Ware & Freidenrich, Palo Alto, Calif. 1992-93, Gray Cary Ware & Freidenrich, Palo Alto 1993–; awards: Special Service Award, Dept. of Army Corps of Engrs. 1983, Award for Excellence, Dept. of Navy 1991. Ofc: Gray Cary Ware & Freidenrich 400 Hamilton Ave Palo Alto 94301

ROBINS, JOHN CALVIN MACGREGOR, physician, surgeon, gynecologist; b. Oct. 10, 1924, Detroit, Mich.; s. John Calvin and Julia May (Knoiihuizen) R.; m. Elizabeth Lou Snow, Aug. 27, 1949; children: Jessica b. 1955, Robert b. 1956, Derek b. 1959, Anthony b. 1961; edn: Univ. Mich. Ann Arbor 1942-43; BA, Hope Coll. Holland Mich. 1946-49; MD, Wayne St. Univ. 1949-54. Career: surgical fellow City of Hope, Duarte 1967-68; head gyn. oncology Naval Hosp., Oakland 1968-69; exec. ofcr., chief ob-gyn. U.S. Naval Hosp., Naples, Italy 1969-72; Kaiser Med. Center, Oakland 1975-78; pvt. practice, San Leandro 1978-85; chief gyn. VA Med. Center Martinez 1985-91; commdg. ofcr. 1st Med. Batt. Vietnam 1966-67; exec. ofcr. Naval Hosp. Lemore 1964-66; v.chief ob-gyn. Naval Hosp. San Diego 1961-64; staff ob-gyn. Naval Hosp. Corpus Christi, Tx. 1958-61; chief resident ob-gyn. Baylor Med. Sch., Houston, Tx. 1954-58; mem: Am. Coll. Ob-gyn. (fellow), Pan Pacific Surgical Assn., St. Andrews Soc. S.F., Clan McGregor Soc. Calif. & Scotland, First Marine Div. Assn. No. Calif. Soc. Med. Friends of Wine, Marines Meml. Club S.F.; mil: capt. USN MC 1942-75; Bronze Star 1967; Republican; Episcopalian; rec: theatre, gardening, sailing.

ROBINSON, ARCHIE STIRLING, lawyer; b. May 28, 1939, Long Beach; s. Archie W. and bonnie May (Noble) R.; m. Susan Hunter, Aug. 19, 1962; children: Jennifer b. 1965, Christopher b. 1967, Matthew b. 1974, Benjamin b. 1976; edn: BA, Columbia Univ. 1960; JD, Stanford Univ. Law Sch. 1963. Career: mng. shareholder Robinson & Wood, San Jose 1964–; advocate Am. Bd. Trial Advocates; fellow Am. Coll. Trial Lawyers; mem: Defense Research Inst. (past pres.), Calif. Defense Counsel (past pres.), Assn. Defense Counsel No. Calif. (past pres.), Stanford Law Soc. (past pres.), Internat. Assn. Defense Counsel, Fedn. Ins. & Corp. Counsel, Am. Ins. Attys., Advent Ministries (dir.); num. articles pub. in profl. jours.; Democrat; Prot.; rec: golf, tennis. Res: 14020 Shadow Oaks Way Saratoga 95070 Ofc: Robinson & Wood 227 N 1st St San Jose 95113

ROBINSON, JEFFREY ALAN, engineering associate; b. March 21, 1955, San Jose; s. James Arthur and Frances Sharon (Amlin) R.; m. Bonnie Marie Deto, Jan. 12, 1978; children: Michelle b. 1979, Scott b. 1983; edn: AS, De Anze Coll. 1979. Career: wafer processor Siltec Corp., Menlo Park 1976-78; machinist Weiss Precision Machining, Redwood City 1978-79; sr. technologist Bendix Field Engring., Livermore 1977-79; Lawrence Livermore Nat. Lab. 1979–, design team member Space Based Sensors 1989–; awards: Dept. Energy Award of Excellence 1988; mem: Am. Vacuum Soc. No. Calif., Elks; articles pub. in tech. jours., 1984 2 engring. notes pub. 1985; Republican; Ch. of Nazareen; rec: carpentry, photog., astronomy. Res: 833 Amber Pl Manteca 95336 Ofc: Lawrence Livermore National Laboratory POB 808 L-273 Livermore 94550

ROBINSON, JOHNNIE DELL, photographer; b. Jan. 26, 1915, Greensboro, Ala.; d. Johnnie Morse and Della (Cain) Miranda; m. Willie Pope, July 29, 1934 (div. 1959); m. James Asa Robinson, July 12, 1966; children: Pamela Jean Pope b. 1950, Rebecca Sue Pope b. 1952; Career: window trimmer Pausons Clothing Store, San Francisco 1951-60; Hinks Dept. Store, Berkeley 1969-85; ret.; photographer Womens C.of C., Berkeley 1984-89; awards: Nat. Council Negro Women Cert. Merit 1976, Internat. Finishing Sch. scholarship 1948; mem: Acorn Camera Club (life), Berkeley Hist. Soc. (bd. mems. 1982-85), Negro Hist. Soc., Berkeley Arch. Heritage Assn., Landmarks Commn., Eastern Star Lodge; 5 photo documentaries including the new St. Paul A.M.E. Ch. in Berkeley, Calif.,1959–; Democrat; African Methodist; rec: architectural photography (collection includes 49 original photos of 1906 earthquake and fire in San Francisco, 64 original photos and 39 original glass plate negatives of Old Franciscan Missions of Calif.). Res: 1428 67th St Berkeley 94702

ROBINSON, MURIEL F. COX, physician, psychiatrist; b. Nov. 6, 1927, Columbus, Ohio; d. Henry Willard and Veola Garry (Isbell) Cox; m. Julius Ceasar Robinson MD, June 2, 1950 (div. 1976); edn: Ohio St. Univ. 1945-48; MD, Meharry Med. Coll. 1952. Career: psychiatry resident Homer G. Phillips Hosp., St. Louis 1953-56; staff psychiatrist St. Louis Child Guidance Clinic, Mo. 1956-57; Napa St. Hosp., Imola 1958; Richmond Health Center, Richmond 1958-75; gen. psychiatry pvt. practice, Richmond and Oakland 1960-79; staff psychiatrist E. Oakland Mental Health Center, Oakland 1976-79; Dept. Youth Authority, Sacto. 1979-92; Locum Tenens Physician Group, 1992-94; biog. listed Who's Who Among Black Am.; mem: Am. Psychiatric Assn. (Life), Black Psychiatrists of Am., Nat. Med. Assn., AMA, AAAS, Sacto. NAACP; Prot.; rec: flute (recorder). Res: PO Box 292148 Sacramento 95829

ROBISON, STEPHEN ELLIOTT, college administrator; b. Sept. 3, 1951, Berkeley; s. James Robert and Lily Rebecca R.; m. Karen Anne Cutter, Sept. 15, 1973; children: Ryan b. 1981, Sara b. 1984; edn: BA political sci., CSU Hayward 1974. Career: dir. Experimental Univ., CSU Hayward, 1973-74, pres. of Arts Letters and Social Sciences Student Council, CSUH 1974-75, pres. Associated Students CSUH 1976; pgm. asst. w. reg. US Dept. Ag., San Francisco 1976; counselor aide Chabot Coll., Hayward 1977; campus activities, resources advisor Ohlone Coll., Fremont 1977-80; coord. student activities Coll. of San Mateo 1980–; guest speaker CSU Hayward 1976, Emeritus Inst. Coll. of San Mateo 1988; honors: BSA Eagle Scout (1968), CSU Hons. List (1971-73); mem: Nat. Assn. Student Personnel Adminstrn., Calif. Comm. Colls. Student Affairs Assn. (state exec. com. 1985–, state treas. 85-86, reg. 3 rep. 86-95), Am. Lung Assn. (p.r. com. 1988); steering com. San Mateo Co. No on Drugs 1987-88; ed. Coll. of San Mateo Student Handbook (1981-95); rec: backpacking, camping, swimming. Res: 1333 Sunnyslope Ave Belmont 94002 Ofc: College of San Mateo Student Activities Office 1700 W Hillsdale Blvd Room 5-125 San Mateo 94002

ROBISON, WILLIAM ROBERT, lawyer; b. May 5, 1947, Memphis, Tenn.; s. Andrew Cliffe, Sr. and Elfrieda (Barnes) R.; m. Hye Sook Park, Dec. 17, 1982 (div. Apr. 1992); edn: AB, Boston Univ. 1970; JD, Northeastern Univ. 1974; admitted bar: Mass. 1974, Dist. Col. 1975, Calif. 1978. Career: atty., assoc. Meyers, Goldstein & Crossland, Boston 1975-76; assoc. Cooley, Shrair, et al Springfield, Mass. 1976-78; assoc. Hertzberg, Koslow & Franzen, Los Angeles 1978-79; assoc. Marcus & Lewi, 1980-81; atty. solo practice, Santa Monica 1981–; judge pro tem L.A. Mncpl. Ct. 1984–, L.A. Superior Ct. 1987–; instr. Northeastern Univ. 1975-76; bd. dirs. Action for Boston Comm. Devel. 1972-76, Boston Legal Assistance Project 1972-76; mem: Am., Mass. 1974-78, Calif., Los Angeles Co., Santa Monica bar assns.; coauthor: Commercial Transactions Desk Book, Inst. for Bus. Planning (1977); Democrat; Unitarian; rec: econs. Res: 2546 Amherst Ave Los Angeles 90064 Ofc: William R. Robison 2546 Amherst Ave Los Angeles 90064

ROBLEDO, GILBERTO, college counselor, professor; b. Sept. 1, 1940, Santa Paula; s. Felix and Virginia (Reyes) R.; m. Joy Moody, Sept. 24, 1966; children: Maya b. 1971, Alma b. 1975; edn: BA sociology, UC Santa Barbara 1964; MA sociology. San Diego St. Univ. 1968; PhD, edn., adminstrn., UC Santa Barbara 1978; AA, liberal studies, Santa Barbara Comm. Coll. 1995; tng. of trainers in multicultural edn. and cultural diversity, Steadson Univ., Deland, Fla. 1995. Career: probation ofcr. Santa Barbara and San Diego Co. Probation Depts., Santa Maria and San Diego 1966-69; prof. Chicano studies San Diego Comm. Coll. and San Diego St. Univ. 1969-72; assoc. dir. Chicano Fedn. San Diego Co.

1972-73; coord. grad. minority program UCSD, La Jolla 1973; extended opportunities dir., counselor Santa Barbara Comm. Coll. 1973-83, coord. student operations/admissions and records 1983-84, coord. disabled student svs. 1984-88, counselor/prof. 1988–; pres. Chicano Research & Resources Inc. 1987–; cons. migrant edn. Santa Barbara Co. Sch. Dist. 1989; evaluator Multicultural Comm. Partnership, So. Santa Barbara Co. through Ctr. for Substance Abuse Prevention, WDC 1991-96; awards: UCSB post doctoral fellowship 1987, City of San Diego mayoral cand. 1971, Santa Barbara City Schs. bd. of edn. cand. 1979; mem: UCSB Alumni Assn. (bd. dirs. 1985-92, exec. com. 1988-89), Fund for Santa Barbara, Raza Advocates/Calif. Higher Edn., CCC EOPS Assn. (v.p. 1974-75), La Casa de la Raza Inc. (pres. 1980-85), Santa Barbara Chicano Scholarship Found. (secty. 1985-86), Calif. 19th Dist. Agri. Assn. (bd. dirs. 1983-86), Human Svs. Commn., Santa Barbara Co. 1990-95, Santa Barbara Hispanic C.of C. (Chicano Res. & Resources Inc. and Sabor Latino are active mems.); contbr. Ghosts in the Barrio, 1973, publs: Job Shadowing in Bus. & Industry & Employees with Disabilities, 1986; MA thesis, 1968, doc. diss., 1978; mil: sp4 USAR 1959-65; Democrat; Prot.; rec: hiking, Latin jazz percussion, band ldr., Sabor Latino, Latin jazz. Res: 1422 W Valerio St Santa Barbara 93101 Ofc: 721 Cliff Dr Santa Barbara 93103

ROCKAS, ELENI (HELEN) ROTOUS, pediatrician; b. Nov. 6, 1933, Aberdeen, Wash.; d. Andreas Nikolaos and Georgia Ionna (Zaniakou) Rotous; m. Chris Evangelos Rockas, Apr. 16, 1961; children: Panayiota b. 1963, Andreas b. 1966; edn: attended Univ. of Wash., Seattle 1951-54; MD, Univ. of Wash. Sch. of Medicine 1958. Career: internship Sacramento Med. Ctr., Sacto., Calif. 1958-59; residency Valley Med. Ctr., Fresno 1961-64; civilian med. ofcr. McClellan AFB, Sacto. 1959-61; pvt. practice pediatrics, Fresno 1964-74; med. dir. Central Valley Regional Ctr. for Developmentally Disabled 1975–; lectr. on developmental disabilities Fresno Pacific Coll.; awards: Outstanding Svc. award Am. Cancer Soc., Dist. Penelope of Yr. award 1974, Chpt. Penelope of Yr. award 1974, Most Outstanding Daughter of Yr. 1981-82; Special Olympics Volunteer award 1989; mem: Fresno Madera Med. Soc. (public relations com., public health com.), CMA, Fresno Madera Women's Med. Assn.; civic: Child Abuse Prevention Council, Epilepsy Soc. (bd. dirs. and profl. advy. com.), VCH Rehab. Ctr. (advy. com.), Assn. for Retarded Citizens, Fresno Philharmonic Assn., Law League of Fresno Co., Daughters of Penelope (pres. 1974-75, 84-85), Saint George Greek Orthodox Ch. and choir, Fresno Comm. Chorus; author: jour. article, 1964; rec: piano, dancing, aerobics, calligraphy, Greek culture, food and music. Res: 2555 W San Ramon Ave Fresno 93711

RODD, EMILY PEARL, documentary photographer, columnist; b. June 6, 1908, Wilton, N.Dak.; d. Morris and Gizella (Glickman) Zvorist; m. Samuel M. Rodd, July 31, 1939; 1 son, Philip b. 1941; edn: N.Y. Univ. 1928-29. Career: exec. secty. Boy Scout HQ, N.Y.C. 1927-41; faculty secty. Barnard Coll. 1960-69; swim instr. ARC, Sun City 1972–; instr. photog. techniques 1978–; awards: Temple Beth Sholom Woman of Year 1972, Sun City News Citizen of Year 1988, Sun City C.of C. hon. mem. 1988, Women Helping Women award Soroptimists Internat. 1989, Photog. Soc. Am. Who's Who in Photog. 1985-88, YMCA Women of Achievement Nominee Certificate 1990, Sun City Hall of Honor Plaque for Outstanding Comm. Svc. 1993, So. Calif. Sr. Life & Opportunities and Svs. for Seniors Inc. Remarkable Senior Award 1994; mem: Photog. Soc. Am., Nat. League Am. Pen Women, Delta Theta Chi; clubs: Gen. Fedn. Women's, Sun City Swim (pres. 1975), Kiwanniannes Service, Sun City Camera (pres. 1976); Republican; Jewish; rec: photog., writing, dancing. Res: 25978 Ridgemoor Rd Sun City 92586-2693

RODGERS, THOMAS PAUL, lawyer; b. May 8, 1950, Midland, Tx.; s. Joseph Paul and Lola Catherine (Thomas) R.; edn: BA, La. St. Univ. 1971; JD, Rutgers Univ. 1974; admitted St. Bar Pa. 1974, Calif. 1981. Career: asst. legal ofcr. Internat. Union for Conservation of Nature, Bonn, W.Germany 1974-75; legal asst. Internat. Council Environ. Law 1974-75; enforcement atty. N.J. Dept. Environ., Trenton 1976-77; sr. atty. U.S. EPA, Phila., Pa. 1978-79; sole practice, San Francisco 1981–; cons. U.S. Govt. 1984–; awards: San Francisco Bar Assn. and/or State Bar of Calif. Outstanding Pro Bono Atty. (1984, 85, 87, 88, 89, 90, 91, 92, 93, 94), Castro Lions Maury Perstein (1988); mem: Am. Bar Assn., Internat. Council Environ. Law, San Francisco Bar Assn., Bay Area Lawyers for Individual Freedom, Castro Lions; articles pub. in profl. jours., 1974-79; Democrat; rec: weight lifting, motorcycling. Ofc: 4510 18th St San Francisco 94114-1832

ROE, BENSON BERTHEAU, retired academic cardiothoracic surgeon; b. July 7, 1918, Los Angeles; s. Hall and Helene (Bertheau) R.; m. Jane F. St. John, Jan. 20, 1945; children: David b. 1948, Virginia b. 1950; edn: AB, UC Berkeley, 1939; MD (cum laude) Harvard Med. Sch., 1943; Bd. cert. Am. Bd. Surgery, 1950, Am. Bd. Thoracic Surgery, 1953. Career: intern and jr. resident in surgery Mass. General Hosp. 1943-44, asst. res. 1947-49, chief resident in surgery 1950; Nat. Research Fellow physiology dept. Harvard Med. Sch. 1948-49; Moseley Travelling Fellow of Harvard Med. sch., Univ. of Edinburgh & Royal Infirmary Edinburgh, 1950-51; instr. surgery Harvard Med. Sch. 1950-51; chief of thoracic surgery St. Lukes Hosp., San Francisco 1953-58, also St. Joseph's Hosp., S.F., 1954-58; asst. clin. prof. surgery UC San Francisco 1952-57, prof. of surgery 1965-89, emeritus prof. 1989–, chief of cardiothoracic surgery UCSF 1958-76, co-chief 1976-87, senior mem. Cardiovascular Research Inst., UCSF, 1958-86; cons. in thoracic surgery VA Hosp., S.F. 1958-87, S.F. Gen. Hosp. 1952-87, Letterman Army Hosp. 1979-91; vis. prof. Univ. Utah 1973, Univ. Ky. 1974, Univ. Gdansk, Poland 1977, 1985, Centro Medico Nacional, Santander, Spain 1977, Univ. Ibadan, Nigeria 1979, Nat. Heart Hosp., London 1979, The Sanger Clinic, Charlotte, N.C. 1980, Rush-Presbyn. Hosp., Chgo. 1981, Penrose Hosp., Colo. Springs, Colo. 1981; dir: Control Laser Corp. 1986-88; cons. Laser Surgery Software Inc. 1989–; cons. Appleton-Davies Pubs., 1981–; editl. bd. Pharos, 1986–; honors: UCB Varsity Crew (NRA Champions), Golden Bear, Winged Helmet, Scabbard and Blade, Psi Upsilon Frat. 1939, Harvard- Alpha Omega Alpha, Aesculapian Club, Boylston Med. Soc., Nu Sigma Nu Frat. 1943; mem: Am. Surgical Assn., Am. Assn. for Thoracic Surgery, Am. Coll. Cardiology, Am. Coll. Surgeons (chmn. advy. coun. thoracic surg. 1975-78, cardiovasc. com. 1978-87), Am. Heart Assn. (nat. coms. 1971-75, pres. S.F. 1964-65), AMA, Am. Soc. for Artificial Internal Organs, Calif. Acad. of Medicine (pres. 1970), Chilean Soc. Cardiology (hon.), Dallas Clin. Soc. (hon.), Internat. Cardiovasc. Soc., Howard C. Naffziger Surg. Soc., Pacific Coast Surg. Assn., S.F. Surg. Soc., Soc. Polish Surgeons (hon.), Soc. Thoracic Surgeons, Soc. Univ. Surgeons, Soc. Vascular Surg., We. Soc. for Clin. Research, We. Thoracic Surgical Assn.; civic bds: Am. Cancer Soc. (chmn. exec. com. S.F. 1964-66), Am. Medico-Legal Found. (cons. 1988–), Avery Fuller Found. (trustee 1979–), Miranda Lux Found. (trustee, pres. 1982–), Internat. Bioethics Found. (dir. 1988–), United Bay Area Crusade (bd., exec. com. 1965-70, spl. gifts com. 1977-81), Planned Parenthood Alameda-S.F. (trustee 1986-90), Point Reyes Bird Observatory (trustee 1989–); clubs: Calif. Tennis, Cruising Club of Am., Pacific Union, St. Francis Yacht, Joyce Island Gun; mil: med. ofcr. USNR, USS Philadelphia 1944-46; author 172+ sci. publs. incl. 2 textbooks, 20 textbook chapters, 1 Presdl. Address; mil: lt. US Naval Reserve 1939-46. Res: 100 Thorndale Dr #346 San Rafael 94903 Ofc: Univ. California M593, San Francisco 94143-0118

ROESCHKE, DONALD FREDERICK, lawyer; b. Mar. 20, 1938, Pago Pago, Samoa; s. Charles Edward and Madeline (McCarty) R.; m. Suzann Hogue, July 12, 1969; 1 son: David, b. 1976 (dec. 1994); edn: BS, CSU Northridge 1961; JD, Southwestern Univ. Sch. of Law 1965; admitted bar: Calif., US Supreme Ct., US Dist. Cts., 9th Cir. Ct. Appeals. Career: self- empl. atty. 1966-72; dep. atty. gen. (IV), Calif. Dept. of Justice, Ofc. of Atty. Gen. 1972-93, writs coord. for L.A. Ofc. of State Atty. Gen.; lectr. on writs, write deputy tng. manuals on state & fed. writ & state appellate procedures; prosecutor, Daniel Caudillo case (described by Preble Stolz in Judging Judges); defender for people when Sirhan Sirhan filed for release in Fed. Ct., various cases in Appellate and Supreme Cts. (state & fed.); civic: L.A. Opera League, Sacto. Opera League, State R.R. Mus. (Sacto.), L.A. Co. Nat. History Mus.; publs: Mastering the Art of the Great Writ, Los Angeles Lawyer (2/81); Contg. Role of the Peace Ofcr. After a Crim. Conviction, Police Ofcr. Law Report (6/81); Hist. Aspects and Procedural Limitations of Fed. Habeas Corpus, Am. Jur. Trials (vol. 39 Lawyers Co-operative, 1989, Bancroft-Whitney Co.); Habeas Corpus: Pretrial Rulings, Am. Jur. Trials (vol. 41, 1990, Bancroft-Whitney Co.); Withdrawal of Guilty Plea, Am. Jur. Trials (vol. 42, 1991 Bancroft-Whitney Co.); Republican (Presdl. Task Force); R.Cath.; rec: model R.R., wt. lifting.

ROGAN, GERALD NEAL, family physician; b. Aug. 21, 1946, Miami, Fla.; s. Albert F. and Elaine (Newman) R.; m. Patricia Cunningham, Nov. 4, 1984; edn: dipl. (academic valedictorian) Interlochen Arts Acad., 1964; BA, philosophy of religion, Univ. Mich., 1968, MD 1972; dipl. Am. Bd. Emergency Med. 1981, recertified 1993; Calif. Comm. Colls. instr. cred. Career: gen. rotating intern San Joaquin Gen. Hosp., Stockton 1972-73; physician/emerg. specialist Calif. Emergency Physicians, Oakland 1973-80; family physician Family & Urgent Care, Walnut Creek 1980–; chmn. dept. of family practice John Muir Med. Ctr. 1989-92; instr. Contra Costa Paramedics, Pittsburg 1977; medico-legal cons. to attys. 1976–; honors: Univ. Mich. Dean's List 1966-67, UM honors sci. pgm. 1964-66, merit scholar UM Med. Sch. 1968-69; mem: Am. Acad. Fam. Physicians, Alameda Contra Costa Med. Soc., Calif. Med. Assn. (delegate), Am. Acad. of Family Physicians (pres. Alameda Contra Costa Chpt. 1993-95), Alameda Contra Costa Med. Assn. (councilor), Rotary Club Walnut Creek (Paul Harris Fellow 1988); rec: legal rev., constrn., equestrian, racquetball. Ofc: Family & Urgent Care of Walnut Creek 112 La Casa Via Ste 130 Walnut Creek 94598

ROGAWAY, BETTY JANE, school system administrator, social worker; b. Sept. 8, 1921, San Francisco; d. Irvine and Dorothy (Nathan) Hyman; m. Roderick Matthew Rogaway, Jan. 16, 1945 (dec. Aug. 1964); children: Stephen, Kathryn Rogaway Farrell; edn: BA, U. Calif., Berkeley, 1942; MA, Calif. State U., San Jose, 1968. Career: Lic. social worker, Calif. Social worker Travelers Aid 1942, Child Welfare Svs. Sutter County, Calif. 1945, ARC, 1942-45; juvenile welfare ofcr. Palo Alto (Calif.) Police Dept. 1945-49; tchr., cons., coord. Palo Alto Unified Sch. Dist. 1958-82, ret., 1982; cons. HeadStart, San Francisco 1966, Calif. State Dept. of Edn., Sacramento 1982. mem: City of Palo Alto Task Force on Child Care 1973, County Task Force on Reasonable Efforts for Child Abuse Prevention, San Jose 1988-90; pres., Palo Alto Hist. Assn. 1989-92; v.p., Calif. Child Devel. Adminstrs. Assn., Sacramento 1981-82; pres., mem. Children's Shelter Assn. of Santa Clara Cty., San Jose 1983–. Rec: reading, gardening, bird watching. Res: 1302 Greenwood Palo Alto 94301-3414

ROGGE, PETER T., physician; b. Aug. 16, 1946, NYC, NY; s. Edmund Arthur and Alice Catherine R.; m. Whitney N., Aug. 1, 1970 (div. 1984); m. 2d. Susan Abbott, Dec. 6, 1987; 1 son Daniel b. 1976; edn: BA, chem., Haverford Coll., Pa. 1968; MBA, finance, Univ. of Chgo. 1970; MD, Northwestern Univ. Sch. Medicine 1976; med. lic. St. of Calif. 1977; diplomate Am. Bd. Ob-Gyn 1982. Career: res. asst. in biology Univ. Chg. 1970-71, asst. to dir. MBA Prog., 1971-72; internship and residency ob-gyn UC Davis, Sacto. Med. Ctr. 1976-80, clin inst. ob-gyn 1980-81; ob-gyn assoc. Sacramento Women's Health Care Med. Group 1981-83; ob-gyn practice, Drs. Rogge, Fritz-Zavacki, and Hays-Partner, Sacto 1983–; assoc. clin. prof. ob-gyn UC Davis Sacto Med. Ctr. 1991–; chief, Sutter Mem. Hosp. Dept. Ob-Gyn, Sutter Comm. Hosps. 1990-91, chmn. gynecology quality assurance com. 1988-89, chmn. obstetrics quality assurance com. 1986-87; dir. residency prog. in ob-gyn UC Davis Med. Sch, Sutter Comm. Hosps. 1988-90; awards: voted Outstanding Surgical Teacher by UC Davis med. students. 1980; mem. Alpha Omega Alpha, No. Calif. OB/GYN Soc., Sacto. El Dorado Co. Med. Soc., CMA; author: jour. article, 1979; contbg. author: Manual of Obstetrics (Little, Brown & Co., 1st, 2nd. 3rd, & 4th Edits., 1980, 83, 87, 91), Advances in Clin. Obstetrics and Gynecology (Williams and Wilkens, 1982), Manual of Preventive Services (Little, Brown & Co., 1988). Res: 2797 Azalea Rd Sacramento 95864 Ofc: Peter Rogge, MD 5030 J St Sacramento 95819

ROGGERO, MIGUEL LEONARDO, consumer product company executive; b. May 17, 1962, San Diego, Calif.; s. Roland Victor and Dinorah S. (Lopez) R.; edn: BS, Univ. of So. Calif., L.A., 1984; MBA, The Wharton Sch., Univ. of Penn., Phila., 1989; lic. real estate broker, Calif. 1992. Career: project analyst, Stephen J. Cannell Productions, Hollywood 1984-85; sr. analyst, Paramount Pictures Corp., L.A. 1985-87; pres. & co-founder, Prolube, Inc., L.A. 1989-90; finance mgr./region controller, Pepsi/Pizza Hut, Irvine 1990-92; mgr. bus. development The Walt Disney Co. 1992–; cons., Oto-Telick, Inc., Sherman Oaks 1987-88; cons., Mgmt. Info. Network, L.A. 1987-88; awards: scholarship, Calif. Masonic Found., L.A. 1982; life mem. Beta Gamma Sigma, L.A. 1983; life mem., Sigma Alpha Mu Frat.; mem: USC Sch. of Bus. Alumni Assn. 1984–, Wharton Club of So. Calif. 1989–, USC Associates, 1992–; Republican; Catholic; rec: skiing, cycling, jogging, exotic travel, photography. Res: 4338 N. Oakglen St. Calabasas 91302

ROHLFING, LAWRENCE DAVID, lawyer; b. Sept. 9, 1960, Las Vegas, Nev.; s. Kenneth Leroy Rohlfing and Judith Ann (Williams) Hainsworth; children: Eric b. 1988, Jessica b. 1992, Maureen b. 1993; edn: BA, Whittier Coll. 1982; JD cum laude, Whittier Coll. Sch. of Law 1985; admitted Calif., 9th Circuit, Central Dist., Eastern Dist. Career: ptnr. Williams & Rohlfing, Norwalk 1985-87; Rohlfing & Donnelly, Santa Fe Springs 1987-89; sole practice, Santa Fe Springs 1989–; honors: Who's Who Am. Law; mem: Am. Bar Assn., Assn. Trial Lawyers of Am., L.A. Trial Lawyers Assn., Nat. Ogn. Social Security Reps., L.A. County Bar (vice chair Social Security sect.); Republican; Christian; rec: historical simulation. Ofc: 12631 E Imperial Hwy Ste C115 Sante Fe Springs 90670

ROHRABACHER, DANA congressman; b. June 21, 1947; s. Donald and Doris R.; edn: student, L.A. Harbor Coll. 1965-67; BA in history, Long Beach State Coll. 1969; MA in Am. Studies, Univ. So. Calif. 1976. Career: reporter City News Svc./Radio West, L.A., 4 yrs.; editorial writer Orange County Register, 1979-80; asst. press sec. Reagan for Pres. Campaign, 1976, 80; speechwriter, spl. asst. to Pres. Reagan White House, Washington, 1981-88; mem. 101st-103rd Congresses from 45th Calif. dist., 1989-92, 103rd-104th Congresses from 45th Calif. dist., 1993–; U.S. del. Young Political Leaders Conf., USSR; disting. lectr. Internat. Terrorism Conf., Paris, 1985; awards: Disting Alumnus award L.A. Harbor Coll. 1987. Ofc: US House of Reps 1027 Longworth Bldg Washington DC 20515-0545*

ROHRBERG, RODERICK GEORGE, company president, manufacturing equipment design consultant; b. Sept. 25, 1926, Minneola, Iowa; s. Charles H. and Emma (Minsen) R.; m. Genevieve Mary Sogard, June 19, 1949; children: Karla b. 1950, Roderick K. b. 1952, Cheries b. 1957, Timothy b. 1959, Christopher b. 1964; edn: B. Naval Scis., Marquette Univ. 1946; BSCE, Iowa State Univ. 1949; Reg. Profl. Engr., Calif. Career: bridge design engr. Alaska Rd. Commn., US Dept. Int. 1949-51; sr. tech. spec. res.engr. No. Am. Rockwell, Los Angeles 1951-69; currently, pres. Creative Pathways Inc.; advanced welding services equipment design & devel., pvt. practice as cons., Torrance 1969–; honors: NASA Commdn. 1965; 1st Nat. Airco welding award 1966; Profl. Achiev. Citation, Iowa State Univ. 1973; 3rd pl., Von Karman Memorial Grand Award, 1974; listed Who's Who in Aviation and Aerospace 1983; mem: Am. Welding Soc., Am. Mfg. Engrs.; mil: USNR 1944-46; pvt. pilot. Res: 2742 W 234th Torrance 90505 Ofc: Creative Pathways Inc., 3121 Fujita St Torrance 90505

ROLAND, CHARLES BUTLER, physician; b. May 30, 1930, Chicago, Ill.; s. Benjamin NMN and Mary Esther (Patterson) R.; m. Lois Virginia Hansen, May 22, 1976; children: Christina b. 1976, Christopher Brian b. 1978, Charla b. 1980; edn: BS, Mich. State Univ. 1952; MD, Univ. of Mich. 1956. Career: internship St. Lawrence Hosp., Lansing, Mich. 1956-57; gen. practice, Lansing Mich. 1957-59; med. ofcr. USAF, Germany 1959-61; gen. practice, Saginaw, Mich. 1961-63; anesthesiology residency UC San Francisco 1963-65; pvt. practice, anesthesiology, Roseville, Calif. 1965–; asst. clin. prof., anesthesiology, UCSF Med. Ctr. 1966-68, UC Davis, Sacramento 1971-75; chief of staff Roseville Hosp. 1976-77; med. staff/hosp. surveyor Calif. Med. Assn., S.F. 1995–; mem: Am. Soc. of Anesthesiology 1966–, Calif. Soc. of Anesthesiology 1966–, Sacto. Co. Med. Soc. 1966–; bd. dirs People Reaching Out, Carmichael, Calif. 1994–; author: med. article pub. in Jour. AMA., 1959; mil: capt. USAF 1959-61; rec: photography. Ofc: C.B. Roland M.D. Prof Corp PO Box 41978 Sacramento 95841-1978

ROLL, DOROTHY (INN YUNG) D(UNG), scientist/federal agency regional data base administrator; b. Feb. 26, 1927, Honolulu; d. William Ah Lien and Agnes Kam Lin (Goo) Dung; m. Frederick M. Stewart, July 30, 1954; 1 son, Lorin D.M. b. 1959; m. 2d. Milton Roll, May 15, 1971; edn: att. Tacoma Catholic Coll., Tacoma, Wash. 1945; BS in zoology, Univ. of Wash., 1949; grad. work Univ. of Hawaii, 1950-51. Career: fishery aide U.S. Bureau of Commercial Fisheries, Pacific Oceanic Fisheries Investigations, Honolulu 1949-57; tech. computer Lockheed Corp. Missiles Div., Sunnyvale 1957; fisheries biologist U.S. Bur. of Comml. Fisheries, Ocean Research Lab. Stanford 1957-70; fisheries biologist U.S. Nat Marine Fisheries Service, Southwest Fisheries Center, La Jolla 1970-74, computer systems analyst 1974-75, chief ADP Ops. 1975-86, chief Information Technology Services, 1987–, mem. (chair 1991-92) Nat. Data Mgmt. Com. 1987–, regional data base adminstr. 1988–; awards: U.S. Fed. Service superior meritorious performance, (1953, 62, 70, 74, 81, 84, 90, 91, 92, 93), U.S. Dept. of Commerce Bronze Medal for superior leadership and out-standing contributions to computer sys. excellence in support of marine fisheries res., 1994;mem: Fed. ADP Council of So. Calif. & Ariz. (treas. 1981-82); clubs: Univ. Wash. Newman 1945-49, Chinese Students 1945-49, Orchesis Modern Dance 1946-48, Pi Alpha 1946-49; publs: spl. sci. reports, U.S. Fish & Wildlife Service, 1953, 58, 67; Democrat; Episcopal; rec: gardening, flower arranging, cooking, needlework. Res: 13886 Mira Montana Dr Del Mar 92014 Ofc: Southwest Fisheries Center 8604 La Jolla Shores Dr La Jolla 92037

ROLLER, ROBERT DOUGLAS, III, psychiatrist; b. Nov. 17, 1928, Charleston, W.Va.; s. Francis Oliver and Mary Elizabeth (Rice) R.; m. Anthonia Ijsselstein, March 7, 1970; children: Robert Douglass IV, Katherine Willis, David Nelson, Anthonia Elizabeth, Alexander Robert, John Richard; edn: BA, Univ. Va. 1950, MD, 1960; postgrad. (philosophy), Univ. Pa. 1953-56. Career: instr. Chestnut Hill Acad., Phila. 1953-56; intern Univ. N.C. Hosp., Chapel Hill 1960-61, resident 1961-62; resident Medical Coll. of Va., Richmond 1963; NIMH research and teaching fellow Univ. Calif. Medical Ctr., San Francisco 1963-66; pvt. practice, Berkeley 1966–; assoc. psychiatrist, research psychiatrist UC Berkeley 1965-71; clin. asst. prof. Univ. Calif. Medical Ctr., San Francisco 1970–; clin. instr. Stanford Univ. Medical Sch., Palo Alto 1969-78; mem. Staff Alta Bates Hosp., Berkeley, Herrick Hosp., Berkeley, Walnut Creek Hosp., Lodi Meml. Hosp., Lodi Community Hosp., 1965-72; chief psychiatrist Clear Water Ranch for Children, Santa Rosa 1964-71; honors: Raven Soc., Univ. Va. Rhodes Scholarship candidate 1949, 54; clubs: Farmington CC (Charlottesville, Va.), Univ. Calif. Faculty, St. Anthony (N.Y.), St. Elmo (Va.), Sleepy Hollow Tennis, Bankers (S.F.), Philadelphia Cricket (1952-58); mil: served with US Navy Reserves, 1950-51. Res: 757 San Diego Rd Berkeley 94707

ROMERO, RICHARD D., auto dealer; b. Sept. 4, 1935, Socorro, N.M.; s. James D. and Clara (McCullough) Romero; m. Valerie A., June 20, 1962; children: Valerie b. 1964, Richard b. 1967, Christine b. 1973; edn: BA in bus. adminstrn., Univ. Mex. Career: jr. auditor 20th Century Fox, Hollywood 1956-57; asst. state auditor State of N.M., Santa Fe. 1957-59; gen. mgr. Bob Wickett Chrysler Plymouth Inc., San Bernardino 1960-70; pres. Pomona Valley Nissan 1970–; J. McCullough Corp., Upland 1973–; B.R.A.S. Internat., Reno, Nev. 1975–; Romero Corp., (Romero Buick), Ontario, Calif. 1976–; Romero AMC/Jeep Renault Inc. 1976–; chmn. bd., CEO Collateral Control Systems, Norwalk 1979–; Norwalk Auto Auction 1979–; chmn. bd. Empire Bank N.A., Rancho Cucamonga 1982–; chmn. Calif. Transp. Commn., Sacto. 1983–; awards: Time Mag. Dealer Quality award 1972, Datsun Quality Dealer 1971–, Mr. Hispanic Businessman of Yr., Hispanic Youth Task Force 1985; mem: So. Calif. Nissan Dealers Assn. (options com.), Pomona Valley Auto Dealers Assn., So. Calif. Datsun Dealers Assn., Outstanding Business Achievement award, Alliance of Latino Business Associates, 1987; Imported Automobile Dealer of Distinction, Am. Internat. Auto Dealers Assn. and Sports Illustrated, 1987; trustee Univ. of LaVerne, counsel of Rose Inst. Claremont McKenna Coll.; active Cath. Social Services So. Calif. (dir), Pomona C. of C., Kiwanis; mil: AUS Tank Reserve Corp 1956-62; Republican; R.Cath. Res: 257 W Clark St Upland 91786 Ofc: Empire Nissan, 1377 Kettering Loop Ontario 91761

ROOT, CHARLES JOSEPH, JR., financial advisor; b. July 26, 1940, Pierre, S.Dak.; s. Charles Joseph and Hazel Ann (Messenger) R.; 1 dau., Roseann Marie; m. Sharon Lee, June 24, 1995; 2 stepdaus., Monique Marie Marcillac, Nichole Marie Marcillac; edn: San Francisco Jr. Coll.; Coll. of Marin La Salle Ext. Univ.; Am. Coll. Life Underwriters; desig: reg. investment advisor (RIA), cert. financial planner (CFP), chartered fin. cons. (ChFC). Career: fin. and estate planner Bankers Life Co., San Francisco 1966-78; Planned Estates Assocs., Corte Madera 1978-81; founder and mng. dir. Double Eagle Financial Corp.,

Santa Rosa 1981–, investment advisor 1983–; awards: Paul Harris fellow 1980; mem: Big Brothers of Am. (v.p. San Rafael 1976-80), Com. to Elect William Filante (treas. 1978), Comm. Health Centers of Marin, Wellspring Found., Center for Attitudinal Healing (treas., bd.dirs.), Pickle Family Circus (bd.dirs.), Redwood Estate Planning Assn. (pres. 1995-96), Internat. Assn. Fin. Planners, Coll. Fin. Planning, Registry of Fin. Planning, Nat. Assn. Life Underwriters (v.p. 1971-76, ed. newsletter 1976-80), Rotary, United Way (Sonoma Mendocino Lake bd. mem. 1993–); mil: USN 1959-63; Republican; rec: flying, downhill skiing, scuba diving. Ofc: 2300 Bethards Dr Ste R Sant Rosa 95405 P.O. Box 2790 Santa Rosa 95405

ROOT, KAPSY (RUSSELL) WEBSTER, administrative law judge; b. Sept. 23, 1919, Kuling, Kiangsi, China; d. Wallace Boyd (BS, BA, MD, FACS) and Elizabeth Mae (Hutchison) Russell, Methodist missionaries stationed at hosps. in Nanking (1909), Wuhu, Soochow, and Changzhou (founded by father in 1918); m. Cornelius Crosby Webster, Jr. Nov. 25, 1942 (div. 1955); 1 child, Grace Katheryne Webster (1946-65); m. Charles M. Root, Mar. 31, 1956; edn: BA, Rockford Coll., 1941; LLB, USC, 1947; admitted Calif. bar 1947. Career: lawyer pvt. practice, Los Angeles 1947-49; staff lawyer Bur. of Reclamation, US Dept. of Interior, Sacto. 1949-54; adminstrv. law judge Calif. Unemployment Insurance Appeals Board, 1954-80; awards: resolutions Calif. State Senate and Assembly 1980, color slide of yr. No. Calif. Camera Clubs 1985; mem: state, nat. and internat. legal assns., Women Lawyers of Sacto. (pres. 1970), Women Lawyers L.A. (treas. 1948), Adminstrv. Law Judges Assn. Calif. (Sacto. br. sec. treas. 1956-66), Calif. State Employees Assn.; civic: YWCA (pub. affairs com. Sacto. 1967), NOW, ACLU, Am. Women for Internat. Understanding, Commonwealth Club of Calif. World Affairs Council No. Calif., Rossmoor Camera Club of Walnut Creek (treas. 1984, 85), Internat. Club Walnut Creek (treas. 1982-83); publs: student ed. So. Calif. Law Rev., 1944-46, contbr. article in book Lushan Memories, 1986; Democrat; Unitarian Universalist; rec: travel, photog., hist., bridge. Res: 1657 Skycrest Dr #16 Walnut Creek 94595

ROSE, E. KASH, physician; b. Oct. 15, 1921, Mize, Ky.; s. S. Lee and Grace Jane (Kash) R.; m. Barbette Pollyanna Browne, Aug. 7, 1941; children: Kenneth b. 1947, Gary b. 1951, Don b. 1959; edn: MD, Univ. of Louisville, Ky. 1943; lic. physician, Calif. Med. Bd. Career: capt. U.S. Army 1944-46; pres. Radiology Med. Group, Napa 1953-91; bd. trustees Queen of Valley Hosp., Napa 1971-85; chmn. of bd. Calif. Med. Assn. 1974-76, pres. 1977-78; pres. Orgn. State Med. Soc. Presidents 1978-79; awards: Man of Year, Queen of Valley Found., Napa 1973; Prof. Emeritus, Napa Co. Med. Soc. 1992; mem: 20-30-Club, Napa (pres. 1955), Napa Rotary Club; mil: capt. U.S. Army 1944-46; Republican; Presbyterian; rec: golf. Res: 8767 W Rosemonte Dr Peoria AZ 85382

ROSE, JACK WARREN, professor emeritus of physical education; b. Nov. 16, 1929, Grand Rapids, Mich.; s. Forrest James and Gladys (Goodwin) R.; m. Susan Jacobsen, June 19, 1955; children: Mike b.1957, Mark b. 1959, Scott b. 1966; edn: BS, Univ. Mich. 1952; MA, 1955; PhD, USC, 1963; postdoctoral, CSU Long Beach 1968. Career: coach, tchr. Univ. Mich., Ann Arbor 1954-55; USC, Los Angeles 1955-56; prof. CSU Long Beach 1956–; vis. prof. W.Va. Coll. Grad. Studies 1977-80; nat. meet dir. Nat. Youth Program, Hershey 1983-89; dir. Track Hall of Fame, Indianapolis 1975-89; tour leader Europe, CSU Long Beach 1981; awards: CSU Assn. Student Body Outstanding Service 1989, Applied Arts & Scis. Prof. 1989, Dept. Athletics 1986, Prof. Excellence 1986, Outstanding Prof. 1983, cert. U.S. Olympic Acad. 1977-89, Internat. Olympic Acad. 1981; mem: NCAA Track Coaches Assn. (pres. 1976), Athletics Congress Officials, So. Calif. Starter Assn. (pres. 1984), Calif. Assn. P.E. Rec. & Dance (student advisor (1977-89); paper pub. 1988, dir. Olympic Ceremony 1984; mil: 1st lt. USAF 1952-54; Republican; Prot.; rec: running (exec. dir. Long Beach marathon 1995). Res: 390 Peralta Ave Long Beach 90807

ROSE, THEODORE G., JR., physician; b. June 2, 1946, Long Branch, N.J. m. Constance Dey, June, 1972 (div. 1990); m. 2d. Joyce Ann Morte, Aug. 24, 1991; children: Ian b. 1978, Julia b. 1994; edn: BA, Johns Hopkins Univ. Sch. of Medicine 1968. MD, 1971; lic. physician St. of Calif.; cert. Am. Bd. Internal Medicine 1975, cert. Cardiopulmonary Resuscitation (advanced) 1978, recert. 1980, 83, (basic) 1986, 88, 90, Advanced Achievement in Internal Medicine 1987, cert. Critical Care Medicine 1987. Career: internship Univ. of So. Calif. Med. Ctr. 1971-72; residency internal medicine, L.A. Co./USC Med. Ctr. 1972-75, chief resident 1974-75; emergency room physician L.A. Co./USC Med. Ctr. and Citizen's Emergency Med. Group, Hollywood 1974-75; instr. in medicine, assoc. dir. undergrad. med. edn. USC Sch. of Medicine 1975-76; resident supr./attending physician L.A. Co./USC Med. Ctr. 1975-76; chief internal medi-cine Natividad Med. Ctr., Salinas 1976-86, med. dir. 1977-86, acting chmn. dept. of family practice, dir. family practice residency prog., acting dir. profl. med. svs., chmn. med.-dental staff 1977-78, dir. intensive care/coronary care unit 1976-86; clin. instr. Ambulatory & Comm. Medicine, UC San Francisco 1976-77, asst. clin. prof. internal medicine 1980-84, family practice 1977-84; instr. health sciences Hartnell Coll., Salinas 1979–; assoc. clin. prof. family practice UCSF 1984-86, assoc. clin. prof. medicine 1984–; chief gen. medicine Highland Gen. Hosp., Oakland 1986–; dir. med. edn. Alameda Co. Med. Ctr.,

Oakland 1986–; chmn. dept. of medicine and dir. internal medicine residency prog. Highland Gen. Hosp., Oakland 1986–; vice chmn. bd. dirs. Special Health Care Authority for Monterey Co., Salinas 1982-83; track physician Laguna Seca Raceway 1978-86; mem. Lib. and Learning Resources Planning Com., Statewide Area Health Edn. Sys. 1979-86; liaison assoc. Commn. on Cancer, Am. Coll. of Surgeons 1983-86; mem. 8th Dist. Med. Quality Review Com., Bd. of Med. Quality Assurance 1979-86, chmn. 1983, mem. 5th Dist. Med. Quality Review Com. 1988-91; chmn. Highland AIDS Task Force, Highland Gen. Hosp. 1988-89, pres. med. staff 1989-90, pres.-elect 1988-89, sec./treas. 1987-88; awards: Physician's Recognition award AMA 1978, Disting. Svc. Citation, Natividad Med. Ctr. 1978, Excellent Leadership in a Clin. Preceptorship award UCSF Class of 1990, 91; mem: Am. Coll. of Physicians (fellow, 1987), Assn. of Program Dirs. in Internal Medicine, CMA 1982-87, Monterey Co. Med. Assn. 1982-86, Johns Hopkins Med. and Surgical Soc., Johns Hopkins Alumni Assn. of the Clin. Faculty of UCSF; author: contr. 8 articles to profl. jours., 1971-93, book chpt. in Becoming a Family Physician, 1988, abstract, 1989; Republican; rec: martial arts. Ofc: 1411 E 31st St Oakland 94602

ROSEN, SANFORD JAY, lawyer; b. Dec. 19, 1937, N.Y.C.; s. Alexander Charles and Viola S. (Grad) R.; m. Catherine Picard, June 22, 1958; children: Caren E. Andrews b. 1961, R. Durelle Schacter b. 1963, Ian D. b. 1965, Melissa S. b. 1969; edn: AB, Cornell Univ., 1969; LLB, Yale Univ., 1962. Career: law clk. Chief Judge Simon E. Sobeloff, U.S. Ct. Appeals, 4th Cir. Balt., Md. 1962-63; prof. Univ. Md. Sch. of Law, Balt. 1963-71; assoc. dir. Council on Legal Edn. Opportunity, Atlanta, Ga. 1969-70; vis. prof. law Univ. Texas, Austin 1970-71; asst. legal dir. national ACLU 1971-73; legal dir. Mex. Am. Legal Defense & Edn. Fund, San Francisco 1973-76; ptnr. Rosen, Remcho & Henderson, S.F. 1976-80; ptnr. Rosen & Remcho 1980-82; prin. Law Ofcs. Sanford Jay Rosen 1982-86; sr. ptnr. Rosen & Phillips 1986-89; prin. Rosen & Assocs. 1990; sr. ptnr. Rosen, Bien & Asaro 1991–; judge pro tem S.F. Superior Ct. 1990–; interim monitor U.S. Dist. Ct., no. dist. Calif., 1989, early neutral evaluator 1987–, mediator 1993–; ad hoc adminstrv. law judge Calif. Agric. Rels. Bd., S.F. 1975-80; awards: Bouton law lectr. Princeton Univ. 1971, Legal svs. honoree Mex. Am. Legal Def. & Edn. Fund Inc. S.F. 1987, Free Person Award Prisoner Rights Union 1993; appt. nat. advy. com. US HEW, W.D.C. 1974-75, Com. on Adminstrn. Crim. Justice, Balt. 1968, commr. Balt. Human Rels. Commn. 1966-69, commr. Patuxent Instn., Balt. 1967-69; mem: ABA, Am. Trial Lawyers Assn., Calif. Attys. for Crim. Justice, Calif. Bar Assn., Bar Assn. S.F., D.C. Bar Assn.; publs: articles in law jours., public press, and cont. legal edn. books; rec: reading, travel, movies.

ROSENBAUM, MICHAEL FRANCIS, fixed income securities specialist, company executive; b. Feb. 9, 1959, New York; s. Francis Fels, Jr. and Joyce (Keefer) R.; m. Elika Sosnick, March 8, 1986; children: Erin Sosnick b. 1989, Sarah Greer b. 1991, Kira Keefor b. 1994; edn: BA, Princeton Univ. 1981; lic. NASD series 3, 7, 8, 24, USALE series 63. Career: summer intern Salomon Brothers, N.Y.C. 1979; specialist clk. Spear Leeds & Kellogg, N.Y.C. summer 1980; mgr. special products, fixed income dept. Sutro & Co. Inc. 1981-85; instnl. salesman fixed income securities/v.p. Pacific Securities Inc., San Francisco 1985-89; br. office mgr. instnl. sales/v.p. Rauscher Pierce Resfnes Inc., S.F. 1989-92;v.p. inst. sales Smith Mitchell Investment Group Inc., San Francisco 1992-93; sr. v.p. inst. mortgage sales Gruntal & Co., San Francisco 1993-94; sr. v.p., mgr. taxable fixed income, Coast Partners Securities Inc. 1994; dir. S.G. Rosenbaum Found. 1977–; clubs: Princeton Univ. Rowing, University Cottage, Princeton (N.Y.), Power Ten (N.Y.), Olympic (S.F.); mem. East Bay Ski Patrol, S.F. Zoological Soc.; publs: The Role of Political Cartoonists post-1940 (1981); Democrat; Jewish; rec: sailing, scuba diving, skiing. Res: PO Box 1035, 14 Madrona Ave Ross 94957 Ofc: Coast Partners Inc. One Embarcadero Center Ste #3550 San Francisco 94111

ROSENBERG, CLAUDE N., JR., investment advisor, author; b. April 10, 1928, San Francisco; s. Claude N. and Elza (Wolff) R.; m. Marjorie Kay Feder (div. 1966); m. Louise Jankelson, Dec. 19, 1968; children: Linda R. b. 1954, Douglas C. b. 1957; edn: BA, Stanford Univ. 1950; MBA, Stanford Grad. Sch. Bus. 1952. Career: ptnr. J. Barth & Co., San Francisco 1955-70; sr. ptnr. RCM Capital Mgmt. 1970–; awards: Stanford Bus. Sch. Ernest C. Arbuckle 1984, Maccabiah Games bronze medal 1989; mem: San Francisco Ballet Assn. (trustee 1975–), Jewish Comm. Fedn. (dir. 1978–), The Family, Calif. Tennis Club (pres. 1968); author 5 books incl. Stock Market Primer, 1962, Investing with the Best, 1987, Wealthy and Wise, 1994; Republican; Jewish; rec: music writing, tennis, fly fishing. Address: San Francisco 94115

ROSENBERG, DAVID, lawyer; b. Nov. 20, 1946, Muenchberg, Germany; s. Harry and Fay (Schweitzer) R.; m. Lea Pepper, June 30, 1968; children: Jason b. 1971, Janis b. 1977; edn: BS journalism, Calif. Polytech. St. Univ. 1968; JD, UC Davis 1974. Career: dep. appointments secty. to gov. Exec. Branch of St. Govt., Sacto. 1976-80, dep. exec. secty. and chief of staff to gov. exec. branch of st. govt., Sacto. 1980-81; ptnr. Felderstein Rosenberg & McManus 1981-86; ptnr. Diepenbrock Wulff Plant & Hannegan 1986–; judicial arbitrator Sacto. Co. Superior Ct., Sacto. 1987–, settlement conf. judge pro tem 1987–; honors: Order of Coif, Calif. Assn. Rehab. Facilities Advocacy Award 1987, Assn. Retarded

Citizens Outstanding Efforts Award 1986; mayor, City of Davis, 1994–, 1986-88; chmn. Calif. Law Revision Commission, 1982-84; mem: Am. Bar Assn., L.A. Co. Bar Assn., Sacto. Co. Bar Assn., Yolo Co. Bar Assn., Exec. Com. of Calif. St. Democratic Party; legislative counsel to Lt. Gov., State of Calif.; author: Endgame, 1986, ed. Calif. Western Law Review, 1973, 76, 78; mil: 1st lt. AUS 1968-71; Democrat; Jewish; rec: writing. Res: The Wildrose House 1112 Westfield Terrace Davis 95616-5725

ROSENBLUM, STEVEN ZVI, physician; b. Feb. 9, 1951, Tel-Aviv, Israel, nat. 1962; s. Dr. David and Dr. Basia (Smolar) R. (both parents MDs); edn: BS chem., UCLA, 1972; MD, Univ. Autonoma Guadalajara, 1976; Fifth Pathway, S. Baltimore Gen. Hosp., Univ. Md., 1976-77; MD lic. Md. 1977, Calif. 1978; cert. Am. Bd. Internal Med. Career: resident surgery Cedars-Sinai Med. Ctr., Los Angeles 1977-80; resident int. med. San Joaquin Gen. Hosp., Stockton, and Stanford Univ. Med. Ctr., Palo Alto, 1980-83; internist pvt. practice, Northridge 1983-85; Hawthorne Comm. Med. Group, Torrance 1985-88; Community Med. Group of the West Valley, Simi Valley 1988–; cons. internal medicine Simi Valley Hosp., Westlake Hosp., Numed Regional Med. Ctr., Humana West Hills Hosp., 1988–, Torrance Mem. Med. Ctr., South Bay Hosp., Redondo Bch., Bay Harbor Hosp., Harbor City, 1986-88; honors: 1st pl. Calif. Fedn. of Chapparal Poets Conv. (1961), life mem. Calif. Scholarship Fedn., B.of A. award english lit., honors at entrance UCLA (1968), AMA phys. recognition (1980, 83, 86, 90, 92); mem: Am. Coll. Physicians, A.C.S. (assoc. 1977-80), AMA, CMA, Calif. House Ofcr. med. Soc. (1980-83), Nat. Assn. Res. & Interns (1980-83), Univ. Autonoma Guadalajara Alumni Assn., Alpha Chi Sigma (UCLA treas. 1971-72), B'nai Brith Youth Orgn. Northridge (v.p. 1969-71); Jewish; rec: swimming, diving, painting, play piano, guitar.

ROSENFELD, IRWIN IRA, physician, psychiatrist; b. Feb. 26, 1951, Brooklyn, N.Y.; s. Rubin Robert and Mildred (Kashtan) R.; m. Sheryl Tally Schwaber, June 24, 1973; children: Elayna b. 1978, Ethan b. 1981; edn: BA cum laude, Cornell Univ. 1972; MD, Med. Coll. Wis. Milwaukee 1976. Career: intern Mercy Hosp., San Diego 1977; psychiatric resident UC Irvine, Orange 1980; pvt. practice, Laguna Hills 1980–; asst. clin. prof. dept. psychiatry UC Irvine, Orange 1982–; chief of staff Capistrano by the Sea Hosp., Dana Point 1986-87; honors: Cornell Univ. Dean's List 1971, 72, Med. Coll. Wis. Valedictorian, Exemplary Psychiatrist award Nat. Alliance for Mentally Ill 1994; mem: Orange Co. Psychiatric Soc. (pres. 1988-90), Am. Psychiatric Assn., AMA, Orange Co. Med. Assn.; Democrat; Jewish; rec: sports, travel, gardening. Ofc: 24022 La Plata Ste 540 Laguna Hills 92653

ROSS, JOHN, physical chemistry professor; b. Oct. 2, 1926, Vienna, Austria; nat. U.S.; m 50; c 2; edn: BS, Queens Coll., 1948; PhD, MIT, 1951; Hon. Degrees: Weizmann Inst. Sci. 1984, Queens Coll., SUNY, 1987, Univ. Bordeaux, France 1987. Career: res. assoc. physical chem., MIT 1950-52; resident fellow Yale Univ. 1952-53; from asst. prof. to prof. of chem., Brown Univ. 1953-66; prof. and chmn. of dept., MIT 1966-71, Frederick George Keyes prof. of chem. 1971-80, prof. of chem. Stanford Univ. 1980–, chmn. of dept. 1983-89, Camille and Henry Dreyfus prof. 1985–; Fellow, NSF 1952-53, Guggenheim Found. 1959-60, Sloan Found. 1960-64; vis. Van der Waals prof., Univ. of Amsterdam 1966; mem. bd. govs. Weizmann Inst. of Sci. 1971–; mem. NSF Advy. Panel 1974–; chmn. of faculty MIT 1975-77; awards: recipient Medal Collège de France, Irving Langmuir Award in Chem. Physics 1992, Dean's Award for Disting. Teaching 1992-93; mem: Nat. Acad. of Scis., Am. Chem. Soc., Am. Physical Soc. (fellow), Am. Acad. of Arts & Scis. (fellow); research: chem. instabilities, oscillatory reactions, thermodynamics of systems far from equilibrium, efficiency of thermal, chem. and biological engines. Ofc: Dept Chemistry Stanford University, Stanford 94305-5080

ROSTVOLD, GERHARD NORMAN, economist, author, lecturer, and financial counselor; b. Oct. 15, 1919, Nashwauk, Minn.; s. Arndt A. and Olive W. (Ness) R.; m. Virginia Faubon, Feb. 3, 1945; children: Roger b. 1949; Laura b. 1950, Christine b. 1951, Ellen b. 1957; edn.: BA., Econ.-Accountancy (with great distinction), Stanford Univ. 1948; MA., Econ., Stanford 1949; PhD, Econ., Stanford 1955. Career: accounting instr., Stanford 1949-51; prof. of econ. and accounting, Pomona Coll. 1952-66; vis. prof., Stanford 1974; econ. newscaster, KHJ, Channel 9's "Ten O'clock News" 1978-82; adjunct prof. of econ., Pepperdine Univ., Presidential/Key Exec. MBA Program; awards: Wig Disting. Professorship Award, Pomona Coll. 1962; NSF Fellow, Stanford 1965-66; Secty. of the Interior's Conservation Award 1975; Am. Men of Sci., Contemporary Authors, Who's Who in Am., Dictionary of Internat. Biog., Men of Achievement and others; mem.: Am. Econ. Assn.; We. Econ. Assn. (pres., 1966-67); Natl. Advy. Bd. on Public Lands (1962-75), chmn. 1971-74; Bd. of Trustees, Mortgage and Realty Trust 1962–; Lambda Alpha Hon. Frat. (Land Econ.), pres., L.A. Chpt. 1976-77; author: textbook, Financing Calif. Govt., 1967; The Econ. of Energy, 1975, Econ. and the Environment, 1975, The Econ. of the Public Utility Enterprise, 1975, Understanding How The Econ. System Works, 1976, Charting Your Path to Econ. and Fin. Survival in the 1980's, 1979, How to Stretch Your Dollars to Cope with the Inflation of the 1980's, 1981, Fin. Planning for Retirement in the 1980's, 1983, New Perspectives on Grazing Fees and Public Land Management in the 1990's (Congl. rept. June 1992), A

Comparative Analysis of the Economic Financial and Competitive Conditions of Montana Ranches Using Federal Forage and Montana Ranches Without Federal Grazing Allotments (Congl. rept July 1993); num. articles, book reviews, and monographs; mil: t/sgt., Army Air Force 1942-45; Lutheran. Res: #4 Montpellier, Laguna Niguel 92677 Ofc: Urbanomics, 23276 South Pointe Dr. Laguna Hills 92653

ROTELLA, SALVATORE G., community college president; b. July 24, 1934, Barcellona, Italy; nat. 1957; s. Sebastiano and Maria (Maio) R.; m. Pilar Vives Selles, July 24, 1961; children: Sebastian b. 1962, Carlo b. 1964, Salvatore b. 1966; edn: BA, internat. relations, Hunter Coll., NY, NY 1955; MA political sci., Univ. of Chicago 1956; DS, Faculty of Political Sci., Univ. of Pavia, Italy; PhD, political sci., Univ. of Chicago 1971. Career: res. assoc. AMA, Chicago, Ill. 1959-60; asst. prof. political sci. Wright Coll. 1960-62; chair dept. of social sci. Loop Coll. 1962-67; asst. dean/dir. Public Svc. Inst., Loop Coll. 1967-70; v.p. career and special programs Loop Coll. 1971-74; assoc. vice chancellor Inst. for City-Wide Programs 1974-75; p.t. adj. prof./dir. grad. prog. Ill. Inst. of Tech., Chgo. 1976-82; pres. Chgo. City-Wide Coll. 1976-80; pres. Loop Coll. and Chgo. City-Wide Coll. 1980-82, vice chancellor 1982-83; chancellor, chief exec. and ednl. ofcr. City Colleges of Chgo. 1983-88; vis. prof. Loyola Univ. of Chgo. 1988-89; v.p. academic affairs Nassau Comm. Coll. SUNY, Garden City, NY 1989-92; pres. Riverside Comm. Coll., Riverside, Calif. 1992–; bd. trustees Saint Xavier Coll.; bd. dirs. Greater State Street Council; bd. mem. Simon Bolivar Found.; commn. mem.: Am. Council on Edn., U.S. Fed. Govt., Am. Assn. of Comm. and Jr. Colls.; awards: Order of Merit, Republic of Italy 1985, Man of Yr., The Gregorians, Chgo. 1985, Chgo. DC Newspaper Educator Annual award 1985, Latino Police Assn. (Chgo.)Educator award 1986, Outstanding Prof. Achievement award, Hunter Coll., NY 1987, listed: Who's Who in Midwest 1969–, Who's Who in Am., Who's Who in Am. Coll. & Univ. Adminstrn., Outstanding Educators of Am.; com. mem.: Ill. Comm. Coll. Trustees Assn., Am. Soc. for Public Adminstrn., Chgo. Assn. of Commerce and Industry, Big Brothers/Big Sisters of Chgo.; mem.: No. Central Assn. of Colls. and Univs. (evaluator/team chmn.), Am. Arbitration Assn. (arbitrators panel), Nat. Assn. of Schools of Public Adminstrn. and Public Affairs, Riverside Co. Philharmonic (bd. dirs.), United Way; author: articles pub. in profl. jours., 1961-95; Catholic. Ofc: Riverside Community College 4800 Magnolia Ave Riverside 92506

ROTHMAN, BARBARA IONA, author, mentor-teacher, lecturer; b. Feb. 1, 1943, Blue Earth, Minn.; d. Alger Milton and Gladys Iona (Furland) Myers; m. Sheldon Rothman, June 27, 1970; son, Trevor David b. 1978; edn: BA, Calif. Luth. Univ., 1965; MA, Univ. San Francisco, 1970. Career: pre-sch. tchr. Nueva Day Sch., Hillsborough 1969-70; kindergarten tchr. Newport-Mesa Unified Sch. Dist., Newport Beach 1966-69, 70-89, 1995– (currently at Lincoln Elem., Corona del Mar), mentor tchr. 1984-92; author: Free To Be Just 4 Years Old, 1977, Free To Be Just 5 Years Old, 1983, newsletter publisher: Free To Be...Newsletter, 1985-90; advr. Early Childhood Edn., lectr. "Free To Be" 1985–; seminar presentor Bur. of Edn. & Research, Bellevue, Wash. 1987–; awards: National PTA Educator of the Year runner-up, S.L.C. 1988, career achiev. Calif. Luth. Univ. 1987; mem: Delta Kappa Gamma -Epsilon Omicron 1985–, Beatrix Potter Soc. Eng. 1985–, P.T.A. Eastbluff Kdg. Ctr. Newport Beach, Calif. Kdg. Assn.; civic: Childrens Home Soc. Calif. (v.p., sec. 1972-78); Republican; Lutheran. Res: 19462 Sierra Raton Rd Irvine 92715

ROWE, RICHARD WORTH, physician; b. Jan. 24, 1952, Boston, Mass.; s. Carter Redd and Mary (Moore) R.; m. Jude McMahon; children: Allison b. 1986, Katherine b. 1988; edn: BA, Univ. of No. Carolina, Chapel Hill 1974; MD, Harvard Med. Sch. 1979; MPH, Harvard Sch. Public Health 1981. Career: pediatric resident Univ. Hosp., San Diego 1979-80; anesthesia resident Brigham & Women's Hosp., Boston, Mass. 1981-83; anesthesia fellow Children's Hosp., Boston 1983-84, staff anesthesiologist 1984-86; staff anesthesiologist Children's Hosp., Oakland, Calif. 1986–; instr. Harvard Med. Sch. 1984-86; asst. prof. UC San Francisco 1988–, Stanford Univ. 1988–, UC Davis 1988–.

ROWLAND, F. SHERWOOD, professor of chemistry, Nobel Prize winner; edn: BS, Ohio Wesleyan Univ.; MS, PhD, Univ. of Chicago. Career: mem. faculty Princeton Univ., Univ. Kansas; first chair dept. chem. Univ. Calif. at Irvine 1964, currently Bren prof. of chem. UC Irvine; specialist in atmospheric chem. and radiochem.; mem. White House com. to evaluate acid rain, 1982-84; Fellow AAAS, Am. Geophysical Union; honors: recipient Tyler World Prize in Ecology and Energy 1983, Am. Chem. Soc.award for Creative Advances in Environmental Sci. and Tech. 1983, Charles A. Dana Award for Pioneering Achievements in Health 1987, Soc. for Environmental Toxicology and Chemistry's Rachel Carson award 1988, Japan Prize in Environmental Sci. and Tech. 1989, UCI Medal 1989, hon. doctorates of sci. by Princeton Univ., Univ. Chgo., Duke Univ. and Whittier Coll., hon. doctorate of law from Ohio Wesleyan Univ., awarded the 1995 Nobel Prize in chemistry (with Mario Molina and Paul Crutzen) for atmospheric studies which led to an understanding of how the ozone layer forms and decomposes; mem: Nat. Acad. of Scis., Am. Acad. of Arts and Scis.; author: 300+ articles in the areas of chem. kinetics, radiochem. and atmospheric chem. Ofc: Univ of California at Irvine Campus Drive Irvine 92717

ROYBAL-ALLARD, LUCILLE, congresswoman; b. June 12, 1941, Boyle Heights, Calif.; d. Edward Roybal; married; 4 children; edn: BA, Calif. State Univ., L.A. Career: former mem. Calif. State Assembly; mem. 103rd-104th Congresses form 33rd Calif. dist. 1993–. Ofc: US House of Reps Washington DC 20515*

ROYCE, EDWARD R. (ED ROYCE), congressman; b. Oct. 12, 1951, Los Angeles; m. Marie Porter; edn: BA, Calif State Univ. Career: tax mgr. Southwestern Portland Cement Co.; U.S. senator from Calif 93rd-103rd Congresses from 32d Calif dist. 1983-93; mem. 103rd-104th Congresses from 39th Calif dist., 1993–; chmn. constitutional. amendments com.; vice chmn. public employment and retirement com.; mem. bus. and profls. com., health and human svs. com., indsl. relations com.; legis. author, campaign co-chmn. Proposition 15 Crime Victims/Speedy Trial Initiative; author nation's 1st felony stalking law, bill creating Foster Family Home Ins. Fund, legis. creating foster parent recruitment and tng. program; awards: named Legis. of Yr. Orange County Rep. Corn. 1986, Child Adv. of Yr. Calif. Assn. Svc. for Children 1987; mem: Anaheim C.of C.; Republican. Ofc: US House of Reps Office of House Members Washington DC 20515*

RUBENKING, NEIL JOHN, computer magazine technical editor, writer; b. July 20, 1953, Alexandria, Va.; s. Earl Marion and Doris Rae (Bjelland) R.; m. Victoria Austin, Apr. 20, 1980, div. 1988; m. Janet Lynn Cooper, Dec. 15, 1988; edn: Univ. Va., 1 yr. Career: Zen Buddhist priest Zen Center of San Francisco, 1978-83; freelance programmer, S.F. 1983-86; contbg. editor PC Mag., N.Y., N.Y. 1987–, technical editor, 1990–; author: PC Mag.'s Turbo Pascal Techniques and Utilities, 1991, PC Mag.'s Turbo Pascal for Windows Techniques and Utilities, 1992, PC Mag. DOS Batch File Lab Notes, 1993, Can Do DOS, 1993, Can Do Windows (Ziff-Davis Press 1993), Delphi Programming for Dummies (IDG Books 1995); contbg. writer Byte, PC Mag., other periodicals, 1985–; bd. dirs. Assn. of Shareware Profls., Bellevue, Wa. 1987-88; author computer programs: Pianoman, 1984, Namegram, 1985, Midiman, 1990, Piano F/X, 1990; Democrat; rec: computer programming. Address: San Francisco

RUBIN, ALAN LEE, physician; b. Sept. 17, 1940, New York; s. Julius Nathan and Edith (Horowitz) R.; m. Enid Jane Feinsilber, Aug. 15, 1965; children: Renee b. 1969, Larry b. 1971; edn: BA, Brandeis Univ. 1962; MD, N.Y. Univ. Sch. Medicine 1966; lic. State Calif. Bd. Med. Examiners 1968. Career: intern Bellevue Hosp., N.Y.C. 1966-67, resident 1967-68; Mt. Zion Hosp., San Francisco 1970-71; fellow in endocrinology UCSF 1971-73; pvt. practice endocrinology, San Francisco 1973–; asst. clin. prof. UCSF 1978–; chmn. cont. edn. St. Francis Hosp. 1983–; mem: Am. Diabetes Assn. (profl. sect.); author: Self-Monitoring Blood Sugar in Diabetes, 1983; mil: major AUS 1968-70; Democrat; Jewish; rec: gardening, backpacking, singing. Res: 25 Via Capistrano Tiburon 94920 Ofc: 490 Post St San Francisco 94102

RUBIN, GERALD M., molecular biologist, genetics educator, administrator; b. Mar. 31, 1950, Boston; s. Benjamin H. and Edith (Weisberg) R.; m. Lynne S. Mastalir, May 7, 1978; 1 son, Alan; edn: BS biology, M.I.T., 1971; PhD molecular biology, Univ. Cambridge, England 1974. Career: tech. asst. lab. of Dr. Boris Magasanik, M.I.T., 1971; Helen Hay Whitney Found. fellow Stanford Univ. Sch. of Med. 1974-76; asst. prof. Harvard Univ. 1977-80; staff dept. embryology Carnegie Instn. of Wash., Balt. 1980-83; John D. MacArthur Prof. Genetics dept. molecular & cell biology UC Berkeley, 1983–, hd. div. genetics, 1987–, assoc. faculty cell & molecular biol. div. Lawrence Berkeley Lab.; investigator Howard Hughes Med. Inst. 1987–; adj. prof. biochem. & biophysics UC Sch. of Med., S.F. 1987–; honors: Phi Beta Kappa 1971, Phi Lambda Epsilon 1971, NSF predoc. fellow 1971-74, US Churchill Found. Fellow 1971-73, Helen Hay Whitney Found. Fellow 1974-76, co-winner Passano Found. Young Scientist Award 1983, co-winner AAAS Newcomb Cleveland Prize 1984, Am. Chem. Soc. Eli Lilly Award in biol. chem. 1985, co-winner NAS-US Steel Found. Award molecular biol. 1985, Genetics Soc. Am. Medal 1986, NAS 1987, AAAS Fellow 1992, Am. Acad. Arts & Scis. Fellow 1992. Ofc: Univ. Calif. Dept. MCB 539 LSA Bldg Berkeley 94720

RUBY, CHARLES LEROY, educator, lawyer, civic leader; b. Carthage, Ind., Dec. 28, 1900; s. Edgar Valentine and Mary Emma (Butler) R.; m. Rachael Elizabeth Martindale, Aug. 30, 1925; children: Phyllis Arline (Mrs. Norman Braskat), Charles L., Martin Dale; edn: certif. Ball State Univ., 1921-22; AB, Central Normal Coll., 1924, LLB, 1926, BS, 1931; BPE, 1932; MA, Stanford Univ., 1929; JD, Pacific Coll. of Law, 1931; PhD, Olympic Univ., 1933; admitted bar: Ind. 1926, U.S. Supreme Ct. 1970. Career: principal Pine Village (Ind.) High Sch., 1923-25; Glenwood (Ind.) Pub. Schs. 1925-26; tchr. El Centro Pub. Sch., Calif. 1926-27, Central Union High Sch., Fresno 1927-29; prof. law Fullerton Coll., 1929-66; life trustee Cont. Learning Experiences pgm. CSUF mem. CSUF Pres.'s Com., hon. chmn. fund com. Gerontology Bldg., Charles L. and Rachael E. Ruby Gerontology Center named in his and late wife's honor; prof. edn. Armstrong Coll., summer 1935, Cent. Normal Coll., summers 1929-33; civic: Ret. Service Vol. Program, North Orange Co. (pres. 1973-76, 83-84), North Orange Co. Vol. Bur. (dir.), Fullerton Sr. Citizens Task Force (dir.), Fullerton Public Forum (founder, dir. 1929-39), Rotary/Fullerton (pres. 1939-40, hon. life mem. 1983–), U.S. Assay Commn. 1968–, Fullerton Sr. Multi-purpose Ctr. (bd. 1981–), O.C. Senior Citizens Advy. Council (bd.), benefactor CSUF Gerontology Ctr.; awards: medal of merit Am. Numismatic Assn. 1954, Special commendn. Calif. State Assembly (1966, 88) and State Senate (1978, 86), recipient commns. from Indiana Sec. of State 1984, Gov. of Calif. 1989, Orange Co. Bd. Suprs. (1985, 86), Exec. Com. Pres. CSUF 1986; mem: Pres.'s Assocs. CSUF, Fullerton Coll. Associates (Spl. Retiree of Yr. 1986), Calif. Tchrs. Assn. (life, pres. So. Sect. 1962-63, treas. 1964-65, dir. 1956-65), O.C. Tchrs. Assn. (pres. 1953-55), Fullerton Coll. Tchrs. Assn. (pres. 1958-60, NEA (life), Stanford Univ. Law Soc. (pres.'s exec. com.), Calif. State Council Edn., Calif. Bus. Educators Assn. (hon. life), Calif. Assn. Univ. Profs., Ind. Bar Found. (fellow), Ind. Bar Assn. (life), Pacific S.W. Bus. Law Assn. (pres. 1959-70, life), Am. Numismatic Assn. (gov. 1951-53, life advy. bd.), Numis. Assn. So. Calif. (life, pres. 1961), Calif. Numis. Assn., Indpls. Coin Club (hon. life), L.A. Coin Club (hon. life), U.S. Supreme Ct. Hist. Soc., Town Hall Calif., North O.C. Mus. Assn. (life, dir., benefactor), Stanford Univ. Alumni Assn. (life), Old Timers Assay Commn., Elks (life), Fullerton Jr. Coll. Vets. (hon. life); contbr. articles to profl. jours.; Democrat (O.C. Dem. Cent. Com. 1962-78). Res: 308 N Marwood Ave Fullerton 92632

RUDIN, ANNE, former mayor; b. Jan. 27, 1924, Passaic, N.J.; d. Philip and Angela Noto; m. Edward Rudin, June 6, 1948; children: Nancy b. 1949, Barbara b. 1950, Carol b. 1950, Jay b. 1953; edn: BS edn., RN, Temple Univ., 1946; MPA, USC, 1983; Reg. Nurse, Pa. 1946, Calif. 1948. Career: nursing instr. Temple Hosp., Phila. 1946-48, Mt. Zion Hosp., San Francisco 1948-49; elected Sacramento City Council, 1971-83, mayor of Sacramento, 1983-92; awards: Girl Scouts Am. Role Model Award 1989, Sacto. History Ctr. Woman of Courage 1989, League Women Voters Civic Contbn. Award 1989; mem: Calif. Elected Women's Assn. 1973–, US Conf. of Mayors 1983-92, World Conf. of Mayors for Peace (v.p. 1985-92), Golden Gate Univ. (trustee), USC Advy. Bd. (chair), Sacramento Symphony Assn. (dir.), Friends of Sacramento River Greenway, Sacramento Theater Co. (dir.), Calif. Common Cause (bd. dirs.), Japan/Am. Conf. of Mayors, Chamber of Commerce Presidents. Address: Sacramento 95822

RUDIN, EDWARD, physician, psychiatrist; b. Sept. 9, 1922, Phila., Pa.; s. Nathan and Rose (Kerek) R.; m. Anna Josephine Noto, June 6, 1948; children: Nanci b. 1949, Barbara b. 1950, Carol b. 1950, Jay b. 1953; edn: AB, biology, Temple Univ. 1943, MD, 1947; lic. physician St. of Calif. 1948; Psychiatry Bd. Cert. 1962. Career: jr. intern Phila. Psychiatric Hosp. 1946; internship Cedars of Lebanon Hosp., Hollywood, Calif. 1948; psychiatric residency, VA Hosp., Palo Alto 1948-51; chief psychiatrist Riverside St. Mental Hygiene Clinic 1953-57; chief of state/local mental health svs., Calif. Dept. of Mental Hygiene 1958-61, dep. dir. comm. svs., 1961-65; dir. Sutter Comm. Hosps. Diagnostic & Treatment Ctr. 1965-69; coord. of planning and dir. Sutter Hosps. Comm. Mental Health Ctr. 1968-78; pvt. psychiatric practice, Riverside 1953-58, and Sacramento, 1959-91; clin. prof. UC Davis Sch. Medicine 1970–; coord. and instr. Sutter Hosps. Mental Health Ctr. 1970-78; faculty advy. com. and course coord. Cont. Edn. in Public Health (through 1960s and early 1970s); instr. Ctr. for Tng. in Comm. and Adminstrv. Psychiatry, Berkeley Dept. of Mental Hygiene, 1960s; clin. tchg. staff Riverside Co. Gen. Hosp., 1950s; instr. March AF Base Leadership Tng. Sch., San Bdo. Valley Coll. ext., UCLA and UC Riverside ext., 1950s; cons.: Sacto. Area Family Svc. Agy., CMA, num. pvt. practice psychiatrists, psychologists and psychiatric social workers, num. voluntary and public social svs. agys; awards: Outstanding Svc. awards Sacto Co. Bd. Suprs. 1985, Sacto Mental Health Assn. 1985, Sacto. Area Family Svc. Agy. 1985, Disting. Svc, award So. Calif. Psychiatric Soc. 1977, Broad Street Pump award Physicians for Social Responsibility 1990, first recipient Edward Rudin Award for Excellence in Govt. Relations, Calif. Psychiatric Soc. 1990; mem: AMA, CMA, Sacto.-El Dorado Med. Soc. (co-chair editl. com., past chair mental health com.), Central Calif. Psychiatric Soc. (life mem., ethics com. 1985–, pres. 1969-70), Am. Psychiatric Assn. (life fellow), Phi Delta Epsilon (life), Physicians for Social Responsibility (founder and current chair of violence study group, pres. Sacto area chpt. 1985-87, 92; prog. dir. 1988-91), Internat. Bioethics Inst., Sacto. Bioethics Group, Bioethics Forum, Sacto. Area Mental Health Assn., Sacto. Assn. for Retarded, United Nations Assn.-USA (bd. dirs. Sacto. chpt.); author: contbr. 12+ articles and guest editls. to Sacto. Medicine and Sutter Medicine, 6 articles to profl. jours.; mil: T/5, U.S. Army 1943-46; capt. USAF 1951-53; rec: reading, writing, theater. Res/Ofc: 1410 Birchwood Lane Sacramento 95822

RUEBNER, BORIS HENRY, academic pathologist; b. Aug. 30, 1923, Germany, nat. U.S. cit. 1964; s. Alfred and Marta (Klein) R.; m. Susan Mautner, Sept. 26, 1957; children: Sally b. 1962, Anthony b. 1964; edn: MB, and MD, Edinburgh Univ., Scotland. Career: prof. pathology Univ. Calif., Davis 1968–, pathologist UCD Medical Ctr., Sacto. 1968–; mem. Assn. of Pathologists, Calif. Med. Assn.; author: Pathology of the Liver 1992, The Gastrointestinal System 1982. Ofc: Dept. Medical Pathology University of California, Davis 95616

RUGANI, FRANK LOUIS, lawyer; b. May 3, 1948, San Mateo; s. Louis Elmo and Franca Elena (Capozza) R.; m. Doborah Jane Holmes, July 10, 1971; children: Paul b. 1981, Jennifer b. 1985; edn: BA, Occidental Coll. 1970; JD, UC

Davis 1978; admitted St. Bar Calif. 1978. Career: atty. O'Melveny & Myers, Newport Beach; awards: Thomas J. Watson fellowship 1970, Calif. St. Assembly fellowship 1970; Democrat; R.Cath.; rec: collecting vintage Calif. wines, presdl. campaign button collecting, marathon running. Ofc: O'Melveny & Myers 610 Newport Center Dr Ste 1700 Newport Beach 92660-6429

RUGGIERI, ALEXANDER F., musician; b. Jan. 10, 1952, Santa Monica; s. Vincent and Ludmilla (Plutalov) R.; edn: B.Music (theory), USC 1976; M.Music (choral music), 1977; Wayne St. Univ. 1980-82. Career: music dir. Orthodox Concert Choir, Los Angeles 1974-77; Musical Arts Choir & Orchestra 1974-77; Bach Chamber Singers, Detroit, Mich. 1980-82; choir dir. Holy Virgin Mary Cathedral, Los Angeles 1982-88; artistic dir. Hollywood Chorale, Hollywood 1986-87; music dir. Cambridge Singers, Los Angeles 1984–; choir dir. First Presbyterian, Newhall 1993-95, Woodland Hills Comm. Ch. 1995–; artistic dir. Little Symphony of Pasadena 1994–; mem: Choral Conductors Guild (treas. 1988-90), So. Calif. Early Music Soc. (pres. 1986-87), Am. Choral Dirs. Assn., Chorus Am., Symphony Orchestra League; ed. Monuments of Russian Choral Music, 1989, composer, arranger of choral music (Holy Note Press 1980-82), reviewer of books and music Orthodox Church Singer, 1980-82; Russian Orthodox. Res: 1557 Lemoyne St Los Angeles 90026

RUMBAUGH, CHARLES EARL, electronics company executive, lawyer; b. Mar. 11, 1943, San Bernardino; s. Max E. and Gertrude M. (Gulker) R.; m. Christina, Mar. 2, 1968; children: Heather, Aaron, Cindy, Eckwood; edn: BS, UCLA 1966; JD, Cal Western Sch. Law 1971; adv. legal studies, USC; Cert. in Advanced Mgmt., Univ. So. Calif. Grad. Sch. of Bus. Admn.; admitted Calif. State Bar 1972, US Dist. Ct. (cent. dist. Calif.), US Ct. of Appeals (9th cir.); Certified Profl. Contracts Mgr., 1987. Career: engr. Westinghouse Electric Corp. 1966-68; corp. counsel Calif. Dept. of Corp. 1971-77; legal counsel Hughes Aircraft Co. 1977-84, asst. to Corporate Contracts Dir. 1984-89, asst. to Corporate Contracts V.P. 1990-95; corporate dir. of contracts & pricing Lear Astronics Corp. 1995–; adj. prof. West Coast Univ.; honors: ed.-in-chief Cal Western Internat. Law Jour. and Appellate Moot Ct. Board, 1970-71; mem: Nat. Contract Mgmt. Assn. (Fellow, South Bay Chpt. pres. 1991, nat. dir. 1992, nat. v.p. Southwestern Region 1993-95, nat. bd. of advisors 1995–), Fed. Bar Assn. (pres. Beverly Hills Chpt. 1992-93), Calif. Bar Assn. (real prop. sect., bus. law sect., franchise law com. 1992–), L.A. Cty. Bar Assn., South Bay Bar Assn., Christian Legal Soc., IEEE, Phi Alpha Delta, Phi Kappa Psi, Nat. Security Industrial Assn. (legal & spl. tasks West Coast Gp., v.ch. 1994–), Aerospace Industries Assn. (chmn. procurement techniques com. 1987-88, 1993-94), Soc. of Professionals In Dispute Resolution; civic: Judge Pro Tem L.A. Superior Court; arbitrator, Am. Arbitration Assn., Christian Conciliation Svs.; Franchise Arbitration & Mediation, Inc. and Arbitration & Mediation Internat.; City of Palos Verdes Estates Citizen Advy. Com. 1986-90; Boy Scouts Am. 1976–; publs. in profl./legal jours.; Christian; rec: jogging, skiing, camping, equestrian. Ofc: PO Box 2636 Rolling Hills 90274 Tel: 310/373-1981

RUMMEL, H. GEORGE, hydroelectric engineer; b. Aug. 4, 1939, Riverton, Wyo.; s. Elmer George and Mary Elizabeth (Sinner) R.; m. Arleen B. Strasheim, June 14, 1987; children: Andrew George b. 1969, Amron Suzanne b. 1974; edn: BSCE, Valparaiso Univ. 1962; MSCE, CSU Sacramento 1972; Reg. Civil Engr. Calif. 1966. Career: asst. civil engr. Calif. Dept. Water Resources Sacto. 1962-72; civil engr. (hydroelectric) Fed. Power Commn. Wash. DC 1972-75; dept. head Harza Engring. Co. Chgo. 1975-80; supr. design of world's largest storage proj.; proj. mgr. (hydroelectric) Sacto. Municipal Utility Dist. 1980–, supr. planning, licensing, design, and initial constrn. for 2 new hydro projects; civic: Little League (team mgr.); Lutheran (Stephen minister, Evangelism chmn.); rec: baseball, skiing, outdoors, fishing. Ofc: SMUD Sacramento 95817

RUMP, MARJORIE ELLEN, librarian; b. Jan. 19, 1919, St. Joseph, Mo.; d. Edward August and Adeline (Boller) Gummig; m. John S. Rump, July 25, 1943; children: Jack b. 1946, Susan b. 1950, Marilyn b. 1953; edn: BA, Univ. Redlands 1941; MS lib. sci., USC 1957; Calif. sec. tchg. cred. (1941). Career: sales, book buyer Sierra Book Store 1953-66; librarian Kern County Lib. Adult Extension 1961-66, East Bakersfield High Sch. 1966-68; Kern County Lib. Shafter Br. 1968-69, KCL Young Adult Ext. and audio-visual supr. 1969-71, KCL Adult & Young Adult Ext. supr. 1972-73, KCL -Beale coord. 1973-79, KCL asst. to County Librarian 1979-82, KCL Adult Ext. supr. 1982-84, KCL acquisitions librn. 1984, KCL Bakersfield Area br. supr. 1985-87, KCL Beale hd. librn., 1987-88, Dep. dir. 1988–; mem. Bakersfield Coll. Pres.'s Advy. Council; dir. Taft Comm. Theater 1949-52; honors: Beta Phi Mu, Theta Alpha Phi, Doubenmeir Award for pub. adminstrn. Am. Soc. for Pub. Adminstrn. 1979, Citizen recogn. City of Bakersfield 1983, Jubilee Medallion Univ. Redlands 1984, Soroptimist Woman of Distinction 1990; mem: Calif. Lib. Assn., Am. Soc. for Pub. Adminstrn. (chpt. pres. 1978), Soc. of Archivists, Conf. of Calif. Hist. Socs. (reg. v.p. 1984-90, CCHS Trust treas. 1986–), Kern Co. Hist. Soc. (pres. 1981), Libraria Sodalitas USC; civic: AAUW (pres. Taft Br. 1948, Bksfld. Br. 1958-9), Women's Assn. First Presbyn. Ch. (pres.), Child Guidance Guild, Assistance League of Bksfld. PEO-MB, Soroptimist Internat. of Bksfld. (pres. 1978-9), Univ. Redlands Alumni Bd., Kern Co. Mus. Alliance, Dorian Soc. CSUB, Wakayama Sister City (bd. 1981-94), Calif Living Mus., Gr.

Bksfld. C.of C. Womens' Div., Beta Lambda Mu Sor.; author: Inside Historic Kern; Presbyterian; rec: travel. Res: 3000 Elmwood Bakersfield 93305 Ofc: Kern County Library 701 Truxtun Ave Bakersfield 93301

RUPERT, DAVID ANDREW, clergyman, administrator; b. Aug. 16, 1940, Oil City, Pa.; s. John Reuben and Wealtha Audrey (Smoyer) R.; m. Lois Martha Annable, June 30, 1962; children: Glenn David b. 1967, Martha Jean b. 1970; edn: BA, Roberts Wesleyan Coll., 1962; BDiv, Western Evangelical Sem., Portland, Or. 1967, MDiv, 1972; DMin, Fuller Theological Sem., Pasadena 1980; ordained deacon, 1965, elder, 1967, Free Methodist Ch. of N.A. Career: Free Methodist Ch. asst. pastor, Herkimer, N.Y. 1962-63, Portland, Or. 1963-64, Salem, Or. 1964-67, pastor, Redmond, Or. 1967-71, sr. pastor (Free Meth.) Willow Vale Community Ch., San Jose, 1971-79, Sacramento, Ca. 1979-84; conf. supt. Calif. Conference Free Methodist Ch., Sacto. 1984-95; conf. supt. Central Ill. Conf. Free Methodist Ch., Greenville 1995–; mem. Gen. Bd. of Adminstrn., Idpls. 1989-95 (secty. Adm. Commn.), del. Gen. Conf. FM Ch. Winona Lake, Ind. 1985, Seattle, Wa. 1989, Anderson, Ind., 1995; mem., secty. Gen. FM Youth Conf., Winona Lake, Ind. 1969; trustee Western Evangelical Sem., Portland 1984-94, trustee Seattle Pacific Univ., Wa. 1987-95; LIFO cons./trainer Stuart Atkins Inc. Beverly Hills 1981–; exec. com. Gr. Sacto. Bill Graham Crusade, 1983; awards: 2d Pres.'s Award for service above self Redmond (Oreg.) Rotary 1971, listed Who's Who in Am. Christian Leadership, Who's Who in Religion, Who's Who in West; mem. Nat. Assn. Evangelicals Nor Cal (1972-94, pres. 1988-91), Calif. Council on Alcohol Problems 1985-95; editor: Celebrating One Hundred Years (1983); Republican (nat. com.); rec: travel, photography, swimming, sports. Res: 9241 Linda Rio Dr Sacramento 95826-2209 Ofc: California Conference Free Methodist Church, 9750 Business Park Dr Ste 212 Sacramento 95827-1716

RUSH, HERMAN E., television executive; b. June 20, 1929, Phila.; s. Eugene and Bella (Sacks) R.; m. Joan Silberman, Mar. 18, 1951; children: James Harrison, Mandie Susan; edn: BBA, Temple Univ., 1950. Career: with Official Films, 1951-57; owner Flamingo Films, 1957-60; with Creative Management Assocs., N.Y.C., 1960-71, pres. TV div. Creative Mgmt. Assocs., 1964-71, exec. v.p. parent co., dir., 1964-71; indep. producer 1971-75; producer Wolper Orgn., 1975-76; pres. Herman Rush Assocs., Inc. (Rush-Flaherty Agy. subs.) 1977-78, Marble Arch TV, Los Angeles 1979-80, pres. Columbia Pictures TV, Burbank 1980-87; chmn. bd. and c.e.o. Coca-Cola Telecomms. 1987-88, Rush Assocs. Inc., Burbank 1988-91; ptnr. Katz Rush Entertainment 1992–; chmn. Entertainment Industries Council; mem. Acad. TV Arts and Scis., Hollywood Radio and TV Soc., Producers Caucus; civic bds: trustee Sugar Ray Robinson Youth Found. 1967-75, pres. Retarded Infant Svs., N.Y.C. 1957-63, bd. dirs. U.S. Marshall's Service Found., STET 1986-93, conferee White House Conf. for a Drug Free America (1987, 88); clubs: Friars, Filmex. Ofc: Katz Rush Entertainment 345 N Maple Dr Beverly Hills 90210

RUSH, JOHN A., insurance agent; b. Oct. 6, 1928, Toledo, Ohio; s. Arnold E. and Bessie A. Rush; m. Patricia Bush, Oct. 1977; children: Leslie b. 1954, Kurt b. 1957, Linda b. 1958, Karl b. 1960, (step) Sana Peterson b. 1956, Eric Peterson b. 1958; edn: AA, Univ. of Toledo 1951. Career: mgr. Ventura Calif. Retail Credit Co. 1951-58; asst. mgr. customer svc. Sears-Roebuck 1958-59; ins. agent State Farm Ins. Co. 1960-94 (ret.); owner/ptnr. New Horizons Travel, Camarillo; appt. Ventura Co. Planning Commn. (commr., chmn. 1963-76), Pleasant Valley Rec. & Parks Dist. (chmn., dir. 1970-86), Calif. Assn. Rec. & Parks Dists. (v.p. 1975-76), elected Camarillo City Council 1976-80 (mayor 1979-80), Camarillo Sanitation Dist. (dir. 1976-80), Ventura Regional Co. Sanitation Dist. 1977-80, Regional Coastal Commn.-Ventura, Santa Barbara, San Luis Obispo (commr., chmn. 1976-79), Calif. State Coastal Commn. (v. chmn. 1979-81); awards: Dunlap Fellow Kiwanis Fund 1988, Hospice Gold Benefactor Award 1990, Hospice Benefactor Award 1990, 91, 92, Camarillo Chamber of Commerce businessman of yr. 1986 C.of C., volunteer of yr. 1992, Caamarillo Man of Yr. 1994; mem.: Lima Bean Soc., Bean Hive No. 1 (pres. 1983), Calif. Macadamia Soc., Calif. Rare Fruit Growers, Internat. Palm Soc.; civic bds: Mayor's Blue Ribbon Com. City of Camarillo 1987, Camarillo Hospice (bd. 1983-89, chmn. 1986-88, pres. Hon. Bd. Dirs. 1988, Hospice Endowment Bd. 1991), Kiwanis Intl. (life fellow, Camarillo Club charter pres. 1966, pres. 1967-68, 1982-83, 1989-90, hon. life mem. 1985, div. 42 lt. gov. 1985-6), Las Posas Prop. Owners Assn. (bd. 1986-95, pres. 1987-95), Camarillo Boys & Girls Club (bd. 1986-95, pres. 1991-92), Boy Scouts Exec. Com. for Fundraising 1992, Pleasant Valley Rec. & Park Dist. Citizens Com. for Park Devel. & Funding 1992, Camarillo Health Care Dist. (pres. 1992-95), Ventura Co. LAFCO (commnr. 1994–), Special Districts Assn. Ventura Co. (v.p. 1994-95), Camarillo C.of C.; mil: sgt. AUS 24th Inf. Div. Japan, 1946-47; Indep.; rec: garden. Res: 1404 Calle Aurora Camarillo 93010

RUSSELL, CAROL (ANN), personnel services company president; b. Dec. 14, 1943, Detroit, Mich.; d. Billy Koud and Ann (Withers) Salerno; m. Victor Rojas; edn: BA Hunter Coll. 1993; reg. employment consultant Calif. Assn. Personnel Consultants, 1974. Career: v.p. Wollborg Michelson, San Francisco, 1974-82; pres., co-owner Russell Staffing Resources, Inc., San Francisco 1983–; firm listed in "Inc. 500" Inc. Mag., Boston (1989, 1990); mem: No. Calif. H.R. Council

(com. chair, mem. 1983–), Calif. Assn. of Temp. Services (pres. Golden Gate chpt. 1983-84), Internat. Assn. for Personnel Women (pres. Bay Area chpt. 1984), Internat. Platform Assn., Soc. for Preservation of Radio Drama, Variety and Comedy, Personnel Assn. of Sonoma Co., Radio Hall of Fame; contbr. articles in trade jours.; media guest host/community producer of JobNet prog. for Viacom Cable; seminar leader; pub. Checkpoint Newsletter; Indep.; D.N.D.; rec: reading, collect Bible commentaries and old time radio cassettes/memorabilia. Ofc: Russell Staffing Resources, Inc. 120 Montgomery St 3d Fl San Francisco 94104

RUTAN, RICHARD GLENN, test pilot, company president; b. July 1, 1938, Loma Linda; s. George A. and Irene (Goforth) R.; children: Holly Lynn b. 1965, Jill Lynn b. 1970; edn: BS, Am. Technological Univ. 1972. Career: served to lt. col. (Ret.) US Air Force 1958-78, awarded the Silver Star, 5 D.F.C., 16 Air Medals and the Purple Heart; prodn. mgr. and chief test pilot of Rutan Aircraft Factory (bro. Burt's co.) 1978-81: test flight devel. pilot of the Defiant, the Beech Starship proof of concept prototype, the European Micro Light, the T-46 scaled demo. for Fairchild Aircraft and the Long-EZ (set num. individual world speed and distance records in 1982); founder, pres. Voyager Aircraft Inc., 1981-1994, with ptnr. Jeana Yeager completed the first around the world, non-stop, non-refueled flight in Voyager, Dec. 14-23, 1986 (more than double prev. absolute world distance record held by a USAF B-52 bomber); awarded Presdl. Citizen's Medal of Honor by Pres. Ronald Reagan (12/27/86) at a spl. ceremony for the Voyager Team; other awards include: Hon. Doctorate Sci. & Technology Central New England Coll. 1987, Hon. Doctorate Humanities Lewis Univ., Ill. 1989, The Collier Trophy Nat. Aviation Club & Nat. Aeronautic Assn. 1986, Iven C. Kincheloe Award Soc. Exptl. Test Pilots 1987, Louis Bleriot Medal 1982, Gold Medal 1986 and The Absolute World Records 1987, Fedn. of Aeronautique Internationale, Nat. Air & Space Mus. Trophy for outstanding achiev. in aerospace tech. 1987, Royal Aero Club of the U.K. gold medal presented by H.R.H. Prince Andrew, Duke of York, with H.R.H., the Duchess of York and Prince Phillip, Royal Consort (May 21, 1987); Paris Aero Club's Grande Medallion & Medalle de Ville Paris, VFW Aviation & Space Award Gold Medal & Citation 1987, Guinness Book of Records Hall of Fame 1988, Nat. Aviation Hall of Fame Spirit of Flight Award 1987, Golden Plate Awrd Am. Acad. of Achiev. 1987, Person of Wk. Peter Jennings ABC World News Tonight 1986, World Record Awards Aero Club of So. Calif., Diamond Wings Award Internat. Order of Characters, Disting. Alumni Dinuba C.of C. 1987, Flying Tiger Pilot Award 1989, Breathe Easy Award Am. Lung Assn. 1989, Eagles of Aviation Embry-Riddle Aero. Univ. 1987, Edward Longstreth Medal of Merit Franklin Inst. 1988, The Hist. of Aviation Award Hawthorne C.of C. 1988, Royal Aero. Soc. Award 1987, The Lindbergh Eagle Chas. A. Lindbergh Fund 1987, Greater LA Citizen of Yr. Boys' Clubs 1988, Internat. Aviation Achiev. Intl. Varieze & Composites Hospitality Club 1989, Ft. Worth Hall of Fame 1987, Meridian Award Children's Mus. 1987; mem: Soc. of Exptl. Test Pilots, Nat. Aeronautic Assn., Exptl. Aircraft Assn., Order of Daedalians (prior Flight Capt. Flt 56 Test Flight Edwards AFB); Republican; rec: aviation. Address: PO Box 359 Mojave 93502

RUTHERFORD, GEORGE WILLIAMS, III, physician; b. Apr. 6, 1952, San Diego, Calif.; s. George Williams Rutherford, II and Anna Gwyn Foster (Dearing) R.; m. Lisa Anderson, Aug. 24, 1974 (div. 1984); m. 2d. Mary Rachel Workman, Feb. 23, 1985; children: Alicia b. 1979, George Williams, IV b. 1982, Alexandra b. 1986, Anne b. 1989, Hugh b. 1991; edn: AB, classics, Stanford Univ. 1974, BS, chem., 1975, AM, history, 1975; MD, Duke Univ. 1978; lic. physician and surgeon, Calif. 1979, N.Y. 1984; cert. Nat. Bd. Med. Examiners 1979; Coll. of Physicians and Surgeons of Ontario ednl. lic. 1980; cert. Am. Bd. Pediatrics 1984. Career: intern, pediatrics, UC Med. Ctr., San Diego 1978-79, resident 1979-80; resident, Hosp. for Sick Children, Toronto, Ontario, Can. 1980-81; chief resident Children's Hosp. and Health Ctr., S.D. 1981, UC Med. Ctr., S.D. 1982; EIS ofcr., epidemiology, Ctrs. for Disease Control, Atlanta 1982-84, med. epidemiologist 1984-85, med. epidemiologist, AIDS prog. 1985-87; chief, AIDS Div., Bureau of Communicable Disease Control, San Francisco Dept. Public Health 1985-86, med. dir. AIDS Ofc. 1986-88, dir. AIDS Ofc. 1988-90; chief, infectious disease br., state epidemiologist, Calif. Dept. Health Svs., Berkeley 1990-92, dep. dir. prevention svs., state epidemiologist 1992-95, state health ofcr. 1993-95; assoc. dean, prof. of epidemiology and health adminstrn. Sch. Public Health, UC Berkeley 1995–; clin. asst. prof. pediatrics Emory Univ. 1982-83, Cornell Univ. 1984-85; asst. clin. prof. UC San Francisco 1986-92, assoc. adj. prof. 1992–; assoc. clin. prof. of comm. health UC Davis 1991–; AIDS advy. com. Episcopal Diocese of Calif. 1986–; co-investigator S.F. Men's Health Study 1990–; bd. of sci. advisors Oral AIDS Ctr., UCSF Sch. of Dentistry 1991–; sci. and profl. advy. com. Bay Area Bus. Group on Health 1992-95; Calif. Dept. Health Svs. coms.: AIDS vaccine R&D advy. com. 1990-95, preventive medicine residency com. (chair) 1992-95, tobacco edn. and res. oversight com. 1994–, childhood lead poisoning prevention implementation task force 1994–, tuberculosis implementation task force (co-chair, exec. com.) 1994–; mem. Calif. EPA Prop. 65 working group 1993-95; mem. UC Berkeley Sch. Public Health Fogarty internat. AIDS tng. prog. 1989–, public health advy. com. 1993–; Dean's adminstrv. council 1995–, space and planning com. (chair) 1995–; founder's bd. Calif. Health Leadership Inst. 1994–; cons.: Pan Am. Health Orgn. 1986-89, Ctrs. for Disease Control, Atlanta

1987–, Calif. Dept. Health Svs. 1987-89, The Pathfinder Fund 1987, World Health Orgn. 1988-90; reviewer, Med. Res. Council of Can. 1993; internat. lectr. in field; awards: Foreign Duty Svc. Ribbon, USPHS 1985; mem: Am. Assn. for History of Medicine 1975–, Am. Soc. Tropical Medicine and Hygiene 1980–, Am. Acad. Pediatrics (fellow 1984–, exec. bd. Sect. on epidemiology 1991–) , Am. Public Health Assn. 1984–, Bay Area Communicable Disease Exchange 1985-95, CMA 1987–, Infectious Diseases Soc. of Am. 1987–, No. Calif. Public Health Assn. 1987–, Internat. AIDS Soc. 1988–, Soc. for Epidemiologic Res. 1989–, Calif./Baja Calif. Binational Health Council 1990–, Conf. of State and Territorial Epidemiologists 1990-95, So. Calif. Public Health Assn. 1990–, U.S.-Mexico Border Health Assn. 1990– (co-pres., state health ofcrs. 1993-95), AIDS and Reproductive Health Network 1991–, Alameda-Contra Costa Med. Assn. 1991–, Bay Area Infectious Disease Soc. 1991–, Assn. St. and Territorial Health Officials 1993-95 (HIV and immunizations coms. 1994-95), Calif. Acad. of Preventive Medicine 1994– (bd. dirs. 1995–); editorial bds: Calif. AIDS Update 1988–, Current Issues in Public Health 1993–, SIDA 1994–; jour. referee: AIDS 1988–, Am. Jour. Public Health 1989–, We. Jour. Medicine 1989–, New England Jour. Medicine 1989–, Jour. of AMA 1989–, Jour. of Acquired Immune Deficiency Syndromes 1990–, Internat. Jour. Epidemiology 1991–, British Med. Jour. 1994–; author: contbr. 43 articles to peer-reviewed jours., 1984-94, 13 book chapters, 1985-93, 113 Govt. health pubs., 1982-94, 160+ abstracts, 1983–, num. review articles and editorials; mil: capt. USPHS (active reserve) 1982–; Republican; Episcopalian; rec: tennis, gardening, cooking. Ofc: University of California School of Public Health 140 Warren Hall Berkeley 94720

RYDER, OLIVER ALLISON, geneticist, educator; b. Dec. 27, 1946, Alexandria, Va.; s. Oliver A. Ryder and Elizabeth Rose (Semans) Paine; m. Cynthia Lou Ryan, Dec. 5, 1970; children: Kerry b. 1978, Ryan b. 1982; edn: BA biology (high honors) UC Riverside, 1968; PhD biology, UC San Diego, 1975. Career: postdoctoral fellow dept. reproductive med. UC San Diego, La Jolla 1975-77, dept. pathology 1977-79, res. assoc. dept. biology 1979-87, adj. prof. 1988–; res. fellow Res. Dept. Zoological Soc. of San Diego, San Diego 1975-79, geneticist 1979-85, Kleberg Chair in Genetics Ctr. for Reproduction of Endangered Species, 1986–; cons. UN, US Congress, San Diego Unified Sch. Dist., Nat. Geographic Soc., Nat. Commn Wildlife & Conservation Kingdom S.A., Sierra Club, County of Orange Dist. Atty., County of San Diego Dist. Atty., others; awards: USPHS trainee genetics 1968-75, Bank Am. Giannini Found. Med. Res. Fellow 1975-76, NIH Nat. Res. Svc. Award 1976-78, San Diego Soc. Natural Hist. fellow, Sci. Fellow of N.Y. Soc. 1990, San Diego Mag. list of 91 San Diegans to Watch in '91 (1991), grantee, prin. investigator NIH (1979-82, 82-85, 85-88), Inst. Mus. Svs. conserv. proj. 1987-88, Calif. Dept. Fish & Game Calif. Condor 1987-89, Marine Mammal Commn. Fla. Manatees 1988-89, John and Beverly Stauffer Trust mgmt. genetic resources 1989-94, J.N. Pew Jr. Memorial Trust 1989-92, Morris Animal Found. mtn. gorillas 1990-92, John and Beverly Stauffer Found. global mgmt. Przewalski's Horse 1992-94; mem: Am. Soc. Mammalogists, Am. Genetics Assn. (assoc. ed. Jour. of Heredity 1990–), Am. Soc. for Cell Biology, Soc. for Systematic Zoology, Am. Soc. for Microbiology, Am. Assn. Zool. Parks and Aquariums (Profl. Fellow), Internat. Soc. for Animal Blood Group Res., Soc. for Conservation Biology, Am. Soc. Human Genetics, Soc. for Study of Evolution; author 130+ books, book chapters, popular and sci. jour. articles and monographs in field; Ofc: Zoological Society of San Diego PO Box 551 San Diego 92112

RYU, EDWIN K. S., financial advisor/planner; b. Nov. 24, 1951, Monterey, Calif.; s. Henry and Helen (Lee) R.; m. Julie Satake; children: Nicole b. 1989, Danielle b. 1991; edn: H.S. diploma, York Sch., Monterey, Calif.; BA in economics, Stanford Univ. 1976; Certified Public Accountant (CPA). Career: supr./mgr. Touche Ross & Co. (now Deloitte & Touche), S.F. 1979-84; v.p. finance Van Kasper & Co., S.F. 1984-85; pres. Ryu and Company, S.F. 1985–; chmn. Kendrick, Stimpfig & Ryu, Ltd. 1995–; bd. dirs. Willow Tree Invest., S.F. 1991–; tchr. Golden Gate Univ., S.F. 1986-89; mem. Stanford Alumni Assn. 1989–; civic: bd. dirs. Stonestown YMCA, S.F. 1989-92; author: International Investments & Taxation (grad. level, Golden Gate Univ.) 1987-89; founder, editor MEDWATCH, newsletter for physicians; rec: basketball, traveling. Res:1094 Marilyn Dr Mountain View 94040

SABELLA, JOSEPH DAVID, retired pathologist, medical company executive; b. July 25, 1929, San Francisco, Calif.; s. Antonio and Katherine (Gelardi) S.; m. Iris Siegel, Dec. 22, 1951; children: Gianna b. 1956, Frank b. 1957, Matthew b. 1965; edn: AB, UC Berkeley 1950; MD, UCSF Sch. of Medicine 1954. Career: intern Kings Co. Hosp., Brooklyn, NY 1954-55; jr. asst. resident gen. surgery, VA Hosp., San Francisco 1955-56; clin fellow, pathology, Mass. Gen. Hosp., Boston, Mass. 1956-59; USAF Med. Corps, Wiesbaden, Germany 1959-63; assoc. pathologist: Franklin Hosp., S.F. 1963-65, Children's and Adult Med. Ctr., S.F. 1965-67, St. Joseph's Hosp., S.F. 1967-69; chief pathologist and dir. lab., Brookside Hosp., San Pablo 1969-82, assoc. pathologist (part-time) 1982-90; chmn., bd. of govs. The Doctor's Co., Santa Monica 1976-94, chmn. and CEO (3/4 time) 1982-90, (full time) 1990-94; cons. pathologist Queen of Valley Hosp., Napa 1990–; fellow, Coll. of Am. Pathologists 1958–; mil: capt. Med. Corps USAF 1959-63; Republican; rec: gardening, cabinet making. Res: 215 Kreuzer Ln Napa 94559

SABHARWAL, RANJIT SINGH, mathematician, educator; b. Dec. 11, 1925, Dhudial, India, nat. US cit. 1981; s. Krishan Chand and Devti (Anand) S.; m. Pritam Chadha, 1948; children: Rajinderpal b. 1949, Armarjit b. 1951, Jasbir b. 1955; edn: BA, honors, Punjab Univ. 1944, MA, 1948; MA, UC Berkeley 1962; PhD, Wash. State Univ. 1966. Career: lectr. in math. Khalsa Coll., Bombay, India 1951-58; tchg. asst. UC Berkeley 1958-62; instr. in math. Portland State Univ. 1962-63; instr. in math. Washington State Univ. 1963-66; asst. prof. Kansas State Univ. 1966-68; assoc. prof. CSU Hayward 1968-74, prof. math. 1974–; mem: Am. Mathematical Soc., Mathematical Assn. of Am., Sigma Xi; research: non-desarguesian geometries. Res: 27892 Adobe Ct Hayward 94542 Ofc: California State University Hayward 94542

SACKETT, DALE MILTON, investor, contractor, engineer, executive; b. May 14, 1923, Long Beach; s. Leonard Frank and Corinne Thelma (Beggs) S.; m. Connie Bawden, Mar. 15, 1987; children: Linda b. 1953, Daniel b. 1957; edn: AA, Pasadena City Coll. 1948; BE mech. engring. (cum laude), USC, 1950. Career: chief air condtg. engr. C.F. Braun & Co., Alhambra 1950-54, designed systems for petroleum and chem. plants; air condtg. contr./engring. cons. D. M. Sackett & Assocs., Los Angeles 1954-60; cons. Chemet Engrs. Inc., Pasadena 1958-60; designed unique process & storage air-condtg. systems using steam refrigeration and utilizing waste coffee bean husks for fuel, for MJB Co., Nicaragua 1959; investor, property devel. & mgmt., 1960–; specialist comml. & indsl. air-condtg. systems, pres./ceo Authorized Service Corp. (contract and service engring.), Los Angeles 1960–; honors: Pi Tau Sigma 1949; mem. ASHRAE 1957–; Rotary Internat. (pres. East L.A. Club 1965-66, Rotarian of Yr. 1967, Dist. 530 Best Club award 1966); mil: non-commd. ofcr. US Army 1943-46, ETO, anti-aircraft unit under Gen. Patton, 3 campaign medals; Republican; Prot.; rec: art collector, photography. Ofc: 1256 S Atlantic Blvd Los Angeles 90022

SADLER, WILLIAM ALAN, JR., professor of sociology and business; b. Mar. 2, 1931, Evanston, Ill.; s. William A. and Marjorie (Eason) S.; m. Sallie I. Off, Apr. 23, 1977; children: William, Lisa, Kirsten and Nelson Green; edn: BA, Univ. Mich., 1953; ThM, General Theol. Sem., 1956, Harvard Univ., 1957; PhD, Harvard Univ., 1962. Career: clergyman Episcopal Church, Diocese of New York, 1959-64; asst. prof. Bishops Univ., Lennoxville, Quebec 1964-68; assoc. prof. Bates Coll., Lewiston, Me. 1968-72; prof. sociology and hd. div. interdisciplinary studies Bloomfield (N.J.) Coll., 1972-85; dean and exec. dir. planning Lock Haven (Pa.) Univ., 1985-89; chief academic ofcr., prof. sociology and bus., dir. human resource mgmt. major, Holy Names Coll., Oakland 1990–; vis. prof. Univ. Victoria, B.C. Canada, 1977, Pacific Sch. Religion, Berkeley 1974, Chapman Coll., Orange 1981; awards: Frederick Sheldon fellow Harvard 1958-59, postdoc. fellow Soc. for Values in Edn., New Haven, Ct. 1973, Danforth Assoc., St. Louis, Mo. 1976, Distinguished Scholar Chapman Coll. 1981, 15 grants from NEH, FIPSE, Kittredge Found., Ford Found., Pa., others; mem.: Am. Sociol. Assn. 1971–, Am. Assn. for Higher Edn. 1975–, Columbia Univ. Education Seminar, N.Y. (dir. 1978-89), Am. Soc. on Aging 1993– (Symposium chair 1994), Outward Bound (advy. bd. 1990–), Sequoyah Hts. HOA (v.p. bd. of dirs.), Inst. for Vitalaging (founding dir.); author: Existence & Love, 1970, Personality & Religion, 1970, 25+ jour. articles; editor: Master Sermons Through Ages, 1962; Democrat; Episcopalian; rec: aquatic sports, running, skiing, camping, hiking. Res: 9377 Skyline Blvd Oakland 94611 Ofc: Holy Names College 3500 Mountain Blvd Oakland 94619

SADUN, ALFREDO ARRIGO, medical scientist, professor, physician; b. Oct. 23, 1950, New Orleans, La.; s. Elvio H. and Lina (Ottolenghi) S.; m. Debra Rice, March 18, 1978; children: Rebecca b. 1980, Elvio b. 1983, Benjamin b. 1987; edn: BS biology, MIT 1972; PhD neurosci., Albert Einstein Coll. Med. N.Y. 1976; MD, 1978; lic. neuro-ophthalmologist, neuroscientist Am. Bd. Ophthalmology 1983. Career: intern Huntington Meml. Hosp., Pasadena 1978-79; resident, ophthalmology Harvard Med. Sch., Boston, Mass. 1979-82, HEED Found. fellow in neuro-ophthalmology Mass. Eye and Ear Inst. 1982-83, instr. ophthalmology 1983-84, asst. prof. ophthalmology 1984, dir. residential tng. prof. Univ. So. Calif. Sch. Med., L.A. 1984-85, asst. prof., ophthalmology and neurosurgery, 1984-87, assoc. prof. 1987-90, full prof. Univ. So. Calif. 1990–; prin. investigator Howe Lab. Harvard Univ., Boston 1981-84, Estelle Doheny Eye Inst., L.A. 1984–; examiner Am. Bd. Ophthalmology; honors: NIH Med. Sci. Tng. award 1972-77, PhD Trainee award 1977-78, Nat. Soc. Preventative Blindness Research award 1981, NIH grantee (1983-85, 1987-91, 1993–), James Adams Scholar 1990-92, Am. Acad. Ophthalmology Honor Award 1994; Fellow, Am. Acad. Ophthalmology, Neuro-Ophthalmologists; mem: Assn. Research in Vision and Opthalmology, Internat. Congress Neuro-ophthalmology, N. Am. Neuro-optalmology Soc. (chmn. membership com.; v.p. 1994–), N.Y. Acad. Scis., Soc. to Prevent Blindness, NIH, Nat. Eye Inst.; author: Optics for Ophthalmologists, 1988, New Methods of Sensory Visual Testing, 1989, 92 peer-reviewed articles pub. 1975–, 120+ other publications, 4 patents, 1986, 20 book chpts, 1982–. Ofc: USC School of Medicine Estelle Doheny Eye Institute 1450 San Pablo Los Angeles 90033-4581

SAHRAKAR, KAMRAN, physician; b. Nov. 19, 1963, Stuttgart, Germany; s. Hadi Sara Kar and Ursula (Kuenzinger) Sahrakar; m. Nancy Elaine Henning, May 6, 1990; 1 dau. Alexandra b. 1993; edn: BS, Univ. of Nevada, Reno 1985;

MD, Univ. of Nevada Sch. Medicine, Reno 1989. Career: physician, UC Davis Sch. Medicine 1989–; honors: AOA Nat. Med. Honor Soc. 1989; mem: AMA, Am. Assn. of Neurologic Surgeons, Congress of Neurologic Surgeons; author: jour. article on traumatic aneurysm, pub. 1995; Greek Orthodox; rec: books, music. Res: PO Box 661983 Sacramento 95866 Ofc: Dept of Neurosurgery 2516 Stockton Blvd Ste 254 Sacramento 95817

SAIDY, ANTHONY FRED, public health physician; b. May 16, 1937, Los Angeles; s. Fred Milhem and Marie Dolores (Mallouk) S.; edn: MS, Fordham Univ. 1958; MD, Cornell Univ. 1962; MPH, UCLA 1968. Career: pub. health physician, tuberculosis splst. L.A. Co. Dept. Health Services, Los Angeles 1967–; founder L.A. Co. Drug Abuse Program 1970; physician U.S. Peace Corps, Jamaica 1963-65; awards: Am. Open Chess Champion 1967, 1992, Canadian Open Chess Champion 1960, U.S. Speed Chess Co-Champion 1956, Internat. Chess Master 1969; mem: U.S. Chess Fedn., Am.-Israel Council for Israeli-Palestinian Peace (advy. bd. 1987–), Coalition for Peace in Middle East (v.chair 1988-92), Am. Arab Anti-Discrimination Com. (pres. L.A. 1987-88, v.p. 1988-89); author: Battle of Chess Ideas, 1972, World of Chess, 1974, The March of Chess Ideas, 1994, contbr. Chess Life & Review, 1964-73; rec: chess, human rights. Ofc: POB 17643 Los Angeles 90017

SAIFER, MARK G., pharmaceutical company research director; b. Sept. 16, 1938, Philadelphia, Pa.; s. Albert and Sylvia (Jolles) S.; m. Phyllis L., Jan. 28, 1961 (div. 1989); children: Scott b. 1963, Alandria b. 1968; m. Merry Sherman, June 26, 1994; edn: BA, Univ. Pa. 1960; PhD, UC Berkeley 1966. Career: sr. cancer research scientist Roswell Park Meml. Inst., Buffalo, N.Y. 1968-70; research dir. Diagnostic Data Inc., Palo Alto 1971-78; v.p. DDI Pharmaceuticals Inc., Mountain View 1978-94; v.p. Oxis International, Inc. 1994–; acting asst. prof. UC Berkeley 1966-67; awards: Am. Cancer Soc. Dernham fellowship 1967; mem: AAAS, N.Y. Acad. Scis., Parenteral Drug Assn.; num. patents in field, num. articles pub. in sci. jours. Ofc: Oxis International Inc. 248-4 Walker Drive Mountain View 94043

SAITO, THEODORE T., physicist; b. Sept. 9, 1942, Poston, Ariz.; s. Frank H. and Akiko (Tsuboi) S.; m. Diane Gail Signorino, Aug. 31, 1968; children: Jennifer b. 1969, Paul b. 1971; edn: BS, USAF Acad. 1964; MS, MIT 1966; PhD, Pa. St. Univ. 1970. Career: tech. area mgr. A.F. Materials Lab., Wright Patterson AFB, Ohio 1980; comdr. Seiler Research Lab., USAF Acad., Colo. 1984; dep. program leader, prec. engring. program Livermore Nat. Lab., Livermore 1984-87, dep. dept. head, def. scis. 1987-88, group leader optics and MODIL leader 1988-92; precision engring. prog. leader (acting) 1992-94, sci. advisor dept. of energy 1994–; honors: Phi Kappa Phi, Sigma Xi, Chennault award and Tech. award SPIE 1980; mem: SPIE (fellow, gov.), Optical Soc. Am. (fellow); mil: lt. col. USAF 1964-84; Republican; Christian; rec: Bible study. Ofc: Lawrence Livermore National Laboratory POB 808 L-32 Livermore 94550

SAKAMOTO, KATSUYUKI, academic administrator; b. Oct. 24, 1938, Los Angeles; m. Edna Christine; children: David b. 1972, Bryce b. 1975; edn: BA, psychol., Calif. State Univ., Fresno 1961, MA, psychol. 1968; PhD, psychol., So. Illinois Univ. 1971; sr. adminstr. coll. mgmt. prog., Carnegie Mellon Univ. 1984. Career: assoc. prof. psychol. Keuka Coll. 1971-78; prof. social psychol. Eastern Oregon State Coll., La Grande, Oreg. 1978-85, assoc. dean 1980-82, acting dean 1982-84, assoc. dean academic affairs 1982-85; prof. psychol. Indiana Univ. East, Richmond, Ind. 1985-91, vice chancellor academic affairs 1985-90, spl. asst. to chancellor 1990-91; chancellor, Calif. Sch. of Profl. Psychology-Alameda 1991–; lectr. So. Ill. Univ. 1970-71; vis. prof. SUNY, Binghamton, NY 1973; adj. prof.: Alfred Univ., NY 1972-76, Eisenhower Coll., Seneca Falls, NY 1975-77, Nazareth Coll. of Rochester, NY 1975-78; bd. dirs. Asian Comm. Mental Health Svs. 1991–; evaluator West. Assn. of Schs. and Colls. 1991–; bd. dirs. Am. Assn. of Univ. Adminstrs. 1991– (exec. com. 1982-91, v.p. 1990-92); bd. dirs. Found. for Ednl. Excellence, Alameda, Calif. 1993–; founding mem./Asian Am. caucus mem. Am. Assn. for Higher Edn. 1987–; mem.: Am. Assn. of State Colls. and Univs., Am. Psychol. Assn., Asian Am. Psychol. Assn. (treas./membership ofcr. 1983-91, pres. 1988-91), Calif. Psychol. Assn., Nat. Assn. of Academic Affairs Adminstrs., Nat. Council of Schs. of Profl. Psychol.; bd. dirs. Alameda Girls Club Inc. 1992–, Rotary Internat.-Alameda 1993–; author: num. profl. presentations and articles in field. Res: 2837 Brown St Alameda 94502 Ofc: Calif. School of Professional Psychology 1005 Atlantic Ave Alameda 94501

SALAMATI, FARSHID, environmental engineer company president; b. May 31, 1949, Tehran, Iran; nat. 1980; s. Plato and Kharman (Yezeshmi) S.; m. Fariba Azari, June 19, 1958; 1 child, Behan b. 1988; edn: BSEE, Univ. Tehran 1974; MS energy, UC Berkeley 1984. Career: field engr. Shahin Factory, Tehran, Iran 1968-72; supr. Irom Engring. Co. 1972-75; project mgr., pres. Techno Band 1975-80; field engr. Eal Corp., Richmond 1980-85; CFO, v.p. Inov Corp., Oakland 1985-87; pres., CFO EIC 1987–; mem: Nat. Asbestos Council (tech. co-chair Calif. chpt. 1988–), Nat. Assn. Environ. Profls., BOMA, Persian Zoroastrian Orgn. (cofounder, secty. 1983-88), Fedn. of Zoroastrian Assns. of No. Am. (v.p. & chair of planning, bus. devel. 1990–), World Safety Orgn. (co-founder No. Calif. chpt. 1993–), Nat. Soc. of Profl. Engrs. 1993-, Am. Indl.

Hygiene Assn. 1992-; mil: lt. col. Tehran 1975-77; rec: swimming, surfing, snorkeling. Res: 6160 Mt Diablo Castro Valley 94552 Ofc: EIC 7901 Oakport St #3100 Oakland 94621

SALINGER, CHARLES, physician, dermatologist; b. April 24, 1945, New York; s. Ernest and Mae (Brenner) S.; m. Donna Marcia Gafford, May 14, 1974 (div. 1992); children: Jennifer b. 1978, Jeffrey b. 1984; edn: BS, Univ. Wis. Madison 1965; MD, St. Univ. N.Y. Health Scis. Center, Syracuse 1968; lic. N.Y. Bd. Med. Examiners 1968, Calif. Bd. Med. Examiners 1974. Career: intern La. St. Univ. Med. Center, New Orleans 1968-69; resident dermatology Charity Hosp., La. St. Univ. Med. Center 1969-72; chief dermatology service USAF Maxwell Regional Hosp., Montgomery, Ala. 1972-74; clin. assoc. prof. dermatology Coll. Osteopathic Medicine of Pacific, Pomona 1977–; chief med. staff Med. Center La Mirada 1987-88, bd. trustees 1985–; Fellow Am. Acad. Dermatology; mem: Los Angeles Met. Dermatologic Soc. (exec. bd. 1987-96, pres. 1994-95), Am. Soc. Dermatologic Surgery (fellow), Internat. Soc. Dermatologic Surgery, Pacific Dermatologic Soc., Internat. Soc. Pediatric Dermatology, AMA, CMA, LACMA; article pub. in profl. jour. 1972; mil: major USAF 1972-74; Jewish; rec: tennis, downhill skiing, billfishing, avocado ranching, managing/coaching Little League. Res: 5440 Emerywood Dr Buena Park 90621 Ofc: 12625 La Mirada Blvd Ste 106 La Mirada 90638

SALK, PETER L., medical research; b. Jan. 21, 1944, Ann Arbor, Mich.; s. Jonas and Donna (Lindsay) S.; m. Ellen Stephanie Schreibman, Oct. 30, 1971; son, Michael; edn: Phillips Exeter Acad. 1957-61; AB, Harvard Coll., 1965; MD, Johns Hopkins Univ. Sch. of Med., 1969. Career: intern, resident in internal med. University Hosps. of Cleveland, Oh. 1969-71; postdoctoral fellow, resrch. assoc., sr. resrch. assoc. Salk Inst. for Biological Studies, La Jolla 1972-84; exec. v.p. Westbridge Research Group, San Diego 1984-90, bd. dirs. 1982-90; assoc., v.p. Jonas Salk Found., La Jolla 1991–; honors: Phi Beta Kappa 1965, Alpha Omega Alpha 1969; contbr. articles in sci. jours.; Maharishi Ayur-Veda physician, past chmn. Age of Enlightenment Transcendental Meditation Ctr. S.D. 1984-86. Ofc: Jonas Salk Foundation 817 Silverado St La Jolla 92037

SALKIN, DAVID, research physician, administrator, educator; b. Aug. 8, 1906, Ukraine; s. Samuel Salkin and Eva Sturman; m. Bess Marguerite Adelman, Sept. 12, 1934; children: Barbara Ruth b. 1938, Robert David b. 1941 (dec. 1947); edn: MD, Univ. of Toronto, Ont., Can. 1929. Career: medical director Hopemont (W.Va.) Sanitarium, 1934-41, medical/hospital dir. 1941-48; med. dir. San Fernando (Calif.) VA Hosp., 1949-67, med./hosp. dir. 1967-71; dir. research La Vina Hosp., Altadena 1972-83; sr. researcher, pulmonary/cancer, Huntington Med. Res. Insts., Pasadena 1984–; asst. prof. medicine Univ. West Va., Morgantown 1934-48; assoc. prof. medicine UCLA, Los Angeles 1949-58; clin. prof. medicine USC, L.A. 1958–, Loma Linda Univ., L.A. 1958–; awards: Veterans Adminstrn. American Acad. TB Physicians 1958, 1962, Gold medal Calif. Thoracic Soc. 1972, Am. Coll. Chest Physicians 1973, Internat. Coccidioides Symp. 1976, Am. Lung Assn. of LA County 1980; staff Huntington Med. Research Insts., Huntington Memorial Hosp., Cedars Sinai Hosp., Barlow Hosp.; mem: Sigma Xi; publs. in med. jours. and texts; Jewish; rec: the Arts. Res: 1820 Linda Vista Ave Pasadena 91103 Ofc: Huntington Medical Research Insts. 660 S Fair Oaks Pasadena 91105

SALMASSI, SADEGH, surgeon; b. Aug. 14, 1946, Baghdad, Iraq; s. Jafar and Kobra (Alavi) S.; m. Tahereh, Jan. 17, 1970; children: Ali b. 1971, Nahal b. 1975; edn: premed., Pahlavi Univ., Shiraz, Iran 1964-66, MD, 1973; bd. certified Am. Bd. Pathol. 1981; lic. Ill. 1978, Mo. 1980, Kans. 1980, Calif. 1983. Career: CC rotating intern Pahlavi Univ. affil. hosps. 1972-73; resident anatomy & clin. pathol. Univ. Ill. 1975-78, chief res. pathol. 1978-79, fellow blood banking and immunohematology 1979-80; emerg. rm. phys. Louise Burg Hosp. Chgo. 1979-80; instr. pathol. Univ. Ill. 1976-80; asst. prof. pathol. Univ. Mo. Kansas City, assoc. dir. anatomic pathol., asst. dir. blood bank Truman Med. Ctr. UMKC 1980-84; dir. Delano Med. Clin. & Lab. Delano, Calif. 1984–; chmn. dept. family practice Delano Regl. Med. Ctr. 1985-87; staff Delano Reg. Med. Center, v.chief staff, chmn. utilization rev. 1988-89, chief of staff 1989-90, pres. Delano Med. Group IPA 1989–; chmn. credential com. 1990-91, chmn pharmacy & therapeutic com. 1990-91; recipient AMA physician recogn. awards; Fellow Am. Coll. Pathologists 1981, Fellow ACIP 1988, mem. AAFP 1988, AMA, AAAS, NY Acad. Scis., Ill. Med. Soc., Chgo. Med. Soc., Iranian Med. Assn., Am. Assn. Blood Banks, Kansas City Soc. Pathols., Pahlavi Univ. Med. Sch. Alumni Assn.; publs: 20+ articles in med. jours., papers presented Univ. Ct., K.C. Soc. Pathols.; mil: 1st lt., physician Rezayeh Mil. Hosp., Iran 1973-75; Muslim; rec: videotaping. Res: 1121 Sussex Circle Bakersfield 93311 Ofc: Delano Med. Clin. 1005 11th Ave Delano 93215

SALMON, NATHAN, philosopher, educator; b. Jan. 2, 1951, Los Angeles; s. Mair and Rebecca (Sene) Ucuzoglu; m. Eileen Mary Conrad, Aug. 28, 1980; edn: AA, El Camino Coll. 1971; BA, UCLA 1973; MA, 1974; PhD, 1979. Career: instr. UCLA, CSU Northridge, CSU Long Beach, 1976-77; lectr. CSU Northridge 1977-78; asst. prof. Princeton Univ. 1978-82, vis. senior research philosopher 1982; assoc. prof. UC Riverside 1982-84; UC Santa Barbara 1984-85; prof. 1985–; awards: Council of Grad. Schs. in U.S. Gustave O Arlt award 1984,

Council Internat. Exchange of Scholars Fulbright Disting. Prof. lecturing grant 1986; mem: Am. Philosophical Assn., Bertrand Russell Soc., Royal Inst. Philosophy Gt. Britain (lifetime hon.); author: Reference & Essence, 1981, Frege's Puzzle, 1986, co-editor: Propositions & Attitudes, 1988. Res: 1105 Orchid Dr Santa Barbara 93111 Ofc: UCSB Dept. Philosophy, Santa Barbara 93106

SALVAGNO, ROB, investment broker; b. Aug. 28, 1947, Corning, Calif.; s. William R. and Annie Sue (Hopkins) S.; m. Ana Maria Salinas, July 5, 1975; children: Robert b. 1976, Lita b. 1980, Alexa b. 1982; edn: BA, Chico State Coll., 1969, MS, Univ. Texas, 1975; reg. rep. SEC, 1981. Career: reg. sanitarian Calif. St. Health Dept., L.A. 1969-71; E-5, environmental splst. US Army, San Antonio, Tx. 1971-74; rsch. assoc. Texas A&M Univ., College Sta. 1974-75; systems mgr. Alamo Area Council of Govts., San Antonio, Tx. 1975-77; pres. Allied Energy Systems Inc., Chico, Calif. 1977-81; senior v.p. investments Paine Webber, Chico 1981–, branch mgr. 1992–; recipient Paine Webber Pacesetter award 1982-88, Pres.'s Council 1989–, Direct Inv. advy. bd. 1982-87, reg. inv. advr. 1991–; civic bds: Chico Youth Football (dir. 1987-88), Chico Youth Soccer (coach 1985-86), Chico Econ. Planning Corp. (dir. 1990–); mem. Rotary 1987–, Elks 1988–, Am. Legion 1990–; publs: book, tech. reports 1975, 2 TV films 1972, 73; Republican; R.Cath.; rec: skiing, travel, tennis, barbershop singing, Arabian horses. Res: 3585 Keefer Rd Chico 95926 Ofc: Paine Webber, 1051 Mangrove Ave Chico 95926

SAMET, MARC KRANE, pharmacologist; b. Apr. 30, 1950, Chgo.; s. Herman and Nora (Krane) S.; edn: BS biochem., No. Ill. Univ., 1973; MS devel. biology, Northwestern Univ., 1975; MS anat. Northwestern Univ. Med. Sch., 1978; MS, PhD pharmacology and toxicology, Kansas Univ., 1983. Career: NIH postdoc. fellowships Univ. Calif. at Berkeley and San Francisco, 1983-85; founding scientist immunology pgm. Applied Immunesciences Inc., Menlo Park 1985-87; assoc. Glenwood Ventures, Menlo Park 1987-88; coord. new technology appls. Vitaphore Corp., 1988-90; dir. new bus. Plan AConsulting Partners, 1991-92; Merck & Co., 1992–; mem: AAAS, Soc. for Neurosci., Am. Assn. Immunologists, N.Y. Acad. Scis., Controlled Release Soc., Internat. Fedn. for Adv. of Genetic Engring. and Biotechnology; publs: 16+ books, chapters, sci. jour. articles re pharm. emerging technology & mktg. strategy Jewish; rec: biking, tennis, photography, hiking. Res: 923 Menlo Ave #1 Menlo Park 94025 Ofc: PO Box 1428 Menlo Park 94026

SAMPLE, STEVEN BROWNING, university president; b. Nov. 29, 1940, St. Louis, Mo.; s. Howard and Dorothy (Cunningham) S.; m. Kathryn Brunkow, Jan. 28, 1961; children: Michelle Sample Smith, Melissa Ann; edn: BS E.E. (highest honors), Univ. of Ill. 1962, MS, 1963, PhD, 1965; reg. profl. engr., State of Nebr. Career: grad. asst./instr. E.E. Dept, Univ. of Ill. 1962-65; sr. scientist Melpar Inc., Falls Ch., Va. 1965-66; asst. prof. Sch. of E.E., Purdue Univ., Lafayette, Ind. 1966-70, assoc. prof. 1970-73; dep. dir. Ill. Bd. Higher Edn, Springfield 1971-74; prof., exec. v.p. acad. affairs, dean Grad. Coll. Univ. Nebr., Lincoln 1974-82; prof. elec. and computer engring. SUNY, Buffalo 1982-91, pres. 1982-91; pres. Univ. of So. Calif., L.A. 1991–, prof. E.E. 1991–; trustee L.A. Ednl. Alliance for Restructuring Now (LEARN) 1991–; bd. dirs: Galaxy Inst. for Edn. 1991–, L.A. World Affairs Council 1991–, Litton Industries. Inc., Beverly Hills 1991–, The Presley Companies, Newport Beach 1991–, First Interstate Bancorp, L.A. 1991–, Rebuild LA 1992–; bd. trustees Univ. So. Calif. 1991–; chmn. The Governor's Conf. on Sci. & Engring Edn., Res. & Devel. 1989-91; bd. dirs.: Regenstrief Med. Found., Indianapolis, Ind. 1982–, Niagara Mohawk Power Corp. 1988-91, Dunlop Tire Corp. 1987-91, Res. Found. of SUNY 1987-91, Marine Midland Bank We. Region, Buffalo, NY 1982-91, Design & Mfg. Corp., Connersville, Inc. 1977-91; vice chmn., bd. dirs. Western N.Y. Tech. Devel. Ctr., Buffalo 1982-91; chmn. bd. dirs. Calspan-UB Res. Ctr., Inc., Buffalo 1983-91; chmn. council of pres. Nat. Assn. of State Univs. and Land-Grant Colls. 1985-86, exec. com. 1987-91, chmn. ednl. telecomms. com. 1982-83; exec. com. Greater Buffalo Devel. Found. Inc. 1982-91; bd. trustees: We. NY Public Broadcasting Assn. 1985-91, Studio Arena Theatre, Buffalo, NY 1983-91, Univ. of Buffalo Found. Inc. 1982-91; chmn. We. NY Regional Econ. Devel. Council 1984-91; awards: Bronze Tablet award and Hamilton Watch Co. Engring award Univ. of Ill. 1962, Sloan Found. Fellow 1962-63, NSF grad. fellow 1963-65, NSF res. grants 1968-73, fellow ACE Adminstrv. Internship Prog. 1970-71, fellow NATO Inst. on Surface Coatings, Imperial Coll., London 1972, Outstanding Paper award IEEE, Purdue Univ. 1976, Disting. Alumnus award Univ. Ill. Dept. E.E. 1980, Engr. of Yr. award NY St. Soc. of Profl. Engrs. 1985, Citation award Buffalo Council on World Affairs 1986, LHD (hon.), Canisius Coll., Buffalo NY 1989, Humanitarian award Nat. Council of Christians and Jews of Buffalo 1991, Walter P. Cook award Univ. of Buffalo 1991, LLD (hon.) Univ. of Sheffield, England 1991, Outstanding Elec. Engr. award Purdue Univ. 1993, EdD. (hon.) Purdue Univ. 1994, LHD (hon.) Hebrew Union Coll. 1994, Humanitarian award Nat. Conf. of Christians and Jews, L.A. 1994, Hollzer Mem. award Jewish Fedn. Council of Greater L.A. 1994; mem: Assn. of Am. Univs. (chair, com. on postdoctoral edn. 1994–), IEEE (ednl. activities bd. 1984–), Project California 1991–, Coalition of 100 Club of L.A. 1991, Calif. Council on Sci. & Tech. 1991–, Council on Fgn. Relations, Sigma XI; bd. dirs. Greater Buffalo C.of C. 1985-91, United Way of Buffalo and Erie Co. 1985-91, Buffalo Philharmonic Orch. 1982-91; bd. mgrs. Buffalo and Erie Co. Hist. Soc.

1982-91; timpanist St. Louis Philharmonic Orch. 1955-58; author: num. articles pub. in profl. jours.; patentee in field; Episcopalian. Res: 1550 Oak Grove Ave San Marino 91108 Ofc: University of Southern Calif Office of the President University Park ADM 110 Los Angeles 90089-0012

SAMPSON, RICHARD ARNIM, security executive; b. June 9, 1927, New Haven, Conn.; s. Richard Arnim Sampson and Ora Viola (Reese) Sampson-Jackson; m. Marilyn Jo Gardner, June 10, 1950 (div. Mar. 1962); children: Gary b. 1951, Susan b. 1955; m. Janet Margaret Battaglia, Jan. 26, 1963 (div. July 1987); children: Cynthia b. 1964, David b. 1965; m. Alice Annette Whitfield, July 23, 1988; children: Shareasa b. 1970, Anthony b. 1972, Erika b. 1976; edn: BS, Mich. State Univ., 1951; MPA, Auburn Univ., 1972; grad. Air War Coll., Montgomery, Ala. 1972. Career: exec. Central Intelligence Agy., W.D.C., 1951-76; mgr. spl. projects Hughes Aircraft Co., El Segundo, Calif. 1976-80; mgr. security Northrop Aircraft Adv. Systems Div., Pico Rivera 1980-83; security mgr. General Dynamics Electronics Div., San Diego 1983-92; dir. of security GDE Systems Inc. 1992–; faculty Southwest L.A. Coll. 1978-79, Webster Univ., San Diego 1991–, Calif. State Univ., San Marcos 1992–; mem. advy. group leadership & mgmt. program in security Mich. St. Univ. 1990–, guest lectr. 1991–, adv. security mgmt. curriculum Palomar Coll., San Marcos 1993–; bd. dirs. Internat. Historical Aviation Search, Inc. 1994–; awards: Order of the Moon Rep. of China, Taiwan 1961, outstanding unit award USAF, Las Vegas 1971, C.I.A. Intel. Medal of Merit, Career Intel. Medal, W.D.C. (1975, 76); mem: Internat. Assn. Chiefs of Police 1957-62, Security Affairs Support Assn. 1989–, Mich. State Univ. Alumni Assn., Am. Soc. for Indsl. Security (1957–, chmn., vice chmn. acad., placement coms. 1994), CIA Retirees Assn. 1976–, Signa Soc. 1976–, Nat. Mgmt. Assn. 1976–, Indsl. Security Working Group 1980–, Contractor SAP/SAR Working Group 1988–, Aerospace Inds. Assn. Security Com. 1987-92, Research Security Assocs. 1987–, Certified Profl. OPSEC Profls. Soc. 1993–, Assn. of Former Intelligence Officers 1993–, Am. Biographical Inst. (research bd. of advisors 1993–), Calif. Crime Prevention Officers 1995, Rancho Bernardo Security Com. 1995–, San Diego Crime Commn. 1995–, Escondido Citizens Patrol 1995–; publs: mag. article "The Police of Taiwan" 1960, manual, Special Projects Security 1965, thesis: Excessive Bureaucracy: Causes and Cures, 1972, "Advanced Ocean Mining & Energy Program", 1975, "The Hughes Glomar Explorer Project", 1994, "The Business Side of Security", 1994; mil: capt. USAR 1949-66; Republican; Congregationalist (trustee, personnel com.); reading, tchg., writing. Res: 1408 Westwood Pl Escondido 92026 Ofc: GDE Systems, Inc. PO Box 1198 Poway 92074

SAMUDIO, JEFFREY BRYAN, urban designer-architectural historian, educator; b. Oct. 3, 1966, San Gabriel; s. Lazaro and Grace (Alvarez) S.; edn: B Architecture, minor in Urban & Regional Planning, USC, 1989, grad. student, cand. M Arch/MURP, 1995; AIA intern. Career: asst. slide curator USC Arch. & Fine Arts Library, Los Angeles 1985-88; sr. ptnr. Design AID, Architecture Planning Preservation, L.A. 1987–; instr. L.A. Trade Tech. Coll. and Rio Hondo Coll., 1989–; instr. arch. history Cal Poly, Pomona; v.p. acquisitions and project devel. Northeast Design and Devel. Group, Inc. 1989-90; assoc. dir. & cofounder USC Sch. of Arch. Program in Historic Preservation 1993–; heritage and econ. adv. for Township of Levvka, Govt. of Fiji 1994–; appt. arch. historian Calif. Historical Resources Commn. 1995–; mem. acad. policy com. and dean search com. USC Sch. of Arch. 1992, Rebuild L.A. Com. 1991; lectr., Japan, Mexico, Fiji, Australia; awards: appreciation City of L.A. 1984, 1989, Parkinson Scholarship for Arch. 1984-85, USC Scholarship for Excellence 1984-89, nat. convention rep. A.I.A. Students USC Chpt. 1985-89, L. Pidgeon Scholarship for Grad. Arch. 1991-92, pres. Assn. of Grad. Arch. Students, USC 1991-92, award of service A.I.A., Pasadena 1991, Phi Beta Phi 1992, Freeman House Fellow, USC Sch. of Arch. 1991-93, Graham Found. grantee 1991, Nat. Trust for Historic Preservation grantee 1992, 93, Getty Conservation Grant 1993, Nat. Park Svc. grantee 1995; mem: Hist. Soc. Sc. Calif. (life), Soc. of Arch. Historians (life, bd. mem.; preservation ofcr. So. Calif. chpt. 1994–; pres. So. Calif. chpt. 1995–), AIA (assoc.), Am. Planning Assn. (assoc.); civic: The Eagle Rock Assn. (bd. 1988-91, chair preservation advocacy 1988), Highland Park Main St. Com. (co-chair 1993-95), mem. Los Angeles Conservancy, Neutra Centennial Com. (advisor 1991), Colorado Blvd. Specific Plan (bd. 1987-90); Republican; rec: preservation advocacy, flying, travel. Ofc: Design AID, Architecture Planning Preservation Whitley Court 1722 N Whitley Ave Hollywood 90028

SANCHEZ, RUBEN DARIO, clergyman, psychotherapist, writer, educator; b. Feb. 12, 1943, Buenos Aires, Argentina, naturalized U.S. citizen 1989; s. Ramon Jose and Maria Concepcion (Pardino) S.; m. Lina Alcira Tabuenca, Feb. 7, 1966; children: Adrian b. 1971, Vivian b. 1973; edn: BA in edn. and theology, River Plate Coll., Entre Rios, Argentina 1968; MA rel. edn., Andrews Univ., Berrien Springs, Mich. 1976; PhD rel. edn., Calif. Graduate Sch. Theology, L.A. 1979; MA clin. psychology, National Univ., L.A. 1992; ordained minister Seventh Day Adventist Ch. Career: minister Calif. Conf., Glendale 1970-71, Ill. Conf., Brookfield, Ill. 1972-77, Oregon Conf., Portland 1977-80; dir. development Adventist Media Ctr., Newbury Park, Calif. 1980-92; leader seminars nat., 1980-95; pres. Advi Internat., Newbury Park 1989-95; clin. counselor pvt. practice, San Fernando, Calif. 1992–; founder, chancellor Pacific Northwest

Christian Sch., Woodburn, Oreg. 1979-80; founder, dir. Christian Bible Inst., Woodburn, Oreg. 1980; dir. Voice of Prophecy Bible Sch., Newbury Park, Calif. 1980-84; awards: Outstanding svs. to the Spanish community radio sta. KROW (1460 AM), Independence, Oreg. 1980, listed Who's Who in Religion 1986, 92, Who's Who in West 1992; mem: Calif. Assn. Marriage and Family Therapists, United Assn. Christian Counselors 1989–, Nat. Fund Raisers Assn. 1991–, Christian Mgmt. Assn. 1980-92, Adventist Theol. Soc.; author: Fascinating Exploration of the Bible, 1977; Intro. to the Old Testament, 1979; Hungry Heart, 1984; Aceptame Asi (Spanish), 1992; rec: sculpture. Res: 2983 Elinor Ct Newbury Park 91320 Ofc: 1100 Rancho Conejo Blvd Newbury Park 91320

SANDELL, JAN RUNE, computer company president and financial consultant; b. May 26, 1954, Kristianstad, Sweden; s. Hugo Leonard and Anna Beata Matilda (Andersson) S.; m. Kathleen Maria Burgi, May 13, 1984; children: Erik Andreas b. 1993; edn: BSEE, Tech. Inst. Hassleholm Sweden 1974; MBA strategic planning, Univ. Lund Sweden 1979; MBA finance, UC Riverside 1980. Career: cons. Mornstam AB, Malmo, Sweden 1978-79; financial analyst, senior fin. anal., mgr. budget & planning Fox & Carskadon Fin. Corp. San Mateo, Calif. 1981-84; dir. fin. planning Homestead Financial Corp. Burlingame 1984; senior dir., senior home office mgr., v.p. Industrial Indemnity Fin. Corp., a Xerox Fin. Services Corp., San Francisco 1984-92; founder and mng. ptnr. Sandell Assoc., a fin. and mgmt. cons. firm 1992-93; pres. Internat. Business Electronics, Inc. 1993–; honors: Cementa Co. Honorary Award (Malmo, Sweden), Calif. Edn. Abroad Scholar (Univ. Lund); mem: Am. Mgmt. Assn. 1985; mil: Swedish Army 1977-78, commendations for computer efficiency improvements (Kristianstad, Sweden); Lutheran; rec: computers, golf, philately, travel, swim, abstract art. Ofc: IBE Inc. 21130 Cabot Blvd Ste A Hayward 94545

SANDERS, AUGUSTA, nurse, county mental health services administrator; b. July 22, 1932, Alexandria, La.; d. James and Elizabeth (Thompson) Swann; m. James Robert Sanders, Jan. 12, 1962 (div. 1969); edn: RN, Morgan State Univ., Provident Hosp. Sch. of Nursing, Balt. 1956; RN, Md. 1956. Career: head nse. VA Hosp., Downey, Ill. 1956-57; staff nse. Huntington Hosp., Pasadena 1957-58; head nse., evening supr. VA Hosp., Los Angeles 1958-60; head nse. NPI-UCLA, 1960-61; staff nse. Am. Red Cross, 1960-64; public health nse. Fed. Govt., W.D.C., 1964-66; staff nse. L.A. County Sheriff's Dept., 1967-72; RN, asst., mental health counselor L.A. County Dept. Mental Health Svs., 1972-89, senior mental health counselor and mental health svc. coordinator, 1989-92; Calif. Gov. appt. mem. 11th Dist. Bd. Med. Quality, 1981-87; awards: Woman of Year Crenshaw/La Tijera B.P.W., L.A. 1987, Wilshire B.P.W., L.A. 1989, Victor Valley B.P.W. 1994, elected pres. Md. State Student Nurses Assn. 1955-56; mem. Internat. Assn. Bus. & Profl. Women (1977–, past chapt. pres., L.A. Sunset Dist. 1988-89), Calif. Fedn. of Bus. and Profl. Women (v.p. membership and mktg. 1995-96); mem. steering com. State Sen. Diane Watson; rec: writing, movies, travel. Res: 13338 Apple Blossom Ln Apple Valley 92308-5415

SANDS, RUSSELL BERTRAM, insurance executive; b. Feb. 14, 1940, Santa Cruz; s. Clarence Russell and Betty Ellyn (Weeks) S.; m. Jacquelyn Hall, Sept. 9, 1960; children: Douglas b. 1962, Gwendolyn b. 1970; edn: undergrad. Wheaton Coll. 1957-59, UCB 1959-61; BA, Western Ill. Univ., 1984. Career: mgr. Insurance Co. of No. Am., San Francisco 1961-69; v.p. Bayly, Martin & Fay, S.F. 1969-76; chmn. bd. and CEO Frank B. Hall & Co., S.F. 1976-92; pres. Rollins Hudig Hall of No. Calif. 1992–; dir. Hammerwell, Inc.; ptnr. San Bro Holdings I; gen. ptnr. Wendy Petroleum; prin. Sands Properties; ptnr. Dixon Oaks MHP; mem.: Nat. Assn. of Ins. Brokers, Western Mobilehome Assn. (ins. com.), World Trade Club, Churchill Club; civic bds.: City Team (dir.), Fellowship Acad. (dir.), Young Life San Francisco (dir.), Mt. Hermon Assn. (advy. council.); Republican; Presbyterian; rec: tennis, golf, travel. Ofc: Frank B. Hall & Co., One Market Plaza San Francisco 94105

SANFORD, RON, travel and wildlife photographer; b. June 13, 1939, Gridley, Calif.; s. Dr. Keith D., DDS, and Ailene (McIntyre) S.; m. Nancy K. Wallace, June 17, 1961; children: Michael b. 1962, Daniel b. 1964; edn: BS, UC Berkeley, 1961. Career: corp. pres. Gridley Growers Inc., Gridley 1965-78; travel and wildlife photographer, internat., 1978-: represented in New York (Black Star), Seattle (Allstock), Tokyo (Imperial Press), Milan (Grazia Neri), Springfield, Vt. (f/STOP); selected credits 1992: N.Y. Times, Washington Post - Insight, U.S.A. Today, Newsweek Mag., Sunset Books, Nat. Geographic WORLD, Nat. Geo. books, Ducks Unlimited Publs., Petersen's Photographic, European Travel & Life, Bon Appetite, Outside, Gourmet, Aloha, Sierra, Glamour, Islands, Stern, Travel- Holiday, Motorland, Harrowsmith, Field & Stream, National Parks, Nat. Wildlife, Backpacker, Buzzworm, Backpacker, Time, Life, Outdoor Photographer, Woman's World, Stock & Commodities, Architectural Digest, Calif. Parklands, Audubon, Vogue, Birder's World, Reader's Digest, Alaska Mag., Popular Photog., Natural History Mag., Airone mag. (Italy), Inflight mags: TWA, US Air, Northwest Orient, American, Calendars: Audubon, Nat. Geographic, Sierra Club, Falcon Press, Nikon, Argus Silver Creek, Nature Conservancy, World Wildlife Fund, Eastman Kodak & others; awards: Wildlife Photographer of Year Calif. Dept. Fish & Game 1984, World Press Photo"Nature Series" Holland Found., Amsterdam (1988, 1990); mem. Am. Soc. of Magazine Photographers, Rotary Internat., Gridley (pres.

1973-74, Paul Harris Fellow 1989); mil: capt. US Army 1962-65; rec: religion, philosophy, mythology. Ofc: Ron Sanford PO Box 248 Gridley 95948 Tel/Fax: 916/846-4687

SANTEE, DALE WILLIAM, lawyer; b. Mar. 28, 1953, Washington, Pa.; s. Robert Erwin and Elsbeth Emma (Bantleon) S.; m. Junko (Mori) S.; children: s. Enri b. 1983; edn: BA, Washington & Jefferson Coll., Pa. 1975; JD, Univ. Pittsburgh Sch. of Law, 1978; MA, No. Arizona Univ., Flagstaff 1982; admitted bar: Pa., 1978, Ct. of Military Appeals, 1979, Calif., 1989. Career: served to major US Air Force, 1979–; asst. staff judge advocate 832CSG/JA, Luke AFB, Ariz. 1979, area def. counsel Det. ULQD5S 1979-81; claims ofcr. 343GSG/JA, Eilson AFB, Ak. 1981-83; staff legal advisor Bd. of Veterans Appeals, W.D.C. 1983-89; asst. staff judge advocate HQ USAF/JAJM, Bolling AFB, D.C. 1986-89; 63CSG/JA, Norton AFB, Calif. 1989-91, 445AW/JA, 1991–; awarded AF Commendation Medal (1981, 89), Meritorious Svc. 1991, Outstanding unit (1979, 91); dep. pub. defender San Diego County, 1990-93, dep. alternate pub. defender 1993–; v.p. Neuer Enterprises, Huntington, Ind. 1984–; honors: Washington & Jefferson Coll. academic scholar 1971-75, Dean's List (1973, 74), Beta scholar 1974, Mathew Brown Ringland Polit. Sci. Award 1975, Pa. Senate law sch. scholar 1975-78, No. Ariz. Univ. Dean's List (1980, 81), Outstanding Young Man in Am. 1981, VA performance award 1988; mem: San Diego Co. Bar Assn. 1989–, Reserve Officer Assn. 1992–, Internat. Platform Assn.; civic: San Diego Comm. Child Abuse Coord. Com. 1990–, Zamorano Elem. Sch. (site com. chmn. 1990-92, PTA pres. 1991-92); Republican; Methodist; rec: sports, coins & stamps. Res: 1156 Corrales Lane Chula Vista 91910 Ofc: Alternate Public Defender of San Diego, 8525 Gibbs Dr Ste 208 San Diego 92123

SANTILLAN, ANTONIO, banker, motion picture finance executive; b. May 8, 1936, Buenos Aires; naturalized, 1966; s. Guillermo Spika and Raphaella C. (Abaladejo) S.; children: Andrea, Miguel, Marcos; edn: grad. Morgan Park Mil. Acad., Chgo. 1954; Coll. of William and Mary, 1958; Calif. lic. real estate broker. Career: asst. in charge of prodn. Wilding Studios, Chgo. 1964; pres. Adams Financial Services, Los Angeles 1965–; writer, producer, dir. (motion pictures) The Glass Cage, co-writer Dirty Mary/ Crazy Larry, Viva Knievel; contbg. writer Once Upon a Time in America; TV panelist Window on Wall Street; contbr. articles to profl. fin. and real estate jours.; recipient Am. Rep. award San Francisco Film Festival, Cork Ireland Film Fest. 1961; mem. Writer's Guild Am., Los Angeles Bd. Realtors, Beverly Hills Bd. Realtors (income, inv. div. steering com.), Westside Realty Bd. (dir.), Los Angeles Ventures Assn. (dir.), Rotary Internat.; Jonathan Club, Round Table, Toastmasters Internat., Wilshire C.C.; mil: USNR 1959. Ofc: Winning Visions, Inc. 425 N Alfred St Los Angeles 90048

SAPAN, YISROEL PINCHAS, obstetrician, gynecologist; b. Feb. 15, 1942, Brooklyn, N.Y.; s. Michel and Basha (Hordes) S.; m. Pnina, Apr. 2, 1967; children: Shaindyl Pia b. 1968, Faivel Yaakov b. 1969, Yonason Yosef b. 1981; edn: BS cum laude, Bklyn Coll. 1961; MD, St. Univ. N.Y. 1965; lic. Am. Bd. Ob-Gyn. Career: intern Long Island Jewish Hosp., New Hyde Park, N.Y. 1965-66; resident North Shore Hosp., Manhasset, N.Y. 1966-69; ob-gyn. USAF Richards-Gebaur AFB, Mo. 1969-70, chief of ob-gyn. 1970-71; staff ob-gyn. Kaiser Permanente Med. Group, San Francisco 1971–; vol. physician Hospice of Marin, San Rafael 1977–; awards: Kaiser Hosp. Tchr. of Year 1984, Chabad of Marin Honoree 1988; mem: S.F. Med. Soc., Am. Coll. Ob-Gyn., Am. Soc. for Coloscopy and Cervical Pathology, CMA, Chabad of Marin (co-founder 1984–); article pub. in profl. jour. 1973; mil: capt. USAF 1969-71; Jewish; rec: Torah study. Address: 2200 O'Farrell St San Francisco 94115

SARTORIS, DAVID JOHN, physician, diagnostic radiologist; b. Nov. 25, 1955; s. Cornelius Ugo and Helen Louise (Lesjak) S.; edn: BS, biology (with distinction), Stanford Univ. 1976; MD, 1980; cert. Am. Bd. Radiology 1984. Career: intern diagnostic radiology Stanford Univ. Med. Ctr. 1980-81, resident 1981-84; fellow musculoskeletal radiology UC San Diego 1984-85, asst. prof. radiology in residence 1985-87, assoc. prof. 1987–, chief, musculoskeletal imaging UCSD Med. Ctr. 1985-91, chief, quantitative bone densitometry 1984–; vis. prof. UC Davis 1985, UC Irvine 1986, Maricopa Med. Ctr. and St. John's Hosp., Phoenix 1986, Univ. of Ottawa 1987, Doris Palmer Arthritis Ctr., Pittsburgh 1988, Univ. of Pittsburgh 1988, 90, VA Med. Ctr., Long Beach 1990, Creighton Univ. Med. Ctr. 1993; com. mem.: UCSD Med. Ctr. JCAH survey com. 1986–, QA com. and QA exec. com. (co-chmn. 1987–), med. ethics com. 1994–, UCSD Dept. Radiology resident selection com. 1985–, lib. com. 1986–, musculoskeletal and MRI fellow selection coms. 1988–, UCSD Sch. of Medicine electives com. 1987– (chmn. 1988–), radioactive drug res. com. 1987–, com. on ednl. policy 1988–, core curriculum com. 1994–, Am. Soc. of Emergency Radiology 1993–, dept. rep. UCSD Acad. Senate Rep. Assembly 1994–, UCSD com. on committees 1994–, core curriculum com. 1994-95, steering com. San Diego Sci. Alliance 1995; vol. advisor Stanford Med. Alumni Assn. 1988–; participant in Low Back Pain Expert Survey, Vermont Rehab. Engring. Ctr. 1988–; mem. sci. advy. bd. Norland Corp. 1990–; reviewer, Am. Fedn. for Aging Res. 1995; editl. advy bds.: Chemical Rubber Co. Press Inc., Theme Med. Pubs. Inc., Year Book Med. Pubs., Applied Radiology; journal reviewer: Jour. Bone and Joint Surgery, Radiology, AJR, Jour. Orthopaedic Res., Jour. Foot Surgery, Investigative Radiology, Med. Physics, Health Tech.: Critical Issues for Decision Makers, Jour. Clin.

Investigation, Infections in Surgery, Jour. Musculoskeletal Medicine, Jour. Bone and Mineral Res., Skeletal Radiology, Jour. Rheumatology, Alcohol Health & Res. World, Jour. Magnetic Resonance Imaging, SCAN; mem. res. grant review bd. The Arthritis Soc., Toronto, Ontario; cons., bd. trustees res. initiatives com., Radiological Soc. No. Am.; lectr. in field (over 548 lectures, 175+ scientific presentations); honors: Phi Beta Kappa, Silver Spoon in Tchg. 1986, UCSD Grad. Students Pride-O-Gram 1986, 87, Am. Coll. Foot Surgeons 3rd place article 1987, Editor's Recognition awards, jour. Radiology 1986, 87, 88, Internat. Skeletal Soc. Pres.'s Medal 1989, Special Recognition award Am. Coll. Foot Surgeons 1989, Cert. of Merit award RSNA 1990, Speakers Bureau award UCSD 1991, 2nd Place Best Article pub Jour. of Foot Surgery 1990, Cert. of Merit award AARS 1991, apt. to Ad Hoc Expert Panel Am. Coll. Radiology 1993, Silver Spoon awards UCSD Sch. Medicine 1993, 94, mem: Internat. Skeletal Soc., Physicians for Social Responsibility, Calif. Radiologic Soc., Radiological Soc. N. Am., Assn. Univ. Radiologists, Am. Roentgen Ray Soc., Am. Coll. Radiology, So. Calif. Bone and Mineral Club, New Bone Densitometry Soc., Bone Dysplasia Soc., San Diego Co. Med. Soc., S.D. Bone Club, Soc. for Advancement of Women's Imaging; co-editor: Am. Coll. Radiology #25-Bone Disease Test and Syllabus (4th series, 1989), Computed Tomography and Magnetic Resonance Imaging of the Whole Body, 1994; editor: The Radiologic Clinics of North America, 1994, Principles of Shoulder Imaging, 1995; author: Contemporary Musculoskeletal Disease: Radiologic-Pathologic Correlation, 1987, Musculoskeletal Imaging Workbook, 1993; co-author: Clinical Magnetic Resonance Imaging, 1990, Imagerie de l'epaule, 1992, MRI and CT of the Musculoskeletal System: A Text-Atlas, 1992, contbr. 425 articles to profl. jours., 46 book chapters, 28 book reviews, 11 abstracts, 15 pub. interviews; Christian; rec: swimming, bicycling, philately. Res: 8585-24 Via Mallorca La Jolla 92037 Ofc: UCSD Medical Center 200 West Arbor Dr San Diego 92103-8756

SASS, JAMES ROBERTUS, international commodities trader, investment manager; b. Mar. 6, 1945, Bartlesville, Okla.; s. Andrew Michael and Norma Bea (Hegwer) S.; m. Diane Marie Quandt, July 12, 1979 (div. 1991); children: Charlene, John, Carridad; edn: AA in Behavioral Sci., Coll. of Marin, 1974; BA, San Francisco State Univ., 1976. Career: devel. fin. mgr. Calif. Equity Investment Group, San Rafael, Calif. 1974-76; v.p. fin. Group 80, Inc., S.F. 1976-80; pres. Mass. Plan, Inc., Pittsfield, Mass. 1980-82, Republic Mortgage & Investment Corp., Cocoa Beach, Fla. 1982-86, InterAmerican Fin. & Trade Group, Miami, Fla. 1986-88, Ocean Star Internat. Corp., San Rafael 1988-90; ptnr. Orchid Internat., San Rafael 1990-94; mng. ptnr. J.R. Sass and Assocs., San Rafael, 1988–; pres. InterAmerican Food Products, San Rafael 1990-93; ptnr. Four C's Internat. Corp., San Rafael 1991-93; gen. ptnr Equity Ptnrs. IV, San Rafael 1991-94; gen. ptnr. Cencal Devel. Fund, San Rafael 1991-92; dir. Firebird Internat. Inc., Petaluma 1991–; gen. ptnr. Cencal Devel. Fund II, San Rafael 1993; bd. dirs. Zelinsky Ctr. and Mus., Moscow, Russian Federation; Cybertech Joint Venture, Minsk, Republic of Belarus; Land and Timber Holdings, Ltd., Belize City, Belize; Internat. Peninsular S.A. de C.V., Mex.; bd. dirs.: Morningstar Farms, Cotati, Calif. 1995–, Petaluma Pacific 1994-95; cons. Mitsui Trading Co., Georgetown, Grand Cayman 1986-94; awards: recipient grant and scholarship NSF, Okla. State Univ. 1962, Tex. Chem. Coun. award 1963; decorated two Bronze Stars, Purple Heart and others, US Army for service in Vietnam 1967-68; appt. chmn. of the US Trade Advy. Bd., WDC 1993; mem.: MENSA, US Coun. for Internat. Bus., Am. Assn. Exporters and Importers, World Trade Ctr. Club, US C. of C., Am. Legion (Nat. HQ, WDC), Union Entrepreneurs Republic Belarus; state v.p. Young Rep., Bishop, Tex. 1963-64; past chpt. pres. US Jaycees, Vacaville, Calif. 1978; mem: Am. Vets, Alliance, San Rafael 1990, Commonwealth Club of Calif., S.F. 1993, San Francisco Internat. Program, S.F. 1993, World Affairs Council, S.F. 1995; author: (pamphlet) Investing in Mexican Real Estate, 1988; (booklet) Business In Kazakhstan, A Handbook for the Commercial Traveler, 1993; mil: sgt., US Army, 1966-72; rec: sailing, travel, martial arts, archaeology, international law study. Res: 325 Fairhills Dr San Rafael 94901-1110

SATO, EUNICE NODA, city administrator; b. June 8, 1921, Livingston, Calif.; d. Bunsaku and Sawa (Maeda) Noda; m. Thomas Takashi Sato, Dec. 9, 1950; children: Charlotte Patricia, Daniel Ryuichi, and Douglas Ryuji (twins); edn: AA, Modesto Jr. Coll., 1941; BA, Univ. No. Colo., 1944; MA, Columbia Univ., 1948. Career: public sch. tchr. Mastodon Twp. Schs., Alpha, Mich., 1944-47; ednl. missionary Reformed Ch. Am., Yokohama, Japan, 1948-51; council mem. City of Long Beach, 1975-86, mayor 1980-82; secty. corp. bd. L.A. Co. Health Systems Agy. 1978-79; past mem. Nat. League of Cities, League of Calif. Cities (pub. safety policy com. 1981-86), So. Calif. Assn. Govts. (community econ. and housing devel. com. 1976-86); civic bds: Am. Red Cross/Long Beach (past pres., dir. 1975–, exec. com. 1978–), Goodwill Industries (dir. 1978-82), St. Mary's Bauer Med. Ctr. (trustee 1977–), Industry Edn. Council/L.B. (pres. 1984-86), Industry Edn. Council of Calif. (dir.), State Advy. Group on Juvenile Justice Delinquency Prevention 1983-91, Calif. Council Criminal Justice 1983–, Girl Scout Council Calif. (legis. com. 1986-92), L.B. Council Girl Scouts U.S., United Way reg. III (1974-88), Asian Pacific Adv. Com. Calif. Dept. Rehab. 1985-87, L.B. Recreation Commn. (commr. 1985-86), Calif. Task Force to Promote Self Esteem and Personal and Social Responsibility 1987-91, NCCJ L.B. (pres. 1987), Internat. Community Council (pres. 1986-87); awards:

Outstanding Service award L.B. Coordinating Council 1969, Silverado United Meth. Ch. Mother of Yr. 1973, Calif. PTA hon. svc., continuing svc. awards 1973, 74, hon. life mem. Nat. PTA 1974, L.B. Area Council Churches Outstanding Laywoman of Yr. 1976, State Women's Council C.of C. Woman of Yr. 1979, Bus. & Profl. Women L.B., D.A.R. Nat. Merit award 1982, YMCA Los Altos Citizen of Yr. 1982, Calif. Community Pool for Handicapped 1982, Outstanding Citizen Torch Club L.B. 1983, Alpha Iota (hon.), Outstanding Contribution-Government award Industry Edn. Council of Calif. 1987, Nat. Conf. Humanitarian of Yr. 1992, appt. by Pres. Bush to Nat. Advy. Council on Ednl. Res. and Improvement 1991-94, elected to Gen. Council on Fin. & Adminstrn. of United Methodist Ch. 1992–, Calif. St. Svc. Council, Am. Red Cross 1995–; Republican (L.A. Co. central com. asst. sec., state exec. com.); Methodist. Res: 551-101 Pittsfield Ct Long Beach 90803

SAUER, RUSSELL FREDRICK, lawyer; b. March 9, 1955, Bayshore, N.Y.; s. Russell F. and Amelia M. (Savarese) S.; m. Kymberley A. Alberts, May 17, 1986; children: Erin b. 1980, Kelly b. 1982, Michelle b. 1987, Kevin b. 1993; edn: BA, Northwestern Univ. 1977, JD, Stanford Univ. 1980. Career: atty., assoc. Latham & Watkins, Los Angeles 1980-87, ptnr. 1987–; honors: Phi Beta Kappa, Chmn. Moot Ct. 1979-80; mem: Calif. Bar Assn., Los Angeles Co. Bar Assn., Am. Bar Assn., Am. Trial Lawyers Assn., Sports Lawyers Assn.; Republican; Cath.; rec: tennis. Ofc: Latham & Watkins 633 W Fifth St Los Angeles 90071

SAUNDERS, DOUGLAS LAURANCE, government lawyer/international trade agency official; b. July 21, 1949, San Francisco; s. Ward Bishop, Jr. and Elaine Kathleen (McDermott) S.; m. Charlton Denise Tarver, Oct. 15, 1987; 1 dau. Hannah Elizabeth Tarver-Saunders b. 1993 edn: undergrad. rel. studies, UCB; JD, Golden Gate Univ., 1986; LLM in internat. commerce & corp. law, Univ. of London, U.K. 1987; admitted bar: Calif. 1986. Career: judicial extern for Judge Thelton E. Henderson, U.S. Dist. Ct., San Francisco 1985; pres. Student Bar Assn. and trustee Golden Gate Univ., S.F. 1985-86; pvt. practice law, Oakland 1986-88; special asst. U.S. District Atty., staff atty. internat. trade and reg. dir. internat. trade, U,S,. Small Bus. Adminstrn., S.F. 1988-93; sr. trade cons. Center for Internat. Trade Development 1993–; private practice, 1993–; adj. prof. internat. bus. law St. Mary's Coll., Moraga 1994–; rec: LandRover mechanic, guitar, photog., backpacking, travel. Res: 5557 Lawton Ave Oakland 94618 Ofc: Center for Internat Trade Development 2201 Broadway Ste 701 Oakland 94612

SAUNDERS, SALLY L., writer, poet, poetry therapist; b. Jan. 15, 1940, Bryn Mawr, Pa.; d. Lawrence W. and Dorothy (Love) Saunders; edn: att. Temple Univ., 1962-63, summer stu. Sophia Univ. (in Tokyo) 1963, We. Ill. Univ. (in Africa) 1964; BS, George Williams Coll., 1965; coursework in tchg., The New Sch. of Soc. Res., N.Y.C. 1968-69. Career: poet; pub. books of poetry: Past the Near Meadows, 1961, Pauses, 1978, Fresh Bread (1982, Golden Quill Press), Random Thoughts, 1992, Patchwork Quilt, 1993; The Times Literary Supplement (London), The New York Times, N.Y. Times Internat. Edit., Empire of The Denver Post, Wormwood Rev., Quaker Life, Mark Twain Jour., New Athenaeum, Villager, The Cristian Sci. Monitor, Univ. Penn. Literary Rev., The Hartford Courant, others; tchr., lectr., num. readings at poetry workshops, bookstores, frequent guest on radio and tv talk shows; group worker Dorchester (Mass.) Settlement House, summer 59, Margaret Fuller House, Cambridge, Mass., summer 51/61; asst. Ten Acre Sch., Wellsley, Mass. 1960-61; group wkr. Univ. House, Phila., 1961-63; vol. Good Shepherd Mission, Fort Defiance, Az., 1963; group wkr. Young Mens Jewish Ctr., Chgo., 1965-66; wkr. Office of Econ. Opp., King Ferry (NY) Migrant Camp, summer 1965; poetry therapist/grant recipient (2) The Inst. of The Penn. Hosp. of Phila.; grantee City of Phila. to tch. poetry writing to children in pub. libraries, U.S. State Dept. to tch. poetry writing schs. in We. Penn., San Francisco YWCA to tch. poetry writing workshops; lectr./tchr. The Miquon (Pa.) Sch., The Montgomery Country Day Sch., Wynnewood, Pa., The Agnes Irwin Sch., Rosemont, Pa., The Shipley Sch., Bryn Mawr, Pa., The Phelps Sch., Malvern, Pa., The Ballard Sch., N.Y., Chestern County (Pa.) Adult Night Sch.; poetry awards include: Pa. Poetry Soc. prize poem 1963, Nat. League of Am. Pen Women best poet 1965, Poetry Soc. of Ga. hon. mention, The Poetry Day Book Award -Spearman Pubs. 1966, The Nutmegger Book Award 1967, Phila. Writers' Conf. 3d prize 1968, Wilory Farm Poetry Contest finalist 1981; mem: Assn. of Am. Poetry Therapy, Internat. Women's Writing Guild, Poets' and Writers' Guild (NYC), Poetry Soc. Am., Pen and Pencil Club, Assn. for Humanistic Psychology, Nat. Writers Club, Press Club S.F., Assn. for Poetry Therapy, Ina Coolbrith Cir., Acad. of Am. Poets; biog. listings in: Who's Who of Am. Women, Who's Who in Am., Ency. of Am. Biography, others. Res: Apt #501 2030 Vallejo St San Francisco 94123 Ofc: 609 Rose Hill Rd Broomall PA 19008 Tel: 610/356-0849

SAUNDERS, WALTER CRUCE, JR., clinical psychologist; b. May 27, 1935, Hollywood; s. Walter Cruce and Anna Maria (Morrill) S.; m. JoAnn Terrana, July 7, 1973; children: Walter Cruce b. 1976, Thomas b. 1978; edn: BA, St. Patricks Coll. 1958; M.Div., 1972; MA, Wright Inst. 1971; PhD, 1974; lic. psychologist Calif. (1980), Neb. (1977). Career: assoc. pastor R.Cath. Diocese of Oakland 1962-71; research asst., tchg. asst. Wright Inst. Grad. Sch., Berkeley 1970-73; prof. psychology Univ. Yucatan, Merida, Mexico 1974-75; clin. psychologist, dir. alcoholism services Panhandle Mental Health Center, Scottsbluff,

Neb. 1976-79; clin. psychologist, supr. Santa Clara Co. Bureau of Mental Health Services, San Jose 1979-85; clin. dir. Alexian Assoc. Psychology & Counseling 1983–; practicum supr. Univ. Wyo. psychology dept., Scottsbluff, Neb. 1977-79; San Jose St. Univ. Sch. Social Work 1979-83; clin. cons. Bridge Counseling Center, Morgan Hill 1983-85; staff Alexian Brothers Hosp., San Jose 1986–; pres. bd. trustees San Antonio Youth Project, Oakland 1967-83; mem: Santa Clara Co. Psychological Assn. (pres. 1989), Am. Psychological Assn., Calif. St. Psychological Assn., Hispanic Inst. Family Devel. (pres. 1982-90), Chicano Mental Health Assn. (chmn. 1983), Hispanic C.of C.; dissertation Theory of Adult Devel. pub. 1974; Democrat; R.Cath.; rec: running, sailing. Ofc: Alexian Associates 3110 Provo Ct Ste A San Jose 95127

SAXENA, AMOL, podiatrist; b. June 5, 1962, Stanford, Calif.; s. Arjun N. and Veera (Saxena) S.; m. Karen Palermo, Aug. 11, 1985; children: Vijay b. 1988, Tara b. 1991; edn: BA, Wash. Univ., St. Louis 1984; BS biol. scis., William M. Scholl Coll. of Podiatric Medicine, 1988; DPM (cum laude); fellow (bd. cert. podiatric surg.) Am. Coll. of Foot Surgeons, 1990. Career: podiatric surgical resident VA Med. Ctr. Westside, Chgo. 1988-89; pvt. podiatric practice specializing in sports medicine, pediatric foot problems, podiatric surgery, 1989-93; podiatrist Dept. Sports Medicine, Palo Alto Med. Found. 1993–; hosp. affils. El Camino and Stanford Univ. Hosps.; team podiatrist Stanford Univ., Univ. of Notre Dame Football, and local high sch. athletic teams, 1989–; podiatrist, med. staff 1992 U.S. Olympic Track & Field Trials; mem. USA Track & Field Sports Medicine Com.; Fellow Am. Acad. Podiat. Sports Medicine 1990; athletic footwear cons. Puma-Etonic-Tretorn, 1986–, Reebok 1993–; guest lectr. podiatric surg. and sports medicine Am. Coll. Foot Surgeons, Calif. and Scholl Colls. of Podiat. Medicine, various orgs.; listed Who's Who in the World 1993, 95; contbr. articles and columns for RunCal mag., others; assoc. editor The Lower Extremity; editl. bd. Jour. of Foot and Ankle Surgery; Republican; rec: running. Res: 3814 Magnolia Drive Palo Alto 94306 Ofc: 1197 Arques Ave Sunnyvale 94086

SAXON, ROBERTA POLLACK, chemical physicist; b. July 19, 1946, Chicago, Ill.; d. Alfred and Blanche B. (Fine) Pollack; edn: BA, Cornell Univ. 1967; MS, Univ. Chgo. 1969; PhD, 1971. Career: research assoc. Argonne Nat. Lab., Argonne, Ill. 1972-73; Univ. Wash., Seattle 1973-74; SRI Internat., Menlo Park 1974-75, chemical physicist 1975-79, sr. chemical physicist 1979-88, program mgr. 1988-91, deputy dir. Physical Scis. Div. 1991-95; dir. Chemistry Lab. 1995–; awards: NATO fellowship (1984-85); mem: Am. Physical Soc.; 50+ articles pub. in profl. jours., 1969–. Ofc: SRI International 333 Ravenswood Ave Menlo Park 94025

SAYLES, CAROL LOUISE, educator; b. May 19, 1937, Danville, Ohio; d. Alton Edgar and Rose Ellen (Gaines) Sayles; edn: BS, Ohio State Univ. 1959; MA, Temple Univ. 1964; Univ. Wash. Seattle 1964-66; UC Riverside 1967-69. Career: tchr. Newark H.S., Ohio 1959-60; Perry H.S., Mich. 1960-62; instr. Beaver Coll., Phila., Pa. 1963; Temple Univ. 1963-64; Univ. Wash., Seattle 1964; Chaffey Coll., Alta Loma 1965-92; dean, social and behavioral scis., Chaffey Coll. 1992-; cons. Mount Baldy 1985–; awards: Chaffey Coll. Faculty of Year 1974, State of Calif. Innovative Grant 1985, Outstanding Educator Am. 1976; mem: Western Speech Assn., CCLC, AACCA, Assn. for Instructioal Administrators (regional ofcr.), Calif. Colls. for Internat. Edn. (regional ofcr.); articles pub. (1974-77), contbr. Realtionships in Inter-personal Comms., 1977; Democrat; rec: painting, sculpting, musical instruments. Ofc: Chaffey College 5885 Haven Ave Alta Loma 91701

SCANNELL, WILLIAM EDWARD, psychologist, management consultant, aerospace company executive; b. Nov. 11, 1934, Muscatine Iowa; s. Mark Edward and Catharine Pearson (Fowler) S.; m. Barbara Hoemann, 1957; children: Cynthia b. 1958, Mark b. 1959, David b. 1961, Terri b. 1962, Stephen b. 1966; edn: BGE, Univ. Nebr., Omaha 1961; BSE indsl. engring., Ariz. St. Univ. 1966; MSE systems engring., So. Methodist Univ. 1969; Western St. Univ. Coll. Law 1981-82; PhD psychology, U.S. Internat. Univ., 1991. Career: master navigator, lt. col. USAF (ret.) 1954-75: aviation cadet, navigator bombardier B-47 Strategic Air Command; chief mgmt. engring. team hdqtrs. USAF Europe; 182 combat missions, forward air controller O-2A DaNang, Vietnam; pgm. mgr. USAF Hq., Air Staff, mem. AF Operating Budget Review Com., asst. to the Dir. Orgn. & Mgmt. Planning Office, US Secty. of Defense, decorated D.F.C. (4), Air Medal (12), Meritorious Service Medal; acct. exec. Merrill Lynch, Pierce, Fenner and Smith; sr. res. engr., econ. analysis, prog. engring. chief ILS Engring., engr. chief, logistic planning/analysis, prog. mgr. CX Aircraft, mgr. sys. support Ground Launched Cruise Missile, mktg. mgr. advanced space pgms., pgm. mgr. MX composite deployment module, General Dynamics 1977-84; mgr. Integrated Logistics Support, Northrop/Electronics, Hawthorne, mgr. pgm. planning & scheduling Northrop B-2 Division, 1984-91; pres. Scannell and Associates, Borrego Springs 1991–; adj. faculty U.S. Internat. Univ., San Diego 1991–; cons. Imperial Co. Mental Health Dept., El Centro 1992–; honors: Psi Chi (psych. hon. soc.), 1st. in class Merrill Lynch Acct. Exec. Tng. Sch.; mem: Am. Inst. Industrial Engrs. (sr. mem.), Nat. Mgmt. Assn., Am. Psychol. Assn. 1992–, Calif. Psychol. Assn. 1992–, Soc. for Indsl. and Organizational Psychology; author: The Nature of Motivation in Aerospace Executives, 1991;

club: Coronado Cays Yacht; Republican; R.Cath. Res: 717 Anza Park Trail Borrego Springs 92004 Ofc: P.O. Box 2392 Borrego Springs 92004 Tel:619/767-3077

SCHACHT, HENRY MEVIS, writer, consultant on public affairs and communications; b. Feb. 28, 1916, Pasadena; s. Henry and Amelia (Claussen) S.; m. Mary Joan Turnbull, Dec. 30, 1937; children: Henry John b. 1944, Linda Joan b. 1947; edn: BA, UC Berkeley 1936. Career: information specialist Univ. Calif., Berkeley 1936-42; dir. agric. and pub. service Nat. Bdcstg. Co., San Francisco 1942-59; dir. agric. Am. Bdcstg. Co., San Francisco 1959-61; dir. agric. info. Univ. Calif., 1961-65; v.p. corp. relations and corp. sec. Calif. Canners & Growers, San Francisco 1965-81; dir. Nat. Canners Assn., Wash. DC 1965-79; agricultural columnist, San Francisco Chronicle, 1959-93; exec. sec., Commn. on Calif. Agriculture and Higher Edn. 1994-95; cons. pub. affairs and communications 1981–; cons. to UN, FAO in Cairo, Tokyo and Mexico City 1963, 65, 66; awards: Am. Seed Trade Assn. 1964, Calif. League Food Processors Service 1985, Calif. Farm Bureau Agric. Newsperson 1988, Pfizer Agric. Editors award 1968; mem: Nat. Canners Assn. (dir. 1965-79), Pub. Rels. Roundtable, Agric. Advy. Council Univ. Calif. 1951-62, UC Alumni Council 1951-62, Big C Soc. UCB 1970–; publs: numerous mag. articles and newspaper columns, 1936–; rec: reading, bonsai, travel. Address: Oakland 94618

SCHACHTER, BONNIE LYNN, publisher; b. Oct. 20, 1952, Flushing, N.Y.; d. Irving and Yetta Schachter; edn: BA comms., Queens Coll. 1974. Career: pres. Multi-Ling Tours, Boston, Mass. 1974; program developer Atpac Tours, N.Y.C. 1975-76; pres. Rent An Event, Breakfast from Tiffanys, N.Y.C. 1978-84; Innovative Amenities, Santa Monica 1984–; mem: Vital Connection (co-chair 1989), United Jewish Fund. (bd. 1988–), Am. Mktg. Assn., Acad. Health Service Mktg., Women in Health Adminstrn.; author: 9 books, pub. 1986–; rec: tennis, skiing, acting. Res: 1021 Lincoln Blvd Santa Monica 90403 Ofc: Informative Amenities POB 1280 Santa Monica 90406

SCHACHTER, RICHARD DENNIS, business executive; b. Mar. 24, 1936, N.Y.C.; s. Irving G. and Rose G. (Coren) S.; div.; children: Adrienne Margo b. 1965, Lynda Renee b. 1969; edn: BA, UCLA 1958; MA candidate, USC 1960-62; BA in metaphysics, Am. Nat. Inst. 1975. Career: engr. Hughes Aircraft Co., Culver City 1958-59; assoc. res. engr. Caltech Jet Propulsion Lab., Pasadena 1959-60; res. engr. N.Am. Aviation, Downey 1960-63; senior electrical engr. Am. Nucleonics Corp., Glendale 1964-65; project engr. Sea Space Systems, Torrance 1965-67; laser physicist Lear Siegler Inc., Santa Monica 1967-69; exec. mgr. WLT, Beverly Hills, real estate 1969-72; currently founder, c.e.o. Centurion II Corp., Marina del Rey; instr. physics USC 1961; v.p., dir. Am. Research Inst. 1983-86; v.p., dir. SAC Inc. 1982-85; advy. cons. Universal Health Inc., Marina del Rey 1984-86; awards: recipient commemorative cert. Gagarin Cosmonaut Tng. Ctr., Star City, Moscow Region, Russia 1992, cert. Israel Assn. of Gen. Aviation for flight from lowest airport on earth (Massada) to Jerusalem, listed Who's Who in West, Comm. Leaders and Noteworthy Americans, mem: Laser Inst. Am., Aircraft Owners and Pilots Assn.; civic: Marina del Rey C.of C., Del Rey Toastmasters (ofcr., CTM 1986-87); devel. original concepts solar flare physics, 1963, res. papers on laser beam propagation, 1968-69; contbr. articles Holistic Health News Media; Republican; Jewish; rec: flying, amateur radio, weightlifting, jogging. Res: The Yacht, Raquel II, Marina del Rey Harbor 90295 Ofc: Centurion II Corp., PO Box 34763 Palms 90034

SCHAG, ERNEST J., JR., lawyer; Jan. 16, 1933, Los Angeles; s. Ernest J. and Lou (Jackson) S.; m. Lucinda Brassell, June 11, 1956 (div. 1979); m. Mary M., Aug. 16, 1980 (div. 1993); children: John b. 1960, Laurie b. 1963, Tracy b. 1964; edn: BA, USC 1954; JD, 1959; LL.M, N.Y. Univ. 1960; admitted St. Bars Calif. and N.Y. (1960). Career: atty. assoc. Lillick Geary & McHose, Los Angeles 1960-63; ptnr. Barnes Schag Johnson Kennedy & Carlson, Newport Beach 1964-78; Meserve Mumper & Hughes 1978-94; Freeman, Freeman & Smiley 1994–; lectr. Univ. Calif. Ext., Orange Co. 1968-84; honors: Skull & Dagger USC 1954, USC Scroll of Hon. 1954, BSA Silver Beaver 1974; mem: Am. Coll. Trust & Estate Counsel (fellow), Orange Co. Bar Assn. (chmn. probate & trust law 1972), Orange Co. Performing Arts Center (dir., fin. chmn.), Orange Coast Coll. Found. (treas., dir.), Girl Scout Trust Orange Co. (chmn., trustee), Orange Co. Council Boy Scouts (v.p. fin., dir. 1975), Hoag Hosp. Found. (chmn. endowment com.); clubs: Newport Harbor Yacht (pres. Anglers, 1978), Big Canyon CC, Ironwood CC; mil: lt. USNR 1954-56; Republican; Prot.; rec: golf. Res: 301 Bay Hill Dr Newport Beach 92660 Ofc:Freeman Freeman & Smiley 20 Corporate Park Irvine 92714

SCHAIBLE, SIEGFRIED, educator; b. Aug. 18, 1940, Marburg, Germany; s. Karl and Lina (Pitzer) S.; m. Ingrid Reuter, May 14, 1967; children: Susanne b. 1969, John b. 1972, Ulrike b. 1973; edn: dipl., Univ. Mainz W. Germany 1967; PhD, Univ. Koln 1971, habilitation, Koln Univ. 1978. Career: wissenschaftlicher asst. Univ. Koln, W. Germany 1967-71, akademischer rat 1971-79; prof. Univ. Alberta, Canada 1979-87; UC Riverside 1987–; vis. prof. Stanford Univ. 1983, 86; Santa Clara Univ. 1986; research, Israel, Italy, France, Greece 1978–; lectr. USA, Canada, Europe 1972–; assoc. ed. sci. jours., W. Germany, Canada, Italy, USA; awards: Univ. Alberta McCalla research professorship 1981-82, Who's

Who in Edn., Internat. Directory Disting. Leadership, 5000 Personalities of World, Five Hundred Leaders of Influence; mem: Ops. Research Soc. Am., Math. Programming Soc.; author: Analysis & Applications of Fractional Programming, 1978, co-ed. Generalized Concavity in Optimization & Econ., 1981, Generalized Concavity Fractional Programming with Econ. Applications, 1990, co-author Generalized Concavity, 1988, 60+ articles pub. in sci. jours.; rec: hiking, classical music, greek, Hebrew. Ofc: Univ. of California Graduate School of Management Riverside 92521

SCHAPIRA, MOREY R., computer networking executive; b. Jan. 4, 1949, Chicago, Ill.; s. Julius and Rose (Schwartz) S.; m. Barbara Joan Stein, May 29, 1977; children: Deborah b. 1979, Rachel b. 1981, Michael b. 1985; edn: BS, physics (with honors), Case Western Reserve Univ. 1970; MBA, Harvard Univ. 1977. Career: staff res. scientist Raytheon Res. Div., Waltham, Mass. 1970-75; sales and mktg. mgmt. for microwave semiconductor and optical comms. divs. Hewlett-Packard Corp., San Jose and Palo Alto 1977-85; nat. distribution sales mgr. Micro Power Systems, Inc., Santa Clara 1985-87; nat. sales mgr. Network General Corp., Menlo Park 1987-89, v.p. worldwide sales 1989-90, gen. mgr. for Asia/Americas sales 1991-93; v.p. mktg. Digital Link Corp., Sunnyvale 1994-; gen. mgr. network gen. Asia, Ams. Div. chmn. United Way Campaign, 1978; nat. v.p. Union of Councils for Soviet Jews 1979-84, nat. pres. 1984-86; pres. Bay Area Council on Soviet Jewry, S.F. 1980-84; honors: listed Who's Who in West; mem: Am. Mgmt. Assn., No. Calif. Venture Capital Assn., Harvard Bus. Sch. Assn. No. Calif., Am. Physics Soc., Churchill Club; editor-in-chief, then pub. A Guide to Jewish Boston, 1974-77; pub., editor-in-chief HarBus News, 1976-77. Res: 1154 Crespi Drive Sunnyvale 94086 Ofc: Digital Link Corp. 217 Humboldt Court Sunnyvale 94089-1300

SCHELCHER, CYNTHIA EYRE, health executive, educator; b. July 15, 1948, Cedar Rapids, Iowa; d. Harlan Ainsworth and Helenruth (Becker) Eyre; m. George Schelcher, Aug. 12, 1972; children: Erin b. 1978, Grant b. 1984, Michael b. 1985; edn: BA, CSU Fresno, 1970; cert. UC Santa Cruz, 1973; MRA, Univ. San Francisco, 1978; cert. fund raising exec. Nat. Soc. Fund Raising Execs. Career: chief exec. Crippled Childrens Soc. of No. Calif., Santa Clara 1973-; faculty Univ. S.F., 1976-; nat. exec. dir. United Scleraderma Found. 1995-; cons. educator/contr. State of Calif. Dept. Health, Sacto. 1980-, City Dept. Health Wash. DC 1982-84, Dept. Community Affairs Austin, Tx. 1980-81; cons. Nat. Inst. for Adv. Studies, Wash. DC 1981-82; faculty Golden Gate Univ., 1984-85, Univ. No. Colo. 1988; state coord. Ky. Ctr. for Edn. Health Resrch., Louisville, Ky. 1971-72; honors: Miss Future Bus. Exec., Phi Beta Lamda, Fresno 1968, Miss Monterey (Calif.) County, Mont. C.of C. 1966, nat. comm. svc. Bonne Bell Corp. 1971, woman of yr. San Jose Jaycees 1978; mem. Nat. Soc. Fund Raising Execs. San Jose (fundraiser of yr. 1988, edn. chair 1986); civic: Nat. Council for the Handicapped (v.p. 1984), Junior League (San Jose, Palo Alto), Rotary Internat.; publs: 2 tng. manuals, 1978, 82; Republican; R.Cath.; rec: family, travel, teaching. Address: CJS & Associates, PO Box 1643 Pebble Beach 93953

SCHENDEL, STEPHEN ALFRED, plastic surgeon, educator; b. Oct. 10, 1947, Mpls.; s. Alfred Reck and Jeanne Shirley (Hagquist) S.; m. Susan, Aug. 15, 1969; children: Elliott b. 1983, Melisande b. 1985; edn: BA, St. Olaf Coll., Northfield, Minn. 1969; DDS, BS (high honors), Univ. of Minn. 1973; asst. etranger, Univ. of Nantes, Fr. 1979-80; MD, Univ. of Hawaii, 1983; diplomate Am. Bd. Dental Examiners 1973, diplomate Am. Bd. Med. Examiners 1984, diplomate Am. Bd. Oral and Maxillofacial Surgery 1983, Am. Bd. Plastic Surgery 1991. Career: oral pathology fellow Univ. Minn. 1972; researcher Univ. Hawaii Sch. Pub. Health, 1973; dental resident Queen's Med. Ctr., Honolulu 1974; oral and maxillofacial surgery resident Parkland Memorial Hosp., Dallas 1975-79; pvt. practice maxillofacial surgery, Honolulu, also asst. clin. prof. surg. Univ. of Hawaii, 1980-83; gen. surgery intern Baylor Univ. Med. Ctr., Dallas 1983; plastic surgery resident Stanford Univ. Med. Ctr., 1984-89; assoc. prof., chief of plastic surgery and chmn. Dept. of Functional Restoration, Stanford Univ. Med. Ctr., currently; asst. Dr. P. Tessier, Paris, Fr. 1987; awards: Omicron Kappa Upsilon 1973, Fulbright Fellow 1979-80, A.E. Carlotti Award 1979, Chateaubriand Fellow French Govt., Paris 1987-88, First prize, jr. clinical research, Plastic Surgery Ednl. Found. 1987; mem: Alliance Francaise (Honolulu chpt. v.p. 1981-82), Baylor Soc. of Surgeons (charter); publs: 34+ sci. jour. articles, 1974-, 3 med. book chapters, 1981, 84, illustrator med. book chpt., surgical/preprosthetic oral surg., 1980; Lutheran; rec: flyfishing. Ofc: Stanford University Dept. Plastic Surgery, Stanford

SCHENKKAN, GERARD VAN DER ZYL, manufacturing company executive; b. April 23, 1956, Austin, Tx.; s. Robert Frederic and Jean (McKenzie) S.; m. Judith Lynn Jones, Aug. 15, 1987; children: Katherine b. 1988, stepson, Aaron Cheris b. 1974; edn: BA hist., Yale Univ. 1978; MBA, Stanford Univ. 1982. Career: asst. to v.chmn. PBS, Wash. D.C. 1978-79; asst. dir. Assn. Pub. Bdcstg. 1979-80; cons. Bain & Co., Palo Alto and Tokyo, Japan 1981-84; exec. Hewlett Packard, 1984-; mem. QED Pub. T.V. and Radio 1980-; honors: Phi Beta Kappa, Arjay Miller scholar Stanford 1982; mem: Stanford Bus. Sch. Alumni Assn., Yale Alumni Assn., Nature Conservancy; Democrat; Episcopalian; rec: singing. Ofc: Hewlett Packard 3000 Hanover St Palo Alto 94304

SCHIELE, PAUL ELLSWORTH, JR., science writer, educator, consultant; b. Nov. 20, 1924, Phila.; s. Paul Ellsworth Sr. and Maud (Barclay) S.; m. Sarah Irene Knauss, Aug. 20, 1946; children: Patricia S. Tiemann, Sandra S. Kicklighter, Deborah S. Hartigan; edn: AT, Temple Univ., 1949; BA, LaVerne Univ., 1955; MA, Claremont Graduate Sch., 1961; PhD, U.S. Internat. Univ., San Diego 1970; Calif. secondary tchg. creds., 1961. Career: tchr. sci. and math. Lincoln High Sch., Phila. 1956-57; tchr., coordinator Ontario School Dist., Ontario, Calif. 1957-65; cons. mathematics and sci., Hacienda La Puente Unified Sch. Dist., 1965-75; asst. prof. CSU Fullerton, 1975-83; owner/pres. Creative Learning Environments and Resources (CLEAR), Glendora 1983-, Sci. Curriculum cons., 1983-; author and writer: Model units for 21 Sci. Activity books-Title III, ESEA project; numerous articles for profl. mags. incl. Teaching Tools, Science Teacher, Nat. Aeronautics, The Instructor, 1960-82; 9+ sound film strips in sci., incl. Western Birds, Processes of Science; 2 sci. educational games; novel: Chasing the Wild Geese (1995 sched.); editor 21 Science Activity books ESEA Title III project; writer & co-director TV series (SCI-TV) Los Angeles; author: Primary Science (science text, tchr.'s manual, 4 film strips) 1972-1976; writer, sci. activities for L.A. Outdoor Edn. Program, 1980-81; editor Living World (sci. text, games), 1974-; appt. advy. com. Sci. and Humanities Symposium, Calif. Mus. Sci. and Industry, 1974; mem: Playhouse 90 (Pasadena), Calif. Elem. Edn. Assn. (hon.), Nat. PTA (hon.), Calif. Inter-Science Council (pres., chmn. 1971), Elem. Sch. Scis. Assn. (pres. advy. bd. 1967), Phi Delta Kappa (charter mem., project dir.), Internat. Platform Assn., ABIRA; Republican; Lutheran; Res: 231 N Catherine Park Dr Glendora 91740

SCHIFF, MARTIN M., physician, author; b. July 16, 1922, Phila.; s. Isidore and Cecelia (Miller) S.; m. Mildred, Jan. 5, 1946; children: Denise b. 1949, Michael b. 1951, David b. 1954; edn: MD, Calif. Coll. of Medicine, 1951. Career: physician pvt. practice, 1951-; author: Eat and Stay Slim, 1968, Doctor Schiff's Miracle Weight-Loss Guide (Parker Pub., 1974), Doctor Schiff's One-Day-At-A-Time Weight-Loss Plan (Stein & Day, 1980), (tape) Weight Loss Plan for Health, Happiness and A Longer Lifespan, 1982, The Thin Connection, 1986, num. self-help pamphlets on weight control, mind and thought control, and how to eliminate forever the "fat between the ears"; mil: lt. jg USNR. Res: 1220 Corsica Dr Pacific Palisades 90272 Ofc: 12900 Venice Blvd Los Angeles 90066

SCHIRMER, JOHN RAYMOND, printer, investor; b. June 28, 1910, Miles City, Mont.; s. John Valentine and Mary Ellen (Danaher) S.; m. Lois Steverson, Dec. 21, 1961; edn: BA, Univ. Wash. Seattle 1941; tchg. cert., Univ. Montana Billings 1936; FCC lic., US Maritime Commn., Boston, Mass. 1943; printing cert., Calif. Comm. Coll., 1953; Hon. degree E. Mont. State Coll. Career: factory sales rep., Liggett & Myers Tobacco Co., Billings, Mont. 1932-34; public sch. educator, Mont. Dept. of Edn. Klein & Big Horn Counties 1936-41; welder Seattle-Tacoma Shipbuilders, Seattle 1942-43; chief radio ofcr. US Maritime Commn., Pacific Ocean Theater 1942-46; equip. engr. Western Elec. Co., Cicero, Ill. 1946-51; journeyman printer Los Angeles Times 1953-75; officer L.A. Superior Ct. 1968; indep. fin. investor assoc. Property Mortgage Co., L.A. area 1975-; mil: pvt. US Army 76th Field Arty. Citizens Mil. Tng. Corps, Ft. Russell, Cheyenne, Wyo. 1928; pvt. Montana Nat. Guard 1936-37; chief radio USN 1942; US Maritime Commn., Gallups Island, Mass., PTO 1942-47; Republican (Presdl. Task Force); Prot.; rec: wildlife, volunteer work, landscaping, reading. Res: 8501 E Drayer Ln South San Gabriel 91770-4209 Ofc: Los Angeles Times Mirror Los Angeles 90053

SCHLAGER, DAN, physician; edn: BA (cum laude), Brandeis Univ. 1977; Nat. Hosp. Ins. of Neurology, Univ. of London, England (summer 1985); MD, Sch. of Medicine and Health Scis., George Wash. Univ. 1986; dept. of plastic surgery and burn unit, Univ. of Copenhagen, Denmark (summer 1987); lic. physician, Calif., Ariz.; cert. Nat. Bd. Med. Examiners. Career: residency, dept. emergency medicine, Univ. of Ariz. Health Scis. Ctr, Tucson 1986-89, chief resident 1988-89; lifeflight helicopter physician Stanford Univ. 1990-92; attending physician emergency dept. Kaiser Found. Hosp., Santa Rosa 1989-; asst. clin prof. medicine UCSF Sch. of Medicine 1994; mem. GATEWAY Com. 1990-; ULTRASOUND course coord., lectr., Diagnostic Ultrasonography for Emergency Physicians, 1992-94; NE Region chairperson Assn. of Am. Colls. 1986; student rep. Assn. of Am. Colls. 1985; awards: Phi Beta Kappa, Brandeis Univ. 1977, Alpha Omega Alpha student res. award, George Wash. Univ. 1984, Best Resident Paper, Marion Lab. 1989; mem: Am. Coll. of Emergency Medicine (fellow), Soc. of Academic Emergency Physicians, Am. Inst. of Ultrasound Medicine; contbg. author: 5 articles to profl. jours. 1987-92; res. in field. Res: 16 Barn Rd Mill Valley 94941 Ofc: Dept of Emergency Medicine Kaiser Foundation Hospital 99 Montecillo Road San Rafael 94903

SCHMALENBERGER, JERRY L., ordained minister and professor; b. Jan. 23, 1934, Greenville, Ohio; s. Harry Henry and Lima (Hormell) S.; m. Carol Ann Walthall, June 8, 1956; children: Stephen b. 1959, Bethany Allison b. 1963, Sarah Layton b. 1965; edn: AB, Wittenberg Univ., Springfield, Ohio 1956; MDiv., Hamma Sch. of Theology, Springfield, Ohio 1959, DMin. 1976; DD, Wittenberg Univ., 1984; ordained Lutheran minister, Jan. 23, 1959. Career: pastor Third Lutheran Ch., Springfield, Ohio 1958-61; pastor First Lutheran, Bellefontaine, Ohio 1961-65; sr. pastor First Lutheran, Tiffin, Ohio 1965-70, Mansfield, Ohio

1970-79; sr. pastor St. Johns Lutheran, Des Moines, Ia. 1979-88; pres., prof. Pacific Lutheran Theol. Seminary, Berkeley, Calif. 1988–; prof. of parish ministry, Pacific Lutheran, Berkeley 1988–; dir. Wittenberg Univ., Springfield, Ohio 1968-88; dir. Grandview Coll., Des Moines, Ia. 1980-90; founding mem. Academy of Evangelists 1984–; mem.: Acad. of Preachers 1984–, Acad. for Homiletics 1990–; convener Grad. Theol. Union Committee of Presidents 1993–; author (13 books): Saints Who Shaped the Church, 1987, Stewards of Creation, 1987, Called to Witness, 1993, Plane Thoughts Parish Ministry, 1994, others; ELCA Lutheran; rec: water skiing, boating. Res: 2770 Marin Ave Berkeley 94708 Ofc: Pacific Lutheran Theological Seminary 2770 Marin Ave Berkeley 94708

SCHMID, RUDI (RUDOLF), professor of medicine and medical school dean emeritus; b. May 2, 1922, Glarus, Switzerland, naturalized Apr. 7, 1954; s. Rudolf and Bertha (Schiesser) S.; m. Sonja D. Wild, Sept. 17, 1949; children: Isabelle b. 1952, Peter R. b. 1955; edn: BA, Gymnasium, Zurich, 1941; MD, Univ. of Zurich, 1947; PhD, Univ. of Minn., 1954. Career: asst. prof. medicine Harvard Med. Sch., Boston 1959-62; prof. medicine Univ. Chicago, Ill. 1962-66; Univ. Calif., San Francisco 1966-91, dean Sch. of Medicine UCSF, 1983-89, assoc. dean for internat. relations UCSF, 1989–, prof. emeritus on recall 1991–; awards: Friedenwald Award, Am. Gastroent. Assn. 1990, Disting. achiev. Am. Gastroent. Assn. 1980, Am. Assn. Study of Liver Disease 1990, Rudolf Aschoff Medal, Univ. of Freiburg, Germany 1979, Canad. Liver Found. gold medal 1985, Disting. Lectr. Assn. Am. Physicians 1976; mem. Nat. Acad. Scis. USA 1974–, Am. Acad. Arts and Scis. (fellow 1982–), Internat. Assn. Study of Liver (1968–, pres. 1980-82), Am. Assn. Study of Liver Disease (1955–, pres. 1965), Assn. Am. Physician (1963–, pres. 1986); clubs: Bohemian (S.F.), mem. Swiss, British, Am. Alpine Clubs; publs: 200+ articles in peer rev. jours. 1950–; mil: senior investigator USPHS 1955-57; rec: reading, internat. travel, history, skiing, mtn. climbing. Res: 211 Woodland Rd Kentfield 94904 Ofc: Univ. of Calif. San Francisco S-224 San Francisco 94143-0410

SCHMIDT, TERRY LANE, health care executive; b. Nov. 28, 1943, Chgo.; s. LeRoy C. and Eunice P.S.; children: Christie Anne, Terry Lane II; edn: BS, Bowling Green State Univ., 1965; MBA health care adminstrn., George Washington Univ., 1971. Career: resident in hosp. adminstrn. Univ. Pittsburgh Med. Ctr., VA Hosp., Pitts. 1968-69; adminstrv. asst. Mt. Sinai Med. Ctr., N.Y.C., 1969-70; asst. dir. Health Facilities Planning Council of Met. Washington, 1970-71; asst. dir. dept. govtl. relations Am. Medical Assn., W.D.C., 1971-74; pres. Terry L. Schmidt Inc., Physician Svs. Group, San Diego 1974–; preceptor Div. of Health Svs. Adminstrn. and adj. prof., Grad. Sch. of Pub. Health, San Diego State Univ. 1989–; guest lectr. Health Care Adminstrn. Prog., Nat. Univ., San Diego 1992–; adj. prof. Coll. of Bus. Adminstrn., U.S. Internat. Univ., San Diego 1994–; exec. director and COO, Emergency Health Assocs., P.C., Phoenix, Az. 1989-91, Charleston Emergency Physicians, S.C., 1990-95, Joplin Emergency Physician Assocs. 1991-92, Big Valley Med. Group 1991-92, Blue Ridge Emergency Physicians, P.C. 1992-93, Berkeley Emergency Physicians, P.C. 1992-93; pres. Med. Cons. Inc., 1983-84; v.p. Crisis Comms. Corp. Ltd. 1982-90; pres. Washington Actions on Health 1975-78; ptnr. Washington counsel Medicine and Health 1979-81; pres. Ambulance Corp. Am., La Jolla 1984-87; chmn., pres. Univ. Inst. 1992–; lectr., p.t. faculty dept. health care adminstrn. George Washington Univ., 1969-84, preceptor 1971-84; asst. prof. Nat. Naval Sch. Health Care Adminstrn. 1971-73; mem. faculty CSC Legislation Insts. 1972-76 (mem. advy. com. on ambulatory care stds. joint commn. on accreditation of hosps. 1971-72), Am. Assn. State Colls. and Univs. Health Tng. Insts.; mem. bd. dirs. Nat. Eye Found. 1976-78; mem. Am. Hosp. Assn., Med. Group Mgmt. Assn., Hosp. Fin. Mgmt. Assn., Med. Group Mgrs., Assn. Venture Capital Groups (bd. 1984-89), Med. Adminstrs. of Calif., San Diego Venture Group (chair 1984-87), UCSD Faculty Club, Alpha Phi Omega (Bowling Green alumni chpt. pres. 1967-70, sec. treas. alumni assn. 1968-71); clubs: Univ. Club (life), Nat. Democratic (life), Nat. Republican (life), Capitol Hill; author: Congress and Health: An Intro. to the Legislative Process and the Key Participants, 1976, A Directory of Fed. Health Resources and Svs. for the Disadvantaged, 1976, Health Care Reimbursement: A Glossary, 1983, num. articles in profl. jours.; mem. editorial advy. bd. Nation's Health 1971-73. Ofc: 9191 Towne Centre Dr Ste 360 San Diego 92122

SCHNAPP, ROGER HERBERT, lawyer; b. Mar. 17, 1946, NY, NY; s. Michael Jay and Beatrice Joan (Becker) S.; m. Candice, Sept. 15, 1979; children: Monica Alexis b. 1992; edn: BS, Cornell Univ. 1966; JD, Harvard Sch. of Law 1969; Univ. Mich. 1978; admitted bar: N.Y. 1970, Calif. 1982, US Dist. Cts. (N.Y., Calif.), US Cts. Appeals, US Supreme Ct. 1974. Career: atty. Civil Aeronautics Bd., Wash. DC 1969-70; labor atty. Western Electric, N.Y.C. 1970-71; mgr. employee relations American Airlines, 1971-74; labor counsel Am. Electric Power Service Corp., N.Y.C. 1974-78, senior labor counsel 1978-80; counsel indsl. rels. Trans World Airlines, 1980-81; sr. assoc. Parker, Milliken, Clark & O'Hara, L.A. 1981-82; ptnr. Rutan & Tucker, Costa Mesa 1983-85; ptnr. Memel, Jacobs, Pierno, Gersh & Ellsworth (later Memel, Jacobs & Ellsworth), Newport Beach 1985-87; sole practice, Newport Beach 1987–; trustee Chapman Univ., Orange 1992–; dir. Dynamic Constrn. Co., Laguna Hills 1986–; mem. US Sec. of Labor's Bus. Research Advy. Council 1989–; mem. Orange County Advy. Council and cons. American Arbitration Assn., 1981–; commentator Financial News Network, Santa Monica, 1982-91; political com-

mentator KOCM, Newport Beach, 1990-91; lectr. Cal. Western Law Sch., San Diego, 1981–; mem: Conf. of Railroad and Airline Labor Lawyers; civic: O.C. Sheriffs Advy. Council 1983–; clubs: Center, Balboa Bay; author: Arbitration Issues for the 1980s (1981); govt. rels. columnist Orange County Business J. 1989-91, chief editor Industrial & Labor Relations Forum J. 1964-66; Republican; Jewish. Res: 20 Vienna Newport Beach 92660 Ofc: 4675 MacArthur Ct Ste 430 Newport Beach 92660

SCHNEIDER, EDWARD LEWIS, physician, university dean, gerontology center administrator; b. June 22, 1940, N.Y.C.; s. Samuel and Ann (Soskin) S.; m. Leah Buturain, June 6, 1987; children: Samuel b. 1989, Isaac b. 1993, Clare b. 1995; edn: BS, Rensselaer Polytech., 1961; MD, Boston Univ., 1966. Career: intern and resident N.Y. Hosp., Cornell Univ., 1966-68; staff fellow Nat. Inst. Allergy & Infectious Diseases, Bethesda, Md. 1968-70; res. fellow Univ. Calif., San Francisco 1970-73; chief sect. on cellular aging Nat. Inst. on Aging, Balt., Md. 1973-79; prof. of med. and dir. Davis Inst. on Aging, Univ. Colorado, Denver 1979-80; assoc. dir. Nat. Inst. on Aging, Bethesda 1980-84, deputy dir. 1984-87; dean and exec. dir. Leonard Davis Sch. of Gerontology, USC, Los Angeles 1986–, prof. med. USC Sch. of Medicine 1987–, William and Sylvia Kugel Prof. Andrus Gerontology Ctr., USC, 1989–; scientific dir. Buck Ctr. for Res. in Aging, Novato, Ca. 1989–; awards: Roche Award, Alpha Omega Alpha, Boston Univ. Alumni Award, Disting. lectr. Sigma Xi, Jacobson lectr. Faculty of Med. Univ. of Newcastle upon Tyne, England; mem. Gerontology Soc. of Am. (Fellow), Am. Soc. of Clinical Investigation, AARP; civic: US Naval Acad. sailing squadron coach 1980-86; editor 10 books incl: The Genetics of Aging, 1978, Biological Markers of Aging, 1982 Handbooks of the Biology of Aging (1985, 90, 95), Eldercare and the Work Force,(1990; rec: sailing, skiing. Ofc: Andrus Gerontology Ctr. 3715 McClintock St Ste 103 Los Angeles 90089-0191

SCHNEIDER, RICHARD C., humanities educator; b. Sept. 20, 1927, Jefferson, Wis.; s. Carl F. and Adele (Gau) S.; edn: BA, Carthage Coll., 1948; MDiv, Luther Sem., St. Paul, Minn. 1951; MEd, Univ. Texas, Austin 1955; Calif. lic. psychotherapist, 1956–. Career: organizer, administrator Lutheran Church, Dallas, Austin, Corpus Christi, Tx. 1951-55; faculty, adminstr. Carthage Coll., Ill. 1955-56; assoc. prof. psychology and humanities Riverside Community Coll., Riv., Calif. 1956-93; awards: NSF psych. seminars, Beloit Coll. 1964, Faculty lectr. Riverside Comm. Coll. 1970, humanities study grantee US Dept. Edn. in India, Egypt, Nigeria 1980, 81, 82; civic: Sierra Club 1979–, Nature Conservancy 1985–, Earthwatch 1985–; publ: (pamphlet) Freedom and Lawful Behavior, 1964; Indep.; Unitarian; rec: backpacking, hiking, biking. Res: 257 Arctoris Circle Bishop 93514-7053

SCHNEIDER, VALERIE ANN, doctor; b. June 3, 1963, Tacoma, Wash.; d. Ted Walter and Marie Ann (Kuran) Lopat; m. William Michael Schneider, July 7, 1990; edn: BA, Spanish, Univ. of Ariz., Tucson 1985; MD, St. George's Univ. Sch. of Medicine, Grenada, West Indies 1991; med. lic. St. of Calif.; cert. Am. Bd. Internal Medicine 1994; FLEX, ECFMG. Career: emergency vol. Hill Ambulance Co., Puyallup, Wash. 1983-84; ground crew operator Destination Tucson, Ariz. 1983-84; lang. tutor Univ. of Ariz. 1983-84; ofc. asst. Farmers Ins. Group, Tacoma, Wash. 1979-86; ofc asst. No. Ariz. Univ., Flagstaff 1987; travel asst. Grenada Internat. travel Svc., West Indies 1987-88; intern and resident, dept. internal medicine, Highland Gen. Hosp., Oakland, Calif. 1991-94; fellow in pulmonary medicine, Calif. Pacific Med. Ctr., S.F. 1994–; mem: Highland Gen. Hosp. contract negotiation com., steering com. Highland Assn. of Interns and Residents, housestaff affairs com., critical care com., Spanish translator; awards: Alpha Epsilon Delta, U.S. Achievement Academy Award 1981, Diploma of Excellence in Spanish 1981, N.Y. Univ. in Spain Scholarship 1984, Outstanding Ariz. Senior Award 1985, Stephen R. Kopycinski Mem. Scholarship to St. George's Univ. Sch. of Medicine 1987-91; Outstanding Senior Award 1991; Resident of Yr., Highland Gen. Hosp. 1994; mem: Am. Med. Women's Assn. 1991–; assoc. mem: Am. Coll. of Physicians 1991–, Am. Thoracic Soc. 1994–, Am. Coll. of Chest Physicians 1994–; contbr. res. papers to profl. assns., jour. article. Ofc: 2351 Clay St #504 San Francisco 94115

SCHNEIDER, WILFRED JOHN, JR., lawyer; b. April 17, 1951, Whittier; s. Wilfred John and Elizabeth (Clay) S.; m. Susan Debra Ann; edn: AA, Rio Hondo Coll. 1972; BA, UCLA 1974; JD, Southwestern Univ. 1978; admitted bar: Calif. 1979, U.S. Dist. Ct. and U.S. Ct. Appeals, 1982. Career: atty., assoc. Chase Rotchford Drukker & Bogust, San Bernardino 1979-87, dir. 1987-94; litigation atty. Law Ofc. of Mary Jo Carlos 1994–; judge pro tem San Bernadino Superior Court, judicial arbitrator San Bernadino, Riverside Counties, Am. Arbitration Assn.; honors: Rio Hondo Coll. student body pres. 1971-72; mem: ABA, San Bernadino Cty. Bar Assn., Los Angeles Cty. Bar Assn., Assn. of So. Calif. Defense Counsel; Republican; Episcopalian. Res: 3749 Ridge Line Dr San Bernardino 92407 Ofc: Law Office of Mary Jo Carlos 2000 Market St 1st Fl Riverside 92501 Tel:909/686-2310

SCHNITZER, GARY ALLEN, company executive; b. Jan. 29, 1942, Portland, Oreg.; s. Gilbert and Thelma S.; children: Andrea b. 1968, Greg b. 1973; edn: BS, USC, 1964. Career: exec. v.p. Schnitzer Steel, Oakland 1964–; West Coast rep. No. Calif. chpt. Scrap Iron & Steel Assn. (pres. 1972-73, nat. dir. 1976, 84-

86); v.chmn. ISRI fgn. trade comm., No. Calif. chpt. (1974-77, 83-84); dir. Island Equipment Co., Guam; bd. mem: Schnitzer Steel Industries, Lasco Shipping Co., Pacific Coast Shipping Co., Trans Pacific Shipping Co., Pacific Chartering Co.; awards: Small bus. Oakland C.of C. 1989, innovative recycling Calif. State Waste Mgmt. Bd., Sacto. 1991, listed Who's Who in the West 1982-94; civic: Bay Area Tumor Inst. (bd. 1989), Oakland Mus., Alameda Co. Hon. Deputy Sheriff, Oakland C.of C., Soc. Prevention of Child Abuse (bd. 1990–), mem. Oakland Mayor's Emergency Economic Task Force 1993, Hon. Consul Gen. of Liberia in S.F. 1995–; clubs: Calif. Tennis (S.F.), Multhomah Athletic (Portland, Oreg.), Silverado Country (Napa), Chaine Des Rotisseurs, Olympic (S.F.); Republican; Jewish; rec: reading, tennis, golf, travel. Ofc: Schnitzer Steel Products PO Box 747 Oakland 94604

SCHOELCH, LAWRENCE FRANCIS, lawyer; b. Oct. 28, 1953, St. Louis, Mo.; s. Wesley Carl and Elizabeth Anne (Higgins) S.; edn: BA in philosophy (magna cum laude), St. Louis Univ., 1976; MA philos., Univ. Notre Dame, 1978; JD, Washington Univ., St. Louis, Mo. 1984; admitted bar: Calif., 1985, Mo., 1986. Career: clk. Arizona Supreme Ct. Justice Jack D.H. Hayes, Phoenix 1984-85; atty., assoc. Kinkle, Rodiger & Spriggs, L.A. 1985-86; Cotkin, Collins & Franscell, L.A., 1986-90; Law Ofcs. Richard Hernandez 1990-92; Law Ofcs. of David Watson 1993-94; Law Ofcs. of Lawrence F. Schoelch and Assocs. 1994–awards: Pres.'s scholar St. Louis Univ. 1976, full tuition scholar Notre Dame, Fisse Scholar, recipient Am. Jurisprudence Award in Property, rep. in S.B.A., law rev. staff Wash. Univ. J. of Urban and Contemporary Law; mem. State Bar Calif., State Bar Mo., L.A. County Bar Assn. Ofc: 3580 Wilshire Blvd 17th Flr Los Angeles 90010

SCHOETTGER, THEODORE LEO, city official; b. Sept. 2, 1920, Burton, Nebr.; s. Frederick and Louise Cecelia (Gierau) S.; m. Kathryn Marguerite Hughey, June 3, 1943; children: Gregory Paul, Julie Anne; edn: BSBA (w. distinction), Univ. Nebr., 1948; C.P.A., Calif. Career: sr. acct. Haskins & Sells, Los Angeles 1948-55; controller Beckman Instruments Inc., Fullerton 1955-58, corp. chief acct., 1958-60; treas. Docummun Inc., L.A. 1960-77; fin. director City of Orange, 1977–; fin. com., treas., bd. dirs. Childrens Hosp.; mem: Calif. Soc. CPAs (nat. dir., v.p., past pres. L.A. chpt.), Fin. Execs. Inst., Mcpl. Fin. Ofcrs. Assn., Town Hall of Calif., Beta Gamma Sigma, Alpha Kappa Psi; club: Jonathan; mil: lt. USNR1942-45. Res: 9626 Shellyfield Rd Downey 90240-3418 Ofc: 300 E Chapman Ave Orange 92666-1591

SCHONFELD, WILLIAM ROST, political science educator, researcher; b. Aug. 28, 1942, NYC, NY; s. William A. and Louise R. (Rost) S.; m. Elena Beortegui, Jan. 23, 1964; children: Natalie Beortegui, Elizabeth Lynn Beortegui; edn: BA (cum laude), govt., NY Univ. 1964; MA, politics, Princeton Univ. 1968, PhD, politics, 1970. Career: res. asst. Ctr. of Internat. Studies, Princeton Univ. 1966-69, res. assoc. 1969-70; vis. lectr., 1970; asst. prof. poli. sci. Univ. of Calif., Irvine 1970-75; dir. grad. studies, Sch. of Social Scis., UC Irvine 1970-73, assoc. prof. poli. sci. 1975-81; co-dir., focused res. prog. in authority studies 1981-84, acting assoc. dean grad. studies, Sch. of Social Scis. 1985-86, 1991, prof. poli. sci. 1981–, dean Sch. of Social Scis. 1982–; vis. asst. prof. UC Berkeley (summer 1972); sr. lectr. Fondation Nationale des Sciences Politiques, Paris 1973-74; researcher Centre de Sociologie des Organisations, Paris 1976-78; univ. com. svc: mem. Chief Exec. Roundtable 1986–, bd. advs. Knowledge and Social Responsibility 1987–, past mem/chair num. other coms.; internat. speaker, lectr. in field; honors: Phi Beta Kappa, Pi Sigma Alpha, Fulbright fellowship (France, 1964-65), Danforth grad. fellowship 1964-69, Summer Faculty fellowship Univ. of Calif. 1971, Fulbright sr. lectr., (France 1973-74), NSF-CNRS Exchange of Scientists Prog. fellow (France 1976-78), Ford Found. grantee 1978-79, Disting. Tchg. award UC Irvine 1984, Prof. of Yr. Finalist, Council for Advancement & Support of Edn. 1984, Outstanding Tchr. Effectiveness award Inter-Frat. Council and Panhellenic Assn. 1987; mem: Am. Poli. Sci. Assn., Assn. Francaise de Sci. Politique, Conf. Group on French Politics and Soc., The Tocqueville Soc.; author: Youth and Authority in France: A Study of Secondary Schools, 1971, Obedience and Revolt: French Behavior Toward Authority, 1976, Ethnographie du PS et du RPR: Les elephants et l'aveugle, 1985; contbr. num. book/manuscript reviews and 20+ articles to profl. jours. Ofc: Sch of Social Sci University of California Irvine 92717

SCHOONHOVEN, CLAUDIA BIRD, professor; b. Oct. 7, 1943, Highland Park, Mich.; d. Claude Marsh and Glenna Jean (May) Bird; m. Gerald R. Schoonhoven, Dec. 27, 1965; son, Scott G. b. 1971; edn: BA (honors history), Univ. Ill.; MA and PhD, sociol., Stanford Univ. Career: asst. traffic operating mgr., service advisor, cons. Bell System Operating Cos.: Mich. Bell, New England T&T, and Pacific Tel., 1965-68; instr. sociology Chabot Coll. 1969-71; fellow orgns. res. tng. pgm., Stanford Univ. 1972-75, postdoc. fellow decision making in orgns., 1975-77, asst. prof. sociol. dept. Stanford Univ. 1976-77, vis. scholar Stanford Grad. Sch. of Bus. 1984-85; vis. prof. Univ. Santa Clara, Leavey Sch. of Bus. 1986; prof. of organization and mgmt. San Jose State Univ. 1977-93; prof. bus. admin. Amos Tuck Sch. of Business, Dartmouth Coll., Hanover, NH 1993–; honors: Univ. of Ill. Phi Alpha Theta scholar, L. Noyes scholar, and E.M. Cartier scholar 1965, PHS pre-doctoral fellow 1971, outstanding prof. SJSU Sch. of Bus. 1981-82, Phi Kappa Phi (mem. 1981, disting. acad.

achiev. award 1984), NASA Faculty Fellow 1983, prin. investigator US Dept. Commerce grants (1985-87, 86-88), Nat. Sci. Found. grantee (1989-91, 1993-95); mem: Acad. of Mgmt. (bd. of governors), Am. Sociol. Assn., We. Acad. of Mgmt. (pres.), Strategic Mgmt. Soc., NOW; author: The Innovation Marathon (1993), and num. res. publs.; rec: skiing, sailing. Res: Los Altos Hills Ofc: Tuck School of Business Dartmouth College Hanover NH 03755

SCHORR, MARTIN M., forensic psychologist; m. Dolores G. Tyson, 1952; edn: AB cum laude, Adelphi Univ., 1949; MS, Purdue Univ., 1953 (pub. Alumni Publications, Purdue Univ. 1952-53); PhD, Denver Univ., 1960; Rhodes Scholarship Balliol Coll., Oxford Univ., England; lic. sch. psychologist 1955, clin. psychologist 1962, forensic splty. 1962; diplomate Am. Bd. of Professional Psychology 1990. Career: chief of clin. psych. services San Diego County Mental Hosp. 1963-67; pvt. practice, specialist forensic examinations, Dektor counterintel. and political violence, 1962–; forensic examiner Superior, Fed. and Mil. Cts., 1962–; assoc. director Timberline Productions, Inc. 1990–; guest prof., abnormal psych., San Diego St. Univ. 1965-68; chief dept. psych. Centre City Hosp. 1976-79; cons. St. Dept. Corrections, Minnewawa 1970-73, Dept. Health, Disability Eval. 1972-75, St. Indsl. Accident Commn. 1972-78, Crim. Justice Adminstrn. 1975-77; cons. Vista Hill Found. (17 yrs), Mercy Hosp. Psychiatric (18 yrs), Foodmaker Corp. (6 yrs), Convent of the Sacred Heart, El Cajon (4 yrs); FAA Examiner, assoc. film dir.; awards: Resolution, Calif. St. Assembly for assistance in formulating Whistleblower Protection Act of 1986, listed Who's Who in Am.; mem: Am. Psychol. Assn., Am. Acad. Forensic Scis., AAAS, Fellow Internat. Assn. of Soc. Psychiat., Internat. Platform Assn., World Mental Health Assn., Mystery Writers Am., PEN Internat., Nat. Writers Club, Mensa Soc.; author, screenplay, Death by Prescription. Address: University City San Diego 92122

SCHROEDER, CORRINE FLORENCE, school psychologist; b. March 3, 1936, Watertown, So.Dak.; d. Leo and Florence Helen (Maher) O'Connor; m. Martin Henry Schroeder, Jr., Aug. 10, 1957; children: Susan b. 1971; edn: BA, San Diego St. Univ. 1958; MA, 1963; Lic. Ednl. Psychologist (LEP), Nat. Cert. Sch. Psychologist (NCSP), Calif. pupil personnel cred. 1965. Career: tchr. San Diego City Schs. 1958-63; Brawley Elem. Sch. Dist. 1963-64; San Diego City Schs. 1964-65, sch. psychologist 1965–; awards: Girl Scouts Silver Service 1982, Green Angel 1983-86, recogn. cert. San Diego City Sch. 1985-86, Bell Jr. H.S. staff person of week/Psychologist Appreciation Day 1989, attendance awards San Diego City Schs. 1987-94; mem: Delta Zeta Sor., CTA, NEA, SDTA, NASP, CASP, SAN CASP, San Diego Imperial Council Girl Scouts, AAUW, Heartland Youth Symphony (treas. 1983-84), San Diego Jr. Womens Club (edn. chmn. 1966-69), St. Martins Ch.; rec: travel, crafts, bridge, theater. Ofc: San Diego City Schools.

SCHROEDER, RITA MOLTHEN, chiropractor; b. Oct. 25, 1922, Savanna, Ill.; d. Frank Joseph and Ruth Jessie (McKenzie) Molthen; m. Richard H. Schroeder, D.C., Apr. 23, 1948; div. 1981; children: Richard b. 1949, Andrew b. 1952, Barbara b. 1953, Thomas b. 1956, Paul b. 1960, Madeline b. 1962; edn: DC, Palmer Sch. of Chiropractic 1949; DC, Cleveland Coll. of Chiro. 1960; Calif. lic. Dr. Chiro., 1961. Career: engring. tooling liaison, Douglas Aircraft Co. 1942-46; chiropractic practice in Brooklyn, NY 1949-59, Fresno, Calif. 1961–, pres. Schroeder Chiropractic, Inc.; bd. dirs. Pacific States Chiropractic Coll. 1978-79, pres. 1980-81; honors: Ambassador Awd., Palmer Coll. of Chiro.; mem: Internat. Chiro. Assn., Internat. Chiro. Assn. of Calif., Fedn. of Chiropractors, Calif. Chiro. Assn., Internat. Platform Assn.; Republican; Cath.; rec: hunting, fishing, swimming, diving. Res: 8701 N Hwy 41 #18 Fresno 93720 Ofc: Schroeder Chiropractic, Inc. 2535 N Fresno, Fresno 93703

SCHROEDER, ROBERT J., veterinarian, public health administrator; b. Nov. 19, 1921, Ft. Collins, Colo.; s. John Henry and Mildred Margaret (McElravy) S.; m. Janice Lorraine Dringman, Aug. 24, 1947; children: Jeryl Lee b. 1948, Craig Reed b. 1951, Curtis John b. 1956; edn: DVM, Colo. St. Univ. Ft. Collins 1947. Career: veterinarian USDA, Mexico 1947-48; staff veterinarian County of Los Angeles, 1948-50, senior veterinarian 1953-57, county veterinarian, dir. 1957-62; dep. dir. L.A. Co. Health Dept. 1972-79; clin. prof. pathology and pub. health USC Sch. of Medicine 1968-79, prof. emeritus 1979–; pres. L.A. Co. Mgmt. Council 1968-69; honors: Colo. St. Univ. hon. alumnus 1969, CSU Coll. Veterinary Medicine hon. alumnus 1969, So. Calif. Veterinary Med. Assn. disting. service 1969, Calif. Regional Med. Program extraordinary service 1973, L.A. Co. Bd. Suprs. disting. service 1979; mem: AVMA (pres. 1967-68), So. Calif. Veterinary Medicine Assn., L.A. Co. Mgmt. Council, Calif. Med. Research Assn. (bd. dirs.), L.A. Zoological Assn. (bd. trustees), Calif. Regional Med. Programs (chmn.); civic: Lions, Speechcrafters, BSA, L.A. C.of C.; article pub. in profl. jour., guest ed. Veterinary Services in Disaster & Emergencies (1987); mil: 1st. lt. AUS 1943-46, 1950-52; Republican; Prot.; rec: camping, fishing, photography. Res: 9738 Tecum Rd Downey 90240

SCHUCK, LAWRENCE ANDREW, manufacturing company executive, pharmacist; b. Aug. 23, 1915, Oxnard; s. John Frank and Anna Francis (Bryant) S.; m. Doris H. Altland, July 26, 1941; children: Lawrence B., b. 1943; Thomas B., b. 1946; Michael R., b. 1959; edn: AA, Ventura Coll. 1935; BS in pharm., UC Berkeley 1938; Ensign USNR, Cornell Univ. 1943. Career: pharmacist, Owl

Drug Co., 1939–, mgr. 1942; pharmacist Parke-Davis & Co., 1946–, dist. mgr. 1951–, gov. sales supr. Parke-Davis Div. Warner Lambert 1965, ret. 1975, devel. corp. clerk training pgm.; honors: Phi Delta Chi (treas. 1938), treas. UC Berkeley Coll. of Pharm. 1938, recipient nat. sales award (new Pontiac) 1947, nat. sales dist. mgr. award 1954, 58; Fellow Am. College Pharmacists 1955; mem. Bay Area Pharmacy Assn., BSA (past councilor), Elks, UC Berkeley Blue & Gold Assn. (life mem. & donor UC Coll. of Pharmacy), American Legion Post 339 (Ventura), V.F.W. Post 1679 Ventura (life); mil: lt. USNR, decorated 2 combat awards, Presdl. Unit citation for Solomon Island Op., then assigned to Staff of Com Ten, San Juan, Puerto Rico as personnel ofcr. under Adm. Griffin; "Plank Owner" U.S. Navy Memorial; Republican (charter mem. Presdl. Task Force, Charter issue Who's Who in Republican Party), recipient Republican Presidential Legion of Merit Award 1993; R.Cath.; rec: workshop, keeping current with pharmaceutical devels. Res: 15711 W Telegraph Rd F-125 Santa Paula 93060

SCHUETZ, JOHN MICHAEL, automotive sales executive; b. Apr. 16, 1947, Chgo.; s. Henry Albert and Ann Delores (Kunst) S.; m. Jacqueline Claire Furneaux, Apr. 22, 1972; children: Michael Richard, Sean David; edn: BS in advt., Marquette Univ., 1969. Career: gen. field mgr. Ford Motor Co., San Jose 1972-85; v.p. western region IVECO Trucks of North America, Huntington Beach 1985-91; Nat. Dealer Devel. mgr. Wynn Oil Co. 1992-95; western regional mgr. Starcraft Automotive, Inc. 1995–; dir. Forsyte Research Group, Santa Rosa 1988–; civic: Boy Scouts Am., El Toro (ldr. 1988–), Am. Youth Soccer Orgn., Saddleback Valley (coach 1988–); mem. Phi Theta Psi; club: Sun and Sail; mil: lt. US Navy 1969-72; Republican; R.Cath. Res: 21821 Ticonderoga Ln El Toro 92630-2313

SCHULTZE, ERNST EUGENE, marketing communications company president; b. Jan. 20, 1944, Columbia, Mo.; s. Andrew Byron and Jeanne V. (Homsley) S.; m. Marlene Diane finke, June 7, 1964 (div. 1981); 1 dau., Nicole b. 1975; edn: BA, Neb. Wesleyan Univ. 1968; MBA, S.D. St. Univ. 1975; Calif. life tchg. credential (1975). Career: mktg. mgr. Ektelon Corp., S.D. 1976-79, project mgr. 1979-80; exec. v.p. Mktg. Group 1980-83; v.p. Jack Lewis Agency 1983-84; market exec. Gable Agency 1984-85; pres. Schultze & Wilson 1985–; awards: Phi Kappa Tau, spl. recogn. S.D.S.U. 1973, listed Who's Who in West 1989-90, Who's Who in World 1990-91, Who's Who in Ind. and Fin., Golden State Award (1989); mem. Killea City Council 1981; mem: Am. Mktg. Assn. (seminar ldr. 1981), Nat. Mgmt. Assn. (pres. 1979), Gaslamp Council (mktg. com. 1988-89); thesis: Marketing a Candidate, 1975, 3 pub. articles in field; Republican; rec: swimming, running, European travel, mountain climbing. Res: 3816 Aragon Dr San Diego 92115

SCHULZ, JOHN CHRISTIAN, manufacturing company executive; b. July 12, 1936, Bklyn.; s. John Valentine and Betty (Dauelsberg) S.; m. Kathleen Brower; children: Alison b. 1963, Christian b. 1968, Amanda b. 1987; edn: BME Rensselaer Polytechnic Inst. 1958; cert. profl. engr., Calif.; cert. mgr. NMA. Career: mgr. quality engring. Bourns Inc., Riverside 1962-64, dir. quality control 1964-68; chief supplier control Gen. Dynamics, Pomona 1969-70, mgr. procurement quality 1970-74, mgr. quality engring. 1974-77, mgr. quality control 1977-80; mgr. quality assur. service Loral Aeronutronic, Newport Beach 1980-93; mgr. quality assur. Safetran Systems Corp., Rancho Cucamonga 1993–; instr. Mt. San Antonio Coll.; current bd. chmn., past pres. Measurement Science Conf. Inc.; mem: ASQC (past chmn., mem. exec. bd.), ASME, Nat. Mgmt. Assn., Riverside Rifle & Pistol Club, Am. Legion; mil: lt. USN, chief engr. USS Pursuit (AGS 17) 1958-62; Rep.; Prot.; rec: photog., shooting. Res: 4492 11th St Riverside 92501 Ofc: Safetran Systems Corp 10655 7th St Rancho Cucamonga 91730

SCHUMACHER, MICHAEL ALLEN, chief probation officer; b. Sept. 1, 1940, Elmhurst, Ill.; s. Allen Arthur and Norah (O'Brien) S.; edn: AA, Cerritos Coll. 1966; BA psychology, CSU Los Angeles 1969; MA, 1973; MPA, USC, 1975; PhD, U.S. Internat. Univ. 1978. Career: subcontract coordinator N. Am. Aviation, Downey 1966-67; accounts analyst Rockwell (space div.), Seal Beach 1967-68, group leader property mgmt. 1968-70; deputy, supr. Orange Co. Probation Dept., Orange 1970-76; ct. adminstr. Orange Co. Juvenile Ct. 1976-79; chief probation ofcr. Orange Co. Probation Dept., Santa Ana 1979–; p.t. instr. USC and Internat. Univ. Mex. 1980–; mem. Calif. Commn. on Drugs, Van Nuys 1989–; Commn. for Revision of Juvenile Ct. Law, Sacto. 1983-84; Calif. Council on Criminal Justice 1984–; State Task Force on Gangs & Drugs 1985-88; awards: Calif. Youth Authority Disting. Service 1985, Chief Probation Office of Year 1987, 1993, Orange County's 20 Most Sensational People of 1993-Orang Coast Mag., Lester Hayes award (pub. article) CPPCA 1994, Community Svc. award Saddleback Coll. 1994; mem: Western Soc. Criminology (fellow), Calif. Probation Parole & Correctional Assn. (st. pres. 1985-86), Chief Probation Ofcrs. Calif. (st.v.p. 1989, st. pres. 1990-92), Calif. Corrections Exec. Council (chmn. 1992-94), Orange Co. Criminal Justice System Advy. Group (chmn. 1992-95), Curriculum Advy. Com. CSU (co-chmn. 1989-90), United Way Orange Co., Family Service Assn. (bd. dirs. 1984-88), Citizens Advy. Bd. (bd. mem. 1985, 86), Walnut Square Homeowners Assn. (pres., treas. 1975, 76), March of Dimes (bd. dirs. 1994), Cambodian Family (bd. dirs. 1989-95), Coalition for Children, Adolescents and Parents (bd. dirs. 1993-95); articles pub. in profl. jours., 1983-93. Ofc: County of Orange 909 N Main St Santa Ana 92701

SCHUNK, ERIC H., lawyer; b. Sept. 12, 1955, Boston, Mass.; s. Henry Frederic and Marian (McAmis) S.; m. Carol Sue; children: Daniel b. 1983, Kirsten b. 1986, Christoffer b. 1988, Evan b. 1991; edn: BS, Georgetown Univ. 1977; MBA, UCLA 1981; JD, 1981; admitted St. Bar Calif.. St. Bar N.Y. Career: clk. Judge Anthony Kennedy 9th Circuit Ct. of Appeals; atty. O'Melveny & Myers, Los Angeles; ptnr. Milbank Tweed, currently mng. ptnr. for L.A. Corporate Dept.; honors: Order of Coif, Psi Chi, Phi Beta Kappa; mem: L.A. Com. of Fgn. Rels. (secty), Am. Bar Assn.; 6 articles pub. in profl. jours. Ofc: Milbank Tweed Hadley & McCloy 601 S Figueroa St Los Angeles 90017

SCHUTZ, JOHN ADOLPH, historian, educator; b. Apr. 10, 1919, Los Angeles; s. Adolph John and Augusta K. (Gluecker) S.; edn: AB, UCLA 1942, MA, 1943, PhD, 1945. Career: asst. prof. Calif. Inst. of Tech., 1945-53; assoc. prof./prof. Whittier College, 1953-65; prof. of history USC, 1965-91, dean 1976-82; vis. prof. (summers) Univ. of Brit. Columbia 1960, Univ. of Waterloo, Ont. 1966, Boston Coll. 1969, CSCLA 1953-65; trustee Citizens Res. Council; awards: grantee Nat. Endowment for Humanities 1971-74, Danforth Fellow 1959; mem: Am. Hist. Assn. (Pacific Coast Br. pres. 1973, sec.treas. 1951-87), New England Historic Geneal. Soc. (trustee 1988–), Orgn. of Am. Historians, So. Calif. Hist. Soc.; author: The American Republic, 1978, The Dawning of America, 1981, William Shirley: King's governor of Massachusetts, 1961, Spain's Colonial Outpost: California (Boyd & Fraser 1985), A Noble Pursuit: A Sesquicentennial History of the New England Genealogical Society, 1995, chpt. in Generations and Changes: Genealogical Perspectives in Social Hist. (Mercer Univ. Press 1986); jt. editor Golden State Series (Boyd & Fraser, 1979–); chpt. in Making of America (US Ofc. Info. 1988, Univ. N.C. 1992); Democrat; R.Cath.; rec: philately, travel. Res: 1100 White Knoll Dr Los Angeles 90012 Ofc: USC, College Park, Los Angeles 90089-0034

SCHUTZ, ROBERT RUDOLPH, editor, writer; b. July 22, 1915, Bixby, Minn.; s. Walter Valentine and Myrtle Esther Lois (Burns) S.; m. Lola Schuelter, Sept. 29, 1939 (div. 1941); m. Marie Hayes, Jan. 22, 1949; children: David b. 1949, Margaret b. 1951, Roberta b. 1953, Karla b. 1955; edn: BS horticulture, Univ. Minn. 1939; MS plant genetics, 1941; cert. meteorology, MIT 1943; PhD econ., UC Berkeley 1952. Career: founder, pub. affairs dir. KPFA Pacifica Radio, Berkeley 1953-60; economist Federal Reserve Bank, San Francisco 1961-63; exec. dir. Am. Soc. Eastern Arts, Berkeley 1966-68; chief exec. Lobby for Peace, San Francisco 1963-66; ed. in chief Annual Reviews, Palo Alto 1968-73; ed. Friends Bulletin, San Francisco 1974-78; treas., dir. Friends Assn. Service Elderly, Santa Rosa 1982-89, ed. Friends in Unity w. Nature 1985-87, treas. Friends Comm. on Unity w. Nature 1985-89; awards: Univ. Minn. sr. gold medal 1939, FASE vol. of year 1989; author: "The $30,000 Solution" (Fithian Press, 1995), Fair Capitalism, 1990, article pub. in profl. jour., 1950; mil: lt. USNR 1942-45; Democrat; Quaker; rec: gardening. Res: 684 Benicia Drive #70 Santa Rosa 95409 Ofc: PO Box 2343 Santa Rosa 95405

SCHUTZ, WILL, psychologist, educator, consultant; b. Dec. 19. 1925, Chicago, Ill.; s. Carl Milton and Ruth Helen Tausig (Burns) S.; m. Ailish Patricia Mellard, Aug. 24, 1985; children: Laurie b. 1953, Caleb b. 1956, Ethan b. 1966, Dana b. 1971, Ari b. 1976; edn: BA, UCLA 1947; MA, 1950; PhD, 1951. Career: tchg. assist. UCLA 1948-50; lectr., exec. secty. Univ. Chgo. 1950-51; research assoc. prof. Tufts Univ., Medford, Mass. 1953-54; lectr., research assoc. Harvard Univ., Cambridge 1954-58; research educator UC Berkeley 1958-62; assoc. prof. Einstein Med., Bronx, N.Y. 1963-67; sr. assoc. Esalen, Big Sur 1967-75; prof., dept. chmn. Antioch Univ., San Francisco 1978-84; pres. Will Schutz Assoc., Mill Valley 1980–; author: The Human Element, 1994, The Truth Option, 1984, Profound Simplicity, 1979, Joy, 1967, FIRO, 1958; mil: lt. USN 1943-45, 1951-53; Jewish; rec: sports, handball. Address: 65 Sunset Way Muir Beach 94965

SCHWAB, CHARLES R., executive, discount broker; b. Woodland, Calif.; m. Helen O'Neil; 5 children; edn: BS Stanford Univ.; Grad. Bus Sch., Stanford Univ.; Career: mutual fund mgr.; founder, chmn. Charles R. Schwab & Co., San Francisco 1971–; author: How To Be Your Own Stockbroker (1984); Republican. Res: Woodside Ofc: Charles R. Schwab & Co 101 Montgomery St 28th fl San Francisco 94104*

SCHWAB, HOWARD JOEL, judge; b. Feb. 13, 1943, Charleston, West Va.; s. Joseph S. and Gertrude J. (Hadas) S.; m. Michelle, July 4, 1970; children: Joshua b. 1976, Bethany b. 1978; edn: AB in hist. (honors), UC Los Angeles 1964, JD, 1967; admitted Calif. St. Bar 1968), U.S. Supreme Ct. Bar (1972). Career: legal adminstrv. clk. Litton Industries, 1967-68; dep. city atty. City of Los Angeles, 1968-69; dep. atty. gen. Calif. St. 1969-84: major litigation personally argued and briefed incl. Faretta v. Calif. (1975, landmark case in US Supreme Ct. estab. indep. right of self-rep. in a crim. trial); Charles Manson Family Cases- People v. Manson,(1976, People v. Manson, 1977, People v. Van Houten, 1980; landmark Calif. Capital Punishment cases- People v. Frierson, 1979, People v. Jackson, 1980, Rockwell v. Superior Ct., 1976; People v. Powell (1974, subject of Joseph Wambaugh's book The Onion Field); People v. Wm. and Emily Harris, 1979; mem. Atty. Gen.'s Prop. 8 Task Force and contbr. to Atty. Gen.'s Guide to Prop. 8, frequent testimony before legislative bodies on crim. law matters; appt. judge

Mcpl. Ct. Los Angeles 1984-85; judge Superior Ct., Los Angeles 1985–; adj. asst. prof. USC Inst. of Psychiatry and Law; publs: 6 pub. opinions authored as assoc. justice pro tem of Ct. of Appeal (1985); num. articles in law jours. and books, Continuing Edn. of the Bar (CEB) and Practicing Law Inst. (PLI); often reprinted article `Diminished Capacity - A Guide' used as ofcl. text for courses at USC Inst. of Psychiatry and Law, CEB, and PLI; frequent lectr. on var. legal topics, lectr. Nat. Homicide Symposium (1977, 79, 82, 84, 89), num. t.v. and radio interviews; mem: Mcpl. Ct. Judges Assn. 1984-85, Calif. St. Bar, Los Angeles Co. Bar Assn. (exec. com. Crim. Justice Sect., mem. Appellate Cts. com.), Assn. of Dep. Attys. Gen. (to 1984), Calif. Dist. Attys. Assn. (to 1984, speakers bur., author var. CDAA programs and publs.), Phi Alpha Delta, Constnl. Rights Found. (vol. speakers bur.); honors: Bancroft-Whitney Award in Torts, UCLA 1965, 1st annual recipient of CDAA Wm. E. James Award for outstanding assistance to local prosecutors statewide 1981, legal career profiled in Prosecutor's Brief, 1980, judicial career profiled in California Living mag. Herald Examiner (2/16/86); Democrat; Jewish; rec: hist., books. Ofc: Los Angeles Superior Ct 6230 Sylmar Ave Van Nuys 91401

SCHWAB, IVAN R., ophthalmologist; b. Jan. 21, 1948, Morgantown, WV; s. Jesse Wayne and Helen Ruth S.; m. Eleanor R., July 16, 1977; 1 son Nathan b. 1983; edn: BA, West Virginia Univ. 1969, MD, 1973. Career: asst. prof. West Virginia Univ. 1982-85, assoc. prof. 1985-89; assoc. prof. UC Davis 1989-92, prof., 1992–; honors: Phi Beta Kappa 1968, Alpha Omega Alpha 1986; pres./elect Ocular Microbiology & Immunology Study Group 1982–; mem: Assn. for Res. in Vision & Ophthalmology 1982–, editor (books): Refractive Keratoplasty, 1988, Clinical Science of Corneal Eye Disease, 1994; rec: bicycling, cross-country skiing, photography. Res: 8664 Ranchwood Ct Fair Oaks 95628 Ofc: UC Davis Dept of Ophthalmology 1603 Alhambra Blvd Sacramento 95816

SCHWARZ, FREDERICK CHARLES, physician, lecturer, writer; b. Jan. 15, 1913, Queensland, Australia; s. Paulus Friedrich Charles and Phoebe (Smith) S.; m. Lillian May Morton, Dec. 26, 1939; children: John Charles Morton, David Frederick, Rosemary Gai Esler; edn: BS, Univ. of Queensland, Australia 1933, BA, 1938, U.O.Q. Bachelor of Medicine Bachelor of Science (MD equivalent) 1944. Career: high sch. tchr., Queensland, Australia 1934-38; lectr. Queensland Teachers Coll., 1939-44; med. practitioner, Sydney, 1946-55; founder, pres., exec. dir. Christian Anti-Communism Crusade, Long Beach, Calif. 1953–; lectr. extensively on Communism in U.S., Australia, and internat., instr. numerous week-long schools; recipient Thomas Jefferson award The Council for Nat. Policy USA 1988; author 2 books: You Can Trust Communists (To Be Communists) (1960, Prentice Hall, 13 printings hard cover, num. printings paper back Chantico Pub. Co.), The Three Faces of Revolution (1972, Capitol Hill Press), various booklets. Ofc: Christian Anti-Communism Crusade 227 E 6th St Long Beach 90802

SCHWARZ, JOYCE, new media executive; b. Jan. 14, 1946, Cleveland, Ohio; d. Frank and Ann (Stefani) Habart; edn: BS journalism, Ohio Univ. 1968; MPW profl. writing, USC, 1984; Robert Redfords Sundance Film Inst. Career: asst. ed. Ladies Home Jour., N.Y. 1968; assoc. ed. Am. Girl Mag. 1969; dir. publications Univ. San Francisco 1970-77; account supr. Foote Cone & Belding 1977-79; v.p. Fawcett McDermott Cavanagh, Honolulu, Hawaii 1979-82; pres. Joyce Communications, Los Angeles 1982–; dir. Star Course Seminars, L.A.; chr. fund raising Women in Film Festival 1985; Blue Ribbon judge Emmy Awards, Acad. T.V. Arts & Scis. 1985–; honors: Am. Bus. Womens Assn. boss of year, listed Outstanding Young Woman in Am.; mem: USC Cinema T.V. Alumni Assn. (pres. 1987-88), Pub. Rels. Soc. Am. (counselors acad.), So. Calif. Publicists Assn., Indep. Feature Project, Am. Booksellers Assn., Book Publicists Club So. Calif., The Fashion Group Inc.; author: Multimedia: Gateway to the New Millenium (Harcourt Brace, 1994), Successful Recareering (Career Press, 1993). Ofc: 1714 Sanborn Ave Los Angeles 90027

SCHWEIKHER, KAREN D., corporate communications executive; b. Jan. 8, 1942, Morristown, N.J.; d. George Wescott and Dorothe (Williams) Dexter; m. Louis E. Terreri, April 20, 1963 (div. 1977); m. Robert Schweikher, Sept. 22, 1984; children: Todd b. 1964, Stacey b. 1968; edn: BS summa cum laude, mktg., Fairleigh Dickinson Univ. 1982. Career: advtg. splst. Allied Corp., 1976-78, advtg. supr. 1978-82, advtg. mgr. 1982-86; mktg. comm. mgr. Ampex Corp. 1986-91, dir. corp. communications Ampex Corp. 1991–; awards: Fairleigh Dickinson Univ. Mktg. Student of Year 1982; Republican; Episcopalian; rec: cooking, handcrafts. Ofc: Ampex Corp. 401 Broadway MS 3A-01 Redwood City 94063

SCOBLE, FRANCIS MATTHEW, engineer; b. Feb. 7, 1949, Teaneck, N.J.; s. Edward James and Doris (Bielitz) S.; m. Lang Trieu, Aug. 7, 1983; edn: BS engring., Univ. Ariz. Tucson 1971; reg. profl. civil engr. Ariz., Calif., Oreg. Career: civil engr. City of Tucson, Ariz. 1972-77; John Carollo Engrs., Phoenix, Ariz. 1978; constrn. mgr. Deleuw Cather Engrs., San Francisco 1978-82; asst. v.p. O'Brien Kreitzberg Assoc. 1982-94; exec. v.p. Consolidated CM, 1994–; rec: antiques, numismatics, book collecting. Res: 700 Broderick St San Francisco 94117

SCOLLARD, JEANNETTE REDDISH, entrepreneur, lecturer, author; b. July 26, 1947, Nashville, Tenn.; d. Andrew Jackson and Ruby Jewel (Wheeler) Mabry; m. Gary Scollard, July 4, 1979; div. 1987; edn: BA, Vanderbilt Univ., Nashville, Tenn. 1968; career: ed., Wall St. Transcript, NY NY 1972-74; sr. ed., Financial World, NY, NY 1974-79; v.p., Chesebrough Pond's, Greenwich, Conn. 1978-79; vice chmn., MMT Sales, NY, NY 1980-87; chmn., Costa Resort Properties, Carlsbad, Calif. 1989–; chmn., SCS Marketing, Carlsbad, Calif. 1987–; Internet host, daily "Millionaire Smarts" on Microsoft Network; tchg. fellow, Woodrow Wilson Found. 1987-88; cons. EKATRA Found., New Delhi, India; awards: Small Biz. Advocate of San Diego, SBA 1992; chief fundraiser, Orgn. of Women in Internat. Trade 1995–; mem. San Diego Host Com. 1996 Republican Convention; mem. advy. com. Nat. Assn. of Women Bus. Owners; dir., Milestone House 1992–; mem: steering com. Mentor Program/SBA 1989–; advy. com., Entrepreneurial Ctr., Manhattanville Coll. 1986-93; trustee and chief fund raiser, Am. Women in Radio & TV 1986-91; trustee, Internat. Radio & TV Found. 1988-90; founding gov., NY Financial Writers, NY, NY 1978-79; author: 3 books: No-Nonsense Mgmt. Tips, 1984; The Self-Employed Woman, 1987; Risk to Win, 1990; columnist, Sounding Off, Entrepreneur Magazine, 1990–; Protestant; rec: piano, Himalayan art. Address: Carlsbad 92009

SCOTT, KELLEY DENISE, lawyer; b. Feb. 13, 1962, Wasco, Calif.; d. Charles Leon and Carol Sue (Williams) Patrick; m. Larry Dean Smith (div. Dec. 1988); m. 2d. Kip Scott, May 21, 1994; children: Jordan b. 1988; edn: AA, Bakersfield Coll., 1985; CSU Bakersfield, 1986; JD, Calif. Pacific Sch. of Law, 1991; admitted bar: Calif. 1991. Career: atty. Kern Co. Public Defenders Ofc., 1989–; mem. Calif. Bar Assn., Kern Co.Bar Assn., Kern Co. Women Lawyers Assn., Small Claims Advisors Assn.; Republican (Kern Co. YR); Calvary Bible Ch.; rec: snow and jet skiing, scuba, crafts. Res: 7116 Bandolero Way Bakersfield 93306 Ofc: 1315 Truxtun Ave Bakersfield 93308

SCOTT, RICHARD THOMAS, corporate trainer, technical writer; b. Oct. 17, 1939, Ogden, Utah; s. Thomas Bradshaw and Reah (Child) S.; m. Connie Greenwood, May 15, 1959; children: Richard T., Jr. b. 1960, Paul S. b. 1961, Stephen B. b. 1962, Aaron D. b. 1965 (dec. 1994); edn: Univ. Utah 1958-59, Weber State Univ. 1959-60, Syracuse Univ. 1969-70. Career: customer engr., system maint. IBM Corp., Salt Lake City 1960-64, advisory instr. IBM Corp., Kingston, NY 1964-71, St. Louis, Mo. 1971-77, San Jose, Calif. 1977-78, senior instr. IBM Corp., Los Angeles 1978-91; owner Conejo SkunkWorks, Thousand Oaks 1991–, dir. of curriculum and instr. development, One Byte At A Tyme (computer tng. & support Ctr.) 1994–; tchr., consultant, and tech. writer, 1964–; mem. Trainers Assn. of So. Calif. (1985–, bd. 1987-91, exec. secty. 1992–); civic: Boy Scouts of Am., St. Louis, San Jose, Thousand Oaks (merit badge counselor: computers, pub. speaking, communications); author and support methodology: Course Devel. System (IBM internal product) 1985-91; mil: E5 USAF Reserves 1957-65; Republican; Latter Day Saints; rec: golf, music DIY puttering. Res/Ofc: Conejo Skunk Works 79 E Avenida de los Arboles Thousand Oaks 91360

SCOTTI, FRANK ANTHONY, ophthalmologist; b. Aug. 23, 1952, Brooklyn, N.Y.; s. Anthony Emil and Christine (Imburgia) S.; edn: BS biol. sci., Rutgers Univ. 1973; MS zoology, Rutgers Grad. Sch. 1974; MD, N.J. Coll. Medicine 1978; cert. Am. Acad. Ophthalmology (1984). Career: gen. surgery intern Balboa Navy Hosp., San Diego 1978-79; preventive medicine physician USN 1979-80; ophthalmology resident Balboa Navy Hosp. 1980-83; chief ophthalmology Navy Hosp. Okinawa, Japan 1983-85; staff ophthalmologist Camp Pendleton (Calif.) Hosp. 1985-87; pvt. practice ophthalmology, Encinitas 1987–; honors: Nat. Hon. Soc. N.J. (1969), outstanding subsplty. cons. Camp Pendleton Hosp. 1986, Southwest Med. Teams Humanitarian of Yr. 1994; mem: Am. Acad. Ophthalmology (fellow), Okinawa Med. Soc., CMA, San Diego Co. Med. Soc., San Diego Eye Bank, S.D. Ophthalmologic Soc., N.J. Med. Sch. Alumni and Century Club; civic: S.D. Big Brothers, S.D. Zool. Soc., S.D. Hash House Harriers, Rotary Club (Encinitas), Southwest Med. Teams; articles pub. in med. jours., 1980, 87; mil: capt. USN 1974–; Cath.; rec: running, scuba diving, carpentry. Res: 2111 Del Mar Heights Rd Del Mar 92014-3019 Ofc: Suite 104 #320 Santa Fe Dr Encinitas 92024-5131

SCOULAR, ROBERT FRANK, lawyer; b. July 9, 1942, Del Norte, Colo.; s. Duane Wm. and Marie Josephine (Moloney) S.; m. Donna Votruba, June 3, 1967; children: Bryan, b. 1971; Sean, b. 1975; Bradley, b. 1980; edn: BS, Aero. Engring., St. Louis Univ. 1964; JD, St. Louis Univ. Sch. of Law 1968; admitted to Calif., Mo., Colo., N.Dak. and US Supreme Court Bars. Career: aerodynamics engr., contract adminstr. Emerson Electric Co., St. Louis, Mo. 1964-66; law clk. Chief Judge Charles J. Vogel, US Ct. of Appeals for the Eighth Circuit, St. Louis 1968-69; ptnr. Bryan, Cave, McPheeters & McRoberts, St. Louis, 1969-89; mng. ptnr., Los Angeles office, 1979-84, sect. leader Tech., Computer and Intellectual Property Law Sect., 1984-89; ptnr. Sonnenschein Nath & Rosenthal, Chicago, mng. ptnr. L.A. office, policy and planning com., co-leader Intellectual Property Sect., 1990–; dir. Corley Printing Co., St. Louis 1973-82; honors: dist. svc Mo. Bar Young Lawyers Sect. 1978, outstanding senior St. Louis Univ. 1964, nat. outstanding cadet and Internat. Air Cadet Exchange Civil Air Patrol 1960; mem: Am. Bar Assn. (nat. dir. Young Lawyers Div. 1977-78), Missouri

Bar (dir. Mo. Lawyers Credit Union 1978-79, chmn. Credit Union Task Force 1977-78, chmn. Young Lawyers Sect. 1976-77), Bar Assn. Met. St. Louis (v.p. 1978-79, chmn. Young Lawyers Sect. 1975-76), St. Louis Bar Found. (dir. 1975-76, 79), Calif. Bar Assn., Am. Judicature Soc., Conf. on Personal Fin. Law, Assn. of Bus. Trial Lawyers, Computer Law Assn., St. Louis Univ. Law Sch. Alumni Assn. (secty. 1970-72), St. Louis Univ. Alumni Council, L.A. C.of C., Boy Scouts of Am. (dir. L.A. Area Council); contbr. articles in law journals; Republican; R.Cath.; rec: golf, tennis, running. Res: 1505 Lower Paseo La Cresta Palos Verdes Estates 90274 Ofc: Sonnenschein Nath & Rosenthal 601 S Figueroa St Ste 1500 Los Angeles 90017

SEAGREN, DANIEL ROBERT, chaplain, clergyman; b. Oct. 31, 1927, Chgo.; s. Elmer Frederich and Selma (Hill) S.; m. Barbara Anne Johnson, Mar. 21, 1959; children: Laurie b. 1960, Scott b. 1964; edn: BA, Univ. Minnesota, 1950; MA, USC, 1959; dipl. North Park Seminary, Ill. 1953; ordained Evangelical Covenant Ch. 1956.; cert. in counseling Univ. of Calif., Santa Barbara 1987. Career: faculty Azusa Coll. 1959-62; admin. No. Park Coll. 1962-66; pastor Evangelical Covenant Ch., Berkeley 1970-74; internat. pastor Immanuel Ch., Sweden 1974-77; pastor Evangelical Covenant Ch., Mich. 1977-82, internat. pastor, Mexico 1982-84; chaplain Samarkand Retirement Community, Santa Barbara 1985-95 (ret.); exec. dir. Conference Ctr. 1957-62; minister of youth/music First Covenant Ch., L.A. 1955-59, minister of youth (Minn.) 1966-69; secty. Morning Song, 1985–; mem: Rotary (Berkeley), Kiwanis (Muskegon, Mich.); author numerous articles, plays, booklets, papers, radio talks, TV scripts, columnist; anchor man The Living Word (weekly TV pgm.) 1977-82; columnist The City Parson (daily newspaper) 1971-74; author 9 books for youth and adult 1969–; mil: U.S. Navy, 1946; Independent ; Protestant Evangelical Covenant; rec: music, writing, sports, travel. Res: 2843 Miradero Dr #B Santa Barbara 93105 Ofc: 2550 Treasure Dr Santa Barbara 93105

SEAMOUNT, DANIEL TAYLOR, land surveyor, forester; b. May 26, 1923, Newton, Kans.; s. Dan and Flossie Mabel (Taylor) S.; m. Janet Underwood, Sept. 9, 1950; children: Daniel, Jr. b. 1951, Ann Marie b. 1953, Nancy b. 1955, Jean b. 1957, Susan b. 1960, Mary b. 1961, David b. 1963; edn: BS in forestry, UC Berkeley 1950, MBA, 1951; Reg. Profl. Forester, Calif. 1974, lic. Land Surveyor in Wash., Calif. 1964, Calif. Std. tchg. cred.- surveying, math., lic. Agricultural Pest Control Advr. 1990, Calif. Peace Officer. Career: forester Union Lumber Co., Fort Bragg 1951-52; instr. South Fork Union High Sch., Miranda 1952-55; logging engr. Crown Zellerbach Corp., Cathlamet, Wash. 1955-57; jr. coll. instr. Olympic Coll., Bremerton, Wash. 1957-60; wage-hour investigator US Dept. of Labor, Riverside, Calif. 1960-62; researcher Tree Crop Harvesting Systems and Farm Labor Efficiency, UC Riverside, 1962-73; timber mgmt. Golden State Building Prods., Redlands 1973-74; forester and land surveyor Calif. Dept. Forestry, 1974–; honors: Lettered in track (3 yrs.) and cross-country (4 yrs.) UC Berkeley, Zi Sigma Phi, Order of the Golden Bear; mem. Soc. of Am. Foresters (chpt. chmn. 1986), Calif. Land Surveyors Assn.; patentee: swing seat used in picking fruit; contbr. 14 research publs. in harvesting efficiency of agricultural tree crops (1965-74); mil: s/sgt. US Army Air Corps 1943-46; Democrat; R.Cath.; rec: road racing, backpacking, x-c skiing. Res: 6655 N Anna St Fresno 93710 Ofc: Calif. Dept. of Forestry and Fire Protection, Ahwahnee Forest Fire Station, PO Box 67, Ahwahnee 93601

SEAWARD, LAURENCE RONALD, financier; b. Nov. 24, 1931, Los Angeles; s. Walter T. and Hildegarde E. (Lossone) S.; m. Mary Louise Dare, May 15, 1949; children: Laurence II b. 1952, Debbi b. 1954, Michael b. 1956; edn: Pierce Coll., 1950. Career: with Pacific Telephone Co., 1954-82: svc. engr. L.A. 1954-64, adminstrv. staff supr. S.F. 1964-66, dist. mgr. L.A. 1966-70, sales and svc. mgr. Pasadena 1970-72, staff supr., mgr. L.A. 1972-76, govt. mgr. So. Calif. area 1976-79; staff mgr. A.T.& T., Basking Ridge, N.J. 1979-80; adminstrv. mgr. Pacific Tel., L.A. 1980-82; financier prin., Palm Desert 1982–; mil: p.o. 2c USN 1951-54, Korean Svc., Nat. Def., UN, Good Conduct, Korean, P.U.C., Commendn. ribbons; rec: tennis, golf. Address: 38-568 Bautista Canyon Way Palm Desert 92260

SEAWRIGHT, MARY SILAN, teacher, promoter of fine arts in education, philanthropist; b. Aug. 17, 1916, Rankin, Pa.; d. Kliment and Bozana (Jovan) Silan; m. Delmar Seawright, Sept. 11, 1943 (dec.); edn: cert. Music Inst., Pgh. 1937-43; BA, CSU Sacto., 1954; MA, and PhD, Century Univ., 1986, 1987. Career: pvt. and pgh. public sch. piano tchr., Pittsburgh, Pa. 1937-43, 46-48; tchr. Trenton (N.Dak.) Sch., 1943-45; Marysville (Ca.) Jt. Unified Schs. 1948-52, (travel Europe 1952-53), 1953–, mem. curriculum com. 1987, 88, 89; mem. Golden Empire Reading Council; advy. bd. Animal Health Technology Pgm., Yuba Coll. 1989-93; honors: pres's award Am. Lung Assn. No. Calif., Chico 1979-80, outstanding tchr. Feather River Service Ctr., Marysville 1986, Lifetime Recognition award Sacto. Opera Assn. 1994; mem: Marysville Unif. Tchrs. Assn., Calif. Tchrs. Assn., NEA, PTA, Delta Kappa Gamma, Century Univ. Alumni Assn. (bd. 1991-93); civic: Arts Council Marysville, Western Soc. of Naturalists (donor 1978–), Trenton St. N. Dak. (scholarship donor 1986–), Veterinary Sch. of Med. UC Davis (scholarship donor 1987–), Endowment Circle Sacramento Opera Assn. (donor), Am. Lung Assn. No. Calif. (bd. 1972-87); Fund for Animals 1976–, Met. Opera Guild, NY (mem. and contbr.), Endowment

Instrumental Music Dept. of Sacramento Country Sch., charter supporter U.S. Holocaust Mus., W.D.C.; Dissertation: Fine Arts in Primary Grades, 1987; Democrat; rec: opera, painting, travels. Res: 229 E 12th St Marysville 95901

SEDLAK, BONNIE JOY, biologist, biotechnology consultant; b. Jan. 30, 1943, Oak Park, Ill.; d. Raymond and Eleanore Mildred (Rada) Sedlak; edn: BA, Northwestern Univ., 1965; MA, Case Western Reserve, 1968; PhD, Northwestern Univ., 1974. Career: res. asst. Case Western, Cleveland, Oh. 1965-68, res. assoc. Northwestern, Evanston, Ill. 1965-74, post-doc. Rush Med. Coll. Chgo. 1974-75; asst. prof. Smith Coll., Northampton, Mass. 1975-77; asst., assoc., tenured prof. State Univ. New York, Purchase, N.Y. 1977-81; assoc. res. scientist Univ. Calif., Irvine, 1981-85; biomed. field sales cons. N. Am. Sci. Assocs., 1986-87; pgm. mgr. Microbics Corp., 1987-88; sr. analyst Fritzsche, Pambianchi and Assocs. Inc., internat. cons. firm in health care bus., 1988-90; cons. prin., San Diego 1990-91; new bus. devel. and licensing mgr. Becton Dickinson Adv. Cellular Biology, San Jose 1991-92; licensing ofcr. Univ. of Calif. 1992-94; listed Who's Who of Am. Men & Women of Sci. (1979, 86); publs: 17 peer rev. sci. papers (1975-86), 9 pub. abstracts (1974-88), 30+ bus. articles (1987-92); rec: painting. Address: PO Box 3021 Half Moon Bay 94019

SEEGALL, MANFRED ISMAR LUDWIG, contract research engineer, educator, freelance and technical writer, retired real estate executive, retired physicist; b. Dec. 23, 1929, Berlin, Germany, came to U.S., 1952, naturalized, 1957; s. Leonhard and Vera Antonie (Vodackova) S.; m. Alma R. Sterner Clarke; 2 stepchildren: James, Mark; edn: BS (magna cum laude), Loyola Coll., 1957; MS, Brown Univ., 1960; PhD, Stuttgart Tech. Univ., Ger. 1965. Career: res. engr. Autonetics Corp. div. of North Am. Aviation, Downey, 1959-61; physicist Astronautics div. Gen. Dynamics, Inc., San Diego 1961-62; res. scientist Max Planck Inst., Stuttgart, 1962-65; instr. statistics and algebra San Diego City Coll., 1966; sr. res. engr. Solar div. Internat. Harvester, San Diego 1967-73; res. cons. in energy and pollution, San Diego 1974-83; sr. scientist Evaluation Res. Corp., San Diego 1981-82; RCS analyst Teledyne Micronetics, 1983-84; sr. design specialist Alcoa Defense Systems, 1984-87; cons. physical scis., 1987-89; independent contr. engring. res., tech. writing, and real estate 1990-93; instr. San Diego City Coll. 1966, Mesa Coll. 1980-81, Grossmont Coll. 1981; mem: IEEE (sr.), Internat. Platform Assn., Calif. Parapsychology Found. (pres. 1994–, secty. res. com.), Cottage of Czechoslovakia of House of Pacific Rels., Rosicrucian Order, Loyola Coll., Brown Univ. alumni assns.; inventions: catalyst for reducing NOx, 1975, App. for Indicating Gas Temp., 1975, Temp. Meas. Apparatus & Method, 1974; publ: Parametric Design Study of Comp., 1987; Republican; R.Cath.; rec: history, philosophy, parapsychology, chess, travel. Res: 8735 Blue Lake Dr San Diego 92119

SEFTON, WILLIAM LEE, certified public accountant; b. Dec. 7, 1943, San Francisco; s. Seibert Lee and Mimi (Stone) S.; m. Wilann Jean, Feb. 14, 1970; children: Robin; edn: BA, Willamette Univ. 1965; M.Acctg., Univ. So. Calif., Los Angeles 1966; CPA, Calif. Career: controller Dataquest Inc., Cupertino 1979-80; pvt. practice public acctg., San Ramon 1980–; mem: Am. Inst. CPAs, Calif. Soc. CPAs, Crow Canyon HOA (past pres.); mil: US Coast Guard 1977; Republican; Mormon. Res: 2011 Saint George Rd Danville 94526 Ofc: 2551 San Ramon Valley Blvd Ste 238 San Ramon 94583

SEGAL, SERAPHINE GEISMAR, art director, painter; b. Oct. 5, 1948, New Orleans, La.; d. Leon Segal and Florette Sera (Geismar) Margolis; m. Alsberg, Sept. 1969 (div. 1979); edn: Univ. SW La. 1967-69; Tualne Univ. 1969; BA, 2-D design, CSU Northridge 1975; BFA, advt. design, Art Center Coll. of Design Pasadena 1984. Career: art dir. Freeman & Assoc., Beverly Hills 1984-85; IAPA & Speciality Automotive Mags., N. Hollywood 1985; owner Geismar, Segal & Moody Design, freelance advt./graphic design firm, Studio City 1984–; freelance painter, Studio City 1967–; instr. graphic design and advt. Glendale Coll. 1987-93, Pierce Coll., Woodland Hills 1985-89, CSU Northridge 1987-88; instr. painting and drawing UCLA 1987-90; instr. visual commns. UC Santa Barbara Ext. 1989–; instr. computer design Moorpark Coll. 1993; art dir. film Return of the Country, 1984, prop maker t.v. series Little House on the Prairie; background artist Hanna-Barbara Studios. Address: Studio City 91604

SEGALL, MARK MELVYN, physician; b. Jan. 20, 1948, NY, NY; s. Solomon Kief and Sylvia (Stangel) S.; m. Nikki Forbes, Feb. 18, 1978; children: Jeremy b. 1979, Eli b. 1982, Leah b. 1984, Noah b. 1990; edn: undergrad. Wayne St. Univ., Univ. Mich., MD, Univ. Mich. Med. Sch., 1972; cert. Am. Bd. Surgery, 1980, Am. Bd. Colon and Rectal Surgery, 1980. Career: family practice of med. So. Calif. Permanente Med. Group, West L.A. 1973-75; surgeon Michigan Colon & Rectal Surgeons, P.C., Southfield, Mich. 1980-83; solo practice of colon and rectal surgery, Los Gatos 1983–; clin. instr. dept. surgery Wayne St. Univ. Sch. of Med., 1981-84, Stanford Univ. Med. Sch., 1985–; awards: Ohio Valley Proctologic Soc. paper award 1980; mem: Soc. Am. Gastrointestinal Endoscopic Surgeons, No. Calif. Soc. Colon and Rectal Surgeons (pres. 1988-89), San Jose Surg. Soc., Santa Clara Surg. Soc., A.C.S. (fellow), Am. Soc. Colon and Rectal Surgeons (fellow), N.W. Soc. Colon and Rectal Surgeons, AMA, CMA, Santa Clara Co. Med. Soc.; publs. in med. literature; Democrat; Jewish. Ofc: 15195 National Ave Ste 202 Los Gatos 95032

SEGEL, KAREN LYNN JOSEPH, attorney, certified tax professional; b. Jan. 15, 1947, Youngstown, Ohio; d. Samuel Dennis and Helen Anita Joseph; grandfather, James Michael Joseph; m. Alvin Gerald Segel, June 9, 1968, div. 1977; 1 son, Adam James b. 1975; edn: BA in Soviet & E. Euro. Studies, Boston Univ., 1968; JD, Southwestern Univ. Sch. Law, 1975. Career: High Sch. Amb. People-To-People Org., 1963; adminstrv. asst. Olds Brunel & Co., NYC 1968-69; U.S. Banknote Corp., NYC 1969-70; tax acct. S.N. Chilkov & Co., CPAs, Beverly Hills 1971-74; intern Calif. Corporations Commr., L.A. 1974-75; tax sr. Oppenheim, Appel & Dixon, L.A. 1977-78; Fox, Westheimer & Co., L.A. 1978; Zebrak, Levine & Mepos, L.A. 1978-79; indep. cons. acct., tax splst., Beverly Hills 1980–; dir. World Wide Motion Picture Corp.; honors: Boston Univ. Dean's List, honors dorm Raleigh House, Disting. Lecture Series 1965-68, listed Who's Who in West 1978; mem. editl. advy. bd. Am. Biog. Inst. (ABI), advy. bd. Women's Inner Cir. of Achiev., named ABI woman of yr. 1991and 1993, listed with issue dedication: 2000 Notable Am. Women (3d), World Who's Who of Women (11th), Internat. Dir. Disting. Leadership 1991, Intl. Who's Who of Intellectuals (9th), listed Comm. Leaders Am., Who's Who in Finance & Industry, Who's Who in World; mem. Nat. Soc. of Tax Profls.; civic: Center Theater Group, Young Symphonians L.A., Nat. Trust for Hist. Preserv., Winterthur Guild, Am. Mus. Natural Hist.; Jewish; rec: travel, collect seashells, raise Lhasa Apso dogs. Address: Beverly Hills

SEIBERT, EVETT P., administrative assistant; b. Aug. 9, 1956, Porterville; d. Gayle Lee and Patsy Ruth (Zellars) Hamma; m. Jeffery Seibert, July 29, 1978; 2 sons: Kyle b. 1989, Trevor b. 1992; edn: BA, CSU Bakersfield, 1988. Career: tchr. Christian Sch., Wilmington 1981-82; instr. San Joaquin Valley Coll., Bakersfield 1985-88; owner Omega Computer Services, 1989–; Republican; Prot.; rec: painting, drawing, sewing. Res: 4825 E Indianapolis Ave Fresno 93726 Ofc: Trans States Airlines Inc 5175 E Clinton Way #10 Fresno 93727

SEIDENGLANZ, KERRY THOMAS, real estate developer; b. Dec. 12, 1949, Glendale, Calif.; s. Robert Leo and Gloria Lucille (Munson) S.; m. Maureen Suzzan Fennell, Jan. 12, 1980; children: Megan b. 1982, Shaun b. 1983, Chelsia b. 1989, Shannon b. 1990; edn: AA, CSU Northridge 1971. Career: real estate agt. Indsl. Security Real Estate, Sun Valley 1971-74, real estate broker 1974-78, co-owner 1978-90; ceo American Diversified Properties 1988–; mem: Am. Indsl. Real Estate Assn., Nat. Assn. Real Estate Appaisers, San Fernando Valley Realty Bd., Internat. Council Shopping Centers, Calif. Manufactured Housing Inst. (bd. dirs.), Sun Valley C.of C. (v.p. 1977-80), Rotary (secty. 1980), Canyon Country C.of C.; Republican; R.Cath.; rec: boating, snow & water skiing. Ofc: American Diversified Properties 9265 Glenoaks Blvd Sun Valley 91352

SEITZ, WALTER STANLEY, cardiologist; b. May 10, 1937, L.A., Calif.; s. Walter and Frances Janette (Schleef) S.; edn: BS, physics & math, UC Berkeley, 1959; Plasma Physics Inst., Princeton, N.J., 1964; PhD, biophysics, Univ. of Vienna, Austria, 1981; MD, Univ. of Vienna Faculty of Medicine, 1982; E.C.F.M.G. Cert. 1982; Med. License, State of Ill., 1983. Career: health physicist, UC Radiation Lab., 1959-61; res. assoc., NIH at Pacific Union Coll., res. physicist at Lockheed Res. Labs., Angwin and Palo Alto, Calif., 1961-63; staff scientist, Xerox Corp., Pasadena, Calif., 1963-66; sr. scientist, Applied Physics Consultants, Palo Alto, 1966-75; grad. student in medicine and biophysics, resident in internal medicine, Univ. of Vienna, Stanford Univ. Hosp. and res. assoc. at the Inst. for Med. Analysis, Vienna, 1975-82; instr., clinical sci., Univ. of Ill. Coll. of Medicine, Urbana, 1983-84; post-doctoral res. scholar, Cardiovascular Res. Inst., UC Sch. of Medicine, S.F., 1984-87; cons. in cardiology, Cardiovascular Res. Inst., UC Sch. of Medicine, S.F., and sr. scientist , Inst. for Med. Analysis and Res., Berkeley, 1987–; honors: Post-Doctoral Res. Fellowship, UC, S.F., 1984; Fellow, Am. Coll. of Angiography, NY, 1987; mem: AAAS, 1983–; NY Acad. of Sciences, 1984–; Physicians for Social Responsibility, 1985–; The Royal Soc. of Medicine, London, 1985–; publs.: over 25 res. and profl. papers pub. in scientific journals, 1964–; patent application: instrument to measure mitral valve pressure gradient and capillary wedge pressure from standard electrocardiogram, 1980; rec: reading, music, painting.

SELANDIA, ELIZABETH, doctor of Oriental medicine, acupuncturist; b. Apr. 3, 1945, Santa Barbara; d. Fredrick Bunnell Pulling, Jr. and Anna LaVerne (Welch) Pulling; m. William Kent Selandia, July 19, 1967 (div. 1977); m. Carsten Hennier, Feb. 4, 1981 (widowed 1986); children: Karina Vanessa Selandia b. 1972 Glostrup, Denmark; edn: grad. San Francisco Coll. of Oriental Medicine & Acupuncture, S.F. 1986; doctor of Oriental medicine, Postgrad. of S.F. Coll. of Oriental Medicine, S.F. 1986; AA in French, Humanities & Behavioral Sciences, College of Marin, Kentfield 1992; BA (with highest honors) in Native Am. studies & linguistics, UC Berkeley 1994; OMD, C.A. Diplomat N.C.C.A. Career: self-employed: astrologer/palmist, worldwide 1967–, importer/exporter, Copenhagen, Denmark 1972-77, gourmet cook & housekeeper, Colo. & Calif. 1977-82; editorial asst. Unix\World Magazine, Mt. View, Calif. 1985-91; doctor of Oriental medicine, self-employed, S.F. Bay Area, No. Calif. 1987–; tchr. of astrology DeKosmos, Amsterdam, Holland 1969; librarian S.F. Coll. of Acupuncture, S.F. 1985-90, tchr. of herbology 1988-89; art show coordinator UAC '95, Monterey; awards: Outstanding Student in Algebra II, French II, Chemistry & Analytical Geometry, Mission Central

H.S., San Luis Obispo 1960-63, lifetime membership Calif. Scholarship Fedn. 1963, Honor Roll Alpha Gamma Sigma, College of Marin 1992, Dean's List UC Berkeley 1992-94, juried art show Best of Show, People's Choice 1995, First and Third Prizes in "One World Under the Stars Art Show", Monterey 1995; mem. Nat. Council for Geocosmic Res. 1980–, Young Scandinavians Club 1985–; author: pub. articles in HALI 1982, 83, Oriental Medicine 1994; editorial asst. (book): Wheel of Times and Mandala by Barry Bryant 1993; ed., compiler & annotator (book): Gently Whispered: Oral Teachings by Kalu Rinpoche 1994; Democrat; Vajrayana Buddhism; rec: I Ching solutions, knitting, cooking, reading. Res: PO Box 827 Larkspur 94977

SELIG, ROBERT W., theatre industry executive; b. Feb. 1, 1910, Cripple Creek, Colo.; s. Adolph and Eva (Cashman) S.; m. Olive McClain Slinde, Dec. 25, 1935; 1 son, Robert W. b. 1939; edn: BA, Univ. Denver 1932; DPS, 1940. Career: advtg. sales 20th Century Fox, Denver, Colo. 1933-36; booker Gaumont British Picture Corp. 1936-37, western div. mgr., San Francisco 1937-40; pres. Intermountain Fox Theatres, Denver, Colo. 1940-61; gen. mgr. Nat. Theatres Amusement Corp., Los Angeles 1961-65, v.p. Pacific Theatres 1965-89; mem: Theatre Assn. Calif. (pres. 1981-89), NATO of Calif. (pres. 1989); mil: U.S. Treasury Dept.; Methodist. Res: 11563 Dona Teresa, N Hollywood 91604 Ofc: NATO of California 116 N Robertson Blvd Ste 706 Los Angeles 90048 also: Pacific Theatres, 120 N Robertson Blvd Los Angeles 90048

SELKIN, CARL MATTHEW, professor of English; b. Nov. 26, 1943, New York, NY; s. William Selkin and Mollie (Lerner) Heiman; m. Carol Elizabeth Wakesberg, June 20, 1965; children: Peter b. 1975, Eli b. 1979; edn: BA, Syracuse Univ. 1965; MA, State Univ. of N.Y., Binghamton 1977, PhD, 1974. Career: lectr. SUNY-Binghamton 1968-69; prof. of English Calif. State Univ., Los Angeles 1970–, English Dept. chair 1991-94, acting dean Sch. of Arts and Letters 1994–; mem Academic Senate, CSU, L.A. 1992–; lectr. in field; awards: Univ. Fellowship 1969-70, CSLA Meritorious Performance and Promise awards 1987, 88, Fulbright Fellow (travel award, France, 1988), invited prof. Universite Blaise Pascal 1989, Fulbright lecture Universite d'haute Alsace 1989, recipient num. grants in the Arts, Humanities and other areas; mem: Modern Lang. Assn. of Am., Art Historians of So. Calif. (life), Assn. for Canadian Studies in U.S., Western States Consortium for Canadian Studies, Nat. Council of Tchrs. of English, Assoc. Depts. of English, CSU English Council, Mus. of Contemporary Art, L.A. Co. Mus. of Art, Southwest Mus., Pacific Asia Mus., Armory Ctr. for the Arts; civic: Luckman Complex (comm. advy. bd. and advy. bd. steering com.), Arts and Letters Angels (bd.), Southwest Chamber Music Soc. (bd.), Dorland Mountain Arts Colony (review bd.), Music Ctr. Edn. Com.; assoc. editor The Altadena Review, 1978-88; author: poems pub. in Yankee Mag., Best U.S. and Canadian Mag. Verse, Gramercy Review; reviews pub. in Mankind: A Mag. of History, Statement; rec: travel, writing. Ofc: School of Arts and Letters Calif. State Univ. Los Angeles 90032

SELLECK, ROBERT DEAN, real estate investor; b. Dec. 27, 1921, Lapeer, Mich.; s. George Samuel and Nellie Louise (Fife) S.; m. Martha Jagger, Apr. 11, 1942; children: Robert II, Thomas, Martha, Daniel; edn: Ohio Wesleyan Univ.; Calif. lic. real estate broker (1948). Career: ptnr. George S. Selleck & Sons, gen. contrs., Detroit, Mich. 1946-48; Coldwell, Banker & Co., Los Angeles 1948-63, v.p./ mgr. 1963-84, sr.v.p./dir. corp. communications Coldwell Banker Commercial Group, 1984-87; owner The Selleck Company, 1987–; honors: recipient w/wife, First Annual Premier Parents Award, March of Dimes Birth Defects Found. 1984, San Fernando Valley Humanitarian Award, Project Heavy 1982 and the Fernando Award 1982; apptd. civic bds: Los Angeles Memorial Coliseum and Sports Arena Commn. (1977-84, pres. 1980), L.A. Olympic Organizing Com. (dir. 1979-86), L.A. Rec. & Parks Commn. (1977-84, pres. 1979 and 1984), Health Dynamics, Inc. (dir., v.chmn.), Valley Presbyterian Hosp. (bd. dirs.); mem: Valley Industry and Commerce Assn. (dir, pres. 1973), L.A. Bd. of Realtors 1948–; clubs: Lakeside Golf (pres. 1976-77), Desert Horizons CC; mil: Army Air Corps 1943-45; Republican; Congregational; rec: golf, gardening. Ofc: The Selleck Company, 21600 Oxnard St Ste 350 Woodland Hills 91367

SELLER, GREGORY EROL, marketing executive, writer; b. Oct. 4, 1953, Denver, Colo.; s. Otto Gustave and Dolores Louise (Crawford) S.; edn: BS in bus., Univ. Colo., 1975. Career: group rep. Great-West Life Corp., Denver, Colo. 1975-78, mgt. group mktg. 1978-82, asst. v.p. 1982-85; pres./chief ops. Benefits Communication Corp. (subs. co. Great-West Life) 1985-88, mem. bd. dirs. 1984–; v.p. major accounts Great-West Life, Los Angeles 1988–; listed Who's Who in Sales & Mktg. 1987-94; Delta Upsilon Frat.; Democrat; Episcopalian. Res: 37 New York Court Monarch Beach 92629 Ofc: Great-West Life Corp. 18101 Von Karman Ave. Suite 1460 Irvine 92715

SELZ, PETER HOWARD, educator; b. Munich, Germany, Mar. 22, 1919; came to US 1936, nat. 1942; s. Eugene and Edith S.; m. Thalia Cheronis, June 10, 1948; div. 1965; children: Tanya Nicole Eugenia, Diana Gabrielle Hamlin; m. Carole Schemmerling, Dec. 14, 1983; edn: student, Columbia Univ., Univ. Paris; MA, Univ. of Chgo., 1949; PhD 1954; DFA, Calif. Coll. Arts and Crafts, 1967. Career: instr, Univ. of Chgo. 1951-56; asst. prof. art history, head art edn.

dept. Inst. Design, Ill. Inst. Tech., Chgo. 1949-55; chmn art dept., dir. art gallery Pomona Coll. 1955-58; curator dept. painting and sculpture exhbns. Mus. Modern Art 1958-65; dir. univ. art mus. UC Berkeley 1965-73, prof. history of art, 1965–; Zaks prof. Hebrew Univ., Jerusalem 1976; vis. prof. CUNY 1987; mem. president's council on art and architecture Yale Univ. 1971-76; trustee Am. Crafts Council 1983-88; pres. Berkeley Art Project 1988–; mem. advy. council archives Am. Art 1971–; project dir. Christo's Running Fence 1973-76; awards: decorated Order of Merit Fed. Republic Germany, Fulbright grantee Paris 1949-50, fellow Belgian-Am. Ednl. Found., sr. fellow Nat. Endowment for Humanities 1972; mem: Coll. Art Assn. (dir. 1959-64, 67-71), AAUP, Internat. Art Critics Assn.; author: German Expressionist Painting, 1957, New Images of Man, 1959, Art Nouveau, 1960, Mark Rothko, 1961, Fifteen Polish Painters, 1961, The Art of Jean Dubuffet, 1962, Emil Nolde, 1963, Max Beckmann, 1964, Alberto Giacometti, 1965, Directions in Kinetic Sculpture, 1966, Funk, 1967, Harold Paris, 1972, Ferdinand Hodler, 1972, Sam Francis, 1975, The American Presidency in Political Cartoons, 1976, Art in Our Times, 1981, Art in a Turbulent France, 1985, Chillida, 1986, Max Beckmann: The Self Portraits, 1992; editor, Art in Am., 1967–; Art Quarterly., 1969-75, Arts, 1981–; contbr articles to art publs.; with OSS AUS 1941-46. Ofc: Dept. Art History Univ. of California, Berkeley 94720

SEPPI, EDWARD JOSEPH, physicist; b. Dec. 16, 1930, Price, Utah; s. Joseph and Fortunata (Seppi); m. Betty Stowell, Aug. 25, 1953; children: Duane b. 1955, Kevin b. 1959, Cynthia b. 1968; edn: BS, Brigham Young Univ., Provo 1952; MS, Univ. Idaho, 1956; PhD, Calif. Inst. of Tech., 1962, Research fellow 1962. Career: staff physicist Inst. for Def. Analysis, W.D.C., 1962-64, cons. 1964-72; head exptl. fac. dept. SLAC, Stanford 1966-68; mgr. medical diagnosis Varian Assocs., Palo Alto 1974-76, senior scientist 1980-91; senior scientist Superconducting Super Collider, Dallas 1990-91; principal scientist Varian, Palo Alto 1991–; honors: Phi Eta Sigma 1952, Phi Kappa Phi 1962; mem.: Am. Physical Soc. 1952–; civic: BSA, Menlo Park (asst. scoutmaster 1969-75), Ladera Comm. Assn., Portola Valley (bd. 1988-90); inventor 22 sci. patents (med. instrumentation), author 82+ sci. publs. and abstracts; Ch. of Jesus Christ of LDS; rec: photography, gardening, computers. Res: 320 Dedalera Dr Portola Valley 94028

SERBEIN, OSCAR NICHOLAS, business educator, consultant; b. Mar.31, 1919, Collins, Iowa; s. Oscar Nicholas and Clara Matilda (Shearer) S.; m. Alice Marie Bigger, Sept. 16, 1952; children: Mary Llewellyn Serbein Parker, John Gregory; edn: BA with highest distinction, Univ. of Iowa 1940, MS, 1941, PhD, Columbia Univ. 1951. Career: grad. asst. math. Univ. of Iowa, Iowa City, 1940-41; clerk Metropolitan Life Ins. Co., N.Y.C. 1941-42; lectr. UC Berkeley, summer 1948, 50; lectr., asst. prof., assoc. prof. Columbia Univ. 1947-59; prof. ins. Stanford Univ. 1959-89, prof. emeritus ins., 1989–; dir. doctoral prog. Grad. Sch. of Bus., Stanford Univ. 1960-64; cons. Ins. Info. Inst., N.Y.C. 1971-78, N. Am. Re-Assurance Life Svc. Co., Palo Alto 1973, SRI Internat., Menlo Park 1980-81, other bus.; cons., expert witness various law firms; bd. dirs. Sr. Citizens Coord. Council, Palo Alto 1986-89, dir. emeritus, 1990–; honors: decorated Bronze Star, 1944; mem: Am. Risk and Ins. Assn., Western Risk and Ins. Assn, Phi Beta Kappa, Sigma Xi, Beta Gamma Sigma; club: Stanford Faculty; author: Paying For Medical Care in the U.S., 1953, Educational Activities of Business, 1961; co-author: Property and Liability Insurance, 4 edit. 1967, Risk Management: Text and Cases, 2 edit., 1983; numerous pub. articles; mil: served to major USAF, WW II; Democrat; Methodist. Res: 731 SanRafael Place Stanford 94305-1007 Ofc: Stanford University Grad Sch Bus Stanford 94305

SERNA, JOE, JR., mayor; b. 1939, Stockton, Calif.; m. Isabel; children: Philip and Lisa; edn: BA in social sci./govt., Sacramento State Coll. 1966; grad. studies in political sci., UC Davis. Career: comm. devel. vol., Peace Corps, Guatemala, 1966; mem. Sacramento City Council representing Dist. 5, 1981-92; mayor, City of Sacramento 1992-; appt. Sacramento's first Council of Economic Advisors, founder Mayor's Summer Reading Camp, Thursday Night Market (downtown Farmer's Market), 1992-; faculty mem. Calif. State Univ., Sacto. 1969-75, 1977- (currently prof. of govt.); co-trustee Crocker Art Museum Assn.; mem. Sacto. Regional Transit Bd. of Dirs., Sacto. Housing and Redevel. Commn., Sacto. City/County Sports Commn. (former chmn.), SETA (former med. of bd.) former mem. Sacto. Metropolitan Cable TV Commn., Sacto. Central Labor Council; dir. United Farmworkers of Am. Support Com., Sacto. Co. 1970-75; former chmn. of several Hispanic organizations; edn. adv. to then-Lt. Gov. Mervyn Dymally 1975-77; chair Sacto. City Council budget & fin. com. 1981-89, transportation & comm. devel. com. 1989-92, mem. law & legislative com. 1989-92, founder Neighborhood Services Dept.; awards: Disting. Faculty award CSU Sacto. 1991, Economic Devel. Leadership award Nat. Council for Urban Econ. Devel. 1994. Ofc: Office of Mayor Sacramento

SERRANTINO, SALVATORE, management consulting company president; b. Aug. 30, 1932, Hartford, Conn.; s. Sebastian and Vencenza (Felichia) S.; m. Margaret Multz, May 14, 1966; dau., Sabrina b. 1973; edn: AA, State Tech. Inst., 1955; BS, Univ. Conn., 1960. Career: asst. v.p., v.p. American Savings Bank, Whittier 1960-64; v.p. Home Savings of Am., Beverly Hills 1964-66; v.p. Ray Burn Inc., L.A. 1966; advt. adminstr. Petersen Pub. Co., L.A. 1966-69; v.p. First Charter Fin. Corp., Beverly Hills 1969-75; exec. v.p. Market Insight Corp.,

San Francisco 1975-77; CFO, dir. California Site Finders, Santa Monica 1977-93; pres., dir. California Research Corp., 1977-93, publisher, mng. editor CRC Report, 1984-93, 94; pres. Calif. Corporate Development Corp., Beverly Hills 1994-; dir. Columbia Nat. Bank 1983-85; chmn. bd., dir. Nat. Lenders Network 1986; chmn. bd., dir. CRC Mortgage Corp., 1987; seminar lectr. UC Berkeley 1981-82, UCLA 1980-84, UC Irvine 1983-84, American Banker 1990; conf. lectr. Grad. Sch. of Mgmt., UC Irvine, 1986; awards: Gold Medal Long Beach Senior Olympics (racquetball, singles) 1992, 2 Silver Medals 1993; mem. Consultants Roundtable (chmn., pres., dir., 1980–); mil: M.I. AUS 1955-57. Res: 1134 Coldwater Canyon Dr Beverly Hills 90210 Ofc: California Corporate Development Corp. 1134 Coldwater Canyon Dr Beverly Hills 90210

SESSLER, ANDREW MARIENHOFF, physicist; b. Dec. 11, 1928, Brooklyn; s. David and Mary (Baron) S.; m. Gladys Lerner, Sept. 23, 1951 (div. 1994); children: Daniel Ira, Jonathan Lawrence, Ruth; edn: BA in math. (cum laude), Harvard Univ., 1949, MA in theoretical physics, 1953. Career: NSF Fellow, Cornell Univ., N.Y. 1953-54; asst. prof. Ohio State Univ., Columbus 1954, assoc. prof. 1960, on lv. Midwestern Univs. Res. 1955-56, vis. physicist Lawrence Radiation Lab. 1959-60, Niels Bohr Inst., Copenhagen summer 1961; res. scientist Univ. Calif. Lawrence Berkeley Lab., Berkeley, 1961–: in theoretical physics 1961-73, energy and environment 1971-73, dir. 1973-80, sr. scientist plasma physics 1980–, sci. policy bd. Stanford Synchrotron Radiation Lab. 1991-92, sci. policy com. Superconducting Super Collider 1992-94; L.J. Haworth dist. scientist Brookhaven Nat. Lab. 1991-92; chmn. sci. policy bd. Stanford Synchrotron Radiation Project 1974-77, mem. advy. com. Lawrence Hall of Sci. 1974-78, EPRI Advanced Fuels Adv. Com. 1978-81, BNL external advy. com. on Isabelle 1980-82; appt. U.S. advisor Punjab Univ. Physics Inst., Chandigarh, India; mem. U.S.-India cooperative pgm. for improvement of sci. edn. in India 1966, high energy physics advy. panel to U.S. AEC 1969-72; mem. hon. advy. bd. Inst. for Adv. Physics Studies, La Jolla Internat. Sch. of Physics 1991–; awards: E.O. Lawrence award U.S. AEC 1970, U.S. Particle Accelerator Sch. prize 1988, fellow Japan Soc. for Promotion of Sci. at KEK 1985, recipient Nicholson Medal for Humanitarian Service, APS 1994; mem: AAAS (fellow, nom. com. 1984-87), Am. Physical Soc. (fellow, chmn. com. internat. freedom scientist 1982, study of directed energy weapons panel 1985-87, chmn. panel public affairs 1988, chmn. div. physics of beams 1990, com. on appls. of physics 1991–), NAS, IEEE (sr. mem.), Fedn. Am. Scientists Council (v.chmn. 1987, chmn. 88–), N.Y. Acad. Sci., Assoc. Univ. Inc. (bd. 1991–); publs: editl. bd. Nuclear Instruments and Methods 1969–, corr. Comments on Modern Physics 1969-71, articles in profl. jours. Res: 225 Clifton St Apt 313 Oakland 94618 Ofc: Univ. California Lawrence Berkeley Lab. 1 Cyclotron Rd MS 71-259 Berkeley 94720 Tel: 415/486-4992

SEVERO, ORLANDO CHARLES, JR., air force officer, space & missile center commander; b. Dec. 22, 1940, Greenwich, Ct.; s. Orlando C., Sr. and Filomena (Ferraro) S.; m. Joan Elza Skogstrom, June 16, 1962; children: Lori b. 1964, Michael b. 1965, Karen b. 1968; edn: BSEE, Va. Mil. Inst., Lexington, Va. 1962; MSEE, AF Inst. Tech., Wright-Patterson AFB, Oh. 1968. Career: served to Col. (0-6) U.S. Air Force, 1962-91: spacecraft proj. mgr. Los Angeles AFB 1972-76; dir. STS computer systems Vandenberg AFB 1977-81, dir. STS engring. 1981-84; dep. pgm. mgr. STS, NASA, Houston, Tx. 1984-85; cmdr. Shuttle Test Group, USAF, Vandenberg AFB 1985-86;cmdr. Western Space & Missile Center, Vandenberg AFB 1986-91, first Air Force Space Command installation cmdr., Vandenberg AFB; co-founder/chmn. Western Commercial Space Ctr., Inc. 1992-93; founder/ pres./c.e.o. Calif. Commercial Spaceport, Inc. (CCSI) 1993–; awards: num. mil. decorations, NASA Exceptional Service Medal, Houston 1985, Manned Flight Awareness Honoree, NASA, WDC 1991, Air Force Assn. meritorious service award 1991, Hon. PhD-Humane Letters Nat. Christian Univ., Mo. 1986, Distinguished Leadership Award CALP 1994; mem: Lompoc Valley C. of C. (v.p.), Lompoc Unified Sch. Dist. (v.p.), Industrial Educ. Council, Western Spaceport Mus. & Sci. Ctr. (v.p., bd. trustees) 1988–; Santa Barbara Co. Economic Dev. Com. (commr.), Kts. Columbus, Odenton, Md. (charter, fin. sec. 1963-66); Republican; R.Cath.; rec: golf, bicycling, backpacking, camping, hunting, fishing. Res: 129 Hercules Ave Lompoc 93436 Ofc: CCSI 3865-A Constellation Rd Lompoc 93436

SEYFERTH, HAROLD HOMER, lecturer, real estate appraiser, retired city planner; b. Jan. 22, 1922, Stockton; s. Lester L. and Beulah May (Perkins) S., father b. in Surprise Valley, Modoc 1896 to pioneer family traveled Oreg. Trail and mother b. 1902 in Chickasaw-Quapaw Reservation, OK; m. Betty Jean Stanley, Apr. 12, 1943; children: Mary B. Hanebuth, Laurence Paul; edn: BA (honors), San Jose State Univ., 1948; MBA, and PhD, Pacific Western Univ., 1981. Career: locomotive engr. Western Pacific R.R., 1939-50 (father was locomotive engr. with co. 43 yrs.); asst. planner City of San Jose, 1950-54; city mgr. Hollister, 1959-63; property mgr. City of Salinas, 1963-68; redevelop. chief land officer City of Seaside, 1968-69; pres. H. Seyferth Assocs., Monterey 1969-92, ret.; teacher, lectr. in field Golden Gate Univ., San Jose State Univ., Hartnell, Monterey Peninsular Coll.; operated orchards, farms, ranches in Santa Clara and San Benito Co.; awards: CORO Found. fellow 1950, grad. fellowship Public Affairs, Who's Who in R.E., Who's Who in the West; mem: San Jose State Univ. Alumni Assn. (pres. Monterey Chpt.), Psy Chi (pres.), Am. Assn. Cert.

Appraisers (cert.), Am. Planning Assn., Calif. Assn. R.E. Tchrs., Internat. Coll. R.E. Cons. Profls., Internat. Inst. Valuers, Internat. Orgn. R.E. Appraisers, Internat. Right of Way Assn., Nat. Assn. Cert. Real Property Appraisers, Nat. Assn. Review Appraisers, R.E. Educators Assn., Urban Land Inst., Assn. Environmental Profl., State Leg. Rep. Railroad Brotherhood, , Am. Philatelic Soc.; civic bds: AARP/VOTE 17th Congl. Dist. Bd., Mariposa Hall (bd. dir.), Enterprise Sch. Dist., Hollister (trustee), Carmel Riviera Mutual Water Co. (chmn.), Boy's City Boy's Club San Jose, Am. Cancer Soc. San Jose, Calif. Historical Soc., Oreg. Historical Soc., Pacheco Club, Sierra (Ventana chpt.), Monterey Peninsula Stamp; mil: USN, amphibious forces Pacific 1942-45. Res: 50 Yankee Point Carmel 93923

SHABOT, MYRON MICHAEL, surgeon, critical care educator; b. Aug. 5, 1945, Houston, Tx.; s. Sam and Mona Doris (Stalarow) S.; 1 son, Samuel Laib b. 1975; edn: BA, Univ. Tx. Austin 1966; MD, Univ. Tx. Dallas 1970; Tulane Univ. New Orleans 1963-64. Career: dir. surgery intensive care unit Harbor UCLA Med. Center, Torrance 1980-82; asst. prof. surgery in residence UC Los Angeles 1980-82; dir. critical care surgery Cedars Sinai Med. Center 1982–; clin. assoc. prof. surgery and anesthesia UCLA 1983–; asst. prof. surgery UCLA Sch. Medicine 1979-82; pres. Computers in Critical Care & Pulmonary Medicine, Norwalk, Conn. 1995–; honors: Phi Eta Sigma; mem: A.C.S. (governor 1994, pres. So. Calif. chpt. 1993–, fellow), Soc. Critical Care Medicine, L.A. Surgical Soc. (secty./treas. 1994–), Western Surgical Assn., Soc. Clin. Data Mgmt. Systems (pres. 1985-86), Pacific Coast Surgical Soc., Temple Beth El (pres. 1991-93); 206 articles, chpts. and abstracts pub. 1975–, editl. bd. Internat. Jour. Clin. Monitoring and Computing, 1984–, Mount Sinai Jour. of Medicine, 1987-88, The Am. Surgeon, 1991–; mil: lt. comdr. USPHS 1971-73; Jewish; rec: radio controlled model aircraft. Ofc: Cedars Sinai Medical Center 8700 Beverly Blvd Ste 8215 Los Angeles 90048

SHAH, JAYENDRA ARVINDLAL, physician; b. Jan. 9, 1937, Nadisar, India, naturalized 1977; s. Arvindlal Harilal and Kamalaben (Arvindlal); m. Usha, Feb. 16, 1963; children: Kenneth, MD b. 1963, Russell, MD b. 1966; edn: inter. sci. undergrad., MB, BS, Gujarat Univ., Ahmedabad, India, 1963; certified Am. Bd. Physical Medicine & Rehabilitation, 1981; diplomate Am. Acad. of Pain Mgmt., 1992; diplomate Am. Bd. Back Surgery 1993. Career: fellow in medicine and rehab. Cornell Univ., N.Y. Med. Coll., UCLA Med. Coll., 1972-75; chief of rehab. services and specialist consultant L.A. County, Long Beach Hosp., 1980-82; facilitator quality improvement, DHS, LBCHC, L.A. Co. 1991-93; special asst. rehab. quality care Rancho LAHC, Downey DHS, L.A. Co. 1994–; rehab. cons. State of Calif. Dept. Disability & Med. Utilization Reviewer 1981-94; dir. Industrial Pain Med. Group (med. service provider co.), Westminster 1981–; neurol. and med. services Beach Neuro Electro Diagnostic Lab., Huntington Beach 1979-86; med. dir. Inst. of Rehabilitative Medicine of So. Calif., Garden Grove 1982-88; recipient recogn. awards Indian Med. Assn. So. Calif. 1985-92, The Gujarati Soc., Norwalk 1984-94, Personalities of Am. "service to profession and community" award; mem: N.Y. Acad. of Sci., Am. Congress Rehab. Medicine, Am. Acad. of Phys. Med. & Rehab. (fellow), Am. Asssn. of Electromyographers, Am. Military Surgeons of U.S., U.S. Flight Surgeons Assn., Internat. Soc. Rehab. Medicine; civic: Fedn. of Indian Assn./F.I.A. (v.p. comm. affairs), The Gujarati Soc. (pres. Norwald R.K. Temple 1992-93), Indian Med. Assn. of So. Calif. (exec. com. 1984-93; organized and managed for Guj. Soc. and Indian Med. Assn. & FIA Health Fair and Cultural Annual Pgm. 1985,88, 90-94), Bharat Vikas Parishad Internat. (founding v.p. Calif. chpt.), Vanik Vaishnav Samaj of So. Calif. (founding pres.), Fedn. of Indian Assns. of So. Calif. (v.p. community affairs 1991-92); mil: major, flt. surgeon USAF Nat. Guard 1979-84, decorated USAF ANG, Wash. DC 1982; rec: table tennis, swimming, travel, flying, cultural programs, Yoga religious festivals-programmer. Res: 1855 S West St Anaheim 92802 Ofc: Jay Shah MD FAA PMR, FAAPM, FABS, Industrial Pain Medical Group, 7960 W McFadden Ave Westminster 90683 Tel: 714-491-9200 FAX 714/897-9384

SHAH, RUGMINI SATHIAPALAN, physician; b. May 25, 1935, Madras, India (nat. 1974); s. U.K. Nair and M.P. Kutty; m. C.K. Sathiapalan, June 2, 2963 (dec. 1972); children: Shalini b. 1966; m. 2. Dhiraj Shah, Aug. 2, 2975; edn: MD, Madras Med. Coll., India 1962. Career: chief, Maternal Child Health Branch, Calif. Dept. Health 1989–; v.p.-health, Sr. Care Action Network, Long Beach 1983-84; mem: Am. Acad. of Pediatrics (fellow 1967–), Am. Soc. of Hematology 1970–, Am. Coll. of Preventive Medicine (fellow 1984–), CMA 1989–, Assn. of Kerala Med. Graduates-USA; group editor (book): Healthy Mom/Healthy Baby, 1993; mil: lt. col. USAR; Republican; Hindu; rec: swimming, traveling. Ofc: California Dept Health 714 P St Rm 750 Sacramento 95814

SHALIT, MARC STANLEY, medical doctor; b. Feb. 17, 1954, Irvington, N.J.; s. Arthur and Holly (Frank) S.; m. Jean Le Chang, DDS, Jan. 27, 1995; edn: BA, psychology, Univ. of Rochester, NY 1977; MD, UC San Francisco 1981; Internal Medicine Bd. cert., Mercy Hosp., San Diego 1981-84; Emergency Medicine Bd. cert., Valley Med. Ctr., Fresno 1984-86. Career: assoc. clin. prof. Dept. of Medicine, UC San Francisco Sch. of Medicine 1986–; asst. chief Dept of Emergency Medicine, Valley Med. Ctr., Fresno 1986–; asst. med. dir. Emergency Med. Svs., Central Calif. Emergency Med. Svs., Fresno 1989–; staff

physician St. Agnes Med. Ctr., Fresno 1988–; indep. medical/legal expert consultation, Fresno 1987–; awards: Teacher of Yr. award Med. Student Assn., Fresno 1987, 88, 91, 93, 94, Outstanding Emergency Medicine Teacher, VMC Emergency Medicine Residency, Fresno 1991, Teacher of Yr. award VMC Family Practice Prog. 1993, 94, Outstanding Faculty Teacher award UCSF/Fresno Med. Edn. Prog. 1993, 94, Kaiser Teaching award UCSF Sch. of Medicine, Fresno 1994; mem: AMA 1981–, Am. Coll. of Physicians 1982–, Am. Coll. of Emergency Physicians 1984–, Soc. for Academic Emergency Medicine 1986–, Am. Acad. of Emergency Medicine 1994–; author: contbr. articles to profl. jours., 1988, 91, 92; rec: soccer, chess, dance, fitness, basketball. Ofc: Dept of Emergency Medicine Valley Medical Center 445 S Cedar Ave Fresno 93702

SHALLAT, RONALD FREDERICK, physician, neurological surgeon; b. May 22, 1941, Chicago, Ill.; s. Charles O. and Minnie A. (Kort) S.; m. Judith Mary McHugh, Aug. 24, 1968; children: Ryan b. 1971, Erin b. 1972, Kevin b. 1976; edn: MD w. honors, Univ. Ill. Sch. Medicine 1966; cert. Am. Bd. Neurosurgery 1976. Career: neurosurgical resident Univ. Ill., Chgo. 1966-73; pvt. practice neurological surgery, Berkeley 1973–; assoc. clin. prof. UCSF Sch. Medicine 1976–; chief div. neurological surgery Children's Hosp., Oakland 1980-86; mem: Am. Assn. Neurological Surgeons, Calif. Assn. Neurological Surgeons, S.F. Neurological Assn., A.C.S. (fellow); num. articles pub. in profl. jours.; mil: capt. USAF 1968-70; rec: golf, jogging. Res: 33 Evergreen Dr Orinda 94563 Ofc: East Bay Medical Group Inc 3000 Colby St Berkeley 94705

SHAM, LU JEU, physicist/educator; b. April 28, 1938, Hong Kong; nat. 1989; s. T. S. and Cecilia Maria (Siu) Shen; m. Georgina Bien, April 25, 1965; children: Kevin, Alisa; edn: BS, ARCS, Imperial Coll. England 1960; PhD physics, Cambridge Univ. England 1963. Career: asst. research physicist UCSD, La Jolla 1963-66; asst. prof. UC Irvine 1966-67; reader Univ. London 1967-68; assoc. prof., prof. UC San Diego, La Jolla 1968–, dean div. nat. sci. UCSD, 1985-89; awards: Gov.'s prize, math. Univ. of London 1960, Churchill scholar Cambridge Univ. 1960-63, Humboldt Found. sci. award 1978, Guggenheim Found. fellow 1984; mem: Am. Physical Soc. (fellow), AAAS; author (theories): Density functionals, Semiconductor heterostructures, Unconventional superconductivity; Democrat; rec: tennis, folk dancing. Ofc: Univ. of Calif. San Diego Dept. of Physics 0319 La Jolla 92093

SHAMES, RICHARD LEIGH, physician; b. June 21, 1945, Norfolk, Va.; s. George Joseph and Rosalie (Weisman) S.; m. Karilee Feibus, Apr. 29, 1979; children: Shauna b. 1979, Georjana b. 1981, Gabriel b. 1986; edn: BA, Harvard Univ. 1967; MD, Univ. Pa. 1971; hypnotherapist, San Francisco Acad. of Hypnosis 1973; Diplomate Nat. Bd. Med. Examiners 1971. Career: researcher Nat. Insts. of Health 1970, intern USPHS, San Francisco 1971; chief clin. physician Marin Co. Health Dept. San Rafael 1972-75; chief med. svcs. The Assn. for Res. and Enlightenment, Edgar Cayce Clin. Phoenix 1979; pvt. practice fam. med., preventive and holistic health Mill Valley 1979–; researcher Nat. Inst. Health 1970; med. dir., founder Wholistic Health & Nutrition Inst., Mill Valley 1975-78; family practice residency instr. UCSF Med. Sch. Family Practice Dept. 1976; bd. dirs. Children's Circle Center Private Sch. 1984; honors: Rose Meadow Levinson Meml. Prize for Cancer Res. 1970; mem: Physicians for Social Responsibility; publ: books: Healing with Mind Power (Rodale Press 1978), The Gift of Health (Bantam Books 1981); contbg. ed. and author of Ask the Family Doctor column for Internat. Jour. of Holistic Health and Med., 1984-85; mil: lt. USPHS 1971; rec: gardening, skiing, sailing. Res: 550 Ethel Ave Mill Valley 94941 Ofc: 10 Willow Ste 4 Mill Valley 94941

SHANDLING, ADRIAN H., physician, medical educator; b. Sept. 29, 1953, Cape Town, South Africa; s. Aaron and Edith Rose (Freedman) S.; m. Gillian Shirley Brenkel, Dec. 2, 1979; children: David and Talia b. 1982, Adam b. 1988; edn: MB ChB, Univ. Cape Town S. Africa 1978. Career: med. resident D.C. Gen. Hosp., Wash. D.C. 1982-85; cardiology fellow UC Irvine 1985-88, asst. clin. prof. 1988-89; honors: Hon. Mention Resident of Year (1985); mem: Am. Coll. Cardiology, N. Am. Soc. Pacing & Electrophysiology; publs: sci. papers in Pace Jour., Cardiac Catherizat. Jour., 1988. Res: 20371 Craimer Ln Huntington Beach 92646 Ofc: Long Beach Memorial Hospital

SHANTHIKUMAR, J. GEORGE, professor of industrial engineering, operations research and business administration; b. July 1, 1950, Sri Lanka; s. Poothathamby Sanders and Grace (Gnanammah) J.; m. Mellony Christa, July 29, 1977; children: Devin b. 1979, Rajan b. 1981, Sohan b. 1986; edn: BS, Univ. Sri Lanka 1972; MA, Univ. Toronto 1977; PhD, 1979. Career: asst. lectr. Univ. Sri Lanka, Peradeniya 1973-75; tchg. asst. Univ. Toronto, Canada 1975-79; asst. prof. Syracuse Univ., N.Y. 1979-82; assoc. prof. Univ. Ariz., Tucson 1982-84; UC Berkeley 1984-88, prof. 1988–, chair Mgt. Sci. Group 1989-91; awards: Canadian Commonwealth scholarship, Schwabacker fellowship, Outstanding Young Man of Am., E.O.E. Periera Gold Medal; mem: Ops. Research Soc. of Am., Inst. Mgmt. Sci.; 200+ tech. papers pub. Res: 80 Los Balcones Dr Alamo 94507 Ofc: Univ. of Calif., Walter A. Haas School of Business Berkeley 94720

SHAPERO, HARRIS JOEL, pediatrician; b. Nov. 22, 1930, Winona, Minn.; s. Charles and Minnie Sara (Ehrlichman) S.; m. Byong Soon Yu, Nov. 6, 1983; children: Bradley b. 1965, Charles b. 1969, Laura b. 1959, James b. 1966; edn: AA, UCLA, 1953; BS, Northwestern Univ. 1954, MD, 1957; diplomate and certified splst. occupational medicine Am. Bd. Preventive Med. 1977, cert. aviation medicine FAA 1976, indep. med. examiner WCAB 1989, indep. med. examiner in preventive and occupational medicine, Calif. Dept. Indsl. Rels., Div. Indsl. Accidents 1989. Career: intern L.A. Co.-Harbor Gen. Hosp. 1957-58, resident in pediatrics, 1958-60, staff physician Harbor-UCLA 1960-64; attdg. physician perceptually Handicapped Children's Clinic, 1960-63; disease control ofcr. for tuberculosis, L.A. Co. Health Dept., 1962-64; pvt. practice splst. in pediatrics and occupational medicine, Cypress, Calif. 1965-85; pediatric cons. L.A. Health Dept., 1963-85, disease control ofcr. sexually transmitted diseases, 1984-85; pediatric cons. Bellflower Clinic, 1962-85; emergency room dir. AMI, Anaheim 1968-78; mem. med. staff Anaheim Gen. Hosp., pediatric staff Hosp. de General, Ensenada, Mex. 1978–; primary care clinician Sacramento Co. Health and a private practice of Medico-Legal Evaluation, 1987-88; founder Calif. Legal Evaluation Med. Group; health care provider/advisor to cities of Anaheim, Buena Park, Cypress, Garden Grove, Cypress Sch. Dist., Magnolia Sch. Dist., Savanna Sch. Dist., Anaheim Unified Sch. Dist., Orange Co. Dept. Edn.; pediatric and tuberculosis cons. var. orgns.; founder Pan American Childrens Mission; named Headliner of year Orange Co. Press Club 1978; mem: Fellow Coll. Preventative Medicine, L.A. Co. Med. Assn., L.A. Co. Indsl. Med. Assn., Am. Coll. Emergency Physicians, L.A. Co. Pediatric Soc., Orange Co. Pediatric Soc., Am. Public Health Assn., Mex.-Am. Border Health Assn.; author: The Silent Epidemic, 1979; Republican; Jewish; rec: antique books and manuscripts, photog., graphics, beekeeper. Res: Rural Box 228 Wilton 95693 MedClinics, Sacramento Area 3160 Folsom Blvd Sacramento 95816

SHAPIRO, BURT JAY, entertainment manager, lawyer; b. June 18, 1947, New York; s. Gustav Samuel and Helen (Futerman) S.; edn: BA, St. Univ. N.Y., Stonybrook 1969; JD, Univ. Houston Law Sch. 1972; admitted St. Bar Tx. 1972, Fed. Dist. Ct. So. Dist. Tx. 1972, 5th Circuit Ct. of Appeals 1972, U.S. Supreme Ct. 1977, U.S. Tax. Ct. 1977. Career: atty. Law Offices W.D. Luther, Houston, Tx. 1972-75; La Vaca Gathering Co. 1975-77; ptnr., sports agent Jerry LeVias Mgmt. Enterprises 1977-80; entertainment mgr., v.p. Wallach Enterprises, Beverly Hills 1980-87; entertainment mgr. Burt Shapiro Mgmt., L.A. 1987–; honors: Who's Who Am. Law, Who's Who Advt., St. Univ. N.Y. Dean's List 1969, Finals Judge, Cable Ace Awards 1991, 92, 93, 94; mem: Acad. TV Arts & Scis., Nat. Cable TV Assn., Radio-TV News Directors Assn., Phi Delta Phi, March of Dimes (bd. mem. 1978-79); Democrat; Jewish. Res: 2147 N Beachwood Dr Los Angeles 90068 Ofc: Burt Shapiro Management POB 69813 Los Angeles 90069

SHAPIRO, ISADORE, chemical consultant, engineer; b. April 25, 1916, Mpls.; s. Jacob and Bessie (Goldman) S.; m. Mae Hirsch, Sept. 4, 1938; children: Stanley Harris b. 1941, Jerald Steven b. 1943; edn: BChE (w. high distinction), Univ. Minn., 1938, PhD 1944, postdoctoral res. fellow 1944-45; Career: asst. instr. chem. Univ. of Minn. 1938-41; res. fellow 1944-45; research chemist E.I. duPont de Nemours & Co., Philadelphia, Penn. 1946; head chem. lab. USN Ordnance Test Sta., Pasadena 1947-52; rater US Civil Svc. Bd. Examiners 1948-52; dir. res. lab. Olin Mathieson Chem. Corp., Pasadena 1952-59; head chem. dept. Hughes Tool Co. Aircraft div., Culver City 1959-62; pres. Universal Chemical Systems, Inc. 1962–; pres. Aerospace Chemical Systems, Inc. 1964-66; dir. contract res. HITCO, 1966-67; prin. scientist McDonnell Douglas Astronautics Co., Santa Monica 1967-70; cons. Garrett AiResearch Mfg. Co., Torrance 1971-82; indep. cons. 1982–; dep. gov. Am. Biographical Inst. Research Assn. 1988, dep. dir. gen. Internat. Biog. Ctr. Eng. 1989; mem: Fellow Am. Inst. of Chemists, Am. Chemical Soc., Am. Physical Soc., Nat. Inst. of Ceramic Engrs., Soc. for Adv. of Materials & Process Engring., Am. Ceramic Soc., AAAS, Am. Ordnance Assn., Am. Inst. Aero. & Astro., Internat. Plansee Soc. for Powder Metal, Am. Assn. Contamination Control, Am. Inst. of Physics, Soc. of Rheology, Am. Powder Metallurgy Inst., Sigma Xi, Tau Beta Pi, Phi Lambda Upsilon; works: 50+ presentations tech. soc. confs. including XVI (Paris), XVII (Munich) and XIX (London) Internat. Congs. for Pure and Appl. Chem.; 5th CIMTEC Italy 1982; XV Latin Am. Chem. Congress, Puerto Rico; Engring. Ceramics, Jerusalem 1984; 6th CIMTEC, Milan 1986; PM '86 in Europe, Dusseldorf 1986; Pittsburgh Conf., Atlantic City 1987; IUPAC Internat. Symp. on Polymers, Jerusalem 1987; First Internat. Conf. on Ceramic Powder Processing, Orlando, Fla. 1987; 3rd Internat. Symp. on Ceramic Materials, Las Vegas 1988; 198th Am. Chem. Soc. Nat. Meeting, Miami Beach 1989; Advances in PM, Chgo. 1991; 1992 Powder Metallurgy World Cong., San Francisco 1992, Internat. Conf. on Powder Metallurgy, Nashville 1993; Internat. Conf. on Powder Metallurgy and Particulate Materials, Toronto, Can. 1994, Seattle, Wash. 1995; contbr. 100+ papers in sci. jours. incl. Jour. of Inorganic and Nuclear Chem., Review Sci. Instr., others; holder 20 patents, others pend.; research: discovered and named Carborane Series of compounds; contbr. catalysis, mass spectrometry, infrared spectroscopy, nuclear magnetic resonance spectrometry, propellant and missile chemistry, boron hydrides, organoboranes, reaction kinetics, surface chemistry, fiber and composites technology incl. Boron Carbide and carbon filaments, compaction of powders; mil: 1st lt. US Army Anti-Aircraft Artillery 1941-44, WWII; rec: European travel. Res: 5624 W 62nd St Los Angeles 90056

SHAPIRO, JAMES STUART, physician, ophthalmologist; b. Mar. 22, 1938, Omaha, Nebr.; s. Morris Myron and Claire (Weitzman) S.; m. Constance Bea Schimmel, June 15, 1963; children: Jay Brian b. 1967, Lori Beth b. 1969; edn: attended Univ. of Mich. 1956-59; BS, medicine, and MD, Univ. of Nebr. Med. Sch. 1959-63; Bd. Cert. in Ophthalmology 1971. Career: internship Highland Alameda Co. Hosp., Oakland, Calif. 1963-64; residency, ophthalmology, Highland Gen. Hosp., Oakland 1966-69; fellowship in ophthalmology, Univ. of Wis. Med. Ctr. 1969; pvt. practice ophthalmology, Oakland 1970–; chmn. ophthalmology, Highland Gen. Hosp. 1972-74; assoc. clin. prof. ophthalmology, Highland Gen. Hosp. and Presbyn. Med. Ctr., S.F. 1972-91; exec. com., dept. ophthalmology, Pacific Presbyn. Med. Ctr. (now Calif. Pacific Med. Ctr.) 1978–; chief ophthalmology Providence Hosp. (now Summit Med. Ctr.) 1985-90, Samuel Merritt Hosp. (now Summit Med. Ctr.) 1986-90; mem. num. hosp. committees 1970–; team ophthalmology cons. Oakland Athletics Baseball and Golden St. Warriors Basketball; mem: Am. Coll. of Surgeons (fellow 1974) East Bay Ophthalmological Soc. (pres. 1978), Alameda Contra Costa Co. Med. Assn. (ethics com.), Big Brothers of East Bay (v.p. 1978), Soc. of Med. Friends of Wine (pres. 1989), advy. bd. Oakland Opera 1989-90, bd. mem. capital campaign fund Calif. Shakespeare Festival 1989-91, bd. mem. and sec. Oakland Ballet 1990–; author: articles pub. in profl. jours, 1969-88; mil: capt. U.S. Army 1964-66. Ofc: Eye Physicians of the East Bay 3300 Webster St Ste 212 Oakland 94609

SHAPIRO, JERALD STEVEN, aerospace company scientist, mortgage banker, executive; b. Dec. 3, 1943, Mnpls.; s. Isadore and Mae (Hirsch) S.; edn: BS, UC Los Angeles 1964, cert. small bus. mgmt., 1970, real estate mgmt. courses, 1969-76; Calif. lic. real estate broker 1970; desig: Cert. Investment Broker 1977, Investment Splst. 1981, Cert. Escrow Ofcr. 1983, CRA (cert. review appraiser, 1986), RMU (reg. mortgage underwriter, 1986). Career: mgr. process engring. and quality control Aerospace Chem. Systems Inc., Gardena 1963-66; chem. engr. HITCO, Gardena 1966-67; mats. & process engr., product reliability engr. McDonnell Douglas Corp., Long Beach 1967-70; chemist Los Angeles Co. Sanitation Dist., 1971-74; staff scientist TRW Def. and Space Systems Gp., Redondo Beach 1974–, team mem. VLBI, Signature appears on MARS via Viking Orbiter (Viking Lander Biol. Instrument); cons. Century 21 Beverlywood Realty Inc., L.A.; pres. Nationwide Mortgage Corp., L.A.; pres. Heritage Realty Group, L.A., exec. v.p. Wilshire Doheny Investments Corp., Beverly Hills, exec. v.p. JSK Capital Group Inc., Beverly Hills; bd. trustees and prof. Internat. Coll. of California, Irvine; bd. dirs. Internat. Wellness Inst., Beverly Hills; advy. bd. First Women's Bank of Calif. 1977-78, bd. dirs: Western Advanced Technology Systems Inc. 1980–, Environmental Protection Polymers Inc. 1980–; mem: Am. Chem. Soc., Nat. Assn. of Mortgage Brokers, Mortgage Bankers Assn. of Am., L.A. Assn. of Realtors, Calif. Assn. Realtors, Calif. Escrow Assn., Nat. Assn. Realtors, Nat. Assn. Review Appraisers and Mortgage Underws., Am. Def. Preparedness Assn.; author: Aware and Beware, Guide to Intelligent Home Buying. Ofc: Nationwide Mortgage Corp. 2800 S Robertson Blvd Los Angeles 90034

SHAPIRO, LUCILLE, molecular biology educator; b. July 16, 1940, N.Y.C.; d. Philip and Yetta (Stein) Cohen; m. Roy Shapiro, Jan. 23, 1960 (div. 1977); 1 child, Peter; m. Harley H. McAdams, July 28, 1978; stepchildren: Paul, Heather; edn: BA, Brooklyn Coll. 1961; PhD, Albert Einstein Coll. Medicine 1966. Career: asst. prof. Albert Einstein Coll. Medicine, N.Y.C. 1967-72, assoc. prof. 1972-77, Kramer prof., chmn. dept. molecular biology 1977-86, dir. biol. scis. div. 1981-86; Eugene Higgins prof., chmn. dept. microbiology, Coll. Physicians and Surgeons Columbia Univ., N.Y.C. 1986-89; Joseph D. Grant prof., chmn. dept. devel. biology Sch. Medicine, Stanford Univ. 1989–; bd. dirs. Silicon Graphics 1993–; bd. sci. counselors NIH, W.D.C. 1980-84, DeWitt Stetten disting. lectr. 1989; bd. sci. advisors G.D. Searle Co., Skokie, Ill. 1984-86; sci. advy. bd. Mass. Gen. Hosp. 1990-93, SmithKline Beecham 1993–; bd. trustees Scientists Inst. for Public Info. 1990–; lectr. Harvey Soc. 1993; commencement address, UC Berkeley 1994; mem. sci. bd. Helen Hay Whitney Found., N.Y.C. 1986–; co-chmn. advy. bd. NSF Biology Directorate 1988-89; vis. com., bd. overseers Harvard Univ., Cambridge, Mass. 1987-90; mem. sci. bd. Whitehead Inst., MIT, Boston 1988-93; mem. sci. review bd. Howard Hughes Med. Inst. 1990-94; mem. sci. review bd. Cancer Ctr. of Mass. Gen. Hosp., Boston 1994–; mem. Presidio Council, City of San Francisco 1991-94; mem. Pres. Council, Univ. of Calif. 1993–; awards: Hirschl Career Scientist award Hirschl Found. 1978, Spirit of Achievement award 1976, Disting. Alumna award Brooklyn Coll. 1983, Excellence in Sci. award Fedn. Am. Socs. of Exptl. Biology 1994, Jane Coffin Child fellow 1966; fellow AAAS, Am. Acad. Arts and Scis.; mem: Am. Acad. Microbiology, Inst. Medicine of Nat. Acad. of Scis. (elected 1991), Nat. Acad. of Scis. (elected 1994), Am. Soc. Biochem. and Molecular Biology (nominating com. 1982, 87, council 1990-93), Am. Heart Assn. (sci. advy. bd. 1984-87); editor: Microbiology Devel. 1984; mem. editorial bd. Jour. Bacteriology 1978-86, Trends in Genetics 1987–, Genes and Devel. 1987-91, Cell Regulation 1990-92, Molecular Biology of the Cell, 1992–, Molecular Microbiology 1991–, Current Opinion on Genetics and Devel. 1991–; contbr. articles to profl. jours.; rec: watercolor painting. Ofc: Stanford Univ Sch Medicine Beckman Ctr Dept Devel Biology Stanford 94305

SHAPIRO, MARTIN AARON, financial planner; b. Aug. 30, 1956, Santa Monica; s. Raymond and Lois Yvonne (Malcolm) S.; m. Joann Janine Goodman, Nov. 14, 1987; children: Natalie b. 1989; edn: BA econ. UCSD 1981; Chartered Fin. Cons. 1989, Chartered Life Underwriter 1989, Cert. Fin. Planner 1992. Career: comm. systems cons. AT&T, L.A. 1981-85; reg. rep. The Equitable, San Diego 1985-88; assoc. Capital Analysts 1988-91; owner Wealth and Tax Specialists 1991–; honors: UCSD Provosts Hons. List 1978-81; mem: UCSD Alumni Assn. (pres. 1989–), Lead San Diego, Arthritis Found. (vice chair 1993–, chair fin. devel.); articles pub. in Cabrillo Chronicle, 1989, La Jolla Light, 1992, Am. Soc. CLU Estate Planning 1994; Republican; Jewish; rec: sports. Res: 11541 Camino Playa Catalina San Diego 92124 Ofc: 4370 La Jolla Village Dr Ste 300 San Diego 92122

SHARMA, ARJUN DUTTA, cardiologist, educator; b. June 2, 1953, Bombay, India; s. Hari D. and Gudrun (Axelsson) S.; m. Carolyn D. Burleigh, May 9, 1981; children: Allira b. 1982, Eric b. 1985, Harrison b. 1991; edn: BSc, Univ. Waterloo, Canada 1972, MD, Univ. Toronto, 1976; desig: FRCPC (1981), FACC (1985), FACP (1989). Career: research assoc. Barnes Hosp., Washington Univ., St. Louis, Mo. 1981-83; asst. prof. medicine Univ. of Western Ontario, London, Can. 1983-88, asst. prof. pharmacol. tox. 1983-89, assoc. prof. medicine 1988-89; assoc. clin. prof. medicine UC Davis, 1989–; dir. interventional electrophysiol. Sutter Memorial Hosp., Sacramento 1990–, mem. research com. 1991–, exec. com. Sutter Heart Inst. 1992–; awards: Dr. C.S. Wainwright Award, Univ. Toronto, 1973, 74, 75; John Melady Award, Univ. Toronto, 1972; 1st Prize research Toronto Gen. Hosp., 1980; career scientist award Ontario Ministry of Heart, 1983-89; med. research grantee MRC, Canada, Ottawa, 1983-89; Fellow Am. Coll. of Cardiology, 1981–, Canadian Cardiovascular Soc., 1981–; mem: Am. Fedn. for Clinical Research, 1981–, NY Acad. of Scis.; civic: Sierra Club, 1991–, Crocker Art Mus., 1989–; publs: 130+ sci. articles; rec: tennis, skiing, philately. Ofc: Diagnostic and Interventional Cardiology Consultants, 3941 J St Ste 260 Sacramento 95864

SHARMAN, WILLIAM, professional basketball player, coach, executive, retired; b. May 25, 1926, Abilene, Tex.; m. Joyce; children by previous marriage: Jerry, Nancy, Janice, Tom; edn: Univ. So. Calif. Career: basketball player Washington Capitols, 1950-51, Boston Celtics, 1951-61; coach Los Angeles/Utah Stars, 1968-71; coach Los Angeles Lakers, 1971-76, gen. mgr., 1976-82, pres., 1982-88; named to Nat. Basketball Assn. All Star First Team (1956-59), 2d Team (1953, 55, 70), All League Team (7t), named Coach of Year NBA (1972), inducted Naismith Basketball Hall of Fame (1976); author: Sharman on Basketball Shooting (1965). Ofc: 4511 Roma Ct Marina Del Rey 90292

SHARP, ULYSSES S. GRANT, retired naval officer; b. Apr. 2, 1906, Chinook, Mont.; s. Ulysses S. G. and Cora (Krauss) S.; m. Patricia O'Connor, Aug. 2, 1930 (dec. 1986); children: Patricia (Mrs. Russell F. Milham) b. 1931, Grant Alexander (Rear Admiral USN-Ret.) b. 1938; m. Nina B. Blake, Feb. 4, 1987; edn: BS, US Naval Acad., 1927; engring. Annapolis Postgrad. Sch., 1934-36; Naval War Coll., 1949-50; Hon. Dr. of Sci. Mont. St. Univ. 1972. Career: served to Admiral U.S. Navy 1923-68: sea assignments abd. USS New Mexico (battle-ship), USS Henderson (transport), USS Sumner, USS Buchanan (destroyers), USS Saratoga (aircraft carrier), 1927-34; abd. USS Richmond (cruiser), USS Winslow (destroyer) 1936-39; Bur. of Ships, 1940-42; Comdg. ofcr. USS Hogan (destroyer-minesweeper) Atlantic 1942-43, USS Boyd (destroyer) PTO, awarded 2 Silver Star medals, 1943-44; staff, Comdr. Destroyer Force, U.S. Pacific Fleet 1944-48; comdg. ofcr. Fleet Sonar Sch., San Diego 1948-49; Comdr. Destroyer Sq. Five Korean War 1950-51, and staff of Comdr. U.S. Seventh Fleet/ fleet planning ofcr. for Inchon invasion; staff of Comdr. U.S. Second Fleet 1951-53; Comdg. Ofcr. USS Macon (cruiser) 1953-54; staff, Comdr.-in-Chief U.S. Pac. Fleet 1954-55; first Flag assignment as Comdr. Cruiser Div. Three 1956-57; dir. strat. plans div. Office of the Chief Naval Ops., Wash. DC 1957-58; Comdr. Cruiser-Destroyer Force, Pacific Fleet, based in San Diego 1959-60, Comdr. U.S. First Fleet 1960; promoted to Vice-Adm., Dep. Chief Naval Ops. Plans and Policy, 1960-63, awarded Navy Distinguished Service Medal; promoted to Adm., Comdr.-in-Chief U.S. Pacific Fleet, 1963-64; apptd. by Pres. Comdr.-in-Chief Pacific (unified command of 1 mil. Army, Navy, Marine Corps and Air Force personnel in 85-mil. sq. mi. area) supr. combat ops. in Vietnam and Pacific, 1964-68; decorated Navy Disting. Service (2d.), Army Disting. Service, decorated by govts. of Thailand, Rep. of China, Rep. of Korea, Rep. of Philippines, Rep. of Vietnam, and Brazil; mem. U.S. Navy League; club: La Jolla CC; author: Strategy for Defeat - Vietnam in Retrospect 1978; Republican; Episcopalian; rec: golf. Res: 876 San Antonio Pl San Diego 92106

SHARPE, ROLAND LEONARD, consulting earthquake engineer; b. Dec. 18, 1923, Shakopee, Minn.; s. Alfred Leonard and Ruth Helen (Carter) S.; m. Jane Esther Steele, Dec. 28, 1946; children: Douglas b. 1954, Deborah b. 1957, Sheryl b. 1965; edn: BSECE, Univ. Mich., Ann Arbor 1947, MSE, 1949; Calif. reg. profl. civil engr., 1952, structural engr., 1954. Career: v.p. 1950-65, exec. v.p. and gen. mgr. J.A. Blume Engineers, San Francisco 1965-73, also technical dir. Aetron-Blume-Atkinson, Palo Alto 1961-66, exec. v.p. J. Blume Engrs.-Iran, Tehran, Iran 1970-73; mng. director Applied Technology Council, Palo Alto 1973-84; pres. Calif. Engring. &.Devel. Co., Las Vegas, Nev. 1976-84;

chmn. and c.e.o. Engring. Decision Analysis Co. Inc., Palo Alto 1974-87; pres. R. Sharpe Consulting Structural Engrs., Cupertino 1987–; mng. dir. EDAC, GmbH, Frankfurt, Ger. 1974-82; chair U.S. Jt. Com. on Earthquake Engring. 1983-88, U.S. nat. advy. com. Nat. Earthquake Hazard Reduction Pgm. 1990-94; honors: Tau Beta Pi 1949, cit. for contbns. to constrn. industry Engring. News Record, NY, NY (1978-79, 86-87), cit. for devel. of improvements in structural design Applied Technology Council 1990)and Japan Struct. Consultants Assn., Tokyo 1990; mem: Am. Soc. Civil Engrs. (1947–, fellow, life, hon. mem. 1994), Am. Concrete Inst. (1947–, life), Struct. Engrs. Assn. of No. Calif. and Calif. (1955–, life), Japan Structural Cons. Assn. (hon. mem.-only non-Japanese, 1992–); civic: Jr. C.of C. Palo Alto (pres. 1954-56); publs: 50+ tech. articles and papers, 1961–, coauthor 3 books: Earthquake Engrg. for Nuclear Power Plants, 1969, Earthquake Mitigation Guidelines for Data Processing Ctrs., 1989, Seismic Safety Guidelines, 1982, 95; mil: sgt. USMC 1942-46; Prot.; rec: skiing, gardening, music. Res: 10320 Rolly Rd Los Altos 94024 Ofc: Sharpe Struct. Engrs. 10051 Pasadena Ave Cupertino 95014

SHATNEY, CLAYTON HENRY, general surgeon, educator; b. Nov. 4, 1943, Bangor, Me.; s. Clayton Lewis and Regina (Cossette) S.; m. Deborah Gaye Hansen, Apr. 1977; children: Anthony, Andrew; edn: grad. (valedictorian) Orono (Me.) H.S., 1961; BA (cum laude, State of Maine Scholar) Bowdoin Coll., 1965; MD, Tufts Univ. Sch. Med., 1969; PhD Cand. Univ. Minn. Grad. Sch., 1974-82; MD lic. Minn. 1970, Calif. 1975, D.C. 1977, Md. 1979, Fla. 1983; bd. cert. Am. Bd. Gen. Surgery 1978, cert. adv. cardiac life support 1979, adv. trauma life support instr. 1981. Career: med. intern Mayo Clinic, Rochester 1969-70, surg. resident Univ. Minn. Hosps., Mpls. 1970-77; served to major US Army Med. Corps, Walter Reed Army Med. Ctr., W.D.C., 1977-79; cons. VA Coop. Studies Pgm., W.D.C. 1980–; asst. prof. surgery Univ. Md. Hosp., Balt. 1979-82; assoc. prof. Univ. Fla. Sch. Med., Jacksonville 1982-87, dir. trauma Univ. Hosp. 1982-85; clin. assoc. prof. surgery Stanford Univ. Sch. of Medicine 1987–; surg. practice Santa Clara Valley Med. Ctr., San Jose; vis. prof. surgery The Upjohn Co., 1974–, Hoechst-Roussel Pharm., 1983–, instr. VALTRAC Anastomosis, Davis & Geck, 1990-91; awards: Garcelon Merit Med. Scholar 1965-69, clin. fellow Am. Cancer Soc. 1971-73, Phi Kappa Phi 1976–, Am. Acad. Fam. Physicians tchg. award 1980, tchg. cit. dept. preventive med. Ohio State Univ. 1981, pres. Fla. Soc. of Critical Care Med. 1987-88, investigator 23+ funded research projects; mem. Assn. for Acad. Surgery, The Shock Soc. (charter), Soc. Critical Care Med., AAAS, Kans. City Surg. Soc. (hon.), So. Med. Assn., SE Surg. Cong., Surg. Infection Soc., A.C.S. (Fellow), Fla. Soc. Critical Care Med., Am. Acad. Surg. Research (charter), Lillehei Surg. Soc., Internat. Platform Assn., Soc. for Surgery of Alimentary Tract, Panamerican Trauma Soc. (charter), Internat. Coll. Surgeons, Am. Assn. for Surgery of Trauma, Santa' Clara Co. Med. Assn., CMA, SW Surg. Cong., Internat. Soc. Surgery, We. Surgical Assn., Pacific Coast Surgical Assn.; publs: 83+ med. jour. articles, 29+ abstracts, 23+ texts & symposia, 3 films, numerous nat., internat. meeting presentations. Ofc: Dept. Surgery Santa Clara Valley Medical Center, 751 S Bascom Ave San Jose 95128 Tel: 408/885-6060

SHAVELSON, LONNY JAY, writer; b. Feb. 14, 1952, Brooklyn, NY; s. Irving Phillip and Roslyn S.; edn: MD, UC San Francisco 1977. Author (4 books): Personal Ad Portraits, 1983, I'm Not Crazy, I Just Lost My Glasses, 1986, Toxic Nation, 1994, A Chosen Death, 1995. Res: 2819 Piedmont Ave Berkeley 94705

SHAW, DONALD J., lawyer; b. Rochester, N.Y.; s. Clarence and Anna (Reichel) S.; m. Peggy Jean; children: Mark, James (Sgt. USMC); edn: stu. acctg./fin. L.A. City Coll., S.F.V. Jr. Coll., CSC Northridge, JD, Southwestern Univ.; admitted bar: Calif., U.S. Dist. Ct. (cent. dist.), U.S. Supreme Ct.; lic. real estate sales agt. Calif. Career: acctg. pos. various cos. including GM, Litton, American Safety and TRW; full charge controller Western Amusement Co. (exhibitor) Film Ventures (distbr. of motion pictures); Chapman and Olson Film Co. (prodn. t.v. commercials); solo law practice, Beverly Hills; corporate counsel USA Video Interactive Corp., Future Media Technologies, Inc., Micron Mining Co., Micron Minerals Corp.; honors: letter of commendn. the White House, resolution Calif. St. Senate (Sen. Alan Robbins) and Assembly (Rep. Richard Katz), commendn. Calif. St. Assembly (Rep. Marion La Follette), L.A. City Mayor Bradley and L.A. Co. Bd. Suprs. (Supr. Michael D. Antonovich); mem: ABA, L.A. Trial Lawyers Assn., Beverly Hills Bar Assn., Century City Bar Assn. (editl. staff), Motion Picture and TV Controller's Assn. (1st v.p.), Forum Com. on Entertainment and Sports Industries, Actor's Fund (life), Am. Film Inst., Variety Club (Tent 25), Internat. Footprinters, British United Svs. Club, Kiwanis (pres. 1985-86); author: Non-Attorney's Trust Handbook. Ofc: 2020 Ave of the Stars Ste 350 Century City 90067

SHAW, RICHARD EUGENE, cardiovascular researcher/biostatistician; b. Jan. 20, 1950, Springfield, Ohio; s. Eugene Russell and Marjorie Caroline (Lewe) S.; m. Christine Costa, Nov. 27, 1976; children: Matthew b. 1985, Brian b. 1987; edn: BA (cum laude), Duquesne Univ., 1972, MA, U.S. Internat. Univ., San Diego 1977; PhD, UC San Francisco Sch. of Medicine, 1984. Career: nuclear med. technologist Scripps Memorial, La Jolla 1975-79; research asst. UC Sch. of Med., San Francisco 1980-85; dir. research and operations San

Francisco Heart Inst., Daly City 1985–; editor The Jour. of Invasive Cardiology, 1990–; lectr., PTCA, San Francisco Heart Inst. 1985–, UC Sch. of Med. 1979-84; mem: Am. Coll. of Cardiology (fellow), Am. Heart Assn., Am. Psychol. Assn., Div. 38 Health Psychology APA, Soc. of Behavioral Medicine, Soc. for Clinical Trials, Am. Soc. of Cardiovascular Interventionists, N.Y. Acad. of Sci., Am. Statistical Assn.; publs: book chapters on angioplasty, recurrence after PTCA (1987–), 150+ articles on PTCA medical and psychological (1985–); rec: computer applications, running, tennis. Ofc: San Francisco Heart Institute, 1900 Sullivan Ave Daly City 94015

SHAW, SUSAN COULTER, school psychologist; b. March 25, 1943, Niagara Falls, N.Y.; d. John Alvah and Elizabeth (Heller) Shaw; edn: BA, Mt. Holyoke Coll. 1965; MS, CSU Hayward 1974; cert. sch. psychologist Calif. (1974), lic. ednl. psychologist Calif. (1983). Career: elem. tchr. Oakland Sch. Dist. 1968-71; sch. psychologist Castro Valley Sch. Dist. 1974-75; Millbrae Sch. Dist. 1977-78; Brisbane Sch. Dist. 1974-78; Laguna Salada Sch. Dist., Pacifica 1978-85; San Mateo Co. Office of Edn., Redwood City 1984–; pvt. practice ednl. psychology, San Francisco 1983–; awards: Fulbright tchg. asst./grad. fellow in Italy (1965-66), NDEA grad. fellowship (1966-67); mem: Nat. Assn. Sch. Psychologists, Sch. Psychologists Assn. San Mateo Co. (past pres.), Calif. Assn. Sch. Psychologists, Calif. Tchrs. Assn., Am. Fedn. Tchrs. Res: 319A Clipper St San Francisco 94114 Ofc: Early Childhood Education 65 Tower Rd San Mateo 94402

SHAW, WILLIAM ALBERT, lawyer; b. Dec. 28, 1943, Fort Dodge, Iowa; s. William Francis and Irene Catherine (Rafferty) S.; edn: BS pharm., Drake Univ. 1966; JD, Univ. Iowa 1969; admitted U.S. Supreme Ct., No. Dist Iowa, Ct. Appeals 9th Circuit. Career: real estate broker Controlled Investment, Beverly Hills 1980–; dep. dist. atty. Los Angeles Co. 1971-74; asst. U.S. atty. So. Dist. Calif., San Diego 1974-76; Kirtland & Packard, Los Angeles 1976-77; ptnr. Reed & Shaw, Beverly Hills 1977-88; atty. sole practice 1988–; pres./CEO, Roxbury Properties, Inc., Beverly Hills 1994–; staff White Hosue Conf. Office, Wash. D.C. 1975-76; dir. Parallax Productions, Beverly Hills 1986–; awards: Gerald R. Ford Presdl. Commend. 1975, City Council of L.A. Commend. 1994, Calif. State Senate Commend. 1994; mem: The Apartment Assn. of Greater L.A. (pres.), Beverly Hills Property Owners (dir. 1986–), Calif. Pharm. Assn., Iowa Bar Assn., Calif. Bar Assn., N.Y. Bar Assn., Wash. D.C. Bar Assn., Los Angeles C.of C. (law and justice exec. com. 1977–), Big Ten Club (immediate past pres.); exec. producer video series The Art of Video, 1986; Republican; Cath.; rec: skiing, biking, travel. Res: 9131 Callejuela Dr Beverly Hills 90210; 2nd home, Lake Tahoe: 730 West Lake Blvd Tahoe City, CA Ofc: 425 S Beverly Dr Beverly Hills 90212

SHAW, WILLIAM JAY, company president, banking executive; b. Jan. 14, 1962, San Francisco; s. William Cooper and Mary Elizabeth (Wolfe) S.; m. Kimberly Ann Kocman, Aug. 24, 1991; son, William Henry b. 1992; edn: BS, Univ. of Pacific, 1984; MPA, USC, 1989. Career: market analyst Am. Savings, Stockton 1984-85; builder account mgr. Bank of Am., San Francisco 1985-88; development specialist L.A. County C.D.C., Monterey Park 1990-93; bus. banking ofcr., Wells Fargo Bank 1993-94; pres. The Mayflower Group 1994–; honors: award of merit USC Graduate Sch. 1989, Outstanding Young Men of Am. 1988, Eagle Scout BSA 1976, listed Who's Who in West 1992, founder pres. Delta Sigma Pi Univ. Of Pacific Lambda Mu (1984, #00001); mem. Soc. of Mayflower Descendants (life), Soc. Calif. Pioneers (life), Soc. Colonial Wars 1990–; Republican; Methodist; rec: golf, tennis, bicycles.

SHEARER, GLENWOOD, realtor, life agent, notary; b. Oct. 4, 1934, Jenkins, Ky.; s. Eddie L. and Bessie (Roberts) S.; m. Lois Jeanette Powell, Nov. 25, 1961; children: Anthony b. 1959, Darryl b. 1962, Brian b. 1964, Curtis b. 1971; edn: AA, Bakersfield Coll. 1969; San Jose St. Univ. 1971-74. Career: mgr. C.I.T. Fin., San Jose 1972-75; realtor Mr. Real Estate 1975–, pres. 1980–; Job Assistance Program 1983–; Shearer Realty 1977-80; mem: NAACP, Urban League, San Jose Real Estate Bd., Emmanuel Male Chorus (secty., v.p.), San Jose C.of C.; mil: USN 1952-72; Republican; Baptist; rec: golf, bowling. Address: Mr. Real Estate 3838 Wiven Place Way San Jose 95121

SHEFRIN, HAROLD MARVIN, economist; b. July 27, 1948, Winnipeg, Canada; s. Samuel and Clara (Danzker) S.; m. Arna P., June 28, 1970; edn: BS hons., Univ. Manitoba Canada 1970; MS math., Univ. Waterloo 1971; PhD, London Sch. of Economics England 1974. Career: asst. prof. Univ. Rochester, N.Y. 1974-79; asst. prof., assoc. prof., prof. Santa Clara Univ. 1979–; cons. Dept. of Energy 1979-82; Syntex Corp. 1983-88. Address: Menlo Park 94025

SHEN, MASON MING-SUN, acupuncturist; b. March 30, 1945, Shanghai, China, nat. US cit. 1975; s. John Kaung-Hao and Mae Chu (Sun) S.; m. Nancy, Aug. 7, 1976; children: Teresa b. 1978, Darren b. 1980; edn: BS, Taiwan Normal Univ. 1968; MS, So. Dakota State Univ. 1971; PhD, Cornell Univ. Med. Coll. 1977; OMD, San Francisco Coll. of Acuppuncture 1984; Hon. A.M.D., Asia Am. Coll., San Diego 1985; MD (Medicina Alternativa), Internat. Univ., Colombo, Sri Lanka 1988; Cert. Acupuncturist, Calif. 1979. Career: Chinese medicine apprenticeship, Taiwan 1962; acupuncturist Acupuncture Inst. of New York, 3 yrs.; pvt. practice Chinese medicine, dir. Pain and Stress Management Center, Pleasanton, 1982–; appt. commr. Acupuncture Com., Medical Bd. of Calif., 1988-92; honors: Nat. Svc. Award for heart research, 1977, Hon. Doctorate, Asian-American Univ., 1985, Hon. Life Pres., Hong-Kong and Kowloon Chinese Medical Assn., 1985, Hon. Pres. S.F. Sch. of Chinese Medicine 1986, Modern Who's Who in Chinese Medicine, 1991, The Internat. Who's Who of Intellectuals, 1989, Disting. Leadership Award, 1988, hon. cons. Second Conf. World Tradition Medicine, Laughlin, Nev. 1995, listed Who's Who in Sci. and Engring,, Who's Who in West, Who's Who in Fin. and Industry, Who's Who in World, Who's Who in Am.; mem: Acupuncture Assn. of Am. (v.p. 1986-89), Am. Assn. Acup. and Oriental Medicine (pres. 1989-90), Calif. Cert. Acup. Assn. (pres. 1984-85), Calif. Acup. Alliance (pres. 1986-87, N. regional chmn. 1985-86), AAAS, NY Acad. of Sci., Am. Found. of Traditional Chinese Med., Rotary Club of Livermore Valley (charter), Contra Costa Chinese Republican Com. (pres. 1988–), Ronald Reagan Trust Fund (charter); publs: 40+ med. papers; cancer res. Cornell Univ. Med. Coll. (5 yrs), heart resrch. UCB (2 yrs), Lawrence Livermore Lab. (1 yr); mil: 2nd lt. Chemical Corps Army R.O.C.; Republican (chairman's advy. bd., Rep. Nat. Com. 1993); rec: travel, equestrian. Res: 3240 Touriga Dr. Pleasanton 94566 Ofc: Acupuncture Center of Pleasanton 3510 Old Santa Rita Rd Ste D Pleasanton 994588

SHENEMAN, JACK M., food and drug scientist; b. March 26, 1927, Grand Rapids, Mich.; s. Ralph M. and Henrietta (Eichhorn) S.; m. Hielke Brugman, Dec. 22, 1957; 1 son b. 1959, 1 dau., Elisa b. 1966; edn: BS, Mich. St. Univ. 1952; MS, 1954; PhD, 1957. Career: research asst. Mich. St. Univ., East Lansing 1954-57; research assoc. Wis. Malting Co., Manitowoc 1957-63, asst. dir. research 1957-63; sr. microbiologist Eli Lilly & Co., Indpls., Ind. 1963-69; Basic Vegetable Co., Vacaville 1969-74; food and drug scientist Calif. Dept. Health Food & Drug Branch, Sacto. 1975-92, expert consultant (food) 1992–; articles pub. in profl. jours. 1957-75; mil: sgt. AUS 1945-47; Presbyterian; rec: piano. Res/Ofc: POB 2476 El Macero 95618

SHEPHERD, ROBIN, educator; b. June 28, 1933; s. Maurice Sidney and Ruby Stevens (Orr) S.; children: Mark b. 1962, Paul b. 1963; m. 2d. Maureen Shackel, Jan. 3, 1986; edn: BS in C.E., Univ. of Leeds, Eng. 1955, MS, 1965, DSc, 1973; PhD, Univ. Canterbury, N.Z. 1971; reg. profl. civil engr., Calif. 1981. Career: asst. engr. De Havilland Aircraft Co., Hatfield, Eng. 1955-57; Ministry of Works, Auckland, N.Z. 1958; faculty Univ. Canterbury, Christchurch, N.Z. 1959-71; assoc. prof. Univ. of Auckland, 1972-79; dir. N.Z. Heavy Engineering Research Assn., 1979-80; prof. UC Irvine, 1980-94, emeritus prof. 1994–; lectr. in civil engring, Calif. Inst. of Technology 1994–; cons. Seismic Resistant Design, N.Z. 1962-80; expert advisor Attorneys & Insurance Assessors, Calif. 1981–; pres. Forensic Expert Advisers Inc., 1990–; awards: E. R. Cooper medal and prize Royal Soc. N.Z. 1972, Erskine Fellow Univ. Canterbury (1969, 87), Fulbright travel grantee, vis. prof. Caltech 1977, vis. res. fellow Imperial Coll. Sci. & Tech., London 1984, vis. overseas fellow St. John's Coll., Cambridge, Eng. 1984; mem: Fellow Am. Soc. of Civil Engrs., Fellow Instn. of Civil Engrs. (U.K.), Nat. Acad. of Forensic Engrs., Earthquake Engring. Res. Ins., Seismol. Soc. of Am., N.Z. Nat. Soc. for Earthquake Engring.; Rotary Club (Auckland 1976-80, Newport/Irvine 1980-89, South Coast Met. 1990–); publs: 150+ tech. jour. papers re earthquake resistant design 1963–; rec: sailboarding, racquetball, golf, opera. Ofc: California Institute of Technology Pasadena 91125

SHERMAN, A. ROBERT, psychologist, educator; b. Nov. 18, 1942, N.Y.C.; s. David R. and Goldie (Wax) S.; m. Llana Sherman, Aug. 14, 1966 (div.); children: J. Colbert b. 1970, Relissa A. b. 1972; edn: BA (w/hons.), Columbia Univ. 1964; MS, Yale Univ. 1966, PhD, 1969; Calif. lic. psych. 1981. Career: faculty dept. of psychology UC Santa Barbara 1969–, clin. psychologist practice, 1981–; res. evaluation cons. Santa Barbara County Schs. 1974-77, cons. and guest lectr. var. orgns.; honors: Phi Beta Kappa 1963, predoctoral res. fellow Nat. Inst. of Mental Health (1964-67, 1968-69), Sigma Xi 1967, Samuel Miller Res. award 1967, Psi Chi Nat. Hon. Soc. in Psychology 1979, vol. of the yr. award Santa Barbara Mental Health Assn. 1979, Teaching Excellence awards UCSB chpts. Delta Delta Delta Sor. 1989, Alpha Chi Omega Sor. 1991, Gamma Phi Beta Sor. 1993, 94; mem: AAUP (chapter pres. 1978-79), Santa Barbara Co. Psychol. Assn. (pres. 1985), Am. Psychol. Assn., Phi Beta Kappa (chap. pres, 1977-78), Assn. for Advancement of Behavior Therapy, Behavior Therapy and Research Soc., Calif. State Psychol. Assn.; Santa Barbara Mental Health Assn. (pres. 1978, 85, 91), Santa Barbara Contg. Edn. Advy. Council, Mountain View Sch. Site Council (pres. 1978-84); publs. include 1 book, sev. book chpts., num. articles in profl. jours. Res: 545 Barling Terr Goleta 93117 Ofc: Dept. Psych. UCSB 93106 also: 5290 Overpass Rd. Ste 232 Santa Barbara 93111

SHERMAN, ERIC, filmmaker, educator; b. June 29, 1947, Santa Monica; s. Vincent and Hedda (Comorau) S.; m. Eugenia Blackiston Dillard, Apr. 1, 1978; children: Cosimo b. 1978, Rocky b. 1982; edn: BA, Yale Univ., 1968. Career: owner/opr. Film Transform, Inc., Los Angeles 1982–; film faculty Art Center Coll. of Design, Pasadena 1976–, Pepperdine Univ., Malibu 1976-86, Mellon lectr. Cal Tech, Pasadena 1978; awards: Peabody Bdcstg., Ga. 1990, Cine Gold Eagle, W.D.C. 1990, CINDY, L.A. 1990, numerous other film festivals; mem.:

Film Forum (bd. dirs. 1988–), American Cinematheque (trustee 1986–); author: The Director's Event (1968), Directing the Film (1976), Frame by Frame (1987), Selling Your Film (1989). Ofc: Film Transform, Inc. 2427 Park Oak Dr Los Angeles 90068

SHERWOOD, ROBERT PETERSEN, educator; b. May 17, 1932, Black Diamond, Wash.; s. James Brazier and Zina (Petersen) S.; m. Merlene Burningham, Nov. 21, 1951; children: Robert Lawrence b. 1953, Richard W. b. 1954, Rolene b. 1956, RaNae b. 1961; edn: BS, and MS, Univ. Utah, 1956, 57; EdD, UC Berkeley, 1965. Career: tchr. Arden-Carmichael Sch. Dist., Carmichael 1957-60; vice prin., principal San Juan Unified Sch. Dist., Sacto. 1960-62, 62-65; assoc. prof. CSU Sacramento, 1965-70; prof. American River Coll., Sacto. 1970–, chair Soc./Anthro. Dept. 1980-86, pres. Academic Senate 1990-91; honors: report to nation Boy Scouts Am., Morgan, Ut., 1950, nat. spirit medal USN, San Diego, 1954, hon. life mem. Calif. P.T.A., Sacto., 1965, merit. svc. West Assn. S. & C., Burlingame, 1981, profl. svc. Phi Delta Kappa, 1987; mem: Calif. Tchrs. Assn., Nat. Edn. Assn. (life), Phi Delta Kappa (life), Calif. Fedn. of Coll. Profs., Faculty Assn. of Calif. Comm. Colls., Toastmasters Club Carmichael (pres. 1966-68); civic: Arden Park Rec. Dist., Sacto. (dir. 1966-72, bd. pres. 69-72); mil: CT2 USN 1953-55; Republican; Latter Day Saints; rec: reading, woodworking, travel. Res: 4053 Esperanza Dr Sacramento 95864 Ofc: American River College 4700 College Oak Dr Sacramento 95841

SHEVOCK, JAMES R., botanist; b. June 7, 1950, Spangler, Pa.; s. Simon Joseph S. and Betty Mae (Elchin) Washington; edn: BS botany, CSU Long Beach 1976; MA biology, 1978. Career: forest botanist Forest Service Sequoia NF, Porterville 1978-82, forest ecologist 1982-84; data base botanist Calif. Dept. Fish & Game, Sacto. 1984-86; regional botanist Forest Service Regional Office, San Francisco 1986–; lectr. botanical groups 1978–; awards: Calif. Acad. Sci. research assoc., Rancho Santa Ana Botanic Garden research assoc., USDA Forest Service cert. of merit 1980, 82, 86, 88, 90, 92, 93; mem: Calif. Native Plant Soc. (v.p. for plant programs 1994–), Am. Soc. Plant Taxonomists, Calif. Botanical Soc., Nature Conservancy; num. articles pub. in botanical jours. 1979–; Democrat; Prot.; rec: classical music, opera, travel. Res: Opera Plaza 601 Van Ness Ave #811 San Francisco 94102 Ofc: U.S. Dept. of Agriculture-Forest Service 630 Sansome St Room 823 San Francisco 94111

SHIELDS, ANDREA L., clinical psychologist; b. Aug. 19, 1947, Montgomery, Alabama; d. Lewis Theodore and Lea (Dawson) Shields; edn: BA (psychol.), Univ. of Ariz. 1965; MA (experimental psychol.), Univ. of Pacific 1971; PhD (clin. psychol.), Fielding Institute, Santa Barbara 1977; exchange student to Greece for People-to-People; lic. Calif. psychologist. Career: trainer So. Ariz. Mental health Ctr., Tucson, Ariz. 1968-69; teaching asst. Univ. of the Pacific, Stockton 1969-70; research asst. and behavioral therapist, Stockton State Hosp., Stockton 1970; instr. psychol., Modesto Jr. Coll., Modesto 1970-71; instr. San Bernardino Valley Coll. 1971-72; instr. for military recruiters, Columbia Coll., Mo. 1974; intern (methadone treatment pgm., child and adolescent svcs., therapy) San Bernardino County Mental Health 1976, clin. psychol. intern 1976-77; clin. psychol. resident San Bernardino Valley Coll. 1977-79; cons. research design, 1978-80; pgm. dir. Mission Valley, Hemet 1979; regional dir. So. Calif., Univ. of San Francisco 1980-81; social services chair Crafton Hills Coll., San Bernardino Comm. Coll. Dist., Yucaipa, prof. psych. 1971-88; private practice clin. and organizational psychol., Rancho Cucamonga, Calif. 1980–; secty., treas. psychol. dept. Rancho Lindo, 1988, 89; listed: Who's Who in Calif. (1981), Who's Who in West (1977), World's Who's Who of Women (1977), Comm. Leaders and Noteworth Am. (1977), Personalities of the West (1977), Notable Am. (1976), Who's Who in American Women of Am. (1976); honors: Outstanding Young Woman (1976); mem: San Antonio Comm. Hosp. psychiatric com., Yucaipa Guidance Clinic (bd. dirs. 1972, 76), Am. Psychol. Assn., Western Psychol. Assn., Western Assn. of Women in Psychol. (ch. 1984), Assn. of Women in Psychol. (registration ch. nat. conf. 1980), Nat. Sci. Foundation Chataqua; author: 13 profl. publications and papers. Res: PO Box 2202 Running Springs 92382 Ofc: Tarika Psychological Services 9045 Haven Ave Ste 107 Rancho Cucamonga 91730

SHIELDS, CHARLES RICHARD, advertising agency creative director/owner; b. July 19, 1944, Lawrence, Kans.; s. Charles Robert and Eloise Margaret (Henson) S.; edn: AA, El Camino Coll. 1965; BFA, Art Center Coll. of Design 1968; MFA, 1969. Career: instr. Colo. Mountain Coll., Glenwood Springs 1971-72; Calif. Coll. Arts & Crafts, Oakland 1974-81; CSU Northridge 1983-85, CSU Fresno 1993-95; creative dir. Wallace Advt., Santa Fe Springs 1985-88; Solutions by Design, Fresno 1988-92; owner Shields Design 1992–; rec: photog. Res: 1330 N Esther Way Fresno 93728 Ofc: Shields Design 415 E Olive Fresno 93728

SHIFFMAN, LESLIE BROWN, administrative executive; b. Dec. 9, 1936, Fresno; d. Albert Brown and Marion Riese Brown-Propp; m. 1957, div. 1972; m.2d. Sidney Shiffman, July 4, 1993; children: Susan b. 1960, Steven b. 1962, David b. 1965, Thomas b. 1965; edn: USC, 1954-56. Career: asst. office mgr. John W. Mitchell, MD, Long Beach 1971-73; cost acctg. clk. Panavision Inc., Tarzana 1973-76; exec. secty. Hartman Galleries, Beverly Hills 1976-78; admin-

strv. asst. Galanos Originals, Los Angeles 1978–; honors: Panhellenic Assn. Alumnae Woman of Year L.A. Area (1978); life mem. Alpha Epsilon Phi Sor.: awarded Emerald lily for 30 yrs. nat. service, elected Woman of Distinction 1993 (highest award for lifetime achievement), nat. pres. 1985-89, nat. v.p. Alumnae 1981-83, nat. treas. 1983-85, nat. v.p. Collegiate chpts. 1979-81, alt. del. Nat. Panhellenic Conf. 1990-91, nat. chair pub. rels. 1962-65, philanthropy 1967-71, pledge pgmg. 1971-75, frat. edn. 1975-77, nat. historian 1989–, reg. dir. 1965-69, USC collegiate chpt. advisor 1960-72, UCLA collegiate chpt. adv. 1976-81, 1989–, ldr. tng. workshops at USC, UCLA, CSU Long Beach, Univ. Colorado, Univ. Ariz.; Life mem., trustee (1985–) Alpha Epsilon Phi Found. Inc. (secty., pres.); mem. bds: Long Beach City Panhellenic Assn. (dir. 1959-66) USC Panhellenic Advisors Assn. (v.p. 1969-70, pres. 1970-71), UCLA Panhellenic Advisors Assn. (pres. 1978-9, 90-1), chair Nat. Panhellenic Conf./ Nat. Pres.'s Meeting (1988); life mem. Brandeis Univ. Nat. Women's Com. (L.B. chpt. pres. 1964-65, regional dir. & treas. 1971-72); active Camp Fire Girls L.B. (ldr. 1968-71), Temple Israel Relig. Sch. Bd. of Edn. L.B. (1966-69), Long Beach Pub. Schs. vol. (reading tutor, PTA bulletin ed. 1968-69), L.B. Jewish Community Ctr. (coms. 1962-70), Nat. Council of Jewish Women L.B. (bd., ofcr. 1960-63); listed Who's Who in West (1989), Who's Who in Am. Women (1989); contbr. articles in ednl. jours.; Republican; Jewish; rec: design hand knit sweaters. Res: 1745 Bentley Ave Apt 1 Los Angeles 90025 Ofc: 2254 S Sepulveda Blvd Los Angeles 90064

SHIFFMAN, MELVIN ARTHUR, physician-surgeon, medical-legal consultant; b. Aug. 23, 1931, Bklyn.; s. Albert and Eva (Krieger) S.; m. Pearl, Aug. 28, 1955; children: Scott b. 1959, Karen b. 1960, Denise b. 1962; edn: BS biochem., Union Coll., 1949; dental med. Harvard Sch., 1953-54; MD, Northwestern Sch. of Med., 1957; JD, Western State Univ., 1976; Dipolmate: Am. Bd. of Surgery 1965, Am. Bd. of Cosmetic Surgery 1989, Am. Bd. of Forensic Examiners 1994. Career: intern med. L.A. County Hosp., Los Angeles 1957-58; lt. comdr. USPHS 1958-60; resident surg. VA Hosp., Long Beach 1960-64; med. practice gen. surgery spec. oncologic surg., reconstrv. and cosmetic surg., 1964–, medico-legal cons. 1976–; asst. clin. prof. surg. UC Irvine 1968-83; past chief surg. Anaheim Gen. Hosp. 1969, chief surg., chief staff, chmn. bd. dirs. Tustin Comm. Hosp. 1974, past chmn. bd. Monte Park Hosp., El Monte 1975; Union of Am. Physicians & Dentists (bd. Calif. Fedn. 1982-86, pres. Orange Co. Local 7802 1982-84); Fellow: Internat. Coll. Surgeons (1966), A.C.S. (liaison); mem: Am. Soc. Cosmetic Breast Surg., Inst. of Bloodless Medicine & Surgery, Royal Soc. of Health 1971, Am. Coll. of Legal Med. 1984; mem: Orange Co. Oncologic Soc. (founder, past pres.), Am. Cancer Soc. (past pres. O.C. chpt. 1971-73), Soc. Head & Neck Surgeons, Am. Soc. Clin. Oncology, So. Calif. Acad. Clin. Oncology, Am. Soc. Abdominal Surgeons, Am. Acad. Cosmetic Surg., Am. Soc. Liposuction Surg., Am. Soc. of Law & Medicine; life fellow Internat. Biog. Assn.; publs: 50+ books and med. jour. articles; rec: wildgame hunting, collector guns, antiques, stamps. Res: 17501 Chatham Tustin 92680 Ofc: 1101 Bryan Ave Ste G Tustin 92680-3883

SHIMER, DONALD ALBERT, foundation president; b. Dec. 5, 1929, Easton, Pa.; s. Arthur Charles and Dora Alice (Uhler) S.; m. Virginia Ries (div.); m. Patricia Nan Worthington, Apr. 12, 1970; children: W. Ralph Lammers b. 1958, Donald A., Jr. b. 1958, Peter A. b. 1962; edn: BA in history, Lafayette Coll., 1951. Career: exec. YMCA, Worcester, Mass., Asbury Park, N.J., Livingston, N.J., Portland, Oreg. 1951-69; sr. v.p. J. Panas & Ptnrs., Chgo. 1969-74; pres. Shimer & Sons Ltd., Chgo., Ill., Walnut Creek, Calif., 1974–; v.p. devel. Childrens Hosp., San Francisco 1975-77; exec. dir. Childrens Hosp. Found., Fresno 1978-82; exec. dir. Marin General Hosp. Found., Greenbrae, Calif. 1982-87; exec. v.p. Gandhi Found., Orinda 1987–; pres. Dollberger & Worthington, Inc. 1992–; pres. Summit Med. Ctr. Found. 1994–; mem. San Francisco YMCA planning & ops. com. 1975–, v.p. YMCA Model Legislature/Court Bd. 1985–; Rotarian; mil: sgt. US Army 1951-53; Republican; Episcopalian; rec: running, golf, travel, reading, computer. Res: 1510 Arkell Rd Walnut Creek 94598-1207

SHIMKHADA, DEEPAK, art history educator; edn: BFA 1968, MFA 1971, Univ. of Baroda, India; MA, USC, 1974; PhD, Ohio State Univ., (ABD) 1979; Languages: Nepali, Sanskrit, English, Hindi, Gujarati, Newari, French. Career: teaching assoc. Ohio State Univ. 1977-81; instr. Scripps Coll. 1981-82; instr. CSU Long Beach 1989, Rio Hondo Coll.; curator "Exhibition of Nepali Art" Montgomery Art Gallery 1973; contbr. Woven Jewels: Tibetan Rugs from So. Calif. Collections (exhibn. cat.) 1992; Tibet: The Contented Heart (book) 1996; coord., contbr. "USC Collects: A Sampling of Taste" (exhib.) USC 1974; organizer, cochair "Himalayan Art & Culture" Univ. Wisc. 1980; organizer, cochair "Innovation Without Loss of Tradition" art history panel, Univ. Mo. 1981; curator "God, Man, Woman and Nature in Asian Art" Scripps Coll. (exhib.), Claremont 1985; curator "Indian Miniatures from the Hariette Von Breton Collection" (exhib.) Pacific Asia Museum, Pasadena, 1986; organizer "Himalayas at the Crossroads" (symposium), Pacific Asia Museum, Pasadena 1987; editor 2 books: Popular Buddhist Mantras in Sanskrit, 1984, Himalayas at the Crossroads: Portrait of a Changing World, 1989; organizer, contbr. "Himalayan Art: Patrons and Public" art history panel CSU-LB 1989; curator "Eye of India: Art of the People" (exhib.) Palos Verdes Art Center, Palos Verdes, 1991; organizer & chair "Art and Religion" Western Conf. of Assn. of Asian Studies, Claremont

McKenna Coll. 1994; pgm. coord. Claremont Grad. Sch. 1987–; editor newsletter: Himalaya, 1987–; lectr. various institutions 1977–; mem: College Art Assn. of Am., Art Historians of So. Calif., Am.-Nepal Soc. of Calif., Assn. for Asian Studies, Assn. for Asian Studies on the West Coast, Nepal Studies Assn., Pacific Asia Museum, Nepal Assn. of Fine Arts, Assn. of Nepalis in the Americas (exec. bd.); awards: Jr. then Sr. Cultural Fellow govt. of India (1962-71), Fulbright fellow U.S. State Dept. (1972-74), tuition fellowship Univ. Chicago 1974-76, Jr. Research Fellow Am. Inst. of Indian Studies for Smithsonian Instn. 1979-80, Ohio State Univ. Grad. Students Alumni Res. Award 1980, Council of South Asia Grant, Assn. for Asian Studies 1989, Honorable Mention in painting Triennale of World Contemporary Art, India 1970, certificate awards, juried exhibs. of Nepal Assn. of Fine Arts, Nepal 1966-69, Dean's List, USC 1973; exhibits: Chicago Public Library 1977, Expo-70 Osaka, Japan, Triennale of World Contemporary Art, India (1967, 70), 1-man show Max Gallery, Kathmandu 1968; publs: numerous articles and papers in profl. jours. Ofc: Claremont Graduate School 165 E 10th St Claremont CA 91711

SHINEFIELD, HENRY ROBERT, pediatrician; b. Oct. 11, 1925, Paterson, N.J.; s. Louis and Sarah (Kaplan) S.; m. Jacqueline Walker; children: Jill, Michael, Kim Strome, Melissa Strome; edn: BA, Columbia Univ. 1945; MD, 1948; dipl. Am. Bd. Pediatrics (examiner 1975–, bd. dirs. 1979–, v.p. 1981–). Career: rotating intern Mt. Sinai Hosp., N.Y.C. 1948-49; pediatric intern Duke Hosp., Durham, N.C. 1949-50; asst. resident pediatrician N.Y. Horp., Cornell 1950-51, pediatrician to outpatients 1953-59, instr. in pediatrics 1959-60, asst. prof. 1960-64, assoc. prof. 1964-65, asst. attdg. pediatrician 1959-63, assoc. attdg. pediatrician 1963-65; pediatrician to outpatients Childrens Hosp., Oakland 1951-53; chief of pediatrics Kaiser-Permanente Med. Center, San Francisco 1965–; assoc. clin. prof. pediatrics Sch. Medicine Univ. Calif. 1966-68, clin. prof. pediatrics 1968–, clin. prof. dermatology 1970–; assoc. attdg. pediatrician Paterson Gen. Hosp., N.J. 1955-59; chief of pediatrics Kaiser Found. Hosp., San Francisco 1967–; pediatrics splst., Paterson 1953-59; cons. San Francisco Gen. Hosp. 1967–, Childrens Hosp., S.F. 1970–, Mt. Zion Hosp., S.F. 1970–; mem. research grants rev. bd. NIH, HEW 1970-74; med. dir. USPHSR 1969–; bd. dirs. S.F. Peer Review Orgn. 1975-80, secty., exec. com. 1976-80; chmn. Calif. St. Child Health Disability Bd. 1973-74; sr. mem. Inst. Medicine Nat. Acad. Scis. 1980–; cons. Bur. Drugs FDA 1970–, Nat. Acad. Scis. 1972–, NIH, HEW 1974–; editl. bds. Western Jour. Medicine 1968-78; Am. Jour. Diseases of Children 1970-80; contbr. writings to profl. pubs.; chmn. S.F. Med. Advy. Com. Nat. Found. March of Dimes 1969-85; mem: Am. Acad. Pediatrics (fellow, com. fetus and newborn 1969-76, com. on drugs 1978-80), AMA, Soc. Pediatric Research, Infectious Diseases Soc. Am., Western Pediatric Soc., Western Soc. Clin. Research, Am. Pediatric Soc., Phi Beta Kappa. Res: 2705 Larkin St San Francisco 94109 Ofc: 2200 O'Farrell St San Francisco 94115

SHIPP, JOSEPH CALVIN, physician, medical educator; b. Feb. 10, 1927, Northport, Ala.; m. Marjorie M. Morris, Nov. 23, 1961; children: Joseph b. 1963, Sherise b. 1967, Dana b. 1970, Michele b. 1974; edn: BS, Univ. Alabama Tuscaloosa 1948; MD, Columbia Univ. Coll. Physicians and Surgeons 1952. Career: instr. Harvard Med. Sch., Boston, Mass. 1958-60; prof. medicine Univ. Fla., Gainesville 1960-70; prof., chmn. regents disting. Univ. Neb. Med. Sch., Omaha 1970-86; prof. medicine in residence UCSF, Fresno 1986–; pres. UCSF Fresno Found. 1994–; bd. of trustees Sansum Med. Research Found. 1993–; honors: Phi Beta Kappa, Alpha Omega Alpha, Univ. Neb. Fulbright-Hayes 1978, Regents Disting. Prof. 1979, 86, Tuscaloosa H.S. Disting. Alumnus 1988; mem: Assn. Am. Physicians, Am. Soc. Clin. Investigation, Am. Fedn. Clin. Res., Am. Coll. of Physicians (Fellow), Endocrine Soc., Am. Diabetes Assn., All India Diabetes Inst., Rotary Fresno; med. research pub. in 250+ publs. (1960–); mil: USN 1944-46; Cath.; rec: photog., music, swimming. Res: 7463 N Laguna Vista Fresno 93711 Ofc: Valley Medical Center 445 S Cedar Ave Fresno 93702

SHIPP, WILLIAM WELDON, certified public accountant; b. June 8, 1927, Los Angeles; s. Pat and Mae (Harris) S.; m. Dorothy Forse, Sept. 23, 1967; children: Karyn b. 1971, William b. 1973; edn: BS, Univ. San Francisco 1952; MBA, Golden Gate Univ. 1963. Career: staff auditor Price Waterhouse, San Francisco 1952-56; acctg. supr. C.C. Moore & Co. 1956-63; chief accountant Westland Life Ins. 1963-66; audit mgr. Soule Steel Co. 1966-67; sr. accountant Bechtel Power Corp. 1967-82; sole practice, Oakland 1982–; instr. UC Berkeley 1983-92; Golden Gate Univ. 1984-85; mem: Am. Inst. CPAs, Calif. Soc. CPAs; mil: sgt. AUS 1945-46; Republican; rec: philately, golf, swimming. Res: 5068 Dublin Ave Oakland 94602 Ofc: 1964 Mountain Blvd Ste 199 Oakland 94611

SHIRE, HAROLD RAYMOND, professor, author, inventor; b. Nov. 23, 1910, Denver, Colo.; s. Samuel and Rose Betty (Herman) S.; m. Cecilia; children: David, Esti, Darcy; edn: Cert. in Bus., UCLA; MBA, Pepperdine Univ.; MLA, USC; JD, Southwestern Univ.; PhD, US Internat. Univ.; admitted bar: Calif., US Supreme Ct. Career: deputy dist. atty. Los Angeles County 1937-39; asst. U.S. atty. 1939-42; pvt. practice law, Los Angeles & Beverly Hills 1946-56; pres. General Connectors Corp., Certified Spotwelding Corp., Quality Aircraft Corp., Quality Trading Corp. 1956-70; chmn. bd. General Connectors Corp., also Bestobel Aircraft Ltd., U.K., 1970-73; prof. structural orgn. & law Pepperdine Univ. 1973-78; investor, builder 1973–; prof. mgmt. & law U.S. Internat. Univ.,

San Diego 1981-85; served in U.S. Army Infantry 1942-46; honors: Companion Royal Aero. Soc. U.K., Chevalier du Vieux Moulin Fr., Service Ofcr. and Adj. Gen.'s Ward & Chenault Post, Am. Legion, Shanghai, China; awards: recipient commendations from U.S. Atty. Gen., Pres. J.F. Kennedy and Pres. L.B. Johnson, Hon. LLD Pepperdine Univ. 1981, Jewish Nat. Fund medal of honor and elected comdr. JNF Legion of Honor 1992; mem. univ. bd. Pepperdine Univ.; mem: Fed., Calif. and Beverly Hills Bar Assns., Am. Soc. Internat. Law, Am. Welding Soc., Material & Process Engrs., Am. Legion, AAUP, AF Assn., Presdl. Round Table, W.D.C. 1989-93, alumni assns., Lambda Delta Beta, Psi Chi, Japan-Am. Soc., Japanese Com. of San Diego (hon. pres.), Urasenke Cha No Yu, The Founders/L.A. Music Ctr., Union of Orthodox Jewish Congregations of Am. (exec. com., bd. govs.), Masons, Scottish Rite, and Shrine; publisher (art): Symbolic Interactionism and Cha No Yu: A Method of Analyzing Japanese Behavior (pub. in Japanese 1982); inventor, high-pressure high-temperature flexible pneumatic, anti-icing, compression & air conditioning sys. used in jet aircraft; research, Japanese behavior, the Way of Tea; Republican; rec: big-game fishing, Chinese ceramics, Japanese bronzes. Ofc: PO Box 1352 Beverly Hills 90213

SHIRLEY, ROBERT BRYCE, corporate lawyer; b. Feb. 5, 1951, Morehead City, N.C.; s. Robert Wayne Shirley and JoAnn Elaine (Shook) Myers; m. Marilyn Jeanette Roy, June 30, 1973; children: Robert b. 1983, James b. 1986, Emma b. 1991; edn: Ba, Stanford Univ., 1973, JD, 1977, MBA, 1977. Career: atty., assoc. McKenna & Fitting, L.A. 1977-79; general counsel The Way International, New Knoxville, 1979-87; ptnr. Morrison & Shirley, Irvine 1987-88; sr. atty. Taco Bell Corp., Irvine 1988-92; corp. counsel Pepsico, Inc. 1993–; mem: ABA 1977–, Calif. Bar Assn. 1977–, Orange County Bar Assn. 1987–; Republican; Christian; rec: skiing, fishing, tennis. Res: 13692 Andele Irvine 92720 Ofc: Taco Bell Corp. 17901 Von Karman Irvine 92714

SHMANSKE, STEPHEN, economist; b. March 11, 1954, New Jersey; s. Bernard Francis and Elizabeth Agnes S.; m. Marian Louise Stevens, Nov. 24, 1979; edn: BS math., Dartmouth Coll. 1976; MA econ., UCLA 1977; PhD, 1982. Career: cons. economist Law Offices of Stevens & Stevens, San Francisco 1979–; economist U.S. Dept. Justice Antitrust Div., Wash. D.C. 1978; prof. CSU Hayward 1979–; editl. cons. W. Pub. Co. 1983; SRA Internat. 1983; D.C. Heath & Co. 1988; cons. Nat. Center for State Cts., S.F. 1980; awards: UCLA Chancellors Intern fellow 1976-80, Smith-Richardson Dissertation fellow 1978-81, CSU Hayward Merit. Performance & Profl. Promise 1985-86; mem: Am. Econ. Assn., Western Econ. Assn., Atlantic Econ. Soc., Indsl. Orgn. Soc.; author: Public Goods, Mixed Goods, and Monopolistic Competition (Tx. A&M Univ. Press), articles pub. in profl. jours.,1982–; Libertarian; Cath.; rec: golf, dogs, woodworking. Ofc: California State University Economics Dept. Hayward 94542

SHONK, ALBERT D., JR., publishers representative; b. May 23, 1932, Los Angeles; s. Albert D., Sr. and Jean (Stannard) S.; edn: BS in bus. adminstrn., USC 1954. Career: field rep., mktg. div. Los Angeles Examiner, 1954-55, asst. mgr. 1955-56, mktg. div. mgr. 1956-57; account exec. Hearst Advt. Svc., 1957-59; acct. exec. Keith H. Evans & Assoc., 1959-63, San Francisco mgr. 1963-65; owner/pres. Albert D. Shonk Co., 1965–; gen. ptnr. Shonk Land Co., Ltd., Charleston, W.V. 1989–; mem: Nat. Assn. of Publishers Reps. (West Coast v.p. 1981-83), Magazine Reps. Assn. of So. Calif., Bus./Profl. Advt. Assn., Town Hall of Calif., Phi Sigma Kappa (dist. gov. 1960-62, nat. v.p. 1962-70, PSK Medallion of Merit 1976, Grand Council 1977-83, Grand Pres. 1979-83, Chancellor 1983-87, 1990-91, Court of Honor -life), Phi Sigma Kappa Found. Inc. (pres., trustee 1984-95, emeritus and honorary trustee 1995–), Alpha Kappa Psi, Skull and Dagger USC, Interfrat. Alumni Assn. So. Calif. (v.p., pres. 1957-61), recipient Nat. Inter-Fraternity Conf. Interfraternal Award 1989, Inter-Greek Soc., USC (founder, v.p., life dir. 1976–, pres. 1984-86), USC Commerce Associates (nat. bd. 1991–, treas. 1995–), USC Assocs., Signet Circle Corp. (hon. life dir., pres. 1977-81, treas. 1989–), Florence Crittenton Center (exec. v.p. 1979-81, pres. 1981-83, bd. chmn. 1983-85, hon. life dir.), Crittenton Assocs. (founding chmn. 1978-80), Junior Advt. Club of L.A. (hon. life mem., past dir., treas., v.p.); Presbyterian. Res: Wilshire Towers 3460 West 7th St Los Angeles 90005 Ofc: 3156 Wilshire Blvd Los Angeles 90010

SHOOTER, ERIC MANVERS, professor of neurobiology; b. Apr. 18, 1924, Mansfield, Nottingham, England; s. Fred and Pattie (Johnson) S.; m. Elaine Staley Arnold, May 28, 1949; dau. Annette b. 1956; edn: BA, MA, PhD, Univ. of Cambridge, England 1945, 1946, 1950. Career: biochemistry lectr. University Coll., London, 1953-63; assoc. prof. genetics Stanford Univ., 1963-68; prof. genetics & biochemistry 1968-75; prof. neurobiology 1975–, chmn. neurobiology dept. 1975-87, chmn. Neurosci. PhD Program Stanford Univ. 1972-82; mem. research advy. com. Childrens Hosp. Med. Center, Boston 1978-90; assoc. Neuroscis. Research Pgm., NY, NY 1979-90; senior cons. Markey Charitable Trust, Miami, Fla. 1985–; permanent teaching staff Internat. Sch. of Neurosci., Praglia, Italy 1987-92; chair sci. advy. bd., dir. Regeneron Pharmaceuticals, Tarrytown, NY 1988–; honors: D.Sc. Univ. of London 1964, Faculty scholar Josiah Macy Jr. Found., NY 1974-75, Sc.D. Univ. of Cambridge 1986, Fellow Royal Soc., London 1988, Wakeman award Duke Univ. 1988, for. assoc. Inst. Medicine 1989; mem: Biochem. Soc., Am. Assn. Biol. Chemistry and Mol.

Biology, AAAS, Am. Soc. for Neurochem., Internat. Soc. Neurochem., Soc. for Neurosci., ACNP, Am. Acad. of Arts & Sci. (fellow 1993); publs: 200+ articles in var. sci. jours.; rec: travel. Res: 370 Golden Oak Dr Portola Valley 94028 Ofc: Dept. Neurobiology Stanford University Sch. of Medicine, Stanford 94305-5401

SHUKLA, PRADIP KANTILAL, educator, management consultant; b. Sept. 7, 1956, Ahmedabad, India, nat. U.S.A. 1978; s. Kantilal T. and Manju K. S.; m. Yatri P. (Thaker), Jan. 6, 1983; children: Monica b. 1985, Amy b. 1989; edn: AA in math., Compton Comm. Coll., 1976; BS in bus. admin./BA econ., CSU Long Beach, 1978, MBA in human resources mgmt., 1979; MS in bus. admin., USC, 1983; MEd, UCLA, 1983; PhD, UCLA, 1989; Calif. Std. secondary tchg. cred., Calif. Comm. Colls. instr., supr., chief adminstr. credentials; cert. in prodn & inventory mgmt. (CPIM) APICS, 1985. Career: lectr. in mgmt. and mktg., Calif. State Univs., Long Beach, L.A., Northridge, Fullerton, 1978-91; assoc. prof. mktg. and mgmt. Chapman Univ., 1991–; dir. instnl. res. Compton Coll., 1986-88; mgmt. cons. prin., 1980–; honors: Alpha Gamma Sigma, Beta Gamma Sigma, Omicron Delta Epsilon, Phi Delta Kappa, Phi Kappa Phi (past chapt. v.p.), Bank of Am. scholar, So. Calif. Edison scholarship finalist, TRW project achiev. scholar, UCLA Grad. Sch. of mgmt. doctoral stipend, CSULB Alumni Assn. Award, 49er gold life pass CSULB, Who's Who Among Students in Am. Univs., UCLA Outstanding Doctoral Graduate Alumni Award; mem: Acad. of Mgmt., We. Mktg. Educators Assn., Am. Mktg. Assn., Am. Ednl. Research Assn., APICS (1983-88); author software pgms.; Republican; Hindu; rec: poetry, photog. Res: 10492 Park Villa Circle Villa Park 92667

SHULMAN, ARTHUR JOSEPH, market research director; b. July 18, 1942, Brooklyn, N.Y.; s. Alex and Ethel S.; m. Rebecca Westberg; children Jennifer b. 1967, Kerrie b. 1971; edn: BS, Bklyn. Coll. 1963; MBA, Baroch Coll. 1966; PhD, City Univ. N.Y. 1973. Career: project dir. Newspaper Advt. Bureau, N.Y.C. 1966-67; research assoc. Advtg. Research Found. 1968-69; project dir. SSC&B 1964-70; research dir. Benton & Bowles, N.Y.C. and L.A. 1970-77; Shulman Research, Los Angeles; mem: Am. Mktg. Assn., Travel Research Assn.; designer Yes... You! game, 1987; author People & Other Animals; playwright: wrote "Joe Carbone's Job", "A Home", and "Afternoon at the Cemetry"; rec: basketball, writing, sports. Ofc: Shulman Research 6621 McLennan Ave Van Nuys 91406

SHULTZ, FRED TOWNSEND, consulting geneticist; b. Mar. 5, 1923, Grinnell, Iowa; s. J. Gordon and Katharine (Townsend) S.; m. Carolyn Covell, June 24, 1961; children: Trina Michele b. 1962, Rebecca Lynn b. 1963, Daniel Kenyon b. 1964, Brian Gregory b. 1965; edn: AB, Stanford Univ., 1947; PhD, UC Berkeley, 1952. Career: pres. Animal Breeding Consultants, Sonoma 1952–; director Biological Frontiers Inst., Sonoma 1962–; pres. Avian Allure, Sonoma 1990–; recipient Poultry Sci. Res. Award 1953; mem.: Poultry Sci. Assn., World Poultry Sci. Assn., World Aquaculture Soc., Am. Genetics Assn., others; inventor: Artificial seeds & nuts, 1992, co-inventor Abalone culture (patents); publs: num. research articles, 1950–; mil: 2d lt. USAF 1942-45; Republican; rec: sailing. Res: Box 313 Sonoma 95476

SHULTZ, GEORGE PRATT, former secretary of state, economics educator; b. Dec. 13, 1920, NYC; s. Birl E. and Margaret Lennox (Pratt) S.; m. Helena M. O'Brien, Feb. 16, 1946; children: Margaret Ann S. Tilsworth, Kathleen Pratt S. Jorgensen, Peter Milton, Barbara Lennox S. White, Alexander George; edn: BA Econs., Princeton Univ., 1942; PhD Indsl. Econs., MIT, 1949; Hon. doctorates Univ. Notre Dame, Loyola Univ., Univ. Pa., Univ. Rochester, Princeton Univ., Carnegie-Mellon Univ., Baruch Coll., NYC, Northwestern Univ. Career: faculty Mass. Inst. Technology 1949-57, assoc. prof. industrial relations 1955-57; prof. indsl. relations Grad. Sch. Bus., Univ. Chicago, 1957-68, dean sch., 1962-68; fellow Ctr. for Advanced Studies in Behavioral Scis., 1968-69; appt. U.S. Sec. Labor, 1969-70; dir. Office of Mgmt. and Budget, 1970-72; U.S. Sec. Treasury, and asst. to the Pres., 1972-74; chmn. Council on Econ. Policy, East-West Trade Policy com.; exec. v.p. Bechtel Corp., San Francisco 1974-75, pres. 1975-77, v.chmn. 1977-81; also dir.; pres. Bechtel Group Inc. 1981-82; prof. mgmt. and public policy Stanford Univ. 1974-82; chmn. Pres. Reagan's Economic Policy Advy. Bd.; U.S. Sec. of State 1982-89; prof. internat. economics Grad. Sch. Bus., Stanford Univ. 1989–, distinguished fellow Hoover Instn., Stanford 1989–; dir: Bechtel Group Inc., Gulfstream Aerospace Corp., AirTouch Commnns., Ziff-Davis Pub. Co.; chmn. J.P. Morgan Internat. Council, chmn. advy. council Inst. Internat. Studies, chmn. State of Calif. Governor's Economic Policy Advy. Bd.; mem. General Motors Corporate Advy. Council; mem: Am. Econ. Assn., Indsl. Relations Res. Assn. (pres. 1968), Nat. Acad. Arbitrators; author: Pressures on Wage Decisions, 1950, The Dynamics of a Labor Market, 1951, Labor Problems: Cases and Readings, 1953, w/T.A. Whisler, Managment Organization and the Computer, 1960, w/Arnold R. Weber, Strategies for the Displaced Worker, 1966, Guidelines, Informal Controls and the Market Place, 1966, w/A. Rees, Workers and Wages in the Urban Labor Market, 1970, w/Kenneth W. Dam, Economic Policy Beyond the Headlines, 1977, Turmoil & Triumph: My Years as Secretary of State, 1993, contbr. chpts. in books, articles; mil: capt. USMCR 1942-45. Ofc: Hoover Institution Stanford University Stanford 94305-6010

SICILIANO, A. VINCENT, bank president; b. July 19, 1950, Washington, D.C.; s. Rocco Carmine and Marian (Stiebel) S.; m. Susan Campbell, May 25, 1974; children: Michael Carmine b. 1983, David Douglas b. 1990; edn: BS environ. engring., BA human biol., Stanford Univ. 1972; MS environ. planning, UC Berkeley 1976. Career: coord. for coastal zone mgmt. Nat. Oceanic Atmospheric Adminstrn., WD. 1972-73; spl. asst. energy planning Calif. Coastal Commn., San Francisco 1974; planning cons. Calif. Coastal Commn. and Govs. Office, Sacto. 1975-76; internat. credit office Bank of Am., Taipei, Taiwan 1976-79, head planning and analysis group, Manila, Philippines 1979-82, v.p., section head, Singapore 1982-83; pres. Internat. Savings Bank, San Diego 1986-94; CEO, Danielson Trust Co., San Diego 1995–; chmn. LISC Adv. Bd.; chmn. Pacific Am. Comm. Found.; honors: Tau Beta Pi, F.E.Terman engring. scholastic achievement 1972, Beatrix Found. UD Regents, UC Berkeley fellowship 1974-76; bd. dirs. YMCA and other civic orgns.; Republican; Christian; rec: amateur radio, skiing. Ofc: Danielson Trust Co 525 B St San Diego 92101

SIDHU, GURMEL SINGH, academic research scientist, geneticist; b. May 23, 1943, Jullundur, India, naturalized U.S. 1991; s. Naranjan Singh and Kartar (Hoti) K.; m. Baljit Kaur, Mar. 23, 1979; children: Vikram b. 1980, Roop b. 1981; edn: BSc, 1960, MSc, 1962; PhD, Univ. British Col., Vancouver 1973. Career: postdoc. fellow S.F. Univ., Burnaby 1973-75, res. scientist, 1975-80; asst. prof. UN, Lincoln 1980-86; res. scientist, prof. CSU Fresno, 1986–; research pathologist Germain's, Fresno 1987–; awards: res. fellow UBC, Vancouver 1972, SFU, Burnaby 1973-75, Univ. Wis., Madison 1985; mem.: AAAS 1987–, Phytopath. Soc. USA (assoc. editor 1980-86), Crop Improvement Soc. India (assoc. editor 1984–); editor: Genetics of Plant Pathogenic Fungi (1989); rec: sports, poetry writing. Res: 1637 Gettysburg Clovis 93612 Ofc: Calif. State Univ. Fresno, Cedar and Shaw Fresno 93740

SIEBERT, ELEANOR DANTZLER, chemistry professor; b. July 18, 1941, Birmingham, Ala.; d. Walter Devotie and Eleanor Marie (Stone) Dantzler; m. Raymond Arthur Siebert, Dec. 30, 1967; children: Cynthia Marie b. 1973, Gregory Scott b. 1976; edn: BA, chem., Duke Univ. 1963; grad. courses, Seton Hall Univ. 1964-65; PhD, UCLA 1969, Grad. Sch. of Edn. 1970-71, postdoctoral, 1973; comm. coll. tchg. cred. 1971, secondary sch. tchg. cred. 1973. Career: res. chemist Gen. Chem. Div., Allied Chem. Corp., Morristown, NJ 1963-65; acting asst. prof. UCLA 1970-71; tchr. Westlake Sch., L.A. 1971-73; asst. prof. dept. physical scis. and math, Mount St. Mary's Coll. 1974-78, chair 1975–, assoc. prof. 1978-83, prof. 1983–; chair president's scholarship com. Mount St, Mary's Coll. 1987–, acad. planning com. 1993-95, pres. faculty assembly 1994-96, past mem num. coms.; vis. scholar UCLA 1981-82, res. assoc. 1982-85, vis. prof. 1989-90; tchr. Westlake Sch (summers 1988-90), pt. time tchr. 1990-91; awards and grants: project dir., 2 NSF grants, Mount St. Mary's Coll. 1976-79, 1987-89, participating faculty NSF grants, Mt. St. Mary's Coll. 1980-82, UCLA 1983-85, 84-85, prin. investigator NIH-MBRS Prog. 1986-89, grantee USC 1990-91, prin. investigator, steering com. NIH-MARC Prog. 1991–, SCST grant 1993, ACS/NSF travel grant 1994, Disting. Svc. Award, So. Calif. ACS 1994, Creative Chemistry award 1994; mem: AAAS, Am. Chemical Soc. (Chem. Edn. Div., chair we. regional conf. 1993, So. Calif. Sect.: chair internal affairs com, chair 1994, chair elect and prog. chair 1993, exec. bd. 1986-92, editor 1988-91, chair ednl. affairs com. 1983-85), Soc. for Coll. Sci. Tchrs. (exec com. 1983, edit. 1983-85, sec.-treas. 1985-88, pres. elect 1989-91, pres. 1991-93), Nat. Sci. Tchrs. Assn. (bd. dirs. 1991-93, budget & fin. com. 1992-94, coll. com. 1991-93, 94-96, jour. advy bd. 1991-93, 94-96, publs. com., chair articulation task force 1994, coll. vision's task force 1992, nat. convention planning com. 1991, ad hoc com. 1989), UCLA Chemists' Assn. (edit. 1982, advy bd. 1982–, pres. 1983-84, alumni council, adv. profl. orgns. 1985), Sigma Xi; author: Study Guide to Accompany CHEM ONE (McGraw-Hill, 1976), Foundations of Chemistry and Instructors' Manual (McGraw-Hill, 1982); co-author: Experimental Studies for General Chemistry (Holden-Day, Inc., 1971), Experiments for General Chemistry (Burgess Internat., 1977-78, 81, 89); contbg. editor: Jour. of Coll. Sci. Tchg. 1991-93, SCST Monograph, 1994; contbr. num. scientific articles to profl. jours. and publs., 1965–. Ofc: Mount St. Mary's College 12001 Chalon Rd Los Angeles 90049-1599

SIEGEL, GILBERT BYRON, educator; b. April 19, 1930, Los Angeles; s. Morris DeSagar and Rose (Vancott) S.; m. Darby Day Smith, Oct. 16, 1954; children: Clark Byron b. 1958, Holly May b. 1960; edn: BS pub. adminstrn., USC 1952; MS, 1957; PhD political sci.; Univ. Pittsburgh 1964. Career: adminstrv. analyst and mgr. County of Los Angeles, 1954-57; vis. asst. prof. USC in Tehran, Iran 1957-59; instr. Univ. Pittsburgh, 1959-61; vis. asst. prof. in Rio de Janeiro, 1961-63; asst., assoc. prof., prof. and assoc. dean Univ. So. Calif., Los Angeles 1965–, dir. USC Productivity Network 1985–; C.C. Crawford Disting. Prof. of Public Productivity 1994; cons. Brazilian govt. 1961, 76, 77, 79; evaluator USN Demonstration Project, China Lake and San Diego 1979-81; cons. UN in Bangkok 1981, USAID in Panama 1986; awards: Olson award So. Calif. Personnel Mgmt. Assn. 1984, Vargas Found. medal of merit 1975, Mosher award Pub. Adminstrn. Rev., W.D.C. 1967; mem: So. Calif. Personnel Mgmt. Assn. (bd.), Internat. Personnel Mgmt. Assn., Am. Am. Soc. Pub. Adminstrn., Pi Sigma ALpha, Pi Alpha Alpha; author: Pub. Employee Compensation and its role in Pub. Sector Strategic Management 1992; co-author Pub. Personnel Adminstrn. 1985, 89; ed. Breaking w. Orthodoxy in Pub. Adminstrn. 1980;

coauthor: Mgmt. in Pub. Systems 1986; editor Human Resource Mgmt. in Pub. Orgns. 1974; mil: sgt. AUS 1952-54; rec: classical music, travel. Res: 208 N Poinsettia Ave Manhattan Beach 90266 Ofc: Univ. So. Calif. School of Public Administration Los Angeles 90089-0041

SIEVERS, TARYN ANNETTE, securities company executive; b. June 24, 1960, Concord; d. Donald Eugene and Kathryn Marie (Doyle) Sievers; edn: BA info. & communications, CSU Chico 1981; BS bus. adminstrn., 1984. Career: v.p., asst. branch mgr. Dean Witter Reynolds, Oakland 1984–; tchr. Acalanes Sch. Dist., Lafayette 1988–; Alameda Sch. Dist. 1988–; Martinez Sch. Dist. 1988–; faculty mem. UC Berkeley Extension; awards: Diablo scholarship 1978, Nat. Sales Achievement Dean Witter 1985; mem: Diablo Scholarship Inc. (pres. bd. dirs. 1989–, v.p. 1988-89), Womens Athletic Club Oakland (bd. dirs. 1989–, asst. treas.), Cath. Charities Oakland; Cath.; rec: skiing, sailing, cooking. Ofc: Dean Witter 1 Kaiser Plaza Ste 1050 Oakland 94612

SIGAL, SANFORD DAVID, commercial and residential developer; b. Jan. 28, 1964, Los Angeles; s. Martin Irving and Gloria Kuth (Blatter) S.; m. Cindy Sisino, Mar. 12, 1988; children: Hayden b. 1991, Thea b. 1993; edn: BA, UCLA, 1987. Career: owner Am. Computer Software, Marina del Rey 1982-85; c.e.o. West Venture Devel., Encino 1994–, dir. commercial devel. 1985-94; mem. Internat. Council of Shopping Centers 1985–; civic: Mar Vista President's Club 1985–, City of Azusa Econ. Devel. Com. 1992–; pub. article (1991); Republican; Jewish; rec: skiing, computers. Ofc: West Venture Development 6345 Balboa Blvd Ste 225 Encino 91316

SIIPOLA, JOHN E(RNEST), business executive, entrepreneur; b. Dec. 22, 1943, Milford, Mass.; s. George Ernest and Doris (Seymour) S.; m. Edna L. Barrett, Apr. 23, 1965; children: Nikki Leigh b. 1976, Jacqueline Danielle b. 1988; edn: Univ. of Texas, Austin; BA (honors) bus. admin. Northeastern Univ., Boston 1972; BS (honors) computer sci. Northeastern Univ. 1976; grad. studies internat. economics. Career: software engr. to cons. mgr. Keane, Inc., Wellesley, Mass., Boston, Mass. and Detroit, Mich. 1965-70; dir. info. systems Dept. Public Health, Boston, Mass. 1970-72; cons. mgr. Arthur D. Little, Inc., 1972-74; sr. exec., dir., Source Services, Inc., Hartford, Conn. and San Francisco, Calif. 1975-84; founder, pres. Computer Alternatives, Inc., San Francisco 1984-87; pres. The Barrett Group, San Francisco 1988-92; pres. Barrett Publishing, Inc. 1992–; dir Big O Tires, Inc. (1988–, chmn. 1991-, ofc. of chief exec. 1994–); mgmt. cons. restructurings 1988–; author: num. prof. articles, 1970-;listed Int. Who's Who, Who's Who in Bus. and Fin., Std. and Poor's; mem: Nat. Assoc. Corp. Dir., Am. Mgmt. Assn., ASM, DPMA, Turnaround Mgt. Assoc., Conference Board, Internat. Platform Assn., Nat. Rifle Assn. (life); civic: C. of C., Booster Club, BPOE 1264; mil: US Navy 1962-68; Republican; Methodist; rec: golf, hunting, skiing. Ofc: 2533 N Carson St Ste1147 Carson City NV 89706

SILKISS, RONA ZEL, ophthalmic plastic surgeon; b. Oct. 19, 1957; d. Emanuel and Rose Silkiss; edn: BS, Northwestern Univ. 1976; MD, Northwestern Univ. Med. Sch., Chgo. 1980; lic. physician St. of Calif. 1981, St. of NY 1982; diplomate Nat. Bd. Med. Examiners 1981; cert.: Am. Bd. Pediatrics 1985, Am. Bd. Ophthalmology 1987. Career: pediatric intern Children's Hosp. of Los Angeles 1980-81, pediatric, PL-2, 1981-82; pediatric, PL-3, The New York Hosp., NY 1982-83; ophthalmology, PL-2, The Jules Stein Eye Inst.-UCLA 1983-84, ophthalmology, PL-3, 1984-85, ophthalmology, PL-4, 1985-86; fellowship in ophthalmic plastic, reconstructive and orbital surgery The Jules Stein Eye Inst./Henry I. Baylis, M.D., 1986-87; mission surgery: Kenya, 1987, Pakistan, 1989, Cambodia, 1992, Uzbekistan, 1993; lectr. Jules Stein Eye Inst.; asst. clin. prof. Calif. Pacific Med. Ctr. and UC Berkeley; cons. and invited speaker in field; honors: Arista Honor Soc., Salutatorian Bronx H.S. Sch. of Sci., Governor's Citation for Excellence, Alpha Lambda Delta, Dean's List Northwestern Univ., Am. Med. Women's Assn. award, Lange award, Parkinson's Disease Found. Fellowship, Merle Carson Prize for Pediatric Res., Jules Stein Inst. Res. award; mem: Alpha Omega Alpha, Am. Acad. Pediatrics (fellow), Am. Acad. Ophthalmology (fellow), Am. Soc. Ophthalmic Plastic and Reconstructive Surgery (fellow), Am. Coll. of Surgeons (fellow), Calif. Soc. Cosmetic Surgeons (advy. bd.), Calif. Assn. Ophthalmology, Am. Med. Women's Assn., CMA, Alameda-Contra Costa Med. Assn., San Francisco Med. Assn., East Bay Ophthalmology Med. Soc.; author: num. pub. articles and abstracts, 1981-94, 15 scientific presentations, 1988-95; contbg. author: Modern Practice in Orthognathic and Reconstructive Surgery (W.B. Saunders Co., 1991); rec: photography, Third World travel. Ofcs: 491 30th Street Ste 103 Oakland 94609, 22 Battery St Ste 905 San Francisco 94111, 122 La Casa Via Ste 221 Walnut Creek 94698, 2675 Stevenson Rd Fremont 94538

SILLS, DAVID GEORGE, jurist; b. Mar. 21, 1938, Peoria, Ill.; s. George Daniel and Mildred Mina (Luthy) S.; m. Susan Mildred La Croix, Dec. 12, 1989; edn: BS, Bradley Univ., 1959; LLB, Univ. of Ill., 1961. Career: pvt. law practice Orange County, Calif. 1965-85; elected Irvine City Council, 1976-85, mayor City of Irvine, 1976-77, 79-82, 84-85; judge Superior Ct., Orange County 1985-90; presiding justice Calif. Court of Appeal, 4th Dist. Div. 3, Santa Ana 1990–; chmn. Irvine Health Found. 1985–; mem: Orange County Bar Assn. 1965–, Banyard Inn 1990–; mil: capt. USMC 1960-62-65; Republican; rec: golf, jogging, history, travel. Ofc: Court of Appeal, 925 Spurgeon Santa Ana 92701

SILVA, RAYMOND ARNOLD, chartered life underwriter, chartered financial consultant; b. June 29, 1930, San Jose; s. Henry Francisco and Emily Eleanor (Fields) S.; m. Carolyn Helms, July 16, 1953; children: Terrence (stepson) b. 1951, Jennifer b. 1954, Jeffrey b. 1955, Laurie b. 1958, Erin b. 1961, Shannon b. 1972; edn: BA, San Jose State Univ. 1952, MA 1956; Chartered Life Underwriter (CLU) The Am. Coll. 1965; Chartered Financial Consultant (ChFC) The Am. Coll. 1984. Career: physical educator, athletic coach Berkeley High Sch., 1955-59, Camden H.S., San Jose 1959-62; field rep. The Guardian Life Insurance Co. of Am., San Jose 1962-95, senior sales cons. The Guardian Life Ins. Co. of Am., NY, NY 1981–; mem. bd. trustees (pres. 1977-79) Campbell Union H.Sch. Dist. 1973-81; dir. San Jose State Univ. Found. 1982-90; dir. (pres. 1974-76) The Spartan Found., San Jose 1968–; honors: agent of yr., San Jose Life Underws. Assn. 1978, Guardian Life Leaders Club (nat. pres. 1978), Guardian Life CLU Assn. (pres. 1977-79), life & qualifying mem. Million Dollar Roundtable 1971–, Top of the Table 1986; elected trustee Am. Coll. 1992-95; mem: Am. Soc. of CLU & ChFC (pres. 1993-94, pres. elect 1992-93, v.p. 1991-92, we. reg. v.p. 1981-82), Assn. for Advanced Underwr., Santa Clara Co. Estate Planning Council (pres. 1982-83), San Jose Rotary (mem. 1972–, bd. 1983-85, pres. 1992-93), Santa Clara Council Boy Scouts Am. (bd. 1985–, Silver Beaver Award 1988, Distinguished Citizen Award 1989); mil: lt. USNR (ret.), active duty 1952-54; Republican; Presbyterian; rec: tennis, raquetball, ski. Res: 185 Surmont Court Los Gatos 95032 Ofc: Guardian Life, 1602 The Alameda Ste 200 San Jose 95126

SILVER, DIANE SOLOMON, physician; b. Sept. 1, 1943, Passaic, N.J.; d. Benjamin and Ethel (Bloomfield) Solomon; m. Brian Robert Silver, June 16, 1968; children: Eli b. 1973, Adam b. 1974, Noah b. 1979; edn: AB, Douglass Coll. (div. of Rutgers Univ.) 1965; MA, Harvard Univ. 1966, post-grad. study 1966-67; med. sch., Tufts Univ. Sch. of Medicine 1967-68; MD, Univ. of So. Calif. Sch. of Medicine 1971; diplomate Am. Bd. of Dermatology. Career: systems analyst and computer programmer U.S. Navy, Bayonne, N.J. (summer) 1964; med. internship St. Mary's Hosp., San Francisco 1971-72; physician VD and family planning clinics/VD controller, Napa Co. Health Dept., Napa, Calif. 1972-76; residency in dermatology Stanford Univ. Med. Ctr. 1976-79; pvt. practice, dermatology, Napa 1979– staff. affiliation, Queen of the Valley Hosp.; lectr. in field; honors: Douglass Coll. Dean's List, Phi Beta Kappa, Pi Mu Epsilon; mem: Napa Co. Med. Soc., CMA, Pacific Dermatologic Assn., S.F. Dermatologic Assn., Am. Acad. of Dermatology; contbg. author: articles pub. in med. jours., 1982. Ofc: 1100 Trancas St Napa 94558

SILVER, LAWRENCE ALAN, psychiatric social worker; b. Oct. 10, 1946, Highland Park, Mich.; s. Herbert Martin and Edna (Keller) S.; m. Hollis Lee Dec, May 2, 1981; edn: BA, Wayne St. Univ. 1971; MSW, Univ. Mich. Ann Arbor 1974; lic. clin. social worker Calif. (1978). Career: clin. social worker Detroit Psychiatric Inst., Mich. 1974-76; St. Joseph Mercy Hosp., Pontiac 1976; VA Mental Hygiene Clinic, San Diego 1977; direct service supr. Harmonium Inc. 1978; social worker San Diego Co. dept. soc. services 1978-80, sr. psychiatric social worker Hillcrest Facility 1980-85, East County Mental Health, El Cajon 1985-94, edn. liaison 1988; med. social worker The Elizabeth Hospice, Escondido 1994–; oral commr. Bd. Behav. Sci. Examiners 1979; honors: Calif. St. Assembly Resolution 1986, San Diego County service award 1988; Nat. Assn. Social Workers (state del. Mich. 1976, chair inservice edn. 1976), Univ. Mich. Alumni Assn., S.D. Zoological Soc.; publs: 2 newspaper articles, 1984; Republican (Rep. Nat. Com.); rec: photog., travel. Res. 1029 Park Hill Dr Escondido 92025 Ofc: The Elizabeth Hospice 1845 E Valley Parkway Escondido 92027

SILVERA, JOHN STEVEN, doctor of chiropractic; b. June 8, 1954, Burbank, Calif.; s. Errol Karl and Mildred Emma (Berry) S.; m. Deborah Ann, Aug. 26, 1979; children: Jordan John b. 1990, Braighlee b. 1993; edn: AA, L.A. Pierce, Woodland Hills, Calif. 1974; BS, UCLA 1977; DC (magna cum laude, Dean's List), L.A. Coll. of Chiropractic, Whittier, Calif. 1982. Career: beach lifeguard (summers), L.A. County 1975-83; chiropractor, private practice, Northridge, Calif. 1983–; mem: Le-Tip Woodland Hills (v.p. 1988-90, 1992-93; pres. 1990-91); Creston Club (Help Youth Found.), Burbank, Calif. 1991-92; author: Life Reflections (in process); rec: exercise, outdoors, gardening, writing, reading. Ofc: Silvera Chiropractic 8555 Reseda Blvd. Northridge 91324

SILVERMAN, EDWARD I., lawyer; b. May 5, 1952, Chicago, Ill.; s. Robert S. and Beverly (Frank) S.; m. Sandra Joan Moss, Nov. 22, 1987; children: Stacey b. 1989, Eric b. 1992; edn: BA with high distinction, Univ. Mich. Ann Arbor 1974; JD, UCLA 1977; admitted St. Bar Calif. (1977), U.S. Dist. Ct. (So. Dist. Calif. 1977, Cent. Dist. Calif. 1984), U.S. Ct. Appeals 9th cir. (1981). Career: law clk. to Hon. L.C. Nielsen Fed. Ct. San Diego 1977-79; assoc. atty. Rogers & Wells 1980-85; self-employed San Diego 1987; assoc. atty. Procopio Cory Hargreaves & Savitch 1988-89, ptnr. 1990–; judge pro tem San Diego Municipal Ct. 1984–; judge pro tem San Diego Superior Ct. 1990–; honors: Phi Eta Sigma, Phi Beta Kappa, UCLA Moot Ct. 1975-77, Wiley W. Manuel Award for pro bono legal services 1991–, Martindale-Hubbell a-v rating; mem: San Diego Co. Bar Assn.; rec: skiing. Ofc: Procopio Cory Hargreaves & Savitch 530 B St Ste 2100 San Diego 92101

SIMMONS, PAULA JOAN, marketing consultant; b. Dec. 1, 1961 Long Beach, Calif.; d. Elton Newman and Joan Marilyn (Perrin) Rockwell; m. Christopher Laird Simmons, July 25, 1992; 1 child: Abby b. 1981; edn: Calif. State Univ. Honors Program, Long Beach, Calif., 1979-81, 1994–. Career: photographic supr., Olan Mills, Inc., Scottsdale, Ariz. 1982-84; asst. mdsg. mgr., Max Factor & Co., Hollywood, Calif. 1984-87; sr. account exec., Transworld Systems, Inc., Long Beach 1987-89; marketing cons., Sebastian Internat., Woodland Hills 1989-91; marketing cons., Rusk, Inc., L.A. 1992-93; acct. mgr. Western Cities Title 1993-94; mktg. cons. Select Graphics 1995–; mem. NAFE, Wash., DC 1986–; awards: Top Regional Sales award, Pacific Div. Transworld Systems, Long Beach 1988; Outstanding Line Devel. award, Sebastian Internat., Woodland Hills 1990, 91; mem: PTA 1986–, Amnesty Internat 1986-90, Parent advy. council 1986-90, Lakewood Artists Guild, Lakewood, Calif. 1976-80; creative works: published poet and writer; Independent; rec: English lit. studies, writing, running. Ofc: 6735 Odessa Ave Van Nuys 91406

SIMON, JOHN J, II, chemist; b.July 8, 1919, New England, No.Dak.; s. John J. and Anna (Stengel) S.; m. Catherine, Jan. 6, 1951 (div.); children: Michael b. 1951, Martin b. 1951, Roberta b. 1954, John b. 1955, Chris b. 1968; edn: AA, N.D. St. Univ. 1941; BS, Univ. Portland 1950. Career: tchr., New England, N.D. 1941-42; chemist, metallurgist Oreg. Steel Mills, Portland 1944-50; chemist Northwest Testing Labs. 1950-55; Nalley Foods, Tacoma, Wash. 1955-60, lab. mgr. Haley Foods, Hillsboro, Oreg. 1960-64; Norbest Turkey Assn., Salt Lake City 1964-69; research mgr. Sun Diamond Corp., Stockton 1969-84; cons.: U.S. Govt., Santiago, Chile 1985, Demsapar, Indonesia 1986, All Foods Consultants, Yuba City 1983–; awards: Internat. Exec. Service Corp. Outstanding Mem. 1985.

SIMONS, ROBERT ALLAN, lawyer; b. Dec. 13, 1947, Chicago, Ill.; s. Harry Lee and Cyrile Rowena (LaVine) S.; m. Linda Lee Treitman, June 28, 1970 (div. 1980); m. Kathleen Ann Flynn, Nov. 9, 1982; edn: BS, So. Ill. Univ. 1969; JD, Loyola Univ. (Chgo.) 1972. Career: asst. contracts mgr. Sperry Univac, Los Angeles 1974-77; gen. counsel Info. Systems Div., Control Data Corp., Santa Clara 1977-81; corp. counsel Dialog Info Services Inc., Palo Alto (now Knight-Ridder Information, Inc.) 1981–; mem: Info. Industry Assn. (co-chair nat. security task force 1987–), Santa Clara Co. Bar Assn. (co-chair corp. counsel sect. 1987–). Ofc: Knight-Ridder Information Inc 2440 El Camino Real Mountain View 94040

SIMPSON, BARCLAY, manufacturing company executive; b. May 25, 1921, Oakland; s. Walter Chapin and Jessie B. (Smith) S.; m. Joan Devine, Oct. 10, 1945; children: John b. 1946, Anne b. 1948, Jean b. 1951, Julie b. 1964, Amy b. 1967, Elizabeth b. 1967; m. 2d. Sharon Hanley, June 8, 1974; edn: BS in bus. admin., UC Berkeley, 1966. Career: chmn./CEO Simpson Mfg. Co., Inc. San Leandro 1956–; dir. Barclay Simpson Fine Arts, Lafayette 1982–; dir: McFarland Energy, Santa Fe Springs 1976–, Civic Bank Corp., Oakland 1985–, Calendar-Robinson Ins., S.F. 1980–; elected dir. Bay Area Rapid Transit 1977-88; bd. trustees: John Muir Hosp. 1962-76, Calif. Coll. of Arts & Crafts 1986–, University Art Museum, Berkeley; mil: lt. cmdr. USN 1942-46, USNR 1946-60; art collector.

SIMPSON, JAMES DELBERT, JR., surgeon; b. Dec. 22, 1943, Estacada, Ore.; s. James Delbert Simpson, Sr. and Fannie Charlotte (Shannon) S.; m. Nancy Elizabeth Wonderly, Aug. 19, 1965 (dec. 1993); children: Gregory b. 1974, Elizabeth b. 1976; edn: BA, Andrews Univ., Berrien Springs, MI 1966; MD, Loma Linda Univ. 1970; diplomate Am. Bd. of Surgery 1977. Career: specialty training-surgery, Loma Linda Univ. 1970-75; surgeon, Loma Linda Univ., Saigon Adventist Hosp., South Vietnam 1975; surgeon, pvt. practice, Centralia, Wash. 1976-79; asst. prof. surgery Loma Linda Univ. 1979-87; surgeon, pvt. practice, St. Helena Hosp., Deer Park, Calif. 1987–; honors: listed Outstanding Young Men of Am. 1966; fellow Am. Coll. of Surgeons 1983–; editor Loma Linda Univ. Surgery Jour. 1980-87; inventor/patentee, water ski instruction device, 1985; rec: flight instr. single & multi-engine/instrument. Res: 660 Sanitarium Rd Deer Park 94576 Ofc: M. Simpson, M.D. PO Box 387 Deer Park 94576

SIMPSON, TIMOTHY WINSTON, teacher; b. Oct. 4, 1957, Los Angeles; s. Walter Lowell and Bessie (Jones) S.; edn: BA sociology, UCLA 1980. Career: physical dir. 28th Street YMCA, Los Angeles 1979-83; asst. mgr. Thrifty Drugs, Santa Monica 1983-85; fitness gym mgr. Jack La Lanne, Inglewood 1985-87; admissions rep. and coll. outreach coord. Watterson Coll., West Covina 1987-88; child care worker Childrens Baptist Home, Inglewood 1988–; teacher, 1988–; math teacher Washington Prep High 1992-93; math tchr. Littlerock H.S. 1993–; awards: Bank of Am. vocat. arts, 1975, Calif. St. scholar, 1975, Phi Beta Sigma; Democrat; Seventh Day Adventist (SDA peer counselor Univ. Ch. 1988–); rec: singing, sailing, marathon (L.A. Marathon finishing times: 1991-5:46, 92- 5:19, 93- 5.21, 94- 5:16, 95- 4:46). Res: 3801 Fernwood Street Rosamond 93560

SIMPSON, WILLIAM BRAND, economist, educator; b. Nov. 30, 1919, Portland, Ore.; s. John Alexander and Janet Christie (Brand) S.; m. Ruth Decker, June 12, 1957; edn: BA, Reed Coll. 1942; MA, Columbia Univ. 1943; PhD, Claremont Grad. Sch. 1971. Career: consultant Nat. Defense Mediation Bd., Portland 1941-42, US Dept. of Interior, Portland 1942, head Economic Sect.

Counter-Intelligence Office, Manila, 1945; spl. representative Supreme Cmdr. of Allied Powers, Japan, 1945-46; cons. U.S. War Dept. Tokyo, 1947; asst. research dir./exec. dir. Cowles Commn. for Resrch in Econ., Univ. of Chgo. 1948-53; co-founder and bd. mem. Inst. of Soc. and Personal Relations, Oakland 1955-61; prof. economics, CSU Los Angeles 1958–; mng. editor and co-ed. Econometrica, 1948-53; cons. to var. univs. and higher edn. agencies, 1954–; honors: Phi Beta Kappa 1942; Fellow Nat. Soc. Sci. Research Council, 1946-48; mem: Econometric Soc. (internat. secty 1948-52); AAUP (state pres. 1975-76, chmn. Com. on Issues and Policy 1981–, Nat. Com. on Econ. Status of Acad. Prof. 1976-79, Nat. Council 1978-81, Com. on Govt. Rels. 1982-88); Am. Economic Assn. (ch. panel on polit. discrimination 1978-80); Am. Assn. for Higher Edn.; ACLU; Cong. of Faculty Assns., Reed "Take Charge" mentor L.A. area 1991–, Claremont Grad Sch. Alumni Council 1993–, advr. Japanese Assn. for Res. on Forcibly Brought Chinese 1991–, advr. Japan Pub. TV 1993; author: Cost Containment in Higher Education (Praeger) 1991; editor: Managing with Scarce Resources (Jossey-Bass) 1993; profl. jour. articles on economics of higher edn.; mil: spl. agt. counter-intell. US Army 1943-46; Democrat; Unitarian; rec: travel, Scottish postal history, pre-Columbian sculpture. Res: POB 41526 Los Angeles 90041 Ofc: California State University 5151 State University Dr Los Angeles 90032

SIMS, RICHARD MAURY, III, appellate court justice; b. Dec. 3, 1943, Oakland; s. Richard M. S.; m. Georgiana Carroll, June 21, 1975; children: Peter b. 1976, Christopher b. 1978; edn: BA, with honors, Amherst Coll. 1965; JD, Harvard Law Sch. 1968. Career: atty. VISTA volunteer S.F. 1968-70; asst. exec. dir. S.F. Com. on Crime 1970-72; gen. counsel & legal ofcr. S.F. Sheriff's Dept. 1972-73; Thelen, Marrin, Johnson & Bridges S.F. 1973-80 (ptnr. 1978-80); superior ct. judge Placer Co. 1980-83; assoc. justice 3rd Dist. Ct. of Appeal Sacto. 1983–; adj. prof. law Univ. S.F. Sch. of Law 1972-75; mem: S.F. Bar Assn. (bd. dirs. 1979-80), S.F. Barristers Club (pres. 1974), S.F. Civil Grand Jury (actg. foreman 1975-76), Rotary Internat.; rec: family, gardening, hiking, painting, skiing. Ofc: Court of Appeals 914 Capitol Mall, Rm 119 Sacramento 95814

SINHA, DIPENDRA KUMAR, mechanical engineer; b. Feb. 18, 1945, Patna, Bihar, India; s. Jogendra Prasad and Saraswati (Varma) S.; m. Basanti Srivastava, July 30, 1971; children: Priyamvada b. 1972, Udayan b. 1986; edn: BSME, Patna Univ., India 1967; Postgrad. Diploma in bus. mgmt. Xavier Labor Relations Inst., India 1976; MSME, Univ. Manchester, U.K. 1978, PhD M.E., 1981. Career: asst. design engr. Tata Steel, Jamshedpur, Bihar, 1970-75, devel. engr. 1975-76; asst. prof. Univ. Manitoba, 1981-84; assoc. prof. Univ. Wis., Platteville 1985-87; assoc. prof., prof. mech. engring. dept. San Francisco State Univ., 1987–; mem: ASEE 1987–, ASME (assoc. 1986–), Am. Orgn. for the Devel. of Bihar (v.p. 1994-96); author: Engineering Graphics With Autocad, 1990, Computer Programming and Applications , 1994; coauthor: FEM by Microcomputers, 1988, Advanced Machine Design by MicroComputer, 1989, Computer Aided Design - An Integrated Approach, 1992, Computer Programming and Applications, 1994; Hinduism; rec: numismatics, photography, Shakespeare. Ofc: San Francisco State University 1600 Holloway Ave San Francisco 94132

SINNOTT, RANDOLPH PAUL, lawyer; b. April 21, 1954, Mineola, N.Y.; s. John and Joan Martha (Guggisberg) S.; m. Denise Shawn Kociemba, July 21, 1979; children: Randolph b. 1984, Erica b. 1985, Alexandra b. 1987; edn: BA, Univ. Mich. 1976; JD, USC, 1982; admitted St. Bar Calif. Career: atty. Gibson Dunn & Crutcher, Los Angeles 1982-92; atty. Sinnott, Dito, Moura & Puebla, L.A. 1993–; mem: Am. Bar Assn., L.A. Co. Bar Assn.; mil: major USMCR 1976–; Lutheran. Ofc: Sinnott Dito Moura & Puebla 550 South Hope St Ste 2000 Los Angeles 90071-2604

SINSHEIMER, ROBERT LOUIS, educator; b. Feb. 5, 1920, Washington, D.C.; s. Allen S. and Rose (Davidson) S.; m. Joan Hirsch, Aug. 6, 1943 (div. 1972); m. Karen B. Keeton, Aug. 1, 1981; children: Lois b. 1948, Kathy b. 1950, Roger b. 1955; edn: BS, MIT 1941; MS, 1942; PhD, 1948. Career: research assoc. MIT, Cambridge, Mass. 1948-49; prof. Iowa State Coll., Ames, Iowa 1949-57; Calif. Inst. Tech., Pasadena 1957-68, prof., chmn. 1968-77; chancellor UC Santa Cruz 1977-87; prof. UCSB 1988–; tchr., researcher Iowa State Coll., Ames 1949-57; Calif. Inst. Tech., Pasadena 1957-77; acad. adminstr. UC Santa Cruz 1977-87; tchr., researcher UCSB 1988–; awards: Calif. Museum of Sci. & Industry Scientist of Year 1968, Royal Acad. Netherlands Beijerinck Medal 1969; mem: Nat. Acad. Sci., Am. Acad. Arts & Sics., Am. Soc. Biochemistry & Molecular Biology, Biophysical Soc.; 250+ articles pub. in sci. jours. 1946–; rec: travel, photog. Res: 4606 Via Cayente Santa Barbara 93110 Ofc: Univ. of Calif. Dept. of Biological Sciences Santa Barbara 93106

SIRI, JEAN BRANDENBURG, community activist; b. Mar. 11, 1920, Lakota, N.Dak.; d. Tunis Orville and Edith Marion (Molloy) Brandenburg; m. William Emil Siri, Dec. 3, 1949; children: Lynn Kimsey b. 1953, Ann Siri b. 1955; edn: BS, Jamestown Coll., 1942; RN, UC San Francisco, 1945; pre-med. UC Berkeley 1945-47. Career: biologist Donner Lab., Lawrence Lab., Berkeley 1947-54; appt. Contra Costa County Grand Jury, Martinez 1967; advy. council Calif. Solid Waste Mgmt./Resource Recovery 1973-75; pub. rep. BA SWM Plan, Oakland 1976, advy. com. EMTF-ABAG 208 Plan, Oakland 1977, mem. EB MUD land use com., wastewater treatment com., Oakland 1977-79; elected bd., chair Stege Sanitary Dist., 1975-79, com. on aging 1985-92; elected El Cerrito City Council 1980-84, 1987-91, mayor 1982-83, 1988-89, chair West County Mayors 1989; Contra Costa Co. bds: Disaster Council 1983, Hazardous Waste Task Force 1984-85, Haz. Mat. Commn. 1986-93, Envir. Health Coord. Council 1985-87, cochair Pub. and Envir. Health Advy. Bd. 1987–, homeless advoc. Wild Women (W. Contra Costa) 1987–, cochair Homeless Advy. Council 1989-93; JPA mem. Solid Waste, West Co. 1988-89, Transp. 1990-91; awards: Sol Feinstone Nat. Environ. Award, Syracuse Univ. 1976-77, Clean Air award Am. Lung Assn. Santa Clara/San Benito Ctys 1976, Pott Award for Individual Achiev. in toxics 1986, Wall of Fame award City of El Cerrito 1995; mem: LWV West Contra Conserv. League (pres., 1968–), LWV-BA Haz. Mats. Com. 1986, Pol. Act. Coal. for Envir. (co-ch.1974-76), People for Open Space (Contra Costa rep. 1967–), Sierra Club 1965–, Audubon Soc., Contra Costa Shoreline Parks Com., Richmond 1965–, NAACP 1980–, Gray Panthers of W.Contra Costa Co. (co-chair, v.p. 1992), Bay Area League of Conserv. Voters (bd. 1979), El Cerrito Hist. Soc. (v.p. 1984), Elmwood Inst. (peer 1989-91), Women's Therapy Ctr. (bd. 1986), Women's Forum (charter 1985–), elected dir. ward 1 E. Bay Reg. Park Bd. 1992–; mil: lt. USNR WVS 1942-45; Democrat; avocation: advocacy. Res: 1015 Leneve Pl El Cerrito 94530

SIRIGNANO, WILLIAM ALFONSO, aerospace and mechanical engineer, educator; b. Apr. 14, 1938, Bronx, NY; s. Anthony P. and Lucy (Caruso) S.; m. Lynn Haisfield, Nov. 26, 1977; children: Jacquelyne Hope b. 1970, Monica Ann b. 1971, Justin Anthony b. 1988; edn: B. Aero. Engring., Rensselaer Poly. Inst. 1959; PhD, Princeton Univ. 1964. Career: mem. res. staff Guggenheim Labs., Aerospace/Mech. Scis., Princeton Univ. 1964-67; asst. prof. to prof. Aerospace/Mech. Scis., Princeton Univ. 1967-79, dept. dir. grad. studies 1974-78; George Tallman Ladd Prof., head of mech. engring. dept., Carnegie-Mellon Univ. 1979-85; dean Sch. of Engring., UC Irvine 1985-94, prof. mech./aerospace engring. 1985–; vis. res. scientist Sandia Nat. Labs., Livermore, Calif. (summers 1978, 84); vis. scholar UC Berkeley (summer 1984); vis. prof. Princeton Univ. 1990; cons: Sandia Labs., Livermore 1972–, Gen. Motors Allison Gas Turbine Div., Indianapolis, Ind. 1987–, Metrolaser, Tustin, Calif. 1989–, United Technologies Res. Ctr., E. Hartford, Ct. 1989–; awards: Guggenheim Fellowship 1959-61, RPI Scholarship 1956-59, Ricketts Price 1959, N.Y. State Regents Scholarship 1955-59, Sigma Xi, Tau Beta Pi and Sigma Gamma Tau 1959, United Aircraft Res. Fellow 1973-74, Edward G. Pendray Aerospace Literature Award, AIAA 1991, Freeman Scholar Award, ASME 1992, Propellants and Combustion Award, AIAA 1992, UC Irvine Alumni Disting. Res. Award 1992, IDERS Oppenheim Award 1993, President's Award, Orange Co. Engring. Council 1994, Am. Electronics Assn., Orange Co. Council 1994; mem: AIAA (fellow 1987, chmn. solid rockets tech. com. 1969-70, mem. propellants and combustion tech. com. 1980-85, publications com. 1989–), ASME (fellow 1989, mem. combustion com., Heat Transfer Div. 1980–), AAAS (fellow 1992), Inst. for Advancement of Engring. (fellow 1994), Combustion Inst. (bd. dirs. and exec. com. 1982–, treas. 1982-84, vice chmn. Ea. Sect. 1977-79, chmn. 1979-81), Inst. for Dynamics of Explosions and Reactive Systems (bd. dirs. and v.p. 1989–), Nat. Acad. of Scis.-Nat. Res. Council (com. on microgravity res. 1990-94, com. chmn. and space studies bd. mem. 1991-94); author or contbg. author: num. sections and articles to books, 1972–, articles to profl. jours.; editl bd. Combustion Sci. and Technology (jour.), 1970-79, 1990–; assoc. tech. editor, Jour. of Heat Transfer, 1986–; editl. advy. bds.: Progress in Energy and Combustion Sci., 1982–, Atomisation and Sprays, 1989–, Numerical Heat Transfer, 1990–, Archivum Combustions, 1992–; co-editor: Modern Research Topics in Aerospace Propulsion, 1990, ICDERS, Progress in Astronautics and Aeronautics, AIAA, 1991, 93; editor: Combustion Science and Technology Book Series, 1991–; prog. reviewer: NSF, 1972–, Army Res. Ofc., 1976–, DOE, 1978–; prog. subcom. for 10 Symposia on Combustion, prog. steering com. for 5 Symposia; reviewer for 15 jours./books. Ofc: Dept of Mechanical and Aerospace Engineering University of California Irvine 92717

SKALA, RICHARD K., doctor of chiropractic; b. Dec. 17, 1950, Queens, N.Y.; s. Richard B. and Katherine J. (Sperling) S.; m. Cynthia M. Camello, Mar. 9, 1974; children: Erin b. 1974, Matthew b. 1976, Lindsay b. 1979, Elizabeth b. 1980; edn: BS in biology, State Univ. N.Y., Albany 1972; doctor of chiropractic, Palmer Coll. of Chiropractic, Davenport, Iowa 1976. Career: assoc. doctor Culver Chiropractic Clinic, Los Altos 1976-77; founding partner Palo Alto Chiropractic Clinic, Palo Alto 1977-80; founder Stanford Chiropractic Clinic, Palo Alto 1980-83; founder East Bay Chiropractic Clinic, Fremont 1983–; partner Key Health Management, Fremont 1989–; state apptd. qualified medical evaluator, Calif. Industrial Med. Council, San Francisco 1992–; awards: Diplomate, Nat. Bd. of Examiners 1976; Diplomate, Internat. Coll. Applied Kinesiology, Detroit, Mich. 1978; Certified Fellow, Am. Acad. of Spinal Biomechanics, Manchester, N.H. 1988; Certified Disability Examiner, Calif. Chiropractic Assn., Sacramento 1990; mem: Am. Chiropractic Assn., Council on Neurology, Council on Roentgenology, Optimist Internat. (life mem., past pres.) 1981-82; Evangelical; rec: reading, flying, skiing. Ofc: 3555 Beacon Ave Fremont 95438

SKOTHEIM, ROBERT ALLEN, educator, museum president; b. Jan. 31, 1933, Seattle; s. Sivert Olaus and Marjorie (Allen) S.; m. Nadine Esther Vail, June 14, 1953; children: Marjorie b. 1956, Kris b. 1957, Julia b. 1961; edn: BA,

Univ. Washington, Seattle, 1955, MA, 1958, PhD, 1962. Career: asst. prof. Wayne State Univ., Detroit 1963-66; assoc. prof. UC Los Angeles, 1966-67; prof. Univ. Colorado, Boulder 1967-72; provost, hobart, Wm. Smith Colls., Geneva, N.Y. 1972-75; pres. Whitman Coll., Walla Walla, Wash. 1975-88; pres. Huntington Library, Art Collections, Botanical Gardens, San Marino 1988–; dir. Pacificorp, Portland 1985-88; awards: John Simon Guggenheim fellow, N.Y. 1967-68; mem. Am. Hist. Assn. 1962–, Org. of Am. Historians 1962–, Am. Antiquarian Soc. 1989–; dir. Forest Lawn Memorial Park 1995–; clubs: Princeton (N.Y.), Rainier (Seattle), Washington Athletic (Seattle), Twilight (Pasadena), Calif. (L.A.), Sunset (L.A.); author: American Intellectual Histories and Historians (Princeton Press, 1966). Res: 1650 Orlando Rd San Marino 91108 Ofc: Huntington Library 1151 Oxford San Marino 91108

SLAUGHTER, JOHN BROOKS, college president; b. Mar. 16, 1934, Topeka, Kans.; m. Ida Bernice Johnson, Aug. 31, 1956; children: John Brooks, Jr. b. 1959, Jacquelyne Michelle b. 1964; edn: undergrad. Washburn Univ. 1951-53, BSEE, Kansas St. Univ., 1956, MS engring., UCLA, 1961, PhD engring. sci., UC San Diego, 1971; reg. profl. engr., Wash. Career: physical sci. adminstr. and hd. Naval Electronics Lab. Ctr., 1960-75; dir. and prof. elec. engring. Applied Physics Lab., Univ. Wash., 1975-77; asst. dir. for Astronomical, Atmospheric, Earth and Ocean Scis., Nat. Sci. Found. 1977-79, dir. 1980-82; acad. v.p. & provost Wash. State Univ. 1979-80; chancellor Univ. of Maryland, Coll. Park 1982-88; pres. Occidental Coll., Los Angeles 1988–; dir: ARCO, Avery Dennison Corp., IBM, Monsanto Co., Northrop Grumman; awards: Whiting scholar 1951-53, Republic Aviation award best speech on airpower 1955, Sigma Tau 1954, Eta Kappa Nu 1954, NELC scientist of yr. 1965, NELC fellow 1969, UCLA engring. alumnus of yr. 1978, disting. svc. NSF 1979, Tau Beta Pi 1980, disting. svc. in engring. Kans. St. Univ. 1981, alumnus of yr. UCSD 1982, Nat. Acad. Engring. 1982, Topeka H.S. Hall of Fame 1983, Unity Media Award Lincoln Univ. 1985, disting. alumnus Washburn Univ. 1985, U.S. Black engr. of yr. 1987, Phi Beta Kappa (hon.) 1988, UCLA Medal 1989, Roger Revelle Award UCSD 1991, Am. Soc. for Engring. Edn. Hall of Fame 1993, named Kansan of Yr. by Kansas Native Sons & Daughters 1994, rec'd. Hon. Doctorates- Washburn Univ. of Topeka 1992, Calif. Lutheran Univ. 1991, Alfred Univ. 1991, Pomona Coll. 1989, Univ. of the Pacific 1989, Kansas State Univ. 1988, HDL, Morehouse Coll. 1988, Bowie St. Coll. 1987, Univ. Miami 1983, Rensselaer Polytech. Inst. 1981, Univ. Ill. 1986, SUNY 1986, Univ. Toledo 1986, Texas Southern Univ. 1984, Univ. Mass. 1983, Wayne State Univ. 1983, Ea. Mich. Univ. 1983, Notre Dame 1982, Univ. Md. 1982, Tuskegee Inst. 1981, USC 1981, ; mem: IEEE (fellow 1977), AAAS (fellow 1978), NAACP (life 1985), Town Hall of Calif. (bd. govs. 1990), LA World Affairs Council (bd. govs. 1990), Am. Acad. of Arts and Scis. 1993; co-editor Computers and Electrical Engring. internat. jour. (Pergamon Press), contbr. num. articles to sci. and higher edn. jours.; Presbyterian; rec: model R.R., tennis. Office of the President, Occidental College 1600 Campus Rd Los Angeles 90041

SLOCUM, CHARLES BRUCE, futurist, strategic planner; b. July 15, 1958, Mt. Holly, N.J.; s. Bruce and Dorothy (McCarraher) S.; edn: BS, TV/Radio, Syracuse Univ., 1980; MBA strat. plng., Wharton Sch. Univ. Pa., 1985. Career: research analyst ABC-TV, NY, NY 1980-81; research supvr. ABC-TV, Los Angeles 1981-83; game show judge NBC-TV, Burbank 1985; senior fin. analyst Paramount Pictures, Hollywood 1986-87; dir. industry analysis Writers Guild of America, L.A. 1987–; cons. entertainment industry 1989–; columnist WGA Jour., L.A. 1988–; guest speaker Writers Connection, Sunnyvale 1989; mem. Acad. of TV Arts & Scis.; Presbyterian. Res: 4735 N Sepulveda Blvd #222 Los Angeles 91403 Ofc: Writers Guild of America 8955 Beverly Blvd West Hollywood 90048

SLOVER, ARCHY F., chemist; b. July 8, 1920, Oshkosh, Wisc.; s. Archie F. and Josephine Petronella (Zindler) S.; m. Mary Beatrice Corkill, May 25, 1946 (dec. June 17, 1987); 1 dau. Mary Kay b. 1947; edn: BA, UCLA 1947. Career: chemist Kelite Products Co., Los Angeles 1946-49; gen. mgr. Delco Chemicals Inc., Los Angeles 1949-57; mgr., Ind. Spec. Pennwalt Corp., Los Angeles and Phila. 1957-75; chemist Custom Chemical Mfg. Co., Cudahy 1976; gen. mgr. Cherokee Chem. Co. Inc., Compton 1977-89; mem: Fellow Am. Inst. of Chemists, Fellow AAAS, Am. Chemical Soc. (senior), Nat. Assn. of Corrosion Engrs. (corrosion splst.), Reserve Ofcrs. Assn., Am. Ordnance Assn., Am. Eletroplaters Soc., Air Force Assn., Kentucky Colonel, Sigma Alpha Epsilon; mil: capt. CAC, 1941, 1942-46; R.Cath. Res: 21 Hacienda Dr Arcadia 91006

SMALLMAN-BUEL, NAN E., architect; b. Dec. 4, 1954, Greenbrae, Calif.; d. Robert Alfred and Patricia Joy (Bates) Smallman; m. Joseph G. Buel, S.E., Nov. 13, 1986; children: Courtney A. Buel b. 1991, Laura J. Buel b. 1993; edn: BS arch., Cal Polytech. Univ. S.L.O., 1980; reg. arch. Calif. Career: draftsperson Milton Chambers Arch. Inc., San Rafael 1980-81; designer Gilbert Murphey & Assocs., San Rafael 1981-82; Wallace Holm Architects, Inc. Monterey 1982-85; architect/prin. Nan E. Smallman & Assocs., San Rafael 1985–; awards: Marin Designer Showcase 1988, Aux. of Marin Co., Tiburon, 1988, Marin Designer Showcase, Novato, 1995; clubs: World Trade Club (S.F.), Marin Bldg. Exchange (San Rafael); Republican; Episcopalian; rec: watercolors.

SMATHERS, JAMES BURTON, medical physicist; b. Aug. 26, 1935, Prairie du Chien, Wis.; s. James Levi and Irma (Stindt) S.; m. Sylvia Lee Rath, Apr. 20, 1957; children: Kristine b. 1958, Kathryn b. 1959, James b. 1961, Ernest b. 1964; edn: BNE, N.C. State Coll., Raleigh 1957, MS, 1959; PhD, Univ. Md., College Park 1967; profl. desig: CHP, PE, DABR, DABMP. Career: res. engr. Atomics Internat., Canoga Park, Calif. 1959; 1st lt. US Army, W.D.C., 1959-61; research scientist U.S. Govt., W.D.C. 1961-67; prof. nuclear engring. Texas A&M Univ., College Station 1967-80; prof. med. physics Univ. Calif. Los Angeles, 1980–; mem.: Am. Assn. Physicists Medicine (treas. 1992-97), Health Physics Soc., Am. Coll. of Med. Physics Am. Coll. of Radiology, Nat. Soc. Profl. Engrs.; publs: 50+ sci. articles; Lutheran. Res: 18229 Minnehaha St Northridge 91326

SMILEY, ROBERT WILLIAM, industrial engineer; b. Oct. 18, 1919, Phila.; s. Albert James and Laura Emma (Hoiler) S.; m. Gloria Morais, June 30, 1990; children: (by previous marriage) Robert, James, Lauralee, Mary, (step) Deborah, Sheila, Vicki, James, Sonja, Michelle; edn: cert. in I.E., Gen. Motors Inst., 1942; stu. Univ. Rochester 1948, Univ. Pitts. grad. Sch. Bus. 1968, CSU San Jose 1969; BSBA, Coll. Notre Dame, Belmont 1972, MBA, 1974; Reg. profl. engr. Calif. Career: with A.S. Hamilton consulting engrs., Rochester, N.Y. 1946-48; Capt. USNR-Ret., active 1942-46, 51-52, LCDR USN 1952, CDR 1960, resigned 1966: tech. contract mgmt. Poseidon/Polaris and Terrier Missile Pgms. 1952-64, ofcr. in charge Polaris Missile Facility Pacific, Bremerton, Wash. 1964-66, chmn. Polaris/ Minuteman/ Pershing Missile Nondestruct Test Com. 1958-64; mgr. product assurance Missile Systems div. Lockheed Missiles and Space Co., Sunnyvale 1966-72, mgr. materiel Missile Systems div. 1972-77; quality control cons. Dragon Missile Pgm., US Army, 1971; mgr. product assurance McDonnell Douglas Astronautics, 1977-78; dir. product assur. Aerojet Tactical Systems, Sacto. 1978-83; dir. quality assurance Aerojet Solid Propulsion Co., Sacto. 1984-92; dir. q.a. Tahoe Surgical Instruments, 1992–; Fellow ASQC (chmn. S.F. sect. 1969-70, exec. bd. 1966–, chmn. reliability div. 1971, 81, nat. v.p. 1984-85), mem. Aircraft Inds. Assn. (chmn. q.a. com.), Navy League, AAAS, Am. Mgmt. Assn., chmn. Sacramento SCORE (Service Corps Retired Execs.) 1993–, docent Calif. State R.R. Museum 1994–; author: Reliability Engineering and Management, 1988, chapters and articles in field. Res/Ofc: 9144 Green Ravine Ln Fair Oaks 95628-4110

SMISEK, THOMAS MILO, certified professional consultant, marketing executive; b. Dec. 15, 1938, Cleveland, Ohio; s. Milo and Adele (Ejze) S.; m. Angela, Aug. 7, 1982; children: Cassandra b. 1963, Brandon b. 1964, Kahana b. 1983; edn: Cleveland Inst. of Art; cert. profl. consultant (CPC), Acad. of Profl. Cons. & Advisors. Career: pres. Tom Smisek Advtg. 1967-80, Tom Smisek Advtg./Mktg. Cons. 1980–; instr. advtg. copywriting Orange Coast Coll.; honors: Scholastic Keys 1957, num. advtg. awards for creativity including 4 Golden Orange Awards from Orange Co. Ad Club; commnr. Orange Co. Sheriff's Advy. Council; assoc. instr. Orange Co. Sheriff's Dept.; mem: Orange Co. Ad Fedn., Am. Ad Fedn., Am. Soc. Profl. Cons.; mil: E-3 USAF (SAC); Republican. Res: Smisek Ranch POB 374 Silverado 92676 Ofc: Tom Smisek Cons. 4000 MacArthur Blvd Ste 3000 Newport Beach 92660

SMITH, CHARLES GILES, SR., pharmaceutical consultant; b. Oct. 26, 1927, Chgo.; s. Charles and Lucille (Bicek) S.; m. Angeline, Apr. 23, 1950; children: C. Giles, Jr. b. 1951, Kevin b. 1953, J. Paul b. 1955, Tracy (Daniels) b. 1956; edn: BS, Ill. Inst. Tech., 1950; MS, Purdue Univ., 1952; PhD biochem., Univ. Wis., Madison, 1954. Career: mgr. biochem. The Upjohn Co., Kalamazoo, Mich. 1954-67; v.p. res. & devel. E.R. Squibb & Sons, and pres. Squibb Inst. Med. Research Co., Princeton, N.J. 1967-75; v.p. res. & devel. Revlon Health Care Group, Tuckahoe, N.Y. 1975-86; pharmaceutical cons., 1986–, cons. pharm. cos., academic groups; dir. Chemex Pharm., Ft. Lee, N.J. 1986–; dir. Dura Pharmaceuticals, San Diego 1988–; dir. Vanguard Medica, Ltd., Surrey, U.K.; awards: DuPont Fellow 1953-54, The Upjohn Prize 1952; mem: Am. Assn. Cancer Res. 1960–, Am. Chem. Soc. 1950–, Fed. Soc. Biol. Chem. 1970–, AAAS; author: The Process of New Drug Discovery and Development (CRC Press) 1992, 45+ biomed. drug res. papers in num. jours. and books, 1954-86; several patents in drug res., 1956-80; mil: pvt. AUS 1946-47; Republican; R.Cath.; rec: handgun/shotgun. Ofc: POB 9814 Rancho Santa Fe 92067-4814

SMITH, CHARLES LEWIS, retired naval commander, association executive; b. Oct. 27, 1920, Clarkston, Ga.; s. Robt. Clyde and Emelyn (Bloodworth) S.; m. Mildred Stilley, Sept. 5, 1947; children: Jan (Vach) b. 1948, Robert Eugene b. 1952; edn: grad. valedictorian Clarkston H.S. 1937, att. Georgia Sch. of Tech., var. mil. schs. Career: enlisted U.S. Navy, 1937-70, served thru ranks to comdr., assigned comdg. ofcr. USS Chicksaw (ATF 83) 1962-64, leadership devel. ofcr. for Amphibious Force, U.S. Pacific Fleet 1964-66 (devel. career counseling pgm. for Amphib. Force, later adopted by USN), comdg. ofcr. USS Tioga County (LST 1158) 1966-68, dept. hd. Amphibious Sch., U.S. Naval Amphibious base, Coronado 1968-70, served in WWII, Korean Conflict and Vietnam, awarded 16 medals and decorations, ret. 1970; joined profl. scouting staff Boy Scouts Am. as dir. public rels. and fin. San Diego County Council, 1971-80, dir. of public rels. 1980-82, planned giving dir. 1982-85, ret.; scout and adult volunteer scouter, 1935–: charter mem. 1st troop in Clarkston, Ga. 1935,

earned 96 merit badges within 3 yrs., rec'd. Eagle Scout from Pres. F.D. Roosevelt at 1st Nat. Jamboree, Wash DC 1937, scout commr. San Diego County Council 1969-71, was scoutmaster for 7th Nat. Jamboree, Farragut St. Park, Ida. 1969, and 13th World Jamboree, Japan 1971, nat. staff Nat. Jamboree, Fort A.P.Hill, Va. 1985, awarded Silver Beaver 1965, Vigil mem. Order of the Arrow 1968, Cross Feathers Award 1970, 4 Silver-Bronze Palm awards, 50-Yr. Veteran 1985, 60-Yr. Veteran 1995, BSA James E. West Fellow 1995, service award Civitan Internat. 1968, resolutions Calif. State Senate for service to community and to to youth 1970, 85, Southwestern Coll. service award 1973, United Way appreciation 1974-82, Kentucky Colonel (1985, bd. 1987), nat. citation for distinguished service Military Order of World Wars (8/87); bd. dirs.: Nat. Soc. of Fundraising Execs. S.D. 1975-1980, United Nations Assn. S.D. 1972-75, Retired Officers Assn. (Sweetwater Chpt. 1972–, pres. 1975, 81), BSA (exec. bd. 1995–); biog. listed 5000 Personalities of the World, Personalities of Am., Internat. Book of Honor, Directory of Disting. Americans, Community Leaders of Am., Who's Who in West; mem: Mil. Order of the World Wars (chpt. v. cdr. 1986-87, sr. v.-cdr. 1987-88, cdr. 1989-90), Nat. Eagle Scout Alumni Assn. (dir. 1986), Masons, Scottish Rite, Shriners, Eastern Star (life 1982), Crazy Horse Mem. Found. 1972, Public Rels. Club of S.D. 1972-85; local civic bds: S.D. Council Navy League of U.S. (dir. 1984), USN Commd. Ofcrs. Mess 1973-89, Kiwanis Club S.D. 1984-87, S.D. Accolades Com. 1988-90, Boys Club Chula Vista 1985-87, devel. com. Alvarado Health Found. Alvarado Hosp. Med. Ctr. 1986-87, charter rev. com. City of Chula Vista 1986-88; Democrat; Methodist; rec: sky diving, scuba, camping, travel. Res: 55 E Sierra Way Chula Vista 91911

SMITH, CHARLES WALTER, educator; b. Jan. 1, 1924, Tulsa, Okla.; s. Silvester and Clara (Greenlaw) S.; m. Jean Lou, Jan. 1946; m. 2d. Lois, Sept. 13, 1947; children: Charlesetta b. 1948, (twins) Marian and Sharian b. 1949, Marietta b. 1950; edn: BS, Langston Univ. 1950; MS, Okla. State Univ. 1958; vocational edn. cert., UC Los Angeles 1983. Career: jet mechanic instr. US Air Force, Amarillo, Tx. 1955; tchr. and athletic dir. high schs. in Holdenville and Bartlesville, Okla. 1950-59; tchr. Los Angeles County Special Sch. 1959-60, Calif. Youth Auth., Whittier 1959-63, L.A. Unified Sch. Dist. 1963-88, ret.; honors: humanitarian Alpha Phi Alpha Frat., Inc. 1984, Y's Men Internat. hon. mention Elmer Crowe award (Denmark 1986), Bill Baker Award (San Diego 1987), Langston Univ. distinguished alumni citation 1988; mem: Am. Edn. Assn., Calif. Tchrs. Assn., Nat. Edn. Assn., Am. Indsl. Edn. Assn., L.A. Indsl. Edn. Assn., Langston Univ. Alumni Assn. (pres. L.A. chpt. 1993-95), Okla. State Univ. Alumni Assn., Alpha Phi Alpha (pres. Beta Psi Lambda chpt., L.A. 1989-91); civic: YMCA, L.A. (bd. mgrs. 1973–), Y's Men Internat. Club (L.A. pres. 1985, lt. regional dir. Western Sect. 1986-87), Holman United Meth. Men Club (secty.); inventor: 'utensits' handles for cooking ware, 1962; articles in edn. jours.; mil: sgt. AUS 1943-45, Bronze Star, Good Conduct Medal; Democrat; Prot.; rec: fishing, hunting, golf, travel. Address: Smith's Construction Co. 3500-366 W Manchester Blvd Inglewood 90305

SMITH, CHESTER, broadcasting executive; b. March 29, 1930, Wade, Okla.; s. Louis L. and Effie S. (Brown) S.; m. Naomi L. Crenshaw, July 19, 1959; children: Lauri, Lorna, Roxanne; Career: recording artist Capitol Records, Los Angeles 1947-61; owner, mgr. KLOC-AM, Modesto 1963-81; owner, ptnr. KCSO-TV, Modesto 1966–, KCBA-TV, Salinas 1981-86, KREN-TV, Reno, Nev. 1986-95, KTA-TV, Santa Maria 1986–, KCVU-TV, Paradise 1989–, KNSO-TV, Merced 1992–, KBVU-TV, Eureka 1992–, and KDS-TV, Chico; mem. Calif. Broadcasters Assn.; elected Hall of Fame, Western Swing Soc.; Republican; Christian. Res: 31110 E Lee Rd Escalon 95320 Ofc: Sainte Limited, 100 Sycamore Ave Ste 3 Modesto 95354

SMITH, CRAIG SCOTT, physician; b. July 16, 1951, San Francisco, Calif.; s. Edward J. and Marjorie Loreen (Bruce) S.; m. Terri Ann Hughes, June 19, 1982; children: Rachel Deanna b. 1984, Jessica Danielle b. 1988, Rebecca Diana b. 1994; edn: BS, Stanford Univ. 1973; MD, UCLA 1977. Career: residency, internal medicine, UC Davis 1978-90; endocrinology and metabolism fellowship, UC Davis 1980-82; physician Endocrine Assn. of Sacramento 1982-84, The Med. Clinic of Sacto. 1984-89, The Permanente Med. Group, Inc., Sacto. 1989–; asst. clin. prof. of medicine UC Davis 1982-89, assoc. clin. prof. of medicine 1989–; honors: Phi Beta Kappa 1972; mem: CMA 1982–, Am. Diabetes Assn. 1982–, The Endocrine Soc. 1990–. Ofc: The Permanente Medical Group Inc. 6600 Bruceville Rd Sacramento 95823

SMITH, DONALD RICHARD, editor, publisher; b. Aug. 20, 1932, Stockton; s. Robert Gordon and Gertrude (Schweitzer) S.; m. Darlene Ruth Thomas, May 7, 1961; children: Douglas Robert b. 1972, Deborah Renae b. 1974; edn: Delta Coll., 1948-50, Coll. of the Pacific 1950. Career: ed., pub. Calif. Odd Fellow & Rebekah, Linden, Calif. 1950–; ed. Elk Grove Citizen 1953-55; asst. dir. Un Pilgrimage, New York, N.Y. 1956, 59; ed., pub. Linden Herald 1959-86; ed., pub. Internat. Rebekah News 1963-86; ed., pub. Internat. Odd Fellow & Rebekah 1986–; pres. IOOF Internat. Press Assn. (Md.) 1962-63, v.p. 1960-61, nominating chmn. (NC) 1986-89; bd. dirs. Three Links Youth Camp 1959-61; pres. Linden Municipal Council 1983, council mem. 1981-90; bd. trustees San Joaquin Co. Historical Soc. 1986-91; honors: Legion of Honor, Order of DeMolay 1961, John R. Williams Award, S.J. Co. Teachers Assn. 1963, 87, Golden Key Award

Stockton Tchrs. Assn. 1971, Achievement Award Stockton Bd. of Supervisors 1970, Citizen of Yr. Lions Internat. 1982; mem: Desktop Pub. Assn., Linden-Peters C.of C. (pres. 1968-69); civic: Odd Fellows of Calif. (Grand Master 1958-59), Charity Odd Fellows Lodge #6, Stockton 1950-, Internat. Odd Fellowship (Sovereign Grand Master 1969-70), Lions Internat. (Linden chpt. 1960-), San Joaquin Co. 4-H Found. (chmn. 1986-); author/pub. "From Statestop to Friendly Comm." 1976, "Three Link Fraternity" 1993, "Six Links of Fellowship", 1995; author book "Leadership Manual Internat. Order Odd Fellows" 1980; Republican; Methodist; rec: Lionel trains, modeling railroad, stamps, coins, history. Ofc: Linden Publications POB 129 Linden 95236

SMITH, E(WART) BRIAN, hazardous waste management executive, engineer; b. Jan. 31, 1938, Poughkeepsie, N.Y.; s. Ewart Gladstone and Genevieve (Contois) S.; m. Betti LaVonne Stoddard, March 26, 1966; children: Samantha, Georgina, Sara, Amanda, Justin; edn: BSEE, Purdue Univ. 1960; MS fin. mgmt., George Washington Univ. 1966; reg. civil engr. Calif., reg. profl. engr. Ind. Career: staff civil engr. USN 1960-66; chief engr. Fluor, Thailand 1966-68; project coordinator Bechtel Co., San Francisco 1968-69; group v.p. Holmes & Narver Inc., Orange 1976-82; v.p., gen. mgr. Fluor Engrs. Inc., Irvine 1982-84; sr.v.p., gen. mgr. 1984-85; pres. Fluor Venture Group, Irvine 1985-86; sr. v.p. Internat. Tech., Torrance 1986-88, pres. & COO, 1988-92; CEO and pres. Smith Environmental Technologies Corp. 1993-; mem: Project Mgmt. Inst., IEEE, Am. Assn. Cost Engrs., Soc. Am. Mil. Engrs., Beavers; mil: served to capt. USNR 1989; Republican; Cath.; rec: skiing, jogging, tennis. Res: 51 Montecito Dr Corona del Mar 92625 Ofc: Smith Environmental Technologies Corp 13455 Noel Rd Ste 1500 Dallas TX 75240 Tel: 214/770-0290

SMITH, GEORGE AUSTIN, surgeon; b. Sept. 19, 1929, Minersville, Utah; s. Othello H. and Addie (Carter) S.; m. Winnafred May, June 19, 1956; children: Nathan b. 1958, Matthew b. 1960, Owen b. 1964, Aaron b. 1964; edn: BA, UCLA 1952; MD, Univ. of Calif. Sch. of Medicine-San Francisco 1956; diplomate Am. Bd. of Surgery 1964. Career: chief of surgery Washington Hosp., Fremont, Calif. 1973-74, chief of med. staff 1976-77; pvt. practice, Fremont 1963-; fellow Am. Coll. of Surgeons 1970-; mil: capt. USAF 1957-59; rec: photography. Ofc: G. Austin Smith, MD, Inc 1900 Mowry Ave Fremont 94536

SMITH, GEORGE IRVING, geologist; b. May 20, 1927, Waterville Me.; s. Joseph Coburn and Ervena (Goodale) S.; m. Patsy Jean Beckstead, Oct. 31, 1953 (div. May 1970); children: Randall b. 1958, Laura b. 1964; m. Teruko Kuwada, Aug. 2, 1974; stepchildren: Michele b. 1963, Marla b. 1967, Mireya b. 1969; edn: AB, Colby Coll., 1949; MS, Calif. Inst. of Tech., 1951, PhD, 1956. Career: instr. Occidental Coll., Eagle Rock 1951-52; geologist, proj. chief US Geol. Survey, Claremont 1952-58; Menlo Park 1958-66; branch chief USGS, Menlo Park 1966-69; project chief 1969-; Fullbright scholar, Australian Nat. Univ., Canberra, 6 mos. 1981; awards: Meritorious svc. US Dept. of Interior, W.D.C. 1983; mem: Geol. Soc. of Am. (1954-, fellow), Mineral. Soc. of Am. (1952-, fellow), Geochemical Soc. 1958-, Am. Quaternary Assn. 1969-, Sigma Xi 1955-; publs: 81+ articles and 24+ abstracts (1953-); mil: p.o.3c USN 1945-46; Independent; rec: photography, travel. Ofc: U.S. Geological Survey 345 Middlefield Rd Menlo Park 94025

SMITH, GERALD W., b. Jan. 17, 1962, Los Angeles, Calif.; s. Louis and Velma (Jones) S.; edn: grad. Pasadena H.S., 1980. Awards: Good Citizenship, 116th St. Sch., Los Angeles 1972-74; mem. Western Riding Club, Burbank; rec: horseback riding, bicycling, camping, theater, movies, travel. Res: 1980 Santa Rosa Ave Pasadena 91104

SMITH, JAMES THOMAS, mathematics educator, author; b. Nov. 8, 1939, Springfield, Oh.; s. Earl Gearhart and Betty Mae (McCartney) S.; m. Helen Marie Patteson, Jan. 26, 1963; 1 son, Jedediah b. 1968; edn: AB, Harvard, 1961, MA, San Francisco State Univ., 1964, MS, Stanford Univ., 1966, PhD, Saskatchewan Univ., 1970. Career: mathematician US Navy, San Francisco 1962-67; lectr. San Francisco St. Univ., 1965-67, prof. math. 1969-; vis. prof. Mills Coll., Oakland 1982-83; software engr. Blaise Computing, Berkeley 1984-85; vis. prof. Inst. Teknologi MARA, Subang Jaya, Malaysia 1988-89; mem. Math. Assn. Am. (1967-, chair No. Calif. 1993), Am. Math. Soc. 1987-, Deutsche Mathematiker Vereinigung (1970-), Harvard Club (SF, v.p. 1989-93); author: C++ Applications Guide, 1992, C++ for Scientists & Engineers, 1991, Advanced Turbo C, 1989, Getting the most from Turbo Pascal, 1987, 9+ res. papers in math., 1970-85. Res: 1363 27th Ave San Francisco 94122 Ofc: Math. Dept. San Francisco State Univ. 1600 Holloway San Francisco 94132

SMITH, JEFFRY ALAN, public health administrator, physician, consultant; b. Dec. 8, 1943, Los Angeles; s. Stanley W. and Marjorie E. S.; m. Jo Anne Hague; edn: BA (philosophy), UCLA 1967, MPH, 1972; BA (biology), CSU Northridge 1971; MD, UACJ, 1977; diplomate am. Bd. Family Practice. Career: resident in family practice WAH, Takoma Park, Md., NIH, Bethesda, Md., Walter Reed Army Hosp., Wash., Children's Hosp. nat. Med. Ctr., Wash.; occupational physician U.S. Dept. of Energy Nevada Test Site, Las Vegas, NV 1980-82; dir. occupational medicine and environ. health Pacific Missile Test Ctr., Point Mugu 1982-84; dist. health ofcr. State Hawaii Dept. Health, Kauai 1984-86; asst. dir.

health Co. of Riverside Dept. Health 1986-87; med. dir. Comm. Human Servises, Monterey 1987-; regional med. dir. Calif. Forensic Med. Group, Salinas 1987-; fellow Am. Acad. Family Physicians; mem: AMA, Am. Occupational Medicine Assn., Flying Physicians, Am. Pub. Health Assn. Res: 27575 Via Sereno Carmel 93923 Ofc: POB 10009 Salinas 93912

SMITH, JUNE MARY, winery public relations executive; b. June 18, 1931, Oak Park, Ill.; d. Edwin Richardson and Constance Margarita (Trimarco) Wright; m. James Smith, July 13, 1957; children: Jeffrey b. 1961, Bradford b. 1964, Jason b. 1965, Joy b. 1966; edn: grad. Oakpark River Forest Township H.S., Oak Park, Ill. 1949. Career: clk. Anderson-McConnell Advt. Agy., Los Angeles 1952-53, Los Angeles Country Club, West L.A. 1953-56, Leon Luxenberg Ins., 1956-57; dep. clerk West L.A. Municipal Ct., 1957-59; order desk Viviane Woodard·Cosmetics, Panorama City 1960-61, cosmetic cons. Viviane Woodard, El Toro 1970-71; dir. pub. relations Roudon-Smith Winery, Santa Cruz 1971-; honors: Proclamation for work with Scotts Valley Hist. Soc. wine festivals Santa Cruz Co. Bd. Suprs. 1983, Scotts Valley C.of C. Woman of Yr. 1990; mem: Santa Cruz Winegrower's Assn. (v.p. 1987), Santa Cruz Mountain Vintner's Assn. 1974, Santa Cruz Area Restaurant Assn. (events com. 1988), Santa Cruz Conv. & Vis. Council 1983, C.of C.: Scotts Valley, Aptos, Capitola, Santa Cruz, Santa Clara, Monterey (mem., Chamber coms. 1983), Rotary Internat./Scotts Valley (bd. dirs. 1990-92, fellowship chr. 1988), Responsible Hospitality Council Santa Cruz (exec. bd. 1989-92), Santa Cruz County Film Advy. Bd. 1994-95; Court Apptd. Special Advocate (CASA) of Santa Cruz Co. 1993-; publs: guest columnist for "Getting Down To Business" col., article Scotts Valley Banner (8/3/88), articles in Taste Mag. (2, 1987), co-writer radio comml. "How the Wines of Roudon-Smith Came to be", 1988; Republican; Cath.; rec: writing, dancing, film extra. Ofc: Roudon-Smith Vineyards, Inc. 2364 Bean Creek Rd Santa Cruz 95066

SMITH, KATHRYN EDEN, lawyer; b. Aug. 14, 1955, Woodbury, N.J.; d. John B. and Eileen S. (Dougherty) Eden; m. Ronald Glen Smith, Sept. 6, 1981; children: Rebecca b. 1988, Patrick b. 1991; edn: BA (magna cum laude), UCSB 1978; JD cum laude, Temple Univ. Sch. Law 1983; admitted St. Bar Calif. 1986. Career: atty., assoc. Montgomery McCracken Walker & Rhoads, Phila., Pa. 1983-85; Hatch & Parent, Santa Barbara 1986-88; sole practice, Santa Barbara 1988-; advy. dir. Santa Barbara Council of Christmas Cheer Inc. 1986-; awards: UCSB Outstanding Grad. 1978, Temple Univ. Sch. Law Catherine Donahue Meml. 1983; mem: S.B. Women Lawyers (bd. dirs. 1988-90), Am. Bar Assn., Santa Barbara Co. Bar Assn. Address: Santa Barbara 93105

SMITH, KERRY CLARK, lawyer; b. July 12, 1935, Phoenix, Ariz.; d. Clark and Fay (Jackson) Smith; m. Michael Waterman, 1958; children: Kevin b. 1964, Ian b. 1966; edn: BA, Stanford Univ. 1957; JD, 1962; admitted U.S. Supreme Ct., St. Bar Calif. Career: atty., assoc. Chickering & Gregory, San Francisco 1962-70, ptnr. 1970-81; ptnr. Pettit & Martin 1981-95; ptnr. Hovis, Smith, Larson, Stewart, Lipscomb & Cross 1995-; dir. Allied Properties 1974-77; ofcr. Pebble Beach Corp. 1974-79; bd. editors Stanford Law Review 1961-62; mem: St. Bar Calif. (bus. law sect., fin. institutions com. 1984-87), San Francisco Bar Assn., Am. Bar Assn. (bus. law sect. banking and savings and loan com.); clubs: University (S.F.), Orinda CC, La Quinta Golf; mil: lt. USN. Ofc: Hovis, Smith, et al 100 Pine St 21st Flr San Francisco 94111 TeL: 415/421-9696

SMITH, LOUIS, equestrian; b. Nov. 2, 1934, Shreveport, La.; s. Louis and Savannah (Durham) S.; m. Velma, Jan. 1, 1962; 1 son, Gerald b. 1962; edn: grad. Freemont H.S., Los Angeles, 1955. Career: maint. engr. L.A. Dept. Water & Power, Pasadena 1968-92; chauffeur Cowboy Limousine Service, 1988-92; civic: mem. Tournament of Roses, equestrian Old Fashioned Day Parades, Pasadena; Altadena Town Council 1982; mem.: Golden West Parade Assn., San Bernardino. Co. 1990-, Internat. Platform Assoc.; awards: Fancy Western Rider, 1st Place, Barstow 1987, 1st, 2d Place, San Bernardino 1990, 92, Leading Rider, Monty Police, Palm Springs 1991, 92, 1st Pl. Western Singleman Rider, Lancaster 1991, Award of Honor State of Calif. 1991, Internat. Man of the Yr. 1992-93, listed in Two Thousand Notable Am. Men, Internat. Who's Who of Intellectuals, featured rider in Palm Springs Feb. 1992, 93, Golden State Award 1992; mil: US Army 1957-58; Democrat; Baptist; rec: Tournament of Dominoes, deer hunting, fresh water fishing, country western guitarist. Res: 1980 Santa Rosa Pasadena 91104

SMITH, MARK LEE, architect; b. Nov. 16, 1957, Los Angeles; s. Selma (Moidel) S.; edn: stu. arch., UC Berkeley 1975-6; BA (hist. of arch.) summa cum laude, UC Los Angeles 1978, MA (arch.) 1980; Reg. Architect, Calif. 1983. Career: designer/drafter John B. Ferguson & Assoc., 1976-83, architect, 1983; architect/prin. Mark L. Smith, AIA, 1984-; awards: National Merit Scholar 1975, UC Regents Scholar 1975-78, Phi Beta Kappa 1978, UCLA Grad. Sch. of Arch. Resrch. Fellow 1979-80, Dean's award- Best Thesis 1980, S.F.V./AIA Design Awards Competition 1988, 89, 90, 91; mem. Am. Inst. of Arch., Calif. Council AIA (dir. 1989-94, v.p. 1991-94, chair cont. edn. 1991-93, chair 1992 conf.), S.F.V. AIA (dir 1986-, treas. 1986, v.p. 1987, pres. 1988, chair, design awards 1994), UCLA John Wooden Ctr. (bd. of govs. 1978-90), Los Angeles Co. Arthitectural Evaluation Bd. 1990-; contbr. articles to profl. jours. Ofc: Mark L. Smith, AIA, 18340 Ventura Blvd Ste 225 Tarzana 91356

SMITH, MARSHALL SAVIDGE, educator, college dean; b. Sept. 16, 1937, East Orange, N.J.; s. Marshall Parsons and Ann Eileen (Zulauf) S.; m. Carol Goodspeed, June 25, 1960 (div. Aug. 1962); m. Louise Nixon Claiborn, Aug. 22, 1964; children: Adam b. 1968, Jennifer b. 1969, Matthew b. 1971, Megan b. 1973; edn: AB, Harvard Univ., 1960, EdM, 1963, EdD, 1970. Career: computer analyst and programmer Raytheon Corp., Andover, Mass. 1959-62; instr., assoc. prof. Harvard Univ., Cambridge 1966-76; asst., assoc. dir. Nat. Inst. of Edn., W.D.C. 1973-76; asst. commr. edn. HEW, 1976-79; chief of staff to Dept. of Edn. Secty., 1980; prof. Univ. Wis., Madison 1980-86; prof. and dean Sch. of Edn. Stanford Univ. 1986-94; Under Sec. Edn. U.S. Dept. of Edn. 1993–; dir: Holmes Group, E.Lansing, Mich.; chmn. bd. Am. Insts. for Res., 1990-94, mem. Nat. Council on Stds. and Testing, 1991-92; cons. US Dept. Edn.; awards: Commnr.'s award and Secty.'s award US Dept. Edn. (1978, 80), 1st vis. scholar Nat. Inst. Edn. 1973; mem: Am. Ednl. Res. Assn. (chair orgn. instl. affiliates 1985-86), Cleve. Conf., Nat. Acad. Edn., NAACP, Amnesty Internat., Madison West Hockey Assn. (pres. 1982-84), dir. Clinton Pres. Transition Team for K-12 Edn 1992-93; author: The General Inquirer (1967), (w/Jencks) Inequality: A Reassessment of the Effect of Family and Schooling in America (1972), 50+ publs. incl. book chapters, profl. jour. articles; Democrat; rec: coaching youth soccer and hockey. Res: 1256 Forest Ave Palo Alto 94301 Ofc: Under Sec. Edn. 400 Maryland Ave SW Washington DC 20202 also School of Education Stanford University, Stanford 94305-3096

SMITH, MICHAEL REID, lawyer; b. April 30, 1941, Los Angeles; s. Roy Andrew and Merlanne (Gardner) S.; edn: BA, UC Berkeley 1963; LL.B, UC Berkeley Boalt Hall 1966. Career: lectr. law Univ. Ife (Peace Corps), Nigeria 1966-68; asst. gen. counsel U.S. Commn. on Civil Rights, Wash. D.C. 1968-73; asst. chancellor legal affairs UC Berkeley 1973–; lectr. constitutional law Armstrong Law Sch., Berkeley; bd. trustees Univ. Art Museum UC Berkeley 1985–; bd. mem. Berkeley City Personnel 1984-86; mem: ACLU (bd. dirs.), Calif. Bar Assn., Am. Bar Assn., U.S. Supreme Ct. Bar Assn.; articles pub. in profl. jours., 1969; Democrat:; Methodist; rec: tennis. Res: 19 Tanglewood Rd Berkeley 94705 Ofc: Univ. California Berkeley 94720-1500

SMITH, NORMAN HENRY, insurance executive; b. Jan. 26, 1937, St. Louis, Mo.; s. Norman Joseph and Helen Ann (Wiedey) S.; m. Susan Sommerfeld, Oct. 5, 1968; children: Carson b. 1977, William b. 1979; edn: BS in Engring., Univ. of Ill. 1960, MBA, honors, 1965; lic. Surplus Lines Broker & Agent Calif. State Dept. of Ins. Career: owner, chmn. bd. Capital Workshop Financial Ins. Services, San Francisco, 1974–; chmn./owner Capital Workshop Internat. Ins. Services Ltd., Grand Turk, B.W.I., 1986–; owner Capital Workshop Gen. Ins. Agy., S.F., 1986–; chmn./owner Professionals Prototype Ins. Cos. Ltd., Grand Turk, B.W.I., 1986–; S.F.; instr. engring. and mgmt. depts. Univ. Ill. 1963-65; honors: valedictorian Monticello (Ill.) H.S. 1955, Univ. of Ill. Ma-Wan-Da and Sachem activity honors 1957, 59, listed Who's Who in U.S. Executives; clubs: San Francisco Yacht, Olympic (S.F.), Snowmobilers (Bear Valley); mem. HOA (Bear Valley); several pub. articles on legal malpracticce; mil: lt. jg USN 1960-63; Republican. rec.: skiing, diving, sailing, art. Res: 2400 Paradise Dr Tiburon 94920 Ofc: Capital Workshop General Insurance Agency, 550 California St, Sacramento Tower 5th Flr San Francisco 94104 also: Capital Workshop International Insurance Serv. Ltd., Hibiscus Sq, Cockburntown, Grand Turk B.W.I.

SMITH, SELMA MOIDEL, lawyer, composer; b. Apr. 3, 1919, Warren, Ohio; d. Louis and Mary (Oyer) Moidel; 1 son, Mark Lee b. 1957; edn: stu. Univ. Calif. 1936-39, USC 1939-41; JD, Pacific Coast Univ. 1942; admitted Calif. State Bar 1943, US Dist. Ct. 1943, US Supreme Ct. 1958. Career: gen. practice law, mem. firm Moidel, Moidel, Moidel & Smith; WWII field dir. civilian advy. com. WAC, 1943; mem. nat. bd. Medical Coll. Penn. (1953–, exec. bd., 1976-80, pres. 1980-82, chair, past pres. com. 1990-92); honors: subject of oral hist. project Women Lawyers Assn. of L.A. 1986, decorated La Order del Merito Juan Pablo Duarte, Dominican Republic; mem: ABA, State Bar of Calif. (servicemen's legal aid com., state bar conf. com. on unauthorized practice of medicine 1964, Disting. Service award 1993), Los Angeles Co. Bar Assn. (Disting. Service award 1993, psychopathic ct. com.), Council Bar Assns. (charter secty. L.A. Co. 1950), L.A. Lawyers Club (pub. defenders com.), Nat. Assn. Women Lawyers (regional dir. W. States, Hawaii 1949-50, judicial adminstrn. com. 1960, chair com. on social commn. of the U.N. 1946, chair com. on unauthorized practice of law 1952, chair world peace through law 1966-67), So. Calif. Women Lawyers Assn. (pres. 1947, 48), Women Lawyers Assn. of L.A. (chair Law Day com.), League of Americas (dir.), Inter-Am. Bar Assn., Calif. Bus. Women's Council (dir. 1951, pres. L.A. chpt. 1952), Calif. Pres.'s Council (1st v.p.), Nat. Assn. Composers USA (dir. 1974-79), Nat. Fedn. Music Clubs (western region chair Amer. music 1971-75, state conv. chair 1972), L.A. Philharmonic Docents (v.p. 1973-83, chair Latin Am. comm. relations 1972-75; press and public relations 1972-75; consultants coord. 1973-75), ASCAP, Euterpe Opera Club (v.p. 1974-75), Plato Soc. UCLA (1981–; Toga editor 1990-93; secty. 1991-92; chair colloquium com. 1992-93, Exceptional Leadership award 1994), Iota Tau Tau (dean L.A., supreme treas.), UCLA Constitution Bicentennial Project discussion ldr. 1985-87, moderator UCLA Ext. Lecture Series 1990, Assn. of Learning in Retirement Orgns. in the West (pres. 1993-94, exec. com. 1994-95, Disting. Service award 1995); composer: Espressivo-Four

Piano Pieces (orch. premiere 1986, performance at Nat. Mus. for Women in the Arts 1989). Res: 5272 Lindley Ave Encino 91316

SMITH, STANLEY THEODORE, physicist; b. Nov. 5, 1927, Rochester, N.Y.; s. Stanley Robin and Beatrice Marie (McDonald) S.; edn: AB, Univ. Rochester 1951; MS, Utah State Univ. 1981. Career: physicist Naval Weapons Center, China Lake 1953-94, missile data analyst 1953, flt. test engr. 1957, infrared systems analyst 1962, dep. program mgr. Optical Signatures Pgm. 1975, ednl. fellowship 1979-81, prin. investigator, performance of electro-optical seekers in global environments 1981, prin. investigator devel. of the spiralling toroidal spectro-interfer, 1982–; prin. investigator hypersonic infrared seeker pgm., 1987–; recipient 3 Sustained Superior Performance awards (1974, 76, 79), Superior Achievement 1978, Spl. Act 1982, Technical Director's award 1988, Patent award 1979, Fellow in sci. and engring. 1990; mem: Internat. Soc. for Optical Engring., Am. Inst. of Aeronautics and Astronautics; author 25+ res. papers, 1974–, numerous tech. presentations; rec: travel, philately, folkdance. Res: 612 Weiman Ave Ridgecrest 93555 Ofc: Eastern Sierra Research Associates Ridgecrest 93555

SMITH, STEVEN ALAN, Oriental medical doctor, psychologist, minister, physiotherapist; b. June 3, 1947, Los Angeles; s. Arthur G. and Minnie (Cohen) S.; edn: physiotherapist, Strong-Berg Inst., Los Angeles 1969; Certified Acupuncturist, Calif. Acupuncture Coll., L.A. 1980, Dr. Oriental medicine 1983; BA Psychology, Ryo Kan Coll., L.A., 1993; MS Psychology Univ. of Santa Monica 1994; MDiv Religious Sci. Theol. Sem. of So. Calif., Thousand Oaks 1994 (Doctoral cand.); cert. in psychoanalysis Calif. Graduate Inst.. Career: body bldg. instr. Palms Jr. High, L.A., 1963; camp counselor Beverly Hills YMCA, 1964; football team strength coach Santa Monica City Coll., 1966; physical conditioning instr. US Navy, 1967-69; body bldg. instr. Riveria CC, L.A., 1970; massage therapist El Cabillero CC, Tarzana, 1971; owner/operator The Gym Club, L.A. 1972-75; physiotherapist, Dr. Joseph Walters, MD, Sherman Oaks, 1975-78; pvt. practice physiotherapist, L.A., 1978-80; pvt. practice trad. Chinese medicine, homeopathic medicine, metabolic nutrition, 1980–; awards: listed Who's Who In Calif. 1983-86; Religious Sci. Service award, Torrance, Calif. 1993; honors: Phi Delta Kappa; mem. Amer. Acupuncture Com., 1990-91; mil: seaman, USN, 1966-69; Jewish, Buddhist, Christian; rec: Chinese and Indian cooking. Res: 3147 Durango Ave Los Angeles 90034

SMITH, STEVEN DENNIS, senior systems engineer; b. Nov. 15, 1945, Charleston, West Va.; s. Dennis Ray and Katherine Mondaine (Sands) S.; edn: BA, Univ. Richmond, 1968; grad. work Va. Polytech. Inst. and State Univ., 1969, 71-72; cert. Astronautical engineering, UCLA 1994. Career: programmer, analyst Hercules Inc., Radford (Va.) Army Ammunition Plant, also Wilmington, Dela. 1968-72; supr. computer systems and ops. Black, Crow and Eidness Inc., Gainsville, Fla. 1972-74; computer scientist Computer Sciences Corp., Silver Springs, Md., London, Eng. and Flensburg, W. Ger., 1974-85; mem. tech. staff TRW, Redondo Beach 1985-88; staff engr. Martin Marietta, Long Beach 1988-92; sr. systems engr. SAIC, 1993–; mem. Am. Inst. Aero. and Astro.; civic: AFS internat. student exchange program (1986–), vol. St. Agnes Hosps., Balt. (1984-85), Hosp. Home Health Care Agy., Calif. (1985-86), AYSO Soccer, Columbia, Md. (1975-79), Howard County Childrens Physical Devel. Clinic (1976-79). Res: 606 N Juanita Ave #3 Redondo Beach 90277 Ofc: SAIC 21151 Western Ave Torrance 90501

SMITH, STEVEN SIDNEY, molecular biologist; b. Feb. 11, 1946, Idaho Falls, Idaho; s. Sidney Ervin and Hermie Phyllis (Robertson) S.; m. Nancy Louise Turner, Dec. 20, 1974; BS, Univ. Idaho, 1968; PhD, UCLA, 1974. Career: asst. res. scientist Beckman Research Inst., City of Hope Nat. Med. Ctr., Duarte 1982-84, staff Cancer Center, 1983–, asst. res. scientist depts. thoracic surgery and molecular biology, 1985-87, assoc. res. scientist div. surgery 1987-90, dir. dept. of Cell & Tumor Biology, 1990–; cons. Am. Inst. Biol. Sci. 1994, Molecular Biosystems Inc., San Diego 1981-84; awards: Phi Beta Kappa, Swiss Nat. Sci. Found. fellow Univ. Bern 1974-77, Scripps Clinic and Research Found., La Jolla 1978-82, NIH fellow Scripps Clinic 1979-81, NIH grantee 1983-93, Council for Tobacco Research grantee 1983-92, Smokeless Tobacco Res. Council grantee 1992–, March of Dimes grantee 1988-91, Office of Naval Res. grantee 1994–, Wellcome vis. prof. of medicine 1995-96; mem: Amer. Crystallographic Assn., Am. Soc. Cellular Biology, Am. Assn. for Cancer Research, Am. Weightlifting Assn.; rec: backpacking. Ofc: City of Hope National Medical Center, 1500 E Duarte Rd Duarte 91010

SMITH, V. ROY, neurosurgeon; b. Feb. 12, 1943, NY, NY; m. Elizabeth Kay Bartlett, June 12, 1971; children: Rebecca b. 1974, Adam b. 1975, Andrew b. 1978; edn: BA, Ohio State Univ. 1964, MD, 1967; lic. physician Ohio, Wis., Minn., Calif.; cert. Am. Bd. Neurological Surgery 1977. Career: internship, surgery, Univ. of Wis. 1967-68, residency, gen. surgery 1968-69; residency, neurologic surgery Mayo Grad. Sch. Medicine, Mayo Clinic 1971-75; neurosurgeon Fresno Neurosurgical Med. Group, Inc.; hosp. affiliations: St. Agnes Med. Ctr. (chmn. dept. of surgery 1983-85, pres. of med. staff 1987-89, chmn. div. of neurosurgery 1993-95), Fresno Comm. Hosp., Valley Children's Hosp., Sierra Hosp., Clovis Comm. Hosp.; lectr. in field; awards: Mayo Clinic Neurological

Travel Award 1975; mem: Am. Coll. of Surgeons (fellow), AMA, CMA, Fresno Co. Med. Soc., Congress of Neurologic Surgeons, Am. Assn. of Neurological Surgeons; author: article pub. in Surgical Neurology, 1975. Ofc: Fresno Neurosurgical Medical Group Inc. 6137 N Thesta Ave Ste 103 Fresno 93710

SMITH, VELMA JONES, teacher; b. Sept. 26, 1936, Heflin, La.; d. Johnnie and Dora (Iverson) Jones; m. Louis Smith; 1 son Gerald b. 1962; edn: BS, Grambling (La.) Coll. 1958; MA, Azusa Pacific Univ. 1974. Career: substitute tchr. Compton Unified Sch. Dist., Compton, Calif. 1963-68, tchr. 1968–; tchr. R.F. Kennedy Sch.. Compton 1968–; mem. Compton Sch. Leadership Team 1994-96, Sch. Site Counci 1994-95, pres. Hospitality Com. 1990-95, chmn. Grade Level Chair.; awards: Best Dressed Western Att., We. Riding Club, L.A. 1976-77, Right From the Start award, Dr. Ralph Parker, Palo Alto 1984, 88, Right to Read award, Garden Grove 1989-90, Effective Tchg. award Compton Unified Sch. Dist. 1994-95, Principal Award of Merit, Kennedy Sch., Compton 1995-96; mem: Internat. Platform Assn. 1990–, Western Riding Club (life), PTA 1968–, NEA (Burlingame, Calif.), CEA (Sacto., Calif.); rec: reading, camping, art, interior decorating, country western, coin collecting, meeting people, helping others. Res: 1980 Santa Rosa Ave Pasadena 91104

SMITH, VIN, piano technician and teacher, sportswriter and editor, newspaper columnist, novelist; b. May 19, 1944, Whittier; s. M. Clifford and Anna Eugenia (Hill) S.; m. Marthea Karen Callaham, May 15, 1969 (div. 1979); children: Jayare, Eric; m. Ginger Hammon, Oct. 20, 1984; children: Amy Michelle, Stacey Erin, Kellie Rae; edn: stu. Columbia Sch. Broadcasting, S.F., 1967; AA, Cuesta Coll., 1974; grad. Am. Sch. of Piano Tuning, 1978. Career: sales mgr. Radio Sta. KTAT, Frederick, Okla., 1967-69; disc jockey KOCY Radio, Okla. City 1969; owner Melmart Markets, San Luis Obispo, Calif. 1971-73; Am. Direct Sales, Grover City, 1973-79; instr. piano Valley View Acad., Arroyo Grande, 1977-78, Long Piano Co., San Luis Obispo, 1977-79, piano technician 1978-79; owner Chocolate Piano, Yreka 1979–; instr. piano Makah Indian Tribe, Neah Bay, Wash. 1981-82; sports editor New Words Digest, Bakersfield 1988- (sports columnist 1987-91); guest columnist Siskiyou Daily News 1991–; nat. publicist Chamber Music Concerts, So. Ore. State Coll. 1993–; stress cons., evaluator Yreka Stress Therapy Clinic, 1985-87; awards: appreciation Siskiyou County Bd. Suprs. 1988, Golden Poet award World of Poetry, Sacto. 1989; mem: Nat. Writers Club (chmn. student com. Yreka chpt. 1988), Author's Guild Inc. (chair, com. for free expression, No. Calif. Chpt. 1995), Author's League of Am., Mystery Writers Am., Soc. Children's Book Writers, Kiwanis, Moose, Jr. C.of C.; rec: horse shoe pitching, photog., reading. Res: 710 Knapp St Yreka 96097-2343 Ofc: Chocolate Piano Svcs PO Box 447 Yreka 96097-0447 Tel: 916/842-7672

SMITH, WILLIAM CLARKE, clergyman; b. Jan. 22, 1926, Bend, Oreg.; s. Jay Harvey Smith and Amelia Grace (Starr) Poor; m. Veta Maxine Davidson of Warren, Ark.; children: Carolyn Jean Aldama, Virginia Ann Bennett, Barbara Lynn Farstad, Rebecca Ruth Sickler, Donald Allen, Patricia Bea Weinbrenner, Dwight David; edn: A.B. Cum laude, Ouachita Baptist U., 1949; postgrad. Golden Gate Baptist Theol. Sem., 1951-53; ordained to ministry So. Baptist Ch., 1948. Career: pastor Owensville Baptist Ch., Ark., 1949-50, Grace Bapt. Ch., Corning, Calif., 1951; assoc. pastor 1st So. Bapt. Ch., Richmond, 1951-53; pastor Montalvin Bapt. Ch., San Pablo, 1953-60, First So. Bapt. Ch., Clovis, 1961-85, Hillside Bapt. Ch., La Puente, 1985, Trinity Bapt. Ch. Modesto, 1986-89, ret.; mem. So. Bapt. Gen. Conv. of Calif. (exec. bd. 1981-85, cons. stewardship dept., 1976-89, parliamentarian, 1964, 69, 74, 78), Calif. So. Bapt. Ministers Conf. (pres. 1979), Clovis Ministerial Fellowship (pres. 1963-65, 67-70, 75-77), So. Bapt. Bd. Child Care (1964-67, chmn. 1966-67), Mid-Valley So. Bapt. Assn. (moderator 1965-66, clk. 1969-78, 1990–), Fresno Bapt. Assn. (moderator 1962-64); civic: Clovis Civic Improvement Bond Com. (chmn. fin. com. 1976), Clovis Bicentennial Com. (chair religion 1975-76), Clovis Parks Advy. Com. (1977-78); listed Who's Who in Religion, Who's Who in the West, Who's Who in Fresno; mil: US Army, 1944-46; Republican; Res: 2644 Crescent Ave Clovis 93612

SMITH, WILLIAM HUGH, municipal internal audit manager; b. Feb. 12, 1920, Peoria, Ill.; s. Hugh Norman (C.P.A.) and Catherine Litta (O'Brien) S.; m. Betty Lou, June 4, 1941; children: Beverly Ann Clark b. 1944, William H., Jr. b. 1948, Mildred Judkins b. 1950, Hugh N. b. 1953, Patrick J. b. 1958; edn: BSBA (hons.), Univ. of Dayton, Ohio 1946; Univ. Ill. Grad. Law Sch. 1940-41; desig: CFE, Cert. Fraud Examiner, Nat. Assn. Cert. Fraud Examiners, 1989. Career: resident mgr. Hugh N. Smith CPAs, Chgo. 1947-75; v.p. and chief auditor United of America Bank, Chgo. 1975-78; audit mgr. internal audit City of Anaheim, Ca. 1979–; chmn. audit com. Hoover Dam Uprate Project; mem. Inst. of Internal Auditors, Inc. Orange Co. (speaker com., bd. govs. 1990-93, Internat. Com. on Govt. Affairs), Nat. Assn. of Cert. Fraud Examiners (bd. regents candidate), V.F.W.; mil: capt. Inf. US Army 1941-46, chief counter intell. SE Procurement Dist., provost marshal Tinian Is. Marianas Islands; Republican (life charter mem. Repub. Presdl. Task Force, Who's Who in Republican Party); R.Cath.; rec: sports. Res: 14415 Baker St Westminster 92683 Ofc: City of Anaheim 200 S Anaheim Blvd Ste 710 Anaheim 92805

SMITH, WILLIAM RICHARD, city official; b. June 24, 1940, New York; s. Harry John and jCatharine Anastatia (Wheeler) S.; m. Judith Ann Carroll, March 18, 1961; children: Shawn b. 1961, Kevin b. 1962, Susan b. 1963, Kurt b. 1966, Eric b. 1970; edn: BA, Iona Coll. 1962; MS, U.S. Naval Postgrad. Sch. 1971; MPA, Golden Gate Univ. 1981. Career: sr. adminstrv. analyst City of Monterey 1981-84; city adminstr. City of Sonora 1984-86; asst. city mgr. City of Monterey 1986-90; city mgr. City of Manhattan Beach 1990–; instr. Golden Gate Univ., San Francisco 1983–; mem: Am. Soc. Pub. Adminstrn., Internat. City Mgmt. Assn.; articles pub. in mil. and profl. jours. (1964-81); mil: lt. col. USMC 1962-81, Silver Star 1968, 2 Bronze Stars 1967, 68, 2 Purple Hearts 1967, 68, Navy Commend. 1972, Defense Merit. Service 1982; Democrat; R.Cath.; rec: flying, sailing, motorcycling. Ofc: City Hall, 1400 Highland Ave Manhattan Beach 90266

SMITHAM, H. BRUCE, real estate broker; b. July 22, 1934, Los Angeles; s. Thomas and Emilie W. (Mac Kinnon) S.; m. Sandra Burke, Sept. 14, 1957; children: Hugh, b. 1961, Andrew, b. 1963, Jane, b. 1965, Bruce, b. 1967, Sarah, b. 1970; BA, UCLA 1961. Career: chmn., Aid to Families w/ Dependent Children, State of Calif. Welfare Dir.'s Assn. 1975-76; asst. dir. Kings Co. & Mendocino Co. 1969-77; owner/ opr. Stage Coach Realty, Ukiah and Redwood Valley, Ca. 1977-83; currently Realtor/owner Smitham Real Estate, Del Mar; mem: Realtors Active in Politics (past chmn.), San Dieguito Assn. Realtors, Mendocino County Bd. Realtors (past chmn. profl. stds. & ethics com.), Nat. Assn. Realtors, past mem. Farm & Land Inst.; clubs: Downtown Ukiah Kiwanis (past pres.), Optimists Del Mar-Solana Beach (past pres.); Democrat; Episcopal; rec: computers, real estate. Ofc: Smitham Real Estate, PO Box 2804 Del Mar 92014

SMOLENSKY, EUGENE, economist, professor and graduate school dean; b. Mar. 4, 1932, Bklyn.; s. Abraham and Jennie (Miller) S.; m. Natalie Joan Rabinowitz, Aug. 16, 1952; children: Paul b. 1955, Beth b. 1958; edn: BA econ., Brooklyn Coll., 1952; MA econ., American Univ., W.D.C. 1956; PhD econ., Univ. Pa., 1961. Career: prof. economics Univ. Wisconsin, Madison 1968-88, chair dept. econ. 1978-80, 86-88, director Inst. for Research on Poverty, 1980-83; prof., dean Grad. Sch. of Public Policy, UC Berkeley, 1988–; mem. Nat. Acad. Scis./Nat. Rsch. Council Panel on Child Care Policy, and NAS Commn. on Women's Employment & Related Issues, 1985-91; editor J. of Human Resources, 1985-88; mem.: Assn. for Pub. Policy Analysis & Mgmt. 1988–, Internat. Inst. for Pub. Finance 1980–; coauthor: Public Expenditures, Taxes and the Distbn. of Income: The U.S., 1950, 1961, 1970 (1977), American Economic Growth (1972), Aggregate Supply and Demand Analysis (1964); mil: USN 1952-56; Democrat; Jewish; rec: collect old master etchings and lithographs. Res: 669 Woodmont Ave Berkeley 94708 Ofc: Graduate School of Public Policy UC Berkeley 2607 Hearst Ave Berkeley 94720

SNAER, SEYMOUR WILLIAM, photographer; b. March 4, 1909, Oakland; s. Seymour Louis and Margaret (McDonald) S.; m. Flora Mary Rudd, June 15, 1938; edn: BA, UC Berkeley 1933. Career: freelance photographer, San Francisco 1936-43; San Francisco Examiner 1943-78; ret.; numerous nat. and local awards incl. Calif. Press Photographer of Yr. 1958, Cigar Inst. of Am. award, S.F. Press Club top award (4t), took the 1st natural color action shots of nat. track meet (1937) for N.Y. Mirror, took a photo of a terrorist bomb explosion in San Francisco which appeared in the Am. Soc. of Media Photographers' book "10,000 Eyes", 1991; mem: Nat. Press Photographers Assn., Calif. Press Photographers Assn., S.F. Bay Area Press Photographers Assn.; author: San Francisco 1939 (1984); commemorative poster: 50th anniversary S.F. World Fair 1939 (1989); Republican; Cath.; rec: amateur radio. Res: 42 Sea Pines Moraga 94556-1029

SNOW, ALAN ALBERT, humanist ministry administrator, author; b. July 20, 1946, Van Nuys; s. Perry William and Virginia (Show) S.; edn: BA, Pepperdine Univ., 1969; MA, Sch. of Theology, Claremont 1974; ThD, Andersonville Baptist Seminary 1994; special studies Univ. of Judaism, L.A.(br. of Jewish Theol. Sem. Am.); Magister Operae Onerosae (hon.) Inst. Antiquity Christianity, Claremont 1972. Career: dir. Independent Humanist Ministries Newport Beach; appt. Mayor's advy. com. L.A.; mem. bd. dirs. Inst. for Judeo-Christian Origins Studies, CSU Long Beach; lectr., cons. at The Whole Life Expo, L.A. on newest discoveries in Dead Sea Scrolls, 1995; listed Who's Who in Religion 1993; mem: Nat. Notary Assn. (ethics com., Cert. Accomplishment), Am. Soc. Notaries, Am. Humanist Assn., Ethical Cultural Soc. L.A., N.Y., Inst. for Dead Sea Scrolls Studies WDC, Biblical Archaeology Soc. WDC (charter mem. Dead Sea Scroll Research Council), The Jesus Seminar, Dead Sea Scrolls Res. Soc. WDC; contbg. author to anthologies: The Book Your Church Doesn't Want You To Read (1993, updated 1995), Sydney Omarr's Astrological Guides For You (1994, 95, 96, 97); Democrat. Res: 518 S Bay Front Balboa Island 92662-1040

SNYDER, JOHN JOSEPH, retired optometrist; b. June 30, 1908, Wonewoc, Wisc.; s. Burt Frederick and Alta Lavinia (Hearn) S.; edn: AB, honors, UCLA 1931, post grad. 1931-32; post grad. Univ. of Colo. 1936, 1938, 1940, 1941; post grad., USC, p.t. 1945-47; BS, Los Angeles Coll. of Optometry 1948, OD, 1949. Career: tchr. Rockvale Jr. Sch. and Mayday Sch., La Plata Co., Colo. 1927-28; supt. pub. schs., h.s. tchr. Marvel, Colo. 1932-33; tchr. biology, physics, chemistry, Durango, Colo. 1933-41; optometrist self-empl., Los Angeles 1952-72,

Torrance 1972-78; vacation and relief optometrist 1979-92; mem: AAAS, Am. Inst. of Biol. Scis., Am. Optometric Assn., Calif. Opt. Assn., L.A. County Opt. Soc., Intl. Biographical Assn. (Fellow), Exchange Club of So. L.A. (pres. 1957, secty. 1962), Francia Boys Club, L.A. (bd. dirs. 1956-64); Republican; rec: fishing, limnology. Address: 25937 Reynolds St Loma Linda 92354

SNYDER, NORMAN GENE, physician; b. Apr. 28, 1923, Adel, Iowa; s. Milo Myran and Phoebe Dillworth (Crouse) S.; m. Delphia Norman, Aug. 13, 1950; children: Michael b. 1951, David b. 1953, Catherine b. 1956, Jonathan Scott b. 1957; edn: undergrad. Drake Univ. 1940-42, Iowa State Univ., Ames 1946-47; MD, Univ. of Iowa 1951; lic. Calif. Career: intern Los Angeles County Harbor Gen. Hosp., Torrance 1951-52; gen. & family medicine practice, West Covina 1953-76; emergency phys. Covina Intercommunity Hosp., 1976-81; gen. & family practice phys. Cigna Health Plans, West Covina 1981–; pres./organizer San Gabriel Valley Hot Line 1969-71; dir. Chase-King Devel. Ctr., Upland 1974-76; elected councilman (mayor 1964-65) City of West Covina 1960-68; named Man of the Year for contbn. to human rights, Covina - W. Covina - La Puente Human Rights Council; mem. Am. Med. Assn.; Rotarian; mil: US Navy 1943-46, lt.jg. Reserve 1947-55; Republican (Rep. Central Com. 49th Assem. Dist. 1962-66); rec: bridge, hiking, boating. Ofc: Community Health Projest HQ, Medical Director, 338 S. Glendale Ave., West Covina 91790

SOELDNER, JOHN STUART, physician, educator; b. Sept. 22, 1932, Boston, Mass.; s. Frank and Mary Amelia (Stuart) S.; m. Elsie Irene Harnish, Aug. 25, 1962; children: Judith b. 1963, Elizabeth b. 1965, Stephen b. 1972; edn: BS (magna cum laude), Tufts Univ. 1954; MD, Dalhousie Univ., Faculty of Medicine, Halifax, N.S., Canada 1959; lic. Med. Council of Canada 1959; diplomate Nat. Bd. of Med. Examiners 1959; registration: Mass. 1961, Calif. 1961, Nova Scotia, Can. 1966; lic. Nuclear Regulatory Commn. 1966. Career: intern then resident Victoria Gen. Hosp., Halifax, N.S., Can. 1958-61; res. fellow in medicine, Dalhousie Univ. Faculty of Medicine and Victoria Gen. Hosp. 1959-60, Harvard Med. Sch. 1961-63; from instr. medicine to assoc. prof. medicine, Harvard Med. Sch., Boston 1964-87; res. assoc. to acting dir. Elliott P. Joslin Res. Lab., Boston 1964-87; prof. of medicine UC Davis Sch. of Medicine1987–; physician, dept. internal medicine, UC Davis Med. Ctr., Sacto. 1988–, mem. diabetes out-patient svc. 1988–, endocrine ward svc. 1989–; cons. Giner, Inc., Waltham, Mass. 1988–; ad hoc cons., NIH Study Sect. on Immunology 1990–; investigator Aoki Diabetes Res. Inst., Sacto. 1992–; cons.: Amsys Corp., Wallingford, Ct. 1993–, St. of Calif. DMV 1994, St. of Calif. Dept. Health Svs. 1994–; mem. UC Davis biostatistics prog. com. 1990–, com. on privilege and tenure 1991–, grad. group in statistics 1992–, affinity group and biostatistics subspeciality standing com. 1992–, med. liaison and collaborative res. task force com. 1993–; mem. UC Davis Sch. of Medicine oversight com. for genetic diseases (chmn. 1990–), res. affairs com. 1992– (chmn. 1993-94), faculty exec. com. 1994–; mem. UC Davis Med. Ctr., Dept. of Internal Medicine intern selection com. 1989–, com. on res. 1989–, fin. council 1991–; founding mem. med. sci. advy bd., Juvenile Diabetes Found., NYC 1980; awards: Alpha Omega Alpha 1959, Juvenile Diabetes Found. Scientific Award 1973, Pfizer Traveling Fellow 1974, U.S. Sr. Scientist Award, Alexander von Humboldt Found. 1975, Upjohn Award of Am. Diabetes Assn. 1986, mem: Am. Diabetes Assn. 1961– (bd. dirs. 1978-84; New Eng. affiliate bd. dirs. 1969-81; Calif. affiliate bd. dirs. 1989–, exec. com. 1992-93, nominating com. 1993–, audit com. 1993–; Sierra-Sacto. Chpt. profl. edn. com. 1988–, bd. dirs. 1990–, chmn. long range planning com. 1990–, pres. 1991-93), Am. Fedn. for Clin. Res. 1961–, European Assn. for Study of Diabetes 1965–, The Endocrine Soc. 1965–, Am. Physiological Soc. 1968–, Soc. for Exptl. Biology and Medicine 1972–, Am. Soc. for Clin. Investigation 1974–, Am. Soc. for Artificial Internal Organs 1975–, Internat. Soc. for Artificial Organs 1977–, Internat. Soc. for Twins 1978–, We. Assn. of Physicians 1991–; author: contbr. 300+ articles to sci. publs.; patentee (3) in field; Democrat; Roman Catholic; rec: family genealogy. Ofc: UC Davis 1625 Alhambra Blvd Ste 2901 Sacramento 95816

SOKOLOFF, ALEXANDER, professor emeritus (biology), b. May 16, 1920, Tokyo; nat. Oct. 8, 1943; s. Dimitri Fyodorovitch and Sofia Alexandrovna Solovieff S.; m. Barbara Bryant, June 24, 1956; children: Alexandra 1961; Elaine 1963; Michael 1964; edn: PhD, U. of Chgo., 1954; AB, UCLA, 1948; AA, UCLA, 1942; career: res. assoc. and instr., U. of Chgo. 1954-55; instr. and asst. prof., Hofstra Coll., Hempstead, NY 1955-58; guest investig., Biology Lab., Cold Spring Harbor, NY 1955-58 and 1961; geneticist, W.H. Miner Agri. Res. Inst., Chazy, NY 1958-60; assoc. res. botanist, UCLA 1960; assoc. res. geneticist, UC, Berkeley 1961-63; geneticist, UC, Berkeley 1966-68; assoc. prof., Calif. State Univ., San Bernardino 1965-68. prof. 1968-90, emeritus prof. 1990–; cons., UC, Berkeley 1967-68; editor, Tribolium Inf. Bull. 1960–; edit.bd., J. Stored Prod. Res. 1965; assoc. ed. and advy. bd., J. Advanced Zool. 1980-92; assoc. ed., Evolution 1972-74; mem. com. maintenance genetic stocks, Genetics Soc. of Am., 1973-86; chmn. subcom. Insect Stocks, 1973-76; hon. mem. editl. bd. Acta Biologica Colombiana; awards: fellow, Royal Entomol. Soc., London 1988–; res. grants NSF, W.D.C. 1957-59 and 1967-73; res. grant, USPHS, W.D.C. 1961; res. grants, U. S. Army Res. Ofc., Triangle Park, SC, 1973-76 and 1976-79; mem: Sigma Xi; Soc. For The Study Of Evolution, Genetics Soc. Am., Am. Genetic Assn., Am. Soc. Naturalists, Am. Soc. Zool.,

Japanese Soc. Population Ecol., Soc. Western Naturalists, Pacific Coast Entomol. Soc.; civic: Elks, San Bernardino; author: The Genetics of Tribolium and Related Species, 1966; The Biology of Tribolium vol. 1, 1972; The Biology of Tribolium vol. 2, 1975; The Biology of Tribolium vol. 3, 1977; over 200 papers and research notes; mil: sgt., USAAF, 1942-46; Democrat; Protestant; rec: travel. Res: 3324 Sepulveda Ave San Bernardino 92404 Ofc: Biology Dept. Calif. State Univ. 5500 N. University Pkwy San Bernardino 92407

SOKOLOV, JACQUE J., founder and chief executive officer healthcare management company, physician; b. Sept. 13, 1954, Los Angeles; s. Albert I. and Frances B. (Burgess) S.; edn: BA in medicine (magna cum laude), USC, 1974, MD (honors), USC Sch. of Med., 1978. Career: intern, resident in internal medicine, Mayo Clinic, Rochester, Minn. 1978-81; cardiologist/ nuclear cardiologist Univ. of Texas Health Sci. Ctr., Dallas 1981-84; healthcare strategic planning cons. 1985-87: Texas Instruments, Southwestern Bell, AT&T, Wang, Rosewood Corp.; chief med. ofcr. Baylor Ctr. for Health Promotion, also Wellness & Lifestyle Corp., Dallas 1985-87; v.p./med. dir. So. Calif. Edison Co., Rosemead 1987-92; founder and CEO, Advanced Health Plans, Inc., Los Angeles 1992–; chmn. of the bd. Coastal Healthcare Group, Inc.; awards: NIH tng. grantee; civic: Nat. Health Policy Council, Nat. Health Found.; co-author 15+ abstracts and med. jour. articles (1983-94). Ofc: Advanced Health Plans, Inc 10100 Santa Monica Blvd Ste1300 Los Angeles 90067

SOLBERG, RONALD LOUIS, investment professional, consultant, banker, international economist, author; b. May 15, 1953, Madison, Wis.; s. Carl Louis and Gladys Irene (Oen) S.; m. Anna Maria Gorgol (div. Aug. 1992), May 16, 1983; edn: BA in econs. (honors), Univ. Wisc., 1975; MA and PhD in econs., UC Berkeley, 1977, 1984. Career: country risk analyst Wells Fargo Bank, N.A., San Francisco 1978-79; asst. v.p./country risk analyst Wells Fargo Bank Ltd., London, Eng. 1979-81; tchg. assoc., actg. instr. econ. UC Berkeley 1981-83; cons. The RAND Corp., 1982-84; adj. asst. prof., econ. devel. and country risk analysis, Grad. Sch. Pub. Adminstrn. USC, 1985-92 v.p./sr. internat. economist Security Pacific Nat. Bank, Los Angeles 1984-87; 1st v.p./ chief internat. economist 1988-90, 1st v.p./portfolio risk mgr. 1991-92; internat. finl. cons. 1992-94; fixed-income credit analyst Pacific Investment Mgmt. Co., Newport Beach 1994–; del. Inst. of Internat. Fin., W.D.C. mission to Malaysia, 1986; advy. com. Cross-Rates, Business Int'l, N.Y. 1988–; advisor on LDC debt swap issues to Sen. Alan J. Dixon; awards: Phi Eta Sigma 1971-72, Newton Booth Fellow in Economics UCB 1975-76, Internat. Res.Fellow Inst. of Internat. Studies UCB 1982-84; mem: Am. Economic Assn., Asia Soc. (Corporate Council So. Calif. chapt. 1989–), Nat. Assn. of Bus. Economists, Soc. for Internat. Devel.; author: Country Risk Analysis: A Handbook (London: Routledge, 1992), Sovereign Rescheduling: Risk and Portfolio Management (London: Unwin Hyman Ltd., 1988); pub. res. papers: RAND (4/83), Shipping Economist (Lloyd's of London Press 12/87), Economic Devel. and World Debt (London: Macmillan Press 9/89), numerous profl. presentations; rec: fishing, x-c skiing, squash, billiards. Res: 765 Avocado Ave Corona Del Mar 92625 Tel: 714/721-5822

SOLOMON, LAURENCE EDWARD, educator, licensed real estate and insurance broker; b. Aug. 22, 1947, Bethesda, Md.; s. Charles and Joan Ruth S.; edn: BA in hist., S.F. St. Univ., 1971, MA in special edn., 1974; life tchg. cred. Dominican Coll. 1972-73, life super. cred. San Jose St. Univ. 1974-75; listed with Calif. Jeweler's Board of Trade 1983–. Career: art pgm. dir. Aid Retarded Children Camp, La Honda 1970; rec. ldr. Recreation Ctr. for Severely Handicapped, San Francisco 1970-72; tchr., asst. prin., principal North Monterey County Sch. Dist., Moss Landing 1972-79; lead elem./sec. pgm. reviewer, special edn. investigator, dist. compliance reviewer Calif. St. Dept. Edn. Sacto. 1980-81; exotic bird importer Orleans Avian Inst., Inc. Slidell, La. 1979-82; real estate broker/mortgage banker Am. Savings & Loan/Unified Mortgage, Santa Cruz Co. 1985-87; insurance agent/ broker rep. Prudential 1981-83, independent 1983–; Life Underwriters Tng. Council grad.- personal ins. 1984; resource specialist Santa Clara and Monterey County Schs., 1987–; awards: Marin County Bd. Edn. scholar 1972, 1st pl. wt.lifting Clark Hatch Fitness Ctr. Singapore 1980, ins. prodn. Prudential Ins. Santa Cruz Co. 1982, world travels and experiences as an exotic bird importer featured in articles in San Jose Mercury, San Jose News, Santa Cruz Sentinel and Watsonville Register-Pajaronian Newspapers, 1981, featured in San Jose Mercure article as an educator, 1995; mem: Nat. Edn. Assn. (1970-82, 88–), Calif. Tchrs. Assn. (1972-76, 88–, elected alt. delegate to nat. conf., Wash. D.C. 1989), Nat. Assn. Life Underwriters 1981–; vol. Special Olympics, Santa Cruz & S.F. 1970–; guest speaker Individualized Instrn. Assn. Conf./No. Calif. 1974, vol. Barrios Unidos, working against gang violence; Jewish; rec: precious gems, dancing, weight tng., photog., guitarist/singer, motorcycling. Res: 1308 El Dorado Ave Santa Cruz 95062

SOLOMON, MARIAN AUDREY, insurance company executive, evaluation research consultant; b. July 31, 1947, New Orleans; d. Ben A. and Jeanette (Arbiter) Solomon; m. Alan M. Schultz, Oct. 19, 1969 (div. 1974); m. Dr. Howard Freeman, Feb. 2, 1979; edn: BS, and MS, Florida State, 1967, 69; PhD, UCLA, 1973, MPH, UCLA, 1944; cert. exec. mgmt. Claremont Grad. Sch. 1986. Career: mgmt. analyst Office of Secty. U.S. Dept. Health, Edn. & Welfare,

W.D.C. 1976-80; senior research mgr. System Development Corp., Los Angeles 1980-82; mgmt. info. systems dir. Los Angeles County Dept. Mental Health 1982-87; assoc. hosp. adminstr. for info. systems UCLA, 1987-88; mgr. strategic planning Blue Cross of Calif., Woodland Hills 1988–; spl. advisor to the Chancellor, Centre de Estuidos Univ. Xochicalco, Ensenada, Mex.; cons. in program eval. The Population Council, Cent. Am. and Mexico City regional office; research advisor mgmt. info. systems Div. of Human Devel., Inst. of Nutrition for Cent. Am. and Panama; honors: editl. bd. Evaluation Review (1980-82), nat. tchg. fellow Fla. A&M Univ. (1968-69), Pi Gamma Mu (soc. scis.), Phi Alpha pres. (soc. work), Tau Kappa Alpha- Delta Sigma Rho (forensic), Phi Lamda Theta (edn.); author 2 sci. books in field, contbr. articles to profl. jours. incl. Drug Intelligence and Clin. Pharmacy (4/82), J. of Health Policy Politics and Law (Winter/81), Health Policy Quarterly (Fall/81), others; rec: yachting. Res: 417 Stuart Court Ojai 93023 Ofc: Blue Cross of California 21555 Oxnard St Woodland Hills 91367

SOLOW, LEE HOWARD, clinical psychologist; b. Jan. 16, 1953, Fairfield; s. Robert Avrom and Marilyn Cynthia (Anes) S.; m. Toni Eileen Gingold, Apr. 5, 1987; children: Max b. 1988, Hannah b. 1990, Sophie b. 1992; edn: BA, UC Irvine, 1974; MA, Calif. Sch. Profl. Psychology, San Diego 1976, PhD, 1978. Career: faculty Coastline Comm. Coll., Fountain Valley 1974–; director Wellness Resources, consultants, 1974–; pvt. practice psychologist, Newport Beach 1978–; divorce mediator 1994–; dir. stress mgmt. Univ. Athletic Club, N.B.; mem. Am. Psy. Assn. 1985–, CSPA 1985–; author: Wellness Resource Guide, 1984; Democrat; Jewish; rec: numismatics, gardening, sports. Res: 702 Heliotrope Corona Del Mar 92625 Tel: 714/955-2575

SOMORJAI, GABOR A., professor of chemistry; b. May 4, 1935, Budapest, Hungary (nat. US, 1962); s. Charles and Livia (Ormos) S.; m. Judith Kaldor, Sept. 2, 1957; children: Nicole b. 1964, John b. 1966; edn: PhD, UC Berkeley, 1960. Career: res. staff, IBM, Yorktown Heights, NY 1960-64; asst. prof. of Chem., UC Berkeley 1964-72; prof. of chem., UC Berkeley 1972–; faculty sr. scientist, Materials Sciences Div., Lawrence Berkeley Lab. 1964–; prog. leader, Surface Sci. and Catalysis Prog., Ctr. for Adv. Materials, Lawrence Berkeley Lab. 1985–; honors: Guggenheim Fellowship 1969, vis. fellow Emmanuel Coll., Cambridge, Eng. 1969, Unilever vis. prof. Univ. of Bristol, Eng. 1972, chmn Div. of Colloid and Surface Chem., Am. Chemical Soc. 1975; recipient Kokes Award, Johns Hopkins Univ., Baltimore, Md. 1976, Emmett Award, Am. Catalysis Soc. 1977; Fellow, Am. Physical Soc. 1976; Baker resident lectr., Cornell Univ. 1977; Miller Professorship, UC Berkeley 1978; recipient, Colloid and Surface Chem. Award, Am. Chemical Soc. 1981, Henry Albert Palladium Award 1986; fellow, Am. Assn. for Advancement of Sci. 1982; Centenary Lectr., Royal Soc. of Chem. 1983; chmn, Gordon Conf. on Catalysis 1983; recipient, Peter Debye Award, Am. Chemical Soc. 1989, Sr. Dist. Scientist Award, Alexander von Humboldt Found. 1989, E.W. Mueller Award, Univ. of Wis. 1989, hon. doctorate Technical Univ., Budapest 1989, Universite Pierre et Marie Curie, Paris, France 1990; hon. mem., Hungarian Acad. of Sciences 1990, Adamson Surface Chemistry Award Am. Chemical Soc. 1994; mem: Nat. Acad. of Sciences 1979–, Am. Acad. of Arts & Sciences 1983–, Cosmos Club., Wash., DC; author: textbooks, Principles of Surface Chem., 1972, Chemistry in Two Dimensions: Surfaces, 1981; monograph, Adsorbed Monolayers on Solid Surfaces, 1979, Introduction to Surface Chemistry and Catalysis, 1994; over 700 scientific papers. Res: 665 San Luis Rd. Berkeley 94707 Ofc: Univ. Calif. Berkeley Dept. of Chemistry Berkeley 94720

SONNENFELD, ALBERT, university professor, department chair; b. July 22, 1934, Berlin, Germany; nat. 1945; s. Dr. Arthur and Dr. Anni (Lichtenstein) S.; m. Portia B. Leys, June 15, 1955 (div. 1986); children: Mark b. 1959, Carole Geithner b. 1962; m. 2d. Dr. Noel Riley Fitch, Aug. 23, 1987; edn: AB., Oberlin Coll., Ohio 1955; AM, Princeton Univ. 1957, PhD, 1958. Career: instr. French, Princeton Univ. 1958-60, from asst. prof. to prof. French & Euro. lit., 1960-76, prof. French & Comp. Lit. 1976-86, chmn. Dept. Romance Langs. 1978-86; Marion Frances Chevalier Prof. of French and Comparative Literatures and dept. chair French and Italian, Univ. of So. Calif., L.A. 1986–; vis. prof. UCLA, Stanford, Rutgers, Wisconsin, London, NYU, CUNY, Dartmouth Coll.; cons. Linguaphone Inst., London 1974–; food critic; restaurant and travel cons.; Fulbright fellow 1966-67; NEH fellow 1978-79, 80, 83; awards: Chevalier des Palmes Academiques, French Govt. 1979, Officer, 1983, named Officier dans l'Ordre des Arts et des Lettres 1989; Zumberge Fellowship for Innovative Res., Univ. So. Calif., Raubenheimer Outstanding Faculty award Univ. So. Calif. 1990; mem: Am. Inst. of Wine and Food (nat. bd. dirs., chair publications bd., nat. speaker on gastronomic subjects), The Athenaeum (London), Phi Beta Kappa; author: L'Oeuvre poetique de Tristan Corbiere (Presses Univ. France, 1961), Crossroads: Studies in the Catholic Novel, 1982, Thirty-six French Poems (Houghton, 1961), 80+ scholarly articles; co-author: Temoins de l'Homme (Scribner, 1965); Independent. Ofc: University of Southern California Taper 126 , University Park Los Angeles 90089-0359

SONNTAG, SELMA KATHERINE, political scientist, educator; b. Oct. 14, 1955, Spokane, Wash.; d. Robert Paul and Selma Margaret (Hultin) Sonntag; m. Robert G. White, March 26, 1988; edn: BA, Univ. Wash. Seattle 1978; MA,

1981; PhD, 1988. Career: profl. assoc. East West Center, Honolulu, Hawaii 1980; vis. asst. prof. Humboldt St. Univ. 1986-89, asst. prof. 1989-92, assoc. prof. 1992–; awards: Fulbright research grant 1993-94; mem: Western Political Sci. Assn.; num. articles pub. in profl. jours., 1980-95; Democrat. Ofc: Humboldt State Univ. Dept. of Political Science Arcata 95521

SOROKIN, CHERYL A., corporate secretary and lawyer; b. May 4; m. Gideon Sorokin; 1 child, David; edn: BA in Spanish/French (w. highest dist.), Indiana Univ., 1966, and MS in edn. (w. highest dist.), 1969; JD (cum laude), Northwestern Univ. Law, 1977. Career: intern Nat. Security Agency, Wash. D.C. 1965; adj. faculty Ind. Univ., Ft. Wayne 1966-69; Spanish tchr. pub. schs. Fairfield, Conn. 1969-71, Wheaton, Ill. 1972-74; atty. Office of the Gen. Counsel, Bank America Corp./Bank of Am., Chgo. and San Francisco 1977-86, corp. secty. and asst. gen. counsel, BAC/B of A, San Francisco 1986–; honors: Order of Coif 1977, Bank Am. Corp. chmn.'s Eagle award 1988, and exceptional performance awards; mem: Am. Bar Assn., Calif. Bar Assn., Am. Soc. Corp. Sectys. (corp. practices com.), Am. Assn. Univ. Women. Ofc: BankAmerica Corp. 555 California St Ste 3018 San Francisco 94104

SORSTOKKE, SUSAN EILEEN, systems engineer; b. May 2, 1955, Seattle; d. Harold William and Carrol Jean (Russ) Sorstokke; edn: BS in sys. engring., Univ. Ariz., 1976; MBA, Univ. Wash., 1983. Career: whse. team mgr. Procter & Gamble Paper Products, Modesto, Calif. 1976-78; quality assurance engr. Westinghouse Hanford Co., Richland, Wa. 1978-80, supv. engring. document ctr. 1980-81; mgr. data control & adminstrn. Westinghouse Electric, Madison, Pa. 1981-82, mgr. data control & records mgmt., 1982-84; prin. engr. Westinghouse Elevator, Morristown, N.J. 1984-87, reg. adminstrn. mgr. Westinghouse Elevator, Arleta, Calif. 1987-90; ops. res. analyst American Honda Motor Co., Torrance 1990-95, project leader, parts systems 1995–; adj. prof. Univ. LaVerne, 1991; c.f.o. Optimist Charities Inc., Acton 1991-94; instr. Excell, L.A. 1991-92; mem. Soc. of Women Engrs. (1975–, past pres. Ea. Wash. sect.), Am. Inst. Industrial Engrs.; civic: Optimist Intl. Santa Clarita 1991-94, Am. Edn. Connection, Santa Clarita (1988-89, 91), Junior Achievement, Greensburg, Pa. 1982-83, Westmoreland Literacy Council 1983-84, EF Found., Santa Clarita 1987-88; Republican; Methodist. Res: 2567 Plaza Del Amo #205 Torrance 90503 Ofc: American Honda Motor Co. Inc. 1919 Torrance Blvd 100-4E-8D Torrance 90501

SOSA-RIDDELL, ADALJIZA, educator; b. Dec. 12, 1937, Colton; d. Luz Paz and Gregoria (Lopez) Sosa; m. William A. Riddell, Aug. 24, 1957; children: Citlali b. 1975; edn: BA, UC Berkeley 1960; MA, 1964; PhD, UC Riverside 1974. Career: tchr. Colton Union H.S., Colton 1961-68; asst. prof. UC Davis 1971-78, prof. of Chicano studies 1978–, coord. Chicana/Latina Research Ctr.; awards: Nat. Assn. Chicano Studies 1989, Sacto. Area YWCA Woman of Year award in edn. 1992; mem: Comision Femenil, Mujeres Activas en Letras y Cambio Social (past chair), Nat. Assn. for Chicano Studies; writer poetry 1974, 75; 5 research articles pub. in profl. jours. 1975-84; Democrat; rec: writing, community service. Res: Sacramento 95827 Ofc: Chicana/o Studies Program University of California Davis 95616

SOUKUP, PAUL ARTHUR, clergyman/professor of communication; b. Aug. 15, 1950, Burbank; s. Frank Kermit and Jeannette Laurette (Ramsey) S.; edn: AB, St. Louis Univ. 1973; M.Div., Jesuit Sch. of Theology 1978; STM, 1980; PhD, Univ. Tx. Austin 1985; ordained priest, 1979. Career: tchr. Loyola H.S., Los Angeles 1973-76; assoc. pastor St. Theresas Ch., Austin, Tx. 1980-85; vis. assoc. pastor St. Joseph of Cupertino 1986–; assoc. prof. comms. Santa Clara Univ. 1985–; cons. U.S. Cath. Conf., Wash. D.C. 1982-88; editl. bd. mem. Jour. of Comms. & Religion 1988–; bd. dirs. Company Mag., Chgo., Ill. 1988–; awards: Univ. Tx. fellowship 1980-83; mem: Soc. of Jesus, UNDA, Speech Comm. Assn., Internat. Comm. Assn.; author: Theology & Communication, 1983, Christian Communication, 1989, monograph: Studies in the Spirituality of Jesuits, 1989, contbr. J. of Comm. & Religion; Democrat; R.Cath.; rec: computers. Ofc: Communication Dept. Santa Clara University, Santa Clara 95053

SOUTHARD, GLENN DONALD, city manager; b. Oct. 1, 1951, Glendale; s. William Arthur Southard and Patricia Lee (Thompson) Ryan; m. Gale deBoers, July 17, 1981; 1 son, Derick; edn: BA, San Diego St. Univ. 1974; MPA, CSU Fullerton 1980. Career: adminstrv. service ofcr. City of Riverside Park & Recreation Dept., Riverside 1977-81; asst. to city mgr. City of W. Covina 1981-85; asst. city mgr. City of San Juan Capistrano 1985-88; city mgr. City of Claremont 1988–; awards: Harry Scoville Disting. Performance Am. Soc. Pub. Adminstrn. 1986, Calif. Jaycees Outstanding Californian 1985, U.S. Congress Recognition Cert. 1984, Outstanding Young Men in Am. 1980; mem: Internat. City Mgmt. Assn., Calif. League of Cities. Ofc: City of Claremont 207 Harvard Claremont 91711

SPAETE, RICHARD ROGER, virologist; bb. Aug. 18, 1947, Rice Lake, Wis.; s. Paul Robert and Helen Margaret S.; edn: BS, Univ. Wis. Eau Claire 1974; MS, Univ. Mont. 1978; PhD, Univ. Chgo. 1982. Career: postdoctoral fellow Stanford Univ., Palo Alto 1983-86; sr. scientist Chiron Corp., Emeryville 1986-92; dir. DNA virus research Aviron, Burlingame 1992–; awards: Pub. Health

Service Predoctoral Traineeship 1978-82, Stanford Univ. Dean's fellow 1983-84, Leukemia Research Found. Postdoctoral Award 1984-85, 85-86; mem: Am. Soc. Microbiology, AAAS; articles pub. in profl. jours., 1982–; patentee in field, 1989–; mil: AUS 1968-70; Republican; Lutheran; rec: skiing. Ofc: Aviron 1450 Rollins Road Burlingame 94010-2307

SPANGLER, CHARLES BISHOP, company president, b. Jan. 7, 1932, Meadows of Dan, Va.; s. Charles Langhorne and Kittie Clyde (Cockram) S.; m. Bettie Smith, Sept. 12, 1954; children: Peggy b. 1955, Charles b. 1957, Thomas b. 1959; edn: AB, Berea Coll. 1953, MS, Univ. of Pittsburgh 1955, PhD, 1963. Career: sr. res. engr. Gen. Dynamics, San Diego 1956-60; asst. prof. math. San Diego St. Univ. 1960-62; mgr. ops. research Litton Data Systems, Van Nuys 1962-69; dir. systems engring. Teledyne Ryan, San Diego 1969-71; dir. advanced sys. 1971-75; pres. Quest Equities Corp. 1976-89; founder and pres. C.B. Spangler Inc. 1989–; founder and pres. Franchise Management Co. of San Diego 1994–; dir: Topaz Div. Intermark Corp. 1962-68, Consumark Corp. 1976-78; awards: Clark Prize in Physics, Berea Coll. 1953, outstanding citizen award Patrick Co., Va. 1975; mem. Am. Math. Soc.; Torrey Pines Christian Ch. (bd. chmn.). Res: 3156 Old Kettle Rd San Diego 92111

SPANIER, JEROME, mathematician, educator, administrator; b. June 3, 1930, St. Paul, Minn.; s. David Howard and Anne (Goldman) S.; m. Bernice Hoffman, Aug. 31, 1952; children: Stephen b. 1956, Ruth b. 1959, Adrienne b. 1959; edn: BA, Univ. Minn., 1951; MS, Univ. Chicago, 1952, PhD, 1955. Career: senior mathematician Bettis Atomic Power Lab., West Mifflin, Pa. 1955-59, Westinghouse fellow 1959-66, advy mathematician 1966-67; mem. tech. staff Science Ctr. No. American Rockwell, Thousand Oaks, Calif. 1967-70; group ldr./math. 1970-71; prof. math. The Claremont Graduate Sch., Claremont 1971–, dean of faculty 1982-87, also v.p. academic affairs 1985-87, v.p. and dean Claremont Grad. Sch., 1987-90; awards: Westinghouse Distinguished svc. 1963, US ERDA and NSF grants, Claremont 1976-80, govt. Siam vis. consultant 1979- and vis. lectr. Siam 1981–, Pres.'s medal CGS, Claremont 1990, Fulbright senior scholar Massey Univ., Palmerston North N.Z. 1990; mem.: editl. bd. J. Statistical Physics 1971–, Mathematical & Computer Modelling 1979–; author: An Atlas of Functions (1987), The Fractional Calculus (1974), Monte Carlo Principles & Neutron Transport Problems (1969); rec: brush painting, music, swimming. Ofc: The Claremont Graduate School 143 E Tenth St Claremont 91711

SPARER, MALCOLM MARTIN, rabbi; b. New York City; m. Erna "Kitty" Reichl (dec. 1990) (fought with the resistance WWII, interpreter at the Nuremburg Trials); children: Ruth, Arthur (dec. 1993), Jennifer, Shoshana; edn: AB, MHL, ordained rabbi, Yeshiva Univ.; MA sociology, City Coll. N.Y., cert. pastoral counselling Des Moines Coll. of Osteopathic Med.; PhD sociology, New York Univ. Career: exec. dir. Rabbinical Council of Calif., Los Angeles 1957-66, adminstr. Torah Univ. (later Yeshiva Univ.) Teacher's Coll. of West Coast, liaison for Union of Orthodox Jewish Congs. of Am., 1957-66, moderator radio series "Lest We Forget" 1962, moderator TV specials on Jewish religion and holiday observances, KNXT Los Angeles, 1964-65; rabbi Beth El Jacob, Des Moines, Iowa 1966-69, TV moderator Des Moines, 1967-69; rabbi, Chevra Thilim, San Francisco, 1969-72; co-chmn. Jerusalem Fair, 25th Ann. of State of Israel, 1973; current: cons. internat. leaders, founder Menorah Inst. (inter-faith activities and communications, devel. econ. interdependence); cons. Commn. on Christian-Jewish and Moslem Relations to European Parliament Nations; fgn. rels. and econ. cons. various govt. and non-govt. orgns.; writer and frequent lectr. on coll. campuses, ch. groups on Judaica and World Affairs; pres. emeritus No. Calif. Board of Rabbis; pres. Menorah Inst.; Rabbi, Jewish Home for Aged, S.F.; chmn. dept. world affairs/internat. politics Community Coll. of S.F.; chaplain Letterman Army VA Hosp., S.F. Presidio; co-founder Black & Jewish Clergy; mem. S.F. Council of Churches (bd. Food Bank Pgm.), Coalition of S.F. (food basket pgm.), Mayor's Commn. on Holocaust Memorial (hon. chmn.), Mayor's Task Force for the Homeless, Gov.'s Fam. Task Force (co-chair), United Jewish Mail: POB 15055 San Francisco 94115 Appeal (Rabbinic Cabinet we. reg.); Ofc: 17350 N Mallard Dr Sonoma 95476 Tel: 415/452-1950

SPECTOR, IRWIN, musicologist; b. Jan. 11, 1916, Garwood, N.J.; s. George and Tillie (Weinberg) S.; m. Jane F. Hoffman, Jan. 22, 1944; children: Jerome b. 1944, Alan b. 1948, Harlan b. 1951, George b. 1956; edn: BS, Trenton St. Coll. 1936; MA, Columbia Univ. 1942; PhD, N.Y. Univ. 1952; dipl., Nat. Conservatory of Music Paris 1954. Career: instr. Monmouth Coll., Long Branch, N.J. 1947-48; vis. prof. Univ. Kans., Lawrence 1968-69; prof. Univ. Grenoble, France 1971; Summer Acad., Nice, France 1972; prof. Ill. St. Univ., Normal 1948-76; bd. mem. Composers Guild of N.J., Ship Bottom 1981-88; Capital Music Festival, Trenton, N.J. 1982-88; awards: Rockefeller Inst. travel grant 1964, Ill. St. Univ. travel grant 1972, Swiss Govt. research grant 1964-65; mem: Am. Musicological Soc., Internat. Musicological Soc., Performing Arts Soc., Presidio Officers Club, B'nai B'rith; author: Instrumental Music of Robert White, 1972, Rhythm & Life, 1989, 20 articles pub., composer 40 musical works; mil: major AUS 1942-46, USAR 1946-62, Bronze Star 1945; Democrat; Jewish; rec: chamber music, chess, tennis. Res: 3064 Rossmoor Parkway #4 Walnut Creek 94595

SPEED, RICHARD BERRY, historian; b. Sept. 27, 1948, Pasadena; s. Richard Berry and Harriet (Caltis) S.; m. Lillian Castillo, Aug. 18, 1976; children: Nathan Richard b. 1977; edn: BA, UC Riverside 1971; MA, CSU Long Beach 1975; PhD, UC Santa Barbara 1987. Career: lectr. dept. of history CSU Hayward 1988–; mem: Am. Hist. Soc., Orgn. of Am. Historians, Soc. Historians of Am. Fgn. Rels., Acad. Political Sci., Center for Study of Presidency; author: Prisoners, Diplomats and the Great War; Republican. Res: 1807 Pheasant Dr Hercules 94547 Ofc: California State University Dept. of History Hayward 94542-3045

SPEIER, KAREN JACQUELINE, lawyer; b. May 14, 1950, San Francisco, Calif.; d. Fred and Nancy Speier; m. Steven Sierra (widowed 1/25/94); children: Jackson Kent Sierra b. 1988, Stephanie Katelin Elizabeth Sierra b. 1994; edn: BA, UC Davis 1972; grad. Hastings Coll. of Law 1976. Career: legal counsel to Congressman Leo J. Ryan, 1978; elected to San Mateo Co. Bd. of Supervisors 1980-86, chair of Bd. 1985; elected 19th Assembly Dist. Calif. 1986–; majority whip of the Assembly 1988–; chair, Assembly Com. on Consumer Protection, Governmental Efficiency and Econ. Devel. 1991–; mem. Assembly coms. on Judiciary and Health; honors: Humanitarian of Yr. award Danny Found. 1994, Legislator of Yr., Girl Scouts of Am. 1994, Nat. Legislator of Yr. by Nat. Assn. of Women Bus. Owners, Consumer Advocate of Yr. by Consumer Action, Legislator of Yr. by: Calif. State Bar Assn., Women Constrn. Owners & Execs., Nat. Mobilization Against Aids, and Nat. Orgn. for Women; inducted San Mateo Co. Women's Hall of Fame, So. San Francisco's Citizen of Yr., Woman of Yr. award Am. Assn. of Univ. Women, saluted by San Mateo Co. Unit Am. Cancer Soc.; author: 149 bills signed into law in Calif., 1986–, which include pro-consumer bills protecting against travel fraud, 900-phone number scams, unfair funeral and cremation practices, and illegal stock transactions; revised workers' compensation laws, nat. guidelines for school lunch progs., state guidelines for children with learning disabilities, creation of statewide early AIDS intervention progs., est. of State Ofc. of Perinatal Substance Abuse, free credit reports to consumers, creation of Women's Bus. Ownership Act & Council, elimination of 1300+ state reports to the legis., others. Ofc: 220 S Spruce Ave #101 South San Francisco 94080 and State Capitol Sacramento 94249-0001

SPELLBERG, NORMAN, judge (retired); b. Apr. 8, 1926, Chgo.; s. Louis and Dora (Rubin) S.; m. Marjorie Francel, Oct. 23, 1954; children: Geoffrey b. 1956, Diane b. 1957; edn: Ill. Inst. Tech., 1943-44; BS, Univ. Ill., Urbana 1948; JD, Golden Gate Univ. 1965. Career: research chemist Sherwin-Williams Paint Co. Inc., Chgo. 1948-51; chief chemist De Soto, Inc., Berkeley 1951-62, resin plant mgr., 1962-65; lawyer, assoc. Hoppe, Mitchell, et al San Francisco 1965-67; ptnr. Hineser & Spellberg, 1967-76; judge Mt. Diablo Municipal Ct., Concord 1976-80; judge Superior Ct., Martinez 1980-91; affiliate (arbitration, mediation, spl. reference), JAMS/Endispute 1991–; prof. law, J.F.K. Univ. 1966–; honors: outstanding faculty J.F.K. Univ. 198), trial judge of yr. Contra Costa Trial Lawyers, Oakland 1984; mem. Calif. Judges Assn.; Century Club (Concord); inventions: Fumaric Acid Polyalkyd (pat. 1967), Short Oil Styrene Alkyd (pat. 1956), Highway Marking Compos. (pat. 1966), num. fgn. counterparts; mil: sgt. USAAC 1944-46; Democrat; Jewish; rec: golf, swim, scuba, ski. Res: 629 Laird Ln Lafayette 94549 Ofc: Superior Court 735 Main St Martinez 94553

SPENCER, DOUGLAS CHARLES, bank executive; b. Aug. 3, 1958, Ogden, Utah; s. Charles Douglas and Geraldine (Austad) S.; m. Sarah Lynn Hanson, April 22, 1981; children: Krysta Nicole b. 1984; Kathryn Blue b. 1988; edn: BS, Brigham Young Univ. 1982; MBA, Univ. Utah 1984; JD, 1985; admitted St. Bar Tx. 1986, Calif. 1988, U.S. Ct. Appeals 9th Dist. 1988. Career: credit analyst InterFirst Bank, Dallas, tx. 1985, sr. credit analyst 1986; loan ofcr. Landmark Bank, La Habra 1986, asst. v.p., loan ofcr. 1987, v.p., sr. credit ofcr. 1987-88, v.p., branch mgr. 1988-94, v.p./SBA div. mgr. 1994-95, sr. v.p./C.O.O. 1995–; awards: Landmark Bank Top Ofcr. 1987, 88, 89; mem: Am. Bar Assn., Orange Co. Bar Assn., World Affairs Council; Republican; Mormon; rec: skiing, weightlifting, running (completed the "last great race on earth", six 100-mile endurance runs, from 6/95 to 9/95). Ofc: Landmark Bank 441 W Whittier Blvd La Habra 90631

SPENCER, ROBERT LEO, merger and acquisition company principal; b. Nov. 12, 1917, NY, NY; s. Leo and Carolyn (Saxe) Sternfeld; m. Grace Seidman, Aug. 27, 1941; children: Kathy S. Freeman b. 1944, Barbara L. Spencer b. 1950; edn: BS comml. sci. (summa cum laude), N.Y. Univ., 1937; LLB, Golden Gate Coll., 1945; C.P.A., Calif.; admitted Calif. State Bar 1945. Career: senior ptnr. Seidman & Seidman, CPAs, N.Y. 1937-41, Beverly Hills 1941-79; ptnr. Spencer-Wittenberg, 1979-83; ptnr. Spencer Niemiec, 1983-86; prin. Spencer Assocs., 1986–; frequent speaker and numerous tax articles; honors: highest g.p.a. in history of coll., class pres., and frat. chancellor, NYU 1937; mem: Am. Inst. CPAs (past governing Council, com. chmn.), Calif. Soc. CPAs (past pres. L.A. Chpt.); civic: Cedars-Sinai Med. Ctr. Bd. Dirs. (exec. com., past bd. chmn.), Jewish Comm. Found. (trustee, past pres.), Jewish Fedn. Council of Gr. L.A. (active 1949–, past dir., v.p.), Hebrew Union Coll. Bd. of Overseers, Pitzer Coll. Bd. Dirs., L.A. United Way (past bd. govs.); club: Hillcrest CC (past pres.); mil: lt.s.g. USNR 1942-46; Democrat; Wilshire Blvd. Temple (past bd. mem., v.p.); rec: golf. Res: 10350 Wilshire Blvd #904 Los Angeles 90024 Ofc: Spencer Associates 10350 Wilshire Blvd #904Los Angeles 90024

SPIEGEL, MARILYN HARRIET, real estate broker; b. April 3, 1935, Brooklyn, N.Y.; d. Harry and Sadie (Oscher) Unger; m. Murray Spiegel, June 12, 1954; children: Eric Lawrence b. 1959, Dana Cheryl b. 1961, Jay Barry b. 1965; edn: grad. Erasmus H.S. 1953; lic. real estate broker 1980. Career: exec. secty. S&W Paper Co., N.Y.C. 1953-54; Japan Paper Co. 1954-59; decorator Royal Decorators, Kans. City, Mo. 1965-70; real estate agent C.P. Realtors, Los Alamitos 1975-79; broker, owner S&S Properties, Garden Grove 1979–; named Realtor of the Yr. CAR (1989); mem: West Orange Bd. of Realtors (dir. 1983–), Calif. Assn. Realtors (dir. 1985–), Summit Orgn., Nat. Council Jewish Women, Toastmasters Intl. (#550, pres.); Republican; Jewish; rec: decorating. Res: 4765 Candleberry Seal Beach 90740 Ofc: S&S Properties 3502 Katella Ave Ste 208 Los Alamitos 90720

SPIELBERG, STEVEN, filmmaker, director and producer; b. 1948, Cincinnati, Ohio; edn: attended Calif. State Univ., Long Beach. Career: made his first film with actors at age 12; made 5 short films while in college, including Amblin (shown at the Atlanta Film Festival 1969); signed 7-yr. contract with Universal Pictures, 1969; dir. t.v. shows for Universal Television including episodes of Night Gallery, Marcus Welby and Columbo; dir., made-for-t.v. feature-length film Duel, 1973; dir. theatrical feature film The Sugarland Express, 1974, Jaws, 1975; writer, dir. Close Encounters of the Third Kind, 1977; dir. Raiders of the Lost Ark, 1981; E.T. The Extra-Terrestrial, 1982; co-writer, co-producer, Poltergeist; dir. Indiana Jones and the Temple of Doom, 1984, The Color Purple, 1986, Empire of the Sun, 1987, Indiana Jones and the Last Crusade, 1989, Always, 1989, Hook, 1991, Jurassic Park, 1993, Schindler's List 1993-94; founder, Amblin Entertainment, Universal City 1984–, producer or exec. producer 12+ films including Gremlins, Goonies, Back to the Future I, II, and III, Who Framed Roger Rabbit?, An American Tail, The Land Before Time, and (as Steven Spielrock) The Flintstones; Amblin Entertainment and Amblin Television productions include Tiny Toon Adventures (Emmy Award winner), Animaniacs (George Foster Peabody Award 1994), seaQuest, DSV (NBC-TV, 1993–), Earth 2 (NBC, 1994–), E.R. (NBC, 1994–) and TNT Screenworks; ptnr., co-founder, Dive!, Los Angeles 1994–; ptnr., co-founder (with Jeffrey Katzenberg and David Geffen), DreamWorks SKG, 1994–; joint venture with Microsoft, Dreamworks Interactive, 1995–; awards: Am. Film Inst. Lifetime Achievement award 1995, Academy Awards for Schindler's List including Best Picture and Best Director, 1994, Directors Guild of Am. Award 1994 (film won 7 Academy Awards, 7 British Academy Awards, Best Picture Awards from NY Film Critics Circle, Nat. Bd. of Review, Producers Guild, L.A. Film Critics, Chicago, Boston & Dallas Film Critics, Christopher Award, and Hollywood Fgn. Press Assn. Golden Globe Awards), Golden Lion Award for Career Achievement, Venice Film Festival 1993, Irving G. Thalberg Award presented at the Acad. Award ceremonies for consistent excellence in filmmaking 1987, Director's Guild of Am. (DGA) Award for direction of The Color Purple, 1986 (film was nominated for 11 Academy Awards), nominated by DGA for Empire of the Sun, Jaws, Close Encounters of the Third Kind, Raiders of the Lost Ark, E.T., nominated by Acad. of Motion Picture Arts & Sciences for Close Encounters of the Third Kind, Raiders of the Lost Ark, E.T., and Schindler's List; featured in Forbes Mag. as one of the year's 40 top-money entertainers, 9/26/94. Ofc: Amblin Entertainment Inc. 100 Universal Plaza, Bungalow 477 Universal City 91608

SPINKS, PAUL, library director, retired; b. Mar. 7, 1922, London, Eng.; m. Clarice Goode, Jan. 27, 1946; son, Philip b. 1954; edn: dipl. Royal Soc. of Arts, Spring Grove Polytechnic, Isleworth, Middlesex, Eng. 1939; BA, Univ. of Okla., 1958, MLS, 1959. Career: library asst. British Museum, London 1939-52; lib. asst. Univ. Okla., 1952-53; research reports librarian Naval Postgraduate Sch., Monterey 1959-61, assoc. lib. dir. 1961-74, library dir. 1974-93; professor emeritus Naval Postgraduate Sch.; honors: Beta Phi Mu; mem. am. Lib. Assn., Special Lib. Assn.; civic: South Net Info. Network, San Jose (bd. 1984-86), British Am. Club, Monterey 1967-68; publs: research reports and articles; mil: warrant ofcr. Royal Air Force 1942-46; rec: writing, walking, swimming. Res: 855 Capistrano Dr Salinas 93901

SPOLTER, PARI DOKHT, author, publisher; b. Jan. 30, 1930, Tehran, Iran; nat. Nov. 18, 1964; m. Herbert Spolter, MD, Aug. 16, 1958; children: David b. 1966, Deborah b. 1967; edn: Licence chimie biologique, Univ. of Geneva, Switzerland 1952; PhD in biochemistry, Univ. of Wisconsin, Madison, Wis. 1961. Career: postdoctoral fellow Temple Univ., Phila. 1961-62; instr. Temple Univ. 1962-66; researcher U.S. Public Health Svc. Hosp., S.F., Calif. 1966-68; writer and publisher of scientific books Orb Publishing Co., Granada Hills, Calif. 1988–; mem: AAAS 1989–, Am. Math. Soc. 1989–, N.Y. Acad. of Scis. 1993–; author: num. jour. articles, 1961-68; books: Gravitational Force of the Sun, 1994, Gravitational Force of the Proton (to be publ.); rec: classical music, opera. Ofc: Orb Publishing Co. 11862 Balboa Bl. #182 Granada Hills 91344-2753

SPRING, DEE, psychotherapist; b. Sept. 22, 1934, Clayton, Ga.; d. James Rusk and Maxie Marie (Thompson) Grant; m. John B. Spring, Mar. 15, 1957 (div. 1981); children: Jay b. 1958, Angela b. 1960, David b. 1965; edn: BA, CSU Fullerton 1976; MA, Vt. Coll. Plainfield 1977; MA clin. psychology, Fielding Inst. S.B. 1985; PhD, 1988. Career: dir. Women's Crisis Center, Placentia 1974-

81; asst. prof., Calif., Mont., Vt. and Ore. 1976–; psychologist, Mont. 1981-83; dir. Earthwood Center, Ventura 1983–; pvt. practice, Calif. and Mont. 1976–; cons. Fullerton Coll. 1977-80; awards: City of Ventura Nat. Cons. Vols. 1984, Am. Mental Health Counselors Assn. Doctoral fellowship 1984, Am. Art Therapy Assn. Nat. Research 1978, Fullerton Coll. Lena & Fay Reynolds scholarships 1974-77, listed: Who's Who Mental Health, Who's Who Among Human Services Profls., Who's Who in West, Who's Who of Am. Women; mem: Am. Art Therapy Assn. (treas. 1984-89), Calif. Soc. for the Study of Dissociation (pres. 1993-95); author pub. book: Shattered Images, 1993; articles, book chpts., and presentations pub. 1980–; rec: art. Ofc: 2021 Sperry Ave Ste 23 Ventura 93003

SPRINGER, PAUL D., film studio executive, lawyer; b. April 27, 1942, New York; s. William W. and Alma (Markowitz) S.; m. Mariann Frankfurt, Aug. 16, 1964; children: Robert b. 1968, William b. 1972; edn: BA, Univ. Bridgeport 1964; JD, Bklyn. Law Sch. 1967; admitted bar: N.Y. 1968, Calif. 1989. Career: atty., assoc. Johnson & Tannenbaum, NYC 1967-70; assoc. counsel Columbia Pictures 1970; sr. v.p. and asst. gen. counsel Paramount Pictures Corp., Los Angeles 1970–; mem: Am. Bar Assn., Acad. Motion Picture Arts and Scis., Los Angeles Copyright Soc., W. Cunningham Park Civic Assn. (trustee 1975–); Jewish. Res: 15915 High Knoll Rd Encino 91436 Ofc: Paramount Pictures Corp. 5555 Melrose Ave Los Angeles 90038

SPRINKEL, RITA L., diplomat, retired executive; b. Aug. 6, 1935, Bergen, Norway; U.S. citizen, 1965; d. Sverre Johannesen Indrebo and Ingeborg N. (Kongsvik) I.; m. Warren Reed Sprinkel, Aug. 12, 1978. Career: former bd. dir. Pritikin Research Found.; former dir. public/employee relations Fontana Paving Inc.; former owner Rita's Tennis Affair, Newport Beach; former v.p. Cort Fox Ford Leasing Inc., Hollywood; representative Royal Norwegian Embassy; clubs: Jonathan (L.A.), Balboa Bay (Newport Beach), Newport Beach Country, Harbor Yacht (Newport Beach), Center (Costa Mesa), Kona Kai Yacht (San Diego), Royal Danish Yacht (Denmark); rec: tennis, sailing. Res: 1026 Santiago Dr Newport Beach 92660

SPRINKEL, WARREN REED, retired engineering contractor, asphalt paving executive; b. June 30, 1922, Los Angeles; s. Walter and Florence Louise (Werdin) S.; m. Rita L., Aug. 12, 1978; 3 children by previous marriage: Steve, Annette and Susan; edn: BS indsl. mgmt., USC 1946. Career: var. pos. family owned asphalt constrn. cos.- L.A. Paving Co. (founded by grandfather E.R. Werdin, 1912), Vernon Paving Co. (founded by father 1936); gen. engring. contr., pres. and chmn. bd. Fontana Paving, Inc. (opr. three rock and asphalt plants, mfr. asphalt paving mats., construct highways, airports, indsl. and residential subdivs.) 1956-88, sold co. to Boral Industries (Australian co.) 1988; mem., chmn. Contractors' State License Bd. (12 years); honors: Blue Key, Skull and Dagger, Kappa Alpha frat. (pres.), Kt. Sovereign Order of the Oak 1990, named Contractor of Year 1974; mem: Am. Road and Transp. Builders Assn./Contractors Div. (sr. v. chmn. 1987-88, ARTBA Award 1989), Fontana C.of C. (past pres.), (current) Assoc. Gen. Contrs. of Calif., Rotary Club (past pres.); mil: command pilot B-24, 15th AF in Italy, WWII, decorated D.F.C., major USAF Korean War, flew B-26 and in chg. Base Ops. and Flying Safety, 60 combat missions in both wars; Republican; cty. campaign chmn. for Gov. Reagan 1965 and 1969, city chmn. Reagan for Pres. 1980; del. Nat. Repub. Conv. (1972, 76), cpgn. chmn. San Bernardino Co. for Pete Wilson for US Senate 1984; Prot. (deacon); rec: tennis, sailing: yacht "Viking Princess" (flagship for Challenger Races for the America's Cup Races, San Diego Apr.-May 1992). Res: 1026 Santiago Dr Newport Beach 92660

SQUARCY, CHARLOTTE VAN HORNE, lawyer; b. June 8, 1947, Chgo., Ill.; d. Charles Marion and Ruth (Van Horne) Squarcy; edn: BA, Smith Coll. 1969; JD, Ind. Univ. 1977; admitted St. Bar Ind. 1977, U.S. Tax Ct. 1977, Mich. 1978, U.S. Supreme Ct. 1980, D.C. 1980, Conn. 1983, Calif. 1986. Career: law clk. to presiding judge Ind. Superior Ct., Hammond, 1976-77; dep. atty. gen. St. Ind. 1977-78; mem. legal staff Gen. Motors Corp., Detroit, Mich. 1978-81; assoc. counsel Olin Corp., Stamford, Conn. 1981-85; sr. assoc. Bishop Barry Howe & Reid, San Francisco 1985-87; sr. assoc. Carroll Burdick & McDonough, San Francisco 1987-91; ptnr. C. Van Horne Squarcy & Assocs. 1991–; bd. dirs. U.S.O., No. Calif.; bd. dirs. Smith Coll., San Francisco; mem: Am. Bar Assn. (v.chmn. products liability com. TIPS, co-chmn. corp. counsel subcom., products liability com.-litigation sec.), The Corporate Bar; Republican; Methodist; rec: golf, music. Res: 51 Sulgrave Ln Peacock Gap San Rafael 94901 Ofc: 100 Pine St 21st Flr San Francisco 94111

SQUIRES, DALE EDWARD, economist; b. Aug. 28, 1950, San Diego; s. Elwin Frank and Christine Minnie (Carter) S.; m. Virginia Shirin Sharifzadeh, Jan. 28, 1986; edn: Am. Univ. Beirut 1970-71; BS hons., UC Berkeley 1973; MS, 1974; PhD, Cornell Univ. 1984. Career: prof. Univ. Agri., Malaysia 1975-77; sr. econ. ofcr. Dept. Fisheries, Sabah, Malaysia 1977-78; industry economist Nat. Marine Fisheries Service, Gloucester, Mass. 1982-84, San Diego 1984–; adj. prof. UCSD 1989–; PhD advisor Centro de Investigacion Sci. Y De Edn. Superior, Esenada, Mex. 1987–; mem. Limited Entry Com., Portland, Oreg. 1987–; Limited Access Alternatives 1984-86; awards: Cornell Univ. Fgn. Language fellowship 1978, Sea Grant scholar 1980; mem: San Diego Oceans

Found., Am. Econ. Assn., Am. Agri. Econ. Assn. Asian Fisheries Soc., Agri. Econ. Assn. SE Asia; articles pub. in profl. jours., 1987–; rec: house renovation, travel, athletics. Ofc: National Marine Fisheries Service POB 271 La Jolla 92038

STACEY, KENNETH ERMES, contractor; b. Oct. 28, 1946, Los Angeles; s. George T. and Erminia R. (Rota) S.; m. Marie Estes, 1989; children: Christine b. 1967; edn: BS, Cal. Poly. Pomona 1969; UCLA 1970. Career: tchr. Moreno Valley High Sch. 1970-72; owner The Stacey Co., cabinet and gen. contractor 1972–; ptnr. D.K. Development 1981–, Miken Co. 1985–, Cost Enterprises 1987–, Stockdale Greens Associates 1988-94; mem: City of Riverside Cultural Heritage Bd. 1981-89 (chmn. 1984-86), The Villages of Palm Springs 1993–, Arabian Horse Assn. of So. Calif. (bd. dirs. 1982-89, pres. 1988), Mission Inn Found. 1984-86, Inland Empire Nat. Bank Advisory Bd. 1987-92, Ronald McDonald House (bldg. com. 1991-94), CCFCHOA (pres. 1991–), Nat. Trust for Historic Preservation, Old Riverside Found. (bd. dir. 1989–), Riverside Ballet Theater (bd.); rec: skiing, racquetball, horse shows. Ofc: The Stacey Co. 2675 3rd St Ste K Riverside 92507-3368

STAHLEY, JOSEPH ROBERT, college professor; b. Aug. 21, 1937, Erie, Pa.; s. Joseph John and Mary Ruth (Unbehaun) S.; m. Ginger Russell-Stahley, Nov. 23, 1948; 1 son Joseph Christopher b. 1970; edn: BS, SUNY, Fredonia, NY 1960; MA, Penn. State Univ. 1965; PhD, UCLA 1976. Career: announcer, TV fir., WICU Radio-TV, Erie, Pa. 1959-62; prof. Calif. Polytechnic St. Univ., Pomona, Calif. 1966-68; exec. dir. Century City Theatre, L.A. 1968-70; instr. English Brighton Sch., Brighton, NY 1970; announcer/TV dir, WHEC Radio/TV, Rochester, NY 1970-72; account exec. KBSC-TV, Los Angeles 1972; prof. and chair, R-TV-Film, L.A. City Coll. 1972–; chair, local Emmys, Nat. Acad. TV Arts & Scis., L.A. 1972-76; cons.: Cartridge Films, Burbank 1971-72, Pacific Media Group, Santa Monica 1984-85; honors: listed Who's Who in Colleges 1960, Who's Who in Am. Edn. 1960; Pendleton Scholar, UCLA 1970; mem: Pioneer Broadcasters/Pacific Pioneer Broadcasters 1972–, Am. Fedn. of TV/Radio Artists 1960–, Internat. Arabian Horse Assn. 1991–; author: (book) History of Erie Playhouse, 1965, (plays) Golden Apples, 1968, One-Eye, 1968; Democrat; Roman Catholic; rec: endurance rider, show horses, actor, director. Res: 11301 Dulcet Ave Northridge 91326-2136 Ofc: 855 N Vermont Ave Los Angeles 90029

STANCILL, JAMES MCNEILL, professor of finance; b. July 30, 1932, Orange, N.J.; s. James McNeill and Anne (Sauter) S.; m. Catherine Jackson, Sept. 25, 1954; children: Martha A., Mary C., Christine; edn: BA, George Washington Univ. 1954; MBA, 1959; PhD, Univ. Pa. 1965. Career: buyer Melpar Inc., Falls Church, Va. 1954-59; adminstrv. ofcr. Univ. Pa., Phila. 1959-64; instr. fin. Wharton, Univ. Pa. 1960-64; asst. prof. fin., assoc. prof. fin., prof. fin. USC, Los Angeles 1964–; prin. Stancill & Assoc., Pasadena 1965–; chmn. Southwest Products Co., Irwindale, Calif.; mem: 20th Century Round Table. Ofc: Univ. Southern California Los Angeles 90089-1421

STANEART, JEFFREY ANSIL, civil engineer/municipal utilities administrator; b. June 12, 1957, Portland, Oreg.; s. Ansil Raymond and Allene Lois (Harrell) S.; m. Jeanne Marie Marston, Aug. 15, 1981 (div. 1987; edn: BSCE, Oreg. St. Univ., 1980. Career: asst., assoc. civil engr. So. Calif. Water Co., Los Angeles 1981-84, water system engr. 1984-85; assoc. civil engr. City of Newport Beach, 1985-87, civil engr. 1987-88, dep. utilities dir. 1988-92; utilities dir. Irvine Ranch Water Dist., Irvine 1992-95, asst. dir. field operations Irvine Ranch Water Dist. 1995–; mem: Orange Co. Water Assn., So. Calif. Water Utility Assn., Am. Water Works Assn., Water Pollution Control Fedn., Am. Pub. Works Assn., Nat. Water Well Assn., Am. Soc. of Civil Engrs., Am. Congress of Surveying and Mapping, Urban & Reg. Information Systems Assn., Fedn. of Outdoor Volleyball Assns., Calif. Beach Volleyball Assn. Ofc: Irvine Ranch Water District, Field Operations Dept, 3512 Michelson Dr Irvine 92716

STANFORD, ROY STANLEY, physician and surgeon; b. Dec. 27, 1925, Stephenville (Huckabay), Tx.; s. Melvin Beverly and Gladys Lillian (Lowe) S.; m. Doris Jean Deaver, Nov. 10, 1945 (div. 1977); children: Robert b. 1952, Donald b. 1954, Catherine b. 1956, Lorraine b. 1963; m. 2d. Patricia Mae Moseley, Nov. 26, 1981; edn: AB, Stanford Univ. 1946; MD, Stanford Sch. of Medicine 1950; lic. physician St. of Calif.; diplomate Am. Bd. of Surgery 1959. Career: internship Stanford Univ. Hosps., San Francisco 1949-50; residencies: gen. surgery Stanford Univ. Hosps., San Francisco 1950-51; med. ofcr. U.S. Navy, Far East Duty 1951-54; gen. surgery Stanford Univ. Hosps. 1954-58, Univ. of Calif. Hosp., S.F. 1956; solo pvt. practice, gen. surgery, Sacramento 1958–; active sr. staff mem: Sutter Gen. Hosp., Mercy Gen. Hosp. and Sutter Mem. Hosp. 1958–; assoc. clin. prof. of surgery UC Davis 1967–; mem: Am. Coll. of Surgeons (fellow 1960–), AMA 1958–, CMA 1958–, Sacto.-El Dorado Med. Soc. 1958– (dir. 1963-72, treas. 1967, 68, 69), Sacto. Surgical Soc. 1958– (pres. 1970-72), Pan-Pacific Surgical Assn.; past dir. Sacto Lions Club, Metropolitan YMCA, Am. Cancer Soc., Stanford Home for Children, others; mil: lt. comdr. U.S. Navy 1943-46, 51-54; Republican; Protestant: Ch. of Christ; rec: real estate, economics. Res: 943 Commons Drive Sacramento 95825-6650 Ofc: 2600 Capitol Ave Ste 411 Sacramento 95816

STANGL, PETER, medical library director; b. Dec. 19, 1936, Budapest, Hungary, nat. 1962; s. Kornel and Anna (Gero) S.; m. Juthica Behura, May 9, 1963; children: Indrani S. b. 1969, P. Anondo b. 1970; edn: BA, Yale Coll. 1962; MS, Sorbonne, Paris 1963; MS, So. Conn. State Univ. 1967. Career: asst. dir. Yale Med. Library, New Haven, Conn. 1967-71; dir. Lane Library, Stanford Univ. Med. Center, Calif. 1971–; mem: Medical Library Assn., ASIS, AAH-SLD; numerous journal articles. Ofc: Lane Library Stanford Univ. Stanford 94305-5323

STANKEVICH, MARK ANTHONY, lawyer; b. Dec. 20, 1953, Trenton, N.J.; s. Anthony and Georgiana (Hajek) S.; edn: BA, Lafayette Coll.1975; JD, UC Berkeley Boalt Hall 1980. Career: atty. Kaplan Livingston et al, Beverly Hills 1980-81; Garey Mason & Sloane, Santa Monica 1981-82; Haldeman Peckerman & Stankevich, Beverly Hills 1983-90; of counsel, Greenberg Glusker Fields Claman & Machtinger, Los Angeles 1990–. Ofc: 1900 Ave of Stars Ste 2000 Los Angeles 90067

STANNARD, RALPH ELY, scientist/engineer/optoelectronics executive; b. Chicago, Ill.; s. Ely Martin and Ina Maude (Perego) S.; edn: BA, San Jose State Univ.; pres. R. Stannard & Assocs., Irvine 1978-86; founder/pres. ODASER Technologies, Newport Beach 1986–; mem: Soc. of Automotive Engrs., IEEE, Optical Soc. Am., Optical Soc. So. Calif., Navy League (dir. Bel Air chpt. 1988); civic: Beverly Hills Pops (bd. 1987–), Opera Pacific, Irvine (founder 1985–), Wagner Soc., Woodland Hills 1987; jour. article "Duane, Prince of Faultland", 1985; aviation cadet Navy Air Corps; Episcopalian; rec: audiophile, opera buff. Ofc: ODASER Technologies PO Box 7458 Newport Beach 92658

STAPLES, ROBERT EUGENE, university professor; b. June 28, 1942, Roanoke, Va.; s. John Ambrose and Anna Theresa (Anthony) S.; edn: AA, L.A. Valley Coll., 1960; AB, Calif. State Univ., Northridge, 1964; MA, San Jose State Univ., 1965; PhD, Univ. of Minn., 1970. Career: asst. prof., Bethune-Cookman Coll., Daytona Beach, Fla. 1967-68; asst. prof., Calif. State Univ., Hayward 1968-69; asst. prof., Fisk Univ., Nashville, Tenn. 1969-70; lectr., UC Irvine 1970-71; assoc. prof., Howard Univ., Wash., DC 1971-73; prof., UC S.F. 1973–;awards: Disting. Achievement Award, Howard Univ. 1979; Simon Bolivar Lectr., Universidad Del Zulia, Venezuela 1979; Disting. Achievement Award, Nat. Council on Family Relations, Mpls., Minn. 1982; Marie Peters Award, Nat. Council on Family Relations, Mpls. 1986; author: World of Black Singles, 1981; Black Family Essays & Studies, 1991; ed., Urban Plantation, 1987; co-author, Black Families at Crossroads, 1993; Independent; rec: tennis reading, travel. Ofc: Univ. of Calif., Box 0612, San Francisco 94143-0612

STAUBUS, GEORGE JOSEPH, educator; b. April 26, 1926, Brunswick, Mo.; s. George W. and Florence (Pittman) S.; m. Sarah Mayer, April 11, 1949; children: Linda b. 1950, Martin b. 1952, Paul b. 1954, Janette b. 1962; edn: BS, Univ. Mo. 1947; MBA, Univ. Chgo. 1949; PhD, 1954; C.P.A. Ill. (1950). Career: instr. Univ. Buffalo, N.Y. 1947-49; instr. Univ. Chgo., Ill. 1949-52; asst. prof., assoc. prof., prof. UC Berkeley 1952–; dir. Research Fin. Acctg. Standards Bd., Stamford, Conn. 1976-78; vis. prof. London Bus. Sch., England 1966-67; awards: Univ. Canterbury N.Z. Erskine fellow 1972, Calif. Soc. CPA Disting. Prof. 1981, Am. Acctg. Assn. Disting. Internat. Lectr. 1982; mem: Am. Acctg. Assn., Am. Inst. C.P.A., Fin. Execs. Inst.; author: Theory of Acctg. to Investors, 1961, Activity Costing & Input-Output Analysis, 1971, Objectives & Concepts Fin. Statements, 1972, Making Acctg. Decisions, 1977, Economic Influences on the Development of Accounting in Firms, 1995, num. articles pub. in profl. jours.; mil: USN 1944-46. Ofc: Univ. California Walter A. Haas School of Business Berkeley 94720

STAUFFER, THOMAS MICHAEL, university president and professor; b. Dec. 4, 1941, Harrisburg, Pa.; s. John Nisley and Louise (Lee) S.; m. Marion Walker, May 13, 1966 (div. 1989); children: Amity b. 1972, Courtney b. 1976, Winston b. 1985; stepchild: Elizabeth b. 1984; m. 2d. Deborah Whisnand, May 16, 1993; edn: BA (cum laude), Wittenberg Univ., Springfield, Ohio 1963; MA, Grad. Sch. of Internat. Studies, Univ. of Denver, Denver, Colo. 1964-66, 67-68, PhD, 1973. Career: asst. dean Keene State Coll., Keene, N.H. 1971-72; prog. dir., v.p. American Council on Education, Wash. DC 1972-82; pres. Univ. of Houston-Clear Lake, Houston, Tx. 1982-91; special asst. to the adminstr., NASA, WDC, 1992; pres. Golden Gate Univ., San Francisco 1992–; pres. St. John Hosp., Houston, Tx. 1982-91; vice chair Texas Sci. and Technology Council, Austin, Tx. 1984-86; chair, Challenger Ctr. for Space Sci. Edn., Wash. DC 1986–; chair Ctr. for Advanced Space Studies, Houston, Tx. 1988-93; awards: Disting. Service awards, Am. Council on Edn. 1989, Greater Houston Hosp. Council 1991 and Texas Senate award 1991; Disting. Alumnus, Univ. of Denver 1990; Space Achievement award, Challenger Ctr., Wash., DC 1991; mem: Council on Foreign Relations, S.F. 1992–, Bay Area Internat. Forum 1992–, Comm. Bd. St. Mary's Hosp., S.F. 1992–,chair Mayor's Blue Ribbon Com. on Econ. Devel., S.F. 1995, S.F. C. of C. (bd. 1995–), S.F. YMCA (bd. 1994–). San Francisco World Trade Assn. (co-chair) 1992–, Rotary; clubs: University Club, S.F. 1992–, World Trade Club, S.F. 1992–; author: num. books and articles. Res: 1806 Green St San Francisco 94123 Ofc: Golden Gate University 536 Mission St San Francisco 94105

STECHMAN, JOHN VANCE, professor of rangeland management; b. Aug. 1, 1934, Peoria, Ill.; s. John Henry and Helen Jean (Vance) S.; m. Dorothy Jean McKowan, Aug. 18, 1956; children: John Carl b. 1960, Jennifer Jean b. 1963; edn: grad. Herbert Hoover H.S., Glendale, Calif. 1952; BS, UC Davis 1957, MS in rangeland mgmt. 1960; cert. consultant range mgmt. 1989, cert. cons. soil erosion control 1993. Career: forest aide US Forest Svc., El Dorado Nat. Forest 1956; range tech. US Agricultural Res. Svc., Davis 1956-57, 59-60; food tech. US Army, QMC Chicago, Ill. 1957-59; prof. Calif. Polytechnic St. Univ., San Luis Obispo, 1960-92; rancher La Cuesta Ranch, San Luis Obispo, 1971-91; cons. La Cuesta Consulting, 1964–; honors: Alpha Zeta hon. agric. frat. 1955, suggestion awards US Army 1958, Hon. chpt. farmer Future Farmers of Am. S.L.O. 1978, Range mgr. of yr. 1991 Calif. sect. Soc. for Range Mgmt.; mem: Soc. for Range Mgmt. (Calif. sect. dir. 1988-90, historian 1990–), S.L.O. Brush Range Improve. Assn. 1972–, Range Sci. Edn. Council 1965-91, Watershed Council of Calif. 1988–, League to Save Lake Tahoe 1988–; civic: Pelican Point Homeowners Assn. Avila Bch. (water bd. 1991–) Montana de Oro State Park Advy. Com. Morro Bay (chmn. 1965-74); author: Common Western Range Plants, 1986, Illustrated History Cal Poly Agriculture, 1985, jour. articles and manuals in field; mil: sp4c USA Quartermaster Corps 1957-59; Republican; Lutheran; rec: reading, art. Res: PO Box 2211 Avila Beach 93424

STEEL, DAWN, motion picture studio executive; b. Aug. 19, New York, NY; d. Nat and Lillian (Tarlow) Steel; m. Charles Roven, May 30, 1988; children: Rebecca b. 1987; edn: mktg. Boston Univ. 1964-65, N.Y.U. 1966-67. Career: sportswriter Major League Baseball Digest and NFL/N.Y.C., 1968-69; editor Penthouse, N.Y.C. 1969-75; pres. Oh Dawn!, N.Y.C. 1975-78; mdsg. cons. Playboy, N.Y.C. 1978-79; v.p. mdsg. Paramount, N.Y.C. 1979-80, v.p. prodn. Paramount, L.A. 1980-83, sr. v.p. prodn. 1983-85, pres. of prodn. 1985-87; pres. Columbia Pictures, 1987-90; formed Steel Pictures, 1990–; (with Charles Roven and Bob Cavallo) formed Atlas Entertainment and signed exclusive movie-production agreement with Turner Pictures 1994; bd. dirs.: Claremont Coll., Home Education Network; dean's advy. bd. UCLA Sch. of Theater, Film and Television 1993–; awards: Crystal award Women in Film, L.A. 1989; mem. Acad. of Motion Picture Arts & Scis., Am. Film Inst. (bd. 1988-90), NOW Legal Def. Fund (NYC); Democrat; Jewish; rec: skiing, tennis, gardening. Ofc: Atlas Entertainment 9169 Sunset Blvd Los Angeles 90069

STEELE, JAN KAY, acupuncturist, doctor of Oriental medicine; b. July 27, 1950, New York, NY; d. Bob and Edy (Kornblum) Steele; edn: BA, CSU Sonoma 1973; grad. acupuncture tng. prog., Am. Coll. of Traditional Chinese Medicine 1985; O.M.D., SAMRA Univ. of Oriental Medicine 1988; Calif. State Teaching Creds. K-9, 7-12 gen. classroom & music edn., CSU Sonoma 1974; lic. realtor, Calif. 1977; lic. private pilot, FAA 1980; cert. acupuncturist State of Calif. 1985; diplomate in acupuncture, Nat. Com. for Certification of Acupuncturists 1985, diplomate of Chinese herbology, NCCA 1994. Career: acupuncture, private practice 1984–; tchr. ESL, Taipei, Taiwan 1985-86; examiner Emperor's Coll. of Traditional Oriental Medicine 1986, tchr., clinic 1986-87; examiner, Calif. Dept. of Consumer Affairs, Med. Bd. of Calif. Acupuncture Com. 1991; guest lectr. Royal Univ. of Am., Sch. of Oriental Medicine 1992; examiner Nat. Comm. for the Certification of Acupuncturists (NCCA) 1993; mem: Calif. Acupuncture Assn. 1990- (chmn. Metro L.A. chpt. 1990, v.p. of legislative affairs 1992), AAAOM 1992–; volunteer, acupuncture clinics: Women's Aids Project 1986, West Hollywood HIV Clinic 1991-93; prog. mgr. acupuncture svcs. Jeffrey Goodman Special Care Clinie 1993-95; volunteer acupuncturist LIGA Internat., Sinaloa, Mexico 1990-91; instr. TCM self-care for HIV+ patients, AIDS Project Los Angeles 1993, 94,95; rec: private pilot, nature. Ofc: 5225 Wilshire Blvd Ste 618 Los Angeles 90036

STEFANO, VINCENT, JR., lawyer; b. Dec. 21, 1938, Burbank; s. Vincent and Mary (Sereno) S.; m. Mary Lou Moore, Nov. 14, 1975; children: Vincent b. 1964, Robert J. b. 1960, Daniel b. 1968, Ann Marie b. 1978, Paige M. b. 1981; edn: BS, USC, 1961; JD, Loyola Univ. 1964; admitted St. Bar Calif. (1965). Career: dep. city atty. City of Los Angeles 1965-67; City of Burbank 1967-69; dep. dist. atty. Co. of Los Angeles 1969-71; atty. sole practice, Van Nuys, Encino, Burbank 1971–; elected councilman City of Burbank 1973-77, mayor 1974-75, pres. Burbank Redevel. Agy. 1974-75; mem. Pub. Service Dept. Com. 1977-79, Police Commn. Burbank (pres. 1980, 85), St. Joseph Med. Center Advy. Bd. (v.p. 1974); mem: Am. Bar Assn., Am. Arbitration Assn., L.A. Co. Bar Assn., Burbank Bar Assn.; Democrat; Cath. Ofc: 1612 W Olive Ave Ste 204 Burbank 91506 Tel: 818-841-0140

STEFFEY, EUGENE PAUL, educator, veterinarian; b. Oct. 27, 1942, Reading, Pa.; s. Paul E. and Mary (Balthaser) S.; children: Michele A. b. 1972, Bret E. b. 1975, Michael R. b. 1978, Brian T. b. 1985; edn: Muhlenberg Coll. 1960-63; VMD, Univ. Pa., Phila. 1967; PhD, UC Davis, 1973. Career: NIH spl. fellowship 1972-73; anesthesia res. fellow UCSF Med. Center 1973; asst. prof. UC Davis 1974-77, assoc. prof. 1977-80, prof. 1980–, chmn. dept. vet. surgery 1980-93; bd. scientific reviewers Am. Jour. Vet. Res. 1984-87; awards: UC Davis Outstanding Intern 1968; mem: num. profl. mems. incl. AVMA, Am. Coll. Vet. Anesthesiologists, Am. Physiolgy Soc., Am. Soc. Pharm. Exptl. Therapeutics, Am. Soc. Anesthesiologists, Calif. Soc. Anesthesiologists; author

85+ articles in profl. jours., 12 textbook chpts.; rec: fishing, outdoor photog., sports. Ofc: Univ. California Dept. of Surgical & Radiological Science, School of Veterinary Medicine Davis 95616

STEGEMEIER, RICHARD JOSEPH, oil company executive; b. Apr. 1, 1928, Alton, Ill.; s. George Henry and Rose Ann (Smola) S.; m. Marjorie Ann Spess, Feb. 9, 1952; children: Richard Michael, David Scott, Laura Ann, Martha Louise; edn: BS in petroleum engring., Univ. Mo., Rolla 1950; cert. petroleum engr. (hon.) 1981; MS in pet. engring., Texas A&M, 1951; Hon. Dr. Engring., Univ. of Missouri - Rolla, 1990; reg. profl. engr. Calif. Career: various nat. and internat. mgmt. pos. with Unocal Corp. (formerly Union Oil Co.), Los Angeles 1951–, pres. sci. and tech. div. 1979-80, senior v.p. corporate devel. 1980-85, pres. and c.o.o. 1985–, c.e.o. 1988–, chmn. bd. 1989–; patentee in field; dir: First Interstate Bancorp, Northrop Corp., Outboard Marine Corp.; apptd. bd. trustees Com. for Economic Devel., bd. overseers Executive Council on Fgn. Diplomats; mem: advy. bds: Northwestern Univ. Kellogg Grad. Sch. of Mgmt., CSU Fullerton, UCLA Anderson Grad. Sch. of Mgmt. (bd. vis.), Harvey Mudd Coll. (trustee), Univ. of Mo. -Rolla (bd. vis.), Loyola Marymount Univ. (trustee), USC (trustee, Sch. of Engring. Bd. of Councilors, Sch. of Business Bd. Advisors, c.e.o.), CSU Long Beach (advy. council); honors: Orange County Engring. Council Outstanding Engr. Merit Award (1980), Inst. for Advancement Engring. Outstanding Engr. Merit Award (1981), Distinguished Achiev. Medal, Texas A & M Univ. (1987), Am. Jewish Com. Human Relations Award (1990), Hugh O'Brian Youth Found. Albert Schweitzer Leadership Award (1990); mem: Nat. Petroleum Council, Am. Petroleum Inst. (dir.), Soc. Petroleum Engrs. (bd., lectr. 1978), Nat. Acad. of Engring., Nat. Assn. of Mfrs. (dir.), Nat. Council of Bus. Advisors (dir.), Am. Inst. Chem. Engrs., 25 Yr. Club Petroleum Industry (past pres.), Town Hall of Calif. (bd. govs.), Bus. Roundtable, Calif. Bus. Roundtable (bd. govs.), Calif. Council on Sci. and Technology (bd. govs.), Calif. C.of C. (dir., chmn.), Conference Board (bd. govs.), Council on Fgn. Relations (bd. govs.), L.A. World Affairs Council (chmn.), World Affairs Council Orange Co. (pres. 1980-82, chmn. 82-84), YMCA L.A. (dir.), Boy Scouts Am. L.A. (chmn. 1991), John Tracy Clinic (dir.), French Found. for Alzheimer Research (dir.), United Way of Gr. L.A. (gen. campaign chmn. 1990-91), Music Center of L.A. Co. (bd. govs.), L.A. Philharmonic Assn. (dir.), Orange County Performing Arts Ctr. (dir.), Huntington Library (bd. overseers), Hugh O'Brian Youth Found. (bd. trustees), Los Angeles Archdiocese Found. (bd. trustees); club: California; Republican; R.Cath. Ofc: Unocal Corp. Unocal Center PO Box 7600 Los Angeles 90051

STEIGERWALD, DOUGLAS GARDINER, economist; b. June 19, 1959, Torrance; s. Joseph Frank and Eileen (Doerr) S.; edn: BA econ., Pomona Coll. 1981; MA statistics, UC Berkeley 1986; PhD econ. 1989. Career: assoc. prof. UC Santa Barbara 1988–; mem: Am. Econ. Assn., Econometric Soc.; articles and newspaper articles pub. 1989. Ofc: Univ. of California Dept. of Economics Santa Barbara 93106

STEIN, KARL NORMAN, plastic surgeon; b. July 1, 1940, Phila.; s. Jack and Lucille (Somoroff) S.; m. Sandra Diane Segal, Aug. 20, 1965; children: Laura b. 1969, Leigh b. 1972; edn: BA chem., Temple Univ., MD, Temple Univ. Sch. of Med.; diplomate Am. Bd. Plastic Surgery. Career: intern Graduate Hosp. Univ. Pa., 1966-67; surgical resident Abington Mem. Hosp., 1967-68; served to capt. USAF 1967-69, gen. surgeon Tinker AFB, Okla. 1968-70; surgical fellow and resident SUNY Up-State Med. Ctr., Syracuse 1970-71; plastic surg. resident Albert Einstein Coll. of Med. affil. hosp., Bronx, NY 1971-74, instr. 1974; pvt. practice physician, spec. reconstrv. and cosmetic surgery, burn therapy, hand surgery, nerve surgery of forearm and arm; employee safety cons. L.A. Dept. Water and Power (prod. film re safety for DWP 1988); past mem. Calif. St. Senate Advy. Commn. on Health & Accident Ins.; founder. non-profit Found. for Plastic and Reconstrv. Surgery (providing free surgical svs. to needy L.A. youngsters incl. removal of gang and drug related tatoos), found. prod. award winning, Emmy nominated videotape re consequences of youthful tattooing; mem: Am. Coll. Surgeons (fellow), Am. Soc. Plastic Surgeons, Am. Burn Assn., Barsky Soc., Am. Soc. Aesthetic Plastic Surgery, Calif. Soc. Plastic Surgeons, AMA, CMA, L.A. Co. Med. Assn., Am. Assn. for Hand Surgery; Jewish; rec: stamps, politics. Ofc: 4910 Van Nuys Blvd Ste 302 Sherman Oaks 91403

STEINBERG, IRWIN I., management consultant; b. Oct. 15, 1926, Brooklyn, N.Y.; s. Samuel and Sophie (Emerman) S.; m. Mollie Deutsch, March 11, 1951; children: Laurence D. b. 1952, Andrew B. b. 1958; edn: BS, U.S. Mil. Acad. West Point 1950; MBA, N.Y. Univ. 1961. Career: v.p. mgmt. Loral Corp., N.Y.C. 1960-70; pres., chmn. Laurand Corp. 1972-77; pres., CEO Gruma Corp., Commerce 1979-82; sr.v.p., c.o.o.., NTS, Calabasas 1983-86; pres. The Steinberg Co., Encino 1986–; adj. prof. bus. mgmt. Woodbury Univ., Burbank 1988-94; Univ. Redlands 1988–; awards: Pub. Rels. Soc. Golden Key 1966, Leather Industry Assn. Man of Year 1973; mem: ADPA, ITEA, TIA, Assn. Grads. USMA, West Point Soc. of L.A.; mil: 1st lt. USA 1950-53; Republican; Jewish; rec: tennis, golf, racquetball. Ofc: The Steinberg Co. 16000 Ventura Blvd 500 Encino 91436

STEINHAUSER, PATRICK TERRY, security executive; March 21, 1951, Springfield, Ill.; s. John Edward and Patricia S.; m. Candace Jean Haave, Oct. 23, 1976; children: Jonathan b. 1981, Trenton b. 1984; edn: AA, Long Beach

Comm. Coll. Career: pres. So. Calif. Taekwon Do. Acad., Long Beach 1975–; pres. Steinhauser Investigations 1982–; hosp. cons. 1978-89; dir. security Long Beach Community Hosp. 1978-88, facilities mgr. 1988-89, sr. admin. dir- gen. services 1989-92, v.p. gen. services 1992–;instr. So. Calif. Taekwon Do Acad. 1975–; awards: Long Beach YMCA Silver Triange, and Man of Year (1983, 86), 5th degree Black Belt Taekwon Do, Master Instructor 1993; mem.: Internat. Assn. Hosp. Security, World Taekwon Do Fedn., Calif. State Taekwon Do Assn. (v.p.); civic: YMCA (bd. dir. 1994), Elks (Long Beach), Seal Beach Rotary, US Olympic Team coach, U.S. Nat. Taekwon Do Union referee, Little League coach & mgr.; rec: martial arts, sports. Address: Long Beach 90815

STEPHENS, WILLIAM LEONARD, university administrator; b. Apr. 19, 1929, Covington, Ky.; s. Leonard Edwin and Mary Blanche (Wright) S.; m. Claire Neall Matsinger, Apr. 12, 1957; edn: AA, New Mexico Military Inst., 1949; BA in biology (hons.), CSU Sacramento, 1957; PhD microbiology, UC Davis, 1963. Career: res. asst. UC Davis, 1957-63; asst. prof. Chico State Coll., 1963-67, assoc. prof. 1967-70, chair dept. biol. scis. 1968-74; prof. CSU Chico, 1970–, dean Coll. of Natural Scis., 1977-91, provost and v.p. acad. affairs, 1991–; honors: CSAA/EOP Award 1985-86, Phi Kappa Phi 1988; mem. Am. Soc. for Microbiol. 1957–, Sigma Xi 1962–, Am. Assn. Univ. Adminstrs.; civic: Science Fair judge, Chico 1963-88, Corning 1973, 74, host numerous elem. and high sch. classes to introduce use of microscope and world of microorganisms, guest lectr. comm. orgs., biol. scis. rep. to Willows H.S. Career Day 1974, 75, 76, mem.: Stansbury Home Preserv. Assn. 1981–, Century Club 1975-89, 91, Univ. Club 1975-89, 91, comm. blood donor 1963–; publs: articles in field (4); mil: HM2 US Navy 1950-54. Res: 1661 Oak Vista Chico 95926 Ofc: Calif. State Univ., Chico 95929

STERN, WOLF HARRY, lawyer, financial executive; b. May 28, 1923, Gelsenkirchen, Germany; nat. 1942; s. Morris and Johanna (Loeb) S.; Edn: BA, UCLA, 1947; LLB, JD, USC, 1950; m. 2d., Alban Ann Weiss, June 13, 1982; children: Lawrence Alan b. 1952, Douglas Wayne b. 1953, William Rodney b. 1955, Wendy Kleeb b. 1956. Career: senior ptnr. law firm Stern, Goldstock, Newport Beach, 1950-88; Law Offices of Wolf H. Stern, 1988–; pres. Bellflower Investment Co., 1964–; dir: Bellflower Natl. Bank 1964-65 (v.chmn. advy. bd. 1962-64), Calif. Pacific Bank 1969-77, Garden State Bank 1973-76, v. chmn. Cerritos Valley Bank 1974-80, chmn. Bellflower Savs. & Loan (now Equitable Svgs. & Loan) 1977-85; honors: Young Man of Year, City of Bellflower (1954); mem: Am. Bar Assn., Calif. State Bar Assn., Orange County Bar Assn., Am. Trial Lawyers Assn., Newport Irvine Profl. Assn. (pres. 1985, 94), Newport C.of C., past mem. Compton Bar Assn. (treas. 1956), Bellflower Jaycees (pres. 1956), Bellflower Elks Lodge, Bellflower Coord. Council (pres. 1953), Bellflower-Lakewood Jewish Comm. Ctr. (pres. 1952), Orange Co. Protocol Found. (dir.); clubs: Performing Arts Frat. (v.p.), Lions Intl. Costa Mesa-Newport Harbor (dist. gov. 1965-66, past pres. Bellflower Club 1954, 58), mil: sgt. US Army Signal Corps, 3 Battle Stars, lt. M.I. USAR; Baha'i (chmn. Local Spiritual Assmbly of Newport Beach); rec: photog., travel. Res: 49 Southampton Ct Newport Beach 92660 Law Offices of Wolf H. Stern, 170 Newport Center Dr Ste 230 Newport Beach 92660

STERNBACH, ROBERT OWEN, neurologist; b. Sept. 9, 1952, Newark N.J.; s. Seymour Bernard and Rosalyn (Blasenstein) S.; m. Debra Beth Freedman, May 16, 1976; edn: AB, Boston Univ. 1973, MD, 1976. Career: chief, dept. of neurology, Kaiser Permanente, Walnut Creek, Calif. 1980–; chmn. ethics com. Kaiser Found. Hosp., Walnut Creek 1987–; mem: Am. Academy of Neurology 1980–. Res: 2825 Prince St Berkeley 94705

STERNITZKE, VINCENT LEO, psychologist; b. July 7, 1925, Boonville, Mo.; s. William Leo and Maurene A. (Knapp) S.; m. Mary Margaret Jones, July 8, 1947; children: David b. 1952, Carol b. 1953; edn: BS, Pittsburg St. Univ. 1948, MS, 1953; Ed.D, Univ. Kans., Lawrence 1957; lic. psychologist Med. Bd. of Calif. 1969. Career: newspaper printer-opr. Southwestern Pub. Co., Joplin, Mo. 1948-49; advtg. sales Corpus Christi Caller-Times, Tx. 1949; instr. graphic arts No. Okla. Coll., Tonkawa 1949-55; asst. reading clinic Univ. Kans., Lawrence 1955-57; asst. prof., assoc. prof. Sam Houston St. Univ., Huntsville 1957-66; test ofcr. CSU Chico 1966-68; sr. psychologist Fairview St. Hosp., Costa Mesa 1968-70, program dir. habilitation 1970-77; counseling psychologist VA Reg. Office, San Francisco 1977-79; staff psychologist Napa St. Hosp. 1979-88; pvt. practice, Vallejo 1988–; mem: Am. Psychol. Assn., Calif. Psychol. Assn., State Mil. Reserve (adj. 1988-92); 2 articles pub. in profl. jours., 1959, 70, booklet pub., 1964, ed. periodical, 1967-68; mil: comdr. USNR 1945; Republican; R.Cath.; rec: Citizens' radio, rubber stamp making. Res: 1424 Granada St Vallejo CA 94591-7633 Ofc: 1516 Napa St Vallejo CA 94590-4493

STETLER, CHARLES EDWARD, professor; b. Sept. 12, 1927, Pitts., Pa.; s. Charles Edward and Katherine (Seidel) S.; m. Ellen Donovan June 25, 1955 (div. Nov., 1981); m. Kristin Jill Brown July 17, 1984 (div. Apr., 1993); m. Mary Grace Aquino, Aug. 25, 1994; children: Peter b. 1959, Paul b. 1963, Casey b. 1966; edn: BA, Duquesne Univ., Pitts., Pa., 1950; MA, Duquesne Univ., 1961; PhD, Tulane Univ., New Orleans, La., 1967. Career: reporter, Pitts. Sun-Telegraph 1951-61; instr., Rollins Coll., Winter Park, Fla. 1961-62; asst. prof., Loyola Univ., New Orleans, La. 1962-67; prof., Calif. State Univ., Long Beach

1967–; exchange prof., Hull Univ., Hull, England, fall term 1984; prof. for Calif. State Univ., Long Beach Students in London, London, England, spring semester, 1991; author: (poetry) Roger, Rick, Karl & Shane Are Friends Of Mine, 1972; approx. 30 essays publ. in profl. journals; approx. 300 poems publ. in magazines and anthologies; book reviews; ed., anthology, New Geography of Poets, 1992. Mil: QM3, USN, 1945-45, 1950-52; Democrat; rec: bridge, golf, tennis. Res: 5912 Bixby Village Dr #62 Long Beach 90803. Ofc: Calif. State Univ. 1250 Bellflower Blvd. Long Beach 90840

STEVENS, WILBUR HUNT, certified public accountant; b. June 20, 1918, Spencer, Ind.; s. John Vosburgh, MD, and Isabelle Jane (Strawser) S.; m. Maxine Dodge, Sept. 28, 1941; children: Linda M. Piffero b. 1950, Deborah A. Augello b. 1952; edn: Milton (Wis.) Coll. 1935-37, BS, UC Berkeley, 1949, MBA, 1949; C.P.A. Calif. 1951. Career: staff acct. McLaren, Goode, West & Co., San Francisco 1949-52; mng. ptnr. Wilbur H. Stevens & Co., Salinas 1952-70; reg. ptnr. (Calif.) Fox & Co. CPAs, Salinas 1970-73; nat. dir. of banking practice Fox & Co., Denver, Colo. 1973-80; pres./chmn. Wilbur H. Stevens, CPA, PC, Salinas 1980–; chmn. Stevens, Sloan & Shah, CPA's, 1994–; chmn. bd./pres. Valley Nat. Bank, Salinas 1963-71; cons. State of Calif. for revision of state's acctg. system 1966; faculty mem. and advy. com. Nat. Banking Sch., Univ. of VA, Charlottesville, Va. 1979-87; adj. prof. acctg. Univ. Denver 1975-78; faculty mem. Assemblies for Bank Directors So. Methodist Univ., Dallas 1976-81; instr. bank auditing, Am. Inst. CPAs, NYC 1969-80, v.p. dir. 1971-75; honors: Frank G. Drum Fellow UCB 1949, Phi Beta Kappa 1949, Beta Gamma Sigma (v.p. 1949), Beta Alpha Psi, Paul Harris Fellow, Rotary Internat. 1977, disting. service Calif. Soc. CPAs 1988; mem: Calif. Soc. CPAs (pres. 1968), Accounting Research Assn. (pres. 1973), Nat. Assn. of State Boards of Accountancy. (pres. 1976), Salinas C.of C. (pres. 1960), Acad. Acctg. Historians, Am. Acctg. Assn., Am. Assn. Coll. Sch. of Bus. (accred. council 1975-78, 81-84), Burma Star Assn. (London), CBI Veterans Assn., Commonwealth Club of Calif., Masons (master 1992, Grand Lodge com. of taxation), Knight Templar, 32 Degree Scottish Rite, Nat. Sojourners (v.p. Monterey Bay Chpt. 1995), Salinas High Twelve Club (pres. 1995), Q.C.C.C. (London), Rotary (dist. gov. 1983, chmn. Internat. Fellowship Accts.), Salinas Valley Exec. Club (pres. 1958), Dir. Council of Indep. Banks (v.p. 1965-67); publs: articles on auditing, 1956-71, banking, 1976-79; Grand Jury Monterey Co. (chmn. audit com. 1989); mil: capt. AUS, Fin. Dept., 1942-53, Fin. Ofcr. 14 AF CBI 1945, Bronze star, China War medal, China Victory medal; Republican; Methodist; rec: travel, Am. hist., literature. Res/Ofc: 38 Santa Ana Dr Salinas 93901-4136

STEVENSON, IVAN KELLY, lawyer, consultant, travel agent, claims administrator; b. Oct. 4, 1949, Quonset Point Naval Air Sta., Wickford Co., R.I.; s. Ivan Julius and Mary Theresa (Schaefer) S.; edn: BA, UC Los Angeles 1971; JD, Southwestern Univ. Sch. of Law 1974; admitted bar Calif (1974), Third Party Adminstr., Dept. Ins. (1983). Career: asst. supr., tech. writer Occidental Life Ins. Co. 1969-72; law clerk, atty. assoc. Martin & Stamp, Long Beach 1972-74, 78-81; Judge Advocate Gen. Corps USN, 1974-79; mng. atty./ptnr. Martin & Stamp, Long Beach, Santa Ana 1981-83; atty. Law Offices of Ivan K. Stevenson, 1983–; ptnr. Benefits Counseling Svc. 1983–; ptnr./ Third Party Administrator, Tayson Ins. Administrators, 1983–; ptnr. Ski Pak, 1990; v.p. Woodson R.R. Devel. Co., 1989–; pres. Sunbolt Travel Inc. 1994–; judge pro tem Orange County Superior Ct.; guest lectr. re med. malpractice: L.A. Co. Med. Assn., Met. Hosp.; lectr. re govt. tort liability: City of Seal Beach, Am. Public Works Assn.; lectr. re client relations: Dispute Resolution Services; cons. on claims administn.; awards: Humanitarian Svc., USN (1975, 76), Outstanding Young Man Am. 1983, listed Who's Who in Calif. (1988, 89, 90, 91, 92, 93, 94); mem: Am. Bar Assn., L.A. Co. Bar Assn. (state bar del. 1989, v. chair atty./client rels. com. 1985-91), Orange Co. Bar Assn., Am. Arbitration Assn., Am. Soc. Law and Med., U.S. Naval Reserves, U.S. Naval Inst., Judge Advocate Assn., U.S. Navy Memorial Found.; civic: Townhall of Calif., Seahill Townhomes HOA, Torrance Windemere HOA, L.A. Co. Judicial Arbitration Panel, L.A. Co./ Orange Co. Fee Mediation Com., Orange County Forum; mil: lt.cdr. USNR 1971–, active duty lt. JAGC USN 1974-78; R.Cath.; rec: triathlete, racquetball, volleyball, marathoner, slalom water skier, golf. Ofc: 959 South Coast Dr Ste 490 Costa Mesa 92626 also: 3868 W Carson St Ste 300-6 Torrance 90503

STEWART, DAVID WAYNE, professor of marketing; b. Oct. 23, 1951, Baton Rouge, La.; s. Wesley A. Stewart, Jr. and Edith L. (Richhart) Moore; m. Lenora Francois, June 6, 1975; children: Sarah b. 1979, Rachel b. 1983; edn: BA, Northeast La. Univ., 1972; MA, PhD, Baylor Univ., 1973, 1974. Career: res. psychologist St. of Louisiana, Pineville 1974-76; res. mgr. Needham, Harper & Steers Advt., Chgo. 1976-78; assoc. prof. Jacksonville State Univ. 1978-80; assoc. prof. Owen Grad. Sch. of Mgmt. Vanderbilt Univ., Nashville, Tenn. 1980-86, assoc. dean 1984-86; prof. mktg. Univ. So. Calif., Los Angeles 1986–, chmn. dept. of mktg. 1995–, The Robert E. Brooker Prof. of Marketing, 1991–, The Ernest W. Hahn Prof. of Marketing, 1990-91; vis. scholar Gen. Motors, Detroit 1988-90; cons. FTC, Wash. D.C. 1986-88, Hewlett Packard, Palo Alto 1986–, Ford Motor Co., Louisville, Ky. 1986, Weyerhauser, Seattle 1986-89; Coca-Cola, Atlanta 1990; awards: Phi Kappa Phi, Alpha Iota Delta, Beta Gamma Sigma, innovation in tchg. Decision Scis. Inst. 1983, Outstanding Young Men of Am. 1985, N.Y. Acad. Sci. 1988, sr. res. fellow Am. Acad. of Advertising 1988; mem:

Soc. for Consumer Psychology (pres. 1985-86), Am. Mktg. Assn., Am. Psychol. Assn. (Fellow 1986, Council of Reps.), Am. Psychol. Soc. (Charter Fellow 1988), Assn. for Consumer Res., Inst. for Mgmt. Scis., Town Hall of Calif.; author 6 books: Secondary Research: Sources and Methods 1984, Effective TV Advertising 1986, Consumer Behavior and The Practice of Mktg. 1987, Nonverbal Communication in Advertising 1988, Focus Groups: Theory and Method 1990, Advertising and Consumer Psychology 1991; mem. editorial bds.: J. of Marketing Research, J. of Marketing, J. of Advertising, Current Issues and Research in Advertising, J. of Promotion Managmt, Management Issues; Republican; Am. Baptist. Res: 9340 La Alba Dr Whittier 90603

STEWART, LELAND PERRY, minister, coordinating council executive, writer; b. Mar. 4, 1928, Detroit, Mich.; s. Hoyt Clifford and Gladys (Woodward) S.; m. Elizabeth Elliot, June 13, 1953; children: Deanna b. 1954, Dana b. 1956, Lynn b. 1958; edn: BSE, Mech. Engring., Univ. of Mich., Ann Arbor, 1949; BSE, Math, Univ. of Mich., 1949; STB, Harvard Div. Sch., 1953; Secondary Life cred., Calif. State Univ., L.A. & Northridge, 1962. Career: founding minister, Unity-and-Diversity Fellowship Center, L.A. 1958–; sec. tchr., L.A. Unified Sch. Dist. 1960-72, 1993–; tchr., Santa Monica/Malibu Unified Sch. Dist. 1993; founder and central coord., Unity-and-Diversity World Council, L.A, 1965–; trumpet player, dance band & Harvard orch. 1945-53; instr., Univ. of Oriental Studies, L.A. 1975-78; ministry trainer, Unity-and-Diversity Fellowship Ctr., L.A. 1973–; tchr., World Univ., L.A. 1988-90; bd. mem. Interfaith Council for UN., L.A. 1988–; life bd. mem. Unity-and-Diversity World Council 1965–; mem: Unitarian Universalist Assn., Boston, Mass.; author: From Industrial Power to Lasting Peace, 1951; author/compiler, Central Scriptures, 1952 and World Scripture, 1953; ed./musician, Creative Music, 1950; ed., Marriage & Other Services, 1953; Democrat and Independent; Universalist; rec: trumpet playing, meditating, swimming, walking, being in nature. Center: 5521 Grosvenor Blvd Ste 22 Los Angeles 90066-6915

STEWART, LUCILLE MARIE, educator, administrator; b. Feb. 24, Pittsburgh, Pa.; d. William H. and Edna (Hoffman) S.; edn: EdB, Duquesne Univ.; EdM, Univ. Pittsburgh; postgrad. Teacher's Coll., Columbia Univ., Univ. Calif., Calif. St. Univ.; tchg. credentials: elem., sec., special edn., supr., adminstr. Career: tchr. Lincoln (Ill.) State Sch., 1953; group leader Retarded Children and Young Adults, Educational Alliance, N.Y.C., 1954-58; tchr. class for mentally retarded, class for emotionally disturbed, Ramapo Sch. Dist. #2, Spring Valley, N.Y. 1958-64; coord. presch. for disadvantaged Ramapo Sch. Dist. 1965-67; program dir. Pomona (N.Y.) Camp for Retarded, summers 1960-63; tchr. mentally retarded students Stockton Sch., San Diego, 1964-65; program specialist in special edn. Palm Springs Unified Sch. Dist., 1967-: Cathedral City Sch. 1967-78, principal elementary summer schs. 1971-72, prin. tchr. Summer Extended Sch. for Special Students, 1979–; mem. exec. com. Univ. Calif. Ext. Area Advy. Com.; Desert Community Mental Health Children's Com.; mem: NEA, Calif. Tchrs. Assn., Palm Springs Tchrs. Assn., Palm Springs Ednl. Leadership Assn., Calif. Assn. of Resource Specialists, Calif. Assn. Program Specialists, AAUW, Assn. for Supervision and Curriculum Devel., Am. Assn. Childhood Edn., Calif. Adminstrs. of Spl. Edn., Internat. Trainers of Communication (Toastmistress), Alpha Kappa Alpha, Phi Delta Kappa. Ofc: Palm Springs Unified School Dist., 333 S Farrell Palm Springs 92262

STEWART, WILFORD ROMNEY, retail sales executive; b. Dec. 22, 1946, White Plains, NY; s. Isaac Mitton and June (Woodruff) S.; m. Sonia Franklin, June 25, 1966; children: Patrick b. 1967, James b. 1968, Shannon b. 1972, Somer b. 1975; edn: BA, Univ. of Redlands, 1968; Calif. real estate sales lic., life/health ins. lic. 1974–. Career: dept. mgr. J.C. Penney Co. in Indio and Palm Springs, 1968-74; founder/chmn. bd. The Instep, Inc. (retail store), Palm Desert 1975–; pres. Stewart-Hoffman, Inc. Laguna Beach 1982–; pres. 4-Seasons Swimwear, Inc. Palm Desert 1983–; real estate sales assoc. Realty Executives 1978–; sustaining mem. BSA 1982; Republican; Mormon. Res: 75-288 Palm Shadow Dr Indian Wells 92210 Ofc: 4-Seasons Swimwear Inc 74-818 Velie Way #7 Palm Desert 92260

STILES, CASSANDRA DANE, international banker; b. Nov. 1, 1953, West Palm Beach. Fla.; d. Philip Henry and Cassandra (Quickel) Stiles; edn: BA econ., Rollins Coll. 1975; MA internat. mgmt., Thunderbird, 1976. Career: fin. analyst F.C.I.A., N.Y.C. 1976; credit analyst Ariz. Bank, Phoenix 1976-78, internat. ofcr., v.p. 1978-84; v.p. trade fin. First Interstate Bank, San Diego 1984-94; v.p. Standard Chartered Bank 1994–; instr. Grossmont Coll., El Cajon 1986-94; apptd. bd. Calif. Export Finance Office L.A. 1988–, commr. Internat. Trade Commn. S.D. 1988-90; mem. San Diego C.of C. (internat. advy. council 1984–), World Trade Assn. S.D. (pres. 1988-90), Dist. Export Council. Ofc: Standard Chartered Bank c/o First Interstate Bank 530 Broadway Ste 1036 San Diego 92101

STINGHEN, DONATO JOSEPH surgeon; b. Oct. 18, 1948, Sacramento, Calif.; s. Joseph Donato and Rita Iola (Salada) S.; edn: BS, UC Davis 1970; MD, Med. Coll. of Wisconsin, Milwaukee 1974. Career: surgeon, pvt. practice, Oakland, Calif.; mem: CMA 1981–, AMA 1980–, Alameda Contra Costa Co. Assn. 1980–, Am. Coll. of Surgeons 1984–, East Bay Surgical 1983–. Res: 338 Wildwood Ave Piedmont 94611 Ofc: 350 30th St #424 Oakland 94609

STOFFEL, DAVID EDMUND, psychologist; b. Feb. 18, 1951, Oakland; s. Charles Edward and Shirley Josephine (Mills) S.; m. Paula Marie Stolinski; children: Julia Leigh b. 1970, Jeffrey Aaron b. 1975; edn: BA in psych., CSU Fullerton, 1973, MS in counseling, 1976; PhD cand. clin. psychol., USIU, San Diego, psychol. intern Orange Co. Mental Health 1994-95. Career: psychologist Westminster Sch. Dist. 1978-86; Capistrano Unified Sch. Dist., 1986–; examiner Calif. Licensing Bd. of Behaviorial Sci. Examiners 1986, 88, 91, 92, 93; ednl. psychologist pvt. practice, Carlsbad 1986–; honors: Psi Chi, Calif. State Fellow CSUF (1975-77), named Outstanding Sch. Psychologist by CASP 1993; mem: Orange Co. Assn. Ednl. Psychologists (past pres.), Calif. Assn. Sch. Psychologists, Calif. Tchrs. Assn., Nat. Educators Assn., Carlsbad Little League (coach, asst. coach 1985-88). Res: 4705 Edinburgh Dr Carlsbad 92008

STOKOS, JAMES, naval officer, dentist, physician-dermatologist; b. Oct. 9, 1928, San Francisco; m. Mary Fern Schisler, Sept. 14, 1950; children: Teres A. (Jacobsen) b. 1952, Julie M. b. 1968; edn: BA, Union Coll., 1952; BS, and DDS, Univ. Nebr., 1957; MD, Loma Linda Univ., 1967; cert. Am. Bd. of Fam. Practice 1973, recert. 1979, 86. Career: dental ofcr. US Army, 1957-62, chief USA Dental Clinic, Pirmasens, Ger. 1959-61, decorated Merit. Svc., Naval Commendn., Civil Def., Humanitarian Svc.; gen. dental pvt. practice, San Bernardino 1962-67; med. ofcr. USN and intern Naval Hosp., Camp Pendleton, Ca. 1967-68; gen. med. pvt. practice, San Bdo. 1968-74; med. ofcr. US Navy, 1974-: resident in radiology, 1976-77, resident in dermatology, 1979-82, dermatology Naval Hosp., San Diego; gen. med. ofcr. Naval Amphibious Base, Coronado 1973-75, 76-78; Op. New Life, Guam, MI 1975; sr. med. ofcr. Marine Corps Recruit Depot, San Diego 1977-79; staff dermatologist Naval Hosp., S.D. 1982, 1984–, hd. dermat. surg. and oncology 1984-85; chief derm. svc. Naval Hosp., Okinawa, Japan 1982-84; asst. prof. Loma Linda Sch. of Dent., 1966-86; clin. instr. comm. med. UC Sch. of Med., San Diego 1979-83, asst. clin. prof. 1988–; mem. Am. Dental Assn.; contbr. articles in med. jours.; Prot.; rec: golf, skiing, tennis. Res: San Diego

STONE, DAVID MARK, physician, facial plastic surgeon; b. Jan. 11, 1956, Chicago, Ill.; s. Milton and Stephanie Caroline (Suzek) S.; edn: BA chemistry, Univ. Ill. 1977; MD, 1981; cert. Am. Bd. Otolaryngology 1986; cert. Am. Bd. of Facial Plastic & Reconstructive Surgery 1991. Career: gen. surgery resident Univ. Ill. Metropolitan Group Hosps., Chgo. 1981-83, dept. otolaryngology Northwestern Univ. 1983-86; fellowship Am. Acad. Facial Plastic & Reconstrv. Surgery/ clin. instr. dept. otolaryngology Univ. Ala., Birmingham 1986-87; chief div. facial plastic surg. Friendly Hills Med. Group, La Habra, Calif. 1987–; asst. clin. prof. dept. otol. UC Irvine, Orange 1988–; honors: Phi Beta Kappa, Univ. Ill. James scholar 1977; mem: Am. Acad. Otol. Head & Neck Surgery (fellow), Am. Acad. Facial Plastic & Reconstructive Surgery (fellow), Am. Coll. of Surgeons (fellow), AMA; articles pub. in sci. jours., 1985-89; rec: swimming, travel. Res: Yorba Linda 92687 Ofc: Friendly Hills Medical Group 951 S Beach Blvd La Habra 90631

STONE, LAWRENCE MAURICE, lawyer, educator; b. March 25, 1931, Malden, Mass.; s. Abraham Jacob and Pauline (Kurtz) S.; m. Dr. Anna Jane Clark, June 15, 1963; children: Abraham Dean b. 1966, Ethan Goldthwaite b. 1968, Katharine Elisheva b. 1970; edn: AB magna cum laude, Harvard Univ. 1953; JD magna cum laude, 1956; admitted St. Bar Mass. 1956, Calif. 1958. Career: research asst. Am. Law Inst., Cambridge, Mass. 1956-57; assoc. Irell & Manella, L.A. 1957-61, ptnr. 1963, 1979–; internat. tax coordinator U.S. Treasury Dept., Wash. D.C. 1961-62, tax legis. counsel 1964-66; prof. law UC Berkeley 1966-78; vis. prof. law Yale Univ., New Haven 1969, Hebrew Univ., Jerusalem 1973-74, Univ. So. Calif., L.A. 1984; mem. advy. group to commr. I.R.S., Wash. D.C. 1973-74; mem. President's Advy. Commn. on Tax Ct. Appointments, Wash. D.C. 1976-80; mem. Commerce Clearing House Tax Advy. Bd. 1985-93; tax advy. bd. Little Brown Co. 1994–; Fellow Am. Coll. Tax Counsel; mem: Am. Law Inst., Am. Bar Assn., Internat. Fiscal Inst., Am. Arbitration Assn., Phi Beta Kappa; bd. editors Harvard Law Review 1955-56; author: (with Doernberg) Fed. Income Taxation of Corporations & Partnerships, 1987, (with Klein, Bankman and Bittker) Federal Income Taxation, 1990. Ofc: Irell & Manella 1800 Ave of Stars Ste 900 Los Angeles 90067

STONE, RONALD SUMNER, educator; b. July 2, 1949, Stamford, Conn.; s. Ervin Bernard and Mildred Helen (Shapiro) Steinberg; m. Arlene Michiel, Oct. 31, 1976; children: Karen Janine b. 1982, Daniel Evan b. 1985; edn: BA, Univ. Wis. 1971; MBA, Rutgers Univ. 1972; PhD, UCLA 1983; C.P.A. Calif. (1974). Career: staff acct. Price Waterhouse, San Jose 1971-74; sr. acct. Coopers & Lybrand, Los Angeles 1977-78; prof. accounting and management information systems CSU Los Angeles, 1980-86, CSU Northridge, 1986–; vis. assoc. prof. and lectr. USC, 1984-93; vis. prof. UCLA 1985; honors: Outstanding Prof. award Laventhol & Horwath 1989, Excellence in Tchg. award CSULA Acctg. Soc. 1985, Arthur Andersen Disting. Tchg. award 1976, 80; mem: Am. Inst. CPA, Calif. Soc. CPA, Am. Acctg. Assn., Inst. of Internal Auditors; publs: Computerized Accounting with Business-Works (McGraw Hill, 1993), articles in profl. jours., 1980–. Res: 11780 Avenida del Sol Northridge 91326 Ofc: School of Business & Economics California State University Northridge 91330-8245

STONE, WESTCOT BELL, III, airline pilot; b. Aug. 23, 1920, Los Angeles; s. Earle Reynolds and Casandra (Bell) S.; m. Bette Werner, Apr. 25, 1956; children: Elizabeth b. 1957, Kimberley b. 1958, Westcot, IV, b. 1962, granddaughter Ashley Elizabeth Bateman, b. 1982; edn: USC. Career: pilot Trans World Airlines Inc. 1946, airline capt. Western Airlines, 1946-80, ret.; mem. Silver Chiefs, Cabrillo Yacht Club, Kaneohe Yacht club (Hawaii), Sigma Alpha Epsilon, Sigma Delta Psi; mil: capt. USAAF 1941-46, decorated Air Medal w/3 o.l.c., D.F.C.; Republican; United Ch. of Christ; rec: pvt. pilot, sailing, travel. Res: 2820 Via de la Guerra Palos Verdes Estates 90274

STOTLER, ALICEMARIE HUBER, federal judge; b. May 29, 1942, Alhambra; d. James Russell and Loretta (Montoya) H.; m. James Allen Stotler, Sept. 11, 1971; edn: BA, USC, 1964, JD, 1967; admitted bar: Calif. 1967, Fed. Ct. no. dist. Calif. 1967, cent. dist. Calif. 1973, US Supreme Ct. 1976; cert. Crim. Law Specialist, 1973. Career: Orange County dep. dist. atty. (first woman hired f.t. O.C.) 1967-73; pvt. practice law, 1973-76, 83-84; appt. municipal ct. judge, Harbor Judicial Dist., Newport Beach 1976-78; appt. judge Superior Ct., Orange Co. 1978-83; appt. judge U.S. Dist. Ct., Central Dist. of Calif., 1984–; instr. Orange Co. Sheriff's Dept. Acad., 1982; instr. CEB State Bar Conf. course in courtroom conduct, 9/83; honors: winner Hale Moot Ct. Competition, statewide Appellate argument compet. 1967, named judge of yr. O.C. Trial Lawyers & Trial Lawyers Sectys. 1978, Franklin G. West Award for contbns. to advance and elevate justice and law Orange Co. Bar Assn. 1985; mem., chair, 1993-96, U.S. Judicial Conf. Coms.: Standing Com. on Rules of Practice and Procedure 1991-94; mem. Ninth Circuit Coms.: Jury Com. 1990-92, Exec. Com., 9th Cir. Jud. Conf. 1989-92, Fed.-State Jud. Council 1989-93; mem: Fed. Judges Assn. (bd. 1989–), Ninth Circuit Dist. Judges Assn., Am. Law Inst., ABA (jud. admin. div. and litigation sect.), Nat. Assn. Women Judges, Calif. Judges' Found. (pres. 1981-82); Orange Co. Bar Assn. (1968–, dir. 1976, sec. 1984, chair 1993-96), O.C. Trial Lawyers Assn. (1973–, dir. 1975); civic: Legion Lex USC (bd. 1981-83), Arthritis Found. Orange Co. (planned giving com. 1976-81), Geo. A. Parker Law Found. (trustee 1979-82); Republican; Prot.; rec: walking, dog shows. Ofc: U.S. District Court 751 W Santa Ana Blvd Ste 403 Santa Ana 92701

STOTTER, LAWRENCE HENRY, lawyer; b. Sept. 24, 1929, Cleveland, Oh.; s. Oscar and Bertha (Lieb) S.; m. Ruth Rapoport, June 30, 1957; children: Daniel, Jennifer, Steven; edn: BBA, Ohio State Univ., 1956, LLB 1958, JD 1967; admitted Calif. St. Bar 1960, U.S. Supreme Ct. 1973, U.S. Tax Ct. 1976. Career: solo law practice, San Francisco 1963-65; ptnr. law firm Stern, Stotter & O'Brien, 1965-75; Stotter, Samuels & Chamberlin, 1975-79; Stotter & Coats, 1979–; faculty Nat. Judicial Coll.; mem. Calif. Family Law Advy. Commn. 1979-80; TV appearances on Phil Donahue Show, and Good Morning America; appt. U.S. State Dept. del. Hague Conf. Pvt. Internat. Law, 1979-80; legal advr. White House Conf. on Families, 1980–; mem: Am. Bar Assn. (past chmn. fam. law sect., editor in chief ABA Family Advocate mag. 1977-82), Am. Bar Found., Am. Acad. Matrimonial Lawyers (past nat. v.p.), Calif. State Bar (past chmn. fam. law sect.); civic: Tamalpais Conservation Club, Marin Co. (pres.); mil: AUS 1950-53. Res: 2244 Vistazo St E, Tiburon 94920 Ofc: 1772 Vallejo St San Francisco 94123

STOTTER, RUTH, storyteller, college instructor; b. July 26, 1936, Madison, Wis.; d. Louis Marvin Rapoport and Jeanne (Michael) R.; m. Lawrence Henry Stotter, June 30, 1957; children: Daniel Jay b.1961, Jennifer Louise b. 1962, Steven Paul b. 1966; edn: BA, Ohio State 1958; MA, Stanford 1959; MA, Sonoma State Univ. 1984; tchg. cert., UC Berkeley, 1961; Calif. Comm. Colls. lifetime teaching credentials in Anthropology, Spl. Edn. Career: freelance storyteller, Artists-in-the-Schools, Renaissance Faire, etc., nationally 1974–; instr. (assoc. prof. ext. ed. dept) Sonoma State Univ. 1982–; dir. Certificate-in-Storytelling program, Dominican Coll., San Rafael 1985–; dir. workshops various storytelling festivals; performances: N.Y. Dance Ctr. 1990, Coll. of Storytellers (London), People's Theatre (San Francisco), etc.; honors: guest artist, Alaska Artist in Schools 1980, performing artist Marin Co. Artist in Schools 1990; mem: Nat. Storytelling Assn., Puppeteers of Am. (cons.), Am. Folklore Soc. (panelist, mem. Aesop Award Com.), L.W.V. of Marin Co. (bd. 1963-66); author: Little Acorns (1976, rev. 1993), About Story, 1994; contbg. author: Family Storytelling Handbook, 1987, Joining In, 1988, prof. jour. (4 issues); pub. and editor annual Storyteller's Calendar, 1988–; audiocassettes: True Tales from California History, 1992, Women of the West, 1994; rec: hiking, kayaking. Ofc: Dominican College, Certificate-in-Storytelling Program 50 Acacia St San Rafael 94901

STOUT, RAY BERNARD, physicist; b. June 16, 1939, Georgetown, Ohio; s. Beryl Bernard and Mary Florence (Edenfield) S.; m. Tanya Karen Kuenzli, Aug. 28, 1965; 1 dau., Natasha Kay b. 1971; edn: BSME, Ohio St. Univ. 1964; MSME, 1969; PhD, Ill. Inst. Tech. 1970; MBA, Univ. Pittsburgh 1972. Career: fellow engr. Westinghouse Electric Corp., Bettis Atomic Power Lab., W. Mifflin, Pa. 1969-79; physicist Lawrence Livermore Nat. Lab., Univ. Calif., Livermore 1979–; mem: Am. Physical Soc., ASME; ed. Techniques & Theory of Stress Measurement for Shock Wave Applications, 1987, Wave Propagation in Granular Material, 1989, patent for triple material stress, 1988, num. articles pub. in tech.

jours.; Democrat; rec: racquet ball, hiking, woodworking. Res: 954 Venus Way Livermore 94550 Ofc: Univ. California POB 808 L-201 Livermore 94550

STOVER, W(ILLARD) ROBERT, temporary services executive; b. June 26, 1921, Philadelphia, Pa.; s. Robert William and Jane (Horton) S.; m. Joan Marie Cote, Dec. 4, 1954; children: Stephen b. 1956, Susan b. 1958, Amy b. 1962; edn: BS, Waynesburg Coll. 1942; Univ. Ill. 1942-43; Univ. Pa.; LHD, Waynesburg Coll. 1991. Career: chmn., CEO Western Temporary Services Inc., Walnut Creek 1948–; advy. bd. San Francisco St. Univ. 1976–; awards: Religious Heritage of Am. businessman of year 1988, Waynesburg Coll. alumnus of year 1985; mem: Young Life Campaign (life bd. mem.), Fuller Theological Seminary (trustee), Mt. Hermon Assn. (dir.), Internat. Students (v.chmn.), Presbyterian Lay Com.; mil: lt.s.g. USN 1942-46; Republican; Presbyterian; rec: golf, philately, skiing. Res: 120 Wildwood Gardens Piedmont 94611 Ofc: Western Temporary Services Inc. 301 Lennon Ln Walnut Creek 94598

STRAATSMA, BRADLEY R., physician; b. Dec. 19, 1917, Grand Rapids, Mich.; s. Clarence Ralph and Lucretia (Nicholson) S.; m. Ruth Reynolds Campbell, June 20, 1951; children: Cary Straatsma Ewing b. 1953, Bradley Derek b. 1955, Greer Ruth b. 1963; edn: combined curriculum, Univ. of Mich., Ann Arbor 1945-47; MD (cum laude), Yale Univ. Sch. of Medicine 1951; cert. Nat. Bd. Med. Examiners, Calif. 1952, Am. Bd. Ophthalmology 1958; DS (hon.) Columbia Univ. 1984. Career: intern New Haven (Ct.) Hosp. 1951-52; vis. scholar Columbia Univ. Coll. of Physicians and Surgeons and Inst. of Ophthal. of Presbyn. Hosp., NY 1952, asst. resident and resident in ophthal. 1955-58; special clin. trainee Nat. Inst. of Neurological Diseases and Blindness, Bethesda, Md. 1958-59; fellow in ophthalmic pathology, Armed Forces Inst. of Pathology, Walter Reed Army Med. Ctr., WDC 1958-59; fellow in ophthal., Wilmer Ophthal. Inst., Johns Hopkins Univ., Baltimore, Md. 1958-59; assoc. prof. to prof. of surgery/ophthal. and chief, Div. of Ophthal., Dept. of Surgery, UCLA Sch. of Medicine 1959-68; dir. Jules Stein Eye Inst., UCLA Sch. of Medicine 1964-68; ophthalmologist-in-chief UCLA Med. Ctr. 1968-94; dir Jules Stein Eye Inst., prof. and chmn. Dept. of Ophthal., UCLA Sch. of Medicine 1968-94; prof. of ophthal., dir. Ctr. for Eye Edn., Dept. Ophthal. and Jules Stein Eye Inst., UCLA Sch. of Medicine 1994–; hosp. med. staff: UCLA Med. Ctr., Harbor/UCLA Med. Ctr., Torrance, VA Med. Ctr., Sepulveda, VA Wadsworth Med. Ctr., L.A., Cedars-Sinai Med. Ctr., L.A., Santa Monica Hosp. Med. Ctr., St. John's Hosp. and Health Ctr., Santa Monica, St. Vincent's Hosp., L.A.; mem. UCLA Sch. Medicine Brain Res. Inst. 1967–, and Jonsson Comprehensive Cancer Ctr. 1992–; sr. faculty assoc. UCLA Ctr. on Aging 1993–; UCLA com. mem.: chmn. Dept. of Ophthal. Com. and Dept. Ophthal Clin. Com. 1968-94, UCLA Sch. Medicine Faculty Council 1968-94, chmn. Jules Stein Eye Inst. Com. 1972-94, UCLA Med. Ctr. Med. staff exec. com. 1975-94, UCLA Clin. Dept. Chairs com. 1981-94, chmn. Dept. of Ophthal. Div. Chiefs com. 1986-94, UCLA Sch. of Medicine Med. Faculty Bd. UCLA Med. Group 1988– (chair 1990-92, chair bylaws com. 1992–, co-chair, regional med. practice com. 1992–), UCLA-Kaiser Permanente Liaison Com. 1989– (chair 1989-90), Neurosci. Advy. Com. 1990–, Chancellor's Ad Hoc Com. 1991–, UCLA Clin. Council, Ofc. of Chancellor 1992–, UCLA Governance Bd., Ofc. of Chancellor 1992–; chmn. Jules Stein Eye Inst. Bd. of Trustees 1977-94; mem. fgn. cons. advs., Instituto Nacional de Investigacion Oftalmologica, Caracas, Venezuela 1973–; bd. dirs. Ophthalmic Pub. Co. 1975– (v.p. 1990-93); mem. nat. bd., Retinitis Pigmentosa Internat. 1983–; chmn. Ocular Melanoma Study Planning Com. 1984-88; bd. dirs. The Heed Ophthalmic Found. 1984–; chmn. sci. advy. bd. Ctr. for the Partially Sighted 1984–; bd. dirs. Pan-Am. Ophthal. Found. 1985–; co-chmn, steering com., exec. com. Collaborative Ocular Melanoma Study 1985–; internat. advy. bd., Internat. Acad. for Res. in Ophthal. 1988–; mem. internat. council of N. African Ctr. for Sight, Tunisia 1989–; bd. trustees Found. of Am. Acad. of Ophthal. 1989– (chmn. bd. trustees 1989-91); chmn., bd. dirs. Heed Ophthal. Found. 1990–; advy bd. One World Sight Project 1991–; mem. Council of Biology Editors, Inc. 1993–; bd. dirs RP Found. Fighting Blindness So. Calif. Affiliate 1994–; internat. lectr. in field; awards: Henry Burr Ferris Award in Anatomy, Yale Univ. Sch. Medicine 1948, and Prosector in Anatomy 1949-50, Alpha Omega Alpha 1950, Wm. Warren Hoppin Award, NY Acad. Medicine 1956, co-recipient sci. exhib. awards from profl. assns. 1956-62, Conrad Berens Award, Internat. Eye Film Festival 1965, Award of Merit, Am. Acad. Ophthal. & Otolaryngology 1967, Cert. of Appreciation, Bd. Trustees AMA 1968, Prof., New Orleans Acad. Ophthal. 1968, Special Cert. NIH 1976, Univ. Svc. Award, UCLA Alumni Assn. 1982, Favaloro Gold Medal, Meridional Ophthal. Soc., Siracusa, Italy 1984, Sr. Honor Award, Bd. Dirs. Am. Acad. Ophthal. 1984, Order of Christopher Columbus, Highest Award, Dominican Republic 1987, Moacyr Alvaro Internat. Award for the Exchange of Ophthal. Knowledge, Brazil 1989, Pan-Am. Assn. of Ophthal. Adminstrv. Ofc. Special Award, Brazil 1989, Gold Medal, Fundacion Oftalmologica Nacional de Columbia 1991, Mildred Weisenfeld Award for Excellence in Ophthal., Assn. for Res. in Vision and Ophthal. 1991, Benjamin F. Boyd Humanitarian Award for Svc. to the Americas, Pan-Am. Assn. Ophthal. 1991, Miguel Aleman Medal, Mexico City 1991, Lucien Howe Medal Award for Disting. Svc. to Ophthal., Am. Ophthal. Soc. 1992, NIH Special Recognition Award, Nat. Eye Health Edn. Prog. 1993, Lifetime Achievement Award, L.A. Soc. Ophthal. 1994, Profl. Achievement Award, UCLA Med. Alumni Assn. 1994, Special Achievement Award, Chinese Am.

Ophthal. Soc. 1995, Sixth Annual S. Rodman Irvine Price, UCLA Dept. Ophthal. Assn. 1995, hon. mem./prof./fellow/guest, num. internat. assns., universities and congresses, 1968-94, res. grantee (4) Nat. Eye Inst. 1966–; mem: Academia Ophthalmologica Internationales, Am. Acad. of Ophthal. and Otolaryngology (sec. for continuing edn. in ophthal. and council mem. 1969-74, pres. 1976-77), Am. Acad. Ophthal. (bd. dirs. 1978-82, bd. councilors 1981, chmn. nat. eye care com 1984-87), Am. Soc. of Cataract and Refractive Surgery, AMA (Sect. on Ophthal. sec. 1963-66, chmn. 1966-67, council mem. 1970-74), Am. Ophthal. Soc. (council mem. 1985-90, chmn. of council 1989-90, v.p. 1991-92, pres. 1992-93), Assn. for Res. in Vision and Ophthal., Assn. of Univ. Professors of Ophthal. (trustee 1969-75, pres. 1973-75, policy devel. com. 1987-89), CMA (ophthal. advy. panel 1972–, panel chmn. 1974-79, sci. bd. 1973-79, House of Delegates 1974, 77, 79), The Jules Gonin Club, L.A. Co. Med. Assn., L.A. Soc. of Ophthal., The Macula Soc., Pan-Am. Assn. of Ophthal. (council mem. 1972-84, constitution and bylaws revision com. 1984-91, pres. 1985-89), The Retina Soc., West Coast Retina Study Club, Chinese Am. Ophthal. Soc.; editl. bd. Am. Jour. of Ophthal. 1974–, editor-in-chief 1993–; author: contbr. over 400 articles, abstracts, reviews, editorials, and forewords to books, profl. jours. and assns., 1949–; mil: lt. (MC), USNR 1952-54. Ofc: Jules Stein Eye Institute 100 Stein Plaza, UCLA Los Angeles 90024-7000

STRAND, CARL LUDVIG, earthquake consultant; b. Nov. 6, 1950, Memphis, Tenn.; s. Sylvester Eugene and Barbara Harris (Maier) S.; edn: BA math. with spec. in earth sciences, Revelle Coll., UCSD, 1973; MS geology, SDSU, 1980; Wilderness trip leadership adminstrn. certificate, Coll. of Extended Studies, SDSU, 1980; UCLA, 1982-84. Career: pres. Strand Earthquake Cons., Los Angeles, 1987–; honors: San Diego Inst. Hist. La Frontera Award, 1980, NCCEM Region IX Executive Citation, 1990, BSA Eagle Scout; mem: Earthquake Engrg. Research Inst., ASCE/TCLEE Earthquake Investigations Com., ASCE Special Stds. Com. on Earthquake Actuated Automatic Gas Shutoff Sys.; author: Pre-1900 earthquakes of Baja California and San Diego County, 1980, articles pub. in profl. jours., 1979-95; Democrat; rec: Masters' water polo, backpacking, scuba diving, genealogy. Ofc: Strand Earthquake Consultants, 1436 S Bentley Ave Ste 6 Los Angeles 90025

STRANG, GEORGE ELLIS, utility company executive; b. Aug. 15, 1939, Monterey Park; s. Warren G. and Opal M. (Holmes) S.; m. Judith Ann, March 21, 1958; children: Steven Ellis b. 1963, Carrie Lynn b. 1960; edn: AA, East L.A. Coll., 1962; BS engring., CSU Los Angeles 1965; MBA, Pepperdine Univ. 1976. Career: engring. and ops. line staff So. Calif. Gas Co. 1965-78; gen. supt. Transmission So. Calif. Gas., Taft 1978-80, project engring. mgr., L.A. 1980-83, chief design engr. 1983, mgr. info. systems 1983-84, v.p. engring. research 1984-90, v.p. engring & operation support 1990-93, v.p. transmission and storage ops. 1993–; mem. Industry Advy. Bd., Sch. Engring. Calif. St. Univ., L.A. 1987–; Industry Tech. Advy. Gas Research Inst., Chgo., Ill. 1985-93; awards: CSULA Disting. Alumnus 1987; mem: Pacific Coast Gas Assn., Am. Gas Assn., Pacific Energy Assn., Calif. St. L.A. Alumni Assn.; mil: sgt. USAR 1958-62; Republican; rec: golf. Res: 1614 Peacock Ln Fullerton 92633 Ofc: Southern California Gas Co. 555 W 5th St Los Angeles 90013

STRANGES, FRANK E., clergyman, educator; b. Oct. 6, 1927, Bklyn.; s. Natale A. and Catherine (Filardo) S.; m. Julie Ann Corcoran, Mar. 12, 1985; children: Sean b. 1974, Michael b. 1975; edn: ThD and PhD in theol., Tenn. Christian Univ., 1962, 1964; PhD psych., Union Univ., 1960; PhD internat. law, 1983. Career: pres. Internat. Evangelism Crusades, 1959–; pres., prof. Internat. Theological Seminary of Calif.; honors: Knight Comdr. Knights of Justice, Knight of Jerusalem, Knight of Malta, FBI Gold Medal Award 1985, American Police Hall of Fame 1985, Gold plaque Republic of South Korea; nat. chaplain Nat. Assn. of Chiefs of Police, W.D.C.; asst. state dir. State Marshalls Assn.; mem: Am. Fedn. of Police, Nat. Chaplains Assn.; publs: author 15 books on space, sci., religion; prod. three TV documentaries and 1 full-length feature film; prod. video, Mysteries of the Dead Sea Scrolls; mil: 4-star gen. and chaplain Chaplains Internat. Assn.; Republican; Prot. Ofc: International Evangelism Crusades, Inc. 14617 Victory Blvd Ste 4 Van Nuys 91411

STRASBURG, LOUIS GLEN, consultant, educator; b. March 22, 1927, Salt Lake City, Utah; s. Joseph Louis and Millie Minerva (Rice) S.; edn: BS, Univ. Utah 1953; MBA, Ohio St. Univ. 1960; PhD, 1962; N.Y. Univ. 1963. Career: prof. UCLA 1962-64; CSU Hayward 1964–; sr. v.p. Lehrer McGovern Bovis, N.Y.C. 1988-89; bd. dirs.: Laurel Grove Hosp., Castro Valley 1970-74, Technicraft Internat., San Mateo 1968-75, Calif. Research Corp., Hayward 1975-88; awards: UCLA Outstanding Prof. 1963, CSU Outstanding Prof. 1965; mem: Am. Inst. Indsl. Engrs. (sr.), Acad. Mgmt., Fin. Mgmt. Assn., Financial Executives Inst.; author: Project Design in Process of Research Mgmt., 1962; mil: capt. USN 1953-63; rec: flying. Ofc: California State University Dept. of Management and Finance Hayward 94542

STRAUBEL, JOHN FREDERICK, advertising and public relations agency executive; b. May 19, 1928, Greenbay, Wis.; s. Clarence Weise and Ethel (Puchner) S.; edn: BS in English, Northwestern Univ., 1950. Career: comms. dir. Hiller Aircraft Corp., Palo Alto 1956-63, Fairchild Hiller Corp., W.D.C.

1963-66; owner/pres. Straubel Communications, Portola Valley 1966–; pub. rels. mgr. Volunteers for Nixon-Lodge, W.D.C., 1960 Campaign; mem.: Pub. Rels. Soc. Am. 1960–; civic: The New Forum, Palo Alto (dir., v.p. 1985-89), Boys & Girls Club Am., Palo Alto (chapt. dir. 1992–); author, editor: One Way Up, 1963, Pacific Diary I, 1952, Pacific Diary II, 1953; mil: lt.j.g. USN 1950-53; Indep.; Presbyterian; rec: comic book artist/writer. Ofc: Straubel Communications, 4370 Alpine Rd Ste 207 Portola Valley 94028

STROM, C. GORDON, physician, otolaryngologist; b. Feb. 6, 1934, Mayville, N.D.; s. Clarence A. and Gladys (Moen) St.; widowed, 1994; children: Peter b. 1958, Kristen b. 1962, Brian b. 1964, Eric b. 1967; edn: BA, Pacific Lutheran Coll., Tacoma, Wash. 1956; MD, Univ. of Wash., Seattle 1961. Career: active duty U.S. Navy 1962–; physician U.S. Naval Hosp., Oakland, Calif. 1972–; asst. clin. prof. UC San Francisco 1977–; awards: Meritorious Svc. award U.S. Navy 1989, 1994; mem: Am. Coll. of Surgeons (fellow 1969–), Am. Acad. of Otolaryngology (fellow 1972–), Triological Soc. (fellow 1972–), AMA 1976–; bd. dirs. Sea West Fed. Credit Union, Oakland 1992–; vice comdr. Treasure Island Yacht Club, S.F.; mil: capt. U.S. Navy 1962–; rec: sailing, skiing, running, music. Res: 3457 Hackamore Drive Hayward 94541 Ofc: Naval Hospital Oakland 94627

STROMME, GARY L., law librarian; b. July 8, 1939, Willmar, Minn.; m. Suzanne Readman, July 21, 1990; edn: BA, philo., Pacific Lutheran Univ. 1965; BLS, Univ. of Brit. Columbia Sch. of Librarianship, 1967; JD, Hastings Coll. of the Law 1973; admitted State Bar of Calif. 1973, US Supreme Ct. Bar, 1977. Career: serials librarian, Univ. of Minn., St. Paul Campus Librarian 1967-69; asst. librarian law firm McCutchen, Doyle, Brown, Enersen, San Francisco 1970-71; asst. librarian Graham & James, S.F. 1971-73; ind. contracting atty., 1973-74; law librarian Pacific Gas & Electric Co., S.F. 1974-94; consultant 1995–; mem: Internat. Soc. Gen. Semantics (S.F. chpt. pres. 1978-80, bd. dir. 1980-81), Am. Assn. Law Libraries (chmn. AALL Com. on indexing of legal periodicals 1986-88), Am. Bar Assn. (chmn. lib. com. Sect. Economics of Law Practice 1978-82); author: An Intro. to the Use of the Law Library, 1974; Basic Legal Research Tech. (rev. 4th ed. 1979); mil: elect. tech. USAF 1959-63. Res: 6106 Ocean View Dr Oakland 94618

STRONG, GARY E., state librarian; b. June 26, 1944, Moscow, Idaho; s. Arthur Dwight and Cleora Anna (Nirk) S.; m. Carolyn Jean Roetker, March 14, 1970; children: Christopher Eric b. 1971, Jennifer Rebecca b. 1974; edn: BS, Univ. of Ida. 1966; MA lib. sci., Univ. of Mich. 1967. Career: instr. in public lib. adminstrn. Div. of Cont. Edn., State of Ore. 1972; ref., adminstrv. asst. Univ. of Ida. Library 1963-66; extension librarian Latah Co. (Ida.) Free Lib. 1966; hd. librarian Markley Residence Lib., Univ. Mich., 1966-67; library dir. Lake Oswego (Ore.) Pub. Lib. 1967-73, Everett (Wa.) Public Lib. 1976-79; assoc. dir. for svs. Washington State Lib. 1976-79, dep. state librarian 1979-80; Calif. State Librarian, 1980–; mem./CEO Calif. Library Svs. Bd.; exec. dir./ex-officio mem. bd. dirs. Calif. State Lib. Found.; mem. bd. dirs. Coop. Lib. Agcy. for Systems and Svs. (v.p. 1981-84); mem. Lib. Adminstrn. and Mgmt. Assn. (pres. 1984-85), Chief Officers of State Lib. Agencies (pres. 1984-86), Calif. Historic Capitol Commn., W. Council of State Libs., No. Reg. Lib. Facility (bd.), Calif., Am. and Spl. Libs. Assn., Calif. State PTA (advsy. bd.), Advsy. Com. to the Lib. of Cong. on Laser Disc Technol.; mem. Book Club of Calif., S.F./Sacto. Book Collectors Club, Book Collectors Club of L.A., Press Club of S.F., Roxborghe Club; past activities: Ore. Lib. Assn. (pres. 1970-71, hon. life mem. 1981), Pacific Northwest Lib. Assn. (pres. 1978-79, hon. life mem. 1981), Pacific Northwest Bibliographic Center (bd. 1977-80), Everett, WA Library Access (prod., host weekly cablevision pgm. 1974-76), Am. Lib. Assn. Commn. on Freedom and Equality of Access to Info. 1984-86, Alpha Phi Omega nat. svc. frat. (sect. chmn. W. Reg. 1967-71); awards: Ore. State Lib. scholarship for grad. study 1966, disting. alumnus Univ. Mich. Sch. of Lib. Sci. 1984, disting. svc. Calif. Literacy Inc. 1985, spl. commendn. Calif. Assn. of Lib. Trustees and Commnrs. 1985; publs: compiler, On Reading - In the Year of the Reader (1987); num. profl. and gen. interest articles, media interviews, frequent keynote speaker. Ofc: State Librarian of California POB 942837 Sacramento 94237-0001

STROUD, SHARRON PATRICIA, minister; b. July 29, 1944, Okemah, Okla.; d. Raymond Dean and Zora Margaret (Woods) Jacobs; widow, Neil Stroud; children: Tricia Lorraine b. 1969. edn: CSU Northridge 1963-64, Pierce City Coll. 1964-65; Ministerial Degree, Un. Ch. Rel. Sci. Sch. of Ministry 1973-75; Master Degree, Motivational Sci. Humanetic Inst. 1976; PhD cand. in behav. psych., La Jolla Univ.; MPhil & religion, Aspen Theol. Univ. 1993, LHD, 1993. Career: religious sci. minister and motivational instr. Self Image Inst., Santa Ana Coll. of Para Medical Arts and Sci. 1972-73; num. self-image seminars, 1972–; founding minister Sci. of Mind Ch. of Positive Thinking 1975-78; minister Rel. Sci. Ch. Ctr., San Diego 1978; minister S.D. Comm. Ch. of Rel. Sci. 1978–; founding minister San Diego Church for the Celebration of Life, Jan. 1, 1989; num. tv and radio appearances, prod. radio show "The Choice is Yours," host local tv ministry "Passport To Life " 1986–, featured in weekly TV prog. "A Course in Miracles" 1992–; tchg. Corporate Am. Cybernetics of Success"; torch carrier First Earth Run, participant Human Unity Conf., and The March for Peace and Hands Across Am., lectr. U.N. Univ. for Peace, Costa Rica, chaired

Planetary Commn., World Peace Event (S.D.); mem. United Clergy of Rel. Sci. (v.p. 1986-87); mem. Rel. Advy. Council, U.S. 42nd Congl. Dist.; recipient speaking awards Nat. Forensic League 1961, United Ch. Rel. Sci. Sch. of Ministry, Resolution San Diego City Council (2/14/75), svc. award Nat. Mgmt. Assn. 1979-80; Beta Sigma Phi Humanitarian sor. (v.p. 1968-72); hon. PhD Heritage Inst. Santa Barbara; Woman of Religion award, Soroptimists Internat.; Hollywood's Salute to Beautiful Women (1972); 1st woman pres. of Sch. of Ministry 1974-75, Internat. Woman of Yr., Internat. Biog. Soc. 1991, 92; listed: Outstanding Young Women of Am. 1970, 80, Who's Who in Calif., Who's Who of the New Thought Movement 1975, Who's Who San Diego Women 1982, Who's Who in Metaphysics; mem: Beta Sigma Pi (v.p. 1968-72), Nat. League of Am. Pen Women, Soroptomist Internat.; publs: The Spiritual Side of Success; The Power of Knowing Who You Are (Herself Mag. 1979); published poet; author: book in progress, Living On The Edge; featured in Time, Newsweek, US News & World Report; Apolitical; Religious Sci.; rec: bicycling, yoga, swimming. Res: Mt. Helix Ofc: 4201 Avenida Gregory Spring Valley 92077

STRUEBING, WILLIAM ELMER, moving company executive; b. April 15, 1938, Los Angeles; s. Elmer H. Struebing and Mina (Stiles) Cunliff; m. Karole Hardt, June 29, 1963; children: Wes b. 1967, Shauna b. 1969; edn: BA, Pomona Coll. 1959; MBA, Northwestern Univ. 1961; Loyola Law Sch. 1966. Career: Westlake Moving & Storage System, Los Angeles 1955-62, v.p. 1962-65, pres., chmn. bd. 1965-81; Westways Inc., Montebello 1979–; Western Moving & Storage Inc. 1982–; awards: L.A. Jaycees outstanding service (1974), Men of Achievement, Notable Am., Who's Who in U.S., Who's Who in West, Who's Who Calif. Bus. & Fin.; mem: Calif. Moving & Storage Assn. (pres. 1966-67, govt. affairs 1978-79), Nat. Moving & Storage Assn. (bd. 1979-89, chmn. 1986-87), Mayflower Warehouse Assn. (bd. 1985-91, chmn. 1988-89), Rotary Internat./L.A., Montebello C.of C., Roger Wagner Chorale, L.A. Master Chorale (bd. dirs.), Crittenton Center (chmn.), Pomona College Alumni Assn. (pres. 1982-83); club: L.A. Athletic; mil: Armed Forces Reserve Data Processing Unit 1962; Republican; Methodist; rec: tennis, racquetball, golf. Ofc: Western Moving & Storage Inc. 1561 Chapin Rd Montebello 90640

STRUNK, HAROLD KENNETH, healthcare executive; b. June 23, 1933, McCreary County, Ky.; s. Obal Edmund and Matilda Luverne (New) S.; m. Nancy Lou Patton, June 12, 1954; children: Nancy Karen b. 1955, Melanie Ann b. 1958, Kenneth Wayne b. 1959; edn: BA psychology, CSU Fullerton 1967; MSW, UCLA, 1969, MPH, 1970; DPH, 1972. Career: proj. mgr. PSRO Support Center for Calif. 1974-78; exec. dir. TakeCare HMO Blue Cross of No. Calif., Oakland 1978-80; sr. health planner Arabian Bechtel Co. Ltd., Jubail, Saudi Arabia 1980-82; hosp. adminstr. Saudi Arabian Mil. Hosp., Dhahran, Saudi Arabia 1982-83; cons. Nat. Med. Enterprises, Al Hada Hosp., Taif, Saudi Arabia 1983-85; physician recruiter Hosp. Staffing System, Pleasanton 1985-87; reg. mgr. Blue Shield of Calif., San Francisco 1987–; awards: British Sub-Aqua Club Per Holmquist 1983; mem: Assn. Mil. Surgeons of U.S., Healthcare Execs. No. Calif., World Affairs Council S.F., British Sub-Aqua Club, Am. Legion, Naval Reserve Assn., Am. Public Health Assn., Middle East Inst., Reserve Ofcrs. Assn., Commonwealth Club of Calif., Assn. of Former Intelligence Ofcrs.; publs: proceedings, Diving Hazards in Persian Gulf, Military Medicine, "Medical Aspects of Persian Gulf Operations"; mil: Capt. USNR 1977– (recalled to active duty U.S. Central Command, Desert Storm, Saudia Arabia/Bahrain); Republican; Presbyterian; rec: scuba diving, competition rifle shooting, photog., Ham radio (WA6JNZ). Res: 4365 Clovewood Ln Pleasanton 94588 Ofc: Blue Shield of California 2 Northpoint San Francisco 94133

STUART, DOROTHY MAE, artist; b. Jan. 8, 1933, Fresno; d. Robert Wesley Williams and Maria Theresa (Gad) Tressler; m. Reginald Ross Stuart, May 18, 1952; children: Doris b. 1954 Darlene b. 1957, Sue b. 1962; edn: grad. Fresno H.S., 1951, student CSU Fresno 1951-52, Fresno City Coll. 1962-64, pvt. courses 1965-68. Career: artist, prin., Fresno 1962–; 1160+ oils, graphics, watercolors, drawings, paintings, 1966–; art demonstrations and judging for schools, fairs and orgns., San Joaquin Valley, 1962–; awards: 53 Fine Art awards art shows Calif., 1966–, Spl. award Soc. of Western Artists- DeYoung Mus., S.F. and Frye Mus., Seattle 1971, invitation 1st Contemporary Western Art Tour to P.R.O.China 1974, degree of honor Soc. of Western Artists, S.F. 1975, nominated Fresno Bus./Profl. Woman of Yr. 1990; mem. Soc. Western Artists, Fresno (bd. 1968-74, v.p. 1968-70), Fresno County Womens Trade Club (1982-93, bd. 1986-92, pres. 1988-90), Fresno Art Mus. (1970–), Patrons for Cultural Arts Fresno (adviser 1987–, bd. 1991-92), Fresno H.S. Centennial (bd. 1988-90); appt. advy. com. State Sen. Ken Maddy's Cent. Calif. Conf. on Women 1989–; publs: art adviser: (book) "A Portrait of Fresno", 1985, artist: (book) "Heritage Fresno", 1975, editor and artist (book) "Fresno High Sch. Centennial 1889-1989" (1989); Republican; christian; rec: travel (40+ countries), collect art and dolls internat. Res/Studio: 326 S Linda Ln Fresno 93727

STUDEMEISTER, ALEX EUGENE, physician; b. March 25, 1955, Caracas, Venezuela; nat. 1977; s. Dr. Alexander Ernst and Marguerite (Preobrajensky) S.; edn: BA, UC Berkeley 1977; MD, Loyola Univ. 1983; cert. Am. Bd. Internal Medicine (1986), and Infectious Diseases (1988). Career: resident Med. Coll. Wis., Milwaukee 1983-86; fellow Loyola Univ., Chgo., Ill. 1986-

88; staff physician San Jose Med. Group 1988–; mem: A.C.P. (diplomate), AMA; publs: 5+ med. jour. articles (1987–); Lutheran; rec: tennis. Ofc: 14651 S Bascom Ave Los Gatos 95032

STUDEMEISTER, PAUL ALEXANDER, geologist; b. Mar. 20, 1954, Caracas, Venez., naturalized U.S. 1966; s. Alexander Ernst and Marguerite (Preobrajensky) S.; edn: BA, UC Berkeley, 1977; PhD, Univ. of Western Ontario, London, Ont., Can. 1982; reg. geologist Calif. (RG4635, 1988), Ariz. (RG26152, 1992), lic. engring. geologist Calif. (CEG1746, 1993), OSHA Supvy. Cert. (29CF12 1910.120). Career: geology prof. Univ. of Ottawa, 1982-83; proj. geologist Dunraine Mines, Toronto, Ont. 1983-84; geology prof. Laurentian Univ., Sudbury, Ont. 1984-85; proj. geologist Agassiz Resources, Toronto 1985; res. petrographer Construction Tech. Labs., Skokie, Ill. 1985-90; proj. geologist Applied GeoSystems, Fremont, Calif. 1990; sr. geologist EVAX Technologies, Scotts Valley, Calif. 1990-93; proj. geologist AGS, Inc. San Francisco 1993; project mgr. The Bentley Co., San Jose 1993-95, Lec Inc., Sunnyvale 1995–; mem. Assn. Engring. Geologists, Groundwater Resources Assn. of Calif.; publs: 14+ articles, thesis: Distbn. of Gold and Copper Occurrences Around an Archean Granitic Stock Near Wawa, Ont., 1982; Conservative Republican; Lutheran; rec: swimming, travel, geol. mapping, exploration. Res: D-105, 2140 Santa Cruz Ave Menlo Park 94025 Ofc: Lec Inc. 1153 Bordeaux Dr Ste 103 Sunnyvale 94089

STUDENMUND, A. HARWOOD, economist; b. Oct. 6, 1944, Cooperstown, NY; s. W.R. and Betsy (Harwood) S.; m. Jaynie M. Miller, July 12, 1980; children: Brent b. 1966, Scott b. 1989, Connell b. 1993; edn: AB, Hamilton Coll., Clinton, NY 1962-66; MA, PhD, Cornell Univ., Ithaca, NY 1966-70. Career: v.p. for student svs. Occidental Coll., Los Angeles; currently Richard W. Millar prof. of economics, Occidental Coll., L.A.; author: Using Econometrics - the best selling econometrics text in the country-2nd edit., 1992; four other books, numerous articles. Ofc: Department of Economics Occidental College Los Angeles 90041

STUMP, NORMAN ALDEN, SR., fire prevention officer, fire marshall; b. Aug. 7, 1940, Beaver Dam, Wisc.; s. Willard Henry and Sylvia (Braun) T.; m. Betty Cleaver, Oct. 19, 1962; children: Norman, Jr. b. 1963, Brenda b. 1965; edn: AA in fire sci., Butte Jr. Coll., 1974; Cert. Fire Investigator, Calif., Cert. Fire Prevention Officer, Calif. Career: fire fighter Fire Dept. City of Salina, Kans. 1961-66, Police Reserve 1963-67; City of Chico Fire Dept. 1967-72, fire engr. 1972–, fire insp./investigator 1979-93; owner Private Security, Chico 1984-87, Private Investigator, 1986–; instr. Butte Junior Coll., Oroville 1976-86; named Fireman of yr. Chico Elks (1986), Chico Exchange Club (1987); mem: Sacramento Valley Fire Prevention Assn., No. Calif. Fire Chiefs Assn. (Fire Prevention Officers Section), Calif. Conf. of Arson Investigators, No. Calif. Burn Found. (dir.), Butte Co. Arson Task Force (past pres.), Sierra Central Credit Union (1st v.p.); civic: Boy Scouts, Elks (ofcr. 1985-90), Exchange Club (bd. 1987-89), Eagles, Toastmasters; mil: airman 2c USAF 1958-61; Republican; Prot.; rec: camping, fishing, hunting, equestrian. Res: 809 Sequoyah Ave Chico 95926 Ofc: City of Chico Fire Dept. 842 Salem Chico 95928

STUTMAN, HARRIS RONALD, pediatrician, educator; b. May 7, 1947, Phila.; s. Sydney and Sally (Press) S.; m. Eileen E. Letson, Apr. 18, 1971; children: Jessica b. 1974, Timothy b. 1978; edn: BA in polit. sci., Univ. Pa., 1968; MD, Penn. State Univ., 1972; MD lic. Pa. 1973, N.J. 1976, Okla. 1982, Calif. 1986; bd. certified Am. Bd. Pediatrics 1977, recert. 1987). Career: pediatric resident Univ. Pittsburgh, 1972-75; infectious disease fellow Univ. Okla., 1982-84; chief resident pediatrics, Childrens Hosp., Pittsburgh 1975-76; pvt. practice, coord. perinatal edn. Kimball Med. Ctr., Lakewood, N.J. 1976-82; attdg. physician Univ. Okla. and Okla. Childrens Hosp. 1984-86; pediatric faculty Univ. of Okla., 1984-86, Univ. Calif. Irvine, 1986–; assoc. dir. res. Miller Childrens Hosp., Long Beach 1986-87, dir. ped. inf. dis./assoc. dir. Cystic Fibrosis Ctr., 1987–; chief of staff Miller Children's Hosp. 1993–; mem. UC Irvine Academic Senate 1986–, Human Subjects Review Com. 1987-90; awards: Mosby Award 1972, Central Okla. Pediatric Soc. Award 1983, So. Med. Assn. Found. Award 1984, Okla. Health Scis. Ctr. pediatrics award 1984, res. grants Nat. Inst. Allergy Inf. Disease, NIH 1987-94, res. grants Cystic Fibrosis Found. 1986–; Fellow Am. Acad. Pediatrics; Fellow Infectious Disease Soc. of Am.; mem.: Am. Soc. for Microbiology, Internat. Soc. for Human Mycology, W. Soc. for Ped. Res., Ped. Infectious Disease Soc., European Soc. for Clin. Microbiology, Mensa (exec. bd. 1985-86); publs: 19+ med. book chpts., 1986–, 37+ jour. articles, 1984–, 64+ res. papers, 1983–; rec: photog., computer pgmg. Res: 5952 Langport Circle Huntington Beach 92649 Miller Childrens Hospital 2801 Atlantic Ave Long Beach 90801

STYLES, BEVERLY, musician/entertainer, non-profit organization executive; b. June 6, 1923, Richmond, Va.; d. John Harry Kenealy and Juanita Russell (Robins) Carpenter; m. Wilbur Cox, Mar. 14, 1942 (div.); m. Robert Marascia, Oct. 5, 1951 (div. 1964); edn: studies w/Ike Carpenter, Hollywood 1965–, Am. Nat. Theatre Acad. 1968-69, w/Paula Raymond, Hollywood 1969-70; diploma, Masterplan Inst., Anaheim, Calif. 1970. Career: freelance performer, musician, 1947-81; owner Beverly Styles Music, Joshua Tree, Calif. 1971–; composer songs: Joshua Tree, 1975, I'm Thankful, 1978, Wow, Wow, Wow, 1986, records include: The Perpetual Styles of Beverly, 1978. Albums include: The Primitive Styles of Beverly, 1977, Colour Chords (And Moods), piano arrangement, 1990, music for The Whispering, pub. 1994; mem: Internat. Platform Assn. 1993-94, ASCAP (Gold pin award); life mem.: Professional Musicians, Local 47, Hollywood, Calif.; civic: v.p. special programs "Lawrence Program" of Calif. (public benefit, non-profit corp. to assist in recovery from alcohol and drug addiction through a structured prog.), Yucca Valley 1992–; talent coord. and co-founder (with Lawrence Rivers), "Quiet Place Studio", Yucca Valley 1994–; author: A Special Plan to Think Upon, The Truth as Seen by a Composer, 1978, A Special Prayer to Think Upon, 1983; Republican; rec: abstract artist. Ofc: PO Box 615 Joshua Tree CA 92252-0615 Tel:619/365-7473 FAX:619/369-1825

SUBOTNICK, STEVEN IRWIN, podiatrist; b. Nov. 14, 1942, Lake Oswego, Oreg.; s. Leonard and Ruth S.; m. Janice, Dec. 28, 1968; children: Mark b. 1972, Ali b. 1974, Kari b. 1976; edn: BS, Lewis and Clark Coll., 1964; grad. sch. Portland St. Univ., 1964-65; DPM (hons.), Calif. Coll. Podiatric Med., San Francisco, 1969, and MS in podiatric med., 1971; Dipl. Am. Bd. Podiatric Surgery. Career: gen. intern Highland Hosp., Oakland 1969-70; resident in foot and ankle surgery, APA fellow, 1970-71; pvt. practice/prin. Hesperian Med. Center, APC, Hayward 1971–; cons. in sports medicine field, past dir. R&D Brooks Shoe Co., podiatric surgical cons. Biomedics Corp., cons. Turn-tec Shoes (Am. Sporting Goods), cons. Viscolas div. Chattanooga Corp.; clin. prof. biomechanics and surg. Calif. Coll. Pod. Medicine, past dir. grad. edn.; adj. prof. kinesiology, CSU Hayward; lectr. family practice med. course UC Med. Ctr., S.F.; podiatric del. to 1984 Olympic Sci. Congress; CEO World Health Found., Berkeley; honors: Outstanding Young Man in Am. 1971, Who's Who in Edn. 1972, appreciation Calif. Podiatry Assn. 1980, Sports Medicine Council of Philippines 1983, Singapore Med. Soc., Malaysian Djarum Badminton Club, Indonesia; Fellow: Am. Acad. Podiatric Sports Medicine (past pres.), Am. Coll. Sports Medicine, Am. Coll. Foot Surgeons, Am. Coll. Foot Orthopedists, Am. Coll. Podopediatrics, Acad. of Ambulatory Foot Surgery, Electrodynogram Soc., Internat. Laser Surgery Soc.; mem. Calif. Pod. Med. Assn. (chmn. sports med. sect.), Aletheia Found. (bd.), Homeopathic Soc., Am. Med. Joggers Assn., Nat. Jogging Assn., Triathlon Fedn./USA (cert. athletic tnr., mem. med. com.), West Valley Track Club, Dolphin Club; numerous TV and radio appearances; author: Podiatric Sports Medicine (Futura Pub. Co., 1975), The Running Foot Doctor (World Publs., 1977), Cures for Common Running Injuries (World Publs., 1979), Sports Medicine of the Lower Extremity (1988), Cures for Comon Walking and Running Injuries (Rodale Press, 1989); mem. editl. staff numerous profl. jours. and re sports medicine and physical therapy, also advy. bd. various gen. circ. mags. of Raben Pub. Co.; lectr. nat. and internat. med. confs.; rec: running, skiing, equestrian. Ofc: 19682 Hesperian Blvd Ste 101 Hayward 94541

SUCHIN, MILTON BERNARD, producer, personal manager; b. Feb. 19, 1944, Bklyn.; s. Martin and Gizela (Mermelstein) S.; m. Vicki L. Rosenberg, June 14, 1981; edn: BS, L.I. Univ., 1971. Career: sr. talent agent Insternat. Creative Mgmt., N.Y.C. and Los Angeles, 1970-79; pres. The Moss and Suchin Corp., personal mgmt./prodn. co., 1979-81; pres./owner The Milton B. Suchin Co., personal mgmt./prodn. co., Beverly Hills, 1981–; exec. producer (interview series) Celebrity Close-Up on Showtime; producer: Gov. William Clement's fund raiser in Dallas 1981; Most Watchable Man TV show for Metromedia TV 1983; co-producer: the Calif. Celebrity 500 Auto Race, Labor Day Weekend 1979; Am. Cancer Research Ctr. show 1981; Human Dolphin Found. show, San Francisco 1981; An Evening with Sammy Davis, Jr. for Temple Emet, Los Angeles; consultant celebrity div. Cerebral Palsy Assn. fund raiser Actor's Temple, N.Y.C.; mem. entertainment commn. 3d annual L.A. Street Scene Festival 1980; awards: certificate of appreciation Mayor of Los Angeles; mem. bd. dirs: Permanent Charities Orgn., Celebrity Outreach Found., the Magic Mirror Found.; pres. Conf. of Personal Mgrs.; mem: Acad. TV Arts and Scis., Hon. Order Ky. Colonels, Friars of N.Y.C., B'nai B'rith (past v.p. Performing Arts lodge N.Y.C., trustee Entertainment Unit #5421 L.A., cert. of appreciation Dist. 1); mil: USN 1963-66. Ofc: The Suchin Co 12747 Riverside Dr Ste 208 Valley Village 91607-3333

SUDDUTH, CHARLES GRAYSON, civil and geotechnical engineer; b. Sept. 16, 1935, Oxnard; s. Charles Franklin and Leilla Eunice (Johnson) S.; edn: BS and MS in civil engring., USC, 1958, 1963, MPA, and cert. in pub. works admins., 1979; reg. civil engr., geotechnical engr. Calif. 1965, 1987. Career: civil engring. asst. Long Beach Water Dept., Long Beach 1962-63; civil engring. asst. L.A. Co. Flood Control Dist. (now Dept. of Pub. Works), Los Angeles 1963-64, senior C.E. asst. 1964-65, C.E. assoc. 1965-66, assoc. civil engr. 1967-70, civil engr. II, L.A. Dept. of County Engr., 1970-80, supvsg. civil engr. III, L.A. Dept. of County Engr. (dept. now merged into Dept. Pub. Works), 1980–; appt. mem. geotech. engring. advy. com. St. Bd. Registration for Profl. Engrs. and Land Surveyors, 1987-, secty. 1987-; apptd. mem. Geotech. Eng. Application Review Com., St. Bd. of Registration for Profl. Engs. & L.S. 1986-87; recipient Daniel Meade Prize for assoc. members Am. Soc. Civil Engrs., NY 1971; mem: ASCE/L.A. Sect. (sect. newsletter ed. & chmn. 1968-69, sect. dir. 1969-70, sec.treas. 1970-71, v.chmn. 1972-73, speakers bur. 1973-80, com. chmn.: soil mechs. 1972-73 conditions of employment 1973-74, student activities 1977-79), Assn. of Engring. Geologists, Nat. Soc. Profl. Engrs., Calif. Soc.

Profl. Engrs., Am. Waterworks Assn., Hillside Village Prop. Owners Assn. (v.p. 1973-); pub. paper: Considering Soc. Value in Engring. Projects, 1972; Republican; Presbyterian; rec: travel. Res: 1851 Boca Ave Los Angeles 90032 Ofc: L.A. Co. Dept. of Public Works 900 S Fremont Ave Alhambra 91803

SUND, MICHAEL WARREN, public and investor relations practioner; b. Sept. 2, 1943, San Diego; s. Warren LeRoy and Patricia (Connors) S.; m. Maureen Ellin Murphy, Apr. 7, 1973; children: Gretchen b. 1980, Gregory b. 1983; edn: AB journ., San Diego State Univ., 1966; MS journ., Northwestern Univ., 1967; Accredited pub. relations practitioner (APR) Pub. Relations Soc. Am., 1984. Career: reporter San Diego Tribune, 1967-69; dist. staff mgr Pacific Bell, San Diego, San Francisco, 1969-80; exec. v.p./prin. The Gable Agency, San Diego 1980-84; dir. pub. rels. Joan B. Kroc Found., San Diego 1984-86; pres./owner Mike Sund Pub. Relations, Rancho Santa Fe 1986-92; dir. corp. comms. Mycogen Corp., 1993–; lectr. UC San Diego Ext., 1984-87; mem. Nat. Investor Relations Inst.; clubs: Rancho Santa Fe Golf; civic bds: Comb. Health Agys. Drive San Diego (dir. 1991–), Roads & Traffic Commn. Rancho Santa Fe (commr. 1990–); mil: capt. USMCR 1968-72; Republican; R.Cath.; rec: golf, gardening. Ofc: Mycogen Corp 5501 Oberlin Drive San Diego 92121-1718

SUNDIN, IMO INSLEY, philanthropist, photographer, educator; b. May 27, 1910, Findlay, Ohio; d. George D. And Cora (Buck) Insley; m. Roy Sundin, 1945; children: Ralph; edn: BS, Kansas State Teachers Coll. 1933; MA in Spanish, Univ. Of Michigan 1940; cert. profl. photographer, N.Y. Inst. Of Photography 1951 (specialty: children's portraits); teacher, H.S. Spanish and Latin, Kansas, Mich., Wyoming 1934-45; mem: Delphian Soc., PEO Chpt. OW, Calif., Eastern Star, El Dorado, Kans.; author: The Uphill Fight; founding donor, Sundin Speech Disorders Found., Santa Monica, Calif.; founding donor, Sundin Leadership Inst. for Student Ambassadors, Literacy Volunteers of America, Inc., Syracuse, N.Y.; Protestant; rec: piano, organ, reading, sewing. Res: Pacific Palisades 90272

SUTTER, JOHN HERBERT, judge; b. July 15, 1928, San Francisco; s. Louis M. and Evelyn M. (Piper) S.; m. Elouise Conte, Sept. 1, 1956; children: Susan b. 1957, Maria b. 1959, Sally b. 1965; edn: BA, Harvard Univ.; LLB, Stanford Univ. Career: dep. dist. atty. Alameda Co., Oakland 1955-59; private law practice in Oakland and San Francisco, 1960-82; judge Superior Ct. Alameda County, Oakland 1982–; lectr. Contg. Edn. of the Bar, Oakland 1970, moderator 1987; lectr. Am. Bar Assn., S.F. 1982; mem. People for Open Space S.F. (1958–, pres. 1963-70), Oakland Citizens Com. for Urban Renewal (1963-71, co-chair 1970), mem. S.F. Bay Conservation & Devel. Commn. 1965-67, Oakland Mus. Assn. 1973, Save the Bay Assn. 1963, Oakland City Council (1971-82, vice mayor 1977-79), Oakland Charter Revision Com. (1962-66, 81-82), Alameda Co. Solid Waste Mgmt. Auth. 1979-82; mem., dir. Calif. Dem. Council, 1960-65, Alameda Co. Dem. Lawyers Club, 1966-67; mem: ABA, Calif. Judges Assn., Alameda Co. Bar Assn. (bd. dirs. 1970, v.chmn. com. on selection of judges 1968), Alameda Co. Lawyers Club, Calif. Judges Assn., League of Calif. Cities (actg. chmn. pub. safety com. 1980-81), Oakland Cultural Affairs Commn. 1991–, Sierra Club; author: Landslide & Subsidence Liability, 1974; mil: tech. AUS 1946-48; Presbyterian; rec: swimming, hiking. Res: 3627 Klamath St Oakland 94602 Ofc: Alameda County Superior Court 1225 Fallon St D-38, Oakland 94612

SUTTERBY, LARRY QUENTIN, physician; b. Sept. 11, 1950, North Kansas City, Mo.; s. John Albert and Wilma Elizabeth (Henry) S.; m. Luciana Risos Magpuri, July 5, 1980; children: Leah b. 1981, Liza b. 1983; edn: BA, William Jewell Coll., Liberty, Mo. 1972; MD, Univ. Missouri, K.C., Mo. 1976; certified (ABIM) Am. Bd. Internal Medicine, 1991; cert. Geriatric Medicine 1993. Career: internal medicine resident Mt. Sinai Hosp., Chgo. 1979; physician Mojave Desert Health Service, Barstow, Calif. 1979-86; physician-internist solo practice, 1986–; medical director: Hospice of Mojave Valley, 1984–, Rimrock Conv. Hosp., 1986-89, 1995–, VNA Hospice, Barstow 1994–, Optioncare Home Health Svs. 1994–; staff Barstow Comm. Hosp. (chief of staff 1983); recipient Loving Care award Visiting Nurse Assn., San Bdo. Co. 1988; mem: Soc. Gen. Internal Medicine 1990–, AMA 1980–, Calif. Med. Assn. 1980–, San Bdo. County Med. Assn. 1980–, Am. Soc. Internal Medicine 1989–, Acad. of Hospice Physicians (founding), Am. Geriatrics Soc. 1990–, Am. Numismatic Assn., Am. Coll. of Physicians, Am. Diabetes Assn., Am. Med. Directors Assn., Calif. Med. Directors Assn.; Democrat; R.Cath.; rec: astronomy, Error Lincoln cents. Ofc: 209 N 2nd Ave Barstow 92311

SWADLEY, BERNADINE HATCH, national association executive, civic volunteer; b. July 21, 1917, Paso Robles; d. Holmer J. and Ruth (Brewer) Hatch; m. Robert Hunter Swadley, June 30, 1946 (dec. Oct. 24, 1990); edn: San Jose State Univ., Stanford Univ., Rudolph Schaeffer Sch. of Design; art degree, Art Inst., Oakland. Career: pres. Swadley Enterprises, Oakland 1983–; mem. Vis. Nurse Assn. (bd. 27 yrs.), Am. Red Cross/Alameda Co. (secty. 1982), Am. Red Cross, Oakland (pres. 1987), T.B. & Health Assn. (past pres.); active Mayor's com. Oakland Clean Community Sys.; bd. dirs. Salvation Army Oakland, 1990–; elected v.p. general Nat. Soc. Daughters of the Am. Revolution, 1991-94 (Calif. State bd. 12 yrs., state regent 1980-82, hon. state regent 1982–), Children of Am.

Colonists (State chaplain 1990-94, state sr. v.p., past pres. S.F. chpt.), Daughters of Am. Colonists, Children Am. Revolution (life, state sr.v.p.), Mary Wessell Soc. CAR (senior leader), author My California Family 1972, DAR Nat. Soc. (life, numerous nat. and chapt. awards), Alameda Co. Hist. Soc. (pres., sec./treas.), mem. Conn. Hist Soc., Founders of Norwich (Conn.), The Colonial Dames of Am. (state pres.), Colonial Clergy, Magna Charta Dames, Mayflower Soc., Soc. of Descendants of Knights of the Most Noble Order of the Sartu, Flagon & Trencher, Ancestral Roster of Sixty Colonists, Order of the Crown of Charlemagne in the United States of Am., The Skyline Garden Club (founder, past pres., 1961–), Calif. Garden Clubs Inc., Calif. Art Research Commn., Rotary Intl. Oakland Sunrise Club, Oakland Mus. (Art Guild art floral com.), Women of St. Paul's Episcopal Ch. (pres. 1959), Beta Sigma Phi (past state pres.), Lakeview Club Oakland (life); Republican. Res: 5461 Fernhoff Rd Oakland 94619-3111

SWANSON, CHRISTIAN ALAN, physician and surgeon; b. Dec. 16, 1959, Oakland, Calif.; s. Stanley Keith and Joan (Danielson) S.; edn: BA, biology, Calif. St. Univ., Chico 1983; MA, cell & molecular biology, Calif. St. Univ., San Francisco 1985; MD, St. Louis Univ. Sch. of Medicine 1990. Career: dried fruit chemist, 1979; employed UC San Francisco 1984-86; Cancer Res. Inst.; physician/surgeon UC Davis Dept. of Surgery 1990–; honors: NIH Normal Volunteer 1982, Arthritis Found. Academic Fellowship 1984, Summer Inst. in Geriatrics (Boston, Mass.) 1989, Outstanding Intern, Dept. Surgery, UC Davis Med. Ctr. 1990-91; mem: Am. Coll. of Surgeons (candidate group), AMA, St. Louis Univ. Alumni Assn.; contbg. author: 4 articles to profl. jours., 1986-95, book chpt. in Modulation of the Immune Response (Marcel-Dekker Publications, NY, 1993), 6 pub. abstracts, 1985-94. Ofc: Dept of Surgery University of California, Davis 95616

SWANSON, ROBERT J., vascular surgeon; edn: undergrad. degree, Johns Hopkins Univ. 1964; MD, Univ. of Miami 1969; lic. physician, St. of Calif.; cert. Am. Bd. of Surgery: gen. surgery 1977, recertified 1987, gen. vascular surgery 1983, recert. 1993. Career: internship, San Francisco Gen. Hosp. 1969-70; gen. surgery residency, UCSF 1970-75; vascular fellowship, UCSF 1975-76; pvt. practice vascular surgery, Berkeley, Calif. 1976–; active staff Alta Bates Hosp., Berkeley; courtesy staff Brookside Hosp., San Pablo; assoc. clin. prof. surgery UCSF; chief, vascular surgery svc. Herrick Hosp. 1982-86; chmn. dept. of surgery Alta Bates Hosp. 1984-86; chmn. dept. surgery utilization mgmt. com., Alta Bates-Herrick Hosp. 1986–, trustee 1989-91; trustee Alta Bates Corp. 1989-90; pres. Alta Bates Med. Group; bd. dirs.: Alta Bates Health Systems, Calif. Health Systems; res. in field; mem: Am. Coll. of Surgeons (fellow), No. Calif. Vascular Soc. (council mem. 1986-89), East Bay Surgical Soc., Howard C. Nafziger Surgical Soc., S.F. Surgical Soc., Internat. Soc. of Cardiovascular Surgery; contbg. author: 16 articles to profl. jours. and orgns., 1968-88. Ofc: 3000 Colby St Ste 301 Berkeley 94705

SWARD, ROBERT STUART, author, poet, academic writer-in-residence; b. June 23, 1933, Chgo.; s. Dr. Irving Michael and Gertrude (Huebsch) S.;m. Sonnie Cox, Jan. 31,1956 (div. 1958); children: Cheryl b. 1957; m. Diane Kaldes, Feb. 26, 1960 (div. 1967); children: Barbara b. 1960, Michael b. 1963; m. Judith Essenson, Mar. 21, 1969 (div. 1972); children: Hannah b. 1970; m. Irina Schestakowich, Aug. 28, 1975 (div. 1987); children: Nicholas b. 1977; edn: BA (hons.), Univ. Ill., Urbana 1956; MA, Univ. Iowa, 1958; postgrad. Univ. of Bristol, Eng. 1960-61, Middlebury Coll., Vt. 1958-62. Career: writer-in-residence Connecticut Coll., New London, Conn. 1958-60, Cornell Univ., Ithaca, N.Y. 1962-64, Univ. of Iowa, Iowa City 1967-68, Univ. of Victoria, B.C., Canada 1969-73, Cabrillo Coll., Aptos, Calif. 1987–, Univ. Calif. Ext., Santa Cruz 1987–; poet-in-residence Univ. Calif. Santa Cruz 1991–; radio bdcstr. Canad. Bdcstg. Corp., Toronto 1982-84; editor, pub. Soft Press, Victoria, Can. 1970-79; assoc. fellow York Univ., Toronto 1964–; awards: Guggenheim Found. fellow 1964-66, D.H. Lawrence fellow, Univ. N.M. 1966-67, Fulbright fellow 1960-61, Canada Council grantee 1981-82, Villa Montalvo Award, Saratoga, Calif. 1990, Djerass Found. fellow 1990-93; mem: Nat. Writers Union 1985–, Modern Poetry Assn. 1992–, Phi Beta Kappa 1956–, League of Canadian Poets 1970–, Calif. St. Teachers Assn. 1987–; civic: creative writing instr. Oak Bay Sr. Citizens, Victoria, B.C., Can., 1970s, Poet In the Schools Pgm., Cultural Council of Santa Cruz Co. 1985–; author fiction, poetry, 16 books incl: Four Incarnations, Poems, 1991, Poet Santa Cruz 1985, Half A Life's History, 1983, Kissing The Dancer, 1964; autobiography: Contemporary Authors Autobiography Series (CAAS), Vol. 13, 1991; mil: Y3c US Navy 1951-54; Democrat; rec: photog., computers. Res: 435 Meder St Santa Cruz 95060 Ofc: PO Box 7062 Santa Cruz 95061

SWARTZLANDER, EARL EUGENE, JR., engineering educator; b. Feb. 1, 1945, San Antonio, TX; s. Earl Eugene and Jane (Nicholas) S.; m. Joan Vickery, June 9, 1968; edn: BS, Purdue Univ., 1967; MS, Univ. of Colo., 1969; PhD, USC, 1972; reg. profl. engr. in Ala., Calif., Colo. and Texas. Career: devel. engr. Ball Bros. Research Corp., Boulder, CO 1967-69; Howard Hughes doctoral fellow Hughes Aircraft Co., Culver City, CA 1969-73; mem. research staff Technology Svc. Corp., Santa Monica 1973-74; chief engr. Geophysical Sys. Corp., Pasadena 1974-75; sr. staff engr. TRW Defense & Space Sys. Gp.,

Redondo Beach 1975-79; asst. mgr. TRW Huntsville Lab., Huntsville, AL 1980-81; mgr. advanced devel. TRW Defense Systems Group, Redondo Bch. 1982-85; mgr. digital processing lab. TRW Electronic Systems Gp., Redondo Bch. 1985-87, dir. IR&D TRW Defense Systems Group, 1987-90; prof. electrical and computer engring. Univ. of Texas, Austin 1990–; speaker univ. seminars at UCLA, Univ. Md., American Univ., Univ. Mich., Auburn Univ., Univ. Minn., George Mason Univ., others 1978–; awards: Howard Hughes doctoral fellow 1969-72, Best Paper award Hawaii conf. on sys. sci. 1983, Tech. Paper award Internat. Systolic Arrays Workshop, Oxford 1986, Purdue Univ. disting. engring. alumnus 1989, Schlumberger Centennial Chair in Engring. 1990–, Louisiana Disting. Lectr. 1991, Purdue Univ. outstanding electrical engr. 1992, Knight, Imperial Russian Order of Saint John of Jerusalem (knights of Malta) 1993; Fellow IEEE 1988, mem. IEEE Computer Soc. (bd. of govs. 1987-91), IEEE Signal Proc. Soc. (bd. of govs. 1992-94), IEEE Solid-State Circuits Council (secty. 1992-93, treas. 1994–); civic: Casiano Estates (dir. 1976-79, pres. 1979-80), Benedict Hills Estates Homeowners Assn. (dir. 1984–, pres. 1991–); author: VLSI Signal Processing Systems (Kluwer Academic Pub. 1985); 100+ papers on signal processing, computer architecture and VLSI; editor-in-chief: J. of VLSI Signal Processing, 1989-95, IEEE Transactions on Computers, 1991-94, IEEE Transactions on Signal Processing, 1995–, ed. IEEE Transactions on Computers, 1982-86, IEEE Transactions on Parallel and Distributed Systems, 1989-90, assoc. ed. IEEE J. of Solid-State Circuits, 1984-88, area ed. ACM Computing Reviews, 1982–; book editor: Computer Design Development, (Hayden Book Co. 1976), Computer Arithmetic (Dowden, Hutchinson & Ross Pub. Co. 1980), Systolic Signal Processing Systems (Marcel Dekker Inc. 1987), Wafer Scale Integration (Kluwer Academic Pub. 1989), Computer Arithmetic Vol. 1 and Vol. 2 (IEEE Computer Soc. Press, 1990). Ofc: Univ. of Texas at Austin, Dept. of Electrical & Computer Engineering, Austin TX 78712

SWEENEY, W(ILLIAM) ALAN, research scientist; b. Sept. 12, 1926, Ocean Falls, B.C., Canada, naturalized U.S. cit., 1958; s. William Patrick and Florence Harriet (Lewthwaite) S.; m. Sally Grant, Apr. 11, 1953; children: Michael A. b. 1954, Peter G. b. 1955, Alison E. b. 1959; edn: B.A.Sc. chem. eng., Univ. British Columbia, Vancouver B.C., 1949; PhD. org. chem., Univ. Washington, Seattle, 1954; 5 ext. courses UC Berkeley 1967-71, also 30+ short courses - human rels., mgmt., personal skills. Career: devel. chemist Canadian Industries Ltd., Toronto, Ontario, Can., 1949-50; res. chemist to res. scientist Chevron Research & Technology Co., Richmond, Calif. 1954-90, mgmt. positions 1964, 75, 84, 86; cons. (internal) Chevron Res. & Tech. Co., 1976-90; cons. Teltech Inc., Mpls., Mn. 1990; cons. D.O.E., Idaho Falls, Id. 1990; awards: scholar Univ. of Brit. Col. (1944, 45), Procter & Gamble fellow Univ. Wash. 1952, Phi Lambda Upsilon 1953, Sigma Xi 1954; mem: Am. Chemical Soc. 1951–, N.Y. Acad. of Scis. 1970–, Chevron Employee Clubs; civic: HOA, Larkspur (pres., bd. 1979-82), United Way - Chevron (chmn., dept. ldr. 72, 73, 86), Marin Co. Canoe Club, PTA; inventor, 100+ Patents in petrochemical area (1961-90); publs: 5 tech. papers on biodegradability (1964-89), Kirk-Othmer Review article on BTX (1991), 9 papers on academic & petrochem. resrch. (1954-69), newsletter articles on technology & org. behavior (1989-90); mil: Canadian OTC 1944-45; Republican; rec: tennis, bridge, travel, boating, hiking. Res: 27 Corte Del Bayo, Larkspur 94939

SWOPE, ALAN JOSEPH, psychologist; b. April 24, 1942, Cleveland, Ohio; s. Floyd Keene and Leone Louise (Davis) S.; m. Bonnie Lee Sokall, June 6, 1976; children: Alison b. 1979, Laura b. 1982; edn: BA, Hiram Coll. 1964: PhD, Columbia Univ. 1969; dipl. Am. Bd. Profl. Psychology 1975. Career: clin. psychologist City of Berkeley 1970-82; pvt. practice, Berkeley 1971–; prof. Wright Inst. 1978–; dir. profl. tng. Calif Sch. Profl. Psychology 1983–; mem. Am. Bd. Profl. Psychology 1983-88; oral commr. and expert cons. Bd. of Psychology, Calif. 1978–; mem: Am. Psychological Assn., Nat. Register Health Providers, Calif. St. Psychological Assn.; articles pub. in profl. jours. Ofc: 3155 College Ave Berkeley 94705

SYDOR, MARCIA LE DUC, teacher, resource specialist program; b. June 11, 1933, Antioch, Calif.; d. Marc Francis and Alice Lela (Lyon) Le Duc; m. Allan Ellsworth Trimble, Dec. 26, 1954; children: Brian b. 1955, Arthur b. 1957, Alysse b. 1959; m. Richard Paul Sydor, Aug. 24, 1984; edn: BA, UC Berkeley, 1954; MA, CSU Sacramento, 1972. Career: secty. Teachers Coll., Columbia Univ., NYC 1963-64; tchr., spl. edn. specialist, Resource Splst. Pgm., Sacramento City Unified Schs., 1967–; life mem. Nat. Edn. Assn.; mem. Toastmasters Internat./Santa Ana (1972–, past internat. dir., internat. awards: DTM 5t, ATM 5t, ATM Bronze 5t, ATM Silver 5t, internat. pres.'s citation 8/89, No. CA/NV Dist. TM of Yr. 1981, 85, Disting. Sustained Svc. award 1995), D.A.R. (regent 1993-95, chair State Com.), Zeta Tau Alpha Alumni (historian 1982–), Sierra Camera Club (past pres. 1981-83, gen. chair N.Am. Internat. Photog. Exh. 1989, service award 1978), PTA Sacto., Sacto. Youth Band Parent's Assn. (service awards 1975, 76), Colonial Daughters of Indian Wars, Boy Scouts (den mother tng. award 1967, den ldr. coach's tng. award 1969); Canadian Polit. Party impartial observer and chair "Western Canada Concept" Annual Conv., Red Deer, Alberta, Can. 1982; Republican; Christian; rec: photography, pub. speaking. Res: 1092 Salmon Dr Roseville 95661

SZEGO, CLARA MARIAN, cell biologist, educator; b. Mar. 23, 1916, Budapest, Hungary, naturalized U.S. 1927; d. Paul S. and Helen (Elek) S.; m. Sidney Roberts, Sept. 14, 1943; edn: AB, Hunter Coll., 1937; MS (Garvan fellow) Univ. Minn., 1939, PhD, 1942. Career: instr. physiology Univ. Minn. 1942-43; Minn. Cancer Res. Inst. fellow 1943-44; rsch. assoc. OSRD, Nat. Bur. Stds. 1944-45, Worcester Found. Exptl. Biology 1945-47; res. instr. physiol. chemistry Yale Univ. Sch. Medicine 1947-48; faculty UC Los Angeles, 1948–, prof. biology, 1960–, res. on steroid protein interactions, mechanisms of hormone action and lysosome participation in normal cell function; awards: Woman of Year in Sci. Los Angeles Times 1957-58, Guggenheim fellow 1956-57, inducted Hunter Coll. Hall of Fame 1987, CIBA award Endocrine Soc. 1953, Phi Beta Kappa (pres. UCLA chpt. 1973-74), Sigma Xi (pres. UCLA chpt. 1976-77); mem.: AAAS (Fellow), Am. Physiol. Soc., Am. Soc. Cell Biology, Endocrine Soc., Soc. for Endocrinology (G.B.), Biochem. Soc. (G.B.), Internat. Soc. Research Reprodn.; numerous sci. publs. in field. Res: 1371 Marinette Rd Pacific Palisades 90272 Ofc: UCLA Dept. Molecular, Cell, and Developmental Biology, Los Angeles 90024-1605

TAEKMAN, MICHAEL SEYMOUR, neurological surgeon, pediatric neurosurgeon; b. June 30, 1937, Chgo., Ill.; s. Harry Joseph and Rose Anne (Sturner) T.; m. Ilene Roberta Erlich, Dec. 18, 1960; children: Jeffrey b. 1964, Jennifer b. 1967, Jessica b. 1970; edn: BS, Univ. of Ill., Chgo. 1958, MD, 1962. Career: internship Univ. of Ill. 1962-63, residency 1963-67; fellowship Univ. of Edinburgh, Scotland 1967; cons. Chgo. Contagious Disease, Chgo., Ill. 1968; pres. East Bay Med. Group, Berkeley 1969–; instr. Univ. of Ill. 1964-67; asst. prof. Univ. of Calif. San Francisco 1969-89, assoc. prof. 1989–; lectr. UC Berkeley 1975–; chief, dept. neurosurgery Alta Bates Hosp., Berkeley 1970–, Children's Hosp. Oakland 1972; chief, dept. surgery Children's Hosp. Oakland 1980-86; awards: Travel Scholarship, Internat. Coll. of Surgeons 1967, fellowship Univ. of Edinburgh 1967; mem: CMA 1969–, ACCMA 1970–, San Francisco Neurological Soc. 1970–, Am. Coll. of Surgeons 1971–, Am. Assn. Neurological Surgeons 1971–, Phi Eta Sigma 1958–, Activities Honorary, Chgo. 1955-58; author: Pituitary Tumor, 1980; contbr. num. neurosurgical articles to profl. jours., 1970–; mil: capt. USAF 1964-71; Republican; Jewish; rec: fly fishing, tennis.

TAFOYA, PETE EDWARD, civil engineering executive; b. Nov. 28, 1948, Visalia; s. Romaldo M. and Jessie (Anguiano) T.; 1 dau., Christina, b. 1976; edn: AA eng., Coll. of the Sequoias, 1968; BS aero. eng., Cal Poly, S.L.O., 1971; MSCE, Univ. Idaho, 1976; grad. NAVFAC Exec. Devel. Pgm., 1986-88; reg. Profl. Engr., Calif. and Ida., 1976; lic. gen. contr., Calif., 1981; Calif. Comm. Colls. instr. cred. (life), 1989. Career: sr. engr. Structures Div., Rockwell Intl. Corp., Downey 1971-75; sr. struct. analyst Applied Mechanics Div., EG&G Corp., Idaho Falls, Ida. 1975-77; consulting engr., owner Paragon Consulting & Constrn., Visalia, Calif. 1977-78, Oxnard 1981–; research struct. engr. Naval Civil Engring. Lab., Port Hueneme 1978-82, shore facilities asst. program mgr. 1982-83, dir. Facilities Engring. Support Office, 1983-86; dept. hd. sealift support, Civil Engring. Support Office, Naval Constrn. Battalion Ctr., Port Hueneme 1986-87; dir. Mech. Systems Div., Naval Civil Engring. Lab., Port Hueneme 1987–; recipient numerous profl. and community svc. awards including: Mexican American Engring. Soc. nat. scholarship 1983-84 and MAES Engr. of Yr. 1984, appreciation Equal Opp. Publs. for articles in "Minority Engineering" 1984, tech. paper and presentation awards 7th Nat. Symp. on Engring. 1983, appreciation for svc. to Mex. Am. community Calif. St. Sen. Gary K. Hart and U.S. Sen. Pete Wilson 1984, appreciation for contbns. to math. engring. and sci. achiev. pgms. Oxnard and Channel Islands High Sch. MESA Pgms. 1981; elected bd. trustees Ventura County Comm. Coll. Dist., 1989–; mem: ASME, Mex. Am. Engr. Soc. (nat. mem. chair 1980-82, we. region v.p. 82-84, Ventura Co. chapt. pres. 1981-82), Future Leaders of Am. (nat. bd. 1989–); R.Cath. Res: 541 Pacific Cove Dr Port Hueneme 93041 Ofc: Naval Facilities Engineering Service Ctr, ESC45, Environmental Dept Port Hueneme 93043

TAIMUTY, SAMUEL ISAAC, physicist; b. Dec. 20, 1917, West Newton, Pa.; s. Elias and Samia (Hawatt) T.; m. Betty Jo Travis, Sept. 12, 1953 (dec.); children: Matthew, Martha; m. Rosalie Richards, Apr. 3, 1976; edn: BS, Carnegie Mellon Univ., 1940; PhD, USC, 1951. Career: sr. physicist U.S. Naval Shipyards, Philadelphia, Pa. and Long Beach, Calif. 1942-46; research asst. USC, 1947-51; sr. physicist U.S. Naval Radiological Defense Lab., 1950-52, SRI Internat., Menlo Park 1952-72; sr. staff engr. Lockheed Missiles & Space Co., Sunnyvale 1972-89; cons. physicist 1971–; mem. Am. Physical Soc., Sigma Xi; patentee, sci. publs. in field. Res: 3346 Kenneth Dr Palo Alto 94303

TAKI, GHAZI H., food scientist; b. Dec. 23, 1933, Baghdad, Iraq; s. Hussni A. and Zainab (Alousi) T.; m. Menal Alousi, Nov. 17, 1958 (div. 1971); m. Beverly Gilliam, Dec. 19, 1981; children: John b. 1962, Adam b. 1983; edn: BS, Univ. Baghdad Iraq 1956; MS, Okla. St. Univ. 1961; PhD, Univ. Fla. 1965. Career: asst. instr. Univ. Baghdad, Iraq 1956-59; grad. asst. Okla. St. Univ., Stillwater 1960-61; research asst. Univ. Fla., Gainesville 1962-65; dir. product devel. Seymour Foods Inc., Topeka, Kans. 1965-68; dir. res. and devel. Frank Tea & Spice Co., Cincinnati, Ohio 1968-70; dir. research Adolphs Food Products, N. Hollywood, Calif. 1970-75; mgr. new product devel. Chesebrough Ponds Inc., Trumball, Conn. 1975-76; mng. dir. Food & Culinary Technologies, Malibu

1976–; pres. Microwave Foods Inc. 1977–; pres. Seasonex 1994–; mem: Inst. Food Technologists, Am. Meat Sci. Assn., Internat. Microwave Power Inst., Shriners; num. papers pub. in sci. jours.; mil: 1st lt. Iraqi Army 1957-58; rec: hiking, music, gardening. Res: 2633 Coal Cyn Rd Malibu 90265

TALLEY, WILSON K., foundation executive, professor emeritus; b. Jan. 27, 1935, St. Louis, Mo.; s. Samuel K. and Isabella G. (McCurtain) T.; m. Helen, July 1, 1981; children: Steve b. 1962, Elaine b. 1964, Edward b. 1965, (stepdau.) Donna b. 1959; edn: BA, UC Berkeley, 1956; MS, Univ. Chgo., 1957; PhD, UC Berkeley, 1963. Career: asst. prof, prof. Dept. Applied Sci. UC Davis 1963-91, prof. emeritus 1991–; asst. to dir. Lawrence Livermore Nat. Lab. 1991-94; White House Fellow 1969-70; hd. theoretical physics div. Lawrence Livermore Nat. Lab. 1971; asst. v.p. Univ. of Calif. statewide, 1971-74; dir., pres. Fannie and John Hertz Found. 1972–; study dir. Commn. on Critical Choices for Americans, N.Y.C. 1974; asst. adminstr. for res. USEPA, Wash. D.C. 1974-77; dir. Helionetics Inc. 1982-86; tech. advy. bds.: Johnson Controls 1981–, Phoenix Laser Systems Inc. 1989-93; awards: disting. pub. adminstr. Denver Univ. 1976, outstanding civilian svc. medal AUS 1986; mem: AAAS (fellow), Army Sci. Bd. (chmn. 1983-86, 1995–), Army Medical Res. Advy. Bd. 1989-93, NSF Math. and Physical Scis. advy. bd. 1993; clubs: Commonwealth, Capitol Hill, Castlewood Country Club; patentee; author 2 books, 36+ research papers; Republican. Ofc: Hertz Foundation, Box 5032 Livermore 94551-5032

TAMAROFF, MARC ALLEN, physician; b. May 22, 1948, Phoenix, Ariz.; s. Sam Al and June Ann T.; m. Sybil Abelsky, Nov. 26, 1978; children: David, b. 1980; Rachael, b. 1986; edn: BS, Univ. of Ariz. 1970, MD, 1974. Career: intern St. Mary Med. Ctr., Long Beach 1974; resident internal med. 1975-7; post-doc. fellow Div. of Clin. Immunology & Allergy, UCLA Med. Ctr. 1977-79; pvt. practice, Allergy 1979–; assoc. dir. for Pgm. Developments, Ctr. for Interdisciplinary Research in Immunologic Diseases (CIRID) UCLA 1979-86; assoc. dir. of Skin Test Svc. and spl. cons. Div. of Clin. Immunol. & Allergy UCLA Med. Ctr. 1979-80; chmn. med. edn. com.Los Altos Hosp., Long Beach 1980-84; chmn. pharmacy & therapeutics com. St. Mary Med. Ctr., Long Beach 1988-91; asst. clin. prof. medicine UC Irvine 1982-85, UCLA 1985–; awards: Phi Kappa Phi 1970, AMA Physician Recognition 1977, Calif. Med. Assn. 1979; Nat. Research Svc. Award, NIH-PHS 1977-79; mem: Am. Coll. of Chest Physicians, Am. Coll. of Allergists, Los Angeles Soc. of Allergy and Clin. Immunology (exec. Council 1990-95, pres. 1993), Long Beach Soc. of Internal Medicine (pres. 1990-92), Immunology Research Group. UCLA Sch. Med., Am. Lung Assn., Asthma & Allergy Found. of Am., Am. Acad. of Allergy, Am. College of Allergy, Asthma & Immunology, Am. College of Chest Physicians; pub. med. research; Democrat; Jewish; rec: tennis, softball. Res: 18171 Ivorycrest Ln Huntington Beach 92648 Ofc: Allergy & Asthma Care Center, 3325 Palo Verde Ste 107 Long Beach 90808

TAN, DIANE MAY LEW, government lawyer; b. Feb. 1, 1951, West Hollywood; d. James Tan and Choon Guey (Louie) Lew; m. King H. Cheung; edn: BA, USC, 1973; grad. studies USC, 1973-75; JD, USC Law Sch. 1978; admitted Calif. Bar (1979). Career: atty., assoc. Fred Hong, Los Angeles 1979-80; dep. pub. defender Office of Calif. State Pub. Defender, L.A. 1980-84; staff atty. Calif. Dept. Fair Employment & Housing, L.A. 1984-92, dep. atty. gen. health quality enforcement sect. Office of the Atty. Gen., L.A. 1992–; awards: Outstanding Young Women of Am. (1986); mem: St. Bar Human Rights Com. (1986-89), Japanese Am. Bar Assn. (bd. 1991, sec. 1990, bd. govs. 1989), St. Bar Juvenile Justice Com. (1982-84), So. Calif. Chinese Lawyers Assn. (bd. 1980-81), L.A. County Bar Assn. (minority rep. in the legal prof. com. 1994–), St. Bar Ethnic Minority Rels. Com. 1992-94, Japanese Am. Bar Assn. (bd. govs. 1992–, Liaison Rep. Multicultural Bar Alliance 1991–), Asian Pacific Am. Women Lawyers Alliance (founding mem/ 1993–), Women Lawyers Assn. of L.A. 1994, Calif. Women Lawyers Assn. 1994–, So. Calif. Chinese Lawyers Assn. 1992–, USC Gen. Alumni Assn.; Democrat; rec: cooking, photog., travel. Ofc: Dept. of Justice, Office of Attorney General, Health Quality Enforcement Sect. 300 S Spring St 5th Flr Los Angeles 90013

TAN, GEORGE C., banking and securities financial information services consultant, real estate investor; b. Mar. 23, 1959, Singapore; s. Richard Cheong-Heong and Sok (Wah) T.; m. Anna S. Luo, Jan. 16, 1985; edn: BA UC Berkeley, 1983; grad. bus. MBA pgm., MIT Sloan School 1995. Career: investor/mgr. real estate props., Burlingame, Calif. 1981-87; system specialist Systematics Inc., San Francisco 1984-86; pgmg. analyst Industrial Indemnity, S.F. 1986-87; technical cons. Interactive Data Corp., S.F. 1987-88, product mgr. 1988-90, senior product mgr. 1990-91; mgmt. cons. to capital mkts., Bank of Am., S.F. 1991-93; systems re-engring. cons. 1994; assoc. ptnr. & sr. prin., American Management Systems Inc. 1995–; honors: 1st string center-fielder Lynx Softball Team Cath. H.S., C.J.C. Singapore 1972-77, Championship Exhib. Games Asia Softball Orgn. in Singapore, Hong Kong, Thailand, Korea 1975, Interactive Data 1988, nominee best prod. mgr. 1989; mem. MIT Real Estate Assn., S.F. 1991-93; rec: MIT's Masters Swimming Team, marathons (NYC 1994), sailing. Res: 2390 39th Ave #1 San Francisco 94116

TANAKA, JEANNIE E., lawyer; b. Jan. 21, 1942; d. Togo W. and Jean M. Tanaka; edn: BA, Internat. Christian Univ., Tokyo 1966; MSW, UCLA, 1968; JD, Washington Coll. of Law, American Univ., W.D.C., 1984. Career: atty., assoc. Seki & Jarvis, Los Angeles 1984-86; Jones, Day et al 1986-87; Reavis & McGrath 1987-89; asst. counsel Union Oil Co., L.A. 1989-91; legal counsel pvt. practice, 1992–; corporations counsel Dept. of Corporations; instr. Aoyama Gakuin; Meiji Gakuin; Sophia Univ.; Tokyo, Japan 1968-75; prog. devel. Encyclopedia Britannica Inst., Tokyo 1976-78; instr. Honda, Mitsubishi, Ricoh Corps., Tokyo 1975-80; with edit. dept. Simul Internat., Tokyo; mem: Japanese Am. Bar Assn., Am. Bar Assn., Calif. Bar Assn., D.C. Bar Assn.; civic: Japan America Soc.; Methodist. Addr: 100 S Doheny Dr Ste 322 Los Angeles 90048

TANAKA, KOUICHI ROBERT, medical educator; b. Dec. 15, 1926, Fresno; s. Kenjiro and Teru (Arai) T.; m. Grace Mutsuko Sakaguchi, Oct. 23, 1965; children: Anne b. 1970, Nancy b. 1973, David b. 1974; edn: BS, Wayne St. Univ. 1949; MD, Wayne St. Univ. Sch. Medicine 1952. Career: intern Los Angeles Co. Gen. Hosp., 1952-53; resident, fellow Detroit Receiving Hosp., Mich. 1953-57; instr. medicine UCLA Sch. Medicine 1957-59, asst. prof. medicine 1959-61, assoc. prof. medicine 1961-68, prof. medicine 1968–; honors: Alpha Omega Alpha, Sigma Xi, Wayne St. Univ. Disting. Alumni Service 1981; mem: Am. Soc. Clin. Investigation, Assn. Am. Physicians, Western Assn. Physicians, Am. Soc. Hematology, Internat. Soc. Hematology, L.A. Soc. Internal Medicine (pres.); 130+ articles pub. in sci. jours.; mil: AUS 1946-48; Republican; Methodist; rec: horticulture. Res: 4 Cayuse Ln Rancho Palos Verdes 90275 Ofc: Harbor-UCLA Medical Ctr. Box 400 Torrance 90509

TANAKA, RICHARD KOICHI, architect/planner; b. Oct. 16, 1931, San Jose; s. Richard Inoru and Mae Yoshiko (Koga) T.; m. Barbara Hisako Kumagai, Oct. 7, 1961; children: Craig Koji b. 1962, Todd Tadashi b. 1963, Sandra Kimi b. 1964, Trent Kiyoshi b. 1974; edn: B.Arch., Univ. Mich. 1954; M.Urban Planning, CSU San Jose 1970. Desig: corporate mem. Am. Inst. Architects, AIA, Am. Inst. of Planning, AIP, Constrn. Specification Inst., CSI. Career: designer, later prin. architect, Newlon Greene Architects, 1954-58; exec. v.p./ptnr. The Steinberg Group, Architects, Planner 1958–; awards: for best comml. project in the West (1982), recipient commendations- S.J. Bicentennial Com., JACL, and Santa Clara Co. Board Supvrs., human relations/ human rights award Santa Clara Co. Human Relations Commn., recogn. awards- City of San Jose, East Side Union H.S. Dist., Asian Am. Educators Assn.; civic: NCCJ (bd. govs.), Boy Scouts Am. Santa Clara Co. (bd. govs.), Alum Rock Park Plng. Com., East Side Union H.S. Dist. (pres. bd. trustees), San Jose Bicentennial Commn. (chmn.), S. J. Tapestry in Talent (pres.), S.J. Parks and Rec. (goals subcom. chmn.), S.J. Symphony (bd.), Santa Clara Co. Human Rels. Commn., Japanese Am. Citizens League (pres. 1971, 72), CSUSJ Counselor Ednl. Com., S.J. Commn. on Internment of local Japanese Americans (chmn.), San Jose/Evergreen Comm. Coll. (trustee 1992, pres. 1993-94), Calif. Comm. Coll. (trustee 1993–); Democrat; rec: painting, golf. Res: 14811 Whipple Ct San Jose 95127 Ofc: The Steinberg Group, San Jose

TANAKA, TOGO WILLIAM, real estate and financial executive; b. Jan 7, 1916, Portland, Oreg.; s. Masaharu and Katsu T.; m. Jean Wada, Nov. 14, 1940; children: Jeannie b. 1942, Christine b. 1944, Wesley b. 1950; edn: BA pol. sci., UC Los Angeles 1936; grad. studies Univ. Chgo. 1944; Career: editor Calif. Daily News 1935-36; L.A. Japanese Daily News 1936-42; Manzanar Relocation Center, Apr.-Dec. 1942; staff Am. Friends Service Com., Chgo. 1943-45; ed./hd. publs. Am. Tech. Soc. (Chgo.) 1945-50; pub. Chicago Publishing Corp. 1950-55; editor American School News, 1949-68; publisher School-Industrial Press, Los Angeles 1955-68; pres./CEO Gramercy Ents., Los Angeles 1960-80, bd. chmn. 1980–; chmn. T.W. Tanaka Co. 1980–; dir: Fed. Reserve Bank of S.F. 1979-88, Los Angeles Wholesale Produce Market Devel. Corp.; advy. council Calif. World Trade Commn. 1985-87; former commnr. Los Angeles Community Redevel. Agy.; honors: Phi Beta Kappa, Pi Gamma Mu, Pi Sigma Alpha, merit award Soc. for Advancement of Mgmt. 1950, 1st award Internat. Council Indsl. Editors 1955, UNESCO Literacy Award 1974, L.A. Catholic Archbishop ecumenical award 1986; civic: Los Angeles Area C.of C. (past dir.), Methodist Hosp. of So. Calif. (bd. dirs.1978-93), L.A. chpt. Nat. Safety Council, Am. Red Cross, Goodwill Industries of So. Calif. (past dir.), L.A. Visitors and Conv. Bur., Wellness Community -Nat., Nat. Strategy Information Ctr. (N.Y.); trustee Whittier Coll.; Commn. on Innovation, Calif. Community Colls., Western Justice Ctr. Found.; clubs: Los Angeles Rotary No. 5 (past pres., dir.), Lincoln, Shriners, Beverly Hills Lodge, Masons; co-author w/ Frank Kern Levin, English Composition & Rhetoric 1948, w/ Dr. Jean Bordeaux, How To Talk More Effectively 1948, w/ Alma Meland, Easy Pathways in English 1950; Republican; United Methodist; rec: gardening, world travel; Res: 949 Malcolm Ave Los Angeles 90024 Ofc: 626 Wilshire Blvd Ste 400 Los Angeles 90017

TANIS, NORMAN EARL, retired dean of university libraries and library expert; b. Aug. 15, 1929, Grand Rapids, Mich.; s. Aaron Orrie and Gertrude (Medendorp) T.; m. Terese Tiernan, Dec. 27, 1981; children: Kathy, b. 1962; Laura, b. 1964; edn: AB, Calvin Coll. 1951; AMLS, Univ. of Mich. 1951; MA, 1956. Career: library coord. Henry Ford Comm. Coll., Dearborn, Mich. 1956-66; library dir. Kans. State Univ., Pittsburgh 1966-9; dir. univ. libs. CSU Northridge 1969-88, dean of university libraries 1988-91; editor/mgr. The Santa Susana Press 1973–; secty. and mem. bd. trustees Univ. San Fernando Coll. of Law 1978-80; v.p./bd. mem. Univ. Club 1988-89; honors: Phi Kappa Phi, Beta Phi Mu, and DHL (hon.) Univ. San Fernando 1975, LLD (hon.) Mid-Valley Coll. Law 1979, Kts. of Col. 1991, Knight Cmdr. Order of the Templars 1989, Ordo Sancti Constantini Magni 1991, Hospitaller Knight of St. Lazarus of Jerusalem 1992–, dist. alumnus Univ. Mich. Sch. of Information & Libr. Sci. (3/28/89), Nat. Libr. Assn. (pres. 1980), Assn. of Calif. & Res. Libraries (pres. 1973-74); mem: Hist. Soc. of So. Calif. 1993–, Order of St. Lawrence-Malta (Duke) 1993–, Catholic Lib. Assn. 1993–, Calif. Academic & Res. Librarians 1989–, Book Club of Calif. 1989–, Publishers Mktg. Assn., Pacific Ctr. for the Book Arts, COS-MEP, Am. Film Inst., Nat. Trust for Preservation, Marine Memorial Club of San Francisco 1976–, Rounce & Coffin Club 1978–, China Inst. (Northridge) 1988–; ed. of the series: People of Achievement in So. Calif.; author books: Cost Analysis of Libr. Functions (Jai Press 1978), Fiscal & Acquisition (Santa Susana Press 1977), Implications of the Tax Reform Act of 1969 (Santa Susana Press 1969), The Faculty Speaks (Kansas State College 1968), Three Hundred Million Books (Tamalpais Press 1974), Libr. Svcs. for Kansas State Coll. (Kansas State Coll. 1968), Lynton R. Kistler: Printer-Lithographer (Santa Susana Press 1976), The Twilight of Orthodoxy in New England (Santa Susana Press 1987); coauthor: Native Americans of North America (Scarecrow Press 1975), Problems in Developing Academic Library Functions (Jai Press 1978), China in Books (Jai Press 1979); mil: cpl. US Army 1952-4, Nat. Defense Medal.; Democrat; Cath.; rec: theatre, travel, swap meets, horsemanship, art collector. Res: 10009 Jovita Chatsworth 91311 Ofc: Calif. State University 18111 Nordhoff Northridge 91330

TANNEN, RICHARD L., university professor and department chairman; b. Aug. 31, 1937, NY, NY; s. Harold and Fannie (Rosenberg) T.; m. Elizabeth W. Harriman, Aug. 8, 1964 (div. 1990); m. 2d. Vivien R. Parkhouse Baraban, Nov. 17, 1990; children: Bradford b. 1965, Whitney b. 1968, Alison b. 1971, Jennifer Baraban b. 1972, Julie Baraban b. 1974; edn: attended Vanderbilt Univ., Nashville, Tenn. 1954-57; MD, Univ. of Tenn., Memphis 1960; med. lic. Tenn., Mass., Maryland, Vermont, Mich., Calif.; diplomate Am. Bd. Internal Medicine. Career: surgical intern, Univ. of Fla., Gainesville 1960-61; med. intern Peter Bent Brigham Hosp., Boston, Mass. 1961-62, jr. resident in medicine 1962-63; res. fellow New England Med. Ctr., Boston, Mass. 1963-65; sr. resident in medicine Peter Bent Brigham Hosp. 1965-66; res. internist Dept. of Metabolism, Walter Reed Army Inst. of Res., W.D.C. 1966-69; asst. in medicine Harvard Med. Sch. 1965-66; asst. prof. and co-dir. nephrology unit, Dept. Medicine, Univ. of Vermont 1969-73, assoc. prof. and dir. 1973-78, acting assoc. chmn. 1975-76; vis. scientist Dept. of Clin. Biochem., The Radcliffe Infirmary, Oxford, England 1976-77; prof. and dir nephrology div., Dept. Internal Medicine, Univ. of Mich. Med. Sch. 1978-88; acting chief nephrology div., VA Hosp., Ann Arbor, Mich. 1978-82; prof. dept. of physiology, Univ. of Mich. Med. Sch. 1982-88; assoc. chmn. res. progs., dept. internal medicine, Univ. of Mich. Med. Sch. 1987-88; dir. George M. O'Brien, Univ. of Mich. Kidney Res. Ctr. 1987-88; chair and prof. dept. of medicine, Univ. of So. Calif. Med. Sch. 1988–; chief, medicine, LAC/USC Med. Ctr. 1988–; prof. dept. of physiology, USC Med. Sch. 1988–; vis. prof.: Case We. Reserve, Univ. of Fla., Penn. State, Cornell, Stoneybrook, 1983-84, Mt. Sinai Med. Sch., Albert Einstein, McGill, Univ. of Chgo., Tufts, 1984-85; Pfizer vis. prof., Boston City Hosp. 1988; Max Martin Salick vis. prof., UCLA 1988; vis. prof.: George Washington Univ. 1992, Emory Univ. 1992, Tulane Univ. 1993, UMDNJ-New Jersey Med. Sch. 1994; Howard P. Lewis vis. prof. Univ. of Ore. 1994; invited speaker/guest speaker, num. universities and profl. assn. meetings, 1983-94; honors: Alpha Omega Alpha, Established Investigator, Am. Heart Assn., NIH Merit Award 1986, President's Award, Nat. Kidney Found. 1986, Disting. Svc. Award, Nat. Kidney Found. 1989, internat. advy. bd. The Jour. of Kuwait Med. Assn. 1986-90, Pasteur Medal, Univ. of Strasbourg 1990, Disting. Alumnus Award, Univ. of Tenn. Coll. Medicine 1991, listed Who's Who in Frontiers of Sci. & Tech., 2nd. edit., Marquis Who's Who 1984, Am. Men and Women of Sci., Who's Who in Tech. Today; mem: Am. Coll. of Physicians (fellow, mem. nephrology com. of MKSAP VIII, 1989), Am. Fedn. for Clin. Res., Am. Soc. of Nephrology (mem. prog. com 1983, chmn. prog. com 1985, councilor 1986-90, chmn. sci. policy com. 1987-91, pres. elect 1991, past pres. 1992), Council on Circulation Am. Heart Assn. (Council on Kidney in CV Diseases: exec. com 1982-90, vice-chmn. 1984-86, chmn. 1986-88; mem. ADDK-D review com. 1986-89; grantee 1973-80), Nat. Kidney Found. (mem. sci. advy. bd. 1980-87, exec. com. sci. advy. bd. 1982-87, chmn. sci. advy. bd. 1984-86, Region III v.p. 1984-87, chmn. public policy com. 1987-89), Internat. Soc. of Nephrology, Am. Soc. of Clin. Investigation, Central Soc. for Clin. Res. (subspecialty sect. chmn. 1985), Assn. of Am. Physicians, We. Assn. of Physicians, We. Soc. for Clin. Investigation, Am. Clin. and Climatological Assn..; grantee: USPHS, 1970–, NIH (prin. investigator 1981-86, 86-91,87-92, prog. dir. of tng. grant 1980-90), Nat. Kidney Found. of Mich. 1983-84, Nat. Kidney Found. 1986-87, Am. Heart Assn. of Mich. 1986-88; editl. bds.: Kidney Internal., Seminars in Nephrology, Am. Jour. of Kidney Diseases, Am. Jour. of Nephrology, Am. Jour. of Physiology, Am. Jour. of Medicine; contbg. editor, jours. and books, 1977-92; contbg. author: 74 peer reviewed and 24 non-peer reviewed articles to profl. jours., 1963–, 30 book chapters, 1977–, 85 abstracts, preliminary commns. and panel discussions, 1967–; mil.: major, USAR 1966-69. Ofc: LAC-USC Medical Center Dept. of Medicine-IRD 220, 2020 Zonal Ave Los Angeles 90033

TANNENBAUM, RICHARD STEPHEN, mortgage banker; b. Sept. 27, 1938, NYC; s. Jerome and Abbie T.; m. Linda, Nov. 8, 1981 (widower 1993); children: Cindy (Holloway) b. 1960, Mark b. 1962; edn: BA, Univ. N.C., 1959; desig: GRI (Grad. Realtors Inst.) Nat. Assn. Realtors; CBC, Inst. Cert. Bus. Counselors. Career: sales, 1959-61; mgmt. pos. 1961-65; pres. Sol Newman Inc. 1965-66; pres. Branford Trousers Co., Ltd. and subs. cos. 1967-71; v.p. Sero Shirts, v.p. College Hall Clothes, v.p. P.J. Brennan, 1972-74; CEO Esquire Sportswear and v.p. L. Greif (div. Genesco) 1975; sales rep. for W. states, Aquascutum, 1976; real estate sales Red Carpet, 1977; broker/owner RTS Realty 1978-88, RTS Mortgage 1984-91; currently mortgage banker, GMAC Mortgage Corp., Riverside; mktg. splst. PRC Realty Systems 1979-80; asst. v.p./broker National First Mortgage Corp., Rancho Cordova 1987-88; mem. Calif. Dept. of R.E. bus. opportunities com. 1984-87; dir. Palm Springs Bd. of Realtors 1994-95; graduate instr. Calif. Assn. of Realtors 1994–; regl. chair Calif. Assn. of Realtors 1995; mem. Federal Strategy Housing Task Force Commn. 1995–; mem: NY Clothing Mfrs. Assn. (dir. 1965-66), Yucca Valley Bd. of Realtors (pres. 1982, 83), Inst. of Cert. Bus. Counselors 1979-92, Am. Inst. of Mortgage Brokers 1987-91; civic: San Bdo. County Water Task Force (conservation com. chair 1989-90), Yucca Valley Sunrise Rotary (pres. 1985-86), Morongo Basin Beautification Corp. (pres. 1987-80), Morongo Basin Jewish Community (founder 1988, pres. 1988-90), Yucca Valley C.of C. (past dir.);Republican; Jewish; Res: 56464 Scandia Lane Yucca Valley 92284 Ofc: The Loan Arranger PO Box 2221 Yucca Valley 92286

TANNER, KATHERINE JEAN, director school facility planning and development; b. Sept. 20, 1948, Denver, Colo.; d. John R. and Olivia F. Tanner; m. Ross Tanner, Sept. 24, 1971; children: Brent b. 1973, Brian b. 1976; edn: Brigham Young Univ. 1966-68; BS in biol. scis., USC 1970; CSU Long Beach 1970-71; med. tech. UC Irvine Med. Ctr. 1972; ednl. facilities plng. cert., UC Riverside 1991; lic. med. technologist, Calif. 1972; desig: MT, Am. Soc. Clin. Path. 1972. Career: clin. lab. technologist UC Irvine Med. Ctr., Orange 1972-76; Scripps Clinic and Research Found., La Jolla 1982-84; elected trustee Del Mar Union Sch. Dist. 1981-86, re-elected 1986-90, board pres. 1983-86, rep. to North City West Jt. Powers Agreement 1986-95; dir. school facility planning and development, Del Mar Union Sch. Dist. 1995–; mem: Am. Soc. of Clin. Pathologists, AAUW, PEO; Republican; Presbyterian; rec: biking, woodwork, garden. Ofc: Del Mar 92014

TANNER, LYNN, actress; b. Mar. 22, 1953, N.Y.C.; d. Harry J. and Barbara Sylvia (Hirschman) Maurer; m. Allen Barry Witz, Aug. 31, 1975; edn: BS, New York Univ., 1975; JD, DePaul Univ., 1980; admitted bar: Ill., 1980. Career: actress, 1980–; appeared in (film) Human Error, 1987, Another Time, Another Place, 1988, (theatre) Pack of Lies, Back at the Blue Dolphin Saloon; British stage debut in Toyer, Redgrave Theater (Michael White Prodns.) 1994, (film) Twisted 1995; mem. Screen Actors Guild, AFTRA, Actors Equity Assn., Women in Film, Women in Theater, Friends and Artists Theatre Ensemble (fmr. mem.).

TANZMANN, VIRGINIA WARD, architect; b. July 6, 1945, Tuxedo, N.Y.; d. John A. Ward and Helen Pfund; m. Carlton M. Davis, Jr.; edn: BA in arch., Syracuse Univ., 1968, BArch, Syracuse Univ. Grad. Sch. 1969; reg. arch. Calif. 1973, Nev. 1987, NCARB 1987. Career: intern arch. Burke Kober Nicolais Archuleta, Los Angeles 1969-72; project arch. Daniel L. Dworsky & Assocs., Los Angeles 1972-74, SUA, Inc., Los Angeles 1974-75; staff architect So. Calif. Rapid Transit Dist., L.A. 1975-78; prin. The Tanzmann Assocs., L.A. 1978–; prin. works include MTA No. Hollywood Station, Los Angeles Mission, Oxnard Housing Authority (430 units), SCRTD Central Maint. Facility (3 of 7 bldgs. L.A.),Metro Rail office renovation (L.A.), L.A. Dept. Water & Power (13 projects Calif., Nev.), Long Beach/L.A. Rail Transit Proj. (6 stations, L.A.), L.A. Conv. Ctr. remodel and expansion, L.A. Bd. Pub. Works Hyperion Pumping Plant, Chevron USA petroleum lab./clinic, L.A. Unified Sch. Dist. rehab. 4 schs., UCLA Med. Ctr. refurbishment 3 flrs., Hollywood Bowl Renovation, Circuit City- 4 retail stores (L.A. & Orange Cos.), Helene Curtis Inds. new retail identity for 50 stores (7 completed), Pizza Hut new Calif. image, SRO Housing Corp. renovation 5 hotels on Skid Row, Chrysalis Ctr. Leonide Hotel rehab., concept design Little Tokyo Svc. Ctr; exhibits: Wash. DC, Monterey Design Conf. (presenter 1981, 87), Los Angeles, Paris, France, Ramsar, Iran; juror Am. Soc. of Landscape Arch., FAIA, AIA; mem: Women's Transportation Coalition (founder, current pres.), Am. Inst. Architects (Fellow, bd. 1981-84, pres. 1994), AIACC (bd. 1983-84, 89-90, Assn. for Women in Arch. (pres. 1987-88, 77-78), USC Architectural Guild (pres. 1990-91), L'Union Internat. des Femmes Architectes, Design Professionals Coalition Advy. Council 1994–; civic: Info Line (bd. 1995), AIA Search for Shelter L.A. (advy. council), E. L.A. Coll. (advy. council), So. Calif. Bldg. Funds (bldg. plans and sites com.), YWCA of L.A. (pres. 1984-87), Volunteer Ctr. of L.A. (pres. 1990-91), United Way (awards and recognition com.), ADPSR (advy. council), L.A. Conservancy, Mus. Contemporary Art, LACMA, Dorland Mountain Arts Colony (exec. com. 1989-91) Ofc: The Tanzmann Associates, 820 E Third St Los Angeles 90013-1820

TARADASH, ROSLYN, electrical supplies distributor; b. Feb. 18, 1927, Chgo.; d. Maurice Charles and Florence (Blumenthal) T.; m. Elmer Finkel, Dec. 4, 1949 (div.); children: Cathy (Beth) b. 1952; edn: BA, Univ. Miami, 1948; lic.

R.E. sales, Calif. 1958. Career: R.E. sales agt., Beverly Hills 1958–, assoc. Mike Silverman, 1960, Mary Robertson & Assocs. 1970; v.p. Hyland Elec. Supply Co., 1965-80, pres./bd. chmn. 1980-81; pres. Tara Electric, Chgo. 1981–; initated successful annexation by City of Beverly Hills (2d largest in B.H.) of so. boundary homesites divided between the Cities of L.A. and B.H. (1975-79), enabling homes to be solely within B.H.; estab. trust fund for diagnostic test and res. in genetically acquired affective illness (1986); involved in affective illness res., nat.; subject of feature article Chicago Tribune Bus. Section (1980); civic: Affective Illness Research, funds res. for manic-depression (founder, pres. 1989), Waif, Carlton Club (Chgo.); mem. Internat. Platform Com., Intl. Biog. Ctr., listed: 2,000 Am. Notable Women, and World Who's Who of Women; Jewish; rec: golf, swimming.

TARG, RUSSELL, physicist; b. April 11, 1934, Chicago, Ill.; s. William and Anne (Jesselson) T.; m. Joan Fischer, Sept. 27, 1958; children: Elisabeth b. 1961, Alexander b. 1962, Nicholas b. 1965; edn: BS physics, Queens Coll. 1954; Columbia Univ. 1954-56. Career: engr. Sperry Gyrascope, Gt. Neck, N.Y. 1956-59; physicist TRG Inc., Syosset, N.Y. 1959-62; engring. splst. Sylvania, Mountain View 1962-72; sr. research physicist SRI Internat., Menlo Park 1972-82; ptnr. Delphi Assocs., San Mateo 1982-86; consulting scientist Lockheed R&D, Palo Alto 1986–; awards: NASA 2 invention awards 1968, 69, IEEE E.V. Taylor Best Tech. Paper 1979; mem: IEEE, Optical Soc. Am., Am. Soc. Psychical Research, Parapsychological Assn; co-author Mind Reach, 1977, Mind Race, 1984, co-ed. Mind at Large, 1979, 50 papers pub. in sci. jours. Ofc: Lockheed Research and Development Ste 97-01 3251 Hanover St Palo Alto 94304

TARI, MEL, religious organization executive, evangelist, author; b. March 18, 1946, Indonesia; nat. 1979; s. Jacob and Theresia (Bees) T.; m. Joyce Purdy, June 21, 1986; children: David Joseph b. 1987, Michael Jacob b. 1990, Joshua John b. 1993; edn: Sekolah Dasar #1, SOE Timor, Indonesia 1952-58; SMP Negeri, 1958-61; SMA Negeri, Kupang Timor Indonesia 1961-64. Career: minister, evangelist, missionary, travel internat. 500,000+ miles yearly for var. Christian orgns.; participate num. confs. incl. World Council of Chs. World Conf. Nairobi 1975, Internat. Conf. for Itinerant Evangelist, sponsored by Dr. Billy Graham, Amsterdam 1986; corp. secty./exec. v.p./dir. All Seasons Resort Inc. 1986–; pres. Christ Ambassadors Fellowship of Indonesia 1965–, founder/pres. Mel Tari Evangelistic Assn., 1976–; mem. Full Gospel Businessmens Fellowship Internat.; author 4 books: Like A Mighty Wind, The Gentle Breeze of Jesus, Am., Jesus is Here, and The Kingdom; Republican (Presdl. Task Force); Christian; rec: collect Bibles in var. languages. Ofc: All Seasons Resort PO Box 3355 Dana Point 92629

TARTER, BLODWEN, brokerage marketing, strategic planning and information technology executive; b. Dec. 2, 1954, Sacto.; d. Bill and Blodwen Edwards (Coburn) T.; m. Alan May; edn: BA, MA, Stanford Univ., 1976; MBA, Univ. Chicago, 1978; PhD, Golden Gate Univ., 1991; lic NASD Series 7, Series 63. Career: mktg. various divs. Mead Corp., Dayton, Oh., N.Y.C., 1978-82; v.p. mktg., v.p. online Info. Access Co., Belmont, Calif. 1982-86; dir. mktg. Channelmark Corp., San Mateo 1986-87; v.p. mktg. Insurance Equities Corp., Palo Alto 1987-89; dir., v.p. Charles Schwab & Co., San Francisco 1989–; mem: Commonwealth Club of Calif. 1990–, Stanford Univ. Alumni (fundraiser 1988–), AIDS Memorial Grove S.F. (vol. 1992–); pub. articles in profl. jours. (1986), The Computer Law Jour. (1992). Res: 1956 Bush St San Francisco 94115 Ofc: Charles Schwab & Co. Inc. 101 Montgomery San Francisco 94104

TATE, L. KENNETH, company president; b. July 18, 1923, Hamilton Co., Ill.; s. Loran Kent and Hattie Wilma (Vantrease) T.; m. Wanda M. (div.); children: Ronald Leroy b. 1946, Kenneth Dean b. 1949, Paulette Nadine b. 1949; m. Dorothy M., Dec. 8, 1960; edn: Aeronautical Engr., Curtis-Wright Tech. Inst., 1948; LLB, Am. Sch. of Law, 1952; spl. courses Univ. Ill., CalTech, Valley Jr. Coll., Contra Costa Jr. Coll., Weaver Coll. Law, USN; reg. Profl. Engr. (#5615) Calif. 1978. Career: quality supr. American Car & Foundry, St. Charles, Mo. 1952-54; insp. and test foreman Bendix Corp., No. Hollywood, Calif. 1955-60; technical sect. mgr. Calif. Inst. of Technology, Pasadena 1960-78; mgr. reliability & quality engring. Fairchild/ Xincom Systems, Canoga Park 1978-82; dir. quality assurance JBL Inc., Northridge 1982-86; owner, pres. Ken Tate Enterprises (wholesale sports orgn., sales worldwide), Reseda 1986–; mem. Am. Soc. for Quality Control (Sr. mem., past sect. chmn. S.F.V. Sect. 0706) 1962–, Am. Numismatic Soc. 1954–, West Valley Coin Club 1978–; lodges: AF&AM, Galatia, Ill. #684 1944–, Masonic, Reseda #666 1982–; publs: articles on statical controls 1978, regression analysis 1982, scrap reduction 1983, spacecraft quality 1986; mil: 1c p.o. USN 1943-46; Democrat; Prot.; rec: bowling, sports cards. Address: 7725 Wilbur Ave Reseda 91335

TATOMER, WILLIAM REEVES, psychiatrist; b. Apr. 29, 1945, Niagara Falls, N.Y.; s. Harry Nicholas and Norma Ethyl (Reeves) T.; m. Mary Catherine Hourican, Sept. 9, 1978; children: Deirdre b. 1980, Meghan b. 1982, Andrew b. 1985; edn: BA, Univ. Va. 1967; MD, 1971; cert. Am. Bd. Psychiatry & Neurology 1983. Career: resident San Mateo Co. Mental Health Services 1974; pvt. practice, San Mateo 1974–; pres. Healthcare Found. San Mateo Co. 1989-91; bd. dirs. Calif. Found. for Med. Care 1990–; councilor No. Calif. Psychiatric

Soc. 1988-91; staff Peninsula Hosp., Burlingame 1974–; Mills Meml. Hosp., San Mateo 1980–; co-host The Celtic Connection radio show 1987-89; mem: Am. Psychiatric Assn. (fellow), San Mateo Psychiatric Soc. (pres. 1985), Calif. Psychiatric Soc., CMA, AMA, Suicide Prevention San Mateo Co. (v.p. 1985-87), San Mateo Co. Medical Assn. (pres. elect); Christian; rec: golf, wine collecting. Ofc: 101 S San Mateo Dr Ste 300 San Mateo 94401

TATUM, THOMAS DESKINS, film and television producer, director; b. Feb. 16, 1946, Pineville, Ky.; s. Clinton Turner and Gaynelle (Deskins) T.; m. Laura Ann Smith, Aug. 15, 1968 (div. 1974); m. Suzanne Pettit, Sept. 29, 1983; children: Rhett Cowden, Walker Edwin; edn: BA, Vanderbilt Univ., 1968; JD, Emory Univ., 1974; admitted bar: Ga. 1974, D.C. 1980. Career: special asst. City of Atlanta, 1974-76; dep. dir. fed. relations National League of Cities, W.D.C., 1977-78; dir. communications Office of Conservation and Solar Energy, 1979-80; chmn. and exec. producer Tatum Communications of Colorado Inc., Telluride and Burbank, Calif. 1981–; chmn., pres. Western Film & Video Inc., Telluride 1987–; appt. mem. advy. bd. Solar Electric Light Fund, W.D.C. (non-profit) 1989–; c.o.o./sr. exec. producer, Planet Central Television 1995–; producer feature film: Winners Take All, 1987; prod./director documentaries: Double High (1982, award), Maui Windsurf, 1983; home videos: Greenpeace in Action, 1988, Girls of Winter/Skiing mag., 1990, Am. Ultra Sports Series with prime network, 1989-93; various cable TV, home video sports pgms., 1982-95; dep. campaign mgr. Maynard Jackson 1973; staff conf. Dem. Mayors 1974-75; nat. urban affairs coord. Carter Mondale campaign 1976 and mem. transition team 1976-77, media cons. Greenpeace 1988; bd. dirs. Atlanta Ballet (v.p. 1975); mem.: Ga. Bar Assn., Washington Bar Assn., Hollywood Film and TV Soc.; club: Los Angeles Tennis; Presbyterian; rec: skiing, sailing, Yoga, tennis, travel. Res: Hollywood and Telluride, CO, ranch Taos, NM; Ofc: Tatum Communications Inc. 2219 W Olive Ave #173 Burbank 91506 and Box 944 Telluride CO 81435

TAYLOR, CLIVE ROY, academic physician; b. July 24, 1944, Cambridge, Eng.; s. Roy and Mildred (Harrison) T.; m. Susan Hoyland, July 29, 1967; children: Matthew b. 1969, Jeremy b. 1970, Ben b. 1974, Emma b. 1978; edn: BA, MA, Cambridge, Eng. 1966, 1970, MB, BS (MD equiv.) 1969; PhD philos., Oxford 1974. Career: lectr. Univ. Oxford, England 1971-75; fellow Medical Res. Council, 1975-76; assoc. prof. USC, L.A. 1976-81, prof. 1981-84, chmn. pathology dept. 1984–; mem. sci. advy. bds.: Techniclone Internat. 1984, Impath 1989, Biogenex 1991; awards: Karger Research Award, Karger, Switz. 1976, Phi Beta publishing award USC 1987, Bachelor scholar Univ. Cambridge 1966, Hobson scholar Univ. Oxford 1969; mem: Royal Coll. Pathologists, Am. Soc. Clin. Pathologists, Planetary Soc.; active AYSO, So. Pasa. (founding commr. 1977); author: Lymph Node Pathology (1979), Immuno Microscopy (1986), Concise Pathology (1992), 10 other books, 200+ sci. papers; rec: soccer coach, tennis, skiing. Res: 1601 Marengo Ave South Pasadena 91030 Ofc: USC Dept. Pathology 2011 Zonal Ave Los Angeles 90033

TAYLOR, EDNA JANE, state employment program counselor; b. May 16, 1934, Flint, Mich.; d. Leonard Lee Harvey and Wynona Ruth (Davis) Belders; m. Bill Frank Taylor, Mar. 17, 1951 (div. 1955); children: Wynona Jane MacDonald b. 1952, Cynthia Lee Zellmer b. 1954; edn: BA, No. Ariz. Univ., 1963; MEd, Univ. Ariz., Tucson 1967. Career: high sch. tchr. Sunnyside School Dist., Tucson 1963-68; employment counselor Calif. State Employment Devel. Dept., Canoga Park, Calif. 1968–; mem. advy. council Pierce Community Coll., Woodland Hills 1979-81; advy. council Van Nuys Community Adult Sch., 1983-95, elected steering com. 1989-90, 90-91; mem. local leadership council Van Nuys Adult Sch., 1991-92; mem: Internat. Assn. Personnel in Employment Security 1968–, Calif. Employment Counselors Assn. (state treas. 1978, 79, state sec. 1980), Delta Psi Kappa (life 1960); rec: writing, tennis, health & fitness. Ofc: State Calif. Employment Development Dept. Canoga Park 91303

TAYLOR, RICHARD EDWARD, physicist; b. Nov. 2, 1929, Medicine Hat, Alberta, Canada; s. Clarence Richard and Delia Alena (Brunsdale) T.; m. Rita Jean Bonneau, Aug. 25, 1951; children: Norman Edward b. 1960; edn: BSc, Univ. Alberta, Edmonton, Can. 1950, MSc, 1952; PhD, Stanford Univ., 1962. Career: boursier Lab de l'Accelerateur, Orsay, France 1958-61; physicist Lawrence Berkeley Lab, Berkeley 1961-62; staff mem. Stanford Linear Accelerator Ctr., 1962-68, prof. (SLAC) Stanford Univ., 1968–, assoc. dir. SLAC, 1982-86; awards: fellow J.S. Guggenheim Found. 1971-72, sr. scientist von Humboldt Found., Bonn, Ger. 1982, W.K.H. Panofsky Prize div. of particles & fields Am. Phys. Soc. 1989, Nobel Prize in Physics, Stockholm, Sweden 1990; mem. Canadian Assn. of Physicists, Nat. Acad. of Sci. (fgn. assoc.); Fellow: Am. Physical Soc., Royal Soc. of Canada, Am. Acad. Arts and Scis., AAAS; publs: num. articles in sci. jours. Ofc: SLAC, PO Box 4349 MS-96 Stanford 94309

TAYLOR, WILLIAM JAMES, lawyer; b. Jan. 26, 1948, Milwaukee, Wis.; s. William Elmer and Elizabeth Emily (Lupinski) T.; m. Marlou Belyea, Sept. 20, 1975; children: Danielle b. 1980, James b. 1986; edn: BA, Yale Univ. 1970; JD, Harvard Law Sch. 1976. Career: law clk. Hon. Shirley M. Hufstedler U.S. Ct. Appeals, L.A. 1976-77; atty., assoc. Brobeck Phleger & Harrison, San Francisco

1977-83, ptnr. 1983-95; dir. Taylor & Jenkins, P.C. 1995–; awards: Bar Assn. S.F. Award of Merit 1984, Legal Services for Children Jean Waldman Child Advocacy award 1988; mem: Am. Bar Assn., Bar Assn. S.F. (bd. mem. 1986-87), ACLU Lawyers Council, Legal Services for Children (bd. mem. 1984-89), Berkeley Law Found. (bd. mem. 1988-91), Attys. Task Force for Children (co-chair 1984-89); ed. No. Dist. Digest, 1978-83, articles and speeches pub. in profl. jours.; 1975–, ed. in chief Harvard Civil Rights-Civil Liberties Law Review, 1976; mil: E-5 AUS 1970-73; Democrat; Prot.; rec: skiing. Res: 842 Mendocino Ave Berkeley 94707 Ofc: Taylor & Jenkins, P.C. 2030 Franklin St 5th Flr Oakland 94612

TAYLOR, WILLIAM P., legislative aide; b. Nov. 7, 1951, Stoneham, Mass.; s. William and Mary Adeline (Pacios) T.; m. Brenda Maria Contreras, Aug. 22, 1978; children: Brenda b. 1974, Karina b. 1981; edn: BS, UC Berkeley 1977-80; San Francisco St. Univ. 1975-76. Career: legis. asst. to Florence McDonald, City council of Berkeley 1982; comm. services asst. Vista Coll., Berkeley 1983-85; legislative asst. to Don Jelinek, City Council of Berkeley 1985-90; legis. asst. to Dona Spring City Council of Berkeley 1993–; mem: St. Calif. Maternal Child & Adolescent Health Bd. 1986-92, City of Berkeley Maternal Child & Adolescent Health Bd. 1982-87, St. Josephs Elem. Sch. Bd. 1988-90; Cath. Ofc: City of Berkeley 2180 Milvia St Berkeley 94704

TEMKO, ALLAN BERNARD, writer; b. Feb. 4, 1924, NY, NY; s. Emanuel and Betty (Alderman) T.; m. Elizabeth Ostroff, July 1, 1950; children: Susannah b. 1955, Alexander Max b. 1957; edn: AB, Columbia Univ., NY, NY, 1947; postgrad. UC Berkeley, 1949-51; Sorbonne, 1948-49, 51-52. Career: lectr., Sorbonne, 1953-54, Ecole des Arts et Metiers, Paris, 1954-55; asst. prof. journalism UC Berkeley, 1956-62; lectr. in city planning and social scis. UC, 1966-70; prof. art, Calif. State Univ., Hayward, 1971-80; lectr. art Stanford Univ., 1981, 82; lectr., Grad. Sch. of Journalism, UC Berkeley, 1991; architecture critic, S.F. Chronicle, 1961-93; West Coast ed., Archtl. Forum, 1959-62; art ed., S.F. Chronicle, 1979-82; archtl. planning cons.; referee in architecture, Guggenheim Found.; awards: recipient, Gold Medal Commonwealth Club Calif. 1956, Silver Medal Commonwealth Club Calif. 1994, Guggenheim fellow 1956-57, journalism award AIA 1961, Rockefeller Found. grantee 1962-63, Twentieth Century Fund grantee 1963-66, Silver Spur award 1985, 1st prize in archtl. criticism Mfrs. Hanover/Art World 1986, Critic's award Mfrs. Hanover/Art World 1987, Profl. Achievement award Soc. Profl. Journalists 1988, Nat. Endowment for the Arts grantee 1988, Pulitzer Prize for Criticism 1990, Inst. Honor award, AIA 1991, appt. Pulitzer Prize juries 1991, 92, Nathaniel Owings Award, Calif. Council AIA 1995; author: Notre Dame of Paris, 1955, Eero Saarinen, 1961, No Way to Build a Ballpark, other essays on architecture, 1993; contbr. articles to US and fgn. magazines and newspapers; civic: environmental adv. to former Pres. John F. Kennedy and former Calif. Gov. Edmund G. Brown; organized the Governor's Design Awards Prog.; chair, Yosemite Falls Design Workshop 1992. Mil: served with USNR 1943-46. Res: 1015 Fresno Ave Berkeley 94707

TEMKO, FLORENCE, author; b. Oct. 20, 1921; edn: attended London Univ., London, England. Career: workshop instr. Metropolitan Mus., N.Y. 1974-81, San Diego Mus. of Art 1985-92, UCSD, La Jolla 1986; cons. Mingei Internat. Mus., La Jolla; seminar leader for teachers of art, reading, math, gifted and learning-disabled; created hundreds of hands-on programs on papercrafts at schools, colleges, museums, libraries in indsl., commercial and convention settings; listed World Who's Who of Women, Who's Who of Am. Women; mem: Author's Guild 1972–, Am. Soc. of Journalists and Authors 1974–, San Diego Press Club 1984–; author: Paperfolding to Begin With, 1968, Papercutting, 1972, Felt Craft, 1974, Self-Stick Craft, 1975, Decoupage Crafts, 1976, Paper Capers, 1974, Paper: Folded, Cut, Sculpted, Folk Crafts for World Friendship, 1976, The Big Felt Burger and 27 Other Craft Projects to Relish, 1977, The Magic of Kirigami, 1978, Paperworks, Let's Take a Trip, Come to My House, Guess Who!, 1982, Chinese Papercuts: Their Story, How to Use Them and Make Them, 1982, elementary Art Games and Puzzles, 1982, New Knitting, 1984, Paper Pandas and Jumping Frogs, 1986, Paper Jewelry, 1990, Paper Tricks 1988, Paper Tricks II, 1990, Scary Things, 1991, Made With Paper, 1991 (French translation, 1994), Origami for Beginners, 1991, Origami for Children, Origami for the Holidays, 1993, Origami Magic, 1993, Bible Origami-New Testament, 1995, Bible Origami, 1995, For Your Eyes Only-13 Ways to Fold Secret Notes, 1995, Folded Money, 1995, Culture Crafts, 1996, others; contbr. N.Y. Sunday Times, Boston Globe Am. Craft, Delta Airlines Inflight Mag., num. other newspapers and magazines; weekly craft column for Berkshire Eagle, others, bi-weekly TV craft prog., num. TV guest appearances; film "Origami" for Film Bd. of Canada, film "Creating with Paper" for CBS Ednl. Films. Res/Ofc: 5050 La Jolla Blvd Ste P-C San Diego 92109

TEMPLE, DIANA HASTINGS, lawyer; b. Aug. 18, 1956, Stockton; d. Walter Andrew and Jane Frances (Goldsberry) Hastings; m. Robert Charles Temple; edn: BA, Univ. Oreg. 1979; MBA, George Washington Univ. 1981; JD, Cornell Law Sch. 1986; note ed. Cornell Internat. Law Jour. 1985-86; admitted bar: N.Y., Calif., U.S. Dist. Ct. no. dist. Calif., U.S. Ct. Appeals 9th cir. Career: economist U.S. Dept. of Commerce, W.D.C. 1980; fin. analyst Econ. Consulting Services 1980-83; atty. Milbank, Tweed, Hadley & McCloy, N.Y.C., 1986-88;

Pillsbury, Madison & Sutro, San Francisco, 1988-90; Orrick, Herrington & Sutcliffe, S.F., 1990-94; princ. Law Offices of Diana Hastings Temple, S.F. 1994–; Lincoln Child Ctr., Oakland (bd. dir.); vol. panelist Early Settlement Prog., Superior Ct., Probate Dept.; mem: Bar Assn. of S.F., St. Bar Calif. (exec. com., estate planning, trust and probate section), Am. Bar Assn. (com. on creditors' rights in decedents' estates); author: (articles) "Informal Preliminary Distributions Under Probate Code Sect. 10520" Estate Planning, Trust & Probate News, 1994, "Recent Tax Court Decision Contradicts Private Letter Rulings" Trusts & Estates mag. (7/93), "Appraisals of Significant Collections" Probate & Property, 1993, "Service Provides Ad Hoc Guidance on New Disclaimers" Trusts & Estates (1/93), "UPC Changes the Rules for Intestate Succession" Estate Planning, Trust & Probate News, 1993. Ofc: One Post Ste 600 San Francisco 94104 Tel: 415/421-3600

TENNEY, JOSEPH RICKS, security executive; b. Sept. 29, 1936, New Orleans, La.; s. Joseph Fosdick and Cecile Clara (Ricks) T.; m. Jean Sherrill Wilcox, Dec. 28, 1963; children: Joseph Wilcox, Laurie Sherrill, Karl Ricks; edn: BS in engring., U.S. Naval Acad. 1960; student USMC Command and Staff Coll. 1970-71; M. in human behavior, USIU, San Diego 1974; JD, Western State Univ. 1984. Career: officer US Marine Corps 1960-80: num. command/staff billets, jt. and naval staff, in combat, recruiting, and recruit training; 10 personal decorations include Silver Star, Vietnamese Cross of Gal. w/Gold Palm, Purple Heart, Joint Svc. Commdn. Medal, Navy Commdn. w/Gold Star & Combat V, N.O.V. 4th CL, DSO 1st CL, Navy Achiev. Medal, Combat Action Ribbon; (his family military history in Am. predates colonial period (1650) forbears fought in Fr. and Indian War, Am. Revolution, War of 1812, Civil War, WWII, Korea and Vietnam, eldest son Marine ofcr. Persian Gulf War); currently dir. security Hyatt Regency Irvine; mem: Army/Navy Co. Club; civic: Collie Club Am. (show rules com. 1978-80, trophy com. 1978-80), Fullerton Booster Club (pres. 1985-87), Fullerton Quarterback Club (v.p. 1981-86), San Diego Collie Club (pres. 1977-80); contbr. article for CCA annual pub., Valley of the Shadow Autobiography, 1974, poem Fame, Am. Poetry Anthol., 1986; Republican; Episcopalian; rec: showing dogs. Res: 601 E Glenwood Fullerton 92631 Ofc: Hyatt Regency Irvine 17900 Jamboree Irvine 92714

TEPLITZ, RAYMOND L., physician, pathologist, cytogeneticist; b. July 20, 1925, Chicago, Ill.; s. Harry and Annette (Duroff) T.; m. Marlyn Ruth Bertman, Feb. 16, 1947; children: Paula Ann b. 1952, Caryl Francis b. 1954; edn: DO, Coll. of OsteopathicPhys. & Surg., L.A. 1949; MD, UC Irvine, 1962. Career: cons. pathologist Monte Sano Hosp., Maywood 1951-63; assoc. prof. City of Hope Hosp., Duarte 1962-63, dir. dept. cytogenetics and cytology 1964-77, chmn. div. cytogenetics and cytology 1977-85; prof., dir. cytopathology UC Davis 1985-94, prof. emeritus 1994–; cons. Vivigen Inc., Santa Fe, N.M. 1983-93; Molecular Diagnostics Inc., Elkhart, Ind. 1983-85; sci. advy. bd. Vestar Research, Pasadena 1981–; med. advy. bd. Nat. Lupus Found., San Gabriel 1981-85; cons. Molecular Biosystems, La Jolla 1984-90; UNESCO 1974; honors: Alpha Omega Alpha, Inst. Pasteur INSERM fellowship 1971-72, City of Hope Med. Center Fred Rosen research fellow 1984-85, Zachary Pitts research fellow 1970, Hadassah Med. Sch. immunology scholar 1979-80; mem: AAAS, Am. Fedn. Clin. Research, AMA, Am. Soc. Cell Biology, Am. Soc. Human Genetics; publs: co-editor (chapt.) 1st internat. conf. on Role of Recombinant DNA in Genetics, 1986, author 5 chapters in med. books including: Path. of Leukemia, 1966, Interventional Ultrasound, 1988; rec: photog., haiku, hiking. Res: 28141 El Camino Winters 95694 Ofc: Univ. California Davis, Dept Med Biochemistry, Davis 95616

TERRANELLA, CHARLES ARTHUR, investment banker; b. May 23, 1944, NY, NY; s. Charles John and Ann (Westuba) T.; m. Mary Ellen, Dec. 24, 1985; children: Sarah b. 1986, Charles F. b. 1989; edn: BBA, City Coll. N.Y., 1967; MBA, Columbia Univ., 1971. Career: fin. exec. Time, Inc. NY, NY 1971-76; fin. officer Calif. Housing Fin. Agy., Sacto. 1977-78; v.p. Lehman Bros. Kuhn Loeb, NY, NY 1979-80; v.p. Dean Witter Reynolds, San Francisco 1981-87; senior v.p. First Calif. Capital Markets Group, S.F. 1988-90; prin. McCarty, Terranella & Carlson, S.F. 1991-93; managing dir. Westhoff-Martin & Associates, Lafayette 1993–; mem. Mensa, Commonwealth Club Calif., World Affairs Council No. Calif. Res: 767 Oak Hollow Ave Vacaville 95687 Ofc: Westhoff-Martin & Associates 3675 Mt. Diablo Blvd Lafayette 94549

TESTA, STEPHEN MICHAEL, geologist, environmental services company president; b. July 17, 1951, Fitchburg, Mass.; s. Guiseppe Alfredo and Angelina Mary (Petitto) T.; m. Lydia Mae Payne, July 26, 1986; son, Brant Ethan Gage; edn: AA, L.A. Valley Jr. Coll., 1971; BS geol., CSU Northridge, 1976, MS geol., 1978; reg. geologist, 1983; reg. environmental assessor, 1989; Cert. profl. geological scientist, 1983; cert. engring. geologist, 1990; cert. environmental insp., 1991. Career: engring. geologist R.T. Frankian & Assocs., Burbank 1976-78; Bechtel, Norwalk 1978-80; Converse Consultants, Seattle 1980-82; senior hydrogeologist Ecology & Environment, Seattle 1982-83; senior geologist Dames & Moore, Seattle 1983-86; v.p. Engineering Enterprises., Long Beach 1986-90; pres. Applied Environmental Services, 1990–; instr. geology and environmental sci. CSU Fullerton 1989-90; instr. environmental sci. USC, 1991; mem: Am. Inst. of Profl. Geologist (profl. dev. com. 1986, cont. edn. com. 1988,

annual meeting com. 1989, program chmn. 1990, presdl. merit award 1987, nat. v.p. 1994), Geological Soc. of Am., L.A. Basin Geol. Soc. (pres. 1990-91), Am. Assn. of Petroleum Geologists (AAPG), AAAS, Assn. of Engring. Geologist, Mineral. Soc. of Amer., Mineral. Soc. of Canada, Hazardous Mats. Control Research Inst., Assn. of Ground Water Scientist and Engrs., Calif. Water Pollution Control Assn., Calif. Groundwater Assn., Sigma Xi, Soc. of Am. Military Engrs.; author: Restoration of Petroleum-Contaminated Aquifers; Principles of Technical Consulting and Project Management; Geological Aspects of Hazardous Waste Management; editor (book) Environmental Concerns in the Petroleum Industry (pub. AAPG Pacific Sect., 1989); 60+ tech. res. papers 1978–; rec: water color artist, collector natural hist. books, minerals. Res: 31232 Belford Dr San Juan Capistrano 92675 Ofc: Applied Environmental Services, 27423 Calle Arroyo San Juan Capistrano 92675

THATCHER, DICKINSON, lawyer; b. May 26, 1919, Huntington Beach; s. Charles Harold and Gladys T. (Dickinson) T.; m. Dale Nadine Mortensen, Feb. 2, 1952; children: Kirk Randolph, b. 1962; Jeffrey Lawrence, b. 1963; edn: BS, UCLA 1941; postgrad., New York Univ. 1943-4; Univ. of Paris 1945-46; JD, Stanford Univ. 1948; LL.M. in Taxation, USC 1962. Career: admitted to Calif. State Bar 1948; Los Angeles Deputy City Atty. 1948-51; credit atty. Union Oil Co. of Calif. 1951-54; trial atty. Tax Div., Dept. Justice, Wash. DC 1954-56; asst. US Atty. Los Angeles 1956-57; lawyer in North Hollywood, Van Nuys, Ojai, 19570-92; mem: St. Bar of Calif. (Disciplinary Bd. 1970-72, Client Security Fund Com. 1973-75), San Fernando Valley Bar Assn. (pres. 1966), Am. Bar Assn, Los Angeles Co. Bar Assn. (Commn. on Arbitration 1963-71, chmn. Council Affiliated Bar Pres. 1968-70, exec. com. Probate and Trust Law Sect. 1985-87), Kiwanis (pres Van Nuys Club 1975-76); mil: US Army 1942-46. Address: 211 Bristol Rd Ojai 93023-2409

THIBAULT, DARRYL ROBERT, lawyer; b. June 16, 1938, Eureka; s. Edgar Exave and Cecilia Marie (Roberts) T.; m. Lori Williams, Apr. 12, 1982; children: Adam b. 1983, Stacey b. 1985; edn: BA in psychology, UC Riverside 1963; Soviet studies, UCLA, 1963-64; internat. law, Univ. Vienna, Austria 1970; JD, George Washington Sch. Law 1979; admitted bar: Dist. Col. 1980, Federal Cts. 1987. Career: intelligence ofcr. Central Intelligence Agency, Washington, D.C. 1970-91, with service in Asia, Europe, and U.S.; v.p. Nationwide Executive Security Services, San Diego 1991-92; pres. PrivIntel, Inc., San Diego 1992–; mem: Am. Bar Assn., D.C. Bar Assn., Fed. Bar Assn., Cal. Assn. Lic. Investigators, Am. Soc. Indus. Security (chm., San Diego Chapt.), Assn. Former Intel. Ofcrs. (pres., San Diego Chapt.); mil: U.S. Army 101st Airborne Div. 1957-59; Republican; R. Cath. Res: 2360 Palo Danzante Alpine 91901

THIBODEAU, PETER, chiropractor, educator; b. Aug. 27, 1942, Sumter, S.Caro.; s. Joseph Harold and Billie (Plowden) T.; (3d. generation chiropractor, both parents, gr.father, sister, uncles, cousins are DCs, gr.father was 2d. DC licentiate in S.Caro.); m. Judyth Ann Errecarte, Jun. 1969; children: Jed b. 1970, Britt b. 1972, Cassie b. 1977, Billie b. 1978; edn: undergrad. Univ. S.C. 1960-61, Cleveland Chiro. Coll. L.A. 1961-62; DC, Logan Chiro. Coll. St. Louis, Mo. 1965; BA, UC Santa Cruz, 1973; lic. DC Calif. 1966; Diplomate, 1982, and Fellow, 1989, Gonstead Clinical Studies Soc. (GCSS), Diplomate Am. Chiropractic Acad. of Neurology (DACAN) cert. 1992, Qualified Medical Educ. (QME) State of Calif. Worker's Compensation System, cert. 1994. Career: GCSS research in computer aided x-ray analysis with Dr. Suh (prof. engring. Univ. Colo.) 1984-87; faculty Los Angeles Chiropractic Coll., preceptor pgm. tchg. spinal adjustive techniques to students and field drs., 1987–; acad. research in biology of the intervertebral disc, immunology, computer aided x-ray analysis; awards: humanitarian in the healing arts Kentuckiana Childrens Ctr. 1979; mem: Internat. Chiropractic Assn., Calif. Chiropractic Assn., Gonstead Clin. Studies Soc., Monterey Bay GCSC (pres. 1991-92), UCSC Alumni, Logan Chiro. Coll. Alumni (life), Rotary Intl. (Santa Cruz Club bd. 1984-86); mil: 1st lt. AUS 1966-69; Republican; rec: sailing, dirt biking, gardening, history. Res: 431 Coyote Ridge Rd Aptos 95003 Ofc: 3121 Park Ave Soquel 95073

THIERS, EUGENE ANDRES, mineral economist; b. Aug. 25, 1941, Santiago, Chile, nat. 1976; s. Eugenio Alva and Elena (Lillo) T.; m. Hilda Pastoriza Stuart, Dec. 23, 1965 (div. 1980); m. Patricia van Metre, Jan. 29, 1983; children: Ximena b. 1966, Eugene b. 1969, Nicholas b. 1976, Alexander b. 1984; edn: BS, Univ. of Chile, 1959; MS, and DESc, Columbia Univ., 1965, 1970. Career: tech. mgr. Minbanco Corp., NY, NY 1966-70; dir. Iron Ctr., Battelle Columbus Labs, Columbus, Oh. 1970-75; senior cons. SRI Internat., Menlo Park 1975-78, dir. Metals Ctr. 1979-83, mgr. Inorganics 1984–; cons. prof. Stanford Univ., 1981–; dir. Small Mines Internat., Montreal, Quebec 1989; advisor Appropriate Technologies, W.D.C. 1987–; honors: fellowships Anaconda, Krumb, Campbell (1962, 64, 65), M.S. citation Columbia Univ. (1965), Tau Beta Pi (1966), U.S. del. to U.S. Acad. of Scis. coal symp. Lima, Peru (1985), outstanding achiev. SRI Internat. (1984); mem: Am. Inst. of Mining Engrs. (chmn. Ohio sect. 1973-74, chmn. No. Calif. 1978-79), AAAS (fellow 1968); publs: tech. articles in field (1985, 88). Res: 426 27th Ave San Mateo 94403 Ofc: SRI International 333 Ravenswood Ave Menlo Park 94025

THIROUX, JACQUES PAUL, professor of philosophy; b. Aug. 7, 1928, Santa Monica, Calif.; s. Jacques and Mary Helen (Garrotto) T.; m. Angelita Solis, July 26, 1952 (div. 1975); m. Emily Louise Lofton Apr. 8, 1984; children: Mark b. 1954, Stephen b. 1956, Paul b. 1959, Jason Ragle b. 1971, Abigale Ragle b. 1972; edn: BA, Pomona Coll., Claremont, Calif., 1949; MA, S.F. State Univ., 1961; AM, Univ. of So. Calif., L.A., 1971. Career: apr. publicist, MGM Studios, Culver City, Calif. 1949-50; T/Sgt., USAF, 1950-61; prof. of Eng., Bakersfield Coll., Bakersfield, Calif. 1961-69; prof. of Philosophy & chair, Bakersfield Coll., 1969-90; lectr. in Philosophy, Calif. State Univ., Bakersfield 1990-; bioethics cons., Delano Reg. Med. Ctr., Delano, Calif. 1988-; bioethics cons., Pacific Regency, Bakersfield, 1989-; mem., bioethics com., Kern Med. Ctr., Bakersfield 1988-; awards: fellowship, NEH, Wash., DC, 1973; mem: (life) Calif. Tchrs. Assn. & NEA 1961-, Calif. Faculty Assn. 1990-, VFW 1984-, AAUW 1990-; author: Practical Eng., 1977, Philosophy: Theory & Practice, 1985, Ethics: Theory & Practice (5th ed.), 1990; Living Fully Through Facing Dying, 1991. Mil: T/Sgt., USAF, 1950-61; rec: acting, singing, dancing. Address: Bakersfield 93311

THODE, JEROME PAUL, information systems management consultant; b. July 26, 1947, Chicago, Ill.; s. Howard Jacob and Lilla Maria (Wojceiowska) T.; m. Kathleen Anne Ferris; children: Christopher b. 1984, Andrew b. 1988; edn: BS math., Ill. Inst. Tech. 1969; MS computer sci., 1972; M.Mgmt., fin. & mktg., Northwestern Grad. Sch. Mgmt. 1979. Career: tech., mgr. Motorola, Chgo., Ill. 1969-76; project mgr. FMC 1976-78; mgr. MIS Morton Norwich 1978-81; prin. Deloitte & Touche, Los Angeles 1981-95; ptnr. Ernst & Young 1995-; guest lectr. UCLA GSM 1988-; mem: Soc. Info. Mgmt. (bd. mem.), Info. Assoc. UCLA Grad. Sch. Mgmt. (exec. bd.), L.A. Athletic Club; articles pub. in profl. jours.; rec: jogging, theatre. Ofc: 515 S Flower St Ste 2500 Los Angeles 90071

THOMAS, ESTHER MERLENE, educator; b. Oct. 16, 1945, San Diego; d. Merton Alfred and Nellie Lida (Von Pilz) T.; edn: AA, Grossmont Coll., 1966; BA, San Diego St. Univ., 1969; MA, Univ. Redlands, 1977; Calif. elem. and adult edn: tchg. creds., Career: teacher Cajon Valley Union Sch. Dist., El Cajon 1969-; tchr. native Amer.(AZ and UT); mem. Nat. Tchrs. Assn., Calif. Tchrs. Assn., Cajon Valley Educators Assn., Christian Bus. & Profl. Women, Lakeside Hist. Soc.; civic: Lakeside Centennial Com. (1985-86), Intl. Christian Women's Club (Seoul 1974), Dir. Bible sch., Sunday Sch. Supt., Cajon Valley Union Sch. Dist. Project AIDS (health articulation com. 1988), Marine Corps Mus. San Diego (charter), Lakeside Hist. Soc. Mus. (curator 1992-1993) contrib. author; mem. Congressman Duncan Hunter's Off Road Adv. Council 1994, Calif. del. to the Republican Senatorial mid-term Conv. W.D.C. 1994; Repub. (U.S. Senatl. Club 1984-, Medal of Merit Ronald Reagan Presdl. Task Force 1986, Presdl. Citizen's Advy. Commn. 1989-92, at large del. Repub. Platform Planning Com. 1988, 92). Res: 13594 Hwy 8 Apt 3 Lakeside 92040 Ofc: Flying Hills Elementary School 1251 Finch St El Cajon 92020

THOMAS, JULIA DESSERY, planner; b. Dec. 4, 1938, Riverside; d. Floyd Gordon and Myrtle (Thomas) Dessery; m. David B. Thomas, Nov. 30, 1963 (div.), children: Leslie; m. Michael Lawrence Bobrow, Mar. 24, 1980, 3 stepchildren, Elizabeth, Erica, David; edn: BA, CSU San Francisco, 1963; MA, Sch. Architecture and Urban Planning UCLA, 1974. Career: dir. communications William L. Pereira Assocs., L.A. 1972-73; sr. assoc. Bobrow/Thomas and Assocs., L.A. 1973-78, pres. 1978-84, chmn. bd. 1984-92, pres./CEO 1992-; guest lectr. USC, Columbia Univ., UCLA, Scripps Coll., Calif. Polytechnic Univ. Pomona, Pepperdine Univ.; prin. works include: Cook Co. Hosp. Repl. Plan, Natividad Med. Ctr., Univ. of Ariz. Cancer Ctr., COH, St. Luke's Med. Ctr., VA Outpatient Clinic Hong Kong Hosp. Authority, San Bernardino Co. Replacement Med. Ctr., Stanford Univ., Palo Alto, Shriners Hosps. for Crippled Children, L.A., Shreveport; Santa Monica Hosp. Med. Ctr.; UCLA Arroyo Bridge; Motion Picture and Television Hosp. and Country Home, Woodland Hills, Calif.; Kings Road Housing for the Elderly, Hollywood; awards include: UCLA Alumni award for excellence in profl. achiev. 1988, AIA/NAVFAC award of merit for US Navy Med. Clinics, Kaneohe, Hawaii 1988 and Port Hueneme, Calif. 1986, Am. Planning Assn./Calif. Chpt. outstanding leadership 1986, DOD design excellence for US Navy Med. Clinic, Port Hueneme, Calif. 1986, L.A. Conservancy award for Parsons-Gates Hall of Adminstrn. Caltech 1984, AIA award for Kings Road Housing for Elderly 1981; mem: Am. Inst. Certified Planners, Am. Planning Assn., L.A. Area C.of C. (bd. and exec. com.); civic: UCLA Grad. Sch. of Arch. and Urban Plng. Dean's Council (exec. com. 1975-), UCLA Found. (bd. trustees 1984-), UCLA John E. Anderson Grad. Sch. of Mgmt. Bd. of Visitors (exec. com. 1986-), UCLA Sch. of Med. The Aesculapians (exec. com. 1988-), Calif. Council for Humanities (v.chair), Mt. St. Mary's Coll. Bd. Regents 1984-, Com. of 200 (past pres.), Julia Dessery Thomas Travelling Fellowship UCLA, public policy com. Blue Cross of Calif., Otis Coll. of Art & Design (trustee); club: Regency (L.A.); contbr. articles to num. profl. publs. Ofc: Bobrow/Thomas and Associates 1001 Westwood Blvd Los Angeles 90024 Ph: 310/208-7017

THOMAS, KEITH RICHARD, advertising executive; b. Feb. 11, 1953, San Francisco; s. Richard Cody and Janet Marie (Cope) T.; m. Marcia Ann Hatch, April 15, 1978; children: Cody b. 1979, Adam b. 1982; edn: BS, San Francisco

St. Univ. 1975. Career: mgr. Gene Comptons Corp., Daly City 1968-71; pres. Joint Commn., San Francisco 1971-73; Pereira Thomas & Assoc. 1973-78; Keith R. Thomas & Co. 1978-87; chmn. bd. and c.e.o. THOMAS/RAHM Inc., Oakland, Sacto., Long Beach, and N.Y. 1987-90; pres., c.e.o. KRT Marketing, Lafayette 1990-; cons. Score, San Francisco 1980-89; awards: Jr. Achievement Am. Entrepreneur of Year 1977; mem: Admark, Am. Advt. Fedn. (past nat. pres.), Oakland Childrens Hosp. (trustee, vice chmn. bd. 1988-), Oakland Festival of Arts (bd. 1987-89), Junior Achievement Bay Area (bd. 1980-87, 1995-), Children's Miracle Network Telethon (No. Calif. chmn. 1989-95), Tony LaRussa's Animal Rescue Found. (bd. 1993-); Republican; Presbyterian. Ofc: KRT Marketing 3685 Mount Diablo Blvd Ste 255 Lafayette 94549

THOMAS, MITCHELL, JR., aerospace engineer; b. Nov. 25, 1936, Terre Haute, Ind.; s. Mitchell and Carolyn Amalia (Wolff) T.; m. Carole Green, 1964 (div. 1967); m. Helen Morris, June 28, 1970; children: Sheri b. 1960, Deborah b. 1964, Mitchell b. 1972; edn: BA, Harvard Coll. 1958; MS, Univ. Ill. 1959; PhD, CalTech. Pasadena 1964. Career: engr. Douglas Aircraft, Santa Monica 1959-70; branch chief McDonnell Douglas, Huntington Beach 1970-75; research and devel. dir. L'Garde Inc., Newport Beach 1975-76, pres., Tustin 1976-95, dir. 1975-; pres./founder, Thomas Dynamics Modeling, Villa Park 1995-; honors: Sigma Xi; mem: AAAS, Am. Inst. Atronautics & Aero. (assoc. fellow), Temple Beth Sholom; 20+ articles pub. in tech. jours.; rec: back packing, motorcycling, camping. Res/Ofc: 9691 Villa Woods Dr Villa Park 92667

THOMAS, WILLIAM BOWEN, manufacturing company executive; b. May 29, 1920, Castleford, Idaho; s. William Warner Thomas and Laura Vivian Taylor; m. Wave Young, Jan. 22, 1951 (div. 1981); m. Miraijana Cvijanovich, Jan. 18, 1983; children: Gail Ann Westwood; edn: Burley H.S., Burley, Idaho. Career: co-founder, Big O Tires, Inc., 1962-92; v.p., Big O Tires, Inc., 1962-85, pres., 1985; bd. of dirs, Big O Tires, Inc., 1962-92; dir., Am. Retreaders Assn., Louisville, Ky. 1968-78, pres. 1978-82; awards: AMF Industry Leadership award, Am. Machine Foundry, 1980; Hall of Fame, Big O Tires, Inc., Englewood, Colo., 1993, Tire Industry Hall of Fame, Nat. Tire Dealers & Retreaders Assn. 1994; President's Club (life), Brigham Young Univ., Provo, Utah; mem: Nat. Tire Dealer & Retreader Assn. (NTDRA), 1950-92; patents: first retractable seat belt, stitcher for laying rubber on tires being retreaded, windshield wiper, ejector impact socket; avocation: rancher, study of history (Winston Churchill). Res: P.O. Box 2468 Portola 96122

THOMAS, WILLIAM MARSHALL, congressman; b. Dec. 6, 1941, Wallace, Idaho; s. Virgil and Gertrude T.; m. Sharon Lynn Hamilton, Jan., 1967; children: Christopher, Amelia; edn: BA San Francisco State Univ. 1963, MA, 1965. Career: mem. faculty dept. Am. govt. Bakersfield (Calif.) Coll., 1965-74, prof. 1965-74; mem. Calif. State Assembly, 1974-78, 96th-104th Congresses from 18th, now 21st Calif. dist., 1979-; vice chmn. of House Task Force on campaign fin. reform; mem. House of Reps. ways and means com.; chmn. com. on House Oversight; chmn. ways & means subcom. on health; mem. ways & means sub-com. on trade; mem. del. to Soviet Union by Am. Council Young Political Leaders 1977; chmn. Kern County Rep. Central Com., 1972-74; mem. Calif. Rep. Com., 1972-80; del. Republican Party Nat. Convention, 1980, 84, 88; mem. Rep. Leader's Task Force on Health Care Reform. Ofc: US House of Reps 2208 Rayburn House Office Bldg Washington DC 20515

THOMASON, PHILLIP BRIAN, linguist, educator; b. dec. 12, 1949, Shawmut, Ala.; s. Marchel Earl and Margaret Evelyn (Wall) T.; m. Cathy Lea Ray, Aug. 19, 1972; 1 son, Brian b. 1977; edn: AB (highest hons.), Univ. of Montevallo, Ala. 1972; MHS in Hispanic studies, Auburn Univ., 1975; PhD, Univ. Ky., Lexington 1987. Career: tchr. of Spanish Kendrick High Sch., Columbus, Ga. 1972-74; Marion (Ala.) Military Inst., 1975-81; grad. asst. Univ. of Ky., 1981-85; instr. Asbury Coll., Ky. 1986; assoc. prof. and coord. of modern languages Pepperdine Univ., Malibu, Calif. 1986-, Language Ctr. director 1990-91; awards: Innovative tchg. ideas Ga. Dept. Edn., Atlanta 1976, fellow Ministry of Culture of Spain, Madrid 1985, Outstanding Young Men of Am. (1977, 88), Who's Who in West 1992-93, Who's Who in Am. Educ. 1993; mem: Fgn. Lang. Alliance of So. Calif. (com. 1991-92), Am. Assn. of Tchrs. of Spanish & Port. 1985-, S.W. Conf. on Lang. Teaching (advy. coun. 1987-), Soc. of the Seven Sages 1983-, Sigma Delta Pi 1972-; publs: diss: El Coliseo de la Cruz Madrid's First Permanent Theatre, 1987; article in Bull. of Hispanic Studies, 1993, translator various religious articles; Ch. of Christ; rec: jogging, gardening. Res: 76 W Avenida de las Flores Thousand Oaks 91360 Ofc: Pepperdine Univ. Modern Language Dept. Malibu 90263-4212

THOMASSON, JORDAN RICHARDS, security industry sales executive; b. Jan. 1, 1958, Alameda; s. Osborne Richards and Muriel Irene (Grunewald) T.; m. Amanda Lynn Martin, Sept. 10, 1978; children: Jordan Matthew b. 1980, Andrea Lynn b. 1985, Joshua Martin b. 1992; edn: grad. Moreau H.S. 1976; Am. Mgmt. Assn. Principles of Profl. Selling 1991, Making More Powerful Presentations 1992. Career: installation mgr. Diablo Alarm Co., Walnut Creek 1979-80; ops. mgr. Transbay 3M Alarm Co., San Leandro 1980-84; br. mgr. Arius Security Inc., Foster City 1984-86, senior br. mgr., North Hollywood 1986-88, regl. mgr. 1988-90, regl. mktg. mgr. 1990; regl. sales mgr. Fire Burglary Instruments Inc.,

Diamond Bar 1990-91; regional sales mgr. Radionics Inc., Diamond Bar 1991-94; regional sales mgr. Ademco Distribution Inc., Orange 1994–, regional v.p., 1995–; edn. com. chmn. Golden Gate Alarm Assn., San Francisco 1985-86; mem: Calif. Alarm Assn., L.A. Burglar & Fire Alarm Assn. (dir. 1993, 94), Security Services Assn. Orange Co. (dir. 1991, 94, program com. chmn. 1991-92, secty. 1992-93), San Diego Burglar & Fire Alarm Assn., Inland Empire Burglar & Fire Alarm Assn.; Republican; Presbyterian; rec: fishing, hunting, golf. Ofc: Ademco Distribution Inc. 1635 N Batavia St Orange 92667

THOMFORD, WILLIAM EMIL, mechanical engineer, railway equipment technical consultant; b. March 15, 1927, San Francisco; s. Emil George and Anna Marie (Robohm) T.; m. Irene Shapoff, March 21, 1948; children: Elaine Margaret b. 1951; John William b. 1955; edn: AA, City Coll. of San Francisco 1949; BA, UC Berkeley 1951; transp. mgmt., Stanford Grad. Sch. of Bus. 1967; Reg. Profl. Engr. Calif. 1978. Career: with So. Pacific Transp. Co., San Francisco 1951-: locomotive and car draftsman 1951, asst. chief draftsman 1958, asst. mgr. mech. engring. & res. 1964, mgr. design engring. 1966, mgr. car engring. 1972, asst. chief mech. ofcr. 1978, mgr. research & test 1980, ret. 1983; currently, tech. cons. railway equip. and transp.; mem. Assn. of Am. Railroads Car Constrn. Com. 1965- (subcom. chmn., 10 yrs., com. chmn. 1981-83); honors: Henderson Medal, The Franklin Inst., Phila. 1964, Best Design In Steel-Transp. Equip., Am. Iron & Steel Inst. 1971, Arnold Stucki Award, ASME, Rail Transp. Div. 1991; mem: Am. Soc. of Mech. Engrs. (Fellow 1986), Nat. Soc. of Profl. Engrs., Car Dept. Ofcrs. Assn., Engrs. Club of San Francisco, Pacific Railway Club; inventor: "Hydra-Cushion" (1st hydraulic impact cushioning device for freight cars), "Vert-A-Pac" (for shipment of 30 autos), Double-Stack Container Car; mil: USN, WWII 1944-46; Lutheran; rec: fishing, golf. Address: Transportation Consulting Services, 1176 Glenwood Dr Millbrae 94030

THOMPSON, CRAIG SNOVER, corporate communications executive; b. May 24, 1932, Bklyn.; s. Craig F. and Edith (Williams) T.; m. Masae Sugizaki, Feb. 21, 1957; children: Lee Anne, Jane Laura; edn: grad. Valley Forge Mil. Acad., 1951; BA, Johns Hopkins Univ., 1954. Career: newspaper and radio reporter Easton (Pa.) Express, 1954-55, 57-59; Wall Street Journal, 1959-60; account exec. Moore, Meldrum & Assocs., 1960; mgr. pub. relations Central Nat. Bank of Cleveland, 1961-62; account exec. Edward Howard & Co., Cleveland 1962-67, v.p. 1967-69, senior v.p. 1969-71; dir. pub. relations White Motor Corp., Cleveland 1971-76; v.p. pub. relations No. Telecom Inc., Nashville 1976-77; v.p. pub. relations White Motor Corp., Farmington Hills, Mich. 1977-80, v.p. corp. comms. 1980-81; dir. exec. communications Rockwell Internat. Corp., Pitts. 1981-86, El Segundo, Calif. 1986-91, Seal Beach 1992–; mem. Pub. Relations Soc. Am. (accredited), Alumni Assn. Valley Forge Mil. Acad. (bd. dirs. 1988-94); civic: Shaker Lakes Reg. Nature Ctr. (bd. 1970-73); mil: 1st lt. Inf. AUS 1955-57. Ofc: Rockwell Intl. Corp. 2201 Seal Beach Blvd Seal Beach 90740-8250

THOMPSON, DAVID ALFRED, industrial engineer; b. Sept. 9, 1929, Chicago, Ill.; s. Clifford James and Christobel Eliza (Sawin) T.; children: Nancy, Brooke, Lynda, Diane, Kristy; edn: BME, Univ. Va. 1951; BS indsl. engring., Univ. Fla. 1955; MS engring., 1956; PhD, Stnaford Univ. 1961; reg. profl. engr. Calif. Career: research asst. Univ. Fla. Engring. and Industries Exptl. Station, Gainesville 1955-56; instr. indsl. engring. Stanford Univ. 1956-58; acting asst prof. 1958-61, asst. prof. 1961-64, assoc. prof. 1964-72, prof. 1972-83, prof. emeritus 1983–; pres. Portola Assocs. 1964–; prin. investigator NASA Ames Research Center, Moffatt Field 1974–; cons. Dept. of St. Fed. EEO Commn.; maj. U.S. and fgn. cos.; cons. emergency comms. center design Santa Clara Co. Criminal Justice Bd. 1975, Bay Area Rapid Transit Control Center 1977; dir., ed. documentary film Rapid Answers for Rapid Transit, Dept. Transp. 1974; contbr. articles profl. jours; editl. advy. bd. Computers and Graphics 1970–; reviewer Indsl. Engring. and IEEE Transactions 1972–; awards: HEW grantee (1967-70); mem: Am, Inst. Indsl. Engrs., Human Factors Soc., IEEE, Am. Soc. Engring. Edn., Am. Soc. Info. Scis., MTM Assn. Standards & Research, Am. Robotics Soc., Soc. Info. Display; mil: served to lt. USNR 1951-58. Res: 121 Peter Coutts Circle Stanford 94305 Ofc: Portola Assocs 2600 El Camino Real Rm 414 Palo Alto 94306

THOMPSON, DENNIS PETERS, plastic surgeon, association president; b. March 18, 1937, Chgo.; s. David John and Ruth Dorothy (Peters) T.; m. Virginia Williams, June 17, 1961; children: Laura Faye b. 1962, Victoria Ruth b. 1964, Elizabeth Jan b. 1969; edn: BS (highest honors in zool.) Univ. of Ill., Urbana 1957; BS, Univ. of Ill., Chgo. 1959, MS and MD, 1961; Univ. of Ill. Dental Sch., Chgo. 1962-63; bd. certified Am. Bd. of Surgery 1971, Am. Bd. of Plastic Surgery 1975, 78. Career: intern Presbyterian St. Luke's Hosp., Chgo. 1961-62, gen. surgery Mayo Clinic, Rochester, Minn. 1964-66, Harbor Gen. Hosp., Torrance 1968-70, plastic surgery UCLA 1971-73; pvt. practice plastic and reconstrv. surgery, aesthetic surgery, Santa Monica; chmn. plastic surg. sect. St. John's Hosp. 1986-91, chief of surg. Beverly Glen Hosp. 1977-79, attdg. staff Olive View Med. Center 1979–; asst. clin. prof. surg. UCLA Med. Center; honors: Phi Kappa Phi, Phi Beta Kappa, Alpha Omega Alpha, clinical faculty of yr. UCLA Plastic Surg. Div. 1985, listed Who's Who in West, Who's Who in Am., Who's Who in World; mem: Am. Coll. of Surgeons, Am. Soc. for Aesthetic

Plastic Surg., Am. Soc. Plastic and Reconstrv. Surgeons, Internat. Soc. Clin. Plastic Surgery, UCLA Plastic Surgery Soc., Lipoplasty Soc. No. Am., Bay Surgical Soc., AMA, CMA, Calif. Soc. Plastic Surgeons, George Webster Soc., Harbor Collegium, L.A. Co. Med. Soc., Los Angeles Soc. of Plastic Surgeons (13 term pres. 1982–), Pan Pacific Surg. Assn., Aesculapians, L.A. West C.of C. (1974- dir. 1981-84, 86-89, past mem. Bev. Hills 1978-80, Santa Monica 1978-89), Cooperative of Am. Physicians (dir. 1980–, treas. 1986–), Fed. Credit Union (pres. 1978-80), Nu Sigma Nu, Delta Sigma Delta; numerous med. publs.; mil: US Navy 1966-68; Congregational (moderator 1975-76, chmn. bd. trustees 1973-74, 1980-82). Ofc: 2001 Santa Monica Blvd Ste 1180-W Santa Monica 90404

THOMPSON, EVON LEE, mortgage broker; b. Dec. 1, 1946, Baltimore; d. Edward W. and Altia (Nixon) Lee; m. Nathan Beams, Nov. 1, 1981 (div. 1987); children: Christopher M.; edn: BS, Morgan State Coll., Balt., 1968; MBA, Atlanta Univ., 1969. Career: pub. service employment coordinator City of Oakland, Calif. 1971-75; dep. dir. recreation, parks and community svsc. City of Berkeley, 1975-79; sales agt. Fox and Carskadon Realtors, Oakland 1979-83; mortgage broker Canty & Assocs., Oakland 1984-90; mortgage broker/prin. Mortgage Loan Professionals, 1990–; awards: Morgan State Coll. grantee 1962-64, Ford Found. fellow 1968, doll maker Blue Ribbons, Alameda Co. Fair 1992, 93, 94, 95, Best of the Show, Manteca Quilt & Doll Show 1994, 95; mem: Am. Mktg. Assn. (sec. 1965-68), Soc. for Advancement of Mgmt. (chartered), Morgan State Coll. Alumni Assn. (v.p. 1985–), Alpha Kappa, Chi Psi Sigma; civic: Bay Area Big Sisters 1975-80, Hope Acad. Parents Assn. 1982-89; clubs: Fairview Home 1990-91, Flying Phoebe Cloth Doll (treas., 1993-95, pres. 1995–); Republican; Methodist; rec: doll maker. Res: 333 Hegenberger Rd #502 Oakland 94621

THOMPSON, GEORGE ALBERT, professor of geophysics; b. June 5, Swissvale, Pa.; s. George Albert and Maude Alice (Harkness) T.; m. Anita Kimmell, July 20, 1944; children: Albert b. 1948, Dan b. 1951, David b. 1953; edn: BS, Pa. State Univ. 1941; MS, MIT 1942; PhD, Stanford Univ. 1949; reg. geophysicist and geologist Calif. Career: geologist U.S. Geological Survey, Wash. D.C. 1942-44, p.t. geologist, geophysicist 1946-76; asst. prof., prof. geophysics Stanford Univ. 1949–, chmn. geophysics dept. 1967-86, chmn. geology dept. 1979-82, dean sch. of earth scis. 1987-89; cons. Advy. Com. on Reactor Safeguards 1974–; bd. dirs. Incorp. Institutions for Seismology 1984–; awards: NSF Postdoctoral fellow 1956-57, Guggenheim fellow 1963-64; Otto Miller Prof. 1980-89, Geological Soc. Am. George P. Woollard award 1983; mem: Geological Soc. of Am. (fellow), AAAS (fellow), Am. Geophysical Union (fellow), Soc. Exploration Geophysicists; 100 research articles pub. in profl. jours.; mil: lt.j.g. USN 1942-44; rec: forestry, beekeeping. Res: 421 Adobe Pl Palo Alto 94306 Ofc: Stanford Univ. Dept. of Geophysics Stanford 94305

THOMPSON, LARRY ANGELO, lawyer, film producer, personal manager; b. Aug. 1, 1944, Clarksdale, Miss.; s. Angelo and Ann (Tuminello) T.; edn: BBA, Univ. Miss., 1966, JD, 1968; admitted bar: Miss. 1968, Calif. 1970. Career: in-house counsel Capitol Records, Hollywood 1969-71; sr. ptnr. in entertainment law, Thompson, Shankman and Bond, Beverly Hills 1971-77; pres. Larry A. Thompson Orgn., Inc. 1977–; co-owner New World Pictures, 1983-85; lectr. entertainment bu. UCLA, USC, SW Univ. of Law Sch., co-chmn. Repub. Nat. Entertainment Com.; apptd. by Gov. to Calif. Entertainment Commn.; recipient Show Bus. Atty. of Yr. award Capitol Records 1971; mem: ABA, Miss. Bar Assn., Calif. Bar Assn., Inter-Am. Bar Assn., Hon. Order Ky. Colonels, Am. Film Inst., Nat. Acad. Recording Arts and Scis., Acad. of TV Arts and Scis., Hollywood Radio and TV Soc. (recipient Vision Award 1993); author: How to Make a Record Deal & Have Your Songs Recorded, 1975; Prime Time Crime, 1982; producer motion pictures: Crimes of Passion, 1984, My Demon Lover, 1987, Quiet Cool, 1987, Breaking the Rules, 1992; prod. TV shows: Jim Nabors Show, 1977, (Emmy nominee), Mickey Spillane's Mike Hammer, 1981, Bring 'Em Back Alive, CBS series, 1984; prod. TV movies: The Other Lover, CBS, 1985, Convicted, ABC, 1986, Intimate Encounters, NBC, 1986, The Woman He Loved, CBS (on Duke & Duchess of Windsor), 1988, Original Sin, NBC, 1989, Class Cruise, NBC, 1989, Little White Lies, NBC, 1989, Lucy & Desi: Before The Laughter, CBS, 1990, Broken Promises, CBS, 1994, Separated by Murder, CBS, 1994; served w/ JAGC, AUS 1966-72; Republican; R.Cath. Res: 9451 Hidden Valley Pl Beverly Hills 90210 Ofc: Larry A. Thompson Organization 345 N Maple Dr Ste 183 Beverly Hills 90210

THOMPSON, THOMAS MICHAEL, naval logistics management executive; b. Dec. 3, 1943, Eureka; s. Henry Clay Harman and Margaret Marion (Lee) T.; edn: BA, Seattle Univ. 1965; MA, Univ. San Francisco, 1989. Career: gen. supply splst. US Army Weapons Command, Rock Island, Ill. 1966-67; inventory mgmt. splst. Sharpe Army Depot, Lathrop 1967-69; inventory mgmt. splst. Naval Ship Weapon Systems Engineering Sta., Port Hueneme 1969-73, logistics mgmt. splst. 1973-83, asst. for logistics tech. ops. 1983-86, div. mgr., 1986-91, dept. mgr., 1991-92, dept. mgr. Port Hueneme Div., Naval Surface Warfare Center, 1992–; recipient Sustained Superior Performance awards; Republican; R.Cath.; rec: teach religious edn. Res: 2507 Grapevine Dr Oxnard 93030 Ofc: PHD, NSWC Code 5B00 Port Hueneme 93043-5007

THOMPSON, WILLIAM HARRELL, marketing executive; b. Aug. 1, 1941, Norfolk, Va.; s. John V. and Dorothy (Harrell) T.; m. Kathie Frazier, Sept. 18, 1976; son, William Nicholas Thompson b. 1978; edn: BS and BA, English, Comms. and Psych., William & Mary, 1964. Career: ofcr. US Navy Special Warfare 1965-70; mktg./pgm. mgr. Atlantic Research Corp. (defense contr.) 1970-72; gen. mgr. four theme attractions incl. the Queen Mary, Specialty Restaurants Corp., 1972-76; dir. franchise devel. Red Carpet Corp. of America (nat. R.E. firm) 1976-82; v.p./franchising ADIA Services Inc. (nat. personnel firm) 1982-84; senior v.p./mktg. & franchising IMI Inc. (nat. mortgage banking firm) 1984-86; v.p./new mkts. and product devel. American Home Shield (ins.), Santa Rosa, Calif. 1986-91; pres. Thompson Company Inc (nat. mktg. cons. firm) 1991–; civic: La Casa Heights HOA, Walnut Creek (pres. 1979-86, treas. 1989-92); Republican; Presbyterian. Ofc: Thompson Company Inc. 3156 Oak Rd Ste 200 Walnut Creek 94596-7723

THOMSEN, ELEANOR A., retired municipal real property manager; b. July 26, 1925, Omaha, Neb.; d. Tony and Rose M. (Pesek) Dimitroff; m. John W. Thomsen, Sept. 11, 1948; children: Gary L. b. 1949, Ronnie K. b. 1952; grandsons, Michael C. b. 1987, Brian M. b. 1991; edn: AA, Chabot Jr. Coll. 1976; BS, Univ. San Francisco 1979; MPA, CSU Hayward 1983; Calif. lic. real estate broker, 1965. Career: clk. Alameda County Public Works Agy. 1964-65, steno., secty. 1965-73, asst. right of way agent 1973-76, assoc. right of way agent 1976-87; real property mgr. City of Hayward, 1987-90; honors: Right of Way Profl. of the Yr. (1982), cert. of achievement in real estate, prop. mgmt. (1974, 77); mem: South Bay Engrs., East Bay Engrs., Am. Public Works Assn., Internat. Right of Way Assn. (pres. 1985); contbr. num. animal rights orgns.; Republican; R.Cath.; rec: crocheting, travel. Res: 909 Regency Court San Ramon 94583-5626

THOMSON, JAMES ALAN, research organization president and chief executive; b. Jan. 21, 1945, Boston, Mass.; s. James Alan and Mary Elizabeth (Pluff) T.; m. Linda Jayne Eggert, June 10, 1967 (div. Dec. 1988); children: Kristen b. 1970, David b. 1972; m. Darlene Marie Weaver, Jan. 5, 1990; edn: BS, Univ. New Hampshire, Durham 1967; MS, Purdue Univ., 1970, PhD, 1972. Career: res. fellow Univ. Wisconsin, Madison 1972-74; systems analyst U.S. Dept. of Def., W.D.C. 1974-77; staff Nat. Security Council, 1977-81; v.p. RAND, Santa Monica, Calif. 1981-89, pres. and CEO 1989–; awarded Hon. Doctorate in Sci., Purdue Univ. 1992; mem.: Internat. Inst. of Strategic Studies, London (1982–, Council mem., trustee 1985–), Council on Foreign Relations; author: Conventional Arms Control and the Security of Europe (1988), chapters in books and pub. articles. Ofc: RAND 1700 Main Street PO Box 2138 Santa Monica 90407-2138

THOMSON, ROBERTA NELSON, genealogical researcher/historian; b. Dec. 11, 1909, San Francisco; d. Robert Elwood and Florence Corle (Rubicam) Nelson; m. John Burnside Thomson, Jr., July 19, 1930 (dec. Aug. 10, 1981); children: Phyllis Lea Sykes b. 1937, Joyce Beth Crowell b. 1941, Victoria Rose Broadhurst b. 1948; edn: grad. Madison Grammar Sch., S.F., Girls' High Sch., S.F., Miss Barclay's Business Sch., S.F., 1926. Career: author: (Suppl.) genealogical book: Patterson-Andrews Register, 1963-73; (family hist.) Roberta Remembers, 4 vols., 1983-94; (family hist.) Ancestral Anthology, 2 vols., 1984; author, compiler: Sequoia Chapter DAR 100 Year History 1891-1991, 4 vols., 1991; researcher Andrews/ Clapp/ Stokes/ Wright/ Van Cleve Genealogy Book, 1975; active Nat. Soc. Daughters of Am. Revolution, Sequoia Chpt. (first DAR chpt. Calif., organized 1891; regent 1975-77, chaplain 1983-85, 88-90, historian/speaker 1980-82, 89-93), Colonial Dames XVII Century, Anne Bradstreet Chpt. (active mem. as chaplain/speaker 1981-93), Chester County Hist. Soc., Pa. (donor/ writer/ manuscripts), Montgomery Clan of N.Am., Calif. (researcher), Calif. Genealogical Soc. (S.F.), Rittenhouse Family Assn. (Pa.), Mechanics Inst. Library, S.F. (life); recipient nat. and Calif. state NSDAR Awards as Sequoia Chpt. regent, chmn. and speaker: Bicentennial Planting and Marking of 5 trees in Golden Gate Park and Parade Grounds of The Presidio of San Francisco; Marking of 4 Revolutionary War Ancestors' Graves in Pa. (1979); Yorktown Com. "World Turned Upside Down" (1981); Two-Volume Ancestral Anthologies (1984); Restoration, Statue of Liberty (1984); Remembrances of old San Francisco (1987); Rittenhouse Tricentennial Reunion (1988); Coit Tower (Lillie Hitchcock Coit: A Pioneer DAR Member) (1989); 100 Year History of Sequoia Chapter DAR (1991); A Past and Present Saga of the Historic Oregon Trail (1994); recipient Martha Washington Medal, Nat. Soc. Sons of the Am. Revolution (1993); Republican; Presbyterian; rec: researching & collecting Old San Francisco memorabilia.

THORPE, JAMES, literary scholar; b. Aug. 17, 1915, Aiken, S.C.; s. James Ernest and Ruby Estelle (Holloway) T.; m. Elizabeth Daniells, July 19, 1941; children: James b. 1942, John b. 1944, Sarah b. 1947; edn: AB, The Citadel 1936; MA, Univ. N.C., 1937; PhD, Harvard Univ. 1941. Career: instr. to prof. eng. Princeton Univ., N.J. 1946-66; senior research assoc. Huntington Library, San Marino 1966–, director Huntington Library, Art Gallery, Botanical Gardens 1966-83; honors: Hon. LittD, Occidental Coll. (1968), LHD, Claremont Grad. Sch. (1968), LittD, The Citadel (1971), HD, Univ. Toledo (1977), Guggenheim fellow (1949-50, 65-66); mem: Am. Philosophical Soc., Am. Acad. Arts & Scis. (fellow), Am. Antiquarian Soc. (fellow), Modern Language Assn., Renaissance

Soc., Milton Soc.; author 14 books; mil: col. AUS Air Corps 1941-46; Democrat; Episcopalian; rec: horticulture. Res: 1199 Arden Rd Pasadena 91106 Ofc: Huntington Library San Marino 91108

TIEN, CHANG-LIN, university chancellor; b. July 24, 1935, Wuhan, China, naturalized U.S. cit. 1969; s. Yun Chien and Yun Di (Lee) T.; m. Di-Hwa Liu, July 25, 1959; children: Norman Chihnan, Phyllis Chihping, Christine Chihyih; edn: BS, Nat. Taiwan Univ., 1955; MME, Univ. Louisville, 1957; MA, PhD, Princeton Univ., 1959. Career: actg. asst. prof. dept. mech. engring. UC Berkeley, 1959-60, asst. prof. 1960-64, assoc. prof. 1964-68, prof. mech. engring. 1968-88, 1990–, A. Martin Berlin Prof. 1987-88, 1990–, dept. chmn. 1974-81; vice chancellor for research UC Berkeley, 1983-85; exec. v. chancellor and UC Irvine distinguished prof. 1988-90; chancellor UC Berkeley, 1990–; tech. cons. Lockheed Missiles & Space, GE Corp.; trustee Princeton Univ. 1991–; mem. bd. of dir: Wells Fargo Bank 1991–; awards: Guggenheim fellow 1965, Heat Transfer Memorial Award 1974, ASME Gustus L. Larson Memorial Award 1975; Fellow: AAAS, ASME, Max Jakob Memorial Award 1981, AIAA (Thermophysics Award 1977), mem. NAE; contbr. articles to profl. jours.; rec: sports. Ofc: Chancellor's Office University of California Berkeley 94720

TILLMAN, DONNA, educator, marketing consultant; b. Dec. 23, 1940, Linn, Mo.; d. Clarence A. and Josephine G. (Bakenbush) Tillman; m. Dr. Mahmood A. Qureshi, July 1974 (div. 1983); 2 children by previous marriage Monica Iven b. 1964, Greg Iven b. 1965; edn: BS in edn., Lincoln Univ., Jefferson City, Mo. 1966; MA research sociology, PhD sociology (dept. fellow 2 yrs.), St. Louis Univ., 1967, 70; MBA, DePaul Univ. Grad. Sch. of Bus., 1980. Career: tenured prof., internat. bus. & mktg., Calif. State Polytechnic Univ., Pomona; p.t. faculty Claremont Grad. Sch. and UC Riverside; former prof. sociol. and dept. chair Northeastern Ill. Univ., Chgo. 10 yrs., also vis. prof. and chair bus. dept. Barat Coll., Lake Forest, Ill.; past asst. prof. We. Ill. Univ., Macomb; hon. res. fellow dept. soc. adminstrn. Univ. Birmingham, U.K.; cons. industry and govt. mktg. agys. (incl. Gen. Motors, Calif. Avocado Commn., Calif. Grape Growers Assn.); frequent speaker profl. confs.; pub. res. and case studies, book reviews; awards: profl. promise Coll. Bus. Adminstrn. CalPoly for excellence in tchg., res. and univ. & comm. svc. 1989, Lottery grant to provide mktg. mgmt. assistance to Women and Minority owned bus. 1988, presdl. merit Northeastern Ill. Univ. 1979-80; mem: Internat. Bus. Assn., We. Mktg. Educators Assn.; rec: sailing, flying, dancing. Res: 1024 S Tait Oceanside 92054

TIMLIN, ROBERT JAMES, judge; b. July 26, 1932, Buffalo, N.Y.; s. John Owen and Loraine Barbara (McCarthy) T.; m. Caroline, Aug. 24, 1963; children: Patrick b. 1967, Sally b. 1968; edn: BA cum laude, Georgetown Univ., 1954; JD, Georgetown Law Ctr., 1959, LLM, 1964. Career: atty. U.S. Dept. of Justice, Wash. DC, 1961-64; asst. U.S. Atty., U.S. Attorney Ofc. Central Dist. of Calif., Los Angeles 1964-66; atty. law firm Hennigan, Ryneal & Butterwick, Riverside 1966-67; city atty. City of Corona 1971-76; city atty. City of Norco 1970-76; atty., sole practitioner, Hunt, Palladino & Timlin, Riverside 1970-76; U.S. magistrate U.S. Dist. Ct. Cent. Dist. Calif., 1971-75; judge Corona Municipal Ct., 1976-80; judge Riverside County Superior Court, 1980-90; assoc. justice Court of Appeal, Fourth Appellate Dist. 1990-94; judge U.S. Dist. Court, Central Dist. of Calif. 1994–; instr. Citrus Belt Law Sch., 1976-77; instr. Calif. Judicial Edn. & Resrch. Ctr., 1976-94, plng. com. 1988-94; bd. trustees Riverside Co. Law Library 1988-89; honors: Trial Judge of Year, CTLA Inland Empire Chpt. 1986, Disting. Service award Leo A. Deegan Inn of Court 1995; mem: ABA, Calif. Judges Assn., Leo A. Deegan Inn of Court 1993–; civic: Notre Dame H.S. Board, Riv. 1982-84, San Bdo. Diocesan Sch. Board (pres. 1978-81), Saint Edwards Sch. Board, Corona (pres. 1977-78), Corona-Norco Family YMCA (bd. 1968-78, pres. 76-77), So. Calif. Comprehensive Health Plng. Council, L.A. 1971-72; contbr. law jour. articles, 1969, 81; mil: pfc AUS 1955-57; Democrat; Cath. Res: 659 W Hacienda Dr Corona 91720 Ofc: U.S. District Court 4100 Main St Riverside 92502-3000

TIMM, ROBERT MERLE, university administrator and extension wildlife specialist; b. Oct. 7, 1949, Pomona; s. Herbert Merle and Mary Elsie (Beasley) T.; m. Janice Howard Hawthorne, May 31, 1986; children: Anna Elizabeth b. 1989, Sarah Beatrice b. 1990; edn: BS biology, Univ. Redlands, 1971; MS ecology, UC Davis, 1973, PhD, 1977; cert. wildlife biologist The Wildlife Soc. 1981. Career: Ext. vertebrate pest specialist and assoc. prof. Univ. Nebraska, Lincoln 1978-87; supt. and Ext. wildlife specialist Hopland Res. and Extension Ctr., Univ. Calif., Hopland, Calif. 1987–; cons. rodent control, USAID and USDA, to Bangladesh 1989; invited speaker 2nd Symposium on Rodent Control, Kuwait City, Kuwait 1985; awards: outstanding book Natural Resource Council of Am., W.D.C. 1983, Rotary Internat. group study exchange fellow to Rep. South Africa 1982, outstanding new specialist Nebr. Coop. Extension Assoc., Lincoln 1982, excellence in pgmg. Nebr. Coop Ext. 1983; mem: Vertebrate Pest Council (chair 1994-96), The Wildlife Soc. 1974–, Am. Soc. of Mammalogists 1985–, Soc. for Range Mgmt. 1987–, Nat. Animal Damage Control Assn. (co-editor newsletter 1991–); publs: 90+ pub. articles on wildlife mgmt. and animal damage control, co-editor proceedings: Predator Mgmt. in North Coastal Calif., 1990, editor (book) Prevention & Control of Wildlife Damage (1983, co-editor 1994); United Ch. of Christ, Congregational (ch. pres.

First Evangelical Covenant Ch., Lincoln, Nebr. 1983-85, Grace Luth. Ch., Ukiah, Ca. 1991-92). Res: 968 Riverside Dr Ukiah 95482 Ofc: UC Hopland Res. and Extension Ctr., 4070 University Rd Hopland 95449

TIMMINS, JAMES DONALD, venture capitalist; b. Oct. 3, 1955, Hamilton, Ontario, Can.; s/ Donald Gardiner and Myrna Letitia (Seymour) T.; edn: BA, Univ. of Toronto, Ontario, Can., 1978; law study, Queen's Univ., Kingston, Ontario, Can., 1979; business study, Stanford Univ., Stanford, Calif., 1981. Career: assoc. Salomon Brothers, S.F., Calif., 1981-84; managing dir. McKewon & Timmins, S.D., Calif., 1984-87; ptnr.Hambrecht & Quist, S.F., Calif., 1987-90; ptnr. Glenwood Capital, Menlo Park, Calif., 1991–; bd. dir. Artios Corp., Irvine 1994–; mem. Olympic Club, S.F., Calif.; Presbyn. Res: 735 Laurelwood Dr. San Mateo 94403 Ofc: Glenwood Capital 3000 Sand Hill Rd. Bldg. 4, Ste. 230, Menlo Park 94025

TINTAREV, KYRIL, mathematician; b. Aug. 9, 1956, St. Petersburg, Russia, naturalized U.S. 1985; s. Alexei P. Sokolov and Samuella A. Tintareva; m. Sonia Pratt, Sept. 1, 1981; children:, Nava b. 1982; edn: MSc, Univ. Leningrad, 1978; PhD, Weizmann Inst., Israel 1986. Career: vis. asst. prof. Purdue Univ., 1985- 86; Univ. Minn., 1986-87; asst. prof. Univ. of Calif. Irvine, 1987-93, assoc. prof. 1993–; lectr. Uppsala Univ., Sweden 1993–, docent 1994–;mem: Am. Mathematical Soc., Swedish Mathematical Soc.; mil: Israel Defence Forces 1980-81; Jewish; rec: ancient Hebrew manuscripts. Ofc: Dept. Math. Univ. California Irvine 92717

TITELBAUM, SYDNEY, biologist; b. Apr. 24, 1913, Rovno, Russia, nat. 1923; s. Aaron and Rebecca (Patles) T.; m. Olga Adler, Mar. 20, 1939; son, Daniel E. b. 1946; edn: PhB (psych.), Univ. Chgo., 1933, PhD (physiology) 1938, JD, 1942. Career: chief physiologist Chicago Biological Research Lab., Chgo. 1939-59; capt. US Army Air Forces 1943-52, aviation physiologist Westover Field, Mass., Heidelberg, Ger. 1943-46; prof. biol. City Colleges of Chicago, 1960-77, Fromm Inst. Univ. of San Francisco, 1978–; honors: Phi Beta Kappa, Sigma Xi, AORC Award Assn. of Ofcl. Racing Chemists, Portland, Oreg. (1960); publs: numerous articles on toxicology (1939-59). Res: 3628 Fillmore St San Francisco 94123-1602

TODD, BLAKE T., financial consultant; b. Aug. 20, 1955, San Diego; s. Roger Grey and Mary Martha (Tramill) T.; m. Darcena Lee Shears, May 24, 1986 (div. Apr. 1, 1989); m. 2d. C.Starlene DeBord (author of "An Occasional Wildflower"), Apr. 29, 1994; edn: undergrad. Pepperdine Univ. 1973-75, study abroad in Heidelberg, Germany 1974-75; BA, hist., UC Santa Cruz, 1977. Career: asst. mgr. Pacific Stereo, Glendale 1977-79; account exec. Dean Witter Reynolds, Pasadena 1979-81; assoc. v.p. Kidder Peabody & Co., Los Angeles 1981-88; portfolio mgr., first v.p. Smith Barney, Glendale 1988–; mem. Pasadena Bond Club (pres. 1991-92), Rotary (past), TRIPOD (treas. 1994–), Newcommen Soc., Los Angeles Bond Club 1992–; Republican. Res: 1801 Cielito Dr Glendale 91207 Ofc: Smith Barney 550 N Brand Blvd Ste 1100 Glendale 91203

TOFTNESS, CECIL GILMAN, lawyer; b. Sept. 13, 1920, Glasgow, Mont.; s. Anton Bernard and Nettie (Pederson) T.; m. Chloe Vincent, 1951; edn: AA, San Diego Evening Jr. Coll. 1943; BS, UCLA, 1947; JD, Southwestern Univ. 1953. Career: pvt. practice of civil law, 1954–, legal splty. Estate Planning; active duty US Navy 1938-46, naval ofcr. USNR 1946–; honors: Class rep. Class 1953 Southwestern Law Sch., listed Who's Who in Am. Law 1985, Who's Who in Am. Fin. and Ind.; mem. Kiwanis (P.V.), Masons (Manhattan Beach-Redondo Beach #742 Blue Lodge, Royal Arch Mason, Knight Templar, LA Commander #9), Phi Delta Legal Frat.; Democrat; Lutheran; rec: travel (partipant in Society Expedition thru the Northwest Passage), gardening, golf. Ofc: 2516 Via Tejon Palos Verdes Estates 90274

TOLLENAERE, LAWRENCE R., chairman (retired); b. Nov. 19, 1922, Berwyn, Ill.: s. Cyrille and Modesta (Van Damme) T.; m. Mary Elizabeth Hansen, Aug. 14, 1948; children: Elizabeth b. 1951, Homer b. 1952, Stephanie b. 1953, Caswell b. 1956, Mary Jennifer b. 1964; edn: BS and MS in engring., Iowa State Univ., 1944, 1949; MBA, USC, 1969; LLD. (hon.), Claremont Grad. Sch., 1977. Career: engr. Aluminum Co. of Am., Huntington Park 1946-47; asst. prof. indsl. engring. Iowa State Univ., Ames 1947-50; sales rep. Am. Pipe and Constrn. Co. (name changed to Ameron, Inc., 1970), South Gate, Calif. 1950-53, specialist rep. to S.Am. 1953-54, 2d v.p./div. mgr. Colombian Div., Bogota 1955-57, v.p./div. mgr. So. Calif. 1957-63, v.p. concrete pipe ops., Monterey Park, 1963-64, pres. corp. hq. 1965-67, dir., pres. and c.e.o. Ameron Inc. 1967-89, chmn. bd., c.e.o. and pres. 1989-93; dir: Avery Dennison, Pasadena; Newhall Land and Farming Co., Valencia; The Parsons Corp., Pasadena; fmr. dir. Pacific Mutual Life Ins. Co., fmr. bd. chmn. Gifford-Hill-American, Inc.; mem: Merchants and Mfrs. Assn./L.A. (fmr. bd. chmn., dir.), The Beavers (hon. dir., past pres.), Calif. C.of C. (dir. 1977-92), Newcomen Soc. in N.Am., Alpha Tau Omega; former mem: Nat. Assn. of Mfrs., Soc. for Advancement of Mgmt., AMA Presidents Assn.; civic bds: The Huntington Library, Art Gal. and Botanical Gardens (bd. trustees), Soc. of Fellows, The Huntington Library (life mem.), Claremont Univ. Ctr. Bd. of Fellows (emeritus 1991), Iowa State Univ.

Found. (bd. of govs., Order of Knoll.); clubs: California (dir., past pres.), Jonathan, Pauma Valley Country, San Gabriel Country, Bohemian (S.F.), Commanderie de Bordeaux (L.A.), Los Angeles Confrerie des Chevaliers du Tastevin, Twilight, Lincoln; mil: ensign to lt.jg USNR 1944-46, WWII; rec: philately, hunting, fishing, equestrian. Res: 1400 Milan Ave South Pasadena 91030 Ofc: 245 S. Los Robles Ave. Pasadena 91101

TOLMACH, JANE LOUISE, civic activist; b. Nov. 12, 1921, Havre, Mont., raised in Ventura, Calif.; d. Robert Francis and Veronica A. (Tracy) McCormick; m. Daniel Michael Tolmach, MD (pediatrician), Sept. 9, 1946; children: James, Richard, Eve Alice, Adam, Jonathan; three grandchildren; edn: AB, UCLA, 1943; MS soc. sci., Smith Coll., 1945; JD, Southwestern Univ. Sch. of Law, 1981. Career: volunteer community service orgns., Oxnard 1948–; mem. Ventura County Grand Jury 1958; Oxnard City Planning Commn. 1957-62; bd. trustees Camarillo State Hosp. 1959-68 (chmn. 1966-68); bd. trustees Oxnard Union H.S. Dist. 1965-72; elected Oxnard City Council 1970-78: bd. dirs. South Coast Area Transit (mem., chmn. 1973-78), So. Calif. Assn. of Govts. (comprehensive transp. steering com. 1974-75, SCAG exec. bd. 1975-76, v.ch. utilities and transp. com. 1977-78), Ventura Co. Energy Com. (1973-74), Ventura Co. Flood Zone II Advy. Com. (1972-77), Ventura Co. Assessment Appeals Bd. 1992–; mem. bds: St. John's Regl. Med. Ctr. (dir. 1986-89), Calif. Comm. Colls. (bd. govs. 1982-87), State Reclamation Bd. (1981-82); Democrat: active local, state and nat. campaigns (mem., chair Ventura Co. Dem. central com. 1953-70, Calif. State central com. 1958-76, 89, Women's Chair South 66-70; del. Nat. Conv. 1960, 68, 76, 88, 92, alt. del. 1956, 64; nom. State Assembly, 36th Dist. 1976); R.Cath. Res: 656 Douglas Ave Oxnard 93030

TOMA, RAMSES BARSOUM, professor; b. Nov. 9, 1938, Cairo, Egypt; nat. 1973; s. Barsoum Khalil and Fieka Ghabriel T.; m. Rosette Roushdy, Sept. 7, 1969; children: Narmer b. 1980, Kamy b. 1985; edn: BS food sci., Ain Shams Univ. Cairo Egypt 1959; MS in food tech., 1965; PhD, La. State Univ. 1971; MPH, Univ. Minn. 1980. Career: food inspr. Ministry of Food Supplies, Cairo, Egypt 1960-68; chemist Crystal Foods Inc., New Orleans, La. 1969; asst. prof. Univ. North Dakota, Grand Forks 1972-74, assoc. prof., dept. chair 1974-80, prof. 1980-84; prof. food science and human nutrition CSU Long Beach, Calif. 1984–; cons. and tchr., Egypt and U.S. 1972–; awards: La. State Univ. scholarship 1969-71, Univ. N.D. faculty research 1974-83, Univ. Minn. Research scholarship 1980, CSU Merit. Performance 1986-89, CSU Long Beach Scholarly and Creative Activities Disting. Award 1991; mem: Am. Inst. Chemist (fellow), Inst. Food Technologists (profl. mem.), Am.Dietitic Assn., Am. Assn. Cereal Chemists, Am. Inst. Nutrition, Egyptian Am. Scholars, Coptic Orthodox Ch., Sigma Xi, Phi Beta Delta; 60 research articles pub. in sci. jours., 1970–; Republican; Coptic Orthodox; rec: swimming, gardening.

TOMBRELLO, THOMAS ANTHONY, JR., professor of physics; b. Sept. 20, 1936, Austin, Tx.; s. Thomas Anthony and Jeanette Lillian (Marcuse) T.; m. Ann Hall, May 30, 1957 (div. 1976); m. Stephanie Russell, Jan. 15, 1977; children: Christopher b. 1958, Susan b. 1962, Karen b. 1964, Kerstin b. 1970; edn: BA physics, Rice Univ. 1958; MA, 1960; PhD, 1961. Career: postdoctoral fellow Rice Univ., Houston, Tx. 1961; Calif. Inst. Tech., Pasadena 1961-62, 1964-65; asst. prof. Yale Univ., New Haven, Conn. 1963; Calif. Inst. Tech. 1965-67, assoc. prof. 1967-71, prof. 1971–; research cons. Schlumberger Doll Research, Ridgefield, Conn. 1981-87, v.p., dir. research 1987-89; awards: NSF Postdoctoral fellow 1961-62, A.P. Sloan Found. fellowship 1971-75, Von Humboldt Found. 1984-85, UC Davis Disting. Vis. Prof. 1984; mem: Am. Physical Soc. (fellow); 200+ papers in sci. jours., 3 patents; Democrat; rec: jogging. Res: 2938 Santa Rosa Altadena 91001 Ofc: California Institute of Technology 200-36 Pasadena 91125

TOMEI, JOEL ALAN, architect; b. May 11, 1941, San Mateo; s. Joseph Ambrose and Grace Leona (Nunes) T.; m. Patricia Hayden Brown, July 12, 1964; children: Amanda H. b. 1978, Elizabeth Y. b. 1983; edn: AA, Santa Rosa Jr. Coll. 1961; BArch, MArch, UC Berkeley, 1966, 1967; Master City Plnng. in Urban Design, Harvard Univ., 1973; reg. arch. Calif. (1970), Ill., Mass.; cert. NCARB. Career: arch. Skidmore, Owings & Merrill, Archs./ Engrs., 1967-78: designer, job captain, Chgo. 1967-70, urban designer Boston 1971-74, San Francisco, also Tehran 1974-80, mem.steering com. chmn. Skidmore, Owings & Merrill 1976; project mgr. Hope Consulting Group, Archs./Engrs., San Francisco 1979- v.p. 1980–, prin. architect 1983–; design team: Sears Tower, Chgo. 1968, U.S. Embassy, Moscow 1977, Bandar Shapour, New Town, Iran 1975, Yanbu, New Town, Saudi Arabia 1976, Saudi Naval Acad., Jeddah, S.A. 1981, project mgr. Moscone Conv. Ctr. Expansion, San Francisco 1987, project mgr. Hall of Justice Expansion, S.F. 1990; design jury critic UC Berkeley 1975; awards: Mellon Scholar Harvard Univ. 1972, 28th annual Progressive Architecture design awd. 1981, AIA award Republic Newspaper Plant, Columbus, Ind. 1980, AIA award Hall of Justice Expansion 1992, U.S. Courts Projects 1993; mem. Am. Inst. of Planners (AIP), Harvard Club (S.F.), S.F. Planning and Urban Research, S.F. Market Street Proj.; Democrat; Episcopalian; rec: photog., film making, gardening. Res: 167 20th Ave San Francisco 94121 Ofc: Fong & Chan Architects 1361 Bush St San Francisco 94109

TOMPKINS, DWIGHT EDWARD, lawyer; b. June 29, 1952, Toledo, Ohio; s. Leonard Charles and Amanda Virginia (Bunce) T.; m. Marilyn Vergara, June 15, 1974; children: Jason b. 1978, Kristin b. 1981; edn: BA anthropology, San Diego St. Univ., 1974; MPA, CSU Long Beach, 1982; JD, Loyola Law Sch., L.A. 1990; admitted bar: Calif. 1990, US Dist. Cts., Cent. Dist. Calif. 1990 and So. Dist. Calif. 1991. Career: mgr. City of South Gate 1976-81; supr. City of Long Beach 1981-85, budget analyst, 1985-89; law clk. Ching, Kurtz & Blix, 1989-90; atty., assoc. Ching & Associates, 1990-91; solo practice Law Offices of Dwight Edward Tompkins, 1991–; gen. counsel Ontrack Management Systems, Inc. 1994–; lectr. CSU Long Beach 1986; honors: Am. Jurisprudence Award for Trial Advocacy, Pi Alpha Alpha, Phi Kappa Phi, Phi Delta Phi; mem: Orange Co. Bar Assn., Order of DeMolay (adv. council Garden Grove chpt. 1992–, master councilor 1969-70), Rotary Internat. (Garden Grove West chpt.), Nat. Rifle Assn., Cypress Nat. Jr. Basketball (bd. 1992-94), Internat DeMolay Alumni Assn., Calif. Bar Assn. Estate Planning Trust & Probate Section, Orange Co. Bar Assn. Estate Planning Probate & Trusts Section; publs: article, J. of Law & Edn. (Summer 1991). Address: PO Box 2817 Seal Beach 90740

TOMPKINS, ROGER BARTON, insurance company executive; b. Dec. 17, 1932, Bloomington, Ill.; s. Arthur Wilson and Dortha (Christopher) T.; m. Elinor Grace Bieneman, June 12, 1954; children: Paul b. 1955, Kathryn b. 1958, Laura b. 1960; edn: BS, Univ. Ill. 1954; LL.B, 1956. Career: agent State Farm, Fla. 1957-59; agency mgr. State Farm Mutual Ins. Co., Miami, Fla. 1960-62, agency dir., St. Petersburg, Fla. 1962-67, exec. asst., Bloominton, Fla. 1967-69, v.p. agency 1969-72, agency v.p. 1972-74, regional v.p., Costa Mesa 1974-90, v.p., Calif. 1991–; mem: Wycliffe Bible Translators Inc. (bd.), Assn. for Calif. Tort Reform (bd.), We. Ins. Info. Svc. (bd.), Personal Ins. Fedn. of Calif. (bd.), Calif. C.of C. (bd.), Calif. Business Roundtable (exec. com.), Neighborhood Housing Svs., L.A. (trustee), Mut. Housing Assn., Sacto. (trustee), Nat. Coalition for the Protection of Children and Families (bd.); Republican; Christian. Res: 1622 Kimberwicke Dr Santa Ana 92705 Ofc: 770 L Street #720 Sacramento 95814

TONG, HOYT CHING, chiropractic physician; b. Apr. 21, 1964, Syracuse, N.Y.; s. Howard Wing Soon Tong; edn: BS, N.C. State Univ., Raleigh 1985; Doctor Of Chiropractic, Palmer Univ., Sunnyvale, Calif. 1988. Career: physician (staff) Neurologic Orthopedic Associates Surgical Group, Los Angeles 1988-93; solo practice Premier Health Center, San Francisco 1993–; lectr. Pacific Coast Hospital, S.F. 1993–; mem: Calif. Chiropractic Assn. 1987–, Academy of Forensic Consultants (fellow) 1993–. Ofc: Premier Health Center, San Francisco 94121

TOOLEY, WILLIAM LANDER, real estate development company executive; b. Apr. 23, 1934, El Paso, Tx.; s. William Lander and Virginia Mary (Ryan) T.; m. Reva Berger, Mar. 5, 1966; children: William b. 1968, Patrick b. 1969, James b. 1972; edn: BA, Stanford Univ. 1956; MBA, Harvard Grad. Sch. 1960. Career: treas., mgr. Pickwick Hotel Co., San Diego 1960-63; David H. Murdock Devel. Co., Phoenix, Ariz. 1963-66; ptnr. Ketchum Peck & Tooley, Los Angeles 1967-74; chmn. Tooley & Co. 1974–; dir. Nat. Realty Com., Wash. D.C. 1975–; bd. dirs. Federal Reserve Bank San Francisco 1988–; mem: Urban Land Inst., Loyola Marymount Univ. Bd. Regents 1982–, Bd. Trustees 1975-82, Calif. Club, Calif. Yacht Club; mil: lt. j.g. USNR 1956-58; Catholic. Ofc: 3303 Wilshire Blvd 12 Floor Los Angeles 90010

TORRES, ESTEBAN EDWARD, congressman, business executive; b. Jan. 27, 1930, Miami, Ariz.; s. Esteban and Rena Baron (Gomez) T.; m. Arcy Sanchez, Jan. 22, 1955; children: Carmen D'Arcy, Rena Denise, Camille Bianca, Selina Andre, Esteban Adrian; edn: student, East Los Angeles Coll., 1960, Calif. State Univ., L.A. 1963, Univ. Md., 1965, Am. Univ., 1966; hon. PhD, Nat. Univ., 1987. Career: chief steward United Auto Workers, local 230, 1954-63, dir. political com., 1963; organizer, internat. rep. United Auto Workers, local 230, Washington, 1964; asst. dir Internat. Affairs Dept., 1975-77; dir. Inter-Am. Bureau for Latin Am., Caribbean, 1965-67; exec. dir. E. L.A. Community Union (TELACU), 1967-74; U.S. ambassador to UNESCO, Paris, 1977-79; chmn. Geneva Group, 1977-78; chmn. U.S. del. Gen. Conf., 1978; spl. asst. to pres. U.S., dir. White House Office Hispanic Affairs, 1979-81; mem. 98th-104th Congresses from 34th Calif. dist., 1983–, mem. appropriations com., subcom. fgn. opinions, veteran HUD and indep. agys.; campaign coord. Jerry Brown for Gov., 1974; Hispanic coord. L.A. County campaign Jimmy Carter for Pres., 1976; mem. Sec. of State Advy. Group, 1979-81; v.p. Nat. Congress Comm. Econ. Devel., 1973-74; pres. Congress Mex.-Am. Univ., 1970-71, L.A. Plaza de la Raza Cultural Ctr., 1974; dir. Nat. Com. on Citizens Broadcasting, 1977; cons. U.S. Congress ofc. of tech. assessment, 1976-77; del. to U.S. Congress European Parliament meetings, 1984–; official congl. observer Geneva Arms Control Talks; chmn. Congl. Hispanic Caucus, 1987; speaker Wrights Del. to USSR, 1987; Dem. dep. whip, 1990; co-chmn. Nat. Hispanic Dems., 1988–; chmn. Japan-Hispanic Inst. Inc.; bd. visitors Sch. Arch., UCLA, 1971-73; bd. dirs. L.A. Co. Econ. Devel. Com., 1972-75, Internat. Devel. Congress, 1976-78; recipient num. awards for public svc.; mem. Americans for Dem. Action (exec. bd. 1975-77); active mem. Veterans of Foreign Wars Post 6315, Pico Rivera, Calif. and Am. Legion Post 0272, Montebello, Calif.; mil: served in AUS, 1949-53, ETO. Ofc: US House of Reps Rm 2368 Rayburn Office Bldg Washington DC 20515-0534

TORTOLANO, JAMES VINCENT, lawyer; b. Aug. 21, 1949, San Jose; s. James and Celia Delores T.; m. Joan Marie Sorci, Aug. 2, 1969 (div. 1970); m. Diane McDermott, Sept. 21, 1991; 1 son, James John b. 1970; edn: BSEE, Univ. Santa Clara 1971; JD, UC Davis 1983; admitted St. Bar Calif. 1983. Career: corp. counsel Advanced Micro Devices, Sunnyvale 1983-90, sr. corp. counsel 1990-94, asst. general counsel 1994-95, assoc. gen. counsel dir. 1995–; mem: Santa Clara Co. Bar Assn., Am. Intellectual Property Assn., Peninsula Patent Law Assn., S.F. Patent Law Assn.; patentee in field; Democrat; rec: golf, music, film, sports. Ofc: Advanced Micro Devices One AMD Place POB 3453 M/S 68 Sunnyvale 94088

TOTTEN, GEORGE OAKLEY, III, political science professor emeritus, author; b. July 21, 1922, W.D.C.; s. George O. Totten Jr. and Vicken (von Post) Totten Barrois; m. Astrid Maria Anderson, June 26 1948 (dec. Apr. 26, 1975); children: Vicken Yuriko, Linnea Catherine; m. Lilia Huiying Li, July 1, 1976; 1 child Blanche Lemes; edn: cert. Univ. Mich., 1943; AB, Columbia Univ., 1946, AM, 1949; MA, Yale Univ., 1950, PhD, 1954; docentur i Japanologi, Univ. Stockholm, 1977. Career: lectr. Columbia Univ., N.Y.C., 1954-55; asst. prof. MIT, Cambridge 1958- 59, Boston Univ. 1959-61; assoc. prof. Univ. Rhode Island Kingston 1961-64; assoc. prof. polit. sci. USC, Los Angeles 1965-68, prof. 1968-92, emeritus 1992–, dept. chmn. 1980-86, dir. East Asian Studies Ctr. 1974-77; affil. scholar Ctr. for Multi-ethnic and Transnat. Studies, USC 1993–; founder/dir. Calif. Pvt. Univs. and Colls. year-in-Japan pgm. Waseda Univ., 1967-73, So. Calif.-UCLA Jt. East Asian Studies Ctr., 1976-77; vis. prof. Univ. Stockholm 1977-79; first dir. for Pacific Asia Studies, 1985-89, sr. counsellor, bd. dirs., 1989–; mem: U.S.-China People's Friendship Assn., W.D.C. 1974–, Com. on U.S.-China Relations, N.Y.C. 1975–, L.A.-Pusan Sister City Assn., L.A. (chmn. 1976-77), L.A.-Guangzhou Sister City Assn. (bd. 1982–), Japan-Am. Soc. L.A. (bd. dir. 1981–), nat. advy. com. of the Japan-Am. Student Conf. 1986–; awards: Social Sci. Res. Council fellow 1952-53, grantee Ford Found. 1955-58, grantee NSF 1979-81, grantee Korea Found. 1993, commendn. award for pgm. on Korean studies Consulate Gen. of Republic of Korea 1975, Philippine Liberation Medal 1994 (awarded for mil. svc. during WWII); mem: founding mem. USC Beta Kappa chpt. Phi Beta Delta nat. honor soc. 1993–, Assn. for Asian Studies, Am. Polit. Sci. Assn., Internat. Polit. Sci. Assn., Internat. Studies Assn., Japanese Polit. Sci. Assn., European Assn. Japanese Studies, China Soc. for People's Friendship Studies, Beijing (adv. bd. 1991–); club: Faculty (USC); author: Social Democratic Movement in Prewar Japan (1966, Chinese edit. 1987), coauthor Socialist Parties in Postwar Japan, 1966, Japan and the New Ocean Regime, 1984, co-editor, author: Developing Nations: Quest for a Model (1970, Japanese edit. 1975), China's Economic Reform: Administering the Introduction of the Market Mechanism, 1992, co-translator: Chien Mu's Traditional Government in Imperial China, 1982, contbg. author: The Politics of Divided Nations (1991, Chinese ed. 1994), co-editor: Community in Crisis: New Directions for the Korean American Community After the Civil Unrest of April 1992 (1994), editor and intro. author: Song of Ariran by Helen Foster Snow (1973, Korean Edit. 1992, Chinese edit. 1993); mil: 1st lt. US Army 1942-46, PTO; Episcopalian; rec: learning languages, jogging, aerobics, dancing. Res: 5129 Village Green Los Angeles 90016-5205 Ofc: Ctr for Multiethnic and Transnational Studies (CMTS) GFS-300 Univ. of Southern California, Los Angeles 90089-1694

TOWNES, CHARLES HARD, astrophysicist; b. July 28, 1915, Greenville, SC; s. Henry Keith and Ellen Sumter (Hard) T.; m. Frances H. Brown, May 4, 1941; children: Linda Lewis b. 1943, Ellen Scriven b. 1946, Carla Keith b. 1949, Holly Robinson b. 1952; edn: BA, BS, Furman Univ. 1935, MA, Duke Univ. 1937, PhD, Calif. Inst. Technol. 1939. Career: mem. tech. staff Bell Telephone Lab. 1939-47; assoc. prof. physics Columbia Univ. 1948-50, prof. 1950-61; exec. dir. Columbia Radiation Lab. 1950-52, chmn. physics dept. 1952-55; provost, prof. physics M.I.T. 1961-66, Inst. Prof. 1966-67; v.p., dir. res. Inst. Def. Analyses Wash. DC 1959-61; univ. prof. physics UC Berkeley 1967–, now prof. grad. sch.; bd. dirs: Gen. Motor (1973-86), Perkin-Elmer, Carnegie Inst., Pacific Sch. of Religion, Calif. Inst. of Tech.; honors: Comstock Prize 1959, Rumford Premium 1961, Thomas Young Medal 1963, Nobel Prize for Physics 1964, Medal of Honor, I.E.E.E. 1966, Earle K. Plyler Prize 1977, Nat. Inventors Hall of Fame 1976, Niels Bohr Internat. Gold Medal 1979, Nat. Medal of Sci. 1982, Engring. & Sci. Hall of Fame 1983, Berkeley Citation 1986, Commonwealth Award 1993; mem: Legion of Honor (Ofcr. 1991–), Am. Physical Soc., Am. Acad. Arts & Scis., Nat. Acad. of Sci., Calif. Acad. of Sci., Am. Phil. Soc., Am. Astron. Soc., The Royal Soc. of London, Ind. Nat. Sci. Acad., Max Planck Soc. 1986, Pontifical Acad. of Scis. (Rome), Russian Acad. of Sci., President's Sci. Advis. Com. 1966-69 (vice chmn. 1967-69); chmn. Sci. & Tech. Advy. Com. for Manned Space Flight NASA 1964-69; inventor MASER, co-inventor LASER; research on nuclear and molecular structure, microwave and infrared astronomy; co-author Microwave Spectroscopy; Prot.; rec: natural history. Res: 1988 San Antonio Ave Berkeley 94707 Ofc: UC Berkeley Dept. of Physics Berkeley 94720

TRACY, BRIAN S., professional speaker, consultant, author; b. Jan. 5, 1944, Charlottown, Canada; s. Arthur J. and Helen Patricia (Kelleher) T.; m. Barbara Anne Klein, June 30, 1979; children: Christina b. 1980, Michael b. 1982, David

b. 1986, Catherine b. 1991; edn: BS in commerce, Univ. Alberta, 1977; MA, Columbia Pacific Univ. Career: sales rep. Steel Office Supplies, Johannesburg, S.A. 1965-66; mgmt. trainee O.K. Bazaars 1966-67; copy writer Lindsay Smithers 1967-68; investment sales Dyavest Internat., Bangkok, Thailand 1968-69; v.p. U.S. Invest Services, Hong Kong 1969-70; investment cons. Invest-Mentor, Mexico City 1971-72; lease agent Knowlton Realty, Vancouver, B.C. 1972-73; real estate developer Allarco Devel., Edmonton 1975-78; gen. mgr. Suzuki Attasco 1978-80; C.O.O. Patrician Land Corp. 1980-81; author (Simon & Schuster): Maximum Achievement, 1993, Advanced Selling Strategies, 1995; author/narrator of Psychology of Achievement, Psychology of Success, Psychology of Selling, How To Start and Build Your Own Successful Business, Peak Performance Woman, Getting Rich In America, The Effective Manager Seminar Series, How To Master Your Time; pres. Inst. for Executive Development, 1975–; chmn. Peak Performance Training, and Brian Tracy Internat.; mem: Nat. Speakers Assn., Am. Soc. for Tng. & Devel., Internat. Platform Assn.; Republican; Prot.; rec: writing, travel (visited 80+ countries). Res: 320 Loma Larga Dr Solana Beach 92075

TRAILL, DAVID ANGUS, classicist, educator; b. Jan. 28, 1942, Helensburgh, Scotland; s. Angus Nicolson and Elizabeth Blyth (Wilson) Traill; edn: MA, classics, Univ. St. Andrews, Scotland, 1964; PhD, classics, UC Berkeley, 1971. Career: lectr. McGill Univ., Montreal, Can. 1964-65; tchg. asst. UC Berkeley 1965-68; asst. prof. UC Davis 1970-78, assoc. prof. 1978-85, prof. 1985–, program dir. Classics, 1985–; prodn. cons. documentaries on Schliemann and Troy, BBC, London 1980-81, 85; mem.: Am. Philol. Assn. 1968–, Archaeol. Inst. Am. 1980–, Medieval Assn. of the Pacific 1972–; author: Walahfrid Strabo's Visio Wettini, 1978; Myth, Scandal and History: The Heinrich Schliemann Controversy, 1986, Excavating Schliemann, 1993, Schliemann of Troy: Treasure and Deceit, 1995. Res: 1351 Monarch Ln Davis 95616 Ofc: Classics Dept. Univ. California, Davis 95616

TRAN, DOUGLAS A., physician; b. Jan. 12, 1950, Saigon, Vietnam, nat. USA 1981; s. Khoe Van and Tram Thi (Nguyen) T.; m. Trang Truong, June 21, 1980; children: Derek b. 1982, Duke b. 1987, Dustin b. 1992, Dylan b. 1993; edn: pre-med. and 5 yrs. medicine, Saigon Univ. 1969-75; MD, Univ. of Calif., Irvine 1979; certified Am. Board of Otolaryngology 1985. Career: intern and resident USC Medical Center 1979-84; pvt. practice otolaryngology in Orange County 1985–; awards: Am. Field Service Scholarship, senior yr. H.Sch. in US, 1967-68; mem. AMA, Orange County Med. Assn., Calif. Med. Assn., Am. Assn. of Otolaryngology, Head & Neck Surgery, USC Alumni Assn.; Republican; Buddhist; rec: fgn. language and cultures, painting, piano, tennis, skiing. Res: 23 Bayporte Irvine 92714

TRAYLOR, WILLIAM ROBERT, author, publisher, printing industry consultant; b. May 21, 1921, Texarkana, Ark.; s. Clarence Edington and Seba Ann (Talley) T.; m. Elvirez Sigler, Oct. 9, 1945; children: Kenneth Warren, Gary Robert, Mark Daniel, Timothy Ryan; edn: student Univ. Houston, 1945-46, Univ. Omaha, 1947-48. Career: Div. mgr. Lily Tulip Cup Corp., N.Y.C., 1948-61; asst. to pres. Johnson & Johnson, New Brunswick, N.J. 1961-63; mgr. we. region Rexall Drug & Chem. subs. Dart Industries, L.A. 1963-67; pres. Prudential Pub. Co., Sebastopol, Calif. 1967–; cons. to printing ind., 1976–; syndicated writer "Bill Friday's Bus. Bull." 1989–; pub. Profl. Estimate and Mgmt. Software for printing ind., 1992; author: Instant Printing (1976, Japanese transl.), Successful Mgmt., 1979, Quick Printing Ency. (1982, 7th edit. 1988), How to Sell Your Product Through (Not to) Wholesalers, 1980; honors: Man of Year Quick Printing Mag. 1987, Who's Who in the World 1993-94; mem. Nat. Assn. Quick Printers (hon. life), C.of C., Kiwanis, Toastmasters; Democrat; rec: skiing, boating. Res/Ofc: 7635 Meadow Court Sebastopol 95472 Tel: 707/824-8416

TRESCHER, SUSAN, lawyer; b. Dec. 18, 1928, Glendale; d. F. George and Susan T. (Shea) Trescher; edn: BA, UC Berkeley 1950; JD, Harvard Univ. 1955; admitted St. Bar Calif. (1956). Career: staff atty. Columbia Pictures, Hollywood 1955-56; law clk. U.S. Dist. Ct., Los Angeles 1956-58; cons. atty. Fund for Republic, Berkeley 1958-60; research atty. Cont. Edn. Bar UC Berkeley 1960-63; Co. of Santa Barbara 1964-82; atty. sole practice, Santa Barbara 1982–; legal counsel Santa Barbara Regional Health Authority 1982–; spl. counsel Santa Barbara Co. Flood Control & Water Conservation Dist. 1982-89; City of Carpinteria 1985-89; mem: Calif. Women Lawyers (dir. 1980-85, v.p. 1981-82), Legal Aid Found. Santa Barbara Co. (dir. 1985-88, pres. 1989), Democratic Central Com., La Mesa Improvement Assn.; ed. Legal Aspects of Competitive Bus. Practices, 1961; rec: gardening, swimming, travel. Res: 1 Mesa Ln Santa Barbara 93101 Ofc: 2600 De La Vina St Ste F Santa Barbara 93105

TRICOLES, GUS PETER, engineer, b. Oct. 18, 1931, San Francisco, Calif.; s. Peter Constantine and Eugenia (Elias) T.; m. Dec. 20, 1953; widowed Dec. 4, 1974; m. Aileen, Apr. 1, 1980; div. Sept., 1980; children: Rosanne b. 1958, Robin b. 1961; edn: BA, physics, UCLA, 1955; MS, applied math, San Diego St. Coll., 1958; MS, physics, UC San Diego, 1962; PhD, applied physics, UC San Diego, 1971; career: design splst. Convair Div., Gen. Dynamics, San Diego, 1955-59; physicist Smyth Res. Assocs., San Diego, 1959-61; res. asst. Scripps Institution, San Diego, 1961-62; sr. engring. staff splst. Gen. Dynamics Electronics, San

Diego, 1962-92; sr. engring. staff splst. GDE Systems, Inc., San Diego, 1992–;cons. to: Aero Geo Industries, San Antonio 1979-80, Transco Industries, L.A. 1972-73, Ministry of Defense, Haifa, Israel 1981, Synergistic Comms., Columbus, Oh. 1989, 1992, Georgia Inst. of Tech., Atlanta 1982, 1984; mem: IEEE (fellow 1956–), Optical Soc. of Am. (fellow 1957–), Am. Geophysical Union 1965–, NY Academy of Sciences 1970, US Comms., Internat. Scientific Radio Union 1965–; civic: San Diego St. Univ. Found.; author: book chpt., Radome Engring. Handbook, 1970; book chpt., Antenna Handbook, 1987; author/inventor: patent, Microwave Holograms, 1965; patent, Anistropic Radomes, 1985; mil: USN, 1951-54; rec: woodworking. Res: 4633 Euclid Ave. San Diego 92115. Ofc: GDE Systems, Inc. P.O. Box 509009 San Diego 92150-9009

TRIEBSCH, ROBERT ERNEST, lawyer; b. Jan. 4, 1939, San Francisco; s. Ernest A. and Virnelle T.; m. Joelle, Feb. 10, 1963; children: Brad b. 1963, Cristina b. 1965, Erin b. 1970; edn: BA, UC Davis 1960; LL.B, UC Berkeley 1963; admitted St. Bar Calif. (1966). Career: ptnr. Muller Pia & Simmons, Salinas 1967-74; pres. Triebsch & Frampton, Turlock 1974–; pres. Calif. St. Univ. Stanislaus Found. bd. dirs. 1995; trustee Turlock Joint Schools Financing Agency 1991–; treas. and v.p. Calif. St. Univ. Stanislaus Statesmen 1976-78; dir. Turlock Refrigerating; bd. dirs. Monterey Co. Bar Assn. 1970-71; mem. Turlock H.S. Bd. Trustees (pres. 1976-88); honors: Blue Key and Calif. Club, UC Davis, Calif. Young Lawyers ed. newspaper 1973-74, dir. 1972-75; mem: Stanislaus Co. Bar Assn., Calif. Bar Assn., Am. Bar Assn., Rotary Club Turlock (pres. 1988-89); mil: capt. AUS 1963-67; Republican; Cath.; rec: tennis, skiing, gardening. Res: 1685 California Ave Turlock 95381 Ofc: Triebsch & Frampton POB 709 Turlock 95381

TRIGIANO, LUCIEN LEWIS, physician; b. Feb. 9, 1926, Easton, Pa.; s. Nicholas L. and Ann (Lewis) T.; m. Elaine J. Eggert; children: Lynn b. 1949, Glenn b. 1951, Robert b. 1953; edn: Ohio Univ., Texas Christian Univ., MD, Temple Univ., 1952; cert. Am. Bd. Physical Med. and Rehab., 1966; cert. instrument pilot FAA. Career: intern Conemaugh Valley Mem. Hosp., Johnstown, Pa. 1952-53; resident gen. medicine Lee Hosp., 1953-54; fellow N.Y.Univ. Inst. of Physical Medicine and Rehab., 1962-64; pvt. med. practice, Johnstown, Pa. 1953-62, 64-71; dist. med. cons. Pa. Bur. Vocat. Rehab., Johnstown, 1955-59; first med. dir. Penn. Rehabilitation Ctr., Johnstown 1959-62; chief rehab. med. 1965-69; dir. dept. rehab. med. Lee Hosp., 1964-71, chief of staff 1966; asst. prof. and dir. client svs. Univ. Pitts. 1965-69; asst. vis. prof. Temple Univ. 1969-73; dir. dept. rehab. med. Ralph K. Davies Med. Ctr., San Francisco 1973-75, St. Joseph's Hosp., S.F. 1975-78, St. Francis Mem. Hosp., S.F. 1978-83; pvt. practice rehabilitative medicine, San Francisco 1983–; mem: AMA, CMA, S.F. Med. Soc., Am. Acad. Physical Med., Nat. Rehab. Assn. (life), Babcock Surgical Soc., A.C.P., Am. Pain Soc., Internat. Soc. for Study of Pain, Am. Acad. of Pain Medicine, Am. Back Soc.; honors: Cotton Bowl Team, Texas Christian Univ. 1945; publs: films (3), med. jour. articles and paper presentations; lectr. UCSF; mil: lt. USN 1943-46; rec: flying, music, lock picking. Ofc: L.L. Trigiano, M.D., Inc., 1150 Bush St Ste 4B San Francisco 94109

TRONAAS, EDWARD MARTIN, college administrator; b. Jan. 19, 1933, Covina; s. Lloyd Oscar (dec.) and Helen Jane (Woodruff) T.; m. Ada Lee Dancer, Apr. 2, 1955; children: Chris b. 1957, Mark b. 1959 (dec.), Alora b. 1961; edn: AA, Mt. San Antonio Coll. 1952; BA (honors), Calif. State Coll. Los Angeles 1958; MA, Claremont Grad. Sch. 1967; EdD, Univ. La Verne 1991; Calif. Comm. Colls. Supr. Cred. 1978. Career: tchr./dept. chmn. West Covina H.S. 1959-66; Citrus Comm. Coll., Glendora 1966-82, dean instrn. 1982-84, v.p. instrn. 1984-86, interim coll. pres. 1985, exec. v.p. 1986-93; statistical and research cons. 1993–; mem. Calif. Comm. Coll. Chief Instructional Ofcrs., Citrus Coll. Found. (exec. bd.), Citrus Coll. Mgmt. Team (pres. 1989); honors: Nat. Sci. Found. Fellowship UCLA 1963-64; civic: Glendora C. of C.,(secty; pres., bd of dir.), Glendora Kiwanis (bd. dirs.), Glendoran For Drug Free Youth (bd. dirs.), Covina 1st Presbyterian Ch. (elder, trustee), Foothill Presbyn. Hosp., Glendora (bd. dirs.); author: Introductory Algebra For College Students (1974 1st ed., Dickenson, 1981 2d ed., Kendall/Hunt), Mathematics For Technicians (1971, Prentice-Hall); mil: USN 1953-55; Republican; Presbyterian; rec: sail, photog., travel. res: 646 Hunters Trail Glendora 91740

TROST, J. RONALD, lawyer; b. Nov. 27, 1932, Fresno; s. David Trost and Betty (Shapiro) Buno; m. Florence Stern; children: Gregory, Larry, Leslie, Jacqueline; edn: BA, Rice Univ. 1954; JD, Univ. Tx. 1957; admitted St. Bars Tx. 1957, Wash. D.C. 1960, Calif. 1963. Career: U.S. Dept. of Justice, Wash. 1957-59; pvt. practice, Wash. 1959-62, Los Angeles 1963–; ptnr. Sidley & Austin 1980–; adj. prof. law UCLA; instr. law USC; contbr. articles to law reveiws and jours.; contbg. ed. Collier on Bankruptcy; mem: Am. Bar Assn., Am. Law Inst., Nat. Bankruptcy Conf., Internat. Bar Assn.; mil: AUS 1957-63. Ofc: Sidley & Austin 2049 Century Park E 35th Flr Los Angeles 90067

TROUT, MONROE E., healthcare executive; b. April 5, 1931, Harrisburg, Pa.; s. David Michael and Florence Margaret (Kashner) T.; m. Sandra Lemke, June 11, 1960; children: Monroe E. b. 1962, Timothy William M. 1966; edn: BA, Univ. Pa. 1953; MD, 1957; LL.B, Dickinson Sch. Law 1964; JD, 1969. Career: dir. drug regulatory affairs Pfizer, NYC; v.p., med. dir. Winthrop Lab.; sr. v.p.

med. and sci. affairs Sterling Drug Inc.; chmn. bd., pres., c.e.o. Am. Healthcare Systems, San Diego; elected New Canaan Town Council, Conn. 1978-86, v.chmn. 1984-86; appt. secty. HEW Commn. on Medical Malpractice 1970-72, jt. commn. Prescription Drug Use 1976-80; awards: recogn. AMA, pres.'s award Am. Coll. Legal Medicine, Dickinson Sch. of Law disting. alumni, Univ. Pa. alumni of merit, Who's Who in Bus. & Fin.; mem: Am. Arbitration Assn. (nat. health advy. bd. 1972–), AMA, Nat. Council Patient Info. & Edn. (advy. bd. 1983–), Am. Coll. Legal Medicine Found. (trustee 1983–), Am. Soc. Med. Adminstrs., Fairbanks Ranch Country Club; 142+ articles pub. in profl. jours.; mil: lt. cmdr. USN; Republican; Lutheran; rec: golf, tennis. Ofc: American Healthcare Systems 12730 High Bluff Dr Ste 300 San Diego 92130-2099

TROVER, DENIS WILLIAM, computer consultant; b. Feb. 1, 1945, Columbus, Ohio; s. Kenneth Harold and Virginia June (Denis) T.; m. Ellen Lloyd, June 12, 1971; 1 dau: Florence Emma, b. 1977; edn: BS, physics, Mich. State Univ. 1967; MBA, Coll. of William and Mary 1972; MS, Vassar Coll. 1973. Career: optical physicist Internat. Business Machines, Fishkill, NY 1967-71; staff assoc. & sys. prgmr. Rockwell Int. Sci. Ctr., Thousand Oaks 1974-8; pres./ dir. Sonix Systems, Inc., Thousand Oaks 1978-83; computer cons. 1983–; mem: Conejo Future Found. 1975- (chmn. Energy Task Force 1980-1); bd. dirs. Vassar Club of So. Calif.; Democrat; Presbyterian; rec: astronomy, photog. Res: 11355 Presilla Rd Camarillo 93012 Ofc: 1107 East Thousand Oaks Blvd Thousand Oaks 91362

TROVER, ELLEN LLOYD, lawyer; b. Nov. 23, 1947, Richmond, Va.;d. Robert VanBuren and Hazel Pauline (Urban) Lloyd; m. Denis W. Trover, 1971; children: Florence, b. 1977; edn: AB, Vassar Coll. 1969; JD, Coll. of William and Mary 1972. Career: assoc. ed. Bancroft-Whitney 1973-74; sole practioner Ellen Lloyd Trover, Atty. at Law 1974-82, 89–; partner Trover & Fisher 1982-89; mem: Com. Law Ofc. Lawout Design of Economics of Law Practice Section 1978-79, Word Processing Applications Com. 1981-84; Conejo Future Found. (trustee 1979-91, chair 1984-88, trustee emeritus 1992–), Hydro Help for the Handicapped (trustee/exec. com. 1980-85), World Affairs Council of Ventura Co. (spl. mem.), Phi Alpha Delta Legal Frat., Am. Bar Assn., Calif. State Bar, Va. Bar Assn., former mem. Conejo Valley Bar Assn. (pres. 1979-80, dir. 1983-85), Atlantis Found. (trustee 1994–); editor Handbooks of State Chronologies 1972-73; Democrat; Presbyterian. Res: 11355 Presilla Rd Camarillo 93012 Ofc: 1107 E Thousand Oaks Blvd 91362

TROWBRIDGE, JEFFERY D., lawyer; b. March 6, 1956, Santa Monica; s. John M. and Betty J. (Taylor) T.; m. Linda P. Olbert, Aug. 5, 1978; children: Brian b. 1985, Daniel b. 1988, Patrice b. 1994; edn: BA, Univ. Colo. Boulder 1978; JD, UCSF Hastings Coll. Law 1981; admitted St. Bar Calif. 1981. Career: atty., assoc. Law Offices Dennis M. Sullivan, Oakland 1981-87; atty., sole practice 1987–; honors: Order of Coif, Thurston Soc., Boettcher Found. scholar 1974-78, Univ. Colo. Pres. Leadership Class 1974-78; mem: Calif. St. Bar Assn., Am. Bar Assn., Alameda Co. Bar Assn., Am. Lung Assn. Alameda Co. (bd. mem. 1989-95, pres. 1992-93), Rotary Club (vocational services dir. 1988-90), Coll. Ave Presbyterian Ch. (deacons bd., treas. 1989-93, session mem. 1993–, corp. bd. 1989–); Republican; Presbyterian; rec: jogging, guitar. Ofc: 2030 Franklin St 5th Floor Oakland 94612

TRUHLAR, OLIVIA MARIE, legal nurse consultant, long term care; b. Sept. 23, 1938, Chgo.; d. Wm. Victor and Olivia Isabel (von Weidmuller) Truhlar; edn: RN, Ill. Masonic Med. Ctr., Chgo., 1959. Career: v.p. Huntington Health Services, Century City 1966-79; pres. Health Systems Educators, Inc. Torrance 1979–; pres. Truhler-Jones Enterprises 1993–; v.p. Hospice of Los Angeles, 1982-86; mem: Am. Coll. of Health Care Adminstrs., Calif. Assn. Health Facilities, Toastmasters Internat.; Republican (Presdl. Com., Presdl. Task Force); Lutheran (pres. Luth. Women Missionary League 1989–), mem. Bd. of Evangelism 1994–; rec: pub. speaking, ballet, theater, reading. Ofc: Health Systems Educators, Inc. Torrance 90504

TRUMAN, EDWARD CRANE, property manager, investor, composer; b. Dec. 28, 1921, Des Moines, IA; s. Wright Edward and Annie Louise (Cate) T.; m. Maxine H., Jun. 28, 1947 (dec. Apr. 25, 1983); children: Robert Edward b. 1949; edn: BA English, Immaculate Heart Coll., L.A. 1978; MA, psychol., Univ. Redlands, Redlands 1980; real est. cert. & labor studies, Univ. Calif., L.A. 1965-66; fine arts, Drake Univ., Des Moines 1936-39. Career: musician/leader., KSO & KRNT, Des Moines, IA 1938-44; music dir. (small groups), ABC-TV, L.A. 1952-55; music dir., NBC-TV, Burbank 1955-59; freelance musician, ASCAP, L.A. 1956–; owner, Truman R.E., L.A. 1965–; owner, Truman Bus. Assoc., L.A. 1975–; co-chair scholarship com., Univ. Calif. Santa Barbara 1992–; dir., General Affiliates of Univ. Calif. Santa Barbara 1987–; chmn., Coldwater Counseling Ctr., Studio City 1992-94; Emmy panelist, Academy of TV Arts & Sci., N. Hollywood 1984–; bd. mem., Episcopal Campus Oversight Com., L.A. 1993-96 (3 yr. term); awards: Career Educ. Citation, U.S. Dept. Educ., Washington 1978; City Atty. Citation, L.A. 1993; R.E. Svc. Citation, Univ. Calif. L.A. 1976; Diamond Circle Award Radio & TV Industry, Pacific Pioneer Broadcasters, Studio City 1992; past pres., Indep. Living Ctr., Van Nuys 1988; mem: Acad. of Television Arts & Scis. 1964–; Am. Soc. Composers Authors & Publ. 1956–;

Pacific Pioneer Broadcasters 1953–; author; many music recordings, 1950-60; television main titles & backgrounds (Ellery Queen, Matinee Theater, Untouchables), 1955-60; mil: s/sgt Signal Corps/AFRS HQ 1944-46; Democrat; Episcopal; rec: coin collecting. Res: 1826 Jewett Dr Los Angeles 90046-7702

TRUMBULL, TERRY ALAN, environmental lawyer; b. Nov. 5, 1945, Berkeley; s. Larry Edward and Emily Josephine (Grote) T.; m. Patricia Vogel (Hon. Magistrate Judge), Aug. 24, 1968; children: Eryn Jennifer b. 1977, Morgann Vogel b. 1985; edn: BA, UC Davis, 1967; JD, Georgetown Univ., 1971; LLM, George Washington Univ., 1973; admitted bar: D.C. 1971, Calif. 1973, U.S. Supreme Ct. 1975. Career: land use atty. Atkinson, Farasyn & Trumbull, Mountain View, Ca. 1978-79; chmn. Calif. Waste Mgmt. Bd., Sacto. 1979-84; environmental atty. The Trumbull Law Firm, Palo Alto 1984-88, San Jose 1992-94, Palo Alto 1995–; Low, Ball & Lynch, Menlo Park 1988-89; Richards, Watson & Gershon, San Francisco 1989-92; appt. chmn., commr. Santa Clara Co. Planning Commn. 1976-79, dir. Calif. Hazardous Waste Mgmt. Council 1982-84, commr. Nat. Commn. on Resource Conservation and Recovery, W.D.C. 1981–; mem. Peninsula Industrial & Bus. Assn. (chmn. govt. affairs com. 1987–), No. Calif. Recycling Assn. and Calif. Resource Recovery Assn. 1979–; author mo. legal column, Refuse News 1985–, 3 chapters on Calif. Solid Waste Law in Calif. Environ. Law and Land Use Practice, 1989–; mil: Nat. Guard/USAR 1979-85; Democrat; rec: computer games, birdwatching. Ofc: The Trumbull Law Firm, 1011 Lincoln Ave Palo Alto 94301-3046

TRYBUS, RAYMOND J., higher education executive, psychologist; b. Jan. 9, 1944, Chicago, Ill.; s. Fred J. and Cecilia (Liszka) T.; m. Sandra A. Noone, Aug. 19, 1967; children: David b. 1970, Nicole b. 1973; edn: BS (cum laude) St. Louis Univ. 1965, MS (Research), 1970, PhD, 1971; lic. psychologist WDC 1973, Md. 1973, Calif. 1989. Career: clin. psychologist Norfolk (Nebr.) St. Hosp. and NE Mental Health Clinic 1967-68; vocational counselor St. Louis Jewish Employment & Vocat. Svc. 1968-69, clin. psychologist 1969-71; clin. psychologist Gallaudet Univ., W.D.C. 1971-72, res. psychologist 1972-74, asst. prof. & dir. demographic studies 1974-78, dean of grad. studies and res. 1978-88; assoc. provost and dean/prof. of psychol. Calif. Sch. of Profl. Psychology, San Diego, Calif. 1988-90, provost 1990-92, chancellor 1992–; dir., Rehabilitation Res. and Training Ctr. on Mental Health for Persons Who Are Hard of Hearing or Late Deafened, 1994–; cons. clin. psychologist St. Elizabeth's Hosp., W.D.C. 1971-78, Family Svc. Found., Lanham, Md. 1982-88; pvt. p.t. clin. and cons. practice San Diego, Calif., W.D.C., Chevy Chase, Md. 1973–; cons. Congl. Res. Svc. 1982-84, McGill Univ. Study of Hearing Impaired Children in Can. 1983-88; mem. nat. advy. council on deafness Univ. of Ark. 1983-86; bd. dirs./pres. Deafness, Speech and Hearing Publs., Inc., W.D.C. 1984-85; cons. UC, S.F. 1989; mem. Sci. Review Bd., Dept. of Veterans Affairs Rehab. Res. & Devel. Svc., W.D.C. 1986–; internat. lectr. and cons.; awards: W.K. Kellogg Found. National Leadership Fellow 1983-86; listed Who's Who in Frontier Sci. & Tech. 1984, in East 1984, in Rehab. 1985, 86, in World 1987-88, 89-90, 93-94, in Calif. 1990, 1995, in West 1990-91, 92-93, 94-95, in Am. Edn. 1989-90, 92-93, 94-95; mem.: San Diego Psychol. Assn. (mem. ethics & standards com. 1994–, chair, 1995–), Calif. Psychol. Assn. (chair div. of edn. & tng. 1990-93, mem. quality edn. com. 1991-93), Am. Psychol. Assn., Am. Psychol. Soc., Am. Council on Edn., Am. Assn. of Higher Edn., Am. Assn. of Univ. Adminstrs. (bd. dirs. 1987-90), Am. Deafness and Rehab. Assn.; co-author A Guide to College/Career Programs for Deaf Students, 1975, 81; editor: The Future of Mental Health Svs. for Deaf People, 1977; co-editor Hearing Impaired Developmentally Disabled Individuals, 1985; editor Jour. of the Am. Deafness and Rehab. Assn. 1988-91; author: 15 book chapters, num. pub. jour. articles and tech. reports in field; Democrat; R. Catholic; rec: hiking, travel, languages. Ofc: Calif. School of Professional Psychology 6212 Ferris Square San Diego 92121

TRYGSTAD, LAWRENCE BENSON, lawyer, educator; b. March 22, 1937, Holton, Mich.; s. Russell and Gussie (Benson) T.; m. Ann J. Quirino, Dec. 21, 1963; children: Michael, Shanon, David; edn: BA, Univ. Mich., 1959; JD, USC 1967; admitted bar: Calif., 1968, U.S. Circuit Ct. Appeals 9th Circuit, 1974, U.S. Dist. Ct., 1968, U.S. Supreme Ct., 1974, U.S. Tax Ct., 1969. Career: tchr. Am. hist. & govt. L.A. Unified Sch. Dist., 1959-68, asst. vice prin. 1965-68; pres. faculty assn. 1965-66, 1967-68; legal counsel Calif. Tchrs. Assn., Los Angeles 1968-71; ptnr. Trygstad & Odell Law Corp., Los Angeles 1971–; instr., tchr. negotiations CSU Northridge; panelist TV show: Law and the Teacher; bd. dirs. George Washington Carver Found.; recipient Am. Jurisprudence award Highest Grade Equity USC, 1967; mem: Am. Bar Assn., L.A. Co. Bar Assn., Calif. Bar Assn., L.A. Trial Lawyers Assn., Nat. Assn. Tchr. Attys., Phi Alpha Delta; write articles for various tchr. organizations. Res: 4209 Aleman Dr Tarzana 91356 Ofc: 1880 Century Park East Ste 517 Century City 90067

TSAI, KUEI-WU, civil engineering educator; b. Jan. 22, 1941, Pei-Kang, China; nat. 1973; s. Chang-Pei and Teh (Huang) T.; m. Leslie Wang, Feb. 2, 1969; children: Felix b. 1971, Gordon b. 1976; edn: BSCE, Nat. Taiwan Univ. Taipei 1962; MSCE, MA, Princeton Univ. 1965; PhD, Princeton Univ. 1967. Career: constrn. engr. Chinese Air Force 1962-63; asst. prof. San Jose St. Univ., San Jose 1967-71, assoc. prof. 1971-76, prof. 1976–, chmn. 1981-89, assoc. dean of engring. 1994–; engring. cons. 1968–; honors: Sigma Xi, Phi Kappa Phi,

Chi Epsilon, San Jose St. Univ. Civil Engring. Prof. of Year 1976, 84, 92, Merit. award 1986, 88, 90, Chinese Inst. Engrs. Inst. award 1987, Outstanding Prof. of San Jose St. Univ. 1991-92, James M. Robbins Nat. Outstanding Tchg. award Chi Epsilon 1993; mem: ASCE; 30+ papers pub. in tech. jours., 1967–; Republican; rec: music. Res: 26510 Purissima Rd Los Altos Hills 94022 Ofc: San Jose State University College of Engineering San Jose 95192

TSAI, WILMAN, chemical engineer; b. Nov. 2, 1960, Hong Kong; s. John Man-Ma and Kathy (Kwei) T.; m. Wen Lee Wen-Hsing, July 1984; children: Jonathan Michael b. 1988, Betsy Rachael b. 1991; edn: BSc chem. engring., BSc environmental engring., Syracuse Univ., 1982; MS chem. engring., Calif. Inst. Tech., 1985, PhD chem. engring., 1987; reg. profl. engr. Calif. Career: research engr. Air Products & Chemicals, Allentown, Pa. 1987-89; research scientist Varian, Palo Alto, Calif. 1989–; awards: Tau Beta Pi, King fellow; mem.: AIChE; rec: astrophotography. Ofc: 4650 Cushing Parkway Fremont 94538

TSCHANG, TAI-PO, pathologist; b. Feb. 14, 1947, Taipei, Taiwan; nat. 1978; s. Hsi-Lin and Ping (Ching) T.; m. Pui-Suen Wong, May 10, 1972 (dec. 1984); m. 2d. Grace C. Huang, Mar. 22, 1986; children: Chi-Chu b. 1975, Chi-Young b. 1976, Chi-Jia b. 1978; edn: BA, So. Illinois Univ. 1969; MD, Duke Univ. 1972. Career: pathologist St. Elizabeth Hosp, Beaumont, Tx. 1977-86; dir. Pathology Dept., St. Agnes Med. Ctr., Fresno, Calif. 1986–; bd. dirs. Central Calif. Blood Ctr., Fresno 1989–; awards: Borden Freshman Prize, So. Ill. Univ. 1966; mem: Coll. Am. Pathologists 1977–, Am. Soc. Clin. Pathologists 1977–, Am. Assn. Blood Bank 1981–, Am. Assn. Clin. Chem. 1989–; contbg. author num. articles to med. jours. 197093; rec: reading, tennis. Ofc: 1303 E Herndon Fresno 93720

TSENG, ANDREW E., acupuncturist, artist; b. Nov. 24, 1917, Shanghai, China, nat. 1984; s. Rev. Shao-yin and Shien-yun Ngi; m. Alice Ma, Sept. 6, 1956; 1 child; edn: BA, Univ. of Shanghai 1939; OMD, Dr. Oriental Medicine, 1983. Career: Chinese medical doctor, acupuncturist, Shanghai, China 1956-78, San Francisco, Calif. 1979-: Haight Ashbury Free Clinic 1980-81, S.F. Coll. of Acupuncture and Oriental Med. 1981–; profl. Chinese landscape painter 1950–, tchr. and cons. in field; contbr. articles on acupuncture techniques; mil: lt. col. Chinese Army 1945; rec: classical music, lit., fine arts. Res: 5095-312 Valley Crest Dr Concord 94521

TUCK, RUSSELL R., college president emeritus; b. June 9, 1934, Martin, Tenn.; s. Russell R. and May (Garrelts) T.; m. Marjorie Gay, June 27, 1959; children: Russell R., Catherine Elizabeth; edn: BS, Union Univ. 1956; MS, George Peebody Sch. for Tchrs. 1957; PhD, 1971. Career: asst. coordinator Korean tchrs. George Peabody Coll., Nashville, Tenn. 1957-59, instr. biology 1959-60; biology tchr., sci. dept. head Univ. City Sr. H.S., Mo. 1965-71, adminstr. 1965-71; prin. Parkway N. Sr. H.S., St. Louis 1971-79; assoc. supt. Parkway Sch. Dist. 1981-84, asst. supt. 1979-81; pres. Calif. Baptist Coll., Riverside 1984–; cons. num. sch. dists. 1984–; mem. Inland Empire Higher Ednl. Council 1984–; honors: Kappa Delta Pi, Phi Delta Kappa, Union Univ. Doctor of Humanics 1975, Disting. Alumnus 1988; mem: Assn. Supervision & Curriculum Devel., Nat. Assn. Secondary Sch. Principals, Am. Assn. Sch. Adminstrs., Am. Assn. of Presidents of Independent Colls. & Univs., ARC (bd. trustees 1984–), Riverside Opera Assn. (bd. trustees 1986–), Riverside C.of C., pres. Riverside Co. Chpt. Am. Red Cross, Rotary; articles pub. in profl. jours.; Baptist. Res: 1242 Coronet Dr Riverside 92506 Ofc: California Baptist College 8432 Magnolia Ave Riverside 92504

TUCKER, MARCUS OTHELLO, judge; b. Nov. 12, 1934, Santa Monica; s. Dr. Marcus Othello, Sr. and Essie Louo (McLendon) T.; m. Indira Hale, May 29, 1965; dau., Angelique b. 1977; edn: BA, USC 1956; JD, Howard Univ. Sch. of Law 1960. Career: pvt. practice of law, Santa Monica 1962-63 and 1967-74; dep. city atty. City of Santa Monica 1963-65; asst. U.S. Attorney, Los Angeles 1965-67; Superior Ct. commr. L.A. Co. 1974-76; judge Long Beach Mcpl. Ct. 1976-85; judge Superior Ct., L.A. Co. 1985–; asst. prof. of law Pacific Coast Univ. Law Sch. (1984, 86); awards: Blackstonian Soc. USC 1956, editl. staff Howard Law Jour. 1958-60, judge of the yr. Juvenile Ct. Dependency Dept. 1986; mem: Juvenile Ct. Lawyers Assn., Santa Monica Bay Dist. Bar Assn. (mem. 1963-74, treas. 1969), Calif. Judges Assn. (chmn. Juvenile Ct. com. 1987), John Langston Bar Assn. (pres. 1972, 73), Lawyers Ref. Svc. (bd. dirs. 1968-72), Legal Aid Found. of L.A. (pres. 1977-78); civic: BSA (advy. bd., 1977–), Vols. of Am. (bd. dirs.), Capitol Classroom (bd. dirs.), Long Beach Comm. Hosp. Found. (bd. dirs., 1977–), Comm. Rehabilitation Industries Found. (pres. 1985-86); mil: sp5 USAR 1960-66; Democrat; Baptist; rec: legal hist. and philosophy of law, travel. Ofc: Superior Court Dept 233 210 W Temple St Los Angeles 90012

TUCKER, MARTIN S., manufacturing and distributing gifts, toys, novelty industry, company president; b. Oct. 4, 1939, St. Louis, Mo.; s. Irwin and Gigi (Schwartz) T., grandparents; Max and Minnie Schwartz, (noted Russian entrepreneur and famous Russian chef Dave and Charlotte Tucker (shoe designer and noted organizer of the Am. Red Cross, St. Louis area); children: Scott b. 1964, Tracy b. 1967; grandchildren; David b. 1990, Megan b. 1992 and Ethan

Irving b. 1994; edn: BS metallurgical engring, Washington Univ. 1961; MS material sci., UCLA 1965, reg. profl. engr Calif. 1967. Career: res. scientist, Hughes Aircraft 1961-65; adj. faculty, Metals-Engineering Institute 1965-1973; sr. scientist, McDonnell-Douglas Aircraft Co. 1965-71; pres. Topco Sales, Taiwan, Hong Kong and Los Angeles 1973–; awards: Engring Edn. Award Mo. Soc. of Profl. Engineers 1961; Fellowship Award Hughes Aircraft 1962-63; Profl. Achievement Award, Douglas Aircraft 1967; listed Who's Who in California 1988–, Who's Who of the American Pacific Rim; mem: Am. Welding Soc. for Metals 1959–, dir./treas. Sheba Medical Ctr., Israel 1993–, Am. Legion (assoc.); clubs: Elks 1990–; patentee, US Patent No. 5,316,605 entitled Inflatable Figure from Flexible Plastic Sheet Materials (May 31, 1994); author: (books) Secret Joys, Crystal Energy; Jewish; rec: tennis, volleyball, basketball. Ofc: Topco Sales, 11960 Borden Ave, PO Box 9010, San Fernando 91341-9010 Tel: (818) 365-9263 Fax: (818) 361-1295

TUCKER, WALTER RAYFORD, III, congressman, lawyer; b. 1957, Compton, Calif.; s. Walter Rayford, Jr. and Martha H. T.; m. Robin; children: Walter Rayford IV, Autumn Monet; edn: BA in poli. sci. (cum laude), Univ. So. Calif. 1978; JD, Georgetown Univ. 1981; ordained Christian minister. Career: staff Segrue, Rothwell, McPeak, Washington; dep. dist. atty. County of Los Angeles, 1984-86; pvt. practice Compton, Calif., 1986–; mayor City of Compton, Calif. 1991-92; mem. 103rd-104th Congresses from 37th Calif. dist. 1993–; mem. public works and trans. com., small bus. com.; active Compton Juvenile Delinquency Panel; Sunday Sch. tchr.; mem: NAACP (life), Calif. Bar Assn., South Central Bar Assn., L.A. Bar Assn., Langston Bar Assn., Kiwanis Club of Compton; Democrat. Ofc: US House of Reps Office of House Members Washington DC 20515

TULAC, JOHN WILLIAM, lawyer, international business transactions and dispute resolution; b. Aug. 9, 1952, Los Angeles; s. Stanley Thomas and Dorothy Gregorine (Fischer) Tulacz; m. Elizabeth Ann Finsterbach, May 11, 1974; children: Megan b. 1983, Shawn Elyse b. 1985, Michelle b. 1988; edn: BS, honors, Calif. State Polytechnic Univ., Pomona 1974; JD, Loyola Law Sch., Los Angeles 1977; admitted bar: Calif. 1977, AV rating Martindale Hubbell Law Directory, Nat. Directory of Preeminent Attys. Internat. Law. Career: economic analyst Congressman Victor V. Veysey, 1974; law clerk, atty. assoc. Nahrwold & Kerr, Los Angeles 1976-78; atty. law office Tom G. Kontos, Los Angeles 1979-81; senior atty. law office John W. Tulac, Newport Beach 1981–; lectr. Cal Poly Pomona Sch. of Bus. 1979–; judge pro tem, arbitrator L.A. Superior Ct., 1989–; judge pro tem L.A. Municipal Ct. 1985–; arbitrator Orange Co. Fee Dispute Pgm. 1984–; internat. business mediator 1991–; dean Irvine Univ. College of Law 1993–; dir: Preston Sports Products Corp. 1990-92, Nulon of America 1988, Artifex Corp. 1986-92, MERCI 1979-82; honors: distinguished alumnus, Sch. of Arts Cal Poly Pomona 1983, disting. alumnus Phi Kappa Phi, Cal Poly chpt. 1984, CalPoly Coll. of Bus. MPPP- merit. performance and profl. promise award 1990, Faculty of Yr. (Law 1992, Internat. Bus. 1993); mem: Am. Bar Assn., Calif. State Bar (conv. del. 1985, 90), L.A. Co. Bar Assn., Orange Co. Bar Assn., Phi Alpha Delta, Delta Sigma Pi, Sigma Phi Epsilon, Cal Poly Alumni Assn. (dir. 1984-88); Republican; R.Cath. Ofc: 1575 S Valley Vista Dr Ste 140 Diamond Bar 91765

TUPIN, JOE PAUL, academic physician-psychiatrist, medical administrator; b. Feb. 17, 1934, Comanche, Texas; s. Joe Henry and Florence Fern (Cauley) T.; m. Betty Ann Thompson, June 19, 1955; children: Paul b. 1957, Rebecca b. 1960, John b. 1968; edn: BS, Univ. of Texas, Austin 1955, MD, Univ. Texas Med. Sch., Galveston 1959. Career: sr. asst. surgeon, lt. comdr. U.S. Pub. Health Service, 1962-64; asst. prof. Univ. of Texas, Galveston 1964-67, assoc. prof. and assoc. dean, 1967-69; assoc. prof. Univ. Calif., Davis 1969-71, prof. 1971-93 prof. emeritus 1994–; chair psychiatry 1976-84, medical dir. UC Davis Med. Ctr., Sacramento 1984-93 (ret. 1994); vis. prof. King's Coll. Med. Sch., London 1974; awards: Friars Soc. Univ. Tex. 1954, Alpha Omega Alpha 1958, Sigma Xi, Rho Chi, Mosby scholar, Ginsberg fellow Group for Adv. of Psychiatry 1960-62, NIMH career tchg. award 1964-66, Nat. Found. Infantile Paralysis fellow 1957, res. grantee Univ. Tex. Med. Br. 1964-69, NIMH 1965-68, UC Davis 1969–; mem: Yolo County Med. Soc. (bd. 1989-93), Calif. Med. Assn. (bd. HMSS 1991-94), Calif. Assn. of Hosps. and Health (bd. 1992–), AMA, Am. Psychiatric Assn. (1962–, Fellow 1969–), Am. Coll Psychiatrists (1969–, Fellow 1978–), AAAS, AAUP; author books, num. sci. papers and jour. articles; mem. editl. bd. Am. Jour. Forensic Psychiatry, 1985-88, Jour. Clin. Psychopharmacology, 1981–, Psychiatry, 1985, Texas,Reports and Biology and Medicine (1965-67, 68-69), Western Jour. Medicine, 1979-89; mil: lt. comdr. USPHS 1962-64, Reserve 1964-80; rec: fishing. Res: 1108 Kent Dr Davis 95616 Ofc: Univ. Calif. Davis Medical Ctr 231 Stockton Blvd Sacramento 95817

TURCHI, PATRICE E.A., physicist; b. June 23, 1952, Lorient, France, naturalized U.S. 1992; s. Pietrino and Solange B.A. (Dubois) T.; m. Michele E. Boyle, Mar. 20, 1986; children: Elodie b. 1987; edn: Dipl. Eng., Nat. Superieure Sch. of Chemistry, Paris 1975; These de Docteur Ingenieur, Univ. Paris VI, 1982, These de Doctorat d'Etat es Scis. Physiques, 1984. Career: asst. prof. Univ. of Paris VI, France 1975-85; vis. res. asst. UC Berkeley 1985-86; sr. vis. scientist Lawrence Livermore Nat. Lab., 1986-89, sr. scientist 1989–; cons.

AGARD-NATO, Chatillon, Fr. 1989; dir. NATO-ASI, Rhodes, Greece 1992; invited prof. Univ. Joseph Fourier, Grenoble, France 1994; regl. ed. (res. jour.) Metal Physics and Advanced Technology 1994; dir. NATO-ASI, Corfu, Greece 1995; awards: medal for highest ranking Alumni of Nat. Sup. Sch. of Chemistry, Paris, Fr. 1975, DOE award for outstanding research accomplishment DOE-OBES1987; mem: Am. Physical Soc. 1986–, Materials Res. Soc. 1989–, The Minerals Metals & Mats. Soc. 1989–, The TMS-Alloy Phases Com. (elected 1991), elected mem. Acta Metallurgica/Hume-Rothery Award Com. of the TMS 1994, Societe des Ingenieurs & Scientifiques de France 1986–; civic: Midori and Kusamura Bonsai clubs, Am. Orchid Soc.; publs: 100+ sci. papers in refereed jours.; mil: Sci. of the Contingent Air Force, Fr. 1977-78; Republican; R.Cath.; rec: history of sci., skiing, tennis, orchidist and bonsai, painting. Ofc: LLNL Materials Science and Technology Div (L-268) PO Box 808 Livermore 94551

TURPIN, PEARL JOYCE, speaker, consultant; b. Oct. 26, 1937, Denison, Tx.; d. Hansel and Laura Elizabeth (Hardy) Fritts; m. Denzel James Cook, Nov. 7, 1954 (div. 1960); m. Peterfield Burleigh Turpin, May 7, 1966; 1 dau., Isabelle b. 1968; edn: Riverside City Coll. 1958-63; Glendale City Coll. 1963-65. Career: collector Med. Bus. Bureau, Riverside 1955-60; collection mgr. Riverside Bus. Mens. Assn. 1960-63; Med. Coll. Service, Glendale 1963-68; Imperial Collection, Sherman Oaks 1968-71; mgr. Gen. Fin., Los Angeles 1971-81; pres., owner Creditors Services of L.A. 1981-91; owner Pearl Turpin SPEAKS, Glendale 1991–; bd. chmn. Consumer Credit Counseling Service of L.A. 1988-90, bd. mem., ofcr. 1976–; spl. cons. Atty. Gen. Task Force Subcom. Consumer Edn. 1979-81; dir. Consumer Edn. Resource Found. 1993–; commr. Senate Advy. Com. of Debt Collection Industry 1984-92; awards: Credit Women Internat. "Credit Woman of Year" (1975-76, 89-90), Consumer Credit Counselors achievement award 1984, Glendale Credit Women Internat. "Boss of Year" 1982-83, Calif. Bur. of Collections recognition award 1991, Calif. Assn. of Collectors "Star" awards (1990, 91, 92), Richard Bullock Award 1992, Chapter 8 Calif. Assn. of Collectors "Cohen-Ferber" outstanding achiev. award 1989-90, Calif. Credit Union Collectors Coun. "Star" award 1991, Nat. Finance Adj. "Special Service" 1991, Nat. Leadership Council "Capitol Award Recipient" 1991, Internat. Credit Conf. Quebec "Internat. Credit Professional of Year" (May 1990); mem: Calif. Assn. Collectors (pres. 1990), Internat. Credit Assn. (bd. mem. 1979-80), Credit Profls. Glendale/L.A. (past pres. & parliamentarian); Republican; Prot.; rec: reading & teaching. Ofc: 3608 Rosemary Ave Glendale 91208

TUTTLE, LEON E., retired financial executive; b. July 24, 1934, Chicago; s. Leon E. Tuttle and Matilda Teresa Perona; m. Roberta Mae Norton, July 20, 1957; children: Katherine b. 1958, Karen b. 1959, John b. 1961, Joe b. 1965; edn: BS, Univ. Wyoming, Laramie 1956; MBA, Mich. State Univ., 1966; M in Bus. Taxation, USC, 1977; C.P.A., Calif. Career: served to Col. US Air Force 1956-80; exec. v.p. Resource Systems Inc., Englewood, Co. 1980-87; mgr. investor relations Tri-Ex Oil & Gas, Denver 1981-82; assoc. director Colorado Lottery, Denver 1983-85; senior cons. Scientific Games Inc., Sacto., Calif. 1985-88, plant controller Sci. Games Inc., Gilroy 1988-93; systems and fin. cons. Scientific Games, Inc.. Sacramento 1993-94; honors: Beta Alpha Psi 1966, Beta Gama Sigma 1966; civic: Gilroy C.of C., Rotary Club; Republican; R.Cath.; rec: golf. Res: 3825 Clover Valley Rd Rocklin 95677

TWISS, ROBERT MANNING, lawyer; b. Aug. 2, 1948, Worcester, Mass.; s. Robert Sullivan and Marion Frances (Manning) T.; m. Joan Marie Callahan, Aug. 4, 1979; edn: BA, Univ. Mass. 1970; JD, Univ. San Francisco 1975; MA, Wichita St. Univ. 1979; LLM, Georgetown Univ. 1981; admitted St. Bar Calif. (1989), Mass. (1976). Career: revenue ofcr., investigator I.R.S., Boston, Mass. 1971-74, atty., Wash. D.C. 1980-86; trial atty. U.S. Dept. Justice 1986-87, asst. U.S. atty., Sacto. 1987-93; United States atty., Sacto., 4/93-12/93; asst. U.S. atty., Sacto, 12/93–; adj. prof. CSU, Sacto. 1988–; adj. asst. prof. Wichita St. Univ. 1977-79; reserve trial judge USAR, Wash. D.C. 1980-86; awards: I.R.S. Markham 1985; mem: Calif. Bar Assn.; 3 articles pub. in profl. jours., 1980-88; mil: capt. AUS 1976-80, USAR 1980-86, Army Commend. Medal 1979, 1980; rec: athletics. Ofc: U.S. Dept. of Justice 650 Capitol Mall Rm 3305 Sacramento 95814

TWITCHELL, KENT, artist; b. Aug. 17, 1942, Lansing, Mich.; s. Robert Edward and Wilma Doris (Berry) T.; m. Susan Catherine Fessler, Dec. 27, 1975 (div. 1986); m. Pandora Seaton, Feb. 23, 1990; children: Rory b. 1986, Art b. 1992; edn: AA, East L.A. Coll., 1969; BA, CSU Los Angeles, 1972; MFA, Otis Art Inst., 1977. Career: illustrator, E4, US Air Force, Hutchinson, Kans. 1960-62, London, England 1962-65: display artist JC Penney Co., Atlanta, Ga. 1965-66; free lance artist, Los Angeles 1968-: abstract espressionist 1968-70, fine artist, muralist, 1971–, portrait artist 1977–; drawing instr. L.A. City Coll. 1979-80, Otis/Parsons Art Inst. 1980-83, painting instr. L.A. County High Sch. for the Arts 1987-90; cons. artist Olympic Murals Pgm., L.A. 1983-84; awards: Outstanding Alumnus CSU L.A. 1987, Hon. Doctor of Arts, Biola Univ. 1989, Artist of year L.A. Co. H.S. for the Arts Found. 1991; mem. advy. bds: Mural Conservancy of L.A. 1988–, Artist Equity Assn. of L.A. 1980–; works incl. design and paintings: 10 story Michael Jackson portrait, Hollywood (1991-93), 9 story mural L.A. Chamber Orch., monument dwntwn. L.A. (1991-94), 3 story mural Julius Erving monument, Phila. (1989), 2 story mural Steve McQueen monument, L.A. (1971); avocation: theology. Ofc: 6480 Lyons Rd Lakeport 95453

TWOREK, MICHAEL LYNN, information technology consultant; b. Aug. 8, 1948, Bremerton, Wash.; s. John Joseph Tworek and Doris Virginia (Bowne) Corcoran; m. Jaunita Marie Walle, Mar. 21, 1970 (div.); children: Cheryl b. 1970, Philip b. 1973; edn: BSE, Arizona State Univ., Tempe 1973; MSEE, Air Force Inst. of Tech., Wright-Patterson AFB, Oh. 1976; MBA, Golden Gate Univ., 1988. Career: served to major USAF 1966-87: program mgr. microcomputer systems USAF Sch. of Aerospace Medicine, Brooks AFB, Tx. 1976-80; asst. prof. Air Force Acad., Colo. 1980-83; project engr. NASA, Kennedy Space Ctr., Fla. 1983-85; chief shuttle fluids div. 6595 Shuttle Test Gp., Vandenberg AFB, Calif. 1985-87, ret. USAF; business devel. mgr. Bechtel Nat. Inc., San Francisco 1987-90; mgr. M&BD Info. Sys., Bechtel Corp., San Francisco 1990-95; sr. mgr. The Automation Group, Redwood City 1995–; honors: Eta Kappa Nu 1971, Tau Beta Pi 1972, Phi Kappa Phi 1972, Outstanding Young Men in Am. 1982, listed Who's Who in the West 1992; mem: Inst. of Electrical & Electronic Engrs. 1971–, Air Force Assn. 1980–, Internat. Platform Assn. 1992–; Republican (mem. Republican Presidential Legion of Merit and Republican Task Force 1992–); rec: running, tennis, backpacking. Res: 1023 Foster City Blvd #C Foster City 94404 Ofc: The Automation Group 230 Twin Dolphin Dr Redwood City 94065

TYLER, STEPHEN HUNTER, lawyer; b. May 17, 1959, Salt Lake City, Utah; s. James Leslie and Carolyn Jean (Crittenden) T.; m. Donna Jeanne Eady, April 24, 1982; children: Stephen J. b. 1984, Rebekah L. b. 1986, Edward H. b. 1988, Matthew K. and Andrew J. b. 1990, Melissa R. b. 1993; edn: BS acctg., Brigham Young Univ. 1982; JD, Pepperdine Univ. 1985; admitted St. Bar Calif. 1985. Career: atty., assoc. Bidart & Assoc., Chino 1985-86; pres. Stephen H. Tyler Inc. 1987–; v.p. Bawden, Tyler & Johnson 1990-93; pres Stephen H. Tyler APLC 1994–; mem bd. dirs. YMCA; Mormon. Ofc: 300 E State St Ste 450 Redlands 92373

UCHIDA, PRENTISS S., entrepreneur, management executive; b. Nov. 30, 1940, San Jose; s. Fred Toshio and Elise Chiyoe (Kurasaki) U.; m. Patricia A. White, Oct. 17, 1981; children: S. Akemi b. 1971, T. Christopher b. 1973, K. Kansai b. 1982; edn: BA, San Jose State Univ. 1963. Career: programmer Lockheed Missile & Space Co., 1963-66; Adage Inc., 1966-69; founder, pres. and chmn. bd. Vector General, Inc. 1969-79; pres. Inner Game Corp., 1979-83; pres. and chmn. bd. Secom General Corp., 1984-86; mgmt. cons., venture capitalist 1986–; dir: Instar Informatique (Paris, Fr. 1981–), Potter Electronics, Nickel Equipment Co., Secom Comms. Co. 1984-86, R.E. Development 1987-88, Commodity Trader 1989-90, Internat. Distbr. Environmental & Nutritional Products 1990–; pres. VanderBolt Company 1995–; civic: United Way (dir. 1977-79). Res: 2504 Sierra Creek Rd Agoura 91301

UDWADIA, FIRDAUS ERACH, scientist, engineer; b. Aug. 28, 1947, Bombay, India; s. Dr. Erach R. and Perin E (Lentin) U.; m. Farida Gagrat, Jan. 6, 1977; children: Shanaira F., b. 1978, Zubin F. b. 1983; edn: BA, Indian Inst. of Tech. 1968; MS, Calif. Inst. of Tech. 1969, PhD 1972; MBA, Univ. of So. Calif. 1985. Career: research fellow, applied science Calif. Inst. of Tech.; asst. prof. Sch. Engring., USC, Los Angeles; prof. civil engring., mech. engring. and bus. adminstrn., USC; bd. dir. firm spec. in applied science, math. and biomechanics; resrch in geophysics, dynamics and biomechanics; cons. Jet Propulsion Lab., Argonne Nat. Labs., Avery Internat., World Health Orgn.; awards: NSF research grantee, 1973–, spl. NSF adv. to Univ. Skopje 1974; mem: Seismological Soc. of Am.; Soc. for Indsl. and Applied Math.; Am. Acad. of Mechanics; Sigma Xi; ASCE; Earthquake Engring. Inst.; orgzr. confs. in areas of System I.D., and Dynamics; publs: 130+ research papers in sci. jours. on earthquake engring., biomechanics, physics and applied mathematics; assoc editor: Applied Mathematics and Computation, Jour. of Optimization Theory and Applications, Jour. of the Franklin Inst., Nonlinear Digest, Jour. of Aerospace Engring., Mathematical Problems in Engring., Jour. of Mathematical Analysis and Applications; Zoroastrian; rec: piano, writing poetry, chess, computers. Res: 2100 S. Santa Anita Ave Arcadia 91006 Ofc: Univ. of So. California, Olin Hall 430K. Los Angeles 90089-1453

UEBERROTH, PETER VICTOR, travel industry executive, former baseball commisioner b. Sept. 2, 1937, Chicago, Ill.; s. Victor C. and Laura (Larson) U.; m. Virginia Nicolaus; four children; edn: CSU, San Jose. Career: founder Transportation Consultants International 1963–, co. went public 1967; chmn. bd./chief exec. First Travel Corp. 1967–; pres. Los Angeles Olympic Organizing Com. 1979-84; commissioner of baseball 1984-89; head, cons. Contrarian Group, Newport Beach 1992; co-chmn. Rebuild Los Angeles 1992-93, bd.dirs. 1992–; dir. Transamerica Corp.; mem: Delta Upsilon, Bel Air CC; Christian; rec: water sports, golf, tennis. Ofc: Los Angeles 90084

UELMEN, GERALD FRANCIS, law professor; b. Oct. 8, 1940, Greendale, Wis.; s. Francis Thomas and Gertrude Louise (Schauer) U.; m. Martha Anne Burns, Apr. 30, 1966; children: Nancy b. 1967, Amelia b. 1968, Matthew b. 1972; edn: BA, Loyola Marymount Univ., Loyola Angeles 1962; JD, Georgetown Univ., Washington, DC 1965, LLM, 1966; admitted Bar Calif. 1967. Career: asst. U.S. atty., Central Dist. Calif., L.A. 1966-70; prof. of law, Loyola Marymount Univ., L.A. 1970-86; dean, Sch. of Law, Santa Clara Univ., Santa

Clara 1986-94, prof. of law, 1994–; pres. Calif. Attorneys for Criminal Justice, L.A. 1982; chair, Ninth Circuit Rules Comm., San Francisco 1984-92; pres. Calif. Acad. of Appellate Lawyers 1989; chair exec. com. Criminal Law Sect., Calif. State Bar 1991; chair Campaign Reform Comm., San Jose 1993; awards: Richard A. Vachon award, Loyola Law Sch., L.A. 1985, Beryl Saltsman award, Santa Clara Co. Bar Assn. 1990; co-author 3 books: Drug Abuse and the Law, 1982, Disorderly Conduct, 1987, Supreme Folly, 1989; Democrat; Roman Catholic; rec: collector of Am. political items; accordion player. Ofc: Santa Clara University School of Law Santa Clara 95053

ULLRICH, DONALD WILLIAM, JR., lawyer, real estate broker; b. Sept. 26, 1952, Pasadena; s. Donald William Ullrich and Laura Elizabeth (Holsinger) McNicol; m. Diane Elizabeth Natale, May 2, 1980 (div. 1983); m. Cynthia Louise Cooke, Nov. 26, 1983; children: Anthony b. 1981, Brittany b. 1985, Austin b. 1987, Evan b. 1990; edn: BA political sci., UC Santa Barbara, 1974; JD, Univ. Pacific McGeorge Law Sch., 1984, LLM bus. and tax law, 1989; MBA cand. UC Davis 1994; admitted bar: Calif. 1985, U.S. Dist. Ct. 1985; Calif. lic. R.E. broker 1990. Career: writer, Lake Tahoe 1974-76; tax examiner I.R.S., San Francisco 1976-77; served to capt. US Marine Corps 1977-88, air support control ofcr. USMC, Cherry Point, N.C. 1977-80, Okinawa, Japan 1980-81, judge advocate, Camp Pendleton 1984-88, major USMC Reserve, San Rafael 1988–; atty. law firm Desmond, Miller & Desmond, Sacto. 1989-93; R.E. broker, 1990–; awards: McGeorge Sch. Law fellowship 1988-89, Merit scholarship 1982-83, Dean's Hon. Roll. 1981-82, USMC law scholar 1981-84, Who's Who Am. Law, Who's Who Am. Law Students, UCSB AUS ROTC scholarship 1972-74, DeAnza Comm. Coll. Dean's Hon. Roll 1970-72; mem: Federalist Soc. Wash., Calif. St. Bar (bus. law, real property and tax sects.), Calif. Assn. of Realtors, Peninsula West Valley Assn. of Realtors; Republican; Prot.; rec: writing, poetry, piano, skiing, horses. Res:15112 Reynosa Dr Murieta 95683 Ofc: PO Box 371, 3331 Rosewood Ln Somerset 95684

UNG, NANCY, orthodontist; b. Oct. 20, 1960, San Francisco; d. Joe Y. and Mary Han (Young) Ung; edn: BS, Stanford Univ. 1982; DMD and MPH, Harvard Univ., 1987; MSD, Univ. Wash., Seattle 1989. Career: jr. asst. health service ofcr. NIH NIDR, Bethesda, Md. 1983-87; Kellogg fellow Harvard Univ., Boston, Mass. 1986-87, dentist 1986-87; orthodontic resident Univ. Wash., Seattle 1987-89; private practice, San Leandro and Berkeley, Calif. 1989–; honors: Phi Eta Sigma, Alpha Lambda Delta, Phi Beta Kappa, Omicron Kappa Upsilon, Harvard Alumni Silver Medal 1987; mem: Am. Assn. Orthodontists, Calif. Dental Assn., Am. Assn. Women Dentists; articles and abstracts pub. in profl. jours., 1983–; rec: travel, hiking, bicycling. Res: 1514 Fernside Blvd Alameda 94501

UNGER, ARLENE KLEIN, behavioral-mental health care executive, company president; b. May 12, 1952, Brooklyn, N.Y.; d. Eli N. and Harriet Barbara (Shapiro) K.; m. Stefan Howard Unger, Aug. 19, 1979; children: Max b. 1981, Elana b. 1989; edn: MS (equivalency), CSU Hayward 1983; BS, Emerson Coll. 1974; MS, So. Conn. State Coll. 1976; PhD, W. Grad. Sch. of Psych. 1991; lic. MFCC (1985). Career: site admin., tchr. splst. Santa Clara Severely Delayed Language Pgm., Santa Clara 1976-81; language & movement splst. Peninsula Children's Ctr., Palo Alto 1981-84; dir. tng. and sales Human Resources Svs., EAP, Sunnyvale 1984-86; employee assistance pgm. mgr. Occupational Health Svs., Inc., Sunnyvale 1986-91; pvt. practice employee assistance pgm. cons., prin. Counseling & Consulting Resources, Palo Alto 1991-93; v.p. clinical svs. Advanced Behavioral Care, Regl. Alliance IPA 1994; pres., CEO, Allied Health Svs., Inc. 1994–; mental health trainer, cons. Decathlon Club, Santa Clara 1986–; leader, splst. Sunnyvale Recreation, Sunnyvale 1976-78; counselor, cons. Pinewood School, Palo Alto 1981-83; therapist Woodside Psychol. Svs., Redwood City 1981-85; awards: CEAP cert. Almaca 1988, Am. Dance Therapy Registry 1986, appointed ch. Almaca "Conf. on AIDS in the Workplace" (1987); mem: Employee Assistance Pgm. Assn., Am. Assn. of Marriage and Family Therapists, Am. Dance Therapy Assn., Am. Speech and Hearing Assn., Am. Assn. of Counseling and Devel., Albert Shultz Jewish Comm. Ctr. (vol.), Decathlon Club, Palo Alto Run Club, EAP Almaca com.; contbr. articles in profl. jours., 1986, 88; founder, creator multicultural nightclub, Cafe Matek, 1976-81; founder, pres. retail jewelry, Boutique Supply, 1983–; creator and dir. Children's Creative Movement & Art Pgm., Sunnyvale 1976-78; rec: consulting, jogging, swimming, guitar playing, painting. Res: 2250 Webster Palo Alto 94301 Ofc: Counseling & Consulting Resources 4151 Middlefield Rd Ste 110 Palo Alto 94303

UNTERMAN, THOMAS EDWARD, lawyer; b. Oct. 23, 1944, Newport, R.I.; s. Dr. Martin D. and Ruth Rose (Marcus) U.; m. Patricia Fogel, June 24, 1969; m. Janet M. Mead, Sept. 27, 1980; children: Rebecca b. 1981, Amy b. 1985; edn: AB, Princeton Univ., 1966; JD, Univ. Chicago Law Sch., 1969; admitted bar: Calif. 1970. Career: atty., assoc. Orrick, Herrington & Sutcliffe, San Francisco 1969-75, ptnr. 1975-86; ptnr. Morrison & Foerster, S.F. 1986-89, Los Angeles, 1989-92; v.p. gen. counsel The Times Mirror Co. L.A. 1989-92; appt. Calif. State Senate Commn. on Corporate Governance, 1986–; civic: Public Counsel (dir. 1992–); Democrat; Jewish. Ofc: The Times Mirror Co. Times Mirror Sq Los Angeles 90053

UNTERMYER, SAMUEL, II, engineer/executive; b. Nov. 25, 1912; s. Irwin and Louise U.; m. Joan Gray, Nov. 25, 1942 (dec. 1961); children: Samuel, III b. 1942, Sylvia b. 1945, Beatrice b. 1948, Daniel b. 1957; edn: BS, M.I.T., 1934; Reg. Profl. Engr., Calif. Career: engr. various diesel engine devel. cos., 1934-42; engr. Oak Ridge Nat. Lab., Oak Ridge, Tenn. 1946-49; asst. to dir. Argonne Nat. Lab., Argonne, Ill. 1949-54; project mgr. Gen. Electric, Pleasanton, Calif. 1954-67; chmn. Nat. Nuclear Corp., Mtn. View 1954-85; pres. Explosive Detection Corp., 1986–; awards: Newcomen Medal, Franklin Inst., Phila. 1981; Fellow Am. Soc. Mech. Engrs., Fellow Am. Nuclear Soc.; inventor: Boiling Water Reactor, 1958; coauthor book: Detecting Fissionable Materials, 1982; mil.: lt. cdr. (USNR) USN 1942-46; Republican; Unitarian; rec: horseback riding. Res: 201 Escobar Rd Portola Valley 94025 Ofc: Explosive Detection Corp., c/o National Nuclear Corp., 1904 Colony St Mountain View 94043

UNWIN, STEPHEN FORMAN, advertising educator; b. Aug. 7, 1927, Higham, Leicestershire, England; s. Phillip Henry and Decima (Forman) U.; m. Pamela Susan Brett, June 6, 1953; children: Phillip b. 1954, Tessa b. 1955, Sam b. 1963; edn: BA, and MA with honors in modern history, Oxford Univ., Eng. 1952, 1968; desig: MIPA, Inst. of Practitioners in Advt., London, 1960. Career: account exec. The London Press Exchange Ltd., London, Eng. 1951-66, dir. The London Press Ex. Org. 1966-67, assoc. dir. LPE Ltd. 1967-69; advt. cons. Illinois Bell, Chgo., Ill. 1974-75; dir. Forest Industries Communications Inst., Atlanta, Ga. 1975-76; publicist British Tourist Auth., London, Eng. 1978-81; advt. cons. J. Walter Thompson Co., San Francisco 1983; sr. analyst Business Dynamics, Carmel, Calif. 1985–; vis. lectr. 1969-70, asst. prof. Univ. Ill., Urbana 1970-74; assoc. prof. Univ. Alabama, Tuscaloosa 1974-79, Washington State Univ., Pullman 1979-81, Univ. Oregon, Eugene 1981-85; mem. Internat. Advt. Edn. Com. Chgo. 1982, Nat. Com. for Advt. Edn. N.Y.C. 1983-84; awards: key to the city of Lubbock, Tx. 1969, vis. prof. Am. Assn. of Advt. Agys., Chgo. 1971, bicentennial judge Advertising Age, Chgo. 1976, vis. prof. Am. Ad Fedn., S.F. 1983; mem: Worcester Coll., Oxford 1952–, Am. Acad. of Advt. 1970–, Kappa Tau Alpha nat. soc. journ. (1973–, Future of Journ. Edn. Com., Eugene, Oreg. 1982-84); Canterbury Cathedral (friend 1985–); author: How Nations Grow Rich (1992), 2 book chapters in The New World of Advertising (1975), contbr. book revs. and articles in jours. and trade mags. 1970–; mil: 2d lt. British Army 1945-48; Episcopalian; rec: travel, genealogy. Ofc: Business Dynamics, 8th & San Carlos, Box S-3197 Carmel 93921

UPP, ROBERT DEAN, lawyer; b. Feb. 6, 1916, Allerton, Ill.; s. Dean Foreman and Ruby (Armstrong) U.; m. Margaret Thiel, July 5, 1939; m. 2d. Jane Dineen, Dec. 26, 1953; children: Dolores b. 1941, Robert Rex b. 1943; edn: BS, Univ. Ill. 1937; MS, MA, USC, 1949; JD, 1948; admitted St. Bar Calif. (1948). Career: atty. pvt. law practise, Solana Beach and Beverly Hills, 1948–; prof. law dept. Los Angeles City Coll. 1949-79; writer West Pub. Co., St. Paul, Minn. 1967–, co-author Business Law, 4 edits. 1967–; cons. Fed. Judicial Center, Wash. D.C. 1982-86; dir., secty. Pan Global Internat. Corp., Solana Beach 1970–; mem. Reserve Ofcrs. Assn. of U.S. (past nat. pres., past Calif. pres.), Senior Army Reserve Commdrs. Assn. (6th Army Retired rep. 1987-88); mil: served to brigadier gen. US Army 1937-74, Inf. Co. comdr. Aleutians, ETO 1942-46, war crimes investigator, Korea 1951-54, decorated Legion of Merit 1972, Meritorious Service medal 1972, Army Commendation 1953, Bronze Star w./V 1945; Democrat; Theocrat; rec: writing, travel. Res: 341 Pacific Ave Solana Beach 92075

UPTON, HENRY YEOMANS, physician, ophthalmologist; b. Feb. 17, 1936, Seattle, Wash.; s. Leland Bickford and Charlotte (Hamblen) U.; m. Virginia Nielson, Feb. 12, 1972 (div. 1980); edn: BS, Stanford Univ. 1959; MD, Univ. Wash. Seattle 1966; diplomate Am. Bd. Ophthalmology. Career: pvt. practice, Auburn, Wash. 1971-72; San Carlos 1972–; assoc. clin. prof., dept. ophthalmology Stanford Univ. 1974–; mem. Am. Acad. Ophthalmology (fellow), Peninsula Eye Soc. (pres. 1986); mil: lt. USN 1959-61, 1966-67; Protestant; rec: skiing. Ofc: 1178 Brittan Ave San Carlos 94070

UTRECHT, PAUL F., lawyer; b. Aug. 31, 1960, The Hague, Netherlands; s. Robert P. and Arnolda (Cohen) U.; edn: BA, Claremont Mens Coll. 1980; Sorbonne Paris 1980; JD, UC Berkeley Boalt Hall 1983. Career: law clk. U.S. Dist. Judge M. Joseph Blumenfeld, Hartford, Conn. 1983-84; atty., assoc. Pillsbury Madison & Sutro, San Francisco 1984-87; Law Office of S.G. Archibald, Paris, France 1987; sole practice, Oakland 1987-94; San Francisco 1994–; book chpt. pub. 1985. Ofc: 235 Montgomery St Ste 810 San Francisco 94104

UYEDA, LANCE D., environmental health specialist, city project manager; b. July 24 1943, Denver; s. John N. and Etsu T. (Kawata) U.; m. Yoshie Susie Takahashi, Jan. 30, 1970; children: Craig b. 1970, Shelley b. 1972, Lauren b. 1974, Scott b. 1975; edn: MBA cand. San Jose State Univ.; Reg. Environ. Health Splst., Calif. Career: prev. med. splst., E5, SP/5, US Army, Fort McArthur, 1967-69; environmental health sanitarian County Health Dept., San Jose 1969-79; envir. health sanitarian City of San Jose, 1979-86, code enforcement supr. 1986-89, 90–, code enforcement div. actg. chief 1989-90, Project Blossom mgr. 1990-92; instr. Health 21, Los Altos Hills; mem.: Calif. Envir.

Health Assn. (p.r. chmn. 1974), SCCO Envir. Health Assn. San Jose (pres. 1975); civic: Am. Youth Soccer Orgn. (commr. region 45 1988); Democrat; rec: photography. Ofc: City of San Jose 801 N First St San Jose 95110

UYEHARA, OTTO ARTHUR, professor emeritus; b. Sept. 9, 1916, Hanford, Calif.; s. Rikichi and Umi (Nakayama) U.; m. Chisako Suda, Aug. 12, 1945; children: Otto Kenneth, Susan Joy Schultheiss, Emi Uyehara Stewart; edn: BS, Univ. Wisconsin, Madison, 1942, MS, 1943; PhD chemical engr., 1946. Career: post doctoral fellow, Univ. Wisconsin, Madison, 1945-46, res. assoc., 1946-47; asst. prof. (mech. engr.), 1947-51, assoc. prof., 1951-57; prof., 1957-81; prof. emeritus, 1982–; awards: Benjamin Smith Reynolds Teaching. Award, Univ. Wisconsin, Madison; SAE Fellow, Soc. of Automotive Engrs., 1985; hon. mem. Japan Soc. of Mechanical Engring., 1986; Scientific Award, Japan Soc. of Automotive Engrs., 1987, Internal Combustion Engine Award ASME Automotive Div. 1994; mem: Soc. of Automotive Engrs. (fellow) 1945–, Am. Soc. of Mechanical Engrs. 1945–, Sigma Xi 1947–; civic: Kiwanis Club of Anaheim (pres. 1987-88); author: three inventions for special valves for IC engines, 1960; low voltage bed wetting sensor, 1975; rec: golf. Res: 544 S. Bond St. Anaheim 92805

VALDEZ, ARNOLD, dentist; b. June 27, 1954, Mojave; s. Stephen Monarez and Mary Lou (Esparza) V.; edn: BS biol. sci., CSU Hayward 1976; BS dental sci., and DDS, UC San Francisco, 1982; MBA, Calif. St. Polytech. Univ. 1985; law student Pacific West Coll. of Law; Calif. State Indep. Med. Examiner and Qualified Med. Examiner. Career: past assoc. dentist Jack E. Bamesberger, Pomona; Robert C. Borland, Claremont; pvt. practice splst. in temporomandibular joint and myofascial pain dysfunction disorders, 1982–; staff Pomona Valley Hosp. Med. Ctr. 1989–; vol. dentist San Antonio Hosp. Dental Clinic, Rancho Cucamonga 1984–, Pomona Valley Assistance League Dental Clinic 1986–; advy. council Chaffee Comm. Coll. 1982–; bd. dir. Pacific West Coll. of Law 1993–; honors: Who's Who Am. H.S. Students 1972, Who's Who Am. Student Leaders 1972, Outstanding Teenagers of Am. 1972, Calif. State scholar 1972-76 and fellow 1978-82; Fellow Acad. of General Dentistry 1991, Master Acad. of Gen. Dentistry 1994, mem. ADA, Calif. Dental Assn., Tri Co. Dental Soc. (chmn. School Screening Com. 1985-87), The Acad. of Gen. Dentistry, Am. Equilibration Soc., USC Sch. of Dentistry Golden Century Club, Psi Omega, Delta Theta Phi, UCSF Alumni Assn., Toastmasters; R.Cath.; rec: Kenpo Karate, racquetsports, gymnastics, volleyball, skiing. Res: 1320 Malaga Upland 91786 Ofc: 410 W Baseline Rd Claremont 91711

VALDEZ, JAMES GERALD, chief operating officer; b. Jan. 26, 1945, Vallejo; s. Charles Arthur and Margaret Ellen (Chavez) V.; m. Catherine Evelyn Gudliewski, Oct. 9, 1970; edn: BS in engring. tech., Cal Poly S.L.O., 1967; MBA, Pepperdine Univ., 1974. Career: sales engr. Shell Oil Co., Los Angeles 1969-70; regional mgr. Ethyl Corp., L.A. 1970-76; dir. product engring. Pennzoil Co., Houston 1976-84; owner Valco Ents., Tustin 1984-86; sr. v.p. mktg. Analysts Inc., Torrance 1986-88; dir. sales & mktg., Castrol Inc., Irvine 1988-93; v.p. & gen. mgr. CSF, Inc., Rialto 1993–; cons. to Amoco Chemical, Lubrizol Corp., and Analysts Inc., L.A. 1984-86; mem: Soc. of Automotive Engrs., Am. Petroleum Inst. (com. chmn. 1977-88), Soc. for Tribology & Lubrication Engring. (L.A. sect. chmn. 1970-88); MA thesis: Mktg. Petroleum Additives to Andean Common Market (1975); mil: major Army Air Def. Arty. 1967-69, 1970-80; Republican; R.Cath.; rec: racquetball, skiing. Res: 5850 E Trapper Trail Anaheim Hills 92807 Ofc: CSF Inc 2941 N Locust Avenue Rialto 92376

VALENTINE, JAMES WILLIAM, professor integrative biology, paleontologist; b. Nov. 10, 1926, Los Angeles; s. Adelbert Cuthbert and Isabel (Davis) V.; m. Diane Mondragon, Mar. 16, 1987; edn: BA, Phillips Univ., Enid, Ok. 1951; MA, UCLA, 1954, PhD, 1958. Career: asst. prof., assoc. prof Univ. Missouri, Columbia 1958-62, 62-64; assoc. prof., prof. UC Davis, 1964-78; prof. geol. scis. UC Santa Barbara, 1978-90; prof. integrative biology UC Berkeley, 1990–; author: Evolutionary Paleoecology (1973), Evolution (1977), Evolving (1979), Phanerozoic Diversity Patterns (1985); mem: Nat. Acad. of Scis. 1984–, Am. Acad. Arts & Scis. (1984–, Fellow), AAAS (Fellow), Geological Soc. of Am. (Fellow), Paleontological Soc. (pres. 1974-75); mil: QM2/c USNR 1944-46; rec: collect works of Charles Darwin.

VALLI, LOUIS PAUL, orthopedic surgeon; b. Feb. 17, 1936, San Jose, Calif.; s. Joseph and Rose (Rabozzi) V.; m. Linda Varnadoe, Apr. 7, 1978 (div. 1988); children: Nicole b. 1972, Brian b. 1980; edn: BA, Stanford Univ. 1958; MD, Marquette Univ. Sch. Medicine 1962; Diplomate, Am. Bd. Orthopaedic Surgery. Career: internship, L.A. County General Hosp. 1962-63; resident, orthopaedic surgery, Univ. of So. Calif. Med. Svs., L.A. Co. Gen. Hosp. 1963-67; asst. chief orthopaedic surgery, 97th Gen. Hosp., Frankfurt, Germany 1968-69; pvt. orthopaedic surgery practice, Sacramento, Calif. 1971–; hosp affiliations: Mercy San Juan Hosp., Mercy Am. River Hosp., Mercy Gen. Hosp., Mercy Folsom Hosp., Roseville Comm. Hosp.; Fellow, Am. Acad. of Orthopaedic Surgery; mem: CMA, We. Orthopaedic Assn., Calif. Orthopaedic Assn., Sacramento-El Dorado Co. Med. Soc.; mil: major U.S. Army 1967-69; Roman Catholic; rec: sports, tennis, skiing, bicycling. Res: 5616 Ridge Park Dr Loomis 95650 Ofc: 6614 Mercy Court Ste B Fair Oaks 95628-3133

VAN BISE, WILLIAM LLOYD LAFITTE, biomedical engineer; b. June 3, 1937, Slidell, La.; s. Lloyd Wm. and Alice Lorena (Gardner) van Lafitte Bise; edn: ASEE, Tulane Univ., Delgado Tech. Inst., 1962; Hon. MD, Oregon Health Scis. Univ. Sch. of Med., Portland, 1975-77; doctoral studies Oreg. Grad. Ctr., Beaverton 1977-79; E.E. biomedical instrumentation. Career: electroacoustic engr. Pendulum Club, New Orleans, La. 1954-57; photographer Van Bise Studios, 1957-60; instrumentation cons. Rad. Sect. Oreg. State Health Div., Portland 1972-78, clin. instr. Sch. of Med. 1975-79; cons. engr., 1976-80, dir., chief res. scientist, founder Pacific Northwest Center, Portland 1980-84, treas. 1988–; chief biomedical res. Tecnic Res. Labs., San Leandro, Calif. 1984–, pres. Tecnic Med. Labs. Inc. 1988–; pres. Electromagnetic Signal Labs., Inc. 1992–; res. cons. Pomona Coll. 1970-71; honors: invited paper and comments U.S. Senate radiation health & safety hearing & com. 1977, guest lectr. Learned Socs. Conf., Ottawa 1980, guest lectr. Kaiser Permanente Hosp., Portland 1981; mem: IEEE, ICWA, AAAS; co-inventor w. Dr. E.A. Rauscher: cardiac (pat. 1988) and pain control (pat. 1989) devices, ELF detection system (pat. 1988), author 56+ tech. papers - ELF, Microwave, Biological effects, Instrumentation measurement techniques (1970–). Ofc: Electromagnetic Signal Laboratories, Inc. 7685 Hughes Dr Golden Valley, Reno NV 89506

VAN BRUNT, EDMUND EWING, physician; b. Apr. 28, 1926, Oakland, Calif.; s. Adrian Wilbur and Kathryn Anne (Shattuck) V.; m. Claire Monod, Feb. 28, 1949; children: Karin b. 1953, Deryk b. 1959, Jahn b. 1965; edn: BA, biophysics, UC Berkeley 1952; MD, UC San Francisco 1959; lic. physician/surgeon St. of Calif. 1959–. Career: staff, internal medicine Kaiser Permanente Med. Ctr., San Francisco 1964-89; dir. Div. of Res., Kaiser Permanente Exec. Ofc., Oakland 1979-91; adj. prof. UC San Francisco 1972-91; honors: Sigma Xi 1968–, hon. ScD, Univ. Paul Sabatier, Toulouse, France 1978; mem: CMA 1964–, Physicians for Social Responsibility 1969-94, Am. Coll. of Physicians (fellow 1974–), Am. Coll. of Med. Informatics (fellow 1978–), French Found. for Med. Res. (pres. 1994–), Berkeley Camera Club; author or co-author 50+ profl. jour. articles and book chpts.; mil: tech. sgt. U.S. Army 1944-46; Independent; rec: photog., flying, swimming.

VAN CLEEF, ROBERT EDWARD, computer specialist; b. May 20, 1946, Fall River, Mass.; s. Jacque Edward and Ellen D. (Fagan) Van C.; m. Mary Bradley, June 5, 1971; children: James, b. 1975, Anna-Marie, b. 1976; edn: AS, Santa Barbara City Coll.; BBA, magna cum laude, National Univ., 1982, MBA, w/distinction 1984. Career: enlisted man US Navy, 1964-76; field engr. Honeywell Corp., Santa Barbara 1976-79; senior tech. support engr. Computer Sciences Corp., San Diego 1979-84; sys. analyst Gateway Computer Sys. Inc., 1984-85; information sys. analyst Gen. Electric Corp. 1985-89; computer specialist NASA, 1989-95; computer spec. MicroUnity Systems Engineering, Inc. 1995–; awards: NASA appreciation cert. 1989, group achiev. NAS projects office 1986, GE profl. recogn. pgm. (4/87), GE recogn. for contbn. NAS/ISC 1986; mem: IEEE, USENIX, Assn. for Computing Machinery (reviewer "ACM Computing Reviews" 1984-90), San Diego Computer Soc. (pres. 1984, ed. journal "Personal Systems" 1984-85), S.D. Osborne Users Gp. (past pres.), Internat. Assn. of Computer Using Gps. (bd. 1984-86), Charismatic Pastoral Service Team (ed. newsletter 1993–) Diocese of San Jose; mil. decorations incl. Vietnam Cpgn. w/8 stars, RVN Armed Forces Meritorious (2), Nat. Def., GCM (2), Unit Commendn. (2), Combat Action Ribbon; Republican; R.Cath.; rec: PC, church choir. Res: PO Box 110578 Campbell 95011 Ofc: MicroUnity Systems Engineering, Inc. 255 Caspian Dr Sunnyvale 94089

VAN DAELE, PATRICK JOSEPH, developer, lawyer; b. April 26, 1960, Whittier; s. John Fredrick and Joan (Cannon) Van D.; m. Robin LeeAnn Ross, Feb. 25, 1989; edn: BS, USC, 1982; JD, Southwestern Univ. Sch. Law, 1986; admitted St. Bar Calif. 1987, lic. real estate broker 1988. Career: law clk. Gilbert Kelly Crowley & Jennett, Los Angeles 1978-85; atty. Reynolds Reider & Bawden, Redlands 1986-87; exec. v.p./C.O.O., Van Daele Devel., Riverside 1987-94, pres./C.O.O., 1994–; mem: Bldg. Industry Assn., USC Alumni Assn.; Republican; R.Cath. Ofc: Van Daele Development Corp. 2900 Adams St Ste C-25 Riverside 92504

VANDENBERGHE, RONALD GUSTAVE, accountant; b. Oakland; s. Anselm Henri and Margaret B. (Bygum) V.; m. Patricia W. Dufour, Aug. 18, 1957; children: Camille, Mark, Matthew; edn: BA, honors, San Jose State Coll. 1959; postgrad., UC Berkeley Extension 1959-60; Golden Gate Coll. 1961-63; CPA Calif. State. Career: real estate developer/investor, Pleasanton 1964–; instr. accounting UC Berkeley, 1963-70; CPA, Pleasanton 1963–; mem. Calif. Soc. CPA's, Masons, Shriners; mil: USAF; Republican; Presbyterian. Res: PO Box 803 Danville 94526 Ofc: POB 728 Pleasanton 94566

VANDERBILT, KERMIT, professor of English (Emeritus); b. Sept. 1, 1925, Decorah, Iowa; s. Lester and Ella (Qualley) V.; m. Vivian Osmundson, Nov. 15, 1947; 1 child: Karen b. 1951; edn: BA, Luther Coll., Decorah, Iowa, 1947; MA, Univ. of Minn., Mpls., Minn., 1949; PhD, Univ. of Minn., 1956; Career: Instr. of Eng., Univ. of Minn., 1954-57; asst. prof. of Eng., Univ. of Wash., Seattle, Wash., 1958-62; asst. prof. of Eng. to prof. of Eng., San Diego State Univ., San Diego, Calif., 1962-91; awards: Outstanding Prof., San Diego State Univ., San

Diego, 1976; LittD, Luther Coll., Decorah, Iowa, 1977; Guggenheim Fellow, 1978; Huntington Lib. Fellow, San Marino, Calif. 1980; Outstanding Academic Book (CHOICE), 1988; author: biography, Charles Eliot Norton, 1959; The Achievement of Howells, 1968; American Literature and the Academy, 1986; ed., La Litterature Americaine (1991, 2nd. edit. 1994); mil: comms. ofcr., USNR, 1943-46. Res: 6937 Coleshill Dr. San Diego 92119-1920

VANDERHOEF, LARRY NEIL, professor of biology, university chancellor; b. March 20, 1941, Perham, Minn.; s. Wilmar James and Ida Lucille (Wothe) V.; m. Rosalie Suzanne Slifka, Aug. 31, 1963; children: Susan Marie, Jonathan Lee; edn: BS, Univ. Wis. 1964; MS, 1965; PhD, Purdue Univ. 1969. Career: postdoctorate Univ. Wis., Madison 1969-70; research assoc. Univ. Wis. 1970-72; asst. prof. biology Univ. Ill., Urbana 1970-74, assoc. prof. 1974-77, prof. 1977–, head dept. plant biology 1977-80; provost agri. and life scis. Univ. Md., College Park 1980-84; exec. v. chancellor UC Davis 1984-94, chancellor 1994–; vis. investigator Carnegie Inst., Edinburgh, Scotland 1976-77; cons. in field; awards: NCR postdoctoral fellow 1969-70 Eisenhower fellow 1987, Dimond travel grantee 1975, NSF grantee (1972, 74, 76, 77, 78, 79), NATO grantee 1980; mem: AAAS, Am. Soc. Plant Physiology (bd. editors Plant Physiology 1977-82, trustee, mem. exec. com., treas. 1982-88), Nat. Assn. St. Univ. & Land Grant Colls. Res: 615 Francisco Pl Davis 95616 Ofc: Univ. of California Office of the Chancellor Davis 95616-8558

VAN DER MEULEN, JOSEPH PIERRE, physician, educator, university hospital administrator; b. Aug. 22, 1929, Boston, Mass.; s. Edward Lawrence and Sarah Jane (Robertson) V.; m. Ann Yadeno, June 18, 1960; children: Elisabeth, Suzanne, Janet; edn: AB, Boston Coll. 1950; MD, Boston Univ., 1954. Career: instr. neurol. Harvard Med. Sch. 1964-65, assoc. 1966-67; asst. prof. neurol. dept. of med. Case Western Reserve Univ. 1967-69, assoc. prof. 1969-71; asst. in neurol. Univ. Hosp., Cleveland 1967-71; asst. nerol. Highland View Hosp.; prof., chmn. dept. neurol. Univ. So. Calif. 1971-79, chief physician L.A. County-USC Med. Center 1971-79, physician specialist neurology 1979–; prof. neurol. USC 1971–, VPHA USC 1977–, dean sch. of med. 1985-86, 1995, sr. v.p. medical affairs 1995, director Allied Health Sciences 1991–; chmn. bd. USC University Hosp. 1990–; appt. Calif. Gov.'s Task Force on Toxics, Waste, and Tech. 1985–; pres. and c.e.o. Kenneth Norris Cancer Hosp. and Research Inst.; bd. dirs: Childrens Hosp., Calif. Hosp., Good Samaritan, Good Hope Med. Found., Doheny Eye Hosp., House Ear Inst., Barlow Respiratory Hosp., Assn. of Academic Health Centers (chmn. elect 1991, bd. 1987–), Thomas Aquinas Coll. (bd. govs. 1987–); awards: clin. tchg. excellence USC 1976, USN Rear Adm. Campbell Chambliss Navy Award 1978, Founders' humanitarian award Myasthenia Gravis Found. 1982, disting. alumnus Boston Univ. 1984, outstanding tchr. USC Dept. Family Medicine 1984, outstanding vol. City of L.A., Alpha Omega Alpha, Phi Kappa Phi 1982; civic: United Way (co-chmn. 1982), Music Center Unified Fund (chmn. med. div.); res. programs: Medical Ethics, Cerebral Death, Computer Assisted Image Analysis of Muscle Biopsies, Hypertension and the CNS, Epidemiological Studies of ALS, Cortical Evoked Potentials, Neurological and Psychological Evaluation in Perinatal Injury; mil: lt. USN med. corps. 1956-58; rec: golf, skier. Res: 39 Club View Ln Rolling Hills Estates 90274 Ofc: USC, 1540 Alcazar St Los Angeles 90033

VANE, SYLVIA BRAKKE, anthropologist, author, publisher, cultural resource management executive; b. Feb. 28, 1918, Fillmore County, Minn.; d. John T. and Hulda Christina (Marburger) Brakke; m. Arthur Bayard Vane, May 17, 1942; children: Ronald Arthur, Linda, Laura V. Ames; edn: AA, Rochester Jr. Coll., 1937; BS (w/distinction), Univ. Minn., 1939; student Radcliffe Coll., 1944; MA, CSU Hayward, 1975. Career: med. tech. Dr. Frost and Hodapp, Willmar, Minn. 1939-41; head labs. Corvallis Gen. Hosp., Oreg. 1941-42; lab. dir. Cambridge Gen. Hosp., Mass. 1942-43, Peninsula Clinic, Redwood City, Calif. 1947-49; v.p. Cultural Systems Res. Inc., Palm Springs and Menlo Park, 1978–; pres. Ballena Press, Menlo Park 1981–; cons. cultural resource mgmt. So. Calif. Edison Co., Rosemead 1978-81, San Diego Gas and Elec. Co., 1980-83, Pacific Gas and Elec. Co., S.F. 1982-83, Wender, Murase & White, W.D.C. 1983-86, Yosemite Indians, Mariposa, Calif. 1982-84, San Luis Rey Band of Mission Indians, Escondido 1986-92, U.S. Ecology, Newport Beach 1986-88, Riverside Co. Flood Control and Water Conservation Dist. 1985–, Met. Water Dist. 1989–, Nat. Park Svc. 1994–; author: (w. L.J. Bean) California Indians, Primary Resources, 1977, 1990, The Cahuilla and the Santa Rosa Mountains, 1981, The Cahuilla Landscape, 1991, Ethnology of the California Indians (2 vol.), Spanish Borderlands Series, 1991, chapters in several books; mem: Soc. Applied Anthropology (fellow), Southwestern Anthropology Assn. (pgm. chair 1976-78, newsletter editor 1976-79), Am. Anthropology Assn. (fellow), Soc. for Am. Archaeology; civic: Girl Scouts U.S. Sequoia Area Council (bd. 1954-61, cons. S.F. Coun. 1962-69), L.W.V. S.San Mateo Co. (bd., v.p., pres. 1960-65); United Ch. of Christ. Ofc: Ballena Press 823 Valparaiso Ave Menlo Park 94025

VAN GUNDY, SEYMOUR DEAN, nematologist, university dean and professor; b. Feb. 24, 1931, Toledo, Ohio; m. Wilma C., June 12, 1954; children: Sue Ann b. 1956, Richard b. 1959; edn: BA, Bowling Green S.U., Ohio, 1953; Ph.D., Univ. Wisconsin, 1957. Career: asst. nematologist UC Riverside 1957-63, assoc. nematologist 1963-68, prof. nematology 1968-73, prof. nematology and

plant pathology 1973–, chmn. dept. nematology UCR, 1972-84; assoc. dean of res. Graduate Div. UCR 1968-70, asst. v. chancellor res. 1970-72; assoc. dean res. Coll. of Natural & Agricultural Scis., 1985-88, actg. dean 1986, interim dean 1988-90, dean 1990-93; lectr., invited spkr. num. campuses and past consultant to various companies; Fellow AAAS 1964–, Am. Phytopathological Soc. 1978–, Soc. of Nematologists 1984–; Rockefeller Found. res. grantee: Cancer Res., Nat. Sci. Found. Res., USDA Competitive Res.; past mem. ed. bd. Revue de Nematologie, Journ. of Nematology and Plant Disease; publs: num. res. papers and articles in profl. jours. Res: 1188 Pastern Rd Riverside 92506 Ofc:Univ. of Calif. Riverside Dept of Nematology Riverside 92521

VAN HOOSER, DAVID BARTON, real estate broker, litigation consultant, arbitrator and mediator; b. July 13, 1939, Oakland; s. Cornelius Barton and Ruth David (Harrison) Van Hooser; m. JoAnn Southwick, July 2, 1979; children: David b. 1960, Lance b. 1963, Aaron b. 1971; edn: BBA, Calif. State Coll. 1970; spl. courses in indsl. suprvn., purchasing, personnel & labor rels., 1957-69; La Salle Ext. Univ. of Law, 1966-9; Northwood Inst. of Mdsg. 1969; cert. specialist: IS, RS, and MS (investment, residential, mgmt. splst.), Century 21, 1985; Graduate Real Estate Inst. (GRI). Career: adminstrv. asst. to the pres. Kaiser Jeep Corp., Oakland 1966-68, dist. sales mgr., So. San Francisco 1968-69; dist. mgr. Winnebago Industries, Concord, Ca. 1970, nat. bus. mgr. in Forrest City, Iowa 1970-71; nat. dealer devel. mgr., 1970-71; we. reg. mgr. Apollo Motor Homes, Reno, Nev. 1979, nat. sales mgr. hdqtrs. Downey, Calif. 1980, v.p. sales 1981, v.p. mktg. & sales, Carson, 1981-84; v.p./mgr. Century 21 Tri Cities Realty, Hesperia 1985-93; pres. Foster Financial Funding, Foster and Associates, Foster Group-Tri Cities Realty, 1992–; broker, gen. mgr. Century 21 Desert Rock, Hesperia 1993–; pres. and gen. mgr. Carl J. Molino Ents. Inc., George Foster Ents. Inc.; prin. broker Utah-Nev.-Calif. Land Exchange (Utah & Calif. co.) 1991; mem: Am. Arbitration Assn. (Panel of Arbitrators), Am. Mgmt. Assn., Calif. Assn. Realtors, Nat. Assn. Realtors, Victor Valley Bd. of Realtors (chmn. profl. & stds. com. 1990-02, past chmn. grievance com.), Century 21 Investment Soc., La Salle Univ. Alumni Assn. (charter); Republican; Ch. of Jesus Christ of Latter Day Saints. Rec: guns/desert survival. Res: 9889 Tradepost Rd Lucerne Valley 92356 Ofc: Century 21 Desert Rock 16061 Bear Valley Rd Ste 1 Hesperia 92345

VAN HOUSE, NANCY ANITA, university professor and acting dean; b. Aug. 3, 1950, Ogden, Utah; edn: AB, English, UC Berkeley 1971; MLS, Sch. of Lib. and Info. Studies, UC Berkeley 1972, PhD, 1979. Career: reference librarian San Mateo Co. Lib., Belmont 1973-76; coord. East Bay Info. Svs. (now Bay Area Lib. & Info. Sys.), Oakland 1976-77; instr. Sch. of Lib. and Info. Studies, UC Berkeley 1977-79; sr. res. assoc. King Res. Inc., Rockville, Md. 1979-81; asst. prof. Sch. of Lib. and Info. Studies, UC Berkeley 1981-87, assoc. prof. 1987-93, prof. 1993–, acting dean 1991–; awards: Assn. for Lib. and Info. Sci. Edn. Res. Competition Winner 1983, 84; grants: prin. investigator: U.S. Dept. of Edn., Higher Edn. Act, lib. career tng. grants (1992-93, 93-94, 94-95), Council on Lib. Resources Cooperative Res. Project 1989, co-prin. investigator U.S. Dept. Edn. Public Lib. Effectiveness Study 1987-88, NSF New Investigators in Info. Sci. grant 1984; mem: Assn. for Lib. and Info. Sci. Edn., Am. Lib. Assn., Calif. Lib. Assn.; assoc. editor Information Systems Res. 1994–; editl. bd. Library Quarterly 1990-95, advy. bd. 1986-89; editl. advy. bd. Lib. and Info. Sci. Res. 1991-92; publications: co-author The Public Library Effectiveness Study (Chg., Ill.: Am. Lib. Assn., 1993), What's Good? Describing the Public Library's Effectiveness: A Practical Approach (Chg., Ill.: Am. Lib. Assn., 1990), Output Measures for Public Libraries 2nd edit. (Chgo., Ill.: Am. Lib. Assn., 1987), Planning and Role Setting for Public Libraries (Chgo., Ill.: Am. Lib. Assn., 1987); author, Public Library User Fees: The Use and Finance of Public Libraries (Westport, Ct.: Greenwood Press, 1983); co-author under name DeWath, A Planning Process for Public Libraries (Chgo., Ill.: Am. Lib. Assn., 1980); num. articles in scholarly jours. Ofc: University of California School of Library & Info. Studies 102 South Hall Berkeley 94720-4600

VAN KIRK, JOHN ELLSWORTH, physician; b. Jan. 13, 1942, Dayton, Ohio; s. Herman Corwin and Dorothy Louise (Shafer) V.K.; children: Linnea b. 1979; edn: BA, cum laude, De Pauw Univ. 1963; BS, Northwestern Univ. 1964; MD, distn., Northwestern Univ. Sch. of Med. 1967; bd. cert. Am. Bd. Internal Med., Cardiovascular Disease. Career: med. internship Evanston Hosp., Northwestern Univ. 1967-68; USPHS staff assoc., NIAID, senior asst. surgeon NIH 1968-70; resident in medicine, fellow in cardiology, Univ. Mich., 1970-74, instr. in internal med. 1973-74; staff cardiologist Mills Memorial Hosp., San Mateo 1974–, dir. critical care and dir. pacemaker clinic; awards: Alpha Omega Alpha, 1st Prize Landscaping, Calif. 1977, Physician's Recogn. Awards (1968, 72, 75, 77, 80, 82, 85, 87, 89, 93); mem: Am. Coll. Cardiology (fellow), Am. Heart Assn., San Mateo Co. Heart Assn. (pres. 1977-79), Calif. Med. Assn., San Mateo Co. Med. Assn.; works: research in devel. of live viral respiratory vaccines for human use; publd. articles in med. journs.; mil: USPHS 1968-70; Republican; United Brethren; rec: gardening, amateur radio, computer science. Res: 235 Amherst Ave San Mateo 94402 Ofc: 50 S San Mateo Dr Ste 270 San Mateo 94401

VANNIX, C(ECIL) ROBERT, programmer and systems analyst; b. June 14, 1953, Glendale; s. Cecil H. Jr. and Gloria Jenny (Zappia) V.; m. 1980, 1 son, Robert Jeremy; edn: AS in plant mgmt., BS in indsl. arts, Loma Linda Univ., 1977; AS in info. systems, Ventura City Coll., 1985. Career: instr. industrial arts Duarte High Sch., 1977-79, Oxnard High Sch., 1979-81; computer cons. Litton Data Command Systems, Agoura 1976-81, senior engr. instr. 1981-85; computer cons. McLaughlin Research Corp., Camarillo 1976-77, senior program analyst 1985-88; senior program analyst Computer Software Analysts, Camarillo 1988-90; V.C. Systems 1990–; mem. Apple PI Computer Club, Litton Computer Club (pres. 1975-76); recipient spl. achiev. award One Way Singers, Glendale 1975; Republican; Adventist. Res: 407 Appletree Ave Camarillo 93012

VAN NOY, TERRY WILLARD, insurance company executive; b. Aug. 31, 1947, Alhambra; s. Barney Willard and Cora Ellen (Simms) V.; m. Betsy Helen Pothen, Dec. 27, 1968; children: Bryan, Mark; edn: BS in bus. mgmt., Calif. State Polytechnic Univ., 1970; MBA, Pepperdine Univ., 1991, CLU, Am. Coll. Career: life underwriter Mutual of Omaha, 1970-: group sales rep. Atlanta 1970-74, dist. mgr. 1974-77, regional mgr. Dallas 1977-82, nat. sales mgr. Hq., Omaha, Nebr. 1982-83, v.p. group mktg. 1983-87, regional v.p. and dir. Mutual of Omaha, Orange, Calif. 1987–; speaker Health Ins. Assn. of Am., Chgo. 1984, Life Ins. Mktg. & Research Assn., S.F. 1987, Toronto 1994; advy. bd. Chapman Univ. Sch. of Business; mem. Am. Soc. CLUs, Orange County Employee Benefit Council, Western Pension & Benefits Conference Bd., Adaptive Business Leaders; Republican; Lutheran (ch. bd. 1987). Res: 381 S Smokeridge Terrace Anaheim 92807 Ofc: Mutual of Omaha 333 S Anita Dr Ste 650 Orange 92668

VAN PRAAG, ALEX, III, engineer consultant; b. June 2, 1918, San Antonio, Tx.; s. S., Sr. and Theda (Farque) Van P.; m. Missie Anne Jones, Oct. 5, 1940 (dec. Dec. 1970); children: Lynne Carole b. 1942, Bruce Alexander b. 1948, Drake Allan b. 1953, Aaron Scott b. 1956; m. Norma Jean Vos-Hellinga, Oct. 23, 1977; stepchildren: Jilda Jayne Hellinga b. 1955, Jeffrey Jon Hellinga b. 1958; edn: BSCE, MS, PhD, Univ. of Ill.; reg. profl. engr. -civil, structural, surveyor; lic. aircraft pvt. pilot, former comml. instr. Career: served to Col. US Army Corps of Engrs. (ret.) 1940-78, active duty 1940-46; v.p. Van Praag Equip. & Mfg. Co., 1946-56; pres. Van Praag Ents. and Mid American Consultants, 1956-58; spl. projects engr. Mark Thomas Consulting Engrs., San Jose 1959-63; pres. Van Praag Assocs., 1963-71; pres. Van Praag Industries, Calif. 1972-76, pres. VPI, Ltd. (res. & devel., sales & prodn. of Praagmatic bldg. system), Calif. 1976-78, VPI, Ltd. (R & D of Transpandable Homes for the Middle East, emphasis on low-cost hsg.) Mont., 1978-79; pres. Van Praag Internat. Ltd., 1980-85, 1988–; exec. ofct. WorldTec Systems, Inc., Minnetonka, Minn. civil engr. US Army Corps Engrs., Presidio San Francisco, 1985-88; awards: Nat. Soc. of Profl. Engrs. 4th annual engr. of year award, Wash. DC, 1983; inventions: The Praagmatic Building System (Pat. #3,818,661, #5,038,535; also Canadian #1,332,866), improved Electro-Mechanical CAM, devel. Dehydrated Fuel for motor vehicles, designer Volumetric Meter Prover Vessels, Nuclear Demolitions, explosives, and Minefield Techn.; mem. Mensa Intl., Masonic A.A.O.N.M.S.; Republican; Prot.; rec: flying. Res: 553 E California St Ripon CA 95366 Ofc: Van Praag Intl. Ltd. PO Box 386 Ripon CA 95366 also WorldTec Systems Inc. 601 Lakeshore Pky Ste 1050 Minnetonka MN 55305

VAN STRALEN, ERIC, title insurance executive; b. Dec. 4, 1952, Montebello; s. Albert Phillip and Evelyn Ruth (Murray) Van S.; m. Linda Kozan Hunt, June 19, 1972 (div. 1979); m. Diane Alene Laizure, May 18, 1980; children: Katrina b. 1974, Rebecca b. 1981, Candice b. 1981; edn: grad. Lakewood H.S., 1971, course work Long Beach City Coll., Solano Comm. Coll., UC Davis. Career: mgr. Title-Tax, Inc., L.A. 1976-79; customer svc. First American Title Co., Fairfield 1980-83; title dept. mgr. Transam. Title Ins. Co., Walnut Creek 1983-87; title ops. mgr. Stewart Title Co., Santa Ana 1987; br. mgr. North Am. Title Co., Glendale 1987-90; title ops. mgr. World Title Co., Burbank 1990-92, county mgr. World Title Co., Pleasanton 1992-93; operations mgr. Guardian Title Co. 1993–; mem. Calif. Land Title Assn. (Speaker's Bur. 1983-85), Calif. Trustees Assn. 1983–; mil: E4 USN 1972-75; Republican; Episcopalian; rec: camping, fishing, hunting. Res: 2249 E Rio Verde Dr West Covina 91791 Ofc: Guardian Title Co 20350 Ventura Blvd #200 Woodland Hills 91346

VAN VELZER, VERNA JEAN, research librarian; b. Jan. 22, 1929, State College, Penn.; d. Harry Leland and Golda Lillian (Cline) V.V.; edn: BS, Univ. Ill. 1950, MLS, Syracuse Univ. 1957. Career: head librarian General Electric Microwave Lab., Palo Alto 1958-64; librarian Research & Devel. Lab., Fairchild Semiconductor Products Co., Palo Alto 1964-65; intelligence librarian Sylvania Electronic Products Co., Mountain View 1965-66; research librarian ESL Inc., Sunnyvale 1966–; honors: Beta Phi Mu, recipient Paul Revere silver bowl Santa Clara Camellia show, biog. listed Internat. Who's Who of Intellectuals, Who's Who in Lib. & Info. Sci., Who's Who in Spl. Libs., Who's Who in West, World Who's Who of Women, others; mem: Spl. Libraries Assn., Assn. for Computing Machinery, IEEE, Am. Defense Preparedness Assn., Am. Inst. Aero. & Astro, Assn. of Old Crows, U.S. Naval Inst., Navy League of the U.S., Am. Biographical Inst. (resrch. bd. advisors, medal of hon.), Nature Conservancy, Am. Horse Protection Assn., Internat. Primate Protection League, Greenpeace, Fund for Animals, PETA, Wildlife Rescue. Res: 4048 Laguna Way Palo Alto 94306

VAN VLIET, STEPHANIE DIANA, numismatist; b. July 20, 1947, Los Angeles; d. Lawrence Joel and Selma Marcia (Kaplan) Misrach; children: Jennifer b. 1969, Adam b. 1970, Jason b. 1974, Jill b. 1976; edn: Fgn. langs., James Monroe H.S., Sepulveda, 1965; AA, L.A. Valley Coll., 1967; cert. CSU Northridge cont. edn. div. bus. and ind. svs., 1989; reg. hypnotherapist, 1991. Career: summer camp counselor Doubs, Fr. 1965; nursery sch. asst., elem. sch. tchr. aide, playground dir., Van Nuys 1966-68; v.p. American Coin Co., Studio City 1968-83; pres. Rubio Medical Center, 1980–; pres. Internat. Gold & Silver, Encino 1983–; honors: capt. of the Saftys, Brentwood Elem. Sch. Playground 1958, ed.-in-chief Sepulveda Jr. H.S. newspaper 1962, student body senator/rep. Fgn. Language Dept., LA Pierce Coll. 1989-90; mem: Am. Numismatic Assn. (life), Am. Numismatic Soc., Nat. Assn. of Watch and Clock Collectors, Israel Numismatic Soc., Casino Chips and Gaming Tokens Collectors Club, Fla. United Numismatics (FUN), ACLU, Older Womens League, N.O.W., NAACP (life), Womens Am. ORT (life), Nat. Council of Senior Citizens (life), ASPCA, Encino C.of C., Lambda Legal Defense and Edn. Fund, Native Am. Rights Fund, Human Rights Campaign Fund, The Acad. of Polit. Sci., L.A. World Affairs Council, Sierra Club, L.A. Co. Mus. of Art, The Nature Conservancy, NRA (life), ICTA, Parents & Friends of Gays & Lesbians, Act-Up, Women Only, So. Calif. Women for Understanding, Women For, Win PAC, B'nai Brith Women, New Jewish Agenda, ARZA, Am. Soc. for Yad Vashem, Jewish Geneal. Soc. L.A., Hillel, Dignity, Longhunter Soc., YWCA, Gene Autry We. Heritage Mus. (founding mem.), Nat. Audubon Soc., Inst. of Noetic Scis., Theta Sigma Tau, Sigma Kappa; Stonewall Democratic Club; Calif. Republican Party (sustaining 1991); publs: her 1st article written in elem. sch., 1957, for Brentwood Sch. newspaper, pub. by LA Times, 2/26/83; volunteer: VA Med. Ctr. (Sepulveda), Childrens Hosp. (L.A.), Gay & Lesbian Comm. Svs. Ctr. (L.A.), Am. Red Cross; Stephen S. Wise Temple; rec: baseball, theater, comedy. Res: 15615 Meadowgate Rd Encino 91436

VAN ZAK, DAVID BRUCE, medical psychologist, educator; b. Nov. 5, 1950, Santa Monica; s. Martin and Anita Van Zak; m. Nina Weinstein, Feb. 15, 1981; edn: AB, UCLA, 1973; MA, Pepperdine Univ., 1976; PsyD, U.S. Internat. Univ., 1983; lic. M.F.C.T. 1977, lic. Psychologist, 1988. Career: dir. of edn. Biofeedback Tng. Inst., Los Angeles 1975-77, also psych. cons. Project Total Push, L.A.; family and marital therapist pvt. practice, West L.A. 1977–, med. psychologist, 1988–; attdg. psychologist Charter Hospitals, Long Beach and Torrance; clin. instr./attdg. psychologist Sch. of Dental Medicine and Pub. Health, USC, 1990–; prof. psych. Profl. Sch. of Psychol. Studies, L.A. 1981-86, adj. prof. psych. U.S. Internat. Univ., San Diego 1984-87; state examiner Calif. Family Therapy Exam, 1985; awards: UCLA Music Dept. staff award (1972, 73), recogn.for outstanding research Am. Psych. Assn. (1976), outstanding tchr. award Coastline Coll. (1981), listed Who's Who in Am. Science & Engring.; mem: Biofeedback Soc. of Am. (nat. examiner 1981-88), Biofeedback Soc. of Calif. (bd. 1987-89, sci. research award finalist 1987), Calif. Assn. of Marital & Family Therapists, Am., Calif. and L.A. Co. Psych. Assns.; presenter Internat. Stress Mgmt. Conf. on Res., Edinburgh (1988); mem. UCLA Band, 1970-73, staff Music Dept., 1971-73; publs: 20+ profl. jour. and book articles; Jewish; rec: musician, bodybuilding, sci-fi. Ofc: David Bruce Van Zak, Psy.D., M.F.C.T., Academy of Biofeedback & Med-Psych, 11600 Wilshire Blvd Ste 210 West Los Angeles 90025 Ph: 310/477-2340

VARTABEDIAN, STEVEN MICHAEL, justice; b. May 8, 1950, Fresno; s. Robt. and Nancy Louise (Joseph) V.; m. Marilyn, Aug. 5, 1972; children: Melanie b. 1979, Stefanie and Pamela b. 1982; edn: BA (summa cum laude), CSU Fresno 1972; JD (magna cum laude), Univ. Santa Clara Sch. Law 1975. Career: atty., ptnr. Vartabedian & Poochigian, Fresno 1976-82; judge Sanger Judicial Dist. 1981-83; Fresno Municipal Ct. 1983-87, presiding judge 1985-87; Fresno Co. Superior Ct. 1987-89; justice Calif. State Ct. Appeals Fifth Dist. 1989–; awards: Phi Kappa Phi 1971, Outstanding Contbn. to Edn. award Sanger Unified Sch. Dist. 1982; contbr. articles Striking a Delicate Balance in Sex Abuse Cases, 1985 and Dismissal and Prearraignment Delay, 1987, Judges Jour., Return of Judicial Comment to Deadlocked Juries, Calif. Cts. Commentary, 1987, Enhancing Sentences with Prior Felony Convictions, Pacific Law Jour., 1992; Republican; First Armenian Presbyterian Ch., elder. Ofc: Court of Appeal 5th Dist 2525 Capitol St Fresno 93721

VASA, HARK MANILAL, software & consulting firm chief executive; b. Feb. 8, 1944, Bombay, India; nat. U.S. citizen, 1976; s. Manilal Panachand and Prabha (Dholakia) V.; m. Kusum B. Doshi, Nov. 8, 1970; children: Anita b. 1972, Sarita b. 1975; edn: BS in elec. engring., V.J.T.I., Bombay, India, 1966; MS, West Va. Univ., 1968. Career: engr. Union Carbide, W.Va. 1968-70; v.p. DSC, Pa. 1970-82; pres. Pac Decision Science Co., Santa Ana 1982–; cons. PDSC, 1982-89; lectr. conferences, 1988; author: articles, 1983, 85, 86, 87, 93, 94, 95; Republican; Jain; rec: social activities, traveling.

VASCONCELLOS, JOHN, legislator, attorney; b. May 11, 1932, San Jose, Calif.; s. John and Teresa (Jacobs) V.; edn: BS, Santa Clara Univ., 1954; LLB, Santa Clara Univ., 1959; admitted Calif. State Bar, 1959. Career: atty., Ruffo & Chadwick, San Jose, 1959; travel sec., Gov. Pat Brown, Sacto., 1960; assemblyman, Calif. State Legislature, Sacto., 1966–; chair, Assembly Ways & Means

Com., Calif. State Legislature, 1980–; founder, Calif. Task Force to Promote Self-Esteem and Personal and Social Responsibility, 1987; chmn., Assembly Democratic Econ. Prosperity Team (ADEPT), 1992–; awards: Legislator of the Decade (1980's), Faculty Assn. of Calif. Comm. Colleges; over 100 other awards during tenure as assemblyman; mem: State Bar of Calif., 1959–; bd. of dir., Calif. Leadership, 1987–; author: A Liberating Vision, 1979; Toward a Healthier State, a 10-yr. comprehensive prog. incl. Human Corps, Sr. Partners, Edn. Reform, Legislative Ethics. Mil: first lt., US Army, 1954-56; Democrat; rec: racquetball, friends, reading, writing. Res: 1915 Bellomy #5 Santa Clara 95050. Ofc: 100 Paseo de San Antonio #106 San Jose 95113

VASQUEZ, GADDI HOLGUIN, county supervisor; b. Jan. 22, 1955, Carrizo Springs, Tex.; s. Guadalupe Garcia Vasquez and Eva V.; m. Elaine Gutierrez, Oct. 14, 1978; children: Jason b. 1979; edn: AA, Rancho Santiago Comm. Coll., Santa Ana 1972; BA, Univ. Redlands, 1980. Career: police ofcr. Orange Police Dept., 1975-79; comm. relations coord. City Mgr.'s Office, Riverside 1979-81; exec. asst. Orange Co. Bd. Suprs., Santa Ana 1981-85; Hispanic liaison Gov.'s Office, Sacto. 1985, dep. appts. sec. 1985-87; apptd. supr. Orange Co. Bd. Suprs. 1987, elected supr. 1988-; mem. Orange Co. Transp. Auth. 1991–, Transp. Corridor Agys. 1987–, Local Agy. Formation Commn. 1988–, Nat. Assn. Latino Elected Officials 1989–, Calif. Council on Crim. Justice 1989; honors: list of 100 most influential Hispanics Hispanic Bus. Mag. 1986-91, Humanitarian award NCCJ 1989, Govt. Hispanic Business Advocate 1991, U.S. Hispanic Chamber 1991, Tree of Life award Jewish Nat. Fund 1991, State Child Devel. Advy. Com. Award 1990; civic bds: Orange County Salvation Army 1991–, Pediatric Cancer Res.Found. 1990–, Orange Co. Boy Scout Council 1988–, Calif. First Amendment Coalition 1991–; Republican; Prot.; rec: reading. Ofc: Orange County Bd. of Supervisors 10 Civic Ctr Plaza Santa Ana 92701

VASU, BANGALORE SESHACHALAM, bioscience and technology educator. administrator; b. Bangalore, India, naturalized U.S., 1982; edn: MA, Univ. of Madras, India 1959, MSc, 1962; PhD, Stanford Univ., 1965. Career: UNESCO specialist in biology, Paris, France and Univ. of Zambia, Lusaka, 1968-73; vis. prof. biology CSU Chico, Calif. 1974-77; professor biology and chair Biosci./Biotech. Mgmt. Menlo Coll., Atherton 1978–; award: Fullbright fellow US Edn. Founds., U.S. and India 1962. Ofc: Menlo College 1000 El Camino Real Atherton 94027

VAUGHAN, CHRISTOPHER MARK, physician; b. Apr. 9, 1952, Boston, Mass.; s. Joseph James and Priscilla M. (Wilkinson) V.; m. Verna Maria Ma, May 24, 1986; children: Jessica b. 1987, Samantha b. 1991; edn: BS (magna cum laude), UC Irvine 1974; MD, Med. Coll. of Wisconsin 1978; lic. physician St. of Calif. 1980; Nat. Bd., Cert. 1980; diplomate Am. Bd. Anesthesiology 1985, diplomate Am. Bd. Pediatrics 1987. Career: internship, pediatrics, UC Irvine 1978-79; residency, pediatric, The Children's Hosp. of San Francisco 1979-81; residency, anesthesia, UCLA Med. Ctr. 1981-82, LAC-USC Med. Ctr. 1982-83; dir. of anesthesiology Tri-Valley Surgery Ctr., Pleasanton, Calif. 1993–; honors: Phi Beta Kappa 1974; mem: Am. Acad. of Pediatrics (fellow, 1989–), Am. Coll. of Anesthesiologists (fellow, 1985–), Soc. of Pediatric Anesthesia 1988–, CMA 1994–, Alameda-Contra Costa Med. Assn. 1994–; Republican; Catholic; rec: running, golf. Res: 3 Coleport Landing Alameda 94502 Ofc: Tri-Valley Surgery Center 4487 Stoneridge Drive Pleasanton 94588

VAUGHAN, DANIEL G., physician-surgeon; b. Mar. 15, 1921, Montana; s. Daniel G. and Katherine (Browne) V.; m. Courtney Sprague, Dec. 3, 1949; children: Laurie b. 1950, Cecilia b. 1952, James b. 1954, Matthew b. 1956, Mary b. 1959, Daniel b. 1960, Katherine b. 1960, Elizabeth b. 1963; edn: BS, Univ. of Wash., Seattle 1942; MD, Univ. of Oregon Med. Sch., Portland 1945; Diplomate Am. Board Ophthalmology 1953. Career: postdoctoral intern King County Hosp., Seattle 1945-46; resident in ophthalmology Univ. of Calif., San Francisco 1948-51; pvt. practice ophthal., San Jose 1951–; staff O'Connor Hosp. (pres. 1964.); founder/pres. Sight Conservation Res. Center, 1960–; clin. prof. UCSF Dept. Ophthal. San Francisco; mem. bd. govs. Francis I. Proctor Found. for Res.in Ophthalmology 1990–; awards: Oregon State Junior Golf Championship 1938, disting. service Francis I. Proctor Found. for Res. in Ophthalmology 1984, outstanding contbn. in med. edn. Santa Clara Co. Med. Soc. 1988; mem: Assn. for Res. in Ophthal. (exec sec. We. Sect. 1961-66), Fellow Am. Coll. of Surgeons (Western US rep. to Advy. Council for Ophthalmic Surgery 1971-74 and chmn. 1974-76), Frederick C. Cordes Eye Soc. (pres. 1965), No. Calif. Soc. for Prevention of Blindness (pres. 1971-73), Pacific Coast Oto-Ophthalmological Soc. (pres. 1980-81), Santa Clara Co. Med. Assn., Santa Clara Univ. (bd. fellows); author eye chapters in 2 med. texts, coauthor: General Ophthalmology, 14th edit. (Lange Med. Pub., transl. 6 langs.), contbr. 30+ sci. articles in ophthalmic jours.; mil: First Marine Div. Med. Corps, China 1946-47. Ofc: 220 Meridian Ave San Jose 95126

VAUGHAN, MICHAEL J., trust company president; b. Jan. 26, 1942, N.Y.; s. Michael J. and Florence R.; m. Sherree R. Vaughan, June 26, 1965; children: Gary R., Andrew M.; edn: AA, Santa Ana Coll. 1962; BA, psychol., CSU Fullerton 1964; postgrad., USC 1966-67; M. in bank trust, Univ. Wash. 1973; lic. real estate Calif. Career: v.p. Union Bank, L.A. 1965-74; Lloyds Bank, Santa

Ana 1974-79; pres. M.J. Vaughan & Co. Inc. 1979-83; sr. v.p. Valencia Bank, Newport Beach 1983-85; pres./CEO Imperial Trust Co., L.A. 1985–; thesis rev. Pacific Coast Banking Sch., Seattle, Wash. 1973-77; mem: Orange Co. Planned Giving Council, So. Calif. Trust Officers. Assn., Internat. Assn. Fin. Planners, Internat. Found. Employee Benefit Plans, Western Pension Conf., Am. Soc. Pension Actuaries, L.A. World Affairs Council, USC Gen. Alumni (life mem.), USC Trojan Club (pres. 1982-83), USC Cardinal & Gold (bd. dirs.), USC Scholarship Club, USC Commerce Assocs. (bd. dirs), USC Cancer Res. Assocs.; active Hoag Hosp. 552, St. Joseph Hosp. Todo's, St. Joseph Hosp. Found. (bd. dirs.), St. Joseph's Hosp. (bd. trustees); clubs: Pacific, City, Tustin Ranch Golf, Santa Ana C.C.; MS thesis: The Devel. of Bus. in Orange Co., hons. recognition 1973; contbr. article, Calif. Planner Mag. (1986); Republican; Lutheran; rec: golf (course record Mission Viejo C.C.). Res: 11581 Ranch Hill Santa Ana 92705 Ofc: Imperial Trust Co. 201 N Figueroa St Ste 610 Los Angeles 90012

VAUGHEN, STEPHEN, stock broker, account executive; b. March 8, 1958, Irving, Tx.; s. Jack Francis and Carol Bird (Ulsrud) V.; m. Lori Jean Duff, July 20, 1983; children: Erin b. 1986, Christine b. 1988; edn: BS bus. adminstrn., CSU Bakersfield 1980. Career: stockbroker, account exec. Crowell Weedon & Co., Encino 1980–; awards: Crowell Weedon & Co. Round Table 1986–); mem: Nat. Assn. Securities Dealers, registered rep. of N.Y.S.E. Member firm, Experimental Aircraft Assn.; mil: Marine Corps Reserves 1977-82; Republican; Methodist; rec: computer programming, technical stockmarket analysis, composite aircraft building. Res: 5439 Seneca Place Simi Valley 93063

VAUGHN, JAMES ENGLISH, JR., neuroscientist; b. Sept. 17, 1939, Kansas City, Mo.; s. James English and Sue Katherine V.; m. Christine Singleton, June 18, 1961; children: Stephanie b. 1965, Stacey b. 1968; edn: BA, Westminster Coll., 1961; PhD, UCLA, 1965. Career: postdoctoral fellow Univ. of Edinburgh, Scotland 1965-66; asst. prof. Boston Univ. Sch. of Med., Mass. 1966-70; assoc. prof. Beckman Research Inst. of City of Hope, Duarte, Calif. 1970-73, prof. 1973–, chmn. div. neurosci. 1987–; awards: res. grantee NIH 1969–, United Cerebral Palsy Found. 1965-66, NSF 1983-87, Huntington's Disease Found. 1987-88, Sadie & Norman Lee Found. 1990-91; mem.: Soc. for Neurosci., Internat. Brain Research Orgn., N.Y. Acad. of Scis., Am. Soc. for Cell Biology, AAAS; publs: book chapters, research articles in profl. jours. (1965–); editl. bd. Synapse (1986–), reviewer J. of Comparative Neurology, Brain Research (1974–), assoc. editor J. of Neurocytology (1978-86). Ofc: Beckman Research Inst. City of Hope 1450 E Duarte Rd Duarte 91010

VEGA, BENJAMIN URBIZO, jurist; b. Jan. 18, 1916, La Ceiba, Honduras; s. Benjamin Urbizo (former Honduras Consul General in Mobile, Ala. and Los Angeles, Ca.) and Catalina (Tablas) V.; m. Janie L. Smith, Oct. 12, 1989; edn: BA, USC, 1938, postgrad. 1938-40; LLB, Pacific Coast Univ. Law, 1941; admitted Calif. St. Bar 1947, US Dist. Ct., So. Dist. 1947, Bd. Immigration Appeals 1948, US Supreme Ct. 1958. Career: atty., assoc. Anderson, McPharlin & Connors, Los Angeles 1947-48, Newman & Newman, 1948-51; deputy dist. atty. County of Los Angeles, 1951-66; judge L.A. Co. Municipal Ct., East L.A. Judicial Dist., 1966-86, retired 1986; awards: distinguished public service L.A. Mayor Sam Yorty 1973, commendation for svs. as Dep. Dist. Atty. Los Angeles County Bd. of Suprs., commendation Municipal Judges Assn., proclamation for svs. Montebello City Council, City of Commerce, Resolution of commendation 55th Assembly Dist. Calif., honored for svc. as judge US Congressman Matthew Martinez 30th Dist. Calif.; mem. Beverly Hills Bar Assn., past mem. ABA, Inter-Amer. Bar Assn., Inglewood, East L.A., Montebello bar assns., Am. Judicature Soc., L.A. Lawyers Club, Conf. of Calif. Judges, Municipal Ct. Judges Assn.; civic: Las Campanitas, League of the Americas, Youth Opportunities Found. (past dir.); Internat. Com. L.A. Philharmonic, Navy League of Beverly Hills. mil: cpl. USAF 1942-46; Democrat; R.Cath.; rec: world travel, collect video cassettes, books. Res: Apt 1207 101 California Ave Santa Monica 90403

VEGA, FRANK, distribution executive, softball association area director; b. July 30, 1954, Havana, Cuba; s. Antonio and Luisa Rosa (Santos Cisneros) V.; m. Cecelia Selayandia, Oct. 7, 1989; children: Liza M. Gallant b. 1969, Mark Asa b. 1980; edn: H.S. dipl. Don Bosco Technical Inst., S. San Gabriel, Calif. 1972; stu. East L.A. Jr. Coll., 1973. Career: documentation draftsman Apollo Motorhomes, Downey 1972-74; design draftsman Robinhood Motorhomes, Carson 1974-75; customer service rep. General Bearings, Vernon 1976-81; br. ops. mgr. Bearings Inc., Pico Rivera 1981-85, sales rep. Bearings Inc., Ontario 1985-86; ADC mgr. Hub City Inc., Santa Fe Springs 1986-93, Anaheim 1993–; area dir. United States Slo-Pitch Softball Assn., San Gabriel Valley 1970–, Antelope Valley 1995–, classification com. chmn. 1985–; rec: softball, reading, golf, boating. Res: 2896 Buckhaven Rd Chino Hills 91709 Ofc: Hub City 1110 N Lemon St Anaheim 92801

VELASQUEZ, RUTH LIND, teacher; b. May 8, 1926, San Francisco; d. Axel and Edith Viola (Carlson) Lind; m. Thomas Aquinas Velasquez, Aug. 14, 1957; children: Laura b. 1959, Donna b. 1962; edn: BA in elem. edn., San Francisco State Univ., 1947, MA, 1953. Calif. std. tchg. credentials: elem. 1947, adminstrv., 1953. Career: tchr. San Francisco Unified Sch. Dist., 1947-90, kindergarten tchr. 1965-70, 1985-90, staff devel. specialist 1970-85; early childhood edn. consultant San Francisco USD 1990-94; honoree, named Outstanding Teacher Delta Phi Upsilon S.F. 1991; mem: Calif. Kindergarten Assn. (profl. devel. leader 1989-92, editor "Take 5" 1989-95, grant com. chair 1989-95, bd. 1995–), Delta Kappa Gamma (co-pres. 1992-94), Delta Phi Upsilon (Grand Council 1989-95), Phi Delta Kappa 1989–; clubs: Margrethe Lodge Danish Sisterhood (S.F.), Epson Salts Computer (Redwood City); author (book, workshop) Recycle for Learning 1995, coauthor (reading pgm.) First Stage Reading Program. Res: 703 Higate Dr Daly City 94015

VENTURA, BRUCE ANTHONY, lawyer; b. July 20, 1959, Petersburg, Va.; s. Luis Santiago and Margaret Louise (Dennison) V.; edn: hons., Univ. Coll. Cardiff Wales 1979-80; BA hons., magna cum laude, Univ. Ill. 1981; JD, UC Berkeley Boalt Hall 1984; admitted St. Bar Calif. 1984, Wash. D.C. 1986. Career: atty., assoc. Paul Hastings Janofsky & Walker, Wash. D.C. 1984-87; Cooley Godward Castro Huddleson & Tatum, Palo Alto 1987-89; v.p. & general counsel (Asia-Pacific) RJR Nabisco Inc., Hong Kong 1989–; vol. E. Palo Alto Vol. Attys. Project 1987-89; exec. ed. Internat. Tax & Bus. Lawyer, Berkeley 1982-84; co-founder, treas. U.N. Assn. Ill., Urbana 1980-81; honors: Who's Who Am. Law Students, Who's Who Am. Coll. Students, Univ. Ill. Bronze Tablet 1981, Edmund S. James scholar 1977-81, Ill. State Scholar, Ill. Nat. Hon. Soc., Phi Beta Kappa; mem: Am. Bar Assn. Ofc: RJR Nabisco 7th Flr Sun Hungkai Centre Wanchai Hong Kong

VERBICA, PETER COE, trustee, real estate principal, developer, financial executive; b. Jan. 31, 1961, San Jose; s. Robert George and Winnifred (Coe) V.; gr. grandson of Henry Willard Coe b. 1820, N.H., opr. cotton textile plant, came overland to Oregon 1847, discovered and worked a gold mine in Amador Co., Calif. 1848-58, married Hannah Smith of N.Y., 1858, settled in 'The Willows' San Jose, Calif., H.W. Coe was first in the region to grow hops, fruit trees, tobacco, and first to produce silk for mfr. (the silk Am. flag he presented US Congress is displayed in the Smithsonian), he ret. to San Felipe Valley where sons Henry Jr. and Charles raised cattle and enlarged Rancho Los Huecos (The Hollows) to include "Pine Ridge Country" (13,000 acres & original Coe ranch bldgs. of 1860s) of the present day Henry Coe State Park, donated in memory of Henry Willard Coe (now the 2d largest state park in Calif. with 79,000 acres, 14 mi. E. of Morgan Hill); m. Karen Kennedy Toole, Sept. 16, 1988; children: d. Vanessa Coe, d. Madeline Marie; edn: Bellarmine Coll. Prep.; BA, Univ. Santa Clara 1983; MS, M.I.T 1992; enrolled Santa Clara Univ. Law School. Career: area mgr. Pacific Bus. Products, Santa Clara 1978; account exec., assoc. v.p. Dean Witter Reynolds, Inc. San Jose 1983-88; fin. cons./2d v.p. Shearson Lehman Hutton, Inc. 1988-89; rancher 1989-94; current: sole trustee fam. bus. holdings and real estate; advisor New England holdings; chief exec./dir. Coe Corp. (real estate holdings incl./or have included the Blue Lakes Ranch; gen. ptnr. CV Equity Partners I, a Calif. Ltd. Ptnrship, gen. ptnr. CV Income Partners I, a Calif. Ltd. Ptnrship); founder, former pres. AMS+; pres. Coe Capital. Inc., a real estate finance co.; lectr., investments, Calif. Comm. Colls., Cupertino 1987; awards: Dean Witter Director's Club 1987, Fox & Carskadon Century Club 1985; writer: mag. articles in Commercial R.E. (3/93), The Pronghorn (Jan.-Feb.); mem. Calif. Cattleman's Assn., Santa Clara Cattleman's Assn., (past) Bldg. Ind. Assn., Nat. Assn. Real Estate Inv. Trusts (acad. assoc.), Nat. Assn. Corp. Dir.; civic bds: (past and current): Santa Clara Univ. (Pres.'s Club, Bd. of Fellows, Kenna Club, Class agt., Internship Pgm. sponsor, writer contbr. Santa Clara Mag., guest lectr.), Bellarmine Coll. Prep. Sch. (St. Robert Cardinal Bellarmine Bd. of Fellows, Pres.'s Club, Reunion Orgnzr.), DeAnza Comm. Coll. (instr.), KTEH-TV (bd. trustees, fin. com., auction com.), The Technology Ctr. of Silicon Valley (mem.), NCCJ (patron), Lucile Salter Packard Children's Hosp. at Stanford (patron), O'Connor Hosp. Found. (patron), Pub. Affairs Council (founding mem.), S.J. Downtown Kiwanis (coms.), Boy Scouts Am. (chmn. Century Club), Am. Heart Assn. (chmn. Planned Giving), KBAY Bus. & Fin. Update (reporter), Junior Achievement (advisor), Music and Arts Found. S.C.V. (patron), San Jose Repertory Theatre (bd. trustees), YMCA (campaign com.), Pineridge Assoc. (life mem.); clubs: Silicon Valley Capital, Commonwealth (S.F.), Rotary, Ducks Unltd., Courtside (Los Gatos), St. Claire; Republican (YR); Episcopal. Ofc: PO Box 7933 San Jose 95150-7933

VERBISCAR, ANTHONY JAMES, chemist, research company executive; b. March 22, 1929, Chgo.; s. Anthony Michael and Anna (Ostronic) V.; m. Sheila M. Walsh, June 27, 1959; children: Stephen, Paul, Ann; edn: Benedictine Coll. 1947-49; BS, De Paul Univ. 1951; PhD organic chem., Univ. Notre Dame 1954; postgrad. Univ. Chgo. 1956-57; UCLA 1964-65. Career: research chemist Hercules Inc., Wilmington, Del. 1954; co-founder, v.p. research Regis Chemical Co., Chgo., Ill. 1957-63; pres. Anver Biosci. Design Inc., Sierra Madre 1965–; prin. investigator grants and contracts NIH, U.S. Army Med. Research & Devel. Command, FDA, Oak Ridge Nat. Lab., NSF; cons., researcher various govt. agencies, cos. and colls.; mem: Am. Chem. Soc., Am.. Inst. Chemists (pres. western sect. 1978-79, local com.), Am. Soc. Pharmacognosy, Oriental Healing Arts Inst.; contbr. num. sci. articles to profl. jours., patentee in field; mil: pvt. AUS 1954-56; R.Cath.; rec: tennis. Res: 491 Crestvale Dr Sierra Madre 91054 Ofc: Anver Biosci. Design 160 E Montecito Ave Sierra Madre 91024-1937

VEREKER, DANIEL A., lawyer; b. Sept. 25, 1943, Hamilton, Oh.; s. Robert Martin and Mary Elizabeth (Kelly) V.; m. Kathy, May 12, 1979; children: Erin, Michael, Richard; edn: JD, Western St. Univ. Coll. of Law, Fullerton 1976. Career: atty. solo practice, Costa Mesa 1977–; instr. Coastline Com. Coll., 1985; lectr. CTLA, Orange Co. Trial Lawyers Assn.; mem: Calif. Trial Lawyers Assn., Orange Co. Trial Lawyers Assn.; past chapt. pres. Calif. Young Republicans; publ: booklet Personal Injury Checklist (1987); mil: USAF 1962-65; rec: fishing, golf, flying. Ofc: Daniel A. Vereker, Atty. 2790 Harbor Blvd Ste 311 Costa Mesa 92626

VERRONE, PATRIC MILLER, writer; b. Sept. 29, 1959, Glendale, N.Y.; s. Pat and Edna (Miller) V.; m. Margaret Williams, July 1, 1989; child: s. Patric Carroll Williams V. b. 1995; edn: BA (magna cum laude) Harvard Coll., 1981; JD, Boston Coll. Law Sch., 1984; admitted bar: Fla. 1984, Calif. 1989. Career: atty. Allen, Knudsen, Swartz, DeBoest, Rhodes & Edwards, P.A., Ft. Myers, Fla. 1984-86; writer "Tonight Show Starring Johnny Carson" Burbank, 1987-90; filmmaker Calloo Callay Inc., Hollywood 1990–; producer, director, writer (film) The Civil War - The Lost Episode, 1992; writer "The Larry Sanders Show Starring Garry Shandling" Hollywood, 1992-93; writer/prod. "The Critic", Culver City, 1993-95; writer/producer "The New Muppet Show", 1995awards: Emmy nom. Acad. TV Arts & Scis., Hollywood 1989, Blue rib. Am. Film & Video Assn., Chgo. 1992, Hon. mention IMAGE Film Fest., Atlanta 1992; mem: Writers Guild West 1986–, California Bar Assn. 1987–, Fla. Bar Assn. 1984–, ABA (1984–; vice chair arts entertainment & sports law com. 1995–), L.A. Co. Bar Assn. (homeless shelter com. 1991–, chmn. artists and the law com. 1992–, Legislative Activity Com. 1992–, Appelate Judicial Eval. Com 1992–, Barristers Sec., Exec. Com. 1993-94, Intellectual Property & Entertainment Law Sect. Exec. Com 1994–), L.A. Municipal Court Temporary Judge 1995, Harvard Club of So. Calif. (interviewer 1991–), Calif. Confederation of the Arts (bd. dir. 1993–), Mus. of Contemporary Art (bd. 1994-95), Los Angeles Lawyer (edit. bd. 1994–); publs: contbr. articles in Baseball and the Am. Legal Mind, 1995, Elysian Fields Quarterly, 1994, Nova Law Review, 1993, Los Angeles Lawyer, 1992-95, ABA Jour., 1990, Boston Coll. Law Rev., 1982-84, Fla. Bar Jour., 1987-89, author, illustrator articles in Harvard Lampoon, 1978-84; Republican; R.Cath.; rec: baseball, movies. Ofc: Calloo Callay Inc. 6466 Odin St Hollywood 90068

VICE, CHARLES LOREN, consulting mechanical engineer; b. Jan. 2, 1921, LaVerne, Okla.; s. Cyrus Christopher and Ethel Segwitch (Hoy) V.; m. Katherine Maxwell, July 16, 1949; children: Katherine Lorene b. 1950, Charles Clark b. 1952, Ann Marie b. 1955; edn: ASTP Cert., Ore. State Univ. 1944, BSME, 1947; grad. wk. USC, 1948-55; Reg. Profl. Engr. (mech.), Calif. Career: mgr. Magnetic Head Div., General Instrument Corp., Hawthorne 1959-62; sr. staff engr. Magnetic Head Div., Ampex Corp., Redwood City 1962-66; chief mech. engr. Collins Radio Corp., Newport Beach 1967-69; pres./bd. chmn. FerraFlux Corp., Santa Ana 1970-78; component engr. & engring. buyer McDonnell Douglas Computer Systems Co., Irvine 1979-90; prin. Precision Consultants Inc., Orange 1990–; cons. Sabor Corp. of Japan 1982–, Teac Corp. of Japan 1974-78, Crown Radio Corp. of Japan 1979-80, Otari Corp. of Japan 1975-77, Univac Corp., Salt Lake City 1975-76, Digital Peripherals Corp. of Taiwan 1989–, Puritan Bennett, El Segundo 1989–; patentee (14) in fields of magnetic recording and profl. sound reproduction, internat. recognized authority on magnetic recording techniques; mem. Nat. Soc. of Profl. Engrs., Toastmasters Internat.; mil: tech. 4/c US Army Engrs. 1943-46, GCM, Victory, Asiatic Pacific Service, Philippine Service with Bronze Star medals; Republican; Christian; rec: piano, singing. Ofc: Precision Consultants, Inc. 5902 E Bryce Ave Orange 92667 Tel: 714/998-5979

VILLEGAS, RICHARD JUNIPERO, artist; b. Apr. 19, 1938, Santa Monica; s. Robert Narciso and Jessie V. (Rodrigues) V.; edn: stu. Art Students League, N.Y.C. 1965-66. Career: artist Joseph Sarosi Inc., N.Y.C. 1961-62; Vozzo & Binetti, 1962-64; Siegman-Ambro, 1964-77; chief artist Greenbaum Bros., Paterson, N.J. 1978-89; owner The Villegas Art Studio, Thousand Oaks 1989–; mem.: C.G. Jung Found. 1960–, Am. Mus. of Natural History 1964–, Nat. Trust for Hist. Preservation 1975–, Westlake Village C.of C. 1989–, Gold Coast Bus. & Profl. Alliance 1991–; rec: Jeffersonian studies, photography, collecting Indian relics, classical music. Res/Studio: The Villegas Art Studio 980 Camino Flores Thousand Oaks 91360-2367

VINSON, THOMAS EUGENE, trust banker; b. Mar. 10, 1945, Oakland; s. Eugene Mullaly and Virginia Phare (Pearson) V.; m. Margaret Kelly, Aug. 16, 1969; edn: BA in pol. sci., CSU Hayward, 1969; cert. trusts, Pacific Coast Banking Sch., Univ. Wash. 1978, num. special courses. Career: Trust/Investment Advisors Wells Fargo Bank, 1969-82; mgr. trust systems analysis, private capital banking, The Crocker Bank, 1982-85; Trust Global Custody and v.p./mgr. No. Calif. Instnl. Trust Services Adminstrn., Bank of America NT&SA, San Francisco 1985-87; v.p. State Street Bank-Calif., Alameda 1988-89; v.p. Bank of America and reg. mgr. Custody Svs. Adminstrn, 1989–; mem: No. Calif. Trust Cos. Assn., Western Pension and Benefits Conf., Securities Indus. Assn., Internat. Ops. Assn.; civic: Commonwealth Club of Calif., Lincoln Child Ctr. Found. (pres. 1981-83, bd., treas., fin. chair), Oakland Mus. Assn.

(dir., asst. treas. 1980-86, 1988-89), Calif. Hist. Soc., Soc. of Calif. Pioneers, Nev. Hist. Soc.; clubs: Dolphin Swimming and Boating, St. Francis Yacht, Lakeview; Republican; R.Cath.; rec: Calif. hist., art, yachting, railroading. Ofc: San Francisco.

VOAKE, RICHARD CHARLES, banker; b. July 21, 1940, Albuquerque, N.M.; s. Charles Frederick and Irene Adelaide (Simms) V.; m. Karen, Sept. 24, 1966; edn: AB econ., Stanford Univ.; MBA fin., UCLA Grad. Sch. of Bus. Career: various pos. Security Pacific Nat. Bank, Los Angeles 1965-73, v.p. 1973-82, first v.p. 1982-84, senior v.p. 1984-87, sr. v.p. Security Pacific Corp., Los Angeles 1987-92; sr. v.p. Bank of America 1992-94; sr. v.p. General Bank 1994–; honors: Beta Gamma Sigma 1965; chm. fin. com., bd. trustees Univ. of La Verne 1988-94; mem. Stanford Alumni Assn., Stanford Block "S", CalTech Associates; clubs: Jonathan (LA), American (Hong Kong), Athenaeum; mil: s/sgt. Calif. Air Nat. Guard 1962-68; Republican; rec: golf, tennis. Address: Pasadena

VOGEL, ERWIN ROYALE, real estate developer; b. May 22, 1922, Alliance, Nebr.; s. Fred John and Aline Sarah (Farquet) V.; m. Georgia Ilene Dilbeck, Sept. 13, 1952; edn: att. L.A. City Coll. 1940-42; B.Arch., USC, 1950; lic. real estate broker, gen. contr., Calif. Career: pres. E. R. Vogel Co., Torrance 1952–; ptnr. Vogel-Kolleck, Vista 1958–; ptnr. Vogel-Singer 1991–; secty. Airtels Inc., Torrance 1959–; recipient 4 merit awards for outstanding buildings Manhattan Beach C.of C.; mem: Realty Boards: Torrance-Lomita-Carson-Greater South Bay 1978–, Aircraft Owners & Pilots Assn., USC Alumni Assn., USC Architl. Guild, Scarab hon. architl. frat. 1950, Am. Bonanza Soc.; civic: BPOE/Redondo Beach, US C.of C., Torrance Airport Boosters Assn.; club: Los Verdes Mens Golf; mil: 1st lt., pilot USAAF 1942-47, AF Reserve 1947-52; Republican (Presdl. Task Force); Prot.; rec: pilot (multi-engine, instrument), golf, gardening. Res: 909 Via Del Monte Palos Verdes Estates 90274 Ofc: E.R. Vogel Co. PO Box 1067 Torrance 90505

VOGT, ROCHUS EUGEN KAMILL, physicist; b. Dec. 21, 1929, Neckarelz, Germany; s. Heinrich and Paula (Schaefer) V.; m. Micheline Alice Yvonne Bauduin, Sept. 6, 1958; children: Michele b. 1963, Nicole b. 1967; edn: cand. phys. Univ. of Karlsruhe, Ger. 1950-52, Univ. Heidelberg, 1952-53; SM, Univ. Chgo., Ill. 1957. PhD. 1961. Career: asst. prof. Calif. Inst. of Technology, Pasadena 1962-65, assoc. prof. 1965-70, prof. physics 1970–, R. Stanton Avery Distinguished Service Prof. 1982–, chmn. of Faculty 1975-77, chief scientist Jet Propulsion Lab. 1977-78, chmn. div. physics, math. and astronomy 1978-83, actg. dir. Owens Valley Radio Observatory 1980-81, v.p. and provost 1983-87, dir. Caltech/MIT Laser Interferometer Gravitational Wave Observatory (LIGO) Project 1987-94; awards: mem. Studienstiftung des deutschen Volkes 1950-53, Fulbright Fellow 1953-54, profl. achiev. award Univ. Chgo. Alumni Assn. 1981, NASA exceptional scientific achiev. medal (1981); mem. Am. Physical Soc. (1961–, fellow), AAAS (1965–, fellow); author: (with R.B. Leighton) Exercises in Intro. Physics (Addison Wesley Pub., 1969), "Cosmic Rays," World Book Ency. (1978), sci. papers in High Energy Astrophysics and Gravitation pub. profl. jours. Ofc: Caltech 102-33, Pasadena 91125

VOICULESCU, DAN VIRGIL, mathematician; b. June 14, 1949, Bucharest, Romania; s. Vlad and Viorica V.; m. Ioana Maria Petrescu, July 30, 1979; edn: Univ. Bucharest Romania 1967-72; PhD math., 1977. Career: asst. dept. math. Univ. Bucharest, Romania 1972-73; research Inst. of Math. 1973-75; Increst Dept. Math. 1975-86; vis. prof. math. dept. UC Berkeley 1986-87, prof. 1987–; mem. Am. Math. Soc.; 45+ research articles pub. in profl. jours. (1972-). Ofc: Univ. of Calif. Berkeley 94720

VOIGT, HARRISON, clinical psychologist; b. Jan. 4, 1940, Philadelphia, Pa.; s. Walter McKinley and Palma (Siano) V.; edn: PhD, Ohio Univ. 1969; lic. clin. psychologist Calif. 1973. Career: staff psychologist Conn. Valley Hosp., Middletown 1968-71; dir. human devel. Univ. Conn. Sch. Nursing, Storrs 1971-72; psychologist pvt. practice, Mill Valley 1973–; dir. clin. psychology training, professor of psychology, Calif. Inst. Integral Studies, San Francisco 1974–; mem: Am. Psychological Assn.; num. articles pub. in profl. jours.; rec: nature. Res: 537 Charles Ln Mill Valley 94941 Ofc: California Institute of Integral Studies 765 Ashbury St San Francisco 94117

VOLCKMANN, DAVID BOYD, professor of psychology; b. Jan. 19, 1942, Kingston, N.Y.; s. Frederick W. and Norma (Hill) V.; m. Jean Pierce, Aug. 27, 1967 (div. 1986); m. Barbara Currier Green, June 6, 1987; children: Matthew, Nicholas, Hannah; edn: BA, Hamilton Coll. 1964; PhD, Ind. Univ. 1970. Career: tchg. asst. Hamilton Coll., Clinton, N.Y. 1963-64; Ind. Univ., Bloomington, Ind. 1964-65, res. asst. 1965-68, tchg. assoc. 1967-70; tchg. faculty Whittier Coll. 1970–, coord. institutional res. 1983–, chmn. psychology 1973-74, 80-83, 89–, dir. CAPHE grant 1988-89; awards: NSF scientific equipment grant 1972, Dept. Health Edn. & Welfare grantee 1975, Lilly Found. vis. scholar 1975, Whittier Coll. tchg. award 1976; mem: Western Psychological Assn., Am. Psychological Assn., Am. Assn. Univ. Profs., Calif. Assn. Institutional Res., Chorale Bel Canto, Cantori Sine Nomine; author Instructors Resource Book in Psych. (1980, 83, 84). Ofc: Whittier College 13406 E Philadelphia Whittier 90608

VON BEROLDINGEN, DOROTHY, judge; b. Feb. 12, 1915, Chgo.; d. Alex R. and Anna (Stastny) Gundelfingen; (div.); son, Paul b. 1944; edn: AA, UC Berkeley, 1934; Northwestern Univ.; LLB, JD, Univ. San Francisco Sch. of Law and S.F. Law Sch., 1954. Career: atty., tax specialist, solo practice, San Francisco 1955-77; judge San Francisco Municipal Ct., 1977–; prof. taxation Lincoln Univ. Sch. of Law, S.F. 1959-69, prof. legal acctg. 1964-69; adj. prof. legal acctg. Hastings Coll. of Law, 1973-74; appt. commr. S.F. Civil Service Commn. 1964-66, v.p./exec. com. Economic Opportunity Council 1964-66; elected San Francisco Bd. Suprs. 1966-77: chair fin. com. 1968-77, chair plng. & devel. com. 1966-68; honors: Order of the Woolsack, Equity Jurisprudence, Univ. S.F. 1952, Am. Jurisprudence awards in contracts, corps., constnl. law, equity, labor law, evidence 1950, 51, 52, 53, Woman of Achiev. Bus. & Profl. Women 1973, Comm. Leadership SF Fellowship 1979, Women Helping Women Soroptomists 1980, Diligence in Crim. Justice Women in Crim. Justice 1984, Queen's Bench Lifetime Achievement Award 1994; mem: ABA, SF Lawyers Club, St. Thomas More Soc., Queen's Bench (bd. 1981-87). Ofc: Hall of Justice, 850 Bryant St San Francisco 94103

VON HOELSCHER, RUSSEL, author, marketeer, consultant; b. Aug. 10, 1942, St. Paul, Minn.; s. Clarence and Francis von Hoelscher; m. Ginger June Julian, Dec. 5, 1980 (div. Oct. 1987); edn: Grossmont Coll., San Diego. Career: bestselling business, investment and motivational writer 1970s–; author: How To Achieve Total Success, 1983, 40+ books and manuals on business, marketing and motivation, also newsletters, reports and articles; copywriter and direct mktg. consultant; seminar/workshop leader; advr. Pres. Carter's Com. on Small Bus. in Am., 1978; honors: Sales & Mktg. Exec. of the Yr. 1986; mem: San Diego Sales & Mktg. Execs., Internat. Writers Guild, Direct Mktg. Assn., Toastmasters Internat.; Libertarian; Metaphysics; rec: chess. Res: 3810 Kenwood Dr Casa de Oro 91977-1023

VONK, DON KELSO, certified public accountant; b. Aug. 13, 1961, San Francisco; s. Abraham Christiaan and Barbara Ann (Kelso) V.; edn: BS in acctg., San Diego St. Univ.; CPA, Calif. 1987. Career: ptnr. Considine & Considine, CPAs, San Diego 1984–; mem. Am. Inst. CPAs, Calif. Soc. CPAs, SDSU Young Alumni (bd., pres. 1992-93), SDSU Aztec Athletic Found. (treas. 1995-96), Sigma Pi Frat. Intl. Alumni Assn. (alumni pres. 1987, chpt. dir. 1988, newsletter ed. 1986-88); Democrat; rec: skiing, golf, baseball, piano, drums, guitar. Res: 7525 Galaxy Ct San Diego 92120 Ofc: Considine & Considine, 1501 5th Ave Ste 400 San Diego 92101

VON STUDNITZ, GILBERT, state official; b. Nov. 24, 1950, Hamburg, Germany; s. Helfrid and Rosemarie Sofie (Kreiten) von S.; m. Erica Lynn Hoot, May 26, 1990; edn: AA, East L.A. Coll., 1971; BA, CSU Los Angeles, 1978. Career: licensing registration examiner Calif. Dept. Motor Veh., L.A. 1982-84, supvg. motor veh. rep., 1984-85, mgr. I, 1985-87, D.M.V. adminstrv. hearing ofcr., Montebello, 1987-91, mgr. III, Sacramento, 1991-93; ops. mgr, Driver Safety Review 1993–; recipient Calif. D.M.V. cert. of quality 1988, appreciation 1989; mem: Calif. State Mgrs. Assn., Sacto. 1986–, Driver Improvement Assn. of Calif., Sacto. (v.p. 1991–), Intertel 1981–, Phi Sigma Kappa 1973–, Mensa 1981–, Assn. of German Nobility in N.Am. (pres. 1985–), West Adams Heritage Assn., L.A. (dir. 1989-91), Benicia Hist. Soc. 1992–, Arts Benicia 1993–; publs: regular contr. to The Blumenbaum mag. (1992–); rec: genealogy research. Res: 1101 W Second Benicia 94510

VON WALDEGG, JAMES, mortgage banker; b. Aug. 23, 1929, Bogota, Colombia, nat. Nov. 13, 1948; s. Hermann and Leonor von W.; m. Jacquelyn Hibbard, Oct. 13, 1946; children: Sherry b. 1947, Vicky b. 1957, Jaime b. 1960; edn: AA, AB, and PhD, Ciudad Univ., 1944-53, Univ. of Bogota, UCLA,, UCB.; lic. pilot comml., single and multi-engine aircraft, FAA cert. flt. instr., CFI, CFII, MEI, AGI, Glider, Sea. Career: lectr. UC Berkeley, 1952-53; pres. West Contra Costa Mortgage Corp., Richmond 1953-70; pres. J & J Mortgage Corp., Orinda 1970–; as student participated in several expeditions to the Amazon Basin and to the San Augustine region of Colombia, was on the UCLA Boxing team, golden gloves and fought 2 profl. matches, holds a black belt in Judo and Karate and his hands are considered lethal weapons; Honorary Lawman Contra Costa Co. Sheriffs Air Squadron (capt.); mem. Bay Area Mortgage Assn. S.F., Mtg. Bankers Assn. W.D.C., Aircraft Owners and Pilots Assn.; zoological resrch. for Pan Amer. Research Assn.- Life cycle of tetra-haimena liminensis; mil: lt. col. Army Air Corps 1944-47, D.F.C.; Republican (del. 1954); R.Cath.; rec: flying, war bird racing. Res: 4847 Northridge Rd Martinez 94553 Ofc: 23 Orinda Way Ste 300 Orinda 94563

VON WIESENBERGER, ARTHUR, beverage industry executive, author, publisher; b. Sept. 13, 1953, N.Y.C.; s. Arthur and Frances Louise (Bayes) V.W.; m. Leslie Sinclair, May 13, 1988; children: Alexander Robert b. 1990, Christopher William b. 1992; edn: grad. Brooks Inst., Motion Picture Div. 1977; art and language studies in Switz. and England, 1968-73. Career: assoc. prod. Swissair, Switz., 1972; prod. Comorian govt./ Air Comores Africa 1973; prod./dir. Aurora Films Worldwide, Switz. 1974; assoc. prod. FMS Prodns., Hollywood 1977; assoc. prod. Warrior's of the Wind, Japan 1978; beverage industry cons. to Anheuser-Busch Inc., Arrowhead Water Co., Ionics Inc., Irons & Sears, Manitou

Corp., Perrier Group of Am., Poland Spring Water, Stanford Wine Co., Valgos Consiel Inc., Vittel (USA) Inc., Wheeler Inc.; bd. chmn. Internat. Source Management, Inc., 1982-87; pub. Best Cellar Books, 1990–; segment host KEYT-TV (ABC) 1993–; dir. American Inst. of Wine and Food; dir. Internat. Festival Du Film De Villars 1975, 76, spkr. Whole Life Expo, Pasadena 1984, 85, 86; contbg. writer Celebrity Society Mag. (travel editor 1988-89), Entree 1984-89, San Francisco Mag.; Epicurean Rendezvous, Private Clubs; awards: Photog. Soc. of Am., Ten Best 1975, MPD travel film award 1975, best menu, NRA 1984, 85; mem: So. Calif. Restaurant Writers Assn. (fmr. pres.), Internat. Food, Wine and Travel Writers Assn.; civic: Westside Boys Club (bd.); clubs: Coral Casino/ Santa Barbara (dir.); publs: Oasis - The Complete Guide to Bottled Water Throughout the World, Capra Press 1978, Charting the Waters, Runner's World 1981, A Guide to Bottled Water, Fit 1982, Shape's Guide to Bottled Water 1984, Delights of Sushi, Centervoice 1982, Mystique of Caviar, In Mag. 1983, Bottled Water 1001 Varieties, Market Watch 1987, H2O The Guide to Quality Bottled Water, Woodbridge Press 1988, Pocket Guide to Bottled Water, Contemporary Books 1990, Shaping Up in Santa Barbara, Valley Mag. 1990, Bed & Breakfasts of Santa Barbara, Valley Mag. 1991, Champagne & Caviar 1992, Capra Press; Republican; Ch. of England; rec: swim, ski, tennis, mountaineering, enology. Res: POB 5658 Santa Barbara 93150

VOORHEES, LORRAINE ISOBEL, college administrator; b. Sept. 23, 1947, Pittsburgh, Pa.; d. Glenn Alvin Jr. and Helen Laverne (Urban) Voorhees; edn: OD, So. Calif. Coll. of Optometry, Fullerton 1971; MS, CSU Fullerton, 1986. Career: faculty So. Calif. Coll. Optometry, Fullerton 1972-80, director admissions & records 1980-86, dir. student affairs 1986-90, dean of student affairs 1990–; mem: Am. Opt. Assn. 1967–, Calif. Opt. Assn. 1967–, Am. Acad. Optometry (Fellow 1974–). Ofc: Southern Calif. College of Optometry, 2575 Yorba Linda Blvd Fullerton 92631

VOS, RICHARD CLARK, college administrator; b. Aug. 16, 1950, Santa Monica; s. William John and Eleanor Gladys (Harpster) V.; m. Nicole Francoise Hamon, Oct. 13, 1976; children: Eric Galen b. 1983, Carl Johann b. 1986; edn: BA, Cornell Univ. 1972; grad. studies, 1972-73. Career: resident advisor Grinnell Coll., Iowa 1973-76, admissions counselor 1976-78, assoc. dir. admission 1978-87; dean of admission and fin. aid Claremont McKenna Coll., Claremont 1987-89, v.p., dean admission and fin. aid 1989–; mem: Nat. Assn., Coll. Admission Counselors, Coll. Bd., Western Assn. Coll. Admission Counselors; rec: camping. Ofc: Claremont McKenna College 890 Columbia Claremont 91711

VOSS, VIRGIL H., physician; b. Feb. 8, 1929, Pekin, Ill.; s. Leo J. and Isabelle E. Voss; m. Lorraine Moorman, Sept. 1, 1956; children: Katherine b. 1958, Carolyn b. 1959, Henry b. 1960, Theresa b. 1962, Helen b. 1963, Lawrence b. 1964, Susan b. 1966, Michael b. 1968, Barbara b. 1970, Daniel b. 1975; edn: BS, Univ. Notre Dame, 1968; MD, Stritch Sch. of Med., Loyola Univ., 1956. Career: capt. Med. Corps US Air Force, chief pediatrics gen. med. outpatient dept. USAF Hosp., Mobile, Ala. 1959-62; resident radiology St. Joseph's and affil. hosps., Denver 1962-65; radiologist The Permanente Med. Group Inc. 1965; chief dept. rad. Kaiser-Permanente Med. Ctr., Santa Clara 1983-88; Fellow emeritus Am. Coll. Radiology; mem: AMA, Calif. Med. Assn., Santa Clara Med. Soc., Am., Calif., Santa Clara Radiol. Socs., Kts. of Columbus; Democrat; R. Cath.; rec: astronomy, golf, bicycling. Res: 14982 Sobey Rd Saratoga 95070

VROOM, DAVID ARCHIE, manufacturing company executive; b. Sept. 12, 1941, Vancouver, Canada; s. Nathaniel Ellenwood and Jean Ferriman (Salsbury) V.; m. Anna Elizabeth Stravers, Sept. 12, 1969; 1 son, Peter b. 1970; edn: BS, Univ. B.C. 1963; PhD, 1967. Career: overseas postdoctoral fellow Nat. Research Council Canada, Amsterdam, Netherlands 1967-68; research scientist Gulf Gen. Atomic Co., San Diego 1969-71; sr. scientist IRT Corp. 1971-74, dept. mgr. 1974-78, tech. and market mgr. 1978-80; sect. dir. Raychem Corp., Menlo Park 1981-84, ops. mgr. 1985-87, dir. radiation services 1987–; mem: Am. Physicial Soc., Am. Chemical Soc.; 75+ papers pub. in sci. and trade jours., 1965–, chpts. pub. in sci. books, 1972-75; mil: lt. Royal Canadian Navy Reserve 1960-66; Lutheran; rec: woodworking, sailing. Res: 107 Walter Hays Dr Palo Alto 94303 Ofc: Raychem Corp. 300 Constitution Dr Menlo Park 94025

WADLEY, HAROLD J., radiologist; b. May 1, 1944, Turlock, Calif.; s. Joseph D. and Mary Jane (Day) W.; m. Clela R. Friesen, June 25, 1966; children: Brian b. 1971, Jay b. 1975; edn: BA, Pasadena Coll. 1966; MD, Loma Linda Univ. 1970; bd. cert. diagnostic radiology, Am. Bd. of Radiology 1975. Career: internship Madigan Army Med. Ctr., Tacoma, Wash. 1970-71; residency Fitzsimons Army Med. Ctr., Denver, Colo. 1971-74; chief of Radiology U/.S. Army Hosp., West Point, NY 1974-77; radiologist Kaiser Permanente, Sacramento 1977–, chief of radiology, 1980-84, chief of ultrasound 1984–, chief of mammography 1994–; honors: listed Who's Who-Am. Colls. & Univs. 1966; mem: Radiological Soc. of N. Am., CMA, Am. Inst. of Ultrasound in Medicine, Calif. Radiological Soc., Soc. of Breast Imaging; mil: major U.S. Army 1970-77; Baptist. Ofc: 2025 Morse Ave Sacramento 95825

WADSWORTH, KEVIN WARREN, retired political consultant, rancher; b. May 22, 1948, Fairmont, W.Va.; s. Warren Wade and Gloria Jean (McClung) W.; edn: AA, Valencia Comm. Coll., Orlando, Fla. 1969; BA comms., Univ. of Central Fla., 1971; grad. studies Fla. A&M Univ., 1975-76. Career: exec. asst. U.S. Senator Ed Gurney, W.D.C., 1972-74; adminstrv. asst. Mayor and City Council, Orlando, Fla. 1976-77; dir. of govt. affairs San Francisco Chamber of Commerce, 1980; asst. v.p. telecomms. adminstrn. Crocker Nat. Bank, S.F. 1981-85; v.p. and CFO, Pinnacle Courseware Inc., San Jose 1985-86, bd. dir. 1983-86; v.p. adminstrv. svs. First Nationwide Bank, S.F. 1986-90; advising and cons. ptnr. Wadsworth & Johnson, Ltd. 1990–; dir., founder and owner Gallery Gloria Jean of S.F.; awards: honoree for Outstanding vol. svc. Nat. Volunteers Service, S.F. 1983, Outstanding Vol. Achievement and Golden Apple Award for AIDS/HIV edn., El Dorado Co. Vol. Ctr. 1993, Ronald Grant Kershaw Award for Meritorious Svc., Log Cabin Rep. Club of S.F. 1993, Champion Volunteer Award of Merit for Making a Difference, United Way-Sacto. Area 1994, past listings in Men of Achievement, Who's Who in West, in Calif., in Computer Mgmt., Emerging Leaders in Am., others; civic bds: El Dorado AIDS Task Force (treas., bd. 1991–), Grassy Run Community Svs. Dist. Placerville (dir., pres. 1991-92); mem: Disabled Am. Veterans 1967–, Am. Legion 1981–, Tau Kappa Epsilon Internat. Frat. (chpt. svs. dir., Knight of Apollo 1971–), Capital Political Action Com. (CAP/PAC), El Dorado Comm. Roundtable on Human Rights, Log Cabin Republicans of Greater Sacto., Marine Corps League (Hangtown Chpt.), Sierra Beacon AIDS Hospice (co-coord.); author books: Circuit Breakers, 1975, Thoughts and Other Transgressions, 1984, song: I Want (by The Lettermen, 1977), editor: White Paper on the Gay Community, 1983; mil: E3 USMC 1966-67; Republican; Met. Community Ch.; rec: politics, non-profit fundraising, vineyard cultivation & sheep raising.

WAETJEN, HERMAN CHARLES, professor of New Testament; b. June 16, 1929, Bremen, Germany; s. Henry and Anna (Ruschmeyer) W.; m. Mary Suzanne Struyk, July 15, 1960; children: Thomas b. 1961 (dec.), Thembisa b. 1963, Elaine b. 1965, David b. 1970; edn: Concordia Jr. Coll., Bronxville, NY; BA, Concordia Sem., St. Louis, Mo., 1950; BD, Concordia Sem., 1953; Dr. Theol., Univ. of Tuebingen, Germany, 1958. Career: instr. Concordia Sem., St. Louis, 1957; asst. prof. Univ. of So. Calif., L.A., 1959-62; assoc. prof. S.F. Sem., San Anselmo, 1962-72; prof. S.F. Sem., 1972–; vis. prof.: Univ. of Nairobi, Kenya, 1973-74, Federal Sem., Pietermaritzburg, So. Africa, 1979-80, Univ. of Zimbabwe, Harare, Zimbabwe, 1986-87; Univ. of Namibia, Windhoek, Namibia 1993-94; awards: scholarships, Hebrew Univ., Jerusalem, Israel, 1954-55, and Lutheran Found., Geneva, Switzerland, 1955-56; fellowships, Assn. of Theol. Schools, 1965-66, 1979-80; mem: Soc. of Biblical Lit. 1959–, Pacific Coast Theol. Soc. 1962–; author: The Origin & Destiny of Humanness, 1976-78, A Reordering of Power, 1989; Democrat; Presbyn.; rec: backpacking, photography, travel. Res: 83 Jordan Ave. San Anselmo 94960. Ofc: S.F. Theol. Sem. San Anselmo 94960

WAGEMAKER, DAVID ISAAC, management consultant, professional seminar leader and speaker; b. Feb. 10, 1949, Grand Rapids, Mich.; s. Raymond Ogden and Inez Loraine W.; edn: BA philos., Grand Valley St. Univ., 1971. Career: owner Education Ctr., Grand Rapids, Mich. 1970-72; speaker and tnr. productivity seminars since 1971–, lead nat. and internat. seminars in time mgmt. and leadership tng., for Fortune 500 cos., small orgns., profit & nonprofit orgns., profl. assns.; cons. American Leadership Coll., WDC 1972-78, Wagemaker Co., Honolulu, 1978-80; ednl. cons. Batten, Batten, Hudson and Swab Inc. (consulting firm), San Diego 1980-81, mgr. 1981; mgmt. cons. The National Mgmt. Inst., and The Podium Inc., San Diego State Univ., 1980–, seminarist Penton Learning Inc., NYC 1982–; securities broker, ins. agt. The Equitable Assurance Co., San Diego 1982; assoc. cons. Pacific Southwest Airlines (now USAir), San Diego 1982-83; mgr. GM Hughes Electronics, Westchester, 1983; v.p. Wagemaker, Inc., Grand Rapids 1984–; sr. cons. Nat. Mgmt. Inst., Flower Mound, Tx. 1985–; publs: (self-help book) Building A Better You, (6-hr. cassette tape series) How To Organize Yourself to Win, (res. paper) Total Quality Mgmt., and num. tng. workbooks; Fellow Acad. Mgmt., mem. Sigma Chi, Zeta Nu (pres. 1968-70), Hughes Golf Club (El Segundo); Republican; Congregationalist. Res: 2227A Robinson St Redondo Beach 90278

WAGNER, C. PETER, seminary professor; b. Aug. 15, 1930, NY, NY; s. C. Graham and Mary (Lewis) W.; m. Doris Mueller, Oct. 15, 1950; children: Karen b. 1954, Ruth b. 1960, Rebecca b. 1964; edn: BS, Rutgers Univ., New Brunswick, N.J., 1952; M. Div., MA, Fuller Theol. Sem., Pasadena, 1955, 1968; Th.M., Princeton Theol. Sem., Princeton, N.J., 1962; PhD, Univ. of So. Calif., L.A., 1977. Career: missionary, S.I.M. Internat., Bolivia, So. Am., 1956-71; prof., Fuller Theol. Sem., Pasadena, 1971–; pres., Global Harvest Ministries, Pasadena, 1991–; awards: Phi Beta Kappa, Rutgers Univ., 1951; author: over 40 books publ. on missions and ch. growth incl.: Your Church Can Grow (1976, 1984) Your Spiritual Gifts (1979, 1994), Warfare Prayer (1992), Churches That Pray (1993), and Spreading the Fire (1995); Congregational. Ofc. Fuller Seminary Pasadena 91182

WAGNER, (HELMUT) REINHARD, physician, anesthesiologist; b. Sept. 26, 1947, Leipzig, Ger.; s. Helmut Paul and Edith Katja (Schmieding) W.; m. Chong Hi Kim, Mar. 1975; children: Yasmin b. 1979, Siegfried Karl b. 1987; edn: MD,

Free Univ., Berlin 1975, PhD in med. (magna cum laude), 1978; cert. Am. Bd. Anesth. 1985. Career: med. intern Free Univ., Berlin 1975-76, Univ. Wisconsin, Madison 1976-77, research fellow Free Univ., Berlin 1977-78, resident anesthesia Penn. St. Univ., Hershey, Pa. 1978-79, Free Univ., Berlin 1980-82, fellow cardiac anesthesia Cleveland Clinic, Oh. 1982-83; asst. prof. Med. Coll., Milw. 1983-84; Oberarzt Med. Hochschule, Hannover, Ger. 1984-85; staff anesthesiologist Meml. Hosp., Bakersfield, Calif. 1985–; San Joaquim Hospital, Physicians Plaza Surgical Ctr.; mem: Am. Soc. Anesth., Berliner Arzte Kammer, CMA, Calif. Soc. Anesth., Kern Co. Med. Soc.; club: Racquet (Bakersfield); publs: num. med. jour. articles; rec: languages, philosophy, history. Ofc: PO Box 2917 Bakersfield 93303-2917

WAGNER, RAY DAVID, aerospace museum historian/archivist; b. Feb. 29, 1924 Phila.; s. James D. and Ethel S. (Shreiber) W.; m. Beatrice Walsh, Apr. 1952 (div. Nov. 1965); m. Mary Davidson, Nov. 17, 1967; children: Roger b. 1952, Wendy b. 1968, David b. 1971; edn: BS, Univ. Pa., 1953, MS Edn., 1955; postgrad. San Diego State Univ., 1958-65. Career: tchr. Crawford High Sch., San Diego 1957-84; instr. USN/Pace, San Diego 1985; archivist San Diego Aerospace Mus., 1985–; awards: research grantee Air Force Hist. Ctr. 1988; mem. Am. Aviation Hist. Soc. 1957–, Air Force Hist. Found. 1980–; author: American Combat Planes (1960, 1968, 1982), North American Sabre, 1963, German Combat Planes, 1970, Mustang Designer, 1990, editor: Soviet Air Force in WWII, 1973; rec: travel, airplane history. Res: 5865 Estelle St San Diego 92115 Ofc: San Diego Aerospace Museum 2001 Pan American Plaza San Diego 92101

WAHDAN, JOSEPHINE BARRIOS, librarian; b. Jan. 11, 1937, Firebaugh; d. Jose and Vera (Balderama) Barrios; div.; children: Dean Burni b. 1959, Laila b. 1975, Nadia b. 1978; edn: BA in foreign langs.(w/distinction), San Diego State Univ. 1970; MLS, Univ. Wis.-Milwaukee 1975. Career: comm. librarian intern Milwaukee Pub. Library 1972-74, comm. librarian 1975-78; acting co. librarian San Benito Co. Library, Hollister 1979, co. librarian 1980–; founder Friends of San Benito Co. Library 1979; pres. Libraries Plus 1983-84; chairwoman S. Bay Cooperative Library System 1984-85; sec./treas. Hollister Barrios Unidos 1994–; mem: World Congress of Poets 1989–, Calif. Library Assn. 1980–, County Librarians Assn. 1980–, REFORMA, Nat. Assn. to Promote Library Svs. to Spanish Speaking 1985–, Youth Svs. Coalition (co-chair 1995–); awards: Library Bookfellow of Yr. Friends Milwaukee Pub. Library, 1974; cert. of appreciation United Comm. Center and Milw. Library Bd. Trustees, 1978; Mex. Am. Com. on Edn. Citizen of Year, 1987; Calif. State Library Award of Merit, 1990; Gavilan College Puente Program, Cert. of Appreciation, 1988, 89; Calif. State Library Recognition of Excellence in Community Partnerships, 1993; poems pub. in American Poetry Anthology, 1986; Hearts On Fire: A Treasury of Poems On Love, 1986; Brisas Poeticas Modernas, 1991 (1st & 2nd edit.); Carta Internacional de Poesia, 1993, Brisas Poeticas Modernas, 1995 (8th edit.); Moslem; rec: Folkloric dancing, tennis, camping. Ofc: San Benito Co Library 470 Fifth St Hollister 95023

WAILES, W. GEORGE, lawyer; b. April 4, 1954, Corona; s. Eugene A. and Mary Margaret (Miller) W.; m. Virginia Hunter Bergman, Aug. 18, 1984; edn: BA, UCSB 1977; JD, UC Davis 1981. Career: atty. So. Pacific Transp. Co., San Francisco 1981-85; Ware Fletcher et al, Palo Alto 1985; Hession & Creedon, San Mateo 1985-88; Carr McClellan et al, Burlingame 1988–; judge pro-tem San Francisco Co. Superior Court 1992–; judge pro-tem San Mateo Co. Superior and Municipal Cts. 1990–; faculty Hastings Coll. of Advocacy 1898– (co-chair 1994–); mem: San Mateo Co. Bar Assn. (chair, labor and employment law sect. 1988-89; chair, business litigation sect. 1993-94), Bar Assn. of San Francisco, Am. Bar Assn., Bay Chamber Symphony Orchestra (bd. dirs. 1986-91, v.p. 1988-91); R.Cath.; rec: sailing, skiing, running. Ofc: Carr McClellan et al 216 Park Road Burlingame 94010

WALKER, CAROLYN LOUISE, nursing professor; b. Apr. 4, 1947, Ft. George Wright, Wash.; d. Marvin John and Louise Olive (Billings) W.; m. Simon Zemel, Apr. 6, 1968 (div. 1981); children: Michelle b. 1971, Brent b. 1971; edn: AA nsg., Fullerton Coll., 1968; BSN, CSU Fullerton, 1976; MSN, CSU Los Angeles, 1979; PhD Nursing, Univ. Utah, 1986. Career: staff nse. CCU, ICU, Burn Unit, Orange County Med. Ctr., 1968-69; staff nse. Children's Hosp. Orange County, 1969-71, summer 1973, ped. oncology hematology unit, 1980-81; office nse. and mgr. Simon I. Zemel MD 1971-77; nsg. instr. Cypress Coll., Cypress 1978-79, instr. obstets. and geriatrics Saddleback Coll., Mission Viejo 1979-80, instr. pediatrics and adv. med.-surg. nsg. Cypress Coll. 1981-82; asst. prof. peds. and obstets. Univ. of Utah, 1984-85; asst. prof. pediatrics San Diego State Univ., 1986-90, assoc. prof. and grad. advisor pediatrics 1990-94; prof. pediatrics, San Diego State Univ. 1994–; co-dir. Ctr. for the Applied Study of the Child, SDSU, 1991–; awards: outstanding student nurse Student Nurse Assn. of Calif. 1967, CSU Fullerton Dean's List 1976, Nat. Deans List 1984, excellence in research Davol Inc. 1986, Outstanding Faculty 1988, research grantee (5, 1988–); mem: Soc. Pediatric Nurses 1991–, Oncology Nsg. Soc. (1988–, ped. spl. interest gp. 1990–), Sigma Theta Tau (faculty advr. 1987-89), Assn. Ped. Oncology Nurses (1983–, chair 1987-91, pres. elect 1994-95, pres. 1995), Am. Nses. Assn., Calif. Nses. Assn. (1978–, alt. nsg. edn. commnr. CNA region II 1990-92), Am. Cancer Soc. (San Diego Children's com. 1989–, psy-

chosocial care cons. 1991–, med. com. 1990–, Camp Reach for the Sky Nse. 1990–, Family Camp com. 1989–, chair 1990); author, editor books and jour. articles in field, sci. presentations at nat. confs. (15+); mem. editl. rev. bds: Am. J. of Cont. Edn. in Nsg. (1987-89), Oncology Nsg. Forum (1988-91), J. of Pediatric Oncology Nsg. (1992–, assoc. res. editor 87-91), Professional Update (1990–); Democrat; Episcopalian; rec: skiing, swimming, golf. Ofc: San Diego State University Sch. of Nursing, San Diego 92182-0254

WALKER, DAVID ALLEN, high technology company executive; b. Aug. 19, 1956, Los Angeles; s. Steve and Florence (Rothman); m. Nancy Anne Taylor, M.D. 1994; edn: BS in engring., UC Los Angeles 1978; MBA fin./mktg., Univ. Chgo. 1982. Career: team mgr. Procter and Gamble Paper Prods. Co., Oxnard 1978-80; sr. fin. analyst Dataproducts Corp., Woodland Hills 1982-83; mgr. bus. plnng. and fin. Burroughs Corp., Camarillo 1983-85; dir. fin. plnng. MICOM Systems Inc., Simi Valley 1985-89; corp. controller TeleTech, Inc., Sherman Oaks 1989; dir. corp. devel. Infonet, El Segundo 1990–; ptnr. DeHart Walker Ents. 1986-91; honors: Gov.'s Scholar 1974, Dean's List (UCLA 1974-77, U.Chgo. 1981), Phi Eta Sigma 1975, Tau Beta Pi 1977; assoc. mem. ASME 1978–, L.A. World Affairs Council 1990–; Republican; Jewish; rec: computer modeling, history, strategy games, golf. Res: 1987 Goldenrod Ct Westlake Village 91361

WALKER, JAMES WALTER, college president; b. June 19, 1936, La Jolla, Calif.; s. James W. and Evangeline (Hargitt) W.; m. Nancy Carol Jewell, Aug. 22, 1959; children: Scott b. 1961, Laura b. 1965; edn: BS, Loyola Univ., Los Angeles 1958; MS, Univ. of Notre Dame, South Bend, Ind. 1964; EdD, Univ. of So. Calif., L.A. 1975. Career: dean, instr. El Camino Coll., Torrance, Calif. 1966-86; v.p. College of the Canyons, Santa Clarita, Calif. 1986-92; pres. Moorpark Coll., Moorpark, Calif. 1992–; dir. Calif. State Univ., Northridge-Ventura campus 1993–; dir. Red Cross, Simi Valley 1993–; dir. Boys & Girls Club, Moorpark 1994–; mem. United Way Allocations 1993–, Redondo Beach Rotary Club (pres. 1984-85), Santa Clarita Rotary Club (pres. 1989-90); Republican; Catholic; rec: jogging, tennis. Res: 1077 Garrido Dr Camarillo 93010 Ofc: Moorpark College 7075 Campus Park Moorpark 93021

WALKER, SALLY C., certified fund raising executive; b. Wash. D.C.; d. William S. and Ellen (Oswald) Walker; edn: BA (cum laude with honors), Stetson Univ., Deland, Fla., 1971. Career: devel. dir. Direct Relief Found., Santa Barbara 1977-82; prin., cons. Walker & Assocs., Santa Barbara 1982–; endowment dir. planned giving United Way Santa Barbara, 1982–; devel. cons. and trainer United Way of Am., Alexandria, Va. 1984-90; steering com., del. Nat. Conf. Planned Giving, 1987-88, Nat. Editorial Bur. chief, 1989; faculty mem. Nat. Acad. for Voluntarism, W.D.C.; contbg. editor: The Endowment Builder; mem.: Nat. Soc. of Fund-Raising Execs. 1984–, Planned Giving Roundtable Santa Barbara County (co-founder, pres. 1986-88, v.p. 1984-86), Santa Barbara Audubon Soc. (bd. 1989–, pres. 1992-93, v.p. 1993–). Ofc: 1423 W Valerio St Santa Barbara 93101

WALKER, WARREN ELLIOTT, policy analyst; b. Apr. 7, 1942, NY, NY; s. David Solomon and Selma Lydia (Goldstein) W.; m. Alpha Hockett, Feb. 1, 1970 (div. 1987); children: Carly b. 1972, Luke b. 1975, Hannah b. 1980; edn: BA, MS, PhD, Cornell Univ., 1963, 64, 68. Career: pres. Compuvisor Inc., Ithaca, N.Y. 1968-70; analyst and project dir. The Rand Inst., N.Y.C. 1970-75; asst. v.p. Chemical Bank, N.Y.C. 1975-76; dir. of research The Urban Acad., N.Y.C. 1976-77; senior policy analyst The Rand Corp., Santa Monica 1977-88, 89–; vis. prof. Delft Univ. of Tech., The Netherlands 1988-89; cons. U.S. EPA, Cinti. 1968-72; adj. prof. Columbia Univ., 1971-77; faculty mem. Rand Graduate Sch., Santa Monica 1981–; editor, pub. sector apps., Mgmt. Sci. J., 1977-85, mem. editorial rev. bd. Fire Technology J., 1979–; awards: Lanchester Prize Ops. Research Soc. of Am. 1974, NATO Science Com. systems sci. prize 1976, TIMS Award for mgmt. sci. achiev., and Edelman Award for mgmt. sci. achiev. The Inst. of Mgmt. Scis. 1974, 84; mem: Ops. Research Soc. of Am. 1963–, The Inst. of Mgmt. Scis. 1963–, L.A. Productivity Advy. Com. 1979-88; author/ed. Fire Department Deployment Analysis, 1979, Building Organizational Decision Support Systems, 1992, contbr. 20+ articles to profl. jours., 1965–; rec: photog., biking. Ofc: The Rand Corp. 1700 Main St Santa Monica 90406

WALL, GLENNIE MURRAY, historic preservation professional; b. Oct. 8, 1931, Roseburg, Ore.; d. James Matheny Corbin and Emily L. Aten; m. Louis Wall, Jan. 3, 1975; 2 daughters; edn: BS, History, Portland State Univ. 1965; Environmental Ed., Univ. of Missouri 1969; Bus. Admin., Univ. of Michigan 1978; Practicing Law Institute 1981-82. Career: historian/park ranger National Park Service, Pipestone, N.M. 1966-68; historian/park supt. Herbert Hoover NHS, West Branch, Iowa 1968-69; historian, Western Regional Ofc., San Francisco 1969-72; historian, Advy. Council on Historic Preservation, Denver, Colo. 1972-74; div. chief National Park Service, Denver Service Ctr. 1974-83; mus. mgr (Maritime) Golden Gate Nat. Recreation Area, San Francisco 1983-89; cultural resources splst./curator, Presidio Project, San Francisco 1989-90; prin. Historic Preservation Planning., 1991–; dir: Council of Am. Maritime Museums, Phila. 1987-88; Nat. Maritime Museum Assn., S.F. 1983-88; chair Equal Opportunity Com., Nat. Park Service, Denver, Colo. 1979-81; instr., lectr.

Nat. Park Svc. preservation law & policy (nationwide) 1972-84; lectr. Nat. Trust for Historic Preservation, Wash., D.C. 1971-88; awards: Hoover Scholar 1992, Nat. Preservation Award, President's Advy. Council 1988, commendation Nat. Park Svc. 1987, Citation for Excellence, U.S. Dept. of Interior 1976, spl. achievement awards Nat. Park Svc. 1969, 72; mem: Am. Assn. of Museums, Internat. Council of Museums, Internat. Cong. of Maritime Museums, Am. Assn. For State and Local History, Am. Decorative Arts Forum, Colo. Corral of the Westerners, Nat. Orgn. of Women; author, ed.:agency standards & guidelines "Cultural Resources Mgmt.", 1983; short course, book "Maritime Preservation", 1987; author "Interpretive Plan, Herbert Hoover NHS", 1968; editor, photographer book, "Pipes on the Plains", 1967; author, photographer "Pictographs & Petroglyphs of Lava Beds National Monument", 1965; rec: travel, photography, writing. Ofc: P.O. Box 370634, Montara CA 94037-0634

WALL, SONJA ELOISE, nurse, nursing registry owner; b. Mar. 28, 1938, Santa Cruz; d. Ray Theothornton and Reva Mattie (Wingo) Wall; m. Edward Gleason Holmes, Aug. 1959 (div. 1968); children: Deborah Lynn, Lance Edward; m. John Aspesi, Sept. 1969 (div. 1977); children: Sabrina Jean, Daniel John; m. Kenneth Talbot LaBoube, Nov. 1, 1977 (div. 1987); 1 dau., Tiffany Amber; edn: BA, San Jose City Coll., 1959, BS, Madonna Coll., 1967, att. Univ. Mich. 1968-70; RN Calif., Mich., Colo. Career: staff nse. Santa Clara Valley Med. Ctr., San Jose 1959-67, Univ. Mich. Hosp., Ann Arbor 1967-73, Porter and Swedish Med. Hosp., Denver 1973-77, Laurel Grove Hosp., Castro Valley, Calif. 1977-79, Advent Hosp., Ukiah 1984-86; motel owner LaBoube Enterprises, Fairfield, Point Arena, Willits 1979-; staff nse. Northridge Hosp., Los Angeles 1986-87, Folsom State Prison, 1987; mng. ptnr. nursing registry Around the Clock Nursing Service, Ukiah 1985-, staff RN Kaiser Permanente Hosp., Sacto. 1986-89; Hospice RN, 1989-93; HSSI Nsg. Reg., 1993 ; owner Royal Plantation petites miniature Horse Farm; mem. Am. Heart Assn. (CPR trainer, recipient awards), Am. Assn. Critical Care Nurses, Calif. Critical Care Nurses Assn., Soc. of Critical Care Medicine, Hospice Nurses Assn., Am. Motel Assn. (beautification and remodeling award 1985), Am. Miniature Horse Assn. (winner nat. grand championship 1981, 82, 83), Internat. Biog. Ctr. England (1990); club: Cameron Park CC; civic: Coloma 4-H (ldr. 1990, asst. 1987-92); contbr. articles to various publs.; Republican; Episcopalian; rec: horses (1/4, pinto-paints, miniatures, thoroughbreds, racing), real estate devel., hiking, golf, swimming. Ofc: Around the Clock Nursing Service PO Box 559 Coloma 95613 Ph: 916/626-3948

WALLACE, DAVID, commercial photographer, fashion, stock, film location scout; s. Gen. William Wallace; edn: student, Univ. Anchorage, 1976, desk top pub. and computer graphics, 1995 . Career: L.S., photographer, Huntington Beach; awards: Univ. Anchorage best of show 1984; mem: Soc. Illustrative Photographers, Advt. & Art Dirs. Orange Co., Costa Mesa Art League; numerous philanthropy projects; photo protrait journalist for Orange County Social Register (Guide to Fundraising Events); 8 inventions, 1983-; lived in Hong Kong and traveled in 21 countries; rec: outdoor mountain sports. Res: 9151 Atlanta Ave Ste 7363 Huntington Beach 92615

WALLER, BRADLEY ALLAN, systems engineer; b. Nov. 17, 1963, Panorama City, Calif.; s. Paul Siegfried and Joan Ruth (Coshever) W.; m. Charlotte Louise (Burger); edn: BS physics, M.I.T., 1986. Career: engring. assoc. IBM Instruments, Danbury, Ct. 1985; research asst. M.I.T. Frances Bitter Nat. Mgmt. Lab., Cambridge 1985-86; systems engr. Hughes, EOS, El Segundo, Calif. 1986-; v.p. mktg. EPage; awards: Wunsch Award M.I.T. mech. engr. dept. 1985, Hughes-EOS personal achiev. award 1991 and team achiev. awards (4); mem: The Nature Friends 1986-; Democrat; Jewish; rec: skiing, classic autos. Res: 417 S Lucia Ave Redondo Beach 90277 Ofc: Hughes EOS PO Box 902 E51/A290 El Segundo 90245

WALLER, LARRY GENE, mortgage banker; b. Nov. 18, 1948, Corpus Christi, Tex.; s. Paul Hobson and Marie (Armellini) W.; m. Mary Sandra Cupp, Dec. 27, 1969 (div. 1987); children: Stacey Ann, Jaime Lynn; m. Sharon Elizabeth Falls, Jan. 28, 1988; 1 child, Lisa Suzanne Cantello; edn: AA, Bakersfield Jr. Coll., 1970; lic. R.E. broker Calif. Career: asst. v.p. Bank of Am., Stockton 1970-78, Wells Fargo Realty Fin. Co., Sacto. 1978-81; regional v.p. Weyerhaeuser Mortgage Co., Sacto. 1981-89; sr. v.p. Koll Realty Advisors, Sacto. 1989-91; pres. and c.f.o. Waller, Kaufman & Sutter, Sacto. 1991-; pres. Brookside Mortgage Corp., Sacto. 1993-94; pres. and c.f.o. Waller Kaufman & Sutter of Nevada, Reno, Nev. 1995-; civic: Com. to Help Attract Major Profl. Sports to Sacto.; mem. Nat. Assn. of Industrial & Office Parks (bd. Sacto.), Mortgage Bankers Assn. (income property com.)., Calif. Mortgage Bankers Assn. Res: 2134 Campton Circle Gold River 95670 Ofc: Waller, Kaufman & Sutter, 2277 Fair Oaks Blvd #400 Sacramento 95825

WALLERSTEIN, LARRY IRA, lawyer; b. June 3, 1950, Baltimore, Md.; s. Rowe H. and Irene Rose (Levin) W.; children: Jennifer b. 1981, Katherine b. 1985; edn: BA english, CSU Northridge 1972, JD, Loyola Univ. 1976; admitted Calif. Bar, 1976, lic. R.E. broker, 1986. Career: trial atty. solo practice, Los Angeles 1976-80; Wallerstein & Stone, L.A. 1980-82; Yettick, Chandler & Schneider, San Jose 1982-83; trial atty./pres. Schneider & Wallerstein Law Corp.,

San Jose 1983-; real estate broker Attorney's Realty, San Jose 1986-91; judge pro tem Santa Clara Superior Ct., San Jose 1984-; arbitrator Santa Clara Co. Bar 1984-, lect. 1986; mem: Santa Clara Co. Bar Assn., Assn. South Bay Brokers, Am. Trial Lawyers Assn., Santa Clara Trial Lawyers Assn., L.A. Bus. Trial Lawyers Assn., San Jose Bd. Realtors; civic: San Jose Atletic Club (pres. bd. adv. 1993), San Jose Downtown Assn. (exec. com. 1993-), San Jose First Housing (bd. dirs.), San Jose Downtown Housing Assn. (co-chair Housing Task Force 1994), Jewish Fedn. of Greater San Jose, YMCA (chief of tribe Indian Princesses); pub. appellate opinions: Farenbaugh v. Belmont (1986), Tate v. Saratoga (1989); Democrat; Jewish; rec: marathons, racquetball, writing, photog. Ofc: Schneider & Wallerstein Law Corp. 111 N Market Ste 1000 San Jose 95113

WALSER, CAROL BEEBE, clinical psychologist; b. Natick, Mass.; d. H. Ward and Margaret (Pardee) Beebe; children: Wendi Michelle b. 1969; edn: BA, Cedar Crest Coll. 1962; MA, Univ. Houston Clear Lake City 1980; PhD, Calif. Sch. Profl. Psychology, Berkeley 1984; lic. clin. psychologist Calif. 1986. Career: dir. comm. services Univ. Tx. Mental Scis. Inst., Tx. Med. Center, Houston 1973-81; family therapist Pathways Agency, San Leandro 1981-82; chief psychology intern Pacific Presbyterian Med. Center, San Francisco 1982-84; NIMH postdoctoral clin. psychology fellow Univ. Tx. Mental Scis. Inst. 1984-85; psychologist John Muir Memorial Hosp., Walnut Creek 1985-86; chief psychologist Davies Med. Center, San Francisco 1986-; adj. faculty Calif. Sch. of Professional Psychology, Berkeley-Alameda 1989-; honors: Who's Who Human Service Profls. (1986-87, 1987-88); mem: Am. Psychol. Assn., San Francisco Psychol. Assn. (pres. 1993), Alameda Co. Psychol. Assn. (pres. 1994), No. Calif. Soc. Psychoanalytic Psychology, No. Calif. Neuropsychology Forum. Ofc: Davies Medical Ctr San Francisco 94114 also: 4283 Piedmont Ave Ste H Oakland 94611 Tel: 510/339-3155

WALSH, KAREN JEAN, insurance agency executive; b. Nov. 8, 1956, Riverside; d. George Robert Lanning and Beverly Diane (Van Huystee) Payne; m. William Matthew Walsh, Jr., Jan. 8, 1977; children: Andrew b. 1982, Patrick b. 1973; 1 grandchild, Austin b. 1991; grad. Riverside Polytechnic H.S., 1974; Lic. ins. agt. and broker, property & cas., life & disability, Calif. (1985), Ariz. non-res. lic. (1991), Nev. non-res. loc. (1993). Career: personal lines underwriter Goldware Ins., Riverside 1975-76; mgr. Beld & Assocs., 1977-84; owner/mgr. Ramco-Calzona Ins., 1984-; awards in advance mgmt., personal lines mgmt., Certified Ins. Counselors (1979, 80); mem: Vocat. Indust. Club of Am. (Riv. chpt. pres. 1974), Insurance Women, Profl. Bus. Women, Am. Mule Assn., Riverside Sheriff Wives Assn.; civic: The Diamond Alliance Baseball Assn. (sec. treas. 1992), Magnolia Center Little League (treas. 1984-, volunteer of yr. 1994); Republican; R.Cath.; rec: equestrian, drawing, bowling. Ofc: Ramco-Calzona Insurance Service, Inc. 5051 Canyon Crest Ste 200 Riverside 92507

WALSH, WILLIAM DESMOND, private investor; b. Aug. 4, 1930, New York; s. William J. and Catherine Grace (Desmond) W.; m. Mary Jane Gordon, April 5, 1951; children: Deborah, Caroline, Michael, Suzanne, Tara Jane, Peter; edn: BA, Fordham Univ. 1951; LL.B., Harvard Univ. 1955; admitted St. Bar N.Y. 1955. Career: asst. U.S. Atty. So. Dist N.Y., N.Y.C. 1955-58; counsel N.Y. Commn. Investigation 1958-61; mgmt. cons. McKinsey & Co. 1961-67; sr. v.p. Arcata Corp., Menlo Park 1967-82; gen. ptnr. Sequoia Assocs. 1982-; pres., c.e.o. Atacra Liquidating Trust 1982-89; chmn. bd.: Newell Indsl. Corp., Lowell, Mich., Deanco, Inc., Ithaca, NY and Champion Rd. Machinery Ltd., Goderich, Ontario; dir. URS Corp., San Francisco; Nat. Edn. Corp., Irvine; Basic Vegetable Products, King City, Calif.; Mikel Yurosek & Son L.P.; Newcourt Credit Group, Inc., Toronto, Ont., Can., Consolidated Freightways, Inc., Palo Alto, Calif.; mem. Com. on univ. resources Harvard Univ.; bd. vis. USC Bus. Sch.; bd. trustees Fordham Univ.; mem: N.Y. St. Bar Assn., Knights of Malta; club: Harvard (N.Y.C., S.F.). Res: 279 Park Ln Atherton 94027 Ofc: 3000 Sand Hill Rd Bldg 2 Ste 140 Menlo Park 94025

WALT, MARTIN, IV, physicist, administrator; b. June 1, 1926, West Plains, Mo.; s. Martin and Dorothy (Mantz) W.; m. Mary Estelle Thompson, Aug. 16, 1950; children: Susan b. 1953, Stephen b. 1955, Anne b. 1959, Patricia b. 1969; edn: BS, Calif. Inst. of Tech. 1950; MS, Univ. Wis. 1951; PhD, 1953. Career: staff Los Alamos Sci. Lab., Los Alamos, N.M. 1953-56; cons. scientist, mgr., dir. of research Lockheed Missiles & Space Co., Palo Alto 1956-92; cons. prof. Stanford Univ., Palo Alto 1986-; gov. bd., exec. com. Am. Inst. Physics, Coll. Park, Md. 1986-; sci. and ednl. advy. com. Lawrence Berkeley Labs. 1984-90; NASA Space and Earth Sci. adv. com. 1984-87; NAS/NRC com. on solar terrestrial research 1983-89 (chmn. 1986-89); bd. of overseers for the superconducting supercollider 1989-93; awards: Univ. Wis. Alumni Research Found. fellowship 1950-51, Atomic Energy Commn. fellowship 1951-53; mem: Am. Physical Soc. (fellow), Am. Geophysical Union (fellow), AAAS, Fremont Hills Country Club; ed. Auroral Phenomena, 1965, Introduction to Geomagnetically Trapped Radiation, 1994, contbr. 100 articles to sci. jours., 1952-; mil: USN 1944-46; Republican; rec: sailing, tennis, running. Res: 12650 Viscaino Ct Los Altos Hills 94022-2517

WALTERS, SYLVIA SOLOCHEK, artist, art educator and administrator; b. Aug. 24, 1938, Milwaukee, Wis.; d. Bernard and Becky (Perlstein) Solochek; m. James H. Walters, Aug. 26, 1963; edn: SS, Nat. Univ.. of Mexico 1959; BS (high honors), Univ. of Wis. 1960, MS, 1961, MFA, 1962. Career: instr. Keuka Coll., NY 1962-63, Univ. of Wis. (summer) 1963, Layton Sch. of Art, Milwaukee, Wis. 1963-64; asst. prodn. mgr. and book designer Univ. of Wis. Press 1964-67; lectr. Univ. of Nebr. (fall) 1967; instr. Doane Coll., Crete, Nee. 1967-68; asst. prof. art edn. St. Louis Univ. 1968-69; prof. art, first chair dept. of art, and gallery dir. Univ. of Missouri 1969-84; prof., art dept. chair San Francisco St. Univ. 1984-93, acting dean Sch. of Creative Arts 1993-94, prof., art dept. chair 1994–; acad. prog. reviewer, UC Santa Barbara 1995; prog. evaluator Nat. Assn. of Schools of Art and Design; juror for profl., comm., and student art exhibitions; vis. artist/lectr.: Univ. N.D. 1980, Cal Poly 1982, Univ. Tx. 1984, Pratt Inst. 1986, Carnegie Mellon 1987, Boston Univ. Sch. for Arts 1987, Calif. St. Summer sch. for Arts, Loyola Marymount 1988, Drake Univ. 1989; bd. dirs.: Comm. of Women Artists, St. Louis 1974-76, Art Coordinating Council for the Area, St. Louis 1976-79, Bay Area Council for Visual Arts 1986-91; fund raising dir. Nat. Women's Caucus for Art 1978-80 (recipient 2 grants from NEA); awards: Sigma Epsilon Sigma (Alpha Chpt.), Phi Kappa Phi, Univ. Wis. fellowship 1960-61, Univ. Wis. tchg. assistantship 1961-62, recipient 3 nat. design awards for books for Univ. Wis. Press, 16 grants and awards for res. & profl. projects 1974-94, num. exhibition awards 1979-94, featured or represented in several jours. and books, represented in 30+ major art collections and Joan Roebuck Gallery, Lafayette, Calif. 1995, listed Who's Who of Am. Women 1995-96, others; mem: Boston Printmakers 1974–, Coll. Art Assn. 1991–, Calif. Soc. of Printmakers 1985– (bd. mem. 1988–); editl. adv. and contbg. writer The Calif. Printmaker Qtly. Jour. 1988–; author: num. articles, reviews, exhibit catalogs., 1959-94; artist: participant in 100+ juried exhibitions, 1960–. Res: 5217 Harbord Drive Oakland 94618 Ofc: Art Dept. San Francisco State University 1600 Holloway Ave San Francisco 94132

WANDER, HARRY JOSEPH, physician, pediatrician; b. March 30, 1933, Emmett, Ida.; s. Harry and Frances pearl (Konoske) W.; m. Eunice Selma Bonnell, July 3, 1954 (div. 1974); m. Ilse Rose Littau, Sept. 9, 1978; children: Douglas b. 1957, Gregory b. 1962, Geoffrey b. 1967; stepchildren: Darin b. 1965, Lisa b. 1970; edn: AA, Boise Jr. Coll. 1953; Coll. Idaho Caldwell 1954; MD, Creighton Univ. Omaha 1958. Career: pediatrician Sutter North Med. Group, Marysville 1967–, pres. and chmn. of the bd., 1995–; clin. prof. pediatrics UC Davis 1972–; med. quality review com. Bd. Med. Quality Assurance Calif. 1982-87; mem: AMA, CMA, Yuba-Sutter-Colusa Med. Soc., Am. Acad. Pediatrics (fellow), Mil. Surgeons of U.S.; mil: USN 1958-67, lt. comdr., USAR 1983-94, COL, Army Achievement Medal 1987, Army Commendation Medal 1988; Republican; R.Cath.; rec: flying, skiing, skin diving. Res: 312 Littlejohn Rd Yuba City 95993 Ofc: Sutter North Medical Group 800 3rd St Marysville 95901

WANG, CHEN CHI, executive - electronics, real estate, and financial corporations; b. Aug. 10, 1932, Taiwan, China, came to U.S. 1959, naturalized 1970; s. Chin-Ting and Chen Kim (Chen) W.; m. Victoria Rebisoff, Mar. 5, 1965; children: Katherine Kim, Gregory Chen, John Christopher, Michael Edward; edn: BA in econ., Nat. Taiwan Univ., 1955, BSEE, San Jose State Coll., 1965, MBA, UC Berkeley, 1961. Career: with IBM Corp., San Jose 1965-72; founder/CEO Electronics Internat. Co., Santa Clara 1968-72; owner, gen. mgr., 1972-81, reorganized as EIC Group, 1982, now chmn. bd./pres.; dir. Systek Electronics Corp., Santa Clara 1970-73; founder/senior ptnr. Wang Enterprises, Santa Clara 1974-80, founder/sr. ptnr. Hanson & Wang Devel. Co., Woodside 1977-85; chmn. bd. Golden Alpha Enterprises, San Mateo 1979–; mng. ptnr. Woodside Acres-Las Pulgas Estates, Woodside 1980-85; founder/sr. ptnr. DeVine & Wang, Oakland 1977-83; Van Heal & Wang, West Village 1981-82; founder/chmn. bd. EIC Fin. Corp., Redwood City 1985–; chmn. bd. Maritek Corp., Corpus Christi, Tx. 1988-89; mem. Internat. Platform Assn., Tau Beta Pi; author: Monetary and Banking System of Taiwan 1955, The Small Car Market in the U.S. 1961; mil: 2d lt. Nationalist Chinese Army 1955-56; Christian Ch. Res: 195 Brookwood Rd Woodside 94062 Ofc: 2075 Woodside Rd Redwood City 94061

WANG, MICHAEL LEE, ophthalmologist; b. June 18, 1960, Portland, Ore.; s. Chan Huan and Katherine Kai Ping (Tsang) W.; m. Susan Carol Wong, DDS, Oct. 25, 1986; children: Jonathan b. 1993, Matthew b. 1994; edn: BS (summa cum laude), psycho-biology, UCLA 1982; MD, Univ. of Calif., San Francisco 1986; med. lic., St. of Calif.; cert. Am. Bd. of Ophthalmology 1991; qualified med. evaluator, St. of Calif., Indsl. Med. Council 1994. Career: internship in medicine, Pacific Presbyn. Med. Ctr., S.F. 1986-87; residency in ophthalmology, UCSF 1987-90; pvt. practice, ophthalmology, Oakland 1990–; asst. clin. prof. ophthal., UCSF Sch. Medicine 1990–; attending clin. faculty, ophthal. Calif. Pacific Med. Ctr. 1991–; tchr./supr. of med. students and residents, UCSF Ophthal. Clinic 1990-95, Highland Gen. Hosp. 1991-94, VA Hosp., S.F. 1991-95, Kaiser Hosp. 1993-95; mem. admissions com. for joint MD/MS prog., UCSF and UC Berkeley 1994-95; cons: Med. Bd. of Calif. 1995, Lerner and Assocs., Krames Commns.; awards: UCLA Alumni Freshman Scholar 1978, UCLA Regent Scholar 1980, Phi Beta Kappa award 1981, UCLA Disting. Scholar award 1981, Phi Eta Sigma award 1981, UCSF Regent Scholar 1982, UCLA Outstanding Senior 1982, Phi Beta Kappa, Highest Honors in Psychology and Dean's Honor List, UCLA 1982, Mortar Board award 1982, Phi Beta Kappa award for grad. students 1985, Alpha Omega Alpha, UCSF 1986; mem: Am. Coll. of Surgeons (Young Surgeon Rep., No. Calif. Chpt. 1994), Chinese Am. Physician Soc., Chinese Am. Ophthal. Soc., Alameda Contra Costa Med. Assn.,

CMA, Calif. Assn. of Ophthal., Am. Acad. of Ophthal. (course monitor, annual mtgs. 1993, 94), AMA, East Bay Ophthal. Soc., S.F. Ophthal. Roundtable, UCLA Alumni Assn., UCSF Clin. Faculty Assn., UCSF Alumni Assn.; civic: Merritt Hosp. Health Access ophthal. lectr. 1991, vol. Oakland Chinatown Health Fair 1991-93, vol. Summit Hosp. Health Access Prog.; contbg. author: 10 sci. articles to profl. jours., 1980-93. Res: 111 Bell Ave Piedmont 94611 Ofc: 3300 Webster #212 Oakland 94609

WANGBERG, ELAINE GREGORY, university administrator; b. Aug. 4, 1942, Huntington, W.Va.; d. Bradford W. and Freda (Smith) Gregory; children: Brigitte M. b. 1966, Leslie G. b. 1971; edn: BS summa cum laude, Univ. Minn. 1964; MA, Univ. Mich. 1970; PhD, 1979. Career: language arts cons. Ann Arbor Pub. Schs., Mich. 1975-78, interim dir. language arts dept. 1977-78; asst. prof. Univ. New Orleans, La. 1979-81, assoc. prof., dir. literacy project 1981-85, dir. res. and devel. 1983-86; v.provost, dean, prof. CSU Chico 1986–; cons. univs. and sch. dists. 1975–; awards: Univ. Mich. Outstanding Dissertation 1979, La. St. Univ. Outstanding Tchr. 1983, U.S. Dept. Edn. Cert. Recog. 1984, Phi Delta Kappa Outstanding Research Award, La. Ednl. Adminstr. of Yr. 1985; mem: Am. Council on Educ., Am. Assn. of Higher Educ., Am. Assn. Univ. Adminstrs., Am. Assn. Univ. Research Parks, Council of Grad. Sch., Western Assn. Grad. Schs. (pres.), Nat. Assn.Women Deans Adminstrs. & Counselors, Council of Graduate Schools (nat. bd mem.), Phi Delta Kappa, Metro. Leadership Forum, Chico C.of C.; num. articles pub. Ofc: California State University 114 Kendall Hall First and Normal Sts Chico 95929-0875

WARD, JAMES DAVID, judge; b. Sept. 8, 1935, Sioux Falls, S.D.; s. Charles David, Jr. and Juanita Marion (Senecal) W.; m. Carole J. Sander, Aug. 4, 1956; children: Kelly, Bruce, Mark; edn: BA, Univ. S.Dak., 1957; JD, Univ. San Francisco, 1959; admitted bar: Calif. Career: deputy dist. atty., Riverside 1960-61; atty., ptnr. Badger, Schulte & Ward, Riverside 1961-64; ptnr. Thompson & Colegate, 1964-93; judge Superior Court, Riverside 1993–; adj. prof. UC Riverside, 1983–, Univ. of LaVerne, 1988-89; mem. Lawyer Representative-Ninth Circuit Judicial Conf. 1992-93; editl. bd. Calif. Lawyer Mag. 1989-94; honors: argued and won 2 cases before U.S. Supreme Ct. Press Enterprise v. Superior Ct., W.D.C. 1984-86, merit. service award Riverside County Bar Assn. 1986, Resolution and appreciation cert. Calif. Legislature, Sacto. 1987; mem.: Calif. State Bar Assn. (1960–, bd. govs. 1981-84, v.p. 1984), Am. Judicature Soc. (1965–, bd. dirs. 1984-87), Am. Board of Trial Advocates 1989–, Riv. County Bar Assn. (1960–, pres. 1973-74), So. Calif. Defense Counsel 1975-93, Calif. Judges Assn. 1994–; civic: Monday Morning Group Riv., Citizens Univ. Com. (pres. 1995), UCR Found., Riverside Comm. Hosp. Found., Riverside Art Assn., Frank Miller Club (Mission Inn); publs: articles Civil Discovery Practice, CEB (1988), contbr. Calif. Lawyer, Calif. Legal Secretaries Mag., other jours.; mil: sgt. Army Reserve 1957-63; Republican; Prot.; rec: skiing. Ofc: Riverside Superior Court 4050 Main St Riverside 92501

WARD, MARY JANE, real estate broker, civic activist; b. Aug. 4, 1952, Saint John, New Brunswick, Canada; d. Clifford Francis and Eileen Elizabeth (Cullinan) Ward; edn: Brookdale Comm. Coll. 1970-72; Univ. San Diego 1972-73; San Diego St. Univ. 1973-75; real estate broker, Anthonys Real Estate Sch. San Diego 1974-81. Career: sales agt. Investor's Realty, San Diego 1975-77; resident mgr. Revere Inn 1977-79; remodeler Sunbelt Fin. Corp. 1979; rental agt. Apartment Selector 1979; property mgr. PLK Realty & Investment 1980-81; project supr., coordinator Dr. Leone 1981–; real estate broker, owner Total Mgmt. Realty 1984–; area leader Mission Beach Town Council 1984-85, secty. 1985-87; honors: Susan Golding cert. of appreciation, 1985; mem. Nat. Audubon Soc. 1995–; civic: initiated State Park Petition Drive, v.p./founder of Californians to Save Belmont Park (Belmont Park Amusement Ctr. blt. by John D. and Adolf B. Spreckels 1928; 4-yr. battle failed to prevent devel. but lead to retention of the original name Belmont Park, also brought 1st Soviet Arts Fest. to San Diego), involved in spearheading the restoration of the Roller Coaster "Big Dipper" 1989–; Democrat; Catholic; rec: windsurfing. Ofc: Total Management Realty Inc 804 Liverpool Ct San Diego 92109

WARD, ROBERT STACY, real estate broker; b. Dec. 15, 1959, Anderson, Ind.; s. Edgar Elmer and Nedra (Smallwood) W.; m. Deborah, May 8, 1982; children: Stacie Ann b. 1984, Robert Jacob b. 1987; edn: BS bus. Indiana Univ. Career: mgr. Cal-Tahoe Realtors, South Lake Tahoe, 1982, owner/broker Century 21 Cal-Tahoe Realtors, 1982-88; mgr. Tahoe Sands Realty, 1988; gen. mgr. for mktg. and sales NaKoro Resorts, Fiji Islands, 1988; owner/broker South Lake Tahoe Realtors, 1988–; mem: Nat. Assn. Realtors, Calif. Assn. Realtors, South Lake Tahoe Bd. of Realtors, Kiwanis Club (sec. 1982-83, treas. 1983-84, 2d v.p. 1991-92, Kiwanis of the Yr. 1993-94, pres. 1994-95), Chamber of Commerce 1983– (ambassador 1991-94); Republican; Presbyterian. Res: 1688 Hekpa South Lake Tahoe 96150 Ofc: South Lake Tahoe Realtors, 1235 Ski Run Blvd South Lake Tahoe 96150

WARD, WILLIAM DUDLEY, designer, university professor; b. Sept.15, 1942, Los Angeles; s. William F. and Evelyn M. (Peterson) W.; m. Carolyn S. Seibert, June 22, 1968; children: Ryan b. 1974, Darrin b. 1976; edn: BS, Calif. Polytechnic Univ., Pomona 1965; MA, UCLA 1967, MFA, 1968. Career: assoc.

prof. UCLA 1969–; freelance system designer 1978–; pres. Control Research, Woodland Hills 1986–; chmn., dept. of theater, UCLA 1989–; designer various lighting, acoustical and studio rigging systems; rec: water sports. Ofc: UCLA Dept of Theater 405 Hilgard Ave Los Angeles 90024

WARE, DAVID JOSEPH, registered investment advisor, expert witness, financial planner; b. Dec. 1, 1928, Oberlin, Ohio; s. Elmer Edwin and Jessie Vanstone (Potter) W.; m. Diane Adams, Sept. 12, 1958 (dec.); children: Stacey b. 1961, Joel b. 1964; m. Mary Spadafora, Aug. 15, 1981; edn: Univ. of Mexico, 1949; BA, DePauw Univ., 1950; bus. sch. Miami Univ., 1950-51, 54-55; grad. course Univ. of Granada, Spain 1957; C.F.P. Coll. Fin. Planning 1984. Career: grain trader Chemurgy Div., Glidden Co., Chgo. 1955-57; commodity dept. mgr. Merrill Lynch, San Francisco 1958-69; br. and regional mgmt., investment sales Dean Witter Reynolds, S.F. 1969-92; mem. bd. dirs. Pacific Commodities Exchange 1972; panelist, research UC Berkeley Bus. Sch., 1970, guest lectr. UCB Grad. Seminar, 1971; instr. grad. sch. Golden Gate Univ., 1987-89; adj. prof. Coll. for Fin. Planning, Denver 1986-87; honors: Alpha Delta Sigma 1949, Phi Beta Kappa 1950, achiev. Chgo. Board of Trade 1956, nat. recognition Junior Achievement, S.F. 1963, regional recognition Jaycees Mill Valley 1964; mem: NASD (arbitrator W.Coast 1985–), Nat. Futures Assn. (arbitrator 1985–), NYSE Disciplinary Com. W. Coast 1975-92, Am. Arbitration Assn. (arb. 1988–), Internat. Assn. Fin. Planners, Registry of Cert. Fin. Planners (CFP), San Francisco C.of C. (chmn. mem. com. 1975-78), Strawberry Dist. (Marin Co., bd. dirs.), Jt. Powers Authority Marin Co., Calif. Spec. Dist. Assn. (Marin Co. Chpt., bd. dirs.); clubs: Olympic (chmn. house com. 1987), S.F. Commodity (pres. 1971); contbr. articles Money Mag. 1987–; mil: lt. AUS Signal Corps 1951-53; Republican; Congregational; rec: bridge, tennis, handball, sailing. Res/Ofc: 248 E Strawberry Dr Mill Valley 94941

WARNER, ROLLIN MILES, JR., educator; b. Dec. 25, 1930, Evanston, Ill.; s. Rollin Miles and Julia Herndon (Polk) W.; edn: English-Speaking Union Schoolboy Exchange to Oundle Sch., Eng.; BA, Yale Univ., 1953; cert. Harvard Law Sch., 1955-56; MBA, Stanford Univ., 1960; supv. cred., Univ. San Francisco, 1974; lic. R.E. broker; Realtor; Cert. Fin. Planner (CFP) Coll. Fin. Plnng., 1977; Registered Investment Adviser. Career: buyer Matson Navigation Co., 1956-58; asst. dir. devel./asst. to VP Fin., Stanford Univ. 1960-63; dean student activities and tchr. Town School, San Francisco 1963-70, 1975–; school prin. and dir. devel. and plant, Katharine Branson Sch., Mt. Tamalpais Sch., 1970-75; ednl. cons. Nat. Center for Fin. Edn.; dep. dir. gen. Internat. Biographical Centre; dep. gov. Am. Biog. Inst. Res. Assn.: honors: Town School Medal, World Decoration of Excellence, Cum Laude Soc., Silver Beaver Award BSA, Scouter's Key, All-America Prep Sch. Swimming, Mt. Tamalpais Sch. Cup, SAR Award (NROTC), Fisher Body Craftsman's Guild 2d prize Ill.; mem: Mathematical Assn. of Am., Inst. of Cert. Fin. Planners, Am. Mgmt. Assn., Am. Swimming Coaches Assn., Am. Camping Assn., Boston Computer Soc., Assn. for Asian Studies, Am. Econ. Assn., Calif. R.E. Edn. Assn., Manteca Bd. of Realtors, R.E. Certificate Inst., Marines Meml. Assn., Chi Psi frat., Lincoln's Inn at Harvard Law Sch., Nautical Res. Guild, Am. Assn. of Individual Investors; civic: Boy Scouts Am. (Troop 14); clubs: University (SF), Grolier (NY), SF Yacht, Old Oundelian (London), Mory's, Book Club of Calif.; author: Free Enterprise at Work 1989, Africa, Asia, Russia 1986, America 1986, Europe 1986, Greece, Rome 1981; mil: lt. USNR 1953-55, Korean, UN, Nat. Service ribbons; Republican; R.Cath.; rec: ship models, computers, bibliophile. Res: 1164 Marion Street Manteca 95337 Ofc: Town School 2750 Jackson St San Francisco 94115

WARREN, THOMAS SPENCER, manufacturing executive; b. July 26, 1903, Anaheim; s. Henry E. and Emily T. (Thomas) W.; m. Barbara Blaisdell, Oct. 28, 1928; children: Paul b. 1933, Bethany b. 1935, Virginia b. 1945; edn: BA, Pomona Coll. 1926. Career: pres. Ultra Violet Products (now UVP, Inc.), Los Angeles 1932-71; chmn. UVP Inc., San Gabriel 1971-83; pres. Black Light Corp. of Am., Los Angeles 1955–; dir., chmn. Ulta Violet Products Ltd., Cambridge, England 1969-83; awards: 1st Thomas S. Warren Award from AGMSA 1993, featured in Lapidary Jour. (3/94 by S.E. Thompson); mem: Pomona Coll. Alumni Assn. (Council 1977-81), East Bay Mineral Soc. (hon.), L.A. Lapidary Soc. (hon.), Fluorescent Mineral Soc. (hon.), San Diego Gem & Mineral Soc. (hon.), Am. Gem & Mineral Suppliers Assn. (founder, pres. 1952-54, dir. 1954-58), Am. Mining Congress (1939–), Rotary Intl. (Hollywood Club 1942-50, dir. 1948, L.A. Club 1950–); coauthor, editor (revised): Ultra-Violet Guide to Minerals (1992), Rainbow Minerals of Franklin, NJ (children's book), contbr., Identification & Qualitative Chemical Analysis of Minerals (O.C. Smith), Collectors Book Fluorescent Minerals (Manuel Robbins), Ultraviolet Light and Fluorescent Minerals (book in progress with Richard Bostwick, Earl Ver Beek); Republican; Prot.; rec: fluorescent minerals. Ofc: PO Box 1501 San Gabriel 91776

WASTE, WILLIAM TEN EYCK, insurance executive; b. Aug. 10, 1925, Oakland; s. Wm. Ewing and Elizabeth (Ten Eyck) W.; m. Laura Piccirillo, Aug. 6, 1949; children: William H. II b. 1951, Ann Elizabeth (Woodbridge) b. 1953, Carlin (McCarthy) b. 1955, Mary Lou (Ashford) b. 1959, Katherine Margaret (Spurlock) b. 1959; edn: Univ. Mich. 1943; BA, Univ. Calif. 1949. Career: various pos. Industrial Indemnity Co., West Coast 1950-74, retired 1974; pres. Beaver Insurance Co., San Francisco, 1974-85, v. chmn./c.e.o. 1985-87, bd. dir.

1974-89; appt. commr. Calif. State Seismic Commn. 1987-91, v.chmn. 1990-91; Oreg. Gov.'s Accident Advy. Com. 1969-72; mem. Oregon Western Ins. Info. Service Bd. 1963-72; recipient pres.'s citation Oregon Ins. Agts. Assn. 1965; mem. Assn. Calif. Ins. Cos. (pres. 1983-85), Workers Compensation Rating Bur. (govng. com.), Calif. Workers Compensation Inst. (pres. 1985-87, dir. 1979-89); mem. bds: The Claremont Colls. (bd. overseers 1981–), Scripps Coll. (v.chmn., chmn. investment com. 1981–), St. Luke's Hosp. (dir. 1988–), Salvation Army (San Francisco advy. bd. chmn. 1977-78, Nat. Advy. Bd. 1980–, v.chmn. 1990-93), USO (S.F. bd. dirs. 1973-82), Episcopal Homes Found. (chmn. fin. com. 1977), Church Divinity Sch. of the Pacific (trustee 1988–), Pacific Rim Soc. (bd. 1990-94); mem: Royal Photographic Soc. (assoc.), SAR, Sigma Phi; clubs: Pacific Union, Bohemian, The California, St. Francis Yacht, Claremont CC, The Club, Kiwanis (pres. S.F. club 1979-80), Masons, K.T.; publs: articles on insurance subjects, and on travels to USSR and China; mil: lst lt. CIC, US Army 1944-47, 51; Republican (v.chmn. Kern Co. Central Com. 1960-63); Episcopalian (sr. warden 1968); rec: photography, skiing, hiking, numismatics. Ofc: 2288 Broadway San Francisco 94115

WATANABE, RICHARD MEGUMI, research fellow, exercise physiologist; b. Sept. 7, 1962, San Fernando, Calif.; s. Takashi and Toshiko (Yamane) W.; edn: BS biol. scis., USC, 1986, MS applied biometry, 1989, postgrad. studies in exercise physiology (in progress). Career: res. asst. dept. physiology & biophysics USC Sch. of Medicine, 1985-87, res. assoc. 1987-89, dir. Kinetic Core, Metabolic Research Unit, 1991–; stats. analyst and computer pgmr. L.A. Co.-USC Med. Ctr. Women's Hosp., 1989-89; honors: Outstanding Young Men of Am. 1983, Outstanding Senior USC 1985, Serono Symposia in-tng. award, 1st prize, Pacific Coast Fertility Soc. 1990, student award for meritorious resrch. Am. Fedn. for Clin. Resrch., Western Soc. 1990, Am. Fed. for Clinical Res. Medical Student Award 1994, Michaela Modan Mem. Award, Am. Diabetes Assn. 1995, NIH predoctoral tng. fellow 1990–; student mem: Am. Diabetes Assn., AAAS, Am. Physiol. Soc.; publs: MS thesis: Mathematical Modeling of Insulin Secretion: Issues of Mode Complexity, 1989, peer reviewed sci. papers and abstracts (20+), med. jour. revs. for Diabetes Care, Diabetologia, Internat. J. of Obesity, others; rec: woodworking, music. Ofc: USC School of Medicine Dept. Physiology & Biophysics, Metabolic Research Unit, 1333 San Pablo St MMR-620 Los Angeles 90033 Tel: 213/342-1939

WATERS, GARY MILES, ophthalmologist; b. June 8, 1941, Hugo, Okla.; s. Gregory Roy Waters, M.D. and Annabelle Lorete (Condak) W.; m. Bonnie Elizabeth Goulden, May 27, 1972; 1 son Gregory b. 1976; edn: BS (with honors), electrical engring., Purdue Univ. 1963; MD, Univ. of Illinois Coll. Medicine, Chgo. 1967; lic. physician St. of Calif.; cert. Am. Bd. Ophthalmology 1976. Career: surgical internship Cook Co. Hosp., Chgo., Ill. 1967-68; surgical residency, Presbyterian-St. Lukes Hosp., Chgo. 1970-71; ophthalmology residency L.A. Co.-Univ. of So. Calif. Med. Ctr., L.A. 1972-75; staff M.D., MacNeal Mem. Hosp., Berwyn, Ill. 1968; staff M.D. Neighborhood Health Ctr., Univ. of Ariz., Tucson 1971-72; solo practice, ophthalmology, Tucson, Ariz. 1975-76; group practice Fresno Med. Group 1976-77, Eye Medical Clinic of Fresno, Inc. 1977–; assoc. staff in ophthalmology Valley Med. Ctr., Fresno 1976–; asst. clin. prof. ophthalmology UC San Francisco 1980–; mem: Am. Coll. of Surgeons (fellow 1982–), AAO 1976–; mil: capt. USAF 1968-70. Ofc: Eye Medical Clinic of Fresno Inc. 1122 S Street Fresno 93721

WATERS, MAXINE, congresswoman; b. Aug. 15, 1938, St. Louis, Mo.; d. Remus and Velma (Moore) Carr; m. Sidney Williams, July 23, 1977; children: Edward, Karen; 2 grandchildren; edn: BA in sociology Calif. State Univ., L.A.; hon. doctorates Spellman Coll., N.C. Agricultural & Tech. State Univ., Morgan State Univ. Career: former tchr. Head Start; mem. Calif. Assembly from dist. 48, 1976-91, Dem. caucus chair, 1984; mem. 102-104th Congresses from 35th Calif. dist., 1991–; mem. House com. on banking, fin., and urban affairs, and com. on veterans' affairs; ranking Democrat on veterans subcom. on edn., employment tng. and housing; mem. banking subcom. on housing and comm. opportunities, and banking subcom. on capital markets, securities and Govt.-sponsored enterprises; sponsored Emergency Devel. Loan Guarantee Prog., 1992, "Youth Fair Chance" prog., 1993, legis. creating a "Center for Women Veterans" within Dept. of Veterans' Affairs, comm. devel. bank bill H.R. 1699; founder Community Build (rebuilding project in L.A., 1992); mem. U.S. delegation to Nelson Mandela's inauguration as Pres. of a free So. Africa; mem: Congl. Black Caucus (organized 1st hearing on AIDS in African Am. comm.), Congl. Caucus for Women's Issues, Congl. Urban Caucus (co-chair), Dem. Nat. Com., Dem. Congl. Campaign Com; del. Dem. Nat. Convention, 1972, 86, 80, 84, 88, 92, mem. rules com. 1984; mem. Nat. Adv. Com. for Women, 1978–; bd. dirs. Essence Mag., TransAfrica Found., Nat. Women's Political Caucus, Ctr. Nat. Policy, Clara Elizabeth Jackson Carter Found., Spellman Coll., Nat. Minority AIDS Project, Women for a Meaningful Summit, Nat. Council Negro Women, Black Women's Agenda; founder Black Women's Forum. Ofc: US House of Reps 330 Cannon Washington DC 20515-0535

WATKINS, CEDRIC LEE, II, television communications executive; b. May 22, 1955, Long beach; s. John B. and Mabel B. (Burkes) W.; children: Cedric L., III, Yasmin Monet, Jade Monique; edn: BS, Wash. St. Univ., Pullman

1978; MBA, Pepperdine Univ., 1980; JD, Univ. of West Los Angeles Law Sch. 1995. Career: account exec. ABC TV, San Francisco 1982-85; CBS TV, Hollywood 1986; western div. mgr. Group WTV Productions, Burbank 1986-87; sr. v.p. We're Rolling Productions, Inglewood 1987–; awards: Nat. Black MBA Assn. MBA of Year 1987, CBS Safe Effort Award, Hollywood 1986; mem: Nat. Black MBA Assn. (nat. membership chmn. 1987–, L.A. Chapt. pres. 1987), NAACP, AFTRA, Christian Youth Assn., First A.M.E. Ch.; rec: tennis, golf, clarinet. Ofc: We're Rolling Productions 8736 Edmonton Pl Inglewood 90305

WATTS, JAMES LAWRENCE, investment banker; b. June 3, 1949, Minot, N.Dak.; s. Lawrence Robert and Deloris Marie (Anderson) W.; edn: BA, econs., Univ. Wisc., 1972; MA, internat. econs., American Univ., W.D.C. 1975, JD, Washington Coll. of Law Am. Univ., 1981; admitted bar: Dist. Col., U.S. Supreme Ct.; lic. NASD Series 7, Series 63. Career: legislative asst. US House of Representatives, W.D.C., 1975-76; assoc. dir. Nat. Assn. of Small Bus. Invesment Cos., W.D.C., 1976-81; of counsel Buchanan Ingersoll, W.D.C., 1981-85; atty. cons. Venture Internat. Inc., Alexandria Va. 1985-86; v.p. corp. fin. FAS/Bekhor Internat., San Diego 1986-87; senior v.p. corp. fin. Cruttenden & Co. (venture fin., mergers & acquisitions, pub. offerings), Newport Beach 1987-92; managing dir. CFI Ltd., Irvine; managing dir. Tuerk & Associates, Irvine 1994–; IRSC Inc., Anaheim 1988–; awards: merit cert. Pres. Jimmy Carter 1980, career achiev. Nat. Assn. Small Bus. Inv. Cos. 1981; mem: Am. Bar Assn.; Republican. Res: 3150 Manistee Dr Costa Mesa 92626

WATTS, VAN, naval philosopher and sea power advocate; b. Aug. 26, 1920, Mooers, N.Y.; s. Bert and Margaret (Baker) W.; m. Lilie Remoreras, 1971; children: Michelle Remie b. 1978, (by previous marriage): Philip b. 1942, Charlotte b. 1946, Britt b. 1947, Lance b. 1948, Douglas b. 1950; Career: U.S. Navy 1937-62; USN travels to 6 continents and pub. author on 2 of them; sailed with Byrd and Michener 1942; his "Our Expanding Language" was read before the Sydney chpt. British Empire Soc., 1944; intro. on return to Norfolk as "a Navy instn." 1952; his televised & broadcasted pgms. sparked goodwill drive placed under civic auspices by the Mayor and endorsed by chamber and churches; activities in N.Y., Wash. and Chicago participated 1952; subject of full-page editorial in OUR NAVY 1953; ideas extolled in Navy Dept. press release to 2,562 ships, stations and overseas commands 1953; producer t.v. and radio navy-slanted shows from Norfolk, Va., 1952-54, and originated the Navy's Sailor of the Week, Month and Year programs, also assisted other svs. in starting pgms.; prod. shows: Norfolk's Sailor of the Week's Big Welcome to Town WTAR-TV 1952-53, WTOV-TV 1954; Sailor of the Week's Bon Voyage WCAV 1952-53, WGH 1954; Navy Guide Cover Girls WLOW 1952-54; Marine of the Month WTAR 1954; Oceana Navy Band WBOF 1954; Portsmouth Sailor of the Week WSAP 1953-54; Sailor of the Year WTOV-TV 1954, WGH 1954; enrollment of all t.v. and radio media in area to promote Norfolk-Navy goodwill drive inspired the formation of the Navy League's Hollywood Council, 1954; created Norfolk's famed Big Ship Welcoming Ceremonies, called by Navy Dept. "centerpiece of Norfolk-Navy rels." 1958; ofcr. courier to NATO Paris Hq. during 1st Lebanon crisis, 1958; LIFE Mag. paid tribute to value of his pgms. in feature "Mighty New Navy" pub. on 10th anniv. of his Sailor of Week, Month and Year pgms., 1962; Nat. Planning Assn's. endorsement of Atlantic Union entered by Rep. Paul Findley in Congl. Record on 14th anniversary of Watts' goodwill drive in NATO's Sea Capital, June 23, 1966; editorialized in Navy Supply Corps OAK LEAF as "Father of an important part of today's people-oriented Navy" 1972; tribute in Congl. Record by Hollywood Rep. Thomas Rees 1973; sponsor Mich.'s USS Mackinac/Byrd Memorial Navy Bicentennial 1975; recipient ltr. of commendn. Nat. Trust for Hist. Preservation 1975; decorated Nat. Def. Serv., Am. Def. Serv., Am. Campaign, Asiatic-Pac. Campaign, WWII Victory, Navy Occup. Serv. (Europe), Armed Forces Exped. (Lebanon), Guadalcanal and New Guinea battle stars, others; recipient num. honors incl. City of Norfolk official thanks 1954 and Royal Mace Pin 1988, Hollywood Council Navy League's gold plaque for the founder of pgms. that spread around the globe, with 3 of his "nautical celebrities" returned from Persian Gulf duty for the ceremonies at Bob Hope Hollywood USO 1988, tribute from ship assn. of USS Enterprise 1988, Navy League Pacific SW Regl. Award 1989, called "Sailor of the Century" by Navy League Hollywood Council Pres. Charles Cabot 1991, advy. bd. WWII Nat. Commemorative Assn. 1992, biographied in The History of Warrant Ofcrs. in the US Navy and Chiefs in the US Navy 1993, portrait and artifacts requested for display by the San Diego Military Heritage Soc., Van Watts Display in Pensacola credited with "vastly enhancing" Navy Mustang Museum's success 1993, credited with "much of the positive civilian awareness of the role and value of the Navy" by historian Kit Bonner in Treasure Island Mus. Assn. Newsletter 1993, 322 Navy League Councils in countries around the globe were reported participating in his programs for honoring outstanding Navymen 1994, achievements noted in Official History of the USN Supply Corps in celebration of Corps Bicentennial 1995; mem: USS Albany CA123 Assn., USS Enterprise CV6 Assn., USS Fremont APA44 Assn., USS Sierra AD18 Assn., NCPO Assn., Tin Can Sailors Assn., Surface Navy Assn. (San Diego Ch.), VFW, Am. Legion (John Philips Sousa Post), Guadalcanal Campaign Vets Assn, US Naval Inst., Naval Hist. Found., Navy Supply Corps Assn., Fleet Reserve Assn., Botsford Family Hist. Assn., New Hampshire Hist. Soc., Brattleboro (Vt.) Hist. Soc.,

Chesterfield (NH) Hist. Soc., Burbank (CA) Hist. Soc., Hollywood Council Navy League (life mem.). Res: 13561 Sherman Way #216 Van Nuys 91405-2874

WAXMAN, HENRY ARNOLD, congressman; b. Sept. 12, 1939, Los Angeles; s. Louis and Esther (Silverman) W.; m. Janet Kessler, Oct. 17, 1971; children: Carol Lynn, Michael David; edn: BA in poli. sci., UCLA 1961, JD, 1964; admitted Bar: Calif. 1965. Career: mem. Calif. State Assembly 1969-74, chmn. com. on health until 1974; mem. 94th-104th Congresses from 24th (now 29th) Calif. Dist. 1975–, chmn. house subcom. on health and environment 1979-94; pres. Calif. Fedn. Young Democrats 1965-67; mem: Calif. Bar Assn., Guardians Jewish Home for Aged, Am. Jewish Congress, Sierra Club, B'nai B'rith, Phi Sigma Alpha. Ofc: US House of Reps 2408 Rayburn House Office Bldg Washington DC 20515

WAY, TSUNG-TO, bank executive; b. Sept. 20, 1912, Fu Ch'in, Fukien Province, China; s. Kuang-Yen and S.P. (Yang) W.; m. Shun-Hwa Chiang, Oct. 16, 1938; children: Helen K.L., Suzanne I.L., Raymond T.Y.; edn: St. John's Sch., Shanghai, Yenching Univ., Peiping. Career: Bank of China 1936–, staff mem. Shanghai Branch 1936-38, hd. Foreign Dept., Kunming Br. 1938-39, hd. Loiwing Agy., Yunnan 1939-40, asst. mgr., sub-mgr. Tientsin 1941-43, sub-mgr. Peiping 1943-44, Tientsin 1944-45, Saigon 1946-51, mgr. Saigon 1951-65, Tokyo 1965-70, asst. gen. mgr. in charge, Bank of China, Tokyo 1970, gen. mgr. Bank of China, Taipei, ROC 1970-71; pres./CEO The Internat. Commercial Bank of China (fmr. Bank of China), Taipei 1971-75, bd. chmn. 1975–, branches throughout E. and S.E. Asia, Panama, USA, Saudi Arabia; mng. dir: China Devel. Corp., China Ins. Co., United World Chinese Comml. Bank (all, Taipei, ROC); apptd. dir. Euro-Asia Trade Orgn., ROC-USA Econ. Council, Assn. of East Asia Rels., China-Netherlands Cultural and Econ. Assn., mem. Chinese Nat. Assn. of Indus. and Commerce/Taipei; clubs: Taipei Internat. Businessmen's, The Yuan Shan (Taipei), Kuo Hwa Golf and CC (Taipei), American (Tokyo), Korean (Taipei); rec: golf, travel, music. Res: 1411 Laguna Ave Burlingame 94010 Ofc: Director, Bank of Canton of California, 555 Montgomery San Francisco 94111

WAYNE, KYRA PETROVSKAYA, actress, author, lecturer; b. Dec. 31, 1918, Crimea, USSR, naturalized U.S. cit. 1952, W.D.C.; d. Vasilly and Zinaida (von Haffenberg) Obolensky; m. George J. Wayne, M.D., Apr. 21, 1961; children: Ronald G. Wayne, M.D. b. 1953; edn: BA, Inst. of Theatre Arts, Leningrad 1939, MA, 1941. Career: actress Leningrad Drama Theatre, Leningrad Theatre of Miniatures, Moscow Satire Theatre, 1939-46; enrichment lectr. Royal Viking Lines cruises, 1978-88; free lance author, 1948–: books: (autobiography) Kyra, 1959, (cookbook) Kyra's Secrets of Russian Cooking, 1960, (juvenile) Quest For The Golden Fleece, 1962, (autobiography) Shurik, 1970, (novel) The Awakening, 1972, The Witches of Barguzin, 1975, (juv.) Max, the Dog that Refused to Die, 1980, (hist. novel) Quest for Empire, 1989, (juv.) Lil' Ol' Charlie, 1990; awards: Red Star For the def. of Leningrad, Red Army USSR 1943, excellence recogn. City Council Leningrad 1945, City Council Moscow 1945, exceptional svc. Crusade for Freedom, W.D.C. 1955, several awards of merit Am. Lung Assn., L.A. County Lung Assn. 1963-88, Best Fiction Book, Dog Writers Assn. of Am. 1980; pres. Med. Faculty Wives UCLA 1970-71; civic bds: Carmel Music Soc. (dir. 1992–), L.A. Co. Lung Assn. (founder, pres. Clean Air Pgm. 1973-75); mil: lt. Red Army Inf. WWII; Republican/Indep.; Russian Orthodox; rec: orchidist, fgn. languages (6), needlepoint.

WAYNE, RONALD GEORGE, physician, anesthesiologist; b. Jan. 29, 1953, York, Pa.; s. George Jerome and Kyra (Petrovskaya) W.; m. Jean C. Henderson, Aug. 15, 1981 (div.); children: Nicholas b. 1982, Christopher b. 1983, Emily b. 1985, Natalie b. 1988; m. 2d. Karen Leigh Bush, Mar. 2, 1995; edn: BA, biology, UC San Diego 1974; MD, USC Sch. of Medicine, L.A. 1978. Career: resident, anesthesiology, Dept. of Anesthesia, Oregon Health Sci. Univ., Portland 1980-81; coord. perinatal anesthesia, Mt. Zion Hosp., San Francisco 1982; staff anesthesiologist Western Med. Ctr., Santa Ana 1983-85, St. Agnes Med. Ctr., Fresno 1985–; Fresno Surgery Ctr. 1985–; ptnr. Anesthesia Consultants of Fresno 1988–; mem: Calif. Soc. of Anesthesiologists 1982–, Am. Soc. of Anesthesiologists 1982–, AMA 1991–; rec: flying, sailing, photography. Ofc: Anesthesia Consultants of Fresno 6760 N West Ave #101 Fresno 93711

WAYRYNEN, GEORGE ALLEN, electronic technician; b. Feb. 17, 1945, Woodland; s. Arthur Einor and Tillie (Schreiner) W.P.M., ret.; m. Sharon Glavin, June 2, 1973; children: Ryan b. 1974, Shawn b. 1976, Casey b. 1979, Megan b. 1981; edn: AS, Sacto. City Coll. 1971; ICS Correspondence Sch. 1977. Career: electronic tech. Fidelity Sound Co., Sacto. 1972; machine repairman Perinati Music & Vending Co. 1972-73; asst. electrician Spreckels Sugar Co., Woodland 1973-79; asst. signalman So. Pacific RR, Sacto. 1979-81; electronic tech. McClellan AFB 1981–; honors: Sacto. St. Coll. Dean's Honor Roll 1972, MAIPAC Sustained Superior Performance 1983, Performance Award (1993, 94), Notable Achievement 1986, Letter of Appreciation (1982, 89); mem: Nat. League of Postmasters, Calif. Rifle & Pistol Assn., NRA, U.S. Shooting Team (sponsor), Woodland Invitational Track Meet; mil: E-4 USAF 1965-69; Republican; Cath.; rec: hiking, photog., hunting. Res: 400 Greenwood Dr Woodland 95695 Ofc: McClellan Air Force Base 95652

WEATHERFORD, ALAN MANN, educator; b. Feb. 6, 1947, Lake Charles, La.; s. Clester Mann and Nell (Birdsong) W.; m. Kathleen Inez Barnhart, Nov. 1, 1969 (div. 1978); m. Elizabeth Ann Dayton, March 9, 1979; children: William b. 1984, Victoria b. 1984; edn: AD nursing, Northwestern St. Univ. 1977; BA, La. St. Univ. 1969; MBA, Univ. Dallas 1981; PhD, Univ. Tx. Dallas 1986. Career: claims adjuster Royal Globe Ins. Co., San Antonio, Tx. 1969-71; reg. nurse Baylor Med. Center, Dallas, Tx. 1918-85; instr. Univ. Tx. Dallas, Richardson 1983-85; assoc. prof. Calif. Polytech. St. Univ., San Luis Obispo 1986–; cons. Maladro Mktg., Dallas, Tx. 1982-85; A. Weatherford Cons., San Luis Obispo 1986–; mem: Am. Fin. Assn., Fin. Mgmt. Assn., So. Fin. Assn., Western Fin. Assn., SW Fin. Assn., Mensa; mil: 1st lt. USAF 1973-75; Democrat; Baptist; rec: microcomputers. Res: PO Box 12108 San Luis Obispo 93406 Ofc: California Polytechnical State University San Luis Obispo 93407

WEATHERUP, ROY GARFIELD, lawyer; b. April 20, 1947, Annapolis, Md.; s. Robert Alexander and Kathryn Crites (Hesser) W.; m. Wendy Gaines, Sept. 10, 1977; children: Jennifer Ruth b. 1980, Christine Ann b. 1983; edn: JD, Stanford Law Sch. 1972; AB, Stanford Univ. 1968. Career: atty., asso. Haight, Brown & Bonesteel, Los Angeles 1972-78, ptnr. 1979–; Moot Ct. judge UCLA Law Sch.; mem: Calif. Acad. of Appellate Lawyers, Los Angeles Co. Bar Assn. (Superior Cts. Com., Economical Litigation Com., Judicial Evaluation Com.), Am. Bar Assn., Town Hall of Calif., BAJI Com. publ. of Calif. Book of Approved Jury Instr.; author: Standing Armies and Armed Citizens: An Historical Analysis of the Second Amendment, Hastings Constl. Law Quarterly Vol. 2, 1975, reprint U.S. Senate Document, 94th Cong. 2d Session; Republican; Methodist; rec: bridge, chess, backpacking. Res: 17260 Rayen St Northridge 91325 Ofc: 1620 26th St, Ste 4000 North, Santa Monica 90404

WEBB, GILBERT ALLEN, obstetrician-gynecologist, clinical professor; b. June 21, 1923, Oakland; s. Frank Gilbert and Allena (Prather) W.; m. Donna Jean Meyer, Feb. 24, 1946; children: Paul Gilbert b. 1949, Pamela Suzanne Eichmann b. 1950, Janet Brunsting b. 1952, Bruce Jeffery b. 1963, William Thomas b. 1964; edn: AB, UC Berkeley, 1943, MD, 1946; Diplomate Am. Bd. Ob-Gyn 1956, re-cert. 1979. Career: rotating intern San Francisco City & Co. Hosp., 1946; postgrad. tng. U.S. Naval Med. Sch., Bethesda 1947-48, asst. resident ob-gyn U.S. Naval Hosp., Bethesda 1948-49; asst. res. psychiatry Langley Porter Clinic, UC Med. Sch., San Francisco 1950, asst. resident through chief resident in ob-gyn, 1951-54; pvt. practice, San Francisco 1955–; chmn. dept. ob-gyn Children's Hosp. of San Francisco 1963-80; clinical prof. ob-gyn UC Med. Sch., S.F., 1973–; Calif. Academy of Medicine, 1985–; med. staff S.S. Hope, Indonesia and Vietnam summer 1961; examiner Am. Bd. of Ob-Gyn 1973-94, residency review com. AMA Council on Res. Edn. 1975-81, editl. advy. bd. OB/Gyn Collected Letters 1975-94, cons. Calif. Dept. Pub. Health 1977-83; awards: outstanding tchr. of yr. Children's Hosp. S.F. 1973-74, outstanding tchr. of yr., clin. faculty tchg. award Dept. Ob-Gyn UC Med. Ctr. S.F. 1977-78, 86, Kaiser award for excellence in tchg. for vol. faculty mem. in a clinical dept. UCSF Sch. of Med. 1983, Ortho OB/GYN Spotlight (1/87), Lifetime Achiev. award Childrens Hosp. of S.F. 1990, Charlotte C. Baer Memorial Award U.C. Med. S.F. 1992; mem: S.F.Co. Med. Soc., AMA, CMA (del. 4t, advy. com. to the pub. 1982-84, advy. panel on ob-gyn 1982-84), S.F. Gynecol. Soc. (pres. 1976-77), Fellow A.C.S. (bd. govs., specialty soc. gov. from Am. Coll. Ob-Gyn 1984-89, advy. council for ob-gyn 1985-89), Fellow Am. Coll. Obstetrics and Gynecology (Calif. sect. chmn. 1980-81, Dist. IX chmn. 1981-84, nat. exec. com. 1981-84, 87-88, v.p. 1987-88, Task Force on Voluntary Rev. 1985-90, Health Care Commn. 1986-90, Capitol Devel. Com. 1986-88), Pacific Coast Obstet. and Gynecol. Soc. (pres. 1992-93); publs: 21+ med. jour. articles and abstracts. Ofc: 3838 California St Ste 812 San Francisco 94118

WEBB, LELAND FREDERICK, professor of mathematics; b. July 27, 1941, Hollywood; s. Robert Wallace and Evelyn Elaine (Gourley) W.; m. Janie Rae Yoder, Jan. 26, 1963; children: Robert Leland, Tamara Lynn Elaine; edn: BA (with high hon.), UC Santa Barbara, 1963; MA, Calif. Polytech. State Univ., 1968; PhD, Univ. Texas, Austin 1971. Career: lectr. dept. edn. Calif. Polytech. State Univ., S.L.O., 1967-68; tchg. asst. dept. math. Univ. Texas, Austin 1970-71; res. assoc. IV Res. and Devel. Ctr. for Tchr. Edn., 1971; asst. prof. CSU Bakersfield 1971-73, assoc. prof. 1973-78, prof. mathematics edn., 1978–, chmn. dept. math. & computer sci., 1982-85, chmn. dept. mathematics 1990–; mem: Calif. State Dept. Edn. math. assessment advy. com. 1985-88, math. framework com. 1983-85, math. test 12th grade writing com. Calif. Assessment Program 1986-87, nat. Math Counts Question writing com. 1987-90; cons. NSF workshops 1972-76, Tokyo, 1975, sch. dists. and county offices of edn. statewide; on sabbatical lv., vis. prof. Agder Regional Coll., Kristiansand, Norway 1980; author K-8 math. texts, Houghton Mifflin Co., 1985-94; awards: grantee NSF 1972-76, fellow U.S. Office Edn. 1968-71, outstanding prof. award CSU Bakersfield 1980, grantee Calif. State Univ. Chancellor's Office 1981-83; mem: Math. Assn. Am., Nat. Council Tchrs. of Math., Calif. Math. Council (central sect. v.p. 1982-84, nat. counc. rep. central sect. 1982-90, nat. coun. state rep. 1986-90), Bakersfield Math. Council (pres. 1976-78), Sch. Sci. and Math. Assn., Sigma Xi, Phi Kappa Phi, Phi Delta Kappa; mil: capt. US Army 1963-67; Unitarian. Res: 7300 Dos Rios Way Bakersfield 93309 Ofc: Math. Dept., California State University, Bakersfield 93311-1099

WEBBER, CARL ENDICOTT EDWARDS, federal administrator; b. Sept. 9, 1908, Salem, Mass.; s. Harry Endicott and Alice Bates (Edwards) W.; m. Catharine Marple (dec.), Dec. 3, 1932; m. 2d Madeline Oliver, Jan. 21, 1984; children: Martha b. 1935, Sandra b. 1937, Carl Jr. b. 1940; edn: B.Journ. Boston Univ. 1930; Yale Univ. Grad. Sch. 1944-45; grad. Sr. Ofcrs. Mil. Mgmt. Sch., Air Univ. 1949; grad. Indsl. Coll. of the Armed Forces 1958. Career: mgr. Social Security Ofc., Santa Monica 1946; asst. regional rep., area dir. Soc. Sec. Regional Ofc., San Francisco 1948-70; supervised Fed. Sec. Sec. Ofc. Networks Wash., Oreg., Alaska, Calif., Ariz., Nev., Hawaii, and Pacific Territories; ret.; appt. Solano County Grand Jury, 1990-92; awards: Commissioner's Citation Dept. Health Edn. Welfare SSA; mem: Reserve Ofcrs. Assn. (Dept. v.p.), Am. Legion (comdr.), Leisure Town Home Assn. (pres.), Redwood Empire Wally Byam Caravan Club Internat. (pres.), Phi Sigma Kappa, Commonwealth Club, Knights Templar, Internat. Caravan Club, Retired Ofcrs. Assn.; mil: reserve ofcr. AUS and USAF 1930-69: maj./insp. gen. Army Inf. WWII, lt. col. air insp., dir. materiel Korean War, decorated combat inf., purple heart, bronze star; Republican; rec: trailering. Res: 430 Yellowstone Dr Vacaville 95687-3360

WEBER, MARVIN JOHN, physicist; b. Feb. 26, 1932, Fresno; s. John William and Louise (Grill) W.; m. Pauline Margaret Sikes, Feb. 2, 1957 (div. 1987); m. Shirley Ann Schultz, Oct. 24, 1987; children: Ann Hilary b. 1959, Eve Kimberley b. 1961; edn: BA, UC Berkeley 1954, MA, 1956; PhD, 1959. Career: physicist Raytheon Co., Waltham, Mass. 1960-73; vis. research assoc. Stanford Univ. 1966; physicist Lawrence Livermore Nat. Lab., Livermore 1973-93; physicist Lawrence Berkeley Nat. Lab. 1994–; temp. staff U.S. Dept. Energy, Wash. D.C. 1984-85; cons. NSF, Wash. D.C. 1973-76, U.S. Dept. Energy 1985-86, 1992-94, Battelle Pacific Northwest Lab., Richland, Wash. 1988-94; regional ed. Jour. Non-Crystalline Solids, Amsterdam 1988–; assoc. ed. Jour. Luminescence 1985–, Jour. Optical Materials 1992–; honors: Phi Beta Kappa, Sigma Xi, Indsl. Research award 1978, Am. Ceramics Soc. George Morey award 1983, Internat. Conf. on Luminescence Prize 1993; mem: Am. Physical Soc. (fellow), Optical Soc. Am. (fellow), Am. Ceramics Soc. (fellow), Materials Research Soc., Am. Assn. for Crystal Growth; ed.-in-chief, CRC Handbook Series of Laser Sci. & Tech., 1982–, 200+ papers pub. in tech. jours., 1960–. Ofc: Lawrence Berkeley National Laboratory, Berkeley 94720

WEBSTER, STEVEN F., general surgeon, medical group administrator; b. April 18, 1948, Lincoln, Nebr.; s. William Wallace and Mary Jane (Stevens) W.; m. Jennifer Lee Kimmel, July 25, 1970; children: Jamie Lynn b. 1966, William Wallace b. 1971; edn: BA, Univ. Neb. Lincoln 1970; MD, Univ. Neb. Omaha 1974. Career: attdg. surgeon Permanente Med. Group, Oakland 1979-87, asst. chief surgery 1988–; mem: A.C.S., CMA, E. Bay Surg. Soc., Alameda Contra Costa Med. Assn.; 2 articles pub. in med. jours., 1985, 89; Republican; Episcopalian. Res: 1054 Silverhill Dr Lafayette 94549 Ofc: Kaiser Permanente 280 W MacArthur Blvd Oakland 94611

WEDBUSH, EDWARD WILLIAM, securities company president; b. Sept. 14, 1932, St. Louis, Mo.; s. Wm. H. and Edith Marie (Herman) Wedbush; m. Jean A. Lawrence, Dec. 18, 1960, Los Angeles; children: Gary Lance, b. 1964, Eric Dean, b. 1967, Leigh Ann, b. 1969; edn: BA mech. engr., Univ. Cincinnati, 1955; MBA (Hughes Fellow), UC Los Angeles, 1957; reg. profl. engr. Calif. Career: engr. in tng. Wagner Elec., 1949-55; engr. Hughes Aircraft Co., 1955-58; assoc. lectr. in engring., UCLA, 1957-59; ptnr. Wedbush, Noble, Cooke, Inc., Los Angeles 1957-67; pres. Wedbush Morgan Securities, 1967–; pres./CEO Wedbush Corp., 1981–; dir: Gt. Amer. 1st Saving Bank San Diego 1987–, Pacific Stock Exchange, S.F. (1973-77, chmn. bd. 1975-77), Pac. Securities Depository Trust Co. (1976-77), Nat. Sec. Clearing Corp (1973-74, dir. and mem. nominating com. 1987-89); mem: N.Y.S.E. (chmn. Reg. Firms Advy. Com. 1986–), Am. Stock Exchange Com., Sec. Ind. Assn. (chmn. exec. com. Calif./Western Dist. 1988–), Reg. Profl. Engrs. Calif. (1958–), Triangle Frat., California Club; advy. bd. Asthma Found.; contbr. articles in engring. jours; rec: tennis. Res: Rancho Santa Fe 92067 Ofc: PO Box 30014 Los Angeles 90030

WEHN, ROBERT ALVIN, stock broker; b. March 3, 1933, Covina; s. Stanley Albert and Mary Jeneva (Sallows) W.; m. Jacquelyne Joanne Kellogg, July 12, 1958; children: Debbie b. 1961, Robert b. 1963, Patrick b. 1964, Lisa b. 1965, Lori b. 1966, Karen b. 1967; edn: AA, Santa Monica Comm. Coll. 1959; BBA, Loyola Univ. 1961. Career: exec. sales rep. UARCO Bus. Forms, Santa Ana 1961-68; stockbroker Dupont Glore Forgan, Orange 1968-73; Dupont Walston, Santa Ana 1973-74; Shearson Am. Express, Orange 1974-83; Securities West Inc., Santa Ana 1983-95 (ret.); supr. Matol Botanical Internat. Ltd. 1988–; mil: airman 1c. USAF 1953-58; Republican; Cath.; rec: hunting, fishing, metal detecting. Res: 18082 Lillian Way Tustin 92680

WEICHSEL, MORTON E., JR., physician; b. June 17, 1933, Pueblo, Colo.; s. Morton E. and Beatrice Clara (Weintraub) W.; children: Kelly b. 1965, Kimberly b. 1966, Courtney b. 1968; edn: BA, Univ. Colo. Boulder 1955; MD, Univ. Buffalo 1962. Career: clin. instr. pediatric neurology Stanford Univ. Med. Center 1968-69; asst. prof. human devel. medicine and psychiatry Mich. State Univ. Coll. Human Medicine, E. Lansing 1971-74; assoc. prof., prof. pediatrics and neurology Harbor-UCLA Med. Center, UCLA Sch. of Medicine, Torrance

1974–; dir. quality assurance, prof. pediatric neurology King-Drew Med. Center, Los Angeles 1989–; chief profl. services Calif. Children's Services, L.A. 1993–; awards: NIH-Stanford Med. Center fellowship neurology 1965-68, NIH-USPHS fellowship devel. neurochemistry 1969-71; mem: Soc. Neuroscis., Soc. Pediatric Research, Am. Coll. Physician Execs., Western Soc. Pediatric Research, Calif. Neurology Soc., Am. Acad. Pediatrics (fellow); 40+ articles pub. in sci. jours. 1974–; mil: lt. j.g. USN 1955-58; rec: interior design, sports, computer technology, financial and estate planning. Res: 650 Avery Long Beach 90807 Ofc: 19720 East Arrow Hwy Covina 91724

WEIL, LEONARD, management consultant, business educator; b. Oct. 14, 1922, New York; s. Max and Pauline (Levy) W.; m. Janice Eileen Hurlburt, May 30, 1953; children: Diane b. 1956, Marilyn b. 1961, Michael b. 1962, Susan b. 1967; edn: BA, UCLA 1943. Career: adminstrv. v.p. Union Bank, Los Angeles 1946-62; pres., CEO Manufacturers Bank 1962-86; pres. emeritus Mitsui Mfrs. 1987–; adj. asst. prof. John E. Anderson Grad. Sch. Mgmt., UCLA 1988–; chmn. bd. Pacific Coast Banking Sch., Wash. 1974-75; mem: Indep. Bankers So. Calif. (pres. 1969-70), Western Indep. Bankers Assn. (pres. 1973-74), Calif. Bankers Assn. (pres. 1976-77), Am. Bankers Assn. (st. v.p. 1972-73, dir. 1980-81), Bond Fund Am. (dir.) Capital World Bond Fund Inc. (dir.), Am. High Income Trust (trustee), Cash Mgmt. Trust of Am. (trustee), Intermediate Bond Fund of Am. (trustee), Braille Inst. (dir.), John E. Anderson Grad. Sch. Mgmt. UCLA (bd. visitors), UCLA Found. (bd. trustees), Am. Econ. Assn., Am. Mgmt. Assn., Town Hall Calif. (bd. mem., past pres.); chpt. pub. in Bankers Handbook, 1978; mil: USAF 1943-45. Ofc: 233 Wilshire Blvd 6th Flr Santa Monica 90401-1312

WEIL, STEVEN MARK, educator; b. Feb. 28. 1949, Chicago; s. Ronald Leo and Leona Ann (Fein) W.; children: Meredith b. 1974; Nethaniel b. 1982; Rachael b. 1984; edn: BS psychology and physical sci. edn., Roosevelt Univ., Chgo. 1980; MS, Univ. Nebraska, Omaha 1982. Career: educ., Chgo. Public Sch. 1980; educ., Fremont Public Sch., Fremont, NE 1981-86; educ., Stockton Unified Sch. District., Stockton 1986–; cons., Stockton 1991–; dir. edn. and exhibits, Children's Museum of Stockton 1992; NSF Grant Proposal Reader, 1987-89; San Joaquin Cty. Sci. Olympiad Judge 1990-92; San Joaquin Cty Sci. Fair Judge 1988-92, Univ. of Pacific, At-Risk Youth Conf. Advy. Com. 1988-92; Nat. Edn. Assn., Jewish Affairs Caucus, vice-chmn. 1991-93; awards: NSF Honors Workshop for Superior Sci. Tchrs. 1985; Who's Who of Emerging Leaders in Am. 1992; Who's Who in the West 1991-92; mem: Nat. Science Tchrs. Assn. (life, spl. edn. advy. bd. 1983-86, spl. edn. advy. bd. chmn. 1986-87, The Sci. Tchr. advy. & manuscript review bds. 1988-91, NSTA Reports! advy bd. 1991-94); Nat. Edn. Assn., del. rep. assembly 1989-93; Phi Delta Kappa (projects dir. 1993-94, foundations rep. 1994-95, 2nd. v.p. 1995-96); author: A Modified Coop Procedure in Gardening, 1984; Untitled Poetry (pub. 1994), assorted poems, 1995, 96; num. presentations and pub. articles; Jewish. Res: 7100 Shoreline Dr #113 Stockton 95219 Ofc: Stockton Unified School District Discovery School 300 N Gertrude Stockton 95215

WEIMERS, LEIGH ALBERT, newspaper columnist; b. Nov. 11, 1935, Napa; s. Leigh and Stella Marie (Heflin) W.; m. Geraldine L. Stone, Aug. 25, 1962; children: Kristin L. b. 1965, Karin L. b. 1968; edn: BA in journ., San Jose St. Univ.,. 1958. Career: sports editor Napa Journal, 1952-53; sports editor Napa Register, 1953-55; reporter San Jose Mercury News, 1958-62, asst. city editor 1962-65, columnist 1965–; dir: Redwood Mutual Water Co. 1971-72, Edgecombe Corp. (bd. chmn. 1982–), San Jose Trolley Corp. 1988–; trustee Centre for Living with Dying 1979-81; trustee Villa Montalvo Ctr. for the Arts 1988-94, 95–; mem. SJSU Alumni Assn. (dir. 1985–), Sigma Chi Frat., Rotary Club (dir. 1988); author: Insider's Guide to Silicon Valley, 1986, 92; librettist (musical comedy) The Ghosts of Sarah Winchester, 1983; mil: sp4 AUS 1958-60; Democrat; Catholic; rec: music, gardening. Ofc: San Jose Mercury News 750 Ridder Park Dr San Jose 95190

WEINBERG, HORST DAVID, pediatrician; b. Feb. 28, 1928, Halle, Germany (nat. 1951); s. Max H. and Käthe (Benjamin) W.; m. Carol Madeline DeSandre, June 2, 1956; children: David b.1958, Susan b. 1963, Carla b. 1967; edn: BS, Univ. of Michigan 1949; MD, Univ. of Chicago Sch. Medicine 1953; lic. physician St. of Calif. 1957; cert. Am. Bd. Pediatrics 1959. Career: internship Cincinnati Gen. Hosp. 1953-54; pediatric residency St. Christopher's Hosp. for Children, Phila. 1954-55, 57-59, Children's Hosp. Med. Ctr., Oakland 1958-59; pvt. practice pediatrics, Fresno, Calif. 1959-93; pt. time pediatric practice, Fresno Pediatric Group 1993–; active staff Valley Children's Hosp. (Pediatric Neurology Clinic, pt. time, 1993–, quality assurance reviewer 1991–, med. dir. Acute Med. Units 1993–, med. dir. Pediatric Intensive Care Unit 1980-84, co-dir. Burn Unit 1970-74, chmn. Med. Staff 1970-72, pediatrician Cardiac Surgical Team 1959-72); courtesy staff: St. Agnes Hosp., Fresno Comm. Hosp., Clovis Comm. Hosp., Valley Med. Ctr. (chmn. pediatrics dept. 1959-61); asst. clin. prof. pediatrics UC San Francisco 1981-88, assoc. clin. prof. pediatrics 1988–; bd. dirs.: Fresno Found. Mentally Retarded 1960-63, Central Valley Heart Assn. 1969-74, Fresno Co. CHDP Bd. (2 yrs.); awards: Disting. Achievement award Am. Heart Assn., Central Valley Heart Assn.; Special Resident Tchg. award Valley Children's Hosp. 1989; mem: Am. Acad. of

Pediatrics, AMA, CMA, Fresno Madera Med. Soc.; host weekly TV prog. "The Doctor Is In", Ch. 24, 1993–; author: contbr. 19 articles to profl. jours., 1970-93; mil: capt. USAF 1955-57; rec: salt water fishing, reading. Ofc: 2983 West Pembrook Loop Fresno 93711

WEINBERG, WILLIAM HENRY, professor of chemical and nuclear engineering, and chemistry; b. Dec. 5, 1944, Columbia, S.C.; s. Vivian Ulric and Ruth W.; m. Ann Elizabeth, Mar. 25, 1989; edn: BS, Univ. South Carolina, 1966; PhD, UC Berkeley, 1970; NATO postdoctoral fellowship Univ. of Cambridge 1971. Career: asst. prof. chem. engring. Calif. Inst. of Technology, Pasadena 1972-74; assoc. prof. 1974-77, prof. chem. engring. and chem. physics, 1977-89, Chevron prof. 1981-86; prof. chem. and nuclear engring. and chem., UC Santa Barbara, 1989–, assoc. dean Coll. of Engring. 1992–; vis. prof. chem. Harvard Univ., 1980, Univ. Pittsburgh, 1987-88; Materials Dept., Univ. of Oxford 1991; Alexander von Humboldt Found. fellow Univ. Munich, 1982; cons. E.I. DuPont Co.; awards: Phi Beta Kappa, Sigma Xi, fellow NSF 1966-69, Alfred P. Sloan Found. 1976-78, Camille and Henry Dreyfus Found. fellow 1976-81, Wayne B. Nottingham Prize Am. Phys. Soc. 1972, Victor K. LaMer Award Am. Chem. Soc. 1973, Allen P. Colburn Award AIChE 1981, Giuseppe Parravano Award Mich. Catalysis Soc. 1989, Kendell Award Am. Chem. Soc. 1991, Arthur W. Adamson Award Am. Chem. Soc. 1995, Disting. Teaching award Coll. of Engring., UC Santa Barbara 1995; mem: Am. Physical Soc. (Fellow), Am. Chem. Soc., AIChE, AAAS, Am. Vacuum Soc. (Fellow), Nat. Acad. of Engring. (USA); author: Low-Energy Electron Diffraction 1986, 430+ journal articles, 1970–, editor 4 books in field, editl. bd. Jour. Applications Surface Sci., 1977-85, Handbook Surfaces and Interfaces, 1978-80, Surface Sci. Reports (1980–, general editor 1992–), Applied Surface Sci., 1985–, Langmuir, 1990–, Surface Sci., 1991–. Ofc: Dept. of Chemical Engineering, Univ. California, Santa Barbara 93106-5080

WEINY, GEORGE AZEM, educator, aquatics consultant; b. July 24, 1933, Keokuk, Iowa; s. George Dunn and Emma Vivian (Kraushaar) W.; m. Jane Louise Eland, Sept. 29, 1956 (div. 1985); children: Tami L., Tomas A., Aaron A., Arden G.; m. Lori Arlene Rowe, Aug. 1985; children: Austin George, Breck Philip; edn: BA, Iowa Wesleyan Coll., 1957; MA, State Univ. Iowa, 1962; PhD, Univ. Beverly Hills, 1980. Career: phys. dir. YMCA, Keokuk, 1956-57; asst. dir. pub. relations Iowa Wesleyan Coll., Mt. Pleasant, Iowa 1957-58; prin., tchr., coach Hillsboro (Iowa) High Sch. 1958-59; tchr., coach Burlington (Iowa) High Sch. and Jr. Coll., 1959-62, Pacific High Sch., San Bernardino 1962-67; prof. phys. edn. CSU San Bernardino 1967–; ednl. cons. Belau Modekngei Sch., West Caroline Islands 1984-85; swim meet dir. Nat. Collegiate Athletic Assn., 1982-84, 86-92; tng. dir. for ofcls. So. Calif. Aquatics Fedn., 1967-78; scuba tour guide Dive Maui Resort, Hawaii 1982-83; salvage diver U.S. Trust Territories, 1973; coach YMCA swim team, San Bernardino 1962-77, 84-93; awards: Who's Who Among Students in Univs. & Colls. 1953, outstanding service So. Calif. Aquatics Fedn. 1978, 25-yr. service NISCA, 1985, 25-yr. service Coll. Swim Coaches Assn. 1987, 40-Yr. Outstanding svc. Commodore Longfellow Award Am. Red Cross, 1991; listed Who's Who in Am. Edn. 1992; mem: Profl. Assn. Diving Instrs. (cert.), Nat. Assn. Underwater Instrs. (cert.), Am. Assn. Health Phys. Edn. Recreation and Dance, Coll. Swim Coaches Assn., Am. Swim Coaches Assn. (cert.), Nat. Interscholastic Swim Coaches Assn. (NISCA); civic: Am. Red Cross (county water safety com. San Bdo. 1968-80), YMCA (bd. 1970-77), Bicentennial Commn. San Bdo. 1975-76; club: Sea Sons Dive, Rialto (pres. 1982-83, sec. 1983-93); ed. Swimming Rules and Case Studies, 1970-73, author Snorkeling Fun for Everyone, 1982, contbr. articles various publs.; mil: sgt. U.S. Army 1953-55, named outstanding trainee US Army 1954, Iowa Nat. Guard (SFC) 1955-58; rec: scuba. Res: PO Box 30393 San Bernardino 92413 Ofc: California State University 5500 University Pkwy San Bernardino 92407

WEISMAN, PAUL HOWARD, tax attorney; b. Oct. 14, 1957, Los Angeles; s. Albert Leon and Rose (Zimman) W.; m. Allison Leigh Minas, Oct. 19, 1985; 2 sons, Alec Bryan b. 1989, Matthew Jason b. 1991; edn: BA, UC Davis 1979; JD, Loyola Law Sch. 1982. Career: tax atty. Office of Chief Counsel I.R.S. Dept. of Treasury, legislation and regulation div., Wash. D.C. 1982-83, sr. tax atty. Dist. Counsel, Los Angeles 1983-87; assoc. tax atty. Goldfarb Sturman Averbach & Sturman, Encino 1990; sole practitioner 1991–; player's contract rep. Nat. Football League Player's Assn.; awards: Ofc. of Chief Counsel Dept. of Treasury Co-Atty. of Year Western Region 1987) Spl. Achievement award 1986) mem: Beverly Hills Bar Assn. (tax sect.), L.A. Co. Bar Assn. (co-chmn. tax court prose pgm.), S.F. Valley Bar Assn.; Republican; Jewish; rec: sports, politics, art. Res: 24425 Fieldmont Pl West Hills 91307 Ofc: 15301 Ventura Blvd #300 Sherman Oaks 91307

WEISS, MALCOLM CHARLES, lawyer; b. Aug. 9, 1956, Richmond, Va.; s. Leo and Iylene Lila (Rosenbaum) W.; edn: BA political sci., UCSB 1979; BA environ., 1979; JD, Law Sch. Lewis & Clark Coll. 1982; admitted St. Bar Calif. (1983). Career: staff asst. U.S. Congress, Wash. D.C. 1977; staff writer Daily Journal, L.A. 1982; cons. Sobotka Inc., Wash. D.C. 1983; environ. splst. U.S. E.P.A. 1983; mgr. AERX div. RMT Inc., Wash. D.C. 1984-86, L.A. 1986-88; atty., ptnr. McClintock Weston Benshoof Rochefort Rubalcava & MacCuish, L.A. 1988–; instr. Air Pollution Control Assn., N.Y. and Phila., Pa. 1981-86;

instr. UCSB extension 1988; awards: UCSB Dean's List Scholar 1978-79, Sch. Law Lewis & Clark Coll. Cert. Environ. & Natural Resources Law 1982, spl. appointment Secty. Envion. Affairs 1988; mem: Air Pollution Control Assn., Am. Bar Assn., Environ. Auditing Forum (steering com. 1986–), L.A. Co. Bar Assn.; 10 articles pub. in profl. jours., 1981-88; Democrat; Jewish; rec: skiing, sports, computers. Res: 10519 Clarkson Rd Los Angeles 90064 Ofc: McClintock Weston Benshoof Rochefort Rubalcava & MacCuish 444 S Flower St 43rd Floor Los Angeles 90071

WEISS, WALTER S., lawyer; b. March 12, 1929, Newark, N.J.; s. Jack and Mollie (Orkin) W.; m. Jacqueline Levit, Sept. 2, 1963 (div. 1984); m. Misty Moore, Sept. 25, 1988; children: Jack b. 1964, Andrew b. 1968; edn: BA, Rutgers Univ. 1949; JD, 1952; admitted St. Bar Calif., N.J., Distr. of Columbia. Career: trial atty. I.R.S., Phila., Pa., and L.A. 1957-61; asst. U.S. atty. chief tax div. U.S. Attys. Office, L.A. 1961-62; ptnr. Goodson & Hannam 1962-67; mng. ptnr. Long & Levit 1967-79; ptnr. Greenberg & Glusker 1979-81; ptnr. Rosenfeld Meyer & Susman, Beverly Hills 1981-93; Law Office of Walter S. Weiss 1993–; arbitrator Nat. Assn. Security Dealers 1975–, Pacific Stock Exchange 1975–; lectr. Univ. of Calif., State Bar of Calif.; chmn. Advy. Council Econ. Devel. St. Calif. 1981-85; mem: Am. Coll. Trial Lawyers (fellow), Conf. Ins. Counsel (pres.), Am. Bar Assn., Beverly Hills Bar Assn., L.A. Co. Bar Assn.; articles pub. in profl. jours.; mil: capt. USAF 1953-56; Democrat; rec: tennis. Ofc: 12424 Wilshire Blvd Los Angeles 90025

WELCH, NANCY RODGER, psychotherapist; b. June 9, 1931, Phila.; d. Alexander Laing and Annie (Patterson) Rodger; m. Clyde Ray Welch, Oct. 31, 1954 (dec. 1966); children: Rodger Laing b. 1956, Scott David b. 1960; edn: BA (magna cum laude), Cal Western Univ., San Diego 1973; MA, US Internat. Univ. Grad. Sch. of Human Behav., 1976; Calif. Comm. Colls. counselor 1977; Marriage Family Therapist (MFT) 1979. Career: field placement intern Juv. Div. Prob. Dept., San Diego 1975-76; intern family case worker Family Service Assn., San Deigo 1976-77, family caseworker 1977-79; marriage family therapist US Navy Family Service Pilot Pgm., S.D. 1979-80, dep. dir. Navy Family Serv. Ctr., San Diego 1980-90, dir. 1990–; appointed specialty advr. to Navy Surgeon General, Bureau of Medicine, Wash., D.C.. in marriage, family therapy 1995; appt. to Commn. of Youth, Families and Children 1995; panel mem. San Diego Commn. on Youth & Children 1986-94, S.D. Welfare Advy. Bd. 1985-86, US Naval Acad. Bd. of Admission, Coronado 1975-90, Armed Services YMCA (1982–, co-chair 1981-82, chair 1989-90, mil. communities task team); honors: Psi Chi Nat. Honor Soc. 1972, listed World Who's Who of Women 1984-85, Who's Who of Am. Women 1984-85, 88-89, Who's Who in Calif. 1990-91; Fellow Am. Orthopsychiatric Assn.; clin. mem: Am. Assn. Marriage Family Therapist; MA thesis: Personality Traits as they relate to the marriage committment, 1976; Republican; Episcopalian; rec: numismatics, philately. Ofc: Director, Family Service Center NAS Miramar San Diego 92145

WELLS, JOHN S., physician; b. June 15, 1934, San Francisco; s. Phillip H. and Marguerite (Brown) W.; m. Retha, 1962 (div. 1971); m. 2d. Judith A. Martois, July 7, 1973; children: Phillip b. 1963, Charles b. 1964, Martin b. 1977, Matthew b. 1979; edn: BA, Stanford Univ. 1956; MD, Univ. Iowa 1965. Career: physician, Arcadia 1969–; deputy dir. Los Angeles Co. Dept Mental Health 1970-93 (ret.); chief of psychiatry Riverside Co. Gen. Hosp. Dept. of Mental Health 1993–; asst. prof. psychiatry USC, L.A. 1977–; mem: Am. Psychiatric Assn. (fellow), So. Calif. Psychiatric Soc. (Councilor 1991-94), Arcadia Police Dept. (res. ofcr. 1980–), BSA (asst. scoutmaster 1988-94); mil: lt. USNR 1958-61; Presbyterian; rec: skiing, computers, hiking. Ofc: 735 Duarte Rd #405 Arcadia 91007

WELSH, WILLIAM DANIEL, physician; b. May 18, 1950, Baltimore, Md.; s. Joseph Leo and Bessie Mary (Tangires) W.; m. Lorraine Lynn Barkhaus; children: Sean William, Ryan Daniel; edn: BS in biol., cum laude, Fairleigh Dickinson Univ. 1972; Russian lang. stu. Johns Hopkins Univ. 1971; D.O. Coll. of Osteopathic Med. and Surg. 1975; lic. Calif., Mich.; bd. cert. Am. Coll. of Osteopathic Family Practitioners; Diplomate Nat. Bds. 1976. Career: tng. clerkships, Mercy Hosp., Baltimore, COMS Coll. Clinics, Des Moines, Haight Ashbury (S.F.) Free Clinic; resident internal medicine Martin Place Hosp., Madison Hts., Mich. 1975-77; physician/ptnr. Family Practice Associates, Whittier 1979–; mem. Friendly Hills Health Network; med. dir. alcohol treatment pgm. Whittier Hosp. Medical Ctr., mem. bd. dirs. 1983-92 (past: exec. com., v.chief staff, dir. emergency dept., chmn. EG and transfusion com.); med. dir. Mirada Hills Rehab. Hosp. 1980-86; admissions com. Coll. of Osteopathic Med. of the Pacific, clin. assoc. prof. 1980-89; A.C.L.S. instr., past med. dir. Family Asthma Forum 1978-85; honors: Phi Zeta Kappa (FDU), Recognition Awards Pathology 1973, 74; mem: Am. Osteopathic Assn., Calif. Osteo. Assn., Los Angeles Co. Osteo. Assn.; patron Coll. of Osteo. Med. & Surg. Alumni, UCLA Alumni, Loyola H.S., Coll. of Osteo. Med. of the Pacific; publs: op-ed NY Times; Christian; rec: ocean boating, skiing. Res: 15705 Gun Tree Dr Hacienda Heights 91745-6346 Ofc: 14350 E Whittier Blvd Ste 100 Whittier 90603

WELTON, MICHAEL PETER, dentist; b. Apr. 19, 1957, Milw.; s. Lloyd Peter and Allegra Irene (Nimmer) W.; m. Etsuko Suehiro, Nov. 21, 1986 (div. 1993); m.2d. Lucia Aldon, Jan. 29, 1994; edn: BS biology, Carroll Coll. 1979;

DDS, Univ. of Minn. Sch. of Dentistry, Mpls. 1983. Career: served to lt. USN 1983-90; gen. practice resident in dentistry Naval Hosp., Camp Pendleton, Oceanside, Calif. 1983-84, periodontics dept. Naval Dental Clinic, Yokosuka, Japan 1984-85, clinic director Negishi Dental Annex, Yokohama, Japan 1985-87, general dentist Br. Dental Clinic Mare Island, Vallejo, Calif. 1987-90, div. officer 1988-90; general practice Gateway Dental Office, Rohnert Park, Calif. 1990-91, Napa Valley Comm. Dental Clinic, Napa 1991-92; awards: legislative extern Am. Student Dental Assn., W.D.C. 1982, outstanding achiev. Delta Sigma Delta 1983; mem.: Am. Dental Assn. 1979–, Calif. Dental Assn. 1987–, Napa Solano Dent. Soc. (com. chmn. 1988–), Commonwealth Club Calif. (S.F.), World Affairs Council No. Calif. (S.F.), Art Deco Soc. Calif. (S.F.), No. Calif. Golf Assn. (Pebble Beach); Republican; rec: golf, skiing. Res: 480 Evelyn Circle Vallejo 94589 Ofc: 3000 Alamo Dr Ste103 Vacaville 95687

WELTY, JOHN D., university president and professor of counselor education; b. Aug. 24, 1944, Amboy, Ill.; s. John Donald and Doris Ellen (Donnelly) W.; children: Anne b. 1970, Elisabeth b. 1973; edn: BS, Western Ill. Univ., Macomb, 1965; MA, Mich. State Univ., E. Lansing, 1967; EdD, Indiana Univ., Bloomington, 1974. Career: asst. dir./admissions counselor Michigan State Univ., E. Lansing, 1966-67; chair, div. of student develop./instr. of edn. Southwest State Univ., Marshall, Minn., 1967-72; doctoral studies, 1972-73; asst. v.p. student affairs/prof. of edn. Southwest State Univ. 1973-74; dir. of residences/adj. asst. prof. State Univ. of N.Y., Albany 1974-77, assoc. dean student affairs/dir. of residences, 1977-80; v.p. student affairs Indiana Univ. of Penn., Indiana, PA 1980-84, pres. 1984-91; pres. Calif. State Univ., Fresno 1991–; cons. Ill. State Univ., Rider Coll., Southwest Minn. State Univ., Thomas Jefferson Univ.; awards: SUNY Chancellor's award for excellence in adminstrn. 1977; ACPA Commission III Outstanding Svc. award 1979; Robert H. Shaffer Dist. Alumnus award Indiana Univ., Bloomington 1986, Distinguished Alumni Award Western Ill. Univ. 1994; listed: Who's Who in Am., Who's Who in the East; mem.: Am. Coll. Personnel Assn., Am. Assn. of State Colls. & Univs., Am. Counsel on Edn., Am. Assn. of Higher Edn.; bd. mem.: Fresno Co. Econ. Devel. Corp., Fresno 1992–, Fresno Comm. Hosp. 1992–, Fresno Bus. Council 1993–; co-author: Five Strategies for Eliminating Alcohol and Other Drug Abuse on Campus: Guide for College Presidents and Governing Boards, 1990; Roman Catholic; rec: golf, jogging, racquetball, reading. Res: 4411 North Van Ness Blvd Fresno 93704 Ofc: Office of the President CSU Fresno 93740-0048

WENDELL, PETER C., venture capitalist, educator; b. May 16, 1950, Englewood, NJ; s. Eugene O. and Virginia M. (Robiolio) W.; m. Lynn Mellen, June 14, 1980; children: Christopher b. 1981, Brian b. 1982, Jennifer b. 1984, Carolyn b. 1985, Patrick b. 1988, Emily b. 1990; edn: AB, magna cum laude, Princeton Univ. 1972; MBA, w/high distinction, Harvard Univ. 1976. Career: asst. to Dr. Geo. Gallup Poll, Inc., Princeton, NJ 1971-72; corporate exec. IBM Corp., held 5 positions Data Processing Div., N.Y.C., White Plains and Chgo., 1972-81; pres., gen. ptnr. Sierra Ventures Mgmt. Co., $250 million venture capital fund, Menlo Park, Calif.; dir.: Intuit, Inc., Menlo Park, Centex Telecommunications Inc., S.F., Providential Corp., S.F.; prof. of entrepreneurship Stanford Univ. Grad. Sch. of Business 1990–; civic bds: Exploratorium (S.F.); clubs: Pacific Union Club, NY Athletic, Harvard (NYC), Princeton (NYC), Univ. Cottage (Princeton); contbr. Journal of Higher Edn. (1980, Ohio St. Univ. Press); R.Cath.; rec: squash, running, lacrosse. Ofc: Sierra Ventures, 3000 Sand Hill Rd Menlo Park 94025

WENDER, FERN Z., lawyer; b. Dec. 6, 1948, Milwaukee, Wis.; d. Benjamin and Nell Sybil (Lubin) Zelonky; m. Ronald H. Wender, Sept. 1, 1968; children: Evan Todd b. 1972, Alison Courtney b. 1974; edn: BA, Barnard Coll. 1970; JD, Southwestern Univ. Sch. Law 1986; admitted St. Bar Calif. (1987). Career: atty. Lichtig, Ellis & Meyberg, Los Angeles, 1986-87; Sheppard, Mullin, Richter & Hampton, 1987-91; Zimmerman, Rosenfeld and Gersh, Beverly Hills, 1991–; Cont. Edn. Bar; Child Custody Visitation Com. St. Bar Calif.; Family Law Exec. Com. L.A. County Bar 1992–; mediator L.A. Superior Court 1991–; Atty. Fee Mediator L.A. Co. Bar 1992–; awards: human relations L.A. Co. (1987), outstanding service City of Beverly Hills (1982-84), outstanding community service City of New Orleans (1970); mem: Southwestern Law Sch. Themis Soc., Am. Bar Assn., Am. Trial Lawyers Assn., L.A. Co. Bar Assn., Beverly Hills Bar Assn., Am. Assn. Bus. Trial Lawyers, Women Lawyers Assn., Columbia Univ. Alumna; rec: sports, theatre, travel. Res: 9577 Lime Orchard Rd Beverly Hills 90210 Ofc: Zimmerman, Rosenfeld and Gersh, 9107 Wilshire Blvd Ste 300 Beverly Hills 90210

WENTWORTH, THEODORE SUMNER, personal injury lawyer; b. July 18, 1938, Brooklyn, NY; s. Theodore S., Sr., and Alice Ruth (Wortmann) W.; m. Sharon Arkush, Mar. 26, 1965 (dec. 1987); children: Christina Linn b. 1968, Kathryn Allison b. 1969; m. Diana von Welanetz, Dec. 9, 1989; stepdau. Lexi b. 1968; edn: JD, UC Hastings Coll. of Law 1962. Career: atty., assoc. Adams, Hunt & Martin, Santa Ana 1963-66; ptnr. Hunt Liljestrom & Wentworth 1967-77; prin. Law Offices of Theodore S. Wentworth, 1978–; pres. InterProfessional Leasing Inc. 1970-78; dir. Don Burns Inc. and Don Burns Prestige Porsche Audi, Garden Grove, 1970-76; owner Rancho Oro Verde, Pauma Valley 1970-78; owner, developer Eagles Ridge, Temecula 1985–; diplomate Nat. Bd. of

Trial Advocates; mem: Calif. Bar Assn., Orange Co. Bar Assn. (bd. dirs. 1972-6), Amer. Trial Lawyers Assn., Calif. Trial Lawyers Assn. (bd. govs. 1968-70), O.C. Trial Lawyers Assn. (pres. 1967-8, Judge pro tem, Attys. Panel 1968-),Lawyer Pilot Bar Assn., Aircraft Owners & Pilots Assn.; civic: Santa Ana -Tustin Comm. Chest (pres. 1972), So. Orange Co. United Way (v.p., dir. 1973-74), Orange Co. Fedn. of Funds (pres. 1972-3), Orange Co. Mental Health Assn. (dir. 1971-74); clubs: Center (Costa Mesa), Pacific (Newport Bch), Balboa Bay (Newport Bch), Bahia Corinthian Yacht (Newport Bch), Corsair Yacht (Emerald Bay, Catalina Is.),Fourth of July Yacht Club (Catalina Is.), Club 33 (Anaheim); works: Vedic researcher & lectr. synthesizing Eastern & Western laws of living in conjunction with num. Vedic scholars in India; Republican; Christian - Vedic; rec: 51 ft. motor yacht "Salute". Res: Corona del Mar Ofc: 4631 Teller Newport Beach 92660

WERDEGAR, DAVID, physician; b. Sept. 16, 1930, NY, NY; m. Kathryn Mickle, Sept. 1, 1961; children: Maurice Clark b. 1965, Matthew Mickle b. 1969; edn: AB, Cornell Univ. 1952, MA, 1953; MD, NY Med. Coll. 1956; MPH, UC Berkeley 1970. Career: prof. and chair, Dept. of Family & Comm. Medicine, UC Sch. of Medicine, San Francisco 1980-85; dir. San Francisco Dept. of Health 1985-90; prof. Health Policy Inst., UC Sch. of Medicine, San Francisco 1990-91; dir. Calif. Ofc. of Statewide Health Planning & Devel. (appt. by Gov. Pete Wilson) 1991–; asst. prof., assoc. prof. to full prof. and dept. chair, Sch. of Medicine, UCSF 1964-94; awards: Deep Springs coll. scholarship, Telluride Assoc. Fellowship, Academic Senate, Disting. Tchg. UCSF Sch. of Medicine; mem: Soc. of Teachers. of Family Medicine, Am. Public Health Assn., Soc. of Med. Administrators, CMA, Am. Coll. of Physicians, Calif. Acad. Family Medicine; author: books and papers related to primary care, preventive medicine and public health, 1963–; mil: capt. U.S. Army 1961-63. Ofc: California Office of Statewide Planning & Development 1600 9th St Sacramento 95814

WERNER, ROGER H., archaeologist; b. Nov. 11, 1950, N.Y.C.; s. Harry Emile Werner and Rena (Roode) Warren; m. Kathleen Diane Engdahl, Feb. 20, 1982; children: Amber F. Parker (stepdau.) b. 1975, Merly L. b. 1982, Sarah M. b. 1985, Jeremy M. b. 1988; edn: BA, Belkap Coll., 1973; MA, CSU Sonoma, Rohnert Park 1982. Career: curatorial asst. Sonoma State Univ., Rohnert Park 1975-77, staff archaeologist 1977-81; staff archaeologist Lake County Planning Dept., Lakeport 1977; Western Archaeological Ctr., Tucson, Az. 1978; pres. Archaeological Services Inc., Stockton 1979–; instr. CSU Fresno, 1992, San Joaquin Delta Coll. 1991–; mem.: Soc. Profl. Archaeologists 1982–, Soc. of Am. Archaeology 1977–, Soc. of Calif. Archaeology 1977–, Soc. of Historic Archaeology 1991–, Great Basin Anthropol. Conf. 1982–, Am. Soc. of Photogrammetry and Remote Sensing, Geological Soc. of Am., URISA; civic: Kiwanis Club (Stockton), Valley Mountain Regl. Ctr. (pres. 1991-92), Stockton Corral (trustee 1992–, treas. 1993), Colonial Hts. PTSA, Stockton (sec. 1982-83, v.p., 1985-88,); contbr. articles in profl. jours. (1979, 91, 92); Democrat; rec: reading, computers, home improve. Res: 1117 Aberdeen Ave Stockton 95209 Ofc: Archaeological Services, Inc. 8027 Lorraine Ave Ste 218 Stockton 95210

WERNER, SANFORD BENSON, physician, epidemiologist; b. Jan. 5, 1939, Newark, N.J.; s. Theodore and Esther (Schneider) W.; m. Carolyn Jean Morrill, June 23, 1968; children: Zoe b. 1972, Max b. 1975; edn: BA, Rutgers Univ. 1960; MD, Wash. Univ. St. Louis 1964; MPH, UC Berkeley 1970. Career: intern, internal medicine Vanderbilt Hosp., Nashville, Tenn. 1964-65; med. epidemiologist Centers for Disease Control and Prevention, Atlanta, Ga. 1965-67; resident internal medicine Univ. Wash. Hosp., Seattle 1967-69; med. epidemiologist Calif. Dept. of Health Services, Berkeley 1969-87, chief disease investigations section 1987–; cons. Nat. Acad. Scis., Wash. D.C. 1984-85; lectr. UC Berkeley 1971–; honors: Phi Beta Kappa, Centers for Disease Control and Prevention Alumni award 1968; mem: Am. Coll. Epidemiology (fellow), Am. Coll. Preventive Medicine (fellow), Bay Area Infectious Disease Soc., Univ. of Calif. Pub. Health Alumni Assn.; author: Epidemiology for Health Scis., 1974, book chpt. on food poisoning (1980, 86, 92); mil: surgeon USPHS 1965-67; rec: squash, jogging. Ofc: Calif. Dept. of Health Services, Div of Communicable Disease Control, 2151 Berkeley Way Berkeley 94704

WEST, BARRY G., lawyer; b. Feb. 3, 1943, New York; s. Irven M. West and Edith (Eisner) Westermann; m. Sheila Blank, Aug. 6, 1966; children: Stephen b. 1967, Karen b. 1970; edn: BA, Queens Coll. 1963; LL.B, St. Johns Law Sch. 1966; LL.M, Harvard Law Sch. 1967; admitted St. Bar Calif. (1973), N.Y. (1967). Career: atty. Paul Weiss Rifkind Wharton & Garrison, N.Y.C. 1967-72; v.p., gen. counsel Technicolor Inc., Los Angeles 1972-73; ptnr. Greenberg & Glusker 1973-86; Hayutin Rubinroit Praw & Kupietzky 1986-87; Bushkin Gaims Gaines & Jonas 1987-88; Gaims Weil West & Epstein 1988–; honors: edit. St. Johns Law Review, 1964-66; mem: Am. Bar Assn., L.A. Co. Bar Assn., Beverly Hills Bar Assn.; rec: skiing, tennis, travel. Res: 4285 Pasadero Place Tarzana 91356 Ofc: Gaims Weil West & Epstein 1875 Century Park E, Ste 1200 Los Angeles 90067

WEST, JOHN BURNARD, professor of medicine; b. Dec. 27, 1928, Adelaide, Australia (US citizen); s. Esmond Frank and Meta Pauline (Spehr) W.; m. Penelope Hall Banks, Oct. 28, 1967; children: Robert b. 1968, Joanna b. 1971;

edn: MBBS, Adelaide Univ., Adelaide, Australia, 1951; MD, Adelaide Univ., 1958; PhD, London Univ., London, Eng., 1960; DSc, Adelaide Univ., 1980. Career: resident Royal Adelaide Hosp., Adelaide, Australia, 1952; resident Hammersmith Hosp., London, Eng., 1953-55; physiologist Sir Edmund Hillary's Himalayan Expedition, 1960-61; dir. Postgraduate Med. Sch., Resp. Res. Group, London, Eng., 1962-67; reader in medicine Postgraduate Med. Sch., London, Eng., 1968; prof. of medicine, physiology, UC San Diego, Calif., 1969–; leader Am. Med. Res. Expedition to Mt. Everest, 1981; US organizer China-US Conf. on Respiratory Failure, Nanjing, 1986; awards: Josiah H. Macy Jr. Found. Faculty Scholar 1974, Ernst Jung Prize for Medicine, Hamburg, W. Germany, 1977, Presidential Citation, Am. Coll. of Chest Physicians 1977, Kaiser Award for Excellence in Tchg. 1980, Orr Reynolds Prize for History, Am. Physiological Soc. 1987, Doctor Honoris Causa, Univ. of Barcelona, Spain 1987, Cosmos Biosatellite award, NASA 1990, Jeffries Med. Res. award, Am. Inst. of Aeronautics and Astronautics 1992, fellow, AAAS 1987–, founding fellow, Am. Inst. for Med. and Biological Engring. 1992–, disting. lectr. at colleges, universities and profl. assns. in US, Canada, England, Russia, the Philippines, So. Africa, Australia and New Zealand 1971–; mem: Am. Physiological Soc., Am. Soc. for Clinical Investigation, Am. Soc. for Gravitation and Space Biology, Am. Thoracic Soc., Assn. of Am. Physicians, Assn. of Chmn. of Depts. of Physiology, Explorers Club, The Fleischner Soc., Harveian Soc. of London, Internat. Soc. for Mountain Medicine, Physiological Soc. (of Great Britain), We. Assn. of Physicians; fellow, Royal Institution of Great Britain, Royal Geographical Soc.(UK), fgn. mem. Russian Acad. of Sciences; clubs: Hurlingham Club, London, Eng., La Jolla Beach & Tennis Club, S.D.; author, books: Ventilation/Bloodflow and Gas Exchange, 1965, 70, 77, 85, 90 (2 fgn. lang. transl. 1980); Respiratory Physiology-The Essentials, 1974, 80, 85, 90 (12 fgn. lang. transl. 1975-90); ed., Translations in Respiratory Physiology, 1975; ed., Regional Differences in the Lung, 1977; ed., Bioengineering Aspects of the Lung, 1977; Pulmonary Pathophysiology-The Essentials, 1977, 82, 87, 91 (7 fgn. lang. transl. 1978-89); Pulmonary Gas Exchange. I. Ventilation, Bloodflow and Diffusion. II. Organism and Environment, 1980; ed., High Altitude Physiology, 1981; co-editor, High Altitude and Man, 1984; Everest-The Testing Place, 1985; ed., Best & Taylor's Physiological Basis of Medical Practice, 1985, 91 (2 fgn. lang. transl. 1986-89), study guide & self-examination review 1985; co-author, High Altitude Medicine and Physiology, 1989; chief ed. with R.G. Crystal, The Lung: Scientific Foundations (2 vols.) 1991, co-ed. Lung Injury 1992. Ofc: UCSD Dept. of Medicine 0623A, 9500 Gilman Dr, La Jolla 92093-0623

WEST, JULIAN RALPH, photographer; b. Dec. 12, 1915, Hot Springs, S.Dak.; s. Joseph C. and Helen E. (Nason) W.; m. Marvel E. Knorr, May 1, 1937, Alliance, Nebr.; children: Stuart J. b. 1938 (dec. Apr. 28, 1988), R. Bruce b. 1940, Judy (Mrs. Donald L. McDermott) b. 1943; edn: BA, Univ. Okla. 1969; Cert. Profl. Contracts Mgr., CPA (Calif., inactive), Cert. Internal Auditor (inactive). Career: public acct. 1946-49; acct. Office of Auditor General, USAF, 1949-62; audit policy div. Ofc. of Secty. of Defense, Pentagon, 1962-67, chief Procurement Review Div. 1967-73; instr. UCLA Ext. Univ. 1977-81; freelance photography and audio/visual presentations, 1979–; pres. Julmik Enterprises, 1980–; mem: Am. Inst. of CPAs, Nat. Contract Mgmt. Assn. (fellow, past nat. dir.), Internat. Freelance Photogs. Orgn., Assoc. Photographers Internat., Photographic Soc. Internat.; civic: Christian Businessmen's Com. of USA, Hollywood YMCA (bd. govs.); sev. travel clubs; Presbyterian (elder). Res: 1955 No Tamarind Ave, No. 14, Hollywood 90068

WEST, SANDI JEAN, real estate loan agent, marketer of trust deeds, and telecommunications reseller; b. Sept. 12, 1945, San Francisco; d. Lyle Hazen and Georgia Arlene (West) Reiswig; edn: AA (bus. administration), San Joaquin Delta Jr. Coll. 1977. Career: eligibility worker San Joaquin County Welfare Dept., Stockton 1968-75; child support collections supr. San Joaquin County Dist. Atty.'s Ofc., Stockton 1975-79; credit mgr. E.D. Wilkinson Grain Co., Stockton 1979-80; agent, estates mgr. Calif. Dept. Devel. Svcs., Sacramento 1980-85; trust ofcr. Sonoma Devel. Ctr., Eldridge 1985-88; pres. West and Associates, Sonoma 1989–; dist. dir. Communications Group of Am. (CGA), Vacaville 1992–; fund raising coord. Sonoma Co. NOW 1993–, Calif. NOW (fundraising com. 1995–, fin./budget com 1995–); loaned executive alumni United Way for North Bay 1990–, loaned exec. United Way for North Bay 1989; vol. police ofcr. Stockton Police Dept. 1968-74; Nonpartisan. Res: POB 1488 Eldridge 95431-1488 Ofc: West and Associates 164 Vista Dr Sonoma 95476 Tel:707/935-0486; Ofc: CGA 479 Mason St #213 Vacaville 95688 Tel: 707/448-1071

WESTERDAHL, JOHN BRIAN, nutritionist, health educator; b. Dec. 3, 1954, Tucson, Ariz.; s. Jay Emanuel and Margaret Camille (Meyer) W.; m. Doris Mui Lian Tan, Nov. 18, 1989; edn: AA, Orange Coast Coll., Costa Mesa, Calif. 1977; BS, Pacific Union Coll., Angwin, Calif. 1979; MPH, Loma Linda Univ., Loma Linda, Calif. 1981; reg. dietitian Am. Dietetic Assn., 1983. Career: nutritionist, health educator Castle Medical Ctr., Kailua, Hawaii, 1981-84, health promotion coord. 1984-87, asst. dir., dir. of health promotion 1987-89; dir. nutrition and health research Health Science, Santa Barbara, Calif. 1989-90; senior nutritionist Shaklee Corp., San Francisco 1990–; talk show host "Nutrition and

You" KGU Radio, Honolulu 1983-89; apptd. mem. nutrition study gp. Gov.'s Conf. on Health Promotion and Disease Prevention for Hawaii, 1985; nutrition com. mem. Am. Heart Assn. Hawaii Div. 1984-87; awards: Outstanding Young Men of Am. US Jaycees 1984, One of 10 Outstanding Young Persons in Hawaii, Hawaii Jaycees 1988; mem: AAAS, Am. Coll. of Sports Medicine, Am. Dietetic Assn., Calif. Dietetic Assn., Am. Coll. of Nutrition, Am. Soc. Pharmacognosy, NY Acad. Scis., Hawaii Nutrition Council (v.p. 1983-86, pres. 1989), Seventh-Day Adventist Dietetic Assn.; Republican; Seventh-Day Adventist; rec: swimming, scuba. Ofc: Shaklee Corp. 444 Market St San Francisco 94111

WESTIN, PHILIP, college president; b. May 6, 1945, Providence, R.I.; s. John Andrew and Gertrude M. (Nelson) W.; m. Barbara Jean Christiansen, Oct. 1, 1966; children: Michele b. 1970, Cynthia b. 1972; m. 2d. Ellisha Marion Bunka, June 7, 1980; stepdaughters: Susan b. 1953, Karen b. 1957; edn: MusB, Univ. of So. Calif., L.A. 1968, MusM, 1970; EdD, Univ. of La Verne, La Verne, Calif., 1990; certificate, Harvard Univ. 1992. Career: instr. Cerritos Coll., Norwalk, Calif. 1970-75, prof. and dept. chair, 1975-85; dean of fine arts El Camino Coll., Torrance, Calif. 1985-86, dean and exec. dir., 1986-91; v.p. instruction Golden West Coll., Huntington Beach, Calif. 1991-93, pres. 1993–; music dir.: Calif. Wind Symphony, Torrance, Calif. 1973-74, Master Symphony Orch., L.A. 1980-84; guest conductor Brown Univ. and Mich. State Univ. 1984; prof. in doctoral prog. Pepperdine Univ., L.A. 1994–; awards: Emmy award nominee CBS-TV 1971, 1st place composition award Nat. Guild of Organists 1979, Comm. Spotlight award La Mirada City Council 1980, Symphony Recognition award Coll. Band Dirs. Assn. 1986, certificate from Comm. Coll. League, Sacto. 1992; mem.: Assn. of Calif. Comm. Coll. Adminstrs. 1989–, Comm. Coll. League 1990–, League for Innovation 1991–, Am. Assn. of Comm. Colls. 1992–, Am. Assn. of Higher Edn. 1992–; composer: symphony, Song of Adoration, 1976, Symphony for Band, 1978; author: dissertation, Experiential Learning in Higher Education Performing Arts, 1990; Democrat; Presbyterian; rec; computing. Ofc: Golden West College 15744 Golden West St Huntington Beach 92647

WESTLAND, JAMES CHRISTOPHER, computer scientist, economist; b. Nov. 17, 1949, Indianapolis, Ind.; s. John Joseph and Mary (Elliott) W.; m. Randa Assad Al-Awar, April 27, 1984; children: Summar b. 1986 Dina b. 1988; edn: BA math., Ind. Univ. 1971; MBA, 1973; PhD, Univ. Mich. 1987. Career: CPA staff, Touche Ross, Chgo. 1973-75; accts. payable mgr. Federated Dept. Store, Dallas 1973; EDP mgr. Republic Life Ins., Dallas 1975-76; Security Plajr, dba Rockwell Internat., Dallas 1976-81; founder, chmn. bd. Synthesis Computer Tech., Long Beach; assoc. prof. Univ. So. Calif.; honors: Beta Alpha Psi, U.S. Dept. Edn. Flas fellow 1987, Arthur Andersen fellow 1986, Univ. Mich. Paton fellow 1981-84, tchg. excellence Dynstra 1985; mem: Am. Inst. C.P.A., Inst. Mgmt. Sci., Assn. Computing Machinery, Am. Statistical Assn.; num. scholarly reports pub. 1980–; Republican; Episcopalian; rec: piano, chess, skiing. Res: 6209 Greenmeadow Lakewood 90713 Ofc: Univ. of So. Calif. 401-F Bridge Hall Los Angeles 90089-1421

WESTLY, STEVEN PAUL, investment banker; b. Aug. 27, 1956, Los Angeles; s. Roy Messell and Sylvia (Snow) Elliott W.; edn: BA, Stanford Univ. 1978; MBA, 1983. Career: asst. to pres. Calif. Pub. Utility Commn., San Francisco 1980-81; mgr. new bus. GTE Sprint, Burlingame 1982-86; dir. mktg. Pacific Concessions, South S.F. 1986-88; mng. dir. Bridgemere Capital, San Francisco 1988-89; faculty, Stanford Grad. Sch. of Business 1991–; bd. trustees Stanford Univ. 1977, 83; advy. bd. Univ. of San Francisco School of Bus.; Stanford Univ. Student Body pres. 1977-78; mem: Youth & Family Assistance, Sequoia YMCA, Center for Econ. Conversion; ed. Energy Efficiency on Utilities: New Directions, Energy Utilities: Next Ten Years; Democrat (Dem. Party st. controller 1983-85, No. Calif. chmn. 1985-87, state v. chmn. 1987-89, Nat. Com. mem. 1988–); Presbyterian; rec: tennis. Res: 2120 Camino de los Robles Menlo Park 94025

WESTON, J. FRED, economist, professor emeritus; b. Feb. 6, 1916, Ft. Wayne, Ind.; s. David Thomas and Bertha (Schwartz) W.; m. June Sherman, May 16, 1942 (dec. 1986); children: Kenneth F. b. 1945, Byron L. b. 1948, Ellen J. b. 1949; m. Eva Dixon, Jan. 3, 1987; edn: AB, MBA, PhD, Univ. of Chicago, 1937, 43, 48. Career: instr. Univ. Chgo. 1940-42; economic cons. to the pres. American Bankers Assn. 1945-46; asst. prof. Univ. Chgo. 1947-48; prof./emeritus UCLA, Los Angeles 1949–, dir. res. pgm. in competition and bus. policy Anderson Grad. Sch. of Mgmt. UCLA 1969–, dir. Res. Ctr. for Managerial Economics and Pub. Policy, AGSM-UCLA 1983-85; awards: Cardinal O'Hara Memorial lectr. Notre Dame Univ. 1965, Disting. Lecture Series- Univ. Okla. 1967, Miss. St. Univ., Univ. Utah 1972, Wright St. Univ., Miami St. Univ. 1975, disting. tchg. UCLA 1978, Cordner Chair, UCLA 1983; mem: Western Economic Assn. (pres. 1960), Am. Finance Assn. (pres. 1966), Western Finance Assn. (honoree for contbns. to fin., S.F., 6/79), Am. Econ. Assn., Econometric Soc., Am. Statistical Assn., Royal Econ. Soc., Financial Analysts Soc., Financial Mgmt. Assn. (pres. 1979-80, exec. bd. 81-83); editl. bds: Business Economics, J. of Financial Res., Managerial and Decision Economics, Southern Business Review; coauthor 5 texts, contbr. articles to profl. jours.; mil: chief warrant ofcr. Ord. D., US Army 1943-45; Indep.; rec: music, walking, tennis, dancing. Res: 258 Tavistock Ave Los Angeles 90049-3229 Ofc: UCLA 110 Westwood Plaza Los Angeles 90095-1481

WETTACH, GEORGE EDWARD, physician; b. June 11, 1940, San Jose; s. George Angevine and Glodine Lillian (Wilks) W.; m. Rose Ann Nemeth, Nov. 24, 1966 (div. Mar. 1988); children: George Randolphe b. 1971, Shannon Elizabeth b. 1977, Robin Scot b. 1978; m. Linda Kay Ridgley, June 10, 1989; edn: pre-med., San Jose State Coll., 1962; MD, St. Louis Univ., 1966. Career: internship St. Louis City Hosp., St. Louis, Mo. 1966-67; USN flight surgeon, RVN, 1968-70; med. resident Highland Gen. Hosp., Oakland, Calif. 1970-71; cardiac fellowship Huntington Meml. Hosp./USC, Pasadena 1971-72; cardiac fellowship Stanford Univ. 1972-73; chief medical resident St. Louis Univ. 1973-74; emergency physician St. Louis (Mo.) City Hosp., 1974-75, St. John's Mercy Med. Ctr., Creve Coeur, Mo. 1975-77; med. dir. St. Louis EMS, 1977-85; emergency physician Nat. Emergency Services Inc., Tiburon, Calif. 1985-90; attdg. physician San Francisco Gen. Hosp., 1988–; clin. instr. Univ. Calif., San Francisco 1989–; sr. flight surgeon Naval Air Reserve, Alameda 1990-94, Naval Air Reserve Santa Clara 1994–, chief of cardiology, USNH Oakland 1995–; Capt. Med. Corps USNR, 1968–; pres. Health Edn. Foundation for Television Inc., Menlo Park 1978–; awards: Tau Delta Phi 1959, Nat. Polaroid Photo Contest Award 1985, US Naval Inst. Maritime Photo Contest 1989, stock car racing award Allied Auto Racing Assn., St. Louis, Mo. 1980; mem: Aerospace Med. Assn. (assoc. fellow 1973–), Assn. of Military Surgeons of U.S., U.S. Naval Inst., Naval Reserve Assn., Reserve Ofcrs. Assn.; civic: Pasadena Community Symphonic Orch. (mem. 1971-72), Menlo Park Art Commn. 1987– (chair 1992-93, 1995–); publs: 20+ med. jour. articles (1973-86); Republican; Prot.; rec: stock car racing, music, voice-overs, photog., art. Res: 193 Willow Rd Menlo Park 94025 Ofc: 500 Shenandoah Plaza Moffett Federal Airfield 94035

WEXLER, JUDIE GAFFIN, vice president of academic affairs; b. Apr. 15, 1945, New York; d. Isaac Pearlman and Sara (Widensky) P.; m. Howard M. Wexler, Mar. 11, 1973; children: Robyn b. 1975, Matthew b. 1978; edn: BA, Sociology, Russell Sage Coll., Troy, NY, 1965; MA, Demography, Univ. of Pa., Phila., 1966; PhD, Sociology, UC Berkeley, 1975; career: dir., NY State Dept. of Mental Hygiene, Albany, NY, 1966-67; demographer and urban sociologist, S.F. Dept. of City Planning, S.F., Calif., 1967-68; prof. of sociology, Holy Names Coll., Oakland, Calif., 1974-91; dean of academic affairs, Holy Names Coll., 1992-93, v.p. of academic affairs 1993–; mem: grant proposal review bd., Sociology Prog., NSF, 1990; Am. Sociological Assn.; Am. Psychological Assn., Div. on Women; Calif. Sociological Assn.; Sociologists for Women in Soc.; awards: S.F. Police Dept. Recognition Award, 1984; Pi Gamma Mu, Nat. Social Sci. Honor Soc.; Population Council Fellowship, Univ. of Calif., 1968-69 and 1970-71; NDEA Fellowship, Univ. of Pa., 1965-66; Milhouse Award in Sociology, 1965; listed in Who's Who in the West 1991, Dictionary of Internat. Biography 1990, Internat. Who's Who of Prof. and Bus. Women 1989–; Two Thousand Notable Amer. Women 1988; Personalities of the Americas 1987, Who's Who of Emerging Leaders in Amer. 1987–, Who's Who of Amer. Women 1982–; editor: Berkeley Jour. of Sociology, 1973-74; author: numerous publs. in prof. jours.; papers and lectures presented to prof. assns. and colleges. Ofc: Holy Names College 3500 Mountain Blvd. Oakland 94619

WEXLER, ROBERT D., college president; b. May 10, 1951, Los Angeles, Calif.; s. Irving J. and Miriam G. (Gribs) W.; m. Dr. Hannah Wexler, Dec. 17, 1972; children: Zev b. 1978, Nili b. 1981, Elisheva b. 1984, Daniella b. 1988; edn: BA, UCLA 1971; MA, Rabbinic ordination, Jewish Theological. Sem., NY, NY 1977; MBA, Baruch Coll., CUNY 1980; PhD, UCLA 1992. Career: lectr. Princeton Univ. 1977-78; assoc. dean, Univ. of Judaism, Los Angeles 1978-86, v.p., 1986-92, pres. 1992–; mem: Rabbinical Assembly, Am. Jewish Com., Bd. of Rabbis. Ofc: University of Judaism 15600 Mulholland Dr Los Angeles 90077

WHANG, SUKOO JACK, clinical pathologist; b. Feb. 3, 1934, Korea; nat. 1963; s. Seung Il and Young Sook (Kim) W.; m. Chung A. Park, Nov. 30 1963; children: Selena b. 1964, Stephanie b. 1970, John b. 1972; edn: BS, Ore. St. Univ. 1957; MS, UCLA 1960; PhD, UCLA 1963; MD, Korea Univ. 1972; diplomate Am. Bd. Pathology, Am. Bd. Tropical Medicine, Am. Bd. Medical Microbiology. Career: asst. prof. CSU, Pomona 1963-64; chief microbiologist Providence Hosp., Southfield, Mich. 1964-65; dir. microbiol. immunol. div. Reference Lab., Newbury Park 1965-69; adj. prof. Pacific Union Coll., 1977-87; currently pathologist/dir. microbiology-serology div., White Meml. Med. Ctr., Los Angeles; honors: Sigma Xi, Am. Men & Women of Sci., Who's Who in West; mem: AMA, Calif. Med. Assn., Coll. of Am. Pathologists (Fellow), Am. Coll. Physicians (Fellow), N.Y. Acad. Scis., Soc. of Hosp. Epidemiologists of Am.; res. in clinical microbiol., syphilis serology & diagnostic tests for detection of inborn errors of metabolism; Republican; Seventh Day Adventist; rec: tennis, swimming, music. Res: 1325 Via Del Rey South Pasadena 91030 Ofc: White Memorial Medical Center 1920 Cesar E. Chavez Ave Los Angeles 90033

WHITE, BRIAN WILLIAM, stockbroker; b. Sept. 5, 1934, Seattle; s. George Carlos and Mae Mary (McCann) W.; m. Christine Catherine Nelson, June 2, 1955 (div. 1970); m. Barbara Maureen Scott, May 21, 1974; children: Catherine b. 1956, Teresa b. 1958, Patrick b. 1959, Melissa b. 1962, Christopher b. 1964, Meghan b. 1980, Erin b. 1982; edn: BS, UC Berkeley, 1958, MBA, 1959. Career: acctg. mgr. Pacific NW Bell Tel. Co., Seattle, Wash. 1959-68; reg. rep. Dominick & Dominick, Sea. 1968-74; dir. Western Search Assocs., San Diego

1974-82; investment exec. Bateman Eichler, San Diego 1982-90; pres. White Securities Inc., La Mesa 1990–; Republican; R.Cath.; rec: golf. Res: 1038 Vista Sierra Dr El Cajon 92019 Ofc: 8363 Center Dr Ste 600 La Mesa 91942

WHITE, BRYAN STANFORD, lawyer; b. Feb. 7, 1956, Orange; s. John A. and Millie C. (Parham) W.; m. Juanita Ramirez; edn: AB, UC Berkeley 1978; JD, Duke Univ. 1981; admitted St. Bar Calif. 1981. Career: atty., assoc. McKenna Conner & Cuneo, Los Angeles 1981-86; sr. atty., asst. secty. Maxxam Inc. 1986-90; counsel and asst. secty. Hilton Hotels Corp. 1990–; honors: Phi Beta Kappa; mem: Am. Bar Assn., Am. Corp. Counsel Assn.; Democrat. Res: 1564 Point View St Los Angeles 90035 Ofc: Hilton Hotels Corp 9336 Civic Center Dr Beverly Hills 90210

WHITE, HALBERT LYNN, JR., professor of economics; b. Nov. 19, 1950, Kansas City, Mo.; s. Halbert Lynn and Emily (Roach) W.; m. Kim Adele Titensor, 1986; edn: AB, Princeton Univ. 1972; PhD, MIT 1976. Career: asst. prof. Univ. Rochester, N.Y. 1976-80; assoc. prof. UCSD 1980-84, prof. 1984–; vis. scholar N.C. State Univ., Raleigh 1984; vis. prof. MIT, Cambridge, Mass. 1984; vis. scholar INSEE, CEPREMAP, Paris, France 1985; vis. fellow Oxford Univ., England 1985; chmn.. La Jolla Data Systems 1988-92; cons. Neural Net R&D Assocs. 1992–; awards: Guggenheim fellow 1988-89, Princeton Univ. Valedictorian 1972; mem: Econometric Soc. (fellow), Am. Mathematical Soc., IEEE, Internat. Neural Network Soc., Jazz Soc. Lower So. Calif.; author: Asymptotic Theory for Econometricians, 1984, Estimation Inference & Specification Analysis, 1994, coauthor: Unified Theory of Estimation & Inference for Nonlinear Dynamic Models, 1988, Artifical Neural Networks: Approximation and Learning Theory, 1992, contbr. 60+ articles to profl. jours.; rec: music composition, jazz trumpet. Ofc: Univ. of Calif. San Diego Dept. of Economics La Jolla 92093

WHITE, JAN, business consultant; b. July 14, 1949, Yonkers, N.Y.; d. Max E. and Shirley D. (Hamburger) Feinberg; children: Shawn b. 1972; edn: BA acctg., Columbia Pacific Univ. 1984. Career: asst. gen. mgr. Greyhound Food Mgmt. Corp.; asst. chief cost acct. United Bank Denver, Colo.; acctg. supr. Payless Stores Corp., corp. offices, Oakland; acctg. mgr. Equitec Fin. Group, Lafayette; controller, cost acctg. mgr. I T Corp., Martinez; cost acctg. mgr. and mgr.- systems design, data processing and budget/forecasting, Membrana Inc., Pleasanton; business consultant, pres. J W Business Solutions; past co-owner/c.f.o. Gamma Graphics, Inc.; appt: comml. arbitrator on behalf of the Am. Arbitration Assn., assoc. ed. of the "Update" (bus. mag.), advsy. bd. of the "Diablo Business" mag.; listed Internat. Who's Who of Profl., Bus. Women, Who's Who in West, 2000 Notable Women in Am., The World Who's Who of Women, Standard & Poor's Register of Corps., Dirs. and Execs.; mem: Nat. Assn. Accts. (dir. 1982-85, 2 tech. manuscript awards), Assoc. Builders & Contractors (referral bus. cons. 1987–), Bay Area Soc. Info. Centers, Entrepreneurs Assn. Diablo Valley, Walnut Creek C.of C., Contra Costa Council, Internat. Trade Assn.; author: Cost Acctg. Principles and Applications for Layman Use (1984); The Break Even Relationship for Cost Conscious Managers; articles: Power of the Word (philosophical), When It's Time To Take The Band-Aids Off, When It's Time To Find The Right Consultant, Paper Flow Problems May Be Costing You More Than You Realize, Purchasing The Perfect Computer & Software Isn't Enough, Handling Substance Abuse In The Workplace, Pricing Your Services For Long Term Survival; pub. author, media interviews, lectr. seminars; rec: equestrienne, x-c skiing, walking. Ofc: 112 Masters Ct Ste 2 Walnut Creek 94598

WHITE, KATHERINE E., physician, pediatrician; b. Mar. 23, 1920, Syracuse, N.Y.; d. Rufus M. and Marguerite Mary (Eselin) White; m. Nicholas V. Oddo, Feb. 12, 1947 (dec. 1966); edn: BA, Syracuse Univ. 1941; MD, 1943. Career: intern Syracuse Univ. Med. Center, Syracuse, N.Y. 1944-45; asst. resident, chief resident Buffalo Children's Hosp. 1945-47; resident, outpatient dept. Los Angeles Children's Hosp. 1947; pediatrician, Long Beach 1947-90; asst. clin. prof. pediatrics UC Irvine Sch. Medicine 1967–; bd. trustees Miller Children's Hosp., Long Beach 1970–; bd. dirs. Children's Clin. 1974-88; bd. med. edn. Meml. Med. Center & Univ. 1987–; honors: Phi Beta Kappa, Citizen of Year Rotary 1967, recogn. Children's Clinic Long Beach 1981, Meml. Med. Center Found. Commend. 1984, Found. Children's Health Care Humanitarian 1987, Soroptimist Woman of Distinction 1987, Soroptimist Hall of Fame 1990, 1st Annual Katherine White MD Humanitarian 1990, Long Beach Kiwanis Club Outstanding Philanthropist Award Meml. Med. Ctr. Found. 1990; mem: Am. Acad. Pediatrics, CMA, L.A. Co. Med. Assn., Long Beach Med. Assn., Am. Women's Med. Assn., L.A. Co. Pediatric Soc., Soroptimist Internat., Found. Children's Health Care, Kappa Delta Alumni Assn.; Republican; Catholic; rec: numismatics, philately. Res: 6354 Riviera Circle Long Beach 90815

WHITE, LAURENS PARK, physician, b. Dec. 21, 1925, St. Louis, Mo.; s. Park Jerauld and Maria (Bain) W.; m. Annette Campbell, May 19, 1983; children: Sonia Helen Pearson b. 1952, Maria Bain Southworth b. 1957; edn: Westminster Coll. 1943-45; MD, Wash. Univ. Med. Sch. 1949. Career: fellow Am. Cancer Soc. 1953-54; instr. med. Stanford 1955-59; Children's Cancer Research Found., Boston, Peter Bent Brigham Hosp. 1959-63; solo practice

Oncol., S.F. 1963–; clin. prof. med. UC San Francisco; mem: Calif. Med. Assn. (chmn. bd. 1984-87, pres. 1988-89), S.F. Med. Soc. (pres. 1979), AMA, Am. Soc. Clin. Oncol., Am. Assn. Cancer Research, Am. Coll. of Physicians, Calif. Acad. Med.; author 2 books and 45+ research papers; mil: sr. surgeon USPHS 1955; Democrat. Ofc: Dr. Laurens White 1580 Valencia St San Francisco 94110

WHITE, RANDALL DONALD, judge; b. Jan. 21, 1952, Indio; s. Walter Donald and Mary Anne (Jorgenson) W.; m. Elisabeth Anne Marie van der Voort, Aug. 7, 1976; children: Alyson Anne Marie b. 1980, Sheldon Randall b. 1982; edn: BA, UCSB 1974; JD, Loyola Univ. 1977; admitted St. Bar Calif. 1978. Career: sr. law clk./atty. Coyle Marrone Robinson, Los Angeles 1975-78; atty. Riverside Co. Dist. Atty. 1979-92; presiding judge Riverside Co. Superior and Municipal Coordinated Courts, Desert Dist. 1993-95; awards: Moose Lodge Prosecutor of Year 1988, Riverside Co. Felony Prosecutor of Year 1987, Merit Svc. 1985, 86, 88; mem: Desert Bar Assn. (trustee 1985-92, pres. elect 1992, treas. 1991, secty. 1990, chmn. edn. com. 1988-92, chmn. law library com. 1987-92), Calif. Dist. Attys. Assn. (training & edn. com. 1983-86, 88-92), United Methodist Ch. (trustee pres. 1992-95, chmn. stewardship com. 1988-90, adminstrv. council past chair), Desert Youth Baseball-Softball (mgr. 1987-92), Desert Youth Soccer (mgr. and bd. mem. 1987-94), Rent Review Commn. City of Palm Desert (chmn. 1987-92), City of Palm Desert Planning Commn., Law League (scholarship com. 1986-88); Republican; Methodist; rec: photog., travel, swimming. Ofc: Riverside County Superior and Municipal Coordinated Courts.

WHITE, ROBERT LEE, university professor; b. Feb. 14, 1927, Plainfield, N.J.; s. Claude and Ruby H. E. (Levick) W.; m. Phyllis Arlt, June 14, 1952; children: Lauren A. b. 1954, Kimberly A. b. 1956, Christopher L. b. 1952, Matthew P. b. 1967; edn: BA, Columbia Coll., NY, 1949; MA, Physics, Columbia Univ., NY, 1951; PhD, Physics, Columbia Univ., 1954. Career: sci. staff Hughes Res. Labs, Malibu, 1954-61; dept. head General Tel. & El. Labs, Palo Alto, 1961-63; assoc. prof EE, Stanford Univ., 1963-67; prof., EE & MS & E, Stanford Univ., 1967-87; dir. The Exploratorium, S.F., 1987-90; prof. EE & MS & E, Stanford Univ., 1990–; dir.: Stanford Ctr. for Res. on Information Storage Materials, 1991–, Spectrotherm Corp., Santa Clara, 1965-70; initial limited ptnr. Mayfield Funds I & II, Menlo Park, 1969-73; dir.: Biostim Corp., Princeton, N.J., 1975-81, Analog Design Tools, Menlo Park, 1981-86; gen. ptnr. Halo Partners, Ft. Lauderdale, Fla., 1985–; awards: Fellow, Amer. Physical Soc., NYC 1962; Fellow, Inst. Elect. & Electronic Engring. NYC. 1975; Guggenheim Fellow, Guggenheim Found., Oxford 1969-70, Zurich 1978; vis. prof. Japan Soc. for Promotion of Sci., Tokyo, 1975; Christensen Fellow, Oxford Univ., Oxford, Eng., 1986; mem: Phi Beta Kappa 1949, Sigma Xi (hon. sci. soc.), 1952; author: 120 tech. articles publ. in profl. journals, 1952–; Basic Quantum Mechanics, 1967; ed., Magnetism & Magnetic Materials, 1965. Mil: ETM 3/C, USN, 1945-46; Independent; Prot.; rec: reading, gardening, travel. Res: 450 El Escarpado Way Stanford 94305

WHITE, ROBERT STEPHEN, physicist, emeritus professor of physics and research physicist; b. Dec. 28, 1920, Ellsworth, Kans.; s. Byron F. and Sebina Ethyl (Leighty) White; m. Freda Marie Bridgewater, Aug. 30, 1942; children: Nancy b. 1945; Margaret b. 1949; John b. 1950; David b. 1953; edn: AB, Southwestern Coll., Winfield, Kans., 1942; MS, Univ. of Ill., 1943; PhD, UC Berkeley, 1951; career: physicist, Lawrence Radiation Lab., Berkeley and Livermore, 1948-61; head, particles and fields dept., Aerospace Corp., El Segundo, 1962-67; prof. of physics, UC Riverside, 1967-92; dir., inst. of geophysics and planetary physics, UC Riverside, 1967-92; chair, physics dept., UC Riverside, 1970-73; emeritus prof. UC Riverside 1992–; Inst. of Geophysics and Planetary Physics, UC Riverside 1992–; awards: NSF Sr. Postdoctoral Fellow, Munich, Germany, 1961-62; Honorary DSc, Southwestern Coll., 1971; grantee numerous grants and contracts, NASA, NSF, ONR, OAR, DOE, others, 1967-92; mem: fellow, mem., Am. Physical Soc., 1951–; Am. Geophysical Union, 1959–; Am. Astronomical Soc., 1970–; AAAS, 1975–; AAUP, 1967–; author: Space Physics, 1970, num. articles pub. in scientific journals, 1949–; mil: lt.jg. USNR, 1944-46. Res: 5225 Austin Rd. Santa Barbara 93111-2905 Ofc: Inst. of Geophysics and Planetary Physics, Univ. of Calif. Riverside 92521

WHITE, STANLEY ARCHIBALD, research electrical engineer; B. Sept. 25, 1931, Providence, R.I.; s. Clarence Archibald White and Lou Ella (Givens) Arford; m. Edda Maria Castano-Benitez, June 6, 1956; children: Dianne, Stanley Jr., Paul, John; edn: BSEE, Purdue Univ., 1957, MSEE, 1959, PhD, 1965; reg. profl. engr. Calif. Career: engr. Rockwell Internat. Corp., Anaheim 1959-68, mgr. 1968-84, senior scientist 1984-90; pres. Signal Processing and Controls Engineering Corp., 1990–; adj. prof. elec. and computer engring. Univ. Calif. 1984–; cons. and lectr. in field; dir: Asilomar Signals Systems, Computer Corp.; awards: N.Am. Aviation Sci. Engring. Fellow 1963-65, Eta Kappa Nu (internat. dir. emeritus, Disting. Fellow), Tau Beta Pi, Sigma Xi (founding pres. Orange Co. Chpt.), Disting. lectr. Nat. Electronics Conf., Chgo. 1973, Engr. of Yr. award Orange Co. Engring. Council 1984, IEEE Centennial Medal 1984, Engr. of Yr. award Rockwell Internat. 1985, Leonardo Da Vinci Medallion 1986, Sci. Achiev. award 1987, Disting. Engring. Alumnus Purdue Univ. 1988, Meritorious Inventor Rockwell Internat. 1989, Disting. Lectr. IEEE Signal Proc. Soc. 1991-92, Outstanding Elec. Engr. award Purdue Univ. 1992; Fellow

AAAS, Am. Inst. of Aeronautics and Astronautics, Inst. Advancement Engring., N.Y. Acad. Scis., IEEE, IEEE/Signal Processing Soc. (founding chmn. Orange County chpt., gen. chmn. Asilomar Conf. on circuits, systems and computers, 1982, v.chmn. internat. 1983 symposium on circuits and systems, gen. chmn. 1984 internat. conf. on acoustics, speech and signal process, gen. chmn. 1992 internat. symposium on circuits and systems), mem: Audio Engring. Soc., Internat. Neural Network Soc., Nat. Mgmt. Assn., Am. Inst. of Physics, Am. Assn. of Physics Teachers, Air Force Assn. (life mem.), Am. Legion; over 50 U.S. patents issued; 100+ publ. articles; contract author for McGraw-Hill Encyclopedia of Science and Technology. Res: 433 E Ave Cordoba San Clemente 92672-2350

WHITE, THOMAS F., stock and bond broker; b. Feb. 14, 1936, Chicago, Ill.; s. Frank H. White and Margaret Norman; child: Shane b. July 25, 1984 edn: BA econ., Beloit Coll. 1960. Career: reg. rep. Merrill Lynch, Cleveland, Ohio 1963-70; First Calif. Co., San Francisco 1970-75; Birr Wilson 1975-78; chmn. Thomas F. White & Co. Inc. 1978–; editor/pub. The White Paper on Municipal Bonds, 1985-92, chmn., co-founder Lombard Instl. Brokerage Inc. 1992–, chmn. Chouteau, Gilmore, & Sheriff Inc. 1992-93; chmn. Lombard Insurance Svs. Inc. 1994–; mem. Calif. Assn. of Independent Brokers Inc. (v.p. and dir. 1991-94); mem. Pacific Stock Exchange Inc.; civic: Beloit Coll. (trustee 1995–), Chanticleer (dir. 1991-92), S.F. Chamber Orch. (dir. 1985-89), S.F. Chamber Symphony. (dir. 1989-90), mem: S.F. Bond Club 1983–, S.F. Genealogy Soc., S.F. Hist. Soc., City Club, Commonwealth Club, S.F. Fine Arts Museum, S.F. MOMA, S.F. Traditional Jazz Found., S.F. Beautiful, Calif. Acad. of Sciences, Signal Soc. (KQED), S.F. Zoological Soc. Federal Club (HRCF), S.F. Model Yacht Club, Nat. Maritime Mus. Assn. Golden Gate Nat. Park Assn., Friends of Rec. & Parks, Nat. Parks & Conservation Assn.; mil: cpl. USMC 1956-58; rec: model yacht racing, travel, camping, Spanish. Ofc: One Second St San Francisco 94105

WHITEHILL, MICHAEL HENRY, lawyer; b. Feb. 20, 1956; s. Fred and Patricia (Badger) W.; m. Robin Michele O'Reilly, Mar. 10, 1989; edn: BA, UC Berkeley 1978; JD, UC Berkeley Boalt Hall Sch. Law 1981. Career: atty., assoc. Lawler Felix & Hall, Los Angeles 1981-84; Gage Mazurksy Schwartz Kussman & Angelo 1984-88; ptnr. Kussman & Whitehill 1988–; mem: Am. Bar Assn., Am. Trial Lawyers Assn., Calif. Trial Lawyers Assn., Los Angeles Trial Lawyers Assn.; articles pub. in profl. jours., 1980-95; Democrat; rec: sports. Ofc: Kussman & Whitehill 10866 Wilshire Blvd Ste 1470 Los Angeles 90024

WHITESCARVER, OLIN DRAVO, oil company executive; b. Jan. 4, 1936, Pasadena; s. Loren and Hannah Olivia (Beatty) W.; m. Jacqueline George, June 24, 1961; children: Laura Lea (Mohun) b. 1963, William Loren b. 1964; edn: Petroleum Engr., Colo. Sch. of Mines, 1958. Career: petroleum engr. Pure Oil Co., Van, Tx. 1959-60, Midland, Tx. 1960-63, area prodn. engr., Lafayette, La. 1963-65; area prodn. engr. Unocal, Houma, La. 1965-73, sr. prodn. engr., Lafayette, La. 1973, dist. prodn. supt., Santa Rosa, Calif. 1973-79, dist. ops. mgr., Indio, 1979-92; v.p. gen. mgr. Unocal Geothermal of Indonesia, Ltd., Jakarta, Indonesia 1992–; mem: Am. Pet. Inst. 1959–, Soc. of Petroleum Engrs. of AIME (1959–, 25 Year Club), Geothermal Resource Council, Geothermal Assn. of Imperial County, Colo. Sch. of Mines Alumni Assn.; civic: Dulac Mission, Dulac, La. (pres. bd. dirs. 1972), Boy Scouts Am., Santa Rosa (troop com. chair 1978); inventor, 5 patents in geothermal; mil: 1st lt. US Army Reserve, C.E. 1958-59; Republican; First United Methodist Ch. (chmn. bd. trustees 1988). Res: Park Royale Apt. No. 1612 Jalan Gatot Subroto Jakarta 10210, Indonesia Ofc: Rata Plaza Office Tower PO Box 1264/JKT Jakarta 10012, Indonesia.

WHITESIDE, CAROL GORDON, state agency executive; b. Dec. 15, 1942, Chgo.; d. Paul George and Helen Louise (Barre) Gordon; m. John Gregory Whiteside, Aug. 15, 1964; children: Brian b. 1970, Derek b. 1973; edn: BA, UC Davis, 1960. Career: personnel mgr. Emporium, Santa Rosa 1965-67; personnel asst. Levi Strauss & Co., San Francisco 1967-69; education counselor Army Edn. Ctr., Landstuhl Germany 1970-72; school trustee Modesto City Schs., Modesto, Ca. 1979-83; elected councilmem. City of Modesto, 1983-87, mayor 1987-91, advy. bd. U.S. Conf. of Mayors, W.D.C. 1990-91, dir. Calif. League of Cities, Sacto. 1990-91, pres. Nat. Republican Mayors & Councilmembers, W.D.C. 1991; gubnatl. exec. appt., State Resources, Sacto., 1991-93; dir. Intergovernmental Affairs, Governor's Ofc., Sacto. 1993–; dir. Lincoln Inst., Cambridge, Mass. 1990–; honors: County outstanding woman Commn. for Women Stanislaus Co. 1988, Woman of Yr. 27th Assem. Dist. Modesto 1991, Soroptimists Modesto 1988; civic bds: United Way Stanislaus Co. 1986-90, Muir Trail Girl Scouts 1983-88; Republican; Lutheran. Res: 1319 Highland Dr Modesto 95354 Ofc:Governor's Office 1400 Tenth St Rm 109 Sacramento 95814

WHITESON, LEON, writer; b. Oct. 19, 1930, Bulawayo, Zimbabwe; s. Charles and Rebecca (Goldman) W.; m. Janine Berman, March 18, 1950 (div. 1979); m. Aviva Cantor, Aug. 7, 1979; children: Paul Charles b. 1950, Karen b. 1954; edn: B.Arch., Univ. Cape Town 1953. Career: arch. asst. London Co. Council, England 1954-67; freelance writer; arch. critic Toronto Star, Canada 1980-84; L.A. Herald Examiner 1984-87; Los Angeles Times 1988–; bd. mem. Watts Towers Trust 1985-87; bd. mem. Greater L.A. Partnership for the

Homeless 1989; pres. Urban Design Adv. Coalition 1986-88; lectr. Art Center Coll. of Design, Pasadena 1987-95; author: Modern Canadian Arch., 1983, The Liveable City, 1983, Watts Towers, 1989, A Garden Story, 1995; rec: gardening. Res: 1350 N Genesee Ave Los Angeles 90046

WHITLATCH, JO BELL, librarian; b. June 21, 1943, Hibbing, Minn.; d. Robert Thompson and Catharine (Neumeier) Bell; m. Norman Whitlatch, Apr. 28, 1972; dau. Catharine b. 1985; edn: BA in hist., Univ. Minn., 1964, MA in lib. sci., 1966; MA in Asian studies, UC Berkeley, 1973, PhD in lib. & info. studies, 1987. Career: acquisitions librarian Coll. of St. Thomas, St. Paul, Minn. 1965-67; acquisitions librarian Stanislaus State Univ., Turlock 1968-72; cataloger San Jose State Univ., 1973-74, circulation librarian 1975-78, access div. head 1979-84, interim university librarian 1985-86, 1991-92, assoc. library dir. access & bibliographic svs. 1987-91, reference librarian and history selector 1992–; faculty SJSU Library Sch., San Jose Fall 1987; honors: Phi Beta Mu, Phi Kappa Phi; mem: ALA, Calif. Library Assn. (pres. Yosemite chpt. 1970, pres. CSU chapt. 1975), Assn. of Asian Studies, Acad. of Mgmt., Calif. Academic & Res. Librarians (pres. 1981), Am. Lib. Assn. Reference and Adult Svs. Assn. (MOPSS section chair 1995-96); author: The Role of the Academic Reference Librarian, 1990, contbr. articles in profl. jours., column editor-govt. docs., 1976-79. Res: 1801 Edgewood Ln Menlo Park 94025 Ofc: San Jose State Univ. San Jose 95192-0028

WHITNEY, DAN, anthropologist; b. July 25, 1937, Alma, Mich.; s. Frank J. Whitney and Ethel Irene (Duffy) Morey; m. Hiroko Saito, Jan. 7, 1958 (div. Feb. 7, 1982); m. Phyllis A. Tubbs, May 7, 1983; children: Teresa b. 1962, Wendi b. 1965; edn: BA journ., Mich. State Univ., E. Lansing 1962, MA sociology/anthropology, 1963, PhD anthropology, 1968; JD (Valedictorian), Western State Univ., San Diego 1976; admitted bar: Calif. 1976. Career: asst. dir. Ctr. for Asian Studies, Mich. State Univ. 1965-66; prof. anthropology and dept. chair San Diego State Univ., 1966–, assoc. dean Arts & Letters, 1969-72, dir. Ctr. for Asian Studies SDSU, 1987-89; ptnr. law firm Gallatin & Whitney, San Diego 1976-83; awards: editor Law Rev. Western State Univ. 1975, Fulbright Prof., Japan 1985-87, Merit. performance San Diego St. Univ. 1989; mem.: Am. Anthropol. Assn. (1966–, newsletter editor 1974-77), Southwestern Anthropol. Assn. 1966–, Calif. Faculty Assn. 1980–, State Bar Calif. (inactive); author: Cultural Context, 1980, monograph, Rhade of South Vietnam, 1962, contbr. articles in anthropol. and law jours.; mil: A/1c USAF 1955-59; Democrat; Prot.; rec: golf, music, reading, fishing, backpacking, camping. Res: 5352 W Falls View Dr San Diego 92115 Ofc: Anthropology, California State Univ., San Diego 92182

WHITNEY, EUGENE BRADLEY, physician; b. Jan. 2, 1924, Long Beach; s. Eugene Bradley Whitney and Frances Helen (Norton) Carhart; m. Ingrid Lavaughn Surges, Aug. 12, 1951; children: Keith Norton b. 1957, Christine Ellen b. 1958; edn: AB, UC Berkeley 1951; MD, Univ. Buffalo Sch. Medicine 1955; dipl. Am. Bd. Internal Medicine (1967). Career: pvt. practice, Pleasant Hill 1959–; attdg. physician Contra Costa Co. Hosp., Martinez 1959-65, pres. med. staff 1964-65; Concord Comm. Hosp. 1969-70, chmn. Utilization Review Com. 1970-79; chmn. geriatrics com. Alameda-Contra Costa Med. Assn., Oakland 1970-81; med. dir. Oak Park Convalescent Hosp., Pleasant Hill 1965–; Lafayette Convalescent Hosp 1965–; Valley Manor Convalescent Hosp., Concord 1975-91; panel mem. Mt. Diablo EKG Panel 1962–; co-dir. cardiac rehab. program Mt. Diablo Hosp. Med. Center 1982–; mem: Alameda Contra Costa Med. Assn., CMA, AMA, E.Bay Soc. Internal Medicine, Calif. Soc. Internal Medicine, Am. Soc. Internal Medicine, Rotary, Diablo Cotillon, Pleasant Hill C.of C., Am. Assn. Med. Dirs., Calif. Assn. Med. Dirs.; mil: pvt. 1c USAAC 1943-46; Republican; Episcopalian; rec: gardening, philately, fishing. Res: 41 Shadow Hill Rd Lafayette 94549

WHITTEMORE, EDWARD WILLIAM, clergyman, retired insurance executive; b. Dec. 21, 1926, San Francisco; s. Edward William and Caroline (Orginos) W.; m. Baroness Margaret Marion Schilling (v. Constatt), Oct. 5, 1962; children: Edward III, Robert, Diane, Linda, Deborah, Dawn, Diane Carol; edn: attended Grace Bible Inst. and Seminary, Long Beach. Career: ins. broker and agt./pres. Ed Whittemore Co., Long Beach 1949-76; ordained minister United Evangelical Churches, pres. Reach Out Ministries, 1977–, pastor Palos Verdes Christ Ch., P.V. Estates; awards: Firemans Fund Ins. Co. Top Producer Western States 1975, Farmers Ins. Exchange Top Producers U.S. 1947, Agri. Ins. Group Top Producer U.S. 1969; mem: Exchange Club (pres.); mil: pvt. 1c. USMC 1942-45; Republican; Prot.; rec: golf. Address: Ed Whittemore & Associates POB 2785, 6336 Paseo Delicias, Rancho Santa Fe 92067

WHORTON, M. DONALD, occupational and environmental health physician; b. Jan. 25, 19143, Las Vegas, N.M.; s. R.H. and Rachel (Siegal) W.; m. Diana L. Obrinsky, Apr. 9, 1972; children: Matthew, R. Laura Elizabeth, Julie Hannah; edn: US Naval Acad. 1961-62; BS biology, New Mexico Highlands Univ., 1964; MD (honors) Univ. New Mexico Sch. of Medicine, 1968; MPH environmental medicine, John Hopkins Univ. Sch. of Hygiene and Pub. Health, 1973; bd. cert. NBME 1969, Am. Bd. of Preventive Med. in Occupational Med. 1975, Am. Bd. of Internal Med. 1975, Am. Bd. of Preventive Medicine 1975, Am. Coll. of Epidemiology 1983. Career: intern Harvard Med. Svc., Boston City Hosp., 1968-

69; resident dept. pathology Univ. N.M. Sch. of Med. Affil. Hosps., 1969-71; staff physician Family Planning Clinic, W.D.C. 1971-72; resident dept. med. Baltimore City Hosp., 1971-74; assoc. dir. div. emergency med. Baltimore City Hosps., 1974-75; instr. anat. Univ. N.M. 1970-71; instr. med. John Hopkins Univ. 1973-75; clin. asst. prof. UC San Francisco 1975-77; lectr. UC Berkeley Sch. of Pub. Hlth. 1975-79, dir. and med. dir. labor occup. hlth. pgm. UCB 1975-77, 77-79, assoc. clin. prof. occup. med. Sch. of Pub. Hlth. UCB 1979-87; prin., sr. occupational physician, epidemiologist Environmental Health Assocs., Oakland 1979-87; exec. v.p./chief med. scientist ENSR Health Sciences, Alameda 1988-94; pvt. practice Donald Whorton, MD, Alameda 1994–; occupational med. staff Franklin Hosp., Ralph K. Davies Med. Ctr. 1984-90; appt. Permanent Commn. and Internat. Assn. on Occup. Hlth. 1983–; corres. NAS Com. of Human Rights 1983–; awards: Fellow Am. Coll. of Epidemiology 1983, elected Inst. of Med. Nat. Acad. Scis., Highlands Univ. Hon. Soc., Alpha Omega Alpha, Upjohn Achiev. Award, Robert Wood Johnson Found. clin. scholar; mem: Am. Pub. Hlth. Assn., Soc. for Occup. and Environ. Hlth., Alameda-Contra Costa County Med. Assn., Calif. Med. Assn., Am. Acad. of Occup. & Environmental Med. (fellow), AAAS; author med. books, book chapts. and numerous jour. articles; mil: midshipman USN 1961-62. Res: 5960 Ascot Dr Oakland 94611 Ofc: Donald Whorton MD 1135 Atlantic Ave Alameda 94501

WIBBELSMAN, NANCY CASTO BENSON, b. Feb. 19, 1949, Lancaster, Ohio; d. Frank S. and Nancy Ann (Casto) Benson Jr.; m. Patrick Nesbitt 1975, div. 1981; m. 2d. Robert John Wibbelsman (stockbroker), Sept. 2, 1984; children: (nee Nesbitt): Elizabeth Paige b. 1977, Patrick Michael Jr. b. 1978; (by spouse's prev. marriage): Robert John Jr. b. 1968, Warren Mahlon b. 1969; edn: Bradford Jr. Coll. 1967-69; Ohio State Univ. 1972, KK7 sorority. Career: campaign chmn. for Reagan, Republican primary, Marina Del Rey, 1976; (postprimary) chmn. People for Ford, in chg of vol. groups, orgns., subcoms. in Calif., 1976; civic: Los Angeles Junior League, DAR; Republican; Episcopal. Res: Los Angeles.

WICKWIRE, PATRICIA JOANNE NELLOR, psychologist, consultant; b. Sioux City, Iowa; d. William McKinley and Clara Rose (Pautsch) N.; m. Robert Wickwire, Sept. 7, 1957; 1 son, William b. 1958; edn: BA, Univ. of Northern Iowa 1951; MA, Univ. of Iowa 1959; PhD, Univ. of Texas Austin 1971; postgrad., USC, UCLA, CSU Long Beach 1951-66. Career: tchr., sch. psychologist, adminstr. South Bay Union H.S. Dist. 1962–; indep. cons. in mgmt. & edn. 1981; pres. The Nellor Wickwire Group, 1982–; univ. lectr.; honors: Psi Chi, Sigma Alpha Iota, Pi Lambda Theta, Alpha Phi Gamma, Kappa Delta Pi; Journalism and English awards; South Bay Woman of the Year; mem: Calif. Interagency Mental Health Council, Am. Assn. of Univ. Women (pres. 1962-72), Beach Cities Symphony Assn., CSU Dominguez Hills, L.A. Co. Dir. of Pupil Svs. (pres. 1974-79), L.A. Co. Directors Spl. Edn., Calif. Personnel & Guidance Assn., L.A. Co. Personnel & Guidance Assn. (pres. 1977-80), Assn. of Calif. Sch. Adminstrs., Calif. Assn. for Measurement & Evaluation in Guidance (exec. bd. pres. 1981–), Calif. Assn. of Sch. Psychologists (exec. bd. 1981–), Internat. Career Assn. Network (dir. 1985–), Am. Assn. Career Edn. (pres. 1990-92, bd. 1988–), Assn. Measurement and Evaluation in Counseling & Devel. (exec. bd. 1987-91), Calif. Assn. for Counseling and Devel. (pres. 1988-89); contbr. articles to profl. jours. Res: 2900 Amby Pl Hermosa Beach 90254

WIDAMAN, GREGORY ALAN, financial advisor; b. Oct. 4, 1955, St. Louis, Mo.; s. Raymond Paul, Sr. and Louise Agnes (Urschler) W.; edn: BS in bus. & econ., Trinity Univ., 1978; C.P.A., 1985. Career: senior auditor Arthur Andersen & Co., Houston 1978-82, audits of Fortune 500 cos.; sr. cons., mgmt. & litigation, Price Waterhouse, Houston 1983-85; mgr. corp. fin. planning Teledyne Inc., Los Angeles 1985-95, fin. advisor to segment pres., Teledyne Inc.; sr. mgr. of operations planning The Walt Disney Co., Burbank 1995–; honors: outstanding student of finance Fin. Executives Inst., San Antonio, Tx. 1978, Blue Key nat. hon. frat. 1978, biog. listings in Marquis Who's Who In The West, Who's Who In Fin. & Ind., Who's Who In The World; mem: Am. Inst. CPAs, Calif. Soc. CPAs, Christian Business Men's Com. of USA, World Affairs Council, MIT/Cal-Tech Ent. Forum; Republican; Christian; rec: white water rafting, skiing, camping, asst. in small bus. startups. Res: 1416 S Barrington #4 Los Angeles 90025 Ofc: The Walt Disney Company 500 S Buena Vista St Burbank 91521-6191

WIECKOWSKI, ROBERT ANTHONY, lawyer; b. Feb. 18, 1955, San Francisco; s. Eugene Anthony and Helen Ann (Gebarowska) W.; edn: BA, UC Berkeley 1977; JD, Santa Clara Univ. 1985; Jagiellonia Univ. Poland 1986-88. Career: legislative asst. U.S. Congressman Don Edwards, Wash. D.C. 1977-82; campaign mgr. Com. to Elect Gus Morrison, Fremont 1985-94; atty. Law Offices Max Cline, San Jose 1988-92; Law Offices of Miller-Wolny, San Jose 1993–; dir. Pan Woda, Sp. 20.0.; mem: Alameda Co. Bar Assn., Tri-City Ecology Center; Democrat; Cath.; rec: acting, sports. Res: 4462 Stevenson Blvd Fremont 94538 Ofc: Law Offices of Miller-Wolny 160 W Santa Clara St Ste 1250 San Jose 95113

WIEMER, ROBERT ERNEST, film and television writer, producer, director; b. Jan. 30, 1938, Highland Park, Mich.; s. Carl Ernest and Marion (Israelian) W.; m. Rhea Dale McGeath, June 14, 1958; children: Robert Marshall, Rhea Whitney; edn: BA, Ohio Wesleyan Univ., 1959. Career: child actor Jam Handy Orgn., Detroit 1946-48; indep. producer 1956-60; dir. documentary ops. WCBS-

TV, N.Y.C. 1964-67; indep. producer of t.v., theatrical and bus. films, N.Y.C. 1967-72; exec. prod. motion pictures and t.v. ITT Corp., N.Y.C. 1973-84, also pres. ITT subs. cos: Blue Marble Co. Inc., Telemontage Inc., Alphaventure Music Inc., Betaventure Music Inc.; founder, pres. and ceo Tigerfilm Inc. 1984-, chmn. bd. Golden Tiger Pictures, Hollywood 1988-; dir. Princeton-American Communications, Inc. 1986-88; exec. producer children's t.v. show "Big Blue Marble" (winner Emmy and Peabody awards); writer, producer, director feature films: My Seventeenth Summer, Witch's Sister, Do Me a Favor, Anna to the Infinite Power, Somewhere, Tomorrow, Night Train to Kathmandu; dir. TV series: Superboy, Star Trek: The Next Generation, Deep Space Nine, Seaquest; recipient CINE award (1974, 76, 77, 79, 81); mem: Directors Guild of Am., Nat. Acad. T.V. Arts and Scis., Information Film Producers Assn. (outstanding prod. award), Nat. Assn. T.V. Programming Execs., Am. Women in Radio and T.V., New Jersey Broadcasters Assn.; mil: capt. USAF 1960-64; Dutch Reform Ch. in Am. (deacon). Ofc: Golden Tiger Pictures 3896 Ruskin St Las Vegas NV 89117 Tel: 702/243-0560 Fax: 702/243-0562

WIENER, HOWARD B., state appellate judge (retired); b. Feb. 1, 1931, Providence, R.I.; s. Henry and Mildred (Woolf) W.; m. Joan, May 23, 1954; children: Daniel b. 1954, Anne b. 1956, Carol b. 1958; edn: AB, cum laude, Brown Univ. 1952; LLB, Harvard 1955; LL.M, Univ. Virginia 1982; admitted Calif. State Bar 1956. Career: clerk Hon. Ben Harrison, U.S. Dist. Ct. L.A. 1955-56; gen. practice atty. Egly & Wiener, L.A. Co. 1956-75; judge San Bernardino Co. Superior Ct., 1975-78; assoc. justice Ct. of Appeal 4th Appellate Dist., Div. 1, 1978-93; pvt. practice in dispute resolution, San Diego 1994–; adj. prof. Univ. San Diego Law Sch., 1979-85, Cal Western Law Sch., 1988–; co-author Rutter Group, Civil Appeals & Writs, lectr. The Rutter Group, Calif. Judges Assn., Ctr. for Jud. Edn. and Res., Claremont Grad. Sch. Exec. Mgmt. Pgm. 1977-78; mem. bd. overseers UC San Diego, bd. vis. USD Law Sch., Calif. Western Sch. of Law (bd. trustees); honors: Phi Beta Kappa 1952, past pres. Pomona Valley Bar Assn. 1968, bd. trustees L.A. Co. Bar Assn. 1969-71, bd. govs., v.p. Calif. State Bar 1972-75, appellate judge of yr. L.A. Trial Lawyers 1981 and San Diego Trial Lawyers 1984; mem: Calif. Judges Assn.; (exec. bd. 1987-90, v.p. 1989-90, past chair appellate cts. com.); founding pres. William B. Enright Am. Inn of Court 1991–; civic: Inter-Comm. Hosp. Covina (bd. trustees 1967-75), Law in a Free Soc. (exec. com. 1975-79), San Diego Univ. Hosp. (comm. advy. bd. 1979-84); Res: 7755 Ludington Pl La Jolla 92037 Ofc: Koll Center 501 W Broadway 19th Flr San Diego 92101 Tel: 619/338-6561

WIENER, ROBIN DALE, lawyer; b. Jan. 11, 1954, New York; d. Jesse Leonard and Celia Wiener; m. Marc David Yablon, June 21, 1987; edn: BA, Brandeis Univ. 1975; BS, Cornell Univ. 1977; JD, Harvard Univ. 1984; admitted St. Bar Calif. (1985). Career: registered nurse N.Y. Hosp., N.Y.C. 1977-81; law clk. Hon. Stephen Reinhardt, U.S. Ct. Appeals, Los Angeles 1984-85; law fellow Center for Law in Pub. Interest 1985-86; atty., assoc. Tuttle & Taylor 198-89; ofcr., shareholder Tuttle & Taylor 1990–; honors: Phi Beta Kappa, Sigma Theta Tau, recipient State Bar of Calif.'s Wiley M. Manuel Award for Pro Bono Legal Service 1994; mem: Calif. Women Lawyers, SacramentoCo. Bar Assn.; editor: Harvard Law Review, 1982-84, Harvard Womens Law Jour., 1983-84; author and edit. of num. articles pub. in profl. jours., 1983-94. Ofc: Tuttle & Taylor 355 S Grand Ave 40th Floor Los Angeles 90071

WIESE, FREDERICK WILLIAM, JR., manufacturing company executive; b. April 22, 1948, Baltimore, Md.; s. Frederick W. and Julia D. (Davis) W.; edn: BS, St. Louis Univ. 1970; MS, Univ. Mo. Rolla 1972. Career: mfg. engr. Procter & Gamble, Cincinnati, Ohio 1973-77; Texas Instruments, Lubbock, Tx. 1977-84; ops. tech. mgr. Johnson Matthey, San Diego 1984–; mem: Soc. Mfg. Engring. (fellow), Internat. Electronic Packaging Soc., Internat. Soc. Hybrid Mfg.; civic: Hispanic Advocacy Com. (S.D.); co-inventor silver/glass attachment, 1985; articles pub. in profl. jours., 1987, 88. Ofc: Johnson Matthey 10080 Willow Creek Rd San Diego 92131

WIJSEN, LOUIS MARINUS, lawyer, writer; b. July 27, 1935, S'Hertogenbosch, Netherlands; nat. 1962; s. Louis Henri Marie and Nellie (Geerts) W.; m. S.C.J. Fransen, Jan. 15, 1959 (div. 1981); children: Mark b. 1963, Seadon b. 1968, Marcella b. 1972; edn: Cert., Maritime Acad., Rotterdam 1955; BA, MIIS 1970; MA, 1971; PhD, UC Berkeley 1977; JD, UC Hastings Coll. Law 1988; admitted St. Bar Calif. 1988. Career: faculty UC Berkeley 1975-79; legal counsel Alamed Co. Pub. Defender, Oakland 1988-89; dep. pub. defender State of Calif., San Francisco 1989-95; atty. 1995–; Ofcr., U.S. Merchant Marine 1964-72, 1979-86; mem: Am. Bar Assn., Calif. St. Bar Assn., Calif. Attys. Criminal Justice; club: Berkeley Yacht (staff commodore); author: Cognition & Image Formation in Literature, 1978, Psychopatholigische Interpretation, 1979, 100+ short stories, essays, articles, 1966–; mil: AUS 1959-62; Democrat; rec: yachting. Law Ofc: 909 Marina Village Pkwy #181 Alameda 94501

WILCK, NADINE BAGLEY HENRY, marketing communications executive; b. Sept. 9, 1949, Avalon, Calif.; d. William A. Bagley and Sherrill Spurgeon; m. Leland Martin Henry, Feb. 15, 1969; children: Jacqueline Leigh Henry Hanson James b. 1969; m. 2d. Carl Thomas Wilck, May 21, 1989; edn: AA in social sci., Saddleback Coll., Mission Viejo, Calif.; profl. designation in public relations,

UCLA 1980; Coro Found. fellowship in public affairs, Orange County, Calif. 1991. Career: publicity coord., publications editor Mission Viejo Company, Mission Viejo 1973-80; dir. mktg. & public relations Saddleback Memorial Med. Ctr., Laguna Hills 1982-86; mktg. mgr. Memorial Health Services, Long Beach 1986-89; sr. cons. health care & edn. Thomas Wilck Assocs., Public Relations/Public Affairs, Irvine 1989–; dir., district & comm. communications Newport-Mesa Unified Sch. Dist., Newport Beach 1994–; chmn. bd. dirs. Calif. Health Decisions, Inc. (mem. bd. dirs. 1992–, chmn.-elect bd. dirs. 1993); bd. dirs. Associates for the Advancement of Nursing Sci. and Research 1992–; awards: Excellence and Merit, Publications, Internat. Assn. of Bus. Comms., Orange Co.; Protos Award for Singularly Outstanding Excellence in Publicity, Public Relations Soc. of Am., Orange Co.; mem: Public Relations Soc. of Am., Healthcare Public Relations and Mktg. Assn. 1984-94, Cortex Pharmaceuticals, Inc. (lay mem., institutional animal care & use com.); civic: Orange Co. Pioneer Council 1990–, Am. Heart Assn., Orange Co. Div. (chmn. bd. dirs. 1994-95, chmn.-elect bd. dirs. 1993-94, v.p. bd. dirs. 1992-93, sec. bd. dirs. 1990-91, mem. bd. dirs. 1982-83, 1987–, comms. com. chair 1981-83, 87-89, 90-94, public affairs com. 1990-94, planned giving com. 1980-81, Am. Heart Assn., Calif. (v.p. comms., bd. dirs. 1991-93, comms. com. 1989-95), Am. Heart Assn., National (comms. com. 1993-96, vol. stroke advy. group 1993-96), Bowers Mus. of Cultural Art, Orange Co. (mem. Governor's advy. council 1992), STOP-GAP Therapeutic Theatre (bd. dirs. 1991-92); editor: Mission Viejo Reporter, Mission Viejo 1974-76; author: feature articles pub. in newspapers and mags., 1973-85; Republican; Christian; rec: piano, sailing, marathon racing, aviation, tennis.

WILCOX, EVLYN, temporary help services company president, former city mayor; children: Wayne, Moire, Marlene. Career: owner, pres. Manpower, Inc. of San Bernardino, Riverside, Corona, Upland, San Gabriel Valley, Victorville; mayor City of San Bernardino, 1985-89; named Citizen of Year Inland Empire Mag. (1979); mem: Exec. Women Internat. Inland Empire Chpt. (pres. 1975), Bus. and Profl. Women USA (pres. San Orco dist.), San Bernardino Area C.of C. (pres. 1978, Athena Award 1986); civic: Arrowhead United Way (campaign chair 1980 & 1990, pres. 1983, 1992), Community Arts Prodns. (pres.), Nat. Orange Show (treas., bd.), YMCA (bd.), CSU San Bernardino Bd. Councillors, Volunteer Ctr. of Inland Empire (pres.), Zonta Internat., Rotary of San Bernardino (pres.), San Bernardino Community Against Drugs (bd. chair), San Bernardino Civic Light Opera Assn. (pres.); rec: gardening, collect porcelain, oriental art and antiques, travel. Ofc: Manpower, Inc. 998 North D St San Bernardino 92410

WILDE, GARY K., hospital administrator; b. Sept. 9, 1955, Los Angeles; s. Virgil J. and Lydia A. (Kezerian) W.; m. Cheryl Anne Harp, Dec. 28, 1978; children: Jaron b. 1979, Kyrsten b. 1982, Daniel b. 1986, John b. 1988, Aricka b. 1992; edn: BA, Brigham Young Univ. 1979; MHSA, Ariz. St. Univ. 1982. Career: pharmaceutical rep. Bristol Myers, Bakersfield 1979-80; fin. asst. St. Lukes Hosp., Phoenix, Ariz. 1981; adminstv. resident Santa Barbara Cottage Hosp. 1982-83, assoc. dir. nursing 1983-84, assoc. v.p. 1984-87, v.p. clin. services 1987–; instr. Univ. LaVerne Ext., Ventura 1985–; v.chair supvy. com. Santa Barbara Co. Fed. Credit Union 1989–; mem: Am. Coll. Healthcare Execs., Healthcare Execs. of So. Calif. (area rep.), LDS BPA (pres. 1984), BSA, Am. Youth Soccer Orgn.; Republican; L.D.S.; rec: computers. Res: 9626 Oneida Ventura 93004 Ofc: Santa Barbara Cottage Hospital POB 689 Santa Barbara 93102

WILDEY, JAMES ALLEN, company owner and executive, licensed real estate broker, general contractor; b. Feb. 13, 1943, Binghamton, N.Y.; s. Leon Earl and Constance Evelyn (Springer) W.; m. Barbara Ann Marold, Sept. 10, 1966; children: J. Dane b. 1968, Eric E. b. 1970; edn: AA, Rochester Inst. Tech. 1964; BS, 1965; MS, Pa. St. Univ. 1967; Calif. lic.: gen. contr., R.E. broker, elderly care facility provider. Career: sr. systems and procedures analyst IBM Corp., Pt. Chester, N.Y. 1967-72; owner Guide Farms, Lebanon, Pa. 1972-77; sr. project mgr. Gen. Public Utilities Service Corp., Reading, Pa. 1977-80; mgr. MIS Quaker Alloy Casting (div. of Harsco), Myerstown, Pa. 1980-83; corp. dir. MIS/EDP Vendo Co., Fresno, Calif. 1983-84; div. mgr. computer services Fresno County, 1984-92; owner, exec. dir. Elim Place, Sanger, Calif. 1992–; owner Fresno Home Services, Clovis 1984–; co-owner Comm. Home Providers-Alzheimers Elderly Care Facility; Fresno Surf 'N Turf, Fresno 1984–; co-owner Affordable Pool Service, Clovis 1988–; honors: Who's Who East, Who's Who Fin. & Industry, Who's Who in Calif. 1992; mem: Assn. Systems Mgmt., Data Processing Mfg. Assn., Fresno Evangelical Free Ch. (bd. mem. 1989-91), Family Life Ctr. (bd. dirs., secty. 1987-89), Lebanon Youth for Christ (bd. dirs. 1979-80); Republican; Prot.; rec: home constrn. & remodeling, sailing. Res: 2390 Alluvial Ave Clovis 93611 Ofc: Elim Place 1808 5th St Sanger 93657

WILHELM, ROBERT OSCAR, lawyer, civil engineer; b. July 7, 1918, Baltimore; s. Clarence Oscar and Agnes Virginia (Grimm) W.; m. Grace Sanborn Luckie, Apr. 4, 1959; edn: BS in C.E., Georgia Inst. of Tech., 1947, MS in Indsl. Mgmt., 1948; JD, Stanford Univ. 1951; admitted bar: Calif. 1952, U.S. Supreme Ct. Career: lawyer, sr. ptnr. law firm Wilhelm, Thompson, Wentholt & Gibbs, Redwood City 1952–; civil engr. and land surveyor in pvt. practice, 1952–; land developer and bldg. contr.; gen. counsel and pres. Bay Counties Builders Escrow Inc., 1972–; mem: Calif. Bar Assn., San Mateo Co. Bar Assn., Calif. Builder's Exchange (past treas.), Peninsula Builder's Exchange

(bd. 1956, pres. 1958, 1971), Bay Counties Civil Engrs. and Land Surveyors Assn. (gen. counsel, pres. 1957), Assn. of Gen. Contrs. S.F. (past dir.), Engring. and Grading Contrs. Assn. (bd., gen. counsel); lodges: Masons, Odd Fellows, Eagles, Elks; author: Constrn. Law for Contractors, Architects and Engineers, (constrn. handbook) Manual of Procedures for the Constrn. Ind. (9th Edit.), columnnist "Law and You" Daily Pacific Builder, 1954–; mil: 1st lt. Army Corps of Engrs. 1942-46. Res: 463 Raymundo Dr Woodside 94062 Ofc: 600 Allerton Redwood City 94063

WILKINS, BURLEIGH TAYLOR, philosophy educator; b. July 1, 1932, Bridgetown, Va.; s. Burleigh and Helen Marie (Taylor) W.; children: Brita Taylor, Carla Cowgill, Burleigh William; edn: BA (summa cum laude), Duke Univ., 1952; MA, Harvard Univ., 1954; MA, Princeton (N.J.) Univ., 1963; PhD, Princeton Univ., 1965. Career: instructor MIT, Cambridge, 1957-60, Princeton Univ., 1960-61, 63; asst. prof. Rice Univ., Houston, 1965-66, assoc. prof. 1966-67; assoc. prof. UC Santa Barbara, 1967-68, professor 1968–; mem: Phi Beta Kappa; author: Carl Becker, 1961, The Problem of Burke's Political Philosophy, 1967, Hegel's Philosophy of History, 1974, Has History Any Meaning?, 1978, Terrorism and Collective Responsibility, 1992. Ofc: Univ of Calif Dept of Philosphy Santa Barbara 93106

WILKINSON, ROSEMARY REGINA CHALLONER, poet, author, lecturer; b. Feb. 21, 1924, New Orleans, La.; d. William Lindsay, Jr. and Julia Regina (Sellen) Challoner; m. Henry B. Wilkinson, Oct. 15, 1949; children: Denis James b. 1952, Marian Regina b. 1954, Paul Francis b. 1959, Richard Challoner b. 1967; edn: tchg. cert. San Francisco St. Univ., 1978, Lifetime tchg. credential, poetry. Career: ten yrs. in hosp. adminstrn., 1939-47, 1957-61; poet and author, Burlingame, Calif. 1965–; secty. gen. (10 yrs.), pres. 1995–, World Acad. of Arts and Culture/ World Congress of Poets (WAAC/WCP), Burlingame 1985-88, and Placerville 1988-95; author 18 poetry books (translations in 35 languages now): A Girl's Will, 1973, California Poet, 1976, Earth's Compromise, 1977, It Happened To Me, 1978, I Am Earth Woman, 1979, The Poet & The Painter, 1981, Gems Within, 1984, In The Pines, 1985, Longing For You, 1986, Purify The Earth, 1988, Sacred In Nature, 1988, Earth's Children, 1990, New Seed, 1990, 91, Angels and Poetry, 1992, Cambrian Zephyr, 1993, Collected Poems, 1994; Prose work: An Historical Epic (trans. into Mandarin 1974), biographer: Epic of the Ship's Captain/Artist; lectures, poetry readings internat.; awards: Dame of Malta (1981- Dame of Grace, Dame of Merit 1985), Dame of St. George (Vt. 1991, Algarve Portugal 1992), Dame of Order of Polonia Restituta, Poland 1989, Dame of St. Sepulcre, Australia 1990, Dame of Knights-St. John of Jerusalem-Portugal 1993, Internat. Order of Merit, England 1993, Gold medal, India 1986, Bronze medal World Poetry Soc. Conf. India 1987, Silver medal Accad. Internaz. Di Pontzen Italy 1988, Schilla Dynasty "Kaya" Crown (gold/jade) Korea 1988, disting. service Nat. League Am. Pen Women USA 1990, Yunus Emre award World Acad. Arts & Culture Taiwan 1991, Yunus Emre award-Turkiye 1992, Acad. Roma- Italy 1991, Unione Della Mondiale Culture- Italy 1991, All India Writers award-Calcutta 1992, Indian Cutlure Ctr.-Calcutta 1992, Acad. Cult/Arte "Il Faro" Italy 1992, Greek Writers award Greece 1993, Internat. Acad. de Lutece Medal D'Or , France 1993, Internat. Woman of 1994-India, XV World Congress of Poets Disting. Service award, Taipei 1994, VI Nat. Encounter of Poets/I Internat. Encounter, Gold Medal, Peru 1994, Internat. Soc. of Greek Writers award 1994, num. others; HDL (hon.) L'Universita Libre, Pakistan 1975, World Acad. Arts & Culture, Taiwan 1981, merit Am. Poets Fellowship Soc. 1973, Poet Laureate Int'l '74 Int'l Woman of 1975, Fellow Internat. Biog. Ctr., Cambridge, Eng. 1981–, Chancellor Internat. Poets Acad., India 1998–; mem: WAAC/WCP (1973–, secty. gen. 1985–), Nat. League Am. Pen Women (mem. 1977–, nat. bd. 1986-90, Berkeley Br. pres. 1988-90), Authors Guild League of Am. N.Y. 1980–, Ina Coolbrith Circle (1966–, dir. emeritus), WPSI-POET India (v.p. 1986–), St. David's Soc. of St. of NY, Internat. Soc. of Greek Writers 1994, Poetry Soc. Am., N.Y. Poetry Forum (life), Poetry Soc. of Japan, London (life), United Writers Assn.-India, World Literary Acad.-England, World Poetry Res. Inst.-Kores (v.p.); civic: founder poetry San Mateo County Fair 1977–, Fine Arts Fair Poetry Workshop (Dr. Williams) Burlingame H.S. (founder 1981-85), Soroptomist (hon. 1981), Avalon Library Assn., Glastonbury, England 1989–; Democrat; R.Cath.; rec: reading, brush painting, gardening. Res: 3146 Buckeye Ct Placerville 95667

WILLARD, ROBERT EDGAR, lawyer; b. Dec. 13, 1929, Bronxville, N.Y.; s. Wm. Edgar and Ethel Marie (Van Ness) W.; m. Shirley Fay Cooper, May 29, 1954; children: Laura Marie, Linda Ann, John Judson; edn: BA in econs., Wash. State Univ., 1954; JD, Harvard Univ., 1958; admitted bar: Calif. 1959. Career: law clk. to U.S. dist. judge 1958-59; atty., assoc. law firm Flint & Mackay, Los Angeles 1959- 61; sole practice, L.A. 1962-64; mem. firm Willard & Baltaxe, L.A. 1964-65, Baird, Holley, Baird & Galen, L.A. 1966-69, Baird, Holley, Galen & Willard, L.A. 1970- 74, Holley, Galen & Willard, L.A. 1975-82, Galvin & Willard, Newport Beach 1982-88; Davis, Punelli, Keathley & Willard, Newport Beach 1989–; mem: ABA, Calif. Bar Assn., L.A. Co. Bar Assn., Assn. Trial Lawyers Am., Am. Judicature Soc., Acacia Frat.; club: Calcutta Saddle and Cycle; mil: AUS 1946-48, 50-51; Congregationalist. Res: 1840 Oriole Costa Mesa 92626 Ofc: Davis, Punelli, Keathley & Willard, 610 Newport Ctr Dr Ste 1000 Newport Beach 92660

WILLIAMS, BEN ALBERT, government administrator; b. Dec. 14, 1946, San Diego; s. Ben Albert and Frances E. (Arnold) W.; m. Gloria Jean Dieken, Sept. 25, 1976; children: Megan b. 1979, Alec b. 1982; edn: BSBA, San Diego St. Univ. 1969; MPA, CSU Hayward 1977. Career: budget analyst Calif. Dept. Indsl. Rels., San Francisco 1973-76; adminstrv. ofcr. Calif. Coastal Commn. 1976-79; dep. dir. adminstrn. Gov.'s. Office of Planning & Research, Sacto. 1979–, interim dir. 1988, military base reuse liaison 1989–; exec. dir. Governor's Base Reuse Task Force 1993-94; mem: Nat. Assn. of Installation Developers (bd. dirs.), Am. Soc. Pub. Adminstrn. (pres. Sacto. chpt. 1988-89), Calif. Forum on Information Tech.; editor Report to Gov. - Calif. Commn. on Ednl. Quality, 1988, contbr. articles to profl. jours.; mil: sp5 AUS 1969-71; Baptist; rec: golf, running. Address: 120 Pawtucket Ct Folsom 95630

WILLIAMS, CHARLES JUDSON, lawyer; b. Nov. 23, 1930, San Mateo; s. John Augustus and Edith (Babcock) W.; children: Patrick b. 1957, Victoria b. 1958, Apphia b. 1981; edn: AB, UC Berkeley, 1952, LLB, 1955; admitted bar: Calif., U.S. Dist. Ct., U.S. Ct. Appeal 1955, U.S. Supreme Ct. 1970. Career: atty., assoc. Kirkbride, Wilson, Harzfeld & Wallace, San Mateo 1956-59, special counsel to cities and districts throughout state re financing of pub. improvements; asssoc. John A. Bohn and Assocs., Benicia 1959-64; solo law practice, 1964-76; assoc. Judith A. Robbins, 1981-90; asst. city atty. City of Benicia 1959-64; city atty. Lafayette 1968–, Moraga 1974-91, Benicia 1980-82, Danville 1982-88, Pittsburg 1984-93, Orinda 1985–; assoc. counsel Central Contra Costa Sanitary Dist. 1959-64; gen. counsel Contra Costa Co. Mcpl. Risk Mgmt. Auth. 1977-88; legal advisor Alaska Supreme Ct. and State Legislature 1959-61; lectr. Cont. Edn. of Bar 1964-65, 77, 88; instr. J.F.K. Univ. Sch. of Law 1965-68, UC Ext. Div. 1974-76; conf. speaker on land use law and planning League of Calif. Cities, 1964–; bd. dirs. County Fair Bd. 1966-68; author: lawbooks on Calif. Code, Calif. Commercial Code Forms, Calif. Govt. Code Forms (West Pub. 1964, 65, 71), Municipal City Code (cities of Pleasant Hill, Benicia, Lafayette, Moraga, Danville, Orinda), Calif. Zoning Practice (CEB, 10 edits. 1977–). Res: 929 Janet Ln Lafayette 94549 Ofc: Law Offices of Charles J. Williams 1320 Arnold Dr Ste 160 Martinez 94553

WILLIAMS, DONALD SPENCER, scientist; b. May 28, 1939, Pasadena; s. Charles G. and Delia S. W.; edn: BS engring. sci., Harvey Mudd Coll., 1961; MS in E.E., Carnegie Mellon Univ., 1962, PhD computer sci., 1969. Career: mgr. computer ctr. Univ. of Pittsburgh, Pa. 1965-67; senior engr. RCA Corp., Palo Alto, Ca. 1969-71; principal investigator JPL, Pasadena 1972-80; chief engr. ops. TRW, Redondo Beach 1980–; cons. prin., 1975–; awards: study grantee Japan Economic Found., Tokyo 1983; mem: AAAS, Assn. for Computing Machinery, Audio Engring. Soc., Nat. Fire Protection Assn., IEEE, Soc. of Motion Picture and TV Engrs.; civic: Town Hall of Calif., Community Assn. Inst., Am. Theatre Organ Soc.; Republican; Presbyterian; rec: theater preservation. Res: PO Box 607 Lawndale 90260-0607 Ofc: TRW Inc., One Space Park Dr. R3-2089, Redondo Beach 90278-1071

WILLIAMS, J(OHN) TILMAN, elected city official, real estate and insurance broker, investor; b. Feb. 26, 1925, Detroit, Mich.; s. Aubrey and Martha Lou W.; m. Sally Jane Robinson, Aug. 22, 1947; children: Leslie Ana, Martha Lou; edn: BS in agri., Mich. State Univ. 1951. Career: pres. Satellite Ins. Brokerage, Garden Grove 1959–; currently pres. Satellite Fin.; Satellite Real Estate, Satellite Mortgage & Loan Co.; elected Garden Grove City Council 1976-84, 1988-92; mayor 1976-78, vice mayor 1980-84, mayor 1987–; mem. ad hoc com. Property Tax to Limit Govt. Spending w/Spirit of 13 Initiative; mem: Bd. Realtors, Indsl. Ins. Agents Assn., Indep. Ins. Agents Assn.; civic: Orange Co. Esperanto Assn. (pres. 1985-88), Garden Grove H.S. Band Boosters (pres.), Am. Legion, VFW; clubs: Lions, Elks, Toastmasters, Fifty-Plus Sr., Citizens of Garden Grove (pres. 1986-88); mil: USAAF WWII PTO; Democrat; Ch. of Active Creativity. Res: 11241 Chapman Ave Garden Grove 92640 Ofc: Satellite Financial 12311 Harbor Blvd Garden Grove 92640

WILLIAMS, MARK TULLY, foundation executive; b. Jan. 20, 1948, Bishop, Calif.; s. Paul Jacob Williams and Gertrude Mary (Melsheimer) W.; m. Paula Marie Fink, June 20, 1970 (div. 1980); 1 son, Joshua Glen b. 1976; m. Melinda Kay Bell, Aug. 14, 1982; children: Brian b. 1986, Mark b. 1992; edn: BA (magna cum laude), Pacific Union Coll. 1970; M.Div. (cum laude), Andrews Univ. SDA Theol. Sem. 1973; MA, health svs. mgmt., Webster Univ. 1987. Career: pastor/tchr. Seventh-Day Adventist Church 1970-80; editor and publisher The Building and Real Estate Journal, Hemet, Calif. 1980-83; asst. adminstr. Anacapa Adventist Hosp. 1983-85; v.p. mktg. and devel. Boulder Memorial Hosp., Colo. 1985-89; v.p. devel. San Antonio Comm. Hosp., Upland, Calif. 1989-90; pres./c.e.o. Riverside Comm. Hosp. Foundation, Riverside 1990–; ptnr., Philanthropic Management Group; honors: pres. sr. class Loma Linda Acad. 1966, certified mem. Nat. Assn. for Healthcare Philanthropy; mem: Riverside Rotary (bd. dirs.), Volunteer Center of Riverside (bd. dirs.), La Sierra Univ. Sch. of Bus. & Mgmt. (advy. council), So. Calif. Assn. for Hosp. Devel., Nat. Soc. of Fund Raising Executives; Republican; Seventh-Day Adventist; rec: mountaineering, skiing, running, cycling. Ofc: Riverside Community Hospital Foundation 4445-A Magnolia Ave Riverside 92501 Tel: 909/788-3471

WILLIAMS, NORMAN HARWOOD, consulting engineer; b. Aug. 4, 1928, Detroit, Mich.; s. Cedric Trevelyan and Eileen Emily (Spicer) W.; m. Lorraine Kreusch, April 11, 1953 (dec. 1983); m. Janet Kay Braverman, Jan. 25, 1985 (dec. 1991); edn: BA physics, UC Berkeley 1951; MS electrical engring., Stanford Univ. 1964. Career: engr. Collins Radio Co., Burbank 1951-56; sr. staff engr. Varian Assoc., Palo Alto 1956-88; cons. engr., San Rafael 1988–; mem: IEEE (sr.), Calif. Soc. Profl. Engrs., Nat. Soc. Profl. Engrs., San Rafael Canal Ministry (exec. bd. 1988–, pres. 1995), Marin Power Squadron (edn. ofcr. 1993–), Elks, Marin Yacht Club (sect. 1993–), St. Aidens Ch., S.F. (sr. warden 1984-86); inventor 12 U.S. patents, co-author (book) Microwave Power Engring., 1963, various articles; mil: 2d asst RO USCG 1945; Democrat; Episcopalian; rec: amateur radio, sailing, hiking. Res: 35 Twin Oaks Ave San Rafael 94901 Ofc: 1537A 4th St Ste 130 San Rafael 94901

WILLIAMS, PATRICIA L., president of a national training corporation; b. Oct. 12, 1941, Slidell, La.; d. Adam A. and Lena M. (Pichon) Faciane; m. John T. Graves (comml. R.E. developer), June 28, 1986; dau. Nikki Renee Williams b. 1973; edn: AA in pol. sci., Los Angeles City Coll. 1970; pol. sci. courses UCLA UCLA Labor Inst.; lic. life & disability ins. agt. Calif. Career: treas. Rosey Grier's Giant Step Inc., cons. Robert Farrell's Recall Campaign 1975-78, We. States staff dir. of Lexington Group of DNC, 1981-83; adminstrv. asst. UAW Local 887, 1962-77; dir. UAW youth Project, 1979-83; dir. UAW Program Planning R&D, 1983-84; comptroller UAW-LETC (Labor Employment and Tng. Corp.) 1984-85, job tng. cons. 1985-88 (only woman on 6-mem. US team during formulation of UAW/ GM-Toyota jt. venture creation of New United Motors Mfg. Inc.), v.p. mktg. res. & devel. 1988-89, senior v. p. UAW-LETC, 1989-92, pres. 1993–; People to People Ambassador Prog., Ambassador to China 1994; established Career Ctr. at World Trade Ctr. N.Y.C. (opened 1/93); owner/pres. Faciane and Assocs. (pub. relations, program plng., mktg.), Los Angeles; co-owner J.T. Graves Commercial R.E. Inc.; apptd. by Spkr. Willie Brown mem. Calif. State Employment Tng. Panel; apptd. by Senate Rules Com. to Calif. State Public Procurement Advy. Com.; apptd. by Supr. Ed Edelmann commr. L.A. Co. Hwy. Safety Commn. (chair 1985); apptd. by Mayor Tom Bradley mem. L.A. Private Industry Council (dir.), mem. L.A. Co. Employment Tng. Action Council, mem. advy. bd. Calif. St. Youth Auth.; honors: appreciation for community interface Rockwell Internat., mother of year Notre Dame Acad. 1987, listed Who's Who in Business & Exec. Women, 5000 Personalities of the World, 2000 Notable Am. Women, L.A. Comm. Colleges Labor Ctr. Award 1993; mem. UAW Local 509; civic: Coro Found. (bd.), L.A. Urban League (bd.), Democratic Lexington Gp. (charter), Nat. Museum of Women in the Arts (charter), Am. Film Inst. (assoc.), Women Aware, Lullaby Guild of Childrens' Home Soc. (chair Ebony Fashion Fair fundraiser 1990, 91), Jack and Jill of Am., L.A. Co. Public Guardian's Office (vol.); Democrat; R.Cath.; rec: writing. Res: 6605 Bedford Ave Los Angeles 90056 Ofc: Faciane & Associates 5150 E Gage Bell 90201

WILLIAMS, RALPH B., services company executive; b. May 30, 1947, Boston, Mass.; s. Ralph B. and Florence (Porter) W.; m. Karen Denise Belville, Jan. 1, 1980; children: Krista B. b. 1981, Lindsay B. b. 1984; edn: BA, Coll. of the Holy Cross, Worchester, Mass. 1969; MBA, Suffolk Univ., Boston 1970; DBA, USC, L.A. 1981; Cert. Mgmt. Acct.; lic. CPA, Mass. Career: in charge acct. Ernst & Whinney, Boston, Mass. 1970-73; v.p. fin. and ops. Coollight Co., Inc., North Hollywood 1976-79; exec. v.p. and chief operating ofcr. K-COMP, Inc., Glendale 1980-82; pres./CEO Technology Solutions Corp., L.A. 1982-84; pres./CEO Omnar Corp., Los Angeles 1984; indep. consultant fin., acctg., systems, and planning, 1985-89; asst. prof. acctg. CSU Bakersfield 1973-74; lectr. in acctg. USC Sch. of Bus. Adminstrn., 1974-78; assoc. prof. acctg. CSU Los Angeles, 1978-89; dir.: Coollight Co. Inc., K-COMP Inc., Tech. Solutions Corp., Omnar Corp.; awards: outstanding professor Iota chapt. Beta Alpha Psi (USC), doctoral fellow Price Waterhouse Found., consortium fellow Am. Acctg. Assn., doctoral fellow Deloitte, Haskins & Sells Found., teaching fellow Suffolk Univ., advisor award Suffolk Univ.; mem: Am. Inst. of CPA's, Calif. Soc. of CPA's, Inst. of Mgmt. Acctg., Alpha Kapa Psi; contbr. articles to profl. jours. Res: 4215 Clubhouse Dr Lakewood 90712

WILLIAMS, RICHARD THOMAS, lawyer; b. Jan. 14, 1945, Evergreen Park, Ill.; s. Raymond Theodore and Elizabeth Dorothy W.; m. Carole Jane Knaul, June 23, 1984; edn: BA, Stanford Univ. 1967; MBA, 1972, JD, 1972; admitted St. Bar Calif. 1972. Career: atty., assoc. Kadison Pfaelzer Woodard Quinn & Rossi, Los Angeles 1972-78, ptnr. 1979-87; Whitman & Ransom 1987-93, mng. ptnr. 1988-90; ptnr. Whitman Breed Abbott & Morgan 1993–; mem: Am. Bar Assn., L.A. Bar Assn.; Methodist. Res: 2721 Club Dr Los Angeles 90064 Ofc: Whitman Breed Abbott & Morgan 633 W 5th St Ste 2100 Los Angeles 90071

WILLIAMS, ROGER A., pathologist; b. Jan. 29, 1939, Dayton, Ohio; s. Harry Roger and D'Esta Marjorie (Humberger) W.; m. Barbara Twist, July 1, 1961; children: Andrew b. 1964, Jason b. 1967; edn: BA, Cornell Univ. 1961; MD, Baylor Univ. 1965; cert. in anatomical and clin. path. Am. Bd. Pathology 1970, blood banking 1973, pediatric pathology 1990. Career: intern, resident in pathology, Harvard Univ., Mass. Gen. Hosp., 1965-66, 1966-69; tchg. fellow Harvard 1967-69; instr. Tufts, 1967-69; pathologist San Diego Inst. of Path. 1971-80;

Coroner's pathologist San Diego Co., 1970-84; lab. dir. El Centro Comm. Hosp., 1971-74; clin. asst. prof. UC San Diego 1972-83; chief pathology Childrens Hosp., San Diego 1974-84, Childrens Hosp., Oakland 1984–; clin. assoc. prof. UCSD 1983-84, UC San Francisco 1985-93; clin. prof. UCD 1993–; honors: Alpha Omega Alpha 1964; mem: AMA, Calif. Med. Assn. (CMA Task Force on Child Abuse 1983), Study Gp. for complications of perinatal care 1983, Children's cancer study gp. 1984, Fellow Coll. of Am. Pathologists (1970, Task Force for Missing and Abused Children 1984), Fellow Am. Soc. of Clin. Path. 1971', Calif. Soc. Path. (bd. dirs. 1978-80), Am. Assn. of Blood Banks, U.S./Canadian Acad. Path., Soc. for Pediatric Path.; civic: Children's Home Soc. (bd. dirs. 1980-81), Rotary Intl.; clubs: San Diego Yacht, Claremont CC; num. publs. in medical literature; mil: lcdr USNR 1969-71; Prot.; rec: trout fishing, tennis, golf. Res: 69 Wildwood Gardens Piedmont 94611-3831 Ofc: Childrens' Hospital 747 Fifty Second St Oakland 94609

WILLIAMS, SPENCER M., federal judge; b. Feb. 24, 1922, Reading, Mass.; m. Kay Bramlage, Aug. 20, 1943; children: Carol, Peter, Spencer, Clark, Janice, and Diane; edn: BA in hist., UC Los Angeles 1943; JD, UCB Boalt Hall Sch. of Law, 1948; admitted Calif. Bar 1949, U.S. Ct. of Appeals 9th cir. 1949, US Dist. Ct. no. dist. Calif. 1949, US Ct. Mil. Appeals 1951, US Supreme Ct. 1952. Career: dep. county counsel Santa Clara County 1949-50, 52-55, county counsel 1955-67; apptd. by Gov. Reagan as adminstr. Calif. State Health and Welfare Agcy. and Calif. Youth and Adult Corrections Agency, 1967-68; secty. Calif. State Human Relations Agency, 1968-70; pvt. law practice w/ Beresford & Adams, Santa Clara Co. 1949, w/Rankin, O'Neal, Center, Luckhardt, Boney, Marlais & Lund, S.C. Co. 1970-71, and w/ Evans, Jackson & Kennedy, Sacto. Co. 1970-71; judge U.S. Dist. Ct., No. Dist. of Calif., 1971–, senior judge 1987–; mem: Fed. Judges Assn. (pres. 1982-87), Ninth Circuit Dist. Judges Assn. (pres. 1981-83), Am. Bar Assn. 1955–, S.C. Co. Bar Assn. 1949–, Sacto. Co. Bar Assn. 1966–, Bar Assn. of S.F. (hon. mem. 1971–), Calif. Dist. Attys. Assn. (pres. 1963-64), Nat. Assn. of Co. Civil Attys. (pres. 1963-64), S.C. Co. Bd. of Law Library Trustees (pres. 1955-56), S.C. Co. Reserve Officers Assn. (pres. 1955); civic: Kiwanis Club, Willow Glen (pres. 1958), YMCA State Com. on Youth & Govt. 1967-68, Boys City Boys' Club, San Jose (bd. 1965-67); Republican; Episcopal (sr. warden St. Phillip's, S.J. 1962-63). Ofc: U.S. Court House 280 South 1st St San Jose 95113

WILLIAMS, STEVE REX, physician; b. Aug. 3, 1953, Henderson, Tx.; s. James Marion and Ruth May (Harrison) W.; m. Toby Barto Richards, 1988; edn: BA cum laude, Southern Methodist, 1973; MD, Univ. Texas Med. Branch, 1977; Fellow Am. Acad. Family Phys. 1982; phys. surgeon lic. Calif. BMQA. Career: intern in gen. surgery L.A. County-USC Med. Center 1977-78; resident in family med. Baylor Coll. of Med. 1979-82; pvt. practice of medicine, Santa Maria 1982-87; dir. Family Practice and Emergency Med. Svs., Valley Hosp. 1983; founder Family Practice Div. at two hosps. in Santa Maria, 1984; pvt. practice, McCloud 1987-91, Valley E.R. Physicians Group, 1991–; awards: full academic scholarship So. Methodist Univ. 1970, Locum Tenens study award at Middlesex Hosp., London 1976; biog. listings in Men of Achievement, 5,000 Personalities of Am., Personalities of World 1989, Internat. Who's Who of Intellectuals, Sterling Who's Who; mem: AMA, Am. Acad. Family Practice, Am. Coll. Emergency Phys., Am. Mensa Assn.; civic: Am. Hydrogen Assn., Citizens for Alternative Tax Structure, Presdl. Repub. Task Force 1986–, Civic Group against Landfill Dumping of Toxic Chems., Keepers of the Flame Frat., Rosecrucian Order; Thebetan Buddhist; rec: equestrian, ski, travel, hiking, camping, flying, soaring. Res: Box 269 McCloud 96057 Ofc: 1032 Cedar Ct McCloud 96057

WILLIAMS, VIVIAN LEWIE, college counselor/marriage-family therapist; b. Jan. 23, 1923, Columbia, S.C.; d. Dr. Lemuel Arthur and Mrs. Ophelia Vivian (McDaniel) Lewie; m. Dr. Charles Warren Williams, Apr. 4, 1947 (dec.); children: Pamela Ann b. 1952, Dr. Charles Warren, Jr. b. 1954 (dec. 1990); edn: BA, Allen Univ., 1942; MA, Univ. Mich., 1946; MS in edn., USC, 1970; lic. Marriage Family Child Counselor, Calif. 1971. Career: asst. prof. psych. Tenn. A&I St. Univ., Nashville 1946-47; asst. prof. edn. Winston Salem St. Coll., 1947-50; reading splst. and language arts coord., project cons., Charlotte-Mecklenburg Schs., Charlotte, N.C. 1963-67; asst. prof. edn./psych. Johnson C. Smith Univ., 1967-69; Teacher Corps team leader USC/Centennial High Sch., Los Angeles 1970-73; prof. counseling and psychology, counselor Compton Community Coll., 1973–, fgn. student advisor 1974-84; awards incl. numerous civic recogn. Columbia, S.C. 1950-53, Charlotte, N.C. 1957-63, recogn. USC Sch. of Edn./Tchr. Corps 1972, achiev. Alpha Gamma Sigma Hon. Soc. Compton 1980, 83, svc. award Allied Health (Nursing Dept.) Compton Coll. 1989; mem: Nat. Acad. of Counselors and Family Therapists (1973–, SW reg. pres. 1989), Nat. Edn. Assn. (life), CTA, Delta Sigma Theta Sor. 1943–, AAUW (life mem.1969–), The Link Inc. (historian Harbor Area chapt. Long Beach 1985-87), Women on Target (L.A.), Afro-American Mus. Found. L.A., NAACP (life); Democrat; Methodist; rec: needlework, crafts, floral arrangements. Res: 6621 E Caro St Paramount 90723 Ofc: Compton Community College 1111 E Artesia Blvd Compton 90221

WILLIAMS, WILLIE, protective services official; b. 1943; m. Evelina; l977; children: Lisa, Willie Jr., Eric; edn: AS Phila. Coll. Textiles and Sci. 1982; postgrad. St. Joseph Univ. 1991. Career: police officer City of Phila. 1964-72, police

detective, 1972-74, police sgt., 1974-76, police lt. juvenile aid div. 1976-84, police capt. 22nd and 23rd dists. 1984-86, police inspector, head training bureau, civil affairs, North police div. 1986-88, dep. commr. adminstrn. 1988, police commr. 1988-92; chief of police L.A. Police Dept. 1992–; lectr, instr. Temple Univ., Univ. Pa., Univ. Del.; mem: West Oak Lane Youth Assn., Pa. Juvenile Officer's Assn., Former scout master Boy Scouts of Am., Southeastern Pa. Chiefs of Police, Nat. Orgn. Black Law Enforcement Execs. (nat. pres.), Internat. Assn. Chiefs of Police, Alpha Sigma Lambda; James Meml. Methodist Ch. Ofc: Office of Police Chief 150 S Los Angeles St Los Angeles 90012

WILLIAMSON, NEIL SEYMOUR, III, aerospace company executive; b. Jan. 5, 1935, Dumont, N.J.; s. Neil Seymour, Jr. and Mary Louise (Bittenbender) W.; m. Sue Carrole Cooper, Dec. 15, 1985; children: Deborah D. b. 1959, Leisa L. b. 1961, Neil S., IV b. 1966, Dirk A. b. 1968, Wendy L. b. 1970; edn: BS, U.S. Mil. Acad., West Point 1958; MSME, Univ. Mich., 1963. Career: commd. 2d lt., served to col. US Army 1958-81: assoc. prof. dept. earth, space and graphic scis. U.S. Mil. Acad., West Point, 1965-68; chief edn. sect. Fort McNair, D.C., 1970-71; analyst armor infantry systems group Army, Pentagon, W.D.C., 1972-73, systems analyst, program analyst requirements office Pentagon, 1974-76; chief adv. systems concept office Redstone Arsenal, Ala. 1976-77; comdr., dir. fire control and small caliber weapon systems lab., Dover, N.J. 1977-78; project mgr. TOW, Redstone Arsenal, 1978-81, retired U.S. Army 1981, decorated Bronze Star with o.l.c., Legion of Merit with o.l.c., Air medal with 7 o.l.c., Purple Heart; mem: Soc. Automotive Engrs., Am. Defense Preparedness Assn., Army Aviation Assn. (pres. Tenn. Valley chpt. 1980), Am. Helicopter Soc., U.S. Armor Assn., Disabled Am. Vets. Ofc: Hughes Aircraft PO Box 902 Bldg E1 M/S F120 El Segundo 90245

WILLIAMSON, RICHARD ARTHUR, English and film educator; b. Oct. 16, 1930, S.F., Calif.; s. Arthur Louis and Edith Lillian (Partridge) W.; edn: AA, City Coll. of S.F., 1950; BA, S.F. State Univ., 1953; MA, S.F. State Univ., 1958; Ctr. for Adv. Film Studies, L.A., 1971; Dirs. Guild of Am. internships: UCLA 1978, Brooklyn Coll., City Univ. of NY 1979-82; career: tchg. asst. S.F. State Univ., 1957; instr. language arts, S.F. State Univ., 1957-58; instr.,Eng., Santa Barbara City Coll., 1958-63; chmn. Eng., Santa Barbara City Coll., 1961-63; lectr. edn., S.F. State Univ., 1966; coord. Film & Composition, Univ. of Calif. Extension, S.F., 1971; instr./prof. of Eng. and film Coll. of San Mateo, 1963–;cons. Coll. Entrance Exam Bd., S.F. 1966-67; juror, Nat. Endowment for the Humanities, S.F. 1973-74, S.F. Internat. Film Festival, 1979-80; judge, Calif. State Student Film Festival, Los Angeles, 1974-75, 1979; writer/cons. Aspen Inst. for Humanistic Studies, Palo Alto, 1974-79; mem: Conf. on Coll. Composition and Comm. 1963- (exec. com. 1969-76, chair coll. comm. 1972-74), Nat. Council of Tchrs. of Eng. 1963–, Bay Area Film/Tape Council 1985–, Film Arts Foundn. 1985; coauthor of 3 books: Anatomy of Reading, 1965, Design For A Composition, 1966, Anatomy of Reading, 2nd. Ed. 1970; author: numerous articles and fiction for newsletters/magazines, 1971-92; The Archaeologist and the Handyman's Wife, (pub. review of The Mother Tongue by Bill Bryson) 1992; mil: PNT3, USN, 1953-55; Democrat; Buddhist; rec: writing. Ofc. Film Department (17-149), College of San Mateo 1700 W. Hillsdale Blvd. San Mateo 94402

WILLIS, CHARLES DUBOIS, neuropsychiatrist; b. Dec. 30, 1925; s. William Charles Willis, M.D. and Alma Anna (Lazear) W.; m. Shirley Mae Clarke, Jan. 28, 1951; children: Carol b. 1951, Nancy b. 1953, John b. 1956, Sarah b. 1963, James b. 1965; edn: BA, Atlantic Union Coll., Lancaster, Mass. 1949; MD, Loma Linda Univ. 1955; diplomate Am. Bd. Psychiatry and Neurology 1964. Career: intern Orange Co. Gen. Hosp., Orange, Calif. 1955-56; resident, psychiatry, Metropolitan St. Hosp., Norwalk, Calif. 1956-57, 60-62; resident, neurology, UCSF Med. Ctr. 1966-68; pvt. practice, Fresno 1968-83; staff psychiatrist St. of Calif., Corcoron, Calif. 1983-93; pres. Ancient World Found. 1991-95; author (book): End of Days; mil: capt. U.S. Army 1957-60; Republican; Protestant; rec: Biblical archeology. Ofc: Ancient World Foundation PO Box 3118 Pinedale 93650

WILSON, BLENDA JACQUELINE, university president; b. Jan. 28, 1941, Woodbridge, N.J.; d. Horace and Margaret (Brogsdale) Wilson; m. Louis Fair, Jr.; edn: AB, Cedar Crest Coll., 1962; AM, Seton Hall Univ., 1965; PhD, Boston Coll., 1979; DHL (hon.), Cedar Crest Coll., 1987, Loretto Heights Coll., 1988, Colo. Tech. Coll., 1988, Univ. Detroit, 1989; LLD (hon.), Rutgers Univ., 1989, Ea. Mich. Univ., 1990, Cambridge Coll., 1991, Schoolcraft Coll., 1992. Career: tchr. Woodbridge Twp. Pub. Schs., 1962-66; exec. dir. Middlesex County Econ. Opportunity Corp., New Brunswick, N.J., 1966-69; exec. asst. to pres. Rutgers Univ., New Brunswick, N.J., 1969-72; sr. assoc. dean Grad. Sch. Edn. Harvard Univ., Cambridge, Mass., 1972-82; v.p. effective sector mgmt. Ind. Sector, Washington, 1982-84; exec. dir. Colo. Commn. Higher Edn., Denver, 1984-88; chancellor and prof. pub. adminstrn. & edn. Univ. Mich., Dearborn, 1988-92; pres. Calif. State Univ., Northridge, 1992–; Am. del. U.S./U.K. Dialogue About Quality Judgments in Higher Edn.; advy. bd. Mich. Consolidated Gas Co., Stanford Inst. Higher Edn. Res., Univ. So. Col. Dist. 60 Nat. Alliance, Nat. Ctr. for Res. to Improve Postsecondary Teaching and Learning, 1988-90; bd. dirs. Alpha Capital Mgmt.; mem. higher edn. colloquium Am. Council Edn., vis.

com. Div. Continuing Edn. in Faculty of Arts & Scis., Harvard Coll., Pew Forum on K-12 Edn. Reform in U.S.; trustee Children's TV Workshop; dir. Univ. Detroit Jesuit High School, Northridge Hosp. Med. Ctr., Arab Community Ctr. for Econ. & Social Svs., Union Bank, J. Paul Getty Trust, Internat. Found. Edn. and Self-Help, James Irvine Found., Achievement Council, L.A.; dir., vice-chair Met. Affairs Corp.; exec. bd. Detroit area council Boy Scouts Am ; bd. dirs. Commonwealth Fund, Henry Ford Hosp.-Fairlane Ctr., Henry Ford Health System, Met. Ctr. for High Tech., United Way for Southeastern Mich.; mem. Nat. Coalition 100 Black Women, Detroit, Race Rels. Council Met. Detroit, Women & Founds. (corp. philanthropy), Greater Detroit Interfaith Round Table NCCJ, advy. bd. Valley Cultural Ctr., Woodland Hills; trustee assoc. Boston Coll., trustee emeritus Cambridge Coll., trustee emeritus/bd. dirs. Found. Ctr.; trustee Henry Ford Mus. & Greenfield Village, Sammy Davis Jr. Nat. Liver Inst.; mem. AAUW, Assn. Governing Bds. (adv. council of pres.'s), Edn. Commn. of the States (student minority task force), Am. Assn. Higher Edn. (chair-elect), Am. Assn. State Colls. & Univs. (com. on policies & purposes, acad. leadership fellows selection com.), Assn. Black Profls. and Adminstrs., Assn. Black Women in Higher Edn., Women Execs. State Govt., Internat. Women's Forum, Mich. Women's Forum, Women's Econ. Club Detroit, Econ. Club, Rotary. Ofc: Calif. State Univ. Northridge Office of President 18111 Nordhoff St Northridge CA 91330

WILSON, CARLOS GUILLERMO (CUBENA), educator, writer (pen name Cubena); b. Apr. 1, 1941, Panama, nat. 1966; s. Henrieta Wilson Williams; m. Colombina Chiru, Feb. 14, 1980; 2 sons: Jaime Jose, Carlos Jose; edn: BA in Spanish, Loyola Marymount Univ., L.A. 1968; MA in Spanish, UCLA 1970; MEd in urban edn., Loyola Marymount Univ. 1982, MA in counseling, 1983; PhD Hispanic languages, UCLA 1975; Calif. Comm. Colls. cred. Spanish instr., 1987; fluent in Spanish, English, Portuguese, French, Latin, Greek (classic). Career: tchr. elem. Spanish Verbum Dei High Sch., Los Angeles 1964-68; prof. Spanish, Loyola Marymount Univ., L.A.1971-91, adj. prof. edn., 1988-91; adj. instr., elem. Spanish, El Camino Coll., 1987-91; prof. San Diego State Univ. 1992–; dir. Hispanic Pastoral Summer Inst., 1989; co-dir. Summer Sch. in Cuernavaca, Mex. 1990; co-founder Afro-Hispanic Review, 1982; dir. Latin Am. Studies Pgm. 1977-79; mem. Latin Am. Studies Assn., Am. Assn. of Tchrs. of Spanish and Portuguese; author: (novels) Los Nietos de Felicidad Dolores, 1990, Chombo, 1981, (short stories) Cuentos del Negro Cubena, 1977, (poems) Pensamientos del Negro Cubena, 1977; profile listed in biographical references, feature subject of various articles; spl. interests: Latin Americans of African ancestry, Minorities in Latin Am., US, Europe and Africa; rec: travel, photography, movies, soccer. Res: 10884 Calle Verde #106 La Mesa 91941 Ofc: San Diego State Univ Dept Spanish and Portuguese San Diego 92182-0440

WILSON, JOHN MURRAY, JR., manufacturing company president; b. May 22, 1933, Los Angeles; s. J. Murray and Elizabeth E. (Reese) W.; m. Marily Anne Purkiss, July 14, 1955 (div. 1971); children: J. Murray b. 1957, Craig A. b. 1959, Kimberley R. b. 1961, Durinda C. b. 1969; edn: BSME, UC Berkeley 1955; MBA, Harvard Bus. Sch. 1960. Career: prodn engr. Hewlett Packard, Palo Alto 1960-61; stock broker Shuman Agnew & Co., San Francisco 1961-63; fin. planning mgr. Ford Motor Co. (aero. div.), Newport Beach 1963-65; gen. mgr. Disc Instruments Inc., Santa Ana 1965-69; pres. Telcor Instruments Inc., Irvine 1969–; founder Biotronic GmbH, W. Germany 1970–; chmn. Cortron Corp., Irvine 1969–; dir. Electro Mechanical Systems, Stuart, Fla. 1975–; mem: Harvard Bus. Sch. Assn., So. Calif. Marine Assn., Nat. Marine Mfrs. Assn., Bohemian Club, S.F.; mil: lt.j.g. USN 1956-58; Republican; Presbyterian; rec: yachting, fly-fishing. Ofc: Telcor Instruments, Inc. 17785 Sky Park Circle Irvine 92714

WILSON, JOHN RICHARD MEREDITH, college professor; b. Feb. 16, 1944, Vancouver, B.C.; nat. 1958; s. John Abraham Ross and Nora Margaret (Mains) W.; m. Mary Ann Ahlberg, Aug. 5, 1967; children: Amy b. 1969, Christine b. 1972; edn: diploma, Santa Barbara H.S., 1961; BA, UC Santa Barbara, 1964; PhD, Northwestern Univ., 1971. Career: instr. to assoc. prof. Minot State Coll., Minot, N.D., 1966-74; contract historian FAA, Wash., DC, 1974-76; assoc. prof. to prof., Mid Am. Nazarene Coll., Olathe, Kans., 1976-89; prof. So. Calif. Coll., Costa Mesa, 1989–; Fellow, Summer Inst., N.E.H., Princeton, N.J., 1980; Fellow, Summer Inst., N.E.H./Christian Coll. Coalition, Boston, Mass., 1984; Malone Fellow, Nat. Council on US-Arab Relations, Cairo, Egypt, 1986; delegate, Witness For Peace, Nicaragua, 1986; adv. placement reader, Ednl. Testing Svc., Princeton, N.J., 1977–; awards: Univ. of Calif. Abroad Pioneer, Bordeaux, France, 1962-63; Hearst Fellowship, Northwestern Univ., Evanston, Ill., 1964-65; Danforth Assoc., Danforth Found., St. Louis, 1980-86; mem: Orgn. of Am. Historians 1976–, Am. Historical Assn. 1976–, Conf. on Faith and History 1976–, Phi Delta Lambda Honor Soc. 1981–, Phi Alpha Theta Honor Soc. 1993–;civic: cand. for House of Representatives, N.D. Democratic party, 1972; Cultural Arts Comm., Costa Mesa, 1990-93; author: Turbulence Aloft, 1979, A New Res. Guide in History, 1986, Herbert Hoover and the Armed Forces, 1993; ed., Forging The American Character, 1991; Democrat; Assemblies of God; rec: baseball fan, softball, mountain hiking, reading. Res: 924 Tanana Place Costa Mesa 92626. Ofc: So. Calif. Coll. 55 Fair Dr. Costa Mesa 92626

WILSON, JON STEPHEN, consultant; b. June 10, 1935, Chickasha, Okla.; s. Marion Alfred and Zella Mae (Eisfelder) W.; m. Nancy Lee, May 31, 1958; children: M. Howard b. 1959, Stephenie b. 1961; edn: BSME, Oklahoma Univ., 1958; M.Automotive E., Chrysler Inst., Detroit 1960; MSE in I.E., Ariz. St. Univ., Tempe 1969. Career: engr. trainee Chrysler Corp., Detroit 1958-60; test engr. 1960-61; test engr. ITT Cannon Elect., Phoenix, Az. 1961-65; environmental lab. mgr. Motorola, S.P.D., Phoenix 1965-74; applications engring. mgr. Endevco div. Allied Signal, San Juan Capistrano, Ca. 1974-78, mktg. mgr. 1978-85; cons. prin. The Dynamic Consultant, 1985–; mem: Am. Consultants League (certified cons. 1986–), Assn. of Profl. Consultants and Advisors (cert. profl. cons. 1991–), Soc. Automotive Engrs. 1958–, Instrument Soc. Am. 1974–, Inst. Environmental Scis. 1965–, Am. Soc. for Tng. & Devel. 1990–, Toastmasters Intl. Dana Point 1984–; author: Climatic Testing Procedures, 1990, Instrumentation for Test & Measurement, 1991, editor (books): Dynamic Pressure Measurement Technology, 1991, Shock & Vibration Measurement Technology, 1986; Indep.; Methodist; rec: photography, computers, philately. Res/Ofc: The Dynamic Consultant 32871 Via Del Amo San Juan Capistrano 92675

WILSON, LAWRENCE PHILIP, newspaper managing editor; b. Nov. 17, 1955, Pasadena; s. Elmer Milton, Jr. and Marka Ann (Oliver) W.; m. Phoebe Wall, Aug. 17, 1985; edn: AB in English, UC Berkeley, 1977; MIM, American Grad. Sch. of Internat. Mgmt., 1982. Career: business mgr. Pasadena Media, Inc. 1984; asst. editor Pasadena Weekly, 1985-87; editorial page editor Star-News, Pasadena 1987-94, managing editor 1994-95, editor 1995–. Ofc: Star-News 911 E Colorado Blvd Pasadena 91109

WILSON, PETE, governor; b. Aug. 23, 1933, Lake Forest, Ill.; s. James Boone and Margaret (Callaghan) W.; m. Betty Robertson (div.); m. Gayle Graham Edlund, May 29, 1983; edn: BA in English lit., Yale Univ., 1955; JD, Boalt Hall UC Berkeley, 1962; Hon. LLD, Grove City Coll., 1983, UC San Diego, 1983, Univ. San Diego, 1984; admitted bar: Calif., 1962. Career: atty. pvt. practice, San Diego 1965-66; elected representative California State Assembly, 1966-71; mayor City of San Diego, 1971-83; U.S. Senator from Calif., 1983-91; Governor, California, 1991–; trustee Conservation Found.; mem. exec. bd. BSA San Diego County Council; hon. trustee So. Calif. Council Soviet Jews; advy. mem. Urban Land Inst., 1985-86; founding dir. Retinitis Pigmentosa Internat.; hon. dir. Alzheimer's Family Ctr. Inc., 1985; hon. bd. dirs. Shakespeare-San Francisco, 1985; awards: Golden Bulldog award (1984, 85, 86), Guardian of Small Bus. 1984, ROTC scholar Yale Univ. 1951-55, Legislator of Year League of Calif. Cities 1985, Man of Yr. Nat. Guard Assn. Calif. 1986, Man of Yr. citation UC Boalt Hall 1986; advy. bd. Nat. Mil. Family Assn.; mem. Phi Delta Phi, Zeta Psi; Republican; Episcopalian. Ofc: State Capitol Office of Governor Sacramento 95814

WILSON, SONJA MARY, business educator, school board official, speaker, consultant, poet; b. Mar. 28, 1938, Lake Charles, La.; d. Albert Ronald and Annelia (DeVille) Molless; m. Willie Williams, Apr. 28, 1956 (div. 1969); m. 2d Howard Brooks Wilson, Nov. 12, 1982; children: William, Dwayne, Rachelle, Devon, Lisa Lewis, Ricardo, stepchildren (by 2d marriage): Howard, Yvonne; 21 grandchildren; edn: grad. Manual Arts High Sch. of L.A., 1956; AA soc. & behav. scis., Mt. San Jacinto Jr. Coll., 1976-92; bus. edn. tchg. cred., UC San Bernardino, 1982; LaVerne Univ., 1984-5, CalPoly 1986; BS educ., So. Ill. Univ., 1995; Calif. tchg. creds.- adult edn., bus. and vocat. edn. Career: sales clerk, National Dollar Stores-1 yr.; sales clk., receptionist Royal Fruit & Produce, L.A. Terminal Annex-4 yrs.; PBX operator, payroll acct., sec., clk. Lake Elsinore Mil. Acad 2 yrs.; steno-typist, telegraph clk., typist Co. of L.A.-5 yrs.; sec., purchasing clk., mgr. General Electric Supply Co.-7 yrs.; with Lake Elsinore Unified Sch. Dist. 34+ yrs.: sec. to prin. Elsinore H.S. 1974-83, tchr. adult vocat. edn. 1979-84, notary pub. 1981-85, coord. vocat. edn. 1983-84, tchr. bus. and vocat. edn., class adviser, 1983-88; elected mem. Lake Elsinore Unified Sch Dist. Board, 1988–, bd. pres. 1988-89, clerk 1991–; Lake Elsinore Sch. Dist. mem. 1979-83, clk., pres., 1982-84, v.p. 1988-89; Calif. Sch. Bds. Assn. (dir. region 18, Golden Bell Award com., audit com., nominations com., conf. planning com., legis. com., by laws com., collective bargaining/bd. task force, media com.); Riverside Co. Sch. Bds. Assn. (1979–, pres. 1989-90, legislative facilitator planner 1988-90); Calif. Coalition of Black School Bd. Members (pres. 1990; presiding ofcr./ speaker Fresno Conf., Bakersfield Conf. 1989, Sacto. City Unified 1990); adv. Black Student Union/Future Leaders of Am. (1983–, appreciation tribute 1989), Nat. Sch. Bd. Assn. (del. Assy. Sargeant/Arms); speaker, panelist and facilitator num. workshops and profl. meetings, Bethel AME Ch. Outstanding Contr. to Educ. 1995, Women's Inner Circle of Achievements 1995; mem. St. Dept. Edn. Hoenig's Tri Council/African-Am. Com. 1990-92; honors: PTA Golden Oak Award for svc. to community and youth 1992, Proclamation City of Lake Elsinore 1989, Proclamation Co. of Riverside 1984, appreciation for comm. service Lake Elsinore C.of C. 1989, 90, Leukemia Soc. of Am. 1989, United Way 1988-89, Lions Club 1976-77, NAACP Outstanding contbns. to comm. services & academic devel. of youth & edn. (4/8/89, 90), Sojourner Truth in Media Network, Hilltop Community Center dedication for excellence in field of edn. 1989, Eta Phi Beta Sor. Inc. for dedication & leadership 1989, Black Art & Social Club for leadership & sensitivity to individual needs of children 1989, Calif. Bus. Edn. Assn., Calif. Elected Women Ofcls. Assn., Calif. Sch.

Employees Assn. (pres., treas., regional rep. asst., state negotiation com., conf. del.), Eta Phi Beta (Gamma Alpha chpt. pres., treas., v.p., reg. ofcr.); civic bds: Girl Scouts (ldr.& camp dir.-2 yrs.), Boy Scouts Am. (leader & den mother); listewd Who's Who in the West (1989, 93, 95), Who's Who in Am. 1991, Who's Who in Am. Educ., Who's Who in the World 1994-95; publs: CSEA President's Column, 1974-78; Valley News local news writer under pen name "Sunshine" 1974; article "Riverside County Schools" in Vision Mag., 1990; poem "Oh To Be Looked In The Eye" Betty Ford Ctr. at Eisenhower "Professional In Residence" Jour.; World of Poetry hon. mention: Double Image-Blackchild; Little Girl, Pain, Outstanding Poet (1994, 95), Nat. Library of Cong. "Mama Green Eyes"; Democrat (Ctr. comm. rep. & del.); rec: travel, gardening, sewing, reading, vintner. Res: 21330 Waite St Lake Elsinore 92530

WILSON, STEVEN AUDIE, lawyer; b. June 14, 1957, Fallon, Nev.; s. James Edward and Joanne Jane (Fister) W.; m. Stephanie Lynn Hamilton, Dec. 30, 1978; 1 dau. Sophie Elizabeth b. 1992; edn: BA, Univ. Nev. Reno 1979; JD, Willamette Univ. Coll. Law 1983; admitted Calif. Supreme Ct. 1983, U.S. Tax Ct. 1983, U.S. Dist. Ct. 1987. Career: adj. mng. ed. Nev. Livestock & Agricultural Jour., Sparks, Nev. 1979; law clk. Oreg. Legal Services, Albany, Oreg. 1982; spl. asst. U.S. Atty., Dept. Justice, San Jose 1987-88; atty. Chief Counsel I.R.S., Jacksonville, Fla. 1983-86; Chief Counsel I.R.S., San Jose 1986-94; special trial atty. Ofc. of Chief Counsel 1994–; awards: I.R.S. Achievement 1986, Willamette Univ. I.H. Van Winkle scholar 1982, Am. Jurisprudence 1981, Speidel Newspaper Charitable Found. scholar 1978, Who's Who Among Am. Law Students, Phi Kappa Phi; mem: Am. Bar Assn., Greenhead Club; Democrat; rec: skiing, backpacking, wine tasting. Address: Fremont 94539

WILSON, SUSANNE BOOTHE, company president; b. Sept. 30, 1928, Gonzales, Tx.; d. Wm. Henry, Jr. and Maurine (Ingraham) Boothe; m. Robert Wilson, 1947; children: William Munsey b. 1949, Robert Howell b. 1952, David Richard b. 1957; 6 grandchildren; edn: Univ. Tx. 1946-48, Coll. of William and Mary 1948-49; BA in polit. sci. (honors), CSU San Jose 1976. Career: politician; elected 2 terms City Council of San Jose 1973-78, v. mayor 1976-78; elected 3 terms Santa Clara Co. Bd. of Suprs. 1979-90, chmn. bd. 1982, 86, 90; Transit Dist. 1983, 87; pres. Solutions by Wilson, San Jose 1994–; leader in residence, prof. pol. sci. San Jose St. Univ., spring 1994; honors: woman of distinction The Woman's Alliance 1984, disting. alumni San Jose St. Univ. 1982, citizen of year Youth Sci. Inst. 1984, named Pub. Health Defender, Silicon Valley Toxics Coalition 1985, Juliette Gordon Low award Girl Scouts Santa Clara Co. 1988, Friend of Labor award COPE 1990, BSA Disting. Citizen of Yr., Mother of Yr. 1991, YWCA residence named Susanne B. Wilson, Friend of Bay Mec 1992, United Way Vol of Yr. 1993; mem: Calif. Elected Women for Edn. and Res. (founding mem., past pres.), Nat. Women's Polit. Caucus (founding mem. 1973–); civic: BSA Advy. Council, S.J.S. Spartan Found., Valley Med. Found., Career Closet (bd.), Friends of Open Space YWCA (advr.), contbr. articles to YWCA Mag., 1972, Women & Crime, 1976, Westplan (Am. Planning Assn., 1982); Democrat; Methodist; rec: garden, philately, skiing, reading, travel. Res: 1743 Valpico Dr San Jose 95124 Ofc: 701 Miller St San Jose 95110

WILSON, TERRY WAYNE, chiropractic doctor; b. May 22, 1961, Downey, Calif.; s. Larry Woodrow and Patricia Anne (Maxwell) W.; m. Carolyn Jane Levy, July 14, 1990; 1 dau. Christine b. 1993; edn: BA in biological scis., CSU Fullerton 1987; DC, Los Angeles Coll. of Chiropractic, Whittier 1987; lic. doctor of chiropractic, Calif. State Bd. of Chiropractic Examiners. Career: chiropractic intern Whittier Health Ctr. 1986-87; post-grad. intern, Robert Hughes, DC, La Habra 1987; assoc. doctor of chiropractic Orange Tree Chiropractic, Corona 1989-91; doctor of chiropractic, pvt. practice Yorba Linda 1992–; mem: Nat. Bd. of Chiropractic Examiners 1987–, Calif. Chiropractic Assn. 1991–, Orange County Chiropractic Assn. 1992–, American Back Soc. 1993–, Nat. Exchange Club NE Orange Co. (bd. dirs.), Diamond Bar Rotary Club, Corona Kiwanis Club; Republican; rec. fitness training. Res: 3343 Braemar Corona 91720 Ofc: East Canyon Chiropractic 24835 La Palma Ste D Yorba Linda 92687

WILSON, THEODORE HENRY, electronics company executive, aerospace engineer; b. Apr. 23, 1940, Eufaula, Okla.; s. Theodore V. and Maggie E. (Buie) W.; m. Barbara Ann Tassara, May 16, 1958 (div. 1982); children: Debbie Marie, Nita Leigh Wilson Axten, Pamela Ann, Brenda Louise, Theodore Henry II, Thomas John; m. Colleen Fagan, Jan. 1, 1983 (div. 1987); m. Karen L. Lerohl, Sept. 26, 1987; edn: BSME, UC Berkeley 1962; MSME, USC 1964, MBA, 1970, MSBA, 1971. Career: sr. res. engr. No. Am. Aviation Co. div. Rockwell Internat., Downey 1962-65; propulsion analyst, supr. div. applied tech. TRW, Redondo Beach 1965-67, mem. devel. staff systems group 1967-71; sr. fin. analyst worldwide automotive dept. TRW, Cleve. 1971-72; contr. systems and energy group TRW, Redondo Beach 1972-79; dir. fin. control equipment group TRW, Cleve. 1979-82, v.p. fin. control indsl. and energy group 1982-85; v.p. fin. space and def. group TRW, Redondo Beach 1985–; lectr., mem. com. acctg. curriculum UCLA Ext. 1974-79; mem: Fin. Execs. Inst. (com. govt. bus.), Machinery and Allied Products Inst. (govt. contracts coun.), Nat. Contract Mgmt. Assn. (bd. advisors), Aerospace Industries Assn. (procurement and fin. coun.), UCLA Chancellors Assocs., Tau Beta Pi, Beta Gamma Sigma, Pi Tau Sigma; Republican. Res: 3617 Via La Selva Palos Verdes Estates 90274

WINCH, GEORGE A., physician; b. Nov. 30, 1921, Springfield, Ill.; s. Anthony and Martha (Stambaugh) W.; m. Esther Shaffer, Oct. 28, 1944; children: Jennifer b. 1951, George, Jr., M.D. b. 1955, John b. 1958; edn: BS in edn., Miami Univ., 1943; MD, Jefferson Med., Phila. 1949. Career: Ob/Gyn resident Univ. Calif. San Francisco, 1953-56, asst. assoc., clin. prof. Ob/Gyn Dept. UCSF Sch. Med., 1953–; med. practice Ob/Gyn, S.F. 1956–; clin. prof. UCSF Ob/Gyn 1984–; awards: residents award to outstanding intern Germantown Hosp. and Dispensary, Phila. 1949-50, Henry J. Kaiser tchg. award, clin. faculty 1975, sect. dist. IX chair ACOG, Wash. DC 1982-88, recogn. 32 yr. tchg. UCSF Ob/Gyn Dept. 1988; mem: UCSF Clin. Faculty (pres. 1980-81), S.F. Gynecol. Soc. (pres. 1985-86), Pacific Coast Ob/Gyn Soc. (sr. mem. 1982–); club: S.F. Yacht; author num. med. papers and seminars, research studies; mil: lt. USN 1949-52; Republican; Episcopalian; rec: sailing, teaching, computers. Ofc: Winch, Smith, Ostermann & Moy, MDs 1700 California St San Francisco 94109

WINCHELL, ROBERT ALLEN, government auditor; b. Oct. 28, 1945, Ft. Monmouth, N.J.; s. Robert Winslow and Mary M. (Allen) W.; edn: BA, UC Santa Barbara, 1967; MBA, Wharton Grad. Div. Univ. Pa., 1969; C.P.A., Calif. Career: fin. analyst, treas. div. S.C. Gas Co., Los Angeles 1975-76; with Defense Contract Audit Agency, 1976–, senior auditor and resident ofcr. Rockwell Internat. B-1 div., El Segundo 1976-79; Hughes Aircraft Co., El Segundo 1979-84; senior auditor Defense Contract Audit Agency regional office, L.A. 1984-86; supvy. auditor, resident office Litton Systems, Woodland Hills 1986-87; Litton Inds. Inc., suboffice, Beverly Hills 1987-89; supvy. auditor AiResearch, Torrance 1989-92; supvy. auditor San Fernando Valley Branch 1993–; mem: Am. Inst. CPAs, Assn. of Govt. Accts.; club: Los Angeles CC; mil: 1st lt. US Army 1969-71, Bronze Star; Republican; Presbyterian; rec: golf, hiking, travel. Res: 2008 California Ave Santa Monica 90403 Ofc: Defense Contract Audit Agency, San Fernando Valley Branch Office, Van Nuys

WINCOR, MICHAEL Z., psychopharmacology educator, clinician, researcher; b. Feb. 9, 1946, Chgo.; s. Emanuel and Rose (Kershner) W.; m. Emily E.M. Smythe; children: Meghan Heather, Katherine Rose; edn: SB in zoology, Univ. Chgo., 1966; PharmD, USC, 1978. Career: research project specialist Univ. Chgo. Sleep Lab, 1968-75; psychiatric pharmacist Brotman Med. Center, Culver City 1979-83; asst. prof. USC, 1983–; cons. Federal Bur. of Prisons Drug Abuse Pgm., Terminal Is., 1978-81; Nat. Inst. Drug Abuse, Bethesda, Md. 1981; The Upjohn Co., Kalamazoo, Mich. 1982-87, 91-92, Area 24 Profl. Stds. Rev. Orgn., L.A. 1983, Brotman Med. Ctr., Culver City 1983-88, SmithKline Beecham Pharms. Phila. 1990-93, Tokyo Coll. of Pharm., Tokyo 1991; G.D. Searle & Co., Chgo. 1992–; mem. bd. dirs. USC Sch. of Pharm. Alumni Assn. 1979–; awards: cert. appreciation Mayor of Los Angeles 1981, Bristol Labs Award 1978, USC Faculty scholar 1978, Rho Chi; mem: Am. Assn. of Colls. of Pharmacy (mem. focus group on liberalization of the profl. curric.), Am. Coll. Clinical Pharmacy (chmn. constn. and bylaws com. 1983-84, mem. credentials com. 1991-93, 95, ednl. affairs com. 1994), Am. Soc. Hosp. Pharmacists (chmn. edn. and tng. advy. working group 1985-88), Am. Pharm. Assn. (del. annual meeting Ho. of Dels. 1989), Sleep Research Soc., Am. Sleep Disorders Assn.; civic: Franklin Avenue School Advy. Council 1986-89, K.I. Children's Ctr. Bd. Dirs. 1988-89, The Sequoyah Sch. Bd. Trustees 1992-93, Ivanhoe School Tech. Com. 1993–; author 30+ jour. articles, book chapters, and papers presented nat. and internat. meetings and reviewer; rec: photography. Ofc: Univ. So. Calif. 1985 Zonal Ave Los Angeles 90033

WINIARSKI, WARREN PAUL, winemaker, vineyardist; b. Oct. 22, 1928, Chgo.; s. Stephen and Lottie (Lacki) W.; m. Barbara Ann Dvorak, Mar. 28, 1958; children: Catherine b. 1960, Stephen b. 1963, Julia b. 1965; edn: BA, St. John's Coll., Annapolis, Md. 1952; grad. studies Univ. of Florence, Croce Inst., Naples, Italy 1954-55; MA, Univ. Chicago, 1964. Career: lectr., liberal arts, Univ. Chicago, 1954-64; cellarman Original Souverain Cellars, Napa Valley 1964-66; asst. winemaker Robert Mondavi Winery, 1966-68; vineyard/winery cons. Napa, Colorado, Sonoma, 1968-72; founder, owner, vineyardist. Stag's Leap Vineyards, Napa Valley 1970–; owner, vineyardist Fay Vineyard, 1986–; dir. Burpee Seed Co., 1991–; mem. bd. St. John's Coll. in Annapolis and Santa Fe, 1989–; awards: Stag's Leap Wine Cellars awarded Gold medals and Harry Waugh trophy as best Calif. wines entered Internat. Wine & Spirit Competition (1982, 83, 88), were the only Calif. wines served by Queen Elizabeth II at dinner for Pres. and Mrs. Reagan's 31st wedding anniversary in S.F. abd. HM Yacht Britannia (1983), wines were served at dinners Pres. Reagan held for Gen. Sec. Mikhail Gorbachev at Summit meetings in Geneva, Reykjavik and W.D.C. (1985, 86, 87), 1978 Cask 23 served at Pres.'s White House dinner for Prime Minister Margaret Thatcher (11/16/88), 1986 Reserve Chardonnay served at Pres.'s White House dinner for Prime Minister Rep. of Poland, Tadeusz Mazowiecki (3/21/90); mem: Congressional Recognition Selection com. Claremont Colls., 1986–; mem: Soc. Enologists, Napa Valley Vintners Assn. (dir. 1988–, chmn. com. for sub-appellations 1987–), Wine Inst. (rules & regulations com. 1980–), Vintners Club S.F., Am. Soc. of Viticulturists & Enologists, Orange County Wine Soc., Internat. Wine & Food Soc., Knights of the Vine Brotherhood (Supreme Kt. 1986); contbg. author: History of Political Philosophy (1963), contbr. articles to trade publs.; Republican; Episcopalian;

rec: Greek folk dancing, fencing, rowing, fishing, classical music. Ofc: Stag's Leap Wine Cellars 5766 Silverado Trail Napa 94558

WINKLER, HOWARD LESLIE, investment banker, business consultant; b. Aug. 16, 1950, NY, NY; s. Martin and Magda (Stark) W.; m. Robin Lynn Richards, Sept. 12, 1976; son, David Menachem; edn: AA in mktg., bus. data proc., and bus. mgmt. degrees, Los Angeles City Coll., 1973, 77, 81. Career: senior cons. Financial Consultants Inc., Los Angeles 1972-81; asst. v.p. Merrill Lynch Inc., L.A. 1981-83; v.p. Drexel, Burnham, Lambert Inc., Beverly Hills 1983-84; pres. Howard Winkler, Investments 1984-90; pres. Landmark Financial Group 1990–; ptnr. N.W.B. Assocs., L.A. 1988-90; nat. political editor B'nai B'rith Messenger, 1986–; chmn. bd. Community Adult Care Ctrs. of America, 1990-91; dir. Federal Home Loan Bank of S.F., 1991-93; chmn. bd. dirs. United Comm. and Housing Devel. Corp., L.A. 1986–; apptd. L.A. Co. Narcotics & Dangerous Drugs Commn. 1987–; Gov. Deukmejian apptd. trustee Minority Health Professions Edn. Found., 1989-94, sec.-treas. 1990-94; recipient awards for community service & leadership- Agudath Israel of Calif., Pres. Reagan, US Sen. Pete Wilson, Gov. G. Deukmejian, US Cong. Bobbi Fiedler 1986, resolution of commendn. Calif. State Assembly 1986, L.A. County Bd. of Suprs. commendn. for 20 yrs. of commitment, leadership & dedication 1994, City of L.A. 1990, comm. leadership Iranian-Jewish Comm. of L.A. 1990, Calif. State Senate Resolution of commendn. spons. Sen. Edward Royce 1992, listed Who's Who in World 1986–, Who's Who in America 1993–, charter issue Who's Who in Republican Party; civic: Calif. Lincoln Clubs PAC (pgm. chair 1987-91), Agudath Israel of Calif. (comm. legis. and civic action 1985–), V.F.W., Jewish War Vets; Republican: Calif. Rep. Party Platform Com. 1988, 90, Calif. YR's 1975-90, Calif. Rep. Assembly 1982-94, full mem. Calif. State Central Com. 1985-93, L.A. Co. Rep. Central Com. 1985-93, chmn. 45th A.D. 1988-90, Nat. Rep. Senatl. Com. nat. fin. bd. 1986-90, state co-chair Pete Wilson for Gov. '90, 1989, state chmn. Kemp for Pres. '88, 1987, mem. Nat. Steering Com. Bush-Quayle '88, 1987, mem. Nat. Exec. Com. Bush-Quayle '92, 1991, fin. com. John Seymour for Senate '92, 1991, mem. Rep. Presdl. Task Force 1985- (Legion of Merit Award 1992), Senatl. Inner Circle 1986- (Republican Senatorial Medal of Freedom award 1994), Golden Circle of Calif. 1986-92, GOP platform planning com. at large del. 1992, appt. del. by Gov. Pete Wilson to GOP nat. conv. Houston 1992; mil: adminstrv. supr. CID US Army 1969-72, SE Asia; Jewish (Orthodox); rec: philanthropies, family time, eating. Ofc: PO Box 480454 Los Angeles 90048 Tel: 213/939-9236

WINNING, ETHAN A., management and human resources consulting executive; b. Dec. 26, 1939, New Bedford, Mass.; s. Edward A. and Ruth W.; m. Sharon Carol Fogel, Jan. 26, 1964; children: Jennifer b. 1967, Amy b. 1969; edn: BA sociology, CSU Northridge, 1963; MS soc. psychology, Univ. Oregon, Eugene 1965, MA edn. and psychology, 1966. Career: psychologist and rehab. counselor State of Calif. and County of L.A., Rancho Los Amigos Hosp., Downey 1966-68; v.p. personnel and tng. Wells Fargo Bank, L.A., Wellsco Data Corp., San Francsco, and Wells Fargo and Co., San Francisco, 1968-73; nat. dir. and v.p. human resources Komatsu America Corp., San Francisco 1974-77; founder, pres. and c.e.o. Ethan A. Winning Associates Inc., Walnut Creek 1977–, estab. Personnel Mediation Services subs. co., 1990–; expert witness in labor, mgmt. disputes, and unemployment claims issues; assoc. ed. for nat. paper, The Personnel News, and monthly columnist for Calif. Job Journal; past secty. Calif. Small Financial Instns. Group; instr. Diablo Valley Coll., 1975-86; past v.p. Contra Costa Execs. Assn.; invited guest radio and TV shows; author: Common Sense Employer-Employee Relations (pub. Merchants and Mfrs. Assn., L.A., 1991), Labor Pains: Employer & Employee Rights & Obligations (TFM Press, 1995); rec: racquetball, biking, writing, tennis, photography, amateur radio (adv. lic. WD6GKF). Ofc: Ethan A. Winning Associates, Inc. 1618 Candelero Dr Walnut Creek 94598 Tel: 510/944-1034

WINSLOW, DAVID ALLEN, naval officer and chaplain, writer; b. July 12, 1944, Dexter, Iowa; s. Franklin Earl and Inez Maude (McPherson) W.; m. Frances Lavinia Edwards, June 6, 1970; children: Frances b. 1975, David b. 1979; edn: BA, Bethany Nazarene Univ., 1968; MDiv, Drew Univ., 1971, STM, 1974; postgrad. N.Y. Univ. 1974-75; ordained United Methodist Ch., 1973. Career: minister of visitation Marble Collegiate Ch., N.Y.C. 1970-71; pastor Trinity United Methodist Ch., Jersey City, N.J. 1971-73; Westside United Methodist Ch., Paterson, N.J. 1973-75; lt. cdr./chaplain US Navy, 1975-95; treas. Santa Clara Valley Council of Churches 1993-94, delegate 1995–; listed Who's Who in Religion, Who's Who in West, Who's Who in the World, Who's Who in Am., Dictionary of Internat. Biog.; mem: Am. Counseling Assn., Am. Mental Health Counselors Assn., The Acad. of Political Sci., Internat. Soc. for Traumatic Stress Studies, The Military Chaplains Assn. of USA; clubs: Dick Richards Breakfast Club 1988-91, Nat. Exchange Club, Navy League (hon.), F&A Masons, Scottish Rite, Salaam Temple, Commonwealth Club of Calif.; civic bds: Am. Red Cross Orange Cty. (disaster service, family service coms. 1989-91), Exchange Club Child Abuse Prevention Ctr. 1990-91; columnist Jersey Jour. 1971-73, The Chaplain 1978, mil. newpapers 1975–; Republican (Greater Irvine Rep. Assembly, Republican Assocs. Orange Co., Assembly Club 69th dist., Santa Clara Valley 1988-92); Republican; United Methodist; rec: sailing, swimming, golf. Res: 20405 Via Volante Cupertino 95014

WINSLOW, FRANCES EDWARDS, public administrator; b. Sept. 12, 1948, Phila.; d. Harry Donaldson and Anna Louise (McColgan) Edwards; m. David A. Winslow, June 6, 1970; children: Frances b. 1975, David b. 1979; edn: BA, Drew Univ., 1969, MA polit. sci., 1971; M Urban Planning, New York Univ., 1974, PhD pub. adminstrn., 1978; cert. hazardous mats. mgmt., UCI Ext., 1991. Career: asst. to city mgr. City of Florham Park, N.J. 1970-73; instr. Kean Coll. N.J., Union 1973-75; public safety asst. Irvine Police Dept. 1984-85, mgmt. analyst 1985-86, senior mgmt. analyst and dir. emergency mgmt. svs. City of Irvine 1986-91; dir. Office of Emergency Svs., City of San Jose, 1991–; adj. prof. National Univ., L.A. campus 1984-86, Orange County 1986-89; cons. Nat. Ctr. for Earthquake Engring. Research, Assn. of Bay Area Gov.; gubnat. appt. mem. Seismic Safety Commn., Calif., Hospital Bldg. Safety Bd., Calif.; mem. Nat. Coordinating Com. on Emergency Mgmt.; Calif. Emergency Svcs. Assn.; awards: Loula D. Lasker Found. fellow 1973-74, Navy League Volunteer Svc. Award 1984, Fire Marshal's Commendn. 1988, outstanding svc. So. Calif. Emergency Svs. Assn. 1991, Soroptimist Intl. Woman of Distinction - Environment 1991, listed Who's Who Among Students in Am. Colls. & Univs., Who's Who in Fin. & Ind., Who's Who Among Women, Who's Who in World, Who's Who Among Emerging Leaders; mem: Orange Cty. Cities Emergency Mgmt. Org. (pres. 1991), Am. Soc. Pub. Adminstrn. (chapter bd. mem., com. chair, ch. secr. 1994-95, ch. pres. 1995-96, nat. policy com. 1995-96, sect. bd. 1993-97), Am. Planning Assn. (com. mem.), Acad. Criminal Justice Scis. (fellow), Internat. City Mgmt. Assn., San Jose Mgmt. Assn. Bd.; civic: Boy Scouts Am. (P.R. com.), Santa Clara Valley Am. Red Cross Disaster Preparedness Com.; editor Urban Resources J. 1989, contbg. writer, Emergency Mgmt. 1990; ASEP Jour. 1995, (book ch.) Cities and Disasters (1990 edit., 1995 edit.); contbr. ed. NCEER Workshop Proceedings, 1990, 92; prod./writer, videos 1986–; Republican; Methodist; rec: church activities, politics, reading, handcrafts. Ofc: City of San Jose 855 M. San Pedro St Ste 404 San Jose 95110

WINTER, PATRICIA SUNDHEIM, science education coordinator; b. June 11, 1938, Chicago, Ill.; d. Harry G. Sundheim, Jr. and Blanche (Langsdorf) S.; m. Richard D. Winter, July 2, 1960 (widowed Apr. 2, 1982); children: Richard, Jr. b. 1966, Melissa b. 1967; edn: BA, sociology, Univ. of Chicago 1960. Career: dir. for alumni and devel. Francis W. Parker Sch., Chgo. 1969-77; market data res. and R.E. appraisal, Keith W. Brownell Co., La Jolla 1978-87; Edn. Outreach coord., General Atomics, San Diego 1993–; initiated Edn. Outreach Prog. and H.S. Sci. Day at Salk Inst. for Biological Studies, San Diego 1990, p.t. vol. 1990–; participated in devel. of 5 science workshops presented at Gen. Atomics 1993–, and San Diego Sci. Educators Assn. Conf. 1994, 95; mem: Calif. Sci. Edn. Advy. Com., San Diego Sci. Alliance (founder, chair steering com.), S.D. Sci. Educators Assn. (industry bd.), S.D. City Schs. Partnerships in Edn. (advy. bd.) and S.D. sci. supervisors com., S.D. Co. Ofc. of Edn. (sci. advy. com.), Reuben H. Fleet Space Theatre and Sci. Ctr. (scholarship com.), So. Calif. Biotech Edn. Consortium, Lincoln Prep. H.S. (med. ROP advy. com.), Southwestern Coll. BEST-ALL Advy. Team, Scripps Ranch H.S. Engring., Tech. and Design Advy. Team; UC San Diego Judaic Studies Bd. Visitors 1993-95; Jewish; rec: cooking, travel, reading, needlework. Res: 6449 Caminito Sinnecock La Jolla 92037 Ofc: General Atomics San Diego

WINTERS, BARBARA ANNE, lawyer; b. June 20, 1947, St. Louis, Mo.; d. Robert Poore Winters and Barbara Anne (Holter) Howell; m. Ronald D. Scales, June 18, 1984; edn: BA w. great distinction, UC Berkeley 1969, PhD 1977, JD 1985. Career: assoc. prof. philosophy UC San Diego, La Jolla 1974-84; extern J. Clifford Wallace, Circuit Judge U.S. Ct. of Appeals 9th Circuit, San Diego 1984; law clk. James R. Browning, Chief Judge, U.S. Ct. Appeals 9th Circuit, San Francisco 1985-86; dir. Howard Rice et al, San Francisco 1992–, assoc. 1986-92; arbitrator Nat. Assn. of Securities Dealers 1989–; awards: 3 Bancroft Whitney Am. Jurisprudence Awards (1983-84), Nat. Endowment for Humanities res. grant 1980, UC Berkeley James Sutton scholarship (1972-73), Order of Coif, Phi Beta Kappa; mem: Am. Bar Assn., Equal Rights Advocates, Bar Assn. San Francisco; publs: articles in profl. jours.; Democrat. Ofc: Howard Rice et al 3 Embarcadero Center 7th Floor San Francisco 94111

WINTERS, KAREN COLE, writer, producer, computer graphics designer; b. Dec. 28, 1948, Long Beach; d. Homer Gray and Kathryne C.; m. Glenn Stuart Winters, Mar. 3, 1974; children: Kelly b. 1981, Michael b. 1985; edn: BA (Phi Beta Kappa), UCLA, 1970, MA journ., UCLA, 1971. Career: assoc. creative dir. Honig-Cooper & Harrington, Los Angeles, 1971-78; assoc. creative dir. Rogers Weiss & Partners, Los Angeles, 1978-79; v.p., creative dir. Winters Productions, La Canada, 1979–, co-prod., interviewer and writer num. shows for ABC-TV news mag. "20/20", 1980–; prod./writer w/Walter Cronkite, documentary on marine pollution, 1990; awards include a Clio (1987, 1st award, outdoor, Sea World of Ohio), an Emmy (1981, Nat. Acad. of TV Arts and Scis., News & Documentary Producers for outstanding individual achiev. ABC-TV news pgm. 20/20), 3 Addy Awards 1988, So. Calif. Newspaper Execs. First Award 1988, Internat. Assn. of Bus. Communicators, Gold Quill Award (1988, for spl. video pgmmg.), PBS "Superfest" selected show (1988, "Changing Roles"), Chgo. Internat. Film Fest. silver plaque (1987, 1/2 hr. PBS show "Changing Roles"), N.Y. Internat. Film Fest. finalist 1987, numerous other creative awards; mem: Women in Design 1988–, Writers Guild 1977–, Verdugo Hills Art Assn. 1989–,

Women in Communications, Crescenta-Canada YMCA 1985–; author: Your Career in Advertising (Nat. Textbook Co., 1980-90), Teach Yourself Photoshop 2.5 (MIS Press/Henry Holt, 1993); rec: watercolor painting, skiing. Ofc: Winters Productions P.O. Box 920 La Canada 91011

WINTON, STEVEN WILLIAM, lawyer; b. May 5, 1957, San Jose; s. Fred B. and Anne (Bush) W.; m. Rita Cecilia cotter, June 6, 1987; edn: U.S. Naval Acad. Annapolis 1975-77; BA, UCSD 1979; JD, UC Berkeley Boalt Hall 1983; admitted St. Bar Calif. 1984. Career: atty., assoc. Alexander Millner, San Francisco 1983-86; Finley Kumble, San Diego 1986-87; Lorenz Alhadeff, San Diego 1988-95; Wittman Mitchell & Skola, San Diego 1995–; awards: U.S.Naval Acad. Outstanding Debater 1977, Boalt Hall Sch. Law Moot Ct. Best Brief 1981; mem: Am. Bar Assn., Bar Assn. San Francisco, San Diego Co. Bar Assn.; mil: USN 1975-77; Democrat. Res: 13303 Bronco Way Poway 92064 Ofc: Wittman Mitchell & Skola 11545 W Bernardo Ct Ste 302 San Diego 92127

WISHEK, MICHAEL BRADLEY, lawyer; b. June 25, 1959, Pasadena; s. Homer Cedric and Donna Jean (Arnold) W.; m. Shari Patrice Rubin, June 7, 1981 (div. 1986); m. Dorothea Jean Palo, Feb. 12, 1988; edn: BA, Claremont Mens Coll. 1981; JD, UC Davis Sch. Law 1985; admitted St. Bar Calif. 1986. Career: assoc. atty. Michael S. Sands Inc., Sacto. 1986-91; ptnr. Rothschild & Wishek 1991–; mem: Calif. Attys. for Criminal Justice, Am. Bar Assn., Sacto. Co. Bar Assn. (co-chair criminal law sect. 1989-90), Criminal Defense Lawyers of Sacto. (bd. mem. 1993–, treas. 1994–), Anthony M. Kennedy Am. Inn of Court 1989-91, Milton L. Schwartz Am. Inn of Court 1992–; edit. Claremont Jour. Philosophy, 1981, 2 articles pub. in profl. jours., 1981, 85; Democrat; rec: sailing, backpacking, skiing. Ofc: Rothschild & Wishek 901 "F" St Ste 200 Sacramento 95814

WITHERSPOON, GREGORY JAY, financial company executive; b. Sept. 30, 1946, Quantico, Va.; s. Thomas S. and Dorothy (Jordan) W.; m. Judith Ann Klein, Feb. 12, 1966 (div.); children: Lisa b. 1966, Michelle b. 1975; edn: BS, CSU Long Beach, 1970; C.P.A., Calif. Career: acctg. senior KMG Peat Marwick, Los Angeles 1969-72; senior mgr. Deloitte & Touche, L.A. 1972-79; c.f.o. Nanco Ents., Santa Barbara 1979-84; ptnr. BWV&P, Santa Barbara 1984-87; pres. Pea Soup Andersens, Buellton 1984-86; senior v.p. and c.f.o. Aames Financial, L.A. 1987–; mem. Am. Inst. CPA 1970–, Calif. Soc. CPAs 1970–; Republican; Presbyterian; rec: all sports.

WITHERUP, RONALD DAVID, seminary graduate school dean; b. May 18, 1950, Franklin, Pa.; s. David Earl and Rose (Malene) W.; edn: BA philosophy, St. Bonaventure Univ. 1972; STM, St. Marys Seminary & Univ. 1976; Th.M, Grad. Theological Union 1979; STL, St. Marys Seminary & Univ. 1981; PhD, Union Theological Seminary 1985. Career: tchr. Kennedy Christian H.S., Sharon, Pa. 1976-78; instr. St. Marys Seminary & Univ., Baltimore, Md. 1979-81; tchg. fellow Union Theological Seminary, Richmond, Va. 1981-85; counseling assoc. Cath. Univ. of Am., Wash. D.C. 1985-86; prof. St. Patricks Seminary, Menlo Park 1986–, academic dean 1987–; adj. faculty St. Marys Seminary & Univ. Cont. Edn. 1979-81; Ecumenical Inst. 1985-86; retreat dir. 1979–; scriptural and counseling workshops 1981–; mem: Soc. Biblical Literature, Cath. Biblical Assn., Catholic Theol. Soc. of Am.Task Force Literary Study of Matthews Gospel, Task Force Narrative Study of New Testament (co-chair 1988-93); book reviews and articles pub. in scholarly jours., 1986–; Cath. Address: 320 Middlefield Rd Menlo Park 94025

WITT, HERBERT, retired federal health and human services executive; b. May 9, 1923, Stockton, Calif.; s. Arnold and Sarah (Peletz) W.; m. Hiala Einhorn, Nov. 17, 1957; children: Heidi b. 1959, Julie b. 1962, Amy b. 1967; edn: AB, Coll. Pacific, Stockton, 1943; MBA, UC Berkeley, 1949; C.P.A., 1955. Career: staff auditor, Price Waterhouse, S.F., Calif. 1953-55; asst. dist. mgr., U.S. Army Audit Agy., 1951-53, 55-65; chief, spl. projects, Defense Contract Audit Agy. 1965-66; reg. inspector gen. audit, Dept. Health & Human Svs., 1966–; instr. auditing, UC Berkeley, 1960–; adj. faculty, Univ. of S.F., 1983–; awards: Assn. Govt. Accountants Presdl. award, 1975; Office Inspector Gen. Profl. Devel. award, 1987; Office Inspector Gen. Thomas D. Morris Leadership award, 1988; Exceptional Achievement award, 1990; We. Intergovtl. Audit Forum Jack Birkholtz Leadership award, 1989; Inst. of Internal Auditors S.F. Area Chpt. Disting. Svc. award, 1992; mem: Inst. Internal Auditors (past pres., S.F. chpt.); Am. Inst. C.P.A.; Calif. Soc. C.P.A.; Am. Acctg. Assn.; We. Intergovtl. Audit Forum; author with V. Brink, Modern Internal Auditing, 1982; with R. Atkisson and V. Brink, Modern Internal Auditing, 1986; mil: lt., USNR 1943-48; Democrat; Jewish; rec: hiking, swimming. Res: LaVerne Ave. Mill Valley 94941

WITTBERGER, RUSSELL GLENN, broadcast executive; b. July 7, 1933, Milwaukee, Wis.; s. Anton George and Libbie Elizabeth (Kresnicka) W.; m. Patricia Elizabeth Bradley, June 26, 1971; children: Steven, Robert, Elizabeth, Gary, Scott, Jennifer; edn: BS journ., Marquette Univ., 1955. Career: gen. sales mgr. WEMP, Milw., Wis. 1968-69; gen. mgr. WNUW-FM, 1970; pres. Rand Broadcasting Corp., Miami, Fla. 1970-73; v.p., gen. mgr. KCBQ Inc., San Diego 1973-78; pres. Downe Communications, 1978; exec. v.p., pres. Charter Broadcasting Co., San Diego, 1978-82; exec. v.p. Cantor Advertising Corp., San Diego 1982-85; v.p. and gen. mgr. Boyd and Farmer Advt., San Diego 1985-86; v.p., gen. mgr., prin. KLZZ-FM, San Luis Obispo, 1987-90; dir. mktg. Metro Traffic Control, San Diego 1990-94; gen. mgr. Metro Networks, San Diego 1994–; prin. Video Passport, San Diego, 1990–; mem: Milwaukee Ad Club (v.p., bd. 1970), Building Industry Assn., San Diego Broadcasters (pres. 1973-75); civic bds: Project Concern Internat. (dir. 1975-78), Radio Advt. Bur. (bd. dirs. 1978), COMBO San Diego (bd. trustees 1981), Food Bank S.L.O. Co. (v.chmn./co-founder 1989-90); Republican. Res: 1061 Abarca Ct Chula Vista 91910 Ofc: Metro Traffic Control 591 Camino De La Reina Ste 525 San Diego 92108

WITTROCK, MERLIN CARL, educational psychologist; b. Jan. 3, 1931, Twin Falls, Idaho; s. Herman C. and Mary Ellen (Baumann) W.; m. Nancy McNulty, Apr. 3, 1953; children: Steven, Catherine, Rebecca; edn: BS biology, Univ. Mo., 1953, MS ednl. psych., 1956; PhD ednl. psych., Univ. Ill., Urbana 1960. Career: prof. grad. sch. edn. UC Los Angeles, 1960–, chmn. div. Educational Psychology, founder Ctr. Study Evaluation 1966, chmn. of the Faculty, 1991-95; fellow Ctr. for Advanced Study in Beh. Scis., 1967-68; vis. prof. Univ. Wis., Univ. Ill., Ind. Univ., Monash Univ., Australia; bd. dirs. Far West Labs., S.F. 1989–; chair com. on evaluation and assessment L.A. Unified Sch. Dist., 1988–; nat. advy. panel for math. scis. Nat. Research Council of Nat. Acad. Sci., 1988-89; chair nat. bd. Nat. Ctr. for Res. in Math. Scis. Edn., 1991-95; awards: Thorndike award for outstanding psychol. res. 1987, UCLA Distinguished Tchr. of the Univ. award Acad. Senate & Alumni Assn. 1990, grantee Ford Found.; Fellow AAAS, Charter Fellow Am. Psychol. Soc., Fellow Am. Psych. Assn. (pres. div. ednl. psych. 1984-85, APA award for outstanding svc. to ednl. psych. 1991, award for outstanding contrb. ednl. psych. 1993, assn. council 1987–), Am. Ednl. Res. Assn. (chmn. ann. conv., chmn. publs. 1980-83, AERA Council 1986-89, bd. dirs. 1987-89, chmn. com. on ednl.-TV 1989–, awards for outstanding contbns. 1986, outstanding service 1989), Phi Delta Kappa; mil: capt. USAF; author, editor: The Evaluation of Instruction, 1970, Changing Education, 1973, Learning and Instruction, 1977, The Human Brain (1977, Danish transl. 1980, Spanish 1982), The Brain and Psychology, 1980, Instrnl. Psychology: Education and Cognitive Processes of the Brain, Neuropsychol. and Cognitive Processes of Reading, 1981, Handbook of Research on Teaching (3d edit. 1986), The Future of Ednl. Psychology, 1989, Research in Learning and Teaching (Macmillan, 1990), Testing and Cognition, 1991, Generative Science Teaching, 1994. Ofc: UCLA 321 Moore Hall L.A. 90095 Ph:310/825-8329

WIVIOTT, LORY DAVID, physician; b. June 15, 1956, Milwaukee, Wis.; s. Howard Hershel and Joanne Sheila (Tugenberg) W.; m. Jodi Ricklen, June 16, 1979 (div. 1983); m. 2d. Margaret Zender-Wiviott, Apr. 11, 1987; children: Lea Lauren b. 1988, Allyana Rachel b. 1991; edn: BA (Honors Coll.), Univ. of Wis., Madison 1978; MD, Albert Einstein Coll. of Medicine, Bronx, NY 1982; diplomate Am. Bd. Internal Medicine 1986; Bd. Cert. in Infectious Diseases 1990. Career: intern and resident, internal medicine Columbia Presbyn. Med. Ctr. Coll. of Physicians and Surgeons, NY 1982-85; res. asst. in infectious diseases Memorial Sloan Kettering Cancer Ctr., NY 1984-85; staff physician internal medicine, emergency rm. Kaiser Permanente Med. Ctr., So. San Francisco 1985-86; fellow in infectious diseases UC San Francisco Med. Ctr. 1986-89; attending physician, tchg. faculty internal medicine and infectious diseases Calif. Pacific Med. Ctr., S.F. 1989–, chmn. internal medicine grand rounds prog. 1990–; clin. instr. in medicine UCSF 1989-93, asst. clin. prof. 1993–; attending physician AIDS Clinic, UCSF 1989-92; adj. prof. Univ. of the Pacific Sch. of Pharmacy, Stockton 1991–; supervising attending, Infectious Diseases Svc.: UCSF Long & Moffitt Hosps. (3/93), UCSF/VA Med. Ctr., S.F. (10/94); vis. postdoctoral fellow in cancer res. UCSF Med. Ctr.; frequent lectr. in field, 1991–; mem. num. hosp. committees; awards: KNAPP Scholarship for Sr. Honors Thesis, Univ. Wis. 1977, Rock-Sleyster Scholarship in Psychiatry, Albert Einstein Coll. Medicine 1980, Alpha Omega Alpha 1981, Universitywide Task Force on AIDS Fellowship Award 1987-89; mem: Bay Area Infectious Diseases Soc., Infectious Diseases Soc. of Am., Physicians Assn. for AIDS Care; author: contbr. 6 articles to profl. jours., 1988-93, 5 abstracts presented, 1985-89. Res: 652 Hilary Drive Tiburon 94920 Ofc: Dept. Medicine/Div. of Infectious Diseases California Pacific Med. Ctr. 2100 Webster St Ste 326 San Francisco 94115

WOELFEL, ROBERT WILLIAM, broadcasting executive; b. Nov. 5, 1944, Los Angeles; s. William Herman and Mary Jane (Hiatt) W.; edn: AA, Mt. San Antonio Coll., 1965; BS in bus., CSU Los Angeles, 1969; MBA, USC, 1972. Career: salesman Burroughs Corp., El Monte 1969-71; sales mgr., announcer radio station KMFB/KPMO, Mendocino 1973-81; gen. mgr. Sta. KOZT, Fort Bragg, 1981-85; Sta. KBLC, Lakeport, 1984-85; v.p., sales mgr. Sta. KZOZ/KKAL, San Luis Obispo, 1985-86; corp. gen. mgr. Visionary Radio Euphonics, Santa Rosa, 1986-87; dir. mktg., gen. sales mgr. Sta. KUBA/KXEZ, Yuba City 1987-88; gen. mgr. Sta. KMRJ, Ukiah 1988-91; broadcast consultancy in Pacific Rim (Lahaina, Hawaii; Hamilton, New Zealand; Hobart, Tasmania) 1991-93; stations mgr., radio div. Mendocino Broadcasting Co. 1993–; principal ptnr. Electoral Target Advertising, 1988-91; instr. advt. comm. colls.; elected councilman City of Ft. Bragg, 1979-85, mayor 1984-85; civic bds: Mendocino Coast Ednl. TV Assn. (dir. 1983-85), Ukiah C.of C. (dir. 1990-91); mil: USN 1966-68; Presbyterian; rec: basketball, reading. Res: PO Box 2538 Mendocino 95460 Ofc: 101-E Boatyard Center Fort Bragg 95437

WOHL, ARMAND JEFFREY, cardiologist, educator; b. Dec. 11, 1946, Phila.; s. Herman L. and Selma (Paul) W.; m. Marylou Giangrossi, Sept. 4, 1977; children: Michael b. 1979, Todd b. 1981; edn: undergrad. Temple Univ. 1964-67; MD, Hahnemann Univ. 1971. Career: intern Bexar County Hosp., San Antonio, Tx. 1971-72; resident in med. Parkland Meml. Hosp., Dallas 1972-74; fellow in cardiol. Univ. of Tx. (Southwestern) Med. Sch. of Dallas 1974-76; chief cardiology USAF Hosp. Elmendorf, Anchorage, Alaska 1976-78; chief of cardiology Riverside Med. Clinic, Riverside, Calif. 1978-79; cardiologist, Grossmont Cardiology Med. Group, La Mesa 1980-84; pvt. practice, La Mesa 1985–; chief of cardiology Grossmont Hosp., La Mesa 1988-90; asst. clin. prof. of med. Univ. Calif., San Diego 1990–; mem: Am. Coll. of Cardiology (Fellow 1979, mem. Health Care Issues Com., Calif. chpt. 1990–, dist. councilor San Diego chpt. 1993–), Am. Coll. of Physicians (Fellow 1979), Council on Clin. Cardiology (Fellow 1981), Am. Heart Assn. (San Diego chpt. bd. 1981-87); publs: 5 abstracts, contbr. 8 articles in med. journals; mil: major USAF 1976-78. Ofc: 5565 Grossmont Center Dr Ste 126, La Mesa 91942

WOLD, ROBERT MILES, optometrist; b. Dec. 5, 1942, Devils Lake, N.D.; s. Anton Miles and Florence (Strommen) W.; m. Margery Wilson, June 13, 1964; children: Peter b. 1968, Dawn b. 1971; edn: AA, Devil's Lake Jr. Coll. 1961; BS, Pacific Univ. Ore. 1963; OD, 1964; MS, 1966. Career: pvt. practice optometry, Los Altos 1965-69; Chula Vista 1969–; awards: Calif. Optometric Assn. Young Optometrist 1970, Best Editorial 1973, S.D. Optometric Soc. Optometrist of Year 1978, Coll. Optometrists A.M. Skeffington award 1974; mem: Am. Acad. Optometry (fellow), Coll. Optometrists in Vision Devel. (fellow, secty. 1970–), Am. Optometric Assn., Calif. Optometric Assn., Am. Optometric Found. (pres. 1991-92), San Diego Co. Optometric Soc. (pres. 1975, 81), Nat. Academies of Practice (disting. practitional 1993–), Rotary (past dir.), Chula Vista C.of C. (past dir.), BSA (scoutmaster 1982-93); 120+ articles pub. in profl. jours; rec: camping, swimming. Res: 627 Mission Ct Chula Vista 92010 Ofc: Drs. Wold and Mason 353 H St Suite C Chula Vista 91910

WOLF, CAROL LYNN, marketing executive; b. Aug. 29, 1956, San Diego; d. William Francis and Elizabeth Carolyn (Kjorlaug) Wolf; edn: BA, San Diego St. Univ. 1978; MS, Colo. St. Univ. 1982; MBA, San Diego State Univ. 1994. Career: chemist Novo Lab., Wilton, Conn. 1982-84; market research 1984-86; chemist Kelco Div., Merck & Co., San Diego 1986-87; product mgr. 1987-90, business mgr. 1990-94, dir. of mktg. 1994–; mem: Inst. Food Techs., Cereal Chemists Soc., Am. Mktg. Assn.; ed. Kelcogel Gellan Gum Update newsletter, 1989; Democrat; Lutheran; rec: aerobics, travel, skiing. Res: 7285 Calabria Ct #12 San Diego 92122 Ofc: Kelco 8355 Aero Dr San Diego 92123

WOLF, SHELDON MARK, physician, neurologist; b. Feb. 26, 1934, New York; s. Herman Leo and Dorothy (Feder) W.; m. Barbara Greenberg, Feb. 7, 1960; children: Jonathan b. 1963, David b. 1966, Daniel b. 1970; edn: BA, Columbia Coll. 1955; MD, 1959. Career: intern Bellevue Hosp., N.Y.C. 1959-60; resident N.Y. Neurological Inst. 1960-63, fellow in neurophysiology 1963-64; attdg. neurologist Kaiser Found. Hosp., L.A. 1964–; clin. prof. neurology UCLA Sch. Medicine, 1980-93; honors: Phi Beta Kappa, Alpha Omega Alpha; mem: Am. Acad. Neurology (fellow), Assn. Research in Nervous & Mental Disease, Am. Neurological Assn.; num. articles pub. in med. and profl. jours.; rec: music, photog. Ofc: 1505 N Edgemont St Los Angeles 90027

WOLFE, CHRISTOPHER LANE, cardiologist, educator; b. Sept. 23, 1951, Saginaw, Mich.; s. Richard Allen and Ellen Marie (Lane) W.; m. Cynthia Marie Soghikian, Sept. 26, 1981; children: Lena Marie, Laura Anne; edn: BA, Am. Univ. Beirut 1974; MD, Wayne State Univ. 1978; Diplomate, Am. Bd. Internal Medicine, subspecialty cardiovascular disease. Career: med. intern and resident Emory Univ. Affiliated Hosps., Atlanta 1978-81; cardiology fell Univ. Tex. Health Sci. Ctr., Dallas 1982-85; asst. prof. medicine UC San Francisco 1986-94, assoc. prof. medicine 1994–; assoc. dir. cardiac care unit Moffitt-Long Hosp.-UCSF 1986-95; med. dir. intensive cardiac care Moffitt-Long Hosp.-UCSF, 1995–; assoc. staff Cardiovascular Res. Ins.-UCSF 1990–; awards: Clinician Scientist award Am. Heart Assn. 1985, British-Am. res. fellow Am. Heart Assn. 1985, Clin. Investigator award Nat. Heart, Lung and Blood Inst. 1986, Nat. Grant-in-Aid Am. Heart Assn. 1992; mem: Am. Heart Assn. (fellow, council clin. res. 1987–), Am. Coll. Cardiology (fellow), Am. Fedn. Clin. Res. (2 Henry Christian Meml. awards 1991), Soc. Nuclear Medicine, Soc. Magnetic Resonance, We. Soc. Clin. Investigation; author: 9 book chpts., num. sci. and review articles, peer-reviewed sci. pubs.; Presbyn. (deacon Westminster Presbyn. Ch., Tiburon 1992-94); rec: hiking, kayaking. Ofc: Univ of California 505 Parnassus Ave San Francisco 94143-0124

WOLFE, CYNTHIA SOGHIKIAN, emergency physician; b. Feb. 17, 1954, Beirut, Lebanon; d. Shahan Katchadour and Juanita (Will) Soghikian; m. Christopher Lane Wolfe, Sept. 26, 1981; children: Lena b. 1988, Laura b. 1990; edn: BA (cum laude), Harvard Univ. 1976; MD, Emory Med. Sch., Atlanta, Ga. 1980; cert. Am. Bd. of Family Practice 1984, Am. Bd. of Emergency Medicine 1989. Career: attending physician (tchg.) John Peter Smith Hosp. E.D., Ft. Worth Tx. 1984-86; clin. prof. emergency medicine UCSF Med. Ctr. 1986-87; assoc. dir emergency dept. Brookside Hosp., San Pablo, Calif. 1987-90; awards:

Armenian Am. Assn. scholarship, Boston 1977; fellow Am. Acad. of Emergency Physicians; author: article on hypothermia pub. Am. Jour. Family Practice, 1994; Presbyterian (deacon Westminster Presbyn. Ch. 1992-93); rec: skiing, hiking, reading, painting, kayaking, biking. Ofc: Pinole Emergency Med Group Doctors Hospital 2151 Appian Way Pinole 94564

WOLFINGER, BARBARA KAYE, research specialist, film-maker; b. Sept. 3, 1929, NY, NY; d. Louis and Margaret (Goodman) Kaye; m. Raymond E. Wolfinger, Aug. 7, 1960; 1 child: Nicholas b. 1966; edn: AB, Univ. of Mich.; grad. study, City Coll. of NY, Mass. Inst. of Tech. Career: dir. design res., McCann-Erickson, Inc., NY, 1954-58; res. cons., Stanford Univ. Inst. for Res. in Political Studies, Langley Porter Inst., Market Planning Corp., Calif. Dept. of Public Health, 1960-70; res. assoc., Inst. for Res. in Social Behavior, Oakland, Calif., 1971-76; res. assoc., Survey Res. Ctr., UC Berkeley, 1976-77; pres., Berkeley Productions, Inc., 1978–; ptnr., Qualitative Res. Assoc., 1978–; awards: CINE Golden Eagle Award, US Indsl. Film Festival, First Prize for film Catch a Falling Star, 1979; Best Film, LEARNING Award, Best in Category, Family Life Video Award for film Black Girl, 1982-83; Red Ribbon, Am. Film Festival, for film Sister of the Bride; author: profl. papers, 1973, 87; pub. articles in Ideology and Discontent, 1964, Design Research, 1957; films: Catch a Falling Star, Black Girl, Chile Penguin, Sister of the Bride, Your Move, Almost Home; video, Nine Months. Res: 715 The Alameda, Berkeley 94707

WOLK, BRUCE ALAN, law professor; b. March 2, 1946, New York; s. Morton and Gertrude W.; m. Lois G., June 22, 1968; children: Adam b. 1975, Daniel b. 1977; edn: BS, Antioch Coll. 1968; MS, Stanford Univ. 1972; JD, Harvard Law Sch. 1975; admitted Wash. D.C. Bar 1975. Career: atty., assoc. Hogan & Hartson, Wash. D.C. 1975-78; prof. of law UC Davis 1978–; dean, Sch. of Law UC Davis 1993–; awards: UC Davis Disting. Tchg. 1987; mem: Am. Bar Assn. Am. Law Inst.; 5 articles pub. in profl. jours., 1980-88; co-author Pension and Employee Benefit Law (2d ed. Foundation Press, 1995); mil: USPHS 1968-70. Res: 1209 Colby Dr Davis 95616 Ofc: Univ. of California School of Law Davis 95616-5201

WOLK, CHARLES JOSEPH, JR., county farm bureau president; b. Feb. 13, 1937, St. Louis, Mo.; s. Charles J. and Catherine E. (Dierker) W.; m. Kathryn James, April 9, 1960; children: Stephen Bennet b. 1961, Joseph Martin b. 1964, Catherine Elizabeth b. 1965; edn: BME, Marquette Univ. 1959; MS mgmt. engring., George Washington Univ. 1971. Career: served to lt. col. US Marine Corps 1959-80; owner Bejoca Co., Fallbrook 1980–; pres. San Diego County Farm Bureau, 1988-90, Farm Bur. rep. San Diego Co. Internat. Trade Commn. 1988–, chmn. San Diego Co. Farm Bur. agri. ednl. program 1983-85; elected commr. Dist. II, Calif. Avocado Commn. 1987-94, chmn. 1995; mem. agri. water advy. com. to Dir. of Calif. Dept. Food & Agri.; bd. dirs. Fallbrook Pub. Utilities Dist. 1981-94, pres. 1984-88; honors: San Diego Union Tribune farmer of year (–1986)–; mem. Calif. Fuyu Growers Assn. (pres. 1986-94), Fallbrook C.of C. (dir. 1991-94, pres. elect 1992, pres. 1993), Fallbrook AG Boosters Club, Fallbrook Youth Baseball (coach 1973), PTA Fallbrook (bd. 1977-79); Republican (del. 74th A.D., San Diego County Rep. Central Com. 1990-93); R.Cath.; rec: western horses. Address: Fallbrook 92028

WOLKOV, HARVEY BRIAN, physician; b. Feb. 8, 1953, Cleveland, Ohio; s. Sidney and Norma (Levin) W.; m. Lauren Cronin, Jan. 9, 1993; edn: BS, honors prog., Purdue Univ. 1975; MS, bionuclear physics, Purdue Univ. 1977; MD, Med. Coll. of Ohio 1979; lic. physician Calif.; DEA registration, diplomate Nat. Bd. of Med. Examiners 1980; cert. Am. Bd. of Radiology 1983. Career: res. asst. neurosci. Purdue Univ. 1973-75; tchg. asst. microbiology 1975-76; internship, medicine/radiation oncology UC Med. Ctr. San Francisco 1979-80; residency, radiation therapy Stanford Univ. Hosp. 1980-83; res. asst. radiobiology Stanford Univ. Med. Ctr. 1982; vis. radiation oncologist Danish Cancer Soc., Inst. of Cancer Res., Aarhus, Denmark 1987; radiation oncologist Radiation Oncology Ctr., Sacramento 1983–; asst. clin. prof. radiology Sch. of Medicine UC Davis 1983-90; med. dir. radiation oncology Mercy Gen. Hosp., Sacto. 1987-90; assoc. clin prof. radiology Sch. of Medicine UC Davis 1990-92, assoc. clin. prof. surgery 1992–; dir. Div. of Radiation Oncology, Radiation Oncology Centers, Sacto. 1990–; honors: Phi Eta Sigma, Phi Kappa Phi, tchg. fellowship Purdue Univ. 1975-76, Eta Sigma Gamma, Am. Cancer Soc. Med. Sch. Fellowship, Am. Cancer Soc. Clin. Fellowship, Am./Euro. Soc. of Therapeutic Radiology and Oncology Travel Award 1987; mem: Am. Soc. for Therapeutic Radiology and Oncology (membership com.), Am. Cancer Soc. (reviewer, res. professorship), Am. Endocurietherapy Soc., Am. Coll. of Radiology (commn. on radiation oncology, com. on radiation therapy oncology group 1987–, com. on stds. and accreditation 1991–, radiation oncology task force on managed care 1994–), Am. Radium Soc., Am. Soc. Clin. Oncology, Sacto.-El Dorado Med. Soc., No. Calif. Radiation therapy Assn., Radiation Therapy Oncology Group (chmn. interoperative radiation therapy com. and new investigators com., mem: exec. com, modality com. publication com. radioimmunoglobulin & radiopharmaceutical com., membership com.), Children's Cancer Study Group 1983-89, Pediatric Oncology Group (co-principle investigator 1989–), Am. Coll. of Surgeons (liaison assoc. commn. on cancer), Sutter Hosps. Med. Res. Found. (bd. dirs 1986-88), Sutter Hosp. Found (bd. trustees 1988–), Sutter Inst. for Med.

Res. 1989– (chmn. grants review com. and policies & procedures com., vice-chmn. res. com. 1990–, editl. bd. "Frontiers"), Sutter Comm. Hosps. (chair radiation oncology quality assurance com., mem: diagnostic imaging/radiation oncology quality assurance, med. advy. com., oncology com., credentials com.); author/contbg. author: 8 book chpts., 1989–, 20 articles to profl. jours., 1982–, num. presentations in field; rec. sculpture, drawing, tennis. Ofc: Radiation Oncology Ctr 5271 F St Sacramento 95819

WOLLMER, RICHARD DIETRICH, professor of operations research and statistics; b. July 27, 1938, Los Angeles; s. Herman Dietrich and Alice Myrtle (Roberts) W.; edn: BA in math., Pomona Coll., Claremont 1960; MA, app. math., Columbia Univ., 1962; MS engring. sci. UC Berkeley 1963; PhD, engring. sci., UC Berkeley, 1965. Career: operations research scientist RAND Corp., Santa Monica 1965-70; prof. ops. res. and statistics, CSU Long Beach, 1970–; lectr. UCLA 1970, 74, vis. assoc. prof. Stanford Univ. 1976, vis. prof. CSU Northridge 1981-82; cons. McDonnell Douglas, Long Beach 1978-80, 82, 1985-91, Logicon, San Pedro 1979-81; awards: NSF fellow Columbia Univ. 1960-61, best paper mil. appls. Operations Res. Soc. Am., Balt. 1969; mem: Ops. Res. Soc. Am. 1965–, The Inst. of Mgmt. Sci. 1965–, So. Calif. TIMS-ORSA (1968–, past chair); pub. jour. articles in Operations Res. Jour. (1992, 70, 64), Annals of Ops. Res., 1991, Mathematical Prog. (1980, 85), Transportation Sci. (1982, 68), Mathematics of Ops. Res., 1977, Mathematical Biosciences, 1976, Networks (1972, 80, 90), Jour. Mathematical Analysis and Applications, 1970, Naval Logistics Res. Quarterly (1970, 69), Mgmt. Sci. Jour., 1968; Republican; Presbyn. (deacon Bel Air Presbyn. 1982-84); rec: sports, music. Res: 6132 Fernwood Dr Huntington Beach 92648 Ofc: Dept. Info. Systems, School of Business CSU Long Beach 1250 Bellflower Blvd Long Beach 90840

WOMACK, THOMAS HOUSTON, manufacturing company executive; b. June 22, 1940, Gallatin, Tenn.; s. Thomas Houston and Jessie (Eckel) W.; m. Linda D. Walker, July 20, 1963 (div. Dec. 1989); children: Britton b. 1969, Kelley b. 1971; m. Pamela Ann Reed, Apr. 20, 1991; edn: BSME, Tenn. Tech. Univ., 1963. Career: project engr. U.S. Gypsum Co., Jacksonville, Fla. 1963-65; project mgr. Maxwell House Div., Gen. Foods Corp., Jacksonville, 1965-68, mfg. mgr., Hoboken, N.J., 1968-71, div. ops. planning mgr., White Plains, N.Y., 1971-73; sales mgr. J.R. Schneider Co., Tiburon, Calif. 1973-79; pres. Womack Internat., Inc. Novato 1979–; listed Who's Who in West, Who's Who in America, Who's Who in the World; mem.: Soc. Tribologists and Lubrication Engrs., Am. Filtration Soc., Soc. of Mfg. Engrs., Am. Soc. of Chemical Engrs.; Republican; Prot. Ofc: Womack International, Inc. One Digital Dr Novato 94949

WONG, ADRIAN MICHAEL, pharmacist, educator; b. May 22, 1951, San Francisco; s. Henry T. and Lillie L. W.; children: Matthew b. 1983; edn: Univ San Francisco 1969-72; BS pharm., Idaho St. Univ. 1975; cert. of residency, UCSF, 1982. Career: pharmacist/owner Los Portales Pharmacy, San Francisco 1978–; co-founder Litigator Software Co., 1985; asst. clin. prof. Sch. Pharm. UC San Francisco, 1986–; adj. prof. pharm. Univ. of Pacific Sch. of Pharmacy, 1989–; appt. Calif. State MEDI-CAL Contract Bd. 1992–; appt. Calif. Pharmacists Employer Task Force, 1989-90; faculty Am. Pharm. Assn. Wm. Apple Memorial Symp. 1990; Calif. State Bd. of Pharm. Competency Com. 1995-2003; mem. owners advy. com. CPhA Acad. of Mgmt.; mem. Pharm. Soc. S.F. (pres. 1988-89, v.p. 1987-88, bd. dirs. 1986-87, 92-94, media spokesman 1986–, Outstanding Pharmacist Award 1989), Am. Pharm. Assn. (educ. affairs com. 1994), Calif. Pharm. Assn. (ho. dels. 1983-88, nominating com. 1986, 88, med. task force 1987-90, chmn. reference com. "B" 1992, chmn. meri-cal advy. com. 1992-94, dir. PAC 1990-94) New Millenium Educ. Inst. (treas.); clubs: Cessna Pilots Assn. /Cessna 150, Rolls Royce Owners, Bentley Drivers; author computer software: The Litigator (1985); R.Cath.; rec: audio engring., flying, auto restoration. Ofc: Los Portales Pharmacy 2480 Mission San Francisco 94110

WONG, DOUGLAS LIM, martial arts teacher, trainer and author; b. Dec. 7, 1948, Los Angeles; son Bing and Mary W.; married Carrie Jean Ogawa, Oct. 24, 1981; children: Travis Todd b. 1985, Tia Alese b. 1988, Cassidy Brooke b. 1994; edn: Aeronautical Engring., Northrop Inst. of Tech., 1967-69, Mktg. Mgmt., Woodbury Bus. Coll., 1969-71. Career: medical record supr. Occupational Health and Safety Div. City of Los Angeles, 1980–; founder White Lotus System of Kung Fu, Master, hd. instr. Sil Lum Kung Fu Studio, Northridge; world lectr., seminars, tng. camps, appearances in movies, TV shows, radio interviews, magazines, newspapers; promoted over 20 tournaments; author: Kung Fu the Way of Life; Shaolin Fighting Theories and Concepts; The Deceptive Hands of Wing Chun; Kung Fu the Endless Journey; Martial Arts editor for nat. physical fitness mag., Exercise for Men Only, 1991–; appt. by AAU Chinese Martial Arts Div. as the Association Chinese Martial Arts Chairperson for So. Pacific area (includes So. Calif.) 1991–; reg. chmn. Pacific Assn. (CA, NV, AZ 1991–); nat. v. chmn. AAU-CMAD elected Sept. 1992; Nat. AAU (life mem. July 1992); Sullivan Nomination Bd.; nat. bd. dirs., prof. ATAMA; founding mem. United Kung Fu Fedn. of N. Am. 1994; adv. to USA Wu Shu-Kung Fu Fedn. 1994; mem. Nat. Assn. of Profl. Martial Artists (NAPMA) 1995–; awards: Inside Kung Fu Mag. list of 100 Most Influential Martial Arts Personalities of All Time (2/91), recipient Commendations and Resolutions - Calif. State Senate and Assembly, Gov. of Calif., L.A. City

Council, L.A. Mayor Bradley, San Diego Mayor, City Council and County Bd. Suprs., U.S. Marine Corps, Am. Red Cross, Lion Internat., Save the Children Found., Ethiopian Famine Relief Project, Kiwanis, Rotary Internat., others; given 8th degree Black Belt ranking Am. Tchr. Assn. of Martial Arts (ATAMA) 1993, listed in Who's Who in Karate and the Other Martial Arts, Who's Who in Am. Martial Arts; Leaders of the Chinese Martial Arts; Masters, Founders and Leaders of Am. Martial Arts; Who's Who of ATAMA 1995; Martial Arts Source Book 1995; featured in over 500 mag. and newspaper articles including Life, Premiere, Runner's World, Natural Physique, Exercise for Men Only, Am. Cinematographer, Asiam, L.A. Times, Daily News, Variety, Inside Kung Fu, Masters & Styles, Profl. Karate, Official Karate, Racquetball Illustrated, others; video series Shaolin Fighting Theories & Concepts, Chinese Martial Arts Fighting Skills, Chinese In-Fighting, 1992, Martial Arts Fundamental & Self Defense (with Carrie Ogawa-Wong), 1992; trained Jason Scott Lee for movie "Dragon-The Bruce Lee Story", 1993; trained Kevin Sorbo for TV series "The Legendary Journey of Hercules"; trained Lucy Lawless for TV series "Xena, Warrior Princess", 1995; members of White Lotus Assn. have appeared in over 1,000 major motion pictures and TV shows from Kung Fu, 1971, to latest Batman movie, 1995. Res: 18215 Chase St Northridge 91325-3731 Ofc: Sil Lum Kung Fu Studio-White Lotus System 8732 Corbin Avenue Northridge 91324 Tel: 818/993-9664

WONG, HING CHUNG, physician; b. 1941, Hong Kong; nat. US citizen 1978; parents: Chui Y. and Shui Man (Tang) Wong (dec.); m. King Y. Wong; 1 son, Kin Wong; edn: B.Med., Nat. Taiwan Univ. 1969; MD, USA, 1976. Career: Family Practice (solo), Chinatown, Los Angeles 1978–; expanded May 1984 Hing C. Wong Med. Clinic, San Gabriel; chief cons. Chaus Jou Assn. in USA, pres. So. Calif. 1986; med. advisor Am. Vietnam Chinese Friendship Assn., Eng Family Ben Assn., Chinese Garment Assn., Elderly Indochinese Assn.; staff French Hosp., chief of staff 1984-85; bd. dirs. Chinatown Service Center 1983-86, mem. Chinatown Comm. Advy. Com. 1988-90; judge Miss L.A. Chinatown Beauty Pageant, 1987, Miss Indochinese Beauty Pageant, 1988; awards: good citizenship City of L.A., service Paralyzed Veterans Assn. 1977; mem. AMA, L.A. Co. Med. Assn.; rec: golf, pool, tennis, karaoke. Ofc: H.C. Wong, MD, 709 N Hill St Ste 19 Los Angeles 90012; also 808 E Valley Blvd San Gabriel 91776

WONG, JAMES BOK, management consultant, economist, engineer; b. Dec. 9, 1922, Canton, China, nat. US cit. 1962; s. Gen Ham and Chen (Yee) W.; m. Wai Ping Lim, Aug. 3, 1946; children: John b. 1948, Jane b. 1955, Julia b. 1956; edn: BS in agric., Univ. Md. 1949, BS in chem. eng. 1950; MS chem. eng., Univ. Ill. 1951, PhD, 1954. Career: research asst. Univ. Ill., Urbana 1950-53; chem. engr. Standard Oil Indiana at Whiting 1953-55; process design & research engr. Shell Devel. Co., Emeryville, Calif. 1955-61; senior plnng. engr., mgr. long range plnng. & econs., chief economist Rexall Drug & Chem. Co., Los Angeles 1961-70, dir. econs. & ops. analysis, dir. internat. technologies Dart Industries (fmrly. Rexall), 1970-81; pres. James B. Wong Associates, Los Angeles 1981–; dir., chmn. exec. com. United Pacific Bank, L.A. 1982–, chmn. bd. dirs. 1988-89; honors: Outstanding Volunteer Svc. award City of Los Angeles 1977, named to Exec. Order of Ohio Commodores, Gov. Ohio 1982, Sigma Xi, Tau Beta Pi, Phi Kappa Phi, Pi Mu Epsilon, Phi Lambda Upsilon, Phi Eta Sigma; mem: Am. Inst. Chem. Engrs., Am. Chem. Soc.; civic: Chinese Am. Citizens Alliance Found. (dir., pres., 1971–), Asian Am. Edn. Commn./L.A. 1971-81; contbr. articles in A.M.A. Archives of Indsl. Hygiene and Occupational Medicine, Indsl. and Engring. Chemistry, and J. Applied Physics; mil: enlisted US Army 14th Air Force (Flying Tigers), 1943-46. Res: 2460 Venus Dr Los Angeles 90046

WONG, JOE, research chemist; b. Aug. 8, 1942, Hong Kong; s. Po Lim and Mildred (Tam) W.; m. Mei-Ngan, Dec. 20, 1969; children: Glenn b. 1971, Christina b. 1974, Theresa b. 1976; edn: BSc, Univ. Tasmania Australia 1965; BSc hons., 1966; PhD, Purdue Univ. 1970; DSc, Univ. Tasmania 1986. Career: staff research chemist G.E. Corp. Research & Devel., Schenectady, N.Y. 1970-86; Lawrence Livermore Nat. Lab., Livermore 1986–; lectr. physical chemistry Hobart Coll., Tasmania, Australia 1966; adj. prof. St. Univ. N.Y., Albany 1982-86; guest lectr. Chinese Acad. Sci., Beijing, China 1982-83; vis. scholar Cambridge Univ., U.K. 1985; RACI lectr. Royal Australian Chem. Inst., Hobart, Melbourne and Sydney 1986; guest lectr. Nat. Taiwan Univ., Taiwan 1989; cons. prof. Stanford Univ. 1993-95; awards: Electolytic Zinc Co. Prize 1966, Am. Ceramic Soc. Prize 1975, 77, Gen. Electric Dushman award 1984, RD-100 awards 1990, 91, Sr. Sci. & Tech. Agency fellowship 1991, Alexander von Humboldt award 1992; mem: SSRL User Orgn. (chmn. 1988), Am. Chemical Soc., Am. Physical Soc., AAAS, Am. Inst. Chemists, Materials Research Soc., Sigma Xi; contbr. 150+ articles pub. in tech. jours., 1970–, author: Glass: Structure by Spectroscopy, 1976, 7 patents in field, 1975-85; Cath.; rec: photog., swimming, travel. Res: 871 El Cerro Blvd Danville 94526 Ofc: Lawrence Livermore National Laboratory POB 808 L-369 Livermore 94551

WONG, KIN-PING, educator, biotechnology researcher, science administrator; b. Aug. 14, 1941, Guangzhou, Guangdong, China; s. Kwok-Keung and Yuan-Kwan (Loo) W.; m. Anna S. K. Koo, Sept. 16, 1968; children: Voon-Chung, 1971; Ming-Chung, 1974; edn: postdoctoral, Duke Univ., Durham, NC, 1968-70;

PhD, Purdue Univ., Lafayette, IN, 1968; BS, Univ. Calif., Berkeley, 1964; teachers diploma, Grantham Teachers Coll., Hong Kong, 1958-59; career: asst./assoc. prof., Univ. South Florida, Tampa, 1970-75; visiting scientist, Max Planck Inst. Molecular Genetics, Berlin, Germany, 1972; visiting prof., Univ. Uppsala, Uppsala, Sweden, 1975; assoc. prof./prof., Univ. Kansas, Kansas City, KS, 1975-83; visiting prof., Univ. Tokyo, Tokyo, Japan, 1979; dean, grad. studies, Univ. Kansas, Kansas City, KS, 1980-83; program dir. biophysics, Nat. Science Found., Washington, 1981-83; science dean/prof., Calif. State Univ., Fresno, 1983–; visiting prof., Stanford Univ. Medical Ctr., Stanford, 1985; adjunct prof. medicine, Univ. Calif. Medical Sch., San Francisco, 1986–; adjunct prof. biochemistry and biophysics, Univ. Calif. Medical Sch., San Francisco, 1987–; trustee, Univ. Calif. San Francisco, Fresno, 1987–; hon. prof., Shantou Univ. Medical, Shantou, People's Republic of China, 1987–; consultant, Dept. Health & Human Resources, Washington, 1985–; managing dir., c.e.o. Hong Kong Onst. of Biotechnology, Hong Kong 1992-93; co-founder, c.e.o., pres. RiboGene, Inc., Dublin 1989-90; awards: res. professorship, Nat. Science Found., Stanford Univ., 1985; sr. res. fellow, European Molecular Biology Orgn., Uppsala, Sweden, 1975; Res. Career Development Award, NIH, Bethesda, 1972-75; Grant on Ribosome, Nat. Inst. General Medical Sciences, Bethesda, 1972-80; Grant on Protein Folding, Nat. Inst. Heart, Lung, and Blood, Bethesda, 1972-87; Health Career Opportunity Grant, Dept. Health & Human Resources, Rockville, MD, 1986-89; Laval Res. Award, Calif. State Univ., Fresno, 1985; hon. mem., Golden Key Hon. Soc., Atlanta, 1986; Pres./Key Executive MBA Prog., Pepperdine Univ., L.A., 1986-88; Calif. Sea Grant, Dept. Commerce, Washington, 1987-90; fellow, Am. Inst. of Chemists, Washington, 1987–; fellow, Royal Soc. of Chemistry, London, England, 1988–; numerous cancer res. grants and awards; mem: Am. Soc. of Biological Chemists, 1976–; Am. Assn. for Advancement of Science, 1975–; Am. Chemical Soc., 1978–; Biophysical Soc., 1970–; Soc. of Sigma Xi, 1969; author: more 50 res. articles in biology, chemistry biochemistry, biophysics, endocrinology; 3 review articles in educational journals, 32 pub. research abstracts; keynote speaker, convocation lecture, symposium, and colloquium lectures; rec: travel; downhill skiing; mountain climbing. Res: Fresno Ofc: Calif. State Univ. Sch. Natural Sciences Fresno 93740-0090

WONG, MAY ANN, bank officer; b. Aug. 14, 1962, Lompoc; d. Ning Hoy and Rosa Kung (Chi) Wong; edn: BA, UC Santa Cruz 1984; Cert. of Bus. Adminstrn., UC Berkeley 1992. Career: asst. mgr. Rice Bowl Restaurant, Lompoc 1975-84; letter of credit processor Bank of the Orient, San Francisco 1984-88, federal funds trader 1988-92, asst operations ofcr. 1992–; awards: UC Santa Cruz Cowell Coll. Service Citation 1984, Elks Student award 1980, Bank of Am. Fgn.Language 1980, Who's Who Among H.S. Students 1980; mem: UC Santa Cruz Alumni Assn. (pres. S.F. Bay Area), Smithsonian Inst., San Francisco Museum Soc., Nat. Geographic Soc.; Democrat; rec: art, literature, music, socializing, travel, walking. Address: San Francisco 94121

WONG, ROBERTA JEAN, pharmacist, educator; b. Nov. 23, 1957, Cleveland, Ohio; d. Robert Young and Ellen Jean (Woo) Wong; m. Michael Wool; edn: UC Davis 1976-79; PharmD, UC San Francisco, 1983. Career: res. pharmacist AIDS Clinic, San Francisco General Hosp., 1984-89; asst. clin. prof. UCSF Sch. of Pharmacy 1985-89; instr. UCLA Sch. of Medicine, Los Angeles 1989-91, drug info. pharmacist UCLA Med. Ctr. 1989-90, investigational drug pharmacist, 1990-94; assoc. mgr. clin. affairs Amgen, Inc. 1994–; awards: fellow ASHP 1991, US Pub. Health Svc. asst. sec. health award, W.D.C. 1991; mem. ASHP (practice advy. panel 1990-92), Am. Pharm. Assn. 1987–, CSHP 1983–; author book chapt. in AIDS Knowledgebase, 1990, Pharmacologic Treatment of HIV Infection, 1988; med. jour. articles; rec: skiing, tennis, golf. Ofc: Amgen Inc 1940 DeHavilland Dr, MS 24-1-B, Thousand Oaks 91320

WOO, SOON HYONG, chiropractor, family practitioner; b. Mar. 28, 1939, Seoul, Korea; s. Soo Chang and Boo-Dug (Kim) W.; m. Soon-Sea Hwang, June 13, 1972; children: Albert, Harold, Jane; edn: DVM, Seoul Nat. Univ., 1963; MD, Chosun Univ., Kwangju, Korea 1975; DC, Cleveland Chiropractic Coll. of L.A., 1985. Career: physician, family practitioner Woo Medical Clinic, Seoul, Korea 1975-82; chiropractor Woo Chiropractic Clinic, Los Angeles 1986–; assoc. prof. of med. sci. South Baylo Univ., Anaheim 1990–; mil: lt. Korean Army 1963-65; rec: photog., travel, music. Res: 1532 3rd Ave Los Angeles 90019 Ofc: Woo Chiropractic Clinic 945 S Western Ave Los Angeles 90006

WOOD, ELDRIDGE DELANO, JR., investment banker; b. Sept. 8, 1938, Cambridge, Mass.; s. Eldridge Delano and Mary Eleanor (Frazier) W.; m. Kim Anh, Sept. 14, 1965; children: Carol b. 1967, Michael b. 1974; edn: BSBA, Northeastern Univ. 1961; MBA, Univ. Chgo. 1963. Career: sales mgr. William H. Rennolds Co., Manila 1965-70; v.p. Purina Taiyo K.K., Tokyo 1971-74; v.p. Private Investment Co. for Asia, Manila 1975-78; senior v.p./COO PICA, Singapore 1978-83; pres./bd. chmn. Inter-Pacific Capital Corp., Los Angeles 1983–; mem. corp. bd. dirs. 20+ cos. in 6 countries, 1965–; mem. Nat. Assn. of Corp. Dirs. (1982–), Jaycees (Internat. Senator); clubs: Elks, Manhattan CC, Army & Navy (Manila), Tokyo Am., Singapore Am.; mil: capt. US Army Signal Corps 1963-65; Republican; R.Cath.; rec: music. Ofc: Inter-Pacific Capital Corp. 6033 W Century Blvd Ste 850 Los Angeles 90045

WOOD, FERGUS JAMES, geophysicist, consultant; b. May 13, 1917, London, Ont., Canada, came to U.S. 1924, naturalized 1932; s. Louis Aubrey and Dora Isabel (Elson) W.; m. Doris M. Hack, Sept. 14, 1946; children: Kathryn Celeste W. Madden, Bonnie Patricia W. Ward; edn: Univ. Oreg. 1934-36; AB, UC Berkeley, 1938, postgrad. 1938-39; postgrad. Univ. Chgo. 1939-40, Univ. Mich. 1940-42, Calif. Inst. Tech. 1946. Career: tchg. asst. Univ. Mich. 1940-42; instr. in physics and astronomy Pasadena City Coll. 1946-48, John Muir Coll. 1948-49; asst. prof. physics Univ. Md. 1949-50; assoc. physicist Johns Hopkins Univ. Applied Physics Lab. 1950-55; sci. editor Ency. Americana, N.Y.C., 1955-60; aeronautical and space res. scientist, sci. asst. to the director Office Space Flight Programs, Hqtrs., NASA, W.D.C., 1960-61; program dir. fgn. sci. info. Nat. Sci. Found., W.D.C., 1961-62; physical scientist, chief sci. and tech. info. staff U.S. Coast and Geodetic Survey (now Nat. Ocean Service), Rockville, Md. 1962-66; phys. scientist Office of Dir., 1967-73, res. assoc. 1973-77; cons. tidal dynamics, Bonita, Calif. 1978–; awards: special achievement Dept. Commerce, NOAA (1970, 74, 76, 77); mem: Sigma Pi Sigma, Pi Mu Epsilon, Delta Phi Alpha, Am. Geophysical Union; writer, tech. dir. documentary film: Pathfinders from the Stars, 1967; contbr. numerous articles to encys., reference sources, profl. jours.; author: The Strategic Role of Perigean Spring Tides in Nautical History and North American Coastal Flooding 1635-1976 (1978), Tidal Dynamics: Coastal Flooding and Cycles of Gravitational Force, 1986, 3rd. edit. Tidal Dynamics: Synergetic Gravitational Forces in Tides and the Solar System, 2 vols. 1995; editor-in-chief: The Prince William Sound, Alaska, Earthquake of 1964 and Aftershocks, vols. 1-2A and sci. coordinator vols. 2B, 2C and 3 (1966-69); mil: capt. USAAF 1942-46; Democrat; Presbyterian. Res: 3103 Casa Bonita Dr Bonita 91902-1735

WOOD, LARRY (MARY LAIRD), journalist, university educator, author, environmental consultant and public relations executive; b. Sandpoint, Idaho; d. Edward Hayes and Alice (McNeel) Small; children: Mary, Marcia, Barry; edn: BA/BEd, summa cum laude (pres. Assoc. Women Students; recipient many campus honors incl. Pasadena Rose Bowl Princess), Univ. Wash., 1938, MA with highest honors, 1940; postgrad. Stanford Univ. 1941-42, postgrad. teaching fellowship 1942-43; postgrad. UC Berkeley 1946-47, cert. in photog. 1971; postgrad. journalism Univ. Wis. 1971-72, Univ. Minn. 1971-72, Univ. Ga. 1972-73; postgrad. in art, arch. and marine biol. UC Santa Cruz, 1974-76, Stanford Hopkins Marine Sta. 1977-80. Career: campus corresp. Seattle Times 1941-42, nat. model for Wonder Bread and store model for I. Magnin, Frederick & Nelson, The Bon Marche; P.R. cons. Seattle and S.F. Bay Area YMCA & YWCA, Eastbay Hosp. Assn., 2-co., 53-park East Bay Reg. Park Dist., Childrens's Hosp. No. Calif., Childrens Home Soc. of No. Calif., Am. Cancer Soc., Forestry Res., 1946–; by-line columnist Oakland Tribune, S.F. Chronicle, 1946-62; Parents' Mag. far west contbg. ed., 1946-65; disting. expert witness Nat. Forensic Ctr., N.J. 1965–; feature writer W. reg. Christian Sci. Monitor, CSM Radio Syn. and Internat. News, 1973–, CSM/Los Angeles Times News Syn., Register and Tribune Syn., Des Moines, 1975–, Times-Mirror Syn., San Jose Mercury News (Nat. Headliner Award), Seattle Times, Chevron USA, Calif. Today mag.; contbg. ed. Travelday Mag., Travelin' Mag., 1976–, Calif. Travel Guides, Fodor (NY and London, David McKay Pubs.) 1981–, Random House, 1987–; coauthor Travelguide to Calif. (jt. pub. Fodor/State of Calif.) 1986–, Focus on Science Series, 3 vol. high sch./univ. texts (Bell & Howell) 1987; 1990-91; feature stories include: Calif.'s Water Wars, Calif.'s New Wilder Ranch State Park, Marvel of Tugs, Nat. Counter-Narcotics Inst. (San Luis Obispo), Calif. Youth Auth. Problems, Sch. Crime in Calif., Calif.'s `Hip' Teens, Jumping Frogs Contest (Calaveras County), Immigration, Youth Gangs, Calif. Lighthouse Hostel Chain, features on Calif. writers Jack London, Mark Twain and Robert Louis Stevenson and their homes in Calif., Mystique of the Migrating Monarch Butterflies, New Nipomo Dunes State Preserve, Elkhorn Slough Nat. Estuarine Reserve at Moss Landing, Ferndale's Victorians (lead, cover article Westways Mag. 6/91); author 22 books including: Wonderful USA! A State by State Guide to Natural Am. (Crown Books, NY, 1989); coauthor: West Winds, anthology of Calif. writers, 1989; 2000+ bylined articles in Sunday Mag. sections, newspapers (syndicates: USIA, Knight Ridder, Times Mirror, Hearst) and mags.; feature writer Linguapress, Paris; book reviewer texts for Bell & Howell, journalism book reviews for Profl. Communicator; prof. journalism (tenure) CSU San Diego 1975–, distinguished vis. prof. CSU San Jose 1976, CSU Hayward, UC Ext. 1979, Univ. Pacific (1979, 82); frequent speaker profl. and ednl. confs.; mem. advy. bd. KRON-TV, NBC, 1987–; press del. Alaska, Ky., Mass., La., Tenn., Wash., Ore., Ida., Hawaii, Mexico, Germany, Hong Kong, Costa Rica, Italy, Jamaica; invited to attend and report major confs. including: Internat. Geographers' Union & Assembly 1992, Internat. Soc. Ecol. Econs., Costa Rica 1992, Internat. Ocean Disposal Symp., Asilomar, Ca. 1986, USN and coop. univs. Marine Medicine: Diving & Health Hazards of Marine and Aquatic Environments, Monterey 1985, IEEE ann. meetings (1985 Ocean Engring. and the Environment), AMA Athletic Assn., HI 1985, Oceans Conf. and Expo. 1985; selected by Am. & Brit. govts. to cover 1983 visit of Queen Elizabeth II and Prince Philip to Calif., also 1986 visit of Prince Charles and Princess Diana to EXPO '86, Vancouver B.C.; work with state and fed. agys. in wildlife mgmt. pgms.; profl. del. EPA del. to Soviet Union and Ea. Europe 1991; VIP press invitee to: Earth Summit, Brazil 1992, Ecol. Soc. Am./Inst. Biol. Scis. ann. conf. Honolulu 1992, Intl. Soc. Ecol. Econs. 1991, Am. Geophys. Union conf. (1982–, press del. AGU annual convs. 1987–, Disting. press del. 1990 nat. conv.), Internat. Conv. Mapping Global Change 1992, Rockefeller Found. Media Seminar "Feeding the World, Protecting the Earth," Commonwealth Awards Banquet (4/92, Wilmington), Conf. Bd. 1995 Corp. Commn. Conf., Calif. Inst. of Tech. Media & Sci. Seminar 1995, Electronic Media Symposium 1994, Nat. Conf. Sci. Writers Am. Heart Assn. 1995, Inat. Cardiologists Symposium for Med. & Sci. Writers 1995, Lake Geneva Reg. Celebration 1994, Canadian Consulate Gen. Dateline Canada 1995, Gorbachev's visit to Stanford Univ., Calif. Gov.'s Conf. on Tourism, trip to Hong Kong by LA Times and Cathay Pacific; press del. AAAS annual convs. 1987–; press del. to Russia, Ukraine and Czech. for Comms. Consortium, 1992; trustee Calif. St. Parks Found., 1976–; 6 works selected by Wolters Noordhoff & Longman, pub. Eng. lang. texts in Europe; 1989-90 works include: Earthquake '89, Oakland Firestorm, Restoration of San Francisco's Chinatown, So. Calif.'s Teens-Trend setters for world fashions, Beverly Hill's High Fund Raising Project, Endangered Species., Calif. Underwater Parks, Calif. Antique Carousels, Yellowstone After the Fire; award winning features include Sea Frontiers, 1983, B.C. Totem Pole series, 1982, "Ebey's Landing" Nat. Hist. Reserve series, 1982; one of 40 top Calif. authors pub. in anthology, West Winds Four, Strawberry Hill Press, 1989; "Columbia: Glacier in Retreat" one of 350 top sci. articles of 1987 and reprinted in Soc. Issues Resources series 1988; honors: recogn. US Forest Svc. 1975, US Nat. Park Svc. List of nation's top environmental writers, award from Oakland Mus. 1979, 81, Port Directors' Assn. 1979, Mortar Bd. honoree 1984, 87, 88, 89, Braodway Hall of Fame 1984 & Broadway Dist. Alumnus 1995 both at Seattle City Ctr., charter mem. planning com. UW Purple & Gold Soc. (charter mem., 1st conf. 1995), Calif. Woman of Achievement (3t), award for article and photographs on California's Underwater Parks, Calif. Writers' Club list of Calif. Top 40 Writers 1989, Lifetime Mem. Nat. Press Photogs. Assn 1994, honoree Oakland C.of C., S.F. C.of C., Chevron USA for features on Bay Area cities; Dict. of Intl. Biography of Cambridge, Eng. (12 books), Am. Biog. Inst. (15 books); listed Who's Who in the West, Who's Who of Am. Women, Who's Who in Am., Who's Who in Fin. and Industry, Who's Who in Advt. and Public Rels., Who's Who in the World, Who's Who Geographical and Prof. Index; mem: Nat. Soc. of Environmental Journalists (charter mem.1990–), Calif. Writers' Club (del. 1989, bd. 1987-88, keynote spkr. All-West Writers Conf. Asilomar 1987, statewide banquet honoree 1990), Public Rels. Soc. Am. (Consultants Acad. 1983–), Women in Commns., Inc. (past sect. v.p., nat. bd. 1968-73, nat. resolutions com. 1983–), Nat. Acad. TV Arts and Scis., World Internat. Environ. Cons., Environ. Cons. No. Am., Am. Mgmt. Assn., Am. Med. Writers Assn., Seattle Advt. & Sales Club (past pres.), Seattle Jr. Ad Club (past pres.), AD/Mark Bay Area (past ofcr.), East Bay Advt. & Mktg. Assn., Oceanic Soc., Internat. Oceanographic Soc., Nat. Parks Assn., World Wildlife Fund, Am. Assn. Edn. in Jour. & Mass Commns. (exec. bd. nat. mag. div., newspaper div. 1978), Investigative Reporters and Editors, Soc. Am. Travel Writers (exec. bd. 1980-82), Soc. Profl. Journalists, Council for Advance. of Sci. Writing, Calif. Acad. Environ. News Writers, Nat. Press Photogs. Assn., Nat. Assn. of Sci. Writers, Calif. Acad. of Scis., Calif. Fine Arts Museums, Nat. Audubon Soc., Smithsonian, UCB Alumni Assn. (life), UW Alumni Assn. (life), UW Oceanscis. Alumni Assn. (charter), UW Sch. of Comms. Alumni, Nat. Sch. PR Assn., Stanford Alumni Assn. (life), Phi Beta Kappa Alumni (scholarship ch. and PR dir. No. Calif. 1969–), Sigma Delta Chi, Theta Sigma Phi, Mortar Board, Totem Club, Pi Lambda Theta; clubs: Nat. Press (W.D.C.), S.F. Press, Eastbay Womens' Press; Ofcs: San Francisco, San Diego, Pebble Beach/Monterey, Seattle and 6161 Castle Dr Piedmont Pines Oakland 94611

WOOD, MICHAEL NEALL, cardiovascular/thoracic surgeon; b. Feb. 15, 1956, Temple, Texas; s. Harold Lee and Betty Jane (Bottomley) W.; m. Sandra Jean Quinn, Aug. 6, 1988; edn: BA chem., Southern Coll., Tenn. 1977; MD, Loma Linda Univ. Sch. of Med., 1981. Career: attdg. surgeon LLU Med. Ctr., Loma Linda 1989–; co-med. dir. cardiovascular surgery San Antonio Comm. Hosp., Upland 1990-93, med. dir. cardiovascular surgery 1993–; mem: Soc. Critical Care Medicine 1989–, Calif. Thoracic Soc., Soc. Thoracic Surgeons, San Bdo. Co. Med. Soc., Am. Coll. Surgeons (assoc. 1986, assoc. fellow 1989), Internat. Coll. Surgeons (fellow 1989), Am. Coll. Chest Phys. (fellow 1995), Am. Coll. Cardiology (fellow 1995), Assn. for Academic Surgery 1990, AMA 1983, Calif. Med. Assn. 1982. Ofc: 1060 E Foothill Blvd Ste 201 Upland 91786

WOOD, RAYMUND FRANCIS, emeritus professor of library science; b. Nov. 9, 1911, London, England, naturalized U.S., 1931; s. George Stephen and Ida Agnes (Lawes) W.; m. Margaret Ann Peed, Feb. 26, 1943; children: Paul George b. 1947, Gregory Leo b. 1952, David Joseph b. 1955; edn: AB, St. Mary's Univ., 1931; MA, Gonzaga Univ., 1939; PhD, UCLA, 1949; MS Libr. Sci., USC, 1950. Career: instr. English, Univ. Santa Clara, 1939-41; tchg asst. history dept. UCLA, 1941-42; registration ofcr. VA Rehab. Pgm., L.A. 1946-48; prin. reference librarian Fresno State Coll., 1950-66; prof. libr. sci. UCLA Grad. Sch. of Library and Info. Sci., Los Angeles 1966-77, asst. dean 1967-70, assoc. dean 1975-77, prof. emeritus 1977–; awards: Del Amo Found. Scholar, travel grantee 1974, merit award Alliance Francaise de Fresno 1966, travel grantee Nat. Book Found., N.Y. 1964, L.A. Mayor's merit award 1983, Knight of St. Gregory 1994; mem.: Jedediah Smith Soc., Stockton (pres. 1987-90, Eager Beaver award 1989), Calif. Libr. Assn., Sacto. 1950–, Fresno County Hist. Soc.

(1952–, hon. life, newsletter editor 1959-66), Mariposa Co. Hist. Soc. (1957–, hon. life), So. Calif. Hist. Soc. 1959–, Friends of Encino/Tarzana Br. Libr. (treas. 1989–, pres. 1977-80, 87-90, newsletter editor 1981–), E Clampus Vitus (Fresno & Bakersfield chapters 1954–), The Westerners (L.A. Corral 1969–), Am. Red Cross (S.F.V. 1977–), Boy Scouts Am. (Encino 1970-75); author: California's Agua Fria, 1954, Life and Death of Peter Lebec, 1956, History of Mission San Jose, 1958, joint author: Ina Coolbrith: Librarian & Laureate, 1973; mil: WOJG US Army 1942-46, ETO; Democrat; Byzantine Catholic; rec: travel, photography, writing. Res: 18052 Rosita St Encino 91316

WOOD, ROBERT WARREN, lawyer, writer; b. July 5, 1955, Des Moines, Iowa; s. Merle Warren and Cecily Ann (Sherk) W.; m. Beatrice R. Lin, Aug. 4, 1979; edn: AB, Humboldt State Univ., 1976; Sheffield Univ. 1975-76; JD, Univ. of Chgo., 1979; admitted bar: Ariz., Calif., N.Y., D.C. Career: atty. law firm Jennings, Strouss & Salmon, Phoenix, Ariz. 1979-80; McCutchen, Doyle, Brown & Enersen, San Francisco 1980-82; Broad, Schulz, Larson & Wineberg (and predecessor firm Broad, Khourie & Schulz), San Francisco 1982-85; Steefel, Levitt & Weiss, 1985-91; Bancroft & McAlister 1992-93; Robert W. Wood, P.C. 1993–; instr. UC Hastings Coll. of Law, 1981-82; mem: ABA, Calif. Bar, N.Y. Bar, Ariz. Bar, Federal Bar Assn., S.F. Bar Assn.; author: The Executive's Complete Guide to Bus. Taxes (Dow Jones-Irwin, 1989); Taxation of Corporate Liquidations: A Complete Planning Guide (Maxwell MacMillan, 1987); Corporate Taxation: Complete Practice and Practice Guide (2nd. ed. Warren Gorham & Lamont 1990); The Ultimate Tax Planning Guide for Growing Companies (Dow Jones-Irwin 1990), S Corporations (Warren Gorham & Lamont 1994); Taxation of Damage Awards and Settlement Payments (Tax Inst., 1991); Tax Strategies for Hiring, Retaining and Terminating Employees (John Wiley 1991); coauthor: Calif. Closely Held Corporations: Tax Planning and Practice Guide (Matthew Bender, 1987); Legal Guide to Independent Contractor Status (John Wiley & Sons 1992); num. law jour. articles re fed. income taxation; num. editorial bds. Ofc: Robert W. Wood, PC 235 Montgomery St Ste 972 San Francisco 94104 Tel: 415/834-1800

WOOD, WAYNE BARRY, freelance photojournalist; b. June 23, 1958, Oakland; s. Byron and Marylaird (Small) W.; edn: cert. photography, UC Berkeley, 1974-79; BS in transp. w. high honors, CSU Hayward and San Francisco, 1980; MBA w. high honors, CSU Hayward, 1982. Career: bylined photojournalist 1971–, with CSM News Syndicate since 1973, with 25+ million readers worldwide and 200 synd. radio stations in U.S. & Can.; coauthor: Fodor's San Francisco, and Fodor's California (guidebooks) 1981-88; photojournalist, specialist in travel, sci., transp., urban renewal, people profiles, and edn.; photos appear in Sea Frontiers (Internat. Oceanographic Found.), Popular Mechanics, Focus On Science textbook series (Charles Merrill Co.), Linguapress, Off Duty, Model Railroader, Fashion Showcase, others; awards: Close scholar and outstanding jr. in econ. and bus., photography awards Railroad Assn., exhib. juried art show CSU Hayward; mem: Soc. of Profl. Journalists, Nat. Press Photogs. Assn.; Presbyterian; rec: magic, natural science. Res: 6161 Castle Dr Oakland 94611

WOODROW, KENNETH M., psychiatrist; b. Mar. 20, 1942, Yonkers, N.Y.; s. Jack H. and Grace (Lewis) W.; m. Mary Mack, June 6, 1968, div. 1985; m. Patricia Stokes July 1, 1989; 1 dau., Laura b. 1975; edn: BA, Wesleyan Univ., 1964; grad. studies UC Davis, 1964; MD, Univ. Md., Balt. 1968; bd. cert. Am. Bd. Psychiatry and Neurology, 1974. Career: research assoc. NIH Lab. of Socioenvironmental Studies, 1963-64; resrch. fellow Univ. Md. Psychiat. Inst., Balt. 1966; intern Kaiser Found. Hosp., Oakland 1969, resident Stanford Univ., 1969-72; staff psychiatrist Atascadero St. Hosp., 1971; clin. assoc. NIMH Lab. of Clin. Psychopharm. USPHS 1972-74; staff psychiatrist Palo Alo VA Hosp., 1974-76; supvg. psychiatrist Santa Clara Valley Med. Ctr., San Jose 1976-77; pvt. practice of psychiatry, Menlo Park; psychiat. cons. Calif. Dept. of Rehabilitation, 1975-81; cons. Job Corps, San Jose 1975-82; clin. assoc. prof. Stanford Univ. Med. Sch., 1975–; awards: Wesleyan Univ., Thorndike Prize for excellence in psychiatry 1963; mem. Am. Psychiatric Assn.; contbr. articles in profl. jours. Ofc: 1225 Crane St Ste 106 Menlo Park 94025

WOODS, ARLEIGH MADDOX, presiding justice State Court of Appeal; b. Aug. 31, 1929, Los Angeles; d. Benjamin Harris and Ida Lota (Evans) Maddox; m. William T. Woods, Aug. 3, 1952; edn: BA, Chapman Coll., 1949; LLB, Southwestern Univ. Sch. of Law, 1953; LLM, Univ. Va., 1984; Hon. LLD, Univ. West L.A. (1984); admitted Calif. St. Bar (1953). Career: general practice of law, 1953-57; atty., prtnr. Levy, Koszdin & Woods, 1957-76; judge Los Angeles Superior Ct., 1976-80; assoc. justice Calif. Ct. of Appeal, 1980-82, presiding justice, 1982–, adminstrv. presiding justice, 1984-87; mem. Judicial Council of Calif. 1985-87, chair Commn. on Judicial Performance 1986-94; honors: Westside Bus. & Profl. Woman of Year 1982, CTLA Apellate Justice of Year 1983, YWCA Silver Medal of Achiev., Profl. Woman of Yr. 1984, honored Black Women Lawyers Assn. 1984, Equal Opp. League life commitment award for judicial excellence 1985, Southwestern Univ. outstanding judicial ofcr. 1987, L.A. Trial Lawyers Assn. Appellate Justice of the Yr. 1989, Bernard Jefferson Award for Judicial Excellence 1990, John Langston Bar Assn. Hall of Fame 1992, Southwestern Univ. Alumna of the Yr. 1995; mem. num. judicial and bar assns., Constl. Rights Found. (v.p., bd. dirs. 1982–), Am. Cancer Res. Found. (bd. dirs. 1981); Southwestern Univ. (trustee 1986–, chair 1995–); rec: painting, needlepoint, youth civic edn. Ofc: Calif. Court of Appeal 300 S Spring St Los Angeles 90013

WOODS, ROBERT DOUGLAS MURRAY, lawyer; b. July 31, 1946, London, England, naturalized U.S., 1966; s. Eric Robert and Dorothea Elizabeth (Armstrong) W.; m. Joan Francis Shoop, 1971 (div. 1973); m. Alexis Jean Perry, May 23, 1975; children: Heidi b. 1964, James b. 1967, Yvette b. 1971 (nee Kone), David Woods b. 1977; edn: BA, Univ. San Diego, 1968, JD, 1973; Grad. Seminary Dipl. Claremont Coll. Episcopal Theol. Sch., 1984; postgrad. studies Kennedy Inst. of Ethics, Georgetown Univ. 1987, 88, 90; admitted bar: Calif. 1973, Fed. Cts. 1973, U.S. Supreme Ct. 1978; ordained Episcopal Priest, 1986, Deacon 1984-86. Career: law clk., civil litigation atty., assoc. Higgs, Fletcher & Mack, San Diego 1973-77; Schall, Boudreau & Gore, 1978-81; ptnr. 1982-86; chief deputy litigation Kern Co. Counsel, Bakersfield 1986-92; chief deputy special litigation 1992–; adj. lectr. Univ. San Diego Law Sch. 1978-81; adj. prof. dept. philosophy & religious studies CSU Bakersfield, 1989–, assoc. Kennedy Inst. of Ethics Georgetown Univ, 1991–. Fellow, Kegley Inst. of Ethics, CSUB, 1988–, lectr. and pub. discussions in areas of legal, med. and govt. ethics, 1989–; instr. Calif. Pacific Sch. of Law, 1990–; judge pro tem. and jud. arbitrator, 1978-86; Am. Arbitration Assn. Nat. Panel, 1980-87; honors: Sigma Psi, Book awards in Constnl. law, evidence and crim. procedure, Varsity swimming, sailing and golf, Outstanding trial lawyer San Diego Trial Lawyers Assn. 1980, State Bar merit certs. 1983, 86, pres.'s award for outstanding Pro Bono Svc. 1985, arbitration service awards 1978, 80; contbg. author: Marine P&I Policy Annotations, ABA Practicing Law Inst., 1980, Effective Direct and Cross-Examination, Calif. CEB, 1984, numerous cont. edn. lectures in trial techniques and splties., 1981–; mil: E4 personnel splst. Adj. Gen. Corps US Army 1969-70; Democrat; Episcopalian (asst. priest St. Luke's, Bksfld. 1988–); rec: mountaineering, backpacking, musician, bicycling, skiing, canoeing. Ofc: Kern County Counsel 1115 Truxtun Ave 4th Fl Bakersfield 93301

WOODWARD, DANIEL HOLT, researcher; b. Oct. 17, 1931, Ft. Worth, Tex.; s. Enos Paul and Jessie Grider (Butts) W.; m. Mary Jane Gerra, Aug. 27, 1954; children: Jeffrey b. 1958, Peter b. 1960; edn: BA, Univ. of Colo. 1951, MA, 1955; PhD, Yale Univ. 1958; MS in L.S., Cath. Univ. of Am. 1969. Career: faculty Mary Washington Coll. Univ. of Va., 1957-72; librarian, 1969-72; librarian Huntington Library, Art Gallery and Botanical Gardens, San Marino 1972-90, sr. res. assoc. 1990–; honors: Phi Beta Kappa, Beta Phi Mu; mem. Bibliog. Soc. Am., Grolier Club, Zamorano Club; editor: The Poems and Translations of Robert Fletcher, 1970; co-editor: New Ellesmere Chaucer Facsimile (2 vols. 1995). mil: AUS 1952-54. Res: 1540 San Pasqual St Pasadena 91106 Ofc: Huntington Library 1151 Oxford Rd San Marino 91108

WOODWORTH, STEPHEN DAVIS, business consultant, investment banker; b. Nov. 4, 1945, Stillwater, Okla.; s. Stanley Davis and Elizabeth (Webb) W.; m. Robin Lee, 1992; children: Lisa b. 1968, Ashley b. 1974; edn: BA, Claremont McKenna Coll. 1967; MBA, Calif. Lutheran Univ. 1975; USC Managerial Policy Inst. 1981. Career: div. mgr. Security Pacific Bank, Los Angeles 1970-87; prin. Woodworth Assoc., Westlake Village 1987-88; pres. Channel Islands Equities, Oxnard 1988–; instr. fin. Grad. Bus. Program Calif. Lutheran Univ. 1978-80; adj. faculty Command & Gen. Staff Coll. Ft. Leavenworth 1985; dir.: Hanson Lab. Furniture Inc., Newbury Park; Hetherington Inc., Ventura; dir. World Affairs Council of Ventura County 1995; bd. trustees Calif. Lutheran Edn. Found., Thousand Oaks 1983-94; So. Calif. bd. dirs. U.S. Olympic Com., L.A. 1982-84; mem: Calif. Lutheran Univ. Alumni Assn. (pres. 1980-82, Outstanding Alumnus honoree 1986), Tower Club, Reserve Ofcr. Assn. (life), Ventura Co. Econ. Devel. Assn., Conejo Future Found., Am. Mgmt. Assn., MIT Enterprise Forum/ Central Coast (dir. 1988–), Conejo Sym. Orch. (former dir.), Alliance for Arts (dir., chmn. 1984–); contbr. numerous articles to bus. jours.; mil: lt. col. USAR 1967–; Republican; R.Cath.; rec: tennis, jogging, travel. Res: 163 Stanislaus Ave Ventura 93004 Ofc: Channel Islands Equities 300 Esplanade Ste 900 Oxnard 93030

WOOLLEY, CHRISTOPHER JOHN, vice president commercial banking sales; b. 1959, England; edn: BA summa cum laude, UCSB 1981; reg. CPA Calif. 1984. Career: accountant Arthur Andersen & Co., Los Angeles 1981-84; controller, CFO Daum/Johnstown Am., L.A. 1984-86; fin. cons. Shearson Lehman Brothers, La Jolla 1987-89; Wells Fargo Bank, San Diego 1990–; lectr. UCSB 1980-81; bus. columnist Calif. Press Bureau, L.A. 1987-89; Republican; rec: running, mountain biking, skiing. Res: San Diego Ofc: Wells Fargo Bank 101 West Broadway #300 San Diego 92101

WOOLSEY, LYNN, congresswoman. Mem. 103rd-104th Congress from 6th Calif. Dist., 1993-. Ofc: US House of Representatives 439 Cannon Washington DC20515-0506*

WOOLSEY, ROY BLAKENEY, electronics company executive; b. June 12, 1945, Norfolk, Va.; s. Roy Blakeney and Louise Stookey (Jones) W.; m. Patricia Bernadine Elkins, Apr. 17, 1988; edn: undergrad. Calif. Inst. Tech., 1962-64; BS (w.distinction), Stanford Univ., 1966, MS, 1967, PhD, 1970. Career: senior

physicist Technology for Communications Internat. (TCI), Mountain View 1970-75, mgr. radio direction finding systems 1975-80, program mgr. 1980-83, dir. strategic systems 1983-88, dir. rsch. & devel. 1988-91, v.p. engring. 1991-92, v.p. programs 1992–; dir: Merit Software Corp., Menlo Park 1990–; awards: grad. fellow NSF 1966-70, Phi Beta Kappa 1966, Sigma Xi 1966; clubs: Stanford, Palo Alto; Sequoia Yacht, Redwood City; YMCA Fitness Ctr., Palo Alto; contbg. author (books): Appls. of Artificial Intelligence to Command and Control Systems, 1988, Antenna Engineering Handbook, 1993, profl. jour. articles, 1968-74; Republican; Presbyterian; rec: sailing, racquetball, tennis, skiing, contract bridge, travel. Res: 26649 Snell Ln Los Altos Hills 94022 Ofc: Technology for Communications Intl. 222 Caspian Dr Sunnyvale 94089

WORELL, AMY BETH, veterinarian; b. Dec. 28, 1954, Vancouver, Wash.; d. Leonard George and Judith Paula (Goldfarb) W.; edn: BS zool., Univ. Ky., 1976; DVM, Auburn Univ., 1982. Career: veterinarian Kray Vet. Clinic, Glendàle 1982-83; Parkwood Pet Clinic, Woodland Hills 1984–; owner, med. dir. All Pets Med. Centre West Hills; honors: Outstanding Young Women Am. 1985; mem: Am. Fedn. of Aviculture (Avy Award 1987, avian resrch. com. mem. 1985–, and state coordinator chairmen 1987–), So. Calif. Vet. Med. Assn. (ethics & griev. com. 1985–), SCVMA Avian Soc. (pres. 1985-89), SCVMA San Fernando Valley Chpt. (pres. 1988, membership chmn. 1995–), West Valley Bird Soc. (v.p. 1989-92); lectr. in avian medicine of Toucans; editl bd. WB Saunders "Avian & Exotic Seminars", 1992–; editl. bd. Mosby "Exotic Pet Practice", 1995–; column ed. "Veterinary Viewpoint," A7-A Watchbird, 1988–, pub. articles in med. and mgmt.; Democrat; Unitarian; rec: aviculturist, jogging. Ofc: All Pets Medical Centre 7606 Fallbrook Ave West Hills 91304

WORKMAN, SCOTT KEITH, pharmacist; b. Nov. 5, 1958, Reedley; s. Donald Gene and Evelyn Marie (Hansen) W.; m. Lori L., Dec. 18, 1977; children: Wesley Scott b. 1981, Candace Dawn b. 1983; edn: BS pharm., Univ. of Pacific 1981; reg. pharmacist. Career: owner, dir. Pharmkee Inc., Fresno 1981–; pres. Fresno-Madera Pharm. Assn. 1988–; dir. Caruthers Pharmacy 1992–; District 5 trustee 1991-94; com. mem. Calif. Pharmacists Assn. Mktg. & Pub. Rels. Task Force, Sacto. (recipient Disting. Young Pharmacist of Yr. 1990); mem: Calif. Pharmacists Assn. (chmn. govtl. affairs reference com. 1989, mem. acad. pharm. mgmt. 1986–, PAC 1986–), Nat. Assn. Retail Druggists, Peoples Ch.; Republican; Prot.; rec: golf, skiing, water skiing. Ofc: Pharmkee Inc. 5796 S Elm Fresno 93706

WORRALL, WENDY J., writer/editor; b. Sept. 11, 1963, Davenport, Ia.; d. Gerald Charles and Joan Margaret (Kraus) Worrall; m. Randy George Helfond, July 11, 1987 (div. 1993); children: Katie Jo b. 1989; edn: BA in bdcst. journalism, USC, 1985; cert., Inst. of Children's Literature, Redding Ridge, Ct. 1994. Career: senior employee communications rep. The Walt Disney Co., Burbank 1985-89; editorial asst., reporter, feature writer The Bernardo News (weekly), Rancho Bernardo, Calif. 1991-93; dir. public rel. Magic Image Films 1993-94; asst. editor Senior World Newsmagazine 1994–; awards: employee of mo. Disney Univ., The Walt Disney Co. (3t), listed Who's Who of Young Am. Women 1985, Who's Who in West 1992, 93, 94, Who's Who in Calif. 1993, 94; mem. USC General Alumni Assn., Town & Gown Jrs., L.A. 1992- (corresp. sec. 1993-94, ed. 92-93), Trojan Jr. Aux., L.A. (1985-92, editor 1987-89, pres. 1990-91, parliamentarian 1991-92), RB Chorale, Rancho Bernardo (1991–, 2d v.p. publicity 1992-93), Disneyland Alumni Assn. 1985–, Athletes & Entertainers for Kids 1986-90; R.Cath.; rec: needlepoint, reading, movies. Res: 17105 W Bernardo Dr #201 San Diego 92127-1501 Ofc: Senior World Newsmagazine P.O. Box 1565, 1000 Pioneer Way El Cajon 92022 Tel: 619/593-2912

WRIGHT, CAROLE YVONNE, chiropractor, chiropractic management consultant; b. July 12, 1932, Long Beach; d. Paul Burt and Mary Leoan (Staley) Fickes; div.; 1 dau. Morgan Michelle b. 1958; edn: DC, Palmer Coll. of Chiropractic, 1976. Career: dir. Environmental Services Alameda Hosp. 1968-73; real estate agt. Esther Weiner Real Estate, Davenport, Iowa 1973-77, during coll. years; chiropractor/prin. Fort Sutter Chiropractic, Sacto. 1986-89; chiropractic mgmt. cons. 1988–, and prin. Wright Chiropractic Health Ctr., 1989–, also Sutter Spinex Ctr., a spinal rehab. & muscle strengthening clinic; instr. Chiropractic Assistants Tng. Pgm. 1981–; honors: Am. Heart Assn. Heart Saver Award 1980, listed Who's Who in Chiropractic Internat. 1980-84; mem: Internat. Chiropractors Assn. 1973–, Internat. Chiropractors Assn. of Calif. (pres. 1983-85, dir. 1979-85), Palmer Coll. Alumni Assn. of Calif. (pres. 1981-83), Soroptimist; guest speaker TV and radio talk shows on chiropractic; Republican; rec: lecturing. Res: 1404 Stonebridge Way Roseville 95661-5456 Ofc: Capitol Chiropractic 1972 Stockton Blvd Sacramento 95816

WRIGHT, HELENE SEGAL, managing editor; b. Jan. 31, 1955, L.A., Calif.; d. Alan and Lila Esther (Hambro) Segal; m. David Scott Wright, May 6, 1979; edn:. Calif. State Univ., Fullerton, Calif., 1973-75; BA, Eng., UC Santa Barbara, 1978. Career: lib. asst., ABC-CLIO, Santa Barbara, 1979-80; editorial asst., ABC-CLIO, Santa Barbara, 1980-81; asst. ed., ABC-CLIO, Santa Barbara, 1981-83; managing ed. ABC Pol. Sci., ABC-CLIO, Santa Barbara, 1983–; advy. bd. mem., Current World Leaders, Santa Barbara, 1989–; mem: Am. Political Sci. Assn.; Democrat; Jewish; rec: swimming, collecting, art, theatre, literature. Ofc: ABC-CLIO 130 Cremona Santa Barbara 93117

WRIGHT, LLOYD GORDON, licensed acupuncturist; b. Sept. 28, 1954, Chgo., Ill.; s. Paul Allen and Frances Aileen (Pollard) W.; m. Jie Min Lin, July 23, 1988; edn: H.S. diploma, Wooster H.S., Reno, Nev., 1972; certified massage therapist, Sonoma Sch. of Holistic Massage, Santa Rosa, Calif., 1979; BA Psychology, S.F. State Univ., 1981; lic. acupuncturist, Am. Coll. of Trad. Chinese Medicine, S.F., Calif., 1985, State of Calif., 1985; Diplomate Nat. Bd. of Acupuncture Orthopedics 1994. Career: mental health worker, Nevada Mental Health Inst., Reno, 1973-76; Peninsula Hosp. & Med. Ctr., Burlingame, Calif., 1978-87; lic. acupuncturist, private practice, Los Altos & Palo Alto, Calif., 1985–; guest lectr. Xian Yang Sch. of Trad. Chinese Medicine, Xian, China, 1986; Stanford Univ., Palo Alto, 1989; Foothill Coll., Los Altos, 1990; examiner, Calif. Acupuncture Lic. Exam, State of Calif., 1991; qualified med. examiner in acupuncture, Ind. Med. Council, State of Calif., 1992; mem. Acupuncture Com., Consumer Affairs, State of Calif., 1993–; awards: Outstanding Svc. and Leadership, Calif. Acupuncture Assn., 1991, 92; mem. Calif. Certified Acupuncture Assn. 1987–; advy. bd. mem. Am. Found. of Trad. Chinese Medicine, 1987–; mem. Calif. Acupuncture Assn. 1987–, bd. of dirs. 1991–; bd. of dirs., Res. Inst. of Chinese Medicine 1993; author: contbg. writer, CAA News Bulletin, 1992-93; Republican; rec: fencing, Chi-Kung. Ofc: 4161 El Camino Way Ste. A-2 Palo Alto 94306

WU, FRANCIS YING WAI, physician; b. June 25, 1936, Shanghai, China; s. Chow Han and Yik Tsee (Wong) W.; m. Amy C.M. Hu, Aug. 24, 1965; children: Rose b. 1966, Justin b. 1967, Andrew b. 1980; edn: MB, BS, Univ. Hong Kong 1963; diplomate Am. Bd. Ob-Gyn. 1974. Career: staff So. Calif. Permanente Med. Group, Bellflower 1970–; asst. clin. prof. ob-gyn. UCLA Sch. Medicine, L.A. 1984–; profl. staff Harbor/UCLA Med. Center 1980–; article pub. in med. jour. 1972; Catholic; rec: swimming, travel, philately. Res: 837 Rivera Pl Palos Verdes Estates 90274 Ofc: Southern California Permanente Medical Group 9449 Imperial Hwy Downey 90242

WU, LI-PEI, banker; b. Sept. 9, 1934, Taiwan; s. Yin-Su and Chiaw-Mei (Hsiao) Wu; m. Jenny S. Lai, March 24, 1964; children: George T. b. 1964, Eugene Y. b. 1967; edn: BA, Nat. Taiwan Univ. 1957; MS bus. admin. Fort Hays State Univ., Hays, KS, 1969; commercial banking exec. pgm., Grad. Sch. of Bus., Columbia Univ., 1974. Career: asst. v.p., v.p. Nat. Bank of Alaska, Anchorage 1969-73, v.p./controller 1973-76, sr. v.p./chief fin. ofcr. 1976-78; chmn. exec. com. Alaska Nat. Bank of the North, Anchorage 1978-79, chief adminstrv. ofcr. 1979-80, pres. 1980-81; pres. & CEO, dir. General Bank & GBC Bankcorp, Los Angeles 1982-84, chmn., pres. & CEO, dir. 1984–; pres. Taiwanese United Fund 1991-92; recipient Outstanding Entrepreneur Award Nat. Assn. of Investment Cos.; mem: Taiwanese Am. Citizens League (founder, past pres.), Nat. Taiwanese Am. Citizens League (pres. 1989-91), Taiwanese Am. Political Action Com. (pres. 1992-93). Ofc: General Bank 800 West Sixth St Los Angeles 90017

WU, SHU-YAU, scientist in ferroelectric materials and related devices; b. Nov. 6, 1936, Taiwan; s. Tang-Chao Wu; m. Chih-Ing Lee, Feb. 8, 1969; children: Lillian b. 1969, Benjamin b. 1971; edn: PhD, Univ. Ill., Urbana 1966. Career: fellow scientist Westinghouse Electric Corp., Pittsburgh, PA 1967-89; sr. tech., prin. scientist McDonnell Douglas Aerospace Corp., Huntington Beach, Calif. 1989–; mem. editl. bd. in integrated ferroelectrics, Gordon and Breach Sci. Pubs., N.Y., N.Y. 1992–; awards: engring. achiev. Westinghouse Research Ctr., Pitts. (1985, 86), recognition award ISIF, Colo. Springs 1991; mem: IEEE 1970–, Sigma Xi 1970–; author 8 U.S. patents, 50+ sci. papers; Republican; rec: fishing, bridge, tennis. Ofc: McDonnell Douglas Space Systems Co. 5301 Bolsa Ave Huntington Beach 92647

WYCOFF, CHARLES COLEMAN, retired physician, anesthesiologist; b. Sept. 2, 1918, Glazier, Texas; s. James Garfield and Ada Sharpe (Braden) W.; m. Gene Marie (Henry), May 16, 1942; children: Michelle, Geoffrey, Brian, Roger, Daniel, Norman, Irene, Teresa; edn: AB, UC Berkeley, 1941; MD, UC San Francisco, 1943; Diplomate Am. Bd. Anesthesiology. Career: founder The Wycoff Group of Anesthesiology, San Francisco 1947-53; chief of anesthesia St. Joseph's Hosp., S.F. 1947-52, San Francisco County Hosp., 1953-54; asst. prof. anesth. Columbia Univ., N.Y.C. 1955-63; founder residency tng. pgms. in anesth. St. Joseph's Hosp., S.F., 1950, S.F. County Hosp., 1954; practice anesth., instr. Presbyterian Med. Ctr., N.Y.C., 1955-63; clin. practice anesth. St. Francis Memorial Hosp., 1963-84; mil: served to capt. Med. Corps US Army 1945-47; producer, dir. films on regional anesthesia; contbr. articles to med. jours.; councilor at lg. Alumni Faculty Assn. Sch. Medicine UCSF 1979-80; scoutmaster Boy Scouts Am., S.F. 1953-55; Democrat; rec: research in evolution of the universe and human behavior. Res: 394 Cross St Napa 94559

WYLIE, JUDITH BABCOCK, author, travel writer, journalist; b. Oct. 7, 1943, Balt.; d. Joseph Brooks and Louise Boynton; m. Frank Winston Wylie, Feb. 19, 1984; edn: BA in biology & English, Univ. of Akron, 1966; MEd, Univ. Kentucky, 1967. Career: pgm. advisor Student Union, Ohio Univ., Athens 1968-71; pgm. dir. Student Union, Univ. Arizona, Tucson 1971-77; program dir. Student Union, CSU Los Angeles, 1977-78, dir. student devel. CSU Los Angeles, 1978-80, asst. to v.p./adminstrn. 1980-83; radio travel commentator Sta. KPCC-

FM, Pasadena 1991-92; radio travel commentator KUSP-FM, Santa Cruz 1993; chief travel writer Pasadena Star News, 1987–, San Gabriel Valley Tribune Newspapers Inc. 1991–; instr. writing seminars Pasadena City Coll. 1985-88, New York Univ., N.Y.C. 1989–; UC Berkeley 1994–; UC Santa Cruz 1995–; travel corresp. for Arlington (Ill.) Herald, Santa Cruz Sentinel; assoc. ed. Romantic Traveling; mem. PEN 1989–, Kappa Kappa Gamma; publs: 100+ travel and gen. lifestyle articles in newspapers and mags. incl. Travel & Leisure, New Woman, San Francisco Focus, Brides, Westways, Diversion; coauthor: The Spa Book, 1983, The Romance Emporium, 1986. Ofc: 1900 Smith Grade Santa Cruz 95060

WYMAN, PHILLIP DAVID, former state senator and assemblyman, rancher; b. Feb. 21, 1945, Hollywood; s. Elliott Sherwood and Rosalie Jane (Mauzy) W.; m. Lynn Dee Larson, May 21, 1977; children: Andrea Dee b. 1978, Elizabeth Frances b. 1982, David Elliott b. 1987; edn: BA, UC Davis 1967; JD, McGeorge Sch. of Law 1973; grad. studies, Ateneo de Manila Univ., Philippines. Career: former exec. v.p. Antelope Valley Board of Trade; mem. Calif. State Assembly 1978-92; elected Calif. Legislature, Senator in special election April 1993; coms: Agriculture and Water Resources, Banking, Commerce, and Internat. Trade, Energy and Public Utilities, Veterans Affairs, Joint Com. on Legis. Audit; mem: Am. Legion, Native Sons of the Golden West, Rotary, Farm Bureau (Kern Co.), Philippine Astronomical Soc. (founder); mil: sgt. USAF; Republican; rec: astronomy. Ofc: PO Box 665 Tehachapi 93581-0665

YAMADA, EILEEN GAYLE, pediatric resident; b. June 17, 1964, Reedley, Calif.; d. Fumio Bill and Ellen Eikue (Kobayashi) Y.; edn: BS, mech. engring. (highest honors), UC Santa Barbara 1987; MD, UC San Francisco Sch. Medicine 1992; diplomate Nat. Bd. Med. Examiners 1993, Calif. Med. Bd. lic. 1993. Career: engring. asst. Diverless Systems Inc., Santa Barbara 1985; res. asst. physiology dept. UCSF 1986; Howard Hughes res. fellow UCSF 1990-91; resident in pediatrics Children's Hospital, Oakland 1992–; honors: Dean's List UCSB 1982-87, Pi Tau Sigma 1984, Tau Beta Pi (life) 1984, Golden Key Nat. Honor Soc., Outstanding Jr. Mem. 1985, Mortar Bd. Sr. Honor Soc. 1986, Inst. for Advancement of Engring. Outstanding Student, UCSB 1986, Japanese Am. Citizen's League undergrad. scholarship 1986, Am. Heart Assn. Student Res. grant 1986, UCSB Thomas More Storke Award for Excellence 1987, Fresno-Madera Cos. Med. Soc. scholarship 1988, 91, Pine Methodist Church: Rodi Ishii scholarship 1991, The Grouch Scholarship award 1991; mem: Am. Acad. of Pediatrics 1992–; contbg. author: sci. abstract and articles to profl. jours. 1991, 92, 94; Democrat; Buddhist; rec: tennis, jogging, hiking.

YAMAHATA, WAYNE ICHIRO, plastic surgeon, educator; b. Sept. 27, 1947, Los Angeles; s. Kyu and May (Suehiro) Y.; m. Pamela, Jan. 26, 1985; children: Jeffery b. 1968, Ashley b. 1987; edn: AB, USC, 1971; MD, UC Davis, 1978; diplomate Am. Bd. Surgery 1987, Am. Bd. Plastic Surgery 1989. Career: intern, resident in surgery, fellow in nutrition, resident in surgery, resident in plastic surgery, Univ. Calif. Davis 1978-86, asst. clin. prof. UC Davis, 1986–; plastic surgeon pvt. practice, Sacto. 1986–; named resident of year UCD 1984; mem: Sacto. El Dorado Med. Soc., Am. Med. Assn., Calif. Med. Assn., Calif. Soc. of Plastic Surgeons, U.C. Davis Surgical Soc., Am. Soc. of Plastic and Reconstrv. Surgeons, Am. Coll. of Surgeons (fellow); author: Clinical Nutrition 1984, contbr. articles in med. jours. 1974, 81. Ofc: 95 Scripps Dr Sacramento 95825

YAO, JOHN S., medical doctor; b. Honolulu, Hawaii; s. Hsin-Nung and Dorothy W. (Wu) Y.; m. Pauline Ann Mysliwiec; edn: BS, Columbia Univ. 1975; MPH, New York, NY 1978; MD, F. Edward Hebert Sch. of Medicine 1983; diplomate Am. Bd. of Internal Medicine 1987. Career: med. dir. Public Health Svc. Hosp., Sells, Ariz. 1986-88; med. dir. Sonoma Co. Indian Health, Santa Rosa, Calif. 1988-90; chief med. ofcr. U.S. Public Health Svc., Sacramento 1990–; adj. asst. clin. prof. UC San Francisco 1988–; mem: N.Y. Acad. of Sci. 1977–, Am. Public Health Assn. 1978–, AMA 1983–, Am. Coll. of Physicians 1983–; author: pub. articles, 1978, 91; Democrat; rec: golf, tennis, skiing. Res: PO Box 4261 San Rafael 94913 Ofc: USPHS 1825 Bell St Ste 200 Sacramento 95825

YARIV, AMNON, physicist, educator; b. Apr. 13, 1930, Tel Aviv, Israel; s. Shraga and Henya (Davidson) Y.; m. Frances; children: Danielle b. 1959, Dana b. 1964, Gabriela b. 1974; edn: BS, UC Berkeley, 1954, MS, 1958, PhD, 1960. Career: staff Bell Labs, Murray Hill, N.J. 1960-64; faculty Calif. Inst. of Tech., Pasadena 1964–; chmn. bd. ORTEL Corp., Alhambra, 1980–, Accuwave, Santa Monica, 1991–; awards: Ives Medal Opt. Soc. Am. 1986, Pender award Univ. Pa. 1985, Quantum Electronics Award IEEE 1980, Nat. Acad. of Engring., Nat. Acad. Scis. 1991, fellow Am. Acad. Arts and Scis. 1982, Harvey Prize 1992; mem.: Opt. Soc. Am., Am. Phys. Soc., IEEE, Am. Acad. Arts & Scis.; mil: sgt. arty. Israel 1948-50; Jewish; rec: hiking, body surfing. Res: 2257 Homet San Marino Ofc: Caltech 1201 California Ave Pasadena 91125

YASNYI, ALLAN DAVID, media communications executive; b. June 22, 1942, New Orleans; s. Ben Z. and Bertha R. (Michalove) Y.; m. Susan K. Manders, artist; children: Benjamin Charles, Judith Evelyn; edn: BBA, Tulane Univ., 1964. Career: indep. film producer, writer, actor, designer for TV, feature films, and stage prodns., performer and producer The Second City, 1961-73; dir. fin. and adminstrn. Quinn Martin Prodns., Hollywood 1973-76, v.p. fin. 1976-77, exec.

v.p. fin. and corp. planning 1977; vice chmn., CEO QM Productions, Beverly Hills 1977-78, bd. chmn./CEO 1978-80; pres./CEO The Synapse Communications Group, Inc. 1981–; exec. dir. Univ. of So. Calif., Entertainment Technology Ctr. 1994-; adj. prof. Univ. of So. Calif., Sch. of Cinema-Television 1994-; exec. producer first live TV & radio broadcast to 120+ nations combining INTELSAT, INTERSPUTNIK, Voice of Am. and Moscow World Radio Svc., 1990; bd. chmn. Found. for Global Bdcstg., Wash. D.C., 1987-93; bd. dirs. Internat. Ctr. for Integrative Studies, NY, NY 1988-92, Assn. of Transpersonal Psychology 1986- (keynote address publ. 1988), bd. trustees Hollywood Arts Council, exec. v.p., trustee Hollywood Hist. Trust 1981-91; publ. participant, ICIS Forum, 1990–; honors: Citizen's State Audience with the Dali Lama, Daramsala, India 1988; Aspen Inst. Exec. Seminars Resource Guest, Global Comms., 1990; inducted Tulane Univ. Hall of Fame 1992; mem: Am. Acad. TV Arts and Scis., Hollywood Radio and TV Soc., Screen Actors Guild, Hollywood C.of C. (dir., exec. com. 1978-93), Asthma & Allergy Found. of Am. (bd. dirs. 1981-85), Inst. of Noetic Scis. 1986–; mil: logistical combat ofcr. US Army 1964-66, Vietnam. Ofc: 4132 Fulton Ave Sherman Oaks 91423

YASSIR, SAID, physician; b. Sept. 13, 1945, Palestine (nat. 1972); s. Momoud and Halima El-Yassir; m. Trisha Ann Peters, Aug. 21, 1993; children: Simone b. 1991, Monica b. 1994; edn: grad. Almakassed H.S., Beirut, Lebanon 1958-65; MD, Ain Shams Univ. Med. Sch., Cairo, Egypt 1971; med. lic. E.C.F.M.G., 1972, St. of Ill., St. of Calif. 1977; cert. Am. Bd. Obstetrics and Gynecology 1980. Career: internship: Eldimmerdash Univ. Hosps, Cairo 1971-72, W. Suburban Hosp., Oak Park, Ill. 1973, Rush Presbyn. St. Luke's Med. Ctr., Chgo., Ill. 1973-74; residency, ob-gyn. Rush Presbyn. St. Luke's Med. Ctr. 1974-77; pvt. practice ob-gyn, Sacramento 1977-80, Carmichael, Calif. 1980-91; gynecologist, dir. women's health svs., VA Clinic, Sacto. 1992-93, pvt. practice ob-gyn, Carmichael 1994–; active staff: Mercy San Juan Hosp. (chmn. dept. ob-gyn 1988-90, chmn. bylaws com. 1990-91), Carmichael, Mercy-Am. River Hosp., Carmichael; courtesy staff: Sutter Mem. Hosp., Sacto., Sutter Gen. Hosp., Sacto., Mercy Gen. Hosp., Sacto.; mem. trauma review com. UC Davis 1990-92; mem. Am. Coll. of Obstetricians and Gynecologists (fellow 1980–), CMA, Am. Assn. of Gynecologic Laparoscopists, Sacto. Co. Med. Soc. (membership com. 1991–). Ofc: 6555 Coyle Ave #220 Carmichael 95608

YAW, ELBERT M., public speaker, counselor, trainer; b. May 5, 1940, Kansas City, Mo.; s. Elbert F. and Juanita F. (Black) Y.; m. Holly H. Chilson, May 16, 1982; children: Kimberly M. b. 1962, Sandi M. b. 1969; edn: pol. sci., Fullerton Coll. 1958-60; L.A. Trade Tech. Coll. 1962-3; BSME, Northrop Univ. 1966; Grad. Sch. Bus., CSU Los Angeles 1968; wholesale mgmt., Stanford Univ. 1980. Career: engr. So. Calif. Gas Co., Los Angeles 1966-67; systems and territory sales Paul-Munroe Co., Pico Rivera 1967-69; western reg. mgr. Fluid Power Systems Div., Ambac Inc., Burlingame 1969-74; area mgr. Paul-Munroe Co., Santa Clara 1974-79, v.p. mktg. and ops./dir. sales, Whittier 1979-85, v.p. No. Calif. area, 1985-87, v.p. distbn., sales and service, 1987-89; speaker, counselor, trainer dba Bert Yaw & Assocs., 1989–; consultant, engr. and bus. 1969-74; honor soc. Northrop Univ. 1965; mem. Auburn C.of C., Grass Valley and Nevada Co. C.of C.; Republican; Christian; rec: hunting, fishing, writing. Res: 24712 Scooterbug Ln Auburn 95603

YEAGER, CHUCK (CHARLES E.), brigadier general (retired), b. Feb. 13, 1923, Myra, West Va.; s. Albert Hal and Susie Mae (Sizemore)Y.; m. Glennis Faye Dickhouse, Feb. 26, 1945; children: Donald C. b. 1946, Michael D. b. 1947, Sharon Yeager Flick b. 1948; Susan F. b. 1953; edn: Hamlin High School 1941; grad. Air Command and Staff Sch. 1952, Air War College, U.S. Air Force (class rank 1) 1961; DSc (hon.), W. Va. Univ. 1948, Marshall Univ., Huntington, W. Va. 1969; D in Aero. Sci., Salem Coll., W. Va. 1975. Career: enlisted U.S. Army Air Corps 1941, later commissioned and rose through the ranks to brig. gen. in the U.S. Air Force, 1969, fighter pilot, ETO 1943-46, experimental flight test pilot 1945-54; various command assignments U.S. Air Force in U.S., Germany, France and Spain 1954-62; comdr. 405th Fighter Wing (127 combat missions, Viet Nam), Seymour Johnson AFB, N.C. 1968-69; vice comdr. 17th Air Force, Ramstein Air Base, Fed. Republic Germany 1969-71; U.S. defense rep. to Pakistan 1971-73; spl. asst. to comdr. Air Force Inspection and Safety Ctr., Norton AFB, Calif. 1973, dir. aerospace safety 1973-75; ret. 1975; WW II double ace (11 kills), 1st USAAF pilot to become an ace in a single mission, 1st pilot to shoot down a jet aircraft (German Junkers JU-88), piloted X-1 research airplane first exceeding the speed of sound Oct. 27, 1947; awarded Collier Trophy by Pres. Harry Truman for breaking the speed of sound 1948; decorated DSM with oak leaf cluster, Silver Star with oak leaf cluster, Legion of Merit with oak leaf cluster, DFC with 2 oak leaf clusters, Bronze Star with V device, Air Medal with 10 oak leaf clusters, Air Force Commendation Medal, Purple Heart, awarded peace time Medal of Honor by Pres. Gerald Ford 1976, recipient Presdl. Medal of Freedom 1985; author: (with Leo Janos) Yeager: An Autobiography, 1985, (with Charles Leerhsen) Press On!, 1988; Protestant; rec: hunting, fishing. Res: PO Box 128 Cedar Ridge 95924-0128

YEAGER, KURT ERIC, research and development executive; b. Sept. 11, 1939, Cleveland, Ohio; s. Joseph Ellsworth and Karolyn Kristine (Pedersen) Y.; m. Rosalie Ann McMillan, Feb. 5, 1960 (div. 1968); m. Regina Ursula Querfurt,

May 12, 1970; children: Geoffrey b. 1961, Phillip b. 1963, Victoria b. 1975; edn: BA chemistry, Kenyon Coll. 1961; MS physics, UC Davis 1964; Industrial College of the Armed Forces 1967; Advanced Mgmt. Program, Univ. of Penn. Wharton Sch. Bus. 1995. Career: ofcr., program mgr. Air Force Tech. Applications Ctr., Alexandria, Va. 1962-68; assoc. dept. dir. Mitre Corp., McLean, Va. 1968-72; dir. energy res. and devel. planning U.S. E.P.A., WDC 1972-74; dir. fossil power plants dept. Electric Power Res. Inst., WDC 1974-79, dir. coal combustion systems div. 1979-83, v.p. generation and storage 1983-91, sr. v.p. EPRI Technical Operations, 1991-95, exec. v.p./c.o.o. EPRI 1995–; bd. mem. Nat. Coal Council, Arlington, Va. 1988-90; mem. Commerce Tech. Advy. Bd., WDC 1974-75; bd. chmn. Coal Quality Inc., Homer City,, Pa. 1989–; tchg. asst. Ohio St. Univ., Columbus 1961-62; mem. bd. ASME Res. Policy Bd., N.Y.C. 1982-84; awards: E.P.A. outstanding service 1974, British Coal Utilization Res. Assn. Robens medal 1989, Fellow ASME 1991; mem. AAAS; Nat. Republican Party, Calif. Republican Party; author: 200 articles and chpts. pub. on energy and environ., 1968–; mil: capt. USAF 1962-68, 2 AF commendation medals 1966; Republican; Episcopalian. Res: 687 Erie Dr Sunnyvale 94087

YEAGER, PHILIP J., real estate executive; b. Mar. 1, 1930, Columbus, Ohio; s. William P. and Anna C. (Meidl) Y.; m. Peggy Wetzler, Nov. 1, 1952; children: Melissa b. 1954, Susan b. 1955, Kurt b. 1956 (dec.), Stephen b. 1959, Christine b. 1961, Jennifer b. 1966; edn: Claremont Men's Coll. 1951; grad. study Ohio State Univ. 1956; Calif. lic. real estate broker (third generation Calif. Realtor); Calif. Comm. Colls. life tchg. credential, real estate; FAA lic. instrument rated pilot (3000 hours). Career: realtor; bd. chmn./CEO Century 21 Region 105 (100 realty offices, adminstrv. hq. Ontario, Calif.), Century 21 Region 113 (190 realty offices, adminstrv. hq. Seattle, Wash.); cons. ptnr./regl. owner Century 21 Mexico (100 realty offices in 44 cities adminstrv. hq. Mexico City); honors: Eagle Scout; mem: Covina Valley Bd. of Realtors (past pres.), Nat. Assn. of Realtors (past dir.); civic: Boy Scouts Am. (former scoutmaster and dist. chmn.), Toastmasters (past pres. 2 clubs); contbr. num. real estate articles in nat. publs.; mil: 1st lt./pilot USAF Korean Campaign 1952-56; Republican; rec: flying, power boating, golf, tennis. Res: 2808 Monte Verde Covina 91724 Ofc: Century 21, Region 105, 3400 Inland Empire Blvd Ontario 91764-5510; Century 21, Region 113, 18000 Pacific Hwy S, Seattle WA 98188; Century 21 Mexico, Monte Libano #245, Lomas de Chapultepec, 11000 Mexico, D.F.

YEE, CARLTON, educator, forestry consultant; b. May 25, 1941, Morenci, Ariz.; s. Joe and Laura (Woo) Y.; m. Linda T., Jan. 24, 1969 (div. 1989); m. Judith Rocha, March 18, 1989; edn: BS, Humboldt State Univ. 1964; MF, Yale Univ. 1965; PhD, Ore. State Univ. 1975; reg. profl. forester Calif. 1973. Career: forester U.S. Forest Service, Calif. 1965-67; instr. Austin State Univ., Nacogdoches, Tx. 1967-70; prof. Humboldt State Univ., Arcata 1970–; v.chmn. Calif. State Bd. Forestry, Sacto. 1983–; cons. forester, Arcata 1975–; mem: Aircraft Owners & Pilots Assn., Soc. Am. Foresters; mil: 1st lt. AUS 1960-62; Republican; rec: flying, bicycling, alpine skiing. Res: POB 360 Bayside 95524

YEE, DONALD H., lawyer; b. Nov. 18, 1960, Sacramento; s. Jimmie H. K. and Gee Suey Y.; edn: BA communications, UCLA 1983; BA political sci. and communications 1983; JD, Univ. Va. 1987; admitted St. Bar Calif. 1987, admitted U.S. Distr. Court, Central Distr.; certified Nat. Football League Players Assn. contract advisor. Career: atty. Lillick & McHose, L.A. 1987-93; of counsel, Mitchell, Silberberg & Knupp (Sports Div.), L.A. 1993–; mem: Constitutional Rights Found. (sports and law advy. council), Assn. Reps. of Profl. Athlets, Sports Lawyers Assn., NCAA, U.S. Volleyball Assn. Grants Program, L.A. Co. Bar Assn., Am. Bar Assn.; rec: sports. Ofc: Mitchell Silberberg & Knupp 11377 W Olympic Blvd Los Angeles 90064

YEE, JAMES MARION, physician; b. Peiping, China; U.S. cit.; m. Carole Jean Mar; children: James Christopher, Alisa Meredith; edn: UC Berkeley; BA, Stanford Univ., 1965; MD, Stanford Med. Sch., 1968; cert. Am. Bd. of Surgery (1974), Am. Bd. of Thoracic Surgery (1976). Career: surgical intern Beth Israel Hosp., Boston 1968-69; gen. surgical resident Univ. Calif. Med. Ctr., San Francisco 1969-73; thoracic surg. res. Highland Gen. Hosp., 1973-75; asst. clin. prof. dept. surgery UC Med. Ctr., S.F.; clin. assoc. UCB-UCSF Jt. Med. Pgm.; med. staff Alta Bates Hosp. (surg. clinic dir.), and Summit Med. Ctr, Oakland; mem: S.F. Surg., Howard C. Naffziger Surg. Soc., Calif. Thoracic Soc., Soc. of Thoracic Surgeons, Am. Coll. of Chest Physicians, Am. Coll. of Surgeons; contbr. articles to med. jours. Ofc: 2900 Telegraph Berkeley 94705

YEEND, WARREN ERNEST, geologist; b. May 14, 1936, Colfax, Wash.; s. Kenneth Edward and Frances Leone (Lynch) Y.; m. Nancy Eloise Neal, June 6, 1965 (div. Dec. 1980); 1 dau., Erica b. 1972; m. Elissa Hirsh, Sept. 29, 1985; edn: BS geology, Wash. State Univ., 1958; MS, Univ. Colo., 1961; PhD geology, Univ. Wis., 1965. Career: geologist US Geological Survey, Menlo Park, Calif. 1965-95 (ret. Jan. 1995); honors: Phi Beta Kappa 1958, Outstanding tchg. asst. Univ. Wis. 1965, USGS special achiev. award 1975, 1980; mem. History of Earth Scis. Soc. 1982–, Geol. Soc. Am. 1976-85, Am. Quaternary Assn. 1974-81; publs: profl. papers (1969, 74), bull., Gold Placers of the Circle Dist., Alaska (1991); rec: books, gardening. Ofc: USGS, 345 Middlefield Rd Menlo Park 94025

YEH, TIMOTHY STEPHEN, physician; b. Dec. 9, 1950, Jersey City, N.J.; s. Shu Tze and Wan (Yuan) Y.; edn: BS, biology, MIT 1972; MD, UC Davis 1976 lic. physician Dist. of Columbia, St. of Calif.; diplomate Nat. Bd. Med. Examiners; bd. cert. pediatrics Am. Bd. Pediatrics 1982, pediatric critical care 1987; Drug Enforcement Adminstrn. cert.; advance trauma life support cert. Am. Coll. Surgeons 1987-95; paramedic basic trauma life support instr. cert. 1987; basic cardiac life support cert. 1989–; pediatric advanced life support instr. cert. 1989–. Career: pediatrics internship UC Davis-Sacto. Med. Ctr. 1976-77, pediatric residency 1977-78, chief resident pediatrics 1978-79; fellow, pediatric intensive care Children's Hosp. Nat. Med. Ctr., W.D.C. 1979-81; dir. pediatric intensive care Children's Hosp. of S.F. 1981-87; assoc. dir. pediatric intensive care Children's Hosp. Oakland 1987-90, dir. 1990–; Children's Hosp. Oakland/UCSF Pediatric Critical Care Fellowship Prog. 1990–; Med. staff Children's Hosp. of S.F. 1981–, Children's Hosp. Oakland 1987–; cons. staff Pacific Presbyn. Med. Ctr. 1982–; assoc. clin. prof. pediatrics UCSF; med. staff Kaiser Hosp., S.F. 1985-87; mem. Children's Hosp Oakland res. com. and resident com. 1987–, trauma morbidity & mortality review 1987–, trauma advy. com 1989–, nutrition com. 1987-90, PICU morbidity & mortality review 1987–, med. svs., review & planning 1990–, continuous quality improvement steering com. 1991–, multicultural com. 1992–; past mem. num. coms. UC Davis Med. Ctr. 1976-79, Children's Hosp. of S.F. 1981-87; awards: Resident of Yr., Pediatrics, UC Davis 1979, Teacher of Yr., Pediatrics, Children's Hosp. of S.F. 1981; mem: Soc. of Critical Care Medicine 1981– (pres. pediatric sect. exec. com. 1986-87, chmn. pediatric sect. subcom. on pediatric IC regionalization & transport 1984-87, co-chmn. sub. on data acquisition in pediatric IC 1985-88; mem. pediatric sect. subcom. on HMO/PICU interactions 1985–, subcom. on multi-instl. studies 1987–, subcom. on near-drowning prevention 1987–; chmn. pediatric sect. subcom. on ethics 1988–), Pediatric Intensive Care Network of No. and Central Calif. 1981– (chmn. 1982-84, 88-89), Am. Acad. of Pediatrics (fellow 1983–; mem. Dist. IX pediatric critical care steering com. 1987–, chpt. I hosp. care com. 1988–; mem. critical care sect. 1985–, exec. com. 1989–) Am. Coll. of Critical Care Medicine (fellow 1989–), Pediatric Critical Care Multi-Instl. Study Group (exec. com. 1987–), Am. Heart Assn. (subcom. on pediatric resuscitation 1992–); author: book chpts in pediatric critical care textbooks, 1981–, jour. articles on severity of illness in pediatric patients, 1982–. Ofc: Children's Hospital Oakland 747 52nd St Oakland 94609

YELNICK, MARC M., lawyer; b. Jan. 30, 1947, New York; s. Louis and Jeanne (Friedman) Y.; m. Linda Sherwin, Dec. 20, 1973; children: Sandy b. 1975, Shauna b. 1978; edn: BA, Bklyn. Coll. 1967; N.Y. Univ. Grad. Bus. Sch. 1967-69; JD, St. John's Univ. 1976. Career: tchr. N.Y.C. Bd. Edn. 1969-77; atty. Billet Billet & Avirom 1977-79; Whitman & Ransom 1979-84; sole practice, San Mateo 1984–; mem: Am. Bar Assn., Am. Immigration Lawyers Assn., San Mateo Co. Bar Assn., Lawyers in Mensa (charter fellow 1979-81); 4 articles pub. in profl. jours. (1982, 83, 90, 92). Ofc: 66 Bovet Rd Ste 353 San Mateo 94402

YEN, TIEN-SZE BENEDICT, virologist, educator; b. Oct. 15, 1953, Taipei, Taiwan, naturalized U.S. cit. 1972; s. Yen-Chen and Er-Ying Chi Y.; m. Maria He, Mar. 26, 1983; children: Cecilia b. 1984, Brian b. 1987; edn: BS, Stanford Univ., 1973; MD, Duke Univ. Sch. of Med., 1982, PhD, 1982. Career: asst. prof. Univ. Calif., San Francisco 1985-91, assoc. prof. 1991–; publs: 50+ jour. articles. Ofc: PO Box 0506 University California, San Francisco 94143

YEN, WEN-HSIUNG, association president, ethnomusicologist, composer, educator, writer; b. June 26, 1934, Tainan, Taiwan, R.O.C.; nat. citizen U.S.A. 1986; m. Yuan-yuan Yen, Jan. 6, 1961; 3 sons; edn: BA, Nat. Taiwan Norman Univ. 1960; MA, Chinese Cluture Univ. 1964; Univ. of Calif. 1971; PhD cand., Chinese Culture Univ., Univ. of Maryland; PhD cand. philosophy, UCLA 1994. Career: instr. Taiwan Provincial Taichung Teacher Coll., 1961-62; prof. Chinese Culture Univ. 1964-69; lectr. West Los Angeles Community Coll., 1978-82; grad. teaching asst. Univ. of Md. 1982-83; instr. L.A. City Coll. 1983–, CSU Los Angeles 1984–, Pasadena City Coll. 1989–; prof. of Chinese, Santa Monica Coll. 1986–, CSU Northridge 1986–; founder Wen Yen Piano Studio, 1972–; founder Chinese Culture Sch. of L.A., 1976–; founder, dir. Chinese Music Orch. of So. Calif., 1974–, TV appearance 1979, and conductor Yue You Chorus of So. Calif.; honors: recognition award Calif. Mus. Found. Bd. of Trustees 1976, recogn. award Chinese Amer. PTA 1980, outstanding tchr. Confucius Commemorative Day Ceremony, L.A. 1984, service award Nat. Taiwan Normal Univ. Alumni Assn. of So. Calif. 1985, recipient Commendations from Pres. George Bush and Pres. Lee Teng-hui (Rep. of China), Calif. Gov. Deukmejian and Lt. Gov. Leo McCarthy on occasion of 10th anniversary of Taiwan Benevolent Assn. of Calif. 1989; musical compositions include: Collection of Works by Mr. Yen, 1969; recordings: Art Songs and Chinese Folk Songs (13 pieces) 1982; Instrumental Ensemble for Chinese Traditional Orch. incl. A Hope of New Spring and San Yang Kai Tai; publs: Taiwan Folk Songs, Vol. 1 (1967), Vol. 2 (1969); A Dictionary of Chinese Music and Musicians (coauthor, 1967), A Collection of Wen-hsiung Yen's Songs (1968, vol. 2 1987); Achievement and Methodology for Comparative Musicology (1968), transl.; Chinese Musical Culture and Folk Songs (Zhong Wen Book Co., Taipei, 1989); organizer concerts in So. Calif. incl. Chinese Musical Culture Concert at CSU Los Angeles (1989, 91), Chinese Art Festival of So. Calif., Evening of Performing Arts at Pasadena City Coll. (6/92), conductor new composition for mixed chorus sung by Yue You Chorus and So. Calif. Catholic Choir; mem: Chinese-Amer. Musicians Assn. of So. Calif. (pres.), Chinese Culture Sch. of L.A. (pres.), Chinese Choral Soc. of So. Calif. (music dir.), Soc. of Ethnomusicol., The College Music Soc., Internat. Council for Traditional Music, Alumni Assn. for Chinese Culture Univ. in USA (pres.), Taiwan Benevolent Assn. of Amer. (bd. 1987–), Taiwan Benevolent Assn. of Calif. (bd. 1985–, v.p. 1986, pres. 1987-89), Chinese Amer. P.T.A. of So. Calif. (supr. 1985–), CSU L.A. Harriet and Chas. Luckman Fine Arts Complex (Gala Steering Com. 1994), v.p. Jt. Tchrs. Coll. and Normal Univ. of Taiwan, Alumni Assn. of So. Calif. 1994; res. presentations China and Confucianism Internat. Conf., CSU L.A. (6/90), 4th Music - Archaeology Symposium, Paris, Fr., Internat. Council for Traditional Music (10/90), Chinese Am.: Origins and Destinations (8/92), Chinese Instrumental Symbolism (10/94); rec: walking, Tai Chi Chuan, table tennis. Address: 482 Los Altos Ave Arcadia 91007

YESKE, DAVID BRENT, financial planner; b. May 21, 1957, Albany, Calif.; s. Ronald A. and JoAnn R. (Huntsman) Y.; m. Virginia Folwell, Jan. 10, 1987; edn: BS applied econs., Univ. San Francisco, 1989; MA econs. U.S.F. 1995; cert. fin. planner (CFP). Career: gen. ptnr. PCM, Ltd., Napa, Calif. 1977-84; wire trader Goldberg Securities, San Francisco 1984-85; brokerage cons. Paul Revere Group, S.F. 1985-90; pres. Yeske & Co., Inc. S.F. 1990–; mem. Inst. of CFP 1990–, Commonwealth Club of Calif., Hermetic Order of the G.D.; rec: Hermeneutics, opera, history. Ofc: Yeske & Company, Inc. 220 Bush St Ste 1109 San Francisco 94104

YOKLEY, RICHARD CLARENCE, firefighter, maintenance chief; b. Dec. 29, 1942, San Diego; s. Clarence Ralph and Dorothy Junese (Sackman) Y.; m. Jean Elizabeth Liddle, July 25, 1964; children: Richard Clarence II, Karin Denise; edn: San Diego City Coll., AS in fire sci., Miramar Coll., 1975; Calif. St. certified fire officer, fire investigator, fire instr. Career: disc jockey Sta. KSDS-FM, San Diego 1966-67; building engr. Consol. Systems Inc., San Diego 1968-72; firefighter Bonita-Sunnyside Fire Dept., 1972–, ops. chief 1991-93; maint. chief 1994–; med. techn. Hartson Ambulance, San Diego 1978-80, Bay Gen. Hosp. (now Scripps Chula Vista Hosp.) 1980-83; chmn. bd. South Bay Emergency Med. Svc. 1988; awards: exemplary svc. award Fire Dept. Directors 1984, Heroism and community svc. Firehouse Mag., N.Y.C. 1987, Chula Vista `Star News Salutes' 1987, Golden svc. San Diego Co. Credit Union 1988; mem: San Diego Co. Fire Prevention Ofcrs. (pres. 1985, mem. 1981-93), S.D. Co. Fire and Arson Investigators 1981-93, Calif. Conf. Arson Investigators 1981-93, Soc. Fire Prevention Engrs. 1981-93, Bonita Bus. and Profl. Assn. (dir. 1991-93, historian award 1987), South Bay Communications 1988, Masons; civic bds: Firehouse Mus., San Diego (asst. curator 1972-88), Boy Scouts Am. Tr. #874 Bonita (scoutmaster 1978-79), Bonita Hist. Mus. (co-founder 1986), So. Div. Deputy Dir. Calif. State Firefighters Assn. 1994–, Calif. Fire Mechanics 1995–; mil: USAF 1962-66, Peshawar, West Pakistan; Republican; Methodist; rec: scuba diving, Sport Chalet Diveclub (v.p. 1990-91), collect firefighting memorabilia, visit fire depts. worldwide (Moscow, Leningrad, Paris, Helsinki, London, others). Res: Box 718 Bonita 91908-0718 Ofc: Bonita-Sunnyside Fire Dept. 4900 Bonita Rd Bonita 91902-1327

YONG, DAVID C., clinical microbiologist, director public health laboratory b. Feb. 9, 1943, Lipis, Pahang, Malaysia; s. Ban Yien and Shin Yin (Ngaw) Y.; m. Lily Lian Loh, Dec. 21, 1968; children: Celina Mei b. 1979, Charles Tat b. 1985; edn: BSc (hons.), Univ. Manitoba, 1968, MSc virology, 1970, PhD med. microbiology, 1973, postdoctoral studies, 1974; Cert. pub. health and clin. microbiologist, Calif. Career: microbiologist, scientist Public Health Lab. Ontario Ministry of Health, Windsor, Ont., Canada 1975-85; instr. St. Clair Coll., Windsor 1976-84; adj. asst. prof. Univ. Windsor, Ont. 1983-84; pub. health lab. dir. Sonoma Co. Health Dept., Santa Rosa, Calif. 1986–; lectr. Sonoma State Univ., Rohnert Park 1986-87, adj. prof. 1991-92; awards: Dr. Stanley Reitman Memorial award for outstanding achiev. in teaching Internat. Soc. Clin. Lab. Technicians and Am. Assn. Bioanalysts 1988, Craftsman and Master of Photographic Arts awards 1984, 1986, Profl. Photog. of Canada; mem: Am. Soc. Microbiology, Calif. Assn. Pub. Health Lab. Dir. (exec. com. 1988-89, pres. 1993-94); Chinese United Methodist Ch.; rec: profl. photog., classical guitarist. Ofc: Sonoma County Public Health Laboratory, 3313 Chanate Rd Santa Rosa 95404

YOUNG, BRYANT LLEWELLYN, lawyer; b. Mar. 9, 1948, Rockford, Ill.; s. Llewellyn Anker and Florence Y.; m. Elizabeth MacMillan, Apr. 16, 1983; children: Kendra, Megan, Lauren; edn: AB, Cornell Univ., 1970; JD, Stanford Univ., 1974. Career: law clk. US Dist. Ct. no. dist. Calif., San Francisco 1974-75; atty., assoc. Dinkelspiel, Pelavin, Steefel & Levitt, S.F. 1975-77; White House fellow, 1977-78, spl. asst. to Secty. of HUD, WDC 1977-79, actg. dep. exec. asst. for ops. 1979; dep. gen. mgr. New Comm. Devel. Corp., 1979, actg. gen. mgr. 1979-80; mgmt. cons. AVCO Corp., 1980; spl. asst. to the c.e.o. and chmn. U.S. Synthetic Fuels Corp., WDC 1980-81, project dir. 1981; pres. Trident Mgmt. Corp., San Francisco 1981-87; counsel Pelavin, Norberg, Harlick & Beck, S.F. 1981-82, ptnr. 1982-87; mng. ptnr. bus. and R.E. sect., Carroll, Burdick & McDonough, S.F. 1987-90; founding ptnr. Young, Vogl, Harlick & Wilson, S.F. 1990–; advy. com. Nat. Multi Housing Council; prin. The Council for Excellence in Govt., WDC 1986-93; honors: Stanford Law Rev., Student Body pres., Hilmer Oehlmann Award for excellence in legal writing, Lawrence Fletcher Award for outstanding contbn. 1974, del. P.R.O.China 1980; mem: White House Fellows Alumni Assn. (chmn. annual meeting 1979, treas., bd. White House Fellows Found. 1980-84), State Bar Calif. (R.E. sect.), State Bar Nev., Dist. Col. Bar Assn., S.F. Bar Assn.; civic: Netherlands-Am. C.of C., Canadian-Am. C.of C. (bd. dirs. 1990–, v.p. 1992–), Chile-Calif. Found. (bd. dirs, exec com. 1993–), S.F. Aid Retarded Citizens Inc. (pub. affairs com. 1977), US-USSR Housing Agreement /New Towns Working Group (US co-chair 1979-80), Am. Field Service Returnees Assn. 1967–, Holland-Am. Soc., Ross Sch. Found. Ofc: Young, Vogl Harlick & Wilson, 425 California St San Francisco 94104

YOUNG, CEDRIC JAN-YEE, public health microbiologist; b. Feb. 23, 1942, Macau, nat. 1954; s. Tim-Oy and Sui-On Y.; m. Selina Chui-Wah, Sept. 1, 1973; children: Derek P.S. b. 1976, Edmund P.W. b. 1978; edn: BA, CSU San Francisco, 1970; MS, CSU Fresno, 1979; cert. pub. health microbiologist Calif. 1970. Career: dir. of lab. Madera County Health Dept., Madera 1973-87, also dir. health edn. 1981-87, mgr. dept. computer system 1983-87; dir. of lab. Stanislaus County Public Health Laboratory., Modesto 1987–; Honors: named to the order of the Golden Sword, Madera 1979; mem: Am. Soc. for Microbiology, Calif. Assn. of P.H. Lab Directors, Am. Cancer Soc. Stanislaus Unit, San Joaquin Valley Health Consortium Fresno 1984-86; Republican; Christian; rec: tennis, photog. Ofc: Stanislaus County Public Health Laboratory 820 Scenic Dr Modesto 95350

YOUNG, CHARLES EDWARD, university chancellor; b. San Bernardino, Calif., Dec. 30, 1931 s. Clayton Charles and Eula May (Walters) Y.; edn: AA San Bernardino Coll. 1954; AB Univ. Calif., Riverside 1955; MA Univ. Calif., Los Angeles 1957, Ph.D., 1960; DHL (hon.), Univ. Judaism, Los Angeles 1969. Career: congl. fellow Washington 1958-59; adminstrv. analyst Office of the Pres., Univ. Calif., Berkeley 1959-60; asst. prof. polit. sci. Univ. Calif., Davis, 1960; asst. prof. polit. sci. UCLA 1960-66, assoc. prof. 1966-69, prof. 1969, asst. to chancellor 1960-62, asst. chancellor, 1962-63, vice chancellor, adminstrn. 1963-68, chancellor 1968–; bd. dirs. Intel Corp.; bd. of governors, Los Angeles Metropolitan Project; Fellow Am. Acad. of Arts and Scis.; cons. Peace Corps. 1961-62, Ford Found. on Latin Am. Activities 1964-66; awards: Named Young Man of Year Westwood Jr. C. of C. 1962; mem: Knight Found. Commn. on Intercollegiate Athletics, Calif. Council on Sci. and Tech., NCAA Pres.'s Commn., Council. for Govt.-Univ.-Industry Res. Roundtable, Nat. Res. Council. Adv. Bd.-issues in Sci. and Tech., Nat. Com. on U.S.-China Rels., chancellor's assocs. UCLA, council. trustees L.A. Ednl. Alliance for Restructuring Now; past chair. Assn. Am. Univs., Nat. Assn. State Univs. and Land-Grant Colls.; mem. adminstrv. bd. Internat. Assn. Univs.; bd. govs. Found. Internat. Exchange Sci. and Cultural Info. by Telecomms., The Theatre Group Inc.; v.p. Young Musicians Found., bd. dirs. Los Angeles Internat. Visitors Council, Greater L.A. Energy Coalition, L.A. World Affairs Council.; trustee UCLA Found.; mil: USAF 1951-52. Ofc: UCLA Office of Chancellor 405 Hilgard Ave Los Angeles 90095-1405

YOUNG, DOUGLAS REA, lawyer; b. July 21, 1948, Los Angeles; s. James Douglas and Dorothy Belle (Rea) Y.; m. Terry Forrest, Jan. 19, 1974; 1 dau: Megann Forrest, b. 1979; edn: BA, cum laude, Yale Univ. 1970/71; JD, UC Berkeley 1976; admitted Calif. State Bar, 1976, US Supreme Ct., 6th and 9th Circuit Cts. of Appeal, Fed. Dist. Cts. (no. and central dists. Calif.), Hawaii. Career: law clerk to US Dist. Judge Alfonso J. Zirpoli 1976-77; assoc. atty. Farella, Braun & Martel 1977-82, partner 1982–; apptd. spl. master in federal litigation (4t), judge pro tem S.F. Municipal Ct. 1984–, S.F. Superior Ct. 1990–; faculty Nat. Inst. for Trial Advocacy 1983–, Hastings Coll. of Advocacy 1985–, Calif. Contg. Edn. of the Bar, Practising Law Inst.; author: (w/ Purver & Davis) California Trial Handbook 2d ed. (Bancroft-Whitney 1987), (w/ Purver, Davis & Kerper) The Trial Lawyer's Book: Preparing and Winning Cases (Lawyers Cooperative 1990), (w/Lynch, Taylor, Purver & Davis) California Negotiation and Settlement Handbook (Lawyers Cooperative 1991), (w/Lynch, Taylor, Purver & Davis) Negotiation and Settlement (Lawyers Cooperative 1992), contbr. articles in legal jours.; lawyer representative from the No. Dist. of Calif. to the Ninth Cir. Judicial Conf., 1992-94; co-founder Berkeley Law Foundation; bd. dir. Legal Aid Soc. of San Francisco 1981–, Public Interest Clearinghouse 1981–; awards: ABA Pro Bono Publico Award 1992, appreciation Berkeley Law Found., appreciation Public Interest Clearinghouse, Award of Merit S.F. Bar Assn., exec. editor Calif. Law Rev. 1975-76; mem: Am. Law Inst., S.F. Am. Inn of Calif. (ofcr.), Calif. St. Bar, Calif. Acad. of Appellate Lawyers (bd.), Berkeley Law Found., ACLU, Bar Assn. of San Francisco, Crim. Justice Act Defense Panel No. Dist. Calif., Environmental Defense Fund, Litigation and Criminal Law Sects. of Am. Bar Assn., Lawyers Club of S.F., Bar Assn. of S.F. (bd. 1990-91, chair litigation sect. 1989), ABA, Calif. Bar Assn.; publs: Cal. L. Rev. 1975; mil: Sgt., USMC 1971-73; Democrat; Prot.; rec: skiing, mountaineering, running. Res: 67 Weybridge Ct Oakland 94611 Ofc: Farella, Braun & Martel, 235 Montgomery St Ste 3000 San Francisco 94104

YOUNG, JAMIE, lawyer; b. Feb. 6, 1956, New York; d. Martin and Arlyne (Levy) Y.; edn: BA summa cum laude, Washington Univ. 1977; JD, N.Y. Univ. 1981; admitted St. Bars N.Y., Calif. Career: atty., assoc. Kurzman Karelsen &

Frank, N.Y.C. 1981-83; Golenbock & Barell 1983-86; sr. counsel CBS Records, L.A. 1986-88; atty., ptnr. Ziffren Brittenham & Branca 1988–; honors: Phi Beta Kappa. Ofc: Ziffren Brittenham & Branca 2121 Ave of Stars Ste 3200 Los Angeles 90067

YOUNG, JEFFREY WILLIAM, mechanical aerospace engineer, consultant; b. Jan. 13, 1947, Pittsburgh, Pa.; s. William Norman and Wilma (Myers) Y.; m. Karen Lynn Young, Nov. 23, 1973; children: Scott N., Witney R.; edn: BS mech. engring., UC Davis, 1969; MS in M.E., M.I.T., 1970; PhD in M.E. (spec. in dynamic systems and controls), UC Davis, 1974; Reg. profl. engr. Calif. Career: lectr. and devel. engr. UC Davis, 1974-75; asst. prof. mech. and aero. engring. Univ. Missouri, Kansas City 1975-79; dir. engring. Structural Dynamics Research Corp., San Diego 1979–; cons. engr. on analysis and design of mech. and aerospace products using computer-aided engring., Space Shuttle, MX Missile, Space Station, high performance computer Disk Drives, Mobile Cmd. Control & Comm. Sys., Radar Def. Unit Veh., proj. mgr. impl. prod. data mgmt. system for airplane config. control; awards: NSF fellow MIT 1964-70, NASA cash award for creative devel. of technical innovation 1983, Tau Beta Pi, Phi Kappa Phi; mem. Am. Soc. Mech. Engrs.; author: (video prodn.) Dynamic Analysis of Space Station Freedom (1990), 20+ tech. publs.; rec: tennis, bicycling. Res: 1482 Sanford Ln Leucadia 92024 Ofc: SDRC 11995 El Camino Real Ste 200 San Diego 92130

YOUNG, KENNETH ROGER, art educator; b. Aug. 25, 1936, Los Angeles; s. John Richardson and Jency Florence (Leman) Y.; m. LaVonne Bonita Kurowski, Mar. 17, 1963 (div. June 1970); m. Suzanne Cecelia Murray, June 20, 1970; children: Christina b. 1971, Steven b. 1974, Joseph b. 1974; edn: AA, Sacto. City Coll., 1956; BA, CSU Sacto., 1958, MA, 1968; Calif. gen. sec. tchg. credential, 1959. Career: art tchr. Roseville High Sch. Dist., 1960-70, Sequoia High Sch. Dist., 1970-82; art resource splst. San Carlos H.S. 1970-73, Morgan Hill Unified Sch. Dist. 1982–, Britton Middle Sch. 1982-85, Live Oak H.S. 1985–; performer-Artists' Theater: San Jose Mus. of Fine Art, Fresno Art Mus., Peninsula Art Mus. (Monterey, Calif.), Kingsley Art Club (Crocker Art Mus., Sacto.), Placer and Nevada Counties Art Docent luncheons, Calif. Art Edn. Assn. confs. and various schs. and orgs. in No. Calif.; awards: tchr. of year San Carlos H.S. 1972, Golden Bell Award (1st) Calif. Sch. Boards Assn. 1987, Calif. Art Educ. Assn. exemplary art educ. 1995; mem.: Am. Fedn. Tchrs. 1982–, Calif. Tchrs. Assn. 1960-82, Nat. Edn. Assn. 1960-82, Calif. Art Edn. Assn. (1970–, no. area sec. rep. 1988-90); civic: Young Audiences of San Jose (bd. 1985-88); mil: sp5 Calif. Army Nat. Guard 1954-65; Democrat; R.Cath.; rec: travel, film study, drawing & painting. Res: 1137-A Reed Ave Sunnyvale 94086-6833

YOUNG, PATRICIA ANN, real estate broker; b. Sept. 26, 1930, Concord; d. John Oscar and Esther Rita (Warren) Whitt; m. Louis Linzy Hudson, Dec. 12, 1947 (div. 1965); m. Haskel Herbert Young, Nov. 1, 1965; children: Gary b. 1948, Steven b. 1950, Linzy b. 1952, Barbara b. 1974; edn: Imperial Valley Coll. 1960-63; real estate, San Francisco Univ. 1985; secretarial, acctg., Am. Sch. 1952. Career: bookkeeper Singer Sewing Center, Porterville 1951; acctg. W.W. McCoullough, Visalia 1952-54; T.V. Channel 26, Tulare 1954; secty. El Centro Sch. Dist., El Centro 1959-63; office mgr. Golden Key Realty, Fresno 1964-65; real estate sales Adobe Realty, Petaluma 1965-66; scoring supr. Harcourt Brace & World West Coast Scoring, Petaluma 1966-67; bookkeeper Red Bud Hosp., Clear Lake Highlands 1968; real estate lic. Boise Cascade, Middletown 1968-69; World Recreation, Hayward 1970-71; co-owner Haskel Young Real Estate, Pioneer 1971–; awards: El Centro Merchants Mother of Year 1963, Fresno Water Ski Club 1st place 1964, Amador Co. Fair Sewing 1st place 1976,; mem: OES Queen Esther (1990 Worthy Matron), Jobs Daughter Bethel, Native Daughters, Daughters of Nile, U.S. Navy League, Jackson Band Boosters, Little League (treas. 1960-63), El Centro PTA (v.p. 1960); Republican; Baptist; rec: oil painting, sewing. Res: 26298 Fairway Dr Pioneer 95666

YOUNG, ROBYN GAIL, neurologist; b. Dec. 24, 1950, Danville, Ill.; d. Martin and Selma Lee (Mervis) Young; m. David Richard Cox, MD., PhD, June 12, 1977 (div. Nov. 1985); 1 child, Ian Richard Cox b. 1984; edn: BS, Stanford Univ., Stanford, Calif., 1973; MD, Yale Univ. Sch. of Medicine, New Haven, Conn., 1977. Career: internship, Pacific Presbyn. Hosp., S.F., 1977-78; residency, internal medicine, Pacific Med. Ctr., S.F., 1978-80; residency, neurology, UC S.F., 1980-83; neurologist, private practice, Oakland, Calif., 1984–; clinical instr., UC S.F. Dept. of Neurology, 1983-94; active staff: Summit Med. Ctr., Oakland, Calif. 1983–; Alameda Hosp., Alameda, Calif. 1988–; courtesy staff: Alta Bates-Herrick Hosp., Berkeley, Calif. 1984–; consulting staff: Pacific Med. Ctr., S.F.; board certification: Diplomate of the Nat. Bd. of Med. Examiners 1978; Am. Bd. of Internal Medicine 1980; Am. Bd. of Psychiatry & Neurology 1986; awards: Nat. Merit Scholarship; Honors in Chem., Stanford, 1973; Nicholas J. Giarman award for outstanding theses, Yale, 1977; mem: Am. Acad. of Neurology 1983–, Alameda-Contra Costa Co. Med. Assn. 1983–, CMA 1983–, AMA 1991–, Profl. Advy. Bd. of the M.S. Soc. 1987–, Easter Seal Soc. of Alameda County 1990- (bd. dir. 1990-93, bd. mgrs. 1993–, chair profl. adv. bd. 1990–); med. dir. Easter Seal Soc., Oakland Ctr. 1993–; publs.: The Interactions of Cholinergic and Anticholinergic Drugs with Nigro-neostriatal Dopaminergic Neurons (Yale thesis) 1977; co-author, Early CT Findings of

Global CNS Hypoperfusion, 1983. Ofc: Robyn G. Young, MD, APC 947 Marina Village Pkwy Alameda 94501; 2832 Summit St. Oakland 94609; and 1900 Telegraph Ave Berkeley 94705 Tel: 510/748-5363

YOUNGBLOOD, RONALD F., seminary professor; b. Aug. 10, 1931, Chgo., Ill.; s. William C. and Ethel V. (Arenz) Y.; m. Carolyn J. Johnson, Aug. 16, 1952; children: Glenn b. 1960, Wendy S. Morrissey b. 1962; edn: BA, Valparaiso Univ., Valparaiso, Ind., 1952; BD, Fuller Theol. Sem., Pasadena, 1955; PhD, Dropsie Coll. for Hebrew & Cognate Learning, Phila., 1961. Career: prof. of Old Testament, Bethel Theol. Sem., St. Paul, Minn., 1961-78; lectr. in Hebrew, Luther Theol. Sem., St. Paul, Minn., 1975-77; dean and prof. of Old Testament, Wheaton Grad. Sch., Wheaton, Ill., 1978-81; prof. of Old Testament, Trinity Evangelical Div. Sch., Deerfield, Ill., 1981-82; adjunct prof. of Old Testament, No. Baptist Theol. Sem., Lombard, Ill., 1981; prof. of Old Testament, Bethel Sem. W., S.D., 1982–; transl., ed., New Internat. Version of the Bible, Wayne, N.J., 1970-78; exec. com., Evangelical Theol. Soc., Lynchburg, Va. 1975–; ed., Journal of Evangelical Theol. Soc., Lynchburg, Va. 1975–; sec. and bd. mem., Near East Archaeological Soc., Madison, Wisc. 1979–; mem., Inst. for Biblical Res., Wheaton, Ill., 1985–; awards: Owen D. Young fellowships in religion, Gen. Electric Found., 1959-61; travel and workshop fellowship, NYU, Israel, 1966; archaeological fellowship, Hebrew Union Coll., Jerusalem, Israel, 1967-68; mem: exec. Com. on Bible Transl., New Internat. Version of the Bible, 1981–; mem, Coll. Ave. Baptist Church, San Diego, 1982–; moderator, SW Baptist Conf., W. Covina, 1992-93; bd. dir., Internat. Bible Soc., Colo. Springs, 1989–; exec. com., bd. of dirs., Internat. Bible Soc., 1992–; author: four books: The Heart of the Old Testament, 1971, Exodus, 1983, Genesis: An Introductory Commentary, 1991, 1 and 2 Samuel, 1992; Republican; Baptist Gen. Conf. Ofc: Bethel Seminary West 6116 Arosa St. San Diego 92115

YOUNGS, JACK MARVIN, cost engineer; b. May 2, 1941, Bklyn.; s. Jack Wm. and Virginia May (Clark) Y.; m. Alexandra Marie Robertson, Oct. 31, 1964; dau., Christine Marie; edn: BE engring., CCNY, 1964; MBA, San Diego State Univ., 1973. Career: mass properties engr. Gen. Dynamics Corp., San Diego 1964-68, res. engr. 1968-69, senior res. engr. 1969-80, senior cost devel. engr. 1980-81, cost devel. engring. specialist 1981–; principal estimator Martin Marietta Astronautics 1994-95; prin. estimator Lockheed Martin Astronautics 1995–; res.in life cycle costing and econ. analysis; awards: 5th pl. World Body Surfing Championships 1987, 6th pl. award 1988, Beta Gamma Sigma, Chi Epsilon, Sigma Iota Epsilon; mem: N.Y. Acad. of Scis., AIAA, Soc. of Cost Estimating and Analysis (pres. San Diego Chpt. 1990-91), Inst. Cost Analysis (cert., charter mem., chapt. treas. 1986-90), Internat. Soc. Parametric Analysts (chapt. bd. 1987-90), Nat. Mgmt. Assn. (space systems div. charter mem. 1985, chapt. award of honor 1975), Assn. MBA Execs., SDSU Business Alumni Assn. (charter 1986); civic bds: Scripps Ranch Civic Assn. (dist. dir. 1976-79), Scripps Ranch Swim Team (pres. 1980-82, dir. 1986-87), Greater San Diego Sci. and Engring. Fair (judge 1981-92), mem. Princeton Univ. Parents Assn.; club: Scripps Ranch Swim and Racquet (dir. 1977-80, treas. 78-79, pres. 79-80); Lutheran. Res: 11461 Tribuna Ave San Diego 92131 Ofc: PO Box 85990 San Diego 92138

YU, DAVID U.L., physicist, engineer, executive; b. Aug. 27, 1940; m. Carolyn A. Mattson; children: Christine b. 1968, Jonathan b. 1972; edn: PhD in physics, Univ. Wash. Seattle 1964; reg. profl. engr. Calif. Career: postdoctoral research Stanford Univ., Palo Alto; sr. postdoctoral research Univ. Surrey, England; prof. Seattle Pacific Univ., Wash.; mgr. sci. and engring. applications Computer Scis. Corp., L.A.; tech. dir., exec. v.p. Basic Tech. Inc.; pres. and CEO, DULY Research Inc.; awards: Sebastian Kerrer Prize NSF 1963, NASA Fellowship 1969, 70, Cottrell Research Corp. grantee; mem: Am. Physical Soc., Sigma Soc., Rolling Hills Covenant Ch.; rec: skiing, photog. Address: Rancho Palos Verdes 90275

ZACHMAN, JOHN A., information management consultant; b. Dec. 16, 1934, Toledo, Ohio; s. Arthur S. and Margaret E. (Morrow) Z.; m. Constance L. DeVito, May 14, 1972; children: Sherri b. 1960, John P. b. 1973; edn: BA in chem., Northwestern Univ., 1957; Tufts Univ. 1960-62. Career: comdr. USNR-Ret., 1957-71, instr. Tufts Univ., USN, 1960-62, exec. ofcr., Long Beach, Calif. 1962-64; with IBM, 1965-91: sales, Chgo. 1965-70, internat. account mgr. in N.Y. and L.A., 1970-74, cons., Los Angeles 1974-91; pres. Zachman Internat., La Canada, 1991–; bd. counsellors USC Sch. of Libr. & Info. Mgmt., 1980-87, bd. advisors Rosary Coll. Sch. of Libr. & Info. Mgmt., River Forest, Ill. 1991–, Emporia State Univ. Sch. Libr. & Info. Mgmt., Kans. 1991–, bd. advisors for info. resource mgmt. Smithsonian Instn., W.D.C. 1992–, bd. dirs. Repository/Architecture/Development Users Gp., Chgo. 1991–, bd. advisors DAMA Internat. 1980–; awards: data resource mgmt. DAMA, N.Y. 1988, ann. excellence award R/AD Cycle Users Gp., Chgo. 1991; mem: Elder Coun. Ch. on the Way, Van Nuys 1978–, Living Way Ministries 1978–, bd. dirs. Marriage Plus Ministries 1980–, Worship Seminars Internat. 1990–; pub. articles "BSP and BICS: A Comparison", 1982, "Framework for Information Systems Architecture", 1987, "Extending and Formalizing the Framework for Information Systems Architecture", 1992; Republican; Prot. Ofc: Zachman International 2222 Foothill Blvd Ste 337 La Canada 91011

ZACKRISON, EDWIN HARRY, university professor; b. Oct. 15, 1941, Hinsdale, Ill.; s. Harry Albin and Esther Virginia (Thorp) Z.; children: Jill b. 1968, Mark b. 1971; edn: BA, La Sierra Univ., Riverside, Calif., 1959-63; MA, Andrews Univ., Berrien Springs, MI, 1963-64; BD, Andrews Univ., 1964-66; PhD, Andrews Univ., 1975-84. Career: youth pastor, Seventh-day Adventist Ch., Alhambra, Calif., 1966-67, Camarillo, Calif., 1967-72; religion prof., Southern Coll., Collegedale, Tenn., 1972-84; chmn., religion dept. La Sierra Acad., Riverside, Calif., 1984-88; religion prof., La Sierra Univ., 1988–; dir., LSA Performing Arts Soc., Riverside, 1984–; pres., La Sierra Comm. Performing Arts Soc., Riverside, 1989–; pres., LSU Alumni Assn., Riverside, 1989-92; dir., Destination Players, Riverside, 1989-92; awards: LSA Faculty Creativity Award, La Sierra Acad. Alumni Assn., 1989; LSA Performing Arts Soc. Comm. Support Award, LSA, 1988; mem: Assn. of Adventist Forums, 1974–; Religious Edn. Assn., 1977–; Amer. Acad. of Religion, 1978–; Evangelical Theol. Soc., 1978–; Ednl. Theatre Assn., 1988–; book ed., La Sierra Univ. Press, 1988–; author: num. articles and periodicals, 1975-91; book, In The Loins of Adam, 1993; Republican; Seventh-day Adventist; rec: producing/directing high sch. plays. Ofc: La Sierra Univ. 4700 Pierce St. Riverside 92515

ZALTA, EDWARD, otorhinolaryngologist, utilization review physician; b. Mar.2, 1930, Houston, Tx.; s. Nouri Louis and Marie Zahde (Lizmi) Z.; m. Carolyn M. Gordon, Oct. 8, 1971; children: Nouri Allan, Lori Ann, Barry Thomas, Ryan David; edn: BS, Tulane Univ., 1952, MD, 1956; Diplomate Am. Bd. of Quality Assurance & Utilization Review Physicians 1986. Career: served to capt. Med. Corps US Army 1957-60, intern Brooke Army Hosp., San Antonio 1956-57, resident in otolaryngology U.S. Army Hosp., Ft. Campbell, 1957-60; practiced medicine spec. in otolaryn. in Glendora, W.Covina and San Dimas, Calif. 1960-82; ENT cons. City of Hope Med. Ctr., 1961-76; current: med. staff Foothill Presbyterian Hosp.; co-founder/CEO/chmn. bd. CAPP CARE INC., Newport Beach; founder/bd. chmn. Medical Data Management; honors: Kappa Nu, Phi Delta Epsilon, award of merit Order St. Lazarus 1981; mem: AMA, Calif. Med. Assn., L.A. Co. Med. Assn. (past pres.), Am. Coll. Medical Quality, Am. Acad. Otolaryn., Am. Council Otolaryn., Am. Assn. Preferred Provider Orgns. (past pres.), Los Angeles Found. Community Service (past pres.), L.A. Poison Info. Ctr., So. Calif. Physicians Council, Inc. (founder Inter-Hosp. Council Continuing Med. Edn.); Republican; Jewish; clubs: Center, Pacific Golf, Glendora Country, Centurion, Sea Bluff Beach and Racquet. Res: 3 Morning Dove Laguna Niguel 92677 Ofc: CAPP CARE, West Tower, 4000 MacArthur Blvd, 10,000, Newport Beach 92660-2526

ZANDERS, CLAUDIA BOND, social worker; b. Oct. 11, 1939, Beaumont, Tx.; d. Charles Senters Bond and Ularae (Reinarz) Herholzer; m. John Zanders, Sept. 4, 1964 (div. 1966); 1 son, Anthony; edn: BA, Trinity Univ. 1960; MSW, Our Lady of Lake Coll. San Antonio 1964; cert. Nat. Assn. Social Workers (1988); lic. clin. social worker Calif. 1977; bd. cert. Diplomate in clin. social wk, Am. Bd. of Examiners 1989. Career: jr. psychiatric social worker Comm. Guidance Clinic, Austin, Tx. 1964-65; Child Guidance Clinic, Lakland AFB, San Antonio, Tx. 1966; med. social worker Foster Grand Parent Project 1966-68; psychiatric social worker Desert Counseling Clinic, China Lake 1968-70; sr. psychiatric social worker Mental Health Clinic Outpatient, Santa Cruz 1970-73; Adoption Unit Santa Cruz Ct. Human Resources Agency 1974–; mem: Mental Health Alliance; Democrat. Address: 2100 Quail Hollow Rd Ben Lomond 95005

ZAX, ADAM, glazing company president, real estate developer; b. June 2, 1962, Houston, Tx.; s. Robert Barney and Elaine Francis (Cohn) Z.; edn: BS bus., Univ. Colo. 1984; Glass Mgmt. Inst., George Mason Univ., 1990. Career: pres. Capistrano Valley Glass, San Juan Capistrano 1979–; pres. Gemini Shower Door 1987–; pres. C.V. Industries, 1991–; mem. Delta Chi (founder Univ. Colo. chapt.); author computer software for glass industry; Republican; Jewish; rec: drumming, horses, dogs, magic, Shaolin Kempo martial arts. Ofc: C.V. Industries 33012 Calle Perfecto San Juan Capistrano 92675

ZEIDMAN, HEYWOOD WILLIAM, psychiatrist, educator; b. Jan. 30, 1941, Brooklyn, N.Y.; s. Irving and Henrietta (Hertz) Z.; m. Ronni Kay Reider, Nov. 27, 1982; children: Jared b. 1985; edn: BA, Bard Coll., 1963; MS, N.Y. Med. Coll., 1969, MD, 1973; Diplomate Am. Bd. Psychiatry & Neurology, 1978, Diplomate Am. Bd. of Adolescent Psychiatry, 1992. Career: ptnr. Psychiatric Centers, San Diego 1976–; med. dir. Broad Horizons, Ramona, Calif. 1986-89; Villa View Hosp., San Diego 1983-90; Adolescent Drug Treatment Pgm., San Diego 1988-90, Adol. Day Pgm. 1991-92; New Life Treatment Ctr., 1990-92; asst. clin. prof. UC San Diego, 1988–; dir. Hosp. Adolescent Svcs. Southwood Hosp., Chula Vista 1992-94; med. dir. Villa View Hosp., San Diego 1994–; cons. Adult Protective Svs., San Diego 1986–; honoree, tchr. of yr. UCSD 1987; mem: AMA 1976–, Calif. Med. Assn. 1976–, San Diego Co. Med. Soc. (del. 1991–), Am. Psychiat. Assn. 1976–, Calif. Psychiat. Assn., San Diego Soc. Psych. Physicians, Am. Soc. Adol. Psychiatry (fellow), San Diego Soc. Adol. Psychiatry (exec. com. 1976–), ASAM, CSAM 1988–, alt. del. Calif. Med. Assn. 1990–; publs: articles, Am. J. Physiology, 1970, We. J. of Medicine, 1975, Fedn. Proceedings, 1968; mil: sp4 US Army Nat. Guard 1963-69; Democrat; Jewish; rec: skiing. Res: 6719 Caminito Prado La Jolla 92037 Ofc: Psychiatric Centers 6719 Alvarado Rd Ste 308 San Diego 92120

ZEITLIN, HERBERT ZAKARY, real estate executive, retired college president; b. N.Y.C.; s. Leonard and Martha Josephine (Soff) Z.; m. Eugenia F. Pawlik, July 3, 1949; children: Mark Clyde, Joyce Therese Harris, Ann Victoria, Clare Katherine; edn: BS, New York Univ., 1947, MA, 1949; EdD, Stanford Univ., 1956. Career: tchr., counselor, dir. testing Phoenix Union High Sch. and Coll. Dist., 1949-57; dean evening coll., prin. high sch. Antelope Valley Union H.S. and Coll. Dist., Lancaster 1957-62; dean instrn. Southwestern Coll., Chula Vista 1962-64; founder, pres. Triton Coll., River Grove, Ill. 1964-76; pres. and dean West Los Angeles Coll., 1976-80; mgmt. cons., pres. Trident Consultants, Los Angeles 1976–; adj. faculty Ariz. State Univ., Flagstaff 1953-55, No. Ill. Univ., DeKalb, 1971-74, UC Santa Barbara, 1979; elected mayor Upper Woodland Hills, Calif.; past pres. Rotary, Maywood, Ill., 1974; awards: recipient spl. commendations Chicago Tribune, Illinois Gov. Richard Ogilvie, named adminstr. of year Ill. Adminstrs. Assn., Triton Coll. Faculty Assn. award, 1974, medal of achiev. Triton Coll. Trustees, 1973; mem: NEA (life), Am. Assn. Community and Jr. Colls., Assn. Calif. Community Coll. Adminstrs., Am. Vocat. Assn.; author, editor in field. Ofc: 21731 Ventura Blvd Woodland Hills 91364

ZELON, LAURIE DEE, lawyer; b. Nov. 15, 1952, Durham, N.C.; d. Irving and Doris Miriam (Baker) Zelon; m. David L. George, Dec. 30,, 1979; children: Jeremy b. 1981, Daniel b. 1983; edn: BA, Cornell Univ. 1974; JD, Harvard Univ. 1977; admitted St. Bar Calif. 1977, Dist. Ct. 9th Circuit 1978,, U.S. Supreme Ct. 1989. Career: atty., assoc. Beardsley Hufstedler & Kemble, Los Angeles 1977-81; Hufstedler Miller Carlson & Beardsley 1981-82, ptnr., atty. 1983-88; Hufstedler Miller Kaus & Beardsley 1988-91; ptnr. Morrison & Foerster 1991–; awards: Harvard Univ. Williston Competition winner 1975; mem: L.A. County Bar Assn. (pres. 1995–), Harvard Vol. Defenders, N.Y. Civil Liberties Union (dir. 1973-74), ACLU So. Calif. (vol. atty. 1977–); ed. in chief Harvard Civil Rights Civil Liberties Law Review, 1976-77, article pub. in profl. jour., 1976; Democrat. Ofc: Morrison & Foerster 355 W Fifth St 35th Flr Los Angeles 90013-1024

ZELTONOGA, WILLIAM LEO, lawyer; b. May 13, 1941, Chicago, Ill.; s. Leo John and Jean (Kereluk) Z.; edn: BA, UCLA 1962; MA, Oxford Univ. 1965; JD, Harvard Univ. 1968. Career: assoc. atty. Wyman Bautzer Rothman & Kuchel, Los Angeles 1968-72; sole practice, Los Angeles 1972–; honors: Rhodes Scholar; mem: Calif. Bar Assn., D.C. Bar Assn., Nat. Trust for Hist. Preservationn, Les Amis du Vin, Sierra Club, Masons; mil: 1st lt. AUS 1969-70, Bronze Star; rec: cooking, art, sports. Res: POB 15128 Beverly Hills 90209-1128 Ofc: 753 N Croft Ave Los Angeles 90069

ZERIN, MARJORY BERNICE, psychotherapist; b. Feb. 17, 1925, Richmond, Va.; d. Frederick Harold and Helen (Helfand) Fisher; m. Edward Zerin, Oct. 27, 1946; children: Jonathan Joseph b. 1948, Wendy Sue b. 1950, Jeffrey Michael b. 1953; edn: BA, Univ. Mich. Ann Arbor 1946; MA, Drake Univ. 1967; PhD clin. psychology, Fielding Inst. Santa Barbara 1982; lic. marriage family child counselor (MFCC) Calif. Career: commr. Commn. on Human Rights & Job Discrimination, Des Moines, Iowa 1964-67; exec. dir. mayor's dept. Community Relations Commn., Newton, Mass. 1968-72; psychotherapist pvt. practice, Westlake Village; lectr. Oxnard Coll., Moorpark Coll., dept. preventive dentistry Sch. Dentistry UCLA; conduct workshops and seminars internat. for medical, mental health, nursing and bus. professionals, incl. Brazil, Finland, Israel, Italy, Singapore, Yugoslavia, USSR also for military forces of U.S. govt.; mem: Calif. Assn. Marriage & Family Therapy, Internat. Transactional Analysis Assn., B'nai B'rith, Conejo C.of C., Westlake Village C.of C., Congregation Adat Elohim; publs: numerous articles pub. profl. jours.; co-author: Six Difficult Personalities; When Your Patient Has a Drinking Problem; The "Q" Model for the Effective Mgmt. of Personal Stress (1986); A Suicide is a Wasted Life (for U.S. Army); dissertation: Family System Factors in Vulnerability to Cults (1982, condensed ms. pub. by AAAS); Democrat; Jewish; rec: skiing, horseback riding, music. Address: Westlake Center for Marital and Family Counseling 3823 Bowsprit Circle Westlake Village 91361

ZHAN, SHERRIE ELLEN, trade consultant; b. Mar. 4, 1946, Chgo., Ill.; d. Bernard Jacob Taub and Rose Rae Ellenhorn; m. Paul Thomas Baldwin, 1971 (div. 1990); children: Marina b. 1976; m. 2d. Jiafu Zhan, 1994; edn: BA, Univ. of Ill. 1967; TESOL cert., UC Irvine 1981-82; cert. internat. bus., Am. Grad. Sch. Internat. Mgmt. (Ariz.) 1986; Calif. tchg. credentials. Career: staff ed. Geol. Soc. of Am., Boulder, Colo. 1972-73; assoc. ed. Newport Life Mag., Newport Bch. 1974-76; public rels. coord. Endevco, San Juan Capistrano 1978-81; lectr. UC Irvine 1982-84, Irvine Valley Coll. 1984-95, Coastline Coll. 1987–; pgm. coord. Am. Grad. Sch. Internat. Mgmt., Orange Co. 1989-93; pres. Baldwin Sai Bei Co., Laguna Hills 1986–; prog. chmn. World Trade Ctr., Santa Ana 1988-89; subject splst. internat. bus., Coastline Comm. Coll. 1989-90; mem. Calif. Community Coll. Statewide Advy. Com. on Bus. Edn. 1990–; honors: recipient grad. scholarship Stanley W. Call Foundation, Costa Mesa 1989-90; mem: World Trade Ctr. Assn. of Orange Co. (moderator China Bus. Forum, 1990); International Mktg. Assn., Am. Grad. Sch. of Internat. Mgmt. (alumni assn. 1986–); author numerous articles profl. jours. 1974-77; rec: travel, horticulture, piano music, writing. Address: 25092 Ericson Way Laguna Hills 92653

ZHANG, ROBINS HONGGUI, doctor of Oriental medicine, professor of Chinese medicine, president of academy; b. Aug. 15, 1948, Xian City, China; s. Yan Zhi and Xuzhan Zhang; m. Aileen Bing Huang, July 28, 1977; children: Jenny Y. Zhang b. 1979; edn: OMD, Beijing Univ. of Traditional Chinese Medicine, Beijing City, China 1975; MS in Western medicine, Univ. of Brussels, Belgium 1986; adv. Western medical training Univs. of London and Birmingham, England; PhD cand., UC Berkeley 1994; lic. acupuncturist Calif. 1993. Career: sr. doctor Beijing Hospital of Chinese Medicine, Beijing, China 1975-86; prof. First Ednl. Hosp., Henan Coll. of Chinese Medicine, Henan, China 1987-90; pres. Tran-America Academy of Chinese Medicine, Albany, Calif. 1991–; deputy dir. Dept. of Chinese Medicine, Ministry of Public Health, Beijing, China 1986-90; med. cons., pres. of Mauritius Govt., Mauritius; med. cons. First Internat. Conf. on Aging, Zhuhai, China 1990; cons. Dept. of Health Policy & Adminstrn., UC Berkeley 1994–; mem: Internat. Red Cross Assn. 1983–, Internat. Hosp. Fedn. (U.K.) 1986–, Calif. Certified Acupuncturists Assn. 1993–; author: journal articles in China Hospital Management 1987, Internat. Hosp. Jour. 1990, Acute Med. Care Jour. 1990; rec: Oigong exercise and dance. Ofc: Tran-America Academy of Chinese Medicine 1284 Solano Ave Albany 94706

ZIEGENBUSCH, TED WAYNE, radio-television personality; b. Mar. 10, 1951, Lima, Ohio; s. Charles Paul and Esther C. (Newman) Z.; m. Ann Pearl Cordell, Aug. 21, 1971 (div. Sept. 1977); m. April Ann Lorenz, Dec. 10, 1977; children: Seth b. 1972, Jeffrey b. 1974, Ryan b. 1980; edn: AA, San Bernardino Valley Coll., 1971. Career: announcer KMEN Radio, San Bdo. 1967-73; KCAL-FM Radio, 1973-80; program director KLAV Radio, Las Vegas, Nev. 1980-81; The Mighty 690, San Diego 1981; announcer KGB Radio, San Diego 1981-82; KOST Radio, Los Angeles 1982–; cons. KIFM Radio, San Diego 1982-83, KOLA Radio, San Bdo. 1980-87; awards: Best actor Nat. Thespians Soc. 1969, Outstanding graduate San Bernardino City Schs. 1984; mem.: Screen Actors Guild 1983–, Am. Fedn. of TV-Radio Artists 1981–; Republican; Prot.; rec: screenwriting, travel, music. Ofc: KOST Radio 610 S Ardmore Los Angeles 90005

ZIEL, DONNA RAE, university administrator; b. Sept. 12, 1943, Santa Barbara; d. Raymond Joseph and Emma Josephine (Osner) Gilbreth; m. T. Brian Ziel, Sept. 8, 1962 (div. Jan. 1976); children: Laura b. 1965, Brian b. 1967; edn: BA (w/distinction), San Jose State Univ., 1973, MA Asian hist., 1979. Career: dept. secty. San Jose State Univ., 1973-76, liberal studies advisor 1976-89, dir. Student Advisement Ctr. SJSU, 1979-89; assoc. dir. San Jose State Univ. Monterey Co. Campus, 1989-92; assoc. dir. Student Outreach 1992–; honors: invited participant Humanities Honors SJSU 1961–, Sourisseau Soc. grantee SJSU 1975, CSU Adminstrv. Fellows Pgm. fellow 1980-81, Phi Kappa Phi Nat. Hon. Soc. (1992, disting. svc. award SJSU chapt. 1992); mem: Calif. Women in Higher Edn. (pres. 1980-81), CSU Women's Council (standing com. on student affairs 1988), Center for Innovative Programs (expert com. 1988), Calif. Advocates for Re-entry Edn. 1980–, Calif. Council of Academic Advisors 1978–, Nat. Assn. Student Personnel Adminstrn. 1978–, Nat. Academic Advisors Assn. 1984–, West. Assn. of Coll. Admissions Counselors 1992–; civic bds: Industry Edn. Council of Monterey County (pres. 1990-91), Sierra Club 1978–, Santa Cruz County Women's Commn. (co-chair 1986-87), Valley Women's Club Boulder Creek, Santa Cruz Women's Network (scholarship com.), Monterey Bay Aquarium (docent 1984–), World Affairs Council; Democrat. Res: 8121 Fremont Ave Ben Lomond 95005 Ofc: San Jose State Univ.One Washington Square San Jose 95192-0011

ZIEMER, ROBERT RUHL, research hydrologist; b. Oct. 25, 1937, Oklahoma City, Okla.; s. Herman Vernon and Floranna (Ruhl) Z.; m. Ruth Puckett, June 24, 1965 (div. 1975); m. Marian Denise Westwick, Jan. 1, 1977; children: Tanya b. 1969, Amy b. 1973, Karen b. 1979, Ryan b. 1982; edn: AA, Fullerton Jr. Coll. 1957; BS, UC Berkeley 1959; MS, 1963; PhD, Colo. St. Univ. 1978; lic. profl. forester Calif. 1973. Career: research and tchg. asst. UC Berkeley 1959-60; res. forester U.S. Dept. Agriculture Forest Service 1960-77; photo-radar intelligence ofcr. Nev. Air Nat. Guard, Reno 1961-67; res. hydrologist U.S. Dept. Agriculture Forest Service, Arcata 1977–; adj. prof. Humboldt St. Univ. 1977–; mem: Am. Geophysical Union (nat. chmn. erosion and sedimentation 1982-88, nat. chmn. evaporation), Internat. Union of Forestry Research Organizations (internat. chmn. 1987–); 65+ research papers pub. in sci. jours.; mil: 1st lt. Nev. Air Nat. Guard 1961-67; rec: carnivorous plant cultivation. Res: 2220 Elizabeth Rd McKinleyville 95521 Ofc: Pacific Southwest Research Station 1700 Bayview Dr Arcata 95521

ZIFFREN, LESTER, lawyer; b. Apr. 13, 1925, Davenport, IA; s. Jacob and Belle (Rothenberg) Z.; m. Paulette C. Rolando; 1 dau. Mimi b. 1959; edn: BA, UCLA 1949; JD, UCLA Law Sch 1952. Career: dep. atty. gen. Calif. Dept. Justice, Atty. Gen. Office 1953-59; partner Greenberg, Ziffren & Shafton 1959-61; partner Ziffren & Ziffren 1961-79; ptnr. Gibson Dunn & Crutcher 1979-90, retired partner/advy. council 1991–; bd. dir. Westminster Capital Inc. (NYSE) 1979–; mem: State Bar Calif., Los Angeles Co. Bar Assn., Beverly Hills Bar Assn.; trustee UCLA Found., bd. vis. UCLA Sch. of Med., UCLA bd. advisors Center on Aging, Chadbourne Fellow Sch. of Law, legal com. Sch. of Law; mem. Brandeis Univ. Pres.'s Council; Hebrew Union Coll.-JIR (nat. v.chmn., bd.

govs. L.A. Campus, v. ch. bd. overseers, exec. com.); L.A. Music Center Opera (bd.), State of Israel Bonds-L.A. (v.chmn. bd., exec. com., past pres. Prime Minister's Club), Cedars Sinai Med. Ctr. (bd. govs.); rec: tennis. Ofc: Gibson, Dunn & Crutcher, 2029 Century Park East 41st Flr Los Angeles 90067

ZIGMAN, PAUL EDMOND, consulting company executive; b. March 10, 1924, Los Angeles; s. Fernand and Rose (ORlijan) Z.; m. Marcia Lee Sokolow, Aug. 15, 1954 (div. 1981); children: Andrea b. 1956, Eric b. 1961; edn: BS chem., UCLA 1948. Career: head tech. mgmt. office U.S. Naval Radiological Defense, San Francisco 1949-59, 61-69; supr. analytical chemistry Atomics Internat., Reseda 1960-61; pres. Environ. Sci. Assocs., San Francisco 1969-94, chmn., bd. dirs. 1969–; mem. subcom. on radioactive standards Nat. Research Council, Wash. D.C. 1964; instr. UC Berkeley Ext. 1979; awards: USN Merit Civilian Service, Assn. Environ. Profls. Outstanding Service 1977, Cert. Appreciation 1984; mem: Am. Chemical Soc., Assn. Environ. Profls. (pres. 1974-76), Nat. Assn. Environ. Profls. (v.p. 1983); 30+ articles pub. in tech. jours., 1953-80; mil: pfc AUS 1943. Res: 2311 Crystal Downs Ct Oxnard 93030 Ofc: Environmental Science Associates 301 Brannan St San Francisco 94107

ZIL, JOHN STEPHEN, psychiatrist-physiologist; b. Oct. 8, 1947, Chgo.; s. Stephen Vincent and Marillyn Charlotte (Jackson) Zilius; dau. Charlene-Elena b. 1984; edn: BS (magna cum laude) Univ. Redlands, 1969; MD, UC San Diego, 1973; MPH in pub. health law (honors), Yale Univ., 1977; JD (w. distinction), Jefferson Coll., 1985. Career: intern, resident in psychiatry and neurology Univ. Ariz. 1973-75; fellow in psychiatry, advanced fellow in social and community psychiatry, Yale Univ. 1975-77; instr., psychiatry and physiology, Yale Univ., Univ. of Mass. 1976-77; Yale Community cons. to Connecticut State Dept. of Corrections 1975-77; chief Inpatient and Day Hosp. Unit, Conn. Mental Health Ctr., Yale-New Haven Hosp. Inc. 1976-77, actg. chief 1975-76; asst. prof. psychiatry UC San Francisco 1977-82, assoc. prof. psychiatry and medicine 1982-86, v. chmn. dept. psychiatry 1983-86; adj. prof. Calif. St. Univ. 1985-87; chief psychiatry and neurology VA Med. Ctr., Fresno 1977-86, prin. investigator Sleep Res. & Physiology Lab 1979-86; chief psychiatrist Calif. Dept. of Corrections, State Capitol 1986–, and clinical faculty UC Davis Sch. of Med. and affil. hosps. 1986–; councillor federally mandated council for Calif. St. Mental Health Plan 1988–; invited faculty contbg. editor Am. Coll. of Psychiat. resident-in-tng. exam. 1981–; assoc. ed. Corrective & Social Psychiatry Jour. 1978–; referee, reviewer Corrections Today, J. of Am. Correctional Assn. 1980–; nat. cons. on Mental Health Svs. in Jails & Prisons, Am. Psychiatric Assn., W.D.C. 1993–; awards: Nat. Merit Scholar 1965, Bank Am. nat. award in Lab. Scis. 1965, Julian Lee Roberts chemistry award, Univ. Redlands 1969, Delta Alpha 1969, Alpha Epsilon Delta nat. medical freshman of yr. 1969, Kendall res. paper award Internat. Symp. in Biochem. Res. 1970, UCSD Pres.'s Scholar in Medicine 1970-71, thesis res. honors Yale 1977, Univ. Calif. Pres.'s Commendn. 1978, Univ. Calif. Alumni Assn. Profl. Achiev. award 1992, Univ. of Redlands Career Achiev. award 1994; mem: Am. Assn. of Mental Health Profls. in Corrections (nat. pres. 1978-82, 1990-94), Fellow Royal Soc. of Health, London 1979, Fellow Am. Assn. for Soc. Psychiat. 1977, Am. Pub. Health Assn., Calif. Scholarship Fedn. (past pres., life, mem., charter pres. UC Sch. of Medicine), Ephebians, AAUP, Am. Psychiat. Assn., Nat. Council on Crime & Delinquency; author: The Case of the Sleep-Walking Rapist (Forensic Monographs, 1992), first author, Mentally Disordered Criminal Offenders, 5 vols. 1989; num. res. publs. and presentations, 1970–. Res: PO Box 163359 Sacramento 95816-9359

ZIMMERMAN, ARNOLD IRA, executive search consultant; b. April 5, 1946, New York; s. Sydney Harry and Gladys (Chitkin) Z.; m. Jianulla Helen Chapralis, Oct. 20, 1978; children: Kevin b. 1963, Timothyb. 1965, Paula b. 1967, Brian b. 1970; edn: BSCE, City Coll. N.Y. 1968; MBA, Iona Coll. 1972. Career: chemical engr. Gen. Foods, White Plains, N.Y. 1969-73; groupleader process engring. Hunt-Wesson, Fullerton 1973-78; exec. search cons. Paul Nursell Assoc., Los Angeles 1978-79; pres. Horizon Assoc., Redondo Beach 1979–; mem: South Bay L.A. Pvt. Industry Council (chmn. 1989–), Beyond War, Nat. Assn. Exec. Cons. (Caif. recruitment chmn. 1987-88), Redondo Beach C.of C.; Democrat; Jewish; rec: bicycling, theatre, racquetball. Address: Horizon Associates 322 S Broadway Redondo Beach 90277

ZIMMERMAN, LINDA, cookbook author, writer, editor; b. Sept. 30, 1946, Chgo.; d. Louis Joseph and Jean (Lakovitz) Zimmerman; m. Gerry Goffin (lyricist); edn: photography, Santa Monica Coll., 1981-83. Career: TV and film prodn., L.A., 1970-84; writer, author, editor 1985-: clients incl. Warner Bros. Pictures, Cannon Films, L.A. Celebrations, Epicurean Cooking Sch., Ma Cuisine Cooking Sch. contbr. articles in numerous magazines and newspapers; books: Chicken Soup, 1994, Grills & Greens, 1993, Cobblers, Buckles & Other Old-Fashioned, Fruit Desserts, 1991, Puddings, Custards & Flans, 1990; editor/pub. source directory, The Food Yellow Pages, 1988, 91; contbg. editor: Low Fat Chicken Breasts by Diane Rozas, 1996, The L.A. Guide to Restaurants, Shops & Gourmet Foods, 1995; editor "The Food Paper," editorial writer, recipe devel. & editing (books): Make-Over Miracles by Michael Maron, 1993, Gault Millau-The Best of Los Angeles, 1992, Entertaining with Robin Leach by Diane Rozas, 1992, Calif. Bistro by Tony DiLembo, 1991, Chicken Breasts II by Diane Rozas,

1990, Fresh from the Freezer by Michael Roberts, 1990, Beauty & Cancer by Peggy Mellody, 1988, Catalon Cuisine by Colman Andrews, 1988; mem. AFTRA, Authors Guild, Ciao Italia (ednl. bd. 1992), Los Angeles Culinary Alliance (founding bd. 1988-89), So. Calif. Culinary Guild (bd. 1989-90). Res: 2720 Nichols Canyon Rd Los Angeles 90046

ZINGG, PAUL JOSEPH, academic administrator; b. July 22, 1947, Newark, N.J.; s. Carl William Zingg and Dolores (Lucking) Dulebohn; m. Candace Adelaide Slater, Aug. 9, 1980; edn: BA, Belmont Abbey Coll., Belmont, NC, 1968; MA, Univ. Richmond, 1969; PhD, Univ. Ga., 1974. Career: instr. history Univ. of Ga. 1970-74; chair dept. history & poli. sci., asst. prof. So. Benedictine Coll., Cullman, Ala. 1975-77; exec. dean Williams Univ., Chgo., 1977-78; asst. dean, coll. arts & scis. Univ. Pa., Phila., 1978-79, vice dean 1979-83; asst. to pres. Univ. Pa., 1983-86; asst. to vice chancellor and provost, UC Berkeley 1986; dean sch. liberal arts and prof. St. Mary's Coll. Calif., Moraga, 1986-93, Calif. Poly. State Univ., San Luis Obispo, 1993–; commn. on human resources and social change, Nat. Assn. St. Univs. and Land-Grant Colls. 1994–; accreditation reviewer: We. Assn. Schs. and Colls. 1991–, Middle Sts. Assn. 1985-86; cons. and contbr: Oakland Mus. exhbn. on Pacific Coast League 1992-94, PBS-TV documentary "Baseball", 1994; editl. cons.: Univ. Neb. Press 1994–, Univ. Pa. Press 1982-86, St. Martins Press, NY 1975-790; editl. com. Council of Fellows, Am. Council on Edn. 1989–, exec. com. 1988-91, advy. com 1986-87; bd. dirs., exec. council Am. Assn. for Advancement of Core Curriculum, 1990-91; reviewer/reader: We. Historical Qtly., Jour. of Sport History, NINE, Internat. Jour. of History of Sport, 1986–; ednl. cons. City of Richmond, Va. public sch. sys. 1979-80, num. colls. and univs.; honors: Alumni Faculty Scholarship award Saint Mary's Coll. 1992, faculty devel. grants 1987, 90, 91, 93; res fellow: Ctr. for Internat. Study/Res., 1980-82, Nat. Endowment for Humanities, 1975, grantee 1989, reviewer summer seminar. prof. 1995; Univ. Pa. Res. Found. awards 1983, 84, Faculty Member of Yr. 1983-84; mem: Orgn. Am. Historians, Soc. for History Edn., N.Am. Soc. for Study of Sport, Am. Studies Assn., Am. Council on Edn. (exec. com. 1988–, fellow 1983-84), Soc. for Am. Baseball Res., Assn. of Am. Colls. and Univs., Phi Alpha Theta, Phi Beta Delta, The Oakland Mus. (bd. of advs. 1994–), Central Coast Performing Arts Ctr. Commn., San Luis Obispo 1993–, Artemis Theater Co. (bd. advs. 1993–), Cal Poly Arts (chmn. 1993–), Hearst Art Gallery, Moraga (bd. dirs 1988-90); author: Runs, Hits and an Era: The Pacific Coast League, 1903-1958 (1994, 2nd edit., 1995), Harry Hooper, 1887-1974: An American Baseball Life, 1993, Pride of the Palestra, 1987; author, editor: The Sporting Image, 1987; co-author: Through Foreign Eyes, 1982, The Academic Penn, 1986; editor: In Search of the American National Character, 1984, Contemporary Topics in Applied Ethics, 1984; cons.: Baseball in America, 1990; contbr. 60+ articles and reviews to profl. publs.; Independent; Catholic; rec: golf, hiking, travel, raising Labrador Retrievers. Res: 1563 Corbett Canyon Rd Arroyo Grande 93420 Ofc: Calif Poly State Univ Coll Liberal Arts San Luis Obispo CA 93407

ZIONY, JOSEPH ISRAEL, consulting geologist; b. Apr. 6, 1935, Los Angeles; s. Aaron and Annie (Mondlin) Z.; m. Denise Pourroy, Sept. 9, 1961; children: David b. 1962, Daniel b. 1967, Sarah b. 1972; edn: undergrad. Univ. Wis. 1951-53; AB, UC Los Angeles 1956, MA, 1959, PhD, 1966; reg. geologist, cert. engring. geologist, Calif. (1970). Career: geologist U.S. Geological Survey 1957-86: Mil. Geology Br., Wash. DC, 1957-59; Fuels Br., Menlo Park, Calif. 1959-60; S.W. States Br., 1960-69; Engring. Geology Br., 1969-73; dep. chief Office of Earthquake Studies USGS, Reston, Va. 1973-76; Earthquake Hazards Br., Menlo Park 1976-77; asst. chief geologist for Western Region, 1977-81; Engring. Seismology and Geology Br., 1981-86, ret. USGS; gubnat. apptd. asst. director for Mining and Geology, Calif. Dept. of Conservation, Sacto. 1988-91; U.S. rep. Central Treaty Orgn. (CENTO) conf. on earthquake hazard mitigation, Tehran, Iran (11/76); awards: Burwell Awd. from Geological Soc. of Am. for USGS Profl. Paper 1360, "Evaluating Earthquake Hazards in the Los Angeles Region"; mem: Geol. Soc. of Am., Assn. of Engring. Geologists, Seismol. Soc. of Am.; publs: 57 reports and maps on earthquake hazards of Western US and on geology and mineral resources of Calif., Nev., and Utah; mil: pfc AUS 1960, USAR 1960-68; Jewish (pres. Cong. Beth Am, Los Altos Hills 1972-73); rec: hiking, fishing, hunting. Res: Palo Alto 94306 Ofc: Palo Alto

ZOHN, MARTIN S., lawyer; b. Oct. 22, 1947, Denver, Colo.; s. William and Alice (Lewis) Z.; m. Carol Falender, June 6, 1980; children: David Joseph, Daniel Robert; edn: BA, Ind.Univ. 1969; JD, Harvard Law Sch. 1972. Career: atty. Cadick Burns Duck & Neighbours, Indianapolis, Ind. 1972-80; ptnr. Pacht Ross Warne Bernard & Sears, Los Angeles 1980-86; Shea & Gould 1986-89; Proskauer Rose Goetz & Mendelsohn 1989–; pres. Indianapolis Settlements Inc. 1977-79; honors: Phi Beta Kappa. Res: 315 22nd St Santa Monica 90402

ZUBAN, ANATOLY TONY, registered investment advisor; b. July 24, 1952, Jersey City, N.J.; s. Gregory and Nina (Grinenko) Z.; edn: BS, UC Irvine, 1974; MBA, Univ. of Utah 1992. Career: claims rep. Farmer's Ins., Anaheim 1976-77; med. sales rep. Wm. H. Rorer Inc., Fort Washington, Pa. 1977-78; profl. med. rep. Abbott Labs., North Chgo. 1978-80, 81-85; regional mktg. rep. Beckman Instruments, Irvine 1980-81; regional sales mgr. Ohaus Scale Corp., Florham Park, N.J. 1985-86; nat. OEM sales engr. Greco Systems, El Cajon 1986-87; fin.

cons. Shearson Lehman Hutton, Rancho Santa Fe 1987-89; account exec. Prudential Bache Securities, Carlsbad 1989-90; A to Z Consulting, San Diego 1992–; Republican; Ukrainian Orthodox; rec: skiing, tennis, sailing, golf. Res/Ofc: 3930 Caminito Del Mar Surf San Diego 92130

ZUCKER, ROBERT STEPHEN, professor of neurobiology; b. Apr. 18, 1945, Phila.; s. Irving Aaron and Dorothy Ruth (Pittenturf) Z.; m. Glenda Anita Teal, Sept. 1, 1968 (div. Apr. 1982); m. Susan Henrietta Schwartz, Jan. 3, 1983; children: David b. 1975, Mark b. 1985, Ariel b. 1986; edn: SB physics, M.I.T., 1966; PhD neurological sci., Stanford Univ., 1971. Career: vis. investigator University College London, London, Eng. 1971-73; Ctr. Nat. de la Recherche Sci., Gif-sur-Yvette, France 1973-74; asst., assoc., prof. physiol. UC Berkeley 1974-80, 80-85, 85-90, prof. neurobiology, 1990–; appt. bd. sci. counselors N.I.N.C.D.S., N.I.H., Bethesda, Md. 1982; mem: study sections NIH, Bethesda (1983-84, 90-91, 93); NIH Reviewer's Reserve 1994–;corp. Marine Biological Lab., Woods Hole, Mass. 1981–; Nachshen Meml. lectr. U. Md. 1992; editl. bds. J. of Neurobiology 1982-86, J. Neurosci. 1988-94; awards: nat. winner Westinghouse Nat. Science Talent Search 1962, predoctoral fellowships NSF, NIH, Woodrow Wilson 1966-71, postdoc. fellowships Helen Hay Whitney Found., NATO, NIH, NSF 1971-74, res. fellow Alfred P. Sloan Found. 1976-80, Javits Award NIH 1987-94; AAAS 1968–, Sigma Xi 1966–, Soc. for Neurosci. 1977–, Biophysical Soc. 1982–, Union of Concerned Scientists 1981–, Amnesty Internat., People for the Am. Way, ACLU, Sierra Club, Common Cause; author 75+ book chpts. and res. articles in Science, Nature, J. of Physiol., J. of Gen. Physiol., Biophysical J., J. Neurophysiol., J. of Neurosci., J. of Neurobiol., Neuron, Proc. Nat. Acad. of Science USA, Annals N.Y. Acad. Sci., Brain Res., J. of Theoretical Biol., J. of Comparative Physiology, Annual Rev. of Neuroscience, Developmental Biol., others; Democrat; Jewish; rec: hiking, sailing, canoeing, skiing. Res: 1236 Oxford St Berkeley 94709 Ofc: University of California MCB Dept 111LSA, Berkeley 94720

ZWICK, BARRY STANLEY, newspaper editor, speechwriter; b. July 21, 1942, Cleveland, OH; s. Alvin Albert and Selma Davidovna (Makofsky) Z.; m. Roberta Joan Yaffe, Mar. 11, 1972; children: Natasha Yvette, Alexander Anatol; edn: BA journalism Ohio State Univ. 1963; MS journalism Columbia Univ. 1965. Career: copy ed. Phila. Inquirer 1964; night news ed. Detroit Free Press 1965-67; west coast ed. L.A. Times/ Washington Post News Svc. 1967-77; makeup ed. L.A. Times 1978–; chmn. Z & Z Ghostwriting 1993–; adj. prof. USC 1975-77; awards: NEH profl. journalism fellow Stanford Univ. 1977-78; author: Hollywood Tanning Secrets, 1980; Jewish. Ofc: L.A. Times, Times Mirror Sq Los Angeles 90053

ZYROFF, ELLEN SLOTOROFF, educator, librarian; b. Aug. 1, 1946, Atlantic City, N.J.; d. Joseph George and Sylvia Beverly (Roth) Slotoroff; m. Jack Zyroff, June 21, 1970; children: Dena b. 1973, David b. 1976; edn: AB (cum laude), Barnard Coll., 1968; MA classics Johns Hopkins, Balt., Md. 1969, PhD classics Johns Hopkins, Balt., Md. 1971; MS (hon.) library svc. Columbia Univ., 1973. Career: instr. classics, Johns Hopkins., 1970-71; Brooklyn Coll., 1971-72; acting chair , classics dept., Yeshiva Univ., N.Y. 1971-72; librarian and instr., UC San Diego, La Jolla 1979, 81, 91; librarian, San Diego State Univ. 1981-85; instr. San Diego Mesa Coll. 1981–; prin. librarian, San Diego Co. Library, 1985–; lectr. classics, San Diego State Univ. 1982, 94; prof. Latin language & literature, San Diego Mesa College; dir. The Reference Desk Research Services, La Jolla 1983–; mem: Calif. Statewide Task Force for Library User Edn. 1989–; honors: life mem. Beta Phi Mu, internat. library sci. hon. soc. 1973–; mem: Calif. Library Assn. 1985- (elected Assembly 1993-95), Am. Library Assn. (com. chair, 1981–), Public Lib. Assn. (rep. to Lib. of Cong. CIP Adv. Com.), San Diego Online Users' Group (exec. bd. 1989-94), Am. Philological Assn. 1970–, World Future Soc. 1991–, Toastmasters Internat. (chpt. v.p. 1991-92), Women's Am. ORT (S.D. pres. 1979-81), Friends of the Lib. for Children's Svs. S.D. Pub. Lib. (first pres.); publs: diss: The Author's Apostrophe in Epic from Homer through Lucan, 1971, curriculum: Project CLIMB: Cooperative Library Instrn. for Maximum Benefit, 1987; rec: bicycling, jogging, writing. Ofc: PO Box 12122 La Jolla 92039